P

OP-Apr 98

R423

WID

The
HUTCHINSON
ENCYCLOPEDIC
DICTIONARY

The HUTCHINSON ENCYCLOPEDIC DICTIONARY

HUTCHINSON

LONDON · MELBOURNE · SYDNEY · AUCKLAND · JOHANNESBURG

035595

Random Century Ltd
20 Vauxhall Bridge Road
London SW1V 2SA

Random Century Australia (Pty) Ltd
20 Alfred Street
Milsons Point
Sydney
NSW 2061, Australia

Random Century Group New Zealand Ltd
PO Box 40-086, Glenfield
Auckland 10, New Zealand

Random Century Group South Africa (Pty) Ltd
PO Box 337, Bergvlei 2012
South Africa

Set in Century Old Style

Data prepared on Telos *and typeset by*
Falcon Typographic Art Ltd, Edinburgh & London
Printed and bound in England

ISBN 0 09 174998 0

Preface

This book is a synthesis: it is both a dictionary and a concise encyclopedia. More than 15,000 entries on people, places, the arts, science, technology, sport, politics, society – and more – from the database of the Hutchinson Encyclopedia have been merged with over 75,000 dictionary definitions from the Oxford Dictionary. In this way, the maximum amount of up-to-the-minute information has been collected in one volume and presented as clearly as possible.

Arrangement of entries

Entries are ordered alphabetically by letter, i.e. as if there were no spaces between words. Thus entries for words beginning 'castor' follow the order:

castor
Castor
Castor and Pollux
castor-oil plant
castrate
castrato

However, we have avoided a purely mechanical alphabetization in cases where a different order corresponds more with human logic. For example, sovereigns with the same name are grouped according to country and then by number, so that King George II of England is placed before George III of England and not next to King George II of Greece. Words beginning with 'Mc' and 'Mac' are treated as if they begin 'Mac'; and 'St' and 'Saint' are both treated as if they were spelt 'Saint'.

Cross-references

Cross-referencing is selective; a cross-reference is shown when another entry contains material directly relevant to the subject matter of an entry, and where the reader may not otherwise think of looking. A cross-reference is indicated by an arrow symbol (◊) immediately preceding the reference.

Parts of speech

For abbreviations of standard parts of speech *see below* **Abbreviations.**
Parts of speech are not given for compound nouns or gazetteer or biographical entries.

Etymologies

These appear in square brackets after the definition(s) of the headword. Their aim is to give a concise and readable account of the origin of the word, so they appear in simplified form.

Abbreviations

The following abbreviations are used throughout the dictionary:

adj./ective etc.	pl./ural
adv./erb etc.	poss./essive
attrib./utive(ly)	prep./osition
c. circa	pron./oun
conj./unction	v. verb
est./imated *etc.*	v.aux. auxiliary verb
fem./inine	v.i. intransitive verb
int./erjection	v.refl. reflexive verb
interrog./ative(ly)	v.t. transitive verb
irreg./ular(ly)	v.t./i. transitive and
n. noun	intransitive verb

Pronunciation key

These are given using the International Phonetic Alphabet (IPA). Where required, alternative pronunciations are also given. The pronunciation for foreign names is generally agreed English form, if there is one: otherwise, an approximation using English sounds is given. When several entries with the same pronunciation occur in succession, the pronunciation is given for the first entry only. For example:

ray[1] /reɪ/ a narrow beam of light
ray[2] a large sea-fish
ray[3] in music, the second note of the major scale
Ray, John (1627-1705). English naturalist.

The rule also applies in lists of identical surnames. The pronunciation is given only in the first occurrence of a name; the ordering of the rest follows the strict alphabetization of the christian names. For example:

Smith /smɪθ/ Adam
Smith Bessie
Smith David
Smith Henry
Smith Ian
etc.

ɑː	father /ˈfɑːðə/, start /stɑːt/	m	minimum /ˈmɪnɪməm/
aɪ	price /praɪs/, high /haɪ/	n	nine /naɪn/
aʊ	mouth /maʊθ/, how /haʊ/	ŋ	sing /sɪŋ/, uncle /ˈʌŋkl/
æ	trap /træp/, man /mæn/	ɒ	lot /lɒt/, watch /wɒtʃ/
b	baby /ˈbeɪbɪ/	ɔː	thought /θɔːt/, north /nɔːθ/
d	dead /ded/	ɔɪ	choice /tʃɔɪs/, boy /bɔɪ/
dʒ	judge /dʒʌdʒ/	p	paper /ˈpeɪpə/
ð	this /ðɪs/, other /ˈʌðə/	r	red /red/, carry /ˈkærɪ/
e	dress /dres/, men /men/	s	space /speɪs/
eɪ	face /feɪs/, wait /weɪt/	ʃ	ship /ʃɪp/, motion /ˈməʊʃən/
eə	square /skweə/, fair /feə/	t	totter /ˈtɒtə/
ɜː	nurse /nɜːs/, pearl /pɜːl/	tʃ	church /tʃɜːtʃ/
ə	another /əˈnʌðə/	θ	thick /θɪk/, author /ˈɔːθə/
əʊ	goat /gəʊt/, snow /snəʊ/	uː	goose /guːs/, soup /suːp/
f	fifty /ˈfɪftɪ/	u	influence /ˈɪnfluəns/
g	giggle /ˈgɪgl/	ʊ	foot /fʊt/, push /pʊʃ/
h	hot /hɒt/	ʊə	poor /pʊə/, cure /kjʊə/
iː	fleece /fliːs/, sea /siː/	v	vivid /ˈvɪvɪd/
i	happy /ˈhæpi/, glorious /ˈglɔːriəs/	ʌ	strut /strʌt/, love /lʌv/
ɪ	kit /kɪt/, tin /tɪn/	w	west /west/
ɪə	near /nɪə/, idea /aɪˈdɪə/	x	loch /lɒx/
j	yellow /ˈjeləʊ/, few /fjuː/	z	zones /zəʊnz/
k	kick /kɪk/	ʒ	pleasure /ˈpleʒə/
l	little /ˈlɪtl/		

Consonants

p b t d k g tʃ dʒ f v θ ð s z ʃ ʒ m n ŋ r l w j ɫ x

Vowels and Diphthongs

iː ɪ e æ ɑː ɒ ŋ ɔː uː u ʌ ɜː ə eɪ əʊ aɪ aʊ ɔɪ ɪə eə ʊə

Stress marks

ˈ (primary word stress)

Editorial Director
Michael Upshall

Pronunciation Editor
J C Wells MA, PhD

Editor
Helen Varley

Editors
Sue Croft, Gian Douglas-Home; Edith Harkness; Ronnie Haydon; Marion Moisy; Frances Lass; Carol Shaw; Ingrid von Essen

Design Consultant
Malcolm Smythe

Design
Terry Cavan
Edna Moore, TEK ART LTD

Database Software
BRS Software Products Ltd

Page Make-Up
Marie Banidol; Helen Bird

Contributors
David Armstrong PhD; Christine Avery MA, PhS; John Ayto MA; Lionel Bender BSc, ChBiol, MIBiol; David Benest; Malcolm Bradbury BA, MA, PhD, Hon D Litt, FRSL; Brendan Bradley MA, MSc, PhD; Roy Brigden BA, FMA; John O E Clark BSc; Mike Corbishley BA, FSA, MIFA; Barbara Taylor Cork; David Cotton BA, PhD; Nigel Davis MSc; Ian D Derbyshire MA, PhD; J Denis Derbyshire BSc, PhD, FBIM; Peter Dews PhD; Dougal Dixon BSc, MSc; Professor George du Boulay FRCR, FRCP, Hon FACR; Robin Dunbar BA, PhD; Suzanne Duke; Jane Farron BA; Peter Fleming BA, PhD; Linda Gamlin BSc, MSc; Derek Gjertsen BA; Lawrence Garner BA; Michael Hitchcock PhD; Jane Insley MSc; H G Jerrard PhD; Brian Jones; Roz Kaveney BA; Robin Kerrod FRAS; Charles Kidd; Stephen Kite BArch, RIBA; Peter Lafferty; Chris Lawn BA, MA; Judith Lewis LLB; Mike Lewis MBCS; Graham Ley BA, MPhil; Carol Lister BSc, PhD; Graham Littler BSc, MSc, FSS; Robin Maconie MA; Roslin Mair MA; Morven MacKilop; Tom McArthur PhD; Karin Mogg BSc, MSc, PhD; Bob Moore BA, PhD; Ian Morrison; David Munro BSc, PhD; Daniel O'Brien MA; Robert Paisley PhD; Carol Place BSc, PhD; Michael Pudlo MSc, PhD; Ian Ridpath FRAS; Adrian Room MA; John Rowlinson BSc, MSc, CChem, FRSC; Jack Schofield BA, MA; Mark Slade MA; Angela Smith BA; Imogen Stoke Wheeler; Glyn Stone; Ingrid von Essen; Stephen Webster BSc, MPhil; Liz Whitelegg BSc; John Woodruff

with special thanks to E M Horsley

a, A (*plural* **as, a's**) **1.** the first letter of the alphabet. **2.** in music, the sixth note of the scale of C major, the reference pitch to which instruments of an orchestra are tuned.

a /ə, *emphatic* eɪ/ *adj.* (called the *indefinite article*) **1.** one person or thing but not any specific one; one like. **2.** per. [Old English]

a- prefix meaning **1.** on (*afoot*), to (*ashore*), towards (*aside*). **2.** in (*nowadays*). **3.** in the process of (*a-begging, a-flutter*). [Old English]

A abbreviation of ampere(s).

Å abbreviation of ångström(s).

A1 1. first class (of ships). **2.** (*colloquial*) first-rate, in perfect condition.

AA abbreviation of British Automobile Association.

Aalborg /'ɔːlbɔːg/ (Danish *Ålborg*) port in Denmark 32 km/20 mi inland from the Kattegat, on the S shore of the Limfjord; population (1988) 155,000. It is one of Denmark's oldest towns and is the capital of Nordjylland county in Jylland (Jutland). It has a castle and the fine Budolfi church.

Aalto /'aːltəu/ Alvar 1898–1976. Finnish architect and designer. He was one of Finland's first Modernists, and his unique architectural style is characterized by asymmetry, curved walls, and contrast of natural materials. His buildings include the Hall of Residence at the Massachusetts Institute of Technology, Cambridge, Massachusetts 1947–49; Technical High School, Otaniemi 1962–65; and Finlandia Hall, Helsinki 1972. He invented a new form of laminated bent plywood furniture in 1932 and won many design awards for household and industrial items.

aardvark /'aːdvaːk/ *n.* a nocturnal African animal *Orycteropus afer*, with a bulky pig-like body, long ears, and a thick tail. It feeds on termites. [Afrikaans = earthpig]

aardwolf *n.* a nocturnal mammal *Proteles cristatus* of ◊hyena family, Hyaenidae. It is found in E and S Africa, usually in the burrows of the aardvark, and feeds on termites.

Aarhus /'aːhuːs/ (Danish *Århus*) second city of Denmark, on the E coast overlooking the Kattegat; population (1988) 258,000. It is the capital of Aarhus county in Jylland (Jutland) and a shipping and commercial centre.

Aaron /'eərən/ *c.*13th century BC. In the Old Testament, the elder brother of Moses and co-leader of the ◊Hebrews in their march from Egypt to the Promised Land of Canaan. He made the Golden Calf for the Hebrews to worship when they despaired of Moses' return from Mount Sinai, but he was allowed to continue as high priest. All his descendants are hereditary high priests, called the *cohanim*, or cohens, and maintain a special place in worship and ceremony in the synagogue. See also ◊Levite.

Aaron Hank (Henry Louis) 1934– . US baseball player. He played for 23 years with the Milwaukee (later Atlanta) Braves (1954–74) and the Milwaukee Brewers (1975–76), hitting a major-league record 755 home runs and 2,297 runs batted in. He was elected to the Baseball Hall of Fame in 1982.

ab- prefix (**abs-** before *c, t*; **a-** before *m, p, v*) giving the meaning off, away, from. [French or from Latin]

aback /ə'bæk/ *adv.* **taken aback,** disconcerted. [Old English]

abacus /'æbəkəs/ *n.* (*plural* **abacuses**) **1.** a frame containing grooves or parallel rods or wires with beads that slide to and fro, used for counting. Familiar to the Greeks and Romans, and used by earlier peoples, possibly even in ancient Babylon, it survives in the more sophisticated beadframe form of the Russian *schoty* and the Japanese *soroban*. **2.** in architecture, the flat upper section of a capital, supporting the architrave. [Latin from Greek *abax* = slab, drawing-board from Hebrew = dust (from use of board sprinkled with sand or dust for drawing geometrical diagrams)]

Abadan /æbə'daːn/ Iranian oil port on the E side of the Shatt-al-Arab; population (1986) 294,000. Abadan is the chief refinery and shipping centre for Iran's oil industry.

abaft *adv.* in the stern half of a ship. —*prep.* nearer to the stern than. [from Old English *be* = by and *æftan* = behind]

abalone /æbə'ləunɪ/ *n.* (*US*) an edible mollusc of the genus *Haliotis*, family Haliotidae, with an ear-shaped shell lined with mother-of-pearl. [American Spanish]

abandon /ə'bændən/ *v.t.* **1.** to go away from without intending to return; to give up, to cease work on. **2.** to yield completely to an emotion or impulse. —*n.* reckless freedom of manner. —**abandonment** *n.* [from Old French *à bandon* = under another's control]

abandoned /ə'bændənd/ *adj.* (of a person or behaviour) showing abandon, depraved.

abase /ə'beɪs/ *v.t.* to humiliate, to degrade. —**abasement** *n.* [from Old French from Latin *bassus* = short]

abashed /ə'bæʃt/ *adj.* embarrassed, disconcerted, ashamed. [from Old French *baïr* = astound]

abate /ə'beɪt/ *v.t./i.* to make or become less, to weaken. —**abatement** *n.* [from Old French from Latin *battuere* = beat]

abattoir /'æbətwaː(ə)/ *n.* a slaughterhouse. [French from Latin *battuere* = beat]

abbacy /'æbəsɪ/ *n.* the office or jurisdiction of an abbot or abbess. [from Latin]

Abbadid dynasty /'æbədɪd/ 11th century. Muslim dynasty based in Seville which lasted from 1023 until 1091. The dynasty was founded by Abu-el-Kasim Mohammed who led the townspeople against the Berbers when the Spanish caliphate fell. The dynasty continued under Motadid (1042–69) and Motamid (1069–91) when the city was taken by the ◊Almoravids.

Abbado /ə'baːdəu/ Claudio 1933– . Italian conductor, long associated with the La Scala opera house, Milan. Principal conductor of the London Symphony Orchestra from 1979, he also worked with the European Community Youth Orchestra from 1977.

Abbas I /'æbəs/ **the Great** *c.*1557–1629. Shah of Persia from 1588. He expanded Persian territory by conquest, defeating the Uzbeks near Herat in 1597 and also the Turks. The port of Bandar-Abbas is named after him. At his death his empire reached from the river Tigris to the Indus. He was a patron of the arts.

Abbas II Hilmi 1874–1944. Last ◊khedive (viceroy) of Egypt, 1892–1914. On the outbreak of war between Britain and Turkey in 1914, he sided with Turkey and was deposed following the establishment of a British protectorate over Egypt.

Abbasid dynasty /'æbəsɪd/ dynasty of the Islamic empire, whose ◊caliphs reigned in Baghdad 750–1258. They were descended from Abbas, the prophet Muhammad's uncle, and some of them, such as Harun al-Rashid and Mamun (reigned 813–33), were outstanding patrons of cultural development. Their power later dwindled, and in 1258 Baghdad was burned by the Tatars.

abbé /'æbeɪ/ n. a Frenchman entitled to wear ecclesiastical dress, with or without official duties. [French from Latin]

abbess /'æbes/ n. a woman who is head of an abbey of nuns. [from Old French]

abbey /'æbɪ/ n. 1. a building occupied by a community of monks or nuns. 2. this community. 3. a church or house that was formerly an abbey. —**the Abbey,** Westminster Abbey. [from Old French from Latin *abbatia* = abbacy]

Abbey Theatre a playhouse in Dublin associated with the Irish literary revival of the early 1900s. The theatre opened in 1904 and staged the works of a number of Irish dramatists, including Lady Gregory, Yeats, J M Synge, and Sean O'Casey. It burned down in 1951, but was rebuilt in 1966.

abbot /'æbət/ n. a man who is head of an abbey of monks (now chiefly in Benedictine and Augustinian orders), usually elected by the monks for life or for a period of years and frequently holding certain episcopal rights. [Old English, ultimately from Aramaic *abba* = father]

Abbott and Costello /'æbət, kɒ'steləʊ/ Stage names of William Abbott (1895–1974) and Louis Cristillo (1906–1959) US comedy duo. They moved to the cinema from vaudeville, and their films, including *Buck Privates* 1941 and *Lost in a Harem* 1944, were showcases for their routines.

abbreviate /ə'briːvɪeɪt/ v.t. to shorten (especially a word or title). —**abbreviation** /-'eɪʃ(ə)n/ n. [from Latin *abbreviare* (*brevis* = short)]

ABC n. 1. the alphabet. 2. the elementary facts of a subject. 3. an alphabetically arranged guide. 4. abbreviation of Australian Broadcasting Corporation (formerly Commission).

Abd Allah /'æbd 'ælə/ the Sudanese dervish leader Abdullah el Taaisha. 1846–1899. Successor to the Mahdi as Sudanese ruler from 1885, he was defeated by the UK general ◊Kitchener at Omdurman in 1898 and later killed in Kordofan.

Abd al-Malik /'æbd æl'maːlɪk/ Caliph who reigned 685–705. Based in Damascus, he waged military campaigns to unite Muslim groups, and battled against the Greeks. He instituted a purely Arab coinage and introduced Arabic as the language for his lands. His reign was turbulent, but he succeeded in extending and strengthening ◊Omayed power. He was a patron of the arts.

Abd el-Krim /'æbd el 'krɪm/ el-Khettabi 1881–1963. Moroccan chief known as the 'Wolf of the ◊Riff'. With his brother Muhammad. he led the **Riff revolt** against the French and Spanish invaders, inflicting disastrous defeat on the Spanish at Anual in 1921, but surrendered to a large French army under Pétain in 1926. Banished to the island of Réunion, he was released in 1947 and died in voluntary exile in Cairo.

abdicate /'æbdɪkeɪt/ v.t./i. to renounce, to resign from a throne, right, or high office. —**abdication** /-'keɪʃ(ə)n/ n. [from Latin *abdicare* (*dicare* = dedicate)]

abdication crisis in British history, the constitutional upheaval of the period 16 Nov 1936 to 10 Dec 1936, brought about by the English king Edward VIII's decision to marry Wallis Simpson, an American divorcee. The marriage of the 'Supreme Governor' of the Church of England to a divorced person was considered unsuitable and the king was finally forced to abdicate on 10 Dec and left for voluntary exile in France. He was created Duke of Windsor and married Mrs Simpson on 3 June 1937.

abdomen /'æbdəmən/ n. 1. the part of the body containing the stomach, bowels, intestines, and other digestive organs; the front surface of the body from waist to groin. 2. the hind part of the body of an insect, crustacean, spider, etc. —**abdominal** /-'dɒmɪn(ə)l/ adj. [Latin]

abduct /æb'dʌkt/ v.t. to carry off (a person) illegally by force or deception. —**abduction** n., **abductor** n. [from Latin *ducere* = lead]

Abdul-Hamid II /'æbdʊl 'hæmɪd/ 1842–1918. Last sultan of Turkey 1876–1909. In 1908 the ◊Young Turks under Enver Pasha forced Abdul-Hamid to restore the constitution of 1876 and in 1909 insisted on his deposition. He

died in confinement. For his part in the ◊Armenian massacres suppressing the revolt of 1894–96 he was known as 'the Great Assassin'; his actions still motivate Armenian violence against the Turks.

Abdullah /æb'dʌlə/ ibn Hussein 1882–1951. King of Jordan from 1946. He worked with the British guerrilla leader T E ◊Lawrence in the Arab revolt of World War I. Abdullah became king of Transjordan in 1946; on the incorporation of Arab Palestine (after the 1948–49 Arab-Israeli War) he renamed the country the Hashemite Kingdom of Jordan. He was assassinated.

Abdullah Sheik Muhammad 1905–1982. Indian politician, known as the 'Lion of Kashmir'. He headed the struggle for constitutional government against the Maharajah of Kashmir, and in 1948, following a coup, became prime minister. He agreed to the accession of the state to India, but was dismissed and imprisoned from 1953 (with brief intervals) until 1966, when he called for Kashmiri self-determination. He became chief minister of Jammu and Kashmir in 1975, accepting the sovereignty of India.

abed /ə'bed/ adv. (*archaic*) in bed. [Old English]

Abel /'eɪbəl/ in the Old Testament, second son of Adam and Eve; as a shepherd, he made burnt offerings of meat to God which were more acceptable than the fruits offered by his brother Cain; he was killed by the jealous Cain.

Abel Frederick Augustus 1827–1902. British scientist and inventor who developed explosives. As a chemist to the War Department, he introduced a method of making gun-cotton and was joint inventor with James ◊Dewar of cordite. He also invented the Abel close-test instrument for determining the ◊flash point (ignition temperature) of petroleum.

Abel John Jacob 1857–1938. US biochemist, discoverer of ◊adrenaline. He studied the chemical composition of body tissues, and this led, in 1898, to the discovery of adrenaline, the first hormone to be identified, which Abel called epinephrine. He later became the first to isolate ◊amino acids from blood.

Abel /'aːbəl/ Niels Henrik 1802–1829. Norwegian mathematician. He demonstrated that the general quintic equation $ax^5 + bx^4 + cx^3 + dx^2 + ex + f = 0$ could not be solved algebraically. Subsequent work covered elliptic functions, integral equations, infinite series, and the binomial theorem.

Abelard /'æbəlaːd/ Peter 1079–1142. French scholastic philosopher, who worked on logic and theology. His romantic liaison with his pupil, ◊Héloïse, caused a medieval scandal. Details of his controversial life are contained in the autobiographical *Historia Calamitatum Mearum/The History of My Misfortunes*.

Abercrombie /'ebəkrʌmbi/ Leslie Patrick 1879–1957. Pioneer of British town planning. He is known for his work replanning British cities after damage in World War II (such as the Greater London Plan, 1944) and for the ◊new town policy. See also ◊garden city.

Aberdeen /æbə'diːn/ city and seaport on the E coast of Scotland, administrative headquarters of Grampian region; population (1986) 214,082. It has shore-based maintenance and service depots for the North Sea oil rigs.

Aberdeen George Hamilton Gordon, 4th Earl of Aberdeen 1784–1860. British Tory politician, prime minister 1852–55; he resigned because of the Crimean War losses.

Aberdeenshire /æbə'diːnʃə/ former county in E Scotland, merged in 1975 into Grampian region.

aberrant /æ'berənt/ adj. departing from the normal type or accepted standard. [from Latin *errare* = stray]

aberration /æbə'reɪʃ(ə)n/ n. 1. departure from what is normal or accepted or regarded as right; a moral or mental lapse. 2. in optics, distortion of an image, the non-convergence of rays of light from a point to a single focus. **Chromatic aberration,** is a form of aberration due to the fact that light of different colours is refracted by different amounts as it passes through a lens, so that the resulting image is fringed with colours. In **spherical aberration** the image is blurred because different parts of a spherical lens or mirror have different focal lengths. In **astigmatism** the image appears elliptical or cross-shaped because of an irregularity in the curvature of the lens. In **coma** the images appear progressively elongated towards the edge of the field of view. 3. in astronomy, the apparent change in the position of a celestial body caused by the combined effects of the speed of light and the speed of the Earth in orbit around the Sun (about 30 kps/18.5 mps).

abet /ə'bet/ *v.t.* (**-tt-**) to encourage or assist (an offender or offence). —**abetter** (in legal use **abettor**) *n.*, **abetment** *n.* [from Old French *à* = to and *beter* = bait]

abeyance /ə'beɪəns/ *n.* the doctrine whereby a peerage falls into a state of suspension between a number of co-heirs or co-heiresses; in the UK the only peerages that can fall into abeyance are baronies that have been created by writ. —**in abeyance**, (of a right or rule or problem etc.) suspended for a time. [from Old French (*à* to, *beer* gape)]

abhor /əb'hɔ:(ə)/ *v.t.* (**-rr-**) to detest, to regard with disgust. —**abhorrence** /-'hɒrəns/ *n.* [from Latin *abhorrere* = shrink in dread]

abhorrent /əb'hɒrənt/ *adj.* disgusting or hateful (*to* a person or one's beliefs); not according *to* (a principle).

abide /ə'baɪd/ *v.t./i.* **1.** to tolerate, to endure. **2.** (*archaic*, *past* **abode** *or* **abided**) to remain, to dwell. —**abide by**, to act in accordance with (a promise etc.). [Old English]

abiding *adj.* enduring, permanent.

Abidja'n /æbi:'dʒɑ:n/ port and capital of the Republic of Ivory Coast, W Africa; population (1982) 1,850,000. Products include coffee, palm oil, cocoa, and timber (mahogany). It is to be replaced as capital by Yamoussoukro.

abigail /'æbɪɡeɪl/ *n.* a lady's maid. [character in Beaumont and Fletcher's *Scornful Lady*; compare 1 Samuel 25]

ability /ə'bɪlɪtɪ/ *n.* the quality that makes an action or process possible; cleverness, talent. [from Old French from Latin *habilis* = deft]

ab initio /æb i'nɪʃɪəʊ/ from the beginning. [Latin]

abiotic factor a nonorganic variable within the ecosystem, affecting the life of organisms. Examples include

aberration
chromatic aberration

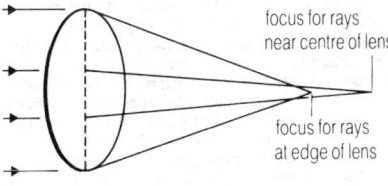

red focus

blue focus

spherical aberration

focus for rays near centre of lens

focus for rays at edge of lens

astigmatism

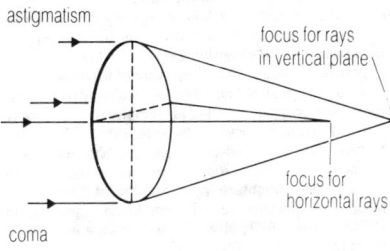

focus for rays in vertical plane

focus for horizontal rays

coma

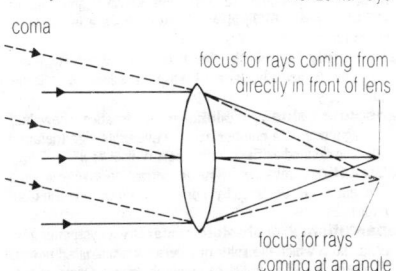

focus for rays coming from directly in front of lens

focus for rays coming at an angle

temperature, light, and soil structure. Abiotic factors can be harmful to the environment, as when sulphur dioxide emissions from power stations produce acid rain.

abject /'æbdʒekt/ *adj.* lacking all pride, made humble; wretched, without resources. —**abjectly** *adv.*, **abjection** /-'dʒekʃən/ *n.* [from Latin *abjectus (jacere* = throw)]

abjure /əb'dʒʊə(ə)/ *v.t.* to renounce or repudiate. —**abjuration** /-'reɪʃ(ə)n/ *n.* [from Latin *abjurare* = deny on oath]

Abkhazia /æb'kɑ:zɪə/ Autonomous Soviet Socialist Republic within Georgia, USSR, situated on the Black Sea; **area** 8,600 sq km/3,320 sq mi; **population** (1989) 526,000; **history** Abkhazia, a Georgian kingdom from the 4th century, was inhabited traditionally by Abkhazis, an ethnic group converted from Christianity to Islam in the 17th century. By the 1980s some 17% of the population were Muslims and two-thirds were of Georgian origin. In March-April and July 1989, Abkhazis demanded secession from Georgia and reinstatement as a full Union republic; violent inter-ethnic clashes erupted in which at least 20 people died. Georgian nationalists want the republic to be incorporated as part of Georgia. The dispute triggered nationalist demonstrations throughout Georgia.

ablative /'æblətɪv/ *n.* in grammar, the case (especially in Latin) that indicates the agent, instrument, or location of an action. —*adj.* of or in the ablative. [from Old French or Latin *ablatus* = carried away]

ablaut /'æblaʊt/ *n.* a change of vowel in related words (e.g. *sing, sang, sung*), characteristic of Indo-European languages. [German]

ablaze /ə'bleɪz/ *predic. adj.* blazing; glittering; greatly excited.

able /'eɪb(ə)l/ *adj.* having the ability or capacity (*to do* something); clever, talented, competent. —**able-bodied** *adj.* fit and strong. —**ably** *adv.* [from Old French from Latin *habilis* = deft]

-able suffix forming adjectives in sense 'that may' (*comfortable, suitable*), now always in passive sense 'that can, may, or must be -d' (*eatable, payable*), 'that can be made the subject of' (*objectionable*), 'that is relevant to or in accordance with' (*fashionable*). [French, from Latin *-abilis*]

ablution /ə'blu:ʃ(ə)n/ *n.* (usually in *plural*) **1.** ceremonial washing for a religious purpose, to purify the soul. For example, Hindus believe that bathing in the river Ganges will purify them. Similar beliefs are found in Christianity and Shinto (for example, the mythical Izanagi purifies himself by diving to the bottom of the sea and washing himself). **2.** (*colloquial*) ordinary washing of the body, a place for doing this. [from Old French or Latin *ablutio* (*luere* = wash)]

ABM abbreviation of anti-ballistic missile; see ◊nuclear warfare.

abnegate /'æbnɪɡeɪt/ *v.t.* to give up or renounce (a pleasure or right etc.). —**abnegation** /-'ɡeɪʃ(ə)n/ *n.* [from Latin *abnegare* = refuse]

abnormal /æb'nɔ:m(ə)l/ *adj.* different from what is normal. —**abnormally** *adv.*, **abnormality** /-'mælɪtɪ/ *n.* [from French from Greek *an-* = not and *homalos* = even]

Abo /'ɔ:bu:/ Swedish name for ◊Turku in Finland.

aboard /ə'bɔ:d/ *adv. & prep.* on or into a ship, aircraft, train, etc.

abode[1] /ə'bəʊd/ *n.* (*archaic* or *literary*) a dwelling-place.

abode[2] past of **abide**.

abolish /ə'bɒlɪʃ/ *v.t.* to put an end to (a custom, institution, etc.). [from French from Latin *abolēre* = destroy]

abolition /æbə'lɪʃ(ə)n/ *n.* abolishing, being abolished, especially with reference to capital punishment or (*historical*) black slavery and the 19th-century movement against this. —**abolitionism** in UK and US history, a movement culminating in the late 18th and early 19th centuries, first to end the slave trade, and then to abolish the institution of ◊slavery and emancipate slaves. In the USA, Benjamin ◊Franklin had argued against slavery as early as 1775. It was officially abolished by the 1863 Emancipation Proclamation of President Abraham ◊Lincoln, but it could not be enforced until 1865 after the Union victory in the civil war. [French or from Latin]

abolitionist *n.* one who favours abolition, especially of capital punishment.

abominable /ə'bɒmɪnəb(ə)l/ *adj.* detestable, loathsome; (*colloquial*) unpleasant. —**abominable snowman**, a large unidentified manlike or bearlike animal said to exist in the

Himalayas, where it is known as a *yeti*. —**abominably** *adv.* [from Old French from Latin]

abominate /ə'bɒmɪneɪt/ *v.t.* to detest, to loathe. [from Latin *abominari* = deprecate]

abomination /əbɒmi'neɪʃ(ə)n/ *n.* 1. detesting, loathing. 2. an object of disgust. [from Old French]

aboriginal /æbə'rɪdʒɪn(ə)l/ *adj.* indigenous, inhabiting a land from an early period, especially before the arrival of colonists; directly descended from early inhabitants. —*n.* an aboriginal inhabitant, especially (**Aboriginal**) of Australia. [from Latin]

aborigines /æbə'rɪdʒɪni:z/ *n.pl.* (*singular* **aborigine** is used informally, but *aboriginal* is preferable) aboriginal inhabitants, especially (**Aborigines**) of Australia. [Latin, probably from *ab origine* = from the beginning]

abort *v.t./i.* 1. to cause an abortion of or to; to undergo abortion. 2. to remain undeveloped, to stop (a growth or disease) in its early stages. 3. to end prematurely and unsuccessfully. [from Latin *aboriri* = miscarry]

abortion /ə'bɔːʃ(ə)n/ *n.* 1. the expulsion (either spontaneous or induced) of a fetus from the womb before it is able to survive, especially in the first 28 weeks of pregnancy. Loss of a fetus at a later gestational age is termed premature stillbirth. Abortion may be accidental (miscarriage) or deliberate (termination of pregnancy). 2. a stunted or misshapen creature or thing.

abortionist *n.* a person who practises abortion, especially illegally.

abortive /ə'bɔːtɪv/ *adj.* 1. producing abortion. 2. unsuccessful. [from Old French from Latin]

Aboukir Bay, Battle of /æbu:'kiə/ also known as the **Battle of the Nile**, the naval battle between the UK and France, in which Admiral Nelson defeated Napoleon's fleet at the Egyptian seaport of Aboukir on 1 Aug 1798.

abound /ə'baʊnd/ *v.i.* to be plentiful; to be rich *in*, to teem *with*. [from Old French from Latin *abundare* = overflow]

about /ə'baʊt/ *prep.* 1. in connection with, on the subject of. 2. at a time near to. 3. all round. 4. near to hand. 5. here and there in, at points throughout. —*adv.* 1. approximately. 2. at points near by, here and there. 3. on the move, in action. 4. all round, in every direction. 5. in rotation or succession. (Tending to be replaced in many uses by *around* and *round*.) —**about turn**, a turn made so as to face the opposite direction; a reversal of opinion or policy etc. **be about to**, to intend to (do something) immediately; to be on the point or verge of. [Old English]

above /ə'bʌv/ *prep.* 1. over, on the top of, higher than; over the level of. 2. more than. 3. higher in rank or importance etc. than. 4. beyond the reach of; too good etc. for. —*adv.* 1. at or to a higher point, overhead. 2. in addition. 3. further back on a page or in a book. 4. (*rhetorically*) in heaven. —*adj.* said, mentioned, or written above. —*n.* that which is above. —**above-board** *adv.* & *adj.* without concealment, open(ly). **above himself** etc., carried away by high spirits or conceit. [from Old English *bufan* (*be* = by and *ufan* = above)]

abracadabra /æbrəkə'dæbrə/ *n.* 1. a supposedly magic formula or spell. 2. gibberish. [Latin from Greek; a cabbalistic word of a Gnostic sect, supposed when written triangularly, and worn, to cure fevers etc.; it is first found in a poem by Q Serenus Sammonicus (late 2nd or early 3rd century AD)]

abrade /ə'breɪd/ *v.t.* to scrape or wear away by rubbing. [from Latin *abradere* (*radere* = scrape)]

Abraham /'eɪbrəhæm/ *c.*2300 BC. In the Old Testament, the founder of the Jewish nation. Jehovah promised him heirs and land for his people in Canaan, (Israel), renamed him Abraham ('father of many nations') and tested his faith by a command (later retracted) to sacrifice his son Isaac.

Abraham, Plains of plateau near Québec, Canada, where the British commander ◊Wolfe defeated the French under ◊Montcalm, 13 Sept 1759, during the French and Indian War (1754–63).

abrasion /ə'breɪʒ(ə)n/ *n.* scraping or wearing away; an area of damage caused thus. [from Latin *radere* = scrape]

abrasive /ə'breɪsɪv/ *adj.* 1. causing abrasion; capable of polishing by rubbing or grinding. 2. harsh and offensive in manner. —*n.* an abrasive substance. There are two types: natural and artificial abrasives, and their hardness is measured using the ◊Mohs' scale. Natural abrasives include quartz, sandstone, pumice, diamond, and corundum; artificial abrasives include rouge, whiting, and carborundum.

abreaction /æbri'ækʃ(ə)n/ *n.* free expression and release of a previously repressed emotion.

abreast /ə'brest/ *adv.* 1. side by side and facing the same way. 2. keeping up, not behind (*of* or *with* developments).

abridge /ə'brɪdʒ/ *v.t.* to shorten into fewer words. —**abridgement** *n.* [from Old French from Latin *abbreviare* (*brevis* = short)]

abroad /ə'brɔːd/ *adv.* 1. in or to a foreign country. 2. over a wide area, in different directions. 3. in circulation.

abrogate /'æbrəgeɪt/ *v.t.* to repeal, to cancel. —**abrogation** /-'geɪʃ(ə)n/ *n.* [from Latin *rogare* = propose law]

abrupt /ə'brʌpt/ *adj.* 1. sudden; disjointed, not smooth; curt. 2. steep, precipitous. —**abruptly** *adv.*, **abruptness** *n.* [from Latin *abruptus* (*rumpere* = break)]

Abruzzi /ə'brutsi/ mountainous region of S central Italy, comprising the provinces of L'Aquila, Chieti, Pescara, and Teramo; area 10,800 sq km/4,169 sq mi; population (1988) 1,258,000; capital L'Aquila. Gran Sasso d'Italia, 2,914 m/ 9,564 ft, is the highest point of the ◊Apennines.

Absalom /'æbsələm/ in the Old Testament, the favourite son of King David; when defeated in a revolt against his father he fled on a mule, but caught his hair in a tree branch and was killed by Joab, one of David's officers.

abscess /'æbsɪs/ *n.* a swollen area of body tissue in which ◊pus gathers in response to infection. Its presence is signalled by pain and inflammation. [from Latin *abscessus* = a going away (*cedere* = go)]

abscissa *n.* (*plural* **abscissae**) in coordinate geometry, the horizontal or *x* coordinate—that is, the distance of a point from the vertical or *y*-axis. For example, a point with the coordinates (3,4) has an abscissa of 3. [from Latin *scindere* = cut]

abscission *n.* in botany, the controlled separation of part of a plant from the main plant body, most commonly, the falling of leaves or the dropping of fruit. In ◊deciduous plants the leaves are shed before the winter or dry season, whereas ◊evergreen plants drop their leaves continually throughout the year. Fruit drop, the abscission of fruit while still immature, is a naturally occurring process.

abscond /əb'skɒnd/ *v.i.* to go away furtively, especially after wrongdoing. —**absconder** *n.* [from Latin *condere* = stow]

abseil /'æbseɪl/ *v.i.* to descend a steep rock-face using a doubled rope fixed at a higher point. —*n.* this process. [from German *ab* = down and *seil* = rope]

absence /'æbs(ə)ns/ *n.* being away, the period of this; non-existence or lack *of*; inattentiveness (*of mind*).

absent /'æbs(ə)nt/ *adj.* not present; not existing. —/əb'sent/ *v.refl.* to keep *oneself* away. —**absent-minded** *adj.* forgetful; with one's mind on other things. —**absently** *adv.* [from Old French or Latin *absens* (*abesse* = be away)]

absentee /æbs(ə)n'ti:/ *n.* one who absents himself. —**absentee landlord**, one not residing at the property he or she leases out. —**absenteeism** *n.*

absinthe /'æbsɪnθ/ *n.* a liqueur originally flavoured with wormwood, now usually with other herbs. [from French from Latin from Greek *apsinthion*]

absolute /'æbsəlu:t, -ju:t/ *adj.* complete, perfect; unrestricted, independent; not relative. —**absolute magnitude**, see ◊magnitude. **absolute majority**, a majority over all rivals combined. **absolute pitch**, the ability to recognize or reproduce exactly the pitch of a note in music. **absolute temperature**, one measured from absolute zero. **absolute zero**, the lowest temperature theoretically possible, zero degrees kelvin, equivalent to –273.15°C/–459.67°F, at which molecules are motionless. [from Latin]

absolutely /'æbsəlu:tlɪ/ *adv.* 1. completely, utterly, unreservedly. 2. actually. 3. in an absolute sense. 4. /-'lu:tlɪ/ quite so, yes.

absolute value or **modulus** in mathematics, the value, or magnitude, of a number irrespective of its sign (denoted $|n|$), and defined as the positive square root of n^2.

absolution /æbsə'lu:ʃ(ə)n/ *n.* formal forgiveness of a penitent's sins, declared by a priest. [from Old French from Latin]

absolutism *n.* or **absolute monarchy** a system of government in which the ruler or rulers have unlimited power. The principle of an absolute monarch, given a right to rule by God (see ◊divine right of kings), was extensively used in Europe during the 17th and 18th centuries. Absolute monarchy is contrasted with limited or constitutional monarchy, in which the sovereign's powers are defined or limited.

absolve /əb'zɒlv/ *v.t.* **1.** to clear *from* or *of* blame or guilt; to give absolution to. **2.** to free *from* an obligation. [from Latin *solvere* = loosen]

absorb /əb'sɔ:b/ *v.t.* to take in, to incorporate as part of itself or oneself; to reduce the effect of, to deal easily with (shock etc.); to engross the attention of. —**absorbency** *n.*, **absorbent** *adj.* & *n.*, **absorption** *n.* in science, the taking up of one substance by another, such as a liquid by a solid or a gas by a liquid. In biology, absorption describes the passing of nutrients or medication into and through tissues such as intestinal walls and blood vessels. In physics, absorption is the phenomenon by which a substance retains radiation of particular wavelengths; it also refers to the partial loss of energy resulting from the passing of light and other electromagnetic waves through a medium. In nuclear physics, absorption is the capture by elements, such as boron, of neutrons produced by fission in a reactor. [from French or Latin *sorbēre* = suck in]

absorptive /əb'sɔ:ptɪv/ *adj.* able to absorb things; engrossing. [from Latin]

abstain /əb'steɪn/ *v.i.* to restrain oneself, especially from drinking alcohol; to decline to use one's vote. —**abstainer** *n.*, **abstention** *n.* [from Anglo-French from Latin *abstinere* = withhold]

abstemious /æb'sti:mɪəs/ *adj.* sparing or not self-indulgent, especially in eating and drinking. —**abstemiously** *adv.*, **abstemiousness** *n.* [from Latin *abstemius* (*temetum* = strong drink)]

abstinence /'æbstɪnəns/ *n.* abstaining, especially from food or alcohol. —**abstinent** *adj.* [from Old French from Latin *abstinere* = withhold]

abstract[1] /'æbstrækt/ *adj.* **1.** having no material existence. **2.** theoretical rather than practical. —*n.* **1.** a summary. **2.** an abstract quality or idea. **3.** an example of ◊abstract art. —**abstract noun**, a noun denoting quality or state. —**abstractly** *adv.*, **abstractness** *n.* [from Old French or Latin *abstractus* (*trahere* = draw)]

abstract[2] /æb'strækt/ *v.t.* **1.** to take out, to remove. **2.** to make a written summary of. —**abstracted** *adj.* inattentive, with one's mind on other things. —**abstractor** *n.*

abstract art nonrepresentational art. Ornamental art without figurative representation occurs in most cultures. The modern abstract movement in sculpture and painting emerged in Europe and North America between 1910 and 1920. Two approaches produce different abstract styles: images that have been 'abstracted' from nature to the point at which they no longer reflect a conventional reality; and nonobjective, or 'pure', art forms, supposedly without reference to reality.

Abstract Expressionism a US movement in abstract art that emphasized the act of painting, the expression inherent in paint itself, and the interaction of artist, paint, and canvas. Abstract Expressionism emerged in New York in the early 1940s. Arshile Gorky, Franz Kline, Jackson Pollock, and Mark Rothko are associated with the movement.

abstraction /æb'strækʃ(ə)n/ *n.* **1.** abstracting, removing. **2.** an abstract idea. **3.** inattentiveness. [French or from Latin]

abstruse /æb'stru:s/ *adj.* hard to understand, profound. —**abstrusely** *adv.*, **abstruseness** *n.* [French or from Latin *abstrudere* = conceal]

absurd /əb'sɜ:d/ *adj.* wildly inappropriate; ridiculous. —**absurdity** *n.*, **absurdly** *adv.* [from French or Latin *surdus* = deaf, dull]

Absurd, Theatre of the avant-garde drama originating with a group of playwrights in the 1950s, including Samuel Beckett, Eugene Ionesco, Jean Genet, and Harold Pinter. Their work expressed the belief that in a godless universe human existence has no meaning or purpose and therefore all communication breaks down. Logical construction and argument gives way to irrational and illogical speech and to its ultimate conclusion, silence, as in Beckett's play *Breath* 1970.

Abu Bakr /æbu:'bækə/ or **Abu-Bekr** 573–634. 'Father of the virgin', name used by Abd-el-Ka'aba from about 618 when the prophet Muhammad married his daughter Ayesha.

He was a close adviser to Muhammad in the period 622–32. On the prophet's death, he became the first ◊caliph, adding Mesopotamia to the Muslim world and instigating expansion into Iraq and Syria.

Abu Dhabi /ˌæbu:'dɑ:bi/ sheikdom in SW Asia, on the Arabian Gulf, capital of the ◊United Arab Emirates. Formerly under British protection, it has been ruled since 1971 by Sheik Zayed Bin al-Nahayan, who is also president of the Supreme Council of Rulers of the United Arab Emirates.

Abuja /ə'bu:dʒə/ city in Nigeria under construction from 1976, intended to replace Lagos as capital. It was designed by the Japanese architect Kenzo Tange in the shape of a crescent.

Abu Musa /ˌæbu:'mu:sɑ:/ a small island in the Persian Gulf, formerly owned by the ruler of Sharjah. It was forcibly occupied by Iran in 1971.

abundant /ə'bʌndənt/ *adj.* more than enough, plenty; rich *in.* —**abundantly** *adv.*, **abundance** *n.* [from Latin *abundare* = overflow]

Abú Nuwás /ˌæbu: 'nu:wæs/ Hasan ibn Háni 762–c.815. Arab poet celebrated for the freedom, eroticism and ironic lightness of touch he brought to traditional forms.

abuse /ə'bju:z/ *v.t.* **1.** to make a bad or wrong use of; to maltreat. **2.** to attack verbally. —/ə'bju:s/ *n.* **1.** misuse; an unjust or corrupt practice. **2.** abusive words, insults. [from Old French from Latin *uti* = use]

Abu Simbel /ˌæbu: 'sɪmbəl/ the former site of two ancient temples in S Egypt, built during the reign of Ramses II and commemorating him and his wife Nefertari; in 1966–67, before the site was flooded by the Aswan High Dam, the temples were moved in sections.

abusive /ə'bju:sɪv/ *adj.* using insulting language, criticizing harshly. —**abusively** *adv.*

abut /ə'bʌt/ *v.t./i.* (-tt-) to adjoin, to border *on*; to touch at one side. [from Old French *but* = end and Latin]

abutment /ə'bʌtmənt/ *n.* a lateral supporting structure of a bridge, arch, etc.

abysmal /ə'bɪzm(ə)l/ *adj.* extremely bad; extreme and deplorable. —**abysmally** *adv.* [from Old French from Latin]

abyss /ə'bɪs/ *n.* a bottomless or deep chasm; an immeasurable depth. [from Latin from Greek *abussos* = bottomless (*a* = not and *bussos* = depth)]

abyssal /ə'bɪs(ə)l/ *adj.* at or of the ocean depths or floor, especially those below 1,000 metres containing relatively little marine life.

abyssal zone dark ocean area 2,000–6,000 m/6,500–19,500 ft deep; temperature 4°C/39°F. Three-quarters of the area of the deep ocean floor lies in the abyssal zone. It is too far from the surface for photosynthesis to take place. Some fish and crustaceans living there are blind or have their own light sources. The region above is the bathyal zone; the region below, the hadyal zone.

Abyssinia /ˌæbi'sɪnɪə/ former name of ◊Ethiopia.

a.c., AC abbreviation of ◊alternating current.

a/c abbreviation of account.

Ac symbol for actinium.

acacia *n.* any tree or shrub of the genus *Acacia* of the legume family Leguminosae. Acacias include the thorn trees of the African savanna and the gum arabic tree *A. senegal* of N Africa, and several North American species of the SW USA and Mexico. Acacias are found in warm regions of the world, particularly Australia. [Latin from Greek]

Academe /'ækədi:m/ *n.* (*literary*) **Groves of Academe**, a university environment. [from Greek]

academic /ækə'demɪk/ *adj.* **1.** of a college or university; scholarly as opposed to technical or practical. **2.** not of practical relevance. —*n.* a member of an academic institution. —**academically** *adv.* [from French or Latin]

academician /əkædə'mɪʃ(ə)n/ *n.* a member of an Academy.

academy /ə'kædəmɪ/ *n.* **1.** a school, especially for specialized training; (*Scottish*) a secondary school. **2.** a society of scholars or artists etc.; **the Academy**, the Royal Academy of Painting, Sculpture, and Architecture. [from Greek *Akadēmia* = name of garden where Plato taught, called after *Akadēmos* = Greek hero]

Academy award an annual cinema award in many categories given since 1927 by the American Academy of Motion Picture Arts and Sciences (founded by Louis B Mayer of Metro-Goldwyn-Mayer in 1927). Arguably cinema's most

Academy Award winners (Oscars)

Year	Award	
1975	Best Picture:	One Flew Over the Cuckoo's Nest
	Best Director:	Milos Forman One Flew Over the Cuckoo's Nest
	Best Actor:	Jack Nicholson One Flew Over the Cuckoo's Nest
	Best Actress:	Louise Fletcher One Flew Over the Cuckoo's Nest
1976	Best Picture:	Rocky
	Best Director:	John G Avildsen Rocky
	Best Actor:	Peter Finch Network
	Best Actress:	Faye Dunaway Network
1977	Best Picture:	Annie Hall
	Best Director:	Woody Allen Annie Hall
	Best Actor:	Richard Dreyfuss The Goodbye Girl
	Best Actress:	Diane Keaton Annie Hall
1978	Best Picture:	The Deerhunter
	Best Director:	Michael Cimino The Deerhunter
	Best Actor:	Jon Voight Coming Home
	Best Actress:	Jane Fonda Coming Home
1979	Best Picture:	Kramer vs Kramer
	Best Director:	Robert Beaton Kramer vs Kramer
	Best Actor:	Dustin Hoffman Kramer vs Kramer
	Best Actress:	Sally Field Norma Rae
1980	Best Picture:	Ordinary People
	Best Director:	Robert Redford Ordinary People
	Best Actor:	Robert De Niro Raging Bull
	Best Actress:	Sissy Spacek Coalminer's Daughter
1981	Best Picture:	Chariots of Fire
	Best Director:	Warren Beatty Reds
	Best Actor:	Henry Fonda On Golden Pond
	Best Actress:	Katharine Hepburn On Golden Pond
1982	Best Picture:	Gandhi
	Best Director:	Richard Attenborough Gandhi
	Best Actor:	Ben Kingsley Gandhi
	Best Actress:	Meryl Streep Sophie's Choice
1983	Best Picture:	Terms of Endearment
	Best Director:	James L Brooks Terms of Endearment
	Best Actor:	Robert Duvall Terms of Endearment
	Best Actress:	Shirley MacLaine Terms of Endearment
1984	Best Picture:	Amadeus
	Best Director:	Milos Forman Amadeus
	Best Actor:	F Murray Abraham Amadeus
	Best Actress:	Sally Field Places in the Heart
1985	Best Picture:	Out of Africa
	Best Director:	Sidney Pollack Out of Africa
	Best Actor:	William Hurt Kiss of the Spiderwoman
	Best Actress:	Geraldine Page The Trip to Bountiful
1986	Best Picture:	Platoon
	Best Director:	Oliver Stone Platoon
	Best Actor:	Paul Newman The Color of Money
	Best Actress:	Marlee Matlin Children of a Lesser God
1987	Best Picture:	The Last Emperor
	Best Director:	Bernardo Bertolucci The Last Emperor
	Best Actor:	Michael Douglas Wall Street
1988	Best Picture:	Rain Man
	Best Director:	Barry Levinson Rain Man
	Best Actor:	Dustin Hoffman Rain Man
	Best Actress:	Jodie Foster The Accused
1989	Best Picture:	My Left Foot
	Best Director:	Oliver Stone Born on the 4th of July
	Best Actor:	Daniel Day-Lewis My Left Foot
	Best Actress:	Jessica Tandy Driving Miss Daisy
1990	Best Picture:	Dances with Wolves
	Best Director:	Kevin Costner Dances with Wolves
	Best Actor:	Jeremy Irons Reversal of Fortune
	Best Actress:	Kathy Bates Misery

prestigious accolade, the award is a gold-plated statuette, which has been nicknamed 'Oscar' since 1931.

Academy, French or *Académie Française*. Literary society founded by ◊Richelieu in 1635 especially concerned with maintaining the purity of the French language; membership is limited to 40 'immortals' at a time.

Academy of Sciences, Soviet a society founded in 1725 by Catherine the Great in St Petersburg. The Academy has been responsible for such achievements as the ◊Sputnik satellite, and has branches in the Ukraine (welding, cybernetics), Armenia (astrophysics), and Georgia (mechanical engineering).

acanthus *n.* any herbaceous plant of the genus *Acanthus* with handsome lobed leaves. Twenty species are found in the Mediterranean region and the Old World tropics, including bear's breech *A. mollis*, whose leaves were used as a motif in classical architecture, especially on Corinthian columns. [Latin from Greek *akantha* = thorn]

a cappella *adj.* & *adv.* (of choral music) sung without instrumental accompaniment. [Italian = in the style of the chapel]

Acapulco /ˌækəˈpʊlkəʊ/ or **Acapulco de Juarez** port and holiday resort in Mexico; population (1985) 638,000.

ACAS /ˈeɪkæs/ acronym from Advisory, Conciliation, and Arbitration Service. The service was set up in 1975 to provide such facilities as a means of avoiding or resolving industrial disputes, and to promote the improvement of collective bargaining.

accede /ækˈsiːd/ *v.i.* 1. to take office, to come *to* the throne. 2. to agree *to* (a proposal etc.). [from Latin *cedere* = go]

accelerate /əkˈseləreɪt/ *v.t./i.* to move faster or happen earlier; to cause to do this; to increase the speed of a motor vehicle. —**acceleration** /-ˈreɪʃən/ *n.* the rate of change of the velocity of a moving body. [from Latin *accelerare* (*celer* = swift)]

accelerated freeze drying see ◊AFD.

accelerator /əkˈseləreɪtə(ə)/ *n.* 1. a device for increasing speed, a pedal that controls the throttle in a motor

vehicle. 2. in physics, a device to bring charged particles (such as ◊protons) up to high speeds and energies, at which they can be of use in industry, medicine, and pure physics.

accelerometer *n.* an apparatus, either mechanical or electromechanical, for measuring acceleration or deceleration—that is, the rate of increase or decrease in the ◊velocity of a moving object.

accent /ˈæksent/ *n.* 1. prominence given to a syllable by stress or pitch. 2. a mark used with a letter or word to indicate pitch, stress, quality of vowel, etc. 3. a particular (especially local or national) mode of pronunciation. 4. a distinctive feature or emphasis. —/ækˈsent/ *v.t.* 1. to pronounce with an accent. 2. to write accents on. 3. to accentuate. —**accentual** /ækˈsentjuːəl/ *adj.* [from Latin *accentus* (*cantus* = song)]

accentor /əkˈsentə(ə)/ *n.* a bird of the genus *Prunella*, e. g. the hedge sparrow. [Latin, from *ad* = to and *cantor* = singer]

accentuate /əkˈsentjuːeɪt/ *v.t.* to emphasize, to make prominent. —**accentuation** /-ˈeɪʃ(ə)n/ *n.* [from Latin]

accept /əkˈsept/ *v.t.* 1. to consent to receive, to take willingly; to answer (an invitation or suitor) affirmatively. 2. to regard favourably; to tolerate or submit to. 3. to take as valid. 4. to undertake (a responsibility etc.). —**acceptance**, *n.* **acceptor** *n.* [from Old French or Latin *acceptare* (*capere* = take)]

acceptable *adj.* worth accepting, welcome; tolerable. —**acceptably** *adv.*, **acceptability** /-ˈbɪlɪtɪ/ *n.*

access /ˈækses/ *n.* 1. a way in, a means of approaching, reaching, or using. 2. an outburst *of* emotion. —*v.t.* 1. to obtain (data) from a computer. 2. to accession. [from Old French or Latin *accedere*]

accessible /əkˈsesɪb(ə)l/ *adj.* that may be reached or obtained. —**accessibility** /-ˈbɪlɪtɪ/ *n.*, **accessibly** *adv.*, [French and from Latin]

accession /əkˈseʃən/ *n.* 1. acceding or attaining (*to* a throne, office, etc.). 2. a thing added. —*v.t.* to record the addition of (a new item) to a library or museum.

accessory /ək'sesərɪ/ *n.* **1.** an additional or extra thing; (usually in *plural*) a small attachment or fitting. **2.** a person who helps in or is privy *to* an act, especially a crime. He or she may be either 'before the fact' (assisting, ordering, or procuring another to commit a crime) or 'after the fact' (giving assistance after the crime). —*adj.* additional, contributing in a minor way. [from Latin]

access time in computing, the 'reaction time': the time taken after being given an instruction before the computer reads from, or writes to, ◊memory.

accidence /'æksɪdəns/ *n.* the part of grammar that deals with the way words are inflected. [from Latin]

accident /'æksɪdənt/ *n.* an event that is unexpected or without apparent cause; an unintentional act, chance; an unfortunate (especially a harmful) event. [from Old French from Latin *accidens* (*cadere* = fall)]

accidental /æksɪ'dentəl/ *adj.* happening or done by accident. —*n.* in music, a sign indicating temporary departure from a key signature. —**accidentally** *adv.* [from Latin]

acclaim *v.t.* to welcome with shouts of approval, to applaud enthusiastically; to hail as. —*n.* a shout of applause or welcome. —**acclamation** /æklə'meɪʃən/ *n.* [from Latin *clamare* = shout]

acclimation *n.* or **acclimatization** the physiological changes induced in an organism by exposure to new environmental conditions. When humans move to higher altitudes, for example, the number of red blood cells rises to increase the oxygen-carrying capacity of the blood in order to compensate for the lower levels of oxygen in the air.

acclimatize /ə'klaɪmətaɪz/ *v.t./i.* to make or become used to a new climate or conditions. —**acclimatization** /-'zeɪʃən/ *n.* [from French *à* = to and *climat* = climate]

acclivity /ə'klɪvɪtɪ/ *n.* an upward slope. [from Latin *clivus* = slope]

accolade /ækə'leɪd/ *n.* **1.** bestowal of praise. **2.** a sign at the bestowal of a knighthood, now usually a tap on the shoulder with the flat of a sword. [French (Latin *collum* = neck)]

accommodate /ə'kɒmədeɪt/ *v.t.* **1.** to provide lodging or room for. **2.** to do a favour to, to oblige or supply (a person *with*). **3.** to adapt, to harmonize. [from Latin *accommodare* (*commodus* = fitting)]

accommodating *adj.* obliging, compliant.

accommodation /əkɒmə'deɪʃən/ *n.* **1.** lodging, living-premises. **2.** adaptation, adjustment; a convenient arrangement. **3.** the ability of the eye to see objects clearly whether they are near or far away. The shape of the eye's lens is changed so that sharp images are focused on the ◊retina, becoming fatter (more biconvex) when focusing the image of a near object. From about the age of 40, the lens in the human eye becomes less flexible, causing the defect of vision known as **presbyopia** or lack of accommodation. —**accommodation address**, one used on letters to a person unable to give a permanent address. [French or from Latin]

accompaniment /ə'kʌmpənɪmənt/ *n.* **1.** an instrumental or orchestral part supporting or partnering a solo instrument, voice, or group. **2.** an accompanying thing. [from French]

accompanist /ə'kʌmpənɪst/ *n.* one who plays a musical accompaniment.

accompany /ə'kʌmpənɪ/ *v.t.* **1.** to go with, to travel with as a companion or helper; to be done or found with. **2.** to provide in addition. **3.** in music, to support or partner with an accompaniment. [from French]

accomplice /ə'kʌmplɪs/ *n.* a partner in crime or wrongdoing. [from French *complice* from Latin *complex* = confederate]

accomplish /ə'kʌmplɪʃ/ *v.t.* to succeed in doing, to complete. [from Old French from Latin *complere* = complete]

accomplished /ə'kʌmplɪʃt/ *adj.* skilled, having many accomplishments.

accomplishment /ə'kʌmplɪʃmənt/ *n.* **1.** an acquired skill, especially a social one. **2.** accomplishing, completion. **3.** a thing achieved.

accord /ə'kɔːd/ *v.t./i.* **1.** to be consistent *with.* **2.** to grant, to give. —*n.* conformity, agreement. —**of one's own accord,** without being asked or compelled. [from French from Latin *cor* = heart]

accordance /ə'kɔːdəns/ *n.* conformity, agreement. —**accordant** *adj.*

according *adv.* **according as,** in a manner or to a degree that varies as. **according to,** in a manner corresponding to; as stated by.

accordingly *adv.* as the (stated) circumstances suggest.

accordion /ə'kɔːdiən/ *n.* a musical instrument of the reed organ type comprising left and right wind-chests connected by a flexible bellows. The right hand plays melody on a piano-style keyboard while the left hand has a system of push-buttons for selecting single notes or chord harmonies. Invented by Cyrill Damien (1772–1847) in Vienna in 1829, it spread throughout the world and can be heard in the popular music of France, China, Russia, and the American South. [from German from Italian *accordare* = tune]

accost /ə'kɒst/ *v.t.* to approach and speak to; (of a prostitute) to solicit. [from French from Italian from Latin *costa* = rib)]

account /ə'kaʊnt/ *n.* **1.** a statement of money, goods, or services received or expended; a credit or similar business arrangement with a bank or firm; a record of this. **2.** a description, a report. **3.** importance, advantage. **4.** a reckoning. —*v.t./i.* to regard as. —**account for,** to give a reckoning of; to provide or serve as an explanation for; to kill or overcome. **on account of,** because of. [from Old French *aconter* (*conter* = count)]

accountable *adj.* having to account (*for* one's actions); explicable. —**accountability** /-'bɪlɪtɪ/ *n.*

accountant *n.* one who keeps or examines business accounts. —**accountancy** *n.* financial management of business and other organizations, from balance sheets to policy decisions.

accounting *n.* keeping or examining accounts; accountancy.

accoutrements /ə'kuːtrəmənts/ *n.pl.* equipment, trappings. [French]

Accra /ə'krɑː/ capital of Ghana; population of greater Accra (including the port, Tema) (1984) 1,420,000. The port trades in cacao, gold, and timber. Industries include engineering, brewing, and food processing. Osu (Christiansborg) Castle is the presidential residence.

accredit /ə'kredɪt/ *v.t.* **1.** to attribute, to credit (*with* a saying etc.). **2.** to send (an ambassador etc.) with credentials. **3.** to gain belief or influence for. —**accreditation** /-'teɪʃən/ *n.,* **accredited** *adj.* [from French]

accretion /ə'kriːʃən/ *n.* a growth or increase by gradual addition; matter added, adhesion of this. [from Latin *accretio* (*crescere* = grow)]

accrue /ə'kruː/ *v.t./i.* to come as a natural increase or advantage; to accumulate. [from Anglo-French from Latin]

accumulate /ə'kjuːmjuːleɪt/ *v.t./i.* to get more and more of; to increase in quantity or mass. —**accumulation** /-'leɪʃən/ *n.* [from Latin *accumulare* (*cumulus* = heap)]

accumulator /ə'kjuːmjuːleɪtə/ *n.* **1.** a rechargeable electric cell, a storage ◊battery. **2.** a collective bet, usually on horse races (normally four or more), such that the winnings from one race are carried forward as the stake on the next, resulting in a potentially enormous return for a small initial outlay. **3.** a storage register in a computer.

accurate /'ækjuərət/ *adj.* precise, conforming exactly to a standard or to truth. —**accuracy** *n.,* **accurately** *adv.* [from Latin *accuratus* = done carefully (*curare* = care)]

accursed /ə'kɜːsɪd/ *adj.* lying under a curse; (*colloquial*) detestable, annoying. [Old English]

accusation /ækjuː'zeɪʃən/ *n.* **1.** a statement accusing a person. **2.** accusing, being accused. [from Old French from Latin *accusare*]

accusative /ə'kjuːzətɪv/ *n.* in grammar, the case expressing the object of a verb or preposition. —*adj.* in grammar, of or in the accusative. [from Old French or Latin]

accusatorial /əkjuːzə'tɔːrɪəl/ *adj.* (of procedure) in which the prosecutor is distinct from the judge (as opposed to *inquisitorial*). [from Latin]

accusatory /ə'kjuːzətərɪ/ *adj.* of or conveying an accusation. [from Latin]

accuse /ə'kjuːz/ *v.t.* to state that one lays the blame for a fault or crime etc. upon. —**accuser** *n.* [from Old French from Latin *accusare* (*causa* = cause)]

accustom /ə'kʌstəm/ *v.t.* to make or become used *to.* [from Old French from Latin]

accustomed /ə'kʌstəmd/ *adj.* customary; used *to.*

ace /eɪs/ *n.* **1.** a playing card etc. with one spot. **2.** one who excels in some activity. **3.** a stroke in tennis (especially a service) that is too good for an opponent to return. **4.** a point scored in rackets, badminton, etc. **—within an ace of,** on the verge of. [from Old French from Latin *as* = one]

Acer /ˈeɪsə/ *n.* a genus of trees and shrubs of N temperate regions with over 115 species, including ◊sycamore and ◊maple.

acerbity /əˈsɜːbɪtɪ/ *n.* **1.** sharpness in speech or manner. **2.** sourness. [from Latin *acerbus* = sour-tasting]

acetaldehyde *n.* common name for ◊ethanal.

acetate /ˈæsɪteɪt/ *n.* common name for ◊ethanoate. [from French from Latin]

acetic /əˈsiːtɪk/ *adj.* of or like vinegar. **—acetic acid,** the common name for ◊ethanoic acid, the acid that gives vinegar its characteristic taste and smell. [from French from Latin *acetum* = vinegar]

acetone /ˈæsɪtəʊn/ *n.* the common name for ◊propanone, a colourless volatile liquid that dissolves organic compounds.

acetylene /əˈsetɪliːn/ *n.* the common name for ◊ethyne.

acetylsalicylic acid the chemical name for the painkilling drug ◊aspirin.

Achaea /əˈkiːə/ in ancient Greece, and also today, an area of the N Peloponnese; the **Achaeans** were the predominant society during the Mycenaean period and are said by Homer to have taken part in the siege of Troy.

Achaean League /əˈkiːən/ the union in 275 BC of most of the cities of the N Peloponnese, which managed to defeat ◊Sparta, but was itself defeated by the Romans in 146 BC.

Achaemenid dynasty /əˈkiːmənɪd/ the family ruling the Persian Empire 550–330 BC, and named after Achaemenes, ancestor of Cyrus the Great, founder of the empire. His successors included Cambyses, Darius I, Xerxes, and Darius III, who, as the last Achaemenid ruler, was killed after defeat in battle against Alexander the Great in 330 BC.

Achates /əˈkeɪtiːz/ a character in the *Aeneid*, an epic poem by the Roman poet Virgil from the 1st century BC. Achates was the friend of the hero Aeneas. The name is proverbial for a faithful companion.

ache /eɪk/ *n.* a continuous or prolonged dull pain or mental distress. **—v.i.** to suffer or be the source of this. **—achy** *adj.* [from Old English]

Achebe /əˈtʃeɪbi/ Chinua 1930– . Nigerian novelist, whose themes include the social and political impact of European colonialism on African people, and the problems of newly independent African nations. His first novel, *Things Fall Apart* 1958, was widely acclaimed; *Anthills of the Savannah* 1987, set in a fictional African country, won the Nobel Prize for Literature in 1989.

achene /əˈkiːn/ *n.* a small dry one-seeded fruit that does not split open to disperse the seed, e.g. the strawberry pip. [from Greek *a* = not and *khainō* = gape]

Acheson /ˈætʃɪsən/ Dean (Gooderham) 1893–1971. US politician; as undersecretary of state 1945–47 in ◊Truman's Democratic administration, he was associated with George C ◊Marshall in preparing the ◊Marshall Plan, and succeeded him as secretary of state 1949–53.

Great Britain has lost an Empire and has not yet found a role.

Dean Acheson
speech at the Military Academy, West Point
5 Dec 1962

---

achieve /əˈtʃiːv/ *v.t.* to reach or attain by effort; to earn (a reputation etc.); to accomplish. [from Old French *a chief* = to a head]

achievement /əˈtʃiːvmənt/ *n.* **1.** something achieved; an act of achieving. **2.** in heraldry, an escutcheon with adjuncts, or a bearing, especially in memory of a distinguished feat.

Achilles /əˈkɪliːz/ Greek hero of Homer's *Iliad*. He was the son of Peleus, king of the Myrmidons in Thessaly, and the sea nymph Thetis, who rendered him invulnerable, except for the heel by which she held him, by dipping him in the river Styx. Achilles killed Hector in the Trojan War and was himself killed by Paris who shot a poisoned arrow into Achilles' heel. **—Achilles' heel,** a weak or

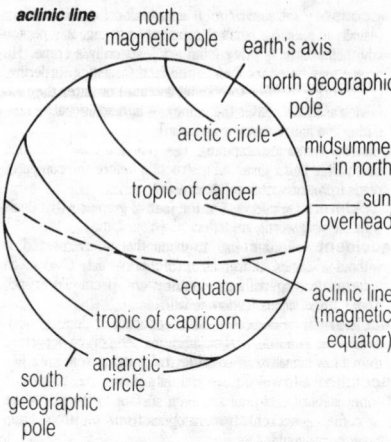

aclinic line / north magnetic pole / earth's axis / north geographic pole / arctic circle / midsummer — in north / tropic of cancer / sun overhead / equator / aclinic line (magnetic equator) / tropic of capricorn / antarctic circle / south geographic pole

vulnerable point. **Achilles' tendon,** a tendon attaching the calf muscles to the heel.

achromatic /ækrəˈmætɪk/ *adj.* in optics, free from colour; transmitting light without decomposing it into constituent colours. **—achromatic lens,** a combination of lenses made from materials of different refractive indexes, constructed in such a way as to minimize chromatic ◊aberration. [from French from Greek *a* = not and *chromatic*]

acid /ˈæsɪd/ *n.* any of a class of substances that contain hydrogen and neutralize alkalis, turn blue litmus red, and of which the principal types are sour and able to corrode or dissolve metals; any sour substance. **—adj.** sharp-tasting, sour; looking or sounding bitter. **—acid house,** a kind of synthesized music with a simple repetitive beat. **acid test,** a crucial and conclusive test. (Acid is applied to a metal to test whether it is gold or not.) **—acidic** /əˈsɪdɪk/ *adj.*, **acidity** /əˈsɪdɪtɪ/ *n.* [from French or Latin *acēre* = be sour]

acidify /əˈsɪdɪfaɪ/ *v.t.* to make or become sour.

acidosis /æsɪˈdəʊsɪs/ *n.* an over-acid condition of blood or body tissue.

acid rain acidic rainfall, thought to be caused principally by the release into the atmosphere of sulphur dioxide (SO_2) and oxides of nitrogen. Sulphur dioxide is formed from the burning of fossil fuels such as coal that contain high quantities of sulphur, and nitrogen oxides are contributed from industrial activities and automobile exhaust fumes.

acid salt a chemical compound formed by the partial neutralization of a dibasic or tribasic ◊acid (one that contains two or three hydrogen atoms). Although a salt, it contains replaceable hydrogen, so it may undergo the typical reactions of an acid. Examples are sodium hydrogen sulphate, $NaHSO_4$, and acid phosphates.

acidulate /əˈsɪdjʊleɪt/ *v.t.* to make somewhat acid. [from Latin *acidulus* = somewhat sour]

acidulous /əˈsɪdʊləs/ *adj.* somewhat acid.

acknowledge /əkˈnɒlɪdʒ/ *v.t.* **1.** to agree to the truth or validity of, to admit. **2.** to report the receipt of. **3.** to show appreciation of. **—acknowledgement** *n.* [from obsolete verb *knowledge*]

aclinic line the magnetic equator, an imaginary line near the equator, where the compass needle balances horizontally, where the attraction of the north and south magnetic poles is equal.

acme /ˈækmɪ/ *n.* the highest point, the point of perfection. [Greek = highest point]

acne /ˈæknɪ/ *n.* inflammation of the oil glands of the skin, occurring mainly among adolescents and young adults, which produces red pimples. [from erroneous Greek *aknas* for *akmas* (*akmē* = facial eruption)]

acolyte /ˈækəlaɪt/ *n.* a person assisting a priest in certain church services; an assistant. [from French or Latin from Greek *akolouthos* = follower]

Aconcagua /ækənˈkægwə/ an extinct volcano in the Argentine Andes, the highest peak in the Americas. Height 6,960 m/22,834 ft. It was first climbed by Vines and Zeebruggen in 1897.

aconite *n.* or **monkshood** a herbaceous Eurasian plant *Aconitum napellus* of the buttercup family Ranunculaceae, with hooded blue-mauve flowers. It produces aconitine, a powerful alkaloid with narcotic and analgesic properties. —**winter aconite,** a yellow-flowered plant of the genus *Eranthis,* blooming in winter. [from French or Latin from Greek]

acorn *n.* the fruit of the oak tree, a ◊nut growing in a shallow cup. [Old English]

acouchi *n.* any of several small S American rodents, genus *Myoprocta.* They have white-tipped tails, and are smaller relatives of the ◊agouti.

acoustic /əˈkuːstɪk/ *adj.* 1. of sound or the sense of hearing; of acoustics. 2. in music, (of a performance or instrument) sounding without electrical amplification or assistance. —*n.* acoustics. —**acoustics** *n.pl.* the properties or qualities (of a room etc.) affecting the transmission of sound; (as *singular*) the science of sound. —**acoustical** *adj.,* **acoustically** *adv.* [from Greek *akouō* = hear]

acoustic ohm the c.g.s. unit of acoustic impedance (the ratio of the sound pressure on a surface to the sound flux through the surface). It is analogous to the ohm as the unit of electrical ◊impedance.

acquaint /əˈkweɪnt/ *v.t.* to make aware or familiar. —**be acquainted with,** to know slightly. [from Old French from Latin *accognitare* (*cognoscere* = know)]

acquaintance *n.* 1. being acquainted. 2. a person one knows slightly.

acquiesce /ækwiˈes/ *v.i.* to agree (tacitly), to raise no objection. —**acquiesce in,** to accept (an arrangement etc.). —**acquiescence** *n.,* **acquiescent** *adj.* [from Latin *quiescere* = rest]

acquire /əˈkwaɪə/ *v.t.* to gain by and for oneself. —**acquired taste,** a liking gained by experience, not instantly. —**acquirement** *n.,* **acquisition** /ækwiˈzɪʃən/ *n.* [from Old French from Latin *acquirere* (*quaerere* = seek)]

acquired character a feature of the body that develops during the lifetime of an individual, usually as a result of repeated use or disuse, such as the enlarged muscles of a weightlifter. ◊Lamarck's theory of evolution assumed that acquired characters were passed from parent to offspring.

acquired immune deficiency syndrome the full name for the disease ◊AIDS.

acquisitive /əˈkwɪzɪtɪv/ *adj.* keen to acquire things. —**acquisitively** *adv.,* **acquisitiveness** *n.* [from Latin]

acquit /əˈkwɪt/ *v.t.* (-tt-) to declare (a person) to be not guilty (*of* an offence etc.). —**acquit oneself,** to perform, to conduct oneself. [from Old French from Latin *acquitare* = pay debt]

acquittal /əˈkwɪtəl/ *n.* 1. in law, the setting free of someone charged with a crime after a trial. 2. performance (*of* a duty).

acre /ˈeɪkə/ *n.* a traditional English measure of land equal to 4,840 square yards (4,047 sq m/0.405 ha). It was originally the size that a yoke of oxen could plough in a day. [Old English = field]

Acre /ˈeɪkə/ or **Akko** seaport in Israel; population (1983) 37,000. Taken by the Crusaders in 1104, it was captured by ◊Saladin in 1187 and retaken by ◊Richard I (the Lionhearted) in 1191. Napoleon failed in a siege in 1799; Gen ◊Allenby captured it in 1918; and it became part of Israel in 1948.

acreage /ˈeɪkərɪdʒ/ *n.* the total number of acres; an extent of land.

acre-foot *n.* a unit sometimes used to measure large volumes of water, such as the capacity of a reservoir (equal to its area in acres multiplied by its average depth in feet). One acre-foot equals 43,560 cu ft/1,233.5 cu m or the amount of water covering one acre to a depth of one foot.

acrid /ˈækrɪd/ *adj.* bitterly pungent; bitter in manner or temper. —**acridity** /əˈkrɪdɪti/ *n.* [from Latin *acer* = keen]

acridine *n.* $C_{13}H_9N$, an organic compound that occurs in coal tar; it is extracted by dilute acids. It is also obtained synthetically. It is used to make dyes and drugs.

acrimonious /ækriˈməʊniəs/ *adj.* bitter in manner or temper. —**acrimoniously** *adv.,* **acrimony** /ˈækrɪməni/ *n.* [from French or Latin]

acrobat /ˈækrəbæt/ *n.* a performer of spectacular gymnastic feats. —**acrobatic** /-ˈbætɪk/ *adj.,* **acrobatically**

adv. [from French from Greek *akron* = summit and *bainō* = walk]

acrobatics /ækrəˈbætɪks/ *n.pl.* acrobatic feats.

acronym /ˈækrənɪm/ *n.* a word formed from the initial letters and/or syllables of other words, intended as a pronounceable abbreviation, for example NATO (North Atlantic Treaty Organization). Many acronyms are so successfully incorporated into everyday language that their original significance is widely overlooked. [from Greek *akron* = extremity and *onoma* = name]

acrophobia *n.* a ◊phobia involving fear of heights.

acropolis /əˈkrɒpəlis/ *n.* the citadel or upper fortified part of an ancient Greek city. —**the Acropolis,** that at Athens, containing the Parthenon, Erechtheum, and other noted buildings, mostly dating from the 5th century BC. The term is also used for analogous structures, such as the massive granite-built ruins of Great ◊Zimbabwe. [from Greek *akron* = summit and *polis* = city]

across /əˈkrɒs/ *prep.* & *adv.* 1. from side to side (of). 2. to or on the other side (of). 3. forming a cross with. 4. so as to be understood or accepted. —**across the board,** applying to all. **come** or **run across,** to meet or find by chance. [from Old French *croix* = cross]

acrostic /əˈkrɒstɪk/ *n.* a word-puzzle or poem in which certain letters (usually the first or first and last in each line) form word(s). A **single acrostic** is formed by the initial letters of lines only, while a **double acrostic** is formed by both initial and final letters. [from French or Greek *akron* = end and *stikhos* = row]

acrylic /əˈkrɪlɪk/ *adj.* of material made from a synthetic polymer derived from acrylic acid. —*n.* an acrylic fibre, plastic, or resin. —**acrylic acid,** common name for ◊propenoic acid, an unsaturated organic acid. [from Latin *acer* = pungent and *olēre* = smell]

act *n.* 1. a thing done; the process of doing something. 2. a piece of entertainment. 3. a pretence. 4. a main division of a play or opera. 5. a decree or law made by a parliament. —*v.t./i.* 1. to perform actions, to behave; to perform functions; to have an effect. 2. to be an actor or actress. 3. to perform (a part) in a play etc.; to portray by actions. —**Acts (of the Apostles),** a book of the New Testament immediately following the Gospels, relating the early history of the Church and dealing largely with the lives and work of St Peter and St Paul. It is traditionally ascribed to St Luke. [from Old French and Latin *actus* (*agere* = do)]

ACT abbreviation of Australian Capital Territory.

ACTH (adrenocorticotropic hormone) a ◊hormone, secreted by the anterior lobe of the ◊pituitary gland, which controls the production of corticosteroid hormones by the ◊adrenal gland. It is commonly produced as a response to stress.

actinic /ækˈtɪnɪk/ *adj.* having photochemical properties, as of short-wavelength radiation. [from Greek *aktis* = ray]

actinide /ˈæktɪnaɪd/ *n.* any of a series of 15 radioactive metallic elements ranging from actinium (atomic number 89) to lawrencium (103). Elements 89 to 95 occur in nature; the rest of the series are synthetic elements only. Actinides are grouped together because of their chemical similarities (for example, they are all bivalent), the properties differing only slightly with atomic number.

actinium /ækˈtɪniəm/ *n.* a white radioactive metallic element, symbol Ac, atomic number 89, selective atomic mass 227. It occurs with uranium and radium in ◊pitchblende, and can be synthesized by bombarding radium with neutrons. Actinium was discovered in 1899 by the French chemist André Debierne. [from Greek *aktis* = ray]

action /ˈækʃən/ *n.* 1. the process of doing or performing, exertion of energy or influence. 2. a thing done; a series of events in a drama etc. 3. a battle, fighting. 4. a way of moving or functioning, the mechanism of an instrument. 5. a lawsuit. —**action replay,** a play-back (at normal speed or in slow motion) of a televised incident in a sports match. **out of action,** not working. [from Old French from Latin]

actionable *adj.* providing ground for an action at law.

action and reaction in physical mechanics, equal and opposite effects produced by a force acting on an object. For example, the pressure of expanding gases from the burning of fuel in a rocket engine (a force) produces an equal and opposite reaction, which causes the rocket to move.

Action Française a French extreme nationalist political movement founded in 1899, first led by Charles Maurras

(1868–1952); it stressed the essential unity of all French people in contrast to the socialist doctrines of class warfare. Its influence peaked in the 1920s.

action painting or **gesture painting** in US art, a dynamic school of ◊Abstract Expressionism. It emphasized the importance of the physical act of painting, sometimes expressed with both inventiveness and aggression, and on occasion performed for the camera. Jackson Pollock was the leading exponent.

action potential in biology, a change in the potential difference (voltage) across the membrane of a nerve-cell when an impulse passes along it. A change in potential (from about –60 to +45 millivolts) accompanies the passage of sodium and potassium ions across the membrane.

Actium, Battle of /'æktɪəm/ a naval battle in which ◊Augustus defeated the combined fleets of ◊Mark Antony and ◊Cleopatra in 31 BC. The site is at Akri, a promontory in W Greece.

activate /'æktɪveɪt/ *v.t.* 1. to make active. 2. to make radioactive. —**activation** /-'veɪʃən/ *n.*, **activator** *n.*

activation energy in chemistry, the energy required to start a chemical reaction.

active /'æktɪv/ *adj.* 1. consisting in or characterized by action, energetic; working, operative; having an effect. 2. radioactive. 3. in grammar, attributing the action of the verb to the person or thing whence it proceeds (e.g. in *we saw him*). —*n.* in grammar, the active voice or form of a verb. —**active voice**, in grammar, that comprising the active forms of verbs. —**actively** *adv.*, **activeness** *n.* [from Old French or Latin]

active transport in cells, the use of energy to move substances, usually molecules or ions, across a membrane.

activist /'æktɪvɪst/ *n.* one who follows a policy of vigorous action in a cause, especially in politics. —**activism** *n.*

activity /æk'tɪvətɪ/ *n.* 1. being active, the exertion of energy. 2. a sphere or kind of action. 3. (especially in *plural*) actions, occupations. 4. radioactivity.

activity series alternative name for ◊reactivity series.

act of Congress in the USA, a bill or resolution passed by both houses of Congress, the Senate and the House of Representatives, which becomes law with the signature of the president. If vetoed by the president, it may still become law if it returns to Congress again and is passed by a majority of two-thirds in each house.

act of God a legal term meaning some sudden and irresistible act of nature that could not reasonably have been foreseen or prevented, such as storms, earthquakes, or sudden death.

act of Parliament in Britain, a change in the law originating in Parliament and called a statute. Such acts may be either public (of general effect), local, or private. Before an act receives the royal assent and becomes law it is a 'bill'. The body of English statute law comprises all the acts passed by Parliament: the existing list opens with the Statute of Merton, passed in 1235. An act (unless it is stated to be for a definite period and then to come to an end) remains on the statute book until it is repealed.

Acton /'æktən/ Eliza 1799–1859. English cookery writer and poet, whose *Modern Cookery for Private Families* 1845 influenced Mrs ◊Beeton.

actor *n.* a performer in a drama, film, etc. —**actress** *n. fem.* [Latin = doer]

Actors Studio a theatre workshop in New York City, established in 1947 by Cheryl Crawford and Elia Kazan. Under Lee Strasberg, who became artistic director in 1948, it became known for the study of Stanislavsky's ◊Method acting.

actual /'æktʃuəl/ *adj.* existing in fact, real; current. [from Old French from Latin]

actuality /æktʃu'ælɪtɪ/ *n.* reality; (in *plural*) existing conditions.

actually /'æktʃuəlɪ/ *adv.* 1. really. 2. at present. 3. strange as it may seem.

actuary /'æktʃuərɪ/ *n.* an expert in statistics, especially one who calculates insurance risks and premiums. —**actuarial** /-'eərɪəl/ *adj.* [from Latin *actuarius* = bookkeeper]

actuate /'æktʃueɪt/ *v.t.* to activate (a movement or process), to cause to function; to cause (a person) to act. —**actuation** /-'eɪʃən/ *n.*, **actuator** *n.* [from Latin]

acuity /ə'kjuːətɪ/ *n.* sharpness, acuteness. [from French or Latin]

acumen /'ækjuːmən/ *n.* shrewdness. [Latin = sharp thing]

acupuncture /'ækjupʌŋktʃə(r)/ *n.* a system of inserting long, thin metal needles into the body at predetermined points to relieve pain, as an anaesthetic in surgery, and to assist healing. The needles are rotated manually or electrically. The method, developed in ancient China and increasingly popular in the West, is thought to work by somehow stimulating the brain's own painkillers, the endorphins. —**acupuncturist** *n.* [from Latin *acu* = with a needle]

acute /ə'kjuːt/ *adj.* 1. sharp or severe in its effect. 2. shrewd, perceptive. 3. in medicine, pertaining to a condition that develops and resolves quickly; not ◊chronic. 4. (of sound) high, shrill. —**acute accent**, a mark over a vowel ´ to show its quality or length. **acute angle**, one of less than 90°. —**acutely** *adv.*, **acuteness** *n.* [from Latin *acutus* (*acuere* = sharpen)]

ad *n.* (*colloquial*) abbreviation of advertisement.

ad- prefix (usually assimilated to **ac-** before *c, k, q,* to **af-** etc. before *f, g, l, n, p, r, s, t;* reduced to **a-** before *sc, sp, st*) implying motion or direction to; change into; addition, adherence, increase; simple intensification. [from Old French or Latin *ad* = to]

AD in the Christian calendar, abbreviation of *anno Domini* [Latin = in the year of the Lord]

ADA *n.* a computer-programming language, developed and owned by the US Department of Defense, designed for use in situations in which the computer controls a process or machine, such as a military aircraft, directly. The language took over five years to specify, and became available for commercial use only in the late 1980s. [from *Ada* Lovelace, regarded as the world's first computer programmer]

adage /'ædɪdʒ/ *n.* a traditional maxim, a proverb. [French from Latin *adagium* (*ad* = to and *aiere* = say)]

adagio /ə'dɑːʒɪəʊ/ *adv.* in music, in slow time. —*n.* (*plural adagios*) in music, a movement to be played in this way. [Italian]

Adam /'ædəm/ a family of Scottish architects and designers. **William Adam** (1689–1748) was the leading Scottish architect of his day, and his son **Robert Adam** (1728–1792) is considered one of the greatest British architects of the late 18th century, who transformed the prevailing Palladian fashion in architecture to a Neo-Classical style. He designed interiors for many great country houses and earned a considerable reputation as a furniture designer.

Adam in Hebrew tradition, the first man. As described in the Old Testament, Adam was formed by God from dust and given the breath of life. He was placed in the Garden of Eden, where ◊Eve was created from his rib and given to

Adams US photographer Ansel Adams.

him as a companion. Because she tempted him, he tasted the forbidden fruit of the Tree of Knowledge of Good and Evil, for which trespass they were expelled from the Garden. —**Adam's apple**, the projection of cartilage at the front of the neck, especially in men. [from Hebrew *adham* = man]

adamant /'ædəmənt/ *adj.* stubbornly resolute. —**adamantine** /-'mæntaɪn/ *adj.* [from Old French from Latin from Greek *adamas* = very hard metal or stone]

Adam de la Halle /æ'dɒm də lɑː 'æl/ *c.*1240–*c.*1290. French poet and composer. His *Jeu de Robin et Marion*, written in Italy about 1282, is a theatrical work with dialogue and songs set to what were apparently popular tunes of the day. It is sometimes called the forerunner of comic opera.

Adams /'ædəmz/ Ansel 1902–1984. US photographer, known for his printed images of dramatic landscapes and organic forms of the American West. He was associated with the ◊Zone System of exposure estimation.

Adams Gerry (Gerard) 1948– . Northern Ireland politician, president of Provisional Sinn Féin (the political wing of the IRA). He was elected a member of Parliament in 1983 but declined to take up his Westminster seat. He has been criticized for failing to denounce IRA violence. In the 1970s he was interned because of his connections with the IRA, he was interned, but later released.

Adams John 1735–1826. second president of the USA 1797–1801, and vice president 1789–97. He was born at Quincy, Massachusetts. He was a member of the Continental Congress 1774–78, and signed the Declaration of Independence. In 1779 he went to France and negotiated the treaties that ended the American Revolution. He was suspicious of the French Revolution, but resisted calls for war with France. In 1785 he became the first US ambassador in London.

Adams John Coolidge 1947– . US composer and conductor, director of the New Music Ensemble 1972–81, and artistic adviser to the San Francisco Symphony Orchestra from 1978. His works include *Electric Wake* 1968, *Heavy Metal* 1971, *Bridge of Dreams* 1982, and the opera *Nixon in China* 1988.

Adams John Couch 1819–1892. English astronomer, who deduced the existence of the planet Neptune in 1845, although it was not found until 1846 by Galle. He also studied the Moon's motion, the Leonid meteors, and terrestrial magnetism.

Adams John Quincy 1767–1848. sixth president of the USA 1825–29. He was born at Quincy, Massachusetts, the eldest son of President John ◊Adams. He at became US minister in The Hague, Berlin, St Petersburg, and London. He negotiated the Treaty of Ghent to end the ◊War of 1812 (fought between Britain and the USA) on generous terms for the USA. In 1817 he became ◊Monroe's secretary of state, formulated the ◊Monroe doctrine in 1823, and was elected president by the house of representatives, despite receiving fewer votes than his main rival, Andrew ◊Jackson. As president, Adams was an advocate of strong federal government.

Adams Neil 1958– . English judo champion. He won two junior and five senior European titles 1974–85, eight senior national titles, and two Olympic silver medals 1980, 1984. In 1981 he was world champion in the 78 kg class.

Adams Richard 1920– . English novelist. A civil servant 1948–72, he wrote *Watership Down* 1972, a tale of a rabbit community, which is read by adults and children. Later novels include *Shardik* 1974, *The Plague Dogs* 1977, and *Girl on a Swing* 1980.

Adams Roger 1889–1971. US organic chemist, known for his painstaking analytical work to determine the composition of naturally occurring substances such as complex vegetable oils and plant ◊alkaloids.

Adams Samuel 1722–1803. US politician, second cousin of President John ◊Adams; he was the chief prompter of the Boston Tea Party (see ◊American Revolution). He was also a signatory to the Declaration of Independence, served in the ◊Continental Congress and anticipated the French emperor Napoleon in calling the British a 'nation of shopkeepers'.

Adamson /'ædəmsən/ Robert R 1821–1848. Scottish photographer who, with David Octavius Hill, produced 2,500 ◊calotypes (mostly portraits) in five years from 1843.

Adana /'ædənə/ capital of Adana (Seyhan) province, S Turkey; population (1985) 776,000. It is a major cotton-growing centre and Turkey's fourth largest city.

adapt /ə'dæpt/ *v.t./i.* to make or become suitable for a new use or situation etc. —**adaptation** /-'teɪʃən/ *n.* [from French from Latin *adaptare* (*aptus* = fit)]

adaptable *adj.* able to be adapted or to adapt. —**adaptability** /-'bɪlɪti/ *n.*

adaptation *n.* in biology, any change in the structure or function of an organism that allows it to survive and reproduce more effectively in its environment. In ◊evolution, adaptation occurs as a result of random variation in the genetic make-up of organisms (produced by ◊mutation and ◊recombination) coupled with natural selection.

adaptive radiation in evolution, the production of several new species, with adaptations to different ways of life, from a single unspecialized ancestor. Adaptive radiation is likely to occur whenever a species enters a new habitat with unoccupied ecological niches.

adaptor *n.* 1. a device for making equipment compatible. 2. a device for connecting several electric plugs to one socket.

ADB abbreviation of Asian Development Bank.

ADC abbreviation of aide-de-camp.

add *v.t./i.* 1. to join (a thing *to* another) as an increase or supplement. 2. to put (numbers or amounts) together to get their total. 3. to make as a further remark. —**add up**, to find the total of; to amount *to*; (*colloquial*) to make sense, to seem reasonable. —**adder** *n.* [from Latin *addere* = put together]

Addams /'ædəmz/ Charles 1912–1988. US cartoonist, creator of the ghoulish family published in the *New Yorker* magazine. A successful television comedy series was based on the cartoon in the 1960s.

Addams Jane 1860–1935. US sociologist and campaigner for women's rights. In 1889 she founded and led the social settlement of Hull House, Chicago, one of the earliest community centres. She was vice president of the National American Women Suffrage Alliance 1911–14, and in 1915 led the Women's Peace Party and the first Women's Peace Congress. She shared the Nobel Peace Prize in 1931.

addax *n.* a light-coloured ◊antelope *Addax nasomaculatus* of the family Bovidae. It lives in the Sahara desert, where it exists on scanty vegetation without drinking. It is about 1.1 m/3.5 ft at the shoulder, and both sexes have spirally twisted horns.

added value in economics, the difference between the cost of producing something and the price at which it is sold. Added value is the basis of VAT or ◊value-added tax, a tax on the value added at each stage of the production process of a commodity.

addendum /ə'dendəm/ *n.* (*plural* **addenda**) something added, usually in writing, which qualifies a foregoing thesis or statement; (in *plural*) additional matter at the end of a book. [Latin, from *addere* = add]

adder *n.* 1. a small venomous European snake, especially the common viper *Vipera berus*. Growing to about 60 cm/ 24 in in length, it has a thick body, a triangular head bearing a characteristic V-shaped mark, and, often, zig-zag markings along the back. It is a shy animal. It feeds on small mammals and lizards. 2. any of various harmless snakes of North America. 3. (also **death adder**) a venomous snake of the cobra family *Acanthophis antarcticus* found in Australia and nearby islands. [Old English, originally *nadder*]

addict /'ædɪkt/ *n.* a person who is addicted, especially to drugs.

addicted /ə'dɪktɪd/ *adj.* having an addiction *to*. [from Latin *addicere* = assign]

addiction *n.* 1. the condition of doing or using something as a habit or compulsively, especially a state of dependence on drugs, alcohol, or other substances. Habitual use of such substances produces changes in chemical processes in the brain; when the substance is withheld, severe neurological manifestations, even death, may follow. These are reversed by the administration of the addictive substance, and mitigated by a gradual reduction in dosage. 2. devotion *to* an interest.

addictive /ə'dɪktɪv/ *adj.* causing addiction.

Addis Ababa /'ædɪs 'æbəbə/ or **Adis Abeba** capital of Ethiopia; population (1984) 1,413,000. It was founded in 1887 by Menelik, chief of Shoa, who ascended the throne of Ethiopia in 1889. The city is the headquarters of the Organization of African Unity.

Addison /ˈædɪsən/ Joseph 1672–1719. English writer. In 1704 he celebrated ◊Marlborough's victory at Blenheim in a poem, 'The Campaign', and subsequently held political appointments, including under-secretary of state and secretary to the Lord-Lieutenant of Ireland in 1708. In 1709 he contributed to the *Tatler*, begun by Richard ◊Steele, with whom he was co-founder in 1711 of the *Spectator*.

Addison's disease a rare deficiency or failure of the ◊adrenal glands to produce corticosteroid hormones; it is treated with hormones. The condition, formerly fatal, is characterized by anemia, weakness, low blood pressure, and brownish pigmentation of the skin. [from T *Addison*, London physician who first described it in 1855]

addition /əˈdɪʃən/ *n.* adding; a thing added. —**in addition**, as something added (*to*). [from Old French or Latin]

additional *adj.* added, extra. —**additionally** *adv.*

addition reaction a chemical reaction in which the atoms of an element or compound react with a double bond or triple bond in an organic compound by opening up one of the bonds and becoming attached to it, for example $CH_2=CH_2$ + HCl → CH_3CH_2Cl. An example is the addition of hydrogen atoms to ◊unsaturated compounds in vegetable oils to produce margarine.

additive /ˈædɪtɪv/ *n.* 1. a thing added, especially a substance with special properties. 2. in food, a chemical added to prolong shelf life (such as salt), alter colour, or improve food value (such as vitamins or minerals). Many chemical additives are used in the manufacture of food. They are subject to regulation since individuals may be affected by constant exposure to even small concentrations of certain additives and suffer side effects such as hyperactivity. Within the European Community, approved additives are given an official ◊E number. —*adj.* involving addition. [from Latin]

addle *v.t./i.* 1. (of an egg) to become rotten and produce no chick. 2. to muddle, to confuse. [Old English = filth]

address /əˈdres/ *n.* 1. the place where a person lives or a company is situated; particulars of this, especially for postal purposes. 2. a speech to an audience. 3. the part of a computer instruction that specifies the location of an item of stored information. A single piece of data can be stored at each address. For microcomputers, this normally amounts to one ◊byte (enough to represent a single character such as a letter or number).—*v.t.* 1. to write postal directions on. 2. to speak or write to; to direct a remark or written statement to. 3. to apply *oneself* or direct one's attention to. 4. to take aim at (the ball, in golf). [from Old French from Latin]

addressee /ædreˈsiː/ *n.* a person to whom a letter etc. is addressed.

adduce /əˈdjuːs/ *v.t.* to cite as an instance or proof. [from Latin *ducere* = bring]

adducible *adj.* that may be adduced.

Adelaide /ˈædɪleɪd/ 1792–1849. Queen consort of ◊William IV of England. Daughter of the Duke of Saxe-Meiningen, she married William, then Duke of Clarence, in 1818. No children of the marriage survived infancy.

Adelaide capital and industrial city of South Australia; population (1986) 993,100. Industries include oil refining, shipbuilding, and the manufacture of electrical goods and cars. Grain, wool, fruit, and wine are exported. Founded in 1836, Adelaide was named after William IV's queen.

Aden /ˈeɪdn/ (Arabic *'Adan*) capital of former South ◊Yemen, on a rocky peninsula at the SW corner of Arabia, commanding the entrance to the Red Sea; population (1984) 318,000. It comprises the new administrative centre Madinet al-Sha'ab; the commercial and business quarters of Crater and Tawahi, and the harbour area of Ma'alla. The city's economy is based on oil refining, fishing, and shipping. A British territory from 1839, Aden became part of independent South Yemen in 1967.

Adenauer /ˈædənaʊə/ Konrad 1876–1967. German Christian Democrat politician, chancellor of West Germany 1949–63. With the French president de Gaulle he achieved the postwar reconciliation of France and Germany and strongly supported all measures designed to strengthen the Western bloc in Europe.

History is the sum total of the things that could have been avoided.

Konrad Adenauer

---

adenoids /ˈædənɔɪdz/ *n.pl.* masses of lymphoid tissue, similar to ◊tonsils, located in the upper part of the throat, behind the nose. They are part of a child's natural defences against the entry of germs but usually shrink and disappear by the age of ten. —**adenoidal** *adj.* [from Greek *adēn* = gland]

adenoma /ædɪˈnəʊmə/ *n.* a gland-like benign tumour.

adept /ˈædept/ *adj.* thoroughly proficient (*in* or *at*). —*n.* an adept person. [from Latin *adipisci* = attain]

adequate *adj.* sufficient, satisfactory; passable but not outstandingly good. —**adequacy** *n.*, **adequately** *adv.* [from Latin *adaequare* = make equal]

Ader /æˈdeə/ Clément 1841–1925. French aviation pioneer and inventor. He demonstrated stereophonic sound transmission by telephone at the 1881 Paris Exhibition of Electricity. His steam-driven aeroplane, the *Éole*, made the first powered takeoff in history (1890), but it could not fly. In 1897, with his *Avion III*, he failed completely, despite false claims made later.

ADH abbreviation of antidiuretic hormone, part of the system maintaining a correct salt/water balance in vertebrates.

adhere /ədˈhɪə/ *v.i.* 1. to stick. 2. to give one's support or allegiance to. 3. to behave according *to* a rule etc. [from French or Latin *haerēre* = stick]

adherent *n.* a supporter (*of* a party or doctrine). —*adj.* adhering or sticking *to*. —**adherence** *n.*

adhesion /ədˈhiːʒən/ *n.* 1. adhering (*literal* or *figurative*). 2. in medicine, the abnormal binding of two tissues as a result of inflammation. The moving surfaces of joints or internal organs may merge together if they have been inflamed. [from French or Latin]

adhesive /ədˈhiːsɪv/ *adj.* having the property of adhering, sticky. —*n.* an adhesive substance. Natural adhesives include gelatin in its crude industrial form (made from bones, hide fragments and fish offal) and vegetable gums. Synthetic adhesives include thermoplastic and thermosetting resins; mixtures of epoxy resin and hardener that set by chemical reaction; and elastomeric (stretching) adhesives for flexible joints. —**adhesive tape**, a strip of paper or transparent material coated with adhesive, used for fastening packages etc. —**adhesiveness** *n.* [from French or Latin *haerēre* = stick]

ad hoc /æd ˈhɒk/ for this purpose, special(ly). [Latin]

adiabatic *n.* in physics, a process that occurs without loss or gain of heat, especially the expansion or contraction of a gas in which a change takes place in the pressure or volume, although no heat is allowed to enter or leave.

adieu /əˈdjuː/ *int.* & *n.* goodbye. [from French *à* = to and *Dieu* = God]

Adi Granth /ɑːdi ˈgrʌnt/ or **Guru Granth Sahib** the single sacred scripture of Sikhism, compiled by religious teachers, containing religious poetry in several languages. [Hindi = first book, from Sanskrit]

ad infinitum /æd ɪnfɪˈnaɪtəm/ without limit, for ever. [Latin]

adipose /ˈædɪpəʊs/ *adj.* of animal fat, fatty. —**adiposity** /-ˈpɒsɪtɪ/ *n.* [from Latin *adeps* = fat]

adipose tissue a type of connective tissue of vertebrates that serves as an energy reserve, and also pads some organs. It is commonly called fat tissue, and consists of large spherical cells filled with fat. In mammals, major layers are in the inner layer of skin and around the kidneys and heart.

adj. in grammar, abbreviation of adjective.

adjacent /əˈdʒeɪsənt/ *adj.* lying near, contiguous (*to*). [from Latin *adjacēre* (*jacēre* = lie)]

Adjani /ɑːˈdʒɑːniː/ Isabelle 1955– . French film actress of Algerian-German descent. She played the title role in Truffaut's *L'Histoire d'Adèle H/The Story of Adèle H* in 1975 and has since appeared in international productions including *Le Locataire/The Tenant; Nosferatu Phantom der Nacht* 1979; and *Ishtar* 1987.

adjective /ˈædʒɪktɪv/ *n.* a word indicating an attribute, used to describe or modify a noun (for example, *new* and *enormous*, as in 'a new hat' and 'an enormous dog'). Adjectives generally have three degrees (grades or levels for the description of relationships): the positive degree (*new, enormous*) the comparative degree (*newer, more enormous*), and the superlative degree (*newest, most enormous*). —**adjectival** /-'taɪvəl/ *adj.*, **adjectivally** *adv.* [from Old French from Latin *adjicere*]

adjoin /ə'dʒɔɪn/ *v.t.* to be next to and joined with. [from Old French from Latin *jungere* = join]

adjourn /ə'dʒɜ:n/ *v.t./i.* to postpone, to break off temporarily for later resumption. —**adjournment** *n.* [from Old French from Latin *diurnum* = day]

adjudge /ə'dʒʌdʒ/ *v.t.* to pronounce judgement on; to pronounce or award judicially. —**adjudg(e)ment** *n.* [from Old French from Latin *adjudicare* (*judex* = judge)]

adjudicate /ə'dʒu:dɪkeɪt/ *v.t./i.* to act as judge; to adjudge. —**adjudication** /-'keɪʃən/ *n.*, **adjudicator** *n.*

adjunct /'ædʒʌŋkt/ *n.* a thing added or attached but subordinate (*to* or *of*). [from Latin]

adjure /ə'dʒʊə/ *v.t.* to command or urge solemnly. —**adjuration** /-'eɪʃən/ *n.* [from Latin *adjurare* = put to an oath]

adjust /ə'dʒʌst/ *v.t./i.* **1.** to arrange, to put into the correct order or position etc.; to regulate. **2.** to make suitable (*to* a need or purpose); to harmonize (discrepancies); to adapt oneself to new conditions. **3.** to assess (loss or damage). —**adjuster** *n.*, **adjustment** *n.* [from French from Latin *juxta* = near]

adjustable *adj.* that may be adjusted.

adjutant /'ædʒʊtənt/ *n.* an army officer assisting a superior officer in administrative duties; an assistant. —**adjutant bird,** a large stork of the genus *Leptoptilus*, of which the largest (*L. dubius*), found in India, is 1.8–2.1 m (6–7 ft.) tall. [from Latin, frequentative of *adjuvare* = help]

Adler /'ɑ:dlə/ Alfred 1870–1937. Austrian psychologist. Adler saw the 'will to power' as more influential in accounting for human behaviour than the sexual drive theory. A dispute over this theory led to the dissolution of his ten-year collaboration with ◊Freud

Adler Larry 1914– . US musician, a virtuoso performer on the harmonica.

ad lib (**-bb-**) (*colloquial*) to speak impromptu, to improvise. —*adj.* (*colloquial*) improvised. —*adv.* as one pleases, to any desired extent. [abbreviation of Latin *ad libitum* = according to pleasure]

admin /'ædmɪn/ *n.* (*colloquial*) abbreviation of administration.

administer /əd'mɪnɪstə/ *v.t./i.* **1.** to manage (business affairs). **2.** to give out (justice, a sacrament) formally; to present (an oath) to; to provide. **3.** to act as administrator. [from French from Latin *ministrare* = minister)]

administrate /əd'mɪnɪstreɪt/ *v.t./i.* to act as administrator (of). [from Latin]

administration /ədmɪni'streɪʃən/ *n.* **1.** administering, especially of public affairs. **2.** the government. [from Old French or Latin]

administrative /əd'mɪnɪstrətɪv/ *adj.* of or involving administration. [from French or Latin]

administrative law law concerning the powers and control of government agencies or those agencies granted statutory powers of administration. These powers include those necessary to operate the agency or to implement its purposes, and making quasi-judicial decisions (such as determining tax liability, granting licences or permits, or hearing complaints against the agency or its officers). The vast increase in these powers in the 20th century in many countries has been widely criticized.

administrator /əd'mɪnɪstreɪtə/ *n.* a manager of business affairs; one who is capable of organizing things; one authorized to manage an estate.

admirable /'ædmərəbəl/ *adj.* worthy of admiration; excellent. —**admirably** *adv.* [French from Latin]

admiral /'ædmərəl/ *n.* the commander-in-chief of a navy; a naval officer of high rank, the commander of a fleet or squadron. There are four grades: *Admiral of the Fleet, Admiral, Vice Admiral, Rear Admiral*. —**red admiral, white admiral,** European species of butterfly (*Vanessa atalanta* and *Ladoga camilla*), perhaps originally called *the admirable*. [from Old French from Latin from Arabic = commander]

Admiral's Cup a sailing series first held in 1957 and held biennially. National teams consisting of three boats compete over three inshore courses (in the Solent) and two offshore courses (378 km/235 mi across the Channel from Cherbourg to the Isle of Wight and 1,045 km/650 mi from Plymouth to Fastnet lighthouse off Ireland, and back). The highlight is the Fastnet race.

Admiralty, Board of the /'ædmərəltɪ/ in Britain, the controlling department of state for the Royal Navy from the reign of Henry VIII until 1964, when most of its functions—apart from that of management—passed to the Ministry of Defence. The 600-year-old office of Lord High Admiral reverted to the sovereign.

admire /əd'maɪə/ *v.t.* to regard with approval, respect, or satisfaction; to express admiration of. —**admiration** /ædmɪ'reɪʃən/ *n.*, **admirer** *n.* [from French or Latin *mirari* = wonder at)]

admissible /əd'mɪsəbəl/ *adj.* (of an idea etc.) worthy of being accepted or considered; (of evidence) allowable in law. —**admissibility** /-i'bɪlɪtɪ/ *n.* [from French or Latin *admittere*]

admission /əd'mɪʃən/ *n.* **1.** an acknowledgement (*of*). **2.** admitting, being admitted; the fee for this.

admit /əd'mɪt/ *v.t./i.* (**-tt-**) **1.** to recognize as true or valid; to confess to. **2.** to allow to enter; to have room for. **3.** to accept (a plea or statement). —**admit of,** to allow a doubt, improvement, etc.) as possible. —**admittance** *n.* [from Latin *mittere* = send)]

admittedly /əd'mɪtɪdlɪ/ *adv.* as an acknowledged fact.

admixture /æd'mɪkstʃə/ *n.* a thing added as an ingredient; the adding of this.

admonish /əd'mɒnɪʃ/ *v.t.* to reprove mildly but firmly; to urge or advise seriously; to warn. —**admonishment** *n.*, **admonition** /-'nɪʃən/ *n.* [from Old French from Latin *monēre* = warn]

admonitory /əd'mɒnɪtərɪ/ *adj.* admonishing.

ad nauseam /æd 'nɔ:zɪæm/ to an excessive or sickening degree. [Latin]

ado /ə'du:/ *n.* fuss, busy activity, trouble. [originally in *much ado* = much to do]

adobe /ə'dəʊbɪ/ *n.* brick made of clay and dried in the sun; clay for this, used extensively in South America, the south-western USA, and Africa. [Spanish from Arabic = the brick]

adolescent /ædə'lesənt/ *adj.* growing up; in the human lifecycle, in the period between the beginning of puberty and adulthood. —*n.* an adolescent person. —**adolescence** *n.* [from Old French from Latin *adolescere* = grow up]

Adonis /ə'dəʊnɪs/ in Greek mythology, a beautiful youth beloved by the goddess ◊Aphrodite. He was killed while boar-hunting but was allowed to return from the lower world for six months every year to rejoin her. The anemone sprang from his blood. [Latin from Greek from Phoenician *adon* = lord]

adopt /ə'dɒpt/ *v.t.* **1.** to take into one's family *as* a relation, especially as one's child with legal guardianship; to choose (a course etc.); to take over (a name, idea, etc.); to choose as a candidate for office. **2.** to accept responsibility for maintenance of (a road etc.). **3.** to approve or accept (a report, accounts). —**adoption** /-ʃən/ *n.* [from French or Latin *optare* = choose]

adoptive *adj.* related by adoption. [from Old French from Latin]

adorable /ə'dɔ:rəbəl/ *adj.* worthy of adoration, very lovable; (*colloquial*) delightful. —**adorably** *adv.*

adore /ə'dɔ:/ *v.t.* **1.** to love deeply. **2.** to worship as divine. **3.** (*colloquial*) to like very much. —**adoration** /-'reɪʃən/ *n.*, **adorer** *n.* [from Old French from Latin *adorare* = worship (*orare* = pray)]

adorn /ə'dɔ:n/ *v.t.* to be an ornament to, to decorate with ornaments. —**adornment** *n.* [from Old French from Latin *adornare* = decorate]

ADP abbreviation of adenosine diphosphate, a raw material in the manufacture of ◊ATP, the molecule used by all cells to drive their chemical reactions.

adrenal /ə'dri:nəl/ *n.* an adrenal gland. —**adrenal** or **suprarenal gland,** either of two ductless glands above the kidneys, secreting adrenalin, each consisting of two parts. The **cortex** (outer part) secretes various steroid hormones, controls salt and water metabolism, and regulates the use of carbohydrates, proteins, and fats. The **medulla** (inner part) secretes the hormones adrenaline and noradrenaline which constrict the blood vessels of the

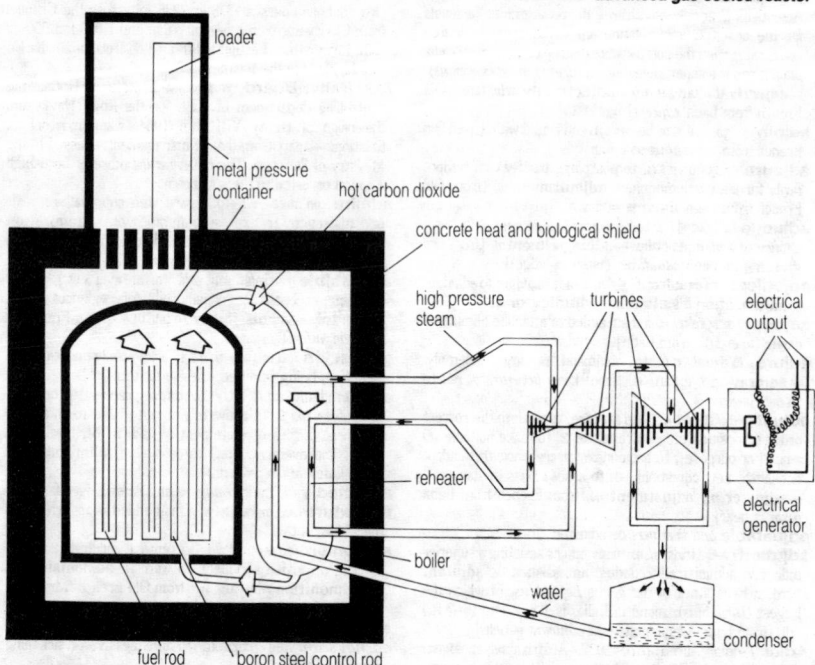

loader

metal pressure container

hot carbon dioxide

concrete heat and biological shield

high pressure steam

turbines

electrical output

reheater

electrical generator

boiler

water

condenser

fuel rod

boron steel control rod

belly and skin so that more blood is available for the heart, lungs, and voluntary muscles, an emergency preparation for the stress reaction 'fight or flight'.

adrenaline /ə'drenəlɪn/ *n.* or **epinephrine** a hormone that stimulates the nervous system, secreted by the medulla of the adrenal glands or prepared synthetically.

adrenocorticotropic hormone see ◊ACTH.

Adrian IV /'eɪdrɪən/ (Nicholas Breakspear) *c.*1100–1159. Pope 1154–59, the only British pope. He secured the execution of the Italian Augustinian monk, Arnold of Brescia, who attacked the holding of property by the Catholic Church; crowned Frederick I Barbarossa as German emperor; refused Henry II's request that Ireland should be granted to the English crown in absolute ownership; and was at the height of a quarrel with the emperor when he died.

Adriatic Sea /eɪdri'ætɪk/ large arm of the Mediterranean Sea, lying NW to SE between the Italian and the Balkan peninsulas. The west shore is Italian; the east is Yugoslav and Albanian. The sea is about 805 km/500 mi long, and its area is 135,250 sq km/52,220 sq mi.

adrift /ə'drɪft/ *adv. & predic. adj.* 1. drifting. 2. (*colloquial*) amiss, out of touch, unfastened.

adroit /ə'drɔɪt/ *adj.* skilful, ingenious. —**adroitly** *adv.*, **adroitness** *n.* [French *à droit* = according to right]

adsorb /æd'sɔːb/ *v.t.* (of a solid) to hold (particles of a gas or liquid) to its surface. —**adsorbent** *adj.*, **adsorption** *n.*, **adsorptive** *adj.*

adulation /ædju'leɪʃən/ *n.* obsequious flattery. —**adulatory** *adj.* [from Latin *adulari* = fawn on]

Adullam /ə'dʌləm/ a biblical city with nearby caves in which David and those who had some grievance took refuge (1 Samuel 22). **Adullamite**, a person who is disaffected or who secedes from a political party; the term was used to describe about 40 British Liberal MPs who voted against their leaders to defeat the 1866 Reform Bill.

adult /'ædʌlt/ *adj.* mature, grown-up. —*n.* an adult person. —**adulthood** *n.* [from Latin]

adulterant /ə'dʌltərənt/ *n.* a substance added in adulterating.

adulterate /ə'dʌltəreɪt/ *v.t.* to make impure or poorer in quality by an admixture of other substance(s). —**adulteration** /-'reɪʃən/ *n.* [from Latin *adulterare* = corrupt]

adulterer /ə'dʌltərə/ *n.* a person (especially a man) who commits adultery. —**adulteress** *n.fem.* [from French from Latin]

adultery /ə'dʌltərɪ/ *n.* voluntary sexual intercourse of a married person with someone other than his or her spouse. —**adulterous** *adj.* [from Old French from Latin]

adumbrate /'ædʌmbreɪt/ *v.t.* 1. to indicate faintly; to foreshadow. 2. to overshadow. —**adumbration** /-'breɪʃən/ *n.* [from Latin *adumbrare* (*umbra* = shade)]

Aduwa, Battle of /'æduaː/ the defeat of the Italians by the Ethiopians at Aduwa in 1896 under Emperor Menelik II. It marked the end of Italian ambitions in this part of Africa until Mussolini's reconquest in 1935.

adv. abbreviation of ◊adverb.

advance /əd'vaːns/ *v.t./i.* 1. to move or put forward; to progress; to rise in rank. 2. to lend, to pay before a due date. 3. to present (a suggestion or claim etc.). 4. to bring (an event) to an earlier date. 5. to raise (a price). —*n.* 1. a forward movement, progress. 2. a rise in price. 3. a loan, payment beforehand. 4. (in *plural*) attempts to establish a friendly or business relationship. —*attrib. adj.* 1. going before others. 2. done or provided in advance. —**in advance**, ahead in time or place. [from Old French from Latin *ab* = away and *ante* = before]

advanced *adj.* 1. far on in progress or life; not elementary. 2. (of ideas etc.) new and not yet generally accepted.

advanced gas-cooled reactor a type of nuclear power generator; see ◊AGR.

advancement *n.* the promotion of a person or plan.

advantage /əd'vaːntɪdʒ/ *n.* 1. a favourable circumstance; benefit; superiority. 2. the next point after deuce in tennis. —*v.t.* to be or give an advantage to. —**take advantage of,** to make use of, to exploit. —**advantageous** /ædvæn'teɪdʒəs/ *adj.*, **advantageously** *adv.* [from Old French]

Advent /'ædvənt/ *n.* 1. the season (with four Sundays) before Christmas Day; the coming of Christ. 2. the arrival of an important person, event, or development. [Old English from Old French from Latin *adventus* = arrival (*venire* = come)]

Adventist /'ædvəntɪst/ *n.* a member of any of various sects believing that the second coming of Christ is imminent. Expectation of the Second Coming of Christ is found in New Testament writings generally. Adventist views are held by the Seventh-Day Adventists, Christadelphians, Jehovah's Witnesses, and the Four Square Gospel Alliance.

adventitious /ædven'tɪʃəs/ *adj.* **1.** accidental, casual. **2.** added from outside. —**adventitious root**, a root developing in an unusual position; for example, ivy roots grow sideways out of the stem and cling to trees or walls. —**adventitiously** *adv.* [from Latin]

adventure /əd'ventʃə/ *n.* **1.** an unusual and exciting or dangerous experience. **2.** willingness to take risks. —**adventure playground**, a playground where children are provided with discarded materials etc. to use imaginatively in play. —**adventurous** *adj.*, **adventurously** *adv.* [from Old French]

adventurer *n.* **1.** one who seeks adventures. **2.** one who is ready to take risks or be unscrupulous for personal gain. —**adventuress** *n.fem.*

adverb /'ædvɜːb/ *n.* a word indicating manner, degree, circumstance, etc., used to modify an adjective (a *beautifully* clear day), verb (she ran *quickly*), or another adverb (they did it *really* well). Most adverbs are formed from adjectives or past participles by adding -*ly* (*quick: quickly*) or -*ally* (*automatic: automatically*). —**adverbial** /əd'vɜːbiəl/ *adj.*, **adverbially** *adv.* [from French or Latin *ad* = to and *verbum* = word]

adversarial /ædvə'seəriəl/ *adj.* **1.** involving adversaries, contested. **2.** opposed, hostile. —**adversarially** *adv.*

adversary /'ædvəsəri/ *n.* an opponent, an enemy.

adverse /'ædvɜːs/ *adj.* unfavourable; harmful. [from Old French from Latin *adversus* (*vertere* = turn)]

adversity /əd'vɜːsɪti/ *n.* misfortune, trouble.

advert /'ædvɜːt/ *n.* (*colloquial*) abbreviation of advertisement.

advertise /'ædvətaɪz/ *v.t./i.* to praise publicly in order to promote sales; to make generally known; to offer or ask *for* by a notice in a newspaper etc. —**advertiser** *n.* **advertising** *n.* any of various methods used by a company to increase the sales of its products or to promote a brand name. Advertising can be seen by economists as either beneficial (since it conveys information about a product and so brings the market closer to a state of ◊perfect competition) or as a hindrance to perfect competition, since it attempts to make illusory distinctions (such as greater sex appeal) between essentially similar products. [from Old French from Latin]

advertisement /əd'vɜːtɪsmənt/ *n.* a public announcement advertising (for) something; advertising. [from French]

Advertising Standards Authority (ASA) an organization founded by the UK advertising industry in 1962 to promote higher standards of advertising in the media (excluding television and radio, which have their own authority). It is financed by the advertisers, who pay 0.1% supplement on the cost of advertisements. It recommends to the media that advertisements which might breach the British Code of Advertising Practice are not published, but has no statutory power.

advice /əd'vaɪs/ *n.* **1.** an opinion given as to future action. **2.** information, news; formal notice of a transaction. —**take advice**, to seek it, to act according to it. [from Old French from Latin *ad* = to and *vidēre* = see]

advisable *adj.* worth recommending, expedient. —**advisability** /-'bɪlɪtɪ/ *n.*

advise /əd'vaɪz/ *v.t./i.* **1.** to give advice (to), to recommend. **2.** to inform. —**adviser** *n.*

advisory /əd'vaɪzərɪ/ *adj.* giving advice.

Advisory, Conciliation, and Arbitration Service (ACAS) in the UK, an independent body set up under the Employment Protection Act 1975 to improve industrial relations. Specifically, ACAS aims to encourage the extension of collective bargaining and, wherever possible, the reform of collective-bargaining machinery.

advocacy /'ædvəkəsɪ/ *n.* **1.** the advocating *of* a policy etc. **2.** the function of an advocate.

advocate /'ædvəkət/ *n.* one who advocates or speaks in favour *of*; one who pleads on behalf of another, especially in a law court. A more common term is ◊barrister or counsel, but advocate is retained in such countries as Scotland and France, whose legal systems are based on Roman law. —/-keɪt/ *v.t.* to recommend, to be in favour of. [from Old French from Latin *advocatus* (*vocare* = call)]

Advocates, faculty of the professional organization for Scottish advocates, the equivalent of English ◊barristers. It was incorporated in 1532 under James V.

adze /ædz/ *n.* an axe-like tool with an arched blade, for trimming large pieces of wood. [Old English]

Aegean civilization /iː'dʒiːən/ the cultures of Bronze Age Greece, including the ◊**Minoan civilization** of Crete and the ◊**Mycenaean civilization** of the E Peloponnese.

Aegean Islands the islands of the Aegean Sea, but more specifically a region of Greece comprising the Dodecanese islands, the Cyclades islands, Lesvos, Samos, and Chios; population (1981) 428,500; area 9,122 sq km/3,523 sq mi.

Aegean Sea branch of the Mediterranean between Greece and Turkey; the Dardanelles connect it with the Sea of Marmara. The numerous islands in the Aegean Sea include Crete, the Cyclades, the Sporades, and the Dodecanese. There is political tension between Greece and Turkey over sea limits claimed by Greece around such islands as Lesvos, Chios, Samos, and Kos.

aegis /'iːdʒɪs/ *n.* protection, sponsorship. [Latin from Greek = mythical shield of Zeus or Athene]

Aelfric /'ælfrɪk/ *c.*955–1020. Anglo-Saxon writer and abbot, author of two collections of *Catholic Homilies* 990–92, sermons, and the *Lives of the Saints* 996–97, written in vernacular Old English prose.

Aeneas /iː'niːəs/ in classical legend, a Trojan prince who became the ancestral hero of the Romans. According to Homer, he was the son of Anchises and the goddess Aphrodite. During the Trojan War he owed his life to the frequent intervention of the gods.

Aeneid /iː'niːɪd/ *n.* an epic poem by Virgil, written in Latin in 12 books of hexameters and composed during the last 11 years of his life (30–19 BC). It celebrates the development of the Roman Empire through the legend of Aeneas. After the fall of Troy, Aeneas wanders for seven years and becomes shipwrecked off Africa. He is received by Dido, queen of Carthage, and they fall in love. Aeneas, however, renounces their love and sails on to Italy where he settles as founder of Latium and the Roman state.

aeolian /iː'əʊliən/ *adj.* wind-borne. —**aeolian harp**, a stringed instrument giving musical sounds on exposure to wind. It was common in parts of central Europe during the 19th century. **Aeolian Islands**, the ancient name of the Lipari Islands. [from *Aeolus*, Greek god of the winds]

aeon /'iːən/ *n.* a long or indefinite period. [from Latin from Greek = age]

aepyornis /iːpɪ'ɔːnɪs/ *n.* a gigantic, flightless, extinct bird of the genus *Aepyornis*, resembling a moa, known from remains found in Madagascar. [Latin from Greek *aipus* = high and *ornis* = bird]

Aequi /'iːkwiː/ *n.pl.* an Italian people, originating around the river Velino, who were turned back from their advance on Rome in 431 BC and were conquered in 304 BC, during the Samnite Wars. Like many other peoples conquered by the Romans, they adopted Roman customs and culture.

aerate /'eəreɪt/ *v.t.* **1.** to expose to the action of air. **2.** to charge with carbon dioxide. —**aeration** /-'reɪʃən/ *n.*, **aerator** *n.* [from Latin *aer* = air]

aerated water water that has had air (oxygen) blown through it. Such water supports aquatic life and prevents growth of bacteria.

aerenchyma *n.* a plant tissue with numerous air-filled spaces between the cells. It occurs in the stems and roots of many aquatic plants, aiding buoyancy and facilitating transport of oxygen around the plant.

aerial /'eəriəl/ *n.* a wire or rod for transmitting or receiving aerial waves; in radio and television broadcasting, a conducting device or **antenna** that radiates or receives electromagnetic waves. The design of an aerial depends principally on the wavelength of the signal. Long waves (hundreds of metres in wavelength) may employ long wire aerials; short waves (several centimetres in wavelength) may employ rods and dipoles; microwaves may also use dipoles – often with reflectors arranged like a toast rack · or highly directional parabolic dish aerials.   —*adj.* **1.** from the air or aircraft. **2.** existing in the air. **3.** like air. [from Latin]

aero- /eərəʊ-/ in combinations, air, aircraft. [from Greek *aēr* = air]

aerobatics /eərə'bætɪks/ *n.pl.* feats of expert flying of aircraft, especially for display.

aeroplane

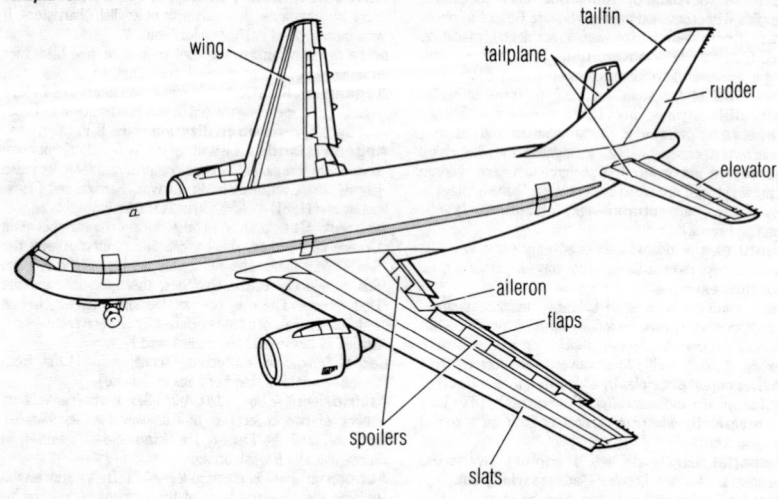

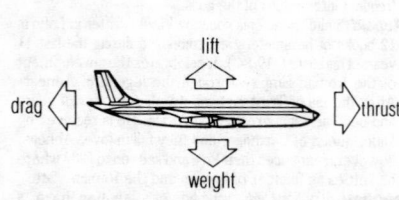

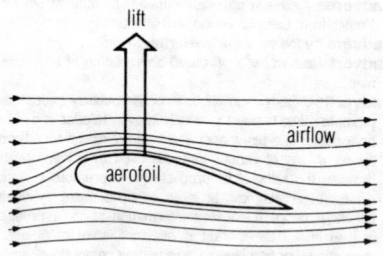

aerobic /eəˈrəʊbɪk/ *adj.* **1.** in biology, a description of those living organisms requiring molecular oxygen (usually dissolved in water) for the efficient release of energy from their food. **2.** (of exercises) designed to increase the intake of oxygen and strengthen the heart and lungs. —**aerobics** *n.pl.* exercises of this kind. [from French from Greek *aēr* = air and *bios* = life]

aerodrome /ˈeərədrəʊm/ *n.* an airfield or airport. [from Greek *aēr* = air and *dromos* = course]

aerodynamics /ˌeərəʊdaɪˈnæmɪks/ *n.* (also as *plural*) the dynamics of solid bodies moving through air, particularly the airflow around bodies (such as land vehicles, bullets, rockets, and aircraft) moving at speed through the atmosphere. —**aerodynamic** *adj.*

aerofoil /ˈeərəfɔɪl/ *n.* a body (e. g. an aircraft wing, fin, or tailplane) shaped to produce a desired aerodynamic reaction (e. g. lift) when it passes through air.

aeronaut /ˈeərənɔːt/ *n.* a balloonist or other aviator. [from Greek *aēr* = air and *nautēs* = sailor]

aeronautics /ˌeərəˈnɔːtɪks/ *n.* the science, art, or practice of the flight of aircraft, including ◊aerodynamics, aircraft structures, jet and rocket propulsion, and aerial navigation. —**aeronautic** *adj.*, **aeronautical** *adj.*

aeroplane /ˈeərəpleɪn/ *n.* a power-driven heavier-than-air aircraft with wings. Aeroplanes are propelled by the thrust of a jet engine or airscrew (propeller). The shape of an aeroplane depends on its use and operating speed—aircraft operating at well below the speed of sound need not be as streamlined as supersonic aircraft. The Wright brothers flew the first powered plane (a biplane) in Kitty Hawk, North Carolina, USA, 1903. [from French]

aerosol /ˈeərəsɒl/ *n.* **1.** particles of liquid or solid suspended in a gas. Fog is a common natural example. **2.** a container holding a liquid or other substance and a propellant gas packed under pressure, dispensing its contents as a fine spray when the pressure is released. Many commercial aerosols use chlorofluorocarbons (CFCs) as propellants, and these are now known to cause destruction of the ◊ozone layer in the Earth's atmosphere. As a consequence, the

international community has agreed to phase out the use of CFCs as propellants. Unfortunately, many so-called 'ozone-friendly' aerosols have the disadvantage of using flammable butane or propane as propellants.

aerospace /ˈeərəʊspeɪs/ *n.* **1.** the Earth's atmosphere and outer space. **2.** the technology of aviation in this.

Aeschines /ˈiːskɪniːz/ lived 4th century BC. Orator of ancient Athens, a rival of ◊Demosthenes.

Aeschylus /ˈiːskələs/ *c.*525–*c.*456 BC. Greek dramatist, widely regarded as the founder of Greek tragedy. By the introduction of a second actor he made true dialogue and dramatic action possible. Aeschylus wrote some 90 plays between 499 and 458 BC, of which seven survive. These are *The Suppliant Women* performed about 490 BC, *The Persians* 472 BC, *Seven against Thebes* 467 BC, *Prometheus Bound* (about 460 BC) and the ◊*Oresteia* trilogy 458 BC.

Every ruler is harsh whose rule is new.

Aeschylus
Prometheus Bound

Aesir /ˈiːsə(r)/ *n.* the principal gods of Norse mythology—Odin, Thor, Balder, Loki, Freya, and Tyr—whose dwelling place was Asgard.

Aesop /ˈiːsɒp/ traditional writer of Greek fables. According to Herodotus, he lived in the reign of Amasis of Egypt (mid-6th century BC) and was a slave of Iadmon, a Thracian. The fables, for which no evidence of his authorship exists, are anecdotal stories using animal characters to illustrate moral or satirical points.

aesthete /ˈiːsθiːt/ *n.* a person who claims to have great understanding and appreciation of what is beautiful, especially in the arts. [from Greek]

aesthetic /iːsˈθetɪk/ *adj.* concerned with or sensitive to what is beautiful; artistic, tasteful. —**aesthetics** *n.pl.* a branch of philosophy dealing with the principles of beauty and tastefulness. It emerged as a distinct branch of enquiry in the mid-18th century. —**aesthetically** *adv.*, **aestheticism** /-sɪzəm/ *n.* [from Greek *aisthanomai* = perceive]

Aesthetic movement an English artistic movement of the late 19th century, dedicated to the doctrine 'art for art's sake' – that is, art as self-sufficient, not needing to justify its existence by serving any particular use. Artists associated with the movement include Beardsley and Whistler. The writer Oscar Wilde was, in his 20s, an exemplary aesthete.

aestivation *n.* in zoology, a state of inactivity and reduced metabolic activity, similar to ◊hibernation, that occurs during the dry season in species such as lungfish and snails. In botany, the term is used to describe the way in which flower petals and sepals are folded in the buds. It is an important feature in ◊plant classification.

aet. abbreviation of *aetatis*. [Latin = of the age]

aether *n.* an alternative form of ◊ether.

aetiology /iːtɪˈɒlədʒɪ/ *n.* 1. the study of causation. 2. the study of the causes of disease. 3. the cause of a disease. —**aetiological** /-pˈlɒdʒɪkəl/ *adj.*, **aetiologically** *adv.* [from Latin from Greek *aitia* = cause]

Aetolia /iːˈtəʊlɪə/ district of ancient Greece on the NW of the gulf of Corinth. **Aetolian League**, a confederation of the cities of Aetolia which, following the death of Alexander the Great, became the chief rival of Macedonian power and the Achaean League.

afar /əˈfɑː/ *adv.* far off, far away.

AFD abbreviation of ◊accelerated freeze drying, a common method of food preservation. See also ◊food technology.

affable /ˈæfəbəl/ *adj.* polite and friendly. —**affability** /-ˈbɪlɪtɪ/ *n.*, **affably** *adv.* [French from Latin *affabilis* (*fari* = speak]

affair /əˈfeə/ *n.* 1. a matter, a concern; a thing done or to be done. 2. a temporary sexual relationship between two persons who are not married to each other. 3. (*colloquial*) a thing or event. 4. (in *plural*) public or private business. [from Anglo-French *à faire* = to do]

affect /əˈfekt/ *v.t.* 1. to produce an effect on; (of disease) to attack; to touch the feelings of. 2. to pretend, to pose as. 3. to make a show of liking or using. [from French or Latin *afficere* = influence (*facere* = do)]

affectation /æfekˈteɪʃən/ *n.* a studied display (*of* modesty etc.); an artificial manner, pretence.

affected /əˈfektɪd/ *adj.* 1. pretended, artificial. 2. full of affectation.

affection /əˈfekʃən/ *n.* 1. love, a liking. 2. a disease or diseased condition.

affectionate /əˈfekʃənət/ *adj.* showing affection, loving. —**affectionately** *adv.*

affiance /əˈfaɪəns/ *v.t.* to promise in marriage. [from Old French from Latin *affidare* = entrust]

affidavit *n.* a legal document, used in court applications and proceedings, in which a person confirms by oath that certain facts are true. [Latin = has stated on oath]

affiliate /əˈfɪlɪeɪt/ *v.t.* to connect as a member or branch. —*n.* an affiliated person or organization. [from Latin *affiliare* = adopt (*filius* = son)]

affiliation /əfɪlɪˈeɪʃən/ *n.* affiliating, being affiliated. —**affiliation order**, in English law, formerly a court order for maintenance against the alleged father of an illegitimate child. Under the Family Law Reform Act 1987, either parent can apply for a court order for maintenance of children, no distinction being made between legitimate and illegitimate children.

affine geometry a geometry that preserves parallelism and the ratios between intervals on any line segment.

affinity /əˈfɪnɪtɪ/ *n.* 1. a liking or attraction. 2. in law, a relationship by marriage not blood, for example between stepparent and stepchild, which may legally preclude their marriage. In Britain, the right to marry was extended to many relationships formerly prohibited, by the Marriage (Prohibited Degrees of Relationship) Act 1986. 3. a resemblance or connection suggesting that there is a relationship. 4. in chemistry, the force of attraction between chemical elements, which helps to keep them in combination in a molecule. [from French from Latin *affinis* = bordering on]

affirm /əˈfɜːm/ *v.t./i.* to assert, to state as a fact; to declare solemnly in place of taking an oath (by a person who has no religious belief or objects to taking an oath on religious grounds). —**affirmation** /-ˈmeɪʃən/ *n.*,

affirmatory /əˈfɜːm-/ *adj.* [from Old French from Latin *affirmare* (*firmus* = strong)]

affirmative /əˈfɜːmətɪv/ *adj.* affirming, answering that a thing is so. —*n.* an affirmative word or statement. —**affirmatively** *adv.*

affirmative action in the USA, a government-endorsed policy of positive discrimination that favours members of minority ethnic groups and women in areas such as employment and education, designed to counter the effects of long-term discrimination against them. The policy has been controversial, and has prompted lawsuits by white males who have been denied jobs or education as a result.

affix /əˈfɪks/ *v.t.* 1. to stick on, to fasten. 2. to add (a signature etc.) in writing. —/ˈæfɪks/ *n.* a thing affixed; in grammar, a prefix or suffix. [from French or Latin *figere* = fix]

afflict /əˈflɪkt/ *v.t.* to distress physically or mentally. [from Latin *fligere* = strike]

affliction /əˈflɪkʃən/ *n.* distress, suffering; a cause of this.

affluent /ˈæfluənt/ *adj.* wealthy; abundant. —*n.* a tributary stream. —**affluence** *n.*, **affluently** *adv.* [from Old French from Latin *fluere* = flow]

affluent society a society in which most people have money left over after satisfying their basic needs such as food and shelter. They are then able to decide how to spend their excess ('disposable') income, and become 'consumers'. The term was popularized by the US economist John Kenneth ◊Galbraith.

afford /əˈfɔːd/ *v.t.* 1. to have enough money, means, or time, etc. for; to be able to spare; to be in a position *to* do. 2. to provide. [from Old English = promote]

afforest /əˈfɒrɪst/ *v.t.* to convert into forest, to plant with trees. —**afforestation** /-ˈteɪʃən/ *n.* [from Latin *foresta* = forest]

affray /əˈfreɪ/ *n.* a breach of the peace by fighting or rioting in public. [from Anglo-French from Latin = remove from peace]

affront /əˈfrʌnt/ *n.* an open insult. —*v.t.* 1. to insult openly. 2. to face, to confront. [from Old French from Latin *frons* = face]

Afghan /ˈæfgæn/ *n.* 1. a native of Afghanistan. 2. the language spoken there, Pashto. **Afghan hound**, a breed of fast hunting dog with long, silky hair, first introduced to the West by British army officers serving on India's North-West Frontier along the Afghanistan border in the late 19th century. The Afghan hound stands about 70 cm/ 28 in tall. [from Pashto]

Afghanistan /æfˈgænɪstɑːn/ Republic of; mountainous, landlocked country in S central Asia, bounded to the N by the USSR, W by Iran, and S and E by Pakistan; **area** 652,090 sq km/251,707 sq mi; **capital** Kābul; **physical** mountainous in centre and NE, desert in SW; **head of state** Najibullah Ahmadzai (president) from 1986; **head of government** Fazl Haq Khaleqiar (prime minister) from 1990; **political system** military emergency republic; **exports** dried fruit, rare minerals, natural gas (piped to USSR), karakul lamb skins, Afghan coats; **population** (1989) 15,590,000 (more than 5 million have become refugees since 1979); **language** Pushtu; **recent history** Full independence recovered 1919 after Third Afghan War with Britain. Constitutional monarchy established 1963, overthrown 1973. Treaty of friendship signed with the USSR in 1978. Reforms introduced, opposed by conservative Muslims. Guerrilla resistance by the mujaheddin led to Soviet invasion in Dec 1979. Partial withdrawal in 1986 was completed in 1989; civil war between government and mujaheddin continued.

Afghan Wars three wars, 1838–42, 1878–80, and 1919, waged between Britain and Afghanistan to counter the threat to British India from expanding Russian influence in Afghanistan.

aficionado /əfɪsjəˈneɪdəʊ/ *n.* (*plural* **aficionados**) a devotee of a sport or pastime. [Spanish]

afield /əˈfiːld/ *adv.* away from home, to or at a distance.

afire /əˈfaɪə/ *adv.* & *predic. adj.* on fire.

aflame /əˈfleɪm/ *adv.* & *predic. adj.* 1. in flames, burning. 2. very excited.

AFL-CIO abbreviation of American Federation of Labor and Congress of Industrial Organizations.

afloat /əˈfləʊt/ *adv.* & *predic. adj.* 1. floating; at sea, on board ship. 2. flooded. 3. out of debt or difficulty. 4. in circulation, current.

afoot /ə'fut/ *adv. & predic. adj.* progressing, in operation.

afore /ə'fɔː/ *adv. & prep. (archaic* or *dialect* except in *nautical* use) before.

aforesaid /ə'fɔːsed/ *adj.* mentioned previously.

aforethought /ə'fɔːθɔːt/ *adj.* premeditated.

a fortiori /eɪ fɔːtiː'ɔːraɪ/ with yet stronger reason (than a conclusion already accepted). [Latin]

afraid /ə'freɪd/ *predic. adj.* **1.** alarmed, frightened, anxious about consequences etc. **2.** (*colloquial*) politely regretful. [originally from *affray*, from Anglo-French from Latin = remove from peace]

afresh /ə'freʃ/ *adv.* anew, beginning again.

Africa /'æfrɪkə/ second largest of the continents, three times the area of Europe; **area** 30,097,000 sq km/ 11,620,451 sq mi; **largest cities** Cairo, Algiers, Lagos, Kinshasa, Abidjan, Tunis, Cape Town, Nairobi; **physical** dominated by a central plateau, which includes the world's largest desert, the ◊Sahara; Nile and Zaïre rivers, but generally there is a lack of rivers, and also of other inlets, so that Africa has proportionately the shortest coastline of all the continents; comparatively few offshore islands; 75% is within the tropics; **products** Africa has 30% of the world's minerals; coffee (Kenya), cocoa (Ghana, Nigeria), cotton (Egypt, Uganda); **population** (1987) 601,000,000; **language** Hamito-Semitic in the N; Bantu below the Sahara; Khosan languages with 'click' consonants in the far S.

African /'æfrɪkən/ *adj.* **1.** of Africa or its people. **2.** (*South African*) Bantu. —*n.* **1.** an African black. **2.** (*South African*) a Bantu of South Africa. —**African marigold,** an annual garden plant *Tagetes erecta* with yellow flowers, originally from Mexico. —**African violet,** an East African plant of the genus *Saintpaulia*, with purple, pink, or white flowers, grown as a houseplant in Britain.

African art the art of sub-Saharan Africa, from prehistory onwards, ranging from the art of ancient civilizations to the new styles of post-imperialist African nations. Among the best-known examples of historic African art are bronze figures from Benin and Ife (in Nigeria) dating from about 1500 and, also on the W coast, in the same period, bronze or brass figures for weighing gold, made by the Ashanti.

Africanize /'æfrɪkənaɪz/ *v.t.* to make African, to place under the control of African blacks. —**Africanization** /-'zeɪʃən/ *n.*

African National Congress (ANC) a multiracial nationalist organization formed in South Africa in 1912 to extend the franchise to the whole population and end all racial discrimination there. Its president is Oliver ◊Tambo and vice president from 1990 Nelson ◊Mandela. Although originally nonviolent, the ANC was banned by the government from 1960 to Jan 1990. In exile in Mozambique it developed a military wing, *Umkhonto we Sizwe,* which engaged in sabotage and guerrilla training. Its leader in exile was Oliver ◊Tambo; former leaders include Albert Luthuli, Nelson Mandela and Solomon Plaatje. State president F W de Klerk lifted the ban in Feb 1990 and the leaders were released from prison. Nelson Mandela, deputy president, now leads ANC activities.

Afrikaans language an official language of the Republic of South Africa (the other is English). Spoken mainly by the ◊Afrikaners, it is a variety of the Dutch language, modified by circumstance and the influence of German, French, and other immigrant as well as local languages. It became a standardized written language about 1875. [Dutch = African]

Afrika Korps the German army in the western desert of N Africa 1941–43 in World War II, commanded by Field Marshal Rommel. They were driven out of N Africa by May 1943.

Afrikaner *n.* (formerly known as **Boer**) an inhabitant of South Africa descended from the original Dutch and ◊Huguenot settlers of the 17th century. Comprising approximately 60% of the white population in the Republic, Afrikaners were originally farmers but have now become mainly urbanized. Their language is Afrikaans. [Afrikaans]

Afro /'æfrəʊ/ *adj.* (of a hairstyle) full and bushy, as that naturally grown by some blacks.

Afro- in combinations, African. [from Latin *Afer* = African]

Afro-American *adj.* of American blacks or their culture. —*n.* an American black.

Afro-Asiatic *adj.* (of languages) Hamito-Semitic.

Afro-Caribbean a West Indian of African descent. Afro-Caribbeans are the descendants of W Africans captured or obtained in trade by European slave-traders, then shipped to the West Indies. Since World War II many Afro-Caribbeans have migrated to Europe, especially to Britain and the Netherlands, and to North America.

afrormosia /æfrɔː'məʊziə/ *n.* an African tree of the genus *Afrormosia*; its teak-like wood, used for furniture. [from *Ormosia*, genus of trees]

aft *adv.* in, near, or to the stern of a ship or the rear of an aircraft. [probably from earlier *baft*]

after *prep.* **1.** behind in place or order; later than. **2.** in spite of. **3.** as a result of. **4.** in pursuit or search of. **5.** about, concerning. **6.** in imitation or honour of. —*adv.* behind; later. —*conj.* at or in a time later than. —*adj.* later, following; nearer the stern in a boat. —**aftercare** *n.* attention after leaving hospital etc. **aftereffect** *n.* an effect that arises or persists after the primary action of something. [Old English]

afterbirth *n.* the placenta and other material, including blood and the fetal membrane, expelled from the mammalian uterus soon after birth.

afterburning *n.* the method of increasing the thrust of a gas turbine (jet) aeroplane engine by spraying additional fuel into the hot exhaust duct between the turbojet and the tail-pipe where it ignites. It is used for short-term increase of power during takeoff or during combat in military aircraft.

after-image *n.* the persistence of an image on the retina of the eye after the object producing it has been removed. This leads to persistence of vision, a necessary phenomenon for the illusion of continuous movement in films and television. The term is also used for the persistence of sensations other than vision.

afterlife *n.* life in a later part of a person's lifetime, or after death.

aftermath /'ɑːftəmæθ/ *n.* **1.** consequences, aftereffects. **2.** new grass growing after mowing or harvest. [from *math* = mowing]

aftermost *adj.* last, furthest aft.

afternoon /ɑːftə'nuːn/ *n.* the time from noon to evening.

after-ripening *n.* the process undergone by the seeds of some plants before germination can occur. It helps seeds to germinate at a time when conditions are most favourable for growth. In some cases the embryo is not fully mature at the time of dispersal and must develop further before germination can take place. Other seeds do not germinate even when the embryo is mature, probably owing to growth inhibitors within the seed that must be leached out or broken down before germination can begin.

afters /'ɑːftəz/ *n.pl.* (*colloquial*) a course following the main course at a meal.

aftershave *n.* a lotion for use after shaving.

afterthought *n.* something thought of or added later.

afterwards /'ɑːftəwədz/ *adv.* US **afterward** *adv.* later, subsequently. [Old English *wards* = in the direction of]

Ag symbol for silver. [from Latin *argentum*]

AG abbreviation of *Aktiengesellschaft.* [German = limited company]

Agadir /ægə'dɪə/ resort and seaport in S Morocco, near the mouth of the river Sus. Population (1984) 110,500. It was rebuilt after being destroyed by an earthquake in 1960.

Agadir Incident an international crisis provoked by Kaiser Wilhelm II of Germany. By sending the gunboat *Panther* to demand territorial concessions from the French, he hoped to drive a wedge into the Anglo-French entente. In fact, German aggression during the second Moroccan crisis merely served to reinforce Anglo-French fears of Germany's intentions. The crisis gave rise to the term 'gunboat diplomacy'.

again /ə'geɪn, ə'gen/ *adv.* **1.** another time, once more; as before; in addition. **2.** furthermore, besides, likewise; on the other hand. [Old English]

against /ə'geɪnst, ə'genst/ *prep.* **1.** in opposition to; to the disadvantage of; in contrast to. **2.** into collision or contact with. **3.** in anticipation of, in preparation for; so as to cancel or lessen the effect of; in return for.

Aga Khan IV /'ɑːgə 'kɑːn/ 1936– . Spiritual head (*imam*) of the **Ismaili** Muslim sect (see ◊Islam). He succeeded his grandfather in 1957.

agama *n.* a lizard of the Old World family Agamidae, especially the genus *Agama.* There are about 280 species, found throughout the warmer regions of the Old World. Many are brilliantly coloured and all are capable of changing the colour of their skin.

Agamemnon /ægə'memnən/ in Greek mythology, a Greek hero, son of Atreus, king of Mycenae. He married Clytemnestra, and their children included ◊Electra, Iphigenia, and ◊Orestes. He led the capture of Troy, received Priam's daughter Cassandra as a prize, and was murdered by Clytemnestra and her lover, Aegisthus, on his return home. His children Orestes and Electra later killed the guilty couple. Aeschylus, Euripides, T S Eliot, O'Neill and Sartre all based plays on the theme.

agapanthus /ægə'pænθəs/ n. an ornamental lily of the genus *Agapanthus*, native to South Africa, with blue or white flowers. [Latin from Greek *agapē* = love and *anthos* = flower]

agape /ə'geɪp/ *predic. adj.* gaping, open-mouthed.

agar /'eɪgɑː/ n. or **agar-agar** any of certain seaweeds of SE Asian seas, especially *Gracilaria lichenoides*, from which a gelatinous substance is extracted, used as a solidifying agent in bacterial culture media, as a laxative and in preserved foods. [Malay]

agaric n. a fungus of typical mushroom shape. Agarics include the field mushroom *Agaricus campestris* and the cultivated edible mushroom *Agaricus brunnesiens*. Closely related is the ◊*Amanita* genus, including the fly agaric *Amanita muscaria*. [from Latin from Greek]

Agassiz /'ægəsi/ Jean Louis 1807–1873. Swiss naturalist who emigrated to the USA and became one of the foremost scientists of the 19th century. He established his name through work on the classification of the fossil fishes. Unlike Darwin, he did not believe that individual species themselves changed, but that new species were created from time to time.

agate n. a kind of hard semiprecious stone, a banded or cloudy type of ◊chalcedony, a silica, SiO_2, that forms in rock cavities. Agates are used as ornamental stones and for art objects. [French from Latin from Greek]

agave /ə'gɑːvɪ/ n. any of several related plants with stiff, sword-shaped, spiny leaves arranged in a rosette. All species of the genus *Agave* come from the warmer parts of the New World. They include *A. sisalina*, whose fibres are used for rope making, and the Mexican century plant *A. americana*. Alcoholic drinks such as ◊tequila and pulque are made from the sap of agave plants. [from Greek *Agaūē* = woman in myth (*agauos* = illustrious)]

age n. **1.** the length of past life or existence. **2.** (*colloquial*, especially in *plural*) a long time. **3.** a historical or other distinct period. **4.** the later part of life, old age. —*v.t./i.* (*participle* ageing) in common usage, the period of deterioration of the physical condition of a living organism that leads to death; in biological terms, the entire life process. —**age-long**, **age-old** *adjs.* having existed for a very long time. **of age,** having reached the age (18, formerly 21) at which one has an adult's legal rights and obligations. **under age,** below this age. [from Old French from Latin *aetas* = age]

aged *adj.* **1.** /eɪdʒd/ of the age of (*aged* 3). **2.** /'eɪdʒɪd/ very old.

ageism n. discrimination against older people in employment, pensions, housing, and health care. To combat it the American Association of Retired Persons (AARP) has 30 million members, and in 1988 a similar organization was founded in the UK. In the USA the association has been responsible for legislation forbidding employers to discriminate; for example, making it illegal to fail to employ, to dismiss, or to reduce working conditions or wages of people aged 40–69.

ageless *adj.* never growing or appearing old or outmoded; eternal.

agency /'eɪdʒənsɪ/ n. **1.** the business or establishment of an agent. **2.** active or intervening action. [from Latin *agere* = do]

agenda /ə'dʒendə/ n. (*plural* agendas) a programme of items of business to be dealt with at a meeting etc. [Latin, from *agere* = do]

agent /'eɪdʒənt/ n. **1.** a person who acts for another in business etc. **2.** one who or that which exerts power or produces an effect. **3.** (also **secret agent**) a spy.

Agent Orange a selective ◊weedkiller, subsequently discovered to contain highly poisonous ◊dioxin. It became notorious after its use in the 1960s during the Vietnam War by US forces to eliminate ground cover which could protect Communists. Thousands of US troops who had handled it later developed cancer or fathered deformed babies. [from the distinctive orange stripe on its packaging]

agent provocateur /æʒɑ̃ prəvɒkə'tɜː/ (*plural agents provocateurs, pronounced* the same) a person employed to detect suspected offenders by tempting them to overt action. [French = provocative agent]

agglomerate /ə'glɒməreɪt/ *v.t./i.* to collect into a mass. —/-ət/ n. a mass, especially of fused volcanic fragments. —/-ət/ *adj.* collected into a mass. —**agglomeration** /-'reɪʃən/ n. [from Latin *agglomerare* (*glomus* = ball)]

agglutinate /ə'gluːtɪneɪt/ *v.t./i.* **1.** to stick or fuse together, to coalesce. **2.** (of language) to combine simple words without change of form to express compound ideas. —**agglutination** /-'eɪʃən/ n., in medicine, the clumping together of ◊antigens, such as blood cells or bacteria, to form larger, visible masses, under the influence of ◊antibodies. As each antigen clumps only in response to its particular antibody, agglutination provides a way of determining ◊blood groups and the identity of unknown bacteria. **agglutinative** /-ətɪv/ *adj.* [from Latin *agglutinare* (*gluten* = glue)]

aggrandize /ə'grændaɪz/ *v.t.* to increase the power, rank, or wealth of; to make seem greater. —**aggrandizement** /-ɪzmənt/ n. [from French from Italian *aggrandire* from Latin *grandis* = large]

aggravate /'ægrəveɪt/ *v.t.* **1.** to increase the gravity of. **2.** (*colloquial, disputed usage*) to annoy. —**aggravation** /-'veɪʃən/ n. [from Latin *aggravare* = make heavy (*gravis* = heavy)]

aggregate /'ægrɪgət/ n. **1.** a total, an amount assembled. **2.** broken stone, gravel, etc., used in making concrete. **3.** a mass of particles or minerals. —*adj.* combined, total. —/-geɪt/ *v.t./i.* to collect or form into an aggregate; to unite; (*colloquial*) to amount to. —**in the aggregate**, as a whole. —**aggregation** /-'geɪʃən/ n. [from Latin *aggregare* = herd together (*grex* = flock)]

aggression /ə'greʃən/ n. **1.** unprovoked attacking or attack; a hostile act or behaviour. **2.** in biology, behaviour used to intimidate or injure another organism (of the same or of a different species), usually for the purposes of gaining a territory, a mate, or food. Aggressive signals include roaring by red deer, snarling by dogs, the fluffing up of feathers by birds, and the raising of fins by some species of fish. **3.** in politics, an unprovoked attack often involving an escalating series of threats aimed at intimidating an opponent. The actions of Nazi Germany, under Adolf Hitler in the 1930s, leading to World War II were considered to be aggressive. The invasion of Kuwait by Iraq in 1990 was condemned as an act of aggression. [from French or Latin *aggressio* = attack (*gradi* = step)]

aggressive /ə'gresɪv/ *adj.* apt to make attacks, showing aggression; forceful, self-assertive. —**aggressively** *adv.*, **aggressiveness** n.

aggressor /ə'gresə/ n. one who makes an unprovoked attack or begins hostilities.

aggrieved /ə'griːvd/ *adj.* having a grievance. [from Old French *agrever* = make heavier]

aghast /ə'gɑːst/ *adj.* filled with consternation or dismay. [from obsolete verb *agast* = frighten]

agile /'ædʒaɪl/ *adj.* nimble, quick-moving; lively. —**agilely** *adv.*, **agility** /ə'dʒɪlɪtɪ/ n. [French from Latin *agere* = do]

Agincourt, Battle of /'ædʒɪnkɔː/ the battle of the Hundred Years' War in which Henry V of England defeated the French on 24 Oct 1415. As a result of the battle, Henry gained France and the French princess, Catherine of Valois, as his wife. The village of Agincourt (modern *Azincourt*) is S of Calais, in N France.

agitate /'ædʒɪteɪt/ *v.t./i.* **1.** to disturb, to excite. **2.** to stir up (public) interest or concern. **3.** to shake briskly. —**agitation** /-'teɪʃən/ n., **agitator** n. [from Latin *agitare*, frequentative of *agere* = drive]

agley /ə'gleɪ/ *adv.* (*Scottish*) askew, awry. [from Scottish *gley* = squint]

aglow /ə'gləʊ/ *predic. adj.* glowing. —*adv.* glowingly.

AGM abbreviation of annual general meeting.

agnail /'ægneɪl/ n. = ◊hangnail. [Old English = tight (metal) nail, hard excrescence in flesh]

Agnew /'ægnjuː/ Spiro 1918– . US vice president 1969–73. A Republican, he was governor of Maryland 1966–69, and vice president under ◊Nixon. He took the lead in a campaign against the press and opponents of the ◊Vietnam war. Although he was one of the few administration officials not to be implicated in the ◊Watergate affair, he resigned in 1973, shortly before pleading 'no contest' to a charge of income-tax evasion.

To some extent, if you've seen one city slum you've seen them all.

Spiro T. Agnew
election speech, Detroit 1968

---

agnostic /æg'nɒstɪk/ *n.* one who believes that nothing can be known of the existence of God or of anything but material phenomena. —*adj.* of this view. —**agnosticism** /-sɪzəm/ *n.* [from Greek *a-* = not and *gnosis* = knowledge]

ago /ə'gəʊ/ *adv.* in the past. [from obsolete *agone* = gone by]

agog /ə'gɒg/ *adv. & predic. adj.* eager, expectant. [from French *en gogues* = in fun]

agonize /'ægənaɪz/ *v.t./i.* **1.** to suffer mental anguish; to suffer agony. **2.** to pain greatly.

agony /'ægənɪ/ *n.* extreme mental or physical suffering; a severe struggle. —**agony aunt,** (*colloquial*) the (female) editor of an agony column. **agony column,** the personal column of a newspaper; a regular newspaper or magazine feature containing readers' questions about personal difficulties, with replies from the columnist. [from Old French or Latin from Greek *agōn* = struggle]

agoraphobia /ægərə'fəʊbɪə/ *n.* a ◊phobia involving fear of open spaces and crowded places. The anxiety produced can be so severe that some sufferers are confined to their homes for many years. —**agoraphobic** *adj. & n.* [from Greek *agora* = marketplace]

Agostini /ægɒ'stiːni/ Giacomo 1943– . Italian motorcyclist. He won a record 122 grand prix and 15 world titles. His world titles were at 350cc and 500cc and he was five times a dual champion.

agouti *n.* a small rodent of the genus *Dasyprocta*, family Dasyproctidae. It is found in the forests of Central and South America. The agouti is herbivorous, swift-running, and about the size of a rabbit.

AGR abbreviation of advanced gas-cooled reactor, a type of ◊nuclear reactor widely used in western Europe, especially Britain. The AGR uses a fuel of enriched uranium dioxide in stainless-steel cladding and a moderator of graphite. Carbon dioxide gas is pumped through the reactor core to extract the heat produced by the ◊fission of the uranium. The heat is transferred to water in a steam generator, and the steam drives a turbogenerator to produce electricity.

Agra /'ɑːgrə/ city of Uttar Pradesh, India, on the river Jumna, 160 km/100 mi SE of Delhi; population (1981) 747,318. A commercial and university centre, it was the capital of the Mogul empire 1527–1628, from which period the ◊Taj Mahal dates.

agrarian /ə'greərɪən/ *adj.* relating to agricultural land or its cultivation, or to landed property. [from Latin *ager* = land]

agree /ə'griː/ *v.t./i.* **1.** to hold a similar opinion; to consent (*to*). **2.** to become or be in harmony, to suit or be compatible *with*. **3.** to approve as correct; to reach agreement about. —**be agreed,** to have reached a similar opinion. [from Old French from Latin *gratus* = pleasing]

agreeable /ə'griːəbəl/ *adj.* **1.** pleasing. **2.** willing to agree. —**agreeably** *adv.*

agreement /ə'griːmənt/ *n.* **1.** agreeing, harmony in opinion or feeling. **2.** a contract or promise.

agribusiness /'ægrɪbɪznɪs/ *n.* the group of industries concerned with the processing and distribution of agricultural produce or with farm machinery.

Agricola /ə'grɪkələ/ Gnaeus Julius AD 37–93. Roman general and politician. Born in Provence, he became Consul of the Roman Republic AD 77, and then governor of Britain AD 78–85. He extended Roman rule to the Firth of Forth in Scotland and won the battle of Mons Graupius. His fleet sailed round the N of Scotland and proved Britain an island.

agricultural revolution the sweeping changes that took place in British agriculture over the period 1750–1850 in response to the increased demand for food from a rapidly expanding population. Changes of the latter half of the 18th century included the enclosure of open fields, the introduction of four-course rotation together with new fodder crops such as turnip, and the development of improved breeds of livestock.

agriculture /'ægrɪkʌltʃə/ *n.* the practice of farming, including the cultivation of the soil (for raising crops) and the rearing of livestock. The units for managing agricultural production vary from small holdings and individually owned farms to corporate-run farms and collective farms run by entire communities. Agriculture developed in Egypt and the Near East at least 7,000 years ago. —**agricultural** /-'kʌltʃərəl/ *adj.*, **agriculturist** /-'kʌl-/ *n.* [French, or from Latin *ager* = field and *cultura* = culture]

agrimony /'ægrɪmənɪ/ *n.* a perennial plant *Agrimonia eupatoria* of the rose family Rosaceae with small yellow flowers. —**hemp agrimony,** a wild perennial plant with mauve flowers and hairy leaves. [from Old French from Latin from Greek *argemonē* = poppy]

Agrippa /ə'grɪpə/ Marcus Vipsanius 63–12 BC. Roman general. He commanded the victorious fleet at ◊Actium and married Julia, daughter of ◊Augustus.

agronomy /ə'grɒnəmɪ/ *n.* the science of soil management and crop production. [from French from Greek *agros* = land and *nemō* = arrange]

aground /ə'graʊnd/ *adv.* on or to the bottom of shallow water.

ague /'eɪgjuː/ *n.* malarial fever; a fit of shivering. [from Old French from Latin *acuta (febris)* = acute fever]

ah interjection expressing surprise, delight, pity, etc. [from French]

AH with reference to the Muslim calendar, abbreviation of *anno Hegirae*. [Latin = year of the flight (of Muhammad, from Mecca to Medina)]

aha interjection expressing surprise or triumph.

Ahab /'eɪhæb/ *c.*875–854 BC. King of Israel. His empire included the suzerainty of Moab, and Judah was his subordinate ally, but his kingdom was weakened by constant wars with Syria. By his marriage with Jezebel, princess of Sidon, Ahab introduced into Israel the worship of the Phoenician god Baal, thus provoking the hostility of Elijah and other prophets. Ahab died in battle against the Syrians at Ramoth Gilead.

Ahasuerus /əhæzju'iərəs/ name of several Persian kings in the Bible, notably the husband of ◊Esther. Traditionally it was also the name of the ◊Wandering Jew. [Latinized Hebrew form of the Persian *Khshayarsha*, Greek *Xerxes*]

ahead /ə'hed/ *adv.* further forward in space, time, or progress etc.; in advance. [origin nautical]

ahimsa *n.* in Hinduism, Buddhism, and Jainism, the doctrine of respect for all life (including the lowest forms and even the elements themselves) and consequently an extreme form of nonviolence. It arises in part from the concept of *karma*, which holds that a person's actions (and thus any injury caused to any form of life) are carried forward from one life to the next, determining each stage of reincarnation. [Sanskrit *a* = without and *himsa* = injury]

Ahmadiyya /ɑːmə'diːə/ *n.* an Islamic religious movement founded by Mirza Ghulam Ahmad (1839–1908). His followers reject the doctrine that Muhammad was the last of the prophets and accept Ahmad's claim to be the Mahdi and Promised Messiah. In 1974 the Ahmadis were denounced by their coreligionists as non-Muslims.

Ahmad Shah Durrani /'ɑːmæd 'ʃɑː/ 1724–1773. Founder and first ruler of Afghanistan. Elected shah in 1747, he had conquered the Punjab by 1751.

Ahmedabad /'ɑːmədəbɑːd/ or **Ahmadabad** capital of Gujarat, India; population (1981) 2,515,195. It is a cotton-manufacturing centre, and has many sacred buildings of the Hindu, Muslim, and Jain faiths.

ahoy /ə'hɔɪ/ *int.* (*nautical*) a call used in hailing.

Ahriman /'ɑːrɪmən/ *n.* in Zoroastrianism, the supreme evil spirit, lord of the darkness and death, waging war with his counterpart Ahura Mazda (Ormuzd) until a time when human beings choose to lead good lives and Ahriman is finally destroyed.

Ahura Mazda /ə'hʊərə 'mæzdə/ or **Ormuzd** in Zoroastrianism, the spirit of supreme good. As god of life and light he will finally prevail over his enemy, Ahriman.

Ahváz /ɑːˈvɑːz/ industrial capital of the province of Khuzestan, W Iran; population (1986) 590,000.

aid *n.* 1. help. 2. one who or that which helps. —*v.t.* to help. [from Old French from Latin *juvare* = help]

AI(D) abbreviation of artificial insemination (by donor). AIH is artificial insemination by husband.

Aidan, St /ˈeɪdn/ *c.*600–651. Irish monk who converted Northumbria to Christianity and founded Lindisfarne monastery on Holy Island off the NE coast of England. His feast day is 31 Aug.

aid, development money given or lent on concessional terms to developing countries or spent on maintaining agencies for this purpose. In the late 1980s official aid from governments of richer nations amounted to $45–$60 billion annually whereas voluntary organizations in the West received about $2.4 billion a year for the Third World. The ◊World Bank is the largest dispenser of aid. All industrialized United Nations (UN) member countries devote a proportion of their gross national product to aid, ranging from 0.21% (Austria) to 1.2% (Norway) (1986 figures).

aide /eɪd/ *n.* an aide-de-camp; an assistant. [French]

aide-de-camp /eɪd də ˈkɑ̃ː/ *n.* (*plural* **aides-de-camp** *pronounced* the same) an officer assisting a senior officer. [French]

aid, foreign another name for development ◊aid.

AIDS or **Aids**, acronym from acquired immune deficiency syndrome, a condition in which a person's natural defences against illness are broken down. It is caused by the human immunodeficiency virus (HIV), now known to be a ◊retrovirus, an organism first identified in 1983. HIV is transmitted in body fluids, mainly blood and sexual secretions.

Aiken /ˈeɪkən/ Howard 1900– . US mathematician. In 1939, in conjunction with engineers from IBM, he started work on the design of an automatic calculator using standard business machine components. In 1944 they completed one of the first computers, the Automatic Sequence Controlled Calculator (known as the Mark 1), a programmable computer controlled by punched paper tape and using ◊punched cards.

aikido *n.* Japanese art of self-defence; one of the ◊martial arts. Two main systems of aikido are tomiki and uyeshiba.

ail *v.t./i.* (*archaic*) to make ill or uneasy; to be in poor health. [Old English *egle* = troublesome]

aileron *n.* a pilot-controlled aerofoil attached to, in, or near the trailing edge of an aeroplane wing, controlling lift and lateral balance. It was invented by US aviation pioneer Glen Curtis (1878–1930) in 1911. [French, diminutive of *aile* = wing from Latin *ala*]

ailing *adj.* ill, in poor health or condition.

ailment *n.* a minor illness.

aim *v.t./i.* 1. to point, direct, or send towards a target; to take aim. 2. to make an attempt, to intend. —*n.* 1. the act of aiming. 2. purpose, intention; goal. [from Old French from Latin *aestimare* = reckon]

aimless *adj.* without a purpose. —**aimlessly** *adv.*, **aimlessness** *n.*

ain't (*colloquial*) am not, is not, are not; has not, have not. [contraction]

Ainu /ˈaɪnuː/ *n.* (*plural* the same or **Ainus**) a member of the non-Mongoloid aboriginal inhabitants of the Japanese archipelago whose physical characteristics (light skin colour, round eyes, and exceptionally thick wavy hair) set them apart dramatically from the majority population of the islands. [Ainu = man]

air *n.* 1. the mixture of gases (mainly oxygen and nitrogen) surrounding the Earth and breathed by all land animals and plants. 2. the atmosphere, open space in this; this as the place where aircraft operate. 3. a light wind. 4. an impression given; an affected manner. 5. a melody, a tune. —*v.t./i.* 1. to expose or be exposed to fresh or warm air so as to remove staleness or damp. 2. to express publicly. —**air bed**, an inflatable mattress. **airbrick** *n.* a brick with holes to allow ventilation. **air-conditioned** *adj.* supplied with **air conditioning**, a system for regulating the humidity and temperature of a building. A complete air-conditioning unit controls the temperature and humidity of the air, removes dust and odours from it, and circulates it by means of a fan. **air cushion**, an inflatable cushion; a layer of air providing support, especially for an **air cushion vehicle** (ACV). The hovercraft is the best-known form of

ACV. **air force**, a branch of the armed forces equipped for attacking and defending by means of aircraft (in Britain, the Royal Air Force, constituted in 1918 by amalgamating the Royal Flying Corps, formed in 1912, with the Royal Naval Air Service). **air freight**, freight carried by air. **air-freight** *v.t.* to send as air freight. **air letter**, a folding sheet of light paper that may be sent cheaply by airmail. **air pocket**, a partial vacuum in the air causing aircraft in flight to drop suddenly. **by air**, in or by aircraft. **in the air**, current, prevalent; uncertain, not yet decided. **on the air**, broadcast or broadcasting by radio or television. —**airer** *n.* [from Old French from Latin from Greek; sense 4 French, probably from Old French *aire* = disposition from Latin *area*; sense 5 from Italian *aria*]

airborne *adj.* 1. transported by air or by aircraft. 2. in flight after taking off.

aircraft *n.* (*plural* the same) any aeronautical vehicle, which may be lighter than air (supported by buoyancy) or heavier than air (supported by the dynamic action of air on its surfaces). ◊Balloons and ◊airships are lighter-than-air craft. Heavier-than-air craft include the ◊aeroplane, glider, autogyro, and helicopter.

aircraft carrier a ship carrying and used as a base for aircraft. After World War II the cost and vulnerability of such large vessels were thought to have outweighed their advantages. However, by 1980 the desire to have a means of destroying enemy aircraft beyond the range of a ship's own weapons led to a widespread revival of aircraft carriers of 20,000–30,000 tonnes.

aircraftman *n.* the lowest rank in the RAF.

aircraftwoman *n.* the lowest rank in the WRAF.

aircrew *n.* the crew manning an aircraft.

Airedale /ˈeədeɪl/ *n.* a terrier of a large rough-coated breed, about 60 cm/2 ft tall. It originated about 1850 in England, as a cross of the otter hound and Irish and Welsh terriers. [place in W Yorkshire]

airfield *n.* an area of land equipped with runways etc. for aircraft.

airflow *n.* a flow of air.

airglow *n.* a faint and variable light in the Earth's atmosphere produced by chemical reactions in the ionosphere.

airgun *n.* a gun using compressed air to propel a missile.

airless *adj.* stuffy; without wind, calm and still.

airlift *n.* large-scale transport of troops, supplies, etc. by air, especially in an emergency. —*v.t.* to transport thus.

airline *n.* a service of air transport for public use; a company providing this.

airliner *n.* a large passenger-carrying aircraft.

airlock *n.* 1. stoppage of a flow by trapped air in a pump or pipe. 2. a compartment with an airtight door at each end, providing access to a pressurized chamber.

airmail *n.* mail carried by air. —*v.t.* to send by airmail.

airman *n.* (*plural* **airmen**) a male member of an air force; a male aviator.

air pollution the contamination of the atmosphere caused by the discharge, accidental or deliberate, of a wide range of toxic substances. The cost of preventing any discharge of pollutants into the air is prohibitive, so attempts are more usually made to reduce gradually the amount of discharge and to disperse this as quickly as possible by using a very tall chimney, or by intermittent release.

airport *n.* an airfield with facilities for passengers and goods.

air raid an aerial attack, usually on a civilian population. In World War II (1939–45), raids were usually made by bomber aircraft, but many thousands were killed in London in 1944 by German V1 and V2 rockets. The air raids on Britain 1940–41 became known as **the Blitz**. The Allies made air raids over European cities.

air sac in birds, a thin-walled extension of the lungs. There are nine of these and they extend into the abdomen and bones, effectively increasing lung capacity. In mammals, it is another name for the ◊alveoli in the lungs, and in some insects, for widenings of the ◊trachea.

airscrew *n.* an aircraft propeller.

airship *n.* a power-driven aircraft that is lighter than air. All airships have streamlined envelopes or hulls, which contain the inflation gas (originally hydrogen, now helium) and are non-rigid, semi-rigid, or rigid.

airsick *adj.* affected with nausea from the motion of an aircraft. —**airsickness** *n.*

airspace *n.* the air above a country and subject to its jurisdiction.

airstrip *n.* a strip of ground prepared for take-off and landing of aircraft.

airtight *adj.* impermeable to air or gas.

air transport a means of conveying goods or passengers by air from one place to another. See ◊aeroplane.

airway *n.* 1. a regular route of aircraft. 2. a ventilating passage in a mine. 3. a passage for air into the lungs; a device to secure this.

airwoman *n.* (*plural* **airwomen**) a female member of an air force; a female aviator.

airworthy *adj.* (of aircraft) fit to fly. —**airworthiness** *n.*

airy *adj.* 1. well-ventilated; breezy. 2. light as air; unsubstantial. 3. casual and light-hearted. —**airy-fairy** *adj.* fanciful, impractical. —**airily** *adv.*, **airiness** *n.*

Airy /'eəri/ George Biddell 1801–1892. English astronomer. He installed a transit telescope at the Cambridge University Observatory at Greenwich, England, and accurately measured ◊Greenwich Mean Time by the stars along the line of zero longitude defined by the position of the observatory.

aisle /ail/ *n.* 1. a side part of a church, divided by pillars from the main ◊nave. 2. a passage between rows of pews or seats. [from Old French from Latin *ala* = wing]

aitch /eitʃ/ *n.* the letter h, H. [from French]

aitchbone /'eitʃbəʊn/ *n.* the rump-bone of an animal; a cut of beef lying over this. [originally *nache-bone* from Old French from Latin *natis* = buttock]

Ajaccio /æ'ʒæksiəʊ/ capital and second largest port of Corsica; population (1982) 55,279. Founded by the Genoese in 1492, it was the birthplace of Napoleon; it has been French since 1768.

ajar /ə'dʒɑː/ *adv. & predic. adj.* slightly open. [from obsolete *char* = turn]

Ajax /'eidʒæks/ Greek hero in Homer's ◊Iliad. Son of Telamon, king of Salamis, he was second only to Achilles among the Greek heroes in the Trojan War. When ◊Agamemnon awarded the armour of the dead Achilles to ◊Odysseus, Ajax is said to have gone mad with jealousy, and then committed suicide in shame.

Ajman /'ædʒmɑːn/ the smallest of the seven states that make up the ◊United Arab Emirates; area 250 sq km/96 sq mi; population (1980) 36,000.

Akbar /'ækbɑː/ Jalal ud-Din Muhammad 1542–1605. Mogul emperor of N India from 1556, when he succeeded his father. He gradually established his rule throughout N India. He is considered the greatest of the Mogul emperors, and the firmness and wisdom of his rule won him the title 'Guardian of Mankind'; he was a patron of the arts.

à Kempis Thomas see ◊Thomas à Kempis, religious writer.

Akhenaton /ækə'nɑːtn/ another name for ◊Ikhnaton, pharaoh of Egypt.

Akhetaton /æki'tɑːtɒn/ capital of ancient Egypt established by the monotheistic pharaoh ◊Ikhnaton as the centre for his cult of the Aton, the sun's disc; it is the modern Tell el Amarna 300 km/190 mi S of Cairo.

Akhmatova /æk'mætəvə/ Anna. Pen name of Anna Andreevna Gorenko 1889–1966. Russian poet. Among her works are the cycle *Requiem* 1963 (written in the 1930s), which deals with the Stalinist terror, and *Poem Without a Hero* 1962 (begun 1940).

Akihito /æki'hiːtəʊ/ 1933– . Emperor of Japan from 1989, succeeding his father Hirohito (Showa). His reign is called the Heisei era ('achievement of universal peace').

akimbo /ə'kimbəʊ/ *adv.* (of arms) with hands on hips and elbows turned outwards. [originally *in kenebow*, probably from Old Norse = bent in a curve]

akin /ə'kin/ *adj.* similar; related.

Akkad /'ækæd/ *n.* the northern Semitic people who conquered the Sumerians in 2350 BC and ruled Mesopotamia. The ancient city of Akkad in central Mesopotamia, founded by ◊Sargon I, was an imperial centre in the 3rd millennium BC; the site is unidentified, but it was on the Euphrates.

Akkaia alternative form of ◊Achaea.

Aksai Chin /æksai/ part of Himalayan Kashmir lying to the E of the Karakoram range. It is occupied by China but claimed by India.

Aksum /'ɑːksʊm/ ancient Greek-influenced Semitic kingdom that flourished 1st–6th centuries AD and covered a large part of modern Ethiopia as well as the Sudan. The ruins of its capital, also called Aksum, lie NW of Aduwa, but the site has been developed as a modern city.

al- for Arabic names beginning with *al-*, see rest of name; for example, for 'al-Fatah', see ◊Fatah, al-.

Al symbol for aluminium.

à la /ɑ: lɑ:/ after the manner of. [French]

Alabama /ælə'bæmə/ state of S USA; **area** 134,700 sq km/51,994 sq mi; **capital** Montgomery; **physical** the Cumberland Plateau in the N; the Black Belt, or Canebrake, in the centre; and S of this, the coastal plain of Piny Woods. The Alabama river is the largest in the state; **products** cotton, soya beans, peanuts, wood products, coal, iron, chemicals, textiles, paper; **population** (1987) 4,149,000; **history** first settled by the French in the early 18th century, it was ceded to Britain in 1763, passed to the USA in 1783, and became a state in 1819. It was one of the ◊Confederate States in the American Civil War.

alabaster /'æləbɑːstə/ *n.* a translucent, usually white form of gypsum, often carved into ornaments. It is a soft material and ranks second on the ◊Mohs' scale of hardness. —*adj.* of alabaster; white or smooth as alabaster. [from Old French from Latin from Greek]

à la carte /ɑ: lɑ: 'kɑːt/ ordered as separate items from a menu. [French]

alacrity /ə'lækriti/ *n.* prompt and eager readiness. [from Latin *alacer* = brisk]

Aladdin /ə'lædin/ in the ◊*Arabian Nights*, a poor boy who obtains a magic lamp: when the lamp is rubbed, a jinn (genie, or spirit) appears and fulfils its owner's wishes.

Alain-Fournier /æ'læŋ 'fʊəniei/ pen name of Henri-Alban Fournier 1886–1914. French novelist. His haunting semi-autobiographical fantasy *Le Grand Meaulnes/The Lost Domain* 1913 was a cult novel of the 1920s and 1930s. His life is intimately recorded in his correspondence with his brother-in-law Jacques Rivière.

Alamein, El, Battles of /'æləmein/ in World War II, two decisive battles in the western desert, N Egypt. In the **First Battle of El Alamein** 1–27 Jul 1942 the British 8th Army under Auchinleck held the German and Italian forces under Rommel. In the **Second Battle of El Alamein** 23 Oct–4 Nov 1942 ◊Montgomery defeated Rommel.

Alamo, the /'æləməʊ/ a mission fortress in San Antonio, Texas, USA. It was besieged 23 Feb–6 Mar 1836 by ◊Santa Anna and 4,000 Mexicans; they killed the garrison of about 180, including Davy ◊Crockett and Jim ◊Bowie.

à la mode /ɑ: lɑ: 'məʊd/ in fashion, fashionable. [French]

Alamogordo /æləmə'gɔːdəʊ/ town in New Mexico, USA, associated with nuclear testing. The first atom bomb was exploded nearby at Trinity Site on 16 July 1945. It is now a test site for guided missiles.

Alanbrooke /'ælənbrʊk/ Alan Francis Brooke, 1st Viscount Alanbrooke 1883–1963. British army officer, chief of staff in World War II and largely responsible for the strategy that led to the German defeat.

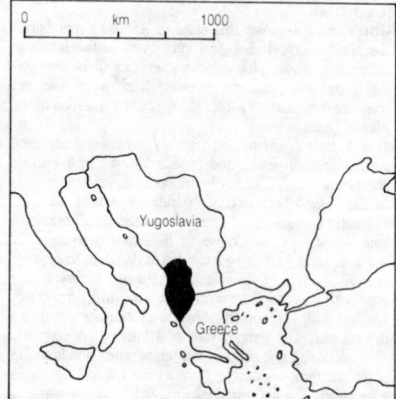

Albania

Alarcón /æla:'kɒn/ Pedro Antonio de 1833–1891. Spanish journalist and writer. The acclaimed *Diario/Diary* was based upon his experiences as a soldier in Morocco. His *El Sombrero de tres picos/The Three-Cornered Hat* 1874 was the basis of Manuel de Falla's ballet.

Alaric /'ælərɪk/ *c.*370–410. King of the Visigoths. In 396 he invaded Greece and retired with much booty to Illyria. In 400 and 408 he invaded Italy, and in 410 captured and sacked Rome, but he died the same year on his way to invade Sicily.

alarm /ə'lɑ:m/ *n.* 1. a warning sound or signal; a device giving this. 2. an alarm clock. 3. fear caused by expectation of danger or difficulty. —*v.t./i.* to frighten; to arouse to a sense of danger. —**alarm clock,** a clock with a device that rings at a set time. [from Old French from Italian *all'arme!* = to arms!]

alarmist *n.* one who raises unnecessary or excessive alarm.

alas /ə'læs/ interjection expressing sorrow or distress. [from Old French from Latin *lassus* = weary]

Alaska /ə'læskə/ largest state of the USA, on the NW extremity of North America, separated from the lower 48 states by British Columbia; **area** 1,531,000 sq km/591,00 sq mi; **capital** Juneau; **physical** much of Alaska is mountainous and includes Mount McKinley, 6,194 m/20,322 ft, the highest peak in North America. Reindeer thrive in the Arctic tundra, and elsewhere there are extensive forests; **products** oil, natural gas, coal, copper, iron, gold, tin, fur, salmon fisheries and canneries, lumber; **population** (1987) 538,000; including 9% American Indians, Aleuts, and Inuits; **history** Alaska was a Russian colony from 1744 until purchased by the USA in 1867 for $7,200,000; it became a state in 1959.

alb *n.* a white vestment reaching to the feet, worn by some priests at church services. [Old English from Latin *albus* = white]

albacore /'ælbəkɔ:(r)/ *n.* a name loosely applied to several species of fishes found in warm regions of the Atlantic and Pacific oceans, in particular to a large tuna, *Thunnus alalunga,* and to several other species of the mackerel family. [from Portuguese from Arabic = the young camel]

Albania /æl'beɪnɪə/ Socialist People's Republic; country in SE Europe, bounded to the W and SW by the Mediterranean sea, to the N and E by Yugoslavia, and to the SE by Greece; **area** 28,748 sq km/11,097 sq mi; **capital** Tiranë; **physical** mainly mountainous, with rivers flowing E–W, and a small coastal plain; **head of state** Ramiz Alia from 1982; **head of government** Adil Carcani from 1982. Hoxha remained premier as first secretary of Albanian Party of Labour until his death 1985; **political system** one-party Socialist republic; **exports** crude oil, bitumen, chrome, iron ore, nickel, coal, copper wire, tobacco, fruit; **population** (1990 est) 3,270,000; **language** Albanian, Greek; **recent history** Communist republic proclaimed under Enver Hoxha in 1946. Albania admitted into Comecon in 1949; broke off relations with USSR 1961 and China 1978. Diplomatic relations with the West restored in 1985. Albania attended the conference of Balkan states in 1988.

Alban, St /'ɔ:lbən/ died AD 303. First Christian martyr in England. In 793 King Offa founded a monastery on the site of Alban's martyrdom, around which the city of St Albans grew up.

albatross /'ælbətrɒs/ *n.* 1. a large seabird, genus *Diomedea,* with long narrow wings adapted for gliding and a wingspan of up to 3 m/10 ft, inhabiting the Pacific and southern Oceans. It belongs to the order Procellariiformes, the same group as petrels and shearwaters. 2. (in golf) a score of 3 under par at a hole. [from Spanish and Portuguese from Arabic = the jug]

albedo /æl'bi:dəʊ/ *n.* (*plural* albedos) the fraction of the incoming light reflected by a body such as a planet. A body with a high albedo, near 1, is very bright, while a body with a low albedo, near 0, is dark. The Moon has an average albedo of 0.07, Venus 0.76, Earth 0.37. [Latin = whiteness (*albus* = white)]

Albee /'ælbi:/ Edward 1928– . US playwright. His plays, performed internationally, are associated with the Theatre of the ◊Absurd and include *The Zoo Story* 1960, *The American Dream* 1961, *Who's Afraid of Virginia Woolf?* 1962, and *Tiny Alice* 1965. *A Delicate Balance* 1966 and *Seascape* 1975 won Pulitzer prizes.

albeit /ɔ:l'bi:ɪt/ *conj.* (*literary*) although. [from *all be it* = let it be completely true that]

Albéniz /æl'beɪnɪθ/ Isaac 1860–1909. Spanish composer and pianist, born in Catalonia. He composed the suite *Iberia* and other piano pieces, making use of traditional Spanish melodies.

Alberoni /ælbə'rəʊni/ Giulio 1664–1752. Spanish-Italian priest and politician, born in Piacenza, Italy. Philip V made him prime minister of Spain in 1715. In 1717 he became a cardinal. He introduced many domestic reforms, but was forced to flee to Italy in 1719, when his foreign policies failed.

Albert /'ælbət/ Prince Consort 1819–1861. Husband of British Queen ◊Victoria from 1840; a patron of the arts, science, and industry. Albert was the second son of the Duke of Saxe-Coburg-Gotha and first cousin to Queen Victoria, whose chief adviser he became. He planned the Great Exhibition of 1851; the profit was used to buy the sites in London of all the South Kensington museums and colleges and the Royal Albert Hall, built 1871. He died of typhoid.

Albert I 1875–1934. King of the Belgians from 1909, the younger son of Philip, Count of Flanders, and the nephew of Leopold II. In 1900 he married Duchess Elisabeth of Bavaria. In World War I he commanded the Allied army that retook the Belgian coast in 1918.

Alberta /æl'bɜ:tə/ province of W Canada; **area** 661,200 sq km/255,223 sq mi; **capital** Edmonton; **physical** the Rocky Mountains; dry, treeless prairie in the centre and S; to N this merges into a zone of poplar, then mixed forest; **products** coal; wheat, barley, oats, sugar beet in the S; more than a million head of cattle; oil and natural gas; **population** (1986) 2,375,000; **history** in the 17th century much of its area was part of a grant to the ◊Hudson's Bay Company for the fur trade. It became a province in 1905.

Alberti /æl'beəti/ Leon Battista 1404–1472. Italian ◊Renaissance architect and theorist who recognized the principles of Classical architecture and their modification for Renaissance practice in *On Architecture* 1452.

Albigenses /ælbi'dʒensi:z/ *n.pl.* a heretical sect of Christians (associated with the ◊Cathars) who flourished in S France near Albi and Toulouse during the 11th–13th centuries. They adopted the Manichean belief in the duality of good and evil and pictured Jesus as being a rebel against the cruelty of an omnipotent God.

albino /æl'bi:nəʊ/ *n.* (*plural* albinos) a person or animal with a congenital lack of colouring pigment in the skin and hair (which are white) and the eyes (usually pink); a plant lacking normal colouring. —**albinism** /'ælbɪnɪzəm/ *n.* [Spanish and Portuguese from Latin *albus* = white]

Albinoni /ælbi'nəʊni/ Tomaso 1671–1751. Italian Baroque composer and violinist, whose work was studied and adapted by ◊Bach. He composed over 40 operas.

Albion /'ælbiən/ ancient name for Britain used by the Greeks and Romans. [mentioned by Pytheas of Massilia (4th century BC) and probably of Celtic origin, but the Romans, having in mind the white cliffs of Dover, assumed it to be derived from *albus* = white]

Ålborg alternative form of ◊Aalborg, Denmark.

Albufeira /ælbu'feərə/ fishing village and resort on the Algarve coast of S Portugal, 43 km/27 mi W of Faro.

album /'ælbəm/ *n.* 1. a blank book in which a collection of postage stamps, photographs, autographs, etc. can be kept. 2. a long-playing gramophone record with several items; a set of records. [Latin = blank tablet (*albus* = white)]

albumen /'ælbjumɪn/ *n.* white of eggs. [Latin *albus* = white]

albumin /'ælbjumɪn/ *n.* or **albumen** any of a group of sulphur-containing ◊proteins. The best known is in the form of egg white; others occur in milk, and as a major component of serum. They are soluble in water and dilute salt solutions, and are coagulated by heat. [from French]

Albuquerque /'ælbəkɜ:ki/ Afonso de 1453–1515. Viceroy and founder of the Portuguese East Indies with strongholds in Ceylon, Goa and Malacca 1508–15, when the king of Portugal replaced him by his worst enemy. He died at sea.

Alcaeus /æl'si:əs/ *c.*611–*c.*580 BC. Greek lyric poet. Born at Mytilene in Lesvos, he was a member of the aristocratic party and went into exile when the popular party triumphed. He wrote odes, and the Alcaic stanza is named after him.

alcázar /æl'kæθɑ:/ *n.* a Moorish palace in Spain; one of five in Toledo was defended by the Nationalists against the Republicans for 71 days in 1936 during the Spanish ◊Civil War. [Arabic = fortress]

Alcazarquivir, Battle of /ælkæθəki'viə/ a battle on 4 Aug 1578 between the forces of Sebastian, king of Portugal (1554–1578), and those of the Berber kingdom of Fez. Sebastian's death on the field of battle paved the way for the incorporation of Portugal into the Spanish kingdom of Philip II.

alchemy /'ælkəmi/ *n.* a medieval form of chemistry, the supposed technique of transmuting base metals, such as lead and mercury, into silver and gold by the philosopher's stone, a hypothetical substance, to which was also attributed the power to give eternal life. **—alchemist** *n.* [from Old French from Latin from Arabic *al-Kimya* = the art of transmuting metals]

Alcibiades /ælsi'baɪədi:z/ 450–404 BC. Athenian general. Handsome and dissolute, he became the archetype of capricious treachery for his military intrigues against his native state with Sparta and Persia; the Persians eventually had him assassinated. He was brought up by ◊Pericles and was a friend of ◊Socrates, whose reputation as a teacher suffered from the association.

Alcock /'ælkɒk/ John William 1892–1919. British aviator. On 14 June 1919, he and Arthur Whitten Brown (1886–1948) made the first nonstop transatlantic flight, from Newfoundland to Ireland.

alcohol /'ælkəhɒl/ *n.* a colourless, volatile liquid, the intoxicant present in wine, beer, and spirits, also used as solvents for gums and resins, in lacquers and varnishes, in the making of dyes, for essential oils in perfumery, and as fuel; liquor containing this. In chemistry, a compound of the same type as alcohol. [French or Latin from Arabic = the kohl]

alcoholic /ælkə'hɒlɪk/ *adj.* of or containing alcohol; caused by alcohol. *—n.* a person who suffers from alcoholism.

alcoholic liquor an intoxicating drink. ◊Ethanol (ethyl alcohol), a colourless liquid, C_2H_5OH, is the basis of all common intoxicants: **wines, ciders, and sherry** contain alcohol produced by direct fermentation with yeasts of the sugar content in the relevant fruit; **malt liquors** are beers and stouts, in which the starch of the grain is converted to sugar by malting, and the sugar then fermented into alcohol by yeasts. Fermented drinks contain less than 20% alcohol; **spirits** are distilled from malted liquors or wines, and can contain up to 55% alcohol. When consumed, alcohol is rapidly absorbed from the stomach and upper intestine and affects nearly every tissue, particularly the central nervous system. Tests have shown that the feeling of elation usually associated with drinking alcoholic liquors is caused by the loss of inhibitions through removal of the restraining influences of the higher cerebral centres. It also results in dilatation of the blood vessels, particularly of the skin.

Alcoholics Anonymous a voluntary self-help organization established in 1934 in the USA to combat alcoholism; branches now exist in many other countries.

alcoholism /'ælkəhɒlɪzəm/ *n.* habitual heavy drinking of alcohol; a diseased condition caused by this.

alcohol strength a measure of the amount of alcohol in a drink. Wine is measured as the percentage volume of alcohol at 20°C; spirits in litres of alcohol at 20°C, although the percentage volume measure is also commonly used. A 75 cl bottle at 40% volume is equivalent to 0.3 litres of alcohol. See also ◊proof spirit.

Alcott /'ɔːlkət/ Louisa M(ay) 1832–1888. US author of the children's classic *Little Women* 1869, which drew on her own home circumstances, the heroine Jo being a partial self-portrait. *Good Wives* 1869 was among its sequels.

alcove /'ælkəʊv/ *n.* a recess in a wall, room, etc. [French from Spanish from Arabic = the vault]

Alcuin /'ælkwɪn/ 735–804. English scholar. Born in York, he went to Rome in 780, and in 782 took up residence at Charlemagne's court in Aachen. From 796 he was abbot of Tours. He disseminated Anglo-Saxon scholarship, organized education and learning in the Frankish empire, gave a strong impulse to the Carolingian Renaissance, and was a prominent member of Charlemagne's academy.

Aldebaran /æl'debərən/ *n.* or **Alpha Tauri** the brightest star in the constellation Taurus and the 13th brightest star in the sky; it marks the eye of the 'bull'. Aldebaran is a red giant 68 light years away, shining with a true luminosity of about 100 times that of the Sun.

aldehyde /'ældɪhaɪd/ *n.* a volatile fluid with a suffocating smell, got by oxidation of alcohol; in chemistry, a compound of the same structure as this. [from Latin = alcohol deprived of hydrogen]

al dente /æl 'dentɪ/ cooked so as to be still firm when bitten. [Italian = to the tooth]

alder *n.* any tree or shrub of the genus *Alnus*, in the birch family Betulaceae, found mainly in cooler parts of the N hemisphere and characterized by toothed leaves and catkins; any of various similar trees (*black, red, white alder*) not related. [Old English]

alderman /'ɔːldəmən/ *n.* (*plural* **aldermen**) **1.** (chiefly *historical*) a senior member of the borough or county councils in England and Wales, elected by the other councillors. The office was abolished in 1974, but the title is still used in the City of London. **2.** (*US & Australian*) an elected governor of a city. [from Old English *aldor* = patriarch (*ald* = old)]

Aldermaston /'ɔːldəmɑːstən/ village in Berkshire, England; site of an atomic and biological weapons research establishment. During 1958–63 the Campaign for Nuclear Disarmament (CND) made it the focus of an annual Easter protest march.

Aldington /'ɔːldɪŋtən/ Richard 1892–1962. British ◊Imagist poet, novelist and critic, who was married to Hilda ◊Doolittle from 1913 to 1937. He wrote biographies of D H Lawrence and T E Lawrence. His novels include *Death of a Hero* 1929 and *All Men are Enemies* 1933.

Aldiss /'ɔːldɪs/ Brian 1925– . English science-fiction writer, anthologist, and critic. His novels include *Non-Stop* 1958, *The Malacia Tapestry* 1976, and the 'Helliconia' trilogy. *Trillion Year Spree* 1986 is a history of science fiction.

ale /eɪl/ *n.* beer, especially (**real ale**) that regarded as brewed and stored in the traditional way, with secondary fermentation in the container from which it is dispensed. [Old English]

aleatory /'eɪliətərɪ/ *adj.* depending on the throw of a die etc. or on chance. **aleatory music,** a method of composition (pioneered by John ◊Cage) dating from about 1945 in which the elements are assembled by chance by using, for example, dice or computer. [from Latin *alea* = die]

alembic /ə'lembɪk/ *n.* an apparatus formerly used in distilling. [from Old French from Latin from Arabic (= the still), from Greek *ambix* = cup]

Alentejo /ælən'teʒuː/ a region of E central Portugal divided into the districts of Alto Alentejo and Baixo Alentejo. The chief towns are Evora, Neja, and Portalegre.

Aleppo /ə'lepəʊ/ (Syrian *Halab*) ancient city in NW Syria; population (1981) 977,000. There has been a settlement on the site for at least 4,000 years.

alert /ə'lɜːt/ *adj.* watchful, vigilant; nimble. *—n.* a warning signal, notice to stand ready; a state or period of special vigilance. *—v.t.* to make alert, to warn of danger. [from French from Italian *all' erta* = to the watchtower]

Aletsch /'ɑːletʃ/ the most extensive glacier in Europe, 23.6 km/14.7 mi long, beginning on the S slopes of the Jungfrau in the Bernese Alps, Switzerland.

Aleutian Islands /ə'luːʃən/ volcanic island chain in the N Pacific, stretching 1,900 km/1,200 mi SW of Alaska, of which it forms part. Population 5,000 Inuit (Eskimo), most of whom belong to the Greek Orthodox Church, 1,600 Aleuts, plus a large US military establishment. There are 14 large and over 100 small islands, running along the Aleutian Trench.

A level or **Advanced level** in the UK, examinations taken by some students in no more than four subjects at one time, usually at the age of 18 after two years' study. Two A-level passes are normally required for entry to a university degree course.

alewife *n.* a fish *Alosa pseudoharengus* of the ◊herring group, up to 30 cm/1 ft long, found in the NW Atlantic and in the Great Lakes of North America.

Alexander /ælɪg'zɑːndə/ Samuel 1859–1938. Australian philosopher who originated the theory of emergent evolution: that the space-time matrix evolved matter; matter evolved life; life evolved mind; and finally God emerged from mind.

Alexander eight popes, including:

Alexander III (Orlando Barninelli) died 1181. Pope 1159–81. His authority was opposed by Frederick I Barbarossa, but Alexander eventually compelled him to render homage in 1178. He supported Henry II of England in his invasion of Ireland, but imposed penance on him after the murder of Thomas à ◊Becket.

Alexander VI (Rodrigo Borgia) 1431–1503. Pope 1492–1503. Of Spanish origin, he bribed his way to the papacy, where he furthered the advancement of his illegitimate children, who included Cesare and Lucrezia ◊Borgia. When ◊Savonarola preached against his corrupt practices Alexander had him executed. Alexander was a great patron of the arts in Italy, as were his children. He is said to have died of poison he had prepared for his cardinals.

Alexander three tsars of Russia:

Alexander I 1777–1825. Tsar from 1801. Defeated by Napoleon at Austerlitz in 1805, he made peace at Tilsit in 1807, but economic crisis led to a break with Napoleon's ◊continental system and the opening of Russian ports to British trade; this led to Napoleon's ill-fated invasion of Russia. After the Congress of Vienna in 1815, Alexander hoped through the Holy Alliance with Austria and Prussia to establish a new Christian order in Europe.

Alexander II 1818–1881. Tsar from 1855. He embarked on reforms of the army, the government, and education, and is remembered as 'the Liberator' for his emancipation of the serfs in 1861. However, the revolutionary element remained unsatisfied, and Alexander became increasingly autocratic and reactionary. He was assassinated by ◊Nihilists.

Alexander III 1845–1894. Tsar from 1881, when he succeeded his father, Alexander II. He pursued a reactionary policy, promoting Russification and persecuting the Jews. He married Dagmar (1847–1928), daughter of Christian IX of Denmark and sister of Queen Alexandra of Britain, in 1866.

Alexander three kings of Scotland:

Alexander I c.1078–1124. King of Scotland from 1107, known as **the Fierce**. He was succeeded by his brother David I.

Alexander II 1198–1249. King of Scotland from 1214, when he succeeded his father William the Lion. Alexander supported the English barons in their struggle with King John after Magna Carta.

Alexander III 1241–1285. King of Scotland from 1249, son of Alexander II. In 1263, by military defeat of Norwegian forces, he extended his authority over the Western Isles, which had been dependent on Norway. He strengthened the power of the central Scottish government.

Alexander I Karageorgevich 1888–1934. Regent of Serbia 1912–21 and king of Yugoslavia 1921–34, as dictator from 1929; assassinated, possibly by Italian Fascists.

Alexander Nevski, St /'nevski/ 1220–1263. Russian military leader, son of the grand duke of Novgorod; in 1240 he defeated the Swedes on the banks of the Neva (hence Nevski), and in 1242 defeated the Teutonic Knights on the frozen Lake Peipus.

Alexander Obrenovich /'brenevits/ 1876–1903. King of Serbia from 1889 while still a minor, on the abdication of his father, King Milan. He took power into his own hands in 1893 and in 1900 married a widow, Draga Mashin. In 1903 Alexander and his queen were murdered, and ◊Peter I Karageorgevich was placed on the throne.

alexanders n. a strong-smelling tall herbaceous plant *Smyrnium olusatrum* of the carrot family Umbelliferae. It is found on hedgebanks and cliffs. Its yellow flowers appear in spring and early summer.

Alexander Severus /si'viərəs/ AD 208–235. Roman emperor from 222, when he succeeded his cousin Heliogabalus. He was born in Palestine. His campaign against the Persians in 232 achieved some success, but in 235, on his way to defend Gaul against German invaders, he was killed in a mutiny.

Alexander the Great 356–323 BC. King of Macedonia and conqueror of the large Persian empire. As commander of the vast Macedonian army he conquered Greece in 336. He defeated the Persian king Darius in Asia Minor in 333, then moved on to Egypt, where he founded Alexandria. He defeated the Persians again in Assyria in 331, then advanced further E to reach the Indus. He

conquered the Punjab before diminished troops forced his retreat.

Alexandra /ælɪg'zɑːndrə/ 1936– . Princess of the UK. Daughter of the Duke of Kent and Princess Marina, she married Angus Ogilvy (1928–), younger son of the earl of Airlie. They have two children, James (1964–) and Marina (1966–).

Alexandra 1872–1918. Last tsarina of Russia 1894–1917. She was the former Princess Alix of Hessen and granddaughter of Britain's Queen Victoria. She married ◊Nicholas II and, from 1907, fell under the spell of ◊Rasputin, a 'holy man' brought to the palace to try to cure her son of haemophilia. She was shot with the rest of her family by the Bolsheviks in the Russian Revolution.

Alexandria /ælɪg'zɑːndriə/ or *El Iskandariya* city, chief port, and second largest city of Egypt, situated between the Mediterranean and Lake Maryut; population (1986) 5,000,000. It is linked by canal with the Nile and is an industrial city (oil refining, gas processing, and cotton and grain trading). Founded in 331 BC by Alexander the Great, Alexandria was for over 1,000 years the capital of Egypt.

Alexandria, Library of a library in Alexandria, Egypt, founded in 330 BC by ◊Ptolemy I Soter. It was the world's first state-funded scientific institution, and comprised a museum, teaching facilities, and a library that contained 700,000 scrolls, including much ancient Greek literature. In 1989 the Egyptian government planned a new library to be the most important Middle Eastern centre for the study of regional civilizations.

Alexandria, School of the writers and scholars of Alexandria, who made the city the chief centre of culture in the Western world from about 331 BC–AD 642. They include the poets Callimachus, Apollonius Rhodius, and Theocritus; Euclid, pioneer of geometry; Eratosthenes, the geographer; Hipparchus, who developed a system of trigonometry; the astronomer Ptolemy; and the Jewish philosopher Philo. The Gnostics and Neo-Platonists also flourished in Alexandria.

alexandrine /ælɪg'zændraɪn/ n. a verse of six iambic feet. —adj. in this metre. [from French from *Alexandre* = Alexander (the Great), subject of a poem in this metre]

Alexeev /æ'leksief/ Vasiliy 1942– . Soviet weightlifter who broke 80 world records 1970–77, a record for any sport.

Alexius /ə'leksiəs/ five emperors of Byzantium, including:

Alexius I /kɒm'niːnəs/ (Comnenus) 1048–1118. Byzantine emperor 1081–1118. The Latin (W European) Crusaders helped him repel Norman and Turkish invasions, and he devoted great skill to buttressing the threatened empire. His daughter ◊Anna Comnena chronicled his reign.

Alexius III (Angelos) died c.1210. Byzantine emperor 1195–1203. He gained power by deposing and blinding his brother Isaac II, but Isaac's Venetian allies enabled him and his son Alexius IV to regain power as co-emperors.

Alexius IV (Angelos) 1182–1204. Byzantine emperor from 1203, when, with the aid of the army of the Fourth Crusade, he deposed his uncle Alexius III. He soon lost the support of the Crusaders (by that time occupying Constantinople), and he was overthrown and murdered by another Alexius, Alexius Mourtzouphlus (son-in-law of Alexius III) in 1204, an act which the Crusaders used as a pretext to sack the city the same year.

alfalfa /æl'fælfə/ n. or **lucerne**, a perennial, tall herbaceous plant *Medicago sativa* of the legume family Leguminosae, with spikes of small purple flowers in late summer. Native to Eurasia, it is now an important worldwide fodder crop, generally processed into hay, meal, or silage. [Spanish from Arabic = a green fodder]

Alfa Romeo /'ælfə rəʊ'meɪəʊ/ Italian car-manufacturing company, known for its racing cars. In 1985 the company was bought by Fiat.

Alfieri /æl'fi'eəri/ Vittorio, Count Alfieri 1749–1803. Italian dramatist. The best of his 28 plays, most of them tragedies, are *Saul* 1782 and *Mirra* 1786.

Alfonsín Foulkes /ælfon'siːn 'fuːks/ Raúl Ricardo 1927– . Argentine politician, president 1983–89, leader of the Radical Union Party (UCR). As president from the country's return to civilian government, he set up an investigation of the army's human-rights violations. Economic problems forced him to seek help from the International Monetary Fund and introduce austerity measures.

Alfred the Great The profile of Alfred the Great, king of Wessex, featured on a coin of about 887.

Alfonso /æl'fɒnseʊ/ six kings of Portugal, including:
Alfonso I 1094–1185. King of Portugal from 1112. He made Portugal independent from León.
Alfonso 13 kings of León, Castile, and Spain, including:
Alfonso VII c.1107–1157. King of León and Castile from 1126, who attempted to unite Spain. Although he protected the Moors, he was killed trying to check a Moorish rising.
Alfonso X called *el Sabio* ('the Wise') 1221–1284. King of Castile from 1252. His reign was politically unsuccessful but he contributed to learning: he made Castilian the official language of the country and commissioned a history of Spain, an encyclopedia, and translations from Arabic of works on, among other subjects, astronomy and games.
Alfonso XI the Avenger 1311–1350. King of Castile from 1312. He ruled cruelly, repressed a rebellion by his nobles, and defeated the last Moorish invasion in 1340.
Alfonso XII 1857–1885. King of Spain from 1875, son of ◊Isabella II. He assumed the throne after a period of republican government following his mother's flight and effective abdication in 1868.
Alfonso XIII 1886–1941. King of Spain 1886–1931. He assumed power in 1906 and married Princess Ena, granddaughter of Queen Victoria of the United Kingdom, in the same year. He abdicated in 1931 soon after the fall of the Primo de Rivera dictatorship 1923–30 (which he supported), and Spain became a republic. His assassination was attempted several times.
Alfred /'ælfrɪd/ **the Great** c.848–c.900. King of Wessex from 871. He defended England against Danish invasion, founded the first English navy, and put into operation a legal code. He encouraged the translation of works from Latin (some of which he translated himself), and promoted the development of the ◊Anglo-Saxon Chronicle.
alfresco /æl'freskəʊ/ *adj. & adv.* in the open air. [from Italian]
algae /'ældʒiː, -giː/ *n.pl.* (usually in *plural, singular* **alga** /'ælgə/) any of a large group of primitive, mainly aquatic, non-flowering photosynthetic plants. Algae range from single-celled forms to multicellular seaweeds of considerable size and complexity. [Latin]
Algarve /æl'gɑːv/ ancient kingdom in S Portugal, the modern district of Faro, a popular holiday resort; population (1981) 323,500. [Arabic *al-gharb* = the west]
algebra /'ældʒɪbrə/ *n.* the branch of mathematics that deals with formulae and equations in which symbols (usually letters) stand for unknown numbers or other entities. —**algebraic** /-'breɪk/ *adj.,* **algebraically** *adv.* [Italian, Spanish, and Latin from Arabic = reunion of broken parts]
Algeciras Conference a conference held in Jan 1906 when France, Germany, Britain, Russia, and Austria-Hungary, together with the USA, Spain, the Low Countries, Portugal, and Sweden, met to settle the question of Morocco. The conference was prompted by increased German demands in what had traditionally been seen as a French area of influence, but it resulted in a reassertion of Anglo-French friendship and the increased isolation of Germany.

Algeria /æl'dʒɪərɪə/ Democratic and Popular Republic of; country in N Africa, bounded to the E by Tunisia and Libya, to the SE by Niger, to the SW by Mali, to the NW by Morocco, and to the N by the Mediterranean Sea; **area** 2,381,741 sq km/919,352 sq mi; **capital** al-Jazair (Algiers); **physical** coastal plains backed by mountains in N; Sahara desert in S; **head of state** Benjedid Chadli from 1979; **political system** one-party socialist republic; **exports** oil, natural gas, iron, wine, olive oil; **population** (1990 est) 25,715,000 (83% Arab, 17% Berber); **language** Arabic (official); Berber, French; **recent history** independence from France achieved in 1962 after eight years of civil war. Ahmed Ben Bella, leader of the National Liberation Front (FLN) elected president of the republic but deposed in 1965 by a military coup. Limited political pluralism introduced in 1989. 1990 elections won by Fundamentalist Islamic Salvation Front.
Algiers /æl'dʒɪəz/ (Arabic *al-Jazair,* French *Alger*) capital of Algeria, situated on the narrow coastal plain between the Atlas mountains and the Mediterranean; population (1984) 2,442,300.
Algiers, Battle of the bitter conflict in Algiers 1954–62 between the Algerian nationalist population and the French colonial army and French settlers. The conflict ended with Algerian independence in 1962.
alginate *n.* a salt of alginic acid $(C_6H_8O)_n$, obtained from brown seaweeds and used in textiles, paper, food products, and pharmaceuticals.
Algol /'ælgɒl/ *n.* or **Beta Persei** an ◊eclipsing binary, a pair of rotating stars in the constellation Perseus, one of which eclipses the other every 69 hours, causing its brightness to drop by two thirds.
ALGOL *n.* or **Algol** in computing, an early high-level programming language, developed in the 1950s and 1960s for scientific applications. A general-purpose language, ALGOL is best suited for mathematical work and has an algebraic style. [from **algo**rithmic **l**anguage]
Algonquin *n.* one of the North American Indians formerly living along the Ottawa River and the northern tributaries of the St Lawrence in E Canada. Many now live on reserves in E Ontario, W Québec, and the NE USA; others have chosen to live among the general populations of Canada and the USA.
algorithm /'ælgərɪðəm/ *n.* a process or rules for calculation, especially by computer, where the term algorithm describes the logical sequence of operations to be performed by a program. [from Old French from Latin from Persian *Al-Khuwārizmī* (name of 9th-century mathematician)]
Alhambra /æl'hæmbrə/ *n.* a fortified palace in Granada, Spain, built on a rocky hill by Moorish kings mainly between 1248 and 1354. It is considered the finest example of Moorish architecture.
Alhazen /æl'hɑːzən/ Ibn al Haytham c.965–1038. Arabian scientist, author of the *Kitab al Manazir/Book of Optics,* translated into Latin as *Perspectiva.* For centuries it remained the most comprehensive and authoritative treatment of optics in both the East and West.
Ali /'ɑːli/ c.600–661. 4th caliph of Islam. He was born in Mecca, the son of Abu Talib, uncle to the prophet Muhammad, who gave him his daughter Fatima in marriage. On Muhammad's death in 632, Ali had a claim to succeed him, but this was not conceded until 656. After a stormy reign, he was assassinated. Around Ali's name the controversy has raged between the Sunni and the Shi'ites (see ◊Islam), the former denying his right to the caliphate and the latter supporting it.
Ali (Ali Pasha) 1741–1822. Turkish politician, known as *Arslan* ('the Lion'). An Albanian, he was appointed pasha (governor) of the Janina region in 1788 (now Ioánnina, Greece). His court was visited by the British poet Byron. He was assassinated on the sultan's order.
Ali /ɑː'liː/ Muhammad. Born Cassius Marcellus Clay, Jr 1942– . US boxer. Olympic light-heavyweight champion in 1960, he went on to become world professional heavyweight champion in 1964, and was the only man to regain the title twice. He was known for his fast footwork and extrovert nature.
Alia /'ælɪə/ Ramiz 1925– . Albanian communist politician, head of state from 1982 and party leader from 1985. He slightly relaxed the isolationist policies of his predecessor

Hoxha and introduced economic reforms following public unrest, thus earning the description of the Albanian Gorbachev.

alias /'eɪlɪəs/ *adv.* called (by a certain name) at other times. —*n.* an assumed name. [Latin = at another time]

alibi /'ælɪbaɪ/ *n.* (*plural* **alibis**) 1. in law, a provable assertion that the accused was at some other place when a crime was committed. 2. (*disputed usage*) an excuse. [Latin = at another place]

Alice's Adventures in Wonderland a children's story by Lewis Carroll, published in 1865. Alice dreams she follows the White Rabbit down a rabbit-hole and meets fantastic characters such as the Cheshire Cat, the Mad Hatter, and the King and Queen of Hearts.

alidade /'ælɪdeɪd/ *n.* a sighting device for angular measurement, formerly used with a quadrant, astrolabe, etc., now with a plane table. [from Latin from Arabic = the revolving radius]

alien /'eɪlɪən/ *n.* 1. a foreign-born resident who is not naturalized in the country where he or she lives. 2. a being from another world. —*adj.* 1. foreign, not one's own, unfamiliar. 2. differing in nature, inconsistent. 3. repugnant. [from Old French from Latin *alius* = other]

Alien and Sedition Acts laws passed by the US Congress in 1798, when war with France seemed likely. The acts lengthened the period of residency required for US citizenship, gave the president the power to expel 'dangerous' aliens, and severely restricted criticism of the government. They were controversial because of the degree of power exercised by central government; they are now also seen as an early manifestation of US xenophobia (fear of foreigners).

alienate /'eɪlɪəneɪt/ *v.t.* 1. to estrange, to make unfriendly or hostile. 2. to transfer the ownership of; to divert. —**alienation** /-'neɪʃən/ *n.* a sense of isolation, powerlessness, and therefore frustration; a feeling of loss of control over one's life; a sense of estrangement from society or even from oneself. [from Latin]

Aligarh /ɑːˈliːɡɑː/ city in Uttar Pradesh, N central India; population (1981) 20,861.

alight[1] /əˈlaɪt/ *predic. adj.* on fire, lit up. [probably from *on a light* (= lighted) *fire*]

alight[2] *v.i.* to get down or off; to descend and settle. [Old English]

align /əˈlaɪn/ *v.t.* 1. to place in or bring into line, to coordinate. 2. to ally with a party or cause. —**alignment** *n.* [from French *à ligne* = into line]

alike /əˈlaɪk/ *predic. adj.* like one another. —*adv.* in a like manner. [from Old English]

alimentary /ælɪˈmentərɪ/ *adj.* of food or nutrition; nourishing. —**alimentary canal**, the tubular passage, about 9 m/30 ft long in a human adult, through which food passes from mouth to anus in being digested and absorbed by the body. It consists of the mouth cavity, pharynx, oesophagus, stomach, and the small and large intestines. [from Latin *alimentarius* (*alere* = nourish)]

alimony /'ælɪmənɪ/ *n.* (*historical*) an allowance (now called ◊maintenance) payable to a woman from her (ex-)husband pending or after a divorce or legal separation; (*US*) an allowance paid to a spouse.

Ali Pasha /ɑːˈliːˈpɑːʃə/ Mehmed Emin 1815–1871. Grand vizier (chief minister) of the Ottoman empire 1855–56, 1858–59, 1861, and 1867–71, noted for his attempts to westernize the Ottoman Empire.

aliphatic /ælɪˈfætɪk/ *adj.* in chemistry (of compounds), related to fats; in which carbon atoms form open chains. [from Greek *aleiphar* = fat]

aliquot /'ælɪkwɒt/ *adj.* that produces a quotient without a fraction when a given larger number is divided by it. —*n.* 1. an aliquot part. 2. a representative portion of a substance. [from French from Latin = several]

alive /əˈlaɪv/ *pred. adj.* 1. living. 2. lively, active; alert or responsive *to*. 3. teeming (*with*). [Old English]

alkali /'ælkəlaɪ/ *n.* (*plural* **alkalis**) 1. any of a class of substances that neutralize acids and form caustic or corrosive solutions in water. The four main alkalis are sodium hydroxide (caustic soda, $NaOH$); potassium hydroxide (caustic potash, KOH); calcium hydroxide (slaked lime or limewater, $Ca(OH)_2$); and aqueous ammonia ($NH_{3\ (aq)}$). 2. a substance with similar but weaker properties, e. g. sodium carbonate. [from Latin from Arabic = the calcined ashes]

alkali metals any of a group of six metallic elements with similar chemical bonding properties: lithium, sodium, potassium, rubidium, caesium, and francium. They are univalent and of very low density (lithium, sodium, and potassium float on water); in general they are reactive, soft, low-melting-point metals.

alkaline /'ælkəlaɪn/ *adj.* having the properties of an alkali. —**alkalinity** /-'lɪnɪtɪ/ *n.*

alkaline-earth metals any of a group of six metallic elements with similar bonding properties: beryllium, magnesium, calcium, strontium, barium, and radium. They are strongly basic, bivalent, and occur in nature only in compounds.

alkaloid /'ælkələ:ɪd/ *n.* any of a large group of nitrogenous bases of plant origin, many of which are used as drugs (e. g. quinine). [from German]

alkane *n.* any member of the group of ◊hydrocarbons having the general formula C_nH_{2n+2} (common name **paraffins**). Lighter alkanes are colourless gases (for example, methane, ethane, propane, butane); in nature they are found dissolved in petroleum. Heavier ones are liquids or solids.

alkene *n.* any member of the group of ◊hydrocarbons having the general formula C_nH_{2n}, commonly known as olefins. Lighter alkenes, such as ethene, $CH_2=CH_2$, and propene, $CH_3CH=CH_2$, are gases, obtained from the cracking of oil fractions (see ◊fractionation). Many useful compounds (such as poly(ethene) and bromoethane) are made from them.

al-Khalil Arabic name for ◊Hebron in the Israeli-occupied West Bank.

alkyl /'ælkɪl/ *n.* (usually *attributive*) derived from or related to a hydrocarbon of the paraffin series. [from German]

alkyne *n.* any member of the group of ◊hydrocarbons with the general formula C_nH_{2n-2}, commonly known as acetylenes. Lighter alkynes are gases (for example, ◊ethyne); heavier ones are liquids or solids.

all /ɔ:l/ *adj.* 1. the whole amount, quantity, or extent of. 2. the greatest possible. 3. any whatever. —*n.* 1. all persons concerned, everything. 2. (in games) on both sides. —*adv.* entirely, quite; (*colloquial*) very. —**after all**, in spite of what has been said, done, or expected. **All Blacks**, the New Zealand international Rugby football team, so called from the colour of their uniforms. **all clear**, a signal that a danger or difficulty is over. **All-Hallows** *n.* All Saints' Day. **all in**, exhausted. **all-in** *attrib.* inclusive of all. **all in all**, when everything is considered; of supreme importance. **all out**, using all possible strength, effort, etc. **all over**, completely finished; in or on all parts (of); typically; (*colloquial*) excessively or effusively attentive to. **all-purpose** *adj.* having many uses. **all right**, (*predicative*) satisfactory, safe and sound, in good condition; satisfactorily, as desired; (as *interjection*) I consent or agree, (*ironically*) you deserve this. **all round**, in all respects; for each person. **all-round** *adj.* (of a person) versatile. **all-rounder** *n.* a versatile person. **all set**, (*colloquial*) ready to start. **all there**, (*colloquial*) mentally alert or normal. **all the same**, in spite of this. **all-time** *adj.* hitherto unsurpassed. **at all**, in any way, to any extent. **in all**, in total, altogether. [Old English]

Allah /'ælə/ the Muslim name of God. [from Arabic *al-Ilah* = the god]

Allahabad /æləhə'bɑ:d/ historic city in Uttar Pradesh state, NE India, 580 km/360 mi SE of Delhi, on the Yamuna River where it meets the Ganges and the mythical Seraswati River; population (1981) 642,000. A Hindu religious festival is held here every 12 years with the participants washing away sin and sickness by bathing in the rivers. [Allahabad = city of god]

allay /əˈleɪ/ *v.t.* to diminish (fear, suspicion, etc.); to relieve or alleviate pain. [Old English]

Allbutt /'ɔ:lbʌt/ Thomas Clifford 1836–1925. British physician who invented a compact medical thermometer, proved that angina is caused by narrowing of the coronary artery, and studied hydrophobia and tetanus.

allegation /ælɪ'geɪʃən/ *n.* an assertion, especially one made without proof; alleging. [from Anglo-French or Latin *allegare* = adduce]

allege /əˈledʒ/ *v.t.* to declare, especially without proof; to advance as an argument or excuse. [from Anglo-French from Latin *litigare* = dispute at law, confused in sense with *allegare* = allege]

allegedly /ə'ledʒɪdlɪ/ *adv.* as is said to be the case.

allegiance /ə'liːdʒəns/ *n.* support of a sovereign, government, or cause etc.; loyalty. [from Anglo-French]

allegorize /'ælɪgəraɪz/ *v.t.* to treat as or by means of an allegory.

allegory /'ælɪgərɪ/ *n.* in literature, the description or illustration of one thing in terms of another; a work of poetry or prose in the form of an extended metaphor or parable that makes use of symbolic fictional characters. —**allegorical** /-'gɒrɪkəl/ *adj.*, **allegorically** *adv.* [from Old French from Latin from Greek *allos* = other and *-agoria* = speaking]

allegretto /ælɪ'gretəʊ/ *adv.* & *adj.* in music, in fairly brisk time. —*n.* (*plural* **allegrettos**) in music, an allegretto passage. [Italian, diminutive of *allegro*]

allegro /ə'legrəʊ/ *adv.* in music, in quick or lively tempo. —*n.* (*plural* **allegros**) in music, an allegro passage. [Italian = lively]

allele *n.* one of two or more alternative forms of a ◊gene at a given locus on a chromosome, caused by a difference in the ◊DNA. Blue and brown eyes in humans are determined by different alleles of the gene for eye colour.

alleluia /ælɪ'luːjə/ *interj.* & *n.* praise to God. [from Latin from Greek from Hebrew = praise the Lord]

allemande /'ælmɑːnd/ *n.* **1.** any of several German dances; music for one of these, especially as a suite movement. **2.** a country-dance figure. [French = German (dance)]

Allen /'ælən/ Woody. Adopted name of Allen Stewart Konigsberg 1935–. US film director and actor, known for his cynical, witty, often self-deprecating parody and off-beat humour. His films include *Sleeper* 1973, *Annie Hall* 1977 (for which he won three Academy Awards), *Hannah and her Sisters* 1986, *Interiors* 1978, *Another Woman* 1988, and *Crimes and Misdemeanours* 1990, which broke with tradition by combining humour and drama.

Bisexuality immediately doubles your chances of a date on Saturday night.

Woody Allen
New York Herald Tribune 1975

Allenby /'ælənbi/ Henry Hynman, 1st Viscount Allenby 1861–1936. British field marshal. In World War I he served in France before taking command in 1917–19 of the British forces in the Middle East. His defeat of the Turkish forces at Megiddo in Palestine in Sept 1918 was followed almost at once by the capitulation of Turkey. He was high commissioner in Egypt 1919–35.

Allende (Gossens) /aɪ'endi/ Salvador 1908–1973. Chilean left-wing politician. Elected president in 1970 as the candidate of the Popular Front alliance, Allende never succeeded in keeping the electoral alliance together in government. His failure to solve the country's economic problems or to deal with political subversion allowed the army, backed by the CIA, to stage the 1973 coup which led to his death.

allergen /'ælədʒən/ *n.* a substance that causes an allergic reaction. —**allergenic** /-'dʒenɪk/ *adj.*

allergic /ə'lɜːdʒɪk/ *adj.* having an allergy or (*colloquial*) antipathy *to*; caused by allergy.

allergy /'ælədʒɪ/ *n.* a condition of special sensitivity of the body that makes it react adversely to certain substances; (*colloquial*) an antipathy. [from German from Greek *allos* = other and *energy*]

alleviate /ə'liːvɪeɪt/ *v.t.* to lessen, to make less severe. —**alleviation** /-'eɪʃən/ *n.*, **alleviator** /-'liː-/ *n.* [from Latin *alleviare* = lighten (*levare* = raise)]

alley *n.* **1.** a narrow passage, especially between or behind buildings. **2.** a channel for balls in bowling etc. **3.** a path bordered by hedges or shrubbery. [from Old French (*aller* = go) from Latin *ambulare* = walk]

alliance /ə'laɪəns/ *n.* a union or agreement to cooperate, especially of a state by treaty or families by marriage. [from Old French from Latin *alligare*]

Alliance, the in UK politics, a loose union 1981–87 formed by the ◊Liberal Party and ◊Social Democratic Party (SDP) for electoral purposes.

allied /'ælaɪd/ *adj.* **1.** having a similar origin or character. **2.** in alliance with foreign states; **Allied**, of the ◊Allies.

Allied Mobile Force (AMF) a permanent multinational military force established in 1960 to move immediately to any NATO country under threat of attack. Its headquarters are in Heidelberg, Germany.

Allies, the in World War I, the 23 countries allied against the Central Powers (Germany, Austria-Hungary, Turkey and Bulgaria), including France, Italy, Russia, the UK and Commonwealth, and, in the latter part of the war, the USA; and in World War II, the 49 countries allied against the ◊Axis powers (Germany, Italy and Japan), including France, the UK and Commonwealth, the USA, and the USSR.

alligator /'ælɪgeɪtə/ *n.* a reptile of the genus *Alligator*, related to the crocodile. There are two species: *A. mississipiensis*, the Mississippi alligator of the S states of the USA, and *A. sinensis* from the swamps of the lower Chang Jiang river in China. The former grows to about 4 m/12 ft, but the latter only to 1.5 m/5 ft. [from Spanish *el lagarto* (Latin *lacerta* = lizard)]

alliteration /əlɪtə'reɪʃən/ *n.* the occurrence of the same letter or sound at the beginning of several words in succession (as in *sing a song of sixpence*). It was a common device in Old English poetry, and its use survives in many traditional English phrases, such as *kith and kin*, *hearth and home*. —**alliterative** /ə'lɪtərətɪv/ *adj.* [from Latin *littera* = letter]

Allium /'ælɪəm/ *n.* a genus of plants belonging to the lily family Liliaceae. Species are usually strong-smelling with a sharp taste, and form bulbs in which sugar is stored. Cultivated species include onion, garlic, chives, and leek.

allocate /'æləkeɪt/ *v.t.* to assign or allot. —**allocable** /'æləkəbəl/ *adj.*, **allocation** /-'keɪʃən/ *n.* [from Latin *allocare* (*locus* = place)]

allometry *n.* in biology, a regular relationship between a given feature (for example, the size of an organ) and the size of the body as a whole, when this relationship is not a simple proportion of body size. Thus, an organ may increase in size proportionately faster, or slower, than body size does.

allopathy *n.* the usual contemporary method of treating disease, using therapies designed to counteract the manifestations of the disease. In strict usage, allopathy is the opposite of ◊homeopathy.

allopurinol *n.* a drug prescribed for the treatment of ◊gout. It acts by reducing levels of ◊uric acid in the blood.

allot /ə'lɒt/ *v.t.* (**-tt-**) to distribute officially; to apportion as a share or task. [from Old French]

allotment /ə'lɒtmənt/ *n.* **1.** a small plot of rented land used for growing vegetables and flowers. Allotments originated in Britain during the 18th and 19th centuries, when much of the common land was enclosed (see ◊enclosures). **2.** apportioning. **3.** a share.

allotrope /'ælətrəʊp/ *n.* an allotropic form (for example, diamond and graphite are allotropes of carbon).

allotropy /ə'lɒtrəpɪ/ *n.* the existence of several forms of a chemical element in the same state (gas, liquid, solid) but with different physical or chemical properties. —**allotropic** /ælə'trɒpɪk/ *adj.* [from Greek *allos* different and *tropos* = manner]

allow /ə'laʊ/ *v.t.* /i.* **1.** to permit, to let happen. **2.** to assign (a fixed sum) to. **3.** to add or deduct in estimating. **4.** to acknowledge as true or acceptable. —**allow for**, to take into consideration; to provide for. [originally = praise, from Old French from Latin (*laudare* = praise and *locare* = place)]

allowable /ə'laʊəbəl/ *adj.* that may be allowed. —**allowably** *adv.*

allowance /ə'laʊəns/ *n.* an amount or sum allowed; a deduction or discount. —*v.t.* to make an allowance to. —**make allowances for**, to regard as a mitigating circumstance.

alloy /'ælɔɪ/ *n.* **1.** any metal blended with some other metallic or nonmetallic substance to give it special qualities, such as resistance to corrosion, or greater hardness, or tensile strength. Useful alloys include bronze, brass, cupronickel, duralumin, German silver, gunmetal, pewter, solder, steel, and stainless steel. The most recent alloys include the superplastics, alloys that can stretch 100% at specific temperatures, permitting, for example, their injection into moulds as easily as plastic. **2.** an inferior metal mixed especially with gold or silver. —*v.t.* **1.** to mix (metals). **2.** to debase by an admixture; to weaken or spoil (pleasure etc. *with*). [from Old French from Latin *alligare*]

All Saints' Day a festival on 1 Nov for all Christian saints and martyrs who have no special day of their own. It is also known as All-Hallows or Hallowmas.

All Souls' Day a festival in the Catholic church, held on 2 Nov (following All Saints' Day) in the conviction that through prayer and self-denial the faithful can hasten the deliverance of souls expiating their sins in purgatory.

allspice *n.* **1.** a spice prepared from dried berries of the pimento tree *Pimenta dioica*, cultivated chiefly in Jamaica. It has an aroma similar to a mixture of cinnamon, cloves, and nutmeg. **2.** the berry of the pimento tree.

Allston /ˈɔːlstən/ Washington 1779–1843. US painter of sea and landscapes, a pioneer of the Romantic movement in the USA. His handling of light and colour earned him the title 'the American Titian'. He also painted classical, religious, and historical subjects.

allude /əˈljuːd/ *v.i.* to refer in passing or indirectly *to* (a thing presumed known). [from Latin *ludere* = play]

allure /əˈljuə/ *v.t.* to entice; to attract or charm. —**allurement** *n.* [from Old French]

allusion /əˈluːʒən/ *n.* a passing or indirect reference (*to*). [French or from Latin *alludere*]

allusive /əˈluːsɪv/ *adj.* containing allusions. —**allusively** *adv.*

alluvium /əˈluːvɪəm/ *n.* (*plural* **alluvia**) a deposit of earth, sand, etc., left by a flood or flow, especially in a river valley. —**alluvial** *adj.* [Latin from *luere* = wash]

ally /ˈælaɪ/ *n.* a state or person cooperating with another for a special purpose, especially by treaty. —*v.t.* to combine in an alliance. [from Old French from Latin *alligare* (*ligare* = bind)]

Allyson /ˈælɪsən/ June. Stage name of Ella Geisman 1917– . US film actress, popular in musicals and straight drama in the 1940s and 1950s. Her work includes *Music for Millions* 1945, *The Three Musketeers* 1948, and *The Glenn Miller Story* 1954.

Alma-Ata /ˌælmə ɑːˈtɑː/ formerly (to 1921) **Vernyi**; capital of the Republic of Kazakh, USSR; population (1987) 1,108,000. Industries include engineering, printing, tobacco processing, textile manufacturing, and leather products.

Almadén /ˌælməˈðen/ mining town in Ciudad Real province, Castilla-La Mancha, central Spain. It has the world's largest supply of mercury, worked since the 4th century BC. Population (1981) 9,700.

Almagest /ˈælmədʒest/ *n.* **1.** the title of an Arabic version of Ptolemy's astronomical treatise, which included the idea of an Earth-centred universe. **2.** (in the Middle Ages; also **almagest**) any of various other celebrated textbooks on astrology and alchemy. [from Arabic *al* = the and Greek *megistē* (*suntaxis*) = the great (system)]

alma mater /ˌælmə ˈmeɪtə/ the title used of a university or school by its past or present members. [Latin = bounteous mother]

almanac /ˈɔːlmənæk/ *n.* or **almanack** **1.** an annual publication containing a calendar with astronomical data and sometimes other information. **2.** a yearbook of sport, theatre, etc. [from Latin from Greek]

Almansa, Battle of /ælˈmænsə/ in the War of the Spanish Succession, battle of 25 April 1707 in which British, Portuguese and Spanish forces were defeated by the French under the Duke of Berwick at a Spanish town in Albacete, about 80 km/50 mi NW of Alicante.

Alma-Tadema /ˈælmə ˈtædɪmə/ Laurence 1836–1912. Dutch painter who settled in the UK in 1870. He painted romantic, idealized scenes from Greek, Roman, and Egyptian life in a distinctive, detailed style.

Almeida /ælˈmeɪdə/ Francisco de *c.*1450–1510. First viceroy of Portuguese India 1505–08.

almighty *adj.* all-powerful; (*colloquial*) very great. —**the Almighty**, God. [Old English]

Almohad /ˈælməhæd/ *n.* a Berber dynasty 1130–1269 founded by the Berber prophet Muhammad ibn Tumart (*c.*1080–1130). They ruled much of Morocco and Spain, which they took by defeating the ◊Almoravids; they later took the area that today forms Algeria and Tunis. Their policy of religious purity involved the forced conversion and massacre of the Jewish population of Spain. They were themselves defeated by the Christian kings of Spain in 1212, and in Morocco in 1269.

almond *n.* a tree *Prunus amygdalus*, family Rosaceae, related to the peach and apricot. Dessert almonds are the kernels of the fruit of the sweet variety *P. amygdalus dulcis*, which is also the source of a low-cholesterol culinary oil. Oil of bitter almonds, from the variety *P. amygdalus amara*, is used in flavouring. Almond oil is also used for cosmetics, perfumes, and fine lubricants. [from Old French from Latin from Greek]

almoner /ˈɑːmənə/ *n.* an official distributor of alms. [from Anglo-French from Latin from Greek *eleos* = pity]

almonry /ˈɑːmənrɪ/ *n.* a place for the distribution of alms.

Almoravid /ˌælˈmɔːrəvɪd/ *n.* a Berber dynasty 1056–1147 founded by the prophet Abdullah ibn Tashfin, ruling much of Morocco and Spain in the 11th–12th centuries. The Almoravids came from the Sahara and in the 11th century began laying the foundations of an empire covering the whole of Morocco and parts of Algeria; their capital was the newly founded Marrakesh. In 1086 they defeated Alfonso VI of Castile to gain much of Spain. They were later overthrown by the ◊Almohads.

almost /ˈɔːlməʊst/ *adv.* all but; as the nearest thing to. [Old English]

alms /ɑːmz/ *n.* (*plural* the same) (*historical*) a donation of food or money given to the poor. [Old English from Latin from Greek *eleos* = pity]

almshouse *n.* a house founded by charity for the accommodation of poor (usually elderly) people.

almucantar /ˌælmjuːˈkæntə/ *n.* a line of constant altitude above the horizon. [from Latin or French from Arabic = sundial (*kantara* = arch)]

aloe /ˈæləʊ/ *n.* a plant of the genus *Aloe*, native to Africa, with erect spikes of flowers and with leaves that yield a bitter juice; (in *plural*) a purgative drug made from this juice. —**American aloe**, a kind of agave. [Old English from Latin from Greek]

aloft /əˈlɒft/ *adv.* high up, overhead; upward. [from Old Norse = in air]

alone /əˈləʊn/ *predic. adj.* without anyone or anything else, without company, assistance, or addition. —*adv.* only, exclusively. [earlier *al one* (*all one*)]

along /əˈlɒŋ/ *adv.* **1.** onward, into a more advanced state. **2.** in company with oneself or others. **3.** beside or through a part or the whole of a thing's length. —*prep.* beside or through (part of) the length of. —**all along**, from the beginning. **along with**, in addition to. [Old English, originally adjective = facing against]

alongshore *adv.* along or beside the shore.

alongside *adv.* at or to the side; close to the side of a ship, pier, or wharf. —*prep.* close to the side of.

aloof /əˈluːf/ *adj.* unconcerned, lacking in sympathy. —*adv.* away, apart. —**aloofness** *n.* [originally nautical, from *luff*]

aloud /əˈlaʊd/ *adv.* in a normal voice so as to be audible; (*archaic*) loudly.

alpaca /ælˈpækə/ *n.* **1.** a domesticated South American hoofed mammal, *Lama pacos*, of the camel family, found in Chile, Peru, and Bolivia, and herded at high elevations in the Andes. About 1 m/3 ft tall at the shoulder, with neck and head another 60 cm/2 ft, it is bred mainly for its long, fine, silky wool. **2.** its wool; fabric made from this. **3.** any of various similar fabrics. [Spanish from Quechua *pako* = reddish-brown]

alpenhorn /ˈælpənhɔːn/ *n.* a long wooden horn formerly used by herdsmen in the Alps. [German = Alpine horn]

alpenstock /ˈælpənstɒk/ *n.* a long iron-tipped staff used in mountain-climbing. [German = Alpine stick]

alpha /ˈælfə/ *n.* **1.** the first letter of the Greek alphabet (α, A) = a. **2.** a first-class mark in an examination. **3.** a designation of the brightest star in a constellation, or sometimes a star's position in a group. —**alpha and omega**, the beginning and the end, or sum total. [Latin from Greek]

alphabet /ˈælfəbet/ *n.* a set of letters used in a language; these in a fixed order; symbols or signs for these. —**phonetic alphabet**, symbols used to represent the sounds of speech. [from Latin from Greek *alpha* (α, A) and *bēta* (β, B), first two letters of Greek alphabet]

alphabetical /ˌælfəˈbetɪkəl/ *adj.* in the order of the letters of the alphabet; using an alphabet. —**alphabetically** *adv.*

alphabetize /ˈælfəbətaɪz/ *v.t.* to put into alphabetical order. —**alphabetization** /-ˈzeɪʃən/ *n.*

Alpha Centauri /ˈælfə senˈtɔːraɪ/ or **Rigil Kent** the brightest star in the constellation Centaurus and the third

alpaca

brightest star in the sky. It is actually a triple star (see ◊binary star); the two brighter stars orbit each other every 80 years, and the third, Proxima Centauri is the closest star to the Sun, 4.3 light years away.

alphanumeric /ˌælfənjuːˈmerɪk/ *adj.* containing both alphabetical and numerical symbols.

alpha particle a positively charged particle emitted from the nucleus of a radio-active ◊atom. It is one of the products of the spontaneous disintegration of radioactive elements such as radium and thorium, and is identical with the nucleus of a helium atom; that is, it consists of two protons and two neutrons. The process of emission, alpha decay, transforms one element into another, decreasing the atomic number by two, and the atomic weight by four. See ◊radioactivity.

Alpine /ˈælpaɪn/ *adj.* of the Alps or other high mountains. —*n.* a plant suited to mountain regions or grown in rock gardens. [from Latin from Greek]

Alps /ælps/ mountain chain, the barrier between N Italy and France, W Germany and Austria; **famous peaks Mont Blanc**, the highest at 4,809 m/15,777 ft, first climbed by Jacques Balmat and Michel Paccard in 1786; **Matterhorn** in the Pennine Alps, 4,479 m/14,694 ft, first climbed by Edward Whymper in 1865; **Eiger** in the Bernese Alps/Oberland, 3,970 m/13,030 ft, with a near-vertical rock wall on the N face, first climbed in 1858; **Jungfrau**, 4,166 m/13,673 ft; and **Finsteraarhorn** 4,275 m/14,027 ft; **famous passes Brenner**, the lowest, Austria/Italy; **Great St Bernard**, the highest, 2,472 m/8,113 ft, Italy/Switzerland (by which Napoleon marched into Italy in 1800); **Little St Bernard**, Italy/France (which Hannibal is thought to have used); and **St Gotthard**, S Switzerland, which Suvorov used when ordered by the tsar to withdraw his troops from Italy. All have been superseded by all-weather road/rail tunnels. The Alps extend into Yugoslavia as the Julian and Dinaric Alps.

already /ɔːlˈredɪ/ *adv.* before the time in question; as early or soon as this.

Alsace region of France; area 8,300 sq km/3,204 sq mi; population (1986) 1,600,000. It consists of the *départements* of Bas-Rhin and Haut-Rhin, and its capital is Strasbourg.

Alsace-Lorraine /ˈælsæs lɒˈreɪn/ area of NE France, lying W of the river Rhine. It forms the French regions of ◊Alsace and ◊Lorraine. The former iron and steel industries are being replaced by electronics, chemicals, and precision engineering. The German dialect spoken does not have equal rights with French, and there is autonomist sentiment. Alsace-Lorraine formed part of Celtic Gaul in Caesar's time, was invaded by the Alemanni and other Germanic tribes in the 4th century, and remained part of the German Empire until the 17th century. In 1648 part of the territory was ceded to France; in 1681 Louis XIV seized Strasbourg. The few remaining districts were seized by France after the French Revolution. Conquered by Germany 1870–71 (chiefly for its iron ores), it was regained by France in 1919, then again annexed by Germany from 1940–44, when it was liberated by the Allies.

Alsatia /ælˈseɪʃə/ the old name for ◊Alsace, formerly part of Germany.

alsatian *n.* a breed of dog known officially from 1977 as the German shepherd. It is about 63 cm/26 in tall, and has a wolflike appearance, a thick coat with many varieties of colouring, and a distinctive gait. Alsatians were introduced from Germany into Britain and the USA after World War I. [from Latin *Alsatia* = Alsace]

also /ˈɔːlsəʊ/ *adv.* in addition, besides. —**also-ran** *n.* a horse or dog not among the first three to finish in a race; a person who has failed to win distinction in his or her activities. [Old English]

Altai /ɑːlˈtaɪ/ territory of the Russian Soviet Federal Socialist Republic in SW Siberia; area 261,700 sq km/101,043 sq mi; population(1985) 2,744,000. The capital is Barnaul.

Altair /ˈælteə/ *n.* or **Alpha Aquilae** the brightest star in the constellation Aquila and the 12th brightest star in the sky. It is a white star 16 light years away and forms the so-called Summer Triangle with the stars Deneb (in the constellation Cygnus) and Vega (in Lyra).

Altamira /ˌæltəˈmiərə/ the site of caves decorated with Palaeolithic wall paintings, the first such to be discovered, in 1879. The paintings are realistic depictions of bison, deer, and horses, in polychrome (several colours). The caves are near the village of Santillana del Mar in Santander province, N Spain; other well-known Palaeolithic cave paintings are in ◊Lascaux in France.

Altamira an Amazonian town in the state of Pará, NE Brazil, situated at the junction of the Trans-Amazonian Highway with the Xingu river, 700 km/400 mi SW of Belem. In 1989 a protest by Brazilian Indians and environmentalists against the building of six dams focused world attention on the devastation of the Amazon rainforest.

altar /ˈɒltə/ *n.* the table on which bread and wine are consecrated in the Eucharist; any structure on which offerings are made to a god. [Old English from Latin *altus* = high]

Altdorfer /ˈæltdɔːfə/ Albrecht *c.*1480–1538. German painter and printmaker, active in Regensburg, Bavaria. Altdorfer's work, inspired by the linear, classical style of the Italian Renaissance, often depicts dramatic landscapes that are out of scale with the figures in the paintings. Many of his works are of religious subjects. His use of light creates tension and effects of movement.

alter /ˈɒltə/ *v.t./i.* to make or become different, to change in character, size, place, etc. —**alteration** /-ˈreɪʃən/ *n.* [from Old French from Latin *alter* = other]

altercate /ˈɒltəkeɪt/ *v.i.* to dispute angrily, to wrangle. —**altercation** /-ˈkeɪʃən/ *n.* [from Latin *altercari*]

alter ego /ˌæltər ˈiːgəʊ/ (*plural* **alter egos**) an intimate friend; another aspect of oneself. [Latin = other self]

alternate[1] /ɒlˈtɜːnət/ *adj.* (of things of two kinds) coming each after one of the other kind; (with *pl.n.*) every second one. —**alternately** *adv.* [from Latin = do things by turns (*alter* = other)]

alternate[2] /ˈɒltəneɪt/ *v.t./i.* to arrange, perform, or occur alternately; to consist of alternate things. —**alternation** *n.*

alternate angle in geometry, one of a pair of angles that lie on opposite sides of a transversal (a line that intersects two or more lines in the same plane). The alternate angles formed by a transversal of two parallel lines are equal.

alternating current (AC) an electric current that flows for an interval of time in one direction and then in the opposite direction, that is, a current that flows in alternately reversed directions through or around a circuit. Electrical energy is usually generated as alternating current in a power station, and alternating currents may be used for both power and lighting.

alternation of generations the typical life cycle of terrestrial plants and some seaweeds, in which two distinct forms occur alternately: **diploid** (having two sets of chromosomes) and **haploid** (one set of chromosomes). The diploid generation produces haploid spores by ◊meiosis, and is called the sporophyte, while the haploid generation produces gametes (sex cells), and is called the gametophyte. The gametes fuse to form a diploid ◊zygote which develops into a new sporophyte; thus the sporophyte and gametophyte alternate.

alternative /ɒlˈtɜːnətɪv/ *adj.* available in place of something else; (of lifestyle, medical treatment, etc.) using practices other than the conventional ones. —*n.* a choice available in place of another; each of two or more possibilities. —**Alternative Service Book,** a book containing the public liturgy of the Church of England published in 1980 for use as the alternative to the Book of Common Prayer. —**alternatively** *adv.*

alternative energy energy from sources that are renewable and ecologically safe, as opposed to sources that are nonrenewable with toxic by-products, such as coal, oil, or gas (fossil fuels), and uranium (for nuclear power). The most important alternative energy source is flowing water, harnessed to ◊hydroelectric power. Other sources include the ocean's tides and waves (see ◊tidal power station and ◊wave power), wind (harnessed by windmills and wind turbines), the Sun (◊solar energy), and the heat trapped in the Earth's crust (◊geothermal energy).

alternative medicine see ◊medicine, alternative.

alternator *n.* an electricity ◊generator that produces an alternating current.

Althing /'ælθɪŋ/ *n.* the parliament of Iceland, established about 930 and the oldest in the world.

although /ɔːl'ðəʊ/ *conj.* though.

Althusser /æltu'seə/ Louis 1918– . French philosopher and Marxist, born in Algeria, who argued that the idea that economic systems determine family and political systems is too simple. He attempted to show how the ruling class ideology of a particular era is a crucial form of class control.

altimeter /'æltɪmiːtə/ *n.* an instrument used in aircraft that measures altitude, or height above sea level. The common type is a form of aneroid ◊barometer, which works by sensing the differences in air pressure at different altitudes. The ◊radar altimeter measures the height of the aircraft above the ground, measuring the time it takes for radio pulses emitted by the aircraft to be reflected. [from Latin *altus* = high]

Altiplano /æltiˈplaːnəʊ/ densely populated upland plateau of the Andes of South America, stretching from S Peru to NW Argentina. Height 3,000–4,000 m/10,000–13,000 ft.

altitude /'æltɪtjuːd/ *n.* **1.** height, especially as measured above sea-level or (of a star) above the horizon. **2.** in geometry, the perpendicular distance from a ◊vertex (corner) of a figure (such as a triangle) to the base (the side opposite the vertex); also the perpendicular line that goes through the vertex to the base. [from Latin *altus* = high]

Altman /'æltmən/ Robert 1922– . US film director. His antiwar comedy *M.A.S.H.* 1970 was a critical and commercial success; subsequent films include *McCabe and Mrs Miller* 1971, *Nashville* 1975, and *Popeye* 1980.

alto /'æltəʊ/ *n.* (*plural* altos) **1.** the highest adult male singing-voice, also known as counter tenor; a female voice of similar range, a contralto; a singer with such a voice; a part written for it. **2.** a viola. **3.** an instrument of the second or third highest pitch in its family. [Italian = high (singing)]

altocumulus /æltəʊˈkjuːmjuːləs/ *n.* (*plural* altocumuli /-laɪ/) cloud like cumulus but at a higher level. [from Latin *altus* = high]

altogether /ɔːltəˈɡeðə/ *adv.* entirely, totally; on the whole. —**in the altogether,** (*colloquial*) nude.

altostratus /æltəʊˈstreɪtəs/ *n.* (*plural* altostrati /-taɪ/) clouds forming a continuous layer at medium altitude. [from Latin *altus* = high]

altruism /'æltruɪzəm/ *n.* **1.** regard for others as a principle of action, unselfishness. **2.** in biology, helping another individual of the same species to reproduce more effectively, as a direct result of which the first individual may leave fewer offspring itself. Female honey bees (workers) behave altruistically by rearing sisters in order to help their mother, the queen bee, reproduce, and forego any possibility of reproducing themselves. —**altruist** *n.*, **altruistic** /-'ɪstɪk/ *adj.*, **altruistically** *adv.* [from French from Italian *altrui* = somebody else]

ALU abbreviation of **arithmetic and logic unit** in a computer, the part of the ◊CPU that performs the basic arithmetic and logical operations on data.

alum /'æləm/ *n.* any double sulphate of a monovalent metal or radical (such as sodium, potassium, or ammonium) with a trivalent metal (such as aluminium or iron). The commonest alum is the double sulphate of potassium and aluminium. Alums are used in medicine, in papermaking and to fix dye in textiles. [from Old French from Latin *alumen*]

alumina /əˈluːmɪnə/ *n.* Al_2O_3, an oxide of aluminium, also called corundum, which is widely distributed in clays,

slates, and shales. It is formed by the decomposition of the feldspars in granite and used as an abrasive. [from Latin *alumen* = alum]

aluminium /æljuˈmɪniəm/ *n.* a light, silvery-white metallic element, symbol Al, atomic number 13, relative atomic mass 26.9815. It is the third most abundant element (and the most abundant metal) in the Earth's crust, of which it makes up about 8.1% by mass. It oxidizes rapidly, the layer of oxide on its surface making it highly resistant to tarnish, and is an excellent conductor of electricity. In its pure state it is a weak metal, but when combined with elements such as copper, silicon, or magnesium, it forms alloys of great strength. [alteration (after *sodium* etc.) from *aluminum*, earlier *alumium* from *alum*]

aluminium ore the raw material from which aluminium is extracted. The main ore is bauxite, a mixture of minerals, found in economic quantities in Australia, Guinea, the West Indies, and several other countries.

aluminize /əˈluːmɪnaɪz/ *v.t.* to coat with aluminium.

aluminum /əˈluːmɪnəm/ *n.* (*US*) aluminium.

alumnus /əˈlʌmnəs/ *n.* (*plural* alumni /-naɪ/) a former pupil or student. [Latin = nursling, pupil (*alere* = nourish)]

Alva /'ælvə/ or **Alba** Ferdinand Alvarez de Toledo, duke of 1508–1582. Spanish politician and general. He successfully commanded the Spanish armies of the Holy Roman emperor Charles V and his son Philip II of Spain. In 1567 he was appointed governor of the Netherlands, where he set up a reign of terror to suppress Protestantism and the revolt of the Netherlands. In 1573 he was recalled by his own wish. He later led a successful expedition against Portugal 1580–81.

Alvarado /ælvəˈrɑːdəʊ/ Pedro de *c.*1485–1541. Spanish conquistador. In 1519 he accompanied Hernándo Cortés in the conquest of Mexico. In 1523–24 he conquered Guatemala.

Alvarez /'ælvarez/ Luis Walter 1911–1988. US physicist who led the research team that discovered the Xi-zero atomic particle in 1959. He had worked on the US atom bomb project for two years, at Chicago and Los Alamos, New Mexico, during World War II. He was awarded a Nobel prize in 1968.

Alvarez Quintero /kɪnˈteərəʊ/ Serafin 1871–1938 and Joaquin 1873–1945. Spanish dramatists. The brothers, born near Seville, always worked together and from 1897 produced some 200 plays, principally on the theme of Andalusia. Among them are *Papá Juan: Centenario* 1909 and *Los Mosquitos* 1928.

alveolus /ælˈviːələs/ *n.* (*plural* alveoli /-laɪ/) **1.** a small cavity such as a tooth-socket or a cell in a honeycomb. **2.** any of the tiny air-filled sacs in the lungs from which oxygen passes into the blood and through which carbon dioxide is removed from it. [Latin, diminutive of *alveus* = cavity]

always /'ɔːlweɪz/ *adv.* at all times, on all occasions; whatever the circumstances; repeatedly.

alyssum /'ælɪsəm/ *n.* any of various cruciferous plants of the genus *Alyssum* etc. with small usually yellow or white flowers. [Latin from Greek = curing (canine) madness]

Alzheimer's disease /'æltshaɪməz/ a common manifestation of ◊dementia, thought to afflict one in 20 people over 65. Attacking the brain's 'grey matter', it is a disease of mental processes rather than physical function, characterized by memory loss and progressive intellectual impairment.

am 1st person singular present of **be.**

Am symbol for americium.

AM in physics, abbreviation of amplitude ◊modulation, one way in which radio waves are altered for the transmission of broadcasting signals. AM is constant in frequency, and varies the amplitude of the transmitting wave in accordance with the signal being broadcast.

a.m. before noon. [abbreviation of Latin *ante meridiem*]

Amal /'æmæl/ *n.* a radical Lebanese ◊Shi'ite military force, established by Musa Sadr in the 1970s; its headquarters are at Borj al-Barajneh. The movement split into extremist and moderate groups in 1982, but both sides agreed on the aim of increasing Shi'ite political representation in Lebanon. The Amal militia under Nabi Berri fought several bloody battles against the Hezbollah (Party of God) in 1988. Amal guerrillas were responsible for many of the attacks and kidnappings in Lebanon during the 1980s, although subsequently the group came to be considered one of the more mainstream elements on the Lebanese political scene.

Amalekite /ə'mæləkaɪt/ *n.* in the Old Testament, a member of an ancient Semitic people of SW Palestine and the Sinai peninsula. According to Exodus 17 they harried the rear of the Israelites after their crossing of the Red Sea, were defeated by Saul and David, and were destroyed in the reign of Hezekiah.

amalgam /ə'mælgəm/ *n.* a mixture or blend; an alloy of mercury with another metal. Amalgam is used in dentistry for filling teeth, and usually contains copper, silver, and zinc as the main alloying ingredients. This amalgam is pliable when first mixed and then sets hard, but the mercury leaches out and causes a type of heavy-metal poisoning. [from French or Latin, probably from Greek *malagma* = emollient]

amalgamate /ə'mælgəmeɪt/ *v.t./i.* to mix, to combine; (of metals) to alloy with mercury. —**amalgamation** /-meɪʃən/ *n.* [from Latin]

Amanita /æmə'naɪtə/ *n.* a genus of fungi (see ◊fungus), distinguished by a ring, or *volva*, round the stem, warty patches on the cap, and a clear white colour of the gills. Many of the species are brightly coloured and highly poisonous. The fly agaric *A. muscaria* is a dangerous, poisonous toadstool with a white-spotted red cap, which grows under birch or pine. The buff-coloured ◊death cap *A. phalloides* is deadly.

amanuensis /əmænju'ensɪs/ *n.* (*plural* **amanuenses**) a literary assistant, especially one who writes from dictation. [Latin, from *a manu* = at hand]

Amanullah Khan /æmə'nulə 'kɑːn/ 1892–1960. Emir (ruler) of Afghanistan 1919–29. Third son of Habibullah Khan, he seized the throne on his father's assassination and concluded a treaty with the British, but his policy of westernization led to rebellion in 1928. Amanullah had to flee, abdicated in 1929, and settled in Rome, Italy.

Amarna tablets a collection of Egyptian clay tablets with cuneiform inscriptions, found in the ruins of the ancient city of ◊Akhetaton on the E bank of the Nile. The majority of the tablets, which comprise royal archives and letters of 1411–1375 BC, are in the British Museum.

amaryllis /æmə'rɪlɪs/ *n.* a South African plant of the genus *Amaryllis*, with lily-like flowers, growing from a bulb; any of various related plants. [Latin from Greek (girl's name)]

amass /ə'mæs/ *v.t.* to heap together, to accumulate. [from French or Latin *massa* = mass]

Amaterasu /əmɑːtə'rɑːsuː/ in Japanese mythology, the sun-goddess, grandmother of Jimmu Tenno, first ruler of Japan, from whom the emperors claimed to be descended.

amateur /'æmətə/ *n.* one who does something as a pastime not as a profession; one who lacks professional skill. —**amateurish** *adj.* [French from Italian from Latin *amator* = lover (*amare* = love)]

Amati /ə'mɑːti/ Italian family of violin-makers, who worked in Cremona, about 1550–1700. Niccolo **Amati** (1596–1684) taught Andrea ◊Guarneri and Antonio ◊Stradivari.

amatol *n.* an explosive consisting of ammonium nitrate and TNT (trinitrotoluene) in almost any proportions.

amatory /'æmətəri/ *adj.* of or showing sexual love. [from Latin *amare* = love]

amaze /ə'meɪz/ *v.t.* to surprise greatly, to overwhelm with wonder. —**amazement** *n.* [from Old English]

Amazon /'æməzən/ South American river, the world's second longest, 6,570 km/4,080 mi, and the largest in volume of water. Its main headstreams, the Marañón and the Ucayali, rise in central Peru and unite to flow E across Brazil for about 4,000 km/2,500 mi. It reaches the Atlantic on the equator, its estuary 80 km/50 mi wide, discharging a volume of water so immense that 64 km/40 mi out to sea, fresh water remains at the surface. [Indian *Amossona* = destroyer of boats]

Amazon[2] *n.* 1. in Greek mythology, a member of a group of legendary female warriors living near the Black Sea, who cut off their right breasts to use the bow more easily. Their queen, Penthesilea, was killed by Achilles at the siege of Troy. The Amazons attacked Theseus and besieged him at Athens, but were defeated, and Theseus took the Amazon Hippolyta captive; she later gave birth to ◊Hippolytus. 2. a tall and strong or athletic woman. —**Amazonian** /-'zəunɪən/ *adj.*

ambassador /æm'bæsədə/ *n.* a diplomat sent by a sovereign or state as a permanent representative or on a mission to another; an official messenger. —**ambassadorial** /-'dɔːrɪəl/ *adj.* [from French, ultimately from Latin *ambactus* = servant]

amber *n.* 1. fossilized resin from coniferous trees of the Middle Tertiary period. It is often washed ashore on the Baltic coast with plant and animal specimens preserved in it; many extinct species have been found preserved in this way. It ranges in colour from red to yellow, and is used to make jewellery. 2. a yellow traffic light used as a cautionary signal between red (= stop) and green (= go). —*adj.* made of or coloured like amber. [from Old French from Arabic]

ambergris /'æmbəgrɪs/ *n.* a grey, waxlike substance found floating in tropical seas and present in the intestines of the sperm whale, used as a fixative in perfumes. [from Old French = grey amber]

ambidextrous /æmbɪ'dekstrəs/ *adj.* able to use either hand equally well. [from Latin *ambi-* on both sides and *dexter* = right-handed]

ambience /'æmbɪəns/ *n.* surroundings.

ambient /'æmbɪənt/ *adj.* surrounding. [from French or Latin *ambi-* = on both sides and *ire* = go]

ambiguous /æm'bɪgjuəs/ *adj.* having more than one possible meaning; doubtful, uncertain. —**ambiguously** *adv.*, **ambiguity** /-'gjuːɪtɪ/ *n.* [from Latin = doubtful (*ambi-* = both ways and *agere* = drive)]

ambit *n.* scope or extent; bounds. [from Latin *ambitus* = circuit]

ambition /æm'bɪʃən/ *n.* desire for distinction or for a specific attainment; its object. [from Old French from Latin = canvassing]

ambitious /æm'bɪʃəs/ *adj.* full of ambition; needing great effort etc., on a large scale. —**ambitiously** *adv.*

ambivalence /æm'bɪvələns/ *n.* coexistence in one person of opposite feelings towards a person or thing. —**ambivalent** *adj.* [from German from Latin *ambo* = both]

amble *v.i.* to walk in a leisurely or casual manner. —*n.* a leisurely pace. [from Old French from Latin *ambulare* = walk]

amblyopia *n.* reduced vision without apparent eye disorder.

Ambrose, St /'æmbrəʊz/ *c.*340–397. One of the early Christian leaders and theologians known as the Fathers of the Church. Feast day 7 Dec.

If you are at Rome live in the Roman style; if you are elsewhere live as they live elsewhere.

St Ambrose

---

ambrosia /æm'brəʊzɪə/ *n.* the food of the gods in classical mythology, supposed to confer eternal life upon all who ate it; something delicious. —**ambrosial** *adj.* [Latin from Greek = elixir of life (*ambrotos* = immortal)]

ambulance /'æmbjʊləns/ *n.* a specially equipped vehicle for conveying the sick or injured to hospital. (The word was used originally of a mobile field hospital.) [French]

ambulant /'æmbjʊlənt/ *adj.* able to walk about, not confined to bed. [from Latin *ambulare* = walk]

ambulatory /'æmbjʊlətərɪ/ *adj.* of or for walking; ambulant. —*n.* a place for walking, as in a cloister. [from Latin]

ambuscade /æmbəs'keɪd/ *n.* an ambush. —*v.t.* to ambush. [from French]

ambush /'æmbʊʃ/ *n.* the placing of troops etc. in concealment to make a surprise attack; such an attack. —*v.t.* to attack from an ambush, to lie in wait for. [from Old French]

ameliorate /ə'miːlɪəreɪt/ *v.t./i.* to make or become better. —**amelioration** /-'reɪʃən/ *n.* [from Old French from Latin *melior* = better]

amen /ɑː'men, eɪ-/ *interjection* (in prayers) signifying so be it, commonly used at the close of a Jewish or Christian prayer or hymn. As used by Jesus in the New Testament it was traditionally translated 'verily'. [from Latin from Greek from Hebrew = certainly]

amenable /ə'miːnəbəl/ *adj.* 1. tractable, responsive. 2. answerable (*to* the law etc.). —**amenability** /-'bɪlɪtɪ/ *n.*, **amenably** *adv.* [Anglo-French from French *amener* =

American Indians: major tribes

Area	Tribe
North America	
Arctic	Inuit, Aleut
Sub-Arctic	Algonquin, Cree, Ottawa
NE Woodlands	Huron, Iroquois, Mohican, Shawnee (Tecumseh)
SE Woodlands	Cherokee, Choctaw, Creek, Hopewell, Natchez, Seminole
Great Plains	Blackfoot, Cheyenne, Comanche, Pawnee, Sioux
NW Coast	Chinook, Tlingit, Tsimshian
Desert West	Apache, Navajo, Pueblo, Hopi, Mojave, Shoshone
Central America	
	Maya, Toltec, Aztec, Mexican

bring (Latin *minare* = drive animals from *minari* = threaten)]

amend /ə'mend/ *v.t.* to correct an error in; to make minor alterations in. —**amendment** *n.* [from Old French from Latin = emend]

amende honorable /æmɑ̃d ɒnɔ:'rɑbl/ a public or open apology and reparation. [French = honourable reparation]

amends /ə'mendz/ *n.pl.* **make amends,** to give compensation. [from Old French = penalties]

Amenhotep /a:mən'həutep/ four Egyptian pharaohs, including:

Amenhotep III *c.* 1400 BC. King of Egypt who built great monuments at Thebes, including the temples at Luxor. Two portrait statues at his tomb were known to the Greeks as the colossi of Memnon; one was cracked, and when the temperature changed at dawn it gave out an eerie sound, then thought supernatural. His son **Amenhotep IV** changed his name to ◊Ikhnaton.

amenity /ə'mi:nɪtɪ/ *n.* a pleasant or useful feature or facility of a place etc.; a pleasant quality. [from Old French or Latin *amoenus* = pleasant]

America /ə'merɪkə/ the W hemisphere of the Earth, containing the continents of North America and South America, with Central America in between. This great land mass extends from the Arctic to the Antarctic, from beyond 75° N to past 55° S. The area is about 42,000,000 sq km/ 16,000,000 sq mi, and the estimated population is over 500,000,000.

American /ə'merɪkən/ *adj.* of the continent of America, especially the USA. —*n.* **1.** a citizen of the USA; a native of America. **2.** the English language as spoken and written in the USA.

American Ballet Theater founded in 1939 as 'Ballet Theater' with co-directors Lucia Chase and Richard Pleasant, then from 1945 Oliver Smith. They aimed to present established and new ballets with frequent celebrity guest appearances, establishing a repertoire of exemplary range and quality.

American Civil War see ◊Civil War, American.

American Federation of Labor and Congress of Industrial Organizations (AFL-CIO) the federation of North American trade unions. The AFL, founded in 1886, was initially a union of skilled craftworkers. The CIO was known in 1935 as the Committee on Industrial Organization (it adopted its present title in 1937 after expulsion from the AFL for its opposition to the AFL policy of including only skilled workers). A merger reunited them in 1955, bringing most unions into the national federation, currently representing about 20% of the workforce in North America.

American Independence, War of alternative name of the ◊American Revolution, the revolt 1775–83 of the British North American colonies that resulted in the establishment of the United States of America.

American Indian one of the aboriginal peoples of the Americas. Columbus named them Indians in 1492 because he believed he had found not the New World, but a new route to India. The Asian ancestors of the Indians are thought to have entered North America on the landbridge, Beringia, exposed by the lowered sea level between Siberia and Alaska during the last Ice Age, 60,000–35,000 BC.

Americanism *n.* a word, sense, or phrase peculiar to or originating in the USA.

Americanize /ə'merɪkənaɪz/ *v.t.* to make American in form or character. —**Americanization** /-'zeɪʃən/ *n.*

Amin Dada *Idi Amin, Ugandan president from 1971 until his overthrow in 1979, surrounded by his bodyguard. He is being asked to explain to reporters how the archbishop of Uganda and two cabinet ministers met a violent death while they were in custody in 1977.*

American Revolution the revolt 1775–83 of the British North American colonies that resulted in the establishment of the United States of America. It was caused by colonial resentment at the contemporary attitude that commercial or industrial interests of any colony should be subordinate to those of the mother country; and by the unwillingness of the colonists to pay for a standing army. It was also fuelled by the colonists' anti-monarchist sentiment and a desire to participate in the policies affecting them.

American Samoa see ◊Samoa, American.

America's Cup an international yacht-racing trophy (named after the US schooner *America*, owned by J L Stevens, who won a race around the Isle of Wight in 1851) contested every three or four years. It is a seven-race series. The USA have dominated the race since its beginning in 1870, losing only once in its 130-year history, to Australia in 1983.

americium /æmə'rɪsɪəm, -ʃɪəm/ *n.* an artificially made transuranic radioactive metallic element, symbol Am, atomic number 95, relative atomic mass 243.13. It was first synthesized in 1944. It is produced from the decay of neutron-bombarded plutonium, can be synthesized in quantity only in nuclear reactors by the bombardment of plutonium with neutrons. It is the element with the highest atomic number occurring naturally: it is found in minute quantities in ◊pitchblende and other uranium ores. [from *America* (where first made)].

Ames /eɪmz/ Adelbert 1880–1955. US scientist, who studied optics and the psychology of visual perception. He concluded that much of what a person sees depends on what he or she expects to see, based (consciously or unconsciously) on previous experience. The Ames Room is often used to conduct experiments and tests on such viewing.

amethyst /'æmɪθɪst/ *n.* a variety of ◊quartz, SiO₂, coloured violet by the presence of small quantities of manganese; used as a semiprecious stone. [from Old French from Latin from Greek = not drunken (the stone being supposed to prevent drunkenness)]

Amhara /æm'hɑ:rə/ *n.* a person of the Amhara culture of the central Ethiopian plateau. The Amhara comprise approximately 25% of Ethiopia's population, and speak Amharic.

Amharic /æm'hærɪk/ n. the official language of Ethiopia. —adj. of or in this language. [from Amhara]

amiable /'eɪmɪəbəl/ adj. friendly and pleasant; likeable. —**amiability** /-'bɪlɪtɪ/ n., **amiably** adv. [from Old French from Latin = amicable (confused with French aimable = lovable]

amicable /'æmɪkəbəl/ adj. friendly, showing friendly feeling. —**amicably** adv. [from Latin amicus = friend]

amice[1] /'æmɪs/ n. a square of white linen worn by celebrant priests, formerly on the neck, now on the neck and shoulders. [ultimately from Latin amictus = garment]

amice[2] n. a cap, hood, or cape of religious orders. [from Old French from Latin amucia]

amicus curiae in law, a barrister advising the court in a legal case as a neutral person, not representing either side. [Latin = friend of the court]

amid /ə'mɪd/ prep. in the middle of, among.

Amida Buddha /'ɑ:mɪdə/ Japanese name for **Amitābha**, the Buddha venerated in Pure Land Buddhism. He presides over the Western Paradise (the Buddha-land of his own creation), and through his unlimited compassion and power to save, true believers can achieve enlightenment and be reborn. [= Buddha of immeasurable light]

amide n. any organic chemical derived from a fatty acid by the replacement of the hydroxyl group by an amino group. One of the simplest amides is acetamide, which has a strong, mousey odour.

amidships /ə'mɪdʃɪps/ adv. in or to the middle of a ship. [from midship(s), after amid]

amidst /ə'mɪdst/ variant of **amid**.

Amies /'eɪmɪz/ Hardy 1909– . British couturier, one of Queen Elizabeth II's dressmakers. Noted from 1934 for his tailored clothes for women, he also designed for men from 1959.

Amin Dada /æ'mi:n 'dɑ:dɑ:/ Idi 1925– . Ugandan politician, president 1971–79. He led the coup that deposed Milton Obote in 1971, expelled the Asian community in 1972, and exercised a reign of terror over his people. He fled when insurgent Ugandan and Tanzanian troops invaded the country in 1979.

amine /'eɪmi:n/ n. a compound in which an alkyl or other non-acidic group replaces a hydrogen atom of ammonia.

amino acid /ə'mi:nəu/ any of a group of organic acids containing a carboxyl group, -COOH, and an amino group, -NH$_2$, attached to the same carbon atom; the general formula is R-CH(NH$_2$)COOH, where R is an organic molecule or hydrogen. In living organisms, about 20 different kinds of amino acids link together into ◊peptides, which join into chains to form polypeptides and ◊proteins.

amir /ə'mɪə/ n. a title of various Muslim rulers. [from Arabic = commander]

Amis /'eɪmɪs/ Kingsley 1922– . English novelist and poet. His works include Lucky Jim 1954, a comic portrayal of life in a provincial university, and Take a Girl Like You 1960. He won the Booker Prize in 1986 for The Old Devils. He is the father of Martin Amis.

It was no wonder that people were so horrible when they started life as children.

Kingsley Amis
Lucky Jim

Amis Martin 1949– . English novelist. His works are characterized by their savage wit and include The Rachel Papers 1974, Money 1984, and London Fields 1989.

amiss /ə'mɪs/ predic. adj. wrong, astray, faulty. —adv. wrongly; inappropriately. [probably from Old Norse á mis = so as to miss]

amity /'æmɪtɪ/ n. friendship, a friendly relationship. [from Old French from Latin amicus = friend]

Amman /ə'mɑ:n/ capital and chief industrial centre of Jordan; population (1980) 1,232,600. It is a major communications centre, linking historic trade routes across the Middle East.

ammeter /'æmɪtə/ n. an instrument for measuring electric current, usually in ◊amperes.

Ammon /'æmən/ in Egyptian mythology, the king of the gods, the equivalent of ◊Zeus or ◊Jupiter. The name is also spelt Amen/Amun, as in the name of the pharaoh

Tutankhamen. In art, he is represented as a ram, as a man with a ram's head, or as a man crowned with feathers.

ammonia /ə'məunɪə/ n. NH$_3$, a colourless, pungent-smelling gas, lighter than air and very soluble in water. It is made on an industrial scale by the ◊Haber process, and used mainly to produce nitrogenous fertilizers, some explosives, and nitric acid.

ammonite /'æmənaɪt/ n. a fossil cephalopod of the order Ammonoidea, related to the modern nautilus. The shell was curled in a plane spiral and made up of numerous gas-filled chambers, the outermost containing the body of the animal. Many species flourished between 200 million and 65 million years ago, ranging in size from that of a small coin to 2 m/ 6 ft across. [from Latin = horn of (Jupiter) Ammon]

ammonium chloride NH$_4$Cl, or **sal ammoniac** a volatile salt that forms white crystals around volcanic craters. It is prepared synthetically for use in 'dry-cell' batteries, fertilizers, and dyes.

ammunition /æmju'nɪʃən/ n. **1.** a supply of projectiles (especially bullets, shells, grenades) fired by guns etc. or hurled. **2.** points that can be used to advantage in an argument etc. [from French la munition taken as l'amunition]

amnesia n. loss or impairment of memory. As a clinical condition it may be caused by disease or injury to the brain, or by shock; in some cases it may be a symptom of an emotional disorder. —**amnesiac** adj. & n. [Latin from Greek = forgetfulness (a- = not and mnaomai = remember)]

amnesty /'æmnɪstɪ/ n. a general pardon, especially for political offences, or the release of a person or group of people from criminal liability for a particular action; for example, the occasional amnesties in Britain for those who surrender firearms that they hold illegally. [from French or Latin from Greek amnēstia = forgetting]

Amnesty International a human-rights organization established in the UK in 1961 to campaign for the release of political prisoners worldwide. It has 700,000 members, and section offices in 43 countries. Amnesty International is politically unaligned. The organization was awarded the Nobel Peace Prize in 1977.

amniocentesis /æmnɪəusen'ti:sɪs/ n. (plural **amniocenteses**) a prenatal diagnostic technique in which a sample of amniotic fluid is withdrawn from the uterus through a hollow needle and analysed for information about the fetus. It is used to detect Down's syndrome and other abnormalities. [from Greek kentēsis = pricking]

amnion /'æmnɪɒn/ n. (plural **amnia**) the innermost of three membranes enclosing the embryo within the egg (reptiles and birds) or within the uterus (mammals). It contains the amniotic fluid which helps to cushion the embryo. —**amniotic** /-'ɒtɪk/ adj. [Greek = caul (amnos = lamb)]

amoeba /ə'mi:bə/ n. (plural **amoebas; amoebae**) one of the simplest living animals, consisting of a single cell and belonging to the group ◊Protozoa. The body consists of colourless protoplasms. Its activities are controlled by its nucleus, and it feeds by flowing round and engulfing organic debris. It reproduces by ◊binary fission. —**amoebic** adj. [Latin from Greek = change]

amok /ə'mɒk/ adv. **run amok**, to run about wildly in violent rage. [Malay = rushing in frenzy]

among /ə'mʌŋ/ prep. in an assembly of, surrounded by; in the number of; between. [Old English = in a crowd]

amongst /ə'mʌŋst/ variant of **among**.

amoral /eɪ'mɒrəl/ adj. not based on or not having moral principles, neither moral nor immoral. —**amoralism** n. [from Greek a- = not and moral]

Amorites /'æməraɪt/ n.pl. an ancient people of Semitic or Indo-European origin, who were among the inhabitants of ◊Canaan at the time of the Israelite invasion. They provided a number of Babylonian kings.

amorous /'æmərəs/ adj. of, showing, or feeling sexual love. —**amorously** adv., **amorousness** n. [from Old French from Latin amor = love]

amorphous /ə'mɔ:fəs/ adj. having no definite shape or form; vague, not organized; in mineralogy, chemistry, uncrystallized. [from Latin from Greek a- = not and morphē = form]

amortize /ə'mɔ:taɪz/ v.t. to pay off a debt gradually by means of a sinking fund; to write off the initial costs of (assets) gradually. —**amortization** /-'zeɪʃən/ n. [from Old French from Latin ad mortem to death]

Amos /'eɪmɒs/ n. a book of the Old Testament written c.750 BC. One of the ◊prophets, Amos was a shepherd who foretold the destruction of Israel because of the people's abandonment of their faith.

amount /ə'maʊnt/ v.i. to be equivalent in total value, quantity, significance, etc., to. —n. the total to which a thing amounts; a quantity. [from French from Latin ad montem = upward]

amour propre /æmuə 'prɒpr/ self-esteem, vanity. [French]

amp abbreviation of 1. ◊ampere. 2. (colloquial) amplifier.

amperage /'æmpərɪdʒ/ n. the strength of electric current, measured in amperes.

ampere n. the basic SI unit (symbol A) of electrical current. Electrical current is measured in a similar way to water current, in terms of an amount per unit time; one ampere represents a flow of about 6.28×10^{18} ◊electrons per second, or a rate of flow of charge of one coulomb per second. [from A Ampère, French physicist (died 1836)]

Ampère's rule a rule developed by André Ampère connecting the direction of an electric current and its associated magnetic currents. Travelling along a current-carrying wire in the direction of the current (from the positive to the negative terminal of a battery), and facing a magnetic needle, the north pole of the needle is deflected to the left-hand side.

ampersand /'æmpəsænd/ n. the sign & (= and). [corruption of '& per se and' = 'the sign & by itself is and']

amphetamine /æm'fetəmi:n/ n. a synthetic drug used as a stimulant and decongestant, known as **speed**. It has been used since World War II to help soldiers overcome fatigue, and until the 1970s was prescribed by doctors as an appetite suppressant for weight loss; also used as an antidepressant, to induce euphoria, and as a stimulant, to increase alertness. Indications for its use today are very restricted because of several side effects, including addiction and distorted behaviour. [abbreviation of chemical name]

amphibian /æm'fɪbiən/ n. 1. an animal living both on land and in water; a vertebrate animal of the class Amphibia, typically having an aquatic larval stage with gills (a tadpole) and an air-breathing four-legged adult stage, generally returning to water to breed. The class includes caecilians, worm-like in appearance; salamanders, frogs, and toads. 2. an amphibious vehicle etc. [from Greek amphi = both and bios = life]

amphibious adj. 1. living or operating both on land and in water. 2. involving military forces landed from the sea.

amphibole n. any one of a large group of rock-forming silicate minerals with an internal structure based on double chains of silicon and oxygen, and with a general formula $X_2Y_5Si_8O_{22}(OH)_2$; closely related to ◊pyroxene. Amphiboles form orthorhombic, monoclinic, and triclinic ◊crystals.

amphioxus n. or **lancelet** a filter-feeding animal about 6 cm/2.5 in long with a fish-like shape and a notochord, or flexible rod, which forms the supporting structure of its body. It lacks organs such as heart or eyes, and lives half-buried on the sea bottom. It is a primitive relative of the vertebrates.

amphitheatre /'æmfɪθɪətə/ n. an oval or circular unroofed building with tiers of seats surrounding a central space. Amphitheatres were used by the Romans for gladiatorial contests, fights of wild animals, and other similar events. [from Latin from Greek amphi = all round and theatron = theatre]

amphora /'æmfərə/ n. (plural **amphorae** /-i:/) a Greek or Roman vessel with a narrow neck and two handles, tapering at the base, used for transporting and storing wine, oil and dry goods. [Latin from Greek amphi- = two and pherō = carry]

ample adj. plentiful, extensive; quite enough; large, of generous proportions. —**ampleness** n., **amply** adv. [from French from Latin amplus]

amplifier /'æmplɪfaɪə/ n. an apparatus for increasing the strength of sounds or electrical signals. The ratio of output signal strength to input signal strength is called the gain of an amplifier. As well as achieving high gain, an amplifier should be free from distortion and able to operate over a range of frequencies. Practical amplifiers are usually complex circuits, although simple amplifiers can be built from single transistors or valves.

amplify /'æmplɪfaɪ/ v.t./i. 1. to increase the strength of (sound or electrical signals). 2. to add detail to (a story

etc.); to expatiate. —**amplification** /-'keɪʃən/ n. [from Old French from Latin]

amplitude /'æmplɪtju:d/ n. 1. spaciousness, abundance. 2. the maximum displacement of an oscillation from the equilibrium position. For a wave motion, it is the height of a crest (or the depth of a trough). With a sound wave, for example, amplitude corresponds to the intensity (loudness) of the sound. In AM (amplitude modulation) radio broadcasting, the required audio-frequency signal is made to modulate (vary slightly) the amplitude of a continuously transmitted radio carrier wave. 3. or **argument**, in mathematics, the angle θ between the position vector of a ◊complex number and the real axis. For the complex number z, the amplitude of $z = r(\cos θ + i \sin θ)$, in which r is the radius and $i = \sqrt{-1}$. [French or from Latin]

ampoule /'æmpu:l/ n. a small sealed glass vessel holding a liquid, especially for injection. [French from Latin ampulla]

ampulla n. 1. a small vessel with a round body and narrow neck, used for holding oil, perfumes, and so on by the ancient Greeks and Romans. 2. in the ◊ear, the slight swelling at the end of each semicircular canal, able to sense the motion of the head. The sense of balance largely depends on sensitive hairs within the ampulla responding to movements of fluid within the inner ear. [Latin]

amputate /'æmpjuteɪt/ v.t. to cut off a limb or other body appendage by surgical operation. —**amputation** /-'teɪʃən/ n. [from Latin amputare (amb- = about and putare = prune)]

amputee /æmpju:'ti:/ n. a person who has had a limb etc. amputated.

Amritsar /æm'rɪtsə/ industrial city in the Punjab, India; population (1981) 595,000. It is the holy city of ◊Sikhism, with the Guru Nanak University (named after the first Sikh guru) and the Golden Temple from which armed demonstrators were evicted by the Indian army under General Dayal in 1984, 325 being killed. Subsequently, Indian prime minister Indira Gandhi was assassinated in reprisal. In 1919 it was the scene of the **Amritsar Massacre**, when British troops under General Edward Dyer (1864–1927) opened fire on a crowd of some 10,000, assembled to protest against the arrest of two Indian National Congress leaders.

Amsterdam /'æmstədæm/ capital of the Netherlands; population (1988) 1,031,000. Canals cut through the city link it with the North Sea and the Rhine, and as a Dutch port it is second only to Rotterdam. There is shipbuilding, printing, food processing, banking, and insurance.

amuck variant of **amok**.

amulet /'æmjulɪt/ n. a thing worn as a charm against evil. [from Latin]

Amundsen /'æmʊndsən/ Roald 1872–1928. Norwegian explorer who in 1903–06 was the first person to navigate the ◊North West Passage. Beaten to the North Pole by ◊Peary in 1910, he reached the South Pole ahead of ◊Scott in 1911.

Amur /ə'muə/ river in E Asia. Formed by the Argun and Shilka rivers, the Amur enters the Sea of Okhotsk. At its mouth the Amur is 16 km/10 mi wide. For much of its course of over 4,400 km/2,730 mi it forms, together with its tributary, the Ussuri, the boundary between the USSR and China.

amuse /ə'mju:z/ v.t. 1. to cause to laugh or smile. 2. to occupy pleasantly. —**amusement** n. [from Old French a = to and muser = stare]

amyl alcohol traditional name for pentanol, $C_5H_{11}OH$. It is a useful solvent, with a distinctive choking odour.

amylase n. one of a group of ◊enzymes that break down ◊starches into their component molecules (sugars) for use in the body. It occurs widely in both plants and animals. In humans, it is found in pancreatic juices and saliva.

an /ən/ emphatic /æn/ adj. the form of a (the indefinite article) used before vowel sounds other than u /ju:, ju/.

ana- /ænə-/ prefix (usually **an-** before a vowel) 1. up (in place or time). 2. again. [from Greek ana = up]

Anabaptist /ænə'bæptɪst/ n. a member of any of various 16th-century religious groups practising adult baptism. They believed in adult rather than child baptism, and sought to establish utopian communities. Anabaptist groups spread rapidly in N Europe, particularly in Germany, and were widely persecuted. [from Latin from Greek baptismos = baptism]

anabolic steroid any ◊hormone of the ◊steroid group of organic compounds that stimulates tissue growth. Its use in medicine is limited to the treatment of some anaemias and breast cancers; it may help to break up blood clots. Side effects include aggressive behaviour, masculinization in women, and, in children, reduced height.

anabolism /ə'næbəlɪzəm/ *n.* the process of building up body tissue, promoted by the influence of certain hormones. It is the constructive side of ◊metabolism, as opposed to catabolism. —**anabolic** /ænə'bɒlɪk/ *adj.* [from Greek *anabolē* = ascent (*ballō* = throw)]

anabranch *n.* a stream that branches from a main river, then reunites with it. For example, the Great Anabranch in New South Wales, Australia, leaves the Darling near Menindee, and joins the Murray below the Darling- Murray confluence. [Greek *ana* = again]

anachronism /ə'nækrənɪzəm/ *n.* the attribution of a custom or event etc. to a period to which it does not belong; a thing thus attributed; a person or thing out of harmony with the period. —**anachronistic** /-'nɪstɪk/ *adj.* [from French or Greek *khronos* = time]

anacoluthon /ænəkə'ljuːθən/ *n.* (*plural* **anacolutha**) a sentence or construction that lacks a proper grammatical sequence. [Latin from Greek *an-* = not and *akolouthos* = following]

anaconda /ænə'kɒndə/ *n.* a South American snake *Eunectes murinus*, a member of the python and boa family, the Boidae. One of the largest snakes, growing to 9 m/30 ft or more, it is found in and near water, where it lies in wait for the birds and animals on which it feeds. The anaconda is not venomous, but kills its prey by coiling round it and squeezing until the creature suffocates. [from Sinhalese = whip-snake; originally of a snake in Sri Lanka]

anaemia /ə'niːmɪə/ *n.* deficiency of red cells or of their haemoglobin in blood. The main symptoms are fatigue, pallor, breathlessness, palpitations, and poor resistance to infection. Treatment depends on the cause. [from Greek = lack of blood]

anaemic /ə'niːmɪk/ *adj.* suffering from anaemia; pale; lacking vitality.

anaerobic *adj.* in biology, a description of those living organisms that do not require oxygen for the release of energy from food (carbohydrates, proteins, and lipids). Anaerobic organisms include many bacteria and yeasts.

anaesthesia /ænɪs'θiːzɪə/ *n.* loss of sensation, especially that induced by anaesthetics. [from Greek *an-* = without and *aisthēsia* = sensation]

anaesthetic /ænɪs'θetɪk/ *n.* a substance (e.g. a drug or gas) that produces loss of sensation and of ability to feel pain. —*adj.* having this effect.

anaesthetize /ə'niːsθətaɪz/ *v.t.* to administer an anaesthetic to. —**anaesthetist** *n.*, **anaesthetization** /-'zeɪʃən/ *n.*

anagram /'ænəgræm/ *n.* a word or phrase formed by transposing the letters of another. [from French and Greek *gramma* = letter]

anal /'eɪnəl/ *adj.* of or near the anus.

Analects /'ænəlekts/ *n.pl.* the most important of the four books that contain the teachings and ideas of ◊Confucianism.

analgesia /ænæl'dʒiːzɪə/ *n.* relief of pain, loss of ability to feel pain while still conscious. ◊Opiates alter the perception or appreciation of pain and are effective in controlling 'deep' visceral (internal) pain. Non-opiates, such as ◊aspirin and ◊paracetamol relieve musculoskeletal pain and reduce inflammation in soft tissues. [from Greek *an-* = without and *algēsia* = pain]

analgesic /ænæl'dʒiːzɪk/ *adj.* producing analgesia. —*n.* an analgesic drug.

analogize /ə'nælədʒaɪz/ *v.t./i.* to represent or explain by analogy; to use analogy.

analogous /ə'næləgəs/ *adj.* partially similar or parallel (*to*). —**analogously** *adv.* [from Latin from Greek]

analogue /'ænəlɒg/ *n.* an analogous thing. [French from Greek *ana-* = according to and *logos* = proportion]

analogue computer a computing device that performs calculations through the interaction of continuously varying physical quantities, such as voltages (as distinct from the more common ◊digital computer, which works with discrete quantities). It is said to operate in 'real time', and can therefore be used to monitor and control events as they happen.

analogy /ə'nælədʒɪ/ *n.* correspondence or partial similarity of things; reasoning from parallel cases. —**analogical** /ænə'lɒdʒɪkəl/ *adj.* [from French or Latin from Greek]

analyse /'ænəlaɪz/ *v.t.* 1. to examine in detail. 2. to ascertain the elements or structure of. 3. to psychoanalyse. —**analysable** *adj.*

analysis /ə'næləsɪs/ *n.* (*plural* **analyses**) 1. the process of analysing; a statement of the result of this. 2. psychoanalysis. 3. the branch of mathematics concerned with limiting processes on axiomatic number systems; ◊calculus of variations and infinitesimal calculus is now called analysis. —**analytic** /ænə'lɪtɪk/ *adj.* in philosophy, a term derived from ◊Kant:the converse of ◊synthetic. In an analytic judgement, the judgement provides no new knowledge; for example: 'all bachelors are unmarried'. **analytical** *adj.*, **analytically** *adv.* [Latin from Greek *luō* = loosen]

analyst /'ænəlɪst/ *n.* 1. one skilled in analysis, especially of chemical substances. 2. a psychoanalyst. [from French]

analytical chemistry the branch of chemistry that deals with the determination of the chemical composition of substances.

analytical engine a programmable computing device, designed by Charles ◊Babbage in the 1830s. It introduced many of the concepts of the digital computer but, because of limitations in manufacturing processes, was never built.

analytical geometry another name for ◊coordinate geometry.

Ananda /ə'nændə/ 5th century BC. Favourite disciple of the Buddha. At his plea, a separate order was established for women. He played a major part in collecting the teachings of the Buddha after his death.

anapaest /'ænəpiːst/ *n.* a metrical foot with two short or unstressed syllables followed by one long or stressed syllable. [from Latin from Greek *anapaistos* (*ana* = reversed (dactyl) and -*paistos* from *paiō* = strike)]

anaphylaxis *n.* in medicine, a severe allergic response. Typically, the air passages become constricted, the blood pressure falls rapidly, and the victim collapses. A rare condition, anaphylaxis can occur following wasp or bee stings or treatment with some drugs.

anarchism /'ænəkɪzəm/ *n.* the political belief that society should have no government, laws, police, or other authority, but should be a free association of all its members. It does not mean 'without order'; most theories of anarchism imply an order of a very strict and symmetrical kind, but they maintain that such order can be achieved by cooperation. Anarchism must not be confused with nihilism (a purely negative and destructive activity directed against society); anarchism is essentially a pacifist movement. —**anarchist** *n.* one who believes that government and law should be abolished. **anarchistic** /-'kɪstɪk/ *adj.* [Greek *anarkhos* = without ruler]

anarchy /'ænəkɪ/ *n.* disorder (especially political), lack of government or control. —**anarchic** /æ'nɑːkɪk/ *adj.* [from Latin from Greek *an-* = without and *arkhē* = rule]

Anastasia /ænə'steɪzɪə/ 1901–1918. Russian Grand Duchess, youngest daughter of ◊Nicholas II. During the Russian Revolution she was presumed shot with her parents by the Bolsheviks after the Revolution of 1917. It was subsequently alleged that Anastasia escaped, but evidence released by the Russian government suggests that she was assassinated with her family.

anastigmatic /ænəstɪg'mætɪk/ *adj.* free from astigmatism. [from Greek]

anastomosis *n.* in medicine, a connection between two vessels (usually blood vessels) in the body. Surgical anastomosis involves the deliberate joining of two vessels or hollow parts of an organ; for example, when part of the intestine has been removed and the remaining free ends are brought together and stitched.

anathema /ə'næθəmə/ *n.* 1. a detested thing. 2. a formal curse of the Church, excommunicating a person or denouncing a doctrine etc. [Latin from Greek = thing assigned (to evil)]

anathematize /ə'næθəmətaɪz/ *v.t.* to curse.

anatomize /ə'nætəmaɪz/ *v.t.* 1. to dissect. 2. to analyse.

anatomy /ə'nætəmɪ/ *n.* 1. the science of body structure; the bodily structure of an animal or plant. 2. analysis. —**anatomical** /ænə'tɒmɪkəl/ *adj.*, **anatomically** *adv.* [from French or Latin from Greek *temnō* = cut]

Anaximander /ænæksi'mændə/ 610–c.547 BC. Greek astronomer and philosopher. He is thought to have been the first to determine solstices and equinoxes, to have invented the sundial, and to have produced the first geographical map. He believed that the universe originated as a formless mass containing the contraries of hot and cold, and wet and dry; land, sea, and air were formed out from the union and separation of these opposites.

ANC abbreviation of African National Congress.

ancestor /'ænsestə/ n. 1. a person from whom one is descended, especially one more remote than grandparents. 2. an early type of animal, plant, or thing from which later ones have evolved. —**ancestral** /-'sestrəl/ adj., **ancestress** /'æn-/ n. fem., **ancestry** n. [from Old French from Latin ante = before and cedere = go]

ancestor worship religious rituals and beliefs oriented towards deceased members of a family or group. Adherents believe that the souls of the dead remain involved in this world, and are capable of influencing current events.

anchor /'æŋkə/ n. 1. a heavy metal weight used to moor a ship to the sea-bottom or a balloon etc. to the ground. 2. a thing that gives stability. —v.t./i. to secure or be moored with an anchor, to cast an anchor; to fix firmly. —**anchor man**, one who coordinates activities, especially the compère in a broadcast; a strong member of a sports team who plays a vital part, e.g. the last runner in a relay race. [from Old English from Latin from Greek agkura]

anchorage /'æŋkərɪdʒ/ n. 1. a place for anchoring. 2. lying at anchor.

Anchorage /'æŋkərɪdʒ/ port and largest town of Alaska, USA, at the head of Cook Inlet; population (1984) 244,030. Established in 1918, Anchorage is a major centre of administration, communication, and commerce. Industries include salmon canning, and coal and gold are mined.

anchorite /'æŋkəraɪt/ n. a hermit, a religious recluse. [from Latin from Greek anakhōreō = retire]

anchovy /'æntʃəvɪ/ n. a small, rich-flavoured fish Engraulis encrasicholus of the (herring family. It is abundant in the Mediterranean and also found on the Atlantic coast of Europea and in the Black Sea, and is fished extensively. It grows to 20 cm/8 in. [from Spanish and Portuguese anchova]

ancien régime the old order; the feudal, absolute monarchy in France before the French Revolution of 1789.

ancient /'eɪnʃənt/ adj. of times long past; having lived or existed for a long time. [from Anglo-French from Latin ante = before]

ancient art the art of prehistoric cultures and the ancient civilizations around the Mediterranean that predate the classical world of Greece and Rome: for example, Sumerian and Aegean art.

ancillary /æn'sɪlərɪ/ adj. subordinate, auxiliary (to). [from Latin ancilla = handmaid]

and /ənd, emphatic ænd/ 1. a conjunction connecting words, clauses, and sentences in a simple relation or implying progression, causation, consequence, duration, number, addition, or variety. 2. (colloquial) to (as in go and, try and). —**and/or**, together with or as an alternative. [Old English]

Andalusia /ændə'luːsɪə/ (Spanish Andalucía) fertile autonomous region of S Spain, including the provinces of Almería, Cádiz, Córdoba, Granada, Huelva, Jaén, Málaga, and Seville; area 87,300 sq km/33,698 sq mi; population (1986) 6,876,000. Málaga, Cádiz, and Algeciras are the chief ports and industrial centres. The Costa del Sol on the S coast has many tourist resorts, including Marbella and Torremolinos.

andalusite n. aluminium silicate, Al_2SiO_5, a white to pinkish mineral crystallizing as square-or rhomb-based prisms. It is common in metamorphic rocks formed from clay sediments under low pressure conditions. Andalusite, kyanite, and sillimanite are all polymorphs of Al_2SiO_5.

Andaman and Nicobar Islands /'ændəmənz/ two groups of islands in the Bay of Bengal, between India and Myanmar (formerly Burma), forming a Union Territory of the Republic of India; area 8,300 sq km/3,204 sq mi; population (1981) 188,000. The economy is based on fishing, timber, rubber, fruit, and rice. The Andamans consist of five principal islands (forming the Great Andaman), the Little Andaman, and about 204 islets; area 6,340 sq km/2,447 sq mi; population (1981) 158,000. The Nicobars,

Andersen *The Danish writer Hans Christian Andersen. He was admired by Charles Dickens, whom he visited in 1857.*

consisting of 19 islands (7 of which are uninhabited), are 120 km/75 mi S of Little Andaman; area 1,953 sq km/754 sq mi; population (1981) 30,500. The main items of trade are coconut and areca nut. The Nicobars were British 1869–1947.

andante /æn'dæntɪ/ adv. in music, in moderately slow tempo. —n. in music, a movement to be played in this way. [Italian = going]

Andean Group /æn'diːən/ (Spanish Grupo Andino) a South American organization aimed at economic and social cooperation between member states. It was established under the Treaty of Cartagena in 1969, by Bolivia, Chile, Colombia, Ecuador, and Peru; Venezuela joined in 1973, but Chile withdrew in 1976. The organization is based in Lima, Peru.

Andean Indian any indigenous inhabitant of the Andes range in South America.

Andersen Hans Christian 1805–1875. Danish writer. His fairy tales such as 'The Ugly Duckling', 'The Emperor's New Clothes', and 'The Snow Queen', gained him international fame and have been translated into many languages.

> 'But the Emperor has nothing on at all!' cried a little child.
>
> **Hans Christian Andersen**
> *The Emperor's New Clothes*

Anderson /'ændəsən/ Carl David 1905– . US physicist, who discovered the positive electron (positron) in 1932; he shared a Nobel prize in 1936.

Anderson Elizabeth Garrett 1836–1917. The first English woman to qualify in medicine. Refused entry into medical school, Anderson studied privately and was licensed by the Society of Apothecaries in London in 1865. She was physician to the Marylebone Dispensary for Women and Children (later renamed the Elizabeth Garrett Anderson Hospital), a London hospital now staffed by women and serving women patients.

Anderson Marian 1902– . US contralto, whose voice was remarkable for its range and richness. She toured Europe in 1930, but in 1939 she was barred from singing at Constitution Hall, Washington, DC, because she was black. In 1955 she sang at the Metropolitan Opera, the first black singer to appear there. In 1958 she was appointed an alternate delegate to the United Nations.

Anderson Sherwood 1876–1941. US writer of sensitive, experimental, and poetic stories of small-town Midwestern life, Winesburg, Ohio 1919.

Andes /'ændi:z/ the great mountain system or *cordillera* that forms the W fringe of South America, extending through some 67° of latitude and the republics of Colombia, Venezuela, Ecuador, Peru, Bolivia, Chile, and Argentina. The mountains exceed 3,600 m/12,000 ft for half their length of 6,500 km/4,000 mi.

andesite *n.* a volcanic igneous rock, intermediate in silica content between rhyolite and basalt. It is characterized by a large quantity of the feldspar ◊minerals, giving it a light colour. Andesite erupts from volcanoes at destructive plate margins (where one plate of the Earth's surface moves beneath another; see ◊plate tectonics). [from *Andes*, where it is found]

Andhra Pradesh /'ændrə prɑː'deʃ/ state in E central India; **area** 276,700 sq km/106,845 sq mi; **capital** Hyderabad; **products** rice, sugar cane, tobacco, groundnuts, cotton; **population** (1981) 53,404,000; **language** Telugu, Urdu, Tamil; **history** formed in 1953 from the Telegu-speaking areas of Madras, and enlarged in 1956 from the former Hyderabad state.

andiron /'ændaɪən/ *n.* a metal stand (usually one of a pair) supporting logs in a fireplace. [from Old French *andier*, assimilated to *iron*]

Andorra /æn'dɔːrə/ Principality of; landlocked country in the E Pyrenees, bounded to the N by France and to the S by Spain; **area** 468 sq km/181 sq mi; **capital** Andorra-la-Vella; **physical** mountainous, with narrow valley; **head of state** Joan Martí y Alanis (bishop of Seo de Urgel, Spain) and François Mitterand (president of France); **head of government** Josep Pintat Solens from 1986; **political system** feudal coprincipality; **exports** main industries tourism and smuggling tobacco; **population** (1990 est) 51,000 (25% Andorrans, 75% immigrant Spanish workers); **language** Catalan (official) 30%, Spanish 59%, French 6%; **recent history** Democratic Party of Andorra formed in 1976 was the first Andorran political organization (the country was ruled jointly by France and the bishops of Urgel since the 13th century). The first prime minister was appointed in 1981.

André /'ɑːndreɪ/ Carl 1935– . US sculptor, a Minimalist, who uses industrial materials to affirm basic formal and aesthetic principles. His *Equivalent VIII* 1976, an arrangement of bricks in Palladian proportion (Tate Gallery, London), was much criticized.

Andrea del Sarto /'ændreɪə del 'sɑːtəʊ/ (Andrea d'Agnola) 1486–1531. Italian Renaissance painter active in Florence, one of the finest portraitists and religious painters of his time. His style is serene and noble, characteristic of High Renaissance art.

Andreas Capellanus /'ændriəs kæpə'leɪnəs/ Latin name for André le Chapelain.

André le Chapelain /'ɒndreɪ lə ʃæ'plæn/ 12th-century French priest and author. He wrote *De Arte Honest Amandi/The Art of Virtuous Love*, a seminal work in ◊courtly love literature, at the request of ◊Marie de France, while he was chaplain at her court in Troyes, E France.

Andress /'ændres/ Ursula 1936– . Swiss actress specializing in glamour leads. Her international career started with *Dr No* 1962. Other films include *She* 1965, *Casino Royale* 1967, *Red Sun* 1971, and *Clash of the Titans* 1981.

Andrew /'ændru:/ (full name Andrew Albert Christian Edward) 1960– . Prince of the United Kingdom, Duke of York, second son of Queen Elizabeth II. He married Sarah Ferguson in 1986, and they have two daughters, Princess Beatrice, (born 1988) and Princess Eugenie, (born 1990).

Andrews /'ændru:z/ John 1813–1885. Irish chemist who conducted a series of experiments on the behaviour of carbon dioxide under varying temperature and pressure. In 1869 he introduced the idea of a critical temperature: 30.9°C in the case of carbon dioxide, beyond which no amount of pressure would liquefy the gas.

Andrews Julie. Stage name of Julia Elizabeth Wells. 1935– . British-born US singer and actress. A child performer with her mother and stepfather in British music halls, she first appeared in the USA in the Broadway production *The Boy Friend* 1954. She was the original Eliza Doolittle in *My Fair Lady* 1956. In 1960 she appeared in Lerner and Loewe's *Camelot* on Broadway. Her films include *Mary Poppins* 1964, *The Americanization of Emily* 1963, *The Sound of Music* 1965, *'10'* 1980, and *Victor/Victoria* 1982.

Andrew, St New Testament apostle, martyred on an X-shaped cross (**St Andrew's cross**). He is the patron saint of Scotland. Feast day 30 Nov.

Andrić /'ændrɪtʃ/ Ivo 1892–1974. Yugoslavian novelist and nationalist. He became a diplomat, and was ambassador to Berlin in 1940. *Na Drini Ćuprija/The Bridge on the Drina* 1945 is an epic history of a small Bosnian town. He was awarded a Nobel prize in 1961.

Androcles /'ændrəkli:z/ traditionally, a Roman slave who fled from a cruel master into the African desert, where he drew a thorn from the paw of a crippled lion. Recaptured and sentenced to combat a lion in the arena, he found his adversary was his old friend. The emperor Tiberius was said to have freed them both.

androecium *n.* the male part of a flower, comprising a number of ◊stamens.

androgen /'ændrəgən/ *n.* a general name for any male sex hormone, of which ◊testosterone is the most important. They are all ◊steroids and are principally involved in the production of male ◊secondary sexual characters (such as facial hair in humans). [from Greek *andro-* = male]

androgynous /æn'drɒdʒɪnəs/ *adj.* hermaphrodite; (of a plant) with stamens and pistils in the same flowers. [from Greek *andro-* = male and *gunē* = woman]

android /'ændrɔːɪd/ *n.* a robot with an apparently human form. [from Greek]

Andromache /æn'drɒməki/ in Greek mythology, the faithful wife of Hector and mother of Astyanax. After the fall of Troy she was awarded to Neoptolemus, Achilles' son; she later married a Trojan seer called Helenus. Andromache is the heroine of Homer's ◊*Iliad* and the subject of a tragedy by Euripides.

Andromeda /æn'drɒmɪdə/ *n.* a major constellation of the N hemisphere, visible in autumn. Its main feature is the Andromeda galaxy. The star Alpha Andromedae forms one corner of the Square of Pegasus. It is named after a princess of Greek mythology who was chained to a rock as a sacrifice to a sea monster and was rescued by Perseus.

Andromeda galaxy a galaxy 2.2 million light years away from Earth in the constellation Andromeda, and the most distant object visible to the naked eye. It is the largest member of the ◊Local Group of galaxies. Like the Milky Way, it is a spiral orbited by several companion galaxies but contains about twice as many stars. It is about 200,000 light years across.

Andropov /æn'drɒpɒf/ Yuri 1914–1984. Soviet communist politician, president of the USSR 1983–84. As chief of the KGB 1967–82, he established a reputation for efficiently suppressing dissent.

anecdote /'ænɪkdəʊt/ *n.* a short account of an entertaining or interesting incident. —**anecdotal** /-'dəʊtəl/ *adj.* [French or from Greek *anekdota* = unpublished things]

anechoic /æni'kəʊɪk/ *adj.* free from echo. —**anechoic chamber**, a room designed to be of high sound absorbency. All surfaces inside the chamber are covered by sound-absorbent materials such as rubber. The walls are often covered with inward-facing pyramids of rubber, to minimize reflections. It is used for experiments in ◊acoustics and for testing audio equipment. [from Greek *an-* = without and *echo*]

anemometer /æni'mɒmɪtə/ *n.* an instrument for measuring the force of wind. A **cup-type anemometer** consists of cups at the ends of arms, which rotate when the wind blows. The speed of rotation indicates the wind speed. **Vane-type anemometers** have vanes, like a small windmill or propellor, that rotate when the wind blows. **Pressure-tube anemometers** use the pressure generated by the wind to indicate speed. The wind blowing into or across a tube develops a pressure, proportional to the wind speed, which is measured by a manometer or pressure gauge. **Hot-wire anemometers** work on the principle that the rate at which heat is transferred from a hot wire to the surrounding air is a measure of the air speed. Wind speed is determined by measuring either the electric current required to maintain a hot wire at a constant temperature, or the variation of resistance while a constant current is maintained. [from Greek *anemos* = wind and *meter*]

anemone *n.* any plant of the genus *Anemone* of the buttercup family Ranunculaceae. The function of petals is performed by its sepals. The garden anemone *A. coronaria* is white, blue, red, or purple. [from Latin from Greek = windflower (*anemos* = wind)]

anemophily *n.* a type of ◊pollination in which the pollen is carried on the wind. The flowers are usually unscented, have either very reduced petals and sepals or lack them altogether, and do not produce nectar. In some species they are borne in ◊catkins. Male and female reproductive structures are commonly found in separate flowers. —**anemophilous** *adj.*

anent /ə'nent/ *prep.* (*Scottish*) concerning. [Old English *an efen* = on a level with]

aneroid /'ænərɔːɪd/ *n.* an **aneroid barometer**, a barometer measuring air pressure by the action of air on the lid of a box containing a vacuum, which causes a pointer to move, not by the height of a fluid column. [from French from Greek *a-* = not and *nēros* = water]

Aneto, Pico /ænetəʊ'piːkəʊ/ highest peak of the Pyrenees mountains, rising to 3,400 m/11,052 ft in the Spanish province of Huesca.

aneurysm /'ænjʊrɪzəm/ *n.* a weakening in the wall of an artery, causing it to balloon outwards, with the risk of rupture and serious, often fatal, blood loss. If detected in time and accessible, some aneurysms can be excised. [from Greek *aneurinō* = widen]

anew /ə'njuː/ *adv.* again; in a different way. [earlier *of newe*]

Angad /'æŋgæd/ 1504–1552. Indian religious leader, second guru (teacher) of Sikhism 1539–52, succeeding Nanak. He popularized the alphabet known as **Gurmukhi**, in which the Sikh scriptures are written.

angel /'eɪndʒəl/ *n.* **1.** in Jewish, Christian, and Muslim belief, a supernatural being intermediate between God and humans. The Christian hierarchy has nine orders: **Seraphim**, **Cherubim**, **Thrones** (who contemplate God and reflect his glory), **Dominations**, **Virtues**, **Powers** (who regulate the stars and the universe), **Principalities**, **Archangels**, and **Angels** (who minister to humanity). Angels are conventionally represented in human form with wings. In traditional Catholic belief every human being has a guardian angel. The existence of angels was reasserted by the Pope in 1986. **2.** a very virtuous, kind, or obliging person. —**angel cake,** very light sponge cake. [from Old French from Latin from Greek *angelos* = messenger]

angel dust the popular name for the anaesthetic phencyclidine.

Angel Falls highest waterfalls in the New World, on the river Caroní in the tropical rainforest of Bolívar Region, Venezuela; total height 978 m/3,210 ft. [named after aviator and prospector J *Angel* who flew over the falls and crash-landed nearby in 1935]

angelfish *n.* the name given to a number of unrelated fishes. The freshwater **angelfish**, genus *Pterophyllum*, of South America, is a tall, side-to-side flattened fish with a striped body, up to 26 cm/10 in long, but usually smaller in captivity. The **angelfish** or **monkfish**, of the genus *Squatina*, is a bottom-living shark up to 1.8 m/6 ft long with a body flattened from top to bottom. The **marine angelfishes**, *Pomacanthus* and others, are long narrow-bodied fish with spiny fins, often brilliantly coloured, up to 60 cm/2 ft long, living around coral reefs in the tropics.

angelic /æn'dʒelɪk/ *adj.* of or like an angel. —**Angelic Doctor**, the nickname of St Thomas Aquinas. —**angelically** *adv.*

angelica *n.* **1.** any plant of the genus *Angelica* of the carrot family Umbelliferae. Mostly Eurasian in distribution, they are tall, perennial herbs with divided leaves and clusters of white or greenish flowers. **2.** its candied stalks, used in cookery. [from Latin = angelic (herb)]

Angelico /æn'dʒelɪkəʊ/ Fra (Guido di Pietro) *c.*1400–1455. Italian painter of religious scenes, active in Florence. He was a monk and painted a series of frescoes at the monastery of San Marco, Florence, begun after 1436. He also produced several altarpieces in a simple style.

Angelou /'ændʒəluː/ Maya (born Marguerite Johnson) 1928– . US novelist, poet, playwright, and short-story writer. Her powerful autobiographical works, *I Know Why the Caged Bird Sings* 1970 and its three sequels, tell of the struggles towards physical and spiritual liberation of a black woman growing up in the South.

angelus /'ændʒɪləs/ *n.* a prayer of the Roman Catholic Church said at morning, noon, and sunset in commemoration of the ◊Incarnation; a bell rung to announce this. [Latin *Angelus Domini* = angel of the Lord, opening words of prayer]

anger /'æŋgə/ *n.* extreme or passionate displeasure. —*v.t.* to make angry. [from Old Norse *angr* = grief]

Anger Kenneth 1932– . US avant-garde filmmaker, brought up in Hollywood. His films, which dispense with conventional narrative, often use homosexual iconography and a personal form of mysticism. They include *Fireworks* 1947, *Scorpio Rising* 1964, and *Lucifer Rising* 1973.

Angevin /'ændʒɪvɪn/ *adj.* relating to the reigns of the English kings Henry II, and Richard I (also known, with the later English kings up to Richard III, as the **Plantagenets**). The **Angevin Empire** comprised the territories (including England) that belonged to the Anjou dynasty. —*n.* a Plantagenet; a native or inhabitant of Anjou in France. [French, from *Anjou*, region of France controlled by Plantagenet kings]

angina /æn'dʒaɪnə/ *n.* or **angina pectoris** pain in the chest brought on by exertion, owing to an inadequate blood supply to the heart because a coronary artery is narrowed. [Latin from Greek *agkhonē* = strangling]

angiography *n.* a technique for X-raying major blood vessels. A radiopaque dye is injected into the bloodstream so that the suspect vessel is clearly silhouetted on the X-ray film.

angiosperm /'ændʒɪəspɜːm/ *n.* a member of the group of flowering plants that have seeds enclosed in an ovary which ripens to a fruit. Angiosperms are divided into ◊monocotyledons (single seed leaf in the embryo) and ◊dicotyledons (two seed leaves in the embryo). They include the majority of flowers, herbs, grasses, and trees except conifers. [from Greek *aggeion* = vessel and *sperma* = seed]

angle[1] /'æŋgəl/ *n.* **1.** the space between two lines or surfaces that meet; the inclination of two lines etc. to each other; a corner. Angles are measured in ◊degrees (°) or ◊radians, and are classified generally by their degree measures. **Acute angles** are less than 90°; **right angles** are exactly 90°; **obtuse angles** are greater than 90° but less than 180°; **reflex angles** are greater than 180° but less than 360°. **2.** a point of view. — *v.t./i.* **1.** to move or place obliquely. **2.** to present (information etc.) from a particular point of view. [from French or Latin *angulus*]

angle[2] *v.i.* **1.** to fish with hook and line. **2.** to seek an objective deviously. —**angler** *n.* **1.** a person who fishes with hook and line. **2.** any of an order of fishes Lophiiformes, with flattened body and broad head and jaws. Many species have small, plant-like tufts on their skin. These act as camouflage for the fish as it waits, either floating among seaweed or lying on the sea bottom, twitching the enlarged tip of the thread-like first ray of its dorsal fin to entice prey. [Old English]

Angle *n.* a member of a N German tribe which came to England in the 5th century, founding kingdoms in Mercia, Northumbria, and East Anglia. The Angles gave their name to England and the English. [from Latin from *Angul*, name of district in Germany]

Anglican /'æŋglɪkən/ *adj.* of the reformed Church of England or any church in communion with it. —*n.* a member of the Anglican Church. —**Anglicanism** *n.* [from Latin *Anglicanus*]

Anglican Communion a family of Christian churches including the Church of England, the US Episcopal Church, and those holding the same essential doctrines, that is the Lambeth Quadrilateral 1888 Holy Scripture as the basis of all doctrine, the Nicene and Apostles' Creeds, Holy Baptism and Holy Communion, and the historic episcopate.

Anglicism /'æŋglɪsɪzəm/ *n.* a peculiarly English word or custom. [from Latin *Anglicus* = of Angles]

Anglicize /'æŋglɪsaɪz/ *v.t.* to make English in form or character.

angling *n.* fishing with rod and line. **Freshwater** and **seafishing** are the most common forms. Angling is the biggest participant sport in the UK.

Anglo- in combinations, English; of English origin; English or British and. [from Latin from *Angul*]

Anglo-Catholic *adj.* of the section of the Church of England that emphasizes its unbroken connection with the early church and seeks maximum accordance with the doctrine of the Catholic Church. —*n.* an adherent of Anglo-Catholic belief.

Anglo-Irish Agreement or **Hillsborough Agreement** the concord reached in 1985 between the UK and Irish premiers, Margaret Thatcher and Garret FitzGerald. One sign of the improved relations between the two countries was increased cooperation between police and security forces across the border with Northern Ireland. The pact also gave the Irish Republic a greater voice in the conduct of Northern Ireland's affairs. However, the agreement was rejected by Northern Ireland Unionists as a step towards renunciation of British sovereignty. In March 1988 talks led to further strengthening of the agreement.

Anglophile /'æŋgləʊfail/ *n.* one who greatly admires England or the English. [Greek *philos* = dear]

Anglo-Saxon *adj.* of English Saxons before the Norman Conquest. —*n.* **1.** an Anglo-Saxon person, one of the several Germanic invaders (Angles, Saxons, and Jutes) who conquered much of Britain between the 5th and 7th centuries. After the conquest a number of kingdoms were set up, commonly referred to as the **Heptarchy**; these were united in the early 9th century under the overlordship of Wessex. The Norman invasion in 1066 brought Anglo-Saxon rule to an end. **2.** the English language of this period, also called Old English. **3.** a person of English descent.

Anglo-Saxon art the painting and sculpture of England from the 7th century to 1066. Carved crosses and ivories, manuscript painting, and gold and enamel jewellery survive. The relics of the Sutton Hoo ship burial, 7th century, and the *Lindisfarne Gospels*, about 690 (both British Museum, London), have typical Celtic ornamental patterns, but in manuscripts of S England a different style emerged in the 9th century, with delicate, lively pen-and-ink figures and heavily decorative foliage borders.

Anglo-Saxon Chronicle a history of England from the Roman invasion to the 11th century, in the form of a series of chronicles written in Old English by monks, begun in the 9th century (during the reign of King Alfred), and continuing to the 12th century.

Angola /æŋ'gəʊlə/ People's Republic of; country in SW Africa, bounded to the W by the Atlantic ocean, to the N and NE by Zaïre, to the E by Zambia, and to the S by Namibia; **area** 1,246,700 sq km/481,226 sq mi; **capital** and chief port Luanda; **physical** narrow coastal plain rises to vast interior plateau with rainforest in NW; desert in S; **head of state and government** José Eduardo dos Santos from 1979; **political system** one-party Socialist republic; **exports** oil, coffee, diamonds, palm oil, sisal, iron ore, fish; **population** (1989 est) 9,733,000 (largest ethnic group Ovimbundu); **language** Portuguese (official); Bantu dialects; **recent history** independence from Portugal achieved in 1975; a struggle for power followed between MPLA, supported by the USSR and Cuba, and FNLA and UNITA supported by the West and South Africa. MPLA gained control in 1976. Guerrilla raids continued until 1988 when a peace treaty providing for the withdrawal of all foreign troops was signed with South Africa and Cuba.

angora /æŋ'gɔːrə/ *n.* **1.** a long-haired variety of cat, goat, or rabbit. **2.** soft fluffy fabric or yarn made from the hair of an angora rabbit or goat. [from *Angora*, the former name of Ankara]

angostura /æŋgə'stjʊərə/ *n.* a flavouring prepared from oil distilled from the bark of *Galipea cusparia*, a South American tree. It is blended with herbs and other flavourings to give **angostura bitters**, which was first used as a stomach remedy and is now used to season food and fruit, to make a 'pink gin', and to prepare other alcoholic drinks. [from *Angostura* (now Ciudad Bolívar), town in Venezuela]

angry /'æŋgrɪ/ *adj.* **1.** feeling or showing anger. **2.** inflamed. —**angrily** *adv.*

Angry Young Men a group of British writers who emerged about 1950 after the creative hiatus that followed World War II. They included Kingsley Amis, John Wain, John Osborne, and Colin Wilson. Also linked to the group were Iris Murdoch and Kenneth Tynan.

angst /æŋst/ *n.* an emotional state of anxiety without a specific cause. In ◊existentialism, the term refers to general human anxiety at having free will, that is, of being responsible for one's actions. [German *angst* = anxiety]

ångström /'æŋgstrəm/ *n.* a unit (symbol Å) of length equal to 10^{-10} metre or one-hundred-millionth of a centimetre, used for atomic measurements and the wavelengths of ◊electromagnetic radiation. [from Swedish physicist A J *Ångström*]

Ångström Anders Jonas 1814–1874. Swedish physicist, who worked in spectroscopy and solar physics.

Anguilla /æŋ'gwɪlə/ island in the E Caribbean; **area** 160 sq km/62 sq mi; **capital** The Valley; **exports** lobster, salt; **population** (1988) 7,000; **language** English, Creole; **government** from 1982, governor, executive council, and legislative house of assembly (chief minister Emile Gumbs from 1984); **recent history** a British colony from 1650, Anguilla was long associated with ◊St Christopher-Nevis but in 1969 declared itself a republic. A small British force restored order, and Anguilla has since 1980 been a separate dependency of the UK.

anguish /'æŋgwɪʃ/ *n.* severe (especially mental) suffering. —**anguished** *adj.* [from Old French from Latin *angustia* = tightness]

angular /'æŋgjʊlə/ *adj.* **1.** having sharp corners or features, not plump or smooth. **2.** forming an angle. **3.** measured by angle. —**angularity** /-'lærɪtɪ/ *n.* [from Latin *angulus* = angle]

angular momentum see ◊momentum.

Angus /'æŋgəs/ former county and modern district on the E coast of Scotland, merged in 1975 in Tayside region.

Anhui /æn'hweɪ/ or **Anhwei** province of E China, watered by the Chang Jiang (Yangtze) river; **area** 139,900 sq km/54,000 sq mi; **capital** Hefei; **products** cereals in the N; cotton, rice, tea in the S; **population** (1986) 52,170,000.

anhydride *n.* a chemical compound obtained by the removal of water from another compound; usually a dehydrated acid. For example, sulphur trioxide SO_3 is the anhydride of sulphuric acid, H_2SO_4.

anhydrite *n.* naturally occurring anhydrous calcium sulphate, $CaSO_4$. It is used commercially for the manufacture of plaster of paris and builders' plaster.

anhydrous *adj.* in chemistry, totally without water, especially water of crystallization.

aniline /'ænɪliːn/ *n.* or **phenylamine**, $C_6H_5NH_2$, one of the simplest aromatic chemicals (a substance related to benzene, with its carbon atoms joined in a ring.) When pure, it is a colourless, oily liquid; it has a characteristic odour, and turns brown in contact with air. It occurs in coal tar, and is used in the rubber industry and to make drugs and dyes. It is highly poisonous. [from German *anil* = indigo, whence originally obtained) from Arabic *al nil* = the indigo]

animadvert /ænɪməd'vɜːt/ *v.i.* to pass hostile criticism or censure (*on*). —**animadversion** /-'vɜːʃən/ *n.* [from Latin *animus* = mind and *vertere* = turn]

animal /'ænɪməl/ *n.* **1.** in zoology, a member of the kingdom Animalia, one of the major categories of living things, or **metazoan**. Animals are all ◊heterotrophs (they obtain their energy from organic substances produced by other organisms); they have ◊eukaryotic cells (the genetic material is contained within a distinct nucleus) bounded by a thin cell membrane rather than the thick cell wall of plants. In the past, it was common to include the single-celled ◊protozoa with the animals, but these are now classified as protists, together with single-celled plants. Thus all animals are multicellular. Most are capable of moving around for at least part of their life cycle. **2.** a member of this kingdom other than man; a quadruped. **3.** a brutish or uncivilized person. —*adj.* **1.** of or like an animal. **2.** bestial; carnal. [from Latin *animalis* = having breath (*anima* = breath)]

animal behaviour the scientific study of the behaviour of animals, either by comparative psychologists (with an interest mainly in the psychological processes involved in the control of behaviour) or by ethologists (with an interest in the biological context and relevance of behaviour).

animalcule /ænɪ'mælkjuːl/ *n.* a microscopic animal. [from *animal* and diminutive *-cule*]

animate /'ænɪmət/ *adj.* having life; lively. —/-eɪt/ *v.t.* **1.** to enliven. **2.** to give life to. **3.** to produce as an animated cartoon. **4.** to motivate. —**animated cartoon**, a film made by photographing a series of drawings or positions of puppets to create an illusion of movement. —**animation** /-'meɪʃən/ *n.*, **animator** *n.* [from Latin *animare* = give life to (*anima* = life)]

animism /'ænɪmɪzəm/ *n.* **1.** in psychology and physiology, the view of human personality that attributes human life and behaviour to a force distinct from matter. **2.** in religious theory, the conception of a spiritual reality behind the material one: for example, belief in the soul as a shadowy duplicate of the body capable of independent activity, both in life and death. **3.** in anthropology, the concept of spirits residing in all natural phenomena and objects. —**animistic** /-'mɪstɪk/ *adj.* [from Latin *anima* = life, soul]

animosity /æni'mɒsɪtɪ/ *n.* a spirit or feeling of hostility. [from Old French or Latin]

animus /'ænɪməs/ *n.* a display of animosity; ill-feeling. [Latin = spirit, mind]

anion /'ænaɪən/ *n.* a negatively charged ion. An electrolyte, such as the salt zinc chloride, $ZnCl_2$, is dissociated in aqueous solution or in the molten state into doubly-charged Zn^{++} zinc ◊cations and singly-charged Cl^-anions. During electrolysis, the zinc cations flow to the cathode (to become discharged and liberate zinc metal) and the chloride anions flow to the anode (to liberate chlorine gas). —**anionic** /-'ɒnɪk/ *adj.*[from Greek *ana* = up and *ion*]

anise *n.* a plant *Pimpinella anisum,* of the carrot family Umbelliferae, whose fragrant seeds are used to flavour foods. See ◊aniseed.

aniseed /'ænɪsiːd/ *n.* the aromatic seed of the ◊anise plant, used for flavouring. Aniseed oil is used in cough medicine. [from Old French from Latin from Greek *anison* = dill]

Ankara /'æŋkərə/ formerly **Angora** capital of Turkey; population (1985) 2,252,000. Industries include cement, textiles, and leather products. It replaced Istanbul (then in Allied occupation) as capital in 1923.

ankh /æŋk/ *n.* a cross with a loop as its upper arm, used in ancient Egypt as a symbol of life. [Egyptian = life]

ankle *n.* the joint connecting the foot with the leg; the part of the leg between this and the calf. [from Old Norse]

anklet /'æŋklɪt/ *n.* an ornament or fetter worn round the ankle. [from *ankle* and *-let* (as in *bracelet*)]

ankylosis /æŋkaɪ'ləʊsɪs/ *n.* the stiffening of a joint by fusion of bones. [from Greek *agkulos* = crooked]

Anna Comnena /'ænə kɒm'niːnə/ 1083–after 1148. Byzantine historian, daughter of the emperor ◊Alexius I, and chiefly remembered as the historian of her father's reign. After a number of abortive attempts to alter the imperial succession in favour of her husband, Nicephorus Bryennius (*c.* 1062–1137), she retired to a convent to write her major work, the *Alexiad.* It describes the Byzantine view of public office, as well as the religious and intellectual life of the period.

Anna Karenina /kə'reninə/ a novel by Leo Tolstoy, published 1873–77. It describes a married woman's love affair with Vronski, a young officer, which ends with her suicide.

annals /'ænəlz/ *n.pl.* a narrative of events year by year; written records. —**annalistic** /-'lɪstɪk/ *adj.* [from French or Latin *annus* = year]

Annapurna /ænə'pɜːnə/ mountain 8,075 m/26,502 ft in the Himalayas, Nepál. The N face was climbed by a French expedition (Maurice Herzog) in 1950 and the S by a British team in 1970.

Anne /æn/ 1665–1714. Queen of Great Britain and Ireland 1702–14. Second daughter of James, Duke of York, who became James II, and Anne Hyde. She succeeded William III in 1702. Events of her reign include the War of the Spanish Succession, Marlborough's victories at Blenheim, Ramillies, Oudenarde, and Malplaquet, and the union of the English and Scottish parliaments in 1707. She was succeeded by George I.

Anne (full name Anne Elizabeth Alice Louise) 1950– . Princess of the UK, second child of Queen Elizabeth II, declared Princess Royal in 1987. She is an excellent horsewoman, winning a gold medal at the 1976 Olympics, and is actively involved in charity work worldwide, especially for children. In 1973 she married Captain Mark Phillips (1949–), of the Queen's Dragoon Guards; they separated in 1989. Their son Peter (1977–) was the first direct descendant of the Queen not to bear a title. They also have a daughter, Zara (1981–).

anneal /ə'niːl/ *v.t.* to heat (metal or glass) for a given time at a given temperature and allow it to cool slowly, especially to toughen it. [Old English = bake]

annelid /'ænəlɪd/ *n.* any segmented worm of the phylum Annelida. Annelids include earthworms, leeches, and

marine worms such as lugworms. [from French from Latin *an(n)ulus* = ring]

Anne of Austria 1601–1666. Queen of France from 1615 and regent 1643–61. Daughter of Philip III of Spain, she married Louis XIII of France (whose chief minister, Cardinal Richelieu, worked against her). On her husband's death she became regent for their son, Louis XIV, until his majority.

Anne of Cleves 1515–1557. Fourth wife of ◊Henry VIII of England, 1540. She was the daughter of the Duke of Cleves, and was recommended to Henry as a wife by Thomas ◊Cromwell, who wanted an alliance with German Protestantism against the Holy Roman Empire. Henry did not like her looks, had the marriage declared void after six months, pensioned her, and had Cromwell beheaded.

Anne of Denmark 1574–1619. Queen consort of James VI of Scotland (later James I of Great Britain 1603). She was the daughter of Frederick II of Denmark and Norway, and married James in 1589. Anne was suspected of Catholic leanings and was notably extravagant.

annex /æ'neks/ *v.t.* **1.** to add or append as a subordinate part. **2.** to incorporate (territory) into one's own. **3.** (*colloquial*) to take without right. —**annexation** /-'seɪʃən/ *n.* [from French from Latin *annectere* (*nectere* = bind)]

annexe /'æneks/ *n.* a building attached to a larger or more important one or forming a subordinate part of a main building.

annihilate /ə'naɪleɪt/ *v.t.* to destroy completely. [from Latin *annihilare* (*nihil* = nothing)]

annihilation /ə'naɪleɪʃ(ə)n/ *n.* **1.** total destruction; the act of such destruction. **2.** in nuclear physics, a process in which a particle and its 'mirror image' particle or ◊antiparticle collide and disappear, with the creation of a burst of energy. The energy created is equivalent to the mass of the colliding particles in accordance with the ◊mass–energy equation. For example, an electron and a positron annihilate to produce a burst of high-energy X-rays.

anniversary /ænɪ'vɜːsərɪ/ *n.* the date on which an event took place in a previous year; a celebration of this. [from Latin *annus* = year and *versus* = turned]

anno Domini /ænəʊ 'dɒmɪnaɪ/ in the Christian chronological system, referring to dates since the birth of Jesus, denoted by the letters AD. There is no year 0, so AD 1 follows immediately after the year 1 BC (before Christ). The system became the standard reckoning in the Western world after being adopted by the English historian Bede in the 8th century. The abbreviations CE (Common Era) and BCE (before Common Era) are often used instead by scholars and writers as objective, rather than religious, terms. [Latin = in the year of the Lord]

annotate /'ænəʊteɪt/ *v.t.* to add explanatory notes to. —**annotation** /-'teɪʃən/ *n.* [from Latin *annotare* (*nota* = mark)]

announce /ə'naʊns/ *v.t.* to make publicly known; to make known the arrival or imminence of; to be a sign of. —**announcement** *n.* [from Old French from Latin *annuntiare* (*nuntius* = messenger)]

announcer *n.* one who announces items in broadcasting.

annoy /ə'nɔɪ/ *v.t.* to anger slightly; to be troublesome to, to molest. —**annoyance** *n.* [from Old French from Latin *in odio* = hateful]

annoyed /ə'nɔɪd/ *adj.* somewhat angry.

annual /'ænjʊəl/ *adj.* **1.** reckoned by the year; recurring once every year. **2.** (of plants) living or lasting only one year or season. —*n.* **1.** a book etc. published in yearly issues. **2.** an annual plant, one that completes its life cycle within one year, during which time it germinates, grows to maturity, bears flowers, produces seed and then dies. Examples include the common poppy *Papaver rhoeas* and groundsel *Senecio vulgaris.* —**annual ring,** or **growth ring,** one of the concentric rings visible on a cut tree trunk or other woody stem, or a ring in the cross-section of a fish etc., from one year's growth. The annual rings may be used to estimate the age of the plant (see ◊dendrochronology), or fish etc., but occasionally more than one growth ring is produced in a given year. —**annually** *adv.* [from Old French from Latin *annus* = year]

annuity /ə'njuːɪtɪ/ *n.* an investment yielding a fixed annual sum; a yearly grant or allowance.

annul /ə'nʌl/ v.t. (-ll-) to declare to be invalid; to cancel, to abolish. —**annulment** n. [from Old French from Latin *annullare* (*nullus* = none)]

annular /'ænjʊlə/ adj. ring-shaped, forming a ring. —**annular eclipse,** see ◊eclipse. [from French or Latin *an(n)ulus* = ring]

annulet /'ænju:lɪt/ n. a small ring; an encircling band. [from Latin *an(n)ulus*]

annulus n. in geometry, the plane area between two concentric circles, making a flat ring. [Latin = ring]

Annunciation n. in the New Testament, the announcement to Mary by the angel Gabriel that she was to be the mother of Christ; the feast of the Annunciation is 25 March (also known as Lady Day). [from Old French from Latin *annuntiare* (*nuntius* = messenger)]

anode /'ænəʊd/ n. the electrode towards which negative particles (anions, electrons) move within a device such as the cells of a battery, electrolytic cells, and diodes. [from Greek *anodos* = way up (*ana* = up and *hodos* = way)]

anodize /'ænədaɪz/ v.t. to coat (a metal, such as aluminium) with a protective oxide layer by electrolysis. This increases the resistance to ◊corrosion.

anodyne /'ænədaɪn/ adj. relieving pain, soothing. —n. an anodyne drug or circumstance. [from Latin from Greek *an-* = without and *odunē* = pain]

anoint /ə'nɔɪnt/ v.t. to apply oil or ointment to, especially as a religious ceremony; to smear (*with* grease etc.). [from Anglo-French from Latin *inungere*]

anomalous /ə'nɒmələs/ adj. deviant, irregular, abnormal. —**anomalously** adv. [from Latin from Greek *an-* = not and *homalos* = even]

anomalous expansion of water the expansion of water as it is cooled from 4°C to 0°C. This behaviour is unusual, because most substances contract when they are cooled. It means that water has a greater density at 4°C than at 0°C. Hence ice floats on water, and the water at the bottom of a pool in winter is warmer than at the surface. As a result large lakes freeze slowly in winter and aquatic life is more likely to survive.

anomaly /ə'nɒməlɪ/ n. an anomalous thing.

anomie n. in the social sciences, a state of 'normlessness' created by the breakdown of commonly agreed standards of behaviour and morality; the term often refers to situations in which the social order appears to have collapsed. The concept was developed by the French sociologist Emil Durkheim.

anon /ə'nɒn/ adv. soon, shortly. [Old English *on an* = into one]

anon. abbreviation of anonymous.

anonymous /ə'nɒnɪməs/ adj. with a name that is not known or not made public; written or given by such a person. —**anonymously** adv., **anonymity** /ænɒ'nɪmɪtɪ/ n. [from Latin from Greek *an-* = without and *onoma* = name]

anorak /'ænəræk/ n. a waterproof jacket, usually with a hood attached. [Eskimo]

anorexia /ænə'reksɪə/ n. lack of appetite for food. It is usually found in adolescent girls and young women, who may be obsessed with the desire to lose weight. Compulsive eating, or ◊bulimia, often accompanies anorexia. —**anorexia nervosa** /nə'vəʊsə/, chronic anorexia caused by a psychological condition. —**anorexic** n. [Latin from Greek *an-* = not and *orexis* = appetite]

another /ə'nʌðə/ adj. additional, one more; a different (*thing* etc.); some other. —n. another person or thing. [earlier *an other*]

Anouilh /ænu:'iː/ Jean 1910–1987. French playwright. His plays, influenced by the Neo-Classical tradition, include *Antigone* 1942, *L'Invitation au château/Ring Round the Moon* 1947, *Colombe* 1950, and *Becket* 1959, about St Thomas Becket and Henry II.

Nobody has a more sacred obligation to obey the law than those who make the law.

Jean Anouilh
Antigone

anoxaemia n. a shortage of oxygen in the lungs and tissues. It may be due to breathing air deficient in oxygen (for instance, at high altitude or where there are noxious fumes), disease of the lungs, or some disorder in which the oxygen-carrying capacity of the blood is impaired.

Anschluss /'ænʃlʊs/ n. the annexation of Austria with Germany, accomplished by the German chancellor Adolf Hitler on 12 March 1938. [German = union]

anserine /'ænsəraɪn/ adj. of or like a goose. [from Latin *anser* = goose]

Ansermet /'ɑ:nseəme/ Ernest 1883–1969. Swiss conductor with Diaghilev's Russian Ballet 1915–23. In 1918 he founded the Swiss Romande Orchestra, conducting many first performances of works by ◊Stravinsky.

ANSI abbreviation of American National Standards Institution, the US national standards body. It sets official procedures in computing, electronics and other areas.

Anson /'ænsən/ George, 1st Baron Anson 1697–1762. English admiral who sailed around the world 1740–44. In 1740 he commanded the squadron attacking the Spanish colonies and shipping in South America; he returned home by circumnavigating the world, with £500,000 of Spanish treasure. He carried out reforms at the Admiralty.

answer /'ɑ:nsə/ n. something said, written, or done in reaction to a question, statement, or circumstance; the solution to a problem. —v.t./i. **1.** to make an answer (to). **2.** to respond to the summons or signal of. **3.** to suit (a need or purpose). **4.** to be responsible *for* or *to*. **5.** to correspond *to* a description. —**answer back,** to answer a rebuke impudently. [Old English = swear against (a charge)]

answerable adj. **1.** responsible *to* or *for*. **2.** that can be answered.

ant n. an insect belonging to the family Formicidae, and to the same order (Hymenoptera) as bees and wasps. Ants are characterized by a conspicuous 'waist' and elbowed antennae. About 10,000 different species are known; all are social in habit, living in highly organized groups, and all construct nests of various kinds. Ants are found in all parts of the world, except the polar regions. [Old English]

Antabuse /'æntəbju:z/ n. trade name of disulfiram, a synthetic chemical used in the treatment of alcoholism. When taken, it produces unpleasant side effects with alcohol, such as nausea, headache, palpitations, and collapse. The 'Antabuse effect' is produced coincidentally by certain antibiotics.

antacid /æn'tæsɪd/ adj. preventing or correcting acidity. —n. an antacid substance that neutralizes stomach acid. It may be taken between meals to relieve symptoms of hyperacidity, such as pain, bloating, nausea, and 'heartburn'. Excessive or prolonged need for antacids should be investigated medically.

antagonism /æn'tægənɪzəm/ n. active opposition, hostility.

antagonist n. an opponent. [from French or Latin from Greek]

antagonistic /æntægə'nɪstɪk/ adj. showing antagonism, hostile.

antagonistic muscle a pair of muscles allowing coordinated movement of the skeletal joints. The extension of the arm, for example, requires one set of muscles to relax, while another set contracts. The individual components of antagonistic pairs can be classified into ◊extensors and ◊flexors.

antagonize /æn'tægənaɪz/ v.t. to arouse antagonism in. [from Greek = struggle against (*agōn* = contest)]

Antakya /æn'tɑ:kjə/ or **Hatay** city in SE Turkey, site of the ancient ◊Antioch; population (1985) 109,200.

Antalya /æn'tɑːljə/ Mediterranean port on the west coast of Turkey and capital of a province of the same name; population (1985) 258,000. The port trades in agricultural and forest produce.

Antananarivo /æntənænə'ri:vəʊ/ formerly **Tananarive** capital of Madagascar, on the interior plateau, with a rail link to Tamatave; population (1986) 703,000.

Antarctic /æn'tɑ:ktɪk/ adj. of the south polar regions. —n. the regions (both land and sea) round the South Pole. [from Old French or Latin from Greek *anti* = opposite and *Arctic*]

Antarctica /æn'tɑ:ktɪkə/ the continent covering the South Pole; **area** 13,727,000 sq km/5,300,000 sq mi; **physical** a vast plateau, of which the highest point is the Vinson Massif in the Ellsworth mountains, 5,139 m/16,866 ft. The Ross Ice Shelf is formed by several glaciers coalescing in the Ross Sea; Mount Erebus on Ross Island is the

anteater

southernmost active volcano. Little more than 1% of the land is ice-free, the temperature falling to –70°C/–100°F and below, and in places the ice is 5,000 m/16,000 ft deep, comprising over two-thirds of the world's fresh water. There are extensive mineral resources, including iron, coal, uranium and other strategic metals, and oil; **population** settlement limited to scientific research stations with changing personnel; **recent history** in 1988, 33 countries signed the Antarctic Minerals Convention, laying Antarctica open to commercial exploitation. Guidelines on environmental protection were included but regarded as inadequate by environmental pressure groups.

Antarctic Circle an imaginary line that encircles the South Pole at latitude 66° 32 | S, south of which the Sun does not rise or set at midsummer. The line encompasses the continent of Antarctica and the Antarctic Ocean.

Antarctic Peninsula a mountainous peninsula of W Antarctica extending 1,930 km/1,200 mi north towards South America. Originally named **Palmer Land** after a US navigator, Captain Nathaniel Palmer, who was the first to explore the region in 1820, it was claimed by Britain in 1832, Chile in 1942 and Argentina in 1940. Its name was changed to the Antarctic Peninsula in 1964.

Antarctic Treaty an agreement signed in 1959 between 12 nations with an interest in Antarctica (including Britain); 35 countries were party to it by 1990. It came into force in 1961 for a 30-year period. Its provisions (covering the area south of latitude 60° S) neither accepted nor rejected any nation's territorial claims, but barred any new ones; imposed a ban on military operations and large-scale mineral extraction; and allowed for free exchange of scientific data from bases. Since 1980 the treaty has been extended to conserve marine resources within the larger area bordered by the Antarctic Convergence.

Antares /æn'teəri:z/ *n.* or **Alpha Scorpii** the brightest star in the constellation Scorpius and the 15th brightest star in the sky. It is a red supergiant several hundred times larger than the Sun, lies about 400 light years away, and fluctuates slightly in brightness.

ante /'ænti/ *n.* a stake put up by a poker player before drawing new cards; an amount to be paid in advance. —*v.t.* to put up (an ante).

ante- prefix meaning before, preceding. [Latin = before]

anteater *n.* a mammal of the family Myrmecophagidae, order Edentata, native to Mexico, Central America, and tropical South America. An anteater lives almost entirely on ants and termites. It has toothless jaws, an extensile tongue, and claws for breaking into the nests of its prey.

antebellum *adj.* in US usage, an adjective referring to the period just before the Civil War (1861–65). [Latin *ante bellum* = before the war]

antecedent /ænti'si:dənt/ *n.* 1. a preceding thing or circumstance. 2. in grammar, a word or phrase to which another word (especially a relative pronoun) refers. 3. (in *plural*) a person's or thing's past history. —*adj.* previous. [from French or Latin (*cedere* = go)]

antechamber *n.* an anteroom.

antedate /ænti'deit/ *v.t.* to be of earlier date than; to give a date earlier than the true one to.

antediluvian /æntidi'lu:viən/ *adj.* of the time before the Flood; (*colloquial*) very old. [from Latin *diluvium* = deluge]

antelope /'æntiləup/ *n.* (*plural* the same or **antelopes**) a swift-running deerlike animal (e. g. chamois, gazelle) belonging to the cow family Bovidae, found especially in Africa. They are grazers or browsers, and chew the cud. They range in size from the dik-diks and duikers, only 30 cm/1 ft high, to the eland, which can be 1.8 m/6 ft at the shoulder. [from Old French or Latin from Greek *antholops*]

antenatal /ænti'neitəl/ *adj.* before birth; relating to pregnancy.

antenna /æn'tenə/ *n.* 1. (*plural* **antennae**) in zoology, an appendage ('feeler') on the head. Insects, centipedes, and millipedes each have one pair of antennae but there are two pairs in crustaceans, such as shrimps. In insects the antennae are usually involved with the senses of smell and touch. They are frequently complex structures with large surface areas that increase the ability to detect scents. 2. (*plural* **antennas**) in radio and television, another name for ◊aerial. [Latin = sail-yard]

antepenultimate /æntipi'nʌltimət/ *adj.* last but two.

ante-post /ænti'pəust/ *adj.* (of racing bets) made before the runners' numbers are displayed.

anterior /æn'tiəriə/ *adj.* 1. nearer the front; prior (*to*). 2. in biology, of or near the head. [from French or Latin, comparative of *ante* = before]

anteroom /'æntiru:m/ *n.* a small room leading to a main one.

anthelmintic *n.* a class of drugs effective against a range of intestinal worms.

anthem /'ænθəm/ *n.* 1. a short choral composition, usually based on a passage of Scripture, for church use; a song of praise or gladness. 2. a national anthem (see ◊national). [Old English from Latin]

anther /'ænθə(r)/ *n.* in a flower, the terminal part of a stamen in which the ◊pollen grains are produced. It is usually borne on a slender stalk or filament, and has two lobes, each containing two chambers or pollen sacs within which the pollen is formed. [from French or Latin from Greek *anthos* = flower]

antheridium *n.* an organ producing the male gametes, ◊antherozoids, in algae, bryophytes (mosses and liverworts), and pteridophytes (ferns, club mosses, and horsetails).

antherozoid *n.* a motile (or independently moving) male gamete produced by algae, bryophytes (mosses and liverworts), pteridophytes (ferns, club mosses, and horsetails), and some gymnosperms (notably the cycads).

anthill /'ænthil/ *n.* a mound of soil formed by ants over their nest.

anthology /æn'θɒlədʒi/ *n.* a collection of passages from literature, especially poetry and song. —**anthologist** *n.* [from French or Latin from Greek *anthos* = flower and *-logia* = collection]

Anthony /'ænθəni/ Susan B(rownell) 1820–1906. US pioneering campaigner for women's rights who also worked for the antislavery and temperance movements. Her causes included equality of pay for women teachers, married women's property rights, and women's suffrage. In 1869, with Elizabeth Cady ◊Stanton, she founded the National Woman Suffrage Association.

Anthony, St /'æntəni/ *c.*251–356. Also known as Anthony of Thebes. Founder of Christian monasticism. Born in Egypt, at the age of 20 he renounced all his possessions and began a hermitic life of study and prayer, later seeking further solitude in a cave in the desert, where he remained for the rest of his life.

anthozoan /ænθə'zəuən/ *n.* a marine animal of the class Anthozoa which includes corals and sea anemones. [from Latin from Greek *anthos* = flower and *zōa* = animals]

anthracene *n.* a white, glistening, crystalline hydrocarbon with a faint blue fluorescence when pure. Its melting point is about 421°F/216°C and its boiling point 644°f/340°C. It occurs in the high-boiling-point fractions of coal tar, where it was discovered in 1832 by the French chemists Auguste Laurent (1808–53) and Jean Dumas (1800–84).

anthracite /'ænθrəsait/ *n.* a hard, dense, glossy variety of ◊coal, containing over 90% of fixed carbon and a low percentage of ash and volatile matter, which causes it to burn without flame, smoke, or smell. [from Greek *anthrax* = coal, carbuncle]

anthrax /'ænθræks/ *n.* a disease of sheep and cattle occasionally transmitted to humans, usually via infected hides and fleeces. It may develop as black skin pustules or severe pneumonia. Treatment is with antibiotics. [Latin from Greek]

anthropocentric /ænθrəpə'sentrik/ *adj.* regarding mankind as the centre of existence. [from Greek *anthrōpos* = human being]

anthropoid /'ænθrəpɔid/ *adj.* like a human in form. —*n.* an anthropoid ape.

anthropology /ænθrə'pɒlədʒɪ/ *n.* the study of human-kind, now usually divided into two main sub-disciplines: study of the social organization and cultural systems of human groups (**social anthropology**), and study of the structure and evolution of humans (**physical** or **biological anthropology**). —**anthropological** /-ə'lɒdʒɪkəl/ *adj.*, **anthropologist** *n.* [from Greek *anthrōpos* = human being and *logos* = discourse]

anthropometry *n.* the science dealing with the measurement of the human body, particularly stature, body weight, cranial capacity, and length of limbs, in samplings of the populations of living peoples and in the remains of buried and fossilized humans.

anthropomorphism /ænθrəpə'mɔːfɪzəm/ *n.* the attribution of human characteristics to animals, inanimate objects, or deities. It appears in the mythologies of many cultures, and as a literary device in fables and allegories. —**anthropomorphic** *adj.*

anthropomorphous /ænθrəpə'mɔːfəs/ *adj.* of human form. [from Greek *anthrōpos* = human being and *morphē* = form]

anti /'æntɪ/ *prep.* opposed to. —*n.* one who is opposed to a policy etc.

anti- prefix meaning opposed to; preventing. [from Greek *anti* = against]

anti-aircraft *adj.* used in attacking enemy aircraft.

antibiotic /æntɪbaɪ'ɒtɪk/ *n.* a drug that kills or inhibits the growth of bacteria and fungi. It is derived from living organisms such as fungi or other bacteria, which distinguishes it from other antibacterials. —*adj.* functioning in this way. [from French from Greek *bios* = life]

antibody /'æntɪbɒdɪ/ *n.* a protein molecule produced in the blood by ◊lymphocytes in response to the presence of invading substances, or ◊antigens, including the proteins carried on the surface of bacteria and viruses. [translation of German *antikörper* (*körper* = body)]

antic *n.* (usually in *plural*) absurd movements intended to cause amusement; odd or foolish behaviour. [from Italian *antico* = antique, used as = grotesque]

anticholinergic *n.* any drug that blocks the passage of certain nerve impulses in the ◊central nervous system by inhibiting the production of acetylcholine, a neurotransmitter.

Antichrist /'æntɪkraɪst/ *n.* in Christian theology, the opponent of Christ, by whom he is finally to be conquered. The Antichrist may be a false messiah, or be connected with false teaching, or be identified with an individual.

anticipate /æn'tɪsɪpeɪt/ *v.t.* **1.** to deal with or use before the proper time. **2.** to forestall. **3.** to be ahead of (a person) in taking some action etc.; to foresee and provide for. **4.** (*disputed usage*) to expect. [from Latin *anticipare* (*anti* = ante and *capere* = take)]

anticipation /æntɪsɪ'peɪʃən/ *n.* anticipating; eager expectation. —**anticipatory** /-'peɪtərɪ/ *adj.*

anticlimax /'æntɪklaɪmæks/ *n.* a trivial conclusion to something significant or impressive, especially when a climax was expected.

anticline /'æntɪklaɪn/ *n.* in geology, a fold in the rocks of the Earth's crust in which the layers or beds bulge upwards to form an arch (seldom preserved intact). —**anticlinal** *adj.* [from Greek *klinō* = lean]

anticlockwise /æntɪ'klɒkwaɪz/ *adj. & adv.* moving in a curve in the opposite direction to the hands of a clock (see ◊clockwise).

anticoagulant *n.* a substance that suppresses the formation of ◊blood clots. Common anticoagulants are heparin, produced by the liver and lungs, and derivatives of coumarin. Anticoagulants are used medically in treating heart attacks, for example. [from Latin *coagulare*]

Anti-Comintern Pact (Anti-Communist Pact) an agreement signed between Germany and Japan on 25 Nov 1936, opposing communism as a menace to peace and order. The pact was signed by Italy in 1937 and by Hungary, Spain, and the Japanese puppet state of Manchukuo in 1939. While directed against the USSR, the agreement also had the effect of giving international recognition to Japanese rule in Manchuria.

anticonvulsant *n.* any drug used to prevent epileptic seizures (convulsions or fits); see ◊epilepsy. [from Latin *convellere* (*vellere* = pull]

Anti-Corn Law League in UK history, an extra-parliamentary pressure group formed in 1838, led by the Liberals ◊Cobden and ◊Bright, which argued for free trade and campaigned successfully against duties on the import of foreign corn to Britain imposed by the ◊Corn Laws, which were repealed in 1846.

anticyclone /æntɪ'saɪkləʊn/ *n.* a system of winds rotating outwards from an area of high barometric pressure, taking a clockwise direction in the N hemisphere and an anticlockwise direction in the S hemisphere. Anticyclones are characterized by clear weather and the absence of rain and violent winds.

antidepressant *n.* any drug used to relieve symptoms in depressive illness. The two main groups are the tricyclic antidepressants (TCADs) and the monoamine oxidase inhibitors (MAOIs), which act by altering chemicals available to the central nervous system.

antidote /'æntɪdəʊt/ *n.* a substance that counteracts the effect of a poison; anything that counteracts unpleasant effects. —**antidotal** *adj.* [French or Latin from Greek *antidotos* = given against]

anti-emetic *n.* any substance that counteracts nausea or vomiting.

antifreeze *n.* a substance added to water (especially in the radiator of a motor vehicle) to lower its freezing-point and therefore make it less likely to freeze. The most common types of antifreeze contain the chemical ethylene glycol, an organic alcohol with a freezing point of about –15°C/5°F.

antifungal *n.* any drug that acts against fungal infection, such as ringworm and athlete's foot.

antigen /'æntɪdʒən/ *n.* any substance that causes the body to produce ◊antibodies. Common antigens include the proteins carried on the surface of bacteria, viruses, and pollen grains. The proteins of incompatible blood groups or tissues also act as antigens. [German (Greek -*genēs* = of a kind)]

Antigone /æn'tɪgənɪ/ in Greek legend, a daughter of Jocasta, by her son ◊Oedipus. She is also the subject of a tragedy by Sophocles, written about 411 BC. The tragedy tells how she buries her brother Polyneices, in defiance of the Theban king Creon, but in accordance with the wishes of the gods. Creon imprisons Antigone in a cave, but after a warning that he has defied the gods, he finds that Antigone has hanged herself.

Antigonus /æn'tɪgənəs/ 382–301 BC. A general of Alexander the Great, after whose death in 323 he made himself master of Asia Minor. He was defeated and slain by ◊Seleucus I at the battle of Ipsus.

Antigua and Barbuda /æn'tiːgə, bɑː'bjuːdə/ State of; country comprising three islands (Antigua, Barbuda, and uninhabited Redonda) in the E Caribbean; **area** Antigua 280 sq km/108 sq mi, Barbuda 161 sq km/62 sq mi, and Redonda 1 sq km/0.4 sq mi; **capital** and chief port St John's; **physical** low-lying tropical islands with volcanic outcrop on W Antigua; **head of state** Elizabeth II from 1981 represented by governor-general; **head of government** Vere C Bird from 1981; **political system** liberal democracy; **exports** sea-island cotton, rum, lobsters; **population** (1989) 83,500; **language** English; **recent history** became an associated state within the Commonwealth in 1967 and fully independent in 1981.

antihero *n.* a central character in a story or drama who noticeably lacks conventional heroic attitudes.

antihistamine /æntɪ'hɪstəmiːn/ *n.* a substance that counteracts the effects of ◊histamine, used in treating allergies. Antihistamines may be naturally produced (such as vitamin C and epinephrin) or synthesized (pseudepinephrin).

antihypertensive therapy any treatment that controls ◊hypertension. The first step is usually exercise and a change in diet to reduce salt and, if necessary, caloric intake. If further measures are required, a drug regimen may be prescribed.

anti-inflammatory *n.* a substance that reduces swelling in soft tissues. Antihistamines relieve allergic reactions; aspirin and ◊NSAIDs are effective in joint and musculoskeletal conditions; rubefacients (counterirritant liniments) ease painful joints, tendons, and muscles; steroids, because of the severe side effects, are only prescribed if other therapy is ineffective, or if a condition is life-threatening. A ◊corticosteroid injection into the affected joint usually gives long-term relief from inflammation.

antiknock *n.* a substance added to motor fuel to prevent or reduce ◊knock.

Antilles /æn'tɪliːz/ the whole group of West Indian islands, divided N–S into the **Greater Antilles** (Cuba, Jamaica, Haiti–Dominican Republic, Puerto Rico) and **Lesser Antilles**, subdivided into the Leeward Islands (Virgin Islands, St Kitts–Nevis, Antigua and Barbuda, Anguilla, Montserrat, and Guadeloupe) and the Windward Islands (Dominica, Martinique, St Lucia, St Vincent and the Grenadines, Barbados, and Grenada).

antilog /'æntɪlɒg/ *n.* (*colloquial*) abbreviation of antilogarithm.

antilogarithm /æntɪ'lɒgərɪðəm/ *n.* the inverse of ◊logarithm, or the number of which a given number is the logarithm. If $y = \log_a x$, then $x = \text{antilog}_a y$.

antimacassar /æntɪmə'kæsə/ *n.* a former name for a short cover put over the backs or arms of chairs etc. to keep them from getting dirty, or as an ornament. [from *Macassar*, because originally used as a protection against the Macassar oil that was used on hair]

antimatter /'æntɪmætə/ *n.* in physics, a (hypothetical) form of matter in which all the attributes of elementary particles, such as electrical charge, magnetic moment, and spin, are reversed. (See ◊antiparticle.)

antimony /'æntɪmənɪ/ *n.* a semi-metallic element, symbol Sb, atomic number 51, relative atomic mass 121.75. It occurs chiefly as the ore stibnite, and is used to make alloys harder; it is also used in photosensitive substances in colour photography, optical electronics, fireproofing, pigment, and medicine. [from Latin *antimonium*]

anting *n.* the rubbing or placing of ants etc. in their feathers by birds, perhaps in order to kill parasites.

antinode *n.* the position in a ◊standing wave pattern at which the amplitude of vibration is greatest. The standing wave of a stretched string vibrating in the fundamental mode has one antinode at its midpoint. A vibrating air column in a pipe has an antinode at the pipe's open end and at the place where the vibration is produced.

antinomy /æn'tɪnəmɪ/ *n.* contradiction between two laws or authorities that are both reasonable.

antinovel *n.* a novel in which the conventions of the form are studiously avoided.

Antioch /'æntɪɒk/ ancient capital of the Greek kingdom of Syria, founded in 300 BC by Seleucus Nicator in memory of his father Antiochus, and famed for its splendour and luxury. Under the Romans it was an early centre of Christianity. The site is now occupied by the Turkish town of ◊Antakya.

Antiochus /æn'taɪəkəs/ four kings of Commagene (69 BC–AD 72), affiliated to the Seleucid dynasty, including:

Antiochus IV Epiphanes 1st century AD. King of Commagene, son of Antiochus III. He was made king in 38 by Caligula, who deposed him immediately. He was restored in 41 by Claudius, and reigned as an ally of Rome against Parthia. He was deposed on suspicion of treason in 72.

Antiochus 13 kings of Syria of the Seleucid dynasty, including:

Antiochus I *c.*324–*c.*261 BC. King of Syria from 281 BC, son of Seleucus I, one of the generals of Alexander the Great. He earned the title of Antiochus Soter, or Saviour, by his defeat of the Gauls in Galatia in 278 BC.

Antiochus II *c.*286–*c.*246 BC. King of Syria 261–246 BC, son of Antiochus I. He was known as Antiochus Theos, the Divine. During his reign the E provinces broke away from the Graeco-Macedonian rule and set up native princes. He made peace with Egypt by marrying the daughter of Ptolemy Philadelphus, but was a tyrant among his own people.

Antiochus III the Great *c.*241–187 BC. King of Syria from 223 BC, nephew of Antiochus II. He secured a loose suzerainty over Armenia and Parthia in 209, overcame Bactria, received the homage of the Indian king of the Kabul valley, and returned by way of the Persian Gulf in 204. He took possession of Palestine, entering Jerusalem in 198. He crossed into NW Greece, but was decisively defeated by the Romans at Thermopylae in 191 and at Magnesia in 190. He had to abandon his domains in Anatolia, and was killed by the people of Elymais.

Antiochus IV *c.*215–164 BC. King of Syria from 175 BC, known as Antiochus Epiphanes, the Illustrious; second son of Antiochus III. He occupied Jerusalem in about 170 BC, seizing much of the Temple treasure, and instituted worship of the Greek type in the Temple in an attempt to eradicate Judaism. This produced the revolt of the Hebrews under the Maccabees; Antiochus died before he could suppress it.

Antiochus VII Sidetes King of Syria from 138 BC. The last strong ruler of the Seleucid dynasty, he took Jerusalem in 134 BC, reducing the Maccabees to subjection, and fought successfully against the Parthians.

Antiochus XIII Asiaticus 1st century BC. King of Syria 69–65 BC, the last of the Seleucid dynasty. During his reign Syria was made a Roman province by Pompey the Great.

antioxidant *n.* a type of food ◊additive, used to prevent fats and oils from becoming rancid, and thus extend their shelf life.

antiparticle *n.* in nuclear physics, a particle corresponding in mass and properties to a given ◊elementary particle but with the opposite electrical charge, magnetic properties, or coupling to other fundamental forces. When a particle and its antiparticle collide, they destroy each other, in the process called 'annihilation', their total energy being converted to lighter particles and/or photons.

antipathy /æn'tɪpəθɪ/ *n.* a strong or deep-seated aversion; its object. —**antipathetic** /-'θetɪk/ *adj.* [from French or Latin from Greek *antipathēs* = opposed in feeling]

antiperspirant /ænti'pɜːspɪrənt/ *n.* a substance that prevents or reduces perspiration.

antiphon /'æntɪfən/ *n.* a hymn or psalm etc. in which versicles or phrases are sung alternately by two sections of a choir; a versicle or phrase from this. [from Latin from Greek *phonē* = sound]

antiphonal /æn'tɪfənəl/ *adj.* sung alternately by two sections of a choir.

antiphony *n.* in music, a form of composition using widely spaced choirs or groups of instruments to create perspectives in sound. It was developed in 17th-century Venice by Giovanni ◊Gabrieli and his pupil Heinrich ◊Schütz.

antipodes /æn'tɪpədiːz/ *n.pl.* places diametrically opposite each other on the Earth; **the Antipodes**, Australasia in relation to Europe. —**antipodal** *adj.*, **antipodean** /-'diːən/ *adj.* [French or Latin from Greek = having the feet opposite]

antipope *n.* a rival claimant to the elected pope for the leadership of the Roman Catholic church, for instance in the Great Schism 1378–1417 when there were rival popes in Rome and Avignon.

antipruritic *n.* any skin preparation or drug administered to relieve itching.

antipsychotic *n.* or **neuroleptic** any drug used to treat the symptoms of severe mental disorder.

antipyretic *n.* any drug, such as aspirin, used to reduce fever.

antiquarian /ænti'kweərɪən/ *adj.* of or dealing in antiques or rare books. —*n.* an antiquary.

antiquary /æn'tɪkwərɪ/ *n.* one who studies or collects antiques or antiquities. [from Latin *antiquus* = ancient]

antiquated /'æntɪkweɪtɪd/ *adj.* old, out of date, old-fashioned. [from Latin]

antique /æn'tiːk/ *n.* an object of considerable age, especially an item of furniture or a decorative object sought by collectors. —*adj.* of or existing from an early date; old; old-fashioned. [French, or from Latin = former, ancient (*ante* = before)]

antiquity /æn'tɪkwɪtɪ/ *n.* **1.** ancient times, especially before the Middle Ages. **2.** great age. **3.** (in *plural*) remains from ancient times. [from Old French from Latin]

antiracism and antisexism active opposition to ◊racism and ◊sexism; positive action or a set of policies, such as 'equal opportunity', can be designed to counteract racism and sexism, often on the part of an official body or an institution, such as a school, a business, or a government agency.

antirrhinum /ænti'raɪnəm/ *n.* a plant of the genus *Antirrhinum* with a flower that has an aperture between closed 'lips'. [Latin, from Greek *anti* = counterfeiting and *rhis* = snout]

antiscorbutic /æntɪskɔː'bjuːtɪk/ *adj.* that prevents or cures scurvy. —*n.* an antiscorbutic medicine. [from Latin *scorbutus* = scurvy]

anti-Semitism /æntisi'mıtız(ə)m/ *n.* literally, prejudice against Semitic people (see ◊Semite), but in practice it has meant prejudice or discrimination against, and persecution of, the Jews as an ethnic group. Anti-Semitism was a tenet of Hitler's Germany, and in the Holocaust of 1933–45 about 6 million Jews died in concentration camps and in local extermination ◊pogroms, such as the siege of the Warsaw ghetto. In the USSR and the Eastern bloc, as well as in Islamic nations, anti-Semitism exists and is promulgated by neofascist groups. It is a form of ◊racism. **anti-Semite** /-'si:maıt/ *n.* a person who discriminates against Jews. **anti-Semitic** /-si'mıtık/ *adj.*

antisepsis /ænti'sepsɪs/ *n.* the process or principles of using antiseptics.

antiseptic /ænti'septɪk/ *n.* any substance that kills or inhibits the growth of microorganisms. The use of antiseptics was pioneered by Joseph ◊Lister. —*adj.* that counteracts sepsis.

antisocial /ænti'səʊʃəl/ *adj.* 1. opposed or harmful to social institutions and laws; interfering with amenities enjoyed by others. 2. not sociable.

antispasmodic *n.* any drug that reduces motility, the spontaneous action of the muscles. ◊Anticholinergics act indirectly by way of the autonomic nervous system, which controls involuntary movement. Other drugs act directly on the smooth muscle to relieve spasm (contraction).

antistatic /ænti'stætɪk/ *adj.* that counteracts the effects of static electricity.

antithesis /æn'tıθəsɪs/ *n.* (*plural* **antitheses** /-əsi:z/) a direct opposite; contrast; contrast of ideas emphasized by the parallelism of contrasted words. —**antithetic** /-'θetɪk/ *adj.,* **antithetical** *adj.* [Latin from Greek *antitithēmi* = set against]

antitoxin /ænti'toksɪn/ *n.* an antibody that counteracts a toxin. —**antitoxic** *adj.*

antitrades /'æntitreɪdz/ *n.pl.* winds blowing above and in the opposite direction to trade winds.

antitrust *adj.* (*US*) opposed to trusts, monopolies or any business practice considered to be unfair or uncompetitive. In the USA, antitrust laws prevent mergers and acquisitions that might create a monopoly situation or ones in which restrictive practices might be stimulated.

antitussive *n.* any substance administered to suppress a cough.

antitype *n.* 1. one of the opposite type. 2. that which a type or symbol represents. [from Greek *antitupos* = corresponding as an impression to the die (*tupos* = stamp)]

antiviral *n.* any drug that acts against viruses, usually preventing them from multiplying. Most viral infections are not susceptible to antibiotics. Antivirals have been difficult drugs to develop, and do not necessarily cure viral diseases.

antivivisection /æntivivi'sekʃ(ə)n/ *adj.* opposed to vivisection, that is, experiments on living animals, which is practised in the pharmaceutical and cosmetics industries on the grounds that it may result in discoveries of importance to medical science. —**antivivisectionist** *n.* one who argues that it is immoral to inflict pain on helpless creatures, and that it is unscientific because results achieved with animals may not be paralleled with human beings.

antler *n.* the 'horn' of a deer, often branched, and made of bone rather than horn. Antlers, unlike true horns, are shed and regrown each year. Reindeer of both sexes grow them, but in all other types of deer, only the males have antlers. —**antlered** *adj.* [from Anglo-French]

antlion *n.* the larva of one of the insects of the family Myrmeleontidae, order Neuroptera, which traps ants by waiting at the bottom of a pit dug in loose, sandy soil. Antlions are mainly tropical, but also occur in parts of Europe and the USA.

Antofagasta /æntəfə'gæstə/ port of N Chile, capital of a region of the same name. The area of the region is 125,300 sq km/48,366 sq mi; its population (1982) 341,000. The population of the town of Antofagasta is 175,000. Nitrates from the Atacama desert are exported.

Antonello da Messina /æntə'neləʊ/ *c.*1430–1479. Italian painter, born in Messina, Sicily, a pioneer of the technique of oil painting, which he is said to have introduced to Italy from N Europe. Flemish influence is reflected in his technique, his use of light, and sometimes in his imagery. Surviving works include bust-length portraits and sombre religious paintings.

Antonine Wall /'æntənaın/ a Roman line of fortification built AD 142–200. The Roman Empire's NW frontier, between the Clyde and Forth rivers, Scotland.

Antoninus Pius /æntənaməs/ AD 86–161. Roman emperor who was adopted in 138 as Hadrian's heir, and succeeded him later that year. He enjoyed a prosperous reign, during which he built the ◊Antonine Wall. His daughter married ◊Marcus Aurelius Antoninus.

Antonioni /æntəuni'əuni/ Michelangelo 1912– . Italian film director, famous for his subtle presentations of neuroses and personal relationships among the leisured classes. His work includes *L'Avventura* 1960, *Blow Up* 1966, and *The Passenger* 1975.

antonym /'æntənɪm/ *n.* a word that is opposite in meaning to another, e. g. *good* and *bad* are antonyms. —**antonymy** *n.,* **antonymous** *adj.* [from French (Greek *onoma* = name)]

Antrim /'æntrɪm/ county of Northern Ireland; **area** 2,830 sq km/1,092 sq mi; **county town** Belfast; **physical** Giant's Causeway of natural hexagonal basalt columns, which, in legend, was built to enable the giants to cross between Ireland and Scotland; Antrim borders Lough Neagh, and is separated from Scotland by the 32 km/ 20 mi wide North Channel; **products** potatoes, oats, linen, synthetic textiles; **population** (1981) 642,000.

antrum *n.* (*plural* **antra**) a cavity of the body, especially one of a pair in the upper jawbone. [Latin from Greek = cave]

Antwerp /'æntwɜ:p/ (Flemish *Antwerpen*, French *Anvers*) port in Belgium on the river Scheldt, capital of the province of Antwerp; population (1988) 476,000. One of the world's busiest ports, it has shipbuilding, oil-refining, petrochemical, textile, and diamond-cutting industries. The home of the artist Rubens is preserved, and many of his works are in the Gothic cathedral. The province of Antwerp has an area of 2,900 sq km/1,119 sq mi; population (1987) 1,588,000.

Anubis /ə'nju:bɪs/ in Egyptian mythology, the jackal-headed god of the dead.

anus /'eɪnəs/ *n.* the excretory opening at the end of the alimentary canal. [Latin]

anvil *n.* an iron block on which a smith hammers metal into shape. [Old English *an* = on and *filt-* = beat]

anxiety *n.* an emotional state of fear or apprehension; something causing this. Anxiety is a normal response to potentially dangerous situations. Abnormal anxiety can either be free-floating, experienced in a wide range of situations, or it may be phobic, when the sufferer is excessively afraid of an object or situation. [from French or Latin]

anxiolytic *n.* any drug that reduces an anxiety state.

anxious /'æŋʃəs/ *adj.* 1. troubled, uneasy in mind. 2. causing or marked by worry. 3. eagerly wanting (*to*). —**anxiously** *adv.* [from Latin *anxius* (*angere* = choke)]

any /'enı/ *adj.* 1. one or some (but no matter which) from three or more or from a quantity. 2. an appreciable or significant (amount etc.). 3. whichever is chosen. —*pron.* any one, any number or amount. —*adv.* at all, in some degree. [Old English]

anybody /'enıbɒdı/ *n. & pron.* 1. any person. 2. a person of importance.

anyhow /'enıhaʊ/ *adv.* 1. anyway. 2. in a disorderly manner.

anyone /'enıwʌn/ *n. & pron.* anybody.

anything *n. & pron.* any thing, a thing of any sort. —**anything but**, not at all. **like anything**, with great intensity.

anyway /'enıweɪ/ *adv.* in any way or manner; in any case.

anywhere /'enı(h)weə/ *adv.* in or to any place. —*pron.* any place.

Anzac /'ænzæk/ *n.* 1. a member of the Australian and New Zealand Army Corps (1914–18). 2. an Australian or a New Zealand person, especially a serviceman. —*adj.* of Anzacs. —**Anzac Day**, 25 April, commemorating the landing of the corps in Gallipoli. [acronym]

Anzio, Battle of /'ænzɪəʊ/ in World War II, the beachhead invasion of Italy 22 Jan–23 May 1944 by Allied troops; failure to use information gained by deciphering German codes (see ◊Ultra) led to Allied troops being stranded temporarily after German attacks. Anzio is a seaport and resort on the W coast of Italy, 53 km/33 mi SE of Rome; population (1984) 25,000.

Anzus /ˈænzəs/ *n.* the combination of Australia, New Zealand, and the USA for the security of the Pacific. [acronym]

aorist /ˈeɪərɪst/ *n.* the unqualified past tense of a verb (especially in Greek), without reference to duration or completion. [from Greek = indefinite]

aorta /eɪˈɔːtə/ *n.* the main artery carrying oxygenated blood from the left ventricle of the heart in birds and mammals. It branches to form smaller arteries, which in turn supply all body organs except the lungs. —**aortic** *adj.* [from Greek *aeirō* = raise]

Aouita /ɑːˈwiːtə/ Said 1960– . Moroccan runner. Outstanding at middle and long distances, he won the 1984 Olympic and 1987 World Championship 5,000-metres title, and has set many world records.

Aoun /ɑːˈuːn/ Michel 1935– . Lebanese soldier and Maronite Christian politician, president 1988–90. As commander of the Lebanese army, he was made president without Muslim support, his appointment precipitating a civil war between Christians and Muslims. His unwillingness to accept a 1989 Arab League–sponsored peace agreement increased his isolation until the following year when he surrendered to military pressure.

Aouzu Strip /ɑːˈuːzuː/ disputed territory 100 km/60 mi wide on the Chad–Libya frontier, occupied by Libya in 1973. Lying to the N of the Tibesti massif, the area is rich in uranium and other minerals.

apace /əˈpeɪs/ *adv.* swiftly. [from Old French *à pas* = at (a considerable) pace]

apache *n.* a violent street ruffian, originally in Paris c.1900.

Apache /əˈpætʃɪ/ *n.* (*plural* the same or **Apaches**) **1.** a member of an Athapaskan-speaking North American Indian tribe. The Apache are related to the Navajo, and now number about 10,000, living in reservations in Arizona, SW Oklahoma, and New Mexico. They were known as fierce raiders and horse warriors in the 18th and 19th centuries. **2.** any of several Athabaskan languages and dialects spoken by these people. [Mexican Spanish]

apart /əˈpɑːt/ *adv.* **1.** separately, not together. **2.** into pieces. **3.** aside, to or at a distance. —**apart from**, excepting, not considering. **tell apart**, to distinguish between. [from Old French *à* = to and *part* = side]

apartheid /əˈpɑːtheɪt/ *n.* the racial-segregation policy of the government of South Africa, which was legislated in 1948, when the Afrikaner National Party gained power. Nonwhites (Bantu, coloured or mixed, or Indian) do not share full rights of citizenship with the 4.5 million whites (for example, the 23 million black people cannot vote in parliamentary elections), and many public facilities and institutions were until 1990 and, in some cases, remain, restricted to the use of one race only. The establishment of ◊Black National States is another manifestation of apartheid. State president F W de Klerk has taken steps to dismantle the apartheid system by lifting the ban on the ◊ANC to enable negotiations on a new multiracial constitution. [Afrikaans = apartness]

apartment /əˈpɑːtmənt/ *n.* **1.** (in *plural*) a suite of rooms, usually rented furnished. **2.** (*US*) a flat. [from French from Italian *a parte* = apart]

apathy /ˈæpəθɪ/ *n.* lack of interest or concern, indifference. —**apathetic** /-ˈθetɪk/ *adj.*, **apathetically** *adv.* [from French from Latin from Greek *a-* = without and *pathos* = suffering]

apatite /ˈæpətaɪt/ *n.* a common calcium phosphate mineral, $Ca_5(PO_4CO_3)_3(F,OH,Cl)$. Apatite occurs widely in igneous rocks, for example pegmatite, and in contact metamorphic rocks, such as marbles. It is used in the manufacture of fertilizer and as a source of phosphorus. Apatite is the chief constituent of tooth enamel. [from German from Greek *apatē* = deceit (from its deceptive forms)]

Apatosaurus /æpətəuˈsɔːrəs/ *n.* a large plant-eating dinosaur, formerly called **Brontosaurus**, which flourished about 145 million years ago. Up to 21 m/69 ft long and 30 tonnes in weight, it stood on four elephant-like legs and had a long tail, long neck, and small head.

ape *n.* any ◊primate closely related to humans, especially of the tailless kind, including gibbon, orang-utan, chimpanzee, and gorilla. —*v.t.* to imitate. —**apeman** *n.* an extinct primate postulated by Haeckel as intermediate between ape and man; a primitive man. [Old English]

Aphrodite A statue in Naples Museum of the Greek goddess of beauty and sexual love.

Apeldoorn /ˈɑːpəldɔːn/ commercial city in Gelderland province, E central Netherlands. Population (1982) 142,400. Het Loo, which is situated nearby, has been the summer residence of the Dutch royal family since the time of William of Orange.

Apennines /ˈæpənaɪn/ chain of mountains stretching the length of the Italian peninsula. A continuation of the Maritime Alps, from Genoa it swings across the peninsula to Ancona on the E coast, and then back to the W coast and into the 'toe' of Italy. The system is continued over the Strait of Messina along the N Sicilian coast, then across the Mediterranean sea in a series of islands to the Atlas mountains of N Africa. The highest peak is Gran Sasso d'Italia at 2,914 m/9,560 ft.

aperient /əˈpɪərɪənt/ *adj.* laxative. —*n.* a laxative medicine. [from Latin *aperire* = to open]

aperitif /əˈperɪtiːf/ *n.* an alcoholic drink taken before a meal. [from French from Latin *aperire* = to open]

aperture /ˈæpətjuə/ *n.* **1.** an opening or gap. **2.** in photography, an opening in the camera that allows light to pass through the lens to strike the film. Controlled by shutter speed and the iris diaphragm, it can be set mechanically or electronically at various diameters. [from Latin]

apex /ˈeɪpeks/ *n.* (*plural* **apexes**) the highest point; the pointed end, the tip. [Latin]

aphasia *n.* difficulty in speaking, writing, and reading, usually caused by damage to the brain.

aphelion /əˈfiːlɪən/ *n.* (*plural* **aphelia**) the point in a planet's or comet's orbit when it is furthest from the Sun. [from Greek *aph' hēliou* = from the Sun]

aphid /ˈeɪfɪd/ *n.* any of the family of small insects, Aphididae, in the order Homoptera, that live by sucking sap from plants. Greenfly and blackfly are aphids.

aphis /ˈeɪfɪs/ *n.* (*plural* **aphides** /-ɪdiːz/) an aphid. [the word was invented by Linnaeus, perhaps a misreading of Greek *koris* = bug]

aphorism /ˈæfərɪzəm/ *n.* a short pithy saying. [from French or Latin from Greek *aphorismos* = definition (*horos* = boundary)]

aphrodisiac /æfrəˈdɪziæk/ *adj.* arousing sexual desire. —*n.* an aphrodisiac substance. [from Greek from *Aphrodite*, Greek goddess of love]

Aphrodite /æfrəˈdaɪti/ in Greek mythology, the goddess of love (Roman Venus, Phoenician Astarte, Babylonian Ishtar); said to be either a daughter of Zeus (in Homer) or sprung from the foam of the sea (in Hesiod). She was the unfaithful wife of Hephaestus, the god of fire, and the mother of Eros. [perhaps from Greek *aphros* = foam]

Apia /'ɑːpiə/ capital and port of Western ◊Samoa, on the N coast of Upolu island, in the W Pacific; population (1981) 33,000.

apiary /'eɪpɪərɪ/ n. a place with a number of hives where bees are kept. —**apiarist** n. [from Latin *apis* = bee]

apical /'eɪpɪkəl/ adj of, at, or forming an apex.

apiculture /'eɪpɪkʌltʃə/ n. beekeeping. —**apiculturist** n. [from Latin *apis* = bee]

apiece /ə'piːs/ adv. for each one. [originally *a piece*]

Apis /'ɑːpɪs/ an ancient Egyptian god with a human body and a bull's head, linked with Osiris (and later merged with him into the Ptolemaic god Serapis); his cult centres were Memphis and Heliopolis, where sacred bulls were mummified.

aplomb /ə'plɒm/ n. assurance, self-confidence. [French = straight as a plummet]

Apocalypse[1] /ə'pɒkəlɪps/ n. **1.** the *Revelation of St John the Divine*, containing a prophetic description of the end of the world. **2.** great and dramatic events like those described in the Apocalypse. —**apocalyptic** /əpɒkə'lɪptɪk/ adj., **apocalyptically** adv. [from Old French from Latin from Greek = uncovering]

Apocalypse[2] n. in literature, a movement which developed from Surrealism in 1938, and included G S Fraser, Henry Treece, J F Hendry, Nicholas Moore, and Tom Scott. Influenced by the work of Dylan Thomas, it favoured Biblical symbolism.

Apocrypha /ə'pɒkrɪfə/ n. an appendix to the Old Testament of the Bible, not included in the final Hebrew canon but recognized by Roman Catholics. There are also disputed New Testament texts known as Apocrypha.

apocryphal /ə'pɒkrɪfəl/ adj. untrue, invented; of doubtful authenticity.

apogee /'æpədʒiː/ n. the highest point, a climax; the point in the orbit of the Moon or any planet or satellite when it is at its furthest point from the Earth. [from French or Greek *apogeion* = away from the Earth (*gē* = Earth)]

apolitical /eɪpə'lɪtɪkəl/ adj. not interested in or concerned with politics. [from Greek *a-* = not and *political*]

Apollinaire /əpɒli'neə/ Guillaume 1880–1918. Pen name of Guillaume Apollinaire de Kostrowitsky. French poet of aristocratic Polish descent. He was a leader of the avant garde in Parisian literary and artistic circles. His novel *Le Poète assassiné/The Poet Assassinated* 1916, followed by the experimental poems *Alcools/Alcohols* 1913 and *Calligrammes/Word Pictures* 1918, show him as a representative of the Cubist and Futurist movements.

Apollo /ə'pɒləʊ/ in Greek and Roman mythology, the god of sun, music, poetry, prophecy, agriculture, and pastoral life, and leader of the Muses. He was the twin child (with Artemis) of Zeus and Leto. Ancient statues show Apollo as the embodiment of the Greek ideal of male beauty.

Apollo asteroid a member of a group of ◊asteroids whose orbits cross that of the Earth. They are named after the first of their kind, Apollo, discovered in 1932, and then lost until 1973. Apollo asteroids are so small and faint that they are difficult to see except when close to Earth (Apollo is about 2 km/1.2 mi across).

Apollonius of Perga /æpə'ləʊniəs/ c.260–c.190 BC. Greek mathematician, called 'the Great Geometer'. In his work *Conic Sections* he showed that a plane intersecting a cone will generate an ellipse, a parabola, or a hyperbola, depending on the angle of intersection. In astronomy, he used a system of circles called epicycles and deferents to explain the motion of the planets; this system, as refined by Ptolemy, was used until the Renaissance.

Apollonius of Rhodes c.220–180 BC. Greek poet, author of the epic *Argonautica*, which tells the story of Jason and the Argonauts.

Apollo of Rhodes the Greek statue of Apollo generally known as the ◊Colossus of Rhodes.

Apollo project US space project to land a person on the Moon, achieved on 20 July 1969, when Neil Armstrong was the first to set foot there. He was accompanied on the moon surface by Col Edwin E Aldrin Jr; Michael Collins remained at the orbiting command controls.

Apollo-Soyuz test project a joint US-Soviet mission begun in 1972 to link a Soviet and a US spacecraft in space. The project culminated in the docking of an *Apollo 18* and *Soyuz 15* craft, both of which were launched on 15 July 1975.

apologetic /əpɒlə'dʒetɪk/ adj. making an apology; diffident. —**apologetics** n.pl. a reasoned defence, especially of Christianity. —**apologetically** adv. [from French from Latin from Greek *apologeomai* = speak in defence]

apologia /æpə'ləʊdʒiə/ n. a formal defence of belief or conduct. [Latin from Greek]

apologist /ə'pɒlədʒɪst/ n. one who makes a formal defence of a belief etc. by argument. [from French from Greek *apologizomai* = render an account]

apologize /ə'pɒlədʒaɪz/ v.i. to make an apology. [from Greek]

apology /ə'pɒlədʒɪ/ n. **1.** regretful acknowledgement of an offence or failure. **2.** an explanation or defence of a belief etc. —**apology for,** a poor or scanty specimen of. [from French or Latin from Greek *apologia* (*apologeomai* = speak in defence)]

Apo, Mount /'ɑːpəʊ/ active volcano and highest peak in the Philippines, rising to 2,954 m/9,692 ft on the island of Mindanao.

apophthegm /'æpəθem/ n. a terse or pithy saying. [from French or Greek *apophtheggomai* = speak out]

apoplectic /æpə'plektɪk/ adj. of, suffering from, or liable to apoplexy; (*colloquial*) liable to fits of rage in which the face becomes very red. —**apoplectically** adv.

apoplexy /'æpəpleksɪ/ n. a sudden inability to feel and move, caused by blockage or rupture of a brain artery. [from Old French from Latin from Greek *apoplēssō* = disable by a stroke]

aposematic coloration in biology, the technical name for ◊warning coloration markings that make a dangerous, poisonous, or foul-tasting animal particularly conspicuous and recognizable to a predator. Examples include the yellow and black stripes of bees and wasps, and the bright red or yellow colours of many poisonous frogs. See also ◊mimicry.

apostasy /ə'pɒstəsɪ/ n. renunciation of one's religious faith or one's principles or party etc. [from Latin from Greek = defection]

apostate /ə'pɒsteɪt/ n. one who renounces his or her former belief, principles, or party, etc. [from Old French or Latin from Greek *apostatēs* = deserter]

apostatize /ə'pɒstətaɪz/ v.i. to become an apostate.

a posteriori /eɪ pɒsteri'ɔːraɪ/ in logic, an argument that deduces causes from their effects; inductive reasoning; the converse of ◊a priori. [Latin = from what comes after]

apostle /ə'pɒsəl/ n. **1.** in the New Testament, any of the chosen 12 ◊disciples sent out by Jesus after his resurrection to preach the Gospel. In the earliest days of Christianity the term was extended to include some who had never known Jesus in the flesh, notably St Paul. **2.** the first successful Christian missionary in a country; the leader of a new faith or reform. —**apostle spoon,** a spoon with a figure of an apostle on the handle. [Old English from Latin from Greek *apostellō* = send forth]

Apostles n.pl. a discussion group founded in 1820 at Cambridge University, England; members have included the poet Tennyson, the philosophers G E Moore and Bertrand Russell, the writers Lytton Strachey and Leonard Woolf, the economist Keynes, and the spies Guy Burgess and Anthony Blunt.

Apostles' Creed one of the three ancient ◊creeds of the Christian church.

apostolic /æpə'stɒlɪk/ adj. of the apostles or their teaching; of the pope. —**apostolic succession,** the doctrine in the Christian church that certain spiritual powers were received by the first apostles directly from Jesus, and have been handed down in the ceremony of 'laying on of hands' from generation to generation of bishops.

apostrophe /ə'pɒstrəfɪ/ n. **1.** a punctuation mark ('). In English it either denotes a missing letter (*mustn't* for *must not*) or number ('*47* for *1947*), or indicates possession ('*John's* camera', 'the *girl's* dress'). **2.** an exclamatory passage addressed to a person or persons or an abstract idea. [Latin from Greek *apostrephō* = turn away]

apostrophize /ə'pɒstrəfaɪz/ v.t. to address in an apostrophe.

apothecaries' weights obsolete units of mass, formerly used in pharmacy: 20 grains made one scruple; three scruples made one drachm; eight drachms made an apothecary's ounce (oz apoth.), and 12 such ounces made an apothecary's pound (lb apoth.). There are 7,000 grains in one pound avoirdupois (0.454 kg).

apothecary /ə'pɒθɪkərɪ/ *n.* (*archaic*) a pharmaceutical chemist. [from Old French from Latin from Greek *apothēkēs* = storehouse]

apotheosis /æpəθɪ'əʊsɪs/ *n.* (*plural* **apotheoses**) 1. deification. 2. a deified ideal; the highest development of a thing. [Latin from Greek *theos* = god]

appal /ə'pɔːl/ *v.t.* (**-ll-**) to fill with horror or dismay, to shock deeply. —**appalling** *adj.* [from Old French *apalir* = grow pale]

Appalachians /æpə'leɪtʃənz/ mountain system of E North America, stretching about 2,400 km/1,500 mi from Alabama to Québec, composed of very ancient eroded rocks. The chain includes the Alleghany, Catskill, and Blue Ridge mountains, the latter having the highest peak, Mount Mitchell, 2,045 m/6,712 ft. The E edge has a fall line to the coastal plain where Philadelphia, Baltimore, and Washington stand.

apparatus /æpə'reɪtəs/ *n.* 1. equipment for performing something, e. g. gymnastics or scientific experiments; bodily organs effecting a natural process. 2. a complicated organization. [Latin *parare* = make ready]

apparel /ə'pærəl/ *n.* (*archaic*) clothing. —*v.t.* (**-ll-**) (*archaic*) to clothe. [from Old French from Romanic = make ready (diminutive of Latin *par* = equal)]

apparent /ə'pærənt/ *adj.* 1. readily visible or perceivable. 2. seeming but not real. —**apparently** *adv.* [from Old French from Latin *apparēre* = come in sight]

apparition /æpə'rɪʃ(ə)n/ *n.* something remarkable or expected that appears; a ghost. [from French or Latin *apparēre*]

appeal /ə'piːl/ *v.t./i.* 1. to make an earnest or formal request; to call attention or resort *to* (evidence etc.) as support; to make a request (*to* a higher court) for alteration of the decision of a lower court; (in cricket) to ask the umpire to declare a batsman out. 2. to be attractive or of interest *to.* —*n.* 1. an act of appealing. 2. an appealing quality, attraction. 3. a request for donations to a cause. [from French from Latin *appellare* = address (*pellere* = drive)]

appear /ə'pɪə/ *v.i.* 1. to become or be visible; to give an impression, to seem. 2. to present oneself formally or publicly. 3. to be published. [from Old French from Latin *apparēre* = come in sight]

appearance *n.* appearing; an outward form as perceived, a semblance. —**keep up appearances,** to maintain a display or pretence of prosperity, good behaviour, etc.

appease /ə'piːz/ *v.t.* to make calm or quiet by making concessions etc. or by satisfying demands. —**appeasement** *n.* historically, the conciliatory policy adopted by the British government, in particular under Neville Chamberlain, towards the Nazi and Fascist dictators in Europe in the 1930s in an effort to maintain peace. It was strongly opposed by Winston Churchill, but the ◊Munich Agreement of 1938 was almost universally hailed as its justification. Appeasement ended when Germany occupied Bohemia–Moravia in March 1939. [from Anglo-French *à* = to and *pais* = peace]

Appel /'æpəl/ Karel 1921– . Dutch painter and sculptor, founder of 'Cobra' 1948, a group of European artists that developed an expressive and dynamic form of abstract painting, with thick paintwork and lurid colours.

appellant /ə'pelənt/ *n.* in law, a person making an appeal to a higher court. [from French from Latin *appellare* = address]

appellation /æpə'leɪʃən/ *n.* a name or title; nomenclature.

append /ə'pend/ *v.t.* to attach; to add, especially to a written document. [from Latin *appendere* (*pendere* = hang)]

appendage /ə'pendɪdʒ/ *n.* a thing attached to or forming a natural part of something larger or more important.

appendicitis /əpendɪ'saɪtɪs/ *n.* inflammation of the ◊appendix. In an acute attack, the pus-filled appendix may burst, causing a potentially lethal spread of infection (see ◊peritonitis). Treatment is by removal (appendectomy).

appendix *n.* (*plural* **appendices** /-ɪsiːz/) 1. a small, blind extension of the bowel in the lower right abdomen, associated with the digestion of cellulose. In herbivores it may be large, containing millions of bacteria secreting enzymes to digest grass. Cellulose is difficult to digest because no

vertebrate can produce the correct digestive enzyme. 2. supplementary matter at the end of a book etc. [from Latin *appendere* (*pendere* = hang)]

appertain /æpə'teɪn/ *v.i.* to belong or relate *to.* [from Old French from Latin *appertinere* (*pertinēre* = pertain)]

appetite /'æpɪtaɪt/ *n.* a natural craving or relish, especially for food or something pleasurable. [from Old French from Latin *appetere* = seek after]

appetizer /'æpɪtaɪzə/ *n.* a small savoury or drink taken before a meal to stimulate the appetite.

appetizing /'æpɪtaɪzɪŋ/ *adj.* (of food) stimulating the appetite, attractive to eat. —**appetizingly** *adv.* [from French]

applaud /ə'plɔːd/ *v.t./i.* to express strong approval (of), especially by clapping; to commend, to praise. —**applause** *n.* [from Latin *plaudere* = clap hands]

apple *n.* a round, firm fruit with juicy flesh; the tree bearing this, *Malus pumila,* of the family Rosaceae. There are several hundred varieties of cultivated apples, grown all over the world, which may be divided into eating, cooking, and cider apples. All are derived from the wild crab apple. —**apple of one's eye,** a cherished person or thing. **apple-pie order,** extreme neatness. [Old English]

Appleseed, Johnny a character in US folk legend who wandered through the country for 40 years sowing apple seeds from which apple trees grew. The legend seems to be based on a historical figure, the US pioneer John Chapman (1774–1845).

Appleton layer a band containing ionized gases in the Earth's upper atmosphere, above the ◊E layer (formerly the Kennelly–Heaviside layer). It can act as a reflector of radio signals, although its ionic composition varies with the sunspot cycle. [from English physicist E *Appleton*]

appliance /ə'plaɪəns/ *n.* a device, a utensil; a fire engine.

applicable /'æplɪkəbəl/ *adj.* that may be applied (*to*), appropriate. —**applicability** /-'bɪlɪtɪ/ *n.* [Old French or from Latin *applicare*]

applicant /'æplɪkənt/ *n.* one who applies for something, especially employment.

application /æplɪ'keɪʃən/ *n.* 1. the act of applying something. 2. a thing applied. 3. a formal request. 4. sustained effort, diligence. 5. relevance. 6. in computing, a program or job designed for the benefit of the end user, such as a payroll system or a ◊word processor. [from French from Latin *applicare*]

applicator /'æplɪkeɪtə/ *n.* a device for applying a substance.

applied /ə'plaɪd/ *adj.* (of knowledge etc.) put to practical use.

appliqué /ə'pliːkeɪ/ *n.* a type of embroidery used to create pictures or patterns by 'applying' pieces of material onto a background fabric. The pieces are cut into the appropriate shapes and sewn on, providing decoration for wall hangings, furnishing textiles, and clothes. —*v.t.* (**appliquéd, appliquéing**) to decorate with appliqué. [French]

apply /ə'plaɪ/ *v.t./i.* 1. to make a formal request. 2. to put into contact, to spread on a surface. 3. to bring into use or action. 4. to be relevant. —**apply oneself,** to give one's attention and energy (*to* a task). [from Old French from Latin *applicare* = fasten to]

appoint /ə'pɔɪnt/ *v.t.* 1. to assign (a person) to a job or office; to seat up (by choosing members. 2. to fix or decide (a date or place etc.). —**well-appointed** *adj.* well-equipped or furnished. [from Old French *à point* = to a point]

appointee /æpɔɪn'tiː/ *n.* a person appointed.

appointment /ə'pɔɪntmənt/ *n.* 1. an arrangement to meet or visit at a particular time. 2. appointing a person to a job; the person appointed. 3. (in *plural*) fittings, furnishings.

Appomattox /æpə'mætəks/ *n.* village in Virginia, USA, scene of the surrender on 9 April 1865 of the Confederate army under Robert E Lee to the Union army under Ulysses S Grant, which ended the American Civil War.

apportion /ə'pɔːʃən/ *v.t.* to share out; to assign as a share (*to*). —**apportionment** *n.* [from French or Latin]

apposite /'æpəsɪt/ *adj.* (of a remark) appropriate. —**appositely** *adv.,* **appositeness** *n.* [from Latin *apponere* = apply]

apposition /æpə'sɪʃən/ *n.* juxtaposition, especially (in grammar) of elements sharing a syntactic function.

appraise /ə'preɪz/ *v.t.* to estimate the value or amount of; to fix a price for (a thing) officially. —**appraisal** *n.* [earlier *apprise,* assimilated to *praise*]

appreciable /əˈpriːʃəbəl/ adj. enough to be seen or felt, considerable. —**appreciably** adv. [French]

appreciate /əˈpriːʃɪeɪt/ v.t./i. 1. to value greatly; to be grateful for. 2. to recognize, to be sympathetically aware of; to assess realistically. 3. to raise or rise in value. —**appreciation** /-ˈeɪʃən/ n. [from Latin *appretiare* = appraise (*pretium* = price)]

appreciative /əˈpriːʃəɪv/ adj. expressing appreciation.

appreciatory /əˈpriːʃətərɪ/ adj. (of remarks etc.) expressing appreciation.

apprehend /æprɪˈhend/ v.t. 1. to arrest, to seize. 2. to understand. 3. to expect with fear or anxiety. [from French or Latin *prehendere* = grasp]

apprehensible /æprɪˈhensɪbəl/ adj. able to be grasped by the mind or perceived by the senses.

apprehension /æprɪˈhenʃən/ n. 1. dread, fearful, expectation. 2. arrest, capture. 3. understanding. [French or from Latin]

apprehensive /æprɪˈhensɪv/ adj. feeling apprehension, anxious. —**apprehensively** adv., **apprehensiveness** n. [from French or Latin]

apprentice /əˈprentɪs/ n. one who is learning a craft and is bound to an employer for a specified term by legal agreement in return for instruction; a novice (jockey). —v.t. to bind as an apprentice. —**apprenticeship** n. [from Old French *apprendre* = learn]

apprise /əˈpraɪz/ v.t. to inform, to notify. [from French *apprendre* = learn]

appro /ˈæprəʊ/ n. (colloquial) abbreviation of approval.

approach /əˈprəʊtʃ/ v.t./i. 1. to come near or nearer (to) in space or time. 2. to be similar or approximate to. 3. to make a tentative proposal to. 4. to set about (a task). —n. 1. an act or means of approaching. 2. a way of dealing with a person or thing. 3. an approximation. 4. the final part of an aircraft's flight before landing. [from Old French from Latin *appropiare* draw near (*prope* = near)]

approachable /əˈprəʊtʃəbəl/ adj. able to be approached; friendly, easy to talk to. —**approachability** /-ˈbɪlɪtɪ/ n.

approbation /æprəˈbeɪʃən/ n. approval, consent. [from Old French from Latin *approbatio* (*probare* = test)]

appropriate[1] /əˈprəʊprɪət/ adj. suitable, proper. —**appropriately** adv., **appropriateness** n. [from Latin *appropriare*]

appropriate[2] /əˈprəʊprɪeɪt/ v.t. to take and use as one's own; to devote (money etc.) to a special purpose. —**appropriation** /-ˈeɪʃən/ n., **appropriator** n. [from Latin *appropriare* (*proprius* = one's own)]

approval /əˈpruːvəl/ n. 1. approving; favourable opinion. 2. consent. —**on approval**, returnable to the supplier (without obligation to purchase) if not suitable.

approve /əˈpruːv/ v.t./i. 1. to give or have a favourable opinion (*of*). 2. to give assent to. [from Old French from Latin *approbare* = test (*probus* = good)]

approx. abbreviation of approximately.

approximate[1] /əˈprɒksɪmət/ adj. almost (but not completely) exact or correct, near to the actual. —**approximately** adv. [from Latin *proximus* = very near]

approximate[2] /əˈprɒksɪmeɪt/ v.t./i. to be or make approximate or near (*to*). —**approximation** /-ˈmeɪʃən/ n. [from Latin *approximare*]

appurtenances /əˈpɜːtɪnənsɪz/ n.pl. belongings, accessories. [from Anglo-French from Latin *appertinere* (*pertinére* = pertain)]

après-ski /æpreɪˈskiː/ adj. done or worn after skiing. [French]

apricot /ˈeɪprɪkɒt/ n. the yellow-fleshed fruit of *Prunus armeniaca*, a tree of the rose family Rosaceae, closely related to the almond, peach, plum, and cherry. Although native to the Far East, it has long been cultivated in Armenia, from where it was introduced into Europe and the USA. [from Portuguese or Spanish from Arabic *al* = the and *barkuk*, from Greek from Latin *praecox* = early-ripe]

April /ˈeɪprəl/ n. the fourth month of the year. —**April fool**, the victim of a hoax on **April Fool's Day,** the first day of April, when it is customary in W Europe and the USA to expose people to ridicule by a practical joke, causing them to believe some falsehood or to go on a fruitless errand. [from Latin *Aprilis*]

a priori /eɪ praɪˈɔːraɪ/ in logic, reasoning from causes to effects; an argument that is known to be true, or false, without reference to experience; the converse of ◊a posteriori. [Latin = from what is before]

apron /ˈeɪprən/ n. 1. a garment worn over the front part of the body to protect the wearer's clothes. 2. a hard-surfaced area on an airfield where aircraft are manœuvred or loaded and unloaded. 3. an extension of a stage in front of a curtain. [originally *naperon*, from Old French *nape* = tablecloth from Latin *mappa*]

apropos /ˈæprəpəʊ, -ˈpəʊ/ adj. & adv. 1. relevant(ly). 2. by the way. —**apropos of**, concerning, with reference to. [from French *à propos* = to the purpose]

apse n. a recess with an arched or domed roof, especially at the end of a church. [Latin from Greek *(h)apsis* = arch, vault]

apsidal /ˈæpsɪdəl/ adj. 1. of the form of an apse. 2. of apsides.

apsis /ˈæpsɪs/ n. (plural **apsides** /ˈæpsɪdiːz/) each of the points, on the orbit of a planet or satellite etc., nearest to or furthest from the body round which it moves. [Latin from Greek *(h)apsis* = arch, vault]

apt adj. 1. suitable, appropriate. 2. having a tendency. 3. quick at learning. —**aptly** adv., **aptness** n. [from Latin *aptus* = fitted]

apteryx /ˈæptərɪks/ n. a kiwi. [from Greek *a-* = without and *pterux* = wing]

aptitude /ˈæptɪtjuːd/ n. a natural ability or skill. [French from Latin *aptus*]

Apuleius /æpjuːˈliːəs/ Lucius lived c. AD 160. Roman lawyer, philosopher, and author of *Metamorphoses*, or ◊*The Golden Ass*.

Apulia /ˈpuːljə/ English form of ◊Puglia, region of Italy.

Aqaba, Gulf of /ˈækəbə/ gulf extending for 160 km/100 mi between the Negev and the Red Sea; its coastline is uninhabited except at its head, where the frontiers of Israel, Egypt, Jordan, and Saudi Arabia converge. Here are the two ports Eilat (Israeli 'Elath') and Aqaba, Jordan's only port.

Aquae Sulis /ˈækwaɪ ˈsuːlɪs/ Roman name of the city of Bath in SW England.

aqualung /ˈækwəlʌŋ/ n. or **scuba**, a portable underwater breathing apparatus. Compressed-air cylinders strapped to the diver's back are regulated by a valve system and by a mouth tube provide air to the diver at the same pressure as that of the surrounding water (which increases with the depth). It was developed in the early 1940s by the French diver Jacques Cousteau. [Latin *aqua* = water]

aquamarine /ækwəməˈriːn/ n. a bluish-green variety of the mineral ◊beryl; its colour. [from Latin *aqua marina* = sea water]

aquaplane /ˈækwəpleɪn/ n. a board on which a person stands for riding on water, pulled by a speedboat. —v.i. 1. to ride on an aquaplane. 2. (of a vehicle) to glide uncontrollably on a wet surface. [Latin *aqua* = water]

aquarium /əˈkweərɪəm/ n. (plural **aquariums**) a tank or artificial pond for keeping and showing living fish and other aquatic life; a building containing such tanks etc. [from Latin *aquarius* = of water]

Aquarius /əˈkweərɪəs/ n. a zodiac constellation a little south of the celestial equator near Pegasus. Aquarius is represented as a man pouring water from a jar. The Sun passes through Aquarius from late Feb to early March. In astrology, the dates for Aquarius are between about 20 Jan and 18 Feb (see ◊precession).

aquatic /əˈkwætɪk/ adj. growing or living in or near water; taking place in or on water. [from French or Latin *aqua* = water]

aquatint /ˈækwətɪnt/ n. 1. a print resembling a watercolour, produced from a copper plate engraved with nitric acid. 2. the technique used to produce such a print. Aquatint became common in the late 18th century. [from French from Italian *acqua tinta* = coloured water]

aqueduct /ˈækwɪdʌkt/ n. an artificial channel or conduit for water, often an elevated structure of stone, wood, or iron built for conducting water across a valley. [from Latin *aquae ductus* = conduit (*aqua* = water and *ducere* = lead)]

aqueous /ˈeɪkwɪəs/ adj. of or like water; produced by water. —**aqueous humour,** a watery fluid found in the space between the cornea and lens of the vertebrate eye. Similar to blood serum in composition, it is renewed every four hours. —**aqueous solution,** a solution in which the solvent is water. [from Latin *aqua* = water]

aquifer n. any rock formation containing water that can be extracted by a well. The rock of an aquifer must be porous and permeable (full of interconnected holes) so that it can absorb water.

Aquila /'ækwɪlə/ n. a constellation on the celestial equator (see ◊celestial sphere), near Capricornus. Its brightest star is first-magnitude ◊Altair, flanked by the stars Beta and Gamma Aquilae. It is represented by an eagle. [Latin *aquila* = eagle]

aquilegia /ækwi'liːdʒjə/ n. a plant of the genus *Aquilegia*, a columbine, especially with blue flowers. [Latin]

aquiline /'ækɪlaɪn/ adj. of or like an eagle; hooked like an eagle's beak. [from Latin *aquila* = eagle]

Aquinas /ə'kwaɪnəs/ St Thomas *c*.1226–1274. Neapolitan philosopher and theologian, the greatest figure of the school of ◊scholasticism. He was a Dominican monk, known as the 'Angelic Doctor'. In 1879 his works were recognized as the basis of Catholic theology. His *Summa contra Gentiles/Against the Errors of the Infidels* 1259–64 argues that reason and faith are compatible. He assimilated the philosophy of Aristotle into Christian doctrine.

Beware of the man of one book.

St Thomas Aquinas

Aquino /ə'kiːnəʊ/ (Maria) Corazón (born Cojuangco) 1933– . President of the Philippines from 1986, when she was instrumental in the nonviolent overthrow of President Ferdinand Marcos. She has sought to rule in a conciliatory manner, but has encountered opposition from left (communist guerrillas) and right (army coup attempts), and her land reforms have been seen as inadequate.

Aquitaine /ækwi'teɪn/ region of SW France; capital Bordeaux; area 41,300 sq km/15,942 sq mi; population (1986) 2,718,000. It comprises the *départements* of Dordogne, Gironde, Landes, Lot-et-Garonne, and Pyrénées-Atlantiques. Red wines (Margaux, St Julien) are produced in the Médoc district, bordering the Gironde. Aquitaine was an English possession 1152–1452.

Ar symbol for argon.

Arab /'ærəb/ n. **1.** a member of a Semitic people originally inhabiting the Arabian peninsula and neighbouring countries, now also other parts of the Middle East and North Africa. **2.** a horse of a breed native to Arabia. —*adj.* of Arabs. [from French, ultimately from Arabic '*arab*]

Arab Emirates see ◊United Arab Emirates.

arabesque /ærə'besk/ n. **1.** an elaborate design using intertwined leaves, branches, and scrolls. **2.** a ballet dancer's position in which one leg is extended horizontally backwards and the arms are outstretched to give the longest possible line from fingertips to toes. **3.** a short, usually florid piece of music. [French from Italian *Arabo* = Arab]

Arabian /ə'reɪbiən/ adj. of Arabia or the Arabs (especially with geographical reference).

Arabian Nights /ə'reɪbiən/ tales in oral circulation among Arab storytellers from the 10th century, probably having their roots in India. They are also known as *The Thousand and One Nights* and include 'Ali Baba', 'Aladdin', 'Sinbad the Sailor', and 'The Old Man of the Sea'.

Arabian Sea the NW branch of the ◊Indian Ocean.

Arabic /'ærəbɪk/ n. a Hamito-Semitic language of W Asia and North Africa, originating among the Arabs of the Arabian peninsula. Arabic script is written from right to left. —*adj.* of or in the Arabic language. [from Old French from Latin from Greek *Arabikos*]

Arabic numerals the symbols 0, 1, 2, 3, 4, 5, 6, 7, 8, 9, early forms of which were in use among the Arabs before being adopted by the peoples of Europe during the Middle Ages in place of Roman numerals. They appear to have originated in India and probably reached Europe by way of Spain.

Arab-Israeli Wars a series of wars between Israel and various Arab states in the Middle East since the founding of the state of Israel in 1948.

Arabistan /ærəbi'staːn/ former name of the Iranian province of Khuzestan, revived in the 1980s by the 2 million Sunni Arab inhabitants who demand autonomy. Unrest and sabotage 1979–80 led to a pledge of a degree of autonomy by Ayatollah Khomeini.

arable /'ærəbəl/ adj. (of land) suitable for growing crops. —*n.* land of this kind. [French or from Latin *arare* = plough]

Arafat *The leader of the Palestine Liberation Organization from 1969, Yasser Arafat.*

Arab League the organization of Arab states established in Cairo in 1945 to promote Arab unity, especially in opposition to Israel. The original members were Egypt, Syria, Iraq, Lebanon, Transjordan (Jordan 1949), Saudi Arabia, and Yemen. In 1979 Egypt was suspended and the League's headquarters transferred to Tunis in protest against the Egypt-Israeli peace, but Egypt was readmitted as a full member in May 1989, and in March 1990 the headquarters returned to Cairo.

Arachne /ə'rækni/ in Greek mythology, a Lydian woman who was so skilful a weaver that she challenged the goddess Athena to a contest. Athena tore Arachne's beautiful tapestries to pieces and Arachne hanged herself. She was transformed into a spider, and her weaving became a cobweb. [Greek = spider]

arachnid /ə'ræknɪd/ n. or **arachnoid**, a member of the class Arachnida, comprising spiders, scorpions, ticks, and mites. They differ from insects in possessing only two main body regions, the cephalophorax and the abdomen. [from French or Latin from Greek *arachnē* = spider]

Arafat /'ærəfæt/ Yasser 1929– . Palestinian nationalist politician, cofounder of al-◊Fatah in 1956 and president of the ◊Palestine Liberation Organization (PLO) from 1969. In the 1970s his activities in pursuit of an independent homeland for Palestinians made him a prominent figure in world politics, but in the 1980s the growth of factions within the PLO effectively reduced his power. He was forced to evacuate Lebanon in 1983, but remained leader of most of the PLO and in 1990 persuaded it to recognize formally the state of Israel.

Arago /ærə'gəʊ/ Dominique 1786–1853. French physicist and astronomer who made major contributions to the early study of ◊electromagnetism. In 1820 he found out that iron enclosed in a wire coil could be magnetized by the passage of an electric current. Later, in 1824, he was the first to observe the ability of a floating copper disc to deflect a magnetic needle, the phenomenon of magnetic rotation.

Aragón /'ærəgən/ autonomous region of NE Spain including the provinces of Huesca, Teruel, and Zaragoza; area 47,700 sq km/18,412 sq mi; population (1986) 1,215,000. Its capital is Zaragoza, and products include almonds, figs, grapes, and olives. Aragón was an independent kingdom 1035–1479.

Aragon /'ærəgɒn/ Louis 1897–1982. French poet and novelist. Beginning as a Dadaist, he became one of the leaders of Surrealism, published volumes of verse, and in 1930 joined the Communist party. Taken prisoner in World

archaeology, chronology

14th–16th centuries	The Renaissance revived interest in classical art, including ruins and buried art and artefacts.
1748	The buried Roman city of Pompeii was discovered.
1784	Thomas Jefferson dug an Indian burial mound on the Rivanna River, Virginia and wrote about it.
1790	John Frere identified Old Stone Age (Palaeolithic) tools together with large extinct animals.
1822	Champollion deciphered Egyptian hieroglyphics.
1836	C J Thomsen devised the Stone, Bronze, and Iron Age classification.
1840s	A H Layard excavated the Assyrian capital of Nineveh.
1868	Great Zimbabwe ruins in E Africa first seen by Europeans.
1871	Heinrich Schliemann began work at Troy.
1879	Stone Age paintings were first discovered at Altamira, Spain.
1880s	A H Pitt-Rivers developed the concept of stratigraphy (identification of successive layers of soil within a site with successive archaeological periods; the most recent at the top).
1891	W M F Petrie began excavating Akhetaton in Egypt.
1899–1935	A J Evans excavated Minoan Knossos in Crete.
1900–44	Max Uhle began the systematic study of the civilizations of Peru.
1911	The Inca city of Machu Picchu discovered by Hiram Bingham in the Andes.
1911–12	Piltdown skull 'discovered'; proved a fake in 1949.
1914–18	Osbert Crawford developed the technique of aerial survey of sites.
1917–27	J E Thompson discovered the great Mayan sites in Yucatán, Mexico.
1922	Tutankhamen's tomb in Egypt opened by Howard Carter.
1926	A kill site in Folsom, New Mexico, was found with spearpoints in association with ancient bison.
1935	Dendrochronology (dating events in the distant past by counting tree rings) developed by A E Douglas; useful when preserved timbers are found.
1939	Anglo-Saxon ship-burial treasure found at Sutton Hoo, England.
1947	The first of the Dead Sea Scrolls discovered.
1948	*Proconsul* prehistoric ape discovered by Mary Leakey in Kenya; several early hominid fossils found by Louis Leakey in Olduvai Gorge 1950s–70s.
1953	Michael Ventris deciphered Minoan Linear B.
1960s	Radiocarbon and thermoluminescence measurement developed as aids for dating remains.
1961	Swedish warship *Wasa* raised at Stockholm.
1963	W B Emery pioneered rescue archaeology at Abu Simbel before it was flooded by the Aswan Dam.
1974	Tomb of Shi Huangdi discovered in China.
1978	Tomb of Philip II of Macedon (Alexander the Great's father) discovered in Greece.
1979	The Aztec capital Tenochtitlán excavated beneath a zone of Mexico City.
1982	The English king Henry VIII's warship *Mary Rose* 1545 was raised and studied with new techniques in underwater archaeology.
1985	The tomb of Maya, Tutankhamen's treasurer, discovered at Saqqara, Egypt.
1988	Turin Shroud established as of medieval date by radiocarbon dating.
1989	Remains of Globe and Rose Theatres, where many of Shakespeare's plays were originally performed, discovered in London.

War II, he escaped to join the Resistance. His experiences are reflected in the poetry of *Le Crève-coeur* 1942 and *Les Yeux d'Elsa* 1944.

The function of genius is to furnish cretins with ideas twenty years later.

Louis Aragon
'Le Porte-Plume', *traité du Style*

Aral Sea /ˈɑːrəl/ inland sea in the USSR; the world's fourth largest lake; divided between Kazakhstan and Uzbekistan; former area 62,000 sq km/24,000 sq mi, but decreasing. Water from its tributaries, the Amu Darya and Syr Darya, has been diverted for irrigation and city use, and the sea is disappearing, with long-term consequences for the climate.

Aramaic /ærəˈmeɪɪk/ *n.* a Hamito-Semitic language of W Asia, the everyday language of Palestine 2,000 years ago. —*adj.* of or in Aramaic. [from *Aram*, biblical name of Syria]

Aran /ˈærən/ *adj.* of a type of patterned knitwear characteristic of the **Aran Islands**, a group of three islands off the W coast of Ireland.

Ararat /ˈærəræt/ double-peaked mountain on the Turkish-Iranian border; the higher, Great Ararat, 5,156 m/16,900 ft, was the reputed resting place of Noah's Ark after the Flood.

araucaria *n.* a coniferous tree of the genus *Araucaria*, allied to the firs, with flat, scalelike needles. Once widespread, araucarias are now native only to the southern hemisphere. They include the monkey-puzzle tree *A. araucana*, the Australian bunya bunya pine *A. bidwillii*, and the Norfolk Island pine *A. heterophylla*.

Arawak /ˈærəwæk/ *n.* a member of an indigenous American people of the Caribbean and NE Amazon Basin. Arawaks lived mainly by shifting cultivation in tropical forests. They were driven out of many West Indian islands by another American Indian people, the Caribs, shortly before the arrival of the Spanish in the 16th century. —**Arawakan** *adj* & *n.*

Arbenz Guzmán /ɑːˈbens ɡʊsˈmæn/ Jácobo 1913–1971. Guatemalan social democratic politician and president from 1951 until his overthrow in 1954 by rebels operating with the help of the US Central Intelligence Agency.

Arbil /ˈɑːbɪl/ Kurdish town in a province of the same name in N Iraq. Occupied since Assyrian times, it was the site of a battle in 331 BC at which Alexander the Great defeated the Persians under Darius III. In 1974 Arbil became the capital of a Kurdish autonomous region set up by the Iraqi government. Population (1985) 334,000.

arbiter *n.* 1. a person with great control or influence over something. 2. a judge, an arbitrator. [Latin]

arbitrageur *n.* in international finance, a person who buys securities (such as currency or commodities) in one country or market for immediate resale in another market, to take advantage of different prices. **Arbitrage** became widespread during the 1970s and 1980s with the increasing ◊deregulation of financial markets.

arbitrary /ˈɑːbɪtrəri/ *adj.* 1. based on random choice or whim; capricious. 2. despotic. —**arbitrarily** *adv.*, **arbitrariness** *n.* [from French or Latin = of an *arbiter*]

arbitrate /ˈɑːbɪtreɪt/ *v.t./i.* to act as an arbitrator, to settle (a dispute) thus. [from Latin *arbitrari* = judge]

arbitration /ɑːbɪˈtreɪʃ(ə)n/ *n.* submission of a dispute to a third, unbiased party for settlement. The dispute may be personal litigation, trade-union issues, or international disputes.

arbitrator /ˈɑːbɪtreɪtə/ *n.* an impartial person chosen to settle a dispute between parties. [Latin]

arbor /ˈɑːbə/ *n.* an axle or spindle on which a wheel etc. revolves in mechanism. [Latin = tree]

arboreal /ɑːˈbɔːrɪəl/ *adj.* of trees; living in trees. [from Latin *arboreus* (*arbor* = tree)]

arboretum /ɑːbəˈriːtəm/ *n.* (*plural* **arboreta**) a place where trees are grown for study and display. An arboretum may have many species or just different varieties of one species – for example, different types of pine tree.

arbour /ˈɑːbə/ *n.* a shady retreat enclosed by trees or climbing plants. [from Anglo-French from Latin *herba* = herb, assimilated to Latin *arbor* = tree]

Arbuthnot /ɑːˈbʌθnət/ John 1667–1735. Scottish physician, attendant on Queen Anne 1705–14. He was a friend of Pope, Gray, and Swift, and was the chief author of the satirical *Memoirs of Martinus Scriblerus*. He created the English national character of John Bull, a prosperous farmer, in his *History of John Bull* 1712, pamphlets advocating peace with France.

arbutus /ɑːˈbjuːtəs/ *n.* 1. an evergreen of the genus *Arbutus*, one with strawberry-like fruits. 2. (*US*) a trailing plant that bears fragrant pink flowers in spring. [Latin]

arc *n.* 1. part of the circumference of a circle or other curve; anything shaped like this. A **minor arc** is less than a semicircle; a **major arc** is greater than a semicircle. 2. a large luminous flow of electric current through gas. —*v.i.* (**arced, arcing** /-k-/) to form an arc, to move in a curve. —**arc lamp,** a lamp in which an arc is used to produce light. [from Old French from Latin *arcus* = bow, curve]

arcade /ɑːˈkeɪd/ *n.* 1. a covered walk, especially one lined with shops. 2. a series of arches supporting or along a wall. [French]

arcane /ɑːˈkeɪn/ *adj.* mysterious, secret, understood by few. [French, or from Latin *arcēre* = shut up and *arca* = chest]

Arc de Triomphe /ˈɑːk də ˈtriːɒmf/ the arch at the head of the Champs Elysées in the Place de l'Etoile, Paris, France, begun by Napoleon in 1806 and completed in 1836. It was intended to commemorate Napoleon's victories of 1805–06. Beneath it rests France's 'Unknown Soldier'.

arch- prefix giving the meaning 1. chief, superior. 2. pre-eminent, extremely bad. [from Old English or Old French, from Latin from Greek *arkhos* = chief]

Arch /ɑːtʃ/ Joseph 1826–1919. English Radical member of Parliament and trade unionist, founder of the National Agricultural Union (the first of its kind) in 1872. He was born in Warwickshire, the son of an agricultural labourer. Entirely self-taught, he became a Methodist preacher, and was Liberal-Labour MP for NW Norfolk.

arch[1] *n.* a structure (usually curved) supporting the weight of what is above it or used ornamentally; something curved like this. —*v.t./i.* to form (into) an arch; to span with or like an arch. [from Old French from Latin *arcus* = arc]

arch[2] *adj.* consciously or affectedly playful. —**archly** *adv.*, **archness** *n.*

Archaean /ɑːˈkiːən/ *adj.* or **Archaeozoic** of the earliest period of geological time; the first part of the Precambrian era, from the formation of Earth up to 2,500 million years ago. Traces of life have recently been found in Archaean rocks.

archaebacteria *n.* three groups of bacteria whose DNA differs significantly from that of other bacteria (called the 'eubacteria'). All are strict anaerobes, that is, they are killed by oxygen. This is thought to be a primitive condition and to indicate that the archaebacteria are related to the earliest life forms, which appeared about 4 billion years ago, when there was little oxygen in the Earth's atmosphere.

archaeology /ɑːkiˈɒlədʒi/ *n.* the study of civilizations through their material remains. —**archaeological** /-əˈlɒdʒɪkəl/ *adj.*, **archaeologist** *n.* [from Greek = ancient history (*arkhaios* = old)]

archaeopteryx *n.* a fossil from the limestone deposits of Bavaria about 160 million years old, and popularly known as 'the first bird', although some earlier bird ancestors are now known. *Archaeopteryx* was about the size of a crow and had feathers and wings, but in many respects its skeleton is reptilian (long, bony tail; teeth) and very like some small meat-eating dinosaurs of the time.

archaic /ɑːˈkeɪɪk/ *adj.* ancient, of an early period in a culture; antiquated; (of a word) no longer in ordinary use. —**archaically** *adv.* [from French from Greek *arkhē* = beginning]

archaism /ˈɑːkeɪɪzəm/ *n.* an archaic word or expression; use of what is archaic. —**archaistic** /-ˈɪstɪk/ *adj.* [from Greek]

archaize /ˈɑːkeɪaɪz/ *v.t./i.* 1. to imitate the archaic. 2. to render archaistic. [from Greek = be old-fashioned]

archangel /ˈɑːkeɪndʒəl/ *n.* an angel of the highest rank. [Old English, ultimately from Greek]

archbishop /ɑːtʃˈbɪʃəp/ *n.* in the Christian church, a bishop of superior rank, who has authority over other bishops in his jurisdiction and often over an ecclesiastical province. The office exists in the Roman Catholic, Eastern Orthodox, and Anglican churches. —**archbishopric** *n.* his office or diocese. [Old English]

archdeacon /ɑːtʃˈdiːkən/ *n.* originally an ordained dignitary of the Christian church charged with the supervision of the deacons attached to a cathedral. Today in the Roman Catholic church the office is purely titular; in the Church of England an archdeacon still has many business duties, such as the periodic inspection of churches. The office is not found in other Protestant churches. —**archdeaconal** /ɑːkɪdiˈækənəl/ *adj.* [Old English, ultimately from Greek]

archdeaconry *n.* an archdeacon's office or residence.

archdiocese /ɑːtʃˈdaɪəsɪs/ *n.* the diocese of an archbishop.

archduchy /ˈɑːtʃdʌtʃi/ *n.* the territory of an archduke.

archduke /ˈɑːtʃdjuːk/ *n.* the chief duke; (*historical*) the title of the son of the Emperor of Austria. —**archduchess** *n.fem.* [from Old French from Latin]

archegonium *n.* (*plural* **archegonai**) the female sex organ found in bryophytes (mosses and liverworts), pteridophytes (ferns, club mosses, and horsetails), and some gymnosperms. It is a multicellular, flask-shaped structure consisting of two parts: the swollen base and venter containing the egg cell, and the long, narrow neck.

archer *n.* 1. one who shoots with bow and arrows. 2. **the Archer,** the constellation or sign of the zodiac Sagittarius. [from Old French from Latin *arcus* = bow]

Archer /ˈɑːtʃə/ Jeffrey 1940– . English writer and politician. A Conservative member of Parliament 1969–74, he lost a fortune in a disastrous investment, but recouped it as a best-selling novelist. Works include *Not a Penny More, Not a Penny Less* 1975, and *First Among Equals* 1984. In 1985 he became deputy chair of the Conservative Party but resigned in Nov 1986 after a scandal.

archerfish *n.* any of a family Toxotidae, especially the genus *Toxotes*, of surface-living fishes native to SE Asia and Australia. The archerfish grows to about 25 cm/10 in and is able to shoot down insects up to 1.5 m/5 ft above the water by spitting a jet of water from its mouth.

archery *n.* the use of the bow and arrow, originally in war and hunting, now as a competitive sport. World Championships were first held in 1931 and were formerly an annual event, now biennial.

archetype /ˈɑːkɪtaɪp/ *n.* 1. the original model from which others are copied. 2. a typical example. —**archetypal** *adj.* [from Latin from Greek *tupos* = stamp]

archiepiscopal /ɑːkiˈpɪskəpəl/ *adj.* of an archbishop or archbishopric. [from Latin from Greek *episkopos* = bishop]

archimandrite /ɑːkiˈmændraɪt/ *n.* the superior of a large monastery in the Orthodox Church. [French or from Latin from Greek *mandra* = monastery]

Archimedes /ɑːkiˈmiːdiːz/ *c.*287–212 BC. Greek mathematician, who made important discoveries in geometry, hydrostatics, and mechanics. He formulated a law of fluid displacement (Archimedes' principle), and is credited with the invention of the Archimedes screw, a cylindrical device for raising water.

Give me where to stand and I will move the earth.
Archimedes

Archimedes' principle in physics, a law discovered by Archimedes stating that an object totally or partly submerged in a fluid displaces a volume of fluid that weighs the same as the apparent loss in weight of the object (which equals the upthrust on it).

Archimedes screw one of the earliest kinds of pump, thought to have been invented by Archimedes. It consists of a spiral screw revolving inside a close-fitting cylinder. It is used, for example, to raise water for irrigation.

archipelago /ɑːkiˈpeləɡoʊ/ *n.* (*plural* **archipelagos**) a group of islands, or an area of sea containing a group of islands. The islands of an archipelago are usually volcanic in origin, and they sometimes reach the tops of peaks in areas around continental margins flooded by the sea. [from Italian from Greek *pelagos* = sea, originally = the Aegean Sea]

Archipenko /ɑːkiˈpeŋkəʊ/ Alexander 1887–1964. Russian-born abstract sculptor who lived in France from 1908 and in the USA from 1923. He pioneered Cubist works composed of angular forms and spaces and later experimented with clear plastic and sculptures incorporating lights.

architect /ˈɑːkɪtekt/ *n.* a designer of buildings and large structures who prepares plans and supervises construction; a designer or creator *of.* [from French, ultimately from Greek *tektōn* = builder]

architectonic /ɑːkɪtekˈtɒnɪk/ *adj.* 1. of architecture or architects. 2. constructive. [from Latin from Greek]

architecture /ˈɑːkɪtektʃə/ *n.* the art or science of designing and constructing buildings. The term covers the design of any structure for living or working in —houses, churches, temples, palaces, and castles —and also the style of building of any particular country at any period of history. —**architectural** /-ˈtektʃərəl/ *adj.*, **architecturally** *adv.* [French or from Latin]

architrave /ˈɑːkɪtreɪv/ *n.* a horizontal beam resting on the tops of columns; a moulded frame round a doorway or window. [French from Italian *trave* from Latin *trabs* = beam]

archive /ˈɑːkaɪv/ *n.* (frequently in *plural*) a collection of the historical documents or records of an institution or community. [from French from Latin from Greek *arkheia* = public records]

archivist /ˈɑːkɪvɪst/ *n.* one in charge of archives.

archon *n.* in ancient Greece, the title of the chief magistrate in many cities. [Greek = ruler]

archway /ˈɑːtʃweɪ/ *n.* an arched entrance or passage.

arc lamp or **arc light** an electric light that uses the illumination of an electric arc maintained between two electrodes. The British scientist Humphry Davy developed an arc lamp in 1808, and its major use in recent years has been in cinema projectors. The lamp consists of two carbon electrodes, between which a very high voltage is maintained. Electric current arcs (jumps) between the two, creating a brilliant light.

arc minute, arc second units for measuring small angles, used in geometry, surveying, map-making, and astronomy. An arc minute is one sixtieth of a degree, and an arc second one sixtieth of an arc minute. Small distances in the sky, as between two close stars or the apparent width of a planet's disc, are expressed in minutes and seconds of arc.

arco *adv.* in music, a direction that cancels a previous instruction to a bowed string player to play *pizzicato* (plucked string.) [Italian = with the bow]

Arctic /ˈɑːktɪk/ region N of the Arctic Circle. There is no Arctic continent, merely pack ice (which breaks into ice floes in summer) surrounding the Pole and floating on the Arctic Ocean. Pack ice is carried by the south-flowing current into the Atlantic Ocean as ◊icebergs. In winter the Sun disappears below the horizon for a time (and in summer, which only lasts up to two months, remains above it), but the cold is less severe than in parts of E Siberia or Antarctica. Land areas in the Arctic have mainly stunted tundra vegetation, with an outburst of summer flowers. Animals include reindeer, caribou, musk ox, fox, hare, lemming, wolf, polar bear, seal, and walrus. There are few birds, except in summer, when insects, especially mosquitoes, are plentiful. The aboriginal people are the ◊Inuit of the Alaskan/Canadian Arctic and Greenland. The most valuable resource is oil. The International Arctic Sciences Committee was established in 1987 by the countries with Arctic coastlines to study ozone depletion and climatic change. —**arctic** *adj.*, of the Arctic; very cold. [from Old French from Latin from Greek *arktos* = bear, Ursa Major]

Arctic Circle an arbitrary line encircling the North Pole at 66° 32′ N.

Arctic Ocean ocean surrounding the North Pole; area 14,000,000 sq km/5,400,000 sq mi. Because of the Siberian and North American rivers flowing into it, it has comparatively low salinity and freezes readily.

Arcturus /ɑːkˈtjʊərəs/ *n.* or **Alpha Boötis** the brightest star in the constellation Boötes and the fourth brightest star

in the sky. Arcturus is a red giant, 36 light years away from Earth. [from Greek *arktus* = bear and *ovros* = guardian, because of its position in a line with the tail of Ursa Major]

Arden /ˈɑːdn/ John 1930– . English playwright. His early plays *Serjeant Musgrave's Dance* 1959 and *The Workhouse Donkey* 1963 show the influence of Brecht. Subsequent works, often written in collaboration with his wife, Margaretta D'Arcy, show increasing concern with the political situation in Northern Ireland and a dissatisfaction with the professional and subsidized theatre world.

Ardennes /ɑːˈden/ wooded plateau in NE France, SE Belgium, and N Luxembourg, cut through by the river Meuse; also a *département* of ◊Champagne-Ardenne. There was heavy fighting here in World Wars I and II (see ◊Bulge, Battle of the).

ardent /ˈɑːdənt/ *adj.* eager, fervent, passionate. —**ardency** *n.*, **ardently** *adv.* [from Old French from Latin *ardens* = burning]

ardour /ˈɑːdə/ *n.* zeal, enthusiasm, passion. [from Old French from Latin *ardēre* = burn]

arduous /ˈɑːdjuəs/ *adj.* hard to accomplish; needing much effort, laborious. —**arduously** *adv.* [from Latin *arduus* = steep, difficult]

are[1] *v.i.* 2nd person singular and 1st, 2nd, and 3rd person plural of **be**.

are[2] /ɑː/ *n.* a metric unit of area, equal to 100 square metres (119.6 sq yd); 100 ares make one ◊hectare. [French from Latin *area*]

area /ˈeərɪə/ *n.* 1. the extent or measure of a surface. 2. a region; a space set aside for a purpose. 3. the field of an activity or subject. 4. a space in front of the basement of a building. [Latin = vacant piece of level ground]

Areca /əˈriːkə/ *n.* a genus of palms native to Asia and Australia. The ◊betel nut comes from the species *A. catechu*. [Portuguese, from Malayalam]

Arecibo /ærɛˈsiːbəʊ/ the site in Puerto Rico of the world's largest single-dish ◊radio telescope, 305 m/1,000 ft in diameter. It is built in a natural hollow, and uses the rotation of the Earth to scan the sky. It has been used both for radar work on the planets and for conventional radio astronomy, and is operated by Cornell University, USA.

arena /əˈriːnə/ *n.* 1. the level area in the centre of an amphitheatre or sports stadium etc. 2. a scene of conflict, a sphere of action. [Latin = sand]

aren't /ɑːnt/ (*colloquial*) contraction of are not.

Arequipa /ærɛˈkiːpə/ city in Peru at the base of the volcano El Misti; population (1988) 592,000. Founded by Pizarro in 1540, it is the cultural focus of S Peru and a busy commercial (soap, textiles) centre.

Ares /ˈeəriːz/ in Greek mythology, the god of war (Roman ◊Mars). The son of Zeus and Hera, he was worshipped chiefly in Thrace.

arête /æˈreɪt/ *n.* a sharp, narrow ridge separating two ◊glacier valleys. The typical U-shaped cross sections of glacier valleys give arêtes very steep sides. Arêtes are common in glaciated mountain regions such as the Rockies, the Himalayas, and the Alps. [French from Latin *arista* = spiny process]

Aretino /ærəˈtiːnəʊ/ Pietro 1492–1556. Italian writer, born in Arezzo. He earned his living, both in Rome and Venice, by publishing satirical pamphlets while under the protection of a highly placed family. His *Letters* 1537–57 are a unique record of the cultural and political events of his time, and illustrate his vivacious, exuberant character. He also wrote poems and comedies.

argali *n.* a wild sheep *Ovis ammon* of Central Asia. The male can grow to 1.2 m/4 ft at the shoulder, and has massive spiral horns.

Argand diagram /ˈɑːɡænd/ in mathematics, a method for representing complex numbers by Cartesian coordinates (x, y). Along the x (horizontal) axis are plotted the real numbers, and along the y (vertical) axis the non-real, or ◊imaginary, numbers.

argent /ˈɑːdʒənt/ *n.* & *adj.* in heraldry, silver or white (colour). [French from Latin *argentum* = silver]

Argentina /ɑːdʒənˈtiːnə/ Republic of; country in South America, bounded by Chile to the W and S, Bolivia to the NW, and Paraguay, Brazil, Uruguay, and the Atlantic Ocean to the E; **area** 2,780,092 sq km/1,073,116 sq mi; **capital** Buenos Aires (to move to Viedma); **physical** mountains in W, forest in N, pampas (treeless plains) in central area,

Patagonian plateau in S; rivers Colorado, Paraná, Uruguay, Rio de la Plata estuary; **territories** Tierra del Fuego; disputed claims to S Atlantic islands; part of Antarctica; **head of state and government** Carlos Menem from 1989; **political system** emergent democratic federal republic; **exports** beef, livestock, cereals, wool, tannin, peanuts, linseed oil, minerals (coal, copper, molybdenum, gold, silver, lead, zinc, barium, uranium); the country has huge resources of oil, natural gas, hydroelectric power; **population** (1989 est) 32,425,000 (mainly Spanish or Italian origin, only about 30,000 American Indians surviving); **language** Spanish (official), English, Italian, German, French; **recent history** independence from Spain achieved in 1816. Juan Perón elected president in 1946, overthrown in 1955. He returned to power in 1973 but died the following year. A coup in 1976 resulted in rule by a military junta. Defeat in the Falklands War with the UK led to General Galtieri's removal from power in 1983. Full diplomatic relations with the UK restored in 1990.

Argentina La Antonia Merce 1890–1936. Spanish dancer, choreographer, and director. She took her artistic name from the land of her birth. She toured as a concert artist with Vicente Escudero and her techniques of castanet playing were revolutionary.

argon *n.* a colourless, odourless, non-metallic, gaseous element, symbol Ar, atomic number 18, relative atomic mass 39.948. It constitutes almost 1% of the Earth's atmosphere, and is used in electric light bulbs and radio tubes. [from Greek *argos* = idle (*a-* = not and *ergon* = work)]

argonaut /'ɑːɡənɔːt/ *n.* or **paper nautilus,** a pelagic octopus, genus *Argonauta.* The 20 cm/8 in female of the common paper nautilus, *A. argo,* secretes a spiralled papery shell for her eggs from the web of the first pair of arms. The male is a 1 cm/0.4 in shell-less dwarf.

Argonauts in Greek legend, the band of heroes who accompanied ◊Jason when he set sail in the *Argo* to find the ◊Golden Fleece.

Argos /'ɑːɡɒs/ city in ancient Greece, at the head of the Gulf of Nauplia, which was once a cult centre of the goddess Hera. In the Homeric age the name 'Argives' was sometimes used instead of 'Greeks'.

argosy /'ɑːɡəsɪ/ *n.* (*poetical*) a merchant-ship; a fleet of these. [probably from Italian *Ragusa nave,* ship of Ragusa (in Dalmatia)]

argot /'ɑːɡəʊ/ *n.* the special jargon of a group. [French]

arguable /'ɑːɡjuəbəl/ *adj.* 1. that may be asserted. 2. open to doubt. **—arguably** *adv.*

argue /'ɑːɡjuː/ *v.t./i.* 1. to exchange views or angry words with expression of disagreement. 2. to reason (*for, against,* or *that*); to treat by reasoning; to prove or indicate; to persuade *into* or *out of.* [from Old French from Latin *argutari* = prattle (*arguere* = prove)]

argument /'ɑːɡjumənt/ *n.* 1. a discussion involving disagreement; a quarrel. 2. a reason advanced; a chain of reasoning. 3. in mathematics, a specific value of the independent variable of a ◊function of *x.* It is also another name for ◊amplitude.

argumentation /ɑːɡjumen'teɪʃən/ *n.* arguing. [French from Latin]

argumentative /ɑːɡju'mentətɪv/ *adj.* fond of arguing. **—argumentatively** *adv.* [from French or Latin]

argy-bargy /'ɑːdʒɪbɑːdʒɪ/ *n.* (*colloquial*) a heated argument. [originally Scottish]

Argyll /ɑː'ɡaɪl/ *n.* the line of Scottish peers who trace their descent to the Campbells of Lochow. The earldom dates from 1457. They include:

Argyll Archibald Campbell, 5th Earl of Argyll 1530–1573. Adherent of the Scottish presbyterian John ◊Knox. A supporter of Mary Queen of Scots from 1561, he commanded her forces after her escape from Lochleven Castle in 1568. He revised his position and became Lord High Chancellor of Scotland in 1572.

aria /'ɑːrɪə/ *n.* an extended piece for solo voice and accompaniment, especially in an opera or oratorio. Arias are often in three sections, the third repeating the first after a contrasting central section. [Italian]

Ariadne /ærɪ'ædnɪ/ in Greek mythology, the daughter of Minos, king of Crete. When Theseus came from Athens as one of the sacrificial victims offered to the Minotaur, she fell in love with him and gave him a ball of thread which enabled him to find his way out of the labyrinth.

Ariane /ærɪ'æn/ *n.* a series of launch vehicles built by the European Space Agency to place satellites into Earth orbit (first flight 1979). The launch site is at Kouru in French Guiana. Ariane is a three-stage rocket using liquid fuels, but small solid-fuel boosters can be attached to its first stage to increase carrying power.

Arianism *n.* a system of Christian theology which denied the complete divinity of Jesus. It was founded in about 310 by ◊Arius, and condemned as heretical at the Council of Nicaea in 325.

Arias Sanchez /'ɑːrɪəs 'sæntʃes/ Oscar 1940– . Costa Rican politician, president from 1986, secretary-general of the left-wing National Liberation Party (PLN). He advocated a neutralist policy and in 1987 was the leading promoter of the Central American Peace Plan (see ◊Nicaragua).

arid /'ærɪd/ *adj.* 1. dry, parched. 2. uninteresting. **—aridly** *adv.,* **aridity** /-'rɪdɪtɪ/ *n.,* **aridness** *n.* [from French or Latin *arēre* = be dry]

arid zone an infertile area with a small, infrequent rainfall that rapidly evaporates because of high temperatures. There are arid zones in Morocco, Pakistan, Australia, USA, and elsewhere.

Aries /'eərɪːz/ *n.* a zodiac constellation in the N hemisphere between Pisces and Taurus, near Auriga, represented as the legendary ram whose golden fleece was sought by Jason and the Argonauts. Its most distinctive feature is a curve of three stars of decreasing brightness. The Sun passes through Aries from late April to mid-May. In astrology, the dates for Aries are between about 21 March and 19 April (see ◊precession). **—Arian** *adj.* & *n.* [Latin = ram]

aright /ə'raɪt/ *adv.* rightly. [Old English]

aril *n.* an accessory seed cover other than a ◊fruit; it may be fleshy and sometimes brightly coloured, woody, or hairy. Examples of arils include the bright-red, fleshy layer surrounding the yew seed and the network of hard filaments that partially covers the nutmeg seed and yields the spice known as mace.

Ariosto /ærɪ'ɒstəʊ/ Ludovico 1474–1533. Italian poet, born in Reggio. He wrote Latin poems and comedies on Classical lines, including the poem *Orlando Furioso* 1516, 1532, an epic treatment of the *Roland* story, and considered to be the perfect poetic expression of the Italian Renaissance.

arise /ə'raɪz/ *v.i.* (*past* **arose,** *past participle* **arisen** /ə'rɪzən/) 1. to come into existence or to people's notice; to originate or result. 2. (*archaic*) to get up; to rise from the dead. [Old English]

Aristarchus of Samos /ærɪ'stɑːkəs/ *c.*280–264 BC. Greek astronomer. The first to argue that the Earth moves around the Sun, he was ridiculed for his beliefs.

Aristides /ærɪ'staɪdɪːz/ *c.*530–468 BC. Athenian politician. He was one of the ten Athenian generals at the battle of ◊Marathon in 490 BC and was elected chief archon, or magistrate. Later he came into conflict with the democratic leader Themistocles, and was exiled in about 483 BC. He returned to fight against the Persians at Salamis in 480 BC and in the following year, commanded the Athenians at Plataea.

aristocracy /ærɪs'tɒkrəsɪ/ *n.* 1. the hereditary upper classes, the nobility or élite. 2. a state governed by these. 3. the best representatives (*of* a category). **—aristocratic** /-tə'krætɪk/ *adj.* [from French from Greek *aristos* = best and *-kratia* = power]

aristocrat /'ærɪstəkræt/ *n.* a member of the aristocracy. [from French]

Aristophanes /ærɪ'stɒfənɪːz/ *c.*448–380 BC. Greek dramatist. Of his 11 extant plays (of a total of over 40), the early comedies are remarkable for the violent satire with which he ridiculed the democratic war leaders. He also satirized contemporary issues such as the new learning of Socrates in *The Clouds* 423 BC and the power of women in ◊*Lysistrata* 411 BC. The chorus plays a prominent role, frequently giving the play its title, as in *The Wasps* 422 BC, *The Birds* 414 BC, and *The Frogs* 405 BC.

Aristotle /'ærɪstɒtl/ 384–322 BC. Greek philosopher who advocated reason and moderation. Aristotle maintained that sense experience is our only source of knowledge, and that by reasoning we can discover the essences of things, that is, their distinguishing qualities. In his works on ethics and politics, Aristotle suggested that human happiness consists in living in conformity with nature.

He derived his political theory from the recognition that mutual aid is natural to humankind, and refused to set up any one constitution as universally ideal. Of Aristotle's works some 22 treatises survive, dealing with logic, metaphysics, physics, astronomy, meteorology, biology, psychology, ethics, politics, and literary criticism.

armadillo

Man is by nature a political animal.

Aristotle
The Politics

arithmetic[1] /əˈrɪθmətɪk/ *n.* **1.** the branch of mathematics that deals with numbers. The fundamental operations of arithmetic are addition, subtraction, multiplication, division, and, dependent on these four, raising to ◊powers and extraction of roots. **2.** calculation by means of numbers. —**arithmetic unit,** the part of a computer where data are processed, as distinct from storage or control units. [from Old French from Latin from Greek *arithmētikē* (*tekhnē* = (art) of counting and *arithmos* = number)]

arithmetic[2] /ærɪθˈmetɪk/ *adj.* or **arithmetical,** of arithmetic. —**arithmetically** *adv.*

arithmetic sequence or **arithmetical progression** or **arithmetical series** a sequence of numbers or terms that have a common difference between any one term and the next in the sequence. For example, 2, 7, 12, 17, 22, 27, ... is an arithmetic sequence with a common difference of 5. The general formula for the *n*th term is $a + (n-1)d$, where *a* is the first term and *d* is the common difference.

Arius /ˈeəriəs/ *c.*256–336. Egyptian priest whose ideas gave rise to ◊Arianism, a Christian belief which denied the complete divinity of Jesus.

Arizona /ærɪˈzəʊnə/ state in SW USA; **area** 294,100 sq km/113,523 sq mi; **capital** Phoenix; **physical** Colorado Plateau in the N and E, desert basins and mountains in the S and W; Colorado River; Grand Canyon; **products** cotton, livestock, copper, molybdenum, silver, electronics, aircraft; **population** (1987) 3,469,000 including over 150,000 American Indians (Navajo, Hopi, Apache), who still own a quarter of the state; **recent history** passed to USA after Mexican War 1848; territory 1863; state 1912.

Arjan /ˈaːdʒən/ Indian religious leader, fifth guru (teacher) of Sikhism from 1581. He built the Golden Temple in ◊Amritsar and compiled the *Adi Granth*, the first volume of Sikh scriptures. He died in Muslim custody.

Arjuna /ˈaːdʒʊnə/ Indian prince, one of the two main characters in the Hindu epic *Mahābhārata*.

ark *n.* **1.** Noah's boat or a model of this. **2. Ark of the Covenant,** in the Old Testament, the chest that contained the Tablets of the Law as given to Moses. It is now the cupboard in a synagogue in which the ◊Torah scrolls are kept. [Old English, from Latin *arca* = chest]

Arkansas /ˈaːkənsɔː/ state in S central USA; **area** 137,800 sq km/53,191 sq mi; **capital** Little Rock; **physical** Ozark Mountains in the W; lowlands in the E; Arkansas River; many lakes; **products** cotton, soya beans, rice, oil, natural gas, bauxite, timber, processed foods; **population** (1986) 2,372,000; **recent history** part of the Louisiana Purchase of 1803; created a state in 1836.

Arkwright /ˈaːkraɪt/ Richard 1732–1792. English inventor and manufacturing pioneer who developed a machine for spinning cotton (he called it a 'spinning frame') in 1768. He set up a water-powered spinning factory in 1771 and installed steam power in another factory in 1790.

arm[1] *n.* **1.** either of the two upper limbs of the human body, from shoulder to hand; something covering this, a sleeve. **2.** a raised side part of a chair, supporting a sitter's arm. **3.** a thing resembling an arm in shape or function. **4.** a control, a means of reaching. —**armband** *n.* a band worn round the arm or sleeve. [Old English]

arm[2] *n.* **1.** (usually in *plural*) a weapon. **2.** a branch of military forces. **3.** (in *plural*) heraldic devices. —*v.t./i.* **1.** to equip with weapons etc.; to equip oneself in preparation for war. **2.** to make (a bomb etc.) ready to explode. —**up in arms,** protesting vigorously. [from Old French from Latin *arma* = weapons]

armada /aːˈmaːdə/ *n.* a fleet of warships, especially (**Armada**) a Spanish naval invasion force sent against

England in 1588 by Philip II of Spain. See ◊Spanish Armada. [Spanish from Romanic = army]

armadillo /aːməˈdɪləʊ/ *n.* (*plural* **armadillos**) a burrowing mammal of the order Dasypodidae, with a body encased in bony plates. Some 20 species live between Texas and Patagonia and range in size from the fairy armadillo at 13 cm/5 in to the giant armadillo, 1.5 m/4.5 ft long. Armadillos feed on insects, snakes, fruit, and carrion. Some can roll into an armoured ball if attacked; others rely on burrowing for protection. [Spanish, diminutive of *armado* = armed man]

Armageddon /aːməˈgedən/ *n.* an ultimate or large-scale conflict, especially that between the forces of good and evil at the end of the world (Revelation 16: 16); the scene of this. It has been identified with ◊Megiddo in Israel.

Armagh /aːˈmaː/ county of Northern Ireland **area** 1,250 sq km/483 sq mi; **county town** Armagh; **physical** flat in the N, with many bogs; low hills in the S; Lough Neagh; **products** chiefly agricultural: apples, potatoes, flax; **population** (1981) 119,000.

armament /ˈaːməmənt/ *n.* **1.** (usually in *plural*) military weapons and equipment. **2.** the process of equipping for war. [from Latin *arma* = weapons]

armature /ˈaːmətʃə/ *n.* **1.** in a motor or generator, the wire-wound coil that carries the current and rotates in a magnetic field. **2.** the moving, iron part of a solenoid, especially if it acts as a switch. **3.** the pole piece of a permanent magnet or electromagnet. **4.** a framework round which a clay or plaster sculpture is modelled. [French from Latin *armatura* = armour]

armchair *n.* **1.** a chair with side supports for a sitter's arms. **2.** (*attributive*) theorizing, not practical or participating; amateur.

Armenia /aːˈmiːniə/ constituent republic of the Soviet Union from 1936; **area** 29,800 sq km/11,506 sq mi; **capital** Yerevan; **physical** mainly mountainous (including Mt Ararat), wooded; **products** copper, molybdenum, cereals, cotton, silk; **population** 3,412,000; **language** Armenian; **recent history** became an independent republic in 1918, was occupied by the Red Army in 1920, and became a constituent republic of the USSR in 1936. In 1988 demands for reunion with Nagorno-Karabakh led to riots, strikes and, during 1989–90, to a civil war quelled by the intervention of Soviet troops.

Armenian church /aːˈmiːniən/ the form of Christianity adopted in Armenia in the 3rd century. The Catholicos, or exarch, is the supreme head, and Echmiadzin (near Yerevan) is his traditional seat.

Armenian language one of the main divisions of the Indo-European language family. Old Armenian, the classic literary language, is still used in the liturgy of the Armenian church. Contemporary Armenian, with modified grammar and enriched with words from other languages, is used by a group of 20th-century writers.

Armenian massacres a series of massacres of Armenians by Turkish soldiers between 1895 and 1915. Reforms promised to Armenian Christians by Turkish rulers never materialized; unrest broke out and there were massacres by Turkish troops 1895. Again in 1909 and 1915, the Turks massacred altogether more than a million Armenians and deported others into the N Syrian desert, where they died of starvation; those who could fled to Russia or Persia. Only some 100,000 were left.

armful *n.* a quantity that is as much as the arm can hold.

armhole *n.* an opening in a garment through which the arm is inserted.

Arminius /aːˈmɪniəs/ 17 BC–AD 21. German chieftain. An ex-soldier of the Roman army, he annihilated a Roman force led by Varus in the Teutoburger Forest area in AD 9, and saved Germany from becoming a Roman province. He thus ensured that the empire's frontier did not extend beyond the Rhine.

Arminius Jacobus. Latinized name of Jakob Harmensen 1560–1609. Dutch Protestant priest who founded Arminianism, a school of Christian theology opposed to Calvin's doctrine of predestination. His views were developed by Simon Episcopius (1583–1643). Arminianism is the basis of Wesleyan ◊Methodism.

armistice /'ɑ:mɪstɪs/ n. a cessation from arms while awaiting a peace settlement. — **the Armistice,** the end of World War I between Germany and the Allies on 11 Nov 1918. — **Armistice Day,** 11 Nov, the anniversary of the Armistice, now replaced by Remembrance Sunday and (in the USA) Veterans Day. [French or from Latin *arma* = arms and *sistere* = make stand]

armlet /'ɑ:mlɪt/ n. a band worn round the arm or sleeve.

armonica n. alternative name for the glass ◊harmonica.

armorial /ɑ:'mɔ:rɪəl/ adj. of coats of arms, heraldic.

armour /'ɑ:mə/ n. 1. a protective covering for the body, formerly worn in battle. Body armour is depicted in Greek and Roman art. Chain mail was developed in the Middle Ages but the craft of the armourer in Europe reached its height in design in the 15th century, when knights were completely encased in plate armour that still allowed freedom of movement. Contemporary bulletproof vests and riot gear are forms of armour. 2. a protective metal covering for an armed vehicle, ship, etc. Since World War II armour for tanks and ships has been developed beyond an increasing thickness of steel plate, becoming an increasingly light, layered composite, including materials such as ceramics. More controversial is 'reactive' armour, consisting of 'shoeboxes' made of armour containing small, quick-acting explosive charges, which are attached at the most vulnerable points of a tank, in order to break up the force of entry of an enemy warhead. 3. armoured fighting vehicles collectively. [from Old French from Latin *arma* = weapons]

armoured /'ɑ:məd/ adj. 1. furnished with armour. 2. equipped with armoured vehicles.

armourer /'ɑ:mərə/ n. 1. an official in charge of small arms. 2. a maker of arms or armour.

armoury /'ɑ:mərɪ/ n. a place where arms are kept.

armpit n. the hollow under the arm below the shoulder.

Armstrong /'ɑ:mstrɒŋ/ Edwin Howard 1890–1954. US radio engineer who developed superheterodyne tuning for reception over a very wide spectrum of radio frequencies and ◊frequency modulation for static-free reception.

Armstrong Louis ('Satchmo') 1901–1971. US jazz cornet and trumpet player and singer, born in New Orleans. His Chicago recordings in the 1920s with the Hot Five and Hot Seven brought him recognition for his warm and pure trumpet tone, his skill at improvisation, and his quirky, gravelly voice. From the 1930s he became equally widely known as a singer, comedian, and film actor.

Armstrong Neil Alden 1930– . US astronaut. In 1969, he was the first person to set foot on the Moon, and said, 'That's one small step for a man, one giant leap for mankind'. The Moon landing was part of the ◊Apollo project.

Armstrong Robert, Baron Armstrong of Ilminster 1927– . British civil servant, cabinet secretary in Margaret Thatcher's government. He received considerable attention as a British Government witness in the 'Spycatcher' trial in Australia in 1987 when, defending the Government's attempts to prevent Peter Wright's book alleging 'dirty tricks' from being published, he was sometimes 'economical with the truth'.

Armstrong William George 1810–1900. English engineer who developed a revolutionary method of making gun barrels in 1855, by building a breech-loading artillery piece with a steel and wrought-iron barrel (previous guns were muzzle-loaded and had cast bronze barrels). By 1880 the 150 mm/16 in Armstrong gun was the standard for all British ordnance.

army n. 1. an organized force armed for fighting on land. 2. a vast group. 3. a body of people organized for a cause. [from Old French]

Arnauld /ɑ:'nəʊ/ French family closely associated with ◊Jansenism, a Christian church movement in the 17th century. **Antoine Arnauld** (1560–1619) was a Parisian advocate, strongly critical of the Jesuits; along with the

philospher Pascal and others, he produced not only Jansenist pamphlets, but works on logic, grammar, and geometry. Many of his 20 children were associated with the abbey of Port Royal, a convent of Cistercian nuns near Versailles which became the centre of Jansenism. His youngest child, **Antoine** (1612–94), the 'great Arnauld', was religious director there.

Arne /ɑ:n/ Thomas Augustus 1710–1778. English composer, whose musical drama *Alfred* 1740 includes the song 'Rule Britannia!'.

Arnhem, Battle of /'ɑ:nəm/ in World War II, an airborne operation by the Allies, 17–26 Sept 1944, to secure a bridgehead over the Rhine, thereby opening the way for a thrust towards the Ruhr and a possible early end to the war. It was only partly successful, with 7,600 casualties. Arnhem is a city in the Netherlands, on the Rhine SE of Utrecht; population (1988) 297,000. It produces salt, chemicals, and pharmaceuticals.

arnica /'ɑ:nɪkə/ n. a composite plant of the genus *Arnica*, with yellow flowers; a substance prepared from this, formerly used to treat bruises.

Arnim /'ɑ:nɪm/ Ludwig Achim von 1781–1831. German Romantic poet and novelist. Born in Berlin, he wrote short stories, a romance (*Gräfin Dolores/Countess Dolores* 1810), and plays, but left the historical novel *Die Kronenwächter* 1817 unfinished. With Clemens Brentano he collected the German folk songs in *Des Knaben Wunderhorn/The Boy's Magic Horn* 1805–08.

Arnold /'ɑ:nld/ Benedict 1741–1801. US soldier and military strategist, who, during the American Revolution won the battle that marked the turning point at Saratoga in 1777 for the Americans. He is chiefly remembered as a traitor to the American side. A merchant in New Haven, Connecticut, he joined the colonial forces but in 1780 plotted to betray the strategic post at West Point to the British.

Arnold Matthew 1822–1888. English poet and critic. His poems, characterized by their elegiac mood and pastoral themes, include *The Forsaken Merman* 1849, *Thyrsis* 1867 (commemorating his friend Arthur Hugh Clough), and *The Scholar Gypsy* 1853. Arnold's critical works include *Essays in Criticism* 1865 and 1888, and *Culture and Anarchy* 1869, which attacks 19th-century philistinism.

aroma /ə'rəʊmə/ n. a smell, especially a pleasant one. [Latin from Greek = spice]

aromatherapy n. the use of aromatic essential oils to relieve tension or to induce a feeling of wellbeing, usually in combination with massage. It is also used to relieve minor skin complaints. Common in the Middle East for centuries, the practice was reintroduced to the West in France during the 1960s.

aromatic /ærə'mætɪk/ adj. fragrant, having a pleasantly strong smell. —n. an aromatic substance. —**aromatically** adv. [from Old French from Latin from Greek]

aromatic compound any organic chemical that incorporates a ◊benzene ring in its structure (see also ◊cyclic compounds). Aromatic compounds undergo chemical substitution reactions.

arose /ə'rəʊz/ v.i. past of **arise**.

around /ə'raʊnd/ adv. 1. on every side, all round; here and there. 2. (*colloquial*) near at hand. —*prep.* 1. on or along the circuit of; on every side of. 2. about, (*US*) approximately at.

arouse /ə'raʊz/ v.t. to rouse; to induce.

Arp /ɑ:p/ Hans or Jean 1887–1966. French abstract painter and sculptor. He was one of the founders of the ◊Dada movement in about 1917, and was associated with the Surrealists. His wood sculptures use organic shapes in bright colours.

arpeggio /ɑ:'pedʒɪəʊ/ n. (*plural* **arpeggios**) the sounding of the notes of a chord in succession; a chord so played. [Italian *arpa* = harp]

arrack /'ærək/ n. a kind of alcoholic spirit, especially that made from coco sap or rice. [from Arabic 'arak]

arraign /ə'reɪn/ v.t. to indict, to accuse; to find fault with (an action or statement), to challenge. —**arraignment** n. [from Anglo-French from Latin *ratio* = reason]

arrange /ə'reɪndʒ/ v.t./i. 1. to put into the required order, to adjust or place. 2. to plan or prepare; to take measures or give instructions. 3. to adapt, especially (music) for performance with different instruments or voices. **—arrangement** *n.* [from Old French *à* = to and *rangier* = range]

arranger *n.* in music, a person who adapts the music of another composer. In film and musical theatre, an assistant in orchestrating a composer's piano score.

arrant /'ærənt/ *adj.* downright, utter. [variant of *errant*, originally in *arrant* (= outlawed roving) *thief*]

arras /'ærəs/ *n.* a richly decorated tapestry or wall-hanging. [from *Arras*, town in France famous in the 13th–16th centuries for tapestry weaving]

Arras, Battle of battle of World War I, April–May 1917. It was an effective but costly British attack on German forces in support of a French offensive, which was only partially successful, on the ◊Siegfried Line. British casualties totalled 84,000 as compared to 75,000 German casualties. In World War II the town of Arras was captured in 1940 by the Germans in their advance on Dunkirk.

Arras, Congress and Treaty of a meeting in N France in 1435 between representatives of Henry VI of England, Charles VII of France, and Philip the Good of Burgundy to settle the Hundred Years' War. The outcome was a diplomatic victory for France. Although England refused to compromise on Henry VI's claim to the French crown, France signed a peace treaty with Burgundy, England's former ally.

array /ə'reɪ/ *n.* an imposing series, a display; an ordered arrangement. **—***v.t.* to arrange in order, to marshal (forces). [from Anglo-French from Latin]

arrears /ə'rɪəz/ *n.* the amount that is still outstanding or uncompleted, especially of a debt or of work to be done. **—in arrears**, not paid or done when it was due. [from Old French from Latin *retro* = backwards]

arrest /ə'rest/ *v.t.* **1.** to seize (a person) by the authority of the law. **2.** to stop or check (a movement or process). **3.** to catch and hold (attention). **—***n.* **1.** an act of arresting, legal seizure of a person to stop commission of a crime or to charge someone with violation of a criminal or civil law. **2.** a stoppage. **—arrester** *n.*, **arrestor** *n.* [from Old French from Latin *restare* = remain]

arrestable /ə'restəbəl/ *adj.* (of an offence) such that the offender may be arrested without a warrant.

arrhythmia *n.* disturbance of the natural rhythm of the heart. There are various kinds of arrhythmia, some harmless, some indicative of heart disease.

arrière-pensée /ærieər'pɑ̃seɪ/ *n.* an ulterior motive; a mental reservation. [French = behind thought]

arris /'ærɪs/ *n.* the sharp edge formed where two surfaces meet to form an angle, especially in architecture. [from French *areste* = *arête*]

arrival /ə'raɪvəl/ *n.* **1.** arriving, appearance on the scene. **2.** a person or thing that has arrived.

arrive /ə'raɪv/ *v.i.* **1.** to reach a destination or a certain point on a journey. **2.** (of a time) to come. **3.** to be recognized as having achieved success in the world. **4.** (*colloquial,* of a baby) to be born. **—arrive at**, to reach (a decision or conclusion). [from Old French from Latin *ripa* = shore]

arrivisie /æri'viːst/ *n.* a person ruthlessly and obsessively aspiring to advancement. [French *arriver* = arrive]

arrogant /'ærəgənt/ *adj.* proud and overbearing through an exaggerated feeling of one's superiority. **—arrogance** *n.*, **arrogantly** *adv.* [from Old French]

arrogate /'ærəgeɪt/ *v.t.* **1.** to claim or seize without right. **2.** to attribute unjustly. **—arrogation** /-'geɪʃən/ *n.* [from Latin *rogare* = ask]

arrow /'ærəʊ/ *n.* a straight, thin, pointed shaft to be shot from a bow; a representation of this, especially to show direction. [Old English]

arrowhead /'ærəʊhed/ *n.* the pointed tip of an arrow.

arrowroot /'ærəʊruːt/ *n.* a starchy substance derived from the roots and tubers of various tropical plants with thick, clumpy roots. The true arrowroot *Maranta arundinacea* was used by the Indians of South America as an antidote against the effects of poisoned arrows.

arse *n.* (*vulgar*) the buttocks. [Old English]

arsenal /'ɑːsənəl/ *n.* a place where weapons and ammunition are stored or manufactured. [French or from Italian from Arabic = workshop]

arsenic /'ɑːsənɪk/ *n.* **1.** a brittle, greyish-white, semi-metallic element (a metalloid), symbol As, atomic number 33, relative atomic mass 74.92. It occurs in many ores and occasionally in its elemental state, and is widely distributed,

being present in minute quantities in the soil, the sea, and the human body. In larger quantities, it is poisonous. **2.** (*popularly*) arsenic trioxide, its main commercial compound. **—arsenical** /ɑː'senɪkəl/ *adj.* [from Old French, ultimately from Persian *zar* = gold]

arson /'ɑːsən/ *n.* the deliberate and criminal act of setting fire to a house or other building. **—arsonist** *n.* [Anglo-French from Latin *ardēre* = burn]

art[1] *n.* **1.** human creative skill or its application; the branch of creative activity concerned with the production of imitative and imaginative designs and expression of ideas, especially in painting; products of this. **2.** any skill; a craft or activity requiring imaginative skill. **3.** (in *plural*) branches of learning (e. g. languages, literature, and history) requiring sympathetic understanding and creative skill as distinct from the technical skills of science. **4.** a specific ability, a knack. **5.** cunning, artfulness; a trick or stratagem. [from Old French from Latin *ars*]

art[2] *v.i.* (*archaic*) 2nd person singular present of ◊be.

Artaud /ɑː'təʊ/ Antonin 1896–1948. French theatre director. Although his play, *Les Cenci/The Cenci* 1935, was a failure, his concept of the **Theatre of Cruelty**, intended to release feelings usually repressed in the unconscious, has been an important influence on modern dramatists such as Albert Camus and Jean Genet and on directors and producers. Declared insane in 1936, Artaud was confined in an asylum.

> We must wash literature off ourselves. We want to be men first of all, to be human.
>
> **Antonin Artaud**
> *Les Oeuvres et les Hommes*

Art Deco /ɑːt 'dekəʊ/ a style in art and architecture that emerged in Europe in the 1920s and continued through the 1930s, using rather heavy, geometrical simplification of form: for example, Radio City Music Hall, New York. It was a self-consciously modern style, with sharp lines, and dominated the decorative arts. The graphic artist Erté (1893–1989) was a fashionable exponent.

artefact /'ɑːtɪfækt/ *n.* an object made by humans, especially a tool, weapon, or vessel as an archaeological item. [from Latin *arte* = by art and *facere* = make]

Artemis /'ɑːtəmɪs/ in Greek mythology, the goddess (Roman Diana) of chastity, the Moon, and the hunt. She is the sister of ◊Apollo. Her cult centre was at Ephesus.

arteriosclerosis /ɑːtɪərɪəʊsklɪə'rəʊsɪs/ *n.* hardening of the walls of arteries, so that blood circulation is hindered. It is associated with smoking, ageing, and a diet high in saturated fats.

artery /'ɑːtərɪ/ *n.* **1.** any of the flexible, elastic tubes conveying blood away from the heart to all parts of the body. Arteries consist of three layers, the middle of which is muscular; its rhythmic contraction aids the pumping of blood around the body. **2.** a main road or railway line. **—arterial** /ɑː'tɪərɪəl/ *adj.* [from Latin from Greek (probably from *airō* = raise)]

artesian well /ɑː'tiːʒən/ a well in which water rises to the surface by natural pressure through a vertically drilled hole. [from French *Artois*, an old province of France]

artful *adj.* crafty, cunningly clever at getting what one wants. **—artfully** *adv.*, **artfulness** *n.*

arthritis /ɑː'θraɪtɪs/ *n.* inflammation of the joints, with pain, swelling, and restricted motion. **—arthritic** /ɑː'θrɪtɪk/ *adj.* & *n.* [Latin from Greek *arthron* = joint]

arthropod /'ɑːθrəpɒd/ *n.* an animal of the phylum Arthropoda, with a segmented body and jointed limbs, and typically encased in a hard outer skeleton which is shed periodically and replaced as the animal grows. Included are arachnids such as spiders and mites, as well as crustaceans, millipedes, centipedes, and insects. [from Greek *arthron* = joint and *pous podos* = foot]

Arthur /'ɑːθə/ 6th century AD. Legendary English king and hero in stories of ◊Camelot and the quest for the ◊Holy Grail. Arthur is said to have been born in Tintagel, Cornwall, and buried in Glastonbury. He may have been a Romano-British leader against pagan Saxon invaders.

Arthur Chester Alan 1830–1886. 21st president of the USA. He was born in Vermont, the son of a Baptist

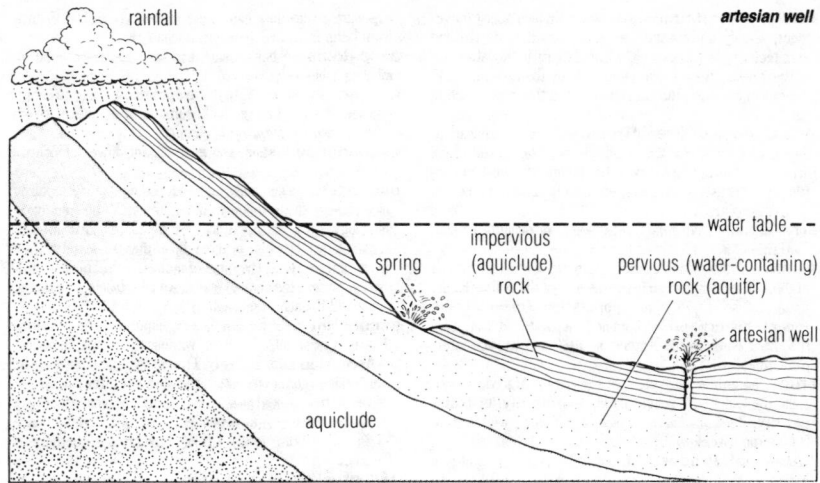

rainfall

artesian well

water table

spring

impervious
(aquiclude)
rock

pervious (water-containing)
rock (aquifer)

artesian well

aquiclude

minister, and became a lawyer and Republican political appointee in New York. In 1880, Arthur was chosen as ◊Garfield's vice president, and was his successor when Garfield was assassinated the following year. Arthur held office until 1885.

Arthur Duke of Brittany 1187–1203. Grandson of Henry II of England and nephew of King ◊John, who is supposed to have had him murdered on 13 April 1203 as a rival for the crown.

Arthur Prince of Wales 1486–1502. Eldest son of Henry VII of England. He married ◊Catherine of Aragon in 1501, when he was 16 and she was 15, but died the next year.

artichoke /ˈɑːtɪtʃəʊk/ *n.* two plants of the composite or sunflower family Compositae. The **common** or **globe artichoke** *Cynara scolymus* is tall, with purplish blue flowers; the bracts of the unopened flower are eaten. The **Jerusalem artichoke** *Helianthus tuberosus* is a kind of sunflower with edible tubers. [from Italian from Arabic; *Jerusalem* is a corruption of Italian *girasole* = sunflower]

article /ˈɑːtɪkəl/ *n.* **1.** a particular item or commodity. **2.** a short, self-contained piece of writing, in a newspaper, journal, etc., or in an encyclopedia. **3.** a clause or item of an agreement. **4.** the definite or indefinite article. (see below). —*v.t.* to bind by articles of apprenticeship. —**definite article**, 'the', **indefinite article**, 'a' or 'an' (or their equivalents in another language). [from Old French from Latin *articulus*, diminutive of *artus* = joint]

articular /ɑːˈtɪkjʊlə/ *adj.* of a joint or joints of the body. [from Latin]

articulate[1] /ɑːˈtɪkjʊlət/ *adj.* **1.** able to express oneself clearly and fluently. **2.** (of speech) spoken clearly, in words. **3.** having joints. —**articulacy** *n.*, **articulately** *adv.*, **articulateness** *n.* [from Latin *articulus*]

articulate[2] /ɑːˈtɪkjʊleɪt/ *v.t./i.* **1.** to speak or express clearly, to pronounce distinctly. **2.** to form a joint *with.* —**articulation** /-ˈleɪʃən/ *n.*

articulated /ɑːˈtɪkjʊleɪtɪd/ *adj.* with parts connected or divided by a (flexible) joint or joints.

artifice /ˈɑːtɪfɪs/ *n.* trickery, a piece of cunning; skill, ingenuity. [French from Latin *ars* = art and *facere* = make]

artificer /ɑːˈtɪfɪsə/ *n.* a skilled workman or mechanic. [from French]

artificial /ɑːtɪˈfɪʃəl/ *adj.* produced by human art or effort, not originating naturally; affected, insincere. —**artificiality** /-ʃɪˈælɪtɪ/ *n.*, **artificially** *adv.* [from Old French or Latin *ars* = art and *facere* = make]

artificial insemination (AI) mating achieved by mechanically injecting semen into the womb without genital contact. It is commonly used with cattle because it allows the farmer to select the type and quality of bull required for the herd, and to control the timing and organization of the breeding programme. The practice of artificially inseminating pigs has also become widespread in recent years.

artificial intelligence (AI) a branch of cognitive science concerned with creating computer programs that can perform actions comparable with those of an intelligent human. Current AI research covers areas such as planning (for robot behaviour), language understanding, pattern recognition, and knowledge representation.

artificial limb a device to replace a limb that has been removed by surgery or one that is malformed because of genetic defects. It is one form of ◊prosthesis.

artificial radioactivity radioactivity arising from human-made radioisotopes (radioactive isotopes or elements that are formed when elements are bombarded with subatomic particles—protons, neutrons, or electrons—or small nuclei).

artificial respiration manual or mechanical stimulation of breathing when the natural process is suspended. If breathing is permanently suspended, as in paralysis, an ◊iron lung is used; in cases of electric shock or apparent drowning, for example, the first choice is the expired-air method, the **kiss of life** by mouth-to-mouth breathing until natural breathing is resumed.

artificial selection in biology, selective breeding of individuals that exhibit particular characteristics that a plant or animal breeder wishes to develop. The development of particular breeds of cattle for improved meat production (such as the Aberdeen Angus) or milk production (such as Jerseys) are examples.

artillery /ɑːˈtɪlərɪ/ *n.* **1.** a collective term for military ◊firearms too heavy to be carried. Artillery can be mounted on ships or aeroplanes and includes cannons and missile launchers. **2.** a branch of an army equipped with these. —**artilleryman** *n.* [from Old French *artiller* = equip]

artisan /ɑːtɪˈzæn, ˈɑː-/ *n.* a skilled worker, a mechanic. [French from Italian from Latin *artire* = instruct in arts]

artist /ˈɑːtɪst/ *n.* **1.** one who practises any of the fine arts, especially painting. **2.** one who does something with skill or taste. **3.** an artiste. —**artistry** *n.* [from French from Italian *arte* = art]

artiste /ɑːˈtiːst/ *n.* a professional performer, especially a singer or dancer. [French]

artistic /ɑːˈtɪstɪk/ *adj.* of art or artists; skilfully or tastefully done; showing aptitude for the fine arts. —**artistically** *adv.*

artless /ˈɑːtlɪs/ *adj.* **1.** free from artfulness, ingenuous. **2.** not resulting from art, natural. **3.** crude, clumsy. —**artlessly** *adv.*, **artlessness** *n.*

Art Nouveau /ɑː nuːˈvəʊ/ an art style of about 1890–1910 in Europe, marked by sinuous lines and stylized flowers and foliage. Also called *Jugendstil* (Germany), *Stile Liberty* (Italy, after the fashionable London department store). Exponents included the illustrator Aubrey Beardsley, the architect and furniture designer Charles Rennie Mackintosh, and the glass and jewellery designer René Lalique. [French = new art]

Arts and Crafts movement an English social movement, largely anti-machine in spirit, based in design and architecture and founded by William Morris in the latter half of the 19th century. It was supported by the architect A W Pugin and by ◊John Ruskin and stressed the importance of hand crafting.

Arts Council of Great Britain a UK arts organization, incorporated in 1945, which aids music, drama, and visual arts with government funds. It has bought the work of contemporary artists since 1942, effectively acting as a patron of promising artists.

arty /'ɑːtɪ/ adj. (colloquial) pretentiously or quaintly artistic. —**artiness** n.

Aruba /ə'ruːbə/ island in the Caribbean, the westernmost of the Lesser Antilles; an overseas part of the Netherlands; **area** 193 sq km/75 sq mi; **population** (1985) 61,000; **recent history** Aruba obtained separate status from the other Netherlands Antilles in 1986 and has full internal autonomy.

arum /'eərəm/ n. any plant of the family Araceae, especially the Old World genus *Arum*. —**arum lily**, or **trumpet lily**, *Zantedeschia aethiopica*, a cultivated white arum. [Latin from Greek *aron*]

Arunachal Pradesh /ɑːrə'nɑːtʃəl prɑː'deʃ/ state of India, in the Himalayas on the borders of Tibet and Myanmar (formerly Burma); **area** 83,600 sq km/32,270 sq mi; **capital** Itanagar; **products** rubber, coffee, spices, fruit, timber; **population** (1981) 628,000; **language** 50 different dialects; **recent history** formerly nominally part of Assam, it became a state in 1986.

Arvand River /ɑː'vɑːnd/ Iranian name for the ◊Shatt al-Arab waterway.

Aryan /'eəriən/ adj. **1.** of the Indo-European family of languages. **2.** of the ancient inhabitants of the Iranian plateau speaking a language of this family. —n. **1.** a member of the Aryan peoples. They are believed to have lived between Central Asia and E Europe, and to have reached Persia and India in one direction and Europe in another sometime in the 2nd century BC. **2.** any of the languages of the Aryan peoples of India; a 19th-century name for the ◊Indo-European languages. **3.** (in Nazi Germany) a non-Jewish European, a person of Nordic racial type. [from Sanskrit *āryas* = noble, earlier used as a national name]

Arya Samaj /'ɑːriə sə'mɑːdʒ/ a Hindu religious sect founded by Dayanand Saraswati (1825–88) in about 1875. He renounced idol-worship and urged a return to the purer principles of the Vedas (Hindu scriptures). For its time the movement was quite revolutionary in its social teachings, which included forbidding ◊caste practices, prohibiting child-marriage, and allowing widows to remarry.

as /əz, emphatic æz/ adv. & conj. **1.** to the same extent; in the manner in which; in the capacity or form of; for instance. **2.** during or at the time of. **3.** for the reason that, seeing that. — rel. pron. that, who, which. —**as from,** on or after (a specified date). **as if,** as would be the case if. **as it were,** as if it was actually so, in a way. **as of,** as from, as at (a specified time). **as though,** as if. **as to,** with regard to. **as well,** advisable, desirable, reasonably. **as well (as),** in addition (to). **as yet,** until now. [from Old English *alswā* = also]

As symbol for arsenic.

ASA n. in photography, a numbering system for rating the speed of films, devised by the American Standards Association. It has now been superseded by ◊ISO, the International Standards Organization.

asafoetida /æsə'fiːtɪdə/ n. a resinous, strong-smelling plant gum formerly used in medicine. [Latin from Persian *azā* = mastic and *fetida* = fetid]

Asante /ə'ʃæntɪ/ n. or **Ashanti,** a person of Asante culture from central Ghana, W of Lake Volta. The Asante language belongs to the Kwa branch of the Niger-Congo family.

a.s.a.p. abbreviation of as soon as possible.

ASAT acronym from antisatellite weapon.

asbestos /æs'bestɒs/ n. any of several related minerals of fibrous structure that offer great heat resistance because of their nonflammability and poor conductivity. Commercial asbestos is generally made from chrysolite, a ◊serpentine mineral, tremolite (a white ◊amphibole) and riebeckite (a blue amphibole, also known as crocidolite when in its fibrous form). Asbestos usage is now strictly controlled because exposure to its dust can cause cancer. [from Old French from Latin from Greek = unquenchable]

asbestosis /æsbes'təʊsɪs/ n. a lung disease caused by inhaling asbestos particles.

ascend /ə'send/ v.t./i. to move upwards, to rise; to climb. —**ascend the throne,** to become king or queen. [from Latin *ascendere* (*scandere* = climb)]

ascendancy /ə'sendənsɪ/ n. dominant power or control (*over*).

ascendant /ə'sendənt/ adj. ascending, rising; gaining ascendancy; in astronomy, rising towards the zenith; in astrology, (of a sign) just above the eastern horizon. —n. in astrology, the point of the ecliptic that is ascendant at a given time, e. g. at the birth of a child. —**in the ascendant,** at or near the peak of one's fortunes; (*popularly*) rising. [from Old French from Latin]

ascension /ə'senʃən/ n. ascent, especially (**Ascension**) that of Christ into Heaven, witnessed by the apostles. —**Ascension Day** or **Holy Thursday,** the Thursday on which this is commemorated, the 40th day after Easter.

Ascension /ə'senʃən/ British island of volcanic origin in the S Atlantic, a dependency of ◊St Helena since 1922; population (1982) 1,625. The chief settlement is Georgetown.

ascent /ə'sent/ n. **1.** ascending; rise. **2.** a way up, an upward path or slope.

ascertain /æsə'teɪn/ v.t. to find out for certain, especially by making enquiries. **ascertainable** adj., **ascertainment** n. [from Old French]

ascetic /ə'setɪk/ adj. severely abstinent, austere; having the appearance of an ascetic. —n. a person leading an ascetic life, especially one doing this in a religious cause. —**ascetically** adv., **asceticism** /-ɪsɪzəm/ n. [from Latin or from Greek *askētēs* = monk and *askeō* = exercise]

Ascham /'æskəm/ Roger c.1515–1568. English scholar and royal tutor, author of *The Scholemaster* 1570 on the art of education.

ascidian /ə'sɪdɪən/ n. a tunicate of the order Ascidiacea, especially a sea-squirt. [from Greek, diminutive of *askos* = wineskin]

ASCII /'æskɪ/ acronym from American Standard Code for Information Interchange. In computing, a coding system in which numbers (between 0 and 127) are assigned to letters, digits, and punctuation symbols. For example, 45 represents a hyphen and 65 a capital A. The system is widely used for the storage of text and for the transmission of data between computers.

ascorbic acid /ə'skɔːbɪk/ or **vitamin C** a relatively simple organic acid found in fresh fruits and vegetables. It is soluble in water and destroyed by prolonged boiling. Lack of ascorbic acid results in scurvy. [from Greek]

ascribable /ə'skraɪbəbəl/ adj. that may be ascribed.

ascribe /ə'skraɪb/ v.t. to attribute. **ascription** /-'skrɪpʃən/ n. [from Latin *scribere* = write]

asdic /'æzdɪk/ n. an early form of sonar. [acronym from Anti-Submarine Detection Investigation Committee]

ASEAN acronym from ◊Association of South East Asian Nations.

asepsis /eɪ'sepsɪs/ n. aseptic methods or conditions (see ◊antiseptic). [from Greek *a*- = not and *sepsis*]

aseptic /eɪ'septɪk/ adj. free from sepsis, especially that caused by microorganisms, surgically sterile; aiming at the absence rather than the counteraction (compare ◊antiseptic) of septic matter. —**aseptically** adv. [from Greek *a*- = not and *septic*]

asexual /eɪ'seksjuəl/ adj. without sex or sexuality; of ◊reproduction not involving the fusion of gametes, —**asexually** adv. [from Greek]

Asgard /'zgɑːd/ in Scandinavian mythology, the place where the gods lived. It was reached by a bridge called Bifrost, the rainbow.

ash[1] n. (frequently in *plural*) the whitish grey powdery residue left after combustion of any substance; (in *plural*) the remains of a human body after cremation. [Old English]

ash[2] n. a tree of the genus *Fraxinus* with silver-grey bark and pinnate foliage with winged fruits, belonging to the olive family Oleaceae. *F. excelsior* is the European species; its timber is of importance. The ◊mountain ash or rowan *Sorbus aucuparia* belongs to the family Rosaceae. [Old English]

ashamed /ə'ʃeɪmd/ adj. (usually predicative) feeling or affected by shame; reluctant or hesitant through shame. [Old English]

Ashbee /'æʃbi/ C(harles) R(obert) 1863–1942. British designer, architect, and writer, one of the major figures of the ◊Arts and Crafts movement. He founded a Guild and School of Handicraft in the East End of London in 1888, but later modified his views, accepting the importance of machinery and design for industry.

ashbin n. a dustbin.

Ashcan school a group of US painters active about 1908–14, also known as the **Eight**. Members included Robert Henri (1865–1929), George Luks (1867–1933), William Glackens (1870–1938), Everett Shinn (1876–1953), and John Sloan (1871–1951). Their style is realist; their subjects centered on city life, the poor, and the outcast. They organized the Armoury Show of 1913, which introduced modern European art to the USA.

Ashcroft /'æʃkrɒft/ Peggy 1907–1991. English actress. Her many leading roles include Desdemona in Othello (with Paul Robeson), Juliet in Romeo and Juliet 1935 (with Laurence Olivier and John Gielgud), and appearances in the British TV play Caught on a Train 1980 (BAFTA award), the series The Jewel in the Crown 1984 and the film A Passage to India 1985.

Ashdown /'æʃdaʊn/ Paddy (Jeremy John Durham) 1941– . English politician. Originally a Liberal MP, he became leader of the Social and Liberal Democrats in 1988. He served in the Royal Marines as a commando, leading a Special Boat Section in Borneo, and was a member of the Diplomatic Service 1971–76.

Ashe /æʃ/ Arthur Robert, Jr 1943– . US tennis player and coach. He won the US national men's singles title at Forest Hills and the first US Open in 1968. Known for his exceptionally strong serve, Ashe turned professional in 1969. He won the Australian men's title in 1970 and Wimbledon in 1975.

ashen adj. of or like ashes, pale as ashes.

Ashes, the a trophy for the winner of a series of test matches in cricket between England and Australia. It is an urn containing the ashes of stumps and bails used in a match when England toured Australia 1882–83.

Ashkenazi /æʃkə'nɑːzɪ/ n. (plural **Ashkenazim**) a Jew of German or E European descent, as opposed to a Sephardi, of Spanish, Portuguese, or N African descent.

Ashkenazy /æʃkə'nɑːzi/ Vladimir 1937– . Soviet-born pianist and conductor. His keyboard technique differs slightly from standard Western technique. In 1962 he was joint winner of the Tchaikovsky Competition with John Ogdon. He excels in Rachmaninov, Prokofiev, and Liszt.

Ashkhabad /æʃkə'bæd/ capital of Republic of Turkmen, USSR; population (1987) 382,000. 'Bukhara' carpets are made here.

ashlar /'æʃlə/ n. square-hewn stones, masonry made of these; thin slabs of this used for facing walls. [from Old French from Latin, diminutive of axis = board]

Ashley /'æʃli/ Laura (born Mountney) 1925–1985. Welsh designer, who established and gave her name to a Neo-Victorian country style in clothes and furnishings beginning in 1953. She founded an international chain of shops.

Ashmole /'æʃməʊl/ Elias 1617–1692. English antiquary, whose collection forms the basis of the Ashmolean Museum, Oxford.

ashore /ə'ʃɔː/ adv. to or on shore; on land.

ashram n. (in India etc.) a place of religious learning or retreat; a community whose members lead a simple life of discipline and self-denial and devote themselves to social service. Noted ashrams are those founded by Mahatma Gandhi at Wardha and the poet Rabindranath Tagore at Santiniketan. [from Sanskrit = hermitage]

Ashton /'æʃtən/ Frederick 1904–1988. British dancer and choreographer. He studied with Léonid Massine and Marie Rambert before joining the Vic-Wells Ballet in 1935 as chief choreographer, creating several roles for Margot Fonteyn. He was director of the Royal Ballet, London, 1963–70.

ashtray n. a receptacle for tobacco ash.

Ash Wednesday the first day of Lent, the period in the Christian calendar leading up to Easter; in the Roman Catholic church the foreheads of the congregation are marked with a cross in ash, as a sign of penitence.

ashy adj. like ash, ashen; covered with ashes.

Asia /'eɪʃə/ largest of the continents, forming the E part of Eurasia to the E of the Ural mountains, one third of the total land surface of the world; **area** 44,000,000 sq km/17,000,000 sq mi; **largest cities** (population over 5 million) Tokyo, Shanghai, Osaka, Beijing, Seoul, Calcutta, Bombay, Jakarta, Bangkok, Tehran, Hong Kong; **physical** five main divisions: (1) central triangular mountain mass, including the Himalayas; to the N the great Tibetan plateau, bounded by the Kunlun mountains, N of which lie further ranges and the Gobi Desert; (2) the SW plateaux and ranges, forming Afghanistan, Baluchistan, Iran; (3) the N lowlands, from the central mountains to the Arctic Ocean, much of which is frozen for several months each year; (4) the E margin and islands; (5) the S plateau and river plains, including Arabia, the Deccan, and the alluvial plains of the Euphrates, Tigris, Indus, Ganges, and Irrawaddy. The climate shows great extremes and contrasts, the heart of the continent becoming bitterly cold in winter and very hot in summer. This accounts for the Asiatic monsoons, bringing heavy rain to all SE Asia, China, and Japan, between May and Oct; **population** (1984) 3,000 million, the most densely populated of the continents; **language** predominantly tonal languages, (Chinese), in the E, Indo-Iranian languages in central India and Pakistan (Hindi/Urdu), Semitic (Arabic) in the SW.

Asia Minor /'eɪʃə 'maɪnə/ historical name for **Anatolia**, the Asian part of Turkey.

Asian /'eɪʃən, 'eɪʒ-/ adj. of the continent of Asia. —n. an Asian person. [from Latin from Greek]

Asian Development Bank (ADB) a bank founded in 1966 to stimulate growth in Asia and the Far East by administering direct loans and technical assistance. Members include 30 countries within the region and 14 countries of W Europe and North America. The headquarters are in Manila, Philippines.

Asia-Pacific Economic Cooperation Conference (APEC) a trade group comprising 12 Pacific Asian countries, formed in Nov 1898 to promote multilateral trade and economic cooperation between member states. Its members are the USA, Canada, Japan, Australia, New Zealand, South Korea, Brunei, Indonesia, Malaysia, the Phillipines, Singapore, and Thailand.

Asiatic /eɪzi'ætɪk/ adj. of Asia.

aside /ə'saɪd/ adv. to or on one side, away from the main part or group. —n. words spoken aside.

Asiento, Treaty of an agreement between the UK and Spain in 1713, whereby British traders were permitted to introduce 144,000 black slaves into the Spanish-American colonies in the course of the following 30 years. In 1750 the right was bought out by the Spanish government for $100,000.

Asimov /'æzɪmɒf/ Isaac 1920– . US science-fiction writer and writer on science, born in the USSR. He has published about 200 books, and is possibly best known for his I, Robot 1950 and the 'Foundation' trilogy 1951–53, continued in Foundation's Edge 1983.

asinine /'æsɪnaɪn/ adj. like an ass, silly, stupid. —**asininity** /-'nɪnɪtɪ/ n. [from Latin asinus = ass]

ask /ɑːsk/ v.t./i. 1. to call for an answer to or about, to address a question to. 2. to seek to obtain from someone. 3. to invite. [Old English]

askance /ə'skæns/ adv. with a sideways look. —**look askance at**, to regard with distrust or disapproval.

askew /ə'skjuː/ adv. & pred. adj. not straight or level, oblique(ly).

aslant /ə'slɑːnt/ adv. on a slant, obliquely. —prep. obliquely across.

asleep /ə'sliːp/ pred. adj. sleeping; (of a limb etc.) numb. —adv. into a state of sleep.

AS Level General Certificate of Education. Advanced Supplementary examinations introduced in the UK in 1988 as the equivalent to 'half an ◊A Level' as a means of broadening the sixth form (age 16–18) curriculum, and including more students in the examination system.

Asmara /æs'mɑːrə/ or **Asmera** capital of Eritrea, Ethiopia; 64 km/40 mi SW of Massawa on the Red Sea; population (1984) 275,385. Products include beer, clothes, and textiles. In 1974, unrest here precipitated the end of the Ethiopian Empire. It has a naval school.

asocial /eɪsəʊʃəl/ adj. not social; not sociable; (colloquial) inconsiderate. [from Greek a- = not and social]

Asoka /ə'səukə/ lived *c.*273–238 BC. Indian emperor, who was a Buddhist convert. He had edicts enjoining the adoption of his new faith carved on pillars and rock faces throughout his dominions, and many survive, among the oldest deciphered texts in India. In Patna there are the remains of a hall built by him.

asp *n.* any of several venomous snakes, including *Vipera aspis* of S Europe, allied to the adder, and the Egyptian cobra *Naja haje*, reputed to have been used by the Egyptian queen Cleopatra for her suicide. [from Old French or Latin from Greek]

asparagus /ə'spærəgəs/ *n.* a plant of the genus *Asparagus*, especially a species (*A. officinalis*) whose young shoots are cooked and eaten as a vegetable; this food. [Latin from Greek]

Aspasia /ə'speɪzɪə/ *c.*440 BC. Greek courtesan, the mistress of the Athenian politician ◊Pericles. As a 'foreigner' from Miletus, she could not be recognized as his wife, but their son was later legitimized. The philosopher Socrates visited her salon, a meeting place for the celebrities of Athens. Her free thinking led to a charge of impiety, from which Pericles had to defend her.

aspect /'æspekt/ *n.* **1.** a person's or thing's appearance, especially to the mind, a feature by which a matter is considered. **2.** the direction a thing faces, the side of a building etc. facing a particular direction. **3.** in astrology, the relative position of planets etc., regarded as influencing events. [from Latin *adspicere* = look at]

aspen *n.* any of several species of ◊poplar tree, genus *Populus*. The quaking aspen *P. tremula* has flattened leaf-stalks that cause the leaves to flutter with every breeze. [Old English (earlier *asp*)]

asperity /ə'sperɪtɪ/ *n.* harshness of temper or tone. [from Old French or Latin *asper* = rough]

aspersion /ə'spɜːʃən/ *n.* a damaging or derogatory remark. —**cast aspersions on,** to attack the reputation of. [from Latin *aspergere* = sprinkle]

asphalt /'æsfælt/ *n.* a tarlike bitumen made from petroleum; a mixture of this with sand and gravel for use in paving etc. —*v.t.* to coat or pave with asphalt. [from Latin from Greek]

asphodel /'æsfədel/ *n.* either of two related Old World genera (*Asphodeline* and *Asphodelus*) of plants of the lily family Liliaceae. *Asphodelus albus*, the white asphodel or king's spear, is found in Italy and Greece; *Asphodeline lutea* is the yellow asphodel. In poetry, an immortal flower growing in Elysium. [from Latin from Greek]

asphyxia /æs'fɪksɪə/ *n.* lack of oxygen in the blood through impaired respiration, causing unconsciousness or death; suffocation. [from Greek *a-* = not and *sphuxis* = pulse]

asphyxiate /æs'fɪksɪeɪt/ *v.t./i.* to cause asphyxia in; to suffocate. —**asphyxiation** /-'eɪʃən/ *n.*

aspic /'æspɪk/ *n.* a savoury jelly for holding meat, fish, egg, etc. [French = asp (the colours of the jelly being compared to those of the asp)]

aspidistra /æspɪ'dɪstrə/ *n.* an Asiatic plant of the genus *Aspidistra*, with broad tapering leaves, often grown as a house plant. [from Greek *aspis* = shield]

aspirant /'æspɪrənt, ə'spaɪər-/ *n.* one who aspires, especially to an honour or position. —*adj.* aspiring. [French or from Latin]

aspirate[1] /'æspɪreɪt/ *v.t.* **1.** to pronounce with an initial *h* or with release of breath. **2.** to draw (fluid) by suction from a cavity etc. [from Latin]

aspirate[2] /'æspərət/ *n.* the sound of *h*; a consonant pronounced with this. —*adj.* pronounced with an aspirate.

aspiration /æspə'reɪʃən/ *n.* **1.** ambition, strong desire. **2.** aspirating. **3.** the drawing of breath.

aspirator /'æspəreɪtə/ *n.* a device for drawing fluid from a cavity etc.

aspire /ə'spaɪə/ *v.i.* to have an ambition or strong desire. [from French or Latin *adspirare* = breathe upon]

aspirin /'æspərɪn/ *n.* a white powder, acetylsalicylic acid, used to relieve pain and reduce fever; a tablet of this. Aspirin is derived from the white willow tree *Salix alba*. [German]

asplenium *n.* a fern of the family Aspleniaceae, generally known as spleenwort.

Asplund /'æsplənd/ (Erik) Gunnar 1885–1940. Swedish architect. His early work, for example at the Stockholm

South Cemetery (1914), was in the Neo-Classical tradition. Later buildings, such as the Stockholm City Library (1924–27) and Gothenburg City Hall (1934–37), developed a refined Modern-Classical style, culminating in the Stockholm South Cemetery Crematorium (1935–40).

Asquith /'æskwɪθ/ Herbert Henry, 1st Earl of Oxford and Asquith 1852–1928. British Liberal politician, prime minister 1908–16. As chancellor of the Exchequer he introduced old-age pensions in 1908. He limited the powers of the House of Lords and attempted to give Ireland Home Rule.

One to mislead the public, another to mislead the Cabinet, and the third to mislead itself.
   Herbert Henry Asquith, 1st Earl of Oxford
(on the reason for the War Office's keeping three sets of figures) quoted in Alastair Horne,
The Price of Glory

---

ass[1] *n.* **1.** a quadruped of the horse genus *Equus* with long ears, a tufted tail and characteristic bray. Donkeys and burros are domesticated asses. The donkey was regarded in ancient times as the embodiment of lust quite as much as stupidity. **2.** a stupid person. [Old English from Latin *asinus*]

ass[2] *n.* (*US, vulgar*) = ◊arse.

Assad /'æsæd/ Hafez al 1930– . Syrian Ba'athist politician, president from 1971. He became prime minister after the bloodless military coup in 1970, and the following year was the first president to be elected by popular vote. Having suppressed dissent, he was re-elected in 1978 and 1985. He is a Shia (Alawite) Muslim.

assail /ə'seɪl/ *v.t.* **1.** to attack physically or verbally. **2.** to begin (a task) resolutely. —**assailant** *n.* [from Old French from Latin *assilire* (*salire* = leap)]

Assam /æ'sæm/ state of NE India; **area** 78,400 sq km/ 30,262 sq mi; **capital** Dispur; **products** tea, oil, rice, jute, sugar, cotton, coal; **population** (1981) 19,903,000, including 12 million Assamese, 5 million Bengalis, Nepális, and 2,000,000 native people; **recent history** after Burmese invasion in 1826, Britain took control; made it a separate province in 1874; included in the Dominion of India, except for most of the Muslim district of Silhet, which went to Pakistan in 1947. Ethnic unrest started in the 1960s when Assamese was declared the official language. The Gara, Khasi, and Jainitia districts became the state of ◊Meghalaya in 1971; the Mizo district became the Union Territory of Mizoram in 1972. There were massacres of Muslim Bengalis by Hindus in 1983. In 1987 members of Bodo ethnic group began fighting for a separate homeland.

assassin /ə'sæsɪn/ *n.* **1.** one who assassinates another. **2. Assassin,** any of a number of Muslim fanatics in the time of the Crusades, notorious for a series of killings of political and religious opponents. [ultimately from Arabic (*plural*) = hashish-takers, so called because they acted as if crazed by hashish]

assassinate /ə'sæsɪneɪt/ *v.t.* to kill (an important person) by violent means, usually for political or religious motives. —**assassination** /-'neɪʃən/ *n.*, **assassinator** *n.*

assault /ə'sɔːlt/ *n.* a violent physical or verbal attack; (*euphemism*) rape; in law, a threat or display of violence against a person. The kinds of criminal assault are common (ordinary); aggravated (more serious, such as causing actual bodily harm); or indecent (of a sexual nature). —*v.t.* to make an assault on, to attack. [from Old French from Latin *assilire* (*salire* = leap)]

assault ship a naval vessel designed to land and support troops and vehicles under hostile conditions.

assay /ə'seɪ/ *n.* a test of metal or ore to determine its ingredients and quality. —*v.t./i.* **1.** to make an assay of (metal). **2.** (*archaic*) to attempt. [from Old French, variant of *essai* = essay]

assegai /'æsɪgaɪ/ *n.* a light, iron-tipped spear of South African peoples. [from French or Portuguese from Arabic = the spear]

assemblage /ə'semblɪdʒ/ *n.* **1.** coming together. **2.** an assembly; things assembled.

assemble /ə'sembəl/ *v.t./i.* to bring or come together; to fit or put (components, or a completed whole) together.

—**assembler** *n.* [from Old French from Latin *ad* = to and *simul* = together]

assembly /ə'semblɪ/ *n.* **1.** assembling. **2.** an assembled group; a deliberative body. —**assembly line,** machinery arranged in a sequence by which a product is progressively assembled; a method of mass production.

assembly code a computer-programming language closely related to the internal codes of the machine itself. It consists chiefly of a set of short mnemonics which are translated, by a program called an assembler, into ◊machine code for the computer's ◊CPU (central processing unit) to follow directly. In assembly language, for example, JMP means 'jump' and LDA is 'load accumulator'. It is used by programmers who need to write very fast or efficient programs.

assent /ə'sent/ *n.* (official) consent or approval. —*v.i.* to express agreement, to consent. —**assenter** *n.* [from Old French from Latin *assentari* (*sentire* = think)]

assert /ə'sɜ:t/ *v.t.* **1.** to declare as true, to state. **2.** to enforce a claim to (rights). —**assert oneself,** to insist on one's rights or recognition; to take effective action. —**assertion** *n.,* **assertive** *adj.* [from Latin *serere* = join]

assess /ə'ses/ *v.t.* to estimate the value of (property) for taxation; to decide or fix the amount of (a tax, penalty, etc.). —**assessment** *n.* [from French from Latin *assidēre* = sit by]

assessor /ə'sesə/ *n.* **1.** one who assesses, especially for tax or insurance. **2.** one who advises a judge in court on technical matters. [from Old French from Latin = assistant judge]

asset /'æset/ *n.* **1.** a possession having value; a useful quality, skill, or person. **2.** a business accounting term that covers the land or property of a company or individual, payments due from bills, investments, and anything else owned that can be turned into cash. On a company's balance sheet, total assets must be equal to liabilities (money and services owed). [from Anglo-French from Latin *ad* = to and *satis* = enough]

asseverate /ə'sevəreɪt/ *v.t.* to state solemnly. —**asseveration** /-'reɪʃən/ *n.* [from Latin *severus* = serious]

assiduous /ə'sɪdjuəs/ *adj.* persevering, working with diligence and close attention. —**assiduity** /æsi'dju:ɪtɪ/ *n.* **assiduously** *adv.,* **assiduousness** *n.* [from Latin *assidēre* = sit by]

assign /ə'saɪn/ *v.t.* to allot; to put aside or specify for a particular purpose; to designate; to ascribe or attribute; in law, to transfer formally. —**assignable** *adj.* [from Old French from Latin *assignare* = mark out to (*signum* =sign)]

assignation /æsɪg'neɪʃən/ *n.* **1.** an appointment to meet, especially by lovers in secret. **2.** assigning.

assignment /ə'saɪnmənt/ *n.* **1.** a thing assigned, especially a task or duty; a share. **2.** assigning.

assimilate /ə'sɪmɪleɪt/ *v.t./i.* **1.** to absorb or become absorbed. **2.** to make alike or similar (*to*). —**assimilable** *adj.,* **assimilation** /-'leɪʃən/ *n.* [from Latin *assimilare* (*similis* = like)]

assist /ə'sɪst/ *v.t./i.* to help. —**assistance** *n.* [from French from Latin *assistere* = take one's stand by]

assistant /ə'sɪstənt/ *n.* one who assists, a helper; one who serves customers in a shop. — *adj.* assisting, helping a senior and ranking next below him or her.

assize *n.* in medieval Europe, the passing of laws, either by the king with the consent of nobles, as in the Constitutions of ◊Clarendon of 1164 by Henry II, or as a complete system, such as the **Assizes of Jerusalem,** a compilation of the law of the feudal kingdom of Jerusalem in the 13th century.

assizes /ə'saɪzɪz/ *n.pl.* a periodical county session, held until 1972, for the administration of civil and criminal justice. [from French from Latin *assidēre* = sit by]

associate[1] /ə'səʊsɪeɪt, -ʃeɪt/ *v.t./i.* **1.** to connect in one's mind. **2.** to join as a companion or colleague etc.; to act together for a common purpose; to have frequent dealings (*with*). **3.** to declare (oneself) as being in agreement with. —**associative** *adj.* [from Latin *associare* (*socius* = sharing, allied)]

associate[2] /ə'səʊsɪət, -ʃiət/ *n.* **1.** a subordinate member of a society etc. **2.** a partner or colleague. —*adj.* **1.** associated. **2.** having subordinate membership.

association /əsəʊsɪ'eɪʃən, -ʃɪ-/ *n.* **1.** a body of persons organized for a common purpose. **2.** a mental connection of

ideas. **3.** associating, companionship. —**Association football,** see ◊football.

Association of Southeast Asian Nations (ASEAN) a regional alliance formed in Bangkok in 1967; it took over the nonmilitary role of the South East Asia Treaty Organization in 1975. Its members are Indonesia, Malaysia, the Philippines, Singapore, Thailand, and (from 1984) Brunei; its headquarters are in Jakarta, Indonesia.

associative law in mathematics, the law that states that the result of performing certain consecutive operations is independent of the order in which they are performed. Thus addition is associative because, for example $3 + (4 + 5)$ gives the same sum as $(3 + 4) + 5$. Multiplication is also associative: for example, $2 \times (3 \times 4)$ gives the same product as $(2 \times 3) \times 4$. Subtraction and division are not associative.

assonance /'æsənəns/ *n.* resemblance of sound between two syllables; a rhyme depending on identity in vowel sounds only (as *sonnet/porridge*) or in consonants only (as *killed/cold*). **assonant** *adj.,* **assonantal** /-'næntəl/ *adj.* [French from Latin *assonare* (*sonus* = sound)]

assort /ə'sɔ:t/ *v.t./i.* **1.** to arrange in sorts, to classify. **2.** to suit or harmonize (*with*). [from Old French *à* = to and *sorte* = sort]

assortative mating in ◊population genetics, selective mating in a population between individuals that are genetically related or have similar characteristics. If sufficiently consistent, assortative mating can theoretically result in the evolution of new species without geographical isolation (see ◊speciation).

assorted /ə'sɔ:tɪd/ *adj.* **1.** of various sorts, mixed. **2.** matched.

assortment /ə'sɔ:tmənt/ *n.* **1.** an assorted group or mixture. **2.** classification.

assuage /ə'sweɪdʒ/ *v.t.* to soothe, to make less severe; to appease (an appetite). —**assuagement** *n.* [from Old French from Latin *suavis* = sweet]

assume /ə'sju:m/ *v.t.* **1.** to take as true or sure to happen. **2.** to put on oneself (a role or attitude etc.); to undertake (an office). [from Latin *sumere* = take]

assuming /ə'sju:mɪŋ/ *adj.* presumptuous, arrogant.

assumption /ə'sʌmpʃən/ *n.* assuming, a thing assumed. —**the Assumption,** the taking of the Virgin Mary in bodily form into heaven; the festival commemorating this (15 Aug).

assurance /ə'ʃʊərəns/ *n.* **1.** a formal declaration or promise, a guarantee. **2.** self-confidence. **3.** certainty. **4.** insurance, especially of life. Insurance companies tend to use the term **assurance** of policies where a sum is payable after a fixed number of years or on the death of the insured person, and **insurance** of policies relating to events such as fire, accident, or death within a limited period. In popular usage the word 'insurance' is used in both cases.

assure /ə'ʃʊə/ *v.t.* **1.** to make (a person) sure (*of* a fact), to convince; to tell confidently. **2.** to ensure the happening etc. of, to guarantee. **3.** to insure (especially life). [from Old French from Latin *securus* = safe]

assured /ə'ʃʊəd/ *adj.* made sure; confident. —**assuredly** /-rɪdlɪ/ *adv.* certainly.

Assyria /ə'sɪrɪə/ empire in the Middle East *c.* 2500–612 BC, in N Mesopotamia (now Iraq); early capital Ashur, later Nineveh. It was initially subject to Sumer and intermittently to Babylon. The Assyrians adopted in the main the Sumerian religion and structure of society. At its greatest extent the empire included Egypt and stretched from the E Mediterranean coast to the head of the Persian Gulf.

Astaire /ə'steə/ Fred. 1899–1987. Stage name of Frederick Austerlitz. US dancer, actor, singer, and choreographer, who starred in numerous films, including *Top Hat* 1935, *Easter Parade* 1948, and *Funny Face* 1957, many of which contained inventive sequences he designed and choreographed himself. He made ten classic films with the most popular of his dancing partners, Ginger Rogers. He later played straight dramatic roles, in films such as *On the Beach* 1959.

Astarte /ə'stɑ:tɪ/ alternative name for the Babylonian and Assyrian goddess ◊Ishtar.

astatine /'æstətiːn/ *n.* a radioactive element, symbol At, atomic number 85. [from Greek *astatos* = unstable]

Astaire *Stylish American dancer Fred Astaire and his most frequent partner, Ginger Rogers.*

aster *n.* any plant of the large genus *Aster*, family Compositae, belonging to the same subfamily as the daisy. All asters have starlike flowers with yellow centres and outer rays (not petals) varying from blue and purple to white. [Latin from Greek = star]

asterisk /ˈæstərɪsk/ *n.* a starlike punctuation mark (*) used to link the asterisked word with a note at the bottom of a page, and to mark that certain letters are missing from a word (especially a taboo word such as 'f**k'). —*v.t.* to mark with an asterisk. [from Latin from Greek = little star]

astern /əˈstɜːn/ *adv.* 1. in or to the rear of a ship or aircraft, behind. 2. backwards.

asteroid /ˈæstərɔɪd/ *n.* 1. or **minor planet**, any of many thousands of small bodies, composed of rock and iron, that orbit the Sun. They range in diameter from under 1 km/0.6 mi to 1,000 km/620 mi. Most asteroids lie in a belt between the orbits of Mars and Jupiter. They are thought to be fragments left over from the formation of the ◊Solar System. About 100,000 may exist, but their total mass is only a few hundredths the mass of the Moon. 2. a starfish. [from Greek *astēr* = star]

asthenosphere *n.* a division of the Earth's structure lying beneath the ◊lithosphere, at a depth of approximately 70 km/45 mi to 260 km/160 mi. It is thought to be the soft, partially molten layer of the ◊mantle on which the rigid plates of the Earth's surface move to produce the motions of ◊plate tectonics.

asthma /ˈæsmə/ *n.* a respiratory disease, often with paroxysms of difficult breathing. Attacks may be provoked by allergy, infection, stress, or emotional upset. It may also be increasing as a result of air pollution and occupational hazards. Treatment is with ◊bronchodilators to relax the bronchial muscles and thereby ease the breathing, and in severe cases by inhaled ◊steroids that reduce inflammation of the bronchi. —**asthmatic** /æsˈmætɪk/ *adj. & n.* [from Latin from Greek *azō* = breathe hard]

astigmatism /əˈstɪgmətɪzəm/ *n.* a defect in an eye or lens. It results when the curvature differs in two perpendicular planes, so that rays in one may be in focus while rays in the other are not. With astigmatic eyesight, the vertical and horizontal cannot be in focus at the same time; correction is by use of a cylindrical lens that reduces the overall focal length of one plane so that both planes are in sharp focus. —**astigmatic** /æstɪgˈmætɪk/ *adj.*, **astigmatically** *adv.* [from Greek *a-* = not and *stigma* = point]

astir /əˈstɜː/ *adv. & pred. adj.* in motion; out of bed.

Aston /ˈæstən/ Francis William 1877–1945. English physicist, who developed the mass spectrometer, which separates ◊isotopes by projecting their ions (charged atoms) through a magnetic field. He received the Nobel Prize for Chemistry in 1922.

astonish /əˈstɒnɪʃ/ *v.t.* to surprise very greatly. —**astonishment** *n.* [from Old French from Latin *tonare* = thunder]

Astor /ˈæstə/ prominent US and British family. **John Jacob Astor** (1763–1848) was a US millionaire. **Waldorf Astor**, 2nd Viscount Astor (1879—1952), was Conservative member of Parliament for Plymouth 1910–19, when he succeeded to the peerage. He was chief proprietor of the British *Observer* newspaper. His wife was Nancy Witcher Langhorne (1879–1964), **Lady Astor**, the first woman member of Parliament to take a seat in the House of Commons in 1919, when she succeeded her husband for the constituency of Plymouth. She was also a temperance supporter and political hostess. Government policy was said to be decided at Cliveden, their country home.

astound /əˈstaʊnd/ *v.t.* to shock with surprise.

astragal /ˈæstrəgəl/ *n.* a small moulding, of semicircular section, placed round the top or bottom of a column. [from Latin from Greek]

astrakhan /æstrəˈkæn/ *n.* the dark, tightly curled fleece of lambs from Astrakhan in Russia; an imitation of this.

astral /ˈæstrəl/ *adj.* of or connected with stars. —**astral body**, a supposed ethereal counterpart of the body. [from Latin *astrum* = star]

astray /əˈstreɪ/ *adv.* out of the right way. —**go astray**, to be missing; to fall into error or wrongdoing. [from Old French from Latin *extra* = away and *vagari* = wander]

astride /əˈstraɪd/ *adv.* with one leg on either side (*of*); with feet wide apart. —*prep.* astride of; extending across.

astringent /əˈstrɪndʒənt/ *adj.* 1. that causes contraction of body tissue and checks bleeding. 2. severe, austere. —*n.* an astringent substance. —**astringency** *n.* [French from Latin *stringere* = bind]

astrolabe /ˈæstrəleɪb/ *n.* an instrument formerly used for measuring the altitudes of stars etc. until replaced by the sextant. Astrolabes usually consisted of a flat disc with a sighting rod that could be pivoted to point at the Sun or bright stars. From the altitude of the Sun or star above the horizon, the local time could be estimated. [from Old French from Latin from Greek = star taking]

astrology /əˈstrɒlədʒɪ/ *n.* the study of the relative positions of the planets and stars in the belief that they influence events on Earth. Astrology has no proven scientific basis, but has been widespread since ancient times. Western astrology is based on the 12 signs of the ◊zodiac; Chinese astrology is based on a 60-year cycle and lunar calendar. —**astrologer** *n.* a person who casts a ◊horoscope based on the time and place of the subject's birth. **astrological** /æstrəˈlɒdʒɪkəl/ *adj.*, **astrologically** *adv.* [from Old French from Latin from Greek *astron* = star]

astrometry *n.* the measurement of the precise positions of stars, planets, and other bodies in space. Such information is needed for practical purposes, such as accurate timekeeping, surveying and navigation, and calculating orbits and measuring distances in space.

astronaut /ˈæstrənɔːt/ *n.* the Western term for a person making flights into space; the Soviet term is **cosmonaut**. [from Greek *astron* = star and *nautēs* = sailor]

astronautics /æstrəˈnɔːtɪks/ *n.* the science of space travel and its technology. —**astronautical** *adj.*

astronomical /æstrəˈnɒmɪkəl/ *adj.* 1. of astronomy. 2. vast in amount. —**astronomically** *adv.*

astronomical unit a unit (symbol AU) equal to the mean distance of the Earth from the Sun: 149,597,870 km/92,955,800 mi. It is used to describe planetary distances. Light travels this distance in approximately 8.3 minutes.

astronomy *n.* the science of the celestial bodies: the Sun, the Moon, and the planets; the stars and galaxies; and all other objects in the universe. It is concerned with their positions, motions, distances, and physical conditions; and with their origins and evolution. Astronomy thus divides into fields such as astrophysics, celestial mechanics, and cosmology. See also ◊gamma-ray astronomy and ◊ultraviolet astronomy. —**astronomer** *n.* [from Old French from Latin from Greek *astron* = star and *nemō* = arrange]

astronomy: chronology

2300 BC	Chinese astronomers made their earliest observations.
2000	Babylonian priests made their first observational records.
1900	Stonehenge was constructed: first phase.
365	The Chinese observed the satellites of Jupiter with the naked eye.
3rd century	Aristarchus argued that the sun is the centre of the solar system.
2nd century	Ptolemy's complicated Earth-centred system was promulgated, which dominated the astronomy of the Middle Ages.
1543	Copernicus revived the ideas of Aristarchus in De Revolutionibus.
1608	Lippershey invented the telescope, which was first used by Galileo 1609.
1609	Kepler's first two laws of planetary motion were published (the third appeared 1619).
1632	Leiden established the world's first official observatory.
1633	Galileo's theories were condemned by the Inquisition.
1675	The Royal Greenwich Observatory was founded in England.
1687	Newton's Principia was published, including his 'law of universal gravitation'.
1718	Halley predicted the return of the comet named after him, observed 1758: it was last seen 1986.
1781	Herschel discovered Uranus and recognized stellar systems beyond our Galaxy.
1796	Laplace elaborated his theory of the origin of the solar system.
1801	Piazzi discovered the first asteroid, Ceres.
1814	Fraunhofer first studied absorption lines in the solar spectrum.
1846	Neptune was identified by Galle, following predictions by Adams and Leverrier.
1859	Kirchhoff explained dark lines in the sun's spectrum.
1887	The earliest photographic star charts were produced.
1889	E E Barnard took the first photographs of the Milky Way.
1890	The first photograph of the spectrum was taken.
1908	Fragment of comet fell at Tungusta, Siberia.
1920	Eddington began the study of interstellar matter.
1923	Hubble proved that the galaxies are systems independent of the Milky Way, and by 1930 had confirmed the concept of an expanding universe.
1930	The planet Pluto was discovered by Clyde Tombaugh at the Lowell Observatory, Arizona, USA.
1931	Jansky founded radioastronomy.
1945	Radar contact with the moon was established by Z Bay of Hungary and the US Army Signal Corps Laboratory.
1948	The 200-inch Hale reflector telescope was installed at Mount Palomar, California, USA.
1955	The Jodrell Bank telescope 'dish' in England was completed.
1957	The first Sputnik satellite (USSR) opened the age of space observation.
1962	The first X-ray source was discovered in Scorpio.
1963	The first quasar was discovered.
1967	The first pulsar was discovered by Jocelyn Bell.
1969	The first manned moon landing was made by US astronauts.
1976	A 236-inch reflector telescope was installed at Mount Semirodniki (USSR).
1977	Uranus was discovered to have rings.
1977	The spacecraft Voyager 1 and 2 were launched, passing Jupiter and Saturn 1979–81.
1978	The spacecraft Pioneer Venus 1 and 2 reached Venus.
1978	A satellite of Pluto, Charon, was discovered by James Christie of the US Naval Observatory.
1979	The UK infrared telescope (UKIRT) was established on Hawaii.
1985	Halley's comet returned.
1986	Voyager 2 flew by Uranus and discovered ten new moons.
1987	Bright supernova visible to the naked eye for the first time since 1604.
1989	Voyager 2 flew by Neptune.

astrophotography *n.* the use of photography in astronomical research. The first successful photograph of a celestial object was the daguerreotype plate of the Moon taken by J W Draper of the USA in March 1840. Modern-day astrophotography uses techniques such as ◊charge-coupled devices.

astrophysics /æstrəʊ'fɪzɪks/ *n.* the branch of astronomy concerned with the physics and chemistry of stars, galaxies, and the universe. It began with the development of ◊spectroscopy in the 19th century, which allowed astronomers to analyse the composition of stars from their light. —**astrophysical** *adj.*, **astrophysicist** *n.* [from Greek *astron* = star]

Asturias /æ'stuəriəs/ autonomous region of N Spain; area 10,600 sq km/4,092 sq mi; population (1986) 1,114,000. Half of Spain's coal is produced from the mines of Asturias. Agricultural produce includes maize, fruit, and livestock. Oviedo and Gijon are the main industrial towns.

Asturias Miguel Ángel 1899–1974. Guatemalan author and diplomat. He published poetry, Guatemalan legends, and novels, such as *El Señor Presidente/The President* 1946, *Men of Corn* 1949, and *Strong Wind* 1950, attacking Latin-American dictatorships and 'Yankee imperialism'. He was awarded the Nobel prize for Literature in 1967.

astute /ə'stju:t/ *adj.* shrewd, seeing how to gain an advantage. —**astutely** *adv.*, **astuteness** *n.* [from French or Latin *astus* = craft]

Asunción /æsu:nsi'ɒn/ capital and port of Paraguay, on the Paraguay river; population (1984) 729,000. It produces textiles, footwear, and food products. It was founded in 1537, the first Spanish settlement in the La Plata region.

asunder /ə'sʌndə/ *adv.* (*formal*) apart, in pieces. [Old English *on sundran* = into pieces]

Aswan /æs'wɑːn/ winter resort town in Upper Egypt; population (1985) 183,000. It is near the High Dam, built 1960–70, which keeps the level of the Nile constant throughout the year without flooding. It produces steel and textiles.

asylum /ə'saɪləm/ *n.* 1. a place of refuge (formerly for criminals). 2. (in full **political asylum**) protection given by a state to a political refugee from another country. 3. (*historical*) an institution for the care and shelter of insane or destitute persons. [from Latin from Greek = refuge (*a-* = not and *sulon* = right of seizure)]

asymmetry /æ'sɪmətri, eɪ-/ *n.* lack of symmetry. —**asymmetric** /-'metrik/ *adj.*, **asymmetrical** *adj.* [from Greek *a-* = not and *symmetry*]

asymptote *n.* in ◊coordinate geometry, a straight line towards which a curve approaches more and more closely but never reaches. If a point on a curve approaches a straight line such that its distance from the straight line is *d*, then the line is an asymptote to the curve if limit *d* tends to zero as the point moves towards infinity.

at /ət, *emphatic* æt/ *prep.* 1. having as position, time of day, state, or price. 2. with motion or aim towards. —**at it**, working, in activity. [Old English]

At symbol for astatine.

Atacama /ætə'kɑːmə/ desert in N Chile; area about 80,000 sq km/31,000 sq mi. Inland are mountains, and the coastal area is rainless and barren. There are silver and copper mines and extensive nitrate deposits.

Atahualpa /ætə'wɑːlpə/ *c.*1502–1533. Last emperor of the Incas of Peru. He was taken prisoner in 1532 when the Spaniards arrived, and agreed to pay a huge ransom, but was accused of plotting against the conquistador Pizarro and sentenced to be burned. On his consenting to Christian baptism, the sentence was commuted to strangulation.

Atatürk /'ætətɜːk/ Kemal. Name assumed in 1934 by Mustafa Kemal Pasha 1881–1938. Turkish politician and general, first president of Turkey from 1923. After World War I he established a provisional rebel government and in 1921–22 the Turkish armies under his leadership expelled the Greeks who were occupying Turkey. He was the founder of the modern republic, which he ruled as virtual dictator, with a policy of consistent and radical westernization. [Atatürk = father of the Turks]

atavism /'ætəvɪzəm/ *n.* resemblance to remote ancestors rather than to parents, reversion to an earlier type; in psychology, the manifestation of primitive forms of behaviour. —**atavistic** /-'vɪstɪk/ *adj.* [from French from Latin *atavus* = ancestor]

ataxia *n.* the loss of muscular coordination due to neurological damage or disease.

ate /et, eɪt/ *v.t./i.* past of eat.

Athanasius, St /æθə'neɪʃəs/ 298–373. Bishop of Alexandria, supporter of the doctrines of the Trinity and Incarnation. He was a disciple of St Anthony the hermit, and an opponent of ◊Arianism in the great Arian controversy. Following the official condemnation of Arianism at the Council of Nicaea in 325, Athanasius was appointed bishop of Alexandria in 328. The **Athanasian creed**, one of the three ancient ◊creeds of the Christian church, was not written by him, although it reflects his views.

atheism /'eɪθiɪzəm/ *n.* nonbelief in, or the positive denial of, the existence of a god or gods. —**atheist** *n.*, **atheistic** /-'ɪstɪk/ *adj.* [from French from Greek *a-* = not and *theos* = god]

Athelney, Isle of /'æθəlni/ an area of firm ground in marshland near Taunton in Somerset, England, in 878 the headquarters of king ◊Alfred the Great when he was in hiding from the Danes.

Athelstan /'æθəlstən/ *c.*895–939. King of the Mercians and West Saxons. Son of Edward the Elder and grandson of Alfred the Great, he was crowned king in 925 at Kingston-upon-Thames. He subdued parts of Cornwall and Wales, and in 937 defeated the Welsh, Scots, and Danes at Brunanburh.

Athena /ə'θiːnə/ in Greek mythology, the goddess (Roman Minerva) of war, wisdom, and the arts and crafts, who was supposed to have sprung fully grown from the head of Zeus. Her chief cult centre was Athens, where the ◊Parthenon was dedicated to her.

Athens /'æθɪnz/ Greek *Athinai* capital city of Greece and of ancient Attica; population (1981) 885,000, metropolitan area 3,027,000. Situated 8 km/5 mi NE of its port of Piraeus on the Gulf of Aegina, it is built around the rocky hills of the Acropolis 169 m/555 ft and the Areopagus 112 m/368 ft. The ◊Acropolis dominates the city. Remains of ancient Greece include the Parthenon, the Erechtheum, and the temple of Athena Nike.

atheroma *n.* (*plural* **atheromas** or **atheromata**) furring-up of the interior of an artery by deposits, mainly of cholesterol, within its walls.

atherosclerosis /æθərəusklɪə'rəusɪs/ *n.* the formation of fatty deposits in arteries, often with thickening and hardening of the artery walls, associated with ◊atheroma. [from German from Greek *athērē* = gruel]

athlete /'æθliːt/ *n.* one who competes or excels in physical games and exercises. —**athlete's foot**, a fungous disease of the feet. [from Latin from Greek *athlon* = prize]

athletic /æθ'letɪk/ *adj.* of athletes; physically strong and active, muscular. —**athleticism** *n.* [from French or Latin]

athletics *n.pl.* **1.** competitive track and field events consisting of running, throwing, and jumping disciplines. **Running events** range from sprint races (100 metres) and hurdles to the marathon (26 miles 385 yards). **Jumping events** are the high jump, long jump, triple jump, and pole vault (men only). **Throwing events** are javelin, discus, shot put, and hammer throw (men only). **2.** (*US*) physical sports and games of any kind.

athwart /ə'θwɔːt/ *adv.* & *prep.* across from side to side. [from Old Norse = transverse]

Atlanta /ət'læntə/ capital and largest city of Georgia, USA; population (1980) 422,000, metropolitan area 2,010,000. There are Ford and Lockheed assembly plants, and it is the headquarters of Coca-Cola.

Atlantic /ət'læntɪk/ *adj.* of the Atlantic Ocean.

Atlantic, Battle of the 1. the German campaign during World War I to prevent merchant shipping from delivering food supplies from the USA to the Allies, especially the UK. By 1917, some 875,000 tons of shipping had been lost. The odds were only turned by the belated use of naval **convoys** and **depth charges** to deter submarine attack. **2.** the continuous battle fought in the Atlantic Ocean throughout World War II (1939–45) by the sea and air forces of the Allies and Germany. The number of U-boats destroyed by the Allies during the war was nearly 800. At least 2,200 convoys of 75,000 merchant ships crossed the Atlantic, protected by US naval forces. Before the US entry into the war in 1941, destroyers were supplied to the British under the Lend-Lease Act of 1941.

Atlantic Charter a declaration issued during World War II by the British prime minister Churchill and the US president Roosevelt after meetings in Aug 1941. It stressed their countries' good intentions and war aims and was largely a propaganda exercise to demonstrate public solidarity between the Allies.

Atlantic Ocean the ocean lying between Europe and Africa to the E and the Americas to the W, probably named after the legendary island ◊Atlantis. The area of its basin is 81,500,000 sq km/31,500,000 sq mi; including the Arctic Ocean, and Antarctic seas, 106,200,000 sq km/41,000,000 sq mi. The average depth is 3 km/2 mi; greatest depth 8,648 m/28,374 ft. The Mid-Atlantic Ridge divides it from N to S. Lava welling up from this central area annually increases the distance between South America and Africa. The N Atlantic is the saltiest of the main oceans, and it has the largest tidal range. In the 1960s–80s average wave heights increased by 25%, the largest from 12 m/39 ft to 18 m/59 ft.

Atlantis legendary island continent, said to have sunk about 9600 BC, following underwater convulsions. Although the Atlantic Ocean is probably named after it, the structure of the sea bottom rules out its ever having existed there.

atlas /'ætləs/ *n.* a book of maps. The atlas was introduced in the 16th century by ◊Mercator, who began work on it in 1585; it was completed by his son in 1594. Early atlases had a frontispiece showing Atlas supporting the globe. [from *Atlas*]

Atlas in Greek mythology, one of the ◊Titans who revolted against the gods; as a punishment, Atlas was compelled to support the heavens on his head and shoulders. Growing weary, he asked ◊Perseus to turn him into stone, and he was transformed into Mount Atlas.

Atlas Mountains mountain system of NW Africa, stretching 2,400 km/1,500 mi from the Atlantic coast of Morocco to the Gulf of Gabes, Tunisia, and lying between the Mediterranean to the N and the Sahara to the S. The highest peak is Mount Toubkal 4,167 m/13,670 ft.

atman /'ætmən/ *n.* in Hinduism, the individual soul or the eternal essential self; the supreme principle of life in the universe. [Sanskrit = self; essence, highest personal principle of life]

atmosphere /'ætməsfɪə/ *n.* **1.** the mixture of gases surrounding the Earth or a heavenly body. Atmospheric pressure decreases with height in the atmosphere. In its lowest layer, the atmosphere of the Earth consists of nitrogen (78%) and oxygen (21%), both in molecular form (two atoms bounded together). The other 1% is largely argon, with very small quantities of other gases, including water vapour and carbon dioxide. The atmosphere plays a major part in the various cycles of nature (the ◊water cycle, ◊carbon cycle, and ◊nitrogen cycle). It is the principle industrial source of nitrogen, oxygen, and argon, which are obtained by fractional distillation of liquid air. **2.** the air in a room etc. **3.** a psychological environment; the tone or mood pervading a book or work of art etc. **4.** in physics, a unit (symbol atm) of pressure equal to 760 torr, 1013.25 millibars, or 1.01325×10^5 newtons per square metre. The actual pressure exerted by the atmosphere fluctuates around this value, which is assumed to be standard at sea level and 0°C, and is used when dealing with very high pressures. —**atmospheric** /-'ferɪk/ *adj.* [from Greek *atmos* = vapour and *sphere*]

atmospherics /ætməs'ferɪks/ *n. or n.pl.* electrical disturbance in the atmosphere; interference in telecommunications caused by this.

atoll /'ætɒl/ *n.* a ring-shaped coral reef enclosing a lagoon. [from Maldive *atolu*]

atom /'ætəm/ *n.* **1.** the smallest unit of matter that can take part in a chemical reaction, and which cannot be broken down chemically into anything simpler; this as a source of atomic energy. There are 109 different types of atom, corresponding with the 109 known elements as listed in the ◊periodic table of the elements. **2.** a minute portion or thing. [from Old French from Latin from Greek *atomos* = indivisible]

atom bomb a bomb deriving its explosive force from nuclear fission (see ◊nuclear energy) as a result of a neutron chain reaction, developed in the 1940s in the USA into a usable weapon.

atomic /ə'tɒmɪk/ *adj.* **1.** of an atom or atoms. **2.** using energy from atoms. —**atomic bomb** an atom bomb. **atomic theory,** the theory that all matter consists of atoms.

atomic clock a timekeeping device regulated by various periodic processes occurring in atoms and molecules, such as atomic vibration or the frequency of absorbed or emitted radiation.

atomic energy another name for ◊nuclear energy.

atomicity *n.* the number of atoms of an ◊element that combine together to form a molecule. A molecule of oxygen (O_2) has atomicity 2; sulphur (S_8) has atomicity 8.

atomic mass unit or **dalton** a unit (symbol amu or u) of mass that is used to measure the relative mass of atoms and molecules. It is equal to one-twelfth of the mass of a carbon-12 atom, which is equivalent to the mass of a proton or 1.66×10^{-27} kg. The ◊relative atomic mass of an atom has no units; thus oxygen-16 has an atomic mass of 16 daltons, but a relative atomic mass of 16.

atomic number the positive charge on (number of protons in) the nucleus of an atom. The elements are numbered 1 (hydrogen) to 109 (unnilennium) in the ◊periodic table of elements.

atomic radiation energy given out by disintegrating atoms during ◊radioactive decay. The energy may be in the form of fast-moving particles, known as ◊alpha particles and ◊beta particles, or in the form of high-energy electromagnetic waves, known as ◊gamma radiation. Overlong exposure to atomic radiation can lead to ◊radiation sickness.

atomic size or **atomic radius** the size of an atom expressed as the radius in ◊ångströms or other units of length. The sodium atom has an atomic radius of 1.57 ångströms (1.57×10^{-8} cm). For metals, the size of the atom is always greater than the size of its ion. For non-metals the reverse is true.

atomic structure the internal structure of an ◊atom. The core of the atom is the **nucleus,** a particle only one ten-thousandth the diameter of the atom itself. The simplest nucleus, that of hydrogen, comprises a single positively charged particle, the **proton.** Nuclei of other elements contain more protons and additional particles of about the same mass as the proton but with no electrical charge, **neutrons.** The nucleus is surrounded by a number of **electrons,** each of which has a negative charge equal to the positive charge on a proton, but which weighs only $1/1839$ times as much. For a neutral atom, the nucleus is surrounded by the same number of electrons as it contains protons. Atoms are held together by the electrical forces of attraction between each negative electron and the positive protons within the nucleus.

atomic time the time as given by ◊atomic clocks.

atomic weight another name for ◊relative atomic mass.

atomism /'ætəmɪzəm/ *n.* the philosophical theory that all matter consists of minute individual particles. —**atomistic** /-'mɪstɪk/ *adj.*

atomize /'ætəmaɪz/ *v.t.* to reduce to atoms or fine particles. —**atomization** /-'zeɪʃən/ *n.*

atomizer *n.* a device for reducing liquids to a fine spray. A vertical tube connected with a horizontal tube dips into a bottle of liquid, and at one end of the horizontal tube is a nozzle, at the other a rubber bulb. When the bulb is squeezed, air rushes over the top of the vertical tube and out through the nozzle. Following ◊Bernoulli's principle, the pressure at the top of the vertical tube is reduced, allowing the liquid to rise. The air stream picks up the liquid, breaks it up into tiny drops and carries it out of the nozzle as a spray.

Aton /'ɑːtn/ *n.* in ancient Egypt, the Sun's disc as an emblem of the single deity whose worship was promoted by ◊Ikhnaton in an attempt to replace the many gods traditionally worshipped.

atonal /eɪ'təʊnəl/ *adj.* in music, not written in any one ◊key; often associated with an expressionist style. —**atonality** /-'nælɪtɪ/ *n.* [from Greek *a-* = not and *tonal*]

atone /ə'təʊn/ *v.i.* to make amends (*for*). —**atonement** *n.* —**the Atonement,** in Christian theology, the doctrine that Jesus suffered on the cross to bring about reconciliation and forgiveness between God and humanity. [from *at one*]

Atonement, Day of Jewish holy day (*Yom Kippur*) held on the tenth day of Tishri (Sept–Oct), the first month of the Jewish year. It is a day of fasting, penitence, and cleansing from sin, ending the Ten Days of Penitence that follow *Rosh Hashanah,* the Jewish New Year.

ATP *n.* (**adenosine triphosphate**) a nucleotide molecule found in all cells. It can yield large amounts of energy, and is used to drive many biological processes, including muscle contraction and the synthesis of complex molecules needed by the cell. ATP is formed during photosynthesis in plants, or by the breakdown of food molecules during metabolism in animals.

atrium /'eɪtrɪəm/ *n.* (*plural* **atria** or **atriums**) **1.** the central court of an ancient Roman house. **2.** either of the two upper cavities in the heart, receiving blood under low pressure as it returns from the body. Atrium walls are thin and stretch easily to allow blood into the heart. On contraction, the atria force blood into the thick-walled ventricles, which then give a second, more powerful beat. [Latin]

atrocious /ə'trəʊʃəs/ *adj.* very bad; wicked. —**atrociously** *adv.* [from Latin *atrox* = cruel]

atrocity /ə'trɒsɪtɪ/ *n.* a wicked or cruel act, wickedness; a repellent thing. [from French or Latin]

atrophy /'ætrəfɪ/ *n.* wasting away through undernourishment or lack of use; emaciation. —*v.t./i.* to cause atrophy in; to suffer atrophy. [from French or Latin from Greek *a-* = without and *trophē* = food]

atropine /'ætrəpɪn, -piːn/ *n.* a poisonous alkaloid found in deadly nightshade. It acts as an ◊anticholinergic and, as atropine sulphate, is administered as a mild antispasmodic drug. [from *Atropos,* one of the three Greek Fates, who cut people's lives short]

attach /ə'tætʃ/ *v.t./i.* **1.** to fix to something else. **2.** to join (oneself) as a companion etc.; to assign (a person) to a particular group. **3.** to accompany or form part of. **4.** to attribute; to be attributable. **5.** to seize by legal authority. —**be attached to,** to be very fond of. [from Old French = fasten]

attachable *adj.* that may be attached.

attaché /ə'tæʃeɪ/ *n.* a person attached to an ambassador's staff and having responsibility in a specific capacity. —**attaché case,** a small rectangular case for carrying documents etc. [French]

attachment *n.* **1.** attaching, being attached. **2.** a thing (especially a device) attached. **3.** affection, devotion. **4.** legal seizure.

attack /ə'tæk/ *v.t./i.* **1.** to act violently against; to make an attack. **2.** to criticize strongly. **3.** to act harmfully on. **4.** to undertake (a task) with vigour. —*n.* **1.** an act of attacking. **2.** strong criticism. **3.** a sudden onset of illness etc. —**attacker** *n.* [from French from Italian = join battle]

attain *v.t./i.* to succeed in accomplishing, obtaining, or reaching. [from Anglo-French from Latin *tangere* = touch]

attainable /ə'teɪnəbəl/ *adj.* that may be attained.

attainder, bill of a legislative device that allowed the English Parliament to declare guilt and impose a punishment on an individual without bringing the matter before the courts. Such bills were used intermittently from the Wars of the Roses until 1798. Some acts of attainder were also passed by US colonial legislators during the American Revolution to deal with 'loyalists' who continued to support the English crown.

attainment /ə'teɪnmənt/ *n.* **1.** attaining. **2.** (usually in *plural*) what is attained, an achievement.

attar /ˈætə/ n. a fragrant oil, especially from rose petals. — **attar of roses**, the perfume derived from the essential oil of roses (especially damask roses), obtained by crushing and distilling the petals of the flowers. [Persian from Arabic *itr* = perfume]

attempt /əˈtempt/ v.t. to make an effort to accomplish. —n. an effort to accomplish, overcome, or surpass something; an attack. In law, a partial or unsuccessful commission of a crime. [from Old French from Latin *temptare* = try]

Attenborough /ˈætnbərə/ Richard 1923– . English film actor, director and producer. He began his acting career in war films and comedies. His later films include *Brighton Rock* 1947 and *10 Rillington Place* 1970 (as actor), and *Oh! What a Lovely War* 1968, *Gandhi* (which won six Academy Awards) 1982, and *Cry Freedom* 1987 (as director).

attend /əˈtend/ v.t./i. 1. to be present (at); to go regularly to. 2. to apply one's mind; to accompany. —**attendance** n. [from Old French from Latin *attendere* (*tendere* = stretch)]

attendant /əˈtendənt/ n. a person attending, especially to provide service. —adj. accompanying; waiting on.

attention /əˈtenʃən/ n. 1. applying one's mind, mental concentration; awareness. 2. consideration, care. 3. putting into good condition. 4. an attitude of concentration or readiness (also as a command). 5. (in *plural*) small acts of kindness or courtesy. —int. an order to take notice or to assume an attitude of attention. [from Latin *attendere*)]

attentive /əˈtentɪv/ adj. paying attention; devotedly courteous or considerate. —**attentively** adv., **attentiveness** n. [from French]

attenuate /əˈtenjueɪt/ v.t. 1. to make slender or thin. 2. to reduce in force or value. —**attenuation** /-ˈeɪʃən/ n. [from Latin *attenuare* (*tenuis* = thin)]

Atterbury /ˈætəbəri/ Francis 1662–1732. English bishop and Jacobite politician. In 1687 he was appointed a royal chaplain by William III. Under Queen Anne he received rapid promotion, becoming bishop of Rochester in 1713. His Jacobite sympathies prevented his further rise, and in 1722 he was sent to the Tower of London and subsequently banished. He was a friend of the writers Pope and Swift.

attest /əˈtest/ v.t./i. 1. to be evidence or proof of. 2. to declare to be true or genuine. —**attestation** /ætesˈteɪʃən/ n. [from French from Latin *attestari* (*testis* = witness)]

attic /ˈætɪk/ n. a room in the top storey of a house, immediately below the roof. [from French, originally used of a small architectural feature above a larger one]

Attic adj. 1. of Athens or Attica. 2. of the ancient Greek dialect used there. —n. this dialect. [from Latin from Greek]

Attica /ˈætɪkə/ (Greek *Attiki*) region of Greece comprising Athens and the district around it; area 3,381 sq km/1,305 sq mi. It is noted for its language, art, and philosophical thought in Classical times. It is a prefecture of modern Greece with Athens as its capital.

Attila /əˈtɪlə/ c.406–453. King of the Huns from 434, called the 'Scourge of God'. He embarked on a career of vast conquests, ranging from the Rhine to Persia. In 451 he invaded Gaul, but was defeated on the ◊Catalaunian Fields by the Roman and Visigoth armies under Aëtius (died 454) and Theodoric I. In 452 Attila led his Huns into Italy and only the personal intervention of Pope Leo I prevented the sacking of Rome.

Attila Line the line dividing Greek and Turkish Cyprus, so called because of a fanciful identification of the Turks with the Huns.

attire /əˈtaɪə/ n. (formal) clothes. [from Old French *à tire* = in order]

attired /əˈtaɪəd/ adj. (formal) clothed.

Attis /ˈætɪs/ in Classical mythology, a Phrygian god whose death and resurrection symbolized the end of winter and the arrival of spring. Beloved by the goddess ◊Cybele, who drove him mad as a punishment for his infidelity, he castrated himself and bled to death.

attitude /ˈætɪtjuːd/ n. 1. a way of regarding, a disposition or reaction (*to*). 2. a position of the body or its parts. 3. the position of an aircraft etc. in relation to given points. [French from Italian from Latin *aptus* = fitted]

Attlee /ˈætli/ Clement (Richard), 1st Earl 1883–1967. British Labour politician. In the coalition government during World War II he was Lord Privy Seal 1940–42, dominions secretary 1942–43, and Lord President of the Council 1943–45, as well as deputy prime minister from 1942.

As prime minister 1945–51 he introduced a sweeping programme of nationalization and a whole new system of social services.

Democracy means government by discussion but it is only effective if you can stop people talking.
Clement Attlee
Anatomy of Britain

---

atto- /ˈætəʊ-/ prefix denoting a factor of 10⁻¹⁸ (*attometre*). [from Danish or Norwegian *atten* = eighteen]

attorney /əˈtɜːnɪ/ n. one appointed to act for another in business or legal affairs; (*US*) a lawyer. —**Attorney-General** n. the chief legal officer, appointed by the government holding office. [from Old French *atorner* = assign]

attract /əˈtrækt/ v.t. 1. to draw towards itself by unseen force. 2. to arouse interest, pleasure, or admiration in. —**attraction** n. [from Latin *trahere* = pull]

attractive /əˈtræktɪv/ adj. 1. that attracts or can attract. 2. good-looking. —**attractively** adv., **attractiveness** n. [from French from Latin]

attributable /əˈtrɪbjuːtəbəl/ adj. that may be attributed.

attribute¹ /əˈtrɪbjuːt/ v.t. (with *to*) to regard as belonging to, caused by, or originated by. —**attribution** /-ˈbjuːʃən/ n. [from Latin *tribuere* = allot]

attribute² /ˈætrɪbjuːt/ n. 1. a quality ascribed to or characteristic of a person or thing. 2. an object associated with or symbolizing a person.

attributive /əˈtrɪbjutɪv/ adj. expressing an attribute; in grammar, (of an adjective) placed before the noun it qualifies (compare ◊predicative). —**attributively** adv. [from French]

attrition /əˈtrɪʃən/ n. 1. wearing away by friction. 2. gradual wearing down of strength and morale by harassment. [from Latin *attritio* (*terere* = rub)]

attune /əˈtjuːn/ v.t. 1. to harmonize or adapt (one's mind etc.) *to* a matter or idea. 2. to bring into musical accord.

Atwood /ˈætwʊd/ Margaret (Eleanor) 1939– . Canadian novelist, short story writer, and poet. Her novels, which often treat feminist themes with wit and irony, include *The Edible Woman* 1969, *Life Before Man* 1979, *Bodily Harm* 1981, *The Handmaid's Tale* 1986, and *Cat's Eye* 1989.

atypical /eɪˈtɪpɪkəl/ adj. not belonging to any type. [from Greek *a-* = not and *typical*]

Au symbol for gold. [from Latin *aurum*]

Auber /ˈəʊbeə/ Daniel François Esprit 1782–1871. French operatic composer who studied under the Italian composer and teacher Cherubini. He wrote about 50 operas, including *La Muette de Portici/The Mute Girl of Portici* 1828 and the comic opera *Fra Diavolo* 1830.

aubergine n. or **eggplant** 1. a plant *Solanum melongena*, a member of the nightshade family Solanaceae. The aubergine is native to tropical Asia. Its purple-skinned, sometimes white, fruits are eaten as a vegetable. 2. its dark-purple colour. [French, ultimately from Sanskrit]

Aubrey /ˈɔːbrɪ/ John 1626–1697. English biographer and antiquary. His *Lives*, begun in 1667, contains gossip, anecdotes, and valuable insights into the celebrities of his time. Unpublished during his lifetime, a standard edition of the work appeared as *Brief Lives* 1898 in two volumes (edited by A Clark). Aubrey was the first to claim Stonehenge as a Druid temple.

aubrietia /ɔːˈbriːʃə/ n. a low-growing perennial rock plant with mauve, purple, or pink flowers. [from Claude *Aubriet*, French botanist (died 1743)]

auburn /ˈɔːbən/ adj. (of hair) reddish-brown. [originally = yellowish-white, from Old French from Latin *albus* = white]

Auckland /ˈɔːklənd/ largest city in New Zealand, situated in the northern part of North Island; population (1987) 889,000. It fills the isthmus that separates its two harbours (Waitemata and Manukau), and its suburbs spread N across the Harbour Bridge. It is the country's chief port and leading industrial centre, having iron and steel plants, engineering, car assembly, textiles, food-processing, sugar-refining, and brewing.

auction /ˈɔːkʃən/ n. a sale in which each article is sold to the highest bidder. —v.t. to sell by auction. [from Latin *augêre* = increase]

auction bridge a card game played by two pairs of players using all 52 cards in a standard pack. The chief characteristic is the selection of trumps by a preliminary bid or auction. It has been succeeded in popularity by ◊contract bridge.

auctioneer /ɔːkʃə'niə/ *n.* one whose business is to conduct auctions. —*v.t.* to sell by auction.

audacious /ɔː'deɪʃəs/ *adj.* daring, bold. —**audaciously** *adv.*, **audacity** /ɔ'dæsɪtɪ/ *n.* [from Latin *audēre* = dare]

Auden /'ɔːdn/ W(ystan) H(ugh) 1907–1973. US poet of British origin. He wrote some of his most original poetry, such as *Look, Stranger!* 1936, in the 1930s when he led the influential left-wing literary group that included Louis MacNeice, Stephen Spender, and Cecil Day Lewis. He moved to the USA in 1939, became a US citizen in 1946, and adopted a more conservative and Christian viewpoint, in *The Age of Anxiety* 1947.

audible /'ɔːdɪbəl/ *adj.* that can be heard (distinctly). —**audibility** /-'bɪlɪtɪ/ *n.*, **audibly** *adv.* [from Latin *audire* = hear]

audience /'ɔːdɪəns/ *n.* 1. a group of listeners or spectators. 2. a formal interview. [from Old French from Latin]

audio /'ɔːdɪəʊ/ *n.* (*plural* **audios**) and in combinations, audible sound reproduced mechanically; its reproduction. —**audio frequency**, a frequency comparable to that of ordinary sound. **audiotypist** *n.* one who types from a recording. **audiovisual** *adj.* using both sight and sound. [from Latin *audire* = hear]

audiometer *n.* an electrical instrument to test hearing.

audit /'ɔːdɪt/ *n.* the official inspection of a company's accounts by a qualified accountant as required each year by law to ensure that the company balance sheet reflects the true state of its affairs. —*v.t.* to conduct an audit of. [from Latin *auditus* = hearing]

Audit Commission an independent body in the UK established by the Local Government Finance Act of 1982. It administers the District Audit Service (established in 1844) and appoints auditors for the accounts of all UK local authorities. The Audit Commission consists of 15 members: its aims include finding ways of saving costs, and controlling illegal local-authority spending.

audition /ɔː'dɪʃən/ *n.* a trial performance to test the suitability of an actor etc. for a part. —*v.t./i.* give an audition to; have an audition. [from Latin *audire* = hear]

auditor /'ɔːdɪtə/ *n.* 1. one authorized to audit accounts. 2. a listener. [from Anglo-French from Latin]

auditorium /ɔːdɪ'tɔːrɪəm/ *n.* (*plural* **auditoriums**) the part of a theatre etc. occupied by an audience. [Latin]

auditory /'ɔːdɪtərɪ/ *adj.* of or concerned with hearing. [from Latin]

auditory canal a tube leading from the outer ◊ear opening to the eardrum. It is found only in animals whose eardrums are located inside the skull, principally mammals and birds.

Audubon /'ɔːdəbɒn/ John James 1785–1851. US naturalist and artist. In 1827, after extensive travels and observations of birds, he published the first part of his *Birds of North America*, with a remarkable series of colour plates. Later he produced a similar work on North American quadrupeds.

au fait /əʊ 'feɪ/ well acquainted *with* a subject. [French]

Augean stables in Greek mythology, one of the labours of ◊Heracles was to clean out the stables of Augeas, king of Elis in Greece. They contained 3,000 cattle and had never been cleaned before. He was given only one day to do the labour and so diverted the river Alpheus through their yard.

auger /'ɔːgə/ *n.* a tool for boring holes in wood, having a long shank with a helical groove, and a transverse handle. [Old English *nafu* = nave of wheel, *gār* = piercer]

aught /ɔːt/ *n.* (*archaic* or *poetical*) anything. [Old English]

augment¹ /ɔːg'ment/ *v.t.* to increase, to make greater. —**augmentation** /-'teɪʃən/ *n.* [from French or Latin *augēre* = increase]

augment² /'ɔːgmənt/ *n.* a vowel prefixed to past tenses in Greek and Sanskrit.

Augrabies Falls /ɔː'xrɑːbiz/ waterfalls in the Orange River, NW Cape Province, South Africa. Height 148 m/480 ft.

au gratin /əʊ 'grætæ̃/ cooked with a crust of breadcrumbs and grated cheese. [French *gratter* = grate]

Augsburg, Confession of /'aʊgzbuəg/ a statement of the Protestant faith as held by the German Reformers,

composed by Philip ◊Melanchthon. Presented to the holy Roman emperor Charles V, at the conference known as the Diet of Augsburg in 1530, it is the creed of the modern Lutheran church.

augur /'ɔːgə/ *n.* 1. a member of a college of Roman priests who interpreted the will of the gods from signs or 'auspices' such as the flight of birds, the condition of entrails of sacrificed animals, and the direction of thunder and lightning. Their advice was sought before battle and on other important occasions. 2. a soothsayer. —*v.t./i.* to portend; to serve as an omen. —**augural** *adj.* [Latin]

august /ɔː'gʌst/ *adj.* majestic, imposing. [from French or Latin = consecrated, venerable]

August /'ɔːgʌst/ *n.* the eighth month of the year. [Old English, from *Augustus*, first Roman emperor]

Augustan age /ɔː'gʌst(ə)n/ the golden age of the Roman emperor ◊Augustus, during which art and literature flourished. The name is also given to later periods which used Classical ideals, such as that of Queen Anne in England.

Augustine of Hippo, St /ɔː'gʌstɪn/354–430. One of the early Christian leaders and writers known as the Fathers of the Church. He was converted to Christianity by Ambrose in Milan and became bishop of Hippo (modern Annaba, Algeria) in 396. Among Augustine's many writings are his *Confessions*, a spiritual autobiography, and *De Civitate Dei/The City of God*, vindicating the Christian church and divine providence in 22 books.

Augustine, St /ɔː'gʌstɪn/ First archbishop of Canterbury, England. He was sent from Rome to convert England to Christianity by Pope Gregory I. He landed at Ebbsfleet, Kent in 597, and soon after baptized Ethelbert, King of Kent, along with many of his subjects. He was consecrated bishop of the English at Arles in the same year, and appointed archbishop in 601, establishing his see at Canterbury. Feast day 26 May.

Augustinian /ɔːgə'stɪnɪən/ *n.* a member of a religious community that follows the Rule of St ◊Augustine of Hippo. It includes the Canons of St Augustine, Augustinian Friars and Hermits, Premonstratensians, Gilbertines, and Trinitarians. —*adj.*, of or relating to the Rule of St Augustine.

Augustus /ɔː'gʌstəs/ BC 63–AD 14. Title of Octavian (Gaius Julius Caesar Octavianus), first of the Roman emperors. He joined forces with Mark Antony and Lepidus in the Second Triumvirate. Following Mark Antony's liaison with the Egyptian Queen Cleopatra, Augustus defeated her troops at Actium in 31 BC. As emperor (from 27 BC) he reformed the government of the empire, the army, and Rome's public services, and was a patron of the arts. The period of his rule is known as the ◊Augustan Age.

auk /ɔːk/ *n.* a marine diving bird of the family Alcidae, including little auks, razorbills, puffins, murres, and guillemots. Confined to the N hemisphere, they feed on fish and use their wings to 'fly' underwater in pursuit. [from Old Norse *álka*]

auld lang syne /ɔːld læŋ 'saɪn/ (*Scottish*) days of long ago. [Scottish = old long since]

aunt /ɑːnt/ *n.* a sister or sister-in-law of one's father or mother; (*colloquial*) an unrelated friend of a parent. —**Aunt Sally**, a figure used as a target in a throwing-game; a target of general abuse. [from Anglo-French from Latin *amita*]

auntie, aunty /'ɑːntɪ/ *n.* (*colloquial*) an aunt.

au pair /əʊ 'peər/ a young person, usually from abroad, helping with housework etc. in return for board and lodging. [French]

aura /'ɔːrə/ *n.* (*plural* **auras**) the distinctive atmosphere attending a person or thing; a subtle emanation. [Latin from Greek = breeze]

aural /'ɔːrəl/ *adj.* of or concerning the ear or hearing. —**aurally** *adv.* [from Latin *auris* = ear]

Aurangzeb /'ɔːrəŋzeb/ or **Aurungzebe** 1618–1707. Mogul emperor of N India from 1658. Third son of Shah Jehan, he made himself master of the court by a palace revolution. His reign was the most brilliant period of the Mogul dynasty, but his despotic tendencies and Muslim fanaticism aroused much opposition. His latter years were spent in war with the princes of Rajputana and Mahrattas.

Aurelian /ɔː'riːlɪən/ (Lucius Domitius Aurelianus) *c.*214–AD 275. Roman emperor from 270. A successful soldier, he was chosen emperor by his troops on the death of Claudius II. He defeated the Goths and Vandals, defeated and captured ◊Zenobia of Palmyra, and was planning a campaign against Parthia when he was murdered. The **Aurelian Wall,** a fortification surrounding Rome, was built by Aurelian in 271. It was made of concrete, and substantial ruins exist. The **Aurelian Way** ran from Rome through Pisa and Genoa to Antipolis (Antibes) in Gaul.

Aurelius Antoninus /ɔːˈriːliəs/ Marcus Roman emperor; see ◊Marcus Aurelius Antoninus.

aureola /ɔːˈriːələ/, *n.* or **aureole** /ˈɔːriəʊl/ **1.** a celestial crown or halo, especially round the head or body of a portrayed divine figure. **2.** a corona round the Sun or Moon. [Latin = golden crown]

au revoir /əʊ rəˈvwɑːr/ goodbye for the moment. [French]

Auric /ɔːˈriːk/ Georges 1899–1983. French composer. He was one of the musical group called ◊Les Six. Auric composed a comic opera, several ballets, and incidental music to films of Jean Cocteau.

auricle /ˈɔːrɪkəl/ *n.* **1.** the external part of the ear. **2.** an atrium of the heart; a small appendage to this. —**auricular** /ɔːˈrɪkjʊlə/ *adj.* [from Latin, diminutive of *auris* = ear]

auricula *n.* a species of primrose *Primula auricula*, a plant whose leaves are said to resemble bear's ears. It is native to the Alps, but often cultivated in gardens.

auriferous /ɔːˈrɪfərəs/ *adj.* yielding gold. [from Latin *aurum* = gold and *ferre* = bear]

Auriga /ɔːˈraɪɡə/ *n.* a constellation of the N hemisphere, represented as a man driving a chariot. Its brightest star is first-magnitude Capella about 45 light years from Earth; Epsilon Aurigae is an ◊eclipsing binary star, with a period of 27 years, the longest of its kind (last eclipse 1983).

Aurignacian /ɔːrɪɡˈneɪʃ(ə)n/ *adj.* in archaeology, of or relating to an Old Stone Age culture that came between the Mousterian and the Solutrian in the Upper Palaeolithic. The earliest cave paintings are attributed to the Aurignacian peoples of W Europe about 16,000 BC. [from *Aurignac* in SW France, where remains were found]

Auriol /ɔːriˈəʊl/ Vincent 1884–1966. French socialist politician. He was president of the two Constituent Assemblies of 1946 and first president of the Fourth Republic 1947–54.

aurochs /ˈɔːrɒks/ *n.* (*plural* **aurochs**) an extinct species of long-horned wild cattle *Bos primigenius* that formerly roamed Europe, SW Asia, and N Africa. It survived in Poland until 1627. Black to reddish or grey, it was up to 1.8 m/6 ft at the shoulder. It is depicted in many cave paintings, and is considered the ancestor of domestic cattle. [German]

aurora /ɔːˈrɔːrə/ *n.* (*plural* **auroras, aurorae** /-iː/) a luminescent display of colours in the atmosphere at high northern latitudes (called **aurora borealis**) and southern latitudes (called **aurora australis**). It arises from electrical interactions between the Earth's magnetic field and streams of energetic charged particles from the Sun. An aurora is usually in the form of a luminous arch with its apex towards the magnetic pole followed by arcs, bands, rays, curtains, and coronas, usually green, but often showing shades of blue and red, and sometimes yellow or white. [from Latin = dawn]

Aurora Roman goddess of the dawn. The Greek equivalent is Eos.

Auschwitz /ˈaʊʃvɪts/ *n.* (Polish *Oswiecim*) town near Kraków in Poland, the site of a notorious ◊concentration camp used by the Nazis in World War II to exterminate Jews and other political and social minorities, as part of the 'final solution'. Each of the four gas chambers could hold 6,000 people.

auscultation /ɔːskʊlˈteɪʃən/ *n.* listening to the sounds of the heart, lungs, etc., for diagnosis, usually with the aid of a stethoscope. [from Latin *auscultare* = listen to]

Ausgleich /ˈaʊsɡlaɪx/ *n.* the compromise between Austria and Hungary of 8 Feb 1867 that established the Austro-Hungarian Dual Monarchy under Habsburg rule. It endured until the collapse of Austria-Hungary in 1918.

auspice /ɔːspɪs/ *n.* **1.** an omen. **2.** (in *plural*) patronage. [originally = observation of bird flight (in divination); French or from Latin *avis* = bird]

auspicious /ɔːˈspɪʃəs/ *adj.* showing signs that promise well, favourable. —**auspiciously** *adv.*, **auspiciousness** *n.*

Aussie /ˈɒzɪ/ *n.* & *adj.* (*colloquial*) abbreviation of Australian.

Austen Jane 1775–1817. British novelist, noted for her domestic novels of manners. All her novels are set within

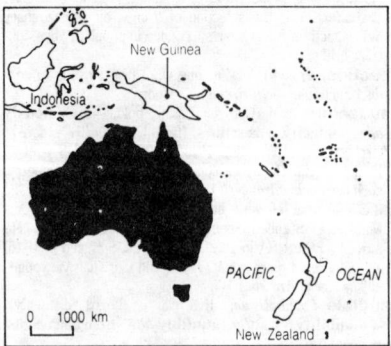

the confines of middle-class provincial society, and show her skill at drawing characters and situations with delicate irony. These include *Sense and Sensibility* 1811, *Pride and Prejudice* 1813, *Mansfield Park* 1814, *Emma* 1816, *Persuasion* and *Northanger Abbey* 1818.

austere /ɔːˈstɪə/ *adj.* stern, grim; severely simple; severe in self-discipline or abstinence. —**austerely** *adv.*, **austerity** /ɔːˈsterətɪ/ *n.* [from Old French from Latin from Greek *austēros* = severe]

Austerlitz, Battle of /ˈaʊstəlɪts/ battle on 2 Dec 1805 in which the French forces of Emperor Napoleon defeated those of Alexander I of Russia and Francis II of Austria at a small town in Czechoslovakia, (formerly in Austria), 19 km/ 12 mi E of Brno.

Austin /ˈɒstɪn/ Alfred 1835–1913. British poet. He made his name with the satirical poem *The Season* 1861, which was followed by plays and volumes of poetry little read today; from 1896 he was poet laureate.

Austin Herbert, 1st Baron Austin 1866–1941. English industrialist who began manufacturing cars in 1905 in Northfield, Birmingham, notably the Austin Seven in 1921.

austral /ˈɔːstrəl/ *adj.* **1.** southern. **2.** Austral, Australian; Australasian. [from Latin *australis* (*Auster* = south wind)]

Australasia /ɒstrəˈleɪziə/ a loosely applied geographical term, usually meaning Australia, New Zealand, and neighbouring islands in the S Pacific. —**Australasian** *adj.* of this area, *n.* an Australasian person. [from *Australia* and *Asia*]

Australia /ɒsˈtreɪliə/ Commonwealth of; country occupying the smallest continent, S of Indonesia, between the Pacific and Indian oceans; **area** 7,682,300 sq km/ 2,966,136 sq mi; **capital** Canberra; **physical** the world's smallest, flattest, and driest continent (40% lies in the Tropics, one third is desert, and one third is marginal grazing); Great Sandy Desert; Great Victoria Desert; Simpson Desert; the Great Barrier Reef (largest coral reef in the world, stretching 1,250 mi/2000 km of E coast of Queensland); Great Dividing Range and Australian Alps in the E; rivers N-S, but Darling River and Murray system E-S; Lake Eyre basin and Nullarbor Plain in S; **territories** Norfolk Island, Christmas Island, Cocos (Keeling) Islands, Ashmore and Cartier Islands, Coral Sea Islands, Heard Island and McDonald Islands, Australian Antarctic Territory; **head of state** Elizabeth II from 1952 represented by governor-general; **head of government** Robert Hawke from 1983; **political system** federal constitutional monarchy; Australia is an independent sovereign nation within the Commonwealth; **exports** world's largest exporter of sheep, wool, alumina, coal, refined lead and zinc ores, and mineral sands; other exports include cereals, beef, veal, mutton, lamb, sugar, nickel, bauxite, iron ore; principal trading partners are Japan, the US, and EC member states; **population** (1990 est) 16,650,000; **language** English, Aboriginal.

Australia Day a public holiday in Australia, the anniversary of Captain Phillip's arrival on 26 Jan 1788 to found Port Jackson (now Sydney), the first colony.

Australian /ɒsˈtreɪliən, ɔː-/ *adj.* of Australia or its people. —*n.* a native or inhabitant of Australia.

Australian Aborigine any of the 500 groups of indigenous inhabitants of the continent of Australia, who

Australia: history

30,000–10,000 BC	Aboriginal immigration from S India, Sri Lanka, and SE Asia.
AD 1606	First European sightings of Australia include Dutch ship *Duyfken* off Cape York.
1770	Captain Cook claimed New South Wales for Britain.
1788	Sydney founded.
19th century	The great age of exploration: coastal surveys (Bass, Flinders), interior (Sturt, Eyre, Leichhardt, Burke and Wills, McDouall Stuart, Forrest). Also the era of the bushrangers, overlanders and squatters, and individuals such as William Buckley and Ned Kelly.
1804	Castle Hill Rising by Irish convicts in New South Wales.
1813	Barrier·of the Blue mountains crossed.
1825	Tasmania seceded from New South Wales.
1829	Western Australia formed.
1836	South Australia formed.
1840–68	Convict transportation ended.
1851–61	Gold rushes (Ballarat, Bendigo).
1851	Victoria seceded from New South Wales.
1855	Victoria achieved government.
1856	New South Wales, South Australia, Tasmania achieved government.
1859	Queensland formed from New South Wales and achieved government.
1860	(National) Country Party founded.
1890	Western Australia achieved government.
1891	Depression gave rise to the Australian Labor Party.
1899–1900	South African War – forces offered by the individual colonies.
1901	Creation of the Commonwealth of Australia.
1911	Site for capital at Canberra acquired.
1914–18	World War I – Anzac troops in Europe including Gallipoli.
1939–45	World War II – Anzac troops in Greece, Crete, and N Africa (El Alamein) and the Pacific (Battle of the Coral Sea).
1941	Curtin's appeal to USA for help in World War II marks the end of the special relationship with Britain.
1944	Liberal Party founded by Menzies.
1948–75	Two million new immigrants, the majority from continental Europe.
1950–53	Korean War – Australian troops formed part of the United Nations forces.
1964–72	Vietnam War – Commonwealth troops in alliance with US forces.
1966–74	Mineral boom typified by the Poseidon nickel mine.
1967	Australia became a member of ASEAN.
1973	Britain entered the Common Market, and in the 1970s Japan became Australia's chief trading partner.
1974	Whitlam abolished 'white Australia' policy.
1975	Constitutional crisis; Prime Minister Whitlam dismissed by the governor general.
1975	United Nations trust territory of Papua New Guinea became independent.
1978	Northern Territory achieved self-government.
1979	Opening of uranium mines in Northern Territory.
1983	Hawke convened first national economic summit to seek consensus on economic policy to deal with growing unemployment.
1986	Australia Act passed by UK government, eliminating last vestiges of British legal authority in Australia.
1988	Labor foreign minister Bill Hayden appointed governor general designate. Free trade agreement signed with New Zealand.
1989	Andrew Peacock returned as Liberal Party leader. National Party leader, Ian Sinclair, replaced by Charles Blunt.
1990	Hawke won a record fourth election victory.

migrated to this region from S Asia about 40,000 years ago. They were hunters and gatherers, living throughout the continent in small kin-based groups before European settlement. Several hundred different languages developed, the most important being Aranda (Arunta), spoken in central Australia, and Murngin, spoken in Arnhem Land. In recent years there has been a movement for the recognition of Aborigine rights and campaigning against racial discrimination in housing, education, wages, and medical facilities.

Australian Antarctic Territory the islands and territories S of 60° S, between 160° E and 45° E longitude, excluding Adélie Land; area 6,044,000 sq km/2,332,984 sq mi of land and 75,800 sq km/29,259 sq mi of ice shelf. The population on the Antarctic continent is limited to research personnel.

Australian Capital Territory territory ceded to Australia by New South Wales in 1911 to provide the site of ◊Canberra, with its port at Jervis Bay, ceded in 1915; area 2,400 sq km/926 sq mi; population (1987) 261,000.

Austral Islands /ˈɒstrəl/ alternative name for ◊Tubuai Islands, part of ◊French Polynesia.

Austria /ˈɒstrɪə/ Republic of; landlocked country in central Europe, bounded by Hungary to the E, Yugoslavia to the SE, Italy to the SW, Switzerland to the W, Germany to the NW, and Czechoslovakia to the NE; **area** 83,920 sq km/32,393 sq mi; **capital** Vienna; **physical** mountainous, with the Alps in W and S and the Danube River basin in E; **head**

of state Kurt Waldheim from 1986; **head of government** Franz Vranitzky from 1986; **political system** democratic federal republic; **exports** manufactured goods, lumber, textiles, chemicals; **population** (1990 est) 7,595,000; **language** German; **recent history** part of the Habsburg empire until 1918. Incorporated into Hitler's Third Reich in 1938. Under Allied occupation the constitution was reinstated in 1945, and independence was formally recognized in 1955. Austria applied for membership of the European Community in 1989.

Austrian Succession, War of the 1740–48 war between Austria (supported by England and the Netherlands) and Prussia (supported by France and Spain)

Austro-Hungarian empire /ˈɒstrəʊ hʌŋˈɡɛərɪən/ the Dual Monarchy established with the ◊Ausgleich by the Habsburg Franz Joseph in 1867 between his empire of Austria and his kingdom of Hungary (including territory that became Czechoslovakia as well as parts of Poland, the Ukraine, Romania, Yugoslavia and Italy.) In 1910 it had an area of 261,239 sq km/100,838 sq mi with a population of 51 million. It collapsed in the autumn of 1918 with the end of World War I. Only two king-emperors ruled: Franz Joseph 1867–1916 and Charles 1916–18.

autarchy /ˈɔːtɑːkɪ/ *n.* despotism, absolute rule. [from Greek *autos* = self and *arkhē* = rule]

autarky /ˈɔːtɑːkɪ/ *n.* self-sufficiency, especially in economic affairs. [from Greek *autos* = self and *arkeō* = suffice]

authentic

authentic /ɔ:'θentɪk/ *adj.* genuine, of legitimate or undisputed origin; trustworthy. —**authentically** *adv.*, **authenticity** /-'tɪsɪtɪ/ *n.* [from Old French from Latin from Greek = principal, genuine]

authenticate /ɔ:'θentɪkeɪt/ *v.t.* to establish as valid or authentic. —**authentication** /-'keɪʃən/ *n.*, **authenticator** *n.* [from Latin]

author /'ɔ:θə/ *n.* 1. the writer of a book or books, article(s), etc. 2. the originator *of* a plan or policy etc. —**authorship** *n.* [from Anglo-French from Latin *auctor* (*augére* = increase)]

authoritarian /ɔ:θɒrɪ'teərɪən/ *adj.* favouring or characterized by unqualified obedience to authority. —*n.* an authoritarian person.

authoritarianism *n.* the rule of a country by a dominant élite who repress opponents and the press to maintain their own wealth and power. They are frequently indifferent to activities not affecting their security, and rival power centres, such as trade unions and political parties, are often allowed to exist, although under tight control. An extreme form is ◊totalitarianism.

authoritative /ɔ:'θɒrɪtətɪv/ *adj.* reliable, as having authority; official. —**authoritatively** *adv.*

authority /ɔ:'θɒrɪtɪ/ *n.* 1. the power or right to enforce obedience. 2. (especially in *plural*) a body having authority. 3. personal influence arising from knowledge or position etc., a testimony based on this. 4. a person to whom knowledge or influence is attributed; an expert. [from Old French from Latin *auctor* (*augére* = increase)]

authorize /'ɔ:θəraɪz/ *v.t.* to give authority to (a person) or for (an action etc.); to recognize officially. —**Authorized Version** the English translation of the Bible (1611), ordered by King James I. —**authorization** /-'zeɪʃən/ *n.*

autism /'ɔ:tɪzəm/ *n.* a mental condition, especially in children, preventing proper response to the environment. Generally present from birth, **infantile autism** is characterized by a withdrawn state and a failure to develop normally in language or social behaviour, although the autistic child may show signs of high intelligence in other areas, such as music. Many have impaired intellect, however, and the causes may range from brain damage to heredity. —**autistic** /ɔ:'tɪstɪk/ *adj.* [from Greek *autos* = self]

auto /'ɔ:təʊ/ *n.* (*plural* **autos**) (*US colloquial*) a motor car. [abbreviation of *automobile*]

auto- /'ɔ:tə(ʊ)/ in combinations, self; own; of or by oneself or itself, automatic. [from Greek *autos* = self]

autobahn /'ɔ:təbɑ:n/ *n.* a German, Austrian, or Swiss motorway. [German *auto* = motor car and *bahn* = road]

autobiography /ɔ:təbaɪ'ɒgrəfɪ/ *n.* the story of a person's life written by himself or herself; the writing of this. An autobiography is distinguished from a journal or diary by being a connected narrative, and from memoirs by dealing less with contemporary events and personalities. *The Boke of Margery Kempe c.*1432–36 is the oldest extant autobiography in English. —**autobiographical** /-'græfɪkəl/ *adj.*

autochrome *n. & adj.* in photography, a single-plate additive colour process devised by the ◊Lumière brothers in 1903. It was the first commercially available process, in use 1907–35.

autochthonous /ɔ:'tɒkθənəs/ *adj.* indigenous, aboriginal. [from Greek = sprung from that land (*khthōn* = land)]

autoclave /'ɔ:təkleɪv/ *n.* 1. a strong vessel used for chemical reactions at high pressures and temperatures. 2. a sterilizer using high-pressure steam. [from Latin *clavus* = nail or *clavis* = key]

autocracy /ɔ:'tɒkrəsɪ/ *n.* absolute government by one person; dictatorship. Russian government under the Tsars was an autocracy extending from the mid-16th century to the early 20th century. The title *Autocratix* (a female autocrat) was assumed by Catherine II of Russia in the 18th century. [from Greek]

autocrat /'ɔ:təkræt/ *n.* a sole ruler with absolute power; an authoritarian person. —**autocratic** /-'krætɪk/ *adj.*, **autocratically** *adv.* [from French from Greek *kratos* = power]

autocross /'ɔ:təkrɒs/ *n.* motor racing across country or on unmade roads.

Autocue /'ɔ:təkju:/ *n.* trade name for a device showing a television speaker the script as an aid to memory.

auto-da-fé /ɔ:təʊdɑ:'feɪ/ *n.* (*plural* **autos-da-fé**) a religious ceremony, including a procession, solemn mass,

and sermon, which accompanied the sentencing of heretics by the Spanish ◊Inquisition before they were handed over to the secular authorities for punishment, usually burning. [Portuguese = act of the faith]

autogiro /ɔ:tə'dʒaɪrəʊ/ *n.* or **autogyro** (*plural* **autogiros, autogyros**) an aircraft with rotating wings which generate lift during flight. The autogiro's rotor provides only lift, not propulsion. The autogiro has been superseded by the helicopter, in which the rotor provides both. [Spanish *giro* = gyration)]

autograph /'ɔ:təgrɑ:f/ *n.* 1. a person's signature, his or her handwriting. 2. a manuscript in the author's handwriting. 3. a document signed by its author. —*v.t.* to sign or write on in one's own hand. [French or from Latin from Greek *graphō* = write]

autoimmunity *n.* in medicine, a condition in which the body's immune responses are mobilized not against 'foreign' matter, such as invading germs, but against the body. Diseases considered to be of autoimmune origin include myasthenia gravis, pernicious anaemia, rheumatoid arthritis, and lupus erythematosus. —**autoimmune** *adj.*

autolysis *n.* in biology, the destruction of a ◊cell after its death by the action of its own ◊enzymes, which break down its structural molecules.

automate /'ɔ:təmeɪt/ *v.t.* to apply automation to, to operate by automation. [back-formation from *automation*]

automatic /ɔ:tə'mætɪk/ *adj.* 1. working of itself without direct human intervention in the process. 2. done from habit without conscious thought. 3. following necessarily. 4. (of a firearm) having a mechanism for continuous loading and firing. —*n.* 1. an automatic gun etc. 2. a motor vehicle with automatic transmission. —**automatic transmission**, a system in a motor vehicle for automatic gear change. —**automatically** *adv.* [Latin from Greek = acting of itself]

automatic pilot a control device that keeps an aeroplane flying automatically on a given course at a given height and speed. The automatic pilot contains a set of ◊gyroscopes that provide references for the plane's course. Sensors detect when the plane deviates from this course and send signals to the control surfaces—the ailerons, elevators, and rudder—to take the appropriate action. Autopilot is also used in missiles.

automation /ɔ:tə'meɪʃən/ *n.* the production of goods etc. by automatic processes; use of automatic equipment in place of human effort.

automatism /ɔ:'tɒmətɪzəm/ *n.* 1. the performance of actions without awareness or conscious intent. It is seen in sleepwalking and in some (relatively rare) psychotic states. 2. unthinking routine. [from French]

automaton /ɔ:'tɒmətən/ *n.* (*plural* **automatons,** *collective* **automata**) 1. a machine responding to automatic (especially electronic) control. 2. a person acting mechanically. [Latin from Greek = acting of itself]

automobile /'ɔ:təməbi:l/ *n.* (*US*) a motor car. [French]

Automobile Association (AA) a motoring organization founded in Britain in 1905. Originally designed to protect motorists from the police, it gradually broadened its services to include signposting, technical and legal services, as well as roadside help for members. In 1914 membership stood at 83,000; it now exceeds 6 million.

automotive /ɔ:tə'məʊtɪv/ *adj.* concerned with motor vehicles.

autonomic /ɔ:tə'nɒmɪk/ *adj.* functioning involuntarily. [from Greek *autos* = self and *nomos* = law]

autonomic nervous system in mammals, the part of the nervous system that controls the involuntary activities of the smooth muscles (of the digestive tract, blood vessels), the heart, and the glands. The **sympathetic** system responds to stress, when it speeds the heart rate, increases blood pressure and generally prepares the body for action. The **parasympathetic** system is more important when the body is at rest, since it slows the heart rate, decreases blood pressure, and stimulates the digestive system.

Autonomisti /aʊtɒnə'mɪstɪ/ *n.* a semi-clandestine amalgam of Marxist student organizations in W Europe, linked with guerrilla groups and such acts as the kidnapping and murder of Italian premier Aldo Moro by the Red Brigades in 1978.

autonomous /ɔ:'tɒnəməs/ *adj.* self-governing, acting independently. [from Greek *auto* = self and *nomos* = law)]

autonomy /ɔːˈtɒnəmɪ/ *n.* the right of self-government, independence.
autopilot /ˈɔːtəʊpaɪlət/ *n.* an automatic pilot.
autopsy /ˈɔːtɒpsɪ/ *n.* or **post-mortem** an examination of the internal organs and tissues of a dead body to try to establish the cause of death. [from French from Greek *autoptēs* = eyewitness]
autoradiography *n.* a technique for following the movement of molecules within an organism, especially a plant, by labelling with a radioactive isotope that can be traced on photographs. It is used to study ◊photosynthesis, where the pathway of radioactive carbon dioxide can be traced as it moves through the various chemical stages.
autosome *n.* any ◊chromosome in the cell other than a sex chromosome. Autosomes are of the same number and kind in both males and females of a given species.
autostrada /ˈɔːtəstrɑːdə/ *n.* (*plural* **autostrade** /-deɪ/) an Italian motorway. [Italian *strada* = road]
auto-suggestion *n.* conscious or unconscious acceptance of an idea as true, without demanding rational proof, but with potential subsequent effect for good or ill. Pioneered by the French psychotherapist Emile Coué (1857–1926) in healing, it is used in modern psychotherapy to conquer nervous habits, and dependence on tobacco, alcohol, and so on.
autotroph *n.* any living organism that synthesizes organic substances from inorganic molecules by using light or chemical energy. All green plants and many planktonic organisms are autotrophs, using sunlight to convert carbon dioxide and water into sugars by ◊photosynthesis.
autumn /ˈɔːtəm/ *n.* the season between summer and winter; a time of incipient decline. —**autumnal** /ɔːˈtʌmnəl/ *adj.* [from Old French from Latin *autumnus*]
autumnal equinox see ◊equinox.
autumn crocus any member of the genus *Colchicum*, family Liliaceae. One species, the mauve meadow saffron *C. autumnale*, yields **colchicine**, which is used in treating gout and in plant breeding.
Auvergne /əʊˈveən/ ancient province of central France, now comprising the *départements* Allier, Cantal, Haute-Loire, and Puy-de-Dôme; **area** 26,000 sq km/10,036 sq mi; **population** (1986) 1,334,000; **capital** Clermont-Ferrand; **physical** it lies on the Central Plateau and is mountainous, composed chiefly of volcanic rocks; **products** cattle, wheat, wine, and cheese.
auxiliary /ɔːgˈzɪljərɪ/ *adj.* giving help; additional, subsidiary. —*n.* **1.** an auxiliary person or thing. **2.** an auxiliary verb. **3.** (in *plural*) foreign or allied troops in the service of a nation at war. —**auxiliary verb,** a verb used to form tenses, moods, etc. of other verbs (e. g. *have* in *they have gone*). [from Latin *auxilium* = help]
auxin /ˈɔːksɪn/ *n.* a substance that stimulates the growth of plants, a growth ◊hormone. **Synthetic auxins** are used in rooting powders for cuttings, and in some weedkillers, where high auxin concentrations cause such rapid growth that the plants die. They are also used to prevent premature fruitdrop in orchards. The most common naturally occurring auxin is known as indoleacetic acid, or IAA. [German, from Greek *auxō* = increase]
AV abbreviation of Authorized Version.
avail /əˈveɪl/ *v.t./i.* to be of use or advantage (to). —*n.* effectiveness, advantage. —**avail oneself of,** to make use of. [from Old French from Latin *valēre* = be strong]
available /əˈveɪləbəl/ *adj.* capable of being used; at one's disposal. —**availability** /-ˈbɪlɪtɪ/ *n.*
avalanche /ˈævəlɑːnʃ/ *n.* **1.** a mass of dislodged snow, rock, etc., sliding rapidly down a mountain. Avalanches occur because of the unstable nature of snow masses in mountain areas. **2.** a great onrush. [French *avaler* = descend]
Avalokiteśvara /ˌævələʊkɪteɪʃˈvɑːrə/ *n.* in Mahāyāna Buddhism, one of the most important ◊bodhisattvas, seen as embodying compassion. Known as *Guanyin* in China and *Kwannon* in Japan, he is one of the attendants of Amida Buddha.
Avalon /ˈævəlɒn/ in Celtic legend, the island of the blessed, or paradise; and in the Arthurian legend the land of heroes, to which the dead king was conveyed. It has been associated with Glastonbury in SW England.
avant-garde /ˌævãˈgɑːd/ *n.* a leading group of innovators, especially in art and literature. The term was introduced

after the French Revolution, when it was used to describe any socialist political movement. —*adj.* (of ideas) new, progressive. [French = vanguard]
avarice /ˈævərɪs/ *n.* greed for wealth or gain. —**avaricious** *adj.*, **avariciously** *adv.* [from Old French from Latin *avarus* = greedy]
Avatar /ˈævətɑː(r)/ *n.* in Hindu mythology, the descent of a deity to earth in a visible form. The ten Avatars of ◊Vishnu are the best known. [from Sanskrit = descent]
Avebury /ˈeɪvbərɪ/ Europe's largest stone circle (diameter 412 m/1,352 ft), Wiltshire, England. It was probably constructed in the Neolithic period 3,500 years ago, and is linked with nearby ◊Silbury Hill. The village of Avebury was built within the circle, and many of the stones were used for building material.
Avebury John Lubbock, 1st Baron Avebury 1834–1913. British banker. A Liberal (from 1886 Liberal Unionist) member of Parliament 1870–1900, he was responsible for the Bank Holidays Act of 1871 introducing statutory public holidays.
Ave Maria /ˈɑːvɪ, ˈɑːveɪ/ a Christian devotional recitation and prayer to the Virgin Mary, which takes its name from the archangel Gabriel's salutation to the Virgin Mary when announcing that she would be the mother of the Messiah (Luke 1: 28) [Latin = Hail, Mary]
avenge /əˈvendʒ/ *v.t.* to take vengeance for (an injury) or on behalf of (a person). —**avenger** *n.* [from Old French from Latin *vindicare* = vindicate]
avens *n.* any of several low-growing plants of the genus *Geum* of the rose family Rosaceae. Species are distributed throughout Eurasia and N Africa. Mountain avens *Dryas octopetala* belongs to a different genus and grows in mountain and arctic areas of Eurasia and North America. A creeping perennial, it has white flowers with yellow stamens.
avenue /ˈævənjuː/ *n.* **1.** a broad main street; a tree-lined approach or path. **2.** a way of approach. [French from *avenir* = come to from Latin *venire* = come]
aver /əˈvɜː/ *v.t.* (**-rr-**) to assert, to affirm. —**averment** *n.* [from Old French *a-* = to and Latin *verus* = true]
average /ˈævərɪdʒ/ *n.* **1.** the generally prevailing rate, degree, or amount. **2.** a number obtained by adding several quantities together and dividing the total by the number of quantities. **3.** in law, damage to or loss of a ship or cargo. —*adj.* of the usual or ordinary standard; calculated by making an average. —*v.t.* to amount to or produce as an average; to calculate the average of. [from French from Italian from Arabic = damaged goods]
Averroës /æˈvɜːrəʊiːz/ (Arabic **Ibn Rushd**) 1126–1198. Arabian philosopher who argued for the eternity of matter and against the immortality of the individual soul. His philosophical writings, including commentaries on Aristotle and on Plato's *Republic*, became known to the West through Latin translations. He influenced Christian and Jewish writers into the Renaissance, and reconciled Islamic and Greek thought.
averse /əˈvɜːs/ *pred. adj.* unwilling, opposed, disinclined (*to* or *from*). [from Latin *vertere* = turn]
aversion /əˈvɜːʃən/ *n.* **1.** a strong dislike (*to* or *from*), unwillingness. **2.** an object of dislike. [French or from Latin]
avert /əˈvɜːt/ *v.t.* **1.** to turn away (eyes, thoughts, etc.). **2.** to prevent (a disaster etc.) from happening. [from Latin *vertere* = turn]
Avery Tex (Frederick Bean) 1907–1980. US cartoon-film director who used violent, sometimes surreal humour. At Warner Brothers he helped develop the characters Bugs Bunny and Daffy Duck, before moving to MGM in 1942 where he created, among others, Droopy and Screwball Squirrel.
Avesta /əˈvestə/ *n.* the sacred scripture of Zoroastrianism, compiled by Zoroaster as a means of reforming an older tradition. (See ◊Zend-Avesta.) —**Avestan** *adj. & n.* [from Persian *avastāk* = text]
aviary /ˈeɪvɪərɪ/ *n.* a large cage or building for keeping birds. [from Latin *avis* bird]
aviation /eɪvɪˈeɪʃən/ *n.* the practice or science of flying aircraft. See ◊flight. [French from Latin *avis* = bird]
aviator /ˈeɪvɪeɪtə/ *n.* a pilot or member of an aircraft crew in the early days of aviation.
avid /ˈævɪd/ *adj.* eager, greedy. —**avidity** /əˈvɪdɪtɪ/ *n.*, **avidly** *adv.* [from French or Latin *avēre* = crave]

Avignon /'ævi:njɒn/ city in Provence, France, capital of Vaucluse *département*, on the river Rhône NW of Marseilles; population (1982) 174,000. It was an important Gallic and Roman city, and has 14th-century walls, a 12th-century bridge (only half still standing), a 13th-century cathedral, and a palace built 1334–42 during the residence here of the popes. Avignon was papal property 1348–1791.

avionics /eɪvi'ɒnɪks/ *n. or n.pl.* the science of electronics applied to aeronautics. [from *avi(ation) and electronics*]

avocado /ævə'kɑ:dəʊ/ *n.* (*plural* **avocados**) **1.** a tree *Persea americana* of the laurel family, native to Central America. The dark green, thick-skinned, pear-shaped fruit has thick skin and creamy flesh. **2.** its dark green colour. [Spanish (= advocate) from Aztec]

avocation /ævə'keɪʃən/ *n.* a secondary activity done in addition to one's main work; (*colloquial*) one's occupation. [from Latin *avocare* = call away]

avocet /'ævəset/ *n.* a wading bird, genus *Recurvirostra*, family Recurvirostridae, with characteristic long, narrow, upturned bill used in sifting water as it feeds in the shallows. It is about 45 cm/18 in long, and has long legs, partly-webbed feet, and black and white plumage. There are four species. [from French from Italian]

Avogadro's hypothesis /ævə'gɑ:drəʊ/ in chemistry, the law stating that equal volumes of all gases, when at the same temperature and pressure, have the same numbers of molecules. This law was first propounded by the Italian physicist, Count Amadeo Avogadro (1776–1856).

Avogadro's number or **Avogadro's constant** the number of carbon atoms in 12 g of the carbon-12 isotope (6.022045×10^{23}). The relative atomic mass of any element, expressed in grams, contains this number of atoms. [from Amadeo *Avogadro*]

avoid /ə'vɔɪd/ *v.t.* to keep away or refrain from; to escape or evade. —**avoidable** *adj.*, **avoidance** *n.* [from Anglo-French = clear out]

avoirdupois /ævədə'pɔɪz/ *n.* a system of weights based on a pound (0.45 kg) of 16 ounces (each of 16 drams) or 7,000 grains (each equal to 65 mg). [French = goods of weight]

Avon /'eɪvɒn/ any of several rivers in England and Scotland. The Avon in Warwickshire is associated with Shakespeare.

Avon county in SW England; **area** 1,340 sq km/517 sq mi; **administrative headquarters** Bristol; **products** aircraft and other engineering products, tobacco, chemicals, printing, dairy products; **population** (1987) 951,000; **recent history** formed in 1974 from the city and county of Bristol, part of S Gloucestershire, and part of N Somerset.

avow /ə'vaʊ/ *v.t.* to declare, to admit. —**avowal** *n.*, **avowedly** /ə'vaʊdlɪ/ *adv.* [from Old French from Latin *vocare* = call]

avuncular /ə'vʌŋkjʊlə/ *adj.* of or like a kindly uncle. [from Latin *avunculus* = maternal uncle (diminutive of *avus* =grandfather)]

AWACS /'eɪwæks/ acronym from Airborne Warning And Control System.

await /ə'weɪt/ *v.t.* to wait for; to be in store for. [from Anglo-French]

awake /ə'weɪk/ *v.t./i.* (*past* **awoke** /ə'wəʊk/, *past participle* **awoken** /ə'wəʊkən/) **1.** to wake, to cease from sleep; to become active. **2.** to rouse from sleep. —*pred. adj.* no longer or not yet asleep; alert. [Old English]

awaken /ə'weɪkən/ *v.t.* to awake; to draw the attention of (a person *to* a fact etc.). [Old English]

award /ə'wɔd/ *v.t.* to give by official decision as a payment, prize, or penalty. —*n.* **1.** a decision of this kind. **2.** an amount or prize etc. awarded. [Anglo-French *awarder*]

aware /ə'weə/ *pred. adj.* having knowledge or realization (*of* or *that*). [Old English]

awash /ə'wɒʃ/ *pred. adj.* washed over by water or waves.

Awash /'a:waː∫/ river that rises to the S of Addis Ababa in Ethiopia and flows NE to Lake Abba on the frontier with Djibouti. Although deep inside present-day Ethiopia, the Awash River is considered by Somalis to mark the eastern limit of Ethiopian sovereignty prior to the colonial division of Somaliland in the 19th century.

away /ə'weɪ/ *adv.* **1.** to or at a distance; into nonexistence. **2.** constantly, persistently. **3.** without delay. —*adj.* played or playing on an opponent's ground. —*n.* an away match or (in football pools) victory in this. [Old English]

awe /ɔː/ *n.* respect or admiration charged with reverence or fear. —*v.t.* to fill or inspire with awe. [Old Norse]

Awe longest of the Scottish freshwater lochs (37 km/23 mi), in Strathclyde, SE of Oban. It is drained by the river Awe into Loch Etive.

aweigh /ə'weɪ/ *adv.* (of an anchor) just lifted from the bottom in weighing anchor.

awesome /'ɔːsəm/ *adj.* inspiring awe.

awestricken, awestruck *adjs.* filled with awe.

awful /'ɔːfəl/ *adj.* **1.** (*colloquial*) very bad or poor; notable of its kind. **2.** awe-inspiring, terrifying.

awfully /'ɔːfʊlɪ, colloquial 'ɔːflɪ/ *adv.* **1.** in a way that inspires awe. **2.** (*colloquial*) very; badly.

awhile /ə'waɪl/ *adv.* for a short time. [Old English = *a while*]

awkward /'ɔːkwəd/ *adj.* **1.** clumsy, having little skill. **2.** difficult to handle, use, or deal with. **3.** embarrassing, inconvenient; embarrassed. —**awkwardly** *adv.*, **awkwardness** *n.* [from obsolete *awk* = perverse, from Old Norse = turned the wrong way]

awl *n.* a small, pointed tool for pricking holes, especially in leather or wood. [Old English]

awn *n.* the bristly head of the sheath of barley, oats, etc. [from Old Norse]

awning *n.* a canvas or plastic sheet stretched by supports from a wall as a shelter against sun and rain.

awoke past of **awake**.

awoken past participle of **awake**.

awry /ə'raɪ/ *adv.* **1.** crookedly, out of the true position. **2.** amiss. —*pred. adj.* crooked.

axe *n.* a chopping-tool with a long handle and a heavy blade. —*v.t.* to eliminate or reduce drastically. —**have an axe to grind**, to have a personal interest involved and to be anxious to take care of it. [Old English]

Axelrod /'æksəlrɒd/ Julius 1912– . US neuropharmacologist, who shared the 1970 Nobel Prize for Medicine with the biophysicists Bernard Katz and Ulf von Euler for his work on ◊neurotransmitters.

axial /'æksɪəl/ *adj.* **1.** of or forming an axis. **2.** round an axis. —**axially** *adv.* [Latin = axle, pivot]

axil *n.* the upper angle where a leaf joins a stem, or between a branch and the trunk of a tree. —**axillary** *adj.* [from Latin *axilla* armpit (diminutive of *ala* = wing)]

axiology /æksɪ'ɒlədʒɪ/ *n.* in philosophy, the theory of value. —**axiological** /-'lɒdʒɪkəl/ *adj.* [from French from Greek *axia* = value]

axiom /'æksɪəm/ *n.* an established or accepted principle; a self-evident truth. —**axiomatic** /-'mætɪk/ *adj.* [from French or Latin from Greek *axios* = worthy]

axis /'æksɪs/ *n.* (*plural* **axes** /-siːz/) **1.** an imaginary line about which an object rotates; a line about which a regular figure is symmetrically arranged. **2.** in mathematics, a reference line from which measurements may be taken, as in a **coordinate axis**; or a line about which an object may be symmetrical, as in an **axis of symmetry**; or a line about which an object or plane figure may revolve. **3.** the relation between countries, regarded as a common pivot on which they revolve, especially the ◊Axis. [Latin = axle, pivot]

Axis *n.* the alliance of Nazi Germany and Fascist Italy before and during World War II. The **Rome–Berlin Axis** was formed in 1936, when Italy was being threatened with sanctions because of its invasion of Ethiopia (Abyssinia). It became a full military and political alliance in May 1939. A ten-year alliance between Germany, Italy, and Japan (**Rome–Berlin–Tokyo Axis**) was signed in Sept 1940 and was subsequently joined by Hungary, Bulgaria, Romania, and the puppet states of Slovakia and Croatia. The Axis collapsed with the surrender of Italy in 1943, followed by Germany and Japan in 1945.

axle *n.* the bar or rod on which a wheel or wheels revolve(s); the rod connecting a pair of wheels of a vehicle. [from Old Norse]

Axminster /'æksmɪnstə/ *n.* a machine-woven tufted carpet with cut pile. [name of town in Devon]

axolotl /æksə'lɒtəl/ *n.* any of several species of newtlike amphibian belonging to the family Ambystomatidae, especially *A. mexicanum*, found in Mexican lakes. Axolotls can breed without changing to the adult form, although individuals occasionally develop into land-dwelling adults. [Nahuatl *atl* = water and *xolotl* servant]

axon /'æksɒn/ *n.* a long, threadlike extension of a nerve-cell, usually carrying signals from it towards other nerve-cells, or an effector organ such as a muscle. [from Greek = axis]

Axum /'a:ksʊm/ alternative transliteration of ◊Aksum, an ancient kingdom in Ethiopia.

Ayacucho /aɪə'ku:tʃaʊ/ capital of a province of the same name in the Andean mountains of central Peru; population (1988) 94,200. The last great battle in the war of independence against Spain was fought near here in Dec 1824.

ayatollah /aɪə'tɒlə/ *n.* a Shi'ite religious leader in Iran. [Persian from Arabic = token of God]

Ayckbourn /'eɪkbɔ:n/ Alan 1939–. English playwright. His prolific output, characterized by comic dialogue, includes *Absurd Person Singular* 1973, the trilogy *The Norman Conquests* 1974 and scripts for television.

Few women care to be laughed at and men not at all, except for large sums of money.

Alan Ayckbourn
The Norman Conquests

---

aye¹ /aɪ/ *adv.* (*archaic, dialect, nautical,* or *formal*) yes, —*n.* an affirmative answer or vote. [probably from pronoun *I* expressing assent]

aye² /aɪ/ *adv.* (*archaic*) always. [from Old Norse]

aye-aye *n.* a nocturnal, tree-climbing prosimian *Daubentonia madagascariensis* of Madagascar, related to the lemurs. It is just over 1 m/3 ft long, including a tail 50 cm/20 in long.

Ayer /eə/ A(lfred) J(ules) 1910–1989. English philosopher. He wrote *Language, Truth and Logic* 1936, an exposition of the theory of 'logical positivism', presenting a criterion by which meaningful statements (essentially truths of logic, as well as statements derived from experience) could be distinguished from meaningless metaphysical utterances (for example, claims that there is a God or that the world external to our own minds is illusory).

Ayers Rock /eəz/ a vast, ovate mass of pinkish rock in Northern Territory, Australia; 335 m/1,100 ft high and 9 km/6 mi around.

Ayesha /'aɪʃə/ 611–678. Third and favourite wife of the prophet Muhammad, who married her when she was nine. Her father, Abu Bakr, became ◊caliph on Muhammad's death in 632, and she bitterly opposed the later succession to the caliphate of Ali, who had once accused her of infidelity.

Ayrshire /'eəʃə/ former county of SW Scotland, with a 113 km/70 mi coastline on the Firth of Clyde. In 1975 the major part was merged in the region of Strathclyde.

Ayub Khan /ɑː'ju:b/ 1907–1974. Pakistani soldier and president from 1958 to 1969. He served in the Burma Campaign 1942–45, and was commander in chief of the Pakistan army in 1951. In 1958 martial law was proclaimed in Pakistan and Ayub Khan assumed power after a bloodless army coup. He won the presidential elections in 1960 and 1965. He established a stable economy and achieved limited land reforms. His militaristic government was unpopular, particularly with Bengalis. He resigned in 1969 after widespread opposition and civil disorder, notably in Kashmir.

Ayurveda /aɪuə'veɪdə/ *n.* an ancient Hindu system of medicine. The main principles are derived from the Vedas of the 1st century AD, and it is still practised in India, using herbs, purgatives, and liniments, in Ayurvedic hospitals and dispensaries.

azalea /ə'zeɪlɪə/ *n.* any of various deciduous flowering shrubs, genus *Rhododendron*, of the heath family Ericaceae. Azaleas are closely related to the evergreen ◊rhododendrons of the same genus. There are several species of azaleas native to Asia and North America, and from these many cultivated varieties have been derived. [from Greek = dry (from the dry soil in which Linnaeus believed that azaleas flourished)]

Azaña /ə'θænjə/ Manuel 1880–1940. Spanish politician and first prime minister 1931–33 of the second Spanish republic. He was last president of the republic during the Civil War 1936–39, before the establishment of a dictatorship under Franco.

Azerbaijan /æzəbaɪ'dʒɑ:n/ constituent republic of the USSR from 1936; **area** 86,600 sq km/33,436 sq mi; **capital** Baku; **physical** Caspian Sea; the country ranges from semidesert to the Caucasus mountains; **products** oil, iron, copper, fruit, vines, cotton, silk, carpets; **population** (1987) 6,811,000; 78% Azerbaijani, 8% Russian, 8% Armenian; **language** Turkic; **recent history** a member of the Transcaucasian Federation in 1917, it became an independent republic in 1918; occupied by the Red Army in 1920. Riots in 1990 led to the death of many Armenians.

Azerbaijan, Iranian /æzəbaɪ'dʒɑ:n/ two provinces of NW Iran, **Eastern Azerbaijan** (capital Tabriz), population (1986) 4,114,000, and **Western Azerbaijan** (capital Orúmiyeh), population 1,972,000. Azeris in Iran, as in the USSR, are Muslim (Shi'ite) ethnic Turks, descendants of followers of the Khans from the Mongol Empire.

Azhar, El /ə'za:/ Muslim university and mosque in Cairo, Egypt. Founded in 970 by Jawhar, commander in chief of the army of the Fatimid caliph, it is claimed to be the oldest university in the world. It became the centre of Islamic learning, with several subsidiary foundations, and is now primarily a school of Koranic teaching.

Azilian /ə'zɪlɪən/ *n.* an archaeological period following the close of the Old Stone (Palaeolithic) Age and regarded as one of the cultures of the Mesolithic Age. It was first recognized by Piette at Mas d'Azil, a village in Ariège, France. —*adj.* of this period.

azimuth /'æzɪməθ/ *n.* **1.** an arc of the sky from the zenith to the horizon. **2.** the distance (measured as an angle) along the horizon clockwise from the N point to the point where the azimuth through a particular object (e. g. a star) meets the horizon. **3.** a directional bearing. —**azimuthal** /-'mu:θəl/ *adj.* [from Old French from Arabic *al* = the and *sumūt* = directions]

azo dye a synthetic dye containing the azo group of two nitrogen atoms (N=N) connecting aromatic ring compounds. Azo dyes are usually red, brown, or yellow, and make up about half the dyes produced. They are manufactured from aromatic ◊amines.

Azores /ə'zɔ:z/ group of nine islands in the N Atlantic, belonging to Portugal; area 2,247 sq km/867 sq mi; population (1987) 254,000. They are outlying peaks of the Mid-Atlantic Ridge and are volcanic in origin. The capital is Ponta Delgada on the main island, San Miguel.

Azov /'eɪzɒv/ Russian (*Azovskoye More*) inland sea of the USSR forming a gulf in the NE of the Black Sea; area 37,555 sq km/14,500 sq mi. Principal ports include Rostov-on-Don, Kerch, and Taganrog. Azov is a good source of freshwater fish.

AZT *n.* or **retrovir**, or **zidovudine** trade names of azidothymidine, an antiviral drug used in the treatment of ◊AIDS.

Aztec /'æztek/ *n.* **1.** a member of an ancient Mexican civilization that migrated S into the valley of Mexico in the 12th century, and in 1325 began reclaiming lake marshland to build their capital, Tenochtitlán, on the site of present-day Mexico City. Under Montezuma I (reigned to 1440), the Aztecs created a tribute empire in central Mexico. **2.** their language, also called Nahuatl. —*adj.* of the Aztecs or their language. [from French or Spanish from Nahuatl = men of the north]

azure /'æʒə, 'æʒuə/ *adj. & n.* sky-blue; (in heraldry) blue. [from Old French from Latin from Arabic *al* = the and *lāzaward* (from Persian) = lapis lazuli]

b, B (*plural* **bs, b's**) *n.* **1.** the second letter of the alphabet. **2.** in music, the seventh note in the scale of C major.

b. abbreviation of born.

B symbol for ◊boron.

Ba symbol for ◊barium.

BA in education, abbreviation of Bachelor of Arts, an academic degree.

Baabda /'bɑbdə/ the capital of the province of Jebel Lubnan in central Lebanon, SE of Beirut, and site of the country's presidential palace.

Baader-Meinhof gang /'bɑːdɑ 'maɪnhɒf/ the popular name for the West German left-wing guerrilla group, the *Rote Armee Fraktion*/Red Army Faction, active from 1968 against what it perceived as US imperialism. [from its two leaders Andreas Baader (1943–1977) and Ulrike Meinhof (1934–1976)]

Baal /beɪl/ a divine title given to their chief male gods by the Phoenicians, or Canaanites. Their worship as fertility gods, often orgiastic and of a phallic character, was strongly denounced by the Hebrew prophets. [Semitic = lord or owner]

Baalbek /'bɑːlbek/ a city of ancient Syria, now in Lebanon, 60 km/36 mi NE of Beirut, 1,150 m/3,000 ft above sea level. It was originally a centre of Baal worship. The Greeks identified Baal with Helios, the Sun, and renamed Baalbek **Heliopolis**. Its ruins, including Roman temples, survive; the Temple of Bacchus, built in the 2nd century AD, is still almost intact.

Ba'ath Party /bɑːθ/ a socialist party aiming at the extended union of all Arab countries, active in Iraq and Syria.

Bab, the /bɑːb/ the assumed name of Mirza Ali Mohammad 1819–1850. Persian religious leader, born in Shiraz, founder of ◊Babism, an offshoot of Islam. In 1844 he proclaimed that he was a gateway to the Hidden Imam, a new messenger of Allah who was to come. He gained a large following whose activities caused the Persian authorities to fear a rebellion, and who were therefore persecuted. The Bab was executed for heresy. [Arabic = gate]

baba /'bɑːbɑː/ *n.* or **rum baba** a sponge cake soaked in rum syrup. [French]

Babangida /bɑː'bæŋɡɪdɑː/ Ibrahim 1941– . Nigerian politician and soldier, president from 1985. He became head of the Nigerian army in 1983 and in 1985 led a coup against President Buhari, assuming the presidency himself.

Babbage /'bæbɪdʒ/ Charles 1792–1871. English mathematician credited with being the inventor of the computer. He designed an ◊analytical engine, a general purpose mechanical computing device for performing different calculations according to a program input on punched cards (an idea borrowed from the Jacquard loom). This device was never built, but it embodied many of the principles on which present digital computers are based.

Babbit metal /'bæbɪt/ a soft, white metal, an ◊alloy of tin, lead, copper, and antimony, used to reduce friction in bearings. [from US inventor Isaac *Babbit* who developed it in 1839]

Babbitt Milton 1916– . US composer. After studying with Roger ◊Sessions he developed a personal style of ◊serialism influenced by jazz. He is a leading composer of electronic

music using the 1960 RCA Mark II synthesizer, which he helped to design.

babble *v.t./i.* **1.** to make incoherent sounds; to talk inarticulately or excessively; to say incoherently. **2.** to repeat or divulge foolishly. **3.** (of a stream etc.) to murmur as it trickles. —*n.* **1.** incoherent or foolish talk. **2.** a confused murmur.

babbler *n.* a bird of the thrush family, Muscicapidae, with a loud babbling cry. Babblers, subfamily Timaliinae, are found in the Old World. There are some 250 species in the group.

babe *n.* **1.** (*poetical*) a baby. **2.** an inexperienced or guileless person. **3.** (*US slang*) a young woman. [imitative of child's *ba ba*]

babel /'beɪbəl/ *n.* **1.** a confused noise, especially of voices. **2.** a scene of confusion. [from Hebrew *babel* = Babylon from Semitic *bab ili* = gate of God]

Babel Hebrew name for the city of ◊Babylon, chiefly associated with the **Tower of Babel** which, in the Genesis story in the Old Testament, was erected in the plain of Shinar by the descendants of Noah. It was a ziggurat, or staged temple, seven storeys high (100 m/300 ft) with a shrine of Marduk on the summit. It was built by Nabopolassar, father of Nebuchadnezzar, and was destroyed when Sennacherib sacked the city in 689 BC.

Babel Isaak Emmanuilovich 1894–1941. Russian writer. Born in Odessa, he was an ardent supporter of the Revolution and fought with Budyenny's cavalry in the Polish campaign of 1921–22, an experience which inspired *Konarmiya*/*Red Cavalry* 1926. His other works include *Odesskie rasskazy*/*Stories from Odessa* 1924, which portrays the life of the Odessa Jews.

Babeuf /bɑː'bɜːf/ François-Noël 1760–1797. French revolutionary journalist, a pioneer of practical socialism. In 1794 he founded a newspaper in Paris, later known as the *Tribune of the People*, in which he demanded the equality of all people. He was guillotined for conspiring against the ruling Directory during the French Revolution.

Babi faith /'bɑːbi/ an alternative name for the ◊Baha'i faith.

babirusa *n.* a wild pig *Babirousa babyrussa*, becoming increasingly rare, found in the moist forests and by the water of Sulawesi, Buru, and nearby Indonesian islands. The male has large upper tusks which grow upwards through the skin of the snout and curve back towards the forehead. The babirusa is up to 80 cm/2.5 ft at the shoulder. It is nocturnal, and swims well.

Babism /'bɑːbɪzəm/ *n.* a religious movement founded in the 1840s by Mirza Ali Mohammad. An offshoot of Islam, it differs mainly in the belief that Muhammad was not the last of the prophets. The movement split into two groups after the death of the Bab; Baha'ullah, the leader of one of these groups, founded the ◊Baha'i faith. [from the *Bab*, assumed name of Mirza Ali Mohammad]

Babi Yar /'bɑːbi 'jɑː/ site of a massacre in World War II of more than 100,000 people (80,000 Jews; the others were Poles, Russians, and Ukrainians) by German troops in 1941, in Kiev, USSR. The poet ◊Yevtushenko drew attention to it in the early 1960s in a poem of the same name.

baboon /bə'buːn/ *n.* a large African and Arabian monkey, genus *Papio*, with a long, doglike muzzle and large canine teeth, spending much of its time on the ground in open country. Males, with head and body up to 1.1 m/3.5 ft long, are larger than females and dominant males rule the 'troops' in which baboons live. [from Old French or Latin]

Babur /'bɑːbə/ the title given to ◊Zahir ud-din Muhammad, founder of the Mogul Empire in N India. [Arabic = lion]

baby /'beɪbɪ/ *n.* **1.** a very young child or animal. **2.** the youngest member of a family etc.; a thing small of its kind; a childish person. **3.** (*slang*) a sweetheart. **4.** (*slang*) one's own concern or activity. —*v.t.* to treat like a baby. —**baby grand,** a small grand piano. **baby-sit** *v.i.* to look after a young child while its parents are out. **baby-sitter** *n.* one who baby-sits. —**babyhood** *n.,* **babyish** *adj.*

Babylon /'bæbɪlən/ capital of ancient Babylonia, on the bank of the lower Euphrates River. The site is now in Iraq, 88 km/55 mi S of Baghdad and 8 km/5 mi N of Hilla, which is built chiefly of bricks from the ruins of Babylon. In 1986–89 President Saddam Hussein constructed a replica of the Southern Palace and citadel of Nebuchadnezzar II, on the plans of the German archaeologist Robert Koldeway. The **hanging gardens of Babylon,** one of the ◊seven wonders of the world, were probably erected on a vaulted stone base, the only stone construction in the mud-brick city. They formed a series of terraces, irrigated by a hydraulic system.

Bacall /bə'kɔːl/ Lauren. Stage name of Betty Joan Perske 1924– . US actress who became an overnight star when cast by Howard Hawks opposite Humphrey Bogart in *To Have and Have Not* 1944. She and Bogart married in 1945, and starred together in *The Big Sleep* 1946. Her other films include *The Cobweb* 1955 and *Harper* 1966.

Baccalauréat /bækələ:reɪɑː/ *n.* the French examination providing the school-leaving certificate and qualification for university entrance, also available on an international basis as an alternative to English ◊A levels. [French]

baccalaureate /bækə'bːrɪət/ *n.* the degree of a Bachelor of Arts or Science etc. [from Latin *baccalaureus* = an advanced student, with pun on *bacca lauri* = laurel berry]

baccarat /'bækərɑː/ *n.* a gambling card game, played against the banker by punters each in turn staking that their hand will total nine. [French]

Bacchus /'bækəs/ in Greek and Roman mythology, the god of fertility (see ◊Dionysus) and of wine; his rites (the **Bacchanalia**) were orgiastic.

Bach /bɑːx/ Johann Sebastian 1685–1750. German composer. His appointments included positions at the courts of Weimar and Anhalt-Köthen, and from 1723 until his death he was musical director at St Thomas's choir school in Leipzig. Bach was a master of ◊counterpoint, and his music epitomizes the Baroque polyphonic style. His orchestral music includes the six *Brandenburg Concertos*, other concertos for clavier and violin, and four orchestral suites. Bach's keyboard music—for clavier and organ—his fugues and his choral music are of equal importance. He also wrote chamber music and songs. He came from a distinguished musical family and three of his sons became noted composers: **Wilhelm Friedemann Bach** (1710–1784), also an organist, improviser and master of ◊counterpoint; **Carl Philip Emmanuel Bach** (1714–1788), who introduced a new homophonic style which influenced Mozart, Haydn, and Beethoven; and **Johann Christian Bach** (1735–1782), celebrated in Italy as a composer of operas, and music master to the British royal family.

bachelor /'bætʃələ/ *n.* **1.** an unmarried man. **2.** one who holds the degree of Bachelor of Arts or Science etc. —**bachelor flat,** one suitable for a person living alone. **Bachelor of Arts** *or* **Science** etc., a person who has obtained a first degree in arts or sciences, or other faculty. [from Old French *bacheler* = aspirant to knighthood]

bacillus /bə'sɪləs/ *n.* (*plural* **bacilli** /-laɪ/) a member of a group of rodlike ◊bacteria that occur everywhere in the soil and air. By entering and multiplying in animal and other tissues, some are responsible for diseases such as anthrax or for causing food spoilage. —**bacillary** *adj.* [Latin, diminutive of *baculus* = stick]

back¹ *n.* **1.** the hinder surface of the human body from shoulder to hip; the corresponding part of an animal's body. **2.** a similar ridge-shaped part, the keel of a ship. **3.** an outer or rear surface; the less active, less important, or less visible part; the side or part normally away from the spectator or direction of motion. **4.** the part of a garment covering the back. **5.** a defensive player near the goal in football etc. —*adj.* **1.** situated behind or in the rear. **2.** of or for past time. **3.** (of vowels) formed at the back of the mouth (as in *hard, hot*). —*adv.* **1.** to the rear, away from the front. **2.** in or into an earlier or normal position or condition; in or into the past. **3.** at a distance; in check. **4.** in return. —**at the back of one's mind,** borne in mind but not consciously thought of. **backbencher** *n.* an MP not entitled to sit on the front benches in Parliament, i.e. one without senior office either in government or in opposition. **back boiler,** a boiler behind a domestic fire. **back formation,** an apparent root word formed from a word that looks like (but is not) its derivative, as *laze* from *lazy*; formation of words in this way. **back of beyond,** (*colloquial*) a remote and benighted region. **back seat,** a seat at the back; a less prominent position. **back-seat driver,** a person who has no responsibility but is eager to advise someone who has. **back slang,** a form of slang using words spelt backwards, as *yob* for *boy*. **back-to-back** *adj.* (of houses) built with juxtaposed backs. **back to front,** with the back placed where the front should be. **get** *or* **put a person's back up,** to annoy or irritate him or her. **get off a person's back,** to stop annoying him or her. **have one's back to the wall,** to be fighting for survival. **put one's back into,** to put all one's strength into (efforts). **see the back of,** to be rid of. **turn one's back on,** to repudiate (former associates etc.). [Old English]

back² *v.t./i.* **1.** to help with money, to give encouragement or support to; to lay a bet on the success of. **2.** to go or cause to go backwards. **3.** to provide with a lining or support at the back; to provide a musical accompaniment to. **4.** to be so situated that its rear abuts *on.* **5.** (of wind) to change gradually in an anticlockwise direction. —**back down,** to abandon a claim, viewpoint etc. **back out,** to withdraw from an agreement. **back up,** to give encouragement or support to; to confirm (a statement). **back water,** to reverse a boat's forward motion by using the oars. —**backer** *n.*

backache *n.* pain in the back.

backbiting *n.* spiteful talk about a person, especially in his or her absence.

backblocks *n.pl.* (*Australian* and *New Zealand*) land in the remote interior.

backbone *n.* **1.** the spine. **2.** the main support of a structure. **3.** firmness of character.

backchat *n.* (*colloquial*) impudent repartee.

backcross *n.* a breeding technique used to determine the genetic makeup of an individual organism.

backdate *v.t.* to assign an earlier date than the actual one to (a document etc.); to make (agreements etc.) retrospectively valid.

backdrop *n.* a flat, painted curtain at the back of a stage set.

backfire *v.i.* **1.** (of an engine or vehicle) to undergo premature explosion in the cylinder or exhaust pipe. **2.** (of a plan etc.) to go wrong, especially so as to recoil on its originator. —*n.* an instance of backfiring.

backgammon /'bækgæmən/ *n.* a board game for two players, often used in gambling, played on a special double board with pieces like draughtsmen moved according to the throw of a dice. It was known in Mesopotamia, Greece and Rome, and in medieval England. [from *back¹* (because pieces go back and re-enter) and obsolete *gamen* = game]

background *n.* ˈ1. the back part of a scene etc., especially as the setting for the chief part; an unimportant or unobtrusive position. **2.** a person's education, knowledge, or social circumstances; explanatory or contributory information or circumstances.

backhand *n.* a stroke, especially in tennis, made with the back of one's hand towards one's opponent; the side of the court or player on which such strokes are made.

backhanded *adj.* **1.** delivered with the back of the hand. **2.** (of a compliment) oblique, ambiguous.

backhander *n.* **1.** a back-handed stroke. **2.** (*slang*) a reward for services rendered, a bribe.

backing *n.* **1.** support, encouragement; a body of supporters. **2.** material used to support or line the back of something. **3.** a musical accompaniment to a singer.

backlash *n.* a violent, usually hostile, reaction.

backless *adj.* without a back; (of a dress) cut low at the back.

backlog *n.* arrears of uncompleted work etc. [originally = a large log placed at the back of a fire to sustain it]

backpack *n.* a rucksack; a package of equipment carried similarly.

back-pedal *v.i.* (-ll-) 1. to work the pedals of a bicycle backwards. 2. to reverse one's previous action or opinion.

backside *n.* (*colloquial*) the buttocks.

backslide *v.i.* to relapse into error or bad ways.

backspace *v.i.* to cause a typewriter carriage or golf ball to move backwards one space.

backstage *adj. & adv.* behind the curtain of a theatre, especially in the wings or dressing rooms.

backstitch *v.t./i.* to sew by inserting the needle each time behind the place where it has just been brought out. —*n.* a stitch made in this way.

backstroke *n.* a swimming stroke performed on the back.

backtrack *v.i.* to retrace one's steps; to reverse one's action.

backward /'bækwəd/ *adj.* 1. directed towards the back or to the starting point. 2. slow to make (mental etc.) progress. 3. lacking confidence to come forward, shy. —*adv.* backwards. —**backwardness** *n.*

backwards /'bækwədz/ *adv.* 1. towards the direction away from one's front; back foremost. 2. (of the motion of a thing) towards its starting point. 3. in the reverse of the usual order; into a worse state; into the past. —**bend** *or* **lean over backwards**, to go to great lengths (*to*). **know something backwards**, to know it exhaustively.

backwash *n.* receding waves created by a moving ship.

backwater *n.* 1. a stretch of stagnant water beside a stream. 2. a place indifferent to progress or new ideas.

backwoods *n.* 1. remote virgin forest, as formerly in North America. 2. a remote or backward area. —**backwoodsman** *n.* (*plural* **backwoodsmen**).

backyard *n.* a yard at the back of a house.

bacon /'beɪkən/ *n.* dried and salted meat from the back or side of a pig. —**bring home the bacon**, (*slang*) to succeed in an undertaking. **save one's bacon**, (*slang*) to escape injury or punishment. [from Old French]

Bacon Francis 1561–1626. English politician, philosopher, and essayist. He became Lord Chancellor in 1618, and the same year confessed to bribe-taking, was fined £40,000 (which was paid by the king), and spent four days in the Tower of London. His works include *Essays* 1597, characterized by pith and brevity; *The Advancement of Learning* 1605, a seminal work discussing scientific method; the *Novum Organum* 1620, in which he redefined the task of natural science, seeing it as a means of empirical discovery and a method of increasing human power over nature; and *The New Atlantis* 1626, describing a utopian state in which scientific knowledge is systematically sought and exploited.

Bacon Francis 1909– . Irish painter, born in Dublin. He came to London in 1925 and taught himself to paint. He practised abstract art, then developed a distorted Expressionist style with tortured figures presented in loosely defined space. From 1945 he focused on studies of figures, as in his series of screaming popes based on the portrait of Innocent X by Velázquez.

bacteria plural of ◊bacterium.

bactericide /bæk'tɪərɪsaɪd/ *n.* a substance that kills bacteria. —**bactericidal** *adj.* [from Latin *caedere* = kill]

bacteriology *n.* the scientific study of bacteria. —**bacteriological** /-'lɒdʒɪkəl/ *adj.*, **bacteriologist** *n.*

bacteriophage *n.* a virus that attacks bacteria. Such viruses are now of use in genetic engineering.

bacterium /bæk'tɪərɪəm/ *n.* (*plural* **bacteria**) any of several types of microscopic or ultramicroscopic single-celled organisms with prokaryotic cells (see ◊prokaryote). They usually reproduce by ◊binary fission, and since this may occur approximately every 20 minutes, a single bacterium is potentially capable of producing 16 million copies of itself in a day. —**bacterial** *adj.* [from Greek *baktērion*, diminutive of *baktron* = stick]

Bactria /'bæktrɪə/ former region of central Asia (now Afghanistan, Pakistan, and Soviet Central Asia) which was partly conquered by ◊Alexander the Great. During the 3rd–6th centuries BC it was a centre of East-West trade and cultural exchange.

Bactrian /'bæktrɪən/ *n.* one of the two species of ◊camel, found in Asia.

badger

American badger

bad *adj.* (*comparative* **worse**, *superlative* **worst**) 1. of poor quality, defective. 2. putrid, decaying. 3. in poor health, injured. 4. morally defective, wicked; (of a child) naughty. 5. unwelcome, disagreeable; harmful, detrimental; (of something unwelcome) serious, severe. —*adv.* (*US*) badly. —**bad blood**, unfriendly feelings. **bad debt**, one not recoverable. **bad language**, swearwords. **feel bad about**, to feel guilt or remorse about. **go to the bad**, to become criminal, dissolute, or immoral. **not bad**, (*colloquial*) good, fairly good. —**badness** *n.*

bade /bæd, beɪd/ past of **bid**.

Baden /'baːdn/ former state of SW Germany, which had Karlsruhe as its capital. Baden was captured from the Romans in 282 by the Alemanni; later it became a margravate and, in 1806, a grand duchy. A state of the German empire 1871–1918, then a republic, and under Hitler a *Gau* (province), it was divided between the *Länder* of Württemberg-Baden and Baden in 1945 and in 1952 made part of ◊Baden-Württemberg.

Baden-Powell /'beɪdn 'pəʊəl/ Robert Stephenson Smyth, 1st Baron Baden-Powell 1857–1941. English general, founder of the Scout Association. He fought in defence of Mafeking (now Mafikeng) during the Second South African War. After 1907 he devoted his time to developing the Scout movement, which rapidly spread throughout the world.

Baden-Württemberg /'baːdn 'vʊətəmbɜːg/ administrative region (German *Land*) of SW Germany; **area** 35,800 sq km/13,819 sq mi; **capital** Stuttgart; **physical** Black Forest; Rhine boundary S and W; source of the Danube; see also ◊Swabia; **products** wine, jewellery, watches, clocks, musical instruments, textiles, chemicals, iron, steel, electrical equipment, surgical instruments; **population** (1988) 9,390,000; **recent history** formed in 1952 (following a plebiscite) by the merger of the *Länder* Baden, Württemberg-Baden, and Württemberg-Hohenzollern.

badge *n.* something worn to show one's rank, membership etc.

badger /'bædʒə/ *n.* a large burrowing animal of the weasel family, with molar teeth of a crushing type adapted to a partly vegetable diet, and short, strong legs with long claws suitable for digging. The Eurasian **common badger** *Meles meles* is about 1 m/3 ft long, with long, coarse, greyish hair on the back, and a white face with a broad, black stripe along each side. Mainly a woodland animal, it is harmless and nocturnal, and spends the day in a system of burrows called a 'sett'. It feeds on roots, a variety of fruits and nuts, insects, worms, mice, and young rabbits. —*v.t.* to pester. [perhaps from *badge*, from the distinctive markings on its head]

badinage /'bædɪnɑːʒ/ *n.* good-humoured mockery. [French]

badlands *n.pl.* a barren landscape cut by erosion into a maze of ravines, pinnacles, gullies and sharp-edged ridges. South Dakota and Nebraska, USA, are examples.

badly *adv.* (**worse**, **worst**) 1. defectively, improperly. 2. so as to inflict much injury, severely. 3. (*colloquial*) very much.

badminton /'bædmɪntən/ *n.* a volleying game played by one or two players opposing an equivalent number across a net, using rackets and a shuttlecock. From the outset it gained popularity with army officers who took it to India and played it out of doors. The first laws were drawn up in Poona in the mid-1870s. [from *Badminton* in Avon, W England, where the game is supposed to have evolved about 1870]

Badoglio /bɑːˈdəʊljəʊ/ Pietro 1871–1956. Italian soldier and Fascist politician. A veteran of campaigns against the peoples of Tripoli and Cyrenaica, in 1935 he became commander in chief in Ethiopia, adopting ruthless measures to break patriot resistance. He was created viceroy of Ethiopia and duke of Addis Ababa in 1936. He resigned during a disastrous World War II campaign into Greece in 1940 and succeeded Mussolini as prime minister of Italy from July 1943 to June 1944, negotiating the armistice with the Allies.

Baedeker /ˈbeɪdɪkə/ Karl 1801–1859. German publisher of foreign travel guides from 1829. These are now published in Hamburg (before World War II in Leipzig).

Baekeland /ˈbeɪklənd/ Leo Hendrik 1863–1944. Belgian-born US chemist who invented ◊Bakelite, the first commercial plastic, made from formaldehyde and phenol. He later made a photographic paper, Velox, which could be developed in artificial light.

Baffin /ˈbæfɪn/ William 1584–1622. English explorer and navigator. In 1616, he and Robert Bylot explored Baffin Bay, NE Canada, and reached latitude 77° 45' N, which for 236 years remained the 'furthest north'.

baffle v.t. 1. to perplex, to bewilder. 2. to frustrate. —n. a screen preventing the passage of sound etc. —bafflement n.

BAFTA /ˈbæftə/ acronym from British Academy of Film and Television Arts.

bag n. 1. a receptacle for carrying things, made of flexible material with an opening at the top; this with its contents. 2. anything resembling this, as loose folds of skin under the eyes. 3. the total number of game shot by one person. 4. (in plural, slang) a great quantity of. —v.t. (-gg-) 1. to put in a bag. 2. (slang) to secure possession of. —bag and baggage, with all one's belongings. in the bag, as good as secured. —bagful n. (plural bagfuls).

bagatelle /bægəˈtel/ n. 1. a board game in which small balls are struck into holes. 2. a thing of no importance. 3. a short piece of music, especially for the piano. [French from Italian]

Bagehot /ˈbædʒət/ Walter 1826–1877. English writer and economist, author of The English Constitution 1867, a classic analysis of the British political system. He was editor of the Economist magazine 1860–77.

baggage /ˈbægɪdʒ/ n. 1. luggage, especially that carried by sea or air. 2. the portable equipment of an army. [from Old French bagues = bundles]

Baggara /ˈbægərə/ n. a Bedouin people of the Nile basin, principally in Kordofan, Sudan, W of the White Nile. They are Muslims, traditionally occupied in cattle breeding and big-game hunting.

baggy adj. hanging in loose folds.

Baghdad /bægˈdæd/ historic city and capital of Iraq, on the Tigris river; population (1985) 4,649,000. Industries include oil refining, distilling, tanning, tobacco processing, and the manufacture of textiles and cement. Founded in 762, it became Iraq's capital in 1921. It was severely bombed during the ◊Gulf War of 1991. A route centre from the earliest times, it was developed by the 8th-century caliph Harun al-Rashid. It was overrun 1258 by the Mongols, who destroyed the irrigation system. In 1639 it was taken by the Turks. During World War I, Baghdad was captured by General Maude 1917. To the SE, on the river Tigris, are the ruins of Ctesiphon, capital of Parthia about 250 BC–AD 226 and of the ◊Sassanian Empire about 226–641.

bagpipe n. (also in plural) an ancient wind instrument used outdoors and incorporating a number of reed pipes powered from a single inflated bag squeezed by the player's arm and fed with air either by breath or by means of small bellows strapped to the waist. Known in Roman times, bagpipes are found in various forms throughout Europe.

bah /bɑː/ interjection expressing contempt or disgust.

Bahadur Shah II /bəˈhɑːdə ˈʃɑː/ 1775–1862. Last of the Mogul emperors of India. He reigned, though in name only, as king of Delhi 1837–57, when he was hailed by the mutineers of the ◊Sepoy Rebellion as an independent emperor in Delhi. After the rebellion he was exiled to Burma with his family.

Baha'i /bɑːˈhɑːɪ/ n. a monotheistic religion, or a follower of this, founded in the 19th century from a Muslim splinter group, ◊Babism, by the Persian ◊Baha'ullah and his son

Abdul Baha (1844–1921). It maintains that all great religious leaders are manifestations of the unknowable God and all scriptures are sacred. There is no priesthood: all Baha'is are expected to teach, and to work towards world unification. There are about 4.5 million Baha'is worldwide. —Baha'ism n. [from Persian bahā = splendour]

Bahamas /bəˈhɑːməz/ Commonwealth of the; a country comprising a group of islands in the Caribbean, off the SE coast of Florida; **area** 13,864 sq km/5,352 sq mi; **capital** Nassau on New Providence; **physical** 700 tropical coral islands (only 30 are inhabited) and about 1,000 cays; **head of state** Elizabeth II from 1973 represented by governor general; **head of government** Lynden Oscar Pindling from 1967; **political system** constitutional monarchy; **exports** cement, pharmaceuticals, petroleum products, crawfish, rum, pulpwood, over half the islands' employment comes from tourism; **population** (1990 est) 251,000; **language** English; **recent history** Independence was achieved from Britain in 1964. The first national assembly elections were held in 1967 and full independence was reached in 1973.

Baha'ullah /bɑːhɑːˈʊlə/ the title of Mirza Hosein Ali 1817–1892. Persian founder of the ◊Baha'i religion. He proclaimed himself as the prophet the ◊Bab had foretold. [Persian = God's glory]

Bahrain /bɑːˈreɪn/ State of; a country comprising a group of islands in the Arabian Gulf, between Saudi Arabia and Iran; **area** 688 sq km/266 sq mi; **capital** Manama on the largest island (also called Bahrain); **physical** 35 islands, composed largely of sand-covered limestone; generally poor and infertile soil; flat and hot; a causeway links Bahrain to mainland Saudi Arabia; **head of state and government** Sheikh Isa bin Sulman al-Khalifa (1933–) from 1961; **political system** absolute emirate; **exports** oil, natural gas, aluminium, fish; **population** (1990 est) 512,000 (two thirds are nationals); **language** Arabic (official), Farsi, English, Urdu; **recent history** British protectorate 1861–1968, Bahrain became an independent state in 1971. A national assembly was elected and dissolved; the Emir assumed virtually absolute power in 1975.

Baikal /baɪˈkæl/ (Russian **Baykal Ozero**) the largest freshwater lake in Asia, (area 31,500 sq km/12,150 sq mi) and deepest in the world (up to 1,740 m/5,710 ft), in S Siberia, USSR. Fed by more than 300 rivers, it is drained only by the Lower Angara. It has sturgeon fisheries and rich fauna, including its own breed of seals, but is threatened by pollution.

Baikonur /baɪkəˈnuə/ the main Soviet launch site for spacecraft, located at Tyuratam, near the Aral Sea.

bail[1] n. 1. money or property pledged as security that an arrested person will appear in court to stand trial if released temporarily. If the person does not attend, the bail may be forfeited. 2. permission for a person's release on such security. —v.t. to procure the release of (an arrested person) by becoming security for him or her. —bail out, to rescue from financial difficulties. —on bail, released after bail is pledged. [from Old French bailler = take charge of, from Latin baiulare = carry a load]

bail[2] n. 1. in cricket, either of the two cross-pieces resting on the three stumps of the wicket. 2. a bar separating horses in an open stable. 3. a bar holding paper against the platen of a typewriter. [from Old French bailler = enclose]

bail[3] v.t. to scoop out (water) that has entered a boat; to clear (a boat) of water. [from French baille = bucket]

bailey /ˈbeɪlɪ/ n. the outer wall of a castle; a court enclosed by this.

Bailey Donald Coleman 1901–1985. English engineer, inventor in World War II of the portable **Bailey bridge**, made of interlocking, interchangeable, adjustable, easily transportable units.

bailie /ˈbeɪlɪ/ n. a municipal officer and magistrate in Scotland.

bailiff /ˈbeɪlɪf/ n. 1. an officer of the court whose job, usually in the county courts, is to serve notices and enforce the court's orders involving seizure of the goods of a debtor; a bailiff can also make arrests. 2. a landlord's agent or steward. 3. the leading civil officer in each of the Channel Islands. [from Old French from Latin baiulus = manager]

bailiwick /ˈbeɪlɪwɪk/ n. the jurisdiction of a bailie or (in the Channel Islands) a bailiff. [from wick = district]

Bainbridge /'beɪnbrɪdʒ/ Beryl 1933– . English novelist, originally an actress, whose works have the drama and economy of a stage play. They include *The Dressmaker* 1973, *The Bottle Factory Outing* 1974, and the collected short stories in *Mum and Mr Armitage* 1985.

bain-marie /bæmæ'riː/ *n.* a vessel of hot water in which a dish of food is placed for slow cooking. [French from Latin *balneum mariae* = bath of Mary (supposed Jewish alchemist)]

Bairam /baɪ'rɑːm/ *n.* either of two annual Muslim festivals, **Greater Bairam**, celebrated concurrently with the annual pilgrimage (*hadj*) in the 12th month of the Muslim lunar calendar and continuing for three or four days, and **Lesser Bairam**, which follows the month of ritual fasting (Ramadan), the ninth month of the year, and lasts two or three days. [Turkish and Persian]

Baird /beəd/ John Logie 1888–1946. Scottish electrical engineer who pioneered television. In 1925 he gave the first public demonstration of television and in 1926 pioneered fibre optics, radar (in advance of Robert ◊Watson-Watt), and 'noctovision', a system for seeing at night by using infrared rays.

bairn /beən/ *n.* (*Scottish*) a child. [Old English]

bait *n.* food (real or sham) used to entice fish etc.; an enticement. —*v.t.* 1. to put bait on or in (a fish-hook, trap etc.). 2. to attack (a chained bear etc.) with dogs for sport; to torment or provoke. [from Old Norse]

baize *n.* a coarse, usually green, woollen material used to cover tables, doors etc. [from French *bai* = chestnut-coloured]

bake *v.t./i.* 1. to cook or be cooked by dry heat, especially in an oven. 2. to harden or be hardened by exposure to heat. —**baked beans**, cooked haricot beans (usually tinned and prepared with tomato sauce). [Old English]

bakehouse *n.* a house or room for baking bread.

Bakelite /'beɪkəlaɪt/ *n.* the first synthetic ◊plastic, created by Leo ◊Baekeland in 1909. Bakelite is hard, tough, and heatproof, and is used as an electrical insulator. It is made by the reaction of phenol with formaldehyde, producing a powdery resin that sets solid when heated. Objects are made by subjecting the resin to compression moulding (simultaneous heat and pressure in a mould). [from L H *Baekeland*]

baker /beɪkə/ *n.* one who bakes and sells bread. —**baker's dozen**, 13 (from the old custom of giving the retailer a free loaf for every 12 bought).

Baker Benjamin 1840–1907. English engineer who, with English engineer John Fowler (1817–1898), designed London's first underground railway (the Metropolitan and District) in 1869, the Forth Bridge, Scotland, 1890, and the original Aswan Dam on the river Nile, Egypt.

Baker James (Addison), III 1930– . US Republican politician. Under President Reagan, he was White House Chief of Staff 1981–85 and Treasury secretary 1985–88. After managing Bush's successful presidential campaign in 1988, Baker was appointed secretary of state in 1989.

Baker Kenneth (Wilfrid) 1934– . English Conservative politician, education secretary 1986–89, chair of the Conservative Party 1989–90, and home secretary from 1990.

bakery *n.* a place where bread is made or sold.

Bakewell tart /'beɪkwel/ a tart containing an almond-flavoured pudding mixture over a layer of jam. [town in Derbyshire, England]

baking *adj.* (*colloquial*, of weather etc.) intolerably hot.

baking powder a mixture of ◊bicarbonate of soda, $NaHCO_3$, and solid tartaric acid, used in cooking as a raising agent. When added to flour, the presence of water and heat causes carbon dioxide to be released, which makes the dough rise.

baksheesh /bæk'ʃiː ʃ/ *n.* (in the Middle East) a gratuity, alms. [Persian]

Bakst /bækst/ Leon. Assumed name of Leon Rosenberg 1886–1924. Russian painter and theatrical designer. He used intense colours and fantastic images from Oriental and folk art, with an Art Nouveau tendency to graceful surface pattern. His designs for Diaghilev's touring *Ballets Russes* made a deep impression in Paris 1909–14.

Baku /bɑː'kuː/ the capital city of the Azerbaijan Republic, USSR, and industrial port on the Caspian Sea; population (1987) 1,741,000. Baku is a centre of the Soviet oil industry and is linked by pipelines with Batumi on the Black Sea.

In Jan 1990 there were violent clashes between the Azeri majority and the Armenian minority, and Soviet troops were sent to the region. Over 13,000 Armenians subsequently fled from the city.

Bakunin /bə'kuːnɪn/ Mikhail 1814–1876. Russian anarchist, active in Europe. In 1848 he was expelled from France as a revolutionary agitator. In Switzerland in the 1860s he became recognized as the leader of the anarchist movement. In 1869 he joined the First International (a coordinating socialist body) but, after stormy conflicts with Karl Marx, was expelled in 1872.

> To *exploit* and to *govern* mean the same thing . . . Exploitation and government are two inseparable expressions of what is called politics.
> **Mikhail Bakunin**
> *The Knouto-Germanic Empire and the Soviet Revolution*

Balaclava /bælə'klɑːvə/ *n.* (in full **Balaclava helmet**) a knitted cap covering the head and neck, with an opening for the face. [from *Balaclava* in the Crimea]

Balaclava, Battle of in the Crimean War, an engagement on 25 Oct 1854 near a town in Ukraine, 10 km/6 mi SE of Sevastopol. It was the scene of the ill-timed **Charge of the Light Brigade** of British cavalry against the Russian entrenched artillery. Of the 673 soldiers who took part, there were 272 casualties.

Balakirev /bə'lɑːkɪref/ Mily Alexeyevich 1837–1910. Russian composer. He wrote orchestral and piano music, songs, and a symphonic poem *Tamara*, all imbued with the Russian national character and spirit. He was leader of the group known as the Five and taught its members: Mussorgsky, Cui, Rimsky-Korsakov, and Borodin.

balalaika /bælə'laɪkə/ *n.* a guitarlike instrument (made in various sizes) with a triangular sound box, ˙frets, and two, three, or four strings played by strumming with the fingers. It is popular in Slavonic countries. [Russian]

balance /'bæləns/ *n.* 1. an apparatus for weighing or measuring mass. The various types include the **beam balance** consisting of a centrally pivoted lever with pans hanging from each end, and the **spring balance**, in which the object to be weighed stretches (or compresses) a vertical coil spring fitted with a pointer that indicates the weight on a scale. Kitchen and bathroom scales are balances. 2. or **balance wheel** a mechanism regulating the speed of a clock or watch. 3. the stable condition arising from even distribution of weight or amount. 4. a preponderating weight or amount. 5. the agreement or difference between credits and debits; a statement of this. 6. the difference between a sum paid and a sum due; the amount left over. —*v.t./i.* 1. to offset, to weigh (considerations etc.) against each other. 2. to distribute (weights) evenly; to be, put, or keep in a state of balance. 3. to compare the credit and debit sides of (an account) and make any necessary entry to equalize them; (of an account) to have its two sides equal. —**in the balance**, with the outcome still undecided. **on balance**, taking all things into consideration. [from Old French from Latin *bilanx* = two-scaled (balance) (*lanx* = scale)]

balance of nature in ecology, the idea that there is an inherent stability in most ◊ecosystems, and that human interference can disrupt this stability. Organisms in the ecosystem are adapted to each other – for example, predator and prey populations keep each other in check; waste products produced by one species are used by another; and resources used by some are replenished by others.

balance of payments in economics, a tabular account of a country's debit and credit transactions with other countries. Items are divided into the **current account**, which includes both visible trade (imports and exports) and invisible trade (such as transport, tourism, interest, and dividends), and the **capital account**, which includes investment in and out of the country, international grants, and loans. Deficits or surpluses on these accounts are brought into balance by buying and selling reserves of foreign currencies.

balance of power in politics, the theory that the best way of ensuring international order is to have power so distributed among states that no single state is able to

Baldwin *Brought up in Harlem, the author James Baldwin started preaching at the Fireside Pentecostal Church at the age of 14.*

achieve a dominant position. The term, which may also refer more simply to the actual distribution of power, is one of the most enduring concepts in international relations. Since the development of nuclear weapons, it has been asserted that the balance of power has been replaced by a **balance of terror.**

balance of trade the balance of trade transactions of a country recorded in its current account; it forms one component of the country's ◊balance of payments.

balance sheet a statement of the financial position of a company or individual on a specific date, showing both ◊assets and ◊liabilities.

Balanchine /bæləntʃiːn/ George 1904–1983. Russian-born choreographer. After leaving the USSR in 1924, he worked with Diaghilev in France. Moving to the USA in 1933, he became a major influence on modern dance, starting the New York City Ballet in 1948. His many works include *Apollon Musagète* 1928 and *The Prodigal Son* 1929 for Diaghilev, several works for music by Stravinsky, such as *Agon* 1957 and *Duo Concertante* 1972, and musicals such as *On Your Toes* 1936 and *The Boys from Syracuse* 1938.

Balboa /bælˈbouə/ Vasco Núñez de 1475–1519. Spanish ◊conquistador, the first European to see the eastern side of the Pacific Ocean, on 25 Sept 1513, from the isthmus of Darien (now Panama). He was made admiral of the Pacific and governor of Panama but was removed by Spanish court intrigue, imprisoned, and executed.

balcony /bælkənɪ/ n. 1. a platform with a rail or balustrade, on the outside of a building, with access from an upper-storey door or window. 2. an upper tier of seats in a cinema or above the dress circle in a theatre. [from Italiᴀɴ]

bald /bɔːld/ adj. 1. with a hairless scalp; (of animals etc.) lacking the usual hairs, feathers etc. of the species. 2. (of a tyre) having its tread worn away. 3. (of style) plain and unelaborated. —**bald eagle,** a kind of eagle *Haliaetus leucocephalus* with white feathers on its head and neck, the emblematic bird of the USA.

baldachin /bældəkɪn/ n. or **baldaquin** a canopy over a throne etc. [from Italian *Baldaco* = Baghdad, where the original brocade of the canopy was made]

Balder /bɔːldə/ in Norse mythology, the son of ◊Odin and ◊Freya and husband of Nanna, and the best, wisest, and most loved of all the gods. He was killed, at ◊Loki's instigation, by a twig of mistletoe shot by the blind god Hodur.

balderdash /bɔːldədæʃ/ n. nonsense.

balding /bɔːldɪŋ/ adj. becoming bald.

baldric /bɔːldrɪk/ n. a strap, worn across the body, on which a shield or sword is hung. [from Old French *baudrei*]

Baldwin /bɔːldwɪn/ James 1924–1987. US writer, born in New York City, who portrayed the condition of black Americans in contemporary society. His works include the novels *Go Tell It on the Mountain* 1953, *Another Country* 1962, and *Just Above My Head* 1979; the play *The Amen Corner* 1955; and the autobiographical essays *Notes of a Native Son* 1955 and *The Fire Next Time* 1963. He was active in the civil-rights movement.

Baldwin Stanley, 1st Earl Baldwin of Bewdley 1867–1947. English Conservative politician, prime minister 1923–24, 1924–29, and 1935–37; he weathered the general strike of 1926, secured complete adult suffrage in 1928, and handled the ◊abdication crisis of Edward VIII in 1936, but failed to prepare Britain for World War II.

Baldwin I 1058–1118. King of Jerusalem. A French noble who joined his brother ◊Godfrey de Bouillon on the First Crusade in 1096, Baldwin established the kingdom of Jerusalem in 1100. It was destroyed by Islamic conquest in 1187.

bale[1] n. a large bundle of merchandise (e.g. cloth) or hay. —v.t. to make into a bale. —**baler** n. [from Middle Dutch]

bale[2] v.i. **bale out,** to escape from an aircraft by parachute. [from Old French *bailler*]

Balearic Islands /bæliˈærɪk/ (Spanish *Baleares*) Group of islands in the Mediterranean forming an autonomous region of Spain; including ◊Majorca, ◊Minorca, ◊Ibiza, Cabrera, and Formentera; **area** 5,000 sq km/1,930 sq mi; **capital** Palma de Mallorca; **products** figs, olives, oranges, wine, brandy, coal, iron, slate; tourism is crucial; **population** (1986) 755,000; **history** a Roman colony from 123 BC, the Balearic Islands were an independent Moorish kingdom 1009–1232. They were conquered by Aragón in 1343.

baleen /bæˈliːn/ n. whalebone. [from Old French from Latin *balaena* = whale]

baleful /beɪlfəl/ adj. having a deadly or malign influence. —**balefully** adv. [from *bale* (Old English *b(e)alu*) = destruction, evil]

Balewa /bəˈleɪwə/ an alternative title of Nigerian politician ◊Tafawa Balewa.

Balfour /bælfə/ Arthur James, 1st Earl of Balfour 1848–1930. British Conservative politician, prime minister 1902–05 and foreign secretary 1916–19, when he issued the Balfour Declaration in 1917 and was involved in peace negotiations after World War I, signing the Treaty of Versailles.

Balfour Declaration a letter, dated 2 Nov 1917, from the British foreign secretary A J Balfour to Lord Rothschild (chair, British Zionist Federation) stating: 'HM government view with favour the establishment in Palestine of a national home for the Jewish people'. It led to the foundation of Israel in 1948.

Bali /bɑːli/ island of Indonesia, E of Java, one of the Sunda Islands; **area** 5,800 sq km/2,240 sq mi; **capital** Denpasar; **physical** volcanic mountains; **products** gold and silver work, woodcarving, weaving, copra, salt, coffee; **population** (1980) 2,470,000; **history** Bali's Hindu culture goes back to the 7th century; the Dutch gained control of the island about 1908.

Baliol /beɪliəl/ John de *c.*1250–1314. King of Scotland 1292–96. As an heir to the Scottish throne on the death of Margaret, the Maid of Norway, his cause was supported by the English king, Edward I, against 12 other claimants. Having paid homage to Edward, Baliol was proclaimed king, but rebelled and gave up the kingdom when English forces attacked Scotland.

balk /bɔːk/ v.t./i. 1. to shy or jib *at.* 2. to thwart. [= *baulk*]

Balkan /bɔːlkən, ˈbɒl-/ adj. of the peninsula of SE Europe, S of the Danube and Sava rivers, or its peoples or countries. [Turkish]

Balkans /bɔːlkənz/ peninsula of SE Europe, stretching into the Mediterranean Sea between the Adriatic and Aegean seas, comprising Albania, Bulgaria, Greece, Romania, Turkey-in-Europe, and Yugoslavia. It is joined to the rest of Europe by an isthmus 1,200 km/750 mi wide between Rijeka to the W and the mouth of the Danube on the Black Sea to the E.

Balkan Wars two wars 1912–13 and 1913 (preceding World War I) which resulted in the expulsion by the Balkan states of Ottoman Turkey from Europe, except for a small area around Istanbul.

ball[1] /bɔːl/ *n.* **1.** a rounded object, solid or hollow, especially for use in a game. **2.** a single delivery of a ball by a bowler in cricket or a pitcher in baseball. **3.** a rounded mass or part; (in *plural, vulgar*) the testicles. —*v.t./i.* to form into a ball. —**ball bearing,** a ◊bearing using small steel balls. **ballpoint (pen),** a pen with a tiny ball as its writing point. **on the ball,** (*colloquial*) alert. **set the ball rolling,** to open a discussion. [from Old Norse]

ball[2] *n.* a formal social gathering for dancing. [from French from Latin from Greek]

Ball John died 1381. English priest, one of the leaders of the ◊Peasants' Revolt of 1381. A follower of John Wycliffe and a believer in social equality, he was imprisoned for disagreeing with the archbishop of Canterbury. During the revolt he was released from prison, and when in Blackheath, London, preached from the text 'When Adam delved and Eve span, who was then the gentleman?' When the revolt collapsed he escaped but was captured near Coventry and executed.

Ball Lucille 1911–1989. US comedy actress. From 1951 to 1957 she starred with her husband, Cuban bandleader Desi Arnaz, in *I Love Lucy*, the first US television show filmed before an audience. It was followed by *The Lucy Show* 1962–68 and *Here's Lucy* 1968–74.

ballad /ˈbæləd/ *n.* a slow, simple song, especially one with a repeated melody; a poem or song in short stanzas telling a story. Of simple metrical form and dealing with some strongly emotional event, the ballad is halfway between the lyric and the epic. Most English ballads date from the 15th century. Poets of the Romantic movement both in England and in Germany were greatly influenced by the ballad revival, as seen in, for example, *Lyrical Ballads* 1798 of Wordsworth and Coleridge. Other later forms are the 'broadsheets' with a satirical or political motive, and the testamentary 'hanging' ballads of the condemned criminal. [from Old French from Provençal *balada* = dancing song]

ballade /bæˈlɑːd/ *n.* **1.** a poem with one or more sets of three verses with seven, eight, or ten lines each ending with the same refrain line, and a short final verse. The form developed in France in the later Middle Ages from the ballad. **2.** in music, an instrumental piece based on a story; a form used in piano works by ◊Chopin and ◊Liszt. [French]

balladeer *n.* a composer or performer of ballads.

ball-and-socket joint a joint allowing considerable movement in three dimensions, for instance the joint between the pelvis and the femur. To facilitate movement, such joints are lubricated by cartilage and synovial fluid. The bones are kept in place by ligaments and moved by muscles.

Ballard /ˈbælɑːd/ J(ames) G(raham) 1930– . British novelist whose works include science fiction on the theme of disaster, such as *The Drowned World* 1962 and *High Rise* 1975, and the partly autobiographical *Empire of the Sun* 1984, dealing with his internment in China during World War II.

ballast /ˈbæləst/ *n.* **1.** heavy material placed in the hold of a ship or the car of a balloon to give it stability. **2.** coarse stones etc. forming the bed of a railway or road. —*v.t.* to weight with ballast. [from Low German or Scandinavian]

ballcock *n.* a device with a floating ball controlling the water level in a cistern; a type of ◊ball valve.

ballerina /bæləˈriːnə/ *n.* a woman ballet dancer, especially one taking leading roles in classical ballet. [Italian (*ballare* = dance)]

Ballesteros /bæliˈstɪərɒs/ Seve(riano) 1957– . Spanish golfer who came to prominence in 1976 and has won several leading tournaments in the USA, including the Masters Tournament. He has also won the British Open three times: in 1979, 1984, and 1988.

ballet /ˈbæleɪ/ *n.* a theatrical representation in dance form in which music also plays a major part in telling a story or conveying a mood. Some such form of entertainment existed in ancient Greece, but Western ballet as we know it today first appeared in Italy. From there it was brought by Catherine de ◊Medici to France in the form of a spectacle combining singing, dancing, and declamation. In the 20th century Russian ballet has had a vital influence on the classical tradition in the West, and modern ballet has developed in the USA through the work of George ◊Balanchine and

Martha ◊Graham, and in the UK through the influence of Marie ◊Rambert. [French from Italian *balletto* = a little dance]

balletomane /ˈbælɪtəmeɪn/ *n.* a ballet enthusiast.

ballista /bəˈlɪstə/ *n.* (*plural* **ballistae**) a machine of ancient warfare for hurling large stones etc. [Latin, from Greek *ballō* = throw]

ballistic /bəˈlɪstɪk/ *adj.* of projectiles. —**ballistic missile,** one powered only during the initial stages of its flight and falling by gravity on its target.

ballistics /bəˈlɪstɪks/ *n.* the study of the motion and impact of projectiles such as bullets, bombs, and missiles. For projectiles from a gun, relevant exterior factors include temperature, barometric pressure, and wind strength; and for nuclear missiles these extend to such factors as the speed at which the Earth turns.

balloon /bəˈluːn/ *n.* **1.** a small inflatable rubber bag with a neck, used as a child's toy or decoration. **2.** a large rounded fabric envelope inflated with hot air or gas to make it rise in the air, often one with a basket etc. for passengers. The first successful human balloon ascent was made by the ◊Montgolfier brothers in 1783 in Paris. During the French Revolution balloons were used for observation; in World War II they were used to defend London against low-flying aircraft. They are now used for recreation and as a means of meteorological, infrared, gamma-ray, and ultraviolet observation. The first transatlantic crossing by balloon was made 11–17 Aug 1978 by a US team. **3.** a balloon-shaped line containing the words or thoughts of a character in a comic strip or cartoon. —*v.t./i.* **1.** to swell out like a balloon. **2.** to travel by balloon. **3.** to hit or kick (a ball) high in the air. [from French or Italian *balla* = ball]

balloonist *n.* one who travels by balloon.

ballot /ˈbælət/ *n.* the process of voting (see ◊vote) to select a representative or course of action etc. usually in secret and on ballot papers; the total of votes cast by this method. —*v.t./i.* to vote or cause to vote by ballot. —**ballot box,** a container for ballot papers. **ballot paper,** a paper used in voting by ballot, usually having the names of candidates etc. printed on it. [from Italian = small ball; such voting was originally by small balls]

ballroom *n.* a large room for formal dancing. —**ballroom dancing,** performing social dances such as the ◊foxtrot, quickstep, ◊tango, and ◊waltz.

ball valve a valve used especially in lavatory cisterns to cut off the water supply when it reaches the correct level. It consists of a flat rubber washer at one end of a pivoting arm and a hollow ball at the other. The ball floats on the water surface, rising as the cistern fills, and at the correct level the rubber washer is pushed against the water-inlet pipe, cutting off the flow.

bally /ˈbælɪ/ *adj.* & *adv.* (*colloquial, dated*) a milder form of intensive 'bloody'. [voicing of *bl—y*, squeamish printing of *bloody*]

ballyhoo /bæliˈhuː/ *n.* loud noise; fuss; extravagant publicity.

balm /bɑːm/ *n.* **1.** a fragrant medicinal gum exuded by certain trees, balsam. **2.** an aromatic ointment. **3.** a healing or soothing influence. **4.** a herb *Melissa officinalis* with lemon-scented leaves. [from Old French from Latin = balsam]

Balmer /ˈbælmə/ Johann 1825–1898. Swiss physicist and mathematician who developed a formula that gave the wavelengths of the hydrogen atom spectrum. This simple formula played a central role in the development of spectral theory.

Balmoral Castle /bælˈmɒrəl/ the residence of the British royal family in Scotland on the river Dee, 10.5 km/6.5 mi NE of Braemar, Grampian region. The castle was rebuilt 1853–55 by Prince Albert, who bought the estate in 1852.

balmy /ˈbɑːmɪ/ *adj.* **1.** resembling balm, fragrant or soothing; (of air) soft and warm. **2.** (*slang*) = ◊barmy.

baloney /bəˈləʊnɪ/ variant of ◊boloney.

balsa /ˈbɔːlsə/ *n.* or **balsawood** a very light strong wood from a tropical American tree *Ochroma pyramidale*, used for models etc. [Spanish = raft]

balsam /ˈbɔːlsəm/ *n.* **1.** a resinous exudation from certain trees, balm, such as balsam of Peru from the Central American tree *Myroxylon pereirae*; an ointment, especially of a substance dissolved in oil or turpentine; a tree producing balsam. **2.** any of various flowering plants of the genus

Impatiens, especially one cultivated for its showy flowers. They are usually annuals with spurred red or white flowers and pods that burst and scatter their seeds when ripe. [Old English from Latin *balsamum*]

Baltic /'bɔːltɪk, 'bɒl-/ *adj.* of the Baltic Sea. —*n.* **Baltic Sea**, a large shallow arm of the North Sea, extending NE from the narrow Skagerrak and Kattegat, between Sweden and Denmark, to the Gulf of Bothnia between Sweden and Finland. Its coastline is 8,000 km/5,000 mi long, and its area, including the gulfs of Riga, Finland, and Bothnia, is 422,300 sq km/163,000 sq mi. Its shoreline is shared by Denmark, Germany, Poland, the USSR, Finland, and Sweden. [from Latin *Balthae* = dwellers near the Baltic Sea]

Baltic, Battle of the a naval battle fought off Copenhagen on 2 April 1801, in which a British fleet under Sir Hyde Parker, with ◊Nelson as second-in-command, annihilated the Danish navy.

Baltimore /'bɔːltɪmɔː/ industrial port and largest city in Maryland, USA, on the W shore of Chesapeake Bay, NE of Washington DC; population (1980) 2,300,000. Industries include shipbuilding, oil refining, food processing, and the manufacture of steel, chemicals, and aerospace equipment. Johns Hopkins University, Goucher College, the Peabody Conservatory of Music, and seven other universities are here.

Baltistan /bæltɪ'stɑːn/ region in the Karakoram range of NE Kashmir held by Pakistan since 1949. It is the home of Balti Muslims of Tibetan origin. The chief town is Skardu, but Ghyari is of greater significance to Muslims as the site of a mosque built by Sayyid Ali Hamadani, a Persian who brought the Shia Muslim religion to Baltistan in the 14th century.

Baluch *adj.* or **Baluchi** or **Baloch** native to Baluchistan, a region in SW Pakistan and SE Iran on the Arabian Sea. —*n.* an inhabitant of Baluchistan. Their common religion is Islam, and they speak Baluchi, a member of the Iranian branch of the Indo-European language family.

Baluchistan /bəluːtʃi'stɑːn/ mountainous desert area, comprising a province of Pakistan, part of the Iranian province of Sīstān and Balūchestan, and a small area of Afghanistan. The Pakistani province has an area of 347,200 sq km/134,019 sq mi and a population (1985) of 4,908,000; its capital is Quetta. Sīstān and Balūchestan has an area of 181,600 sq km/70,098 sq mi and a population (1986) of 1,197,000; its capital is Zahedan. The port of Gwadar in Pakistan is strategically important, on the Indian Ocean and the Strait of Hormuz.

baluster /'bæləstə/ *n.* a short pillar with a curving outline, especially in a balustrade; a post helping to support a rail. [from French, ultimately from Greek *balaustion* = flower of wild pomegranate, from resemblance in shape]

balustrade /bælə'streɪd/ *n.* a row of balusters with a rail or coping as an ornamental parapet to a balcony, terrace etc. [French]

Balzac /bæl'zæk/ Honoré de 1799–1850. French novelist. His first success was *Les Chouans*/*The Chouans* and *La Physiologie du mariage*/*The Physiology of Marriage* 1829, inspired by Scott. This was the beginning of the long series of novels *La Comédie humaine*/*The ◊Human Comedy*. He also wrote the Rabelaisian *Contes drolatiques*/*Ribald Tales* 1833.

Bamako /bæmə'kəʊ/ capital and port of Mali on the river Niger; population (1976) 404,022. It produces pharmaceuticals, chemicals, textiles, tobacco, and metal products.

bamboo /bæm'buː/ *n.* 1. any of numerous plants of the subgroup Bambuseae within the grass family Gramineae, mainly found in tropical and subtropical countries. Some species grow as tall as 36 m/120 ft. The young shoots are edible. 2. the hollow stem of such a plant. The stems are jointed and can be used in furniture, house, and boat construction, and in the making of paper. [from Dutch from Portuguese *Mambu*, from Malay]

bamboozle /bæm'buːzəl/ *v.t.* (*colloquial*) to hoax, to cheat; to mystify, to perplex. —**bamboozlement** *n.*

ban *v.t.* (**-nn-**) to prohibit officially (*from*); to forbid. —*n.* an official prohibition. [Old English = summon]

banal /bə'nɑːl/ *adj.* commonplace, trite. —**banality** /bə'nælɪtɪ/ *n.* [French from Old English; originally = compulsory, hence = common to all]

banana /bə'nɑːnə/ *n.* a long, crescent-shaped, yellow fruit; the treelike tropical plant of the genus *Musa*,

especially *M. sapientum*, bearing it. The trees grow up to 8 m/25 ft high. The edible banana is the fruit of a sterile hybrid form. —**banana republic**, (*derogatory*) a small tropical country dependent on its fruit exports and regarded as economically unstable. [Portuguese or Spanish, from African name]

Bananarama /bənɑːnə'rɑːmə/ *n.* a British pop group formed in 1981, a vocal trio comprising, from 1988, founder members Sarah Dallin (1962–) and Keren Woodward (1963–), with Jackie O'Sullivan (1966–). They were the top-selling female group of the 1980s.

Bancroft /'bænkrɒft/ George 1800–1891. US diplomat and historian. A Democrat, he was secretary of the navy in 1845 when he established the US Naval Academy at Annapolis, Maryland, and as acting secretary of war (May 1846) was instrumental in bringing about the occupation of California and the ◊Mexican war. He wrote a *History of the United States* 1834–76.

band[1] *n.* 1. a narrow strip, hoop, or loop. 2. a range of values, wavelengths etc. between two given limits. —*v.t.* to put a band on or round. —**band saw**, a power saw consisting of a toothed steel belt running over wheels. [from Old Norse]

band[2] *n.* 1. an organized group of people with a common purpose. 2. a group of musicians organized for playing together; for example, **military**, comprising woodwind, brass, and percussion; **brass**, solely of brass and percussion; **marching**, a variant of brass; **dance**, often like a small orchestra; **jazz** and **rock and pop**, generally electric guitar, bass, and drums variously augmented; and **steel**, from the West Indies, in which percussion instruments made from oildrums sound like marimbas. —*v.t./i.* to unite in an organized group. [from Old French]

Band, the a North American rock group 1961–76. They acquired their name when working as Bob Dylan's backing band, and made their solo debut in 1968 with *Music from Big Pink*. Their unostentatious ensemble playing and strong original material set a new trend.

Banda /'bændə/ Hastings Kamuzu 1902– . Malawi politician, president from 1966. He led his country's independence movement and was prime minister of Nyasaland (the former name of Malawi) from 1963. He became Malawi's first president in 1966 and in 1971 was named president for life; his rule has been authoritarian.

bandage /'bændɪdʒ/ *n.* a strip of material used to bind a wound. —*v.t.* to bind with a bandage. [French]

bandanna /bæn'dænə/ *n.* a large handkerchief with spots or other pattern. [from Hindi = tie-dyeing]

Bandaranaike /bændərə'naɪkə/ Sirimavo (born Ratwatte) 1916– . Sri Lankan politician, who succeeded her husband Solomon Bandaranaike to become the world's first female prime minister 1960–65 and 1970–77, but was expelled from parliament in 1980 for abuse of her powers while in office. She was largely responsible for the new constitution of 1972.

Bandaranaike Solomon West Ridgeway Dias 1899–1959. Sri Lankan nationalist politician. In 1951 he founded the Sri Lanka Freedom party and in 1956 became prime minister, pledged to a socialist programme and a neutral foreign policy. He failed to satisfy extremists and was assassinated by a Buddhist monk.

Bandar Seri Begawan /'bændə 'seri bə'gɑːwən/ formerly **Brunei Town** capital of Brunei; population (1983) 57,558.

bandbox *n.* a box for hats etc.

bandeau /'bændəʊ/ *n.* (*plural* **bandeaux** /-əʊz/) a strip of material worn round the hair or inside a hat. [French]

bandicoot /'bændikuːt/ *n.* 1. a kind of very large rat *Bandicota indica* in India. 2. a small marsupial mammal inhabiting Australia and New Guinea. There are about 11 species, family Peramelidae, rat-or rabbit-sized and living in burrows. They have long snouts, eat insects, and are nocturnal. A related group, the **rabbit bandicoots** or **bilbys**, is reduced to a single species that is now endangered and protected by law. [Telugu = pig-rat]

banding *n.* in UK education, the division of school pupils into broad streams by ability. Banding is used by some local authorities to ensure that comprehensive schools receive an intake of children spread right across the ability range. It is used internally by some schools as a means of avoiding groups of widely mixed ability.

bandit *n.* a robber or outlaw, especially one of a gang attacking travellers. —**banditry** *n.* [from Italian = outlawed]

bandmaster *n.* the conductor of a musical band.

bandoleer, bandolier /bændə'liə/ *n.* a shoulder belt with loops for ammunition. [from Dutch or French]

bandstand *n.* a platform for musicians, especially outdoors.

Bandung /'bænduŋ/ commercial city and capital of Jawa Barat province on the island of Java, Indonesia; population (1980) 1,463,000. Bandung is the third largest city in Indonesia and was the administrative centre when the country was the Netherlands East Indies. —**Bandung Conference,** the first conference (1955) of the Afro-Asian nations, proclaiming anticolonialism and neutrality between East and West.

bandwagon /'bændwægən/ *n.* a wagon for a band of musicians to ride in, as in a parade. —**climb** *or* **jump on the bandwagon,** to attach oneself to a successful party or cause.

bandwidth *n.* in telecommunications etc., a range of frequencies.

bandy[1] *v.i.* to exchange (words etc. *with*); to pass on (a rumour etc.) thoughtlessly. —*n.* a game resembling ice hockey but played with a ball not a puck. [perhaps from French *bander* = take sides, oppose]

bandy[2] *adj.* (of legs) curving apart at the knees. [perhaps from obsolete *bandy* = hockey stick]

bandy-bandy *n.* a venomous Australian snake *Vermicella annulata* of the cobra family, which grows to about 75 cm/ 2.5 ft. It is banded in black and white. It is not aggressive towards humans.

bane *n.* 1. a cause of ruin or trouble. 2. (*archaic*) a poison (now only in plant names, as *henbane*). —**baneful** *adj.* [Old English]

Banffshire /'bænfʃə/ former county of NE Scotland, now in Grampian region.

bang *v.t./i.* 1. to make a sudden, loud noise like an explosion; to strike or shut noisily. 2. to collide. —*n.* 1. a banging noise. 2. a sharp blow. —*adv.* 1. with a banging sound. 2. (*colloquial*) abruptly, exactly. [imitative]

Bangalore /bæŋgə'lɔ:/ capital of Karnataka state, S India; population (1981) 2,914,000. Industries include electronics, aircraft, machine tools, and coffee.

banger *n.* anything that makes a loud bang, as a firework; (*colloquial*) a noisy old car; (*slang*) a sausage.

Bangkok /bæŋ'kɒk/ capital and port of Thailand, on the river Chao Phraya; population (1987) 5,609,000. Products include paper, ceramics, cement, textiles, and aircraft. It is the headquarters of the South-East Asia Treaty Organization (SEATO).

Bangladesh /bæŋglə'deʃ/ People's Republic of; country in S Asia, surrounded on three sides by India and bounded to the S by the Bay of Bengal; **area** 144,000 sq km/55,585 sq mi; **capital** Dhaka (formerly Dacca); **physical** flat delta of rivers Ganges and Brahmaputra; some 75% of the land is less than 3 m/10 ft above sea level; hilly in extreme SE and NE; **head of state and government** Begum Khaleda Zia; **political system** restricted democratic republic; **exports** jute (50% of world production), tea, garments; **population** (1990 est) 117,980,000; **language** Bangla (Bengali); **recent history** formed into E province of Pakistan on partition of British India in 1947. Bangladesh emerged from civil war as an independent nation in 1971; under martial law 1975–76, 1982–86.

bangle *n.* a large decorative ring worn round the arm or ankle. [from Hindi *bangri*]

Bangui /bɒŋ'gi:/ capital and port of the Central African Republic, on the river Ubangi; population (1988) 597,000. Industries include beer, cigarettes, office machinery, and timber and metal products.

banian /'bænjən/ *n.* a tropical fig tree; see ◊banyan.

banish *v.t.* 1. to condemn to exile. 2. to dismiss from one's mind or presence. —**banishment** *n.* [from Old French]

banister /'bænɪstə/ *n.* any of the posts supporting a stair handrail; (in *plural*) these posts together with the rail. [corruption of *baluster*]

banjo /'bændʒəʊ/ *n.* (*plural* **banjos**) a stringed instrument like a guitar, with a long fretted neck and circular drum-type sound box covered on the topside only by stretched skin (now usually plastic). It is played with a

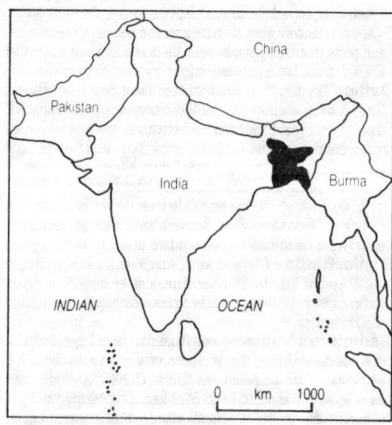

Bangladesh

plectrum. —**banjoist** *n.* [corruption of earlier *bandore*, ultimately from Greek *pandoura* = three-stringed lute]

Banjul /bæn'dʒu:l/ capital and chief port of Gambia, on an island at the mouth of the river Gambia; population (1983) 44,536. It was known as **Bathurst** until 1973. It was established as a settlement for freed slaves in 1816.

bank[1] *n.* 1. a stretch of sloping ground, especially that on either side of a river. 2. a raised mass of sand etc. in the bed of the sea or of a river. 3. a flat-topped mass of snow or cloud. —*v.t./i.* 1. to provide with or form a bank. 2. to heap; to pile coal dust etc. on (a fire) so that it burns slowly. 3. to tilt laterally in rounding a curve. [from Old Norse]

bank[2] *n.* 1. a financial institution that uses funds deposited with it to lend money to companies or individuals, and that also provides financial services to its customers. 2. a place for storing a reserve supply (e.g. of blood). 3. the pool of money in a gambling game. —*v.t./i.* to deposit (money) at a bank; to have an account *at* or *with* a bank. —**bank holiday,** in the UK, a weekday kept as a public holiday, when banks are officially closed. [from French or Italian, referring to the fact that early bankers transacted their business at a bench (*banco*) in the marketplace]

bank[3] *n.* a series of similar objects grouped in a row; a tier of oars in a galley. [from Old French *banc* = bench]

banker *n.* 1. one who runs a bank. 2. the keeper of the bank in a gambling game.

Bank for International Settlements (BIS) a bank established in 1930 to handle German reparations settlements from World War I. The BIS (based in Basel, Switzerland) is today a centre for economic and monetary research and assists cooperation between central banks. Its financial activities are essentially short-term.

Bankhead /'bæŋkhed/ Tallulah 1903–1968. US actress, renowned for her wit and flamboyant lifestyle. Her stage appearances include *Dark Victory* 1934, *The Little Foxes* 1939, and *The Skin of Our Teeth* 1942. Her films include Hitchcock's *Lifeboat* 1943.

banking *n.* the business of running a bank.

banknote *n.* a strip of paper serving as currency, originally a promissory note from a bank.

Bank of England the UK central bank founded by Act of Parliament in 1694. It was entrusted with note issue in 1844 and nationalized in 1946. It is banker to the UK government and assists in implementing financial and monetary policies through intervention in financial and foreign exchange markets.

bank rate an interest rate fixed by the Bank of England as a guide to mortgage, hire purchase rates, and so on, which was replaced in 1972 by the **minimum lending rate** (lowest rate at which the Bank acts as lender of last resort to the money market), which from 1978 was again a 'bank rate' set by the Bank.

bankrupt /'bæŋkrʌpt/ *adj.* 1. declared by a court of law to be unable to meet debts in full; financially ruined, insolvent. 2. destitute *of*. —*n.* a person officially declared bankrupt. —*v.t.* to make bankrupt. —**bankruptcy** *n.* the process by which the property of a person (in legal terms, an individual or corporation) unable to pay debts is taken away under a court order and divided fairly among the person's creditors, after preferential payments such as taxes and wages. Proceedings may be instituted either by the debtor (voluntary bankruptcy) or by any creditor for a substantial sum (involuntary bankruptcy). Until 'discharged', a bankrupt is severely restricted in financial activities. [from Italian = broken bench]

Banksia /'bæŋksɪə/ n. a genus of shrubs and trees, family Proteaceae, native to Australia. They have spiny evergreen leaves and include the honeysuckle tree.

banner n. **1.** a large cloth carrying an emblem or slogan, carried on a crossbar or between two poles at public demonstrations. **2.** the flag of a king, knight etc., serving as a rallying point. —**banner headline,** one extending across a newspaper page. [from Anglo-French from Latin *bandum* = standard]

Bannister /'bænɪstə/ Roger (Gilbert) 1929– . English track and field athlete, the first person to run a mile in under four minutes. He achieved this feat at Oxford, England, on 6 May 1954 in a time of 3 min 59.4 sec.

bannock /'bænək/ n. (*Scottish* and *north of England*) a round flat loaf, usually unleavened. [Old English]

Bannockburn, Battle of /'bænəkbɜːn/ a battle on 24 June 1314 in which ◊Robert I of Scotland (known as Robert the Bruce) defeated the English under ◊Edward II, who had come to relieve the besieged Stirling Castle.

banns n.pl. an announcement in church, usually read out on three successive Sundays, of an intended marriage, to give opportunity of objection.

banquet /'bæŋkwɪt/ n. a sumptuous meal; an elaborate and formal dinner. —v.i. to take part in a banquet. —**banqueter** n. [from French, diminutive of *banc* = bench]

banshee /'bænʃiː/ n. (*Irish* and *Scottish*) a female spirit whose wail outside a house is superstitiously believed to portend death within. [Irish = woman of the fairies]

bantam /'bæntəm/ n. a small variety of domestic chicken. This can either be a small version of one of the large breeds, or a separate type. Some are prolific layers, and bantam cocks have a reputation as spirited fighters. [from *Bantam*, seaport in Java]

bantamweight n. a boxing weight between flyweight and featherweight.

banter n. playful good-humoured teasing. —v.t./i. to exchange banter, to joke in a good-humoured way; to chaff.

Banting /'bæntɪŋ/ Frederick Grant 1891–1941. Canadian physician who discovered a technique for isolating the hormone insulin in 1921 when, experimentally, he and his colleague Charles ◊Best tied off the ducts of the ◊pancreas to determine the function of the cells known as the islets of Langerhans. This allowed for the treatment of diabetes. Banting and, from John J R Macleod, his mentor, shared the 1923 Nobel Prize for Medicine, and Banting divided his prize with Best.

Bantu /bæn'tuː/ n. (*plural* the same or **Bantus**) **1.** a large group of peoples in central and southern Africa; a member of this group. **2.** the group of languages spoken by them, including Swahili, Xhosa, and Zulu. —adj. of the Bantu or their languages. [Zulu = people]

banyan n. a tropical Asian fig tree *Ficus benghalensis* of the family Moraceae. It produces aerial roots that grow down from its spreading branches, forming supporting pillars that have the appearance of separate trunks. [Portuguese from Sanskrit = trader (from such a tree under which traders built a pagoda)]

baobab /'beɪəʊbæb/ n. an African tree *Adansonia digitata*, family Bombacaceae. It has rootlike branches, hence its nickname 'upside-down tree', and edible fruit known as monkey bread. [probably native name]

bap n. a soft, flat bread roll. [Scottish]

baptism /'bæptɪzəm/ n. immersion in or sprinkling with water as a religious rite of initiation. It was practised long before the beginning of Christianity. In the Christian baptism ceremony, sponsors or godparents make vows on behalf of the child, which are renewed by the child 'at confirmation. It is one of the seven sacraments. The **amrit** ceremony in Sikhism is sometimes referred to as baptism. —**baptism of fire,** initiation in a painful experience, such as exposure to gunfire. —**baptismal** /-'tɪzməl/ adj.

baptist /'bæptɪst/ n. **1.** a member of any of several Protestant and evangelical sects that practise baptism by immersion only upon profession of faith. Bap[tists seek their authority in the Bible. Baptism originated among English Dissenters who took refuge in the Netherlands in the early 17th century, and spread by emigration and, later missionary activity. Of the world total of approximately 31 million, some 26.5 million are in the USA and 265,000 in the UK. **2. the Baptist,** the title of St. John who baptized Jesus.

baptistery /'bæptɪstərɪ/ n. a part of a church, or (formerly) a separate building, used for baptism; an immersion receptacle in a Baptist chapel. [from Greek *baptistērion* = bathing place]

baptize /bæp'taɪz/ v.t. **1.** to administer baptism to, to christen. **2.** to name or nickname. [from Old French from Latin from Greek *baptizō* = immerse, baptize]

bar[1] n. **1.** a long piece of rigid material; an oblong piece (of chocolate, soap etc.); the heating element of an electric fire. **2.** a strip of silver below the clasp of a medal, serving as an extra distinction. **3.** a band of colour etc., a stripe. **4.** a rod or pole that fastens, confines, or obstructs something; a barrier; a sandbank or shoal at the mouth of a harbour or estuary; a restriction. **5.** in music, any of the vertical lines dividing a piece of music into equal units; a section between two of these. **6.** a partition (real or imaginary) across a lawcourt, separating the judge, jury, and certain lawyers from the public; **the Bar,** barristers. **7.** a counter across which alcoholic drinks are served; the room containing this; a counter for special service (e.g. *heel bar* for shoe repairs). —v.t. (-**rr**-). **1.** to fasten with a bar, bolt etc.; to shut *in* or *out.* **2.** to obstruct, prevent, or prohibit; to exclude. —prep. excluding. [from Old French *barre*]

bar[2] n. a c.g.s. unit of pressure equal to 10^5 pascals or 10^6 dynes/cm², approximately 750 mmHg or 0.987 atm. Its diminutive, the **millibar** (one-thousandth of a bar), is commonly used by meteorologists. [from Greek *baros* = weight]

Bara /'bɑːrə/ Theda. Stage name of Theodosia Goodman 1890–1955. US actress, the first movie sex symbol. Appearing first in a silent film entitled *A Fool There Was* 1915, she went on to play a series of sultry roles in the films *Salome, Cleopatra,* and *The Vampire,* the movie from which the term 'vamp' originated. As the most popular star of the Fox studios, Bara made more than 40 films before retiring in 1920.

Barabbas /bə'ræbəs/ in the New Testament, a condemned robber released by Pilate at Passover instead of Jesus to appease a mob.

barathea /bærə'θiːə/ n. a kind of fine cloth, especially of wool woven with silk.

barb n. **1.** a small spine curving back from the point of an arrow or fish-hook, making it difficult to withdraw from what it has pierced. **2.** a wounding remark. **3.** a fleshy appendage from the mouth of some fishes. **4.** a lateral filament branching from the shaft of a feather. **5.** a fish of the genus *Barbus* and some related genera of the family Cyprinidae. As well as the ◊barbel, barbs include many small tropical Old World species, some of which are familiar aquarium fish. [from Old French from Latin *barba* = beard]

Barbados /bɑː'beɪdɒs/ island country in the Caribbean, one of the Lesser Antilles; **area** 430 sq km/166 sq mi; **capital** Bridgetown; **physical** most easterly island of the West Indies; surrounded by coral reefs; subject to hurricanes June-Nov; **head of state** Elizabeth II from 1966 represented by governor general Hugh Springer from 1984; **head of government** prime minister Erskine Lloyd Sandiford from 1987; **political system** constitutional monarchy; **exports** sugar, rum, electronic parts, clothing; **population** (1990 est) 260,000; **language** English; **recent history** British colony in 1627; developed as a sugar plantation economy. Independence from Britain was achieved in 1961; full independence within the Commonwealth was reached in 1966.

barbarian /bɑː'beərɪən/ n. an uncivilized person. —adj. uncivilized.

barbaric /bɑː'bærɪk/ adj. typical of a barbarian, rough and unrefined.

barbarism /'bɑːbərɪzəm/ n. **1.** an uncivilized condition or practice. **2.** an unacceptable linguistic usage.

barbarity /bɑː'bærɪtɪ/ n. savage cruelty; a savagely cruel act.

Barbarossa /bɑːbə'rɒsə/ a nickname given to the Holy

Barbie Klaus Barbie, the Nazi SS commander in Lyon, France, during World War II.

Roman emperor ◊Frederick I, and also to two brothers, Horuk and Khair-ed-Din, who were Barbary pirates. Horuk was killed by the Spaniards in 1518; Khair-ed-Din took Tunis in 1534 and died in Constantinople in 1546. [= red beard]

barbarous /'bɑːbərəs/ *adj.* uncivilized; savagely cruel. —**barbarously** *adv.* [from Latin from Greek, originally = non-Greek, then = outside the Romano-Greek world]

Barbary ape /'bɑːbəri/ a tailless yellowish-brown macaque monkey *Macaca sylvanus*, found in the mountains and wilds of Algeria and Morocco. It was introduced to Gibraltar, where legend has it that the British will leave if the colony dies out. [from Barbary, region of N Africa]

barbastelle *n.* an insect-eating bat *Barbastella barbastellus* with 'frosted' black fur and a wingspan of about 25 cm/10 in, occasionally found in the UK but more common in mainland Europe.

barbecue /'bɑːbɪkjuː/ *n.* a metal frame or portable grill for cooking meat, especially over an open fire; meat so cooked; an open-air party using this. —*v.t.* to cook on a barbecue. [from Spanish from Haitian]

barbed *adj.* 1. furnished with a barb or barbs. 2. (of remarks) having cruel undertones. —**barbed wire**, fencing material made of strands of galvanized wire (see ◊galvanizing), twisted together with sharp barbs at close intervals. In 1873 an American, Joseph Glidden, devised a machine to mass-produce barbed wire.

barbel /'bɑːbəl/ *n.* 1. a beardlike filament at the mouth of some fishes. 2. a large European freshwater fish of the genus *Barbus* with such filaments. [from Old French]

barbell *n.* a metal rod used in weightlifting, with adjustable weighted discs at either end.

barber /'bɑːbə/ *n.* a men's hairdresser. —**barbershop** *adj.* of a style of highly chromatic part singing by male quartets, revived in the USA during the 19th century. [Anglo-French from Latin *barba* = beard]

Barber Samuel 1910–1981. US composer of works in a restrained Neo-Classical style, including *Adagio for Strings* 1936 and the opera *Vanessa* 1958.

barbet *n.* a small, tropical bird, often brightly coloured. There are some 78 species of barbet in the family Capitonidae, about half living in Africa. Barbets eat insects and fruits and, being distant relations of woodpeckers, drill nest holes with their beaks. [diminutive of Latin *barba* = beard, from the bristles at the base of the beak]

barbican /'bɑːbɪkən/ *n.* an outer defence of a castle or city, especially a double tower over a gate or bridge. —**the Barbican**, arts and residential complex in the City of London, built in 1982. [from Old French]

Barbie /'bɑːbi/ Klaus 1913– . German Nazi, a member of the ◊SS from 1936. During World War II he was involved in the deportation of Jews from the occupied Netherlands 1940–42 and in tracking down Jews and Resistance workers in France 1942–45. Having escaped capture in 1945, Barbie was employed by the US intelligence services in Germany before moving to Bolivia in 1951. Expelled from there in 1983, he was arrested and convicted of crimes against humanity in France in 1987.

Barbirolli /bɑːbɪ'rɒli/ John 1899–1970. English conductor. He made his name as a cellist, and in 1937 succeeded Toscanini as conductor of the New York Philharmonic Orchestra. He returned to England in 1943, where he remained conductor of the Hallé Orchestra, Manchester, until his death.

barbiturate /bɑː'bɪtjʊrət/ *n.* a soporific and sedative drug consisting of any salt or ester of barbituric acid, $C_4H_4O_3N_2$. It works by depressing brain activity. Highly addictive, most barbiturates are no longer prescribed and are listed as controlled substances. [from French from German]

barbituric acid /bɑːbɪ'tjuərɪk/ an acid, malonyl urea, from which barbiturates are derived. [from French from German, from *Barbara*, woman's name]

Barbizon school /bɑːbiː'zɒn/ French school of landscape painters of the mid-19th century. Members included Jean-François Millet, Diaz de la Peña (1807–1876), and Théodore Rousseau (1812–1867). They aimed to paint fresh, realistic scenes, sketching and painting their subjects in the open air. [from *Barbizon* in the forest of Fontainebleau, near Paris, where they worked]

Barbour /'bɑːbə/ John *c.*1316–1395. Scottish poet, whose chronicle poem *The Brus* is among the earliest Scottish poetry.

Barbuda /bɑː'bjuːdə/ one of the islands that form the state of ◊Antigua and Barbuda.

barbule /'bɑːbjuːl/ *n.* a filament branching from the barb of a feather. [from Latin diminutive of *barba* = beard]

barcarole /bɑːkə'rɒl, -'rəʊl/ *n.* 1. a gondolier's song. 2. a piece of music with steady lilting rhythm, especially for piano. [from French from Italian *barca* = boat]

Barcelona /bɑːsə'ləʊnə/ capital, industrial city (textiles, engineering, chemicals), and port of Catalonia, NE Spain; population (1986) 1,694,000. As the chief centre of anarchism and Catalonian nationalism, it was prominent in the overthrow of the monarchy in 1931 and was the last city of the republic to surrender to Franco in 1939.

bar chart in statistics, a way of displaying data. The heights or lengths of the bars are proportional to the quantities they represent.

bar code a pattern of bars and spaces which can be read by a computer. Bar codes are widely used in retailing, industrial distribution, and public libraries. The code is read by a ◊scanning device, and the computer interprets it from the widths of the bars and spaces.

bard[1] *n.* 1. a Celtic minstrel; a Welsh poet honoured at an ◊Eisteddfod. 2. (*archaic*) a poet. —**the Bard of Avon**, ◊Shakespeare. [Celtic]

bard[2] *v.i.* to place slices of bacon over (meat etc.) before roasting. [from French *barde* (originally = horse's breastplate), ultimately from Arabic]

Bardeen /bɑː'diːn/ John 1908– . US physicist who won a Nobel prize in 1956, with Walter Brattain and William Shockley, for the development of the transistor in 1948. In 1972 he became the first double winner of a Nobel prize in the same subject (with Leon Cooper and John Schrieffer) for his work on superconductivity.

Bardot /bɑː'dəʊ/ Brigitte 1934– . French film actress, whose sensual appeal did much to popularize French cinema internationally. Her films include *Et Dieu créa la Femme/ And God Created Woman* 1950, *Viva Maria* 1965, and *Shalako* 1968.

Bardo Thodol /'bɑːdəʊ 'θəʊdɒl/ also known as the *Book of the Dead*, a Tibetan Buddhist text giving instructions to the newly dead about the Bardo, or state between death and rebirth.

bare *adj.* 1. not clothed, not covered; scantily furnished. 2. empty. 3. plain, not elaborated. 4. scanty, only just sufficient. —v.t. to uncover, to reveal. —**barely** adv., **bareness** n. [Old English]

bareback adj. & adv. on a horse without a saddle.

Barebones Parliament /'beəbəʊnz/ in English history, an assembly called by Oliver ◊Cromwell to replace the 'Rump Parliament' in July 1653. It consisted of 140 members nominated by the army. Although they attempted to pass sensible legislation (civil marriage; registration of births, deaths, and marriages; custody of lunatics), its members' attempts to abolish tithes, patronage, and the court of chancery, and to codify the law led to the resignation of the moderates and its dissolution in Dec 1653. [from Praise-God *Barbon*, one of its members]

barefaced adj. shameless, impudent.

barefoot adj. & adv. without shoes, stockings etc., on the feet.

bareheaded adj. without a hat.

barely adv. scarcely, only just.

Barenboim /'bærənbɔɪm/ Daniel 1942– . Israeli pianist and conductor, born in Argentina. Pianist and conductor with the English Chamber Orchestra from 1964, he became conductor of the New York Philharmonic Orchestra in 1970 and musical director of the Orchestre de Paris in 1975. Appointed artistic director of the Opéra Bastille, Paris, from July 1987, he was fired from his post a few months before the Opéra's opening in July 1989. He is a celebrated interpreter of Mozart and Beethoven.

Barents /'bærənts/ Willem c. 1550–1597. Dutch explorer and navigator. He made three expeditions to seek the ◊Northeast Passage; he died on the last voyage. The **Barents Sea**, part of the Arctic Ocean N of Norway, is named after him.

bargain /'bɑːgɪn/ n. an agreement made with obligations on both sides, or on the terms of a sale; something obtained as a result of this, a thing got cheaply. —v.i. **1.** to discuss the terms of a sale or agreement. **2.** to expect or be prepared *for*. [from Old French *bargaignier*]

barge n. a long flat-bottomed boat carrying freight on rivers or canals; a large ornamental boat for state occasions etc. —v.i. to lurch or move clumsily *into*, *around* etc. —**barge in**, to intrude without ceremony. [from Old French, perhaps from Latin *barca* = ship's boat]

bargeboard n. a board or ornamental screen under the edge of a gable.

bargee /bɑːˈdʒiː/ n. a person in charge of a barge (for freight); a member of its crew.

Bari /'bɑːri/ capital of Puglia region, S Italy, and industrial port on the Adriatic; population (1988) 359,000. It is the site of Italy's first nuclear power station; the part of the town known as Tecnopolis is the Italian equivalent of ◊Silicon Valley.

Barikot /bɑːriˈkɒt/ garrison town in Konar province, E Afghanistan, near the Pakistan frontier. Besieged by Mujaheddin rebels in 1985, the relief of Barikot by Soviet and Afghan troops was one of the largest military engagements of the Afghan war during Soviet occupation.

Barisal /bʌriˈsɑːl/ river port and capital city of Barisal region, S Bangladesh; population (1981) 142,000. It trades in jute, rice, fish, and oilseed.

baritone /'bærɪtəʊn/ n. a male voice between tenor and bass; a singer having such a voice; a part written for it. [from Italian from Greek *barus* = heavy]

barium /'beəriəm/ n. a soft, silver-white, metallic element, symbol Ba, atomic number 56, relative atomic mass 137.33. It is one of the alkaline-earth metals, found in nature as barium carbonate and barium sulphate. As the sulphate it is used in medicine; barium is also used in alloys, pigments, and safety matches and, with strontium, forms the emissive surface in cathode-ray tubes. It was first discovered in barytes or heavy spar. —**barium meal**, a mixture including barium sulphate, which is opaque to X-rays, used in radiography of the alimentary canal. [from Greek *barus* = heavy]

bark[1] n. the protective outer layer on the stems and roots of woody plants, composed mainly of dead cells. To allow for expansion of the stem, the bark is continually added to from within, and the outer surface often becomes fissured or is shed as scales. —v.t. **1.** to strip bark from (trees). **2.** to scrape the skin off (part of the body) accidentally. [from Scandinavian]

bark[2] v.t./i. **1.** (of a dog or fox) to utter a sharp explosive cry. **2.** to speak or utter in a sharp commanding tone. —n. a sound of or like barking. —**bark up the wrong tree**, to direct one's efforts to the wrong quarter. [Old English]

barley /'bɑːli/ n. a cereal plant of the genus *Hordeum*, or its grain. The cultivated barley *Hordeum vulgare* comprises three varieties: six-rowed barley, four-rowed barley, and two-rowed barley. Barley was one of the earliest cereals to be cultivated, and no other cereal can thrive in so wide a range of climate. Polar barley is sown and reaped well within the Arctic Circle in Europe. Barley is no longer much used in breadmaking, but its high-protein varieties are used widely as animal feed. Its main importance is in brewing and distilling, for which low-protein varieties are used. —**barley sugar**, a sweet made of boiled sugar. **barley water**, a drink made from barley. [Old English]

barmaid n. a woman who serves behind the bar of a public house etc.

barman n. (*plural* **barmen**) a man who serves behind the bar of a public house etc.

bar mitzvah /'mɪtzvə/ **1.** a Jewish boy aged 13 when he takes on the responsibilities of an adult under the Jewish law. **2.** the solemnization of this event by calling upon the boy to read from the Torah in a synagogue service. Less common is the **bat** or **bas mitzvah** for girls aged 12. The child is subsequently regarded as a full member of the congregation. [Hebrew = son of commandment]

barmy adj. (*slang*) crazy. [from Old English *barm* = froth on top of fermenting liquor]

barn n. a simple roofed building for the storage and processing of corn or hay etc. on a farm. —**barn dance**, a kind of country dance; a social gathering for dancing, originally held in a barn. **barn owl**, a kind of ◊owl, brownish above with white underparts. [Old English = barley house]

Barnabas, St /'bɑːnəbəs/ in the New Testament, a 'fellow labourer' with St Paul; he went with St Mark on a missionary journey to Cyprus, his birthplace. Feast day 11 June.

barnacle /'bɑːnəkəl/ n. a marine crustacean of the subclass Cirripedia. The larval form is free-swimming, but when mature it fixes itself by the head to rock or floating wood. The animal then remains attached, enclosed in a shell through which the cirri (modified legs) protrude to sweep food into the mouth. Barnacles include the stalked **goose barnacle** *Lepas anatifera* found on ships' bottoms and the **acorn barnacles**, such as *Balanus balanoides*, common on rocks. —**barnacle goose**, an Arctic goose *Branta leucopsis* visiting Britain in winter.

Barnard /'bɑːnɑːd/ Christiaan (Neethling) 1922– . South African surgeon who performed the first human heart transplant in 1967 in Cape Town. The patient, 54-year-old Louis Washkansky, lived for 18 days.

Barnardo /bəˈnɑːdəʊ/ Thomas John 1845–1905. Irish philanthropist who was known as Dr Barnardo, although not medically qualified. He opened the first of a series of homes for destitute children in 1867 in Stepney, E London.

Barnard's star the second closest star to the Sun, six light years away in the constellation Ophiuchus. It is a faint red dwarf of 9th magnitude, visible only through a telescope. It is named after the US astronomer Edward E Barnard (1857–1923), who discovered in 1916 that it has the fastest proper motion of any star, crossing 1 degree of sky every 350 years.

Barnet, Battle of in the English Wars of the ◊Roses, the defeat of Lancaster by York on 14 April 1471 in Barnet (now in NW London).

barney /'bɑːnɪ/ n. (*slang*) a noisy dispute.

barnstorm v.i. to travel through rural areas as an actor or political campaigner. —**barnstormer** n.

Barnum /'bɑːnəm/ Phineas T(aylor) 1810–1891. US circus owner. In 1871, after an adventurous career, he established the 'Greatest Show on Earth', which included the midget 'Tom Thumb', a circus, a menagerie, and an exhibition of 'freaks', conveyed in 100 rail cars. He coined the phrase 'there's a sucker born every minute'.

How were the receipts today in Madison Square Garden?

Phineas Taylor Barnum
(last words)

barograph /'bærəgrɑːf/ n. a device for recording variations in atmospheric pressure. A pen, governed by the movements of an aneroid barometer, makes a continuous line on a paper strip on a cylinder that rotates over a day or week to create a **barogram**, or permanent record of variations in atmospheric pressure. [from Greek *graphō* = write]

barometer /bə'rɒmɪtə(r)/ n. an instrument that measures atmospheric pressure as an indication of weather. Most often used are the **mercury barometer** and the **aneroid barometer**. —**barometric** /b&r'metrik/ adj. [from Greek *baros* = weight and *metron* = measure]

baron /'bærən/ n. 1. a member of the lowest order of the British ◊peerage, styled *Lord* —; a foreign nobleman of equivalent rank (styled *Baron* —). 2. one who controls the trade in a specified commodity, a magnate. 3. (*historical*) one who held land from the king in the Middle Ages. —**baroness** n.fem. [from Anglo-French from Latin *baro* = man]

baronet /'bærənɪt/ n. a member of the lowest hereditary titled British order, ranking next below a baron; the first creations were in 1611 by James I. A baronet does not have a seat in the House of Lords, but is entitled to the style *Sir* before his name. —**baronetcy** n.

baronial /bə'rəunɪəl/ adj. of or suitable for a baron.

Barons' Wars civil wars in England: **1215–17** between King ◊John and his barons, over his failure to honour ◊Magna Carta; **1264–67** between ◊Henry III (and the future ◊Edward I) and his barons (led by Simon de ◊Montfort); **1264** 14 May **Battle of Lewes** at which Henry III was defeated and captured **1265** 4 Aug Simon de Montfort was defeated by Edward I at Evesham and killed.

barony /'bærənɪ/ n. the rank or domain of a baron.

Baroque /bə'rɒk/ adj. or baroque of a style of art and architecture characterized by extravagance in ornament, asymmetry of design, and great expressiveness; of comparable musical developments. —n. Baroque style or ornamentation; Baroque art collectively. It dominated European art for most of the 17th century, with artists such as the painter Rubens and the sculptor Bernini. In architecture, it often involved large-scale designs, such as Bernini's piazza in Rome and the palace of Versailles in France. In music, the Baroque period lasted from about 1600 to 1750, and its major composers included Monteverdi, Vivaldi, J S Bach, and Handel. [French from Portuguese, originally = misshapen pearl]

Barotseland /bə'rɒtsɪlænd/ former kingdom in Western Province of ◊Zambia.

barouche /bə'ruːʃ/ n. a four-wheeled horse-drawn carriage with seats for two couples facing each other. [from German from Italian from Latin *birotus* (*rota* = wheel)]

barque /bɑːk/ n. a sailing ship square-rigged on the foremast and mainmast and fore-and-aft rigged on the mizen. [from French, probably from Latin *barca* = ship's boat]

barquentine /'bɑːkəntiːn/ n. a three-masted vessel with the foremast square-rigged, the main and mizen fore-and-aft rigged. [after *brigantine*]

barrack /'bærək/ v.t./i. (of spectators etc.) to shout derisively (at).

barracks /'bærəks/ n. a large building or group of buildings in which soldiers are housed; a large, plain and ugly building. —**barrack-room lawyer**, a pompously argumentative person. [from French from Italian or Spanish = soldier's tent]

barracuda /bærə'kuːdə/ n. 1. a large voracious tropical sea fish of the family Sphyraenidae, especially *Sphyraena barracuda*, which can grow over 2 m/6 ft long and has a superficial resemblance to a pike. Young fish shoal but the older ones are solitary. The barracuda has very sharp shearing teeth, and may attack people. 2. or **barracouta** /-'kuːtə/ a long slender sea fish *Thyrsites atun* of the Pacific etc. (In South Africa the same fish is called **snoek**.) [American Spanish]

Barragán /bærə'gɑːn/ Luis 1902–1988. Mexican architect, known for his use of rough wooden beams, cobbles, lava, and adobe, his simple houses with walled gardens, and his fountains.

barrage /'bærɑːʒ/ n. 1. a heavy continuous artillery bombardment; a rapid succession of criticisms, questions etc. 2. an artificial barrier in a river, acting as a dam. —**barrage balloon**, a large balloon anchored to the ground, as part of a barrier against aircraft. [French, from *barre* = bar]

Barrancabermeja /bəræŋkəbəmeɪxə/ port and oil-refining centre on the Magdalena River in the department of Santander, NE Colombia. It is a major outlet for oil from the De Mares fields, which are linked by pipeline to Cartagena on the Caribbean coast.

Barranquilla /bærən'kiːljə/ seaport in N Colombia, on the river Magdalena; population (1985) 1,120,900. Products include chemicals, tobacco, textiles, furniture, and footwear.

Barras /bæ'rɑːs/ Paul François Jean Nicolas, Count 1755–1829. French revolutionary. He was elected to the National Convention in 1792 and helped to overthrow Robespierre in 1794. In 1795 he became a member of the ruling Directory (see ◊French Revolution). In 1796 he brought about the marriage of his former mistress Joséphine de Beauharnais with Napoleon and assumed dictatorial powers. After Napoleon's coup d'état on 19 Nov 1799, Barras fell into disgrace.

barratry /'bærətrɪ/ n. fraud or culpable negligence by a ship's master or crew at the expense of the owner or insurer. [from Old French *barat* = deceit]

Barrault Jean Louis 1910– . French actor and director. His films include *La Symphonie fantastique* 1942, *Les Enfants du paradis* 1944, and *La Ronde* 1950.

barre /bɑː/ n. a horizontal bar at waist level, used by dancers to steady themselves when exercising. [French]

Barre Raymond 1924– . French politician, member of the centre-right *Union pour la Démocratie Française*; prime minister 1976–81, when he also held the Finance Ministry portfolio and gained a reputation as a tough and determined budget-cutter.

barrel /'bærəl/ n. 1. a large rounded usually wooden container for liquids etc., with slightly bulging sides and flat circular ends. 2. a unit of liquid capacity, the value of which depends on the liquid being measured. It is used for petroleum, a barrel of which contains 160 litres/35 imperial gallons; a barrel of alcohol contains 189 litres/41.5 imperial gallons; in brewing 164 litres/36 imperial gallons; in the oil industry 35 imperial or 42 US gallons. 3. a cylindrical tubelike part, especially the part of a gun through which the shot is fired. —v.t. (**-ll-**) to store in a barrel. —**barrel vault**, a vault with a uniform concave roof. [from Old French]

barrel organ 1. a pipe organ, played by turning a handle. This works a pump and drives a replaceable cylinder upon which music is recorded as a pattern of ridges controlling the passage of air to the pipes. It was much used in churches in the 18th and 19th centuries. 2. or **barrel piano** or **street piano** a street instrument (not of the organ type) producing notes by means of metal tongues struck by pins fixed in the barrel.

barren /'bærən/ adj. 1. (of land) unable to produce crops or vegetation, infertile. 2. unable to bear young; not producing fruit. 3. not productive of results. [from Anglo-French]

Barrett Browning /'braʊnɪŋ/ Elizabeth 1806–1861. English poet. In 1844 she published *Poems* (including 'The Cry of the Children'), which led to her friendship with and secret marriage to Robert Browning in 1846. The *Sonnets from the Portuguese* 1847 were written during their courtship. Later works include *Casa Guidi Windows* 1851 and the poetic novel *Aurora Leigh* 1857.

barricade /bæri'keɪd/ n. a barrier, especially one hastily erected across a street. —v.t. to block or defend with a barricade. [French, from Spanish *barrica* = cask]

Barrie /'bæri/ J(ames) M(atthew) 1860–1937. Scottish playwright and novelist, author of *The Admirable Crichton* 1902 and the children's fantasy *Peter Pan* 1904.

barrier /'bæriə/ n. 1. a fence, rail etc., barring advance or preventing access. 2. a gate at a railway station where tickets have to be shown. 3. a circumstance that prevents progress or communication etc. —**barrier reef**, a ◊coral reef cut off from the nearest land by a channel or shallow lagoon. [from Anglo-French]

barrister /'bæristə/ n. in the UK, a lawyer qualified by study at the ◊Inns of Court to plead for a client in court. In Scotland he or she is called an ◊advocate. Barristers act for clients through the intermediary of ◊solicitors. In the highest courts, only barristers can represent litigants but this distinction between barristers and solicitors seems

Barrymore *US actor John Barrymore was the youngest of the three talented Barrymores, whose parents were also actors.*

likely to change in the 1990s. In the USA an attorney (lawyer) may serve both functions. When pupil barristers complete their training they are 'called to the bar': this is the name of the ceremony in which they are admitted as members of the profession. A ◊Queen's Counsel (silk) is a senior barrister appointed on the recommendation of the Lord Chancellor. [from Old French *barre*]

barrow[1] /'bærəʊ/ *n.* **1.** a two-wheeled handcart, especially for selling things in the street. **2.** a wheelbarrow. [Old English]

barrow[2] *n.* a mound of earth or sometimes stones constructed in ancient times to cover one or more burials. Examples are found in many parts of the world. The two main types are **long**, dating from the New Stone Age, or Neolithic, and **round**, from the later Mesolithic peoples of the early Bronze Age. [Old English = hill, hillock]

Barrow Clyde 1900–1934. US criminal; see ◊Bonnie and Clyde.

Barrow Isaac 1630–1677. English mathematician, theologian, and classicist. His *Lectiones geometricae* 1670 contains the essence of the theory of ◊calculus, which was later expanded by Isaac ◊Newton and Gottfried ◊Leibniz.

Barry /'bæri/ Charles 1795–1860. English architect of the Neo-Gothic Houses of Parliament at Westminster, London, 1840–60, in collaboration with ◊Pugin.

Barry Comtesse du. See ◊Du Barry, mistress of Louis XV of France.

Barrymore /'bærɪmɔ:/ US family of actors, the children of British-born Maurice Barrymore and Georgie Drew, both stage personalities. **Lionel Barrymore** (1878–1954) first appeared on the stage with his grandmother, Mrs John Drew, in 1893. He played numerous film roles from 1909, including *A Free Soul* 1931 and *Grand Hotel* 1932, but was perhaps best known for his annual radio portrayal of Scrooge in Dickens's *A Christmas Carol*. **Ethel Barrymore** (1879–1959) played with the British actor Henry Irving in London in 1898 and in 1928 opened the Ethel Barrymore Theatre in New York; she also appeared in many films from 1914, including *None but the Lonely Heart* 1944. **John Barrymore** (1882–1942) was a flamboyant actor who often appeared on stage and screen with his brother and sister. In his early years he was a Shakespearean actor. From 1923 he acted almost entirely in films, including *Dinner at Eight* 1933, and became a screen idol, nicknamed 'the Profile'.

Barstow /'bɑ:stəʊ/ Stan 1928– . English writer whose novels describe northern working-class life and include *A Kind of Loving* 1960.

Bart /bɑ:/ Jean 1651–1702. French naval hero who harassed the British fleet in many daring exploits.

bartender /'bɑ:tendə/ *n.* a barman or barmaid.

barter /'bɑ:tə/ *v.t./i.* to part with (goods) in exchange for others of equivalent value; to trade in this way. —*n.* such trade or exchange.

Barth /bɑ:θ/ John 1930– . US novelist, influential in experimental writing in the 1960s. Chief works include *The Sot-Weed Factor* 1960, *Giles Goat-Boy* 1966, and *Lost in the Funhouse* 1968, interwoven fictions based on language games.

Barth /bɑ:t/ Karl 1886–1968. Swiss Protestant theologian. Socialist in his political views, he attacked the Nazis. His *Church Dogmatics* 1932–62 makes the resurrection of Jesus the focal point of Christianity.

Barthes /bɑ:t/ Roland 1915–1980. French critic and theorist of ◊semiology, the science of signs and symbols. One of the French 'new critics', he attacked traditional literary criticism in his early works, including *Sur Racine/On Racine* 1963, and set out his own theories in *Eléments de sémiologie* 1964. He also wrote an autobiographical novel, *Roland Barthes sur Roland Barthes* 1975.

Bartholomew, Massacre of St /bɑ:'θɒləmju:/ see ◊St Bartholomew, Massacre of.

Bartholomew, St in the New Testament, one of the apostles. Legends relate that after the Crucifixion he took Christianity to India, or that he was a missionary in Anatolia and Armenia, where he suffered martyrdom by being flayed alive. Feast day 24 Aug.

Bartók /'bɑ:tɒk/ Béla 1881–1945. Hungarian composer. Regarded as a child prodigy, he studied music at the Budapest Conservatory, later working with ◊Kodály in recording and and transcribing local folk music for a government project. This led him to develop a personal musical language combining folk elements with mathematical concepts of tone and rhythmic proportion. His large output includes six string quartets, a ballet *The Miraculous Mandarin* 1919, which was banned because of its subject matter, concertos, an opera, and graded teaching pieces for piano. He died in the USA, having fled from Hungary in 1940.

Barton /'bɑ:tn/ Edmund 1849–1920. Australian politician. He was leader of the federation movement from 1896 and first prime minister of Australia 1901–03.

Baruch /bə'ru:k/ Bernard (Mannes) 1870–1965. US financier. He was a friend of British prime minister Churchill and a self-appointed, unpaid adviser to US presidents Wilson, F D Roosevelt, and Truman. He strongly advocated international control of nuclear energy.

baryon /'bærɪɒn/ *n.* a subatomic ◊particle, either a nucleon or a hyperon. [from Greek *barus* = heavy; so called because their mass is greater than, or equal to, that of the proton]

Baryshnikov /bə'rɪʃnɪkɒf/ Mikhail 1948– . Soviet dancer, now in the USA. He joined the Kirov Ballet in 1967 and became one of their most brilliant soloists. After defecting in Canada in 1974, he joined the American Ballet Theatre as a principal dancer, leaving to join the New York City Ballet 1978–80. He rejoined the American Ballet Theatre as director 1980–90. From 1990 he has danced for various companies.

baryta /bə'raɪtə/ *n.* barium oxide or hydroxide. [from Greek *barus* = heavy]

barytes /bə'raɪti:z/ *n.* barium sulphate, $BaSO_4$, the most common mineral of barium. It is white or light-coloured, and has a comparatively high density (specific gravity 4.6); the latter property makes it useful in the production of high-density drilling muds. It is also used in some white paints. Barytes occurs mainly in ore veins, where it is often found with calcite and with lead and zinc minerals. It crystallizes in the ◊orthorhombic system and can form tabular crystals or radiating fibrous masses.

baryton *n.* a bowed stringed instrument producing an intense singing tone. It is based on an 18th-century viol and modified by the addition of sympathetic (freely vibrating) strings. [from French]

basal /'beɪsəl/ *adj.* of or forming the base of something.

basal metabolic rate (BMR) the amount of energy needed by an animal just to stay alive. It is measured when the animal is awake but resting, and includes the

base

binary (base 2)	octal (base 8)	decimal (base 10)	hexadecimal (base 16)
0	0	0	0
1	1	1	1
10	2	2	2
11	3	3	3
100	4	4	4
101	5	5	5
110	6	6	6
111	7	7	7
1000	10	8	8
1001	11	9	9
1010	12	10	A
1011	13	11	B
1100	14	12	C
1101	15	13	D
1110	16	14	E
1111	17	15	F
10000	20	16	10
1111111	377	255	FF
11111010001	3721	2001	7D1

energy required to keep the heart beating, sustain breathing, repair tissues, and keep the brain and nerves functioning. Measuring the animal's consumption of oxygen gives an accurate value for BMR, because oxygen is needed to release energy from food.

basalt /'bæsɔːlt/ *n.* the commonest volcanic ◊igneous rock, and the principal rock type on the ocean floor; it is basic, that is, it contains relatively little silica: under 50%. It is usually dark grey, but can also be green, brown, or black, and often forms columnar strata. —**basaltic** /bə'sɔːltɪk/ *adj.* [from Latin from Greek *basanos* = touchstone]

bascule /'bæskjuːl/ *n.* a lever apparatus used in a **bascule bridge**, a type of drawbridge in which one or two counterweighted deck members pivot upwards to allow shipping to pass underneath. One example is the double bascule Tower Bridge in London. [French = seesaw]

base[1] *n.* **1.** the lowest part of anything, the part on which it rests. **2.** a basis; a main principle or starting point. **3.** the headquarters of an expedition or military force etc., from where its operations are directed. **4.** the main or underlying ingredient of a mixture. **5.** in chemistry, a substance (not necessarily soluble in water) that can combine with an acid to form a salt; that is, a substance that accepts protons. Bases can contain negative ions such as the hydroxide ion, OH^-, which is the strongest base, or be molecules such as ammonia, NH_3. Ammonia is a weak base, as only some of its molecules accept protons. Bases that dissolve in water are called ◊alkalis. **6.** in mathematics, the number on which a system of calculation is based, e.g. 10 in decimal counting, 2 in the ◊binary system. A base is also a number that, when raised to a particular power (that is, when multiplied by itself a particular number of times as in $10^2 = 10 \times 10 = 100$), has a ◊logarithm equal to the power. For example, the logarithm of 100 to the base ten is 2. **7.** in baseball, any of the four stations that a batsman must reach in turn in scoring a run. —*v.t.* to use as a base or foundation, or as evidence for a conclusion etc. [French, or from Latin from Greek *basis* = stepping]

base[2] *adj.* **1.** lacking moral worth, cowardly, contemptible. **2.** (of metals) not precious; (of coins) adulterated with inferior metal. —**basely** *adv.*, **baseness** *n.* [from French *bas* = of low height, from Latin *bassus* = short]

baseball *n.* the national summer game of the USA, derived in the 19th century from the English game of ◊rounders. Baseball is played between two teams, each of nine players, on a pitch ('field') marked out in the form of a diamond, with a base at each corner. The ball is struck with a cylindrical bat, and the players try to score ('make a run') by circuiting the bases. A 'home run' is a circuit on one hit.

Basel /'bɑːzəl/ or **Basle** (French *Bâle*) financial, commercial, and industrial city in Switzerland; population (1987) 363,000. Basel was a strong military station under the Romans. In 1501 it joined the Swiss confederation and later developed as a centre for the Reformation.

base lending rate the rate of interest to which most bank lending is linked, the actual rate depending on the status of the borrower. A prestigious company might command a rate only 1% above base rate while an individual would be charged several points above. An alternative method of interest rates is ◊LIBOR.

baseless *adj.* with no foundation in fact.

baseline *n.* a line used as a base or starting point; the line at each end of a tennis court.

basement /'beɪsmənt/ *n.* a storey below ground level.

basenji /bə'sendʒɪ/ *n.* a breed of dog originating in Central Africa, where it is used as a hunter. About 41 cm/1.3 ft tall, it has a wrinkled forehead, curled tail, and short glossy coat. It has no true bark. [from a Bantu language]

base pair in biochemistry, the linkage of two base (purine or pyrimidine) molecules in ◊DNA. They are found in nucleotides, and form the basis of the genetic code.

bash *v.t.* **1.** to strike violently. **2.** to attack violently with blows, words, or hostile actions. —*n.* a heavy blow. —**have a bash**, (*colloquial*) to have a try. [imitative]

bashful *adj.* self-consciously shy. —**bashfully** *adv.*, **bashfulness** *n.* [from obsolete *bash* v. = abash]

Bashkir /bæʃ'kɪə/ autonomous republic of the USSR, with the Ural Mountains on the E; **area** 143,600 sq km/ 55, 430 sq mi; **capital** Ufa; **products** minerals, oil; **population** (1982) 3,876,000; **recent history** annexed by Russia in 1557; became the first Soviet autonomous republic in 1919.

Bashō /'bɑːʃəʊ/ the pen name of Matsuo Munefusa 1644–1694. Japanese poet who was a master of the **haiku**, a 17-syllable poetic form with lines of 5, 7, and 5 syllables, which he infused with subtle allusiveness and made the accepted form of poetic expression in Japan. *Oku no hosomichi/The Narrow Road to the Deep North* 1694, an account of a visit to northern Honshu, consists of haikus interspersed with prose passages.

basic /'beɪsɪk/ *adj.* **1.** forming a base or starting point; forming a standard minimum before additions. **2.** of fundamental importance. **3.** (of rock or soil) having a low silica content in proportion to the lime or other bases present. —**Basic English**, a simplified form of English with a select vocabulary of 850 words, devised in the 1920s as an international auxiliary language; as a route into Standard English for foreign learners; and as a reminder to the English-speaking world of the virtues of plain language. **basic slag**, a fertilizer containing phosphates, formed as a by-product in steel manufacture. —**basically** *adv.*

BASIC /'beɪsɪk/ acronym from Beginner's All-purpose Symbolic Instruction Code; a computer-programming language, developed in 1964. Most versions use an ◊interpreter program, which allows programs to be entered and run with no intermediate translation, although recent versions have been implemented as a ◊compiler. The language is relatively easy to learn, and is popular among users of microcomputers.

basicity *n.* the number of replaceable hydrogen atoms in an acid. Nitric acid, HNO_3, is monobasic; sulphuric acid, H_2SO_4, is dibasic; and phosphoric acid, H_3PO_4, is tribasic.

basic-oxygen process the most widely used method of steelmaking, involving the blasting of oxygen at supersonic speed into molten pig iron.

basidiocarp *n.* the spore-bearing body, or 'fruiting body', of all basidiomycete ◊fungi except the rusts and smuts. A well-known example is the edible mushroom. Other types include globular basidiocarps (puffballs) and flat ones that project from tree trunks (brackets). They are made up of a mass of tightly packed, intermeshed ◊hyphae.

Basie /'beɪsi/ Count (William) 1904–1984. US jazz band leader, pianist, and organist who developed the big-band sound and a simplified, swinging style of music. He led impressive groups of musicians in a career spanning more than 50 years.

basil /'bæzəl/ *n.* a plant *Ocimum basilicum* of the mint family Labiatae. A native of the tropics, it is cultivated in Europe as a culinary herb. [from Old French from Latin from Greek *basilikos* = royal]

Basil II /'bæzl/ *c.*958–1025. Byzantine emperor from 976. His achievement as emperor was to contain, and later decisively defeat, the Bulgarians, earning for himself the title 'Bulgar-Slayer' after a victory in 1014. After the battle he blinded almost all 15,000 of the defeated, leaving only a few men with one eye to lead their fellows home. The Byzantine empire had reached its largest extent at the time of his death.

basilica /bə'zılıkə/ *n.* an oblong hall or church with a double colonnade and an apse. Originally a type of Roman public building, used for judicial or other public business, this architectural form was adopted by the early Christians for their churches. The earliest known basilica, at Pompeii, dates from the 2nd century BC. [Latin from Greek = royal (house)]

Basilicata /bəzılı'kɑːtə/ mountainous region of S Italy, comprising the provinces of Potenza and Matera; area 10,000 sq km/3,860 sq mi; population (1988) 622,000. Its capital is Potenza. It was the Roman province of **Lucania**.

basilisk /'bæzılısk/ *n.* 1. or **cockatrice** a mythical reptile, hatched by a serpent from a cock's egg. Its breath, and even its glance, was fatal. 2. a South American lizard, genus *Basiliscus*. It is able to run on its hind legs when travelling fast (about 11 kph/7 mph) and may dash a short distance across the surface of water. The male has a well-developed crest on the head, body, and tail. [from Latin from Greek, diminutive of *basileus* = king]

Basil, St /'bæzl/ *c.*330–379. Cappadocian monk, known as 'the Great', founder of the Basilian monks. Elected bishop of Caesarea in 370, Basil opposed the heresy of ◊Arianism. He wrote many theological works and composed the 'Liturgy of St Basil', in use in the Eastern Orthodox Church. Feast day 2 Jan.

basin /'beisən/ *n.* 1. a rounded open vessel for liquids etc.; a washbasin. 2. a depression where water collects; the tract of country drained by a river. 3. an almost landlocked harbour. —**basinful** *n.* [from Old French from Latin *ba(s)cinus*]

basis /'beisis/ *n.* (*plural* **bases** /'beisiːz/) 1. a foundation or support. 2. a main principle, a starting point. [Latin from Greek *basis* = stepping]

bask /bɑːsk/ *v.i.* (usually with *in*) to lie or rest comfortably in a pleasant warmth; to enjoy (one's popularity, glory etc.). —**basking shark**, a very large shark *Cetorhinus maximus* accustomed to lie near the surface of water. [from Old Norse]

Baskerville /'bæskəvıl/ John 1706–1775. English printer and typographer, who experimented in casting types from 1750 onwards. The Baskerville typeface is named after him.

basket /'bɑːskıt/ *n.* a container made of interwoven cane, wire etc.; the amount contained in it. —**basket weave**, one with a pattern resembling basketwork. —**basketful** *n.* [Anglo-French and Old French]

basketball *n.* a ball game between two teams of five or six players on an indoor enclosed court. The object is, via a series of passing moves, to throw the large inflated ball through a circular hoop and net, 3.05 m/10 ft above the ground, at the opposing side's end of the court. Basketball was invented by YMCA instructor James Naismith in Springfield, Massachusetts, in 1891. The ◊Harlem Globetrotters have helped to popularize the game worldwide. The first world championship for men was held in 1950 and in 1953 for women. They are now held every four years.

basketry /'bɑːskıtrı/ *n.* 1. baskets and other objects made by interweaving or plaiting rushes, cane, or other equally strong, natural fibres. 2. the art of weaving these.

basketwork *n.* basketry.

Basle /bɑːl/ an alternative form of ◊Basel, city in Switzerland.

Basov /'bɑːsɒf/ Nikolai Gennadievich 1912– . Soviet physicist who in 1953, with his compatriot Aleksandr Prokhorov, developed the microwave amplifier called a ◊maser. They were awarded the 1964 Nobel Prize for Physics, which they shared with Charles Townes of the USA.

Basque /bɑːsk, bæsk/ *n.* 1. a member of a people living in the Basque region of N Spain (created in 1980) and the adjoining French *département* of Pyrénées-Atlantiques. The Basques are a pre-Indo-European people, who largely maintained their independence until the 19th century and speak their own tongue. During the Spanish Civil War

1936–39 they were on the Republican side and were defeated by Franco. The Basque separatist movement ETA (*Euskadi ta Azkatasuna*/Basque Nation and Liberty) and the French organization *Enbata*/Ocean Wind engaged in guerrilla activity from 1968 in an unsuccessful attempt to secure a united Basque state. 2. their language, **Euskara**, apparently unrelated to any other language in the world. It is spoken by some half a million people around the Bay of Biscay ('the Basque bay'), as well as by emigrants in both Europe and the Americas. —*adj.* of the Basques or their language. [French from Latin *Vasco*]

Basque Country (French *Pays Basque*) the homeland of the Basque people in the W Pyrenees. The Basque Country includes the Basque Provinces of N Spain and the French *arrondissements* of Bayonne and Maulaon.

Basque Provinces (Spanish *Vascongadas*, Basque *Euskadi*) autonomous region of N Spain, comprising the provinces of Vizcaya, Alava, and Guipuzcoa; area 7,300 sq km/2,818 sq mi; population (1986) 2,133,000.

Basra /'bæzrə/ (Arabic *al-Basrah*) principal port in Iraq, in the Shatt-al-Arab delta, 97 km/60 mi from the Persian Gulf; population (1985) 617,000. Exports include wool, oil, cereal, and dates. It was heavily bombed during the Gulf War in 1991.

bas-relief /'bæsrıliːf/ *n.* low ◊relief; a sculpture or carving in low relief. [from Italian *basso rilievo*]

bass[1] /beis/ *adj.* deep-sounding; of the lowest musical pitch. —*n.* 1. a male voice of the lowest range; a singer with such a voice; a part written for it. 2. bass pitch. 3. (*colloquial*) a double bass (see ◊violin); a bass guitar. —**bass viol**, a viola da gamba. [ultimately from Greek *basis* = stepping, alteration after Italian *basso*]

bass[2] /bæs/ *n.* (*plural* **basses**, *collective* **bass**) any of several marine fish of the perch family, especially *Morone labrax* found in the N Atlantic and Mediterranean. They grow to 1 m/3 ft, and are often seen in shoals. [Old English]

Bassein /bɑː'sein/ port in Myanmar (Burma), in the Irrawaddy delta, 126 km/78 mi from the sea; population (1983) 355,588. Bassein was founded in the 13th century.

Basse-Normandie /'bæs nɔ:mɒn'diː/ or **Lower Normandy** coastal region of NW France lying between Haute-Normandie and Brittany (Bretagne). It includes the *départements* of Calvados, Manche, and Orne; area 17,600 sq km/6,794 sq mi; population (1986) 1,373,000. Its capital is Caen. Apart from stock farming, dairy farming, and the production of textiles, the area produces Calvados (apple brandy).

basset /'bæsıt/ *n.* (in full **basset hound**) a short-legged dog with a long body, wrinkled forehead, and long pendulous ears, originally bred in France for hunting hares. [French, diminutive of *bas* = low]

Basseterre /bæs 'teə/ capital and port of St Kitts–Nevis, in the Leeward Islands; population (1980) 14,000. Industries include data processing, rum, clothes, and electrical components.

basset horn /'bæsıt/ a musical ◊woodwind instrument resembling a clarinet, pitched in F and ending in a brass bell.

bassinet /bæsı'net/ *n.* a child's wicker cradle with a hood. [French, diminutive of *bassin* = basin]

bassoon /bə'suːn/ *n.* a double-reed ◊woodwind instrument, the bass of the oboe family. It doubles back on itself in a tube about 2.5 m/7.5 ft long. Its tone is rich and deep. —**bassoonist** *n.* [from French from Italian *bassone* (*basso* = deep from Latin *bassus* = low)]

Bass Strait /bæs/ channel between Australia and Tasmania, named after British explorer George Bass (1763–1808); oil was discovered there in the 1960s.

bast /bæst/ *n.* fibrous material obtained from the inner bark of the lime tree or other sources and used for matting etc.; phloem. [Old English]

bastard /'bɑːstəd/ *adj.* 1. born of parents not married to each other. 2. hybrid. 3. in botany and zoology, resembling (the species whose name is appropriated). —*n.* 1. a bastard person. 2. (*colloquial*) a disliked or difficult person or thing. [from Old French from Latin]

bastardize *v.t.* to declare (a person) illegitimate.

bastardy *n.* the condition of being a bastard, illegitimacy.

baste[1] /beist/ *v.t.* to moisten (roasting meat) with melted fat to prevent it from drying.

baste[2] /beɪst/ *v.t.* to stitch loosely together (preparatory to regular sewing). [from Old French = sew lightly]

Bastille /bæsˈtiːl/ *n.* the castle of St Antoine, built about 1370 as part of the fortifications of Paris, which was used for centuries as a state prison; it was singled out for the initial attack by the mob that set the French Revolution in motion on 14 July 1789. Only seven prisoners were found in the castle when it was stormed; the governor and most of the garrison were killed, and the Bastille was razed.

bastinado /bæstiˈnɑːdəʊ/ *n.* (*plural* **bastinados**) a torture consisting of repeated blows with a cane on the soles of the feet. —*v.t.* to torture in this way. [from Spanish *baston* = stick]

bastion /ˈbæstiən/ *n.* 1. a projecting part of a fortification. 2. a fortified place near hostile territory. 3. an institution etc. serving as a stronghold. [French from Italian *bastire* = build]

Basutoland /bəˈsuːtəʊlænd/ the former name (until 1966) of ◊Lesotho.

bat[1] *n.* 1. an implement (usually of wood) with a handle and a flat or curved surface for striking the ball in games; a turn at using this. 2. a batsman. —*v.t.* (-**tt**-) to use a bat; to hit with a bat. —**off one's own bat,** without prompting or assistance. [from Old English *batt* = club from Old French *battre* = hit]

bat[2] *n.* a furry, flying mammal in which the forelimbs are developed as wings capable of rapid and sustained flight. There are two main groups of bats: **megabats,** or **flying foxes,** which eat fruit, and **microbats,** which mainly eat insects. Although by no means blind, many microbats rely largely on echolocation for navigation and finding prey, sending out pulses of high-pitched sound and listening for the echo. Bats are nocturnal, and those native to temperate countries hibernate in winter. There are about 1,000 species of bats forming the order Chiroptera, making this the second-largest mammalian order; bats make up nearly one quarter of the world's mammals. Although bats are widely distributed, bat populations have declined alarmingly and many species are now endangered. —**blind as a bat,** completely blind. [from Scandinavian, originally *bakke*]

bat[3] *v.t.* (-**tt**-) to flutter. —**not bat an eyelid,** (*colloquial*) to show no surprise or alarm. [variant of obsolete *bate* = flutter]

Bataan /bəˈtɑːn/ peninsula in Luzon, the Philippines, which was defended against the Japanese in World War II by US and Filipino troops under General MacArthur from 1 Jan to 9 April 1942. MacArthur was evacuated, but some 67,000 Allied prisoners died on the **Bataan Death March** to camps in the interior.

Batak /ˈbɑːtæk/ *n.* a member of any of the several distinct but related peoples of N Sumatra in Indonesia. Numbering approximately 2.5 million, the Batak speak languages belonging to the Austronesian family.

batch /bætʃ/ *n.* 1. a quantity of loaves or cakes produced at a single baking. 2. a quantity or number of persons or things coming or dealt with together; an instalment. [from Old English]

batch system in computing, a system for processing data with little or no operator intervention. Batches of data are prepared in advance, and processed during regular 'runs' (for example, each night, or at weekends). This enables efficient use of the computer and is well suited to applications of a repetitive nature, such as a company payroll.

bated /ˈbeɪtɪd/ *adj.* **with bated breath,** holding one's breath in anxiety or suspense. [from *abate*]

Bateman /ˈbeɪtmən/ H(enry) M(ayo) 1887–1970. Australian cartoonist who lived in England. His cartoons are based on themes of social embarrassment and confusion, in such series as *The Man who …* (as in *The Guardsman who dropped his rifle*).

Bates /beɪts/ Alan 1934– . English actor, a versatile male lead in over 60 plays and films. His films include *Zorba the Greek* 1965, *Far from the Madding Crowd* 1967, *Women in Love* 1970, *The Go-Between* 1971, *The Shout* 1978, and *Duet for One* 1986.

Bates H(enry) W(alter) 1825–1892. English naturalist and explorer, who spent 11 years collecting animals and plants in South America and identified 8,000 new species of insects. He made a special study of ◊camouflage in animals, and his observation of insect imitation of species unpleasant to predators is known as 'Batesian mimicry'.

Bates H(erbert) E(rnest) 1906–1974. English author. Of his many novels and short stories, *The Jacaranda Tree* 1949 and *The Darling Buds of May* 1958 demonstrate the fineness of his natural observation and compassionate portrayal of character. *Fair Stood the Wind for France* 1944 was based on his experience as a squadron leader in World War II.

bath /bɑːθ/ *n.* (*plural* **baths** /bɑːðz/) 1. a long, open vessel in which one sits to wash the body; water for this; the process of washing in it; (in *plural*) a building where baths may be taken by the public. 2. (in *plural*) a public swimming pool. 3. a liquid in which something is immersed; its container. —*v.t./i.* to immerse in a bath; to take a bath. —**Order of the Bath,** a British order of knighthood, believed to have been founded in the reign of Henry IV (1399–1413). Formally instituted in 1815, it included civilians from 1847 and women from 1970. It is so called from the ceremonial bath which originally preceded installation. [Old English]

Bath bun a round, spiced bun with currants and icing. [from *Bath,* spa town in Avon, England]

bath chair a kind of wheelchair for invalids.

bathe /beɪð/ *v.t./i.* 1. to immerse in or treat with liquid; to lie immersed in water etc. 2. to go swimming. 3. (of light or warmth) to envelop. —*n.* an instance of bathing. —**bathing suit,** a garment worn for swimming. —**bather** *n.*

Báthory /ˈbɑːtəri/ Stephen 1533–1586. King of Poland, elected by a diet convened in 1575 and crowned in 1576. Báthory succeeded in driving the Russian troops of Ivan the Terrible out of his country. His military successes brought potential conflicts with Sweden, but he died before these developed.

bathos /ˈbeɪθɒs/ *n.* unintentional descent from the sublime to the commonplace or absurd. [Greek = depth]

bathroom *n.* a room with a bath, washbasin etc.; (*euphemism*) a lavatory.

Bathurst /ˈbæθɜːst/ the former name (until 1973) of ◊Banjul, capital of the Gambia.

Bathurst town in New South Wales, on the Macquarie River, Australia; population (1981) 19,600. It dates from the 1851 gold rush.

Bathurst port in New Brunswick, Canada; population (1981) 19,500. Industries include copper and zinc mining. Products include paper and timber.

bathyal zone the upper part of the ocean, which lies on the continental shelf at a depth of between 200 and 2,000 metres/650 and 6,500 ft. [from Greek *bathus* = deep]

bathyscaph /ˈbæpθɪskæf/ *n.* or **bathyscaphe** or **bathyscape** a free-moving deep-sea diving apparatus used for exploration at great depths in the ocean. In 1960, Jacques Piccard and Don Walsh took the bathyscaph *Trieste* to a depth of 10,917 m/35,820 ft in the Challenger Deep in the ◊Mariana Trench off the island of Guam in the Pacific Ocean. [French, from Greek *bathus* = deep and *skaphos* = ship]

bathysphere /ˈbæθɪsfɪə/ *n.* a spherical diving vessel for deep-sea observation. It is lowered into the ocean by cable to a maximum depth of 900 m/3,000 ft. [from Greek *bathus* = deep]

batik /ˈbætɪk/ *n.* a method, originally Javanese, of printing coloured designs on textiles by waxing the parts not to be dyed, so as to repel the pigment; fabric treated thus. Practised throughout Indonesia, the craft was introduced to the West by the Dutch. [Javanese = painted]

Batista /bəˈtiːstə/ Fulgencio 1901–1973. Cuban dictator 1933–44 and 1952–59, whose authoritarian methods enabled him to jail his opponents and amass a large personal fortune. He was overthrown by rebel forces led by Fidel ◊Castro in 1959.

batiste /bæˈtiːst/ *n.* a fine, light cotton or linen fabric. [French, from *Baptiste* of Cambrai, first maker]

batman /ˈbætmən/ *n.* (*plural* **batmen**) a soldier acting as personal servant to an officer. [from Old French from Latin *bastum* = pack saddle]

baton /ˈbætən/ *n.* 1. a long, thin stick used by a conductor to direct performers; a short stick carried and passed on in a relay race; a drum major's stick; a staff of office; a police officer's truncheon. 2. in heraldry, a narrow bend truncated at each end. 3. a stroke replacing a figure on the face of a clock or watch. —**baton sinister,** in heraldry, a baton from sinister to dexter, used as a mark of bastardy. [from French from Latin *bastum* = stick]

batrachian /bəˈtreɪkɪən/ n. any of a class of amphibians (Batrachia or Salientia) that discard gills and tails, e.g. ◊frog and ◊toad. —adj. of these animals. [from Greek *batrachos* = frog]

batsman /ˈbætsmən/ n. (plural **batsmen**) a player who is batting in cricket or baseball; one who is good at this.

battalion /bəˈtælɪən/ n. a large body of soldiers ready for battle, especially an infantry unit forming part of a brigade; a large group of persons with a common purpose. [from French from Italian *battaglia* = battle]

batten[1] /ˈbætən/ n. **1.** a long, narrow piece of squared timber. **2.** a strip of wood or metal fastening or holding something in place. —v.t. to strengthen or fasten with battens. [from Old French *battre* = beat]

batten[2] v.i. to grow fat or prosperous *on*. [Old Norse]

Batten Jean 1909–1982. New Zealand aviator who made the first Australia–Britain return solo flight by a woman in 1935, and established speed records.

Battenberg /ˈbætənbɜːɡ/ n. (in full **Battenberg cake**) a kind of cake made in a rectangular shape with alternating pink and yellow squares, covered with marzipan. [perhaps from name of village in W Germany]

batter[1] v.t./i. to hit with repeated hard blows; to knock heavily and insistently *at*. —n. a beaten mixture of flour, eggs, and milk for cooking. —**battered baby, wife**, etc., one subjected to repeated violence. [from Anglo-French from Latin *battuere* = beat]

batter[2] n. a batsman in baseball.

battering ram a swinging beam, formerly with an iron ram's-head end, used to breach walls etc.

battery /ˈbætərɪ/ n. **1.** any energy storage device allowing release of electricity on demand. A battery is made up of one or more cells, each containing two conducting ◊electrodes (one positive, one negative) immersed in an ◊electrolyte, in a container. When an outside connection (such as through a light bulb) is made between the electrodes, a current flows through the circuit, and chemical reactions releasing energy take place within the cells. **2.** a series of cages for the intensive keeping of poultry or cattle etc. **3.** a set of connected similar units of equipment. **4.** in law, unlawful physical violence inflicted on a person. —**battery acid**, ◊sulphuric acid of 70% concentration used in lead-cell batteries (as in motor vehicles). [from French from Latin *battuere* = beat]

battle n. **1.** a fight between large organized forces. **2.** a contest; a hard struggle. —v.i. to struggle hard. —**battle cry**, a war cry; a slogan. [from Old French from Latin = gladiatorial exercises]

battleaxe n. **1.** a heavy axe used in ancient warfare. **2.** (colloquial) a formidable or domineering woman.

battledore /ˈbætəldɔː/ n. a small racket used with a shuttlecock in the volleying game of **battledore and shuttlecock**. [perhaps from Provençal *batedor* = beater, originally a paddlelike instrument used in washing etc.]

battledress n. the everyday uniform of a soldier etc.

battlefield n. the site of a battle.

battleground n. a battlefield.

battlement /ˈbætəlmənt/ n. (usually in plural) a parapet with lower sections at intervals, originally for firing from. [from Old French *batailler* = fortify]

battleship n. a warship with the heaviest armour and largest guns.

batty /ˈbætɪ/ adj. (slang) crazy; eccentric.

bauble /ˈbɔːbəl/ n. a showy but valueless ornament. [from Old French *ba(u)bel* = toy]

baud /bɔːd/ n. in telecommunications and computers, a unit of signal transmission speed equal to one electrical pulse per second; (loosely) a unit of data transmission speed of one bit per second: 300 bauds is about 300 words a minute. [from J M E *Baudot*, French engineer (died 1903)]

Baudelaire /bəʊdəˈleə/ Charles (Pierre) 1821–1867. French poet whose work combined rhythmical and musical perfection with a morbid romanticism and eroticism, finding beauty in decadence and evil. His first book of verse was *Les Fleurs du mal/ Flowers of Evil* 1857.

Baudouin /bəʊduˈæn/ 1930– . King of Belgium from 1951. In 1950 his father, ◊Leopold III, abdicated and Baudouin was known until his succession in July 1951 as *Le Prince Royal*. In 1960 he married Fabiola de Mora y Aragón (1928–), member of a Spanish noble family.

Bauhaus /ˈbaʊhaʊs/ n. a German school of architecture and design founded in 1919 by the architect Walter ◊Gropius in Weimar, Germany, in an attempt to fuse all arts, design, architecture, and crafts into a unified whole. Moved to Dessau under political pressure in 1925, it was closed by the Nazis in 1933 because of 'decadence'. Associated with the Bauhaus were the artists Klee and Kandinsky and the architect Mies van der Rohe. Gropius and Marcel Breuer worked together in the USA 1937–40. The international style of Modern architecture spread worldwide from there and in 1972 the **Bauhaus Archive** was installed in new premises in Berlin. [German = building house]

Bāul /ˈbɑːul/ n. a member of a Bengali mystical sect that emphasizes freedom from compulsion, from doctrine, and from social caste; they avoid all outward forms of religious worship. They are not ascetic, but aim for harmony between physical and spiritual needs.

baulk /bɔːk/ n. **1.** a strip of ground left unploughed; a strip of earth left between excavation trenches. **2.** the area of a billiard table within which the cue balls are placed at the start of a game. **3.** a roughly squared length of timber. [Old English from Old Norse]

Baum /bɔːm/ L(yman) Frank 1856–1919. US writer, author of the children's fantasy *The Wonderful Wizard of Oz* 1900 and its 13 sequels. The series was continued by another author after his death. The film *The Wizard of Oz* 1939 achieved lasting popularity.

bauxite /ˈbɔːksaɪt/ n. the principal ore of ◊aluminium, consisting of a mixture of hydrated aluminium oxides and hydroxides, generally contaminated with compounds of iron, which give it a red colour. Chief producers of bauxite are Australia, Guinea, Jamaica, the USSR, Suriname, and Brazil. [French, from *Les Baux* in S France]

Bavaria /bəˈveərɪə/ (German **Bayern**) administrative region (German *Land*) of S Germany; **area** 70,600 sq km/ 27,252 sq mi; **capital** Munich; **physical** largest of the German *Länder*; forms the Danube basin; **products** beer, electronics, electrical engineering, optics, cars, aerospace, chemicals, plastics, oil refining, textiles, glass, toys; **population** (1988) 11,083,000; **recent history** became a state of the German Empire in 1871. The last king, Ludwig III, abdicated in 1918, and Bavaria declared itself a republic.

bawdy /ˈbɔːdɪ/ adj. humorously indecent. —n. bawdy talk or writing. —**bawdily** adv., **bawdiness** n. [from obsolete *bawd* = woman brothelkeeper]

bawl /bɔːl/ v.t./i. to call out loudly; to weep noisily. —**bawl out**, (colloquial) to reprimand severely. [imitative]

Bax /bæks/ Arnold Edward Trevor 1883–1953. English composer. His works were often based on Celtic legends and include seven symphonies, *The Garden of Fand* (a symphonic poem), and *Tintagel* (an orchestral tone poem). He was Master of the King's Musick 1942–53.

bay[1] n. a broad inlet of the sea where the land curves inwards. [from Old French from Spanish *bahia*]

battery

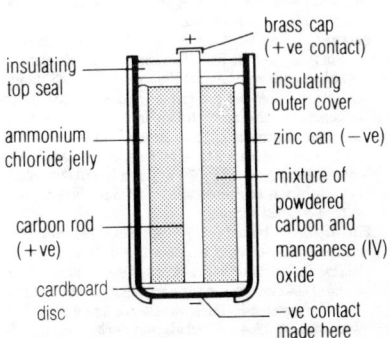

brass cap
(+ve contact)
insulating top seal
insulating outer cover
ammonium chloride jelly
zinc can (−ve)
mixture of powdered carbon and manganese (IV) oxide
carbon rod (+ve)
cardboard disc
−ve contact made here

bay² *n.* **1.** a section of wall between buttresses or columns. **2.** a recess in a room or building, especially one formed by a projecting window. **3.** any of a series of compartments in a building or structure; a partitioned or marked area forming a unit. **4.** the cul-de-sac where a side line terminates at a railway station. —**bay window,** a window projecting from the line of a building. [from Old French *ba(y)er* = gape]

bay³ *n.* any of various species of ◊laurel, genus *Laurus*. The aromatic evergreen leaves are used for flavouring in cookery. There is also a golden-leaved variety. —**bay rum,** perfume (especially for the hair) originally distilled from rum and bayberry leaves. [from Old French from Latin *baca* = berry]

bay⁴ *n.* the deep, drawn-out cry of a large dog or of hounds in pursuit of a hunted animal. —*v.i.* to utter this cry. —**at bay,** facing one's attackers, as a cornered animal. **hold** *or* **keep at bay,** to fight off (pursuers). [from Old French *ba(y)er* = gape]

bay⁵ *adj.* (especially of a horse) reddish-brown. —*n.* a reddish-brown horse. [from Old French from Latin *badius*]

Bayard /'beɪɑːd/ Pierre du Terrail, Chevalier de 1473–1524. French soldier. He served under Charles VIII, Louis XII, and Francis I and was killed in action at the crossing of the Sesia in Italy. His heroic exploits in battle and in tournaments, and his chivalry and magnanimity, won him the accolade of 'knight without fear and without reproach'.

bayberry *n.* a fragrant West Indian tree, *Pimenta acris*.

Bayern /'baɪən/ German name for ◊Bavaria, region of Germany.

Bayesian statistics /'beɪziən/ a form of statistics that uses the knowledge of prior probability together with the probability of actual data to determine posterior probabilities, using Bayes' theorem.

Bayes's theorem in statistics, a theorem relating the ◊probability of particular events taking place to the probability that events conditional upon them have occurred. [from English mathematician Thomas *Bayes* (1702–1761)]

Bayeux Tapestry a linen hanging 70 m/231 ft long and 50 cm/20 in wide, made about 1067–70, which gives a vivid pictorial record of the invasion of England by ◊William I (the Conqueror) in 1066. It is an embroidery rather than a true tapestry, sewn with woollen threads in blue, green, red, and yellow, containing 72 separate scenes with descriptive wording in Latin. It is exhibited at the museum of Bayeaux in Normandy, France.

Bayliss /'beɪlɪs/ William Maddock 1860–1924. English physiologist, who discovered the digestive hormone secretin with E H ◊Starling in 1902. During World War I, Bayliss introduced the use of saline (salt water) injections to help the injured recover from ◊shock.

Bay of Pigs inlet on the S coast of Cuba about 145 km/90 mi SW of Havana, the site of an unsuccessful invasion attempt by 1,500 US-sponsored Cuban exiles on 17–20 April 1961; 1,173 were taken prisoner.

bayonet /'beɪənɪt/ *n.* a stabbing blade that can be attached to the muzzle of a rifle for use in hand-to-hand fighting. The bayonet was placed inside the barrel of the muzzle-loading muskets of the late 17th century. The **sock** or **ring bayonet,** invented in 1700, allowed a weapon to be fired without interruption. —*v.t.* to wound with a bayonet. —**bayonet fitting,** a type of attachment in which a cylindrical part is pushed into a socket and twisted slightly so that it is secured by engagement of parts. [from French, perhaps from *Bayonne* in SW France, where the weapon is said to have first been made or used]

bazaar /bə'zɑː/ *n.* **1.** a market in oriental countries. **2.** a sale of goods to raise funds for charity. [from Persian]

Bazaine /bæ'zeɪn/ Achille François 1811–1888. Marshal of France. From being a private soldier in 1831 he rose to command the French troops in Mexico 1862–67 and was made a marshal in 1864. In the Franco-Prussian War Bazaine allowed himself to be taken in the fortress of Metz, surrendering on 27 Oct 1870 with nearly 180,000 soldiers. For this he was court-martialled in 1873 and imprisoned but in 1874 escaped to Spain.

Bazalgette /'bæzldʒet/ Joseph 1819–1890. English civil engineer who, as chief engineer to the London Board of Works, designed London's sewer system, a total of 155 km/83 mi of sewers, covering an area of 256 sq km/100 sq mi. It was completed in 1865. He also designed the Victoria Embankment 1864–70, which was built over the river

Thames and combined a main sewer, a water frontage, an underground railway, and a road. helen

bazooka /bə'zuːkə/ *n.* a tubular antitank rocket launcher. [originally = trombonelike instrument]

BBC abbreviation of ◊British Broadcasting Corporation.

BC abbreviation of before Christ (in dating).

BCE abbreviation of before the Common Era (in dating); see ◊calendar.

B cell or **B** ◊**lymphocyte** an immune cell that produces ◊antibodies. Each B cell produces just one type of antibody, specific to a single ◊antigen.

BCG abbreviation of bacillus of ◊Calmette and Guérin, used as a vaccine to confer active immunity to ◊tuberculosis (TB).

bdellium /'delɪəm/ *n.* a resin used especially as a perfume; the tree (especially of the genus *Commiphora*) yielding this. [Latin from Greek from Hebrew]

be /biː, *emphatic* biː/ *v.i.* (*present* am, are, is; *past* was, were; *past participle* been; *participle* being) **1.** to exist; to occur; to occupy a given position in space or time. **2.** to have a certain quality, identity, meaning, cost etc. —*v.aux.* used with parts of other verbs to form passive, continuous tenses, or (with infinitive) to express destiny, duty etc. —**be-all (and end-all)** *n.* one's consuming purpose. **be that as it may,** whatever the facts of the matter may be. **for the time being,** for the moment. **have been,** (*colloquial*) to have come or gone as a visitor. **let be,** to leave undisturbed. **the —to be,** the future (person of a named function). [Old English]

Be symbol for ◊beryllium.

be- prefix **1.** forming verbs implying transitive action (*bemoan*), completeness (*becalm*), thoroughness (*belabour*), attitude or treatment (*befriend*). **2.** forming adjectives with the suffix *-ed* in sense 'having' (*bespectacled*). [Old English = *by*]

beach *n.* a pebbly or sandy shore, especially of the sea between high and low watermark. —*v.t.* to haul up (a boat) on the beach. —**beachhead** *n.* a fortified position set up on a beach by landing forces.

Beach Boys, the a US pop group formed in 1961. They began as exponents of vocal-harmony surf music with Chuck Berry guitar riffs (their hits include 'Surfin' USA' 1963 and 'Help Me, Rhonda' 1965) but the compositions, arrangements, and production by Brian Wilson (1942–) became highly complex under the influence of psychedelic rock, peaking with 'Good Vibrations' in 1966. Wilson spent most of the next 20 years in retirement but returned with a solo album in 1988.

beachcomber /'biːtʃkəʊmə/ *n.* one who lives by salvaging objects washed up on the beach; a loafer who lives on what they can earn casually on a waterfront. —**beachcombing** *n.*

beacon /'biːkən/ *n.* **1.** a signal fire set up in a high or prominent position; a high hill suitable for such a fire. **2.** a warning or guiding light; a Belisha beacon. **3.** a signal station such as a lighthouse. [Old English]

bead *n.* **1.** a small piece of perforated hard material for making necklaces etc.; (in *plural*) a necklace or string of beads, a rosary. **2.** a drop of moisture; a bubble. **3.** a small knob forming the sight of a gun. **4.** a strip on the inner edge of a pneumatic tyre for gripping the wheel. **5.** a small globular moulding, often applied in rows like a series of beads. —*v.t.* **1.** to adorn with beads. **2.** to coat (a surface) with beads of moisture. —**draw a bead on,** to take aim at. [Old English = prayer (from its use in rosaries)]

beading *n.* **1.** a decoration of beads. **2.** a moulding or carving like a series of beads. **3.** a strip of material with one side rounded, used to trim the edge of wood. **4.** the bead of a tyre.

beadle /'biːdəl/ *n.* **1.** a ceremonial officer of a church, college etc. **2.** (*Scottish*) a church officer attending on a minister. **3.** (*historical*) a minor officer of a parish, dealing with petty offenders etc. [from Old French from Germanic]

beady *adj.* (of eyes) small and glittering.

beagle /'biːgəl/ *n.* a short-haired hound with pendant ears, sickle tail, and bell-like voice, originally used in hunting hares etc. on foot. [from Old French *beegueule* = noisy person]

beagling *n.* hunting with beagles.

beak *n.* **1.** a bird's horny projecting jaws. The beaks of birds are adapted by shape and size to specific diets. **2.** a similar mouthlike part or other projection. —**beaked** *adj.* [from Old French, of Celtic origin]

beaker /'bi:kə/ *n.* **1.** a tall narrow drinking cup, often without a handle. **2.** an open glass vessel with straight sides and a lip for pouring liquids, used in laboratories. **3.** in archaeology, a wide-mouthed pottery vessel. [Old Norse, perhaps from Greek *bikos* = drinking vessel]

Beaker people a people thought to be of Iberian origin who spread out over Europe in the 2nd millennium BC, and who began Stonehenge in England. They were skilled in metal-working, and their remains include the earthenware beakers that distinguish them from other cultures of that time.

beam *n.* **1.** a long sturdy piece of timber or other solid material used in building houses etc. **2.** the crossbar of a balance. **3.** (in *plural*) the horizontal cross timbers of a ship; a ship's greatest breadth. **4.** a ray or stream of light or other radiation. **5.** radio waves transmitted undispersed, especially as used to guide aircraft or missiles. **6.** a radiant look, a smile. —*v.t./i.* **1.** to radiate (light, affection etc.). **2.** to direct (radio signals); to shine. **3.** to smile radiantly. —**on one's beam ends**, (*colloquial*) near the end of one's resources. [Old English = tree]

beam balance an instrument for measuring mass (or weight). A simple form consists of a beam pivoted at its midpoint with a pan hanging at each end. The mass to be measured, in one pan, is compared with a variety of standard masses placed in the other. When the beam is balanced, the masses' turning effects or moments under gravity, and hence the masses themselves, are equal.

beam weapon a weapon capable of destroying a target by means of a high-energy beam. Beam weapons similar to the 'death ray' of science fiction have been explored, most notably during Ronald Reagan's presidential term in the 1980s in the USA.

bean *n.* **1.** any of the oval edible seeds of various leguminous plants; a plant producing beans. Beans are rich in nitrogenous or protein matter and are grown both for human consumption and as food for cattle and horses. Varieties of bean are grown throughout Europe, the USA, South America, China, Japan, and SE Asia. **2.** a similar-shaped seed of other plants (cocoa, coffee). —**full of beans**, (*colloquial*) lively, in high spirits. **spill the beans**, (*slang*) to divulge secrets. [Old English]

beanfeast *n.* a festive entertainment, originally one given annually by an employer to the employees. [beans and bacon were regarded as an indispensable dish]

beano /'bi:nəʊ/ *n.* (*plural* **beanos**) (*slang*) a party, a merry time.

bear[1] /beə/ *v.t./i.* (*past* **bore**; *past participle* **borne**) **1.** to carry; to support. **2.** to bring or take. **3.** to have as a visible feature or as a name, meaning etc. **4.** to hold or cherish in the mind. **5.** to give birth to; to produce (fruit or flowers). **6.** to hold up (a load) without collapsing; to sustain (a cost); to endure, to tolerate; to be fit for. **7.** to make one's way in a given direction. **8.** to exert pressure, to thrust. —**bear on**, to be relevant to. **bear out**, to confirm. **bear up**, to remain cheerful, not despair. **bear with**, to tolerate patiently. **bear witness to**, to provide evidence of the truth of. **bring to bear**, to focus (pressure etc.). **be borne in upon**, to become convincing to. [Old English]

bear[2] *n.* **1.** a large, heavy, powerful mammal of the family Ursidae, with thick fur and a very short tail. Bears breed once a year, producing one to four cubs. In northern regions they hibernate, and the young are born in the winter den. They are found mainly in North America and N Asia. **2.** a rough uncouth or surly person. **3.** one who sells shares on the Stock Exchange for future delivery, hoping to buy them at a lower price in the meantime; the opposite of a ◊bull. In a bear market, prices fall, and bears prosper. The term (which dates from the 18th century) is probably derived from the proverb 'to sell the bear's skin before one has caught the bear'. —**bearhug** *n.* a powerful hug. **Great Bear, Little Bear**, the constellations ◊Ursa Major and ◊Ursa Minor. [Old English]

bearable *adj.* endurable.

bearberry *n.* any of several species of evergreen trailing shrub, genus *Arctostaphylos*, of the heath family, found on uplands and rocky places. Most bearberries are North American but *A. uva-ursi* is also found in Asia and Europe in northern mountainous regions. It bears small pink flowers in spring, followed by red berries that are edible but dry.

beard /biəd/ *n.* hair on the chin etc. of an adult man; similar hair in certain animals; for example, goats. —*v.t.* to confront boldly. —**bearded** *adj.* [Old English]

Beardsley /'biədzli/ Aubrey (Vincent) 1872–1898. English illustrator. His meticulously executed black-and-white work displays the sinuous line and decorative mannerisms of Art Nouveau and was often charged with being grotesque and decadent.

bearer *n.* **1.** one who carries or helps to carry a load, especially equipment on an expedition. **2.** one who brings a letter or message; the actual presenter of a cheque.

beargarden *n.* (*colloquial*) a scene of rowdy behaviour.

bearing *n.* **1.** bodily attitude as expressing character. **2.** relationship, relevance. **3.** (usually in *plural*) the part of a machine bearing the friction to allow free movement between two parts, typically the rotation of a shaft in a housing. **Ball bearings** consist of two rings, one fixed to a housing, one to the rotating shaft. Between them is a set, or race, of steel balls. They are widely used to support shafts, as in the spindle in the hub of a bicycle wheel. **4.** the compass direction of one point in relation to another; (in *plural*) relative position. Bearings are measured in degrees and given as three-digit numbers increasing clockwise. For instance, NW would be denoted as 045M or 045T, depending whether the reference line were magnetic (M) or true (T) north. **5.** a heraldic charge or device.

bearskin *n.* in the British army, the tall, furry cap worn by members of the ◊Guards.

beast *n.* **1.** an animal, especially a wild, four-footed kind. **2.** an offensively brutal or sensuous man; (*colloquial*) any objectionable person. [from Old French from Latin *bestia*]

beastly *adj.* **1.** of or like a beast, especially in obedience to animal instincts. **2.** (*colloquial*) objectionable, highly unpleasant.

beat *v.t./i.* (*past* **beat**; *past participle* **beaten**) **1.** to hit repeatedly, especially with a stick; to strike persistently; to shape or flatten by blows. **2.** to mix vigorously to a frothy or smooth consistency. **3.** (of the heart) to pulsate rhythmically. **4.** to overcome, to do better than; to be too difficult for. **5.** to sail to windward by a series of alternate tacks across the wind. —*n.* **1.** a regular repeated stroke, a sound of this; the rhythmic pulsation of the heart. **2.** the principal recurring accent in music or verse. **3.** a route regularly patrolled by a police officer or sentinel. —*pred. adj.* (*slang*) exhausted, tired out. —**beat about the bush**, to approach a subject in a roundabout way. **beat a retreat**, to withdraw to a safer position. **beat down**, to force (a seller) to lower his price; (of the sun, rain etc.) to come down with great force. **beaten track**, a well-worn or frequented route. **beat it**, (*slang*) to go away. **beat off**, to repel (an attacker). **beat the bounds**, to perform the ancient English ceremony of going round a parish boundary striking certain points with willow rods. **beat time**, to wave a stick or tap in time with music. **beat up**, to assault systematically with punches, kicks etc. [Old English]

beater *n.* **1.** an implement for beating things; a device for tapping a triangle (percussion instrument). **2.** a person employed to rouse game at a shoot.

beat generation the beatniks of the 1950s and 1960s, characterized by dropping out of conventional life styles and opting for life on the road, drugs, and antimaterialist values; and the associated literary movement whose members included William S Burroughs, Allen Ginsberg, and Jack Kerouac (who is credited with coining the term).

beatific /bi:ə'tɪfɪk/ *adj.* **1.** (of smiles etc.) showing great happiness. **2.** making blessed. [from French or Latin *beatus* = blessed and *facere* = make]

beatify /bi:'ætɪfaɪ/ *v.t.* to make blessed; in the Catholic church, (of the pope) to declare (a person) to be in heaven (the first step to ◊canonization). People who have been beatified can be prayed to, and the title 'Blessed' can be put before their names. —**beatification** /-fɪ'keɪʃən/ *n.*

beatitude /bi:'ætɪtju:d/ *n.* **1.** blessedness. **2.** (in *plural*) in the New Testament, the sayings of Jesus reported in Matthew 5: 3–11 and Luke 6: 20–38, listing the spiritual qualities that characterize members of the kingdom of God. [from Latin *beatus* = blessed]

Beatles, the /'bi:tlz/ English pop group 1960–70. The members, all born in Liverpool, were John Lennon

Beaufort scale

Number and description	Features	Air speed mi per hr	m per sec
0 calm	smoke rises vertically; water smooth	less than 1	less than 0.3
1 light air	smoke shows wind direction; water ruffled	1–3	0.3–1.5
2 slight breeze	leaves rustle; wind felt on face	4–7	1.6–3.3
3 gentle breeze	loose paper blows around	8–12	3.4–5.4
4 moderate	branches sway	13–18	5.5–7.9
5 fresh breeze	small trees sway, leaves blown off	19–24	8.0–10.7
6 strong breeze	whistling in telephone wires; sea spray	25–31	10.8–13.8
7 moderate gale	large trees sway	32–38	13.9–17.1
8 fresh gale	twigs break from trees	39–46	17.2–20.7
9 strong gale	branches break from trees	47–54	20.8–24.4
10 whole gale	trees uprooted, weak buildings collapse	55–63	24.5–28.4
11 storm	widespread damage	64–72	28.5–32.6
12 hurricane	widespread structural damage	above 73	above 32.7

(1940–1980, rhythm guitar, vocals), Paul McCartney (1942– , bass, vocals), George Harrison (1943– , lead guitar, vocals), and Ringo Starr (formerly Richard Starkey, 1940– , drums). Using songs written largely by Lennon and McCartney, the Beatles dominated rock music and pop culture in the 1960s.

beat music a style of pop music that evolved in the UK in the early 1960s, known in its purest form as ◊Mersey beat, and as British Invasion in the USA. The beat groups characteristically had a simple, guitar-dominated line-up, vocal harmonies, and catchy tunes. They included the Beatles, the Hollies (1962–), and the Zombies (1962–67).

Beaton /'biːtn/ Cecil 1904–1980. English portrait and fashion photographer, designer, illustrator, diarist, and conversationalist. He produced portrait studies and also designed scenery and costumes for ballets, and sets for plays and films.

Beaton David 1494–1546. Scottish nationalist cardinal and politician, adviser to James V. Under Mary Queen of Scots, he was opposed to the alliance with England and persecuted reformers such as George Wishart, who was condemned to the stake; he was killed by Wishart's friends.

Beatrix /'biətriks/ 1936– . Queen of the Netherlands. The eldest daughter of Queen ◊Juliana, she succeeded to the throne on her mother's abdication in 1980. In 1966, she married German diplomat Claus von Amsberg (1926–).

beats *n.pl.* regular variations in the loudness of the sound when two notes of nearly equal pitch or ◊frequency are heard together. The beats result from the ◊interference between the sound waves of the notes. The frequency of the beats equals the difference in frequency of the notes.

Beatty /'beɪti/ Warren. Stage name of Warren Beaty 1937– . US film actor and director, popular for such films as *Bonnie and Clyde* 1967 and *Heaven Can Wait* 1978. His more recent productions include *Reds* 1981, *Ishtar* 1987, and *Dick Tracy* 1990.

Beauclerk /'bəʊkleə/ the family name of the dukes of St Albans; descended from King Charles II by his mistress Eleanor Gwyn.

Beaufort /'bəʊfət/ Henry 1375–1447. English priest, bishop of Lincoln from 1398, of Winchester from 1405. As chancellor of England, he supported his half-brother Henry IV, and made enormous personal loans to Henry V to finance war against France. As a guardian of Henry VI from 1421, he was in effective control of the country until 1426. In the same year he was created a cardinal. In 1431 he crowned Henry VI as king of France in Paris.

Beaufort scale a system of recording wind velocity, devised in 1806 by Francis Beaufort (1774–1857). It is a numerical scale ranging from 0 to 17, calm being indicated by 0 and a hurricane by 12; 13–17 indicate degrees of hurricane force.

Beaujolais /'bəʊʒəleɪ/ *n.* light, fruity red wine produced in the area S of Burgundy in E France. Beaujolais is best drunk while young; the broaching date is

the third Thursday in Nov, when the new vintage is rushed to the USA, the UK, Japan and other countries, so that the Beaujolais *nouveau* (new Beaujolais) may be marketed.

Beaumarchais /bəʊmɑːˈʃeɪ/ Pierre Augustin Caron de 1732–1799. French dramatist. His great comedies *Le Barbier de Seville*/*The Barber of Seville* 1775 and *Le Mariage de Figaro*/*The Marriage of Figaro* (1778, but prohibited until 1784) form the basis of operas by ◊Rossini and ◊Mozart.

Beaumont /'bəʊmɒnt/ Francis 1584–1616. English dramatist and poet. From about 1608 he collaborated with John ◊Fletcher. Their joint plays include *Philaster* 1610, *The Maid's Tragedy* about 1611, and *A King and No King* about 1611. *The Woman Hater* about 1606 and *The Knight of the Burning Pestle* about 1607 are ascribed to Beaumont alone.

Beauregard /bəʊrəˈgɑː/ Pierre 1818–1893. US Confederate general whose opening fire on ◊Fort Sumter, South Carolina, started the American Civil War in 1861.

beautician /bjuːˈtɪʃən/ *n.* one who gives beautifying treatments to the face or body.

beautiful /'bjuːtɪfəl/ *adj.* 1. having beauty, pleasing to the eye, ear, or mind. 2. admirable or excellent of its kind. —**beautifully** *adv.*

beautify /'bjuːtɪfaɪ/ *v.t.* to make beautiful. —**beautification** /-fɪˈkeɪʃən/ *n.*

beauty /'bjuːtɪ/ *n.* 1. qualities of form, face etc., that together please one or more of the senses or the mind; a person or thing having these. 2. a fine specimen; a pleasing or advantageous feature. —**beauty parlour,** an establishment giving beautifying treatments. **beauty queen,** a woman judged the most beautiful in a contest. **beauty sleep,** sleep that is said to make or keep a person beautiful. **beauty spot,** a place famous for its beautiful scenery; a birthmark or artificial patch on the face, said to heighten beauty. [from Anglo-French from Latin *bellus* = pretty]

Beauvoir /bəʊˈvwɑː/ Simone de 1908–1986. French socialist, feminist, and writer, who taught philosophy at the Sorbonne university in Paris 1931–43. Her book *Le Deuxième sexe*/*The Second Sex* 1949 became a seminal work for many feminists.

beaver[1] *n.* 1. an amphibious rodent *Castor fiber* with webbed hind feet, a broad flat scaly tail, and thick waterproof brown fur. It has very large incisor teeth and fells trees to feed on the bark and to use the logs to construct dams and the 'lodge', in which the young are reared, food is stored, and where much of the winter is spent. 2. its fur; a hat made of this. 3. **Beaver,** a member of a junior branch of the Scout Association, consisting of boys aged six and seven. —*v.i.* **beaver away,** to work hard. [Old English]

beaver[2] *n.* (*historical*) the lower portion of the face guard of a helmet, when worn with a visor. [from Old French *baviere* = bib]

Beaverbrook /'biːvəbrʊk/ (William) Max(well) Aitken, 1st Baron Beaverbrook 1879–1964. British newspaper proprietor and politician, born in Canada. He bought a majority interest in the *Daily Express* in 1919, founded the *Sunday Express* in 1921, and bought the London *Evening Standard* in 1929. He served in Lloyd George's World War I cabinet and Churchill's World War II cabinet.

bebop /'bi:bɒp/ *n.* or **bop** a rhythmically complex, virtuosic, highly improvisational, 'hot' jazz style that was developed in the USA 1945–55 by Charlie Parker, Dizzy Gillespie, Thelonius Monk, and other disaffected black musicians. [imitative]

becalm /bi'kɑːm/ *v.t.* (usually in *passive*) to keep (a ship) motionless through absence of wind.

became past of become.

because /bi'kɒz/ *conj.* for the reason that, since. —*adv.* by reason of.

béchamel sauce /'beʃəməl/a kind of fine white sauce. [invented by Marquis de *Béchamel* (died 1703), courtier of Louis XIV]

Bechet /be'ʃeɪ/ Sidney (Joseph) 1897–1959. US jazz musician, born in New Orleans. He played clarinet and was the first to forge an individual style on the soprano saxophone. Bechet was based in Paris in the late 1920s and the 1950s, where he was recognized by classical musicians as a serious artist.

Bechuanaland /betʃu'ɑːnəlænd/ the former name (until 1966) of ◊Botswana.

beck[1] *n.* (*archaic*) a gesture. —**at the beck and call of,** subject to constant orders from.

beck[2] *n.* (*N England*) a brook, a stream. [Old Norse]

Becker /'bekə/ Boris 1967– . German lawn-tennis player. In 1985 he became the youngest winner of a singles title at Wimbledon at the age of 17. He has won the title three times and helped West Germany to win the Davis Cup in 1988 and 1989. He also won the US Open in 1989.

Becket /'bekɪt/ St Thomas à 1118–1170. English priest and politician. He was chancellor to ◊Henry II 1155–62, when he was appointed archbishop of Canterbury. The interests of the church soon conflicted with those of the crown and Becket was assassinated; he was canonized in 1172.

Beckett /'bekɪt/ Samuel 1906–1989. Irish novelist and dramatist, who wrote in French and English. His *En attendant Godot/Waiting for Godot* 1952 is possibly the most universally known example of Theatre of the ◊Absurd (in which life is taken to be meaningless). This genre is taken to further extremes in *Fin de Partie/Endgame* 1957 and *Happy Days* 1961. He received the Nobel Prize for Literature in 1969.

beckon /'bekən/ *v.t./i.* to signal or summon by a gesture. [Old English, related to *beacon*]

become /bi'kʌm/ *v.t./i.* (*past* **became**; *past participle* **become**) 1. to come or grow to be, to begin to be. 2. to suit, to be becoming to. —**become of,** to happen to. [Old English]

becoming *adj.* giving a pleasing appearance or effect, suitable. —**becomingly** *adv.*

becquerel /'bekərəl/ *n.* the SI unit (symbol Bq) of ◊radioactivity, equal to one radioactive disintegration (change in the nucleus of an atom when a particle or ray is given off) per second. [from A H *Becquerel*]

Becquerel /bekə'rel/ Antoine Henri 1852–1908. French physicist who discovered penetrating radiation coming from uranium salts, the first indication of ◊radioactivity, and shared a Nobel prize with Marie and Pierre ◊Curie in 1903.

bed *n.* 1. a base or support to sleep or rest on, a piece of furniture with a mattress and covering. 2. a garden plot in which plants are grown. 3. the bottom of the sea or a river etc.; the foundation of a road or railway. 4. in geology, a single ◊sedimentary rock unit with a distinct set of physical characteristics or contained fossils, readily distinguishable from those of beds above and below. Well-defined partings called **bedding planes** separate successive beds or strata. —*v.t./i.* (**-dd-**) 1. to put or go to bed. 2. to plant in a garden bed. 3. to place or fix in a foundation. [Old English]

bedaub /bi'dɔːb/ *v.t.* to smear all over, especially with paint.

bedbug *n.* a small, flat, evil-smelling, wingless, red-brown insect *Cimex lectularius* with piercing mouthparts. It hides by day in dirty crevices or bedclothes and emerges at night to suck human blood.

bedclothes *n.pl.* sheets, blankets etc., used on a bed.

bedding *n.* 1. things used to make a bed (e.g. mattress, bedclothes; straw and hay for horses etc.). 2. geological strata. —**bedding plant,** a plant suitable for a garden bed.

Bede /bi:d/ *c.*673–735. English theologian and historian, known as **the Venerable Bede,** active in Durham and Northumbria. He wrote many scientific, theological, and historical works. His *Historia Ecclesiastica Gentis Anglorum/Ecclesiastical History of the English People* 731 is a seminal source for early English history.

bedevil /bi'devəl/ *v.t.* (**-ll-**) to trouble or vex; to confuse or perplex; to torment or abuse. —**bedevilment** *n.*

bedfellow *n.* one occupying the same bed; an associate.

Bedfordshire /'bedfədʃə/ county in central S England; area 1,240 sq km/479 sq mi; products cereals, vegetables, agricultural machinery, electrical goods; population (1987) 526,000.

bedizen /bi'daɪzən/ *v.t.* to deck out gaudily. [from obsolete *dizen* = deck out]

bedlam /'bedləm/ *n.* a scene of wild confusion or uproar. [from St Mary of *Bethlehem,* the earliest mental hospital in Europe, opened in the 14th century in London]

Bedouin /'beduɪn/ *n.* (*plural* the same) a member of a nomadic people of Arabia and N Africa, now becoming increasingly settled. Their traditional trade was the rearing of horses and camels. [from Old French ultimately from Arabic *bedw* = desert]

bedpan *n.* a pan for use as a lavatory by a person confined to bed.

bedpost *n.* any of the upright supports of a bedstead.

bedraggled /bi'drægəld/ *adj.* wet and dishevelled. [Old English]

bedridden /'bedrɪdən/ *adj.* permanently confined to bed by infirmity.

bedrock *n.* 1. solid rock beneath loose soil. 2. basic facts or principles.

bedroom *n.* a room with a bed or other furniture for sleeping in.

Beds. abbreviation of ◊Bedfordshire.

bedside *n.* a position by a bed.

bedsit, bedsitter (*colloquial*) a bedsitting room.

bedsitting room a room serving as bedroom and sitting room.

bedsore *n.* a sore caused by prolonged lying in bed.

bedspread *n.* a cloth or cover put over a bed when this is not in use.

bedstead /'bedsted/ *n.* the framework of a bed.

bedstraw *n.* a herbaceous plant of the genus *Galium,* formerly used as straw for beds.

bee *n.* a four-winged insect of the super-family Apoidea in the order Hymenoptera, usually with a sting. There are over 12,000 species, of which fewer than 1 in 20 are social in habit. The **hive** or **honey bee** *Apis mellifera* establishes perennial colonies of about 80,000, the majority being infertile females (workers), with a few larger fertile males (drones), and a single very large fertile female (the queen). Hive bees communicate by a form of dance, and collect nectar and pollen to produce wax and honey. —**a bee in one's bonnet,** (*colloquial*) an obsession. [Old English]

beech *n.* 1. a forest tree of the genus *Fagus.* The **common beech** *Fagus sylvaticus,* found in European forests, has a smooth grey trunk and edible nuts, or 'mast', which are used as animal feed or processed for oil. The timber is used in furniture. 2. any of various similar chiefly evergreen trees of the genus *Notofagus,* growing in cooler regions of the countries of the southern hemisphere. 3. the wood of any of these. [Old English]

Beecham /'bi:tʃəm/ Thomas 1879–1961. English conductor and impresario. He established the Royal Philharmonic Orchestra in 1946 and fostered the works of composers such as Delius, Sibelius, and Richard Strauss.

Beecher /'bi:tʃə/ Lyman 1775–1863. US Presbyterian cleric, one of the most popular pulpit orators of his time. He was the father of Harriet Beecher ◊Stowe and Henry Ward Beecher. As pastor from 1847 of Plymouth church, Brooklyn, New York, he was a leader in the movement for the abolition of slavery.

Beeching /'bi:tʃɪŋ/ Richard, Baron Beeching 1913–1985. English scientist and administrator. He was chair of the British Railways Board 1963–65, producing the controversial **Beeching Report** 1963, planning concentration on

beechmast

98

Beeton, Mrs *Isabella Beeton, whose name became a byword for household management.*

intercity passenger traffic and a freight system, at the cost of closing many rural and branch lines.

beechmast /'bi:tʃmɑːst/ *n.* beech nuts collectively.

bee-eater *n.* a bird *Merops apiaster* found in Africa, S Europe, and Asia. It feeds on a variety of insects, including bees, which it catches in its long narrow bill. Chestnut, yellow, and blue-green, it is gregarious, and generally nests in river banks and sandpits.

beef *n.* **1.** the meat of an ox, bull, or cow; (*plural* beeves) an ox etc. bred for meat. **2.** (*colloquial*) muscular strength, brawn. **3.** (*slang*) a complaint. —*v.i.* (*slang*) to grumble. —**beef tea,** stewed extract of beef, given to invalids etc. **beef up,** (*slang*) to strengthen, to reinforce. [from Anglo-French from Latin *bos bovis* = ox]

beefeater /'bi:fi:tə/ *n.* a guard at the Tower of London, or a member of the Yeomen of the Guard, wearing Tudor dress as uniform. [from obsolete sense = dependant, well-fed menial]

beefy *adj.* like beef; brawny, muscular. —**beefiness** *n.*

beehive *n.* a hive.

beeline *n.* a straight line of travel between two points. —**make a beeline for,** to head directly for.

Beelzebub /bi'elzɪbʌb/ in the New Testament, the leader of the devils, sometimes identified with Satan and sometimes with his chief assistant (see ◊devil). In the Old Testament Beelzebub was a god worshipped by the Philistines. [Hebrew = lord of the flies]

been past participle of be.

beep *n.* a short high-pitched sound, especially that of a car horn. —*v.i.* to make this sound. [imitative]

beer *n.* an alcoholic drink made from malt (fermented barley or other grain), flavoured with hops. Beer contains between 1% and 6% alcohol. One of the oldest alcoholic drinks, it was brewed in ancient Egypt and Babylon. The medieval distinction between beer (containing hops) and ale (without hops) has now fallen into disuse and beer has come to be used as a generic term including ale, stout, and lager. —**small beer,** something insignificant. —**beery** *adj.* [Old English]

Beersheba /bɪə'ʃi:bə/ industrial town in Israel; population (1987) 115,000. It is the chief centre of the Negev desert and has been a settlement from the Stone Age.

beeswax /'bi:zwæks/ *n.* wax secreted by bees for honeycombs and used for polishing wood.

beeswing /'bi:zwɪŋ/ *n.* a filmy crust on old port wine.

beet *n.* (*plural* the same or beets) a plant of the genus *Beta*. The common beet *B. vulgaris* is used in one variety to produce sugar, and another, the mangelwurzel, is grown as cattle fodder. For red beet, see ◊beetroot. [Old English from Latin]

Beethoven /'beɪthəʊvən/ Ludwig van 1770–1827. German composer and pianist, whose mastery of musical expression in every genre made him the dominant influence on 19th-century music. Beethoven's repertoire includes concert overtures; the opera *Fidelio*; five piano concertos and two for violin (one unfinished); 32 piano sonatas, including the *Moonlight* and *Appassionata*; 17 string quartets; the *Mass in D* (*Missa solemnis*); and nine symphonies, as well many youthful works. He usually played his own

piano pieces and conducted his orchestral works until he was hampered by deafness from 1801; nevertheless he continued to compose.

beetle[1] *n.* an insect of the order Coleoptera with leathery forewings folding down in a protective sheath over the membranous hindwings, which are those used for flight. They pass through a complete metamorphosis. They include some of the largest and smallest of all insects: the largest is the **Hercules beetle** *Dynastes hercules* of the South American rainforests, 15 cm/6 in long; the smallest is only 0.05 cm/0.02 in. Comprising more than 50% of the animal kingdom, beetles number some 370,000 named species, with many not yet described. [Old English]

beetle[2] *n.* a heavy-headed tool for crushing or ramming things. [Old English]

beetle-browed *adj.* with brows projecting in a threatening way.

beetling *adj.* projecting threateningly, overhanging.

Beeton, Mrs /'bi:tn/ (Isabella Mary Mayson) 1836–1865. English writer on cookery and domestic management. She produced *Beeton's Household Management* 1859, the first comprehensive work on domestic science.

beetroot *n.* the red root of the garden beet *Beta rubra*, used in salads etc.

befall /bi'fɔ:l/ *v.i.t.* (*past* befell; *past participle* befallen) to happen (to).

befit /bi'fɪt/ *v.t.* (-tt-) to be suited to or proper for.

befog /bi'fɒg/ *v.t.* (-gg-) to envelop as with fog, to confuse.

before /bi'fɔ:/ *adv. & prep.* **1.** ahead (of), in front (of); in the presence of. **2.** at a time previous (to). **3.** in preference to. —*conj.* earlier than the time when. —**before Christ,** (of a date) reckoned backwards from the birth of Christ.

beforehand *adv.* in advance, in readiness or anticipation.

befriend /bi'frend/ *v.t.* to act as a friend to, to help.

befuddle /bi'fʌdəl/ *v.t.* to stupefy, to confuse with or as with alcoholic drink.

beg *v.t./i.* (-gg-) **1.** to ask for as a gift or favour, to request earnestly or humbly; to live by seeking charity, usually for money and food. Begging is prohibited in many Western countries and stringent measures are taken against it in the USSR. In the Middle East and Asia, almsgiving is often considered a religious obligation. **2.** to ask for formally; to take or ask leave to do something. —**beg the question,** to assume the truth, in reasoning, of a thing that is still to be proved. **go begging,** to be available but unwanted.

began past of begin.

beget /bi'get/ *v.t.* (-tt-; *past* begot (*archaic* begat); *past participle* begotten) to be the father of; to give rise to (an effect).

beggar /'begə/ *n.* **1.** one who lives by begging; a very poor person. **2.** (*colloquial*) a person, a fellow. —*v.t.* **1.** to reduce to extreme poverty. **2.** to render (description etc.) inadequate. —**beggarly** *adj.*, **beggary** *n.*

begin /bi'gɪn/ *v.t./i.* (-nn-; *past* began; *past participle* begun) **1.** to perform the earliest or first part of (an activity or process etc.). **2.** to be the first to do something; to take the first step, to start speaking; (*colloquial*) to show any likelihood. **3.** to come into existence. **4.** to have its first element or starting point (at some point in space or time). [Old English]

Begin /'beɪgɪn/ Menachem 1913– . Israeli politician, born in Poland. He was a leader of the extremist Irgun Zvai Leumi organization in Palestine from 1942; was prime minister of Israel 1977–83, as head of the right-wing Likud party; and in 1978 shared a Nobel Peace Prize with President Sadat of Egypt for work on the ◊Camp David Agreements for a Middle East peace settlement.

beginner *n.* one who is just beginning, especially to learn a skill. —**beginner's luck,** good luck supposed to attend a beginner.

beginning *n.* the first part of something; the time or place at which something begins; source, origin. —**beginning of the end,** the first clear signs of an (often unfavourable) outcome.

begone /bi'gɒn/ *interjection* meaning go away at once!

begonia /bi'gəʊnɪə/ *n.* any plant of the genus *Begonia* of the tropical and subtropical plant family Begoniaceae. Begonias have fleshy and succulent leaves, and some have large, brilliant flowers. There are numerous species native to the tropics, in particular South America and India. [from M *Bégon*, French patron of science (died 1710)]

begot, begotten past and past participle of **beget.**

begrudge /bɪ'grʌdʒ/ *v.t.* to grudge.

beguile /bɪ'gaɪl/ *v.t.* **1.** to charm or divert; to make (time) pass pleasantly. **2.** to deceive, to trick. **—beguilement** *n.* [from obsolete *guile* = deceive]

beguine /bɪ'giːn/ *n.* a dance of West Indian origin; its music or rhythm. [from French *béguin* = infatuation]

begum /'beɪgəm/ *n.* in Pakistan and India, the title of a Muslim married woman, = Mrs; a Muslim woman of high rank. [from Urdu from Turkish = princess]

begun past participle of **begin.**

behalf /bɪ'hɑːf/ *n.* **on behalf of,** in the interests of, as the representative of. [earlier *bihalve* = on the part of (*half* = side)]

Behan /'biːən/ Brendan 1923–1964. Irish dramatist. His early experience of prison and knowledge of the workings of the ◊IRA (recounted in his autobiography *Borstal Boy* 1958) provided him with two recurrent themes in his plays. *The Quare Fellow* 1954 was followed by the tragicomedy *The Hostage* 1958, first written in Gaelic.

behave /bɪ'heɪv/ *v.i.* **1.** to act or react (in a specified way). **2.** to show good manners; to conduct (oneself) well.

behaviour /bɪ'heɪvjə/ *n.* a way of behaving, manners.

behavioural *adj.* of or concerned with behaviour. **—behavioural science,** any discipline that studies behaviour, e.g. sociology.

behaviourism *n.* the study of actions by analysis into stimulus and response; advocacy of this as the only valid method in psychology. Behaviourism originated in the USA, where the leading exponent was John Broadus ◊Watson. Behaviourists maintain that all human activity can ultimately be explained in terms of conditioned reactions or reflexes and habits formed in consequence. Leading behaviourists include ◊Pavlov and B F ◊Skinner. **—behaviourist** *n.,* **behaviouristic** /-'rɪstɪk/ *adj.*

behaviour therapy in psychology, the application of behavioural principles, derived from learning theories, to the treatment of clinical conditions such as ◊phobias, ◊obsessions, sexual and interpersonal problems. For example, in treating a phobia the person is taken into the feared situation in gradual steps. Over time, the fear typically reduces, and the problem becomes less acute.

behead /bɪ'hed/ *v.t.* to cut off the head of, especially in execution.

beheld past of **behold.**

behemoth *n.* in the Old Testament (Job 40), an animal cited by God as evidence of his power; usually thought to refer to the hippopotamus. It is used proverbially to mean any giant creature. [Hebrew = beasts]

behest /bɪ'hest/ *n.* (*literary*) a command, a request. [Old English]

behind /bɪ'haɪnd/ *adv. & prep.* **1.** to the rear (of); further back in space or time (than). **2.** in an inferior position (to). **3.** in support (of). **4.** remaining after others have left. **5.** in arrears (with). **—***n.* (*colloquial*) the buttocks. **—behind the times,** antiquated in ideas or practices. **behind time,** late, unpunctual. [Old English]

behindhand /bɪ'haɪndhænd/ *adv. & pred. adj.* in arrears; behind time; out of date.

Behn /ben/ Aphra 1640–1689. English novelist and playwright, the first woman in England to earn her living as a writer. Her writings were criticized for their explicitness; they frequently present events from a woman's point of view. Her novel *Oronooko* 1688 is an attack on slavery.

behold /bɪ'həʊld/ *v.t.* (*past* and *past participle* **beheld**) (*archaic* or *literary*) to observe, to see.

beholden /bɪ'həʊldən/ *pred. adj.* under an obligation (to).

behoove /bɪ'huːv/ *v.t. impers.* (*US*) = **behove.**

behove /bɪ'həʊv/ *v.t. impers.* to be incumbent on; to be fitting for. [from Old English *hof*]

Behrens /'beərənz/ Peter 1868–1940. German architect. He pioneered the adaptation of architecture to industry, and designed the AEG turbine factory in Berlin 1909, a landmark in industrial design. He influenced ◊Le Corbusier and ◊Gropius.

Behring /'beərɪŋ/ Emil von 1854–1917. German physician who discovered that the body produces antitoxins, substances able to counteract poisons released by bacteria.

Using this knowledge, he developed new treatments for diseases such as ◊diphtheria.

Beiderbecke /'baɪdəbek/ Bix (Leon Bismarck) 1903–1931. US jazz cornetist, composer, and pianist. A romantic soloist with King Oliver, Louis Armstrong, and Paul Whiteman's orchestras, Beiderbecke was the first acknowledged white jazz innovator. He was inspired by the classical composers Debussy, Ravel, and Stravinsky.

beige /beɪʒ/ *adj. & n.* sandy fawn. [French]

Beijing /beɪ'dʒɪŋ/ formerly **Peking** capital of China; part of its NE border is formed by the Great Wall of China; population (1986) 5,860,000. The municipality of Beijing has an area of 17,800 sq km/6,871 sq mi and a population (1986) of 9,750,000. Industries include textiles, petrochemicals, steel, and engineering.

being /'biː.ɪŋ/ *n.* **1.** existence. **2.** essence or nature, constitution. **3.** something (especially a person) that exists and has life.

Beirut /beɪ'ruːt/ or **Beyrouth** capital and port of Lebanon, population (1980) 702,000. Until the civil war 1975–76, Beirut was an international financial centre, with four universities (Lebanese, Arab, French, and US), and a centre of espionage. It was besieged and virtually destroyed by the Israeli army July–Sept 1982 to enforce the withdrawal of forces of the Palestinian Liberation Organization. After the ceasefire, 500 Palestinians were massacred in the Sabra–Chatila camps 16–18 Sept, 1982, by dissident ◊Phalangist and ◊Maronite troops, with alleged Israeli complicity. Civil disturbances continued. In 1987 Syrian troops were sent in. The installation of a broad-based government in Dec 1990 gave promise of a more settled future. Western hostages are still held at unknown locations in Beirut.

bejewelled /bɪ'dʒuː.əld/ *adj.* adorned with jewels.

Bekka, the /be'kɑː/ or **El Beqa'a** a governorate of E Lebanon separated from Syria by the Anti-Lebanon mountains. The Bekka Valley has been of strategic importance in the Syrian struggle for control of N Lebanon. In the early 1980s the valley was penetrated by Shia Muslims who established an extremist Hezbollah stronghold with the support of Iranian Revolutionary Guards. Zahlé and the ancient city of Baalbek are the chief towns.

bel *n.* a unit of sound measurement equal to ten ◊decibels. [from Alexander Graham *Bell*]

belabour /bɪ'leɪbə/ *v.t.* **1.** to attack physically or verbally. **2.** to labour (a subject).

belated /bɪ'leɪtɪd/ *adj.* coming late or too late. **—belatedly** *adv.*

Belaúnde Terry /belɑː'ʊndeɪ 'teri/ Fernando 1913– . President of Peru 1963–1968 and 1980–1985. He championed land reform and the construction of roads to open up the Amazon valley. He fled to the USA in 1968 after being deposed by a military junta. After his return, his second term in office was marked by rampant inflation, enormous foreign debts, terrorism, mass killings, and human-rights violations by the armed forces.

Belgium

Belau /bəˈlaʊ/ Republic of, formerly **Palau**; self-governing island group in Micronesia; area 500 sq km/193 sq mi, consisting of 26 larger islands (8 inhabited) and about 300 islets; population (1988) 14,000. It is part of the US Trust Territory, and became internally self-governing in 1980. Since then, a number of referendums have shown that Belau wishes to remain a nuclear-free zone, although the USA is exerting strong pressure to secure nuclear facilities for itself.

belay /bɪˈleɪ/ v.t. to secure (a rope) by winding it round a peg or spike etc. —n. the securing of a rope in this way. [from Dutch *beleggen*]

bel canto /ˈbel ˈkæntəʊ/ a style of operatic singing concentrating on beauty of sound and vocal technique. The style originated in the 18th century and reached its peak in the operas of Rossini, Donizetti, and Bellini. [Italian = beautiful song]

belch v.t./i. **1.** to emit wind from the stomach through the mouth. **2.** (of a chimney, gun etc.) to discharge (smoke etc.). —n. an act of belching. [Old English]

beleaguer /bɪˈliːgə/ v.t. (*literary*) **1.** to besiege. **2.** to harass or oppress. [from Dutch *belegeren* = camp round (*leger* = camp)]

belemnite /ˈbeləmnaɪt/ n. a common fossil; an extinct relative of the squid, with rows of little hooks rather than suckers on the arms. The parts of belemnites most frequently found as fossils are the bullet-shaped shells that were within the body. Like squid, belemnites had an ink sac which could be used to produce a smokescreen when attacked. [from Greek *belemnon* = dart]

Belfast /belˈfɑːst/ industrial port (shipbuilding, engineering, electronics, textiles, tobacco) and capital of Northern Ireland since 1920; population (1985) 300,000. From 1968 it has been heavily damaged by guerrilla activities.

belfry /ˈbelfrɪ/ n. a bell tower (chiefly attached to a church); the bell-chamber in this. [originally = siege tower; from Old French from Germanic]

Belgian Congo the former name (1908–60) of ◊Zaïre.

Belgium /ˈbeldʒəm/ kingdom of; country in N Europe, bounded to the NW by the North Sea, to the SW by France, to the E by Luxembourg and Germany, and to the NE by the Netherlands; **area** 30,510 sq km/11,784 sq mi; **capital** Brussels; **physical** flat coastal plain in NW, central rolling hills, hills and forest in SE; forested plateau of the Ardennes; rivers Scheldt and Meuse; **head of state** King Baudouin from 1951; **head of government** Wilfried Martens from 1981; **political system** liberal democracy; **exports** iron, steel, textiles, manufactured goods, petrochemicals; **population** (1990 est) 9,895,000 (comprising Flemings and Walloons); **language** in the N (Flanders) Flemish (a Dutch dialect, known as *Vlaams*) 55%; in the S (Wallonia) Walloon (a French dialect) 32%; bilingual 11%; German (E border) 0.6%; all are official; **recent history** became an independent kingdom in 1830. Invaded by Germany in 1914 and £940. Since 1945 Belgium has been a major force for international cooperation in Europe, being a founding member of the ◊Benelux Economic Union; of the the Council of Europe and NATO in 1949, and of the European Community (◊EC) in 1957. Steps towards regional autonomy were taken in 1971, 1974, and 1980, when regional assemblies were created for Flanders and Wallonia and a three-member executive for Brussels.

Belgrade /belˈgreɪd/ (Serbo-Croat *Beograd*) capital of Yugoslavia and Serbia, and Danube river port linked with the port of Bar on the Adriatic; population (1981) 1,470,000. Industries include light engineering, food processing, textiles, pharmaceuticals, and electrical goods.

Belgrano /belˈgrɑːnəʊ/ Manuel 1770–1820. Argentine revolutionary. He was a member of the military group that led the 1810 revolt against Spain. Later, he commanded the revolutionary army until he was replaced by José de ◊San Martín in 1814.

belie /bɪˈlaɪ/ v.t. (*past* and *past participle* belied; *present participle* belying) **1.** to fail to confirm, to show to be untrue; to fail to live up to (one's reputation, promise etc.). **2.** to give a false idea of.

belief /bɪˈliːf/ n. **1.** the act of believing. **2.** something firmly believed. **3.** trust, confidence *in*. **4.** acceptance of a doctrine etc., one's religion.

believable /bɪˈliːvəbəl/ adj. that may be believed.

believe /bɪˈliːv/ v.t./i. **1.** to accept as true or conveying

Bellini *The Doge Leonardo Loredan painted by Venetian artist Giovanni Bellini about 1459.*

truth. **2.** to think, to suppose. **3.** to have (religious) faith; to have faith *in*; to have confidence *in*. —**believer** n. [Old English]

Belisarius /beliˈsɑːrɪəs/ c.505–565. Roman general under Emperor ◊Justinian I.

Belisha beacon /bɪˈliː ʃə/ in the UK, a flashing orange globe on a striped post, marking a pedestrian crossing. [from L Hore-*Belisha*, minister of transport in 1934]

belittle /bɪˈlɪtəl/ v.t. to imply to be of little consequence. —**belittlement** n.

Belize /bəˈliːz/ country in Central America, bounded to the N by Mexico, to the W and S by Guatemala, and to the E by the Caribbean Sea; **area** 22,963 sq km/8,864 sq mi; **capital** Belmopan; **physical** tropical swampy coastal plain, Maya Mountains in S, over 90% under forest; world's second largest barrier reef; **head of state** Elizabeth II from 1981 represented by governor general; **head of government** George Price from 1989; **political system** constitutional monarchy; **exports** sugar, citrus, rice, lobster; **population** (1990 est) 180,400 (including Mayan minority in the interior); **language** English (official), Spanish (widely spoken), native Creole dialects; **recent history** became a British colony (British Honduras) in 1862. Self-government was achieved in 1964. In 1970 the capital was moved from Belize City to the new town of Belmopan. In 1974 the name Belize was adopted. In 1975 British troops were sent to defend the long-disputed frontier with Guatemala; negotiations begun in 1977 were inconclusive. Full independence was achieved in 1981.

Belize City chief port of Belize; population (1980) 40,000. After the city, then capital of the British colony of British Honduras, was destroyed by a hurricane in 1961 it was decided to move the capital inland to Belmopan.

bell[1] n. **1.** an ancient musical instrument in all sizes comprising a suspended hollow metal container with a beater attached, which rings when shaken. Church bells are massive instruments, cast in bronze, and mounted in towers from where their sound can be heard over a wide area. Their shape is a flared bowl with a thickened rim engineered to produce a clangorous mixture of tones. Orchestral **tubular bells**, made of brass or steel, offer a chromatic scale of pitches of reduced power, and are played by striking with a wooden mallet. **2.** the sound of a bell, used as a signal, indicating the half-hours of a nautical watch. A day is divided into seven watches, five of four hours each and two, called dogwatches, of two hours. Each half-hour of each watch is indicated by the striking of a bell, eight bells signalling the end of the watch. **3.** a bell-shaped object or flower. 4. a device making a ringing or buzzing sound for attracting attention in a house etc. —**bell-bottomed** *adj.* (of trousers) widening from the knee down. [Old English]

bell² *n.* the bay of a stag. —*v.i.* to make this sound. [Old English]

Bell Alexander Graham 1847–1922. Scottish scientist and inventor of the telephone. He patented his invention in 1876, and later experimented with a type of phonograph and, in aeronautics, invented the tricycle undercarriage.

belladonna /belə'dɒnə/ *n.* or **deadly nightshade** a poisonous plant *Atropa belladonna* with purple flowers and black berries; found in Europe and Asia. The dried powdered leaves contain ◊alkaloids. Belladonna extract acts medicinally as an ◊anticholinergic, and is highly toxic in large doses. [from Italian = beautiful lady]

Bellay /be'leɪ/ Joachim du *c.*1522–1560. French poet and prose writer, who published the great manifesto of the new school of French poetry, the Pléiade: *Défense et illustration de la langue française* 1549.

belle /bel/ *n.* a beautiful or the most beautiful woman. [French from Latin *bellus* = beautiful]

belle époque /bel i'pɒk/ in Europe, the period of settled and comfortable life preceding World War I. [French = fine period]

belles-lettres /bel'letr/ *n.pl.* literature that is appreciated more for its aesthetic qualities than for its content; writings or studies of a literary nature. [French = fine letters]

bellflower *n.* a general name for many plants of the family Campanulaceae, notably those of the genus *Campanula*. The Canterbury bell *C. medium* is the garden variety, originally from S Europe. The ◊harebell is also a *Campanula*.

bellicose /'belɪkəʊz/ *adj.* eager to fight, warlike. —**bellicosity** /-'kɒsɪtɪ/ *n.* [from Latin *bellum* = war]

belligerent /bɪ'lɪdʒərənt/ *adj.* engaged in a war or conflict; bellicose. —*n.* a person or nation participating in a war. —**belligerence** *n.*, **belligerency** *n.* [from Latin *bellum* = war and *gerere* = wage]

Bellingshausen /'belɪŋzhaʊzən/ Fabian Gottlieb von 1779–1852. Russian Antarctic explorer, the first to sight and circumnavigate the Antarctic continent 1819–21, although he did not realize what it was.

Bellini /be'li:ni/ a family of Italian Renaissance painters, founders of the Venetian school. **Giovanni Bellini** (*c.*1430–1516) produced portraits and various religious subjects. He introduced softness in tone, harmony in composition, and a use of luminous colour that influenced the next generation of painters (including his pupils Giorgione and Titian). He worked in oil rather than tempera.

Bellini Vincenzo 1801–1835. Italian composer, born in Catania, Sicily. His operas include *La Sonnambula* 1831, *Norma* 1831, and *I Puritani* 1835.

bellow /'beləʊ/ *v.i./t.* to emit a deep loud roar; to utter loudly. —*n.* a loud roar, originally that of a bull.

Bellow Saul 1915– . US novelist, born in Canada, who settled in Chicago with his family in 1924. His works include the picaresque *The Adventures of Augie March* 1953, the philosophically speculative *Herzog* 1964, *Humboldt's Gift* 1975, *The Dean's December* 1982, and *The Bellarosa Connection* 1989. He was awarded the Nobel Prize for Literature in 1976.

bellows /'beləʊz/ *n.pl.* 1. a device which, when squeezed, drives a blast of air into a fire, through organ pipes etc. 2. the expandable part of a camera etc.

bell ringing or **campanology** the art of ringing church bells by hand, by means of a rope fastened to a wheel rotating the entire bell mechanism. **Change ringing** is an English art of ringing all the possible sequences of a number of bells in strict order, using one player to each bell. Fixed permutations of 5–12 bells are rung. In Europe and the USA, the **carillon** performs arrangements of well-known music for up to 70 static bells. It is played by a single operator using a keyboard system of levers and pulleys acting on the striking mechanisms only. **Handbell ringing** is played solo or by a team of ringers selecting from a range of lightweight bells of pure tone resting on a table.

belly /'belɪ/ *n.* 1. the abdomen; the stomach. 2. the underside of a four-legged animal. 3. the cavity or bulging part of anything. —*v.i./t.* to swell out. —**bellyache** *n.* stomach pain; *v.i.* (*slang*) to complain querulously. **belly dance,** an oriental dance by a woman, with voluptuous movements

of the belly. **belly dancer,** a woman who performs such a dance. [Old English = bag]

Belmopan /belmə'pæn/ capital of Belize from 1970; population (1980) 3,000. It replaced Belize City as administrative centre of the country.

Belo Horizonte /'beləʊ hɒri'zɒnteɪ/ industrial city (steel, engineering, textiles) in SE Brazil, capital of the fast-developing state of Minas Gerais; population (1985) 3,060,000. Built in the 1890s, it was Brazil's first planned modern city.

belong /bɪ'lɒŋ/ *v.i.* 1. (with *to*) to be the property of; to be rightly assigned to as a duty, right, part etc.; to be a member of (a club, family etc.). 2. to fit an environment etc.; to be rightly placed. [from obsolete *long* = belong]

belongings *n.pl.* personal possessions.

Belorussia an alternative spelling of ◊Byelorussia.

beloved /bɪ'lʌvɪd/ *adj.* much loved (*predicative* /-'lʌvd/). —*n.* a beloved person.

below /bɪ'ləʊ/ *adv.* 1. at or to a lower point or level. 2. further down a page, further on in a book etc. —*prep.* lower in position, amount, rank etc., than; downstream from.

Belsen /'belsən/ site of a Nazi ◊concentration camp in Lower Saxony, Germany.

Belshazzar /bel'ʃæzə/ in the Old Testament, the last king of Babylon, son of Nebuchadnezzar. During a feast (known as **Belshazzar's Feast**) he saw a message which appeared on the wall, interpreted by ◊Daniel as prophesying the fall of Babylon and death of Belshazzar.

belt *n.* 1. a strip of leather etc. worn round the waist or diagonally across the chest to secure clothes or hold weapons etc. 2. a strip of colour, a special surface, trees etc., round or on something; a zone or region. 3. a flexible strip carrying machine-gun cartridges; an endless strap connecting pulleys etc. 4. (*slang*) a heavy blow. —*v.t.* 1. to put a belt round. 2. to thrash with a belt; (*slang*) to hit with force. 3. to move rapidly. —**below the belt,** unfair, unfairly. **belt up,** to fasten one's safety belt; (*slang*) to stop talking. **tighten one's belt,** to live more frugally. [Old English from Latin *balteus*]

beluga /bɪ'lu:gə/ *n.* 1. a large white sturgeon *Huso huso*; caviare from this. 2. a white whale *Delphinapterus leucas.* [Russian *belyi* = white]

belvedere /'belvɪdɪə/ *n.* a raised turret or summerhouse from which to view scenery. [Italian = beautiful view]

Bemba /'bembə/ *n.* (*plural* the same or **Bembas**) a member of a people native to NE Zambia and neighbouring areas of Zaïre and Zimbabwe, although many live in urban areas such as Lusaka and Copperbelt. The Bemba language belongs to the Bantu branch of the Niger-Congo family.

bemoan /bɪ'məʊn/ *v.t.* to lament, complain of.

bemuse /bɪ'mju:z/ *v.t.* to stupefy or bewilder.

Ben Ali /ben 'æli/ Zine el Abidine 1936– . Tunisian politician, president from 1987. After training in France and the USA, he returned to Tunisia and became director-general of national security. He was made minister of the interior and then prime minister under the ageing president for life, Habib ◊Bourguiba, whom he deposed in 1987 by a bloodless coup with the aid of ministerial colleagues.

Benares /bɪ'nɑ:rɪz/ transliteration of ◊Varanasi, holy city in India.

Ben Barka /ben 'bɑ:kə/ Mehdi 1920–1965. Moroccan politician. He became president of the National Consultative Assembly in 1956 on the country's independence from France. He was assassinated by Moroccan agents with the aid of French secret-service men as a result of his alleged involvement in an attempt on King Hassan's life and for supporting Algeria in Algerian-Moroccan border disputes.

Ben Bella /ben 'belə/ Ahmed 1916– . Algerian leader of the National Liberation Front (FLN) from 1952; prime minister of independent Algeria 1962–65, when he was overthrown by ◊Boumédienne and detained until 1980. He founded a new party, *Mouvement pour la Démocratie en Algérie*, in 1985. In 1990 he returned to Algeria.

bench *n.* 1. a long seat of wood or stone. 2. a worktable for a carpenter, scientist etc. 3. a judge's seat in court; a lawcourt; (*collective*) judges and magistrates. —**bench mark,** a surveyor's mark indicating a point in a line of levels; a standard or point of reference. **King's** *or* **Queen's Bench,** a division of the High Court of Justice. **on the bench,** serving as a judge or magistrate. [Old English]

bencher *n.* in English law, a senior member of any of the Inns of Court.

bend[1] *v.t./i. (past* and *past participle* **bent** except in *bended knee*) **1.** to force (what was straight) into a curve or angle; to become curved or angular; to modify (rules) to suit oneself. **2.** to direct (one's energies) *to.* **3.** to incline from the vertical; to submit or bow *(to, before);* to force to submit. **4.** to turn (one's steps etc.) in a new direction. —*n.* **1.** a curve, departure from a straight course; the bent part of a thing. **2.** (in *plural*) sickness due to too rapid decompression e.g. after deep-sea diving, arising from too rapid a release of nitrogen from solution in the diver's blood under pressure. [Old English]

bend[2] *n.* **1.** any of various knots used to tie one rope to another. **2.** in heraldry, a stripe from the dexter chief to the sinister base. —**bend sinister,** in heraldry, a stripe from the sinister chief to the dexter base, sometimes used as a sign of bastardy. [Old English = band, bond]

beneath /bɪ'ni:θ/ *adv. & prep.* **1.** below, under. **2.** not worthy of. —**beneath contempt,** not even worth despising. [Old English]

Benedict XV /'benɪdɪkt/ 1854–1922. Pope from 1914. During World War I he endeavoured to bring about a peace settlement, and during his papacy British, French, and Dutch official relations were renewed with the Vatican.

Benedictine order a religious order of monks and nuns in the Roman Catholic church, founded by St ◊Benedict at Subiaco, Italy, in the 6th century. It had a stong influence on medieval learning and reached the height of its prosperity early in the 14th century.

benediction /beni'dɪkʃən/ *n.* a spoken blessing, especially at the end of a Christian service, particularly the Mass, or as a special Roman Catholic service. —**benedictory** *adj.* [from Old French from Latin *benedicere* = bless]

Benedict, St /'benɪdɪkt/ *c.*480–*c.*547. Founder of Christian monasticism in the West and of the ◊Benedictine order. He founded the monastery of Monte Cassino, Italy. Here he wrote out his rule for monastic life, and was visited shortly before his death by the Ostrogothic king Totila, whom he converted to the Christian faith. Feast day 11 July.

benefaction /beni'fækʃən/ *n.* a charitable gift or endowment, especially to an institution.

benefactor /'benɪfæktə/ *n.* one who has given financial or other help, especially to an institution. —**benefactress** *n. fem.* [from Latin]

benefice /'benɪfɪs/ *n.* **1.** a living held by a Christian cleric. **2.** in the early Middle Ages, a donation of land or money to the Christian church as an act of devotion. [from Old French from Latin *beneficium* = kind deed]

beneficent /bɪ'nefɪsənt/ *adj.* conferring blessings or favours. —**beneficence** *n.* [from Latin]

beneficial /beni'fɪʃəl/ *adj.* advantageous, having benefits. —**beneficially** *adj.*

beneficiary /beni'fɪʃərɪ/ *n.* a recipient of benefits, especially as designated in a will.

benefit /'benɪfɪt/ *n.* **1.** a favourable, helpful, or profitable factor or circumstance. **2.** a payment to which one is entitled from an insurance policy or government funds. **3.** a public performance or game of which the proceeds go to a charitable cause etc. —*v.t./i.* **1.** to do good to. **2.** to receive benefit *(from* or *by).* —**benefit of clergy,** the privilege, to which Christian clerics were formerly entitled, of being tried before an ecclesiastical court not a secular one, or (in certain cases) of being exempt from the sentence imposed. **benefit of the doubt,** concession that a person is innocent, correct etc., although doubt exists. **benefit society,** a society for mutual insurance against illness or the effects of old age. [from Anglo-French from Latin *benefactum (bene facere* = do well)]

Benelux /'benɪlʌks/ *n.* the customs union of Belgium, the Netherlands, and Luxembourg (agreed in 1944, fully effective from 1960); the precursor of the European Community.

Beneš /'beneʃ/ Eduard 1884–1948. Czechoslovak politician. He worked with Thomas ◊Masaryk towards Czechoslovak nationalism from 1918 and was foreign minister and representative at the League of Nations. He was president of the republic from 1935 until forced to resign by the Germans; he headed a government in exile in London during World War II. He returned home as president in 1945 but resigned again after the Communist coup of 1948.

benevolent /bɪ'nevələnt/ *adj.* wishing to do good to others, friendly and helpful; (of a fund) charitable. —**benevolence** *n.,* **benevolently** *adv.* [from Old French from Latin *bene volens* = well wishing]

Bengal /ben'gɔ:l/ former province of British India, divided in 1947 into ◊West Bengal, a state of India, and East Bengal, from 1972 ◊Bangladesh. The famine in 1943, caused by a slump in demand for jute and a bad harvest, resulted in over 3 million deaths.

Bengali language a member of the Indo-Iranian branch of the Indo-European language family, the official language of Bangladesh and of the state of Bengal in E India.

Benghazi /ben'gɑ:zi/ or **Banghazi** historic city and industrial port in N Libya on the Gulf of Sirte; population (1982) 650,000. It was controlled by Turkey between the 16th century and 1911, and by Italy 1911–1942; a major naval supply base during World War II.

Ben-Gurion /ben 'gʊəriən/ David. Adopted name of David Gruen 1886–1973. Israeli statesman and socialist politician, one of the founders of the state of Israel, the country's first prime minister 1948–53, and again 1955–63.

benighted /bɪ'naɪtɪd/ *adj.* **1.** overtaken by night. **2.** intellectually or morally ignorant.

benign /bɪ'naɪn/ *adj.* kindly; propitious; (of climate) mild; (of disease) mild, not malignant. —**benignly** *adv.* [from Old French from Latin *benignus*]

benignant /bɪ'nɪgnənt/ *adj.* kindly, especially to inferiors; beneficial. —**benignancy** *n.,* **benignantly** *adv.*

benignity /bɪ'nɪgnɪtɪ/ *n.* kindliness.

Benin /be'ni:n/ People's Republic of; country in W Africa, sandwiched between Nigeria on the E and Togo on the W, with Burkina Faso to the NW, Niger to the NE, and the Atlantic Ocean to the S; **area** 112,622 sq km/ 43,472 sq mi; **capital** Porto Novo (official), Cotonou (de facto); **physical** flat, humid, with dense vegetation; **head of state and government** Mathieu Kerekou from 1972; **political system** one-party Socialist republic; **exports** cocoa, peanuts, cotton, palm oil, petroleum; **population** (1990 est) 4,840,000; **language** French (official); Fan 47%; **history** Under French control in 1893; independence was achieved in 1960. A period of acute political instability was followed by a military regime in 1972; this was replaced by civilian rule from 1977. The country's name was changed from Dahomey to Benin in 1975.

Benin former African kingdom 1200–1897, now part of Nigeria. It reached the height of its power in the 14th–17th centuries when it ruled the area between the Niger Delta and Lagos. Benin traded in spices, ivory, palm oil, and slaves until its decline and eventual incorporation into Nigeria. The oba (ruler) of Benin continues to rule his people as a divine monarch. The present oba is considered an enlightened leader and one who is helping his people to become part of modern Nigeria.

benison /'benɪzən/ *n. (archaic)* a blessing. [from Old French from Latin *benedictio* = benediction]

Benjamin /'bendʒəmɪn/ Arthur 1893–1960. Australian pianist and composer who taught composition at the Royal College of Music in London from 1925, where ◊Britten was one of his pupils. His works include *Jamaican Rumba,* inspired by a visit to the West Indies in 1937.

Benjamin George (William John) 1960– . English composer, conductor, and pianist. He was a pupil of Messiaen, and his colourful and sonorous works include *Ringed by the Flat Horizon* 1980, *At First Light* 1982, *Antara* 1987, and *Cascade* 1990.

Benn /ben/ Tony (Anthony Wedgwood) 1925– . English Labour politician, formerly the leading figure on the party's left wing. He was minister of technology 1966–70 and of industry 1974–75, but his campaign against entry to the European Community led to his transfer to the Department of Energy 1975–79. He unsuccessfully contested Neil Kinnock for the party leadership in 1988.

Bennett /'benɪt/ Alan 1934– . English playwright. His works (set in his native north of England) treat subjects such as senility, illness, and death with macabre comedy. They include TV films, for example *An Englishman Abroad* 1982; the cinema film *A Private Function* 1984; and plays like *Forty Years On* 1968 and *Getting On* 1971.

Life is rather like a tin of sardines – we're all of us looking for the key.

Alan Bennett
Beyond the Fringe

Bennett (Enoch) Arnold 1867–1931. English novelist. He became a London journalist in 1893 and editor of *Woman* in 1896. His books include *Anna of the Five Towns* 1904, *The Old Wives' Tale* 1908, and the trilogy *Clayhanger, Hilda Lessways*, and *These Twain* 1910–16.

Bennett Richard Rodney 1936– . English composer of jazz, film music, symphonies, and operas. His film scores for *Far from the Madding Crowd* 1967, *Nicholas and Alexandra* 1971, and *Murder on the Orient Express* 1974 all received Oscar nominations. His operas include *The Mines of Sulphur* 1963 and *Victory* 1970.

Ben Nevis /ben 'nevɪs/ highest mountain in the British Isles (1,342 m/4,406 ft), in the Grampians, Scotland.

bent[1] *v.t./i.* past participle of **bend[1]**. —*adj.* curved or having an angle; (*slang*) dishonest, illicit. —*n.* a natural tendency or bias; a talent (*for*). —**bent on**, determined on, seeking to do.

bent[2] *n.* **1.** any of various coarse stiff grasses of the genus *Agrostris*. Creeping bent grass *A. stolonifera*, also known as fiorin, is common in N North America and Eurasia, including lowland Britain. It spreads by ◊stolons and bears large attractive ◊panicles of yellow or purple flowers on thin stalks. It is often used on lawns and golf courses. **2.** the flower stalk of grasses, especially when old and dry. [= Old English *beonet*]

Bentham /'benθəm/ Jeremy 1748–1832. English philosopher, legal and social reformer, and founder of ◊utilitarianism. The essence of his moral philosophy is found in the pronouncement of his *Principles of Morals and Legislation* (written in 1780, published in 1789): that the object of all legislation should be 'the greatest happiness for the greatest number'.

benthos /'benθɒs/ *n.* the flora and fauna found at the bottom of a sea or lake. [Greek = depth of sea]

Bentinck /'bentɪŋk/ Lord William Cavendish 1774–1839. English colonial administrator, first governor general of India 1828–35. He acted against the ancient Indian rituals of thuggee and suttee, and established English as the medium of instruction.

Bentiu /'bentiu:/ an oil-rich region to the W of the White Nile, in the Upper Nile province of S Sudan.

Bentley /'bentli/ John Francis 1839–1902. British architect, a convert to Catholicism, who designed Westminster Cathedral, London (1895–1903). It is outwardly Byzantine but inwardly shaped by shadowy vaults of bare brickwork. The campanile is the tallest church tower in London.

bentwood *n.* wood artificially curved for making furniture. It was originally a country style of wooden furniture, mainly chairs, made by steam-heating and then bending rods of wood to form the back, legs, and seat frame. Twentieth-century designers such as Marcel ◊Breuer and Alvar ◊Aalto developed a different form by bending sheets of plywood.

benumb /bɪ'nʌm/ *v.t.* to make numb; to paralyse or deaden.

Benz /bents/ Karl 1844–1929. German automobile engineer, who produced the world's first petrol-driven motor vehicle. He built his first model engine in 1878 and the petrol-driven car in 1885.

benzaldehyde *n.* C_6H_5CHO, a clear colourless liquid with the characteristic odour of almonds. It is used as a solvent and to make perfumes and dyes. It occurs in certain leaves, such as the cherry, laurel, and peach, and in a combined form in certain nuts and kernels. It can be extracted from such natural sources, but is usually made from ◊toluene.

Benzedrine /'benzədri:n/ *n.* a trade name for ◊amphetamine, a stimulant drug.

benzene /'benzi:n/ *n.* C_6H_6, a clear liquid hydrocarbon of characteristic odour, occurring in coal tar. It is used as a solvent, in the synthesis of many chemicals, and in the manufacture of plastics. [from *benzoin*]

benzine /'benzi:n/ *n.* a spirit obtained from petroleum and used as a cleansing agent. [from *benzoin*]

Berg *Austrian composer Alban Berg was taught by Schoenberg, and did much to popularize his master's 12-tone system by combining it with a lyrical style.*

benzoic acid C_6H_5COOH, a white crystalline solid, sparingly soluble in water, that is used as a preservative for certain foods and as an antiseptic. It is obtained chemically by the direct oxidation of benzaldehyde and occurs in certain natural resins, some essential oils, and as hippuric acid.

benzoin /'benzəʊɪn/ *n.* the aromatic resin of an East Indian tree *Styrax benzoin*; a white crystalline constituent of this. Benzoin is used in the preparation of cosmetics, perfumes, and incense. —**benzoic** /-'zəʊɪk/ *adj.* [from French from Arabic *lubān jāwī* = incense of Java]

benzol /'benzɒl/ *n.* benzene, especially in its unrefined state.

Ben Zvi /ben 'zvi:/ Izhak 1884–1963. Israeli politician, president 1952–63. He was born in Atpoltava, Russia, and became active in the Zionist movement in the Ukraine. In 1907 he went to Palestine but was deported in 1915 with ◊Ben-Gurion. They served in the Jewish Legion under General Allenby, who commanded the British forces in the Middle East.

Beograd /'beɪəʊgræd/ the Serbo-Croatian form of ◊Belgrade, capital of Yugoslavia.

Beowulf /'beɪəʊwʊlf/ *n.* an Anglo-Saxon poem (composed about 700), the only complete surviving example of Germanic folk epic. It exists in a single manuscript copied about 1000 in the Cottonian collection of the British Museum.

bequeath /bɪ'kwi:ð/ *v.t.* to leave (personal estate) to a person by will; to transmit to posterity. [Old English]

bequest /bɪ'kwest/ *n.* bequeathing; a thing bequeathed.

berate /bɪ'reɪt/ *v.t.* to scold or rebuke severely.

Berber /'bɜːbə/ *n.* a member of a non-Semitic Caucasoid people of N Africa, who since prehistoric times inhabited Barbary, the Mediterranean coastlands from Egypt to the Atlantic. Their language, modern Berber (a member of the Afro-Asiatic language family), is spoken by about one-third of Algerians and nearly two-thirds of Moroccans, ten million people. Berbers are mainly agricultural, but some are still nomadic.

berberis /'bɜːbərɪs/ *n.* a cultivated prickly yellow-flowered shrub of the genus *Berberis*. [from Latin and Old French]

berceuse /beə'sɜːz/ *n.* an instrumental piece of music in the style of a lullaby. [French (*bercer* = rock to sleep)]

Berchtold /'beəxtəʊlt/ Count Leopold von 1863–1942. Prime minister and foreign minister of Austria-Hungary 1912–15 and a crucial figure in the events that led to World War I, because his indecisive stance caused tension with Serbia.

bereave /bɪ'ri:v/ *v.t.* (chiefly in *passive*; *past participle* **bereaved**) to deprive of a near relative, spouse etc., by death. [from Old English *reave* = take away forcibly]

bereft /bɪ'reft/ *adj.* deprived (*of*).

Berengaria of Navarre 1165–1230. The only English queen never to set foot in England. Daughter of King Sancho VI of Navarre, she married Richard I of England in Cyprus in 1191, and accompanied him on his crusade to the Holy Land.

Berenson /'berənsən/ Bernard 1865–1959. US art expert, born in Lithuania, once revered as a leading scholar of the Italian Renaissance. He amassed a great fortune, and many of his attributions of previously anonymous Italian paintings were later disproved.

beret /'bereɪ/ n. a round flat cap of felt or cloth. [French]

berg n. an iceberg. [abbreviation]

Berg /beəg/ Alban 1885–1935. Austrian composer. He studied under ◊Schoenberg and was associated with him as one of the leaders of the serial, or 12-tone, school of composition. His output includes orchestral, chamber, and vocal music as well as two operas, *Wozzeck* 1925, a grim story of working-class life, and the unfinished *Lulu* 1929–35.

Berg Paul 1926– . US molecular biologist. In 1972, using gene-splicing techniques developed by others, Berg spliced and combined into a single hybrid ◊DNA from an animal tumour virus (SV40) and DNA from a bacterial virus. Berg's work aroused fears in other workers and excited continuing controversy. For his work on recombinant DNA, Berg shared the 1980 Nobel Prize for Chemistry with Walter ◊Gilbert and Frederick ◊Sanger.

bergamot /'bɜːgəmɒt/ n. 1. a perfume from the rind of a citrus fruit; the tree *Citrus bergamia* bearing this fruit. 2. an aromatic herb, especially *Monardia didyma*. [from *Bergamo* in Italy]

Bergen /'beəgən/ industrial port (shipbuilding, engineering, fishing) in SW Norway; population (1988) 210,000. Founded in 1070, Bergen was a member of the Hanseatic League.

Bergius /'beəgiəs/ Friedrich Karl Rudolph 1884–1949. German research chemist who invented processes for converting coal into oil and wood into sugar. He received the Nobel Prize for Chemistry in 1931.

Bergman /'beəgmən/ Ingmar 1918– . Swedish film producer and director. His work deals with complex moral, psychological, and metaphysical problems and is often heavily tinged with pessimism. His films include *Wild Strawberries* 1957, *Persona* 1966, and *Fanny and Alexander* 1982.

Bergman Ingrid 1917–1982. Swedish actress, whose early films include *Intermezzo* 1939, *Casablanca*, *For Whom the Bell Tolls* both 1943, and *Gaslight* 1944, for which she won an Academy Award. By leaving her husband to have a child with director Roberto Rossellini, she broke an unofficial moral code of Hollywood-star behaviour and was ostracized for many years. During that period, she made films in Europe such as *Stromboli* 1949 (directed by Rossellini). Later films include *Anastasia* 1956, for which she won an Academy Award.

Bergson /'beək'sɒn/ Henri 1859–1941. French philosopher who believed that time, change, and development were the essence of reality. He thought that time was not a succession of distinct and separate instants but a continuous process in which one period merged imperceptibly into the next. He was awarded the Nobel Prize for Literature in 1928.

Beria /'beəriə/ Lavrenti 1899–1953. Soviet politician who became head of the Soviet police force and minister of the interior in 1938. On Stalin's death in 1953, he attempted to seize power but was foiled and shot after a secret trial.

beriberi /beri'beri/ n. a tropical disease of the nervous system, caused by deficiency of vitamin B. [Sinhalese, from *beri* = weakness]

Bering /'beərɪŋ/ Vitus 1681–1741. Danish explorer, the first European to sight Alaska. He died on Bering Island in the Bering Sea, both named after him, as is the Bering Strait.

Bering Sea section of the N Pacific between Alaska and Siberia, from the Aleutian Islands N to Bering Strait.

Bering Strait strait between Alaska and Siberia, separating Asia from North America and linking the N Pacific and Arctic oceans.

Berio /'beəriəʊ/ Luciano 1925– . Italian composer. His style has been described as graceful ◊serialism, and he has frequently experimented with electronic music and taped sound. His works include nine *Sequenzas/Sequences* 1957–75 for various solo instruments or voice, *Sinfonia* 1969 for voices and orchestra, *Points on the curve to find* ... 1974, and a number of dramatic works, including the opera *Un re in ascolto/A King Listens* 1984, loosely based on Shakespeare's *The Tempest*.

Beriosova /beri'ɒsəvə/ Svetlana 1932– . British ballerina. Born in Lithuania and brought up partly in the USA, she danced with the Royal Ballet from 1952. Her style had a lyrical dignity and she excelled in *The Lady and the Fool*, *Ondine*, and *Giselle*.

Berkeley /'bɜːkli/ Busby. Stage name of William Berkeley Enos 1895–1976. US choreographer and film director who made use of ingenious and extravagant sets, choreography, and costumes. After he choreographed more than 20 Broadway musicals, producer Samuel Goldwyn engaged him for the musical film *Whoopee* 1930. His musical extravaganzas include the films *Gold Diggers of 1933* and *Footlight Parade* 1933.

Berkeley town on San Francisco Bay in California, USA; population (1980) 103,500. It is the headquarters of the University of California, renowned for its nuclear research.

Berkeley Lennox (Randal Francis) 1903–1989. English composer. His works for the voice include *The Hill of the Graces* 1975, verses from Spenser's *Fairie Queene*; and his operas *Nelson* 1953 and *Ruth* 1956.

berkelium n. a synthesized, radioactive, metallic element of the ◊actinide series, symbol Bk, atomic number 97, relative atomic mass 247. It was first produced in 1949 by Glenn Seaborg and his team by bombarding americium with helium ions. [from *Berkeley* in California, where first made]

Berks. abbreviation of Berkshire.

Berkshire /'bɑːkʃə/ or **Royal Berkshire** county in south central England; **area** 1,260 sq km/486 sq mi; **physical** rivers Thames and Kennet; Inkpen Beacon, 297 m/975 ft; Bagshot Heath; Ridgeway Path, walkers' path (partly prehistoric) running from Wiltshire across the Berkshire Downs into Hertfordshire; Windsor Forest; **products** general agricultural and horticultural goods, electronics, plastics, pharmaceuticals; **population** (1987) 741,000.

Berlin /bɜː'lɪn/ industrial city (machine tools, electrical goods, paper, printing) and capital of Germany; population (1990) 3,102,500. The Berlin Wall divided the city from 1961 to 1989, but in Oct 1990 Berlin became the capital of a unified Germany once more with East and West Berlin reunited as the 16th *Land* (state) of the Federal Republic.

Berlin Irving. Adopted name of Israel Baline 1888–1989. Russian-born US composer, whose hits include 'Alexander's Ragtime Band', 'Always', 'God Bless America', and 'White Christmas', and the musicals *Top Hat* 1935, *Annie Get Your Gun* 1950, and *Call Me Madam* 1953. He also wrote film scores such as *Blue Skies* and *Easter Parade*.

Berlin blockade the closing of entry to Berlin from the west by Soviet forces between June 1948 and May 1949. It was an attempt to prevent the other Allies (USA, France, and Britain) unifying the western part of Germany. The British and US forces responded by sending supplies to the city by air for over a year (the **Berlin airlift**). In May 1949 the blockade was lifted; the airlift continued until Sept. The blockade ultimately resulted in the division of Berlin, and consequently Germany, into Eastern and Western sectors.

Berlin, Conference of a conference 1884–85 of European powers (France, Germany, the UK, Belgium, and Portugal) called by Chancellor Otto von Bismarck to decide on the colonial partition of Africa.

Berlin, Congress of a congress of European powers (Russia, Turkey, Austria-Hungary, Britain, France, Italy, and Germany) held in Berlin in 1878 to determine the boundaries of the Balkan states after the Russo-Turkish war.

Berlinguer /beəlɪŋ'gweə/ Enrico 1922–1984. Italian Communist who freed the party from Soviet influence. By 1976 he was near to the premiership, but the murder of Aldo Moro, a former prime minister, by Red Brigade guerrillas prompted a move of support to the socialists.

Berlin Wall the dividing barrier between East and West Berlin 1961–89, erected by East Germany to keep its citizens in. Escapers from East to West were shot on sight. On 9 Nov 1989 the East German government opened its borders to try to halt the mass exodus of its citizens to the West via other Eastern bloc countries, and the wall was gradually dismantled.

Berlioz /'beəliəuz/ (Louis) Hector 1803–1869. French romantic composer and the founder of modern orchestration. Much of his music was inspired by drama and literature and has a theatrical quality. He wrote symphonic works, such as *Symphonie fantastique* and *Roméo et*

Juliette; dramatic cantatas including *La Damnation de Faust* and *L'Enfance du Christ*; sacred music; and three operas, *Béatrice et Bénédict, Benvenuto Cellini*, and *Les Troyens*.

Bermuda /bə'mju:də/ British colony in the NW Atlantic; **area** 54 sq km/21 sq mi; **capital** and chief port Hamilton; **physical** consists of about 150 small islands, 20 inhabited, linked by bridges and causeways; **products** Easter lilies, pharmaceuticals; tourism and banking are important; **head of government** John Swan from 1982; **population** (1988) 58,100; **language** English; **recent history** the islands were settled by British colonists in 1609. Racial violence in 1977 led to intervention, at the request of the government, by British troops.

Bern /beən/ (French *Berne*) capital of Switzerland and of Bern canton in W Switzerland on the Aare River; population (1987) 300,000. It joined the Swiss confederation in 1353 and became the capital in 1848. Industries include textiles, chocolate, pharmaceuticals, light metal, and electrical goods.

Bernadette, St /bɜ:nə'det/ 1844–1879. French saint, born in Lourdes in the French Pyrenees. In Feb 1858 she had a vision of the Virgin Mary in a grotto, which subsequently became a centre of pilgrimage. Many sick people who were dipped in the water of a spring there were said to have been cured. Feast day 16 April.

Bernadotte /bɜ:nə'dɒt/ Jean-Baptiste Jules 1764–1844. Marshal in Napoleon's army who in 1818 became ◊Charles XIV of Sweden. Hence, Bernadotte is the family name of the present royal house of Sweden.

Bernard /beə'nɑ:/ Claude 1813–1878. French physiologist and founder of experimental medicine. Bernard first demonstrated that digestion is not restricted to the stomach, but takes place throughout the small intestine. He discovered the digestive input of the pancreas, several functions of the liver, and the vasomotor nerves which dilate and contract the blood vessels and thus regulate body temperature. This led him to the concept of the *milieu intérieur* ('internal environment') whose stability is essential to good health.

Bernard of Clairvaux, St /kleə'vəʊ/ 1090–1153. Christian founder in 1115 of Clairvaux monastery in Champagne, France. He reinvigorated the ◊Cistercian order, preached in support of the Second Crusade in 1146, and had the scholastic philosopher Abelard condemned for heresy. He is often depicted with a beehive. Feast day 20 Aug.

I have freed my soul.

St Bernard of Clairvaux
Epistle 371

Bernard of Menthon, St /mɒn'tɒn/ or **Bernard of Montjoux** 923–1008. Christian priest, founder of the hospices for travellers on the Alpine passes that bear his name. The large, heavily built **St Bernard** dogs, formerly employed to find travellers lost in the snow, were also named after him. He is the patron saint of mountaineers. Feast day 28 May.

Bernese Oberland /'bɜ:ni:z 'əʊbəlænd/ or **Bernese Alps** mountainous area in the S of Berne canton, Switzerland. It includes the Jungfrau, Eiger, and Finsteraarhorn peaks. Interlaken is the chief town.

Bernhard /'beənɑ:t/ Prince of the Netherlands 1911– . Formerly Prince Bernhard of Lippe-Biesterfeld, he married Princess ◊Juliana in 1937. When Germany invaded the Netherlands in 1940, he escaped to England and became liaison officer for the Dutch and British forces, playing a part in the organization of the Dutch Resistance.

Bernhardt /'bɜ:nhɑ:t/ Sarah. Stage name of Rosine Bernard 1845–1923. French actress who dominated the stage of her day, frequently performing at the Comédie-Française in Paris. She excelled in tragic roles, including Cordelia in Shakespeare's *King Lear*, the title role in Racine's *Phèdre*, and the male roles of Hamlet and of Napoleon's son in Edmond ◊Rostand's *L'Aiglon*.

Bernini /beə'ni:ni/ Giovanni Lorenzo 1598–1680. Italian sculptor, architect, and painter, a leading figure in the development of the ◊Baroque style. His work in Rome includes the colonnaded piazza in front of St Peter's Basilica 1656, fountains (as in the Piazza Navona), and

papal monuments. His sculpture includes *The Ecstasy of St Theresa* 1645–52 (Sta Maria della Vittoria, Rome) and numerous portrait busts.

Bernoulli /bɜ:'nu:li/ Swiss family that produced many capable mathematicians and scientists in the 17th, 18th, and 19th centuries, in particular the brothers **Jakob** (1654–1705) and **Johann** (1667–1748), also **Daniel** (1700–1782), son of Johann.

Bernoulli's principle the statement that the speed of a fluid varies inversely with the pressure, an increase in speed producing a decrease in pressure (such as a drop in hydraulic pressure as the fluid speeds up flowing through a constriction in a pipe) and vice versa. The principle also explains the pressure differences on each surface of an aerofoil, which gives lift to the wing of an aircraft. [from Daniel *Bernoulli*]

Bernstein /'bɜ:nstaɪn/ Leonard 1918–1990. US composer, conductor, and pianist. His works, which established a vogue for realistic, contemporary themes, include symphonies such as *The Age of Anxiety* 1949; ballets such as *Fancy Free* 1944; scores for musicals including *Wonderful Town* 1953 and *West Side Story* 1957; and *Mass* 1971 in memory of President J F Kennedy.

Berri /'beri/ Nabih 1939– . Lebanese politician and soldier, leader of Amal ('Hope'), the Syrian-backed Shi'ite nationalist movement. He was minister of justice in the government of President ◊Gemayel from 1984. In 1988 Amal was disbanded after defeat by the Iranian-backed Hezbollah ('Children of God') during the Lebanese civil wars, and Berri joined the cabinet of Selim Hoss in 1989.

berry *n.* any small, roundish, juicy fruit without a stone; in botany, a fleshy, many-seeded ◊fruit that does not split open to release the seeds. The outer layer of tissue, the exocarp, forms an outer skin that is often brightly coloured to attract birds to eat the fruit and thus disperse the seeds (e.g. banana, tomato). [Old English]

Berry /'beri/ Chuck (Charles Edward) 1926– . US rock-and-roll singer, prolific songwriter, and guitarist. His characteristic guitar riffs became staples of rock music, and his humorous storytelling lyrics were also emulated. He had a string of hits in the 1950s and 1960s beginning with 'Maybellene' 1955 and enjoyed a revival in the 1980s.

Berryman /'berimən/ John 1914–1972. US poet whose complex and personal works include *Homage to Mistress Bradstreet* 1956, *77 Dream Songs* 1964 (Pulitzer Prize), and *His Toy, His Dream, His Rest* 1968.

berserk /bə'sɜ:k/ *adj.* uncontrollably violent. —**go berserk,** to fly into a violent rage, to lose control. —**berserker** *n.* in Scandinavian legend, a warrior who went into a frenzy in battle. [originally = Norse warrior, from Icelandic = bear coat]

berth *n.* **1.** a fixed bunk on a ship, train etc., for sleeping in. **2.** a ship's place at a wharf; room for a ship to swing at anchor. —*v.t./i.* **1.** to moor (a ship) in a berth; to come to a mooring. **2.** to provide with a sleeping berth. —**give a wide berth to,** to keep at a safe distance from. [from Old English *bear*]

Berthelot /beətə'ləʊ/ Pierre Eugène Marcellin 1827–1907. French chemist and politician who carried out research into dyes and explosives, and proved that hydrocarbons and other organic compounds can be synthesized from inorganic materials.

Bertholet /beətə'leɪ/ Claude Louis 1748–1822. French chemist who carried out research on dyes and bleaches (introducing the use of ◊chlorine as a bleach) and determined the composition of ◊ammonia. Modern chemical nomenclature is based on a system worked out by Bertholet and Antoine ◊Lavoisier.

Bertolucci /beətəu'lu:tʃi/ Bernardo 1940– . Italian film director whose work combines political and historical perspectives with an elegant and lyrical visual appeal. His films include *The Spider's Stratagem* 1970, *Last Tango in Paris* 1972, *The Last Emperor* 1987 (Academy Award), and *The Sheltering Sky* 1990.

Bertrand de Born /beə'trɒn də 'bɔ:n/ *c.*1140–*c.*1215. Provençal ◊troubadour. He was viscount of Hautefort in Périgord, accompanied Richard the Lionheart to Palestine, and died a monk.

Berwickshire /'berɪkʃə/ former county of SE Scotland, a district of Borders region from 1975.

beryl /'berɪl/ n. a mineral, beryllium aluminium silicate, $Be_3Al_2Si_6O_{18}$, which forms crystals chiefly in granite. It is the chief ore of beryllium. Two of its gem forms are aquamarine (light-blue crystals) and emerald (dark-green crystals). [from Old French from Latin from Greek *bērullos*]

beryllium /bə'rɪliəm/ n. a hard, light-weight, silver-white, metallic element, symbol Be, atomic number 4, relative atomic mass 9.012. It is one of the ◊alkaline-earth metals, with chemical properties similar to those of magnesium; in nature it is found only in combination with other elements. It is used to make sturdy, light alloys and to control the speed of neutrons in nuclear reactors. It was discovered in 1798 by French chemist Louis-Nicolas Vauquelin (1763–1829).

Berzelius /bə'ziːliəs/ Jöns Jakob 1779–1848. Swedish chemist who accurately determined more than 2,000 relative atomic and molecular masses. He devised (1813–14) the system of chemical symbols and formulae now in use and proposed oxygen as a reference standard for atomic masses. His discoveries include the elements selenium (1817), cerium, and thorium (1828); he was the first to prepare silicon in its amorphous form and to isolate zirconium.

beseech /bɪ'siːtʃ/ v.t. (past and past participle besought /-'sɔːt/) to implore, to ask earnestly for.

beset /bɪ'set/ v.t. (-tt-; past and past participle beset) to surround, to hem in; (of troubles etc.) to assail persistently.

beside /bɪ'saɪd/ prep. 1. by the side of; near. 2. compared with. —**beside oneself**, frantic with worry, anger etc. **beside the point**, irrelevant.

besides /bɪ'saɪdz/ adv. & prep. in addition (to).

besiege /bɪ'siːdʒ/ v.t. 1. to lay siege to. 2. to crowd round oppressively, to harass with requests etc.

besom /'biːzəm/ n. a broom made of twigs tied round a stick. [Old English]

besot /bɪ'sɒt/ v.t. (-tt-; especially in *passive*) to infatuate.

bespeak /bɪ'spiːk/ v.t. (past **bespoke**; past participle **bespoken**, as *adjective* **bespoke**) 1. to engage beforehand; to commission (a product). 2. to be an indication of.

bespectacled /bɪ'spektəkəld/ adj. wearing spectacles.

bespoke /bɪ'spəʊk/ adj. (of clothes etc.) made to order; (of a tailor etc.) dealing in such goods.

Bessarabia /besə'reɪbɪə/ territory in SE Europe, annexed by Russia in 1812, which broke away at the Russian Revolution to join Romania. The cession was confirmed by the Allies, but not by Russia, in a Paris treaty of 1920; Russia reoccupied it in 1940 and divided it between the Moldovan and Ukrainian republics. Romania recognized the position in the 1947 peace treaty.

Bessel /'besl/ Friedrich Wilhelm 1784–1846. German astronomer and mathematician, the first person to find the approximate distance to a star by direct methods when he measured the ◊parallax (annual displacement) of the star 61 Cygni in 1838. In mathematics, he introduced the series of functions now known as **Bessel functions**.

Bessemer /'besɪmə/ Henry 1813–1898. English civil engineer who invented a method of converting molten pig iron into steel.

Bessemer process the first cheap method of making ◊steel, invented in England in 1856. It has since been superseded by more efficient steelmaking processes, such as the ◊basic-oxygen process. In the Bessemer process compressed air is blown into the bottom of a converter, a furnace shaped like a cement mixer, containing molten pig iron. The excess carbon in the iron burns out, other impurities form a slag, and the furnace is emptied by tilting. [from Henry *Bessemer*, inventor of the process]

best adj. (*superlative* of **good**) of the most excellent or desirable kind. —adv. (*superlative* of **well**) in the best manner; to the greatest degree; most usefully. —n. that which is best; the chief merit; (colloquial) one's best clothes. —v.t. (colloquial) to defeat or outwit. —**at best**, on the most hopeful or favourable view. **best end**, the rib end of neck of lamb, meatier than the scrag end. **best man**, a bridegroom's chief attendant. **best part**, most of. **best seller**, a book that sells in very large numbers. **do one's best**, do all one can. **get** or **have the best of**, to win (a fight etc.). **make the best of**, to be as contented as possible with; to do what one can with (something of limited potential). [Old English *betest*]

Best /best/ Charles Herbert 1899–1978. Canadian physiologist, one of the team of Canadian scientists including Frederick ◊Banting whose research resulted in the discovery of insulin as a treatment for diabetes in 1922.

bestial /'bestɪəl/ adj. of a beast; beastlike in cruelty, blind lust etc. —**bestiality** /-'ælɪtɪ/ n. [from Old French from Latin *bestia* = beast]

bestiary /'bestɪərɪ/ n. in medieval Europe, a book with stories and illustrations which depicted real and mythical animals or plants to illustrate a (usually Christian) moral. The stories were initially derived from the Greek *Physiologus*, a collection of 48 such stories, written in Alexandria around the 2nd century AD. [from Latin]

bestir /bɪ'stɜː/ v.t. (-rr-) to rouse or exert (*oneself*).

bestow /bɪ'stəʊ/ v.t. to confer. —**bestowal** n.

bestrew /bɪ'struː/ v.t. (past participle **bestrewed**, **bestrewn**) to strew; to lie scattered over.

bestride /bɪ'straɪd/ v.t. (past **bestrode**; past participle **bestridden**) 1. to sit astride on. 2. to stand astride over.

bet v.i./t. (-tt-; past and past participle **bet**, **betted**) 1. to risk one's money against another's on the outcome of an event; to risk (an amount) thus. 1. (colloquial) to think most likely. —n. 1. an act of betting. 2. a sum staked. —**you bet**, (slang) you may be sure.

beta /'biːtə/ n. 1. the second letter of the Greek alphabet (β, B) = b. 2. a second-class mark in an examination. 3. a designation of the second brightest star in a constellation, or sometimes a star's position in a group. [from Greek]

beta-blocker n. any of a class of drugs that block impulses that stimulate certain nerve endings (**beta receptors**) serving the heart muscles. This reduces the heart rate and the force of contraction, which in turn reduces the amount of oxygen (and therefore the blood supply) required by the heart. Beta-blockers are banned from use in competitive sports. They may be useful in the treatment of angina, arrhythmia, and raised blood pressure, and following myocardial infarctions. They must be withdrawn from use gradually.

beta decay the disintegration of the nucleus of an atom to produce a ◊beta particle, or high-speed electron, and an antineutrino. During beta decay, a proton in the nucleus changes into a neutron, thereby increasing the atomic number by one while the mass number stays the same. The mass lost in the change is converted into kinetic (movement) energy of the beta particle. Beta decay is caused by the weak nuclear force, one of the fundamental ◊forces of nature operating inside the nucleus.

betake /bɪ'teɪk/ v.refl. (past **betook**; past participle **betaken**) to go *to*.

beta particle an electron ejected with great velocity from a radioactive atom that is undergoing spontaneous disintegration. Beta particles do not exist in the nucleus but are created on disintegration when a neutron converts to a proton to emit an electron.

betatron /'biːtətrɒn/ n. an apparatus for accelerating electrons in a circular path. [from *beta* and (*elec*)*tron*]

betel /'biːt(ə)l/ n. the leaf of the plant *Piper betle*, chewed with ◊betel nut. [from Portuguese from Malayalam]

Betelgeuse /'biːtldʒɜːz/ n. or **Alpha Orionis** a red supergiant star in the constellation of Orion and the tenth brightest star in the sky, although its brightness varies. It is over 300 times the diameter of the Sun, about the same size as the orbit of Mars, and lies 650 light years from Earth.

betel nut the fruit of the areca palm *Areca catechu*, used together with lime and betel pepper as a masticatory stimulant in parts of Asia. Chewing it results in blackened teeth and a mouth stained deep red.

bête noire /beɪt 'nwɑː/ (*plural* **bêtes noires** pronounced the same) a person's chief dislike. [French, literally = black beast]

bethink /bɪ'θɪŋk/ v.refl. (past and past participle **bethought**) to stop to think, to recollect.

Bethlehem /'beθlɪhem/ (Hebrew **Beit-Lahm**) town on the W bank of the river Jordan, S of Jerusalem. Occupied by Israel in 1967; population (1980) 14,000. In the Bible it is mentioned as the birthplace of King David and Jesus.

Bethmann Hollweg /'beɪtmæn 'hɒlveg/ Theobald von 1856–1921. German politician, imperial chancellor 1909–17, largely responsible for engineering popular support for World War I in Germany, but his power was overthrown by a military dictatorship under ◊Ludendorff and ◊Hindenburg.

betide /bɪˈtaɪd/ v.t./i. to happen (to), now chiefly in **woe betide** (a person), originally a curse, now a warning. [from obsolete *tide* = befall]

betimes /bɪˈtaɪmz/ adv. (*literary*) in good time, early.

Betjeman /ˈbetʃəmən/ John 1906-1984. English poet and essayist, originator of a peculiarly English light verse, nostalgic and delighting in Victorian and Edwardian architecture. His *Collected poems by* appeared in 1968 and a verse autobiography *Summoned by Bells* in 1960. He became poet laureate in 1972.

> One cannot assess in terms of cash or exports and imports an imponderable thing like the turn of a lane or an inn or a church tower or a familiar skyline.
> **John Betjeman**
> *The Observer* 1969

betoken /bɪˈtəʊkən/ v.t. to be a sign of, to indicate.

betony /ˈbetənɪ/ n. a purple-flowered plant *Betonica officinalis*, formerly used in medicine. A hedgerow weed in Britain, it has a hairy stem and leaves. [from Old French from Latin, perhaps from name of Iberian tribe]

betray /bɪˈtreɪ/ v.t. 1. to be disloyal to; to give up or reveal disloyally (to an enemy). 2. to reveal involuntarily; to be evidence of. 3. to lead astray. —**betrayal** n., **betrayer** n. [from obsolete *tray* from French from Latin *tradere* = hand over]

betroth /bɪˈtrəʊð/ v.t. to engage to marry a specified person. —**betrothal** n., **betrothed** adj. & n. [from *truth*]

Bettelheim /ˈbetlhaɪm/ Bruno 1903–1990. Austrian-born US child psychologist. He was imprisoned at Dachau and Buchenwald concentration camps for two years 1933–35, but emigrated to the USA in 1939. There he founded a treatment centre for autistic children. His books include *Love is Not Enough* 1950, *The Uses of Enchantment* 1976, and *A Good Enough Parent* 1987.

better adj. (*comparative* of **good**) 1. of a more excellent or desirable kind. 2. partly or fully recovered from illness. 3. greater (*part* etc.). —adv. (*comparative* of **well**[1]) in a better manner; to a greater degree; more usefully. —n. that which is better; (in *plural*) one's superiors. —v.t. to improve; to surpass (a feat). —v.refl. to improve one's position in life. —**better half**, (*colloquial*) one's spouse. **get the better of**, to defeat or outwit. **had better**, would find it more advantageous to. [Old English]

betterment n. improvement.

betting shop a bookmaker's shop or office.

between /bɪˈtwiːn/ adv. & prep. 1. in the space, time, condition etc., bounded by (two limits). 2. to and from; reciprocally felt or done by. 3. by the sharing or joint action of. 4. taking one and rejecting the other of. —**between ourselves, between you and me,** speaking in confidence. **in between,** in an intermediate position. [Old English]

betwixt /bɪˈtwɪkst/ prep. & adv. between, now only in **betwixt and between,** (*colloquial*) neither one thing nor the other. [from Old English]

Beuys /bɔɪs/ Joseph 1921–1986. German sculptor and performance artist, one of the leaders of avant-garde art in Europe during the 1970s and 1980s. His sculpture makes use of unusual materials such as felt and fat. He was strongly influenced by his wartime experiences.

Bevan /ˈbevən/ Aneurin 1897–1960. Welsh Labour politician. Son of a Welsh miner, and himself a miner at 13, he became member of Parliament for Ebbw Vale 1929–60. As minister of health 1945–51, he inaugurated the National Health Service (NHS); he was minister of labour Jan–April 1951, when he resigned (with Harold Wilson) on the introduction of NHS charges and led a Bevanite faction against the government.

bevel /ˈbevəl/ n. 1. a joiner's or mason's tool for adjusting angles. 2. a slope from the vertical or horizontal; a sloping edge or surface. —v.t./i. (-ll-) to reduce (a square edge) to a sloping one; to slope at an angle. [from Old French *baer* = gape]

beverage /ˈbevərɪdʒ/ n. any drink. [from Old French from Latin *bibere* = drink]

Beveridge /ˈbevərɪdʒ/ William Henry, 1st Baron Beveridge 1879–1963. British economist. A civil servant, he acted as Lloyd George's lieutenant in the social legislation of the

Betjeman The poet John Betjeman was regarded with much affection for his ability to capture the popular mood and for his care for England's architectural heritage.

Liberal government before World War I. The Beveridge Report 1942 formed the basis of the welfare state in Britain.

Beveridge Report, the in British history, the 1942 findings and recommendations of an official committee which formed the basis for the social-reform legislation of the Labour government of 1945–50. It proposed a scheme of social insurance from 'the cradle to the grave', and recommended a national health service, social insurance and assistance, family allowances and full-employment policies. [from William *Beveridge*, who chaired the committee]

Bevin /ˈbevɪn/ Ernest 1881–1951. English Labour politician. Chief creator of the Transport and General Workers' Union, he was its general secretary from 1921 to 1940, when he entered the war cabinet as minister of labour and National Service. He organized the 'Bevin boys', chosen by ballot to work in the coal mines as war service, and was foreign secretary in the Labour government 1945–51.

bevy /ˈbevɪ/ n. a large group (*of*).

bewail /bɪˈweɪl/ v.t. to wail over, to mourn for.

beware /bɪˈweə/ v.i. (only *imperative* and *infinitive*) to be on one's guard. —**beware of,** to be cautious of, to guard against. [from obsolete *ware* = cautious]

Bewick /ˈbjuːɪk/ Thomas 1753–1828. English wood engraver, excelling in animal subjects. His illustrated *A General History of Quadrupeds* 1790 and *A History of British Birds* 1797–1804 display his skill.

bewilder /bɪˈwɪldə/ v.t. to perplex or confuse. —**bewilderment** n. [from obsolete *wilder* = to lose one's way]

bewitch /bɪˈwɪtʃ/ v.t. 1. to captivate, to delight greatly. 2. to cast a spell on.

beyond /bɪˈjɒnd/ adv. & prep. 1. at or to the far side (of). 2. outside the scope or understanding of. 3. in addition (to). —n. the unknown after death. [Old English *be* = by, related to *yon*]

bezel /ˈbezəl/ n. 1. the sloping edge of a chisel; an oblique face of a cut gem. 2. a rim holding a glass cover etc. or a gem in position. [from Old French]

Bezier curve a curved line that connects a series of points (or 'nodes') in the smoothest possible way. The shape of the curve is governed by a series of complex mathematical formulae. They are used in ◊computer graphics and design (◊CAD).

bezique /bɪˈziːk/ n. a card game for two players, using a double pack of 64 cards (ace to seven only); a combination of the queen of spades and jack of diamonds in this game. [French]

BFI abbreviation of ◊British Film Institute.

BFPO abbreviation of British Forces Post Office.

Bhagavad-Gītā /ˈbʌgəvəd ˈgiːtə/ n. a religious and philosophical Sanskrit poem, dating from around 300 BC, forming an episode in the sixth book of the *Mahābhārata*, one of the two great Hindu epics. It is the supreme religious work of Hinduism. [Hindu = the song of the blessed]

bhakti /'bɑːktɪ/ *n.* in Hinduism, a tradition of worship that emphasizes love and devotion rather than ritual, sacrifice, or study. It is directed to one supreme deity, usually Vishnu (especially in his incarnations as Rama and Krishna) or Siva, by whose grace salvation may be attained by all regardless of sex, caste, or class. [Sanskrit = devotion]

bhang /bæŋ/ *n.* Indian ◊hemp; its dried leaves smoked or chewed for their mood-changing properties. [from Portuguese from Sanskrit]

bhangra *n.* a type of pop music evolved in the UK in the late 1970s from traditional Punjabi music, combining electronic instruments and ethnic drums.

bhikku *n.* a Buddhist monk who is totally dependent on alms and the monastic community (*sangha*) for support.

Bhindranwale /'bɪndrəwʊlə/ Sant Jarnail Singh 1947–1984. Indian Sikh fundamentalist leader, who campaigned for the creation of a separate state of Khalistan during the early 1980s, precipitating a bloody Hindu-Sikh conflict in the Punjab. Having taken refuge in the Golden Temple complex in Amritsar and built up an arms cache for guerrilla activities, Bhindranwale, along with around 500 followers, died at the hands of Indian security forces who stormed the temple in June 1984.

Bhopal /bəʊ'pɑːl/ industrial city; capital of Madhya Pradesh, central India; formerly capital of the princely state of Bhopal; population (1981) 672,000; products: textiles, chemicals, electrical goods, jewellery. The nearby Bhimbetka Caves have the world's largest collection of prehistoric paintings, which are about 10,000 years old. In 1984 2,600 people died from an escape of poisonous gas from a factory owned by the US company Union Carbide; long-term health problems may be suffered by up to 300,000 people.

Bhumibol Adulyadej 1927– . King of Thailand from 1946. Born in the USA and educated in Bangkok and Switzerland, he succeeded to the throne on the assassination of his brother. In 1973 he was active, with popular support, in overthrowing the military government of Marshal Thanom Kittikachorn and thus ended a sequence of army-dominated regimes in power from 1932.

Bhutan /buːˈtɑːn/ Kingdom of; mountainous, landlocked country in SE Asia, bordered to the N by China and to the S by India; **area** 46,500 sq km/17,954 sq mi; **capital** Thimbu (Thimphu); **physical** occupies S slopes of the Himalayas; cut by valleys formed by tributaries of the Brahmaputra; thick forests in S; **head of state and government** Jigme Singye Wangchuk from 1972; **political system** absolute monarchy; **exports** timber, talc, fruit, cement; **population** (1990 est) 1,566,000; **language** official Dzongkha (a Tibetan dialect), Nepali, and English; **recent history** first hereditary monarchy installed in 1907. National assembly installed in 1953; the first cabinet was established in 1968. Pro-democracy demonstrations took place in 1990.

Bhutto /'buːtəʊ/ Benazir 1953– . Pakistani politician, leader of the Pakistan People's Party from 1984 (in exile until 1986), and prime minister of Pakistan 1988–90. She was the first female leader of a Muslim state.

Bhutto Zulfikar Ali 1928–1979. Pakistani politician, president 1971–73; prime minister from 1973 until the 1977 military coup led by General ◊Zia ul Haq. In 1978 he was sentenced to death for conspiring to murder a political opponent and was hanged the following year.

Bi symbol for ◊bismuth.

bi- /baɪ-/ prefix meaning two, twice (e.g. *bilateral, biweekly*). [Latin]

Biafra /biˈæfrə/ Republic of; African state 1967–70. Fears that Nigerian central government was increasingly in the hands of the rival Hausa ethnic group led the predominantly Ibo Eastern Region of Nigeria to secede in 1967 under Lt Col Odumegwu Ojukwu. On the proclamation of Biafra, civil war with the rest of the federation ensued. In a bitterly fought campaign federal forces confined the Biafrans to a shrinking area of the interior by 1968, and by 1970 Biafra ceased to exist. An estimated 1–2 million people died in the conflict, half of them civilians.

biannual /baɪˈænjuəl/ *adj.* twice-yearly.

bias /'baɪəs/ *n.* **1.** a predisposition or prejudice. **2.** distortion of a statistical result by a neglected factor. **3.** in bowls, the oblique course of a bowl or the lopsided form causing it. **4.** an oblique direction in cutting cloth. —*v.t.* (*past tense* and *past participle* biased) to give a bias to, to influence unfairly. —**bias binding**, a strip of material cut diagonally, used to bind edges. [from Old French]

bib *n.* **1.** a cloth etc. tied over a child's chest at meals to protect its clothes. **2.** the part of an apron or overall covering the chest. [perhaps from archaic *bib* = drink (from Latin *bibere*)]

Bible /'baɪbl/ *n.* **1.** the sacred book of the Jewish and Christian religions. The Hebrew Bible, recognized by both Jews and Christians, is called the ◊Old Testament by Christians. The ◊New Testament comprises books recognized by the Christian church from the 4th century as canonical. The Roman Catholic Bible also includes the ◊Apocrypha. The first English translation of the entire Bible was by a priest, Miles Coverdale, in 1535; the Authorized Version or **King James Bible** of 1611 was long influential for the clarity and beauty of its language. A revision of the Authorized Version carried out in 1959 produced the widely used Revised Standard Version. A completely new translation into English from the original Hebrew and Greek texts was published as the New English Bible (New Testament 1961, Old Testament and Apocrypha 1970). Another English translation is the Jerusalem Bible, completed by Catholic scholars in 1966. **2.** a copy of these books; the scriptures of another religion; an authoritative book. [from Old French from Latin from Greek *biblia* = books, originally diminutive of *bublos* = papyrus]

biblical /'bɪblɪkəl/ *adj.* of or in the Bible.

bibliography /bɪbliˈɒgrəfɪ/ *n.* **1.** a list of books by a given author or on a given topic. **2.** the study of the history of books and their production. —**bibliographer** *n.,* **bibliographical** /-'græfɪkəl/ *adj.* [from Greek *biblia* and *graphia* = writing]

bibliophile /'bɪbliəfaɪl/ *n.* a lover of books. [from French (Greek *biblia* = books and *philos* = friend)]

bibulous /'bɪbjuləs/ *adj.* addicted to alcoholic drink. [from Latin *bibere* = drink]

bicameral /'baɪkæmərəl/ *adj.* having two legislative chambers. [from Latin *camera* = chamber]

bicarbonate /baɪˈkɑːbəneɪt/ *n.* common name for ◊hydrogen carbonate. —**bicarbonate of soda**, $NaHCO_3$ (technical name **sodium hydrogencarbonate**), a white crystalline solid that neutralizes acids and is used in medicine to treat acid indigestion. It is also used in baking powders and effervescent drinks.

bicentenary /baɪsenˈtiːnərɪ/ *n.* a 200th anniversary.

bicentennial /baɪsenˈteniəl/ *adj.* occurring every 200 years. —*n.* a bicentenary.

biceps /'baɪseps/ *n.* a muscle with two attachments, especially that which bends the elbow. [Latin = two-headed]

Bichat /biːˈʃɑː/ Marie François Xavier 1771–1802. French physician and founder of ◊histology, the study of tissues. He studied the organs of the body, their structure, and the ways in which they are affected by disease. This led to his discovery and naming of 'tissue', a basic biological and medical concept; he identified 21 types. He argued that disease does not affect the whole organ but only certain of its constituent tissues.

bicker *v.i.* to quarrel pettily.

biconcave /baɪˈkɒnkeɪv/ *adj.* (of a lens) concave on both sides.

biconvex /baɪˈkɒnveks/ *adj.* (of a lens) convex on both sides.

bicuspid /baɪˈkʌspɪd/ *adj.* having two cusps. —*n.* any of the eight bicuspid teeth (between the molars and canines). —**bicuspid valve**, in the left side of the ◊heart, a flap of tissue that prevents blood flowing back into the atrium when the ventricle contracts. [from Latin *cuspis* = sharp point]

bicycle /'baɪsɪkəl/ *n.* a road vehicle with two wheels one behind the other, driven by pedals worked by the rider. —*v.i.* to ride on a bicycle. —**bicycle clip**, each of a pair of clips for securing a cyclist's trouser leg at the ankle. —**bicyclist** *n.* [from French (Greek *kuklos* = wheel)]

bid *v.t./i.* (**-dd-**; *past* and *past participle* **bid**) **1.** to offer (a certain sum) as the price one is willing to pay, especially at an auction; to make a bid or bids; in card games, to state (the number of tricks) one undertakes to win in a given suit. **2.** (*past* **bade,** *past participle* **bidden** or **bid**) to instruct or invite to; to utter (a greeting, farewell). —*n.* **1.** an act of bidding; a sum etc. bid. **2.** an attempt. —**bid fair to,** to seem likely to. **make a bid for,** to attempt to secure. [Old English]

biddable /'bɪdəbəl/ *adj.* docile, obedient.

bidding *n.* **1.** a person's command or invitation. **2.** the bids made at an auction or in a card game.

biddy *n.* **old biddy,** (*slang*) an elderly woman. [pet form of woman's Christian name *Bridget*]

bide *v.t./i.* (*archaic* or *dialect*) to remain. —**bide one's time,** to await one's best opportunity. [Old English]

bidet /'bi:deɪ/ *n.* a low basin for sitting astride to wash the genital and anal regions. [French = pony]

Biedermeier /'bi:dəmaɪə/ *adj.* of or in a mid-19th-century Germanic style of art and furniture design. [derogatorily named after Gottlieb *Biedermeier*, a fictitious character embodying bourgeois taste]

biennial /baɪ'eniəl/ *adj.* **1.** lasting or living for two years. **2.** happening every second year. —*n.* a plant that completes its life cycle in two years. During the first year it grows vegetatively and the surplus food produced is stored in its ◊perennating organ, usually the root. In the following year these food reserves are used for the production of leaves, flowers, and seeds, after which the plant dies. Many root vegetables are biennials, including the carrot *Daucus carota* and parsnip *Pastinaca sativa*. Some garden plants that are grown as biennials are actually perennials, for example, the wallflower *Cheiranthus cheiri*. [from Latin *annus* = year]

bier /bɪə/ *n.* a movable stand on which a coffin or corpse rests. [Old English]

biff *n.* (*slang*) a smart blow. —*v.t.* to strike (a person). [imitative]

bifid /'baɪfɪd/ *adj.* divided by a deep cleft into two parts. [from Latin *findere* = split]

bifocal /baɪ'fəukəl/ *adj.* having two foci (of spectacle lenses having part for near and part for distant vision). —**bifocals** *n.pl.* spectacles with such lenses.

bifurcate /'baɪfɜ:keɪt/ *v.t./i.* to divide into two branches. —**bifurcation** /-'keɪʃən/ *n.* [from Latin *bifurcare* (*furca* = fork)]

big *adj.* (**-gg-**) **1.** large in size, amount, or intensity; outstandingly large of its kind; grown up, elder. **2.** important, outstanding. **3.** boastful; (*colloquial*) ambitious, generous. **4.** advanced in pregnancy (especially of animals). —*adv.* (*colloquial*) on a grand scale, ambitiously. —**Big Brother,** a seemingly benevolent but in fact ruthless dictator (character in George Orwell's novel *1984*). **big end,** the end of a connecting rod in an engine, encircling the crankshaft. **bighead** *n.* (*colloquial*) a conceited person. **big-hearted** *adj.* generous. **big time,** (*slang*) the highest rank among entertainers etc. **big top,** the main tent at a circus.

bigamy /'bɪgəmɪ/ *n.* in law, the offence of marrying a person while already lawfully married to another. In some countries marriage to more than one wife or husband is lawful; see also ◊polygamy. —**bigamist** *n.*, **bigamous** *adj.* [from Old French from Latin (Greek *gamos* = marriage)]

big-band jazz dance and ◊swing music created in the late 1930s and 1940s by orchestras such as those of Duke ◊Ellington and Benny ◊Goodman. Big bands (upwards of a dozen musicians) relied on arrangement rather than improvisation. Their music was extremely popular in the UK and USA.

Big Bang in astronomy, the hypothetical 'explosive' event that marked the origin of the universe as we know it. At the time of the Big Bang, the entire universe was squeezed into a hot, super-dense state, which was, according to some calculations, 300 million times smaller than the universe is today. The Big Bang explosion threw this compacted material outwards, producing the expanding universe (see ◊red shift). The cause of the Big Bang is unknown; observations of the current rate of expansion of the universe suggest that it took place almost 20 billion years ago. See also ◊cosmology.

Big Bang in economics, the major changes instituted in late 1986 to the organization and practices of the City of London as Britain's financial centre, with the aim of ensuring that London retained its place as one of the leading world financial centres. Facilitated in part by computerization and

on-line communications, the changes included the liberalization of the London ◊Stock Exchange. This involved merging the functions of jobber (dealer in stocks and shares) and broker (who mediates between the jobber and the public), introducing negotiated commission rates, and allowing foreign banks and financial companies to own British brokers/jobbers, or themselves to join the London Stock Exchange.

Big Ben the bell in the clock tower of the Houses of Parliament in London, cast at the Whitechapel Bell Foundry in 1858. It weighs 13.7 tonnes. [from *Benjamin* Hall, first commissioner of works at the time]

Big Bertha any of three large German howitzer guns that were mounted on railway wagons during World War I.

Big Dipper the North American name for the Plough, the seven brightest and most prominent stars in the constellation ◊Ursa Major.

Biggin Hill /'bɪgɪn/ an airport in the SE London borough of Bromley. It was the most famous of the Royal Air Force stations in the Battle of Britain in World War II.

bighorn *n.* either of two North American sheep *Ovis canadensis* and *O. dalli* with transversely ribbed horns, which, in the male, may curve in a huge spiral.

bight /baɪt/ *n.* **1.** a loop of rope. **2.** a wide shallow bay on a coast. [Old English]

bigot /'bɪgət/ *n.* an obstinate and intolerant adherent of a creed or view. —**bigoted** *adj.*, **bigotry** *n.* [French]

bigwig *n.* (*colloquial*) an important person.

Bihar /bɪ'hɑ:/ or **Behar** state of NE India; **area** 173,900 sq km/67,125 sq mi; **capital** Patna; **physical** river Ganges in the N, Rajmahal Hills in the S; **products** copper, iron, coal, rice, jute, sugar cane, grain, oilseed; **population** (1981) 69,823,000; **language** Hindi, Bihari.

Bijapur /bɪdʒə'puə/ ancient city in Karnataka, India. It was founded around AD 1489 by Yusuf Adil Shah (died 1511), the son of Murad II, as the capital of the Muslim kingdom of Biafra. The city and kingdom was annexed by the Mogul emperor Aurangzeb in 1686.

bijou /'bi:ʒu:/ *adj.* small and elegant. [French = jewel]

bike *n.* (*colloquial*) a bicycle or motor cycle. —*v.i.* (*colloquial*) to ride on this. [abbreviation]

bikini /bɪ'ki:nɪ/ *n.* a woman's scanty two-piece beach garment. [from *Bikini* atoll]

Bikini atoll in the ◊Marshall Islands, W Pacific, where the USA carried out 23 atom-bomb tests 1946–63. In 1990 a US plan was announced to remove radioactive topsoil, allowing 800 islanders to return home.

Biko /'bi:kəʊ/ Steve (Stephen) 1946–1977. South African civil-rights leader. An active opponent of ◊apartheid, he was arrested in Sept 1977; he died in detention six days later. Since his death in the custody of South African police he has been a symbol of the anti-apartheid movement.

bilateral /baɪ'lætərəl/ *adj.* of, on, or having two sides; involving two parties. —**bilateralism** *n.* in economics, a trade agreement between two countries or groups of countries in which they give each other preferential treatment. Usually the terms agreed result in balanced trade and are favoured by countries with limited foreign exchange reserves. Bilateralism is incompatible with free trade. **bilaterally** *adv.* [from Latin *latus* = side]

Bilbao /bɪl'baʊ/ industrial port (iron and steel, chemicals, cement, food) in N Spain, capital of Biscay province; population (1986) 378,000.

bilberry /'bɪlbərɪ/ *n.* several species of shrubs of the genus *Vaccinium* of the heath family Ericaceae, closely related to North American blueberries; its purple-black berry. [Scandinavian]

bilby *n.* a rabbit-eared bandicoot *Macrotis lagotis*, a lightly built marsupial with big ears and long nose. This burrowing animal is mainly carnivorous, and its pouch opens backwards.

Bildungsroman *n.* a novel that deals with the psychological and emotional development of its protagonist, tracing his or her life from inexperienced youth to maturity. The first example of the type is generally considered to be ◊Wieland's *Agathon* 1765–66, but it was ◊Goethe's *Wilhelm Meisters Lehrjahr/Wilhelm Meister's Apprenticeship* 1795–96 that established the genre. Although taken up by writers in other languages, it remained chiefly a German form, and later notable examples have included ◊Mann's

Der Zauberberg/The Magic Mountain 1924. [German = education novel]

bile *n.* **1.** a bitter yellowish fluid produced by the liver. In most vertebrates, it is stored in the gall bladder and emptied into the small intestine as food passes through. Bile consists of bile salts, bile pigments, cholesterol, and lecithin. **Bile salts** assist in the breakdown and absorption of fats; **bile pigments** are the breakdown products of old red blood cells that are passed into the gut to be eliminated with the faeces. **2.** (*archaic*) one of the four ◊humours. —**bile duct,** a duct conveying bile to the duodenum. [from French from Latin *bilis*]

bilge /bɪldʒ/ *n.* **1.** the nearly flat part of a ship's bottom. **2.** or **bilge water** the foul water that collects there. **3.** (*slang*) worthless ideas or talk.

bilharzia *n.* or **schistosomiasis** a disease that causes anaemia, inflammation, formation of scar tissue, dysentery, enlargement of the spleen and liver, and cirrhosis of the liver. It is contracted by bathing in water contaminated with human sewage, and caused by a parasitic flatworm. Some 300 million people are thought to suffer from this disease in the tropics. [from T *Bilharz*, German physician (1825–1862)]

bilingual /baɪˈlɪŋgwəl/ *adj.* speaking or written in two languages. [from Latin *lingua* = language]

bilious /ˈbɪljəs/ *adj.* **1.** affected by sickness assumed to be caused by a disorder of the bile. **2.** of a sickly yellowish hue. —**biliousness** *n.*

bilk *v.t.* to cheat (*of* what is due); to avoid paying (a creditor etc.).

bill[1] *n.* **1.** a statement of charges for goods or services supplied. **2.** the draft of a proposed law. **3.** a poster or placard; a programme of entertainment. **4.** (*US*) a banknote. —*v.t.* **1.** to announce on a poster or in a programme. **2.** to advertise *as.* **3.** to send a note of charges to. —**bill of exchange,** a written order to pay a sum on a given date to the drawer or a named person; it is a form of commercial credit instrument, or IOU, used in international trade. **bill of fare,** a menu. **bill of lading,** an inventory of goods to be shipped, signed by the carrier. [from Anglo-French from Latin *bulla* = seal]

bill[2] *n.* **1.** a bird's beak, especially when slender or flattened. **2.** a narrow promontory. —*v.i.* (of doves) to stroke each other's bills. —**bill and coo,** to exchange caresses. [Old English]

bill[3] *n.* (*historical*) a weapon with a hooked blade. [Old English]

billabong /ˈbɪləbɒŋ/ *n.* (*Australian*) a river branch forming a backwater or stagnant pool; a waterhole formed by the drying up of the channel that connnected it to a river. [from Aboriginal *Bilibang* Bell River (*billa* = water and *bung* = dead)]

billboard *n.* a hoarding for advertisements.

billet[1] /ˈbɪlɪt/ *n.* **1.** an order to a householder to lodge and board soldiers etc.; a place so provided. **2.** (*colloquial*) a job. — *v.t.* to place (soldiers etc.) in a billet. [from Anglo-French, diminutive of *bille* = from Latin *bulla* = seal]

billet[2] *n.* **1.** a thick piece of firewood. **2.** a small bar of metal. [from French, diminutive of *bille* = tree trunk]

billet-doux /bɪliˈduː/ *n.* (*plural* **billets-doux** -ˈduːz/) (*jocular*) a love letter. [French = sweet note]

billhook *n.* a tool with a hooked blade, used for pruning etc.

billiards /ˈbɪljədz/ *n.* an indoor game played, normally by two players, with tapered poles called cues and composition balls (one red, two white) on a rectangular table covered with a green baize cloth with six pockets, one at each corner and in each of the long sides at the middle. Scoring strokes are made by potting the red ball, potting the opponent's ball, or potting another ball off one of these two. The cannon (when the cue ball hits the two other balls on the table) is another scoring stroke. —**bar billiards,** a game in which balls are to be struck into holes on a table. [from French *billard* = cue, diminutive of *bille* = tree trunk]

billingsgate /ˈbɪlɪŋzgeɪt/ *n.* coarse abuse. [from *Billingsgate*, a London fish market dating from the 16th century, known for the invective traditionally ascribed to the fish porters]

billion /ˈbɪljən/ *adj. & n.* (*plural* **billion** except as below) **1.** (*US* and increasingly *British*) a thousand million (1,000,000,000). **2.** (formerly *British*) a million million. **3.**

Billy the Kid *The US outlaw William Bonney, Billy the Kid, who was shot by Sheriff Pat Garrett in 1881.*

billions (*plural, colloquial*) great numbers *of.* —**billionth** *adj.* [from French]

Bill of Rights any law guaranteeing citizens' rights, especially the first ten amendments to the US ◊Constitution: 1. guarantees freedom of worship, of speech, of the press, of assembly, and to petition the government; 2. grants the right to keep and bear arms (which has hindered recent attempts to control illicit use of arms); 3. prohibits billeting of soldiers in private homes in peacetime; 4. forbids unreasonable search and seizure; 5. guarantees none be 'deprived of life, liberty or property without due process of law' or be compelled in any criminal case to be a witness against oneself; 6. grants the right to speedy trial, to call witnesses, and to have defence counsel; 7. grants the right to trial by jury; 8. prevents the infliction of excessive bail or fines, or 'cruel and unusual punishment'; 9. 10. provide a safeguard to the states and people for all rights not specifically delegated to the central government. Not originally part of the draft of the Constitution, the Bill of Rights emerged during the period of ratification. Twelve amendments were proposed by Congress in 1789; the ten now called the Bill of Rights were ratified in 1791.

billow /ˈbɪləʊ/ *n.* a large wave. —*v.i.* to rise or roll like waves. —**billowy** *adj.* [from Old Norse]

billy abbreviation of ◊billycan.

billycan /ˈbɪlikæn/ *n.* a tin or enamelled container with a lid and handle, used as a cooking vessel, especially in Australia. [perhaps from Aboriginal *billa* = water]

billy goat /ˈbɪligəʊt/ a male goat. [from *Billy*, pet form of *William*]

Billy the Kid /ˈbɪli/ nickname of William H Bonney 1859–1881. the US outlaw, a leader in the Lincoln County cattle war in New Mexico, who allegedly killed his first victim at the age of 12 and is reputed to have killed 22 people in all. He was sentenced to death for murdering a sheriff, but escaped (killing two guards), and was finally shot by Sheriff Pat Garrett while trying to avoid recapture.

bimah /biːmɑː/ *n.* in Judaism, a raised platform in a synagogue from which the ◊Torah scroll is read.

bimetallic /baɪmɪˈtælɪk/ *adj.* using or made of two metals. —**bimetallic strip,** a strip made from two metals each having a different coefficient of thermal expansion; it therefore bends when subjected to a change in temperature. Such strips are used widely for temperature measurement and control.

bimodal distribution in statistics, a frequency distribution of data having two distinct peaks.

bin *n.* a large rigid container, usually with a lid, for storing coal, grain, flour etc.; a receptacle for rubbish. [Old English]

binary /'baɪnərɪ/ *adj.* involving a pair or pairs. —*n.* **1.** a ◊binary star. **2.** in music, a form in two matching sections. —**binary compound**, one containing two chemical elements or radicals. **binary digit**, either of the two digits used in the ◊binary number system. [from Latin *bini* = two together]

binary fission in biology, a form of ◊asexual reproduction, whereby a single-celled organism divides into two smaller 'daughter' cells. It can also occur in a few simple multicellular organisms, such as sea anemones, producing two smaller sea anemones of equal size.

binary number system or **binary number code** a system of numbers to ◊base 2 using combinations of the two digits 1 and 0. Binary numbers play a key role in digital computers, where they form the basis of the internal coding of information, the values of ◊bits (short for 'binary digits') being represented as on/off (1 and 0) states of switches and high/low voltages in circuits.

binary star a pair of stars moving in orbit around their common centre of mass. Observations show that most stars are binary, or even multiple; for example, the nearest star system to the Sun, ◊Alpha Centauri.

binary weapon in chemical warfare, a weapon consisting of two substances that in isolation are harmless but when mixed together form a poisonous nerve gas. They are loaded into the delivery system separately and combine after launch.

binaural /baɪn'ɔ:rəl, bɪ-/ *adj.* of or used with both ears; (of sound) recorded by two microphones and usually transmitted separately to the two ears. [from *bi-* and *aural*]

bind /baɪnd/ *v.t./i.* (*past* and *past participle* **bound**) **1.** to tie or fasten together; to encircle *with*; to bandage (*up*). **2.** to secure or restrain by fastening; to fasten sheets of (a book) into a cover (see ◊bookbinding); to cover the edge of (a thing) with strengthening or decorative material. **3.** to be obligatory; to compel, to impose a duty on. **4.** to stick together. **5.** to constipate. **6.** (*slang*) to grumble. —*n.* (*slang*) a nuisance, a bore. —**bind over**, in law, to put under an obligation (*to* keep the peace etc.). [Old English]

binder /'baɪndə/ *n.* **1.** a loose cover for papers. **2.** a bookbinder. **3.** a substance that binds things together. **4.** a machine that binds harvested corn into sheaves.

bindery *n.* a bookbinder's workshop.

binding /'baɪndɪŋ/ *n.* something that binds, especially the gluing etc. and covers of a book. —*adj.* obligatory (*on*). —**binding energy**, in physics, the amount of energy needed to break the nucleus of an atom into the neutrons and protons of which it is made up.

bindweed /'baɪndwi:d/ *n.* a ◊convolvulus plant.

bine *n.* the twisting stem of a climbing plant, especially the hop. [dialect form of *bind*]

binge /bɪndʒ/ *n.* (*slang*) a drinking or eating bout or spree. —*v.i.*

bingo[1] /'bɪŋgəʊ/ an exclamation at a sudden action or event.

bingo[2] *n.* a gambling game, a type of lotto played with cards on which numbered squares have to be covered as the numbers are called at random. The player to cover all or a set of these first wins a prize.

binnacle /'bɪnəkəl/ *n.* a case or stand for a ship's compass. [earlier *bittacle*, from Spanish or Portuguese from Latin *habitaculum* = lodging]

binocular /bi'nɒkjʊlə, baɪ-/ *n.* (usually in *plural* and /bɪ-/) an optical instrument for viewing an object in magnification with both eyes; for example, field glasses and opera glasses. Binoculars consist of two telescopes containing lenses and prisms, which produce a stereoscopic effect as well as magnifying the image. Use of prisms has the effect of 'folding' the light path, allowing for a compact design. —/usually baɪ-/ *adj.* for or using both eyes. [from Latin *bini* = two together and *oculus* = eye]

binomial /baɪ'nəʊmɪəl/ *n.* an algebraic expression consisting of two terms linked by a plus or minus sign. —*adj.* consisting of two terms so linked. —**binomial system of nomenclature**, in biology, the system in which all organisms are identified by a two-part Latinized name. Devised by the biologist ◊Linnaeus, it is also known as the Linnaean system. The first name is capitalized and identifies the ◊genus; the second identifies the ◊species within that genus. **binomial theorem**, a formula for finding any power of a binomial without multiplying at length. It was discovered by Isaac ◊Newton and first published in 1676. [from French (Greek *nomos* = part)]

binturong /'bɪntjʊərɒŋ/ *n.* a shaggy-coated mammal *Arctitis binturong*, the largest member of the mongoose family, nearly 1 m/3 ft long excluding a long muscular tail with a prehensile tip. Mainly nocturnal and tree-dwelling, the binturong is found in the forests of SE Asia, feeding on fruit, eggs, and small animals. [Malay]

bio- /baɪəʊ-/ prefix meaning of life or living things. [from Greek *bios* = life]

biochemistry /baɪəʊ'kemɪstrɪ/ *n.* the study of the chemistry of living organisms: the structure and reactions of proteins such as enzymes, nucleic acids, carbohydrates, and lipids. —**biochemical** *adj.*, **biochemist** *n.*

biodegradable /baɪəʊdɪ'greɪdəbəl/ *n.* capable of being broken down by living organisms, principally bacteria and fungi. Biodegradable substances, such as fruit, vegetables, and sewage, can be rendered harmless by natural processes. Nonbiodegradable substances, such as most plastics and heavy metals, accumulate in the environment and may cause serious problems of ◊pollution.

bioengineering /baɪəʊendʒɪ'nɪərɪŋ/ *n.* the application of engineering techniques to biological processes. Common applications include the design and use of artificial limbs, joints, and organs, including hip joints and heart valves.

biofeedback *n.* the modification or control of a biological system by its results or effects. For example, a change in the position or ◊trophic level of one species affects all levels above it.

biog. abbreviation of biography.

biogenesis *n.* in biology, the hypothesis that living matter always arises out of other similar forms of living matter. This superseded the opposite idea of ◊spontaneous generation or abiogenesis (that is, that living things may arise out of nonliving matter). [term coined in 1870 by T H Huxley]

biogeography *n.* the study of how and why plants and animals are distributed around the world, in the past as well as in the present; more specifically, a theory describing the geographical distribution of ◊species developed by Robert MacArthur and E O ◊Wilson. The theory argues that for many species, ecological specializations mean that suitable habitats are patchy in their occurrence. Thus for a dragonfly, ponds in which to breed are separated by large tracts of land, and for edelweiss adapted to alpine peaks the deep valleys between cannot be colonized.

biography /baɪ'ɒgrəfɪ/ *n.* a written account of a person's life (when it is written by that person, it is an ◊autobiography); the writing of biographies. —**biographer** *n.*, **biographical** /baɪə'græfɪkəl/ *adj.* [from Greek *graphia* = writing]

Bioko /bi'əʊkəʊ/ island in the Bight of Bonny, W Africa, part of Equatorial Guinea; area 2,017 sq km/786 sq mi; produces coffee, cacao, and copra; population (1983) 57,190. Formerly a Spanish possession, as *Fernando Po*, it was known 1973–79 as *Macías Nguema Bijogo*.

biological /baɪə'lɒdʒɪkəl/ *adj.* of or relating to biology. —**biologically** *adv.*

biological clock a regular internal rhythm of activity, produced by unknown mechanisms, and not dependent on external time signals. Such clocks are known to exist in almost all animals, and also in many plants, fungi, and unicellular organisms. In higher organisms, there appears to be a series of clocks of graded importance. For example, although body temperature and activity cycles in human beings are normally 'set' to 24 hours, the two cycles may vary independently, showing that two clock mechanisms are involved. Exposing humans to bright light can change the biological clock and help, for example, people suffering from jet lag.

biological computer a proposed technology for computing devices based on growing complex organic molecules (biomolecules) as components. Its theoretical basis is that cells, the building blocks of all living things, have chemical systems that can store and exchange electrons and therefore function as electrical components. It is currently the subject of long-term research.

biological control the control of pests such as insects and fungi through biological means, rather than the use of chemicals. This can include breeding resistant crop strains; inducing sterility in the pest; infecting the pest species with disease organisms; or introducing the pest's natural predator. Biological control tends to be naturally self-regulating, but because ecosystems are so complex, it is difficult to predict all the consequences of introducing a biological controlling agent.

biological oxygen demand (BOD) the amount of dissolved oxygen taken up by microorganisms in a sample of water. Since these microorganisms live by decomposing organic matter, and the amount of oxygen used is proportional to their number and metabolic rate, BOD can be used as a measure of the extent to which the water is polluted with organic compounds.

biological shield the shield around a nuclear reactor to protect personnel from the effects of ◊radiation. It usually consists of a thick wall of steel and concrete.

biological warfare the use of living organisms, or of infectious material derived from them, to bring about death or disease in humans, animals, or plants. It was condemned by the Geneva Convention of 1925, to which the United Nations has urged all states to adhere. Nevertheless research in this area continues; the Biological Weapons Convention permits research for defence purposes but does not define how this differs from offensive weapons development. In 1990 the US Department of Defense allocated $60 million to research, develop, and test defence systems. Advances in genetic engineering make the development of new varieties of potentially offensive biological weapons more likely. At least ten countries have this capability. See also ◊chemical warfare.

biology n. the science of living organisms. Strictly speaking, biology includes all the life sciences – or example, anatomy and physiology, cytology, zoology and botany, ecology, genetics, biochemistry and biophysics, animal behaviour, embryology, and plant breeding. —**biologist** n. [from Greek bios = life]

bioluminescence n. the production of light by living organisms. It is a feature of many fishes, crustaceans, and other marine animals, especially deep-sea organisms. On land, bioluminescence is seen in some nocturnal insects such as glowworms and fireflies, and in certain bacteria and fungi. Light is usually produced by the oxidation of luciferin, a reaction catalysed by the ◊enzyme luciferase. This reaction is unique, being the only known biological oxidation that does not produce heat. Animal luminescence is involved in communication, camouflage, or the luring of prey, but its function in other organisms is unclear.

biomass n. the total dry weight of organisms present in a given area. It may be specified for one species (such as earthworm biomass), for a category of species (for example, herbivore biomass), or for all species (total biomass).

biome n. a broad natural assemblage of plants and animals shaped by common patterns of vegetation and climate. Examples include the tundra biome and the desert biome.

biometry /baɪˈɒmɪtrɪ/ n. the analysis of biological phenomena by statistical methods. The term is now largely obsolete, since mathematical or statistical work is an integral part of most biological disciplines. —**biometric** /baɪəˈmetrɪk/ adj. [from Greek metron = measure]

bionic /baɪˈɒnɪk/ adj. forming or possessing an electronically operated body part or parts. The bionic arm, for example, is an artificial limb that uses electronics to amplify minute electrical signals generated in body muscles to work electric motors, which operate the joints of fingers and wrist. —**bionics** n. the design and development of electronic or mechanical artificial systems that imitate those of living things. [from bio-, after electronic]

biophysics /baɪəˈfɪzɪks/ n. the science of the physical properties of living organisms and their constituents, and the investigation of biological phenomena in general by means of the techniques of modern physics. Examples include using the principles of ◊mechanics to calculate the strength of bones and muscles, and ◊thermodynamics to

study plant and animal energetics. —**biophysical** adj., **biophysicist** n.

biopsy /ˈbaɪɒpsɪ/ n. an examination of tissue cut from the living body, as a means of diagnosis; surgical removal of such tissue. [from bio-after autopsy]

biorhythm /ˈbaɪəʊrɪðəm/ n. any of the internal cycles mediated by ◊hormones, in the physical state and activity patterns of certain plants and animals that have seasonal activities. Examples include winter hibernation, spring flowering or breeding, and periodic migration. The hormonal changes themselves are often a response to changes in day length (◊photoperiodism); they signal the time of year to the animal or plant. Other biorhythms are innate and continue even if external stimuli such as day length are removed. These include a 24-hour or ◊circadian rhythm, a 28-day or circalunar rhythm (corresponding to the phases of the Moon), and even a year-long rhythm in some organisms. Biorhythms are said to govern a person's physiological, emotional, and intellectual activity.

biosensor n. a device based on microelectronic circuits that can directly measure medically significant variables for the purpose of diagnosis or monitoring treatment. One such device measures the blood sugar level of diabetics using a single drop of blood, and shows the result on a liquid crystal display within a few minutes.

biosphere /ˈbaɪəsfɪə(r)/ n. or **ecosphere** that region of the Earth's surface (land and water), and the atmosphere above it, which can be occupied by living organisms.

biosynthesis n. the synthesis of organic chemicals from simple inorganic ones by living cells—for example, the conversion of carbon dioxide and water to glucose by plants during ◊photosynthesis. Other biosynthetic reactions produce cell constituents including proteins and fats.

biotechnology n. the industrial use of living organisms, to manufacture food, drugs, or other products. Historically biotechnology has largely been restricted to the brewing and baking industries, using ◊fermentation by yeast. The most recent advances include ◊genetic engineering, in which single-celled organisms with modified ◊DNA are used to produce substances such as insulin.

biotic /baɪˈɒtɪk/ adj. of life or living things. —**biotic factor** n. any organic variable affecting an ecosystem, for example the changing population of elephants and its effect on the African savanna. [from French or Latin from Greek bios = life]

biotin /ˈbaɪətɪn/ n. a vitamin of the B-complex, also called vitamin H, controlling growth. It is found in many different kinds of food; egg yolk, liver, and yeast contain large amounts. [German]

biotite n. a dark mica, $K(Mg,Fe)_3Al\ Si_3O_{10}(OH,F)_2$, a common silicate mineral. It is colourless to silvery white with shiny surfaces, and like all micas, it splits into very thin flakes along its one perfect cleavage. Biotite is a mineral of igneous rocks such as granites, and metamorphic rocks such as schists and gneisses.

bipartisan /baɪpɑːtiˈzæn/ adj. involving or agreed to by two parties.

bipartite /baɪˈpɑːtaɪt/ adj. consisting of two parts; shared by two parties. [from Latin partiri = divide]

biped /ˈbaɪped/ n. a two-footed animal. —adj. two-footed. [from Latin pes = foot]

biplane /ˈbaɪpleɪn/ n. an aeroplane with two sets of wings, one above the other.

bipolar /baɪˈpəʊlə/ adj. having two poles or extremities.

birch /bɜːtʃ/ n. 1. a tree of the genus Betula with smooth bark and slender branches, including about 40 species found in cool temperate parts of the northern hemisphere. Birches grow rapidly, and their hard, beautiful wood is used for veneers and cabinet work. 2. a rod of birch twigs, used for flogging delinquents. —v.t. to flog with a birch. [Old English]

bird /bɜːd/ n. 1. a backboned animal of the class Aves, the biggest group of land vertebrates, characterized by warm blood, feathers, wings, breathing through lungs, and egg-laying by the female. There are nearly 8,500 species of birds. 2. (slang) a person (especially a strange one); (derogatory) a young woman. 3. (rhyming slang, from birdlime = time) a prison sentence. —**bird of passage**, a migrant, a transient visitor. **bird-watcher** n. one who studies birds in their natural surroundings.

Bird Isabella 1832–1904. British traveller and writer who wrote extensively of her journeys in the USA, Persia, Tibet, Kurdistan, China, Japan, and Korea.

birdie /'bɜːdɪ/ *n.* **1.** (*children's colloquial*) a bird. **2.** in golf, a hole played in one stroke under par.

bird of paradise one of 40 species of crowlike birds, family Paradiseidae, native to New Guinea and neighbouring islands. Females are drably coloured, but the males have bright and elaborate plumage used in courtship display. Hunted almost to extinction for their plumage, they are now subject to conservation.

Birdseye /'bɜːdzaɪ/ Clarence 1886–1956. US inventor who pioneered food refrigeration processes by rapidly freezing prepared food between two refrigerated metal plates. To market his products he founded the General Sea Foods Company in 1924, which he sold to General Foods in 1929.

biretta /bɪ'retə/ *n.* a square cap worn by (especially Roman Catholic) priests. [from Italian or Spanish diminutive from Latin *birrus* = cape]

Birkenhead /'bɜːkənhed/ Frederick Edwin Smith, 1st Earl of Birkenhead 1872–1930. English Conservative politician. A flamboyant character, known as 'FE', he joined with Edward Carson in organizing armed resistance in Ulster to Irish Home Rule. He was Lord Chancellor 1919–22 and a much criticized secretary for India 1924–28.

The world continues to offer glittering prizes to those who have stout hearts and sharp swords.
Frederick Edwin Smith, 1st Earl of Birkenhead
rectorial address, Glasgow University,
7 November 1923

Birmingham /'bɜːmɪŋəm/ **1.** industrial city in West Midlands, second largest city of the UK; population (1989) 998,200, metropolitan area 2,632,000. Industries include motor vehicles, machine tools, aerospace control systems, plastics, chemicals, and food. **2.** industrial city (iron, steel, chemicals, building materials, computers, cotton textiles) and commercial centre in Alabama, USA; population (1980) 847,000.

Biro /'baɪrəʊ/ *n.* the trade name of a kind of ballpoint pen. [from Lazlo *Biró*, Hungarian inventor (1900–1985)]

birth *n.* **1.** the emergence of young from the mother's body. **2.** origin, parentage. —**birth certificate,** an official document giving the date and place etc. of a person's birth. **birth control,** prevention of undesired pregnancy; see ◊contraceptive. **birth rate,** the number of births in one year for every 1,000 people. **give birth to,** to produce (young); to cause. [from Old Norse]

birthday *n.* the anniversary of the day of one's birth.

birthmark *n.* an unusual coloured mark on a person's skin at or from the time of birth.

birthplace *n.* the place of a person's birth.

birthright *n.* rights belonging to a person by birth, especially as the eldest son.

birthstone *n.* in astrology, a gemstone associated with a particular month or sign of the zodiac and thought to bring good luck if worn by a person born then.

Birtwistle /'bɜːtwɪsl/ Harrison 1934– . English avant-garde composer. He has specialized in chamber music, for example, his chamber opera *Punch and Judy* 1967 and *Down by the Greenwood Side* 1969.

Biscay, Bay of /'bɪskeɪ/ bay of the Atlantic Ocean between N Spain and W France, known for rough seas and exceptionally high tides.

biscuit /'bɪskɪt/ *n.* **1.** a flat, thin, unleavened cake, usually dry and crisp. **2.** porcelain after firing but before glazing. **3.** a light-brown colour. [from Old French from Latin *biscoctus* = twice baked]

bise *n.* a cold dry northerly wind experienced in southern France and Switzerland. [from Old French]

bisect /baɪ'sekt/ *v.t.* to divide into two (strictly, equal) parts. —**bisection** *n.,* **bisector** *n.* [from Latin *secare* = cut]

bisexual /baɪ'seksjuəl/ *adj.* **1.** sexually attracted both to men and women. **2.** having male and female sexual organs in one individual. —**bisexuality** /-'aelɪtɪ/ *n.*

bishop /'bɪʃəp/ *n.* **1.** a priest next in rank to an archbishop

in the Roman Catholic, Eastern Orthodox, Anglican, or episcopal churches. A bishop has charge of a district called a diocese. **2.** a mitre-shaped chess piece. [Old English, ultimately from Greek *episkopos* = overseer]

bishopric /'bɪʃəprɪk/ *n.* the office or diocese of a bishop.

Bismarck /'bɪzmɑːk/ Otto Eduard Leopold, Prince von 1815–1898. German politician, prime minister of Prussia 1862–90 and chancellor of the German Empire 1871–90. He pursued an aggressively expansionist policy, waging wars against Denmark 1863–64, Austria in 1866, and France 1870–71, which brought about the unification of Germany.

Bismarck Archipelago /'bɪzmɑːk/ group of over 200 islands in SW Pacific Ocean, part of ◊Papua New Guinea; area 49,660 sq km/19,200 sq mi. The largest island is New Britain.

bismuth /'bɪzməpθ/ *n.* a hard, brittle, pinkish-white, metallic element, symbol Bi, atomic number 83, relative atomic mass 208.98. It is the last of the stable elements; all from atomic number 84 up are radioactive. Bismuth occurs in ores and occasionally as a free metal. It is a poor conductor of heat and electricity, and is used in alloys of low melting point and in medical compounds to soothe gastric ulcers. [from German *Wismut*]

bison /'baɪsən/ *n.* (*plural* the same) a large, hoofed mammal of the bovine family. There are two species, both brown. **1.** the European wild ox or **wisent** *Bison bonasus,* of which only a few protected herds survive; it is about 2 m/7 ft high and weighs a tonne. **2.** the North American buffalo *Bison bison,* slightly smaller than the European bison, with a heavier mane and more sloping hindquarters. Formerly roaming the prairies in vast numbers, it was almost exterminated in the 19th century, but survives in protected areas. [from Latin from Germanic]

bisque[1] /bɪsk/ *n.* an extra turn, stroke etc., allowed to an inferior player in some games. [French]

bisque[2] *n.* unglazed white porcelain. [from *biscuit*]

bisque[3] *n.* rich soup made from shellfish. [French]

Bissau /bi'saʊ/ capital and chief port of Guinea-Bissau, on an island at the mouth of the Geba river; population (1988) 125,000. Originally a fortified slave-trading centre, Bissau became a free port in 1869.

bistre /'bɪstə/ *n.* a brown pigment prepared from soot; the colour of this. [French]

bistro /'biːstrəʊ/ *n.* (*plural* **bistros**) a small restaurant. [French]

bit[1] *n.* a small piece or quantity; a short distance or time; a small coin. —**a bit,** (*colloquial*) somewhat. **bit by bit,** gradually. **bit part,** a small part in a play or film. [Old English]

bit[2] *n.* **1.** the mouthpiece of a bridle. **2.** the part of a tool that cuts, grips etc.; the boring piece of a drill. [Old English]

bit[3] *n.* in computing, the smallest unit of information, expressed as a choice between two possibilities: a binary digit or place in a binary number. A ◊byte is eight bits. [from *b(inary dig)it*]

bit[4] past of **bite.**

bitch *n.* **1.** a female dog; a female fox, otter etc. **2.** (*derogatory*) a spiteful or unpleasant person. —*v.i.* to speak spitefully; (*colloquial*) to grumble. [Old English]

bitchy /'bɪtʃɪ/ *adj.* spiteful, catty. —**bitchiness** *n.*

bite *v.t./i.* (*past* **bit**; *past participle* **bitten**) **1.** to cut into or wound with the teeth; to take (a piece) *off* with the teeth. **2.** (of an insect) to sting; (of a snake) to pierce with its fangs. **3.** to snap *at*; (of a fish) to accept bait. **4.** to cause smarting pain. **5.** (of a wheel, screw etc.) to grip the surface. —*n.* **1.** an act of biting; a wound made by biting etc. **2.** a mouthful of food; a snack. **3.** the taking of bait by a fish. **4.** incisiveness, pungency. [Old English]

bit pad a computer input device; see ◊graphics tablet.

bitter *adj.* **1.** having a sharp, astringent taste, not sweet; (of beer) strongly flavoured with hops. **2.** piercingly cold. **3.** painful to the mind. **4.** showing grief or resentment; virulent, resentful. —*n.* bitter beer; (in *plural*) liquors impregnated with bitter herbs. —**bittersweet** *adj.* sweet but with a bitter element. **to the bitter end,** to the last extremity however painful. —**bitterly** *adv.,* **bitterness** *n.* [Old English]

bittern /'bɪtɜːn/ *n.* a marsh bird of the genus *Botaurus,* allied to herons, especially the **common bittern** *B. stellaris* of Europe and Asia. It is shy, stoutly built, has a streaked camouflage pattern and a loud, booming call. It is now quite rare in Britain. [from Old French from Latin *butio* = bittern and *taurus* = bull]

bittersweet *n.* an alternative name for the woody ◊night-shade plant.

bitty *adj.* made up of bits, scrappy.

bitumen /'bɪtjumɪn/ *n.* an impure mixture of hydrocarbons, including such deposits as petroleum, asphalt, and natural gas, although sometimes the term is restricted to a soft kind of pitch resembling asphalt. —**bituminous** /-'tju:mɪnəs/ *adj.* [Latin]

bivalent *n.* in biology, the pair of homologous chromosomes during reduction division (◊meiosis). —*adj.* in chemistry, (of an element or group) having a ◊valency of two (the term **divalent** is more common).

bivalve /'baɪvælv/ *adj.* (of shellfish) having two shells hinged together by a ligament on the dorsal side of the body. —*n.* a bivalve shellfish, such as the oyster. The bivalves form one of the five classes of molluscs, the Lamellibranchiata, otherwise known as Bivalvia or Pelycypoda, containing about 8,000 species.

bivouac /'bɪvuæk/ *n.* an encampment without tents, as of troops in the field. —*v.i.* (**-ck-**) to camp thus. [from French]

bizarre /bɪ'zɑ:/ *adj.* strikingly odd in appearance or effect. [French, originally = brave, soldierly]

Bizet /'bi:zeɪ/ Georges (Alexandre César Léopold) 1838–1875. French composer of operas, among them *Les Pêcheurs de perles/The Pearl Fishers* 1863, and *La jolie Fille de Perth/The Fair Maid of Perth* 1866. He also wrote the concert overture *Patrie* and incidental music to Daudet's *L'Arlésienne.* His operatic masterpiece *Carmen* was produced a few months before his death in 1875.

Bjelke-Petersen /'bjelkə 'pɪtəsən/ Joh(annes) 1911– . Australian right-wing politician, leader of the Queensland National Party (QNP) and premier of Queensland 1968–87.

Bk symbol for ◊berkelium.

blab *v.t./i.* (**-bb-**) to talk indiscreetly, to let out (secrets) by indiscreet talk.

black *adj.* **1.** colourless from the absence or absorption of light, of the colour of coal or soot. **2.** of African descent or culture etc. In the UK and some other countries (but not in North America) the term is sometimes also used for people originally from the Indian subcontinent, Australian Aborigines, and peoples of Melanesia. **3.** (of the sky) dusky, overcast. **4.** sinister, wicked; dismal, sullen, frowning; portending trouble or difficulty; (of humour) morbid, cynical. **5.** (of goods etc.) banned by workers on strike from being handled by other trade-unionists. —*n.* **1.** black colour or pigment; black (especially mourning) clothes or material. **2.** a black ball or piece in a game. **3.** the credit side of an account; *in the black,* solvent. **4.** or **Black,** a black person. —*v.t.* **1.** to make black. **2.** to polish with blacking. **3.** to declare (goods) to be 'black'. —**black and blue,** discoloured by bruises. **black and white,** photographed etc. in shades of grey and not in colour; comprising only opposite extremes; *in black and white,* recorded in writing or print. **black bread,** coarse rye bread. **black coffee,** coffee without milk. **black eye,** one with the surrounding skin darkened by bruises. **Black Friars,** monks of the ◊Dominican order, so called from their black cloaks. **black ice,** thin transparent ice on a road etc. **black letter,** a heavy style of type used by early printers. **black magic,** ◊witchcraft involving the invocation of devils. **Black Maria,** a police vehicle for conveying prisoners. **black mark,** a mark of discredit. **black market,** illicit traffic in rationed or officially restricted goods. **black mass,** a sacrificial rite in honour of Satan, parodying the Eucharist. **Black Monk,** a member of the ◊Benedictine order, so called from the colour of the habit. **blackout** *n.* a covering of all windows etc. to prevent light being seen by enemy aircraft; loss of electrical power; a temporary ban on the release of news; (*colloquial*) a momentary loss of consciousness. **black out,** to impose a blackout on; to suffer a blackout. **black pepper,** ◊pepper from the unripe berries complete with husks. **black sheep,** a discreditable character in an otherwise well-behaved group. **black tie,** a man's black bow tie worn with a dinner jacket. —**blackly** *adv.,* **blackness** *n.* [Old English]

Black Joseph 1728–1799. Scottish physicist and chemist, who in 1754 discovered carbon dioxide (which he called 'fixed air'). By his investigations in 1761 of latent heat and

Black *Scottish chemist and physicist Joseph Black, a medallion by Tassie 1788.*

specific heat, he laid the foundation for the work of his pupil James Watt.

Black and Tans (*colloquial*) a special force of military police employed by the British in 1920–21 to combat the Sinn Feiners (Irish nationalists) in Ireland. [from the colours of the uniforms, khaki (*tan*) with *black* hats and belts]

blackball *v.t.* to reject (a proposed member of a club etc.) in a ballot, originally by voting with a black ball.

blackberry *n.* a prickly shrub *Rubus fruticosus* of the rose family; its fruit. Closely allied to raspberries and dewberries (all ◊brambles), the blackberry is native to northern parts of Europe. It produces pink or white blossoms and edible black compound fruits.

blackbird *n.* **1.** a songbird *Turdus merula* of the thrush family. The male is black with yellow bill and eyelids, the female dark brown with a dark beak. About 25 cm/10 in long, it lays three to five blue-green eggs with brown spots. Its song is rich and flutelike. **2.** (*US*) the grackle or a similar bird.

blackboard *n.* a board with a smooth dark surface, used in classrooms etc. for writing on in chalk.

black body in physics, a hypothetical object that completely absorbs all thermal (heat) radiation striking it. It is also a perfect emitter of thermal radiation.

black box 1. the unit containing an aeroplane's flight and voice recorders. These monitor the plane's behaviour and the crew's conversation, thus providing valuable clues to the cause of a disaster. The box is nearly indestructible and usually painted orange for easy recovery. **2.** any compact electronic device that can be quickly connected or disconnected as a unit.

blackbuck *n.* an antelope *Antilope cervicapra* found in central and NW India. It is related to the gazelle, from which it differs in having spirally-twisted horns. The male is black above and white beneath, whereas the female and young are fawn-coloured above. It is about 76 cm/2.5 ft in height.

Blackburn /'blækbɜ:n/ industrial town in Lancashire, England, 32 km/20 mi NW of Manchester. It was preeminently a cotton-weaving town until World War II; today, engineering is its main product. Population (1981) 88,000.

blackcap *n.* a bird *Sylvia atricapilla* of the warbler family. The male has a black cap, the female a reddish-brown one. About 14 cm/5.5 in long, the blackcap likes wooded areas, and is a summer visitor to N Europe.

blackcock *n.* a male black ◊grouse.

Black Country central area of England, around and to the N of Birmingham. Heavily industrialized, it gained its name in the 19th century from its belching chimneys, but antipollution laws have changed its aspect.

blackcurrant *n.* the small, dark, edible berry of the shrub *Ribes nigrum*; this shrub.

Black Death a great epidemic of bubonic ◊plague that ravaged Europe in the 14th century, killing between one third and half of the population. The cause of the plague was the bacterium *Pasteurella pestis*, transmitted by fleas borne by migrating Asian black rats. The name Black Death was first used in England in the early 19th century.

black earth exceedingly fertile soil, a kind of ◊loess, that covers a belt of land in NE North America, Europe, and Asia.

black economy the unofficial economy of a country, which includes undeclared earnings from a second job (moonlighting), and enjoyment of undervalued goods and services (such as company perks) designed for tax-evasion purposes. In industrialized countries, the black economy has been estimated to equal about 10% of gross domestic product.

blacken /'blækən/ *v.t./i.* 1. to make or become black. 2. to speak ill of, to defame.

blackfly *n.* a plant-sucking insect, a type of ◊aphid.

Blackfoot /'blækfut/ *n.* a member of a ◊Plains American Indian people, some 10,000 in number and consisting of three subtribes: the Blackfoot proper, the Blood, and the Piegan, who live in Montana, USA, and Saskatchewan and Alberta, Canada. They were skilled, horse-riding buffalo hunters until their territories were settled by Europeans. Their language belongs to the Algonquian family. [from their black moccasins]

Black Forest (German *Schwarzwald*) a mountainous region of coniferous forest in Baden-Württemberg, W Germany. Bounded to the W and S by the Rhine, which separates it from the Vosges, it has an area of 4,660 sq km/1,800 sq mi and rises to 1,493 m/4,905 ft in the Feldberg. Parts of the forest have recently been affected by ◊acid rain.

Black Friday in US history, the day, 24 Sept 1869, on which Jay Gould (1836–1892) and James Fisk (1834–1872), stock manipulators, attempted to corner the gold market by trying to prevent the government from selling gold. President Grant refused to agree, but they spread the rumour that the president was opposed to the sales. George S Boutwell (1818–1905) with Grant's approval ordered the sale of $4 million in gold. The gold price plunged and many speculators were ruined. The two men made about $11 million.

blackguard /'blægɑːd/ *n.* an unprincipled villain, a scoundrel. —**blackguardly** *adj.* [originally collect. n. = royal scullions, vagrants etc.]

blackhead *n.* a black-topped pimple on the face etc.

black hole an object in space whose gravity is so great that nothing can escape from it, not even light. Thought to form when massive stars shrink at the ends of their lives, a black hole sucks in more matter, including other stars, from the space around it. Matter that falls into a black hole is squeezed to infinite density at the centre of the hole. Black holes can be detected because gas falling towards them becomes so hot that it emits X-rays.

Black Hole of Calcutta an incident in Anglo-Indian history: according to tradition, the nawab (ruler) of Bengal confined 146 British prisoners on the night of 20 June 1756 in one small room, of whom only 23 allegedly survived. Later research reduced the death count to 43, assigning negligence rather than intention.

blacking *n.* black polish for shoes.

black lead another word for ◊graphite.

blackleg *n.* (*derogatory*) a person who refuses to join an appropriate trade union, or who participates in strike-breaking by working for an employer whose regular workers are on strike. —*v.i.* (**-gg-**) to act as a blackleg.

blacklist *n.* a list of persons etc. in disfavour. —*v.t.* to put on a blacklist.

blackmail *n.* exaction of payment in return for not carrying out a threat, especially to reveal discreditable secrets; payment exacted thus; use of threats or moral pressure. —*v.t.* to exact payment by blackmail; to threaten, to coerce. —**blackmailer** *n.* [from obsolete *mail* = rent]

Black Monday a worldwide stockmarket crash that began on 19 Oct 1987, prompted by the announcement of worse than expected US trade figures and the response by the US secretary of the Treasury, James Baker, that the sliding dollar needed to decline further. This caused a world panic as fears of the likely impact of a US recession were voiced by the major industrialized countries. Between 19 and 23 Oct, the New York Stock Exchange fell by 33%, the London Stock Exchange Financial Times 100 Index by 25%, the European index by 17%, and Tokyo by 12%. The total paper loss on the London Stock Exchange and other City of London institutions was £94 billion. The expected world recession did not occur; by the end of 1988 it was clear that the main effect had been a steadying in stock-market activity and only a slight slowdown in world economic growth.

Blackmore /'blækmɔː/ R(ichard) D(oddridge) 1825–1900. English novelist, author of *Lorna Doone* 1869, a romance set on Exmoor, SW England, in the late 17th century.

Black Muslim a member of a religious group founded in 1929 in the USA and led, from 1934, by Elijah Muhammad (then Elijah Poole) (1897–1975) after he had a vision of ◊Allah. Its growth from 1946 as a black separatist organization was due to Malcolm X (1926–1965), who in 1964 broke away and founded his own Organization for Afro-American Unity, preaching 'active self-defence'.

Black National State an area in the Republic of South Africa set aside for development towards self-government by black Africans in accordance with ◊apartheid. Before 1980 these areas were known as **black homelands** or **bantustans**. They make up less than 14% of the country and tend to be in arid areas (though some have mineral wealth), and may be in scattered blocks. Those that have so far achieved nominal independence are Transkei in 1976, Bophuthatswana in 1977, Venda in 1979, and Ciskei in 1981. They are not recognized outside South Africa because of their racial basis.

Blackpool /'blækpuːl/ seaside resort in Lancashire, England, 45 km/28 mi N of Liverpool; population (1981) 148,000. The largest holiday resort in N England, it has amusement facilities that include 11 km/7 mi of promenades, known for their 'illuminations' of coloured lights, fun fairs, and a tower 152 m/500 ft high. Political party conferences are often held here.

Black Power a movement towards black separatism in the USA during the 1960s, embodied in the **Black Panther Party** founded in 1966 by Huey Newton and Bobby Seale. Its declared aim was the establishment of a separate black state in the USA established by a black plebiscite under the aegis of the United Nations. Following a National Black Political Convention in 1972, a National Black Assembly was established to exercise pressure on the Democratic and Republican parties.

Black Prince the nickname of ◊Edward, Prince of Wales, eldest son of Edward III of England.

Black Sea (Russian *Chernoye More*) inland sea in SE Europe, linked with the seas of Azov and Marmara, and via the Dardanelles with the Mediterranean. Uranium deposits beneath it are among the world's largest.

Black September a guerrilla splinter group of the ◊Palestine Liberation Organization formed in 1970. Operating from bases in Syria and Lebanon, it was responsible for the kidnappings at the Munich Olympics of 1972 that led to the deaths of 11 Israelis, and more recent hijack and bomb attempts. [from the month in which Palestinian guerrillas were expelled from Jordan by King Hussein]

Blackshirts *n.pl.* any fascist paramilitary organization. Originating with Mussolini's fascist Squadristi in the 1920s, the term was also applied to the Nazi SS (*Schutzstaffel*) and to the followers of Oswald Mosley's British Union of Fascists.

blacksmith *n.* a smith who works in iron.

blacksnake *n.* any of several species of snake. The blacksnake *Pseudechis porphyriacus* is a venomous snake of the cobra family found in damp forests and swamps in E Australia. The blacksnake *Coluber constrictor* from the E USA is a relative of the grass snake, growing up to 1.2 m/4 ft long, and without venom.

Black Stone in Islam, a sacred stone built into the E corner of the ◊Kaaba which is a focal point of the *hajj*, or pilgrimage, to Mecca. There are a number of stories concerning its origin, one of which states that it was sent to Earth at the time of the first man, Adam; Muhammad declared that it was given to Abraham by Gabriel. It has been suggested that it is of meteoric origin.

black stump in Australia, an imaginary boundary between civilization and the outback, as in the phrase *this side of the black stump*.

blackthorn *n.* a densely branched spiny European bush *Prunus spinosa*, family Rosaceae. It produces white blossom on black and leafless branches in early spring. Its sour, plumlike, blue-black fruit, the sloe, is used to flavour gin.

Black Thursday the day of the Wall Street stock-market crash, 29 Oct 1929, which precipitated the ◊Depression in the USA and throughout the world.

Blackwall Tunnel a road tunnel under the river Thames, London, linking the Bugsby Marshes (S) with the top end of the Isle of Dogs (N). The northbound tunnel, 7,056 km/4,410 ft long with an internal diameter of 24 ft, was built 1891–97 to a design by Sir Alexander Binnie; the southbound tunnel, 4,592 km/2,870 ft long with an internal diameter of 27.5 ft, was built 1960–67 to a design by Mott, Hay and Anderson.

Blackwell /'blækwel/ Elizabeth 1821–1910. US physician, born in England, the first woman to qualify in medicine in the USA (1849) and the first woman to be recognized as a qualified physician in the UK (1869).

black widow a North American spider *Latrodectus mactans*. The male is small and harmless, but the female is 1.3 cm/0.5 in long with a red patch below the abdomen and a powerful venomous bite. The bite causes pain and fever in human victims, but they usually recover.

bladder *n.* a sac in the bodies of humans and animals for holding liquids, especially the urinary bladder (see ◊urinary system); an animal's bladder, or a bag resembling this, inflated or otherwise prepared for various uses. —**bladderwort** *n.* any of a large genus *Utricularia* of carnivorous aquatic plants of the family Lentibulariaceae. They have leaves with bladders that entrap small aquatic animals. **bladderwrack** *n.* a seaweed with air-filled swellings among its fronds. [Old English]

blade *n.* 1. the cutting part of a knife etc.; the flat wide part of a spade, oar etc. 2. the flat narrow leaf of grasses; the broad part of a leaf, as distinct from its stalk. 3. a broad flattish bone. [Old English]

Blake /bleɪk/ William 1757–1827. English painter, engraver, poet, and mystic, a leading figure in the Romantic period. His visionary, symbolic poems include *Songs of Innocence* 1789 and *Songs of Experience* 1794. He engraved the text and illustrations for his works and hand-coloured them, mostly in watercolour. He also illustrated works by others, including John Milton and William Shakespeare, and created a highly personal style.

A Robin Red breast in a Cage
Puts all of Heaven in a Rage.

William Blake
Auguries of Innocence

---

blame *v.t.* to hold responsible and criticize (*for*); to fix the responsibility for (misfortunes etc.) *on* a person. —*n.* responsibility for a bad result or attribution of it to a person. —**blameless** *adj.*, **blameworthy** *adj.* [from Old French, ultimately = *blaspheme*]

Blamey /'bleɪmi/ Thomas Albert 1884–1951. The first Australian field marshal. Born in New South Wales, he served at Gallipoli, Turkey, and on the Western Front in World War I. In World War II he was commander in chief of the Allied Land Forces in the SW Pacific 1942–45.

Blanc /blɒŋ/ Louis 1811–1882. French socialist and journalist. In 1839 he founded the *Revue du progrès*, in which he published his *Organisation du travail*, advocating the establishment of cooperative workshops and other socialist schemes. He was a member of the provisional government of 1848 (see ◊revolutions of 1848) and from its fall lived in the UK until 1871.

blanch /blɑːntʃ/ *v.t./i.* 1. to make white by extracting the colour from or by depriving (plants) of light. 2. to peel (almonds) by scalding; to dip (vegetables) in boiling water. 3. to become pale with fear etc. [from Old French *blanc* = white]

blancmange /blə'mɒnʒ/ *n.* a flavoured jellylike pudding made with cornflour and milk. [from Old French = white food]

bland *adj.* mild in flavour or properties; insipid, dull; soothing in manner, suave. —**blandly** *adj.*, **blandness** *n.* [from Latin *blandus* = soft, caressing]

blandish /'blændɪʃ/ *v.t.* to flatter, to cajole. —**blandishment** *n.* (usually in *plural*) [from Old French *blandir* = flatter from Latin]

blank *adj.* 1. not written, printed, or recorded on; with spaces left for details or signature. 2. showing no interest or emotion. 3. sheer, unadorned. —*n.* 1. a blank space in a document etc.; an empty surface. 2. a dash put in place of an omitted word. 3. a blank cartridge. —*v.t.* to screen *off* or *out.* —**blank cartridge,** one containing no bullet. **blank cheque,** one with the amount left for the payee to fill in. **blank verse,** unrhymed verse, usually in iambic pentameter, or ten-syllable lines of five stresses. First used by the Italian Gian Giorgio Trissino in his tragedy *Sofonisba* 1514–15, it was introduced to England about 1540 by the Earl of Surrey, and developed by Christopher Marlowe. More recent exponents of blank verse in English include Thomas Hardy, T S Eliot, and Robert Frost. **draw a blank,** to be unsuccessful, to get no response. [from Old French *blanc* = white from Germanic]

blanket /'blæŋkɪt/ *n.* 1. a thick covering made of woollen or other fabric, used for warmth, chiefly as bedding. 2. a thick covering mass or layer. —*adj.* general, covering all cases or classes. —*v.t.* 1. to cover with a blanket. 2. to suppress (a scandal etc.). [from Old French diminutive of *blanc* = white]

Blanqui /blɒŋ'kiː/ Louis Auguste 1805–1881. French revolutionary politician. He formulated the theory of the 'dictatorship of the proletariat', used by Karl Marx, and spent a total of 33 years in prison for insurrection. Although in prison, he was elected president of the Commune of Paris in 1871. His followers, the Blanquists, joined with the Marxists in 1881.

Blantyre-Limbe /'blæntaɪə 'lɪmbeɪ/ chief industrial and commercial centre of Malawi, in the Shire highlands; population (1985) 355,000. It produces tea, coffee, rubber, tobacco, and textiles.

blare /bleə/ *v.i./t.* to make a loud sound like a trumpet; to utter loudly. —*n.* a blaring sound. [from Dutch, imitative]

blarney /'blɑːni/ *n.* deceptive flattery. —*v.t./i.* to use or subject to such flattery. [from *Blarney* Castle near Cork, Republic of Ireland, a stone of which is said to confer a cajoling tongue on anyone kissing it]

blasé /'blɑːzeɪ/ *adj.* bored or unimpressed, especially through familiarity. [French]

Blashford-Snell /'blæʃfəd 'snel/ John 1936– . English explorer and soldier. His expeditions have included the first descent and exploration of the Blue Nile in 1968; the journey from Alaska to Cape Horn, crossing the Darien Gap between Panama and Colombia for the first time 1971–72; and the first complete navigation of the Zaïre River, Africa, 1974–75.

Blasis /blæ'siː/ Carlo 1797–1878. Italian ballet teacher of French extraction. He was successful as a dancer in Paris and in Milan, where he established a dancing school in 1837. His celebrated treatise on the art of dancing, *Traité élémentaire, théoretique et pratique de l'art de la danse* 1820, forms the basis of classical dance training.

blaspheme /blæs'fiːm/ *v.t./i* to utter blasphemy against, to talk impiously. —**blasphemer** *n.* [from Old French from Latin from Greek *blasphēmeō* = speak ill of]

blasphemy /'blæsfəmi/ *n.* a written or spoken insult directed against religious belief or sacred things with deliberate intent to outrage believers. —**blasphemous** *adj.*

blast /blɑːst/ *n.* 1. an explosion, a destructive wave of air from this; a strong gust of wind etc. 2. the loud sound made by a trumpet, car horn etc. —*v.t.* 1. to blow up (rocks etc.) with explosives. 2. to blow destructively on, to wither or blight (*literary*, and in curses or as interjection of annoyance). —**(at) full blast,** at full capacity or speed. **blast off,** (of a rocket or spacecraft) to launch into space. **blastoff** *n.* this launching. [Old English]

blasted /'blɑːstɪd/ *adj.* cursed, damnable. —*adv.* damnably.

blast furnace a smelting furnace in which temperature is raised by the injection of an air blast. It is employed in the extraction of metals from their ores, chiefly pig iron from iron ore.

blastocyst *n.* in mammals, a stage in the development of

blast furnace

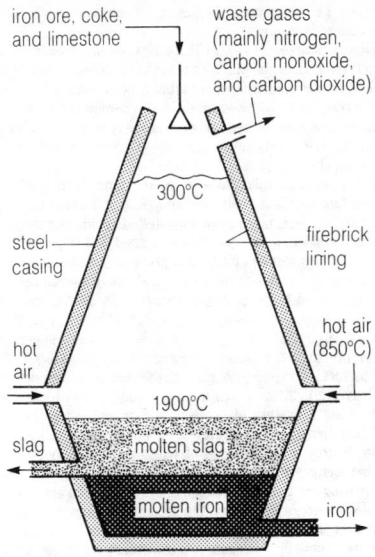

iron ore, coke, and limestone

waste gases (mainly nitrogen, carbon monoxide, and carbon dioxide)

300°C

steel casing

firebrick lining

hot air

hot air (850°C)

1900°C

slag   molten slag

molten iron   iron

the ◊embryo that is roughly equivalent to the ◊blastula of other animal groups.

blastomere *n*. in biology, a cell formed in the first stages of embryonic development, after the splitting of the fertilized ovum, but before the formation of the blastula or blastocyst.

blastula *n*. an early stage in the development of a fertilized egg, when the egg changes from a solid mass of cells (the morula) to a hollow ball of cells (the blastula), containing a fluid-filled cavity (the blastocoel). See also ◊embryology.

blatant /'bleɪtənt/ *adj*. flagrant, unashamed; loudly obtrusive. —**blatantly** *adv*. [originally = clamorous; coined by the poet Edmund Spenser]

blather /'blæðə/ *v.i.* (*colloquial*) to chatter foolishly. —*n*. (*colloquial*) foolish chatter. [from Old Norse]

Blaue Reiter, der /'blaʊə 'raɪtə/ a group of German Expressionist painters based in Munich, some of whom had left *die* ◊*Brücke*. They were interested in the value of colours, in folk art, and in the necessity of painting 'the inner, spiritual side of nature', but styles were highly varied. Wassily Kandinsky and Franz Marc published a book of their views in 1912, and there were two exhibitions (1911, 1912). [German = the blue rider]

blaze[1] *n*. 1. a bright flame or fire. 2. a brilliant display (*of* lights, colours, publicity). 3. a sudden outburst of emotion. —*v.i.* 1. to burn or shine fiercely. 2. to display sudden emotion, usually anger. —**blaze away**, to fire a gun continuously. [Old English = torch]

blaze[2] *n*. 1. a white mark on the face of an animal, especially a horse. 2. a mark made in the bark of a tree to indicate a route. —*v.t.* to mark (a tree or path) with blazes. —**blaze a trail**, to show the way for others to follow.

blaze[3] *v.t.* to proclaim. [from Middle Low German and Middle Dutch]

blazer /'bleɪzə/ *n*. a light jacket often in the colours, or with the badge, of a team or school.

blazon /'bleɪzən/ *n*. a heraldic shield, a coat of arms. —*v.t.* to proclaim; to describe or paint (a coat of arms); to inscribe with arms, names etc., in colours. —**blazonry** *n*. [from Old French *blason* = shield]

bleach *v.t./i.* to whiten by chemicals or exposure to sunlight. —*n*. a bleaching substance or process. [Old English]

bleaching *n*. the decolorization of coloured materials. The two main types of bleaching agent are the **oxidizing bleaches**, which add oxygen and remove hydrogen, and include the ultraviolet rays in sunlight, hydrogen peroxide, and chlorine in household bleaches, and the **reducing**

bleaches, which add hydrogen or remove oxygen, for example sulphur dioxide.

bleaching powder a substance made by reacting chlorine with solid slaked lime (calcium hydroxide, $Ca(OH)_2$). It is an oxidizing bleach, the active ingredient of which is the chlorate(I) ion (hypochlorite, OCl^-). Under the action of light this ion slowly releases oxygen, which prevents the growth of bacteria. The same reaction makes the addition of chlorine an effective treatment for drinking water and swimming baths, as chlorine and water react to form hypochloric acid, $HOCl$, and hydrochloric acid.

bleak[1] *adj*. 1. cold and windswept. 2. unpromising, dreary, grim. —**bleakly** *adv.*, **bleakness** *n*. [originally = pale]

bleak[2] *n*. a freshwater fish *Alburnus alburnus* of the carp family. It grows up to to 20 cm/8 in long and lives in still or slow-running clear water in Europe, including Britain.

bleary *adj*. dim-sighted from watering of the eyes. —**blearily** *adv*. [from Low German]

bleat *n*. the tremulous cry of a sheep, goat, or calf. —*v.i.* to utter this cry; to say or speak feebly or plaintively. [Old English, imitative]

bleed *v.t./i* (*past and past participle* **bled**) 1. to leak blood or other fluid; to run. 2. to draw off blood or surplus fluid from; (*colloquial*) to extort money from. —*n*. an act of bleeding; see ◊haemorrhage. [Old English]

bleep *v.i.* to emit an intermittent high-pitched signal. —*n*. such a signal. [imitative]

blemish /'blemɪʃ/ *v.t.* to spoil the beauty or perfection of. —*n*. a defect, a flaw. [from Old French *blesmir* = make pale]

blench *v.i.* to flinch. [Old English = deceive]

blend *v.t./i.* 1. to mix (different varieties) to get a required flavour, texture etc. 2. to mingle or merge (*with*). 3. (of colours etc.) to pass imperceptibly into each other. 4. to harmonize. —*n*. a mixture of different varieties. [from Old Norse]

blende /blend/ *n*. native zinc sulphide. [German (*blenden* = deceive, because while often resembling lead ore it yielded no lead)]

blender *n*. a device for blending soft or liquid foods.

blenny *n*. any fish of the family Blenniidae, mostly small fishes found near rocky shores, with elongated slimy bodies tapering from head to tail, no scales, and long pelvic fins set far forward. [from Latin from Greek *blennos* = mucus]

Blériot /'bleriəʊ/ Louis 1872–1936. French aviator who, in a 24-horsepower monoplane of his own construction, made the first flight across the English Channel on 25 July 1909.

blesbok *n*. an African antelope *Damaliscus albifrons* about 1 m/3 ft high, with curved horns, brownish body, and a white blaze on the face. It was seriously depleted in the wild at the end of the 19th century. A few protected herds survive in South Africa. It is farmed for meat.

bless *v.t.* 1. to invoke God's favour on; to sanctify by the sign of the cross; to consecrate (food etc.). 2. to glorify (God); to attribute one's good luck to (one's stars etc.). —**be blessed with**, to be fortunate enough to possess. [Old English]

blessed /'blesɪd/ *pred. adj.* holy; beatified; (*ironic slang*) cursed.

blessing *n*. 1. an invocation of God's favour; a grace before or after a meal. 2. something one is thankful for, a benefit.

blew past of **blow**.

blewits /'bluːɪts/ *n*. an edible mushroom with a lilac stem.

Bligh /blaɪ/ William 1754–1817. English admiral. Bligh accompanied Captain James ◊Cook on his second voyage around the world 1772–74, and in 1787 commanded HMS *Bounty* on an expedition to the Pacific. On the return voyage the crew mutinied in 1789, and Bligh was cast adrift in a boat with 18 men. He was appointed governor of New South Wales in 1805, where his discipline again provoked a mutiny in 1808 (the Rum Rebellion). He returned to Britain, and was made an admiral in 1811.

blight /blaɪt/ *n*. 1. a disease causing plants to shrivel up etc.; a fungus or aphid causing it. 2. an obscure malignant influence. —*v.t.* 1. to affect (plants) with blight. 2. to frustrate or spoil.

blighter /'blaɪtə/ *n*. (*colloquial*) a person or thing, especially an annoying one.

Blighty /'blaɪtɪ/ *n*. (*military slang*) home (especially Britain) after service abroad; a wound ensuring one's return home.

[from Hindi = foreign, European]

blimey /'blaɪmɪ/ interjection of astonishment, contempt etc. [corruption of *(God) blind me*]

blimp n. 1. or **dirigible** a small nonrigid ◊airship. 2. a soundproof cover for a cine camera. 3. **(Colonel) Blimp,** a die-hard reactionary (named after a cartoon character representing a pompous obese elderly man).

blind /blaɪnd/ adj. 1. lacking the power of sight; (of a corner etc.) not allowing a clear view of the road ahead; (of flying) relying solely on instruments. 2. without foresight or discernment; reckless; not governed by purpose. —v.t. to deprive of sight; to dazzle with bright light; to beguile so as to rob of judgement; to overawe. —n. 1. a screen for a window; a shop's awning. 2. a pretext, a ruse. —**blind alley,** a street closed at one end. **blind date,** a social engagement between a man and woman who have not previously met. **blind spot,** a spot in the ◊eye insensitive to light; an area in which discernment is lacking. Where the optic nerve and blood vessels pass through the retina no visual image can be formed since there are no light-sensitive cells in this part of the retina. **blind stitch** etc., sewing visible on one side only. **turn a blind eye to,** to pretend not to notice. —**blindly** adv., **blindness** n. [Old English]

blindfold adj. & adv. with the eyes bandaged. —n. a cloth placed over a person's eyes. —v.t. to block the sight of with a blindfold. [originally *blindfelled* = struck blind]

blindworm n. another name for a ◊slowworm. [from its small eyes]

blink v.t./i. 1. to move the eyelids quickly down and up; to look with eyes opening and shutting. 2. to shine with an unsteady or intermittent light. 3. to shirk consideration of (facts etc.). —n. 1. an act of blinking. 2. a momentary gleam. [Old English]

blinkers n.pl. screens on a horse's bridle to prevent it seeing sideways.

blinking adj. & adv. (slang, euphemism) bloody (= damned).

blip n. a spot of light on a radar screen; a quick popping sound. —v.i. (**-pp-**) to make a blip. [imitative]

bliss /blɪs/ n. perfect happiness; the perfect joy of heaven. —**blissful** adj., **blissfully** adv. [Old English from Germanic = blithe]

Bliss Arthur (Drummond) 1891–1975. English composer who became Master of the Queen's Musick in 1953. Works include *A Colour Symphony* 1922, music for ballets *Checkmate* 1937, *Miracle in the Gorbals* 1944, and *Adam Zero* 1946; an opera *The Olympians* 1949; and dramatic film music, including *Things to Come* 1935.

blister n. a bubble on the skin filled with watery fluid, caused by friction etc.; a similar swelling on painted wood etc. —v.t./i. 1. to develop blisters; to raise blisters on. 2. to criticize sharply.

blithe /blaɪð/ adj. joyous, carefree; casual, careless. [Old English]

blitz /blɪts/ n. a sudden intensive (usually aerial) attack; **the Blitz,** in Britain during World War II, the attempted saturation bombing of London by the German air force between Sept 1940 and May 1941. —v.t. to attack or destroy by a blitz. [abbreviation of *blitzkrieg*]

blitzkrieg /'blɪtskriːg/ n. an intensive campaign intended to bring about a speedy victory, especially as used by Germany against various countries of Europe at the beginning of World War II 1939–41. [German = lightning war]

Blixen /'blɪksən/ Karen, born Karen Dinesen 1885–1962. Danish writer. Her autobiography *Out of Africa* 1937 is based on her experience of running a coffee plantation in Kenya. She wrote fiction, mainly in English, under the pen name Isak Dinesen.

blizzard /'blɪzəd/ n. a severe snowstorm.

bloat v.t. to cause to swell out, to make turgid. [from obsolete *bloat* = swollen]

bloated adj. puffed up with pride of wealth, self-indulgence etc.

bloater n. a herring half-dried in smoke.

blob n. a thick drop; a small round mass. [imitative]

bloc /blɒk/ n. a combination of countries, parties etc., to foster a common interest. [French = block]

Bloch /blɒk/ Ernest 1880–1959. US composer, born in Geneva, Switzerland. He went to the USA in 1916 and became founder-director of the Cleveland Institute of Music 1920–25. Among his works are the lyrical drama *Macbeth*

1910, *Schelomo* for cello and orchestra 1916, five string quartets, and *Suite Hébraique*, for viola and orchestra 1953. He often used themes based on Jewish liturgical music and folk song.

Bloch Konrad 1912– . US chemist whose research concerned cholesterol. Making use of the ◊radioisotope carbon-14 (the radioactive form of carbon), he was able to follow the complex steps by which the body chemically transforms acetic acid into cholesterol. For his ability in this field Bloch shared the 1964 Nobel Prize for Medicine with Feodor Lynen (1911–).

block n. 1. a solid piece of wood, stone, or other hard substance; this as used for chopping or hammering on, or from which horses are mounted; **the block,** that on which condemned people were beheaded. 2. a large building divided into flats or offices. 3. a group of buildings bounded by streets. 4. an obstruction; an inability or mental resistance caused by psychological factors. 5. a large section of seats, shares etc. as a unit; (*attributive*) made or treated as a large unit. 6. a piece of wood or metal engraved for printing. 7. a pulley mounted in a case. —v.t. 1. to obstruct or impede; to restrict the use or conversion of (currency). 2. to sketch *in* or *out* roughly. —**block and tackle,** a system of ◊pulleys and ropes, especially for lifting things. **blockbuster** n. a bomb powerful enough to destroy a whole block of buildings; a film, book etc. that has great commercial success. **block diagram,** one showing the general arrangement of parts in an apparatus. **block letters,** letters written separately as in print, usually in capitals. **block mountain,** one formed by faults. **block vote,** a vote by a delegate to a conference etc. proportional in value to the number of persons represented. [from Old French from Low Dutch]

blockade n. the cutting-off of a place by hostile forces by land, sea or air so as to prevent any movement to or fro, in order to compel a surrender without attack. No nation has the right to declare a blockade unless it has the power to enforce it, according to international law. The Declaration of London 1909 laid down that a blockade must not be extended beyond the coasts and ports belonging to or occupied by an enemy. See also ◊Berlin blockade. —v.t. to subject to a blockade.

blockage /'blɒkɪdʒ/ n. 1. something that blocks. 2. the state of being blocked.

blockhead n. a slow-witted person.

blockhouse n. a reinforced concrete military shelter; a timber building used as a fort, with loopholes for guns.

Bloemfontein /'bluːmfənteɪn/ capital of the Orange Free State and judicial capital of the Republic of South Africa; population (1985) 204,000. The city, founded in 1846, produces canned fruit, glassware, furniture, and plastics.

Blok /blɒk/ Alexander Alexandrovich 1880–1921. Russian poet who, as a follower of the French Symbolist movement, used words for their symbolic rather than actual meaning. He backed the 1917 Revolution, as in his poems *The Twelve* 1918 and *The Scythians* 1918, the latter appealing to the West to join in the revolution.

bloke n. (*colloquial*) a man, a fellow. [Shelta]

Blomberg /'blɒmbeək/ Werner von 1878–1946. German soldier and Nazi politician, minister of defence 1933–35, minister of war, and head of the *Wehrmacht* (army) 1935–38 under Hitler's chancellorship. He was discredited by his marriage to a prostitute and dismissed in Jan 1938, enabling Hitler to exercise more direct control over the armed forces. In spite of his removal from office, Blomberg was put on trial for war crimes in 1946 at Nuremberg.

Blomdahl /'blɒmdɑːl/ Karl-Birger 1916–1968. Swedish composer of ballets and symphonies in expressionist style. His opera *Aniara* 1959 incorporates electronic music and is set in a spaceship.

blond adj. (of a woman or her hair usually **blonde**) fair-haired; (of hair) fair. —n. a fair-haired person. [from French from Latin = yellow]

blood /blʌd/ n. 1. the fluid, usually red, circulating in the arteries, veins, and capillaries of vertebrate animals. In humans it makes up 5% of the body weight, occupying a volume of 5.5 l/10 pt in the average adult. It consists of a colourless, transparent liquid called **plasma**, containing microscopic cells of three main varieties. **Red cells** (erythrocytes) form nearly half the volume of the blood, with 5 billion cells per litre. Their red colour is caused by ◊haemoglobin. **White cells** (◊leucocytes) are of various kinds. Some (phagocytes) ingest invading bacteria and so protect the body from disease; these also help to repair injured tissues. Others (◊lymphocytes) produce antibodies, which help provide immunity. Blood **platelets** (thrombocytes) assist in the clotting of blood. **2.** the taking of life. **3.** passion, temperament. **4.** race, descent, parentage; blood relations. **5.** a dandy. —*v.t.* to give (hounds) their first taste of blood; to initiate (a person). —**blood bath,** a massacre. **blood count,** the number of corpuscles in a given volume of blood. **blood-curdling** *adj.* extremely horrific. **blood money,** a fine paid by a killer to the victim's next of kin. **blood orange,** a variety of orange with red-streaked pulp. **blood poisoning,** infection of the bloodstream by bacteria. **blood relation,** one related by birth, not marriage. **blood sports,** sports involving the killing of animals. **blood-stained** *adj.* stained with blood; guilty of bloodshed. **in cold blood,** with premeditated violence. [Old English]

Blood Thomas 1618–1680. Irish adventurer, known as Colonel Blood, who attempted to steal the crown jewels from the Tower of London, England, in 1671.

blood clotting a complex series of events that prevents excessive bleeding after injury. The result is the formation of a net of fibres over the cut blood vessels, made up of the protein ◊fibrin.

blood group the classification of human blood types according to antigenic activity. Red blood cells of one individual may carry molecules on their surface that act as ◊antigens in another individual whose red blood cells lack these molecules. The two main antigens are designated A and B. These give rise to four blood groups: having A only (A), having B only (B), having both (AB), and having neither (O). Each of these groups may or may not contain the ◊rhesus factor. Correct typing of blood groups is vital in transfusion, since incompatible types of donor and recipient blood will result in blood clotting, with possible death of the recipient.

bloodhound *n.* an ancient breed of dog. Black and tan in colour, it has long, pendulous ears and a distinctive wrinkled head and face. It grows to a height of about 65 cm/26 in at the shoulder. The breed originated as a hunting dog in Belgium in the Middle Ages, and its excellent powers of scent have been employed in tracking and criminal detection from very early times.

bloodless *adj.* **1.** without blood, pale from loss of blood. **2.** involving no bloodshed. **3.** without vitality; unemotional.

blood pressure the pressure, or tension, of the blood against the inner walls of blood vessels, especially the arteries, due to the muscular pumping activity of the heart. Abnormally high blood pressure (see ◊hypertension) may be associated with various conditions or arise with no obvious cause; abnormally low blood pressure occurs in ◊shock.

bloodshed *n.* the spilling of blood, slaughter.

bloodshot *adj.* (of eyeballs) tinged with blood.

bloodstock *n.* pedigree horses.

bloodstream *n.* the blood circulating in the body.

bloodsucker *n.* **1.** a creature that sucks blood, a leech. **2.** an extortionate person.

blood test the laboratory evaluation of a blood sample. There are numerous blood tests, from simple typing to establish the ◊blood group to sophisticated biochemical assays of substances, such as hormones, present in the blood only in minute quantities.

bloodthirsty *adj.* eager for bloodshed.

blood vessel a specialist tube that carries blood around the body of multicellular animals. Blood vessels are highly evolved in vertebrates, where the three main types, the arteries, veins, and capillaries, are all adapted for their particular role within the body.

bloody /'blʌdɪ/ *adj.* **1.** of, like, or smeared with blood. **2.** involving bloodshed; cruel, bloodthirsty. **3.** (*slang*) cursed, damnable. —*adv.* (*slang*) damnably. —*v.t.* to stain with blood. **bloody-minded** *adj.* deliberately uncooperative. —**bloodily** *adv.,* **bloodiness** *n.*

bloom *n.* **1.** the flower of a plant (especially one grown chiefly for this). **2.** greatest beauty or perfection; freshness; flush, glow. **3.** the whitish powdery or waxlike coating over the surface of certain fruits that easily rubs off when handled. It often contains ◊yeasts that live on the sugars in

blood

red cells

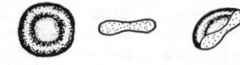

white cells

platelets

blood allowed to stand

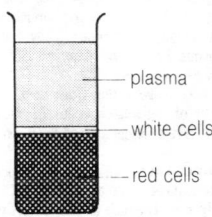

the fruit. **4.** a rapid increase in number of certain species of algae found in lakes and ponds. —*v.i.* **1.** to bear blooms, to be in bloom. **2.** to be in full beauty or vigour. —**in bloom,** flowering. [from Old Norse]

Bloom /blu:m/ Claire 1931– . British actress who first made her reputation on the stage in Shakespearean roles. Her films include *Richard III* 1956 and *The Brothers Karamazov* 1958, and television appearances include *Brideshead Revisited* 1980.

bloomer /'blu:mə/ *n.* (*slang*) a blunder.

Bloomer Amelia Jenks 1818–1894. US campaigner for women's rights. In 1849, when unwieldy crinolines were the fashion, she introduced a costume called 'rational dress' for women, consisting of a short jacket, full skirt reaching to just below the knee, and loose trousers gathered at the ankles, which became known as bloomers. She published the magazine *The Lily* 1849–54, which campaigned for women's rights and dress reform, and lectured with Susan B ◊Anthony in New York, USA.

bloomers *n.pl.* **1.** (*colloquial*) knickers with legs. **2.** loose knee-length trousers formerly worn by women. [from Amelia *Bloomer*]

blooming *adj.* & *adv.* **1.** in bloom; flourishing. **2.** (*slang,* expressing mild annoyance or dislike) confounded.

Bloomsbury Group a group of writers and artists based in ◊Bloomsbury, London, in the early 20th century. The group included the artists Duncan Grant and Vanessa Bell, and the writers Lytton ◊Strachey and Leonard and Virginia ◊Woolf. [from *Bloomsbury,* central London district]

blossom /'blɒsəm/ *n.* a flower or mass of flowers, especially of a fruit tree. —*v.i.* **1.** to open into blossom. **2.** to evolve or mature *into.* **3.** to thrive. [Old English]

blot *n.* **1.** a small stain of ink etc. **2.** a disfiguring feature. **3.** something bringing disgrace. —*v.t.* (-tt-) **1.** to stain with ink or other liquid. **2.** to dry with blotting paper. —**blot out,** to obliterate; to obscure from view. **blotting paper,** absorbent paper for drying wet ink.

blotch /blɒtʃ/ *n.* a discoloured patch on the skin; any large irregular patch of colour. —**blotchy** *adj.* [from obsolete *plotch* and *blot*]

blotter *n.* a pad of blotting paper.

blotto /'blɒtəʊ/ *adj.* (*slang*) very drunk.

blouse /blaʊz/ *n.* 1. a shirtlike garment worn by women. 2. a waist-length jacket forming part of a soldier's or aviator's battledress. [French]

blow[1] /bləʊ/ *v.t./i* (*past* **blew** /blu:/; *past participle* **blown** /bləʊn/) 1. to direct a current of air from the mouth; to move rapidly as a current of air; to breathe hard; (of a whale) to eject air and water when surfacing. 2. to sound (a wind instrument), (of such an instrument) to sound; to send out (bubbles etc.) or clear (the nose) by breathing. 3. to break open with explosives, to send flying (*off* etc.) by explosion; to melt (a fuse) or be melted under an overload. 4. to propel by a current of air; to shape (molten glass) by blowing. 5. (*slang*) to reveal (a secret etc.). 6. (*slang*, especially as *interjection*) to curse. 7. (*slang*) to squander; to bungle. —*n.* an act of blowing; exposure to fresh air. —**blow-dry** *v.t.* to use a hand-held drier to style washed hair while drying it. **blowhole** *n.* a hole for blowing or breathing through; an outlet for the escape of air or gas etc. **blow one's own trumpet**, to boast. **blowout** *n.* an uncontrolled eruption of oil or gas from a well; a burst in a tyre; (*colloquial*) a large meal. **blow up**, to shatter or be shattered in an explosion; to inflate with air; (*colloquial*) to enlarge (a photograph). [Old English]

blow[2] *n.* a hard stroke with the hand or a weapon; a sudden shock or misfortune.

Blow John 1648–1708. English composer. He taught ◊Purcell, and wrote church music, for example the anthem 'I Was Glad when They Said unto Me' 1697. His masque *Venus and Adonis* 1685 is sometimes called the first English opera.

blowfly *n.* a fly, genus *Calliphora*, also known as bluebottle, or of the related genus *Lucilia*, when it is greenbottle. It lays its eggs in dead flesh, on which the maggots feed.

blowlamp *n.* a portable burner producing a very hot flame that can be directed on to a small area.

blowpipe *n.* 1. a tube for blowing air through, to increase the heat of a flame or in glass-blowing. 2. a tube through which poisonous darts are blown.

blowzy /blaʊzi/ *adj.* red-faced, coarse-looking; slatternly. [from obsolete *blowze* = beggar's wench]

blubber *n.* a thick layer of ◊fat under the skin of marine mammals, which provides an energy store and an effective insulating layer, preventing the loss of body heat to the surrounding water. Blubber has been used (when boiled down) in engineering, food processing, cosmetics, and printing, but all of these products can now be produced synthetically, thus saving the lives of animals. —*v.i.* to sob noisily. —*adj.* (of lips) thick, swollen. [probably imitative]

Blücher /blu:kə/ Gebhard Leberecht von 1742–1819. Prussian general and field marshal, popular as 'Marshal Forward'. He took an active part in the patriotic movement, and in the War of German Liberation defeated the French as commander in chief at Leipzig in 1813, crossed the Rhine to Paris in 1814, and was made prince of Wahlstadt (Silesia).

bludgeon /blʌdʒən/ *n.* a short stick with a heavy end. —*v.t.* 1. to beat with a bludgeon. 2. to coerce.

blue /blu:/ *adj.* 1. having the colour of the clear sky. 2. sad, despondent. 3. indecent. —*n.* 1. blue colour or pigment; blue clothes or material. 2. the distinction of representing Oxford or Cambridge University in a sport; one holding this. 3. (in *plural*) a despondent state; ◊blues music. —*v.t.* (*participle* **blueing**) 1. to make blue. 2. (*colloquial*) to squander. —**blue baby**, one with congenital blueness of the skin from a heart defect. **blue blood**, aristocratic birth. **blue book**, in the UK, a Parliamentary or Privy Council report. **blue cheese,** cheese with veins of blue mould. **blue-collar worker,** a manual or industrial worker. **blue-eyed boy,** (*colloquial*) a favourite. **blue-pencil** *v.t.* to delete with a blue pencil, to censor. **Blue Peter,** a blue flag with a white square raised when a ship leaves port. **Blue Riband** (*or* **Ribbon**) **of the Atlantic,** a trophy for the ship making the fastest sea crossing of the Atlantic. **blue ribbon,** the ribbon of the Garter; a small strip of blue ribbon formerly worn by certain abstainers from alcoholic beverages; (*or* **riband**) the highest honour in any sphere; for example, the blue riband of horse racing in the UK is held by the winner of the Derby. **blue tit,** a tit with bright blue tail, wings, and top of head. **blue whale,** a rorqual, the largest known living mammal. **once in a blue moon,** very rarely. **out of the**

blue, unexpectedly. —**blueness** *n.* [from Old French *bleu* from Germanic]

Bluebeard /blu:biəd/ a folk-tale character, popularized by the writer Charles Perrault in France about 1697, and historically identified with Gilles de ◊Rais. He murdered six wives for disobeying his command not to enter a locked room, but was himself killed before he could murder the seventh.

bluebell *n.* a plant with blue bell-shaped flowers, the wild hyacinth *Endymion nonscriptus* or (*Scottish*) harebell *Campanula rotundifolia*.

bluebird *n.* three species of a North American bird, genus *Sialia*, belonging to the thrush subfamily, Turdinae. The eastern bluebird *S. sialis* is regarded as the herald of spring. About 18 cm/7 in long, it has a reddish breast, the upper plumage being sky-blue, and a distinctive song.

bluebottle *n.* a large buzzing ◊blowfly with a blue body.

bluebuck *n.* any of several species of antelope, including the blue ◊duiker *Cephalophus monticola* of South Africa, about 33 cm/13 in high. The male of the Indian ◊nilgai antelope is also known as the bluebuck.

blue chip in business and finance, a stock that is considered strong and reliable in terms of the dividend yield and capital value. Blue-chip companies are favoured by stock-market investors more interested in security than risk taking.

bluegrass *n.* 1. a dense, spreading grass of the genus *Poa*, which is blue-tinted and grows in clumps. Various species are known from the northern hemisphere. Kentucky bluegrass *P. pratensis*, introduced from Europe, provides pasture for horses. 2. a country-music style of the Kentucky region, typically featuring fast banjo and guitar picking and harmony singing.

blue-green algae single-celled, primitive organisms that resemble bacteria in their internal cell organization, sometimes joined together in colonies or filaments. Blue-green algae are among the oldest known living organisms; remains have been found in rocks up to 3.5 billion years old. They are widely distributed in aquatic habitats, on the damp surfaces of rocks and trees, and in the soil.

blue gum an Australian tree *Eucalyptus globulus* of the myrtle family, with bluish bark, a chief source of eucalyptus oil. It is cultivated extensively in California.

Blue Mountains part of the ◊Great Divide, New South Wales, Australia, ranging 600–1,100 m/2,000–3,600 ft and blocking Sydney from the interior until the crossing in 1813 by surveyor William Lawson, Gregory Blaxland, and William Wentworth.

Blue Nile (Arabic *Bahr el Azraq*) river rising in the mountains of Ethiopia. Flowing W then N for 2,000 km/1,250 mi, it eventually meets the White Nile at Khartoum. The river is dammed at Roseires where a hydroelectric scheme produces 70% of Sudan's electricity.

blueprint *n.* a blue-and-white photographic print of plans, technical drawings etc.; a detailed plan.

Blue Ridge Mountains range extending from West Virginia to Georgia, USA, and including Mount Mitchell 2,045 m/6,712 ft; part of the ◊Appalachians.

blues *n.pl.* African-American music that originated in the rural South in the late 19th century, characterized by a 12-bar construction and often melancholy lyrics. Blues guitar and vocal styles have played a vital part in the development of jazz and pop music in general.

blue shift in astronomy, a manifestation of the ◊Doppler effect in which an object appears bluer when it is moving towards the observer or the observer is moving towards it (blue light is of a higher frequency than other colours in the spectrum). The blue shift is the opposite of the ◊red shift.

bluestocking *n.* an intellectual woman. [from the '*Blue Stocking* Club', 18th-century English literary coterie]

bluff[1] *v.t./i.* to make pretence of strength etc. to gain an advantage; to deceive by this. —*n.* an act of bluffing. [originally a term in the game of poker, from Dutch *bluffen* = brag]

bluff[2] *adj.* 1. (of cliffs etc.) having a vertical or steep broad front. 2. frank or abrupt and hearty in manner. —*n.* a bluff cliff or headland.

bluish /blu:ɪʃ/ *adj.* fairly blue.

Blum /blu:m/ Léon 1872–1950. French politician. He was converted to socialism by the ◊Dreyfus affair in 1899 and in 1936 became the first socialist prime minister of France.

He was again premier for a few weeks in 1938. Imprisoned under the ◊Vichy government in 1942 as a danger to French security, he was released by the Allies in 1945. He again became premier for a few weeks in 1946.

blunder *v.i.* to make a serious or foolish mistake; to move clumsily and uncertainly. —*n.* a serious or foolish mistake.

blunderbuss /'blʌndəbəs/ *n.* a type of muzzle-loading, usually flintlock, gun for close-range use, common in the 18th century, with a flared muzzle, firing many balls at one shot. [from Dutch = thunder-gun]

blunt /'blʌnt/ *adj.* **1.** without a sharp edge or point, not sharp. **2.** abrupt and outspoken. —*v.t.* to make blunt or less sharp. —**bluntly** *adv.*, **bluntness** *n.*

Blunt Anthony 1907–1983. British art historian and double agent. As a Cambridge lecturer, he recruited for the Soviet secret service and, as a member of the British Secret Service 1940–45, passed information to the USSR. In 1951 he assisted the defection to the USSR of the British agents Guy ◊Burgess and Donald Maclean (1913–1983). He was the author of many respected works on French and Italian art. Unmasked in 1964, he was given immunity after his confession.

blur *v.t.* (-rr-) to make or become less distinct; to smear (writing etc.). —*n.* **1.** a thing seen or heard indistinctly. **2.** a smear.

blurb *n.* descriptive or commendatory matter, especially a description of a book printed on its jacket. [said to have been originated in 1907 by Gelett Burgess (1866–1951), US humorist]

blurt *v.t.* (usually with *out*) to utter abruptly or tactlessly. [imitative]

blush *v.i.* **1.** to develop a pink tinge in the face from shame or embarrassment; to be ashamed or embarrassed *to*. **2.** to be red or pink. —*n.* an act of blushing; a rosy glow. [Old English]

bluster *v.i.* to behave noisily or boisterously; (of winds etc.) to blow fiercely. —*n.* noisy self-assertive talk, threats. —**blustery** *adj.* [imitative]

Blyth /blaɪð/ Charles 'Chay' 1940– . British sailing adventurer who rowed across the Atlantic with Capt John Ridgeway in 1966 and sailed solo around the world in a westerly direction 1970–71. In 1973–74 he sailed around the world with a crew in the opposite direction, and in 1977 he made a record-breaking transatlantic crossing from Cape Verde to Antigua.

Blyton /'blaɪtn/ Enid 1897–1968. English writer of children's books. She created the character Noddy and the adventures of the 'Famous Five' and 'Secret Seven', but has been criticized by educationalists for social, racial, and sexual stereotyping.

BMA abbreviation of British Medical Association.

BMR abbreviation of ◊basal metabolic rate.

BMX *n.* **1.** organized bicycle racing on a dirt track. **2.** a kind of bicycle for use in this. [abbreviation of *bicycle moto-cross*]

BNF abbreviation of British Nuclear Fuels.

boa /'bəʊə/ *n.* any of various nonvenomous snakes of the family Boidae, found mainly in tropical and subtropical parts of the New World. Boas feed mainly on small mammals and birds. They catch these in their teeth or kill them by constriction (crushing the creature within their coils until it suffocates). The **boa constrictor** *Constrictor constrictor* can grow up to 5.5 m/18.5 ft long, but rarely reaches more than 4 m/12 ft. Other boas include the **anaconda** and the **emerald tree boa** *Boa canina*, about 2 m/6 ft long and bright green. **2.** a woman's long furry or feathered wrap for the throat. [Latin]

Boadicea /bəʊədi'siːə/ an alternative spelling of British queen ◊Boudicca.

boar *n.* **1.** a wild member of the pig family, such as the Eurasian wild boar *Sus scrofa*, from which domestic pig breeds derive. The wild boar is sturdily built, being 1.5 m/4.5 ft long and 1 m/3 ft high, and possesses formidable tusks. Of gregarious nature and mainly woodland-dwelling, it feeds on roots, nuts, insects, and some carrion. It was formerly common in forested areas of Europe. **2.** an uncastrated male domestic pig. [Old English]

board *n.* **1.** a flat, thin piece of sawn timber, usually long and narrow; a flat piece of wood or other firm substance used in games, for posting notices etc. **2.** material resembling boards, made of compressed fibres; thick, stiff card used for book covers. **3.** provision of meals, usually for

payment. **4.** the directors of a company or other official group meeting together. **5.** (in *plural*) a theatre stage, the acting profession. —*v.t./i.* **1.** to go aboard (a ship, aircraft etc.). **2.** to cover or close *up* with boards. **3.** to provide with or receive meals, usually for payment. —**board game,** a game played on a specially marked board. **on board,** on or on to a ship, aircraft, oil rig etc. [Old English]

boarder *n.* one who boards with a person, especially a pupil who boards at a boarding school.

boarding house a house at which board and lodging may be obtained for payment.

boarding school a school offering board and lodging as well as tuition to its students.

boardroom *n.* a room in which a board of directors etc. regularly meet.

boardsailing *n.* another name for ◊windsurfing, a watersport combining elements of surfing and sailing, also called sailboarding.

boast *v.t./i.* to speak with great pride and try to impress people, to extol one's own excellence etc.; to be the proud possessor of. —*n.* an act of boasting; something one boasts of. [from Anglo-French]

boastful *adj.* boasting frequently, full of boasting. —**boastfully** *adv.*, **boastfulness** *n.*

boat *n.* **1.** a small vessel propelled on water by paddle, oars, sail, or engine; (*loosely*) a ship; (*US*) a sea-going vessel. **2.** a boat-shaped vessel for gravy etc. —*v.i.* to go in a boat, especially for pleasure. —**boathook** *n.* a long pole with a hook and spike at the end for moving boats. **boathouse,** a shed at the water's edge in which boats are kept. **boat train,** one timed to catch a boat. **in the same boat,** suffering the same troubles. [Old English]

boater *n.* a flat-topped straw hat with a brim.

boatman *n.* (*plural* boatmen) one who conveys by boat or hires out boats.

boat people any who leave their country surreptitiously by boat, especially the Vietnamese who left after the reunification of Vietnam in 1975. 160,000 Vietnamese fled to Hong Kong, many being attacked at sea by Thai pirates, and in 1989 50,000 remained there in cramped, squalid refugee camps. The UK government began forced repatriation in 1990.

Boat Race an annual UK rowing race between the crews of Oxford and Cambridge universities. It is held during the Easter vacation over a 6.8 km/4.25 mi course on the river Thames between Putney and Mortlake, SW London.

boatswain /'bəʊsən/ *n.* a ship's officer in charge of the crew, rigging etc.

bob¹ *v.i.* (-bb-) to make a jerky movement, to move quickly up and down; to curtsy quickly. —*n.* a bobbing movement. —**bob up,** (*colloquial*) to appear or re-emerge suddenly.

bob² *n.* **1.** a hairstyle in which the hair is cut short to hang evenly. **2.** a weight on a pendulum. —*v.t.* to cut (the hair) in a bob.

bob³ *n.* (*plural* the same) (*slang*) a shilling, five pence.

bobbin /'bɒbɪn/ *n.* a cylinder holding a spool of thread in machine sewing, lace-making etc. [from French]

bobble *n.* a small, ornamental woolly ball.

bobby /'bɒbi/ *n.* (*British, colloquial*) a policeman. [from Sir Robert Peel, home secretary at the passing of the Metropolitan Police Act, 1828]

bobcat *n.* a wild cat *Felis rufa* living in a variety of habitats from S Canada through to S Mexico. It is similar to the lynx, but only 75 cm/2.5 ft long, with reddish fur and less well-developed ear tufts.

bobolink *n.* a North American songbird *Dolichonyx oryzivorus*. [from the distinctive call of the male]

bobsleigh /'bɒbsleɪ/ *n.* or **bobsled** a sleigh with two axles, each of which has two runners, steered either by ropes or by a wheel; the winter sport in which such sleighs, normally crewed by four or two persons, are guided down a specially prepared descending track of solid ice with banked bends at speeds of up to 130 kph/80 mph. —**bobsleighing, bobsledding** *n.* It was introduced as an Olympic event in 1924 and world championships were held every year since 1931.

bobstay *n.* a rope holding the bowsprit down.

bobtail *n.* a docked tail, a horse or dog having such a tail.

Boccaccio /bɒ'kɑːtʃiəʊ/ Giovanni 1313–1375. Italian poet, chiefly known for the collection of tales called the ◊*Decameron* 1348–53.

Boccherini /bɒkə'riːni/ (Ridolfo) Luigi 1743–1805. Italian composer and cellist. He studied in Rome, made his mark in Paris in 1768, and was court composer in Prussia and Spain. Boccherini composed some 350 instrumental works, an opera, and oratorios.

Boccioni /bɒtʃi'əuni/ Umberto 1882–1916. Italian painter and sculptor. One of the founders of the ◊Futurist movement, he was a pioneer of abstract art.

bode *v.t./i.* to be a sign of, to portend. —**bode ill or well,** to be a bad or good sign. [Old English]

Bode /'bəudə/ Johann Elert 1747–1826. German astronomer, director of the Berlin observatory. He published the first atlas of all stars visible to the naked eye, *Uranographia* 1801, and devised Bode's Law.

bodega /bə'diːgə/ *n.* a cellar or shop selling wine. [Spanish]

Bodhidharma /bəudi'dɑːmə/ 6th century AD. Indian Buddhist. He entered China from S India about 520, and was the founder of Zen, the school of Mahāyāna Buddhism in which intuitive meditation, prompted by contemplation, leads to enlightenment.

bodhisattva *n.* in Mahāyāna Buddhism, someone who seeks ◊enlightenment in order to help other living beings. A bodhisattva is free to enter ◊nirvana but voluntarily chooses to be reborn until all other beings have attained that state.

bodice /'bɒdɪs/ *n.* 1. the upper part of a woman's dress, down to the waist. 2. a woman's vestlike undergarment. [originally *pair of bodies* = whalebone corset]

Bodichon /'bəudɪʃɒn/ Barbara (born Leigh-Smith) 1827–1891. English feminist and campaigner for women's education and suffrage. She wrote *Women and Work* 1857, and was a founder of the magazine *The Englishwoman's Journal* in 1858.

bodily /'bɒdɪlɪ/ *adj.* of the human body or physical nature. —*adv.* 1. as a whole. 2. in the body, in person.

Bodin /bəu'dæn/ Jean 1530–1596. French political philosopher whose six-volume *De la République* 1576 is considered the first work on political economy.

bodkin /'bɒdkɪn/ *n.* a blunt, thick needle for drawing tape etc. through a hem.

Bodoni /bə'dəuni/ Giambattista 1740–1813. Italian printer who managed the printing press of the Duke of Parma and produced high-quality editions of the classics. He designed several typefaces, including one bearing his name, which is in use today.

body /'bɒdɪ/ *n.* 1. the physical structure, including bones, flesh, and organs, of a human being (see ◊human body) or animal (alive or dead). 2. a corpse. 3. the trunk apart from the head and limbs; the main or central part of something; the majority *of.* 4. a group of persons or things regarded as a unit. 5. (*colloquial*) a person. 6. a distinct piece of matter. 7. solidity, substantial character etc. —**body blow,** a very severe setback. **body building,** strengthening of the body by exercises. **body language,** involuntary movements or attitudes by which a person communicates his feelings or moods etc. (usually unwittingly) to others. **bodyline bowling,** in cricket, persistent fast bowling on the leg side, threatening the batsman's body. **body politic,** the nation in its corporate character. **in a body,** collectively. [Old English]

bodyguard *n.* a person or group of persons escorting and guarding a dignitary etc.

body snatcher (*historical*) one who illicitly disinterred corpses for dissection. —**body snatching.**

bodywork *n.* the structure of a vehicle body.

Boeing /'bəuɪŋ/ William Edward 1881–1956. US industrialist, founder of the Boeing Airplane Company in 1917. Its military aircraft include the flying fortress bombers used in World War II, and the Chinook helicopter; its commercial craft include the ◊jetfoil and the Boeing 707 and 747 jets.

Boeotia /bi'əuʃə/ ancient district of central Greece, of which ◊Thebes was the chief city; the **Boeotian League** (formed by ten city states in the 6th century BC) superseded ◊Sparta in the leadership of Greece in the 4th century BC.

Boer /'bəuə(r), buə(r)/ *n.* a Dutch settler or descendant of Dutch and Huguenot settlers in South Africa; see also ◊Afrikaner. —*adj.* of Boers. [Dutch = farmer]

Boer War the second of the ◊South African Wars 1889–1902; war between the Dutch settlers in South Africa and the British.

Bodichon *English feminist Barbara Bodichon, probably the model for the heroine of George Eliot's novel* Romola.

Boethius /bəu'iːθiəs/ Anicius Manilus Severinus AD 480–524. Roman philosopher. While imprisoned on suspicion of treason by the emperor ◊Theodoric, he wrote treatises on music and mathematics and *De Consolatione Philosophiae/The Consolation of Philosophy*, a dialogue in prose. It was translated into European languages during the Middle Ages; English translations by Alfred the Great, Geoffrey Chaucer, and Queen Elizabeth I.

boffin /'bɒfɪn/ *n.* (*British, colloquial*) a person engaged in (especially secret) scientific research.

bog *n.* an area of soft, wet, spongy ground consisting of decaying vegetable matter or ◊peat. Bogs occur on the uplands of cold or temperate areas where drainage is poor. —*v.t.* (**-gg-**; usually in *passive* with *down*) to stick fast in wet ground; to impede the progress of. —**bog myrtle,** a fragrant-leaved shrub found in bogs. **bog oak,** wood of oak etc. preserved in peat. —**boggy** *adj.* [from Irish or Gaelic *bogach*]

Bogarde /'bəugɑːd/ Dirk. Stage name of Derek van den Bogaerde 1921– . English film actor, who appeared in comedies and adventure films such as *Doctor in the House* 1954 and *Campbell's Kingdom* 1957, before acquiring international recognition for complex roles in films such as *The Servant* 1963 and *Accident* 1967, made with director Joseph Losey, and Luchino Visconti's *Death in Venice* 1971.

Bogart /'bəugɑːt/ Humphrey 1899–1957. US film actor, who achieved fame with his portrayal of a gangster in *The Petrified Forest* 1936. He became an international cult figure as the romantic, tough loner in such films as *The Maltese Falcon* 1941 and *Casablanca* 1943, and won an Academy Award for his role in *The African Queen* 1952.

bogbean *n.* or **buckbean** an aquatic or bog plant *Menyanthes trifoliata* of the gentian family, with a creeping rhizome and leaves and pink flower spikes held above water. It is found over much of the northern hemisphere.

Bogdanovich /bɒg'dænəvɪtʃ/ Peter 1939– . US film director, screenwriter, and producer, formerly a critic. *The Last Picture Show* 1971 was followed by two films that attempted to capture the style of old Hollywood, *What's Up Doc?* 1972 and *Paper Moon* 1973. Both made money but neither was a critical success. In 1990 he made *Texasville*, a follow-up to *The Last Picture Show*.

bogey /'bəugɪ/ *n.* in golf, a score of one stroke above par at a hole.

boggle *v.i.* to take alarm or hesitate (*at*). [from dialect *bogle* = bogy]

bogie /'bəugɪ/ *n.* a wheeled undercarriage pivoted below a locomotive etc.

Bogotá /bɒgə'tɑː/ capital of Colombia, South America; 2,640 m/8,660 ft above sea level on the edge of the plateau

Bolivia

of the E Cordillera; population (1985) 4,185,000. It was founded in 1538.

bogus /'bəʊgəs/ *adj.* sham, spurious.

bogy /'bəʊgi/ *n.* an evil spirit; an object of dread. [originally (*Old*) *Bogey* = the Devil]

bogyman /'bəʊgɪmæn/ *n.* (*plural* **bogymen**) a person (often imaginary) causing fear or difficulty.

Bohemia /bəʊ'hi:mɪə/ area of W Czechoslovakia, a kingdom of central Europe from the 9th century. It was under Habsburg rule 1526–1918, when it was included in Czechoslovakia. [from the Celtic *Boii*, its earliest known inhabitants]

Bohemian /bəʊ'hi:mɪən/ *adj.* 1. of Bohemia, an area of Czechoslovakia. 2. or **bohemian** irregular and socially unconventional habits. —*n.* a person of bohemian habits. [from *Bohemia*]

Böhm /bɜ:m/ Karl 1894–1981. Austrian conductor known for his interpretation of Beethoven, Mozart and Strauss.

Bohr /bɔ:/ Niels (Henrik David) 1885–1962. Danish physicist. After work with Ernest ◊Rutherford at Manchester, he became professor at Copenhagen in 1916, and founded there the Institute of Theoretical Physics, of which he became director in 1920. He was awarded the Nobel Prize for Physics in 1922. During World War II he worked on the atomic bomb in the USA. In 1952, he helped to set up ◊CERN, the European nuclear research organization, in Geneva. His son, **Aage Bohr** (1922–), produced a new model of the nucleus in 1952, known as the collective model, and for this work shared the 1975 Nobel Prize for Physics.

boil[1] *v.t./i.* 1. (of liquid) to reach the temperature at which vapour bubbles form within the body of the liquid (whereas ◊evaporation occurs only at the surface); to bring to ◊boiling point; to cook or be cooked in boiling liquid, to subject to the heat of boiling liquid. 2. (of the sea etc.) to seethe like boiling liquid. 3. to be greatly disturbed by anger or other strong emotion. —*n.* the act or point of boiling. —**boil over,** to spill over in boiling. [from Anglo-French from Latin *bullire* (*bulla* = bubble)]

boil[2] *n.* an inflamed pus-filled swelling under the skin. [Old English]

Boileau /bwæ'ləʊ/ Nicolas 1636–1711. French poet and critic. After a series of contemporary satires, his *Epîtres/Epistles* 1669–77 led to his joint appointment with Racine as royal historiographer in 1677. Later works include *L'Art poétique/The Art of Poetry* 1674 and the mock-heroic *Le Lutrin/The Lectern* 1674–83.

boiler *n.* 1. a tank in which a house's hot water is stored; any vessel that converts water into steam. Boilers are used in conventional power stations to generate steam to feed steam ◊turbines, which drive the electricity generators. They are also used in steamships, which are propelled by steam turbines, and in steam locomotives. Every boiler has a furnace in which fuel (coal, oil, or gas) is burned to produce hot gases, and a system of tubes in which heat is

transferred from the gases to the water. 2. a large tub for boiling laundry.

boiling point 1. for any given liquid, the temperature at which the application of heat raises the temperature of the liquid no further, but converts it to vapour. The boiling point of water under normal pressure is 100°C/212°F. The lower the pressure, the lower the boiling point, and vice versa. 2. a state of great anger or excitement.

boisterous /'bɔɪstərəs/ *adj.* noisily exuberant; (of the wind or sea) stormy, turbulent.

Bokassa /bɒ'kæsə/ Jean-Bédel 1921– . President and later self-proclaimed emperor of the Central African Republic 1966–79. Commander in chief from 1963, in Dec 1965 he led the military coup that gave him the presidency. On 4 Dec 1976 he proclaimed the Central African Empire and one year later crowned himself as emperor for life. His regime was characterized by arbitrary state violence and cruelty. Overthrown in 1979, Bokassa was in exile until 1986. Upon his return he was sentenced to death, but this was commuted to life imprisonment in 1988.

Bokhara /bɒ'kɑ:rə/ another form of ◊Bukhara, city in Asian USSR.

Bol /bɒl/ Ferdinand 1610–1680. Dutch painter, a pupil and for many years an imitator of ◊Rembrandt. After the 1660s he developed a more independent style and prospered as a portraitist.

bold /bəʊld/ *adj.* 1. confident and courageous, adventurous; shameless, impudent. 2. standing out distinctly, conspicuous. —**bold face,** type with thick heavy lines. —**boldly** *adv.*, **boldness** *n.* [Old English]

bole *n.* the trunk of a tree. [from Old Norse]

bolero *n.* (*plural* **boleros**) 1. /bə'leərəʊ/ a Spanish dance in triple time for a solo dancer or a couple, usually with castanet accompaniment; the music for this. 2. /'bɒlərəʊ/ a short jacket with no front fastening. [Spanish]

boletus *n.* a genus of fleshy fungi belonging to the class Basidiomycetes, with thick stems and caps of various colours. The European *Boletus edulis* is edible, but some species are poisonous.

Boleyn /bə'lɪn/ Anne 1507–1536. Queen of England, the woman for whom Henry VIII broke with the pope and founded the Church of England (see ◊Reformation). Second wife of Henry, she was married to him in 1533 and gave birth to the future Queen Elizabeth I in the same year. Accused of adultery and incest with her half-brother (a charge invented by Thomas ◊Cromwell), she was beheaded.

Bolívar /bɒ'li:vɑ:/ Simón 1783–1830. South American nationalist, leader of revolutionary armies, known as **the Liberator.** He fought the Spanish colonial forces in several uprisings and eventually liberated his native Venezuela in 1821, Colombia and Ecuador in 1822, Peru in 1824, and Bolivia (a new state named after him, formerly Upper Peru) in 1825.

Bolivia /bə'lɪvɪə/ Republic of; landlocked country in South America, bordered N and E by Brazil, SE by Paraguay, S by Argentina, and W by Chile and Peru; **area** 1,098,581 sq km/424,052 sq mi; **capital** La Paz (seat of government), Sucre (legal capital and seat of judiciary); **physical** high plateau of the Andes in the W between mountain ridges (the Altiplano), forest and lowlands in the E; lakes Titicaca and Poopó; **head of state and government** Jaime Paz Zamora from 1989; **political system** emergent democratic republic; **population** (1990 est) 6,730,000; (Quechua 25%, Aymara 30%, Mestizo 30%, European 14%); **language** Spanish, Aymara, Quechua (all official); **recent history** liberated from Spanish rule by Simón ◊Bolívar in 1825; name changed from Upper Peru to Bolivia. The country has suffered from repeated army coups to overthrow elected presidents, including the uprising by Che ◊Guevara in 1967. A worsening economy has made necessary economic aid from the USA and Europe.

Bolkiah /'bɒlkiə/ Hassanal 1946– . Sultan of Brunei from 1967, following the abdication of his father, Omar Ali Saifuddin (1916–1986). On independence, in 1984, Bolkiah also assumed the posts of prime minister and defence minister.

boll /bəʊl/ *n.* a round seed vessel (of cotton, flax etc.). —**boll weevil,** a small American beetle *Anthonomus grandis* of the weevil group. The female lays her eggs in the unripe pods, or bolls, of the cotton plant, and on these the larvae feed, causing great destruction. [from Middle Dutch *bolle*]

Böll /bɜːl/ Heinrich 1917–1985. West German novelist. A radical Catholic and anti-Nazi, he attacked Germany's political past and the materialism of its contemporary society. His many publications include poems, short stories, and novels which satirize German society, for example *Billard um Halbzehn/Billiards at Half-Past Nine* 1959 and *Gruppenbild mit Dame/Group Portrait with Lady* 1971. He received the Nobel Prize for Literature in 1972.

bollard /'bɒləd/ *n.* 1. each of a line of short posts for keeping traffic off a path etc. 2. a post on a ship or quay to which a mooring rope may be tied.

Bologna /bə'lɒnjə/ industrial city and capital of Emilia-Romagna, Italy, 80 km/50 mi N of Florence; population (1988) 427,000. It was the site of an Etruscan town, later of a Roman colony, and became a republic in the 12th century. It came under papal rule in 1506 and was united with Italy in 1860.

bolometer *n.* a sensitive ◊thermometer that measures the energy of radiation by registering the change in electrical resistance of a fine wire when it is exposed to heat or light. The US astronomer Samuel Langley devised it in 1880 for measuring radiation from stars.

boloney /bə'ləʊnɪ/ *n.* (*slang*) nonsense.

Bolshevik /'bɒlʃɪvɪk/ *n.* 1. a member of the majority of the Russian Social Democratic Party who split from the ◊Mensheviks in 1903. The Bolsheviks, under ◊Lenin, advocated the destruction of capitalist political and economic institutions, and the setting up of a socialist state with power in the hands of the workers. The Bolsheviks set in motion the ◊Russian Revolution in 1917. 2. (*loosely*) any socialist extremist. —**Bolshevism** *n.*, **Bolshevist** *n.* [Russian = member of the majority]

Bolshie /'bɒlʃɪ/ *adj.* (*slang*) 1. Bolshevik, left-wing. 2. rebellious, uncooperative. —*n.* (*slang*) a Bolshevik. [abbreviation]

bolster /'bəʊlstə/ *n.* 1. a long underpillow across a bed. 2. a pad or support in a machine or instrument. —*v.t.* to support or prop (*up*), to strengthen. [Old English]

bolt[1] /bəʊlt/ *n.* 1. a bar sliding into a socket, for fastening a door. 2. a heavy pin for holding metal plates etc. together, usually secured with a nut. 3. an act of bolting. 4. a discharge of lightning. 5. an arrow shot from a crossbow. —*v.t./i.* 1. to secure (a door) with bolts, to keep *in* or *out* by bolting a door; to fasten together with metal bolts. 2. to eat (food) very rapidly. 3. to dash off suddenly, (of a horse) to run off out of control. 4. to run to seed prematurely. —**bolthole** *n.* a means or place of escape. **bolt upright**, rigidly upright. [Old English]

bolt[2] /bəʊlt/ *v.t.* to sift (flour etc.). [from Old French *bul(e)ter*]

Boltzmann constant in physics, the constant (symbol *k*) that relates the kinetic energy (energy of motion) of a gas atom or molecule to temperature. Its value is 1.380662×10^{-23} joules per Kelvin. It is equal to the gas constant *R*, divided by ◊Avogadro's number. [from Austrian physicist Ludwig *Boltzmann* (1844–1906)]

bolus *n.* a mouthful of chewed food mixed with saliva, ready for swallowing. Most vertebrates swallow food immediately, but grazing mammals chew their food a great deal, allowing a mechanical and chemical breakdown to begin.

bomb /bɒm/ *n.* a destructive device containing explosive or chemical material and generally used in warfare. There are also ◊incendiary bombs and nuclear bombs and missiles (see ◊nuclear warfare). Any object designed to cause damage by explosion can be called a bomb (car bombs, letter bombs). Initially dropped from aeroplanes (from World War I), bombs were in World War II also launched by rocket (◊V1, V2). The 1960s saw the development of missiles that could be launched from aircraft, land sites, or submarines. In the 1970s laser guidance systems were developed to hit small targets with accuracy. **the bomb**, a nuclear bomb. —*v.t.* to attack with bombs, especially from the air. [from French, ultimately from Greek *bombos* = loud humming]

bombard /bɒm'bɑːd/ *v.t.* 1. to attack persistently with heavy guns. 2. to assail *with* questions, abuse etc. 3. in physics, to direct a stream of high-speed particles at. —**bombardment** *n.* [from French]

bombardier /bɒmbə'dɪə/ *n.* 1. a noncommissioned officer in the artillery. 2. (*US*) a person in an aircraft who releases bombs. [from French]

bombast /'bɒmbæst/ *n.* pompous or grandiloquent language. —**bombastic** /-'bæstɪk/ *adj.*, **bombastically** *adv.* [from obsolete *bombace* = cotton wadding]

Bombay /bɒm'beɪ/ 1. former province of British India; the capital was the city of Bombay. The major part became in 1960 the two new states of ◊Gujarat and ◊Maharashtra. 2. industrial port (textiles, engineering, pharmaceuticals, diamonds), commercial centre, and capital of Maharashtra, W India; population (1981) 8,227,000.

bombay duck or **bummalo** a small fish *Harpodon nehereus* found in the Indian Ocean. It has a thin body, up to 40 cm/16 in long, and sharp, pointed teeth. It feeds on shellfish and other small fish. It is valuable as a food fish, and is eaten, salted and dried, with dishes such as curry. [corruption of *bombil*, Indian name of the fish]

bombazine /'bɒmbəziːn/ *n.* a twilled, worsted dress material, especially the black kind formerly much used for mourning. [from French ultimately from Greek *bombux* = silk]

bomber /'bɒmə/ *n.* 1. an aircraft used to drop bombs. 2. a person using bombs illegally.

bombshell *n.* an overwhelming surprise or disappointment.

bona fide /bəʊnə 'faɪdɪ/ genuine, sincere. —**bona fides** /-iːz/, honest intention, sincerity. [Latin = (in) good faith]

bonanza /bə'nænzə/ *n.* a source of wealth or prosperity, an unexpected success (originally a mining term). [Spanish = fair weather, prosperity]

Bonaparte /'bəʊnəpɑːt/ Corsican family of Italian origin that gave rise to the Napoleonic dynasty: see ◊Napoleon I, ◊Napoleon II, and ◊Napoleon III. Others were the brothers and sister of Napoleon I: **Joseph** 1768–1844, whom Napoleon made king of Naples in 1806 and Spain in 1808; **Lucien** 1775–1840, whose handling of the Council of Five Hundred on 10 Nov 1799 ensured Napoleon's future; **Louis** 1778–1846, made king of Holland 1806–10, who was the father of Napoleon III; **Caroline** 1782—1839, who married Joachim ◊Murat in 1800; **Jerome** 1784–1860, made king of Westphalia in 1807.

Bonar Law British Conservative politician. See ◊Law, Andrew Bonar.

Bonaventura, St /bɒnəven'tʊərə/ (John of Fidanza) 1221–1274. Italian Roman Catholic theologian. He entered the Franciscan order in 1243, became professor of theology in Paris, and in 1256 general of his order. In 1273 he was created cardinal and bishop of Albano. Feast day 15 July.

bonbon *n.* a sweet. [French *bon* = good]

bond *n.* 1. something that binds together or (usually in *plural*) restrains. 2. a binding agreement; a deed by which a person binds himself to pay another; a certificate issued by a government or company, undertaking to repay borrowed money together with fixed interest. Usually a long-term security, a bond may be irredeemable, secured or unsecured. Property bonds are non-fixed securities with the yield fixed to property investment. See also ◊Eurobond. 3. in chemistry, the result of the forces of attraction that hold together atoms of an element or elements to form a molecule. The principle types of bonding are ◊ionic, ◊covalent, ◊metallic, and ◊intermolecular (such as hydrogen bonding). 4. any of various methods (*English bond, Flemish bond,* etc.) of holding a wall together by making bricks overlap. —*v.t.* 1. to unite or reinforce with a bond. 2. to place goods in bond. —**bond (paper)**, a high-quality writing paper. **in bond**, stored by the Customs in special warehouses until the importer has paid the duty. [variant of *band*[1]]

Bond /bɒnd/ Alan 1938– . Australian entrepreneur and yacht owner, whose company, Bond Corporation, had interests in newspapers, breweries, television, oil, gas, and gold-mining. His yacht *Australia II* won the 1983 America's Cup from the USA. By the late 1980s it was clear that the Bond empire had overstretched itself and in Sept 1990 he relinquished control of the group.

Bond Edward 1935– . British dramatist, whose work has aroused controversy because of the savagery of some of his themes, for example the brutal killing of a baby, symbol of a society producing unwanted children, in *Saved* 1965. His later works include *Black Mass* 1970 about apartheid, *Bingo* 1973, and *The Sea* 1973.

bondage *n.* slavery, captivity; subjection to any constraining force. [from Old English *bonda* = husbandman]

bonded *adj.* (of goods) placed in bond; (of warehouses) containing such goods.

Bondfield /'bɒndfiːld/ Margaret Grace 1873–1953. British socialist who became a trade-union organizer to improve working conditions for women. She was a Labour member of Parliament 1923–24 and 1926–31, and was the first woman to enter the cabinet—as minister of labour, 1929–31.

Bondi Beach Australian beach on the E coast of the S side of Sydney Harbour, celebrated for its surf.

bondservant *n.* (*historical*) a slave or serf in the Caribbean in the 18th and 19th centuries; a person who was offered a few acres of land in return for some years of compulsory service. The system was a means of obtaining labour from Europe.

bone *n.* **1.** the hard connective tissue of most vertebrate animals; (in *plural*) a skeleton, especially as remains. Bone consists of a network of collagen fibres impregnated with calcium phospate. Enclosed within this solid matrix are bone cells, blood vessels, and nerves. In strength, the toughest bone is comparable with reinforced concrete. There are two types of bone: those that develop by replacing ◊cartilage and those that form directly from connective tissue. The latter are usually platelike in shape, and form in the skin of the developing embryo. Humans have about 206 distinct bones in the ◊skeleton. **2.** the material of which bones consist or a similar substance. **3.** (in *plural*) the basic essentials of a thing. —*v.t.* to remove the bones from. —**bone-dry** *adj.* completely dry. **bonemeal** *n.* ground bones used as fertilizer. **bone of contention**, the subject of a dispute. **boneshaker** *n.* an old jolting vehicle; (historical) an early type of bicycle. **have a bone to pick**, to have something to complain about or dispute *with*. **make no bones about**, to admit or allow without fuss. **to the bone**, to the bare minimum. [Old English]

bone china or **soft paste** semi-porcelain made of 5% bone ash added to 95% kaolin; first made in the West in imitation of Chinese porcelain.

bone marrow in vertebrates, soft tissue in the centre of some large bones that manufactures red and white blood cells.

bonfire *n.* a large open-air fire. —**Bonfire Night,** in the UK, that of 5 November, when bonfires are lit in memory of the Gunpowder Plot (see Guy ◊Fawkes). [earlier *bonefire* = fire in which bones are burnt]

bongo[1] /'bɒŋgəʊ/ *n.* (*plural* the same) a Central African antelope *Boocercus eurycerus*, living in dense, humid forests. Up to 1.4 m/4.5 ft at the shoulder, it has spiral-shaped horns which may be 80 cm/2.6 ft or more in length. The body is rich chestnut, with narrow white stripes running vertically down the sides, and a black belly.

bongo[2] (*plural* **bongos, bongoes**) each of a pair of small drums usually held between the knees and beaten with the fingers. [American Spanish]

Bonhoeffer /'bɒnhɜːfə/ Dietrich 1906–1945. German Lutheran theologian and opponent of Nazism. Involved in an anti-Hitler plot, he was executed by the Nazis in Flossenbürg concentration camp. His *Letters and Papers from Prison* 1953 became the textbook of modern radical theology, advocating the idea of a 'religionless' Christianity.

bonhomie /'bɒnəmi/ *n.* friendly geniality. [French (from *bonhomme* = good-natured man)]

Boniface /'bɒnɪfeɪs/ the name of nine popes, including:

Boniface VIII Benedict Caetani *c.*1228–1303. Pope from 1294. He clashed unsuccessfully with Philip IV of France over his taxation of the clergy, and also with Henry III of England.

Boniface, St Wynfrith 680–754. English Benedictine monk, known as the 'Apostle of Germany'. After a missionary journey to Frisia in 716, he was given the task of bringing Christianity to Germany by Pope Gregory II in 718, and was appointed archbishop of Mainz in 746. He returned to Frisia in 754 and was martyred near Dockum. Feast day 5 June.

bonito *n.* any of various medium-sized tuna, predatory fish of the genus *Sarda*, in the mackerel family. The ocean bonito *Katsuwonus pelamis* grows to 1 m/3 ft and is

common in tropical seas. The Atlantic bonito *Sarda sarda* is found in the Mediterranean and tropical Atlantic and grows to the same length but has a narrower body.

bon mot a witty remark. [French]

Bonn /bɒn/ industrial city (chemicals, textiles, plastics, aluminium) and seat of government of Germany, 18 km/15 mi SSE of Cologne, on the left bank of the Rhine; population (1988) 292,000.

Bonnard /bɒ'nɑː/ Pierre 1867–1947. French Post-Impressionist painter. With other members of **les ◊Nabis**, he explored the decorative arts (posters, stained glass, furniture). He painted domestic interiors and nudes.

Bonner /'bɒnə/ Yelena 1923– . Soviet human-rights campaigner. Disillusioned by the Soviet invasion of Czechoslovakia in 1968, she resigned from the Communist Party after marrying her second husband, Andrei ◊Sakharov, in 1971, and became active in the dissident movement.

bonnet /'bɒnɪt/ *n.* **1.** an outdoor headdress tied with strings below the chin, now chiefly worn by babies. **2.** a Scotch cap. **3.** a hinged cover over the engine of a motor vehicle. [from Old French *bonet* (originally = the material of which caps were made)]

Bonneville Salt Flats /'bɒnəvɪl/ bed of a prehistoric lake in Utah, USA, of which the Great Salt Lake is the surviving remnant. A number of world land-speed records have been set here.

Bonnie and Clyde /'bɒni, klaɪd/ Bonnie Parker (1911–1934) and Clyde Barrow (1900–1934). US criminals who carried out a series of small robberies in Texas, Oklahoma, New Mexico, and Missouri between Aug 1932 and May 1934. They were eventually betrayed and then killed in a police ambush.

bonny /'bɒni/ *adj.* (chiefly *Scottish*) **1.** handsome, healthy-looking. **2.** pleasant. [perhaps from French *bon* = good]

bonsai /'bɒnsaɪ/ *n.* an artificially dwarf potted tree or shrub; the method of growing these. It originated in China over 700 years ago and later spread to Japan. Some specimens in the imperial Japanese collection are over 300 years old. [Japanese = bowl cultivation]

bonus /'bəʊnəs/ *n.* something paid or given in addition to the normal amount; an extra benefit. [Latin = good]

bon voyage an expression of good wishes to someone beginning a journey. [French]

bony /'bəʊni/ *adj.* of or like bone; thin with prominent bones; (of fish) having a skeleton of bone rather than cartilage. —**boniness** *n.*

bonze *n.* a Buddhist priest in Japan or adjacent countries. [from French or Portuguese from Japanese]

boo interjection expressing disapproval or contempt. —*n.* the sound *boo*. —*v.t./i.* to utter boos, to jeer at. [imitative]

boob[1] *n.* (*slang*) **1.** a silly mistake. **2.** a foolish person. —*v.i.* (*slang*) to make a silly mistake. [from *booby*]

boob[2] *n.* (usually in *plural*; *slang*) a woman's breast. [from earlier *bub, bubby*]

boobook *n.* an owl *Ninox novaeseelandiae* found in Australia. [from its call]

booby *n.* **1.** a stupid or childish person. **2.** a tropical seabird of the genus *Sula*, in the same family, Sulidae, as the northern ◊gannet. There are six species, including the circumtropical brown booby *Sula leucogaster*. They inhabit coastal waters, and dive to catch fish. The name was given to them by sailors who saw their tameness as stupidity. —**booby prize,** a prize awarded to the person coming last in a contest. **booby trap,** a hidden trap rigged up for a practical joke; a disguised explosive device. **booby-trap** *v.t.* to place a booby trap in or on. [from Spanish *bobo* from Latin *balbus* = stammering]

boogie-woogie /buː'giːwuːgɪ/ *n.* a style of playing jazz or blues on the piano, using a repeated motif for the left hand. It was common in the USA from around 1900 to the 1950s. Boogie-woogie players included Pinetop Smith (1904–1929), Meade 'Lux' Lewis (1905–1964), and Jimmy Yancey (1898–1951).

book /bʊk/ *n.* **1.** a set of printed sheets bound together in a cover for reading; a written work intended for printing as a book. **2.** a bound set of blank sheets for writing notes, accounts, exercises etc. in; (in *plural*) a set of accounts. **3.** a series of cheques, stamps, tickets etc., bound together like a book. **4.** a main division of a literary work, or of the Bible. **5.** a record of bets made. **6.** a libretto, the script of a play. —*v.t./i.* **1.** to enter the name of in a book or list; to record a charge against. **2.** to reserve in advance; to make a reservation. —**bookcase** *n.* a piece of furniture with shelves for books. **book club,** a society supplying its members with selected books on special terms. **book ends,** a pair of props designed to keep a row of unshelved books upright. **book in,** to register one's arrival at a hotel etc. **bookplate** *n.* a label with the owner's name etc. pasted at the front of a book. **book token,** a voucher exchangeable for books of a given value. **bring to book,** to call to account. **by the book,** strictly in accordance with regulations. [Old English]

bookbinder *n.* one who binds books professionally. —**bookbinding** *n.* the securing of the pages of a book between protective covers by sewing and/or gluing. Cloth binding was first introduced in 1822, but from the mid-20th century synthetic bindings have been increasingly used, and most hardback books are bound by machine.

Booker Prize /'bʊkə/ British literary prize of £20,000 awarded annually (from 1969) by the Booker company (formerly Booker McConnell) to a novel published in the UK during the previous year. The winner for 1990 was A S Byatt with her novel *Possession.*

bookie /'bʊkɪ/ *n.* (*colloquial*) a bookmaker. [abbreviation]

bookish /'bʊkɪʃ/ *adj.* addicted to reading; deriving one's knowledge from books, not from experience.

bookkeeper *n.* one who keeps accounts, especially as a profession. —**bookkeeping** *n.*

booklet /'bʊklɪt/ *n.* a small, thin, usually paper-covered book.

booklouse *n.* any of numerous species of tiny wingless insects of the order Psocoptera, especially *Atropus pulsatoria,* that live in books and papers, feeding on starches and moulds.

bookmaker *n.* a professional taker of bets. —**book-making** *n.*

bookmark *n.* a strip of card, leather etc. inserted in a book to mark the reader's place.

Book of Hours see ◊Hours, Books of.

Book of the Dead an ancient Egyptian book, known as the *Book of Coming Forth by Day,* buried with the dead as a guide to reaching the kingdom of Osiris, the god of the underworld.

bookseller *n.* a dealer in books.

bookshop *n.* a shop selling books.

bookworm *n.* **1.** a person addicted to reading. **2.** a larva or ◊booklouse that feeds on paper etc. in books.

Boole /buːl/ George 1814–1864. English mathematician, whose work *The Mathematical Analysis of Logic* 1847 established the basis of modern mathematical logic, and whose **Boolean algebra** can be used in designing computers.

boom[1] *n.* a deep resonant sound. —*v.i.* to make or speak with a boom. [imitative]

boom[2] *n.* a period of sudden prosperity or commercial activity. —*v.i.* to enjoy a boom.

boom[3] *n.* **1.** a long pole fixed at one end to support the bottom of a sail, microphone etc. **2.** a barrier across a harbour. [from Dutch = beam]

boomerang /'buːməræŋ/ *n.* **1.** a hand-thrown, flat, wooden hunting missile shaped in a curved angle, developed by the Australian Aborigines. It is used to kill game and as a weapon; some are specifically made to return to the thrower if the target is missed. **2.** a scheme etc. that recoils unfavourably on its originator. —*v.i.* (of a scheme) to recoil thus. [Aboriginal]

boomslang *n.* a rear-fanged venomous African snake *Dispholidus typus,* often green but sometimes brown or blackish. It lives in trees, and feeds on tree-dwelling lizards such as chameleons. Its venom can be fatal to humans; however, boomslangs rarely attack people. [Afrikaans = tree snake]

boon[1] *n.* something to be thankful for, a blessing. [from Old Norse = prayer]

boon[2] *adj.* **boon companion,** a pleasant sociable companion. [from Old French from Latin *bonus* = good]

Boone /buːn/ Daniel 1734–1820. US pioneer, who explored the Wilderness Road (East Virginia–Kentucky) in 1775 and paved the way for the first westward migration of settlers.

boor /bʊə/ *n.* an ill-mannered person. —**boorish** *adj.*, **boorishness** *n.* [from Low Dutch]

Boorman /'bɔːmən/ John 1933– . English film director who, after working in television, directed successful films

Booth William Booth, *founder of the Salvation Army in 1878, and its first general.*

both in Hollywood (*Deliverance* 1972, *Point Blank* 1967) and in Britain (*Excalibur* 1981, *Hope and Glory* 1987).

boost *v.t.* to increase the strength or reputation of; (*colloquial*) to push from below. —*n.* an act of boosting.

booster *n.* a device for increasing voltage or signal strength; an auxiliary engine or rocket for initial acceleration; an injection etc. renewing the effect of an earlier one.

boot[1] *n.* **1.** an outer foot covering, often of leather, coming above the ankle. **2.** a luggage compartment at the back of a car. —*v.t.* **1.** to kick. **2.** or **bootstrap** to start up a computer. Most computers have a small, built-in boot program whose only job is to load a slightly larger program, usually from a disc, which in turn loads the main ◊operating system. [from Old Norse]

boot[2] *n.* **to boot,** as well, into the bargain. [Old English = advantage]

bootee /buː'tiː/ *n.* a baby's knitted or crocheted boot.

Boötes /bəʊ'əʊtiːz/ *n.* a constellation of the northern hemisphere represented by a herder driving a bear (Ursa Major) around the pole. Its brightest star is ◊Arcturus (or Alpha Boötis) about 36 light years from Earth.

booth /buːð/ *n.* a small temporary shelter for a stall etc. at a market or fair; an enclosure or compartment for telephoning, voting etc. [from Old Norse]

Booth John Wilkes 1839–1865. US actor and fanatical Confederate sympathizer who assassinated President Abraham ◊Lincoln on 14 April 1865; he escaped with a broken leg and was later shot in a barn in Virginia when he refused to surrender.

Booth William 1829–1912. English evangelist and itinerant preacher. He established a mission among the poor in Whitechapel, London, but the churches were reluctant to accept his converts and in 1878 he founded the ◊Salvation Army and became its first general.

Boothby /'buːðbi/ Robert John Graham, Baron Boothby 1900–1986. Scottish politician. He became a Unionist member of Parliament in 1924 and was parliamentary private secretary to Churchill 1926–29. He advocated Britain's entry into the European Community.

bootleg *adj.* smuggled, illicit, produced without authorization (originally of liquor). —**bootlegger** *n.* [from the former practice of smugglers of concealing liquor bottles in their boots]

bootless *adj.* unavailing.

booty /'buːti/ *n.* plunder gained in war etc., loot. [from German = exchange]

booze *n.* (*colloquial*) alcoholic drink. —*v.i.* (*colloquial*) to drink heavily. —**boozer** *n.*, **boozy** *adj.* [from Dutch = drink to excess]

bop abbreviation of ◊bebop, a style of jazz.

Bophuthatswana /ˌbəupuːˈtətˈswɑːnə/ Republic of; self-governing black 'homeland' within South Africa; **area** 40,330 sq km/15,571 sq mi; **capital** Mmbatho or Sun City, a casino resort frequented by many white South Africans; **government** executive president elected by the assembly: Chief Lucas Mangope; **exports** platinum, chrome, vanadium, asbestos, manganese; **population** (1985) 1,627,000; **language** Setswana, English; **recent history** first 'independent' Black National State from 1977, but not recognized by any country other than South Africa.

Bora-Bora /bɔːrəˈbɔːrə/ *n.* one of the 14 Society Islands of French Polynesia, situated 225 km/140 mi NW of Tahiti. Area 39 sq km/15 sq mi. Exports include mother-of-pearl, fruit, and tobacco.

boracic /bəˈræsɪk/ *adj.* of borax. —**boracic acid,** boric acid.

borage /ˈbɒrɪdʒ/ *n.* a salad plant *Borago officinalis* cultivated in Britain and occasionally naturalized. It has small blue flowers and hairy leaves. [from Old French, ultimately from Arabic = father of sweat (from its use as a diaphoretic)]

borax /ˈbɔːræks/ *n.* hydrous sodium borate, $Na_2B_4O_7.10H_2O$, found as soft, whitish crystals or encrustations on the shores of hot springs and in the dry beds of salt lakes in arid regions, where it occurs with other borates, halite, and ◊gypsum. It is used in making glass, enamels, and detergents. [from Old French, ultimately from Persian]

Bordeaux /bɔːˈdəu/ port on the Garonne, capital of Aquitaine, SW France, a centre for the wine trade, oil refining, and aeronautics and space industries; **population** (1982) 640,000. Bordeaux was under the English crown for three centuries until 1453. In 1870, 1914, and 1940 the French government was moved here because of German invasion.

border /ˈbɔːdə/ *n.* **1.** an edge or boundary; the part near this. **2.** the dividing line between two countries; the district on either side of this. **3.** a strip of ground round the edge of a garden. **4.** an edging to a garment etc. —*v.t./i.* **1.** to provide with a border; to serve as a border to. **2.** (with *on*) to adjoin; to come close to (a condition). —**the Border,** that between England and Scotland. [from Old French *bordure*]

Border Allan 1955– . Australian cricketer, captain of the Australian team from 1985. He has played for New South Wales and Queensland, and in England for Gloucestershire and Essex. He made his test debut for Australia 1978–79.

borderland *n.* **1.** the district near a border. **2.** a condition between two extremes. **3.** an area for debate.

borderline *n.* a boundary; the limit of a category etc. —*adj.* on or near the borderline.

Borders /ˈbɔːdəz/ region of Scotland; **area** 4,700 sq km/1,815 sq mi; **towns** Newtown St Boswells (administrative headquarters); **physical** river Tweed; Lammermuir, Moorfoot, and Pentland hills; **products** knitted goods, tweed, electronics, timber; **population** (1987) 102,000.

Bordet /bɔːˈdeɪ/ Jules 1870–1961. Belgian bacteriologist and immunologist who researched the role of blood serum in the human immune response. He was the first to isolate, in 1906, the whooping-cough bacillus.

bore[1] *v.t./i.* **1.** to make (a hole or well etc.), especially with a revolving tool; to make a hole (in) thus; to drill (the shaft of a well). **2.** to hollow out (a tube) evenly. **3.** (of a racehorse) to push another horse out of the way. —*n.* **1.** the hollow of a gun barrel or of the cylinder in an internal-combustion engine; its diameter. **2.** a borehole made to find water etc. [Old English; compare Old Norse *bora* = borehole]

bore[2] *v.t.* to weary by tedious talk or dullness. —*n.* a dull or wearisome person or thing. —**boredom** *n.*, **boring** *adj.*

bore[3] *n.* a high tidal wave with a steep front that occurs when two tides meet or when the spring flood tide rushes up a narrowing estuary. [from Scandinavian]

bore[4] past of **bear**[1].

borehole *n.* a deep hole bored in the ground especially to find water.

Borelli /bəˈreli/ Giovanni Alfonso 1608–1679. Italian scientist who explored the links between physics and medicine, and showed how mechanical principles could be applied to animal ◊physiology. This approach, known as iatrophysics, has proved basic to understanding how the mammalian body works.

Borg /bɔːg/ Björn 1956– . Swedish lawn-tennis player who won the men's singles title at Wimbledon five times 1976–80, a record since the abolition of the challenge system in 1922. In 1990 Borg announced tentative plans to return to professional tennis.

Borges /ˈbɔːxes/ Jorge Luis 1899–1986. Argentine poet and short-story writer. In 1961 he became director of the National Library, Buenos Aires, and was professor of English literature at the university there. He is known for his fantastic and paradoxical work *Ficciones/Fictions* 1944.

The Falklands thing was a fight between two bald men over a comb.

Jorge Luis Borges
Time 1983

Borgia /ˈbɔːdʒə/ Cesare 1476–1507. Italian general, illegitimate son of Pope ◊Alexander VI. Made a cardinal at 17 by his father, he resigned to become captain-general of the papacy, campaigning successfully against the city republics of Italy. Ruthless and treacherous in war, he was an able ruler (the model for Machiavelli's *The Prince*), but his power crumbled on the death of his father. He was a patron of artists, including Leonardo da Vinci.

Borgia Lucrezia 1480–1519. Duchess of Ferrara from 1501. She was the illegitimate daughter of Pope ◊Alexander VI and sister of Cesare Borgia. She was married at 12 and again at 13 to further her father's ambitions, both marriages being annulled by him. At 18 she was married once more, but her husband was murdered in 1500 on the order of her brother, with whom (as well as with her father) she was said to have committed incest. Her final marriage was to the duke of Este, the son and heir of the duke of Ferrara. She made the court a centre of culture and was a patron of authors and artists such as Ariosto and Titian.

boric acid /ˈbɔːrɪk/ or **boracic acid** H_3BO_3, an acid formed by the combination of hydrogen and oxygen with nonmetallic boron. It is a weak antiseptic and is used in the manufacture of glass and enamels. It is also an efficient insecticide against cockroaches.

Boris III /ˈbɒrɪs/ 1894–1943. Tsar of Bulgaria from 1918, when he succeeded his father, Ferdinand I. From 1934 he was virtual dictator until his sudden and mysterious death following a visit to Hitler. His son Simeon II was tsar until deposed in 1946.

Boris Godunov 1552–1605. See Boris ◊Godunov, tsar of Russia from 1598.

Bormann /ˈbɔːmæn/ Martin 1900–1945. German Nazi leader. He took part in the abortive Munich ◊putsch (uprising) of 1923 and rose to high positions in the Nazi (National Socialist) Party, becoming party chancellor in May 1941. He was believed until 1973 to have escaped the fall of Berlin in May 1945 and was tried in his absence and sentenced to death at the ◊Nuremberg trials 1945–46.

born —past participle of **bear**[1]. —*adj.* **1.** existing as a result of birth. **2.** qualified by natural disposition or ability. **3.** destined or of a certain status or origin by birth. —**born of,** owing its origin to.

Born /bɔːn/ Max 1882–1970. German physicist, who received a Nobel prize in 1954 for fundamental work on the ◊quantum theory. He left Germany for the UK during the Nazi era.

-borne with prefixed noun in sense 'carried or transported by'. [past participle of *bear*[1].]

Borneo /ˈbɔːnɪəu/ third largest island in the world, one of the Sunda Islands in the W Pacific; area 754,000 sq km/290,000 sq mi. It comprises the Malaysian territories of ◊Sabah and ◊Sarawak; ◊Brunei; and, occupying by far the largest part, the Indonesian territory of ◊Kalimantan. It is mountainous and densely forested. In coastal areas the people of Borneo are mainly of Malaysian origin, with a few Chinese, and the interior is inhabited by the indigenous Dayaks. The island was formerly under both Dutch and British colonial influence until Sarawak was formed in 1841.

Bornu /bɔːˈnuː/ kingdom of the 9th–19th centuries to the W and S of Lake Chad, west central Africa. Converted to Islam in the 11th century, it reached its greatest strength in the 15th–18th centuries. From 1901 it was absorbed in the British, French, and German colonies in this area, which became the states of Niger, Cameroon, and Nigeria. The largest section of ancient Bornu is now the **state of Bornu** in Nigeria.

Borodin /'bɒrədɪn/ Alexander Porfir'yevich 1833–1887. Russian composer. His principal work is the opera *Prince Igor*, left unfinished, it was completed by Rimsky-Korsakov and Glazunov and includes the Polovtsian Dances.

Borodino, Battle of /bɒrə'di:nəʊ/ battle 110 km/70 mi NW of Moscow on 7 Sept 1812, in which French troops under Napoleon defeated the Russian army under Kutusov.

boron /'bɔ:rɒn/ *n.* a nonmetallic element, symbol B, atomic number 5, relative atomic mass 10.811. In nature it is found only in compounds, as with sodium and oxygen in borax. It exists in two allotropic forms: a brown amorphous powder and very hard, brilliant crystals. Its compounds are used in the preparation of boric acid, water softeners, soaps, enamels, glass, and pottery glazes. In alloys it is used to harden steel. Because it absorbs slow neutrons, it is used to make boron carbide control rods for nuclear reactors. It is a necessary trace element in the human diet. [from *borax* with ending of *carbon*, which it resembles in some respects]

borough /'bʌrə/ *n.* **1.** an administrative division of London or of New York City; a territorial division in Alaska, corresponding to a county. **2.** a unit of local government in the UK from the 8th century until 1974, when it continued as an honorary status granted by royal charter to a district council, entitling its leader to the title of mayor; (*historical*) a town sending representatives to Parliament. [Old English; originally = fortress, fortified town]

Borromini /bɒrəu'mi:ni/ Francesco 1599–1667. Italian ◊Baroque architect who worked under Bernini on St Peter's Basilica, Rome. Later he became his rival, and created the oval-shaped church of San Carlo alle Quattro Fontane, Rome.

borrow /'bɒrəʊ/ *v.t./i.* to get the temporary use of (a thing) on condition that it is returned; to obtain money thus; to adopt or use (ideas etc. originated by another). [Old English]

Borstal institution /'bɔ:stəl/ (*British, historical*) a place of detention for offenders aged 15–21. From 1983 Borstals were officially known as youth custody centres, and were subsequently replaced by **young offender institutions**. [from *Borstal* prison near Rochester, Kent, where the system was first introduced in 1908]

bortsch /bɔ:tʃ/ *n.* a highly seasoned Russian or Polish soup of various ingredients including beetroot and cabbage. [from Russian *borshch*]

borzoi /'bɔ:zɔɪ/ *n.* a large breed of dog originating in Russia, 75 cm/2.5 ft or more at the shoulder. It is of the greyhound type, white with darker markings, with a thick, silky coat. [Russian = swift]

Bosch /bɒs/ Hieronymus (Jerome) 1460–1516. Early Netherlandish painter. His fantastic visions of weird and hellish creatures, as shown in *The Garden of Earthly Delights* about 1505–10 (Prado, Madrid), show astonishing imagination and a complex imagery. His religious subjects focused not on the holy figures but on the mass of ordinary witnesses, placing the religious event in a contemporary Netherlandish context and creating cruel caricatures of human sinfulness.

Bosch Juan 1909– . President of the Dominican Republic in 1963. His left-wing Partido Revolucionario Dominicano won a landslide victory in the 1962 elections. In office, he attempted agrarian reform and labour legislation. Opposed by the USA, he was overthrown by the army. His achievement was to establish a democratic political party after three decades of dictatorship.

Boscovich /'bɒskəvɪtʃ/ Ruggiero 1711–1787. Italian scientist. An early supporter of Newton, he developed a theory of the atom as a single point with surrounding fields of repulsive and attractive forces that was popular in the 19th century.

bosh *n.* & *int.* (*slang*) nonsense. [from Turkish = empty]

bos'n /'bəʊsən/ contraction of ◊boatswain.

Bosnia and Herzegovina /'bɒzniə hɜ:tsɪgə'vi:nə/ constituent republic of Yugoslavia; **area** 51,100 sq km/

19,725 sq mi; **capital** Sarajevo; **physical** barren, mountainous country; **population** (1986) 4,360,000; including 30% Serbs, 17% Croats; **language** Serbian variant of Serbo-Croat; **recent history** ruled by the Ottoman Empire 1463–1878 and Austria 1878–1918, when it was incorporated in what was to be Yugoslavia. In 1943 Marshal Tito set up a provisional government at liberated Jajce and declared the Yugoslav Federal Republic in 1945, after the expulsion of remaining German forces. Islamic nationalist unrest broke out in the 1980s, and Muslim–Serb violence worsened in 1989–1990.

bosom /'buzəm/ *n.* the breast, especially of a woman, or the part of a dress covering it; the enclosing space formed by the breast and arms. —**bosom friend,** an intimate friend. [Old English]

boson /'bəʊzɒn/ *n.* a particle obeying the relations stated by Bose and Einstein, with integral spin. [from S N *Bose*, Indian physicist (1894–1974)]

Bosporus /'bɒspərəs/ (Turkish *Karadeniz Boğazi*) strait 27 km/17 mi long joining the Black Sea with the Sea of Marmara and forming part of the water division between Europe and Asia. Istanbul stands on its W side. The **Bosporus Bridge** 1973 links Istanbul and Turkey-in-Asia (1,621 m/5,320 ft). In 1988 a second bridge across the straits was opened, linking Asia and Europe.

boss[1] *n.* (*colloquial*) an employer or manager. —*v.t.* (*colloquial*) to be the boss of; to order *about*. [from Dutch *baas* = master]

boss[2] *n.* a round projecting knob or stud, as in the centre of a shield; a carved projection where ribs of vaulting cross. [from Old French]

boss-eyed *adj.* cross-eyed, having only one good eye. [from *boss* = miss a shot]

bossy *adj.* (*colloquial*) fond of ordering people about. —**bossiness** *n.*

Boston /'bɒstən/ industrial and commercial centre, capital of Massachusetts, USA; population (1980) 563,000; metropolitan area 2,800,000. Harvard University and Massachusetts Institute of Technology, also Amhurst, Williams, and Wellesley colleges, are nearby.

Boston Tea Party a protest in 1773 against the British tea tax by colonists in Massachusetts, America, before the ◊American Revolution.

bosun, bo'sun /'bəʊsən/ contraction of ◊boatswain.

Boswell /'bɒzwəl/ James 1740–1795. Scottish biographer and diarist. He was a member of Samuel ◊Johnson's London Literary Club, and in 1773 the two men travelled to Scotland together, as recorded in Boswell's *Journal of the Tour to the Hebrides* 1785. His classic English biography, *Life of Samuel Johnson*, was published in 1791. His long-lost personal papers were acquired for publication by Yale University in 1949, and the *Journals* are of exceptional interest.

Bosworth, Battle of /'bɒzwəθ/ the last battle of the Wars of the ◊Roses, fought on 22 Aug 1485. Richard III, the Yorkist king, was defeated and slain by Henry of Richmond, who became Henry VII. The battlefield is near the village of Market Bosworth, 19 km/12 mi W of Leicester, England.

botanic garden a place where a wide range of plants is grown, providing the opportunity to see a botanical diversity not likely to be encountered naturally. Among the earliest forms of botanic garden was the **physic garden**, devoted to the study and growth of medicinal plants; an example is the Chelsea Physic Garden in London, established in 1673 and still in existence.

botanize /'bɒtənaɪz/ *v.i.* to collect or study plants.

botany /'bɒtənɪ/ *n.* the study of plants. It is subdivided into a number of specialized studies, such as the identification and classification of plants (taxonomy), their external formation (plant morphology), their internal arrangement (plant anatomy), their microscopic examination (plant histology), their functioning and life history (plant physiology), and their distribution over the Earth's surface in relation to their surroundings (plant ecology). Palaeobotany concerns the study of fossil plants, while economic botany deals with the utility of plants. Horticulture, agriculture, and forestry are specialized branches of botany. —**botanical** /bə'tænɪkəl/ *adj.* [from French or Latin from Greek *botanē* = plant]

Botany Bay an inlet on the E coast of Australia, 8 km/5 mi S of Sydney, New South Wales. Chosen in 1787 as the site for a penal colony, it proved unsuitable. Sydney now stands on the site of the former settlement. 2. (*historical, colloquial*) any convict settlement in Australia.

botch *v.t.* to bungle, to do badly; to patch or put together clumsily. —*n.* bungled or spoilt work.

botfly *n.* any fly of the family Oestridae. The larvae are parasites that feed on the skin (warblefly of cattle) or in the nasal cavity (nostril flies of sheep and deer). The horse botfly belongs to another family, the Gasterophilidae. It has a parasitic larva that feeds in the horse's stomach.

both /bəʊθ/ *adj. & pron.* the two, not only one. —*adv.* with equal truth in two cases. [from Old Norse]

Botha /ˈbəʊtə/ Louis 1862–1919. South African soldier and politician, a commander in the Second South African War. In 1907 Botha became premier of the Transvaal and in 1910 of the first Union South African government. On the outbreak of World War I in 1914 he rallied South Africa to the Commonwealth, suppressed a Boer revolt, and conquered German South West Africa.

Botha P(ieter) W(illem) 1916– . South African politician. Prime minister from 1978, he initiated a modification of ◊apartheid, which later slowed in the face of Afrikaner (Boer) opposition. In 1984 he became the first executive state president. In 1989 he unwillingly resigned both party leadership and presidency after suffering a stroke, and was succeeded by F W de Klerk.

Botham /ˈbəʊθəm/ Ian (Terrence) 1955– . English cricketer. His total of 376 test wickets was a record until surpassed by Richard ◊Hadlee (New Zealand) in 1989. A prolific all-rounder, he also scored 5,119 runs and took 112 catches during his 97 test-match appearances. He has played county cricket for Somerset and Worcestershire (for which he currently plays) as well as playing in Australia. He played for England 1977–89.

Bothe /ˈbəʊtə/ Walther 1891–1957. German physicist who showed in 1929 that the cosmic rays bombarding the Earth are composed not of photons but of more massive particles. He was awarded the Nobel Prize for Physics in 1954.

bother /ˈbɒðə/ *v.t./i.* 1. to give trouble, worry, or annoyance to. 2. to take trouble. 3. to concern oneself *with*. —*n.* a person or thing causing bother.

bothersome /ˈbɒðəsəm/ *adj.* troublesome.

Bothwell /ˈbɒθwəl/ James Hepburn, 4th Earl of Bothwell *c.*1536–1578. Scottish noble, third husband of ◊Mary Queen of Scots, 1567–70, alleged to have arranged the explosion that killed Darnley, her previous husband, in 1567.

bo tree /ˈbəʊ ˈtriː/ or **peepul** the Buddhist name for a large Indian fig tree *Ficus religiosa* related to the banyan, sometimes worshipped as a symbol of the Buddha since he is said to have attained enlightenment beneath such a tree. [Sinhalese *bo* (Sanskrit *boahi* = perfect knowledge)]

Botswana /bɒtˈswɑːnə/ Republic of; landlocked country in central southern Africa, bounded to the S and E by South Africa, to the W and N by Namibia, and to the NE by Zimbabwe; **area** 582,000 sq km/225,000 sq mi; **capital** Gaborone; **physical** Kalahari Desert in SW, plains in E, fertile lands and Okavango Swamp in N, remarkable for its wildlife; **head of state and government** Quett Ketamile Joni Masire from 1980; **exports** diamonds, copper, nickel, meat; **population** (1990 est) 1,218,000 (80% Bamangwato, 20% Bangwaketse); **language** English (official); Setswana (national); **recent history** became a British protectorate in 1885. Independence achieved in 1966; new constitution came into effect; name changed from Bechuanaland to Botswana.

Botticelli /bɒtiˈtʃeli/ Sandro 1445–1510. Italian painter of religious and mythological subjects. He was patronized by the ruling ◊Medici family, for whom he painted *Primavera* 1478 and *The Birth of Venus* about 1482–84 (both in the Uffizi, Florence). From the 1490s he was influenced by the religious fanatic ◊Savonarola and developed a harshly expressive and emotional style.

bottle *n.* 1. a narrow-necked glass or plastic container for storing liquid; the amount that will fill it. 2. a hot-water bottle. 3. a baby's feeding bottle. 4. (*slang*) courage. —*v.t.* 1. to seal or store in bottles or jars. 2. (with *up*) to confine; to restrain (feelings etc.). —**bottlebrush** *n.* a cylindrical brush for cleaning inside bottles; any of various plants with flowers of this shape. **bottle-green** *adj.* dark green. **bottleneck** *n.* a narrow stretch of road where traffic cannot flow freely. **bottle party**, one to which each guest brings a bottle of drink. [from Old French]

bottom /ˈbɒtəm/ *n.* 1. the lowest part of anything, that on which it rests; the buttocks. 2. the lowest or most distant point; the less honourable end of a table, class etc. 3. the ground under a stretch of water. 4. a ship's keel or hull; a ship. —*adj.* lowest in position, rank, or degree. —*v.t./i.* 1. to provide with a bottom. 2. (of prices, usually with *out*) to reach the lowest level. —**at bottom**, basically. **bottom line**, the amount of total assets after profit and loss etc. are calculated; (*figurative*) the essential thing. **get to the bottom of**, to find the real cause of. [Old English]

botulism /ˈbɒtjʊlɪzəm/ *n.* a rare, often fatal type of ◊food poisoning. Symptoms include muscular paralysis and disturbed breathing and vision. It is caused by a toxin produced by the bacterium *Clostridium botulinum*, sometimes found in improperly canned food. [from Latin *botulus* = sausage]

Boucher /buːˈʃeɪ/ François 1703–1770. French Rococo painter, court painter from 1765. He was much patronized for his light-hearted, decorative scenes: for example *Diana Bathing* 1742 (Louvre, Paris).

bouclé /ˈbuːkleɪ/ *n.* yarn with looped or curled ply; a fabric made from this. [French = curled]

Boudicca /ˈbuːdɪkə/ died AD 60. Queen of the Iceni (native Britons), often referred to by the Latin form **Boadicea**. Her husband, King Prasutagus, had been a tributary of the Romans, but on his death in AD 60 the territory of the Iceni was violently annexed. Boudicca was scourged and her daughters raped. Boudicca raised the whole of SE England in revolt, and before the main Roman armies could return from campaigning in Wales she burned London, St Albans, and Colchester. Later the Romans under governor Suetonius Paulinus defeated the British somewhere between London and Chester; they were virtually annihilated and Boudicca poisoned herself.

Boudin /buːˈdæŋ/ Eugène 1824–1898. French artist, a forerunner of the Impressionists, known for his fresh seaside scenes painted in the open air.

boudoir /ˈbuːdwɑː/ *n.* a woman's private room. [French (*bouder* = sulk)]

Bougainville /ˈbuːɡənvɪl/ Louis Antoine de 1729–1811. French navigator. After service with the French in Canada during the Seven Years' War, he made the first French circumnavigation of the world 1766–69 and the first systematic observations of longitude.

bougainvillea /buːɡənˈvɪlɪə/ *n.* a South American tropical shrub of the genus *Bougainvillaea*, now cultivated in warm countries throughout the world for the red and purple bracts that cover the flowers. [from L A de *Bougainville*]

bough /baʊ/ *n.* any of the main branches of a tree. [Old English]

bought past and past participle of **buy**.

bouillon /ˈbuːjɔ̃/ *n.* thin clear soup. [French (*bouillir* = boil)]

Boulanger /buːlɒnˈʒeɪ/ Nadia (Juliette) 1887–1979. French music teacher and conductor. A pupil of Fauré and admirer of Stravinsky, she included among her composition pupils at the American Conservatory in Fontainebleau (from 1921) Aaron Copland, Roy Harris, Walter Piston, and Philip Glass.

boulder /ˈbəʊldə/ *n.* a large stone worn smooth by weather or water. [from Scandinavian]

boules /buːl/ *n.pl.* or **pétanque** or (in Italy) **boccie** a game similar to bowls; see ◊bowl³. [French = balls]

boulevard /ˈbuːləvɑːd/ *n.* a broad often tree-lined street (in France etc.); (*US*) a broad main road. [French from German = bulwark (originally of promenade on demolished fortification)]

Boulez /ˈbuːlez/ Pierre 1925– . French composer and conductor. He studied with ◊Messiaen and promoted contemporary music with a series of innovative *Domaine Musical* concerts and recordings in the 1950s, as conductor of the BBC Symphony and New York Philharmonic orchestras during the 1970s, and as founder and director of IRCAM, a music-research studio in Paris opened in 1976.

boulle /buːl/ *n.* or **buhl** a type of ◊marquetry in brass and tortoiseshell. It originated in Italy. [from its most skilful exponent, the French artisan André-Charles *Boulle* (1642–1732)]

boult variant of ◊bolt².

Boulting /ˈbəʊltɪŋ/ John 1913–85 and Roy 1913– . British film director and producer team that was successful in the late 1940s and 1950s. Their films include *Brighton Rock*

1947, *Lucky Jim* 1957, and *I'm All Right Jack* 1959. They were twins.

Boulton Matthew 1728–1809. British factory-owner, who helped to finance James Watt's development of the steam engine. Boulton had an engineering works at Soho near Birmingham, and in 1775 he went into partnership with Watt to develop engines to power factory machines that had previously been driven by water.

I sell here, Sir, what all the world desires to have
—POWER.

Matthew Boulton
to Boswell
(of his engineering works, in 1776)

Boumédienne /buːˈmeɪdjen/ Houari. The adopted name of Mohammed Boukharouba 1925–1978. Algerian politician who brought the nationalist leader Ben Bella to power by a revolt in 1962, and superseded him as president in 1965 by a further coup.

bounce *v.t./i.* 1. to rebound or cause to rebound; (*slang*, of a cheque) to be returned by the bank as worthless. 2. to rush noisily or boisterously. —*n.* 1. an act or the power of bouncing. 2. a self-confident manner, swagger. —**bouncy** *adj.*

bouncer *n.* 1. a ◊bumper in cricket. 2. a person employed to eject troublesome people from a nightclub etc.

bouncing *adj.* (usually of a baby) big and healthy.

bound[1] *v.i.* to spring or leap, to move by leaps; (of a ball etc.) to recoil from a wall or the ground. —*n.* a springy upward or forward movement; the recoil of a ball etc. [from Anglo-French, originally = resound]

bound[2] *n.* (usually in *plural*) the limit of a territory; a limitation, a restriction. —*v.t.* to set bounds to; to be the boundary of. —**beat the bounds**, see ◊beat[1]. **out of bounds**, beyond one's permitted area. [from Anglo-French from Latin]

bound[3] *adj.* heading *for* a place or in a given direction. [from Old Norse = ready]

bound[4] past participle of **bind**. —*adj.* 1. obliged by law or duty *to*; certain *to*. 2. tied or fastened. —**bound up with**, closely associated with.

boundary /ˈbaʊndərɪ/ *n.* 1. a line marking the limit of land etc. 2. in cricket, the limit of the field; a hit to this, scoring four or six runs. —**boundary layer**, the layer of fluid adjacent to the surface of a moving body, or of air to an aircraft in motion.

Boundary Peak highest mountain in Nevada, USA, rising to 4,006 m/13,143 ft on the Nevada–California frontier.

bounden /ˈbaʊndən/ *adj.* (of duty etc.) obligatory. [archaic past participle of *bind*[1]]

boundless *adj.* unlimited.

bountiful /ˈbaʊntɪfʊl/ *adj.* 1. generous in giving. 2. ample.

bounty /ˈbaʊntɪ/ *n.* 1. liberality in giving; a generous gift. 2. a sum paid as an official reward, especially by the state. [from Old French from Latin *bonus* = good]

Bounty Mutiny on the; a naval mutiny in the Pacific in 1789 against British captain William ◊Bligh.

bouquet /buːˈkeɪ/ *n.* 1. a bunch of flowers for carrying in the hand. 2. a compliment. 3. the perfume of a wine. —**bouquet garni** /ˈgɑːnɪ/, a bunch or bag of mixed herbs for flavouring a stew etc. [French, from Old French *bois* = wood]

bourbon /ˈbɜːbən/ *n.* (US) whisky distilled from maize and rye. [from *Bourbon* County, Kentucky, where first made]

Bourbon /ˈbuəbən/ Charles, Duke of 1490–1527. Constable of France, honoured for his courage at the Battle of Marignano in 1515. Later he served the Holy Roman Emperor Charles V, and helped to drive the French from Italy. In 1526 he was made duke of Milan, and in 1527 allowed his troops to sack Rome. He was killed by a shot the artist Cellini claimed to have fired.

Bourbon, duchy of /ˈbuəbən/ originally a seigneury (feudal domain) created in the 10th century in the county of Bourges, central France, held by the Bourbon family. It became a duchy in 1327.

Bourbon, house of French royal dynasty (succeeding that of ◊Valois) beginning with Henry IV in 1589 and ending with Louis XVI in 1792, with a brief revival under Louis

XVIII, Charles X, and Louis Philippe. The Bourbons also ruled Spain almost uninterruptedly from Philip V to Alfonso XIII and were restored in 1975 (◊Juan Carlos); at one point they also ruled Naples and several Italian duchies.

Bourdon gauge /ˈbuədən/ an instrument for measuring pressure. The gauge contains a C-shaped tube, closed at one end and oval in cross-section, which straightens and changes circumference slightly when a gas or liquid under pressure flows into it. Levers and gears make the movement at the end of the tube work a pointer, which indicates pressure on a circular scale. [from its inventor in 1849, French hydraulic engineer Eugène *Bourdon* (1808–1884)]

bourgeois /ˈbuəʒwɑː/ *adj.* of or associated with the middle classes; conventional, materialistic. —*n.* a bourgeois person. [French = burgess]

bourgeoisie /buəʒwɑːˈziː/ *n.* the middle classes: those above the workers and peasants, and below the nobility. Bourgeoisie (and bourgeois) has also acquired a contemptuous sense, implying commonplace, philistine respectability. By socialists it is applied to the whole propertied class, as distinct from the proletariat. [French, originally = the freemen of a borough]

Bourgogne /buəˈɡɔɲ/ region of France that includes the *départements* of Côte-d'Or, Nièvre, Sâone-et-Loire, and Yonne; area 31,600 sq km/12,198 sq mi; population (1986) 1,607,000. Its capital is Dijon. It is renowned for its wines, such as Chablis and Nuits-Saint-Georges, and for its cattle (the Charolais herdbook is maintained at Nevers). A former independent kingdom and duchy (English name ◊Burgundy), it was incorporated into France in 1477.

Bourguiba /buəˈɡiːbə/ Habib ben Ali 1903– . Tunisian politician, first president of Tunisia 1957–87. Educated at the University of Paris, he became a journalist and was frequently imprisoned by the French for his nationalist aims as leader of the Néo-Destour party. He became prime minister in 1956, president (for life from 1974) and prime minister of the Tunisian republic in 1957; he was overthrown in a coup in 1987.

bourn /buən/ *n.* a small stream.

bourne /bɔːn/ *n.* (*archaic*) a limit. [from French *borne* from Old French *bodne*]

Bournonville /buənɒŋˈviːl/ August 1805–1879. Danish dancer and choreographer. He worked with the Royal Danish Ballet for most of his life, giving Danish ballet a worldwide importance. His ballets, many of which were revived in the later 20th century, include *La Sylphide* 1836 (music by Lövenskjöld) and *Napoli* 1842.

bourse /buəs/ *n.* a money market; **Bourse**, the Paris stock exchange. [French = purse, from Latin *bursa*]

bout *n.* 1. a turn or spell of an activity; an attack *of* an illness. 2. a boxing or wrestling match. [from obsolete *bought* = bending]

boutique /buːˈtiːk/ *n.* a small shop or department selling clothes and other items of fashion. [French]

Bouts /baʊts/ Dierick *c.*1420–1475. Early Netherlandish painter. Born in Haarlem, he settled in Louvain, painting portraits and religious scenes influenced by Rogier van der Weyden. *The Last Supper* 1464–68 (St Pierre, Louvain) is one of his finest works.

Bouvines, Battle of /buːˈviːn/ a victory for Philip II (Philip Augustus) of France in 1214, near the village of Bouvines in Flanders, over the Holy Roman emperor Otto IV and his allies. The battle, one of the most decisive in medieval Europe, ensured the succession of Frederick II as emperor and confirmed Philip as ruler of the whole of N France and Flanders; it led to the renunciation of all English claims to the region.

bouzouki /buːˈzuːkɪ/ *n.* a Greek stringed instrument of the lute family, plucked with a plectrum, played in popular music. [modern Greek]

bovine /ˈbəʊvaɪn/ *adj.* of or like an ox; dull, stupid. [from Latin *bos* = ox]

bovine somatotropin (BST) a hormone that increases an injected cow's milk yield by 10–40%. It is a protein naturally occurring in milk, and breaks down within the human digestive tract into harmless amino acids. However, following trials in the UK in 1988, doubts have arisen whether such a degree of protein addition could in the long term be guaranteed harmless either to cattle or to humans.

bovine spongiform encephalopathy (BSE) a disease of cattle, allied to ◊scrapie, that renders the brain spongy and may drive an animal mad. It has been identified only in the UK, where more than 14,000 cases had been confirmed between the first diagnosis, in Nov 1986, and June 1990.

bow[1] /baʊ/ *n.* **1.** a shallow curve or bend; a thing of this form. **2.** a weapon for shooting arrows, with string stretched across the ends of a curved piece of wood etc. **3.** a flexible stick with stretched horsehair for playing a violin etc. **4.** a knot made with a loop or loops, a ribbon etc. so tied. —*v.t.* to use the bow on (a violin etc., or *absolute*). —**bow-legged** *adj.* having bandy legs. **bow tie,** a necktie tied in a bow. **bow window,** a curved bay window. [Old English]

bow[2] /baʊ/ *v.t./i.* **1.** to incline the head or body, especially in formal salutation; to incline (the head) thus. **2.** to cause to bend under a weight. —*n.* an act of bowing. —**bow and scrape,** to be obsequiously polite. **take a bow,** to acknowledge applause. [Old English]

bow[3] *n.* (often in *plural*) the fore end of a boat or ship; the rower nearest the bow. [from Low German or Dutch]

Bow /baʊ/ Clara 1905–1965. US silent-film actress, known as the 'It Girl' after her vivacious performance in *It* 1927. Her other films included *Wings* 1927 and *The Wild Party* 1929. Scandals about her romances and her mental and physical fragility led to the end of her career.

Bow Bells the bells of St Mary-le-Bow church, Cheapside, London; a person born within the sound of Bow Bells is traditionally considered a true Cockney. The bells also feature in the legend of Dick ◊Whittington.

Bowdler /ˈbaʊdlə/ Thomas 1754–1825. English editor, whose prudishly expurgated versions of Shakespeare and other authors gave rise to **bowdlerize** *v.t.* to expurgate (a book or author). —**bowdlerization** /-ˈzeɪʃən/ *n.*

bowel /ˈbaʊəl/ *n.* a division of the alimentary canal below the stomach, the ◊intestine; (in *plural*) innermost parts. [from Old French from Latin (diminutive of *botulus* = sausage)]

bower /ˈbaʊə/ *n.* a leafy shelter, an arbour. [Old English = dwelling]

bowerbird *n.* a New Guinean and N Australian bird of the family Ptilonorhynchidae, related to the ◊birds of paradise. The males are dull-coloured and build elaborate bowers of sticks and grass, decorated with shells, feathers, or flowers, and even painted with the juice of berries, to attract the females. There are 17 species.

bowfin *n.* a North American fish *Amia calva* with a swim bladder highly developed as an air sac, enabling it to breathe air. It is the only surviving member of a primitive group of bony fishes.

bowhead *n.* an Arctic whale *Balaena mysticetus* with strongly curving upper jawbones supporting the plates of baleen with which it sifts planktonic crustaceans from the water. Averaging 15 m/50 ft long and 90 tonnes in weight, these slow-moving, placid whales were once extremely common, but by the 17th century were already becoming scarce through hunting. Only an estimated 3,000 remain, and continued hunting by the Inuit may result in extinction.

Bowie /ˈbaʊi/ David. Stage name of David Jones 1947– . English pop singer, songwriter, and actor, born in Brixton, London. He became a glam-rock star in the early 1970s with the release of *The Rise and Fall of Ziggy Stardust and the Spiders from Mars* album in 1972, and collaborated in the mid-1970s with the electronic virtuoso Brian Eno (1948–) and Iggy Pop. He has also acted in plays and films, including Nicolas Roeg's *The Man Who Fell to Earth* 1976.

Bowie James 'Jim' 1796–1836. US frontier scout and folk hero. A colonel in the Texan forces during the Mexican War, he is said to have invented the single-edge, curved hunting and throwing knife known as a **bowie knife**. He was killed in the battle of the ◊Alamo.

bowl[1] /baʊl/ *n.* **1.** a round, open vessel for food or liquid. **2.** the rounded part of a tobacco pipe, spoon etc. **3.** the contents of a bowl. **4.** (*US*) an outdoor stadium (originally bowl-shaped) for football. [Old English]

bowl[2] *n.* a hard ball weighted or shaped so as to run in a curve; (in *plural*) a game played with these on grass, or with round balls in tenpin bowling or skittles. It has been played in Britain since the 13th century at least. —*v.t.* **1.** to play bowls; to roll (a ball etc.) along the ground. **2.** in cricket, to deliver (a ball); to dismiss (a batsman) by delivering a ball that hits the wicket. **3.** to move (*along*) rapidly in a vehicle

Bowie *British pop singer and songwriter. David Bowie has also acted in films, notably* The Man Who Fell to Earth *1976*

etc. —**bowling alley,** one of a series of enclosed channels for playing skittles; a building containing these. **bowling green,** a lawn for playing bowls. **bowl over,** to knock down; to amaze or disconcert. [from French from Latin *bulla* = bubble]

bowler[1] /ˈbaʊlə/ *n.* **1.** one who plays bowls. **2.** in cricket, the player who delivers the ball.

bowler[2] *n.* a stiff felt hat with a rounded crown. [from J *Bowler*, London hatter who designed it in 1850]

bowline /ˈbaʊlɪn/ *n.* **1.** a rope from a ship's bow keeping the sail taut against the wind. **2.** a knot forming a nonslipping loop at the end of a rope.

bowling /ˈbaʊlɪŋ/ *n.* or **tenpin bowling** an indoor game for individual players or for teams, in which a player tries to knock down with a ball ten 'pins' placed in a triangle.

Bowman's capsule /ˈbaʊmən/ in the vertebrate kidney, a microscopic filtering device used in the initial stages of waste removal and urine formation.

bowsprit /ˈbaʊsprɪt/ *n.* a long spar running forward from a ship's bow. [from Middle Low German or Middle Dutch]

box[1] *n.* **1.** a container for solids, usually with flat sides and a lid; the quantity contained in this. **2.** a separate compartment, as for several people in a theatre, for horses in a stable etc., or witnesses in a lawcourt. **3.** a boxlike shelter, as for a sentry, person telephoning etc.; a small country house for shooting, fishing etc. **4.** a confined space. **5.** a receptacle at a newspaper office for replies to an advertisement. **6.** a coachman's seat. —*v.t.* to put in or provide with a box. —**box girder,** a girder made of plates fastened in a box shape. **box in** or **up,** to shut into a small space restricting movement. **box junction,** a road intersection with a yellow-striped area which a vehicle may not enter (except when turning right) until its exit is clear. **box number,** the number of a box in a newspaper office. **box office,** an office for booking seats at a theatre etc. **box pleat,** a combination of two parallel pleats forming a raised strip. **boxroom** *n.* a room for storing boxes etc. **box spring,** each of a set of vertical springs in a mattress. [Old English, from Latin *pyxis, buxis*]

box[2] *v.t./i.* **1.** to fight with the fists, especially in ◊boxing gloves as a sport. **2.** to slap (a person's ears). —*n.* a hard slap on the ears etc.

box[3] *n.* an evergreen shrub of the genus *Buxus*, especially *B. sempervirens*, much used in hedging and topiary; its wood. [Old English from Latin *buxus*, variant of Latin *pyxis* = box of boxwood]

boxer *n.* **1.** one who boxes for sport. **2.** a dog of a breed of medium size with a smooth coat and a set-back nose. The tail is usually docked. Boxers are usually brown but may be brindled or white.

Boxer *n.* a member of the *I ho ch'üan* ('Righteous Harmonious Fists'), an antiforeign society of Chinese nationalists who in 1900, at the instigation of the empress dowager, besieged the European and US legations in Beijing and murdered missionaries and thousands of Chinese Christian converts (the **Boxer Rebellion** *or* **Uprising**). An international punitive force was dispatched, Beijing was captured on 14 Aug 1900, and China agreed to pay a large indemnity.

boxfish *n.* any fish of the family Ostraciodontidae, with scales that are hexagonal bony plates fused to form a box covering the body, only the mouth and fins being free of the armour.

boxing *n.* fighting with fists, almost entirely a male sport. It dates from the 18th century, when fights were fought with bare knuckles and untimed rounds. Each round ended with a knockdown. Fighting with gloves became the accepted form in the latter part of the 19th century after the formulation of the Queensberry Rules in 1867. —**boxing glove,** a padded glove worn in the sport of boxing. **boxing weight,** the weight at which boxers are matched. British professional scale, upper weight limits: flyweight 8 stone, bantamweight 8 stone 6 lbs, featherweight 9 stone, lightweight 9 stone 9 lbs, light welterweight 10 stone, welterweight 10 stone 7 lbs, light middleweight 11 stone, middleweight 11 stone 6 lbs, light heavyweight 12 stone 7 lbs, heavyweight (no limit; any weight above 12 stone 7 lbs). The weights and divisions are modified in the amateur scale.

Boxing Day in Britain, the first weekday after Christmas, when Christmas boxes used to be presented.

boy *n.* 1. a male child. 2. a young man. 3. (*derogatory*) a (young) male employee or servant. —**the boys,** a group of men, especially in a social context. **boyfriend** *n.* a girl's or woman's regular male companion. —**boyhood** *n.*, **boyish** *adj.*

boyar *n.* a landowner in the Russian aristocracy. During the 16th century boyars formed a powerful interest group threatening the tsar's power, until their influence was decisively broken in 1565 when Ivan the Terrible confiscated much of their land. [from Russian]

boycott /'bɔɪkɒt/ *v.t.* to combine in refusing to have dealings with (a person, group etc.) or handle (goods etc.). —*n.* an act of boycotting. [from Charles *Boycott*]

Boycott Charles Cunningham 1832–1897. English land agent in County Mayo, Ireland, who strongly opposed the demands for agrarian reform by the Irish Land League 1879–81, with the result that the peasants refused to work for him.

Boycott Geoffrey 1940– . English cricketer born in Yorkshire, England's most prolific run-maker with 8,114 runs in test cricket. He was banned as a test player in 1982 for taking part in matches against South Africa.

Boyd-Orr /'bɔɪd 'ɔː/ John 1880–1971. Scottish nutritionist and health campaigner. He was awarded the Nobel Prize for Peace in 1949 in recognition of his work towards alleviating world hunger.

Boyle's law in physics, the principle that the volume of a given mass of gas at a constant temperature is inversely proportional to its pressure. [from Irish chemist Robert *Boyle* (1627–1691) who discovered it in 1662]

Boyne /bɔɪn/ river in the Irish Republic. Rising in the Bog of Allen in County Kildare, it flows 110 km/69 mi NE to the Irish Sea near Drogheda.

Boyne, Battle of the battle fought on 1 Jul 1690 in E Ireland, in which James II was defeated by William III and fled to France. It was the decisive battle of the War of English Succession, confirming a Protestant monarch. It was fought at Oldbridge near the mouth of the river Boyne.

Boy Scout a member of the ◊Scout organization.

Bo Zhu Yi /'bəʊ 'dʒuː 'jiː/ 772–846. Chinese poet (formerly known as *Po Chu-i*). President from 841 of the imperial war department, he criticized government policy. He is said to have checked his work with an old peasant woman for clarity of expression.

BP abbreviation of 1. British Pharmacopoeia. 2. British Petroleum. 3. before the present (especially in geological dating).

Br symbol for ◊bromine.

BR abbreviation of British Rail.

bra /brɑː/ *n.* a brassière. [abbreviation]

Brabant /brə'bænt/ (Flemish *Braband*) former duchy of W Europe, comprising the Dutch province of ◊North Brabant and the Belgian provinces of Brabant and Antwerp. They were divided when Belgium became independent in 1830. The present-day Belgian province of Brabant has an area of 3,400 sq km/1,312 sq mi and a population (1987) of 2,222,000.

brace *n.* 1. a device that clamps things together or holds and supports them in position. 2. (in *plural*) straps to hold up the trousers, fastened to the waistband and passing over the shoulders. 3. (especially of game; *plural* same) a pair. 4. a rope attached to the yard of a ship for trimming a sail. 5. a connecting mark { or } in printing.—*v.t.* 1. to clamp or hold up by a brace, to fasten tightly, to steady against pressure or shock. 2. to invigorate. —**brace and bit,** a revolving tool with a D-shaped handle, for boring holes. [from Old French from Latin *bracchia* = arms]

bracelet /'breɪslɪt/ *n.* an ornamental band or chain worn on the wrist or arm. [from Old French, diminutive of *bracel* from Latin *bracchiale*]

brachiopod /'brækɪəpɒd/ *n.* an invertebrate of the phylum Brachiopoda with two shells, resembling but totally unrelated to bivalves, found especially as a fossil. There are about 300 living species; they were much more numerous in past geological ages. They are suspension feeders, ingesting minute food particles from water. A single internal organ, the iophophore, handles feeding, aspiration, and excretion. [from Greek *brakhiōn* = arm and *pous podos* = foot]

brachiosaurus /brækɪə'sɔːrəs/ *n.* a huge dinosaur of the genus *Brachiosaurus*, with the forelegs longer than the hind legs. [from Greek *brakhiōn* = arm and *sauros* = lizard]

brachycephalic /ˌbrækɪsɪ'fælɪk/ *adj.* having a short rounded skull. —**brachycephalous** /-'sefələs/ *adj.*, **brachycephaly** *n.* [from Greek *brakhus* = short and *kephalē* = head]

bracken /'brækən/ *n.* a large fern of heaths and hillsides, especially *Pteridium aquilinum*, abundant in the northern hemisphere; a mass of such ferns. A perennial rootstock throws up coarse fronds. [from Old Norse]

bracket /'brækɪt/ *n.* 1. a flat-topped projection from a wall supporting a statue, arch etc.; a shelf fixed with an angled prop to a wall. 2. a mark used in pairs ( ) [ ] to enclose words or figures. 3. a group of people classified together as similar or falling between given limits. —*v.t.* 1. to enclose (words etc.) in brackets. 2. to group in the same category. —**bracket clock,** a clock designed to stand on a shelf or wall bracket. **bracket fungus,** any ◊fungus of the class Basidiomycetes, with fruiting bodies that grow like shelves from trees. [from Spanish from Latin *bracae* = breeches]

brackish *adj.* (of water) slightly saline. [from Low German or Dutch]

bract *n.* a leaflike structure in whose ◊axil a flower or inflorescence develops. Bracts are generally green and smaller than the true leaves. However, in some plants they may be brightly coloured and conspicuous, taking over the role of attracting pollinating insects to the flowers, whose own petals are small; examples include poinsettia *Euphorbia pulcherrima* and bougainvillea. [from Latin *bractea* = thin metal sheet]

Bracton /'bræktən/ Henry de, died 1268. English judge, writer on English law, and chancellor of Exeter cathedral from 1264. He compiled an account of the laws and customs of the English, *De Legibus et consuetudinibus Anglie,* the first of its kind.

brad *n.* a thin, flat nail with the head in the form of a slight enlargement at the top. [from Old Norse = spike]

bradawl /'brædɔːl/ *n.* a small, non-spiral hand tool for boring holes for brads and screws.

Bradbury /'brædbəri/ Malcolm 1932– . English novelist and critic, whose writings include comic and satiric portrayals of academic life. Professor of American studies at the University of East Anglia from 1970. His major work is *The History Man* 1975, set in a provincial English university; other works include *Rates of Exchange* 1983.

Marriage is the most advanced form of warfare in the modern world.

Malcolm Bradbury
The History Man

Bradbury Ray 1920– . US writer, one of the first science-fiction writers to make the genre 'respectable' to a wider readership. His work shows nostalgia for small-town Midwestern life, and includes *The Martian Chronicles* 1950, *Something Wicked This Way Comes* 1962, and *Fahrenheit 451* 1953.

Bradford /'brædfəd/ industrial city (engineering, machine tools, electronics, printing) in West Yorkshire, England, 14 km/9 mi W of Leeds; population (1981) 281,000.

Bradlaugh /'brædlɔː/ Charles 1833–1891. English free-thinker and radical politician. In 1880 he was elected Liberal member of Parliament for Northampton, but was not allowed to take his seat until 1886 because, as an atheist, he (unsuccessfully) claimed the right to affirm instead of taking the oath. He was associated with the feminist Annie Besant.

Bradley /'brædli/ Omar Nelson 1893–1981. US general in World War II. In 1943 he commanded the 2nd US Corps in Tunisia and Sicily, and in 1944 led the US troops in the invasion of France. He was chief of staff of the US Army 1948–49 and chair of the joint chiefs of staff 1949–53. He was appointed general of the army in 1950.

Bradman /'brædmən/ Donald George 1908– . Australian test cricketer with the highest average in test history. From 52 test matches he averaged 99.94 runs per innings. He only needed four runs from his final test innings to average 100 but was dismissed at second ball.

Bradshaw /'brædʃɔː/ George 1801–1853. English publisher who brought out the first railway timetable in 1839. Thereafter *Bradshaw's Railway Companion* appeared at regular intervals.

brae /breɪ/ n. (*Scottish*) a steep slope, a hillside. [from Old Norse = eyelash]

brag v.t./i. (-gg-) to talk boastfully; to boast. —n. boastful talk.

Bragança /brə'gænsə/ 1. capital of a province of the same name in NE Portugal, 176 km/110 mi NE of Oporto. Population (1981) 13,900. It was the original family seat of the royal house of Bragança. 2. the royal house of Portugal whose members reigned 1640–1853; another branch were emperors of Brazil 1822–89.

braggart /'brægət/ n. boastful person. —adj. boastful

Brahe /'braːhə/ Tycho 1546–1601. Danish astronomer, who made accurate observations of the planets from which the German astronomer and mathematician Johann ◊Kepler proved that planets orbit the Sun in ellipses. His discovery and report of the 1572 supernova brought him recognition, and his observations of the comet of 1577 proved that it moved on an orbit among the planets, thus disproving the Greek view that comets were in the Earth's atmosphere.

Brahma /'braːmə/ in Hinduism, the creator of the cosmos, who forms with Vishnu and Siva the Trimurti, or three aspects of the absolute spirit.

Brahman /'braːmən/ 1. in Hinduism, the supreme being, an abstract, impersonal world-soul into whom the *atman*, or individual soul, will eventually be absorbed when its cycle of rebirth is ended. 2. variant of ◊brahmin. [Sanskrit = sacred knowledge]

Brahmanism n. the earliest stage in the development of ◊Hinduism. Its sacred scriptures are the ◊Vedas, with their accompanying literature of comment and explanation known as Brahmanas, Aranyakas, and Upanishads.

Brahmaputra /braːmə'puːtrə/ river in Asia 2,900 km/ 1,800 mi long, a tributary of the Ganges.

Brahma Samaj /'braːmə sə'maːdʒ/ Indian monotheistic religious movement, founded in 1830 in Calcutta by Ram Mohun Roy, who attempted to recover the simple worship of the Vedas and purify Hinduism. The movement had split into a number of sects by the end of the 19th century and is now almost defunct.

brahmin /'braːmɪn/ n. a member of the Hindu priestly class, versed in sacred knowledge (the ◊Veda). —**brahminical** /-'mɪnɪkəl/ adj., **brahminism** n. [Sanskrit = sacred knowledge]

Brahms /braːmz/ Johannes 1833–1897. German composer, pianist, and conductor, considered one of the greatest composers of symphonic music and songs. His works include four symphonies; ◊lieder (songs); concertos for piano and for violin; chamber music; sonatas; and the choral *A German Requiem* 1868. He performed and conducted his own works.

braid n. 1. a woven band of silk or thread used for trimming. 2. a plaited tress of hair. —v.t. 1. to trim with braid. 2. to plait. 3. (especially in *past participle*; of a stream) to divide (especially at low water) into several channels. [Old English]

Braille /breɪl/ n. a system of writing for the blind. Letters are represented by a combination of raised dots on paper or other materials, which are then read by touch. —v.t. to represent in Braille. [from Louis *Braille*, its inventor (1809–1852), a blind French teacher who perfected his system in 1834]

brain n. 1. in higher animals, a mass of interconnected ◊nerve cells, forming the anterior part of the ◊central nervous system, whose activities it coordinates and controls. In ◊vertebrates, the brain is contained by the skull. An enlarged portion of the upper spinal cord, the **medulla oblongata**, contains centres for the control of respiration, heartbeat rate and strength, and blood pressure. Overlying this is the **cerebellum**, which is concerned with coordinating complex muscular processes such as maintaining posture and moving limbs. The cerebral hemispheres (**cerebrum**) are paired outgrowths of the front end of the forebrain, in early vertebrates mainly concerned with the senses, but in higher vertebrates greatly developed and involved in the integration of all sensory input and motor output, and in intelligent behaviour. 2. an intelligent person; (also in *plural*) one who organizes a complex plan or idea. 3. (often in *plural*) intellectual power. 4. an electronic device with functions comparable to the brain's. —v.t. to kill by a heavy blow on the head. —**brainchild** n. a person's inspired idea. **brain drain,** the loss of talented or professional people by emigration. **brain stem,** the stemlike portion of the brain connecting the cerebral hemispheres with the spinal cord. **brains trust,** a group of experts giving impromptu answers to questions (as a form of entertainment). **on the brain,** obsessively in one's thoughts. [Old English]

Braine /breɪn/ John 1922–1986. English novelist. His novel *Room at the Top* 1957 created the character of Joe Lampton, one of the first of the northern working-class antiheroes.

brainless adj. lacking intelligence.

brainpower n. mental ability or intelligence.

brainstorm n. 1. a sudden extreme mental disturbance. 2. (*US*) a sudden bright idea.

brainstorming n. (*US*) a spontaneous discussion in a search for new ideas.

brainwash v.t. to implant new ideas in the mind of (a person) and eliminate established ones by subjecting him or her systematically to great mental pressure.

brainwave n. 1. an electrical impulse in the brain. 2. (*colloquial*) a sudden bright idea.

brainy adj. intellectually active or clever. —**braininess** n.

braise /breɪz/ v.t. to cook (meat) slowly in fat or with very little liquid in a closed vessel. [from French *braise* = live coals]

Braithwaite /'breɪθweɪt/ Eustace Adolph 1912– . Guyanese author. His experiences as a teacher in London prompted *To Sir with Love* 1959. His *Reluctant Neighbours* 1972 deals with black–white relations.

brake[1] n. a device for checking the motion of a wheel, vehicle etc. The mechanically applied caliper brake used on bicycles uses a scissor action to press hard rubber blocks against the wheel rim. The main braking system of a car works hydraulically: when the driver depresses the brake pedal, liquid pressure forces pistons to apply brakes on each wheel. —v.t./i. to apply a brake; to retard by a brake. —**brake drum,** a cylinder attached to a wheel, on which the brake shoe presses. **brake horsepower,** the power of an engine measured by the force needed to

brake

disc brake

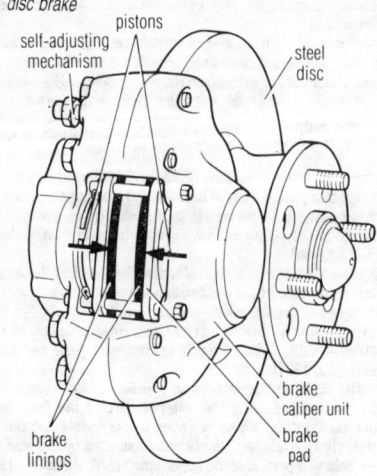

self-adjusting
mechanism
pistons
steel
disc
brake
caliper unit
brake
pad
brake
linings

drum brake

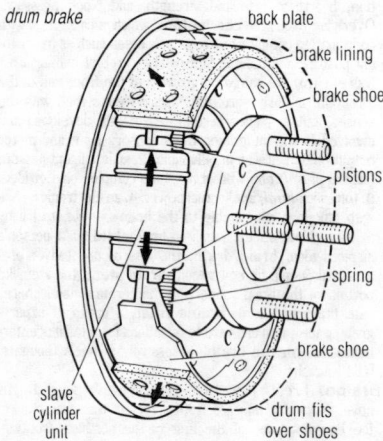

back plate
brake lining
brake shoe
pistons
spring
brake shoe
slave
cylinder
unit
drum fits
over shoes

brake it. **brake shoe,** a long curved block acting on a wheel to brake it.

brake[2] *n.* a clump of bushes, a thicket. [from Old English = branch, stump]

brake[3] *n.* (*British*) an estate car. [variant of *break* = carriage frame, wagonette]

Bramah /ˈbrɑːmə/ Joseph 1748–1814. English inventor of a flushing water closet in 1778, an 'unpickable' lock in 1784, and the hydraulic press in 1795. The press made use of ◊Pascal's principle (that pressure in fluid contained in a vessel is evenly distributed) and employed water as the hydraulic fluid; it enabled the 19th-century bridge builders to lift massive girders.

Bramante /brəˈmænti/ Donato *c.*1444–1514. Italian Renaissance architect and artist. Inspired by Classical designs, he was employed by Pope Julius II in rebuilding part of the Vatican and St Peter's in Rome.

bramble *n.* a rough prickly shrub of the genus *Rubus* with long trailing shoots; its fruit. Examples are ◊blackberry, raspberry, and dewberry. —**brambly** *adj.* [Old English]

brambling *n.* a brightly coloured bird *Fringilla montifringilla* belonging to the finch family, about 15 cm/6 in long. It breeds in N Europe and Asia. [from German]

bran *n.* ground husks of grain, sifted out from the flour. —**bran tub,** (British) a lucky dip with prizes hidden in bran. [from Old French]

Branagh /ˈbrænə/ Kenneth 1960– . Irish actor and director. He launched his Renaissance Theatre Company in 1987, was a notable Hamlet and Touchstone in 1988,

and in 1989 directed and starred in a film of Shakespeare's *Henry V.*

branch /brɑːntʃ/ *n.* **1.** a limb from the trunk or bough of a tree. **2.** a lateral extension of a river, road, railway etc. **3.** a subdivision of a family, study etc. **4.** a local establishment of a bank or other central organization. —*v.t.* to diverge from the main part; (often with *off*) to divide into branches; to put out branches. —**branch out,** to extend one's field of interest. [from Old French from Latin *branca* = paw]

Brancusi /brænˈkuːzi/ Constantin 1876–1957. Romanian sculptor, active in Paris from 1904, a pioneer of abstract forms and conceptual art. He was one of the first sculptors in the 20th century to carve directly from his material, working with marble, granite, wood, and other materials. By the 1930s he had achieved monumental simplicity with structures of simple repeated forms (*Endless Column* and other works in Tirgu Jiu public park, Romania).

brand *n.* **1.** a trade mark, identifying label etc., on goods; a particular make of goods. **2.** a mark of ownership burned on livestock with a hot iron, the iron used for this. **3.** a stigma, mark of disgrace. **4.** a piece of burning or charred wood. —*v.t.* **1.** to assign a trade mark or proprietary label to (goods). **2.** to mark with a hot iron as a mark of ownership or disgrace; to stigmatize. **3.** to impress on the memory. —**brand-new** *adj.* completely new. [Old English]

Brandenburg /ˈbrændənbɜːg/ administrative *Land* (state) of Germany; **area** 25,000 sq km/10,000 sq mi; **capital** Potsdam; **products** iron and steel, paper, pulp, metal products, semiconductors; **population** (1990) 2,700,000; **recent history** at the end of World War II, Brandenburg lost over 12,950 sq km/5,000 sq mi of territory when Poland advanced its frontier to the line of the Oder and Neisse rivers. The remainder, which became a region of East Germany, was divided in 1952 into the districts of Frankfurt-on-Oder, Potsdam, and Cottbus. When Germany was reunited in 1990, Brandenburg reappeared as a state of the federal republic.

brandish /ˈbrændɪʃ/ *v.t.* to wave (weapons etc.) threateningly or in display. [from Old French from Germanic]

Brando /ˈbrændəʊ/ Marlon 1924– . US actor whose casual, mumbling speech and use of ◊Method acting earned him a place as one of the most distinctive screen actors. His films include *A Streetcar Named Desire* 1951, *The Wild One* 1954, *On the Waterfront* 1954 (Academy Award), *The Godfather,* and *Last Tango in Paris* both 1972.

Brandt /brænt/ Bill 1905–1983. English photographer who produced a large body of richly printed and romantic black-and-white studies of people, London life, and social behaviour.

Brandt Willy. The adopted name of Karl Herbert Frahm 1913– . West German socialist politician, federal chancellor (premier) 1969–74. He played a key role in the remoulding of the Social Democratic Party (SPD) as a moderate socialist force (leader 1964–87). As mayor of West Berlin 1957–66, Brandt became internationally known during the Berlin Wall crisis of 1961. He received the Nobel Peace Prize in 1971.

brandy /ˈbrændi/ *n.* a strong spirit distilled from fermented grape juice (notably that of France, for example Armagnac and Cognac), or that of other fruits such as calvados (from apples) and Kirschwasser (from cherries). Brandy contains up to 55% alcohol. —**brandy snap,** a crisp rolled gingerbread wafer. [from Dutch *brandewijn* = burnt (distilled) wine]

Branson /ˈbrænsən/ Richard 1950– . British entrepreneur, whose Virgin company developed quickly, diversifying from retailing records to the airline business.

Braque /brɑːk/ Georges 1882–1963. French painter who, with Picasso, founded the Cubist movement around 1907–10. They worked together at L'Estaque in the south of France and in Paris. Braque began to experiment in collages and invented a technique of gluing paper, wood, and other materials to canvas. His later work became more decorative.

brash *adj.* vulgarly or obnoxiously self-assertive, impudent. [dialect]

Brasília /brəˈzɪliə/ capital of Brazil from 1960, 1,000 m/3,000 ft above sea level; population (1980) 411,500. It was designed by Lucio Costa (1902–63), with Oscar Niemeyer as chief architect, as a completely new city to bring life to the interior.

Braşov /brɑːˈsɒv/ (Hungarian *Brassó*, German *Krondstadt*) industrial city (machine tools, industrial equipment, chemicals, cement, woollens) in central Romania at the foot of the Transylvanian Alps; population (1985) 347,000. It belonged to Hungary until 1920.

brass /brɑːs/ *n.* 1. a widely used metal ◊alloy of copper and zinc, with not more than 5% or 6% of other metals. The zinc content ranges from 20% to 45%, and the colour of brass varies accordingly from coppery to whitish yellow. Brasses are characterized by the ease with which they may be shaped and machined; they are strong and ductile, resist many forms of corrosion, and are used for electrical fittings, ammunition cases, screws, household fittings, and ornaments. 2. brass objects or wind instruments made of brass or other metal, which are directly blown through a 'cup' or 'funnel' mouthpiece; a brass memorial tablet in a church; a brass ornament worn by a horse. In a symphony orchestra brass instruments comprise: the French horn, a descendant of the natural hunting horn, valved, and curved into a circular loop, with a wide bell; the trumpet, a cylindrical tube curved into an oblong, with a narrow bell and three valves (the state fanfare trumpet has no valves); the trombone, an instrument with a 'slide' to vary the effective length of the tube (the sackbut, common from the 14th century, was its forerunner); and the tuba, normally the lowest-toned instrument of the orchestra; valved and with a very wide bore to give sonority, it has a bell that points upward. 3. (*historical*) bronze. 4. (*colloquial*) money. 5. (*slang*) impudence. —*adj.* made of brass. —**brass band**, a band playing brass instruments. In descending order of pitch, they comprise: the cornet, a three-valved instrument, looking like a shorter, broader trumpet, and with a wider bore; the flugelhorn, a valved instrument, rather similar in range to the cornet; the tenor horn; B-flat baritone; euphonium; trombone; and bombardon (bass tuba). A brass band normally also includes bass and side drums, triangle, and cymbals. **brass rubbing**, the taking of impressions on paper of memorial brasses. **brass tacks**, (*colloquial*) essential details. [Old English]

Brassaï /bræsɑːˈiː/ the adopted name of Gyula Halesz 1899–1986. French photographer of Hungarian origin. From the early 1930s on, he documented the nightlife of Paris (mainly by flash) before turning to more abstract work.

brasserie /ˈbræsərɪ/ *n.* a bar where food can be obtained as well as drinks; an informal licensed restaurant. [French = brewery (*brasser* = brew)]

Brassica /ˈbræsɪkə/ *n.* a genus of plants of the family Cruciferae. The most familiar species is the common cabbage *Brassica oleracea*, with its varieties broccoli, cauliflower, kale, and brussels sprouts. [Latin]

brassière /ˈbræsɪeə/ *n.* a woman's undergarment supporting the breasts. [French]

brassy /ˈbrɑːsɪ/ *adj.* 1. bold and vulgar; pretentious, showy. 2. loud and strident. —**brassiness** *n.*

brat *n.* (*derogatory*) a child.

Bratislava /ˈbrætɪslɑːvə/ (German *Pressburg*) industrial port (engineering, chemicals, oil refining) in Czechoslovakia, on the river Danube; population (1986) 417,000. It was the capital of Hungary 1526–1784 and is now capital of the Slovak Socialist Republic and second largest city in Czechoslovakia.

Brattain /ˈbrætn/ Walter Houser 1902–1987. US physicist. In 1956 he was awarded a Nobel prize jointly with William Shockley and John Bardeen for their work on the development of the transistor, which replaced the comparatively costly and clumsy vacuum tube in electronics.

bravado /brəˈvɑːdəʊ/ *n.* an outward display of fearlessness. [Spanish]

brave *adj.* able or ready to face danger, pain etc. 2. splendid, spectacular. —*v.t.* to face bravely or defiantly. —*n.* a North American Indian warrior. —**bravely** *adj.*, **bravery** /ˈbreɪvərɪ/ *n.* [from French from Spanish]

bravo[1] /ˈbrɑːvəʊ/ *n.* (*plural* **bravos**) interjection of approval; well done! [French from Italian]

bravo[2] *n.* (*plural* **bravoes**) a hired ruffian or killer. [French from Italian]

bravura /brəˈvʊərə/ *n.* a brilliant or ambitious performance; a piece of vocal etc. music calling for technical virtuosity. [Italian]

brawl *n.* a noisy quarrel or fight. —*v.i.* 1. to take part in a brawl. 2. (of a stream) to flow noisily. —**brawler** *n.* [from Provençal]

brawn *n.* 1. muscle, muscular strength. 2. pressed jellied meat made from a pig's head etc. —**brawny** *adj.* [from Anglo-French from Germanic]

bray *n.* a donkey's loud strident cry; any loud harsh sound. —*v.i.* to emit a bray. [from Old French]

braze *v.t.* to join two metals by melting an ◊alloy into the joint. It is similar to soldering but takes place at a much higher temperature. Copper and silver alloys are widely used for brazing, at temperatures up to about 900°C/1,650°F. [from French *braser* (*braise* = live coals)]

brazen /ˈbreɪzən/ *adj.* 1. shameless and defiant. 2. of or like brass; harsh in tone or colour. —*v.t.* to face (a situation) *out* boldly and defiantly after doing wrong. [Old English]

brazier[1] /ˈbreɪzɪə/ a metal stand with burning coal as a portable heater. [from French *brasier*]

brazier[2] /ˈbreɪzɪə/ *n.* a worker in brass. [probably from *brass*, after *glass, glazier*]

Brazil /brəˈzɪl/ Federative Republic of; country in South America, bounded SW by Uruguay, Argentina, Paraguay and Bolivia; W by Peru and Colombia; N by Venezuela, Guyana, Suriname, and French Guiana; and E by the Atlantic Ocean; **area** 8,511,965 sq km/3,285,618 sq mi; **capital** Brasília; **physical** the densely forested Amazon basin covers the northern half of the country with a network of rivers; the south is fertile; enormous energy resources both hydroelectric and nuclear (uranium ore); **head of state and government** Fernando Affonso Collor de Mello from 1989; **political system** emergent democratic federal republic; **exports** coffee, sugar, soya beans, cotton, textiles, timber, motor vehicles, iron, chrome, manganese, tungsten and other ores, as well as quartz crystals, industrial diamonds, gemstones; the world's sixth largest arms exporter; **population** (1990 est) 153,770,000 (including 200,000 Indians, survivors of 5 million, especially in Rondonia and Mato Grosso, mostly living on reservations); **language** Portuguese (official); 120 Indian languages; **recent history** independence achieved from Portugal in 1822; monarchy abolished and republic established in 1889. Free political parties abolished by President Gen Castelo Branco in 1964; legalized again in 1979. Power was transferred from the president to the congress in 1988.

Brazil nut the seed, rich in oil and highly nutritious, of the gigantic South American tree *Bertholletia excelsa*. The seeds are enclosed in a hard outer casing, each fruit containing 10–20 seeds arranged like the segments of an orange. The timber of the tree is also valuable.

brazing a method of joining two metals by melting an ◊alloy into the joint.

Brazzaville /ˈbræzəvɪl/ capital of the Congo, industrial port (foundries, railway repairs, shipbuilding, shoes, soap,

Brazil

furniture, bricks) on the river Zaïre, opposite Kinshasa; population (1984) 595,000.

breach *n.* **1.** a breaking of or failure to observe a law, contract etc. **2.** a breaking of relations, estrangement. **3.** a gap or opening (in fortifications etc). —*v.t.* to make a breach in. —**breach of the peace,** a disturbance, an affray. **breach of promise,** the breaking of a promise to marry. [from Old French from Germanic]

bread *n.* a food made with ground cereals and a moistening agent, such as wheat and water; many variations of ingredients are possible. The dough (the mixture of flour and moisture) is usually kneaded and baked; it may be unleavened or raised (usually with yeast). Bread has been a staple of human diet in many civilizations as long as agriculture has been practised, and some hunter-gatherer peoples made it from crushed acorns or beech nuts. Potatoes, banana and cassava bread are among some local varieties, but most breads are made from fermented cereals which form glutens when mixed with water. The earliest bread was unleavened and was made from a mixture of flour and water and dried in the sun on flat stones. The Egyptians first used ovens and made leavened bread. The yeast creates gas making the dough rise. —*v.t.* to coat with breadcrumbs for frying. [Old English]

breadboard *n.* **1.** a board for cutting bread on. **2.** a board on which an experimental electric circuit is set out.

breadcrumbs *n.pl.* bread crumbled for use in cooking.

breadfruit *n.* the fruit of the tropical trees *Artocarpus communis* and *A. altilis* of the mulberry family Moraceae. It is highly nutritious and when baked is said to taste like bread. It is native to many South Pacific islands.

breadth /bredθ/ *n.* **1.** the distance or measurement from side to side of a thing. **2.** great extent. **3.** freedom from limitations set by prejudice, intolerance etc. [from Old English]

breadwinner *n.* the member of a family who earns the money to support the other(s).

break /breɪk/ *v.t.i.* (*past* **broke**; *past participle* **broken**) **1.** to separate or cause to separate into pieces under a blow or strain; to damage, to make or become inoperative; to break the bone in (a part of the body). **2.** to stop for a time, to make or become discontinuous; (of weather) to change suddenly after a fine spell. **3.** to fail to keep (a law or promise etc.). **4.** to make a way suddenly or violently. **5.** to emerge or appear suddenly (from); to reveal (news etc.); to become known. **6.** to surpass (a record). **7.** to solve (a cipher). **8.** to make or become weak; to overwhelm with grief etc.; to destroy the spirit etc. of (a person). **9.** to change course etc. suddenly; (of a voice) to change its even tone, either with emotion or (of a boy's voice) by becoming suddenly deeper at puberty; (of waves) to fall in foam. **10.** (of boxers) to come out of a clinch. —*n.* **1.** the act or process of breaking. **2.** a point where a thing is broken, a gap. **3.** an interval, an interruption, a pause in activity. **4.** a sudden dash. **5.** (*slang*) a piece of luck. **6.** in cricket, a change of direction of a ball on bouncing. **7.** points scored continuously in billiards etc. —**break away,** to free oneself from constraint; to secede. **break the bank,** to exhaust its funds (in gambling etc.). **break dancing,** a kind of street dancing to a loud beat, with wriggling and bending of the arms and legs, in which the dancers may spin to the floor and revolve on their backs. **break down,** to experience mechanical failure; to make or become ineffective; to suffer an emotional collapse; to reduce to its constituent parts by chemical action or analysis. **break even,** to emerge from a transaction with neither profit nor loss. **break in,** to enter forcibly; to interpose a remark; to accustom to a habit or duties etc.; to wear until comfortable. **break-in** *n.* a forcible entry by a thief etc. **breaking point,** the point at which a person or thing gives way under stress. **break into,** to enter forcibly; to begin suddenly to utter, perform etc. **break off,** to detach by breaking; to bring abruptly to an end; to cease talking etc. **break open,** to use force to open. **break out,** to escape by force from prison etc.; to begin or develop suddenly; to become suddenly covered *in* a rash. **break-out** *n.* a forcible escape. **break up,** to break into small pieces; to separate, (of schoolchildren) to disperse for the holidays. **break wind,** to emit wind from the anus. **break with,** to end one's friendship with. [Old English]

breakable *adj.* easily broken.

breakage *n.* damage by breaking; an instance of this.

breakaway *n.* a breaking of one's ties, secession. —*adj.* that has broken away or seceded.

breakdown *n.* **1.** a failure of mechanical action health, mental stability etc. **2.** an analysis of statistics.

breaker *n.* a heavy wave breaking on a coast or over a reef.

breakfast /'brekfəst/ *n.* the first meal of the day. —*v.i.* to have breakfast.

breakneck *adj.* (of speed) dangerously fast.

Breakspear /'breɪkspɪə/ Nicholas. Original name of ◊Adrian IV, the only English pope.

breakthrough *n.* **1.** a major advance or discovery. **2.** the act of breaking through an obstacle etc.

breakup *n.* disintegration, collapse; dispersal.

breakwater *n.* a barrier protecting a harbour etc. against heavy waves.

bream *n.* (*plural* the same) a deep-bodied flattened freshwater fish of the genus *Abramis*, especially *A. brama*, growing to about 50 cm/1.6 ft, typically found in lowland rivers across Europe; or **sea bream** a similarly shaped fish of the family Sparidae. [from Old French]

breast /brest/ *n.* **1.** either of the two protuberant milk-secreting organs on the upper front of a woman's body, also known as a ◊mammary gland; the corresponding (usually rudimentary) part of a man's body. **2.** the upper front of the human body or of a garment covering it; the corresponding part in animals. **3.** the breast as a source of emotion. —*v.t.* to advance to meet with one's breast; to reach the top of (a hill). —**breast-feed** *v.t.* to feed (a baby) with milk from the breast. **breaststroke** *n.* a swimming stroke performed face downwards, with sweeping movements of the arms. [Old English]

breastbone *n.* the flat vertical bone in the chest joined to the ribs.

breastplate *n.* a piece of armour covering the chest.

breastwork *n.* a low temporary defensive wall or parapet.

breath /breθ/ *n.* **1.** air drawn into and expelled from the lungs; exhaled air as perceived by the senses. **2.** a breathing in; breathing, ability to breathe. **3.** a slight movement of air; a whiff (of perfume). **4.** a hint or slight rumour (of suspicion etc.). —**breath test,** a test of breath to discover the amount of alcohol in the body. **hold one's breath,** to cease breathing temporarily from excitement etc. **out of breath,** panting after strenuous exercise. **under one's breath,** in a whisper. [Old English]

breathalyse /'breθəlaɪz/ *v.t.* to test with a Breathalyzer.

Breathalyzer *n.* or **Breathalyser** the trade name of an instrument for on-the-spot checking by the police of the amount of alcohol consumed by a suspect driver. The driver breathes into a plastic bag connected to a tube containing a chemical (such as a diluted solution of potassium dichromate in 50% sulphuric acid) which changes colour. Another method is to use a gas chromatograph, again from a breath sample. [from *breath* and *analyse*]

breathe /briːð/ *v.t.i.* **1.** to draw air into and expel it from the lungs for ◊gas exchange; to be alive; to draw into or expel from the lungs on the breath. Breathing is sometimes referred to as external respiration, for true respiration is a cellular (internal) process. **2.** to utter or mention; to speak softly. **3.** to pause for breath. **4.** to exude or instil (a quality or feeling). —**breathe again** *or* **freely,** to feel relieved of fear etc. **breathing space,** time to breathe, a chance to recover from effort.

breather /'briːðə/ *n.* a pause for rest; a spell of fresh air.

breathless *adj.* panting after exertion; holding one's breath with excitement.

breathtaking *adj.* spectacular, very exciting.

breccia /'bretʃɪə/ *n.* a coarse clastic ◊sedimentary rock, made up of broken fragments (clasts) of pre-existing rocks. It is similar to ◊conglomerate but the fragments in breccia are large and jagged.

Brecht /brext/ Bertolt 1898–1956. German dramatist and poet, who aimed to destroy the 'suspension of disbelief' usual in the theatre and to express Marxist ideas. He adapted John Gay's *Beggar's Opera* as *Die Dreigroschenoper/The Threepenny Opera* 1928, set to music by Kurt Weill. Later plays include *Mutter Courage/Mother Courage* 1941, set during the Thirty Years' War, and *Der kaukasische Kreidekreis/The Caucasian Chalk Circle* 1949.

Brecknockshire /'breknɒkʃə/ former county of Wales, merged in ◊Powys in 1974.

bred past and past participle of **breed**.

Breda, Treaty of /breɪ'dɑː/ the 1667 treaty that ended the Second Anglo-Dutch War (1664–67). By the terms of the treaty, England gained New Amsterdam, which was renamed New York.

breech *n.* 1. the back part of a rifle or gun barrel. 2. (*archaic*) the buttocks. —**breech birth,** a birth in which the baby's buttocks or feet emerge first. [Old English]

breeches /'brɪtʃɪz/ *n.pl.* knee-length trousers, now worn for riding or in ceremonial dress. —**breeches buoy,** a lifebuoy with canvas breeches, slung on a rope for hauling people off a wreck etc.

breed *v.t./i.* (*past* and *past participle* **bred**) 1. to bear young. 2. to keep (animals) in order to produce young. 3. to train or bring up. 4. to give rise to. 5. to produce (fissile material) in a breeder reactor. —*n.* 1. a strain of an animal or plant species evolved by selective breeding (see ◊artificial selection). 2. family, lineage. 3. a sort or kind. [Old English]

breeder *n.* one who breeds animals.

breeder reactor or **fast reactor** alternative names for ◊fast breeder, a type of nuclear reactor.

breeding *n.* 1. the production of young from animals, propagation; in biology, the crossing and selection of animals and plants to change the characteristics of an existing ◊breed or ◊cultivar (variety), or to produce a new one. 2. good manners resulting from training or background. 3. in nuclear physics, a process in a reactor in which more fissionable material is produced than is consumed in running the reactor.

breeze[1] *n.* a cool or gentle wind. —*v.i.* (*colloquial*) to come *in*, to move *along* etc., in a casual jaunty manner. [from Spanish *briza* = NE wind]

breeze[2] *n.* small cinders. —**breeze block,** a lightweight building block made from breeze with sand and cement. [from French *braise* = live coals]

breezy *adj.* 1. pleasantly windy or windswept. 2. casual and jaunty in manner.

Bremen /'breɪmən/ 1. administrative region (German *Land*) in N Germany, consisting of the cities of Bremen and Bremerhaven; area 400 sq km/154 sq mi; population (1988) 652,000. 2. industrial port (iron, steel, oil refining, chemicals, aircraft, shipbuilding, cars) in N Germany on the river Weser, 69 km/43 mi from the open sea; population (1988) 522,000.

Brendel /'brendl/ Alfred 1931– . Austrian pianist, known for his fastidious and searching interpretations of Beethoven, Schubert, and Liszt.

Brenner /'brenə/ Sidney 1927– . South African scientist, one of the pioneers of genetic engineering. Brenner discovered messenger ◊RNA (a link between ◊DNA and the ◊ribosomes in which proteins are synthesized) in 1960.

Brenner Pass lowest of the Alpine passes, 1,370 m/ 4,495 ft; it leads from Trentino–Alto Adige, Italy, to the Austrian Tirol, and is 19 km/12 mi long.

brent goose or **brent** the smallest kind of wild ◊goose, *Branta bernicla*.

Brenton /'brentən/ Howard 1942– . English dramatist, whose works include *The Romans in Britain* 1980 and a translation of Brecht's *The Life of Galileo*.

Brescia /'breʃə/ ancient **Brixia** historic and industrial city in N Italy, 84 km/52 mi E of Milan. Its medieval walls are still standing and it has a 12th-century and a 17th-century cathedral. Products: textiles, engineering, firearms, metal products; population (1988) 199,000.

Breslau /'breslaʊ/ the German name of ◊Wrocław, town in Poland.

Brest /brest/ naval base and industrial port (electronics, engineering, chemicals) on *Rade de Brest* (Brest Roads), a great bay at the western extremity of Brittany, France; population (1983) 201,000. Occupied as a U-boat base by the Germans 1940–44, the town was destroyed by Allied bombing and rebuilt.

Brest-Litovsk, Treaty of a bilateral treaty signed on 3 March 1918 between Russia and Germany, Austria-Hungary, and their allies. Under it, Russia agreed to recognize the independence of Georgia, the Ukraine, Poland and the Baltic States, and pay heavy compensation. Under the Nov 1918 Armistice that ended World War I, it was annulled.

Bretagne /bre'tən/ region of NW France, see ◊Brittany.

brethren /'breðrɪn/ *n.pl.* brothers (*archaic* except with reference to monastic orders, certain sects etc.).

Brétigny, Treaty of /bretɪn'jiː/ an agreement made between Edward III of England and John II of France in 1360 at the end of the first phase of the Hundred Years' War, under which Edward received Aquitaine and its dependencies in exchange for renunciation of his claim to the French throne.

Breton /'bretɒn/ *adj.* of the Bretons or their language. —*n.* 1. a native or inhabitant of Brittany. 2. the language of the Bretons, a member of the Celtic branch of the Indo-European language family; the language of Brittany in France, related to Welsh and Cornish, and descended from the speech of Celts who left Britain as a consequence of the Anglo-Saxon invasions of the 5th and 6th centuries. Officially neglected for centuries, Breton is now a recognized language of France. [Old French = Briton]

Breton André 1896–1966. French author, among the leaders of the ◊Dada art movement. *Les Champs magnétiques/ Magnetic Fields* 1921, an experiment in automatic writing, was one of the products of the movement. He was also a founder of ◊Surrealism, publishing *Le Manifeste de surréalisme/Surrealist Manifesto* 1924. Other works include *Najda* 1928, the story of his love affair with a medium.

Breuer /'brɔɪə/ Josef 1842–1925. Viennese physician, one of the pioneers of psychoanalysis. He applied it successfully to cases of hysteria, and collaborated with Freud in *Studien über Hysterie/Studies in Hysteria* 1895.

Breuer Marcel 1902–1981. Hungarian-born architect and designer, who studied and taught at the ◊Bauhaus school in Germany. His tubular steel chair of 1925 was the first of its kind. He moved to England, then to the USA, where he was in partnership with Walter Gropius 1937–40. His buildings show an affinity with natural materials; the best known is the Bijenkorf, Rotterdam (with Elzas), 1953.

Breuil /'brɔɪ/ Henri 1877–1961. French prehistorian, professor of historic ethnography and director of research at the Institute of Human Palaeontology, Paris, from 1910. He established the genuine antiquity of Palaeolithic cave art and stressed the anthropological approach to human prehistory.

breve /briː'v/ *n.* 1. a mark (˘) placed over a short or unstressed vowel. 2. in music, a note equal to two semibreves. [variant of *brief*]

brevity /'brevɪtɪ/ *n.* conciseness of written or spoken expression; shortness, especially of duration. [from Latin *brevis* = brief]

breviary /'briːvɪərɪ/ *n.* in the Roman Catholic Church, the book of instructions for reciting the daily services. It is usually in four volumes, one for each season. [from Latin *breviarium* = summary]

brew /bruː/ *v.t./i.* 1. to make (◊beer etc.) by infusion, boiling, and fermentation; to make (tea etc.) by infusion; to undergo such processes. 2. (of evil results) to develop, to gather force. —*n.* a liquid or amount of liquid made by brewing; the process of brewing; the quality of what is brewed. —**brewer** *n.* [Old English]

brewery /'bruːərɪ/ *n.* a place where beer is brewed commercially.

brewster *n.* a unit (symbol B) for measuring the reaction of optical materials to stress, defined in terms of the slowing down of light passing through the material when it is stretched or compressed.

Brezhnev /'breʒnef/ Leonid Ilyich 1906–1982. Soviet leader. A protégé of Stalin and Khrushchev, he came to power (after he and ◊Kosygin forced Khrushchev to resign) as general secretary of the Soviet Communist Party (CPSU) 1964–82 and was president 1977–82. Domestically he was conservative; abroad, the USSR was established as a military and political superpower during the Brezhnev era, extending its influence in Africa and Asia.

Brian /'brɑɪən/ known as **Brian Boru** ('Brian of the Tribute') 926–1014. High king of Ireland from 976, who took Munster, Leinster, and Connacht to become ruler of all Ireland. He defeated the Norse at Clontarf, thus ending Norse control of Dublin, although he was himself killed. He was the last high king with jurisdiction over most of Scotland. His exploits were celebrated in several chronicles.

Briand /bri'ɒn/ Aristide 1862–1932. French radical socialist politician. He was prime minister 1909–11, 1913, 1915–17, 1921–22, 1925–26 and 1929, and foreign minister 1925–32. In 1925 he concluded the ◊Locarno Pact (settling Germany's western frontier) and in 1928 the ◊Kellogg-Briand Pact renouncing war; in 1930 he outlined a scheme for a United States of Europe.

briar[1,2] variant of ◊brier[1,2].

bribe *n.* money etc. offered to procure a corrupt action or decision in favour of the giver. —*v.t.* to give a bribe to. —**bribery** /'braɪbərɪ/ *n.* [from Old French *briber* = beg]

bric-à-brac /'brɪkəbræk/ *n.* odds and ends, usually old, ornamental, less valuable than antiques. [from obsolete French = at random]

brick *n.* 1. a small, usually rectangular, block of baked or dried clay, used in building; the material of this; building work consisting of such blocks. Bricks are made by kneading a mixture of crushed clay and other materials into a stiff mud and extruding it into a ribbon. The ribbon is cut into individual bricks, which are fired at a temperature of up to about 1,000°C/1,800°F. Bricks may alternatively be pressed into shape in moulds. 2. a brick-shaped loaf, block of ice cream etc. —*adj.* made of brick. —*v.t.* to block *up* or fill *in* with bricks. —**brick red** *adj.* having the red colour of bricks. [from Low German or Dutch]

brickbat *n.* 1. a piece of brick, especially as a missile. 2. an uncomplimentary remark.

bricklayer *n.* a worker who builds with bricks.

brickwork *n.* a structure of or building in bricks.

bridal /'braɪdəl/ *adj.* of a bride or wedding. [Old English, originally as noun = wedding feast]

bride *n.* a woman on or just before her wedding day; a newly married woman. [Old English]

bridegroom *n.* a man on or just before his wedding day; a newly married man.

bridesmaid *n.* an unmarried woman or girl attending the bride at a wedding.

bridewealth *n.* or **brideprice** goods or property presented by a man's family to the family of his prospective wife as part of the marriage agreement. It is the usual practice among many societies in Africa, Asia, and the Pacific, and among many American Indian groups. In most S European and S Asian countries the corresponding custom is ◊dowry.

bridge[1] /brɪdʒ/ *n.* 1. a structure that provides a continuous path or road over water, valleys, ravines, or above other roads; a thing joining or connecting parts. Bridges can be designed according to four principles: **arch** for example, Sydney Harbour bridge (steel arch), Australia, with a span of 503 m/1,650 ft; **beam** *or* **girder** for example, Rio–Niteroi, Guanabara Bay, Brazil, centre span 300 m/984 ft; length 13,900 m/8 mi 3,380 ft; ◊**cantilever** for example, Forth rail bridge, Scotland, 1,658 m/5,440 ft long with two main spans, two cantilevers each, one from each tower; **suspension** for example, Humber bridge, England, with a centre span of 1,410 m/4,628 ft. 2. the upper bony part of the nose. 3. a piece of wood etc. over which the strings of a violin etc. are stretched. 4. the raised platform on a ship from which the captain directs its course. 5. a false tooth or teeth supported by the natural teeth on each side. —*v.t.* to connect by or as by a bridge. —**Bridge of Sighs**, a 16th-century covered bridge in Venice between the doge's palace and the state prison, crossed by prisoners on their way to torture or execution. **bridging loan,** a loan to cover the short interval between buying one thing and selling another (especially houses). [Old English]

bridge[2] *n.* a card game derived from whist, in which one player's cards are exposed and played by his or her partner. First played among members of the Indian Civil Service about 1900, bridge was brought to England in 1903 and played at the Portland Club in 1908. It is played in two forms: ◊auction bridge and ◊contract bridge.

bridgehead *n.* a fortified position established in hostile territory, especially on the far side of a river as a base for further advance.

Bridgetown /'brɪdʒtaʊn/ port and capital of Barbados, founded in 1628; population (1987) 8,000. Sugar is exported through the nearby deep-water port.

Bridget, St /'brɪdʒɪt/ 453–523. A patron saint of Ireland, also known as **St Brigit** or **St Bride.** She founded a church and monastery at Kildare, and is said to have been the daughter of a prince of Ulster. Feast day 1 Feb.

Bridgewater /'brɪdʒwɔːtə/ Francis Egerton, 3rd Duke of 1736–1803. Pioneer of British inland navigation. With James ◊Brindley as his engineer, he constructed 1762–72

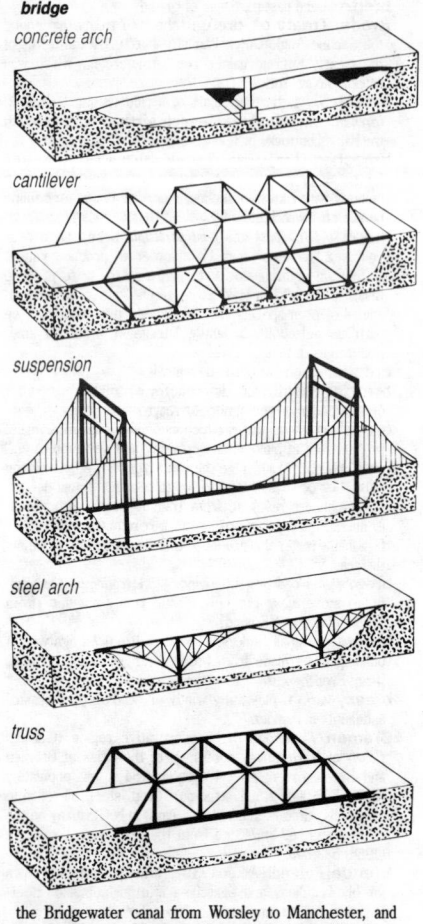

bridge

concrete arch

cantilever

suspension

steel arch

truss

the Bridgewater canal from Worsley to Manchester, and from there to the Mersey, a distance of 67.5 km/42 mi.

bridle /'braɪdəl/ *n.* the harness round a horse's head by which the rider controls it; a restraining thing or influence. —*v.t./i.* 1. to put a bridle on; to curb or restrain. 2. to draw up the head in pride or resentment. —**bridle path,** one suitable for horse-riding. [Old English]

Brie /briː/ *n.* a kind of soft, ripe cheese. [from *Brie* in N France]

brief *adj.* 1. of short duration. 2. concise. —*n.* 1. a summary of the facts of a case drawn up for a barrister; a case taken on by a barrister. 2. (in *plural*) very short pants. —*v.t.* to give a brief to (a barrister); to provide with the essential facts beforehand. —**briefly** *adv.,* **briefness** *n.* [from Anglo-French from Latin *breve* = dispatch (*brevis* = short)]

briefcase *n.* a flat case for carrying documents.

brier[1] /'braɪə/ *n.* a wild rose or other prickly bush. [Old English]

brier[2] *n.* a shrubby heath *Erica arborea* of S Europe; a tobacco pipe made from its woody root. [from French *bruyère* = heath]

brig *n.* a square-rigged sailing ship with two masts. [abbreviation of *brigantine*]

brigade /brɪ'geɪd/ *n.* 1. a military unit forming part of a division. 2. a body of people organized for a special purpose. [from French from Italian *brigata* = company (*brigare* = be busy with, from *briga* = strife)]

brigadier /brɪgə'dɪə/ *n.* an officer commanding a brigade; a staff officer with similar status, next in rank above a colonel. [French]

brigand /'brɪgənd/ *n.* a member of a robber gang, a bandit. —**brigandage** *n.* [from Old French from Italian]

brigantine /'brɪgənti:n/ *n.* a sailing ship with two masts, the foremast square-rigged, used in the 18th and 19th centuries for short coastal and trading voyages. [from Old French or Italian]

bright /braɪt/ *adj. n.* **1.** emitting or reflecting much light, shining. **2.** (of colour) intense, conspicuous. **3.** intelligent, talented. **4.** cheerful, vivacious. *–adv.* brightly. *–***brightly** *adv.*, **brightness** *n.* [Old English].

Bright John 1811–1889. English Liberal politician, a campaigner for free trade, peace, and social reform. A Quaker mill-owner, he was among the founders of the Anti-Corn Law League in 1839, and was largely instrumental in securing the passage of the Reform Bill of 1867.

England is the mother of Parliaments.
John Bright
Birmingham 18 Jan 1865

Bright /braɪt/ Richard 1789–1858. British physician who described many conditions and linked oedema to kidney disease. Bright's disease, an inflammation of the kidneys, is named after him; see ◊nephritis.

brighten /'braɪtən/ *v.t./i.* to make or become brighter.

brill *n.* a flatfish *Scophthalmus rhombus*, living in shallow water over sandy bottoms in the NE Atlantic and Mediterranean.

Brillat-Savarin /bri'ja: sævə'ræŋ/ Jean Anthelme 1755–1826. French gastronome, author of *La Physiologie du Goût* 1825, a compilation of observations on food and drink regarded as the first great classic of gastronomic literature. Most of his professional life was spent as a politician.

brilliant /'brɪliənt/ *adj.* **1.** bright, sparkling. **2.** strikingly talented or intelligent. **3.** showy. *–n.* a diamond of the finest cut and brilliance, with many facets. *–***brilliance** *n.*, **brilliancy** *n.* [from French *brillant* = shining, from Italian *brillare*]

brilliantine /'brɪjənti:n/ *n.* a substance to make the hair glossy. [from French]

brim *n.* the edge or lip of a cup or other vessel; the projecting edge of a hat. *–v.t./i.* (-**mm**-) to fill or be full to the brim. *–***brim over,** to overflow.

brimstone *n.* (*archaic*) sulphur.

brindled /'brɪndəld/ *adj.* (especially of dogs or cattle) brownish or tawny with streaks of other colour. [from Scandinavian]

Brindley /'brɪndli/ James 1716–1772. English canal builder, the first to employ tunnels and aqueducts extensively, in order to reduce the number of locks on a direct-route canal. His 580 km/360 mi of canals included the Bridgewater (Manchester–Liverpool) and Grand Union (Manchester–Potteries) canals.

brine *n.* water saturated with salt: a solution of sodium chloride, NaCl, in water. Brines are used extensively in the food-manufacturing industry for canning vegetables, pickling vegetables (sauerkraut, for example), and curing meat. Industrially, brine is the source from which chlorine, caustic soda (sodium hydroxide), and sodium carbonate are made. *–v.t.* to soak in brine. *–***briny** *adj.* [Old English]

Brinell hardness test /bri'nel/ a test for the hardness of a substance according to the area of indentation made by a 10-mm/0.4-in hardened steel or sintered tungsten carbide ball under standard loading conditions in a test machine. The resulting Brinell number is equal to the load (kg) divided by the surface area (mm^2). [from its inventor, Swedish engineer Johann *Brinell* (1849–1925)]

bring *v.t./i.* (*past* and *past participle* **brought** /brɔ:t/) **1.** to come carrying, leading etc. **2.** to cause to be present, to result in. **3.** to put forward (charges etc.) in court. **4.** to cause to reach a given state. **5.** to induce *to*. *–***bring about,** to cause to happen. **bring-and-buy sale,** a sale at which people bring items for sale and buy those brought by others. **bring down,** to cause to fall; to lower (prices). **bring forth,** to give birth to. **bring forward,** to move to an earlier time; to transfer from a previous page or account. **bring in,** to introduce; to yield as income or profit. **bring off,** to attempt successfully. **bring on,** to cause to develop rapidly. **bring out,** to bring into prominence; to publish. **bring up,** to supervise the education etc. of (a growing

child); to call attention to (a subject); to vomit; to come to a sudden halt. [Old English]

brink *n.* **1.** the edge of a steep place or stretch of water. **2.** the point immediately before some dangerous action, experience etc. [from Old Norse]

brinkmanship *n.* the art of pursuing a dangerous policy to the brink of war etc. before desisting. [after *sportsmanship*]

brio /'bri:əʊ/ *n.* vivacity. [Italian]

briquette /bri'ket/ *n.* a block of compressed coal dust. [French, diminutive of *brique* = brick]

Brisbane /'brɪzbən/ industrial port (brewing, engineering, tanning, tobacco, shoes; oil pipeline from Moonie), capital of Queensland, E Australia, near the mouth of Brisbane river, dredged to carry ocean-going ships; population (1986) 1,171,300. [from Thomas *Brisbane*]

Brisbane Thomas Makdougall 1773–1860. Scottish soldier, colonial administrator, and astronomer. After serving in the Napoleonic Wars under Wellington, he was governor of New South Wales 1821–25. He catalogued over 7,000 stars.

brisk *adj.* moving quickly, active, lively. *–***briskly** *adv.*, **briskness** *n.*

brisket /'brɪskɪt/ *n.* a joint of meat cut from an animal's breast. [from Anglo-French]

brisling /'brɪzlɪŋ/ *n.* a small herring or sprat. [Norwegian and Danish]

Brissot /bri:'səʊ/ Jacques Pierre 1754–1793. French revolutionary leader, born in Chartres. He became a member of the legislative assembly and the National Convention, but his party of moderate republicans, the ◊Girondins, or Brissotins, fell foul of Robespierre, and Brissot was guillotined.

bristle /'brɪsəl/ *n.* **1.** a short, stiff hair. **2.** one of the stiff pieces of hair or wire etc. in a brush. *–v.t./i.* **1.** to show anger or temper. **2.** (of hair or feathers) to stand upright; (of an animal etc.) to make the hair bristle. *–***bristle with,** to have in abundance. [Old English]

bristlecone pine a type of ◊pine tree.

bristletail *n.* a primitive wingless insect of the order Thysanura. Up to 2 cm/0.8 in long, bristletails have a body tapering from front to back, two long antennae, and three 'tails' at the rear end.

bristly /'brɪsli/ *adj.* full of bristles; rough and prickly.

Bristol /'brɪstəl/ industrial port (aircraft engines, engineering, microelectronics, tobacco, chemicals, paper, printing), administrative headquarters of river Avon, SW England; population (1986) 391,000. The old docks have been redeveloped for housing, industry, and yachting facilities; a new city centre has Brunel's Temple Meads railway station at its focus and a weir across the Avon nearby.

Bristow /'brɪstaʊ/ Eric 1957– . English darts player nicknamed 'the Crafty Cockney'. He has won all the game's major titles, including the world professional title a record five times between 1980 and 1986.

Britain /'brɪtn/ *n.* or **Great Britain** island off the NW coast of Europe, one of the British Isles. It consists of ◊England, ◊Scotland, and ◊Wales, and is part of the ◊United Kingdom. [from the Roman *Britannia*, from the ancient Celtic name of the inhabitants, *Bryttas*]

Britain, ancient the period in the British Isles, excluding Ireland, from prehistory to the Roman occupation. After the last glacial retreat of the Ice Age about 15,000 BC, Britain was inhabited by hunters who became neolithic farming villagers. They built stone circles and buried their chiefs in ◊barrow mounds. Around 400 BC Britain was conquered by the ◊Celts and 54 BC by the Romans under Julius Caesar; ◊Boudicca led an uprising against their occupation.

Britain, Battle of World War II air battle between German and UK air forces over Britain lasting from 10 July to 12 Oct 1940.

Britannic /bri'tænɪk/ *adj.* of Britain (chiefly in *His* or *Her Britannic Majesty*).

Britannicus /bri'tænɪkəs/ Tiberius Claudius *c.* AD 41–55. Roman prince, son of Emperor Claudius and Messalina; so called from his father's expedition to Britain. He was poisoned by Nero.

Briticism /'brɪtɪsɪzm/ *n.* an idiom used in Britain but not in the USA etc. [after *Gallicism*]

British /'brɪtɪʃ/ *adj.* of Great Britain or the United Kingdom. —**the British,** the people of Great Britain or the United Kingdom. [Old English]

British Antarctic Territory a colony created in 1962 and comprising all British territories S of latitude 60° S: the South Orkney Islands, the South Shetland Islands, the Antarctic Peninsula and all adjacent lands, and Coats Land, extending to the South Pole; total land area 660,000 sq km/ 170,874 sq mi. Population (exclusively scientific personnel) about 300.

British Broadcasting Corporation (BBC) the state-owned broadcasting network in the UK. It operates television and national and local radio stations, and is financed solely by the sale of television viewing licences. It is not allowed to carry advertisements, but overseas radio broadcasts (World Service) have a government subsidy.

British Columbia /kə'lʌmbiə/ province of Canada on the Pacific; **area** 947,800 sq km/365,851 sq mi; **capital** Victoria; **physical** Rocky Mountains and Coast Range; deeply indented coast; rivers include the Fraser and Columbia; over 80 lakes; more than half the land is forested; **products** fruit and vegetables; timber and wood products; fish; coal, copper, iron, lead; oil and natural gas; hydroelectricity; **population** (1986) 2,889,000; **history** Captain Cook explored the coast in 1778; a British colony was founded on Vancouver Island in 1849, and the gold rush of 1858 extended settlement to the mainland; it became a province in 1871. In 1885 the Canadian Pacific Railroad linking British Columbia to the E coast was completed.

British Commonwealth of Nations former official name of the ◊Commonwealth.

British Council a semi-official organization set up in 1935 (royal charter 1940) to promote a wider knowledge of the UK, excluding politics and commerce, and to develop cultural relations with other countries.

British Empire the various territories all over the world conquered or colonized by Britain from about 1600, most now independent or ruled by other powers; the British Empire was at its largest at the end of World War I, with over 25% of the world's population and area. The ◊Commonwealth is composed of former and remaining territories of the British Empire.

British Empire, Order of the a British order of chivalry, instituted by George V in 1917. There are military and civil divisions, and the ranks are GBE, Knight Grand Cross or Dame Grand Cross; KBE, Knight Commander; DBE, Dame Commander; CBE, Commander; OBE, Officer; MBE, Member. In 1974 awards for civilian gallantry previously made within the order were replaced by the Queen's Gallantry Medal (QGM), which ranks after the George Cross and George Medal.

British Honduras /'brɪtn/ former name of ◊Belize, a country in Central America.

British Film Institute (BFI) an organization founded in 1933 to promote the cinema as a means of entertainment and instruction.

British Indian Ocean Territory British colony in the Indian Ocean directly administered by the Foreign and Commonwealth Office. It consists of the Chagos Archipelago some 1,900 km/1,200 mi NE of Mauritius; **area** 60 sq km/23 sq mi; **physical** lagoons; **products** copra, salt fish, tortoiseshell; **population** (1982) 3,000; **history** purchased in 1965 for $3 million by Britain from Mauritius to provide a joint US/UK base.

British Isles a group of islands off the NW coast of Europe, consisting of Great Britain (England, Wales, and Scotland), Ireland, the Channel Islands, the Orkney and Shetland islands, the Isle of Man, and many other islands that are included in various counties, such as the Isle of Wight, Isles of Scilly, Lundy Island, and the Inner and Outer Hebrides. The islands are divided from Europe by the North Sea, Strait of Dover, and the English Channel, and face the Atlantic to the west.

British Legion an organization to promote the welfare of British veterans of war service and their dependants. Established under the leadership of D Haig in 1921 (royal charter 1925) it became the **Royal British Legion** in 1971; it is nonpolitical. The sale on Remembrance Sunday of Flanders poppies made by disabled members raises much of its funds.

British Library the national library of the UK. Created

in 1973, it comprises the **reference division** (the former library departments of the British Museum, being rehoused at the Euston Road, London, site); **lending division** at Boston Spa, Yorkshire, from which full text documents and graphics can be sent, using a satellite link, to other countries; **bibliographic services division** (incorporating the British National Bibliography); and the **National Sound Archive** in South Kensington, London.

British Museum the largest museum of the UK. Founded in 1753, it opened in London in 1759. Rapid additions led to the construction of the present buildings by 1852. In 1881 the Natural History Museum was transferred to South Kensington.

British Somaliland /'səmɑlilænd/ a former British protectorate comprising over 176,000 sq km/67,980 sq mi of territory on the Somali coast of Africa from 1884 until the independence of Somalia in 1960. British authorities were harassed by a self-proclaimed messiah known as the 'Mad Mullah' from 1901 until 1910.

British Standards Institute (BSI) the UK national standards body. Although government-funded, the institute is independent. The BSI interprets international technical standards for the UK, and also sets its own.

British Technology Group a UK corporation exploiting inventions derived from public or private sources, usually jointly with industrial firms. It was set up in 1967 under the Development of Inventions Acts 1948–65 and known as the National Research Development Council until 1981.

British Telecom a British company that formed part of the Post Office until 1980, and was privatized in 1984. It is responsible for ◊telecommunications, including the telephone network, and radio and television broadcasting. Previously a monopoly, it now faces commercial competition for some of its services. It operates Britain's ◊viewdata network called ◊Prestel.

British thermal unit an imperial unit (symbol Btu) of heat, now replaced in the SI system by the ◊joule (one British thermal unit is approximately 1,055 joules). Burning one cubic foot of natural gas releases about 1,000 Btu of heat.

British Virgin Islands part of the ◊Virgin Islands group in the West Indies.

Briton /'brɪtən/ *n.* **1.** a member of the people living in South Britain before the Roman conquest. **2.** a native of Great Britain. [from Latin from Celtic]

Brittain /'brɪtn/ Vera 1894–1970. English socialist writer, a nurse to the troops overseas 1915–19, as told in her *Testament of Youth* 1933; *Testament of Friendship* 1950 commemorated Winifred ◊Holtby. She married political scientist Sir George Catlin (1896–1979); their daughter is Shirley ◊Williams.

Brittan /'brɪtn/ Leon 1939– . English Conservative politician and lawyer. Chief secretary to the Treasury 1981–83, home secretary 1983–85, secretary for trade and industry 1985–86 (he resigned over his part in the ◊Westland affair) and senior European Commissioner from 1988.

Brittany /'brɪtəni/ French *Bretagne* region of NW France in the Breton peninsula between the Bay of Biscay and the English Channel; area 27,200 sq km/10,499 sq mi; population (1987) 2,767,000. Its capital is Rennes and it includes the *départements* of Côte-du-Nord, Finistère, Ille-et-Vilaine, and Morbihan. It is a farming region.

Britten /'brɪtn/ (Edward) Benjamin 1913–1976. English composer. He often wrote for the individual voice; for example, the role in the opera *Peter Grimes* 1945, based on verses by Crabbe, was created for Peter ◊Pears. Among his many works are the *Young Person's Guide to the Orchestra* 1946, the chamber opera *The Rape of Lucretia* 1946, *Billy Budd* 1951, *A Midsummer Night's Dream* 1960, and *Death in Venice* 1973.

brittle *adj.* hard but fragile; easily destroyed. —**brittleness** *n.* [Old English]

brittle-star *n.* any member of the echinoderm class Ophiuroidea. A brittle-star resembles a starfish, and has a small, central, rounded body and long, flexible, spiny arms used for walking. The small brittle-star *Amphipholis squamata* is greyish, about 4.5 cm/2 in across, and found on sea bottoms worldwide. It broods its young, and its arms can be luminous.

Brno /'bɜːnəʊ/ industrial city in central Czechoslovakia (chemicals, arms, textiles, machinery); population (1984)

380,800. Now the third largest city in Czechoslovakia, Brno was formerly capital of the Austrian crown land of Moravia.

broach[1] *v.t.* 1. raise (a subject) for discussion. 2. to pierce (a cask) to draw liquor. —*n.* 1. a tool for enlarging holes. 2. a roasting spit. —**broach spire,** a church spire rising from a square tower without a parapet. [from Old French from Latin *broccus* = projecting]

broach[2] *v.t./i.* (usually with *to*) to veer or cause (a ship) to veer and present its side to the wind and waves.

broad /brɔːd/ *adj.* 1. large in extent from one side to the other, wide; (after measurements) in breadth; extensive. 2. full and complete; (of hints) explicit; (of accent) strongly regional. 3. tolerant, liberal. 4. in general terms, not detailed. 5. (of humour) somewhat coarse. —*n.* the broad part. —**broad bean,** an edible bean *Vicia faba* or one of its large flat seeds. **Broad Church,** the section of the Anglican Church favouring toleration, not strict adherence to dogma. **broad-minded** *adj.* having tolerant views. [Old English]

broadbill *n.* a primitive perching bird of the family Eurylaimidae, found in Africa and S Asia. Broadbills are forest birds and are often found near water. They are gregarious and noisy, have brilliant coloration and wide bills, and feed largely on insects.

broadcast *v.t./i* (*past* and *past participle* broadcast) 1. to transmit (programmes or information) by radio or television; to speak or perform thus. 2. to disseminate (information) widely. 3. to scatter (seed) at random rather than in rows. —*n.* a radio or television programme or transmission. —*adv.* by random sowing. —**broadcaster** *n.*

broadcloth *n.* a fine woollen or worsted cloth used in tailoring (originally woven on a wide loom).

broaden /ˈbrɔːdən/ *v.t./i.* to make or become broad.

broad-leaved tree a tree belonging to the ◊angiosperms, such as ash, beech, oak, maple, or birch. Their leaves are generally broad and flat, in contrast to the needlelike leaves of most ◊conifers. See also ◊deciduous tree.

broadloom *adj.* (of carpets) woven in broad widths.

Broadmoor /ˈbrɔːdmɔː/ *n.* a special hospital (established in 1863) in Crowthorne, Berkshire, England, for those formerly described as 'criminally insane'.

broadsheet *n.* a large sheet of paper printed on one side only, especially with information.

broadside *n.* 1. the firing of all the guns on one side of a ship. 2. a fierce verbal attack. 3. the side of a ship above the water between bow and quarter. —**broadside on,** sideways on.

Broads, Norfolk /brɔːdz/ area of freshwater lakes in England, see ◊Norfolk Broads.

broadsword *n.* a sword with a broad blade for cutting rather than thrusting.

Broadway /ˈbrɔːdweɪ/ an avenue in New York running NW from the tip of Manhattan and crossing Times Square at 42nd Street, at the heart of the theatre district, where Broadway is known as 'the Great White Way'. New York theatres situated outside this area are described as **off-Broadway;** those even smaller and farther away are **off-off-Broadway.**

brocade /brəˈkeɪd/ *n.* a fabric woven with raised pattern. —*v.t.* to weave thus. [from Spanish and Portuguese from Italian *brocco* = twisted thread]

broccoli *n.* a variety of ◊cabbage with greenish flower heads. [Italian]

broch /brɒk/ *n.* a circular dry-stone tower of a type found in northern Scotland and the adjacent islands, dating from about 100 BC–AD 100. [from Old Norse *borg* = castle]

brochure /ˈbrəʊʃʊə/ *n.* a booklet or pamphlet giving descriptive information. [French = stitching (*brocher* = stitch)]

broderie anglaise /brəʊdri æɡˈleɪz/ a type of embroidery on white linen or cotton, in which holes are cut in patterns and oversewn, often to decorate lingerie, shirts, and skirts. [French = English embroidery]

Brodsky /ˈbrɒdski/ Joseph 1940– . Russian poet, who emigrated to the USA in 1972. His work, often dealing with themes of exile, is admired for its wit and economy of language, particularly in its use of understatement. Many of his poems, written in Russian, have been translated into English (*A Part of Speech* 1980). More recently he has also written in English. He was awarded the Nobel Prize for Literature in 1987.

Broglie, de /də ˈbrəʊli/ Louis, 7th Duc de Broglie 1892–1987. French theoretical physicist. He established that all subatomic particles can be described either by particle equations or by wave equations, thus laying the foundations of wave mechanics. He was awarded the 1929 Nobel Prize for Physics.

Broglie, de Maurice, 6th Duc de Broglie 1875–1960. French physicist. He worked on X-rays and gamma rays, and helped to establish the Einsteinian description of light in terms of photons. He was the brother of Louis de Broglie.

brogue[1] /brəʊɡ/ *n.* a strong outdoor shoe with ornamental perforated bands; a rough shoe of untanned leather. [from Irish and Gaelic from Old Norse]

brogue[2] *n.* a strong regional, especially Irish, accent.

broil *v.t./i.* to cook (meat) on a fire or gridiron; to make or become very hot, as from sunshine. [from Old French *bruler* = burn]

broiler *n.* a young chicken reared for broiling or roasting.

broke past of **break.** —*adj.* (*colloquial*) having no money, bankrupt.

broken past participle of **break.** —*adj.* that has been broken; (of a person) crushed in spirit, beaten; (of a language) spoken imperfectly (by a foreigner); (of sleep or time) disturbed, interrupted. —**broken chord,** in music, a chord in which the notes are played successively, not simultaneously. **broken-down** *adj.* worn or sick, inoperative through mechanical failure. **brokenhearted** *adj.* overwhelmed by grief. **broken home,** a family lacking one parent, as by divorce or separation. **broken reed,** a person who proves unreliable in an emergency.

broker *n.* 1. an agent buying and selling for others; a dealer on the Stock Exchange. 2. an official licensed to sell or appraise distrained goods. [from Anglo-French]

brokerage /ˈbrəʊkərɪdʒ/ *n.* a broker's fee or commission.

brolga *n.* or **native companion** an Australian crane *Grus rubicunda*, about 1.5 m/5 ft tall, mainly grey with a red patch on the head.

brolly *n.* (*colloquial*) an umbrella. [abbreviation]

brome grass any annual grass of the genus *Bromus* of the temperate zone; some are used for forage, but many are weeds.

bromeliad *n.* any tropical or subtropical plant of the pineapple family Bromeliaceae, usually with stiff leathery leaves and bright flower spikes.

bromide /ˈbrəʊmaɪd/ *n.* 1. a salt of the halide series containing the Br⁻ ion, which is formed when a bromine atom gains an electron. It is used in sedatives. 2. a soothing statement.

bromine /ˈbrəʊmiːn/ *n.* a dark reddish-brown, non-metallic element, a volatile liquid at room temperature, symbol Br, atomic number 35, relative atomic mass 79.904. It is a member of the ◊halogen group, has an unpleasant odour, and is very irritating to mucous membranes. Its salts are known as bromides. [from French from Greek *brōmos* = stench]

bromocriptine *n.* a drug that mimics the actions of the naturally occurring biochemical substance dopamine, a neurotransmitter. Bromocriptine acts on the pituitary gland to inhibit the release of prolactin, the hormone that regulates lactation, and thus reduces or suppresses milk production. It is also used in the treatment of ◊Parkinson's disease.

bronchial /ˈbrɒŋkɪəl/ *adj.* of the bronchi (see ◊bronchus) or the smaller tubes into which they divide. [from Latin from Greek]

bronchiole *n.* a small-bore air tube found in the vertebrate lung responsible for delivering air to the main respiratory surfaces. Bronchioles lead off from the larger bronchus and branch extensively before terminating in the many thousand alveoli that form the bulk of lung tissue.

bronchitis /brɒŋˈkaɪtɪs/ *n.* inflammation of the bronchi (air passages) of the lungs, usually caused initially by a viral infection, such as a cold or flu. It is aggravated by environmental pollutants, especially smoking, and results in a persistent cough, irritated mucus-secreting glands, and large amounts of sputum.

bronchodilator *n.* any drug that relieves obstruction of the airways by causing the bronchi and bronchioles to relax and widen. It is most useful in the treatment of ◊asthma.

bronchus *n.* (*plural* bronchi /-kaɪ/) either of a pair of large tubes splitting off from the windpipe and passing into the vertebrate lung. Apart from their size, bronchi differ from the bronchioles in possessing cartilaginous rings, which give rigidity and prevent collapse during breathing movements. [Latin from Greek]

bronco /ˈbrɒŋkəʊ/ n. (plural **broncos**) a wild or half-tamed horse of the western USA. [Spanish = rough]

Bronson /ˈbrɒnsn/ Charles. Stage name of Charles Bunchinsky 1922– . US film actor. His films are mainly violent thrillers such as Death Wish 1974. He was one of the seven in The Magnificent Seven 1960.

Brontë /ˈbrɒnti/ family of English writers, including the three sisters **Charlotte** (1816–1855), **Emily Jane** (1818–1848), and **Anne** (1820–49), and their brother **Patrick Branwell** (1817–1848). Their most enduring works are Charlotte Brontë's Jane Eyre 1847 and Emily Brontë's Wuthering Heights 1847. Later works include Anne's The Tenant of Wildfell Hall 1848 and Charlotte's Shirley 1849 and Villette 1853.

brontosaurus /ˌbrɒntəˈsɔːrəs/ n. the former name of a type of large, plant-eating dinosaur, now known as ◊apatosaurus. [from Greek brontē = thunder and sauros = lizard]

bronze n. 1. an alloy of copper and tin. It is harder than pure copper, more suitable for ◊casting, and also resists ◊corrosion. Bronze may contain as much as 25% tin, together with small amounts of other metals, mainly lead. 2. its brownish colour. 3. an object (especially a work of art) made of bronze. —adj. made of or coloured like bronze. —v.t. to give a bronze surface or colour to; (of the Sun etc.) to tan. —**bronze medal**, one awarded as the third prize. [from French from Italian, probably from Persian birinj = copper]

Bronze Age the stage of prehistory and early history when bronze became the first metal worked extensively and used for tools and weapons. It developed out of the Stone Age, preceded the Iron Age and may be dated 5000–1200 BC in the Middle East and about 2000–500 BC in Europe. Recent discoveries in Thailand suggest that the Far East, rather than the Middle East, was the cradle of the Bronze Age.

Bronzino /brɒndˈziːnəʊ/ Agnolo 1503–1572. Italian painter active in Florence, court painter to Cosimo I, Duke of Tuscany. He painted in an elegant, Mannerist style and is best known for portraits and the allegory Venus, Cupid, Folly and Time about 1545 (National Gallery, London).

brooch /brəʊtʃ/ n. an ornamental clasp fastening by a pin at the back. [from Latin broccus = projecting]

brood n. 1. the young of a bird or other creature produced at one hatching or birth. 2. the children in a family. —v.i. 1. to ponder anxiously or resentfully. 2. to sit as a hen on eggs to hatch them. [Old English]

broody adj. 1. (of a hen) wanting to brood. 2. engrossed and thoughtful.

brook[1] /brʊk/ n. a small stream. [Old English]

brook[2] v.t. (usually with negative) to tolerate, to allow. [Old English]

Brook Peter 1925– . English theatrical producer and director. Known for his experimental productions with the Royal Shakespeare Company in England, he began working with the Paris-based Le Centre International de Créations Théâtrales in 1970. Films he has directed include Lord of the Flies 1962 and Meetings with Remarkable Men 1979.

Brooke /brʊk/ Peter Leonard 1934– . British Conservative politician, a member of Parliament from 1977. He was appointed chair of the Conservative Party by Margaret Thatcher in 1987, and was made Northern Ireland secretary in 1989.

Brooke Rupert Chawner 1887–1915. English poet, symbol of the World War I 'lost generation'. His poems, the most popular being five war sonnets (including 'Grantchester' and 'The Great Lover'), were published posthumously.

Brookeborough /ˈbrʊkbərə/ Basil Brooke, Viscount Brookeborough 1888–1973. Unionist politician of Northern Ireland. He entered Parliament in 1929, held ministerial posts 1933–45, and was prime minister of Northern Ireland 1943–63. He was a staunch advocate of strong links with Britain.

Brookner /ˈbrʊknə/ Anita 1928– . English novelist and art historian, whose novels include Hotel du Lac 1984,

winner of the Booker Prize, A Misalliance 1986, and Latecomers 1988.

Brooks /brʊks/ Louise 1906–1985. US actress, known for her roles in silent films such as Die Büchse der Pandora/Pandora's Box 1928 and Das Tagebuch einer Verlorenen/Diary of a Lost Girl 1929, both directed by G W ◊Pabst. She retired from the screen in 1938.

Brooks Mel. The assumed name of Melvin Kaminsky 1926– . US film director, comedian and actor, whose madcap and verbal slapstick humour is featured in films such as The Producers 1968, Blazing Saddles, Young Frankenstein both 1974, Silent Movie 1976, High Anxiety 1977, History of the World Part I 1981, To Be Or Not to Be 1983 and the Star Wars spoof Spaceballs 1987.

broom n. 1. any shrub of the legume family Leguminosae, especially species of the genera Cytisus, Genista, and Spartium, often cultivated for their bright yellow flowers. 2. a long-handled implement for sweeping floors, originally made with twigs from this. —**new broom**, a newly appointed person eager to make changes. [Old English]

broomstick n. a broom handle.

broth /brɒθ/ n. the water in which meat or fish has been boiled; a soup made from this. [Old English]

brothel /ˈbrɒθəl/ n. a house where prostitutes may be visited. [originally = worthless man, prostitute, from Old English]

brother /ˈbrʌðə/ n. 1. a man or boy in relation to the other sons and daughters of his parents. 2. a man who is a close friend or associate; a male fellow member of the same church, trade union, or other association, or of the human race. 3. a monk who is not a priest. —**brother-in-law** n. (plural **brothers-in-law**) the brother of one's husband or wife; the husband of one's sister. —**brotherly** adj. [Old English]

brotherhood /ˈbrʌðəhʊd/ n. 1. friendly feeling as between brothers. 2. an association of men with common (often religious) beliefs or interests.

brougham /ˈbruːəm/ n. (historical) a one-horse closed carriage with the driver's seat outside; a motor car with the driver's seat open. [from Lord Brougham (1778–1868)]

brought /brɔːt/ past and past participle of **bring**.

Brouwer /ˈbraʊə/ Adriaen 1605–1638. Flemish painter who studied with Frans Hals. He excelled in scenes of peasant revelry.

brow /braʊ/ n. 1. (usually in plural) an eyebrow. 2. the forehead. 3. the projecting upper part or edge of a hill or cliff. [Old English]

browbeat v.t. to intimidate.

brown /braʊn/ adj. of a colour between orange and black; dark-skinned, suntanned; (of bread) brown from the colour of the wholemeal or other coarse flour used. —n. brown colour or pigment; brown clothes or material. —v.t./i. to make or become brown. —**brown bear**, a large ◊bear Ursus arctos of the northern hemisphere with shaggy usually brownish fur. **brown paper**, unbleached paper used for packing. **brown sugar**, sugar only partially refined. [Old English]

Brown 'Capability' (Lancelot) 1715–1783. English landscape gardener. He acquired his nickname because of his continual enthusiasm for the 'capabilities' of natural landscapes, which he adapted or simulated for the gardens and parks of stately homes including Stowe, Powys; Blenheim Palace, Oxfordshire; and Petworth House, West Sussex.

Brown Charles Brockden 1771–1810. US novelist and magazine editor. He is called the 'father of the American novel' for his Wieland 1798, Ormond 1799, Edgar Huntly 1799, and Arthur Mervyn 1800. His works also pioneered the Gothic and fantastic traditions in US fiction.

Brown Earle 1926– . US composer who pioneered ◊graphic notation and mobile form during the 1950s. He was an associate of John ◊Cage.

Brown Ford Madox 1821–1893. English painter associated with the ◊Pre-Raphaelite Brotherhood. His pictures include The Last of England 1855 (Birmingham Art Gallery) and Work 1852–65 (City Art Gallery, Manchester), packed with realistic detail and symbolic incident.

Brown George, Baron George-Brown 1914–1985. English Labour politician. He entered Parliament in 1945, was briefly minister of works in 1951, and contested the leadership of the party on the death of Gaitskell, but was defeated by Harold Wilson. He was secretary for economic affairs

Browning Admired for his innovative works incorporating psychological analysis and obscure historical characters, Robert Browning was one of the most popular Victorian poets.

1964–66 and foreign secretary 1966–68. He was created a life peer in 1970.

Brown (James) Gordon 1951–. Scottish Labour politician. He entered Parliament in 1983, rising quickly to the opposition front bench, with a reputation as an outstanding debater.

Brown John 1800–1859. US slavery abolitionist. With 18 men, on the night of 16 Oct 1859, he seized the government arsenal at Harper's Ferry in W Virginia, apparently intending to distribute weapons to runaway slaves who would then defend the mountain stronghold, which Brown hoped would become a republic of former slaves. On 18 Oct the arsenal was stormed by US Marines under Col Robert E ◊Lee. Brown was tried and hanged on 2 Dec, becoming a martyr and the hero of the popular song 'John Brown's Body'.

Brown Robert 1773–1858. Scottish botanist, a pioneer of plant classification and the first to describe and name the cell nucleus.

Browne /braʊn/ Hablot Knight 1815–1882. English illustrator, pseudonym Phiz, known for his illustrations of Charles Dickens's works.

Browne Thomas 1605–1682. English author and physician. Born in London, he travelled widely in Europe before settling in Norwich in 1637. He displayed a richness of style in *Religio Medici/The Religion of a Doctor* 1643, a justification of his profession; *Vulgar Errors* 1646, an examination of popular legend and superstition; *Urn Burial* and *The Garden of Cyrus* 1658; and *Christian Morals*, published posthumously in 1717.

Brownian movement the continuous random motion of particles in a fluid medium (gas or liquid) as they are subject to impact from the molecules of the medium. [from Robert *Brown* who observed the phenomenon in 1827]

brownie /ˈbraʊnɪ/ *n.* **1.** a benevolent elf. **2.** a heavy flat chocolate cake cut into squares. **3.** a junior member of the ◊Girl Guides.

browning /ˈbraʊnɪŋ/ *n.* browned flour or other additive to colour gravy.

Browning Robert 1812–1889. English poet, married to Elizabeth ◊Barrett Browning. His work is characterized by the use of dramatic monologue and an interest in obscure literary and historical figures. It includes the play *Pippa Passes* 1841 and the poems 'The Pied Piper of Hamelin' 1842, 'My Last Duchess' 1842, 'Home Thoughts from Abroad' 1845, and 'Rabbi Ben Ezra' 1864.

brown ring test an analytical chemistry test for the detection of ◊nitrates.

Browns Ferry /braʊnz ˈferɪ/ site of a nuclear power station on the Alabama River, central Alabama. A nuclear accident in 1975 resulted in the closure of the plant for 18 months. This incident marked the beginning of widespread disenchantment with nuclear power in the USA.

Brownshirts *n.pl.* the SA (*Sturmabteilung*), or Storm Troops, the private army of the German Nazi party. [from the colour of the uniform]

browse /braʊz/ *v.i.* **1.** to read or inspect items on display etc. casually. **2.** (of animals) to crop or feed *on* leaves and young shoots. —*n.* an act or spell of browsing. [from Old French *broust* = young shoot]

Bruce /bruːs/ one of the chief Scottish noble houses. Robert I (Robert the Bruce) and his son, David II, were both kings of Scotland descended from Robert de Bruis (died 1094), a Norman knight who came to England with William the Conqueror in 1066.

Bruce James 1730–1794. Scottish explorer, the first European to reach the source of the Blue Nile, in 1770, and to follow the river downstream to Cairo in 1773.

Bruce Robert de, 5th Lord of Annandale 1210–1295. Scottish noble, one of the unsuccessful claimants to the throne at the death of Alexander II in 1290. His grandson was ◊Robert I (the Bruce).

Bruce Robert. King of Scotland; see ◊Robert I.

Bruce Stanley Melbourne, 1st Viscount Bruce of Melbourne 1883–1967. Australian National Party politician, prime minister 1923–29. He was elected to parliament in 1918. As prime minister he introduced a number of social welfare measures.

brucellosis /bruːsəˈləʊsɪs/ *n.* a bacterial disease causing abortion in domestic animals and recurrent fever in humans consuming their products. [from D *Bruce*, Scottish physician (1855–1931)]

Brücke, die /ˈbrʊkə/ German Expressionist art movement 1905–13, formed in Dresden. Ernst Ludwig Kirchner was one of its founders, and Emil Nolde, a member 1906–07. Influenced by African art, they strove for spiritual significance, using raw colours to express different emotions. In 1911 the ◊Blaue Reiter took over as the leading group in German art. [German = the bridge]

Bruckner /ˈbrʊknə/ (Joseph) Anton 1824–1896. Austrian Romantic composer. He was cathedral organist in Linz 1856–68, and from 1868 he was professor at the Vienna Conservatoire. His works include many choral pieces and ten symphonies, the last unfinished. His compositions were influenced by Richard ◊Wagner and Beethoven.

Brüderhof *n.* a Christian Protestant sect with beliefs similar to the Mennonites. They live in groups of families (single persons are assigned to a family), marry only within the sect (divorce is not allowed), and retain a 'modest' dress for women (cap or headscarf, and long skirts). [German = Society of Brothers]

Brueghel /ˈbrɜːxəl/ family of Flemish painters. **Pieter Brueghel** 'the elder' (c.1525–1569) was one of the greatest artists of his time. He painted satirical and humorous pictures of peasant life, many of which include symbolic details illustrating folly and inhumanity, and a series of Months (five survive), including *Hunters in the Snow* (Kunsthistorisches Museum, Vienna). His son **Pieter Brueghel** 'the younger' (c.1564–1636) was known for his nightmare scenes of hell, while **Jan Brueghel** (1568–1625) painted landscapes and still lifes.

Bruges /bruːʒ/ (Flemish *Brugge*) historic city in NW Belgium; capital of W Flanders province, 16 km/10 mi from the North Sea, with which it is connected by canal; population (1985) 117,700. Bruges was the capital of medieval ◊Flanders and was the chief European wool-manufacturing town and its chief market.

bruise /bruːz/ *n.* an injury caused by a blow etc. that discolours the skin without breaking it. —*v.t./i.* to injure in this way; to be susceptible to bruises; to hurt mentally. [originally = crush, from Old English]

bruit /bruːt/ *v.t.* (*archaic*) to spread (a report) *abroad* or *about*. [French = noise]

Brulé /ˈbruːle/ Étienne c.1592–1632. French adventurer and explorer. He travelled with ◊Champlain to the New World in 1608 and settled in Québec, where he lived with the Algonquin Indians. He explored the Great Lakes and travelled as far south as Chesapeake Bay. Returning north, he was killed and eaten by Huron Indians.

Brummell /ˈbrʌməl/ Beau (George Bryan) 1778–1840. British dandy and leader of fashion. He introduced long trousers as conventional day and evening wear for men. A friend of the Prince of Wales, the future George IV, he later quarrelled with him, and was driven by gambling losses to exile in France in 1816 and died in an asylum.

brunch *n.* (*colloquial*) a meal combining breakfast and lunch.

Brundtland /'brʌntlænd/ Gro Harlem 1939– . Norwegian Labour politician. Environment minister 1974–76, she briefly took over as prime minister in 1981, and was elected prime minister in 1986 and again in 1990.

Brunei /bru:'naɪ/ Islamic Sultanate of; country on the N coast of Borneo, surrounded to the landward side by Sarawak and bounded to the N by the South China Sea; **area** 5,765 sq km/2,225 sq mi; **capital** and chief port Bandar Seri Begawan; **physical** flat coastal plain with hilly lowland in W and mountains in E; 75% of the area is forested; the Limbang valley splits Brunei in two, and its cession to Sarawak in 1890 is disputed by Brunei; **head of state and of government** HM Muda Hassanal Bolkiah Mu'izzaddin Waddaulah, Sultan of Brunei, from 1968; **political system** absolute monarchy; **exports** liquefied natural gas (world's largest producer) and oil, both expected to be exhausted by the year 2000; **population** (1990 est) 372,000; **language** Malay (official), Chinese (Hokkien), English; **history** Brunei became a British protectorate in 1888; independence was achieved in 1984.

Brunei Town the former name (until 1970) of ◊Bandar Seri Begawan, Brunei.

Brunel /bru:'nel/ Isambard Kingdom 1806–1859. English engineer and inventor. In 1833 he became engineer to the Great Western Railway, which adopted the 2.1 m/7 ft gauge on his advice. He built the Clifton Suspension Bridge over the river Avon at Bristol and the Saltash Bridge over the river Tamar near Plymouth. His shipbuilding designs include the *Great Western* 1838, the first steamship to cross the Atlantic regularly; the *Great Britain* 1845, the first large iron ship to have a screw propeller; and the *Great Eastern* 1858, which laid the first transatlantic telegraph cable.

Brunel Marc Isambard 1769–1849. French-born English engineer and inventor, and father of Isambard Kingdom Brunel. He constructed the Rotherhithe tunnel under the river Thames in London from Wapping to Rotherhithe 1825–43.

Brunelleschi /bru:nə'leski/ Filippo 1377–1446. Italian Renaissance architect. One of the earliest and greatest Renaissance architects, he pioneered the scientific use of perspective. He was responsible for the construction of the dome of Florence Cathedral (completed in 1438), a feat deemed impossible by many of his contemporaries.

brunette /bru:'net/ *n.* a woman with dark brown hair. [French, diminutive of *brun* = brown]

Bruno /'bru:nəʊ/ Giordano 1548–1600. Italian philosopher. He entered the Dominican order of monks in 1563, but his sceptical attitude to Catholic doctrines forced him to flee Italy in 1577. After visiting Geneva and Paris, he lived in England 1583–85, where he wrote some of his finest works. When he returned to Europe, he was arrested by the ◊Inquisition in 1593 in Venice and burned at the stake for his adoption of Copernican astronomy and his heretical religious views.

Bruno, St 1030–1101. German founder of the monastic Catholic ◊Carthusian order. He was born in Cologne, became a priest, and controlled the cathedral school of Rheims 1057–76. Withdrawing to the mountains near Grenoble after an ecclesiastical controversy, he founded the monastery at Chartreuse in 1084. Feast day 6 Oct.

Brunswick /'brʌnzwɪk/ (German *Braunschweig*) industrial city (chemical engineering, precision engineering, food processing) in Lower Saxony, W Germany; population (1988) 248,000. It was one of the chief cities of N Germany in the Middle Ages and a member of the ◊Hanseatic League. It was capital of the duchy of Brunswick from 1671.

brunt *n.* the chief stress or strain (*of* an attack or responsibility etc.).

brush *n.* **1.** an implement with bristles, hairs etc., set in a solid base for cleaning, painting, dressing the hair etc.; an application of this. **2.** a fox's bushy tail. **3.** a brushlike piece of carbon or metal for making an electrical connection, especially with a moving part. **4.** a short, usually unpleasant, encounter *with*. —*v.t.* **1.** to sweep clean, arrange etc., with a brush. **2.** to touch lightly in passing. **3.** to apply or remove with a brush. —**brush aside**, to dismiss as irrelevant. **brush off**, to dismiss abruptly. **brushoff** *n.* an abrupt

dismissal, a rebuff. **brush up**, to clean or smarten up; to revive one's former knowledge of. [from Anglo-French *brousse*, Old French *brosse*]

brushed *adj.* (of fabrics) finished with a nap.

brushwood *n.* cut or broken twigs etc.; undergrowth.

brushwork *n.* manipulation of the brush in painting; a painter's style in this.

brusque /brʊsk/ *adj.* abrupt or offhand in manner. —**brusquely** *adv.*, **brusqueness** *n.* [French, from Italian *brusco* = sour]

Brussels /'brʌsəlz/ (Flemish *Brussel* French *Bruxelles*) capital of Belgium, industrial city (lace, textiles, machinery, chemicals); population (1987) 974,000 (80% French-speaking, the suburbs Flemish-speaking). It is the headquarters of the European Economic Community and, since 1967, of the international secretariat of NATO. First settled in the 6th century, and a city from 1321, Brussels became the capital of the Spanish Netherlands in 1530 and of Belgium in 1830.

Brussels sprout one of the small edible buds along the stem of a variety (*Brassica oleracea* var. *gemmifera*) of ◊cabbage.

Brussels, Treaty of a pact of economic, political, cultural, and military alliance established on 17 March 1948, for 50 years, by the UK, France, and the Benelux countries, joined by West Germany and Italy in 1955. It was the forerunner of the North Atlantic Treaty Organization and the European Community.

Brussilov /bru:'si:lɒf/ Aleksei Alekseevich 1853–1926. Russian general, military leader in World War I who achieved major successes against the Austro-Hungarian forces in 1916. Later he was commander of the Red Army in 1920, which drove the Poles to within a few miles of Warsaw before being repulsed by them.

brutal /'bru:təl/ *adj.* very cruel, merciless. —**brutality** /-'tælɪtɪ/ *n.*, **brutally** *adv.*

brutalize *v.t./i.* to make or become brutal; to treat brutally.

brute *n.* a brutal or (*colloquial*) disagreeable person. —*adj.* unable to reason; animal-like in stupidity, sensuality etc.; unthinking, exerted etc. without mental effort. —**brutish** *adj.* [from French from Latin *brutus* = stupid]

Brutus /'bru:təs/ Marcus Junius *c.*78–42 BC. Roman soldier, a supporter of ◊Pompey (against Caesar) in the civil war. Pardoned by ◊Caesar and raised to high office by him, he nevertheless plotted Caesar's assassination to restore the purity of the Republic. Brutus committed suicide when he was defeated (with ◊Cassius) by ◊Mark Antony, Caesar's lieutenant, at Philippi in 42 BC.

Bruxelles French form of ◊Brussels, capital of Belgium.

Brynner /'brɪnə/ Yul. Stage name of Youl Bryner 1915–1985. US actor who made baldness his trademark. He played the king in *The King and I* both on stage 1951 and on film 1956; he is also memorable as the leader in *The Magnificent Seven* 1960.

bryony /'braɪənɪ/ *n.* either of two hedgerow climbing plants found in Europe including Britain: **white bryony** *Bryonia dioica* belonging to the gourd family Cucurbitaceae, and **black bryony** *Tamus communis* of the yam family Dioscoreaceae. [from Latin from Greek]

bryophyte /'braɪəfaɪt/ *n.* a member of the Bryophyta, a division of the plant kingdom containing three classes, the Hepaticae (◊liverwort), Musci (◊moss), and Anthocerotae (◊hornwort). Bryophytes are generally small, low-growing, terrestrial plants with no vascular (water-conducting) system as in higher plants. Their life cycle shows a marked ◊alternation of generations. Bryophytes chiefly occur in damp habitats and require water for the dispersal of the male gametes (◊antherozoids). [ultimately from Greek *bruon* = moss and *phuton* = plant]

Brythonic /braɪ'θɒnɪk/ *adj.* of the Celts of southern Britain or their languages. —*n.* the southern group of the Celtic languages, including Welsh, Cornish, and Breton. [from Welsh *Brython* = Britons]

Brzezinski /brə'ʒɪnski/ Zbigniew 1928– . US Democrat politician, born in Poland; he taught at Harvard University, USA, and became a US citizen in 1949. He was national security adviser to President Carter 1977–81 and chief architect of Carter's human-rights policy.

BSc abbreviation of Bachelor of Science, an academic degree.

BSE abbreviation of ◊bovine spongiform encephalopathy, popularly known as 'mad cow disease'.

BSI abbreviation of ◊British Standards Institute.

BST abbreviation of **1**. British Summer Time. **2**. ◊bovine somatotropin.

BT abbreviation of ◊British Telecom.

Btu symbol for ◊British thermal unit.

bubble *n*. **1**. a globular film of liquid enclosing air or gas; an air-filled cavity in glass etc. **2**. a transparent domed canopy. —*v.t.* to send up or rise in bubbles; to make the sound of bubbles. —**bubble and squeak,** cooked potato and cabbage fried together in a cake. —**bubble gum,** chewing gum that can be blown into bubbles. —**bubbly** *adj*.

bubble chamber in physics, a device for observing the nature and movement of atomic particles, and their interaction with radiations. It is a vessel filled with a highly superheated liquid through which ionizing particles move and collide. The paths of these particles are shown by strings of bubbles which can be photographed and studied. By using a pressurized liquid medium instead of a gas, it overcomes drawbacks inherent in the earlier ◊cloud chamber. It was invented by Donald ◊Glaser in 1952.

bubble memory in computing, a memory device based on the creation of small 'bubbles' on a magnetic surface. Bubble memories typically store up to four megabits (4 million ◊bits) of information. They are not sensitive to shock and vibration, unlike other memory devices such as disc drives, yet, like magnetic discs, they do not lose their information when the computer is switched off.

Bubiyan /buːˈbiʲɑn/ an island off Kuwait, occupied by Iraq in 1990 after an ultimatum to Kuwait to give it up was refused.

bubonic /bjuːˈbɒnɪk/ *adj.* **bubonic plague,** a contagious bacterial disease characterized by inflamed swellings (*buboes*) in the groin or armpit; see ◊plague. [from Greek *boubōn* = groin]

Bucaramanga /buːkaːrəˈmæŋɡə/ industrial (coffee, tobacco, cacao, cotton) and commercial city in north central Colombia; population (1985) 493,929. It was founded by the Spanish in 1622.

buccaneer /bʌkəˈnɪə(r)/ *n*. a member of various groups of seafarers who plundered Spanish ships and colonies on the Spanish American coast in the 17th century. Unlike true pirates, they were acting on (sometimes spurious) commission. —**buccaneering** *adj.* & *n*. [from French *boucan* = barbecue, of Brazilian origin]

Buchan /ˈbʌxən, ˈbʌkən/ John, Baron Tweedsmuir 1875–1940. Scottish politician and author. Called to the Bar in 1901, he was Conservative member of Parliament for the Scottish universities 1927–35, and governor general of Canada 1934–40. His adventure stories include *The Thirty-Nine Steps* 1915, *Greenmantle* 1916, and *The Three Hostages* 1924.

Bucharest /buːkəˈrest/ (Romanian *Bucureşti*) capital and largest city of Romania; population (1985) 1,976,000, the conurbation of Bucharest district having an area of 1,520 sq km/587 sq mi and a population of 2,273,000. Originally a citadel built by Vlad the Impaler (see ◊Dracula) to stop the advance of the Ottoman invasion in the 14th century, it became the capital of the princes of Wallachia in 1698 and of Romania in 1861. Savage fighting took place in the city during Romania's 1989 revolution.

Buchenwald /ˈbuːxənvælt/ site of a Nazi ◊concentration camp 1937–45 at a village NE of Weimar, E Germany.

Buchner Eduard 1860–1917. German chemist who researched the process of fermentation. In 1897 he observed that fermentation could be produced mechanically, by cell-free extracts. Buchner argued that it was not the whole yeast cell that produced fermentation, but only the presence of the enzyme he named zymase. He was awarded the Nobel Prize for Chemistry in 1907.

buck[1] /bʌk/ *n*. **1**. a male deer, rabbit, or hare. **2**. (*archaic*) a fashionable young man. —*v.t./i.* (of a horse) to jump vertically with back arched; to throw (the rider) thus. —**buck up,** (*slang*) to hurry up; to cheer up. [Old English]

buck[2] *n*. in poker, an object placed as a reminder before the player whose turn it is to deal. —**pass the buck,** (*colloquial*) to shift responsibility (and possibly blame) to another.

buck[3] *n*. (*US slang*) a dollar.

Buck Pearl S 1892–1973. US novelist. Daughter of missionaries to China, she spent much of her life there and wrote novels about Chinese life, such as *East Wind–West Wind* 1930 and *The Good Earth* 1931. She received the Nobel Prize for Literature in 1938.

bucket /ˈbʌkɪt/ *n*. **1**. a round flat-bottomed container with a handle, for carrying liquids etc.; the amount contained in this. **2**. a scoop in a dredger etc.; a compartment in a water wheel. —*v.t./i.* **1**. to travel or drive fast and bumpily. **2**. to rain or pour down heavily. [perhaps from Old English = pitcher]

Buckingham /ˈbʌkɪŋəm/ George Villiers, 1st Duke of Buckingham 1592–1628. English courtier, adviser to James I and later Charles I. After Charles's accession, Buckingham attempted to form a Protestant coalition in Europe, which led to war with France, but he failed to relieve the Protestants (◊Huguenots) besieged in La Rochelle in 1627. This added to his unpopularity with Parliament, and he was assassinated.

Buckingham George Villiers, 2nd Duke of Buckingham 1628–1687. English politician, a member of the ◊Cabal under Charles II. A dissolute son of the first duke, he was brought up with the royal children. His play *The Rehearsal* satirized the style of the poet Dryden, who portrayed him as Zimri in *Absalom and Achitophel*.

Buckingham Palace the London home of the British sovereign, built in 1703 for the duke of Buckingham, but bought by George III in 1762 and reconstructed by ◊Nash 1821–36; a new front was added in 1913.

Buckinghamshire /ˈbʌkɪŋəmʃə/ a county in southeast central England; **area** 1,880 sq km/726 sq mi; **features** ◊Chequers (country seat of the prime minister); Burnham Beeches; Open University at Walton Hall; **products** furniture, chiefly beech; agricultural goods; **population** (1987) 621,000.

buckle *n*. a metal clasp with a hinged pin for securing a strap, belt etc. —*v.t./i.* **1**. to fasten with a buckle. **2**. to crumple or cause to crumple under pressure. [from Old French from Latin *buccula* = cheek strap of helmet]

buckler *n*. a small, round shield with a handle.

buckram /ˈbʌkrəm/ *n*. coarse linen or cloth stiffened with paste, used for binding books etc. [from Anglo-French]

Bucks abbreviation of ◊Buckinghamshire.

buckshee /bʌkˈʃiː/ *adj.* & *adv.* (*slang*) free of charge. [corruption of *baksheesh*]

buckshot *n*. coarse lead shot.

buckskin *n*. leather from a buck's skin; a thick, smooth cotton or woollen fabric.

buckthorn *n*. any of various thorny shrubs of the family Rhamnaceae, of which two species, the buckthorn *Rhamnus cathartica* and the alder buckthorn *Frangula alnus*, are native to Britain.

buckwheat *n*. a highly nutrititious grain plant of the genus *Fagopyrum*, especially *F. esculentum*, of the family Polygonaceae. The plant grows to about 1 m/3 ft, and the seeds are either eaten whole or ground into flour. It is eaten both by humans and animals. Buckwheat can grow in poor soil in a short summer. [Dutch = beech wheat]

bucolic /bjuːˈkɒlɪk/ *adj.* of herders or shepherds, pastoral. —*n*. a pastoral poem. [from Latin from Greek *boukolos* = herdsman]

bud *n*. the rudiment of a shoot, foliage, or flower; a leaf or flower not fully open; an asexual growth separating from an organism to form a new animal. A plant bud is usually enclosed by protective scales; inside is a very short stem and numerous undeveloped leaves, or flower parts, or both. **Terminal buds** are found at the tips of shoots, while **axillary buds** develop in the ◊axils of the leaves, often remaining dormant unless the terminal bud is removed or damaged. **Adventitious buds** may be produced anywhere on the plant, their formation sometimes stimulated by an injury, such as that caused by pruning. —*v.t./i.* (-**dd**-) **1**. to put forth buds. **2**. to graft the bud of (a plant) on another plant. **3**. (especially in *participle*) to begin to grow or develop.

Budapest /bjuːdəˈpest/ capital of Hungary, industrial city (chemicals, textiles) on the river Danube; population (1985) 2,089,000. Buda, on the right bank of the Danube, became the Hungarian capital in 1867 and was joined with Pest, on the left bank, in 1872.

Buddha /ˈbuːdə/ the title of Prince Gautama Siddhārtha *c.*563–483 BC. a religious leader, founder of Buddhism, born at Lumbini in Nepal. At the age of 29, he left his wife

Buddhism

Buddha *A 13th-century Thai bronze statue of the Buddha.*

and son and a life of luxury, to escape from the material burdens of existence. After six years of austerity he realized that asceticism, like overindulgence, was futile, and chose the middle way of meditation. He became enlightened under a bo tree near Buddh Gaya in Bihar, India. He began teaching at Varanasi, and founded the Sangha, or order of monks. He spent the rest of his life travelling around N India, and died at Kusinagara in Uttar Pradesh. [Sanskrit = enlightened (*budh* = wake up, know)]

Buddhism *n.* one of the great world religions, which originated in India about 500 BC. It derives from the teaching of Buddha, who is regarded as one of a series of such enlightened beings; there are no gods. The chief doctrine is that of **karma**, good or evil deeds meeting an appropriate reward or punishment either in this life or (through reincarnation) a long succession of lives. The main divisions in Buddhism are **Theravāda** (or **Hīnayāna**) in SE Asia and **Mahāyāna** in N Asia; **Lamaism** in Tibet and **Zen** in Japan are among the many Mahāyāna sects. Its symbol is the lotus. There are over 247.5 million Buddhists worldwide. —**Buddhist** *n. & adj.*

budding *n.* 1. a type of ◊asexual reproduction in which an outgrowth develops from a cell to form a new individual. Most yeasts reproduce in this way. 2. in horticulture, a method of ◊grafting.

buddleia *n.* a tropical genus of shrubs and trees, family Buddleiaceae, to which the butterfly bush *Buddleia davidii* belongs. Its purple or white flower heads are attractive to insects and it is widely cultivated. [from *A Buddle*, English botanist (died 1715)]

buddy *n.* a friend, a mate.

budge /bʌdʒ/ (chiefly in negative contexts) 1. to move in the least degree. 2. to abandon or cause to abandon an opinion. [from French *bouger*]

Budge Donald 1915– . US tennis player. He was the first to perform the Grand Slam when he won the Wimbledon, French, US, and Australian championships all in 1938.

budgerigar /ˈbʌdʒərɪgɑː(r)/ *n.* a small Australian parakeet *Melopsittacus undulatus* that feeds mainly on grass seeds. Normally it is bright green, but yellow, white, blue, and mauve varieties have been bred for the pet market. [Aboriginal = good cockatoo]

budget /ˈbʌdʒɪt/ *n.* an estimate or plan of income and expenditure, especially those of a country; the amount of

money needed or available. National budgets set out estimates of government income and expenditure and generally include projected changes in taxation and growth. —*v.t./i.* to allot or allow *for* in a budget. —**budgetary** *adj.* [from Old French from Latin *bulga* = bag]

budgie /ˈbʌdʒɪ/ *n.* (*colloquial*) a ◊budgerigar. [abbreviation]

Buenos Aires /ˈbweɪnɒs ˈaɪrɪz/ capital and industrial city of Argentina, on the S bank of the Rio de la Plata; population (1980) 2,922,829, metropolitan area 9,969,826. It was founded in 1536 and became the capital in 1853.

buff *n.* 1. a velvety, dull-yellow leather; the colour of this. 2. (*colloquial*) an enthusiast. [originally for going to fires, from the buff uniforms once worn by New York volunteer fire fighters] —*v.t.* to polish (metal etc.) by rubbing; to make velvety like buff. —**in the buff**, naked. [originally = buffalo, from French *buffle*]

buffalo *n.* (*plural* **buffaloes**, *collectively* **buffalo**) two species of wild cattle. The Asiatic water buffalo *Bubalis bubalis* is found domesticated throughout S Asia and wild in parts of India and Nepal. It likes moist conditions. Usually grey or black, up to 1.8 m/6 ft high, both sexes carry large horns. The African buffalo *Syncerus caffer* is found in Africa, S of the Sahara, where there is grass, water, and cover in which to retreat. There are a number of subspecies, the biggest up to 1.6 m/5 ft high, and black, with massive horns set close together over the head. The name buffalo is also commonly applied to the American ◊bison. [probably from Portuguese from Latin from Greek *boubalos*]

buffer[1] *n.* 1. thing that deadens impact, especially a shock absorber fitted (in pairs) on a railway vehicle or at the end of a track. 2. in chemistry, a substance that maintains the degree of acidity in a solution (see ◊pH). 3. in computing, part of the memory used to hold data while it is waiting to be used. —**buffer state,** a small country between two powerful ones, thought to reduce the chance of war between these. [from *buff* = sound as of a soft body when struck]

buffer[2] *n.* (*slang*) a man, a fellow.

buffet[1] /ˈbʊfeɪ/ *n.* 1. a place where light meals may be bought (usually at a counter) and eaten. 2. /also ˈbʌfɪt/ a sideboard or recessed cupboard for dishes etc. 3. provision of food where guests serve themselves. —**buffet car,** a railway coach in which refreshments are served. [French = stool]

buffet[2] /ˈbʌfɪt/ *n.* a blow, especially with the hand. —*v.t.* to deal such blows to; to contend with (waves etc.). [from Old French, diminutive of *bufe* = blow]

Buffon /buːˈfɔ̃/ George Louise Leclerc, Comte de 1707–1778. French naturalist and author of the 18th century's most significant work of natural history, the 44-volume *Histoire naturelle* (1749–1804), 36 volumes of which he completed before his death. In *The Epochs of Nature*, one of the volumes, he questioned biblical chronology for the first time, and raised the Earth's age from the traditional figure of 6,000 years to the seemingly colossal estimate of 75,000 years.

buffoon /bəˈfuːn/ *n.* a jester, a clown. —**buffoonery** *n.* [from French from Italian from Latin *buffo* = clown]

bug *n.* 1. any insect belonging to the order Hemiptera; any small insect. All hemipterous insects have two pairs of wings with forewings partly thickened. They also have piercing mouthparts adapted for sucking the juices of plants or animals, the 'beak' being tucked under the body when not in use. 2. (*colloquial*) a virus, an infection; an obsessive enthusiasm or enthusiast. 3. (*slang*) a concealed microphone. 4. (*slang*) a defect in a machine etc.; in computing, an error in a program. It can be an error in the logical structure of a program or a syntactic error, such as a spelling mistake. Some bugs cause a program to fail immediately; others remain dormant, causing problems only when a particular combination of events occurs. —*v.t.* (-gg-) (*slang*) 1. to conceal a microphone in. 2. to annoy.

Bugatti /bjuːˈgæti/ *n.* a racing and sports-car company, founded by the Italian Ettore Bugatti (1881–1947). The first car was produced in 1908, but it was not until 1924 that one of the great Bugattis, Type 35, was produced. Bugatti cars are credited with more race wins than any other. The company was taken over by Hispano Suiza after Bugatti's death in 1947.

bugbear *n.* a cause of annoyance; an object of baseless fear, a bogy. [from obsolete *bug* = bogy]

bugger *n.* **1.** (*vulgar*) a hateful or contemptible person or thing; a sodomite. **2.** (*vulgar*) interjection expressing annoyance. [from Dutch, ultimately from Latin *Bulgarus* = Bulgarian heretic]

buggery *n.* sodomy.

buggy *n.* a light, horse-drawn vehicle for one or two persons; a small, sturdy motor vehicle.

bugle[1] /'bju:gəl/ *n.* in music, a valveless brass instrument with a shorter tube and less expanded bell than the trumpet. Constructed of copper plated with brass, it has long been used as a military instrument for giving a range of signals based on the tones of a harmonic series. —*v.i.* to sound a bugle. —**bugler** *n.* [originally = buffalo; from Old French from Latin *buculus* = young bull]

bugle[2] *n.* any plant of a low-growing genus *Ajuga* of the mint family Labiatae, with spikes of white, pink, or blue flowers. They are often grown as ground covers. [from Latin *bugula*] helen

bugloss /'bju:glɒs/ *n.* **1.** a plant related to borage, of various genera, distinguished by its rough, bristly leaves and small blue flowers. **2.** a plant of the genus *Echium*, especially *E. vulgare* (also called **viper's bugloss**) with white, bristly hairs and blue flowers. [from French or Latin from Greek *bouglossos* = ox-tongued, with reference to the shape and roughness of its leaves]

buhl *n.* an alternative spelling of ◊boulle, a type of marquetry.

build /bɪld/ *v.t.* (*past* and *past participle* **built** /bɪlt/) to construct by putting parts or material together; to develop or establish (a reputation etc.). —*n.* style of construction; proportions of the body. —**build up**, to establish or be established gradually. [Old English]

builder *n.* one who builds, especially a contractor who builds houses.

building *n.* **1.** the construction of houses etc. **2.** a permanent built structure that can be entered.

building society in the UK, a financial institution that attracts investment in order to lend money, repayable at interest, for the purchase or building of a house on security of a ◊mortgage. Since the 1970s building societies have considerably expanded their services and in many ways now compete with clearing banks.

build-up *n.* **1.** a favourable description in advance. **2.** a gradual approach to a climax.

built /bɪlt/ past and past participle of **build**. —*adj.* having a specified bodily build. —**built-up** *adj.* increased in height etc. by the addition of parts; (of an area) fully occupied by houses etc.

Bukharest an alternative form of ◊Bucharest, capital of Romania.

Bukharin /bu'xɑ:rɪn/ Nikolai Ivanovich 1888–1938. Soviet politician and theorist. A moderate, he was the chief Bolshevik thinker after Lenin. Executed on Stalin's orders for treason in 1938, he was posthumously rehabilitated in 1988.

Bulawayo /bulə'weɪəʊ/ industrial city and railway junction in Zimbabwe; population (1982) 415,000. It lies at an altitude of 1,355 m/4,450 ft on the river Matsheumlope, a tributary of the Zambezi, and was founded on the site of the kraal (enclosed village), burned down in 1893, of the Matabele chief, Lobenguela. It produces agricultural and electrical equipment. The former capital of Matabeleland, Bulawayo developed with the exploitation of goldmines in the neighbourhood.

bulb *n.* **1.** in some plants, an underground bud with fleshy leaves containing a reserve food supply and with roots growing from its base. Bulbs function in vegetative reproduction and are characteristic of many monocotyledenous plants such as the daffodil, snowdrop, and onion. Bulbs are grown on a commercial scale in temperate countries, such as England and the Netherlands. **2.** an object or part shaped like this; an electric lamp, its glass container. —**bulbous** /'bʌlbəs/ *adj.* [from Latin from Greek *bolbos* = onion]

bulbul *n.* a small, fruit-eating, passerine bird of the family Pycnonotidae. There are about 120 species, mainly in the forests of the Old World tropics.

Bulgakov Mikhail Afanasyevich 1891–1940. Russian novelist and playwright. His novel *The White Guard* 1924, dramatized as *The Days of the Turbins* 1926, deals with the Revolution and the civil war.

Bulganin /bul'gɑ:nɪn/ Nikolai 1895–1975. Soviet military leader and politician. He helped to organize Moscow's defence in World War II, became a marshal of the USSR in 1947, and was minister of defence 1947–49 and 1953–55. On the fall of Malenkov he became prime minister (chair of Council of Ministers) 1955–58 until ousted by Khrushchev.

Bulgaria /bʌl'geəriə/ People's Republic of; country in SE Europe, bounded to the N by Romania, to the W by Yugoslavia, to the S by Greece, to the SW by Turkey, and to the E by the Black Sea; **area** 110,912 sq km/42,812 sq mi; **capital** Sofia; **physical** Balkan and Rhodope mountains; Danube River in N; Bulgaria is in a key position on the land route from Europe to Asia; **head of state** Zhelyo Zhelev from 1990; **head of government** Dimitar Popov from 1990; **political system** Socialist pluralist republic; **exports** textiles, chemicals, nonferrous metals, timber, minerals, machinery; **population** (1990 est) 8,978,000; **language** Bulgarian, Turkish; **recent history** became a kingdom independent of Turkish rule in 1908. Soviet invasion of German-occupied Bulgaria in 1944; monarchy abolished and communist-dominated people's republic proclaimed in 1946. A Soviet-style constitution was adopted in 1947. Multicandidate elections were introduced in 1987; opposition parties allowed to form in 1989.

bulge *n.* **1.** an irregularly rounded swelling. **2.** (*colloquial*) a temporary increase in numbers. —*v.i.* to form a bulge. [from Latin *bulga* = bag]

Bulge, Battle of the or **Ardennes offensive** in World War II, Hitler's plan, code-named 'Watch on the Rhine', for a breakthrough by his field marshal ◊Rundstedt aimed at the US line in Ardennes from 16 Dec 1944 to 28 Jan 1945. There were 77,000 Allied casualties and 130,000 German, including Hitler's last powerful reserve, his panzer elite.

bulimia *n.* a condition of continuous, uncontrolled hunger. Considered a counteraction to stress or depression, this eating disorder is found chiefly in young women. When compensated for by forced vomiting or overdoses of laxatives, the condition   called **bulimia nervosa**. It is sometimes associated with ◊anorexia. [Greek = ox hunger]

bulk *n.* **1.** size or magnitude, especially when great. **2.** the greater part *of*. **3.** a large shape, body, or person. **4.** a large quantity. —*v.t./i.* **1.** to increase the size or thickness of. **2.** to seem (*large* etc.) in size or importance. —**bulk buying**, buying in large amounts, especially by one buyer of much of a producer's output. [Old Norse]

bulkhead *n.* an upright partition between compartments in a ship, aircraft etc. [from *bulk* = stall]

bulky *adj.* taking up much space, inconveniently large. —**bulkiness** *n.*

bull[1] /bul/ *n.* **1.** an uncastrated male of the ox family; the male of the whale, elephant, and other large animals. **2.** **the Bull**, the constellation or sign of the zodiac Taurus. **3.** the bull's-eye of a target. **4.** one who buys shares on the Stock Exchange in the hope of selling them at a higher price later; the opposite of a ◊bear. In a bull market, prices rise and bulls profit. —**bull-nosed** *adj.* with a rounded end. [from Old Norse]

bull[2] /bul/ a papal edict. Important bulls include Leo X's condemnation of Luther in 1520 and Pius IX's proclamation of papal infallibility in 1870. [from Latin *bulla* = seal]

Bull John. A typical Englishman, as represented in cartoons and caricatures: a stocky figure, regarded as stubborn and honest.

Bull John *c.*1562–1628. English composer, organist, and virginalist. Most of his output is for keyboard, and includes ◊'God Save the King'. He also wrote sacred vocal music.

bulldog *n.* a dog of strong, courageous breed with a broad head and short thick neck. It has deeply wrinkled cheeks, small folded ears, and the nose laid back between the eyes. The bulldog grows to about 45 cm/18 in at the shoulder. The breed is British, of ancient but uncertain origin.

bulldoze /'buldəuz/ *v.t.* **1.** to move or clear with a bulldozer. **2.** (*colloquial*) to intimidate; to force one's *way*. [originally = coerce by threats of violence]

Buller /'bulə/ Redvers Henry 1839–1908. English commander against the Boers in the South African War 1899–1902. He was defeated at Colenso and Spion Kop, but relieved Ladysmith; he was superseded by Lord Roberts.

bullet /'bulɪt/ *n.* a small cylindrical projectile fired from a gun etc. [from French diminutive of *boule* = ball]

bulletin /'bʊlɪln/ n. a short official statement of news, the condition of a patient etc. [French from Italian diminutive of *bulletta* = passport (Latin *bulla* = seal)]

bullfighting n. the sport of baiting and usually killing a bull, the national sport of Spain. Originally popular in Greece and Rome, bullfighting was introduced into Spain by the Moors in the 11th century. —**bullfighter** n.

bullfinch n. a Eurasian songbird *Pyrrhula pyrrhula*, with a thick head and neck, and short heavy bill. It is small and blue-grey or black, the males reddish and the females brown on the breast. Bullfinches are 15 cm/6 in long, and usually seen in pairs. They feed on tree buds as well as seeds and berries, and are usually seen in woodland. They also live in the Aleutians and on the Alaska mainland.

bullfrog n. a large American frog with a bellowing cry.

bullhead n. or **miller's thumb** a small fish *Cottus gobio* found in fresh water in the northern hemisphere, often under stones. It has a large head, a spine on the gill cover, and grows to 10 cm/4 in.

bullion /'bʊljən/ n. gold or silver in bulk before coining, or valued by weight. [Anglo-French = mint]

bullock /'bʊlək/ n. a castrated bull. [Old English, diminutive of *bull*[1]]

Bull Run, Battles of /'bʊl rʌn/ in the American Civil War, two victories for the Confederate army under General Robert E Lee at Manassas Junction, NE Virginia: **1st Battle of Bull Run** 21 July 1861; **2nd Battle of Bull Run** 29–30 Aug 1862.

bull's-eye n. 1. the centre of a target. 2. a large, hard, minty sweet. 3. a hemisphere or thick disc of glass as a window in a ship, a small circular window; a hemispherical lens, a lantern with this; a boss at the centre of a sheet of blown glass.

bull terrier a heavily built, smooth-coated breed of dog, usually white, originating as a cross between terrier and bulldog. It grows to about 40 cm/16 in tall, and was formerly used in bull baiting. Pit bull terriers are used in illegal dog fights.

bully[1] /'bʊlɪ/ n. a person using strength or power to hurt or coerce others by intimidation. —*v.t.* to behave as a bully towards, to intimidate.

bully[2] n. the start of play in hockey, at which two opposing players tap the ground and each other's sticks three times before hitting the ball. —*v.i.* to start play thus.

Bülow /'bju:ləʊ/ Bernhard, Prince von 1849–1929. German diplomat and politician. He was chancellor of the German Empire 1900–09 under Kaiser Wilhelm II and, holding that self-interest was the only rule for any state, adopted attitudes to France and Russia that unintentionally reinforced the trend towards opposing European power groups: the ◊Triple Entente (Britain, France, Russia) and ◊Triple Alliance (Germany, Austria-Hungary, Italy).

bulrush /'bʊlrʌʃ/ n. either of two plants: the great reed mace or cat's-tail *Typha latifolia* with chocolate-brown, tight-packed flower spikes reaching up to 15 cm/6 in long; and a type of sedge *Scirpus lacustris* with tufts of reddish-brown flowers at the top of a rounded, rushlike stem. [from *bull*[1] in sense 'coarse']

bulwark /'bʊlwək/ n. 1. a defensive wall, especially of earth; a protecting person or thing. 2. (usually in *plural*) a ship's side above deck. [from Middle Dutch]

bum[1] n. (*slang*) the buttocks.

bum[2] n. (*US slang*) a loafer, a dissolute person. [from German *bummler* = loafer]

bumble *v.i.* 1. to blunder, to act ineptly. 2. to ramble *on* in speaking. 3. to buzz loudly.

bumblebee n. any large ◊bee, usually dark-coloured but banded with yellow, orange or white, belonging to the genus *Bombus*.

bummalo /'bʌmələʊ/ n. (*plural* the same) another name for ◊bombay duck.

bump n. 1. a dull-sounding blow or impact. 2. a swelling produced by this. 3. any lump or unevenness on a surface; a prominence on the skull, associated by phrenologists with mental faculties. —*v.t./i.* to hit or come (*against* or *into*) with a bump; to hurt thus; to travel with jolts. —**bump into**, (*colloquial*) to meet by chance. **bump off**, (*slang*) to murder. **bump up**, to increase (prices etc.). —**bumpily** *adv.*, **bumpiness** n., **bumpy** *adj.* [imitative]

bumper n. 1. a horizontal bar attached at either end of a motor vehicle to reduce damage in a collision. 2. in cricket, a ball that rises high after pitching. 3. a wine glass filled to the brim. —*adj.* (of crops etc.) exceptionally abundant.

bumpkin n. an awkward or simple country person. [from Dutch]

bumptious /'bʌmpʃəs/ *adj.* offensively self-confident. [from *bump* after *fractious*]

bun n. 1. a small, round cake often with currants. 2. hair fastened in a rounded mass at the back of the head.

bunch n. 1. a set of things growing or fastened together. 2. (*slang*) a gang or group. —*v.t./i.* 1. to make into a bunch. 2. to gather into close folds. 3. to form a group or crowd. —**bunchy** *adj.*

Bunche /bʌntʃ/ Ralph 1904–1971. US diplomat, principal director of the United Nations Department of Trusteeship 1947–54, and UN undersecretary acting as mediator in Palestine 1948–49 and as special representative in the Congo in 1960. In 1950 he was awarded the Nobel Peace Prize, the first ever awarded to a black person.

bundle n. a collection of things fastened or wrapped together. —*v.t.* 1. to make into a bundle. 2. to throw hastily *into* a receptacle; to send (a person) unceremoniously *out* etc.

bung n. a large stopper, especially for the mouth of a cask. —*v.t.* 1. to stop with a bung. 2. (*slang*) to throw, to put. —**bunged up**, blocked. [from Dutch]

bungalow /'bʌŋgələʊ/ n. a one-storeyed house. [originally in India, from Gujarati from Hindi = of Bengal]

bungle *v.t.* to mismanage, to blunder through lack of skill. —n. a bungled attempt. —**bungler** n. [imitative]

bunion /'bʌnjən/ n. a swelling on the foot, especially on the big toe. [from Old French *buigne* = bump on head]

bunk[1] n. a shelflike bed, usually one in a tiered series, as in a ship etc.

bunk[2] n. **do a bunk,** (*slang*) to go away hurriedly.

bunk[3] n. (*slang*) bunkum. [abbreviation]

bunker n. 1. a compartment for coal; a reinforced underground shelter. 2. a sandy hollow constructed as an obstacle on a golf course. —*v.t.* to fill the bunkers of (a ship) with fuel.

Bunker Hill, Battle of the first considerable engagement in the ◊American Revolution, on 17 June 1775, near a small hill in Charlestown (now part of Boston), Massachusetts, USA; although the colonists were defeated they were able to retreat to Boston and suffered fewer casualties than the British.

bunkum n. nonsense, claptrap. [from a verbose US congressman from *Buncombe* County in North Carolina about 1820]

bunny n. (*children's colloquial*) a rabbit. [from dialect *bun* = rabbit]

Bunsen /'bʊnzən/ Robert Wilhelm von 1811–1899. German chemist, credited with the invention of the **Bunsen burner**. His name is also given to the carbon-zinc electric cell, which he invented in 1841 for use in arc lamps. In 1859 he discovered two new elements, caesium and rubidium.

Bunshaft /'bʌnʃaft/ Gordon 1909–1990. US architect whose Modernist buildings include the first to be completely enclosed in curtain walling (walls which hang from a rigid steel frame), the Lever Building 1952 in New York. He also designed the Heinz Company's UK headquarters 1965 in Hayes Park, London.

bunting[1] n. flags and similar festive decorations; a loosely woven fabric used for these.

bunting[2] n. any of a number of sturdy finchlike passerine birds with short, thick bills, of the family Emberizidae, especially the genera *Passerim* and *Emberiza*. Most of these brightly coloured birds are native to the New World.

Buñuel /bu:'njuel/ Luis 1900–1983. Spanish ◊Surrealist film director. He collaborated with Salvador Dali in *Un Chien andalou* 1928, and established his solo career with *Los Olvidados/The Young and the Damned* 1950. His works are often anticlerical, with black humour and erotic imagery.

Bunyan /'bʌnjən/ John 1628–1688. English author. A Baptist, he was imprisoned in Bedford 1660–72 for unlicensed preaching. During a second jail sentence in 1675 he started to write *The Pilgrim's Progress*, the first part of which was published in 1678. Other works include *Grace Abounding* 1666, *The Life and Death of Mr Badman* 1680, and *The Holy War* 1682.

He that is down need fear no fall;
He that is low, no pride.

John Bunyan
The Pilgrim's Progress

bunyip *n.* mythical animal of the Australian Aborigines; it is a river creature, rather like a slender, long-necked hippopotamus. The word has been adopted in Australian English to mean 'fake' or 'impostor'.

buoy /bɔɪ/ *n.* **1.** an anchored float marking a navigable course or reefs etc. Buoys come in different shapes, such as a pole (spar buoy), cylinder (car buoy), and cone (nun buoy). Light buoys carry a small tower surmounted by a flashing lantern, and bell buoys house a bell, which rings as the buoy moves up and down with the waves. Mooring buoys are heavy and have a ring on top to which a ship can be tied. **2.** a lifebuoy. —*v.t.* **1.** to mark with a buoy. **2.** (also with *up*) to keep afloat, to sustain and encourage (a person, courage etc.).

buoyant /'bɔɪənt/ *adj.* **1.** able to stay afloat. **2.** constantly cheerful or light-hearted. —**buoyancy** *n.* the lifting effect of a fluid on a body wholly or partly immersed in it. [from French or Spanish]

bur *n.* or **burr** a seed or seed head with hooked bristles, especially a 'false fruit' or ◊pseudocarp like that of burdock *Arctium.* Burs catch in the feathers or fur of passing animals, and thus may be dispersed over considerable distances. [from Scandinavian]

Burbage /'bɜːbɪdʒ/ Richard *c.*1567–1619. English actor, thought to have been ◊Shakespeare's original Hamlet, Othello, and Lear. He also appeared in first productions of works by Ben Jonson, Thomas Kyd, and John Webster. His father **James Burbage** (*c.*1530–1597) built the first English playhouse, known as 'the Theatre'; his brother **Cuthbert Burbage** (*c.*1566–1636) built the original ◊Globe Theatre in 1599 in London.

burble *v.i.* to make a murmuring noise; to speak ramblingly. [imitative]

burbot /'bɜːbət/ *n.* a long, rounded fish *Lota lota* of the cod family, the only one living entirely in fresh water. Up to 1 m/3 ft long, it lives on the bottom of clear lakes and rivers, often in holes or under rocks, throughout Europe, Asia, and North America.

burden *n.* **1.** a thing carried, especially something heavy; an oppressive responsibility, expense etc. **2.** a ship's carrying capacity. **3.** the refrain of a song; the main theme of a speech etc. —*v.t.* to place a heavy load on, to encumber; to oppress. —**burden of proof,** in court proceedings, the duty of a party to produce sufficient evidence to prove that his or her case is true. [Old English]

burdensome *adj.* troublesome, oppressive.

burdock /'bɜːdɒk/ *n.* any of the bushy herbs belonging to the genus *Arctium* of the family Compositae, characterized by hairy leaves and ripe fruit enclosed in ◊burs with strong hooks.

bureau /'bjuərəu/ *n.* (*plural* **bureaux**) **1.** a writing desk with drawers. **2.** an office or department for transacting specific business; a government department. [French = desk, originally its baize covering, ultimately from Greek *purros* = red]

bureaucracy /bjuə'rɒkrəsɪ/ *n.* an organization whose structure and operations are governed to a high degree by written rules and a hierarchy of offices; in its broadest sense, all forms of administration, and in its narrowest, rule by officials. [after *aristocracy* etc.]

bureaucrat /'bjuərəkræt/ *n.* an official in a bureaucracy. —**bureaucratic** /-'krætɪk/ *adj.*

burette /bjuə'ret/ *n.* in chemistry, a long, narrow, calibrated glass tube, with a tap at the bottom, used in ◊titrations for the controlled delivery of measured variable quantities of a liquid. [French]

burgee /bɜː'dʒiː/ *n.* a small triangular or swallow-tailed flag on a yacht.

Burgenland /'buəgənlænd/ federal state of SE Austria, extending from the Danube S along the W border of the Hungarian plain; area 4,000 sq km/1,544 sq mi; population (1987) 267,000. It is a largely agricultural region adjoining the Neusiedler See, and produces timber, fruit,

sugar, wine, lignite, antimony, and limestone. Its capital is Eisenstadt.

burgeon /'bɜːdʒən/ *v.i.* (*literary*) to begin to grow rapidly, to flourish. [from Old French from Latin *burra* = wool]

Burges /'bɜːdʒɪz/ William 1827–1881. English Gothic revivalist architect. His chief works are Cork Cathedral 1862–76, additions to and remodelling of Cardiff Castle 1865, and Castle Coch near Cardiff 1875. His style is characterized by sumptuous interiors with carving, painting, and gilding.

burgess /'bɜːdʒɪs/ *n.* a citizen of a town or borough; (*historical*) an MP for a borough, corporate town, or university. [from Old French from Latin *burgus* = borough]

Burgess Anthony. Pen name of Anthony John Burgess Wilson 1917– . English novelist, critic, and composer. His prolific work includes *A Clockwork Orange* 1962, set in a future London terrorized by teenage gangs, and the panoramic *Earthly Powers* 1980. His vision has been described as bleak and pessimistic, but his work is also comic and satiric, as in his novels featuring the poet Enderby.

Burgess Guy (Francis de Moncy) 1910–1963. English spy, a diplomat recruited by the USSR as an agent; he was linked with Kim ◊Philby, Donald Maclean (1913–1983), and Anthony ◊Blunt.

Burgess Shale Site the site of unique fossil-bearing rock formations, 530 million years old, in Yoho National Park, British Colombia, Canada. The shales in this corner of the Rocky Mountains contain more than 120 species of marine invertebrate fossils. Although discovered in 1909 by Charles Walcott, the Burgess Shales have only recently been used as evidence in the debate concerning the evolution of life. In 1990 Stephen Jay Gould drew attention to a body of scientific opinion interpreting the fossil finds as evidence of parallel early evolutionary trends extinguished by chance rather than natural selection.

burgh /'bʌrə/ *n.* **1.** (*historical*) originally a fortified settlement, usually surrounding a monastery or castle, in Germanic lands in the 9th–10th centuries. Later, it was used to mean new towns, or towns that enjoyed particular privileges relating to government and taxation. **2.** a former unit of Scottish local government, abolished in 1975. [Scottish form of *borough*]

Burgh /də 'bɜːg/ Hubert de; died 1243. English ◊justiciar and regent of England. He began his career in the administration of Richard I, and was promoted to the justiciarship by King John; he remained in that position under Henry III from 1216 until his dismissal. He was a supporter of King John against the barons, and ended French intervention in England by his defeat of the French fleet in the Strait of Dover in 1217. He reorganized royal administration and the Common Law.

burgher /'bɜːgə(r)/ *n.* (*historical*) a citizen of a ◊burgh who was a freeman of the burgh and had the right to participate in its government. A burgher usually had to possess a house within the burgh. [from German or Dutch *burg* = borough]

Burghley /'bɜːli/ William Cecil, Baron Burghley 1520–1598. English politician, chief adviser to Elizabeth I as secretary of state from 1558 and Lord High Treasurer from 1572. He was largely responsible for the religious settlement of 1559, and took a leading role in the events preceding the execution of Mary Queen of Scots in 1587.

burglar /'bɜːglə/ *n.* one who commits burglary. —**burglarious** /-'gleərɪəs/ *adj.* [from Anglo-French *burgler* = plunderer]

burglary /'bɜːglərɪ/ *n.* in law, the offence of breaking into a building as a trespasser with the intent to commit theft or other serious crime.

burgle *v.t.* to enter and rob (a house), to rob the house of (a person). [from *burglar*]

burgomaster /'bɜːgəmɑːstə/ *n.* the mayor of a Dutch or Flemish town. [from Dutch *burg* = borough]

Burgoyne /bɜː'gɔɪn/ John 1722–1792. English general and dramatist. He served in the American Revolutionary War and surrendered in 1777 to the colonists at Saratoga, New York State, in one of the pivotal battles of the war. He wrote comedies, among them *The Maid of the Oaks* 1775 and *The Heiress* 1786.

burgundy /'bɜːgəndɪ/ *n.* a red or white wine from Burgundy in E France; a similar wine from elsewhere.

Burgundy ancient kingdom and duchy in the valleys of the rivers Saône and Rhône, France. The Burgundi were a Teutonic tribe that overran the country about 400. From the 9th century to the death of Duke ◊Charles the Bold in 1477, it was the nucleus of a powerful principality. On Charles's death the duchy was incorporated into France. The capital of Burgundy was Dijon. Today the region to which it corresponds is ◊Bourgogne.

burial /'beriəl/ *n.* 1. the burying of a dead body; a funeral. 2. in archaeology, a grave or its remains.

burin /'bjuərin/ *n.* a tool for engraving on copper or wood; a prehistoric flint tool with a narrow chisel edge. [French]

Burke /bɜ:k/ Edmund 1729–1797. British Whig politician and political theorist, born in Dublin, Ireland. In Parliament from 1765, he opposed the government's attempts to coerce the American colonists, for example in *Thoughts on the Present Discontents* 1770, and supported the emancipation of Ireland, but denounced the French Revolution, for example in *Reflections on the Revolution in France* 1790.

Burke Robert O'Hara 1820–1861. Australian explorer who made the first south–north crossing of Australia (from Victoria to the Gulf of Carpentaria), with William Wills (1834–1861). Both died on the return journey, and only one of their party survived.

Burke William 1792–1829. Irish murderer. He and his partner William Hare, living in Edinburgh, dug up the dead to sell for dissection. They increased their supplies by murdering at least 15 people. Burke was hanged on the evidence of Hare.

Burke's Peerage the popular name of the *Genealogical and Heraldic History of the Peerage, Baronetage, and Knightage of the United Kingdom*, first issued by John Burke in 1826. The most recent edition was in 1970.

Burkina Faso /bɜ:'ki:nə 'fæsəu/ People's Democratic Republic of; landlocked country in W Africa, bounded to the E by Niger, to the NW and W by Mali, to the S by Ivory Coast, Ghana, Togo, and Benin; **area** 274,122 sq km/ 105,811 sq mi; **capital** Ouagadougou; **physical** landlocked plateau with hills in W and SW; headwaters of the river Volta; tropical savanna exposed to overgrazing and deforestation; **head of state and government** Blaise Compaore from 1987; **political system** one-party military republic; **exports** cotton, groundnuts, livestock, hides, skins, sesame; **population** (1990 est) 8,941,000; **language** French (official); about 50 native Sudanic languages spoken by 90% of population; **recent history** independence achieved from France in 1960. A series of coups has rocked the country between military and civilian rule. Previously known as Upper Volta, Burkina Faso was given its present name in 1984.

burlesque /bɜ:'lesk/ *n.* 1. a composition in which a serious subject is treated comically or a trivial one with mock solemnity; this as a branch of literature etc. 2. in the USA, a type of sex and comedy show invented in 1866 with acts including acrobats, singers, and comedians. During the 1920s striptease was introduced in order to counteract the growing popularity of the movies. Burlesque was frequently banned in the USA. 3. (*historical*) a form of satirical comedy of the 17th and 18th centuries, parodying a particular play or dramatic genre. For example, ◊Gay's *The Beggar's Opera* 1728 is a burlesque of 18th-century opera, and ◊Sheridan's *The Critic* 1777 satirizes the sentimentality in contemporary drama. —*adj.* of the nature of burlesque. —*v.t.* to make or give a burlesque of. [French from Italian *burla* = mockery]

Burlington /'bɜ:lɪŋtən/ Richard Boyle, 3rd Earl of 1694–1753. Anglo-Irish architectural patron and architect; one of the premier exponents of the Palladian style in Britain. His buildings, such as Chiswick House in London (1725–29), are characterized by absolute adherence to the Classical rules. His major protégé was William ◊Kent.

burly *adj.* of strong sturdy build. [originally = stately]

Burma the former name (to 1989) of ◊Myanmar.

Burmese /bɜ:'mi:z/ *adj.* of Myanmar (Burma) or its people or language. —*n.* (*plural* the same) 1. a native or inhabitant of Myanmar, a state with over 20 ethnic groups, all of whom have the right to Burmese nationality. The largest group are the Burmans, speakers of a Sino-Tibetan language, who migrated from the hills E of Tibet, settling in the area around Mandalay by the 11th century AD. 2. the official language of Myanmar.

burn[1] *v.t./i.* (*past* and *past participle* **burned, burnt**) 1. to consume or be consumed by fire; to blaze or glow with fire. 2. to use or be used as fuel; to give out or cause to give out light or heat. 3. to injure by fire or great heat, to suffer such injury; to scorch or char in cooking. 4. to produce (a mark etc.) by fire; to harden (bricks) by fire. 5. to feel a hot sensation. 6. to be filled *with* a violent emotion. —*n.* a mark or injury caused by the destruction of body tissue by extremes of temperature, corrosive chemicals, electricity, or radiation. **First-degree burns** may cause reddening; **second-degree burns** cause blistering and irritation but usually heal spontaneously; **third-degree burns** are disfiguring and may be life-threatening. —**burn down**, to destroy or be destroyed by burning. **burning glass,** a lens to concentrate the Sun's rays on an object and burn it. [Old English]

burn[2] *n.* (*Scottish*) a brook. [Old English]

Burne-Jones /'bɜ:n 'dʒəunz/ Edward Coley 1833–1898. English painter. In 1856 he was apprenticed to the Pre-Raphaelite painter ◊Rossetti, who remained a dominant influence. His paintings, inspired by legend and myth, were characterized by elongated forms as in *King Cophetua and the Beggar Maid* 1880–84 (Tate Gallery, London). He later moved towards Symbolism. He also designed tapestries and stained glass in association with William ◊Morris.

Burnell /bɜ:'nel/ (Susan) Jocelyn (Bell) 1943– . British astronomer. In 1967 she discovered the first ◊pulsar (rapidly flashing star) with Antony ◊Hewish and colleagues at Cambridge University, England.

burner *n.* the part of a lamp, gas cooker etc., that emits and shapes the flame.

burnet /'bɜ:nit/ *n.* a herb *Sanguisorba minor* of the rose family, also known as **salad burnet.** It smells of cucumber and can be used in salads. The term is also used for other members of the genus *Sanguisorba*.

Burnet Gilbert 1643–1715. Anglo-Scottish historian and bishop, author of *History of His Own Time* 1723–24. His Whig views having brought him into disfavour, he retired to the Netherlands on the accession of James II and became the confidential adviser of William of Orange, with whom he sailed to England in 1688. He was appointed bishop of Salisbury in 1689.

Burnett /bɜ'net/ Frances (Eliza) Hodgson 1849–1924. English writer, living in the USA from 1865, whose novels for children include the rags-to-riches tale *Little Lord Fauntleroy* 1886 and *The Secret Garden* 1909.

Burney /'bɜ:ni/ Fanny (Frances) 1752–1840. English novelist and diarist, daughter of the musician Dr Charles Burney (1726–1814). She achieved success with *Evelina*, published anonymously in 1778, became a member of Dr ◊Johnson's circle, received a post at court from Queen Charlotte, and in 1793 married the émigré General d'Arblay. She published three further novels, *Cecilia* 1782, *Camilla* 1796, and *The Wanderer* 1814, and her diaries and letters appeared in 1842.

Burnham /'bɜ:nəm/ Forbes 1923–1985. Guyanese Marxist-Leninist politician. He was prime minister 1964–80, leading the country to independence in 1966 and declaring it the world's first cooperative republic in 1970. He was executive president 1980–85. Resistance to the US landing in Grenada in 1983 was said to be due to his forewarning the Grenadans of the attack.

burning *adj.* 1. that burns; ardent, intense. 2. (of a question) hotly discussed.

burnish /'bɜ:nɪʃ/ *v.t.* to polish by rubbing. [from Old French *brunir* (*brun* = brown)]

burnous /bɜ:'nu:s/ *n.* an Arab or Moorish hooded cloak. [French from Arabic from Greek *birros* = cloak]

Burns /bɜ:nz/ John 1858–1943. English labour leader, sentenced to six weeks' imprisonment for his part in the Trafalgar Square demonstration on 'Bloody Sunday', 13 Nov 1887, and leader of the strike in 1889 securing the dockers' tanner (wage of 6d per hour). An Independent Labour member of Parliament 1892–1918, he was the first person from the labouring classes to be a member of the cabinet, as president of the Local Government Board 1906–14.

Burns Robert 1759–1796. Scottish poet, notable for his use of the Scots dialect at a time when it was not considered suitably 'elevated' for literature. Burns's first volume, *Poems, Chiefly in the Scottish Dialect*, appeared in 1786. In

Burne-Jones *The Burne-Jones and Morris families, photographed by Frederick Hollyer in 1874. Burne-Jones (rear, left) and William Morris (standing) became close friends at Oxford.*

addition to his poetry, Burns wrote or adapted many songs, including 'Auld Lang Syne'.

burnt past and past participle of **burn**[1]. —*adj.* **burnt ochre, sienna,** etc., pigment darkened by burning. **burnt offering,** a sacrifice offered by burning.

burp *v.t./i. (colloquial)* to belch; to cause (a baby) to belch. —*n. (colloquial)* a belch. [imitative]

burr[1] *n.* 1. a whirring sound; a rough pronunciation of the letter r; a regional accent characterized by this. 2. a rough edge on metal or paper. 3. a small drill. —*v.i.* to make a burr.

burr[2] variant of ◊bur.

Burra /'bʌrə/ Edward 1905–1976. English painter devoted to themes of city life, its hustle, humour, and grimy squalor. *The Snack Bar* 1930 (Tate Gallery, London) and his watercolour scenes of Harlem, New York, 1933–34, are characteristic. Postwar works include religious paintings and landscapes.

Burroughs /'bʌrəuz/ Edgar Rice 1875–1950. US novelist, born in Chicago. He wrote *Tarzan of the Apes* 1914, the story of an aristocratic child lost in the jungle and reared by apes, and followed it with over 20 more books about the Tarzan character. He also wrote about life on Mars.

Burroughs William S 1914– . US novelist, born in St Louis, Missouri. He 'dropped out' and, as part of the ◊beat generation, wrote *Junky* 1953, *The Naked Lunch* 1959, *The Soft Machine* 1961, and *Dead Fingers Talk* 1963. Later novels include *Queer* 1986.

Burroughs William Steward 1857–1898. US industrialist who invented the first hand-operated adding machine to give printed results.

burrow /'bʌrəu/ *n.* a hole or tunnel dug by a fox, rabbit etc. as a dwelling. —*v.t./i.* 1. to dig a burrow; to form by burrowing. 2. to investigate or search (*into*). [variant of *borough*]

Bursa /'bɜːsə/ city in NW Turkey, with a port at Mudania; population (1985) 614,000. It was the capital of the Ottoman Empire 1326–1423.

bursar /'bɜːsə/ *n.* 1. a person who manages the finances of a college etc. 2. a student holding a bursary. [from French or Latin *bursa* = bag]

bursary *n.* 1. a grant or scholarship awarded to a student. 2. the bursar's office in a college.

burst *v.t./i. (past* and *past participle* **burst**) 1. to force open by internal pressure; to be full to overflowing. 2. to

make one's way with sudden violence; to appear or come suddenly. —*n.* 1. a bursting, a split. 2. a sudden outbreak or explosion. 3. a sudden effort, a spurt. —**burst into,** to break into (blossom, flame, tears etc.). **burst out,** to exclaim suddenly; to begin suddenly. [Old English]

Burt /bɜːt/ Cyril Lodowic 1883–1971. English psychologist. A specialist in child and mental development, he argued in *The Young Delinquent* 1925 the importance of social and environmental factors in delinquency. After his death it was discovered that he had falsified some of his experimental results in an attempt to prove his theory that intelligence is largely inherited. In 1989 this evidence of his guilt was further questioned.

Burton /'bɜːtn/ Richard (Francis) 1821–1890. English explorer and translator (he knew 35 oriental languages). He travelled mainly in the Middle East and NE Africa, often disguised as a Muslim; made two attempts to find the source of the Nile, in 1855 and 1857–58 (on the second, with ◊Speke, he reached Lake Tanganyika); and wrote many travel books. He translated oriental erotica and the *Arabian Nights* 1885–88.

Burton Richard. The stage name of Richard Jenkins 1925–1984. Welsh actor, remarkable for the dramatic quality of his voice. He appeared in several films with Elizabeth Taylor, including *Cleopatra* 1962 and *Who's Afraid of Virginia Woolf?* 1966. Among his later films are *Equus* 1977 and *1984* 1984.

Burton Robert 1577–1640. English philosopher who wrote an analysis of depression, *Anatomy of Melancholy* 1621, a compendium of information on the medical and religious opinions of the time, much used by later authors.

Burundi /bu'rundi/ Republic of; country in east central Africa, bounded to the N by Rwanda, to the W by Zaïre, to the S by Lake Tanganyika, and to the SE and E by Tanzania; **area** 27,834 sq km/10,744 sq mi; **capital** Bujumbura; **physical** landlocked grassy highland straddling watershed of Mile and Congo; Lake Tanganyika, Great Rift Valley; **head of state and government** Pierre Buyoya from 1987; **political system** one-party military republic; **exports** coffee, cotton, tea, nickel, hides, livestock; **population** (1990 est) 5,647,000 (of whom 15% are the Nilotic Tutsi, still holding most of the land and political power, 1% are Pymy Twa, and the remainder Bantu Hutu; **language** Kirundi (a Bantu language) and French (official); Kiswahili; **recent history** separated from Ruanda-Urundi as Burundi

Bush *US president from 1989, George Bush.*

in 1962; given independence as a monarchy under King Mwambutsa IV. Declared a republic in 1966. The constitution of 1981 provided for a national assembly.

bury /'berɪ/ *v.t.* 1. to deposit (a corpse) in the earth, a tomb, or the sea; to put underground; to put out of sight. 2. to involve *oneself* deeply *in* (a study etc.). —**bury the hatchet,** to cease quarrelling. [Old English]

bus *n.* (*plural* **buses**) a long-bodied passenger vehicle, especially one serving the public on a fixed route. —*v.t./i.* (**bused, busing**) to go by bus; to transport by bus, especially to counteract racial segregation. [abbreviation of *omnibus*]

busby /'bʌzbɪ/ *n.* a tall fur cap worn by hussars as part of military ceremonial uniform.

bush[1] /buʃ/ *n.* 1. a shrub or clump of shrubs; a thick growth (of hair etc.). 2. wild uncultivated country, forest (in Australia, Africa etc.). —**bushbaby** *n.* a small African tree-climbing lemur. [from Old English and Old Norse]

bush[2] *n.* 1. a metal lining for a round hole in which something fits or revolves. 2. an electrically insulating sleeve. —*v.t.* to fit with a bush. [from Middle Dutch *busse* = box]

Bush George 1924– . 41st president of the USA from 1989, a Republican. He was director of the Central Intelligence Agency (CIA) 1976–81 and US vice president 1981–89. Evidence came to light in 1987 linking him with the ◊Irangate scandal. His responses as president to the Soviet leader Gorbachev's diplomatic initiatives were initially criticized as inadequate, but sending US troops to depose his former ally, General Noriega of Panama, proved a popular move at home. He faced economic recession in the USA and was the driving force behind international opposition to Iraq's invasion of Kuwait 1990. The military victory over Iraq in the 1991 Gulf War strengthened his position.

bushbuck *n.* an antelope, *Tragelaphus scriptus*, found over most of Africa S of the Sahara. Up to 1 m/3 ft high, the males have keeled horns twisted into spirals, and are brown to blackish. The females are generally hornless, lighter, and redder. All have white markings, including stripes or vertical rows of dots down the sides. Rarely far from water, bushbuck live in woods and thick brush.

bushel /'buʃəl/ *n.* a measure of capacity equal to eight gallons or four pecks (2,219.36 cu in/36.37 litres) in the UK; some US states have different standards according to the goods measured. [from Old French *buissel*]

bushido *n.* the chivalric code of honour of the Japanese military caste, the ◊samurai. The code stresses simple living, integrity, self-discipline, and bravery. [Japanese = the way of the warrior].

bushman *n.* (*plural* **bushmen**) 1. a dweller or traveller in the Australian bush. 2. **Bushman,** a former term for the ◊Kung, an aboriginal people of S Africa.

bushmaster *n.* a large snake *Lachesis muta* found in wooded areas of South and Central America. Up to 4 m/ 12 ft long, it is the largest venomous snake in the New World. It is a type of pit viper, and is related to the rattlesnakes. When alarmed, it produces a noise by vibrating its tail among dry leaves.

bushranger *n.* (*historical*) an Australian armed robber of the 19th century. The first bushrangers were escaped convicts. The last gang was led by Ned ◊Kelly and his brother Dan 1878–80. They form the subject of many Australian ballads.

bushy /'buʃɪ/ *adj.* 1. growing thickly like a bush. 2. covered with bushes.

business /'bɪznɪs/ *n.* 1. a person's regular occupation or profession. 2. a thing that is one's concern, a task or duty. 3. a thing or things needing to be dealt with. 4. (*derogatory*) an affair, subject, or device. 5. buying and selling, trade; a commercial house or firm. —**business man** *or* **woman,** one engaged in commerce. **mean business,** to be in earnest. **mind one's own business,** to refrain from meddling. [Old English]

businesslike *adj.* practical, methodical.

busker *n.* a singer or other entertainer who performs in the street. —**busking** *n.* [from obsolete *busk* = peddle]

buskin *n.* a thick-soled boot worn by tragic actors in ancient Greece.

Busoni /bu:'sɔʊni/ Ferruccio (Dante Benvenuto) 1866–1924. Italian pianist, composer, and music critic. Much of his music was for the piano, but he also composed several operas, including *Doktor Faust*, completed by a pupil after his death.

bust[1] *v.t./i.* (*past* and *past participle* **bust, busted**) (*colloquial*) to break or burst. —*adj.* (*colloquial*) broken, burst; bankrupt. —*n.* (*colloquial*) a sudden (especially financial) failure. —**bust-up** *n.* a quarrel. [from *burst*]

bust[2] *n.* 1. a sculptured representation of the head, shoulders, and chest. 2. the upper front of a woman's etc. body; the measurement round this. [from French from Italian]

Bustamante /bʌstə'mænti/ (William) Alexander (born Clarke) 1884–1977. Jamaican socialist politician. As leader of the Labour Party, he was the first prime minister of independent Jamaica 1962–67.

bustard *n.* a large, tall, ostrichlike, swift-running bird of the family Otididae, related to cranes but with a rounder body, a thicker neck, and a relatively short beak. Bustards are found on the ground on open plains and fields.

bustle[1] /'bʌsəl/ *v.i.* to make a show of activity, to hurry (*about*). —*n.* excited activity.

bustle[2] *n.* (*historical*) a pad used to puff out a woman's skirt at the back.

busy /'bɪzɪ/ *adj.* 1. actively engaged in doing something; ceaselessly active, always employed; meddlesome. 2. full of business or activity. —*v.t.* to occupy or keep busy. —**busily** *adv.* [Old English]

busybody *n.* a meddlesome person.

but /bət, *emphatic* bʌt/ *conj.* nevertheless, however; on the other hand; otherwise than; without the result that. —*prep.* except, apart from, other than. —*adv.* only, no more than. —*n.* an objection. [Old English (from *by* and *out*); originally = outside]

butadiene *n.* or **buta-1,3-diene** CH_2:$CHCH$:CH_2, an inflammable gas derived from petroleum, used in making synthetic rubber and resins.

butane /'bju:teɪn/ *n.* C_4H_{10}, one of two gaseous alkanes (paraffin hydrocarbon) having the same formula but differing in structure. Normal butane is derived from natural gas; **isobutane** is a by-product of petroleum manufacture. Liquefied under pressure, it is used as a fuel for industrial and domestic purposes (for example in portable cookers). [from *butyl*]

butch /butʃ/ *adj.* (*slang*) masculine, tough-looking.

butcher /'butʃə/ *n.* 1. a dealer in meat; one who slaughters animals for food. 2. one who kills or has people killed needlessly or brutally. —*v.t.* 1. to slaughter or cut up (an animal) for meat. **2.** to kill needlessly or cruelly. **3.** to perform or deal with very ineptly. [from Old French *bo(u)chier* (*boc* = buck)]

Bute /bjuːt/ John Stuart, 3rd Earl of Bute 1713–1792. Scottish Tory politician, prime minister 1762–63. On the accession of George III in 1760, he became the chief instrument in the king's policy for breaking the power of the Whigs and establishing the personal rule of the monarch through Parliament.

Buthelezi /buːtəˈleɪzi/ Chief Gatsha 1928– . Zulu leader and politician, chief minister of KwaZulu, a black 'homeland' in the Republic of South Africa from 1970. He is founder and president from 1975 of ◊Inkatha, a paramilitary political organization.

butler /ˈbʌtlə/ *n.* the chief manservant of a household, in charge of the wine cellar. [from Anglo-French *buteler* (*bouteille* = bottle)]

Butler Josephine (born Gray) 1828–1906. English social reformer. She promoted women's education and the Married Women's Property Act, and campaigned against the Contagious Diseases Acts of 1862–70, which made women in garrison towns liable to compulsory examination for venereal disease. As a result of her campaigns the acts were repealed in 1883.

Butler Richard Austen ('Rab'), Baron Butler 1902–1982. English Conservative politician. As minister of education 1941–45, he was responsible for the Education Act 1944; he was chancellor of the Exchequer 1951–55, Lord Privy Seal 1955–59, and foreign minister 1963–64. As a candidate for the premiership, he was defeated by Harold Macmillan in 1957 (under whom he was home secretary 1957–62), and by Douglas-Home in 1963. He was master of Trinity College, Cambridge, 1965–78.

Butler Samuel 1612–1680. English satirist. His poem *Hudibras*, published in three parts in 1663, 1664, and 1678, became immediately popular for its biting satire against the Puritans.

Butler Samuel 1835–1902. English author who made his name in 1872 with his satiric attack on contemporary utopianism, *Erewhon* (*nowhere* reversed), but is now remembered for his autobiographical *The Way of All Flesh* written 1872–85 and published in 1903.

It has been said that although God cannot alter the past, historians can.

Samuel Butler
Erewhon

Butlin /ˈbʌtlɪn/ Billy (William) 1899–1980. British holiday-camp entrepreneur. Born in South Africa, he went in early life to Canada, but later entered the fairground business in the UK. He originated a chain of camps that provide accommodation, meals, and amusements at an inclusive price.

butt[1] *v.t./i.* **1.** to push with the head like a ram or goat. **2.** to meet or cause to meet edge to edge. —*n.* **1.** an act of butting. **2.** a butted join. —**butt in,** to interfere. [from Anglo-French *buter* = strike, thrust]

butt[2] *n.* **1.** an object *of* ridicule etc.; a person habitually mocked or teased. **2.** a mound behind a target; (in *plural*) a shooting range. [from Old French *but* = goal]

butt[3] *n.* the thicker end of a tool or weapon; the stub of a cigarette or cigar. [from Dutch *bot* = stumpy]

butt[4] *n.* a large cask. [from Anglo-French from Latin *buttis*]

butter *n.* a foodstuff made from the fatty portion of milk. Inside a single machine, the cream is churned, the buttermilk drawn off, and the butter washed, salted, and worked, to achieve an even consistency. —*v.t.* to spread, cook, or serve with butter. —**butter bean,** a large dried white Lima bean. **butterfingers** *n.* a clumsy person always dropping things. **butter muslin,** thin loosely woven cloth originally used for wrapping butter. **butter up,** (*colloquial*) to flatter. [Old English, ultimately from Greek *bouturon*]

buttercup *n.* a plant of the genus *Ranunculus* with divided leaves and yellow flowers. Species include the common buttercup *R. acris* and the creeping buttercup *R. repens*.

butterfly *n.* any of a large group of insects of the order Lepidoptera, distinguished from moths in most instances by diurnal behaviour, clubbed or dilated antennae, thin bodies, and the usually erect position of the wings when at rest.

The wings are covered with tiny scales, often brightly coloured. There are some 15,000 species of butterfly, many of which are under threat throughout the world because of the destruction of habitat. —**butterfly fish,** any of several fishes, not all related. The freshwater butterfly fish *Pantodon buchholzi* of W Africa can leap from the water and glide for a short distance on its large winglike pectoral fins. Up to 10 cm/4 in long, it lives in stagnant water. The tropical marine butterfly fishes, family Chaetodontidae, are brightly coloured with laterally flattened bodies, often with long snouts which they poke into crevices in rocks and coral when feeding. **butterfly nut,** a kind of wing nut. **butterfly stroke,** in swimming, a stroke in which both arms are lifted forwards simultaneously.

buttermilk *n.* the somewhat acid liquid left after churning butter.

butterscotch *n.* a hard kind of toffee.

butterwort *n.* an insectivorous plant, genus *Pinguicula*, of the bladderwort family, with purplish flowers and a rosette of flat leaves covered with a sticky secretion that traps insects.

buttery[1] /ˈbʌtəri/ *adj.* like or containing butter.

buttery[2] *n.* a place in a college etc. where provisions are kept and supplied.

buttock /ˈbʌtək/ *n.* (usually in *plural*) either of the two fleshy rounded parts on the lower rear of a human or animal body. [diminutive of *butt* = ridge]

button /ˈbʌtən/ *n.* **1.** a small disc or knob attached to a garment etc. to fasten it by passing through a hole, or to serve as an ornament or badge. **2.** a small rounded object of similar form, especially a knob to operate an electrical device. —*v.t./i.* to fasten (*up*) with buttons. —**button mushroom,** a small unopened mushroom. [from Old French *bouton*]

buttonhole *n.* **1.** a slit through which a button is passed to fasten clothing etc. **2.** a flower worn in the buttonhole of a coat lapel. —*v.t.* to accost and detain (a reluctant listener).

buttress /ˈbʌtrɪs/ *n.* **1.** a projecting support built against a wall. **2.** a support or reinforcement. —*v.t.* **1.** to support with a buttress or buttresses. **2.** to give support and help to. [from Old French (*ars*) *bouterez* = thrusting (arch)]

butyl /ˈbjuːtɪl/ *n.* the radical C_4H_9 derived from butane. [from Latin *butyrum* = butter]

buxom /ˈbʌksəm/ *adj.* (especially of women) plump and healthy-looking. [earlier = *pliant*]

Buxtehude /bʊkstəˈhuːdə/ Diderik 1637–1707. Danish composer and organist at Lübeck, Germany, who influenced ◊Bach and ◊Handel. He is remembered for his organ works and cantatas, written for his evening concerts or *Abendmusiken*.

buy /baɪ/ *v.t.* (*past* and *past participle* **bought** /bɔːt/) **1.** to obtain in exchange for money etc.; to win over by bribery. **2.** (*slang*) to believe, to accept the truth of. —*n.* a purchase. —**buy off,** to pay to be rid of. **buy out,** to pay (a person) to give up an ownership etc. **buy up,** to buy all available stock of; to absorb (a firm) by purchase. [Old English]

buyer *n.* one who buys; an agent who selects and purchases stock for a large shop. —**buyer's market,** a market having an excess of goods and services on offer and where prices are likely to be declining. The buyer benefits from the wide choice and competition available.

buzz *v.t./i.* **1.** to make a sibilant hum like a bee; to be filled with a confused murmur. **2.** to be filled with activity or excitement; to move excitedly *about* etc. **3.** to threaten (an aircraft) by flying close to it. —*n.* a buzzing sound; (*slang*) a telephone call. —**buzz off,** (*slang*) to go away. **buzz word,** a word (especially technical or jargon) used more to impress than to inform. [imitative]

buzzard /ˈbʌzəd/ *n.* any of a number of species of hawks of the genus *Buteo*, with broad wings, often seen soaring. [from Old French from Latin *buteo* = falcon]

buzzer *n.* an electrical device producing a buzzing sound as a signal.

by /baɪ/ *prep.* **1.** near, beside. **2.** along, via, passing through or beside; avoiding. **3.** in circumstances of, during. **4.** through the agency or means of; (of an animal) having as its sire. **5.** as soon as, not later than. **6.** according to, using a standard or unit. **7.** succeeding, with a succession of. **8.** to the extent of. **9.** concerning, in respect of. **10.** as surely as one believes in (God etc.). —*adv.* **1.** close at hand. **2.** aside, in reserve. **3.** past. —*adj.* subordinate, incidental; secondary, side. —*n.* = ◊bye¹. —**by and by**, before long. **by the by** (*or* **bye**), incidentally. **by and large**, on the whole. **by oneself**, without companions; by one's own unaided efforts. [Old English]

Byblos /'bɪblɒs/ ancient Phoenician city (modern Jebeil), 32 km/20 mi N of Beirut, Lebanon. Known to the Assyrians and Babylonians as **Gubla**, it had a thriving export of cedar and pinewood to Egypt as early as 1500 BC. In Roman times it had an amphitheatre, baths, and a temple dedicated to an unknown male god, and was known for its celebration of the resurrection of Adonis, worshipped as a god of vegetation.

bye¹ /baɪ/ *n.* **1.** in cricket, a run scored from a ball that passes the batsman without being hit. **2.** the status of an unpaired competitor in a game, who proceeds to the next round as if having won.

bye² /baɪ/ *or* **bye-bye** (*colloquial*) goodbye. [abbreviation]

by-election *n.* in the UK, the election of a member of Parliament in place of one who has died or resigned.

Byelorussia /bieləu'rʌʃə/ *or* **Belorussia** constituent republic of western USSR; **area** 207,600 sq km/80,154 sq mi; **capital** Minsk; **physical** more than 25% forested; rivers W Dvina, Dnieper and its tributaries, including the Pripet and Beresina; the Pripet Marshes in the E; mild and damp climate; **products** peat, agricultural machinery, fertilizers, glass, textiles, leather, salt, electrical goods, meat, dairy produce; **population** (1987) 10,078,000; 79% Byelorussian, 12% Russian, 4% Polish, 2% Ukrainian, 1% Jewish; **recent history** Byelorussia became a republic of the USSR in 1919. In a series of mass executions ordered by Stalin 1937–41, more than 100,000 people were shot. The republic suffered severely under German invasion and occupation during World War II. A Byelorussian Popular Front was established in Feb 1989 and a more extreme nationalist organization, the Tolaka group, in Nov 1989. [Russian *Belaruskaya* = White Russia]

bygone *adj.* past, antiquated. —*n.* (in *plural*) a past offence or injury (in phrase *let bygones be bygones*).

by-law *n.* a regulation made by a local authority or corporation. [perhaps from Scandinavian *by* = town]

byline *n.* a line in a newspaper etc. naming the writer of an article.

Byng /bɪŋ/ John 1704–1757. English admiral. Byng failed in the attempt to relieve Fort St Philip when in 1756 the island of Minorca was invaded by France. He was court-martialled and shot. The French writer Voltaire ironically commented that it was done 'to encourage the others'.

bypass *n.* **1.** a main road taking through traffic round a town or congested area. **2.** a secondary channel, pipe etc. for use when the main one is closed. —*v.t.* **1.** to avoid by means of a bypass; to provide with a bypass. **2.** to avoid consulting (a person) or omit (procedures etc.) in order to act quickly.

by-play *n.* subsidiary action in a play, usually without speech.

by-product *n.* a producť arising incidentally in the manufacture of something else; a secondary result.

Byrd /bɜːd/ Richard Evelyn 1888–1957. US aviator and explorer. The first to fly over the North Pole, in 1926, he also flew over the South Pole in 1929, and led five overland expeditions in Antarctica.

Byrd William 1543–1623. English composer. His church choral music (set to Latin words, as he was a firm Catholic) represents his most important work. He also composed secular vocal and instrumental music.

Byrds, the /bɜːdz/ US pioneering folk-rock group 1964–73. Remembered for their 12-string guitar sound and the hits 'Mr Tambourine Man' (a 1965 version of Bob Dylan's song) and 'Eight Miles High' 1966, they moved towards country rock in the late 1960s.

byre /'baɪə/ *n.* a cow shed. [Old English]

byroad *n.* a minor road.

Byron /'baɪrən/ Augusta Ada 1815–1851. British mathematician, daughter of ◊Lord Byron. She was the world's first computer programmer, working with ◊Babbage's mechanical invention. In 1983 a new, high-level computer language, ADA, was named after her.

Byron George Gordon, 6th Baron Byron 1788–1824. English poet who became the symbol of Romanticism and political liberalism throughout Europe in the 19th century. His reputation was established with the first two cantos of *Childe Harold* 1812. Later works include *The Prisoner of Chillon* 1816, *Beppo* 1818, *Mazeppa* 1819, and, most notably, *Don Juan* 1819–24. He left England in 1816, spending most of his later life in Italy.

byssinosis /bɪsɪ'nəʊsɪs/ *n.* a lung disease caused by prolonged inhalation of textile-fibre dust. [from Greek *bussinos* = made of linen]

bystander *n.* one who stands by but does not take part in something, a spectator.

byte /baɪt/ *n.* in computing, a basic unit of storage of information. A byte is eight ◊bits and can hold either a single character (letter, digit or punctuation symbol) or a number between 0 and 255. Not all computers use bytes, although the unit is widely used in microcomputers.

byway *n.* a minor road or path.

byword *n.* a person or thing cited as a notable example; a familar saying.

Byzantine /bɪ'zæntaɪn, baɪ-/ *adj.* of Byzantium or the Eastern Roman Empire; resembling its complicated and devious politics. —*n.* a native or inhabitant of Byzantium.

Byzantine Empire the **Eastern Roman Empire** 395–1453, with its capital at Constantinople (formerly Byzantium).

Byzantine style a style in the visual arts and architecture that originated in the 4th–5th centuries in Byzantium (the capital of the Eastern Roman Empire), and spread to Italy, throughout the Balkans, and to Russia, where it survived for many centuries. It is characterized by heavy stylization, strong linear emphasis, the use of rigid artistic stereotypes and rich colours such as gold. Byzantine artists excelled in mosaic work and manuscript painting. In architecture, the dome supported on pendentives was in widespread use.

Byzantium /baɪ'zæntiəm/ ancient Greek city on the Bosphorus (modern Istanbul), founded as a colony of the Greek city of Megara, near Corinth, about 660 BC. In AD 330 the capital of the Roman Empire was transferred there by Constantine the Great, who renamed it ◊Constantinople.

c, C (**cs, c's**)**1.** the third letter of the alphabet. **2.** in music, the first note of the natural major scale. **3.** (as a Roman numeral) 100.

c. abbreviation of **1.** century. **2.** chapter. **3.** cent.

c. abbreviation of circa, about.

C abbreviation of **1.** centum. **2.** century. **3.** centigrade. **4.** ◊Celsius. **5.** coulomb.

C *n.* a general-purpose computer-programming language popular on minicomputers and microcomputers. Developed in the early 1970s from an earlier language called BCPL, C is closely associated with the operating system ◊Unix. It is good for writing fast and efficient systems programs, such as operating systems (which control the operations of the computer).

C symbol for **1.** carbon. **2.** or © copyright.

°C symbol for degrees ◊Celsius, commonly called centigrade.

Ca symbol for calcium.

cab *n.* **1.** a taxi; (*historical*) a cabriolet or its improved successor the hansom; any of various types of horse-drawn public carriage with two or four wheels. **2.** the driver's compartment in a train, lorry, or crane. [abbreviation of *cabriolet*]

cabal /kə'bæl/ *n.* **1.** a secret intrigue. **2.** a political clique. [from French from Latin = *cabbala*]

Cabal, the a group of politicians, the English king Charles II's counsellors 1667–73, whose initials made up the word by coincidence—Clifford (Thomas Clifford 1630–1673), Ashley (Anthony Ashley Cooper, 1st Earl of ◊Shaftesbury), ◊Buckingham (George Villiers, 2nd Duke of Buckingham), Arlington (Henry Bennett, 1st Earl of Arlington 1618–1685), and ◊Lauderdale (John Maitland, Duke of Lauderdale).

cabaletta *n.* in music, a short aria with repeats which the singer could freely embellish as a display of virtuosity. In the 19th century the term came to be used for the final section of an elaborate aria.

cabaret /'kæbəreɪ/ *n.* an entertainment provided in a restaurant or nightclub while guests eat or drink at tables; such a nightclub etc. [French = tavern]

cabbage /'kæbɪdʒ/ *n.* **1.** a plant *Brassica oleracea* of the cress family Cruciferae, allied to the turnip and wild mustard, or charlock. It is a major table vegetable, cultivated as early as 2000 BC, and the numerous commercial varieties include kale, Brussels sprouts, common cabbage, savoy, cauliflower, sprouting broccoli, and kohlrabi. **2.** (*colloquial*) a person who lives inactively or without interest. [from Old French *caboche* = head]

cabbala /kə'bɑːlə/ *n.* a pretended tradition of mystical interpretation of the Old Testament, using esoteric methods (including ciphers), that reached the height of its influence in the later Middle Ages. [Latin from Hebrew = tradition]

cabbalistic /kæbə'lɪstɪk/ *adj.* of or like the cabbala; having a mystical sense, occult.

cabby, cabbie /'kæbɪ/ *n.* (*colloquial*) a taxi driver.

caber /'keɪbə/ *n.* a roughly-trimmed tree trunk used in the Scottish Highland sport of **tossing the caber**, a ◊Highland Games event. The caber (about 6 m/20 ft long, weighing about 100 kg/220 lb) is held in the palms of the cupped hands and rests on the shoulder. The thrower runs forward and tosses the caber, rotating it through 180 degrees so that it lands on its opposite end and falls forward. The best competitors toss the caber about 12 m/40 ft. [from Gaelic *cabar* = pole]

cabin /'kæbɪn/ *n.* **1.** a small shelter or house, especially of wood. **2.** a room or compartment in a ship, aircraft, etc., for passengers or crew. **3.** a driver's cab. —**cabin boy,** a man or boy waiting on officers or passengers on a ship. **cabin cruiser,** a large motor boat with a cabin. [from Old French from Latin *capanna*]

Cabinda /kə'bɪndə/ or **Kabinda** African coastal enclave, a province of ◊Angola; area 7,770 sq km/3,000 sq mi; population (1980) 81,300. The capital is Cabinda. There are oil reserves. Cabinda, which was attached to Angola in 1886, has made claims to independence.

cabinet /'kæbɪnɪt/ *n.* **1.** a cupboard or container with drawers, shelves, etc., for storing or displaying articles; a piece of furniture housing a radio or television set etc. **2.** the group of ministers holding a country's highest executive offices who decide government policy. In Britain the cabinet system originated under the Stuarts. Under William III it became customary for the king to select his ministers from the party with a parliamentary majority. The US cabinet, unlike the British, does not initiate legislation, and its members, appointed by the president, must not be members of Congress. —**cabinet-maker** *n.* a skilled joiner.

cable /'keɪbl/ *n.* **1.** a thick rope of wire or hemp; an encased group of insulated wires for transmitting electricity or for telecommunications; the anchor chain of a ship. **2.** (in full **cable stitch**) a knitted pattern looking like twisted rope. **3.** a unit of length used on ships, originally the length of a ship's anchor cable or 120 fathoms (720 ft/219 m), but now taken as one-tenth of a ◊nautical mile (608 ft/185.3m). —*v.t./i.* to communicate with or transmit by cablegram. —**cable car,** any of the cars in a **cable railway,** mounted on an endless cable and drawn up and down a mountain side etc. by an engine at one end. **cable television,** transmission of television programmes by cable to subscribers. [from Anglo-French from Latin *caplum* = halter, from Arabic]

cablegram *n.* a telegram message sent by undersea cable.

caboose /kə'buːs/ *n.* (*US*) a guard's van, especially on a goods train. [from Dutch]

Cabot /'kæbət/ Sebastian 1474–1557. Italian navigator and cartographer, the second son of Giovanni ◊Caboto. He explored the Brazilian coast and the River Plate in 1526–30 for Charles V.

Caboto /kæ'bəutəu/ Giovanni or **John Cabot** 1450–1498. Italian navigator. Commissioned, with his three sons, by Henry VII of England to discover unknown lands, he arrived at Cape Breton Island on 24 June 1497, and became the first European to reach the North American mainland (he thought he was in NE Asia). In 1498 he sailed again, touching Greenland, and probably died on the voyage.

Cabral /kə'brɑːl/ Pedro Alvarez 1460–1526. Portuguese explorer. He set sail from Lisbon for the East Indies in March 1500, and accidentally reached Brazil by taking a course too far west. He claimed the country for Portugal on 25 April as Spain had not followed up Vicente Pinzón's (c.1460–1523) landing there earlier in the year. Continuing around Africa, he lost seven of his fleet of 13 ships (the explorer Bartolomeu ◊Diaz being one of those drowned), and landed in Mozambique. Proceeding to India, he negotiated the first Indo-Portuguese treaties for trade, and returned to Lisbon in July 1501.

cabriole /'kæbriəʊl/ *n*. a kind of curved leg characteristic of 17th–18th-century furniture, especially that of Chippendale type. [French, from Italian *capriolare* = leap in the air; from resemblance to a leaping animal's foreleg]

cabriolet /'kæbriəleɪ/ *n*. a light two-wheeled carriage with a hood, drawn by one horse, introduced into London from Paris in the early 19th century. [French, from *cabriole* = goat's leap]

cacao /kə'keɪəʊ/ *n*. (*plural* cacaos) the seed from which ◊cocoa and chocolate are made; the tree *Theobroma cacao* producing it. It grows to some 6 m/20 ft high and begins producing fruit about the fifth year. This matures rapidly as a pod, 12.5–22.5 cm/5–9 in long, containing 20 to 40 seeds (beans) embedded in juicy white pulp. The tree bears fruit all year round and there are two, sometimes three, harvests. [Spanish from Nahuatl]

cachalot /'kæ∫əlɒt/ *n*. a sperm whale. [French from Spanish and Portuguese]

cache /kæ∫/ *n*. a place for hiding treasures or stores; things so hidden. —*v.t.* to put in a cache. [French (*cacher* = hide)]

cachet /'kæ∫eɪ/ *n*. 1. a distinguishing mark or seal. 2. prestige. 3. internal evidence of authenticity. 4. a wafer enclosing an unpleasant medicine. [French (*cacher* = press, from Latin *coactare* = constrain)]

cackle *n*. 1. the clucking of a hen. 2. noisy, inconsequential talk. 3. a loud, silly laugh. —*v.i.* to emit a cackle; to utter or express with a cackle. —**cut the cackle,** (*colloquial*) to come to the point.

cacophony /kə'kɒfənɪ/ *n*. harsh, discordant sound. —**cacophonous** *adj.* [from French from Greek *kakos* = bad and *phōnē* = sound]

cactus /'kæktəs/ *n*. (*plural* cacti /-aɪ/, cactuses) a succulent plant of the family Cactaceae, although the term is commonly applied to many different succulent and prickly plants. True cacti have a woody axis (central core) overlaid with an enlarged fleshy stem, which assumes various forms and is usually covered with spines (actually reduced leaves). They all have special adaptations to growing in dry areas. Some species have been introduced to the Old World, for example, in the Mediterranean area. [Latin from Greek]

cad *n*. a person (especially a man) who behaves dishonourably. —**caddish** *adj.* [abbreviation of *caddie* in the sense 'odd-job man']

CAD acronym from computer-aided design, the use of computers for creating and editing design drawings. CAD also allows such things as automatic testing of designs and multiple or animated three-dimensional views of designs. CAD systems are widely used in architecture, electronics, and engineering, for example in the motor vehicle industry where cars designed with the assistance of computers are now commonplace. A related development is ◊CAM (computer-assisted manufacture).

cadaver /kə'deɪvə/ *n*. a corpse. [from Latin *cadere* = fall]

cadaverous /kə'dævərəs/ *adj.* corpselike, gaunt and pale.

caddie /'kædɪ/ *n*. 1. a person who assists a golfer during a match, carrying his clubs etc. 2. a small container holding articles ready for use. —*v.i.* to act as caddie. [originally Scottish, from French *cadet*]

caddis fly /'kædɪsflaɪ/ an insect of the order Trichoptera. Adults are generally dull brown, mothlike, with wings covered in tiny hairs. Mouthparts are poorly developed, and many do not feed as adults. They are usually found near water. —**caddis worm,** its larva.

caddy[1] /'kædɪ/ *n*. a small box for holding tea. [earlier *catty* = weight of 1⅓ lb, from Malay *kāti*]

caddy[2] variant of **caddie.**

Cade /keɪd/ Jack died 1450. English rebel. He was a prosperous landowner who led a revolt in 1450 in Kent against the high taxes and court corruption of Henry VI and demanded the recall from Ireland of Richard, Duke of York. The rebels defeated the royal forces at Sevenoaks and occupied London. After being promised reforms and pardon they dispersed, but Cade was hunted down and killed.

cadence /'keɪdəns/ *n*. 1. the fall of the voice, especially at the end of a phrase or sentence; tonal inflection. 2. rhythm in sound. 3. a melodic or harmonic progression or device conventionally associated with the end of a musical composition, section, or phrase. [from Italian *cadenza* from Latin *cadere* = fall]

cadency /'keɪdənsɪ/ *n*. the status of a younger branch of a family.

cadenza /kə'denzə/ *n*. a flourish inserted into the final cadence of any section of a vocal aria or a movement in a concerto, sonata, or other solo instrumental work.

cadet /kə'det/ *n*. 1. a member of a corps receiving elementary military or police training. 2. a younger son. [French, from diminutive of Latin *caput* = head]

cadge /kædʒ/ *v.t./i.* to ask for as a gift; to beg. —**cadger** *n*.

Cádiz /kə'dɪz/ Spanish city and naval base, capital and seaport of the province of Cádiz, standing on Cádiz Bay, an inlet of the Atlantic, 103 km/64 mi S of Seville; population (1986) 154,000. After the discovery of the Americas in 1492, Cádiz became one of Europe's most vital trade ports. The English seaman Francis Drake burned a Spanish fleet here in 1587 to prevent the sailing of the ◊Armada.

cadmium /'kædmɪəm/ *n*. a soft, silver-white, ductile and malleable, metallic element, symbol Cd, atomic number 48, relative atomic mass 112.40. Cadmium occurs in nature as a sulphide or carbonate in zinc ores. It is a toxic metal that, because of industrial dumping, has become an environmental pollutant. Its uses include batteries, electroplating, and as a constituent of alloys used for bearings with low coefficients of friction; it is also a constituent of an alloy with a very low melting point. [from obsolete *cadmia* = calamine, ultimately from Greek *kadm(e)ia (gē)* = Cadmean (earth), from *Cadmus* in Greek legend]

Cadmus /'kædməs/ in Greek mythology, a Phoenician from ◊Tyre, brother of ◊Europa. He founded the city of Thebes in Greece. Obeying the oracle of Athena, Cadmus slew the sacred dragon which guarded the spring of Ares. He then sowed the teeth of the dragon from which sprang a multitude of fierce warriors. These armed men then fought among themselves and the survivors were considered to be the ancestors of the Theban aristocracy. Cadmus married ◊Harmonia and was credited with the introduction of the Phoenician alphabet into Greece.

cadre /'kɑːdə/ *n*. a group forming a nucleus of trained persons round which a military or political unit can be formed. [French from Italian from Latin *quadrus* = square]

Cadwalader /kæd'wɒlədə/ 7th century. Welsh hero. The son of Cadwallon, king of Gwynedd, N Wales, he defeated and killed Eadwine of Northumbria in 633. About a year later he was killed in battle.

caecilian /si'sɪlɪən/ *n*. a tropical amphibian of rather wormlike appearance. There are about 170 species known, forming the amphibian order Apoda (also known as Caecilia or Gymnophiona). Caecilians have a grooved skin that gives a 'segmented' appearance, have no trace of limbs, and mostly live below ground. Some species bear live young, others lay eggs. [from Latin *caecilia*, a kind of lizard]

caecum /'siːkəm/ *n*. (*plural* caeca) in the ◊digestive system of animals, a blind-ending tube branching off from the first part of the large intestine, terminating in the appendix. It has no function in humans but is used for the digestion of cellulose by some grass-eating mammals. [Latin *caecus* = blind]

Caedmon /'kædmən/ 7th century. Earliest known English poet. According to the Northumbrian historian Bede, when Caedmon was a cowherd at the Christian monastery of Whitby, he was commanded to sing by a stranger in a dream, and on waking produced a hymn on the Creation. The original poem is preserved in some manuscripts. Caedmon became a monk and may have composed other religious poems.

Caernarvon /kə'nɔːvən/ (Welsh *Caernarfon*) administrative headquarters of Gwynedd, N Wales, situated on the SW shore of the Menai Strait; **population** (1981) 10,000.

Caernarvonshire /kə'nɑːvən∫ə/ former county of N Wales, merged in ◊Gwynedd in 1974.

Caesar /'siːzə/ a powerful family of ancient Rome, which included Gaius Julius Caesar (see separate entry), whose grandnephew and adopted son ◊Augustus assumed the name of Caesar and passed it on to his adopted son

Caesar Roman statesman and military commander, Gaius Julius Caesar.

◊Tiberius. Henceforth, it was used by the successive emperors, becoming a title of the Roman rulers. The titles 'tsar' in Russia and 'kaiser' in Germany were both derived from the name Caesar.

Caesar Gaius Julius *c.*102–44 BC. Roman statesman and general. He formed with Pompey and Crassus the First Triumvirate in 60 BC. He conquered Gaul 58–50 and invaded Britain in 55 and 54. He fought against Pompey 49–48, defeating him at Pharsalus. After a period in Egypt Caesar returned to Rome as dictator from 46. He was assassinated by conspirators on the ◊Ides of March in the year 44.

Caesarea /siːzəˈriə/ ancient city in Palestine (now ◊Qisarya) built by Herod the Great 22–12 BC, who also constructed a port (*portus Augusti*). It was the administrative capital of the province of Judaea.

Caesarea Mazaca /siːzəˈrɛə məˈzɑːkə/ the ancient name for the Turkish city of ◊Kayseri.

Caesarean /siˈzeəriən/ *adj.* **Caesarean birth** *or* **section,** the delivery of a child by cutting into the mother's womb through the wall of the abdomen. It may be recommended for almost any obstetric complication implying a threat to mother or baby. [from the story that Julius Caesar was born in this way] section.

caesium /ˈsiːziəm/ *n.* a soft, silvery-white, ductile, metallic element, symbol Cs, atomic number 55, relative atomic mass 132.905. It is one of the ◊alkali metals, and is the most electropositive of all the elements. In air it ignites spontaneously, and it reacts vigorously with water. It is used in the manufacture of photoelectric cells. The name comes from the blueness of its spectral line. [from Latin *caesius* = bluish-or greyish-green, from its spectrum lines]

caesura /siˈzjuərə/ *n.* a short pause in the rhythm of a line of verse. [Latin (*caedere* = cut)]

Caetano /kaɪˈtɑːnəʊ/ Marcello 1906–1980. Portuguese right-wing politician. Professor of administrative law at Lisbon from 1940, he succeeded the dictator Salazar as prime minister from 1968 until his exile after the military coup of 1974. He was granted political asylum in Brazil.

café /ˈkæfeɪ/ *n.* a teashop or small restaurant. [French = coffee (-house)]

cafeteria /kæfiˈtiəriə/ *n.* a restaurant in which customers serve themselves from a counter or display. [from American Spanish = coffee shop]

caffeine /ˈkæfiːn/ *n.* an alkaloid stimulant found in tea leaves and coffee beans. [from French *café* = coffee]

caftan /ˈkæftən/ *n.* **1.** a long coatlike garment, often with a sash or belt, worn by men in countries of the Near East. **2.** a woman's long loose dress. [from Turkish]

cage /keɪdʒ/ *n.* **1.** a structure with bars or wires, especially for containing animals or birds. **2.** any similar framework, an enclosed platform in which people travel in a lift or the shaft of a mine. —*v.t.* to confine in a cage. [from Old French from Latin *cavea*]

Cage John 1912– . US composer. A pupil of ◊Schoenberg and ◊Cowell, he joined others in reacting against the European music tradition in favour of a more realistic idiom open to non-Western attitudes. During the 1930s, he assembled and toured a percussion orchestra incorporating ethnic instruments and noise-makers. His effect on contemporary musical thinking is summed up by the piano piece *4 minutes 33 seconds* 1952, in which a performer holds an audience in expectation without playing a note.

cagey /ˈkeɪdʒɪ/ *adj.* (*colloquial*) cautious about giving information, secretive. —**cagily** *adv.,* **caginess** *n.*

Cagliari /kælˈjɑːri/ capital and port of Sardinia, Italy, on the Gulf of Cagliari; population (1988) 222,000.

Cagney /ˈkægni/ James 1899–1986. US actor who moved to films from Broadway. Usually associated with gangster roles in films such as *The Public Enemy* 1931, he was an actor of great versatility, playing Bottom in *A Midsummer Night's Dream* 1935 and singing and dancing in *Yankee Doodle Dandy* 1942.

cagoule /kəˈguːl/ *n.* a thin, hooded waterproof jacket reaching to the knees. [French]

cahier *n.* the working notes or drawings of a writer or artist. [French = notebook]

cahoots /kəˈhuːts/ *n.pl.* (*US slang*) **in cahoots with,** in collusion with.

Cahora Bassa /ˈkəhɒɪrɑ ˈbæsə/ the largest hydroelectric scheme in Africa, created as a result of the damming of the Zambezi River to form a reservoir 230 km/144 mi long in W Mozambique.

Cain /keɪn/ in the Old Testament, the first-born son of Adam and Eve. Motivated by jealousy, he murdered his brother Abel as the latter's sacrifice was more acceptable to God than his own.

Caine /keɪn/ Michael. Stage name of Maurice Micklewhite 1933– . English actor, whose long career has seen him mature from cheeky, Cockney roles to an artist of great range and versatility. His cinematic history includes the films *Alfie* 1966, *California Suite* 1978, *Educating Rita* 1983, and *Hannah and her Sisters* 1986.

Cainozoic /kaɪnəˈzəʊɪk/ *adj.* of the most recent era of geological time, following the Mesozoic era and lasting from about 65 million years ago to the present day. —*n.* this era. [from Greek *kainos* = new and *zōion* = animal]

caique /kaɪˈiːk/ *n.* a light rowing boat used on the Bosporus; a Levantine sailing ship. [French from Italian from Turkish *kayik*]

cairn *n.* a mound of rough stones set up as a monument or landmark. —**cairn terrier,** a small, shaggy terrier with short legs, formerly used for flushing out foxes and badgers. [from Gaelic *carn*]

cairngorm *n.* a yellow or wine-coloured semiprecious stone from the Cairngorm mountains in Scotland. [from Gaelic *carn gorm* = blue cairn]

Cairo /ˈkaɪrəʊ/ capital of Egypt, on the E bank of the Nile 13 km/8 mi above the apex of the Delta and 160 km/100 mi from the Mediterranean; the largest city in Africa and in the Middle East; population (1985) 6,205,000, Greater Cairo (1987) 13,300,000. El Fustat (Old Cairo) was founded by Arabs about AD 64, Cairo itself about 1000 by the ◊Fatimid ruler Gowhar. The Great Pyramids and Sphinx are nearby at Giza. [Arabic *el Qahira*]

caisson /ˈkeɪsən/ *n.* a watertight chamber inside which work can be carried out on underwater structures. [French from Italian *cassone*]

cajole /kəˈdʒəʊl/ *v.t.* to coax. —**cajolery** *n.* [from French *cajoler*]

Cajun /ˈkeɪdʒən/ *n.* a member of a French-speaking community of Louisiana, USA, descended from French-Canadians who, in the 18th century, were driven there from Nova Scotia. **Cajun music** has a lively rhythm and features steel guitar, fiddle, and accordion. [from *Acadia*, former name of Nova Scotia]

cake *n.* **1.** a baked, sweet, breadlike food made from a mixture of flour, fats, sugar, eggs, etc. **2.** other food cooked in a flat, round shape. **3.** a flattish, compact mass. **4.** cattlecake. —*v.t./i.* to form into a compact mass; to encrust *with* a hardened or sticky mass. [Old Norse]

CAL acronym from computer-assisted learning, the use of computers in education and training, where the computer displays instructional material to a student and asks questions about the information given. The student's answers determine the sequence of the lessons.

calabash /'kæləbæʃ/ *n.* **1.** a tropical American tree of the genus *Crescentia*, with fruit in the form of large gourds. **2.** this or a similar gourd whose shell serves for holding liquid etc. **3.** a bowl or pipe made from a gourd. [from French from Spanish, perhaps from Persian *karbuz* = melon]

calabrese /kælə'breɪseɪ/ *n.* a variety of sprouting broccoli. [Italian = Calabrian]

Calabria /kə'læbrɪə/ mountainous earthquake region occupying the 'toe' of Italy, comprising the provinces of Catanzaro, Cosenza, and Reggio; capital Catanzaro; area 15,100 sq km/5,829 sq mi; population (1988) 2,146,000. Reggio is the industrial centre.

calamine /'kæləmaɪn/ *n.* ZnCO₃, zinc carbonate, an ore of zinc. The term also refers to a pink powder made up of a mixture of zinc oxide and iron(II) oxide used in lotions and ointments as an astringent for treating, for example, eczema, measles rash, and insect bites and stings. [from French from Latin *cadmia*]

calamity /kə'læmɪtɪ/ *n.* a grievous disaster or adversity. —**calamitous** /-mɪtəs/ *adj.* [from French from Latin]

Calamity Jane nickname of Martha Jane Burke *c.*1852–1903. US heroine of Deadwood, South Dakota. She worked as a teamster, transporting supplies to the mining camps, adopted male dress and, as an excellent shot, promised 'calamity' to any aggressor. Many fictional accounts of the 'wild west' featured her exploits.

calcareous /kæl'keərɪəs/ *adj.* of or containing calcium carbonate. [from Latin *calx* = lime]

calceolaria /kælsɪə'leərɪə/ *n.* a plant of the *Calceolaria* figwort genus, family Scrophulariaceae, with brilliantly coloured, slipper-shaped flowers. Native to South America, they were introduced to Europe and the USA in the 1830s. [from Latin, diminutive of *calceus* = shoe]

calcify /'kælsɪfaɪ/ *v.t./i.* to harden by a deposit of calcium salts; to convert or be converted into calcium carbonate. —**calcification** /-'keɪʃən/ *n.* [from Latin *calx* = lime]

calcine /'kælsaɪn/ *v.t./i.* to reduce (a substance) or be reduced to quicklime or powder by heating to a high temperature without melting it. —**calcination** /-si'neɪʃən/ *n.* [from Old French or Latin]

calcite /'kælsaɪt/ *n.* a common, colourless, white, or light-coloured rock-forming mineral, calcium carbonate, CaCO₃. It is the main constituent of ◊limestone and marble, and forms many types of invertebrate shell.

calcium /'kælsɪəm/ *n.* a soft, silvery-white, metallic element, symbol Ca, atomic number 20, relative atomic mass 40.08. It is one of the ◊alkaline-earth metals. One of the most widely distributed elements, it is the fifth most abundant element (the third most abundant metal) in the Earth's crust. It is found mainly as its carbonate CaCO₃, which occurs in a fairly pure condition as chalk and limestone (see ◊calcite). Calcium is an essential component of bones, teeth, shells, milk and leaves, and it forms 1.5% of the human body by mass. [from Latin *calx* = lime]

calculable /'kælkjʊləbəl/ *adj.* that may be calculated.

calculate /'kælkjʊleɪt/ *v.t./i.* **1.** to ascertain, especially by using mathematics or by reckoning. **2.** .. plan deliberately; to rely *on.* **3.** (*US colloquial*) to suppose, to believe. —**calculation** /-'leɪʃən/ *n.* [from Latin]

calculated *adj.* **1.** done with awarenesss of the likely consequences. **2.** designed or suitable *to* do.

calculating *adj.* (of a person) shrewd, scheming.

calculator *n.* a pocket-sized, electronic computing device for performing numerical calculations. It can add, subtract, multiply, and divide; many also have squares, roots, and advanced trigonometric and statistical functions. Input is by a small keyboard and results are shown on a one-line screen which is typically a ◊liquid crystal display (LCD). The first electronic calculator was manufactured by the Bell Punch Company, USA, in 1963. [from Latin]

calculus /'kælkjʊləs/ *n.* **1.** a branch of mathematics that permits the manipulation of continuously varying quantities, used in practical problems involving such matters as changing speeds, problems of flight, varying stresses in the framework of a bridge, and alternating current theory. **Integral calculus** deals .. the method of summation or adding together the effects of continuously varying quantities. **Differential calculus** deals in a similar way with rates of change. Many of its applications arose from the study of the gradients of the tangents to curves. **2.** (*plural* **calculi**) a stone or concretion found

Calderón de la Barca *Don Pedro Calderón de la Barca combined raw emotion with detailed examinations of intellectual themes in his plays.*

in some part of the body. [Latin = small stone (used on an abacus)]

Calcutta /kæl'kʌtə/ the largest city of India, on the river Hooghly, the westernmost mouth of the river Ganges, some 130 km/80 mi N of the Bay of Bengal. It is the capital of West Bengal; population (1981) 9,166,000. It is chiefly a commercial and industrial centre (engineering, shipbuilding, jute, and other textiles). Calcutta was the seat of government of British India 1773–1912.

Caldecott /'kɔːldɪkət/ Randolph 1846–1886. British artist and illustrator of books for children, including *John Gilpin* 1848.

Calder /'kɔːldə/ Alexander 1898–1976. US abstract sculptor, the inventor of **mobiles**, suspended shapes that move in the lightest current of air. In the 1920s he began making wire sculptures with movable parts; in the 1960s he created **stabiles**, large coloured sculptures of sheet metal.

caldera *n.* in geology, a very large, basin-shaped ◊crater. Calderas are found at the tops of volcanoes, where the original peak has collapsed into an empty chamber beneath. The basin, many times larger than the original volcanic vent, may be flooded, producing a crater lake, or the flat floor may contain a number of small volcanic cones, produced by volcanic activity after the collapse.

Calderón de la Barca /kældə'rɒn deɪ lɑː 'bɑːkə/ Pedro 1600–1681. Spanish dramatist and poet. After the death of Lope de Vega in 1635, he was considered to be the leading Spanish dramatist. Most celebrated of the 118 plays is the philosophical *La Vida es sueño/Life is a Dream* 1635.

Caldwell /'kɔːldwel/ Erskine (Preston) 1903–1987. US novelist, whose *Tobacco Road* 1932 and *God's Little Acre* 1933 are earthy and vivid presentations of poverty-stricken Southern sharecroppers.

Caledonian /kælɪ'dəʊnɪən/ *adj.* of Scotland or (in Roman times) Caledonia (northern Britain). —*n.* (usually *jocular*) a Scotsman. [from Latin *Caledonia*]

calendar /'kælɪndə/ *n.* **1.** the division of the ◊year into months, weeks, and days and the method of ordering the years. From year one, an assumed date of the birth of Jesus, dates are calculated backwards (BC 'before Christ', or BCE 'before common era') and forwards (AD, Latin *anno domini* 'in the year of the Lord' or CE 'common era'). The **lunar month** (period between one new moon and the next) naturally averages 29.5 days, but the Western calendar uses for convenience a **calendar month** with a complete number of days, 30 or 31 (Feb has 28). For adjustments, since there are slightly fewer than six extra hours a year left over, they are added to Feb as a 29th day every fourth year (**leap year**), century years being excepted unless they are divisible by 400. For example 1896 was a leap year; 1900 was not. **2.** a chart showing the days, weeks, and months of a particular year; an adjustable device showing the day's date etc. **3.** a register or list of special dates or events, documents chronologically arranged, etc. —*v.t.* **1.** to enter in a calendar. **2.** to analyse and index (documents). [from Anglo-French from Latin *calendarium* = account book]

calender /'kælɪndə/ *n.* a machine for rolling cloth, paper, etc. to glaze or smooth it. —*v.t.* to press in a calender. [from French]

calends /'kælɪndz/ *n.pl.* the first day of the month in the ancient Roman calendar. [from Old French from Latin *calendae*]

calf[1] /kɑ:f/ *n.* (*plural* **calves** /kɑ:vz/) the young of cattle, also of the deer, elephant, whale, and certain other animals; calfskin. —**calf love** *n.* immature romantic love. [Old English]

calf[2] /kɑ:f/ *n.* (*plural* **calves** /kɑ:vz/) the fleshy hind part of the human leg below the knee. [Old Norse]

calfskin *n.* leather made from the skin of calves.

Calgary /'kælgəri/ city in Alberta, Canada, on the Bow River, in the foothills of the Rockies; at 1,048 m/3,440 ft it is one of the highest Canadian towns; population (1986) 671,000. It is the centre of a large agricultural region and is the oil and financial centre of Alberta and W Canada.

Cali /kæ'li:/ city in SW Colombia, in the Cauca Valley 975 m/3,200 ft above sea level, founded in 1536. Cali has textile, sugar, and engineering industries. Population (1985) 1,398,276.

calibrate /'kælɪbreɪt/ *v.t.* **1.** to mark (a gauge) with a scale of readings; to correlate the readings of (an instrument etc.) with a standard. A mercury ◊thermometer, for example, can be calibrated with a Celsius scale by noting the heights of the mercury column at two standard temperatures (the freezing point, 0°C, and boiling point, 100°C) and dividing the distance between them into 100 equal parts and continuing these divisions above and below. **2.** to find the calibre of. —**calibration, calibrator** *n.*

calibre /'kælɪbə/ *n.* **1.** the internal diameter of a gun barrel or tube; the diameter of a bullet or shell. **2.** strength or quality of character; ability, importance. [from French, ultimately from Arabic = mould]

calico /'kælɪkəʊ/ *n.* (*plural* **calicoes**) cotton cloth, especially plain white or unbleached; (*US*) printed cotton fabric. —*adj.* **1.** of calico. **2.** (*US*) multicoloured. [from *Calicut*, town in India]

California /kælɪ'fɔ:nɪə/ Pacific state of the USA; **area** 411,100 sq km/158,685 sq mi; **capital** Sacramento; **physical** Sierra Nevada (including Yosemite and Sequoia National Parks, Lake Tahoe and Mount Whitney, 4,418 m/14,500 ft); and the Coast Range; Death Valley 86 m/282 ft below sea level; Colorado and Mojave deserts; Monterey Peninsula; Salton Sea; offshore in the Pacific there are vast underwater volcanoes with tops 8 km/5 mi across; **products** leading agricultural state with fruit, nuts, wheat, vegetables, cotton, rice, all mostly grown by irrigation; beef cattle, timber, fish, oil, natural gas, aerospace, electronics (Silicon Valley), food processing, films and television programmes; **population** (1987) 27,663,000, 66% non-Hispanic white; 20% Hispanic; 7.5% Black; 7% Asian (including many Vietnamese); **recent history** California became a state in 1850. Gold had been discovered in the Sierra Nevada in Jan 1848, and was followed by the gold rush 1849–56.

California current the cold ocean ◊current in the East Pacific Ocean flowing southwards down the W coast of North America. It is part of the North Pacific ◊gyre (a vast, circular movement of ocean water).

californium /kælɪ'fɔ:nɪəm/ *n.* a synthesized, radioactive, metallic element of the ◊actinide series, symbol Cf, atomic number 98, relative atomic mass 251. It is produced in very small quantities and used in nuclear reactors as a neutron source. The longest-lived isotope, Cf-251, has a half-life of 800 years. [from *California* (where first made)]

Caligula /kə'lɪgjʊlə/ nickname of Gaius Caesar 12–AD 41. Roman emperor, son of Germanicus and successor to Tiberius in AD 37. Caligula was a cruel tyrant and was assassinated by an officer of his guard. Believed to have been mentally unstable, he is remembered for giving a consulship to his horse Incitatus. [= little boot;

he was given the name because of the military boots he wore as a baby]

calima *n.* a dust cloud in Europe, coming from the Sahara Desert, which sometimes causes heatwaves and eye irritation. [Spanish = haze]

caliph /'kælɪf, 'keɪ-/ *n.* (*historical*) the title of civic and religious heads of the world of Islam. The first caliph was ◊Abu Bakr. Nominally elective, the office became hereditary, held by the Ummayyad dynasty 661–750 and then by the ◊Abbasid. During the 10th century the political and military power passed to the leader of the caliph's Turkish bodyguard; about the same time, an independent ◊Fatimid caliphate sprang up in Egypt. After the death of the last Abbasid in 1258, the title was claimed by a number of Muslim chieftains in Egypt, Turkey, and India. The most powerful of these were the Turkish sultans of the Ottoman Empire. —**caliphate** *n.* [from Old French from Arabic = successor (i.e. one succeeding Muhammad)]

calix /'keɪlɪks/ *n.* (*plural* **calices** /-ɪsi:z/) a cuplike cavity or organ. [Latin = cup]

call /kɔ:l/ *v.t./i.* **1.** to shout or speak *out* loudly to attract attention; (of a bird etc.) to utter its call. **2.** to summon; to order to take place; to invite (attention etc.). **3.** to rouse deliberately from sleep, to summon to get up. **4.** to name, describe, or regard as. **5.** to communicate or converse with by telephone or radio. **6.** to name (a suit) in bidding at cards; to attempt to predict the result of tossing a coin etc. **7.** to make a brief visit (*at* a place, *on* a person). —*n.* **1.** a shout or cry; the characteristic cry of a bird etc.; a signal on a bugle etc. **2.** a summons, an invitation; a demand or claim; a need, an occasion. **3.** a player's right or turn to bid or call trumps at cards; a bid etc. thus made. **4.** an act of telephoning, a conversation over the telephone. **5.** the option of buying stock at a given date. —**call box,** a telephone kiosk. **call girl,** a prostitute accepting appointments by telephone. **call up,** to summon to do military service. **call-up** *n.* a summons to do military service. **on call,** ready or available when needed. —**caller** *n.* [Old English from Old Norse]

Callaghan /'kæləhæn/ (Leonard) James, Baron Callaghan 1912–. British Labour politician. As chancellor of the Exchequer 1964–67, he introduced corporation and capital-gains taxes, and resigned following devaluation. He was home secretary 1967–70 and prime minister 1976–79 in a period of increasing economic stress.

When I am starving in the morning, I say to myself that if I were a young man I would emigrate. By the time I am sitting down to breakfast, I ask myself 'Where would I go?'

James Callaghan

Callao /kaɪ'aʊ/ chief commercial and fishing port of Peru, 12 km/7 mi SW of Lima; population (1988) 318,000. Founded in 1537, it was destroyed by an earthquake in 1746. It is Peru's main naval base, and produces fertilizers.

Callas /'kæləs/ Maria. Adopted name of Maria Kalogeropoulos 1923–1977. US lyric soprano, born in New York of Greek parents. With a voice of fine range and a gift for dramatic expression, she excelled in operas including *Norma, Madame Butterfly, Aïda, Lucia di Lammermoor,* and *Medea.*

Callicrates /kə'lɪkrəti:z/5th century BC. Athenian architect (with Ictinus) of the ◊Parthenon on the Acropolis.

calligraphy /kə'lɪgrəfɪ/ *n.* the art of handwriting, regarded in China and Japan as the greatest of the visual arts, and playing a large part in Islamic art because the depiction of the human and animal form is forbidden. —**calligrapher** *n.*, **calligraphist** *n.*, **calligraphic** /kælɪ'græfɪk/ *adj.* [from Greek *kallos* = beauty and *graphē* = writing]

Callimachus /kə'lɪməkəs/ 310–240 BC. Greek poet and critic known for his epigrams. Born in Cyrene, he taught in Alexandria, where he is reputed to have been head of the great library.

calling *n.* a profession or trade; a vocation.

calliper /'kælɪpə/ *n.* (usually in *plural*) **1.** a pair of hinged arms for measuring diameters. **2.** a metal support for a weak or injured leg.

callisthenics /kælɪs'θenɪks/ *n.pl.* exercises to develop elegance and grace of movement. [from Greek *kallos* = beauty and *sthenos* = strength]

Callisto /kə'lɪstəʊ/ *n.* the second-largest moon of Jupiter, 4,800 km/3,000 mi in diameter, orbiting every 16.7 days at a distance of 1.9 million km/1.2 million mi from the planet. Its surface is covered with large craters.

callosity /kə'lɒsɪtɪ/ *n.* abnormal hardness of the skin; a callus. [from French or Latin]

callous /'kæləs/ *adj.* 1. unfeeling, unsympathetic. 2. (of skin) hardened. [from Latin *callosus*]

callow /'kæləʊ/ *adj.* immature and inexperienced. —**callowly** *adv.*, **callowness** *n.* [Old English]

callus /'kæləs/ *n.* 1. an area of hard, thickened skin or tissue. 2. bony material formed when a bone fracture heals. 3. in botany, a tissue that forms at a damaged plant surface. Composed of large, thin-walled ◊parenchyma cells, it grows over and around the wound, eventually covering the exposed area. [Latin]

calm /kɑːm/ *adj.* 1. quiet and still, not windy. 2. not excited or agitated. 3. confident. —*n.* a calm condition or period. —*v.t./i.* to make or become calm. —**calmly** *adv.*, **calmness** *n.* [from Latin from Greek *kauma* = heat]

Calmette /kæl'met/ Albert 1863–1933. French bacteriologist. A student of Pasteur, he developed (with Camille Guérin (1872–1961)) the ◊BCG vaccine against tuberculosis in 1921.

calomel /'kæləmel/ *n.* Hg_2Cl_2 (technical name mercury(I) chloride), a white, heavy powder formerly used as a laxative, now used as a pesticide and fungicide. [perhaps from Greek *kalos* = beautiful and *melas* = black]

Calor gas /'kælə/ trade name for liquefied butane etc. stored under pressure in containers for use where mains gas is not available. [Latin *calor* = heat]

caloric /'kælərɪk/ *adj.* of heat; of calories. [from French]

calorie /'kælərɪ/ *n.* a c.g.s. unit of heat, now replaced by the ◊joule (one calorie is approximately 4.2 joules). It is the heat required to raise the temperature of one gram of water by 1°C. In dietetics, the calorie or kilocalorie is equal to 1,000 calories. [French from Latin *calor* = heat]

calorific /kælə'rɪfɪk/ *adj.* producing heat. —**calorific value**, the amount of heat generated by a given mass of fuel when it is completely burned. It is measured in joules per kilogram. Calorific values are measured experimentally with a bomb calorimeter.

calorimeter /kælə'rɪmɪtə(r)/ *n.* an instrument used in physics to measure heat. A simple calorimeter consists of a heavy copper vessel that is polished (to reduce heat losses by radiation) and covered with insulating material (to reduce losses by convection and conduction).

calotype *n.* a paper-based photograph using a wax-paper negative, the first example of the ◊negative/positive process, invented by the English photographer Fox Talbot around 1834.

caltrop or **caltrap** 1. (*historical*) a four-spiked iron ball thrown on the ground to impede cavalry horses; in heraldry, a representation of this. 2. a plant with spined flowerheads resembling caltrops. [from Old French *cauchir* = tread and *trappe* = trap]; sense 2 from Old English]

calumniate /kə'lʌmnɪeɪt/ *v.t.* to slander, to defame. —**calumniation** /-'eɪʃən/ *n.* [from Latin *calumniari*]

calumny /'kæləmnɪ/ *n.* slander; malicious representation. —**calumnious** /kə'lʌmnɪəs/ *adj.* [from Latin]

Calvary /'kælvərɪ/ in the New Testament, the site of Jesus's crucifixion at Jerusalem. Two chief locations are suggested: the site where the Church of the Sepulchre now stands, and the hill beyond the Damascus gate. [from Latin *calvaria* = skull, translation of Greek *golgotha* from Aramaic]

calve /kɑːv/ *v.i.* to give birth to a calf. [Old English]

Calvin /'kælvɪn/ John (also known as **Cauvin** or **Chauvin**) 1509–1564. French-born Swiss Protestant church reformer and theologian. He was a leader of the Reformation in Geneva and set up a strict religious community there. His theological system is known as Calvinism, and his church government is ◊Presbyterianism. Calvin wrote (in Latin) *Institutes of the Christian Religion* 1536 and commentaries on the New Testament and much of the Old Testament.

Calvin Melvin 1911– . US chemist who, using radioactive carbon-14 as a tracer, determined the biochemical processes of ◊photosynthesis, in which green plants use

◊chlorophyll to convert carbon dioxide and water into sugar and oxygen. He was awarded the Nobel Prize for Chemistry in 1961.

Calvinism /'kælvɪnɪzəm/ *n.* a Christian doctrine as interpreted by John Calvin and adopted in Scotland, parts of Switzerland, and the Netherlands; by the ◊Puritans in England and New England, USA; and by the subsequent Congregational and Presbyterian churches in the USA. Its central doctrine is predestination, under which certain souls (the elect) are predestined by God through the sacrifice of Jesus to salvation, and the rest to damnation. Although Calvinism is rarely accepted today in its strictest interpretation, the 20th century has seen a Neo-Calvinist revival through the work of Karl ◊Barth. —**Calvinist** *n.*, **Calvinistic** *adj.* [from *Calvin*]

calx *n.* (*plural* **calces** /'kælsiːz/) the powdery or friable substance left after the burning of a metal or mineral. [Latin = lime]

calypso /kə'lɪpsəʊ/ *n.* (*plural* **calypsos**) a West Indian song with a variable rhythm and topical, usually improvised, lyrics.

Calypso in Greek mythology, a sea ◊nymph who waylaid the homeward-bound Odysseus for seven years.

calyx /'keɪlɪks/ *n.* (*plural* **calyces** /-ɪsiːz/) the collective term for the ◊sepals of a flower, forming the outermost whorl of the ◊perianth. It surrounds the other flower parts and protects them while in bud. In some flowers, for example, the campions *Silene*, the sepals are fused along their sides, forming a tubular calyx. [Latin from Greek *kaluptō* = hide]

cam *n.* a part of a machine that converts circular motion to linear motion or vice versa. The **edge cam** in a car engine is in the form of a rounded projection on a shaft, the camshaft. When the camshaft turns, the cams press against linkages (plungers or followers) that open the valves in the cylinders. [from Dutch *kam* = comb (*kamrad* = cogwheel)]

CAM acronym from computer-aided manufacture, the use of computers to control production processes; in particular, the control of machine tools and ◊robots in factories. In some factories, the whole design and production system has been automated by linking ◊CAD (computer-aided design) to CAM.

camaraderie /kæmə'rɑːdərɪ/ *n.* comradeship, mutual trust and friendship. [French]

Camargo /kæmɑː'gəʊ/ Marie-Anne de Cupis de 1710–1770. French ballet dancer of Spanish descent. Born in Brussels, she became a ballet star in Paris in 1726. She was the first ballerina to wear a shortened skirt, which allowed freedom of movement and increased visibility. She was the first to attain the ◊entrechat quatre.

Camargue /kæ'mɑːg/ marshy area of the ◊Rhône delta, S of Arles, France; about 780 sq km/300 sq mi. Bulls and horses are bred there, and the nature reserve, which is known for its bird life, forms the southern part.

camber /'kæmbə/ *n.* a convex or arched shape given to the surface of a road, deck, etc.; the banked outer curve of a bend in a road etc. —*v.t.* to construct with a camber. [from French (= arched) from Latin *camurus* = curved inwards]

cambium /'kæmbɪəm/ *n.* a layer of actively dividing cells (lateral ◊meristem), found within stems and roots, that gives rise to ◊secondary growth in perennial plants, causing an increase in girth. There are two main types of cambium: vascular cambium which gives rise to secondary ◊xylem and ◊phloem tissues, and cork cambium (or phellogen) which gives rise to secondary cortex and cork tissues (see ◊bark). [Latin = exchange]

Cambodia /kæm'bəʊdɪə/ State of; country in SE Asia, bordered N and NW by Thailand, N by Laos, E and SE by Vietnam, and SW by the South China Sea; **area** 181,035 sq km/69,880 sq mi; **capital** Phnom Penh; **physical** mostly flat forested plains with mountains in SW and N; Mekong River runs N–S; **head of state** Heng Samarin from 1979; **head of government** Hun Sen from 1985 (neither are officially recognized); **political system** communism; **population** (1990 est) 6,993,000; **language** Khmer (official), French; **recent history** independence was achieved from France in 1953. Vietnamese invasion in 1978; the country was known as the People's Republic of Kampuchea 1979–89, until Vietnamese forces were fully withdrawn.

Cambrai, Battles of /kɒm'breɪ/ two battles in World War I at Cambrai in NE France: **First Battle** Nov-Dec 1917; the town was almost captured by the British when large numbers of tanks were used for the first time. **Second Battle** 26 Aug–5 Oct 1918; the town was taken during the final British offensive.

Cambrian /'kæmbriən/ *adj.* **1.** Welsh. **2.** of the first period of the Palaeozoic era, 590–505 million years ago. All invertebrate animal life appeared, and marine algae was widespread. The earliest fossils with hard shells, such as trilobites, date from this period. —*n.* this period. [from Latin *Cambria*, variant of *Cumbria* from Welsh]

cambric /'kæmbrɪk/ *n.* thin linen or cotton cloth. [from *Cambrai*, town in N France where it was originally made]

Cambridge /'keɪmbrɪdʒ/ city in England, on the river Cam (a river sometimes called by its earlier name, Granta), 80 km/50 mi N of London; population (1989) 101,000. It is the administrative headquarters of Cambridgeshire. The city is centred on Cambridge University (founded in the 12th century).

Cambridgeshire /'keɪmbrɪdʒʃə/ county in E England; **area** 3,410 sq km/1,316 sq mi; **administrative headquarters** Cambridge; **physical** rivers: Ouse, Cam, Nene; Isle of Ely; **products** mainly agricultural; **population** (1989) 642,000

Cambs. abbreviation of Cambridgeshire.

Cambyses /kæm'baɪsiːz/ 6th century BC. Emperor of Persia 529–522 BC. Succeeding his father Cyrus, he assassinated his brother Smerdis and conquered Egypt in 525 BC. There he outraged many of the local religious customs and was said to have become insane. He died in Syria on his journey home, probably by suicide.

Camden /'kæmdən/ William 1551–1623. English antiquary. He published his topographical survey *Britannia* in 1586, and was headmaster of Westminster School from 1593. The **Camden Society** (1838) commemorates his work.

Camden Town Group a school of British painters 1911–13, based in Camden Town, London, inspired by W R ◊Sickert. The work of Spencer Gore (1878–1914) and Harold Gilman (1876–1919) is typical of the group, rendering everyday town scenes in Post-Impressionist style.

came past of come.

camel /'kæməl/ *n.* **1.** a large, cud-chewing mammal of the even-toed hoofed order Artiodactyla. Unlike typical ruminants, it has a three-chambered stomach. It has two toes which have broad soft soles for walking on sand, and hoofs resembling nails. There are two species, the single-humped **Arabian camel** *Camelus dromedarius*, and the twin-humped **Bactrian camel** *Camelus bactrianus* from Asia. They carry a food reserve of fatty tissue in the hump, can go without drinking for long periods, can feed on salty vegetation, and withstand extremes of heat and cold, thus being well adapted to desert conditions. **2.** fawn colour. —**camel('s) hair**, fabric made of this or similar hair; fine, soft hair used in artists' brushes. [Old English from Latin from Greek from Semitic]

camellia /kə'meliə/ *n.* any oriental evergreen shrub with roselike flowers of the genus *Camellia*, tea family Theaceae. Numerous species, including *C. japonica* and *C. reticulata*, have been introduced into Europe and the USA. [from J *Camellus*, 17th-century Jesuit and botanist]

Camelot /'kæməlɒt/ the legendary seat of King ◊Arthur.

Camembert /'kæməmbeə/ *n.* a kind of small, soft, rich cheese. [name of town in Normandy, France, where it was originally made]

cameo /'kæmiəʊ/ *n.* (*plural* **cameos**) **1.** a small relief carving of semiprecious stone, shell or glass. A pale-coloured surface layer is carved to reveal a darker ground. Fine cameos were produced in ancient Greece and Rome, during the Renaissance, and in the Victorian era. They were used for decorating goblets and vases, and as jewellery. **2.** something small but well executed, especially a short descriptive literary sketch or an acted scene. [from Old French and Latin]

camera /'kæmərə/ *n.* an apparatus for taking photographs, motion pictures, or television pictures. —*in camera*, in law, in a judge's private room; privately, not in public. [Latin = vault, from Greek *kamara* = thing with arched cover]

cameraman *n.* or **camerawoman** (*plural* **cameramen** *or* **camerawomen**) a person whose job is to operate a camera, especially in film making or television.

camera obscura /əb'skjuərə/ an apparatus that uses a darkened box or room with an aperture for projecting an image of a distant object on a screen within. [Latin = dark chamber]

Cameron Julia Margaret 1815–1879. British photographer. She made lively, revealing portraits of the Victorian intelligentsia using a large camera, five-minute exposures, and wet plates. Her subjects included Darwin and Tennyson.

Cameroon /kæmə'ruːn/ Republic of; country in W Africa, bounded NW by Nigeria, NE by Chad, E by the Central African Republic, S by Congo, Gabon, and Equatorial Guinea, and W by the Atlantic; **area** 475,440 sq km/ 183,638 sq mi; **capital** Yaoundé; **physical** desert in far N in the Lake Chad basin, mountains in W, dry savanna plateau in the intermediate area, and dense tropical rainforest in S; **head of state and government** Paul Biya from 1982; **political system** one-party authoritarian nationalism; **exports** cocoa, coffee, bananas, cotton, timber, rubber, groundnuts, gold, aluminium; **population** (1990 est) 11,109,000; **language** French and English in pidgin variations (official); 163 indigenous languages; **recent history** German rule was established by treaty in 1884. The country was captured by Allied forces in World War I and divided between Britain and France. French Cameroon became an independent republic in 1960; the S part of British Cameroon joined in 1961 (the N part merged with Nigeria).

camisole /'kæmɪsəʊl/ *n.* a woman's bodicelike garment or undergarment. [French from Italian or Spanish = shirt]

Camoëns /'kæməʊenz/ or **Camões**, Luís Vaz de 1524– 1580. Portuguese poet and soldier. He went on various military expeditions, and was shipwrecked in 1558. His poem, *Os Lusiades/The Lusiads*, published in 1572, tells the story of the explorer Vasco da Gama and incorporates much Portuguese history; it has become the country's national epic. His posthumously published lyric poetry is also now valued.

camomile /'kæməmaɪl/ *n.* an aromatic composite plant of the genus *Anthemis* or *Matricaria* with flowers that are used as a tonic. [from Old French from Latin from Greek = earth apple (from the apple-like smell of the flowers)]

Camorra /kə'mɒrə/ *n.* an Italian secret society formed about 1820 by criminals in the dungeons of Naples and continued once they were freed. It dominated politics from 1848, was suppressed in 1911, but many members eventually surfaced in the US ◊Mafia. The Camorra still operates in the Naples area.

camouflage /'kæməflɑːdʒ/ *n.* colours or structures that allow an animal or object to blend with its surroundings to avoid detection. Camouflage can take the form of matching the background colour, of countershading (darker on top, lighter below, to counteract natural shadows), or of irregular patterns that break up the outline of the animal or object. More elaborate animal camouflage involves closely resembling a feature of the natural environment; this is akin to ◊mimicry. —*v.t.* to hide by camouflage. [French *camoufler* = disguise, from Italian]

camp[1] *n.* **1.** a place where troops are lodged or trained. **2.** an ancient fortified site. **3.** temporary accommodation of tents, huts, etc. for holiday-makers, detainees, etc. **4.** the adherents of a doctrine or party. —*v.i.* to live in a camp; to make a camp. —**camp bed**, a folding portable bed. **camp follower**, a hanger-on providing services to a military camp etc. or sympathetic to a group or theory. —**camper** *n.* [French from Italian from Latin *campus* = level ground]

camp[2] *adj.* affectedly exaggerated for theatrical effect; effeminate, homosexual. —*n.* a camp manner or style. —*v.t./i.* to act in a camp way.

campaign /kæm'peɪn/ *n.* **1.** a series of military operations in a definite area or for a particular objective. **2.** an organized course of action for a particular purpose, especially to arouse public interest. —*v.i.* to take part in a campaign. —**campaigner** *n.* [from French = open country]

Campaign for Nuclear Disarmament (CND) a nonparty-political British organization advocating the abolition of nuclear weapons worldwide: CND seeks unilateral British initiatives to help start the multilateral process and end the arms race.

Campania /kæm'peɪnɪə/ agricultural region (wheat, citrus, wine, vegetables, tobacco) of S Italy, including the volcano ◊Vesuvius; **capital** Naples; industrial centres Benevento, Caserta, and Salerno; **area** 13,600 sq km/ 5,250 sq mi; **population** (1988) 5,732,000. There are ancient sites at Pompeii, Herculaneum, and Paestum.

campanile *n.* originally a bell tower erected near, or attached to, churches or town halls in Italy. The leaning tower of Pisa is a renowned example; another is the great campanile of Florence, 90 m/275 ft high.

campanology /kæmpə'nɒlədʒɪ/ *n.* the study of bells and their founding, ringing, etc. See also ◊bell ringing. —**campanologist** *n.* [from Latin *campana* = bell]

campanula /kəm'pænjʊlə/ *n.* a plant of the genus *Campanula* with bell-shaped usually blue, pink, or white flowers. [diminutive of Latin *campana* = bell]

Campbell /'kæmbəl/ family name of the dukes of Argyll; seated at Inveraray Castle, Argyll.

Campbell Colin, 1st Baron Clyde 1792–1863. British field marshal. He commanded the Highland Brigade at ◊Balaclava in the Crimean War and, as commander in chief during the Indian Mutiny, raised the siege of Lucknow and captured Cawnpore.

Campbell Donald Malcolm 1921–1967. English car and speedboat enthusiast, son of Malcolm Campbell, who simultaneously held the land-speed and water-speed records. In 1964 he set the world water-speed record of 444.57 kph/ 276.3 mph on Lake Dumbleyung, Australia, with the turbojet hydroplane *Bluebird*, and achieved the land-speed record of 648.7 kph/403.1 mph at Lake Eyre salt flats, Australia. He was killed in an attempt to raise his water-speed record on Coniston Water, England.

Campbell Malcolm 1885–1948. English racing driver who, at one time, held both land-speed and water-speed records. His car and boat were both called *Bluebird*. His son Donald Campbell emulated his feats.

Campbell Mrs Patrick (born Beatrice Stella Tanner) 1865–1940. English actress, whose roles included Paula in Pinero's *The Second Mrs Tanqueray* 1893 and Eliza in *Pygmalion*, written for her by G B Shaw, with whom she had an amusing correspondence.

Campbell Roy 1901–1957. South African poet, who established his reputation with the *The Flaming Terrapin* 1924. Born in Durban, he became a professional jouster and bullfighter in Spain and Provence, France. He fought for Franco in the Spanish Civil War, and was with the Commonwealth forces in World War II.

Campbell-Bannerman /'bænəmən/ Henry 1836–1908. British Liberal politician, prime minister 1905–08. It was during his term of office that the South African colonies achieved self-government, and the Trades Disputes Act 1906 was passed.

Camp David /'kæmp 'deɪvɪd/ the official country home of US presidents, situated in the Appalachian mountains, Maryland; it was originally named Shangri-la by F D Roosevelt, but was renamed Camp David by Eisenhower (after his grandson).

Camp David Agreements two framework agreements signed at Camp David, Maryland, USA, in 1978 by the Israeli prime minister Begin and Egyptian president Sadat, under the guidance of US president Carter, covering an Egypt–Israel peace treaty and phased withdrawal of Israel from Sinai, which was completed in 1982, and an overall Middle East settlement including the election by the West Bank and Gaza Strip Palestinians of a 'self-governing authority'. The latter issue stalled over questions of who should represent the Palestinians and what form the self-governing body should take.

Camperdown /'kæmpədaʊn/ (Dutch *Kamperduin*) village on the NW Netherlands coast, off which a British fleet defeated the Dutch on 11 Oct 1797 in the Revolutionary Wars.

camphor /'kæmfə/ *n.* $C_{10}H_{16}O$, a volatile, aromatic ◊ketone substance obtained from the camphor tree *Cinnamomum camphora*. It is distilled from chips of the wood, and is used in insect repellents and in the manufacture of celluloid. [from Old French or Latin from Arabic from Sanskrit]

camphorated /'kæmfəreɪtɪd/ *adj.* containing camphor.

Campin /kɒm'pæn/Robert, also known as the **Master of Flémalle** *c.*1378–1444. Netherlandish painter of the early Renaissance, active in Tournai from 1406, one of the first

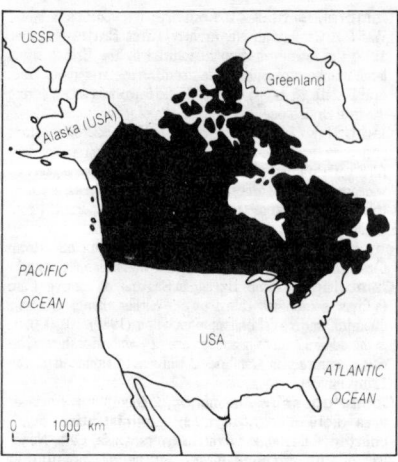

Canada

northern masters to use oil. Several altarpieces are attributed to him. Rogier van der Weyden was his pupil.

campion /'kæmpɪən/ *n.* any of several plants of the genera *Lychnis* and *Silene*, belonging to the pink family Caryophyllaceae, which include the garden campion *L. coronaria*, the wild white and red campions *S.· alba* and *S. dioica*, and the bladder campion *S. vulgaris*.

Campion Edmund 1540–1581. English Jesuit and Roman Catholic martyr. He took orders in the English church, but fled to Douai, France, where in 1571 he recanted Protestantism. In 1573 he became a Jesuit in Rome, and in 1580 was sent to England as a missionary. He was betrayed as a spy in 1581, imprisoned in the Tower of London, and hanged, drawn, and quartered as a traitor.

Campion Thomas 1567–1620. English poet and musician. He was the author of the critical *Art of English Poesie* 1602, and four *Bookes of Ayres*, for which he composed both words and music.

Campo-Formio, Treaty of /'kæmpəʊ 'fɔːmɪəʊ/ the peace settlement made in 1797 during the Revolutionary Wars between Napoleon and Austria, by which France gained the region that is now Belgium and Austria was compensated with Venice and part of that area which is now Yugoslavia.

campsite *n.* a camping site, especially one equipped for holiday-makers.

campus /'kæmpəs/ *n.* the grounds of a university or college; a university, especially as a teaching institution. [Latin = field]

camshaft *n.* a shaft carrying cams.

Camus /kæ'mjuː/ Albert 1913–1960. Algerian-born French writer. A journalist in France, he was active in the Resistance during World War II. His novels, which owe much to ◊existentialism, include *L'Etranger/The Outsider* 1942, *La Peste/The Plague* 1948, and *L'Homme Révolté/The Rebel* 1952. He was awarded the Nobel Prize for Literature in 1957.

can[1] /kən, emphatic kæn/ *v.aux.* (*singular present* can; *past* could) 1. to be able to, to know how to. 2. to have the right to, to be permitted to. [Old English = know]

can[2] *n.* a metal or plastic container for liquids; a tin container in which food or drink is hermetically sealed for preservation. —*v.t.* (-nn-) to put or preserve in a can. —**canned music**, music recorded for reproduction. [Old English]

Canaan /'keɪnən/ the ancient region between the Mediterranean and the Dead Sea, called in the Bible the 'Promised Land' of the Israelites. Occupied as early as the 3rd millennium BC by the Canaanites, a Semitic speaking people who were known to the Greeks of the 1st millennium as Phoenicians. The capital was Ebla (now Tell Mardikh, Syria).

Canada /'kænədə/ Dominion of; country occupying the northern part of the North American continent, bounded to the S by the USA, to the N by the Arctic Ocean, to the NW by Alaska, to the E by the Atlantic Ocean, and to the W by the Pacific Ocean; **area** 9,970,600 sq km/3,849,803 sq mi; **capital** Ottawa; **physical** Rocky Mountains in W, with low-lying plains in interior and rolling hills in E; Great Lakes in the S. The climate varies from temperate in the S to arctic in the N; **head of state** Elizabeth II from 1952 represented by governor general; **head of government** Brian Mulroney from 1984; **political system** federal constitutional monarchy; **exports** wheat, timber, pulp, newsprint, fish (salmon), furs, oil, natural gas, aluminium, asbestos, coal, copper, iron, nickel, motor vehicles and parts, industrial and agricultural machinery, fertilizers; **population** (1990 est) 26,527,000, including 300,000 North American Indians, some 300,000 Meltis (people of mixed race), and 19,000 Eskimo; **language** English, French (both official), North American Indian languages and the Eskimo Inuktitut; **recent history** the Dominion of Canada, a member of the British Commonwealth, was founded in 1867 (having been ceded to Britain by France in 1763); Newfoundland joined in 1949. The Canada Act of 1982 removed Britain's last legal control over Canadian affairs.

Canadian /kə'neɪdɪən/ *adj.* of Canada or its people. —*n.* a native or inhabitant of Canada.

canaille /kæ'naɪ/ *n.* the mob, rabble. [French]

canal /kə'næl/ *n.* **1.** an artificial waterway constructed for drainage, irrigation, or navigation. **Irrigation canals** carry water for irrigation from rivers, reservoirs, or wells, and are carefully designed to maintain an even flow of water over the whole length. **Navigation and ship canals** are constructed at one level between ◊locks, and frequently link with other forms of waterway, such as rivers and sea links, to form a waterway system. The world's two major international ship canals are the Suez Canal 1869 and the Panama Canal 1914, which provide invaluable short cuts for shipping between Europe and the East and between the E and W coasts of the Americas. **2.** a tubular passage in a plant or animal body. [from Old French or Italian from Latin *canalis*]

Canaletto /kænə'letəʊ/ Antonio (Giovanni Antoni Canal) 1697–1768. Italian painter celebrated for his paintings of views (*vedute*) of Venice (his native city) and of the river Thames and London 1746–56.

canalize /'kænəlaɪz/ *v.t.* **1.** to make a canal through; to provide with canals. **2.** to channel. —**canalization** /-'zeɪʃən/ *n.* [from French]

canapé /'kænəpeɪ/ *n.* a small piece of bread, pastry, or biscuit with a savoury topping. [French]

Canaries current the cold ocean current in the North Atlantic Ocean flowing SW from Spain along the NW coast of Africa. It meets the northern equatorial current at a latitude of 20° N.

canary /kə'neərɪ/ *n.* a bird *Serinus canaria* of the finch family, found wild in the Canary Islands and Madeira. It is greenish with a yellow underside. Canaries have been bred as cage birds in Europe since the 15th century, and many domestic varieties are yellow or orange. [from *Canary* Islands]

Canary Islands /kə'neərɪ/ (Spanish *Canarias*) group of volcanic islands 100 km/60 mi off the NW coast of Africa, forming the Spanish provinces of Las Palmas and Santa Cruz de Tenerife; **area** 7,300 sq km/2,818 sq mi; **population** (1986) 1,615,000; **features** the province of Santa Cruz comprises Tenerife (which has the highest peak, Pico de Teide 3,713 m/12,186 ft), Palma, Gomera, and Hierro; the province of Las Palmas comprises Gran Canaria, Lanzarote, and Fuerteventura. There are also six uninhabited islets. [from Latin *canis* = dog, one of the islands being noted in Roman times for large dogs]

canasta /kə'næstə/ *n.* a card game of Uruguayan origin, resembling rummy. [Spanish = basket]

Canberra /'kænbərə/ capital of Australia (since 1908), situated in Australian Capital Territory, enclosed within New South Wales, on a tributary of the Murrumbidgee River; **area** (Australian Capital Territory including the port at Jervis Bay) 2,432 sq km/939 sq mi; **population** (1986) 285,800.

cancan /'kænkæn/ *n.* a high-kicking stage dance for women (solo or line of dancers) originating in Paris about 1830. The music usually associated with the cancan is the *galop* from Offenbach's *Orpheus in the Underworld*.

cancel /'kænsəl/ *v.t./i.* (-ll-) **1.** to state that (a previous arrangement or decision) will not take place or be executed;

to discontinue; to annul, to make void. **2.** to neutralize, to counterbalance. **3.** to obliterate or delete (writing etc.); to mark so as to prevent further use. **4.** in mathematics, to strike out (an equal factor) on each side of an equation etc. —**cancellation** /-'leɪʃən/ *n.* [from French from Latin *cancelli* = crossbars]

cancer /'kænsər/ *n.* **1.** a group of diseases characterized by abnormal proliferation of cells. Cancer (malignant) cells are usually degenerate, capable only of reproducing themselves (tumour formation) until they outnumber the surrounding healthy cells. Malignant cells tend to spread from their site of origin by travelling through the bloodstream or lymphatic system. **2.** an evil influence or corruption. —**cancerous** *adj.*, **cancroid** /'kæŋkrɔɪd/ *adj.* [Latin = crab]

Cancer *n.* the faintest of the zodiac constellations (its brightest stars are fourth magnitude). It lies in the northern hemisphere, near Ursa Major, and is represented as a crab. Cancer's most distinctive feature is the star cluster Praesepe, popularly known as the Beehive. The Sun passes through the constellation during late July and early Aug. In astrology, the dates for Cancer are between about 22 June and 22 July (see ◊precession). —**tropic of Cancer**, see ◊tropic [Latin = crab]

candela /kæn'di:lə/ *n.* the SI unit (symbol cd) of luminous intensity, the luminous intensity, in the perpendicular direction, of a surface of 1/600,000 square metre of a black body at the temperature of freezing platinum under a pressure of 101,325 newtons per square metre. It replaced the old units of candle and standard candle. [Latin = candle (*candēre* = shine)]

candelabrum /kændɪ'lɑ:brəm/ *n.* (*plural* **candelabra**) a large branched candlestick or light holder. [Latin]

candid *adj.* **1.** frank, not hiding one's thoughts. **2.** in photography, informal, of a picture taken usually without the subject's knowledge. —**candidly** *adv.*, **candidness** *n.* [from French or Latin *candidus* = white]

Candida albicans /'kændɪdə 'ælbɪkænz/ a yeastlike fungus that is present in the human digestive tract and in the vagina, which causes no harm in most healthy people. It can cause problems if it multiplies excessively, as in vaginal candidiasis or ◊thrush, the main symptom of which is intense itching. The most common form of thrush is oral, which often occurs in those taking steroids or prolonged courses of antibiotics.

candidate /'kændɪdət/ *n.* **1.** a person who seeks or is nominated for an office, award, etc. **2.** a person or thing likely to gain a specified distinction or position. **3.** one taking an examination. —**candidacy** *n.*, **candidature** *n.* [from French or Latin = white-robed, from the white robes worn by Roman candidates for office]

candle *n.* a usually cylindrical stick of wax or tallow enclosing a wick for giving light when burning. —**candlelight** *n.* the light of candles. **cannot hold a candle to**, is very inferior to. [Old English from Latin *candēre* = shine]

Candlemas /'kændəlməs/ *n.* the feast of the Purification of the Virgin Mary (2 Feb), when candles are blessed. [Old English]

candlepower *n.* a unit of luminous intensity.

candlestick *n.* a holder for one or more candles.

candlewick *n.* a fabric with a raised, tufted pattern worked in thick, soft cotton yarn; this yarn.

candour /'kændə/ *n.* candid speech or quality, frankness. [from French or Latin *candor* = whiteness]

candy *n.* **1.** sugar crystallized by repeated boiling and slow evaporation. **2.** (*US*) sweets, a sweet. —*v.t.* to preserve (fruit etc.) by coating or impregnating with candy. —**candyfloss** *n.* a fluffy mass of spun sugar round a stick. **candy stripes**, alternate stripes of white and colour. **candy-striped** *adj.* [earlier *sugar candy*, from French from Arabic *kand* = sugar, ultimately from Sanskrit]

candytuft *n.* a garden plant of the genus *Iberis* with white, pink, or purple flowers in flat tufts. [from *Candia*, Crete]

cane *n.* **1.** the hollow, jointed stem of tall reeds and grasses (e. g. bamboo, sugar cane); the solid stem of slender palms (e. g. Malacca); a plant with such a stem; the stems of these used as material for wickerwork etc. **2.** a stem or a length of it, or a slender rod, used as a walking stick or to support a plant etc. or as a stick for use in corporal punishment. —*v.t.* **1.** to beat with a cane. **2.** to weave cane into (a chair etc.). —**cane sugar**, sugar obtained from the juice of sugar cane.

Canetti *The first Bulgarian to win the Nobel Prize for Literature was Elias Canetti in 1981.*

[from Old French from Latin from Greek *kanna* = reed, from Semitic]

Canes Venatici /ˈkeɪniːz viˈnætɪsaɪ/ a constellation of the northern hemisphere near Ursa Major, representing the hunting dogs of ◊Boötes, the herdsman. Its stars are faint, and it contains the Whirlpool galaxy (M51), the first spiral galaxy to be recognized.

Canetti /kəˈneti/ Elias 1905– . Bulgarian-born writer who was exiled from Austria as a Jew in 1938 and settled in England in 1939. His books, written in German, include the novel *Die Blendung/Auto da Fé* and an autobiography *The Tongue Set Free* (translated in 1988). He was concerned with crowd behaviour and the psychology of power. He was awarded the Nobel Prize for Literature in 1981.

canine /ˈkeɪnaɪn/ *adj.* of a dog or dogs. —*n.* 1. a dog. 2. a canine tooth. —**canine tooth**, a strong, pointed tooth between the incisors and molars used for catching prey, for killing, and for tearing flesh. Canines are absent in herbivores such as rabbits and sheep, and are much reduced in humans. [from Latin *caninus* (*canis* = dog)]

Canis Major /ˈkeɪnɪs/ a brilliant constellation of the southern hemisphere, representing one of the two dogs following at the heel of Orion. Its main star, Sirius, is the brightest star in the sky.

Canis Minor a small constellation along the celestial equator, representing the second of the two dogs of Orion (the other dog is represented by Canis Major). Its brightest star is Procyon.

canister /ˈkænɪstə/ *n.* a metal box or other container; a cylinder, filled with shot or tear gas, that bursts and releases its contents on impact. [from Latin from Greek *kanastron* = wicker basket]

canker /ˈkæŋkə/ *n.* 1. a disease that destroys the wood of trees and plants; a disease causing ulcerous sores in animals. 2. a corrupting influence. —**cankerous** *adj.* [Old English from Latin]

canna /ˈkænə/ *n.* a tropical plant of the genus *Canna*, with ornamental leaves and bright yellow, red, or orange flowers. [Latin]

cannabis /ˈkænəbɪs/ *n.* a hemp plant of the genus *Cannabis*; a preparation of this for smoking or chewing as an intoxicant or hallucinogenic drug. [Latin from Greek]

cannery /ˈkænərɪ/ *n.* a canning factory.

cannibal /ˈkænɪbəl/ *n.* a person who eats human flesh; an animal that eats its own species. —**cannibalism** *n.*, **cannibalistic** /-ˈlɪstɪk/ *adj.* [from Spanish, variant of *Caribes*, name of West Indian tribe (Caribs) formerly noted for their practice of cannibalism]

cannibalize /ˈkænɪbəlaɪz/ *v.t.* to use (a machine etc.) as a source of spare parts for others. —**cannibalization** /-ˈzeɪʃən/ *n.*

canning /ˈkænɪŋ/ *n.* the preservation of food in hermetically sealed containers by the application of heat. Originated by Nicolas Appert in France in 1809 with glass containers, it was developed by Peter Durand in England in 1810 with cans made of sheet steel thinly coated with tin to delay corrosion.

Canning Charles John, 1st Earl 1812–1862. English administrator, first viceroy of India from 1858. As governor general of India from 1856, he suppressed the Indian Mutiny with a fair but firm hand which earned him the nickname 'Clemency Canning'. He was the son of George Canning.

Canning George 1770–1827. English Tory politician, foreign secretary 1807–10 and 1822–27, and prime minister in 1827 in coalition with the Whigs. He was largely responsible, during the Napoleonic Wars, for the seizure of the Danish fleet and British intervention in the Spanish peninsula.

Cannizzaro /kæniˈzɑːrəʊ/ Stanislao 1826–1910. Italian chemist who revived interest in the work of Avogadro in 1811 that had revealed the difference between ◊atoms and ◊molecules, and so established atomic and molecular weights as the basis of chemical calculations.

cannon /ˈkænən/ *n.* 1. (*plural* the same) an old type of large heavy gun of a size which required it to be mounted for firing, discharging solid metal balls. 2. an automatic shell-firing gun used in aircraft. 3. the hitting of two balls successively by a player's ball in billiards. —*v.i.* to collide heavily *against* or *into*. —**cannon bone**, a tube-shaped bone between a horse's hock and fetlock. **cannon fodder**, people regarded merely as material to be expended in war. [from French from Italian = great tube; sense 3 formerly *carom*]

Cannon Annie Jump 1863–1941. US astronomer who, from 1896, worked at Harvard College Observatory and carried out revolutionary work on the classification of stars by examining their spectra. Her system, still used today, has spectra arranged according to temperature and runs from O through B, A, F, G, K, and M. O-type stars are the hottest, with surface temperatures of 35,000K. She also discovered over 300 ◊variable stars and five ◊novae.

cannonade /kænəˈneɪd/ *n.* continuous heavy gunfire. —*v.t.* to bombard with a cannonade.

cannot /ˈkænɒt/ = can not.

canny /ˈkænɪ/ *adj.* shrewd and cautious; worldly-wise. —**cannily** *adv.*, **canniness** *n.*

Cano /ˈkɑːnəʊ/ Juan Sebastian del *c.*1476–1526. Spanish voyager. It is claimed that he was the first sea captain to sail around the world. He sailed with Magellan in 1519 and, after the latter's death in the Philippines, brought the *Victoria* safely home to Spain.

canoe /kəˈnuː/ *n.* a keelless boat, pointed at both ends and propelled by a paddle or paddles, in which the paddler faces forward, often in a kneeling position. —*v.i.* (*participle* **canoeing**) to go in or paddle a canoe. —**canoeist** *n.* [from Spanish and Haitian *canoa*]

canoeing *n.* the sport of propelling a canoe by paddles or sails. Canoeing was popularized as a sport in the 19th century. The Royal Canoe Club in Britain was founded in 1866.

canon /ˈkænən/ *n.* 1. a general rule, law, principle, or criterion; a church decree or law. 2. a member of a cathedral chapter. 3. a body of sacred or other writings accepted as genuine. 4. the central unchanging part of the Roman Catholic Mass. 5. a passage or piece of music in which a theme is taken up by several parts successively. [Old English from Latin from Greek *kanōn* = rule]

canonical /kəˈnɒnɪkəl/ *adj.* 1. according to or ordered by canon law. 2. included in the canon of Scripture; authoritative, accepted. 3. of a cathedral canon or chapter. 4. (*in plural*) the canonical dress of clergy. [from Latin]

canonical hours in the Roman Catholic church, seven set periods of devotion: **matins** and **lauds**, **prime**, **terce**, **sext**, **nones**, **evensong** or **vespers**, **compline**. In the Anglican church, it is the period 8 am–6 pm within which marriage can be legally performed in a parish church without a special licence.

canonization *n.* in the Roman Catholic Church, the admission of one of its members to the Calendar of ◊Saints.

The evidence of the candidate's exceptional piety is contested before the Congregation for the Causes of Saints by the Promotor Fidei, popularly known as the **devil's advocate**. Papal ratification of a favourable verdict results in ◊beatification, and full sainthood (conferred in St Peter's basilica, the Vatican) follows after further proof. —**canonize** v.t. [from Latin]

canon law the rules and regulations of the Christian church, especially the Greek Orthodox, Roman Catholic, and Anglican churches. Its origin is sought in the declarations of Jesus and the apostles. In 1983 Pope John Paul II issued a new canon law code reducing offences carrying automatic excommunication, extending the grounds for annulment of marriage, removing the ban on marriage with non- Catholics, and banning trade union and political activity by priests.

Canopus /kə'nəʊpəs/ n. the second brightest star in the sky (after Sirius), lying in the constellation Carina. It is a yellow-white supergiant about 200 light years from Earth, and thousands of times more luminous than the Sun.

canopy /'kænəpɪ/ n. **1.** a hanging cover forming a shelter above a throne, bed, or person etc.; any similar covering. **2.** the expanding part of a parachute. —v.t. to supply or be a canopy to. [from Latin from Greek = mosquito net (kōnōps = gnat)]

Canossa /kə'nɒsə/ n. a ruined castle 19 km/12 mi SW of Reggio, Italy. The Holy Roman emperor Henry IV did penance here before Pope ◊Gregory VII in 1077 for having opposed him in the question of investitures.

Canova /kə'nəʊvə/ Antonio 1757–1822. Italian Neo-Classical sculptor, based in Rome from 1781. He received commissions from popes, kings, and emperors for his highly finished marble portrait busts and groups. He made several portraits of Napoleon.

Cánovas del Castillo /'kænəvæs del kæ'stɪljəʊ/ Antonio 1828–1897. Spanish politician and chief architect of the political system known as the *turno politico* through which his own Conservative party, and that of the Liberals under Práxedes Sagasta, alternated in power. Elections were rigged to ensure the appropriate majorities. Cánovas was assassinated in 1897 by anarchists.

can't /kɑːnt/ cannot.

cant[1] n. **1.** insincere pious or moral talk. **2.** jargon. —v.i. to use cant. [probably from Latin *cantare* = sing]

cant[2] n. a tilted or sloping position; a sloping surface, a bevel. —v.t./i. to tilt, to slope. [Low German or Dutch = edge, from Latin *cant(h)us* = iron tyre]

Cantab. abbreviation of Cantabrigian, of Cambridge University.

cantabile /kæn'tɑːbɪlɪ/ adv. in music, in a smooth flowing style. —n. a piece to be performed in this way. [Italian = suitable for singing]

Cantabria /kæn'tæbrɪə/ autonomous region of N Spain; area 5,300 sq km/2,046 sq mi; **capital** Santander; **population** (1986) 525,000.

Cantabrigian /kæntə'brɪdʒɪən/ adj. of Cambridge or Cambridge University. —n. a citizen of Cambridge; a member of Cambridge University. [from *Cantabrigia*, Latinized name of Cambridge]

cantaloup /'kæntəluːp/ n. or **cantaloupe** any of several small varieties of muskmelon, *Cucumis melo*, distinguished by their round, ribbed fruits with orange-coloured flesh. [French, from *Cantaluppi* near Rome, where first grown in Europe]

cantankerous /kæn'tæŋkərəs/ adj. bad-tempered, quarrelsome. —**cantankerously** adv., **cantankerousness** n. [perhaps from Irish *cant* = outbidding and rancorous]

cantata /kæn'tɑːtə/ n. in music, an extended work for voices, from the Italian, meaning 'sung', as opposed to ◊sonata ('sounded') for instruments. A cantata can be sacred or secular, sometimes uses solo voices, and usually has orchestral accompaniment. The first printed collection of sacred cantata texts dates from 1670. [Italian = sung (air) from *cantare* = sing]

canteen /kæn'tiːn/ n. **1.** a restaurant for the employees of a factory, office, etc.; a shop for provisions or liquor in a barracks or camp. **2.** a case or box containing a set of cutlery. **3.** a soldier's or camper's water flask. [from French or Irish = cellar]

canter n. a gentle gallop. —v.t./i. to go or cause to go at a canter. [short for *Canterbury gallop* etc., from the supposed easy pace of medieval pilgrims to Canterbury in Kent]

Canterbury /'kæntəbərɪ/ city in Kent, England, on the river Stour, 100 km/62 mi SE of London; population (1984) 39,000.

Canterbury, archbishop of the primate of all England, archbishop of the Church of England (Anglican), and first peer of the realm, ranking next to royalty. He crowns the sovereign, has a seat in the House of Lords, and is a member of the Privy Council. He is appointed by the prime minister. Formerly selected by political consultation, since 1980 the new archbishops have been selected by a church group, the Crown Appointments Commission (formed in 1977). The first holder of the office was St Augustine 601–04; his 20th-century successors have been: Randal T Davidson in 1903, C G Lang in 1928, William Temple in 1942, G F Fisher in 1945, A Michael Ramsey in 1961, D Coggan in 1974, Robert A K Runcie in 1980, and George L Carey from April 1991. The archbishop's official residence is at Lambeth Palace, London, and second residence at the Old Palace, Canterbury.

Canterbury Tales an unfinished collection of stories in prose and verse (c.1387) by Geoffrey ◊Chaucer, told by a group of pilgrims on their way to Thomas à ◊Becket's tomb at Canterbury. The tales and preludes are remarkable for their vivid character portrayal and colloquial language. Each pilgrim has to tell two stories on the way to Canterbury, and two on the way back, but only 24 tales were written.

cantharides /kæn'θærɪdiːz/ n.pl. the dried remains of a kind of beetle *Lytta vesicatoria*. It has been used in medicine for its irritant action on the skin, and as an aphrodisiac. [Latin from Greek]

canticle /'kæntɪkəl/ n. **1.** a song or chant with words taken from the Bible. **2. Canticles,** the Song of Solomon. [from Old French or Latin, diminutive of *canticum* (*cantus* = song)]

cantilever /'kæntɪliːvə(r)/ n. a beam or structure that is fixed at one end only, though it may be supported at some point along its length; for example, a diving board. The cantilever principle, widely used in construction engineering, eliminates the need for a second main support at the free end of the beam, allowing for more elegant structures and reducing the amount of materials required. Many large-span bridges have been built on the cantilever principle.

cantle n. the upward-curving hind part of a saddle. [from Anglo-French from Latin *cantellus*, diminutive of *canthus* = iron tyre]

canto /'kæntəʊ/ n. (*plural* **cantos**) any of the sections into which a long poem is divided. [Italian = song, from Latin *cantus*]

canton /'kæntɒn/ n. a subdivision of a country; a state of the Swiss confederation. [Old French = corner]

Canton former name of *Kwangchow* or ◊**Guangzhou** in China.

Cantonese /kæntə'niːz/ n. (*plural* the same) **1.** a native or inhabitant of the city of Canton (now ◊Guangzhou in China. **2.** a Chinese language spoken in S China and in Hong Kong. —adj. of Canton or its people or language.

cantor /'kæntɔː/ n. the leader of the liturgical singing of a church choir; a precentor in a synagogue. —**cantorial** /-'tɔːrɪəl/ adj. [Latin = singer (*canere* = sing)]

cantus firmus in music, any familiar melody used by an early composer as the basis for musical invention. [Latin = fixed voice part]

Canute /kə'njuːt/ c.995–1035. King of England from 1016, Denmark from 1018, and Norway from 1028. Having invaded England in 1013 with his father, Sweyn, king of Denmark, he was acclaimed king on his father's death in 1014 by his ◊Viking army. Canute defeated ◊Edmund Ironside at Assandun, Essex, in 1016, and became king of all England on Edmund's death. He succeeded his brother Harold as king of Denmark in 1018, compelled King Malcolm to pay homage by invading Scotland in about 1027, and conquered Norway in 1028. He was succeeded by his illegitimate son Harold I.

Canute VI (Cnut VI) 1163–1202. King of Denmark from 1182, son and successor of Waldemar Knudsson. With his brother and successor, Waldemar II, he resisted Frederick I's northward expansion, and established Denmark as the dominant power in the Baltic.

canvas /'kænvəs/ *n*. **1.** strong, coarse cloth used for making tents and sails and as a surface for oil painting; a painting on canvas. **2.** a racing boat's covered end. [from Old French from Latin *cannabis*]

canvass /'kænvəs/ *v.t./i.* **1.** to solicit votes (from); to ascertain the opinions of; to ask for custom from. **2.** to propose (an idea or plan etc.). —*n*. canvassing, especially of electors. —**canvasser** *n*. [originally = toss in a sheet, hence = shake up, agitate]

canyon /'kænjən/ *n*. a deep, narrow valley or gorge running through mountains. Canyons are formed by stream down-cutting, usually in areas of low rainfall, where the stream or river receives water from outside the area. [from Spanish = tube, from Latin]

Cao Chan /'tsaʊ 'tʃæn/ or **Ts'ao Chan** 1719–1763. Chinese novelist. His tragic love story *Hung Lou Meng/The Dream of the Red Chamber* involves the downfall of a Manchu family and is semi-autobiographical.

caoutchouc /'kaʊtʃʊk/ *n*. unvulcanized rubber. [French from Carib *cahuchu*]

cap *n*. **1.** a soft brimless head covering, usually with a peak. **2.** a head covering worn in a particular profession; an academic mortarboard; a cap awarded as a sign of membership of a sports team. **3.** a caplike cover or top. **4.** a ◊diaphragm contraceptive. —*v.t.* (**-pp-**) **1.** to put a cap on; to cover the top or end of. **2.** to award a sports cap to. **3.** to form the top of. **4.** to surpass, to excel. [from Old English from Latin *cappa*, perhaps from *caput* = head]

cap. abbreviation of capital.

CAP abbreviation of Common Agricultural Policy (of the EC), a system for establishing common prices for most agricultural products, a single fund for price supports, and levies on imports.

capable /'keɪpəbəl/ *adj*. having a certain ability or capacity *of*; competent. —**capability** /-'bɪlɪtɪ/ *n*., **capably** *adv*. [French from Latin *capere* = hold]

capacious /kə'peɪʃəs/ *adj*. roomy, able to hold much. —**capaciously** *adv*., **capaciousness** *n*. [from Latin *capax* (*capere* = hold)]

capacitance /kə'pæsɪtəns/ *n*. ability to store an electric charge; the measure of this, the ratio of the change in the electric charge of a body to a corresponding change in its potential.

capacitor /kə'pæsɪtə/ *n*. or **condenser** a device having capacitance, usually consisting of conductors separated by an insulator.

capacity /kə'pæsɪtɪ/ *n*. **1.** the ability to contain or accommodate. **2.** ability, capability. **3.** the maximum amount that can be contained or produced etc. **4.** function, position, legal competency. —**to capacity**, fully, to the full. [from French from Latin *capere* = hold]

caparison /kə'pærɪsən/ *n*. a horse's trappings; equipment, finery. —*v.t.* to adorn. [from French from Spanish = saddlecloth]

cape[1] *n*. a cloak; a similarly shaped part or garment covering the shoulders. [French from Latin *cappa* = cap]

cape[2] *n*. a coastal promontory. —**the Cape**, the Cape of Good Hope; the province containing it, Cape Province. [from Old French from Latin *caput* = head]

Cape Canaveral /'keɪp kə'nævərəl/ promontory on the Atlantic coast of Florida, USA, 367 km/228 mi N of Miami, used as a rocket launch site by ◊NASA. First mentioned in 1513, it was known in 1963–73 as Cape Kennedy. The ◊Kennedy Space Center is nearby.

Cape Cod /'keɪp 'kɒd/ hook-shaped peninsula in SE Massachusetts, USA; 100 km/60 mi long and 1.6–32 km/1–20 mi wide; population (1980) 150,000. Its beaches and woods make it a popular tourist area. It is separated from the rest of the state by the Cape Cod Canal. [named after the cod which were caught in the dangerous shoals of the cape]

Cape gooseberry a plant *Physalis peruviana* of the potato family. Originating in South America, it is grown in South Africa, from where it takes its name. It is cultivated for its fruit, a yellow berry surrounded by a papery ◊calyx.

Cape Horn /'keɪp hɒn/ southernmost point of South America, in the Chilean part of the archipelago of ◊Tierra del Fuego; notorious for gales and heavy seas. [named in 1616 by its Dutch discoverer Willem Schouten (1580–1625) after his birthplace (Hoorn)]

Čapek /'tʃæpek/ Karel (Matelj) 1890–1938. Czech writer whose works often deal with social injustice in an imaginative, satirical way. *R.U.R.* 1921 is a play in which robots (a term he coined) rebel against their controllers; the novel *Valka s Mloky/War With the Newts* 1936 is a science-fiction classic.

Capella /kə'pelə/ *n*. the brightest star in the constellation Auriga and the sixth brightest star in the sky. It consists of a pair of yellow giant stars 45 light years from Earth, orbiting each other every 104 days.

Cape of Good Hope /'keɪp əv gʊd 'həʊp/ South African headland forming a peninsula between Table Bay and False Bay, Cape Town. The first European to sail around it was Bartholomew Diaz in 1488. Formerly named Cape of Storms, it was given its present name by King John II of Portugal.

Cape Province /'keɪp 'prɒvɪns/ (Afrikaans *Kaapprovinsie*) largest province of the Republic of South Africa, named after the Cape of Good Hope; **area** 641,379 sq km/247,638 sq mi, excluding Walvis Bay; **capital** Cape Town; **physical** Orange River, Drakensberg, Table Mountain (highest point Maclear's Beacon, 1087 m/3567 ft); Great Karoo Plateau, Walvis Bay; **products** fruit, vegetables, wine; meat, ostrich feathers; diamonds, copper, asbestos, manganese; **population** (1985) 5,041,000; officially including 44% coloured; 31% black; 25% white; 0.6% Asian; **recent history** the Cape achieved self-government (from Britain) in 1872. It was an original province of the Union of South Africa in 1910.

caper[1] /'keɪpə/ *v.i.* to jump or run about playfully. —*n*. **1.** a playful jump or leap. **2.** a prank. **3.** (*slang*) an activity. [from Italian *capriolare* = leap in the air]

caper[2] /'keɪpə/ *n*. a trailing shrub *Capparis spinosa*, native to the Mediterranean and belonging to the family Capparidaceae; (in *plural*) its buds pickled for use in sauces etc. [from Latin from Greek *kapparis*]

capercaillie /kæpə'keɪlɪ/ *n*. the largest kind of European grouse, *Tetrao urogallus*. [from Gaelic = horse of the forest]

Capet /'kæ'pet/ Hugh 938–996. King of France from 987, when he claimed the throne on the death of Louis V. He founded the **Capetian dynasty**, of which various branches continued to reign until the French Revolution, for example, ◊Valois and ◊Bourbon.

Cape Town /'keɪp taʊn/ (Afrikaans *Kaapstad*) port and oldest town in South Africa, situated in the SW on Table Bay; population (1985) 776,617. Industries include horticulture and trade in wool, wine, fruit, grain, and oil. It is the legislative capital of the Republic of South Africa and capital of Cape Province; it was founded in 1652.

Cape Verde /'vɜːd/ Republic of; group of islands in the Atlantic, off the coast of Senegal; **area** 4,033 sq km/1,557 sq mi; **capital** Praia; **physical** archipelago of ten volcanic islands; **head of state and government** Aristides Pereira from 1975; **political system** one-party socialist state; **exports** bananas, coffee, salt, fish; **population** (1990 est) 375,000, including 100,000 Angolan refugees; **language** Creole dialect of Portuguese; **recent history** independence was achieved from Portugal in 1975. Union with Guinea-Bissau was provided for, but abandoned in 1981.

capillarity *n*. the spontaneous movement of liquids up or down narrow tubes, or capillaries. The movement is due to unbalanced molecular attraction at the boundary between the liquid and the tube. If liquid molecules near the boundary are more strongly attracted to molecules in the material of the tube than to other nearby liquid molecules, the liquid will rise in the tube. If liquid molecules are less attracted to the material of the tube than to other liquid molecules, the liquid will fall. [from Latin]

capillary /kə'pɪlərɪ/ *adj*. like a hair, hairlike in diameter. —*n*. **1.** in physics, a very narrow, thick-walled tube, usually made of glass, such as in a thermometer. Properties of fluids, such as surface tension and viscosity, can be studied using capillary tubes. **2.** in anatomy, a fine blood vessel, between 8 and 20 thousandths of a millimetre in diameter, that connects the ◊arteries and veins of vertebrates. Water, proteins, soluble food substances, gases, and white blood cells pass through the capillary wall (consisting of a single layer of cells) between the fluid (◊lymph) bathing the body tissue outside the capillary and the blood within the capillary. —**capillary attraction, repulsion,** the tendency of liquid to be drawn up or down in a capillary tube. [from Latin *capillus* = hair]

capital /'kæpɪtəl/ *n.* **1.** the most important town or city of a country or region, usually its seat of government and administrative centre. **2.** the money or other assets with which a company starts business; accumulated wealth; capitalists collectively. **3.** a capital letter. **4.** the head of a column or pillar. —*adj.* **1.** principal, most important; (*colloquial*) excellent. **2.** involving punishment by death; very serious. **3.** (of letters of the alphabet) of the form and size used to begin a name or sentence. —**capital gain,** profit from the sale of investment or property. **capital sum,** a lump sum of money, especially that payable to an insured person. **make capital out of,** to use (a situation etc.) to one's own advantage. [from Old French from Latin *caput* = head]

capital bond an investment bond, which is purchased by a single payment, set up for a fixed period, and offered for sale by a life insurance company. The emphasis is on capital growth of the lump sum invested rather than on income.

capital expenditure spending on fixed assets such as plant and equipment, trade investments, or the purchase of other businesses.

capital gains tax an income tax levied on the change of value of a person's assets, often property.

capitalism /'kæpɪtəlɪzəm/ *n.* an economic system in which the principal means of production, distribution, and exchange are in private (individual or corporate) hands and competitively operated for profit.

capitalist /'kæpɪtəlɪst/ *n.* **1.** a person using or possessing capital, a rich person. **2.** a believer in capitalism. —*adj.* of or favouring capitalism. —**capitalistic** /-'ɪstɪk/ *adj.*

capitalize /'kæpɪtəlaɪz/ *v.t./i.* **1.** to convert into capital; to provide with capital. **2.** to write or print with a capital letter; to begin (a word) with a capital letter. —**capitalize on,** to use to one's advantage. —**capitalization** /-'zeɪʃən/ *n.* [from French]

capital punishment punishment by death. Capital punishment, abolished in the UK in 1965 for all crimes except treason, is retained in many countries, including the USA (37 states), France, and the USSR. Methods of execution include electrocution, lethal gas, hanging, shooting, lethal injection, garrotting, and decapitation. In Britain, the number of capital offences was reduced from over 200 at the end of the 18th century, until capital punishment was abolished in 1866 for all crimes except murder, treason, piracy, and certain arson attacks. Its use was subject to the royal prerogative of mercy. The punishment was carried out by hanging (in public until 1866).

capitation /kæpi'teɪʃən/ *n.* a tax or fee levied per person. [French or from Latin = poll tax (*caput* = head)]

capitulate /kə'pɪtjuleɪt/ *v.i.* to surrender. —**capitulation** /-'leɪʃən/ *n.* [from Latin *capitulare* = put under headings, from *capitulum,* diminutive of *caput* = head]

capitulum *n.* in botany, a flattened or rounded head (inflorescence) of numerous, small, stalkless flowers. The capitulum is surrounded by a circlet of petal-like bracts and has the appearance of a large, single flower. It is characteristic of plants belonging to the daisy family (Compositae) such as the daisy *Bellis perennis* and the garden marigold *Calendula officinalis* but is also seen in parts of other families, such as scabious *Knautia* and teasels *Dipsacus.* The individual flowers are known as ◊florets.

Capodimonte /'keɪpəu di 'montei/ village, N of Naples, Italy, where porcelain known by the same name was first produced under King Charles III of Naples about 1740. The porcelain is usually white, painted with colourful folk figures, landscapes, or flowers.

capon /'keɪpən/ *n.* a domestic cock castrated and fattened for eating. [Old English from Anglo-French from Latin *capo*]

Capone /kə'pəun/ Al(phonse) 1898–1947. US gangster, born in Brooklyn, New York, the son of an Italian barber. His nickname was **Scarface.** During the ◊Prohibition period, Capone built a formidable criminal organization in Chicago. He was brutal in his pursuit of dominance, killing seven members of a rival gang in the St Valentine's Day massacre. He was imprisoned 1931–39 for income-tax evasion, the only charge that could be sustained against him.

Capote /kə'pəuti/ Truman. Pen name of Truman Streckfus Persons 1924–1984. US novelist, short-story writer, and playwright. He wrote *Breakfast at Tiffany's* 1958; set a trend with the first 'non-fiction novel', *In Cold Blood* 1966, reconstructing a Kansas killing; and mingled recollection and fiction in *Music for Chameleons* 1980.

> Venice is like eating an entire box of chocolate liqueurs at one go.
>
> **Truman Capote**
> The *Observer* 1961

Cappadocia /kæpə'dəuʃə/ ancient region of Asia Minor, in E central Turkey. It was conquered by the Persians in 584 BC but in the 3rd century BC became an independent kingdom. The region was annexed as a province of the Roman Empire in AD 17.

Capra /'kæprə/ Frank 1897– . Italian-born US film director. His films, satirical social comedies which often have idealistic heroes, include *It Happened One Night* 1934, *Mr Deeds Goes to Town* 1936, and *You Can't Take It With You* 1938, for which he received Academy Awards.

capriccio /kə'prɪtʃiəu/ *n.* in music, a short instrumental piece, often humorous or whimsical in character. [Italian = sudden start (originally = horror)]

caprice /kə'priːs/ *n.* **1.** a whim; a tendency to capricious behaviour. **2.** a work of lively fancy in art or music. [French from Italian *capriccio* = sudden start]

capricious /kə'prɪʃəs/ *adj.* guided by caprice, impulsive; unpredictable. —**capriciously** *adv.*, **capriciousness** *n.*

Capricorn /'kæprɪkɔːn/ *n.* or **Capricornus** a zodiac constellation in the southern hemisphere near Sagittarius. It is represented as a fish-tailed goat, and its brightest stars are third magnitude. The Sun passes through it late Jan to mid-Feb. In astrology, the dates for Capricorn are between about 22 Dec and 19 Jan (see ◊precession). —**tropic of Capricorn,** see ◊tropic. [from Old French from Latin *caper* = goat and *cornu* = horn]

Caprivi /kə'priːvi/ Georg Leo, Graf von 1831–1899. German soldier and politician. While chief of the admiralty (1883–88) he reorganized the German navy. He became imperial chancellor 1890–94, succeeding Bismarck, and renewed the Triple Alliance but wavered between European allies and Russia. Although he strengthened the army he alienated the conservatives.

Caprivi Strip NE access strip for ◊Namibia to the Zambezi River.

capsicum /'kæpsɪkəm/ *n.* any pepper plant of the genus *Capsicum* of the nightshade family Solanaceae, native to Central and South America. The differing species produce green to red fruits that vary in size. The small ones are used whole to give the hot flavour of chilli, or ground to produce cayenne pepper; the large, pointed or squarish pods, known as sweet peppers, are mild-flavoured and used as a vegetable. [perhaps from Latin *capsa* = case]

capsize /kæp'saɪz/ *v.t./i.* to overturn (a boat); to be overturned. [perhaps from Spanish *capuzar* = sink by the head (*cabo* = head, *chapuzar* = dive)]

capstan /'kæpstən/ *n.* **1.** a thick revolving post round which a cable or rope is wound as it turns, e. g. to raise a ship's anchor. **2.** a revolving spindle carrying the spool on a tape recorder. —**capstan lathe,** a lathe with a revolving tool hold er. [from Provençal from Latin *capere* = seize]

capsule /'kæpsjuːl/ *n.* **1.** a small soluble case in which a dose of medicine is enclosed for swallowing. **2.** in botany, a dry, usually many-seeded fruit formed from an ovary composed of two or more fused ◊carpels, which splits open to release the seeds; the spore-containing structure of mosses and liverworts. **3.** a detachable compartment of an aircraft or nose cone of a rocket. —*adj.* concise, highly condensed. [French from Latin *capsa* = case]

capsulize /'kæpsjulaɪz/ *v.t.* to put (information etc.) into a compact form.

captain /'kæptɪn/ *n.* **1.** a person given authority over a group or team. **2.** the person commanding a ship; a naval officer ranking next below commodore. **3.** an army officer ranking next below major. **4.** the pilot of a civil aircraft.

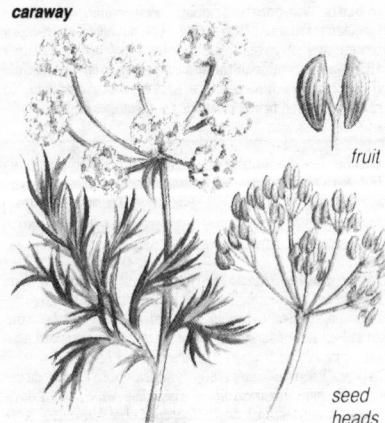

caraway

fruit

seed
heads

—*v.t.* to be captain of. —**captaincy** *n.* [from Old French from Latin = chief (*caput* = head)]

caption /'kæpʃən/ *n.* a short title or heading; a description or explanation printed with an illustration etc.; words shown on a cinema or television screen. —*v.t.* to provide with a caption. [from Latin *capere* = take]

captious /'kæpʃəs/ *adj.* fond of finding fault, raising petty objections. —**captiously** *adv.*, **captiousness** *n.* [from Old French or Latin]

captivate /'kæptɪveɪt/ *v.t.* to capture the affection or fancy of, to charm. —**captivation** /-'veɪʃən/ *n.* [from Latin *captivare* = take captive]

captive /'kæptɪv/ *adj.* taken prisoner; restrained, confined; (of an audience or market) having no choice but to listen or comply. —*n.* a captive person or animal. [from Latin *captivus* (*capere* = take)]

captivity /kæp'tɪvɪtɪ/ *n.* the state of being held captive. —**the Captivity**, that of the Jews in Babylon, to which they were deported by Nebuchadnezzar in 586 BC and from which they were released by Cyrus in 538 BC.

captor /'kæptə/ *n.* one who captures. [Latin]

capture /'kæptʃə/ *v.t.* **1.** to take prisoner, to seize; to obtain by force, trickery, attraction, or skill. **2.** to portray (a likeness etc.) in permanent form. **3.** to absorb (an atomic particle). **4.** (of a stream) to divert the upper course of (another) into its own waters by encroaching on the other's basin. **5.** (of a star or planet) to bring (an object) within its gravitational field. **6.** to put (data) into a form accessible by computer. —*n.* **1.** the act of capturing. **2.** a thing or person captured. [French from Latin]

Capuchin /'kæpjʊtʃɪn/ *n.* **1.** a member of the Franciscan order of monks in the Roman Catholic church, instituted by the Italian monk Matteo di Bassi (died 1552), who wished to return to the literal observance of the rule of St Francis. The Capuchin rule was drawn up in 1529 and the order recognized by the pope in 1619. The order has been involved in missionary activity. **2.** a monkey, genus *Cebus*, found in Central and South America, so called because the hairs on the head resemble the cowl of a Capuchin monk; a pigeon with a hoodlike crown of feathers. [French from Italian *cappuccio* = cowl]

capybara /kæpɪ'bɑːrə/ *n.* the largest rodent *Hydrochoerus hydrochaeris*, up to 1.3 m/4 ft long and 50 kg/110 lb in weight. It is found in South America, and belongs to the guinea pig family. The capybara inhabits marshes and dense vegetation around water. It has thin, yellowish hair, swims well, and can rest under water with just eyes, ears, and nose above the surface. [Tupi]

car *n.* or **motor car** **1.** a small, driver-guided, passenger-carrying motor vehicle; originally the automated version of the horse-drawn carriage, meant to convey people and their goods over streets and roads. Most are four-wheeled and have water-cooled, piston-type internal-combustion engines fuelled by petrol or diesel. Variations have existed for decades that use ingenious and often nonpolluting power plants, but the motor industry long ago settled on this general formula for the consumer market. Experimental and sports models are streamlined, energy-efficient, and hand-built. **2.** a railway carriage of a specified type; (*US*) any railway carriage or van. **3.** the passenger compartment of an airship, balloon, cable railway, or lift. —**car park**, an area for parking cars. [from Anglo-French from Latin *carrum*]

Caracalla /kærə'kælə/ Marcus Aurelius Antoninus 186–AD 217. Roman emperor. He succeeded his father Septimus Severus in 211, ruled with cruelty and extravagance, and was assassinated. [so-called from the Gallic cloak (caracalla) that he wore]

Caracas /kə'rækəs/ chief city and capital of Venezuela; situated on the Andean slopes, 13 km/8 mi S of its port La Guaira on the Caribbean coast; population of metropolitan area (1981) 1,817,000. Founded in 1567, it is now a major industrial and commercial centre, notably for oil companies.

Caractacus /kə'ræktəkəs/ died *c.* AD 54. British chieftain who headed resistance to the Romans in SE England AD 43–51, but was defeated on the Welsh border. Shown in Claudius's triumphal procession, he was released in tribute to his courage and died in Rome.

caracul variant of **karakul**.

carafe /kə'ræf/ *n.* a glass container in which water or wine is served at table. [French, ultimately from Arabic = drinking vessel]

caramel /'kærəməl/ *n.* **1.** burnt sugar or syrup used for colouring or flavouring food. **2.** a kind of toffee tasting like this. **3.** light-brown colour. [French from Spanish]

caramelize /'kærəməlaɪz/ *v.t./i.* to turn into caramel. —**caramelization** /-'zeɪʃən/ *n.*

carapace /'kærəpeɪs/ *n.* the upper shell of a tortoise or crustacean. [French from Spanish]

carat /'kærət/ *n.* a unit of weight for precious stones, 0.2 g/0.00705 oz; a unit of measurement for the purity of gold (*US* **karat**), pure gold being 24 carat. [French, ultimately from Greek *keration* = fruit of carob (diminutive of *keras* = horn)]

Caravaggio /kærə'vædʒɪəʊ/ Michelangelo Merisi da 1573–1610. Italian early Baroque painter, active in Rome 1592–1606, then in Naples, and finally in Malta. His life was as dramatic as his art (he had to leave Rome after killing a man). He created a forceful style, using contrasts of light and shade and focusing closely on the subject figures, sometimes using dramatic foreshortening.

caravan /'kærəvæn/ *n.* **1.** an enclosed carriage equipped for living in, able to be towed by a vehicle; a covered cart used similarly, towed by a horse. **2.** a company (especially of merchants) travelling together, especially across desert country. —*v.i.* (**-nn-**) to travel or live in a caravan. [from French from Persian]

caravanserai /kærə'vænsəraɪ/ *n.* (in eastern countries) an inn with a large central courtyard for accommodation of travelling caravans. [from Persian = caravan place]

caraway /'kærəweɪ/ *n.* a herb *Carum carvi* of the carrot family Umbelliferae. It is grown for its spicy, aromatic seeds, which are used in cookery, medicine, and perfumery. [from Spanish from Arabic, perhaps from Greek *caron* = cumin]

carbide /'kɑːbaɪd/ *n.* a binary compound of carbon, especially **calcium carbide** which is used in making acetylene gas.

carbine /'kɑːbaɪn/ *n.* a short rifle, originally for cavalry use. [earlier and French *carabine* = weapon of the *carabin* = mounted musketeer]

carbohydrate /kɑːbə'haɪdreɪt/ *n.* **1.** an energy-producing compound of carbon with oxygen and hydrogen with the basic formula $C_m(H_2O)_n$, e.g. starch, sugar, glucose. **2.** starchy food, considered to be fattening.

carbolic /kɑː'bɒlɪk/ *adj.* **carbolic acid**, ◊**phenol**. **carbolic soap**, soap containing this.

carbon /'kɑːbən/ *n.* **1.** a non-metallic element, symbol C, atomic number 6 relative atomic mass 12.011. It occurs on its own as diamond and graphite (the allotropes), in carbonaceous rocks such as chalk and limestone, as carbon dioxide in the atmosphere, as hydrocarbons in petroleum, coal, and natural gas, and as a constituent of all organic substances. **2.** carbon copy; carbon paper. **3.** a rod of carbon used in an arc lamp. —**carbon copy**, a copy made with carbon paper; an exact copy. **carbon 14**, a radioisotope with mass 14 used in dating prehistoric objects. **carbon paper**, thin, pigmented paper placed between sheets of paper for reproducing what is written or typed on the top sheet. **carbon tetrachloride**, a colourless liquid used as a solvent in dry cleaning etc. [from French from Latin *carbo* = charcoal]

carbonaceous /kɑ:bə'neɪʃəs/ *adj.* consisting of or containing carbon; of or like coal or charcoal.

carbonade /kɑ:bə'neɪd/ *n.* a rich beef stew containing beer. [French]

Carbonari /kɑ:bə'nɑ:ri/ *n.* a secret revolutionary society in S Italy in the first half of the 19th century that advocated constitutional government. The movement spread to N Italy but support dwindled after the formation of ◊Mazzini's nationalist 'Young Italy' movement, although it helped prove the way for the unification of Italy (see ◊Risorgimento).

carbonate /'kɑ:bəneɪt/ *n.* CO_3^{2-}, an ion formed when carbon dioxide dissolves in water, and any salt formed by this ion and another chemical element, usually a metal. Carbonates give off carbon dioxide when heated or treated with dilute acids. —*v.t.* to impregnate with carbon dioxide; to make (drinks) effervescent with this. [from French]

carbon cycle the sequence by which carbon circulates and is recycled through the natural world. The carbon element from carbon dioxide in the atmosphere is taken up during the process of ◊photosynthesis, and the oxygen component is released back into the atmosphere. Today, the carbon cycle is being altered by the increased consumption of fossil fuels, and the burning of large tracts of tropical forests, as a result of which levels of carbon dioxide are building up in the atmosphere and probably contributing to the ◊greenhouse effect.

carbon dating an alternative name for ◊radiocarbon dating.

carbon dioxide CO_2, a colourless gas formed by the complete oxidation of carbon. It is produced during the process of respiration by living things and by the decay of organic matter.

carbon fibre a fine, black, silky filament of pure carbon produced by heat treatment from a special grade of Courtelle acrylic fibre, used for reinforcing plastics. The resulting composite is very stiff and, weight for weight, has four times the strength of high-tensile steel. It is used in aerospace, cars, and electrical and sports equipment.

carbonic /kɑ:'bɒnɪk/ *adj.* of carbon. —**carbonic acid**, a weak acid formed from carbon dioxide and water.

carboniferous /kɑ:bə'nɪfərəs/ *adj.* producing coal. [from Latin *carbo* = coal and *ferous* = bearing]

Carboniferous *adj.* of the period of geological time 360–286 million years ago, the fifth period of the Palaeozoic era. —*n.* this period. Typical of the lower-Carboniferous rocks are shallow-water ◊limestones, while upper-Carboniferous rocks have ◊delta deposits with ◊coal. Amphibians were abundant, and reptiles evolved. [from French from Latin *carbo* = coal]

carbonize /'kɑ:bənaɪz/ *v.t.* 1. to convert into carbon; to reduce to charcoal or coke. 2. to coat with carbon. —**carbonization** /-'zeɪʃən/ *n.*

carbon monoxide CO, a colourless, odourless gas formed when carbon is oxidized in a limited supply of air. It is a poisonous constituent of car exhaust fumes, forming a stable compound with haemoglobin in the blood, thus preventing the haemoglobin from transporting oxygen to the body tissues.

carborundum /kɑ:bə'rʌndəm/ *n.* a compound of carbon and silicon, used especially as an abrasive.

carboy /'kɑ:bɔɪ/ *n.* a large, globular bottle enclosed in a frame, used for transporting liquids safely. [from Persian = large glass flagon]

carbuncle /'kɑ:bʌŋkəl/ *n.* 1. a severe abscess in the skin. 2. a bright-red gem cut in a knoblike shape. [from Old French from Latin = small coal (*carbo* = coal)]

carburation /kɑ:bju'reɪʃən/ *n.* the process of charging air with a spray of liquid hydrocarbon fuel.

carburettor /kɑ:bju'retə/ *n.* an apparatus for the carburation of air in an internal-combustion engine.

carcass /'kɑ:kəs/ *n.* 1. the dead body of an animal, especially one prepared for cutting up as meat; the bony part of the body of a bird before or after cooking. 2. a framework; the foundation structure of a tyre. [from Anglo-French]

Carchemish /'kɑ:kəmɪʃ/ (now **Karkamis**, Turkey) centre of the ◊Hittite New Empire (*c.*1400–1200 BC) on the river Euphrates, 80 km/50 mi NE of Aleppo, and taken

by Sargon II of Assyria in 717 BC. Nebuchadnezzar II of Babylon defeated the Egyptians here in 605 BC.

carcinogen /kɑ:'sɪnədʒən/ *n.* a substance that induces cancer. —**carcinogenic** /-'dʒenɪk/ *adj.*

carcinoma /kɑ:si'nəʊmə/ *n.* (*plural* **carcinomata**) a cancerous tumour arising from the skin, the glandular tissues, or the mucous membranes that line the gut and lungs. [Latin from Greek *karkinos* = crab]

card[1] *n.* 1. thick, stiff paper or thin cardboard; a piece of this for writing or printing on, especially to send messages or greetings or to record information; a flat usually rectangular piece of thin pasteboard, plastic, etc., recording membership or identifying the bearer; (in *plural, colloquial*) an employee's documents held by his employer. 2. a playing card; (in *plural*) card playing. 3. a programme of events at a race meeting etc. 4. (*colloquial*) an odd or amusing person. —**card-carrying** *adj.* being a registered member of a political party, trade union, etc. **cardsharp** *n.* a swindler at card games. **card vote,** a block vote (see ◊block). **on the cards,** likely, possible. [from Old English from Latin from Greek *khartēs* = papyrus leaf]

card[2] *n.* a toothed instrument or wire brush for raising nap on cloth or for disentangling fibres before spinning. —*v.t.* to brush or comb with a card. [from Old French from Latin *carere* = card]

cardamom /'kɑ:dəməm/ *n.* a spice from the seed capsules of various East Indian plants, especially *Elettaria cardamomum*, a plant of the ginger family. [from Latin or French from Greek *kardamon* = cress and *amōmon* = a spice plant]

cardboard *n.* stiff paper or pasteboard, especially for making cards or boxes.

Cárdenas /'kɑ:dɪnæs/ Lázaro 1895–1970. Mexican centre-left politician and general, president 1934–40, minister of defence 1943–45.

cardiac /'kɑ:dɪæk/ *adj.* of the heart. [from French or Latin from Greek *kardia* = heart]

Cardiff /'kɑ:dɪf/ capital of Wales (from 1955) and administrative headquarters of South and Mid Glamorgan, at the mouth of the Taff, Rhymney, and Ely Rivers; population (1983) 279,800. Besides steelworks, there are automotive component, flour milling, paper, cigar, and other industries.

Cardiff Arms Park a Welsh rugby ground officially known as the National Stadium, situated in Cardiff. The stadium became the permanent home of the Welsh national team in 1964 and has a capacity of 64,000.

cardigan /'kɑ:dɪgən/ *n.* a knitted jacket. [named after the 7th Earl of Cardigan (died 1868), who led the disastrous Charge of the Light Brigade in the Crimean War]

Cardiganshire /'kɑ:dɪgənʃə/ former county of Wales which in 1974 was merged, together with Pembrokeshire and Carmarthenshire, into Dyfed.

Cardin /'kɑ:dæn/ Pierre 1922– . French fashion designer; the first women's designer to show a collection for men, in 1960.

cardinal /'kɑ:dɪnəl/ *adj.* 1. chief, fundamental. 2. deep scarlet as worn by cardinals. —*n.* 1. a member of the Sacred College of the Roman Catholic Church. Cardinals hold the highest rank next to the pope, who is chosen from their number. 2. a small scarlet American songbird of the genus *Richmondena*. —**cardinal numbers,** the whole numbers (1, 2, 3, etc.) representing a quantity, as opposed to ordinal numbers. **cardinal points,** the four main points of the compass, N, S, E, and W. **cardinal virtues,** justice, prudence, temperance, fortitude, faith, hope, charity. [from Old French from Latin *cardo* = hinge]

cardioid *n.* a heart-shaped curve traced out by a point on the circumference of a circle that rolls around the edge of another circle of the same diameter. The polar equation of the cardioid is of the form $r = a(1 + \cos \theta)$. It is also the pattern of response of an undirectional microphone.

cardiology /kɑ:dɪ'ɒlədʒɪ/ *n.* the branch of medicine concerned with diseases and abnormalities of the heart. —**cardiological** *adj.*, **cardiologist** *n.* [from Greek *kardia* = heart]

Cardwell /'kɑ:dwel/ Edward. Viscount Cardwell 1813–1886. British Liberal politician. He entered Parliament as a supporter of the Conservative prime minister ◊Peel in 1842, and 1868-74 was secretary for war under Gladstone, when he carried out many reforms, including the abolition of the purchase of military commissions and promotions.

care /keə/ n. 1. serious attention and thought; caution to avoid damage or loss. 2. protection, charge, supervision. 3. a thing to be done or seen to. —v.t./i. 1. to feel concern or interest. 2. to feel affection or a liking for or willingness to do. 3. to provide for. —care of, at the address of (one who will deliver or forward things). in care, taken into the care of a local authority. [Old English = sorrow]

careen /kə'ri:n/ v.t. 1. to tilt, to lean over. 2. (US) to swerve. [from French from Italian from Latin carina = keel]

career /kə'riə/ n. 1. one's advancement through life, especially in a profession; a profession or occupation, especially one offering advancement. 2. swift forward movement. —v.i. to move swiftly or wildly. [from French, ultimately from Latin carrus = car]

careerist n. a person who is predominantly concerned with advancement in a career.

carefree adj. light-hearted through being free from anxiety or responsibility.

careful adj. giving serious attention and thought, painstaking; done with care and attention; cautious. —**carefully** adv., **carefulness** n.

careless adj. not giving or given serious attention and thought; unthinking, insensitive; casual and lighthearted. —**carelessly** adv., **carelessness** n.

care order in Britain, a court order that places a child in the care of a local authority.

carer n. one who looks after a sick or disabled person at home.

caress /kə'res/ v.t. to touch or stroke lovingly. —n. a loving touch, a kiss. [from French from Latin carus = dear]

caret /'kærət/ n. a mark showing an omission (and intended insertion) in something printed or written. [Latin = is lacking]

caretaker n. 1. a person employed to look after a house or building etc. 2. (attributive) exercising temporary power.

Carew /kə'ru:/ Thomas c.1595–c.1640. English poet. He was a gentleman of the privy chamber to Charles I in 1628, and a lyricist as well as member of the school of ◊Cavalier poets.

careworn adj. showing the effects of prolonged worry.

Carey Peter 1943– . Australian novelist. He has combined work in advertising with a writing career since 1962, and his novels include Bliss 1981, Illywhacker (Australian slang for 'con man') 1985, and Oscar and Lucinda 1988, which won the Booker prize.

cargo n. (plural cargoes) goods carried on a ship or aircraft. [Spanish]

cargo cult a Melanesian religious movement, dating from the 19th century. Adherents believe the arrival of cargo is through the agency of a messianic spirit figure, and heralds a new paradise free of white dominance. The movement became especially active during World War II with the apparently miraculous dropping of supplies from aeroplanes.

Carib /'kærɪb/ n. a member of a group of ◊American Indian people of the N coast of South America and the islands of the S West Indies in the Caribbean. Those who moved north to take the islands from the Arawak Indians were reputedly fierce cannibals. In 1796, the English in the West Indies deported most of them to Roatan Island, off Honduras.

Caribbean Community and Common Market (CARICOM) an organization for economic and foreign policy coordination in the Caribbean region, established by the Treaty of Chaguaramas in 1973 with headquarters in Georgetown, Guyana. The leading member is Trinidad and Tobago; other members are Antigua, Barbados, Belize, Dominica, Grenada, Guyana, Jamaica, Montserrat, St Christopher– Nevis, Anguilla, St Lucia, and St Vincent. Following a left-wing Grenadan coup in 1979, a progressive regional subgroup was formed including St Lucia and Dominica.

Caribbean Sea /kærɪ'bi:ən/ part of the Atlantic Ocean between the N coasts of South and Central America and the West Indies, about 2,740 km/1,700 mi long and between 650 km/400 mi–1,500 km/900 mi wide. It is here that the Gulf Stream turns towards Europe.

caribou /'kærɪbu:/ n. (plural the same) a North American reindeer. [French, probably from American Indian]

caricature /'kærɪkətjuə/ n. a grotesque representation, especially of a person by exaggeration of characteristics; a ridiculously poor imitation or version. — v.t. to make or give a caricature of. —**caricaturist** n. [French from Italian caricare = exaggerate]

CARICOM /'kærɪkom/ acronym from ◊Caribbean Community and Common Market.

caries /'keəri:z/ n. (plural the same) decay in bones or teeth. [Latin]

carillon /kə'rɪljən, 'kæ-/ n. a set of bells sounded either from a keyboard or mechanically. [French]

Carina /kə'ri:nə/ n. a constellation of the southern hemisphere, representing a ship's keel. Its brightest star is Canopus; it also contains Eta Carinae, a massive and highly luminous star embedded in a gas cloud. It has varied unpredictably in the past; some astronomers think it is likely to explode as a supernova within 10,000 years.

Carinthia /kə'rɪnθiə/ (German Kärnten) alpine federal province of SE Austria, bordering Italy and Yugoslavia in the S; capital Klagenfurt; area 9,500 sq km/3,667 sq mi; population (1987) 542,000. It was an independent duchy from 976 and a possession of the Habsburg dynasty 1276–1918.

carioca /kæri'əukə/ n. a Brazilian dance resembling the samba; music for this. [Portuguese]

Carissimi /kə'rɪsɪmi/ Giacomo 1605–1674. Italian composer, a pioneer of the oratorio.

Carl XVI Gustaf /ka:l/ 1946– . King of Sweden from 1973. He succeeded his grandfather Gustaf VI, his father having been killed in an air crash in 1947. Under the new Swedish constitution, which became effective on his grandfather's death, the monarchy was stripped of all power at his accession.

Carlist /'ka:lɪst/ n. a supporter of the claims of the Spanish pretender Don Carlos de Bourbon (1788–1855), and his descendants, to the Spanish crown. The Carlist revolt continued, primarily in the Basque provinces, until 1839. In 1977 the Carlist political party was legalized and Carlos Hugo de Bourbon Parma (1930–) renounced his claim as pretender and became reconciled with King Juan Carlos. See also ◊Bourbon. —adj.

Carlos /ka:los/ four kings of Spain. See ◊Charles.

Carlos I 1863–1908. King of Portugal, of the Braganza-Coburg line, from 1889 until he was assassinated in Lisbon with his elder son Luis. He was succeeded by his younger son Manuel.

Carlos Don 1545–1568. Spanish prince. Son of Philip II, he was recognized as heir to the thrones of Castile and Aragon but became mentally unstable and had to be placed under restraint following a plot to assassinate his father. His story was the subject of plays by Schiller, Alfieri, Otway, and others.

Carlow /'ka:ləu/ county in the Republic of Ireland, in the province of Leinster; county town Carlow; area 900 sq km/347 sq mi; population (1986) 41,000. Mostly flat except for mountains in the S, the land is fertile, and well suited to dairy farming.

Carlson /'ka:lsən/ Chester 1906–1968. US scientist who invented ◊xerography. A research worker with Bell Telephone, he lost his job in 1930 during the Depression and set to work on his own to develop an efficient copying machine. By 1938 he had invented the Xerox photocopier.

Carlsson /'ka:lsən/ Ingvar (Gösta) 1934– . Swedish socialist politician, leader of the Social Democratic Party, deputy prime minister 1982–86 and prime minister from 1986.

Carlucci /ka:'lu:tʃi/ Frank (Charles) 1930– . US politician, a pragmatic moderate. A former diplomat and deputy director of the CIA, he was national security adviser 1986–87 and defence secretary 1987–89 under Reagan, supporting Soviet-US arms reduction.

Carlyle /ka:'laɪl/ Thomas 1795–1881. Scottish essayist and social historian. His work included Sartor Resartus 1833–34, describing his loss of Christian belief, French Revolution 1837, Chartism 1839, and Past and Present 1843. He was a friend of J S ◊Mill and Ralph Waldo ◊Emerson.

The true University of these days is a collection of books.

Thomas Carlyle
The Hero as Man of Letters

Carmarthenshire /kəˈmɑːðənʃə/ former county of S Wales, now part of ◊Dyfed. The county town was Carmarthen.

Carmelite /ˈkɑːməlaɪt/ n. a member of the Carmelite order of friars or nuns founded on Mount Carmel in Palestine by Berthold, a crusader from Calabria, about 1155, and spread to Europe in the 13th century. The Carmelites have devoted themselves largely to missionary work and mystical theology. They are known as **White Friars** because of the white overmantle they wear (over a brown habit). —*adj.* of the Carmelite order. [from Latin, from Mount *Carmel*]

Carmichael /ˈkɑːˈmaɪkəl/ Hoagy (Hoagland Howard) 1899–1981. US jazz composer, pianist, singer, and actor. His songs include 'Stardust' 1927, 'Rockin' Chair' 1930, 'Lazy River' 1931, and 'In the Cool, Cool, Cool of the Evening' 1951 (Academy Award).

Carmina Burana /ˈkɑːmɪnə buˈrɑːnə/ a medieval lyric miscellany compiled from the work of wandering 13th-century scholars and including secular (love songs and drinking songs) as well as religious verse. A cantata (1937) by Carl ◊Orff is based on the material.

carminative /ˈkɑːmɪnətɪv/ *adj.* curing flatulence. —*n.* a carminative drug. [from French or Latin *carminare* = heal (by incantation)]

carmine /ˈkɑːmaɪn/ *adj.* of vivid crimson colour. —*n.* **1.** this colour. **2.** a red pigment made from cochineal. [from French or Latin]

carnage /ˈkɑːnɪdʒ/ *n.* great slaughter. [French from Italian from Latin *caro* = flesh]

carnal /ˈkɑːnəl/ *adj.* of the body or flesh, not spiritual; sensual, sexual. —**carnality** /-ˈnælɪtɪ/ *n.*, **carnally** *adv.* [from Latin]

Carnarvon variant of ◊Caernarvon.

carnassial /kɑːˈnæsɪəl/ *n.* a carnassial tooth. —*adj.* **carnassial tooth,** a carnivore's premolar tooth, adapted for cutting. [from French *carnassier* = carnivorous]

carnation /kɑːˈneɪʃən/ *n.* a double-flowered cultivated variety of a plant *Dianthus caryophyllus* of the pink family. The flowers smell like cloves; they are divided into flake, bizarre, and picotees, according to whether the petals exhibit one or more colours on their white ground, have the colour dispersed in strips, or have a coloured border to the petals. [earlier *coronation*]

carnauba *n.* a palm *Copernicia cerifera* native to South America. It produces fine timber and a hard wax, used for polishes and lipsticks.

Carné /kɑːˈneɪ/ Marcel 1906– . French director of the films *Le Jour se lève*/*Daybreak* 1939 and *Les Enfants du paradis*/*Children of Paradise* 1944.

Carnegie /kɑːˈneɪgɪ/ the family name of the earls of Northesk and Southesk and of the Duke of Fife, who is descended from Queen Victoria.

Carnegie Andrew 1835–1919. US industrialist and philanthropist, born in Scotland, who developed the Pittsburgh iron and steel industries, making the USA the world's leading producer. He endowed public libraries, education and various research trusts.

carnelian /kɑːˈniːlɪən/ variant of **cornelian**[2].

carnet /ˈkɑːneɪ/ *n.* the documents of identification etc. that are needed to permit a vehicle to be driven across a frontier or to use a camping site. [French = notebook]

carnival /ˈkɑːnɪvəl/ *n.* **1.** festivities and public merry-making, usually with a procession. **2.** (*US*) a funfair or circus. [from Italian from Latin *carnelevarium* = Shrovetide, from *caro* = meat and *levare* = put away, with reference to the austerities of Lent]

carnivore /ˈkɑːnɪvɔː/ *n.* a carnivorous animal or plant.

carnivorous /kɑːˈnɪvərəs/ *adj.* feeding on flesh or other animal matter; belonging to the Carnivora, a large order of mainly carnivorous mammals (bears, cats, dogs, foxes, seals, etc.). [from Latin *caro* = flesh]

Carnot /ˈkɑːnəʊ/ Lazare Nicolas Marguerite 1753–1823. French general and politician. A member of the National Convention in the French Revolution, he organized the armies of the republic. He was war minister 1800–01 and minister of the interior in 1815 under Napoleon. His work on fortification, *De la défense de places fortes* 1810, became a military textbook. Minister of the interior during the ◊hundred days, he was proscribed at the restoration of the monarchy and retired to Germany.

Carnot Marie François Sadi 1837–1894. French president from 1887, grandson of Lazare Carnot. He successfully countered the Boulangist anti-German movement (see ◊Boulanger) and in 1892 the scandals arising out of French financial activities in Panama. He was assassinated by an Italian anarchist at Lyons.

Carnot (Nicolas Leonard) Sadi 1796–1832. French scientist and military engineer who founded the science of ◊thermodynamics; his pioneering work was *Réflexions sur la puissance motrice du feu*/*On the Motive Power of Fire*.

Carnot cycle the changes in the physical condition of a gas in a reversible heat engine, necessarily in the following order: **a.** isothermal expansion (without change of temperature), **b.** adiabatic expansion (without change of heat content), **c.** isothermal compression, and **d.** adiabatic compression. [from Sadi *Carnot*, who discovered it in 1824].

carnotite *n.* potassium uranium vanadate, $K_2(UO_2)_2(VO_4)_2 \cdot 3H_2O$, a radioactive ore of vanadium and uranium with traces of radium. A yellow powdery mineral, it is mined chiefly in the Colorado Plateau, USA; Radium Hill, Australia; and Shaba, Zaïre.

Caro /ˈkɑːrəʊ/ Anthony 1924– . British sculptor who made bold, large abstracts using ready-made angular metal shapes, often without bases. Works include *Fathom* (outside the Economist Building, London).

carob /ˈkærəb/ *n.* a small Mediterranean tree *Ceratonia siliqua* of the legume family Leguminosae. Its 20 cm/8 in pods are used as animal fodder; they are also the source of a chocolate substitute. [from French, ultimately from Arabic]

carol /ˈkærəl/ *n.* a joyful song, especially a Christmas hymn. —*v.t./i.* **(-ll-)** to sing carols; to sing joyfully. —**caroller** *n.* [from Old French]

Carol two kings of Romania:

Carol I 1839–1914. First king of Romania 1881–1914. A prince of the house of Hohenzollern-Sigmaringen, he was invited to become prince of Romania, then part of the Ottoman Empire, in 1866. In 1877, in alliance with Russia, he declared war on Turkey, and the Congress of Berlin 1878 recognized Romanian independence.

Carol II 1893–1953. King of Romania 1930–40. In 1938 he introduced a new constitution under which he practically became an absolute ruler. He was forced to abdicate by the pro-Nazi ◊Iron Guard in Sept 1940.

Carolina /kærəˈlaɪnə/ two separate states of the USA; see ◊North Carolina and ◊South Carolina.

Caroline of Anspach /ˈkærəlaɪn, ˈænspæx/ 1683–1737. Queen of George II of Great Britain and Ireland. The daughter of the Margrave of Brandenburg-Anspach, she married George, Electoral Prince of Hanover in 1705, and followed him to England in 1714 when his father became King George I. She was the patron of many leading writers and politicians, she supported Sir Robert Walpole and kept him in power, and she acted as regent during her husband's four absences.

Carnot *Founder of the science of thermodynamics, Sadi Carnot.*

Caroline of Brunswick /'brʌnzwɪk/ 1768–1821. Queen of George IV of Great Britain, who unsuccessfully attempted to divorce her on his accession to the throne in 1820.

Carolines /'kærəlaɪmz/ a scattered archipelago in Micronesia, Pacific Ocean, consisting of over 500 coral islets; area 1,200 sq km/463 sq mi. The chief islands are Ponape, Kusai, and Truk in the eastern group, and Yap and Belau in the western group.

Carolingian dynasty /kærə'lɪndʒɪən/ a Frankish dynasty descending from ◊Pepin the Short (died 768) and named after his son Charlemagne; its last ruler was Louis V of France (reigned 966–87), who was followed by Hugh ◊Capet.

carotene n. a naturally occurring pigment of the ◊carotenoid group. Carotenes produce the orange, yellow, and red colours of carrots, tomatoes, oranges, and crustaceans. They are also involved in ◊photosynthesis as adjuncts to ◊chlorophyll. In vertebrates, carotenes are converted to vitamin A and retinal pigments important in vision.

carotenoid n. one of a group of yellow, orange, red, or brown pigments found in many living organisms, particularly in the ◊chloroplasts of plants. There are two main types, the **carotenes** and the **xanthophylls**. Both types are long-chain ◊lipids (fats).

Carothers /kə'rʌðəz/ Wallace 1896–1937. US chemist, who carried out research into polymerization. By 1930 he had discovered that some polymers were fibre forming, and in 1937 he produced ◊nylon.

carotid /kə'rɒtɪd/ adj. of the two main arteries, one on each side of the neck, carrying blood to the head. —n. a carotid artery. [from French from Greek karoō = stupefy, compression of these arteries being thought to cause stupor]

carouse /kə'raʊz/ v.i. to have a noisy or lively drinking party. —n. such a party. —**carousal** n. [from German gar aus = (drunk) right out]

carousel /kæru'sel/ n. 1. (US) a merry-go-round. 2. a rotating conveyor or delivery system. [French from Italian]

carp[1] n. (plural the same) a fish Cyprinus carpio found all over the world. It commonly grows to 50 cm/1.8 ft and 3 kg/7 lb, but may be even larger. It lives in lakes, ponds, and slow rivers. The wild form is drab, but cultivated forms may be golden, or may have few large scales (mirror carp) or be scaleless (leather carp). **Koi** carp are highly prized and can grow up to 1 m/3 ft long with a distinctive pink, red, white or black colouring. [from Old French from Provençal or Latin]

carp[2] v.i. to find fault, to complain pettily. [from Old Norse = brag]

Carpaccio /kɑː'pætʃɪəʊ/ Vittorio 1450/60–1525/26. Italian painter known for scenes of his native Venice. His series The Legend of St Ursula 1490–98 (Accademia, Venice) is full of detail of contemporary Venetian life. His other great series is the lives of saints George and Jerome 1502–07 (S Giorgio degli Schiavoni, Venice).

carpal /'kɑːpəl/ adj. of the wrist bone. [from Greek karpos = wrist]

Carpathian Mountains /kɑː'peɪθɪən/ Central European mountain system, forming a semicircle through Czechoslovakia–Poland–USSR–Romania, 1,450 km/900 mi long. The central **Tatra mountains** on the Czechoslovakia–Poland frontier include the highest peak, Gerlachovka, 2,663 m/8,737 ft.

Carpeaux /kɑː'pəʊ/ Jean-Baptiste 1827–1875. French sculptor whose lively naturalistic subjects include La Danse 1865–69 for the Opéra, Paris.

carpe diem live for the present. [Latin = seize the day]

carpel /'kɑːpəl/ n. any of the segments of a compound pistil of a flower; a simple pistil, in which the seeds develop. [from French from Greek karpos = fruit]

carpenter /'kɑːpɪntə/ n. a craftsman in woodwork, one who makes or repairs wooden structures. —v.t./i. to do or make by carpenter's work. —**carpentry** n. [from Old French from Latin carpentum = wagon]

Carpenter /'kɑːpəntə/ John 1948– . US director of horror and science fiction films. His career began with Dark Star 1974 and Halloween 1978, and continued with such films as The Thing 1982, Christine 1983, Starman 1984, and They Live 1988. He also composes his own film scores.

carpet /'kɑːpɪt/ n. 1. a thick textile covering for floors or stairs. 2. a carpetlike expanse, a thick layer underfoot.

—v.t. 1. to cover with or as with a carpet. 2. (colloquial) to reprimand. —**carpetbag** n. a travelling bag of the kind formerly made of carpetlike material. **carpetbagger** n. a political candidate without local connections; (historical) any of the adventurers from the northern states who went into the southern states after the American Civil War, in order to profit from the postwar reorganization (so called from the carpetbag which held all their possessions). **carpet- sweeper** n. a household device with revolving brushes for sweeping carpets. **on the carpet,** (colloquial) being reprimanded. [from Old French or Latin carpere = pull to pieces]

Carpini /kɑː'piːni/ Johannes de Plano 1182–1252. Franciscan friar and traveller. Sent by Pope Innocent IV on a mission to the Great Khan, he visited Mongolia 1245–47 and wrote a history of the Mongols.

carport n. an open-sided shelter for a car, projecting from the side of a house.

carpus /'kɑːpəs/ n. (plural **carpi** /-paɪ/) the set of small bones connecting the hand and forearm, especially the wrist in humans. [from Greek karpos = wrist]

Carracci /kə'rɑːtʃi/ Italian family of painters in Bologna, whose forte was murals and ceilings. The foremost of them, **Annibale Carracci** (1560–1609), decorated the Farnese Palace, Rome, with a series of mythological paintings united by simulated architectural ornamental surrounds (completed in 1604).

Carradine /'kærədiːn/ John (Richmond Reed) 1906–1988. US film actor who often played sinister roles. He appeared in many major Hollywood films, such as Stagecoach 1939 and The Grapes of Wrath 1940, but was later seen mostly in 'B' horror films, including House of Frankenstein 1944.

carragheen n. a species of deep-reddish, branched seaweed Chondrus crispus. It is found on rocky shores on both sides of the Atlantic, and is exploited commercially in food and medicinal preparations and as cattle feed. [from Carragheen in Ireland]

Carrel /kə'rel/ Alexis 1873–1944. US surgeon born in France, whose experiments paved the way for organ transplantation. Working at the Rockefeller Institute in New York City, he devised a way of joining blood vessels end to end (anastomosing). This was a key move in the development of transplant surgery, as was his work on keeping organs viable outside the body, for which he was awarded the Nobel Prize for Medicine in 1912.

carriage /'kærɪdʒ/ n. 1. a wheeled passenger vehicle, usually horse-drawn. 2. a railway passenger vehicle. 3. the conveying of goods etc.; the cost of this. 4. a moving part carrying or holding something in a machine. 5. a gun carriage. 6. the posture of the body when walking. —**carriage clock,** a small portable clock with a rectangular case and a handle on top.

carriageway n. the part of the road on which vehicles travel.

carrier /'kærɪə/ n. 1. a person or thing that carries something; a person or company conveying goods or passengers for payment. 2. a support or receptacle for carrying something; a carrier bag. 3. a person or animal that transmits a disease without being affected by it. 4. an aircraft carrier. —**carrier bag,** a paper or plastic bag, with handles, for holding shopping etc. **carrier pigeon,** a homing pigeon used to carry messages tied to its leg or neck. **carrier wave,** a high-frequency electromagnetic wave modulated in amplitude or frequency to convey a telecommunications signal.

Carrington /'kærɪŋtən/ Peter Alexander Rupert, 6th Baron Carrington 1919– . British Conservative politician. He was defence secretary 1970–74, and led the opposition in the House of Lords 1964–70 and 1974–79. While foreign secretary in 1979–82, he negotiated independence for Zimbabwe, but resigned after failing to anticipate the Falklands crisis. He was secretary general of NATO 1984–88.

carrion /'kærɪən/ n. dead, putrefying flesh. —**carrion crow,** a black crow Corvus corone that feeds on carrion and small animals. [from Anglo-French from Latin caro = flesh]

Carroll /'kærəl/ Lewis. Pen name of Charles Lutwidge Dodgson 1832–1898. English mathematician and writer of children's books. He wrote the children's classic Alice's Adventures in Wonderland 1865 and its sequel Through the

Looking Glass 1872. He also published mathematics books under his own name.

'If everybody minded their own business,' said the Duchess in a hoarse growl, 'the world would go round a deal faster than it does.'

Lewis Carroll
Alice's Adventures in Wonderland

---

carrot /ˈkærət/ *n.* **1.** an umbelliferous plant *Daucus carota* with a tapering orange-coloured edible root; this root, used as a vegetable. Cultivated since the 16th century, it has a high sugar content and also contains carotene, which is converted by the human liver to vitamin A. **2.** a means of enticement. —**carroty** *adj.* [from French from Latin from Greek *karōton*]

carry /ˈkærɪ/ *v.t./i.* **1.** to hold up or support while moving; to take with one from one place to another. **2.** to support the weight or responsibility of. **3.** to be pregnant with. **4.** to conduct or transmit. **5.** to take (a process etc.) to a specified point. **6.** to involve, to entail or imply. **7.** to transfer (a figure) to a column of higher value. **8.** to hold (the body or oneself) in a specified way. **9.** (of a newspaper or broadcast etc.) to include in its contents; (of a shop) to keep a regular stock of. **10.** (of sound) to be audible at a distance; (of a gun etc.) to propel to a specified distance. **11.** to win or capture; to win over (an audience); to win victory or acceptance for (a proposal etc.). — *n.* an act of carrying; in golf, the flight of a ball before pitching. —**be carried away,** to be uncontrollably excited. **carrycot** *n.* a portable cot for a baby. **carry forward,** to transfer to a new page or account. **carry off,** to take away (especially by force); (of a disease) to cause the death of; to win (a prize); to deal with (a situation) successfully. **carry on,** to continue; to engage in; (*colloquial*) to behave excitedly, to complain lengthily; to flirt or have an affair (*with*). **carry out,** to put (an idea etc.) into practice. **carry over,** to carry forward; to postpone. **carry weight,** to be influential or important. [from Anglo-French]

carrying capacity in ecology, the maximum number of animals of a given species that a particular area can support. When the carrying capacity is exceeded, there is insufficient food (or other resources) for the members of the population. The population may then be reduced by emigration, reproductive failure, or death through starvation.

Carson /ˈkɑːsən/ Christopher 'Kit' 1809–68. US frontiersman, guide, and Indian agent, who later fought for the Federal side in the Civil War. Carson City was named after him.

Carson Edward Henry, Baron Carson 1854–1935. Irish politician and lawyer who played a decisive part in the trial of the writer Oscar Wilde. In the years before World War I he led the movement in Ulster to resist Irish ◊Home Rule by force of arms if need be.

Carson Willie (William) 1942– . British jockey, born in Scotland, who has ridden three Epsom Derby winners as well as the winners of most major races in England and abroad.

cart *n.* a small, strong vehicle with two or four wheels for carrying loads, usually drawn by a horse; a light vehicle for pulling by hand. —*v.t.* **1.** to convey in a cart. **2.** (*slang*) to carry or take laboriously. —**carthorse** *n.* a horse of heavy build, fit for drawing carts. **cartwheel** *n.* a handspring in which the body turns with limbs spread like the spokes of a wheel, balancing on each hand in turn. **cartwright** *n.* a maker of carts. [Old Norse and Old English]

Cartagena /kɑːtəˈdʒiːnə/ (Spanish *Cartagena de los Indes*) port, industrial centre, and capital of the department of Bolívar, NW Colombia; population (1985) 531,000. Plastics and chemicals are produced here.

carte blanche /kɑːt blɑːʃ/ full discretionary power given to a person. [French = blank paper]

cartel /kɑːˈtel/ *n.* an association of firms that remain independent but which enter into agreement to set mutually acceptable prices for their products. A cartel may restrict output or raise prices in order to prevent entrants to the market and increase member profits. [from German from French from Italian, diminutive of *carta* = card]

Carter /ˈkɑːtə/ Angela 1940– . English writer of the ◊magic realist school. Her novels include *The Magic Toyshop* (filmed by David Wheatley in 1987) and *Nights at the Circus* 1984. She co-wrote the script for the film *The Company of Wolves* 1984, based on one of her stories.

Carter Elliott (Cook) 1908– . US composer. His early music shows the influence of ◊Stravinsky, but after 1950 it became increasingly intricate and densely written in a manner resembling ◊Ives. He invented 'metrical modulation' which allows different instruments or groups to stay in touch while playing at different speeds. He has written four string quartets, the *Symphony for Three Orchestras* 1967, and the song cycle *A Mirror on Which to Dwell* 1975.

Carter Jimmy (James Earl) 1924– . 39th president of the USA 1977–81, a Democrat. In 1976 he narrowly wrested the presidency from Gerald Ford. Features of his presidency were the return of the Panama Canal Zone to Panama, the Camp David Agreements for peace in the Middle East, and the Iranian seizure of US embassy hostages. He was defeated by Ronald Reagan in 1980.

Carter Doctrine the assertion in 1980 by President Carter of a vital US interest in the Persian Gulf region (prompted by the Soviet invasion of Afghanistan and instability in Iran): any outside attempt at control would be met by military force if necessary.

Cartesian /kɑːˈtiːzjən/ *adj.* of ◊Descartes (1596–1650). —*n.* a follower of Descartes. —**Cartesian coordinates,** in ◊coordinate geometry, the components of a system used to represent vectors or to denote the position of a point on a plane (two dimensions) or in space (three dimensions) with reference to a set of two or more axes. The Cartesian coordinate system can be extended to any finite number of dimensions (axes), and is used thus in theoretical mathematics. **Cartesian diver,** a toy device that rises and falls in liquid when the cover of a vessel is subjected to varying pressure. [from Latin *Cartesius* = Descartes]

Carthage /ˈkɑːθɪdʒ/ ancient Phoenician port in N Africa; it lay 16 km/10 mi N of Tunis, Tunisia. A leading trading centre, from the 6th century BC it was in conflict with Greece, and then with Rome, and was destroyed by Roman forces in 146 BC at the end of the ◊**Punic Wars**. About 45 BC, Roman colonists settled in Carthage, and it became the wealthy capital of the province of Africa. After its capture by the Vandals in AD 439 it was little more than a pirate stronghold. From 533 it formed part

Carter *thirty-ninth president of the USA, Jimmy Carter.*

caryatid *The Erectheon, Porch of the Caryatids at the Parthenon, Athens, Greece.*

of the Byzantine Empire until its final destruction by Arabs in 698.

Carthusian /kɑːˈθjuːzɪən/ *n.* a member of the Carthusian order of monks or nuns founded by St Bruno in 1084 at Chartreuse, near Grenoble, France. Living chiefly in unbroken silence, they ate one vegetarian meal a day and supported themselves by their own labours; the rule is still one of severe austerity. —*adj.* of the Carthusian order. [from Latin *Cart(h)usia* = Chartreuse]

Cartier /kɑːˈtiˈeɪ/ Georges Étienne 1814–1873. French-Canadian politician. He fought against the British in the rebellion of 1837, was elected to the Canadian parliament in 1848, and was joint prime minister with John A Macdonald 1858–62. He brought Québec into the Canadian federation in 1867.

Cartier Jacques 1491–1557. French navigator who was the first European to sail up the St Lawrence river in 1534. He named the site of Montreal.

Cartier-Bresson /breˈsɒn/ Henri 1908– . French photographer, considered one of the greatest photographic artists. His documentary work was shot in black and white, using a small format camera.

cartilage /ˈkɑːtɪlɪdʒ/ *n.* a flexible bluish-white connective ◊tissue made up of the protein collagen. In cartilaginous fish it forms the skeleton; in other vertebrates it forms the greater part of the the embryonic skeleton, and is replaced by ◊bone in the course of development, except in areas of wear such as bone endings, and the discs between the back-bones. It also forms structural tissue in the larynx, nose, and external ear of mammals. [French from Latin *cartilago*]

cartilaginous /kɑːtɪˈlædʒɪnəs/ *adj.* of or like cartilage; (of fish) having a cartilaginous skeleton.

Cartland /ˈkɑːtlənd/ Barbara 1904– . English romantic novelist. She published her first book *Jigsaw* in 1921 and since then has produced a prolific stream of stories of chastely romantic love, usually in idealized or exotic settings, for a mainly female audience (such as *Love Climbs In* 1978 and *Moments of Love* 1981).

cartography /kɑːˈtɒgrəfɪ/ *n.* map drawing. —**cartographer** *n.*, **cartographic** /-ˈgræfɪk/ *adj.* [from French *carte* = map]

cartomancy *n.* the practice of telling fortunes by cards, often ◊tarot cards.

carton /ˈkɑːtən/ *n.* a light box or container made of cardboard or plastic. [French]

cartoon /kɑːˈtuːn/ *n.* 1. a humorous drawing in a newspaper etc., especially as a topical comment; a sequence of such drawings telling a comic or serial story; an animated cartoon on film. 2. an artist's full-size drawing as a sketch for a work of art. —*v.t.* to draw a cartoon of. —**cartoonist** *n.* [from Italian *carta* = card]

cartouche /kɑːˈtuːʃ/ *n.* 1. a scroll-like ornamentation in architecture etc. 2. an oval emblem containing hieroglyphics that give the birth name and coronation name of an ancient Egyptian king. [French = cartridge]

cartridge /ˈkɑːtrɪdʒ/ *n.* 1. a case containing a charge of propellant explosive for firearms or blasting, with bullet or shot if for small arms. 2. a sealed container holding film, magnetic tape, etc., ready for insertion as a unit. 3. a

component on the pick-up head of a record player, carrying the stylus. —**cartridge paper,** thick, strong paper for drawing etc.

Cartwright /ˈkɑːtraɪt/ Edmund 1743–1823. English inventor. He patented the power loom in 1785, built a weaving mill in 1787, and patented a wool-combing machine in 1789.

Caruso /kəˈruːsəʊ/ Enrico 1873–1921. Italian operatic tenor. In 1902 he starred, with Nellie Melba, in Puccini's *La Bohème.* He was one of the first opera singers to profit from gramophone recordings

carve *v.t./i.* 1. to produce or shape by cutting; to cut designs etc. in (hard material). 2. to cut (meat) into slices for serving. 3. to make (a career etc.) by effort. —**carve up,** to divide into parts or shares. [Old English]

carvel-built /ˈkɑːvəlˈbɪlt/ *adj.* (of a boat) made with planks joined smoothly and not overlapping. [from French, ultimately from Greek *karabos* = light ship]

carver /ˈkɑːvə/ *n.* 1. one who carves. 2. a knife or (in *plural*) knife and fork for carving meat. 3. a chair with arms that forms one of a set of dining-room chairs.

Carver George Washington 1864–1943. US agricultural chemist. Born a slave in Missouri, he was kidnapped and raised by his former owner, Moses Carver. He devoted his life to improving the economy of the US South and the condition of blacks.

Carver Raymond 1939–1988. US short-story writer and poet, author of vivid tales of contemporary US life, a collection of which were published in *Cathedral* 1983; *Fires* 1985 includes his essays and poems.

carving *n.* a carved object or design.

Cary /ˈkeərɪ/ (Arthur) Joyce (Lunel) 1888–1957. English novelist. He used his experiences gained in Nigeria in the Colonial Service (which he entered in 1918) as a backdrop to such novels as *Mister Johnson* 1939. Other books include *The Horse's Mouth* 1944.

caryatid /kærɪˈætɪd/ *n.* a sculptured female figure used as a supporting pillar in a building; a male figure is a *telamon* or *atlas.* [from French, ultimately from Greek = priestess of Caryae in Greece]

caryopsis *n.* a dry, one-seeded ◊fruit in which the wall of the seed becomes fused to the carpel wall during its development. It is a type of ◊achene, and therefore develops from one ovary and does not split open to release the seed. Caryopses are typical of members of the grass family (Gramineae), including the cereals.

Casablanca /kæsəˈblæŋkə/ (Arabic *Dar el-Beida*) port, commercial and industrial centre on the Atlantic coast of Morocco; population (1981) 2,409,000. It trades in fish, phosphates, and manganese. The Great Hassan II Mosque, completed in 1989, is the world's largest; it is built on a platform (40,000 sq m/430,000 sq ft) jutting out over the Atlantic, with walls 60 m/200 ft high, topped by a hydraulic sliding roof, and a minaret 175 m/574 ft high.

Casablanca Conference the World War II meeting of the US and UK leaders Roosevelt and Churchill, 14–24 Jan 1943, at which the Allied demand for the unconditional surrender of Germany, Italy, and Japan was issued.

Casals /kəˈsɑːlz/ Pablo 1876–1973. Catalan cellist, composer, and conductor. As a cellist, he was celebrated for his interpretations of J S Bach's unaccompanied suites. He wrote instrumental and choral works, including the Christmas oratorio *The Manger.*

Casanova de Seingalt /kæsəˈnəʊvə də sæŋˈgælt/ Giovanni Jacopo 1725–1798. Italian adventurer, spy, violinist, librarian, and, according to his *Memoirs,* one of the world's great lovers. From 1774 he was a spy in the Venetian police service. In 1785 he was appointed librarian to Count Waldstein at his castle of Dúx in Bohemia. Here Casanova wrote his *Memoirs* (published 1826–38, although the complete text did not appear until 1960–61). His name is used to signify a man notorious for many love affairs.

cascade /kæsˈkeɪd/ *n.* a small waterfall, especially one in a series; something arranged like this. —*v.i.* to fall in or like a cascade. [French, ultimately from Latin *casus* = case]

Cascais /kəʃˈkaɪʃ/ fishing port and resort town on the Costa do Sol, 25 km/16 mi W of Lisbon, Portugal.

cascara /kæsˈkɑːrə/ *n.* the bark of a North American buckthorn, used as a laxative. [Spanish = sacred bark]

case[1] *n.* 1. an instance of a thing's occurring; an actual or hypothetical situation. 2. a condition of disease or injury, a

person suffering from this. **3.** an instance or condition of one receiving professional guidance, especially by a doctor. **4.** a matter under investigation e. g. by police. **5.** a lawsuit; the sum of arguments on one side in this; a set of facts or arguments supporting something. **6.** in grammar, the relation of a word to others in a sentence; the form of a noun, adjective, or pronoun expressing this. —**case law** law as established by cases decided. **in any case,** whatever the facts are. **in case,** lest something should happen; in the event of. [from Old French from Latin *casus* (*cadere* = fall)]
case[2] *n.* **1.** a container or protective covering; this with its contents. **2.** a suitcase or other item of luggage. **3.** in printing, a partitioned receptacle for type. —*v.t.* to enclose in a case. —**case-harden** *v.t.* to harden the surface of (metal, especially iron by carbonizing); to make unfeeling or unsympathetic. **lower case,** noncapital letters in printing type. **upper case,** capital letters in printing type. [from Old French from Latin *capsa* = box (*capere* = hold)]
case grammar a theory of language structure that proposes that the underlying structure of language should contain some sort of functional information about the roles of its components; thus in the sentence 'The girl opened the door', the phrase *the girl* would have the role of agent, not merely that of grammatical subject.
casein *n.* the main protein of milk, from which it can be separated by the action of acid, the enzyme rennin, or bacteria (souring); it is also the main component of cheese. Casein is used commercially in cosmetics, glues, and as a sizing for coating paper.
casemate /ˈkeɪsmeɪt/ *n.* **1.** a room built inside the thick wall of a fortification. **2.** an armoured enclosure for guns on a warship. [French and Italian, perhaps from Greek *khasma* = gap]
casement /ˈkeɪsmənt/ *n.* a window hinged to open at the side; (*poetical*) a window. [from Latin *cassimentum*]
Casement Roger David 1864–1916. Irish nationalist. While in the British consular service, he exposed the ruthless exploitation of the people of the Belgian Congo and Peru, for which he was knighted in 1911 (degraded in 1916). He was hanged for treason by the British for his part in the Irish republican Easter Rising.
cash *n.* money in coin or notes; immediate payment at the time of purchase; (*colloquial*) wealth. —*v.t.* to give or obtain cash for. —**cash and carry,** a system of (especially wholesale) trading in which the buyer pays for goods in cash and takes them away himself. **cash flow,** movement of money out of and into a business, affecting its ability to make payments. **cash in (on),** to profit (from); to use to one's advantage. **cash on delivery,** a system of paying for goods when they are delivered. **cash register,** a machine in a shop etc. with mechanism for recording the amount of each sale. [from French]
Cash /kæʃ/ Johnny 1932– . US country singer, songwriter, and guitarist. His early hits, recorded for Sun Records in Memphis, Tennessee, include the million-selling 'I Walk the Line' 1956. Many of his songs have become classics. He is also known as 'The Man in Black' because of his penchant for dressing entirely in black clothes.
Cash Pat 1965– . Australian tennis player. He won the 1986 Davis Cup for Australia and won Wimbledon in 1987.
cash crop a crop grown solely for sale rather than for the farmer's own use, for example, coffee, cotton, or sugar beet. Many Third World countries grow cash crops to meet their debt repayments rather than grow food for their people. The price for these crops depends on financial interests, such as those of the multinational companies and the International Monetary Fund. In Britain, the most widespread cash crop is the potato.
cashew /ˈkæʃuː/ *n.* an edible, kidney-shaped nut; the tropical tree *Anacardium occidentale* producing this. [from Portuguese from Tupi]
cashier[1] /kæˈʃɪə/ *n.* ra person in charge of cash transactions in a bank or shop etc. [from Dutch or French]
cashier[2] /kæˈʃɪə/ *v.t.* to dismiss from service, especially with disgrace. [from Flemish from French from Latin *cassare* = quash]
cashmere /kæʃˈmɪə/ *n.* a very fine, soft wool, especially that of the Kashmir goat; fabric made from this. [from *Kashmir* in Asia]
casing /ˈkeɪsɪŋ/ *n.* a protective covering.

casino /kəˈsiːnəʊ/ *n.* (*plural* **casinos**) a public room or building for gambling and other amusements. [Italian, diminutive of *casa* = house from Latin *casa* = cottage]
cask /kɑːsk/ *n.* a barrel, especially one for alcoholic liquor; its contents. [from French or Spanish *casco* = helmet]
casket /ˈkɑːskɪt/ *n.* **1.** a small, usually ornamental, box for holding valuables etc. **2.** (*US*) a coffin. [perhaps from Anglo-French, ultimately from Latin *capsa*]
Caslavska /ˈtʃɑːslæfskə/ Vera 1943–. Czechoslovak gymnast, the first of the great present-day stylists. She won a record 21 world, Olympic and European gold medals 1959–68; she also won eight silver and three bronze medals.
Caspian Sea /ˈkæspɪən/ the world's largest inland sea, divided between Iran and the USSR. It covers an area of about 400,000 sq km/155,000 sq mi, with a maximum depth of 1,000 m/3,250 ft. The chief ports are Astrakhan and Baku. It is now approximately 28 m/90 ft below sea level due to drainage in the N, and the damming of the Volga and Ural rivers for hydroelectric power.
Cassandra /kəˈsændrə/ in Greek mythology, the daughter of ◊Priam, king of Troy. Her prophecies (for example, of the fall of Troy) were never believed, because she had rejected the love of Apollo. She was murdered with Agamemnon by his wife Clytemnestra.
cassata /kəˈsɑːtə/ *n.* an ice-cream cake containing fruit and nuts. [Italian]
Cassatt /kəˈsæt/ Mary 1845–1926. US Impressionist painter and printmaker. In 1868 she settled in Paris. Her popular, colourful pictures of mothers and children show the influence of Japanese prints, for example *The Bath* 1892 (Art Institute, Chicago).
cassava /kəˈsɑːvə/ *n.* or **manioc** a plant *Manihot utilissima*, belonging to the spurge family Euphorbiaceae. Native to South America, it is now widely grown throughout the tropics for its starch-containing roots, from which tapioca and bread are made. [from American Indian *casavi*]
Cassavetes /kæsəˈveɪtiːz/ John 1929–1989. US film director and actor, who directed experimental, apparently improvised films, including *Shadows* 1960, and *The Killing of a Chinese Bookie* 1980. His acting appearances included *The Dirty Dozen* 1967, and *Rosemary's Baby* 1968.
casserole /ˈkæsərəʊl/ *n.* a covered dish in which meat etc. is cooked and served; food cooked in this. —*v.t.* to cook in a casserole. [French, ultimately from Greek *kuathion* = little cup]
cassette /kəˈset/ *n.* a small, sealed case containing a reel of film or magnetic tape. [French, diminutive of *casse*]
cassia /ˈkæsɪə/ *n.* the bark of a SE Asian plant *Cinnamomum cassia*, of the laurel family Lauraceae. It is aromatic and closely resembles true cinnamon, for which it is a widely used substitute. *Cassia* is also a genus of pod-bearing tropical plants of the family Caesalpiniaceae, many of which have strong purgative properties; *Cassia senna* is the source of the laxative drug senna. [from Latin from Greek from Hebrew]
Cassini /kæˈsiːni/ Giovanni Domenico 1625–1712. Italian-French astronomer, who discovered four of the moons of Saturn and the gap in the rings of Saturn now called the **Cassini division.**
Cassiopeia /kæsɪəˈpeɪə/ *n.* a prominent constellation of the northern hemisphere, representing the mother of Andromeda. It has a distinctive W-shape, and contains one of the most powerful radio sources in the sky, Cassiopeia A, the remains of a ◊supernova (star explosion), as well as open and globular clusters.
cassiterite *n.* or **tinstone** the chief ore of tin, consisting of reddish-brown to black stannic oxide, SnO_2, usually found in granite rocks. When fresh it has a bright ('adamantine') lustre. It was formerly mined extensively in Cornwall, England; today Malaysia is the world's major supplier. Other sources of cassiterite are in Africa, Indonesia, and South America.
Cassius /ˈkæsɪəs/ Gaius died 42 BC. Roman soldier, one of the conspirators who killed Julius ◊Caesar in 44. He fought at Carrhae in 53, and with the republicans against Caesar at Pharsalus in 48, was pardoned and appointed praetor, but became a leader in the conspiracy of 44, and after Caesar's death joined Brutus. He committed suicide after his defeat at ◊Philippi in 42 BC.

Cassivelaunus /kæsɪvəˈlaʊnəs/ chieftain of the British tribe, the Catuvellauni, who led the British resistance to the Romans under Caesar in 54 BC.

cassock /ˈkæsək/ n. a long, usually black or red garment worn by certain clergy and members of a church choir. [from French from Italian *cassaca* = horseman's coat]

Casson /ˈkæsən/ Hugh 1910–. English architect, professor at the Royal College of Art 1953–75, and president of the Royal Academy 1976–84. His books include *Victorian Architecture* 1948. He was director of architecture for the Festival of Britain 1948–51.

The British love permanence more than they love beauty.

Hugh Casson
The Observer 1964

---

cassowary /ˈkæsəweərɪ/ n. a large flightless bird, genus *Casuarius*, found in New Guinea and N Australia, usually in forests. Cassowaries are related to emus, but have a bare head with a horny casque, or helmet, on top, and brightly coloured skin on the neck. The loose plumage is black and the wings are tiny, but cassowaries can run and leap well, defending themselves by kicking. They stand up to 1.5 m/5 ft tall. [from Malay]

cast /kɑːst/ v.t./i. (past and past participle cast) 1. to throw, to emit; to shed. 2. to send, direct, or cause to fall (on, over, etc.). 3. to record or register (a vote). 4. to shape (molten metal or plastic material) in a mould; to make (a product) thus. 5. to assign (an actor) as a character; to allocate roles in (a play or film etc.). 6. to utter (aspersions on). 7. to reckon or add up (figures); to calculate (a horoscope). —n. 1. the throwing of a missile, dice, fishing line or net, etc. 2. an object of metal, clay, etc., made in a mould; a moulded mass of solidified material, especially plaster protecting a broken limb. 3. a set of actors taking parts in a play or film etc. 4. the form, type, or quality (of features, the mind, etc.). 5. a tinge of colour. 6. a slight squint. —cast about for, to try to find or think of. cast down, to depress, to deject. casting vote, the deciding vote when votes on two sides are equal. cast off, to discard; to release a ship from its moorings; in knitting, to loop stitches off a needle to form an edge. castoff n. an abandoned thing; a garment that the owner will not wear again. cast on, in knitting, to make the first row of loops on a needle. [from Old Norse]

Castagno /kæˈstænjəʊ/ Andrea del c.1421–1457. Italian Renaissance painter, active in Florence. In his frescoes in Sta Apollonia, Florence, he adapted the pictorial space to the architectural framework and followed ◊Masaccio's lead in perspective.

castanet /kæstəˈnet/ n. (usually in *plural*) a small, concave piece of hardwood, ivory, etc., struck against another by the fingers as a rhythmic accompaniment, especially to a Spanish dance. [from Spanish from Latin *castanea* = chestnut]

castaway /ˈkɑːstəweɪ/ n. a shipwrecked person. —adj. 1. discarded. 2. shipwrecked.

caste /kɑːst/ n. 1. one of the four main groups into which Hindu society has been divided from ancient times and from which over 3,000 subsequent divisions derive: **Brahmans** (priests), **Kshatriyas** (nobles and warriors), **Vaisyas** (traders and farmers), and **Sudras** (servants). There is also a fifth group, **Harijan** (untouchables). No upward or downward mobility exists, as in classed societies. 2. a more or less exclusive social class or system of classes. —casteism /-tɪzəm/ n. [from Spanish and Portuguese *casta* = lineage, feminine of *casto* = pure]

castellated /ˈkæstəleɪtɪd/ adj. built with battlements; castlelike. —castellation /-ˈleɪʃən/ n. [from Latin]

Castelo Branco /kəʃˈtelu ˈbræŋku/ Camilo 1825–1890. Portuguese novelist. His work fluctuates between mysticism and bohemianism, and includes *Amor de perdição/Love of Perdition* 1862, written during his imprisonment for adultery.

caster variant of **castor**.

castigate /ˈkæstɪgeɪt/ v.t. to rebuke or punish severely. —castigation /-ˈgeɪʃən/ n., castigator n. [from Latin *castigare* = reprove]

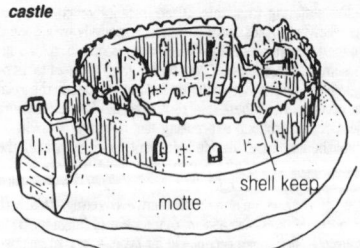

castle

shell keep
motte

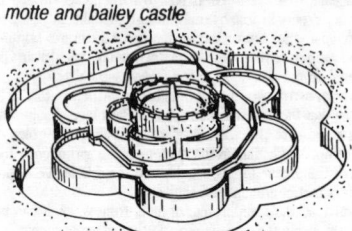

motte and bailey castle

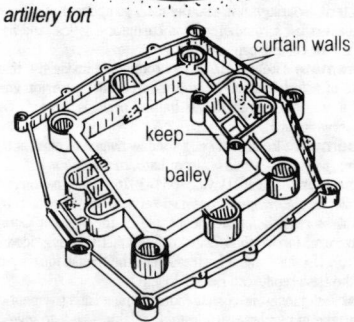

artillery fort

curtain walls
keep
bailey

concentric castle

Castiglione /kæstiːliˈəʊni/ Baldassare, Count Castiglione 1478–1529. Italian author and diplomat who described the perfect Renaissance gentleman in *Il Cortegiano/The Courtier* 1528.

Castile /kæsˈtiːl/ kingdom founded in the 10th century, occupying the central plateau of Spain. Its union with ◊Aragon in 1479, based on the marriage of ◊Ferdinand and Isabella, effected the foundation of the Spanish state, which at the time was occupied and ruled by the ◊Moors. Castile comprised the two great basins separated by the Sierra de Gredos and the Sierra de Guadarrama, known traditionally as Old and New Castile. The area now forms the regions of ◊Castilla-León and ◊Castilla-La Mancha.

Castilian language /kæsˈtɪliən/ a member of the Romance branch of the Indo-European language family originating in NW Spain, in the provinces of Old and New Castile. It is the basis of present-day standard Spanish (see ◊Spanish language) and is often seen as the same language, the terms *castellano* and *español* being used interchangeably in both Spain and the Spanish-speaking countries of the Americas.

Castilla /kæˈstiːljə/ Ramón 1797–1867. President of Peru 1841–51 and 1855–62. He dominated Peruvian politics for over two decades, bringing political stability. Income from guano exports was used to reduce the national debt and improve transport and educational facilities. He abolished black slavery and the head tax on Indians.

Castilla-La Mancha /kæˈstiːljə lɑː ˈmæntʃə/ autonomous region of central Spain, covering an area of 79,200 sq km/30,571 sq mi; population (1986) 1,665,000. It includes the provinces of Albacete, Ciudad Real, Cuenca, Guadalajara, and Toledo. Irrigated land produces grain and chickpeas, and merino sheep graze here.

Castilla-León /leɪˈɒn/ autonomous region of central Spain, covering an area of 94,100 sq km/36,323 sq mi; population (1986) 2,600,000. It includes the provinces of Ávila, Burgos, León, Palencia, Salamanca, Segovia, Soria, Valladolid, and Zamora. Irrigated land produces wheat and rye. Cattle, sheep, and fighting bulls are bred in the uplands.

cast iron a cheap but invaluable constructional material, most commonly used for car engine blocks. Cast iron is partly refined pig (crude) ◊iron, which is very fluid when molten and highly suitable for shaping by casting, as it contains too many impurities, such as carbon, to be readily shaped in any other way. Solid cast iron is heavy and can absorb great shock but is very brittle. **—cast-iron** *adj.* made of cast iron; very strong, unchallengeable.

castle /'kɑ:səl/ *n.* 1. a large fortified building or group of buildings. 2. in chess, a rook. **—***v.t./i.* in chess, to move (the king) two squares towards a rook and the rook to the square which the king has crossed; (of the king or player) to make such a move. **—castles in the air,** a visionary unattainable scheme, a daydream. [from Anglo-French from Latin, diminutive of *castrum* = fort]

Castle /'kɑ:səl/ Barbara, Baroness Castle (born Betts) 1911– . English Labour politician, a cabinet minister in the Labour governments of the 1960s and 1970s. She led the Labour group in the European Parliament 1979–89.

Castlemaine /'kɑ:səlmeɪn/ Lady (born Barbara Villiers) 1641–1709. Mistress of Charles II of England 1660–70 and mother of his son, the Duke of Grafton (1663–1690).

Castlemaine town in Victoria, Australia, about 105 km/65 mi NW of Melbourne, on the river Loddon. Site of the earliest gold strikes in 1851, its population rose to 30,000 at that period. It survives as an agricultural marketing centre.

Castlereagh /'kɑ:səlreɪ/ Robert Stewart, Viscount Castlereagh 1769–1822. Anglo-Irish Tory politician. As chief secretary for Ireland 1797–1801, he suppressed the rebellion of 1798 and helped the younger Pitt secure the union of England, Scotland, and Ireland in 1801. As foreign secretary 1812–22 he coordinated European opposition to Napoleon and represented Britain at the Congress of Vienna 1814–15.

castor /'kɑ:stə/ *n.* 1. a small swivelled wheel (often one of a set) fixed to the leg or underside of a piece of furniture so that this can be moved easily. 2. a small container for sugar or salt, with a perforated top for sprinkling the contents. **—castor sugar,** finely granulated white sugar.

Castor /'kɑ:stə/ *n.* or **Alpha Geminorum** the second brightest star in the constellation Gemini and the 23rd brightest star in the sky. Along with ◊Pollux, it forms a prominent pair at the eastern end of Gemini.

Castor and Pollux/Polydeuces /pɒlʌks, pɒli'dju:si:z/ in Greek mythology, the twin sons of Leda (by ◊Zeus), brothers of ◊Helen and ◊Clytemnestra. Protectors of mariners, they were transformed at death into the constellation Gemini.

castor-oil plant a tall, tropical and subtropical shrub *Ricinus communis* of the spurge family Euphorbiaceae. The seeds (*North American* **castor beans**) yield the purgative castor oil and also ricin, one of the most powerful poisons known, which can be targeted to destroy cancer cells, while leaving normal cells untouched.

castrate /kæ'streɪt/ *v.t.* 1. to remove the testicles of, to geld. 2. to deprive of vigour. **—castration** *n.* removal of the testicles. Male domestic animals may be castrated to prevent reproduction, make them larger or more docile, or remove a disease site. The effects of castration can also be achieved by chemical means, by administration of hormones, in humans and animals. [from Latin *castrare*]

castrato /kæ'strɑ:təʊ/ *n.* (*plural* **castrati** /-ti:/) (*historical*) a male singer castrated in boyhood to preserve a soprano or alto voice. [Italian]

Castries /kæ'stri:z/ port and capital of St Lucia, on the NW coast of the island in the Caribbean; population (1988) 53,000. It produces textiles, chemicals, tobacco, and wood and rubber products.

Castro /'kæstrəʊ/ Cipriano 1858–1924. Venezuelan dictator 1899–1908, known as 'the Lion of the Andes'. When he refused to pay off foreign debts in 1902, British, German, and Italian ships blockaded the country. He presided over a corrupt government. There were frequent rebellions during his rule, and opponents of his regime were exiled or murdered.

Castro (Ruz) /'ru:s/ Fidel 1927– . Cuban Communist politician, prime minister 1959–76 and president from 1976. He led two unsuccessful coups against the right-wing Batista regime and led the revolution that overthrew the dictator in 1959. From 1979 he was also president of the non-aligned movement, although promoting the line of the USSR, which subsidized his regime. The Castro regime introduced a centrally planned economy based on the production for export of sugar, tobacco, and nickel. By nationalizing US-owned businesses in 1960, Castro gained the enmity of the USA, which came to a head in the ◊Cuban missile crisis of 1962. His regime became socialist and he espoused Marxism-Leninism until, in 1974, he rejected Marx's formula 'from each according to his ability and to each according to his need' and decreed that each Cuban should 'receive according to his work'.

casual /'kæzjʊəl/ *adj.* 1. happening by chance. 2. unconcerned, made or done without great care or thought. 3. not regular or permanent. 4. (of clothes) informal. **—** *n.* 1. a casual worker. 2. (usually in *plural*) casual clothes or shoes. **—casually** *adv.,* **casualness** *n.* [from Old French and Latin]

casualty /'kæzjʊəltɪ/ *n.* 1. a person killed or injured in war or in an accident; a thing lost or destroyed in some occurrence. 2. an accident or mishap. [from Latin]

casuarina /kæzjʊə'ri:nə/ *n.* a tree or shrub of the genus *Casuarina*, family Casuarinaceae, which includes many species native to Australia and New Guinea but is also found in Africa and Asia. [from *cassowary*, from fancied resemblance to its feathers]

casuistry /'kæzjuːɪstrɪ/ *n.* clever but often false reasoning, especially about moral issues. **—casuist** *n.,* **casuistic** /-'ɪstɪk/ *adj.* [from French from Spanish from Latin]

casus belli a justification for war, grounds for a dispute. [Latin]

cat *n.* 1. a small, furry, domesticated, carnivorous quadruped, *Felis catus*; a member of the genus *Felis* (e. g. lion, tiger, leopard (*the big/great cats*); a catlike animal of other species. 2. (*colloquial*) a malicious or spiteful woman. 3. the cat-o'-nine-tails. **—cat-and-dog life,** one full of quarrels. **cat-and-mouse game,** the practice of taking slight action repeatedly against a weaker party. **cat burglar,** one who enters by climbing a wall or drainpipe etc. to an upper storey. **cat-o'-nine-tails** *n.* a whip with nine knotted lashes. **cat's cradle,** a child's game with string forming looped patterns between the fingers. **Catseye** *n.* trade name of any of a line of reflector studs marking the centre or edge of a road (patented in 1934). **cat's-paw** *n.* a person used as a tool by another (from the fable of the monkey who used the paw of his friend the cat to rake roasted chestnuts out of the fire). [Old English from Latin *cattus*]

cata- /kætə-/ prefix (usually **cat-** before a vowel or h) meaning 1. down (e. g. *cataract*). 2. wrongly (e. g. *catachresis*). [from Greek *kata* = down]

catabolism /kə'tæbəlɪzəm/ *n.* in biology, the destructive part of ◊metabolism where living tissue is changed into energy and waste products. It is the opposite of anabolism. It occurs continuously in the body, but is accelerated during many disease processes, such as fever, and in starvation. **—catabolic** /kætə'bɒlɪk/ *adj.* [from Greek *bolē* = throwing]

catachresis /kætə'kri:sɪs/ *n.* incorrect use of words. **—catachrestic** *adj.* [Latin from Greek *khrēsis* from *khraomai* = use]

cataclysm /'kætəklɪzəm/ *n.* a violent upheaval or disaster; a sudden great change caused by this. [from French from Greek *klusmos* = flood]

cataclysmic /kætə'klɪzmɪk/ *adj.* of or involving a cataclysm. **—cataclysmic variable,** a class of variable star which includes dwarf novae, classical novae, and others exhibiting single or repeated outbursts.

catacomb /'kætəku:m/ *n.* a subterranean place for burial of the dead, consisting of galleries of passages with recesses excavated in their sides for tombs. [from French from Latin *catacumbas*]

catafalque /'kætəfælk/ *n.* a decorated platform for supporting the coffin of a distinguished person during a funeral or lying-in-state. [French from Italian]

Catalan language /'kætələn, -lən/ a member of the Romance branch of the Indo-European language family, an Iberian language closely related to Provençal in France. It is spoken in Catalonia in NE Spain, the Balearic Isles, Andorra, and a corner of SW France.

Catalaunian Fields /kætə'lɔːniən/ plain near Troyes, France, scene of the defeat of Attila the Hun by the Romans and Goths under the Roman general Aëtius (died 454) in 451.

catalepsy /'kætəlepsɪ/ n. a trance or seizure with unconsciousness and rigidity of the body. —**cataleptic** /-'leptɪk/ adj. & n. [from French or Latin from Greek lēpsis = seizure]

Catal Hüyük /tʃæ'tɑːlhuː'juːk/ a Neolithic site (6000 BC) in Turkey-in-Asia, SE of Konya. It was a fortified city and had temples with wall paintings and objects such as jewellery and mirrors. Finds at Jericho and Catal Hüyük together indicated much earlier development of urban life in the ancient world than was previously imagined.

catalogue /'kætəlɒg/ n. a list of items, usually in systematic order and often with a description of each. —v.t. to make a catalogue of; to enter in a catalogue. —**cataloguer** n. [French from Latin from Greek legō = choose]

Catalonia /kætə'ləʊnɪə/ (Spanish **Cataluña**) autonomous region of NE Spain, covering an area of 31,900 sq km/12,313 sq mi; population (1986) 5,977,000. It includes Barcelona (the capital), Gerona, Lérida, and Tarragona. Industries include wool and cotton textiles; hydroelectric power is produced.

catalpa n. any of a genus Catalpa of trees belonging to the trumpet creeper Bignoniaceae family, found in North America, China, and the West Indies. The northern catalpa C. speciosa of North America grows to 30 m/100 ft and has heart-shaped, deciduous leaves and tubular white flowers with purple borders.

catalyse /'kætəlaɪz/ v.t. to accelerate or produce by catalysis.

catalysis /kə'tælɪsɪs/ n. (plural catalyses /-siːz/) the action of a catalyst. [from Greek = dissolution (luō = set free)]

catalyst /'kætəlɪst/ n. a substance that aids or accelerates a chemical reaction without itself undergoing change; a person or thing that precipitates a change.

catalytic /kætə'lɪtɪk/ adj. of or using a catalyst; of catalysis. —**catalytic converter**, a device with a catalyst for converting pollutant gases, for example toxic emissions from the internal-combustion engine, into harmless products. **catalytic cracker**, a device in which catalytic cracking is carried out. **catalytic cracking**, the cracking of petroleum oils by a process using a catalyst.

catamaran /kætəmə'ræn/ n. 1. a boat with twin hulls side by side. 2. a raft of yoked logs or boats. [from Tamil = tied wood]

catamite /'kætəmaɪt/ n. the passive partner (especially a boy) in homosexual practices. [from Latin from Greek]

Cat and Mouse Act the popular name for the **Prisoners, Temporary Discharge for Health, Act** 1913; an attempt by the UK Liberal government under Herbert Asquith to reduce embarrassment caused by the incarceration of ◊suffragettes accused of violent offences against property. The government was accused of playing cat to suffragette mice by its adoption of powers of release and rearrest.

Catania /kə'tɑːnɪə/ industrial port in Sicily; population (1988) 372,000. It exports local sulphur.

catapult /'kætəpʌlt/ n. 1. a forked stick etc. with elastic for shooting small stones. 2. an ancient type of military machine for hurling large stones etc. 3. a mechanical device for launching a glider, an aircraft from a ship's deck, etc. —v.t./i. 1. to launch with or hurl from a catapult. 2. to fling forcibly. 3. to leap or be hurled forcibly. [from French or Latin from Greek pellō = hurl]

cataract /'kætərækt/ n. 1. a large waterfall; a rush of water. 2. a condition in which the lens of the eye becomes progressively opaque. [from Latin from Greek = down-rushing; sense 2 probably from obsolete sense = portcullis]

catarrh /kə'tɑː/ n. inflammation of mucous membrane; a watery discharge in the nose or throat due to this. —**catarrhal** adj. [from French from Latin from Greek rheō = flow]

catastrophe /kə'tæstrəfɪ/ n. a great and usually sudden disaster; a disastrous end. **catastrophic** /kætə'strɒfɪk/ adj., **catastrophically** adv. [from Latin from Greek strephō = turn]

catastrophe theory a mathematical theory developed by René Thom in 1972, in which he showed that the growth of an organism proceeds by a series of gradual changes that are triggered by, and in turn trigger, large-scale changes or 'catastrophic' jumps. It also has applications in engineering (for example, the gradual strain on the structure of a bridge that can eventually result in a sudden collapse) and has been extended to economic and psychological events.

catastrophism n. the theory that the geological features of the Earth were formed by a series of sudden, violent 'catastrophes' beyond the ordinary workings of nature. The theory was largely the work of Georges ◊Cuvier. It was later replaced by the concepts of ◊uniformitarianism and ◊evolution.

catatonia /kætə'təʊnɪə/ n. schizophrenia with intervals of catalepsy and occasionally violence; catalepsy. —**catatonic** /-'tɒnɪk/ adj. & n. [from Greek tonos = tension]

catcall n. a shrill whistle of disapproval. —v.i. to make a catcall.

catch v.t./i. (past and past participle **caught** /kɔːt/) 1. to capture in a trap, in the hand(s) etc., or after a chase; to lay hold of; to catch out (a batsman). 2. to be in time for and board (a train etc.). 3. to detect or surprise; to trap into a mistake or contradiction etc. 4. to get or contract by infection, contagion, or example. 5. to grasp with the senses or mind; to perceive and reproduce (a likeness etc.). 6. to become or cause to become fixed or entangled; to check suddenly. 7. to draw the attention of, to captivate. 8. to begin to burn. —n. 1. the act of catching. 2. something caught or worth catching. 3. a concealed difficulty or disadvantage; a question etc. involving this for a victim. 4. a device for fastening something. 5. in music, a round, especially with words arranged to produce a humorous effect. —**catch-all** n. a thing for including many items. **catch-as-catch-can** n. wrestling in which few or no holds are barred. **catch crop**, a crop that grows quickly and is harvested while the main crop is growing. **catch hold of**, to grasp, to seize in the hand(s). **catch it**, (colloquial) to be scolded or punished. **catch on**, (colloquial) to become popular; to understand what is meant. **catch out**, to detect in a mistake; to get (a batsman) out by catching the ball direct from his bat. **catch phrase**, a phrase in frequent current use; a slogan. **catch up**, to come abreast with (a person etc. ahead); to make up arrears. [from Anglo-French from Latin captare = try to catch]

catch-22 n. (colloquial) a dilemma where the victim is bound to suffer, no matter which course of action etc. he takes. [title of a comic novel by J Heller 1961, set in the Second World War, in which the hero wishes not to fly any more missions and decides to go crazy, only to be told that anyone who wants to get out of combat duty is not really crazy]

catcher n. one who catches; a baseball fielder who stands behind the batter.

catching adj. infectious; catchy.

catchment n. collection of rainfall. —**catchment area**, an area from which rainfall drains into a river or reservoir; an area served by a school, hospital, etc.

catchpenny adj. intended to sell quickly.

catchweight adj. & n. in sport, accepting a contestant at the weight he happens to be, not a fixed weight.

catchword n. 1. a memorable word or phrase in frequent current use, a slogan. 2. a word so placed as to draw attention.

catchy adj. 1. (of a tune etc.) easy to remember. 2. tricky, involving a catch.

Cateau-Cambresis, Treaty of /kæ'təʊ kæm'breɪsɪs/ the treaty that ended the dynastic wars between the Valois of France and the Habsburg Empire, 2–3 April 1559.

catechism /'kætɪkɪzəm/ n. a summary of the principles of a religion in the form of questions and answers; a series of questions. [from Latin]

catechize /'kætɪkaɪz/ v.t. to put a series of questions to; to instruct by use of the church catechism. [from Latin from Greek katēkheō = make clear]

catecholamine n. a chemical that functions as a ◊neurotransmitter or a ◊hormone. Dopamine, epinephrine (adrenaline), and norepinephrine (noradrenaline) are catecholamines.

catechumen /kætɪ'kjuːmən/ n. a convert to Christianity who is being instructed before baptism.

categorical /kætɪ'gɒrɪkəl/ adj. unconditional, explicit. —**categorical imperative**, a technical term in ◊Kant's moral philosophy designating the supreme principle of morality for rational beings. The imperative orders us to act only in such a way that we can wish a maxim, or subjective principle, of our action to be a universal law. —**categorically** *adv.*

categorize /'kætɪɡəraɪz/ *v.t.* to place in a category. —**categorization** /-'zeɪʃən/ *n.*

category /'kætɪɡərɪ/ *n.* a class or division (of things etc.); in philosophy, a fundamental concept applied to being that cannot be reduced to anything more elementary. Aristotle listed ten categories: substance, quantity, quality, relation, place, time, position, state, action, passion. [from French or Latin from Greek = statement (*katēgoros* = accuser)]

catenary /kə'ti:nərɪ/ *n.* a curve formed by a uniform chain hanging freely from two points that are not in the same vertical line. —*adj.* forming or like such a curve, [from Latin *catena* = chain]

cater /'keɪtə/ *v.i.* **1.** to supply food; to provide meals, amusements, etc. *for.* **2.** to pander *to* (bad inclinations). [from obsolete *cater* (now *caterer*), from Old French *acater* = buy]

caterer /'keɪtərə/ *n.* one whose trade is to supply food for social events.

caterpillar /'kætəpɪlə/ *n.* the larva of a butterfly or moth; a similar larva of various insects. [from French, literally = hairy cat]

Caterpillar track trade name of an endless flexible belt of metal plates on which certain vehicles such as tanks and bulldozers run, which takes the place of ordinary tyred wheels. A track-laying vehicle has a track on each side, and its engine drives small cogwheels that run along the top of the track in contact with the ground. The advantage of such tracks over wheels is that they distribute the vehicle's weight over a wider area and are thus ideal for use on soft and waterlogged as well as rough and rocky ground.

caterwaul /'kætəwɔ:l/ *v.i.* to make a cat's shrill, howling cry.

catfish *n.* a fish belonging to the order Siluriformes, in which barbels (feelers) on the head are well developed, so giving a resemblance to the whiskers of a cat. Catfishes are found worldwide, mainly but not exclusively in fresh water, and are plentiful in South America.

catgut *n.* fine, strong thread made from the dried intestines of sheep etc., used for the strings of musical instruments and for surgical suture.

Cathar /'kæθə/ *n.* a member of a sect in medieval Europe usually numbered among the Christian heretics. Influenced by ◊Manichaeism, the Cathars started about the 10th century in the Balkans where they were called 'Bogomils', spread to SW Europe where they were often identified with the ◊Albigenses, and by the middle of the 14th century had been destroyed or driven underground by the Inquisition. The Believers, or *Credentes*, could approach God only through the Perfect (the ordained priesthood), who were implicitly obeyed in everything, and lived lives of the strictest self-denial and chastity. [Medieval Latin = the pure]

catharsis /kə'θɑ:sɪs/ *n.* **1.** purgation. **2.** relief of strong feelings or tension, e. g. by giving vent to these in drama or art (the emotional effect of tragedy described in Aristotle's *Poetics*). [from Greek *kathairō* = cleanse]

cathartic /kə'θɑ:tɪk/ *adj.* effecting catharsis; purgative. —*n.* a cathartic substance.

cathedral /kə'θi:drəl/ *n.* the principal church of a bishop's see, containing the throne of a bishop or archbishop, which is usually situated on the south side of the choir. A cathedral is governed by a dean and chapter. —*adj.* of or having a cathedral. [from Old French or Latin from Greek *kathedra* = seat]

Catherine I /'kæθrɪn/ 1684–1727. Empress of Russia from 1725. A Lithuanian peasant girl, born Martha Skavronsky, she married a Swedish dragoon and eventually became the mistress of Peter the Great. In 1703 she was rechristened as Katarina Alexeievna, and in 1711 the tsar divorced his wife and married Catherine in 1712. In 1724 she was proclaimed empress, and after Peter's death in 1725 she ruled capably with the help of her ministers. She allied Russia with Austria and Spain in an anti-English bloc.

Catherine II the Great 1729–1796. Empress of Russia from 1762, and daughter of the German prince of Anhalt-Zerbst. In 1745, she married the Russian grand duke Peter.

Six months after he became Tsar Peter III in 1762, he was murdered in a coup and Catherine ruled alone. During her reign Russia extended its boundaries to include territory from wars with the Turks 1768–72, 1787–92, and from the partitions of Poland 1772, 1793, and 1795.

I shall be an autocrat: that's my trade. And the good Lord will forgive me: that's his.

Catherine II
(attrib.)

Catherine de' Medici /deɪ 'medɪtʃi/ 1519–1589. French queen consort of Henry II, whom she married in 1533; daughter of Lorenzo de' Medici, duke of Urbino; and mother of Francis II, Charles IX, and Henry III. At first outshone by Henry's mistress Diane de Poitiers (1490–1566), she became regent 1560–63 for Charles IX and remained in power until his death in 1574.

Catherine of Alexandria, St Christian martyr who, according to legend, disputed with 50 scholars, refusing to give up her faith and marry Emperor Maxentius. Her emblem is a wheel, on which her persecutors tried to kill her (the wheel broke and she was beheaded). Feast day 25 Nov.

Catherine of Aragon /'ærəgən/ 1485–1536. First queen of Henry VIII of England, 1509–33, and mother of Mary I; Henry divorced her without papal approval, thus beginning the English ◊Reformation.

Catherine of Braganza /brə'gænzə/ 1638–1705. Queen of Charles II of England 1662–85. The daughter of John IV of Portugal (1604–1656), she brought the Portuguese possessions of Bombay and Tangier as her dowry to England. Her childlessness and practice of her Catholic faith were unpopular, but Charles resisted pressure for divorce. She returned to Lisbon in 1692, after his death.

Catherine of Siena /si'enə/ 1347–1380. Italian mystic, born in Siena, Italy. She persuaded Pope Gregory XI to return to Rome from Avignon in 1376. In 1375 she is said to have received on her body the stigmata, the impression

Catherine II *Catherine the Great of Russia, remembered as a benevolent despot.*

of Jesus' wounds. Her *Dialogue* is a classic mystical work. Feast day 29 April.

Catherine of Valois /væl'wɑ:/ 1401–1437. Queen of Henry V of England, whom she married in 1420; the mother of Henry VI. After the death of Henry V, she secretly married Owen Tudor (*c*.1400–1461) in about 1425, and their son Edmund Tudor became the father of Henry VII.

Catherine wheela firework that rotates when lit. [from St *Catherine* of Alexandria]

catheter /'kæθɪtə/ *n.* a fine tube inserted into the body to introduce or remove fluids. The original catheter was the urinary one, passed by way of the urethra (the duct that leads urine away from the bladder). In today's practice, catheters can be inserted into blood vessels, either in the limbs or trunk, to provide blood samples and local pressure measurements, and to deliver drugs and/or nutrients directly into the bloodstream. [from Greek *kathiēmi* = send down]

cathode /'kæθəʊd/ *n.* the electrode by which current leaves a device. —**cathode-ray tube,** a vacuum tube in which a beam of electrons from the cathode produces a luminous image on a fluorescent screen (as in a television set and an oscilloscope). [from Greek *kathodos* = way down]

catholic /'kæθəlɪk/ *adj.* universal, including many or most things. —**catholicity** /-'lɪsɪtɪ/ *n.* [from Old French or Latin from Greek *kata* = in respect of and *holos* = whole]

Catholic *adj.* 1. including all Christians, or all of the Western Church. 2. Roman Catholic. — *n.* a Roman Catholic. —**Catholicism** /-'θɒlɪsɪzəm/ *n.*

Catholic Emancipation in British history, acts of Parliament passed in 1780–1829 to relieve Catholics of civil and political restrictions imposed from the time of Henry VIII and the Reformation.

Catiline /'kætɪlaɪn/ (Lucius Sergius Catilina) *c.*108–62 BC. Roman politician. Twice failing to be elected to the consulship in 64/63 BC, he planned a military coup, but ◊Cicero exposed his conspiracy. He died at the head of the insurgents.

cation /'kætaɪən/ *n.* a positively charged ion (as opposed to *anion*). —**cationic** /-'ɒnɪk/ *adj.* [from Greek *kata* = down]

catkin *n.* a spike of small, soft flowers (usually hanging) on trees such as willow and hazel. [from Dutch = kitten]

Catlin /'kætlɪn/ George 1796–1872. US painter and explorer. From the 1830s he made a series of visits to the Great Plains, painting landscapes and scenes of American Indian life.

catmint *n.* a blue-flowered plant *Nepeta cataria* with a strong smell that is attractive to cats.

catnap *n.* a short sleep. —*v.i.* (-**pp-**) to have a catnap.

catnip *n.* catmint.

Cato /'keɪtəʊ/ Marcus Porcius 234–149 BC. Roman politician. Appointed censor (senior magistrate) in 184, he excluded from the Senate those who did not meet his high standards. He was so impressed by the power of ◊Carthage, on a visit in 157, that he ended every speech by saying 'Carthage must be destroyed.' His farming manual is the earliest surviving work in Latin prose.

Cato Street Conspiracy in British history, an unsuccessful plot hatched in Cato Street, London, to murder the Tory foreign secretary Castlereagh and all his ministers on 20 Feb 1820. The leader, the Radical Arthur Thistlewood (1770–1820), who intended to set up a provisional government, was hanged with four others.

CAT scan or **CT scan** acronym from computerized axial tomography, in medicine, a sophisticated method of X-ray imaging. Quick and noninvasive, CAT scanning is an aid to diagnosis, helping to pinpoint problem areas without the need for exploratory surgery.

catsuit *n.* a close-fitting garment covering the body from neck to feet, with sleeves and trouser legs.

cattle *n.pl.* large, ruminant, even-toed, hoofed mammals of the family Bovidae, including wild species such as buffalo, bison, yak, gaur, gayal, and banteng, as well as domestic breeds. —**cattle-grid** *n.* a grid covering a ditch, allowing vehicles to pass over but not cattle, sheep, etc. [from Old French *chatel*]

catty *adj.* catlike; malicious, speaking spitefully. —**cattily** *adv.*, **cattiness** *n.*

Catullus /kə'tʌləs/ Gaius Valerius *c.*84–54 BC. Roman lyric poet, born in Verona of a well-to-do family. He moved in the literary and political society of Rome and wrote lyrics describing his unhappy love affair with Clodia, probably the wife of the consul Metellus, calling her Lesbia. His longer poems include two wedding songs. Many of his poems are short verses to his friends.

catwalk /'kætwɔ:k/ *n.* a raised, narrow pathway.

Caucasoid /'kɔ:kəsɔɪd/ *adj.* or **Caucasian** a former racial classification used for any of the light-skinned peoples. [so named because the German anthropologist J F Blumenbach (1752–1840) theorized that they originated in the *Caucasus*]

Caucasus /'kɔ:kəsəs/ series of mountain ranges between the Caspian and Black Seas, USSR; 1,200 km/750 mi long. The highest is Elbruz, 5,633 m/18,480 ft.

Cauchy /'kəʊʃi/ Augustin Louis 1789–1857. French mathematician, celebrated for his rigorous methods of analysis. His prolific output included work on complex functions, determinants, and probability, and on the convergence of infinite series. In calculus, he refined the concepts of the limit and the definite integral.

caucus /'kɔ:kəs/ *n.* 1. (often *derogatory*) the committee of a local branch of a political party, making plans, decisions, etc. 2. (*US*) a meeting of party leaders to decide policy etc. 3. (*Australian*) the parliamentary members of a political party who decide policy etc.; a meeting of these. [US word, perhaps from Algonquin = adviser]

caudal /'kɔ:dəl/ *adj.* of, like, or at the tail. [from Latin *cauda* = tail]

caudate /'kɔ:'deɪt/ *adj.* having a tail.

caught past and past participle of **catch.**

caul /kɔ:l/ *n.* a membrane enclosing a fetus in the womb; part of this sometimes found on a child's head at birth. [perhaps from Old French = small cap]

cauldron /'kɔ:ldrən/ *n.* a large, deep cooking pot for boiling things in. [from Anglo-French from Latin *caldarium* = hot bath]

cauliflower /'kɒlɪflaʊə/ *n.* a variety of ◊cabbage *Brassica oleracea*, distinguished by its large, flattened head of fleshy, aborted flowers. —**cauliflower ear,** an ear thickened by repeated blows. [from French *chou fleur* = flowered cabbage]

caulk /kɔ:k/ *v.t.* to make watertight by filling seams or joints with waterproof material, or by driving edges of plating together. [from Old French from Latin *calcare* = tread]

causal /'kɔ:zəl/ *adj.* of or forming a cause; relating to cause and effect. —**causally** *adv.* [from Latin]

causality /kɔ:'zælɪtɪ/ *n.* the relationship between cause and effect; the principle that everything has a cause.

causation /kɔ:'zeɪʃən/ *n.* the act of causing; causality. [French or from Latin]

causative /'kɔ:zətɪv/ *adj.* acting as or expressing a cause. [from Old French or Latin]

cause /kɔ:z/ *n.* 1. a thing that produces an effect; a person or thing that makes something happen. 2. a reason or motive; justification. 3. a principle, belief, or purpose for which efforts are made, a movement or charity. 4. a matter to be settled at law; a case offered at law. —*v.t.* to be the cause of, to produce, to make happen. [from Old French from Latin *causa*]

cause célèbre /kɔ:z se'lebrə/ (*plural* **causes célèbres** pronounced the same) a lawsuit or other issue that rouses great interest. [French]

causeway /'kɔ:zweɪ/ *n.* a raised road across low or wet ground. [earlier *cauce(way)*, from Old French from Latin *calx* = limestone]

caustic /'kɔ:stɪk/ *adj.* 1. that burns or corrodes things by chemical action. 2. sarcastic. —**caustic curve,** a curve formed by the intersection of rays reflected or refracted from a curved surface. **caustic soda,** sodium hydroxide. —**causticity** /-'tɪsɪtɪ/ *n.*, **caustically** *adv.* [from Latin from Greek *kaustos* = burnt]

cauterize /'kɔ:təraɪz/ *v.t.* to burn (tissue) with a caustic substance or hot iron to destroy infection or stop bleeding. —**cauterization** /-'zeɪʃən/ *n.* [from French from Latin from Greek *kautērion* = branding iron]

Cauthen /'kɔ:θən/ Steve 1960– . US jockey. He rode Affirmed to the US Triple Crown in 1978 at the age of 18 and won 487 races in 1977. He has ridden in England since 1979 and has twice won the Derby, on Slip Anchor in 1985 and on

Reference Point in 1987. He was UK champion jockey in 1984, 1985, and 1987.

caution /'kɔːʃən/ n. 1. avoidance of rashness, attention to safety. 2. a warning against danger etc.; a warning and reprimand. 3. (*colloquial*) an amusing person or thing. —*v.t.* to warn; to warn and reprimand. [from Old French from Latin *cavere* = take heed]

cautionary /'kɔːʃənərɪ/ adj. that gives or serves as a warning.

cautious /'kɔːʃəs/ adj. having or showing caution. —**cautiously** adv., **cautiousness** n.

Cauvery /'kɔːvərɪ/ or **Kaveri** river of S India, rising in the W Ghats and flowing 765 km/475 mi SE to meet the Bay of Bengal in a wide delta. A major source of hydroelectric power since 1902 when India's first hydropower plant was built on the river.

Cavaco Silva /kə'væːkəʊ 'sɪlvə/ Anibal 1939– . Portuguese politician, finance minister 1980–81, and prime minister and Social Democratic Party (PSD) leader from 1985. Under his leadership Portugal joined the European Community in 1985 and the Western European Union in 1988.

Cavafy /kə'vɑːfɪ/ Constantinos. Pen name of Konstantínos Pétrou 1863–1933. Greek poet. An Alexandrian, he shed light on Greek history, recreating the classical period with zest. He published only one book of poetry and remained almost unknown until translations of his works appeared in 1952.

cavalcade /'kævəlkeɪd/ n. a procession or company of people on horseback or in cars etc. [French from Italian *cavalcare* = ride, from Latin *caballus* = horse]

cavalier /kævə'lɪə/ n. a courtly gentleman. —*adj.* arrogant, offhand.

Cavalier n. a supporter of Charles I in the English Civil War. [French from Italian]

Cavalier poets poets of Charles I's court, including Thomas Carew, Robert Herrick, Richard Lovelace, and John Suckling. They wrote witty, light-hearted love lyrics.

Cavalli /kə'vælɪ/ (Pietro) Francesco 1602–1676. Italian composer, organist at St Mark's, Venice, and the first to make opera a popular entertainment with such works as *Xerxes* 1654, later performed in honour of Louis XIV's wedding in Paris. Twenty-seven of his operas survive.

cavalry /'kævəlrɪ/ n. (usually as *plural*) troops who fight on horseback or in armoured vehicles. [from French from Italian from Latin *caballus* = horse]

Cavan /'kævən/ agricultural county of the Republic of Ireland, in the province of Ulster; **area** 1,890 sq km/730 sq mi; **capital** Cavan; **population** (1986) 54,000.

cave /keɪv/ n. a hollow in the side of a hill or cliff, or underground usually produced by the action of underground water or by waves on a seacoast. —*v.i.* to explore caves. —**cave painting**, picture(s) of animals etc. on the interior of a cave, especially by prehistoric peoples. **cave in**, to fall or cause to fall inwards, to collapse; to withdraw one's opposition. [from Old French from Latin *cavus* = hollow]

Cave Edward 1691–1754. British printer and founder, under the pseudonym Sylvanus Urban, of *The Gentleman's Magazine* 1731–1914, the first periodical to be called a magazine. Dr Samuel ◊Johnson was a contributor 1738–44.

caveat /'kævɪæt/ n. a warning; a proviso. [Latin = let him beware]

caveat emptor dictum that professes the buyer is responsible for checking the quality of nonwarrantied goods purchased. [Latin = let the buyer beware]

cave canem beware of the dog. [Latin]

Cavell /'kævəl/ Edith Louisa 1865–1915. British matron of a Red Cross hospital in Brussels, Belgium, in World War I, who helped Allied soldiers escape to the Dutch frontier. She was court-martialled by the Germans and condemned to death.

Standing as I do, in the view of God and eternity I realize that patriotism is not enough. I must have no hatred or bitterness towards anyone.

Edith Cavell
to chaplain before her execution by a firing squad

---

caveman n. or **cavewoman** (*plural* **cavemen** or **cavewomen**) a prehistoric human living in caves. —**caveman,** a man with a rough primitive manner towards women.

Cavendish /'kævəndɪʃ 'lævəndɪʃ/ family name of the dukes of Devonshire; the family seat is at Chatsworth, Derbyshire.

Cavendish Henry 1731–1810. English physicist, grandson of the 2nd Duke of Devonshire. He discovered hydrogen (which he called 'inflammable air') in 1766, and determined the compositions of water and of nitric acid.

Cavendish Spencer see ◊Hartington, Spencer Compton Cavendish, British politician.

Cavendish-Bentinck /'bentɪŋk/ the family name of the dukes of Portland.

Cavendish experiment the measurement of the gravitational attraction between lead and gold spheres, which enabled the calculation of a mean value for the mass and density of the Earth, using Newton's Law of Universal Gravitation. [from Henry *Cavendish*]

cavern /'kævən/ n. a large cave. —**cavernous** adj. [from Old French or Latin *cavus* = hollow]

cave temple an example of rock architecture, such as Ajanta in western India and Alamira, near Santander, in Spain.

caviare /'kævɪɑː/ n. the salted roe of sturgeon or other large fish. [from Italian from Turkish]

cavil /'kævɪl/ v.i. (**-ll-**) to raise petty objections (*at*). —*n.* a petty objection. [from French from Latin *cavilla* = mockery]

cavitation n. the formation of partial vacuums in fluids at high velocities, produced by propellers or other machine parts in hydraulic engines, in accordance with the ◊Bernoulli effect. When these vacuums collapse, pitting, vibration, and noise can occur in the metal parts in contact with the fluids.

cavity /'kævɪtɪ/ n. a hollow within a solid body. —**cavity wall,** a double wall with an internal space. [from French or Latin]

cavort /kə'vɔːt/ v.i. to prance or caper excitedly.

Cavour /kə'vʊə/ Camillo Benso di, Count 1810–1861. Italian nationalist politician, editor of *Il ◊Risorgimento* from 1847. As prime minister of Piedmont 1852–59 and 1860–61, he enlisted the support of Britain and France for the concept of a united Italy, achieved in 1861; after expelling the Austrians in 1859, he assisted Garibaldi in liberating Southern Italy in 1860.

cavy n. a type of short-tailed South American rodent, family Caviidae, of which the **guinea-pig** *Cavia porcellus* is an example. Wild cavies are greyish or brownish with rather coarse hair. They live in small groups in burrows, and have been kept for food since ancient times.

caw n. the harsh cry of a rook, raven, or crow etc. —*v.i.* to make a caw.

Cawley Evonne Fay (born Evonne Goolagong) 1951– . Australian Aboriginal tennis player. She won the Wimbledon singles title in 1971 and 1980 and the doubles in 1974. She was the Australian singles title holder 1974-76 and doubles champion 1971, 1974 and 1975.

Cawnpore /kɔːn'pɔː/ former spelling of ◊Kanpur, Indian city.

Caxton /'kækstən/ William *c.*1422–1491. First English printer. He learned the art of printing in Cologne, Germany in 1471 and set up a press in Belgium, where he produced the first book printed in English, his own version of a French romance, *Recuyell of the Historyes of Troye* 1474. Returning to England in 1476 he established himself in London, where he produced the first book printed in England, *Dictes or Sayengis of the Philosophres* 1477.

cayenne /keɪ'en/ n. (in full **cayenne pepper**) pungent, red, powdered pepper made from the dried fruits of various species of ◊capsicum (especially *Capsicum frutescens*), a tropical American genus of plants of the family Solanaceae. It is wholly distinct in its origin from black or white pepper, which is derived from an East Indian plant (*Piper nigrum*). [from Tupi, assimilated to *Cayenne*]

Cayenne capital and chief port of French Guiana, on Cayenne island at the mouth of the river Cayenne; population (1982) 38,135.

Cayley /'keɪlɪ/ Arthur 1821–1895. English mathematician, who developed matrix algebra, used by ◊Heisenberg in his elucidation of quantum mechanics.

Ceauşescu *Former Romanian communist leader, Nicolae Ceauşescu.*

Cayley George 1773–1857. British aviation pioneer, inventor of the first piloted glider in 1853, and the caterpillar tractor.

cayman /ˈkeɪmən/ *n.* (*plural* **caymans**) a South American alligator, especially of the genus *Caiman.* [from Spanish and Portuguese from Carib]

Cayman Islands British island group in the West Indies; **area** 260 sq km/100 sq mi; **physical** comprises three low-lying islands: Grand Cayman, Cayman Brac, and Little Cayman; **government** governor, executive council, and legislative assembly; **exports** seawhip coral, a source of ◊prostaglandins; shrimps; honey; jewellery; **population** (1988) 22,000; **language** English; **recent history** administered with Jamaica until 1962, when the Caymans became a separate colony, they are now a tourist resort, international financial centre, and tax haven.

CB abbreviation of ◊citizens' band (radio).

CBI abbreviation of Confederation of British Industry, the employers' federation in the UK, founded in 1965.

cc abbreviation of carbon copy/copies; symbol for cubic centimetre.

CC abbreviation of **1.** county council. **2.** cricket club.

cd abbreviation of ◊candela.

Cd symbol for ◊cadmium.

CD abbreviation of **1.** *Corps Diplomatique.* [French = Diplomatic Corps] **2.** compact disc.

CD-ROM *n.* in computing, a storage device, consisting of a metal disc with a plastic coating, on which information is etched in the form of microscopic pits. A CD-ROM typically holds about 550 ◊megabytes of data. CD-ROMs cannot have information written on to them by the computer, but must be manufactured from a master.

CDU abbreviation of Christian Democratic Union, the centre-right party in the Germany.

Ce symbol for ◊cerium.

CE abbreviation of **1.** Common Era (see under ◊calendar). **2.** Church of England (often C of E).

céad míle fáilte a conventional form of greeting in Ireland. [Irish = a hundred thousand welcomes]

cease /siːs/ *v.t./i.* to bring or come to an end; to stop. —**ceasefire** *n.* a signal (in war) to stop firing; a halt in hostilities. [from Old French from Latin *cessare*]

ceaseless *adj.* without cease, not ceasing.

Ceauşescu /tʃaʊˈʃesku/ Nicolae 1918–1989. Romanian politician, leader of the Romanian Communist Party (RCP), in power 1965–89. He pursued a policy line independent of and critical of the USSR. He appointed family members, including his wife **Elena Ceauşescu**, to senior state and party posts, and governed in an increasingly repressive

manner, zealously implementing schemes that impoverished the nation. The Ceauşescus were overthrown in a bloody revolutionary coup in Dec 1989 and executed.

Cebu /seɪˈbuː/ chief city and port of the island of Cebu in the Philippines; population (1980) 490,000; area of the island 5,086 sq km/1,964 sq mi.

Cecil /ˈsesəl/ Henry Richard Amherst 1943– . Scottish-born racehorse trainer with stables at Warren Place, Newmarket. The most successful English trainer of all time in terms of prize money, he has been the top trainer nine times, winning the most prize money in a season.

Cecil /ˈsɪsəl/ Robert, 1st Earl of Salisbury 1563–1612. Secretary of state to Elizabeth I of England, succeeding his father, Lord Burghley; he was afterwards chief minister to James I, who created him Earl of Salisbury in 1605.

Cecilia, St /səˈsiːliə/ Christian patron saint of music, martyred in Rome in the 2nd or 3rd century, who is said to have sung hymns while undergoing torture. Feast day 22 Nov.

CEDA (abbreviation of Spanish *Confederación Español de Derechas Autónomas*) a federation of right-wing parties under the leadership of José Maria Gil Robles, founded during the Second Spanish Republic in 1933 to provide a right-wing coalition in the Spanish Cortes. Supporting the Catholic and Monarchist causes, the federation was uncommitted as to the form of government.

cedar /ˈsiːdə/ *n.* an evergreen coniferous tree of the genus *Cedrus*; its hard fragrant wood. [from Old French from Latin from Greek *kedros*]

cede /siːd/ *v.t.* to give up one's rights to or possession of. [from Latin *cedere* = yield]

cedilla /sɪˈdɪlə/ *n.* a mark written under *c* especially in French, to show that it is sibilant (as in *façade*). [from Spanish, diminutive of *zeda* = z]

Ceefax /ˈsiːfæks/ *n.* one of Britain's two ◊teletext systems (the other is Oracle), or 'magazines of the air', developed by the BBC and first broadcast in 1973. [= see facts]

CEGB abbreviation of the former (until 1990) Central Electricity Generating Board.

ceilidh /ˈkeɪli/ *n.* (originally *Scottish* and *Irish*) an informal gathering for traditional music, dancing, etc. [Gaelic]

ceiling /ˈsiːlɪŋ/ *n.* **1.** the undersurface of the top of a room etc. **2.** the maximum altitude a given aircraft can normally reach. **3.** an upper limit (of prices, performance, etc.).

Cela /ˈθelə/ Camilo José 1916– . Spanish novelist. Among his novels, characterized by their violence and brutal realism, are *La familia de Pascual Duarte*/*The Family of Pascal Duarte* 1942, and *La colmena*/*The Hive* 1951. He was awarded the Nobel Prize for Literature in 1989.

celandine /ˈselændaɪn/ *n.* either of two yellow-flowered plants, **greater celandine** *Chelidonium majus* and **lesser celandine** *Ranunculus ficaria*. [from Old French from Latin from Greek *chelidon* = the swallow]

Celebes /səˈliːbɪz/ English name for ◊Sulawesi, an island of Indonesia.

celebrant /ˈselɪbrənt/ *n.* an officiating priest, especially at the Eucharist.

celebrate /ˈselɪbreɪt/ *v.t./i.* **1.** to mark (an occasion) with festivities; to engage in such festivities. **2.** to perform (religious rites); to officiate at the Eucharist etc. **3.** to praise widely, to extol. —**celebration** /-ˈbreɪʃən/ *n.* [from Latin *celebrare* (*celeber* = renowned)]

celebrated *adj.* widely known.

celebrity /sɪˈlebrɪti/ *n.* a well-known person; fame.

celeriac /sɪˈleriæk/ *n.* a variety of celery with a large edible root. It is a member of the family Umbelliferae.

celerity /sɪˈlerɪti/ *n.* (*archaic* and *literary*) swiftness. [from Latin *celer* = swift]

celery /ˈseləri/ *n.* a plant *Apium graveolens* of the carrot family Umbelliferae which grows wild in ditches and salt marshes and has a coarse texture and acrid taste. Cultivated varieties of celery are grown under cover to make them less bitter; blanched stems are eaten raw in salads or cooked. [from French, ultimately from Greek *selinon* = parsley]

celesta /sɪˈlestə/ *n.* a small keyboard instrument with hammers striking metal plates to give a bell-like sound. It was invented by Auguste Mustel in 1886 and first used to effect by Tchaikovsky in *The Nutcracker* ballet music. [from French *céleste*]

cell

plant cell

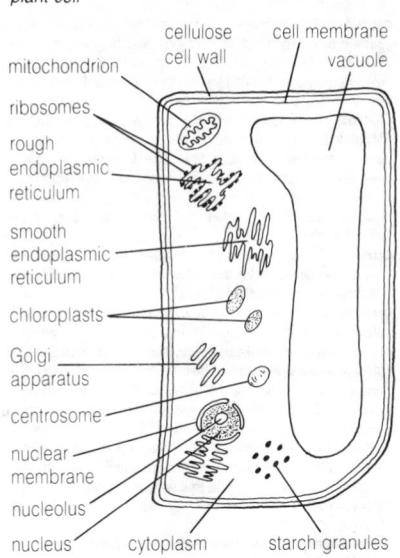

animal cell

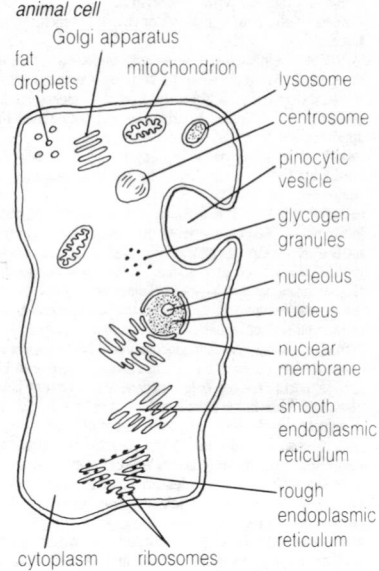

celestial /si'lestiəl/ *adj*. 1. of the sky or heavenly bodies. 2. of heaven, divine. —**celestially** *adv*. [from Latin *caelum* = sky]

celestial mechanics the branch of astronomy that deals with the calculation of the orbits of celestial bodies, their gravitational attractions (such as those that produce the Earth's tides), and also the orbits of artificial satellites and space probes. It is based on the laws of motion and gravity laid down by ◊Newton.

Celestial Police a group of astronomers in Germany 1800–15, who set out to discover a supposed missing planet thought to be orbiting the Sun between Mars and Jupiter, a region now known to be occupied by types of ◊asteroid. Although they did not discover the first asteroid (found in 1801), they discovered the second, Pallas (1802), third, Juno (1804), and fourth, Vesta (1807).

celestial sphere the imaginary sphere surrounding the Earth, on which the celestial bodies seem to lie. The positions of bodies such as stars, planets, and galaxies are specified by their coordinates on the celestial sphere. The equivalents of latitude and longitude on the celestial sphere are called ◊declination and right ascension (see ◊right) (which is measured in hours from 0 to 24). The **celestial poles** lie directly above the Earth's poles, and the **celestial equator** lies over the Earth's equator. The celestial sphere appears to rotate once around the Earth each day, actually a result of the rotation of the Earth on its axis.

celibate /'selɪbət/ *adj*. remaining unmarried or abstaining from sexual relations, especially for religious reasons. In some religions, such as Christianity and Buddhism, celibacy is a requirement for certain religious roles, such as the priesthood or a monastic life. Other religions, including Judaism, strongly discourage celibacy. —*n*. a celibate person. —**celibacy** *n*. [from Latin *caelebs* = bachelor]

Céline /se'li:n/ Louis Ferdinand. Pen name of Louis Destouches 1884–1961. French novelist, whose writings (the first of which was *Voyage au bout de la nuit*/*Journey to the End of the Night* 1932) aroused controversy over their cynicism and misanthropy.

cell *n*. 1. a very small room, e. g. for a monk in a monastery or for confining a prisoner. 2. a compartment in a honeycomb. 3. a microscopic structure which is effectively the unit of life. All living organisms consist of one or more cells, with the exception of ◊viruses. Bacteria, protozoa, and many other microorganisms consist of single cells, whereas a human is made up of billions of cells. Essential features of a cell are the membrane, which encloses it and restricts the flow of substances in and out; the jellylike material within, often known as ◊protoplasm; the

◊ribosomes, which carry out protein synthesis; and the ◊DNA, which forms the hereditary material. 4. a container with materials for producing electricity by chemical action; a device for converting chemical or radiant energy into electrical energy. 5. a small group of people forming a centre or nucleus of political (often subversive) activities. [from Latin *cella* = storeroom]

cellar /'selə/ *n*. 1. a room below ground level, used for storage (especially of wine). 2. a person's or institution's stock of wine. [from Anglo-French from Latin *cellarium*]

cell division the process by which a cell divides, either ◊meiosis, associated with sexual reproduction, or ◊mitosis, associated with growth, cell replacement or repair. Both forms involve the duplication of DNA and the splitting of the nucleus.

Cellini /tʃe'li:ni/ Benvenuto 1500–1571. Italian sculptor and goldsmith working in the Mannerist style; author of an arrogant autobiography (begun in 1558). Among his works are a graceful bronze *Perseus* 1545–54 (Loggia dei Lanzi, Florence) and a gold salt cellar made for Francis I of France 1540–43 (Kunsthistorisches Museum, Vienna), topped by nude reclining figures.

cell membrane or **plasma membrane** the thin layer of protein and fat surrounding cells that controls substances passing between the cytoplasm and the intercellular space. Cell membrane is 'semi-permeable', allowing some substances to pass through and others not.

cello /'tʃeləʊ/ *n*. (*plural* **cellos**) a violoncello, an instrument like a large violin with four strings and a range of over three octaves, played supported on the floor in an upright or slanting position between the seated player's knees. —**cellist** *n*. [abbreviation of *violoncello*]

Cellophane /'seləfeɪn/ *n*. trade name of a thin, transparent wrapping material made from wood ◊cellulose, widely used for packaging, first produced by Swiss chemist Jacques Edwin Brandenberger in 1908.

cellphone *n*. a telephone based on a cellular radio network.

cell sap a dilute fluid found in the large central vacuole of many plant cells. It is made up of water, amino acids, glucose, and salts. The sap has many functions, including storage of useful materials, and provides mechanical support for nonwoody plants.

cellular /'seljʊlə/ *adj*. consisting of cells; (of blankets etc.) woven with an open mesh. —**cellularity** /-'lærɪti/ *n*.

cellular radio or **cellphone** a mobile radio telephone, one of a network connected to the telephone system by a computer-controlled communication system. Service areas are divided into small 'cells', about 5 km/3 mi across, each with a separate low-power transmitter.

cellule /'selju:l/ *n.* a small cell or cavity. [French, or from Latin *cellula*]

cellulite /'seljulait/ *n.* a fatty compound alleged by some dietitians to be produced in the body by liver disorder and to cause lumpy deposits on the hips and thighs. Medical opinion generally denies its existence, attributing the lumpy appearance to a type of subcutaneous fat deposit.

cellulitis *n.* inflammation of body tissue, especially subcutaneous tissue, accompanied by swelling, redness, and pain.

celluloid /'seljuloid/ *n.* a transparent or translucent, highly inflammable, plastic material (a ◊thermoplastic made from nitrocellulose and camphor) once used for toilet articles, novelties, and photographic film. It has been replaced by the noninflammable substance cellulose acetate.

cellulose /'selju:ljəuz, -əus/ *n.* **1.** the principal constituent of the cell wall of higher plants; a complex ◊carbohydrate composed of long chains of glucose units. Molecules of cellulose are organized into long, unbranched microfibrils that give support to the cell wall. Cellulose is the most abundant substance found in the plant kingdom. It has numerous uses in industry: in rope-making; as a source of textiles (linen, cotton, viscose, and acetate) and plastics (cellophane and celluloid); in the manufacture of nondrip paint; and in food additives such as whipped dessert toppings. **2.** (*popularly*) paint or lacquer made from solutions of cellulose acetate or nitrate. [from French or Latin]

cellulose nitrate an ◊ester made by the action of nitric acid and sulphuric acid on cellulose and used to make lacquers and explosives ('guncotton'). See also ◊nitrocellulose.

Celsius /'selsiəs/ *adj.* of or using the Celsius (centigrade) temperature scale in which one division or degree is taken as one hundredth part of the interval between the freezing point (0°C) and the boiling point (100°C) of water at standard atmospheric pressure. [from Anders *Celsius* (1701–1744), Swedish astronomer who advocated this scale]

Celt /kelt/ *n.* a member of a people of alpine Europe and Iberia whose first known territory was in central Europe about 1200 BC, in the basin of the upper Danube, the Alps, and parts of France and S Germany. In the 6th century they spread into Spain and Portugal. Over the next 300 years, they also spread into the British Isles (see ◊Britain, ancient), N Italy (sacking Rome in 390 BC), Greece, the Balkans, and parts of Asia Minor, although they never established a united empire. In the 1st century BC they were defeated by the Roman Empire and by Germanic tribes, and confined largely to Britain, Ireland, and N France. Between the Bronze and Iron Ages, in the 9th–5th centuries BC, they developed a transitional culture (named the **Hallstatt** culture after its archaeological site SW of Salzburg). They farmed and raised cattle, and were pioneers of ironworking, reaching their peak in the period from the 5th century to the Roman conquest (the **La Tène** culture). Celtic languages survive in Ireland, Wales, Scotland, the Isle of Man, and Brittany. [from Latin from Greek *Keltoi*] [Greek *Keltoi*]

Celtic /'keltik/ *adj.* of the Celts and kindred peoples, or their languages. —*n.* a subgroup of the Indo-European language group, today spoken in the British Isles and in Brittany, divided into two groups, Goidelic (consisting of Irish, Scots Gaelic, and Manx) and Brythonic (consisting of Welsh, Cornish, and Breton). [from Latin or French]

Celtic League a nationalist organization based in Ireland, aiming at an independent Celtic federation. It was founded in 1975 with representatives from Alba (Scotland), Breizh (Brittany), Eire, Kernow (Cornwall), Cymru (Wales), and Ellan Vannin (Isle of Man).

cembalo *n.* an accompanying keyboard instrument in classical music.

cement /si'ment/ *n.* a grey powder made by burning lime and clay, which sets to a stonelike mass when mixed with water and is used as a building material, mortar, etc.; any soft substance that sets firm. In geology, a chemically precipitated material such as carbonate that occupies the interstices of clastic rocks is called cement. —*v.t.* to join with or like cement; to apply cement to, to line with cement. —**cementation** /-'teiʃən/ *n.* [from Old French from Latin *caementum* = quarry stone]

cemetery /'semitəri/ *n.* a burial ground other than a churchyard. [from Latin from Greek *koimētērion* = dormitory]

cenotaph /'senətɑ:f/ *n.* a monument to commemorate a person or persons not actually buried at the site, as in the Whitehall Cenotaph, London, designed by Edwin Lutyens to commemorate the dead of both world wars. [from Greek = empty tomb]

Cenozoic /si:nəu'zəuik/ *adj.* or **Caenozoic** of the era of geological time that began 65 million years ago and is still in process. —*n.* this era. The Cenozoic is divided into the Tertiary and Quaternary periods and marks the emergence of mammals as a dominant group, including humans, and the formation of the mountain chains of the Himalayas and the Alps.

censer /'sensə/ *n.* a small container in which incense is burnt, swung on chains in a religious ceremony to disperse its fragrance. [from Anglo-French]

censor /'sensə/ *n.* **1.** an official with the power to suppress parts of books, films, letters, news, etc., on grounds of obscenity, risk to security, etc. **2.** in ancient Rome, either of two senior magistrates, high officials elected every five years to hold office for 18 months. Their responsibilities included public morality, a census of the citizens, and a revision of the Senatorial list. **3.** in Freudian psychology, the psychic function that prevents unacceptable unconscious impulses from reaching the conscious mind. —*v.t.* to suppress (books, films, etc.) in this way. *n.* [Latin]

censorious /sen'sɔ:riəs/ *adj.* severely critical, faultfinding.

censorship *n.* the suppression by authority of material considered immoral, heretical, subversive, libellous, damaging to state security, or otherwise offensive. It is generally more stringent under totalitarian or strongly religious regimes and in wartime.

censorship, film control of the content and presentation of films. Film censorship dates back almost as far as the cinema. In Britain, censorship was established in 1912, in the USA in 1922. Censorship in Britain was the responsibility of the British Board of Film Censors (now the British Board of Film Classification) which gives each film a rating. In Britain, children were not prevented from seeing certain films until 1933, when the 'H' (for 'horrific') certificate was introduced (replaced by 'X' in 1951).

censure /'senʃə/ *n.* strong criticism or condemnation, a rebuke. —*v.t.* to blame and rebuke. [from Old French from Latin *censēre* = assess]

census /'sensəs/ *n.* an official count of the population of a country, originally for military call-up and taxation, later for assessment of social trends as other information regarding age, sex, and occupation of each individual was included. The first US census was taken in 1790 and the first in Britain in 1801. [Latin]

cent *n.* one hundredth of a US dollar or certain other metric units of currency; a coin of this value. [from French, Italian or Latin *centum* = hundred]

Centaur /'sentɔ:/ *n.* in Greek mythology, a member of a tribe of wild creatures with the upper part of a man and the hindquarters of a horse.

Centaurus /sen'tɔ:rəs/ *n.* a large, bright constellation of the southern hemisphere, represented as a centaur. It contains the closest star to the Sun, Proxima Centauri. Omega Centauri, the largest and brightest globular cluster of stars in the sky, is 16,000 light years away. Centaurus A, a peculiar galaxy 15 million light years away, is a strong source of radio waves and X-rays.

centaury /'sentɔ:ri/ *n.* a plant of the genus *Centaurium* with small pink flowers usually in clusters, especially the common centaury of the herbalists *C. erythraea*. [from Latin from Greek = centaur, because said to have been discovered and used medicinally by Chiron the Centaur, tutor of Achilles]

CentCom abbreviation of US ◊Central Command, a military strike force.

centenarian /senti'neəriən/ *n.* a person who is 100 or more years old.

centenary /sen'ti:nəri/ *n.* a 100th anniversary. —*adj.* of such an anniversary. [from Latin *centeni* = 100 each]

centennial /sen'teniəl/ *adj. & n.* centenary.

centesimal /sen'tesiməl/ *adj.* reckoning or reckoned by hundredths. [from Latin *centum* = hundred]

centi- in combinations, **1.** one hundredth. **2.** a hundred. [from Latin *centum* = hundred]

centigrade /'sentɪgreɪd/ *adj.* of or having a temperature scale of 100 degrees, 0° being the freezing point and 100° the boiling point of water. [from Latin *gradus* = step]

centigram /'sentɪgræm/ *n.* one hundredth of a gram.

centilitre /'sentɪli:tə/ *n.* one hundredth of a litre.

centimetre /'sentɪmi:tə/ *n.* one hundredth of a metre, about 0.4 in.

centipede /'sentɪpi:d/ *n.* a many-legged arthropod of the class Chilopoda, members of which have a distinct head and a single pair of long antennae. Their bodies are composed of segments (which may number nearly 200), each of similar form and bearing a single pair of legs. Most are small, but the tropical *Scolopendra gigantea* may reach 30 cm/1 ft in length. **Millipedes**, class Diplopoda, have fewer segments (up to 100), but have two pairs of legs on each. [from French or Latin *centum* = hundred and *pes pedis* = foot]

CENTO abbreviation of ◊Central Treaty Organization.

central /'sentrəl/ *adj.* **1.** of, at, from, or forming the centre. **2.** chief, most important. —**central bank**, a national (not commercial) bank, issuing currency. **central heating**, a method of warming a building from one source by circulating hot water, hot air, or steam in pipes, or by linked radiators. **Central Intelligence Agency (CIA)**, a federal agency in the USA, established in 1947, responsible for coordinating government intelligence activities. **Central Powers**, Germany and Austria-Hungary before 1914. —**centrality** /-'trælɪtɪ/ *n.*, **centrally** *adv.* [French or from Latin *centrum* = centre]

Central African Republic /'sentrəl 'æfrɪkən rɪ'pʌblɪk/ landlocked country in Central Africa, bordered NE and E by Sudan, S by Zaïre and the Congo, W by Cameroon, and NW by Chad; **area** 622,436 sq km/240,260 sq mi; **capital** Bangui; **physical** most of the country is on a plateau, with rivers flowing N and S. Dry in N, rainforest in SW; **head of state and government** Andrel Kolingba from 1981; **political system** one-party military republic; **exports** diamonds, uranium, coffee, cotton, timber, tobacco; **population** (1990 est) 2,879,000; **language** Sangho (national), French (official); **recent history** independence was achieved from France in 1960. A military coup in 1965 led to Col Bokassa declaring himself president for life and emperor. He was deposed by former president David Dacko in 1979, in turn deposed by Gen André Kolingba in 1981.

Central America /'sentrəl ə'merɪkə/ the part of the Americas that links Mexico with the isthmus of Panama, comprising Belize, Costa Rica, El Salvador, Guatemala, Honduras, Nicaragua, and Panama.

Central American Common Market ODECA (*Organización de Estados Centro-americanos*) an economic alliance established in 1960 by El Salvador, Guatemala, Honduras (seceded in 1970), and Nicaragua; Costa Rica joined in 1962.

Central Command (CentCom) a military strike force consisting of units from the US army, navy, and air force, which operates in the Middle East and North Africa. Its headquarters are in Fort McDill, Florida. It was established in 1979, following the Iranian hostage crisis and the Soviet invasion of Afghanistan, and was known as the Rapid Deployment Force until 1983.

Central Criminal Court in the UK, the Crown Court in the City of London, able to try all treasons and serious offences committed in the City or Greater London. First established in 1834, it is popularly known as the Old Bailey after part of the medieval defences of London; the present building is on the site of Newgate Prison.

central dogma in genetics and evolution, the fundamental belief that ◊genes can affect the nature of the physical body, but that changes in the body (for example, through use or accident) cannot be translated into changes in the genes.

centralism /'sentrəlɪzəm/ *n.* a centralizing policy, especially in administration. —**centralist** *n.*

centralize /'sentrəlaɪz/ *v.t.* to concentrate (administration etc.) at a single centre; to subject to such a system. —**centralization** /-'zeɪʃən/ *n.*

Central Lowlands one of the three geographical divisions of Scotland, occupying the fertile and densely populated plain that lies between two geological fault lines,

which run nearly parallel NE–SW across Scotland from Stonehaven to Dumbarton and from Dunbar to Girvan.

central nervous system the part of the nervous system with a concentration of ◊nerve cells which coordinates various body functions. In ◊vertebrates, the central nervous system consists of a brain and a dorsal nerve cord (the spinal cord) within the spinal column. In worms, insects, and crustaceans, it consists of a paired ventral nerve cord with concentrations of nerve cells, known as ganglia (see ◊ganglion) in each segment, and a small brain in the head.

Central Scotland a region of Scotland, formed in 1975 from the counties of Stirling, S Perth, and W Lothian; **area** 2,600 sq km/1,004 sq mi; **administrative headquarters** Stirling; **physical** Loch Lomond; wooded valley called the Trossachs; **products** agriculture; industries including brewing and distilling, engineering, electronics; **population** (1987) 272,000.

Central Treaty Organization (CENTO) a military alliance that replaced the ◊Baghdad Pact in 1959; it collapsed when the withdrawal of Iran, Pakistan, and Turkey in 1979 left the UK as the only member.

centre /'sentə/ *n.* **1.** the middle point or part; a pivot or axis of rotation. **2.** a point towards which interest is directed or from which administration etc. is organized; a main source of dispersal. **3.** a place where certain activities or facilities are concentrated. **4.** those members of a political party or group holding moderate opinions, between two extremes. **5.** a centre forward. —*adj.* of or at the centre. —*v.t./i.* **1.** to place in or at the centre. **2.** to concentrate or be concentrated *in* or *on*. **3.** to kick or hit from the wing towards the middle of the pitch in football or hockey. —**centre forward, centre half** *ns.* the middle player in the forward (or halfback) line in football etc. **centre of gravity**, the point round which the mass of a body is evenly distributed. **centrepiece** *n.* an ornament for the middle of a table etc., a principal item. [from Old French or Latin from Greek *kentron* = sharp point]

Centre /sɒntr/ region of N central France, covering an area of 39,200 sq km/15,131 sq mi; population (1986) 2,324,000. It includes the *départements* of Cher, Eure-et-Loire, Indre, Indre-et-Loire, Loire-et-Cher, and Loiret. Its capital is Orléans.

centre of mass or **centre of gravity** the point in or near an object from which its total weight appears to originate and can be assumed to act. A symmetrical homogeneous object such as a sphere or cube has its centre of mass at its physical centre; a hollow shape (such as a cup) may have its centre of mass in space inside the hollow.

Centre Party (German *Zentrumspartei*) a German political party established in 1871 to protect Catholic interests. Although alienated by Chancellor Bismarck's ◊*Kulturkampf* 1873–78, in the following years the *Zentrum* became an essential component in the government of imperial Germany. The party continued to play a part in the politics of Weimar Germany before being barred by Hitler in the summer of 1933.

centrifugal /sen'trɪfjʊgəl, -'fju:-/ *adj.* moving away from the centre or axis. —**centrifugal force**, a useful concept in physics, based on an apparent (but not real) force. It may be regarded as a force that acts radially outwards from a spinning or orbiting object, thus balancing the ◊centripetal force (which is real). For an object of mass *m* moving with a velocity *v* in a circle of radius *r*, the centrifugal force *F* equals mv^2/r (outwards). **centrifugal machine**, one in which the rotation causes this. —**centrifugally** *adv.* [from Latin *centrum* = centre and *fugere* = flee]

centrifuge /'sentrɪfju:dʒ/ *n.* a machine using centrifugal force to separate substances of different densities (e. g. milk and cream). —*v.t.* to subject to centrifugal motion; to separate by using a centrifuge. [French]

centriole *n.* a structure found in the ◊cells of animals that plays a role in the processes of ◊meiosis and ◊mitosis (cell division).

centripetal /sen'trɪpɪtəl, -'pi:-/ *adj.* moving towards the centre or axis. —**centripetal force**, a force that acts radially inwards on an object moving in a curved path. For example, with a weight whirled in a circle at the end of a length of string, the centripetal force is the tension in the string. For an object of mass *m* moving with a velocity *v* in a circle of radius *r*, the centripetal force *F* equals mv^2/r (inwards). The reaction to this force is the ◊centrifugal force. [from Latin *centrum* = centre and *petere* = seek]

centrist /'sentrist/ *n.* one who adopts a middle position in politics etc. —**centrism** *n.*

centromere *n.* the part of a ◊chromosome where there are no ◊genes. Under the microscope, it usually appears as a constriction in the strand of the chromosome, and is the point at which the spindle fibres are attached during ◊meiosis and ◊mitosis (cell division).

centurion /cen'tjuəriən/ *n.* an officer in the Roman army, originally one commanding 100 infantrymen. [from Latin]

century /'sentjuri, -tʃəri/ *n.* 1. a period of 100 years, especially one reckoned from the birth of Christ. 2. a score of 100; in cricket, a batsman's score of at least 100 runs in an innings. [from Latin *centuria* (*centum* = hundred)]

cephalic /si'fælik/ *adj.* of or in the head. —**cephalic index**, the ratio of the maximum skull width to maximum skull length, multiplied by 100. [from French from Latin from Greek *kephalē* = head]

cephalopod /'sefələpɒd/ *n.* a type of predatory marine mollusc with the mouth and head surrounded by tentacles. They are the most intelligent, the fastest-moving, and the largest of all animals without backbones, and there are remarkable luminescent forms which swim or drift at great depths. Cephalopods have the most highly developed nervous and sensory systems of all invertebrates, the eye in some closely paralleling that found in vertebrates. Examples include octopus, squid, and cuttlefish. Shells are rudimentary or absent in most cephalopods. [from Greek *kephalē* = head and *pous podos* = foot]

cephalosporin *n.* any of a class of broad-spectrum antibiotics derived from a fungus (genus *Cephalosporium*). It is similar to penicillin and is used on penicillin-resistant infections.

Cepheid variable /'si:fiɪd/ a yellow supergiant star that varies regularly in brightness every few days or weeks as a result of pulsations. The time that a Cepheid variable takes to pulsate is directly related to its average brightness; the longer the pulsation period, the brighter the star.

Cepheus /'si:fiəs/ *n.* a constellation of the north polar region, representing King Cepheus of Greek mythology, husband of Cassiopeia and father of Andromeda. It contains the Garnet Star (Mu Cephei), a red supergiant of variable brightness that is one of the reddest-coloured stars known, and Delta Cephei, prototype of the ◊Cepheid variables.

ceramic /si'ræmik/ *adj.* of pottery or similar substances. —*n.* 1. a ceramic article or substance. Ceramics are divided into heavy clay products (bricks, roof tiles, drainpipes, sanitary ware), refractories or high-temperature materials (linings for furnaces used to manufacture steel, fuel elements in nuclear reactors), and ◊pottery, which uses china clay, ball clay, china stone, and flint. Super-ceramics, such as silicon carbide, are lighter, stronger, and more heat-resistant than steel for use in motor and aircraft engines and have to be cast to shape since they are too hard to machine. 2. (in *plural*) the art of making pottery etc. [from Greek *keramos* = pottery]

Cerberus /'sɜ:bərəs/ in Greek mythology, the three-headed dog guarding the entrance to ◊Hades, the underworld.

cereal /'siəriəl/ *adj.* of edible grain. —*n.* 1. edible grain or the grass producing it. 2. a breakfast food made from this. [from Latin *cerealis* from *Ceres*, ancient Italian corn goddess]

cerebellum /seri'beləm/ *n.* a small part of the brain, located in the back of the skull of ◊vertebrate animals which controls muscular movements, balance, and coordination. It is relatively small in lower animals such as newts and lizards, but large in birds since flight demands precise coordination. The human cerebellum is also well developed, because of the need for balance when walking or running, and for coordinated hand movements. [Latin, diminutive of *cerebrum*]

cerebral /'seribrəl/ *adj.* of the brain; intellectual. [from Latin *cerebrum* = brain]

cerebral haemorrhage or **apoplectic fit** in medicine, a stroke in which a blood vessel bursts in the brain, caused by factors such as high blood pressure combined with hardening of the arteries (an ◊aneurysm), or chronic poisoning with lead or alcohol. It may cause death or damage parts

of the brain, leading to paralysis or mental impairment. The effects are usually long-term and the condition may recur.

cerebral palsy any abnormality of the brain caused by oxygen deprivation before birth, injury during birth, haemorrhage, meningitis, viral infection, or faulty development. It is characterized by muscle spasm, weakness, lack of coordination, and impaired movement. Intelligence is not always affected.

cerebration /seri'breiʃən/ *n.* activity of the brain.

cerebro-spinal /seribrəu'spainəl/ *adj.* of the brain and spinal cord.

cerebrum /'seribrəm/ *n.* the principal part of the vertebrate ◊brain, formed from the two paired cerebral hemispheres. In birds and mammals it is the largest part of the brain. It is covered with an infolded layer of grey matter, the cerebral cortex, which integrates brain functions. The cerebrum coordinates the senses, and is responsible for learning and other higher mental faculties. [Latin]

ceremonial /seri'məuniəl/ *adj.* of a ceremony, used in ceremonies; formal. —*n.* ceremony; a system of rules for ceremonies. —**ceremonially** *adv.* [from Latin]

ceremonious /seri'məuniəs/ *adj.* full of ceremony; elaborately performed. —**ceremoniously** *adv.*

ceremony /'seriməni/ *n.* 1. a set of formal acts, especially those used on a religious or public occasion. 2. formal or elaborate politeness. [from Old French or Latin *caerimonia* = religous worship]

Ceres /'siəri:z/ *n.* 1. in Roman mythology, the goddess of agriculture; see ◊Demeter. 2. the largest asteroid, 1,020 km/634 mi in diameter, and the first to be discovered (by Giuseppe Piazzi in 1801). Ceres orbits the Sun every 4.6 years at an average distance of 420 million km/260 million mi. Its mass is about one-sixtieth (0.017) of that of the Moon. 2. in Roman mythology, the goddess of agriculture; see ◊Demeter.

cerise /sə'ri:z/ *adj. & n.* light, clear red. [French = cherry]

cerium /'siəriəm/ *n.* a malleable and ductile, grey, metallic element, symbol Ce, atomic number 58, relative atomic mass 140.12. It is the most abundant member of the ◊lanthanide series, and is used in alloys, electronic components, nuclear fuels, and lighter flints. It was discovered in 1804 by Jöns Berzelius and Wilhelm Hisinger (1766–1852). [from the asteroid *Ceres* discovered just before the element]

cermet *n.* a bonded material containing ceramics and metal, widely used in jet engines and nuclear reactors. Cermets behave much like metals but have the great heat resistance of ceramics. Tungsten carbide, molybdenum boride, and aluminium oxide are among the ceramics used; iron, cobalt, nickel, and chromium are among the metals.

CERN acronym for a nuclear research organization founded in 1954 as a cooperative enterprise among European governments. It has laboratories at Meyrin, near Geneva, Switzerland. It was originally known as the *Conseil Européen pour la Recherche Nucléaire* but subsequently renamed *Organisation Européenne pour la Recherche Nucléaire*, although still familiarly known as CERN. It houses the world's largest particle ◊accelerator, the ◊Large Electron–Positron Collider (LEP), with which notable advances have been made in ◊particle physics.

certain /'sɜ:tən/ *adj.* 1. feeling sure, convinced. 2. known without doubt; that can be relied on to happen, be effective, etc. 3. that will not be further specified or defined. 4. small in amount but definitely there. [from Old French from Latin *certus* = settled]

certainly *adv.* without doubt; yes.

certainty *n.* 1. an undoubted fact; an indubitable prospect. 2. absolute conviction. [from Anglo-French]

certifiable /'sɜ:tifaiəbəl/ *adj.* that can be certified.

certificate /sə'tifikət/ *n.* an official written or printed statement attesting certain facts. —**certificated** *adj.*, **certification** /-'keiʃən/ *n.* [from French or Latin]

certify /'sɜ:tifai/ *v.t.* to state formally on a certificate; to declare (a person) officially to be insane. [from Old French from Latin]

certitude /'sɜ:titju:d/ *n.* a feeling of certainty.

cerulean /sə'ru:liən/ *adj.* sky-blue. [from Latin *caeruleus* (*caelum* = sky)]

Cervantes /sɜ:'vænti:z/ Saavedra, Miguel de 1547–1616. Spanish novelist, playwright, and poet, whose masterpiece, ◊*Don Quixote* (in full *El ingenioso hidalgo Don*

Quixote de la Mancha) was published in 1605. In 1613, his *Novelas Ejemplares/Exemplary Novels* appeared, followed by *Viaje del Parnaso/The Voyage to Parnassus* 1614. A spurious second part of *Don Quixote* prompted Cervantes to bring out his own second part in 1615, often considered superior to the first in construction and characterization.

There are only two families in the world, as an old grandmother of mine used to say: the Haves and the Have-nots.

Miguel de Cervantes Saavedra
Don Quixote

---

cervical cancer cancer of the cervix (the neck of the womb).

cervical smear the removal of a small sample of tissue from the cervix (neck of the womb) to screen for changes implying a likelihood of cancer. The procedure is also known as the **Pap test** after its originator, George Papanicolau.

cervix /'sɜ:vɪks/ *n.* (*plural* **cervices** /-visi:z/) the neck; a necklike structure, especially the opening of the womb. —**cervical** /sə'vaɪkəl, 'sɜ:vɪkəl/ *adj.* [Latin]

César /se'zɑ:/ adopted name of César Baldaccini 1921– French sculptor who uses iron and scrap metal and, in the 1960s, crushed car bodies. His subjects are imaginary insects and animals.

cessation /se'seɪʃən/ *n.* ceasing; a pause. [from Latin *cessare* = cease]

cession /'seʃən/ *n.* the act of ceding. [from Old French or Latin]

cesspit /'sespɪt/ *n.* a covered pit for temporary storage of liquid waste or sewage.

cesspool /'sespu:l/ *n.* = cesspit. [perhaps from earlier *cesperalle* from *suspiral* = water pipe]

c'est la vie that's life. [French]

CET abbreviation of Central European Time.

cetacean /si'teɪʃən/ *n.* a member of the mammalian order Cetacea, containing whales, dolphins, and porpoises. —*adj.* of cetaceans. [from Latin from Greek *kētos* = whale]

cetane /'si:teɪn/ *n.* a hydrocarbon of the paraffin series, found in petroleum.

Cetewayo /ketʃ'waɪəʊ/ (Cetshwayo) *c.*1826–1884. King of Zululand, South Africa 1873–83, whose rule was threatened by British annexation of the Transvaal in 1877. Although he defeated the British at Isandhlwana in 1879, he was later that year defeated by them at Ulundi. Restored to his throne in 1883, he was then expelled by his subjects.

Cetus /'si:təs/ *n.* a constellation straddling the celestial equator (see ◊celestial sphere), representing the whale. Its brightest star is Diphda (Beta Ceti), about 69 light years from Earth. Cetus contains the long-period variable star ◊Mira, and ◊Tau Ceti, one of the nearest stars visible with the naked eye.

Ceylon /si'lɒn/ former name of ◊Sri Lanka.

Cézanne /seɪ'zæn/ Paul 1839–1906. French Post-Impressionist painter, a leading figure in the development of modern art. He broke away from the Impressionists' spontaneous vision to develop a style that captured not only light and life, but the structure of natural forms in landscapes, still lifes, portraits, and his series of bathers.

cf. compare. [abbreviation of Latin *confer*]

Cf symbol for ◊californium.

CFC abbreviation of chloro-fluorocarbon, any of various usually gaseous substances thought to be harmful to the ozone layer in the Earth's atmosphere.

CFE abbreviation of conventional forces in Europe. Talks between government representatives began in Vienna, Austria, in March 1989 designed to reduce the 'conventional' (non-nuclear) forces (US, Soviet, French, British, and German) in Europe.

c.g.s. system or **C.G.S. system** a system of units based on the centimetre, gram, and second, as units of length, mass, and time, respectively. It has been replaced for scientific work by the ◊SI system to avoid inconsistencies in definition of the thermal calorie and electrical quantities.

Chablis /'ʃæbli:/ *n.* a white burgundy wine. [from *Chablis* in E France]

Chabrol /ʃæ'brɒl/ Claude 1930– . French film director. Originally a critic, he was one of the French 'New Wave'

of directors. His works of murder and suspense, which owe much to Hitchcock, include *Les Biches/The Girlfriends* 1968, *Le Boucher/The Butcher* 1970, and *Cop au Vin* 1984.

Chaco /'tʃɑ:kəʊ/ province of Argentina, covering an area of 99,633 sq km/38,458 sq mi; population (1980) 701,400. Its capital is Resistencia, in the SE. The chief crop is cotton, and there is forestry.

chacun à son goût each to his own taste. [French]

Chad /tʃæd/ Republic of; landlocked country in central N Africa, bounded to the N by Libya, to the E by Sudan, to the S by the Central African Republic, and to the W by Cameroon, Nigeria, and Niger; **area** 1,284,000 sq km/ 495,624 sq mi; **capital** N'djamena; **physical** mountains in the NW, savanna and part of Sahara Desert in the N; rivers in the S flow N to Lake Chad in marshy E; **head of state and government** Idriss Deby from 1990; **political system** emergent democracy; **exports** cotton, meat, livestock, hides, skins, bauxite, uranium, gold, oil; **population** (1990 est) 5,064,000; **language** French, Arabic (both official), over 100 African dialects; **recent history** independence was achieved from France in 1960; violent opposition from the Chadian National Liberation Front, backed by Libya, eventually drove the government into exile in 1981. Fighting continued between Libyan-backed and French-backed forces until 1987. Full diplomatic relations were restored with Libya in 1988.

chadar, chador variants of ◊chuddar.

Chad, Lake /tʃæd/ lake on the NE boundary of Nigeria. It once varied in extent between rainy and dry seasons from 50,000 sq km/20,000 sq mi to 20,000 sq km/7,000 sq mi, but a series of droughts in 1979–89 reduced its area by 80%. The Lake Chad basin is being jointly developed for oil and natron by Cameroon, Chad, Niger, and Nigeria.

Chadli /ʃæd'li:/ Benjedid 1929– . Algerian socialist politician, president from 1979. An army colonel, he supported Boumédienne in the overthrow of Ben Bella in 1965, and succeeded Boumédienne in 1979, pursuing more moderate policies. He prevailed in a power struggle in Sept 1989 with Prime Minister Kasdi Merbah, replacing him with Mouloud Hamrouche.

Chadwick /'tʃædwɪk/ James 1891–1974. English physicist. In 1932 he discovered the particle in the nucleus of an atom that became known as the neutron because it has no electric charge. He was awarded the Nobel Prize for Physics in 1935.

chafe /tʃeɪf/ *v.t./i.* **1.** to rub (the skin etc.) to restore warmth. **2.** to make or become sore by rubbing. **3.** to become irritated or impatient. [from Old French *chauffer* from Latin *calefacere* = make warm]

chafer /'tʃeɪfə/ *n.* a type of beetle, family Scarabaeidae. The adults eat foliage or flowers, and the underground larvae feed on roots, especially of grasses and cereals, and can be very destructive. Examples include the ◊cockchafer and the **rose chafer** *Cetonia aurata*, about 2 cm/ 0.8 in long and bright green. [Old English]

chaff /tʃɑ:f/ *n.* **1.** corn husks separated from the seed by threshing etc.; chopped hay or straw as cattle food; worthless stuff. **2.** good-humoured teasing or joking. —*v.t.* to tease or joke in a good-humoured way. [Old English]

chaffer /'tʃæfə/ *v.i.* to bargain or haggle. [Old English]

chaffinch /'tʃæfɪntʃ/ *n.* a bird *Fringilla coelebs* of the finch family, common throughout much of Europe and W Asia. About 15 cm/6 in long, the male is olive-brown above, with a bright chestnut breast, a bluish-grey cap, and two white bands on the upper part of the wing; the female is duller. [Old English]

chafing dish /'tʃeɪfɪŋ/ a pan with a heater under it for cooking food or keeping it warm at the table.

Chagall /ʃæ'gæl/ Marc 1887–1985. Russian-born French painter and designer; much of his highly coloured, fantastic imagery was inspired by the village life of his boyhood. He also designed stained glass, mosaics (for Israel's Knesset (parliament) in the 1960s), tapestries, and stage sets.

chagrin /'ʃægrɪn/ *n.* a feeling of annoyance and embarrassment or disappointment. —*v.t.* to affect with chagrin. [French]

chain /tʃeɪn/ *n.* **1.** a series of connected metal links or rings, used for hauling, supporting, or restraining things or worn as an ornament; a connected series or sequence. **2.** a number of shops, hotels, etc., owned by a single company. **3.** a unit of length for measuring land, 66 ft. —*v.t.* to fasten

chalk These chalk cliffs near Lulworth, Dorset, provide some of the finest coastal scenery in England.

or restrain with a chain. —**chain gang**, a group of prisoners chained together for manual work. **chain letter**, a letter of which the recipient is asked to make copies and send these to others, who will do the same. **chain mail**, armour made from interlaced rings. **chain reaction**, a chemical or nuclear reaction the products of which themselves cause further reactions; a series of events in which each causes or influences the next. **chain saw**, a saw consisting of an endless loop of chain with teeth set in it. **chain-smoke** *v.i.* to smoke many cigarettes in a continuous succession. **chain stitch**, an ornamental sewing or crochet stitch like a chain; a stitch made by a sewing machine using a single thread that is hooked through its own loop on the underside of the fabric sewn. **chain store**, one of a series of shops owned by the same firm and selling similar goods. [from Old French from Latin *catena*]

Chain Ernst Boris 1906–1979. German-born British biochemist who worked on the development of ◊penicillin. Chain fled to Britain from the Nazis in 1933. After the discovery of penicillin by Alexander Fleming, Chain worked to isolate and purify it. For this work, he shared the 1945 Nobel Prize for Medicine with Fleming and Howard Florey. Chain also discovered penicillinase, an enzyme that destroys penicillin.

chair *n.* 1. a movable seat with a back, for one person. 2. a position of authority at a meeting, the chairmanship. 3. a professorship. 4. (*US*) the electric chair. —*v.t.* 1. to seat in a chair of honour. 2. to carry in triumph on the shoulders of a group. 3. to act as chairman or chairwoman of. —**chair lift**, a series of chairs suspended from an endless cable for carrying passengers up a mountain etc. [from Anglo-French from Latin from Greek *cathedra*]

chairman *n.* or **chairwoman** (*plural* **chairmen** or **chairwomen**) the person presiding over a meeting; the regular president of a committee, board of directors, etc. —**chairperson** *n.*, **chairmanship** *n.*

chaise longue /'ʃeɪz 'lɒŋg/ a low chair with the seat long enough to support the sitter's legs. [French = long chair]

Chaka /'ʃɑːgə/ alternative spelling of ◊Shaka, Zulu chief.

Chalatenango /tʃələætiˈnæŋgəʊ/ department on the N frontier of El Salvador; **area** 2,507 sq km/968 sq mi; **capital** Chalatenango; **population** (1981) 235,700.

chalaza *n.* a glutinous mass of transparent albumen supporting the yolk inside birds' eggs. The chalaza is formed as the egg slowly passes down the oviduct, when it also acquires its coiled structure.

Chalcedon, Council of /'kælˈsiːdən/ an ecumenical council of the early Christian church, convoked in 451 by the Roman emperor Marcian, and held at Chalcedon (now Kadiköy, Turkey). The council, attended by over 500 bishops, resulted in the **Definition of Chalcedon**, an agreed doctrine for both the eastern and western churches.

chalcedony /kælˈsedənɪ/ *n.* a form of quartz, SiO_2, in which the crystals are so fine-grained that they are impossible to distinguish with a microscope (cryptocrystalline). Agate, onyx, tiger's eye, and carnelian are gem varieties (see ◊gem) of chalcedony. [from Latin from Greek]

chalcolithic /kælkəˈlɪθɪk/ *adj.* of a period in which both stone and bronze implements were used. [from Greek *khalkos* = copper and *lithos* = stone]

chalcopyrite *n.* copper iron sulphide, Cu_2FeS_2, the most common ore of copper. It is brassy-yellow in colour and

may have an iridescent surface tarnish. It occurs in many different types of mineral vein, in rocks ranging from basalt to limestone.

Chaldea /kælˈdiːə/ an ancient region of Babylonia. —**Chaldean,** *adj.* [from Assyrian *Kaldu*]

chalet /'ʃæleɪ/ *n.* 1. a Swiss mountain hut or cottage; a house in similar style. 2. a small hut in a holiday camp etc. [Swiss French]

Chaliapin /ʃæliˈæpɪn/ Fyodor Ivanovich 1873–1938. Russian bass singer, born in Kazan of peasant parentage. His greatest role was that of Boris Godunov in Mussorgsky's opera of the same name. Chaliapin left the USSR in 1921 to live and sing in the capital cities of the world.

chalice /'tʃælɪs/ *n.* a vessel like a large goblet for holding wine, one from which wine is drunk at the Eucharist. [from Old French from Latin *calix* = cup]

chalk /tʃɔːk/ *n.* 1. a soft, fine-grained, whitish rock composed of calcium carbonate, $CaCO_3$, extensively quarried for use in cement, lime, and mortar, and in the manufacture of cosmetics and toothpaste. 2. a stick of this or similar substance, white or coloured, used for writing or drawing. —*v.t.* to mark, draw, rub, etc., with a stick of chalk. —**by a long chalk**, by far. **chalk stripe**, a textile pattern of thin white stripes on a dark background. **chalk up**, to register (a success etc.). —**chalky** *adj.* [Old English from Latin *calx*]

challenge /'tʃælɪndʒ/ *n.* 1. a call to demonstrate one's ability or strength, especially in a contest. 2. a call or demand to respond, a sentry's call for a person to identify himself. 3. a formal objection, e. g. to a juryman. 4. a challenging task. —*v.t.* 1. to issue a challenge to. 2. to raise a formal objection to. 3. to question the truth or rightness of. 4. (*absolute,* usually in *participle*) to offer problems that test one's abilities, to be stimulating. —**challenger** *n.* [from Old French from Latin *calumnia* = calumny]

Chalmers /'tʃɑːməz/ Thomas 1780–1847. Scottish theologian. At the Disruption of the ◊Church of Scotland in 1843, Chalmers withdrew from the church along with a large number of other priests, and became principal of the Free Church college, thus founding the ◊Free Church of Scotland.

chalybeate /kəˈlɪbɪət/ *adj.* (of water or springs) impregnated with iron salts. [from Latin from Greek *khalups* = steel]

chamber /'tʃeɪmbə/ *n.* 1. an assembly hall; the council or other body that meets in it. 2. (in *plural*) a set of rooms in a larger building, a judge's room for hearing cases that do not need to be taken in court. 3. a cavity or compartment in the body of an animal or plant, or in machinery. 4. (*archaic*) a room, especially a bedroom. —**chamber music**, music written for a small number of players, suitable for performing in a room or small hall. **Chamber of Commerce**, an association of businessmen and women to promote social commercial interests. **chamber pot**, a receptacle for urine etc., used in the bedroom. [from Old French from Latin *camera* = vaulted chamber]

chamberlain /'tʃeɪmbəlɪn/ *n.* an official managing a royal or noble household. [from Old French from Germanic]

Chamberlain (Arthur) Neville 1869–1940. British Conservative politician, son of Joseph Chamberlain. He was prime minister 1937–40; his policy of appeasement towards the fascist dictators Mussolini and Hitler (with whom he concluded the ◊Munich Agreement in 1938) failed to prevent the outbreak of World War II. He resigned in 1940 following the defeat of the British forces in Norway.

In war, whichever side may call itself the victor, there are no winners, but all are losers.

Neville Chamberlain
speech at Kettering 3 July 1938

Chamberlain (Joseph) Austen 1863–1937. British Conservative politician, elder son of Joseph Chamberlain; as foreign secretary 1924–29 he negotiated the Pact of ◊Locarno, for which he won the Nobel Peace Prize in 1925, and signed the ◊Kellogg–Briand pact to outlaw war in 1928.

Chamberlain Joseph 1836–1914. British politician, reformist mayor of and member of Parliament for Birmingham; in 1886, he resigned from the cabinet over

Gladstone's policy of home rule for Ireland, and led the revolt of the Liberal-Unionists.

Chamberlain Owen 1920– . US physicist whose graduate studies were interrupted by wartime work on the Manhattan project at Los Alamos. After World War II, working with Italian physicist Emilio Segrè, he discovered the existence of the antiproton. Both men were awarded the Nobel Prize for Physics in 1959.

Chamberlain, Lord in the UK, chief officer of the royal household, who engages staff and appoints retail suppliers. Until 1968 the Lord Chamberlain licensed and censored plays before their public performance. The office is temporary, and appointments are made by the government.

Chamberlain, Lord Great in the UK, the only officer of state whose position survives from Norman times; responsibilities include the arrangements for the opening of Parliament, assisting with the regalia at coronations, and organizing the ceremony when bishops and peers are created.

chambermaid *n.* a woman employed to clean and tidy bedrooms in a hotel etc.

Chambers /'tʃeɪmbəz/ William 1726–1796. British architect and popularizer of Chinese influence (for example, the pagoda in Kew Gardens, London) and designer of Somerset House, London.

chameleon /kə'mi:liən/ *n.* 1. a type of lizard, some 80 or so species of the family Chameleontidae. Some species have highly developed colour-changing abilities, which are caused by changes in the intensity of light, temperature, and emotion, which affect the dispersal of pigment granules in the layers of cells beneath the outer skin. 2. a changeable or inconstant person. [from Latin, from Greek = ground lion]

chamfer /'tʃæmfə/ *v.t.* to bevel symmetrically. —*n.* a chamfered edge or corner. [from French *chant* = edge and *fraint* = broken]

chamois /'ʃæmwæ:/ *n.* 1. (*plural* the same /-wɑ:z/) a goatlike mammal *Rupicapra rupicapra* found in mountain ranges of S Europe and Asia Minor; it is brown, with dark patches running through the eyes, and can be up to 80 cm/2.6 ft high. 2. /'ʃæmɪ/ or **chamois leather** soft yellowish leather from sheep, goats, deer, etc., or a piece of this, used for washing or polishing things. [French]

chamomile variant of ◊camomile.

champ *v.t./i.* 1. to munch noisily; to make a chewing action or noise. 2. to show impatience.

champagne /ʃæm'peɪn/ *n.* 1. a naturally sparkling white wine from Champagne in France; a similar wine from elsewhere. 2. a pale straw colour. [from *Champagne*, former province in E France]

Champagne-Ardenne /ʃæmpeɪnɑ:'den/ region of NE France, covering an area of 25,600 sq km/9,882 sq mi; population (1986) 1,353,000. Its capital is Reims, and it comprises the *départements* of Ardennes, Aube, Marne, and Haute-Marne. It has sheep and dairy farming and vineyards.

Champaigne /ʃæm'peɪn/ Philippe de 1602–1674. French artist, the leading portrait painter of the court of Louis XIII. Of Flemish origin, he went to Paris in 1621 and gained the patronage of Cardinal Richelieu. His style is elegant, cool, and restrained.

champignon *n.* a fungus *Marasmius oreades*, family Agaricaceae, which is edible and a popular food in parts of Europe. It is known as the fairy ring champignon because the fruiting bodies (mushrooms) occur in rings around the outer edge of the underground mycelium (threadlike tubes) of the fungus. Several other edible agarics are also called champignons.

champion /'tʃæmpiən/ *n.* 1. (frequently *attributive*) a person or thing that has defeated or surpassed all rivals in a competition. 2. a person who fights or argues in support of another or of a cause. —*v.t.* to support as a champion. [from Old French from Latin *campio* = fighter (*campus* = field)]

championship *n.* 1. the status of a champion in a sport etc.; a contest held to decide the champion. 2. advocacy, defence (of a cause etc.).

Champlain /ʃæm'pleɪn/ Samuel de 1567–1635. French pioneer, soldier, and explorer in Canada. Having served in the army of Henry IV and on an expedition to the West Indies, he began his exploration of Canada in 1603. In a third expedition in 1608 he founded and named Québec, and was appointed Lieutenant-Governor of French Canada in 1612.

champlevé /'ʃɑləveɪ/ *adj.* of or using a style of enamelwork decoration in which hollows are made in a metal surface and filled with enamel. —*n.* this style. [French = raised field]

Champollion /ʃɒmpɒl'jɒn/ Jean François, le Jeune 1790–1832. French Egyptologist who in 1822 deciphered Egyptian hieroglyphics with the aid of the ◊Rosetta Stone.

chance /tʃɑ:ns/ *n.* 1. the way things happen without known cause or agency; the supposed force governing such happenings, luck, fate. 2. a possibility, likelihood. 3. an opportunity. —*adj.* happening by chance. —*v.t./i.* 1. to happen by chance. 2. to take one's chance of, to risk. —**by chance**, as it turns or turned out; without being planned. **chance on**, to come upon or find by chance. **chance one's arm**, (*colloquial*) to take a chance although failure is possible. **take a chance**, to take a risk, to act in the hope that a particular thing will (or will not) happen. **take chances**, to behave riskily. **take one's chance**, to trust to luck. [from Anglo-French from Latin *cadere* = fall]

chancel /'tʃɑ:nsəl/ *n.* the part of a church, often screened off, containing the altar. [from Old French from Latin *cancelli* = grating]

chancellery /'tʃɑ:nsələrɪ/ *n.* 1. a chancellor's department, residence, or staff. 2. = Chancery.

chancellor /'tʃɑ:nsələ/ *n.* 1. a state or law official of various kinds; the chief minister of state in Germany and Austria. 2. the nonresident head of a university. [from Anglo-French from Latin *cancellarius* = secretary]

Chancellor, Lord a UK state official, originally the royal secretary, today a member of the cabinet, whose office ends with a change of government. The Lord Chancellor acts as speaker of the House of Lords, may preside over the court of appeal, and is head of the judiciary.

chancellor of the Duchy of Lancaster in the UK, an honorary post held by a cabinet minister who has other nondepartmental responsibilities. The chancellor of the Duchy of Lancaster was originally the monarch's representative controlling the royal lands and courts within the duchy.

chancellor of the Exchequer in the UK, a senior cabinet minister responsible for the national economy and the preparation of the budget. The office, established under Henry III, originally entailed keeping the Exchequer seal.

chancery /'tʃɑ:nsərɪ/ *n.* 1. a public records office. 2. an office attached to an embassy or consulate.

Chancery *n.* in the UK, a division of the high court that deals with such matters as the administration of the estates of deceased persons, the execution of trusts, the enforcement of sales of land, and foreclosure (see ◊foreclose) of mortgages. Before reorganization of the court system in 1875, it administered the rules of ◊equity as distinct from ◊common law.

chancy /'tʃɑ:nsɪ/ *adj.* risky, uncertain.

Chandelā /tʃʌn'deɪlɑ:/ *n.* or **Candella** a Rajput dynasty that ruled the Bundelkhand region of central India from the 9th to the 11th century. The Chandelās fought against Muslim invaders, until they were replaced by the Bundelās.

chandelier /ʃændə'liə/ *n.* an ornamental, branched support for a number of lights, hung from a ceiling. [from French]

Chandigarh /tʃʌndi'gɑ:/ city of N India, in the foothills of the Himalayas; population (1981) 421,000. It is also a Union Territory; **area** 114 sq km/44 sq mi; **population** (1981) 450,000.

chandler /'tʃɑ:ndlə/ *n.* a dealer in ropes, canvas, and other supplies for ships. [from French]

Chandler Raymond 1888–1959. US crime writer, who created the hard-boiled private eye Philip Marlowe in books that include *The Big Sleep* 1939, *Farewell, My Lovely* 1940, and *The Long Goodbye* 1954.

Chandragupta Maurya /'tʃʌndrəguptə 'mauriə/ ruler of N India c.321–c.297 BC, founder of the Maurya dynasty. He overthrew the Nanda dynasty in 325 and then conquered the Punjab in 322 after the death of ◊Alexander the Great, expanding his empire west to Persia. He is credited with having united most of India.

Chanel /ʃæ'nel/ Coco (Gabrielle) 1883–1971. French fashion designer, the creator of the 'little black dress', the informal cardigan suit, costume jewellery, and perfumes.

Chaney /'tʃeɪnɪ/ Lon (Alonso) 1883–1930. US star of silent films, often in grotesque or monstrous roles such as *The Phantom of the Opera* 1925. A master of make-up,

Chanel The French couturier 'Coco' Chanel in 1929.

he was nicknamed 'The Man of a Thousand Faces'. He sometimes employed extremely painful devices for added effectiveness, as in the title role in *The Hunchback of Notre Dame* 1923, when he carried over 70 lbs of costume in the form of a heavy hump and harness.

Chaney Lon, Jr (Creighton) 1906–1973. US actor, son of Lon Chaney, who gave an acclaimed performance as Lennie in *Of Mice and Men* 1940. He went on to star in many 1940s horror films, including the title role in *The Wolfman* 1941. His other work includes *My Favorite Brunette* 1947 and *The Haunted Palace* 1963.

Chang Ch'ien /ˈdʒæŋ ˈtʃen/ lived 2nd century BC. Chinese explorer who pioneered the ◊Silk Road.

Changchun /tʃæŋˈtʃun/ industrial city and capital of Jilin province, China; population (1986) 1,860,000. Machinery and motor vehicles are manufactured. It is also the centre of an agricultural district.

change /tʃeɪndʒ/ *v.t./i.* 1. to make or become different; to pass from one form or phase into another. 2. to take or use another instead of; to put fresh clothes or coverings etc. on; to go from one (vehicle, route, etc.) to another; to exchange. 3. to give small money in change for; to give different currency for. —*n.* 1. changing, alteration; substitution of one thing for another, variety; a reserve (of clothing etc.); a fresh occupation or surroundings. 2. money in small units; money returned as the balance when the price is less than the amount tendered. 3. the menopause. 4. (usually in *plural*) in bell-ringing, the different orders in which the bells of a peal may be rung. —**change hands,** to pass to a new owner. **change of heart,** a great alteration in one's attitude or feelings. **change of life,** the menopause. **change one's mind,** to adopt a new purpose or way of thinking. **change over,** to change from one system or situation to another. **change-over** *n.* such a change. **change-ringing** *n.* ringing a peal of bells in a series of different orders. [from Anglo-French from Latin *cambire* = barter]

changeable /ˈtʃeɪndʒəbəl/ *adj.* liable to change, inconstant.

changeling /ˈtʃeɪndʒlɪŋ/ *n.* a child or thing believed to have been substituted secretly for another, especially by elves etc.

change of state in physics, when a gas condenses to a liquid or a liquid freezes to a solid. Similar changes take place when a solid melts to form a liquid or a liquid vaporizes (evaporates) to produce gas. The first set of changes are brought about by cooling, the second set by heating. In the unusual change of state called *sublimation*, a solid changes directly to a gas without passing through the liquid state. For example, solid carbon dioxide (dry ice) sublimes to carbon dioxide gas.

Chang Jiang /ˈtʃæŋ dʒiˈæŋ/ longest river (formerly Yangtze Kiang) of China, flowing about 6,300 km/3,900 mi from Tibet to the Yellow Sea. It is a major commercial waterway.

Changsha /tʃæŋˈʃɑː/ river port, on the river Chang Jiang, capital of Hunan province, China; population (1986) 1,160,000. It trades in rice, tea, timber, and nonferrous metals; works antimony, lead, and silver; and produces chemicals, electronics, porcelain, and embroideries.

channel /ˈtʃænl/ *n.* 1. the sunken bed of a watercourse; the navigable part of a waterway. 2. a piece of water (wider than a strait) connecting two seas. 3. a passage along which a liquid may flow; a sunken course or line along which something may move. 4. any course by which news or information etc. may travel. 5. a band of broadcasting frequencies reserved for a particular programme. 6. a path for transmitting electrical signals or (in computers) data. —*v.t.* (-ll-) 1. to form channels or grooves in. 2. to direct along a channel or desired route. [from Old French from Latin *canalis* = canal]

Channel, English stretch of water between England and France, leading in the west to the Atlantic Ocean, and in the east via the Strait of Dover to the North Sea; also known as La Manche (French 'the sleeve') from its shape.

Channel Islands a group of islands in the English Channel, off the NW coast of France, a possession of the British crown; **area** 194 sq km/75 sq mi; **physical** comprising the islands of Jersey, Guernsey, Alderney, Great and Little Sark, with the lesser Herm, Brechou, Jethou, and Lihou; **exports** flowers, early potatoes, tomatoes, butterflies; **population** (1981) 128,878.

Channel swimming a popular test of endurance since Captain Matthew Webb (1848–1883) first swam across the English Channel from Dover to Calais in 1875. His time was 21 hr 45 min for the 34 km/21 mi journey.

Channel tunnel a tunnel built beneath the English Channel, linking Britain with mainland Europe. It comprises twin rail tunnels, 50 km/31 mi long and 7.3 m/24 ft in diameter, located 40 m/130 ft beneath the seabed. Specially designed shuttle trains carrying cars and lorries will run between terminals at Folkestone, Kent, and Sangatte, W of Calais, France. It was begun in 1986 and is scheduled to be operational in 1993.

chanson de geste /ˈʃɑːsɒn də ˈʒest/ the epic poetry of the High Middle Ages. It probably developed from oral poetry recited in royal or princely courts, and takes as its subject the exploits of heroes, such as those associated with Charlemagne and the Crusades.

Chanson de Roland /ʃɑːˈsɒn də rəʊˈlɒn/ an early 12th-century epic poem which tells of the real and imaginary deeds of Roland and other knights of Charlemagne, and their last stand against the Basques at Roncesvalles.

chant /tʃɑːnt/ *n.* 1. a melody for psalms and other unmetrical texts, in which an indefinite number of syllables are sung to one opening note. 2. a measured monotonous song. —*v.t.* to sing, especially a chant; to shout or call rhythmically. [from Old French from Latin *cantare* = sing]

chanter *n.* 1. one who chants. 2. the melody pipe of bagpipes.

chanterelle /ʃɑːntəˈrel/ *n.* a yellow, edible, funnel-shaped fungus *Cantharellus cibarius*. [French, from Latin from Greek *kantharos* = drinking vessel]

chantry /ˈtʃɑːntrɪ/ *n.* 1. in medieval Europe, a religious ceremony in which, in return for an endowment of land, the souls of the donor, his family, and his friends would be prayed for. A chantry could be held at an existing altar, or in a specially constructed chantry chapel, in which the donor's body was usually buried. 2. a chapel endowed for the saying of masses for the founder's soul. [from Anglo-French *chanter* = chant]

chaos /ˈkeɪɒs/ *n.* 1. utter confusion or disorder. 2. formless primordial matter. —**chaos theory** or **chaology,** a branch of mathematics used to deal with chaotic systems, an engineered structure, such as an oil platform, that is subjected to irregular, unpredictable wave stress. —**chaotic** /-ˈɒtɪk/ *adj.*, **chaotically** *adv.* [French or Latin from Greek]

chap[1] *n.* (*colloquial*) a man, a fellow. [abbreviation of archaic *chapman* = pedlar]

chap[2] *v.t.* (-pp-) (of skin) to split or crack, (of wind etc.) to cause to develop chaps. —*n.* (usually in *plural*) a crack in the skin.

chap[3] *n.* the lower jaw or half of the cheek, especially of a pig, as food. [variant of *chop*[3]]

chaparral /tʃæpəˈræl, ʃæ-/ *n.* (*US*) dense tangled brushwood, especially in the SW USA and Mexico. [Spanish *chaparra* = evergreen oak]

chapati, chapatti variants of ◊chupatty.

chapbook *n.* (*historical*) a small pamphlet of tales, ballads, tracts, etc., hawked by chapmen.

chapel /ˈtʃæpəl/ *n.* 1. a place used for Christian worship, other than a cathedral or parish church; a service in this. 2. a separate part of a cathedral or church, with its own altar.

3. a section of a trade union in a printing works. [from Old French from Latin, diminutive of *cappa* = cloak; the first chapel was a sanctuary in which St Martin's sacred cloak was kept by *capellani* (chaplains)]

Chapel Royal in the UK, the royal retinue of priests, singers, and musicians (including Tallis, Byrd, and Purcell) of the English court from 1135.

chaperon /'ʃæpərəʊn/ *n.* an older or married woman in charge of a young unmarried woman on social occasions. —*v.t.* to act as a chaperon to. —**chaperonage** *n.* [French = hood]

chaplain /'tʃæplɪn/ *n.* a clergyman attached to a private chapel, institution, regiment, ship, etc. —**chaplaincy** *n.* [from Anglo-French from Latin]

chaplet /'tʃæplɪt/ *n.* 1. a wreath for the head. 2. a short rosary. [from Old French from Latin *cappa* = cap]

Chaplin /'tʃæplɪn/ Charlie (Charles Spencer) 1889–1977. English film actor-director. He made his reputation as a tramp with a smudge moustache, bowler hat, and twirling cane in silent comedies from the mid-1910s, including *The Rink* 1916, *The Kid* 1921, and *The Gold Rush* 1925. His work often contrasts buffoonery with pathos, and his later films combine dialogue with mime and music, as in *The Great Dictator* 1940, and *Limelight* 1952. He was one of cinema's most popular stars.

chapman /'tʃæpmən/ *n.* (*plural* **chapmen**) (*historical*) a pedlar. [from Old English *cēap* = barter]

Chapman Frederick Spencer 1907–1971. British explorer, mountaineer, and writer, who explored Greenland, the Himalayas, and Malaysia. He accompanied Gino Watkins on the British Arctic Air Routes Expedition 1930–31 and in 1935 joined a climbing expedition to the Himalayas. For two years he participated in a government mission to Tibet, before setting out to climb the 7,315 m/24,000 ft peak, Chomollari.

Chapman George 1559–1634. English poet and dramatist. His translations of Homer (completed in 1616) were celebrated; his plays include the comedy *Eastward Ho!* (with Jonson and Marston) 1605 and the tragedy *Bussy d'Amboise* 1607.

chapter /'tʃæptə/ *n.* 1. a division of a book; (*figurative*) a period of time. 2. the canons of a cathedral or the monks of a particular order etc.; a meeting of these. —**chapter house**, a building used for such meetings. [from Old French from Latin *capitulum*, diminutive of *caput* = head]

char[1] *v.t.* (**-rr-**) to make or become black by burning; to burn to charcoal.

char[2] *n.* a charwoman. —*v.i.* (**-rr-**) to work as a charwoman. [earlier *chare* from Old English *cerr* = a turn]

char[3] *n.* (*plural* the same) a fish *Salvelinus alpinus* related to the trout, living in the Arctic coastal waters, and also in Europe and North America in some upland lakes. It is one of Britain's rarest fish, and is at risk from increasing acidification.

charabanc /'ʃærəbæŋ/ *n.* a long vehicle, originally horse-drawn and open, later an early form of motor coach, with seating on transverse benches facing forward. [from French *char-à-bancs* = benched carriage]

characin *n.* a freshwater fish belonging to the family Characidae. There are over 1,300 species, mostly in South and Central America, but also in Africa. Most are carnivores. In typical characins, unlike the somewhat similar carp family, the mouth is toothed, and there is a small dorsal adipose fin just in front of the tail.

character /'kærɪktə/ *n.* 1. the distinguishing qualities of a person, group, or thing; a person's moral qualities; moral strength. 2. reputation; good reputation. 3. a person having specified qualities; an eccentric. 4. a person in a play, novel, etc. 5. a description of a person's qualities, a testimonial. 6. (often in *plural*) an inscribed letter or graphic symbol, as in an alphabet. 7. a physical characteristic of a biological species. [from Old French from Latin from Greek = stamp, impression]

characteristic /kærɪktə'rɪstɪk/ *adj.* distinctive of a particular individual, class, etc. —*n.* 1. a characteristic feature or quality. 2. in mathematics, the integral part (whole number) of a ◊logarithm. For example, in base ten, $10^0 = 1$, $10^1 = 10$, $10^3 = 100$, and so on; the powers to which 10 is raised are the characteristics. —**characteristically** *adv.* [from French or Latin]

characterize /'kærɪktəraɪz/ *v.t.* 1. to sum up the qualities of. 2. to be characteristic of. —**characterization** /-'zeɪʃən/ *n.* [from French or Latin from Greek]

charade /ʃə'rɑ:d/ *n.* 1. (in *plural*) a game in which a word has to be guessed from clues to each syllable given in acted scenes. 2. an absurd pretence. [French from Provençal *charra* = chatter]

charcoal /'tʃɑ:kəʊl/ *n.* the black carbonized residue of partially burnt wood etc., used as a filtering material, as fuel, or for drawing. —**charcoal grey,** very dark grey.

Charcot /ʃɑ:'kəʊ/ Jean-Martin 1825–1893. French neurologist who studied hysteria, sclerosis, locomotor ataxia, and senile diseases, examining the way certain mental illnesses cause physical changes in the brain. He exhibited hysterical women at weekly public lectures, which became highly fashionable events. Sigmund ◊Freud was one of his pupils.

Chardin /ʃɑ:'dæn/ Jean-Baptiste-Siméon 1699–1779. French painter of naturalistic still lifes and quiet domestic scenes that recall the Dutch tradition. His work is a complete contrast to that of his contemporaries, the Rococo painters. He developed his own technique using successive layers of paint to achieve depth of tone and is generally considered one of the finest exponents of the genre.

Chardonnet /ʃɑ:dɒ'neɪ/ Hilaire Bernigaud 1839–1924. French chemist who developed artificial silk in 1883, the first artificial fibre.

charge *n.* 1. the price asked for goods or services. 2. a formal accusation. 3. an admonition given about one's duty or responsibility; a task or duty. 4. custody. 5. an impetuous attack in battle etc. 6. the quantity of material used in an apparatus in a single operation, especially of explosive in a gun. 7. the amount of electricity contained in a substance; energy stored chemically for conversion into electricity. 8. a heraldic device or bearing. —*v.t./i.* 1. to ask as a price; to ask (a person) for a price; to debit (a cost) *to* an account. 2. to accuse formally of a crime. 3. to entrust *with* a task; to admonish *to.* 4. to advance impetuously; to attack thus. 5. to give an electric charge to; to store energy in; to load with the requisite amount of explosive etc. 6. to saturate with liquid, vapour, or chemical. —**in charge,** in command. **take charge,** to take control. [from Old French from Latin *carricare* = load (*carrus* = car)]

charge-coupled device (CCD) a device which usually consists of alternate layers of metal, silicon dioxide, and silicon, used by astronomers to detect solid photons of light. Charge-coupled devices contain large numbers of light-sensitive electric circuits known as picture elements (or pixels). Each pixel stores an electronic charge proportional to the amount of light reaching it from the telescopic image focused on to the CCD.

chargé d'affaires /ʃɑ:ʒeɪ dæ'feə/ (*plural* **chargés** /-eɪ/) an ambassador's deputy; an envoy to a minor country. [French = entrusted with affairs]

charged particle beam a high-energy beam of electrons or protons that does not burn through the surface of its target like a ◊laser, but cuts through it. Such beams are being developed as weapons.

Charge of the Light Brigade the disastrous attack by the British Light Brigade of cavalry against the Russian entrenched artillery on 25 Oct 1854 during the Crimean War at ◊Balaclava.

charger *n.* 1. a cavalry horse. 2. an apparatus for charging a battery.

chariot /'tʃærɪət/ *n.* a horse-drawn carriage with two wheels, used in ancient Egypt, Greece, and Rome, for fighting, processions, and races; it is thought to have originated in Asia. —**charioteer** /-ɪə'tɪə/ *n.* [from Old French *char* = car]

charisma /kə'rɪzmə/ *n.* the capacity to inspire devotion and enthusiasm; divinely conferred power or talent. —**charismatic** /kærɪz'mætɪk/ *adj.* [Latin from Greek *kharis* = favour, grace]

charismatic movement a recent movement within the Christian church that emphasizes the role of the Holy Spirit in the life of the individual believer and in the life of the church. See ◊Pentecostal movement.

charitable /'tʃærɪtəbəl/ *adj.* 1. generous in giving to those in need; lenient in judging others. 2. connected with organized charities. —**charitably** *adv.*

charity

charity /'tʃærɪtɪ/ *n.* **1.** kindness or voluntary giving to those in need; an organization for helping those in need; help so given. **2.** leniency in judging others; love towards others. [from Old French from Latin *caritas* (*carus* = dear)]

charlady *n.* a ◊charwoman.

charlatan /'ʃɑːlətən/ *n.* one falsely claiming to have a special knowledge or skill. —**charlatanism** *n.* [French from Italian = babbler]

Charlemagne /ʃɑːləˈmeɪn/ Charles I **the Great** 742–814. King of the Franks from 768 and Holy Roman emperor from 800. By inheritance (his father was ◊Pepin the Short) and extensive campaigns of conquest, he united most of W Europe by 804, when after 30 years of war the Saxons came under his control. He reformed the legal, judicial, and military systems; established schools; and promoted Christianity, commerce, agriculture, arts, and literature. In his capital, Aachen, scholars gathered from all over Europe.

Charles /tʃɑːlz/ (Mary) Eugenia 1919– . Dominican politician, prime minister from 1980; cofounder and first leader of the centrist Dominica Freedom Party (DFP).

Charles Jacques Alexandre César 1746–1823. French physicist, who studied gases and made the first ascent of a hydrogen-filled balloon in 1783. His work on the expansion of gases led to the formulation of ◊Charles's law.

Charles Ray 1930– . US singer, songwriter, and pianist, whose first hits were 'I've Got A Woman' 1955, 'What'd I Say' 1959, and 'Georgia on My Mind' 1960. He has recorded gospel, blues, rock, soul, country, and rhythm and blues.

Charles two kings of Britain:

Charles I 1600–1649. King of Great Britain and Ireland from 1625, son of James I of England (James VI of Scotland). He accepted the ◊Petition of Right 1628 but then dissolved Parliament and ruled without one 1629–40. His advisers were ◊Strafford and ◊Laud, who persecuted the Puritans and provoked the Scots to revolt. The ◊Short Parliament, summoned in 1640, refused funds, and the ◊Long Parliament later that year rebelled. Charles declared war on Parliament in 1642 but surrendered in 1646 and was beheaded 1649.

Charles II 1630–1685. King of Great Britain and Ireland from 1660, when Parliament accepted the restoration of the monarchy; son of Charles I. His chief minister Clarendon, who arranged his marriage in 1662 with Catherine of Braganza, was replaced in 1667 with the ◊Cabal of advisers. His plans to restore Catholicism in Britain led to war with the Netherlands 1672–74 and a break with Parliament, which he dissolved in 1681. He was succeeded by James II.

. . . my words are my own, and my actions are my ministers.

Charles II

Charles (full name Charles Philip Arthur George) 1948– . Prince of the United Kingdom, heir to the British throne, and Prince of Wales since 1958 (invested in 1969). He is the first-born child of Queen Elizabeth II and the Duke of Edinburgh. He studied at Trinity College, Cambridge, 1967–70, before serving in the Royal Air Force and Royal Navy. He is the first royal heir since 1659 to have an English wife, Lady Diana Spencer, daughter of the 8th Earl Spencer. They have two sons and heirs, William (1982–) and Henry (1984–).

Charles ten kings of France:

Charles I better known as the emperor ◊Charlemagne.

Charles II the Bald; see ◊Charles II, Holy Roman emperor.

Charles III the Simple 879–929. King of France 893–922, son of Louis the Stammerer. He was crowned at Reims. In 911 he ceded what later became the duchy of Normandy to the Norman chief Rollo.

Charles IV the Fair 1294–1328. King of France from 1322, when he succeeded Philip V as the last of the direct Capetian line.

Charles V the Wise 1337–1380. King of France from 1364. He was regent during the captivity of his father, John II, in England 1356–60, and became king on John's death. He reconquered nearly all France from England 1369–80.

Charles VI the Mad or **the Well-Beloved** 1368–1422. King of France from 1380, succeeding his father Charles V, he was under the regency of his uncles until 1388. He became mentally unstable in 1392, and civil war broke out between the dukes of Orléans and Burgundy. Henry V of England invaded France in 1415, conquering Normandy, and in 1420 forcing Charles to sign the Treaty of Troyes, recognizing Henry as his successor.

Charles VII 1403–1461. King of France from 1429. Son of Charles VI, he was excluded from the succession by the Treaty of Troyes, but recognized by the South of France. In 1429 Joan of Arc raised the siege of Orléans and had him crowned at Reims. He organized France's first standing army and by 1453 he had expelled the English from all of France except Calais.

Charles VIII 1470–1498. King of France from 1483, when he succeeded his father, Louis XI. In 1494 he unsuccessfully tried to claim the Neapolitan crown, and when he entered Naples in 1495 was forced to withdraw by a coalition of Milan, Venice, Spain, and the Holy Roman Empire. He defeated them at Fornovo, but lost Naples. He died while preparing a second expedition.

Charles IX 1550–1574. King of France from 1560. Second son of Henry II and Catherine de' Medici, he succeeded his brother Francis II at the age of ten but remained under the domination of his mother's regency for ten years while France was torn by religious wars. In 1570 he fell under the influence of the ◊Huguenot leader Admiral Coligny (1517–1572); alarmed by this, Catherine instigated his order for the Massacre of ◊St Bartholomew, which led to a new religious war.

Charles X 1757–1836. King of France from 1824. Grandson of Louis XV and brother of Louis XVI and Louis XVIII, he was known as the *comte d'Artois* before his accession. He fled to England at the beginning of the French Revolution, and when he came to the throne on the death of Louis XVIII, he attempted to reverse the achievements of the Revolution. A revolt ensued in 1830, and he again fled to England.

Charles seven rulers of the Holy Roman Empire:

Charles I better known as ◊Charlemagne.

Charles II the Bald 823–877. Holy Roman emperor from 875 and (as Charles II) king of France from 843. Younger son of Louis I (the Pious), he warred against his eldest brother, Emperor Lothair I. The Treaty of Verdun 843 made him king of the West Frankish Kingdom (now France and the Spanish Marches).

Charles III the Fat 839–888. Holy Roman emperor 881–87; he became king of the West Franks in 885, thus uniting for the last time the whole of Charlemagne's dominions, but was deposed.

Charles IV 1316–1378. Holy Roman emperor from 1355 and king of Bohemia from 1346. Son of John of Luxembourg, king of Bohemia, he was elected king of Germany in 1346 and ruled all Germany from 1347. He was the founder of the first German university in Prague in 1348.

Charles V 1500–1558. Holy Roman emperor 1519–56. Son of Philip of Burgundy and Joanna of Castile, he inherited vast possessions, which led to rivalry with Francis I of France, whose alliance with the Ottoman Empire brought Vienna under siege in 1529 and 1532. Charles was also in conflict with the Protestants in Germany until the Treaty of Passau in 1552, which allowed the Lutherans religious liberty.

Charles VI 1685–1740. Holy Roman emperor from 1711, father of ◊Maria Theresa, whose succession to his Austrian dominions he tried to ensure, and himself claimant to the Spanish throne in 1700, thus causing the War of the ◊Spanish Succession.

Charles VII 1697–1745. Holy Roman emperor from 1742, opponent of ◊Maria Theresa's claim to the Austrian dominions of Charles VI.

Charles (Karl Franz Josef) 1887–1922. Emperor of Austria and king of Hungary from 1916, the last of the Habsburg emperors. He succeeded his great-uncle, Franz Josef in 1916 but was forced to withdraw to Switzerland in 1918, although he refused to abdicate. In 1921 he attempted unsuccessfully to regain the crown of Hungary and was deported to Madeira, where he died.

Charles V Holy Roman emperor and king of Spain, Charles V.

Charles (Spanish *Carlos*) four kings of Spain:

Charles I 1500–1558. See ◊Charles V, Holy Roman emperor.

Charles II 1661–1700. King of Spain from 1665; second son of Philip IV, he was the last of the Spanish Habsburg kings. Mentally handicapped from birth, he bequeathed his dominions to Philip of Anjou, grandson of Louis XIV, which led to the War of the ◊Spanish Succession.

Charles III 1716–1788. King of Spain from 1759. Son of Philip V, he became duke of Parma in 1732 and in 1734 conquered Naples and Sicily. On the death of his half-brother Ferdinand VI (1713–1759), he became king of Spain, handing over Naples and Sicily to his son Ferdinand (1751–1825). During his reign, Spain was twice at war with Britain: during the Seven Years' War, when he sided with France and lost Florida; and when he backed the colonists in the American Revolution and regained it. At home he carried out a programme of reforms and expelled the Jesuits.

Charles IV 1748–1819. King of Spain from 1788, when he succeeded his father, Charles III, but left the government in the hands of his wife and her lover, the minister Manuel de Godoy (1767–1851). In 1808 Charles was induced to abdicate by Napoleon's machinations in favour of his son Ferdinand VII (1784–1833), who was subsequently deposed by Napoleon's brother Joseph. Charles was awarded a pension by Napoleon and died in Rome.

Charles (Swedish *Carl*) 15 kings of Sweden (the first six were local chieftains) including:

Charles VIII King of Sweden from 1448. He was elected regent of Sweden in 1438, when Sweden broke away from Denmark and Norway. He stepped down in 1441 when Christopher III of Bavaria (1418–1448) was elected king, but after his death became king. He was twice expelled by the Danes and twice restored.

Charles IX 1550–1611. King of Sweden from 1604, the youngest son of Gustavus Vasa. In 1568 he and his brother John led the rebellion against Eric XIV (1533–1577); John became king as John III and attempted to catholicize Sweden, and Charles led the opposition. John's son Sigismund, king of Poland and a Catholic, succeeded to the Swedish throne in 1592, and Charles led the Protestants. He was made regent in 1595 and deposed Sigismund in 1599. Charles was elected king of Sweden in 1604 and was involved in unsuccessful wars with Russia, Poland, and Denmark. He was the father of Gustavus Adolphus.

Charles X 1622–1660. King of Sweden from 1654, when he succeeded his cousin Christina. He waged war with Poland and Denmark and in 1657 invaded Denmark by leading his army over the frozen sea.

Charles XI 1655–1697. King of Sweden from 1660, when he succeeded his father Charles X. His mother acted as regent until 1672 when Charles took over the government. He was a remarkable general and reformed the administration.

Charles XII 1682–1718. King of Sweden from 1697, when he succeeded his father, Charles XI. From 1700 he was involved in wars with Denmark, Poland, and Russia. He won a succession of victories until, in 1709 while invading Russia, he was defeated at Poltava in the Ukraine, and forced to take refuge in Turkey until 1714. He was killed while besieging Fredrikshall.

Charles XIII 1748–1818. King of Sweden from 1809, when he was elected; he became the first king of Sweden and Norway in 1814.

Charles XIV (Jean Baptiste Jules ◊Bernadotte) 1763–1844. King of Sweden and Norway from 1818. A former marshal in the French army, in 1810 he was elected crown prince of Sweden under the name of Charles John (*Carl Johan*). Loyal to his adopted country, he brought Sweden into the alliance against Napoleon in 1813, as a reward for which Sweden received Norway. He was the founder of the present dynasty.

Charles XV 1826–1872. King of Sweden and Norway from 1859, when he succeeded his father Oscar I. A popular and liberal monarch, his main achievement was the reform of the constitution.

Charles Albert /'ælbət/ 1798–1849. King of Sardinia from 1831. He showed liberal sympathies in early life, and after his accession introduced some reforms. On the outbreak of the 1848 revolution he granted a constitution and declared war on Austria. His troops were defeated at Custozza and Novara. In 1849 he abdicated in favour of his son Victor Emmanuel and retired to a monastery, where he died.

Charles Augustus /ɔː'gʌstəs/ 1757–1828. Grand Duke of Saxe-Weimar in Germany. He succeeded his father in infancy, fought against the French in 1792–94 and 1806, and was the patron and friend of the writer Goethe.

Charles Edward Stuart /'edwəd'stjuːət/ 1720–1788. British prince, known as the **Young Pretender** or **Bonnie Prince Charlie**, grandson of James II. In the Jacobite rebellion of 1745 Charles won the support of the Scottish Hi ghlanders; his army invaded England but was beaten back by the Duke of ◊Cumberland and routed at ◊Culloden in 1746. Charles went into exile.

Charles Martel /mɑː'tel/ *c.*688–741. Frankish ruler (Mayor of the Palace) of the E Frankish kingdom from 717 and the whole kingdom from 731. His victory against the Moors at Moussais-la-Bataille near Tours in 732 earned him his nickname of Martel, 'the Hammer', because he halted the Islamic advance by the ◊Moors into Europe. An illegitimate son of Pepin of Heristal (Pepin II, Mayor of the Palace *c.*640–714), he was a grandfather of Charlemagne.

Charles's law a law stated by Jacques Charles in 1787, and independently by Joseph Gay-Lussac (1778–1850) in 1802, which states that the volume of a given mass of gas at constant pressure is directly proportional to the absolute temperature: it increases by 1/273 of its volume at 0°C for each 1°C rise of temperature. This means that the coefficient of expansion of all gases is the same. The law is only approximately true and the coefficient of expansion is generally taken as 0.003663 per 1°C.

Charles the Bold Duke of Burgundy 1433–1477. Son of Philip the Good, he inherited Burgundy and the Low Countries from him in 1465. He waged wars attempting to free the duchy from dependence on France and restore it as a kingdom. He was killed in battle.

Charleston /'tʃɑːlstən/ *n.* a lively American dance of the 1920s, with side kicks from the knee. [from *Charleston* in S Carolina]

charlock /'tʃɑːlɒk/ *n.* or **wild mustard** an annual plant *Sinapis arvensis* of the family Cruciferae. It is a common weed in Britain, reaching a height of 60 cm/2 ft, with yellow flowers. [Old English]

charlotte /'ʃɑːlɒt/ *n.* **1.** a pudding made of stewed apple or other fruit with a covering or layer of crumbs, biscuits, etc. **2.** a moulded dessert consisting of a creamy filling enclosed in sponge fingers. [French]

Charlotte Amalie /'ʃɑːlət ə'mɑːljə/ capital and tourist resort of the US Virgin Islands; population (1980) 11,756.

Charlotte Augusta /'ʃɑːlət ɔː'gʌstə/ Princess 1796–1817. Only child of George IV and Caroline of Brunswick, and heir to the British throne. In 1816 she married Prince Leopold of Saxe-Coburg (later Leopold I of the Belgians), but died in childbirth 18 months later.

Charlotte Sophia /'sə'faɪə/ 1744–1818. British queen consort. The daughter of the German duke of Mecklenburg-Strelitz, she married George III of Great Britain and Ireland in 1761, and bore him nine sons and six daughters.

Charlottetown /'ʃɑːləttaʊn/ capital of Prince Edward Island, Canada; population (1986) 16,000. The city trades in textiles, fish, timber, vegetables, and dairy produce. It was founded by the French in the 1720s.

Charlton /'tʃɑːltən/ Bobby (Robert) 1937– . English footballer, younger brother of Jack Charlton, who scored a record 49 goals in 106 appearances. He spent most of his playing career with Manchester United.

Charlton Jack 1935– . English footballer, older brother of Robert (Bobby) and nephew of Jackie Milburn. He spent all his playing career with Leeds United and played more than 750 games for them.

charm n. 1. attractiveness, the power of arousing love or admiration; an attractive feature. 2. an act, object, or words believed to have occult power; a trinket on a bracelet etc. 3. in physics, a property possessed by one type of ◊quark (very small particles found inside protons and neutrons), called the charm quark. The effects of charm are only seen in experiments with particle ◊accelerators.. See ◊elementary particles. —v.t. 1. to delight; to influence by personal charm. 2. to influence by or as if by magic. —**charmer** n. [from Old French from Latin carmen = song, spell]

charming adj. delightfully attractive. —**charmingly** adv.

charnel house /'tʃɑːnəl/ a place where the bodies or bones of the dead are kept. [French from Latin]

Charollais /'ʃærəleɪ/ n. a French breed of large, white beef cattle; an animal of this breed. [from Monts du Charollais in E France]

Charon /'keərən/ in Greek mythology, the boatman who ferried the dead over the river Styx to the underworld.

Charpentier /ʃɑː'pɒntieɪ/ Gustave 1860–1956. French composer who wrote an opera about Paris working-class life, Louise 1900.

Charpentier Marc-Antoine 1645–1704. French composer who wrote sacred music including a number of masses; other works include instrumental theatre music and the opera Médée 1693.

chart n. 1. a map for those navigating on water or in the air; an outline map for showing special information. 2. a diagram, graph, or table giving information in tabular form; (in plural) those listing the recordings currently most popular. —v.t. to make a chart of, to map. [from French from Latin charta = card]

charter n. 1. a document from a ruler or government, conferring rights or laying down a constitution. 2. the chartering of an aircraft, ship, etc. —v.t. 1. to grant a charter to; to found by charter. 2. to let or hire (an aircraft, ship, etc.) for private use. —**chartered accountant, surveyor,** etc., one belonging to a professional body that has a royal charter. **charter flight,** a flight by chartered aircraft. [from Old French from Latin, diminutive of charta = card]

Charter 88 a British political campaign begun in 1988, calling for a written constitution to prevent what it termed the development of 'an elective dictatorship'. Those who signed the charter, including many figures from the arts, objected to what they saw as the autocratic premiership of Margaret Thatcher.

Chartism n. a popular movement in Britain for electoral and social reform, 1837–48, whose principles were set out in a manifesto called The People's Charter, a six-point programme comprising: universal male suffrage, equal electoral districts, secret ballot, annual parliaments, abolition of the property qualification for, and payment of, members of Parliament. Greater prosperity, lack of organization, and rivalry in the leadership led to its demise. —**Chartist** n.

chartreuse /ʃɑː'trɜːz/ n. 1. a pale green or yellow, aromatic brandy liqueur. 2. its green colour. 3. fruit enclosed in jelly. [from La Grande Chartreuse]

Chartreuse, La Grande the original home of the Carthusian order of Roman Catholic monks, established by St Bruno around 1084, in a remote valley near Grenoble, France. The present buildings date from the 17th century.

charwoman n. (plural charwomen) a woman hired by the hour to clean a house or other building.

chary /'tʃeərɪ/ adj. cautious, wary; sparing of. [Old English]

Charybdis /kə'rɪbdɪs/ in Greek mythology, a whirlpool formed by a monster of the same name on one side of the narrow straits of Messina, Sicily, opposite the monster Scylla.

chase[1] v.t./i. /tʃeɪs/ 1. to go quickly after in order to capture, overtake, or drive away. 2. to hurry. 3. (colloquial) to try to attain. —n. 1. chasing, pursuit; hunting, especially as a sport. 2. unenclosed parkland, originally for hunting. [from Old French from Latin captare (capere = catch)]

chase[2] v.t. /tʃeɪs/ to engrave or emboss (metal). [from French]

chaser n. 1. a horse for steeplechasing. 2. a drink taken after another of a different kind.

chasm /'kæzəm/ n. 1. a very deep cleft in the ground etc. 2. a wide difference of feeling, interests, etc. [from Latin from Greek = gaping hollow]

chassis /'ʃæsɪ, -iː/ n. (plural chassis /-iːz/) the base frame of a motor vehicle, carriage, etc.; a metal frame to carry radio etc. equipment. [from French from Latin]

chaste /tʃeɪst/ adj. 1. virgin, celibate; not having sexual intercourse except with one's spouse. 2. simple in style, not ornate. —**chastely** adv. [from Old French from Latin castus]

chasten /'tʃeɪsən/ v.t. to subdue the pride of. [from Old French from Latin castigare = castigate]

chastise /tʃæ'staɪz/ v.t. to punish, especially by beating. —**chastisement** n.

chastity /'tʃæstɪtɪ/ n. 1. virginity, celibacy. 2. simplicity of style. [from Old French from Latin castus = chaste]

chasuble /'tʃæzjʊbəl/ n. a loose sleeveless outer vestment worn by a priest celebrating the Eucharist. The colour of the chasuble depends on which feast is being celebrated. [from Old French, ultimately from Latin casula = hooded cloak]

chat n. a friendly informal conversation. —v.i. (-tt-) to hold a chat. —**chat up,** (colloquial) to chat to a person flirtatiously or with a particular motive. **chat show,** a television programme in which people are interviewed.

château /'ʃætəʊ/ n. (plural châteaux /-əʊz/) a large French country house or castle. The château was first used as a domestic building in the late 15th century; by the reign of Louis XIII (1610–43) fortifications such as moats and keeps were no longer used for defensive purposes, but merely as decorative features. [French = castle]

Chateaubriand /ʃætəʊbrɪ'ɒn/ François René, vicomte de 1768–1848. French author. In exile from the French Revolution 1794–99, he wrote Atala 1801 (written after his encounters with North American Indians); and the autobiographical René , which formed part of Le Génie du christianisme/The Genius of Christianity 1802.

chatelaine /'ʃætəleɪn/ n. 1. the mistress of a large house. 2. (historical) a set of short chains attached to a woman's belt, for carrying keys etc. [French]

chattel /'ʃætəl/ n. (usually in plural) a movable possession (as opposed to a house or land). [from Old French]

chatter /'ʃætə/ v.i. 1. to talk quickly, incessantly, trivially, or indiscreetly. 2. (of a bird) to emit short quick notes. 3. (of the teeth) to click repeatedly together. —n. chattering talk or sound.

chatterbox n. a talkative person.

Chatterton /'tʃætətən/ Thomas 1752–1770 English poet whose medieval-style poems and brief life were to inspire English Romanticism. Born in Bristol, he studied ancient documents he found in the Church of St Mary Redcliffe and composed poems he ascribed to a 15th-century monk, Thomas Rowley, which were at first accepted as genuine. He committed suicide in London, after becoming destitute.

chatty adj. 1. fond of chatting. 2. resembling chat. —**chattily** adv., **chattiness** n.

Chatwin /'tʃætwɪn/ Bruce 1940–1989. English writer. His works include The Songlines 1987, written after living with Aborigines, Utz 1988, about a manic porcelain collector in Prague, and What Am I Doing Here? 1989.

Chaucer /'tʃɔːsə/ Geoffrey c.1340–1400. English poet, author of *The Canterbury Tales* about 1387, a collection of tales told by pilgrims on their way to the Thomas à Becket shrine. He was the most influential English poet of the Middle Ages. Chaucer's other work includes the French-influenced *Romance of the Rose* and *Troilus and Criseyde* based on Boccaccio's *Il Filostrato*.

> He was a verray, parfit genteel Knyght.
> **Geoffrey Chaucer**
> *The Canterbury Tales (Prologue)*

chauffeur /'ʃəufə, ʃəu'fɜː/ n. a person employed to drive a car. —v.t. to drive as chauffeur. —**chauffeuse** /-z/ n.fem. [French = stoker]

chauvinism /'ʃəuvɪnɪzəm/ n. 1. exaggerated or aggressive patriotism. 2. excessive or prejudiced support or loyalty for one's cause or group. In the mid-20th century the expression **male chauvinism** was coined to mean an assumed superiority of the male sex over the female. —**chauvinist** n., **chauvinistic** /-'nɪstɪk/ adj. [from Nicolas *Chauvin*, Napoleonic veteran who exhibited fanatical patriotism]

Chávez /'tʃɑːves/ Carlos 1899–1978. Mexican composer. A student of the piano and of the complex rhythms of his country's folk music, he founded the Mexico Symphony Orchestra. He composed a number of ballets, seven symphonies, and concertos for both violin and piano.

Chayefsky /tʃeɪ'efski/ (Sidney) 'Paddy' 1923–1981. US writer. He established his reputation with the television plays *Marty* 1955 (for which he won an Oscar when he turned it into a film), and *Bachelor Party* 1957. He also won Oscars for *The Hospital* 1971 and *Network* 1976.

cheap adj. 1. low in price, worth more than it cost; charging low prices, offering good value. 2. poor in quality, of low value; showy but worthless, silly. —**cheaply** adv., **cheapness** n. [from obsolete *cheap* = bargain, from Old English]

cheapen v.t./i. to make or become cheap; to depreciate, to degrade.

cheapjack n. a seller of shoddy goods at low prices. —adj. of poor quality, shoddy.

cheat v.t./i. to trick or deceive, to deprive *of* by trickery; to act fraudulently or dishonestly. — n. 1. one who cheats. 2. a deception, a trick.

check[1] n. 1. a stopping or slowing of motion, a pause; a loss of the scent in hunting. 2. a restraint. 3. a control to secure accuracy; a test or examination to see that something is correct or in good working order. 4. a receipt; a bill in a restaurant. 5. (*US*) a cheque. 6. in chess, exposure of a king to possible capture. —v.t./i. 1. to stop or slow the motion of suddenly, to restrain; to make a sudden stop. 2. to test or examine for correctness or good working order. 3. (*US*) to correspond when compared. 4. in chess, to threaten (an opponent's king). —**check in**, to register one's arrival at a hotel, airport, etc. **check on** *or* **up** *or* **up on**, to examine or investigate the correctness, honesty, etc., of. **check out**, to leave a hotel, airport, etc., with proper formalities; to test (a possibility). **checkout** n. checking out; a place where goods are paid for by customers in a supermarket. **checkup** n. a thorough examination, especially a medical one. [from Old French, ultimately from Persian = king]

check[2] n. a cross-lined pattern of small squares. [probably from *chequer*]

check digit in computing, a digit added to important codes for ◊error detection.

checked adj. having a check pattern.

checkers n.pl. (usually treated as *singular*) (*US*) the game of draughts.

checkmate n. 1. in chess, a check from which the king cannot escape. 2. a final defeat. —v.t. 1. to put in checkmate. 2. to defeat finally, to foil. [from Old French, ultimately from Persian *shāh māt* = the king is dead]

check-off n. in industrial relations, the procedure whereby an employer, on behalf of a trade union, deducts union subscriptions at source from its employees' wages.

Cheddar /'tʃedə/ n. a hard cheese of a kind originally made at Cheddar in Somerset.

cheek n. 1. either side of the face below the eye. 2. impudent speech; quiet arrogance. —v.t. to speak impudently to. —**cheekbone** n. the bone below the eye. **cheek by jowl**, in juxtaposition. [Old English]

cheeky adj. impertinent, saucy. —**cheekily** adv., **cheekiness** n.

cheep n. the weak, shrill cry of a young bird. —v.i. to make this cry. [imitative]

cheer n. 1. a shout of encouragement or applause. 2. cheerfulness. —v.t./i. 1. to raise a cheer; to applaud or urge *on* with cheers. 2. to comfort or gladden. —**cheer up**, to make or become more cheerful. [from Anglo-French = face, ultimately from Greek *kara* = head]

cheerful adj. in good spirits, visibly happy; pleasantly bright. —**cheerfully** adv., **cheerfulness** n.

cheerio /tʃɪəri'əu/ (*colloquial*) interjection expressing good wishes on parting; goodbye.

cheerless adj. gloomy, comfortless.

cheery adj. ebulliently cheerful. —**cheerily** adv.

cheese /tʃiːz/ n. 1. a food made from milk curds or occasionally from whey; a shaped mass of this. 2. a thick, stiff jam. —**cheeseparing** adj. & n. stingy, stinginess. —**cheesy** adj. [Old English, from Latin *caseus*]

cheesecake n. a tart filled with sweetened curds.

cheesecloth n. a thin, loosely woven, cotton fabric.

cheetah /'tʃiːtə/ n. a large wild cat *Acinonyx jubatus* native to Africa, Arabia, and SW Asia, but now rare in some areas. Yellowish with black spots, it has a slim, lithe build. It is up to 1 m/3 ft tall at the shoulder, and up to 1.5 m/ 5 ft long. It can reach 110 kph/70 mph, but tires after about 400 metres. Cheetahs live in open country where they hunt small antelopes, hares, and birds. [Hindi, perhaps from Sanskrit *chitraka* = speckled]

Cheever /'tʃiːvə/ John 1912–1982. US writer. His short stories and novels include *The Wapshot Chronicle* 1937, *Bullet Park* 1969, *World of Apples* 1973, and *Falconer* 1977.

chef /ʃef/ n. a cook (especially the head cook) in a restaurant etc. [French = head]

chef-d'œuvre /ʃeɪ'dœvr/ (*plural* **chefs-d'œuvre**, pronounced the same) a masterpiece. [French]

Cheka n. a secret police organization operating in the USSR 1918–23. It originated from the tsarist Okhrana and became successively the OGPU (GPU) 1923–34, NKVD 1934–46, and MVD 1946–53, before its present form, the ◊KGB.

Chekhov /'tʃekɒf/ Anton (Pavlovich) 1860–1904. Russian dramatist and writer. He began to write short stories and comic sketches as a medical student. His plays concentrate on the creation of atmosphere and delineation of internal development, rather than external action. His first play *Ivanov* 1887 was a failure, as was *The Seagull* 1896 until revived by Stanislavsky in 1898 at the Moscow Art Theatre, for which Chekhov went on to write his major plays: *Uncle Vanya* 1899, *The Three Sisters* 1901, and *The Cherry Orchard* 1904.

chela n. in Hinduism, a follower or pupil of a guru (teacher).

chelate n. a type of chemical compound whose molecules consist of one or more metal atoms or charged ions joined to chains of organic residues by coordinate (or dative covalent) chemical ◊bonds.

Chelsea /'tʃelsɪ/ a historic area of the Royal Borough of Kensington and Chelsea, SW London. —**Chelsea bun**, a kind of rolled currant bun. **Chelsea pensioner**, an inmate of Chelsea Royal Hospital for old or disabled soldiers.

Chekhov Russian dramatist and writer Anton Chekhov.

Chelsea porcelain factory thought to be the first porcelain factory in England. Based in SW London, it dated from the 1740s, when it was known as the Chelsea Porcelain Works. Chelsea porcelain includes plates and other items decorated with botanical, bird, and insect paintings. The factory was taken over by William Duesbury of Derby in 1769, and pulled down in 1784.

Chelyabinsk /tʃeli'æbɪnsk/ industrial town and capital of Chelyabinsk region, W Siberia, USSR; population (1987) 1,119,000. It has iron and engineering works and makes chemicals, motor vehicles, and aircraft.

chemical /'kemɪkəl/ adj. of, using, or produced by chemistry or chemicals. —n. a substance obtained by or used in a chemical process. —**chemical engineering,** the industrial applications of chemistry. —**chemically** adv. [from French from Latin]

chemical change the change that occurs in a chemical reaction. A new substance is formed, with properties different from those of the starting materials; significant energy changes are involved; and the change cannot easily be reversed. A simple example of chemical change is the burning of carbon.

chemical equation a method of indicating the reactants and products of a chemical reaction by using chemical symbols and formulae. A chemical equation gives two basic pieces of information: (1) the reactants (on the left-hand side) and products (right-hand side); and (2) the reacting proportions (stoichiometry), that is how many units of each reactant and product are involved. The equation must balance; that is, the total number of atoms of a particular element on the left-hand side must be the same as the number of atoms of that element on the right-hand side.

chemical equilibrium the condition in which the products of a reversible chemical reaction are formed at the same rate at which they decompose back into the reactants, so that the concentration of each reactant and product remains constant.

chemical family a collection of elements that have very similar chemical and physical properties. In the ◊periodic table of the elements such collections are to be found in the vertical columns (groups). The groups that contain the most markedly similar elements are group I, the ◊alkali metals; group II, the ◊alkaline-earth elements; group VII, the ◊halogens; and group 0, the noble or ◊inert gases.

chemical warfare the use in war of gaseous, liquid, or solid substances intended to have a toxic effect on humans, animals, or plants. Together with biological warfare, it was banned in 1925 by the Geneva Convention. In 1989, when the 149-nation Conference on Chemical Weapons unanimously voted to outlaw chemical weapons, the total US stockpile was estimated at 30,000 tonnes and the Soviet stockpile at 300,000 tonnes.

chemiluminescence n. an alternative term for ◊bioluminescence.

chemise /ʃə'miːz/ n. a loose-fitting undergarment formerly worn by women, hanging straight from the shoulders; a dress of similar shape. [from Old French from Latin camisia = shirt]

chemisorption n. the attachment, by chemical means, of a single layer of molecules, atoms, or ions of gas to the surface of a solid or, less frequently, a liquid. It is the basis of catalysis (see ◊catalyst) and of great industrial importance.

chemist /'kemɪst/ n. 1. a dealer in medicinal drugs etc. 2. a scientist specializing in chemistry. [from French]

chemistry /'kemɪstrɪ/ n. 1. the scientific study of substances and their elements and of how they react when combined, etc. 2. the chemical properties, reactions, etc., of a substance.

chemosynthesis n. a method of making ◊protoplasm (contents of a living cell) using the energy from chemical reactions, in contrast to the use of light energy employed for the same purpose in ◊photosynthesis. The process is used by certain bacteria, which can synthesize organic compounds from carbon dioxide and water using the energy from special methods of ◊respiration.

chemotherapy /keməʊ'θerəpɪ/ n. treatment of disease by drugs and other chemical substances. It usually refers to treatment of cancer with cytotoxic and other drugs. The term was coined by the German bacteriologist Paul Ehrlich for the use of synthetic chemicals against infectious diseases.

chemotropism n. the movement by part of a plant in response to a chemical stimulus. The response by the plant is termed 'positive' if the growth is towards the stimulus or 'negative' if the growth is away from the stimulus.

Chengdu /tʃeŋ'duː/ formerly **Chengtu** ancient city, capital of Sichuan province, China; population (1986) 2,580,000. It is a busy rail junction and has railway workshops, and textile, electronics, and engineering industries. There are well-preserved temples.

chenille /ʃə'niːl/ n. a tufty, velvety cord or yarn, used for trimming furniture; a fabric made from this. [French = hairy caterpillar, from Latin canicula = little dog]

cheongsam /tʃiɒŋ'sæm/ n. a Chinese woman's garment with a high neck and slit skirt. [Chinese]

cheque /tʃek/ n. (US **check**) a written order for a bank to pay a stated sum from the drawer's account; a printed form for writing this. —**chequebook** n. a book of printed forms for writing cheques. **cheque card,** a card issued by a bank, guaranteeing payment of cheques up to a stated amount.

chequer /'tʃekə/ n. (chiefly in plural) a pattern of squares of alternating colours, as on a chessboard. —v.t. 1. to mark with such a pattern; to variegate. 2. to vary with different elements; (in past participle) marked by vicissitudes of fortune.

Chequers /'tʃekəz/ n. the country home of the prime minister of the UK. It is an Elizabethan mansion in the Chiltern hills near Princes Risborough, Buckinghamshire, and was given to the nation by Lord Lee of Fareham under the Chequers Estate Act 1917, which came into effect in 1921.

Cherenkov /tʃi'reŋkɒf/ Pavel 1904– . Soviet physicist. In 1934 he discovered **Cherenkov radiation**; this occurs as a bluish light when charged atomic particles pass through water or other media at a speed in excess of that of light. He shared the Nobel Prize for Physics in 1958 with his colleagues Ilya ◊Frank and Igor Tamm.

cherish /'tʃerɪʃ/ v.t. to tend lovingly; to be fond of; to cling to (a hope or feeling). [from Old French cher from Latin carus = dear]

Chernenko /tʃɜ:'neŋkəʊ/ Konstantin 1911–1985. Soviet politician, leader of the Soviet Communist Party (CPSU) and president 1984–85. He was a protégé of Brezhnev and from 1978 a member of the Politburo.

Chernobyl /tʃə'nɒubəl/ town in Ukraine, USSR. In April 1986 a leak, caused by overheating, occurred in a nonpressurized boiling-water nuclear reactor. The resulting clouds of radioactive isotopes were traced as far away as Sweden; over 250 people were killed, and thousands of square miles contaminated.

Cherokee /'tʃerəkiː/ n. (plural the same) a member of a North ◊American Indian people, formerly living in the S Allegheny Mountains of what is now Alabama, the Carolinas, Georgia, and Tennessee. Their scholarly leader Sequoyah (c.1770–1843) devised the syllabary used for writing their language, which belongs to the Iroquoian family. [native name]

cheroot /ʃə'ruːt/ n. a cigar with both ends open. [from French from Tamil]

cherry /'tʃerɪ/ n. 1. a small, soft, round stone fruit. 2. a tree of the genus Prunus bearing this or grown for its ornamental flowers; the wood of this tree. Cultivated cherries are derived from two species, the sour cherry P. cerasus, and the gean P. avium, which grow wild in Britain. The former is the ancestor of morello, duke, and Kentish cherries; the latter of the sweet cherries: hearts, mazzards, and bigarreaus. 3. the bright red colour of ripe cherries. —adj. bright red. —**cherry brandy,** a liqueur of brandy in which cherries have been steeped. [from Old French from Latin perhaps from Greek kerasos]

chert /tʃɜːt/ n. a flintlike form of quartz.

cherub /'tʃerəb/ n. 1. (plural **cherubim**) an angelic being of an order usually grouped with the seraphim. 2. a representation, in art, of a winged, chubby child; a pretty or well-behaved child. —**cherubic** /-'ruːbɪk/ adj. [Old English, from Hebrew]

chervil /'tʃɜːvɪl/ n. any of several plants of the carrot family Umbelliferae. The garden chervil Anthriscus cerefolium has leaves with a sweetish odour, resembling parsley. It is used as a garnish and in soups. [Old English from Latin from Greek khairephullon]

Ches. abbreviation of Cheshire.

Chesapeake Bay /'tʃesəpiːk/ largest of the inlets on the Atlantic coast of the USA, bordered by Maryland and Virginia. Its wildlife is threatened by urban and industrial development.

Cheshire /'tʃeʃə(r)/ county in NW England; **area** 2,320 sq km/896 sq mi; **administrative headquarters** Chester; **physical** chiefly a fertile plain; rivers: Mersey, Dee, Weaver; **products** textiles, chemicals, dairy products; **population** (1987) 952,000. —**Cheshire cheese,** a crumbly cheese originally made in Cheshire. **like a Cheshire cat,** with a broad fixed grin.

chess *n.* 1. a board game originating as early as the 2nd century AD. Two players use 16 pieces each, on a board of 64 squares of alternating colour, to try to force the opponent into a position where the main piece (the king) is threatened, and cannot move to another position without remaining threatened. [from Old French *esches*, plural of *eschec*]

chessboard *n.* the board used in chess.

chest *n.* 1. a large, strong box for storing or transporting things. 2. the part of the body enclosed by the ribs and breastbone; the upper front surface of the body. —**chest of drawers,** a piece of furniture consisting of a set of drawers in a frame, for storing clothes etc. [Old English from Latin from Greek *kistē*]

chesterfield /'tʃestəfiːld/ *n.* a sofa with padded back, seat, and ends. [from 19th-century Earl of *Chesterfield*]

Chesterfield Philip Dormer Stanhope, 4th Earl of Chesterfield 1694–1773. English politician and writer, author of *Letters to his Son* 1774 – his illegitimate son, Philip Stanhope (1732–1768).

Chesterton /'tʃestətən/ G(ilbert) K(eith) 1874–1936. English novelist, essayist, and satirical poet, author of a series of novels featuring the naïve priest-detective Father Brown. Other novels include *The Napoleon of Notting Hill* 1904 and *The Man Who Knew Too Much* 1922.

One bears great things from the valley, only small things from the peak.

G K Chesterton
The Hammer of God

---

chestnut /'tʃesnʌt/ *n.* 1. a tree with hard brown nuts, those of the Spanish or sweet chestnut *Castanea sativa* being edible; its nut; the wood of this tree. 2. deep reddish-brown. 3. a horse of reddish-brown or yellowish-brown colour. 4. a small, hard patch on a horse's leg. 5. an old joke or anecdote. —*adj.* deep reddish-brown or (of horses) yellowish-brown. [from obsolete *chesten* (from Old French from Latin from Greek *kastanea*)]

Chetnik /'tʃetnɪk/ *n.* a member of a Serbian nationalist group that operated underground during the German occupation of Yugoslavia during World War II. Led by Col Draza ◊Mihailovič, the Chetniks initially received aid from the Allies, but this was later transferred to the communist partisans led by Tito.

cheval glass /ʃə'væl/ a tall mirror swung on an upright frame. [from French *cheval* = horse, frame]

chevalier /ʃevə'liə/ *n.* a member of certain orders of knighthood, or of the French Legion of Honour etc. [from Anglo-French from Latin *caballus* = horse]

Chevalier /ʃə'væliei/ Maurice 1888–1972. French singer and actor. He began as dancing partner to the revue artiste ◊Mistinguette at the ◊Folies-Bergère, and made numerous films including *Innocents of Paris* 1929, which revived his song 'Louise', *The Merry Widow* 1934, and *Gigi* 1958.

Chevreul /ʃə'vrɜːl/ Michel-Eugene 1786–1889. French chemist who studied the composition of fats and identified a number of fatty acids, including 'margaric acid', which became the basis of margarine.

chevron /'tʃevrən/ *n.* a V-shaped line, stripe, or bar, especially one worn on the sleeve of a uniform to denote rank. [from Old French from Latin *caper* = goat; compare Latin *capreoli* = pair of rafters]

chew *v.t.* to work or grind between the teeth; to make this movement. —*n.* the act of chewing; something for chewing. —**chewing gum** *n.* flavoured gum for prolonged chewing. **chew over,** (*colloquial*) to think over. [Old English]

chez /ʃei/ *prep.* at the home of. [French, from Old French from Latin *casa* = cottage]

chi /kai/ *n.* the 22nd letter of the Greek alphabet = χ, X.

Chiang Ching /dʒi'æŋ 'tʃɪŋ/ former name of the Chinese actress ◊Jiang Qing, third wife of Mao.

Chiang Ching-kuo /tʃi'æŋ tʃɪŋ 'kwəʊ/ 1910–1988. Taiwanese politician, son of Chiang Kai-shek, prime minister 1971–78, president 1978–88.

Chiang Kai-shek /'tʃæŋ kai 'ʃek/ Pinyin *Jiang Jie Shi* 1887–1975. Chinese Nationalist ◊Guomindang (Kuomintang) general and politician, president of China 1928–31 and 1943–49, and of Taiwan from 1949, where he set up a US-supported right-wing government on his expulsion from the mainland by the Communist forces. He was a commander in the civil war that lasted from the end of imperial rule in 1911 to the Second ◊Sino-Japanese War and beyond, having split with the Communist leader Mao Zedong in 1927.

Chianti /ki'ænti/ *n.* a dry, usually red, Italian wine. [name of town in Tuscany]

chiaroscuro /kiɑːrə'skuərəʊ/ *n.* treatment of light and shade in painting; light and shade effects in nature. [Italian *chiaro* = bright and *oscuro* = dark]

Chiba /'tʃiːbə/ industrial city (paper, steel, textiles) in Kanton region, E Honshu island, Japan, 40 km/25 mi W of Tokyo; population (1987) 793,000.

chic /ʃiːk/ *n.* fashionable elegance or stylishness in dress etc. —*adj.* fashionably elegant, stylish. [French]

Chicago /ʃi'kɑːgəʊ/ financial and industrial (iron, steel, chemicals, textiles) city in Illinois, USA, on Lake Michigan; population (1980) 3,005,000. It contains the world's first skyscraper (built 1887–88) and some of the world's tallest skyscrapers, including the Sears Tower, 443 m/1,454 ft. The famous stockyards are now closed.

chicane /ʃi'kein/ *v.t./i.* to practise or subject to chicanery; to trick. —*n.* 1. chicanery. 2. an artificial barrier on a motor-racing course etc. [French = quibble]

chicanery /ʃi'keinəri/ *n.* quibbles or subterfuges used to gain an advantage. [from French]

Chicano /tʃi'kɑːnəʊ/ *n.* a citizen or resident of the USA of Mexican descent. The term was originally used for those who became US citizens after the ◊Mexican War.

Chichén Itzá /tʃi'tʃen ɪt'sɑː/ Toltec city situated among the Mayan city-states of Yucatán, Mexico. It flourished AD 900–1200 and displays Classic and Post-Classic architecture of the Toltec style. The site has temples and sculptures and colour reliefs, an observatory, and a sacred well into which sacrifices, including human beings, were cast.

Chichester /'tʃitʃistə/ Francis 1901–1972. English sailor and navigator. In 1931 he made the first E–W crossing of the Tasman Sea in *Gipsy Moth*, and in 1966–67 circumnavigated the world in his yacht *Gipsy Moth IV*.

chick *n.* 1. a young bird before or after hatching. 2. (*slang*) a young woman.

chicken /'tʃɪkɪn/ *n.* 1. a young bird, especially of the domestic fowl. 2. the flesh of the domestic fowl as food. —*adj.* (*slang*) afraid to do something, cowardly. —*v.i.* (*slang*) to opt *out* through cowardice. —**chicken feed,** (*colloquial*) an unimportant or small amount of money etc. **chicken-hearted** *adj.* cowardly. **chicken wire,** light wire netting with hexagonal mesh. [Old English]

chickenpox *n.* or **varicella** a common acute disease, caused by a virus of the ◊herpes group and transmitted by airborne droplets. Chickenpox chiefly attacks children under ten. The incubation period is two to three weeks. One attack normally gives immunity for life.

chickpea *n.* an annual plant *Cicer arietinum*, family Leguminosae, which is grown for food in India and the Middle East. Its short, hairy pods contain edible pealike seeds. [*chick* for earlier *chich* from French from Latin *cicer*]

chickweed *n.* a small weed *Stellaria media* with tiny white flowers.

Chiclayo /tʃi'klaiəʊ/ capital of Lambayeque department, NW Peru; population (1988) 395,000.

chicle /'tʃɪkəl/ *n.* a gumlike substance obtained from the sapodilla tree *Achras zapota*, used chiefly in chewing gum. [Spanish, from Nahuatl]

chicory /'tʃɪkəri/ *n.* 1. a blue-flowered plant *Cichorium intybus* grown for salads etc.; its root ground for use with or instead of coffee. Its crown is known in the USA as *endive*. [from French from Latin from Greek]

chide *v.t.* (*past* **chided**, **chid**; *past participle* **chided**, **chidden**) (*archaic and literary*) to scold. [Old English]

chief *n.* **1.** a leader or ruler; the head of a tribe, clan, etc.; a person with the highest authority. **2.** in heraldry, the upper third of a shield. —*adj.* highest in rank or authority; most important. [from Old French from Latin *caput* = head]

chiefly *adv.* pre-eminently, above all; mainly but not exclusively.

chieftain /'tʃiːftən/ *n.* the chief of a clan or tribe. [from Old French from Latin *capitaneus* = captain]

chiffchaff *n.* a bird *Phylloscopus collybita* of the warbler family, found in woodlands and thickets in Europe and N Asia during the summer, migrating south for the winter. About 11 cm/4.3 in long, olive above, greyish below, with an eye stripe and usually dark legs, it looks similar to a willow warbler but has a distinctive song. [imitative]

chiffon /'ʃɪfɒn/ *n.* **1.** a light, diaphanous fabric of silk, nylon, etc. **2.** a very light-textured pudding made with beaten egg white. [French (*chiffe* = rag)]

chiffonier /ʃɪfəˈnɪə/ *n.* **1.** a movable, low cupboard with a top used as a sideboard. **2.** (*US*) a tall chest of drawers. [from French = rag picker, chest of drawers for odds and ends]

Chifley /'tʃɪfli/ Ben (Joseph Benedict) 1885–1951. Australian Labor prime minister 1945–49. He united the party in fulfilling a welfare and nationalization programme 1945–49 (although he failed in an attempt to nationalize the banks in 1947) and initiated an immigration programme and the Snowy Mountains hydroelectric project.

chigger *n.* or **harvest mite** a scarlet or rusty brown ◊mite of the family Trombiculidae, common in summer and autumn. The tiny red larvae cause intensely irritating bites. [variant of *chigoe*]

chignon /'ʃiːnjɔ̃/ *n.* a coil or mass of hair worn by women at the back of the head. [French, originally = nape]

chigoe /'tʃɪgəʊ/ *n.* a tropical flea that burrows into the skin. [Carib]

chihuahua /tʃɪˈwɑːwə/ *n.* the smallest breed of dog, developed in the USA from Mexican origins. It may weigh only 1 kg/2.2 lb. The domed head and wide set ears are characteristic, and the skull is large compared to the body. It can be almost any colour, and occurs in both smooth (or even hairless) and long-coated varieties. [from *Chihuahua*]

Chihuahua capital of Chihuahua state, Mexico, 1,285 km/800 mi NW of Mexico City; population (1984) 375,000. Founded in 1707, it is the centre of a mining district.

chilblain /'tʃɪlbleɪn/ *n.* an inflamed swelling on a finger, toe, etc., caused by exposure to cold and by poor blood circulation. [from Old English *blain* = swelling, sore]

child /tʃaɪld/ *n.* (*plural* **children** /'tʃɪldrən/) **1.** a young person of either sex before puberty; an unborn or newborn human being; a childish person. **2.** a son or daughter; a descendant; a product *of.* —**child's play,** something very easy to do. [Old English]

child abuse the molesting of children by parents and other adults. It can give rise to various criminal charges and has become a growing concern since the early 1980s. A local authority can take abused children away from their parents by obtaining a care order from a juvenile court under the Children's and Young Persons Act 1969 (replaced by the Children's Act 1989). Controversial methods of diagnosing sexual abuse led to a public inquiry in Cleveland, England in 1988, which severely criticized the handling of such cases.

childbirth *n.* the process of giving birth to a child.

Child, Convention on the Rights of the a United Nations document designed to make the wellbeing of children an international obligation. It was adopted in 1989 and covers·children from birth up to 18.

Childe /tʃaɪld/ Gordon 1892–1957. Australian archaeologist, director of the London Institute of Archaeology 1946–57. He discovered the prehistoric village of Skara Brae in the Orkneys, and published *The Dawn of European Civilization* 1939.

Childers /'tʃɪldəz/ (Robert) Erskine 1870–1922. Irish Sinn Féin politician, author of the spy novel *The Riddle of the Sands* 1903. He was executed as a Republican terrorist.

childhood *n.* the period or condition of being a child.

childish *adj.* immature like a child; unsuited to an adult. —**childishly** *adv.*, **childishness** *n.*

childless *adj.* having no children.

childlike *adj.* having the good qualities of a child, simple and innocent.

child prodigy a young person who has developed a remarkable talent for one or more subjects or pursuits. ◊Mozart was a child prodigy of musical genius.

Children's Crusade a ◊Crusade by some 10,000 children from France, the Low Countries, and Germany in 1212, to recapture Jerusalem for Christianity. They were motivated by religious piety. Many of them were sold into slavery or died of disease.

Chile /'tʃɪli/ Republic of; South American country, bounded to the N by Peru and Bolivia, to the E by Argentina, and to the S and W by the Pacific Ocean; **area** 756,950 sq km/292,257 sq mi; **capital** Santiago; **physical** Andes mountains along E border, Atacama Desert in N, arable land and forest in S; territories Easter Island, Juan Fernandez Islands of Tierra del Fuego, part of Antarctica; **head of state and government** Patricio Aylwin Azodar from 1990; **political system** emergent democratic republic; **exports** copper, iron, nitrate (Chile is the chief mining country of South America), pulp and paper; **population** (1990 est) 13,000,000 (the majority mestizo, of mixed American Indian and Spanish descent); **language** Spanish; **recent history** independence from Spain was achieved in 1818. An extensive programme of nationalization and social reform launched by Dr Salvador Allende in 1970 was halted by Gen Pinochet's military takeover in 1973. In 1989 he agreed to constitutional changes to allow pluralist politics.

Chilean Revolution /'tʃɪliən/ in Chile, the presidency of Salvador ◊Allende 1970–73, the Western hemisphere's first democratically elected Marxist-oriented president of an independent state.

chiliasm *n.* another term for millenarianism; see ◊millennium.

chill *n.* **1.** unpleasant coldness. **2.** an illness with feverish shivering. **3.** coldness of manner. —*adj.* chilly. —*v.t./i.* **1.** to make or become cold; to harden (molten metal) by contact with cold material; to preserve (meat etc.) at a low temperature without freezing. **2.** to depress or dispirit. [Old English]

chilli /'tʃɪli/ *n.* (*plural* **chillies**) the small, red, hot-tasting dried pod of a type of capsicum, *Capsicum frutescens*, used as a relish or made into seasoning. [from Spanish from Aztec]

chilly *adj.* rather cold, unpleasantly cold; cold and unfriendly in manner.

Chiltern Hundreds, stewardship of /'tsɪltən/ in the UK, a nominal office of profit under the crown. British members of Parliament must not resign; therefore, if they wish to leave office during a Parliament, they may apply for this office, a formality that disqualifies them from being an MP.

chimaera *n.* a fish of the group Holocephali. They have thick bodies that taper to a long, thin tail, large fins, smooth skin, and a cartilaginous skeleton. They can grow to 1.5 m/4.5 ft. Most chimaeras are deep-water fish, and even *Chimaera monstrosa*, a relatively shallow-living form caught around European coasts, lives at a depth of 300–500 m/1,000–1,600 ft.

Chimbote /tʃɪmˈbəʊti/ the largest fishing port in Peru; population (1981) 216,000.

chime *n.* a tuned set of bells; a series of notes sounded by these. —*v.t./i.* (of bells) to sound; (of a clock) to indicate (the hour) by chiming. —**chime in,** to interject a remark; to agree or correspond *with.* [Old English from Latin from Greek *kumbalon* = cymbal]

chimera /kɪˈmɪərə/ *n.* in biology, an organism composed of tissues that are genetically different. Chimeras can develop naturally if a ◊mutation occurs in a cell of a developing embryo, but are more commonly produced artificially by implanting cells from one organism into the embryo of another. —**chimerical** /-ˈmerɪkəl/ *adj.* [from Latin from Greek]

Chimera or **Chimaera** in Greek mythology, a fire-breathing animal with a lion's head, a goat's body, and a serpent's tail; hence any apparent hybrid of two or more creatures. The Chimera was killed by the hero Bellerophon on the winged horse Pegasus. [from Latin from Greek = she-goat]

Chinese dynasties

Dynasty	Dates	Major Events
Hsia	1994–1523 BC	Agriculture, bronze, first writing
Shang or Yin	1523–1027	First major dynasty; first Chinese calendar
Chou	1027–255	Developed society using money, iron, written laws; age of Confucius.
Qin	255–206	Unification after period of Warring States, building of Great Wall begun, roads built.
Han	AD 206–220	First centralized and effectively administered empire; introduction of Buddhism.
San Kuo (Three Kingdoms)	220–265	Division into three parts, prolonged fighting and eventual victory of Wei over Chu and Wu; Confucianism superseded by Buddhism and Taoism.
Tsin	265–420	Beginning of Hun invasions in the N
Sui	581–618	Reunification; barbarian invasions stopped; Great Wall refortified
T'ang	618–906	Centralized government; empire greatly extended; period of excellence in sculpture, painting and poetry.
Wu Tai (Five Dynasties)	907–960	Economic depression and loss of territory in N China, central Asia and Korea; first use of paper money
Sung	960–1279	Period of calm and creativity; printing developed (movable type); central government restored; N and W frontiers neglected and Mongol incursions begun.
Yüan	1260–1368	Beginning of Mongol rule in China, under Kublai Khan; Marco Polo visited China; dynasty brought to an end by widespread revolts, centred in Mongolia.
Ming	1368–1644	Mongols driven out by native Chinese, Mongolia captured by 2nd Ming emperor; period of architectural development; Beijing flourished as new capital.
Manchu	1644–1912	China once again under non-Chinese rule, the Qing conquered by nomads from Manchuria; trade with the West, culture flourished, but conservatism eventually led to the dynasty's overthrow by nationalistic revolutionaries under Sun Yatsen.

chimney /'tʃɪmnɪ/ *n.* **1.** a structure carrying off the smoke or steam of a fire, furnace, engine etc.; the part of this projecting above a roof. **2.** a glass tube protecting the flame of a lamp. **3.** a narrow vertical cleft in a rock face. —**chimney breast**, the projecting part of a wall round a chimney flue. **chimneypot** *n.* an earthenware or metal tube at the top of a chimney. **chimney stack**, a number of chimneys standing together. **chimney sweep**, one who removes soot from inside chimneys. [from Old French from Latin from Greek *kaminos* = oven]

chimpanzee /tʃɪmpən'ziː/ *n.* a Central and West African ape of the genus *Pan*, of which there are two species: *P. troglodytes*, which resembles man more closely than does any other ape, and the pygmy chimpanzee *P. paniscus*. They are covered in thin but long black body hair, except for the face, hands, and feet, which may have pink or black skin. Chimpanzees normally walk on all fours, supporting the front of the body on the knuckles of the fingers, but can stand or walk upright for a short distance. *P. troglodytes* can grow to 1.4 m/4.5 ft tall, and weigh up to 50 kg/110 lb. They are strong, and climb well, but spend time on the ground. They live in loose social groups. The bulk of the diet is fruit, with some leaves, insects, and occasional meat. Chimpanzees can use 'tools', fashioning twigs to extract termites from their nests. [from French from African native name]

Chimu /'tʃiːmuː/ *n.* a South American civilization that flourished on the coast of Peru from about 1250 to about 1470, when the Chimu were conquered by the Incas. They produced fine work in gold, realistic portrait pottery, savage fanged feline images in clay, and possibly a system of writing or recording by painting patterns on beans. They built aqueducts carrying water many miles, and the huge, mazelike city of Chan Chan, 36 sq km/14 sq mi, on the coast near Trujillo.

chin *n.* the front of the lower jaw. [Old English]

china /'tʃaɪnə/ *n.* fine earthenware, porcelain. —**china clay**, a clay mineral formed by the decomposition of ⊘feldspars. The alteration of aluminium silicates results in the formation of **kaolinite**, $Al_2Si_2O_5(OH)_2$, from which **kaolin**, or white china clay, is derived. Kaolinite is economically important in the ceramic and paper industries. It is mined in the UK, the USA, France, and Czechoslovakia.

China People's Republic of; country in SE Asia, bounded to the N by Mongolia; NW and NE by the USSR; SW by India and Nepál; S by Bhutan, Myanmar (Burma), Laos, and Vietnam; SE by the South China Sea; E by the East China Sea, North Korea, and the USSR; **area** 9,596,960 sq km/3,599,975 sq mi; **capital** Beijing (Peking); **physical** two-thirds of China is mountains or desert (N and W), including the Gobi Desert in the N; the low-lying E is irrigated by rivers Huang He (Yellow River), Chang Jiang (Yangtze-Kiang), Xi Jiang (Si Kiang); **head of state** Yang Shangkun from 1988; **head of government** Li Peng from 1987; **political system** communist republic; **exports** tea, livestock and animal products, silk, cotton, oil, minerals (China is the world's largest producer of tungsten), chemicals, light industrial goods; **population** (1990 est) 1,130,065,000 (the majority are Han or ethnic Chinese; other ethnic groups include Tibetan, Uigur, and Zhuang); **language** Chinese, including Mandarin (official), Cantonese and other dialects; **recent history** the People's Republic of China was proclaimed by Mao Zedong in 1949; a Soviet-style constitution was adopted and steps were taken to centralize the economy, the USSR providing economic aid. The Great Leap Forward 1958 intended to hasten the achievement of the Marxist ideal of true communism by the creation of self-sufficient agricultural and industrial communes. A breach in Sino-Soviet relations brought a withdrawal of Soviet technical advisers in 1960, and a Sino-Soviet border war in 1962. The failure of the plan resulted in a recovery programme, including privatisation schemes, under President Liu Shaoqi, against which Mao launched the Great Proletarian Cultural Revolution (1966-69), to re-establish the supremacy of his ideology. The death of Mao Zedong and Prime Minister Zhou Enlai in 1976 initiated a violent succession struggle between left and right; by 1979 the 'rightist' Den Xiaoping had gained effective control of the government; economic reforms were introduced, including the dismantling of the commune system. During the 1980s contact with the West led to mounting pressure for democratization, and an austerity budget introduced in 1989 led

China

to student unrest. A student-led prodemocracy movement organized mass demonstrations leading up to Soviet leader Mikhail Gorbachev's visit in June 1989; in a single incident more than 2,000 unarmed protesters were massacred by army troops in Beijing's Tiananmen Square. International protest was answered by a crackdown on dissidents and a return to conservative policies. The West imposed sanctions, but during the 1990s contact was re-established and most sanctions withdrawn.

chinagraph /'tʃaɪnəgrɑːf/ n. a kind of pencil that can write on china and glass.

China Sea /'tʃaɪnə/ area of the Pacific Ocean bordered by China, Vietnam, Borneo, the Philippines, and Japan. Various groups of small islands and shoals, including the Paracels, 500 km/300 mi E of Vietnam, have been disputed by China and other powers because they lie in oil-rich areas.

chincherinchee n. a poisonous plant *Ornithogalum thyrsoides* of the lily family Liliaceae. It is native to South Africa, and has spikes of long-lasting, white or yellow, waxlike flowers.

chinchilla /tʃɪn'tʃɪlə/ n. **1.** a small South American rodent of the genus *Chinchilla*, about the size of a small rabbit, with long ears and a long bushy tail; its soft grey fur. **2.** a variety of silver-coloured domestic cat. **3.** a variety of rabbit bred for its fur; this fur. [Spanish, diminutive of *chinche* = bug]

Chindit /'tʃɪndɪt/ n. a member of the allied forces fighting behind Japanese lines in Burma 1943–5. [from Burmese *chinthé* = a mythical creature]

chine[1] n. **1.** an animal's backbone; a joint of meat containing part of this. **2.** a mountain ridge. —v.t. to cut through the backbone of (a carcass). [from Old French from Germanic (related to Latin *spina* = spine)]

chine[2] n. a deep narrow ravine on the Isle of Wight or Dorset coast. [Old English *cinu* = chink]

Chinese /tʃaɪ'niːz/ n. (*plural* the same) **1.** a native of China; a person of Chinese descent. **2.** the language spoken in China; a language of the Sino-Tibetan family. Chinese languages are also spoken in Taiwan, Hong Kong, Singapore, and Chinese communities throughout the world. Varieties of spoken Chinese differ greatly, but all share a written form using thousands of ideographic symbols (characters). Nowadays, *putonghua* ('common speech'), based on the educated Beijing dialect known as Mandarin Chinese, is promoted throughout China as the national spoken and written language. —adj. of China or its people or language. —**Chinese lantern**, a collapsible paper lantern; a plant *Physalis alkekengi* grown for its inflated papery orange calyx.

Chinese Revolution a series of major political upheavals in China 1911–49 that eventually led to Communist party rule and the establishment of the People's Republic of China.

chink[1] n. a narrow opening or slit.

chink[2] n. a sound like glasses or coins being struck together. —v.t./i. to make or cause to make this sound. [imitative]

chinoiserie /ʃɪn'wɑːzərɪ/ n. imitation of Chinese motifs in furniture or decoration; examples of this. [French]

chinook /tʃɪ'nʊk/ n. a warm, dry wind which blows down the eastern slopes of the Rocky Mountains; (*erroneous*) a warm, wet oceanic wind west of them. [from *Chinook*, tribe of N American Indians]

chintz n. a cotton fabric with a printed pattern, usually glazed, used for furnishings. [from Hindi from Sanskrit *citra* = variegated]

chip v.t./i. (**-pp-**) **1.** to knock or break (a piece) *off, away*; to break the edge or surface of; to shape or carve thus. **2.** to make (potatoes) into chips. —n. **1.** a piece chipped off; the mark left by this. **2.** a long fried strip of potato. **3.** a counter used in a game. **4.** a microchip; a complete electronic circuit on a slice of silicon (or other ◊semiconductor) crystal only a few millimetres square. —**chip off the old block**, a child who is very like his or her father. **chip on one's shoulder**, a feeling of resentment or bitterness about something. **chip in**, (*colloquial*) to interrupt; to contribute money. [from Old English *cipp, cyp* = beam]

chipboard n. material made of compressed wood chips and resin.

chipmunk /'tʃɪpmʌŋk/ n. any of several species of small ground squirrel with characteristic stripes along their sides.

Chipmunks live in North America and E Asia, in a variety of habitats, usually wooded, and take shelter in burrows. They have pouches in their cheeks for carrying food. They climb well but spend most of their time on or near the ground.

chipolata /tʃɪpə'lɑːtə/ n. a small spicy sausage. [French from Italian *cipolla* = onion]

Chippendale /'tʃɪpəndeɪl/ Thomas *c*.1718–1779. English furniture designer who set up his workshop in St Martin's Lane, London in 1753. His book *The Gentleman and Cabinet Maker's Director* 1754, was a significant contribution to furniture design. He favoured Louis XVI, Chinese, Gothic, and Neo-Classical styles, and worked mainly in mahogany.

Chirac /'ʃɪəræk/ Jacques 1932– . French conservative politician, prime minister 1974–76 and 1986–88. He established the neo-Gaullist *Rassemblement pour la République* (RPR) in 1976, and became mayor of Paris in 1977.

Chirico /'kɪərɪkəʊ/ Giorgio de 1888–1978. Italian painter born in Greece, whose style presaged Surrealism in its use of enigmatic imagery and dreamlike settings, for example, *Nostalgia of the Infinite* 1911, Museum of Modern Art, New York.

chiromancy /'kaɪrəmænsɪ/ n. palmistry. —**chiromancer** n. [from Greek *kheir* = hand]

Chiron /'kaɪrən/ n. an outer asteroid discovered by Charles Kowal in 1977, orbiting between Saturn and Uranus. It appears to have a dark surface resembling that of asteroids in the inner solar system, probably consists of a mixture of ice and dark stony material, and may have a diameter of about 200 km/120 mi.

chiropody /kɪ'rɒpədɪ/ n. treatment of ailments of the foot. —**chiropodist** n. [from Greek *kheir* = hand and *pous* = foot]

chiropractic /kaɪrə'præktɪk/ n. treatment of disease by manipulation of the spine and joints. —**chiropractor** n. [from Greek *kheir* = hand and *praktikos*]

chirp n. the short sharp note of a small bird or a grasshopper. —v.i. to make this sound.

chirrup /'tʃɪrəp/ n. a series of chirps. —v.i. to make this sound.

chisel /'tʃɪzəl/ n. a tool with a bevelled cutting edge for shaping wood, stone, or metal. —v.t. (**-ll-**) to cut or shape with a chisel. [from Old French from Latin *caedere* = cut]

Chissano /ʃi'sɑːnəʊ/ Joaquim 1939–. Mozambique nationalist politician, president from 1986; foreign minister 1975–86.

chit[1] n. a shoot, a sprout. —v.i. (of seed) to sprout, to germinate.

chit[2] n. a young child; a small young woman. [originally = whelp, cub, kitten]

chit[3] n. a short written note, especially of an order made, a sum owed etc. [earlier *chitty*, from Hindi from Sanskrit *citra* = mark]

chitchat n. chat, gossip.

chitin /'kaɪtɪn/ n. a complex long-chain compound, or ◊polymer; a nitrogenous derivative of glucose. Chitin is found principally in the ◊exoskeleton of insects and other arthropods. It combines with protein to form a covering that can be hard and tough, as in beetles, or soft and flexible, as

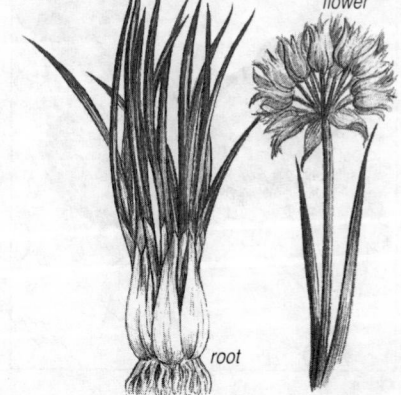

chive

flower

root

in caterpillars and other insect larvae. In crustaceans such as crabs, it is impregnated with calcium carbonate giving extra strength. —**chitinous** adj. [from French from Greek khitō = garment]

Chittagong /'tʃitəgoŋ/ city and port in Bangladesh, 16 km/10 mi from the mouth of the Karnaphuli River, on the Bay of Bengal; population (1981) 1,388,476. Industries include steel, engineering, chemicals, and textiles.

chitterlings n.pl. the smaller intestines of a pig, cooked as food.

chivalry /'ʃivəlrɪ/ n. courtesy and consideration, especially to weaker people; the medieval knightly system with its ethical and social code. —**chivalrous** adj. [from Old French from Latin = horseman]

chive n. (chiefly in plural) a bulbous perennial plant Allium schoenoprasum of the lily family Liliaceae. It has long, tubular leaves and dense, round flower heads in blue or lilac, and is used as a garnish for salads. [from Old French from Latin cepa = onion]

chivvy /'tʃivi/ v.t. to keep urging (a person) to hurry, to harass. [from chevy, probably from ballad of Chevy Chase, place on Scottish border]

chlamydia n. (plural chlamydiae) a single-celled bacterium that can only live parasitically in animal cells. Chlamydiae are thought to be descendants of bacteria that have lost certain metabolic processes. In humans, they cause ◊trachoma, a disease found mainly in the tropics (a leading cause of blindness), and psittacosis, which is contracted from birds by inhaling particles of dried droppings.

chloral /'klɔːrəl/ n. or **trichloroethanal**, CCl_3CHO, an oily colourless liquid with a characteristic pungent smell, produced by the action of chlorine on ethanol. It is soluble in water and its compound chloral hydrate is a powerful sleep-inducing agent. [French chlore = chlorine and alcool = alcohol]

chloramphenicol n. the first of the broad-spectrum antibiotics to be used commercially. It was discovered in a Peruvian soil sample containing the bacillus Streptomyces venezuelae, which produces the antibiotic substance $C_{11}H_{12}Cl_2N_2O_5$, now synthesized. Because of its toxicity, its use is limited to treatment of life-threatening infections, such as meningitis and typhoid fever.

chlorate n. any salt from an acid containing both chlorine and oxygen, ClO, ClO_2, ClO_3, and ClO_4. Common chlorates are those of sodium, potassium, and barium. Certain chlorates are used in weedkillers.

chloride /'klɔːraɪd/ n. Cl^-, a negative ion formed when hydrogen chloride dissolves in water, and any salt containing this ion, commonly formed by the action of hydrochloric acid, HCl, on various metals or by direct combination of a metal and chlorine. Sodium chloride, NaCl, is common table salt.

chlorinate /'klɔːrɪneɪt/ v.t. to treat or disinfect with chlorine. —**chlorination** /-'neɪʃən/ n.

chlorine /'klɔːriːn/ n. a greenish-yellow, gaseous, nonmetallic element with a pungent odour, symbol Cl, atomic number 17, relative atomic mass 35.453 (a mixture of two isotopes: 75% Cl-35, 25% Cl-37). It is the second member of the ◊halogen group (group VII of the periodic table). In nature it is widely distributed in combination with the ◊alkali metals, as chlorates or chlorides; in its pure form the gas is a diatomic molecule (Cl_2). It is a very reactive element, and combines with most metals, some nonmetals, and a wide variety of compounds. [Greek khlōros = green]

chlorofluorocarbon n. (CFC) a synthetic chemical, which is odourless, nontoxic, nonflammable, and chemically inert. CFCs are used as propellants in ◊aerosol cans, refrigerants in refrigerators and air conditioners, in the manufacture of foam boxes for take-away food cartons, and as cleaning substances in the electronics industry. They are partly responsible for the destruction of the ◊ozone layer. In June 1990 representatives of 93 nations, including the UK and the USA, agreed to phase out production of CFCs and other ozone-depleting chemicals by the end of the 20th century.

chloroform /'klɒrəfɔːm/ n. or **trichloromethane**, CCl_3, a clear, colourless, toxic, carcinogenic liquid with a characteristic, pungent, sickly-sweet smell and taste, formerly used as an anaesthetic (now superseded by less harmful substances). It is used as a solvent and in the synthesis of organic chemical compounds. —v.t. to make unconscious with chloroform. [from French]

chlorophyll /'klɒrəfɪl/ n. a green pigment present in the majority of plants, which is responsible for the absorption of light energy during the light reaction of ◊photosynthesis. It absorbs the red and blue-violet parts of sunlight but reflects the green, thus giving plants their most characteristic colour. [from French from Greek khlōros = green and phullon = leaf]

chloroplast n. a structure within a plant cell containing the green pigment chlorophyll. Chloroplasts occur in most cells of the green plant that are exposed to light, often in large numbers. Typically, they are flattened and disclike, with a double membrane enclosing the stroma, a gel-like matrix. Within the stroma are stacks of fluid-containing cavities, or vesicles, where ◊photosynthesis occurs.

chlorosis n. an abnormal condition of green plants in which the stems and leaves turn pale green or yellow. The yellowing is due to a reduction in the levels of the green chlorophyll pigments. It may be caused by a deficiency in essential elements (such as magnesium, iron, or manganese), a lack of light, genetic factors, or virus infection.

choc n. (colloquial) abbreviation of chocolate; a chocolate. —**choc-ice** n. a small bar of ice cream coated with chocolate.

chock n. a block or wedge used to prevent something from moving. —v.t. to wedge with a chock or chocks. —**chock-a-block** adj. & adv. crammed or crowded together. **chock-full** adj. crammed full.

chocolate /'tʃɒkələt/ n. 1. an edible powder, paste, or solid block made from cacao seeds; a sweet made of or coated with this; a drink made with it. 2. dark-brown colour. —adj. 1. made of chocolate; flavoured or coated with chocolate. 2. chocolate-coloured. [from French or Spanish from Aztec chocolatl]

choice n. the act or power of choosing; a person or thing chosen; a variety from which to choose. —adj. of special quality. [from Old French from Germanic]

choir /kwaɪə/ n. 1. an organized body of singers especially in a church. 2. the part of a church etc. where they sit. [from Old French from Latin chorus]

Choiseul /ʃwæ'zɜːl/ Étienne François, duc de Choiseul 1719–1785. French politician. Originally a protégé of Mme de Pompadour, the mistress of Louis XV, he became minister for foreign affairs in 1758, and held this and other offices until 1770. He banished the Jesuits, and was a supporter of the Enlightenment philosophers Diderot and Voltaire.

choke /tʃəuk/ v.t./i. 1. to stop the breathing of by compressing or blocking the windpipe or (of smoke etc.) by being unfit to breathe; to be unable to breathe from such a cause; to make or become speechless from emotion. 2. to clog, to smother. —n. 1. choking, a choking sound. 2. a valve controlling the flow of air into a petrol engine. 3. an inductance coil to smooth variations of alternating current. —**choke off**, (colloquial) to silence or discourage, usually by snubbing. [from Old English ācēocian (cēoce = cheek)]

choker n. a high collar; a close-fitting necklace.

cholecystectomy n. the surgical removal of the ◊gall bladder.

choler /'kɒlə/ n. 1. (historical) one of the four humours. 2. (poetical or archaic) anger, irascibility. [from Old French from Latin from Greek kholē = bile]

cholera /'kɒlərə/ n. any of several intestinal diseases, especially **Asiatic cholera**, an infection caused by a bacterium Vibrio cholerae, transmitted in contaminated water and characterized by violent diarrhoea and vomiting. It is prevalent in many tropical areas. [from Latin]

choleric /'kɒlərɪk/ adj. irascible; angry.

cholesterol /kə'lestərɒl/ n. a waxy, fatty, ◊steroid substance that is ubiquitous and vital in the body. It is made by the liver, and also provided in the diet by foods such as eggs, meat, and butter. A high level of cholesterol in the blood is thought to contribute to atherosclerosis (hardening of the arteries). [from Greek kholē = bile and stereos = stiff]

Chomsky /'tʃɒmski/ Noam 1928–. US professor of linguistics. He proposed a theory of transformational generative grammar, which attracted widespread interest because of the claims it made about the relationship between language and the mind and the universality of an underlying language structure. He is also a leading voice against the imperialist tendencies of the US government.

Colourless green ideas sleep furiously.
Noam Chomsky
Syntactic Structures
(example of a grammatically acceptable
sentence that makes no sense)

chondrite /'kɒndraɪt/ *n.* a meteorite containing granules (*chondrules*), the most abundant type of meteorite in the solar system. [from German from Greek *khondros* = granule]

Chongjin /tʃʊŋ'dʒɪn/ capital of North Hamgyong province on the NE coast of North Korea; population (1984) 754,000.

Chongqing /tʃʊŋ'tʃɪŋ/ or **Chungking**, also known as Pahsien city in Sichuan province, China, that stands at the the ◊Chang Jiang and Jialing Jiang rivers; population (1984) 2,733,700. Industries include iron, steel, chemicals, synthetic rubber, and textiles.

chook /tʃuk/ *n.* (*Australian* and *New Zealand*) a domestic fowl, a chicken. [probably from dialect *chuck* = chick]

Choonhavan Chatichai 1922– . Thai conservative politician, prime minister of Thailand from 1988. He has promoted a peace settlement in neighbouring Cambodia as part of a vision of transforming Indochina into a thriving open-trade zone.

choose /tʃuːz/ *v.t./i.* (*past* chose /tʃəʊz/; *past participle* chosen /tʃəʊzən/) to select from a greater number; to decide or desire as a matter of preference. [Old English]

choosey /'tʃuːzɪ/ *adj.* (*colloquial*) careful and cautious in choosing, hard to please.

chop[1] *v.t./i.* (-pp-) 1. to cut with a heavy blow, usually with an axe or knife; to cut up small in cookery; to make a chopping blow *at.* 2. to strike (a ball) with a heavy edgewise blow. —*n.* 1. a chopping stroke or blow. 2. a thick slice of meat, usually including a rib.

chop[2] *v.t./i.* (-pp-) **chop and change**, to keep changing. [perhaps variation of obsolete *chap* = barter]

chop[3] *n.* (usually in *plural*) the jaws of a person or animal.

Chopin /'ʃɒpæn/ Frédéric (François) 1810–1849. Polish composer and pianist. He made his debut as a pianist at the age of eight. As a performer, Chopin revolutionized the technique of pianoforte playing, and concentrated on solo piano pieces. His compositions for piano are characterized by their lyrical and poetic quality.

Chopin /'ʃəʊpæn/ Kate 1851–1904. US novelist and short-story writer. Her novel *The Awakening* 1899, the story of a married New Orleans woman's awakening to her sexuality, is now regarded as a classic of feminist sensibility.

chopper *n.* 1. a short axe with a large blade; a butcher's cleaver. 2. (*slang*) a helicopter.

choppy *adj.* 1. (of the sea) full of short, broken waves. 2. jerky, abrupt. —**choppiness** *n.*

chopsticks *n.pl.* a pair of sticks held in one hand and used in China etc. to lift food to the mouth. [from pidgin English *chop* = quick]

chop suey /tʃɒp'suːɪ/ a Chinese dish of small pieces of meat fried with rice and vegetables. [Chinese = mixed bits]

choral /'kɔːrəl/ *adj.* written for a choir or chorus; sung or spoken by these. —**choral society**, a society formed to sing choral music. [from Latin]

chorale /kɒ'rɑːl/ *n.* a metrical hymn sung in unison, originally in the Lutheran Church; a harmonized form of this. [from German]

chord[1] /kɔːd/ *n.* a group of notes sounded together in harmony. [originally *cord* from *accord*]

chord[2] *n.* 1. a straight line joining the ends of an arc. 2. (*poetical*) a string of a harp etc.

chordate /'kɔːdeɪt/ *adj.* of the phylum Chordata, having a notochord, a supporting rod of tissue running down the body. —*n.* a member of this phylum, which includes all the vertebrates as well as a few invertebrate groups, characterized by having a notochord at some stage of the life cycle. [from Latin *chorda*]

chore /tʃɔː/ *n.* a recurrent or tedious task.

chorea *n.* a disease of the nervous system marked by involuntary movements of the face muscles and limbs,

formerly called St Vitus's dance. ◊Huntington's chorea is also characterized by such movements.

choreograph /'kɒriəgrɑːf/ *v.t.* to provide choreography for.

choreography /kɒri'ɒgrəfɪ/ *n.* the composition of ballet or stage dances. —**choreographer** *n.*, **choreographic** /-'græfɪk/ *adj.* [from Greek *khoreia* = choral dancing to music]

chorion *n.* the outermost of the three membranes enclosing the embryo of reptiles, birds, and mammals; the ◊amnion is the innermost membrane.

chorister /'kɒrɪstə/ *n.* a member of a church choir. [from Old French *quer* = choir]

choroid *n.* the black layer found at the rear of the ◊eye beneath the retina. By absorbing light that has already passed through the retina, it stops back reflection and so aids vision.

chortle *n.* a loud gleeful chuckle. —*v.i.* to utter a chortle. [blend of *chuckle* and *snort*]

chorus /'kɔːrəs/ *n.* 1. an organized group of singers; a group of singing dancers in an opera, musical comedy, etc. or in an ancient Greek play. 2. a thing sung or said by many at once; the refrain of a song, which the audience join the performer in singing. 3. a character speaking the prologue etc. in a play. —*v.t./i.* to say or sing in chorus. [Latin from Greek]

chose, chosen past and past participle of **choose**.

Chou En-lai /'tʃəu en 'laɪ/ alternative transcription of ◊Zhou Enlai.

chough /tʃʌf/ *n.* a bird *Pyrrhocorax pyrrhocorax* of the crow family, about 38 cm/15 in long, black-feathered, and with red bill and legs. It lives on sea cliffs and mountains from Europe to E Asia, but is now rare. [imitative].

choux pastry /ʃuː/ a very light pastry enriched with eggs. [French]

chow /tʃaʊ/ *n.* a breed of dog originating in China in ancient times. About 45 cm/1.5 ft tall, it has a broad neck and head, round catlike feet, a soft, woolly undercoat with a coarse outer coat, and a mane. Its coat should be of one colour, and it has an unusual blue-black tongue. [short for *chow-chow*, perhaps from pidgin English]

chowder /'tʃaʊdə/ *n.* (*US*) a thick soup of clams (or fish) and vegetables. [perhaps from French *chaudière* = pot]

chow mein /tʃaʊ 'meɪn/ a Chinese dish of fried noodles usually with shredded meat and vegetables. [from Chinese = fried flour]

Chrétien de Troyes /kreti'æn də 'trwɑː/ medieval French poet, born in Champagne about the middle of the 12th century. His epics, which include *Le Chevalier de la charrette*; *Perceval*, written for Philip, Count of Flanders; *Erec*; *Yvain*; and other Arthurian romances, introduced the concept of the ◊Holy Grail.

chrism /'krɪzəm/ *n.* consecrated oil. [Old English from Latin from Greek *khrisma* = anointing]

Christ /kraɪst/ the Messiah of Jewish prophecy; the title (now treated as a name) of Jesus, regarded as fulfilling this prophecy. [Old English from Latin from Greek *khristos* = anointed one (translation of Hebrew = Messiah)]

christen /'krɪsən/ *v.t.* to admit to the Christian church by baptism; to give a name or nickname to. [Old English = make Christian]

Christian /'krɪstjən/ *adj.* 1. of the doctrines of Christianity, believing in or based on these. 2. showing the qualities of a Christian, kindly, humane. —*n.* 1. an adherent of Christianity. 2. a kindly or humane person. —**Christian era**, the era reckoned from the birth of Christ. **Christian name**, a personal name given at baptism. [from Latin *Christus* = Christ]

Christian ten kings of Denmark and Norway, including:

Christian I 1426–1481. King of Denmark from 1448, and founder of the Oldenburg dynasty. In 1450 he established the union of Denmark and Norway that lasted until 1814.

Christian IV 1577–1648. King of Denmark and Norway from 1588. He sided with the Protestants in the Thirty Years' War (1618–48), and founded Christiania (now Oslo, capital of Norway). He was succeeded by Frederick II in 1648.

Christian VIII 1786–1848. King of Denmark 1839–48. He was unpopular because of his opposition to reform. His attempt to encourage the Danish language and culture in Schleswig and Holstein led to an insurrection there shortly after his death. He was succeeded by Frederick VII.

Christian IX 1818–1906. King of Denmark from 1863. His daughter Alexandra married Edward VII of the UK and another, Dagmar, married Tsar Alexander III of Russia; his second son, George, became king of Greece. In 1864 he lost the duchies of Schleswig and Holstein after a war with Austria and Prussia.

Christian X 1870–1947. King of Denmark and Iceland from 1912, when he succeeded his father Frederick VIII. He married Alexandrine, Duchess of Mecklenburg-Schwerin, and was popular for his democratic attitude. During World War II he was held prisoner by the Germans in Copenhagen. He was succeeded by Frederick IX.

Christiania /krɪstiˈɑːniə/ n. in skiing, a turn in which the skis are kept parallel, used for stopping short. [former name of Oslo]

Christianity /krɪstiˈænɪti/ n. the world religion derived from the teaching of Jesus in the first third of the 1st century, with a present-day membership of about 1 billion. Its main divisions are the ◊Roman Catholic, ◊Eastern Orthodox, and ◊Protestant churches. An omnipotent God the Father is the fundamental concept, together with the doctrine of the Trinity, that is, the union of the three persons of the Father, Son, and Holy Spirit in one Godhead (though sects differ on how this is interpreted). Christians believe that Jesus died for the sins of humanity, and his divinity is based on the belief in his resurrection after death and his ascension into Heaven. The main commandments are to love God and to love one's neighbour as oneself, which, if followed successfully, lead to an afterlife in heaven. [from Old French]

Christian Science a sect, the Church of Christ, Scientist, established in the USA by Mary Baker Eddy in 1879. Christian Scientists believe that since God is good and is a spirit, matter and evil are not ultimately real. Consequently they refuse all medical treatment. It has its own daily newspaper, the *Christian Science Monitor*.

christie /ˈkrɪsti/ n. ◊Christiania. [abbreviation]

Christie Agatha 1890–1976. English detective novelist who created the characters Hercule Poirot and Miss Jane Marple. She wrote more than 70 novels including *The Murder of Roger Ackroyd* 1926 and *Ten Little Indians* 1939, and the play *The Mousetrap* 1952.

Christie Julie 1940– . English film actress, who became a star in the 1960s following her award-winning performance in *Darling* 1965. She also appeared in *Doctor Zhivago* 1965; *The Go-Between* 1971; *Don't Look Now* 1973; *Memoirs of a Survivor* 1982; and *Power* 1986.

Christie Linford 1960– . Jamaican-born English sprinter. In 1986, Christie won the European 100 metres championship and finished second to Ben Johnson in the Commonwealth Games. At the 1988 Seoul Olympics, he won two silver medals in the 100 metres and 4 × 100 metres relay. In 1990 he won gold medals in the Commonwealth Games for the 100 metres and 4 × 100 metres relay.

Christina /krɪsˈtiːnə/ 1626–1689. Queen of Sweden 1632–54. Succeeding her father Gustavus Adolphus at the age of six, she assumed power in 1644, but disagreed with the former regent Oxenstjerna. Refusing to marry, she eventually nominated her cousin Charles Gustavus (Charles X) as her successor. As a secret convert to Roman Catholicism, which was then illegal in Sweden, she had to abdicate in 1654, and went to live in Rome, twice returning to Sweden unsuccessfully to claim the throne.

Christine de Pisan /ˈkrɪstiːn də ˈpiːzɒn/ 1364–1430. French poet and historian. Her works include love lyrics, philosophical poems, a poem in praise of Joan of Arc, a history of Charles V, and various defences of women, including *La cité des dames/The City of Ladies*.

Christingle /krɪˈstɪŋgəl/ n. a lighted candle set in an orange received at a Christingle service. —**Christingle service,** a children's Advent service, originally in the Moravian church and recently popularized outside it, at which each participant is given an orange (symbolizing the world) set with a candle (symbolizing Christ as the Light of the World) and other symbolical decorations. [from *Christ*]

Christmas /ˈkrɪsməs/ n. 25 Dec, a Christian religious holiday, observed throughout the Western world and traditionally marked by feasting and the giving of gifts. In the Christian church, it is the day on which the birth of Jesus is celebrated, although the actual birth date is unknown. Many of its customs have a non-Christian origin and were adapted from celebrations of the winter ◊solstice. —**Christmas box,** a present or gratuity given at Christmas, especially to employees. **Christmas card,** a card sent with greetings at Christmas. **Christmas Day,** 25 Dec. **Christmas Eve,** 24 Dec. **Christmas pudding,** rich plum pudding eaten at Christmas. **Christmas rose,** a white-flowered winter-blooming hellebore, *Helleborus niger*. **Christmas tree,** a young conifer (or imitation of one) decorated with lights etc. at Christmas. The custom was a medieval German tradition and is now practised in many Western countries. Christmas trees were introduced to Britain in the 19th century by Albert, the Prince Consort. The tree most commonly used is the Norway spruce *Picea abies*.

Christo /ˈkrɪstəʊ/ adopted name of Christo Javacheff 1935–. US sculptor, born in Bulgaria, active in Paris in the 1950s and in New York from 1964. He is known for his wrapped works: structures such as bridges and buildings, and even areas of coastline, are temporarily wrapped in synthetic fabric tied down with rope. The *Running Fence* 1976 across California was another temporary work.

Christophe /kriːˈstɒf/ Henri 1767–1820. West Indian slave, one of the leaders of the revolt against the French in 1791, who was proclaimed king of Haiti in 1811. His government distributed plantations to military leaders. He shot himself when his troops deserted him because of his alleged cruelty.

Christopher, St /ˈkrɪstəfə/ the patron saint of travellers, traditionally a martyr in Syria in the 3rd century. He is depicted carrying the child Jesus across a river. His feast day on 25 July was dropped from the Roman Catholic liturgical calendar in 1969.

chromatic /krəˈmætɪk/ adj. **1.** of colour, in colours. **2.** in music, with notes not belonging to the diatonic scale. —**chromatic scale,** one that proceeds by semitones. All 12 notes in the octave are used rather than the 7 notes of the diatonic scale. [from French or Latin from Greek *khrōma* = colour]

chromatin /ˈkrəʊmətɪn/ n. a readily stained constituent of the nucleus of a cell. [German, from Greek *khrōma* = colour]

chromatography /krəʊməˈtɒgrəfi/ n. separation of a mixture into its component substances by passing it over material which absorbs these at different rates so that they appear as layers, often of different colours. The technique is used for both qualitative and quantitive analyses in biology and chemistry. [from German]

chrome /krəʊm/ n. chromium, especially as a plating; a yellow pigment obtained from a compound of chromium. [French, from Greek *khrōma* = colour, from the brilliant colours of its compounds]

chromite n. iron chromium oxide, $FeCr_2O_4$, the main ore of chromium. It is one of the spinel group of minerals, and crystallizes in dark coloured octahedra of the cubic system. Chromite is usually found in association with ultrabasic and basic rocks; for example in Cyprus it occurs with serpentine, and in South Africa it forms continuous layers in a layered intrusion.

chromium /ˈkrəʊmiəm/ n. a hard, brittle, grey-white, metallic element, symbol Cr, atomic number 24, relative atomic mass 51.996. It takes a high polish, has a high melting point, and is very resistant to corrosion. It is used in chromium electroplating, to make stainless steel and other alloys, and as a catalyst. Its compounds are used for tanning leather and for ◊alums. In human nutrition it is a vital trace element. In nature, it occurs chiefly as a chrome–iron ore $FeCr_2O_4$. The USSR, Zimbabwe, and Brazil are sources.

chromosome /ˈkrəʊməsəʊm/ n. a structure in a cell nucleus that carries the ◊genes. Each chromosome consists of one very long strand of DNA, coiled and folded to produce a compact chromosome. The point on a chromosome where a particular gene occurs is known as its locus. Most higher organisms have two copies of each chromosome (they are ◊diploid) but some have only one (they are ◊haploid). See also ◊mitosis and ◊meiosis. [German, from Greek *khrōma* = colour and *sōma* = body]

chromosphere n. a layer of mostly hydrogen gas about 10,000 km/6,000 mi deep above the visible surface of the Sun (the photosphere). It appears pinkish-red during ◊eclipses of the Sun.

chronic /'krɒnɪk/ adj. (of diseases etc.) long-lasting, persistent; suffering from a chronic disease. —**chronically** adv. [from French from Latin from Greek khronos = time]

chronicle /'krɒnɪkəl/ n. a record of events in the order of their occurrence. —v.t. to record in a chronicle. —**Chronicles**, either of two books of the Old Testament recording the history of Israel and Judah from the Creation until the return from Exile (536 BC). —**chronicler** n. [from Anglo-French from Latin from Greek khronika]

chronicles, medieval books modelled on the Old Testament Books of Chronicles. Until the later Middle Ages, they were usually written in Latin by clerics, who borrowed extensively from one another.

chronogram /'krɒnəgræm/ n. a phrase etc. of which the Roman numeral letters, when added, give a date, e. g. LorD haVe MerCIe Vpon Vs = 50 + 500 + 5 + 1000 + 100 + 1 + 5 + 5 = 1666. [from Greek khronos = time]

chronology /krə'nɒlədʒɪ/ n. arrangement of events according to date or in order of occurrence. —**chronological** /krɒnə'lɒdʒɪkəl/ adj., **chronologically** adv. [from Greek khronos = time]

chronometer /krə'nɒmɪtə/ n. a time-measuring instrument, especially one keeping accurate time in spite of movement or of variations in temperature, humidity, and air pressure. The first accurate marine chronometer, capable of an accuracy of half a minute a year, was made in 1761 by John Harrison in England. The term is now applied to scientific time-keeping devices. [from Greek khronos = time]

chrysalis /'krɪsəlɪs/ n. (plural **chrysalides** /-'sælɪdiːz/) a butterfly or moth at the quiescent stage between the larval and adult phases; the case enclosing it. [from Latin from Greek khrusos = gold]

chrysanthemum /krɪ'sænθəməm/ n. any plant of the genus Chrysanthemum of the family Compositae, with about 200 species. There are hundreds of cultivated varieties, whose exact wild ancestry is uncertain. In the Far East the common chrysanthemum has been cultivated for more than 2,000 years and is the national emblem of Japan. Chrysanthemums may be grown from seed, but are more usually reproduced by cutting or division. They were introduced into England in 1789. [Latin from Greek khrusos = gold and anthemon = flower]

chryselephantine /krɪseli'fæntaɪn/ adj. (of sculpture) overlaid with gold and ivory. [from Greek khrusos = gold and elephas = ivory]

chrysoberyl /'krɪsəu'berɪl/ n. a yellowish-green gem. [from Latin from Greek]

chrysolite /'krɪsəlaɪt/ n. a precious stone, a variety of olivine. [from Old French from Latin from Greek khrusos = gold and lithos = stone]

chub n. (plural the same) a freshwater fish Leuciscus cephalus of the carp family. Rather thickset and cylindrical, it grows up to 60 cm/2 ft, is dark greenish or grey on the back, silvery yellow below, with metallic flashes on the flanks. It lives generally in clean rivers, from Britain to the USSR.

chubby adj. plump, plump-faced.

Chubu /'tʃuːbuː/ mountainous coastal region of central Honshu island, Japan, covering an area of 66,774 sq km/ 25,791 sq mi; population (1986) 20,694,000. The chief city is Nagoya.

chuck[1] v.t. 1. (colloquial) to throw carelessly or casually. 2. to touch playfully (under the chin). —n. an act of chucking. —**chuck out**, (slang) to expel; to throw away. [perhaps from French chuquer = knock]

chuck[2] n. 1. the part of a lathe holding the workpiece; the part of a drill holding the bit. 2. a cut of beef from the neck to the ribs.

chuckle n. a quiet or suppressed laugh. —v.i. to give a chuckle.

chuddar /'tʃʌdə/ n. or **chadar** or **chador** a large piece of cloth worn as a kind of cloak, leaving only the face exposed, by Muslim women in certain countries. [from Persian]

chug n. the dull, short, repeated sound of an engine running slowly. —v.i. (-gg-) to move with or make this sound.

Chugoku /tʃuː'gəuku:/ SW region of Honshu island, Japan, covering an area of 31,881 sq km/12,314 sq mi; population (1986) 7,764,000. The chief city is Hiroshima.

chukker /'tʃʌkə/ n. or **chukka** a period of play in polo. [from Hindi from Sanskrit cakra = wheel]

church

Norwich Cathedral (plan)

chum n. (colloquial) a close friend. —v.i. (-mm-) —**chum up**, (colloquial) to form a close friendship. [probably abbreviation of chamber fellow]

chummy adj. (colloquial) friendly. —**chumminess** n.

chump n. 1. the thick blunt end of loin of lamb etc. 2. (colloquial) a stupid person. [blend of chunk and lump]

Chun Doo-hwan /'tʃʌn duː'hwɑːn/ 1931– . South Korean military ruler who seized power in 1979; president 1981–88 as head of the newly formed Democratic Justice Party.

chunk n. a thick lump cut off; a substantial amount.

chunky adj. 1. in chunks, containing chunks. 2. short and thickset.

chupatty /tʃʌ'pætɪ/ n. a small, flat, thin cake of coarse unleavened bread. [from Hindi]

church n. a building for public Christian worship; a service in this. —v.t. to perform the church service of thanksgiving for (a woman after childbirth). —**the Church**, the whole body of Christian believers; a particular group of these; the clergy, the clerical profession. [Old English from Greek kuriakon = Lord's (house)]

Church Army a religious organization within the Church of England founded in 1882 by Wilson Carlile (1847–1942), an industrialist converted after the failure of his textile firm, who took orders in 1880. Originally intended for evangelical and social work in the London slums, it developed along Salvation Army lines, and has done much work among ex-prisoners and for the soldiers of both World Wars.

Churchill /'tʃɜːtʃɪl/ Caryl 1938– . British playwright, whose predominantly radical and feminist works include Cloud Nine 1979, Top Girls 1982, and Serious Money 1987.

Churchill Randolph (Henry Spencer) 1849–1895. English Conservative politician, chancellor of the Exchequer and leader of the House of Commons in 1886; father of Winston Churchill.

Churchill Winston (Leonard Spencer) 1874–1965. English Conservative politician. In Parliament from 1900, as a Liberal until 1923, he held a number of ministerial offices, including First Lord of the Admiralty 1911–15 and chancellor of the Exchequer 1924–29. Absent from the cabinet in the 1930s, he returned in Sept 1939 to lead a coalition government 1940–45, negotiating with Allied leaders in World War II; he was again prime minister in 1951–55. He won the Nobel Prize for Literature in 1953.

Never in the field of human conflict was so much owed by so many to so few.

Winston Churchill
speech 20 Aug 1940

churchman *n.* or **churchwoman** (*plural* **churchmen** or **churchwomen**) 1. a member of the clergy. 2. a member of a church.

Church of England the established form of Christianity in England, a member of the Anglican Communion. It was dissociated from the Roman Catholic Church in 1534. There were approximately 1,100,000 regular worshippers in 1988. In England the two archbishops head the provinces of Canterbury and York, which are subdivided into bishoprics. The Church Assembly of 1919 was replaced in 1970 by a **General Synod** with three houses (bishops, other clergy, and laity) to regulate church matters, subject to Parliament and the royal assent. A **Lambeth Conference** (first held in 1867), attended by bishops from all parts of the Anglican Communion, is held every ten years and presided over in London by the archbishop of Canterbury. It is not legislative but its decisions are often put into practice. The **Church Commissioners** for England (1948) manage the assets of the Church (in 1989 valued at £2.64 billion) and endowment of livings.

The main parties, all products of the 19th century, are: the **Evangelical** or **Low Church**, which maintains the Church's Protestant character; the **Anglo-Catholic** or **High Church**, which stresses continuity with the pre-Reformation church and is marked by ritualistic practices, the use of confession, and maintenance of religious communities of both sexes; and the **Liberal** or **Modernist**, concerned with the reconciliation of the Church with modern thought. There is also the **Pentecostal Charismatic** movement, emphasizing spontaneity and speaking in tongues.

Church of Scotland the established form of Christianity in Scotland, first recognized by the state in 1560. It is based on the Protestant doctrines of the reformer Calvin and governed on Presbyterian lines. The Church went through several periods of episcopacy in the 17th century, and those who adhered to episcopacy after 1690 formed the Episcopal Church of Scotland, an autonomous church in communion with the Church of England. In 1843 there was a split in the Church of Scotland (the Disruption), in which almost a third of its ministers and members left and formed the Free Church of Scotland. Its membership in 1988 was about 850,000.

churchwarden *n.* 1. a lay representative of a parish who helps with the business of a church. 2. a long-stemmed clay pipe.

churchyard *n.* the enclosed ground round a church, especially as used for burials.

churlish *adj.* rude and unfriendly, ungracious; mean, grudging. —**churlishly** *adv.*, **churlishness** *n.* [Old English]

churn *n.* 1. a vessel in which milk or cream is shaken to produce butter. 2. a large milk can in which milk is carried from a farm. —*v.t./i.* 1. to shake (milk or cream) in a churn; to produce (butter) thus. 2. to stir or swirl violently, to break *up* the surface of. —**churn out**, to produce in quantity. [Old English]

Churrigueresque /tʃʌrɪgəˈrɛsk/ *adj.* of the lavishly ornamented late Spanish baroque style. [from José de *Churriguera*, Spanish architect (1650–1725)]

chute /ʃuːt/ *n.* a sloping or vertical channel or slide for conveying things to a lower level. [French = fall]

chutney /ˈtʃʌtnɪ/ *n.* a pungent relish of fruits, vinegar, spices, etc. [from Hindi]

chyme *n.* a general term for the stomach contents. It resembles a thick, creamy fluid and is made up of partly-digested food, hydrochloric acid, and a range of enzymes.

CIA abbreviation of Central Intelligence Agency.

Ciano /ˈtʃɑːnəʊ/ Galeazzo 1903–1944. Italian Fascist politician. Son-in-law of Mussolini, he was foreign minister 1936–43, when his loyalty became suspect. He voted against Mussolini at the meeting of the Grand Council in July 1943 that overthrew the dictator, but was later tried for treason and shot by the Fascists.

Cibachrome *n.* in photography, trade name for a process of printing directly from transparencies. Distinguished by rich, saturated colours, it can be home-processed and the colours are highly resistant to fading. It was introduced in 1963. It is marketed by Ilford UK Ltd.

ciborium /sɪˈbɔːrɪəm/ *n.* (*plural* **ciboria**) 1. in architecture, a canopy; a canopied shrine. 2. a covered receptacle

for the reservation of the Eucharist. [Latin from Greek = seed vessel of the water lily, cup made from it]

cicada /sɪˈkɑːdə/ *n.* an insect of the family Cicadidae. Most species are tropical, but a few occur in Europe and North America. Young cicadas live underground, for up to 17 years in some species. The adults live on trees, from which they such the juices. The males produce a loud, almost continuous, chirping by vibrating membranes in resonating cavities in the abdomen. The rare *Cicadetta montana*, about 2 cm/0.8 in long, lives in the New Forest, England. [Latin]

cicatrice /ˈsɪkətrɪs/ *n.* the scar left by a healed wound. [from Old French or Latin]

cicely /ˈsɪsəlɪ/ *n.* or **sweet cicely** an aromatic umbelliferous herb, *Myrrhis odorata*. [from Latin from Greek *seselis*, assimilated to the woman's name *Cicely*]

Cicero /ˈsɪsərəʊ/ 106–43 BC. Roman orator, writer, and politician. His speeches and philosophical and rhetorical works are models of Latin prose, and his letters provide a picture of contemporary Roman life. As consul in 63 BC he exposed Catiline's conspiracy in four major orations.

There is nothing so absurd but some philosopher has said it.

Cicero
De Divinatione

cicerone /tʃɪtʃəˈrəʊnɪ, sɪs-/ *n.* (*plural* **ciceroni** /-niː/) a guide who shows antiquities to visitors. [Italian from Latin *Cicero*]

cichlid *n.* a freshwater fish of the family Cichlidae. Cichlids are somewhat perchlike, but have a single nostril on each side instead of two. They are mostly predatory, and have deep, colourful bodies, flattened from side to side so that some are almost disc shaped. Many are territorial in the breeding season and may show care of the young. There are more than 1,000 species found in South and Central America, Africa, and India.

CID abbreviation of Criminal Investigation Department.

-cide suffix giving the meaning of person or substance that kills (e. g. *regicide, insecticide*); killing (e. g. *homicide*). [from Latin *caedere* = kill]

Cid, El /sɪd/ Rodrigo Díaz de Bivar 1040–1099. Spanish soldier, nicknamed **El Cid** by the ◊Moors. Born in Castile of a noble family, he fought against the king of Navarre and won his nickname *el Campeador* ('the Champion') by killing the Navarrese champion in single combat. Essentially a mercenary, fighting both with and against the Moors, he died while defending Valencia against them, and in subsequent romances became Spain's national hero. [= the lord]

cider /ˈsaɪdə/ *n.* in the UK, a fermented drink made from the juice of the apple; in the USA the term cider usually refers to unfermented (nonalcoholic) apple juice. Cider has been known for more than 2,000 years, and for many centuries has been a popular drink in France and England, which are now its main centres of production. [from Old French, ultimately from Hebrew = strong drink]

Cierva /θɪˈeəvə/ Juan de la 1895–1936. Spanish engineer. In trying to produce an aircraft that would not stall and could fly slowly, he invented the ◊autogiro, the forerunner of the helicopter but differing from it in having unpowered rotors that revolve freely.

cif in economics, abbreviation of cost, insurance, and freight or charged in full. Many countries value their imports on this basis, whereas exports are usually valued ◊fob. For balance of payments purposes, figures are usually adjusted to include the freight and insurance costs.

cigar /sɪˈgɑː/ *n.* a compact roll of tobacco leaves for smoking. It was originally a sheath of palm leaves filled with tobacco, smoked by the Indians of Central and North America. Cigar smoking was introduced into Spain soon after 1492, and spread all over Europe in the next few centuries. From about 1890 cigar smoking was gradually supplanted in popularity in Britain by cigarette smoking. [from French or Spanish]

cigarette /sɪgəˈrɛt/ *n.* a thin paper tube stuffed with shredded tobacco for smoking, usually plugged with a filter. The first cigarettes were the *papelitos* smoked in South America about 1750. The habit spread to Spain, and then throughout the world, and is today the most general form of tobacco smoking. [French, diminutive of *cigare*]

ciliary muscle a ring of muscle surrounding and controlling the lens inside the vertebrate eye, used in ◊accommodation (focusing). Suspensory ligaments, resembling the spokes of a wheel, connect the lens to the cilinary muscle and pull the lens into a flatter shape when the muscle relaxes. On contraction, the lens returns to its normal spherical state.

ciliate /'sɪliət/ *adj.* having cilia. —*n.* a member of the class Ciliata consisting of protozoa which have a relatively complex body structure and are characterized by possessing cilia.

Cilicia ancient region of Asia Minor, now forming part of Turkey, situated between the Taurus Mountains and the Mediterranean.

cilium /'sɪliəm/ *n.* (*plural* cilia) a minute hair fringing a leaf, an insect's wing, etc; a small threadlike organ on the surface of some cells, composed of contractile fibres that produce rhythmic waving movements. Some single-celled organisms move by means of cilia. In multicellular animals, they keep lubricated surfaces clear of debris. They also move food in the digestive tracts of some invertebrates. [Latin = eyelid]

Cimabue /tʃiːməˈbuːeɪ/ Giovanni (Cenni de Peppi) *c.*1240–1302. Italian painter, active in Florence, traditionally styled the 'father of Italian painting'. Among the works attributed to him are *Madonna and Child* (Uffizi, Florence), a huge Gothic image of the Virgin that nevertheless has a softness and solidity that points forwards to Giotto.

cimbalom *n.* in music, a type of ◊dulcimer.

Cimino /tʃiˈmiːnəʊ/ Michael 1943– . US film director, who established his reputation with *The Deer Hunter* 1978 (which won five Academy Awards). His other films include the financially and critically disastrous *Heaven's Gate* 1981 and *The Year of the Dragon* 1986.

cinchona /sɪŋˈkəʊnə/ *n.* any shrub or tree of the tropical American genus *Chinchoua* of the madder family Rubiaceae. ◊Quinine is produced from the bark of some species, and these are now cultivated in India, Sri Lanka, the Philippines, and Indonesia. [from Countess of *Chinchón* who introduced the drug to Spain in 1640]

Cincinnatus /sɪnsiˈnɑːtəs/ Lucius Quintus 5th century BC. Roman general. Appointed dictator in 458 BC, he defeated the Aequi (an Italian people) in a brief campaign, then resumed life as a yeoman farmer.

cincture /'sɪŋktʃə, -tʃuə/ *n.* (*literary*) a girdle, belt, or border. —*v.t.* to surround with a cincture. [from Latin *cinctura* (*cingere* = gird)]

cinder /'sɪndə/ *n.* the residue of coal, wood, etc., after it has ceased to flame; (in *plural*) ashes. [Old English]

Cinderella /sɪndə'relə/ the heroine of a traditional fairy tale of the same name, of which about 700 versions exist. Cinderella is an ill-treated youngest daughter who is enabled by a fairy godmother to attend the royal ball. She captivates Prince Charming but must flee at midnight, losing a tiny glass slipper by which the prince later identifies her.

cine- /sɪni-/ prefix meaning cinematographic.

cine camera a camera that takes a rapid sequence of still photographs – 24 frames (pictures) each second. When the pictures are projected one after the other at the same speed on to a screen, they appear to show movement, because our eyes hold on to the image of one picture before the next one appears.

cinema /'sɪnəmə/ *n.* 1. a theatre where motion-picture films are shown. 2. films as an art or industry. Cinema borrows from the other arts, such as music, drama, and literature, but is entirely dependent for its origins on technological developments, including the technology of action photography, projection, sound reproduction, and film processing and printing (see ◊photography). —**cinematic** /-'mætɪk/ *adj.* [from French *cinéma*, abbreviation of *cinématographe*]

CinemaScope /'sɪnəməskəʊp/ *n.* trade name for a wide-screen process in which anamorphic lenses are used to compress a wide image into a standard frame and then expand it again during projection. The first film to be made in CinemaScope was *The Robe* 1953.

cinémathèque /sɪnəmə'tek/ *n.* a film library or repository; a small cinema. [from French *cinéma* and *bibliothèque* = library)]

cinematograph /sɪnə'mætəgrɑːf/ *n.* a machine for projecting motion-picture films on to a screen. [from French *cinématographe* (machine patented by the Lumière brothers in 1895), from Greek *kinēma* = motion]

cinematography /sɪnɪmə'tɒgrəfɪ/ *n.* the art of making motion-picture films. —**cinematographer** *n.*, **cinematographic** /-'græfɪk/ *adj.*

cinéma-vérité /sɪnɪmə 'verɪteɪ/ *n.* a style of documentary film-making developed in the late 1950s and early 1960s that aims to capture truth on film by observing, recording, and presenting real events and situations as they occur without major directorial, editorial, or technical control. [French = film truth]

Cinerama /sɪnə'rɑːmə/ *n.* trade name for a wide-screen process devised in 1937 by Fred Waller of Paramount's special effects department. Originally three 35-mm cameras and three projectors were used to record and project a single image. Three aspects of the image were recorded and then projected on a large curved screen with the result that the images blended together to produce an illusion of vastness. The first Cinerama film was *How the West Was Won* 1962. It was eventually abandoned in favour of a single-lens 70-mm process.

cineraria /sɪnə'reəriə/ *n.* a composite plant, a variety of *Senecio cruentus*, with bright daisylike flowers. [Latin = of ashes, from the hoary leaves of allied species]

cinerary urn /'sɪnərərɪ/ an urn for holding a dead person's ashes after cremation. [from Latin]

cinnabar /'sɪnəbɑː/ *n.* 1. red mercuric sulphide, HgS, the only commercially useful ore of mercury. It is deposited in veins and impregnations near recent volcanic rocks and hot springs. The pigment obtained from this, vermilion. 2. a moth with reddish-marked wings. [from Latin from Greek]

cinnamon /'sɪnəmən/ *n.* a spice from the aromatic inner bark of a SE Asian tree *Cinnamomum zeylanicum* of the laurel family; its colour, a yellowish-brown. [from Old French from Latin, ultimately from Semitic]

cinquefoil /'sɪŋkfɔɪl/ *n.* 1. a plant of the genus *Potentilla*, with a compound leaf of five leaflets. 2. a five-cusped ornament etc. [from Latin *quinque* = five and *folium* = leaf]

Cinque Ports /sɪŋk/ a group of ports in S England, originally five, Sandwich, Dover, Hythe, Romney, and Hastings, later including Rye, Winchelsea, and others. Probably founded in Roman times, they rose to importance after the Norman conquest and until the end of the 15th century were bound to supply the ships and men necessary against invasion.

cipher /'saɪfə/ *n.* 1. a set of letters or symbols representing others, used to conceal the meaning of a message etc. 2. the symbol O, representing nought or zero. 3. any Arabic numeral. —*v.t.* to write in cipher. [from Old French from Latin from Arabic = zero]

circa /'sɜːkə/ *prep.* about (a specified date or number). [Latin]

circadian /sɜː'keɪdɪən/ *adj.* (of physiological activities etc.) occurring about once every 24 hours. The most obvious manifestation of **circadian rhythm** is the regular cycle of sleeping and waking, but body temperature and the concentration of ◊hormones that influence mood and behaviour also vary over the day. In humans, alteration of habits (such as rapid air travel round the world) may result in the circadian rhythm being out of phase with actual activity patterns, causing malaise until it has had time to adjust. [from Latin *circa* = about and *dies* = day]

Circe /'sɜː.si/ in Greek mythology, an enchantress. In the *Odyssey* of Homer she turned the followers of Odysseus into pigs when she held their leader captive.

circle /'sɜːkəl/ *n.* 1. the path followed by a point that moves so as to keep a constant distance, the **radius**, from a fixed point, the **centre**. The longest distance in a straight line from one side of a circle to the other, passing through the centre, is called the **diameter**, and its measure is twice that of the radius. The ratio of the distance all the way around the circle (the **circumference**) to the diameter is an ◊irrational number called π (pi), roughly equal to 3.14159. A circle of radius r and diameter d has a circumference $C = \pi d$, or $C = 2\pi r$, and an area $A = \pi r^2$. 2. a circular or roundish structure, enclosure, etc.; a curved upper tier of seats at a theatre etc.; a road or railway without ends, on which traffic circulates continuously. 3. persons grouped round a centre of interest; a restricted group or set. —*v.t./i.* **1.** to move in a circle; to revolve round. **2.** to form a circle round, to surround. [from Old French from Latin *circulus*, diminutive of *circus* = ring]

circlet /'sɜːklɪt/ *n.* an ornamental band worn round the head.

circuit /'sɜːkɪt/ *n.* **1.** a line enclosing an area, the route or distance round; a motor-racing track. **2.** in physics or electrical engineering, an arrangement of electrical components through which a current can flow. In a **series circuit** the components are connected end-to-end so that the current flows through all components one after the other. In a **parallel circuit** the components are connected side-by-side so that part of the current passes through each component. A **circuit diagram** shows in graphical form how components are connected together, using standard symbols for the components. **3.** a judge's itinerary through a district to hold courts, such a district; a group of Methodist churches served by a set of itinerant preachers. **4.** a chain of theatres, cinemas, etc., under a single management. **5.** a sequence of sporting events. [from Old French from Latin *circuitus* (*circum* = round and *ire* = go)]

circuit breaker a switching device designed to protect an electric circuit from excessive current. It has the same action as a ◊fuse, and many houses now have a circuit breaker between the incoming main supply and the domestic circuits. They usually work by means of ◊solenoids. The circuit breakers at electricity-generating stations have to be specially designed to prevent dangerous arcing (the release of luminous discharge) when the high-voltage supply is switched off. They may use an air blast or oil immersion to quench the arc.

circuitous /sɜː'kjuːɪtəs/ *adj.* going a long way round, indirect. [from Latin]

circuitry /'sɜːkɪtrɪ/ *n.* a system of electric circuits; the equipment forming this.

circular /'sɜːkjʊlə/ *adj.* **1.** in the form of a circle. **2.** travelling in a circle; (of reasoning) following a vicious circle. **3.** (of letters etc.) addressed to a number of people, not individual. —*n.* a circular letter, leaflet, etc. —**circular**

circle

diameter
radius
centre
circumference

minor arc

minor segment
chord
major segment

tangent

major sector
minor sector

major arc

16b
16a

3 4 5 6 7 8 9 10 11 12 13 14 15 2 1 16b

1 3 5 7 9 11 13 15
16a 2 4 6 8 10 12 14 16b

πr

saw, a rotating toothed disc for sawing wood etc. —**circularity** /-'lærɪtɪ/ *n.* [from Anglo-French from Latin *circularis* (*circulus* = circle)]

circularize /'sɜːkjʊləraɪz/ *v.t.* to send circulars to.

circulate /'sɜːkjʊleɪt/ *v.t./i.* **1.** to go round continuously; to hand or be passed from person to person. **2.** to send circulars to. [from Latin]

circulation /sɜːkjʊ'leɪʃən/ *n.* **1.** movement from and back to a starting point, especially that of the blood from and to the heart. **2.** transmission or distribution (of information, books, etc.). **3.** the number of copies of a newspaper etc. sold or distributed.

circulatory /'sɜːkjʊ'leɪtərɪ/ *adj.* of the circulation of the blood. —**circulatory system,** the system of vessels in an animal's body that transports blood (or other circulatory fluid) to and from the different parts of the body. Except for simple animals such as sponges and coelenterates (jelly-fishes, sea anemones, corals), all animals have a circulatory system.

circumcise /'sɜːkəmsaɪz/ *v.t.* to cut off the foreskin of (a male person) as a religious rite or surgically; to cut off the clitoris of (a female person), to perform the operation of infibulation on. —**circumcision** /-'sɪʒən/ *n.* [from Old French from Latin *circum* = round and *caedere* = cut]

circumference /sɜː'kʌmfərəns/ *n.* the line enclosing a plane figure, especially a circle, or a circular object; the distance round this. Its length varies according to the nature of the curve, and may be ascertained by the appropriate formula. The circumference of a circle is $2\pi r$, where r is the radius and π is the constant pi, approximately equal to 3.1416. [from Old French from Latin *circum* = round and *ferre* = carry]

circumflex /'sɜːkəmfleks/ *n.* or **circumflex accent** a mark (ˆ) over a vowel to show contraction, length, or special quality. [from Latin *circum* = round and *flexus* = bent]

circumlocution /sɜːkəmlə'kjuːʃən/ *n.* speaking in a roundabout or indirect way; a roundabout expression. —**circumlocutory** /-'lɒkjʊtərɪ/ *adj.* [from Latin *circum* = round and *locutio* = speaking]

circumnavigate /sɜːkəm'nævɪgeɪt/ *v.t.* to sail round (the world etc.). The first ship to sail around the world was the *Victoria*, one of the Spanish squadron of five vessels that sailed from Seville in Aug 1519 under the Portuguese navigator Ferdinand Magellan. —**circumnavigation** /-'geɪʃən/ *n.* [from Latin *circum* = round and *navigare* = navigate]

circumscribe /'sɜːkəmskraɪb/ *v.t.* **1.** to draw a line round; in geometry, to draw (a figure) round another so as to touch it at points without cutting it. **2.** to mark the limits of, to restrict. —**circumscription** /-'skrɪpʃən/ *n.* [from Latin *circum* = round and *scribere* = write]

circumspect /'sɜːkəmspekt/ *adj.* cautious, taking everything into account. —**circumspection** /-'spekʃən/ *n.* [from Latin *circum* = round and *specere* = look]

circumstance /'sɜːkəmstəns/ *n.* **1.** a fact or occurrence. **2.** (in *plural*) the conditions connected with or affecting an event or person or action, financial position. **3.** ceremony, fuss. [from Old French from Latin *circum* = round and *stare* = stand]

circumstantial /sɜːkəm'stænʃəl/ *adj.* **1.** giving full details. **2.** (of evidence) consisting of facts that strongly suggest something without providing direct proof. —**circumstantiality** /-ʃɪ'ælɪtɪ/ *n.*, **circumstantially** *adv.* [from Latin]

circumvent /sɜːkəm'vent/ *v.t.* to evade or find a way round (a difficulty); to outwit. —**circumvention** *n.* [from Latin *circum* = round and *venire* = come]

circus /'sɜːkəs/ *n.* **1.** a travelling show of performing animals, acrobats, clowns, etc. Performances are often held in a large tent ('big top'). The popularity of animal acts decreased in the 1980s and 1990s. **2.** (*colloquial*) a scene of lively action. **3.** (*colloquial*) a group of people in a common activity, especially sport. **4.** an open space in a town, on which streets converge. **5.** (*historical*) an arena for sports and games. [Latin = ring]

cire perdue /siər 'pɜːdjuː/ a method of casting bronze by using an inner and an outer mould, with molten metal poured in after the wax layer between these has been melted away. [French = lost wax]

cirque /sɜːk/ *n.* a deep bowl-shaped hollow at the head of a valley or on a mountainside. [French from Latin *circus* = ring]

cirrhosis /sɪˈrəʊsɪs/ *n.* any degenerative disease in an organ of the body, especially the liver, characterized by excessive development of connective tissue, causing scarring and painful swelling. Cirrhosis of the liver may be caused by an infection such as viral hepatitis, by chronic alcoholism or drug use, blood disorder, or malnutrition. If cirrhosis is diagnosed early, it can be arrested by treating the cause; otherwise it will progress to jaundice, oedema, vomiting blood, coma, and death. [from Greek *kirrhos* = tawny]

cirriped /ˈsɪrɪped/ *n.* a marine crustacean in a valved shell, e. g. a barnacle. [from Latin *cirrus* = curl (from form of legs) and *pes* = foot]

cirrocumulus /sɪrəʊˈkjuːmjuːləs/ *n.* (*plural* **cirrocumuli** /-laɪ/) a form of usually high cloud consisting of small, roundish, fleecy clouds in contact with one another, known as 'mackerel sky'.

cirrostratus /sɪrəʊˈstreɪtəs/ *n.* (*plural* **cirrostrati** /-taɪ/) thin, usually high, white cloud composed mainly of fine ice crystals and producing halo phenomena.

cirrus /ˈsɪrəs/ *n.* (*plural* **cirri** /-raɪ/) 1. a form of cloud, usually high, with diverging filaments or wisps. 2. a tendril or appendage of a plant or animal. [Latin = curl]

Cisalpine Gaul /sɪsˈælpaɪn/ a region of the Roman province of Gallia (N Italy) S of the Alps; **Transalpine Gaul**, the region N of the Alps, comprised Belgium, France, the Netherlands, and Switzerland.

Ciskei, Republic of /sɪsˈkaɪ/ a Bantu homeland in South Africa, one of the two homelands of the Xhosa people created by South Africa (the other is Transkei). It became independent in 1981, although this is not recognized by any other country; **area** 7,700 sq km/2,974 sq mi; **capital** Bisho; **government** president (Brig Oupa Gqozo from 1990) with legislative and executive councils; **products** pineapples, timber, metal products, leather, textiles; **population** (1984) 903,681; **language** Xhosa.

cissy variant of **sissy**.

cist /kɪst/ *n.* a prehistoric burial chest or chamber excavated in rock or formed of stones or hollowed tree trunks, especially a stone coffin formed of slabs placed on edge and covered on the top by one or more horizontal slabs. [Welsh = chest]

Cistercian /sɪsˈtɜːʃən/ *n.* a member of the Cistercian order. —*adj.* of the Cistercian order. [from French from Latin *Cistercium* = Cîteaux]

Cistercian order a Roman Catholic monastic order established at Cîteaux, near Dijon in France, in 1098 by St Robert de Champagne, abbot of Molesme, as a stricter form of the Benedictine order. Living mainly by agricultural labour, the Cistercians made many advances in farming methods in the Middle Ages. The ◊Trappists, so called from the original house at La Trappe in Normandy (founded by Dominique de Rancé in 1664), followed a particularly strict version of the rule.

cistern /ˈsɪstɜːn/ *n.* a tank for storing water (especially in a roof space) supplying taps, or as part of a flushing lavatory; an underground reservoir. [from Old French from Latin *cista* = box, from Greek *kistē*]

cistron *n.* in genetics, the segment of ◊DNA that is required to synthesize a complete polypeptide chain. It is the molecular equivalent of a gene.

cistus *n.* a shrub of the genus *Cistus* with large white, pink, or purple flowers. [from Greek]

citadel /ˈsɪtədəl/ *n.* 1. a fortress, usually on high ground, protecting or dominating a city. 2. a meeting hall of the Salvation Army. [from French or Italian, from Latin *civitas* = city]

cite /saɪt/ *v.t.* 1. to quote or mention as an example or to support an argument. 2. to mention in an official dispatch. 3. to summon to appear in a lawcourt. —**citation** /-ˈteɪʃən/ *n.* [from French from Latin *ciēre* = set moving]

CITES abbreviation of Convention on International Trade in Endangered Species, an international agreement signed by 81 countries under the auspices of the ◊IUCN to regulate the trade in endangered species of animals and plants.

cithara *n.* an ancient musical instrument, resembling a lyre but with a flat back. It was strung with wire and plucked with a plectrum or (after the 16th century) with the fingers. The bandurria and laud, still popular in Spain, are instruments of the same type.

citizen /ˈsɪtɪzən/ *n.* a native or naturalized member *of* a state; an inhabitant of a city. —**citizenship** *n.* status as a member of a state. In most countries citizenship may be acquired either by birth or by naturalization. The status confers rights such as voting and the protection of the law and also imposes responsibilities such as military service, in some countries. **citizenry** *n.* [from Anglo-French from Latin *civitas* = city]

Citizens Advice Bureau (CAB) a UK organization established in 1939 to provide information and advice to the public on any subject, such as personal problems, financial, house purchase, or consumer rights. If required, the bureau will act on behalf of citizens, drawing on its own sources of legal and other experts. There are more than 600 bureaus located all over the UK.

citizens' band (CB) a short-range radio communication (around 27 MHz) facility used by members of the public in the USA and many European countries to talk to one another or call for emergency assistance. Use of a form of citizens' band called Open Channel (above 928 MHz) was legalized in the UK in 1980.

citrate /ˈsɪtreɪt/ *n.* a salt of citric acid.

citric /ˈsɪtrɪk/ *adj.* derived from citrus fruit. —**citric acid**, $CH_2(COOH)$ $C(OH)(COOH)CH_2COOH$, an organic acid widely distributed in the plant kingdom, found in high concentrations in citrus fruits, with a sharp, sour taste. At one time it was commercially prepared from concentrated lemon juice, but now the main source is the fermentation of sugar with certain moulds. [from French from Latin *citrus* = citron]

citron /ˈsɪtrən/ *n.* a large, yellow-skinned fruit like a lemon; the tree *Citrus medica* bearing it. [French from Latin *citrus*]

citronella /sɪtrəˈnelə/ *n.* a fragrant oil obtained from a grass *Cymbopogon nardus* of S Asia; this grass.

citrus /ˈsɪtrəs/ *n.* a tree of the genus *Citrus*, including citron, lemon, and orange; the fruit of such a tree. [Latin]

city /ˈsɪtɪ/ *n.* a large town, especially one created by royal charter and containing a cathedral. —**the City**, the part of London governed by the Lord Mayor and Corporation; the business quarter of this; commercial circles. **city fathers**, the officials administering a city. **city-state** *n.* (*historical*) a city that is also an independent state, characteristic of ancient Greece. [from Old French from Latin *civitas* (*civis* = citizen)]

cityscape *n.* a view of a city, city scenery.

city technology college in the UK, a planned network of some 20 schools, financed jointly by government and industry, designed to teach technological subjects in inner-city areas to students aged 11–18.

Ciudad Juárez /sjuːˈðaːð ˈxwaːres/ city on the Rio Grande, in Chihuahua, N Mexico, on the US border; population (1986) 596,000. It is a centre for cotton.

civet /ˈsɪvɪt/ *n.* 1. or **civet cat** any of various small catlike animals of the family Viverridae, especially *Civettictis civetta* of central Africa. 2. the strong musky perfume obtained from its anal glands. [from French, ultimately from Arabic = the perfume]

civic /ˈsɪvɪk/ *adj.* of a city; of citizens or citizenship. —**civic centre**, the area where municipal offices are situated. [from Old French or Latin]

Civic Forum (Czech *Občanske Forum*) a Czech democratic movement, formed in Nov 1989, led by Vaclav ◊Havel. In Dec 1989 it participated in forming a coalition government after the collapse of communist rule in Czechoslovakia. Its Slovak counterpart is ◊Public Against Violence.

civics /ˈsɪvɪks/ *n.pl.* the study of the rights and duties of citizenship.

civil /ˈsɪvəl, -ɪl/ *adj.* 1. of or belonging to citizens. 2. of ordinary citizens, nonmilitary. 3. polite, obliging, not rude. 4. in law, concerning private rights and not criminal offences. 5. (of the length of the day, year, etc.) fixed by custom or law, not natural or astronomical. —**civil defence**, an organization for protecting civilians in an air raid or other enemy action. **civil liberty**, freedom of action subject to the law. **civil marriage**, one solemnized with a civil (not religious) ceremony. **civil war**, war between people of the same country. —**civilly** *adv.* [from Old French from Latin *civilis*]

civil aviation the operation of passenger and freight transport by air. With increasing traffic, control of air space is a major problem, and in 1963 Eurocontrol was established by Belgium, France, West Germany, Luxembourg, the Netherlands, and the UK to supervise both military and civil movement in the air space over member countries. There is also a tendency to coordinate services and other facilities between national airlines; for example, the establishment of Air Union by France (Air France), West Germany (Lufthansa), Italy (Alitalia) and Belgium (Sabena) in 1963.

civil disobedience the deliberate breaking of laws considered unjust, a form of nonviolent direct action; the term was coined by the US writer Thoreau in an essay of that name in 1849. It was advocated by Mahatma ◊Gandhi to prompt peaceful withdrawal of British power from India. Civil disobedience has since been employed by, for instance, the US civil-rights movement in the 1960s and the peace movement in the 1980s.

civil engineering the branch of engineering that is concerned with the construction of roads, bridges, aqueducts, waterworks, tunnels, canals, irrigation works, and harbours. The professional organization in Britain is the Institution of Civil Engineers, which was founded in 1818 and is the oldest engineering institution in the world. —**civil engineer** a person who works in civil engineering.

civilian /si'viljən/ *n.* a person not in the armed forces or police force. —*adj.* of or for civilians.

civility /si'viliti/ *n.* politeness; an act of politeness. [from Old French from Latin]

civilization /ˌsɪvɪlaɪ'zeɪʃən/ *n.* **1.** an advanced stage or system of social development; those peoples of the world regarded as having this. **2.** a people or nation (especially of the past) regarded as an element of social evolution.

civilize /'sɪvɪlaɪz/ *v.t.* to bring out of a barbarous or primitive stage of society to a more developed one; to refine and educate. [from French *civiliser*]

civil law the legal system based on Roman law, one of the two main European legal systems, English (common) law being the other; the law relating to matters other than criminal law, such as ◊contract and ◊tort.

civil list in the UK, the annual sum provided from public funds to meet the official expenses of the sovereign and immediate dependants. Three-quarters of the this sum goes on wages for the royal household. Private expenses are met by the ◊privy purse.

civil-list pension in the UK, a pension paid to persons in need who have just claims on the royal beneficence, who have rendered personal service to the crown, or who have rendered service to the public by their discoveries in science and attainments in literature, art, or the like. The recipients are nominated by the prime minister, and the list is approved by Parliament.

civil rights the rights of the individual citizen. In many countries they are specified (as in the Bill of Rights of the US constitution) and guaranteed by law to ensure equal treatment for all citizens. In the USA, the struggle to obtain civil rights for former slaves and their descendants, both through legislation and in practice, has been a major theme since the Civil War.

civil service the body of administrative staff appointed to carry out the policy of a government. Members of the UK civil service may not take an active part in politics, and do not change with the government. The two main divisions of the British civil service are the **Home** and **Diplomatic** services, the latter created in 1965 by amalgamation of the Foreign, Commonwealth, and Trade Commission services. All employees are paid out of funds voted annually for the purpose by Parliament. —**civil servant**, a member of the civil service.

civil society the part of a society or culture outside the government and state-run institutions. For Marx and Hegel, civil society was that part of society where self-interest and materialism were rampant, although Adam ◊Smith believed that enlightened self-interest would promote the general good. Classical writers and earlier political theorists such as John ◊Locke used the term to describe the whole of a civilized society.

Civil War, American also called **War Between the States** the war of 1861–65 between the Southern or Confederate states of America and the Northern or Union states. The former wished to maintain certain 'states'

rights', in particular the right to determine state law on the institution of slavery, and claimed the right to secede from the Union; the latter fought primarily to maintain the Union, with slave emancipation (1863) a secondary issue.

Civil War, English in British history, the struggle in the middle years of the 17th century between the king, Charles I, and the Royalists (Cavaliers) on one side, and the Parliamentarians (also called Roundheads) on the other. The Parliamentarians under ◊Cromwell dealt a series of defeats to Charles, executing him in 1649, and Cromwell made himself Protector (ruler) until the restoration of the monarchy in 1660.

Civil War, Spanish the war of 1936–39 precipitated by a military revolt led by Gen Franco against the Republican government. Inferior military capability led to the gradual defeat of the Republicans by 1939.

civvies /'sɪvɪz/ *n.pl.* (*slang*) civilian clothes. [abbreviation]

Civvy Street civilian life. [abbreviation]

cl abbreviation of centilitre(s).

Cl symbol for chlorine.

clack *v.i.* to make a sharp sound as of boards struck together; to chatter. —*n.* a clacking noise or talk.

clad[1] past and past participle of **clothe**.

clad[2] *v.t.* (**-dd-**) to provide with cladding.

cladding *n.* a protective coating or covering on a structure, material, etc.

clade /kleɪd/ *n.* a group of organisms that have evolved from a common ancestor. [from Greek *klados* = branch]

cladistics /klə'dɪstɪks/ *n.* the systematic classification of groups of organisms on the basis of the order of their assumed divergence from ancestral species.

cladode *n.* a flattened stem that is leaflike in appearance and function. It is an adaptation to dry conditions because a stem contains fewer ◊stomata than a leaf, and water loss is thus minimized. The true leaves in such plants are usually reduced to spines or small scales. Examples of plants with cladodes are butcher's-broom *Ruscus aculeatus*, asparagus, and certain cacti. Cladodes may bear flowers or fruit on their surface, and this distinguishes them from leaves.

claim *v.t.* **1.** to demand as one's due or property. **2.** to represent oneself as having; to profess *to*; to assert *that*. **3.** to have as an achievement or victim etc.; to deserve (attention etc.). —*n.* **1.** a demand for a thing considered one's due. **2.** the right or title (*to*). **3.** an assertion. **4.** a thing (especially land) claimed. [from Old French from Latin *clamare* = call out]

claimant *n.* a person making a claim, especially in a lawsuit.

Clair /kleə/ René. Adopted name of René-Lucien Chomette 1898–1981. French film-maker, originally a poet, novelist, and journalist. His *Sous les toits de Paris*/*Under the Roofs of Paris* 1930 was one of the first sound films.

clairvoyance /kleə'vɔɪəns/ *n.* the supposed faculty of seeing mentally things in the future or out of sight; exceptional insight. —**clairvoyant** *n.* & *adj.* [French *clair* = clear and *voyant* = seeing]

clam *n.* an edible bivalve mollusc, especially *Mercenaria mercenaria* and *Mya arenaria*. The giant clam *Tridacna gigas* of the Indopacific can grow to 1 m/3 ft across in 50 years and weigh, with the shell, 500 kg/1,000 lb. —*v.i.* (**-mm-**) **clam up**, (*slang*) to become silent. [apparently from *clam* = clamp]

clamber *v.i.* to climb laboriously with hands and feet. —*n.* a difficult climb. [probably from *clamb* (obsolete past tense of *climb*)]

clammy *adj.* unpleasantly damp and sticky. —**clammily** *adv.*, **clamminess** *n.* [from *clam* = daub]

clamour /'klæmə/ *n.* a loud or vehement shouting or noise; a loud protest or demand. —*v.t./i.* to make a clamour; to utter with a clamour. —**clamorous** *adj.* [from Old French from Latin *clamare* = call out]

clamp[1] *n.* a device, especially a brace or band of iron etc., for strengthening, pressing, or holding things together. —*v.t.* to strengthen or fasten with a clamp; to fix firmly. —**clamp down on**, to become strict about; to suppress. **clampdown** *n.* [from Low German or Dutch]

clamp[2] *n.* a pile of bricks for burning; potatoes etc. stored in the open under straw and earth, peat, etc. [probably from Dutch]

clan *n.* a group of families with a common ancestor, especially in Scotland; a large family or social group; a group with

Clapton *Eric Clapton (right) with George Harrison (left) at the Live Aid concert, 1985.*

a strong common interest. —**clannish** *adj.,* **clansman** *n.* [from Gaelic from Latin *planta* = sprout]

clandestine /klæn'destɪn/ *adj.* surreptitious, secret. —**clandestinely** *adv.* [from French or Latin *clam* = secretly]

clang *n.* a loud, resonant, metallic sound. — *v.t./i.* to make or cause to make a clang. [compare Latin *clangere* = resound]

clangour /'klæŋgə/ *n.* prolonged clanging. —**clangorous** *adj.* [from Latin]

clank *n.* a metallic sound as of metal striking metal. —*v.t./i.* to make or cause to make a clank.

clap *v.t./i.* (**-pp-**) **1.** to strike the palms (or *hands*) repeatedly together, especially in applause; to applaud thus. **2.** to put or place with vigour or determination. —*n.* **1.** an act of clapping, especially as applause; an explosive sound, especially of thunder. **2.** a friendly slap. —**clap eyes on,** (*colloquial*) to catch sight of. **clapped out,** (*slang*) worn out, exhausted. [Old English = throb, beat]

clapper *n.* the tongue or striker of a bell. —**clapperboard** *n.* a device in film-making that makes a sharp clap for synchronizing picture and sound.

clapper bridge a rough bridge consisting of a series of slabs or planks resting on piles of stones. [perhaps from Latin *claperius* = heap of stones]

Clapton /'klæptən/ Eric 1945– . English blues and rock guitarist, singer, and composer, member of the British blues boom groups the Yardbirds and Cream in the 1960s. One of the pioneers of heavy rock, he later adopted a more laid-back style in his solo career which gave rise to his nickname 'Slowhand'. His song 'Layla' 1973 recorded under the name Derek And The Dominos has become a rock classic.

claptrap *n.* insincere or pretentious talk, nonsense.

claque /klæk/ *n.* a hired group of applauders in a theatre etc. [French *claquer* = clap]

Clare /kleə/ county on the W coast of the Republic of Ireland, in the province of Munster, covering an area of 3,190 sq km/1,231 sq mi; population (1986) 91,000. Shannon airport is here.

Clare John 1793–1864. English poet. His work includes *Poems Descriptive of Rural Life* 1820, *The Village Minstrel* 1821, and *Shepherd's Calendar* 1827. Clare's work was largely rediscovered in the 20th century.

Clarence /'klærəns/ English ducal title, which has been conferred on a number of princes. The last was Albert Victor 1864–92, eldest son of Edward VII.

Clarendon /'klærəndən/ Edward Hyde, 1st Earl of Clarendon 1609–1674. English politician and historian, chief adviser to Charles II 1651–67. A member of Parliament in 1640, he joined the Royalist side in 1641. The **Clarendon Code** (1661–65), a series of acts passed by the government, was directed at Nonconformists (or Dissenters) and designed to secure the supremacy of the Church of England.

Clarendon, Constitutions of in English history, a series of resolutions agreed by a council summoned by Henry II at Clarendon in Wiltshire in 1164. The Constitutions aimed at limiting the secular power of the clergy, and were abandoned after the murder of Thomas à Becket. They form an early English legal document of great historical value.

Clare, St /kleə/ *c.*1194–1253. Christian saint. Born in Assisi, Italy, she became at 18 a follower of St Francis, who founded for her the convent at San Damiano. Here she gathered the first members of the **Order of Poor Clares**. In 1958 she was proclaimed by Pius XII the patron saint of television, since in 1252 she saw from her convent sickbed the Christmas services being held in the Basilica of St Francis in Assisi. Feast day 12 Aug.

claret /'klærət/ *n.* **1.** red wine, especially from Bordeaux. **2.** reddish-violet colour. [French, originally = clarified wine (Latin *clarus* = clear)]

clarify /'klærɪfaɪ/ *v.t./i.* **1.** to make or become clear to see or easier to understand. **2.** to free (a liquid etc.) from impurity or opaqueness. —**clarification** /-fɪ'keɪʃən/ *n.* [from Old French from Latin *clarus* = clear]

clarinet /klærɪ'net/ *n.* a single-reed woodwind instrument developed in Germany in the 18th century. At the lower end of its range it has a rich 'woody' tone, which becomes increasingly brilliant towards the upper register. Its ability both to blend and to contrast with other instruments make it popular for chamber music and as a solo instrument. It is also heard in military and concert bands and as a jazz instrument. —**clarinettist** *n.* [from French, diminutive of *clarine* = a kind of bell]

clarion /'klærɪən/ *n.* **1.** a clear rousing sound. **2.** (*historical*) a shrill war trumpet. [from Latin *clarus* = clear]

clarity /'klærɪtɪ/ *n.* clearness.

Clark /klɑːk/ Jim (James) 1936–1968. Scottish-born motor racing driver, one of the finest in the postwar era. He was twice world champion in 1963 and 1965. He spent all his Formula One career with Lotus.

Clark Joe (Joseph) Charles 1939– . Canadian Progressive Conservative politician, born in Alberta. He became party leader in 1976, and in May 1979 defeated ◊Trudeau at the polls to become the youngest prime minister in Canada's history. Following the rejection of his government's budget, he was defeated in a second election in Feb 1980. He became Secretary of State for External Affairs (foreign minister) in the ◊Mulroney government (1984–).

Clark Kenneth, Lord Clark 1903–1983. English art historian, director of the National Gallery, London, 1934–45. His books include *Leonardo da Vinci* 1939 and *The Nude* 1956.

Clarke /klɑːk/ Arthur C(harles) 1917– . English science fiction and nonfiction writer, who originated the plan for the system of communications satellites in 1945. His works include *Childhood's End* 1953 and *2001: A Space Odyssey* 1968 (which was made into a film by Stanley Kubrick), and *2010: Odyssey Two* 1982.

Clarke Jeremiah 1659–1707. English composer. Organist at St Paul's, he composed 'The Prince of Denmark's March', a harpsichord piece that was arranged by Sir Henry ◊Wood as a 'Trumpet Voluntary' and wrongly attributed to Purcell.

Clarke Kenneth (Harry) 1940– . British Conservative politician, member of Parliament from 1970, a cabinet minister from 1985, minister of health 1988–90, and education secretary from 1990.

Clarke Marcus Andrew Hislop 1846–1881. Australian writer. Born in London, he went to Australia when he was 18 and worked as a journalist in Victoria. He wrote *For the Term of his Natural Life* in 1874, a novel dealing with life in the early Australian prison settlements.

Clarke orbit an alternative name for the ◊geostationary orbit, an orbit 35,900 km/22,300 mi high, in which satellites circle at the same speed as the Earth turns. This orbit was first suggested by space writer Arthur C Clarke in 1945.

Clarkson /'klɑːksən/ Thomas 1760–1846. English philanthropist. From 1785 he devoted himself to a campaign against slavery. He was one of the founders of the Anti-Slavery Society in 1823 and was largely responsible for the abolition of slavery in British colonies in 1833.

clash *v.t./i.* **1.** to strike making a loud harsh sound as of light metal objects struck together. **2.** to conflict, to disagree; to coincide inconveniently (*with*). **3.** (of colours) to produce an unpleasant visual effect by not being harmonious. —*n.* **1.** a sound of clashing. **2.** conflict, a disagreement. **3.** a clashing of colours. [imitative]

clasp /klɑːsp/ *n.* **1.** a device with interlocking parts for fastening. **2.** a grasp, a handshake, an embrace. **3.** a bar on a medal ribbon. —*v.t.* **1.** to fasten with a clasp. **2.** to grasp, to hold closely or embrace. —**clasp knife,** a folding knife with a catch to hold the blade open.

class /klɑːs/ *n.* **1.** a set of persons or things grouped together, or graded or differentiated (especially by quality) from others; a division or order of society; a division of candidates by merit in an examination. **2.** in biology, a group of related ◊orders. For example, all mammals belong to the class Mammalia and all birds to the class Aves. Among plants, all class names end in 'idae' (such as Asteridae) and among fungi in 'mycetes'; there are no equivalent conventions among animals. Related classes are grouped together in a ◊phylum. **3.** distinction, high quality. **4.** a set of students taught together; the occasion when they meet. —*v.t.* to place in a class, to classify. [from Latin *classis* = division of Roman people]

class action in law, a court procedure where one or more claimants represent a larger group of people who are all making the same kind of claim against the same defendant. The court's decision is binding on all the members of the group.

classic /'klæsɪk/ *adj.* **1.** of acknowledged excellence; outstandingly important, remarkably typical. **2.** of ancient Greek and Roman art, literature, and culture; resembling this, especially in harmony, restraint, and strict adherence to form. **3.** having historic associations. —*n.* **1.** a classic work, example, writer, etc. **2.** (in *plural*) the study of ancient Greek and Roman literature, culture, etc. [from Latin *classicus* = of the highest class]

classical /'klæsɪkəl/ *adj.* **1.** of ancient Greek and Roman art, literature, culture, etc. **2.** simple and harmonious in style. **3.** (of music) serious, following established forms; of the period about 1750–1800. —**classical scholar,** an expert in ancient Greek and Roman languages and culture. —**classically** *adv.*

classical economics a school of economic thought that dominated 19th-century thinking. It originated with Adam ◊Smith's *The Wealth of Nations* 1776, which embodied many of the basic concepts and principles of the classical school. Central to the theory were economic freedom, competition, and *laissez faire* government. The idea that economic growth could best be promoted by free trade, unassisted by government, was in conflict with ◊mercantilism.

classicism /'klæsɪsɪzəm/ *n.* following of the classic style. —**Classicism,** a term often used to characterize the culture of 18th-century Europe, and contrasted with 19th-century Romanticism. See also ◊Neo-Classicism.

classicist /'klæsɪsɪst/ *n.* a classical scholar.

classifiable /'klæsɪfaɪəbəl/ *adj.* that can be classified.

classification /ˌklæsɪfɪˈkeɪʃən/ *n.* **1.** arrangement in classes or categories; the assignment of a class to. **2.** in biology, the arrangement of organisms into a hierarchy of groups, on the basis of their similarities in biochemical, anatomical or physiological characters. The basic grouping is a ◊species, several of which may constitute a ◊genus, which in turn are grouped into families, and so on up through orders, classes, phyla (in plants, sometimes called divisions), to kingdoms. **3.** the designation of a document, information, etc. as officially secret or not for general disclosure.

classificatory /klæsɪfɪˈkeɪtərɪ/ *adj.* of or involving classification.

classify /'klæsɪfaɪ/ *v.t.* **1.** to arrange according to a system of classification. **2.** to designate as officially secret or not for general disclosure.

class interval in statistics, the range of each class of data, used when dealing with large amounts of data. To obtain an idea of the distribution, the data are broken down into convenient classes, which must be mutually exclusive and are usually equal. The class interval defines the range of each class; for example if the class interval is five and the data begin at zero, the classes are 0–4, 5–9, 10–14, and so on.

classless *adj.* without distinctions of social class.

classroom *n.* a room where a class of students is taught.

classy /'klɑːsɪ/ *adj.* (*colloquial*) superior, stylish. —**classily** *adv.*, **classiness** *n.*

clathrate *n.* a compound formed by small molecules filling in the holes in the structural lattice of another compound, for example, sulphur dioxide molecules in ice crystals. Clathrates are therefore intermediate between mixtures and compounds.

clatter *n.* a sound as of hard objects struck together or falling; noisy talk. —*v.i.* to make a clatter; to fall, move, etc., with a clatter. [Old English]

Claude /kləʊd/ Georges 1870–1960. French industrial chemist, responsible for inventing neon signs. He discovered in 1896 that acetylene, normally explosive, could be safely transported when dissolved in acetone. He later demonstrated that neon gas could be used to provide a bright red light in signs.

Claudel /kləʊˈdel/ Paul 1868–1955. French poet and dramatist. A fervent Catholic, he was influenced by the Symbolists and achieved an effect of mystic allegory in such plays as *L'Annonce faite à Marie/Tidings Brought to Mary* 1912 and *Le Soulier de satin/The Satin Slipper* 1929, set in 16th-century Spain. His verse includes *Cinq grandes odes/Five Great Odes* 1910.

Claude Lorrain /kləʊd lɒˈræn/ (Claude Gellée) 1600–1682. French landscape painter, active in Rome from 1627. His distinctive, luminous, Classical style had great impact on late 17th-and 18th-century taste. His subjects are mostly mythological and historical, with insignificant figures lost in great expanses of poetic scenery, as in *The Enchanted Castle* 1664 (National Gallery, London).

Claudian /'klɔːdiən/ or **Claudius Claudianus** *c.*370–404. Last of the great Latin poets of the Roman Empire, probably born in Alexandria. He wrote official panegyrics, epigrams, and the epic *The Rape of Proserpine.*

Claudius /'klɔːdiəs/ Tiberius Claudius Nero 10 BC–AD 54. Nephew of ◊Tiberius, made Roman emperor by his troops in AD 41, after the murder of his nephew Caligula. Claudius was a scholar, historian, and able administrator. During his reign the Roman Empire was considerably extended, and in 43 he took part in the invasion of Britain.

Each man is the smith of his own fortune.

Claudius

clause /klɔːz/ *n.* **1.** a distinct part of a sentence, containing a finite verb. **2.** a single part in a treaty, law, contract, etc. [from Old French from Latin *clausula* = conclusion]

Clause 28 in British law, section 28 of the Local Government Act 1988 that prohibits local authorities promoting homosexuality by publishing material, or by promoting the teaching in state schools of the acceptability of homosexuality as a 'pretended family relationship'. There was widespread opposition to the introduction of the provision.

Clausewitz /'klaʊzəvɪts/ Karl von 1780–1831. Prussian officer and writer on war, born near Magdeburg. His book *Vom Kriege/On War* 1833, translated into English in 1873, gave a new philosophical foundation to the art of war and put forward a concept of strategy that was influential until World War I.

clausius /'klaʊzɪəs/ *n.* in engineering, a unit of ◊entropy (the loss of energy as heat in any physical process). It is defined as the ratio of energy to temperature above absolute zero.

Clausius Rudolf Julius Emaneul 1822–1888. German physicist, one of the founders of the science of thermodynamics. In 1850 he enunciated its second law: heat cannot pass from a colder to a hotter body.

claustrophobia /ˌklɔːstrəˈfəʊbiə/ *n.* abnormal fear of being in a confined space. —**claustrophobic** *adj.* [from Latin *claustrum* = enclosed space]

claves *n.pl.* a musical percussion instrument of Latin American origin, consisting of small hardwood batons struck together.

clavichord /'klævɪkɔːd/ *n.* a stringed keyboard instrument with a very soft tone, developed in the 14th century and in use from the early 15th century. Notes are sounded by a metal blade striking the string. The clavichord was a forerunner of the pianoforte. [from Latin *clavis* = key and *chorda* = string]

clavicle /'klævɪkəl/ *n.* the collar bone of many vertebrates. In humans it is vulnerable to fracture; falls involving a sudden force on the arm may result in excessive stress passing into the chest region by way of the clavicle and other bones. [from Latin, diminutive of *clavis* = key]

clavier /'kleɪvɪə/ *n.* a keyboard; an instrument with this; an organ manual. [French, or from German from Latin, originally = key bearer (*clavis* = key)]

claw *n.* **1.** the pointed nail of an animal's or bird's foot; a foot armed with claws. **2.** the pincers of a shellfish. **3.** a device for grappling and holding things. —*v.t.* to scratch or maul or pull with the claws; to scratch with the fingernails. —**claw back,** to recoup (money etc.) that has just been given away, e. g. in taxation. **claw hammer,** a hammer with one side of the head forked for extracting nails. [Old English]

clay /kleɪ/ *n.* a very fine-grained ◊sedimentary deposit that has undergone a greater or lesser degree of consolidation. When moistened it is plastic, and it hardens on heating, which renders it impermeable. It may be white, grey, red, yellow, blue, or black, depending on its composition. Clay minerals consist largely of hydrous silicates of aluminium and magnesium together with iron, potassium, sodium, and organic substances. The crystals of clay minerals have a layered structure, capable of holding water, and are responsible for its plastic properties. According to international classification, in mechanical analysis of soil, clay has a grain size of less than 0.002 mm/0.00008 in. —**clay pigeon,** a breakable disc thrown up from a trap as a target for shooting. [Old English]

Clay Cassius Marcellus, Jr the original name of boxer Muhammad ◊Ali.

Clay Henry 1777–1852. US politician. He supported the War of 1812 against Britain, and tried to hold the Union together on the slavery issue by the Missouri Compromise of 1820, and again in the compromise of 1850. He was secretary of state 1825–29, and is also remembered for his 'American system', which favoured the national bank, internal improvements to facilitate commercial and industrial development, and the raising of protective tariffs.

clay mineral one of a group of hydrous silicate minerals that form most of the fine-grained particles in clays. Clay minerals are normally formed by weathering or alteration of other silicates. Virtually all have sheet silicate structures similar to the micas. They exhibit the following useful properties: loss of water on heating, swelling and shrinking in different conditions, cation exchange with other media, and plasticity when wet. Examples are kaolinite, illite, and montmorillonite.

claymore *n.* **1.** a Scottish two-edged broadsword. **2.** a broadsword (often single-edged) with a basketlike structure protecting the hilt. [Gaelic = great sword]

clean *adj.* **1.** free from dirt or impurities, not soiled; not yet used, preserving what is regarded as the original state; free from obscenity or indecency; attentive to personal hygiene and cleanness; (of a nuclear weapon) producing relatively little fallout; containing nothing dishonourable, (of a licence) without endorsements. **2.** complete, clear-cut; evenly shaped, without projections or roughness. —*adv.* **1.** completely, entirely. **2.** in a clean manner. —*v.t./i.* to make or become clean. —*n.* a process of cleaning. —**clean-cut** *adj.* sharply outlined. **clean out,** to clean the inside of; (*slang*) to use up all the supplies or money of. **clean-shaven** *adj.* with beard or moustache shaved off. **clean sheet,** a record not showing any offences. **clean up,** to make clean or tidy; to restore order or morality to; (*colloquial*) to make a gain or profit. **make a clean breast of,** to confess fully about. —**cleanness** *n.* [Old English]

cleaner *n.* **1.** a person employed to clean rooms. **2.** (usually in *plural*) an establishment for cleaning clothes. **3.** a device or substance for cleaning things.

cleanly[1] /ˈkliːnlɪ/ *adv.* in a clean manner.

cleanly[2] /ˈklenlɪ/ *adj.* habitually clean, with clean habits. —**cleanliness** *n.*

cleanse /klenz/ *v.t.* to make clean or pure. —**cleanser** *n.*

clear *adj.* **1.** not clouded or murky or spotted; transparent; (of the conscience) free from guilt. **2.** readily perceived by the senses or mind. **3.** able to discern readily and accurately; confident or convinced (*about, that*). **4.** (of a road etc.) unobstructed, open. **5.** net, without deduction, complete; unhampered, free (*of* debt, commitments, etc.). —*adv.* clearly; completely; apart, out of contact. —*v.t./i.* **1.** to make or become clear. **2.** to free from or *of* obstruction, suspicion, etc.; to show or declare to be innocent (*of*); to approve (a person) for special duty, access to information, etc.; to pass (a cheque) through a clearing house. **3.** to pass over or by without touching; to pass through (a customs office etc.). **4.** to make (an amount of money) as a net gain or to balance expenses. —**clear away,** to remove

Cleese *English actor and comedian John Cleese in* A Fish Called Wanda *1988.*

completely; to remove used crockery etc. after a meal; (of mists etc.) to disappear. **clear-cut** *adj.* sharply defined. **clearing bank,** a large bank belonging to a clearing house. **clearing house,** a bankers' establishment where cheques etc. are exchanged, only the balances being paid in cash; an agency for collecting or distributing information etc. **clear off,** to get rid of, to complete payment of (a debt etc.); (*colloquial*) to go away. **clear out,** to empty; to remove; (*colloquial*) to go away. **clear up,** to tidy up; to solve (a mystery etc.); (of weather) to become fine. **clear a thing with,** to get approval or authorization of it from (a person). —**clearly** *adv.,* **clearness** *n.* [from Old French from Latin *clarus* = bright, clear]

clearance *n.* **1.** the act or process of clearing or being cleared; permission, authorization. **2.** a space allowed for one object to move within or past another.

clearing *n.* an open space in woodland from which trees have been cleared.

clearway *n.* a main road (other than a motorway) on which vehicles may not ordinarily stop.

cleat *n.* **1.** a projecting piece of metal, wood, etc., bolted on for securing ropes to, or to strengthen woodwork. **2.** a projecting piece fastened to a spar, gangway, boat etc., to prevent slipping. **3.** a wedge serving as a support. [Old English]

cleavage *n.* **1.** the process of splitting, the way in which a thing tends to split; in geology, the tendency of a rock, especially slate, to split along parallel or subparallel planes that result from re-alignment of component minerals during deformation or metamorphism. **2.** the hollow between full breasts.

cleave[1] *v.t./i.* (*past* clove, cleft, cleaved; *past participle* cloven /ˈkləʊvən/, cleft, cleaved) to chop, to split or become split, especially along the grain or line of cleavage; to make a way through (the air etc.). [Old English]

cleave[2] *v.i.* (*literary*) to stick fast or adhere *to.* [Old English]

cleaver *n.* a heavy chopping tool used by butchers.

cleavers *n.* (as *singular* or *plural*) a plant *Galium aparine* with hooked bristles on its stem that catch in clothes etc.

Cleese /kliːz/ John 1939– . English actor and comedian, who has appeared in both television and films. He has written and appeared in the satirical television programmes *That Was The Week That Was* and *The Frost Report* as well as the anarchic comedy series *Monty Python's Flying Circus* and *Fawlty Towers* which he co-wrote with his ex-wife Connie Booth. His films include *Monty Python and the Holy Grail* 1974, *The Life of Brian* 1979, and *A Fish Called Wanda* 1988.

clef *n.* a symbol on a staff in a musical score, locating a particular note on it and showing the pitch of the notes following that symbol, e. g. **alto** (*or* C) **clef, bass** (*or* F) **clef, treble** (*or* G) **clef.** [French = key]

cleft past participle of **cleave**[1]. —*adj.* split, partly divided. —*n.* a space made by cleaving, a fissure. —**cleft palate,** a congenital split in the roof of the mouth. **in a cleft stick,** in a dilemma.

Cleisthenes /'klaɪsθəniːz/ ruler of Athens. Inspired by Solon, he is credited with the establishment of democracy in Athens in 507 BC.

cleistogamy n. the production of flowers that never fully open and which are automatically self-fertilized. Cleistogamous flowers are often formed late in the year, after the production of normal flowers, or during a period of cold weather, as seen in several species of violet *Viola*.

Cleland /'klelənd/ John 1709–1789. English author. He wrote *Fanny Hill, the Memoirs of a Woman of Pleasure* 1748–49 to try to extricate himself from the grip of his London creditors. The book was considered immoral. Cleland was called before the Privy Council, but was granted a pension to prevent further misdemeanours.

clematis /'klemətɪs/ n. a climbing plant of the genus *Clematis*, chiefly with white, pink, or purple flowers. The wild traveller's joy or old man's beard, *Clematis vitalba*, is the only British species, although many have been introduced and garden hybrids bred. [Latin from Greek *klēma* = vine branch]

Clemenceau /klemɒn'səʊ/ Georges 1841–1929. French politician and journalist (prominent in the defence of ◊Dreyfus). He was prime minister 1906–09 and 1917–20. After World War I he presided over the Peace Conference in Paris that drew up the Treaty of ◊Versailles, but failed to secure for France the Rhine as a frontier.

Clemens /'klemənz/ Samuel Langhorne. Real name of the US writer Mark ◊Twain.

clement /'klemənt/ adj. 1. (of weather) mild. 2. merciful. —**clemency** n. [from Latin]

Clement VII 1478–1534. Pope 1523–34. He refused to allow the divorce of Henry VIII of England and Catherine of Aragon. Illegitimate son of a brother of Lorenzo di Medici, the ruler of Florence, he commissioned monuments for the Medici chapel in Florence from the Renaissance artist Michelangelo.

Clementi /kle'menti/ Muzio 1752–1832. Italian pianist and composer. He settled in London in 1782 as a teacher and then as proprietor of a successful piano and music business. He was the founder of the new technique of piano playing, and his series of studies, *Gradus AD Parnassum* 1817 is still in use.

clementine /'kleməntiːn/ n. a kind of small orange. It has a flowery taste and scent and is in season in winter. It is commonly grown in N Africa and Spain. [French]

Clement of Rome, St /'klemənt/ late 1st century AD. One of the early Christian leaders and writers known as the Fathers of the Church. According to tradition, he was the third or fourth bishop of Rome and a disciple of St Peter. He wrote a letter addressed to the church at Corinth (First Epistle of Clement), and many other writings have been attributed to him.

clench v.t. 1. to close (the teeth or fingers) tightly; to grasp firmly. 2. to clinch (a nail or rivet). —n. a clenching action, a clenched state. [Old English]

Cleon /'kliːɒn/ Athenian demagogue and military leader in the Peloponnesian War (431–404 BC). After the death of Pericles, to whom he was opposed, he won power as representative of the commercial classes and leader of the party, advocating a vigorous war policy. He was killed fighting the Spartans at Amphipolis.

Cleopatra /kliːə'pætrə/ c.68–30 BC. Queen of Egypt 51–48 and 47–30 BC. When the Roman general Julius Caesar arrived in Egypt, he restored her to the throne from which she had been ousted. Cleopatra and Caesar became lovers and she went with him to Rome. After Caesar's assassination in 44 BC she returned to Alexandria and resumed her position as queen of Egypt. In 41 BC she was joined there by Mark Antony, one of Rome's rulers. In 31 BC Rome declared war on Egypt and scored a decisive victory in the naval Battle of Actium off the W coast of Greece. Cleopatra fled with her 60 ships to Egypt; Antony abandoned the struggle and followed her. Both he and Cleopatra committed suicide.

Cleopatra's Needle either of two ancient Egyptian granite obelisks erected at Heliopolis in the 15th century BC by Thothmes III, and removed to Alexandria by the Roman emperor Augustus about 14 BC. They have no connection with Cleopatra's reign. One of the pair was taken to England in 1878 and erected on the Victoria Embankment in London. The other was given by the

khedive of Egypt to the USA and erected in Central Park, New York, in 1881.

clerestory /'klɪəstəri/ n. the part of the wall of a cathedral or large church, with a series of windows, above the aisle roof.

clergy n. (usually as *plural*) the body of those ordained for religious service. [from Old French]

clergyman n. (*plural* **clergymen**) a member of the male clergy, especially of the Church of England.

cleric /'klerɪk/ n. a member of the clergy. [from Latin from Greek *klēros* = heritage, priestly order]

clerical /'klerɪkəl/ adj. 1. of the clergy or a cleric. 2. of or done by clerks. —**clerical collar**, an upright white collar fastening at the back, worn by clergy.

clerihew /'klerɪhjuː/ n. a short witty, comic, or nonsensical verse, usually in two rhyming couplets with free metre in lines of unequal length. [from Edmund *Clerihew* Bentley, English writer (1875–1956), its inventor]

clerk /klɑːk/ n. 1. a person employed in an office, bank, etc., to keep records, accounts, etc. 2. a secretary or agent of a local council (**town clerk**), court, etc. 3. a lay officer of a church (**parish clerk**). —**clerk of (the) works**, an overseer of building works etc. [from Old English and Old French]

Clermont-Ferrand /'kleəmɒn fe'rɒn/ city, capital of Puy-de-Dôme *département*, in the Auvergne region of France; population (1983) 256,000. It is a centre for agriculture, and its rubber industry is the largest in France.

Cleveland /'kliːvlənd/ 1. county in NE England; **area** 580 sq km/224 sq mi; **administrative headquarters** Middlesbrough; **features** river Tees; North Yorkshire Moors National Park; **products** steel, chemicals; **population** (1987) 555,000. 2. largest city of Ohio, USA, on Lake Erie at the mouth of the river Cuyahoga; population (1981) 574,000. Its chief industries are iron and steel, and petrol refining.

Cleveland, Ohio largest city of Ohio, USA, on Lake Erie at the mouth of the river Cuyahoga: **population** (1981) 574,000, metropolitan area 1,899,000. Its chief industries are iron and steel, and petroleum refining.

Cleveland (Stephen) Grover 1837–1908. 22nd and 24th president of the USA, 1885–89 and 1893–97; the first Democratic president elected after the Civil War, and the only president to hold office for two nonconsecutive terms.

The lessons of paternalism ought to be unlearned and the better lesson taught that while the people should patriotically and cheerfully support their government, its functions do not include the support of the people.

Stephen Grover Cleveland
inaugural address 1893

---

clever /'klevə/ adj. quick at learning or understanding things, skilful; ingenious. —**cleverly** adj., **cleverness** n.

clevis /'klevɪs/ n. a U-shaped piece of metal at the end of a beam for attaching tackle etc. [from Old English]

clew /kluː/ n. the lower or after corner of a sail; the small cords suspending a hammock. —v.t. to draw the lower ends of (a sail) *up* to the upper yard or mast for furling. [Old English, originally = ball of thread]

cliché /'kliː ʃeɪ/ n. a hackneyed phrase or opinion. [French, originally = metal casting of stereotype]

click n. a slight sharp sound as of a dropping latch. —v.t./i. 1. to make or cause to make a click; to fasten with a click. 2. (*slang*) to become clear or understandable; to be successful; to become friendly *with*.

client /'klaɪənt/ n. a person using the services of a lawyer, architect, or professional person other than a doctor, or of a business; a customer. [from Latin *cliens* (*cluere* = hear, obey)]

clientele /kliːɒn'tel/ n. clients or customers collectively. [from Latin and French]

cliff /klɪf/ n. a steep rock face, especially on the coast. —**cliffhanger** n. in which the viewer etc. is left in suspense at the end of each episode. [Old English]

Cliff Clarice 1899–1972. English pottery designer. Her Bizarre ware, characterized by brightly coloured floral and geometric decoration on often geometrically shaped china, became increasingly popular in the 1930s.

Clift /klɪft/ Montgomery (Edward) 1920–1966. US film and theatre actor. A star of the late 1940s and 1950s in films such as *Red River* 1948, *A Place in the Sun* 1951, and *From Here To Eternity* 1953, he was disfigured in a car accident in 1957 but continued to make films. He played the title role in *Freud* 1962.

climacteric /klaɪˈmæktərɪk/ *n.* the period of life when physical powers begin to decline. [from French or Latin from Greek]

climactic /klaɪˈmæktɪk/ *adj.* of a climax.

climate /ˈklaɪmət/ *n.* 1. the prevailing weather conditions of an area; a region with certain weather conditions. Climate encompasses all the meteorological elements and the factors that influence them. The primary factors that determine the variations of climate over the surface of the Earth are: (a) the effect of latitude and the tilt of the Earth's axis to the plane of the orbit abut the Sun (66.5°C); (b) the large-scale movements of different wind belts over the Earth's surface; (c) the temperature difference between land and sea; (d) contours of the ground; and (e) location of the area in relation to ocean currents. Catastrophic variations to climate may be caused by the impact of another planetary body, or by clouds resulting from volcanic activity. 2. the prevailing trend of opinion or feeling. —**climatic** /-ˈpˈmætɪk/ *adj.* [from Old French or Latin from Greek *klima* = slope]

climatology *n.* the study of climate, its global variations and causes.

climax /ˈklaɪmæks/ *n.* 1. the event or point of the greatest intensity or interest, culmination. 2. sexual orgasm. —*v.t./i.* to reach or bring to a climax. [Latin from Greek = ladder]

climax community an assemblage of plants and animals that is relatively stable in its environment (for example, oak woods in Britain). It is brought about by ecological ◊succession, and represents the point at which succession ceases to occu, providing conditions remain unaltered.

climb /klaɪm/ *v.t./i.* 1. to go up or over by effort. 2. to move upwards, to go higher; (of a plant) to grow up a support. 3. to rise in social rank etc. by one's own efforts. —*n.* 1. the action of climbing. 2. a hill etc. climbed or to be climbed. —**climb down,** to go downwards by effort; to retreat from a position taken up in argument. **climb-down** *n.* such a retreat. **climbing frame,** a structure of jointed bars etc. for children to climb on. [Old English]

climber *n.* 1. a mountaineer. 2. a climbing plant. 3. one who strives to rise socially.

clime *n.* (*literary*) a region; a climate. [from Latin *clima*]

clinch *v.t./i.* 1. to confirm or settle (an argument or bargain) conclusively. 2. (of boxers) to come too close together for a full-arm blow; (*colloquial*) to embrace. 3. to secure (a nail or rivet) by driving the point sideways when it is through. —*n.* a clinching action, a clinched state.

clincher *n.* a decisive point that settles an argument, proposition, etc.

cling *v.i.* (*past and past participle* **clung**) 1. to maintain one's grasp, to hold on tightly. 2. to become attached, to stick fast. 3. to be stubbornly faithful. [Old English]

clingstone *n.* a kind of peach or nectarine in which the stone is difficult to separate from the flesh.

clinic /ˈklɪnɪk/ *n.* 1. a private or specialized hospital. 2. a place or session at which specialized medical treatment or advice is given. [from French from Greek]

clinical /ˈklɪnɪkəl/ *adj.* 1. of or for the treatment of patients; taught or learnt at the hospital bedside. 2. dispassionate, coldly detached. —**clinical death,** death judged by observation of a person's condition. —**clinically** *adv.* [from Latin from Greek *klinē* = bed]

clinical psychology a discipline dealing with the understanding and treatment of health problems, particularly mental disorders. The main problems dealt with include anxiety, phobias, depression, obsessions, sexual and marital problems, drug and alcohol dependence, childhood behavioural problems, psychoses (such as schizophrenia), mental handicap, and brain damage (such as dementia).

clinician /klɪˈnɪʃən/ *n.* one who is skilled in the practice of clinical medicine, psychiatry, etc.

clink[1] *n.* a sharp ringing sound. —*v.t./i.* to make or cause to make this sound. [from Dutch]

Clive Known as 'Clive of India', Robert Clive has been called the founder of the British Empire in India.

clink[2] *n.* (*slang*) prison.

clinker *n.* a mass of slag or lava; the stony residue from burnt coal. [from Dutch]

clinker-built *adj.* (of a boat) having its external planks overlapping and secured with clinched nails. [from *clink*, dialect variant of *clinch*]

clinometer *n.* a hand-held surveying instrument for measuring angles of slope.

clip[1] *n.* 1. a device for holding things together or affixing something. 2. a piece of jewellery fastened by a clip. 3. a set of attached cartridges for a firearm. —*v.t.* (**-pp-**) to grip tightly; to fix with a clip. —**clip-on** *adj.* attached by a clip. [Old English]

clip[2] *v.t.* (**-pp-**) 1. to cut or trim with shears or scissors. 2. to punch a small piece from (a ticket etc.) to show that it has been used; to cut from a newspaper etc. 3. to omit (letters etc.) from (a word pronounced). 4. (*colloquial*) to hit sharply. —*n.* 1. the act of clipping. 2. something clipped; a yield of wool clipped from sheep; an extract from a film. 3. (*colloquial*) a sharp blow. 4. (*colloquial*) a rapid pace. [from Old Norse]

clipboard *n.* a small portable board with a spring clip for holding papers.

clipper *n.* 1. a fast sailing ship. 2. (usually in *plural*) an instrument for clipping hair.

clipping *n.* a piece clipped off; a newspaper cutting.

clique /kliːk/ *n.* a small exclusive group of people. —**cliquish** *adj.*, **cliquy** *adj.* [French, originally = clicking noise]

clitoris /ˈklɪtərɪs/ *n.* a small erectile part of the female genitals, at the upper end of the vulva. —**clitoral** *adj.* [Latin from Greek]

Clive /klaɪv/ Robert, Baron Clive of Plassey 1725–1774. English soldier and administrator, who established British rule in India by victories over the French in 1751 and over the nawab of Bengal in 1757. On his return to Britain his wealth led to allegations that he had abused his power. Although acquitted, he committed suicide.

cloaca /kləʊˈeɪkə/ *n.* (*plural* **cloacae** /-iː/) the excretory opening at the end of the intestinal canal in birds, reptiles, etc. [Latin = sewer]

cloak *n.* a sleeveless outdoor garment hanging loosely from the shoulders. —*v.t.* 1. to cover with a cloak. 2. to conceal, to disguise. —**cloak-and-dagger** *adj.* involving intrigue and espionage. [from Old French *cloke*, variant of *cloche* = bell (from its shape)]

cloakroom *n.* a room where outdoor clothes and luggage may be left by visitors; (*euphemism*) a lavatory.

clobber[1] *n.* (*slang*) clothing, personal belongings.

clobber[2] *v.t.* (*slang*) 1. to hit repeatedly, to beat up. 2. to defeat. 3. to criticize severely.

cloche /klɒʃ/ n. 1. a portable, translucent cover for protecting outdoor plants. 2. a woman's close-fitting, bell-shaped hat. [French = bell, from Latin]

clock¹ n. 1. an instrument measuring and recording the passage of time, with a regulating device (so that it operates at a uniform speed) and constant motive power, usually indicating hours, minutes, etc., by hands on a dial or by displayed figures. 2. a clocklike measuring device; (colloquial) a speedometer, taximeter, or stopwatch. 3. the seed head of a dandelion. —v.t. to time (a race) with a stopwatch; (also with up) to attain or register (a stated time, distance, or speed). **clock golf**, a game in which a golf ball is putted into a hole from successive points round a circle. **clock in** or **on**, to register one's arrival at work, especially by means of an automatic clock. **clock off** or **out**, to register one's departure similarly. [from Low German or Dutch from Latin clocca = bell]

clock² n. an ornamental pattern on the side of a stocking or sock.

clockwise adj. & adv. moving in a curve from left to right, corresponding in direction to the hands of a clock.

clockwork n. a mechanism with spring and gears, like that used (from the 15th century, instead of weights) to drive clocks; (attributive) driven by clockwork.

clod n. a lump of earth, clay, etc.

clodhoppers n.pl. (colloquial) large, heavy shoes.

clog n. a shoe with a thick wooden sole. —v.t./i. (-gg-) to cause an obstruction in; to become blocked.

cloisonné /klwɑːˈzɒneɪ/ n. an ornamental craft technique in which thin metal strips are soldered in a pattern on to a metal surface, and the resulting compartments (cloisons) filled with coloured enamels and fired. Cloisonné vases and brooches were made in medieval Europe, but the technique was perfected in Japan and China during the 17th, 18th, and 19th centuries. —adj. of or using this technique. [French, from cloison = partition, ultimately from Latin claudere = close]

cloister n. 1. a covered walk, often round a quadrangle with a wall on the outer side and a colonnade on the inner side, especially in a monastery, convent, college, or cathedral. 2. monastic life or seclusion. —v.t. to seclude in a convent etc. —**cloistral** adj. [from Old French from Latin claustrum = enclosed place (claudere = shut)]

cloistered adj. secluded, sheltered; monastic.

clone n. a group of plants or organisms produced asexually from one stock or ancestor; one such organism; (colloquial) a person regarded as identical with another. The term has been adopted by computer technology, in which it describes a (nonexistent) device that mimics an actual one to enable certain software programs to run correctly. —v.t. to propagate as a clone. —**clonal** /ˈkləʊnəl/ adj. [from Greek klōn = twig]

clonk n. a sharp, heavy sound of an impact. —v.t./i. 1. to make this sound. 2. (colloquial) to hit. [imitative]

close¹ /kləʊs/ adj. 1. near in space or time; near in relationship or association; nearly alike; (of a race or contest) in which the competitors are almost equal. 2. dense, compact, with only slight intervals; detailed, leaving no gaps or weaknesses. 3. oppressively warm or humid. 4. closed, shut; limited to certain persons. 5. hidden, secret; secretive. 6. niggardly. —adv. at a short distance or interval. —n. 1. a street closed at one end. 2. a precinct of a cathedral. —**at close quarters**, very close together. **close harmony**, harmony in which the notes of a chord are close together. **close-hauled** adj. with sails hauled aft to sail close to the wind. **close-knit** adj. closely united. **close season**, the season when the killing of game etc. is illegal. **close shave**, a narrow escape. **close-up** n. a photograph etc. taken at close range. —**closely** adv., **closeness** n. [from Old French from Latin clausus (claudere = shut)]

close² /kləʊz/ v.t./i. 1. to shut, to block up. 2. to bring or come to an end; to be or declare to be not open to the public. 3. to bring or come closer or into contact; to make (an electric circuit etc.) continuous. —n. a conclusion, an end. —**closed-circuit** adj. (of television) transmitted by wires to a restricted circuit of receivers. **close down**, to cease working, trading, or transmitting. **close in**, to approach from all sides so as to shut in or entrap; (of days) to get successively shorter. **close with**, to accept the offer made by (a person); to join battle or start fighting with. **closing time**, the time when a public

house etc. ends business. [from Old French clos from Latin claudere = shut]

closed adj. in mathematics, descriptive of a set of data for which an operation (such as addition or multiplication) done on any members of the set gives a result that is also a member of the set.

closed-circuit television (CCTV) a localized television system in which programmes are sent over relatively short distances, the camera, receiver, and controls being linked by cable. Closed-circuit TV systems are used in department stores and large offices as a means of internal security, monitoring people's movements.

closed shop any company or firm, public corporation, or other body that requires its employees to be members of the appropriate trade union. Usually demanded by unions, the closed shop may be preferred by employers as simplifying negotiation, but it was condemned by the European Court of Human Rights in 1981.

closet /ˈklɒzɪt/ n. a cupboard or small room; a water closet. —v.t. to shut away, especially in private conference or study. [from Old French, diminutive of clos = enclosed space]

closure /ˈkləʊʒə/ n. a closing or closed state; a decision in Parliament to take a vote without further debate. —v.t. to apply closure to (a motion, speaker, etc.). [from Old French from Latin clausura (claudere = close)]

clot n. a thick mass of coagulated liquid, especially of blood exposed to air. —v.i. (-tt-) to form into clots. —**clotted cream**, thick cream obtained by slow scalding. [Old English]

cloth n. 1. woven or felted material; a piece of this for a special purpose; a dishcloth, tablecloth, etc. 2. clerical clothes, the clergy. [Old English]

clothe /kləʊð/ v.t. (past and past participle **clothed** or **clad**) to put clothes on, to provide with clothes; to cover as with clothes. [Old English]

clothes /kləʊðz, -əʊz/ n.pl. things worn to cover the body and limbs; bedclothes. —**clotheshorse** n. a frame for airing washed clothes. **clothesline** n. a rope or wire on which washed clothes are hung out to dry. **clothes peg**, a clip or forked device for securing clothes to a clothesline. [Old English (originally plural of cloth)]

clothier /ˈkləʊðɪə/ n. a seller of clothes.

clothing /ˈkləʊðɪŋ/ n. clothes collectively.

cloud n. 1. a visible mass of condensed watery vapour floating high above the ground. Clouds, like fogs or mists which occur at lower levels, are formed by the cooling of air charged with water vapour, which generally condenses around tiny dust particles. 2. a mass of smoke or dust; a large moving mass of insects etc. in the sky. 3. a state of gloom, trouble, or suspicion. —v.t./i. to cover or darken with clouds or gloom or trouble; to become overcast or gloomy. —**cloud-cuckoo-land** n. a realm of fantasy or unrealistic ideas (translation of Greek name of realm in Aristophanes' Birds built by the birds to separate the gods from mankind). [Old English]

cloudburst n. a sudden, violent rainstorm.

cloud chamber an apparatus for tracking ionized particles. It consists of a vessel filled with air or other gas, supersaturated with water vapour. When suddenly expanded, the vapour cools and a cloud of tiny droplets forms on any nuclei, dust, or ions present. As single, fast-moving, ionizing particles collide with the air or gas molecules, they show as visible tracks.

cloudless adj. without clouds.

cloudy adj. 1. covered with clouds, overcast. 2. not clear, not transparent. —**cloudiness** n.

Clouet /ˈkluːeɪ/ François c.1515–1572. French portrait painter who succeeded his father Jean Clouet as court painter. He worked in the Italian style of Mannerism. His half-nude portrait of Diane de Poitiers, The Lady in Her Bath 1499–1566 (National Gallery, Washington), is also thought to be a likeness of Marie Touchet, mistress of Charles IX (1550–74).

Clouet Jean (known as **Janet**) 1486–1541. French artist, court painter to Francis I. His portraits and drawings, often compared to Holbein's, show an outstanding naturalism.

Clough /klʌf/ Arthur Hugh 1819–1861. English poet. Many of his lyrics are marked by a melancholy scepticism that reflects his struggle with his religious doubt.

clout *n.* **1.** a heavy blow. **2.** (*archaic*) a piece of cloth or clothing. —*v.t.* to hit hard. [Old English]

clove[1] *n.* the dried, unopened flower bud of the clove tree *Eugenia caryophyllus*. A member of the myrtle family Myrtaceae, the clove tree is a native of the Moluccas. Cloves are used for flavouring in cookery and confectionery. Oil of cloves, which has tonic and carminative qualities, is employed in medicine. The aromatic quality of cloves is shared to a large degree by the leaves, bark, and fruit of the tree. [from Old French from Latin *clavus* = nail (from the shape)]

clove[2] *n.* a small segment of a compound bulb, especially of garlic. [Old English]

clove[3] past of **cleave**[1].

clove hitch a knot used for securing a rope to a spar or to another rope.

cloven past participle of **cleave**[1]. —*adj.* split, partly divided. —**cloven hoof,** a hoof that is divided, as of oxen, sheep, or goats.

clover *n.* any of numerous species of plants (mostly of the Old World genus *Trifolium* but also including several related genera) of the legume family Leguminosae. Found mainly in temperate regions, clover plants have trifoliate leaves and roundish flowerheads or a spike of small flowers. Many species are cultivated as fodder crops for cattle. Eighteen species are native to Britain. —**in clover,** in ease and luxury. [Old English]

Clovis /ˈkləʊvɪs/ 465–511. Merovingian king of the Franks from 481. He succeeded his father Childeric as king of the Salian (northern) Franks; defeated the Gallo-Romans (Romanized Gauls) near Soissons in 486, ending their rule in France; and defeated the Alemanni, a confederation of Germanic tribes, near Cologne in 496. He embraced Christianity and subsequently proved a powerful defender of orthodoxy against the Arian ◊Visigoths, whom he defeated at Poitiers in 507. He made Paris his capital.

clown *n.* a performer, especially in a circus, who does comical tricks and actions; a person acting like a clown. —*v.i.* to behave like a clown. —**clownish** *adj.*

cloy *v.t.* to satiate or sicken, especially with richness, sweetness, or excess. [from Anglo-French]

club *n.* **1.** a heavy, stick thick at one end, used as a weapon etc.; a stick with a shaped head, used in golf. **2.** a playing card of the suit (**clubs**) marked with black clover leaves. **3.** an association of persons meeting periodically for a shared activity; an organization or premises offering its members social amenities, meals, temporary accommodation, etc.; an organization offering subscribers certain benefits. Many of the London men's clubs developed from the taverns and coffee-houses of the 17th and 18th centuries. Clubs based on political principles were common in the late 18th and early 19th centuries, for example the Jacobin Club in Paris in the 1790s and the English Carlton Club, founded in 1832 to oppose the Great Reform Bill. Sports and recreational clubs also originated in the 19th century, with the creation of working mens' clubs in Britain and workers' recreation clubs elsewhere in Europe. —*v.t./i.* (**-bb-**) **1.** to strike with a club etc. **2.** to combine, especially in making up a sum of money for a purpose. —**club foot,** a congenitally deformed foot. **club moss,** a pteridophyte with upright spikes of spore cases. **club root,** a disease of cabbages etc. with a swelling at the base of the stem. [Old Norse]

clubbable *adj.* sociable, fit for membership of a club.

clubhouse *n.* the premises used by a club.

Club of Rome an informal international organization, set up after a meeting at the Accademia dei Lincei, Rome, in 1968, which aims to promote greater understanding of the interdependence of global economic, political, natural, and social systems.

cluck *n.* a guttural cry like that of a hen. —*v.i.* to emit a cluck. [imitative]

clue *n.* a fact or idea that gives a guide to the solution of a problem; a word or words indicating what is to be inserted in a crossword puzzle. —*v.t.* to provide with a clue. —**not to have a clue,** (*colloquial*) to be ignorant or incompetent.

Cluj /kluːʒ/ (German *Klausenberg*) city in Transylvania, Romania, located on the river Someş; population (1985) 310,000. It is a communications centre for Romania and the Hungarian plain. Industries include machine tools, furniture, and knitwear.

clump *n.* a cluster or mass (of trees, tall plants, etc.). —*v.t.* **1.** to form a clump, to arrange in a clump. **2.** to walk with a heavy tread. **3.** (*colloquial*) to hit. [from Low German or Dutch]

clumsy /ˈklʌmzɪ/ *adj.* heavy and lacking in dexterity or grace; large and difficult to handle or use; done without tact or skill. —**clumsily** *adv.*, **clumsiness** *n.* [from obsolete *clumse* = be numb with cold, probably from Scandinavian]

clung past and past participle of **cling**.

cluster *n.* **1.** a small, close group. **2.** a group of stars bound together by gravity. **3.** in music, the effect of playing simultaneously and without emphasis all the notes within a chosen interval. Invented by ◊Cowell for the piano, it was adopted by ◊Penderecki for string orchestra; in radio and film an organ cluster is the traditional sound of reverie. —*v.t./i.* to gather in a cluster. [Old English]

clutch[1] *v.t./i.* to seize eagerly, to grasp tightly; try to grasp *at*. —*n.* **1.** a tight grasp; (in *plural*) grasping hands, cruel or relentless grasp or control. **2.** (in motor vehicles) a device for connecting the engine to the transmission; the pedal operating this. [Old English]

clutch[2] *n.* a set of eggs for hatching; the chickens hatched from these. [variant of north of England *cletch*, from Old Norse]

clutter *n.* a crowded, untidy collection of things; untidy state. —*v.t.* to crowd untidily, to fill with clutter.

Clwyd /ˈkluːɪd/ county in N Wales; **area** 2,420 sq km/ 934 sq mi; **administrative headquarters** Mold; **physical rivers:** Dee, Clwyd; Clwydian Range with Offa's Dyke along the main ridge; **products** dairy and meat products, optical glass, chemicals, limestone, microprocessors, plastics; **population** (1987) 403,000; **language** 19% Welsh, English.

Clyde /klaɪd/ river in Strathclyde, Scotland; 170 km/ 103 mi long. The Firth of Clyde and Firth of Forth are linked by the Forth and Clyde canal, 56 km/35 mi long. The shipbuilding yards have declined in recent years.

Clydesdale /ˈklaɪdzdeɪl/ *n.* a breed of heavy draught horses originally bred near the River Clyde; an animal of this breed.

Clytemnestra /klaɪtəmˈniːstrə/ in Greek mythology, the wife of ◊Agamemnon. With her lover Aegisthus, she murdered her husband and was in turn killed by her son Orestes.

cm abbreviation of centimetre(s).

Cm symbol for ◊curium.

CMOS abbreviation of complementary metal oxide semiconductor, a family of digital ◊integrated circuits. They are widely used in building electronic systems because they can operate on any voltage between 3 and 15 volts, and have relatively low power consumption and heat dissipation.

CND abbreviation of ◊Campaign for Nuclear Disarmament.

Cnossus alternative form of ◊Knossos.

Cnut alternative spelling of ◊Canute.

co- prefix meaning together with, jointly. [Latin]

c/o abbreviation of care of.

Co symbol for cobalt.

Co. abbreviation of company.

CO abbreviation of Commanding Officer.

coach *n.* **1.** a single-decker bus, usually comfortably equipped for longer journeys; a railway carriage; a closed horse-drawn carriage. **2.** an instructor or trainer in sport; a private tutor. —*v.t.* to train or teach as a coach. —**coach screw,** a large screw with a square head, turned by a spanner. [from French from Magyar]

coachwork *n.* the bodywork of a road or railway vehicle.

coagulant /kəʊˈægjʊlənt/ *n.* a substance that causes coagulation.

coagulate /kəʊˈægjʊleɪt/ *v.t./i.* to change from a liquid to a semisolid; to clot, to curdle. —**coagulation** *n.* [from Latin *coagulare* (*coagulum* = rennet)]

coal *n.* a hard black mineral, found below ground and used as fuel and in making gas, tar, etc.; a piece of this, one that is burning. Coal is classified according to the proportion of carbon and volatiles it contains. The main types are ◊anthracite (shiny, with more than 90% carbon), **bituminous coal** (shiny and dull patches, more than 80% carbon), and ◊lignite (woody, grading into ◊peat, 70% carbon). —*v.t./i.* to put coal into (a ship etc.); to take in a supply of coal. —**coalface** *n.* the exposed surface of coal in a mine. **coal measures,** a series of rocks formed by seams of coal and intervening strata. **coals to Newcastle,** a thing brought to a place where it is already plentiful, an unnecessary action. **coal scuttle,** a container for coal to supply a domestic fire. **coal tar,** tar extracted from bituminous coal. **coal tit,** a small greyish bird with a dark head. [Old English]

coalesce /kəuə'les/ *v.i.* to come together and form one whole. —**coalescence** *n.,* **coalescent** *adj.* [from Latin *coalescere* (*alescere* = grow up)]

coalfield *n.* an area yielding coal.

coal gas gas produced when coal is destructively distilled or heated out of contact with the air. Its main constituents are methane, hydrogen, and carbon monoxide. Coal gas has been superseded by ◊natural gas for domestic purposes.

coalition /kəu'lɪʃən/ *n.* fusion into one whole; a temporary alliance of political parties. [from Latin]

coaming *n.* a raised border round a ship's hatches etc. to keep out water.

coarse *adj.* **1.** rough or loose in texture, made of large particles. **2.** lacking refinement of manner or perception, crude, vulgar; (of language) obscene. **3.** inferior, common. —**coarse fish,** freshwater fish other than salmon and trout. —**coarsely** *adv.,* **coarseness** *n.*

coarsen *v.t./i.* to make or become coarse.

coast *n.* the border of the land nearest the sea, the seashore. —*v.i.* **1.** to ride or move, usually downhill, without the use of power. **2.** to sail along the coast. —**coastal** *adj.* [from Old French from Latin *costa* = rib, flank]

coastal erosion the erosion of the land by the constant battering of the waves of the sea. This produces two effects. The first is a hydraulic effect, in which the force of the wave compresses air pockets in coastal rocks and cliffs, and the air then expands explosively. The second is the effect of abrasion, in which rocks and pebbles are flung against the cliffs, wearing them away.

coaster *n.* **1.** a ship that travels along the coast. **2.** a small tray or mat for a bottle or glass.

coastguard *n.* a body of persons employed to keep watch on coasts, prevent smuggling, assist distressed vessels, watch for oil slicks, and so on; a member of this.

coastline *n.* the line of the seashore, especially with regard to its configuration.

coat *n.* **1.** an outer garment with sleeves and often extending below the hips, an overcoat, jacket, etc. **2.** a natural covering, especially an animal's fur or hair. **3.** a covering of paint etc. laid on a surface at any one time. —*v.t.* to cover *with* a coat or layer; (of paint etc.) to form a covering to. —**coat of arms,** the heraldic bearings or shield of a person or corporation. **coat of mail,** see ◊mail[2]. [from Old French from Germanic]

coati *n.* or **coatimundi** any of several species of carnivores of the genus *Nasua,* in the same family, Procyonidae, as the raccoons. A coati is a good climber and has long claws, a long tail, a good sense of smell, and a long, flexible piglike snout used for digging. Coatis live in packs in the forests of South and Central America.

coating *n.* **1.** a covering layer. **2.** material for coats.

coauthor *n.* a joint author. —*v.t.* to be joint author of.

coax *v.t.* **1.** to persuade gradually or by flattery; to obtain by such means. **2.** to manipulate carefully or slowly. [from 'make a *cokes* of' (obsolete *cokes* = fool)]

coaxial /kəu'æksɪəl/ *adj.* having a common axis; (of an electric cable or line) transmitting by means of two concentric conductors separated by an insulator.

cob *n.* **1.** a roundish lump. **2.** a corn cob. **3.** a sturdy riding horse with short legs. **4.** a male swan. **5.** a large hazelnut. **6.** a loaf rounded on the top.

cobalt /'kəubɔːlt, -ɒlt/ *n.* **1.** a hard, lustrous, grey, metallic element, symbol Co, atomic number 27, relative atomic mass 58.933. It is found in various ores (the main ones being smaltite, linnaeite, cobaltite, and glaucodot) and occasionally as a free metal, sometimes also in metallic meteorite fragments. It is used in the preparation of magnetic, wear-resistant, and high-strength alloys; its compounds are used in inks, paints, and varnishes. **2.** a pigment made from cobalt. —*adj.* the deep-blue colour characteristic of this pigment. [from German *kobalt,* probably = *kobold* = goblin or demon of the mines, the ore having been so called by the miners on account of its worthlessness (as then supposed) and from its bad effects upon their health and upon the silver ores with which it occurred,

cobra

Indian cobra

effects due mainly to the arsenic and sulphur with which it was combined]

Cobb /kɒb/ Ty(rus Raymond), nicknamed 'the Georgia Peach' 1886–1961. US baseball player, one of the greatest batters and base runners of all time. He played for Detroit and Philadelphia 1905–28, and won the American League batting average championship 12 times. He holds the record for runs scored, 2,254, and batting average, 0.367. He had 4,191 hits in his career—a record that stood for almost 60 years.

cobber *n.* (*Australian* and *New Zealand colloquial*) a friend, a mate. [perhaps from dialect *cob* = take a liking to]

Cobbett /'kɒbɪt/ William 1763–1835. English Radical politician and journalist, who published the weekly *Political Register* 1802–35. He spent much time in North America. His crusading essays on farmers' conditions were collected as *Rural Rides* 1830.

Give me Lord, neither poverty nor riches.

William Cobbett

---

cobble[1] *n.* (in full **cobblestone**) a small, rounded stone used for paving. —*v.t.* to pave with cobbles.

cobble[2] *v.t.* to mend or patch up (especially shoes); to repair or put together roughly. [back formation from *cobbler*]

cobbler *n.* **1.** a shoe repairer. **2.** an iced drink of wine, sugar, and lemon. **3.** a fruit pie topped with scones.

Cobden /'kɒbdən/ Richard 1804–1865. English Liberal politician and economist, cofounder with John Bright of the Anti-Corn Law League 1839. A member of Parliament from 1841, he opposed class and religious privileges and believed in disarmament and free trade.

COBOL /'kəubɒl/ *n.* a computer programming language, designed in the late 1950s for business use. COBOL facilitates the writing of programs that deal with large computer files and handle business arithmetic. It has become the major language for commercial data processing. [acronym from **Co**mmon **B**usiness **O**riented **L**anguage]

cobra /'kəubrə, 'kɒ-/ *n.* any of several poisonous snakes, including the genus *Naja,* of the family Elapidae, found in Africa and S Asia, species of which can grow from 1 m/ 3 ft to over 4.3 m/14 ft. The neck stretches into a 'hood' when the snake is alarmed. Cobra venom contains nerve toxins powerful enough to kill humans. [Portuguese from Latin *colubra* = snake]

Coburn /'kəubɜːn/ James 1928– . US film actor, popular in the 1960s and 1970s. His films include *The Magnificent Seven* 1960, *Our Man Flint* 1966, and *Cross of Iron* 1977.

cobweb *n.* the fine network spun by a spider; a thread of this. —**cobwebby** *adj.* [from obsolete *coppe* = spider]

coca /'kəukə/ *n.* a South American shrub *Erythroxylon coca* whose dried leaves are the source of cocaine; its leaves, chewed as a stimulant. [Spanish from Quechua]

Coca-Cola /kəukə'kəulə/ *n.* trade name of a sweetened, fizzy drink, originally flavoured by coca and cola nuts, containing caramel and caffeine. Invented in 1886, Coca-Cola was sold in every state of the USA by 1895 and in 155 countries around the world by 1987.

cocaine /kɒ'keɪn, kəu-/ *n.* an alkaloid, $C_{17}H_{21}NO_4$, extracted from the leaves of the coca tree. It has limited medical application, mainly as a local anaesthetic agent that is readily absorbed by mucous membranes (lining tissues) of the nose and throat. It is both toxic and addictive. Its use as a stimulant is illegal. ◊Crack is a derivative of cocaine.

coccyx /'kɒksɪks/ n. (plural **coccyges** /-dʒiːz/) a small triangular bone at the base of the spinal column. [Latin from Greek kokkux = cuckoo (from being shaped like its bill)]

Cochabamba /kɒtʃə'bæmbə/ city in central Bolivia, SE of La Paz; population (1985) 317,000. Its altitude is 2,550 m/8,370 ft; it is a centre of agricultural trading and oil refining.

cochineal /'kɒtʃɪniːl/ n. a bright-red colouring matter made from the dried bodies of a Mexican insect Dactylopius coccus. [from French or Spanish from Latin coccinus = scarlet from Greek]

cochlea /'kɒkliə/ n. (plural **cochleae** /-liːɪ/) the spiral cavity of the inner ear. It is equipped with approximately 10,000 hair cells, which move in response to sound waves and thus stimulate nerve cells to send messages to the brain. [Latin = snail shell, from Greek]

Cochran /'kɒkrən/ C(harles) B(lake) 1872–1951. English impresario who promoted entertainment ranging from wrestling and roller skating to Diaghilev's Ballets Russes.

cock[1] 1. a male bird, especially of the domestic fowl. 2. the firing lever in a gun, raised to be released by the trigger; a cocked position. 3. a tap or valve controlling the flow of a liquid. —v.t. 1. to make upright or erect; to move (the eye or ear) attentively or knowingly; to set aslant or turn up the brim of (a hat). 2. to raise the cock of (a gun). —**cock-a-doodle-doo**, the sound of a cock crowing. **cock-a-hoop** adj. exultant. **cock-a-leekie** n. a Scottish soup of cock boiled with leeks. **cock-and-bull story**, one that is absurd or incredible. **cock a snook**, see ◊snook. **cockcrow** n. dawn. **cocked hat**, a brimless triangular hat pointed at front, back, and top. **cockeyed** adj. (colloquial) crooked, askew; absurd, not practical. **cockfight** n. a fight between cocks as a sport. **cockshy** n. a target for throwing at, a throw at this; an object of ridicule or criticism. [from Old English and French]

cock[2] a small conical pile of hay or straw.

cockade /kɒ'keɪd/ n. a rosette etc. worn in the hat as a badge. [from French]

cockatiel n. an Australian parrot Nymphicus hollandicus, about 20 cm/8 in long, with greyish plumage, yellow cheeks, a long tail, and a crest like a cockatoo. They are popular as pets and aviary birds.

cockatoo /kɒkə'tuː/ n. any of several crested parrots, in particular of the genus Cacatua. They usually have light-coloured plumage with tinges of red, yellow, or orange on the face, and an erectile crest on the head. They are native to Australia, New Guinea, and nearby islands. [from Dutch from Malay]

cockchafer /'kɒktʃeɪfə/ n. or **maybug** European beetle Melolontha melolontha of the scarab family, up to 3 cm/1.2 in long, with clumsy, buzzing flight, seen on early summer evenings. Cockchafers damage trees by feeding on the foliage and flowers.

Cockcroft /'kɒkrɒft/ John Douglas 1897–1967. English physicist. In 1932 he and the Irish physicist Ernest Walton succeeded in splitting the nucleus of an atom for the first time. In 1951 they were jointly awarded the Nobel Prize for Physics.

cocker n. (in full **cocker spaniel**) a small spaniel with a golden-brown coat. [from cock[1], as starting woodcock]

cockerel /'kɒkərəl/ n. a young cock.

Cockerell Charles 1788–1863. English architect who built mainly in a Neo-Classical style derived from antiquity and from the work of Christopher Wren. His buildings include the Ashmolean Museum and the Taylorian Institute in Oxford 1841–45.

Cockerell Christopher 1910– . English engineer who invented the ◊hovercraft in 1959.

cockle n. 1. any of over 200 species of bivalve mollusc with ribbed, heart-shaped shells. Some are edible and are sold in W European markets. The common cockle Cerastoderma edule is up to 5 cm/2 in across, and is found in sand or mud on shores and in estuaries around N European and Mediterranean coasts. 2. a pucker or wrinkle in paper, glass, etc. 3. (in full **cockleshell**) a small shallow boat. —v.t./i. to make or become puckered. [from Old French coquille = shell from Latin from Greek]

cockney /'kɒkni/ n. 1. a native of London, especially of the East End (according to Minsheu (early 17th century) 'one born within the sound of Bow Bells'). 2. the dialect or accent historically associated with this area. —adj. of cockneys or their dialect. [from obsolete cokeney = cock's egg, original sense probably small or ill-shaped egg, hence 'milksop', 'townsman']

cock-of-the-rock n. a South American bird Rupicola peruviana of the family Cotingidae, which also includes the cotingas and umbrella birds. The male cock-of-the-rock has brilliant orange plumage including the head crest, the female is a duller brown. Males clear an area of ground and use it as a communal display ground, spreading wings, tail, and crest to attract mates.

cockpit n. 1. the compartment for the pilot (and crew) of an aircraft or spacecraft; the driver's seat in a racing car; a space for the helmsman in some small yachts. 2. an arena of war or other conflict. 3. a place made for cockfights.

cockroach n. any of numerous insects of the family Blattidae, distantly related to mantises and grasshoppers. There are 3,500 species, mainly in the tropics; they infest kitchens and bathrooms. They have long antennae and biting mouthparts. They can fly, but rarely do so. [from Spanish cucaracha]

cockscomb n. the crest of a cock.

cocksure adj. presumptuously or arrogantly confident; absolutely sure. [from cock = God]

cocktail n. 1. a mixed alcoholic drink, especially of spirit with bitters etc. 2. an appetizer containing shellfish or fruit.

cocktail effect the effect of two toxic, or potentially toxic, chemicals when taken together rather than separately. Such effects are known to occur with some mixtures of chemicals, with one ingredient making the body more sensitive to another ingredient. This sometimes occurs because both chemicals require the same ◊enzyme to break them down.

cocky adj. pertly self-confident. —**cockily** adv., **cockiness** n.

coco /'kəʊkəʊ/ n. a tropical palm tree Cocos nucifera from which coconuts come. [Spanish and Portuguese = grimace]

cocoa /'kəʊkəʊ/ n. a powder made with crushed ◊cacao seeds, often with other ingredients; a drink made from this. Chocolate was introduced to Europe as a drink in the 16th century; eating chocolate was first produced in the late 18th century. Cocoa and chocolate are widely used in confectionery, drinks, and some savoury dishes. —**cocoa bean**, a cacao seed. **cocoa butter**, a fatty substance obtained from this. [alteration of cacao]

coconut /'kəʊkənʌt/ n. the fruit of the coco palm Cocos nucifera of the family Arecaceae, which grows throughout the lowland tropics. The fruit has a large outer husk of fibres, which is split off and used for coconut matting and ropes. Inside this is the nut exported to temperate countries. Its hard shell contains white flesh and a milky juice, both of which are nourishing and palatable. —**coconut shy**, a fairground amusement where balls are thrown to dislodge coconuts from a stand.

cocoon /kə'kuːn/ n. the silky case spun by an insect larva to protect itself as a chrysalis, especially that of a silkworm; a protective covering. —v.t. to wrap or coat in a cocoon. [from French from Provençal coca = shell]

Cocos Islands /'kəʊkɒs/ or **Keeling Islands** group of 27 small coral islands in the Indian Ocean, about 2,770 km/1,720 mi NW of Perth, Australia, covering an area of 14 sq km/5.5 sq mi; population (1986) 616. They are owned by Australia.

cocotte /kə'kɒt/ n. a small, fireproof dish for serving food. [French]

Cocteau /'kɒktəʊ/ Jean 1889–1963. French poet, dramatist, and film director. A leading figure in European Modernism, he worked with Picasso, Diaghilev, and Stravinsky. He produced many volumes of poetry, ballets such as Le Boeuf sur le toit/The Nothing Doing Bar 1920, plays, for example, Orphée/Orpheus 1926, and a mature novel of bourgeois French life, Les Enfants terribles/Children of the Game 1929, which he made into a film in 1950.

Victor Hugo ... a madman who thought he was Victor Hugo.

Jean Cocteau
Opium

---

cod n. (plural the same) or **codfish** any fish of the family Gadoidea, in particular the Atlantic cod, Gadus morhua

Cocteau *French playwright, novelist, poet, film director, and artist Jean Cocteau in 1929.*

found in the N Atlantic and Baltic. Brown to grey with spots, white below, it can grow to 1.5 m/5 ft. —**cod-liver oil**, oil from cod livers, rich in vitamins A and D.

COD abbreviation of cash (*US* collect) on delivery.

coda *n.* the final passage of a movement or piece of music, often elaborate and distinct; the concluding section of a ballet. [Italian from Latin *cauda* = tail]

coddle *v.t.* **1.** to treat as an invalid; to protect attentively, to pamper. **2.** to cook (an egg) in water just below boiling point.

code *n.* **1.** a system of words, letters, or symbols used to represent others for secrecy or brevity. **2.** a system of prearranged signals for transmitting messages. **3.** a set of instructions used in programming a computer. **4.** a systematic set of laws or rules; in law, the body of a country's civil or criminal law. The *Code Napoléon* in France 1804–10 was widely copied in European countries with civil law systems. **5.** a prevailing standard of moral behaviour. —*v.t.* to put into code. [from Old French from Latin *codex*]

codeine /'kəʊdiːn/ *n.* an alkaloid obtained from opium, used to relieve pain or induce sleep. [from Greek *kōdeia* = poppyhead]

codex /'kəʊdeks/ *n.* (*plural* **codices** /-dɪsiːz/) **1.** an ancient manuscript text in the book form which between the 1st and 4th centuries AD gradually replaced the continuous roll previously used for written documents. **2.** a collection of pharmaceutical descriptions of drugs etc. [Latin = wood block, tablet, book (as these tablets were often coated with wax and inscribed)]

codger /'kɒdʒə/ *n.* (*colloquial*) a person, especially a strange one.

codicil /'kɒdɪsɪl/ *n.* an addition to a will explaining, modifying, or revoking it or part of it. [from Latin, diminutive of *codex*]

codify /'kəʊdɪfaɪ/ *v.t.* to arrange (laws etc.) systematically into a code. —**codification** /-'keɪʃən/ *n.*, **codifier** *n.*

codling[1] *n.* or **codlin** **1.** a kind of cooking apple, usually oblong and yellowish. **2.** a moth whose larva feeds on apples. [from French *quer de lion* = lionheart]

codling[2] *n.* a small codfish.

codon *n.* in genetics, a triplet of bases (see ◊base pair) in a molecule of DNA or RNA that directs the placement of a particular amino acid during the process of protein synthesis. There are 64 codons in the ◊genetic code.

codpiece *n.* an appendage like small bag or a flap at the front of a man's breeches in 15th–16th-century dress. [from obsolete *cod* = scrotum]

Cody /'kəʊdi/ Samuel Franklin 1862–1913. US aviation pioneer. He made his first powered flight on 16 Oct 1908 at Farnborough, England, in a machine of his own design. He was killed in a flying accident.

Cody William Frederick 1846–1917. US scout and performer, known as **Buffalo Bill** from his contract to supply buffalo carcasses to railway labourers (over 4,000 in 18 months). From 1883 he toured the USA and Europe with a Wild West show which featured the recreation of Indian attacks and, for a time, the cast included Chief ◊Sitting Bull as well as Annie ◊Oakley.

Coe /kəʊ/ Sebastian 1956– . English middle-distance runner. He was Olympic 1,500-metre champion in 1980 and

1984. Between 1979 and 1981 he broke eight individual world records at 800 metres, 1,000 metres, 1,500 metres, and one mile. In 1990 he announced his retirement after failing to win a Commonwealth Games title and is now pursuing a political career with the Conservative party.

coeducation /kəʊedjuː'keɪʃən/ *n.* the education of both boys and girls in one institution. There has been a marked switch away from single-sex education and in favour of coeducation over the last 20 years in the UK, although there is some evidence to suggest that girls perform better in a single-sex institution, particularly in maths and science. In 1954, the USSR returned to its earlier coeducational system, partly abolished in 1944. In the USA, 90% of schools and colleges are coeducational. In Islamic countries, coeducation is discouraged beyond the infant stage. —**coeducational** *adj.*

coefficient /kəʊɪ'fɪʃənt/ *n.* **1.** in mathematics, a quantity placed before and multiplying another quantity for example, in the expression $4x^2 + 2xy - x$, the coefficient of x^2 is 4 (because $4x^2$ means $4 \times x^2$), that of xy is 2, and that of x is –1 (because $-1 \times x = -x$). **2.** in physics, a multiplier or factor by which a property is measured.

coefficient of relationship the probability that any two individuals share a given gene by virtue of being descended from a common ancestor. In sexual reproduction of diploid species, an individual shares half its genes with each parent, with its offspring, and (on average) with each sibling; but only a quarter (on average) with its grandchildren or its siblings' offspring; an eighth with its great-grandchildren, and so on.

coelacanth /'siːləkænθ/ *n.* a fish of the family Coelacanthidae, originally thought to have a hollow spine, extinct but for one species *Latimeria chalumnae* which grows up to 2 m/6 ft long. It has bone and muscle at the base of the fins, and is distantly related to the freshwater lobefins, which were the ancestors of all land animals with backbones. Coelacanths live in deep water surrounding the Comoros Islands, off the coast of Madagascar. They are now under threat; a belief that fluid from the spine has a life-extending effect has made them much sought after. [from Greek *koilos* = hollow and *acantha* = spine]

coelenterate /siː'lentəreɪt/ *n.* a member of the phylum Coelenterata, aquatic animals (including sea anemones, hydras, jellyfish, and corals) with a simple tube-shaped or cup-shaped body and a digestive system with a single opening surrounded by a ring of tentacles. —*adj.* of coelenterates. [from Greek *koilos* = hollow and *enteron* = intestine]

coeliac /'siːliæk/ *adj.* of the belly. —**coeliac disease**, an intestinal disease causing defective digestion of fats, usually in young children, due to disorder of the absorptive surface of the small intestine. It is mainly associated with an intolerance to gluten (a constituent of wheat) and characterized by diarrhoea and malnutrition. [from Latin from Greek *koilia* = belly]

coelom *n.* in all but the simplest animals, the fluid-filled cavity that separates the body wall from the gut and associated organs, and allows the gut muscles to contract independently of the rest of the body.

coenobite /'siːnəbaɪt/ *n.* a member of a monastic community. —**coenobitic** /-'bɪtɪk/ *adj.*, **coenobitical** *adj.* [from Old French or Latin from Greek *koinobion* = convent (*koinos* = common and *bios* = life)]

coequal /kəʊ'iːkwəl/ *adj. & n.* (*archaic* or *literary*) equal.

coerce /kəʊ'ɜːs/ *v.t.* to impel or force (*into* obedience etc.). —**coercion** *n.* [from Latin *coercēre* (*arcēre* = restrain)]

coercive /kəʊ'ɜːsɪv/ *adj.* using coercion.

Coetzee /ku:t'siə/ J(ohn) M 1940– . South African author whose novel *In the Heart of the Country* 1975 dealt with the rape of a white woman by a black man. In 1983 he won Britain's prestigious ◊Booker Prize for *The Life and Times of Michael K*.

coeval /kəʊ'iːvəl/ *adj.* having the same age, existing at the same epoch. —*n.* a coeval person, a contemporary. [from Latin *coaevus* (*aevum* = age)]

coexist /kəʊɪg'zɪst/ *v.i.* to exist together (*with*). [from Latin *existere* = exist]

coexistence *n.* coexisting. —**peaceful coexistence**, mutual tolerance of nations with different ideologies or political and social systems. —**coexistent** *adj.*

coextensive /kəʊɪk'stensɪv/ *adj.* extending over the same space or time.

C. of E. abbreviation of Church of England.

coffee /'kɒfɪ/ *n.* **1.** a drink made from the roasted and ground beanlike seeds of a tropical shrub; a cup of this. Coffee drinking began in Arab countries in the 14th century but did not become common in Europe until 300 years later. **2.** the seeds of a tropical shrub of the genus *Coffea*; this shrub. Naturally about 5 m/17 ft tall, it is pruned to about 2 m/7 ft, is fully fruit-bearing in five or six years, and continues for 30 years. Coffee grows best on frost-free hillsides with moderate rainfall. The world's largest producers are Brazil, Colombia, and the Ivory Coast; others include Indonesia, Ethiopia, India, the Philippines, and Cameroon. **3.** the pale brown colour of coffee mixed with milk. —**coffee bar,** a place serving coffee and light refreshments from a counter. **coffee morning,** a morning social gathering at which coffee is served, usually in aid of a good cause. **coffee shop,** an informal restaurant, especially at a hotel. **coffee table,** a small low table. **coffee-table book,** a large expensive illustrated book, too large for a bookshelf. [from Turkish from Arabic]

coffer *n.* **1.** a large, strong box for valuables; (in *plural*) a treasury, funds. **2.** a sunken panel in a ceiling etc. —**cofferdam** *n.* a watertight enclosure pumped dry for work in building bridges etc., or for repairing a ship. [from Old French from Latin from Greek *kophinos* = basket]

coffin *n.* a box in which a corpse is buried or cremated. —*v.t.* to put in a coffin. [from Old French = little basket]

cog *n.* any of a series of projections on the edge of a wheel or bar transferring motion by engaging with another series; an unimportant member of an organization etc. —**cogwheel** *n.* a wheel with cogs. [probably from Scandinavian]

cogent /'kəʊdʒənt/ *adj.* convincing, compelling. —**cogency** *n.,* **cogently** *adv.* [from Latin *cogere* = compel]

cogging *n.* the process of passing heated metal ingots between a pair of rollers as the first stage in rolling them into the shape required.

cogitate /'kɒdʒɪteɪt/ *v.t./i.* to ponder, to meditate. —**cogitation** /-'teɪʃən/ *n.,* **cogitative** *adj.* [from Latin *cogitare* = think]

cogito, ergo sum 'I think, therefore I am'; quotation from French philosopher René Descartes. [Latin]

cognac /'kɒnjæk/ *n.* brandy, especially that distilled in the town of Cognac in western France. [from *Cognac*]

cognate /'kɒgneɪt/ *adj.* related or descended from a common ancestor; (of a word) having the same linguistic family or derivation. —*n.* a relative; a cognate word. [from Latin *gnatus* = born]

cognition /kɒg'nɪʃən/ *n.* knowing, perceiving, or conceiving as an act or faculty distinct from emotion and volition; the result of this. —**cognitional** *adj.,* **cognitive** /'kɒgnɪtɪv/ *adj.* [from Latin *gnoscere* = know]

cognitive therapy a treatment for emotional disorders such as ◊depression and ◊anxiety, developed by Professor Aaron T Beck in the USA. The treatment includes ◊behaviour therapy and has been most helpful for people suffering from depression.

cognizance /'kɒgnɪzəns/ *n.* **1.** knowledge or awareness, perception. **2.** sphere of observation or concern. **3.** a distinctive device or mark. [from Old French from Latin]

cognizant /'kɒgnɪzənt/ *adj.* having knowledge or taking note of.

cognomen /kɒg'nəʊmen/ *n.* a nickname; an ancient Roman's personal name or epithet. [Latin]

cognoscente /kɒnjəʊ'ʃentɪ/ *n.* (*plural* **cognoscenti**) a connoisseur. [Italian]

cohabit /kəʊ'hæbɪt/ *v.i.* to live together as husband and wife (usually of a couple who are not married to each other). —**cohabitation** /-'teɪʃən/ *n.* [from Latin *habitare* = dwell]

Cohan /'kəʊhæn/ Robert Paul 1925–. US choreographer and founder of the London Contemporary Dance Theatre 1969–87; now artistic director of the Contemporary Dance Theatre. He was a student of Martha ◊Graham and codirector of her company 1966–69. His ballets include *Waterless Method of Swimming Instruction* 1974 and *Mass for Man* 1985.

cohere /kəʊ'hɪə/ *v.i.* **1.** (of parts or a whole) to stick together, to remain united. **2.** (of reasoning etc.) to be logical or consistent. [from Latin *haerēre* = stick]

coherence *n.* in physics, the property of two or more waves of a beam of light or other ◊electromagnetic radiation having the same frequency and the same ◊phase, or a constant phase difference.

coherent /kəʊ'hɪərənt/ *adj.* cohering; (of reasoning) connected logically; not rambling in speech or in reasoning. —**coherence** *n.,* **coherently** *adv.*

cohesion /kəʊ'hiːʒən/ *n.* sticking together; in physics, a phenomenon in which interaction between two surfaces of the same material in contact makes them cling together (with two different materials the similar phenomenon is called adhesion). According to kinetic theory, cohesion is caused by attraction between particles at the atomic or molecular level. Surface tension (see ◊surface), which causes liquids to form spherical droplets, is caused by cohesion. —**cohesive** *adj.*

cohort /'kəʊhɔːt/ *n.* **1.** a Roman military unit, one tenth of a legion; a band of warriors. **2.** persons banded or grouped together; a group having a common statistical characteristic. [from French or Latin *cohors*]

COI abbreviation of Central Office of Information.

coif *n.* (*historical*) a close-fitting cap. [from Old French from Latin *cofia* = helmet]

coiffeur /kwɑː'fɜː/ *n.* a hairdresser. —**coiffeuse** *n.fem.* [French]

coiffure /kwɑː'fjuə/ *n.* a hairstyle. [French]

coign /kɔɪn/ *n.* a projecting corner, chiefly in **coign of vantage,** a place from which a good view can be obtained. [old form of *coin*]

coil *v.t./i.* to arrange or be arranged in spirals or concentric rings; to move sinuously. —*n.* a coiled length of rope etc.; a coiled arrangement; a single turn of a coiled thing; a flexible loop as a contraceptive device in the womb; a coiled wire for the passage of an electric current. [from Old French from Latin *colligere* = collect]

coin *n.* a small stamped disc of metal as official money; coins collectively. The right to make and issue coins is a state monopoly, and the great majority are tokens in that their face value is greater than that of the metal of which they consist. A milled edge, originally used on gold and silver coins to avoid fraudulent 'clipping' of the edges of precious metal coins, is retained in some present-day token coinage. —*v.t.* **1.** to make (money) by stamping metal; to make (metal) into coins. **2.** to invent (a new word or phrase). [from Old French = stamping die, from Latin *cuneus* = wedge]

coinage /'kɔːnɪdʒ/ *n.* **1.** coining; coins; a system of coins in use. **2.** a coined word or phrase.

coincide /kəʊɪn'saɪd/ *v.i.* **1.** to occur at the same time; to occupy the same portion of space. **2.** to agree or be identical (*with*). [from Latin *incidere* = fall on]

coincidence /kəʊ'ɪnsɪdəns/ *n.* coinciding; a remarkable concurrence of events or circumstances without apparent causal connection. —**coincident** *adj.*

coincidental /kəʊɪnsɪ'dentəl/ *adj.* occurring by coincidence; in the nature of a coincidence. —**coincidentally** *adv.*

Cointreau /'kwæntrəʊ/ *n.* trade name of a colourless, orange-flavoured liqueur.

coir /kɔɪə/ *n.* coconut fibre used for ropes, matting, etc. [from Malayalam = cord]

coition /kəʊ'ɪʃən/ *n.* coitus. [from Latin *coire* (*ire* = go)]

coitus /'kəʊɪtəs/ *n.* sexual intercourse. —**coital** *adj.* [Latin]

coke /kəʊk/ *n.* a clean, light fuel produced by the carbonization of certain types of coal. Coke comprises 90% carbon together with very small quantities of water, hydrogen, and oxygen, and makes a useful industrial and domestic fuel. The process was patented in England in 1622, but it was only in 1709 that Abraham Darby devised a commercial method of production. —*v.t.* to convert (coal) into coke. [probably from dialect = core]

Coke Edward 1552–1634. Lord Chief Justice of England 1613–17. He was a defender of common law against royal prerogative; against Charles I he drew up the ◊Petition of Right 1628, which defines and protects Parliament's liberties.

221

For a man's house is his castle.

Edward Coke
Third Institute

Coke Thomas William 1754–1842. English pioneer and promoter of the improvements associated with the Agricultural Revolution. His innovations included regular manuring of the soil, the cultivation of fodder crops in association with corn, and the drilling of wheat and turnips.

col /kɒl/ n. 1. a depression in a chain of mountains. 2. a region of low pressure between anticyclones. [French from Latin = neck]

col- prefix see ◊com-.

cola /'kəʊlə/ n. or **kola** any tropical tree of the genus *Cola*, especially *C. acuminata*, family Sterculiaceae. Cola nuts are chewed in W Africa for their high caffeine content, and in the West are used to flavour soft drinks.

colander /'kʌləndə/ n. a perforated, bowl-shaped vessel used to strain off liquid in cooking. [from Latin *colare* = strain]

Colbert /kɒl'beə/ Claudette. Stage name of Claudette Lily Cauchoin 1905– . French-born film actress, who lived in Hollywood from childhood. She was ideally cast in sophisticated, romantic roles, but had a natural instinct for comedy and appeared in several of Hollywood's finest, including *It Happened One Night* 1934 and *The Palm Beach Story* 1942.

Colbert Jean-Baptiste 1619–1683. French politician, chief minister to Louis XIV, and controller-general (finance minister) from 1665. He reformed the Treasury, promoted French industry and commerce by protectionist measures, and tried to make France a naval power equal to England or the Netherlands, while favouring a peaceful foreign policy.

cold adj. 1. of or at a low temperature, especially when compared with the human body; not heated, cooled after heat; feeling cold. 2. dead; (slang) unconscious. 3. lacking geniality, affection, or enthusiasm. 4. depressing, dispiriting. 5. (of colour) suggestive of cold. 6. remote from the thing sought; (of the scent in hunting) grown faint. 7. unrehearsed. —adv. in a cold state. —n. 1. prevalence of low temperature; cold condition. 2. the common cold (see entry below). —**cold-blooded** adj. having a body temperature that varies with that of the environment; callous, cruel. **cold chisel,** a toughened steel chisel. **cold comfort,** poor consolation. **cold cream,** an ointment for cleansing and softening the skin. **cold frame,** an unheated frame for growing small plants. **cold shoulder,** deliberate unfriendliness. **cold-shoulder** v.t. to be unfriendly to. **cold storage,** storage in a refrigerator; *in cold storage,* put aside but still available. **cold war,** hostilities short of armed conflict, consisting in threats, violent propaganda, subversive political activities or the like. **get** *or* **have cold feet,** to feel afraid or reluctant. **throw** *or* **pour cold water on,** to be discouraging about, to belittle. —**coldly** adv., **coldness** n. [Old English, cognate with Latin *gelu* = frost]

cold, common a minor disease of the upper respiratory tract, caused by a variety of viruses. Symptoms are headache, chill, nasal discharge, sore throat, and occasionally cough. Research indicates that the virulence of a cold depends on psychological factors and either a reduction or an increase of social or work activity, as a result of stress, in the previous six months.

Cold Harbor, Battle of /'kəʊld 'hɑːbə/ in the American Civil War, an engagement near Richmond, Virginia, 1–12 June 1864, in which the Confederate Army under Robert E Lee repulsed Union attacks under Ulysses S Grant.

Colditz /'kəʊldɪts/ town in Germany, near Leipzig, site of a castle used as a high-security prisoner-of-war camp (Oflag IVC) in World War II. Among daring escapes was that of British Captain Patrick Reid and others in Oct 1942. It became a museum in 1989. In 1990 the castle was being converted to a hotel.

Cold War the relations from about 1945–90 between the USSR and Eastern Europe on the one hand, and the USA and Western Europe on the other. The Cold War was exacerbated by propaganda, covert activity by intelligence agencies, and economic sanctions, and intensified at times of conflict. Arms reduction agreements between the USA and USSR in the late 1980s, and a diminution of Soviet

influence in Eastern Europe, symbolized by the opening of the ◊Berlin Wall in 1989, led to a reassessment of positions. The formal end of the Cold War occurred in November 1990.

cole n. any of various plants of the cabbage family, especially (**cole-seed**) rape. [from Old Norse from Latin *caulis*]

Coleman /'kəʊlmən/ Ornette 1930– . US alto saxophonist and jazz composer. In the late 1950s he rejected the established structural principles of jazz for free avant-garde improvisation. He has worked with small and large groups, ethnic musicians of different traditions, and symphony orchestras.

Cole, Old King /kəʊl/ legendary British king, supposed to be the father of St Helena, who married the Roman emperor Constantius, father of Constantine; he is also supposed to have founded Colchester. The historical Cole was possibly a North British chieftain named Coel, of the 5th century, who successfully defended his land against the Picts and Scots. The nursery rhyme is only recorded from 1709.

coleopterous /kɒli'ɒptərəs/ adj. of the order Coleoptera (comprising beetles and weevils) of insects with front wings serving as sheaths for the hinder wings. [from Greek *koleon* = sheath and *pteron* = wing]

coleoptile n. the protective sheath that surrounds the young shoot tip of a grass during its passage through the soil to the surface. Although of relatively simple structure, most coleoptiles are very sensitive to light, ensuring that seedlings grow upwards.

Coleridge /'kəʊlərɪdʒ/ Samuel Taylor 1772–1834. English poet, one of the founders of the Romantic movement. A friend of Southey and Wordsworth, he collaborated with the latter on *Lyrical Ballads* 1798. His poems include 'The Ancient Mariner', 'Christabel', and 'Kubla Khan'; critical works include *Biographia Literaria* 1817.

Coleridge-Taylor /'teɪlə/ Samuel 1875–1912. English composer, the son of a West African doctor and an English mother. He wrote the cantata *Hiawatha's Wedding Feast* 1898, a setting in three parts of Longfellow's poem. He was a student and champion of traditional black music.

coleslaw /'kəʊlslɔ:/ n. a salad of sliced raw cabbage coated in dressing. [from *cole*]

Colette /kɒ'let/ Sidonie-Gabrielle 1873–1954. French writer. At 20 she married Henri Gauthier-Villars, a journalist known as 'Willy', under whose name and direction her four 'Claudine' novels, based on her own early life, were written. Divorced in 1906, she worked as a striptease and mime artist for a while, but continued to write. Works from this later period include *Chéri* 1920, *La Fin de Chéri/The End of Chéri* 1926, and *Gigi* 1944.

coleus /'kəʊliəs/ n. a plant of the genus *Coleus* with variegated coloured leaves. [from Greek *koleos* = sheath]

colic /'kɒlɪk/ n. a severe spasmodic abdominal pain. —**colicky** adj. [from French from Latin]

colitis /kə'laɪtɪs/ n. inflammation of the lining of the colon (large intestine) with diarrhoea (often bloody). It may be caused by food poisoning or some types of bacterial dysentery.

collaborate /kə'læbəreɪt/ v.i. to work jointly (with), especially at a literary or artistic production; to cooperate with the enemy. —**collaboration** /-'reɪʃən/ n., **collaborator** n. [from Latin *laborare* = work]

collage /kɒ'lɑ:ʒ/ n. a form or work of art in which various materials are arranged and glued to a backing. [French = gluing]

collagen /'kɒlədʒən/ n. a strong, rubbery ◊protein that plays a major structural role in the bodies of ◊vertebrates. Collagen supports the ear flaps and the tip of the nose in humans, as well as being the main constituent of tendons and ligaments. Bones are made up of collagen, with the mineral calcium phosphate providing increased rigidity. [from French from Greek *kolla* = glue]

collapse /kə'læps/ v.t./i. 1. to fall down or in suddenly. 2. to lose strength, force, or value suddenly; to cause to collapse. —n. the act or process of collapsing; a breakdown. [from Latin *collapsus* (*labi* = slip)]

collapsible /kə'læpsɪbəl/ adj. made so as to fold compactly.

collar /'kɒlə/ n. 1. a neckband, upright or turned over, of a coat, dress, shirt, etc. 2. a strap of leather etc. put round an animal's neck. 3. a restraining or connecting band, ring, or pipe in a machine etc. —*v.t.* (*slang*) to seize, to appropriate. —**collar beam,** a horizontal beam connecting two rafters. **collarbone** *n.* the bone joining the breastbone and shoulder blade, the clavicle. [from Anglo-French from Latin *collum* = neck]

collate /kə'leɪt/ *v.t.* to compare (texts etc.) in detail (*with*); to collect and arrange systematically. —**collator** *n.* [from Latin *collat-*, past participle stem of *conferre* = bring together]

collateral /kə'lætərəl/ *adj.* 1. side by side, parallel; additional but subordinate, contributory; connected but aside from the main subject, course, etc. 2. descended from the same stock but by a different line. — *n.* a collateral person or security. —**collateral security,** an additional security pledged; a security lodged by a third party, or consisting of stocks, shares, property, etc., as opposed to a personal guarantee. —**collaterally** *adv.* [from Latin *lateralis* = lateral]

collation /kə'leɪʃən/ *n.* 1. collating, being collated. 2. a light meal. [from Latin; sense 2 from *Collationes Patrum* (= *Lives of the Fathers*) read in Benedictine monasteries and followed by a light repast]

colleague /'kɒliːg/ *n.* a fellow official or worker, especially in a profession or business. [from French from Latin *collega* = partner in office (*legare* = depute)]

collect[1] /kə'lekt/ *v.t.i./i.* 1. to bring or come together, to assemble, to accumulate; to seek and obtain (books, stamps, etc.) systematically for addition to others; to get (contributions, tax, etc.) from a number of people. 2. to call for, to fetch. 3. to regain control of, to concentrate, to recover (*oneself,* one's thoughts, courage, etc.); (in past participle) not perturbed or distracted. —*adj.* & *adv.* (*US*) to be paid for by the recipient (of a telephone call, parcel, etc.). —**collection** *n.,* **collector** *n.* [from Old French from Latin *colligere* (*legere* = pick)]

collect[2] /'kɒlekt/ *n.* a short prayer of the Anglican or Roman Catholic Church, usually to be read on an appointed day.

collectable /kə'lektəbəl/ *adj.* suitable for being collected. —*n.* (usually in *plural*) a collectable item.

collective /kə'lektɪv/ *adj.* formed by, constituting, or denoting a collection; taken as a whole, aggregate, common. —*n.* 1. a collective farm. 2. a collective noun. —**collective bargaining,** negotiation of wages etc. by an organized body of employees. **collective farm,** a jointly operated amalgamation of several smallholdings. **collective noun,** a singular noun denoting a collection or number of individuals (e.g. *cattle, flock, troop*). **collective ownership,** ownership of land etc. by all for the benefit of all. —**collectivity** /-'tɪvɪtɪ/ *n.,* **collectively** *adv.* [from French or Latin *colligere*]

collective security a system for achieving international stability by an agreement among all states to unite against any aggressor. Such a commitment was embodied in the post-World War I League of Nations and also in the United Nations, although neither body was able to live up to the ideals of its founders.

collective unconscious in psychology, the term used for the shared pool of memories inherited from ancestors that Carl Jung suggested coexisted with individual ◊unconscious recollections, and which might affect individuals both for ill in precipitating mental disturbance, or for good in prompting achievements (for example, in the arts).

collectivism *n.* the theory or practice of collective ownership of land and means of production. —**collectivist** *n.*

collectivization *n.* the policy pursued by Stalin in the USSR after 1928 to reorganize agriculture by taking land into state or collective ownership. Much of this was achieved during the first two ◊Five-Year Plans but only with much coercion and loss of life among the peasantry.

colleen /kə'liːn/ *n.* (*Irish*) a girl. [Irish, diminutive of *caile* = countrywoman]

college /'kɒlɪdʒ/ *n.* 1. an establishment for higher or professional education; a body of teachers and students within a university, their premises; a small university; a school. 2. an organized body of persons with shared functions and privileges. [from Old French or Latin]

College of Arms or **Heralds' College** an English heraldic body formed in 1484 by Richard III incorporating the heralds attached to the Royal Household; reincorporated by Royal Charter of Philip and Mary in 1555. There are three Kings of Arms, six Heralds, and four Pursuivants, who specialize in genealogical and heraldic work. The College establishes the right to bear Arms, and the Kings of Arms grant Arms by letters patent. In Ireland the office of Ulster King of Arms was transferred in 1943 to the College of Arms in London and placed with that of Norroy King of Arms, who now has jurisdiction in Northern Ireland as well as in the north of England.

collegiate /kə'liːdʒiət/ *adj.* of a college or college student. —**collegiate church,** a church (other than a cathedral) with a chapter of canons but without bishops, or (*Scottish* and *US*) associated jointly with others under a group of pastors. [from Latin]

collenchyma *n.* a plant tissue composed of relatively elongated cells with thickened cell walls, in particular at the corners where adjacent cells meet. It is a supporting and strengthening tissue found in nonwoody plants, mainly in the stems and leaves.

collide /kə'laɪd/ *v.i.* to come into collision or conflict (*with*). [from Latin *collidere* (*laedere* = strike and hurt)]

collie /'kɒli/ *n.* a type of sheepdog originally bred in Britain. The **rough** and **smooth collies** are about 60 cm/2 ft tall, and have long narrow heads and muzzles. They may be light to dark brown or silver-grey, with black and white markings. The **border collie** is a working dog, often black and white, about 50 cm/20 in tall, with a dense coat. The **bearded collie** is about the same size, and is rather like an Old English sheepdog in appearance. [perhaps from coll = coal (as being originally black)]

collier /'kɒliə/ *n.* 1. a coal miner. 2. a ship that carries coal as its cargo.

Collier Lesley 1947– . British ballerina, a principal dancer of the Royal Ballet from 1972.

colliery *n.* a coal mine and its buildings.

collimator *n.* 1. a small telescope attached to a larger optical instrument to fix its line of sight. 2. an optical device for producing a nondivergent beam of light. 3. any device for limiting the size and angle of spread of a beam of radiation or particles.

collinear *adj.* in mathematics, lying on the same straight line.

Collingwood /'kɒlɪŋwʊd/ Cuthbert, Baron Collingwood 1748–1810. English admiral who served with Horatio Nelson in the West Indies against France and blockaded French ports in 1803–05; after Nelson's death he took command at the Battle of Trafalgar.

Collingwood Robin George 1889–1943. English philosopher who believed that any philosophical theory or position could only be properly understood within its own historical context and not from the point of view of the present. His aesthetic theory is outlined in *Principles of Art* 1938.

Collins /'kɒlɪnz/ Michael 1890–1922. Irish nationalist. He was a Sinn Féin leader, a founder and director of intelligence of the Irish Republican Army in 1919, minister for finance in the provisional government of the Irish Free State in 1922 (see ◊Ireland, Republic of), commander of the Free State forces in the civil war and for ten days head of state before being killed.

Collins Phil(lip David Charles) 1951– . English pop singer, drummer, and actor. A member of the group Genesis since 1970, he has also pursued a successful solo career since 1981, with hits (often new versions of old songs) including 'In the Air Tonight' 1981 and 'Groovy Kind of Love' 1988.

Collins (William) Wilkie 1824–1889. English author of mystery and suspense novels. He wrote *The Woman in White* 1860 (with its fat villain Count Fosco), often called the first English detective novel, and *The Moonstone* 1868 (with Sergeant Cuff, one of the first detectives in English literature).

collision /kə'lɪʒən/ *n.* colliding, the striking of one body against another. —**collision course,** a course or action that is bound to end in a collision. [from Latin]

collision theory a theory that explains chemical reactions and the way in which the rate of reaction alters when the conditions alter. For a reaction to occur the reactant particles must collide. Only a certain fraction of the total collisions cause chemical change; these are called **fruitful collisions**. These fruitful collisions have sufficient energy (activation energy) at the moment of impact to break the

Collins *English rock star Phil Collins*

existing bonds and form new bonds, resulting in the products of the reaction. Increasing the concentration of the reactants and raising the temperature bring about more collisions and therefore more fruitful collisions, increasing the rate of reaction.

collocate /'kɒləkeɪt/ *v.t.* to place (especially words) together or side by side. —**collocation** /-'keɪʃən/ *n.* [from Latin *locare* = place]

Collodi /kɒ'ləʊdi/ Carlo. Pen name of Carlo Lorenzini 1826–1890. Italian journalist and writer, who in 1881–83 wrote *The Adventure of Pinocchio*, the children's story of a wooden puppet that became a human boy.

colloid /'kɒlɔɪd/ *n.* **1.** a gluey substance. **2.** a noncrystalline substance composed of extremely small particles, forming a viscous solution with special properties; a finely divided substance dispersed in a gas, liquid, or solid. There are various types of colloids: those involving gases include an aerosol (a dispersion of a liquid or solid in a gas, as in fog or smoke) and a foam (a dispersion of a gas in a liquid). Liquids form both the dispersed and continuous phases in an **emulsion.** —**colloidal** *adj.* [from Greek *kolla* = glue]

collop /'kɒləp/ *n.* a slice of meat, an escalope. [from Scandinavian = fried bacon and eggs]

colloquial /kə'ləʊkwɪəl/ *adj.* belonging or proper to ordinary or familiar conversation, not formal or literary. —**colloquially** *adv.*

colloquialism *n.* a colloquial word or phrase; use of these.

colloquy /'kɒləkwɪ/ *n.* talk, a conversation. [from Latin *colloquium* (*loqui* = speak)]

collusion /kə'luː.ʒən/ *n.* a secret agreement or cooperation, especially for fraud or deceit. —**collusive** *adj.* [from Old French or Latin *collusio* (*ludere* = play)]

collywobbles /'kɒlɪwɒbəlz/ *n.pl.* (*colloquial*) rumblings or pain in the stomach; an apprehensive feeling.

cologne /kə'ləʊn/ *n.* eau-de-Cologne or other lightly scented liquid, used to cool or scent the skin.

Cologne (German *Köln*) industrial and commercial port in North Rhine–Westphalia, Germany, on the left bank of the Rhine, 35 km/22 mi from Düsseldorf; population (1988) 914,000. To the N is the Ruhr coalfield, on which many of Cologne's industries are based. They include motor vehicles, railway wagons, chemicals, and machine tools.

Colombia /kə'lɒmbɪə/ Republic of; country in South America, bounded N and W by the Caribbean and the Pacific and having borders with Panama to the NW, Venezuela to the E and NE, Brazil to the SE, and Peru and Ecuador to the SW; **area** 1,141,748 sq km/440,715 sq mi; **capital** Bogotá; **physical** the Andes mountains run N–S; flat coastland in the W and plains in the E; the Magdalena River runs N to the Caribbean Sea; **head of state and government** Virgilio Barco Vargas from 1986; **political system** emergent democratic republic; **exports** emeralds (world's largest producer), coffee (second largest world producer), cocaine (country's largest export), bananas, cotton, meat, sugar, oil, skins, hides; **population** (1990 est) 32,598,800

(mestizo 68%, white 20%, Amerindian 1%); **language** Spanish; **recent history** full independence was achieved from Spain in 1886. Civil war broke out in 1949; the Conservatives and Liberals formed a National Front. Civil unrest continued because of disillusionment with the government; Virgilio Barco Vargas was elected by a record margin in 1986.

Colombo /kə'lʌmbəʊ/ capital and principal seaport of Sri Lanka, on the W coast near the mouth of the Kelani; population (1981) 588,000, Greater Colombo about 1,000,000. It trades in tea, rubber, and cacao. It has iron-and steelworks and an oil refinery.

Colombo /kə'lɒmbəʊ/ Matteo Realdo *c.*1516–1559. Italian anatomist who discovered pulmonary circulation, the process of blood circulating from the heart to the lungs and back.

Colombo Plan a plan for cooperative economic development in S and SE Asia, established in 1951. The member countries meet annually to discuss economic and development plans such as irrigation, hydroelectric schemes, and technical training.

colon[1] /'kəʊlən/ *n.* a punctuation mark (:), used (i) to show that what follows is an example, list, or summary of what precedes it, or a contrasting idea; (ii) between numbers that are in proportion. [from Latin from Greek *kōlon* = limb, clause]

colon[2] *n.* the lower and greater part of the large intestine. —**colonic** /-'lɒnɪk/ *adj.* [from Old French or Latin from Greek]

Colón /kɒ'lɒn/ second largest city in Panama, at the Caribbean end of the Panama Canal; population (1980) 60,000.

colonel /'kɜːnəl/ *n.* an officer commanding a regiment, of rank next below brigadier. —**colonelcy** *n.* [from French from Italian *colonna* = column]

colonial /kə'ləʊnɪəl/ *adj.* of a colony or colonies. —*n.* an inhabitant of a colony. [French]

colonialism *n.* the policy of acquiring or maintaining colonies; (*derogatory*) an alleged policy of exploitation of colonies. —**colonialist** *n.*

colonist /'kɒlənɪst/ *n.* a settler in or inhabitant of a colony.

colonize /'kɒlənaɪz/ *v.t./i.* to establish a colony (in); to join a colony. —**colonization** /-'zeɪʃən/ *n.*

colonnade /kɒlə'neɪd/ *n.* a row of columns, especially supporting entablature or roof. [French *colonne* = column]

colony /'kɒlənɪ/ *n.* **1.** a settlement or settlers in a new country fully or partly subject to the mother country; their territory. **2.** a group of one nationality, occupation, etc., forming a community in a city. **3.** a group of animals that live close together. [from Latin *colonus* = farmer, from *colere* = cultivate]

colophon /'kɒləfən/ *n.* a tailpiece in a manuscript or book, giving the writer's or printer's name, date, etc.; a publisher's or printer's imprint, especially on a title page. [Latin from Greek = summit, finishing touch]

Colorado /kɒlə'rɑːdəʊ/ state of the central W USA; nicknamed Centennial State; **area** 269,700 sq km/104,104 sq mi; **capital** Denver; **physical** Great Plains in the E; the main ranges of the Rocky Mountains; high plateaux of the Colorado Basin in the W; **products** cereals, meat and dairy products, oil, coal, molybdenum, uranium, iron, steel, machinery; **population** (1986) 3,267,000; **history** Denver was founded following the discovery of gold in 1858; Colorado became a state in 1876.

coloration /kʌlə'reɪʃən/ *n.* colouring; an arrangement of colours. [French or from Latin *colorare* = colour]

coloratura /kɒlərə'tuərə/ *n.* an elaborate ornamentation of a vocal melody; a soprano skilled in coloratura singing. [Italian from Latin]

colossal /kə'lɒsəl/ *adj.* immense; (*colloquial*) remarkable, splendid. —**colossally** *adv.* [French *colosse* = colossus]

Colosseum /kɒlə'siːəm/ *n.* an amphitheatre in ancient Rome, begun by the emperor Vespasian to replace the one destroyed by fire during the reign of Nero, and completed by his son Titus in AD 80. It was 187 m/615 ft long and 49 m/160 ft high, and seated 50,000 people. Early Christians were martyred there by lions and gladiators. It could be flooded for mock sea battles.

colossus /kə'lɒsəs/ n. (plural **colossi**) 1. a statue of more than life size. 2. a gigantic person or personified empire etc. [Latin from Greek]

Colossus of Rhodes /ɒv 'rəʊdz/ a bronze statue of Apollo erected at the entrance to the harbour at Rhodes in 292–280 BC. Said to have been about 30 m/100 ft high, it was counted as one of the Seven Wonders of the World, but in 224 BC it fell as a result of an earthquake.

colostomy /kə'lɒstəmi/ n. an artificial opening through which the bowel can empty, made surgically by bringing part of the colon to the surface of the abdomen. [from *colon*[2] and Greek *stoma* = mouth]

colour /'kʌlə/ n. 1. the sensation produced on the eye by rays of light resolved (as by a prism) into different wavelengths or by selective reflection (*black* being the effect produced by no light or by a surface reflecting no rays, and *white* the effect produced by rays of unresolved light). From long to short wavelengths (from about 700 to 400 nanometres) the colours are red, orange, yellow, green, blue, indigo, and violet. 2. a particular variety of this. 3. the use of all colours (not only black and white), e. g. in photography. 4. a colouring substance. 5. pigmentation of the skin, especially when dark. 6. ruddiness of complexion. 7. (in *plural*) a coloured ribbon etc. given to regular or leading members of a sports team; the flag of a ship or regiment. 8. a show of reason; a pretext. 9. quality, mood, or variety in music, literature, etc. —*v.t./i.* 1. to put colour on, to paint, stain, or dye; to take on colour, to blush. 2. to give a special character or bias to. —**colour bar**, discrimination between white and nonwhite persons. **colour scheme**, a systematic combination of colours. **primary colours**, (of light) red, green, and violet, (of paints etc.) red, blue, and yellow, giving all others by mixture. **secondary colour**, a mixture of two primary colours. [from Old French from Latin]

colourant /'kʌlərənt/ n. colouring matter.

colour blindness a hereditary defect of vision that reduces the ability to discriminate certain colours, especially red and green. The condition is sex-linked, affecting men more than women. In the most common types there is confusion among the red–yellow–green range of colours; for example, many colour-blind observers are unable to distinguish red from yellow or yellow from green. The physiological cause of congenital colour blindness is not known, although it probably arises from some defect in the retinal receptors.

coloured adj. having colour; wholly or partly of nonwhite descent, or (**Coloured**, in South Africa) of mixed white and non white descent. —n. a coloured person; **Coloured**, (in South Africa) a person of mixed white and nonwhite descent.

colourful adj. full of colour or interest; with vivid details. —**colourfully** adv.

colouring n. 1. the disposition of colours; additives used to alter or improve the colour of processed foods. 2. a substance giving colour. 3. an artist's use of colour. 4. facial complexion.

colourless adj. without colour; lacking character or vividness.

colours, military flags or standards carried by military regiments, so-called because of the various combinations of colours employed to distinguish one country or one regiment from another.

colt /kəʊlt/ n. 1. a young male horse. 2. an inexperienced player in a team. [Old English = young donkey or camel]

Coltrane /kɒl'treɪn/ John (William) 1926–1967. US jazz saxophonist, who first came to prominence in 1955 with the Miles ◊Davis quintet, later playing with Thelonius Monk in 1957. A powerful and individual artist, Coltrane's performances featured much experimentation. His 1960s quartet was highly regarded for its innovations in melody and harmony.

coltsfoot /'kəʊltsfʊt/ n. a plant *Tussilago farfara* with large leaves and yellow flowers. Its Latin name refers to the fact that a cough medicine (Latin *tussis* = cough) was formerly made from it.

colugo n. a SE Asian climbing mammal of the genus *Cynocephalus*, order Dermoptera, about 60 cm/2 ft long including tail. It glides between forest trees using a flap of

Columbus An engraving of the portrait by Sebastiano del Piombo.

skin that extends from head to forelimb to hindlimb to tail. It may glide 130 m/425 ft or more, losing little height. It feeds largely on buds and leaves, and rests hanging upside down under branches.

Colum /'kɒləm/ Padraic 1881–1972. Irish poet and playwright who was associated with the foundation of the Abbey Theatre, Dublin, where his plays *Land* 1905 and *Thomas Muskerry* 1910, were performed. His *Collected Poems* 1932 show his gift for lyrical expression.

Columban, St /kə'lʌmbən/ 543–615. Irish Christian abbot. He was born in Leinster, studied at Bangor, and in about 585 went to the Vosges, France, with 12 other monks and founded the monastery of Luxeuil. Later, he preached in Switzerland, then went to Italy, where he built the abbey of Bobbio in the Apennines. Feast day 23 Nov.

Columba, St /kə'lʌmbə/ 521–597. Irish Christian abbot, missionary to Scotland. He was born in County Donegal of royal descent, and founded monasteries and churches in Ireland. In 563 he sailed with 12 companions to Iona, and built a monastery there that was to play a leading part in the conversion of Britain. Feast day 9 June. [Latin form of *Colum-cille* = Colum of the cell]

Columbia, District of /kə'lʌmbiə/ seat of the federal government of the USA, bordering the capital, Washington; area 178 sq km/69 sq mi. Situated on the Potomac River, it was ceded by Maryland as the national capital site in 1790.

Columbia Pictures /kə'lʌmbiə/ a US film production and distribution company founded in 1924. It grew out of a smaller company founded in 1920 by Harry and Jack Cohn and Joe Brandt. Under Harry Cohn's guidance, Columbia became a major studio by the 1940s, producing such commercial hits as *Gilda* 1946. After Cohn's death in 1958 the studio remained successful, producing international films such as *Lawrence of Arabia* 1962.

columbine /'kɒləmbaɪn/ n. any plant of the genus *Aquilegia* of the buttercup family Ranunculaceae. All are perennial herbs with divided leaves and flowers with spurred petals. In Britain *A. vulgaris* grows wild in woods and is a familiar garden plant. [from Old French from Latin *columba* = pigeon, from the resemblance of the flower to clustered pigeons]

columbium n. (Cb) former name for the chemical element ◊niobium. The name is still used occasionally in metallurgy.

Columbus /kə'lʌmbəs/ Christopher (Spanish *Cristobal Colón*) 1451–1506. Italian navigator and explorer who made four voyages to the New World: 1492 to San Salvador Island, Cuba, and Haiti; 1493–96 to Guadaloupe, Montserrat, Antigua, Puerto Rico, and Jamaica; 1498 to Trinidad and the mainland of South America; 1502–04 to Honduras and Nicaragua.

I must sail on until with the help of our Lord,
I discover land.

Christopher Columbus
to crew the day before sighting America 1492

column /'kɒləm/ n. **1.** a pillar, usually of circular section and with a base and capital. Cretan paintings reveal the existence of wooden columns in Aegean architecture, about 1500 BC. The Hittites, Assyrians, and Egyptians also used wooden columns, and they are a feature of the monumental architecture of China and Japan. In classical architecture there are five principal types of column; see ◊order **2.** something shaped like a pillar. **3.** a vertical division of a page in printed matter; a part of a newspaper devoted to a particular subject or by a regular writer. **4.** a vertical row of figures in accounts etc. **5.** a long, narrow formation of troops or vehicles etc. —**columnar** /kə'lʌmnə/ adj. [from Old French and Latin = pillar]
columnist /'kɒləmɪst/ n. a person regularly writing a newspaper column.
com- prefix (becoming **col-**before l, **cor-**before r, and **con-**before other consonants) with, jointly; altogether. [from Latin cum = with]
coma[1] /'kəumə/ n. (plural **comas**) in medicine, a state of deep unconsciousness from which the subject cannot be roused and in which the subject does not respond to pain. [from Latin from Greek kóma = deep sleep] = hair]
coma[2] n. (plural **comae**) **1.** in astronomy, the hazy cloud of gas and dust that surrounds the nucleus of a ◊comet. **2.** in optics, one of the geometrical aberrations of a lens, whereby skew rays from a point object make a comet-shaped spot on the image plane instead of meeting at a point. [from Latin from Greek komē = hair]
Comanche /kə'mæntʃɪ/ n. **1.** a North American Indian people of Texas and Oklahoma. **2.** their language. —adj. of this people or their language. [Spanish]
Comaneci /kɒmə'netʃ/ Nadia 1961– . Romanian gymnast. She won three gold medals at the 1976 Olympics at the age of 14, and was the first gymnast to record a perfect score of 10 in international competition.
comatose /'kəumətəus/ adj. in a coma, drowsy.
comb /kəum/ n. **1.** a toothed strip of rigid material for tidying and arranging the hair or for keeping it in place; part of a machine having a similar design or purpose. **2.** the red, fleshy crest of a fowl, especially the cock. **3.** a honeycomb. —v.t./i. to draw a comb through (hair); to dress (wool etc.) with a comb; (colloquial) to search (a place etc.) thoroughly. —**comb out,** to remove with a comb; (colloquial) to search out and get rid of (anything unwanted). [Old English]
combat /'kɒmbæt/ n. a fight, struggle, or contest. —v.t./i. to engage in a contest (with); to oppose, to strive against. [from French from Latin batuere = fight]
combatant /'kɒmbətənt/ adj. fighting, for fighting. —n. a person engaged in fighting.
combative /'kɒmbətɪv/ adj. pugnacious.
combe /kuːm/ variant of **coomb.**
combination /kɒmbɪ'neɪʃən/ n. **1.** combining, being combined; a combined state. **2.** a combined set of persons or things; a sequence of numbers or letters used to open a combination lock. **3.** in mathematics, a selection of a number of objects from some larger number of objects when no account is taken of order within any one arrangement, for example, 123, 213, and 312 are regarded as the same combination of three digits from 1234. **4.** (in plural) a one-piece undergarment for body and legs. —**combination lock,** a lock which can be opened only by a specific sequence of movements. —**combinative** /'kɒmbɪnətɪv/ adj.
Combination Laws laws passed in Britain in 1799 and 1800 making trade unionism illegal, introduced after the French Revolution for fear that the unions would become centres of political agitation. The unions continued to exist, but claimed to be friendly societies or went underground, until the acts were repealed in 1824, largely owing to the radical Francis Place.
combine[1] /kəm'baɪn/ v.t./i. to join or be joined into a group, set, or mixture; to cooperate. [from Old French or Latin combinare (bini = two together)]

combine[2] /'kɒmbaɪn/ n. a combination of persons or firms acting together in business. —**combine harvester,** a combined reaping and threshing machine.
combings /'kəumɪŋz/ n.pl. loose hair removed by a brush or comb.
combust /kəm'bʌst/ v.t. to subject to combustion.
combustible /kəm'bʌstɪbəl/ adj. capable of or used for burning. —n. a combustible thing. —**combustibility** /-'bɪlɪtɪ/ n.
combustion /kəm'bʌstʃən/ n. the process of burning, a chemical process (accompanied by heat and light) in which substances combine with oxygen. [from French or Latin combustere = burn up]
come /kʌm/ v.i. **1.** to move, be brought towards, or reach a place thought of as near or familiar to the speaker or hearer. **2.** to reach a specified point, condition, or result. **3.** to occur, to happen, to become present instead of future. **4.** to take or occupy a specified position in space or time. **5.** to become perceptible or known. **6.** to be available. **7.** to be descended, to be the result (of). **8.** (colloquial) to behave like. **9.** (in imperative) an exclamation of mild protest or encouragement. —**come about,** to happen. **come across,** to meet or find unexpectedly. **come along,** to make progress; (as imperative) hurry up. **comeback** n. a return to one's former successful position; (colloquial) a retort or retaliation. **come by,** to obtain. **comedown** n. a downfall; an anticlimax. **come-hither** adj. flirtatious, inviting. **come out,** to emerge, to become known; to go on strike; to be published; to declare oneself (for or against); to be satisfactorily visible in a photograph etc.; to erupt, to become covered in (a rash etc.); to emerge from an examination etc. with a specified result; to be solved. **come out with,** to say, to disclose. **come over,** (of a feeling etc.) to affect (a person); (colloquial) to be affected with (a feeling). **come round,** to pay an informal visit; to recover consciousness; to be converted to another person's opinion; (of a date) to recur. **come to,** to amount to, to be equivalent to; to recover consciousness. **come to pass,** to happen. **come up,** to arise for discussion etc., to occur. **comeuppance** n. (colloquial) a deserved punishment or rebuke. **come up with,** to present or produce (an idea etc.); to draw level with. —**comer** n. [Old English]
Comecon /'kɒmɪkɒn/ or CMEA the English name for an economic organization of Soviet-bloc countries, founded in 1949 and analogous to the European Economic Community. [acronym from Council for Mutual Economic Aid (or Assistance), translation of Russian title]
comedian /kə'meɪdɪən/ n. a humorous performer on the stage, television, etc.; an actor who plays comic parts. —**comedienne** /-'en/ n.fem.
Comédie Française /kɒmeɪ'di: frɒn'seɪz/ the French national theatre (for both comedy and tragedy) in Paris, founded in 1680 by Louis XIV. Its base is the Salle Richelieu on the right bank of the river Seine, and the Théâtre de l'Odéon, on the left bank, is a testing ground for avant-garde ideas.
comedy /'kɒmɪdɪ/ n. **1.** a light, amusing play or film, usually with a happy ending; the branch of drama that consists of such plays. The earliest comic tradition developed in ancient Greece, in the farcical satires of Aristophanes. Great comic playwrights include Shakespeare, Molière, Goldoni, Marivaux, George Bernard Shaw, and Oscar Wilde. Genres of comedy include pantomime, satire, farce, black comedy, and ◊commedia dell'arte. **2.** humour, humorous incidents in life. [from Old French from Latin from Greek komos = revel]
comely /'kʌmlɪ/ adj. handsome, good-looking. **comeliness** n.
comestibles /kə'mestɪbəlz/ n.pl. (formal or jocular) things to eat. [from French from Latin comedere = eat]
comet /'kɒmɪt/ n. a luminous object seen in the night sky, consisting of an icy nucleus and a tail of evaporated gas and dust particles. —**cometary** adj. [from French from Latin from Greek = long-haired]
comfit /'kʌmfɪt/ n. (archaic) a sweet consisting of a nut etc. in sugar. [from Old French from Latin confectum (facere = make)]
comfort /'kʌmfət/ n. **1.** a state of physical or mental wellbeing or contentment. **2.** relief of suffering or grief, consolation; a person or thing that gives this. **3.** (in plural) things that allow ease or wellbeing in life. —v.t. to give

comfort to, to soothe in grief, to console. —**comforter** *n*. [from Old French from Latin *confortare* = strengthen (*fortis* = strong)]

comfortable /'kʌmfətəbəl/ *adj*. 1. giving or feeling ease and contentment; not close or restricted. —**comfortably** *adv*.

comfrey /'kʌmfrɪ/ *n*. any plant of the genus *Symphytum* of the borage family Boraginaceae with rough, hairy leaves and small bell-shaped flowers, found in Europe and W Asia. Up to 1.2 m/4 ft tall, it has hairy, winged stems, lanceolate (tapering) leaves, and white, yellowish, purple, or pink flowers in drooping clusters. [from Anglo-French from Latin *conferva* (*fervē* = boil)]

comfy /'kʌmfɪ/ *adj*. (*colloquial*) comfortable.

comic /'kɒmɪk/ *adj*. of or like comedy; causing amusement or laughter. —*n*. 1. a comedian. 2. a paper (usually for children) with series of strip cartoons. —**comical** *adj*., **comically** *adv*. [from Latin]

comic strip or **strip cartoon** a sequence of several frames of drawings in ◊cartoon style. Strips, which may work independently or form instalments of a serial, are usually humorous or satirical in content. Longer stories in comic strip form are published separately as comic books.

Comines /kɒ'miːn/ Philippe de *c*.1445–1509. French diplomat in the service of Charles the Bold, Louis XI, and Charles VIII; author of *Mémoires* 1489–98.

Cominform /'kɒmɪnfɔːm/ the **Communist Information Bureau** 1947–56, established by the Soviet politician Andrei Zhdanov (1896–1948) to exchange information between European communist parties. Yugoslavia was expelled in 1948. [acronym]

coming /'kʌmɪŋ/ *adj*. approaching next; likely to be important in the near future. —*n*. arrival.

Comintern /'kɒmɪntɜːn/ acronym from **Communist International**.

comity /'kɒmɪtɪ/ *n*. courtesy, friendship; an association of nations etc. for their mutual benefit. —**comity of nations**, nations' friendly recognition of each other's laws and customs. [from Latin *comis* = courteous]

comma *n*. the punctuation mark (,), indicating a slight pause or break between parts of a sentence, or separating words or figures in a list. [from Latin from Greek = clause]

command /kə'mɑːnd/ *n*. 1. a statement, given with authority, that some action must be performed. 2. the right to control others, authority. 3. ability to use something, mastery. 4. forces or a district under a commander. —*v.t./i.* 1. to give a command or order to; to have authority over. 2. to deserve and get. 3. to dominate (a strategic position) from a superior height, to look down over. —**Command paper**, a paper laid before Parliament by royal command. **command performance**, a performance of a film, show, etc., by royal request. [from Anglo-French from Latin = commend]

commandant /'kɒməndænt/ *n*. a commanding officer, especially of a military academy or prisoner-of-war camp. [French]

commandeer /kɒmən'dɪə/ *v.t.* to seize for military use; to seize for one's own purposes. [from South African Dutch from French = command]

commander /kə'mɑːndə/ *n*. 1. one who commands, especially a naval officer of rank next below captain. 2. (in full **Knight Commander**) a member of the higher class in some orders of knighthood. —**commander-in-chief** *n*. the supreme commander. [from Old French]

command language in computing, a set of commands and the rules governing their use by which users control a program. For example, an ◊operating system may have commands such as SAVE and DELETE, or a payroll program may have commands for adding and amending staff records.

commandment /kə'mɑːndmənt/ *n*. a divine command, especially (**Commandment**) one of the ten given to Moses (Exodus 20: 1–17).

commando /kə'mɑːndəʊ/ *n*. (*plural* **commandos**) 1. a party called out for military purposes. 2. in the Boer War, a unit of the Boer army composed of the militia of an electoral district. 3. in the Second World War, a member of a military unit specially trained for making raids and assaults; such a unit. [Portuguese]

commedia dell'arte a popular form of Italian improvised drama in the 16th and 17th centuries, performed by trained troupes of actors and involving stock characters and situations. It exerted considerable influence on writers such as Molière and Goldoni, and on the genres of ◊pantomime, harlequinade, and the ◊*Punch and Judy* show. It laid the foundation for a tradition of mime, strong in France, that has continued with the contemporary mime of Jean-Louis Barrault and Marcel Marceau.

comme il faut /kɒm iːl 'fəʊ/ proper, properly, as it should be. [French = as is necessary]

commemorate /kə'meməreɪt/ *v.t.* to keep in memory by a celebration or ceremony; to be a memorial to. —**commemoration** /-'reɪʃən/ *n*., **commemorative** *adj*. [from Latin *commemorare* (*memor* = mindful)]

commence /kə'mens/ *v.t.* to begin. —**commencement** *n*. [from Old French from Latin (*initiare* = initiate)]

commend /kə'mend/ *v.t.* 1. to praise; to recommend. 2. to entrust, to commit. —**commendation** /-'deɪʃən/ *n*., **commendatory** /-'men-/ *adj*. [from Latin *commendare* (*mandare* = entrust)]

commendable /kə'mendəbəl/ *adj*. praiseworthy. —**commendably** *adv*. [from Old French]

commensal /kə'mensəl/ *adj*. living in a form of symbiosis that is beneficial to one species and neither harmful nor beneficial to the other. —*n*. a plant or animal living thus. —**commensalism** *n*. [from French or Latin *mensa* = table]

commensurable /kə'menʃærəbəl/ *adj*. measurable by the same standard (*with* or *to*); proportionate *to*. [from Latin]

commensurate /kə'menʃərət/ *adj*. coextensive (*with*); proportionate (*to* or *with*).

comment /'kɒment/ *n*. a brief critical or explanatory remark or note, an opinion. —*v.i.* to utter or write comments. [from Latin = contrivance, interpretation (*comminisci* = devise)]

commentary /'kɒmentərɪ/ *n*. a series of descriptive comments on an event or performance; a set of explanatory notes on a text etc.

commentate /'kɒmənteɪt/ *v.i.* to act as a commentator.

commentator *n*. the speaker or writer of a commentary; one who comments on current events. [Latin]

commerce /'kɒmɜːs/ *n*. buying and selling, all forms of trading, including banking, insurance, etc. [French or from Latin *commercium* (*merx* = merchandise)]

commercial /kə'mɜːʃəl/ *adj*. of or engaged in commerce; concerned chiefly with financial profit; (of broadcasting) in which advertisements are included to provide finance. —*n*. a broadcast advertisement. —**commercial traveller**, a firm's representative visiting shops etc. to obtain orders. —**commercially** *adv*.

commercialism *n*. commercial practices and attitudes.

commercialize *v.t.* to make commercial; to seek to make profitable. —**commercialization** /-'zeɪʃən/ *n*.

commie /'kɒmɪ/ *n*. (*slang, derogatory*) a communist.

commination /kɒmɪ'neɪʃən/ *n*. threatening of divine vengeance. —**comminatory** /'kɒmɪneɪtərɪ/ *adj*. [from Latin *minare* = threaten]

commingle /kə'mɪŋgəl/ *v.t./i.* (*literary*) to mix together.

comminute /'kɒmɪnjuːt/ *v.t.* 1. to reduce to small fragments. 2. to divide (property) into small portions. —**comminuted fracture**, one producing multiple fragments of bone. —**comminution** /-'njuːʃən/ *n*. [from Latin *minuere* = lessen]

commiserate /kə'mɪzəreɪt/ *v.i.* to express pity, to sympathize. —**commiseration** /-'reɪʃən/ *n*., **commiserative** *adj*. [from Latin *miserari* = pity]

commissar /'kɒmɪsɑː/ *n*. (*historical*) a head of a government department of the USSR. [from Russian from French]

commissariat /kɒmɪ'seərɪət/ *n*. 1. the department responsible for the supply of food etc. for an army; the food supplied. 2. (*historical*) a government department of the USSR. [French]

commissary /'kɒmɪsərɪ/ *n*. 1. a deputy, a delegate. 2. (*US*) a store where food and other supplies are sold at a military base. 3. (*US*) a restaurant in a film studio or factory etc. [from Latin = person in charge]

commission /kə'mɪʃən/ *n*. 1. the giving of authority to a person to perform a task; the task so given; such a person's authority or instructions. 2. a body or board of persons constituted to perform certain duties. 3. a warrant conferring authority, especially that of an officer in the armed forces above a certain rank. 4. the payment or percentage received by an agent. 5. committing, performance (e.g. of a crime). —*v.t.* 1. to give a commission to; to employ (a person) *to* do a piece of work. 2. to prepare (a ship) for active service. 3. to bring (a machine etc.) into operation. —**commission agent**, a bookmaker. **in** *or* **out of commission**, ready or not ready for use. [from Old French from Latin]

commissionaire /kəmɪʃəˈneə/ *n.* an attendant at the door of a theatre, office, etc. [French]

commissioner /kəˈmɪʃənə/ *n.* 1. one who is appointed by commission (e.g. the head of Scotland Yard). 2. a member of a commission. 3. an official representing the government in a district, department, etc. —**Commissioner for Oaths**, a solicitor authorized to administer oaths in affidavits etc. [from Latin]

commissure /ˈkɒmɪsjuə/ *n.* the joint between two bones; a junction or seam. [from Latin = junction]

commit /kəˈmɪt/ *v.t.* (**-tt-**) 1. to be the doer of (a crime etc.). 2. to entrust for safe keeping or treatment. 3. to pledge, to bind with an obligation. —**commit to memory**, to memorize. [from Latin *committere* = entrust (*mittere* = send)]

commitment /kəˈmɪtmənt/ *n.* 1. committing, being committed. 2. an engagement or involvement that restricts freedom of action or choice. 3. an obligation or pledge.

committal /kəˈmɪtəl/ *n.* the action of committing, especially to prison or for burial or cremation.

committal proceedings in the UK, a preliminary hearing in a magistrate's court to decide whether there is a case to answer before a higher court.

committee /kəˈmɪtɪ/ *n.* a group of persons appointed by (and usually out of) a larger body, to attend to special business or manage the business of a club etc.

Committee of Imperial Defence an informal group established in 1902 to coordinate planning of the British Empire's defence forces. Initially meeting on a temporary basis, it was established permanently in 1904. Members were usually cabinet ministers concerned with defence, military leaders, and key civil servants.

commode /kəˈməud/ *n.* 1. a chamber pot mounted in a chair or box with a cover. 2. a chest of drawers. [French from Latin *commodus* = convenient]

commodious /kəˈməudiəs/ *adj.* roomy. [from French from Latin]

commodity /kəˈmɒdɪtɪ/ *n.* an article of trade, especially a product as opposed to a service. —**commodity market**, a market dealing in raw or semiraw materials that are amenable to grading and that can be stored for considerable periods without deterioration. [from Old French or Latin]

commodore /ˈkɒmədɔː/ *n.* a naval officer next below rear admiral; the commander of a squadron or other division of a fleet; the president of a yacht club. [from Dutch from French = commander]

Commodus /ˈkɒmədəs/ Lucius Aelius Aurelius AD 161–192. Roman emperor from 180, son of Marcus Aurelius Antoninus. He was a tyrant, spending lavishly on gladiatorial combats, confiscating the property of the wealthy, persecuting the Senate, and renaming Rome 'Colonia Commodia'. He was strangled at the instigation of his mistress and advisors, who had discovered themselves on the emperor's death list.'

common /ˈkɒmən/ *adj.* 1. shared by, coming from, or affecting all concerned; of or belonging to the whole community, public. 2. occurring often; ordinary, of the most familiar or numerous kind. 3. without special rank or position; (in *plural*) the common people. 4. of inferior quality; ill-bred, unrefined. 5. in grammar, (of a noun) referring to any one of a class; (of gender) referring to individuals of either sex. —*n.* unenclosed wasteland and pasture used in common by the inhabitants of a parish or district or the community at large. Commons originated in the Middle Ages, when every manor had a large area of unenclosed, uncultivated land over which freeholders had rights to take the natural produce. All common land (such as village greens) must now be registered under the Commons Registration Act 1965; otherwise the rights of common are lost. —**Common Era**, the Christian era. **common law**, unwritten law based on custom and precedent. **common-law husband** *or* **wife**, one recognized by common law without

an official ceremony, usually after a period of cohabitation. **Common Market**, the European Economic Community. **common or garden**, (*colloquial*) ordinary. **common room** *n.* a room for social use by students or teachers at a college etc. **common sense**, good practical sense in everyday matters. **common time**, in music, four crotchets in a bar. **in common**, shared by several (especially as an interest or characteristic); in joint use. **the Commons**, the House of Commons. **commonly** *adv.*, **commonness** *n.* [from Old French from Latin]

Common Agricultural Policy (CAP) a system that allows the member countries of the European Community (EC) jointly to organize and control agricultural production within their boundaries. The objectives of the CAP were outlined in the Treaty of Rome: to increase agricultural productivity, to provide a fair standard of living for farmers and their employees, to stabilize markets, and to assure the availability of supply at a price that was reasonable to the consumer.

commonality /kɒməˈnælɪtɪ/ *n.* 1. the sharing of an attribute. 2. a common occurrence.

commonalty /ˈkɒmənəltɪ/ *n.* the common people; the general body (of humankind etc.).

commoner /ˈkɒmənə/ *n.* 1. a member of the common people (below the rank of peer). 2. a student without financial support from a college.

common logarithms ◊logarithms to the base ten.

commonplace *adj.* ordinary, usual; lacking in originality or individuality. —*n.* a commonplace event, topic, etc., or remark. [translation of Latin and Greek (literally common place) = general theme]

Common Prayer, Book of the service book of the Church of England, based largely on the Roman breviary. The first service book in English was known as the *First Prayer Book of Edward VI*, published in 1549, and is the basis of the *Book of Common Prayer* still, although not exclusively, in use.

commonsensical /kɒmənˈsensɪkəl/ *adj.* having or marked by common sense.

Commons, House of the lower but more powerful of the two parts of the British and Canadian ◊parliaments. In the UK, the House of Commons consists of 650 elected members of Parliament each of whom represents a constituency. Its functions are to debate, legislate, and to scrutinize the activities of government.

commonwealth /ˈkɒmənwelθ/ *n.* 1. an independent state or community. 2. a republic or democratic state. 3. a federation of states. —**the Commonwealth**, (i) the republican government of Britain between the execution of Charles I in 1649 and the Restoration in 1660; (ii) see ◊Commonwealth, the (British), below. **New Commonwealth**, those countries which have achieved self-government within the Commonwealth since 1945.

Commonwealth conference any consultation between the prime ministers (or defence, finance, foreign, or other ministers) of the sovereign independent members of the Commonwealth. These are informal discussion meetings, and the implementation of policies is decided by individual governments. Recent Commonwealth conferences have been in Singapore 1971, the first outside the UK; Sydney 1978, the first regional meeting; Lusaka 1979, the first regular session in Africa; and Vancouver 1987.

Commonwealth Day a public holiday in parts of the Commonwealth, celebrated on the second Monday in March (the official birthday of Elizabeth II). It was called **Empire Day** until 1958 and celebrated on 24 May (Queen Victoria's birthday) until 1966.

Commonwealth Development Corporation an organization founded as the Colonial Development Corporation in 1948 to aid the development of dependent Commonwealth territories; the change of name and extension of its activities to include those now independent were announced in 1962.

Commonwealth Games a multisport gathering of competitors from British Commonwealth countries. Held every four years, the first meeting (known as the British Empire Games) was at Hamilton, Canada, Aug 1930.

Commonwealth Immigration Acts successive Acts which attempted to regulate the entry into the UK of

Commonwealth, British

Country	Capital	(Area in 1,000 sq km)
IN AFRICA		
Botswana	Gaborone	(575)
British Indian Ocean Terr.	Victoria	(0.2)
Gambia	Banjul	(11)
Ghana	Accra	(239)
Kenya	Nairobi	(583)
Lesotho	Maseru	(30)
Malawi	Zomba	(117)
Mauritius	Port Louis	(2)
Nigeria	Lagos	(924)
St Helena	Jamestown	(0.1)
Seychelles	Victoria	(65)
Sierra Leone	Freetown	(73)
Swaziland	Mbabane	(17)
Tanzania	Dodoma	(943)
Uganda	Kampala	(236)
Zambia	Lusaka	(752)
Zimbabwe	Salisbury	(391)
IN THE AMERICAS		
Anguilla	The Valley	(0.09)
Antigua	St John's	(0.4)
Bahamas	Nassau	(14)
Barbados	Bridgetown	(0.4)
Belize	Belmopan	(23)
Bermuda	Hamilton	(0.05)
Brit. Virgin Is.	Road Town	(0.2)
Canada	Ottawa	(9,976)
Cayman Islands	Georgetown	(0.3)
Dominica	Roseau	(0.7)
Falkland Is.	Stanley	(12)
Grenada	St George's	(0.3)
Guyana	Georgetown	(210)
Jamaica	Kingston	(12)
Montserrat	Plymouth	(0.1)
St Christopher-Nevis	Basseterre Charlestown	(0.4)
St Lucia	Castries	(0.6)
St Vincent and the Grenadines	Kingstown	(0.2)
Trinidad and Tobago	Port of Spain	(0.5)
Turks and Caicos Is.	Grand Turk	(0.4)
IN THE ANTARCTIC		
Australian Antarctic Terr.		(5,403)
Brit. Antarctic Terr.		(390)
Falklands Is. Dependencies		(1.6)
(N.Z.) Ross Dependency		(453)

Country	Capital	(Area in 1,000 sq km)
IN ASIA		
Bangladesh	Dacca	(143)
Brunei	Bandar Seri Begawan	(6)
Cyprus	Nicosia	(9)
Hong Kong	Victoria	(1.2)
India	Delhi	(3,215)
Malaysia, Rep. of	Kuala Lumpur	(332)
Maldives	Malé	(0.3)
Singapore	Singapore	(0.6)
Sri Lanka	Colombo	(66)
IN AUSTRALASIA AND THE PACIFIC		
Australia	Canberra	(7,704)
Norfolk Island		(0.03)
Fiji	Suva	(18)
Kiribati	Tarawa	(0.7)
*Nauru		(0.02)
New Zealand	Wellington	(269)
Cook Islands		(0.2)
Niue Island		(0.3)
Tokelau Islands		(0.01)
Papua New Guinea	Port Moresby	(475)
Pitcairn		(0.005)
Solomon Islands	Honiara	(30)
Tonga	Nuku'alofa	(0.7)
*Tuvalu	Funafuti	(0.02)
Vanuatu	Vila	(15)
Western Samoa	Apia	(3)
IN EUROPE		
*United Kingdom		
England	London	(131)
Wales	Cardiff	(21)
Scotland	Edinburgh	(79)
N. Ireland	Belfast	(14)
Isle of Man	Douglas	(0.5)
Channel Islands		(0.2)
Gibraltar	Gibraltar	(0.006)
Malta	Valletta	(0.3)
TOTAL		(33,932)

*Special members

British subjects from the Commonwealth. The Commonwealth Immigration Act passed by the Conservative government in 1962 ruled that Commonwealth immigrants entering Britain must have employment or be able to offer required skills.

Commonwealth, the (British) a voluntary association of 48 states that have been or still are ruled by Britain (see ◊British Empire). Independent states are full members of the Commonwealth, while dependent territories, such as colonies and protectorates, rank as Commonwealth countries. Small self-governing countries, such as Nauru, may have special status. The Commonwealth is founded more on tradition and sentiment than political or economic factors. Queen Elizabeth II is the formal head but not the ruler of member states. The Commonwealth secretariat, headed from Oct 1989 by Nigerian Emeka Anyaoko as secretary general, is based in London.

commotion /kə'məʊʃən/ n. uproar, fuss and disturbance. [from Old French or Latin]

communal /'kɒmjunəl/ adj. shared between the members of a group or community. —**communally** adv., **communalistic** /-'lɪstɪk/ adj. [French from Latin]

commune[1] /'kɒmju:n/ n. 1. a group of people, not all of one family, sharing living arrangements and goods. 2. a small district of local government in France and certain other European countries. [from Latin communia (communis = common)]

commune[2] /kɒ'mju:n/ v.i. to communicate mentally or spiritually, to feel in close touch (with). [from French = share]

Commune, Paris /'kɒmju:n/ two periods of government in France; see ◊Paris Commune.

communicable /kə'mju:nɪkəbəl/ adj. that can be communicated. [from Old French or Latin]

communicant /kə'mju:nɪkənt/ *n.* **1.** a person who receives Holy Communion; one who does this regularly. **2.** one who communicates information.

communicate /kə'mju:nɪkeɪt/ *v.t./i.* **1.** to impart, to transmit; to make known; to succeed in conveying information. **2.** to have social dealings (*with*). **3.** to be connected. **4.** to receive Holy Communion. [from Latin *communicare*]

communication /kəmju:nɪ'keɪʃən/ *n.* **1.** communicating; in biology, the signalling of information by one organism to another, usually with the intention of altering the recipient's behaviour. Signals used in communication may be visual, auditory, olfactory (such as the odours released by the scent glands of a deer), electrical (as in the pulses emitted by electric fish), or tactile. **2.** something that communicates information, sent or transmitted from one person to another; a letter or message. **3.** a means of communicating (connecting); e. g. a road, railway, telegraph line, radio, etc. **4.** (in *plural*) the science and practice of transmitting information.

communications satellite a relay station in space for sending telephone, television, telex, and other messages around the world. Messages are sent to and from the satellites via ground stations. Most communications satellites are in ◊geostationary orbit, appearing to hang fixed over one point on the Earth's surface.

communicative /kə'mju:nɪkətɪv/ *adj.* ready and willing to talk and impart information.

communion /kə'mju:nɪən/ *n.* **1.** fellowship, having ideas and beliefs in common. **2.** a body of Christians of the same denomination. **3.** social dealings. —(**Holy**) **Communion**, the Eucharist. **communion of saints**, fellowship of Christians past and present. [from Old French or Latin]

communiqué /kə'mju:nɪkeɪ/ *n.* an official communication or report. [French = communicated]

communism /'kɒmju:nɪzəm/ *n.* **1.** a system of society with vesting of property in the community, each member working for the common benefit according to his capacity and receiving according to his needs. **2.** or **Communism**, a movement or political party advocating communism, especially as derived from Marxism; a communistic form of society established in the 20th century. The first communist state was the USSR after the revolution of 1917. Revolutionary socialist parties and groups united to form communist parties in other countries (in the UK in 1920). After World War II, communism was enforced in those countries that came under Soviet occupation. China emerged after 1961 as a rival to the USSR in world communist leadership, and other countries attempted to adapt communism to their own needs. The late 1980s saw a movement for more individual freedom in many communist countries, culminating in the abolition or overthrow of communist rule in some Eastern European countries, and further state repression in China. [from French (*commun* = common)]

Communism Peak (Russian *Pik Kommunizma*) the highest mountain in the USSR, in the Pamir range in Tadzhikistan; 7,495 m/24,599 ft.

communist /'kɒmjʊnɪst/ *n.* **1.** a supporter of communism. **2. Communist**, a member or supporter of a communist party. —**communistic** /-'nɪstɪk/ *adj.*

community /kə'mju:nɪtɪ/ *n.* **1.** a body of people living in one place, district, or country; a group having a religion, race, profession, etc., in common; a commune. **2.** fellowship (*of* interest etc.); the state of being shared or held in common; joint ownership or liability. **3.** in ecology, an assemblage of plants, animals, and other organisms living within a circumscribed area. Communities are usually named by reference to a dominant feature such as characteristic plant species (for example, a beech wood community), or a prominent physical feature (for example, a freshwater pond community). —**community centre**, a place providing social, recreational, and educational facilities for a neighbourhood. **community council**, in Wales, the name for a ◊parish council. **community charge**, a form of local tax introduced in Scotland in 1989 and in England and Wales in 1990, replacing domestic rates; commonly known as the ◊poll tax. **community home**, a centre for housing young offenders. **community singing**, organized singing in chorus by a large gathering of people. [from Old French from Latin]

community architecture a movement enabling people to work directly with architects in the design and building of their own homes and neighbourhoods. It is an approach strongly encouraged by the Prince of Wales.

community school/education the philosophy asserting that educational institutions are more effective if they involve all members of the surrounding community. It was pioneered by Henry Morris during his time as chief education officer for Cambridgeshire 1922–54.

community service a provision under which minor offenders are sentenced to work in the service of the community (aiding children, the elderly, or the handicapped), instead of prison.

commutative /kə'mju:tətɪv/ *adj.* (of a mathematical operation) producing the same result regardless of the order in which the quantities are taken (e. g. $3 + 4 = 7$, $4 + 3 = 7$). [from French or Latin]

commutator *n.* a device in a DC (direct current) electric motor that reverses the current flowing in the armature coils as the armature rotates. A DC generator, or ◊dynamo, uses a commutator to convert the AC (alternating current) generated in the armature coils into DC. A commutator consists of opposite pairs of conductors insulated from one another, and contact to an external circuit is provided by carbon or metal brushes.

commute /kə'mju:t/ *v.t./i.* **1.** to travel regularly by train, bus, or car to and from one's daily work in a city etc. **2.** to exchange *for*; to change (one form of payment or obligation) *for* or *into* another; to change (a punishment) *to* another less severe. —**commutation** /-'teɪʃən/ *n.* [from Latin *mutare* = change]

commuter *n.* one who commutes to and from work.

Comoros /'kɒmərəʊz/ Federal Islamic Republic of; group of islands in the Indian Ocean between Madagascar and the E coast of Africa. Three of them, Njazidja, Nzwani, and Mwali, form the republic of Comoros. The fourth island in the group, Mayotte, is a French dependency; **area** 1,862 sq km/719 sq mi; **capital** Moroni; **physical** the islands are volcanic; they lie at the N end of the Mozambique Channel; **head of state and government** Said Mohammad Djohar (interim adminstration); **political system** authoritarian nationalism; **exports** copra, vanilla, cocoa, sisal, coffee, cloves, essential oils; **population** (1990 est) 459,000; **language** Comorian (Swahili and Arabic dialect), Makua, French, Arabic (official); **recent history** independence was achieved in 1975, but Mayotte remained part of France; the Comoros joined the United Nations the same year. Two presidents have been killed in attempts to gain control of the government; an interim president is in power.

compact[1] /kəm'pækt/ *adj.* closely or neatly packed together; concise. —*v.t.* to make compact. —/'kɒm-/ *n.* a small, flat case for face powder. —**compactly** *adv.*, **compactness** *n.* [from Latin *pingere* = fasten]

compact[2] /'kɒmpækt/ *n.* an agreement, a contract. [from Latin *compactum*]

compact disc a disc for digital information storage, about 12 cm/4.5 in across, mainly used for music, when it has up to an hour's playing time on one side. It is made of aluminium with a transparent plastic coating; the metal disc underneath is etched by a ◊laser beam with microscopic pits that carry a digital code representing the sounds. During playback, a laser beam reads the code and produces signals that are changed into near-exact replicas of the original sounds.

companion /kəm'pænjən/ *n.* **1.** one who associates with or accompanies another; (formerly) a woman paid to live with and accompany another. **2.** a member of the lowest grade of some orders of knighthood. **3.** a handbook or reference book dealing with a specified subject. **4.** a thing that matches or accompanies another. —**companionway** *n.* a staircase from a ship's deck to the saloon or cabins. —**companionship** *n.* [from Old French from Latin]

companionable *adj.* sociable, friendly. —**companionably** *adv.*

Companion of Honour a member of a British order of chivalry, founded by George V in 1917. The order is of one class only, and carries no title, but Companions append 'CH' to their names. The number is limited to 65 and the award is made to both men and women.

company /'kʌmpənɪ/ *n.* **1.** being with another or others. **2.** a number of people assembled, guests; a person's associates; a body of persons assembled for a common (especially commercial) object; a group of actors etc.; a subdivision of an infantry battalion. —**part company**, to go different ways after being together; to cease associating (*with*). [from Anglo-French]

comparable /'kɒmpərəbəl, (disputed usage) -'pær-/ *adj.* that can be compared (*with* or *to*). —**comparability** /-'bılıtı/ *n.*, **comparably** *adv.* [from Old French]

comparative /kəm'pærətıv/ *adj.* perceptible or estimated by comparison; of or involving comparison; considered in relation to each other. —*n.* in grammar, the comparative degree. —**comparative adjective, adverb**, one in the comparative degree. **comparative degree**, the form expressing a higher degree of a quality (e. g. *braver, more quickly*). [from Latin]

comparative advantage a law of international trade first elaborated by David Ricardo (1772–1823) showing that trade becomes advantageous if the cost of production of particular items differs between one country and another.

compare /kəm'peə/ *v.t./i.* 1. to estimate the similarity of (one thing *with* or *to* another; two things); to liken or regard as similar (*to*); to bear comparison *with*. 2. to form the comparative and superlative degrees of (an adjective or adverb). —*n.* (*literary*) comparison. [from Old French from Latin *comparare* (*par* = equal)]

comparison /kəm'pærısən/ *n.* comparing. —**bear comparison**, to be able to be compared favourably **with. degrees of comparison**, in grammar, the positive, comparative, and superlative (of adjectives and adverbs).

compartment /kəm'pɑːtmənt/ *n.* a division separated by partitions, e. g. in a railway carriage; a watertight division of a ship. [from French from Italian from Latin *partiri* = share]

compartmental /kɒmpɑ:'mentəl/ *adj.* of or divided into compartments or categories.

compartmentalize /kɒmpɑ:t'mentəlaız/ *v.t.* to divide into compartments or categories.

compass /'kʌmpəs/ *n.* 1. an instrument showing the magnetic north and bearings from it. The most commonly used is a magnetic compass, consisting of a thin piece of magnetic material with the north-seeking pole indicated, free to rotate on a pivot and mounted on a compass card on which the points of the compass are marked. When the compass is properly adjusted and used, the north-seeking pole will point to the magnetic north, from which true north can be found from tables of magnetic corrections. 2. (often in *plural*) an instrument for taking measurements and describing circles, with two legs connected at one end by a movable joint. 3. circumference, boundary; area, extent, scope; the range of a voice or musical instrument. —**compass rose**, a circle showing the 32 principal points of the compass. [from Old French from Latin *passus* = step]

compassion /kəm'pæʃən/ *n.* a feeling of pity inclining one to be helpful or show mercy. [from Old French from Latin *pati* = suffer]

compassionate /kəm'pæʃənət/ *adj.* sympathetic, showing compassion. —**compassionate leave**, leave granted on grounds of bereavement etc. —**compassionately** *adv.*

compatible /kəm'pætıbəl/ *adj.* 1. able to coexist (*with*); mutually tolerant. 2. (of equipment etc.) able to be used in combination. —**compatibility** /-'bılıtı/ *n.* [French from Latin]

compatriot /kəm'pætrıət/ *n.* a fellow countryman. [from French from Latin *patria* = mother country]

compeer /kəm'pıə/ *n.* a person of equal standing; a comrade. [from Old French]

compel /kəm'pel/ *v.t.* (-ll-) 1. to use irresistible force or influence so as to cause (a person etc.) to do something; to allow no choice of action. 2. to arouse (a feeling) irresistibly. [from Latin *pellere* = drive]

compelling *adj.* arousing strong interest or admiration.

compendious /kəm'pendiəs/ *adj.* comprehensive but brief. [from Old French from Latin]

compendium /kəm'pendiəm/ *n.* (*plural* **compendia**) 1. a concise summary or abridgement. 2. a collection of table games etc. [Latin = saving, short cut (*pendere* = weigh)]

compensate /'kɒmpənseıt/ *v.t./i.* 1. to make suitable payment in return for (loss, damage, etc.); to recompense.

2. to counterbalance. —**compensatory** *adj.* [from Latin *compensare* (*pendere* = weigh)]

compensation /kɒmpən'seıʃən/ *n.* compensating, being compensated; a thing (especially money) that compensates. [from Old French from Latin]

compensation point in biology, the point at which there is just enough light for a plant to survive. At this point all the food produced by ⃝photosynthesis is used up by ⃝respiration. For aquatic plants, the compensation point is the depth of water at which there is just enough light to sustain life (deeper water = less light = less photosynthesis).

compere /'kɒmpeə/ *n.* a person who introduces artistes at a variety show etc. —*v.t.* to act as compere to. [French *compère* = godfather]

compete /kəm'piːt/ *v.i.* to take part in a contest, race, etc.; to strive (*with* or *against*). [from Latin *competere* = strive after]

competence /'kɒmpıtəns/ *n.* or **competency** 1. being competent, ability; legal capacity. 2. a comfortably adequate income. 3. in linguistics, the set of internalized rules in a person's brain that makes it possible to understand and produce language.

competent /'kɒmpıtənt/ *adj.* having the required knowledge, ability, or authority; effective, adequate. —**competently** *adv.* [from Old French or Latin]

competition /kɒmpı'tıʃən/ *n.* 1. an event in which people compete. 2. competing (*for*) by examination, in trade, etc.; in ecology, the interaction between two or more organisms, or groups of organisms (for example, species), that use a common resource which is in short supply. 3. those competing with a person or group of people.

competition, perfect in economics, a market situation in which there are many potential and actual buyers and sellers, each being too small to be an individual influence on the price; the market is open to all and the products being traded are homogeneous. At the same time, the producers are seeking the maximum profit and consumers the best value for money.

competitive /kəm'petıtıv/ *adj.* of or involving competition; (of prices etc.) comparing favourably with those of rivals. —**competitively** *adv.*

competitor /kəm'petıtə/ *n.* one who competes; a rival, especially in trade.

compile /kəm'paıl/ *v.t.* to collect and arrange (information) into a list, volume, etc.; to produce (books etc.) thus. —**compilation** /-'leıʃən/ *n.*, **compiler** *n.* [from Old French or Latin *compilare* = plunder]

compiler *n.* a computer program that translates other programs into a form in which they can be run by the computer. Most programs are written in high-level languages, designed for the convenience of the programmer. The compiler converts these into the ⃝machine code, which the computer understands.

complacent /kəm'pleısənt/ *adj.* self-satisfied, calmly content. —**complacency** *n.*, **complacently** *adv.* [from Latin *placēre* = please]

complain /kəm'pleın/ *v.i.* to express dissatisfaction. —**complain of**, to say that one is suffering from (a pain etc.); to state a grievance concerning. [from Old French from Latin *plangere* = lament]

complainant /kəm'pleınənt/ *n.* the plaintiff (in certain lawsuits).

complaint /kəm'pleınt/ *n.* 1. a statement of dissatisfaction, utterance of a grievance, a formal accusation. 2. a cause of dissatisfaction; an illness.

complaisant /kəm'pleızənt/ *adj.* inclined to please or defer to others; acquiescent. —**complaisance** *n.* [French]

complement /'kɒmpləmənt/ *n.* that which makes a thing complete; the full number required to man a ship, fill a conveyance, etc.; the word or words added to a verb to complete the predicate; the deficiency of an angle from 90°. —*v.t.* to complete; to form a complement to. [from Latin]

complementary /kɒmplə'mentərı/ *adj.* completing, forming a complement; (of two or more things) complementing each other. —**complementary colour**, a colour of light that when combined with a given colour makes white light (e. g. blue with yellow).

complementary angles in geometry, two angles that add up to 90°.

complementation *n.* in genetics, the interaction that can occur between two different mutant alleles of a gene in a ◊diploid organism, to make up for each other's deficiencies and allow the organism to function normally.

complete /kəm'pli:t/ *adj.* having all its parts, entire; finished; thorough, in every way. —*v.t.* to make complete; to finish; to fill in (a form etc.). —**complete with,** having as an important feature or addition. —**completely** *adv.,* **completeness** *n.* [from Old French or Latin *complere* = fill]

completion /kəm'pli:ʃən/ *n.* completing, being completed.

complex /'kɒmpleks/ *adj.* consisting of several parts, composite; complicated. —*n.* **1.** a complex whole. **2.** a group of usually repressed ideas etc. causing abnormal behaviour or mental state. **3.** a set of buildings. —**complexity** *n.* [from French or Latin *complecti* = embrace, associated with *complexus* = plaited]

complexion /kəm'plekʃən/ *n.* **1.** the natural colour, texture, and appearance of the skin, especially of the face. **2.** character, aspect. [from Old French from Latin]

complex number in mathematics, a number written in the form $a + ib$, where a and b are ◊real numbers and i is the square root of –1 (that is, $i^2 = -1$); i used to be known as the 'imaginary' part of the complex number. Some equations in algebra, such as those of the form $x^2 + 5 = 0$, cannot be solved without recourse to complex numbers, because the real numbers do not include square roots of negative numbers.

compliance *n.* in the UK, abiding by the terms of the Financial Services Act 1986. Companies undertaking any form of investment business are regulated by the Act and must fulfil their obligations to investors under it, under four main headings: efficiency, competitiveness, confidence, and flexibility.

compliant /kəm'plaɪənt/ *adj.* complying, obedient. —**compliance** *n.*

complicate /'kɒmplikeit/ *v.t.* to make involved, intricate, or difficult. [from Latin *plicare* = fold]

complication /kɒmpli'keiʃən/ *n.* **1.** an involved condition, an entangled state of affairs. **2.** a complicating circumstance; a secondary disease or condition aggravating an already existing one.

complicity /kəm'plisiti/ *n.* partnership in evil action. [from obsolete *complice* = accomplice]

compliment /'kɒmplimənt/ *n.* a polite expression of praise; an act implying praise; (in *plural*) formal greetings accompanying a note, present, etc. —/-ment/ *v.t.* to pay a compliment to. [French from Latin]

complimentary /kɒmpli'mentəri/ *adj.* expressing a compliment; given free of charge by way of compliment.

compline /'kɒmplin/ *n.* the last of the canonical hours of prayer; the service said at this. [from Old French from Latin]

comply /kəm'plai/ *v.i.* to act in accordance (*with*). [from Italian from Latin *complēre* = fill up]

component /kəm'pəunənt/ *adj.* forming one of the parts of a whole. —*n.* a component part; in mathematics, one of the vectors produced when a single vector is resolved into two or more parts. [from Latin]

componential analysis in linguistics, the analysis of the elements of a word's meaning. The word *boy,* for example, might be said to have three basic meaning elements (or semantic properties): 'human', 'young,' and 'male'; and so might the word *murder:* 'kill', 'intentional', and 'illegal'.

comport /kəm'pɔ:t/ *v.t./i.* (*literary*) to conduct or behave *oneself.* —**comport with,** to suit, to befit. —**comportment** *n.* [from Latin *portare* = carry]

compose /kəm'pəuz/ *v.t.* **1.** to create in music or writing. **2.** to form, to make up. **3.** (in printing) to set up (type), to arrange (an article etc.) in type. **4.** to arrange artistically, neatly, or for a specified purpose. **5.** to make (oneself, one's feelings, etc.) calm. —**composed of,** made up of, consisting of. [from French from Latin *ponere* = put]

composed *adj.* calm, self-possessed. —**composedly** /-idli/ *adv.*

composer *n.* one who composes (especially music).

Compositae /kəm'pɒziti:/ *n.* the daisy family; dicotyledonous flowering plants characterized by flowers borne in composite heads (see ◊capitulum). It is the largest family of flowering plants, the majority being herbaceous. Birds seem to favour the family for use in nest 'decoration', possibly because many species either repel or kill insects (see ◊pyrethrum). Species include the daisy and dandelion; food

plants such as the artichoke, lettuce, and safflower; and the garden varieties of chrysanthemum, dahlia, and zinnia.

composite /'kɒmpəzit, -zait/ *adj.* **1.** made up of various parts. **2.** of a plant, of the family ◊Compositae. **3.** in architecture, of mixed Ionic and Corinthian style. —*n.* a composite thing or plant; in industry, any purpose-designed engineering material created by combining single materials with complementary properties into a composite form. [French from Latin]

composite function in mathematics, a function made up of two or more other functions carried out in sequence, usually denoted by * or ○, as in the relation $(f * g) x = f[g(x)]$.

composition /kɒmpə'ziʃən/ *n.* **1.** an act or method of putting together into a whole, composing. **2.** a thing composed, a piece of writing or (especially) music. **3.** the constitution of a substance etc.; the arrangement of parts in a picture etc. **4.** a compound artificial substance, especially one serving the purpose of a natural one. **5.** a financial compromise. —**compositional** *adj.* [from Old French from Latin]

compositor /kəm'pɒzitə/ *n.* one who sets up type for printing. [from Anglo-French from Latin]

compos mentis of sound mind. [Latin]

compost /'kɒmpɒst/ *n.* a mixture of decayed organic matter used as a fertilizer; a mixture usually of soil and other ingredients for growing seedlings, cuttings, etc. —*v.t.* to make into compost; to treat with compost. [from Old French from Latin]

composure /kɒm'pəuʒə/ *n.* tranquil demeanour, calmness.

compote /'kɒmpəut, -pɒt/ *n.* fruit preserved or cooked in syrup. [French]

compound[1] /'kɒmpaund/ *n.* a thing made up of two or more ingredients; a substance consisting of two or more elements chemically united in fixed proportions; a word formed by a combination of words. —/kəm'paund/ *v.t./i.* **1.** to mix or combine (ingredients or elements); to make up (a composite whole); to increase or complicate (difficulties etc.). **2.** to settle (a matter) by mutual agreement; to condone or conceal (an offence or liability) for personal gain; to come to terms (*with* a person). —/'kɒmpaund/ *adj.* made up of two or more ingredients; combined, collective. —**compound fracture,** one complicated by a wound. **compound time,** in music, that with a ternary subdivision of the unit (e.g. into three, six, nine). [from Old French from Latin *componere* = put together]

compound[2] *n.* an enclosure or fenced-in space; (in India, China, etc.) the enclosure in which a house or factory stands. [from Portuguese or Dutch from Malay *kampong*]

compound interest interest calculated by increasing the original capital by the amount of interest each time the interest becomes due. When simple interest is calculated, only the interest on the original capital is added.

comprehend /kɒmpri'hend/ *v.t.* **1.** to grasp mentally, to understand. **2.** to include. —**comprehensible** *adj.,* **comprehension** *n.* [from Old French or Latin *prehendere* = grasp, seize]

comprehensive *adj.* including much or all, inclusive. —*n.* a comprehensive school. —**comprehensive school,** a large secondary school providing courses for children of all abilities. —**comprehensively** *adv.*

compress /kəm'pres/ *v.t.* to squeeze together; to bring into a smaller space. —/'kɒmpres/ *n.* a pad of lint etc. pressed on to some part of the body to stop bleeding, relieve inflammation, etc. [from Old French or Latin *compressare,* frequentative of *comprimere* (*premere* = press)]

compression /kəm'preʃən/ *n.* compressing; reduction in the volume of fuel mixture in an internal-combustion engine before ignition.

compressor /kəm'presə/ *n.* a machine for compressing air or other gases commonly used to power pneumatic tools, such as road drills, paint sprayers, and dentist's drills.

comprise /kəm'praiz/ *v.t.* to include, to consist of. [from French]

compromise /'kɒmprəmaiz/ *n.* **1.** a settlement made by each side giving up part of its demands; the process of making this. **2.** an intermediate way *between* conflicting courses, opinions, etc. —*v.t./i.* **1.** to settle (a dispute) or modify (principles) by compromise; to make a compromise. **2.** to

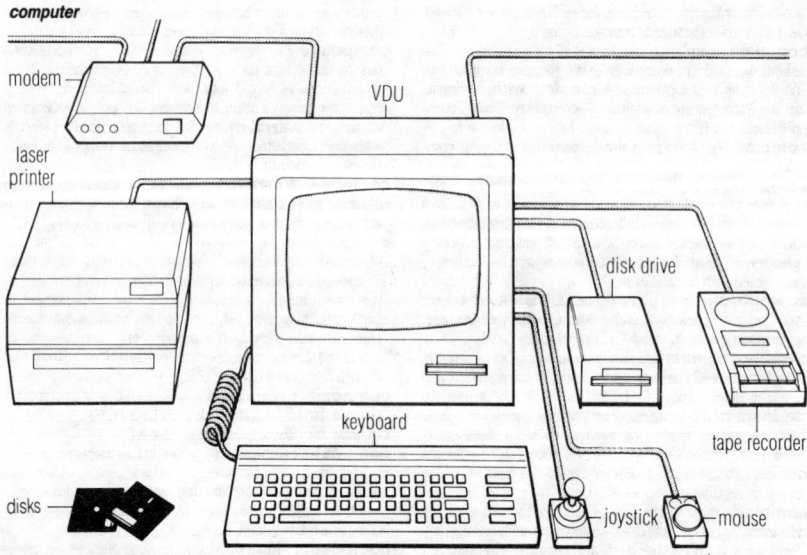

computer

modem

laser printer

VDU

disk drive

keyboard

tape recorder

disks

joystick — mouse

bring under suspicion or into danger by indiscreet action. [from Old French from Latin *promittere* = put forth]

Compton /ˈkɒmptən/ Arthur Holly 1892–1962. US physicist known for his work on X-rays. Working in Chicago in 1923, he found that X-rays scattered by such light elements as carbon increased their wavelengths. Compton concluded from this unexpected result that the X-rays were displaying both wavelike and particlelike properties, since named the **Compton effect**. He shared the 1927 Nobel Prize for Physics with British physicist Charles ◊Wilson (1869-1959).

Compton-Burnett /ˈkʌmptən ˈbɜːnɪt/ Ivy 1892–1969. English novelist. She used dialogue to show reactions of small groups of characters dominated by the tyranny of family relationships. Her novels, set at the turn of the century, include *Pastors and Masters* 1925, *More Women Than Men* 1933, and *Mother and Son* 1955.

'We may as well imagine the scene.'
'No my mind baulks at it.'
'Mine does worse. It constructs it.'

Ivy Compton-Burnett
A Family and a Fortune

---

comptroller *n.* variant of **controller** (in titles of some financial officers).

compulsion /kəmˈpʌlʃən/ *n.* compelling, being compelled; an irresistible urge. [from French from Latin]

compulsive /kəmˈpʌlsɪv/ *adj.* tending to compel; resulting or acting from or as if from compulsion, especially contrary to one's conscious wishes; irresistible.

compulsory /kəmˈpʌlsəri/ *adj.* that must be done, required by the rules etc. —**compulsorily** *adv.*

compulsory purchase in the UK the right of the state and authorized bodies to buy land required for public purposes even against the wishes of the owner. Under the Land Compensation Act 1973, fair recompense is payable.

compunction /kəmˈpʌŋkʃən/ *n.* pricking of the conscience; a slight regret or scruple. [from Old French from Latin *pungere* = prick]

computable /kəmˈpjuːtəbəl/ *adj.* that can be computed. —**computability** /-ˈbɪlɪtɪ/ *n.*

compute /kəmˈpjuːt/ *v.t./i.* to reckon or calculate; to use a computer. —**computation** /kɒmpjuːˈteɪʃən/ *n.* [from French or Latin *computare* = reckon]

computer /kəmˈpjuːtə/ *n.* **1.** a programmable electronic device that processes data and performs calculations and other symbol manipulation tasks. There are three types: the ◊**digital computer**, which manipulates information coded as ◊binary numbers, the ◊**analogue computer**, which works with continuously varying quantities, and the **hybrid computer**, which has characteristics of both analogue and digital computers. **2.** one who or that which computes.

computer game or **video game** a computer-controlled game in which the computer (usually) opposes the human player. Computer games typically employ fast, animated graphics on a ◊VDU (screen) and synthesized sound.

computer generation one of five broad groups into which computers can be classified: first generation (the earliest computers, developed in the 1940s and 1950s, made from valves and wire circuits); second generation (from the early 1960s, based on transistors and printed circuits); third generation (from the late 1960s, using integrated circuits, and often sold as families of computers, such as the IBM 360 series); fourth generation (using ◊microprocessors and large-scale integration, still in current use); and fifth generation (based on parallel processors and very large-scale integration, currently under development).

computer graphics the techniques involved in creating images by computer. These are widely used in the film and television industries for producing animated charts and diagrams.

computerize /kəmˈpjuːtəraɪz/ *v.t.* to equip with, perform, or produce by computer. —**computerization** /-ˈzeɪʃən/ *n.*

computer literacy the ability to understand and make use of computer technology in an everyday context.

computer numerical control the control of machine tools, most often milling machines, by a computer. The pattern of work for the machine to follow, which often involves performing repeated sequences of actions, is described using a special-purpose programming language.

computer simulation the representation of a real-life situation in a computer program. For example, the program might simulate the flow of customers arriving at a bank. The user can alter variables, such as the number of cashiers on duty, and see the effect.

computing device any device built to perform or help perform computations, such as the ◊abacus, ◊slide rule, or ◊computer.

comrade /ˈkɒmrəd/ *n.* an associate or companion in some activity; a fellow socialist or communist. —**comradely** *adj.*, **comradeship** *n.* [from French from Spanish, originally = roommate]

Comte /kɒmt/ Auguste 1798–1857. French philosopher, regarded as the founder of sociology, a term he coined in 1830. He sought to establish sociology as an intellectual discipline, using a scientific approach ('positivism') as the basis of a new science of social order and social development.

con[1] *v.t.* (**-nn-**) (*slang*) to persuade or swindle (a person) after winning his or her confidence. —*n.* (*slang*) a confidence trick. [abbreviation of *confidence*]

con[2] *v.t.* (**-nn-**) to peruse, study, or learn by heart. [form of *can*[1]]

con[3] *v.t.* (**-nn-**) to direct the steering of (a ship). [originally *cond* from French *conduire*]

con[4] *adv. & prep.* (of an argument or reason) against. —*n.* a reason against (see ◊*pro*[2]). [from Latin *contra* = against]

con- prefix see com-.

Conakry /kɒnəˈkri:/ capital and chief port of the Republic of Guinea; population (1980) 763,000. It is on the island of Tumbo, linked with the mainland by a causeway and by rail with Kankan, 480 km/300 mi NE. Bauxite and iron ore are mined nearby.

concatenate /kənˈkætɪneɪt/ *v.t.* to link together, to form a sequence of. —**concatenation** /-ˈneɪʃən/ *n.* [from Latin *concatenare* (*catena* = chain)]

concave /kɒnˈkeɪv/ *adj.* curved like the interior of a circle or sphere. —**concavity** /-ˈkævɪtɪ/ *n.* [from Latin *cavus* = hollow]

concave lens a converging ◊lens – that is, a parallel beam of light gets wider as it passes through such a lens. A concave lens is thinner at its centre than at the edges.

conceal /kənˈsiːl/ *v.t.* to keep secret or hidden. —**concealment** *n.* [from Old French from Latin *concelare* = hide]

concede /kənˈsiːd/ *v.t.* 1. to admit to be true. 2. to grant (a privilege, right, etc.) 3. to admit defeat in (a contest, election, etc.). [from French or Latin *cedere* = cede]

conceit /kənˈsiːt/ *n.* 1. excessive pride in oneself. 2. a fanciful notion.

conceited *adj.* having too high an opinion of one's qualities or attributes.

conceivable /kənˈsiːvəbəl/ *adj.* that can be (mentally) conceived. —**conceivably** *adv.*

conceive /kənˈsiːv/ *v.t./i.* 1. to become pregnant (with). 2. to form (ideas etc.) in the mind; to imagine, to think *of*. [from Old French from Latin *concipere* (*capere* = take)]

concentrate /ˈkɒnsəntreɪt/ *v.t./i.* 1. to employ all one's thought, attention, efforts, etc. (*on*); to bring or come together to one place. 2. to increase the strength of (a liquid etc.) by removing water etc. —*n.* a concentrated substance. [from French *concentrer*]

concentrated *adj.* 1. (of a liquid) having more than the natural or original strength, not diluted. 2. intense.

concentration /kɒnsənˈtreɪʃən/ *n.* 1. concentrating, being concentrated. 2. the amount or strength of a substance in a mixture; a mental state of exclusive attention.

concentration camp a prison camp devised by the British during the Second Boer War in South Africa in 1899 for the detention of Afrikaner women and children A system of approximately 5,000 concentration camps was developed by the Nazis in Germany and occupied Europe (1933–45) to imprison political and ideological opponents after Hitler became chancellor in Jan 1933. Several hundred camps were established in Germany and occupied Europe, the most infamous being the extermination camps of Auschwitz, Belsen, Dachau, Maidanek, Sobibor, and Treblinka. The total number of people who died at the camps exceeded six million, and some inmates were subjected to medical experimentation before being killed.

concentric /kənˈsentrɪk/ *adj.* having a common centre. —**concentrically** *adv.* [from Old French from Latin]

concept /ˈkɒnsept/ *n.* a generalized idea or notion. [from Latin]

conceptacle *n.* a flask-shaped cavity found in the swollen tips of certain brown seaweeds, notably the wracks, *Fucus*. The gametes are formed within the conceptacles and released into the water via a small pore known as an ostiole.

conception /kənˈsepʃən/ *n.* 1. conceiving, being conceived. 2. the result of this, an idea. —**conceptional** *adj.* [from Old French from Latin]

conceptual /kənˈseptjuəl/ *adj.* of mental concepts.

conceptualism /kənˈseptjuəlɪzəm/ *n.* the theory that universals exist, but only as mental concepts. —**conceptualist** *n.*

conceptualize /kənˈseptjuəlaɪz/ *v.t.* to form a mental concept of.

concern /kənˈsɜːn/ *v.t.* to be relevant or important to; to affect or worry; to relate to, to be about. — *n.* 1. a

thing of interest or importance to one. 2. anxiety, worry. 3. (in *plural*) one's affairs. 4. a business or firm; (*colloquial*) a thing. —**be concerned in**, to take part in. **concern oneself**, to feel an interest or anxiety (*in, about,* etc.); to have a desire to deal *with*. —**concernment** *n.* [from French or Latin *cernere* = sift, discern]

concerned *adj.* 1. anxious, troubled. 2. involved, interested. —**concernedly** /-ɪdlɪ/ *adv.*, **concernedness** /-ɪdnɪs/ *n.*

concerning *prep.* about, with regard to.

concert /ˈkɒnsət/ *n.* 1. a musical entertainment by several performers. 2. a combination of voices or sounds. 3. agreement, working together. —**concert pitch**, a pitch, slightly higher than the ordinary, internationally agreed for concert performances. [French from Italian]

concerted /kənˈsɜːtɪd/ *adj.* 1. effected by mutual agreement, done in cooperation. 2. in music, arranged in parts for voices or instruments.

concertina /kɒnsəˈtiːnə/ *n.* a portable reed organ related to the ◊accordion but smaller in size and rounder in shape, with buttons for keys. It was invented in England in the 19th century. —*v.t./i.* to compress or collapse in folds like those of a concertina.

concert master in music, the leader of an orchestra, usually the principal violinist.

concerto /kənˈtʃɜːtəʊ/ *n.* (*plural* **concertos** or **concerti** /-iː/) a composition (usually in three movements) for one or more solo instruments accompanied by an orchestra. —**concerto grosso** /ˈgrəʊsəʊ/, a composition with a small group of solo instruments accompanied by an orchestra. [Italian, from *concertare* = bring into harmony and *grosso* = big]

concession /kənˈseʃən/ *n.* 1. conceding. 2. a thing conceded, especially a grant of land for extraction of minerals, trading rights, etc.; a reduction in price for certain categories of person. —**concessionary** *adj.* [from French or Latin]

concessionaire /kənseʃəˈneə/ *n.* the holder of a concession. [French]

concessive /kənˈsesɪv/ *adj.* in grammar, expressing a concession, of words such as *although* or *even if.* [from Latin]

conch /kɒntʃ/ *n.* the spiral shell of certain shellfish; such a shellfish, especially a large gastropod. [from Latin *concha* from Greek]

Conchobar /ˈkɒnuə/ in Celtic mythology, a king of Ulster whose intended bride, Deirdre, eloped with Noísi. She died of sorrow when Conchobar killed her husband and his brothers.

conchology /kɒŋˈkɒlədʒɪ/ *n.* the study of shells and shellfish. —**conchologist** *n.*

concierge /ˈkɒnsieəʒ/ *n.* (in France and French speaking areas) a doorkeeper or porter (especially of a block of flats). [French, from Latin *conservius* = fellow slave]

conciliate /kənˈsɪlɪeɪt/ *v.t.* to win over from anger or hostility, to win the goodwill of; to reconcile (disagreeing parties). —**conciliation** /-ˈeɪʃən/ *n.* **conciliator** *n.*, **conciliatory** *adj.* [from Latin *conciliare* = combine, gain (*concilium* = council)]

concilliar movement the 15th-century attempt to urge the supremacy of church councils over the popes, with regard to the ◊Great Schism and the reformation of the church. Councils were held in Pisa in 1409, Constance 1414–18, Pavia-Siena 1423–24, Basle 1431–49, and Ferrara-Florence-Rome 1438–47.

concise /kənˈsaɪs/ *adj.* brief but comprehensive in expression. —**concisely** *adv.*, **conciseness** *n.*, **concision** /-ˈsɪʒən/ *n.* [from French or Latin *caedere* = cut]

conclave /ˈkɒnkleɪv/ *n.* a private meeting; a meeting place or assembly of cardinals for the election of a pope. [from Old French from Latin = lockable room (*clavis* = key)]

conclude /kənˈkluːd/ *v.t./i.* 1. to bring or come to an end; to arrange or settle (a treaty etc.) finally. 2. to draw a conclusion (*that*). [from Latin *concludere* (*claudere* = shut)]

conclusion /kənˈkluːʒən/ *n.* 1. ending, an end. 2. a settling or concluding (of peace etc.). 3. a judgement or opinion based on reasoning; a proposition in logic reached from previous ones.

conclusive /kənˈkluːsɪv/ *adj.* decisive, completely convincing. —**conclusively** *adv.*

concoct /kən'kɒkt/ *v.t.* to prepare, especially by mixing a variety of ingredients; to invent (a story or plot). —**concoction** /-'kɒkʃən/ *n.* [from Latin *coquere* = cook]

concomitant /kən'kɒmɪtənt/ *adj.* accompanying. —*n.* an accompanying thing. —**concomitance** *n.* [from Latin *concomitari* (*comes* = companion)]

concord /'kɒŋkɔːd/ *n.* 1. agreement, harmony. 2. in music, a chord or interval satisfactory in itself. 3. in grammar, agreement between words in gender, number, etc. —**concordant** /kən'kɔːdənt/ *adj.* [from Old French from Latin *cor* = heart]

concordance /kən'kɔːdəns/ *n.* 1. agreement. 2. an alphabetical index of the words used by an author or in a book. The first concordance was one prepared to the Latin Vulgate Bible by a Dominican in the 13th century.

concordat /kən'kɔːdæt/ *n.* an official agreement, especially between church and state. [from French or Latin past participle of *concordare*]

Concorde /'kɒŋkɔːd/ *n.* the only ◊supersonic airliner, which cruises at Mach 2, or twice the speed of sound, about 2,170 kph/1,350 mph. Concorde, the result of Anglo-French cooperation, made its first flight in 1969 and entered commercial service seven years later. It is 62 m/202 ft long and has a wing span of nearly 26 m/84 ft.

concourse /'kɒŋkɔːs/ *n.* 1. a crowd, a gathering. 2. a large open area in a railway station etc. [from Old French from Latin]

concrete /'kɒŋkriːt/ *n.* a mixture of cement with sand or gravel, used in building since Roman and Egyptian times. —*adj.* 1. existing in material form, real. 2. definite, positive. 3. in grammar, of a noun, denoting a thing, not a quality or state etc. —*v.t./i.* 1. to cover with or embed in concrete. 2. /kən'kriːt/ to form into a mass, to solidify. —**concrete music,** music prepared from recorded (natural or man-made) sounds. **concrete poetry,** poetry using typographical devices to enhance its effect. [from French from Latin *concrescere* = grow together]

concretion /kən'kriːʃən/ *n.* a hard solid mass; the forming of this by coalescence.

concubine /'kɒŋkjʊbaɪn/ *n.* a woman cohabiting with a man to whom she is not married; a secondary wife in polygamous societies. —**concubinage** /kən'kjuːbɪnɪdʒ/ *n.* [from Old French from Latin *cubare* = lie]

concupiscence /kən'kjuːpɪsəns, kɒnkjuːˈpɪ-/ *n.* intense sexual desire. —**concupiscent** *adj.* [from Latin *concupiscere* = begin to desire]

concur /kən'kɜː/ *v.i.* (**-rr-**) 1. to agree in opinion. 2. to happen together, to coincide. [from Latin *currere* = run]

concurrence /kən'kʌrəns/ *n.* 1. agreement. 2. simultaneous occurrence of events.

concurrent /kən'kʌrənt/ *adj.* 1. existing or acting together or at the same time. 2. running in the same direction; (of three or more lines) meeting at or tending to one point. —**concurrently** *adv.*

concuss /kən'kʌs/ *v.t.* to subject to concussion. [from Latin *concutere* (*quatere* = shake)]

concussion /kən'kʌʃən/ *n.* 1. injury to the brain caused by a heavy blow, fall, etc. 2. violent shaking.

Condé /kɒn'deɪ/ Louis de Bourbon, Prince of Condé 1530–1569. Prominent French ◊Huguenot leader, founder of the house of Condé and uncle of Henry IV of France. He fought in the wars between Henry II and the Holy Roman emperor Charles V, including the defence of Metz.

Condé Louis II 1621–1686. Prince of Condé called the **Great Condé** . French commander, who won brilliant victories during the Thirty Years' War at Rocroi in 1643 and Lens in 1648, but rebelled in 1651 and entered the Spanish service. Pardoned in 1660, he commanded Louis XIV's armies against the Spanish and the Dutch.

condemn /kən'dem/ *v.t.* 1. to express utter disapproval of. 2. to pronounce guilty, to convict; to sentence *to* a punishment; to assign an unpleasant future or fate to. 3. to pronounce unfit for use or habitation. —**condemnation** /kɒndem'neɪʃən/ *n.,* **condemnatory** /kən'demnətəri/ *adj.* [from Old French from Latin *condemnare* (*damnare* = damn)]

condensation /kɒnden'seɪʃən/ *n.* 1. condensing. 2. condensed material (especially water on cold windows etc.). 3. abridgement. [from Latin]

condor

condensation number in physics, the ratio of the number of molecules condensing on a surface to the total number of molecules touching that surface.

condense /kən'dens/ *v.t./i.* 1. to make denser or more concentrated. 2. to change or be changed from gas or vapour into liquid. 3. to express in few words. —**condensed milk,** milk thickened by evaporation and sweetened. [from French or Latin *condensare* (*densus* = thick)]

condenser *n.* 1. an apparatus or vessel for condensing vapour. 2. a capacitor. 3. in optics, a short-focal-length convex ◊lens or combination of lenses used for concentrating a light source on to a small area, as used in a slide projector or microscope substage lighting unit.

condescend /kɒndi'send/ *v.i.* to be gracious enough (*to* do), especially while showing one's feeling of dignity or superiority; to disregard one's superiority (*to* a person). —**condescension** *n.* [from Old French from Latin *descendere* = descend]

condign /kən'daɪn/ *adj.* (of punishment etc.) severe and well-deserved. [from Old French from Latin *dignus* = worthy]

condiment /'kɒndɪmənt/ *n.* a seasoning or relish for food. [from Latin *condire* = pickle]

condition /kən'dɪʃən/ *n.* 1. a stipulation, a thing upon the fulfilment of which depends something else. 2. the state of being of a person or thing. 3. a state of physical fitness or (of things) fitness for use. 4. an ailment or abnormality. 5. (in *plural*) circumstances, especially those affecting the functioning or existence of something. —*v.t.* 1. to bring into the desired state or condition; to make fit; to train or accustom. 2. to modify, to have a strong effect on. —**conditioned reflex,** a reflex response to a non-natural stimulus, established by training. **on condition that,** with the condition that. [from Old French from Latin = thing agreed on (*dicere* = say)]

conditional *adj.* 1. dependent (*on*); not absolute, containing a condition or stipulation. 2. in grammar, of a clause, mood, etc., expressing a condition. —**conditionally** *adv.*

conditioning *n.* in psychology, two major principles of behaviour modification. In **classical conditioning,** described by Ivan Pavlov, a new stimulus can evoke an automatic response by being repeatedly associated with a stimulus that naturally provokes a response. For example, a bell repeatedly associated with food will eventually trigger salivation, even if presented without food. In **operant conditioning,** described by Edward Lee Thorndike (1874–1949) and B F Skinner, the frequency of a voluntary response can be increased by following it with a reinforcer or reward.

condole /kən'dəʊl/ *v.i.* to express sympathy (*with* a person *on* a loss etc.). —**condolence** n. [from Latin *dolēre* = grieve]

condom /'kɒndəm/ *n.* a contraceptive sheath.

condominium /kɒndə'mɪnɪəm/ *n.* 1. joint control of a state's affairs by two or more other states. 2. in North America, a type of joint property ownership of, for example, a block of flats. [Latin *dominium* = sovereignty]

condone /kən'dəʊn/ *v.t.* to forgive or overlook (an offence or wrongdoing). —**condonation** /kɒndə'neɪʃən/ *n.* [from Latin *donare* = give]

condor /ˈkɒndə/ *n.* a very large vulture *Vultur gryphus* of South America with a wingspan up to 3 m/10 ft; it is black with some white on the wings and a white frill at the base of the neck; a smaller (and rare) vulture, the California condor *Gymnogyps californianus* of North America. [Spanish from Quechua *cuntur*]

Condorcet /kɒndɔːˈseɪ/ Marie Jean Antoine Nicolas Caritat, Marquis de Condorcet 1743–1794. French philosopher, mathematician, and politician, associated with the ◊Encyclopédistes. One of the ◊Girondins, he opposed the execution of Louis XVI, and was imprisoned and poisoned himself. His *Esquisse d'un tableau des progrès de l'esprit humain/Historical Survey of the Progress of Human Understanding* 1795 envisaged inevitable future progress, though not the perfectibility of human nature.

conduce /kənˈdjuːs/ *v.i.* to tend to lead or contribute *to* (a result). —**conducive** *adj.* [from Latin]

conduct /ˈkɒndʌkt/ *n.* 1. behaviour (especially in its moral aspect). 2. the manner of directing and managing (a business or war). —/kənˈdʌkt/ *v.t.* 1. to lead or guide. 2. to direct or manage (a business etc.). 3. to be conductor of (an orchestra etc.). 4. to transmit (heat, electricity, etc.) by conduction. —**conduct oneself,** to behave (*well, badly,* etc.). [from Old French from Latin *ducere* = lead]

conductance /kənˈdʌktəns/ *n.* the ability of a material to carry an electrical current, usually given the symbol *G*. For a direct current, it is the reciprocal of resistance: a conductor of resistance *R* has a conductance of $1/R$. For an alternating current, conductance is the resistance *R* divided by the impedence Z: $G = R/Z$. Conductance was formerly expressed in reciprocal ohms (or mhos); the SI unit is the Siemens (S).

conduction /kənˈdʌkʃən/ *n.* the transmission or conducting of heat, electricity etc.

conductive /kənˈdʌktɪv/ *adj.* having the property of conducting heat or electricity. —**conductivity** /kɒndʌkˈtɪvɪtɪ/ *n.*

conductor /kənˈdʌktə/ *n.* 1. a person who directs the performance of an orchestra, choir, etc. 2. one who collects fares in a bus etc. 3. a material that conducts heat or electricity (as opposed to a nonconductor or insulator). A good conductor has a high electrical or thermal conductivity, and is generally a substance rich in free electrons such as a metal. A poor conductor (such as the nonmetals glass and porcelain) has few free electrons. Carbon is exceptional in being nonmetallic and yet (in some of its forms) is a relatively good conductor of heat and electricity. [from French from Latin]

conductress /kənˈdʌktrɪs/ *n.fem.* a woman bus conductor.

conduit /ˈkɒndɪt, -djuɪt/ *n.* a channel or pipe for conveying liquids; a tube or trough for protecting insulated electric wires. [from Old French from Latin]

condyle /ˈkɒndaɪl/ *n.* a rounded process at the end of a bone, forming an articulation with another bone. [French from Latin from Greek *kondulos* = knuckle]

cone *n.* 1. a solid figure with a circular plane base, narrowing to a point; a thing of similar shape, solid or hollow. 2. in geometry, a solid or surface generated by rotating an isosceles triangle or framework about its line of symmetry; it can also be formed by the set of all straight lines passing through a fixed point and the points of a circle or ellipse whose plane does not contain the point. 3. in biology, the reproductive structure of the conifers and cycads; also known as a ◊strobilus; it consists of a central axis surrounded by numerous, overlapping, scale-like sporophylls, modified leaves that bear the reproductive organs. Usually there are separate male and female cones, the former bearing pollen sacs containing pollen grains, and the larger female cones bearing the ovules that contain the ova or egg cells. 4. an ice-cream cornet. [from French from Latin from Greek]

coney variant of ◊cony.

confabulate /kənˈfæbjuleɪt/ *v.i.* to converse, to chat. —**confabulation** /-ˈleɪʃən/ *n.* [from Latin *confabulari* (*fabula* = tale)]

confection /kənˈfekʃən/ *n.* a dish or delicacy made with sweet ingredients; a cake or sweet. [from Old French from Latin *conficere* = prepare]

confectioner *n.* a maker or retailer of confectionery.

confectionery *n.* confections, especially sweets.

confederacy /kənˈfedərəsɪ/ *n.* a league or alliance, especially (**the Confederacy**) that of the Confederate States. [from Anglo-French]

confederate /kənˈfedərət/ *adj.* allied. —*n.* 1. an ally, especially (in bad sense) an accomplice. 2. **Confederate,** a supporter of the Confederate States. —/-reɪt/ *v.t./i.* to bring or come into alliance (*with*). —**Confederate States,** the 11 southern states which seceded from the United States in 1860–61 and formed a confederacy of their own (thus precipitating the American Civil War) which was finally overthrown in 1865, after which they were reunited to the USA. [from Latin]

confederation /kənfedəˈreɪʃən/ *n.* 1. forming or being formed in alliance etc. 2. a union or alliance of states. In US history, the initial means by which the 13 former British colonies created a form of national government. Ratified in 1781, the Articles estalished a unicameral legislature, Congress, with limited powers of raising revenue, regulating currency, and conducting foreign affairs. But because the individual states retained significant autonomy, the confederation was unmanageable. The articles were superseded by the US Constitution in 1788.

Confederation, Articles of in US history, the initial means by which the 13 former British colonies created a form of national government. Ratified in 1781, the Articles established a unicameral legislature, Congress, with limited powers of raising revenue, regulating currency, and conducting foreign affairs. But because the individual states retained significant autonomy, the confederation was unmanageable. The articles were superseded by the US Constitution in 1788.

Confederation of British Industry (CBI) a UK organization of employers, established in 1965, combining the former Federation of British Industries (founded in 1916), British Employers' Confederation, and National Association of British Manufacturers.

confer /kənˈfɜː/ *v.t./i.* (**-rr-**) 1. to grant, to bestow. 2. to hold a conference or discussion. —**conferrable** *adj.* [from Latin *ferre* = bring]

conference /ˈkɒnfərəns/ *n.* consultation; a meeting (especially a regular one) for discussion.

conferment /kənˈfɜːmənt/ *n.* the conferring (of a degree, honour, etc.).

confess /kənˈfes/ *v.t./i.* 1. to acknowledge, own, or admit (a fault, wrongdoing, etc.); to admit reluctantly. 2. to declare one's sins formally, especially to a priest. 3. (of a priest) to hear the confession of. [from Old French from Latin *confitēri* (*fatēri* = declare, avow)]

confessedly /kənˈfesɪdlɪ/ *adv.* by personal or general admission.

confession /kənˈfeʃən/ *n.* 1. the confessing (of an offence etc., or of sins to a priest). 2. a thing confessed; a declaration of one's religious beliefs, a statement of one's principles.

confessional *n.* an enclosed stall in a church, in which a priest sits to hear confessions. —*adj.* of a confession.

confessor *n.* 1. a priest who hears confessions and gives spiritual counsel. 2. one who avows his religion in the face of danger. [from Anglo-French from Latin]

confetti /kənˈfetɪ/ *n.* small bits of coloured paper thrown by wedding guests at the bride and bridegroom. [Italian]

confidant /kɒnfiˈdænt/ *n.* (*feminine* **confidante** *pronounced* the same) a person trusted with knowledge of one's private affairs.

confide /kənˈfaɪd/ *v.t./i.* 1. to tell (secrets *to*). 2. to entrust (an object of care or a task *to*). —**confide in,** to talk confidentially to. [from Latin *fidere* = trust]

confidence /ˈkɒnfɪdəns/ *n.* 1. firm trust; a feeling of certainty, sense of self-reliance, boldness. 2. something told confidentially. —**confidence man,** one who robs by means of a confidence trick. **confidence trick,** a swindle in which the victim is persuaded to trust someone who gives a false impression of honesty. **in a person's confidence,** trusted with his or her secrets. [from Latin]

confident *n.* feeling or showing confidence, bold. [French from Italian]

confidential /kɒnfiˈdenʃəl/ *adj.* 1. spoken or written in confidence. 2. entrusted with secrets. 3. confiding. —**confidentiality** /-ʃiˈælɪtɪ/ *n.*, **confidentially** *adv.*

configuration /kənfɪgjuə'reɪʃən/ *n.* manner of arrangement, shape, outline. [from Latin *configuratio* (*figurare* = fashion)]

Confindustria /kɒnfɪn'dustriə/ *n.* in European history, a general confederation of industry established in Italy in 1920 with the aim of countering working-class agitation. It contributed large funds to the fascist movement, which, in turn, used its *squadristi* against the workers. After Mussolini's takeover of power in 1922, Confindustria became one of the major groups of the fascist corporative state.

confine /kən'faɪn/ *v.t.* to keep or restrict within certain limits; to imprison. —/'kɒnfaɪn/ *n.* (usually in *plural*) a limit or boundary of an area. —**be confined,** to be undergoing childbirth. [from French from Latin *finis* = limit]

confinement *n.* 1. confining, being confined. 2. the period of childbirth.

confirm /kən'fɜːm/ *v.t.* 1. to provide support for the truth or correctness of. 2. to establish more firmly; to encourage (*in* an opinion etc.). 3. to make formally definite or valid. 4. to administer the rite of confirmation to. —**confirmative** *adj.*, **confirmatory** /-'fɜː-/ *adj.* [from Old French from Latin *confirmare* (*firmus* = firm)]

confirmation /kɒnfə'meɪʃən/ *n.* 1. confirming; corroboration. 2. a religious rite practised by a number of Christian denominations, including Roman Catholic, Anglican, and Orthodox, in which a previously baptized person is admitted to full membership of the church. In Reform Judaism there is often a confirmation service several years after the bar or bat mitzvah (initiation into the congregation).

confirmed *adj.* firmly settled in some habit or condition.

confiscate /'kɒnfɪskeɪt/ *v.t.* to take or seize by authority. —**confiscation** /-'keɪʃən/ *n.* [from Latin *confiscare* (*fiscus* = treasure)]

conflagration /kɒnflə'greɪʃən/ *n.* a great and destructive fire. [from Latin *conflagratio* (*flagrare* = blaze)]

conflate /kən'fleɪt/ *v.t.* to blend or fuse together (especially two variant texts into one). —**conflation** *n.* [from Latin *flare* = blow]

conflict /'kɒnflɪkt/ *n.* 1. a fight, a struggle. 2. the clashing (*of* opposed principles etc.). —/kən'flɪkt/ *v.i.* 1. to struggle (*with*). 2. to clash or be incompatible. [from Latin *fligere* = strike]

confluence /'kɒnfluəns/ *n.* flowing together; the place where the two rivers unite.

confluent /'kɒnfluənt/ *adj.* flowing together, uniting. —*n.* a stream joining another. [from Latin *fluere* = flow]

conform /kən'fɔːm/ *v.t./i.* 1. to comply *with* rules or general custom. 2. to make or be conformable. —**conform to** *or* **with,** to comply or be in accordance with. [from Old French from Latin *conformare* (*forma* = shape)]

conformable *adj.* 1. similar (*to*). 2. consistent (*with*), adaptable (*to*). —**conformably** *adv.*

conformation /kɒnfə'meɪʃən/ *n.* the way in which a thing is formed, its structure.

conformist /kən'fɔːmɪst/ *n.* one who conforms to an established practice. —**conformism** *n.*

conformity *n.* conforming with established practice; agreement, suitability. [from Old French from Latin]

confound /kən'faʊnd/ *v.t.* 1. to perplex, to baffle; to confuse. 2. (*archaic*) to defeat or overthrow. —*interjection* expressing annoyance (*confound it!*). [from Anglo-French from Latin *confundere* = mix up]

confounded *adj.* (*colloquial*) damned.

confrère /'kɒnfreə/ *n.* a fellow member of a profession etc. [French = fellow brother]

confront /kən'frʌnt/ *v.t.* 1. to meet or stand facing; to face in hostility or defiance. 2. (of a difficulty etc.) to present itself to. 3. to bring (a person) face to face *with* (accusers etc.). —**confrontation** /kɒnfrʌn'teɪʃən/ *n.* [from French from Latin *confrontare* (*frons* = face)]

Confucianism /kən'fjuːʃənɪzəm/ *n.* a system of philosophical and ethical teachings founded by the Chinese philospher Confucius in the 6th century BC. For about 2,500 years most of the Chinese people have derived from Confucianism their ideas of cosmology, political government, social organization, and individual conduct. Human relationships follow the patriarchal pattern. The origin of things is seen in the union of **yin** and **yang,** the passive and active principles. [from *Confucius*]

Confucius /kən'fjuːʃəs/ Latinized form of *Kong Zi,* 'Kong the master' 551–479 BC. Chinese sage who devoted his life to relieving suffering among the poor through governmental and administrative reform. His emphasis on tradition and ethics attracted a growing number of pupils during his lifetime. *The Analects of Confucius,* a compilation of his teachings, was published after his death.

Study the past, if you would divine the future.
Confucius

---

confuse /kən'fjuːz/ *v.t.* 1. to bring into disorder, to mix up. 2. to throw the mind or feelings of (a person) into disorder; to destroy the composure of. 3. to mix up in the mind, to fail to distinguish between. 4. to make unclear. —**confusedly** /-'fjuːzɪdlɪ/ *adv.*

confusion *n.* the act or result of confusing; a confused state.

confute /kən'fjuːt/ *v.t.* to prove (a person or thing) to be in error. —**confutation** /kɒnfju:'teɪʃən/ *n.* [from Latin *confutare* = restrain]

conga /'kɒŋgə/ *n.* a Latin American dance of African origin, usually with a number of persons in a single line. —**conga drum,** a tall, narrow, low-toned drum beaten with the hands. [American Spanish, from Spanish *conga* = of the Congo]

congé /'kɔːʒeɪ/ *n.* unceremonious dismissal; leave-taking. [from Old French from Latin *commeatus* = leave of absence (*commeare* = go and come)]

congeal /kən'dʒiːl/ *v.t./i.* to become or cause to become semisolid by cooling; (of blood etc.) to coagulate. —**congelation** /kɒndʒə'leɪʃən/ *n.* [from Old French from Latin *congelare* = freeze (*gelu* = ice)]

congener /'kɒndʒenə/ *n.* a thing or person of the same kind or class. [from Latin]

congenial /kən'dʒiːniəl/ *adj.* pleasant because like oneself in temperament or interests; suited or agreeable (*to*). —**congeniality** /-'ælɪtɪ/ *n.*, **congenially** *adv.*

congenital /kən'dʒenɪtəl/ *adj.* existing or as such from birth. —**congenitally** *adv.* [from Latin *genitus* = begotten)]

congenital disease in medicine, a disease that is present at birth. It is not necessarily genetic in origin; for example, congenital herpes may be acquired by the baby as it passes through the mother's birth canal.

conger /'kɒŋgə/ *n.* any of a family, Congridae, of large marine eels, in particular the genus *Conger.* Conger eels live in shallow water, hiding in crevices during the day and active by night, feeding on fish and crabs. They are valued for food and angling.

congeries /kən'dʒɪəriːz/ *n.* (*plural* the same) a disorderly collection, a mass or heap. [Latin]

congest /kən'dʒest/ *n.* (usually in *past participle*) to affect with congestion. [from Latin *congere* (*gerere* = bring)]

congestion /kən'dʒestʃən/ *n.* abnormal accumulation or obstruction, especially of traffic etc. or of blood in a part of the body.

conglomerate /kən'glɒmərət/ *adj.* gathered into a rounded mass. —*n.* 1. a conglomerate mass. 2. a group or corporation formed by the merging of separate firms. 3. a coarse clastic ◊sedimentary rock, composed of rounded fragments (clasts) of pre-existing rocks cemented in a finer matrix, usually sand. —/-reɪt/ *v.t.* to collect into a coherent mass. —**conglomeration** /-'reɪʃən/ *n.* [from Latin *conglomerare* (*glomus* = ball)]

Congo /'kɒŋgəʊ/ People's Republic of the; country in W central Africa, bounded to the N by Cameroon and the Central African Republic, to the E and S by Zaïre, to the W by the Atlantic Ocean, and to the NW by Gabon; **area** 342,000 sq km/132,012 sq mi; **capital** Brazzaville; **physical** narrow coastal plain rises to central plateau then falls into northern basin. Zaïre (Congo) River on the border with Zaïre; half the country is rainforest; **head of state and government** Denis Sassou-Nguesso from 1979; **political system** one-party Socialist republic; **exports** timber, potash, petroleum, coffee, tobacco; **population** (1990 est) 2,305,000 (chiefly Bantu); **language** French (official), many African dialects spoken; **recent history** independence from France was achieved in 1960, since when government of the country has been unsettled. Multiparty politics were promised in 1990.

congratulate /kən'grætjʊleɪt/ v.t. to express pleasure at the happiness, excellence, or good fortune of (a person on an event etc.). —**congratulate oneself**, to think oneself fortunate. —**congratulatory** adj. [from Latin gratulari = show joy]

congratulation /kəngrætju'leɪʃən/ n. congratulating; an expression of this.

congregate /'kɒŋgrɪgeɪt/ v.t./i. to collect or gather into a crowd. [from Latin congregare (grex = flock)]

congregation /kɒngrɪ'geɪʃən/ n. a gathering of persons, especially for religious purposes; a body of persons regularly attending a particular church etc. [from Old French or Latin]

congregational adj. 1. of a congregation. 2. **Congregational**, of or adhering to Congregationalism.

Congregationalism /kɒngrɪ'geɪʃəlɪzəm/ n. a form of church government adopted by those Protestant Christians known as Congregationalists, who let each congregation manage its own affairs. The first Congregationalists were the Brownists, named after Robert Browne, who defined the congregational principle in 1580. In the 17th century they were known as Independents and their members included Cromwell and many of his followers. They were persecuted under the Act of Uniformity 1622. The Congregational Church in England and Wales and the Presbyterian Church in England merged in 1972 to form the United Reformed Church. —**Congregationalist** n.

congress /'kɒŋgres/ n. 1. a formal meeting of delegates for discussion. 2. a national legislative assembly. [from Latin gradi = walk]

Congress n. the national legislature of the USA, consisting of the House of Representatives (435 members, apportioned to the states of the Union on the basis of population, and elected for two-year terms) and the Senate (100 senators, two for each state, elected for six years, one-third elected every two years). Both representatives and senators are elected by direct popular vote. Congress meets in Washington DC, in the Capitol. An ◊act of Congress is a bill passed by both houses.

Congress Party, Indian see ◊Indian National Congress Party.

congressional /kən'greʃənəl/ adj. of a congress.

Congress of Industrial Organizations (CIO) a branch of the ◊American Federation of Labor and Congress of Industrial Organizations, the federation of US trade unions.

Congress of Racial Equality (CORE) a US nonviolent civil-rights organization, founded in Chicago in 1942.

congress system developed from the Congress of Vienna 1814–15, a series of international meetings in Aachen, Germany in 1818, Troppali, Austria in 1820, and Verona, Italy in 1822. British opposition to the use of congresses by ◊Metternich as a weapon against liberal and national movements inside Europe brought them to an end as a system of international arbitration, although congresses continued to meet into the 1830s.

Congreve /'kɒŋgri:v/ William 1670–1729. English dramatist and poet. His first success was the comedy *The Old Bachelor* 1693, followed by *The Double Dealer* 1694, *Love for Love* 1695, the tragedy *The Mourning Bride* 1697, and *The Way of the World* 1700. His plays, which satirize the social affectations of the time, are characterized by elegant wit and wordplay.

congruent /'kɒŋgruənt/ adj. 1. suitable, consistent (with). 2. in geometry, having the same shape and size, as applied to two-dimensional or solid figures. With plane congruent figures, one figure will fit on top of the other exactly, though this may first require rotation and/or reflection (making a mirror image) of one of the figures. —**congruence** n., **congruency** n. [from French or Latin congruere = agree]

congruous /'kɒŋgruəs/ adj. suitable, agreeing; fitting. —**congruity** /-'gruɪti/ n. [from Latin congruus]

conic /'kɒnɪk/ adj. of a cone. —**conic section**, a curve obtained when a conical surface is intersected by a plane. If the intersecting plane cuts both extensions of the cone, it yields a ◊hyperbola; if it is parallel to the side of the cone, it produces a ◊parabola. Other intersecting planes produce ◊circles or ◊ellipses. [from Latin from Greek]

conical /'kɒnɪkəl/ adj. cone-shaped.

conidium n. (plural **conidia**) an asexual spore formed by some fungi at the tip of a specialized ◊hypha or conidiophore. The conidiophores grow erect, and cells from their ends round off and separate into conidia, often forming long chains. Conidia easily become detached and are dispersed by air movements.

conifer /'kɒnɪfə, 'kəʊn-/ n. a tree or shrub of the class Coniferales, in the gymnosperm or naked-seed-bearing group of plants. They are often pyramidal in form, with leaves that are either scaled or made up of needles; most are evergreen. Conifers include pines, spruces, firs, yews, junipers, monkey puzzles, and larches. —**coniferous** /-'nɪfərəs/ adj. [from Latin (ferre = bear)]

conjectural /kən'dʒektʃərəl/ adj. based on or involving conjecture.

conjecture /kən'dʒektʃə/ n. 1. formation of an opinion on incomplete grounds; guessing. 2. a guess. —v.t./i. to guess. [from Old French or Latin conjicere (jacere = throw)]

conjoin /kən'dʒɔɪn/ v.t./i. to join or combine. [from Old French from Latin jungere = join]

conjoint /'kɒndʒɔɪnt/ adj. associated, conjoined.

conjunctiva /kɒndʒʌŋk'taɪvə/ n. the membrane covering the vertebrate ◊eye. It is continuous with the epidermis of the eyelid, and lies on the surface of the ◊cornea. [Latin]

conjugal /'kɒndʒʊgəl/ adj. of marriage or the relationship of husband and wife. —**conjugally** adv. [from Latin conjunx = spouse]

conjugate /'kɒndʒʊgeɪt/ v.t./i. 1. to give the different forms of (a verb). 2. to unite; to become fused. —adj. joined together, coupled, fused; in mathematics, indicating that two elements are reciprocally related, for example (a + ib) and (a − ib) are conjugate complex numbers. —n. a conjugate word or thing. [from Latin conjugare = yoke together (jugum = yoke)]

conjugate angle in geometry, one of two angles that add up to 360°.

conjugation /kɒndʒʊ'geɪʃən/ n. 1. in grammar, a system of verbal inflection. 2. in biology, the bacterial equivalent of sexual reproduction. A fragment of the ◊DNA from one bacterium is passed along a thin tube, the pilus, into the cell of another bacterium.

conjunct /kən'dʒʌŋkt/ adj. joined together; combined; associated. [from Latin]

conjunction /kən'dʒʌŋkʃən/ n. 1. joining, connection. 2. in grammar, a word used to connect clauses or sentences, or words in the same clause (e. g. and, but, if). 3. a combination of events or circumstances. 4. in astronomy, the alignment of two celestial bodies so that they have the same position as seen from Earth. **Inferior conjunction** occurs when an ◊inferior planet (or other object) passes between the Earth and Sun, and has an identical right ascension to the Sun. **Superior conjunction** occurs when a ◊superior planet (or other object) passes behind or on the far side of the Sun, and has the same right ascension as the Sun. **Planetary conjunction** takes place when a planet is closely aligned with another celestial object, such as the Moon, a star, or another planet, as seen from Earth.

conjunctive /kən'dʒʌŋktɪv/ adj. serving to join; in grammar, of the nature of a conjunction.

conjunctivitis /kɒndʒʌŋktɪ'vaɪtɪs/ n. inflammation of the conjunctiva.

conjuncture /kən'dʒʌŋktʃə/ n. a combination of events; a state of affairs. [French from Italian]

conjure /'kʌndʒə/ v.t./i. 1. to perform tricks which appear to be magical, especially by movements of the hands. 2. to summon (a spirit) to appear. —**conjure up**, to produce as if from nothing; to evoke. [from Old French conjurer = plot, exorcize, from Latin conjurare = bind together by oath]

conjuror n. a skilled performer of conjuring tricks.

conker n. a horse chestnut fruit; (in plural) a children's game played with these on strings. [from dialect conker = snail shell]

Connacht /'kɒnɔ:t/ province of the Republic of Ireland, comprising the counties of Galway, Leitrim, Mayo, Roscommon, and Sligo; area 17,130 sq km/6,612 sq mi; population (1986) 431,000. The chief towns are Galway, Roscommon, Castlebar, Sligo, and Carrick-on-Shannon. Mainly lowland, it is agricultural and stock-raising country, with poor land in the west.

Connery *Actor Sean Connery shot to fame as the first James Bond in* Dr No *1962.*

connate /'kɒneɪt/ *adj.* **1.** born with a person, innate. **2.** formed at the same time. **3.** (of leaves etc.) united from the start of life. [from Latin *connatus* (*nasci* = be born)]

connect /kə'nekt/ *v.t./i.* **1.** to join, to be joined; to construct a line etc. from (one point to another). **2.** to associate mentally or practically; (usually in *passive*) to unite or associate in a relationship etc. **3.** (of a train etc.) to be synchronized at its destination *with* another, allowing passengers to transfer. **4.** to be meaningful or relevant; to form a logical sequence. —**connecting rod,** the rod between the piston and the crankpin etc. [from Latin *nectere* = bind]

Connecticut /kə'netikət/ state in New England, USA; nicknamed Constitution State/Nutmeg State; **area** 13,000 sq km/5,018 sq mi; **capital** Hartford; **physical** highlands in the NW; Connecticut River; **products** dairy, poultry, and market garden products; tobacco, watches, clocks, silverware, helicopters, jet engines, nuclear submarines; **population** (1983) 3,138,000; **history** settled by Puritan colonists from Massachusetts in 1635, it was one of the Thirteen Colonies, and became a state in 1788.

connection /kə'nekʃən/ *n.* **1.** connecting; being connected or related. **2.** a relationship or association of ideas. **3.** a connecting part. **4.** a relative or close associate. **5.** a group of associates or clients. **6.** a connecting train etc.

connectionist machine a computing device built from a large number of interconnected simple processors, which are able both to communicate with each other and process information separately. The underlying model is that of the human brain.

connective *adj.* serving to connect, especially of body tissues connecting and supporting organs etc.

connective tissue in animals, tissue made up of a noncellular substance, the ◊extracellular matrix, in which some cells are embedded. Skin, bones, tendons, cartilage, and adipose tissue (fat) are the main connective tissues. There are also small amounts of connective tissue in organs such as the brain and liver, where they maintain shape and structure.

connector *n.* a thing that connects others.

Connell /'kɒnl/ James Irish socialist who wrote the British Labour Party anthem 'The Red Flag' during the 1889 London strike.

Connery /'kɒnəri/ Sean 1930– . Scottish film actor, the first, and arguably the best, interpreter of James Bond in several films based on the novels of Ian Fleming. His films include *Dr No* 1962, *From Russia with Love* 1963, *Marnie* 1964, *Goldfinger* 1964, *Diamonds are Forever* 1971, *A Bridge Too Far* 1977, *The Name of the Rose* 1986, *The Untouchables* 1987, and *The Russia House* 1990.

conning tower a raised structure on a submarine, containing the periscope; an armoured pilot house on a warship.

connive /kə'naɪv/ *v.i.* **connive at,** to disregard or tacitly consent to (wrongdoing). —**connivance** *n.* [from French or Latin *connivēre* = shut the eyes to]

connoisseur /kɒnə'sɜ:/ *n.* an expert judge (*of* or *in* matters of taste, especially in the fine arts). [from French *connaître* = know]

Connolly /'kɒnəli/ Cyril 1903–1974. English critic and author. As founder-editor of the literary magazine *Horizon* 1930–50, he had considerable critical influence. His books include *The Rock Pool* 1935, a novel of artists on the Riviera, and *The Unquiet Grave* 1945.

Connors /'kɒnəz/ Jimmy 1952– . US lawn tennis player. He won the Wimbledon title in 1974, and has since won ten Grand Slam events. He was one of the first players to popularize the two-handed backhand.

connote /kə'nəut/ *v.t.* (of words) to imply in addition to the literal meaning; to mean, to signify. —**connotation** /kɒnə'teɪʃən/ *n.,* **connotative** /'kɒnəteɪtɪv/ *adj.* [from Latin *notare* = note]

connubial /kə'nju:bɪəl/ *adj.* of marriage or the relation of husband and wife. [from Latin *nubere* = marry]

conquer /'kɒŋkə/ *v.t./i.* to overcome and control militarily; to be victorious; to overcome by effort. —**conqueror** *n.* [from Anglo-French from Latin *conquirere* = win]

conquest /'kɒŋkwest/ *n.* **1.** conquering. **2.** conquered territory; something won; a person whose affections have been won. —**the Conquest** *or* **Norman Conquest,** the conquest of England by William of Normandy in 1066.

conquistador /kɒn'kwɪstədɔ:/ *n.* (*plural* **conquistadores** /-ɔ:ri:z/) a conqueror, especially one of the Spanish soldiers and adventurers who conquered South and Central America in the 16th century. [Spanish]

Conrad /'kɒnræd/ Joseph 1857–1924. British novelist of Polish parentage, born Teodor Jozef Konrad Korzeniowski in the Ukraine. His novels include *Almayer's Folly* 1895, *Lord Jim* 1900, *Heart of Darkness* 1902, *Nostromo* 1904, *The Secret Agent* 1907, and *Under Western Eyes* 1911. His works vividly evoke the mysteries of sea life and exotic foreign settings and explore the psychological isolation of the 'outsider'.

> The terrorist and the policeman come from the same basket.
>
> **Joseph Conrad**
> *The Secret Agent*

Conrad /'kɒnræd/ several kings of the Germans and Holy Roman emperors, including:

Conrad I King of the Germans from 911, when he succeeded Louis the Child, the last of the German Carolingians. During his reign the realm was harassed by ◊Magyar invaders.

Conrad II King of the Germans from 1024, Holy Roman emperor from 1027. He ceded the Sleswick (Schleswig) borderland, S of the Jutland peninsula, to King Canute, but extended his rule into Lombardy and Burgundy.

Conrad III 1093–1152. Holy Roman emperor from 1138, the first king of the Hohenstaufen dynasty. Throughout his reign there was a fierce struggle between his followers, the Ghibellines, and the Guelphs (see ◊Guelphand Ghibelline) the followers of Henry the Proud, duke of Saxony and Bavaria (1108–1139), and later of his son Henry the Lion (1129–1195).

Conrad IV 1228–1254. Elected king of the Germans 1237. Son of the Holy Roman emperor Frederick II, he had to defend his right of succession against Henry Raspe of Thuringia (died 1247) and William of Holland (1227–1256).

Conrad V (Conradin) 1252–1268. Son of Conrad IV, recognized as king of the Germans, Sicily, and Jerusalem by German supporters of the ◊Hohenstaufens in 1254. He led Ghibelline (see ◊Guelph and Ghibelline) forces against Charles of Anjou at the battle of Tagliacozzo, N Italy in 1266, and was captured and executed.

Conran /'kɒnrən/ Terence 1931– . British designer and retailer of furnishings, fashion, and household goods. He was founder of the Habitat and Conran companies, with retail outlets in the UK, USA, and elsewhere. He also developed Mothercare, and his Storehouse group of companies gained control of British Home Stores in 1986.

consanguineous /ˌkɒnsæŋˈgwɪnɪəs/ adj. descended from the same ancestor, akin. —**consanguinity** n. [from Latin sanguis = blood]

conscience /ˈkɒnʃəns/ n. the moral sense of right and wrong, especially as felt by a person and affecting his behaviour. —**conscience clause**, a clause in a law, ensuring respect for the consciences of those affected. **conscience money**, a sum paid to relieve one's conscience. **conscience-stricken** adj. made uneasy by a bad conscience. [from Old French from Latin]

conscientious /ˌkɒnʃɪˈenʃəs/ adj. obedient to conscience; showing or done with careful attention. —**conscientious objector**, a person who for reasons of conscience objects to military service etc. —**conscientiously** adv., **conscientiousness** n.

conscious /ˈkɒnʃəs/ adj. 1. awake and aware of one's surroundings and identity. 2. knowing, aware (of or that). 3. (of actions, emotions, etc.) realized or recognized by the doer etc., intentional. —n. the conscious mind. —**consciously** adv. [from Latin conscire = be privy to (scire = know)]

consciousness n. awareness; a person's conscious thoughts and feelings as a whole.

conscript /kənˈskrɪpt/ v.t. to summon for compulsory state (especially military) service. —/ˈkɒnskrɪpt/ n. a conscripted person. [from Latin conscribere = enrol]

conscription n. legislation requiring all able-bodied male citizens (and female in some countries, such as Israel) to serve with the armed forces. It originated in France in 1792, and in the 19th and 20th centuries became the established practice in almost all European states.

consecrate /ˈkɒnsɪkreɪt/ v.t. 1. to make or declare sacred, to dedicate formally to a religious or divine purpose. 2. to devote to a purpose. —**consecration** /-ˈkreɪʃən/ n. [from Latin consecrare (sacrare = dedicate)]

consecutive /kənˈsekjʊtɪv/ adj. 1. following continuously, in unbroken or logical order. 2. in grammar, expressing consequence. —**consecutively** adv. [from French from Latin sequi = follow]

consensus /kənˈsensəs/ n. agreement in opinion; a majority view. [Latin]

consent /kənˈsent/ v.i. to express willingness or agree (to), to give permission (that). —n. voluntary agreement, permission. —**age of consent**, the age at which a girl's or boy's consent to sexual intercourse is valid in law. In the UK it is 16 (21 for male homosexual intercourse). [from Old French from Latin consentire = agree (sentire = feel)]

consequence /ˈkɒnsɪkwəns/ n. 1. what follows logically or effectively from some causal action or condition. 2. importance.

consequent /ˈkɒnsɪkwənt/ adj. following as a consequence (on or upon); logically consistent. —n. a thing that follows another. —**consequently** adv. [from Old French from Latin consequi]

consequential /ˌkɒnsɪˈkwenʃəl/ adj. 1. consequent; resulting indirectly. 2. self-important. —**consequentially** adv. [from Latin consequentia = consequence]

conservancy /kənˈsɜːvənsɪ/ n. a body controlling a port, river, etc., or concerned with the preservation of natural resources. [from Anglo-French from Latin]

conservation /ˌkɒnsəˈveɪʃən/ n. preservation, especially of the natural environment. Since the 1950s there has been a growing realization that the Earth, together with its atmosphere, animal and plant life, mineral and agricultural resources, form an interdependent whole, which is in danger of irreversible depletion and eventual destruction unless positive measures are taken to conserve a balance.

conservationist n. a supporter or advocate of environmental conservation.

conservation of energy the principle that states that in a chemical reaction, the total amount of energy in the system remains unchanged.

conservation of mass the principle that states that in a chemical reaction the sum of all the masses of the substances involved in the reaction (reactants) is equal to the sum of all of the masses of the substances produced by the reaction (products), that is, no matter is gained or lost.

conservative /kənˈsɜːvətɪv/ adj. 1. tending to conserve, averse to rapid changes; (of views, taste, etc.) avoiding extremes. 2. (of an estimate etc.) purposely low. —n. 1. a conservative person. 2. **Conservative**, a member or supporter of the Conservative Party. —**Conservative Party**, a political party disposed to maintain existing institutions and promote private enterprise; the name replaced **Tory** in general use from 1830 onwards. Traditionally the party of landed interests, it broadened its political base under Disraeli's leadership in the 19th century. The present Conservative Party's free-market capitalism is supported by the world of finance and the management of industry. —**conservatism** n., **conservatively** adv. [from Latin]

conservatoire /kənˈsɜːvətwɑː/ n. a (usually European) school of music or other arts. [French]

conservatory /kənˈsɜːvətərɪ/ n. a greenhouse for tender plants, especially one with a communicating entrance from a house.

conserve /kənˈsɜːv/ v.t. to keep from harm, decay, or loss, especially for future use. —n. jam, especially that made from fresh fruit. [from Old French from Latin servare = keep safe]

consider /kənˈsɪdə/ v.t. 1. to think about, especially in order to reach a conclusion; to examine the merits of; (in past participle, of an opinion etc.) formed after careful thought. 2. to make allowances or be thoughtful for. 3. to think to be; to have the opinion that. 4. to look attentively at. [from Old French from Latin considerare (originally an augural term, from sidus = star)]

considerable /kənˈsɪdərəbəl/ adj. not negligible, fairly great in amount or extent etc.; of some importance. —**considerably** adv.

considerate /kənˈsɪdərət/ adj. thoughtful for others, careful not to cause inconvenience or hurt. —**considerately** adv. [from Latin]

consideration /kənˌsɪdəˈreɪʃən/ n. 1. careful thought. 2. being considerate, kindness. 3. a factor influencing a decision or course of action. 4. a compensation, reward. —**in consideration of**, in return for, on account of. **take into consideration**, to make allowance for. [from Old French from Latin]

considering prep. in view of, taking into consideration; (colloquial) in view of the circumstances.

consign /kənˈsaɪn/ v.t. to hand over or deliver; to assign or commit to; to send (goods) to. [from French or Latin consignare = mark with a seal]

consignee /ˌkɒnsaɪˈniː/ n. a person to whom something is consigned.

consignment n. 1. consigning. 2. a batch of goods etc. consigned.

consist /kənˈsɪst/ v.i. 1. to be composed of. 2. to be consistent with. —**consist in**, to have as its basis or essential feature. [from Latin consistere = exist]

consistency /kənˈsɪstənsɪ/ n. 1. degree of density, firmness, or solidity, especially of thick liquids. 2. being consistent. [from French or Latin]

consistent /kənˈsɪstənt/ adj. 1. compatible or in harmony (with). 2. (of a person) constant to the same principles of thought or action. —**consistently** adv.

consistory /kənˈsɪstərɪ/ n. 1. a council of cardinals, or of the pope and cardinals. 2. **Consistory (Court)**, an Anglican bishop's court to deal with ecclesiastical problems and offences. [from Old French from Latin]

consolation /ˌkɒnsəˈleɪʃən/ n. consoling; a consoling circumstance. —**consolation prize**, a prize given to a competitor who just fails to win one of the main prizes. —**consolatory** adj.

console[1] /kənˈsəʊl/ v.t. to comfort, especially in grief or disappointment. [from French from Latin consolari]

console[2] /ˈkɒnsəʊl/ n. 1. a bracket supporting a shelf etc. 2. a frame containing the keys and stops of an organ; a panel for switches, controls, etc. 3. a cabinet for radio etc. equipment. [French]

consolidate /kənˈsɒlɪdeɪt/ v.t./i. 1. to make or become strong or solid. 2. to combine into one whole. —**consolidation** /-ˈdeɪʃən/ n. [from Latin consolidare (solidus = solid)]

consols /ˈkɒnsɒlz/ n.pl. British government securities. [abbreviation of consolidated annuities]

consommé /kənˈsɒmeɪ/ n. clear meat soup. [French]

consonance /ˈkɒnsənəns/ n. agreement or harmony.

consonant /ˈkɒnsənənt/ n. a speech sound in which the breath is at least partially obstructed, combining with a vowel to form a syllable; a letter representing this. —adj. in agreement or harmony with; agreeable to. —**consonantal** /-ˈnæntəl/ adj. [from French from Latin sonare = sound]

consort[1] /'kɒnsɔːt/ n. 1. a wife or husband, especially of a reigning monarch. 2. a ship sailing with another. —/kən'sɔːt/ v.i. 1. to associate or keep company (with, together). 2. to be in harmony (with). [from French from Latin consors = sharer (sors = lot)]

consort[2] n. an ensemble of voices and/or instruments in English music from about 1570 to 1720. [earlier form of concert]

consortium /kən'sɔːtiəm/ n. (plural consortia) an association, especially of several business companies. [Latin]

conspectus /kən'spektəs/ n. a general view or survey; a synopsis. [Latin (conspicere = look at attentively)]

conspicuous /kən'spɪkjuəs/ adj. clearly visible, attracting attention; noteworthy, striking. —conspicuously adv., conspicuousness n. [from Latin]

conspicuous consumption the selection and purchase of goods for their social rather than their inherent value. The term was coined by US economist Thorsten Veblen.

conspiracy /kən'spɪrəsɪ/ n. an act of conspiring; an unlawful combination or plot. —conspiracy of silence, an agreement not to talk about something.

conspirator /kən'spɪrətə/ n. a person who conspires. —conspiratorial /-'tɔːriəl/ adj., conspiratorially adv.

conspire /kən'spaɪə/ v.i. 1. to plan secretly with others, especially for some unlawful purpose. 2. (of events) to seem to be working together. [from Old French from Latin conspirare = agree, plot (spirare = breathe)]

constable /'kʌnstəbəl, 'kɒn-/ n. 1. a policeman or policewoman; a police officer of the lowest rank. 2. the governor of a royal castle. 3. (historical) the principal officer of the royal household. —Chief Constable, the head of the police force of an area. [from Old French from Latin comes stabuli = count of the stable]

Constable /'kʌnstəbəl/ John 1776–1837. English landscape painter. He painted scenes of his native Suffolk including The Haywain 1821 (National Gallery, London), and he travelled widely in Britain, depicting castles, cathedrals, landscapes, and coastal scenes. His many sketches are often considered among his best work. The paintings are remarkable for their freshness and influenced French painters such as Delacroix. In Nov 1990 The Lock 1824 was sold at Sotheby's, London, to a private collector for the record price of £10.78 million.

constabulary /kən'stæbjʊlərɪ/ n. a police force.

Constance, Council of /'kɒnstəns/ a council held by the Roman Catholic Church 1414–17 in Constance, Germany. It elected Pope Martin V, which ended the Great Schism 1378–1417 when there were rival popes in Rome and Avignon.

constancy /'kɒnstənsɪ/ n. the quality of being unchanging and dependable; faithfulness.

constant /'kɒnstənt/ adj. 1. continuous; frequently occurring. 2. unchanging, faithful, dependable. —n. anything that does not vary; in mathematics and physics, a quantity or number of constant value. —constantly adv. [from Old French from Latin stare = stand]

Constanţa /kɒn'stæntsə/ chief Romanian port on the Black Sea, capital of Constanţa region, and third largest city of Romania; population (1985) 323,000. It has refineries, shipbuilding yards, and food factories.

constantan n. a high-resistance alloy of approximately 40% nickel and 60% copper with a very low temperature coefficient. It is used in electrical resistors.

constant composition, law of in chemistry, the law that states that the proportions of the amounts of the elements in a pure compound are always the same and are independent of the method used to produce it.

Constant de Rebecque /kɒn'stɒn də rə'bek/ (Henri) Benjamin 1767–1830. French writer and politician. An advocate of the Revolution, he opposed Napoleon and in 1803 went into exile. Returning to Paris after the fall of Napoleon in 1814 he proposed a constitutional monarchy. He published the autobiographical novel Adolphe 1816, which reflects his affair with Madame de Staël, and later wrote the monumental study De la Religion 1825–31.

Constantine II /'kɒnstəntaɪn/ 1940– . King of the Hellenes (Greece). In 1964 he succeeded his father Paul I, went into exile in 1967, and was formally deposed in 1973.

Constantine the Great /'kɒnstəntaɪn/ AD 274–337. First Christian emperor of Rome and founder of Constantinople. He defeated Maxentius, joint emperor of Rome in 321, and in 313 formally recognized Christianity. As sole emperor of the West of the Empire, he defeated Licinius, emperor of the East, to become ruler of the Roman world in 324. He presided over the church's first council at Nicaea in 325. In 330 Constantine moved his capital to Byzantium, renaming it Constantinople.

Constantinople /kɒnstænti'nəupəl/ former name of Istanbul, Turkey, from 330 to 1453. It was named for the Roman emperor Constantine the Great when he enlarged the Greek city of Byzantium in 328 and declared it the capital of the Byzantine Empire 330. Its elaborate fortifications enabled it to resist a succession of sieges, but it was captured by crusaders in 1204, and was the seat of a Latin (Western European) kingdom until recaptured by the Greeks in 1261. An attack by the Turks in 1422 proved unsuccessful, but it was taken by another Turkish army on 29 May 1453 after nearly a year's siege, and became the capital of the Ottoman Empire.

constant prices a series of prices adjusted to reflect real purchasing power. If wages were to rise by 15% from 100 per week (to 115) and the rate of inflation was 10% (requiring 110 to maintain spending power), the real wage would have risen by 5%. Also an index used to create a constant price series, unlike current prices.

constellation /kɒnstə'leɪʃən/ n. one of the 88 areas into which the sky is divided for the purposes of identifying and naming celestial objects; a group of stars forming a recognizable pattern in the sky and identified by some imaginative name describing their form or identifying them with a mythological figure. [from French from Latin constellatio (stella = star)]

consternation /kɒnstə'neɪʃən/ n. amazement or dismay causing mental confusion. [from French or Latin sternere = throw down]

constipate /'kɒnstɪpeɪt/ v.t. to affect with constipation. [from Latin stipare = stuff full]

constipation /kɒnstɪ'peɪʃən/ n. a condition with hardened faeces and difficulty in emptying the bowels.

constituency /kən'stɪtjuənsɪ/ n. a body of voters who elect a representative; an area so represented.

constituent /kən'stɪtjuənt/ adj. 1. composing or helping to make a whole. 2. able to make or change a constitution; electing a representative. — n. 1. a constituent part. 2. a member of a constituency.

constitute /'kɒnstɪtjuːt/ v.t. 1. to compose, to be the essence or components of. 2. to appoint or set up (an assembly etc.) in legal form. 3. to form or establish. [from Latin constituere (statuere = set up)]

constitution /kɒnstɪ'tjuːʃən/ n. 1. an act or method of constituting, composition. 2. the condition of a person's body as regards health, strength, etc. 3. the form in which a state is organized; the body of fundamental principles by which a state or organization is governed. Since the French Revolution almost all countries (the UK is one exception) have adopted written constitutions; that of the USA (1787) is the oldest.

constitutional adj. of, in harmony with, or limited by the constitution. —n. a walk taken regularly as healthy exercise. —constitutionality /-'nælɪtɪ/ n., constitutionally adv.

constitutive /'kɒnstɪtjuːtɪv/ adj. 1. able to form or appoint, constituent. 2. essential.

constrain /kən'streɪn/ v.t. 1. to urge irresistibly or by necessity. 2. to confine forcibly, to imprison. 3. (in past participle) forced, embarrassed. [from Old French from Latin stringere = bind]

constraint /kən'streɪnt/ n. constraining, being constrained; a restriction; restraint of natural feelings, a constrained manner.

constrict /kən'strɪkt/ v.t. to compress, to make narrow or tight. —constriction n., constrictive adj. [from Latin]

constrictor n. 1. a muscle that draws together or narrows a part. 2. a snake that kills by compressing its prey.

construct /kən'strʌkt/ v.t. 1. to make by fitting parts together, to build or form. 2. in geometry, to delineate (a figure). —/'kɒn-/ n. a thing constructed, especially by the mind. —constructor /-'strʌktə/ n. [from Latin struere = pile, build]

construction /kən'strʌkʃən/ n. 1. constructing; a thing constructed. 2. the syntactical connection of words in a sentence. 3. an interpretation or explanation of a statement or action. —constructional adj.

constructive /kən'strʌktɪv/ adj. tending to form a basis for ideas, positive, helpful. —**constructively** adv.

Constructivism /kɒn'strʌktɪvɪzm/ n. a revolutionary art movement founded in Moscow in 1917 by the Russians Naum ◊Gabo, Antoine Pevsner (1886–1962), and Vladimir Tatlin (1885–1953). Tatlin's abstract sculptures, using wood, metal, and clear plastic, were hung on walls or suspended from ceilings. The brothers Gabo and Pevsner soon left the USSR and joined the European avant-garde. —**Constructivist** n. [from Russian *konstruktivizm*]

construe /kən'stru:/ v.t. 1. to interpret (words or actions). 2. to combine (words *with* others) grammatically. 3. to analyse the syntax of (a sentence). 4. to translate word for word.

consubstantial /kɒnsəb'stænʃəl/ adj. of one substance. [from Latin]

consubstantiation /kɒnsəbstænʃi'eɪʃən/ n. the doctrine, associated especially with Luther, that in the Eucharist, after consecration of the elements, the real substances of the body and blood of Christ coexist with the those of the bread and wine.

consul /'kɒnsəl/ n. 1. an official appointed by the state to live in a foreign city and protect the state's citizens and other interests there. 2. (*historical*) either of the two annually elected chief magistrates in ancient Rome. —**consular** /'kɒnsjulə/ adj. [Latin]

consulate /'kɒnsjulət/ n. the position, office, or residence of a consul.

consult /kən'sʌlt/ v.t./i. 1. to seek information or advice from (a person, book, etc.); to take counsel (*with*). 2. to take (feelings etc.) into consideration. [from French from Latin *consultare*, frequentative of *consulere* = take counsel]

consultant /kən'sʌltənt/ n. a person qualified to give expert professional advice, especially in a branch of medicine. —**consultancy** n.

consultation /kɒnsəl'teɪʃən/ n. consulting; a meeting for this purpose. [from Old French or Latin]

consultative /kən'sʌltətɪv/ adj. of or for consultation.

consume /kən'sju:m/ v.t. 1. to eat or drink; to use up; to destroy. 2. (in *past participle*) possessed *by* or entirely preoccupied *with* (envy etc.). —**consumable** adj. [from Latin *sumere* = take up]

consumer n. one who consumes, especially one who uses a product; a person who buys or uses goods or services; any organism that obtains its food by consuming organic material.

consumer durable a commodity that is required to satisfy personal requirements and that has a long life, such as furniture and electrical goods, as opposed to food and drink, which are **perishables** and have to be replaced frequently.

consumerism n. 1. protection or promotion of consumers' interests. 2. high consumption of goods, the belief in this.

consumer protection laws and measures designed to ensure fair trading for buyers. Responsibility for checking goods and services for quality, safety, and suitability has in the past few years moved increasingly away from the consumer to the producer.

consumers' association a group formed to protect consumer interests usually where the quality and price of goods or services is concerned.

consummate /kən'sʌmɪt/ adj. complete; perfect; supremely skilled. —/'kɒnsəmeɪt/ v.t. to make perfect or complete; to complete (a marriage) by sexual intercourse. —**consummation** /kɒnsə'meɪʃən/ n. [from Latin *consummare* = complete (*summus* = utmost)]

consumption /kən'sʌmpʃən/ n. 1. consuming; the amount consumed. In economics, a country's total expenditure over a given period (usually a year) on goods and services (including expenditure on raw materials and defence). 2. the purchase and use of goods etc. 3. pulmonary tuberculosis.

consumptive /kən'sʌmptɪv/ adj. tending to or affected with pulmonary tuberculosis. —n. a consumptive person.

contact /'kɒntækt/ n. 1. the condition or state of touching, meeting, or communicating. 2. a person who is or may be contacted for information, assistance, etc. 3. a person likely to carry a contagious disease through being near an infected person. 4. a connection for the passage of an electric current. —/also kən'tækt/ v.t. to get in touch with (a person); to begin communication or personal dealings with. —**contact lens**, a small, usually plastic, lens placed against the eyeball to correct faulty vision. [from Latin *contingere* (*tangere* = touch)]

contact process the main industrial method of manufacturing the chemical ◊sulphuric acid. Sulphur dioxide and air

are passed over a hot (450°C) ◊catalyst of vanadium(V) oxide. The sulphur trioxide produced is then absorbed in concentrated sulphuric acid to make fuming sulphuric acid (oleum). Unreacted gases are recycled. The oleum is diluted with water to give concentrated sulphuric acid (98%).

contado n. in northern and central Italy from the 9th to 13th centuries, the territory under a count's jurisdiction. During the 13th century, this jurisdiction passed to the cities, and it came to refer to the rural area over which a city exerted political and economic control.

Contadora /kɒntə'dɔ:rə/ Panamanian island of the Pearl Island group in the Gulf of Panama. It was the first meeting place, in 1983, of the foreign ministers of Colombia, Mexico, Panama, and Venezuela (now known as the **Contadora Group**) who came together to discuss the problems of Central America.

contagion /kən'teɪdʒən/ n. the spreading of disease by bodily contact; a disease so transmitted; a corrupting moral influence. [from Latin *contagio*]

contagious /kən'teɪdʒəs/ adj. (of a person) likely to transmit disease by bodily contact; (of a disease) transmitted in this way. [from Latin *contagiosus*]

contain /kən'teɪn/ v.t. 1. to have, hold, or be able to hold within itself; to include or comprise; to consist of, to be equal to; (of a number) to be divisible by (a factor) without remainder. 2. to enclose, to prevent from moving or extending; to control or restrain (feelings etc.). [from Old French from Latin *continēre* (*tenēre* = hold)]

container n. 1. a box, jar, etc., for containing particular things. 2. a large boxlike receptacle of standard design for the transport of goods.

containerize v.t. to transport by container; to convert to this method of transporting goods. —**containerization** /-'zeɪʃən/ n.

containment n. the action or policy of preventing the expansion of a hostile country or influence. —**Containment** n. a US policy dating from 1947 designed to prevent the spread of communism beyond the borders of the USSR.

contaminate /kən'tæmɪneɪt/ v.t. to pollute, especially with radioactivity; to infect. —**contaminant** n., **contamination** /-'neɪʃən/ n., **contaminator** n. [from Latin *contaminare* (*tamin-* related to *tangere* = touch)]

contemn /kən'tem/ v.t. (*literary*) to despise; to disregard. [from Old French or Latin *contemnere* = despise]

contemplate /'kɒntəmpleɪt/ v.t./i. 1. to survey with the eyes or mind. 2. to regard (an event) as possible; to intend. 3. to meditate. —**contemplation** /-'pleɪʃən/ n. [from Latin *contemplari* (*templum* = area within which an augur took the auspices)]

contemplative /kən'templətɪv/ adj. of or given to (especially religious) contemplation, meditative. —n. a person devoted to religious contemplation. [from Old French from Latin]

contemporaneous /kəntempə'reɪnɪəs/ adj. existing or occurring at the same time (*with*). —**contemporaneity** /-'ni:ɪtɪ/ n. [from Latin *contemporaneus* (*tempus* = time)]

contemporary /kən'tempərərɪ/ adj. 1. belonging to the same time or period; of the same age. 2. modern in style or design. —n. a contemporary person or thing. [from Latin]

contempt /kən'tempt/ n. 1. the feeling that a person or thing is worthless or beneath consideration, or deserving extreme reproach or scorn; the condition of being held in contempt.

contemptible /kən'temptɪbəl/ adj. deserving contempt. —**contemptibility** /-'bɪlɪtɪ/ n., **contemptibly** adv.

contempt of court behaviour that shows contempt for the authority of a court, such as disobeying a court order; behaviour that disrupts, prejudices, or interferes with court proceedings; and abuse of judges, inside or outside a court. The court may punish contempt with a fine or imprisonment.

contemptuous adj. feeling or showing contempt. —**contemptuously** adv., **contemptuousness** n.

contend /kən'tend/ v.i. 1. to struggle or compete; to argue (*with*). 2. to assert or maintain (*that*). —**contender** n. [from Old French or Latin *tendere* = stretch, strive]

content[1] /'kɒntent/ n. 1. (usually in *plural*) what is contained in a thing, especially in a vessel, book, or house. 2. capacity, volume. 3. the amount (of a constituent) contained. 4. the substance (of a speech etc.) as distinct from the form. [from Latin]

content[2] /kən'tent/ *predic.* adj. satisfied, adequately

continent

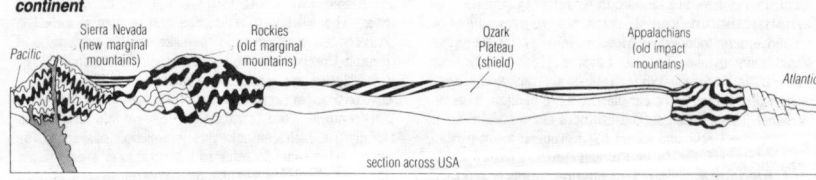

Sierra Nevada (new marginal mountains) — Rockies (old marginal mountains) — Ozark Plateau (shield) — Appalachians (old impact mountains)

Pacific — Atlantic

section across USA

happy; willing (*to* do). —*v.t.* to make content, to satisfy. —*n.* a contented state, satisfaction. [from Old French from Latin]

contented /kən'tɛntɪd/ *adj.* satisfied; willing to be content *with.* —**contentedly** *adv.*

contention /kən'tɛnʃən/ *n.* **1.** contending, argument or dispute. **2.** the point contended for in an argument.

contentious /kən'tɛnʃəs/ *adj.* **1.** quarrelsome. **2.** likely to cause argument.

contentment *n.* a contented state, tranquil happiness.

conterminous /kɒn'tɜːmɪnəs/ *adj.* having a common boundary (*with*). [from Latin *terminus* = boundary]

contest /'kɒntɛst/ *n.* contending, strife; a competition. —/kən'tɛst/ *v.t.* **1.** to dispute (a claim or statement). **2.** to contend or compete for (a prize, a seat in parliament, etc.) or in (an election). [from Latin *contestari* (*testis* = witness)]

contestant /kən'tɛstənt/ *n.* one who takes part in a contest.

context /'kɒntɛkst/ *n.* **1.** the parts that precede and follow a word or passage and fix its precise meaning. **2.** attendant circumstances. —**contextual** /kən'tɛkstjʊəl/ *adj.* [from Latin *texere* = weave]

Conti /'kɒnti/ Tom' 1945– . British stage and film actor specializing in character roles. His films include *The Duellists* 1977, *Merry Christmas Mr Lawrence* 1983, *Reuben, Reuben* 1983, *Beyond Therapy* 1987, and *Shirley Valentine* 1989.

contiguous /kən'tɪgjʊəs/ *adj.* next (*to*); touching, in contact. —**contiguity** /kɒnti'gju:ɪtɪ/ *n.*, **contiguously** *adv.*

continent[1] /'kɒntɪnənt/ any of the main continuous bodies of land (Europe, Asia, Africa, North America, South America, Australia, Antarctica). —**the Continent,** the mainland of Europe as distinct from the British Isles. [from Latin *terra continens* = continuous land]

continent[2] able to control the movements of the bowels and bladder. —**continence** *n.* [from Latin]

continental /kɒnti'nɛntəl/ *adj.* **1.** of or characteristic of a continent. **2.** Continental, characteristic of the Continent. —**Continental breakfast,** a light breakfast of coffee and rolls etc. **continental quilt,** a duvet. **continental shelf,** the shallow sea bed bordering a continent. **continental slope,** the relatively steep slope between the outer edge of the continental shelf and the ocean bed.

Continental Congress in US history, the federal legislature of the original 13 states, acting as a provisional revolutionary government during the War of ◊American Independence. It was convened in Philadelphia in 1774–89, when the constitution was adopted. The second Continental Congress, convened in May 1775, was responsible for drawing up the Declaration of Independence.

continental drift in geology, a theory proposed by the German meteorologist Alfred Wegener in 1915 that, about 200 million years ago, Earth consisted of a single large continent (◊Pangaea) that subsequently broke apart to form the continents known today. Such vast continental movements could not be satisfactorily explained until the study of ◊plate tectonics in the 1960s.

Continental System the system of economic preference and protection within Europe created by the French emperor Napoleon in order to exclude British trade. Apart from its function as economic warfare, the system also reinforced the French economy at the expense of other European states. It lasted from 1806 to 1813 but failed due to British naval superiority.

contingency /kən'tɪndʒənsɪ/ *n.* an event that may or may not occur; an unknown or unforeseen circumstance.

contingent /kən'tɪndʒənt/ *adj.* conditional or dependent (*on* or *upon* especially an uncertain event or circumstance); that may or may not occur; fortuitous. —*n.* a body of troops, ships, etc., forming part of a larger group. —**contingently** *adv.* [from Latin]

continual /kən'tɪnjʊəl/ *adj.* constantly or frequently recurring; always happening. —**continually** *adv.*

continuance /kən'tɪnjʊəns/ *n.* continuing in existence or operation; duration.

continuation /kəntɪnjʊ'eɪʃən/ *n.* continuing; a thing that continues something else.

continue /kən'tɪnju:/ *v.t./i.* **1.** to maintain or keep up, not to stop (an action etc.). **2.** to resume or prolong (a narrative, journey, etc., or *absolute*); to prolong, to be a sequel to. **3.** to remain, to stay; not to become other than. [from Old French from Latin *continuare*]

continuity /kɒntɪ'nju:ɪtɪ/ *n.* **1.** being continuous; unbroken succession; logical sequence. **2.** maintenance of consistency in successive shots or scenes of a film etc. **3.** linkage between broadcast items.

continuo /kən'tɪnjʊəʊ/ *n.* (*plural* **continuos**) abbreviation of *basso continuo*; in music, the bass line on which a keyboard player, often accompanied by a bass stringed instrument, built up a harmonic accompaniment in 17th-century Baroque music. [Italian]

continuous /kən'tɪnjʊəs/ *adj.* without an interval or break, uninterrupted; connected throughout in space or time. —**continuously** *adv.* [from Latin]

continuum /kən'tɪnjʊəm/ *n.* (*plural* **continua**) **1.** a thing of continuous structure. **2.** in mathematics, a set (see under ◊set[2], sense 7) that is infinite and everywhere continuous, such as the set of points on a line. [Latin]

contort /kən'tɔːt/ *v.t.* to twist or force out of normal shape. —**contortion** *n.* [from Latin *torquêre* = twist]

contortionist /kən'tɔːʃənɪst/ *n.* a performer who can twist his body into unusual positions.

contour /'kɒntʊə/ *n.* **1.** an outline. **2.** a line on a map joining points at the same altitude. **3.** a line separating differently coloured parts of a design. —*v.t.* to mark with contour lines. [from French from Italian *contornare* = draw in outline]

Contra /'kɒntrə/ *n.* a member of a Central American right-

continental drift

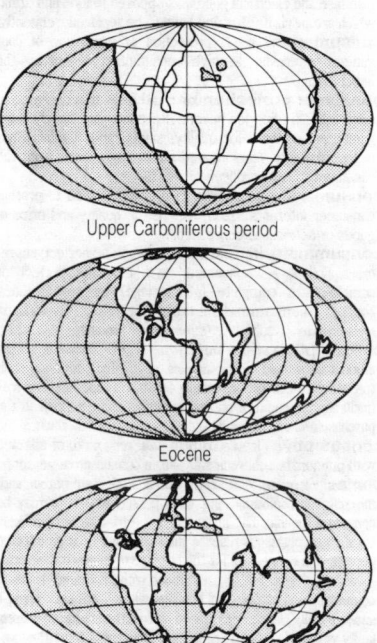

Upper Carboniferous period

Eocene

Lower Quaternary

wing guerrilla force attempting to overthrow the democratically elected Nicaraguan Sandinista government 1979–90. The Contras, many of them mercenaries or former members of the deposed Somota's guard (see ◊Nicaraguan Revolution), have operated mainly from bases outside Nicaragua, especially in Honduras, with covert US funding as revealed by the ◊Irangate hearings 1986-87. In 1989 US president Bush announced an agreement with Congress to provide $41 million in aid to the Contras until Feb 1990. The Sandinista government was defeated by the National Opposition Union, a US-backed coalition, in the Feb 1990 elections.

contra- prefix meaning against, opposed to. [from Latin *contra* = against]

contraband /'kɒntrəbænd/ *n.* smuggled goods, smuggling; prohibited trade. —*adj.* forbidden to be imported or exported. [from Spanish from Italian *bando* = proclamation]

contrabassoon *n.* a larger version of the ◊bassoon, sounding an octave lower.

contraception /kɒntrə'sepʃən/ *n.* prevention of pregnancy, the use of contraceptives.

contraceptive /kɒntrə'septɪv/ *adj.* preventing pregnancy. —*n.* a contraceptive device or drug. The contraceptive pill (the ◊Pill) contains female hormones that interfere with egg production or the first stage of pregnancy. The 'morning-after' pill can be taken after unprotected intercourse. Barrier contraceptives include condoms (sheaths) and caps, also called Dutch caps or diaphragms, which prevent the sperm entering the cervix (neck of the womb). ◊Intrauterine devices, also known as IUDs or coils, cause a slight inflammation of the lining of the womb; this prevents the fertilized egg from becoming implanted. See also ◊family planning.

contract /'kɒntrækt/ *n.* a written or spoken agreement, especially one enforceable by law; the document recording it. —/kən'trækt/ *v.t./i.* 1. to make or become smaller; to draw (muscles, the brow, etc.) together. 2. to shorten (a word) by combination or elision. 3. to make a contract (*with*); to form or enter into (a marriage, debt, etc.); to arrange for (work) to be done by contract. **contract in** *or* **out**, to elect to enter or not to enter a scheme or commitment. [from Old French from Latin *contractus* (*trahere* = draw)]

contractable *adj.* (of disease) that may be contracted.

contract bridge a form of bridge in which only tricks bid and won count towards the game. First played in 1925, from 1930 it quickly outgrew ◊auction bridge in popularity. The game originated on a steamer en route from Los Angeles to Havanna, and was introduced by Harold Stirling Vanderbilt (1884–1970), one of the players.

contractible *adj.* able to be made smaller or drawn together.

contractile /kən'træktaɪl/ *adj.* capable of or producing contraction. —**contractile root**, in botany, a thickened root at the base of a corm, bulb, or other organ that helps position it at an appropriate level in the ground. Contractile roots are found, for example, on the corms of *Crocus*. After they have become anchored in the soil, the upper portion contracts, pulling the plant deeper into the ground. **contractile vacuole**, a tiny organelle found in many single-celled freshwater organisms which slowly fills with water, and then contracts, expelling the water from the cell. —**contractility** /kɒntræk'tɪlɪti/ *n.*

contraction /kən'trækʃən/ *n.* 1. contracting. 2. shortening a word or words by combination or elision; a contracted form. 3. the contracting of a muscle, especially the muscles of the womb in childbirth.

contractor /kən'træktə/ *n.* one who makes a contract, especially to build houses.

contractual /kən'træktjuəl/ *adj.* of or in the nature of a contract. —**contractually** *adv.*

contradict /kɒntrə'dɪkt/ *v.t.* to deny; to deny the statement made by; (of facts, statements, etc.) to be at variance or conflict with. —**contradiction** *n.*, **contradictory** *adj.* [from Latin *dicere* = say]

contradistinction /kɒntrədɪs'tɪŋkʃən/ *n.* distinction by contrast; contrast.

contraflow *n.* a flow (especially of road traffic) in a direction opposite to, and alongside, that of the usual or established flow.

contralto /kən'træltəʊ/ *n.* (*plural* **contraltos**) the lowest female singing voice; a singer with such a voice; a part written for it. [Italian]

contraption /kən'træpʃən/ *n.* a machine or device, especially a strange or cumbersome one.

contrapuntal /kɒntrə'pʌntəl/ *adj.* of or in counterpoint. —**contrapuntally** *adv.* [from Italian *contrappunto* = counterpoint]

contrariwise /kən'treərɪwaɪz/ *adv.* on the other hand, in the opposite way; perversely.

contrary[1] /'kɒntrərɪ/ *adj.* opposed in nature, tendency, or direction; in opposition *to* ; (of a wind) impeding, unfavourable. —*n.* the opposite of a person or thing. —*adv.* in opposition or contrast *to*. —**on the contrary**, in contrast to what has just been implied or stated. [from Anglo-French from Latin *contrarius*]

contrary[2] /kən'treɪrɪ/ *adj.* doing the opposite of what is expected or advised, wilful. —**contrariness** *n.*

contrast /'kɒntrɑːst/ *n.* 1. juxtaposition or comparison showing striking differences; a difference so revealed. 2. a person or thing having noticeably different qualities (*to*). 3. the degree of difference between tones in a photograph or television picture. —/kən'trɑːst/ *v.t./i.* to set in opposition to reveal a contrast; to have or show a contrast (*with*). [from French from Italian from Latin *stare* = stand]

contravene /kɒntrə'viːn/ *v.t.* to violate or infringe (a law); to contradict, to conflict with. —**contravention** /- 'venʃən/ *n.* [from Latin *venire* = come]

contretemps /'kɒtrɒtɑ̃/ *n.* an unfortunate occurrence; an unexpected mishap. [French]

contribute /kən'trɪbjuːt, disputed usage 'kɒn-/ *v.t./i.* to give jointly with others (*to* a common fund); to supply (an article) for publication with others. —**contribute to**, to help to bring about. —**contributor** *n.* [from Latin *tribuere* = bestow]

contribution /kɒntrɪ'bjuːʃən/ *n.* contributing; a thing contributed. [from Old French or Latin]

contributory /kən'trɪbjutərɪ/ *adj.* that contributes; using contributions.

contrite /'kɒntraɪt/ *adj.* penitent, feeling great guilt. —**contritely** *adv.*, **contrition** /kən'trɪʃən/ *n.* [from Old French from Latin *contritus* = bruised (*terere* = rub)]

contrivance /kən'traɪvəns/ *n.* contriving; something contrived, especially a device or plan.

contrive /kən'traɪv/ *v.t./i.* to devise, plan, or make resourcefully or with skill; to manage (*to* do). —**contriver** *n.* [from Old French *controver* = find, imagine, from Italian]

control /kən'trəʊl/ *n.* 1. the power of directing or restraining; self-restraint; a means of restraining or regulating; (usually in *plural*) switches and other devices by which a machine is controlled. 2. a place where something is controlled or verified. 3. a standard of comparison for checking the results of an experiment. 4. a personality said to direct the actions and words of a spiritualist medium. —*v.t.* 1. to have control of, to regulate; to serve as a control to. 2. to check or verify. —**control tower**, a tall building at an airport from which air traffic is controlled. **in control**, in charge (*of*). **out of control**, unrestrained, without control. —**controllable** *adj.* [from Anglo-French *contreroller* = keep copy of accounts, from Latin *rotulus* = roll]

control experiment an essential part of a scientifically valid experiment, designed to show that the factor being tested is actually responsible for the effect observed. In the control experiment all factors, apart from the one under test, are exactly the same as in the test experiments, and all the same measurements are carried out. In drug trials, a placebo (a harmless substance) is given alongside the substance being tested in order to compare effects.

controller *n.* a person or thing that controls; a person in charge of expenditure.

controversial /kɒntrə'vɜːʃəl/ *adj.* causing or subject to controversy.

controversy /'kɒntrəvɜːsɪ, kən'trɒvəsɪ/ *n.* a prolonged argument or dispute.

controvert /'kɒntrəvɜːt/ *v.t.* to dispute or deny. [from French from Latin *vertere* = turn]

contumacy /'kɒntjuməsɪ/ *n.* stubborn refusal to obey or comply. —**contumacious** /kɒntju'meɪʃəs/ *adj.* [from Latin *contumax*]

contumely /'kɒntjuːmlɪ/ *n.* insulting language or treatment; disgrace. —**contumelious** /kɒntjuː'miːlɪəs/ *adj.* [from Latin]

contuse /kən'tju:z/ v.t. to bruise. —**contusion** n. [from Latin tundere = thump]

conundrum /kə'nʌndrəm/ n. a riddle or hard question, especially one with a pun in its answer.

conurbation /kɒnɜ:'beɪʃən/ n. an extended urban area, especially consisting of several towns and merging suburbs. [from Latin urbs = city]

convalesce /kɒnvə'les/ v.i. to recover health after an illness. [from Latin valescere = grow strong]

convalescent /kɒnvə'lesənt/ adj. recovering from an illness. —n. a convalescent person. —**convalescence** n.

convection /kən'vekʃən/ n. 1. the transmission of heat by movement of a fluid (gas or liquid). According to kinetic theory, molecules of fluid in contact with the source of heat expand and tend to rise within the bulk of the fluid. Less energetic, cooler molecules sink to take their place, setting up convection currents. This is the principle of natural convection in many domestic hot-water systems and space heaters. 2. in meteorology, a vertical movement of air. —**convective** adj. [from Latin convectio (vehere = carry)]

convector /kən'vektə/ n. a heating appliance that circulates warm air.

convene /kɒn'vi:n/ v.t./i. to summon or arrange (a meeting etc.); to assemble. —**convener** n. [from Latin venire = come]

convenience /kən'vi:nɪəns/ n. 1. the quality of being convenient, suitability; freedom from difficulty or trouble; advantage. 2. a useful thing; a lavatory, especially a public one. —**convenience food,** food requiring very little preparation.

convenient /kən'vi:nɪənt/ adj. serving one's comfort or interests, suitable, free of trouble or difficulty; available or occurring at a suitable time or place. —**conveniently** adv. [from Latin convenire = suit, agree with]

convent /'kɒnvənt/ n. a religious community, especially of nuns, under vows; a building occupied by this. [from Anglo-French from Latin]

conventicle /kən'ventɪkəl/ n. (chiefly historical) a secret meeting, especially of religious dissenters. [from Latin]

convention /kən'venʃən/ n. 1. a formal assembly or conference. 2. a formal agreement or treaty. 3. general agreement on social behaviour etc. by the implicit consent of the majority. 4. a custom or customary practice. [from Old French from Latin]

conventional adj. depending on or according with a convention; (of a person) attentive to social conventions; usual, of agreed significance; not spontaneous or sincere or original; (of weapons or a power) non-nuclear. —**conventionalism** n., **conventionality** /-'nælɪtɪ/ n., **conventionally** adv. [from French or Latin]

converge /kən'vɜ:dʒ/ v.i. to come together or towards the same point. —**converge on,** to approach from different directions. —**convergence** n., **convergent** adj. [from Latin vergere = incline]

convergence n. in mathematics, the property of a series of numbers in which the difference between consecutive terms gradually decreases. The sum of a converging series approaches a limit as the number of terms tends to ◊infinity.

convergent evolution the independent evolution of similar structures in species (or other taxonomic groups) that are not closely related, as a result of living in a similar way. Thus, birds and bats have wings, not because they are descended from a common winged ancestor, but because their respective ancestors independently evolved flight.

conversant /kən'vɜ:sənt/ adj. well acquainted (with a subject etc.). [from Old French]

conversation /kɒnvə'seɪʃən/ n. the informal exchange of ideas by spoken words; an instance of this. [from Old French from Latin]

conversational adj. of or in a conversation; colloquial. —**conversationally** adv.

conversationalist n. a person fond of or good at conversation.

converse[1] /kən'vɜ:s/ adj. to hold a conversation, to talk (with). —/'kɒnvɜ:s/ n. (archaic) conversation. [from Old French from Latin conversari = keep company]

converse[2] /'kɒnvɜ:s/ adj. opposite, contrary, reversed. —n. a converse statement, idea or proposition. —**conversely** /kən'vɜ:slɪ/ adv. [from Latin]

convert /kən'vɜ:t/ v.t./i. 1. to change or be able to be changed in form or function (into). 2. to cause (a person) to change his beliefs, opinion, party, etc. 3. to change (money etc.) into a different form or currency. 4. to make structural alterations in (a building) for a new purpose. 5. to complete (a try in Rugby football) by kicking a goal. —/'kɒnvɜ:t/ n. a person converted, especially to a new religion. —**conversion** n., **converter** n. [from Old French from Latin vertere = turn]

convertible /kən'vɜ:tɪbəl/ adj. able to be converted. —n. a car with a folding or detachable roof. —**convertibility** /-'bɪlɪtɪ/ n. [Old French from Latin]

convertiplane n. a type of ◊vertical takeoff aircraft with rotors on its wings that spin horizontally for takeoff, but tilt to spin in a vertical plane for forward flight.

convex /'kɒnveks/ adj. with the outline or surface curved like the exterior of a sphere or circle. —**convexity** /kɒn'veksɪtɪ/ n. [from Latin convexus = vaulted]

convex lens a converging ◊lens, a parallel beam of light passing through which converges and is eventually brought to a focus; it can therefore produce a real image on a screen. Such a lens is wider at its centre than at the edges. Common forms include **biconvex** (with both surfaces curved outwards) and **plano-convex** (with one flat surface and one convex). The whole lens may be further curved overall, making a **concavo-convex** or converging meniscus lens, as in some lenses used in corrective eyewear.

convey /kən'veɪ/ v.t. 1. to transport or carry (goods, passengers, etc.). 2. to communicate (an idea, meaning, etc.). 3. to transfer the legal title to (property). 4. to transmit (sound etc.). —**conveyable** adj. [from Old French from Latin conviare (via = way)]

conveyance n. 1. conveying. 2. a means of transport, a vehicle. 3. the transfer of property; a deed effecting this. —(in legal sense) **conveyancing** n. the administrative process involved in transferring title to land, usually on its sale or purchase. In England and Wales, conveyancing is usually done by solicitors, but, since 1985, can also be done by licensed conveyancers. Conveyancing has been simplified by the registration of land with the ◊Land Registry. **conveyancer** n.

conveyor n. or **conveyer** a person or thing that conveys. —**conveyor belt,** an endless moving belt for conveying articles in a factory etc. Trough-shaped belts are used, for example in mines, for transporting ores and coal. **Chain conveyors** are also used in coal mines to remove coal from the cutting machines. Overhead endless chain conveyors are used to carry components and bodies in car assembly works. Other types include **bucket conveyors** and **screw conveyors,** powered versions of ◊Archimedes screw.

convict /kən'vɪkt/ v.t. to prove or find guilty (of). —/'kɒnvɪkt/ n. a convicted prisoner. [from Latin vincere = conquer]

convict system British penal system of transporting convicted people to the British colonies, usually Australia. The ◊First Fleet arrived at Sydney Cove in Jan 1788. Altogether about 137,000 male and 25,000 female convicts were transported to Australia between 1788 and 1868.

conviction /kən'vɪkʃən/ n. 1. convicting, being convicted. 2. being convinced, a convinced state; a firm belief.

convince /kən'vɪns/ v.t. to persuade firmly (of, that). —**convincible** adj. [from Latin]

convivial /kən'vɪvɪəl/ adj. fond of good company, sociable and lively. —**conviviality** /-'ælɪtɪ/ n. **convivially** adv. [from Latin convivium = feast]

convocation /kɒnvə'keɪʃən/ n. convoking; an assembly convoked, especially the provincial synod of Anglican clergy or the legislative assembly of a university. —**convocational** adj.

convoke /kən'vəʊk/ v.t. to call together; to summon to assemble. [from Latin vocare = call]

convoluted /'kɒnvəlu:tɪd/ adj. coiled, twisted; complex. [from Latin convolutus (volvere = roll)]

convolution /kɒnvə'lu:ʃən/ n. coiling; a coil or twist; complexity; a sinuous fold in the surface of the brain.

convolvulus /kən'vɒlvjʊləs/ n. or **bindweed** any plant of the genus Convolvulus of the morning-glory family Convolvulaceae. They are characterized by their twining stems and by their petals, which are united into a funnel-shaped tube. The field bindweed C. arvensis, a trailing plant with white or pink-and-white-streaked flowers, is a common weed in Britain.

Cook English navigator and explorer Captain James Cook.

convoy /'kɒnvɔɪ/ *v.t.* to escort as a protection. —*n.* 1. convoying. 2. a group of ships, vehicles, etc., travelling together or escorted. [from Old French]

convoy system the grouping of ships to sail together under naval escort in wartime. In World War I (1914–18) navy escort vessels were at first used only to accompany troopships, but the convoy system was adopted for merchant shipping when the unrestricted German submarine campaign began in 1917.

convulse /kən'vʌls/ *v.t.* (usually in *passive*) to affect with convulsions; to cause to laugh uncontrollably. —**convulsive** *adj.* [from Latin *vellere* = pull]

convulsion /kən'vʌlʃən/ *n.* 1. (often in *plural*) a violent, irregular motion of the limbs or body caused by involuntary contraction of the muscles. 2. a violent disturbance. 3. (in *plural*) uncontrollable laughter.

cony /'kəʊnɪ/ *n.* a rabbit; its fur. [from Anglo-French from Latin *cuniculus*]

coo *n.* a soft murmuring sound like that of the dove. —*v.t./i.* to emit a coo; to talk or say in a soft or amorous voice. [imitative]

cooee /'kuːiː/ *n.* a cry used to attract attention. —*v.i.* to emit a cooee. —*interjection* (*colloquial*) used to attract attention. [imitative, originally Aboriginal]

cook /kʊk/ *v.t./i.* 1. to prepare (food) by heating; to undergo cooking. 2. (*colloquial*) to alter or falsify (accounts etc.). —*n.* one who cooks, especially professionally or in a specified way. —**cook up,** (*colloquial*) to invent or concoct (a story, an excuse, etc.). [Old English from Latin *coquus*]

Cook James 1728–1779. English naval explorer. After surveying the St Lawrence 1759, he made three voyages: 1769–71 to Tahiti, New Zealand, and Australia; 1772–75 to the South Pacific; and 1776–79 to the South and North Pacific, attempting to find the Northwest Passage and charting the Siberian coast. He was killed in Hawaii.

Cook Thomas 1808–1892. Pioneer British travel agent and founder of Thomas Cook & Son. He introduced traveller's cheques (then called 'circular notes'), in the early 1870s.

Cooke /kʊk/ Sam 1931–1964. US soul singer and songwriter who began his career as a gospel singer and turned to pop music in 1956. His hits include 'You Send Me' 1957 and 'Wonderful World' 1960 (re-released 1986).

cooker *n.* 1. an appliance or vessel for cooking food. 2. a fruit (especially an apple) suitable for cooking.

cookery *n.* the art or practice of cooking.

cookie /'kʊkɪ/ *n.* 1. (*US*) a sweet biscuit. 2. (*Scottish*) a plain bun. [from Dutch *koekje*, diminutive of *koek* = cake]

Cook Islands /kʊk/ group of six large and a number of smaller Polynesian islands 2,600 km/1,600 mi NE of Auckland, New Zealand, covering an area of 290 sq km/ 112 sq mi; population (1986) 17,000. Their main products include fruit, copra, and crafts. They became a self-governing overseas territory of New Zealand in 1965.

Cook, Mount highest point, 3,764 m/12,353 ft, of the Southern Alps, a range of mountains running through New Zealand.

Cook Strait strait dividing North Island and South Island, New Zealand. A submarine cable carries electricity from South to North Island.

cool *adj.* 1. of or at a fairly low temperature, fairly cold, not hot; suggesting or achieving coolness. 2. calm, unexcited; lacking enthusiasm, restrained; calmly audacious. —*n.* coolness; cool air, a cool place. —*v.t./i.* (often with *down* or *off*) to make or become cool. —**cooling tower,** a tall structure for cooling hot water before reuse, especially in industry. **cooling-off period,** an interval to allow for a change of mind before action. **cool off,** to calm down. —**coolly** /'kuːllɪ/ *adv.*, **coolness** *n.* [Old English]

coolant /'kuːlənt/ *n.* a cooling agent, especially a fluid to remove heat from an engine.

cooler *n.* 1. a vessel in which a thing is cooled. 2. (*slang*) a prison cell.

Coolidge /'kuːlɪdʒ/ (John) Calvin 1872–1933. 30th president of the USA 1923–29, a Republican. As Warren ◊Harding's vice president 1921–23, he succeeded to the presidency upon Harding's death (2 Aug 1923). He won the 1924 presidential election, and his period of office was marked by great economic prosperity.

> The business of America is business.
> **(John) Calvin Coolidge**
> speech 17 Jan 1925

coolie /'kuːlɪ/ *n.* an unskilled native labourer in Eastern countries. [perhaps from *Kuli*, tribe in India]

coomb /kuːm/ *n.* a valley on the side of a hill; a short valley running up from the coast. [Old English]

coop *n.* a cage for keeping poultry. —*v.t.* to keep in a coop; (often with *in* or *up*) to confine (a person). [from Low German or Dutch, ultimately from Latin *cupa* = cask]

cooper /'kuːpə/ *n.* a maker or repairer of casks and barrels.

Cooper a Grand Prix motor racing team formed by John Cooper (1923–) which built Formula Two and Formula Three cars before building the revolutionary rear-engined Cooper T45 in 1958.

Cooper Gary 1901–1962. US film actor. He epitomized the lean, true-hearted Yankee, slow of speech but capable of outdoing the 'bad guys' in *Lives of a Bengal Lancer* 1935, *Mr Deeds Goes to Town* (Academy Award for best picture 1936), *Sergeant York* 1940 (Academy Award for best actor 1941), and *High Noon* (Academy Award for best actor 1952).

Cooper James Fenimore 1789–1851. US writer of 50 novels, becoming popular with *The Spy* 1821. He wrote volumes of *Leatherstocking Tales* about the frontier hero Leatherstocking and American Indians before and after the American Revolution, including *The Last of the Mohicans* 1826.

Cooper Leon 1930– . British physicist who in 1955 began work on the puzzling phenomena of ◊superconductivity. He proposed that at low temperatures electrons would be bound in pairs (since known as **Cooper pairs**) and in this state electrical resistance to their flow through solids would disappear. He shared the 1972 Nobel Prize for Physics with ◊Bardeen and Schrieffer.

Cooper Susie. Married name Susan Vera Barker 1902– . English pottery designer. Her style has varied from colourful Art Deco to softer, pastel decoration on more classical shapes. She started her own company in 1929, which later became part of the Wedgwood factory, where she was senior designer from 1966.

cooperate /kəʊ'ɒpəreɪt/ *v.i.* to work or act together (*with*). —**cooperation** /-'reɪʃən/ *n.*, **cooperator** *n.* [from Latin *cooperari* (*opus* = work)]

cooperative /kəʊ'ɒpərətɪv/ *adj.* 1. of or providing cooperation; willing to cooperate. 2. (of a business) owned and run jointly by its members with profits shared among them. —*n.* a cooperative farm or society. —**cooperatively** *adv.*

cooperative movement the banding together of groups of people for mutual assistance in trade, manufacture, the supply of credit, or other services. The original principles of cooperative movement were laid down in 1844 by the Rochdale Pioneers, under the influence of Robert Owen, and by Charles Fourier in France.

Cooperative Party a political party founded in Britain in 1917 by the cooperative movement to maintain its principles in parliamentary and local government. A written constitution was adopted in 1938. The party had strong links with the Labour Party; from 1946 Cooperative Party candidates stood in elections as Cooperative and Labour Candidates and, after the 1959 general election, agreement was reached to limit the party's candidates to 30.

Cooperative Wholesale Society (CWS) a British concern, the largest cooperative organization in the world, owned and controlled by the numerous cooperative retail societies, which are also its customers. Founded in 1863, it acts as wholesaler, manufacturer, and banker, and owns factories, farms, and estates, in addition to offices and warehouses.

coopt /kəʊˈɒpt/ v.t. to appoint to membership of a body by the invitation or votes of the existing members. —**cooption** n., **cooptive** adj. [from Latin cooptare (optare = choose)]

coordinate /kəʊˈɔːdɪnət/ adj. equal in rank or importance (especially of the parts of a compound sentence); consisting of coordinate things. —n. 1. a coordinate thing. 2. in mathematics, each of a system of magnitudes used to fix the position of a point, a line, or a plane. 3. (in plural) matching items of clothing. —/-neɪt/ v.t. to make coordinate; to bring (parts, movements, etc.) into a proper relationship; to cause (the limbs, parts, etc.) to function together or in proper order. —**coordinately** adv., **coordination**/-ˈneɪʃən/ n., **coordinative** adj., **coordinator** n. [from Latin ordinare = arrange, order]

coordinate geometry or **analytical geometry** a system of geometry in which points, lines, shapes, and surfaces are represented by algebraic expressions. In plane (two-dimensional) coordinate geometry, the plane is usually defined by two axes at right angles to each other, the horizontal x-axis and the vertical y-axis, meeting at O, the origin. A point on the plane can be represented by a pair of ◊Cartesian coordinates, which define its position in terms of its distance along the x-axis and along the y-axis from O. These distances are respectively the x and y coordinates of the point.

coot n. any of various freshwater birds of the genus Fulica in the rail family. Coots are about 38 cm/1.2 ft long, and mainly black. They have a white bill, extending up the forehead in a plate, and big feet with lobed toes.

Coote /kuːt/ Eyre 1726–1783. Irish general in British India whose victory in 1760 at Wandiwash, followed by the capture of Pondicherry, ended French hopes of supremacy. He returned to India as commander in chief in 1779, and several times defeated ◊Hyder Ali, sultan of Mysore.

cop n. (slang) a policeman. —v.t. (-pp-) (slang) 1. to catch or arrest (an offender). 2. to receive, to obtain or suffer. —**cop out**, (slang) to withdraw, to give up. **cop-out** n. (slang) a cowardly evasion or escape. [perhaps from obsolete French cap = arrest from caper = seize]

copal /ˈkəʊpəl/ n. the resin of various tropical trees, used for varnish. [Spanish from Aztec]

copartner /kəʊˈpɑːtnə/ n. a partner or associate. —**copartnership** n.

cope[1] v.i. to deal effectively or contend with; (colloquial) to manage successfully. [from Old French from Latin from Greek kolaphos = blow with fist]

cope[2] n. a long cloaklike vestment worn by priests in ceremonies and processions. —v.t. to cover with a cope or coping. [Old English, from Latin cappa = cap, cape]

copeck /ˈkəʊpek/ n. a Russian coin, one hundredth of a rouble. [from Russian kopeika]

Copenhagen /kəʊpənˈheɪɡən/ (Danish **København**) capital of Denmark, on the islands of Zealand and Amager; population (1988) 1,344,000 (including suburbs). Copenhagen was a fishing village until 1167, when the bishop of Roskilde built the castle on the site of the present Christiansborg Palace. A settlement grew up, and it became the Danish capital in 1443. The university was founded in 1497. The city was under German occupation from April 1940–May 1945.

Copenhagen, Battle of naval victory on 2 April 1801 by a British fleet under Sir Hyde Parker (1739–1807) and ◊Nelson over the Danish fleet. Nelson put his telescope to his blind eye and refused to see Parker's signal for withdrawal.

copepod n. a crustacean of the subclass Copepoda, mainly microscopic and found in plankton.

Coperario /kəʊpəˈrɑːrɪəʊ/ John c.1570–1626. English composer of songs with lute or viol accompaniment.

Copernicus /kəˈpɜːnɪkəs/ Nicolaus 1473–1543. Polish astronomer, who believed that the Sun, not Earth, is at the centre of the solar system, thus defying the church doctrine of the time. For 30 years he worked on the hypothesis that the rotation and the orbital motion of Earth were responsible for the apparent movement of the heavenly bodies. His great work De Revolutionibus Orbium Coelestium/About the Revolutions of the Heavenly Spheres was not published until the year of his death.

Finally we shall place the Sun himself at the centre of the Universe.

Nicolaus Copernicus
De Revolutionibus Orbium Coelestium

copier /ˈkɒpɪə/ n. a person or machine that copies (documents etc.).

copilot /ˈkəʊpaɪlət/ n. the second pilot in an aircraft.

coping /ˈkəʊpɪŋ/ n. the top (usually sloping) row of masonry in a wall. —**coping stone**, a stone used in a coping.

coping saw a D-shaped saw for cutting curved outlines in wood. [from Old French coper = cut]

copious /ˈkəʊpɪəs/ adj. abundant, plentiful; producing much. —**copiously** adv. [from Old French or Latin copia = plenty]

coplanar adj. in geometry, describing lines or points that all lie in the same plane.

Copland /ˈkəʊplənd/ Aaron 1900–1990. US composer. Copland's early works, such as the piano concerto of 1926, were in the jazz idiom but he gradually developed a gentler style with a regional flavour drawn from American folk music.

Copley /ˈkɒpli/ John Singleton 1738–1815. US painter. He was the leading portraitist of the colonial period, but from 1775 he lived mainly in London, where he painted lively historical scenes such as *The Death of Major Pierson* 1783 (Tate Gallery, London).

copper[1] /ˈkɒpə/ n. 1. a reddish-brown ductile metallic element, symbol Cu, atomic number 29, relative atomic mass 63.546. It is used for its toughness, softness, pliability, high thermal and electrical conductivity, and resistance to corrosion. 2. a bronze coin; a penny. 3. a large metal vessel for boiling things, especially laundry. —adj. made of or coloured like copper. —v.t. to cover with copper. —**Copper Age**, the prehistoric period when some weapons and tools were made of copper, either before or in place of bronze. **copper beech**, a variety of beech with copper-coloured leaves. **copper-bottomed** adj. having the bottom sheathed with copper (especially of a ship or pan); reliable; genuine. **copper ore**, any mineral from which copper is extracted, including native copper, chalcocite, chalcopyrite, bornite, azurite, malachite, and chrysocolla. [Old English from Latin cuprum = cyprium aes = Cyprus metal (Cyprus was the principal source of copper in Roman times)]

copper[2] n. (slang) a policeman.

copperhead n. a venomous American or Australian snake with a reddish-brown head.

copperplate n. 1. a polished copper plate for engraving or etching; a print made from this. 2. a fine style of handwriting.

coppice /ˈkɒpɪs/ n. an area of small trees and undergrowth. —v.t. to cut trees down to near ground level at regular intervals, typically every 3–20 years, to promote the growth of numerous shoots from the base for use as firewood, fencing and so on. [from Old French from Latin]

Coppola /ˈkɒpələ/ Francis Ford 1939–. US film director and screenwriter. He directed *The Godfather* 1972, which became one of the biggest money-making films of all time, and its sequel *The Godfather Part II* 1974, which gained seven Academy Awards. His other films include *Apocalypse Now* 1979, *One From the Heart* 1982, *Rumble Fish* 1983, *The Outsiders* 1983, *The Cotton Club* 1984, *Gardens of Stone* 1987, *Tucker: The Man and His Dream* 1988, and *The Godfather Part III* 1990.

copra /ˈkɒprə/ *n.* dried coconut kernels. [Portuguese from Malayalam]

copse *n.* a coppice.

Copt *n.* 1. a native Egyptian in and after the Hellenistic period. 2. a member of the Coptic Church. Copts now form a small minority (about 5%) of Egypt's population. [from French from Arabic, ultimately from Greek *Aiguptios* = Egyptian]

Coptic /ˈkɒptɪk/ *adj.* of the Copts or Coptic. —*n.* the language of the Copts, now used only in the Coptic Church. A member of the Hamito-Semitic language family, it is descended from the language of the ancient Egyptians and is written in the Greek alphabet with some additional characters derived from ◊demotic script. —**Coptic Church**, the native Christian church in Egypt, traditionally founded by St Mark. The head of the Coptic Church is the Patriarch of Alexandria, currently Shenonda III (1923–   ), 117th pope of Alexandria. Imprisoned by President Sadat in 1981, he is opposed by Muslim fundamentalists.

copula /ˈkɒpjʊlə/ *n.* a connecting word, especially a part of the verb *to be* connecting the predicate with the subject. [Latin = fastening]

copulate /ˈkɒpjʊleɪt/ *v.i.* to come together sexually (*with*), as in the act of mating. —**copulation** /-ˈleɪʃən/ *n.* [from Latin *copulare* = fasten together]

copy /ˈkɒpɪ/ *n.* 1. a thing made to look like another; a specimen of a book, magazine, etc. 2. matter to be printed; material for a newspaper article. 3. the text of an advertisement. —*v.t./i.* to make a copy (of); to imitate, to do the same as. —**copy typist**, one who makes typewritten copies of documents etc. **copywriter** *n.* a writer of copy for publication, especially publicity material. [from Old French from Latin *copia* = abundance, in medieval sense = transcript, from phrase *facere copiam describendi* = give permission to transcribe]

copybook *n.* a book containing models of handwriting for learners to imitate. —*adj.* tritely conventional; exemplary.

copyhold *n.* (*historical*) tenure of land in accordance with the transcript of manorial records; land so held.

copyist *n.* a person who makes copies; an imitator.

copyright *n.* the exclusive legal right to print, publish, perform, film, or record literary, artistic, or musical material (including plays, recordings, films, photographs, radio and television broadcasts, and, in the USA and Britain, computer programs), normally vested in the creator of such material.

coquette /kɒˈket/ *n.* a flirtatious woman or girl. —*v.i.* to flirt. —**coquettish** *adj.*, **coquetry** /ˈkɒkɪtrɪ/ *n.* [French = wanton, diminutive of *coq* = cock]

cor- prefix see ◊com-.

coracle /ˈkɒrəkəl/ *n.* a small boat, constructed of wickerwork and made watertight originally with animal hides but more recently with pitch or some other watertight material, used for river and coastal transport by the ancient Britons and still used by fishermen on the rivers and lakes of Wales and Ireland. [from Welsh *corwgl* (*corwg* = Irish *currach* = boat)]

coral /ˈkɒrəl/ *n.* 1. a hard usually red, pink, or white calcareous substance secreted by many species of coelenterates for support or habitation, and sometimes building up to form reefs and islands; that forming the skeleton of the precious coral (*corallium*) of the Mediterranean and Red Sea; (*loosely*) a similar substance produced by marine algae etc. 2. a structure formed of such substances. 3. any of numerous species of usually colonial marine coelenterates producing a horny, calcareous, or soft skeleton; an individual polyp or colony of these, especially of the order Madreporaria (the stony or true corals) which have a calcareous skeleton and are the main reef-forming types. 3. the yellowish-or reddish-pink colour of some corals. —*adj.* 1. made of coral. 2. yellowish-or reddish-pink. [from Old French from Latin from Greek *korallion*, probably of Semitic origin]

Coralli /kɒrəˈliː/ Jean 1779–1854. French dancer and choreographer of Italian descent. He made his debut as a dancer in 1802. He choreographed *Le Diable boiteux* 1836

for the Austrian ballerina Fanny Elssler, *Giselle* 1841 and *La Péri* 1843 for the Italian ballerina Grisi; and many other well-known ballets.

coralline /ˈkɒrəlaɪn/ *adj.* of or like coral. —*n.* a seaweed with a hard, jointed stem. [from Italian *corallino*, diminutive of *corallo*]

Coral Sea /ˈkɒrəl/ or **Solomon Sea** part of the Pacific Ocean lying between NE Australia, New Guinea, the Solomon Islands, Vanuatu, and New Caledonia. It contains numerous coral islands and reefs. The Coral Sea Islands are a Territory of Australia; they comprise scattered reefs and islands over an area of about 1,000,000 sq km. They are uninhabited except for a meteorological station on Willis Island. The ◊Great Barrier Reef lies along its western edge.

cor anglais /kɔːr ˈɑ̃gleɪ/ an alto woodwind instrument of the oboe family. [French = English horn]

corbel /ˈkɔːbəl/ *n.* a stone or timber projection from a wall, acting as a supporting bracket. —**corbelled** *adj.* [from Old French, diminutive of *corp* = crow]

corbie /ˈkɔːbɪ/ *n.* (*Scottish*) a raven, a black crow. [from Old French *corb*, *corp* from Latin *corvus*]

Corbière /kɔːbiˈeə/ Tristan 1845–1875. French poet. His *Les Amours jaunes/Yellow Loves* 1873 went unrecognized until Verlaine called attention to it in 1884. Many of his poems, such as *La Rhapsodie Foraine/Wandering Rhapsody*, deal with life in his native Brittany.

Adulterous mixture of everything.

Tristan Corbière
Epitaph

cord *n.* 1. thick string or a piece of this; a similar structure in the body; electric flex. 2. a ribbed fabric, especially corduroy; (in *plural*) corduroy trousers. 3. a measure of cut wood; one cord equals 128 cubic feet (3.456 cubic metres), or a stack 8 feet (2.4 m) long, 4 feet (1.2 m) wide, and 4 feet high. —*v.t.* 1. to secure with cord. 2. (in *past participle*, of cloth) ribbed. [from Old French from Latin from Greek *khordē* = string of musical instrument]

Corday /kɔːˈdeɪ/ Charlotte 1768–1793. French Girondin (right-wing republican during the French Revolution). After the overthrow of the Girondins by the more extreme Jacobins in May 1793, she stabbed to death the Jacobin leader, Marat, with a bread knife as he sat in his bath in July of the same year. She was guillotined.

cordial /ˈkɔːdɪəl/ *adj.* heartfelt, sincere; warm, friendly. —*n.* a fruit-flavoured drink. —**cordiality** /-ˈælɪtɪ/ *n.*, **cordially** *adv.* [from Latin *cordialis* (*cor* = heart)]

cordierite *n.* a silicate mineral, $(Mg,Fe)_2Al_4Si_5O_{18}$, blue to purplish in colour, characteristic of metamorphic rocks formed from clay sediments under conditions of low pressure but moderate temperature; it is the mineral that forms the spots in spotted slate and spotted hornfels.

cordillera *n.* a group of mountain ranges and their valleys, all running in a specific direction, formed by the continued convergence of two ◊tectonic plates along a line.

Cordilleras, the /kɔːdɪlˈjeərəz/ mountainous western section of North America, with the Rocky mountains and the coastal ranges parallel to the contact between the North American and the Pacific plates.

cordite /ˈkɔːdaɪt/ *n.* a cordlike smokeless explosive.

cordon /ˈkɔːdən/ *n.* 1. a line or circle of police, soldiers, guards, etc., especially one preventing access to or from an area. 2. an ornamental cord or braid. 3. a fruit tree trained to grow as a single stem. —*v.t.* (often with *off*) to enclose or separate with a cordon of police. [from Italian and French]

cordon bleu /kɔːdɔ̃ ˈblɜː/ 1. of the highest class in cookery. 2. a cook of this class. [French = blue ribbon, originally that worn by Knights-grand-cross of the French order of the Holy Ghost, the highest order of chivalry under the Bourbon kings; hence extended to other first-class distinctions]

corduroy /ˈkɔːdərɔɪ/ *n.* a thick cotton fabric with velvety ribs; (in *plural*) corduroy trousers. [from *cord* = ribbed fabric and obsolete *duroy* = coarse woollen fabric]

core *n.* 1. the horny central part of certain fruits, containing the seeds. 2. the central or most important part of anything. 3. the central region of the Earth, which is divided into an inner core, the upper boundary of which is 1,700 km/1,060 mi from the centre, and an outer core, 1,820 km/1,130 mi thick. Both parts are thought to consist of iron-nickel alloy, with the inner core being solid and the outer core being liquid. The temperature may be 3,000°C/5,400°F. **4.** the region of fissile material in a nuclear reactor. **5.** a unit of structure in a computer, storing one bit (see ◊bit³) of data. **6.** the inner strand of an electric cable. **7.** the piece of soft iron forming the centre of a magnet or induction coil. —*v.t.* to remove the core from.

Corelli /kəˈreli/ Arcangelo 1653–1713. Italian composer and violinist. He was one of the first virtuoso violinists and his music, marked by graceful melody, includes a set of *concerti grossi* and five sets of chamber sonatas.

coreopsis /kɒriˈɒpsɪs/ *n.* a plant of the genus *Coreopsis*, with daisylike, usually yellow, flowers. [Latin, from Greek *koris* = bug and *opsis* = appearance (from the shape of the seed)]

co-respondent /kəʊriˈspɒndənt/ *n.* the person (especially the man) said to have committed adultery with the respondent in a divorce case.

Corfu /kɔːˈfuː/ (Greek *Kérkira*) northernmost, and second largest of the Ionian islands, off the coast of Epirus in the Ionian Sea; area 1,072 sq km/414 sq mi; population (1981) 96,500. Its businesses include tourism, fruit, olive oil, and textiles. Its largest town is the port of Corfu (*Kérkira*), population (1981) 33,560. Corfu was colonized by the Corinthians in about 700 BC. Venice held it from 1386–1797, Britain from 1815–64.

Corfu incident an international crisis 27 Aug–27 Sept 1923 which marked the first assertion of power in foreign affairs by the Italian Fascist government.

corgi /ˈkɔːgɪ/ *n.* a dog of short-legged Welsh breed with a foxlike head. [Welsh]

coriander /kɒriˈændə/ *n.* an aromatic herb, *Coriandrum sativum*; its seeds used as flavouring in meat products, bakery goods, tobacco, gin, and curry powder. Coriander is much used in cooking in the Middle East, India, Mexico, and China. [from Old French from Latin from Greek]

Corinna /kəˈrɪnə/ lived 6th century BC. Greek lyric poet, said to have instructed Pindar. Only fragments of her poetry survive.

Corinth /ˈkɒrɪnθ/ (Greek *Kórinthos*) port in Greece, on the isthmus connecting the Peloponnese with the mainland; population (1981) 22,650. The rocky isthmus is bisected by the 6.5 km/4 mi Corinth canal, opened in 1893. The site of the ancient city-state of Corinth lies 7 km/4.5 mi to the SW.

Corinthian /kəˈrɪnθiən/ *adj.* **1.** of ancient Corinth in S Greece. **2.** in architecture, of the order characterized by acanthus leaf capitals and ornate decoration, used especially by the Romans. [from Latin from Greek *Korinthios*]

Coriolis effect /kɒriˈəʊlɪs/ a result of the deflective force of the Earth's west to east rotation. Winds, ocean currents, and aircraft are deflected to the right of their direction of travel in the northern hemisphere and to the left in the southern hemisphere.

cork /kɔːk/ *n.* **1.** the light, waterproof outer layers of the bark of the stems and roots of almost all trees and shrubs. The **cork oak** *Quercus suber*, a native of S Europe and North Africa, is cultivated in Spain and Portugal; the exceptionally thick outer layers of its bark provide the cork that is used commercially. **2.** a bottle stopper of cork or other material. **3.** a float made of cork. —*v.t.* (often with *up*) to stop or confine; to restrain (the feelings etc.). [from Low German or Dutch from Spanish *alcorque*]

Cork largest county of the Republic of Ireland, in the province of Munster, covering an area of 7,460 sq km/2,880 sq mi; population (1986) 413,000. It is agricultural, but there is also some copper and manganese mining, marble quarrying, and river and sea fishing. Natural gas and oilfields are found off the S coast at Kinsale. The county town is Cork.

corkage /ˈkɔːkɪdʒ/ *n.* a charge made by a restaurant etc. for serving wine (especially when brought from elsewhere).

corked *adj.* stopped with cork; (of wine) spoilt by a decayed cork.

corkscrew *n.* **1.** a spiral steel device for extracting corks from bottles. **2.** (often *attributive*) a thing with a spiral shape. —*v.i.* to move spirally, to twist.

corm *n.* a short, swollen, underground plant stem, surrounded by protective scale leaves, as seen in *Crocus*. It stores food, provides a means of ◊vegetative reproduction, and acts as a ◊perennating organ. [from Latin from Greek *kormos* = trunk with boughs lopped off]

Corman /ˈkɔːmən/ Roger 1926– . US film director and producer. He directed a stylish series of Edgar Allan Poe films starring Vincent Price that began with *The House of Usher* 1960. After 1970 Corman confined himself to production and distribution.

cormorant /ˈkɔːmərənt/ *n.* any of various diving seabirds, mainly of the genus *Phalacrocorax*, about 90 cm/3 ft long, with webbed feet, long neck, hooked beak, and glossy black plumage. There are some 30 species of cormorants worldwide. Cormorants generally feed on fish and shellfish. Some species breed on inland lakes and rivers. [from Old French from Latin *corvus marinus* = sea raven]

Corn. abbreviation of Cornwall.

corn¹ *n.* a cereal before or after harvesting, especially wheat, oats, barley, or (*US*) maize; a grain or seed of a cereal plant. —**corn circle**, see ◊crop circle. **corncob** *n.* the cylindrical centre of an ear of maize, to which the grains are attached. **corn on the cob**, maize cooked and eaten in this form. **corn dolly**, a symbolic or decorative figure made of plaited straw. [Old English]

corn² *n.* a small, tender, horny place on the skin, especially on the toe. [from Anglo-French from Latin *cornu* = horn]

corncrake *n.* a bird *Crex crex* of the rail family. About 25 cm/10 in long, it is drably coloured, shy, and has a persistent rasping call. It lives in meadows and crops in temperate regions, but has become rare where mechanical methods of cutting corn are used.

cornea /ˈkɔːniə/ *n.* the transparent membrane covering the iris and pupil of the eyeball. The cornea is curved and behaves as a fixed lens, so that light entering the eye is partly focused before it reaches the lens. —**corneal** *adj.* [from Latin *cornea* (*tela* = horny tissue)]

corned *adj.* (of beef) preserved in salt or brine.

Corneille /kɔːˈneɪ/ Pierre 1606–1684. French dramatist. His many tragedies, such as *Oedipe* 1659, glorify the strength of will governed by reason, and established the French classical dramatic tradition for the next two centuries. His first play, *Mélite*, was performed in 1629, followed by others that gained him a brief period of favour with Cardinal Richelieu. *Le Cid* 1636 was attacked by the Academicians, although it received public acclaim. Later plays were based on Aristotle's unities.

cornel /ˈkɔːnəl/ *n.* a tree of the genus *Cornus*, e. g. cornelian cherry, dogwood. [from German, ultimately from Latin *cornus* = horn]

cornelian /kɔːˈniːliən/ *n.* a dull red variety of chalcedony. [from Old French, after Latin *caro* = flesh]

cornelian cherry /kɔːˈniːliən/ a European berry-bearing tree, *Cornus mas*.

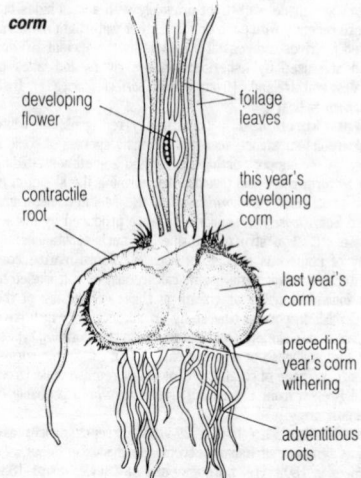

corm

developing flower

foilage leaves

contractile root

this year's developing corm

last year's corm

preceding year's corm withering

adventitious roots

corner *n.* 1. a place where converging sides or edges meet; a projecting angle, especially where two streets meet. 2. an internal space or recess formed by the meeting of two walls etc.; an angle of a ring in boxing etc., especially one where a contestant rests between rounds; a difficult position, especially one with no escape. 3. a secluded or remote place; a region or quarter, especially a remote one. 4. the action or result of buying the whole available stock of a commodity. 5. a free kick or hit from the corner of the field in football and hockey. —*v.t./i.* 1. to force (a person) into a difficult or inescapable position. 2. to establish a corner in (a commodity). 3. (especially of or in a vehicle) to go round a corner. —**cornerstone** *n.* a stone in the projecting angle of a wall, a foundation stone; an indispensable part or basis. [from Anglo-French from Latin *cornarium*]

cornet /'kɔːnɪt/ *n.* 1. a brass instrument resembling a trumpet but shorter with a wider bore and mellower tone, and without fixed notes. Notes of different pitch are obtained by over-blowing and by means of three pistons. 2. a conical wafer for holding ice cream. —**cornettist**, **cornetist** /-'netɪst/ *n.* [from Old French diminutive from Latin *cornu* = horn, trumpet]

cornett *n.* a 17th-century woodwind instrument with a cup mouthpiece which produces a trumpetlike tone.

cornflakes *n.pl.* a breakfast cereal of toasted maize flakes.

cornflour *n.* in the UK, the purified starch content of maize, used as a thickener in cooking; in the USA it is called cornstarch.

cornflower *n.* a plant (especially a blue-flowered kind, *Centaurea cyanus* now commonly grown in gardens as a herbaceous plant) that grows wild in cornfields.

Cornforth /'kɔːnfɔːθ/ John 1917– . Australian chemist who settled in England in 1941. In 1975 he shared the Nobel Prize for Chemistry with Vladimir Prelog for work using ◊radioisotopes as 'markers' to find out how enzymes synthesize chemicals that are mirror images of one another (stereo ◊isomers).

cornice /'kɔːnɪs/ *n.* a horizontal moulding in relief, especially along the top of an internal wall or as the topmost part of an entablature. [from French from Italian]

Cornish /'kɔːnɪʃ/ *adj.* of Cornwall or its people or language. —*n.* the ancient Celtic language spoken in Cornwall until 1777. Written Cornish first appeared in 10th-century documents; some religious plays were written in Cornish in the 15th and 16th centuries, but later literature is scanty, consisting mainly of folk tales and verses. —**Cornish pasty**, seasoned meat and vegetables baked in a pastry envelope. [from *Cornwall*, county of SW England]

Corn Laws in Britain until 1846, laws used to regulate the export or import of cereals in order to maintain an adequate supply for consumers and a secure price for producers. For centuries the Corn Laws formed an integral part of the mercantile system in England; they were repealed because they became an unwarranted tax on food and a hindrance to British exports. After the Napoleonic wars, with mounting pressure from a growing urban population, the Corn Laws aroused strong opposition because of their tendency to drive up prices. They were modified in 1828 and 1842 and, partly as a result of the Irish potato famine, repealed by Robert Peel in 1846. A remaining nominal duty was removed in 1869.

cornucopia /kɔːnju'kəʊpiə/ *n.* in Greek mythology, one of the horns of the goat Amaltheia, which was caused by Zeus to refill itself indefinitely with food and drink. In paintings, the cornucopia is depicted as a horn-shaped container spilling over with fruit and flowers. [Latin *cornu copiae* = horn of plenty]

Cornwall /'kɔːnwɔːl/ county in SW England including the ◊Scilly Islands (Scillies); **area** (excluding Scillies) 3,550 sq km/1,370 sq mi; **administrative headquarters** Truro; **physical** Bodmin Moor (including Brown Willy 419 m/1,375 ft), Land's End peninsula, St Michael's Mount, rivers Tamar, Fowey, Fal, Camel; **products** electronics, spring flowers, tin (mined since Bronze Age, some workings renewed in 1960s, though the industry has all but disappeared), kaolin (St Austell), fish; **population** (1987) 453,000; **history** the Stannary or Tinners' Parliament, established in the 11th century, ceased to meet in 1752 but its powers were never rescinded at Westminster, and it was revived in 1974 as a separatist movement.

Cornwallis /kɔːn'wɒlɪs/ Charles, 1st Marquess 1738–1805. English general in the ◊American Revolution until 1781, when his defeat at Yorktown led to final surrender and ended the war. He then served twice as governor general of India and once as viceroy of Ireland.

corny *adj.* (*colloquial*) trite; feebly humorous; sentimental, old-fashioned. —**cornily** *adv.*, **corniness** *n.*

corolla /kə'rɒlə/ *n.* the whorl of petals forming the inner envelope of a flower. In some plants the petal margins are partially or completely fused to form a **corolla tube**, for example in bindweed *Convolvulus arevensis*. [Latin, diminutive of *corona*]

corollary /kə'rɒlərɪ/ *n.* a proposition that follows from one already proved; the natural consequence (*of*). [from Latin *corollarium* = money paid for garlands, gratuity]

corona /kə'rəʊnə/ *n.* (*plural* **coronae** /-iː/) 1. the outermost region of the Sun, normally visible only during a total solar eclipse, when it is seen as a pearly glow round the disc of the obscuring Moon, extending for several times the radius of the Sun. It consists of an extremely rarefied gas of electrically charged particles, heated to a temperature of about 2,000,000°C/3,600,000°F by sound waves originating in the surface layers of the Sun. There is evidence of such regions in other stars. 2. a glow round an electric conductor. 3. any of various crownlike parts of the body. 4. (in a flower) an appendage on top of a seed or on the inner side of a corolla. —**coronal** *adj.* [Latin = garland, crown]

Corona Australis or **Southern Crown**, a constellation of the southern hemisphere, located near the constellation Sagittarius.

Corona Borealis or **Northern Crown**, a constellation of the northern hemisphere, between Hercules and Boötis, representing the headband of Ariadne that was cast into the sky by Bacchus. Its brightest star is Alphecca (or Gemma), which is 78 light years from Earth.

Coronado /kɒrə'nɑːdəʊ/ Francisco de *c.*1500–1554. Spanish explorer who sailed to the New World in 1535 in search of gold. In 1540 he set out with several hundred men from the Gulf of California on an exploration of what are today the Southern states. Although he failed to discover any gold, his expedition came across the impressive Grand Canyon of the Colorado and introduced the use of the horse to the indigenous Indians.

coronary /'kɒrənərɪ/ *adj.* of the arteries supplying blood to the heart. —*n.* a coronary artery or thrombosis. —**coronary thrombosis**, blockage of a coronary artery by a clot of blood.

coronary artery disease a condition in which the fatty deposits of ◊atherosclerosis form in the coronary arteries that supply the heart muscle, making them too narrow.

coronation /kɒrə'neɪʃən/ *n.* the ceremony of investing a sovereign with the emblems of royalty, as a symbol of inauguration in office. Since the coronation of Harold in 1066, English sovereigns have been crowned in Westminster Abbey, London. The kings of Scotland were traditionally crowned in Scone; French kings in Rheims. [from Old French from Latin *coronatio* (*coronare* = crown)]

coroner /'kɒrənə(r)/ *n.* an official who investigates the deaths of persons who have died suddenly by acts of violence, or under suspicious circumstances, by holding an inquest or ordering a post-mortem examination.

coronet /'kɒrənɪt, -net/ *n.* 1. a small crown; a band of jewels worn as a headdress. 2. the lowest part of a horse's pastern. [from Old French, diminutive of *corone* = crown]

Corot /'kɒrəʊ/ Jean-Baptiste-Camille 1796–1875. French painter, creator of a distinctive landscape style with cool colours and soft focus. His early work, including Italian scenes in the 1820s, influenced the Barbizon school of painters. Like them, Corot worked outdoors, but he also continued a conventional academic tradition with more romanticized paintings.

corpora /'kɔːpərə/ plural of **corpus**.

corporal[1] *n.* a noncommissioned army or RAF officer next below a sergeant. [from French from Italian]

corporal[2] *adj.* of the human body. —**corporal punishment**, that inflicted on the body, especially by beating. It is still used as a punishment for criminals in many countries, especially under Islamic law. It was abolished as a punishment for criminals in Britain in 1967 but only became illegal for punishing schoolchildren in state schools in 1986. —**corporality** /-'ælɪtɪ/ *n*. [from Old French from Latin *corpus* = body]

corporate /'kɔːpərət/ *adj*. forming a corporation or group; of or belonging to a group. [from Latin *corporare* = form into a body]

corporation /kɔːpə'reɪʃən/ *n*. 1. a group of people authorized to act as an individual, especially in business. 2. the civic authorities of a borough, town, or city. 3. (*colloquial*) a protruding abdomen.

corporation tax a tax levied on a company's profits by public authorities. It is a form of income tax, and rates vary according to country, but there is usually a flat rate. It is a large source of revenue for governments.

corporatism *n*. the belief that the state in capitalist democracies should intervene to a large extent in the economy to ensure social harmony.

corporative /'kɔːpərətɪv/ *adj*. of a corporation; governed by or organized in corporations, especially of employers and employed.

corporative state a state in which the members are organized and represented not on a local basis as citizens, but as producers working in a particular trade, industry, or profession. Originating with the syndicalist workers' movement, the idea was superficially adopted by the fascists during the 1920s and 1930s. Catholic social theory, as expounded in some papal encyclicals, also favours the corporative state as a means of eliminating class conflict.

corporeal /kɔː'pɔːrɪəl/ *adj*. bodily, physical; material. —**corporeality** /-'ælɪtɪ/ *n*., **corporeally** *adv*. [from Latin *corpus* = body]

corposant /'kɔːpəzənt/ *n*. or **St Elmo's fire** a luminous electrical discharge sometimes seen on a ship or aircraft during a storm. [from Spanish *corpo santo* = holy body]

corps /kɔː/ *n*. (*plural* the same /kɔːz/) 1. a military force or division. 2. a group of persons engaged in some activity. [French]

corps de ballet /kɔː də 'bæleɪ/ a company of ballet dancers. [French]

corps diplomatique /dɪpləmæ'tiːk/ the diplomatic corps (see ◊diplomatic). [French]

corpse *n*. a dead (usually human) body. [from Old French from Latin *corpus* = body]

corpulent /'kɔːpjʊlənt/ *adj*. bulky in body, fat. —**corpulence** *n*. [from Latin *corpulentus*]

corpus /'kɔːpəs/ *n*. (*plural* **corpora** /'kɔːpərə/) a body or collection of writings, texts, etc.

Corpus Christi /'krɪstɪ/ a feast celebrated in the Roman Catholic and Orthodox Churches, and to some extent in the Anglican Church, on the Thursday after Trinity Sunday. It was instituted in the 13th century through the devotion of St Juliana, prioress of Mount Cornillon, near Liège, Belgium, in honour of the Real Presence of Christ in the Eucharist.

corpuscle /'kɔːpʌsəl/ *n*. a minute body or cell in an organism, especially (in *plural*) the red or white cells in the blood of vertebrates. —**corpuscular** /-'pʌskjʊlə/ *adj*. [from Latin *corpusculum*, diminutive of *corpus* = body]

corpuscular theory a hypothesis about the nature of light championed by Isaac Newton, who postulated that it consists of a stream of particles or corpuscles. The theory was superseded at the beginning of the 19th century by Thomas ◊Young's wave theory. ◊Quantum theory and wave mechanics embody both concepts.

corpus luteum (plural **corpora lutea**) a temporary endocrine gland found in the mammalian ◊ovary. It is formed after ovulation from the Graafian follicle, a group of cells associated with bringing the egg to maturity, and secretes the hormone progesterone.

corral /kɒ'rɑːl/ *n*. an enclosure for wild animals or (*US*) cattle or horses. —*v.t*. (**-ll-**) to put or keep in a corral. [Spanish and Portuguese *curral*]

correct /kə'rekt/ *adj*. 1. true, accurate. 2. (of conduct) proper, in accordance with taste or a standard. —*v.t*. 1. to set right (an error, omission, etc.); to mark the errors in; to substitute the right thing for (a wrong one). 2. to admonish; to punish (a person or fault). 3. to counteract (a harmful or divergent tendency etc.); to eliminate an aberration from (a lens etc.); to bring into accordance with a standard. —**correctly** *adv*., **correctness** *n*., **corrector** *n*. [from Latin *corrigere* (*regere* = guide)]

correction /kə'rekʃən/ *n*. 1. correcting. 2. a thing substituted for what is wrong. 3. (*archaic*) punishment. [from Old French from Latin]

correctitude /kə'rektɪtjuːd/ *n*. consciously correct behaviour.

corrective /kə'rektɪv/ *adj*. serving to correct or counteract something harmful. —*n*. a corrective measure or thing. [French or from Latin]

Correggio /kɒ'redʒɪəʊ/ Antonio Allegri da *c*.1494–1534. Italian painter of the High Renaissance, whose style followed the classical grandeur of Leonardo and Titian but anticipated the Baroque in its emphasis on movement, softer forms, and contrasts of light and shade.

correlate /'kɒrəleɪt/ *v.t./i*. to have or bring into a mutual relation or dependence (*with* or *to*). —*n*. each of two related or complementary things. —**correlation** /-'leɪʃən/ *n*. [from Latin *relatio* = relation]

correlation *n*. a relation or form of interdependence between two sets of data. In ◊statistics, such relations are measured by the calculation of ◊coefficients. These generally measure correlation on a scale with 1 indicating perfect positive correlation, 0 no correlation at all, and –1 perfect inverse correlation.

correlative /kɒ'relətɪv/ *adj*. having a mutual relationship; in grammar, (of words) corresponding to each other and used regularly together (as *neither* and *nor*). —**correlativity** /-'tɪvɪtɪ/ *n*. [from Latin *relativus* = relative]

correspond /kɒrɪ'spɒnd/ *v.i*. 1. to be analogous (*to*) or in agreement (*with*). 2. to communicate by interchange of letters (*with*). [from French from Latin *respondere* = answer]

correspondence *n*. 1. agreement or similarity. 2. in mathematics, the relation between two sets where an operation on the members of one set maps some or all of them on to one or more members of the other. For example, if *A* is the set of members of a family and *B* is the set of months in the year, *A* and *B* are in correspondence if the operation is: '… has a birthday in the month of …'. 3. communication by letters; the letters sent or received. —**correspondence course**, a course of study conducted by post. [from Old French from Latin]

correspondent *n*. 1. a person writing letters to another, especially regularly. 2. a person employed by a newspaper to write regularly on a particular subject.

corridor /'kɒrɪdɔː/ *n*. 1. a passage from which doors lead into rooms; a passage in a train giving access to compartments along its length. 2. a strip of territory of one state passing through that of another. 3. a route which aircraft must follow, especially over foreign territory. [French from Italian *correre* = run]

corrie *n*. (Welsh *cwm*; French, American *cirque*) the Scottish term for a steep-walled hollow in the mountainside of a glaciated area representing the source of a melted glacier. The weight of the ice has ground out the bottom and worn back the sides. It is open at the front, and its sides and back are formed of ◊arêtes. There may be a lake in the bottom. [Gaelic]

corrigendum /kɒrɪ'gendəm/ *n*. (*plural* **corrigenda**) a thing to be corrected, especially an error in a book. [Latin *corrigere* = correct]

corrigible /'kɒrɪdʒɪbəl/ *adj*. able to be corrected; submissive. —**corrigibly** *adv*. [from French from Latin]

corroborate /kə'rɒbəreɪt/ *v.t*. to confirm or give support to (a person, a statement or belief). —**corroboration** /-'reɪʃən/ *n*., **corroborative** /kə'rɒbərətɪv/ *adj*. **corroborator** *n*., **corroboratory** /kə'rɒbərətərɪ/ *adj*. [from Latin *corroborare* (*robur* = strength)]

corroboree /kə'rɒbərɪ/ *n*. a festive or warlike dance of Australian aboriginals; a noisy party. [Aboriginal]

corrode /kə'rəʊd/ *v.t./i*. to wear away, especially by chemical action; to destroy gradually; to decay. —**corrosion** *n*. The rusting of ordinary iron and steel is the most common form of corrosion. Rusting takes place in moist air: the iron combines with oxygen and water to form a brown-orange deposit of rust, hydrated iron oxide. The rate of corrosion is increased where the atmosphere is polluted with sulphur dioxide. Salty road and air conditions accelerate the rusting of car bodies. [from Latin *rodere* = gnaw]

corrosive /kə'rəʊsɪv/ *adj*. tending to corrode. —*n*. a corrosive substance. [from Old French]

corrugated /'kɒrʊgeɪtɪd/ *adj*. formed into regular alternate folds and grooves, especially so as to strengthen (iron etc., or for use as roofing) or make (cardboard or paper) more resilient. —**corrugation** /-'geɪʃən/ *n*. [from Latin *corrugare* (*ruga* = wrinkle)]

corrupt /kə'rʌpt/ *adj*. **1**. morally depraved, wicked; influenced by or using bribery. **2**. (of a text etc.) made suspect or unreliable by errors or alterations. —*v.t./i*. to make or become corrupt. —**corruption** *n*., **corruptive** *adj*. [from Old French or Latin *corruptus* (*rumpere* = break)]

corruptible /kə'rʌptɪbəl/ *adj*. able to be (especially morally) corrupted. —**corruptibility** /-'bɪlɪtɪ/ *n*.

corsage /kɔː'sɑːʒ/ *n*. (*US*) a small bouquet worn by a woman. [from Old French]

corsair *n*. a pirate ship; a pirate based on the North African Barbary Coast. From the 16th century the corsairs plundered shipping in the Mediterranean and Atlantic, holding hostages for ransom or selling them as slaves. Although many punitive expeditions were sent against them, they were not suppressed until France occupied Algiers in 1830. [from French from Latin *cursarius*]

corselette /'kɔːslɪt/ *n*. a woman's foundation garment combining corset and brassière.

corset /'kɔːsɪt/ *n*. a close-fitting undergarment worn to compress and shape the figure or as a surgical support. —*v.t*. **1**. to provide with a corset. **2**. to control closely. —**corsetry** *n*. [from Old French diminutive of *cors* = body]

Corsica /'kɔːsɪkə/ (French *Corse*) island region of France, in the Mediterranean off the W coast of Italy, N of Sardinia; it comprises the *départements* of Haute Corse and Corse du Sud; **area** 8,700 sq km/3,358 sq mi; **capital** Ajaccio (port); **physical** mountainous, with ◊maquis vegetation; **government** its special status involves a 61-member regional parliament with the power to scrutinize French National Assembly bills applicable to the island and propose amendments; **products** wine, olive oil; **population** (1986) 249,000; including just under 50% native Corsicans. There are about 400,000 *émigrés*, mostly in Mexico and Central America, who return to retire; **language** French (official); the majority speak Corsican, an Italian dialect; **recent history** from 1962, French *pieds noirs* (Algerian refugees) were settled in Corsica, and their prosperity helped to fan nationalist feeling, which demands an independent Corsica. This fuelled a 'national liberation front' (FNLC), banned in 1983.

corslet /'kɔːslɪt/ *n*. **1**. a garment (usually tight-fitting) covering the body. **2**. (*historical*) armour covering the trunk of the body. [from Old French]

Cort /kɔːt/ Henry 1740–1800. English iron manufacturer. For the manufacture of ◊wrought iron, he invented the puddling process and developed the rolling mill, both of which were significant in the Industrial Revolution.

Cortázar /kɔː'tɑːzə/ Julio 1914–1984. Argentine writer, born in Brussels, whose novels include *The Winners* 1960, *Hopscotch* 1963, and *Sixty-Two: A Model Kit* 1968. His several volumes of short stories include 'Blow-up', adapted for a film by the Italian director Antonioni.

cortège /kɔː'teɪʒ/ *n*. a procession, especially for a funeral. [French]

Cortés /'kɔːtez/ Hernán (Ferdinand) 1485–1547. Spanish conquistador. He conquered the Aztec empire in 1519–21, and secured Mexico for Spain. His conquests eventually included most of Mexico and N Central America.

cortex /'kɔːteks/ *n*. (*plural* **cortices** /-isɪːz/) the outer covering of the kidney or other organ; the outer grey matter of the brain. In botany the cortex includes nonspecialized cells lying just beneath the surface cells of the root and stem. —**cortical** *adj*., **corticated** *adj*. [Latin = bark]

corticosteroid *n*. any of several steroid hormones secreted by the cortex of the ◊adrenal glands; also synthetic forms with similar properties. Corticosteroids have anti-inflammatory and ◊immunosuppressive effects and may be used to treat a number of conditions including rheumatoid arthritis, severe allergies, asthma, some skin diseases, and some cancers.

cortisone /'kɔːtɪzəʊn/ *n*. a natural corticosteroid produced by the ◊adrenal gland, now synthesized for its anti-inflammatory qualities and used in the treatment of rheumatoid arthritis, inflammation, and allergy.

corundum /kə'rʌndəm/ *n*. aluminium oxide, Al_2O_3, the hardest naturally occurring mineral known apart from dia-

Cortés *Spanish soldier and conqueror of Mexico, Ferdinand Cortés.*

mond (corundum rates 9 on the Mohs' scale); lack of ◊cleavage also increases its durability. Gem quality corundum is ruby (red) or sapphire (any other colour including blue). Material of lesser quality is used as an abrasive and for other industrial purposes; synthetic corundum is also used in industry. [from Tamil from Sanskrit = ruby]

coruscate /'kɒrəskeɪt/ *v.i*. to sparkle, to shine. —**coruscation** /-'skeɪʃən/ *n*. [from Latin *coruscare* = glitter]

corvette /kɔː'vet/ *n*. a small naval escort vessel; (*historical*) a flush-decked warship with one tier of guns. [French, from Middle Dutch *corf* = kind of ship]

corymb /'kɒrɪmb/ *n*. a flat-topped cluster of flowers on a long stem with the stems lengthening away from the centre. [from French or Latin from Greek = cluster]

cos¹ /kɒs/ *n*. a crisp lettuce with narrow leaves. [from *Cos*, island in the Aegean, where it originated]

cos² /kɒs, -z/ abbreviation of ◊cosine.

cos³ /kɒz/ *conj*. (*colloquial*) because.

cosec. /'kəʊsek/ abbreviation of ◊cosecant.

cosecant /kəʊ'siːkənt/ *n*. in trigonometry, a ◊function of an angle in a right-angled triangle found by dividing the length of the hypotenuse (the longest side) by the length of the side opposite the angle. Thus the cosecant of an angle A, usually shortened to cosec A, is always greater than 1. It is the reciprocal of the sine of the angle, that is, cosec $A = 1/\sin A$.

Cosgrave /'kɒzgreɪv/ Liam 1920– . Irish Fine Gael politician, prime minister of the Republic of Ireland 1973–77. As party leader 1965–77, he headed a Fine Gael–Labour coalition government from 1973. Relations between the Irish and UK governments improved under his premiership.

Cosgrave William Thomas 1880–1965. Irish politician. He took part in the ◊Easter Rising of 1916 and sat in the Sinn Féin cabinet of 1919–21. Head of the Free State government 1922–33, he founded and led the Fine Gael opposition 1933–44. His eldest son is Liam Cosgrave.

cosh *n*. (*colloquial*) a heavy blunt weapon. —*v.t*. (*colloquial*) to hit with a cosh.

cosine /'kəʊsaɪn/ *n*. in trigonometry, a function of an angle in a right-angled triangle found by dividing the length of the side adjacent to the angle by the length of the hypotenuse (the longest side). It is usually shortened to cos.

cosmetic /kɒz'metɪk/ *adj*. **1**. designed to beautify the skin, hair, etc.; (of a body treatment or surgery) improving or restoring the normal appearance. **2**. superficially improving or beneficial. —*n*. a cosmetic preparation, especially for the face. —**cosmetically** *adv.* [from French from Greek *kosmeō* = adorn]

cosmic /'kɒzmɪk/ *adj.* of the cosmos, especially as distinct from the Earth; of or for space travel. —**cosmic rays** *or* **radiation,** high energy radiation from outer space.

cosmic background radiation the electromagnetic radiation, also known as the 3° radiation, left over from the original formation of the universe in the Big Bang around 15 billion years ago. It corresponds to an overall background temperature of 3K (–270°C/–454°F), or 3°C above absolute zero.

cosmic radiation streams of high-energy particles from outer space, consisting of protons, alpha particles, and light nuclei, which collide with atomic nuclei in the Earth's atmosphere.

cosmogony /kɒz'mɒgənɪ/ *n.* the origin of the universe; a theory about this. [from Greek *cosmos* = universe and *-gonia* = begetting]

cosmology /kɒz'mɒlədʒɪ/ *n.* the science of the creation and development of the universe. Modern cosmology began in the 1920s with the discovery that the universe is expanding, which suggested that it began in an explosion, the ◊Big Bang. An alternative view, the ◊**steady-state theory,** claimed that the universe has no origin, but is expanding because new matter is being continually created. —**cosmological** /-'lɒdʒɪkəl/ *adj.,* **cosmologist** *n.*

cosmonaut /'kɒzmənɔ:t/ *n.* a Russian astronaut.

cosmopolitan /kɒzmə'pɒlɪtən/ *adj.* of or from many parts of the world; free from national limitations or prejudices. —*n.* a cosmopolitan person. —**cosmopolitanism** *n.* [from Greek *kosmopolitēs* = citizen of the world]

cosmos[1] /'kɒzmɒs/ *n.* the universe as a well-ordered whole. [Greek = order, ornament, world, or universe]

cosmos[2] *n.* a garden plant of the genus *Cosmos,* with pink, white, or purple flowers.

Cosmos /'kɒzmɒs/ *n.* the name used since the early 1960s for nearly all Soviet artificial satellites. Nearly 2,000 Cosmos satellites have been launched.

Cossack /'kɒsæk/ *n.* a member of any of several, formerly horse-raising, Tatar groups of S and SW Russia, the Ukraine, and Poland, who took in escaped serfs, and lived in independent communal settlements (military brotherhoods) from the 15th to the 19th centuries. Later they held land in return for military service in the cavalry under Russian and Polish rulers. After 1917, the various Cossack communities were incorporated into the Soviet administrative and collective system. [ultimately from Turki = nomad, adventurer (first used of an unrelated nomadic people, the Kzaakhs of S Siberia)]

cosset /'kɒsɪt/ *v.t.* to pamper. [from earlier n. = pet lamb, from Anglo-French from Old English *cotsǣta* = cottager]

cost *v.t.* 1. (*past* and *past participle* **cost**) to be obtainable for (a certain sum), to have as a price; to require as an effort; to involve as a loss or sacrifice. 2. (*past* and *past participle* **costed**) to fix or estimate the cost of. —*n.* what a thing costs, a price; an expenditure of time or effort; a loss or sacrifice; (in *plural*) legal expenses. —**at all costs,** no matter what the cost or risk may be. **cost-effective** *adj.* effective in relation to its cost. **cost price,** the price paid for a thing by one who later sells it. [from Old French from Latin *constare* = stand at a price]

costal /'kɒstəl/ *adj.* of the ribs. [from French from Latin *costa* = rib]

co-star *n.* a cinema or stage star appearing with another or others of equal importance. —*v.t.* (**-rr-**) to include as a co-star.

Costa Rica /'kɒstə 'ri:kə/ Republic of; country in Central America, bounded N by Nicaragua, S by Panama, E by the Caribbean, and W by the Pacific Ocean; **area** 51,100 sq km/19,735 sq mi; **capital** San José; **physical** high central plateau and tropical coasts; Costa Rica was once entirely forested but by 1983 only 17% of the forest remained; half of the arable land had been cleared for cattle ranching; **head of state and government** Rafael Calderón from 1990; **political system** liberal democracy; **exports** coffee, bananas, cocoa, sugar, beef; **population** (1990 est) 3,032,000 (including 1,200 Guaymi Indians); **language** Spanish (official); **recent history** independence was achieved from Spain in 1821. A new constitution was adopted in 1949. Deterioration in the economy was faced by a harsh austerity programme. Despite US pressure,

Costa Rica remained neutral towards the Sandinista regime in Nicaragua during the 1980s.

cost benefit analysis the process whereby a project is assessed for its social and welfare benefits in addition to considering the financial return on investment. For example, this might take into account the environmental impact of an industrial plant or convenience for users of a new railway.

Costello /kɒ'steləʊ/ Elvis. Stage name of Declan McManus 1954– . English rock singer, songwriter, and guitarist, renowned for his stylistic range and intricate lyrics. His albums with his group the Attractions include *Armed Forces* 1979, *Trust* 1981, *Blood and Chocolate* 1986, and *Spike* 1989.

coster *n.* a costermonger. [abbreviation]

Coster /'kɒstə/ Laurens Janszoon 1370–1440. Dutch printer. According to some sources, he invented moveable type, but after his death an apprentice ran off to Mainz with the blocks and, taking ◊Gutenberg into his confidence, began a printing business with him.

costermonger /'kɒstəmʌŋgə/ *n.* a person who sells fruit, vegetables, etc., from a barrow in the street. [from *costard* = large apple from Old French]

costive /'kɒstɪv/ *adj.* constipated. [from Old French from Latin]

costly *adj.* costing much, expensive. —**costliness** *n.*

cost of living the cost of goods and services needed for an average standard of living. In Britain the cost-of-living index was introduced in 1914 and based on the expenditure of a working-class family of man, woman, and three children; the standard is 100. Known from 1947 as the Retail Price Index (RPI), it is revised to allow for inflation.

costume /'kɒstju:m/ *n.* a style of dress, especially as associated with a particular place or time; a set of clothes; clothes or a garment for a particular activity; an actor's clothes for a part. —**costume jewellery,** jewellery made of inexpensive materials. [French from Italian, from Latin *consuetudo* = custom]

costumier /kɒ'stju:mɪə/ *n.* one who makes or deals in costumes. [French]

cosy /'kəʊzɪ/ *adj.* comfortable and warm, snug. —*n.* a cover to keep hot a teapot or boiled egg. —*v.t.* (often with *along*) (*colloquial*) to reassure, to delude. —**cosily** *adv.,* **cosiness** *n.* [originally Scottish]

cot[1] *n.* a bed with high sides for a baby or very young child; a small, light bed. —**cot death,** the death of an apparently healthy baby during sleep, also known as **sudden infant death syndrome** (SIDS). It is most common in the winter months, and strikes boys more than girls. The cause is not known. [from Hindi = bedstead, hammock]

cot[2] *n.* a small shelter; a cote; (*poetic*) a cottage. [Old English]

cot[3] abbreviation of cotangent.

cotangent /'kəʊtændʒənt/ *n.* in trigonometry, a ◊function of an angle in a right-angled triangle found by dividing the length of the side adjacent to the angle by the length of the side opposite it. It is usually written as cotan, or cot and it is the reciprocal of the tangent of the angle, so that cot A = 1/tan A, where A is the angle in question.

cote *n.* a shed, stall, or shelter, especially for birds or animals. [Old English]

coterie /'kəʊtərɪ/ *n.* an exclusive group of people sharing an interest. [French, originally = association of tenants]

Cotman /'kɒtmən/ John Sell 1782–1842. English landscape painter, with Crome a founder of the **Norwich school,** a group of realistic landscape painters influenced by Dutch examples. His early watercolours were bold designs in simple, flat washes of colour, for example *Greta Bridge, Yorkshire* 1805 (British Museum, London).

cotoneaster /kətəʊni'æstə(r)/ *n.* any plant of the Eurasian genus *Cotoneaster* of trees and shrubs of the rose family Rosaceae, closely allied to the hawthorn and medlar. The fruits, though small and unpalatable, are usually bright red and conspicuous, often persisting through the winter. Some of the shrubs are cultivated for their attractive appearance. [from Latin *cotoneum* = quince]

Cotonou /kɒtə'nu:/ chief port and largest city of Benin, on the Bight of Benin; population (1982) 487,000. Palm products and timber are exported.

Cotopaxi /kɒtə'pæksi/ an active volcano, situated to the S of Quito in Ecuador. It is 5,897 m/19,347 ft high and was first climbed in 1872. [Quechua = shining peak]

cottage /'kɒtɪdʒ/ n. a small, simple house, especially in the country. —**cottage cheese**, a soft white cheese made from curds of skim milk without pressing. **cottage industry**, one carried on at home. **cottage pie**, a dish of minced meat topped with mashed potato. [from Anglo-French]

cottager n. one who lives in a cottage.

cottar /'kɒtə/ n. or **cotter** (*historical* and *Scottish*) a farm labourer having free use of a cottage.

cotter n. a bolt or wedge for securing parts of machinery etc. —**cotter pin**, a cotter, a split pin put through a cotter to keep it in place.

cotton /'kɒtən/ n. a soft, white, fibrous substance covering the seeds of tropical plants of the genus *Gossypium*; such a plant; thread or cloth made from this. —*v.i.* **cotton on (to)**, (*slang*) to understand; to form a liking or attachment for. —**cotton wool**, fluffy wadding of a kind originally made from raw cotton. —**cottony** *adj.* [from Old French from Arabic]

Cotton /'kɒtn/ Joseph 1905– . US actor, who was brought into films by Orson Welles. He appeared in many international productions, until the early 1980s, often in leading or important roles, including *Citizen Kane* 1941, *The Third Man* 1949, and *The Abominable Dr Phibes* 1971.

cotton gin a machine that separates cotton fibres from the seed boll. The production of the gin (then called an **engine**) by US inventor Eli Whitney in 1793 was a milestone in textile history.

cottonwood n. any of several species of North American poplar (genus *Populus*) with seeds topped by a thick tuft of silky hairs. The **eastern cottonwood** *P. deltoides*, growing to 30 m/100 ft, is native to the eastern USA. The name cottonwood is also given to the downy-leaved Australian tree *Bedfordia salaoina*.

cotyledon /kɒti'li:dən/ n. a structure in the embryo of a seed plant that may form a 'leaf' after germination and is commonly known as a seed leaf. The number of cotyledons present in an embryo is an important character in the classification of flowering plants (◊angiosperms). [Latin from Greek *kotulē* = cup]

couch[1] /kaʊtʃ/ n. **1.** a piece of furniture like a sofa but with the back extending along half its length and only one raised end; a sofa or settee. **2.** a bedlike structure on which a doctor's patient can lie for examination. —*v.i.* **1.** to express *in* words of a certain kind. **2.** to lay as on a couch. **3.** to lie in a lair etc. or in ambush. **4.** to lower (a spear) to the position for attack. [from Old French from Latin *collocare* = lay in place]

couch[2] /kuːtʃ, kaʊtʃ/ n. (in full **couch grass**) a European grass *Agropyron repens* of the family Gramineae. It spreads rapidly by underground stems. It is considered a troublesome weed in North America, where it has been introduced.

couchant /'kaʊtʃənt/ adj. in heraldry, (of an animal) lying with the body resting on the legs and the head raised. [French]

couchette /kuː'ʃet/ n. a railway carriage with seats that are convertible into sleeping berths; a berth in this. [French = little bed]

cougar /'kuːgə/ n. (*US*) a puma. [French, from Guarani]

cough /kɒf/ v.t./i. **1.** to expel air or other matter from the lungs with a sudden sharp sound; (of an engine etc.) to make a similar sound. **2.** (*slang*) to confess. —*n.* the act or sound of coughing; a condition of the respiratory organs causing coughing. —**cough mixture**, a medicine to relieve a cough. **cough up**, to eject or say with coughs; (*slang*) to bring out or give (money or information) reluctantly. [imitative, related to Dutch *kuchen*]

could /kʊd/ v.aux. **1.** past of *can*[1]. **2.** to feel inclined to. —**could be**, (*colloquial*) might be; that may be true.

couldn't /'kʊdənt/ = could not.

coulomb /'kuːlɒm/ n. the SI unit (symbol C) of electrical charge. One coulomb is the quantity of electricity conveyed by a current of one ◊ampere in one second. [from C A de *Coulomb*]

Coulomb Charles Augustin de 1736–1806. French scientist, inventor of the torsion balance for measuring the force of electric and magnetic attraction.

coulter /'kəʊltə/ n. a vertical blade in front of a ploughshare. [Old English from Latin *culter* = knife]

council /'kaʊnsəl/ n. an advisory, deliberative, or administrative body; a meeting of the local administrative body of a county, city, town etc. —**council house**, a house owned and let by a local council. [from Anglo-French from Latin *concilium* = assembly]

Council for Mutual Economic Assistance (CMEA) the full name of ◊Comecon, an organization established in 1949 by Eastern bloc countries.

councillor /'kaʊnsələ/ n. a member of a council, especially of a local administrative council.

Council of Europe a body constituted in 1949 at Strasbourg, France (still its headquarters) to secure 'a greater measure of unity between the European countries'. The widest association of European states, it has a **Committee** of foreign ministers, a **Parliamentary Assembly** (with members from national parliaments), and a **European Commission** investigating violations of human rights.

counsel /'kaʊnsəl/ n. **1.** advice formally given; consultation, especially to seek or give advice; professional guidance. **2.** a legal adviser (especially a barrister); a group of these. —*v.t.* (**-ll-**) **1.** to advise, to recommend. **2.** to give professional guidance to (a person in need of psychological help). —**counsel of despair**, an action to be taken when all else fails. **counsel of perfection**, ideal but impracticable advice. **keep one's own counsel**, not to confide in others. **King's** or **Queen's Counsel**, counsel to the Crown, taking precedence over other barristers. **take counsel**, to consult *with*. [from Old French from Latin *consilium* (*consulere* = consult)]

counsellor /'kaʊnsələ/ n. an adviser; one who gives counsel.

count[1] /kaʊnt/ v.t./i. **1.** to find the number of (things etc.), especially by assigning successive numerals; to repeat numerals in order. **2.** to include or be included in a reckoning or consideration. **3.** to have a certain value or significance. **4.** to regard or consider. —*n.* **1.** counting, a calculation. **2.** a total. **3.** any of the points being considered. **4.** each of the charges in a legal indictment. —**count on**, to rely on, to expect. **count out**, to exclude, to disregard; to complete a count of ten seconds over (a fallen boxer etc.); to procure an adjournment of (the House of Commons) for lack of a quorum. **count up**, to find the total of. **keep** or **lose count**, to know or not know how many there have been. **out for the count**, defeated, unconscious. [from Old French from Latin *computare* = compute]

count[2] /kaʊnt/ n. a foreign nobleman equivalent in rank to an earl. [from Old French from Latin *comes* = companion]

countdown n. counting numerals backwards to zero, especially before launching a spacecraft etc.

countenance /'kaʊntɪnəns/ n. **1.** a facial expression; the face; composure of the face. **2.** moral support or approval. —*v.t.* to give approval to (an act); to encourage or connive at (a person or practice). —**keep one's countenance**, to maintain composure, to refrain from laughing. [from Old French *contenir* = contain]

counter[1] /'kaʊntə/ n. **1.** a flat-topped fitment in a shop etc. over which goods are sold or served or business is conducted with customers. **2.** a small disc used in table games for scoring etc. **3.** a token representing a coin. **4.** a device for counting. —**under the counter**, surreptitiously, illegally. [from Old French from Latin *computatorium*]

counter[2] /'kaʊntə/ v.t./i. **1.** to oppose, to contradict. **2.** to make or meet by a countermove; to baffle or frustrate thus. **3.** to give a return blow in boxing. —*adv.* in the opposite direction or manner. —*adj.* opposite. —*n.* **1.** a return action or blow; a countermove. **2.** the stiff part of a shoe or boot round the heel. **3.** the curved part of a ship's stern.

counter- prefix forming verbs, nouns, adjectives, and adverbs, implying retaliation or reversal (e.g. *counterstroke*, *counterclockwise*), rivalry or opposition (e.g. *counterattraction*, *countercurrent*), reciprocity or correspondence (e.g. *countersign*, *counterpart*). [from Old French *contre* from Latin *contra* = against]

counteract /kaʊntə'rækt/ v.t. to neutralize, hinder, or defeat by contrary action. —**counteraction** n., **counteractive** adj.

counterattack n. an attack made to meet an enemy's or opponent's attack. —*v.t./i.* to make a counterattack (on).

counterbalance *n.* a weight or influence that balances another. —*v.t.* to be a counterbalance to, to neutralize thus.

countercheck *n.* **1.** an obstruction checking movement or operating against another check. **2.** a second test for verifying another. —*v.t.* to verify by a second test.

counterclockwise *adj.* & *adv.* anticlockwise.

counterespionage *n.* action taken to uncover and frustrate enemy espionage.

counterfeit /'kaʊntəfɪt, -fiːt/ *adj.* made in imitation and of inferior material, usually to defraud; not genuine, forged. —*n.* a counterfeit thing. —*v.t.* to make a counterfeit of in order to defraud, to forge. [from past participle of Old French *contrefaire* from Latin = make in opposition]

counterfoil /'kaʊntəfɔɪl/ *n.* the part of a cheque, receipt, etc., retained as a record by the person issuing it.

counterintelligence *n.* counterespionage.

countermand /kaʊntə'mɑːnd/ *v.t.* to revoke or cancel (a command). —*n.* a command cancelling a previous one. [from Old French from Latin *mandare* = order]

countermarch *n.* a march in the opposite direction. —*v.t./i.* to march or cause to march back.

countermeasure *n.* an action taken to counteract a danger or threat.

countermove *n.* a move or action taken in opposition to another.

counterpane /'kaʊntəpeɪn/ *n.* a bedspread. [from Old French from Latin *culcita puncta* = quilted mattress]

counterpart /'kaʊntəpɑːt/ *n.* a person or thing like or naturally complementary to another; a duplicate.

counterpoint *n.* a melody added as an accompaniment to a given melody; the art or mode of adding melodies as an accompaniment according to fixed rules. ◊Palestrina and J S ◊Bach were masters of counterpoint. —*v.t.* to add counterpoint to; to set in contrast. [from Old French from Latin *contrapunctum* = pricked or marked opposite, i.e. to the original melody]

counterpoise /'kaʊntəpɔɪz/ *n.* the balancing of each other by two weights or forces; a counterbalancing weight or force. —*v.t.* to counterbalance; to compensate for. [from Old French from Latin *pensum* = weight]

counterproductive *adj.* having the opposite of the desired effect.

Counter-Reformation *n.* a movement initiated by the Catholic Church at the Council of Trent 1545–63 to counter the spread of the ◊Reformation. Extending into the 17th century, its dominant forces included the rise of the Jesuits as an educating and missionary group and the deployment of the Spanish ◊Inquisition in other countries.

counter-revolution *n.* a revolution opposing a former one or reversing its results.

countersign /'kaʊntəsaɪn/ *v.t.* to add a confirming signature to (a document already signed by another). —*n.* a word required in answer to a sentry's challenge; an identificatory mark. —**countersignature** /-sɪg-/ *n.* [from French from Italian]

countersink /'kaʊntəsɪŋk/ *v.t.* (*past* and *past participle* **countersunk**) to shape the top of (a screw hole) with a tapered enlargement so that a screw head lies level with or below the surface; to sink (a screw etc.) in such a hole.

counterstroke /'kaʊntəstrəʊk/ *n.* a stroke given in return.

countertenor *n.* the highest natural male voice, favoured by the Elizabethans and revived in the UK by Alfred Deller (1912–1979); a singer with such a voice; a part written for it.

countervail /'kaʊntəveɪl/ *v.t.* to counterbalance; to avail against. [from Anglo-French from Latin *contra valēre* = be of worth against]

countervailing power in economics, the belief that too much power held by one group or company can be balanced or neutralized by another, creating a compatible relationship, such as trade unions in the case of strong management in a large company, or an opposition party facing an authoritarian government.

counterweight /'kaʊntəweɪt/ *n.* a counterbalancing weight.

countess /'kaʊntɪs/ *n.* the wife or widow of an earl or count; a woman holding the rank of an earl or count. [from Old French from Latin *comitissa*]

countless /'kaʊntlɪs/ *adj.* too many to be counted.

countrified /'kʌntrɪfaɪd/ *adj.* rustic in appearance or manners.

country /'kʌntrɪ/ *n.* **1.** the territory of a nation; the state of which one is a member. **2.** the national population (especially as electors). **3.** a land or region with regard to its aspect or associations. **4.** open regions of fields and woods etc. as distinct from towns or the capital (often *attributive*). **country club**, a sporting social club in a rural area. **country dance**, a traditional English dance, often with couples face to face in lines. **go to the country**, to appeal to the body of electors after an adverse or doubtful vote in the House of Commons, or at the end of a government's term of office, by effecting the dissolution of Parliament and holding a general election. [from Old French from Latin *contrata (terra)* = land lying opposite]

country and western the popular music of the white US South and West; it evolved from the folk music of the English, Irish, and Scottish settlers and has a strong blues influence. Lyrics typically extol family values and traditional sex roles. Characteristic instruments are the slide guitar, mandolin, and fiddle.

countryman *n.* or **countrywoman** (*plural* **countrymen** or **countrywomen**) **1.** a person living in rural parts. **2.** a fellow member of a state or district.

Country Party (official name **National Country Party** from 1975) the Australian political party representing the interests of the farmers and people of the smaller towns; it holds the power balance between Liberals and Labor. It developed from about 1860, gained strength after the introduction of preferential voting (see ◊vote) in 1918, and has been in coalition with the Liberals from 1949.

countryside *n.* country districts.

Countryside Commission an official conservation body, created for England and Wales under the Countryside Act 1968. It replaced the National Parks Commission, and had by 1980 created over 160 Country Parks.

countrywide *adj.* extending throughout a nation.

county /'kaʊntɪ/ *n.* **1.** the administrative unit of a country or state. In the UK it is nowadays synonymous with 'shire', although historically the two had different origins. Many of the English counties can be traced back to Saxon times. In the USA a county is a subdivision of a state; the power of counties differs widely between states. The Republic of Ireland has 26 geographical and 27 administrative counties. **2.** the people of a county; long-established families of a high social level. **county town**, a town that is the administrative centre of a county. [from Anglo-French from Latin *comitatus*]

county council in the UK, a unit of local government, whose responsibilities include broad planning policy, highways, education, personal social services, and libraries; police, fire, and traffic control; and refuse disposal. Since the Local Government Act of 1972, the county councils in England and Wales consist of a chair and councillors (the distinction between councillors and aldermen has been abolished). Councillors are elected for four years, the franchise being the same as for parliamentary elections, and elect the chair from among their own number.

county court an English court of law created by the County Courts Act 1846 and now governed by the Act of 1984. It exists to try civil cases, such as actions on ◊contract and ◊tort where the claim does not exceed £5,000, and disputes about land, such as between landlord and tenant. County courts are presided over by one or more circuit judges. An appeal on a point of law lies to the Court of Appeal.

County Palatine see ◊Palatine.

coup /kuː/ *n.* a successful stroke or move, a ◊coup d'état. [French from Latin *colpus* = blow]

coup de grâce /kuː də 'grɑːs/ a finishing stroke. [French]

coup d'état /deɪ'tɑː/ or **coup** the forcible takeover of the government of a country by elements from within that country, generally carried out by violent or illegal means. It differs from a revolution in typically being carried out by a small group (for example, of army officers or opposition politicians) to install its leader as head of government, rather than being a mass uprising by the people. [French]

coupé /'kuːpeɪ/ *n.* a closed two-door car with a sloping back. [from French *couper* = cut]

Couperin /'kuːpəræn/ François *le Grand* 1668–1733. French composer who held various court appointments under Louis XIV and wrote vocal, chamber, and harpsichord music.

couple /'kʌpəl/ *n.* **1.** a man and woman who are in a steady relationship, engaged, or married to each other. **2.** a pair of partners in a dance etc. **3.** two things, or (*loosely*) several things. —*v.t./i.* **1.** to link or associate together. **2.** to copulate. [from Old French from Latin *copula* = fastening]

couplet /'kʌplɪt/ *n.* two successive lines of verse, especially when rhyming and of the same length. [French]

coupling /'kʌplɪŋ/ *n.* **1.** a link connecting two railway vehicles or two parts of machinery. **2.** the arrangement of items on a gramophone record.

coupon /'ku:pɒn/ *n.* **1.** a small, often detachable, piece of printed paper entitling the holder to specified goods or a service or some concession. **2.** a small printed form of application or entry for a competition etc. [from French *couper* = cut]

courage /'kʌrɪdʒ/ *n.* readiness to face and endure danger or difficulty; the ability to control or suppress fear or its disturbing effects; a courageous mood or inclination. —**have the courage of one's convictions**, to have the courage to do what one believes to be right. [from Old French from Latin *cor* = heart]

courageous /kə'reɪdʒəs/ *adj.* having or showing courage. —**courageously** *adv.*

Courbet /'kuəbeɪ/ Gustave 1819–1877. French artist, a portrait, genre, and landscape painter. Reacting against academic trends, both Classicist and Romantic, he sought to establish a new realism based on contemporary life. His *Burial at Ornans* 1850 (Louvre, Paris), showing ordinary working people gathered round a village grave, shocked the public and the critics with its 'vulgarity'.

courgette /kuə'ʒet/ *n.* a small green or yellow vegetable marrow. [from French *courge* = gourd]

courier /'kuriə/ *n.* **1.** a special messenger. **2.** a person employed to guide and assist a group of tourists. [from French from Italian *corriere* from Latin *currere* = run]

Courrèges /ku'reɪʒ/ André 1923– . French couturier. Originally with Balenciaga, he founded his own firm in 1961 and is credited with inventing the miniskirt in 1964.

course /kɔːs/ *n.* **1.** an onward movement in space or time; a direction taken or intended; the direction or channel followed by a river etc. **2.** the successive development *of* events, the ordinary sequence or order; a line of conduct or action. **3.** a series *of* lectures, lessons etc., in a particular subject; a sequence *of* medical treatment. **4.** each successive part of a meal. **5.** a golf course; a racecourse. **6.** a continuous row of masonry at one level in a building. —*v.t./i.* **1.** to use hounds to hunt (especially hares). **2.** to move or flow freely. —**in the course of**, in the process of. **in due course**, at about the expected time. **of course**, as is or was to be expected, without doubt, admittedly. [from Old French from Latin *cursus* (*currere* = run)]

courser /'kɔːsə/ *n.* **1.** a fast-running African or Asian bird. **2.** (*poetic*) a swift horse. [from Latin]

court /kɔːt/ *n.* **1.** a courtyard; a yard surrounded by houses, with entry from the street. **2.** an enclosed or marked area for some games, e. g. squash and tennis. **3.** or **Court** a sovereign's establishment with courtiers and attendants; this as representing a country; a reception at court. **4.** (in full **court of law**) a judicial body hearing legal cases; the place where this meets; **the court**, judges of a court. See ◊law courts and particular kinds of court, e. g. ◊county court, ◊small claims court, and ◊Diplock court. —*v.t.* to treat flatteringly or with special attention; to seek to attract the favour or love of; to seek to win; to make oneself vulnerable to. —**court card**, a playing card that is a king, queen, or jack. **courthouse** *n.* the building in which a court of law is held; (*US*) the building containing the administrative offices of a county. **court martial**, (*plural* **courts martial**) a judicial court of naval, military, or air force officers for trying charges involving offences against military law; trial by such a court. **court-martial** *v.t.* (-ll-) to try by court martial. **court shoe**, a woman's light shoe with a low-cut upper. **go to court**, to take legal action. **hold court**, to preside over one's admirers. **out of court**, (of a settlement) without reaching trial; not worth discussing. **pay court to**, to court (a person) to win favour. **put out of court**, to refuse or make it inappropriate to consider. [from Anglo-French from Latin *cohors* = yard, retinue]

Court Margaret (born Smith) 1942– . Australian tennis player. The most prolific winner in the women's game, she won a record 64 Grand Slam titles, including 25 at singles.

Courtauld /'kɔːtəuld/ Samuel 1793–1881. English industrialist who developed the production of viscose rayon and other synthetic fibres from 1904. He founded the firm of Courtaulds in 1816 in Bocking, Essex, and at first specialized in silk and crêpe manufacture. His great-nephew, **Samuel Courtauld** (1876–1947), was chair of the firm from 1921, and in 1931 gave his house and art collection to the University of London as the Courtauld Institute. The Courtauld collection was moved to Somerset House in 1990.

courteous /'kɜːtiəs/ *adj.* polite, considerate. —**courteously** *adv.* [from Old French]

courtesan /kɔːti'zæn/ *n.* a prostitute with clients among the wealthy or nobility. [from French from Italian *cortigiano* = courtier]

courtesy /'kɜːtəsɪ/ *n.* courteous behaviour, a courteous act. —**by courtesy of**, by permission of. **courtesy light**, a light in a car that is switched on automatically by opening the door. [from Old French]

courtesy title in the UK, a title given to the progeny of members of the peerage. For example, the eldest son of a duke, marquess, or earl may bear one of his father's lesser titles; thus the Duke of Marlborough's son is the Marquess of Blandford. Those with courtesy titles are not peers and do not sit in the House of Lords.

courtier /'kɔːtiə/ *n.* a companion of the sovereign at court. [from Anglo-French]

courtly /'kɔːtlɪ/ *adj.* polished or refined in manners. —**courtly love**, the conventional medieval tradition of knightly love and etiquette. —**courtliness** *n.*

Courtneidge /'kɔːtnɪdʒ/ Cicely 1893–1980. English comic actress and singer, who appeared both on stage and in films. She married comedian Jack Hulbert (1892–1978), with whom she formed a successful variety partnership.

Court of Session the supreme Civil Court in Scotland, established in 1532. Cases come in the first place before one of the judges of the Outer House, and from that decision an appeal lies to the Inner House which sits in two divisions called the First and Second Division. From the decisions of the Inner House an appeal lies to the House of Lords. The court sits in Edinburgh.

Court of the Lord Lyon a Scottish heraldic authority composed of one King of Arms, three Heralds, and three Pursuivants who specialize in genealogical work. It embodies the High Sennachie of Scotland's Celtic kings.

courtship *n.* courting, especially of an intended wife; a period of courting; behaviour exhibited by animals as a prelude to mating.

courtyard *n.* a space enclosed by walls or buildings.

couscous /'ku:sku:s/ *n.* a North African dish of crushed wheat or coarse flour steamed over broth, often with meat or fruit added. [French from Arabic *kaskasa* = to pound]

cousin /'kʌzən/ *n.* or **first cousin** or **cousin german** a son or daughter of one's uncle or aunt; **first cousin once** (*or twice* etc.) **removed**, a son or daughter (or grandson etc.) of one's first cousin, one's parent's (or grandparent's etc.) cousin; **second cousin**, a son or daughter of one's parent's first cousin. **2.** (*historical*) the title used by one sovereign addressing another. —**cousinly** *adj.* [from Old French from Latin *consobrinus*]

Cousteau /'ku:stəu/ Jacques-Yves 1910– . French oceanographer, celebrated for his researches in command of the *Calypso* from 1951, his film and television documentaries, and his many books; he pioneered the invention of the aqualung in 1943 and developed techniques in underwater filming.

couture /ku:'tjuə/ *n.* the design and making of high-quality fashionable clothes. [French = sewing, dressmaking]

couturier /ku:'tjuriei/ *n.* a fashion designer. —**couturière** /-ieə/ *n.fem.* [French]

couvade /ku:'vɑːd/ *n.* a custom of some primitive peoples by which the husband feigns illness and is put to bed when his wife is giving birth to a child. It has been observed since antiquity in many cultures, and may have begun either as a magic ritual or as a way of asserting paternity. [French *couver* = hatch from Latin *cubare* = lie down]

covalent bond a chemical ◊bond produced when two atoms each contribute an electron for mutual sharing. It

Cousteau French naval officer and underwater explorer Jacques Cousteau.

is composed of two electrons and is often represented by a single line drawn between the two atoms. This type of bonding always produces a ◊molecule. Covalently bonded substances include hydrogen (H_2) and water (H_2O).

cove[1] *n.* 1. a small bay or inlet of the coast; a sheltered recess. 2. a curved moulding at the junction of a ceiling and a wall. —*v.t.* 1. to provide (a room etc.) with a cove. 2. to slope (the sides of a fireplace) inwards. [Old English = chamber]

cove[2] *n.* (*slang*) a fellow, a man.

coven /ˈkʌvən/ *n.* an assembly of witches. [from Old French *covent*]

covenant /ˈkʌvənənt/ *n.* a formal agreement, in law, a sealed contract; the biblical compact between God and the Israelites. —*v.t./i.* to agree, especially by legal covenant (*with* a person). [from Old French *co(n)venir*]

covenanter *n.* 1. one who covenants. 2. **Covenanter**, a supporter of the Scottish National Covenant of 1638 and the Solemn League and Covenant (1643), proclamations defending Presbyterianism and resisting the religious policies of Charles I.

Coventry /ˈkɒvəntri/ industrial city in West Midlands, England; population (1981) 313,800. Manufacturing includes cars, electronic equipment, machine tools, and agricultural machinery. —**send to Coventry,** to refuse to speak to or associate with.

cover /ˈkʌvə/ *v.t.* 1. to lie or extend over, to form or occupy the whole surface of. 2. to conceal or protect (a thing) by placing something on or in front of it; to provide (a person) with something that covers; to protect, to clothe; to strew thoroughly *with*. 3. to enclose or include; to deal with (a subject). 4. to travel (a specified distance etc.). 5. to be enough money to pay for. 6. to investigate or describe as a reporter. 7. (of a fortification or gun etc.) to have within its range; to protect from a commanding position; to keep a gun aimed at; to have within one's range of fire; to protect by firing against the enemy. 8. to protect or oppose (another player) in field games. 9. (of a stallion etc.) to mate with. 10. to deputize temporarily *for*. 11. (in *past participle*) wearing a hat, having a roof. —*n.* 1. a thing that covers, a lid, a top. 2. the binding of a book; one board of this. 3. an envelope or other postal wrapping. 4. shelter, protection. 5. a screen, a pretence; a pretended identity. 6. funds from an insurance to meet a liability or contingent loss, protection by insurance. 7. a supporting force protecting another from attack. 8. an individual place setting at a meal. 9. cover point. —**cover charge,** an extra charge

per person in a restaurant etc. **cover girl,** a girl whose picture appears on magazine covers. **covering letter** *or* **note,** one sent with and explaining goods or documents. **cover note,** a temporary certificate of current insurance. **cover point,** a cricket fieldsman covering point. **cover-up** *n.* a concealment, especially of facts. **take cover,** to seek shelter. **under cover,** in secret, sheltered from the weather. **under cover of,** hidden or protected by (e. g. darkness); with an outward show of (e. g. friendship). [from Old French from Latin *operire* = cover]

coverage /ˈkʌvərɪdʒ/ *n.* the area or amount covered or reached; the reporting of events in a newspaper etc.

coverall /ˈkʌvərɔːl/ *n.* a thing that covers entirely; (usually in *plural*) a full-length protective garment.

coverlet /ˈkʌvəlɪt/ *n.* a covering, especially a bedspread. [from Anglo-French *lit* = bed]

covert /ˈkʌvət/ *adj.* disguised, not open or explicit. —*n.* 1. a wood or thicket affording cover for game. 2. a feather covering the base of a bird's wing feather or tail feather. —**covertly** *adv.*

covet /ˈkʌvɪt/ *v.t.* to envy another the possession of, to long to possess. [from Old French from Latin]

covetous /ˈkʌvɪtəs/ *adj.* coveting, avaricious, grasping. —**covetously** *adv.*, **covetousness** *n.*

covey /ˈkʌvɪ/ *n.* 1. a brood of partridges (especially flying together). 2. a small group of people. [from Old French from Latin *cubare* = lie]

cow[1] *n.* (*plural* **cows,** *archaic* **kine**) 1. the fully grown female of any bovine animal, especially of the domestic species used as a source of milk and beef. 2. the female of other large animals, especially the elephant, whale, or seal. —**cowlick** *n.* a projecting lock of hair. **cowpat** *n.* a flat, round piece of cow dung. [Old English]

cow[2] *v.t.* to intimidate, to dispirit. [from Old Norse *kúga* = oppress]

coward /ˈkaʊəd/ *n.* a person easily giving way to fear and lacking courage. [from Old French from Latin *cauda* = tail]

Coward Noël 1899–1973. English playwright, actor, producer, director, and composer, who epitomized the witty and sophisticated man of the theatre. From his first success with *The Young Idea* 1923, he wrote and appeared in plays and comedies on both sides of the Atlantic such as *Hay Fever* 1925, *Private Lives* 1930 with Gertrude Lawrence, *Design for Living* 1933, and *Blithe Spirit* 1941.

cowardice /ˈkaʊədɪs/ *n.* cowardly feelings or conduct.

cowardly *adj.* of or like a coward, lacking courage; (of an action) done against one who cannot retaliate. —**cowardliness** *n.*

cowbell *n.* a bell hung round a cow's neck.

cowboy *n.* 1. in the western USA, a man in charge of cattle. 2. (*colloquial*) an unscrupulous or reckless business man.

cowcatcher *n.* a fender fitted on the front of a locomotive to push aside cattle or other obstacles on the line.

Cowell /ˈkaʊəl/ Henry 1897–1965. US composer and writer. He experimented with new ways of playing the piano, strumming the strings in *Aeolian Harp* 1923 and introducing clusters, using a ruler on the keys in *The Banshee* 1925.

I believe a composer must forge his own forms out of the many influences that play upon him and never close his ears to any part of the world of sound . . .
Henry Cowell

cower *v.i.* to crouch or shrink back, especially in fear; to huddle up. [from Low German *küren* = lie in wait]

cowfish *n.* a kind of ◊boxfish.

cowherd *n.* a person who looks after cows at pasture.

cowhide *n.* a cow's hide; leather or a whip made from this.

cowl *n.* 1. a monk's hood or hooded garment. 2. a hood-shaped covering, especially of a chimney or shaft. [Old English from Latin *cucullus* = hood of cloak]

Cowley /ˈkaʊli/ Abraham 1618–1667. English poet. He introduced the Pindaric ode (based on the Greek poet Pindar) to English poetry, and published metaphysical verse with elaborate imagery, as well as essays.

cowling *n.* a removable cover over the engine of a vehicle or aircraft.

co-worker *n.* one who works in collaboration with another.

cow parsley or **keck** a tall perennial plant *Anthriscus sylvestris* of the carrot family. Up to 1 m/3 ft tall, with pinnate leaves, hollow furrowed stems, and heads of white flowers, it is widespread in hedgerows and shady places. It grows in Europe, N Asia, and N Africa.

Cowper /'ku:pə/ William 1731–1800. English poet. He trained as a lawyer, but suffered a mental breakdown in 1763 and entered an asylum, where he underwent an evangelical conversion. He later wrote hymns (including 'God moves in a mysterious way'). His verse includes the six books of *The Task* 1785.

cowpox *n.* a disease of cows, caused by a virus which is used in vaccination against smallpox.

cowrie /'kaurɪ/ *n.* a marine snail of the family Cypreidae, in which the interior spiral form is concealed by a double outer lip. The shells are hard, shiny, and often coloured. Most cowries are shallow-water forms, and are found in many parts of the world, in particular the tropical Indo Pacific. Cowries have been used as ornaments and fertility charms, and also as currency, for example the Pacific money cowrie *Cypraea moneta*. [from Urdu and Hindi]

cowslip *n.* a wild plant *Primula veris* with small yellow flowers. [Old English *slyppe* = slimy substance, i.e. dung]

cox *n.* a coxswain, especially of a racing boat. —*v.t./i.* to act as cox (of). [abbreviation]

coxcomb /'kɒkskəum/ *n.* 1. a conceited, showy person. 2. (*historical*) a medieval jester's cap. —**coxcombry** *n.* [= *cock's comb*]

coxswain /'kɒkswein, 'kɒksən/ *n.* 1. the steersman of a rowing boat or other small boat. 2. the senior petty officer in a small ship. —*v.t./i.* to act as coxswain (of). [from obsolete *cock* = small boat]

coy *adj.* affectedly modest or bashful; archly reticent. —**coyly** *adv.*, **coyness** *n.* [from Old French from Latin *quietus* = quiet]

coyote /kɔɪ'əutɪ, 'kɔɪəut/ *n.* a wild dog *Canis latrans*, in appearance like a small wolf, living from Alaska to Central America and E to New York. Its head and body are about 90 cm/3 ft long and brown, flecked with grey or black. Coyotes live in open country and can run at 65 km/40 mph. Their main foods are rabbits and rodents. Although persecuted by humans for over a century, the species is very successful. [Mexican Spanish from Aztec]

coypu /'kɔɪpu:/ *n.* a South American water rodent *Myocastor coypus*, about 60 cm/2 ft long and weighing up to 9 kg/20 lb. It has a scaly, ratlike tail, webbed hind feet, a blunt-muzzled head, and large orange incisors. The fur is reddish brown. It feeds on vegetation, and lives in burrows in river and lake banks. [native name in Chile]

Coysevox /kwæz'vɒks/ Antoine 1640–1720. French Baroque sculptor. He was employed at the palace of Versailles, contributing a stucco relief of a triumphant Louis XIV to the Salon de la Guerre.

cozen /'kʌzən/ *v.t./i.* (*literary*) to cheat, to defraud; to act deceitfully. —**cozenage** *n.*

Cozens /'kʌzənz/ John Robert 1752–1797. British landscape painter, a watercolourist, whose Romantic views of Europe, painted on tours in the 1770s and 1780s, influenced both Thomas Girtin and J M W Turner.

c.p. abbreviation of candlepower.

Cpl. abbreviation of Corporal.

CPP abbreviation of current purchasing power.

c.p.s. abbreviation of cycles per second.

CPU abbreviation of central processing unit, the part of a computer that executes individual program instructions and controls the operation of other parts.

CPVE abbreviation of Certificate of Pre-Vocational Education; in the UK, an educational qualification introduced in 1986 for students over 16 in schools and colleges who require a one-year course of preparation for work or further vocational study.

Cr symbol for ◊chromium.

crab *n.* 1. any decapod (ten-legged) crustacean of the division Brachyura, with a broad, rather round, upper body shell (carapace) and a small ◊abdomen tucked beneath the body. Crabs are related to lobsters and crayfish and are mainly marine, though some crabs live in fresh water or on land. They are alert carnivores and scavengers. They have a typical sideways walk, and strong pincers on the first pair of legs, the other four pairs being used for walking. Periodically, the outer shell is cast to allow for growth. The name crab is sometimes used for similar arthropods, such as the horseshoe crab, which is neither a true crab nor a crustacean. 2. **the Crab**, the constellation or sign of the zodiac Cancer. —*v.t./i.* (*colloquial*) (**-bb-**) to criticize adversely or captiously; to act so as to spoil. —**catch a crab**, to get an oar jammed underwater by a faulty stroke in rowing. **crab louse**, a parasite infesting the hairy parts of the body. [Old English, related to Low German *krabben* and Old Norse *krafla* = scratch]

crab apple any of 25 species of wild ◊apple trees (genus *Malus*) native to temperate regions of the northern hemisphere; the fruit of these trees. Numerous varieties of cultivated apples have been derived from *M. pumila*, the common native crab apple of SE Europe and central Asia. The fruit of native species is smaller and more bitter than that of cultivated varieties.

Crabbe /kræb/ George 1754–1832. English poet. Originally a doctor, he became a clergyman in 1781, and wrote grimly realistic verse on the poor of his own time: *The*

CPU

CPU

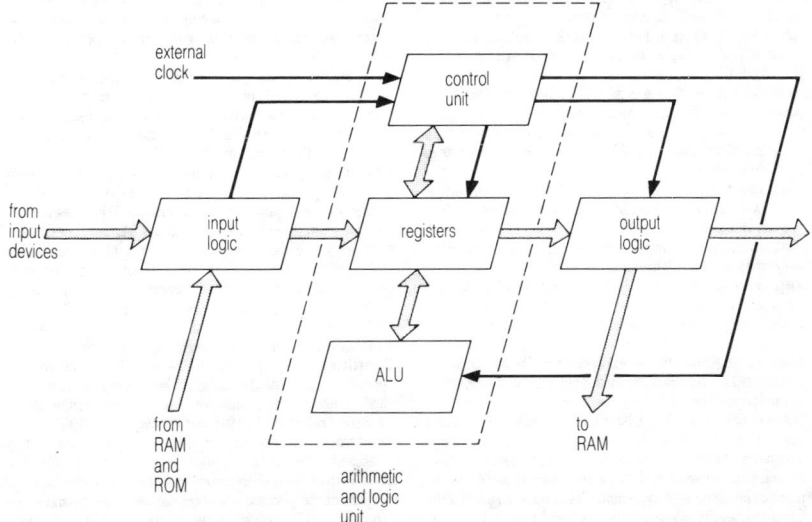

external clock

from input devices

control unit

input logic

registers

output logic

ALU

from RAM and ROM

to RAM

arithmetic and logic unit

Village 1783, *The Parish Register* 1807, *The Borough* 1810 (which includes the story used in the Britten opera *Peter Grimes*), and *Tales of the Hall* 1819.

crabbed /'kræbɪd/ *adj.* 1. bad-tempered, crabby. 2. (of writing) difficult to read or decipher.

crabby *adj.* irritable, morose. —**crabbily** *adv.*, **crabbiness** *n.*

Crab nebula a cloud of gas 6,000 light years from Earth, in the constellation Taurus. It is the remains of a star that exploded as a ◊supernova (observed as a brilliant point of light on Earth in 1054). At its centre is a ◊pulsar that flashes 30 times a second. The name comes from its crablike appearance.

crabwise *adv. & adj.* sideways or backwards like the movement of a crab.

crack *n.* 1. a sudden sharp explosive sound. 2. a sharp blow. 3. a narrow opening; a line of division where something is broken but has not come completely apart. 4. (*colloquial*) a wisecrack, a joke. 5. a chemical (bicarbonate) derivative of ◊cocaine in hard, crystalline lumps; it is heated and inhaled (smoked) and is highly addictive. —*adj.* (*colloquial*) first-rate. —*v.t./i.* 1. to break without coming completely apart; to become broken thus; to gape with cracks. 2. to make or cause to make the sound of a crack; to hit sharply. 3. to break the case of (a nut); to break into (a safe etc.); to find the solution to (a code or problem). 4. (of the voice) to become suddenly harsh, as with emotion. 5. to yield suddenly or cease to resist under strain. 6. to tell (a joke). 7. to break down (heavy oils) in order to produce lighter ones. 8. (in *past participle*, *colloquial*) crazy, infatuated. —**crack a bottle**, to open it and drink the contents. **crack-brained** *adj.* crazy. **crack down on**, (*colloquial*) to take severe measures against. **crack of dawn**, daybreak. **crack up**, (*colloquial*) to have a physical or mental breakdown; to praise highly (usually in *passive*, especially in *not all it* etc. *is cracked up to be*). **get cracking**, (*colloquial*) to make a start. **have a crack at**, (*colloquial*) to attempt. [Old English = resound]

cracker *n.* 1. an explosive firework. 2. a small paper toy in the form of a roll that makes a cracking sound when pulled apart. 3. a thin, crisp, savoury biscuit; (*US*) a biscuit.

crackers *predic. adj.* (*slang*) crazy.

crackle /'krækəl/ *n.* a series of repeated slight cracks as of burning wood. —*v.i.* to emit a crackle.

crackling *n.* the crisp skin of roast pork.

cracknel /'kræknəl/ *n.* a light, crisp kind of biscuit. [from French from Middle Dutch]

crackpot *adj.* (*colloquial*) eccentric, unpractical. —*n.* (*colloquial*) an eccentric or unpractical person.

Cracow /'krækau/ alternative form of ◊Kraków, Polish city.

-cracy /krəsɪ/ suffix with sense 'rule or ruling body of'. [from French from Greek *kratos* = strength]

cradle /'kreɪdəl/ *n.* 1. a small bed or cot for a baby, usually on rockers. 2. a place regarded as the origin of something. 3. a supporting framework or structure. —*v.t.* to place in a cradle; to contain or shelter as in a cradle. [Old English]

craft /krɑːft/ *n.* 1. a special skill or technique; an occupation needing this. 2. cunning, craftiness. 3. (*plural* same) a ship or boat, an aircraft or spacecraft. —*v.t.* to make in a skilful manner. [Old English = Old High German *kraft* = strength]

craftsman *n.* or **craftswoman** (*plural* **craftsmen** or **craftswomen**) one who practises a craft; a skilled person. —**craftsmanship** *n.*

crafty *adj.* cunning, using underhand methods; ingenious. —**craftily** *adv.*, **craftiness** *n.*

crag *n.* a steep rugged rock. —**craggy** *adj.*, **cragginess** *n.* [Celtic]

Craig /kreɪg/ Edward Gordon 1872–1966. English director and stage designer. His innovations and theories on stage design and lighting effects, expounded in *On the Art of the Theatre* 1911, had a profound influence on stage production in Europe and the USA.

Craig James 1871–1940. Ulster Unionist politician, the first prime minister of Northern Ireland 1921–40. Craig became a member of Parliament in 1906, and was a highly effective organizer of Unionist resistance to Home Rule. As prime minister he carried out systematic discrimination against the Catholic minority, abolishing proportional representation in

1929 and redrawing constituency boundaries to ensure Protestant majorities.

crake *n.* a bird of the rail family, especially the corncrake. [from Old Norse, imitative of cry]

cram *v.t./i.* (**-mm-**) 1. to fill to excess; to force (*in* or *into*). 2. to feed to excess. 3. to study intensively for an examination. [Old English]

cramp *n.* 1. a sudden painful involuntary contraction of muscle(s). 2. (in full **cramp iron**) a kind of clamp, especially for holding masonry or timbers. —*v.t.* 1. to affect with cramp. 2. to restrict or confine narrowly. 3. to fasten with a cramp. —**cramp a person's style**, to prevent him from acting freely or to his best ability. [from Old French from Middle Dutch]

cramped *adj.* (of a space) too narrow; (of handwriting) small and with the letters close together.

crampon /'kræmpɒn/ *n.* an iron plate with spikes fixed to a boot for climbing on ice. [from French]

Cranach /'krɑːnæx/ Lucas 1472–1553. German painter, etcher, and woodcut artist, a leading light in the German Renaissance. He painted many full-length nudes and precise and polished portraits, such as *Martin Luther* 1521 (Uffizi, Florence).

cranberry /'krænbərɪ/ *n.* a small, acid, red berry; the shrub bearing it *Vaccinium oxycoccus* or *V. macrocarpon*. [after German *kranbeere* = crane berry]

crane /kreɪn/ *n.* 1. a machine for moving heavy objects, usually by suspending them from a projecting arm or beam. The three main types are the **jib crane**, the **overhead travelling crane**, and the **tower crane**. Most cranes have the machinery mounted on a revolving turntable which may be mounted on trucks or be self-propelled. 2. a large wading bird of the family Gruidae, with long legs, neck, and bill. Cranes are marsh-and plains-dwelling birds, feeding on plants as well as insects and small animals. They fly well and are usually migratory. Their courtship includes frenzied, leaping dances. They are found in all parts of the world except South America. —*v.t./i.* to stretch (one's neck) in order to see something. [Old English]

Crane (Harold) Hart 1899–1932. US poet. His long mystical poem *The Bridge* 1930 uses the Brooklyn Bridge as a symbol. In his work he attempted to link humanity's present with its past, in an epic continuum. His poetry is highly original. He drowned after jumping overboard from a steamer bringing him back to the USA after a visit to Mexico.

Crane Stephen 1871–1900. US journalist and writer, who introduced grim realism into the US novel. His book *The Red Badge of Courage* 1895 deals vividly with the US Civil War.

crane fly or **daddy-longlegs** any fly of the family Tipulidae, with long, slender, fragile legs. They look like giant mosquitoes, but the adults are quite harmless. The larvae live in soil or water. Some species, for example the **common crane fly** *Tipula paludosa*, have soil-living larvae known as **leatherjackets**, which cause crop damage by eating roots.

cranesbill *n.* any plant of the genus *Geranium*, which contains about 400 species. The plants are named after the long, beaklike process attached to the seed vessels. When ripe, this splits into coiling spirals, which jerk the seeds out, assisting in their distribution.

craniotomy *n.* an operation to remove or turn back a small flap of skull bone to give access to the living brain.

cranium /'kreɪnɪəm/ *n.* (*plural* **crania**) the bones enclosing the brain; the skull. —**cranial** *adj.* [Latin from Greek]

crank[1] *n.* the part of an axle or shaft bent at right angles for converting reciprocal into circular motion, or vice versa. —*v.t.* to move by means of a crank; to start (*up*) (a car engine) by turning a crank. [Old English]

crank[2] *n.* an eccentric person.

crankcase *n.* the case enclosing a crankshaft.

Cranko /'kræŋkau/ John 1927–1973. British choreographer. Born in South Africa, he joined Sadler's Wells in 1946, and excelled in the creation of comedy characters, as in the *Tritsch-Tratsch Polka* 1946 and *Pineapple Poll* 1951.

crankpin *n.* the pin by which the connecting rod is attached to the crank.

crankshaft *n.* a shaft driven by a crank, an essential component of the piston engine that converts the up-and-down (reciprocating) motion of the pistons into useful rotary motion. The car crankshaft carries a number of cranks. The pistons are connected to the cranks by connecting rods and ◊bearings; when the pistons move up and down, the connecting rods force the offset crank pins to describe a circle, thereby rotating the crankshaft.

cranky *adj.* 1. shaky. 2. crotchety, eccentric; ill-tempered. —**crankily** *adv.*, **crankiness** *n.*

Cranmer /'krænmə/ Thomas 1489–1556. English cleric, archbishop of Canterbury from 1533. A Protestant convert, under Edward VI he helped to shape the doctrines of the Church of England. He was responsible for the issue of the Prayer Books of 1549 and 1552, and supported the succession of Lady Jane Grey. Condemned for heresy under the Catholic Mary Tudor, he at first recanted, but when his life was not spared, resumed his position and was burned at the stake, first holding to the fire the hand which had signed his recantation.

This was the hand that wrote it, therefore it shall suffer punishment.

Thomas Cranmer
at the stake 21 March 1556

---

crannog /'krænəg/ *n.* a lake dwelling in Scotland or Ireland, examples of which are found from the Neolithic period until medieval times. [Irish *crann* = tree, beam]

cranny *n.* a crevice. —**crannied** *adj.* [from Old French from Latin *crena* = notch]

crap *n.* (*vulgar*) faeces; nonsense, rubbish. —*v.i.* (**-pp-**) (*vulgar*) to defecate. —**crappy** *adj.* [from Dutch; originally = chaff, refuse from fat boiling]

crape *n.* crêpe, usually of black silk etc., especially for mourning dress.

craps *n.pl.* a game of chance played with dice, popular in the USA. —**shoot craps**, to play this. [perhaps from *crab* = lowest throw at dice]

crapulent /'kræpulənt/ *adj.* suffering or resulting from intemperance. —**crapulence** *n.*, **crapulous** *adj.* [from Latin from Greek *kraipalē* = drunken headache]

crash[1] *n.* 1. a sudden, violent, percussive noise as of something breaking by impact; a fall or impact accompanied by this; a burst of loud sound. 2. a sudden downfall or collapse (especially of a government or a business). 3. (*attributive*) done rapidly or urgently. —*v.t./i.* 1. to fall, collide, or proceed with a crash, to cause to do this; to make the noise of a crash. 2. (of an aircraft or pilot) to fall violently to land or sea. 3. to collapse financially. 4. to pass (an instruction etc. to stop, especially a red light). 5. (*colloquial*) to enter or take part in (a party etc.) uninvited. —*adv.* with a crash. —**crash-dive** *v.i.* (of a submarine) to submerge hurriedly in an emergency; (of an aircraft) to dive and crash; (*n.*) the action of this. **crash helmet**, a helmet worn to protect the head in case of a crash. **crash-land** *v.t./i.* (of an aircraft or pilot) to land hurriedly with a crash. [imitative]

crash[2] *n.* a coarse, plain linen or cotton fabric. [from Russian *krashenina*]

Crashaw /'kræʃɔ:/ Richard 1613–1649. English religious poet of the metaphysical school. He published a book of Latin sacred epigrams in 1634, then went to Paris, where he joined the Roman Catholic Church; his collection of poems *Steps to the Temple* appeared in 1646.

crashing *adj.* (*colloquial*) overwhelming.

crass /kræs/ *adj.* gross; grossly stupid. —**crassly** *adv.*, **crassness** *n.* [from Latin *crassus* = thick]

Crassus /'kræsəs/ Marcus Licinius *c.*108–53 BC. Roman general who crushed the ◊Spartacus uprising in 71 BC. In 60 he joined with Caesar and Pompey in the First Triumvirate and obtained command in the East in 55. Invading Mesopotamia, he was defeated by the Parthians at the battle of Carrhae, captured, and put to death.

-crat suffix forming nouns meaning 'a supporter or member of a -cracy'. [from French from Greek]

crate *n.* 1. a packing case made of wooden slats, for conveying fragile goods. 2. a divided container for holding milk bottles. 3. (*slang*) an old aircraft or car. —*v.t.* to pack in a crate. [perhaps from Dutch *krat* = basket]

crater /'kreɪtə/ *n.* the mouth of a volcano; a bowl-shaped cavity, especially that made by the explosion of a shell or bomb. [Latin from Greek = mixing bowl]

Crawford US film star Joan Crawford.

-cratic, **-cratical** suffixes forming adjectives from nouns ending in *-crat*.

craton *n.* or **shield** the core of a continent, a vast tract of highly deformed ◊metamorphic rock around which the continent has been built. Intense mountain-building periods shook these shield areas in Precambrian times before stable conditions set in.

cravat /krə'væt/ *n.* 1. a short scarf. 2. a broad necktie. [from French from German from Serbo-Croatian = Croat]

crave *v.t./i.* to desire greatly, to long *for*; to ask earnestly for. [Old English]

craven /'kreɪvən/ *adj.* cowardly, abject. —*n.* a craven person. [perhaps from Old French *cravanté* from Latin *crepare* = burst]

craving *n.* a strong desire, an intense longing.

craw *n.* the crop of a bird or insect. —**stick in one's craw**, to be unacceptable. [from Middle Low German or Dutch]

crawfish *n.* a large, spiny sea lobster, *Palinurus vulgaris*, sometimes called crayfish, without pincers, growing up to 50 cm/1.8 ft. [variant of *crayfish*]

Crawford /'krɔ:fəd/ Joan. Stage name of Lucille Le Seur 1908–1977. US film actress. She began her career as a chorus girl in 1924, and her first film appearance was in 1925. She became a star with her performance as a 'flapper' in *Our Darling Daughter* 1928. In later films she appeared as a sultry, mature woman. Her films include *Mildred Pierce* 1945 (for which she won an Academy Award), *Password* 1947, and *Whatever Happened to Baby Jane?* 1962.

crawl *v.i.* 1. to progress with the body on or close to the ground or other surface, or on hands and knees. 2. to walk or move or (of time) pass slowly. 3. (*colloquial*) to seek favour by behaving in a servile way. 4. to be covered or filled *with*. 5. (of the skin etc.) to creep. —*n.* 1. crawling. 2. a slow rate of motion. 3. a high-speed overarm swimming stroke.

crawling peg in economics, also known as a **sliding peg** or **sliding parity** or **moving parity**, a method of achieving a desired adjustment in a currency exchange rate (up or down) by small percentages over a given period, rather than by major revaluation or devaluation.

Craxi /'kræksi/ Bettino 1934– . Italian socialist politician, leader of the Italian Socialist Party (PSI) from 1976, prime minister 1983–87.

crayfish *n.* a freshwater decapod (ten-limbed) crustacean belonging to several families structurally similar to, but smaller than, the lobster. Crayfish are brownish-green scavengers and are found in all parts of the world except Africa. They are edible, and some species are farmed. [from Old French *crevice* = crab from German]

crayon /'kreɪən/ n. a stick or pencil of coloured wax etc. for drawing. —v.t. to draw or colour with crayons. [French craie = chalk]

craze n. a great but usually temporary enthusiasm; the object of this. —v.t. to make crazy. [originally = break, shatter; perhaps from Old Norse]

crazy /'kreɪzɪ/ adj. 1. insane; foolish, lacking sense. 2. (colloquial) extremely enthusiastic (about). 3. (of a building etc.) unsound. —**crazy paving**, paving made up of irregular pieces. —**like crazy**, (colloquial) like mad, very much. —crazily adv., craziness n.

Crazy Horse 1849–1877. Sioux Indian chief, one of the Indian leaders at the massacre of ◊Little Bighorn. He was killed when captured.

creak n. a harsh strident noise, as of an unoiled hinge. —v.i. to make or move with a creak; to be in poor condition. —creaky adj., creakily adv. [imitative]

cream n. 1. the part of milk with a high fat content; its yellowish-white colour. 2. a creamlike preparation or ointment; a food or drink with the consistency of or compared to cream. 3. the best part of. —v.t./i. 1. to remove the cream from (milk). 2. to make creamy; to beat to a creamy consistency. 3. to apply cosmetic cream to. 4. to form cream, froth, or scum. —**cream cheese**, a soft, rich cheese made of cream or unskimmed milk without pressing. **cream off**, to remove the best or a required part of. **cream of tartar**, purified tartar used in medicine and cooking. [from Old French from Latin]

creamery /'kriːmərɪ/ n. a place where dairy products are processed or sold.

creamy adj. like cream; rich in cream. —creamily adv., creaminess n.

crease n. 1. a line caused by folding or crushing. 2. a line defining the position of the bowler or batsman in cricket. —v.t./i. 1. to make creases in; to develop creases. 2. (slang) to stun, to tire out. [earlier creast = crest]

create /kriː'eɪt/ v.t./i. 1. to bring into existence, to give rise to; to originate. 2. to invest (a person) with a rank. 3. (slang) to make a fuss. [from Latin creare]

creation /kriː'eɪʃən/ n. 1. creating. 2. all created things. 3. a thing created, especially by human intelligence. —**the Creation**, the creation of the world. [from Old French from Latin]

creationism n. a theory concerned with the origins of matter and life, claiming, as does the Bible in Genesis, that the world and humanity were created by a supernatural Creator, not more than 6,000 years ago. It was developed in response to Darwin's theory of ◊evolution, and it is not recognized by most scientists as having a factual basis.

creation myth a legend of the origin of the world. All cultures have ancient stories of the creation of the Earth or its inhabitants. Often this involves the violent death of a primordial being from whose body everything then arises; the giant Ymir in Scandinavian mythology is an example. Marriage between heaven and earth is another common explanation, as in Greek mythology (Uranus and Gaia).

creative /kriː'eɪtɪv/ adj. able to create; inventive, imaginative. —creativity /-'tɪvɪtɪ/ n., creatively adv.

creative accounting the practice of organizing and presenting company accounts in a way that, though desirable for the company concerned, relies on a liberal and unorthodox interpretation of general accountancy procedures.

creator /kriː'eɪtə/ n. one who creates something; **the Creator**, God. [from Old French from Latin]

creature /'kriːtʃə/ n. 1. a created being, especially an animal; a person. 2. one in a subservient position. —**creature comforts**, good food, clothes, surroundings etc. [from Old French from Latin]

crèche /kreɪʃ/ n. a day nursery for babies. [French]

Crécy, Battle of /'kresi/ the first major battle of the Hundred Years' War, 1346. Philip VI of France was defeated by Edward III of England at the village of Crécy-en-Ponthieu, now in Somme département, France, 18 km/11 mi NE of Abbeville.

credence /'kriːdəns/ n. 1. belief. 2. a small table, shelf, or niche for the Eucharistic elements before consecration. [from Old French from Latin]

credentials /krɪ'denʃəlz/ n.pl. a letter or letters of introduction; evidence of achievement or trustworthiness. [from Latin]

credibility /kredɪ'bɪlɪtɪ/ n. being credible. —**credibility gap**, the seeming difference between what is said and what is true.

credible /'kredɪbəl/ adj. believable, worthy of belief. —credibly adv. [from Latin]

credit /'kredɪt/ n. 1. belief or confidence in a person, his or her words, or actions. 2. a source of honour or good reputation; the power or influence it gives. 3. acknowledgement of merit or achievement; (usually in plural) the acknowledgement of a contributor's services to a book, film etc. 4. trust that a person will pay later for goods supplied; power to buy in this way; a person's financial standing. 5. the sum at a person's disposal in a bank; an entry in an account of a sum paid into it; this sum. 6. the side of an account recording such entries. 7. (US) a certificate of the completion of a course by a student. —v.t. 1. to believe, to take to be true or reliable. 2. to enter on the credit side of an account (an amount to a person, a person with an amount). 3. to attribute. —**credit with**, to ascribe (a quality or feeling) to. **give credit for**, to recognize that (a person) has a quality etc. **on credit**, by arrangement to pay later. **to one's credit**, in one's favour. [from French from Latin credere = believe, trust]

creditable adj. praiseworthy, bringing honour or respect. —creditably adv.

credit card a card issued by a credit company, retail outlet, or bank, which enables the holder to obtain goods or services on credit (usually to a specified limit), payable on specified terms. The first credit card was introduced in 1950 in the USA.

creditor /'kredɪtə/ n. a person to whom money is owed. [from Anglo-French from Latin]

credit rating a measure of the willingness or ability to pay for goods, loans, or services rendered by an individual, company, or country. A country with a good credit rating will attract loans on favourable terms.

credo /'kriːdəʊ, 'kreɪ-/ n. (plural credos) a creed. [Latin = I believe]

credulity /krɪ'djuːlɪtɪ/ n. an inclination to believe too readily.

credulous /'kredjʊləs/ adj. too ready to believe; (of behaviour) showing credulity. —credulously adv. [from Latin]

Cree /kriː/ n. 1. a member of a North American Indian people whose language belongs to the Algonquian family. The Cree are distributed over a vast area in Canada from Québec to Alberta. In the USA the majority of Cree live in the Rocky Boys reservation in Montana. 2. the language of the Cree. —adj. of the Cree people or their language.

creed /kriːd/ n. in general, any system of belief; in the Christian Church the verbal confessions of faith expressing the accepted doctrines of the Church. The different forms are the ◊Apostles' Creed, the ◊Nicene Creed, and the Athanasian Creed ◊Athanasius). The only creed recognized by the Orthodox Church is the Nicene. —creedal adj. [Old English from Latin credo]

Creed Frederick George 1871–1957. Canadian inventor who developed the ◊teleprinter. He perfected the Creed telegraphy system (teleprinter), first used in Fleet Street, the headquarters of the British press, in 1912 and subsequently, usually under the name Telex, in offices throughout the world.

creek n. an inlet on the sea coast; a short arm of a river; (Australian and New Zealand) a stream, a brook; (US) a tributary of a river. —**up the creek**, (slang) in difficulties; crazy. [from Old Norse or Middle Dutch]

creel n. a fisherman's large wicker basket. [originally Scottish]

creep v.i. (past and past participle crept) 1. to move slowly with the body prone and close to the ground; to move stealthily or cautiously, to advance very gradually; (of a plant) to grow along the ground or up a vertical surface. 2. to experience a shivering sensation due to repugnance or fear. 3. to develop gradually. —n. 1. creeping. 2. (slang) an unpleasant person. 3. the property of a solid, typically a metal, under continuous stress that causes it to deform below its yield point (the point at which any elastic solid normally stretches without any increase in load or stress). —**the creeps**, (colloquial) a nervous feeling of revulsion or fear. [Old English]

creeper *n.* a person or thing that creeps; a creeping or climbing plant; a small, short-legged passerine bird of the family Certhidae which spirals with a mouselike movement up tree trunks, searching for insects and larvae with its thin, down-curved beak.

creepy *adj.* causing nervous revulsion or fear; having this feeling. —**creepy-crawly** *n.* (*colloquial*) a small creeping insect. —**creepily** *adv.*, creepiness *n.*

creese variant of ◊kris.

cremate /krɪˈmeɪt/ *v.t.* to dispose of a corpse by burning it to ashes. —**cremation** *n.* the custom of cremation was universal among ancient Indo-European peoples, for example, the Greeks, Romans, and Teutons. It was discontinued among Christians until the late 19th century because of their belief in the bodily resurrection of the dead. Overcrowded urban cemeteries gave rise to its revival in the West. It has remained the usual method of disposal in the East. [from Latin *cremare* = burn]

crematorium /kremə'tɔːrɪəm/ *n.* (*plural* **crematoria**) a place where corpses are cremated. [Latin]

crematory /'kremətərɪ/ *adj.* of or pertaining to cremation. —*n.* (*US*) a crematorium.

crème de la crème the elite, the very best. [French = the cream of the cream]

crème de menthe /krem də 'mæt/ a green peppermint liqueur. [French = cream of mint]

crenate /'kriːneɪt/ *adj.* with a notched edge or rounded teeth. —**crenated** *adj.* [from Latin *crena* = notch]

crenel /'krenəl/ *n.* an open space or indentation in an embattled parapet, originally for shooting through. [from Old French from diminutive of Latin *crena* = notch]

crenellate /'krenəleɪt/ *v.t.* to furnish with battlements or loopholes. —**crenellation** /-'leɪʃən/ *n.* [from French]

Creole /'kriːəʊl/ *n.* 1. a descendant of European settlers in the West Indies or Central or South America; a white descendant of French settlers in the southern USA. 2. a person of mixed European and black descent. 3. a creolized language; any ◊pidgin language that has ceased to be simply trade jargon in ports and markets and has become the mother tongue of a particular community. —*adj.* 1. that is a Creole; of Creole or Creoles. 2. **creole**, of local origin or descent. [from French from Spanish, probably from Portuguese *crioulo* = home-born slave]

creolize /'kriːəlaɪz/ *v.t.* to make (the language of a dominant group, in modified form) into the sole language of the group dominated.

creosote /'kriːəsəʊt/ *n.* a dark-brown oil distilled from coal tar, used as a wood preservative; a colourless oily fluid distilled from wood tar, used as an antiseptic. —*v.t.* to treat with creosote. [from German from Greek = flesh preserver]

crêpe /kreɪp/ *n.* 1. a gauzelike fabric with a wrinkled surface. 2. a durable, wrinkled, sheet rubber used for shoe soles etc. —**crêpe paper**, a thin, crinkled paper. **crêpe Suzette**, a small, sweet pancake served flambé. [French from Latin]

crepitate /'krepɪteɪt/ *v.i.* to make a crackling sound. —**crepitation** /'teɪʃən/ *n.* [from Latin *crepitare* (frequentative of *crepare* = creak)]

crept past and past participle of **creep**.

crepuscular /krɪˈpʌskjʊlə/ *adj.* 1. of twilight; (of animals) appearing or active in twilight. 2. dim, not yet fully enlightened. [from Latin *crepusculum* = twilight]

crescendo /krɪˈʃendəʊ/ *adv.* in music, with a gradual increase of loudness. —*n.* (*plural* **crescendos**) 1. a passage to be played this way. 2. progress towards a climax. [Italian]

crescent /'kresənt/ *n.* 1. the waxing Moon; the Moon as seen in the first or last quarter; this as an emblem of Turkey or Islam. The **Red Crescent** is the Muslim equivalent of the Red Cross. 2. anything of crescent shape, especially a street of houses. —*adj.* 1. increasing. 2. crescent-shaped. [from Anglo-French from Latin *crescere* = grow]

cress *n.* any of various cruciferous plants with pungent edible leaves. The common European **garden cress** *Lepidium sativum* is cultivated worldwide. The young plants are grown along with white mustard to be eaten while in the seed-leaf stage as 'mustard and cress'.

crest *n.* 1. a comb or tuft on a bird's or animal's head. 2. a plume, as on a helmet etc. 3. the top of a mountain, roof, or ridge; the surface line of the neck in animals; a curl of foam

on a wave. 4. a device above the shield and helmet on a coat of arms, or on notepaper etc. —*v.t./i.* 1. to reach the crest of. 2. (of a wave) to form a crest. 3. to serve as a crest to, to crown. [from Old French from Latin *crista*]

crestfallen *adj.* dejected, abashed.

cretaceous /krɪˈteɪʃəs/ *adj.* 1. of the nature of chalk. 2. **Cretaceous**, of the final period of the Mesozoic era, lasting from about 144 to 65 million years ago, during which angiosperm (seed-bearing) plants evolved, and dinosaurs and other reptiles reached a peak before almost complete extinction at the end of the period. —**Cretaceous** *n.* this period. [from Latin *cretaceus* (*creta* = chalk)]

Crete /kriːt/ (Greek *Kríti*) largest of the Greek islands, in the E Mediterranean Sea, 100 km/62 mi SE of mainland Greece; **area** 8,378 sq km/3,234 sq mi; **capital** Iráklion; **products** citrus fruit, olives, wine; **population** (1981) 502,000; **language** Cretan dialect of Greek; **history** it has remains of the ◊Minoan civilization 3000–1400 BC, (see ◊Knossos) and was successively under Roman, Byzantine, Venetian, and Turkish rule. The island was annexed by Greece in 1913.

cretin /'kretɪn/ *n.* a person with deformity and mental retardation caused by thyroid deficiency; (*colloquial*) a stupid person. —**cretinism** *n.*, **cretinous** *adj.* [from Swiss French]

cretonne /'kretɒn/ *n.* a colour-printed cotton cloth used for chair covers etc. [French, from *Creton* in Normandy]

crevasse /krɪˈvæs/ *n.* a deep, open crack, especially in the ice of a glacier. [French]

crevice /'krevɪs/ *n.* a narrow opening or fissure especially in a rock or wall. [from Old French *crevace* (*crever* = burst)]

crew[1] /kruː/ *n.* 1. the body of persons manning a ship, aircraft, etc.; these other than the officers. 2. a group of people, especially working together. —*v.t./i.* to act as a crew (for); to supply a crew for. —**crew cut,** a closely cropped man's haircut. **crew neck**, a close-fitting round neckline, especially of a pullover. [originally = reinforcement; from Old French *creue* = increase from Latin *crescere* = grow]

crew[2] past of **crow**.

crewel /'kruːəl/ *n.* a thin worsted yarn for tapestry and embroidery. —**crewelwork** *n.* a design in this on linen.

crib *n.* 1. a wooden framework for holding animals' fodder. 2. a child's bed or cot. 3. a model of the manger scene at Bethlehem. 4. the cards given by other players to the dealer at cribbage; (*colloquial*) cribbage. 5. a literal translation for the use of students; (*colloquial*) an instance of plagiarism. —*v.t./i.* (**-bb-**) 1. to confine in a small space. 2. to pilfer; to copy unfairly or without acknowledgement. [Old English]

cribbage *n.* a card game for two or more persons, with a 'crib' (see ◊crib[4]).

crick /krɪk/ *n.* a sudden painful stiffness in the neck or back. —*v.t.* to cause a crick in.

Crick Francis 1916– . English molecular biologist. From 1949 he researched the molecular structure of DNA, and the means whereby characteristics are transmitted from one generation to another. For this work he was awarded the Nobel Prize for Physiology or Medicine (with Maurice Wilkins (1916–) and James D ◊Watson).

cricket[1] /'krɪkɪt/ *n.* the national summer sport in England. The game is played between two sides of 11 players each on a field 20 m/22 yd long with a wicket at each end. The object of the game is to score more runs than the opponents. A run is normally scored by the batsman after striking the ball and exchanging ends with his or her partner, or by hitting the ball to the boundary line for an automatic four or six runs. A batsman stands at each wicket and is bowled a stipulated number of balls (usually six), after which another bowler bowls from the other wicket. A batsman is usually got 'out' by being bowled, caught, run out, stumped or l.b.w. (leg before wicket) - when the ball hits his leg or her leg which is placed before the wicket. The exact origins of cricket are unknown, but it certainly dates back to the 16th century. It became popular in southern England in the late 18th century. Rules were drawn up in 1774 and modified following the formation of the Marylebone Cricket Club (MCC) in 1787. Every year a series of Test Matches is played among member countries of the Commonwealth, where the game has its greatest popularity: Australia, India, New Zealand, Pakistan, England, Sri Lanka, and the West Indies. Test matches take several days, but otherwise the majority of matches last one, three, or four days. —**not cricket**, (*colloquial*) not fair play (from the game's tradition of fair play and generous applause for the achievements of players of both sides). **cricketer** *n.*

cricket[2] *n.* an insect belonging to various families, in particular the Grillidae, of the order Orthoptera. They are related to grasshoppers. Crickets are somewhat flattened and have long antennae. The males make a chirping noise by rubbing together special areas on the forewings. The females have a long needlelike egglaying organ (ovipositor). There are some 900 species known worldwide. [from Old French *criquer* = creak]

cri de coeur /kri: də kɜ:/ a passionate appeal, a complaint or protest. [French = cry from the heart]

cried past and past participle of **cry**.

crier /ˈkraɪə/ *n.* one who cries, especially an official making public announcements in lawcourts or in the street. [from Anglo-French]

crikey /ˈkraɪkɪ/ (*slang*) interjection expressing astonishment. [euphemism for *Christ*]

crime *n.* an act (usually a serious offence) punishable by law; an evil act; such acts collectively; (*colloquial*) a shame, a senseless act. [from Old French from Latin *crimen* = accusation, offence]

Crimea /kraɪˈmɪə/ northern peninsula on the Black Sea, a region of ◊Ukraine Republic, USSR, from 1954; **area** 27,000 sq km/10,425 sq mi; **capital** Simferopol; **physical** mainly steppe, but S coast is a holiday resort; **products** iron, oil; **recent history** under Turkish rule 1475–1774; a subsequent brief independence was ended by Russian annexation in 1783. It was the republic of Taurida 1917–20 and the Crimean Autonomous Soviet Republic from 1920 until occupied by Germany from July 1942–May 1944. It was then reduced to a region, its Tatar people being deported to Uzbekistan for collaboration. Although they were exonerated in 1967 and some were allowed to return, others were forcibly re-exiled in 1979.

Crimean War the war 1853–56 between Russia and the allied powers of England, France, Turkey, and Sardinia. The war arose from British and French mistrust of Russia's ambitions in the Balkans. The battles of the River Alma, Balaclava (including the charge of the Light Brigade), and Inkerman in 1854 led to a siege which, due to military mismanagement, lasted for a year until Sept 1855. The war was ended by the Treaty of Paris of 1856. The scandal surrounding French and British losses through disease led to the organization of proper military nursing services by Florence Nightingale.

criminal /ˈkrɪmɪnəl/ *n.* a person guilty of crime. —*adj.* of, involving, or concerning crime; guilty of crime. —**criminality** /-ˈnælɪtɪ/ *n.* **criminally** *adv.* [from Latin]

Criminal Injuries Compensation Board a UK board established in 1964 to administer financial compensation by the state for victims of crimes of violence. Victims can claim compensation for their injuries, but not for damage to property. The compensation awarded is similar to the amount that would be obtained for a court in damages (see ◊damage) for personal injury.

Criminal Investigation Department (CID) the detective branch of the London Metropolitan Police, established in 1878 and comprising a force of about 4,000 men and women, recruited entirely from the uniformed police and controlled by an assistant commissioner. Such branches are now also found in the regional police forces.

criminal law the body of law that defines the public wrongs (crimes) that are punishable by the state and establishes methods of prosecution and punishment. It is distinct from ◊civil law, which deals with legal relationships between individuals (including organizations), such as contract law.

criminology /krɪmɪˈnɒlədʒɪ/ *n.* the scientific study of crime. —**criminologist** *n.*

crimp *v.t.* to press into small folds or ridges; to corrugate; to make waves in (hair). —*n.* a crimped thing or form. [probably from Middle Dutch or Middle Low German]

crimson /ˈkrɪmzən/ *adj.* of a rich, deep red inclining to purple. —*n.* crimson colour. [ultimately from Arabic]

cringe /krɪndʒ/ *vi.* to shrink back in fear, to cower; to behave obsequiously (*to*).

crinkle *n.* a wrinkle, a crease. —*v.t./i.* to form crinkles (in). —**crinkly** *adj.* [frequentative of Old English *crincan* = yield]

crinoid /ˈkrɪnɔɪd/ *adj.* lily-shaped. —*n.* a crinoid echinoderm. [from Greek *krinoeidēs* (*krinon* = lily)]

crinoline /ˈkrɪnəlɪn, -li:n/ *n.* **1.** a stiffened or hooped petticoat formerly worn to make a long skirt stand out. **2.** a stiff fabric of horsehair etc. used for linings, hats etc. [French from Latin *crinis* = hair and *linum* = thread]

cripes /kraɪps/ (*vulgar*) interjection expressing astonishment. [perversion of *Christ*]

cripple *n.* a person who is permanently lame. —*v.t.* to make a cripple of, to lame; to disable, to weaken or damage seriously. [Old English]

Cripps /krɪps/ (Richard) Stafford 1889–1952. British Labour politician, expelled from the Labour party 1939–45 for supporting a 'Popular Front' against Chamberlain's appeasement policy. He was ambassador to Moscow 1940–42, minister of aircraft production 1942–45, and chancellor of the Exchequer 1947–50.

crisis /ˈkraɪsɪs/ *n.* (*plural* **crises** /-si:z/) a decisive moment; a time of danger or great difficulty. [Latin from Greek = decision]

crisp *adj.* **1.** hard but brittle, breaking with a snap; slightly stiff. **2.** (of air) cold and bracing. **3.** (of style or manner) brisk and decisive. —*n.* a thin, fried slice of potato (sold in packets etc.). —*v.t./i.* to make or become crisp. —**crisply** *adv.*, **crispness** *n.*, **crispy** *adj.* [from Latin *crispus* = curled]

crispbread *n.* a thin, crisp biscuit of crushed rye etc.

Crispi /ˈkrɪspi/ Francesco 1819–1907. Italian prime minister 1887–91 and 1893–96. He advocated the ◊Triple Alliance of Italy with Germany and Austria, but was deposed in 1896.

crisscross *n.* a pattern of crossing lines. —*adj.* crossing, in cross lines. —*adv.* crosswise, at cross purposes. —*v.t./i.* to mark or form or move in a crisscross pattern. [originally from *Christ's cross*]

criterion /kraɪˈtɪərɪən/ *n.* (*plural* **criteria**) a principle or standard by which a thing is judged. [Greek = means of judging]

crith *n.* a unit of mass used for weighing gases. One crith is the mass of one litre of hydrogen gas (H_2) at standard temperature and pressure.

critic /ˈkrɪtɪk/ *n.* **1.** one who censures. **2.** one who reviews or judges the merit of literary, artistic etc., works. [from Latin from Greek *kritēs* = judge]

critical /ˈkrɪtɪkəl/ *adj.* **1.** fault-finding, censorious; expressing criticism. **2.** of or at a crisis, decisive, crucial. **3.** marking the transition from one state etc. to another; (of a nuclear reactor) maintaining a self-sustaining chain reaction. —**critical path**, the sequence of stages determining the minimum time needed for a complex operation. —**critically** *adv.* [from Latin]

critical angle in optics, for a ray of light passing from a denser to a less dense medium (such as from glass to air), the smallest angle of incidence at which the emergent ray grazes the surface of the denser medium – at an angle of refraction of 90°.

critical mass in nuclear physics, the minimum mass of fissile material that can undergo a continuous chain reaction (see ◊chain). Below this mass, too many ◊neutrons escape from the surface for a chain reaction to carry on; above the critical mass, the reaction may accelerate into a nuclear explosion.

critical temperature temperature above which a particular gas cannot be converted into a liquid by pressure alone. It is also the temperature at which a magnetic material loses its magnetism (the Curie temperature or point).

criticism /ˈkrɪtɪsɪzəm/ *n.* **1.** finding fault, censure. **2.** the work of a critic; a critical article, essay, or remark.

criticize /ˈkrɪtɪsaɪz/ *v.t./i.* **1.** to find fault (with), to censure. **2.** to discuss critically.

critique /krɪˈtiːk/ *n.* **1.** a critical essay or analysis. **2.** a criticism. [French]

Crivelli /krɪˈveli/ Carlo 1435/40–1495/1500. Italian painter in the early Renaissance style, active in Venice. He painted extremely detailed, decorated religious works, sometimes festooned with garlands of fruit. His figure style is strongly Italian, reflecting the influence of Mantegna.

CRO abbreviation of ◊cathode-ray oscilloscope, a common laboratory instrument.

croak *n.* a deep, hoarse cry or sound as of a raven or frog. —*v.t./i.* **1.** to utter or speak with a croak. **2.** (*slang*) to die; to kill.

Croat /'krəʊæt/ *n.* **1.** a native or inhabitant of Croatia in Yugoslavia. **2.** the language of the Croats. —**Croatian** /-'eɪʃən/ *adj. & n.* [from Latin from Serbo-Croatian *Hrvat*]

Croatia /krəʊ'eɪʃə/ (Serbo-Croat *Hrvatska*) constituent republic of Yugoslavia; **area** 56,500 sq km/21,809 sq mi; **capital** Zagreb; **physical** Adriatic coastline with large islands; very mountainous, with part of the Karst region and the Julian and Styrian Alps; some marshland; **population** (1985) 4,660,000; including 75% Croats, 11% Serbs, and 0.5% Hungarians; **language** the Croatian variant of Serbo-Croat; **recent history** Croatia was included in the kingdom of the Serbs, Croats, and Slovenes (called Yugoslavia from 1931) in 1918. It was a Nazi puppet state during World War II, and has been a centre for nationalist and separatist demands from the 1970s. Tension between majority Croat and minority Serbian populations increased following the election April–May 1990 of a right-wing Croat nationalist government led by Franje Tudman, which asserted regional autonomy. A multiparty system was adopted, and in Feb 1991 the new government called for secession. Worsening Serb–Croatia hostilities led to clashes in May 1991. The federal army intervened, but fighting continued.

Croce /'krəʊtʃi/ Benedetto 1866–1952. Italian philosopher, historian, and literary critic; an opponent of fascism. His *Philosophy of the Spirit* 1902–17 was a landmark in idealism. Like Hegel, he held that ideas do not represent reality but *are* reality; but unlike Hegel, he rejected every kind of transcendence.

crochet /'krəʊʃeɪ/ *n.* needlework in which the yarn is looped into a pattern of stitches by means of a hooked needle. —*v.t./i.* to make in or do crochet. [French (*croc* = hook)]

crock[1] *n.* (*colloquial*) a person who suffers from ill health or lameness etc.; a worn-out vehicle, ship etc. [originally Scottish, perhaps from Flemish]

crock[2] *n.* an earthenware pot or jar; a broken piece of this. [Old English]

crockery *n.* earthenware vessels, plates etc.

crocket /'krɒkɪt/ *n.* a small ornamental carving on the inclined side of a pinnacle etc. [from Old French]

Crockett /'krɒkɪt/ Davy 1786–1836. US folk hero. Born in Tennessee, he became a Democratic Congressman 1827–31 and 1833–35. A series of books, of which he may have been part-author, made him into a mythical hero of the frontier, but their Whig associations cost him his office. He died in the battle of the ◊Alamo during the war for Texan independence.

crocodile /'krɒkədaɪl/ *n.* **1.** a large aquatic carnivorous reptile of the family Crocodiliae, related to alligators and caimans, but distinguished from them by a more pointed snout and a notch in the upper jaw into which the fourth tooth in the lower jaw fits. Crocodiles can grow up to 6 m/ 20 ft, and have long, powerful tails that propel them when swimming. They can live up to 100 years. **2.** the skin of a crocodile, used to make bags, shoes etc. **3.** (*colloquial*) a line of schoolchildren etc. walking in pairs. —**crocodile tears**, insincere grief (from the belief that the crocodile wept while devouring, or to allure, its victim). [from Old French from Latin from Greek *krokodilos*]

crocus /'krəʊkəs/ *n.* a dwarf spring-flowering plant of the genus *Crocus*, growing from a corm, with yellow, purple, or white flowers. —**autumn crocus**, a similar plant blooming in autumn after its leaves have died down. [Latin from Greek, of Semitic origin]

Croesus /'kriːsəs/ the last king of Lydia, famed for his wealth. His court included ◊Solon, who warned him that no man could be called happy until his life had ended happily. When Croesus was overthrown by Cyrus the Great in 546 BC and condemned to be burned to death, he called out Solon's name. Cyrus, having learned the reason, spared his life.

croft *n.* an enclosed piece of (usually arable) land; a small rented farm, especially in the Highlands of Scotland, traditionally farming common land cooperatively. The 1886 Crofters Act gave security of tenure to crofters. Today, although grazing land is still shared, arable land is typically

Cromwell A portrait after Samuel Cooper 1656, National Portrait Gallery, London.

enclosed. —*v.i.* to farm a croft; to live as a crofter. [Old English]

crofter *n.* one who rents a croft.

Crohn's disease /krəʊn/ a chronic inflammatory bowel disease, also known as **regional ileitis** or **regional enteritis**. It tends to flare up for a few days at a time, causing diarrhoea, abdominal cramps, loss of appetite, and mild fever. The cause of Crohn's disease is unknown, although stress may be an factor.

croissant /'krwɑːsɑ̃/ *n.* a crescent-shaped bread roll. [French = crescent]

Cro-Magnon /krəʊ'mænjə/ *n.* a prehistoric human, believed to be ancestral to Europeans, the first skeletons of which were found in 1868. They are thought to have superseded the Neanderthals about 40,000 years ago. Although biologically advanced, they were more robust in build than present-day humans. They hunted bison, reindeer, and horses, and are associated with two successive Upper Paleolithic cultures (Aurignacian and Magdalenian). [from *Cro-Magnon* cave near Les Eyzies, in the Dordogne region of France, where first found]

Crome /krəʊm/ John 1768–1821. English landscape painter, founder of the **Norwich school** with John Sell Cotman in 1803. His works include *The Poringland Oak* of about 1818 (Tate Gallery, London), showing Dutch influence.

cromlech /'krɒmlek/ *n.* **1.** a megalithic chamber tomb, a dolmen. **2.** in Brittany, a circle of upright prehistoric stones. [Welsh *crwm* = curved and *llech* = flat stone]

Crompton Samuel 1753–1827. English inventor at the time of the Industrial Revolution. He invented the 'spinning mule' in 1779, combining the ideas of ◊Arkwright and ◊Hargreaves. Though widely adopted, his invention brought him little financial return.

Cromwell /'krɒmwel/ Oliver 1599–1658. English general and politician, Puritan leader of the Parliamentary side against Charles I in the ◊Civil War. He raised cavalry forces (later called **Ironsides**) which aided the victories at Edgehill in 1642 and ◊Marston Moor in 1644, and organized the New Model Army, which he led (with General Fairfax) to victory at Naseby in 1645. He signed the king's death warrant in 1648 and in the power struggle that followed sided with the army and the establishment of the ◊Commonwealth. He expelled Parliament and established the Protectorate. As Lord Protector (ruler) from 1653, Cromwell established religious toleration and raised Britain's prestige in Europe on the basis of an alliance with France against Spain.

Cromwell Richard 1626–1712. Son of Oliver Cromwell, he succeeded his father as Lord Protector but resigned in May 1659, having been forced to abdicate by the army. He lived in exile in France after the Restoration until 1680.

Cromwell Thomas, Earl of Essex *c.*1485–1540. English politician who drafted the legislation making the Church of

England independent of Rome. Originally in Lord Chancellor Wolsey's service, he became secretary to Henry VIII in 1534 and the real director of government policy; he was executed for treason.

crone *n.* a withered old woman. [from Dutch *croonje* = carcass]

crony *n.* a close friend. [from Greek *khronios* = of long standing (*khronos* = time)]

crook /krʊk/ *n.* **1.** the hooked staff of a shepherd or bishop. **2.** a bent or curved thing; a hook; a bend, a curve. **3.** (*colloquial*) a rogue, a swindler; a professional criminal. —*adj.* (*Australian* and *New Zealand*) unsatisfactory, unpleasant; ailing, injured. —*v.t./i.* to bend, to curve. [from Old Norse]

crooked /ˈkrʊkɪd/ *adj.* **1.** not straight or level; bent, curved, twisted. **2.** not straightforward, dishonest. —**crookedly** *adv.*, **crookedness** *n.*

Crookes /krʊks/ William 1832–1919. English scientist, whose many chemical and physical discoveries included the metallic element thallium in 1861, the radiometer in 1875, and Crookes' high-vacuum tube used in X-ray techniques.

croon *v.t./i.* to hum or sing in a low subdued voice and sentimental manner. —*n.* such singing. —**crooner** *n.* [originally Scottish and north of England, from Middle Dutch, Middle Low German *kronen* = groan, lament]

crop *n.* **1.** the produce of cultivated plants, especially cereals; a season's total yield; a group or amount produced at one time. **2.** the handle of a looped whip. **3.** hair cut very short. **4.** the pouch in a bird's gullet where food is prepared for digestion. —*v.t./i.* (**-pp-**) **1.** to cut or bite off; to cut (hair) very short. **2.** to sow (land) *with* a crop; to bear crops. —**crop-eared** *adj.* with the ears or hair cut short. **crop up**, to occur unexpectedly or by chance. [Old English]

crop circle a circular pattern of flattened corn (or other crop) which appears mysteriously in fields just before harvest time. The circles can have diameters up to 200ft. In 1990, over 200 circles were sighted in Britain, but they have appeared in more than 30 countries. Scientists believe they are caused by a type of whirlwind, which occurs when a mini-frontal pressure system passes over a hill in the right temperature conditions, triggering a powerful vortex of air, which flattens the crop.

cropper *n.* a crop producing plant of a specified quality. —**come a cropper**, (*slang*) to fall heavily, to fail badly.

crop rotation the system of regularly changing the crops grown on a piece of land. The crops are grown in a particular order to utilize and add to the nutrients in the soil and to prevent the buildup of insect and fungal pests.

croquet /ˈkrəʊkeɪ/ *n.* **1.** a game played on a lawn measuring 27 m/90 ft by 18 m/60 ft in which wooden balls are driven with mallets through square-topped hoops. Played in France in the 16th and 17th centuries, it gained popularity in England in the 1850s, and was revived 100 years later. **2.** an act of croqueting. —*v.t./i.* to drive away (an opponent's ball) by placing one's own against it and striking one's own. [perhaps dialect variant of French *crochet* = hook]

croquette /krəʊˈket/ *n.* a roll of potato, meat etc. coated in breadcrumbs and fried. [French (*croquer* = crunch)]

crore /krɔː/ *n.* in India, ten million, one hundred lakhs. [from Hindi from Sanskrit *koti* = apex]

Crosby /ˈkrɒzbi/ Bing (Harry Lillis) 1904–1977. US film actor and singer, who achieved world success with his distinctive style of crooning in such songs as 'Pennies from Heaven', and 'White Christmas', featured in films of the same names. He won an acting Oscar for *Going My Way* 1944, and made a series of 'road' film comedies with Dorothy Lamour and Bob Hope, the last being *Road to Hong Kong* 1962.

crosier /ˈkrəʊzɪə, -ʒə/ *n.* the hooked staff carried by a bishop as a symbol of office. [from Old French *crossier* = crook bearer, *croisier* = cross bearer]

cross[1] *n.* **1.** an upright post with a transverse bar, as used in antiquity for crucifixion, especially (**the Cross**) that on which Christ was crucified; a representation of this as the emblem of Christianity, a staff surmounted by a cross; a monument in the form of a cross. **2.** a thing or mark of similar shape, especially the figure made by two short intersecting lines (+ or ×). **3.** a decoration indicating rank in some orders of knighthood or awarded for personal valour. **4.** an intermixture of breeds, a hybrid; a mixture or compromise *between* two or more things. **5.** a crosswise movement of an actor, football, boxer's fist etc. **6.** a

trouble or annoyance. —*adj.* **1.** transverse, reaching from side to side; intersecting. **2.** contrary, opposed, reciprocal. **3.** annoyed or angry (*with*) —**be at cross purposes**, to misunderstand or conflict with one another. **on the cross**, diagonally. —**crossly** *adv.*, **crossness** *n.* [Old English, ultimately from Latin *crux*]

cross[2] *v.t./i.* **1.** to go across (a road, river, sea, any area), to cross a road etc. **2.** to intersect or be across one another; to cause to be in this position. **3.** to draw a line or lines across. **4.** to make the sign of the cross over (especially *oneself*). **5.** to pass in opposite or different directions. **6.** to thwart, to frustrate; to anger by refusing to acquiesce. **7.** to interbreed; to cross-fertilize. —**cross one's heart**, to make the sign of the cross over it as a sign of sincerity. **cross one's mind**, (of an idea etc.) to occur to one. **cross off**, to remove from a list etc. **cross out**, to cancel, to obliterate.

crossbar *n.* a horizontal bar, especially between uprights.

cross-bench *n.* a bench in Parliament for members not belonging to the government or main opposition.

crossbill *n.* a species of bird, a ◊finch of the genus *Loxia*, in which the hooked tips of the upper and lower beak cross one another, an adaptation for extracting the seeds from conifer cones. The **red crossbill** *Loxia curvirostra* is found in parts of Eurasia and North America.

crossbow *n.* a bow fixed across a wooden stock, with a groove for the arrow and a mechanism for drawing and releasing the string.

crossbreed *v.t.* to produce a hybrid of. —*n.* a hybrid animal or plant. —**crossbred** *adj.* hybrid.

crosscheck *v.t./i.* to check by an alternative method of verification. —*n.* a check of this kind.

cross-country *adj.* & *adv.* across fields, not keeping to main or direct roads.

crosscut *n.* a diagonal cut, path etc. —**crosscut saw**, a saw for cutting across the grain of wood.

crosse *n.* the netted crook used in lacrosse. [French]

cross-examine *v.t.* to examine (especially an opposing witness in a lawcourt) so as to check or extend previous testimony. —**cross-examination** *n.*

cross-eyed *adj.* having one or both eyes turned towards the nose.

cross-fertilize *v.t.* to fertilize (an animal or plant) from one of a different species. —**cross-fertilization** *n.*

crossfire *n.* a firing of guns in two crossing directions; opposition, interrogation etc., from several sides at once.

cross-grained *adj.* **1.** (of wood) with the grain in crossing directions. **2.** (of a person) perverse, intractable.

crossing *n.* **1.** place where things cross. **2.** a place at which one may cross. **3.** a journey across water.

crossing over in biology, a process that occurs during ◊meiosis. While the chromosomes are lying alongside each other in pairs, each partner may twist around the other and exchange corresponding chromosomal segments. It is a form of genetic ◊recombination, which increases variation and thus provides the raw material of evolution.

cross-legged *adj.* with the legs crossed, or with the ankles crossed and knees apart.

Crossman /ˈkrɒsmən/ Richard (Howard Stafford) 1907–1974. British Labour politician. He was minister of housing and local government 1964–66 and of health and social security 1968–70. His pòsthumous *Crossman Papers* 1975 revealed confidential cabinet discussion.

He certainly does not confide in me any profound thoughts about the future of the Labour Party, and I am prepared to say as of today, I don't think he has any.

Richard Crossman on Harold Wilson, *Diaries* 1966

---

crosspatch *n.* a bad-tempered person.

cross-ply *adj.* (of a tyre) having the fabric layers with the cords lying crosswise.

cross-question *v.t.* to cross-examine.

cross-reference *n.* a reference from one part of a book etc. to another.

crossroads *n. pl.* the intersection of two roads. —**at the crossroads**, at the point where a decision must be made or a course of action chosen.

cross section 1. a transverse section; a representation or diagram of a thing as if cut through. 2. a representative sample. —**cross-sectional** *adj.*

cross-stitch *n.* a stitch formed by two crossing stiches.

crosstalk *n.* 1. unwanted transfer of signals between communication channels. 2. repartee.

crossways *adv.* = ◊crosswise.

crosswind *n.* a wind blowing across the direction of travel.

crosswise *adv.* or **crossways** in the manner of a cross, across, with one crossing the other.

crossword *n.* a puzzle in which a grid of open and blacked-out squares must be filled with interlocking words, to be read horizontally and vertically, according to numbered clues. The first crossword was devised by Arthur Wynne of Liverpool, England, in the *New York World* 1913.

crotch *n.* the place where things (especially the legs of a body or a garment) fork. [perhaps from Old French *croc(he)* = hook]

crotchet /'krotʃɪt/ *n.* in music, a note equal to two quavers or half a minim. [from Old French]

crotchety *adj.* peevish.

crouch *v. i.* to lower the body with the knees bent close against the chest; to be in this position. —*n.* crouching. [from Old French *crochir* = be bent]

croup[1] /kru:p/ *n.* an inflammation of the larynx and trachea of children, with a hard cough and difficult breathing. [from *croup* = to croak]

croup[2] *n.* the rump (especially of a horse). [from Old French]

croupier /'kru:piə/ *n.* a person in charge of a gambling table raking in and paying out money. [French, originally = rider on the croup]

croûton /'kru:tɒn/ *n.* a small piece of fried or toasted bread served with soup etc. [French]

crow /krəʊ/ *n.* 1. a large black bird of the genus *Corvus* or family Corvidae, including the jackdaw, raven, and rook. Crows are usually about 45 cm/1.5 ft long, black, with a strong bill feathered at the base, and omnivorous with a bias towards animal food. They are considered to be very intelligent. 2. the cry of a crow, the crowing of a cock. —*v. i.* (*past* in 1st sense also **crew** /kru:/) 1. (of a cock) to utter a loud shrill cry. 2. (of a baby) to utter happy sounds. 3. to express gleeful satisfaction (*over*). —**as the crow flies**, in a straight line. **crow's foot**, a wrinkle at the outer corner of the eye. **crow's nest**, a barrel fixed at the masthead of a sailing ship as a shelter for the lookout. [Old English]

crowbar *n.* an iron bar with a flattened end, used as a lever.

crowd *n.* a large number of people gathered together without orderly arrangement; a mass of spectators, an audience; (*colloquial*) a company, a set, a lot. —*v. t./i.* to come or cause to come together in a crowd; to fill, to occupy, to cram (*into* or *with*); to inconvenience by crowding or coming aggressively close to. —**crowd out**, to keep out by crowding. —**crowded** *adj.* [Old English *crūdan* = press, drive]

crowding out in economics, a situation in which an increase in government expenditure, by generating price increases and thus a reduction in the real money supply, results in a fall in private consumption and/or investment. Crowding out has been used in recent years as a justification for privatization of state-owned services and industries in the UK and other countries.

crown *n.* 1. a monarch's ornamental and usually jewelled headdress. 2. (often **the Crown**) the monarch (especially as head of state); the power or authority of the monarch. 3. a wreath for the head, as an emblem of victory; a reward for or consummation of effort. 4. the top part of a thing, especially of the head or a hat; the highest or central point of an arched or curved thing; the part of a tooth projecting from the gum, an artificial replacement for this or a part of this. 5. a figure of a crown as a mark or emblem. 6. a British coin worth 25p (formerly five shillings). 7. a former size of paper, 504 × 384 mm. —*v. t.* 1. to put a crown on; to invest with a regal crown or office; to be a crown to, to encircle or rest on the top of; to be the consummation, reward, or finishing touch to. 2. (*slang*) to hit on the head. 3. to

promote (a piece in draughts) to king. —**Crown Derby**, a kind of china made at Derby and often marked with a crown.

crown jewels, the sovereign's regalia, including a crown, sceptre, and orb, used on ceremonial occasions. **crown prince**, the male heir to a throne. **crown princess**, the wife of a crown prince; the female heir to a throne. **crown wheel**, a wheel with teeth or cogs at right angles to its plane. [from Anglo-French from Latin *corona*]

crown colony any British colony that is under the direct legislative control of the crown and does not possess its own system of representative government. Crown colonies are administered by a crown-appointed governor or by elected or nominated legislative and executive councils with an official majority. Usually the crown retains rights of veto and of direct legislation by orders in council.

Crown Court in England and Wales, a court that hears serious criminal cases referred from ◊magistrates' courts after ◊committal proceedings. Crown Courts replaced ◊quarter sessions and assizes, which were abolished in 1971. Appeals against conviction or sentence at magistrates' courts may be heard in Crown Courts. Appeal from a Crown Court is to the Court of Appeal.

Crown Estate the title (from 1956) of land in the UK formerly owned by the monarch but handed to Parliament (by George III in 1760) in exchange for an annual payment (called the civil list). It owns valuable sites in central London and 268,400 acres in England and Scotland.

crozier variant of **crosier**.

CRT abbreviation of ◊cathode-ray tube.

cruces plural of **crux**.

crucial /'kru:ʃəl/ *adj.* decisive, critical; (*colloquial*) (disputed usage) very important. —**crucially** *adv.* [French, from Latin *crux* = cross]

crucible /'kru:sɪbəl/ *n.* a melting pot for metals etc.; a severe test. [from Latin *crucibulum*]

cruciferous /kru:'sɪfərəs/ *adj.* of the family Cruciferae, having flowers with four equal petals arranged crosswise. [from Latin = cross-bearing]

crucifix /'kru:sɪfɪks/ *n.* a model of the cross, especially with a figure of Christ on it. [from Old French from Latin = fixed to a cross]

crucifixion /kru:sɪ'fɪkʃən/ *n.* death by fastening to a cross, a form of capital punishment used by the ancient Romans, Persians, and Carthaginians, and abolished by the Roman emperor Constantine; **the Crucifixion**, that of Christ. [from Latin]

cruciform /'kru:sɪfɔ:m/ *adj.* cross-shaped. [from Latin *crux* = cross]

crucify /'kru:sɪfaɪ/ *v. t.* 1. to put to death by fastening to a cross. 2. to persecute, to torment; to destroy in argument etc. [from Old French from Latin]

cruck /krʌk/ *n.* one of the paired curved timbers extending to the ground in the framework of a house roof.

crude /kru:d/ *adj.* in the natural state, not refined; lacking finish, unpolished; rude, blunt. —**crudely** *adv.*, **crudity** *n.* [from Latin *crudus* = raw, rough]

cruel /'kru:əl/ *adj.* indifferent to or gratified by another's suffering; causing pain or suffering. —**cruelly** *adv.*, **cruelty** *n.* [from Old French from Latin *crudelis*]

Cruelty, Theatre of a theory advanced by Antonin ◊Artaud in his book *Le Théâtre et son double* 1938 and adopted by a number of writers and directors. It aims to shock the audience into an awareness of basic, primitive human nature through the release of feelings usually repressed by conventional behaviour.

cruet /'kru:ɪt/ *n.* a small glass bottle for holding oil or vinegar for use at table; a stand holding this and salt, pepper, and mustard pots. [from Old French, diminutive of *crue* = pot]

Cruft /krʌft/ Charles 1852–1938. British dog expert. He organized his first dog show in 1886, and from that year annual shows bearing his name were held in Islington, London.

Cruikshank /'krʊkʃæŋk/ George 1792–1878. English painter and illustrator, remembered for his political cartoons and illustrations for Charles Dickens's *Oliver Twist* and Daniel Defoe's *Robinson Crusoe*.

cruise /kru:z/ *v. i.* 1. to sail about without precise destination, or calling at a series of places. 2. (of a motor vehicle or aircraft) to travel at a moderate economical speed. 3. (of a vehicle or driver) to travel at random, especially slowly. —*n.* a cruising voyage. [probably from Dutch *kruis* = cross]

cruise missile a long-range guided missile that has a terrain-seeking radar system and flies at moderate speed and low altitude. It is descended from the German V-1 of World War II.

cruiser /'kru:zə/ *n.* a warship of high speed and medium armament; a cabin cruiser (see ◊cabin). [from Dutch]

cruiserweight *n.* light heavyweight (see ◊heavyweight).

crumb /krʌm/ *n.* 1. a small fragment, especially of bread; a small particle or amount *of.* 2. the soft inner part of bread. —*v.t.* 1. to cover with breadcrumbs. 2. to crumble (bread). —**crumby** *adj.* [Old English]

crumble *v.t./i.* to break or fall into small fragments; (of power, reputation etc.) to collapse gradually. —*n.* a dish of cooked fruit with a crumbly topping. —**crumbly** *adj.*

crumbs /krʌmz/ *interjection* expressing dismay or surprise. [euphemism for *Christ*]

crummy *adj.* (*slang*) dirty, squalid; inferior, worthless. —**crumminess** *n.*

crumpet /'krʌmpɪt/ *n.* 1. a flat, soft cake of yeast mixture, toasted and eaten with butter. 2. (*slang*) the head. 3. (*slang*) a sexually attractive person.

crumple *v.t./i.* to crush or become crushed into creases; to collapse, to give way. [from obsolete *crump* = curl up]

crumple zone the region at the front and rear of a motor vehicle that is designed to crumple gradually during a collision, so reducing the risk of serious injury to passengers. The progressive crumpling absorbs the kinetic energy of the vehicle more gradually than would a rigid structure, thereby diminishing the forces of deceleration acting on the vehicle and on the people inside.

crunch *v.t./i.* to crush noisily with the teeth; to grind underfoot (gravel, dry snow etc.); to make a crunching sound. —*n.* 1. crunching; a crunching sound. 2. (*colloquial*) a decisive event. —**when it comes to the crunch,** (*colloquial*) when there is a showdown. [imitative]

crupper *n.* a strap holding a harness back by passing under a horse's tail. [from Anglo-French]

crusade *n.* 1. Crusade, any of a series of military expeditions undertaken by Christian western Europe in the 11th–13th centuries to recover the Holy Land from the Saracens. 2. a vigorous campaign in favour of a cause. —*v.t./i.* to engage in a crusade. [earlier *croisade* (French, from *croix* = cross] **1st Crusade 1095–99** led by Baldwin of Boulogne, Godfrey of Bouillon, and Peter the Hermit. Motivated by occupation of Anatolia and Jerusalem by the Seljuk Turks. The crusade succeeded in recapturing Jerusalem and establishing a series of Latin kingdoms on the Syrian coast. **2nd Crusade 1147–49** led by Louis VII of France and Emperor Conrad III; a complete failure. **3rd Crusade 1189–92** led by Philip II Augustus of France and Richard I of England. Failed to recapture Jerusalem, which had been seized by Saladin in 1187. **4th Crusade 1202–04** led by William of Montferrata, and Baldwin of Hainault. Directed against Egypt but diverted by the Venetians to sack and divide Constantinople. **Children's Crusade 1212** thousands of children crossed Europe on their way to the Holy Land but many were sold into slavery at Marseille, or died of disease and hunger. **5th Crusade 1218–21** led by King Andrew of Hungary, Cardinal Pelagius, King John of Jerusalem, and King Hugh of Cyprus. Captured and then lost Damietta, Egypt. **6th Crusade 1228–29** led by the Holy Roman emperor Frederick II. Jerusalem recovered by negotiation with the sultan of Egypt, but the city was finally lost in 1244. **7th and 8th Crusades 1249–54, 1270–72** both led by Louis IX of France. Acre, the last Christian fortress in Syria, was lost in 1291.

crusader *n.* 1. Crusader, one who took part in the Crusades. 2. one who engages in a crusade.

cruse /kru:z/ *n.* (*archaic*) an earthenware pot or jar. [Old English]

crush *v.t./i.* 1. to press heavily or with violence so as to break, injure or wrinkle; to squeeze tightly; to press or pound into small fragments. 2. to become crushed. 3. to defeat or subdue completely. —*n.* 1. a crowded mass of people pressed together. 2. a drink made from the juice of crushed fruit. 3. (*slang*) an infatuation. [from Old French *croissir* = gnash (the teeth)]

crushable /'krʌʃəbəl/ *adj.* that can be crushed; easily crushed.

crust *n.* 1. the hard outer part of bread; the similar casing of anything. 2. the rocky outer skin of the Earth, consisting of the **oceanic crust** and the **continental crust.** The oceanic crust is on average about 10 km/6.2 mi thick and consists mostly of basaltic types of rock. The continental crust is primarily granitic in composition and more complex in its structure. Because of the movements of ◊plate tectonics, the oceanic crust is in no place older than about 200 million years. Parts of the continental crust are over three billion years old. 3. a deposit, especially from wine on a bottle. 4. (*slang*) impudence. —*v.t./i.* to cover with or form into a crust; to become covered with a crust. —**crustal** *adj.* [from Old French from Latin *crusta* = rind, shell]

crustacean /krʌ'steɪʃən/ *n.* a member of the Crustacea, a large class of hard-shelled mainly aquatic animals including crabs, lobsters, shrimps, woodlice etc. The external skeleton is made of protein and chitin hardened with lime. Each segment bears a pair of appendages that may be modified as sensory feelers (antennae), as mouthparts, or as swimming, walking, or grasping structures. —*adj.* of crustaceans. [from Latin]

crusty *adj.* 1. having a crisp crust. 2. irritable, curt. —**crustily** *adv.,* **crustiness** *n.*

crutch *n.* 1. a support for a lame person, usually with a crosspiece fitting under the armpit or shaped so that the weight is supported on the forearm; any support. 2. the crotch. [Old English]

crux /krʌks/ *n.* (*plural* **cruces** /'kru:si:z/) the decisive point, the crucial element of a problem. [Latin = cross]

Crux *n.* a constellation of the southern hemisphere, popularly known as the Southern Cross, the smallest of the 88 constellations. Its brightest star, Alpha Crucis (or Acrux), is a ◊double star about 360 light years from Earth. Near Beta Crucis lies a glittering star cluster known as the Jewel Box. The constellation also contains the Coalsack, a dark cloud of dust silhouetted against the bright starry background of the Milky Way.

cry /kraɪ/ *v.t./i.* (*past* and *past participle* **cried**) 1. to make a loud shrill sound; to call out loudly in words; (of an animal) to utter its cry. 2. to shed tears. 3. (often with *out*) to appeal, demand, or show need *for.* 4. (of a hawker etc.) to proclaim (wares) for sale. —*n.* 1. a loud inarticulate utterance of pain, grief, joy etc.; a loud excited utterance of words; the loud natural utterance of an animal, that of hounds on a scent. 2. an urgent appeal or entreaty; a public demand. 3. a watchword, a rallying call. 4. a spell of weeping. —**crybaby** *n.* a person who weeps easily or without good reason. **cry down,** to disparage. **cry off,** to withdraw from a promise or undertaking. **cry up,** to praise, to extol. **cry wolf,** see ◊wolf. **in full cry,** in close pursuit. [from Old French from Latin *quiritare* = wail]

crying *adj.* (especially of injustice) flagrant, demanding redress.

cryogenics /kraɪə'dʒeniks/ *n.* the science of very low temperatures (approaching ◊absolute zero), including the production of very low temperatures and the exploitation of special properties associated with them, such as the disappearance of electrical resistance (◊superconductivity). [from Greek *kruos* = frost]

cryolite *n.* a rare granular crystalline mineral, Na_3AlF_6, used in the electrolyte reduction of ◊bauxite to aluminium. It is chiefly found in Greenland.

cryosurgery /kraɪəu'sɜ:dʒəri/ *n.* surgery in which local application of intense cold is used for anaesthesia or therapy. [from Greek *kruos* = frost]

crypt /krɪpt/ *n.* a vault, especially one beneath a church, used as a burial place. [from Latin from Greek *kruptē* (*kruptos* = hidden)]

cryptic /'krɪptɪk/ *adj.* secret, mysterious; obscure in meaning. —**cryptically** *adv.*

cryptogam /'krɪptəgæm/ *n.* an obsolete name applied to the lower plants. It included the algae, liverworts, mosses, and ferns (plus the fungi and bacteria in very early schemes of classification). In such classifications seed plants were known as ◊phanerogams. —**cryptogamous** /-'tɒgəməs/ *adj.* [from French]

cryptogram /'krɪptəgræm/ *n.* a thing written in cipher.

cryptography /krɪp'tɒgrəfi/ *n.* the science of creating and reading codes; for example, those produced by the

Enigma coding machine used by the Germans in World War II (as in ◊Ultra) and those used in commerce by banks encoding electronic fund-transfer messages, business firms sending computer-conveyed memos between headquarters, and in the growing field of electronic mail. No method of encrypting is completely unbreakable, but decoding can be made extremely complex and time consuming. —**cryptographer** *n.*, **cryptographic** /-tə'græfɪk/ *adj.*

cryptorchism *n.* or **cryptochidism** a condition marked by undescended testicles; failure of the testes to complete their descent into the scrotum before birth. When only one testicle has descended, the condition is known as monorchism.

crystal /'krɪstəl/ *n.* 1. a kind of clear, transparent, colourless mineral; a piece of this. 2. highly transparent glass, flint glass; articles made of this. 3. an aggregation of molecules with a definite internal structure and the external form of a solid enclosed by symmetrically arranged plane faces. —*adj.* made of crystal; like or clear as crystal. —**crystal ball,** a glass globe used in crystal gazing. **crystal gazing,** concentrating one's gaze on a crystal to obtain a picture by hallucination etc. [Old English from Old French, ultimately from Greek *krustallos* = ice, crystal]

crystalline /'krɪstəlaɪn/ *adj.* 1. of, like, or clear as crystal. 2. having the structure and form of a crystal. —**crystallinity** /-'lɪnɪtɪ/ *n.* [from Old French]

crystallize /'krɪstəlaɪz/ *v.t./i.* 1. to form into crystals. 2. (of ideas or plans) to become definite. —**crystallized fruit,** fruit preserved in sugar. —**crystallization** /-'zeɪʃən/ *n.*

crystallography /krɪstə'lɒgrəfɪ/ *n.* the scientific study of crystals. In 1912, it was found that the shape and size of the unit cell of a crystal can be discovered by X-rays, thus opening up an entirely new way of 'seeing' atoms. This means of determining the atomic patterns in a crystal is known as X-ray diffraction. By this method it has been found that many substances have a unit cell that exhibits all the symmetry of the whole crystal. In table salt (sodium chloride, NaCl), for instance, the unit cell is an exact cube. Many materials were not even suspected of being crystals until they were examined by X-ray crystallography. —**crystallographer** *n.*

crystalloid /'krɪstəlɔɪd/ *n.* a substance having a crystalline structure.

Crystal Palace a glass and iron building designed by Joseph ◊Paxton, housing the Great Exhibition of 1851 in Hyde Park, London; it was later rebuilt in a modified form at Sydenham Hill in 1854 (burned down in 1936).

crystal system one of seven classification categories into which crystalline substances are placed by definition of their symmetry. The elements of symmetry used for this purpose are: (1) planes of mirror symmetry, across which a minor image is seen, and (2) axes of rotational symmetry, about which, in a 360° rotation of the crystal, equivalent faces are seen twice, three, four, or six times.

The crystal systems are: cubic, tetragonal, orthorhombic, monoclinic, triclinic, trigonal, and hexagonal. In US terminology only six crystal systems are recognized since the trigonal is regarded as a class of the hexagonal.

c/s abbreviation of cycles per second.

Cs symbol for ◊caesium.

CSCE abbreviation of Conference on Security and Cooperation in Europe, popularly known as the ◊Helsinki Conference.

CSE abbreviation of Certificate of Secondary Education; in the UK, the examinations taken by the majority of secondary school pupils who were not regarded as academically capable of GCE ◊O Level, until the introduction of the common secondary examination system, ◊GCSE, in 1988.

Ctesiphon /'tesɪfən/ the ruined royal city of the Parthians, and later capital of the Sassanian Empire, 19 km/12 mi SE of Baghdad, Iraq. A palace of the 4th century still has its throne room standing, spanned by a single vault of unreinforced brickwork some 24 m/80 ft across.

CT scanner or **CAT scanner** a medical device used to obtain detailed X-ray pictures of the inside of a patient's body. The body is examined in slices, and an overall picture is built up from the results by computer. This technique is called ◊tomography.

cu or **cu.** abbreviation of cubic (measure).

Cu symbol for copper.

cub *n.* 1. the young of a fox, bear, lion etc. 2. an ill-mannered young man. 3. (*colloquial*) an inexperienced reporter. 4. **Cub,** a Cub Scout. —*v.t./i.* (**-bb-**) 1. to bring forth (cubs). 2. to hunt fox cubs. —**Cub Scout,** a member of a junior branch of the Scout Association, consisting of boys aged eight to eleven.

Cuba /'kjuːbə/ Republic of; island in the Caribbean, the largest of the West Indies, off the S coast of Florida; **area** 110,860 sq km/42,820 sq mi; **capital** Havana; **physical** comprises Cuba and smaller islands including Isle of Youth; low hills; Sierra Maestra mountains in the SE; Cuba has deep bays, sandy beaches, coral islands and reefs; **head of state and government** Fidel Castro Ruz from 1959; **political system** communist republic; **exports** sugar (largest producer after USSR), tobacco, coffee, iron, copper, nickel; **population** (1990 est) 10,582,000 (37% are white of Spanish descent, 51% mulatto, and 11% are of African origin); **language** Spanish; **recent history** independence was achieved from Spain in 1901. Cuba became a communist state under Fidel Castro. With Soviet help, the country made considerable economic and social progress, also becoming involved in international commitments (Angola, Argentina). Overseas military interventions were reduced in 1989.

Cuban missile crisis a crisis in international relations in 1962 when Soviet rockets were installed in Cuba and US President Kennedy compelled Khrushchev, by an ultimatum, to remove them. The drive by the USSR to match the USA in nuclear weaponry dates from this event.

cubbyhole /'kʌbɪhəʊl/ *n.* a very small room; a small, snug place. [from dialect *cub* = stall from Low German]

cube /kjuːb/ *n.* 1. in geometry, a solid figure whose faces are all squares. It has six equal-area faces and 12 equal-length edges. If the length of one edge is *l*, the volume *V* of the cube is given by $V = l^3$ and its surface area $A = 6l^2$. 2. a cube-shaped block. 3. the product of a number multiplied by its square. —*v.t.* 1. to find the cube of (a number). 2. to cut (food) into small cubes. —**cube root,** the number which produces a given number when cubed. [French or Latin from Greek]

cubic /'kjuːbɪk/ *adj.* 1. of three dimensions. 2. involving the cube (and no higher power) of a number. —**cubic metre** etc., the volume of a cube whose edge is one metre etc. [from French or Latin]

cubical /'kjuːbɪkəl/ *adj.* cube-shaped.

cubicle /'kjuːbɪkəl/ *n.* a small separate sleeping compartment; an enclosed space screened for privacy. [from Latin *cubare* = lie]

cubic measure a measure of volume, indicated either by the prefix 'cubic' followed by a linear measure, as in 'cubic foot', or the suffix 'cubed', as in 'metre cubed'.

Cubism /'kjuːbɪzəm/ *n.* a revolutionary movement in early 20th century painting, pioneering abstract art. Its founders, Braque and Picasso, were admirers of Cézanne and were inspired by his attempt to create a structure on the surface of the canvas. About 1907–10 the Cubists began to 'abstract' images from nature, gradually releasing themselves from the imitation of reality. Cubism announced that a work of art exists in its own right rather than as a representation of the real world, and it attracted such artists as Juan Gris, Fernand Léger, and Robert Delaunay. —**Cubist** *n.* & *adj.* [from French]

cubit /'kjuːbɪt/ *n.* the earliest-known unit of length, which originated between 2800 and 2300 BC. It is approximately 50.5 cm/20.6 in long, which is about the length of the human forearm, measured from the tip of the middle finger to the elbow. [from Latin *cubitum* = elbow]

cuboid /'kjuːbɔɪd/ *adj.* cube-shaped, like a cube. —*n.* a six-sided three-dimensional prism whose faces are all rectangles. [from Greek]

Cuchulain /ku'hulɪn/ in Celtic mythology, a legendary hero, the chief figure in a cycle of Irish legends. He is associated with his uncle Conchobar, king of Ulster; his most famous exploits are described in *Taín Bó Cuailnge/The Cattle Raid of Cuchulain*.

cuckold /'kʌkəʊld/ *n.* a husband whose wife is unfaithful to him. —*v.t.* to make a cuckold of. —**cuckoldry** *n.* [from Old French *cucu* = cuckoo]

cuckoo /'kuku/ *n.* a species of bird, any of about 200 members of the family Cuculidae, commonly the **Eurasian cuckoo** *Cuculus canorus*, whose name derives from its

characteristic call. Somewhat hawklike, it is about 33 cm/
1.1 ft long, bluish-grey and barred beneath (females sometimes reddish), and has a long, typically rounded tail. It is a
'brood parasite', laying its eggs singly, at intervals of about
48 hours, in the nests of small insectivorous birds. As soon
as the young cuckoo hatches, it ejects all other young birds
or eggs from the nest and is tended by its 'foster parents'
until fledging. Cuckoos feed on insects, including hairy caterpillars that are distasteful to most birds. **cuckoo spit**,
a froth exuded by the larvae of certain insects on leaves,
stems etc. [from Old French]

cuckoo flower or **lady's smock** a perennial plant
Cardamine pratensis, family Cruciferae. Native to Britain,
it is common in damp meadows and marshy woods. It bears
pale lilac flowers, which later turn white from April to June.

cuckoopint *n.* or **lords-and-ladies** a perennial plant
Arum maculatum of the Araceae family. The large arrow-
shaped leaves appear in early spring, and the flower-bearing
stalks are enveloped by a bract, or spathe. In late summer
the bright red, berrylike fruits, which are poisonous, make
their appearance.

cucumber /'kjuːkʌmbə/ *n.* a trailing annual plant *Cucumis
sativus* of the gourd family Cucurbitaceae, producing long,
green-skinned fruit with crisp, translucent, edible flesh.
Small cucumbers, called gherkins, usually the fruit of
C. anguria, are often pickled. [from Old French from
Latin *cucumer*]

cud *n.* the half-digested food that a ruminant chews at leisure. —**chew the cud**, to reflect, to ponder. [Old English,
related to Old High German *kuti*, *quiti* = glue]

cuddle *v.t./i.* to hug, to embrace fondly; to lie close and
snug; to nestle together. —*n.* a prolonged and fond hug.
—**cuddlesome** *adj.*, **cuddly** *adj.* [perhaps from dialect
couth = snug]

cudgel /'kʌdʒəl/ *n.* a short, thick stick used as a weapon.
—*v.t.* (-ll-) to beat with a cudgel. —**cudgel one's brains**,
to think hard about a problem. **take up the cudgels for**,
to defend vigorously. [Old English]

cue[1] *n.* something said or done (especially by an actor in
a play) which serves as a signal for another to say or do
something; a stimulus to perception etc.; a signal, a hint.
—*v.t.* to give a cue to. —**cue in**, to insert a cue for; to give
information to.

cue[2] *n.* a billiard player's rod for striking the ball. —*v.t./i.*
to use a cue; to strike with a cue. [variant of *queue*]

cuff[1] *n.* 1. the thicker end part of a sleeve; a separate band
worn round the wrist. 2. (in *plural*, *colloquial*) handcuffs.
—**cuff link**, one of a pair of fasteners for shirt cuffs. **off
the cuff**, extempore, without preparation.

cuff[2] *v.t.* to strike with the open hand. —*n.* a cuffing blow.

Cugnot /kuː'njəʊ/ Nicolas-Joseph 1728–1804. French engineer who produced the first high-pressure steam engine.
While serving in the French army, he was asked to design
a steam-operated gun carriage. After several years, he
produced a three-wheeled, high-pressure carriage capable
of carrying 1,800 l/400 gallons of water and four passengers
at a speed of 5 kph/3 mph. Although he worked further on the
carriage, the political upheavals of the French revolutionary
era obstructed progress and his invention was ignored.

Cui /kwiː/ Casar Antonovich 1853–1918. Russian composer of operas and chamber music. A professional soldier, he joined ◊Balakirev's Group of Five and promoted a
Russian national style.

cuirass /kwɪ'ræs/ *n.* a piece of armour consisting of a
breastplate and backplate fastened together. [from Old
French from Latin *coriaceus* (*corium* = leather)]

cuisine /kwiː'ziːn/ *n.* a style or method of cooking. [French
= kitchen]

cuius regio, eius religio those who live in a country should
adopt the religion of its ruler. [Latin]

Cukor /'kjuːkɔː/ George 1899–1983. US film director. He
moved to the cinema from the theatre, and was praised
for his skilled handling of stars such as Greta ◊Garbo (in
Camille 1937) and Katharine Hepburn (in *The Philadelphia
Story* 1940). His films were usually sophisticated dramas or
light comedies.

cul-de-sac /'kʌldəsæk, 'kʊl-/ *n.* (*plural* **culs-de-sac**
pronounced the same) a street or passage closed at one
end. [French = sack bottom]

culinary /'kʌlɪnərɪ/ *adj.* of or for cooking. [from Latin
culina = kitchen]

cull *v.t.* 1. to pick (a flower etc.), to select. 2. to select
from a herd etc. and kill (surplus animals). —*n.* culling;
an animal or animals culled. [from Old French from Latin
colligere = collect]

Culloden, Battle of /kə'lɒdn/ the defeat in 1746 of the
Jacobite rebel army of the British Prince ◊Charles Edward
Stuart by the Duke of ◊Cumberland on a stretch of moorland
in Inverness-shire, Scotland. This battle effectively ended
the military challenge of the Jacobite rebellion.

culminate /'kʌlmɪneɪt/ *v.i.* to reach its highest point
(*in*). —**culmination** /-'neɪʃən/ *n.* [from Latin *culminare*
(*culmen* = summit)]

culottes /kjuː'lɒts/ *n.pl.* women's trousers styled to
resemble a skirt. [French = knee breeches]

culpable /'kʌlpəbəl/ *adj.* deserving blame. —**culpability** /-'bɪlɪtɪ/ *n.*, **culpably** *adv.* [from Old French from Latin
culpare = to blame]

culprit /'kʌlprɪt/ *n.* a person accused of or guilty of an
offence. [perhaps abbreviation of Anglo-French formula
said by Clerk of Crown to prisoner pleading Not Guilty,
Culpable: prest d'averrer etc. (You are) guilty: (I am)
ready to prove it]

cult *n.* a system of religious worship especially as expressed
in ritual; devotion or homage to a person or thing. [from
French or from Latin *colere* = cultivate, worship]

cultivar *n.* a variety of a plant developed by horticultural or
agricultural techniques. [from *culti*vated *variety*]

cultivate /'kʌltɪveɪt/ *v.t.* 1. to prepare and use (soil) for
crops. 2. to produce (crops) by tending them. 3. to apply
oneself to improving or developing (the mind, an acquaintance, etc.). 4. to spend time and care in developing; to
develop the friendship of. —**cultivation** /-'veɪʃən/ *n.*
[from Latin *cultivare* (*cultiva* (*terra*) = arable land]

cultivator /'kʌltɪveɪtə/ *n.* 1. a device for breaking up
ground. 2. one who cultivates.

Cultural Revolution a mass movement begun by Chinese Communist party chairman Mao Zedong in 1966,
directed against the upper middle class, bureaucrats, artists, and university intellectuals, who were killed, imprisoned, humiliated, or 'resettled'. Intended to 'purify' Chinese
communism, it was also an attempt by Mao to renew his
political and ideological pre-eminence inside China.

culture /'kʌltʃə/ *n.* 1. refined understanding of the arts
and other human intellectual achievement. 2. the customs
and civilization of a particular time or people. 3. improvement by care and training. 4. the cultivation of plants,
rearing of bees, silkworms etc. 4. a quantity of bacteria
grown for study. —*v.t.* to grow bacteria, living cells and
tissues for study. —**cultural** *adj.* [from French or Latin]

cultured *adj.* having or showing culture. —**cultured
pearl**, a pearl formed by an oyster after the insertion of
a foreign body into its shell.

culvert /'kʌlvət/ *n.* a drain that crosses under a road,
canal, etc.

cum /kʊm/ *prep.* with, together with; also used as. [Latin]

Cumae /'kjuːmiː/ ancient city in Italy, on the coast about
16 km/10 mi W of Naples. In was the seat of the oracle of
the Cumaean Sibyl.

Cuman /'kjuːmən/ *n.* a member of a powerful Turki federation of the Middle Ages, which dominated the steppes
in the 11th and 12th centuries and built an empire reaching
from the Volga to the Danube.

cumber *v.t.* (*literary*) to hamper, to hinder, to inconvenience.

Cumberland /'kʌmbələnd/ former county of NW England, merged in 1974 with ◊Cumbria.

Cumberland Ernest Augustus, Duke of Cumberland
1771–1851. King of Hanover from 1837, the fifth son of
George III of Britain. A high Tory and an opponent of all
reforms, his attempts to suppress the constitution met with
open resistance that had to be put down by force.

Cumberland William Augustus, Duke of Cumberland
1721–1765. English general who ended the Jacobite rising
in Scotland with the Battle of Culloden in 1746; his brutal
repression of the Highlanders earned him the nickname
of 'Butcher'.

cumbersome /'kʌmbəsəm/ *adj.* hampering; inconvenient in size, weight, or shape.

Cumbria /'kʌmbrɪə/ county in NW England; **area**
6,810 sq km/2,629 sq mi; **administrative headquarters**
Carlisle; **physical** Lake District National Park, including

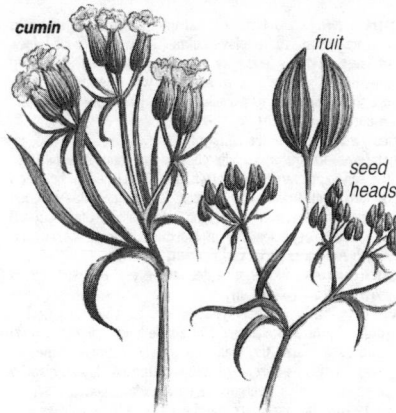

cumin

fruit

seed
heads

Scafell Pike 978 m/3,210 ft, highest mountain in England; Helvellyn 950 m/3,118 ft; Lake Windermere, the largest lake in England, 17 km/10.5 mi long, 1.6 km/1 mi wide, also Derwentwater, Ullswater; **products** the traditional coal, iron, and steel industries of the coast towns have been replaced by newer industries including chemicals, plastics, and electronics; in the N and E there is dairying, and West Cumberland Farmers is the country's largest agricultural cooperative; **population** (1987) 487,000.

cumin /'kʌmɪn/ n. a herb *Cuminum cyminum* of the carrot family Umbelliferae, with aromatic seeds used as a spice in cooking. [from Old French from Latin from Greek (probably of Semitic origin)]

cummerbund /'kʌməbʌnd/ n. a sash worn round the waist. [from Hindi and Persian = loin band]

Cumming /'kʌmɪŋ/ Mansfield 1859–1923. British naval officer, first head of the British Secret Intelligence Service. The head of the service has always since been known by the initial letter 'C'.

cummings /'kʌmɪŋz/ e(dward) e(stlin) 1894–1962. US poet, whose published collections of poetry include *Tulips and Chimneys* 1923. His poems were initially notorious for their idiosyncratic punctuation and typography (he always wrote his name in lower case letters, for example), but their lyric power has gradually been recognized.

Listen: there's a hell of a good universe next door: let's go.

e e cummings
Pity this busy monster, manunkind

---

cumquat variant of **kumquat**.

cumulate /'kju:mjʊleɪt/ v.t./i. to accumulate; to combine (catalogue entries etc.). [from Latin *cumulare* (*cumulus* = heap)]

cumulative /'kju:mjʊlətɪv/ adj. increasing or increased in amount, force etc., by successive additions. —**cumulatively** adv.

cumulative frequency in statistics, the total frequency up to and including a certain point. It is used to draw the cumulative frequency curve, the ogive.

cumulonimbus /ˌkju:mjʊləʊˈnɪmbəs/ n. a form of cloud consisting of a tall, dense mass, present during thunderstorms.

cumulus /'kju:mjʊləs/ n. (*plural* **cumuli**) a form of cloud consisting of rounded masses heaped on a horizontal base. [Latin = heap]

cuneiform /'kju:nɪfɔ:m/ adj. of or using an ancient system of writing with wedge-shaped marks impressed on soft clay with a straight length of reed, bone, wood, or metal, or incised into stone etc. —n. this writing. It was probably invented by the Sumerians, and was in use in Mesopotamia as early as the middle of the 4th millennium BC. [from French from Latin *cuneus* = wedge and *forma* = shape]

Cunene /ku:'neɪni/ or **Kunene** river rising near Nova Lisboa in W central Angola. It flows south to the frontier with Namibia, then west to the Atlantic; length 250 km/15 mi.

Cunha /'ku:njə/ Euclydes da 1866–1909. Brazilian writer. His novel *Os Sertões/Rebellion in the Backlands* 1902 describes the Brazilian *sertão* (backlands), and how a small group of rebels resisted government troops.

cunning adj. 1. skilled in ingenuity or deceit, selfishly clever or crafty; ingenious. 2. (*US*) attractive, quaint. —n. craftiness, skill in deceit. [from Old Norse = knowing]

Cunningham Andrew Browne, 1st Viscount Cunningham of Hyndhope 1883–1963. British admiral in World War II, commander in chief in the Mediterranean 1939–42, maintaining British control; as commander in chief of the Allied Naval Forces in the Mediterranean Feb–Oct 1943 he received the surrender of the Italian fleet.

Cunningham John 1885–1962. British admiral in World War II. He was commander in chief in the Mediterranean 1943–46, First Sea Lord 1946–48, and became admiral of the fleet in 1948.

Cunningham /'kʌnɪŋhæm/ Merce 1919– . US dancer and choreographer. Influenced by Martha ◊Graham, with whose company he was a soloist from 1939–45, he formed his own dance company and school in New York in 1953. His works include *The Seasons* 1947, *Antic Meet* 1958, *Squaregame* 1976, and *Arcade* 1985.

Cunninghame-Graham /ˈɡreɪəm/ Robert Bontine 1852–1936. Scottish writer, politician, and adventurer. Author of essays and short stories such as *Success* 1902, *Faith* 1909, *Hope* 1910, and *Charity* 1912. He wrote many travel books based on his experiences as a rancher in Texas and Argentina 1869–83, and as a traveller in Spain and Morocco 1893–98. He was president of the Scottish Labour Party in 1888 and became first president of the Scottish National Party in 1928.

Cuno /ˈku:nʊ/ Wilhelm 1876–1933. German industrialist and politican who was briefly chancellor of the Weimar Republic 1923.

cunt n. (*vulgar*) the female genitals. [from Old Norse *kunta*, Middle Low German, Middle Dutch *kunte*]

cup n. 1. a small bowl with a handle, used for drinking from; its contents, the amount that it holds. 2. a cup-shaped thing. 3. flavoured wine, cider etc. 4. an ornamental vessel as the prize for a race or contest. 5. one's fate or fortune. —v.t. (-pp-) to form (especially one's hands) into the shape of a cup; to take or hold as in a cup. —**Cup Final,** the final football etc. match in a competition for a cup. —**cupful** n. (*plural* **cupfuls**) [Old English]

cupboard /'kʌbəd/ n. a recess or piece of furniture with a door and (usually) shelves, in which things may be stored. —**cupboard love,** a display of affection meant to secure some gain.

Cupid /'kju:pɪd/ in Roman mythology, the god of love, identified with the Greek god ◊Eros.

cupidity /kju:'pɪdɪtɪ/ n. greed for gain. [from Old French or Latin *cupiditas* = desire]

cupola /'kju:pələ/ n. 1. a small dome on a roof. 2. a furnace for melting metals. 3. a ship's or fort's revolving gun turret. [Italian from Latin *cupa* = cask]

cuppa /'kʌpə/ n. (*colloquial*) a cup of (tea).

cupreous /'kju:prɪəs/ adj. of or like copper. [from Latin *cuprum* = copper]

cupric /'kju:prɪk/ adj. of copper.

cuprite n. Cu$_2$O, a copper ore (copper(I) oxide) found in crystalline form or in earthy masses. It is red to black in colour, and is often called ruby copper.

cupronickel /ˌkju:prəʊˈnɪkəl/ n. a copper alloy (75% copper and 25% nickel), used in hardware products and for coinage.

cur n. 1. a worthless or bad-tempered dog. 2. a contemptible person. [perhaps from Old Norse *kurr* = grumbling]

curable /'kjʊərəbəl/ adj. that can be cured.

curaçao /'kjʊərəsəʊ/ n. a liqueur flavoured with the peel of bitter oranges. [name of Caribbean island producing these oranges]

Curaçao /ˌkjʊərəˈsəʊ/ island in the West Indies, one of the ◊Netherlands Antilles, with an area of 444 sq km/171 sq mi; population (1981) 147,000. The principal industry, dating from 1918, is the refining of Venezuelan petroleum. Curaçao was colonized by Spain in 1527, annexed by the Dutch West India Company in 1634, and gave its name from 1924 to the group of islands renamed Netherlands Antilles in 1948. Its capital is the port of Willemstad.

curacy /'kjʊərəsɪ/ n. a curate's office; the tenure of it.

curare /kjʊəˈrɑːrɪ/ n. a black, resinous poison extracted from the bark and juices of various South American trees and plants. Originally used on arrowheads by Amazonian hunters to paralyse prey, it blocks nerve stimulation of the muscles. Alkaloid derivatives (called curarines) are used in medicine as muscle relaxants during surgery. [from Carib]

curate /ˈkjʊərət/ n. in the Christian Church, literally, a priest who has the cure of souls in a parish; the term is so used in Europe. In the Church of England, a curate is an unbeneficed cleric who acts as assistant to a parish priest. [from Latin]

curative /ˈkjʊərətɪv/ adj. tending or able to cure. —n. a curative thing. [French from Latin]

curator /kjʊəˈreɪtə/ n. a person in charge of a museum or other collection.

curb n. 1. a check, a restraint. 2. a strap or chain fastened to a bit and passing under a horse's lower jaw, used as a check. 3. a border or edging, the frame round the top of a well; a kerb. —v.t. 1. to restrain. 2. to put a curb on (a horse). [from Old French from Latin curvare]

curd n. (often in plural) a coagulated substance formed by the action of acids on milk, made into cheese or eaten as food.

curdle v.t./i. to congeal, to form into curds. —make one's blood curdle, to fill one with horror.

cure v.t. 1. to restore to health; to relieve of a disease; to eliminate (a disease, evil etc.). 2. to preserve (meat, fruit, tobacco, or skins) by salting, drying etc. 3. to vulcanize (rubber). —n. a thing that cures; a restoration to health; a course of medicinal or healing treatment. [from Old French from Latin curare = take care of (cura = care)]

curé /ˈkjʊəreɪ/ n. a parish priest in France etc. [French]

curette /kjʊəˈret/ n. a surgeon's small scraping instrument. —v.t. to scrape with this. —curettage n. [French, from curer = cleanse]

curfew /ˈkɜːfjuː/ n. a signal or time after which people must remain indoors; (historical) a signal for the extinction of fires at a fixed evening hour. [from Anglo-French coeverfu = cover fuel]

Curia /ˈkjʊəriə/ n. or **Curia Romana** the papal court, especially those functionaries through whom the government of the Roman Catholic Church is administered. It includes certain tribunals; the chancellery, which issues papal bulls; various offices including that of the cardinal secretary of state; and the congregations, or councils of cardinals, each with a particular department of work. [Latin = senate house at Rome]

curie /ˈkjʊərɪ/ n. 1. a former unit (symbol Ci) of radioactivity, equal to 37 × 10⁹ becquerels. One gram of radium has a radioactivity of about one curie. 2. a quantity of radioactive substance having this activity. [from P Curie]

Curie Marie (born Sklodovska) 1867–1934. Polish physicist and chemist, who investigated radioactivity in Paris with her husband, French physicist and chemist **Pierre Curie** (1859–1906). They discovered radium and polonium in 1898, isolating the pure elements in 1902. They were jointly awarded the Nobel Prize for Physics with A H ◊Becquerel in 1903, and Marie Curie received the Nobel Prize for Chemistry in 1911. She died a victim of radiation poisoning.

Curie temperature the temperature above which a magnetic material cannot be strongly magnetized. Above the Curie temperature, the energy of the atoms is too great for them to join together to form the small areas of magnetized material, or ◊domains, which combine to produce the strength of the overall magnetization. [from P Curie]

curio /ˈkjʊərɪəʊ/ n. (plural curios) a rare or unusual object. [abbreviation of curiosity]

curiosity /kjʊəriˈɒsɪtɪ/ n. 1. an eager desire to know; inquisitiveness. 2. a strange or rare thing.

curious /ˈkjʊərɪəs/ adj. 1. eager to know or learn; inquisitive. 2. strange, surprising, odd. —curiously adv. [from Old French from Latin curiosus = careful]

curium /ˈkjʊərɪəm/ n. a synthesized, radioactive, metallic element of the ◊actinide series, symbol Cm, atomic number 96, relative atomic mass 247. It is produced by neutron irradiation of plutonium or americium. The longest-lived isotope has a half-life of 1.7 × 10⁷ years. Curium is used to generate heat and power in satellites or in remote places. It was first synthesized in 1944. [from M Curie and P Curie]

curl v.t./i. 1. to bend or coil into a spiral; to move in a spiral form. 2. to play curling. —n. 1. a coiled lock of hair; anything spiral or curved inwards. 2. a curling movement. —curl up, to lie or sit with the knees drawn up; to writhe with horror, shame etc. [from obsolete crulle = curly from Dutch]

curler n. a device for curling the hair.

curlew /ˈkɜːljuː/ n. a wading bird of the genus Numenius of the sandpiper family, Scolopacidae. The curlew is between 36 cm/14 in and 55 cm/1.8 ft in length, and has mottled brown plumage, long legs, and a long, thin, down-curved bill. Several species live in Northern Europe, Asia, and North America. [from Old French]

curlicue /ˈkɜːlɪkjuː/ n. a decorative curl or twist. [from curly and cue² (= pigtail)]

curling n. a game played on ice, in which large, flat, rounded stones are hurled along a defined space (the rink) towards a mark (the tee). One of the national games of Scotland, it has spread to many countries. It can also be played on artificial (cement or tarmacadam) ponds.

curly adj. having or arranged in curls; moving in curves.

curmudgeon /kɜːˈmʌdʒən/ n. a bad-tempered person.

Curragh 'Mutiny' the demand in March 1914 by the British general Hubert Gough and his officers, stationed at Curragh, Ireland, that they should not be asked to take part in forcing Protestant Ulster to participate in Home Rule. They were subsequently allowed to return to duty, and after World War I the solution of partition was adopted.

Curragh, The a horse-racing course in County Kildare where all five Irish Classic races are run. At one time used for hurdle races, it is now used for flat racing only.

currant /ˈkʌrənt/ n. 1. the dried fruit of a small seedless grape Vitis vinifera, used in cookery. 2. any of various shrubs of the genus Ribes producing black, red, or white berries; such a berry. The **redcurrant** Ribes rubrum is a native of S Europe and Asia and occasionally grows wild in Britain. The **whitecurrant** is a cultivated, less acid variety. The **blackcurrant** R. nigrum is the most widely used for cooking. The **flowering currant** R. sanguineum is a native of North America. [from Anglo-French = (grapes of) Corinth, the original source)]

currawong /ˈkʌrəwɒŋ/ n. a small, crowlike Australian bird of the genus Strepera, with a resonant call. [Aboriginal]

currency /ˈkʌrənsɪ/ n. 1. the money in use in a country. 2. being current, prevalence.

current /ˈkʌrənt/ adj. 1. belonging to the present time, happening now. 2. (of money, an opinion, rumour, word) in general circulation or use. —n. 1. a body of water, air, etc., moving in a definite direction, especially through a stiller surrounding body. There are three basic types of oceanic current: **drift currents** are broad and slow-moving; **stream currents** are narrow and swift-moving; and **upwelling currents** bring cold, nutrient-rich water from the ocean bottom. 2. the general tendency or course of events or opinions. 3. the movement of electrically charged particles; a quantity representing the intensity of this. [from Old French from Latin currere = run]

current account a bank account from which money may be drawn without notice; in economics, that part of the balance of payments concerned with current transactions, as opposed to capital movements. It includes trade (visibles) and service transactions, such as investment, insurance, shipping, and tourism (invisibles). The state of the current account is regarded as a barometer of overall economic health.

currently adv. at the present time.

current prices a series of prices that express values pertaining to a given time but that do not take account of the changes in purchasing power, unlike ◊constant prices.

curricle /ˈkʌrɪkəl/ n. a light, open horse-drawn carriage, usually with two horses abreast. [from Latin curriculum]

curriculum /kəˈrɪkjʊləm/ n. (plural curricula) a course of study; in education, the range of subjects offered within an institution or course. Until 1988, the only part of the school curriculum prescribed by law in the UK was religious education. The Education Reform Act 1988 introduced a compulsory **National Curriculum**, which applies to all children of school age (5–16) in state schools. There are three core subjects in the curriculum: English, maths, and science, and seven foundation subjects: technology, history, geography, music, art, physical education, and a foreign language. —**curriculum vitae** /'viːtaɪ/ , an account of one's previous career. [Latin = racecourse (*currere* = run)]

currier /'kʌriə/ *n.* a leather dresser. [from Old French from Latin *corium* = leather]

curry[1] *n.* a dish of meat, fish, eggs etc., cooked with hot-tasting spices, usually served with rice. —*v.t.* to make (meat etc.) into a curry. —**curry powder,** a preparation of turmeric and other spices for making curry. [from Tamil *kari* = sauce]

curry[2] *v.t.* **1.** to groom (a horse) with a currycomb. **2.** to treat (tanned leather) to improve its properties. —**currycomb** *n.* a pad with rubber or plastic projections for grooming a horse. —**curry favour,** to ingratiate oneself. [from Old French from Latin *conredare* from Germanic]

curse *n.* **1.** a solemn utterance wishing a person to suffer destruction or punishment; an evil resulting from this. **2.** a violent exclamation of anger, a profane oath. **3.** a thing that causes evil or harm. —*v.t./i.* to utter a curse against; to utter expletive curses. —**the curse,** (*colloquial*) menstruation. **be cursed with,** to have as a burden or source of harm. [Old English]

cursed /'kɜːsid/ *adj.* damnable, abominable.

cursive /'kɜːsɪv/ *adj.* (of writing) done with joined characters. —*n.* cursive writing. [from Latin (*scriptura*) *cursiva* from *currere* = run]

cursor /'kɜːsə/ *n.* **1.** a transparent slide with a hairline, forming part of a slide rule. **2.** the indicator on a VDU screen, showing a particular position in displayed matter. [Latin = runner]

cursory /'kɜːsəri/ *adj.* hasty, hurried. —**cursorily** *adv.* [from Latin = of a runner]

curt *adj.* noticeably or rudely brief. —**curtly** *adv.,* **curtness** *n.* [from Latin *curtus* = cut short]

curtail /kɜːˈteɪl/ *v.t.* to cut short, to reduce. —**curtailment** *n.* [from obsolete *curtal* = horse with docked tail from Old French]

curtain /'kɜːtən/ *n.* a piece of cloth etc. hung up as a screen, usually movable sideways or upwards, especially at a window or between the stage and auditorium of a theatre; the rise or fall of the stage curtain at the beginning or end of an act or scene; (in *plural, slang*) the end. —*v.t.* to furnish or cover with curtains; to shut off with a curtain or curtains. —**curtain call,** an audience's summons to an actor or actors to take a bow after the fall of the curtain. **curtain-raiser** *n.* a short opening theatre piece; a preliminary event. **curtain wall,** the plain wall of a fortified place, connecting two towers etc. [from Old French from Latin *cortina,* translation of Greek *aulaia* (*aulē* = court)]

Curtin /'kɜːtɪn/ John 1885–1945. Australian Labor politician, prime minister and minister of defence 1941–45. He was elected leader of the Labor Party in 1935. As prime minister, he organized the mobilization of Australia's resources to meet the danger of Japanese invasion during World War II.

Curtis /'kɜːtɪs/ Tony. Stage name of Bernard Schwartz 1925– . US film actor, who starred in the 1950s and 1960s in such films as *The Vikings* 1958, and *The Boston Strangler* 1968, as well as specialising in light comedies such as *Some Like it Hot* 1959, with Jack Lemmon and Marilyn Monroe.

Curtiz /'kɜːtɪz/ Michael. Adopted name of Mihaly Kertesz, 1888–1962. Hungarian-born film director who worked in Austria, Germany, and France before moving to the USA in 1926 where he made several films with Errol Flynn, directed *Mildred Pierce* 1945, which revitalized Joan Crawford's career, and *Casablanca* 1942, for which he won an Academy Award.

curtsy /'kɜːtsi/ *n.* a woman's or girl's salutation made by bending the knees and lowering the body. —*v.i.* to make a curtsy. [variant of *courtesy*]

curvaceous /kɜːˈveɪʃəs/ *adj.* (*colloquial*) (of a woman) having a shapely, curved figure.

curvature /'kɜːvətʃə/ *n.* curving; curved form. [from Old French from Latin]

curve *n.* **1.** a line of which no part is straight; a surface of which no part is flat; a curved form or thing; a curved line on a graph. **2.** in geometry, the ◊locus of a point moving according to specified conditions. The circle is the locus of all points equidistant from a given point (the centre). Other common geometrical curves are the ◊ellipse, ◊parabola, and ◊hyperbola, which are also produced when a cone is cut by a

plane at different angles. —*v.t./i.* to bend or shape so as to form a curve. —**curvy** *adj.* [from Latin *curvus* = curved]

curvet /kɜːˈvet/ *n.* a horse's short, frisky leap. —*v.i.* to perform a curvet. [from Italian diminutive of *corva*]

curvilinear /kɜːviˈlɪniə/ *adj.* contained by or consisting of curved lines.

Curwen /'kɜːwin/ John 1816–1880. English musician. In about 1840 he established the **tonic sol-fa** system of music notation (originated in the 11th century by Guido d'Arezzo) in which the notes of a scale are named by syllables (doh, ray, me, fah, soh, lah, te) to simplify singing by sight.

Curzon /'kɜːzən/ George Nathaniel, 1st Marquess Curzon of Kedleston 1859–1925. English Conservative politician, viceroy of India 1899–1905. During World War I, he was a member of the cabinet from 1916–19. As foreign secretary 1919–22, he set up a British protectorate over Persia.

Curzon Line the Polish-Russian frontier proposed after World War I by the territorial commission of the Versailles conference of 1919, based on the eastward limit of areas with a predominantly Polish population. The frontier established in 1945 in general follows the Curzon Line. [from Lord *Curzon* who suggested in 1920 that the Poles, who had invaded Russia, should retire to this line pending a Russo-Polish peace conference]

Cusack /'kjuːsæk/ Cyril 1910– . Irish actor who joined the Abbey Theatre, Dublin, in 1932 and appeared in many of its productions, including Synge's *The Playboy of the Western World.* In Paris he won an award for his solo performance in Beckett's *Krapp's Last Tape.* In the UK he has played many roles as a member of the Royal Shakespeare Company and the National Theatre Company.

Cushing /'kuʃɪŋ/ Harvey Williams 1869–1939. US neurologist who pioneered neurosurgery, developed a range of techniques for the surgical treatment of brain tumours, and also studied the link between the ◊pituitary gland and conditions such as dwarfism.

Cushing Peter 1913– . British actor who specialized in horror roles in films made at Hammer studios in 1957–73, including *Dracula* 1958, *The Mummy* 1959, and *Frankenstein Must be Destroyed* 1969. Other films include *Doctor Who and the Daleks* 1966, *Star Wars* 1977, and *Top Secret* 1984.

Cushing's syndrome a condition in which the body chemistry is upset by excessive production of ◊steroid hormones from the adrenal cortex.

cushion /'kuʃən/ *n.* **1.** a fabric case filled with a mass of soft or springy material, used to make a seat etc. more comfortable. **2.** a soft pad or other means of support or of protection against jarring; a means of protection against shock; the elastic lining of the rim of a billiard table, from which the balls rebound. **3.** the body of air supporting a hovercraft etc. —*v.t.* **1.** to provide or protect with a cushion or cushions. **2.** to mitigate the adverse effects of. [from Old French from Latin *culcita* = mattress]

cushy /'kuʃi/ *adj.* (*colloquial*, of a job etc.) pleasant and easy. [from Hindi = pleasant]

cusp *n.* a point where two branches of a curve meet and the tangents to each branch coincide; a projecting point between small arcs in Gothic tracery; the horn of a crescent moon etc. [from Latin *cuspis* = point, apex]

cuss *n.* (*colloquial*) **1.** a curse. **2.** an awkward or difficult person. —*v.t./i.* (*colloquial*) to curse. [vulgar pronunciation of *curse*]

cussed /'kʌsid/ *adj.* (*colloquial*) awkward and stubborn. —**cussedness** *n.*

custard /'kʌstəd/ *n.* a dish or sauce made with milk and beaten eggs, usually sweetened; a sweet sauce made with milk and flavoured cornflour. [from Anglo-French from Old French *crouste* = crust]

custard apple any of several tropical fruits produced by trees and shrubs of the family Annonaceae, often cultivated for their large, edible, heart-shaped fruits. The **bullock's heart** *Annona reticulata* bears a large dark-brown fruit containing a sweet, reddish-yellow pulp; it is a native of the West Indies.

Custer /'kʌstə/ George A(rmstrong) 1839–1876. US Civil War general, the Union's youngest brigadier general as a result of a brilliant war record. Reduced in rank in the regular army at the end of the Civil War, he campaigned against the Sioux from 1874, and was killed with a detachment of his troops by the forces of Sioux chief Sitting Bull in the Battle of the Little Big Horn, Montana, also called **Custer's last stand**, on 25 June 1876.

On foot or on horseback he was one of the most perfect types of physical manhood I ever saw.
George Custer of 'Wild Bill' Hickock

custodian /kʌs'təudiən/ n. a guardian or keeper, especially of a public building.

custody /'kʌstədɪ/ n. 1. guardianship, protective care. 2. imprisonment. —**take into custody,** to arrest. —**custodial** /-'stəudiəl/ adj. [from Latin *custodia* (*custos* = guardian)]

custody of children the legal control of a minor by an adult. Parents often have joint custody of their children, but this may be altered by a court order, which may be made in various different circumstances. In all cases, the court's role is to give the welfare of the child paramount consideration.

custom /'kʌstəm/ n. 1. the usual way of behaving or acting; established usage as a power or as having the force of law. 2. a business patronage, regular dealings or customers. 3. (in *plural*) the duty levied on imports; (often treated as *singular*) the government department or officials administering this. —**custom-built** adj. built to a customer's order. **custom house**, an office at a port or frontier etc. at which customs duties are levied. [from Old French from Latin *consuetudo*]

customary adj. in accordance with custom, usual. —**customarily** adv. [from Latin]

customer n. a person who buys goods or services from a shop or business; (*colloquial*) a person one has to deal with. [from Anglo-French]

Customs and Excise the government department responsible for taxes levied on imports. Excise duties are levied on goods produced domestically or on licences to carry on certain trades (such as sale of wines and spirits) or other activities (theatrical entertainments, betting, and so on) within a country.

cut v. t. /i. (-tt-) (*past* and *past participle* **cut**) 1. to penetrate or wound with a sharp-edged instrument (also *figurative*) 2. to divide or detach with a knife etc.; to shape, make, or shorten thus; to be able to cut or be cut; to have (a tooth) appear through the gum. 3. to execute (a *caper* etc.) or make (a *sorry figure* etc.). 4. to reduce by removing part of; to cease to provide; to switch off (electricity, an engine, etc.). 5. to divide a pack of cards; to select (a card) thus. 6. to absent oneself from; to renounce (a connection), to ignore or refuse to recognize (a person). 7. to edit (a film); to go quickly *to* another shot. 8. to hit (a ball) with a chopping motion in cricket etc. 9. to pass *through* etc. as a shorter way. 10. (*US*) to dilute (spirits for drinking). —*n.* 1. the act of cutting; a division, wound, or hurt made by this; a stroke with a sword, whip, or cane. 2. a piece of meat cut from a carcass. 3. the way a thing is cut, the style in which clothes are made. 4. a reduction or cessation. 5. an excision of part of a play, film, book etc. 6. (*slang*) a commission, a share of the profits etc. 7. a stroke made by cutting a ball in cricket etc. 8. a cutting remark. 9. the ignoring of or refusal to recognize a person etc. —**a cut above**, noticeably superior to. **cut and dried,** prepared in advance, ready; inflexible. **cut and run**, (*slang*) to run away. **cut back**, to reduce, to prune. **cutback** n. a reduction. **cut both ways**, to serve both sides of an argument. **cut corners**, to do a task etc. perfunctorily or incompletely. **cut down**, to reduce (expenses etc.). **cut in**, to interrupt; to move in front of another vehicle (especially in overtaking) leaving too little space. **cut it out**, (*slang*, in *imperative*) stop doing that. **cut line**, a line above which service must be made in squash. **cut one's losses**, to abandon an unprofitable scheme before the losses become too great. **cut no ice**, (*slang*) to be of no importance or effect. **cut off**, to end abruptly; to intercept, to interrupt; to prevent from continuing; to disinherit. **cutoff** n. the point at which a thing is cut off; a device for stopping a flow. **cut out**, to remove, to omit; to outdo or supplant; to cease or cause to cease functioning; (in *passive*) to be suited (*for, to* be or do). **cutout** n. a thing cut out; a device for automatic disconnection; the

release of exhaust gases etc. **cut-price** adj. for sale at a reduced price. **cut-rate** adj. available at a reduced rate. **cut a tooth**, to have a tooth beginning to emerge from the gum. **cut one's teeth on**, to acquire experience from. **cut up**, to cut into small pieces; (in *passive*) to be greatly distressed. **cut up rough**, to show anger or resentment. [perhaps Old English]

cutaneous /kju:'teiniəs/ adj. of the skin. [from Latin]

cutaway adj. 1. (of a diagram etc.) having some parts absent to reveal the interior. 2. (of a coat) with the front below the waist cut away.

cute /kju:t/ adj. (*colloquial*) clever, ingenious; (*US*) attractive, quaint. —**cutely** adv., **cuteness** n. [from *acute*]

Cuthbert, St /'kʌθbət/ died 687. Christian saint. A shepherd in Northumbria, England, he entered the monastery of Melrose, Scotland after receiving a vision. He travelled widely as a missionary and because of his alleged miracles was known as the 'wonderworker of Britain'. In 684 he became bishop of Hexham and later of Lindisfarne. Feast day 20 March.

cuticle /'kju:tikəl/ n. 1. the skin at the base of the fingernail or toenail. 2. in zoology, the horny noncellular surface layer of many invertebrates such as insects; in botany, the waxy surface layer on those parts of plants that are exposed to the air, continuous except for ◊stomata and ◊lenticels. All types are secreted by the cells of the ◊epidermis. A cuticle reduces water loss and, in arthropods, acts as an ◊exoskeleton. [from Latin *cuticula*]

cutis /'kju:tis/ n. the true skin beneath the epidermis. [Latin = skin]

cutlass /'kʌtləs/ n. (*historical*) a short sword with a slightly curved blade. [from French from Latin]

cutlery /'kʌtləri/ n. knives, forks, and spoons for use at table. [from Old French from Latin *cultellus*, diminutive of *culter* = knife]

cutlet /'kʌtlit/ n. a neck chop of mutton or lamb; a small piece of veal etc. for frying; a flat cake of minced meat etc. [from Old French from Latin *costa* = rib]

cutter n. 1. a tailor etc. who takes measurements and cuts cloth. 2. a small, fast sailing ship. 3. a small boat carried by a large ship.

cutthroat n. 1. a murderer. 2. a razor with a long blade set in a handle. —*adj.* 1. intense and ruthless. 2. (of a card game) three-handed.

cutting n. 1. a piece cut from a newspaper etc. 2. a piece cut from a plant for propagation. 3. an excavated channel through high ground, for a railway or road.

cuttlefish /'kʌtəlfɪʃ/ n. any of a family, Sepiidae, of cephalopods with an internal calcareous shell (cuttlebone). The common cuttle *Sepia officinalis* of the Atlantic and Mediterranean is up to 30 cm/1 ft long. It swims actively by means of the fins into which the sides of its oval, flattened body are expanded, and jerks itself backwards by shooting a jet of water from its 'siphon'. Cuttlefish eject a black fluid when threatened. [Old English]

Cutty Sark a British sailing ship, built in 1869, one of the tea clippers that used to compete in the 19th century to bring their cargoes fastest from China to Britain. The ship is preserved in dry dock at Greenwich, London. [the name, meaning 'short chemise', comes from the witch in Robert Burns's poem 'Tam O'Shanter']

cutwater n. 1. the forward edge of a ship's prow. 2. a wedge-shaped projection from a pier or bridge.

Cuvier /'kju:viei/ Georges, Baron Cuvier 1769–1832. French comparative anatomist who in 1799 showed that some species have become extinct by reconstructing extinct giant animals that he believed were destroyed in a series of giant deluges. These ideas are expressed in *Recherches sur les ossaments fossiles de quadrupèdes* 1812 and *Discours sur les révolutions de la surface du globe* 1825.

Cuyp /kaip/ Aelbert 1620–1691. Dutch painter of countryside scenes, seascapes, and portraits whose idyllically peaceful landscapes are bathed in golden light: for example, *A Herdsman with Cows by a River* (of about 1650, National Gallery, London). His father, **Jacob Gerritsz Cuyp** (1594–1652), was also a landscape and portrait painter.

Cuzco /'kuskəu/ city in S Peru, capital of Cuzco department, in the Andes, over 3,350 m/11,000 ft above sea level and 560 km/350 mi SE of Lima; population (1988) 255,000. It was founded in the 11th century as the ancient capital of the ◊Inca empire and was captured by Pizarro in 1533.

CV or **c.v.** abbreviation of curriculum vitae.

cwm /kuːm/ n. (in Wales) = ◊coomb; a cirque. [Welsh]

cwo abbreviation of cash with order.

cwt symbol for ◊hundredweight, a unit of weight equal to 112 pounds (50.802 kg).

cyan /ˈsaɪən/ adj. & n. in photography, greenish-blue. [from Greek kuan(e)os = dark blue]

cyanic /saɪˈænɪk/ adj. of or containing cyanogen.

cyanide /ˈsaɪənaɪd/ n. CN-, an ion derived from hydrogen cyanide (HCN), and any salt containing this ion (produced when hydrogen cyanide is neutralized by alkalis), such as potassium cyanide (KCN). The principal cyanides are potassium, sodium, calcium, mercury, gold, and copper. Certain cyanides are poisons.

cyanocobalamin n. the chemical name for ◊vitamin B12, which is normally produced by microorganisms in the gut. The richest natural source is raw liver. The deficiency disease, pernicious anaemia, is the poor development of red blood cells with possible degeneration of the spinal chord. Sufferers develop extensive bruising and recover slowly from even minor injuries.

cyanogen /saɪˈænədʒɪn/ n. an inflammable poisonous gas. [from French from Greek kuanos = dark-blue mineral]

cyanosis /saɪəˈnəʊsɪs/ n. a bluish discoloration of the skin or mucous membranes, usually around the mouth, due to diminished uptake of oxygen. It is most often seen in diseases of the heart, lungs, or blood.

Cybele /ˈsɪbəli/ in Phrygian mythology, an earth goddess, identified by the Greeks with ◊Rhea and honoured in Rome.

cybernetics /saɪbəˈnetɪks/ n. the science of the systems of control and communications in animals and machines. In the laboratory, inanimate objects are created that behave like living systems. Applications range from the creation of electronic artificial limbs to the running of the fully automated factory where decision-making machines operate up to managerial level. —**cybernetic** adj. [from Greek kubernētēs = steersman]

cycad n. a plant of the order Cycadales, belonging to the gymnosperms. Some have a superficial resemblance to palms, others to ferns. Their large cones contain fleshy seeds. There are ten genera and about 80–100 species, native to tropical and subtropical countries. The stems of many species yield an edible starchy substance resembling sago. Cycads were widespread during the Mesozoic era.

cyclamate /ˈsaɪkləmeɪt, ˈsɪk-/ n. an artificial sweetening agent.

cyclamen /ˈsɪkləmən/ n. a plant of the genus Cyclamen, of the primrose family Primulaceae, with heart-shaped leaves and petals that are twisted at the base and bent back. The flowers are usually white or pink, and several species are cultivated. [Latin from Greek (perhaps from kuklos = circle)]

cycle /ˈsaɪkəl/ n. **1.** a recurrent round or period (of events, phenomena etc.); the time needed for one such round or period; cycles per second, hertz. **2.** a recurrent series of operations or states; a series of songs, poems etc., usually on a single theme. **3.** a bicycle, a tricycle, or motor cycle. —v.i. **1.** to ride a bicycle or tricycle. **2.** to move in cycles. [from Old French, or from Latin from Greek kuklos = circle]

cyclic /ˈsaɪklɪk/ adj. **1.** recurring in cycles; belonging to a chronological cycle. **2.** in chemistry, with the constituent atoms forming a ring. **3.** in geometry, describing a polygon of which each vertex (corner) lies on the circumference of a circle. [from French or Latin]

cyclist /ˈsaɪklɪst/ n. a rider of a bicycle.

cyclo- combination form of **cycle**.

cyclo-cross /ˈsaɪkləʊkrɒs/ n. cross-country racing on bicycles.

cycloid n. in geometry, a curve resembling a series of arches traced out by a point on the circumference of a circle that rolls along a straight line. Its applications include the study of the motion of wheeled vehicles along roads and tracks.

cyclone /ˈsaɪkləʊn/ n. a system of winds rotating inwards to an area of low barometric pressure; a violent hurricane of a limited diameter. —**cyclonic** /-ˈklɒnɪk/ adj. [from Greek kuklōma = wheel, coil of snake]

Cyclopean /saɪkləˈpiːən/ adj. (of ancient masonry) made of massive, irregular blocks. [from Latin from Greek Kuklōps = Cyclops, mythical giant]

Cyclops /ˈsaɪklɒps/ in Greek mythology, one of a legendary nation of giants who lived in Sicily, had one eye in the middle of the forehead, and lived as shepherds; Odysseus fought and overcame the Cyclopes in Homer's Odyssey.

cyclosporin n. an ◊immunosuppressive drug derived from a fungus (Tolypocladium inflatum). In use by 1978, it revolutionized transplant surgery by reducing the incidence and severity of rejection of donor organs.

cyclostyle /ˈsaɪkləstaɪl/ n. an apparatus printing copies of writing from a stencil. —v.t. to print or reproduce with this.

cyclotron /ˈsaɪklətron/ n. an apparatus for accelerating charged atomic particles by subjecting them repeatedly to an electric field as they revolve in orbits of increasing diameter in a constant magnetic field.

cygnet /ˈsɪgnɪt/ n. a young swan. [from Anglo-French from Latin]

Cygnus /ˈsɪgnəs/ n. a large, prominent constellation of the northern hemisphere, representing a swan. Its brightest star is first-magnitude ◊Deneb.

cylinder /ˈsɪlɪndə/ n. a uniform solid or hollow body with straight sides and a circular section; a thing of this shape, e. g. a container for liquid gas etc., or a part of a machine, especially the piston chamber in an engine. —**cylindrical** /-ˈlɪndrɪkəl/ adj. [from Latin from Greek kulindō = to roll]

cymbal /ˈsɪmbəl/ n. each of a pair of concave brass plates forming a musical instrument, clashed together or struck to make a ringing sound. Smaller finger cymbals or crotala, used by Debussy and Stockhausen, are more solid and have loose rivets to extend the sound. —**cymbalist** n. [from Latin from Greek kumbē = cup]

Cymbeline or **Cunobelin** 1st century AD. King of the Catuvellauni AD 5–40, who fought unsuccessfully against the Roman invasion of Britain. His capital was at Colchester.

cyme /saɪm/ n. a flower group with a single terminal flower on each stem. [French, variant of cime = summit from Latin from Greek]

Cymric /ˈkɪmrɪk/ adj. Welsh. [from Welsh Cymru = Wales]

Cymru /ˈkʌmri/ Celtic name for ◊Wales.

Cynewulf /ˈkɪnɪwʊlf/ early 8th century. Anglo-Saxon poet who is thought to have been a Northumbrian monk and is the undoubted author of 'Juliana' and part of the 'Christ' in the Exeter Book (a collection of poems now in Exeter Cathedral), and of the 'Fates of the Apostles' and 'Elene' in the Vercelli Book (a collection of Old English manuscripts housed at Vercelli, Italy), in all of which he inserted his name by using runic acrostics.

cynic /ˈsɪnɪk/ n. one who has little faith in human sincerity or goodness. —**cynical** adj., **cynically** adv., **cynicism** n.

Cynic n. a member of an ancient Greek sect of philosophers founded in Athens about 400 BC by Antisthenes, a disciple of Socrates, who advocated a stern and simple morality and a complete disregard of pleasure and comfort. —adj. of the Cynics. [from Latin from Greek Cynosarges, place where the sect was founded]

cynosure /ˈsaɪnəzjʊə, ˈsɪn-/ n. a centre of attraction or admiration. [French, or from Latin from Greek = dog's tail (name for Ursa Minor)]

cypher variant of **cipher**.

cypress /ˈsaɪprəs/ n. a coniferous tree or shrub of the genera Cupressus and Chamaecyparis, family Cupressaceae. There are about 20 species, found mainly in the temperate regions of the northern hemisphere. They have minute, scalelike leaves and small cones made up of woody, wedge-shaped scales and containing an aromatic resin. [from Old French from Latin from Greek]

Cyprian, St /ˈsɪprɪən/ c.210–258. Christian martyr, one of the earliest Christian writers, and bishop of Carthage about 249. He wrote a treatise on the unity of the church. Feast day 16 Sept.

He cannot have God for his father who has not had the church for his mother.

St Cyprian,
De Cath Eccl Unitate

Czechoslovakia *Czechoslovak protesters demonstrating against the Soviet invasion 1968.*

Cypriot /'sɪprɪət/ *n.* 1. a native or inhabitant of Cyprus. 2. the dialect of Greek used there. —*adj.* of Cyprus or its people or language. [from *Cyprus*]

Cyprus /'saɪprəs/ Greek Republic of (in S), Turkish Republic of Northern (in N); island in the Mediterranean, off the S coast of Turkey; **area** 9,251 sq km/3,571 sq mi, 37% in Turkish hands; **capital** Nicosia (divided between Greeks and Turks); **physical** central plain between two E–W mountain ranges; beaches; **heads of state and government** Georgios Vassilou (Greek) from 1988, Rauf Denktaş (Turkish) from 1976; **political system** democratic divided republic; **exports** citrus, grapes, Cyprus sherry, potatoes, copper, pyrites; **population** (1990 est) 708,000 (Greek Cypriot 78%, Turkish Cypriot 18%); **language** Greek and Turkish (official); English; **recent history** independence was achieved from Britain in 1960. The Turks set up their own government in N Cyprus; fighting broke out between the Greek and Turkish communities. A UN peacekeeping force was installed in 1964. Talks began in 1988 on future reunification, under UN auspices.

Cyrano de Bergerac /'sɪrənəu də 'bɜːʒəræk/ Savinien de 1619–1655. French writer. He joined a corps of guards at 19 and performed heroic feats which brought him fame. He is the hero of a classic play by Edmond ◊Rostand, in which his excessively long nose is used as a counterpoint to his chivalrous character.

Cyrenaic /saɪrɪ'neɪɪk/ *adj.* of or related to a school of Greek hedonistic philosophy (see ◊hedonism)founded about 400 BC by Aristippus of Cyrene. He regarded pleasure as the only absolutely worthwhile thing in life but taught that self-control and intelligence were necessary to choose the best pleasures. —*n.* a philosopher or follower of this school.

Cyrenaica /saɪrə'neɪɪkə/ area of E Libya, colonized by the Greeks in the 7th century BC; later held by the Egyptians, Romans, Arabs, Turks, and Italians. Present cities in the region are Benghazi, Derna, and Tobruk.

Cyril and Methodius, Sts /'sɪrəl, mɪ'θəʊdɪəs/ two brothers, both Christian saints: Cyril 826–869 and Methodius 815–885. Born in Thessalonica, they were sent as missionaries to what is today Moravia. They invented a Slavonic alphabet, and translated the Bible and the liturgy from Greek to Slavonic.

Cyrillic /sɪ'rɪlɪk/ *adj.* of one of the two principal Slavonic alphabets (the other is the Roman) in use today. [from St *Cyril*]

Cyril of Alexandria, St /'sɪrəl/ 376–444. Bishop of Alexandria from 412, persecutor of Jews and other non-Christians, and suspected of ordering the murder of Hypatia (*c.*370–*c.*415), a philosopher whose influence was increasing at his expense. He was violently opposed to ◊Nestorianism.

Cyrus the Great /'saɪrəs/ died 529 BC. Founder of the Persian Empire. As king of Persia, originally subject to the ◊Medes whose empire he overthrew in 550 BC, he captured ◊Croesus in 546 BC and conquered all Asia Minor, adding Babylonia (including Syria and Palestine) to his empire in 539 BC, allowing exiled Jews to return to Jerusalem. He died fighting in Afghanistan.

cyst /sɪst/ *n.* a sac containing fluid or soft matter formed on or in the body. [from Greek *kustis* = bladder]

cystic *adj.* 1. of the bladder. 2. like a cyst. [from French]

cystic fibrosis a hereditary disease involving defects of various tissues, including the sweat glands, the mucous glands of the bronchi (air passages), and the pancreas. The sufferer experiences repeated chest infections and digestive disorders and generally fails to thrive.

cystitis /sɪs'taɪtɪs/ *n.* inflammation of the bladder, usually caused by bacterial infection, and resulting in frequent and painful urination. Treatment is by antibiotics and copious fluids with vitamin C. [from Greek *kustis* = bladder]

-cyte /-saɪt/ suffix denoting a mature biological cell.

cytochrome *n.* a type of protein responsible for part of the process of ◊respiration by which food molecules are broken down in ◊aerobic organisms. Cytochromes are part of the electron transport chain, which uses energized electrons to reduce molecular oxygen (O_2) to oxygen ions (O^{2-}). These combine with hydrogen ions (H^+) to form water (H_2O), the end product of aerobic respiration. As electrons are passed from one cytochrome to another energy is released and used to make ◊ATP.

cytokine *n.* in biology, a chemical messenger that carries information from one cell to another, for example the ◊lymphokines.

cytology /saɪ'tɒlədʒɪ/ *n.* the study of biological ◊cells and their functions. Major advances have been made possible in this field by the development of ◊electron microscopes. —**cytological** /-'lɒdʒɪkəl/ *adj.* [from Greek *kutos* = vessel]

cytoplasm /'saɪtəplæzəm/ *n.* the protoplasmic content of a cell other than the nucleus. Strictly speaking, this includes all the ◊organelles (mitochondria, chloroplasts, and so on), but often cytoplasm refers to the jellylike matter in which the organelles are embedded (correctly termed the cytosol). —**cytoplasmic** *adj.*

cytoskeleton *n.* in a living cell, a matrix of protein filaments and tubules that occurs within the cytosol (the liquid part of the cytoplasm). It gives the cell a definite shape, transports vital substances around the cell, and may also be involved in cell movement.

cytotoxic drug any drug used to kill the cells of a malignant tumour, or as an ◊immunosuppressive following organ transplantation; it may also damage healthy cells. Side effects include nausea, vomiting, hair loss, and bone marrow damage.

czar variant of **tsar**, an emperor of Russia.

Czech /tʃek/ *n.* 1. a native of the western and central parts of Czechoslovakia. 2. the Slavonic language of people in these parts. 3. a Czechoslovakian. —*adj.* of the Czechs or their language. [Polish spelling of Bohemian *Cech*]

Czechoslovak /tʃekə'sləʊvæk/ *n.* or **Czechoslovakian** (/-vækɪən/) a native of Czechoslovakia. —*adj.* of Czechoslovakia or its people.

Czechoslovakia /tʃekəslə'vækɪə/ Czech and Slovak Federative Republic; landlocked country in eastern central Europe, bounded NE by Poland, E by the USSR, S by Hungary and Austria, W and NW by Germany; **area** 127,903 sq km/49,371 sq mi; **capital** Prague; **physical** Carpathian Mountains, rivers Morava, Labe (Elbe), Vltava (Moldau); hills and plateau; Danube plain in S; **head of state** Václav Havel from 1989; **head of government** Marián Čalfa from 1989; **political system** liberal democracy; **exports** machinery, timber, ceramics, glass, textiles; **population** (1990 est) 15,695,000 (63% Czech, 31% Slovak, with Hungarian, Polish, German, Russian, and other minorities); **language** Czech and Slovak (official); **recent history** independence was achieved from the Austro-Hungarian Empire in 1918. Czechoslovakia was occupied by Germany 1938–45 and the USSR from 1968. The Communist monopoly of power ended in the bloodless revolution of 1989; complete withdrawal of Soviet troops was agreed by May 1991.

Czerny /'tʃɛəni/ Carl 1791–1857. Austrian composer and pianist. He wrote an enormous quantity of religious and concert music, but is chiefly remembered for his books of graded studies and technical exercises used in piano teaching.

d, D *n.* (*plural* **ds, d's**) **1.** the fourth letter of the alphabet. **2.** in music, the second note in the scale of C major. **3.** (as a Roman numeral) 500.

d abbreviation of **1.** daughter. **2.** died. **3.** (until 1971) penny, pence (short for Latin *denarius*).

DA abbreviation of district attorney.

dab[1] *v.t./i.* (**-bb-**) **1.** to press briefly and lightly. **2.** to aim a feeble blow (*at*), to strike lightly. —*n.* **1.** an act of dabbing, a light blow. **2.** a small amount of a soft substance applied to a surface. **3.** (*in plural, slang*) fingerprints.

dab[2] *n. & adj.* (*colloquial*) or **dab hand** an adept.

dab[3] *n.* a small marine flatfish of the flounder family, including the genus *Limanda*. Dabs live in the N Atlantic and around the coasts of Britain and Scandinavia. Species include the dab *L. limanda* which grows to about 40 cm/16 in, and the American dab *L. proboscida*, which grows to 30 cm/12 in. Both have both eyes on the right side of their bodies. The left, or blind, side is white, while the rough-scaled right side is light-brown or grey, with dark-brown spots.

dabble *v.t./i.* **1.** to wet partly or intermittently; to move the feet, hands, or bill lightly in water or mud. **2.** to study or work casually (*in* a subject).

dabchick *n.* a small water bird of the grebe family.

Dacca /'dækə/ alternative spelling of ◊Dhaka, capital of Bangladesh.

dace /deɪs/ *n.* (*plural* the same) a small freshwater fish, especially of the genus *Leuciscus*, related to the carp.

Dachau /'dæxau/ *n.* the site of a Nazi ◊concentration camp during World War II, in Bavaria, Germany.

dachshund /'dækshund/ *n.* a small dog of German origin, bred originally for digging out badgers. It has a long body and short legs. Several varieties are bred: standard size (up to 10 kg/22 lb), miniature (5 kg/11 lb or less), long-haired, smooth-haired, and wire-haired. [German = badger-dog]

Dacia /'deɪʃə/ an ancient region forming much of modern Romania. The various Dacian tribes were united around 60 BC, and for many years posed a threat to the Roman empire; they were finally conquered by the Roman emperor Trajan AD 101–106, and the region became a province of the same name. It was abandoned to the invading Goths in about 275.

dacoit *n.* historically a member of an armed gang of robbers, formerly active in India and Myanmar (Burma).

dactyl /'dæktɪl/ *n.* a metrical foot with one long or stressed syllable followed by two short or unstressed syllables. —**dactylic** /-'tɪlɪk/ *adj.* [from Greek *dactulos* = finger]

dad *n.* (*colloquial*) father.

Dada /'dɑːdɑː/ *n.* an artistic and literary movement founded in 1915 in Zürich, Switzerland, by the Romanian poet Tristan Tzara (1896–1963) and others in a spirit of rebellion and disillusionment during World War I. Other Dadaist groups were soon formed by the artists ◊Duchamp and ◊Man Ray in New York, and Picabia in Barcelona. Dada had a considerable impact on early 20th-century art, questioning established artistic rules and values. —**Dadaism** /-dɑɪzəm/ *n.*, **Dadaist** *n.* [from French *dada* = hobby-horse]

Dadd /dæd/ Richard 1817–1887. British painter. In 1843 he murdered his father and was committed to an asylum, but continued to paint minutely detailed pictures of fantasies and fairy tales, such as *The Fairy Feller's Master-Stroke* 1855–64 (Tate Gallery, London).

daddy *n.* (*colloquial*) father; the oldest or most important person or thing.

daddy-long legs *n.* a ◊crane fly.

dado /'deɪdəʊ/ *n.* (*plural* **dados**) **1.** the lower part of the wall of a room etc. when it is coloured or faced differently from the upper part. **2.** the plinth of a column. **3.** the cube of a pedestal. [Italian]

Dadra and Nagar Haveli /də'drɑː 'nɡə'veli/ since 1961 a Union Territory of W India; capital Silvassa; area 490 sq km/189 sq mi; population (1981) 104,000. Formerly part of Portuguese Daman, it produces rice, wheat, millet, and timber.

Daedalus /'diːdələs/ in Greek mythology, an Athenian artisan supposed to have constructed for King Minos of Crete the labyrinth in which the ◊Minotaur was imprisoned. He fled from Crete with his son ◊Icarus using wings made from feathers fastened with wax.

Daedalus *n.* in space travel, a futuristic project proposed by the British Interplanetary Society to send a ◊robot probe to nearby stars. The probe, 20 times the size of the Saturn V moon rocket, would be propelled by thermonuclear fusion; in effect, a series of small hydrogen-bomb explosions. Interstellar cruise speed would be about 40,000 km/25,000 mi per second.

daemon *n.* see ◊demon.

daffodil /'dæfədɪl/ *n.* any of several Old World species of the genus *Narcissus*, family Amaryllidaceae, distinguished by their trumpet-shaped flowers. The common daffodil of N Europe *N. pseudonarcissus* has large yellow flowers and grows from a large bulb. There are numerous cultivated forms. [earlier *affodil*, as *asphodel*]

daft /dɑːft/ *adj.* (*colloquial*) silly, foolish, crazy. [Old English = mild]

Dafydd ap Gwilym /'dævɪð æp 'ɡwɪlɪm/ *c.*1340–*c.*1400. Welsh poet whose work is notable for its complex but graceful style, its concern with nature and love rather than with heroic martial deeds, and for its references to Classical and Italian poetry. He was born into an influential Dyfed family, and is traditionally believed to have led a life packed with amorous adventures.

Dagestan /dæɡɪ'stɑːn/ autonomous republic of western USSR, situated E of the ◊Caucasus, bordering the Caspian Sea. Capital Makhachkala; area 50,300 sq km/19,421 sq mi; population (1982) 1,700,000. It is mountainous, with deep valleys, and its numerous ethnic groups speak a variety of distinct languages. Annexed in 1723 from Iran, which strongly resisted Russian conquest, it became an autonomous republic in 1921.

dagger *n.* **1.** a short pointed two-edged weapon used for stabbing. **2.** an ◊obelus. —**at daggers drawn,** hostile and on the point of quarrelling. **look daggers,** to glare angrily. [perhaps from *dag* = pierce]

Daguerre /dæ'ɡeə/ Louis Jacques Mande 1789–1851. French pioneer of photography. Together with Niepce, he is credited with the invention of photography (though others were reaching the same point simultaneously). In 1838 he invented the ◊daguerreotype, a single image process, superseded ten years later by ◊Talbot's negative/positive process.

daguerreotype /dəˈgerəʊtaɪp/ n. an early kind of photograph taken on a silver-coated copper plate and developed by exposure to mercury vapour, giving a positive image of white on silver. [from Louis *Daguerre*]

Dahl /dɑːl/ Johann Christian 1788–1857. Norwegian landscape painter in the Romantic style. He trained in Copenhagen but was active chiefly in Dresden from 1818. He was the first great painter of the Norwegian landscape, in a style that recalls the Dutch artist ◊Ruisdael.

Dahl Roald 1916–1990. British writer, celebrated for short stories with a twist, for example, *Tales of the Unexpected* 1979, and for children's books, including *Charlie and the Chocolate Factory* 1964.

dahlia /ˈdeɪlɪə/ n. any perennial plant of the genus *Dahlia*, family Compositae, comprising 20 species and many cultivated forms. Dahlias are stocky plants with showy flowers that come in a wide range of colours. They are native to Mexico and Central America. [from A *Dahl*, Swedish botanist]

Dahomey /dəˈhəʊmi/ former name (until 1975) of the People's Republic of ◊Benin.

Dáil /dɔɪl/ n. or **Dáil Éireann** /ˈeɪrən/ the lower house of parliament in the Republic of Ireland. It consists of 148 members elected by adult suffrage on a basis of proportional representation. [Irish = assembly (of Ireland)]

daily /ˈdeɪli/ adj. done, produced, or occurring every day or weekday. —adv. every day. —n. **1.** a daily newspaper. **2.** (*colloquial*) a charwoman employed on a daily basis. —**daily bread,** one's livelihood.

Daimler /ˈdeɪmlə/ Gottlieb 1834–1900. German engineer who pioneered the modern car. In 1886 he produced his first motor vehicle and a motorbicycle. He later joined forces with Karl ◊Benz and was one of the pioneers of the high-speed four-stroke petrol engine.

dainty adj. **1.** small and pretty, delicate. **2.** fastidious, especially about food. —n. a delicacy. —**daintily** adv., **daintiness** n. [from Old French from Latin *dignitas* = worth]

daiquiri /ˈdaɪkɪri/ n. a cocktail of rum, limejuice, etc. [from *Daiquiri*, a rum-producing district in Cuba]

dairy n. a room or building where milk and milk products are processed; a shop where these are sold. —**dairy farm,** a farm producing chiefly milk and its derivatives. [Old English = kneader of dough]

dairymaid n. a woman employed in a dairy.

dairyman n. (*plural* **dairymen**) a dealer in milk etc.

dais /ˈdeɪɪs/ n. a low platform, especially at one end of a room or hall. [from Latin *discus* = disc, in medieval Latin = table]

daisy /ˈdeɪzi/ n. any of numerous species of perennial plants in the family Compositae, especially the field daisy of Europe *Chrysanthemum leucanthemum* and the English common daisy *Bellis perennis*, with a single white or pink flower rising from a rosette of leaves. —**daisy wheel,** a disc with characters on its circumference used as a printer in word processing. [Old English = day's eye]

Dakar /ˈdækɑː/ capital and chief port (with artificial harbour) of Senegal; population (1984) 1,000,000.

Daladier /dælædˈjeɪ/ Edouard 1884–1970. French Radical politician. As prime minister April 1938–March 1940, he signed the ◊Munich Agreement in 1938 (by which the Sudeten districts of Czechoslovakia were ceded to Germany) and declared war on Germany in 1939. He resigned in 1940 because of his unpopularity for failing to assist Finland against Russia; arrested on the fall of France in 1940, he was a prisoner in Germany from 1943–45. Following the end of World War II he was re-elected to the Chamber of Deputies 1946–58.

Dalai Lama /ˈdælaɪ ˈlɑːmə/ 14th incarnation 1935– . Spiritual and temporal head of the Tibetan state until 1959, when he went into exile in protest against Chinese annexation and oppression. Tibetan Buddhists believe that each Dalai Lama is a reincarnation of his predecessor and also of Avalokiteśvara, an important ◊bodhisattva, embodying compassion. [Mongolian *dalai* = ocean and *lama*]

dale n. a valley, especially in N England. [Old English]

Dalen /dɑːˈleɪn/ Nils 1869–1937. Swedish industrial engineer who invented the light-controlled valve. This allowed lighthouses to operate automatically and won him the 1912 Nobel Prize for Physics.

Dalgarno /dælˈgɑːnəʊ/ George 1626–1687. Scottish schoolteacher and inventor of the first sign-language alphabet in 1680.

Dalhousie /dælˈhaʊzi/ James Andrew Broun Ramsay, 1st Marquess and 10th Earl of Dalhousie 1812–1860. British administrator, governor-general of India 1848–56. In the second Sikh War he annexed the Punjab in 1849, and, after the second Burmese War, Lower Burma in 1853. He reformed the Indian army and civil service and furthered social and economic progress.

Dali /ˈdɑːli/ Salvador 1904–1989. Spanish painter. In 1928 he collaborated with Buñuel on the film *Un chien andalou*. In 1929 he joined the Surrealists and became notorious for his flamboyant eccentricity. Influenced by the psychoanalytic theories of Freud, he developed a repertoire of dramatic images, such as the distorted human body, limp watches, and burning giraffes. They are painted with a meticulous, polished clarity. He also painted religious themes and many portraits of his wife Gala.

It's either easy or impossible.

Salvador Dali (attrib.)

Dallapiccola /dæləˈpɪkələ/ Luigi 1904–1975. Italian composer. In his early years he was a Neo-Classicist in the manner of Stravinsky, but he soon turned to Serialism, which he adapted to his own style. His works include the operas *Il Prigioniero/The Prisoner* 1949 and *Ulisse/Ulysses* 1968, as well as many vocal and instrumental compositions.

Dallas /ˈdæləs/ commercial city in Texas, USA; population (1980) 904,000, metropolitan area (with Fort Worth) 2,964,000. Industries include banking, insurance, oil, aviation, aerospace, and electronics. Dallas–Fort Worth Regional Airport (opened 1973) is one of the world's largest. John F ◊Kennedy was assassinated here in 1963.

dally v. i. **1.** to dawdle, to waste time. **2.** to amuse oneself; to flirt. —**dalliance** n. [from Old French *dalier* = chat]

Dalmatian /dælˈmeɪʃən/ adj. of Dalmatia, the central region of the coast of Yugoslavia. —n. a breed of dog, about 60 cm/2 ft tall at the shoulder, white with spots that are black or brown. Dalmatians are born white; the spots appear later on. They were formerly used as coach dogs, walking beside horse-drawn carriages to fend off highwaymen.

dalmatic /dælˈmætɪk/ n. a long, loose vestment with slit sides and wide sleeves, worn by deacons and bishops on ceremonial occasions. [from Latin *dalmatica* (*vestis*) = robe of Dalmatian wool]

Dalton /ˈdɔːltən/ Hugh, Baron Dalton 1887–1962. British Labour politician and economist. Chancellor of the Exchequer from 1945, he oversaw nationalization of the Bank of England, but resigned in 1947 after making a disclosure to a lobby correspondent before a budget speech.

Dalton John 1766–1844. British chemist, the first in modern times to propose the existence of atoms, which he considered to be the smallest parts of matter. He produced the first list of relative atomic masses in *Absorption of Gases* 1805. He was the first scientist to note and record colour blindness (he was himself colour-blind).

dam[1] n. a barrier built across a river etc. to hold back water and control its flow. —v.t. (**-mm-**) **1.** to hold back with a dam. **2.** to obstruct, to block (*up*). [from German *tam*] The biggest dams are of the earth-and rock-fill type, also called **embankment dams**. Early dams in Britain, built before about 1800, had a core made from puddle clay (clay which has been mixed with water to make it impervious). Such dams are generally built on broad valley sites. Deep, narrow gorges dictate a **concrete dam**, where the strength of reinforced concrete can withstand the water pressures involved. The first major all-concrete dam in Britain was built at Woodhead in 1876. The first dam where concrete was used to seal the joints in the rocks below was at Tunstall in 1879. The earliest dam in Britain is at the Roman Dolaucothi gold mine in Dyfed, Wales, dating from the 1st century AD.

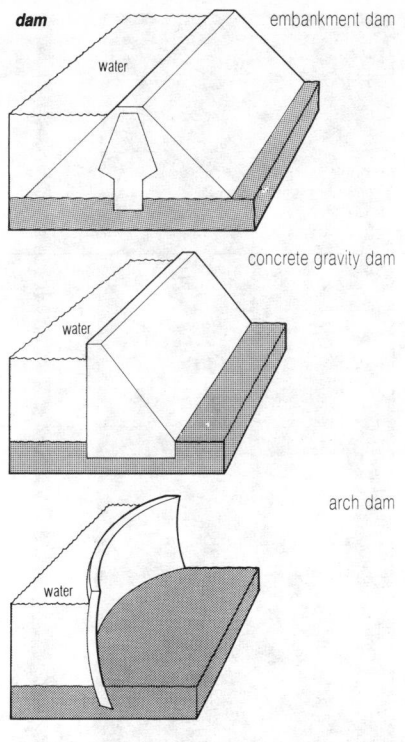

dam

embankment dam

concrete gravity dam

arch dam

buttress dam

dam² *n.* the mother especially of a quadruped. [variant of *dame*]

Dam /dæm/ Carl 1895–1976. Danish biochemist who discovered vitamin K. For his success in this field he shared the 1943 Nobel Prize for Medicine with US biochemist Edward Doisy (1893–1986).

damage /'dæmɪdʒ/ *n.* 1. something done or suffered that reduces the value or usefulness of the thing affected or spoils its appearance. 2. (*slang*) the cost. 3. (in *plural*) money claimed or awarded as compensation for a ◊tort (such as personal injuries caused by negligence) or breach of contract. In the case of breach of contract the complainant can claim all the financial loss he or she has suffered. Damages for personal injuries include compensation for loss of earnings, as well as for the injury. —*v.t.* to cause damage to. [Old French from Latin *damnum* = loss]

damascene /'dæməsi:n/ *v.t.* to decorate (metal) with inlaid or wavy patterns. [from *Damascus* capital of Syria]

Damascus /də'mæskəs/ (Arabic **Dimashq**) capital of Syria, on the river Barada, SE of Beirut; population (1981) 1,251,000. It produces silk, wood products, and brass and copper ware. Said to be the oldest continuously inhabited city in the world, Damascus was an ancient city even in Old Testament times; most notable of the old buildings is the Great Mosque, completed as a Christian church in the 5th century.

damask /'dæməsk/ *n.* figured woven silk or linen, especially white table-linen with designs shown up by reflection of light. —*adj.* 1. made of damask. 2. coloured like a damask rose, velvety pink. —**damask rose,**

a fragrant rose grown especially to make attar. [from *Damascus*]

dame *n.* 1. a comic middle-aged female character in modern pantomime, usually played by a man. 2. (*archaic, jocular,* or *US slang*) a woman. —**dame school,** (*historical*) a small primary school of the 18th century, usually kept by one female teacher, for the children of poor families. [from Old French from Latin *domina* = lady]

Dame *n.* in the UK honours system, the title of a woman who has been awarded the Order of the Bath, Order of St Michael and St George, Royal Victorian Order, or Order of the British Empire. It is also the legal title of the wife or widow of a knight or baronet, placed before her name.

daminozide *n.* (trade name *Alar*) a chemical used by fruit growers to make apples redder and crisper. It was found to be linked to cancer, and the US Environment Protection Agency (EPA) called for an end to its use.

damn /dæm/ *int.* an exclamation of anger or annoyance. —*v.t.* 1. to curse. 2. to condemn as a failure, to censure. 3. to doom to hell. 4. to be the ruin of; to show to be guilty. —*n.* an uttered curse. —*adj.* & *adv.* (*colloquial*) damned. —**damn all,** (*slang*) nothing at all. [from Old French from Latin *damnum* = loss]

damnable /'dæmnəbəl/ *adj.* hateful, annoying. —**damnably** *adv.*

damnation /dæm'neɪʃən/ *n.* eternal punishment in hell. —*int.* damn.

damned /dæmd/ *adj.* hateful, annoying. —*adv.* extremely. —**do one's damnedest,** to do one's utmost.

Damocles /'dæməkliːz/ lived 4th century BC. In Classical legend, a courtier of the elder Dionysius, ruler of Syracuse, Sicily. Having extolled the happiness of his sovereign, Damocles was invited by him to a feast, during which he saw above his head a sword suspended by a single hair. He recognized this as a symbol of the insecurity of the great.

damp *adj.* slightly or moderately wet. —*n.* 1. diffused moisture, especially as an inconvenience or danger. 2. foul or explosive gas in a mine. —*v.t.* 1. to make damp. 2. to make sad or dull, to discourage; to reduce the vigour of. 3. to reduce the vibration of. —**dampcourse,** a layer of damp-proof material built into a wall near the ground to prevent damp from rising. —**damply** *adv.,* **dampness** *n.* [from German = vapour]

dampen *v.t.* to damp.

damper *n.* 1. a device that reduces shock, noise, vibration, or oscillation; a pad that silences a piano-string except when removed by a note's being struck or by use of a pedal. 2. a movable metal plate that regulates the flow of air into the fire in a stove or furnace.

Dampier /'dæmpiə/ William 1652–1715. English explorer and hydrographic surveyor. He was born in Somerset, and went to sea in 1668. He led a life of buccaneering adventure, circumnavigated the globe, and published his *New Voyage Round the World* in 1697. In 1699 he was sent by the government on a voyage to Australia and New Guinea, and again circled the world. He accomplished a third circumnavigation in 1703–07, and on his final voyage in 1708–11 rescued Alexander Selkirk (on whose life ◊Defoe's *Robinson Crusoe* is based) from Juan Fernandez in the S Pacific.

damsel /'dæmzəl/ *n.* (*archaic* or *literary*) a young woman. [from Old French, diminutive of Latin *domina*]

damselfly /'dæmz(ə)lflaɪ/ *n.* a long, slender, colourful dragonfly of the suborder Zygoptera, with two pairs of similar wings that are generally held vertically over the body when at rest, unlike those of other dragonflies.

damson /'dæmzən/ *n.* a cultivated variety of ◊plum tree *Prunus domestica* var. *institia,* distinguished by its small, oval, edible fruit, which is dark purple or blue to black in colour. [from Latin *damascenum (prunum)* = Damascus plum]

dan *n.* a degree of proficiency in judo etc.; one who reaches this. [Japanese]

Danby /'dænbi/ Thomas Osborne, Earl of Danby 1631–1712. British Tory politician. He entered Parliament in 1665, acted from 1673–78 as Charles II's chief minister and in 1674 was created earl of Danby, but was imprisoned in the Tower of London from 1678–84. In 1688 he signed the invitation to William of Orange to take the throne. Danby was again chief minister from 1690–95, and in 1694 was created duke of Leeds.

dance /dɑ:ns/ v.t./i. 1. to move with rhythmical steps or movements, usually to music; to perform (a specified dance). 2. to move in a lively way, to bob up and down. —n. 1. a piece of dancing, a special form of this. The primary purpose of dance may be religious, magical, martial, social, or artistic—the last two being characteristic of nontraditional societies. Ancient Greek dance still exerts an influence on dance movement today. Although Western folk and social dances have a long history, the Eastern dance tradition long predates the Western. The European Classical tradition dates from the 15th century in Italy, the first printed dance text from 16th-century France, and the first dance school in Paris from the 17th century. The 18th century saw the development of European classical ballet as we know it today, and the 19th century saw the rise of Romantic ballet. In the 20th century many divergent styles and ideas have grown from a willingness to explore a variety of techniques and amalgamate different traditions. 2. a social gathering for dancing. 3. a piece of music for dancing to. —dance attendance on, to follow about and help dutifully. lead a person a dance, to cause him much trouble. —dancer n. [from Old French danser]

Dance /dɑ:ns/ Charles 1946- . English film and television actor who achieved fame in The Jewel in the Crown 1984. He has also appeared in Plenty 1986, Good Morning Babylon, The Golden Child 1987, and White Mischief 1988.

dandelion /'dændɪlaɪən/ n. a common composite plant Taraxacum officinale with jagged leaves and a large bright-yellow flower on a hollow stalk, succeeded by a globular head of seeds with downy tufts. [from French dent-de-lion = lion's tooth]

dander n. (colloquial) anger, fighting spirit.

Dandie Dinmont /'dændi 'dɪnmənt/ a breed of ◊terrier that originated in the Scottish border country. It is about 25 cm/10 in tall, short-legged and long-bodied, with drooping ears and a long tail. Its hair, about 5 cm/2 in long, can be greyish or yellowish. It is named after the character Dandie Dinmont in Walter Scott's novel Guy Mannering 1815.

dandified /'dændɪfaɪd/ adj. like a dandy.

dandle v.t. to dance (a child) on one's knees or in one's arms.

Dandolo /'dændələʊ/ Venetian family that produced four doges (rulers), of whom the most outstanding, Enrico (c.1120–1205), became doge in 1193. He greatly increased the dominions of the Venetian republic and accompanied the crusading army that took Constantinople in 1203.

dandruff /'dændrʌf/ n. flakes of scurf on the scalp and in the hair.

dandy n. 1. a man who pays excessive attention to the smartness of his appearance and clothes. 2. (colloquial) an excellent thing. —adj. (colloquial) splendid, first-rate.

Dane n. 1. a native of Denmark. 2. (historical) a Northman invader of England in the 9th–11th centuries —Great Dane, a dog of a large short-haired breed. [from Old Norse Danir (Latin Dani)]

Danegeld /'deɪngeld/ n. a land-tax levied in Anglo-Saxon England (especially 991–1016), originally to bribe the invading Danes to go away, turned into a permanent levy for national defence by the Norman kings. [Old English = Dane payment]

Danelaw /'deɪnlɔ:/ 11th-century name for the area of N and E England settled by the Danes in the 9th century. It occupied about half of England, from the river Tees to the river Thames. Within its bounds, Danish law, customs, and language prevailed. Its linguistic influence is still apparent. [Old English = Danes' law]

danger n. liability or exposure to harm or death; a thing that causes this. [from Old French from Latin dominus = lord]

dangerous /'deɪndʒərəs/ adj. involving or causing danger. —dangerously adv.

dangle v.t./i. 1. to hang loosely; to hold or carry (a thing) so that it sways loosely. 2. to hold out (a bait or temptation) enticingly.

dangling participle see ◊participle.

Daniel /'dæniəl/ 6th century BC. Jewish folk hero and prophet at the court of Nebuchadnezzar; also the name of a book of the Old Testament, probably compiled in

Dante Alighieri Italian poet Dante Alighieri by Andrea del Castagno.

the 2nd century BC. It includes stories about Daniel and his companions Shadrach, Meshach, and Abednego, set during the Babylonian captivity of the Jews.

Daniel Glyn 1914–1986. British archaeologist. Prominent in the development of the subject, he was Disney professor of archaeology, Cambridge, 1974–81. His books include Megaliths in History 1973 and A Short History of Archaeology 1981.

Daniell John Frederic 1790–1845. British chemist and meteorologist who invented a primary electrical cell in 1836. The Daniell cell consists of a central zinc cathode dipping into a porous pot containing zinc sulphate solution. The porous pot is, in turn, immersed in a solution of copper sulphate contained in a copper can, which acts as the cell's anode. The use of a porous barrier prevents polarization (the covering of the anode with small bubbles of hydrogen gas) and allows the cell to generate a continuous current of electricity.

Danish /'deɪnɪʃ/ adj. of Denmark or its people or language. —n. the official language of Denmark. —Danish blue, a soft white cheese with veins of blue mould. Danish pastry, a yeast cake topped with icing, nuts, etc. [from Latin Danensis]

Danish language a member of the North Germanic group of the Indo-European language family, spoken in Denmark and Greenland and related to Icelandic, Faroese, Norwegian, and Swedish. As one of the languages of the Vikings, who invaded and settled in parts of Britain during the 9th to 11th centuries, Old Danish had a strong influence on English. They, their, and them, as well as such sk-words as sky, skill, skin, scrape, and scrub, are of Danish origin. Danish place-name endings include by (a farm or town), as in Derby, Grimsby, and Whitby.

dank adj. unpleasantly cold and damp. [probably from Scandinavian (Swedish dank = marshy spot)]

Dante Alighieri /'dænti æli'gjeəri/ 1265–1321. Italian poet. His masterpiece La Divina Commedia/The ◊ Divine

Comedy 1307–21 is an epic account in three parts of his journey through Hell, Purgatory, and Paradise, during which he is guided part of the way by the poet Virgil; on a metaphorical level the journey is also one of Dante's own spiritual development. Other works include the philosophical prose treatise *Convivio/The Banquet* 1306–08, the first major work of its kind to be written in Italian rather than Latin; *Monarchia/On World Government* 1310–13, expounding his political theories; *De vulgari eloquentia/Concerning the Vulgar Tongue* 1304–06, an original Latin work on Italian, its dialects, and kindred languages; and *Canzoniere/Lyrics*, containing his scattered lyrics.

There is no greater sorrow than to recall a time of happiness in misery.

Dante Alighieri
Inferno

Danton /dɒnˈtɒn/ Georges Jacques 1759–1794. French revolutionary. Originally a lawyer, during the early years of the Revolution he was one of the most influential people in Paris. He organized the uprising on 10 Aug 1792 that overthrew the monarchy, roused the country to expel the Prussian invaders, and in April 1793 formed the revolutionary tribunal and the **Committee of Public Safety**, of which he was the leader until July of that year. Thereafter he lost power to the ◊Jacobins, and, when he attempted to recover it, was arrested and guillotined.

Danube /ˈdænjuːb/ (German *Donau*) the second longest of European rivers, rising on the E slopes of the Black Forest, and flowing 2,858 km/1,776 mi across Europe to enter the Black Sea in Romania by a swampy delta.

Danzig /ˈdæntsɪg/ German name for the Polish port of ◊Gdańsk.

Dão a river in central Portugal that flows 80 km/50 mi through a region noted for its wine.

daphne /ˈdæfnɪ/ *n.* a flowering shrub of the genus *Daphne* (e. g. spurge laurel, mezereon. [from Greek = laurel]

Daphne /ˈdæfnɪ/ in Greek mythology, a nymph who was changed into a laurel tree to escape from Apollo's amorous pursuit.

dapper /ˈdæpə/ *adj.* neat and smart, especially in dress. [from Middle Low German, Middle Dutch = strong, stout]

dapple *v.t.* to mark with spots or patches of colour or shade.

dapple-grey *adj.* grey with darker markings. —*n.* a dapple-grey horse.

Darby /ˈdɑːbi/ Abraham 1677–1717. English iron manufacturer who developed a process for smelting iron ore using coke instead of the more expensive charcoal.

Darby and Joan a devoted old married couple. The source of the names is usually considered to be a poem in the *Gentleman's Magazine* 1735 containing the lines 'Old Darby, with Joan by his side, You've often regarded with wonder: He's dropsical, she is sore-eyed, Yet they're never happy asunder'.

darcy *n.* the ◊c.g.s. unit (symbol D) of permeability, used mainly in geology to describe the permeability of rock (for example, to oil, gas, or water).

Dardanelles /ˌdɑːdəˈnelz/ Turkish strait connecting the Sea of Marmara with the Aegean Sea (ancient name Hellespont, Turkish name *Canakkale Boğazi*; its shores are formed by the ◊Gallipoli peninsula on the NW and the mainland of Turkey-in-Asia on the SE. It is 75 km/47 mi long and 5–6 km/3–4 mi wide.

dare /deə/ *v.t.* (*third person singular present* usually **dare** before an expressed or implied infinitive without *to*) **1.** to have the courage or impudence (*to*); to face as a danger. **2.** to challenge to do something risky. —*n.* a challenge to do something risky. — **I dare say**, I am prepared to believe, I do not deny, it is very likely. [Old English]

daredevil *n.* a recklessly daring person.

Dar es Salaam /ˈdɑːr es səˈlɑːm/ chief seaport in Tanzania, on the Indian Ocean, capital of Tanzania until its replacement by ◊Dodoma in 1974, and still the functional capital; population (1985) 1,394,000. [Arabic = haven of peace]

daring /ˈdeərɪŋ/ *n.* adventurous courage. —*adj.* bold, adventurous; boldly dramatic or unconventional.

dariole /ˈdæriəʊl/ *n.* a savoury or sweet dish cooked and served in a small mould; this mould. [from Old French]

Darius I /dəˈraɪəs/ **the Great** *c.*558–486 BC. King of Persia 521–48 BC. A member of a younger branch of the Achaemenid dynasty, he won the throne from the usurper Gaumata (died 522 BC) and reorganized the government. In 512 BC he marched against the Scythians, a people N of the Black Sea, and subjugated Thrace and Macedonia.

dark *adj.* **1.** with little or no light. **2.** (of colour) of a deep shade closer to black than to white; having a brown or black skin, complexion, or hair. **3.** gloomy, dismal. **4.** secret; mysterious; remote and unexplored. —*n.* **1.** absence of light; a time of darkness, night or nightfall. **2.** a dark colour or area. —**Dark Ages** the period (*c.* 500–1100) between the fall of the Roman Empire and the high Middle Ages. **Dark Continent**, Africa. **dark horse**, a competitor of whose abilities little is known before the contest. **darkroom** *n.* a room where light is excluded so that photographs can be processed. **in the dark**, with no light; lacking information. —**darkly** *adv.*, **darkness** *n.* [Old English]

darken *v.t./i.* to make or become dark. —**never darken a person's door**, to stay away from him or her because one is unwelcome.

darling *n.* a beloved or lovable person or thing, a favourite. —*adj.* beloved; (*colloquial*) charming. [Old English = little dear]

Darling /ˈdɑːlɪŋ/ Grace 1815–1842. British heroine. She was the daughter of a lighthouse keeper on the Farne Islands, off Northumberland. On 7 Sept 1838 the *Forfarshire* was wrecked, and Grace Darling and her father rowed through a storm to the wreck, saving nine lives. She was awarded a medal for her bravery.

darn *v.t.* to mend by weaving yarn across a hole. —*n.* a place mended by darning. —**darning** *n.* a piece of such mending; things to be darned. **darning needle** *n.* a long sewing needle used in darning.

darn², **darned** /dɑːnd/ *n.* = damn, damned. [corruption]

darnel /ˈdɑːnəl/ *n.* a grass *Lolium temulentum* that grows in some countries as a weed among corn. [from French dialect *darnelle*]

Darnley /ˈdɑːnli/ Henry Stewart or Stuart, Lord Darnley 1545–1567. British aristocrat, second husband of Mary Queen of Scots from 1565, and father of James I of England (James VI of Scotland). On the advice of her secretary, David ◊Rizzio, Mary refused Darnley the crown matrimonial; in revenge, Darnley led a band of nobles who murdered Rizzio in Mary's presence. Darnley was assassinated in 1567.

Darrow /ˈdærəʊ/ Clarence (Seward) 1857–1938. US lawyer, born in Ohio, a champion of liberal causes and defender of the underdog. He defended many trade-union leaders, including Eugene ◊Debs in 1894. He was counsel for the defence in the Nathan Leopold and Richard Loeb murder trial in Chicago in 1924, and in the Scopes monkey trial in 1925 in Dayton, Tennessee. He was an opponent of capital punishment.

dart *n.* **1.** a small, pointed missile used as a weapon or in the game of ◊darts. **2.** a darting movement. **3.** a tapering, stitched tuck in a garment. —*v.t./i.* **1.** to spring or move suddenly (*out, past,* etc.). **2.** to direct (a glance etc.) rapidly. —**dartboard** *n.* the target in the game of darts, a board marked with concentric circles. [from Old French *dars*]

Dart /dɑːt/ Raymond 1893–1988. Australian-born South African paleontologist and anthropologist, who discovered in 1924 the first fossil remains of the Australopithecenes, early hominids, near Taungs in Botswana. He named them *Australopithecus africanus*, and spent many years trying to prove to sceptics that they were early humans, since their cranial and dental characteristics were not apelike in any way. In the 1950s and 1960s, the ◊Leakey family found more fossils of this type and of related types in the Olduvai Gorge of E Africa, establishing that Australopithecines were hominids, walked erect, made tools, and lived as early as 5.5 million years ago. After further discoveries in the 1980s, they are today classified as *Homo sapiens australopithecus*, and Dart's assertions have been validated.

darts *n.* an indoor game played on a circular board. Darts (like small arrow shafts) about 13 cm/5 in long are thrown at segmented targets and score points according to their landing place. The present-day numbering system was designed by Brian Gamlin of Bury, Lancashire, England, in 1896. The world championship was inaugurated in 1978 and is held annually.

Darwin /'dɑːwɪn/ capital and port in Northern Territory, Australia, in NW Arnhem Land; population (1986) 69,000. It serves the uranium mining site at Rum Jungle to the S. Destroyed in 1974 by a cyclone, the city was rebuilt on the same site.

Darwin Charles Robert 1809–1882. English scientist who developed the modern theory of ◊evolution and proposed, with Alfred Russel Wallace, the principle of ◊natural selection. After research in South America and the Galápagos Islands as naturalist on HMS *Beagle* 1831–36, Darwin published *On the Origin of Species by Means of Natural Selection or the Preservation of Favoured Races in the Struggle for Life* 1859. This explained the evolutionary process through the principles of natural and sexual selection. It aroused bitter controversy because it disagreed with the literal interpretation of the Book of Genesis in the Bible.

I have tried lately to read Shakespeare, and found it so intolerably dull that it nauseated me.

Charles Robert Darwin
Autobiography

Darwinism, social in US history, an influential but misleading social theory, based upon the work of Charles Darwin and Herbert Spencer, which claimed to offer a scientific justification for late 19th-century *laissez-faire* capitalism (the principle of unrestricted freedom in commerce).

Dasam Granth /'dʌsəm 'grɑːnt/ a collection of the writings of the tenth Sikh guru (teacher), Gobind Singh, and of poems by a number of other writers. It is written in a script called Gurmukhi, the written form of Punjabi popularized by Guru Angad. It contains a retelling of the Krishna legends, devotional verse, and amusing anecdotes.

dash *v.t./i.* 1. to run rapidly, to rush. 2. to knock, drive, or throw forcefully, to shatter thus; to destroy (hopes etc.); to daunt. 3. to write hastily. 4. (*slang*) damn. 5. (*slang*) to give as a bribe. —*n.* 1. a short rapid run, a rush; (*US*) a sprinting-race. 2. impetuous vigour; lively spirit or appearance. 3. a slight admixture (*of* liquid or flavouring). 4. a horizontal stroke (—) in writing or printing to mark a break in the sense, omitted words etc. 5. the longer of the two signals used in the Morse code. 6. a dashboard. —**cut a dash**, to make a brilliant show in appearance or behaviour.

dashboard *n.* a board below the windscreen of a motor vehicle, carrying various instruments and controls.

dashing *adj.* spirited, lively; showy.

Das Kapital Karl Marx's exposition of his theories on economic production, published in three volumes 1867–95. It focuses on the exploitation of the worker and appeals for a classless society where the production process and its rewards are shared equally.

dastardly /'dæstədlɪ/ *adj.* contemptible and cowardly.

dasyure *n.* any ◊marsupial of the family Dasyuridae, also known as a 'native cat', found in Australia and New Guinea. Various species have body lengths from 25 cm/10 in to 75 cm/2.5 ft. Dasyures have long, bushy tails and dark coats with white spots. They are agile, nocturnal carnivores, able to move fast and climb.

data /'deɪtə, 'dɑː-/ *n.pl.* (also (*disputed usage*) as *singular*, although the singular form is **datum**) facts or information used as a basis for inference or reckoning, or prepared for being processed by a computer; quantities or characters for such processing. —**data bank**, a large store or source of data. [Latin = things given (*dare* = give)]

database /'deɪtəbeɪs/ *n.* in computing, a structured collection of data. The database makes data available to the various programs that need them, without those programs needing to be aware of how the data are actually stored. There are three main types (or 'models'): hierarchical, network, and relational, the most widely used (see ◊relational database). A **free-text database** is one that holds the text of articles or books in a form that permits rapid searching.

datable /'deɪtəbəl/ *adj.* capable of being dated.

data compression in computing, techniques for reducing the amount of storage needed for a given amount of data. They include word tokenization, in which frequently

used words are stored as shorter codes; variable bit lengths, in which common characters are represented by fewer bits than less common ones (see bit³); and run-length encoding, in which a repeated value is stored once along with a count.

data processing (DP) the use of computers for performing clerical tasks such as stock control, payroll, and dealing with orders. DP systems are typically ◊batch systems, running on mainframe computers. DP is sometimes called EDP (electronic data processing).

data protection the safeguarding of information about individuals stored on computers, ensuring privacy. The Council of Europe adopted in 1981 a Data Protection Convention, which led in the UK to the Data Protection Act 1984. This requires computer databases containing personal information to be registered, and users to process only accurate information and to retain the information only for a necessary period and for specified purposes. Subject to certain exemptions, individuals have a right of access to their personal data and to have any errors corrected.

date¹ *n.* 1. the numbered day of the month. 2. a statement (usually day, month, and year) on a document, coin etc., of when it was composed or issued; the period to which something belongs; the time at which a thing happens or is to happen. 3. (*colloquial*) an appointment to meet; (*US*) a person of the opposite sex with whom one has a social engagement. —*v.t./i.* 1. to mark with a date; to assign a date *to.* 2. to have existed *from.* 3. to be or become out of date; to show up the age of. 4. (*colloquial*) to make a social engagement with. —**out of date**, no longer fashionable, current, or valid. **to date**, until now. **up to date**, in current fashion; in accordance with what is now known or required. [from Old French from Latin *data* = (letter) given (at specified time and place)]

date² *n.* the oblong, brown, sweet, edible fruit of a palm tree *Phoenix dactylifera* of W Asia and N Africa; (also **date palm**) this tree. [from Old French from Latin from Greek *daktulos* = finger, from the shape of its leaf]

dateline *n.* 1. the imaginary N–S line through the Pacific Ocean, partly along the meridian farthest (i.e. 180°) from Greenwich, E and W of which the date differs (E being one day earlier).

datestamp *n.* an adjustable rubber stamp for marking the date of receipt etc. on a document; its mark. —*v.t.* to mark with a date-stamp.

dative /'deɪtɪv/ *n.* in grammar, the case expressing the indirect object or a recipient. —*adj.*in grammar, of or in the dative. [from Latin (*casus*) *dativus* = (case) of giving]

datum /'deɪtəm, 'dɑː-/ *n.* 1. (*plural* data) see ◊data. 2. (*plural* **datums**) the starting-point from which something is measured or calculated.

datura *n.* a genus of plants *Datura*, family Solanaceae, such as the thorn apple, with handsome, trumpet-shaped blooms. They have narcotic properties.

daub /dɔːb/ *v.t.* 1. to coat or smear roughly with a soft substance; to lay on (such a substance). 2. to paint crudely or unskilfully. —*n.* 1. plaster or other substance daubed on a surface, a smear. 2. a crude painting. [from Old French from Latin *dealbare* = to whitewash (*albus* = white)]

daughter /'dɔːtə/ *n.* 1. a female child in relation to her parent(s); a female descendant or product *of.* 2. in physics and biology, (attributive) an element or cell etc. produced by disintegration or division of another. —**daughter-in-law** *n.* a son's wife. [Old English]

Daumier /dəʊmi'eɪ/ Honoré 1808–1879. French artist. His sharply dramatic and satirical cartoons dissected Parisian society. He produced over 4,000 lithographs and, mainly after 1860, powerful satirical oil paintings that were little appreciated in his lifetime.

daunt /dɔːnt/ *v.t.* to discourage, to intimidate. [from Old French from Latin *domitare* (*domare* = tame)]

dauntless *adj.* not to be daunted, intrepid.

dauphin /'dɔːfɪn/ *n.* the title borne by the eldest son of the king of France from 1349 to 1830, derived from the personal name of a count, whose lands, the **Dauphiné** (capital Grenoble), traditionally passed to the heir to the throne. [from Latin *delphinus* = dolphin]

davenport /'dævənpɔːt/ *n.* 1. a writing-desk with drawers and a hinged flap. 2. (*US*) a large sofa. [sense 1 from Captain *Davenport*, said to have commissioned the first made]

David /dæ'vi:d/ c.1060–970 BC. Second king of Israel. According to the Old Testament he played the harp for King Saul to banish Saul's melancholy; he later slew the Philistine giant Goliath with a sling and stone. After Saul's death David was anointed king at Hebron, took Jerusalem, and made it his capital. David was celebrated as a secular poet and probably wrote some of the psalms attributed to him. David sent Uriah (a soldier in his army) to his death in the front line of battle in order that he might marry his widow, Bathsheba. Their son Solomon became the third king. In both Jewish and Christian belief, the messiah would be a descendant of David; Christians hold this prophecy to have been fulfilled by Jesus.

David Elizabeth 1914– . British cookery writer. Her *Mediterranean Food* 1950 and *French Country Cooking* 1951 helped to spark an interest in foreign cuisine in Britain, and also inspired a growing school of informed, highly literate writing on food and wine.

David Félicien César 1810–1876. French composer. His symphonic fantasy *Desert* 1844 was inspired by travels in Palestine. He was one of the first Western composers to introduce oriental scales and melodies into his music.

David Jacques Louis 1748–1825. French painter in the Neo-Classical style. He was an active supporter of and unofficial painter to the republic during the French Revolution, for which he was imprisoned 1794–95.

David two kings of Scotland:

David I 1084–1153. King of Scotland from 1124. The youngest son of Malcolm III Canmore and St ◊Margaret, he was brought up in the English court of Henry I, and in 1113 married ◊Matilda, widow of the 1st earl of Northampton. He invaded England in 1138 in support of Queen Matilda, but was defeated at Northallerton in the Battle of the Standard, and again in 1141.

David II 1324–1371. King of Scotland from 1329, son of ◊Robert I (the Bruce). David was married at the age of four to Joanna, daughter of Edward II of England. After the defeat of the Scots by Edward III at Halidon Hill in 1333, the young David and Joanna were sent to France for safety. They returned in 1341. In 1346 David invaded England, was captured at the battle of Neville's Cross and imprisoned for 11 years. On Joanna's death 1362 David married Margaret Logie, but divorced her in 1370.

David Copperfield /'deivid 'kopəfi:ld/ a novel by Charles Dickens, published 1849–50. The story follows the orphan David Copperfield from his schooldays and early poverty to eventual fame as an author. Among the characters he encounters are Mr Micawber, Mr Peggotty, and Uriah Heep.

David, St /'deivid/ or **Dewi** 5th–6th century. Patron saint of Wales, Christian abbot and bishop. According to legend he was the son of a prince of Dyfed and uncle of King Arthur; he was responsible for the adoption of the leek as the national emblem of Wales, but his own emblem is a dove. Feast day 1 Mar.

Davies /'deivis/ Peter Maxwell 1934– . English composer and conductor. His music combines medieval and serial codes of practice with a heightened Expressionism as in his opera *Taverner* 1962–68. After training alongside the British composers Goehr and Birtwistle, he studied with the Italian composer Petrassi and later with the US composer Sessions. He has composed music-theatre works for the group the Pierrot Players, later the Fires of London. He moved to Orkney in the 1970s where he has done much to revitalize music, composing for local groups and on local themes.

Davies Robertson 1913– . Canadian novelist. He gained an international reputation with *Fifth Business* 1970, the first novel of his Deptford trilogy, a panoramic work blending philosophy, humour, the occult, and ordinary life. Other works include *A Mixture of Frailties* 1958, *The Rebel Angels* 1981, and *What's Bred in the Bone* 1986.

Da Vinci see ◊Leonardo da Vinci, Italian Renaissance artist.

Davis /'deivis/ Angela 1944– . US left-wing activist for black rights, prominent in the student movement of the 1960s. In 1970 she went into hiding after being accused of supplying guns used in the murder of a judge who had been seized as a hostage in an attempt to secure the release of three black convicts. She was captured, tried,

and acquitted. She was was assistant professor of philosophy at UCLA 1969–70. In 1980 she was the Communist vice-presidential candidate.

Davis Bette 1908–1989. US actress. She entered films in 1930, and established a reputation as a forceful dramatic actress with *Of Human Bondage* 1934. Later films included *Dangerous* 1935 and *Jezebel* 1938, both winning her Academy Awards, *All About Eve* which won the 1950 Academy Award for best picture, and *Whatever Happened to Baby Jane?* 1962. She continued to make films throughout the 1980s such as *How Green Was My Valley* for television, and *The Whales of August* 1987, in which she co-starred with Lillian Gish.

Davis Jefferson 1808–1889. US politician, president of the short-lived Confederate States of America 1861–65. He was a leader of the Southern Democrats in the US Senate from 1857, and a defender of 'humane' slavery; in 1860 he issued a declaration in favour of secession from the USA. During the Civil War he assumed strong political leadership, but often disagreed with military policy. He was imprisoned for two years after the war, one of the few cases of judicial retribution against Confederate leaders.

Davis Miles (Dewey, Jr) 1926– . US jazz trumpeter, composer, and bandleader. He recorded bebop with Charlie Parker in 1945, pioneered 'cool jazz' in the 1950s and jazz-rock fusion beginning in the late 1960s. His significant albums include *Birth of the Cool* 1949, *Sketches of Spain* 1959, and *Bitches' Brew* 1970.

Davis Steve 1957– . English snooker player, who has won every major honour in the game since turning professional in 1978. He has been world champion six times, and has won as many major titles as all the other professionals between them.

Davis Stuart 1894–1964. US abstract painter. He used hard-edged geometric shapes in primary colours and experimented with collage. Much of his work shows the influence of jazz tempos. In the 1920s he produced paintings of commercial packaging, such as *Lucky Strike* 1921 (Museum of Modern Art, New York), that foreshadow Pop art.

Davis Cup an annual tennis tournament for men's international teams, first held in 1900 after Dwight Filley Davis (1879–1945) donated the trophy.

Davison /'deivisən/ Emily 1872–1913. English militant suffragette, who died while trying to stop the king's horse at the Derby at Epsom (she was trampled by the horse). She joined the Women's Social and Political Union in 1906 and served several prison sentences for militant action such as stone throwing, setting fire to pillar boxes, and bombing Lloyd George's country house. Her coffin was carried through London draped in the colours of the suffragette movement, purple, white, and green. It was escorted by 2,000 uniformed suffragettes. She was a teacher with degrees from Oxford and London universities.

Davis Hollywood legend Bette Davis.

davit /'dævɪt/ n. a kind of small crane on board ship. [from Anglo-French, diminutive of *Davi* = David]

Davitt /'dævɪt/ Michael 1846–1906. Irish nationalist. He joined the Fenians (forerunners of the Irish Republican Army) in 1865, and was imprisoned for treason 1870–77. After his release, he and the politician Charles Parnell founded the ◊Land League in 1879. Davitt was jailed several times for agitating for land reform. He was a member of Parliament 1895–99, advocating the reconciliation of extreme and constitutional nationalism.

Davy /'deɪvi/ Humphry 1778–1829. English chemist. As a laboratory assistant in Bristol in 1799, he discovered the respiratory effects of laughing gas (nitrous oxide). He discovered, by electrolysis, the elements sodium and potassium in 1807, and calcium, boron, magnesium, strontium, and barium in 1808. In addition, he established that chlorine is an element and proposed that hydrogen is present in all acids. In 1816, he invented the 'safety lamp' for use in mines where methane was present, enabling the miners to work in previously unsafe conditions. In 1802 he became professor at the Royal Institution, London. He was elected President of the Royal Society in 1820.

Davy lamp an early type of safety lamp for miners, with wire gauze enclosing the flame. [from Sir Humphry *Davy*]

daw n. a jackdaw. [Old English]

dawdle v.i. to proceed slowly and idly.

Dawes /dɔːz/ Charles Gates 1865–1951. US Republican politician. In 1923 he was appointed by the Allied Reparations Commission president of the committee that produced the Dawes Plan, a $200 million loan that enabled Germany to pay enormous war debts after World War I. It reduced tensions temporarily in Europe but was superseded by the Young Plan (which reduced the total reparations bill) in 1929. Dawes was elected US vice president (under Calvin Coolidge) in 1924, received the Nobel Peace Prize in 1925, and was ambassador to Britain from 1929–32.

dawn n. 1. the first light of day. 2. the beginning of. —v.i. 1. to begin to grow light. 2. to begin to appear or become evident. —**dawn chorus,** early-morning bird-song. **dawn on,** to begin to be understood by. [from Old English]

dawn raid in business, the sudden and unexpected buying of a significant proportion of a company's shares, usually as a prelude to a takeover bid. The aim is to prevent the target company having time to organize opposition to the takeover. In the UK the number of shares bought is often just below 5%, the figure above which the ownership of a block of shares must be disclosed under the Companies Act of 1985.

day n. 1. the time between sunrise and sunset; daylight; the hours given to work; the **solar day,** the time for one rotation of the Earth, 24 hours, especially from one midnight to the next; the **sidereal day,** the time that the Earth takes to rotate once relative to the stars, which is 3 minutes 56 seconds shorter than the solar day, because the Sun's position against the background of stars as seen from Earth changes as the Earth orbits it. 2. a specified or appointed date; a period, era, or lifetime. 3. a period of prosperity or success. 4. a day's endeavour, especially as bringing success. —**day bed** n. a bed for daytime rest. **dayboy, daygirl** ns. a school pupil attending a boarding school but living at home. **day centre,** a place where social and other facilities are provided for elderly or handicapped people during the day. **day in, day out,** continuously. **day nursery,** a place where young children are looked after while their parents are at work. **day release,** a system of allowing employees days off work for education. **day return** n. a ticket sold at a reduced rate for a journey both ways in one day. **day room** n. a room for use during the day only. **day star** n. the sun or other morning star. [Old English]

Day /deɪ/ Doris. Stage name of Doris von Kappelhoff 1924– . US film actress and singing star of the 1950s and early 1960s, mostly in musicals and, later, rather coy sex comedies. Her films include *Tea for Two* 1950, *Calamity Jane* 1953, and *Lover Come Back* 1962.

Dayak n. an alternative spelling of ◊Dyak.

Dayan /daɪˈæn/ Moshe 1915–1981. Israeli general and politician. As minister of defence in 1967 and from 1969–74, he was largely responsible for the victory over neighbouring Arab states in the 1967 Six-Day War, but he was criticized for Israel's alleged unpreparedness in the 1973 October War

and resigned along with Prime Minister Golda Meir. Foreign minister from 1977, Dayan resigned in 1979 in protest over the refusal of the Begin government to negotiate with the Palestinians.

daybreak n. the first light of day, dawn.

daydream n. a pleasant fantasy or reverie. —v.i. to indulge in daydreams.

Day Lewis /deɪ ˈluːɪs/ Cecil 1904–1972. Irish poet, British poet laureate 1968–1972. With Auden and Spender, he was one of the influential left-wing poets of the 1930s. He also wrote detective novels under the pseudonym **Nicholas Blake**. In 1968 he succeeded Masefield as poet laureate. His autobiography, *The Buried Day* 1960, was followed by a biography written by his eldest son Sean in 1980.

> There's a kind of release And a kind of torment in every Goodbye for every man.
>
> **Cecil Day Lewis**
> 'Departure in the Dark', *Short is the Time*

daylight n. 1. the light of day; dawn. 2. understanding or knowledge that has dawned. —**daylight robbery,** (colloquial) an excessive charge. **daylight saving,** the achieving of longer evening daylight, especially in summer, by making clocks show a later time. **scare the (living) daylights out of,** (slang) to terrify.

daytime n. the time of daylight.

daze v.t. to stupefy, to bewilder. —n_ a state of being dazed. [from Old Norse = weary]

dazzle v.t. 1. to make temporarily unable to see by excess of light. 2. to impress or overpower by a display of knowledge, ability etc. —n. bright, dazzling light.

dB abbreviation of decibel(s).

dBASE n. a family of microcomputer programs for manipulating large quantities of data; also, a related ◊fourth-generation language. The first version, dBASE II, appeared in the early 1980s, since when it has become widely used. By 1989 the current version had become dBase IV.

DBE abbreviation of Dame Commander of the Order of the British Empire.

DC abbreviation of 1. (also **d.c.**) direct current. 2. District of Columbia. 3. in music, da capo.

DD abbreviation of Doctor of Divinity.

D-day /'diːdeɪ/ n. or **Normandy landings 1.** 6 June 1944, the day of the Allied invasion of Normandy under the command of General Eisenhower, with the aim of liberating Western Europe from German occupation. The Anglo-American invasion fleet landed on the Normandy beaches on the stretch of coast between the Orne River and St Marcouf. Artificial harbours known as 'Mulberries' were constructed and towed across the Channel so that equipment and armaments could be unloaded onto the beaches. After overcoming fierce resistance the allies broke through the German defences; Paris was liberated on 25 August, and Brussels on 2 September. **2.** the day on which an important operation is to begin. [*D* for *day*]

DDT abbreviation of **dichloro-diphenyl-trichloroethane,** $(ClC_6H_4)_2CHCHCl_2$, an insecticide discovered in 1939 by Swiss chemist Paul Müller. It is useful in the control of insects that spread malaria, but resistant strains develop. DDT is highly toxic and persists in the environment and in living tissue. Its use is now banned in most countries.

de- prefix with the meaning **1.** down, away. **2.** completely. **3.** removing, reversing. [from Latin *de* = off, from]

deacon n. in the Roman Catholic and Anglican churches an ordained minister who ranks immediately below a priest. In the Protestant churches a deacon is in training to become a minister or is a lay assistant. The lay order of women deaconesses was revived in 1962 (legally recognized in 1968); in England they may not administer the sacraments, but may conduct public worship and preach. In 1985 the General Synod voted to allow ordination of women as deacons, enabling them to perform marriages and baptisms, but not to take communion or give absolution and the blessing. Male deacons become priests after a year but women do not. —**deaconess**n.fem. [Old English from Latin from Greek *diakonos* = servant]

dead /ded/ *adj.* 1. no longer alive. 2. numb, having lost sensation. 3. unappreciative, insensitive *to*. 4. no longer effective or in use, extinct; inactive; lacking vigour, interest, or activity; (of a ball in games) out of play. 5. abrupt, complete; exact, unqualified. —*adv.* completely, exactly. —*n.* an inactive or silent time. —**dead-alive** *adj.* very dreary. **dead beat**, (*colloquial*) exhausted. **dead-beat escapement**, one that stops 'dead' without recoil. **dead end**, the closed end of a passage etc.; a course etc. with no prospects. **dead heat**, the result of a race in which two or more competitors finish exactly level. **dead letter**, a law or practice that is no longer observed. **dead man's handle**, a controlling-handle on an electric train etc. that disconnects the power supply if released. **dead march**, a funeral march. **dead-nettle**, a plant of the genus *Lamium* with nettle-like leaves but not stinging. **dead-pan** *adj.* & *adv.* with an expressionless face. **dead reckoning**, calculation of a ship's position by log and compass etc. when observations are impossible. **dead set**, a determined attack. **dead shot**, one who never misses the target. **dead water**, the water in a ship's wake close to the stern. **dead weight**, a heavy inert weight. **dead wood**, useless persons or things. [Old English]
deaden /'dedən/ *v.t./i.* to deprive of or lose vitality, loudness, feeling etc.; to make insensitive *to*.
deadline *n.* a time limit. [originally = the line round a military prison (at Andersonville, Georgia, USA; *c.*1864) beyond which a prisoner was liable to be shot down]
deadlock *n.* a situation in which no progress can be made. —*v.t./i.* to bring or come to a deadlock.
deadly /'dedlɪ/ *adj.* 1. causing or able to cause fatal injury, death, or serious damage. 2. intense; deathlike. 3. accurate. —*adv.* as if dead; extremely. —**deadly nightshade**, see ◊belladonna. **seven deadly sins**, those held to result in damnation for a person's soul (traditionally pride, covetousness, lust, envy, gluttony, anger, sloth. —**deadliness** *n.*
Dead Sea a large lake, partly in Israel and partly in Jordan; area 1,020 sq km/394 sq mi; lying 394 m/1,293 ft below sea level. The chief river entering it is the Jordan; it has no outlet and the water is very salty.
Dead Sea Scrolls a collection of ancient scrolls (rolls of writing) and fragments of scrolls found in 1947–56 in caves on the W side of the Jordan 12 km/7 mi S of Jericho and 2 km/1 mi from the N end of the Dead Sea, at ◊Qumran. They include copies of Old Testament books 1,000 years older than those previously known to be extant. Other documents date mainly from about 150 BC–AD 68, when the monastic community that owned them, the ◊Essenes, was destroyed by the Romans because of its support for a revolt against their rule. Some scrolls were found still intact in their storage jars.
deaf /def/ *adj.* 1. wholly or partly without hearing. 2. refusing to listen. —**deaf aid** *n.*, a hearing aid. **deaf-mute** *n.* a person who is both deaf and dumb. —**deafness** *n.* [Old English]
deafen /'defən/ *v.t.* to overwhelm with sound; to make deaf or temporarily unable to hear by a very loud noise. —**deafening** *adj.*
Deakin /'diːkɪn/ Alfred 1856–1919. Australian Liberal politician, prime minister 1903–04, 1905–08, and 1909–10. In his second administration, he enacted legislation on defence and pensions.
deal[1] *v.t./i.* (*past* and *past participle* **dealt** /delt/) 1. to distribute or hand *out* among several people etc.; to distribute cards to players. 2. to assign as a share or deserts; to inflict. 3. to do business; to trade *in*. —*n.* 1. dealing or a player's turn to deal at cards; the round of play following this. 2. (*colloquial*) a business transaction or agreement. 3. (*colloquial*) treatment. 4. (*colloquial*) a large amount. —**deal with**, to do business with; to take action about; to be what is needed by (a situation etc.); to discuss (a subject) in a book or speech etc. [Old English]
deal[2] *n.* sawn fir or pine timber; a deal board of standard size. [from Middle Low German, Middle Dutch *dele* = plank]
dealer *n.* 1. a person dealing at cards. 2. a trader. 3. a jobber on the Stock Exchange.
dealings *n.pl.* a person's conduct or transactions *with* another.
deamination *n.* the removal of the amino group, -NH2, from an unwanted ◊amino acid. This is the nitrogen-containing part, and it is converted into ammonia, uric acid,

Dean *The American cult hero James Dean.*

or urea (depending on the type of animal) to be excreted in the urine. In vertebrates, deamination occurs in the ◊liver.
dean /diːn/ *n.* 1. a clergyman who is head of the chapter of a cathedral or collegiate church. 2. a college fellow responsible for student discipline; the head of a university faculty or department or of a medical college. —**area** *or* **rural dean**, the head of clergy in a division of an archdeaconry. [from Anglo-French from Latin *decanus* (*decem* = ten); originally = chief of group of ten]
Dean Basil 1888–1978. British founder and director-general in 1939 of ◊ENSA, which provided entertainment for the Allied forces in World War II.
Dean James (Byron) 1931–1955. US actor. Killed in a car accident after only his first film, *East of Eden* 1955, had been shown, he posthumously became a cult hero with *Rebel Without a Cause* and *Giant*, both 1956. He became a symbol of teenage rebellion against American middle-class values and is now regarded as a 1950s style icon.
deanery *n.* 1. a dean's house or office. 2. a rural dean's group of parishes.
dear *adj.* 1. much loved; cherished; precious *to*. 2. (as a polite form of address) esteemed. 3. costing more than it is worth; having high prices. —*n.* a dear person. —*adv.* dearly, at a high price. —*int.* expressing as an expression of surprise, distress, or pity. —**dearly** *adv.*, **dearness** *n.* [Old English]
dearth /dɜː θ/ *n.* scarcity, lack.
death /deθ/ *n.* 1. the process of dying, the end of life; final cessation of vital functions; the state of being dead. 2. an event etc. that ends life, a cause of death. 3. the ending or destruction of something. —**at death's door**, close to death. **death cap**, a poisonous toadstool *Amanita phalloides*. **death certificate**, an official statement of the date, place, and cause of a person's death. **death duty**, (*historical*) a tax levied on property after the owner's death. **death knell**, the tolling of a bell to mark a person's death; an event that heralds a thing's extinction. **death mask** *n.* a cast taken of a dead person's face. **death penalty**, punishment by being put to death. **death rate**, the number of deaths per thousand of population per year. **death-roll** *n.* a list or number of those killed in an accident, battle etc. **death's-head**, a picture of a skull as a symbol of death. **deathtrap** *n.* a dangerous place, vehicle etc. **death warrant** *n.* an order for the execution of a condemned person; something that causes the end of an established practice etc. **death wish** *n.* a desire (usually unconscious) for the death of oneself or another. **put to death**, to kill, to execute. **to death**, extremely, to the utmost limit. **to the death**, until one or other is killed. [Old English]
deathbed *n.* a bed on which a person is dying or dies.
deathly *adj.* suggestive of death. —*adv.* in a deathly way.
Death Valley /'deθ 'vælɪ/ depression 225 km/140 mi long and 6–26 km/4–16 mi wide, in SE California, USA. At 85 m/280 ft below sea level, it is the lowest point in North America. Bordering mountains rise to 3,000 m/10,000 ft. It is one of the world's hottest and driest places, with temperatures sometimes exceeding 125°F/51.7°C and

death-watch beetle

an annual rainfall of less than 2 in/5.1 cm. Borax, iron ore, tungsten, gypsum, and salts are extracted.

death-watch beetle any of the family Anobiidae, of wood-boring beetles, in particular *Xestobium rufovillosum*. The larvae live in oaks and willows, and sometimes cause damage by boring in old furniture or structural timbers. To attract the female, the male beetle produces a ticking sound by striking his head on a wooden surface, and this is taken by the superstitious as a warning of approaching death.

deb *n.* (*colloquial*) abbreviation of débutante.

débâcle /deɪˈbɑːkl/ *n.* a sudden disastrous collapse, rout, etc. [French *débâcler* = unbar]

debar /dɪˈbɑː/ *v.t.* (-rr-) to exclude, to prohibit.

debase /dɪˈbeɪs/ *v.t.* to lower in quality or value; to depreciate (coins) by use of an alloy etc. —**debasement** *n.* [from obsolete *base* = abase]

debatable /dɪˈbeɪtəbəl/ *adj.* open to dispute.

debate /dɪˈbeɪt/ *n.* a formal discussion, an open argument. —*v.t./i.* to hold a debate about; to discuss, to consider. [from French]

debauch /dɪˈbɔːtʃ/ *v.t.* to make dissolute; to lead into debauchery. —*n.* a bout of debauchery. [from French]

debauchery /dɪˈbɔːtʃərɪ/ *n.* excessive sensual indulgence.

debenture /dɪˈbentʃə/ *n.* a certificate or bond acknowledging a debt and providing for payment of interest at fixed intervals. [from Latin *debentur* = are owing (*debēre* = owe)]

debilitate /dɪˈbɪlɪteɪt/ *v.t.* to cause debility in. [from Latin]

debility /dɪˈbɪlɪtɪ/ *n.* feebleness, weakness, especially of health. [from Old French from Latin *debilis* = weak]

debit /ˈdebɪt/ *n.* an entry in an account-book of a sum owed; the sum itself, the total of such sums. —*v.t.* to enter as a debit (in). [from French from Latin *debitum* = debt]

debonair /debəˈneə/ *adj.* having a carefree self-assured manner. [from Old French *de bon aire* = of good disposition]

de Bono /də ˈbəʊnəʊ/ Edward 1933– . British medical doctor and psychologist, whose concept of lateral thinking, first expounded in *The Use of Lateral Thinking* 1967, involves thinking round a problem rather than tackling it head-on.

Deborah /ˈdebərə/ in the Old Testament, a prophet and judge (leader). She helped lead an Israelite army against the Canaanite general Sisera, who was killed trying to flee; her song of triumph at his death is regarded as an excellent example of early Hebrew poetry.

debouch /dɪˈbaʊtʃ/ *v.i.* to come out from a ravine or wood etc. into open ground; (of a river or road) to merge into a larger or wider one. [from French *bouche* = mouth]

Debray /dəˈbreɪ/ Régis 1941– . French Marxist theorist who was associated with Che ◊Guevara in the revolutionary movement in Latin America in the 1960s. In 1967 he was sentenced to 30 years' imprisonment in Bolivia but was released after three years. His writings on Latin American politics include *Strategy for Revolution* 1970. He became a specialist adviser to President Mitterrand of France on Latin American affairs.

Debrecen /ˈdebrətsen/ third largest city in Hungary, 193 km/120 mi E of Budapest, in the Great Plain (*Alföld*) region; population (1988) 217,000. It produces tobacco, agricultural machinery, and pharmaceuticals. ◊Kossuth declared Hungary independent of the ◊Habsburgs here in 1849. It is a commercial centre and has a university founded in 1912.

Debrett /dəˈbret/ John 1753–1822. English publisher of a directory of the peerage from 1802, baronetage in 1808, and knightage 1866–73/4; the books are still published under his name.

debridement *n.* the removal of dead or contaminated tissue from a wound to prevent infection.

debrief /diːˈbriːf/ *v.t.* to interrogate (a person) about a completed undertaking in order to obtain information about it.

debris /ˈdebriː, ˈdeɪ-/ *n.* scattered broken pieces, rubbish, wreckage. [from French *briser* = break]

de Broglie see ◊Broglie, de.

Debs /debz/ Eugene Victor 1855–1926. US labour leader and socialist, who organized the Social Democratic Party in 1897. He was the founder and first president of the American Railway Union in 1893, and was imprisoned for six months in 1894 for defying a federal injunction to end

the Pullman strike in Chicago. He was socialist candidate for the presidency in every election from 1900 to 1920, except that of 1916.

debt /det/ *n.* something that is owed by a person or organization, usually money, goods, or services. Debt usually occurs as a result of borrowing **credit**. **Debt servicing** is the payment of interest on a debt. The **national debt** of a country is the total money owed by the national government to private individuals, banks, and so on; **international debt**, the money owed by one country to another, began on a large scale with the investment in foreign countries by newly industrialized countries in the late 19th–early 20th centuries. International debt became a global problem as a result of the oil crisis of the 1970s. [from Old French from Latin *debitum* (*debēre* = owe)]

debt crisis any situation in which an individual, company, or country owes more to others than it can repay or pay interest on; more specifically, the massive indebtedness of many Third World countries that became acute in the 1980s, threatening the stability of the international banking system as many debtor countries became unable to service their debts.

debtor /ˈdetə/ *n.* a person owing money etc.

debug /diːˈbʌg/ *v.t.* (-gg-) **1.** to remove bugs from. **2.** (*slang*) to remove concealed listening devices from (a room etc.) or defects from (a machine etc.).

debunk /diːˈbʌŋk/ *v.t.* (*colloquial*) to show the good reputation of (a person etc.) to be false; to expose the falseness of (a claim etc.).

Debussy /dəˈbuːsi/ (Achille-) Claude 1862–1918. French composer. He broke with the dominant tradition of German Romanticism and introduced new qualities of melody and harmony based on the whole-tone scale, evoking oriental music. His work includes *Prélude à l'après-midi d'un faune* 1894 and the opera *Pelléas et Mélisande* 1902.

début /ˈdeɪbuː, -bjuː/ *n.* a first appearance (as a performer, in society etc.). [French *débuter* = lead off]

débutante /ˈdebjuːtɑːnt/ *n.* a young woman making her social début. [French]

Dec. abbreviation of December.

deca- in combinations **1.** tenfold, having ten. **2.** ten (especially of a unit in the metric system, as *decagram*). [from Greek *deka* = ten]

decade /ˈdekeɪd/ *n.* a ten-year period; a series or group of ten. [from French from Latin from Greek *deka* = ten]

decadence /ˈdekədəns/ *n.* **1.** deterioration, decline (especially of a nation, art or literature after reaching a peak). **2.** decadent attitude or behaviour. [from French from Latin]

decadent /ˈdekədənt/ *adj.* **1.** declining, of a period of decadence. **2.** self-indulgent. [from French from Latin]

decaffeinated /diːˈkæfɪneɪtɪd/ *adj.* having had the caffeine removed or reduced.

decagon /ˈdekəgən/ *n.* a plane figure with ten sides and ten angles. —**decagonal** /-ˈkægənəl/ *adj.* [from Latin from Greek *-gōnos* = angled]

decagram /ˈdekəgræm/ *n.* a metric unit of mass, equal to 10 grams.

decalitre /ˈdekəliːtə/ *n.* a metric unit of capacity, equal to 10 litres.

Decalogue /ˈdekəlɒg/ *n.* the Ten Commandments. [from Old French or Latin from Greek *hoi deka logoi* = the ten commandments]

Decameron, The /dɪˈkæmərən/ a collection of tales by the Italian writer Boccaccio, brought together in 1348–53. Ten young people, fleeing plague-stricken Florence, amuse their fellow travellers by each telling a story on the ten days they spend together. The work had a great influence on English literature, particularly on Chaucer's *Canterbury Tales*.

decametre /ˈdekəmiːtə/ *n.* a metric unit of length, equal to 10 metres.

decamp /dɪˈkæmp/ *v.i.* **1.** to break up or leave camp. **2.** to take oneself off, to abscond. [from French]

decanal /dɪˈkeɪnəl, ˈdekə-/ *adj.* of a dean; of the dean's or S side of a choir. [from Latin *decanus* = dean]

decant /dɪˈkænt/ *v.t.* to pour off (wine, liquid, a solution) leaving a sediment behind; to transfer as if by pouring. [from medieval Latin *decanthare* from Greek *kanthos* = lip of beaker]

decanter /dɪ'kæntə/ n. a stoppered glass bottle into which wine or spirit is decanted.

decapitate /dɪ'kæpɪteɪt/ v.t. to behead. —**decapitation** /-'teɪʃən/ n. [from Latin *caput* = head]

decapod /'dekəpɒd/ n. a ten-footed crustacean, e.g. a crab. [from French from Latin from Greek *pous pod-* = foot]

decarbonize /diː'kɑːbənaɪz/ v.t. to remove the carbon from (an internal-combustion engine etc.). —**decarbonization** /-'zeɪʃən/ n.

de Castella Robert. Australian marathon runner. He set a world record of 2 hr 8 min 18 sec in the 1981 Japanese marathon and is the only person to have won the Commonwealth Games marathon title twice, in 1982 and 1986. He was voted Australian of the Year in 1983.

decathlon /dɪ'kæθlɒn/ n. a two-day athletic competition for men consisting of ten events: 100 metres, long jump, shot put, high jump, 400 metres (day one); 110 metres hurdles, discus, pole vault, javelin, 1,500 metres (day two). Points are awarded for performances and the winner is the athlete with the greatest aggregate score. The decathlon is an Olympic event. [from Greek *deka* = ten and *athlon* = contest]

decay /dɪ'keɪ/ v.t./i. **1.** to rot or decompose, to cause to do this. **2.** to decline or cause to decline in quality, power, wealth, energy, beauty etc. **3.** (of a substance) to undergo change by radioactivity. —n. **1.** a rotten or ruinous state. **2.** decline in health, loss of quality. **3.** radioactive change. [from Old French from Latin *cadere* = fall]

decease n. chiefly in law, death. —v.i. to die. [from Old French from Latin *decessus* (*cedere* = go)]

deceased adj. dead. —n. a person who has died (especially recently).

deceit /dɪ'siːt/ n. the concealing of truth in order to mislead, a dishonest trick; the tendency to use deceit. —**deceitful** adj., **deceitfully** adv., **deceitfulness** n.

deceive /dɪ'siːv/ v.t./i. **1.** to make (a person) believe what is false, to mislead purposely; to use deceit. **2.** to be unfaithful to, especially sexually. —**deceive oneself,** to persist in a mistaken belief. —**deceiver** n. [from Old French from Latin *decipere* (*capere* = take)]

decelerate /diː'seləreɪt/ v.t./i. to reduce the speed (of). —**deceleration** /-'reɪʃən/ n.

December /dɪ'sembə/ n. the twelfth month of the year. [from Old French from Latin *decem* = ten, because originally the tenth month in the Roman calendar]

decency /'diːsənsɪ/ n. correct and tasteful behaviour; compliance with recognized propriety; avoidance of obscenity; (in *plural*) the requirements of correct behaviour. [from Latin]

decennial /dɪ'senɪəl/ adj. lasting for ten years; recurring every ten years. [from Latin *decem* = ten and *annus* = year]

decent /'diːsənt/ adj. **1.** seemly, not immodest or obscene or indelicate; respectable. **2.** acceptable, quite good. **3.** (*colloquial*) kind, obliging. —**decently** adv. [from French or Latin *decēre* = be seemly]

decentralize /diː'sentrəlaɪz/ v.t. to transfer from a central to a local authority; to distribute among local centres. —**decentralization** /-'zeɪʃən/ n.

deception /dɪ'sepʃən/ n. deceiving, being deceived; a thing that deceives. [from Old French or Latin]

deceptive /dɪ'septɪv/ adj. apt to mislead, easily mistaken for something else. —**deceptively** adv.

deci- in combinations, one-tenth. [from Latin *decimus* = tenth]

decibel /'desɪb(e)l/ n. (dB) a unit of measure, used originally to compare sound densities, and subsequently electrical or electronic power outputs; now also used to compare voltages. An increase of 10 dB is equivalent to a 10-fold increase in intensity or power, and a 20-fold increase in voltage. A whisper has an intensity of 20 dB; 140 dB (a jet aircraft taking off nearby) is the threshold of pain.

decide /dɪ'saɪd/ v.t./i. to bring or come to a resolution; to settle (an issue etc.) in favour of one side or another; to give a judgement. [from French or Latin *caedere* = cut]

decided adj. **1.** (usually *attributive*) definite, unquestionable. **2.** having clear opinions, determined. —**decidedly** adv.

decider n. a game, race etc., to decide between competitors finishing equal in a previous contest.

deciduous /dɪ'sɪdjuəs/ adj. (of a tree) shedding its leaves annually; (of leaves, horns, teeth etc.) shed periodically or normally. [from Latin *cadere* = fall]

decigram /'desɪgræm/ n. a metric unit of mass, equal to one-tenth of a gram.

decilitre /'desɪliːtə/ n. a metric unit of capacity, equal to one-tenth of a litre.

decimal /'desɪməl/ adj. of tenths or ten, proceeding or reckoning by tens; of decimal coinage. —n. a decimal fraction. —**decimal coinage** *or* **currency,** that in which the units are decimal multiples or fractions of each other. **decimal fraction,** one with a power of 10 as the denominator, especially when written as figures after the decimal point. **decimal point,** the dot placed after the unit figure in the decimal notation. **decimal system,** that in which each denomination, weight, or measure is 10 times the value of the one immediately below it. [from Latin *decimus* = tenth (*decem* = ten)]

decimalize /'desɪməlaɪz/ v.t. to express as a decimal, to convert to a decimal system. —**decimalization** /-'zeɪʃən/ n.

decimate /'desɪmeɪt/ v.t. to destroy one-tenth of; (disputed usage) to destroy a large proportion of. —**decimation** /-'meɪʃən/ n. [from Latin *decimare* = take the tenth man (*decimus* = tenth), referring to the ancient Roman custom of putting to death one in every ten soldiers taking part in a mutiny or similar crime]

decimetre /'desɪmiːtə/ n. a metric unit of length, equal to one-tenth of a metre.

decipher /dɪ'saɪfə/ v.t. to convert (a text written in cipher or unfamiliar script) into an understandable script or language; to establish the meaning of (poor writing, anything puzzling). —**decipherment** n.

decipherable adj. able to be deciphered.

decision /dɪ'sɪʒən/ n. **1.** an act of deciding. **2.** settlement (of an issue etc.). **3.** a conclusion reached, a resolve made. **4.** the tendency to decide firmly. [from Old French or Latin]

decision table in computing, a method of describing a procedure for a program to follow, based on comparing possible decisions and the consequent actions to be taken. It is often used as an aid in systems design.

decisive /dɪ'saɪsɪv/ adj. **1.** that decides an issue or contributes to a decision. **2.** showing decision and firmness, positive. —**decisively** adv. [from French from Latin]

deck n. **1.** a platform in a ship covering the hull's area (or part of this) at any level and serving as a floor; a ship's accommodation on a particular deck. **2.** a floor or compartment of a bus etc. **3.** the component that carries the magnetic tape, disc etc., in sound-reproduction equipment or a computer. **4.** (*US*) a pack of cards. **5.** (*slang*) the ground. —v.t. **1.** to furnish with or cover as a deck. **2.** (often with *out*) to array, to adorn. —**below deck(s),** in(to) the space under the main deck. **deck chair** n. a portable folding chair (originally used on deck in passenger ships). **deck hand** n. a man employed on a ship's deck in cleaning and odd jobs. [from Middle Dutch = roof, cloak]

-decker in combinations, having a specified number of decks.

declaim /dɪ'kleɪm/ v.t./i. to speak or utter rhetorically or affectedly; to practise oratory; to inveigh *against.* —**declamation** /deklə'meɪʃən/ n., **declamatory** /dɪ'klæmətərɪ/ adj. [from French or Latin]

declaration /deklə'reɪʃən/ n. declaring; an emphatic or deliberate statement; a formal announcement. [from Latin]

Declaration of Independence a historic US document stating the theory of government on which the USA was founded, based on the right 'to life, liberty, and the pursuit of happiness'. The statement was issued by the American Continental Congress on 4 July 1776, renouncing all allegiance to the British crown and ending the political connection with Britain.

Declaration of Rights in Britain, the statement issued by the Convention Parliament of Feb 1689, laying down the conditions under which the crown was to be offered to ◊William III and Mary. Its clauses were later incorporated in the ◊Bill of Rights.

declare /dɪ'kleə/ v.t./i. **1.** to announce openly or formally; to pronounce; to assert emphatically; (in *past participle*) that is such by his own admission. **2.** to acknowledge the possession of (dutiable goods, income etc.). **3.** (in cricket) to choose to close one's side's innings before all the wickets have fallen. **4.** to name the trump suit in a card game. —**declare oneself,** to reveal one's intentions or identity. —**declarative** /-'klærətɪv/ *adj.*, **declaratory** /-'klærətərɪ/ *adj.* [from Latin *declarare* (*clarus* = clear)]

declension /dɪ'klenʃən/ *n.* **1.** variation of the form of a noun etc. to give its grammatical case; the class by which a noun etc. is declined. **2.** falling-off, deterioration. [from Old French]

declination /deklɪ'neɪʃən/ *n.* **1.** a downward bend. **2.** the angular distance of a star etc. N or S of the celestial equator. **3.** the deviation of a compass needle E or W from the true north. —**declinational** *adj.* [from Latin]

decline /dɪ'klaɪn/ *v.t./i.* **1.** to deteriorate, to lose strength or vigour, to decrease. **2.** to refuse (an invitation or challenge) formally and courteously; to give or send a refusal. **3.** to slope downwards; to bend down, to droop. **4.** in grammar, to give the forms of (a noun or adjective) corresponding to the cases. —*n.* **1.** declining, a gradual loss of vigour etc. **2.** deterioration, decay. [from Old French from Latin *declinare* (*clinare* = bend)]

Decline and Fall of the Roman Empire, The History of the a historical work by Edward Gibbon, published in the UK 1776–88. Arranged in three parts, the work spans 13 centuries and covers the history of the empire from Trajan and the Antonines through to the Turkish seizure of Constantinople in 1453.

declivity /dɪ'klɪvɪtɪ/ *n.* a downward slope. [from Latin *declivitas* (*clivus* = slope)]

declutch /diː'klʌtʃ/ *v.i.* to disengage the clutch of a motor vehicle.

decoct /dɪ'kɒkt/ *v.t.* to make a decoction of. [from Latin *decoquere* = boil down]

decoction /dɪ'kɒkʃən/ *n.* boiling down to extract an essence; the essence produced. [from Old French or Latin]

decode /diː'kəud/ *v.t.* to convert (a coded message) into an understandable language.

decoke /diː'kəuk/ *v.t.* (*colloquial*) to decarbonize. —*n.* (*colloquial*) the process of decarbonizing.

décolletage /deɪkɒl'tɑːʒ/ *n.* a low neckline of a woman's dress etc. [French (*collet* = collar of dress)]

décolleté /deɪ'kɒlteɪ/ *adj.* having a low neckline. [French]

decolonization *n.* the gradual achievement of independence by former colonies of the European imperial powers which began after World War I. The process of decolonization accelerated after World War II and the movement affected every continent: India and Pakistan gained independence from Britain in 1947; Algeria gained independence from France in 1962.

decompose /diːkəm'pəuz/ *v.t./i.* **1.** to decay, to rot. **2.** to separate (a substance) into its elements. —**decomposition** /-kɒmpə'zɪʃən/ *n.*

decomposer *n.* in biology, an organism that feeds on excrement, or dead plant and animal matter. Decomposers include dung-beetle larvae, earthworms, many bacteria, and fungi. They play a vital role in ecological systems by freeing important chemical substances, such as nitrogen compounds, locked up in dead organisms or excrement.

decompress /diːkəm'pres/ *v.t.* to subject to decompression.

decompression /diːkəm'preʃən/ *n.* release from compression; the gradual reduction of air pressure on a person who has been subjected to it (especially underwater). —**decompression chamber,** an enclosed space for this. **decompression sickness,** the condition caused by a sudden and substantial change in atmospheric pressure which permits a too-rapid release of nitrogen that has been dissolved in the bloodstream under pressure; when the nitrogen bubbles it causes the bends, a condition whose symptoms include breathing difficulties, joint and muscle pain, and cramps. It is experienced mostly by deep-sea divers who surface too quickly.

decongestant /diːkən'dʒestənt/ *n.* a medicinal substance that relieves congestion.

decontaminate /diːkən'tæmɪneɪt/ *v.t.* to remove (especially radioactive) contamination from. —**decontamination** /-'neɪʃən/ *n.*

decontamination factor in radiological protection, a measure of the effectiveness of a decontamination process. It is the ratio of the original contamination to the remaining radiation after decontamination: 1,000 and above is excellent; 10 and below is poor.

décor /'deɪkɔː, de-/ *n.* the furnishing and decoration of a room or stage. [French]

decorate /'dekəreɪt/ *v.t.* **1.** to furnish with adornments; to serve as an adornment to. **2.** to paint or paper etc. (a room or house). **3.** to invest with an order, medal, or other award. —**Decorated style,** a style of English Gothic architecture (*c.*1250–1350) with increasing use of decoration. —**decorative** /'dekərətɪv/ *adj.* [from Latin *decorare* (*decus* = beauty)]

decoration /dekə'reɪʃən/ *n.* **1.** decorating; a thing that decorates; (in *plural*) flags etc. put up on a festive occasion. **2.** a medal etc. conferred and worn as an honour. [from French or Latin]

decorator /'dekəreɪtər/ *n.* a person who decorates, especially one who paints or papers houses professionally.

decorous /'dekərəs/ *adj.* having or showing decorum. —**decorously** *adv.* [from Latin *decorus* = seemly]

decorum /dɪ'kɔːrəm/ *n.* behaviour or usage conforming with decency or politeness, seemliness. [Latin]

decoy /'diːkɔɪ/ *n.* a thing or person used to lure an animal or other person into a trap or danger; a bait, an enticement. —/dɪ'kɔɪ/ *v.t.* to lure by means of a decoy.

decrease /dɪ'kriːs/ *v.t./i.* to make or become smaller or fewer. —/'diː-/ *n.* decreasing; the amount by which a thing decreases. [from Old French from Latin *decrescere* (*crescere* = grow)]

decree /dɪ'kriː/ *n.* an official or authoritative order having legal force; a judgement or decision of certain lawcourts. —*v.t.* to ordain by decree. —**decree nisi** /'naɪsɑɪ/, a provisional order for divorce, made absolute unless cause to the contrary is shown within a fixed period (Latin *nisi* = unless). [from Old French from Latin *decretum* = thing decided]

decrepit /dɪ'krepɪt/ *adj.* weakened by age or hard use, dilapidated. —**decrepitude** *n* . [from Latin *crepare* = creak]

decretal /dɪ'kriːt(ə)l/ *n.* in medieval Europe, a papal ruling on a disputed point, sent to a bishop or abbot in reply to a request or appeal. The earliest dates from Siricius in 385. [from Latin]

decretum *n.* a collection of papal decrees. The best known is that collected by Gratian (died 1159) in about 1140, comprising some 4,000 items. The decretum was used as an authoritative source of canon law (the rules and regulations of the church).

decry /dɪ'kraɪ/ *v.t.* to disparage, to depreciate.

dedicate /'dedɪkeɪt/ *v.t.* to devote to a sacred person or purpose; to devote (especially *oneself*) to a special task or purpose; (of an author or composer) to address (a book, piece of music etc.) *to* a person as an honour or recognition; (in *past participle*) devoted to a vocation etc., having single-minded loyalty. —**dedicator** *n.* [from Latin *dedicare* (*dicare* = declare)]

dedicated computer a computer built into another device for the purpose of controlling or supplying information to it. The uses of dedicated computers has increased dramatically since the advent of the ♀microprocessor: washing machines, digital watches, cars, and video recorders all have their own processors. —**dedicated system,** a general-purpose computer system confined to performing only one function for reasons of efficiency or convenience, for instance, a word processor.

dedication /dedɪ'keɪʃən/ *n.* dedicating; the words with which a book etc. is dedicated. [from Old French or Latin]

dedicatory /'dedɪkeɪtərɪ/ *adj.* of or forming a dedication.

deduce /dɪ'djuːs/ *v.t.* to infer, to draw as a logical conclusion. —**deducible** *adj.* [from Latin *deducere* (*ducere* = lead)]

deduct /dɪ'dʌkt/ *v.t.* to subtract, to take away; to withhold (a portion or amount). [from Latin]

deductible *adj.* that may be deducted, especially from one's tax or taxable income.

deduction /dɪ'dʌkʃən/ *n.* **1.** deducting; an amount deducted. **2.** deducing, the inferring of particular instances from a general law. **3.** a conclusion reached. [from Old French or Latin]

deductive *adj.* of or reasoning by deduction. [from Latin]

Dee /diː/ river in Grampian region, Scotland; length 139 km/ 87 mi. From its source in the Cairngorms, it flows E into the

North Sea at Aberdeen (by an artificial channel). It is noted for salmon fishing. Also a river in Wales and England; length 112 km/70 mi. Rising in Lake Bala, Gwynnedd, it flows into the Irish Sea W of Chester. There is another Scottish river Dee (61 km/38 mi) in Kirkcudbright.

deed *n.* 1. a thing consciously done; a brave, skilful, or conspicuous act. 2. actual fact, performance. 3. a document effecting the legal transfer of ownership and bearing the disposer's signature. —**deed-box** *n.* a strong box for keeping deeds and other documents. **deed of covenant,** an agreement to pay a regular amount annually to a charity etc., enabling the charity to recover the tax paid by the donor on this amount of his outcome. **deed poll,** a deed made by one party only, especially to change a name. [Old English]

deem *v.t.* to regard, to consider, to judge. [Old English]

deemster /'di:mstə/ *n.* either of the two judges in the Isle of Man.

deep *adj.* 1. extending far down or in from the top, surface, or edge; extending to or lying at a specified depth. 2. situated far down, back, or in. 3. coming or brought from far down or in; low-pitched, full-toned, not shrill. 4. intense, vivid, extreme. 5. heartfelt, absorbing; fully absorbed or overwhelmed. 6. profound, penetrating, difficult to understand. —*n.* 1. a deep place (especially *the* sea) or state. 2. the position of a fieldsman distant from the batsman in cricket. —*adv.* deeply; far down or in. —**deep-fry** *v.t.* to fry (food) in fat or oil that covers it. **deep-laid** *adj.* (of a scheme) secret and elaborate. **deep-rooted, deep-seated** *adjs.* (of feelings or convictions) firmly established, profound. **go off the deep end,** to give way to anger or emotion. **in deep water,** in trouble or difficulty. —**deeply** *adv.*, **deepness** *n.* [Old English]

deepen *v.t./i.* to make or become deep or deeper.

deepfreeze /di:p'fri:z/ *n.* a freezer; storage in a freezer. —*v.t.* (*past* **deepfroze**; *past participle* **deepfrozen**) to store in a deepfreeze.

Deep-Sea Drilling Project a research project initiated by the USA in 1968 to sample the rocks of the ocean ◊crust. The operation became international in 1975, when Britain, France, Germany, Japan, and the USSR also became involved.

deep-sea trench a long and narrow, deep trough (◊ocean trench) in the seafloor, marking the line where one of the plates of the ◊lithosphere is sliding beneath another (see ◊plate tectonics). At this depth (below 6 km/3.6 mi) there is no light and very high pressure; deep-sea trenches are inhabited by crustaceans, coelenterates (for example, sea anemones), polychaetes (a type of worm), molluscs, and echinoderms.

deer *n.* (*plural* the same) a four-footed ruminant animal of the family Cervidae, of which the male usually has antlers. Most species of deer are forest-dwellers and are distributed throughout Eurasia and North America, but are absent from Australia and Africa S of the Sahara. Native to Britain are red deer *Cervus elaphus* and roe deer *Capreolus capreolus*. The fallow deer *Dama dama* came originally from the Mediterranean region, and was probably introduced to Britain by William the Conqueror. The little ◊muntjac has been introduced in more recent years from East Asia, and is spreading. Other species in the deer family include the ◊elk, ◊wapiti, ◊reindeer, and the musk deer *Moschus moschiferus* of Central Asia, which yields musk and has no antlers. [Old English]

deerhound *n.* a large, rough-coated dog, formerly used for hunting and killing deer. Slim and long-legged, it grows to 75 cm/2.5 ft or more, usually with a bluish-grey coat.

deerskin *n.* leather from a deer's skin.

deerstalker /'diəstɔ:kə/ *n.* a soft cloth cap with peaks in front and behind.

deface /di'feis/ *v.t.* to spoil the appearance of; to make illegible. —**defacement** *n.*

de facto /di: 'fæktəʊ, dei/ in fact, existing in fact (whether by right or not). [Latin]

defalcate /'di:fælkeit/ *v.i.* to misappropriate money. —**defalcator** *n.* [from Latin *defalcare* = lop with a sickle (*falx* = sickle)]

defalcation /di:fæl'keiʃən/ *n.* 1. misappropriation of money; the amount misappropriated. 2. a shortcoming.

de Falla Manuel. See ◊Falla, Manuel de.

defame /di'feim/ *v.t.* to attack the good reputation of, to speak ill of. —**defamation** /defə'meiʃən/ *n.*, **defamatory** /di'fæmətəri/ *adj.* [from Old French from Latin *diffamare* (*fama* = report)]

default /di'fɔ:lt, -'fɒlt/ *n.* failure to fulfil an obligation, especially to appear, pay, or act in some way. —*v.i.* to fail to meet an (especially pecuniary) obligation. —**go by default,** to be absent, to be ignored because of absence. **in default of,** because of or in case of the lack or absence of. [from Old French from Latin]

defaulter *n.* one who defaults, especially a soldier guilty of a military offence.

defeat /di'fi:t/ *v.t.* to overcome in a battle or other contest; to frustrate, to baffle. —*n.* defeating, being defeated. [from Anglo-French from Latin *disfacere* (*facere* = do)]

defeatist *n.* one who expects or accepts defeat too readily. —**defeatism** *n.*

defecate /'di:fikeit/ *v.i.* to expel faeces from the bowels. —**defecation** /-'keiʃən/ *n.* [from Latin *defaecere* = purify (*faex* = dregs)]

defect /di'fekt/ *n.* /also 'di:-/ a lack of something essential to adequacy or completeness, an imperfection; a shortcoming, a failing. —*v.i.* to abandon one's country or cause in favour of another. —**defector** *n.* [from Latin *deficere* = fail]

defection /di'fekʃən/ *n.* the abandonment of one's country or cause. [from Latin]

defective /di'fektiv/ *adj.* 1. having defects, imperfect, incomplete. 2. mentally subnormal. —**defectively** *adv.*, **defectiveness** *n.* [from Old French or Latin]

defence /di'fens/ *n.* 1. defending from or resistance against attack; a means of achieving this; (in *plural*) fortifications etc. 2. a justification put forward in response to an accusation. 3. the defendant's case in a lawsuit; counsel for the defendant. 4. the players in the defending position in a game. —**defence mechanism,** the body's reaction against disease organisms; a mental process avoiding conscious conflict. [from Old French from Latin]

defenceless *adj.* having no defence, unable to defend oneself.

Defence, Ministry of a British government department created in 1964 from a temporary Ministry of Defence established after World War II together with the Admiralty, Air Ministry, and War Office. It is headed by the secretary of state for defence with undersecretaries for the Royal Navy, the Army, and the Royal Air Force. This centralization was influenced by the example of the US Department of ◊Defense.

defend /di'fend/ *v.t./i.* 1. to resist an attack made on, to protect. 2. to uphold by argument, to speak or write in favour of; to conduct the defence in a lawsuit. —**defender** *n.* [from Old French from Latin *defendere* (*fendere* = strike)]

defendant *n.* the person accused or sued in a lawsuit.

Defender of the Faith one of the titles of the English sovereign, conferred on Henry VIII in 1521 by Pope Leo X in recognition of the king's treatise against the Protestant Luther. It appears on British coins in the abbreviated form **F.D.** (Latin = *Fidei Defensor*).

Defense, Department of a US government department presided over by the secretary of defence, headquartered in the ◊Pentagon. The secretary holds a seat in the president's cabinet; each of the three military services has a civilian secretary, not of cabinet rank, at its head. It was established when the army, navy, and air force were unified by the National Security Act of 1947.

defensible /di'fensibəl/ *adj.* able to be defended or justified. —**defensibility** /-'biliti/ *n.*, **defensibly** *adv.* [from Latin]

defensive *adj.* done or intended for defence, protective. —**on the defensive,** in an attitude or position of defence; expecting criticism. —**defensively** *adv.* [from French from Latin]

defer[1] /di'fɜ:/ *v.t.* (**-rr-**) to put off to a later time, to postpone. —**deferred payment,** payment by instalments for goods supplied. **deferred shares** (*or* **stock**), shares or stock with the least entitlement to a dividend. —**deferment** *n.*, **deferral** *n.*

defer[2] *v.i.* (**-rr-**) to yield or make concessions in opinion or action (*to* a person). [from French from Latin *deferre* = confer, give]

deference /'defərəns/ *n.* courteous regard, compliance with another's wishes or advice. —**in deference to,** out of respect for. [from French]

deferential /defə'renʃəl/ *adj.* showing deference. —**deferentially** *adv.*

defiance /di'faɪəns/ *n.* defying, open disobedience, bold resistance. [from Old French]

defiant /di'faɪənt/ *adj.* showing defiance. —**defiantly** *adv.*

defibrillation *n.* the use of electrical stimulation to restore a chaotic heartbeat to a rhythmical pattern. In fibrillation, which may occur in most kinds of heart disease, the heart muscle contracts irregularly; the heart is no longer working as an efficient pump. Paddles are applied to the chest wall, and one or more electric shocks are delivered to normalize the beat.

deficiency /di'fɪʃənsɪ/ *n.* being deficient; a lack or shortage (of); a thing lacking, a deficit. —**deficiency disease,** a disease caused by lack of some essential element in the diet.

deficient /di'fɪʃənt/ *adj.* incomplete or insufficient in some essential respect. [from Latin *deficere* = be lacking]

deficit /'defɪsɪt/ *n.* the amount by which a total falls short of what is required; the excess of liabilities over assets. [from French from Latin]

deficit financing in economics, a planned excess of expenditure over income, dictated by government policy, creating a shortfall of public revenue which is met by borrowing. The decision to create a deficit is taken to stimulate an economy by increasing consumer purchasing and at the same time to create more jobs.

defile[1] /di'faɪl/ *v.t.* to make dirty, to pollute; to corrupt. —**defilement** *n.* [for earlier *defoul* from Old French = trample down]

defile[2] *n.* /also 'di:-/ a gorge or pass through which troops etc. can pass only in file. —*v.i.* to march in file. [from French]

definable /di'faɪnəbəl/ *adj.* able to be defined.

define /di'faɪn/ *v.t.* 1. to give the exact meaning of (a word etc.). 2. to describe or explain the scope of. 3. to outline clearly, to mark out the boundary of. [from Old French from Latin *definire* = finish (*finis* = boundary)]

definite /'defɪnɪt/ *adj.* having exact and discernible limits; clear and distinct, not vague. —**definite article,** see ◊article. —**definitely** *adv.* [from Latin]

definition /defɪ'nɪʃən/ *n.* 1. defining; a statement of the precise meaning of a word etc. 2. the degree of distinctness in the outline of an object or image. [from Old French from Latin]

definitive /di'fɪnɪtɪv/ *adj.* (of an answer, treaty, verdict, etc.) final, decisive, unconditional; (of an edition of a book etc.) most authoritative.

deflate /di'fleɪt/ *v.t./i.* 1. to let out the air or gas from (a balloon, tyre etc.). 2. to lose or cause to lose confidence or conceit. 3. to apply deflation to (the economy), to pursue a policy of deflation.

deflation /di'fleɪʃən/ *n.* deflating; reduction of the amount of money in circulation to increase its value as a measure against inflation. —**deflationary** *adj.*

deflect /di'flekt/ *v.t./i.* to turn aside from a straight course or intended purpose; to deviate or cause to deviate (*from*). —**deflexion, deflection** *ns.,* **deflector** *n.* [from Latin *deflectere* (*flectere* = bend)]

deflower /di:'flaʊə/ *v.t.* 1. to deprive (a woman) of virginity; to ravage. 2. to remove the flowers from (a plant). [from Old French from Latin]

Defoe /di'fəʊ/ Daniel 1660–1731. English novelist and journalist, who wrote *Robinson Crusoe* 1719, which was greatly influential in the development of the novel. An active pamphleteer and political critic, he was imprisoned from 1702–04 following publication of the ironic *The Shortest Way With Dissenters.* Fictional works include *Moll Flanders* 1722 and *A Journal of the Plague Year* 1724. Altogether he produced over 500 books, pamphlets, and journals.

defoliate /di:'fəʊlɪeɪt/ *v.t.* to remove the leaves from, especially as a military tactic. —**defoliant** *n.,* **defoliation** /-'eɪʃən/ *n.* [from Latin *defoliare* (*folium* = leaf)]

De Forest /də 'fɒrɪst/ Lee 1873–1961. US physicist who was able to exploit the commercial value of radio. Ambrose ◊Fleming invented the diode valve in 1904. De Forest saw that if a third electrode were added, the triode valve would serve as an amplifier and radio communications would become a practical possibility. He patented his discovery in 1906.

deforestation *n.* the destruction of forest for timber (see ◊forestry) and clearing for agriculture, without planting new trees to replace those lost (reafforestation). Deforestation causes fertile soil to be blown away or washed into rivers, leading to soil ◊erosion, drought, and flooding.

deform /di'fɔ:m/ *v.t.* to spoil the appearance or form of, to put out of shape. —**deformation** /di:fɔ:'meɪʃən/ *n.* [from Latin *deformare* (*forma* = shape)]

deformed *adj.* misshapen.

deformity /di'fɔ:mɪtɪ/ *n.* deformed state; a malformation, especially of a body or limb.

defraud /di'frɔ:d/ *v.t.* to cheat by fraud. [from Old French or Latin (*fraus* = fraud)]

defray /di'freɪ/ *v.t.* to provide the money to pay (a cost or expense). —**defrayal** *n.* [from French from Latin *fredum* = fine]

defrost /di:'frɒst/ *v.t.* to remove the frost or ice from; to unfreeze (frozen food).

deft *adj.* neatly skilful or dextrous, adroit. —**deftly** *adv.,* **deftness** *n.*

defunct /di'fʌŋkt/ *adj.* no longer existing or in use; extinct, dead. [from Latin (past participle of *fungi* = perform)]

defuse /di:'fju:z/ *v.t.* to remove the fuse from (an explosive, a bomb); to reduce the tension or potential danger in (a crisis, difficulty etc.).

defy /di'faɪ/ *v.t.* 1. to resist openly, to refuse to obey. 2. (of a thing) to present insuperable obstacles to. 3. to challenge (a person) to do or prove something. [from Old French from Latin *fides* = faith]

Degas /'deɪɡɑ:/ (Hilaire Germain) Edgar 1834–1917. French Impressionist painter and sculptor. He devoted himself to lively, informal studies, often using pastels, of ballet, horse racing, and young women working. From the 1890s he turned increasingly to sculpture, modelling figures in wax in a fluent, naturalistic style.

de Gaulle /də 'ɡəʊl/ Charles André Joseph Marie 1890–1970. French general and first president of the Fifth Republic 1959–69. He organized the ◊Free French troops fighting the Nazis 1940–44, was head of the provisional French government 1944–46, and leader of his own Gaullist party. In 1958 the national assembly asked him to form a government during France's economic recovery and to solve the crisis in Algeria. He became president at the end of 1958, having changed the constitution to provide for a presidential system, and served until 1969.

degauss /di:'ɡaʊs/ *v.t.* to demagnetize; to neutralize the magnetism of (a ship) by means of an encircling current-carrying conductor, as a precaution against magnetic mines.

degenerate[1] /di'dʒenərət/ *adj.* having lost the qualities that are normal and desirable or proper to its kind. —*n.* a degenerate person or animal. —**degeneracy** *n.*

degenerate[2] *v.i.* to become worse or lower in standard; to become degenerate. —**degeneration** /-'reɪʃən/ *n.* [from Latin *degener* = ignoble, from *genus* = race]

degrade /di'ɡreɪd/ *v.t.* 1. to reduce to a lower rank. 2. to bring into dishonour or contempt. 3. to reduce to a lower organic type or a simpler structure. —**degradation** /degrə'deɪʃən/ *n.* [from Old French from Latin *degradare* (*gradus* = step)]

degrading /di'ɡreɪdɪŋ/ *adj.* humiliating, lowering one's self-respect.

degree /di'ɡri:/ *n.* 1. a stage in an ascending or descending series; a stage in intensity or amount etc.; a category of crime or criminality; a step in direct genealogical descent. 2. a unit of measurement in an angle or arc; a unit in a scale of temperature, hardness etc. 3. an academic diploma awarded for proficiency in a specified subject, or as an honour. —**by degrees,** a little at a time, gradually. [from Old French from Latin *gradus* = step]

de Havilland /də 'hævɪlənd/ Geoffrey 1882–1965. British aircraft designer who designed and whose company produced the Moth biplane, the Mosquito fighter-bomber of World War II, and the postwar Comet, the world's first jet-driven airliner to enter commercial service.

De Havilland Olivia 1916– . US actress, a star in Hollywood from the age of 19, when she appeared in *A Midsummer Night's Dream* 1935. She later successfully played more challenging dramatic roles in films such as *Gone with the Wind* 1939, *Dark Mirror* 1946, and *The Snake Pit* 1948.

De Klerk South African state president and National Party leader F W De Klerk. Since coming to power in 1989 he has embarked on a programme of reform.

dehisce /dɪˈhɪs/ *v.i.* to gape, to burst open (especially of a seed vessel). —**dehiscence** *n.*, **dehiscent** *adj.* [from Latin *dehiscere* (*hiscere* = begin to gape)]

dehumanize /diːˈhjuːmənaɪz/ *v.t.* to remove human characteristics from; to make impersonal. —**dehumanization** /-ˈzeɪʃən/ *n.*

dehydrate /diːˈhaɪdreɪt/ *v.t./i.* to remove the water or moisture from; to make or become dry. —**dehydration** /-ˈdreɪʃən/ *n.* [from Greek *hudōr* = water]

dehydrating agent a substance that will remove water from another substance where the water is chemically bonded, such as water of crystallization in a hydrated salt. Powerful dehydrating agents such as concentrated sulphuric acid will even remove the elements of water from some organic compounds (for example sucrose).

de-ice /diːˈaɪs/ *v.t.* to remove the ice from; to prevent the formation of ice on. —**de-icer** *n.*

deify /diːˈɪfaɪ/ *v.t.* to make a god of; to regard or worship as a god. —**deification** /-fɪˈkeɪʃən/ *n.* [from Old French from Latin *deificare* (*deus* = god)]

Deighton /ˈdeɪtn/ Len 1929– . British author of spy fiction, including *The Ipcress File* 1963, the trilogy *Berlin Game, Mexico Set*, and *London Match* 1983–85, and its sequel *Spy Hook, Spy Line*, and *Spy Sinker* 1988–90, featuring the spy Bernard Samson.

deign /deɪn/ *v.i.* to think fit or condescend *to* do. [from Old French from Latin *dignari* (*dignus* = worthy)]

Dei gratia by the grace of God. [Latin]

Deimos /ˈdaɪmɒs/ *n.* one of the two moons of Mars. It is irregularly shaped, 15 × 12 × 11 km/9 × 7.5 × 7 mi, orbits at a height of 24,000 km/15,000 mi every 1.26 days, and is not as roughly featured as the other moon, Phobos. Deimos was discovered by US astronomer Asaph Hall in 1877, and is thought to be an asteroid captured by Mars' gravity.

deindustrialization *n.* a decline in the share of manufacturing industries in a country's economy. Typically, industrial plants are closed down and not replaced, and service industries increase.

Deirdre /ˈdɪədri/ in Celtic mythology, the beautiful intended bride of ◊Conchobar.

deism /ˈdiːɪzəm/ *n.* belief in the existence of a god (creator of the world) without accepting revelation (compare ◊Theism); a movement of religious thought in the 17th and 18th centuries, characterized by the belief in a rational 'religion of nature' as opposed to the orthodox beliefs of Christianity. —**deist** *n.*, **deistic** /-ˈɪstɪk/ *adj.* [from Latin *deus* = god]

deity /ˈdiːɪtɪ, (*disputed usage*) ˈdeɪ-/ *n.* divine status or nature; a god; **the Deity**, God. [from Old French from Latin]

déjà vu /ˈdeɪʒɑː ˈvuː/ the illusory feeling of having already experienced a present situation; something tediously familiar. [French = already seen]

deject /dɪˈdʒekt/ *v.t.* (often in *past participle*) to put in low spirits, to depress. —**dejectedly** *adv.*, **dejection** *n.* [from Latin *dejicere* = cast down (*jacere* = throw)]

de jure /diː ˈdʒʊərɪ, deɪ ˈjuəreɪ/ rightful; by right. [Latin]

Dekker /ˈdekə/ Thomas *c.*1572-1632. English dramatist and pamphleteer, who wrote mainly in collaboration with others. His play *The Shoemaker's Holiday* 1600 was followed by collaborations with Thomas Middleton, John Webster, Philip Massinger, and others. His pamphlets include *The Gull's Hornbook* 1609, a satire on contemporary fashions.

dekko /ˈdekəʊ/ *n.* (*slang*) a look. [from Hindi]

De Klerk /də ˈkleək/ F(rederik) W(illem) 1936– . South African National Party politician, president from 1989. He trained as a lawyer, and entered the South African parliament in 1972. He served in the cabinets of B J Vorster and P W Botha 1978–89, and in Feb and Aug 1989 successively replaced Botha as National Party leader and state president. Projecting himself as a pragmatic conservative who sought gradual reform of the apartheid system, he won the Sept 1989 elections for his party, but with a reduced majority. In Feb 1990 he ended the ban on the ◊African National Congress opposition movement and released its effective leader, Nelson Mandela.

de Kooning /də ˈkuːnɪŋ/ Willem 1904– . Dutch-born US painter who immigrated to the USA in 1926 and worked as a commercial artist. After World War II he became, together with Jackson Pollock, one of the leaders of the Abstract Expressionist Movement. His *Women* series, exhibited in 1953, was criticized for its grotesque figurative style.

Delacroix /deləˈkrwɑː/ Eugène 1798–1863. French Romantic painter whose prolific output included religious and historical subjects and portraits of friends, among them the musicians Paganini and Chopin. Against French academic tradition, he evolved a highly coloured, fluid style, as in *The Death of Sardanapalus* 1827 (Louvre, Paris).

de la Mare /delə ˈmeə/ Walter 1873–1956. English poet, known for his verse for children, such as *Songs of Childhood* 1902, and the novels *The Three Royal Monkeys* 1910 for children and, for adults, *The Memoirs of a Midget* 1921.

de la Roche /delə ˈrɒʃ/ Mazo 1885–1961. Canadian novelist, author of the 'Whiteoaks' family saga.

Delaunay /dələʊˈneɪ/ Robert 1885–1941. French painter, a pioneer in abstract art. With his wife Sonia Delaunay-Terk he invented Orphism, an early variation on ◊Cubism, focusing on the effects of pure colour.

Delaunay-Terk /dələʊneɪˈteək/ Sonia 1885–1979. French painter and textile designer born in Russia, active in Paris from 1905. With her husband Robert Delaunay, she was a pioneer of abstract art.

De Laurentis /deɪ lɔːˈrentɪs/ Dino 1919– . Italian film producer. His early films, including Fellini's *La Strada/The Street* 1954, brought more acclaim than later epics such as *Waterloo* 1970. He then produced a series of Hollywood films: *Death Wish* 1974, *King Kong* (remake) 1976, and *Dune* 1984.

Delaware /ˈdeləweə/ state in NE USA; nickname First State/Diamond State; **area** 5,300 sq km/2,046 sq mi; **capital** Dover; **physical** divides into three areas: hilly; wooded; and gently undulating; **products** dairy, poultry, and market-garden produce; chemicals, motor vehicles, textiles; **population** (1987) 644,000; **history** Delaware was made a separate British colony in 1702 and organized as a state in 1776, one of the original 13 states of the USA.

de la Warr /ˈdeləweə/ Thomas West, Baron de la Warr 1577–1618. US colonial administrator, known as Delaware. Appointed governor of Virginia in 1609, he arrived in 1610 just in time to prevent the desertion of the Jamestown colonists, and by 1611 had revitalized the settlement. He fell ill, returned to England, and died during his return voyage to the colony in 1618. Both the river and state are named after him.

delay /dɪˈleɪ/ *v.t./i.* to make or be late, to hinder; to postpone, to defer; to wait, to loiter. —*n.* an act or process of delaying; a hindrance; the time lost by inaction or inability to proceed. —**delayed action** *adj.* operating after an interval of time. [from Old French]

Delbruck /ˈdelbrʊk/ Max 1906–1981. German-born US biologist who pioneered techniques in molecular biology, studying genetic changes occurring when viruses invade bacteria. He was awarded the Nobel Prize for Medicine in 1969.

Delcassé /delkæ'seɪ/ Théophile 1852–1923. French politician. He became foreign minister in 1898, but had to resign in 1905 because of German hostility; he held that post again from 1914–15. To a large extent he was responsible for the ◊*Entente Cordiale* with Britain.

delectable /dɪ'lektəbəl/ *adj.* delightful, enjoyable. —**delectably** *adv.* [from Old French from Latin *delectare* = delight)]

delectation /diːlek'teɪʃən/ *n.* enjoyment, delight. [from Old French]

delegacy /'delɪgəsɪ/ *n.* a body of delegates.

delegate /'delɪgət/ *n.* a person appointed as a representative; a member of a deputation or committee. —/-geɪt/ *v.t.* to appoint or send as a representative; to entrust (a task) *to* an agent. [from Latin *delegare* (*legare* = depute)]

delegation /deli'geɪʃən/ *n.* 1. delegating. 2. a body of delegates.

De Lesseps /dəle'seps/ Ferdinand, Vicomte. See de ◊Lesseps.

delete /dɪ'liːt/ *v.t.* to cross out or remove (a letter, word, etc.). —**deletion** *n.* [from Latin *delēre* = efface]

deleterious *adj.* harmful to the body or mind. [from Latin from Greek]

delft *n.* or **delftware** a kind of glazed earthenware, usually decorated in blue, made at Delft in Holland.

Delhi /'delɪ/ Union Territory of the Republic of India from 1956; capital New Delhi; area 1,500 sq km/579 sq mi; population (1981) 6,196,000. It produces grains, sugar cane, fruits, and vegetables.

deliberate /dɪ'lɪbərət/ *adj.* 1. intentional, fully considered. 2. unhurried, slow and careful. —/-reɪt/ *v.i.* to think carefully (about); to take counsel. —**deliberately** *adv.* [from Latin *deliberare* (*librare* = weigh from *libra* = balance)]

deliberation /dɪlɪbə'reɪʃən/ *n.* careful consideration; careful slowness. [from Old French from Latin]

deliberative /dɪ'lɪbərətɪv/ *adj.* of or for deliberation. [from French or Latin]

Delibes /də'liːb/ (Clement Philibert) Léo 1836–1891. French composer. His works include the ballet *Coppélia* and the opera *Lakmé* .

delicacy /'delɪkəsɪ/ *n.* 1. delicateness. 2. avoidance of immodesty or giving offence. 3. a choice food.

delicate /'delɪkət/ *adj.* 1. fine or pleasing in texture or construction etc.; (of colour or taste etc.) pleasantly subtle, not strong. 2. deft, sensitive; (especially of actions) considerate. 3. tender, easily harmed; liable to illness; requiring deftness or tact. 4. avoiding coarseness or impropriety. —**delicately** *adv.*, **delicateness** *n.* [from Old French or Latin]

delicatessen /delɪkə'tesən/ *n.* a shop selling prepared foods and delicacies; such food. [Dutch or German from French *délicatesse*]

delicious /dɪ'lɪʃəs/ *adj.* highly pleasing, especially to the taste or smell. —**deliciously** *adv.* [from Old French from Latin *deliciae* = delight]

delight /dɪ'laɪt/ *v.t./i.* 1. to please greatly. 2. to take great pleasure *in*; to be highly pleased *to* do. —*n.* great pleasure; a thing that gives it. [from Old French from Latin *delectare*]

delightful *adj.* giving delight. —**delightfully** *adv.*

Delilah /də'laɪlə/ *n.* in the Old Testament, the Philistine mistress of ◊Samson, who cut his hair and thereby stole his power.

delimit /dɪ'lɪmɪt/ *v.t.* to fix the limits or boundaries of. —**delimitation** /-'teɪʃən/ *n.* [from French from Latin *delimitare* (*limes* = boundary)]

delineate /dɪ'lɪnɪeɪt/ *v.t.* to show by a drawing or description. **delineation** /-'eɪʃən/ *n.* [from Latin *delineare* (*linea* = line)]

delinquent /dɪ'lɪŋkwənt/ *adj.* committing an offence; failing in a duty. —*n.* an offender (especially **juvenile delinquent**). —**delinquency** *n.* [from Latin *delinquere* = offend]

deliquesce /deli'kwes/ *v.i.* to become liquid, to melt; to dissolve in moisture absorbed from the air. —**deliquescence** *n.*, **deliquescent** *adj.* [from Latin *deliquescere* = begin to be liquid]

delirious /dɪ'lɪrɪəs/ *adj.* affected with delirium; raving, wildly excited; ecstatic. —**deliriously** *adv.*

delirium /dɪ'lɪrɪəm/ *n.* a disordered state of mind with incoherent speech and hallucinations; a mood of frenzied

Delphi Tholos in the Sanctuary of Athena ('Marmaria') in Delphi, Greece.

excitement. —**delirium tremens** /'triː menz/, a form of delirium with tremors and terrifying delusions due to prolonged consumption of alcohol. [Latin, from *delirare* = be deranged, originally = deviate from a ridge in ploughing]

Delius /'diːlɪəs/ Frederick (Theodore Albert) 1862–1934. English composer. His works include the the opera *A Village Romeo and Juliet* 1901; the choral pieces *Appalachia* 1903, *Sea Drift* 1904, *A Mass of Life* 1905; orchestral works such as *In a Summer Garden* 1908, *A Song of the High Hills* 1911; chamber music; and songs.

deliver /dɪ'lɪvə/ *v.t.* 1. to convey or distribute (letters or goods etc.) to a destination or destinations; to transfer possession of, to give *up* or hand *over* to another. 2. to utter (a speech or sermon); to aim or launch (a blow, attack, ball). 3. to set free, to rescue (*from*). 4. to assist at the birth of or in giving birth; (also **be delivered of**) to give birth to. —**deliver the goods**, (*colloquial*) to carry out one's part of a bargain. —**deliverer** *n.* [from Old French]

deliverance *n.* rescue, setting free.

delivery *n.* delivering, being delivered; the periodical distribution of letters or goods etc.; the manner of delivering a ball, speech etc. [from Anglo-French]

dell *n.* a small wooded hollow. [Old English]

Delon /də'lɒn/ Alain 1935– . French actor, who appeared in the films *Rocco e i suoi Fratelli/Rocco and his Brothers* 1960, *Il Gattopardo/The Leopard* 1963, *Texas across the River* 1966, *Scorpio* 1972, and *Swann in Love* 1984.

Deiors /də'lɔː/ Jacques 1925– . French socialist politician, finance minister 1981–84. As president of the European Commission from 1984 he has overseen significant budgetary reform and the move towards a free European Community market in 1992, with increased powers residing in Brussels.

delouse /diː'laus/ *v.t.* to rid of lice.

Delphi /'delfɪ/ *n.* city of ancient Greece, situated in a rocky valley N of the gulf of Corinth, on the S slopes of Mount Parnassus, site of a famous ◊oracle in the temple of Apollo. In the same temple was the *Omphalos*, a conical stone supposed to stand at the centre of the Earth. The oracle was interpreted by priests from the inspired utterances of the Pythian priestess until it was closed down by the Roman emperor Theodosius in AD 390. A European Cultural Centre was built nearby in 1966–67.

Delphic /'delfɪk/ *adj.* of or like the ancient Greek oracle at Delphi; obscure, enigmatic. [from *Delphi*]

delphinium /del'fɪnɪəm/ *n.* any plant of the genus *Delphinium* belonging to the buttercup family Ranunculaceae. There are some 250 species, including the great flowered larkspur *D. grandiflorum*, an Asian form and one of the ancestors of the garden delphinium. Most species have blue, purple, or white flowers in a long spike. [Latin from Greek = larkspur]

del Sarto /del 'sɑː tou/ Andrea 1486–1531. See ◊Andrea del Sarto, Italian Renaissance painter.

delta *n.* 1. the fourth letter of the Greek alphabet, = δ, Δ. 2. a triangular alluvial tract at a river's mouth enclosed or watered by diverging outlets; the shape of the Nile delta is like the Greek letter, and thus gave rise to the name. 3. a designation of the fourth-brightest star in a constellation, or sometimes the star's position in a group. —**deltaic** /del'teɪk/ *adj.* [Greek, from Phoenician *daleth* = door]

Delta Force US antiguerrilla force, based at Fort Bragg, North Carolina, and modelled on the British ◊Special Air Service.

delta wing an aircraft wing shaped like the Greek letter (Δ). Its design enables an aircraft to pass through the

◊sound barrier with little effect. The supersonic airliner Concorde and the US Space Shuttle have delta wings.

delude /dɪ'luːd/ v.t. to fool, to deceive. [from Latin *deludere* (*ludere* = play)]

deluge /'delju:dʒ/ n. 1. a great flood; **the Deluge,** Noah's flood. 2. a heavy fall of rain. 3. an overwhelming rush. —v.t. to flood; to overwhelm. [from Old French from Latin *diluvium*]

delusion /dɪ'luːʒən/ n. a false belief or impression; a vain hope; a hallucination. —**delusive** adj. [from Latin]

de luxe /də 'lʌks, 'luks/ of a superior kind or quality; sumptuous. [French = of luxury]

delve v.t./i. 1. to search (*into* books etc.) for information. 2. (*archaic*) to dig. [Old English]

demagnetize /diː'mægnɪtaɪz/ v.t. to remove the magnetization of. —**demagnetization** /-'zeɪʃən/ n.

demagogue /'deməgɒg/ n. a political agitator appealing to popular wishes or prejudices. —**demagogic** /-'gɒgɪk/ adj., **demagogy** /'dem-/ n. [from Greek *dēmos* = people and *agōgos* = leading]

de Maiziere Lothar 1940– . German politician, leader from 1989–90 of the conservative Christian Democratic Union in East Germany. He became premier after East Germany's first democratic election in April 1990 and negotiated the country's reunion with West Germany.

demand /dɪ'mɑːnd/ n. 1. a request made as of right or peremptorily; an urgent claim. 2. popular desire for goods or services. —v.t. 1. to make a demand for. 2. to insist on being told. 3. to require, to call for. —**in demand,** much sought after. **on demand,** as soon as asked for. [from Old French from Latin *demandare* (*mandare* = to commission)]

demanding adj. requiring much skill or effort; making many demands.

demarcation /diːmɑː'keɪʃən/ n. the marking of a boundary or limits, especially between work considered by trade unions to belong to different trades. [from Spanish *demarcar* = mark bounds of]

démarche /'deɪmɑːʃ/ n. a step or proceeding in diplomacy, especially one initiating a fresh policy. [French *démarcher* = take steps]

dematerialize /diːmə'tɪəriəlaɪz/ v.t./i. to make or become non-material or spiritual.

demean /dɪ'miːn/ v.t. to lower the dignity of.

demeanour /dɪ'miːnə/ n. bearing, outward behaviour. [from Old French from Latin *minare* = drive animals from *minari* = threaten]

demented /dɪ'mentɪd/ adj. driven mad, crazy. [from Old French or Latin *demens* = out of one's mind]

dementia /dɪ'menʃə/ n. insanity with loss of intellectual power due to brain disease or injury. —**dementia praecox** /'priː'kɒks/, schizophrenia. [Latin]

demerara /demə'reərə/ n. a kind of raw cane-sugar, originally and chiefly from Demerara, a region of Guyana, the crystals of which have a yellowish-brown colour.

demerit /diː'merɪt/ n. a fault, an undesirable quality. [from Old French or Latin *demerēri* = deserve]

demesne /dɪ'miːn, -meɪn/ n. 1. the land attached to a mansion etc.; territory, a domain; landed property, an estate. 2. possession (of land) as one's own. 3. a region or sphere (*of*). [from Anglo-French = belonging to a lord, from Latin *dominus* = lord]

Demeter /dɪ'miːtə/ in Greek mythology, goddess of agriculture (identified with Roman ◊Ceres), daughter of Kronos and Rhea, and mother of Persephone by Zeus. She is identified with the Egyptian goddess Isis and had a temple dedicated to her at Eleusis where ◊mystery religions were celebrated.

Demetrius /dɪ'miːtriəs/ Donskoi ('of the Don') 1350–1389. Grand prince of Moscow from 1363. He achieved the first Russian victory over the Tatars on the plain of Kulikovo, next to the river Don (hence his nickname) in 1380.

demi- /'demɪ/ prefix meaning half. [from French from Latin *dimidius*]

demigod /'demɪgɒd/ n. a partly divine being; the offspring of a mortal and a god or goddess; a godlike person.

demijohn /'demɪdʒɒn/ n. a large bottle in a wicker case. [corruption of French *dame-jeanne* = Lady Jane]

demilitarize /diː'mɪlɪtəraɪz/ v.t. to remove military organization or forces from (a zone etc.). —**demilitarization** /-'zeɪʃən/ n.

De Mille /də 'mɪl/ Agnes 1909– . US dancer and choreographer. One of the most significant contributors to the American Ballet Theater with dramatic ballets like *Fall River Legend* 1948, she also led the change on Broadway to new-style musicals with her choreography of *Oklahoma!* 1943, *Carousel* 1945, and others.

De Mille Cecil B(lount) 1881–1959. US film director and producer. He entered films in 1913 with Jesse L Lasky (with whom he later established Paramount Pictures), and was one of the founders of Hollywood. He specialized in biblical epics, such as *The Sign of the Cross* 1932 and *The Ten Commandments* 1923; remade in 1956. He also made the 1952 Academy Award-winning *The Greatest Show on Earth*.

demimondaine /demɪmɔ̃'deɪn/ n. a woman of the *demimonde*.

demimonde /'demɪmɒnd/ n. 1. women of doubtful repute in society. 2. a group behaving with doubtful legality etc. [French = half-world]

Demirel /demi'rel/ Suleyman 1924– . Turkish politician. Leader from 1964 of the Justice Party, he was prime minister 1965–71, 1975–77, and 1979–80. He favoured links with the West, full membership in the European Community, and foreign investment in Turkish industry.

demise /dɪ'maɪz/ n. 1. death. 2. transfer of an estate by lease or a will. —v.t. to transfer (an estate or title) to another. [from Anglo-French = abdicate]

demisemiquaver /demi'semɪkweɪvə/ n. a note in music equal to half a semiquaver.

demist /diː'mɪst/ v.t. to clear mist from (a windscreen etc.). —**demister** n.

De Mita /de'miːtə/ Luigi Ciriaco 1928– . Italian conservative politician, leader of the Christian Democratic Party (DC) from 1982, prime minister 1988–1990. He entered the Chamber of Deputies in 1963 and held a number of ministerial posts in the 1970s before becoming DC secretary-general.

demo /'deməu/ n. (*plural* **demos**) (*colloquial*) a demonstration, especially to express opinion.

demob /diː'mɒb/ v.t. (**-bb-**) (*colloquial*) to demobilize.

demobilize /diː'məubɪlaɪz/ v.t. to release from military service. —**demobilization** /-'zeɪʃən/ n.

democracy /dɪ'mɒkrəsɪ/ n. 1. government by all the people, direct or representative; a state having this. 2. a form of society ignoring hereditary class distinctions and tolerating minority views. [from French from Latin from Greek *dēmos* = the people]

democrat /'deməkræt/ n. 1. an advocate of democracy. 2. Democrat, (*US*) a member of the Democratic Party. [from French]

democratic /demə'krætɪk/ adj. of or according to democracy; supporting or constituting democracy. —**Democratic Party,** one of the two chief political parties in the USA (the other being the Republican Party). —**democratically** adv. [from French from Latin from Greek]

democratize /dɪ'mɒkrətaɪz/ v.t. to make democratic. —**democratization** /-'zeɪʃən/ n.

demodulation /diːmɒdju'leɪʃən/ n. the process of extracting a modulating radio signal from a modulated wave etc.

demography /dɪ'mɒgrəfɪ/ n. the study of statistics of births, deaths, diseases etc., as illustrating the conditions of life in communities. —**demographic** /demə'græfɪk/ adj., **demographically** adv. [from Greek *dēmos* = the people]

demolish /dɪ'mɒlɪʃ/ v.t. 1. to pull or knock down (a building); to destroy. 2. to refute (a theory); to overthrow (an institution). 3. (*jocular*) to eat up. —**demolition** /demə'lɪʃən/ n. [from French from Latin *demoliri* (*moliri* = construct]

demon /'diːmən/ n. 1. a devil, an evil spirit; a cruel or forceful person; a personified evil passion. 2. or **daemon** a supernatural being in Greek mythology. —**demonic** /dɪ'mɒnɪk/ adj. [from Latin from Greek *daimōn* = inferior deity, spirit]

demonetize /diː'mɒnɪtaɪz/ v.t. to withdraw (a coin etc.) from use as money. —**demonetization** /-'zeɪʃən/ n. [from French from Latin *moneta* = money]

demoniac /dɪ'məuniæk/ adj. 1. possessed by an evil spirit. 2. of or like a demon. 3. fiercely energetic, frenzied. —n. a demoniac person.

Dempsey *A fearless, aggressive fighter, 'Jack' Dempsey, known as the Manassa Mauler, was world heavyweight boxing champion from 1919–26.*

—**demoniacal** /di:məˈnaɪəkəl/ *adj.* [from Old French from Latin from Greek *daimonion* diminutive of *daimōn* = inferior deity]

demonology /di:məˈnɒlədʒɪ/ *n.* the study of beliefs about demons.

demonstrable /ˈdemənstrəbəl/ *adj.* able to be shown or proved. —**demonstrably** *adv.* [from Latin]

demonstrate /ˈdemənstreɪt/ *v.t./i.* 1. to show evidence of; to describe and explain by help of specimens or experiments; to prove the truth of logically. 2. to take part in a public demonstration. [from Latin *demonstrare* (*monstrare* = show)]

demonstration /demənˈstreɪʃən/ *n.* 1. demonstrating; an instance of this. 2. a show of feeling. 3. an organized gathering or procession to express the opinion of a group publicly. 4. a display of military force. [from Old French or Latin]

demonstrative /dɪˈmɒnstrətɪv/ *adj.* 1. showing or proving. 2. given to or marked by the open expression of feelings. 3. in grammar, of an adjective or pronoun, indicating the person or thing referred to (e.g. *this, those*). —**demonstratively** *adv.* [from Old French from Latin]

demonstrator /ˈdemənstreɪtə/ *n.* one who demonstrates; one who teaches by demonstration, especially in a laboratory. [from Latin]

demoralize /dɪˈmɒrəlaɪz/ *v.t.* to weaken the morale of, to dishearten. —**demoralization** /-ˈzeɪʃən/ *n.* [from French]

de Morgan /də ˈmɔːgən/ William Frend 1839–1917. English pottery designer who set up his own factory in 1888 in Fulham, London, producing tiles and pottery painted with flora and fauna in a style typical of the Arts and Crafts Movement.

Demosthenes /dɪˈmɒsθəniːz/ *c.*384–322 BC. Athenian orator and politician. From 351 BC he led the party that advocated resistance to the growing power of ◊Philip II of Macedon, and in his *Philippics* incited the Athenians to war. This policy resulted in the defeat of Chaeronea in 338, and the establishment of Macedonian supremacy. After the death of Alexander he organized a revolt; when it failed, he took poison to avoid capture by the Macedonians.

demote /diːˈməʊt/ *v.t.* to reduce to a lower rank or class. —**demotion** *n.*

demotic /dɪˈmɒtɪk/ *adj.* (of language or writing) of the popular form. —*n.* 1. demotic script, the popular simplified form of ancient Egyptian writing derived from Egyptian hieratic script, itself a cursive form of ◊hieroglyphic. Demotic documents are known from the 6th century BC to about AD 470. It was written horizontally, from right

to left. 2. the popular form of modern Greek. [from Greek *dēmos* = people]

Dempsey /ˈdempsi/ 'Jack' (William Harrison); nicknamed 'the Manassa Mauler'. 1895–1983. US heavyweight boxing champion. He beat Jess Willard in 1919 to win the title and held it until losing to Gene Tunney in 1926. He engaged in the 'Battle of the Long Count' with Tunney in 1927.

demur /dɪˈmɜː/ *v.t.* (**-rr-**) to raise objections, to be unwilling. —*n.* objecting (usually in *without demur*). [from Old French from Latin *morari* = delay]

demure /dɪˈmjʊə/ *adj.* quiet and serious or affectedly so. —**demurely** *adv.*, **demureness** *n.*

demurrer /dɪˈmʌrə/ *n.* a legal objection to the relevance of an opponent's point. [from Anglo-French]

den *n.* 1. a wild beast's lair. 2. a place of crime or vice. 3. a small private room for study etc. [Old English]

denarius /dɪˈneəriəs/ *n.* (*plural* **denarii** /-riaɪ/) an ancient Roman silver coin. [Latin *deni* = ten each]

denary *adj.* of ten, decimal. [from Latin]

denationalize /diːˈnæʃənəlaɪz/ *v.t.* to transfer (an industry, institution etc.) from national to private ownership. —**denationalization** /-ˈzeɪʃən/ *n.*

denature /diːˈneɪtʃə/ *v.t.* 1. to change the nature or properties of. 2. to make (alcohol) unfit for drinking. **denaturation** *n.* irreversible changes occurring in the structure of proteins such as enzymes, usually caused by changes in pH or temperature. An example is the heating of egg albumen resulting in solid egg white. [from French]

Denbighshire /ˈdenbiʃə/ former county of Wales, largely merged in 1974, together with Flint and part of Merioneth, in Clwyd; a small area along the W border was included in Gwynedd. Denbigh, in the Clwyd valley (population about 9,000), was the county town.

Dench /dentʃ/ Judi 1934– . British actress who made her professional debut as Ophelia in *Hamlet* in 1957 with the Old Vic Company. Her Shakespearean roles include Portia in *Twelfth Night*, Lady Macbeth, and Cleopatra. She is also a versatile comedy actress and has appeared in films, for example *A Room with a View* 1986, and on television.

dendrite *n.* part of a ◊nerve cell or neuron. The dendrites are slender filaments projecting from the cell body. They receive incoming messages from many other nerve cells and pass them on to the cell body. If the combined effect of these messages is strong enough, the cell body will send an electrical impulse along the axon (the threadlike extension of a nerve cell). The tip of the axon passes its message to the dendrites of other nerve cells.

dendrochronology /dendrəʊkrəˈnɒlədʒɪ/ *n.* a method of dating timber by study of its annual growth-rings. Samples of wood are obtained by means of a narrow metal tube that is driven into a tree to remove a core extending from the bark to the centre. Samples taken from timbers at an archaeological site can be compared with cores from old, living trees; the year when they were felled can be determined by locating the point where the rings of the two samples correspond. [from Greek *dendron* = tree and *chronology*]

dendrology /denˈdrɒlədʒɪ/ *n.* the study of trees. [from Greek *dendron* = tree]

dene /diːn/ *n.* a narrow wooded valley. [Old English]

Dene /ˈdeni/ *n.* a term applied to distinct but related indigenous people. In Canada, since the 1970s, it has been used to describe the Native Americans (Athabaskan Indians) in the Northwest Territories. The official body representing them is called the Dene Nation.

Deneb /ˈdeneb/ *n.* the brightest star in the constellation Cygnus, and the 19th brightest star in the sky. It is one of the greatest supergiant stars known, with a true luminosity of about 60,000 times that of the Sun. Deneb is about 1,800 light years from Earth.

Deneuve /dəˈnɜːv/ Catherine 1943– . French actress acclaimed for her performance in Roman Polanski's film *Repulsion* 1965. She also appeared in *Les Parapluies de Cherbourg/Umbrellas of Cherbourg* 1964, *Belle de jour* 1967, *Hustle* 1975, and *The Hunger* 1983.

dengue /ˈdengi/ *n.* an infectious tropical fever causing acute pain in the joints. [West Indian Spanish from Swahili]

Deng Xiaoping /ˈdʌŋ ʃaʊˈpɪŋ/ or **Teng Hsiao-ping** 1904– . Chinese political leader. A member of the Chinese Communist Party (CCP) from the 1920s, he took part in the Long March 1934–36. He was in the Politburo from 1955 until ousted in the Cultural Revolution 1966–69. Reinstated

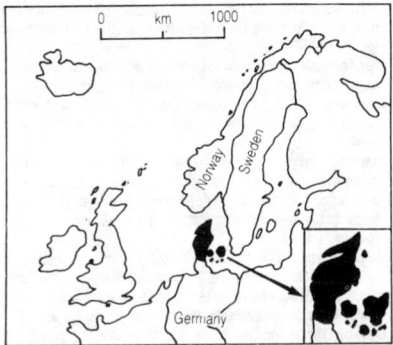

Denmark

in the 1970s, he gradually took power and introduced a radical economic modernization programme. He retired from the Politburo in 1987 and from his last official position (as chair of State Military Commission) in March 1990, but remained influential behind the scenes.

Den Haag /den 'hɑːx/ Dutch form of The ◊Hague town in the Netherlands.

deniable /dɪ'naɪəbəl/ *adj.* able to be denied.

denial /dɪ'naɪəl/ *n.* 1. denying. 2. refusal of a request or wish. 3. a statement that a thing is not true or existent. 4. a disavowal.

denier /'denjə/ *n.* a unit of weight for measuring the fineness of silk, rayon, or nylon yarn. [originally name of small coin; from Old French from Latin *denarius*]

denigrate /'denɪgreɪt/ *v.t.* to blacken the reputation of; to defame. —**denigration** /-'greɪʃən/ *n.*, **denigrator** *n.* [from Latin *denigrare* (*niger* = black)]

Denikin /dɪ'niːkɪn/ Anton Ivanovich 1872–1947. Russian general who distinguished himself in the ◊Russo-Japanese War 1904–05 and World War I. After the outbreak of the Bolshevik Revolution in 1917 he organized a volunteer army of 60,000 Whites (loyalists) but in 1919 was routed and escaped to France. He wrote a history of the Revolution and the Civil War.

denim /'denɪm/ *n.* a twilled cotton fabric used for overalls, jeans etc.; (in *plural*) a garment made of this. [for *serge de Nim* (*Nîmes* in S. France)]

De Niro /də 'nɪərəʊ/ Robert 1943– . US actor. He won Oscars for *The Godfather Part II* 1974 and *Raging Bull* 1979.

denitrification *n.* a process occurring naturally in soil, where bacteria break down ◊nitrates to give nitrogen gas, which returns to the atmosphere.

denizen /'denɪzən/ *n.* 1. an inhabitant or occupant (of a place). 2. a foreigner admitted to residence and certain rights. 3. a naturalized foreign word, animal, or plant. [from Anglo-French *deinz* = within from Latin *de intus*]

Denktash /'deŋktæʃ/ Rauf R 1924– . Turkish-Cypriot politician. In 1975 the Turkish Federated State of Cyprus (TFSC) was formed in the N third of the island, with Denktash as its head, and in 1983 he became president of the breakaway Turkish Republic of Northern Cyprus (TRNC).

Denmark /'denmɑːk/ Kingdom of; peninsula and islands in N Europe, bounded to the N by the Skagerrak, to the E by the Kattegat, to the S by Germany, and to the W by the North Sea; **area** 16,627 sq mi/43,075 sq km; **capital** Copenhagen; **physical** comprises the Jutland peninsula and about 500 islands (100 inhabited); the land is flat and cultivated; sand dunes and lagoons on the W coast and long inlets on the E; **head of state** Queen Margarethe II from 1972; **head of government** Poul Schlüter from 1982; **exports** bacon, dairy produce, eggs, fish, mink pelts, car and aircraft parts, electrical equipment, textiles, chemicals; **population** (1990 est) 5,134,000; **language** Danish (official); **recent history** occupied by Germany 1940. Recognized the independence of Iceland 1945 and granted home rule to the Faeroe Islands 1948. Founder member of NATO 1949; member of European Free Trade Association (EFTA) 1960–1973; joined European Community 1973. In 1972 Margrethe II became Denmark's first

queen in nearly 600 years; inconclusive general elections, minority governments and coalitions have dogged Danish politics since 1987.

Denning /'denɪŋ/ Alfred Thompson, Baron Denning of Whitchurch 1899– . British judge, Master of the Rolls 1962–82. In 1963 he conducted the inquiry into the ◊Profumo scandal. A vigorous and highly innovative civil lawyer, he was controversial in his defence of the rights of the individual against the state, the unions, and big business.

denominate /dɪ'nɒmɪneɪt/ *v.t.* to give a name to; to call or describe (a person or thing) as. [from Latin *denominare*]

denomination /dɪnɒmɪ'neɪʃən/ *n.* 1. a name or designation, especially a characteristic or class name. 2. a church or religious sect. 3. a class of units of measurement or money. [from Old French or Latin]

denominational /dɪnɒmɪ'neɪʃənəl/ *adj.* of a particular religious denomination.

denominator /dɪ'nɒmɪneɪtə/ *n.* the number below the line in a vulgar fraction, showing how many parts the whole is divided into, the divisor. —**least** *or* **lowest common denominator,** the lowest common multiple of the denominators of several fractions; the common feature of the members of a group. [from French or Latin]

denote /dɪ'nəʊt/ *v.t.* 1. to be the name for, to be the sign or symbol of. 2. to indicate, to give to understand; to signify. —**denotation** /dɪ:nəʊ'teɪʃən/ *n.* [from French or Latin *denotare* (*notare* = mark)]

dénouement /deɪ'nuːmɑ̃/ *n.* the unravelling of a plot, especially the final resolution in a play, novel etc. [French = unknotting]

denounce /dɪ'naʊns/ *v.t.* 1. to inform against, to accuse publicly. 2. to announce withdrawal from (a treaty etc.). [from Old French from Latin *denuntiare* = make known (*nuntius* = messenger)]

de novo /di: 'nəʊvəʊ/ afresh, starting again. [Latin]

Denpasar /den'pɑːsɑː/ capital of Bali in the Lesser Sunda Islands of Indonesia. Population (1980) 88,100.

dense *adj.* 1. closely compacted in substance; crowded together. 2. crass, stupid. —**densely** *adv.*, **denseness** *n.* [from French or Latin *densus*]

density /'densɪtɪ/ *n.* 1. closeness of substance. 2. the degree of consistency measured by the quantity of mass in a unit volume. 3. the opacity of a photographic image. —**relative density,** the ratio of the density of a substance to that of water at 4°C. [from French or Latin]

dent *n.* a depression in a surface left by a blow or pressure. —*v.t./i.* to make a dent in; to become dented.

dental /'dentəl/ *adj.* 1. of or for the teeth; dentistry. 2. (of a consonant) pronounced with the tongue-tip against the upper front teeth or the ridge of the teeth. —**dental floss,** fine, strong thread used to clean between the teeth. **dental surgeon,** a dentist. [from Latin *dentalis* (*dens* = tooth)]

dentate /'denteɪt/ *adj.* toothed, having toothlike notches. [from Latin *dentatus*]

dentifrice /'dentɪfrɪs/ *n.* a powder, paste etc., for cleaning the teeth. [French from Latin *dens* = tooth and *fricare* = rub]

dentine /'denti:n/ *n.* the hard, dense tissue forming the main part of teeth. [from Latin *dens* tooth]

dentist /'dentɪst/ *n.* a person who is qualified to treat the teeth, extract them, fit artificial ones etc. [from French from Latin *dens* = tooth]

dentistry *n.* the care and treatment of the teeth and gums. **Orthodontics** deals with the straightening of the teeth for aesthetic and clinical reasons, and **periodontics** with care of the supporting tissue (bone and gums).

dentition /den'tɪʃən/ *n.* 1. the type and arrangement of teeth in a species. There are several types of teeth, each having different functions. A grass-eating animal, for example, has well-developed molars for grinding its food; a meat-eater has large canines with which to catch and kill its prey. A species may have several types of teeth, but those that are least useful may be reduced in size or fail to develop. An animal's dentition is represented diagrammatically by a dental formula. 2. teething. [from Latin *dentire* = teethe]

denture /'dentʃə/ *n.* a set of artificial teeth. [French from Latin]

denude /dɪ'njuːd/ *v.t.* to make naked or bare; to strip of a covering, property etc. —**denudation** /di:nju:'deɪʃən/ *n.* [from Latin *denudare* = strip (*nudus* = naked)]

denunciation /dɪnʌnsɪ'eɪʃən/ *n.* denouncing. —**denunciatory** /dɪ'nʌnsɪətərɪ/ *adj.* [from French or Latin]

Denver /'denvə/ city and capital of Colorado, USA, on the South Platte river, near the foothills of the Rocky mountains; population (1980) 492,365, Denver-Boulder metropolitan area 1,850,000. It is a processing and distribution centre for a large agricultural area and for natural resources (minerals, oil, gas). It was the centre of a gold and silver boom in the 1870s and 1880s, and for oil in the 1970s.

deny /dɪ'naɪ/ *v.t.* 1. to declare untrue or nonexistent. 2. to disavow or repudiate. 3. to refuse (a request, applicant, thing *to* a person). —**deny oneself**, to restrict (one's food, drink, or pleasure). [from Old French from Latin *denegare* (*negare* = say no)]

deodar /'diːədɑː/ *n.* the Himalayan cedar *Cedrus deodara*, the tallest of the cedars (sometimes 60 m/200 ft in height), with pendulous tips to its slightly drooping branches and bearing large barrel-shaped cones. [from Hindi from Sanskrit = divine tree]

deodorant /diː'əʊdərənt/ *adj.* that removes or conceals unwanted odours. —*n.* a deodorant substance.

deodorize /diː'əʊdəraɪz/ *v.t.* to destroy the odour of. —**deodorization** /-'zeɪʃən/ *n.* [from Latin *odor* = smell]

Deo gratias thanks to God. [Latin]

deontology *n.* the ethical theory that the rightness of an action consists in its conformity to duty, regardless of the consequences that may result from it. Deontological ethics is thus opposed to any form of utilitarianism or pragmatism.

deoxyribonucleic acid /dɪɒksɪraɪbəʊnjuː'kliːɪk/ see ◊DNA.

dep. abbreviation of 1. departs. 2. deputy.

Depardieu /də'pɑːdjɜː/ Gerard 1948– . Versatile French actor who has appeared in the films *Deux hommes dans la ville* 1973, *Le camion* 1977, *Mon oncle d'Amérique* 1980, *The Moon in the Gutter* 1983, *Jean de Florette* 1985, and *Cyrano de Bergerac* 1990.

depart /dɪ'pɑːt/ *v.i.* to go away, to leave; (of a train, bus, etc.) to set out, to leave; to diverge or deviate. —**depart this life**, to die. [from Old French from Latin *dispertire* = divide]

departed *adj.* & *n.* bygone; (*the*) deceased.

department *n.* 1. a separate part of a complex whole, a branch, especially of a municipal or state administration, university, or shop. 2. an administrative district in France etc. 3. an area of activity. —**department store**, a large shop supplying many kinds of goods from various departments. —**departmental** /diːpɑːt'mentəl/ *adj.* [from French]

Department of Employment (DE) the UK government department responsible for manpower policies, the promotion of equal employment opportunities, the payment of unemployment benefits, the collection of labour statistics, the overseeing of industrial relations and the administration of employment legislation.

departure /dɪ'pɑːtʃə/ *n.* 1. going away; a deviation *from* (the truth, a standard); the starting of a train, aircraft etc. 2. setting out on a course of action or thought. [from Old French]

depend /dɪ'pend/ *v.i.* 1. (with *on* or *upon*, or *absolute*) to be controlled or determined by. 2. (with *on* or *upon*) to be unable to do without, to need for success etc. 3. to trust confidently, to feel certain about. 4. (*archaic*) to hang down. [from Old French from Latin *dependēre* (*pendēre* = hang)]

dependable *adj.* that may be depended on. —**dependability** /-'bɪlɪtɪ/ *n.*, **dependably** *adv.*

dependant *n.* one who depends on another for support. [from French]

dependence *n.* depending, being dependent; reliance.

dependency *n.* a country or province controlled by another.

dependent *adj.* 1. depending (*on*). 2. unable to do without something (especially a drug). 3. maintained at another's cost. 4. (of a clause, phrase, or word) in a subordinate relation to a sentence or word. —*n.* (*US*) = ◊dependant.

depict /dɪ'pɪkt/ *v.t.* to represent in drawing or colours; to portray in words, to describe. —**depiction** *n.* [from Latin *depingere* (*pingere* = paint)]

depilate /'depɪleɪt/ *v.t.* to remove hair from. —**depilation** /-'leɪʃən/ *n.* [from Latin *depilare* (*pilus* = hair)]

depilatory /dɪ'pɪlətərɪ/ *adj.* that removes unwanted hair. —*n.* a depilatory substance.

deplete /dɪ'pliːt/ *v.t.* to empty, to exhaust; to reduce the numbers or quantity of. —**depletion** *n.* [from Latin *deplere* (*plēre* = fill)]

deplorable /dɪ'plɔːrəbəl/ *adj.* lamentable, regrettable; exceedingly bad, shocking. —**deplorably** *adv.*

deplore /dɪ'plɔː/ *v.t.* to regret deeply; to find deplorable. [from French or Italian from Latin *deplorare* (*plorare* = bewail)]

deploy /dɪ'plɔɪ/ *v.t.* 1. to spread (troops) out from a column into a line. 2. to bring (forces, arguments etc.) into effective action. —**deployment** *n.* [from French from Latin *displicare* = scatter and *deplicare* = explain (*plicare* = fold)]

deponent /dɪ'pəʊnənt/ *adj.* (of a verb, especially in Greek and Latin) passive in form but active in meaning. —*n.* 1. a deponent verb. 2. a person making a deposition under oath. [from Latin *deponere* = put down, lay aside]

depopulate /diː'pɒpjʊleɪt/ *v.t.* to reduce the population of. —**depopulation** /-'leɪʃən/ *n.* [from Latin *depopulari* = lay waste (*populus* = people)]

deport /dɪ'pɔːt/ *v.t.* 1. to remove (an unwanted person) from a country. 2. to behave or conduct *oneself* (in a specified manner). [from Old French from Latin *deportare* (*portare* = carry)]

deportation /diːpɔː'teɪʃən/ *n.* the removal of an unwanted person from a country.

deportee /diːpɔː'tiː/ *n.* a person who has been or is to be deported.

deportment /dɪ'pɔːtmənt/ *n.* bearing, behaviour. [from French]

depose /dɪ'pəʊz/ *v.t.i.* 1. to remove from power; to dethrone. 2. to bear witness *that*, to testify *to*, especially on oath in court. [from Old French from Latin]

deposit /dɪ'pɒzɪt/ *n.* 1. a thing stored or entrusted for safe-keeping; a sum placed in a bank. 2. a sum required and paid as a pledge or first instalment. 3. a layer of precipitated matter, a natural accumulation. —*v.t.* 1. to store or entrust for keeping (especially a sum in a bank). 2. to pay as a pledge. 3. to lay down; (of water etc.) to leave (matter) lying. —**deposit account**, a savings account at a bank requiring notice for withdrawal. [from past participle of Latin *deponere* = put down, lay aside]

depositary /dɪ'pɒzɪtərɪ/ *n.* a person to whom a thing is entrusted. [from Latin]

deposition /depə'zɪʃən, diː-/ *n.* 1. deposing; a dethronement. 2. sworn evidence, the giving of this. 3. the taking down of Christ from the Cross. [from Old French from Latin]

depositor *n.* a person who deposits money or property.

depository /dɪ'pɒzɪtərɪ/ *n.* a storehouse; = ◊depositary. [from Latin]

depot /'depəʊ/ *n.* 1. a storehouse, especially one for military supplies. 2. the headquarters of a regiment. 3. a place where goods are deposited or from which goods, vehicles, etc., are dispatched; a bus station; (*US*) a railway station. [from French]

deprave /dɪ'preɪv/ *v.t.* to make morally bad, to corrupt. —**depravation** /deprə'veɪʃən/ *n.* [from Old French or Latin *depravare* (*pravus* = crooked)]

depravity /dɪ'prævɪtɪ/ *n.* moral corruption, wickedness. [from Latin]

deprecate /'deprɪkeɪt/ *v.t.* 1. to express a wish against or disapproval of. 2. to try to avert (a person's anger etc.). —**deprecation** /-'keɪʃən/ *n.*, **deprecatory** /'deprɪkətərɪ/ *adj.* [from Latin *deprecari* = pray (a thing) away]

depreciate /dɪ'priːʃɪeɪt/ *v.t.i.* 1. to diminish in value, price, or purchasing power. 2. to disparage, to belittle. [from Latin *depretiare* (*pretiare* = value from *pretium* = price)]

depreciation /dɪpriːsɪ'eɪʃən/ *n.* a decline in value, especially that due to wear and tear; the allowance made for this.

depreciatory /dɪ'priːʃətərɪ/ *adj.* disparaging.

depredation /deprɪ'deɪʃən/ *n.* (usually in *plural*) plundering, destruction. [from French from Latin *praedari* = plunder]

depress /dɪ'pres/ *v.t.* 1. to lower the spirits of, to sadden. 2. to reduce the activity of (especially trade). 3. to press down (a lever etc.). —**depressed area**, an area of economic depression. [from Old French from Latin *depressare* (*premere* = press)]

depression *A soup kitchen in Chicago during the Depression.*

depressant *adj.* causing depression. —*n.* a depressant agent or influence.

depression /dɪ'preʃən/ *n.* **1.** a state of extreme dejection, often with physical symptoms; clinical depression, which is prolonged or unduly severe, often requires treatment, such as antidepressant medication, ◊cognitive therapy, or, in very rare cases, electroconvulsive therapy (ECT), in which an electrical current is passed through the brain. **2.** a long period of financial and industrial slump. Specifically, the term the Depression describes two periods of crisis in the world economies: 1873–96 and 1929–mid-1930s. **3.** a lowering of atmospheric pressure; the winds caused by this. **4.** a sunken place or hollow on a surface. **5.** pressing down.

depressive *adj.* tending to depress; involving mental depression. —*n.* a person suffering from depression. [from French or Latin]

deprivation /deprɪ'veɪʃən/ *n.* depriving; loss of a desired thing.

deprive /dɪ'praɪv/ *v.t.* to prevent from the use or enjoyment *of*; to dispossess or strip *of*. —**deprived child**, one lacking a normal home life. [from Old French from Latin *deprivare* (*privare* = deprive)]

de profundis a cry from the depths of misery. From the Bible, Psalm 130: *De profundis clamavi AD te*; 'Out of the depths have I cried to thee'. [Latin = from the depths]

Dept. abbreviation of Department.

depth *n.* **1.** deepness; the measurement from the top down, from the surface inwards, or from the front to the back. **2.** profundity, abstruseness; sagacity. **3.** intensity of a colour, darkness etc. **4.** (often in *plural*) the deepest or most central part. —**depth charge**, a bomb exploding under water, for dropping on a submerged submarine etc. **in depth**, thoroughly. **in-depth** *adj.* thorough. **out of one's depth**, in water too deep to stand in; engaged on a task beyond one's powers.

deputation /depjʊ'teɪʃən/ *n.* a body of persons appointed to represent others. [from Latin]

depute /dɪ'pjuːt/ *v.t.* to delegate (a task) to a person; to appoint as one's deputy. [from Old French from Latin *deputare* = regard as, allot]

deputize /'depjʊtaɪz/ *v.i.* to act as deputy (*for*).

deputy /'depjʊtɪ/ *n.* **1.** a person appointed to act as a substitute for another. **2.** a parliamentary representative

in some countries. [from past participle of Old French *deputer*]

de Quincey /də 'kwɪnsi/ Thomas 1785–1859. English author, whose works include *Confessions of an English Opium-Eater* 1821 and the essays 'On the Knocking at the Gate in Macbeth' 1823 and 'On Murder Considered as One of the Fine Arts' 1827. He was a friend of the poets Wordsworth and Coleridge.

derail /dɪ'reɪl/ *v.t.* to cause (a train) to leave the rails. —**derailment** *n.* [from French]

derange /dɪ'reɪndʒ/ *v.t.* to throw into confusion, to disrupt; to make insane. —**derangement** *n.* [from French *rang* = rank, order]

Derby /'dɑːbi/ industrial city in Derbyshire, England; population (1981) 216,000. **products** rail locomotives, Rolls-Royce cars and airplane engines, chemicals, paper, electrical, mining and engineering equipment.

Derby *n.* **1.** an annual horse-race for three-year-olds, run over 2.4 km/1.5 mi on Epsom Downs in England on the last Wednesday in May or the first Wednesday in June. It was established in 1780 and named after the 12th earl of Derby. **2.** a similar race elsewhere. **3.** an important sporting contest.

Derby. abbreviation of Derbyshire.

Derby Edward (George Geoffrey Smith) Stanley, 14th Earl of Derby 1799–1869. British politician, prime minister 1852, 1858–59, and 1866–68. Originally a Whig, he became secretary for the colonies in 1830, and introduced the bill for the abolition of slavery. He joined the Tories in 1834, and the split in the Tory Party over Robert Peel's free-trade policy gave Derby the leadership for 20 years.

Derbyshire /'dɑːbiʃə/ county in N central England; **area** 2,630 sq km/1,015 sq mi; **administrative headquarters** Derby; **physical** 636 m/2,088 ft); rivers: Derwent, Dove, Rother, Trent; **products** cereals; dairy and sheep farming. There have been pit and factory closures, but the area is being redeveloped, and there are large reserves of fluorspar; **population** (1987) 919,000.

deregulation *n.* action to abolish or reduce state controls and supervision over private economic activities, as with the deregulation of the US airline industry in 1978. Its purpose is to improve competitiveness. In Britain the major changes in the City of London in 1986 (the ◊Big Bang) were in part deregulation.

derelict /ˈderɪlɪkt/ adj. abandoned, left to fall into ruin (especially of a ship at sea or decrepit property). —n. an abandoned property, especially a ship; a person forsaken by society, a social misfit. [from Latin *derelictus* (*relinquere* = leave behind)].

dereliction /deriˈlɪkʃən/ n. **1.** abandoning, being abandoned. **2.** neglect *of duty*. **3.** a shortcoming. [from Latin]

derestrict /diːriˈstrɪkt/ v.t. to remove a restriction (especially a speed-limit) from. —**derestriction** n.

deride /dɪˈraɪd/ v.t. to laugh scornfully at; to treat with scorn. [from Latin *deridēre* (*ridēre* = laugh)]

de rigueur /də riˈgɜː/ required by custom or etiquette. [French = of strictness]

derision /dɪˈrɪʒən/ n. scorn, ridicule. [from Old French from Latin]

derisive /dɪˈraɪsɪv/ adj. scornful, showing derision. —**derisively** adv.

derisory /dɪˈraɪsərɪ/ adj. **1.** showing derision. **2.** deserving derision; too insignificant for serious consideration. [from Latin]

derivation /deriˈveɪʃən/ n. **1.** deriving. **2.** the formation of a word from a word or root; the tracing or a statement of this. [from French or Latin]

derivative /dɪˈrɪvətɪv/ adj. derived from a source, not original. —n. **1.** a derivative word or thing. **2.** or **differential coefficient** in mathematics, the limit of the gradient of a chord between two points on a curve as the distance between the points tends to zero; a quantity measuring the rate of change of another. [from French from Latin]

derive /dɪˈraɪv/ v.t./i. **1.** to trace or obtain *from* a source. **2.** to originate, to be descended, *from*. **3.** to show or assert the descent or formation of (a word etc.) *from*. [from Old French or Latin *derivare* (*rivus* = stream)]

dermatitis /dɜːməˈtaɪtɪs/ n. inflammation of the skin (see ḍeczema), usually related to allergy. **Dermatosis** refers to any skin disorder and may be caused by contact or systemic problems. [from Greek *derma* = skin]

dermatology /dɜːməˈtɒlədʒɪ/ n. the study of the skin and its diseases. —**dermatologist** n.

dermis /ˈdɜːmɪs/ n. the layer of skin below the epidermis.

De Roburt /dəˈrɒbət/ Hammer 1923– . President of Nauru 1968–89, out of office 1976–78 and briefly in 1986. During the country's occupation 1942–45, he was deported to Japan. He became head chief of Nauru in 1956 and was elected the country's first president in 1968. In 1989 he was ousted on a no-confidence motion.

derogate /ˈderəgeɪt/ v.i. to detract *from* (a merit, right, etc.). —**derogation** /-ˈgeɪʃən/ n. [from Latin *derogare* (*rogare* = ask)]

derogatory /dɪˈrɒgətərɪ/ adj. involving disparagement or discredit; depreciatory.

derrick /ˈderɪk/ n. **1.** a kind of crane with an arm pivoted at the base of a central post or to a floor. **2.** the framework over an oil-well etc., holding the drilling machinery. [originally = gallows, from name of London hangman *c.*1600]

derring-do /ˈderɪŋˈduː/ n. (*literary*) heroic courage or action. [originally = *daring to do*]

derris /ˈderɪs/ n. **1.** a tropical climbing plant of the genus *Derris*. **2.** an insecticide made from its powdered root. [Latin from Greek = leather covering (in allusion to its pods)]

Derry /ˈderɪ/ county of Northern Ireland; **area** 2,070 sq km/799 sq mi; **county town** Derry (formerly Londonderry); Coleraine, Portstewart; **physical** rivers Foyle, Bann, and Roe; **products** mainly agricultural, but farming is hindered by the very heavy rainfall; flax, cattle, sheep, food processing, textiles, light engineering; **population** (1981) 187,000.

Derry /ˈderɪ/ (Gaelic *doire*, 'a place of oaks') historic city and port on the river Foyle, County Derry, Northern Ireland; population (1981) 89,100. Known as Londonderry until 1984, Derry dates from the foundation of a monastery by St Columba in AD 546. James I of England granted the borough and surrounding land to the citizens of London and a large colony of imported Protestants founded the present city which they named Londonderry. Textiles and chemicals are produced.

derv n. a fuel oil used in heavy road-vehicles. [from *diesel-engined road vehicle*]

dervish /ˈdɜːvɪʃ/ n. a member of any of several Sufi religious groups, vowed to poverty and austerity and holding

Descartes *An engraving of French philosopher and mathematician René Descartes from a portrait by Frans Hals.*

esoteric beliefs. There are various orders of dervishes, each with its rule and special ritual. The 'whirling dervishes' claim close communion with the deity through ecstatic dancing; the 'howling dervishes' gash themselves with knives to demonstrate the miraculous feats possible to those who trust in Allah. [from Turkish from Persian = poor, a mendicant]

Derwent /ˈdɜːwənt/ river in N Yorkshire, NE England; length 112 km/70 mi. Rising in the N Yorkshire moors, it joins the river Ouse SE of Selby. Other rivers of the same name in the UK are found in Derbyshire (96 km/60 mi), Cumbria (56 km/35 mi), and Northumberland (26 km/16 mi).

Desai /deˈsaɪ/ Morarji 1896– . Indian politician. An early follower of Mahatma Gandhi, he was prime minister from 1977–79, as leader of the ◊Janata party, after toppling Indira Gandhi. Party infighting led to his resignation of both the premiership and the party leadership.

desalinate /diːˈsælɪneɪt/ v.t. to remove the salt from (especially sea-water) to produce fresh water for irrigation or drinking. Distillation has usually been the method adopted, but in the 1970s a cheaper process, using certain polymer materials that filter the molecules of salt from the water by reverse osmosis, was developed. —**desalination** /-ˈneɪʃən/ n.

descant /ˈdeskænt/ n. a free soprano part added to a tune; (*poetic*) a song, a melody. —/dɪsˈkænt/ v.i. to talk lengthily *upon*. [from Old French from Latin *cantus* = song]

The greatest spirits are capable of the greatest vices as well as of the greatest virtues.

René Descartes
Discourse on Method

Descartes /deɪˈkɑːt/ René 1596–1650. French mathematician and philosopher who believed that commonly accepted knowledge was doubtful because of the subjective nature of the senses, and attempted to rebuild human knowledge using as his foundation '*cogito ergo sum*' ('I think, therefore I am'). He also believed that the entire material universe could be explained in terms of mathematical physics. He is regarded as the discoverer of analytical geometry and the founder of the science of optics, and also helped to shape contemporary theories of astronomy and animal behaviour.

descend /dɪ'send/ v.t./i. 1. to go or come down; to slope downwards. 2. to make a sudden attack or unexpected visit (on). 3. to sink or stoop to (an unworthy act), to pass by inheritance to. —**be descended from**, to come by descent from (a specified person etc.). [from Old French from Latin descendere (scandere = climb)]

descendant n. a person descended from another. [from French]

descent /dɪ'sent/ n. 1. the act of descending. 2. a way by which one may descend; a downward slope. 3. lineage, family origin. 4. a sudden attack. 5. decline, fall.

Deschamps /deɪ'ʃɒm/ Eustache 1346–1406. French poet, born in Champagne, who was the author of more than 1,000 ballades, and the Miroir de mariage/The Mirror of Marriage, an attack on women.

describe /dɪ'skraɪb/ v.t. 1. to set forth in words; to recite the characteristics of. 2. to mark out, to draw, to move in (a specified line or curve). [from Latin describere (scribere = write)]

description /dɪ'skrɪpʃə)n/ n. 1. describing; an account or verbal picture. 2. a sort or class.

descriptive /dɪ'skrɪptɪv/ adj. serving or seeking to describe; (of linguistics or grammar etc.) studying the structure of a language at a given time, avoiding comparisons with other languages or other historical phases and without social evaluations.

descry /dɪ'skraɪ/ v.t. to catch sight of, to succeed in discerning. [from Old French descrier; originally = announce, proclaim]

desecrate /'desɪkreɪt/ v.t. to treat (a sacred thing) with irreverence or disrespect. —**desecration** /-'kreɪʃən/ n., **desecrator** n.

desegregate /di:'segrɪgeɪt/ v.t. to abolish racial segregation in. —**desegregation** /-'geɪʃən/ n.

deselection n. in Britain, the removal or withholding of a sitting member of Parliament's official status as a candidate for a forthcoming election. The term came into use in the 1980s with the efforts of many local Labour parties to revoke the candidature of MPs viewed as too right-wing.

desert[1] /dɪ'zɜ:t/ v.t./i. to abandon, to leave without intention of returning; to leave military service unlawfully. —**deserter** n., **desertion** n. [from French from Latin deserere = forsake]

desert[2] /'dezət/ n. an area without sufficient rainfall and, consequently, vegetation to support human life. Scientifically, this term includes the ice areas of the polar regions. Almost 33% of Earth's land surface is desert, and this proportion is increasing. —adj. uninhabited, barren. [from Old French from Latin desertus]

desert[3] /dɪ'zɜ:t/ n. 1. deserving, being worthy of reward or punishment. 2. (in plural) a deserved recompense. [from Old French]

desertification n. the creation of deserts by changes in climate, or by human-aided processes such as overgrazing, destruction of forest belts, and exhaustion of the soil by too intensive cultivation without restoration of fertility; all usually prompted by the pressures of expanding populations. The process can be reversed by special planting (marram grass, trees) and by the use of water-absorbent plastic grains (a polymer absorbent of 40 times its own weight of water), which, added to the sand, enable crops to be grown. About 135 million people are directly affected by desertification, mainly in Africa, the Indian subcontinent, and South America.

Desert Orchid one of the most popular steeplechase horses in Britain. It has won more than 30 National Hunt races, including the King George VI Chase 1986, 1988–89, Cheltenham Gold Cup 1989, and the 1990 Irish Grand National.

deserve /dɪ'zɜ:v/ v.t. to be entitled to, especially by one's conduct or qualities. [from Old French from Latin deservire (servire = serve)]

deservedly /dɪ'zɜ:vɪdlɪ/ adv. as deserved, justly.

deserving adj. worthy (of), worth rewarding or supporting.

déshabillé /deɪzæ'bi:eɪ/ n. the state of being only partly dressed. [French = undressed]

de Sica /deɪ'si:kə/ Vittorio 1902–1974. Italian film director and actor. He won his first Oscar with Bicycle Thieves

1948, a film of subtle realism. Later films included Umberto D 1952, Two Women 1960, and The Garden of the Finzi-Continis 1971.

desiccate /'desɪkeɪt/ v.t. to remove the moisture from; to dry (a foodstuff) to preserve it. —**desiccation** /-'keɪʃən/ n., **desiccator** n. [from Latin desiccare (siccus = dry)]

desiccator n. an airtight vessel, traditionally made of glass, in which materials may be stored either to dehydrate them or to prevent them, once dried, from reabsorbing moisture.

desideratum /dɪsɪdə'reɪtəm/ n. (plural **desiderata** /-'rɑ:-/) a thing that is lacking but needed or desired. [Latin]

design /dɪ'zaɪn/ n. 1. a preliminary outline or drawing for something that is to be made; the art of producing these. 2. a scheme of lines or shapes forming a decoration. 3. a general arrangement or layout; an established form of a product. 4. an intention or purpose; a mental plan, a scheme of attack or approach. —v.t./i. 1. to prepare a design for; to be a designer. 2. to intend or set aside for some purpose. —**by design**, on purpose. **have designs on**, to plan to harm or appropriate. [from French from Latin]

designate /'dezɪgneɪt/ v.t. 1. to specify, to indicate as having some function. 2. to describe as, to give or serve as a name or distinctive mark to. 3. to appoint to a position. —/-nət/ adj. appointed to but not yet installed in office. [from Latin designare (signum = mark)]

designation /dezɪg'neɪʃən/ n. designating; a name or title. [from Old French or Latin]

Design Centre exhibition spaces in London and Glasgow established in 1956 by the Council of Industrial Design (set up by the government in 1944 to improve standards in British products) to act as a showcase for goods deemed to be of a high standard of design.

designedly /dɪ'zaɪnɪdlɪ/ adv. intentionally.

designer n. one who makes designs, especially for clothes or manufactured products.

designing adj. crafty, scheming.

desirable adj. worth having or wishing for; causing desire; (of a course of action) advisable.

desire /dɪ'zaɪə/ n. 1. an unsatisfied longing, a feeling of potential pleasure or satisfaction in obtaining or possessing something. 2. an expression of this, a request. 3. an object of desire. 4. strong sexual urge. —v.t./i. to have a desire for; to ask for; (archaic) to wish. —**leaves much to be desired**, is very imperfect. [from Old French from Latin desiderare = long for]

desirous predic. adj. having a desire, desiring. [from Anglo-French]

desist /dɪ'zɪst, -'sɪst/ v.i. to cease (from). [from Old French from Latin desistere (sistere = stop)]

desk n. 1. a piece of furniture with a flat or sloped surface serving as a rest for writing or reading at. 2. a counter behind which a receptionist or cashier sits. 3. the section of a newspaper office dealing with specified topics. 4. the position of the music-stand at which a player (especially of a stringed instrument) sits in an orchestra. [from Latin]

desktop publishing (DTP) the use of microcomputers for small-scale typesetting and page make-up. DTP systems are capable of producing camera-ready pages (pages ready for photographing and printing), made up of text and graphics, with text set in different typefaces and sizes. The page can be previewed on the screen before final printing on a laser printer.

Desmoulins /deɪmu:'læn/ Camille 1760–1794. French revolutionary who summoned the mob to arms on 12 July 1789, so precipitating the revolt that culminated in the storming of the Bastille. A prominent ◊Jacobin, he was elected to the National Convention in 1792. His Histoire des Brissotins was largely responsible for the overthrow of the ◊Girondins, but shortly after he was sent to the guillotine as too moderate.

desolate /'desələt/ adj. 1. left alone, solitary. 2. deserted, uninhabited, barren, dismal. 3. forlorn and wretched. —/-leɪt/ v.t. 1. to depopulate, to devastate. 2. to make (a person) wretched. [from Latin desolatus (solus = alone)]

desolation /desə'leɪʃən/ n. 1. a desolate or barren state. 2. being forsaken, loneliness. 3. grief, wretchedness.

de Soto /də 'səʊtəʊ/ Hernando c.1496–1542. Spanish explorer who sailed with d'Avila (c.1400–1531) to Darien, Central America, 1519, explored the Yucatán Peninsula

1528, and travelled with Pizarro in Peru 1530–35. In 1538 he was made governor of Cuba and Florida. In his expedition of 1539, he explored Florida, Georgia, and the Mississippi River.

despair /dɪs'peə/ n. complete loss or absence of hope; a thing that causes this. —v.i. to lose all hope (of). [from Old French from Latin desperare (sperare = hope)]

despatch variant of **dispatch**.

desperado /despə'rɑːdəʊ/ n. (plural **desperadoes**) a desperate or reckless person, especially a criminal.

desperate /'despərət/ adj. 1. leaving no or little room for hope; extremely dangerous or serious. 2. reckless from despair; violent, lawless. 3. staking all on a small chance. —**desperately** adv.

desperation /despə'reɪʃən/ n. despair; a reckless state of mind, readiness to take any way out of a desperate situation. [from Latin]

despicable /'despɪkəbəl, dɪ'spɪk-/ adj. deserving to be despised, contemptible. —**despicably** adv. [from Latin despicari = despise]

despise v.t. to regard as inferior or worthless; to feel contempt for. [from Old French from Latin despicere = look down on (specere = look at)]

despite /dɪ'spaɪt/ prep. in spite of. —n. (literary) 1. disdain. 2. malice, hatred. [from Old French from Latin despectus]

despoil /dɪ'spɔɪl/ v.t. (literary) to plunder, to rob. —**despoliation** /dɪspəʊli'eɪʃən/ n. [from Old French or Latin]

despond /dɪ'spɒnd/ v.i. to lose heart, to be dejected. [from Latin despondēre = abandon (spondēre = promise)]

despondent /dɪ'spɒndənt/ adj. having lost heart, dejected. —**despondency** n., **despondently** adv.

despot /'despɒt/ n. an absolute ruler; a tyrant. [from French from Latin from Greek despotēs = master]

despotic /de'spɒtɪk/ adj. having unrestricted power, tyrannous. —**despotically** adv.

despotism /'despətɪzəm/ n. rule by a despot; a country ruled by a despot.

Desprez /deɪ'preɪ/ Josquin Franco-Flemish composer; see ◊Josquin Desprez.

Dessalines /desæ'liːn/ Jean Jacques c.1758–1806. Emperor of Haiti 1804–06. Born in Guinea, he was taken to Haiti as a slave, where in 1802 he succeeded ◊Toussaint L'Ouverture as leader of the black revolt against the French. After defeating the French, he proclaimed Haiti's independence and made himself emperor. He was killed when trying to suppress an uprising provoked by his cruelty.

dessert /dɪ'zɜːt/ n. the sweet course of a meal; a course of fruit, nuts etc., at the end of dinner. [from French desservir = clear the table]

dessertspoon n. a spoon between a tablespoon and a teaspoon in size. —**dessertspoonful** n. (plural **dessertspoonfuls**)

destination /destɪ'neɪʃən/ n. a place to which a person or thing is going. [from Old French and Latin]

destine /'destɪn/ v.t. to settle or determine the future of; to appoint, to set apart for a purpose. [from French from Latin destinare]

destiny /'destɪnɪ/ n. fate considered as a power; what is destined to happen to a person etc.; the predetermined course of events. [from Old French]

destitute /'destɪtjuːt/ n. adj. without resources, in great need of food, shelter etc.; devoid of. —**destitution** /-'tjuːʃən/ n.[from Latin destituere = forsake (statuere = place)]

destroy /dɪ'strɔɪ/ v.t. 1. to pull or break down; to make useless. 2. to kill (especially a sick or unwanted animal) deliberately. 3. to nullify, to neutralize the effect of; to put out of existence. [from Old French from Latin destruere (struere = build)]

destroyer n. 1. a person or thing that destroys. 2. a fast warship designed to protect other ships. Destroyers played a critical role in the ◊convoy system in World War II. Modern destroyers often carry guided missiles and displace 3,700–5,650 tonnes.

destruct /dɪ'strʌkt/ v.t./i. (US) to destroy (one's own equipment) deliberately; to be destroyed thus. —n. (US) the action of destructing. [from Latin]

destructible adj. able to be destroyed. [French or from Latin]

destruction /dɪ'strʌkʃən/ n. destroying, being destroyed; a cause of this. [from Old French from Latin]

destructive /dɪ'strʌktɪv/ adj. 1. destroying, causing destruction. 2. (of criticism etc.) merely negative, refuting etc. without offering amendments or alternatives.

desuetude /dɪ'sjuːɪtjuːd/ n. a state of disuse. [from French or Latin desuetudo (suescere = be accustomed)]

desultory /'desəltərɪ/ adj. going constantly from one subject to another; disconnected, unmethodical. —**desultorily** adv., **desultoriness** n. [from Latin desultor = one who vaults, from salire = leap]

detach /dɪ'tætʃ/ v.t. 1. to unfasten or separate and remove (from). 2. to send (part of a force) on a separate mission. [from French]

detached adj. 1. separate, standing apart. 2. unemotional, impartial.

detachment n. 1. detaching, being detached. 2. a lack of emotion or concern, impartiality. 3. a portion of an army etc. separately employed. [from French]

detail /'diːteɪl/ n. 1. an item, a small or subordinate particular; these collectively, the treatment of them. 2. minor decoration in a building, picture etc. 3. a small military detachment. —v.t. 1. to give particulars of, to describe fully. 2. to assign for special duty. —**in detail**, describing the individual parts or events fully. [from French tailler = cut]

detailed adj. having or involving many details; thorough.

detain /dɪ'teɪn/ v.t. 1. to keep in confinement or under restraint. 2. to keep waiting, to delay. [from Old French from Latin detinēre (tenēre = hold)]

detainee /diːteɪ'niː/ n. a person detained in custody, usually on political grounds.

detect /dɪ'tekt/ v.t. to discover the existence or presence of; to discover (a person) in the performance of some wrong or secret act. —**detector** n. [from Latin detegere (tegere = cover)]

detectable adj. that may be detected.

detection /dɪ'tekʃən/ n. detecting, being detected; the work of a detective.

detective /dɪ'tektɪv/ n. a person, especially a member of a police force, employed to investigate crimes. —adj. serving to detect.

détente /deɪ'tɑːt/ n. the easing of strained relations, especially between states. [French = relaxation]

detention /dɪ'tenʃən/ n. detaining, being detained; being kept in school after hours as a punishment. —**detention centre**, an institution for the brief detention of young offenders. [from French or Latin]

deter /dɪ'tɜː/ v.t. (-rr-) to discourage or prevent (from) through fear or dislike of the consequences. —**determent** n. [from Latin deterrēre (terrēre = frighten)]

detergent /dɪ'tɜːdʒənt/ n. a cleansing agent, especially a synthetic substance used with water for removing dirt etc. The common detergents are made from fats (hydrocarbons) and sulphuric acid, and their long-chain molecules have a type of structure similar to that of soap molecules: a salt group at one end attached to a long hydrocarbon 'tail'. They have the advantage over soap in that they do not produce scum by forming insoluble salts with the calcium and magnesium ions present in hard water. —adj. cleansing. [from Latin detergēre (tergēre = wipe)]

deteriorate /dɪ'tɪərɪəreɪt/ v.t./i. to make or become worse. —**deterioration** /-'reɪʃən/ n. [from Latin deterior = worse]

determinant /dɪ'tɜːmɪnənt/ adj. determining, decisive. —n. 1. a determining factor. 2. the quantity obtained by adding the products of the elements of a square matrix according to a certain rule. [from Latin]

determinate /dɪ'tɜːmɪnət/ adj. limited, of definite scope or nature.

determination /dɪtɜːmɪ'neɪʃən/ n. 1. firmness of purpose, resoluteness. 2. the process of deciding, determining, or calculating. [from Old French from Latin]

determinative /dɪ'tɜːmɪnətɪv/ adj. serving to define, qualify, or direct. —n. a determinative thing. [from French]

determine /dɪ'tɜːmɪn/ v.t./i. 1. to find out or calculate precisely; to settle, to decide; to be the decisive factor in regard to. 2. to decide firmly, to resolve. —**be determined**, to have decided firmly. [from Old French from Latin determinare (terminus = end, limit)]

determined *adj.* showing determination, resolute, unflinching. —**determinedly** *adv.*

determinism /diˈtɜːmɪnɪzəm/ *n.* the theory that human action is not free but is determined by motives regarded as external forces acting on the will. —**determinist** *n.*, **deterministic** /-ˈnɪstɪk/ *adj.*

deterrence *n.* the belief that a potential aggressor will be discouraged from launching a 'first strike' nuclear attack by the knowledge that the adversary is capable of inflicting 'unacceptable damage' in a retaliatory strike. This doctrine is widely known as that of **mutual assured destruction (MAD)**. Three essential characteristics of deterrence are: the 'capability to act', 'credibility', and the 'will to act'. **deterrent** /diˈterənt/ *adj.* deterring. —*n.* a deterrent thing or factor. [from Latin]

detest /diˈtest/ *v.t.* to hate, to loathe. —**detestation** /-ˈsteɪʃən/ *n.* [from Latin *detestari* = call to witness]

detestable *adj.* intensely disliked, hateful.

dethrone /diːˈθrəʊn/ *v.t.* to remove from a throne, to depose. —**dethronement** *n.*

de Tocqueville Alexis. See ◊Tocqueville, Alexis de.

detonate /ˈdetəneɪt/ *v.t./i.* to explode or cause to explode with a loud report. —**detonation** /-ˈneɪʃən/ *n.* [from Latin *detonare* (*tonare* = thunder)]

detonator *n.* or **blasting cap** or **percussion cap** a small explosive charge used to trigger off a main charge of high explosive. The relatively unstable compounds mercury fulminate and lead acid are often used in detonators, being set off by a lighted fuse or, more commonly, an electric current.

detour /ˈdiːtʊə/ *n.* a divergence from one's direct or intended route, a roundabout course. [from French *détourner* = turn away]

detract /diˈtrækt/ *v.t./i.* to take away (some amount) *from* a whole. —**detract from**, to reduce the credit due to, to depreciate. —**detraction** *n.*, **detractor** *n.* [from Latin *detrahere* (*trahere* = draw)]

detriment /ˈdetrɪmənt/ *n.* harm, damage; a thing causing this. —**detrimental** /-ˈmentəl/ *adj.*, **detrimentally** *adv.* [from Old French or Latin *detrimentum* (*deterere* = wear away)]

detritus /diˈtraɪtəs/ *n.* matter produced by erosion, as gravel or rock-debris; in biology, the organic debris produced during the ◊decomposition of animals and plants. [from French from Latin]

Detroit /diˈtrɔɪt/ city in Michigan, USA, situated on Detroit River; population (1980) 1,203,339, metropolitan area 4,353,000. It is an industrial centre with the headquarters of Ford, Chrysler, and General Motors, hence its nickname, Motown (from 'motor town'). Other manufactured products include metal products, machine tools, chemicals, office machines, and pharmaceuticals. Detroit is a port on the St Lawrence Seaway and the home of Wayne State University and its Medical Center complex. The University of Detroit and the Detroit Institute of Arts are also here.

de trop /də ˈtrəʊ/ not wanted, in the way. [French = excessive]

deuce[1] /djuːs/ *n.* 1. (in tennis) the score of 40 all, at which two consecutive points are needed to win. 2. the two on dice. [from Old French from Latin *duos* (*duo* = two)]

deuce[2] /djuːs/ *n.* misfortune, the Devil (*colloquial* used especially as an exclamation of surprise or annoyance). [from Low German *duus*, the two at dice being the worst throw]

deuced /ˈdjuːsɪd, djuːst/ *adj. & adv.* damned.

deus ex machina /ˈdeɪəs eks ˈmækɪnə/ an unexpected power or event saving a seemingly impossible situation, especially in a play or novel. [Latin translated from Greek = god from the machinery (with reference to the machinery by which, in ancient Greek theatre, gods were shown in the air)]

deuterium /djuːˈtɪəriəm/ *n.* a naturally occuring heavy isotope of hydrogen, mass number 2 (one proton and one neutron), discovered by Harold Urey in 1932. In nature, about one in every 6,500 hydrogen atoms is deuterium. The symbol D is sometimes used for it. Combined with oxygen, it produces 'heavy water', D_2O, used in the nuclear industry. [from Greek *deuteros* = second]

deuteron /ˈdjuːtərɒn/ *n.* the nucleus of an atom of deuterium (heavy hydrogen). It consists of one proton and

one neutron, and is used in the bombardment of chemical elements to synthesize other elements.

Deuteronomy /djuːtəˈrɒnəmi/ *n.* a book of the Old Testament; fifth book of the ◊Torah. It contains various laws, including the ten commandments, and gives an account of the death of Moses.

Deutschmark /ˈdɔɪtʃmɑːk/ *n.* the currency unit in Germany. [German = German mark]

de Valera /də vəˈleərə/ Eamon 1882–1975. Irish nationalist politician, prime minister of the Irish Free State/Eire/Republic of Ireland 1932–48, 1951–54, and 1957–59, and president 1959–73. Repeatedly imprisoned, he participated in the Easter Rising 1916 and was leader of the nationalist ◊Sinn Féin party 1917–26, when he formed the republican ◊Fianna Fáil party; he directed negotiations with Britain in 1921 but refused to accept the partition of Ireland until 1937.

de Valois /də ˈvælwɑː/ Ninette. Stage name of Edris Stannus 1898– . Irish dancer, choreographer, and teacher. A pioneer of British national ballet, she worked with Diaghilev in Paris before opening a dance academy in London in 1926. Collaborating with Lilian Baylis at the ◊Old Vic, she founded the Vic-Wells Ballet 1931, which later became the Royal Ballet and Royal Ballet School. Among her works are *Job* in 1931 and *Checkmate* 1937.

devalue /diːˈvæljuː/ *v.t.* to reduce the value of, to reduce the value of (a currency) in relation to other currencies or to gold. —**devaluation** /-ˈeɪʃən/ *n.*

Devanagari /deɪvəˈnɑːɡəri/ *n.* the alphabet in which Sanskrit, Hindi, and several North Indian languages are usually written. [Sanskrit = of the divine town]

devastate /ˈdevəsteɪt/ *v.t.* to lay waste, to cause great destruction to. —**devastation** /-ˈsteɪʃən/ *n.* [from Latin *devastare* (*vastare* = lay waste)]

devastating *adj.* crushingly effective, overwhelming.

develop /diˈveləp/ *v.t./i.* 1. to make or become bigger, fuller, or more elaborate or systematic; to bring or come to an active or visible state or to maturity, to reveal or be revealed. 2. to begin to exhibit or suffer from. 3. to construct new buildings on (land); to convert (land) to a new use so as to use its resources. 4. to treat (a photographic film etc.) to make the picture visible. —**developing country**, a poor or primitive country that is developing better economic and social conditions. —**developer** *n.* [from French *développer*]

development *n.* 1. developing, being developed. 2. a thing that has developed, especially an event or circumstance. 3. developed land. 4. in music, elaboration of a theme, especially in the second part of a movement in sonata form. —**development area**, one where new industries are encouraged in order to counteract unemployment there. —**developmental** /-ˈmentəl/ *adj* .

development aid see ◊aid, development.

developmental psychology the study of the development of cognition and behaviour from birth to adulthood.

deviance *n.* abnormal behaviour; that is, behaviour that deviates from the norms or the laws of a society or group, and so invokes social sanctions, controls, or stigma. The term may refer to minor abnormalities (such as nail-biting) as well as to criminal acts.

deviant /ˈdiːviənt/ *adj.* that deviates from the normal. —*n.* a deviant person or thing.

deviate /ˈdiːvieɪt/ *v.i.* to turn aside or diverge (*from* a course of action, rule etc.). —**deviator** *n.* [f Latin *deviare* (*via* = way)]

deviation /diːviˈeɪʃən/ *n.* deviating; departing from an accepted political (especially Communist) doctrine. —**deviationist** *n.* [from French from Latin]

device /diˈvaɪs/ *n.* 1. a thing made or adapted for a particular purpose. 2. a plan, a scheme; a trick. 3. an emblematic or heraldic design. —**leave a person to his or her own devices**, to do as he or she wishes without help or advice. [from Old French from Latin]

devil /ˈdevəl/ *n.* 1. the supreme spirit of evil (usually **the Devil**); an evil spirit, a demon, a superhuman malignant being; a personified evil spirit, force, or quality. 2. a wicked or cruel person; a mischievously energetic, clever, or self-willed person. 3. (*colloquial*) a person, a fellow. 4. fighting spirit, mischievousness. 5. (*colloquial*) something difficult or awkward. 6. a literary hack used by an employer; a junior legal counsel. —*v.t./i.* (**-ll-**) 1. to cook (food) with hot seasoning. **2.** to act as a devil (for an author or barrister). **3.** (*US*) to harass, to worry. —**between the devil and the deep blue sea**, in a dilemma. **a devil of**, (*colloquial*) a considerable or remarkable. **devil-may-care** *adj.* cheerful and reckless. **devil's advocate**, one who tests a proposition by arguing against it. **devil's coach horse**, a large rove-beetle. **the devil's own**, very difficult or unusual. **the devil to pay**, trouble to be expected. **give the Devil his due**, to acknowledge the merits or achievement of a person otherwise disfavoured. **play the devil with**, to cause severe damage to. [Old English from Latin from Greek *diabolos* = slanderer]

devilish *adj.* of or like a devil; mischievous. —*adv.* (*colloquial*) very, extremely.

devilment *n.* mischief, wild spirits.

devil ray any of several large rays of the genera *Manta* and *Mobula*, fish in which two 'horns' project forward from the sides of the huge mouth. These flaps of skin guide the plankton on which the fishes feed into the mouth. The largest of these rays can be 7 m/23 ft across, and weigh 1,000 kg/2,200 lb. They live in warm seas.

devilry *n.* wickedness, reckless mischief; black magic.

Devil's Island /'devəlz 'aɪlənd/ (French *Île du Diable*) smallest of the Îles du Salut, off French Guiana, 43 km/27 mi NW of Cayenne. The group of islands was collectively and popularly known by the name Devil's Island and formed a penal colony notorious for its terrible conditions.

devious /'diːvɪəs/ *adj.* winding, circuitous; not straightforward, underhand. —**deviously** *adv.*, **deviousness** *n.* [from Latin *devius* (*via* = way)]

devise /dɪ'vaɪz/ *v.t.* **1.** to plan or invent by careful thought. **2.** in law, to leave (real estate) by will. [from Old French from Latin *dividere* = divide]

devoid /dɪ'vɔɪd/ *predic. adj.* (with *of*) quite lacking or free from. [from Old French]

devolution /diːvə'luːʃən/ *n.* delegation of power, especially by a central government to a local or regional administration. [from Latin]

Devolution, War of the war waged unsuccessfully from 1667–68 by Louis XIV of France to gain Spanish territory in the Netherlands, of which ownership had allegedly 'devolved' on his wife Maria Theresa.

devolve /dɪ'vɒlv/ *v.i.* (of work or duties) to pass or be passed on to another; (of property etc.) to descend or pass (*to* or *upon*). [from Latin *devolvere* (*volvere* = roll)]

Devon /'devən/ or **Devonshire** county in SW England; **area** 6,720 sq km/2,594 sq mi; **administrative headquarters** Exeter; **physical** rivers: Dart, Exe, Tamar; National Parks: Dartmoor, Exmoor; **products** mainly agricultural, with sheep and dairy farming; cider and clotted cream; kaolin in the S; Honiton lace; Dartington glass; **population** (1987) 1,010,000;

Devonian *adj.* of a period of geological time 408–360 million years ago, the fourth period of the Palaeozoic era. Many desert sandstones from North America and Europe date from this time. The first land plants flourished in the Devonian period, corals were abundant in the seas, amphibians evolved from air-breathing fish, and insects developed on land.

Devonshire, 8th Duke of see ◊Hartington, Spencer Compton Cavendish, British politician.

devote /dɪ'vəʊt/ *v.t.* to apply or give over *to* a particular activity or purpose. [from Latin *devovēre* (*vovēre* = vow)]

devoted *adj.* showing devotion, very loyal or loving. —**devotedly** *adv.*

devotee /devə'tiː/ *n.* a person who is devoted to something, an enthusiast.

devotio moderna a movement of revived religious spirituality which emerged in the Netherlands at the end of the 14th century and spread into the rest of W Europe. Its emphasis was on individual, rather than communal, devotion, including the private reading of religious works.

devotion /dɪ'vəʊʃən/ *n.* **1.** great love or loyalty, enthusiastic zeal. **2.** religious worship; (in *plural*) prayers. —**devotional** *adj.* [from Old French or Latin]

devour /dɪ'vaʊə/ *v.t.* **1.** to eat hungrily or greedily. **2.** (of fire etc.) to engulf, to destroy. **3.** to take in greedily with the eyes or ears. **4.** to absorb the attention of. [from Old French from Latin *devorare* (*vorare* = swallow)]

devout /dɪ'vaʊt/ *adj.* earnestly religious; earnest, sincere. —**devoutly** *adv.* [from Old French from Latin *devotus*]

De Vries /friːs/ Hugo 1848–1935. Dutch botanist, who conducted important research on osmosis in plant cells and was a pioneer in the study of plant evolution. His work led to the rediscovery of ◊Mendel's laws and the discovery of spontaneously occurring ◊mutations.

devsirme *n.* a levy of one in four males aged 10–20 taken by the Ottoman rulers of their Balkan provinces. All were brought to Constantinople and converted to Islam before being trained for the army or the civil service. This practice lasted from the 14th to the mid-17th centuries.

dew *n.* atmospheric vapour condensing in small drops on cool surfaces between evening and morning; beaded or glistening moisture resembling this. —**dewclaw** *n.* the rudimentary inner toe of some dogs. **dew point** *n.* the temperature at which the air can hold no more water vapour, and dew forms. **dew pond** *n.* a shallow, usually artificial, pond once supposed to be fed by atmospheric condensation. —**dewy** *adj.* [Old English]

dewar /'djuːə/ *n.* a double-walled flask with the space between its walls evacuated to reduce transfer of heat. [from Sir J *Dewar*]

Dewar /'djuːə/ James 1842–1923. Scottish chemist and physicist who invented the ◊vacuum flask (Thermos) 1872, during his research into the properties of matter at extremely low temperatures.

dewberry *n.* a bluish fruit like a blackberry; the shrub *Rubus caesius* bearing it.

dewdrop *n.* a drop of dew.

Dewey /'djuːi/ Melvil 1851–1931. US librarian. In 1876, he devised the **Dewey Decimal System** of classification for books, now widely used in libraries.

dewlap *n.* a fold of loose skin hanging from the throat of cattle and other animals.

dexter *adj.* (in heraldry) of or on the right-hand side (the observer's left) of a shield etc. [Latin = on the right]

dexterity /dek'steriti/ *n.* skill in handling things; manual or mental adroitness. [from French from Latin]

dexterous variant of **dextrous**.

dextrous /'dekstrəs/ *adj.* having or showing dexterity. —**dextrously** *adv.* [from Latin]

DFC abbreviation of Distinguished Flying Cross.

DFM abbreviation of Distinguished Flying Medal.

Dhaka /'dækə/ or **Dacca** capital of Bangladesh from 1971, in Dhaka region, W of the river Meghna; population (1984) 3,600,000. It trades in jute, oilseed, sugar, and tea and produces textiles, chemicals, glass, and metal products.

dharma /'dɑːmə/ *n.* **1.** the Hindu moral law; right behaviour; social rules. **2.** (in Buddhism) truth. [Sanskrit = law, custom]

Dhaulagiri /daʊlə'giəri/ mountain in the ◊Himalayas of W central Nepál, rising to 8,172 m/26,811 ft.

Dhofar /'dəʊfɑː/ mountainous western province of ◊Oman, on the border with ◊Yemen; population (1982) 40,000. South Yemen supported guerrilla activity here in the 1970s, while Britain and Iran supported the government's military operations. The capital is Salalah, which has a port at Rasut.

dhole *n.* a wild dog *Cuon alpinus* found in Asia from Siberia to Java. With head and body up to 1 m/3 ft long, variable in colour but often reddish above and lighter below, the dhole lives in groups of from 3 to 30 individuals. The species is becoming rare and is protected in some areas.

dhoti /'dəʊti/ *n.* the loincloth worn by male Hindus. [Hindi]

dhow /daʊ/ *n.* a lateen-rigged ship of the Arabian Sea.

DHSS abbreviation of Department of Health and Social Security, a UK government department until divided in 1988.

di- prefix meaning two, double. [Greek *dis* = twice]

dia- (**di-** before a vowel) prefix meaning **1.** through. **2.** apart. **3.** across. [Greek *dia* = through]

diabetes /daɪə'biːtiːz/ *n.* a disease (also called **diabetes mellitus**) in which a disorder of the islets of Langerhans in the ◊pancreas prevents the body producing the hormone ◊insulin, so that sugars cannot be used properly. Treatment is by strict dietary control and oral or injected insulin. [originally = siphon; Latin from Greek *diabainō* = go through]

diabetic /daɪə'betɪk/ *adj.* of or having diabetes, for diabetics. —*n.* a person suffering from diabetes.

diabolic, diabolical /daɪəˈbɒlɪk, -kəl/ of the Devil; devilish, inhumanly cruel or wicked; fiendishly clever or cunning or annoying. —**diabolically** adv. [from Old French or Latin]

diabolism /daɪˈæbəlɪzəm/ n. worship of the Devil; sorcery. [from Greek]

diachronic /daɪəˈkrɒnɪk/ adj. concerned with the historical development of a subject. —**diachronic linguistics**, historical linguistics (see ◊historical). [from French (Greek *khronos* = time)]

diaconal /daɪˈækənəl/ adj. of a deacon. [from Latin]

diaconate /daɪˈækənət/ n. 1. the office of a deacon. 2. a body of deacons.

diacritical /daɪəˈkrɪtɪkəl/ adj. distinguishing, distinctive. —**diacritical mark** (*or* **sign**), a sign used to indicate different sounds or values of a letter (an accent, diaeresis, cedilla etc.). [from Greek]

diadem /ˈdaɪədem/ n. 1. a crown or headband worn as a sign of sovereignty. 2. sovereignty. 3. a crowning distinction or glory. [from Old French from Latin from Greek *deō* = bind]

diaeresis /daɪˈɪərəsɪs/ n. (*plural* **diaereses** /-siːz/) a mark (as in *naïve*) over a vowel indicating that it is sounded separately. [Latin from Greek = separation]

diagenesis n. or **lithification** in geology, the physical and chemical changes by which a sediment becomes a ◊sedimentary rock. The main processes involved include compaction of the grains, and the cementing of the grains together by the growth of new minerals deposited by percolating groundwater.

Diaghilev /diˈægəlef/ Sergei Pavlovich 1872–1929. Russian ballet impresario, who in 1909 founded the *Ballets Russes*/Russian Ballet (headquarters in Monaco), which he directed for 20 years. Through this company he brought Russian ballet to the West, introducing and encouraging a dazzling array of dancers, choreographers, and composers, such as Pavlova, Nijinsky, Fokine, Massine, Balanchine, Stravinsky, and Prokofiev.

diagnose /ˈdaɪəgnəʊz/ v.t. to make a diagnosis of (a disease, a mechanical fault etc.); to infer the presence of (a specified disease etc.) from symptoms.

diagnosis /daɪəgˈnəʊsɪs/ n. (*plural* **diagnoses** /-siːz/) the identification of a disease by means of the patient's symptoms, a formal statement of this; the ascertainment of the cause of a mechanical fault etc. [Latin from Greek *gignōskō* = recognize]

diagnostic /daɪəgˈnɒstɪk/ adj. of or assisting diagnosis. —n. a symptom. —**diagnostician** /-ˈstɪʃən/ n. [from Greek]

diagonal /daɪˈægənəl/ adj. crossing a straight-sided figure from corner to corner, slanting, oblique. —n. a straight line joining two opposite corners. —**diagonally** adv. [from Latin from Greek *gōnia* = angle]

diagram /ˈdaɪəgræm/ n. a drawing showing the general scheme or outline of an object and its parts; a graphic representation of a course or the results of an action or process. —**diagrammatic** /-ˈmætɪk/ adj., **diagrammatically** adv. [from Latin from Greek]

dial /ˈdaɪəl/ n. 1. the plate on the front of a clock or watch, marking the hours etc.; a similar flat plate marked with a scale for the measurement of something, and having a movable pointer indicating the amount registered. 2. a movable disc with finger holes over a circle of numbers, manipulated in order to make a connection with another instrument; a plate or disc etc. on a radio or television set for selecting a wavelength or channel. 3. (*slang*) a person's face. —v.t./i. (-ll-) to select or regulate by means of a dial; to make a telephone connection by using a dial or numbered buttons; to ring up (a number etc.) thus. [from Latin *dies* = day]

dialect /ˈdaɪəlekt/ n. a form of speech peculiar to a district or class; a subordinate variety of a language showing sufficient differences from the standard language in vocabulary, pronunciation, or idiom for it to be considered as distinct. —**dialectal** /-ˈlektəl/ adj., **dialectology** n. [from French or Latin from Greek = discourse (*dialegomai* = converse)]

dialectic /daɪəˈlektɪk/ n. 1. (also in *plural*, occasionally treated as *singular*) the art of investigating the truth of opinions; the testing of truth by discussion, logical disputation. 2. criticism dealing with metaphysical contradictions and their solutions; the existence or action of opposing social forces etc. —**Hegelian dialectic**, an interpretive method

in which the contradiction between a thesis and its antithesis is resolved through synthesis. —adj. of disputation or dialectics. [from Old French or Latin from Greek *dialektikē* (*tekhnē* = art) of debate]

dialectical /daɪəˈlektɪkəl/ adj. of dialectic. —**dialectical materialism**, the theory propagated by Marx and Engels according to which political events or social phenomena are to be interpreted as a conflict of social forces (the 'class struggle') produced by the operation of economic causes.

dialogue /ˈdaɪəlɒg/ n. a conversation; the written form of this; a passage of conversation in a novel etc.; a discussion between the representatives of two groups etc. [from Old French from Latin from Greek *dialegomai* = converse]

dialysis /daɪˈælɪsɪs/ n. (*plural* **dialyses** /-siːz/) the separation of particles by differences in their ability to pass through a suitable membrane; the process of allowing blood to flow past such a membrane on the other side of which is another liquid, so that certain dissolved substances in the blood may pass through the membrane and the blood itself be purified or cleansed in cases of renal failure, poisoning, etc.; an occasion of undergoing this process. [from Latin from Greek = dissolution (*luō* = set free)]

diamanté /dɪəˈmɑːteɪ/ adj. decorated with powdered crystal or other sparkling substance. [French = set with diamonds]

diameter /daɪˈæmɪtə/ n. a straight line passing from side to side through the centre of a circle or sphere; a transverse measurement, width, or thickness; the unit of linear magnifying power. [from Old French from Latin from Greek = measuring across]

diametrical /daɪəˈmetrɪkəl/ adj. 1. of or along a diameter. 2. (of opposites etc.) complete, direct. —**diametrically** adv. [from Greek]

diamond /ˈdaɪəmənd/ n. 1. a very hard, transparent, precious stone of pure crystallized carbon, the hardest natural substance known (10 on the ◊Mohs' scale). Industrial diamonds are used for cutting, grinding, and polishing. 2. a rhombus; a rhombus-shaped thing. 3. a playing-card of the suit (**diamonds**) marked with red rhombuses. —**diamond wedding**, the 60th (or 75th) anniversary of a wedding. [from Old French from Latin from Greek *adamas* = adamant]

Diana /daɪˈænə/ in Roman mythology, the goddess of chastity, hunting, and the moon (Greek ◊Artemis), daughter of Jupiter and twin of Apollo.

Diana Princess of Wales 1961– . The daughter of the 8th Earl Spencer, she married Prince Charles at St Paul's Cathedral, London, in 1981, the first English bride of a royal heir since 1659. She is descended from the only sovereigns from whom Prince Charles is not descended, Charles II and James II.

DIANE the collection of information suppliers or 'hosts' for the European computer network. [acronym from *Direct Information Access Network for Europe*.

dianthus /daɪˈænθəs/ n. a flowering plant of the genus *Dianthus*, including the carnation. [from Greek *Dios* = of Zeus and *anthos* = flower]

diapason /daɪəˈpeɪsɒn, -z-/ n. the entire compass of a musical instrument or voice; a fixed standard of musical pitch; either of the two main organ-stops extending through the whole compass. [from Latin from Greek = through all (notes)]

diapause n. a period of suspended development that occurs in some species of insects, characterized by greatly reduced metabolism. Periods of diapause are often timed to coincide with the winter months, and improve the insect's chances of surviving adverse conditions.

diaper /ˈdaɪəpə/ n. (*US*) a baby's nappy. [from Old French from Latin from Greek]

diaphanous /daɪˈæfənəs/ adj. (of a fabric etc.) light and delicate and almost transparent. [from Latin from Greek *-phanēs* = showing]

diaphragm /ˈdaɪəfræm/ n. 1. the muscular partition between the thorax and the abdomen in mammals. 2. a thin sheet used as a partition etc.; a vibrating disc in a microphone, telephone, loudspeaker etc., and acoustic systems etc. 3. a device for varying the lens aperture in a camera etc. 4. a thin contraceptive cap fitting over the cervix of the uterus. [from Latin from Greek *phragma* = fence]

diarist /ˈdaɪərɪst/ n. one who keeps a diary.

diarrhoea /daɪəˈriːə/ n. the condition of excessively frequent and loose bowel movements caused by intestinal irritants (including some drugs and poisons), infection with harmful organisms (as in dysentery, salmonella, or cholera), or allergies. [from Latin from Greek *rheô* = flow]

diary /'daɪərɪ/ *n.* a daily record of events or thoughts; a book for this or for noting future engagements. One of the earliest diaries extant is that of a Japanese noblewoman, the *Kagerô Nikki* 954–974, and the earliest diary in English is that of Edward VI (ruled 1547–53). Notable diaries include those of Samuel Pepys, the writer John Evelyn, the Quaker George Fox, and in the 20th century those of Anne ◊Frank and the writers André Gide and Katherine Mansfield. [from Latin *diarium* (*dies* = day)]

Diaspora /daɪ'æspərə/ *n.* the dispersion of the Jews, initially from Palestine after the Babylonian conquest in 586 BC, and then following the Roman sack of Jerusalem in AD 70 and their crushing of the Jewish revolt in 135. The term has come to refer to all the Jews living outside Israel. [Greek, from *dia* = through and *speirô* = scatter]

diastase /'daɪəsteɪs/ *n.* the enzyme converting starch to sugar, important in digestion. [French from Greek = separation]

diastole /daɪ'æstəlɪ/ *n.* the dilatation of the heart rhythmically alternating with systole to form the pulse. —**diastolic** /daɪə'stɒlɪk/ *adj.* [Latin from Greek *stellô* = send]

diathermy /'daɪəθəmɪ/ *n.* the application of high-frequency electric currents to produce heat within the body. —**diathermic** *adj.* [from German from Greek *dia* = through, *thermon* = heat]

diatom /'daɪətəm/ *n.* a microscopic one-cell alga of the division Bacillariophyta, found as plankton and forming fossil deposits. [from Latin from Greek = cut in half]

diatomic /daɪə'tɒmɪk/ *adj.* consisting of two atoms; having two replaceable atoms or radicals.

diatomic molecule a molecule composed of two identical atoms joined together, such as oxygen, O_2.

diatonic /daɪə'tɒnɪk/ *adj.* in music, (of a scale, interval etc.) involving only notes proper to the prevailing key without chromatic alteration. [from French or Latin from Greek *tonikos* = tonic]

diatribe /'daɪətraɪb/ *n.* a forceful verbal attack, abusive criticism. [French from Latin from Greek *diatribê*= spending of time, discourse]

Diaz /'diːæʃ/ Bartolomeu *c.*1450–1500. Portuguese explorer, the first European to reach the Cape of Good Hope 1488, and to establish a route around Africa. He drowned during an expedition with Pedro ◊Cabral.

Díaz /'diːæs/ Porfirio 1830–1915. Dictator of Mexico 1877–80 and 1884–1911. After losing the 1876 election, he overthrew the government and seized power. He was supported by conservative landowners and foreign capitalists, who invested in railways and mines. He centralized the state at the expense of the peasants and Indians, and dismantled all local and regional leadership. He faced mounting and revolutionary opposition in his final years and was forced into exile in 1911.

Diaz de Solís /'diːæs deɪ 'səʊlɪs/ Juan 1471–*c.*1516. Spanish explorer in South America, who reached the estuary of the River Plate and was killed and eaten by cannibals.

dibber /'dɪbə/ *n.* a handtool for making holes in the ground for seeds or young plants.

dibble /'dɪbl/ *n.* a dibber. —*v.t./i.* to prepare (soil) with a dibble, to sow or plant with a dibble.

dice *n.* (properly *plural* of die[2] but often as *singular*) a small cube with the faces bearing usually 1–6 spots used in games of chance; a game played with one or more of these. —*v.t./i.* 1. to gamble with dice. 2. to cut into small cubes. —**no dice**, (*slang*) no success or prospect of it.

dicey /'daɪsɪ/ *adj.* (*slang*) risky, unreliable.

dichotomy /daɪ'kɒtəmɪ/ *n.* a division into two parts or kinds. [from Latin from Greek *dikho-* = apart and -*tomia* = cutting]

dichromatic /daɪkrə'mætɪk/ *adj.* 1. two-coloured. 2. having vision sensitive to only two of the three primary colours. [from Greek *khrôma* = colour]

Dick /dɪk/ Philip K(endred) 1928–1982. US science-fiction writer, whose works often deal with religion and the subjectivity of reality; his novels include *The Man in the High Castle* 1962 and *Do Androids Dream of Electric Sheep?* 1968.

dickens /'dɪkɪnz/ *n.* (*colloquial*) deuce, the Devil (especially in exclamations).

Dickens *English novelist Charles Dickens.*

Dickens /'dɪkɪnz/ Charles 1812–1870. English novelist, popular for his memorable characters and his portrayal of the social evils of Victorian England. In 1836 he published the first number of the *Pickwick Papers*, followed by *Oliver Twist* 1838, the first of his 'reforming' novels; *Nicholas Nickleby* 1839; *Barnaby Rudge* 1840; *The Old Curiosity Shop* 1841; and *David Copperfield* 1849. Among his later books are *A Tale of Two Cities* 1859 and *Great Expectations* 1861.

Dickensian /di'kenziən/ *adj.* of the novelist Charles Dickens or his works; resembling situations described in them.

dicker *v.i.* to bargain, to haggle. [perhaps from *dicker* = set of ten (hides), as unit of trade]

Dickinson /'dɪkɪnsən/ Emily 1830–1886. US poet. Born in Amherst, Massachusetts, she lived in near seclusion there from 1862. Hardly any of her many short, mystical poems were published during her lifetime. Her work became well known only in the 20th century.

dicky *adj.* (*slang*) unsound, likely to collapse or fail. —*n.* (*colloquial*) a false shirt-front.

dicotyledon /daɪkɒtɪ'liːd(ə)n/ *n.* a major subdivision of the ◊angiosperms, containing the great majority of flowering plants. Dicotyledons are characterized by the presence of two seed leaves, or ◊cotyledons, in the embryo, which is usually surrounded by an ◊endosperm. They generally have broad leaves with netlike veins. Dicotyledons may be small plants such as daisies and buttercups, shrubs, or trees such as oak and beech. The other subdivision of the angiosperms is the ◊monocotyledons. —**dicotyledonous** *adj.*

Dictaphone /'dɪktəfəʊn/ *n.* trade name of a machine for recording and playing back dictated words.

dictate /dɪk'teɪt/ *v.t./i.* 1. to say or read aloud (words to be written down or recorded). 2. to state or order with the force of authority; to give peremptory orders. —/'dɪkteɪt/ *n.* (usually in *plural*) an authoritative instruction. —**dictation** /-'teɪʃən/ *n.* [from Latin *dictare* (*dicere* = say)]

dictator *n.* a ruler (often a usurper) with unrestricted authority; a person with supreme authority in any sphere; a domineering person. In ancient Rome a dictator was a magistrate invested with emergency powers for six months. —**dictatorship** *n.* Dictatorships were common in Latin America during the 19th century, but the only European example during this period was the rule of Napoleon III. The crises following World War I produced many dictatorships, including the regimes of Atatürk and Pilsudski (nationalist); Mussolini, Hitler, Primo de Rivera, Franco, and Salazar (all right-wing); and Stalin (Communist). [from Latin]

dictatorial /dɪktə'tɔːrɪəl/ *adj.* of or like a dictator; imperious, overbearing. —**dictatorially** *adv.*

dictatorship of the proletariat the Marxist term for a revolutionary dictatorship established during the transition from capitalism to ◊communism after a socialist revolution.

diction /'dɪkʃən/ n. **1.** a person's manner of enunciation in speaking or singing. **2.** the choice of words and phrases in speech or writing. [from French or Latin *dictio* (*dicere* = say)]

dictionary /'dɪkʃənərɪ/ n. a book that lists (usually in alphabetical order) and explains the words of a language (often with information on pronunciation, inflected forms, and etymology) or gives the equivalent words in another language; a similar book explaining the terms of a particular subject. [from Latin]

dictum /'dɪktəm/ n. (*plural* **dicta**) a formal expression of opinion; a saying. [Latin (past participle of *dicere* = say)]

did past of do[1].

didactic /dɪ'dæktɪk, daɪ-/ adj. meant to instruct; (of a person) tediously pedantic. —**didactically** adv., **didacticism** /-tɪsɪzəm/ n. [from Greek *didaskō* = teach]

diddle v.t. (*slang*) to cheat, to swindle. [from Jeremy *Diddler*, character in play (1803)]

Diderot /'diːdərəʊ/ Denis 1713–1784. French philosopher who is closely associated with the Enlightenment, the European intellectual movement for social and scientific progress, and was editor of the ◊*Encyclopédie* 1751–1780. An expanded and politicized version of Ephraim Chamber's English encyclopedia of 1728, this work exerted an enormous influence on contemporary social thinking with its materialism and anticlericalism. Its compilers were known as *Encyclopedistes*.

didjeridu n. a musical wind instrument, made from a hollow bamboo section 1.5 m/4 ft long and blown to produce rhythmic, booming notes. First developed and played by Australian Aborigines.

didn't (*colloquial*) = did not.

Dido /'daɪdəʊ/ a Phoenician princess, legendary founder of Carthage, who committed suicide in order to avoid marrying a local prince. In the Latin epic *Aeneid*, Virgil claims that it was because ◊Aeneas deserted her.

die[1] /daɪ/ v.i. (*participle* **dying** /'daɪɪŋ/) **1.** to cease to live, to expire, to lose vital force. **2.** to cease to exist or function, to disappear, to fade away; (of flame) to go out. **3.** to wish longingly or intently. **4.** to be exhausted or tormented. —**die away**, to become weaker or fainter to the point of extinction. **die back**, (of a plant) to decay from the tip towards the root. **die down**, to become less loud or strong. **die-hard** n. a conservative or stubborn person. **die out**, to become extinct, to cease to exist. **never say die**, keep up courage, not give in. [probably from Old Norse]

die[2] **1.** see ◊dice. **2.** an engraved device for stamping a design on coins, medals etc.; a device for stamping, cutting, or moulding material into a particular shape. —**diecasting** n. a process or product of casting from metal moulds. **die-sinker** n. an engraver of dies. **die-stamping** n. embossing paper etc. with a die. **straight as a die**, quite straight, very honest. [from Old French from Latin *datum* past participle of *dare* = give]

Diefenbaker /'diːfənbeɪkə/ John George 1895–1979. Canadian Progressive Conservative politician, prime minister from 1957–63, when he was defeated after criticism of the proposed manufacture of nuclear weapons in Canada.

dielectric /daɪə'lektrɪk/ adj. that does not conduct electricity. —n. a dielectric substance usable for insulating.

Dien Bien Phu, Battle of /'diːen bːen fuː/ a decisive battle in the ◊Indo-China War at a French fortress in North Vietnam, near the Laotian border. French troops were besieged from 13 Mar–7 May 1954 by the Communist Vietminh. The fall of Dien Bien Phu resulted in the end of French control of Indochina.

diesel /'diːzəl/ n. **1.** or **diesel engine** a type of internal-combustion engine in which ignition of fuel is produced by the heat of air that has been highly compressed. **2.** a vehicle driven by such an engine. **3.** the fuel for this. —**diesel-electric** adj. driven by electric current from a generator driven by a diesel engine. **diesel oil,** the heavy petroleum fraction used in diesel engines. [from R *Diesel*]

Diesel Rudolf 1858–1913. German engineer who patented the diesel engine. He began his career as a refrigerator engineer and, like many engineers of the period, sought to develop a more efficient power source than the conventional steam engine. Able to operate with greater efficiency and economy, the diesel engine soon found a ready market. The

diesel engine operates by compressing air until it becomes sufficiently hot to ignite the fuel. It is a piston-in-cylinder engine, like the ◊petrol engine, but just air (rather than an air-and-fuel mixture) is taken into the cylinder on the first piston stroke (down). The piston moves up and compresses the air until it is at a very high temperature. The fuel oil is then injected into the hot air, where it burns, driving the piston down on its power stroke. For this reason the engine is called a compression-ignition engine.

diet[1] /'daɪət/ n. the sort of foods one habitually eats; a prescribed course of food to which a person is restricted. A special diet may be recommended for medical reasons, to limit or increase certain nutrients; undertaken to lose weight, by a reduction in calorie intake; or observed on religious, moral, or emotional grounds. An adequate diet is one that fulfils the body's nutritional requirements and gives an energy intake proportional to the person's activity level (the average daily requirement is 2,400 calories). Some 450 million people in the world subsist on less than 1,500 calories, whereas in the developed countries the average daily intake is 3,300. —v.t./i. to restrict oneself to a special diet, especially in order to control one's weight; to restrict (a person) to a special diet. —**dietary** adj. [from Old French from Latin from Greek *diaita* = way of life]

diet[2] n. a conference or congress (especially as the English name for some foreign parliamentary assemblies); a meeting or convention of the princes and other dignitaries of the Holy Roman (German) Empire, for example, the Diet of Worms which met in 1521 to consider the question of Luther's doctrines and the governance of the empire under Charles V. [from Latin *dieta* (*dies* = day)]

dietetic /daɪə'tetɪk/ adj. of diet and nutrition. [from Latin from Greek]

dietetics n.pl. the scientific study of diet and nutrition.

dietitian /daɪə'tɪʃən/ n. an expert in dietetics.

Dietrich /'diːtrɪk/ Marlene. Stage name of Magdalene von Losch 1904–. German-born US actress and singer, who first won fame by her appearance with Emil Jannings in both the German and American versions of the film *The Blue Angel* 1930. She stayed in Hollywood, becoming a US citizen in 1937. Her husky, sultry singing voice added to her appeal. Her other films include *Blonde Venus* 1932 and *Destry Rides Again* 1939, and *Just a Gigolo* 1978. She also starred in *Judgment at Nuremberg* 1961 and was the subject of Maximilian Schell's frank documentary *Marlene* 1983.

Dieu et mon droit the motto of the royal arms of Great Britain. [French = God and my right]

differ v.i. **1.** to be unlike; to be distinguishable *from*. **2.** to disagree in opinion (*from*). [from Old French from Latin *differre* originally = bear apart]

difference n. **1.** being different or unlike. **2.** a point in which things differ; the amount or degree of unlikeness. **3.** the quantity by which amounts differ, the remainder left after subtraction. **4.** a disagreement in opinion, a dispute, a quarrel. —**make all the difference,** to be very important or significant. **split the difference,** to take the average of two proposed amounts. [from Old French from Latin]

different adj. unlike, of other nature, form, or quality (*from* or (*disputed usage*) *to*); separate, distinct; unusual. —**differently** adv. [from Old French from Latin]

Dietrich *Marlene Dietrich in* The Blue Angel *1930, the film that won her international fame.*

differential /dɪfə'renʃəl/ *adj.* 1. of or showing or depending on a difference; constituting or relating to specific differences. 2. in mathematics, relating to infinitesimal differences. —*n.* 1. an agreed difference in wage between industries or between different classes of workers in the same industry. 2. a difference between rates of interest etc. 3. a differential gear. —**differential calculus**, a branch of ◊analysis involving the differentiation of functions (see ◊differentiate) with applications such as determination of maximum and minimum points and rates of change. **differential gear**, a gear enabling a motor vehicle's driven wheels to revolve at different speeds in rounding corners. The differential consists of sets of bevel gears and pinions within a cage attached to the crown wheel. When cornering, the bevel pinions rotate to allow the outer wheel to turn faster than the inner. [from Latin]

differentiate /dɪfə'renʃieɪt/ *v.t.* 1. to constitute the difference between or in. 2. to recognize as different, to distinguish, to discriminate. 3. to develop differences, to become different; in embryology, to become increasingly specialized, giving rise to more complex structures that have particular functions in the adult organism. 4. in mathematics, to calculate the derivative of. —**differentiation** /-'eɪʃən/ *n.*

difficult /'dɪfɪkəlt/ *adj.* needing much effort or skill; troublesome, perplexing; not easy to please or satisfy.

difficulty /'dɪfɪkəltɪ/ *n.* being difficult; a difficult problem or thing, a hindrance to progress; (often in *plural*) trouble or distress, especially shortage of money. [from Latin *difficultas*]

diffident /'dɪfɪdənt/ *adj.* lacking self-confidence, hesitating to put oneself or one's ideas forward. —**diffidence** *n.*, **diffidently** *adv.* [from Latin *diffidere* = mistrust (*fidere* = trust)]

diffract /dɪ'frækt/ *v.t.* to break up (a beam of light) into a series of dark and light bands or coloured spectra, or (a beam of radiation or particles) into a series of high and low intensities. —**diffractive** *adj.* [from Latin = break apart (*frangere* = break)]

diffraction /dɪ'frækʃən/ *n.* diffracting. —**diffraction grating**, a plate of glass or polished metal ruled with very close equidistant parallel lines, producing a spectrum by means of the transmitted or reflected light.

diffuse /dɪ'fjuːs/ *adj.* spread out, not concentrated; wordy, not concise. —/-'fjuːz/ *v.t.* to spread widely or thinly; (especially of fluids) to intermingle by diffusion. —**diffusible** /-z-/ *adj.*, **diffusive** /-s-/ *adj.* [from French or Latin *diffusus* = extensive (*fundere* = pour)]

diffusion *n.* diffusing, being diffuse; the interpenetration of substances by the natural movement of their particles. In physical chemistry, any of at least three processes: the spontaneous mixing of gases or liquids (classed together as **fluids** in scientific usage) when brought into contact without mechanical mixing or stirring; the spontaneous passage of fluids through membranes; and the spontaneous passage of dissolved materials both through the material in which they are dissolved and also through membranes. [from Latin]

dig *v.t./i.* (-gg-; *past* and *past participle* dug) 1. to break up and remove or turn over (ground etc.) with a tool, the hands, claws etc.; to make (a way, hole etc.) or obtain by digging; to excavate archaeologically. 2. to thrust (a sharp object) *into* or *in*; to prod or nudge. 3. to make a search (*for* or *into*). —*n.* 1. a piece of digging; an archaeological excavation. 2. a prod or nudge. 3. a cutting or sarcastic remark. 4. (in *plural, colloquial*) lodgings. —**dig one's heels** *or* **toes in**, to be obstinate, to refuse to give way. **dig in**, to mix into the soil by digging; (*colloquial*) to begin eating. **dig oneself in**, to dig a defensive trench or pit; to establish one's position.

Digambara /dɪ'gʌmbərə/ *n.* a member of a sect of Jain monks (see ◊Jainism) who practise complete nudity. [= sky-clad]

digest /dɪ'dʒest/ *v.t.* 1. to assimilate food in the stomach and bowels. 2. to understand and assimilate mentally. 3. to summarize. —/'daɪdʒest/ *n.* a methodical summary, especially of laws; a periodical synopsis of current literature or news. [from Latin *digerere* = distribute, dispose]

digestible /dɪ'dʒestɪbəl/ *adj.* able to be digested.

digestion /dɪ'dʒestʃən/ *n.* the process of digesting; the power of digesting food.

digestive /dɪ'dʒestɪv/ *adj.* of or aiding digestion. —*n.* a digestive substance. —**digestive biscuit**, a sweet kind of wholemeal biscuit. [from Old French or Latin]

digestive system the mouth, stomach, gut, and associated glands of animals, which are responsible for digesting food. The food is broken down by physical and chemical means in the ◊stomach; digestion is completed, and most nutrients are absorbed in the small intestine; what remains is stored and concentrated into faeces in the large intestine. In birds, additional digestive organs are the ◊crop and ◊gizzard.

digger *n.* 1. one who digs; a mechanical excavator. 2. (*colloquial*) a term coined in Australia to describe goldminers, but adopted by Australian and New Zealand soldiers in France in 1916-17 and now generally used to mean an Australian soldier, especially one who fought in World War I, or, more generally, an Australian or New Zealander. In Australia it is also a term of friendly address, in the sense of 'mate'.

Diggers *n.* also called **true** ◊**Levellers**. An English 17th-century radical sect that attempted to dig common land. It became prominent in April 1649 when, headed by Gerrard Winstanley (*c.*1609–1660), it set up communal colonies near Cobham, Surrey, and elsewhere. These colonies were attacked by mobs and, being pacifists, the Diggers made no resistance. The support they attracted alarmed the government and they were dispersed in 1650. Their ideas influenced the early ◊Quakers.

diggings *n. pl.* 1. a mine or goldfield. 2. (*colloquial*) lodgings.

digit /'dɪdʒɪt/ *n.* 1. any of the numerals from 0 to 9. In computing, different numbering systems have different ranges of digits. For example, ◊hexadecimal has digits 0 to 9 and A to F, whereas binary has two digits (or ◊bits), 0 and 1. 2. a finger or toe. [from Latin *digitus* = finger, toe]

digital /'dɪdʒɪt(ə)l/ *n. & adj.* in electronics and computing, a term meaning 'coded as numbers'. A digital system uses two-state, either on/off or high/low voltage pulses, to encode, receive, and transmit information. —**digital clock, watch**, one showing the time by displayed digits, not by hands. **digital display** one which shows discrete values as numbers. —**digitally** *adv.* [from Latin *digitalis*]

digital audio tape (DAT) tape used to record sounds in digital or numerical form. DAT is a compact medium, as a cassette the size of a credit card can hold four hours of sound.

digital computer a computing device that operates on a two-state system, using symbols that are internally coded as binary numbers (numbers made up of combinations of the digits 0 and 1); see ◊computer.

digital data transmission in computing, a way of sending data by converting all signals (whether pictures, sounds, or words) into numeric (normally binary) codes before transmission and then reconverting them on receipt. This virtually eliminates any distortion or degradation of the signal during transmission, storage, or processing.

digitalis /dɪdʒɪ'teɪlɪs/ *n.* a plant of the genus *Digitalis* of the figwort family Scrophulariaceae, which includes the ◊foxgloves; a drug prepared from dried foxglove leaves, that increases the efficiency of the heart by strengthening its muscle contractions and slowing its rate.

digital recording a technique whereby the pressure of sound waves is sampled more than 30,000 times a second and the values recorded as numbers which, during playback, are reconverted to sound waves. This gives very high-quality reproduction. In digital recording the signals picked up by the microphone are converted into precise numerical values by computer. These values, which represent the original sound wave form exactly, are recorded on compact disc. When it is played back by ◊laser, the exact values are retrieved. When fed via an amplifier to a loudspeaker, sound waves exactly like the original ones are reproduced.

digital sampling an electronic process used in ◊telecommunications for transforming a constantly varying (analogue) signal into one composed of discrete units, a digital signal. In the creation of recorded music, sampling enables the composer, producer, or remix engineer to borrow discrete vocal or instrumental parts from other recorded work (it is also possible to sample live sound).

dignified *adj.* having or showing dignity.

dill

flower

seed
head

seed

dignify /'dɪgnɪfaɪ/ v.t. to confer dignity on, to ennoble; to give a high-sounding name to. [from Old French from Latin *dignus* = worthy]

dignitary /'dɪgnɪtərɪ/ n. a person holding a high rank or position, especially ecclesiastical.

dignity /'dɪgnɪtɪ/ n. 1. a composed and serious manner or style, showing suitable formality. 2. worthiness of honour or respect. 3. a high rank or position. **beneath one's dignity**, not worthy enough for one to do. **stand on one's dignity**, to insist on being treated with respect. [from Latin *dignitas* (*dignus* = worthy)]

digraph /'daɪgrɑːf/ n. a union of two letters representing one sound (as *ph*, *ea*). [from Greek *-graphos* = written]

digress /daɪ'gres/ v.i. to depart from the main subject temporarily in speech or writing. —**digression** n. [from Latin *digredi* = depart (*gradus* = step)]

dik-dik n. any of several species of tiny antelope, genus *Madoqua*, found in Africa S of the Sahara in dry areas with scattered brush. Dik-diks are about 60 cm/2 ft long and 35 cm/1.1 ft tall, and often seen in pairs. Males have short, pointed horns. The dik-dik is so named because of its alarm call.

dike /daɪk/ n. a long wall or embankment against flooding; a ditch; a low wall of turf or stone. —v.t. to provide or protect with dikes. [from Old Norse or Dutch]

diktat /'dɪktɑːt/ n. a categorical statement or decree. [German = *dictate*]

dilapidated /dɪ'læpɪdeɪtɪd/ adj. in a state of disrepair or ruin. —**dilapidation** /-'deɪʃən/ n. [from Latin *dilapidare* = squander (*lapis* = stone)]

dilatation and curettage (D and C) a common gynaecological procedure in which the cervix (neck of the womb) is widened, or dilated, giving access so that the lining of the womb can be scraped away (curettage). It may be carried out to terminate a pregnancy, treat an incomplete miscarriage, discover the cause of heavy menstrual bleeding, or for biopsy.

dilate /daɪ'leɪt/ v.t./i. 1. to make or become wider or larger. 2. to speak or write at length. —**dilation** n. [from Old French from Latin *dilatare* = spread out (*latus* = wide)]

dilatory /'dɪlətərɪ/ adj. 1. slow to act, not prompt. 2. designed to cause delay. [from Latin *dilatorius* (*dilator* = delayer)]

dilemma /dɪ'lemə, daɪ-/ n. a situation in which a choice has to be made between alternatives that are both undesirable; (*disputed usage*) a difficult situation. [Latin from Greek = double proposition]

dilettante /dɪlɪ'tæntɪ/ n. (*plural* **dilettanti** /-tiː/, **dilettantes**) a person who dabbles in a subject without serious study of it. —**dilettantism** n. [Italian, from *dilettare* (from Latin *delectare* = delight]

diligent /'dɪlɪdʒənt/ adj. careful and hard-working; showing care and effort. —**diligence** n., **diligently** adv. [from Old French from Latin *diligens* = assiduous from *diligere* = love]

dill n. a herb *Anethum graveolens* of the carrot family Umbelliferae, whose bitter seeds and aromatic leaves are used for culinary and medicinal purposes. [Old English]

dilly-dally v.i. to waste time by indecision etc.

dilute /daɪ'ljuːt/ v.t. 1. to reduce the strength of (a fluid) by adding water or other solvent. 2. to weaken or reduce the forcefulness of. —adj. diluted. —**dilution** n. [from Latin *diluere* = wash away, dilute]

dim adj. 1. faintly luminous or visible, not bright. 2. indistinct, not clearly perceived or remembered. 3. not seeing clearly; (*colloquial*) stupid. —v.t./i. (**-mm-**) to become or make dim. —**dimly** adv., **dimness** n. [Old English]

DiMaggio /dɪ'mɑːdʒɪəʊ/Joe 1914– . US baseball player with the New York Yankees 1936–51. In 1941 he set a record by getting hits in 56 consecutive games. He was an outstanding fielder, hit 361 home runs, and had a career average of .325. He was once married to the actress Marilyn Monroe.

dime /daɪm/ n. (*US*) a ten-cent coin. [originally = tithe, from Old French from Latin *decima* (*pars*) = tenth part]

dime novel a melodramatic paperback novel of a series started in the US in the 1850s by Erastus F Beadle and frequently dealing with frontier adventure. Like British 'penny dreadfuls', dime novels attained massive sales. Dime novels were especially popular with troops during the American Civil War. The 'Nick Carter' Library added detective stories to the genre.

dimension /daɪ'menʃən/ n. a measurable extent of any kind, as length, breadth, thickness, area, or volume; (in *plural*) size; extent or scope in a particular aspect. —**dimensional** adj. [from Old French from Latin (*mensio* = measure)]

dimidiate /dɪ'mɪdɪət/ adj. halved, split in two. —**dimidiation** /-'eɪʃən/ n. [from Latin *dimidiare* (*midium* = half)]

diminish /dɪ'mɪnɪʃ/ v.t./i. to make or become smaller or less (in fact or appearance); to lessen the reputation of (a person). —**law of diminishing returns**, the fact that expenditure, taxation etc., beyond a certain point does not produce a proportionate yield. [from earlier *minish* (from Old French, and *diminue* from Old French from Latin *diminuere* = break up small]

diminuendo /dɪmɪnjuː'endəʊ/ adv. in music, with a gradual decrease of loudness. —n. (*plural* **diminuendos**) in music, a passage to be played in this way. [Italian]

diminution /dɪmɪ'njuːʃən/ n. diminishing, being diminished; decrease. [from Old French from Latin]

diminutive /dɪ'mɪnjʊtɪv/ adj. 1. remarkably small, tiny. 2. (of a derivative or suffix) used to imply something small (actually or in token of affection etc.) of the kind denoted by the simple word. —n. a diminutive word.

Dimitrov /dɪmɪ'trɒf/ Georgi 1882–1949. Bulgarian communist, prime minister from 1946. He was elected a deputy in 1913 and from 1919 was a member of the executive of the Comintern, an international communist organization (see the ◊International). In 1933 he was arrested in Berlin and tried with others in Leipzig for allegedly setting fire to the parliament building (see ◊Reichstag fire). Acquitted, he went to the USSR, where he became general secretary of the Comintern until its dissolution in 1943.

dimity /'dɪmɪtɪ/ n. a cotton fabric woven with checks or stripes of heavier thread. [from Italian or Latin from Greek *dimitos* = of double thread]

dimple n. a small hollow or dent, especially in the cheek or chin. —v.t./i. to produce dimples in; to show dimples.

din n. a prolonged loud and distracting noise. —v.t./i. (**-nn-**) 1. to force (information) *into* a person by continually repeating it. 2. to make a din. [Old English]

dinar /'diːnɑː/ n. a currency unit in Yugoslavia and in several countries of the Middle East and North Africa. [from Arabic and Persian from Greek from Latin *denarius* = silver coin]

dine v.t./i. 1. to eat dinner. 2. to give dinner to (especially socially). —**dining car** n. a railway coach in which meals are served. **dining room** n. a room in which meals are eaten. [from Old French *di(s)ner* from Latin *disjejunare* = break one's fast *jejunare* = fast]

Dine /daɪn/ Jim 1935– . US Pop artist. He experimented with combinations of paintings and objects, such as a sink attached to a canvas.

diner n. 1. a person who dines. 2. a small dining room. 3. a dining car on a train.

Dinesen /'dɪnɪsən/ Isak 1885–1962. Pen name of Danish writer Karen ◊Blixen, born Karen Christentze Dinesen.

Dingaan /'dɪŋgɑːn/ died 1840. Zulu chief from 1828. He obtained the throne by murdering his predecessor, Shaka, and became noted for his cruelty. In warfare with the Boer immigrants into Natal he was defeated on 16 Dec 1838 – 'Dingaan's Day'. He escaped to Swaziland, where he was deposed by his brother Mpande and subsequently assassinated.

ding-dong *n.* the sound of alternating strokes as of two bells. —*adj.* (of a contest) in which each contestant alternately has the advantage. —*adv.* with vigour and energy.

dinghy /'dɪŋgɪ, -ɡɪ/ *n.* a ship's small boat; a small pleasure boat; a small inflatable rubber boat. [from Hindi = Indian river boat]

dingle *n.* a deep wooded valley or dell.

dingo /'dɪŋgəʊ/ *n.* (*plural* **dingoes**) a wild or half-domesticated Australian dog *Canis dingo*. Descended from domestic dogs brought from Asia by Aborigines thousands of years ago, it belongs to the same family, Canidae, as domestic dogs. It is reddish brown with a bushy tail, and often hunts at night. It cannot bark. [Aboriginal]

dingy /'dɪndʒɪ/ *adj.* dull-coloured, drab; dirty-looking. —**dingily** *adv.*, **dinginess** *n.*

Dinkins /'dɪŋkɪnz/ David 1927– . Mayor of New York City from Jan 1990, a Democrat. He won a reputation as a moderate and consensual community politician and was Manhattan borough president before succeeding Ed Koch to become New York's first black mayor.

dinkum /'dɪŋkəm/ *adj.* (*Australian* and *New Zealand colloquial*) genuine, real.

dinky *adj.* (*colloquial*) neat and attractive; small, dainty. [diminutive of Scottish *dink* = neat, trim]

dinner *n.* the chief meal of the day, whether at midday or evening; a formal evening meal in honour of a person or event. —**dinner jacket,** a man's short, usually black, jacket for evening wear. [from Old French]

Dinorwig /dɪ'nɔːwɪg/ *n.* the location of Europe's largest pumped-storage hydroelectric scheme, completed in 1984, in Gwynedd, North Wales. Six turbogenerators are involved, with a maximum output of some 1,880 megawatts. The working head of water for the station is 530 m/1,740 ft.

dinosaur /'daɪnəsɔː(r)/ *n.* any of a group (sometimes considered as two separate orders) of extinct reptiles living between 215 million and 65 million years ago. Their closest living relations are crocodiles and birds, the latter perhaps descended from the dinosaurs. Many species of dinosaur evolved during the millions of years they were the dominant large land animals. Most were large (up to 27 m/90 ft), but some were as small as chickens. They disappeared 65 million years ago for reasons not fully understood, although many theories exist. [from Latin from Greek *deinos* = terrible and *sauros* = lizard]

dint *n.* a dent. —*v.t.* to mark with dints. —**by dint of,** by force or means of. [from Old English and Old Norse]

diocese /'daɪəsɪs/ *n.* the district under the pastoral care of a bishop. —**diocesan** /daɪ'ɒsɪsən/ *adj.* [from Old French from Latin from Greek *dioikēsis* = administration]

Diocletian /daɪə'kliːʃən/ Gaius Valerius Diocletianus AD 245–313. Roman emperor from 284–305, when he abdicated in favour of Galerius. He reorganized and subdivided the empire, with two joint and two subordinate emperors, and in 303 initiated severe persecution of Christians.

diode /'daɪəʊd/ *n.* a thermionic valve having two electrodes; a semiconductor rectifier having two terminals.

dioecious /daɪ'iːʃəs/ *adj.* **1.** in botany, with male and female organs on separate plants. **2.** in zoology, having the two sexes in separate individuals. [from Greek *-oikos* = -housed]

Diogenes /daɪ'ɒdʒəniːz/ *c.*412–323 BC. Ascetic Greek philosopher of the ◊Cynic school. He believed in freedom and self-sufficiency for the individual, and that the virtuous life was the simple life; he did not believe in social mores.

Dion Cassius /'daɪən 'kæsɪəs/ AD 150–235. Roman historian. He wrote, in Greek, a Roman history in 80 books (of which 26 survive), covering the period from the founding of the city to AD 229, including the only surviving account of the invasion of Britain by Claudius in AD 43.

Dionysius /daɪə'nɪzɪəs/ two tyrants of the ancient Greek city of Syracuse in Sicily. **Dionysius the Elder** (432–367 BC) seized power in 405. His first two wars with Carthage further extended the power of Syracuse,

but in a third (383–378 BC) he was defeated. He was a patron of ◊Plato (see also ◊Damocles). He was succeeded by his son, **Dionysius the Younger,** who was driven out of Syracuse by Dion in 356; he was tyrant again in 353, but in 343 returned to Corinth.

Dionysus /daɪə'naɪsəs/ in Greek mythology, the god of wine (son of Semele and Zeus), and also of orgiastic excess. He was identified with ◊Bacchus, whose rites were less savage. Attendant on him were the ◊maenads.

dioptre /daɪ'ɒptə/ *n.* an optical unit in which the power of a ◊lens is expressed as the reciprocal of its focal length in metres. The usual convention is that convergent lenses are positive and divergent lenses negative. Short-sighted people need lenses of power about -0.66 dioptre; a typical value for long sight is about $+1.5$ dioptre. [from French from Latin from Greek *dioptra* = optical instrument]

Dior /'diːɔː/ Christian 1905–1957. French couturier who established his own Paris salon in 1947 and made an impact with the 'New Look' – long, cinch-waisted, and full-skirted—after wartime austerity.

diorama /daɪə'rɑːmə/ *n.* **1.** a scenic painting in which changes in colour and direction of illumination simulate sunrise etc. **2.** a small representation of a scene with three-dimensional figures, viewed through a window etc. **3.** a small-scale model or film set. [from Greek *dia* = through and *horama* = thing seen]

diorite *n.* an igneous rock intermediate in composition; the coarse-grained plutonic equivalent of ◊andesite.

Diouf /di'uːf/ Abdou 1935– . Senegalese politician, president from 1980. He became prime minister in 1970 under President Leopold Senghor and, on his retirement, succeeded him, being re-elected in 1983 and 1988.

dioxide /daɪ'ɒksaɪd/ *n.* an oxide containing two atoms of oxygen.

dioxin *n.* any of a family of over 200 organic chemicals, all of which are heterocyclic hydrocarbons (cyclic compounds, i.e. having rings of atoms in their molecules), of which 2,3,7,8-tetrachlorodibenzodioxin (2,3,7,8-TCDD) is the most widespread. A highly toxic chemical, it occurred as an impurity in a defoliant (Agent Orange) used in the Vietnam War, and in the weedkiller 2,4,5-T. It has been associated with a disfiguring skin complaint (chloracne), birth defects, miscarriages, and cancer.

dip *v.t./i.* (-**pp**-) **1.** to put or let down into a liquid, to immerse; to dye (a fabric) thus; to wash (sheep) in vermin-killing liquid; to go under water and emerge quickly; to go down, to go below any surface or level. **2.** to lower for a moment and then raise again; to lower the beam of (a vehicle's headlights) to reduce dazzle. **3.** to slope or extend downwards. **4.** to put a hand or ladle etc. *into* to take something out; to look cursorily *into* (a book etc.). —*n.* **1.** dipping, being dipped. **2.** (*colloquial*) a bathe in the sea etc. **3.** a liquid in which a thing is dipped; a sauce or dressing in which food is dipped before eating. **4.** the downward slope of a road etc.; a depression in the skyline etc. —**dipstick** *n.* a rod for measuring the depth of a liquid, especially oil in a vehicle's engine. **dip switch** *n.* a switch for dipping a vehicle's headlights. [Old English]

dip, magnetic the angle between the horizontal and that taken up by a freely pivoted magnetic needle (the dip needle) mounted vertically in the Earth's magnetic field. It is also called the angle of inclination. The dip needle parallels the lines of force of the magnetic field at any point. Thus at the magnetic north and south poles, the needle dips vertically and the angle of dip is 90°.

diphtheria /dɪf'θɪərɪə/ *n.* an acute infectious bacterial disease with inflammation of a mucous membrane especially of the throat. The organism responsible is a bacterium (*Corynebacterium diptheria*). Its incidence has been reduced greatly by immunization. [from French from Greek *diphthera* = piece of leather, from the toughness of the false membrane developed]

diphthong /'dɪfθɒŋ/ *n.* a union of two vowels (letters or sounds) pronounced in one syllable (as in *coin, loud, toy*). —**diphthongal** /-'θɒŋgəl/ *adj* [from French from Latin from Greek *phthongos* = sound]

Diplock court /'dɪplɒk/ in Northern Ireland, a type of court established in 1972 by the British government under Lord Diplock (1907–1985) to try offences linked with guerrilla violence. The right to jury trial was suspended and the court consisted of a single judge, because allegedly

magnetic dip

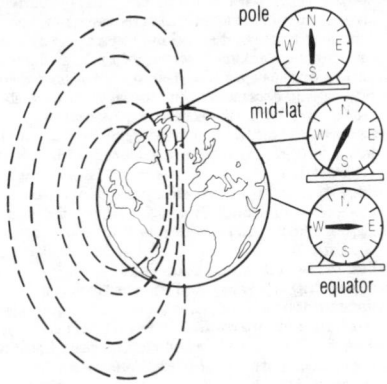

pole

mid-lat

equator

magnetic lines of force

potential jurors were being intimidated and were unwilling to serve. Despite widespread criticism, the Diplock courts have remained in operation.

diplodocus /dɪˈplɒdəkəs/ *n.* a giant herbivorous dinosaur of the order Sauropoda that lived about 145 million years ago, the fossils of which have been found in the W USA. Up to 27 m/88 ft long, most of this neck and tail, it weighed about 11 tonnes. It walked on four elephantine legs, had nostrils on top of the skull, and peg-like teeth at the front of the mouth. [from Greek *diploos* = double and *dokos* = beam]

diploid /ˈdɪplɔɪd/ *adj.* having two sets of ◊chromosomes in each cell. In sexually reproducing species, one set is derived from each parent, the ◊gametes, or sex cells, of each parent being ◊haploid (having only one set of chromosomes) due to ◊meiosis (reduction cell division). —*n.* a diploid cell or organism. [German, from Greek *diplous* = double and *eidos* = form]

diploma /dɪˈpləʊmə/ *n.* 1. a certificate awarded by a college etc. to a person who has successfully completed a course of study; a document conferring honour or privilege. 2. an official document, a charter. [Latin from Greek = folded paper (*diplous* = double)]

diplomacy /dɪˈpləʊməsɪ/ *n.* the management of international relations or skill in this; tact. [from French]

diplomat /ˈdɪpləmæt/ *n.* 1. a member of the diplomatic service. 2. a tactful person. [from French]

diplomatic /dɪpləˈmætɪk/ *adj.* of or involved in diplomacy; tactful. —*n.* (in *singular* or *plural*) the palaeographic and critical study of diplomas (sense 2). —**diplomatic immunity,** exemption of diplomatic staff etc. abroad from arrest, taxation etc. **diplomatic service,** the branch of public service concerned with the representation of a country abroad. —**diplomatically** *adv.* [from French]

diplomatist /dɪˈpləʊmətɪst/ *n.* a diplomat.

diplopia *n.* double vision occurring due to a lack of coordination of the movements of the eyes. It may arise from disorder in, or damage to, the nerve supply or muscles of the eye, or from intoxication.

dipole *n.* in chemistry, a pair of equal and opposite charges located apart, as in some ionic molecules. The product of one charge and the distance between them is the **dipole moment.**

dipper *n.* 1. a thing that dips. 2. any of various passerine birds of the family Cinclidae, found in hilly and mountainous regions across Eurasia and North America. The Eurasian dipper *Cinclus cinclus* is about 18 cm/7 in long, has blackish plumage, chestnut below, with white chin and breast, and a tail shaped and cocked like a wren's.

dipsomania /dɪpsəˈmeɪnɪə/ *n.* an uncontrollable craving for alcohol. —**dipsomaniac** *n.* [from Greek *dipsa* = thirst]

dipterous /ˈdɪptərəs/ *adj.* two-winged, belonging to the order Diptera (insects with one pair of membranous wings, e.g. fly, mosquito). [from Greek *pteron* = wing]

diptych /ˈdɪptɪk/ *n.* a painting, especially an altar-piece, on two leaves closing like a book. [from Latin from Greek = pair of writing tablets (*ptukhē* = fold)]

Dirac /dɪˈræk/ Paul Adrien Maurice 1902–1984. British physicist who worked out a version of quantum mechanics consistent with special ◊relativity. The existence of the positron (positive electron) was one of its predictions. He shared the Nobel Prize for Physics in 1933.

dire *adj.* dreadful, calamitous, ominous; extreme and requiring urgent remedy. [from Latin *dirus*]

direct /dɪˈrekt, daɪ-/ *adj.* 1. extending or moving in a straight line or by the shortest route, not crooked or oblique. 2. straightforward, going straight to the point; frank, not ambiguous. 3. without intermediaries; personal. 4. (of descent) linear, not collateral. 5. complete, greatest possible. —*adv.* in a direct way or manner; by a direct route. —*v.t.* 1. to control, to manage, to govern the actions of; to command; to supervise the acting etc. of (a play or film etc.). 2. to tell (a person) the way (*to*); to address (a letter etc. *to*). 3. to cause (a blow, remark, effort, attention etc.) to have a specified direction or target. —**direct action,** exertion of pressure on the community by action (e.g. a strike or sabotage) seeking an immediate effect, rather than by parliamentary means. **direct current,** an electric current flowing in one direction only. **direct debit,** the regular debiting of a person's bank account at the request of a creditor. **direct-grant school,** one receiving money from the government and not from a local authority, and in return observing certain conditions as to the admission of pupils. **direct object,** the primary object of action of a transitive verb. **direct speech,** words quoted as actually spoken, not modified by being reported. **direct tax,** one levied on income as distinct from one on goods or services. —**directness** *n.* [from Latin *dirigere* (*regere* = keep straight, rule)]

directed numbers ◊integers with a positive (+) or negative (–) sign attached. On a graph, a positive sign shows a movement to the right or upwards; a negative sign indicates movement downwards or to the left.

direction *n.* 1. directing, supervision. 2. (usually in *plural*) an order or instruction. 3. a line along which or a point to or from which a person or thing moves or looks; the tendency or scope of a subject, aspect. [from French or Latin]

directional *adj.* 1. of or indicating direction. 2. sending or receiving radio signals in one direction only.

directive *n.* a general instruction for a procedure or action. —*adj.* serving to direct.

directly *adv.* in a direct line or manner; at once, without delay. —*conj.* as soon as.

director *n.* one who directs, especially a member of the board managing the affairs of a company etc.; a person who directs a play, film etc.; a spiritual advisor. —**directorial** /-ˈtɔːrɪəl/ *adj.*, **directorship** *n.*, **directress** *n. fem.* [from Anglo-French from Latin = governor]

directorate *n.* 1. the office of director. 2. a board of directors.

Director of Public Prosecutions (DPP) in the UK, the head of the Crown Prosecution Service (established in 1985), responsible for the conduct of all criminal prosecutions in England and Wales. The DPP was formerly responsible only for the prosecution of certain serious crimes, such as murder.

directory *n.* a book with a list of telephone subscribers, inhabitants of a district, members of a profession etc., with various details.

dirge *n.* a slow mournful song; a lament for the dead. [from Latin *dirige* imperative of *dirigere* = direct, first word in Latin antiphon (from Psalm 5: 8) in Office of the Dead]

dirigible /ˈdɪrɪdʒɪbəl/ *adj.* capable of being guided. —*n.* a dirigible balloon airship.

dirk *n.* a kind of dagger, especially of a Scottish Highlander.

dirndl /ˈdɜːndəl/ *n.* a woman's dress imitating Alpine peasant costume, with a fitted bodice and full skirt; or **dirndl skirt,** a full gathered skirt with a tight waistband. [German, diminutive of *dirne* = girl]

dirt *n.* 1. unclean matter that soils something. 2. earth, soil. 3. foul or malicious words or talk. 4. excrement. —**dirt-cheap,** (*colloquial*) very cheap. **dirt road,** a road without a made surface. **dirt track** *n.* a racing track made of earth or rolled cinders etc. **treat like dirt,** to treat (a person) with contempt. [Old Norse = excrement]

dirty *adj.* 1. soiled by dirt, unclean; (of a nuclear weapon) causing considerable fall-out. 2. obscene, lewd. 3. dishonourable, unfair. 4. (of weather) rough, squally. 5. (of a colour) not pure or clear. —*v.t./i.* to make or become dirty. —**dirty look,** (*colloquial*) a look of disapproval or disgust. **dirty word,** an obscene word; a word for something disapproved of. —**dirtily** *adv.*, **dirtiness** *n.*

dis- prefix (**di-**before certain consonants) implying reversal of an action or state, the direct opposite of the simple word, the removal of a thing or quality, completeness or intensification of the action, expulsion from. [Latin]

disability /dɪsə'bɪlɪtɪ/ *n.* something that disables or disqualifies a person; a physical incapacity caused by injury, disease etc.

disable /dɪs'eɪbəl/ *v.t.* to deprive of an ability; (especially in *past participle*) to cripple, to deprive of or reduce the power of acting, walking etc. —**disablement** *n.*

disabuse /dɪsə'bjuːz/ *v.t.* to free of a false idea etc., to disillusion.

disaccharide *n.* a ◊sugar made up of two monosaccharide units. Sucrose, $C_{12}H_{22}O_{11}$, or table sugar, is a disaccharide.

disadvantage /dɪsəd'vɑːntɪdʒ/ *n.* an unfavourable circumstance or condition; damage to one's interest or reputation. —*v.t.* to put at a disadvantage. —**disadvantageous** /-'teɪdʒəs/ *adj* .

disadvantaged *adj.* in unfavourable conditions; lacking normal social etc. opportunities.

disaffected /dɪsə'fektɪd/ *adj.* discontented; disloyal. —**disaffection** *n.*

disagree /dɪsə'griː/ *v.i.* 1. to hold a different opinion; to quarrel. 2. (of factors or circumstances) to fail to correspond. —**disagree with,** to differ in opinion from; to have an adverse effect on. —**disagreement** *n.*

disagreeable *adj.* unpleasant, not to one's liking; (of a person) not amiable. —**disagreeably** *adv.*

disallow /dɪsə'laʊ/ *v.t.* to refuse to allow or accept as valid.

disappear /dɪsə'pɪə/ *v.i.* to cease to be visible, to pass from sight or existence. —**disappearance** *n.*

disappoint /dɪsə'pɔɪnt/ *v.t.* to fail to fulfil the desire or expectation of; to frustrate (a hope, purpose etc.). [from Old French]

disappointment *n.* a person, thing, or event that proves disappointing; the resulting distress.

disapprobation /dɪsæprə'beɪʃən/ *n.* disapproval.

disapprove /dɪsə'pruːv/ *v.i.* to have or express an unfavourable opinion (*of*). —**disapproval** *n.*

disarm /dɪ'sɑːm/ *v.t./i.* 1. to deprive of weapons or the means of defence; to reduce or give up one's own armaments. 2. to defuse (a bomb). 3. to pacify the hostility or suspicions of. [from Old French]

disarmament /dɪs'ɑːməmənt/ *n.* the reduction of a country's weapons of war. Most disarmament talks since World War II have been concerned with nuclear-arms verification, but biological, chemical, and conventional weapons have also come under discussion at the United Nations and in other forums.

disarrange /dɪsə'reɪndʒ/ *v.t.* to undo the arrangement of, to disorganize. —**disarrangement** *n.*

disarray /dɪsə'reɪ/ *n.* disorder. —*v.t.* to throw into disorder.

disassociate /dɪsə'səʊsɪeɪt/ *v.t.* = ◊dissociate.

disaster /dɪ'zɑːstə/ *n.* a sudden or great misfortune; a complete failure. —**disastrous** *adj.*, **disastrously** *adv.* [from French from Italian (Latin *astrum* = star, planet)]

disavow /dɪsə'vaʊ/ *v.t.* to disclaim knowledge of or responsibility for. —**disavowal** *n.*

disband /dɪs'bænd/ *v.t./i.* to break up (a group etc.); (of a group) to disperse. —**disbandment** *n.*

disbar /dɪs'bɑː/ *v.t.* (**-rr-**) to deprive (a barrister) of the right to practise law. —**disbarment** *n.*

disbelieve /dɪsbɪ'liːv/ *v.t./i.* to refuse or be unable to believe; to be sceptical. —**disbelief** *n.*, **disbeliever** *n.*

disburden /dɪs'bɜːdən/ *v.t.* to relieve of a burden; to remove (a load, anxieties etc.).

disburse /dɪs'bɜːs/ *v.t.* to pay out (money). —**disbursal** *n.*, **disbursement** *n.* [from Old French *bourse* = purse]

disc *n.* 1. a thin circular plate of any material; something shaped or looking like this, as the sun's face. 2. a layer of cartilage between the vertebrae. 3. a gramophone record. 4. in computing, a disc with a surface on which data can be recorded (usually magnetically) and stored; there are several types, including ◊floppy discs, ◊hard discs, and ◊CD-ROM. —**disc brake,** a brake consisting of a disc operated by the action of friction pads on it. **disc drive,** in computing, a device for controlling and using discs, having a rotation mechanism. **disc jockey,** a presenter of a broadcast programme featuring recordings of popular music. **disc pack,** a data storage medium consisting of an assembly of rigid magnetic discs mounted on a spindle, with a removable protective cover. [from French or from Latin *discus*]

discard /dɪs'kɑːd/ *v.t.* to put aside as useless or unwanted; to reject (a playing card) from a hand. —/'dɪs-/ *n.* a discarded thing.

discern /dɪ'sɜːn/ *v.t.* to perceive clearly with the mind or senses; to make out by thought or by gazing, listening, etc. [from Old French from Latin *discernere* (*cernere* = separate)]

discernible *adj.* able to be discerned.

discerning *adj.* having good judgement or insight.

discernment *n.* good judgement or insight.

discharge /dɪs'tʃɑːdʒ/ *v.t./i.* 1. to send out or emit (missiles, liquids etc.), (of a wound etc.) to emit a liquid; to unload from a ship. 2. to release (a prisoner); to allow (a patient, jury etc.) to leave; to relieve (a bankrupt) of residual liability; to dismiss from employment or office. 3. to acquit oneself of, to pay or perform (a duty or obligation). 4. to fire (a gun); to release the electric charge of; to remove the cargo from (a ship etc.). —/also 'dɪs-/ *n.* 1. discharging, being discharged. 2. that which is discharged, especially matter from a wound or sore. 3. the release of an electric charge, especially with a spark. 4. a written certificate of release, dismissal etc. [from Old French]

discharge tube a device in which a gas conducting an electric current emits visible light. It is usually a glass tube from which virtually all the air has been removed (so that it 'contains' a near vacuum), with electrodes at each end. When a high-voltage current is passed between the electrodes, the few remaining gas atoms in the tube (or some deliberately introduced ones) ionize and emit coloured light as they conduct the current along the tube. The light originates as electrons change energy levels in the ionized atoms.

disciple /dɪ'saɪpəl/ *n.* a follower or adherent of a leader, teacher etc.; one of Christ's original followers. [from Latin *discipulus* (*discere* = learn)]

disciplinarian /dɪsɪplɪ'neərɪən/ *n.* one who enforces or believes in strict discipline.

disciplinary *adj.* of or for discipline.

discipline /'dɪsɪplɪn/ *n.* 1. training or a way of life aimed at self-control and obedience; order maintained or observed among pupils, soldiers, and others under control; control exercised over the members of an organization. 2. punishment given to correct a person or enforce obedience. 3. a branch of instruction or learning. —*v.t.* to train to obedience and order; to punish. [from Latin *discere* = learn]

disclaim /dɪs'kleɪm/ *v.t.* to renounce a claim to, to disown, to deny (responsibility etc.).

disclaimer *n.* a statement disclaiming something; a renunciation.

disclose /dɪs'kləʊz/ *v.t.* 1. to make known. 2. to expose to view. —**disclosure** *n.* [from Old French]

disco *n.* (*plural* **discos**) (*colloquial*) a discothèque; a dancing-party with records; equipment for this.

discolour /dɪs'kʌlə/ *v.t./i.* to spoil the colour of, to stain; to become changed in colour or stained. —**discoloration** /-'reɪʃən/ *n.* [from Old French or Latin *colorare* = colour]

discomfit /dɪs'kʌmfɪt/ *v.t.* to humiliate or disconcert completely. —**discomfiture** /-fɪtʃə/ *n.* [from Old French *desconfire* from Latin *conficere* = put together]

discomfort /dɪs'kʌmfət/ *n.* lack of comfort; a thing causing this. —*v.t.* to make uncomfortable.

discompose /dɪskəm'pəʊz/ *v.t.* to disturb the composure of. —**discomposure** *n.*

disconcert /dɪskən'sɜːt/ *v.t.* to disturb the self-possession of, to fluster. [from French]

disconnect /dɪskə'nekt/ *v.t.* to break the connection of; to put out of action by disconnecting parts. —**disconnection** *n.*

disconnected *adj.* (especially of speech or writing) lacking orderly connection, having abrupt transitions.

disconsolate /dɪs'kɒnsələt/ *adj.* forlorn, downcast, disappointed. [from Latin *disconsolatus* (*consolare* = console)]

discontent /dɪskən'tent/ n. dissatisfaction, lack of contentment; a grievance. —v.t. to make dissatisfied. —**discontentment** n.

discontented adj. dissatisfied, feeling discontent.

discontinue /dɪskən'tɪnjuː/ v.t./i. to cease, to cause to cease; to cease from, to give up. —**discontinuance** n. [from Old French from Latin discontinuare (continuare = continue)]

discontinuous /dɪskən'tɪnjuəs/ adj. lacking continuity in space or time, intermittent. —**discontinuity** /-'juːɪtɪ/ n.

discord /'dɪskɔːd/ n. 1. opposition of views, strife; a harsh noise, clashing sounds. 2. in music, a lack of harmony between notes sounded together. [from Old French from Latin cor = heart]

discordant /dɪs'kɔːdənt/ adj. disagreeing; not in harmony, clashing. —**discordance** n.

discothèque /'dɪskəʊtek/ n. a club etc. where amplified recorded popular music is played for dancing; the equipment for playing such records. [French = record-library]

discount /'dɪskaʊnt/ n. an amount deducted from the full or normal price; an amount deducted for the immediate payment of a sum not yet due (e. g. on a bill of exchange. —v.t. 1. /-'kaʊnt/ to disregard partly or wholly. 2. /'dɪs-/ to buy or sell at a discount; to deduct an amount from (a price etc.). —**at a discount**, below full or normal price; (figurative) not at the true value. [from French or Italian]

discountenance /dɪs'kaʊntənəns/ v.t. 1. to refuse to approve of. 2. to disconcert.

discourage /dɪs'kʌrɪdʒ/ v.t. to deprive of courage or confidence; to dissuade, to deter; to show disapproval of. —**discouragement** n. [from Old French]

discourse /'dɪskɔːs/ n. 1. conversation; a speech or lecture. 2. a written treatise on a subject. —/-'kɔːs/ v.i. 1. to converse; to speak or write at length on a subject. 2. to utter a discourse. [from Latin discursus]

discourteous /dɪs'kɜːtɪəs/ adj. lacking courtesy. —**discourteously** adv., **discourtesy** n.

discover /dɪs'kʌvə/ v.t. to acquire knowledge or sight of by effort or chance; to be the first to do this in a particular case. [from Old French from Latin discooperire (cooperire = cover)]

discovery n. discovering; a thing discovered.

discredit /dɪs'kredɪt/ v.t. 1. to harm the good reputation of. 2. to refuse to believe; to cause to be disbelieved. —n. 1. harm to a reputation, a person or thing causing this. 2. lack of credibility.

discreditable adj. bringing discredit, shameful. —**discreditably** adv.

discreet /dɪs'kriːt/ adj. 1. showing caution and good judgement in what one does; not giving away secrets. 2. unobtrusive. —**discreetly** adv. [from Old French from Latin discretus = separate, discretio = discernment]

discrepancy /dɪs'krepənsɪ/ n. a difference, failure to correspond, inconsistency. —**discrepant** adj. [from Latin = discordance of sound]

discrete /dɪs'kriːt/ adj. separate, individually distinct; discontinuous. [from Latin discernere = distinguish, separate]

discretion /dɪs'kreʃən/ n. 1. good judgement, prudence; ability to keep secrets. 2. freedom or authority to act according to one's judgement. —**years** or **age of discretion,** the age at which a person is considered capable of managing his or her own affairs. [from Old French from Latin]

discretionary adj. done or used at a person's discretion.

discriminate /dɪs'krɪmɪneɪt/ v.t./i. 1. to make or see a distinction (between); to distinguish unfairly against or in favour of a person on grounds of sex, race, colour, etc. 2. to have good taste or judgement. —**discrimination** /-'neɪʃən/ n., **discriminatory** /-'krɪm-/ adj. **negative discrimination**, often based on ◊stereotype, includes anti-Semitism, apartheid, caste, racism, sexism, and slavery. **positive discrimination**, or 'affirmative action', is sometimes practised in an attempt to counteract the effects of previous long-term discrimination. Minorities and, in some cases, majorities have been targets for discrimination. National legislation in the UK includes the ◊Race Relations Acts 1965 and 1976 and the Sex Discrimination Act of 1975. [from Latin discrimen = distinction].

discriminating adj. showing good judgement, discerning.

discursive /dɪs'kɜːsɪv/ adj. wandering from topic to topic. [from Latin discurrere = run to and fro]

discus /'dɪskəs/ n. a circular disc thrown by athletes from within a circle 2.5 m/8 ft in diameter. The men's discus weighs 2 kg/4.4 lb and the women's 1 kg/2.2 lb. Discus throwing was a competition in ancient Greece at gymnastic contests, especially at the Olympic Games. It is an event in modern Olympics and track and field meets. [Latin from Greek diskos]

discuss /dɪs'kʌs/ v.t. to consider (a subject) by talking or writing about it; to hold a conversation about. —**discussion** n. [from Latin discutere = shake to pieces]

disdain /dɪs'deɪn/ n. scorn, contempt. —v.t. to regard with disdain; to refrain or refuse from disdain. —**disdainful** adj., **disdainfully** adv. [from Old French from Latin dedignare = think unworthy]

disease /dɪ'ziːz/ n. an unhealthy condition of the body, a plant, or some part thereof, caused by infection, diet, or faulty functioning of a physiological process; a particular kind of this; an abnormal mental condition. [from Old French]

diseased adj. affected with disease; abnormal, disordered.

disembark /dɪsɪm'bɑːk/ v.t./i. to go or put ashore. —**disembarkation** /-'keɪʃən/ n.

disembarrass /dɪsɪm'bærəs/ v.t. 1. to free from embarrassment. 2. to rid or relieve (of). —**disembarrassment** n.

disembody /dɪsɪm'bɒdɪ/ v.t. to free (a soul, spirit etc.) from the body or concrete form. —**disembodiment** n.

disembowel /dɪsɪm'baʊəl/ v.t. (-ll-) to remove the bowels or entrails of. —**disembowelment** n.

disenchant /dɪsɪn'tʃɑːnt/ v.t. to free from enchantment or illusion. —**disenchantment** n.

disencumber /dɪsɪn'kʌmbə/ v.t. to free from encumbrance.

disengage /dɪsɪn'geɪdʒ/ v.t./i. to detach, to loosen, to release from engagement; to become detached. —**disengagement** n.

disengaged adj. at leisure, uncommitted; detached.

disentangle /dɪsɪn'tæŋgəl/ v.t./i. to free or become free of tangles or complications. —**disentanglement** n.

disestablish /dɪsɪ'stæblɪʃ/ v.t. to end the established state of, to deprive (the church) of its state connection. —**disestablishment** n.

disfavour /dɪs'feɪvə/ n. dislike, disapproval; being disliked. —v.t. to regard or treat with disfavour.

disfigure /dɪs'fɪgə/ v.t. to spoil the appearance of. —**disfigurement** n.

disfranchise /dɪs'fræntʃaɪz/ v.t. to deprive of rights as a citizen or of a franchise held. —**disfranchisement** n.

disgorge /dɪs'gɔːdʒ/ v.t. to eject from the throat; to pour forth.

disgrace /dɪs'greɪs/ n. loss of favour or respect, downfall from a position of honour; a thing that causes this. —v.t. to bring disgrace to, to degrade; to dismiss from favour or honour. [from French from Italian]

disgraceful adj. causing disgrace, shameful. —**disgracefully** adv.

disgruntled /dɪs'grʌntəld/ adj. sulkily discontented.

disguise /dɪs'gaɪz/ v.t. to conceal the identity of, to make unrecognizable; to conceal or obscure. —n. something worn to disguise one's identity; a disguised state. [from Old French]

disgust /dɪs'gʌst/ n. strong dislike, repugnance. —v.t. to cause disgust in. [from Old French from Italian]

dish n. 1. a shallow flat-bottomed container for holding food; its contents; (in plural) all the utensils used at a meal. 2. a particular kind of food. 3. a dish-shaped object or cavity. 4. (colloquial) an attractive young woman. —v.t. 1. to make dish-shaped. 2. (colloquial) to frustrate, to ruin. —**dish out**, (slang) to distribute (carelessly). **dish up**, to put (food) in dishes ready for serving, to prepare to serve a meal; (slang) to present as fact or argument. **dishwater** n. water in which dishes have been washed. [Old English from Latin discus = disc]

dishabille /dɪsə'biːl/ variant of **déshabillé** .

disharmony /dɪs'hɑːmənɪ/ n. lack of harmony, discord. —**disharmonious** /-'məʊnɪəs/ adj.

dishcloth n. a cloth for washing dishes.

dishearten /dɪs'hɑːtən/ v.t. to make despondent, to cause to lose courage or confidence. —**disheartenment** n.

dishevelled /dɪ'ʃevəld/ adj. ruffled and untidy. —**dishevelment** n. [from Old French chevel = hair]

dishonest /dɪs'ɒnɪst/ adj. not honest. —**dishonestly** adv., **dishonesty** n.

dishonour /dɪs'ɒnə/ n. loss of honour or respect, shame or disgrace; a thing that causes this. —v.t. 1. to bring dishonour upon, to disgrace. 2. to refuse to accept or pay (a cheque etc.). [from Old French from Latin dishonorare]

dishonourable /dɪs'ɒnərəbəl/ adj. bringing dishonour, shameful, ignominious. —**dishonourably** adv.

dishwasher n. 1. a machine for washing dishes. 2. a water wagtail.

disillusion /dɪsɪ'luːʒən/ v.t. to free from illusion or mistaken belief. —n. being disillusioned. —**disillusionment** n.

disincentive /dɪsɪn'sentɪv/ n. a thing or factor discouraging a particular action.

disincline /dɪsɪn'klaɪn/ v.t. to make unwilling. —**disinclination** /-kli'neɪʃən/ n.

disinfect /dɪsɪn'fekt/ v.t. to cleanse of infection, to remove bacteria from. —**disinfection** n.

disinfectant adj. having disinfecting properties. —n. a disinfecting substance that kills, or prevents the growth of, bacteria and other microorganisms. Chemical disinfectants include carbolic acid (phenol, used by ◊Lister in surgery in the 1870s) acetaldehyde (ethanal), formaldehyde (methanal), chlorine, and iodine.

disinflation /dɪsɪn'fleɪʃən/ n. a policy designed to counteract inflation without producing the disadvantages of deflation. —**disinflationary** n.

disingenuous /dɪsɪn'dʒenjuəs/ adj. insincere, giving a false appearance of candour. —**disingenuously** adv., **disingenuousness** n.

disinherit /dɪsɪn'herɪt/ v.t. to reject as one's heir, to deprive of the right of inheritance (especially by making a new will). —**disinheritance** n. [from inherit in obsolete sense 'make heir']

disintegrate /dɪ'sɪntɪgreɪt/ v.t./i. to separate or cause to separate into component parts, to break up; to deprive of or lose cohesion; (of a nucleus) to emit one or more particles or divide into smaller nuclei. —**disintegration** /-'greɪʃən/ n., **disintegrator** n.

disinter /dɪsɪn'tɜː/ v.t. (-rr-) to dig up (especially a corpse) from the ground. —**disinterment** n.

disinterest /dɪs'ɪntərest/ n. 1. impartiality. 2. (disputed usage) lack of concern.

disinterested adj. 1. impartial, not influenced by involvement or advantage. 2. (disputed usage) uninterested. —**disinterestedly** adv., **disinterestedness** n.

disinvestment n. the withdrawal of investments in a country for political reasons; in economics, non-replacement of stock as it wears out.

disjoin /dɪs'dʒɔɪn/ v.t. to separate, to disunite, to part. [from Old French from Latin disjungere (jungere = join)]

disjoint /dɪs'dʒɔɪnt/ v.t. to take to pieces at the joints; to dislocate; to disturb the working or connection of.

disjointed adj. (of talk) disconnected.

disjunction /dɪs'dʒʌŋkʃən/ n. disjoining, separation. [from Old French or Latin]

disjunctive /dɪs'dʒʌŋktɪv/ adj. involving separation; (of conjunctions such as or and but) introducing an alternative or contrast. [from Latin]

disk variant of disc.

diskette /dɪs'ket/ n. a floppy disc, not necessarily of small size.

dislike /dɪs'laɪk/ n. a feeling that a person or thing is unpleasant, unattractive etc.; the object of this. —v.t. to have a dislike for, not to like.

dislocate /'dɪsləkeɪt/ v.t. to disturb the normal connection of, to displace a bone in (a joint); to disrupt, to put out of order. —**dislocation** /-'keɪʃən/ n. [from Old French or Latin dislocare (locare = place)]

dislocation n. in chemistry, a fault in the atomic structure of a crystal.

dislodge /dɪs'lɒdʒ/ v.t. to disturb or move from an established position. —**dislodgement** n.

disloyal /dɪs'lɔɪəl/ adj. unfaithful, lacking loyalty. —**disloyally** adv., **disloyalty** n.

dismal /'dɪzməl/ adj. causing or showing gloom, miserable, dreary; (colloquial) feeble, inept. —**dismally** adv. [from Old French from Latin dies mali = unlucky days (of which there were held to be two in each month)]

dismantle /dɪs'mæntəl/ v.t. to pull down, to take to pieces; to deprive of defences, equipment etc.

dismay n. a feeling of helplessness and alarm in the face of some danger or difficulty. —v.t. to fill with dismay. [from Old French]

dismember /dɪs'membə/ v.t. 1. to remove the limbs from. 2. to partition (a country etc.), to divide up. —**dismemberment** n. [from Old French from Latin membrum = limb]

dismiss /dɪs'mɪs/ v.t. 1. to send away, to cause to leave one's presence; to disperse. 2. to order to terminate employment or service (especially with dishonour). 3. to put out of one's thoughts, to cease to feel or discuss; to treat (a subject) summarily; to reject (a lawsuit etc.) without further hearing. 4. to put out (a batsman or side) in cricket (for a stated score). —**dismissal** n., **dismissive** adj. [from Old French from Latin dimissus (mittere = send)]

dismount /dɪs'maʊnt/ v.t./i. 1. to get off or down from an animal one is riding; to cause to fall off, to unseat. 2. to remove (a thing, especially a gun) from its mounting.

Disney /'dɪznɪ/ Walt(er Elias) 1901–1966. US film-maker and animator, a pioneer of family entertainment. He established his own studio in Hollywood in 1923, and his first Mickey Mouse cartoons (Plane Crazy which was silent, and Steamboat Willie which had sound) appeared in 1928. In addition to short cartoons the studio made feature-length animated films, including Snow White and the Seven Dwarfs 1938, Pinocchio 1940, and Dumbo 1941. Disney's cartoon figures, for example Donald Duck, also appeared in comic books worldwide. In 1955 Disney opened the first theme park, Disneyland, in California.

disobedient /dɪsə'biːdɪənt/ adj. disobeying, rebellious. —**disobedience** n., **disobediently** adv.

disobey /dɪsə'beɪ/ v.t./i. fail or refuse to obey; to disregard (a rule, order etc.).

disorder /dɪs'ɔːdə/ n. 1. lack of order, confusion; a commotion, a riot. 2. disturbance of a normal state or function; an ailment, a disease. —v.t. to put into disorder, to upset. [from Old French]

disorderly adj. untidy, confused; riotous, contrary to public order or morality. —**disorderly house,** a brothel.

disorganize /dɪs'ɔːgənaɪz/ v.t. to upset the order or system of, to throw into confusion. —**disorganization** /-'zeɪʃən/ n.

disorient /dɪs'ɔːrɪənt/ v.t. to disorientate.

disorientate /dɪs'ɔːrɪənteɪt/ v.t. to confuse (a person) as to his or her bearings. —**disorientation** /-'teɪʃən/ n.

disown /dɪs'əʊn/ v.t. to refuse to recognize or acknowledge, to repudiate; to reject connection with.

disparage /dɪs'pærɪdʒ/ v.t. to speak slightingly of, to belittle. —**disparagement** n., **disparagingly** adv. [from Old French desparagier = marry unequally (parage = equality of rank from Latin par = equal)]

disparate /'dɪspərət/ adj. essentially different, unrelated, not comparable. [from Latin disparare = separate, influenced in sense by dispar = unequal]

disparity /dɪs'pærɪtɪ/ n. inequality, difference, incongruity. [from French from Latin dispar = unequal]

dispassionate /dɪs'pæʃənət/ adj. free from emotion, impartial. —**dispassionately** adv.

dispatch /dɪ'spætʃ/ v.t. 1. to send off to a destination or for a purpose. 2. to give the deathblow to, to kill; to finish or dispose of promptly or quickly. —n. 1. dispatching, being dispatched. 2. promptness, efficiency. 3. a written (official) message; a news report sent to a newspaper or news agency. —**dispatch box** n. a case for carrying official documents. **dispatch rider** n. an official messenger on a motorcycle. [from Italian dispacciare or Spanish despachar]

dispel /dɪ'spel/ v.t. (-ll-) to drive away, to scatter (darkness, fog, fears etc.). [from Latin dispellere (pellere = drive)]

dispensable /dɪ'spensəbəl/ adj. that can be dispensed with. [from Latin]

dispensary /dɪ'spensərɪ/ n. a place (especially a room) where medicines are dispensed. [from Latin]

dispensation /dɪspen'seɪʃən/ n. 1. dispensing, distributing. 2. ordering or management, especially of the world by Providence. 3. an exemption from a penalty, rule, or obligation. [from Old French or Latin]

dispense /dɪˈspens/ *v.t./i.* to distribute, to deal out, to administer; to make up and give out (medicines etc.) according to prescriptions. —**dispense with,** to do without; to make unnecessary. [from Old French from Latin *dispensare*, frequentative of *dispendere* = weigh or pay out]

dispenser *n.* 1. a person who dispenses (especially medicine). 2. a device for dispensing commodities in fixed quantities.

disperse /dɪˈspɜːs/ *v.t./i.* 1. to scatter; to drive, go, or send in different directions. 2. to send to or station at different points. 3. to put in circulation, to disseminate. 4. to separate (white light) into coloured constituents. —**dispersal** *n.*, **dispersive** *adj.* [from Latin *dispergere* (*spargere* = scatter)]

dispersion /dɪˈspɜːʃən/ *n.* 1. dispersing, being dispersed; in optics, the splitting of white light into a spectrum; in chemistry, the distribution of the microscopic particles of a ◊colloid. 2. **the Dispersion,** the scattering of Jews among Gentiles from the time of the Captivity onwards; the Jews thus scattered. See also ◊Diaspora.

dispirit /dɪˈspɪrɪt/ *v.t.* (often in *past participle*) to make despondent.

displace /dɪsˈpleɪs/ *v.t.* to move from its place; to oust, to take the place of; to remove from office. —**displaced person,** one removed from his or her home country by military or political pressure; originally, a civilian deported from a German-occupied country to work in Germany during the World War II, and thereafter homeless.

displacement *n.* 1. displacing, being displaced. 2. the amount of fluid displaced by a thing floating or immersed in it; the amount by which a thing is shifted from its place.

displacement activity in animal behaviour, an action that is performed out of its normal context, while the animal is in a state of stress, frustration, or uncertainty. Birds, for example, often peck at grass when uncertain whether to attack or flee from an opponent; similarly, humans scratch their heads when nervous.

displacement reaction a chemical reaction in which a less reactive element is replaced in a compound by a more reactive one.

display /dɪˈspleɪ/ *v.t.* to exhibit, to show; to reveal, to betray, to allow to appear. —*n.* 1. displaying. 2. a thing or things displayed, a show; ostentation. 3. a bird's special pattern of behaviour as a means of visual communication. [from Old French from Latin *displicare* (*plicare* = fold)]

displease /dɪsˈpliːz/ *v.t.* to arouse the disapproval or indignation of, to offend; to be unpleasing to. [from Old French from Latin *placēre* = please]

displeasure /dɪsˈpleʒə/ *n.* a displeased feeling, indignation, dissatisfaction.

disport /dɪˈspɔːt/ *v.t./i.* to play, to frolic; to enjoy *oneself.* [from Old French from Latin *portare* = carry]

disposable *adj.* able to be disposed of; at one's disposal; designed to be thrown away after use. —*n.* a disposable article.

disposal *n.* disposing, disposing of. —**at one's disposal,** available for one's use.

dispose /dɪˈspəʊz/ *v.t./i.* 1. to place suitably or in order, to arrange. 2. to incline, to make willing or desirous; to bring (a person, the mind) into a certain state; (in *passive*) to have a specified tendency of mind. 3. to determine the course of events. —**dispose of,** to get rid of; to deal with, to finish; to prove (an argument etc.) incorrect. [from Old French]

disposition /dɪspəˈzɪʃən/ *n.* 1. setting in order, arrangement. 2. the relative position of parts. 3. a temperament; a natural tendency, an inclination. 4. (usually in *plural*) a plan, preparations. [from Old French from Latin *disponere* = arrange]

dispossess /dɪspəˈzes/ *v.t.* to deprive (a person) of the possession *of*; to oust, to dislodge. —**dispossession** *n.*

disproof /dɪsˈpruːf/ *n.* disproving, a refutation.

disproportion /dɪsprəˈpɔːʃən/ *n.* lack of proportion; being out of proportion.

disproportionate /dɪsprəˈpɔːʃənət/ *adj.* out of proportion, relatively too large or too small. —**disproportionately** *adv.*

disprove /dɪsˈpruːv/ *v.t.* to prove to be false.

disputable /dɪsˈpjuːtəbl/ *adj.* open to dispute, not certainly true. [French, or from Latin]

disputant /dɪsˈpjuːtənt/ *adj.* a person involved in disputation.

disputation /dɪspjuːˈteɪʃən/ *n.* 1. an argument, a debate. 2. a formal discussion of a set question or thesis. [from French or Latin]

disputatious /dɪspjuːˈteɪʃəs/ *adj.* fond of argument.

dispute /dɪsˈpjuːt/ *v.t./i.* 1. to argue, to debate. 2. to quarrel. 3. to question the truth or validity of. —*n.* 1. an argument, a debate. 2. a quarrel. —**in dispute,** being argued about. [from Old French from Latin *disputare* = estimate (*putare* = reckon)]

disqualify /dɪsˈkwɒlɪfaɪ/ *v.t.* to make or declare ineligible or unsuitable; to debar from a competition. —**disqualification** /-ˈkeɪʃən/ *n.*

disquiet /dɪsˈkwaɪət/ *n.* uneasiness, anxiety. —*v.t.* to cause disquiet to.

disquietude /dɪsˈkwaɪətjuːd/ *n.* a state of disquiet.

disquisition /dɪskwɪˈzɪʃən/ *n.* a long elaborate treatise or discourse upon a subject. [French from Latin *quaerere* = seek]

Disraeli /dɪzˈreɪli/ Benjamin, Earl of Beaconsfield 1804–1881. British Conservative politician and novelist. Elected to Parliament in 1837, he was chancellor of the Exchequer under Lord ◊Derby in 1852, 1858–59, and 1866–68, and prime minister in 1868 and 1874–80. His imperialist policies brought India directly under the crown, and he personally purchased control of the Suez Canal. The central Conservative Party organization is his creation. His popular, political novels reflect an interest in social reform and include *Coningsby* 1844 and *Sybil* 1845.

There is no waste of time in life like that of making explanations.

Benjamin Disraeli
speech March 11 1873.

disregard /dɪsrɪˈɡɑːd/ *v.t.* to pay no attention to, to treat as of no importance. —*n.* lack of attention, indifference, neglect.

disrepair /dɪsrɪˈpeə/ *n.* bad condition due to lack of repairs.

disreputable /dɪsˈrepjʊtəbəl/ *adj.* of bad repute, not respectable in character or appearance; discreditable. —**disreputably** *adv.*

disrepute /dɪsrɪˈpjuːt/ *n.* lack of good repute, discredit.

disrespect /dɪsrɪˈspekt/ *n.* lack of respect, discourtesy. —**disrespectful** *adj.*, **disrespectfully** *adv.*

disrobe /dɪsˈrəʊb/ *v.t./i.* to remove clothes (from).

disrupt /dɪsˈrʌpt/ *v.t.* to interrupt the flow or continuity of, to bring disorder to; to break apart. —**disruption** *n.*, **disruptive** *adj.* [from Latin *disrumpere* (*rumpere* = break)]

dissatisfaction /dɪsætɪsˈfækʃən/ *n.* lack of satisfaction or contentment; a cause of this.

dissatisfy /dɪˈsætɪsfaɪ/ *v.t.* to fail to satisfy, to make discontented.

dissect /dɪˈsekt/ *v.t.* 1. to cut into pieces, especially so as to examine parts or structure. 2. to analyse, to examine or criticize in detail. —**dissection** *n.*, **dissector** *n.* [from Latin *dissecare* (*secare* = cut)]

dissemble /dɪˈsembəl/ *v.t./i.* to conceal or disguise (intention, character, feeling etc.); to talk or act hypocritically or insincerely. [from Old French from Latin *dissimulare* (*simulare* = simulate)]

disseminate /dɪˈsemɪneɪt/ *v.t.* to scatter about, to spread (ideas etc.) widely. —**dissemination** /-ˈneɪʃən/ *n.*, **disseminator** *n.* [from Latin *disseminare* (*semen* = seed)]

dissension /dɪˈsenʃən/ *n.* discord arising from dissent. [from Old French from Latin]

dissent /dɪˈsent/ *v.i.* to disagree openly, to hold a different view or belief (*from*). —*n.* such a difference of view or belief; an expression of this. [from Latin *dissentire* (*sentire* = feel)]

dissenter *n.* one who dissents; **Dissenter,** a member of a sect that has separated from the Church of England, a Nonconformist. [from prec.]

dissentient /dɪ'senʃɪənt, -ʃənt/ adj. dissenting from an established view. —n. a dissentient person.

dissertation /dɪsə'teɪʃən/ n. a detailed discourse, especially as submitted for a higher degree in a university. [from Latin dissertare, frequentative of disserere = examine]

disservice /dɪs'sɜːvɪs/ n. a harmful action, especially one done in a misguided attempt to help.

dissident /'dɪsɪdənt/ adj. disagreeing, at variance. —n. a person who is at variance, especially with established authority. —**dissidence** n. [French, or from Latin dissidēre (sedēre = sit)]

dissimilar /dɪ'sɪmɪlə/ adj. unlike, not similar. —**dissimilarity** /-'lærɪtɪ/ n.

dissimulate /dɪ'sɪmjʊleɪt/ v.t./i. to dissemble. —**dissimulation** /-'leɪʃən/ n. [from Latin dissimulare (simulare = simulate)]

dissipate /'dɪsɪpeɪt/ v.t./i. to dispel, to disperse; to squander, to fritter away. [from Latin dissipare = scatter around]

dissipated adj. given to dissipation, dissolute.

dissipation /dɪsɪ'peɪʃən/ n. dissipating; a frivolous or dissolute way of life.

dissociate /dɪ'səʊsɪeɪt, -ʃɪ-/ v.t./i. to separate or disconnect in thought or fact; to become dissociated. —**dissociate oneself from**, to declare oneself unconnected with. —**dissociation** /-'eɪʃən/ n., **dissociative** adj. [from Latin dissociare (socius = companion)]

dissociation /dɪ'səʊsɪeɪʃ(ə)n/ n. in chemistry, the process whereby a single compound splits into two or more smaller products that can easily recombine to form the reactant.

dissoluble /dɪ'sɒljʊbəl/ adj. that can be disintegrated, loosened, or disconnected. [French, or from Latin]

dissolute /'dɪsəluːt, -ljuːt/ adj. morally lax, licentious. [from Latin]

dissolution /dɪsə'luːʃən, -'ljuː-/ n. 1. dissolving, being dissolved, especially of a partnership or of a parliament for a new election; the breaking up or abolition (of an institution). 2. death. [from Old French or Latin]

dissolve /dɪ'zɒlv/ v.t./i. 1. to make or become liquid, especially by immersion or dispersion in a liquid. 2. to disappear gradually; to cause to do this. 3. to dismiss or disperse (an assembly, especially a parliament). 4. to annul or put an end to (a marriage or partnership). —**dissolve into**, to give way to (tears, laughter). [from Latin dissolvere (solvere = loosen)]

dissonant /'dɪsənənt/ adj. not in harmony, harsh-toned; incongruous. —**dissonance** n. [from Old French or Latin dissonare (sonare = sound)]

dissuade /dɪ'sweɪd/ v.t. to give advice or exercise influence to discourage or divert (a person from). —**dissuasion** n., **dissuasive** adj. [from Latin dissuadēre (suadēre = persuade)]

distaff /'dɪstɑːf/ n. a cleft stick holding wool or flax for spinning. —**distaff side**, the branch of a family descended from a female parent or ancestor. [Old English (as Middle Low German dise(ne) = bunch of flax and staff]

distance /'dɪstəns/ n. 1. the length of space between one point and another; a space of time. 2. a distant point, a remoter field of vision. 3. being far off; remoteness, reserve. —v.t. 1. to place or cause to seem far off. 2. to leave far behind in a race etc. —**keep one's distance**, to remain apart or aloof. [from Old French from Latin (distare = stand apart)]

distance ratio or **velocity ratio** in a machine, the distance moved by the output force divided by the distance moved by the input force. The ratio indicates the movement magnification achieved by the machine, and also the speed or velocity magnification possible.

distant adj. 1. far away, at a specified distance; remote in position, time, relationship, or concept. 2. avoiding familiarity, aloof. —**distantly** adv.

distaste /dɪs'teɪst/ n. a dislike, an aversion (for).

distasteful adj. causing distaste, disagreeable to. —**distastefully** adv.

distemper[1] /dɪ'stempə/ n. a disease of dogs and some other animals, with catarrh and weakness. —v.t. (archaic, usually in past participle) to upset, to derange. [from Latin distemperare (temperare = mix in correct proportion)]

distemper[2] n. a kind of paint using glue or size instead of an oil-base, for use on walls. —v.t. to paint with this. [from Old French or Latin distemperare = soak]

distend /dɪ'stend/ v.t./i. to swell or stretch out by pressure from within. —**distensible** adj., **distension** n. [from Latin distendere (tendere = stretch)]

distich /'dɪstɪk/ n. a verse couplet. [from Latin from Greek stikhos = line]

distil /dɪ'stɪl/ v.t. 1. to purify, to extract the essence from (a substance) by vaporizing it with heat then condensing it with cold and re-collecting the resulting liquid; to make (whisky, an essence etc.) by distilling raw materials. 2. to fall or cause to fall in drops. —**distillation** /-'leɪʃən/ n. [from Latin distillare (stilla = drop)]

distillate /dɪ'stɪleɪt/ n. a product of distillation.

distiller n. one who distils, especially a maker of alcoholic liquor.

distillery n. a place where alcoholic liquor is distilled.

distinct adj. 1. not identical, separate, different in quality or kind. 2. clearly perceptible, definite, and unmistakable. —**distinctly** adv., **distinctness** n. [from past participle of Latin distinguere]

distinction /dɪ'stɪŋkʃən/ n. 1. seeing or making a difference, discrimination. 2. a difference seen or made; a thing that differentiates. 3. distinguished character, excellence. 4. the showing of special consideration. 5. a title or mark of honour. [from Old French from Latin]

distinctive adj. distinguishing, characteristic. —**distinctively** adv.

distingué /dɪ'stæŋgeɪ/ adj. having a distinguished air or manners. [French]

distinguish /dɪ'stɪŋgwɪʃ/ v.t./i. 1. to observe or identify a difference in; to differentiate, to draw distinctions (between); to characterize, to be a mark or property of. 2. to make out by listening, looking etc. 3. to make oneself prominent or noteworthy (by some achievement). [from French or Latin distinguere (stinguere = extinguish)]

distinguishable adj. able to be distinguished.

distinguished adj eminent, having distinction.

distort /dɪ'stɔːt/ v.t. to pull or twist out of shape; to transmit (a sound etc.) inaccurately; to misrepresent (facts etc.). —**distortion** n. [from Latin distorquēre (torquēre = twist)]

distract /dɪ'strækt/ v.t. to draw away the attention of (a person, the mind etc.); to confuse, to bewilder. [from Latin trahere = draw]

distraction /dɪ'strækʃən/ n. 1. distracting, being distracted. 2. a thing that distracts the attention or impairs concentration. 3. an amusement, a relaxation. 4. mental confusion or distress. [from Old French or Latin]

distrain /dɪ'streɪn/ v.i. to levy distraint (upon a person or goods). [from Old French from Latin distringere (stringere = draw tight)]

distraint /dɪ'streɪnt/ n. the seizure of goods as a method of enforcing payment.

distrait /dɪ'streɪ/ adj. (feminine distraite /-eɪt/) inattentive; distraught. [French]

distraught /dɪ'strɔːt/ adj. much troubled in mind; demented with worry etc.

distress /dɪ'stres/ n. 1. anguish or suffering caused by pain, sorrow, worry, or exhaustion; a state of difficulty or helplessness; lack of money or necessaries. 2. in law, distraint. —v.t. to cause distress to, to make unhappy. [from Old French]

distressed adj. affected by distress, impoverished. —**distressed area**, a region of much poverty and unemployment.

distributary /dɪ'strɪbjʊtərɪ/ n. a river or glacier branch that does not return to the main stream after leaving it (as in a delta).

distribute /dɪ'strɪbjuːt, (disputed usage) 'dɪs-/ v.t. to divide and give a share of to each of a number; to spread about, to scatter, to put at different points; to arrange, to classify. —**distribution** /-'bjuːʃən/ n. [from Latin distribuere (tribuere = assign)]

distributive /dɪ'strɪbjʊtɪv/ adj. of, concerned with, or produced by distribution; in mathematics, descriptive of any operation * for which, when it is performed with another operation ∘, a * (b ∘ c) = (a * b) ∘ (a * c); in grammar and logic, referring to each individual within a class, not to the class collectively. —n. a distributive word (e. g. each, neither, every). [from French or Latin]

distributive law in mathematics, the law that states that if there are two binary operations '×' and '+' on a set, '×' distributes over '+' as in multiplication, so that, for example, 3 × (4 + 5) is the same as (3 × 4) + (3 x 5). See also ◊associative law and ◊commutative law.

distributor /di'strɪbjutə/ *n.* **1.** one who distributes things, especially an agent who markets goods. **2.** a device in an internal-combustion engine for passing the current to each sparking-plug in turn. The electricity is passed to the plug leads by the tip of a rotor arm, driven by the engine camshaft, and current is fed to the rotor arm from the ignition coil. The distributor also houses the contact point or breaker, which opens and closes to interrupt the battery current to the coil, thus triggering the high-voltage pulses. In modern cars with electronic ignition, it is absent.

district /'dɪstrɪkt/ *n.* a region or territory regarded as a geographical or administrative unit; a division of a county. —**district attorney,** (*US*) the prosecuting officer of a district. **district nurse,** a local nurse visiting patients at their homes. [French from Latin = territory of jurisdiction]

district council a unit of local government in England and Wales. The district councils are headed by an annually elected chair or, in an honorary borough or city, a mayor or lord mayor. Councillors are elected for four years, according to one of the following practices: either one-third of the councillors retire at a time, so that district elections are held in three out of four years, and county-council elections taking place in the fourth; or the whole council retires midway between county-council elections. The responsibilities of district councils cover housing, local planning and development, roads (excluding trunk and classified), bus services, environmental health (refuse collection, clean air, food safety and hygiene, and enforcement of the Offices, Shops and Railway Premises Act), local taxation, museums and art galleries, parks and playing fields, swimming facilities, cemeteries, and so on. In metropolitan district councils education, personal social services, and libraries are also included.

District of Columbia /kə'lʌmbiə/ federal district of the USA, see ◊Washington.

distrust /dɪs'trʌst/ *n.* lack of trust, suspicion. —*v.t.* to feel distrust in. —**distrustful** *adj.*

disturb /di'stɜ:b/ *v.t.* **1.** to break the rest or quiet or calm of; to agitate, to worry. **2.** to move from a settled position. **3.** (in *past participle*) emotionally or mentally unstable or abnormal. [from Old French from Latin *disturbare* (*turbare* = to disorder)]

disturbance *n.* an interruption of tranquillity; agitation; a tumult, an uproar.

disunion /dɪs'ju:niən/ *n.* separation, lack of union; discord.

disunite /dɪsju:'naɪt/ *v.t./i.* to remove unity from; to cause to separate, to experience separation. —**disunity** /-'ju:nɪti/ *n.*

disuse /dɪs'ju:z/ *v.t.* to cease to use. —/-'ju:s/ *n.* a disused state.

disyllable /dɪ'sɪləbəl, daɪ-/ *n.* a word or metrical foot of two syllables. —**disyllabic** /-'læbɪk/ *adj.*

ditch *n.* a long, narrow excavated channel, especially for drainage or to mark a boundary. —*v.t./i.* **1.** to make or repair ditches. **2.** to drive (a vehicle) into a ditch; (*slang*) to make a forced landing on the sea, to bring (an aircraft) down thus. **3.** (*slang*) to abandon, to discard, to leave in the lurch; to frustrate. —**dull as ditchwater,** very dull. [Old English]

dither /'dɪðə/ *v.i.* to be nervously hesitant or unsure; to tremble, to quiver. —*n.* a state of dithering, nervous excitement or apprehension.

dithyramb /'dɪθɪræm/ *n.* a Greek choric hymn, wild in character; a passionate or inflated poem, speech, or writing. —**dithyrambic** /-'ræmbɪk/ *adj.* [from Latin from Greek]

dittany /'dɪtəni/ *n.* a herb of the genus *Dictamnus,* formerly supposed to be of medicinal value. [from Old French from Latin *dictamnus* from Greek, perhaps from *Diktē* mountain in Crete where (among other places) the herb grew]

ditto /'dɪtəʊ/ *n.* (*plural* dittos) the aforesaid, the same (in accounts, inventories etc.), symbolized by two small marks (*ditto marks* ,,) placed under the word or item repeated; (*colloquial*) an expression of agreement. [Italian from Latin]

ditty *n.* a short, simple song. [from Old French *dité* = composition from Latin *dicere* = say]

diuretic /daɪə'retɪk/ *adj.* causing an increased secretion of urine. —*n.* a diuretic drug. [from Old French or Latin from Greek *oureō* = urinate]

diurnal /daɪ'ɜ:nəl/ *adj.* **1.** of the day, not nocturnal. **2.** daily; occupying one day. [from Latin *dies* = day]

diva /'di:və/ *n.* a great woman singer, a prima donna. [Italian from Latin = goddess]

divalent /daɪ'veɪlənt/ *adj.* in chemistry, having a valence of two.

divan /di'væn/ *n.* a low couch or bed without a back or ends. [from French or Italian ultimately from Persian = bench]

dive *v.t./i.* **1.** to plunge, especially head first, into water; (of an aircraft) to plunge steeply downwards; (of a submarine or diver) to submerge; to go down or out of sight suddenly. **2.** to rush or move suddenly. **3.** to put (one's hand) *into* one's pocket, handbag etc. —*n.* **1.** an act of diving; a sharp downward movement or fall. **2.** (*colloquial*) a disreputable place, a drinking-den. —**dive-bomb** *v.t.* to drop bombs on from a diving aircraft. **diving bell** an open-bottomed structure supplied with air, in which a diver can be lowered into deep water. **diving board** a springboard for diving from. **diving suit** a watertight suit, usually with a helmet and an air supply for work underwater. [Old English]

diver *n.* **1.** one who dives, especially a person who works underwater in a diving suit. **2.** a diving bird, especially of the genus *Gavia,* also called **loon**. Their legs are set so far back that walking is almost impossible, and they come to land only to nest, but divers are powerful swimmers and good flyers. They have straight bills and long bodies, and feed on fish, crustaceans, and some water plants. Of the four species, the largest is the white-billed diver *Gavia adamsii,* an Arctic species 75 cm/2.5 ft long.

diverge /daɪ'vɜ:dʒ/ *v.i.* to go in different directions from a common point, to become further apart; to go aside *from* a track or path. —**divergent** *adj.,* **divergence** *n.* [from Latin *vergere* = incline]

divers /'daɪvəz/ *adj.* (*archaic*) various, several. [from Old French]

diverse /daɪ'vɜ:s/ *adj.* of different kinds, varied. [from Latin *diversus* (*vertere* = turn)]

diversify /daɪ'vɜ:sɪfaɪ/ *v.t.* to make diverse, to vary; to spread (an investment) over several enterprises or products. —**diversification** /-fɪ'keɪʃən/ *n.* [from Old French from Latin]

diversion /daɪ'vɜ:ʃən/ *n.* **1.** diverting something from its course. **2.** the diverting of attention, a manœuvre to achieve this; a pastime, a recreation. **3.** an alternative route when a road is temporarily closed to traffic. —**diversionary** *adj.* [from Latin]

diversity /daɪ'vɜ:sɪti/ *n.* being diverse; a variety. [from Old French]

divert /daɪ'vɜ:t/ *v.t.* **1.** to turn aside from its course; to cause to go by a different route. **2.** to distract (the attention); to entertain or amuse. [from French from Latin *vertere* = turn]

diverticulitis *n.* an inflammation of the diverticula (pockets of herniation) in the large intestine. The condition is usually controlled by diet and antibiotics.

divertissement /di:vɜ:'ti:smɑ̃/ *n.* a short ballet etc. between acts or longer pieces; a diversion or entertainment. [French]

divest /daɪ'vest/ *v.t.* to strip (a person) *of* clothes; to deprive or rid *of.* [from Old French from Latin *vestire* = clothe]

divide /di'vaɪd/ *v.t./i.* **1.** to separate *into* parts, to split or break up; to separate (one thing) from another; to become or be able to be divided. **2.** to mark out into parts or groups, to classify. **3.** to cause to disagree, to set at variance. **4.** to distribute, to share out. **5.** to find how many times a number contains another. **6.** to separate (an assembly etc.) into two sets in voting, to be thus separated. —*n.* **1.** a watershed. **2.** (*figurative*) a dividing line. —**divided skirt,** culottes. [from Latin *dividere* = force apart]

dividend /'dɪvɪdend/ *n.* **1.** a number to be divided. **2.** a share of profits paid to shareholders or to winners in a football pool. **3.** the benefit from an action. [from Anglo-French from Latin]

divider *n.* **1.** a screen etc. dividing a room. **2.** (in *plural*) measuring compasses.

divination *n.* the art of ascertaining future events or eliciting other hidden knowledge by supernatural or nonrational means. Divination played a large part in the ancient civilizations of the Egyptians, Greeks (see ◊oracle), Romans, and Chinese (see ◊*I Ching*), and is still practised throughout the world. [from Old French or from Latin]

divine¹ /dɪˈvaɪn/ *adj.* 1. of, from, or like God or a god; sacred. 2. (*colloquial*) excellent, delightful. —*n.* a theologian or clergyman. —**divinely** *adv.* [from Old French from Latin *divus* = god]

divine² *v.t./i.* to discover by intuition, inspiration, or guessing; to foresee; to practise divination. —**divining rod** *n.* a dowsing rod (see ◊dowse). —**diviner** *n.* [from French from Latin *divinare*]

Divine Comedy, The an epic poem by Dante Alighieri 1307–21, describing a journey through Hell, Purgatory, and Paradise. The poet Virgil is Dante's guide through Hell and Purgatory; to each of the three realms, or circles, Dante assigns historical and contemporary personages according to their moral (and also political) worth. In Paradise Dante finds his lifelong love Beatrice. The poem makes great use of symbolism and allegory, and influenced many English writers including Milton, Byron, Shelley, and TS Eliot.

Divine Light Mission a religious movement founded in India in 1960, which gained a prominent following in the USA in the 1970s. It proclaims Guru Maharaj Ji as the present age's successor to the gods or religious leaders Krishna, Buddha, Jesus, and Muhammad, who can provide his followers with the knowledge required to attain salvation.

divine right of kings the Christian political doctrine that hereditary monarchy is the system approved by God, hereditary right cannot be forfeited, monarchs are accountable to God alone for their actions, and rebellion against the lawful sovereign is therefore blasphemous.

diving *n.* the sport of entering water either from a springboard (3 m/10 ft) above the water, or from a platform (10 m/33 ft) above the water. Various differing starts are adopted, and twists and somersaults performed in midair. Points are awarded and the level of difficulty of each dive is used as a multiplying factor.

diving apparatus any equipment used to enable a person to spend time underwater. Diving bells were in use in the 18th century, the diver breathing air trapped in a bell-shaped chamber. This was followed by cumbersome diving suits in the early 19th century. Complete freedom of movement came with the ◊aqualung, invented by Jacques ◊Cousteau in the early 1940s. For work at greater depths the technique of saturation diving was developed in the 1970s, where divers live for a week or more breathing a mixture of helium and oxygen at the pressure existing on the seabed where they work (as in tunnel building).

divinity /dɪˈvɪnɪtɪ/ *n.* 1. being divine; a god; godhead. 2. theology. [from Old French from Latin]

divisible /dɪˈvɪzɪbəl/ *adj.* able to be divided. —**divisibility** /-ˈbɪlɪtɪ/ *n.* [French or from Latin]

division /dɪˈvɪʒən/ *n.* 1. dividing, being divided; a process of dividing a number by another; a disagreement or discord; (in Parliament) the separation of members into two sections for counting votes. 2. one of the parts into which a thing is divided; a major unit of administration or organization. —**division sign**, the sign ÷ indicating that one quantity is to be divided by another. —**divisional** *adj.* [from Old French from Latin]

divisive /dɪˈvaɪsɪv/ *adj.* tending to cause disagreement. [from Latin]

divisor /dɪˈvaɪzə/ *n.* the number by which another is to be divided. [from French or from Latin]

divorce /dɪˈvɔːs/ *n.* 1. legal dissolution of a marriage. 2. severance, separation. —*v.t.* 1. to separate by divorce; to end a marriage with (one's husband or wife) by divorce. The ease with which a divorce can be obtained in different countries varies considerably and is also affected by different religious practices. In England, divorce could only be secured by the passing of a private act of Parliament until 1857, when the Matrimonial Causes Act set up the Divorce Court and provided limited grounds for divorce. The grounds for divorce were gradually liberalized by further acts of Parliament, culminating in the Divorce Reform Act 1969, under which the sole ground for divorce is the irretrievable breakdown of the marriage. 2. to

detach, to separate. [from Old French from Latin *vortere* = *vertere* = turn]

divorcee /dɪvɔːˈsiː/ *n.* a divorced person.

divot /ˈdɪvət/ *n.* a piece of turf cut out by a blow, especially by the head of a golf-club. [originally Scottish]

divulge /daɪˈvʌldʒ/ *v.t.* to disclose or reveal (a secret etc.). —**divulgence** *n.* [from Latin *vulgare* = publish]

divvy *n.* (*colloquial*) a dividend. —*v.t.* (*colloquial*, with *up*) to share out. [abbreviation of *dividend*]

Diwali /diˈwɑːlɪ/ *n.* a Hindu festival in Oct/Nov celebrating Lakshmi, goddess of light and wealth. It is marked by the lighting of lamps and candles, feasting, and exchange of gifts. [from Hindi from Sanskrit = row of lamps (*dīpa* = lamp)]

dixie *n.* a large iron cooking-pot used by campers etc. [from Hindi *degchī* from Persian, diminutive of *deg* = pot]

Dixie /ˈdɪksɪ/ the southern states of the USA.

Dixieland /ˈdɪksɪlænd/ *n.* 1. Dixie. 2. a kind of jazz with a strong two-beat rhythm that originated in New Orleans, USA, in the early 20th century, dominated by cornet, trombone, and clarinet. The trumpeter Louis Armstrong emerged from this style. The **trad jazz** movement in the UK in the 1940s–50s was a Dixieland revival.

DIY abbreviation of do-it-yourself.

dizzy *adj.* giddy, feeling confused; making giddy. —*v.t.* to make dizzy, to bewilder. —**dizzily** *adv.*, **dizziness** *n.* [Old English]

DJ abbreviation of 1. a disc jockey. 2. a dinner jacket.

Djakarta variant spelling of ◊Jakarta, capital of Indonesia.

Djibouti /dʒɪˈbuːtɪ/ chief port and capital of the Republic of Djibouti, on a peninsula 240 km/149 mi SW of Aden and 565 km/351 mi NE of Addis Ababa; population (1988) 290,000.

Djibouti Republic of; a country on the E coast of Africa, at the S end of the Red Sea, bounded to the E by the Gulf of Aden, to the SE by the Somali Republic, and to the S, W, and N by Ethiopia; **area** 23,200 sq km/8,955 sq mi; **capital** (and chief port) Djibouti; **physical** mountains divide an inland plateau from a coastal plain; climate hot and arid; **head of state and government** Hassan Gouled Aptidon from 1977; **exports** acts mainly as a transit port for Ethiopia; **population** (1990 est) 337,000 (Issa 47%, Afar 37%, European 8%, Arab 6%); **language** Somali, Afar, French (official), Arabic; **recent history** achieved independence from France in 1977. In 1979 all political parties combined to form the People's Progress Assembly (RPP), made the only legal party in a new constitution 1981. A policy of neutrality has been in force throughout Hassan Gouled's presidency; treaties of friendship have been signed with Ethiopia, Somalia, Kenya and Sudan.

Djilas /ˈdʒɪləs/ Milovan 1911– . Yugoslav political writer and dissident. A former close wartime colleague of Marshal Tito, in 1953 he was dismissed from high office and subsequently imprisoned because of his advocacy of greater political pluralism. He was released in 1966 and formally rehabilitated in 1989.

dl abbreviation of decilitre(s).

D.Litt. abbreviation of Doctor of Letters. [from Latin *Doctor Litterarum*]

dm abbreviation of decimetre(s).

DM abbreviation of Deutschmark, the unit of currency in Germany.

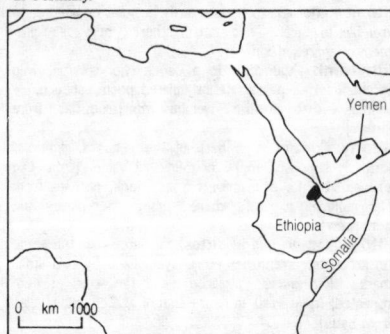

Djibouti

DNA abbreviation of deoxyribonucleic acid, a complex two-stranded molecule that contains, in chemically coded form, all the information needed to build, control, and maintain a living organism. DNA is a ladderlike double-stranded ◊nucleic acid that forms the basis of genetic inheritance in all organisms, except for a few viruses that have only ◊RNA. In ◊eukaryotic organisms, it is organized into ◊chromosomes and contained in the cell nucleus.

Dnepropetrovsk /nɪprəpiˈtrɒfsk/ city in Ukraine, USSR, on the right bank of the river Dnieper; population (1987) 1,182,000. It is the centre of an major industrial region, with iron, steel, chemical, and engineering industries. It is linked with the Dnieper Dam, 60 km/37 mi downstream.

Dnieper /ˈniːpə/ or **Dnepr** Russian river rising in the Smolensk region and flowing S past Kiev, Dnepropetrovsk, and Zaporozhe, to enter the Black Sea E of Odessa. Total length 2,250 km/1,400 mi.

D-notice *n.* an official request to news editors not to publish items on specified subjects, for reasons of security. [from defence + notice]

do[1] /du/, *emphatic* du:/ *v.t./i.* (*third person singular present* **does** /dʌz/; *past* **did** ; *past participle* **done** /dʌn/; *participle* **doing**) 1. to perform, to carry out, to fulfil or complete. 2. to produce, to make; to bring about, to provide. 3. to deal with, to set in order; to work out, to solve; to work at, to be occupied with; to cook; to translate or transform; (*slang*) to cheat, to rob or burgle; to prosecute or convict. 4. to cover in travelling; (*colloquial*) to visit, to see the sights of. 5. to undergo. 6. to provide food etc. for; (*colloquial*) to satisfy, to be suitable or convenient to. 7. to produce (a play etc.); to play the part of, to act like. 8. to fare, to get on, to achieve something. 9. to be suitable or acceptable, to serve a purpose. 10. to be in progress. —*v.aux.*, with infinitive or elliptically, for emphasis, in inversion, in questions and negations, or in place of the verb. —**do away with**, to get rid of, to abolish, to kill. **do down**, (*colloquial*) to overcome, to cheat, to swindle. **do for**, to be satisfactory or sufficient for; (*colloquial*) to destroy, to ruin, to kill; (*colloquial*) to act as a housekeeper for. **do-gooder** *n.* person meaning to do social good but unrealistic or intrusive in the process. **do in**, (*slang*) to ruin, to kill; (*colloquial*) to exhaust, to tire out. **do-it-yourself** *adj. & n.* (work) done or to be done by an amateur handyman at home. **do or die**, to persist regardless of danger. **do out**, to clean or redecorate (a room). **do over**, (*slang*) to attack, to beat up. **do something for**, (*colloquial*) to enhance the appearance or quality of. **do up**, to fasten, to wrap up; to refurbish, to renovate. **do with**, to use, to treat. **do without**, to forgo, to manage without. **to do with**, in connection with, related to. [Old English]

do[2] /du:/ *n.* (*plural* **dos, do's**) 1. an elaborate event, party, or operation. 2. (*colloquial*) a swindle, a hoax. —**dos and don'ts**, the rules of behaviour. **fair dos**, fair shares.

do[3] variant of **doh**.

do. abbreviation of ditto.

Dobell /dəʊˈbel/ William 1899–1970. Australian portraitist and genre painter, born in New South Wales. In 1929–39 he studied art in the UK and the Netherlands. His portrait of *Joshua Smith* 1943 (Sir Edward Hayward, Adelaide) provoked a court case (Dobell was accused of caricaturing his subject).

Dobermann *n.* or **Dobermann Pinscher** /ˈdəʊbəmən ˈpɪnʃə(r)/ a smooth-coated dog with a docked tail, much used as a guard dog. It stands up to 70 cm/2.2 ft tall, has a long head with a flat, smooth skull, and is often black with brown markings. [from L *Dobermann* (19th-century German dog-breeder) and German *pinscher* = terrier]

Döblin Alfred 1878–1957. German novelist. His *Berlin-Alexanderplatz* 1929 owes much to James Joyce in its minutely detailed depiction of the inner lives of a city's inhabitants, and is considered by many to be the finest 20th-century German novel. Other works include *November 1918: Eine deutsche Revolution/A German Revolution* 1939–50 (published in four parts) about the formation of the Weimar Republic.

Dobrynin /dəˈbriːnɪn/ Anataloy Fedorovich 1919– Soviet diplomat, ambassador to the USA 1962–86, emerging during the 1970s as a warm supporter of ◊detente.

Dobzhansky /dɒbˈʒaːnski/ Theodosius 1900–1975. US geneticist of Ukrainian origin. A pioneer of modern genetics and evolutionary theory, he showed that genetic variability

between individuals of the same species is very high and that this diversity is vital to the process of evolution. His book *Genetics and the Origin of Species* was published in 1937.

doc (*colloquial*) abbreviation of doctor.

docile /ˈdəʊsaɪl/ *adj.* submissive, easily managed. —**docilely** *adv.*, **docility** /-ˈsɪlɪtɪ/ *n.* [from Latin *docēre* = teach]

dock[1] *n.* an artificially enclosed body of water for the loading, unloading, and repair of ships; (in *plural*) a range of docks with wharves and offices. —*v.t./i.* 1. to bring or come into dock. 2. to join (two or more spacecraft) together in space, to become joined thus. —**in dock**, (*colloquial*) in hospital or (of a vehicle) laid up for repairs. [from Middle Dutch *docke*]

dock[2] *n.* an enclosure in a criminal court for the accused. [probable from Flemish *dok* = cage]

dock[3] *n.* a number of plants of the genus *Rumex* of the buckwheat family Polygonaceae. They are tall, annual to perennial herbs, often with lance-shaped leaves and small, greenish flowers. [Old English]

dock[4] *v.t.* 1. to cut short (an animal's tail). 2. to reduce or take away a part of (wages, supplies etc.). [from *dock* = fleshy part of tail]

dock[5] *n.* 1. the solid fleshy part of an animal's tail. 2. the crupper of a saddle or harness. [perhaps from Middle Low German *dokke* = bundle of straw]

docker *n.* a person employed to load and unload ships.

docket /ˈdɒkɪt/ *n.* a document or label listing goods delivered or the contents of a package, or recording the payment of customs dues etc. —*v.t.* to enter on a docket, to label with a docket.

dockland *n.* the district near docks.

dockyard *n.* an area with docks and equipment for building and repairing ships.

doctor /ˈdɒktə/ *n.* 1. a qualified practitioner of medicine, a physician. 2. a person who holds a doctorate. —*v.t.* 1. to treat medically. 2. to castrate or spay (an animal). 3. to patch up (machinery etc.); to tamper with or falsify. [from Old French from Latin *docēre* = teach]

doctoral /ˈdɒktərəl/ *adj.* of or for the degree of doctor.

doctorate /ˈdɒktərət/ *n.* the highest university degree in any faculty.

Doctor Faustus, The tragical history of a drama by Christopher Marlowe, published (in two versions) 1604 and 1616, first performed in England in 1594. The play, based on a medieval legend, tells how Faustus surrenders his soul to the Devil in return for 24 years of life and the services of Mephistopheles, who will grant his every wish.

doctrinaire /dɒktriˈneə/ *n.* a person who applies principles pedantically without allowance for circumstances. —*adj.* theoretical and unpractical. [French]

doctrine /ˈdɒktrɪn/ *n.* what is taught, a body of instruction; a principle of religion, a political etc. belief, a set of such principles. —**doctrinal** /-ˈtraɪnəl/ *adj.* [from Old French from Latin]

document /ˈdɒkjʊmənt/ *n.* a thing, especially a title-deed, writing, or inscription, that provides a record or evidence. —*v.t.* to prove by or provide with documents. —**documentation** /-ˈteɪʃən/ *n.* [from Old French from Latin = proof]

documentary /dɒkjuˈmentərɪ/ *adj.* consisting of documents; providing a factual record or report. —*n.* a documentary film.

dodder[1] *v.i.* to tremble or totter, especially from age. —**dodderer** *n.*, **doddery** *adj.*

dodder[2] *n.* a threadlike, climbing parasitic plant of the genus *Cuscuta*. [= Middle Low German *dod(d)er*, Middle High German *toter*]

dodecagon /dəʊˈdekəgən/ *n.* a plane figure with twelve sides and angles. [from Greek *dōdeka* = twelve and -*gonos* = angled]

dodecahedron /dəʊdekəˈhiːdrən/ *n.* a solid figure with twelve faces. [from Greek *dōdeka* = twelve and *hedra* = base]

dodecaphonic /dəʊdekəˈfɒnɪk/ *adj.* of a compositional method, in which the twelve notes of the octave are treated equally, without the focusing on a 'home-note' (the tonic) of traditional harmony. [from Greek *dōdeka* twelve and *phonic*]

dodge /dɒdʒ/ *v.t./i.* to move quickly to one side, or *round*, *about*, or *behind* an obstacle, to elude a pursuer, blow etc.;

to evade by cunning or trickery. —*n.* a quick movement to avoid something; a clever trick or expedient.

dodgem /'dɒdʒəm/ *n.* a small electrically driven car in an enclosure at a funfair, in which the driver tries to bump other cars and dodge those trying to bump his or her car.

Dodgson /'dɒdsən/ Charles Lutwidge. Real name of writer Lewis ◊Carroll.

dodgy *adj.* (*colloquial*) awkward, unreliable, tricky.

dodo /'dəʊdəʊ/ *n.* (*plural* **dodos**) an extinct bird *Raphus cucullatus* formerly found on the island of Mauritius, but exterminated before the end of the 17th century. Related to the pigeons, it was larger than a turkey, with a bulky body and very short wings and tail. Flightless and trusting, it was easy prey to humans. —**as dead as the dodo**, entirely obsolete. [from Portuguese = simpleton]

Dodoma /'dəʊdəmə/ official capital of Tanzania since 1974, when it replaced Dar-es-Salaam; 1,132 m/3,713 ft above sea level; population (1984) 180,000. It is a centre of communications, linked by rail with Dar-es-Salaam and Kigoma on Lake Tanganyika, and by road with Kenya to the N and Zambia and Malawi to the S.

doe /dəʊ/ *n.* the female of the fallow deer, reindeer, hare, or rabbit. [Old English]

Doe Samuel Kenyon 1950–1990. Liberian politician and soldier, head of state 1980–90 who seized power in a coup. Having successfully put down an uprising in April 1990, Doe was later deposed and killed by rebel forces in Sept 1990.

DOE abbreviation of Department of the Environment.

doer /'duː.ə/ *n.* one who does something; one who acts rather than merely talking or thinking.

does /dʌz/ third person singular present of **do.**

doeskin *n.* the skin of a fallow deer; leather made from this.

doesn't /'dʌznət/ = does not.

doff *v.t.* to take off (a hat or clothing). [= *do off*]

dog *n.* **1.** a four-legged carnivorous animal of the genus *Canis*, of many breeds (wild and domesticated); the male of this or of a fox or wolf. The domestic dog *Canis familiaris* is descended from the wolf or jackal, and bred into many different varieties for use as working animals and pets. There are over 400 different breeds of dog throughout the world. The UK Kennel Club (1873) groups those eligible for registration (150 breeds) into sporting breeds (hound, gundog, and terrier) and non-sporting (utility, working, and toy). **2.** a person, a despicable person. **3.** a mechanical device for gripping something. —*v.t.* to follow closely and persistently, to pursue, to track. —**dog collar** *n.* a collar for a dog; (*colloquial*) a clerical collar. **dog days,** the hottest period of the year. **dog-eared** *adj.* (of a book) with the corners worn or battered with use. **dog-eat-dog** *n.* ruthless competition. **dog-end** *n.* (*slang*) a cigarette-end. **dog in the manger,** one who clings to a thing he or she cannot use, preventing others from enjoying it. **dog's breakfast,** (*colloquial*) a mess. **dog's life,** a life of misery or harassment. **dog star** *n.* the chief star of the constellation Canis Major or Minor, especially Sirius. **dog-tired** *adj.* tired out. **dogwatch** *n.* one of the two-hour watches on a ship (4–6 or 6–8 p.m.). **go to the dogs,** (*slang*) to deteriorate, to be ruined. [Old English]

dogcart *n.* a two-wheeled driving cart with cross seats back to back.

doge /dəʊdʒ/ *n.* (*historical*) the chief magistrate in the former republics of Venice and Genoa. The first doge of Venice was appointed in 697 with absolute power (modified in 1297), and from his accession dates Venice's prominence in history. The last Venetian doge, Lodovico Manin, retired in 1797 and the last Genoese doge in 1804. [French from Italian from Latin *dux* = leader]

Dōgen /'dəʊgen/ 1200–1253. Japanese Buddhist monk, pupil of Eisai; founder of the Sōtōschool of Zen. He did not reject study, but stressed the importance of *zazen*, seated meditation, for its own sake.

dogfight *n.* **1.** a close combat between fighter aircraft. **2.** an uproar, a fight like that between dogs.

dogfish *n.* (*plural* usually the same) any of several small sharks found in the NE Atlantic, Pacific, and Mediterranean. The sandy dogfish *Scyliorhinus caniculus* is found around the coasts of Britain, Scandinavia, and Europe. Bottom-living, it is sandy brown and covered with spots, and grows to about 75 cm/2.5 ft. It is edible, and is known

in restaurants as 'rock eel' or 'rock salmon'. Various other species of small shark may also be called dogfish.

dogged /'dɒgɪd/ *adj.* tenacious, grimly persistent. —**doggedly** *adv.*

doggerel /'dɒgərəl/ *n.* poor or trivial verse. [apparently from *dog* (with disparaging force as in *dogrose*)]

doggie /'dɒgɪ/ *n.* (*children's colloquial*) a dog.

doggo *adv.* **lie doggo,** (*slang*) to lie motionless or hidden.

doggy *adj.* of or like a dog; devoted to dogs. —*n.* = ◊doggie.

doghouse *n.* (*US*) a dog's kennel. —**in the doghouse,** (*slang*) in disgrace.

dogma /'dɒgmə/ *n.* **1.** a principle or tenet; a system of these, especially as laid down by the authority of a church. **2.** an arrogant declaration of opinion. [Latin from Greek *dokeō* = seem]

dogmatic /dɒg'mætɪk/ *adj.* **1.** of or in the nature of a dogma. **2.** asserting or given to asserting dogmas or opinions; intolerantly authoritative. —**dogmatically** *adv.*

dogmatism /'dɒgmətɪzəm/ *n.* the tendency to be dogmatic.

dogmatize /'dɒgmətaɪz/ *v.t./i.* to speak dogmatically; to express (a principle etc.) as a dogma. [from French from Latin from Greek]

Dogon /'dəʊgɒn/ *n.* a member of the W African Dogon culture from E Mali and NW Burkina Faso. The Dogon number approximately 250,000, and their language belongs to the Voltaic (Gur) branch of the Niger-Congo family.

dogrose *n.* a wild hedge-rose *Rosa canina*.

dogsbody /'dɒgzbɒdɪ/ *n.* (*colloquial*) a drudge.

dogwood *n.* any deciduous tree or shrub of the genus *Cornus* of the dogwood family Cornaceae, native to temperate regions of North America and Eurasia. *C. sanguinea* grows up to 4 m/12 ft high. Several of the species are notable for their coloured bark: the Westonbirt dogwood *C. alba* has brilliant red stems in winter.

doh /dəʊ/ *n.* in music, the first note of a major scale in ◊tonic sol-fa. [from Italian *do*]

Doha /'dəʊhɑː/ (Arabic *Ad Dawḥah*) capital and chief port of Qatar; population (1986) 217,000. Industries include oil refining, refrigeration plants, engineering, and food processing. It is the centre of vocational training for all the Persian Gulf states.

Doi /'dɔɪ/ Takako 1929– . Japanese socialist politician, leader of the Japan Socialist Party (JSP) from 1986 and responsible for much of its recent revival. She is the country's first female major party leader.

Doi Inthanon /dɔɪnˈθænən/ highest mountain in Thailand, rising to 2,595 m/8,513 ft SW of Chiang Mai in NW Thailand.

doily /'dɔɪlɪ/ *n.* a small ornamental lace or paper mat used on a plate for cakes etc.

doing /'duː.ɪŋ/ participle of do¹. —*n.* **1.** activity, effort. **2.** (in *plural, slang*) adjuncts, things needed.

Doisy /'dɔɪzɪ/ Edward 1893–1986. US biochemist. In 1939 Doisy succeeded in synthesizing vitamin K, a compound earlier discovered by Carl ◊Dam, with whom he shared the 1943 Nobel Prize for Medicine.

Dolby /'dɒlbɪ/ *n.* trade name of a system used in tape-recording to reduce unwanted sounds at high frequency. [from R *Dolby* the inventor]

Dolci /'dɒltʃi/ Carlo 1616–1686. Italian painter of the late Baroque period, active in Florence. He created intensely emotional versions of religious subjects, such as *The Last Communion of St Jerome.*

doldrums /'dɒldrəmz/ *n.pl.* **1.** low spirits; a period of inactivity. **2.** an equatorial ocean region often marked by calms.

dole *n.* **1.** a charitable distribution, a thing given sparingly or reluctantly. **2. the dole,** (*colloquial*) a state benefit payable to insured persons who are unable to obtain employment. —*v.t.* to deal *out* sparingly. —**on the dole,** (*colloquial*) receiving state benefit for the unemployed. [Old English, related to *deal*¹]

doleful /'dəʊlfəl/ *adj.* mournful, sad; dreary, dismal. —**dolefully** *adv.* [from *dole* grief from Old French from Latin *dolēre* = grieve]

dolerite /'dɒləraɪt/ *n.* a coarse basaltic rock. [from French from Greek *doleros* = deceptive (because its contents are difficult to distinguish)]

dolphin

dolichocephalic /dɒlɪkusɪ'fælɪk/ *adj.* having a skull that is longer than it is wide. —**dolichocephalous** /-'sefələs/ *adj.*, **dolichocephalism** /-'sef-/ *n.*, **dolichocephaly** /-'sef-/ *n.* [from Greek *dolikhos* = long and *cephalic*]

Dolin /'dɒlɪn/ Anton. Stage name of Patrick Healey-Kay 1904–1983. British dancer and choreographer, a pioneer of UK ballet. After studying under Nijinsky, he was a leading member of Diaghilev's company 1924–27. He formed the Markova–Dolin Ballet with Alicia Markova 1935–38, and was a guest soloist with the American Ballet Theater 1940–46.

doll /dɒl/ *n.* **1.** a small model of a human figure, especially a baby or child, as a child's toy; a ventriloquist's dummy. **2.** (*slang*) a young woman. —*v.t.* (*colloquial*) to dress *up* smartly. [pet form of name *Dorothy*]

Doll William Richard 1912– . British physician who, working with Professor Bradford Hill (1897–) provided the first statistical proof of the link between smoking and lung cancer in 1950. In a later study of the smoking habits of doctors, they were able to show that stopping smoking immediately reduces the risk of cancer.

dollar /'dɒlə/ *n.* the currency unit in the USA and certain other countries. [from Low German from German *thaler* (*Joachimsthaler*, coin from *Joachimstal* in Germany)]

Dollfuss /'dɒlfuːs/ Engelbert 1892–1934. Austrian Christian Socialist politician who was appointed chancellor in 1932, and in 1933 suppressed parliament and ruled by decree. In Feb 1934 he crushed a protest by the socialist workers by force, and in May Austria was declared a 'corporative' state. The Nazis attempted a coup d'état on 25 July; the Chancellery was seized and Dollfuss murdered.

dollop /'dɒləp/ *n.* (*colloquial*) a shapeless lump of food etc.

Doll's House, The a play by Henrik Ibsen, first produced in Norway in 1879. It describes the blackmail of Nora, the sheltered wife of a successful lawyer, the revelation of her guilty secret to her husband, and subsequent marital breakdown.

dolly *n.* **1.** (*children's colloquial*) a doll. **2.** a movable platform for a cine-camera. —**dolly-bird** *n.* (*colloquial*) an attractive and stylish young woman.

dolman sleeve /'dɒlmən/ a loose sleeve cut in one piece with the body of a garment. [from Turkish]

dolmen *n.* a prehistoric monument in the form of a chamber built of large stone slabs, roofed over by a flat stone that they support. Dolmens are grave chambers of the Neolithic period, found in Europe and Africa, and occasionally in Asia as far E as Japan. In Wales they are known as **cromlechs**. [French, perhaps from Cornish *tolmēn* = hole of stone]

Dolmetsch /'dɒlmetʃ/ Arnold 1858–1940. French-born musician and instrument-maker who settled in England in 1914 and became a leading figure in the revival of early music.

dolomite /'dɒləmaɪt/ *n.* **1.** calcium magnesium carbonate, $CaMg(Co_{32})$, which is similar to calcite but often forms rhombohedral crystals with curved faces. Dolomite occurs with ore minerals in veins; it can form by replacement of other carbonates in rocks, and can also precipitate from seawater. **2.** a sedimentary rock containing a high proportion of the mineral dolomite; a variety of limestone, or marble (if metamorphosed). The magnesian limestone of N England is a dolomite. —**dolomitic** /-'mɪtɪk/ *adj.* [French, from D de *Dolomieu* French geologist (died 1802)]

dolour /'dɒlə/ *n.* (*literary*) sorrow, distress. —**dolorous** *adj.* [from Old French from Latin]

dolphin *n.* any of various highly intelligent aquatic mammals of the family Delphinidae, which also includes porpoises. There are about 60 species. The common dolphin *Delphinus delphis* is found in all temperate and tropical seas. It is up to 2.5 m/8 ft long, and is dark above and white below, with bands of grey, white, and yellow on the sides. It has up to 100 teeth in its jaws, which make the 15 cm/6 in 'beak' protrude forward from the rounded head. The corners of its mouth are permanently upturned, giving the appearance of a smile. Dolphins feed on fish and squid. The river dolphins, of which there are only five species, belong to the family Platanistidae. All river dolphins are threatened by dams and pollution, and some, such as the whitefin dolphin *Lipotes vexillifer* of the Chiang Jiang River, China, are in danger of extinction. [from Latin *delphinus* from Greek]

dolt /dəult/ *n.* a stupid person.

Dom /dɒm/ a title prefixed to the names of some Roman Catholic dignitaries, and Benedictine and Carthusian monks. [from Latin *dominus* = master]

-dom suffix forming nouns, (1) from nouns or adjectives, denoting rank, condition, or domain (*earldom, freedom, kingdom*), (2) from nouns, denoting collective plural or in sense 'the ways of- -s' (*officialdom*). [Old English]

Domagk /'dəumæk/ Gerhard 1895–1964. German pathologist, discoverer of antibacterial sulphonamide drugs. He found in 1932 that a coal-tar dye called Prontosil red contains chemicals with powerful antibacterial properties. Sulphanilamide became the first of the sulphonamide drugs, used before ◊antibiotics were discovered to treat a wide range of conditions, including pneumonia and septic wounds. He was awarded the Nobel Prize for Physiology and Medicine in 1939.

domain /də'meɪn/ *n.* an area under one rule, a realm; an estate or lands under one control; a sphere of control or influence; a small area in a magnetic field that behaves like a tiny magnet. [from French, variant of *demesne*]

dome /dəum/ *n.* a rounded vault forming a roof; a dome-shaped thing. [from French from Italian *duomo* = cathedral from Latin *domus* = house]

domed *adj.* having a dome or domes; shaped like a dome.

Domenichino /dəmeni'kiːnəu/ real name Domenico Zampieri 1582–1641. Italian Baroque painter and architect, active in Bologna, Naples, and Rome. He began as an assistant to the ◊Carracci family of painters and continued its early Baroque style in, for example, frescoes painted from 1624–28 in the choir of S Andrea della Valle, Rome.

Dome of the Rock a building in Jerusalem dating from the 7th century AD enshrining the rock from which, in Muslim tradition, Muhammad ascended to heaven on his ◊Night Journey. It stands on the site of the Jewish national Temple and is visited by pilgrims.

Domesday Book a record of the survey of England carried out in 1086 by officials of William the Conqueror in order to assess land tax and other dues, ascertain the value of the crown lands, and enable the king to estimate the power of his vassal barons.

domestic /də'mestɪk/ *adj.* of the home or household or family affairs; of one's own country, not foreign or international; fond of home life; (of an animal) kept by or living with man. —*n.* a household servant. —**domestic science**, home economics (see ◊home). —**domestically** *adv.* [from French from Latin *domus* = house]

domesticate *v.t.* to tame (an animal) to live with humans; to accustom to home life and management. [from Latin]

domesticity /dɒmes'tɪsɪti/ *n.* being domestic; domestic or home life.

domestic service paid employment in the household of another person, as maid, butler, cook, gardener, and so on. It is traditionally a poorly paid occupation, reserved for those without other job skills. The social and economic conditions of the 20th century, and the introduction of labour-saving technology, have narrowed this field of employment, and work by domestic cleaners, baby-sitters, and *au pairs* in the West is mostly part-time and unregulated.

domicile /'dɒmɪsaɪl/ *n.* a dwelling-place; in law, a place of permanent residence, the fact of residing. [from Old French from Latin *domus* = house]

domiciled *adj.* having a domicile at or in.

domiciliary /dɒmi'sɪliəri/ *adj.* of a dwelling-place (especially of the visit of a doctor, officials etc., to a person's home). [from French from Latin]

dominance in genetics, the masking of one ◊allele by another allele. For example, if a ◊heterorygous person has one allele for blue eyes and one for brown eyes, his or her eye colour will be brown. The allele for blue eyes is described as ◊recessive (see ◊recessive) and the allele for brown eyes as dominant.

dominant /'dɒmɪnənt/ *adj.* dominating, prevailing; (of an inherited characteristic) appearing in offspring even when a corresponding opposite characteristic is also inherited. —*n.* in music, the fifth note of the diatonic scale of any key. [French from Latin *dominari*]

dominate /'dɒmɪneɪt/ *v.t./i.* to have a commanding influence over; to be the most influential or conspicuous; (of a high place) to have a commanding position over. —**domination** /-'neɪʃən/ *n.* [from Latin *dominari* (*dominus* = lord)]

domineer /dɒmɪ'nɪə/ *v.i.* to behave in an arrogant and overbearing way. [from Dutch from French *dominer*]

Domingo /də'mɪŋgəʊ/ Placido 1937– . Spanish tenor who excels in romantic operatic roles. A member of a musical family, he emigrated with them to Mexico in 1950. He made his debut in 1960 as Alfredo in Verdi's *La Traviata*, then spent four years with the Israel National Opera. He sang at the New York City Opera in 1965 and has since performed diverse roles in opera houses worldwide. In 1986 he starred in the film version of *Otello*.

Dominica /dɒmɪ'niːkə/ Commonwealth of; island in the West Indies, between Guadeloupe and Martinique, the largest of the Windward Islands, with the Atlantic to the E and the Caribbean to the W; **area** 290 sq mi/751 sq km; **capital** Roseau, with a deepwater port; **physical** second largest of the Windward Islands; mountainous central ridge with tropical rainforest; **head of state** Clarence Seignoret from 1983; Mary Eugenia Charles from 1980; **exports** bananas, coconuts, citrus, lime, bay oil; **population** (1990 est) 94.200 (mainly black African in origin, a small Carib reserve of some 500; **language** English (official); Dominican *patois*; **recent history** independence achieved from Britain 1978, with Patrick John as prime minister. After defeat in 1980 general election, John was implicated in a plot to overthrow the government, tried and acquitted 1982, retried and found guilty 1985. Regrouping of left-of-centre parties resulted in new Labour Party of Dominica (DFP), led by Eugenia Charles, reelected.

Dominican order a Roman Catholic order of friars founded in 1215 by St Dominic; they are also known as Friars Preachers, Black Friars, or Jacobins. The order is worldwide and there is also an order of contemplative nuns; the habit is black and white.

Dominican Republic /də'mɪnɪkən/ country in the West Indies, occupying the E of the island of Hispaniola, with Haiti to the W. The island is surrounded by the Caribbean Sea; **area** 18,700 sq mi/48,442 sq km; **capital** Santo Domingo; **physical** comprises E two-thirds of island of Hispaniola; central mountain range; fertile valley in N; **head of state and government** Joaquín Ricardo Balaguer from 1986; **exports** sugar, gold, silver, bauxite, tobacco, coffee, ferro-nickel; **population** (1989 est) 7,307,000; **language** Spanish (official); **recent history** military coup established dictatorship under Rafael Trujillo from 1930 until 1961, when Trujillo was assassinated; the first democratic elections were held in 1962. In 1963 elected President Bosch was overthrown in a military coup. A period of political instability and economic difficulties led to pressure from the International Monetary Fund to adopt austerity measures to save the economy in 1985.

Dominic, St /'dɒmɪnɪk/ 1170–1221. Founder of the Roman Catholic Dominican order of preaching friars. Feast day 7 Aug.

dominion /də'mɪnjən/ *n.* **1.** sovereignty, control. **2.** the territory of a sovereign or government, a domain. **3.** (*historical*) the title of the self-governing territories of the British Commonwealth. [from Old French from Latin *dominus* = lord]

domino¹ /'dɒmɪnəʊ/ *n.* a loose cloak with a mask for the upper part of the face, formerly worn at masquerades. [French]

domino² each of 28 small oblong pieces marked with (usually) 0–6 pips in each half; (in *plural*) the game played with these. —**domino theory,** the theory that one (especially a political) event precipitates others in a causal sequence, like a row of dominoes falling over. [perhaps named from the semblance of the black back of the domino to the masquerade garment of the same name]

Domino 'Fats' (Antoine) 1928– . US rock-and-roll pianist, singer, and songwriter, exponent of the New Orleans style. His hits include 'Ain't That A Shame' 1955 and 'Blueberry Hill' 1956.

Domitian /də'mɪʃən/ Titus Flavius Domitianus AD 51–96. Roman emperor from AD 81. He finalized the conquest of Britain (see ◊Agricola), strengthened the Rhine–Danube frontier, and suppressed immorality as well as freedom of thought (see ◊Epictetus) in philosophy and religion (Christians were persecuted). His reign of terror led to his assassination.

don¹ *n.* **1.** a head, fellow, or tutor of a college, especially at Oxford or Cambridge. **2. Don,** a Spanish title prefixed to a man's Christian name. [Spanish from Latin *dominus* = lord]

don² *v.t.* (**-nn-**) to put on (clothing etc.). [= do on]

Don /dɒn/ river in the USSR, rising to the S of Moscow and entering the NE extremity of the Sea of Azov; length 1,900 km/1,180 mi. In its lower reaches the Don is 1.5 km/1 mi wide, and for about four months of the year it is closed by ice. Its upper course is linked to the river Volga by a canal.

Donald /'dɒnld/ Ian 1910–1987. English obstetrician who introduced ultrasound scanning, using very high-frequency sound waves. He pioneered its use in obstetrics as a means of scanning the growing foetus without exposure to the danger of X-rays. Donald's experience of using radar in World War II suggested to him the use of ultrasound for medical purposes.

donate /dəʊ'neɪt/ *v.t.* to give or contribute (money etc.), especially voluntarily to a fund or institution.

Donatello /dɒnə'teləʊ/ (Donato di Niccolo) 1386–1466. Italian sculptor of the early Renaissance, born in Florence. He was instrumental in reviving the Classical style, as in his graceful bronze statue of the youthful *David* (Bargello, Florence) and his equestrian statue of the general *Gattamelata* 1443 (Padua). The course of Florentine art in the 15th century was strongly influenced by his style.

donation /dəʊ'neɪʃən/ *n.* an act of donating; an amount donated. [from Old French from Latin *donum* = gift]

Donau /'dəʊnaʊ/ German name for the ◊Danube.

done /dʌn/ past participle of do¹. —*adj.* **1.** completed; cooked. **2.** (of an action or behaviour etc.) socially acceptable. **3.** (as *interjection* in reply to an offer etc.) accepted. **4.** (*colloquial*) tired out (often with *in* or *up*). —**be done with,** to have finished with. **done for,** in serious trouble. **have done with,** to finish dealing with.

Donegal /dɒni'gɔːl/ mountainous county in Ulster province in the NW of the Republic of Ireland, surrounded on three sides by the Atlantic; **area** 4,830 sq km/1,864 sq mi; population (1986) 130,000. The county town is Lifford; the market town and port of Donegal is at the head of Donegal Bay in the SW. Commercial activities include sheep and cattle raising, tweed and linen manufacture, and some deep-sea fishing. The river Erne hydroelectric project (1952) involved the building of large power stations at Ballyshannon.

Donellan /'dɒnələn/ Declan 1953– . British theatre director, co-founder of the **Cheek by Jowl** theatre company in 1981, and associate director of the National Theatre from 1989. His irreverent and audacious productions include many classics, such as Racine's *Andromaque.*

Donen /'dəʊnən/ Stanley 1924– . US film director, formerly a dancer, who codirected two of Gene Kelly's best musicals, *On the Town* 1949 and *Singin' in the Rain* 1952. His other films include *Charade* 1963 and *Two for the Road* 1968.

Donetsk /dɒ'nets/ city in Ukraine, USSR; capital of Donetsk region, situated in the Donets Basin, a major coal mining area, 600 km/372 mi SE of Kiev; population (1987) 1,090,000. It has blast furnaces, rolling mills, and other heavy industries.

Dönitz /'dɜːnɪts/ Karl 1891–1980. German admiral, originator of the wolf-pack submarine technique, which sank 15 million tonnes of Allied shipping in World War II. He succeeded Hitler in 1945, capitulated, and was imprisoned from 1946–56.

Donizetti /dɒnɪd'zeti/ Gaetano 1797–1848. Italian composer who created more than 60 operas, including *Lucrezia Borgia* 1833, *Lucia di Lammermoor* 1835, *La Fille du régiment* 1840, *La Favorite* 1840, and *Don Pasquale* 1843.

They show the influence of Rossini and Bellini, and are characterized by a flow of expressive melodies.

donjon /'dɒndʒən/ *n.* the great tower or keep of a castle. [archaic spelling of *dungeon*]

Don Juan /'dʒuːən/ character of Spanish legend, Don Juan Tenorio, supposed to have lived in the 14th century and notorious for his debauchery. Tirso de Molina, Molière, Mozart, Byron, and George Bernard Shaw have featured the legend in their works.

donkey /'dɒŋkɪ/ *n.* 1. a domestic ass (see ◊ass[1]). 2. (*colloquial*) a stupid person. —**donkey engine,** a small auxiliary engine. **donkey jacket,** a workman's thick weatherproof jacket. **donkey's years,** (*colloquial*) a very long time. **donkey-work** *n.* the laborious part of a job.

Donna /'dɒnə/ *n.* the title of an Italian, Spanish, or Portuguese lady. [Italian from Latin *domina* = mistress]

Donne /dʌn/ John 1571–1631. English metaphysical poet whose work is characterized by subtle imagery and figurative language. In 1615 Donne took orders in the Church of England and as dean of St Paul's Cathedral, London, was noted for his sermons. His poetry includes the sonnets 'Batter my heart, three person'd God' and 'Death be not proud', elegies, and satires.

For God's sake hold your tongue, and let me love.
John Donne
The Canonization

---

donnish *adj.* like a college don; pedantic.

Donnybrook /'dɒnɪbrʊk/ former village, now part of Dublin, Republic of Ireland, notorious until 1855 for riotous fairs.

donor /'dəʊnə/ *n.* one who gives or donates something; one who provides blood for transfusion, semen for insemination, or an organ or tissue for transplantation. [from Anglo-French from Latin *donator*]

Don Quixote de la Mancha a satirical romance by Cervantes, published in two parts in 1605 and 1615. Don Quixote, a self-styled knight, embarks on a series of chivalric adventures accompanied by his servant Sancho Panza. Quixote's imagination leads him to see harmless objects as enemies to be fought, as in his tilting at windmills.

don't /dəʊnt/ (*colloquial*) = do not. —*n.* a prohibition.

doodle *v.t./i.* to scribble or draw, especially absentmindedly. —*n.* a scribble or drawing made by doodling. [originally = foolish person; compare Low German *dudelkopf*]

Doolittle /'duːlɪtl/ Hilda, pen name **HD** 1886–1961. US poet. She went to Europe in 1911, and was associated with Ezra Pound and the British writer Richard ◊Aldington (to whom she was married 1913–37) in founding the Imagist school of poetry, advocating simplicity, precision, and brevity. Her work includes the *Sea Garden* 1916 and *Helen in Egypt* 1916.

doom *n.* a grim fate or destiny, death or ruin; a condemnation. —*v.t.* to condemn or destine *to*. [Old English = statute]

doomsday /'duːmzdeɪ/ *n.* the day of the Last Judgement. —**till doomsday,** for ever.

Doomsday Book variant spelling of ◊Domesday Book.

door /dɔː/ *n.* 1. a hinged, sliding, or revolving barrier for closing the entrance to a building, room, cupboard etc.; this as representing a house etc.; a doorway. 2. an entrance or exit, the means of access or approach. —**doorkeeper** *n.* a doorman. **door-to-door** *adj.* (of selling etc.) done at each house in turn. [Old English]

doorbell *n.* a bell in a house rung at the front door by visitors to signal arrival.

doorknob *n.* a knob for turning to release the latch of a door.

doorman *n.* (*plural* **doormen**) a person on duty at the entrance to a large building.

doormat *n.* 1. a mat at an entrance, for wiping the shoes. 2. a feebly submissive person.

Doors, the a US psychedelic rock group formed in 1965 in Los Angeles by Jim Morrison (1943–1971, vocals), Ray Manzarek (1935– , keyboards), Robby Krieger (1946– , guitar), and John Densmore (1944– , drums). Their first hit was 'Light My Fire' from their debut album *The Doors*

1967. They were noted for Morrison's poetic lyrics and flamboyant performance.

doorstep *n.* 1. a step leading to the outer door of a house etc.; a point in front of this. 2. (*slang*) a thick slice of bread. —**on one's doorstep,** very close.

doorstop *n.* a device for keeping a door open or to prevent it from striking a wall etc. when opened.

doorway *n.* an opening filled by a door.

dope *n.* 1. a thick liquid used as a lubricant etc.; varnish. 2. (*slang*) a drug, especially a narcotic; a drug or stimulant given to an athlete etc. to affect performance. 3. (*slang*) information. 4. (*slang*) a stupid person. —*v.t./i.* 1. to treat with dope. 2. to give a drug or stimulant to; to take addictive drugs. [from Dutch *doop* = sauce]

dopey /'dəʊpɪ/ *adj.* (*slang*) half asleep; stupefied by or as by a drug; stupid. —**dopiness** *n.*

doppelgänger /'dɒpəlgeŋə/ *n.* the wraith of a living person. [German = double-goer]

Doppler effect /'dɒplə/ the apparent increase (or decrease) in the frequency of sound, light, and other waves when the source and the observer become closer (or more distant). It is responsible for the perceived change in pitch of a siren as it approaches and then recedes, and for the ◊red shift of light from distant stars. [from C J *Doppler* Austrian physicist (died 1853)]

dorado /dɒˈrɑːdəʊ/ *n.* (*plural* **dorados**) a blue and silver sea-fish of the genus *Coryphaena*, showing brilliant colours when it dies out of water. [Spanish = gilt]

Dorado /dəˈrɑːdəʊ/ *n.* a constellation of the S hemisphere, represented as a goldfish. It is easy to locate, since the Large ◊Magellanic Cloud marks its southern border. Its brightest star is Alpha Doradus, just under 200 light years from Earth.

Dorati /dɒˈrɑːti/ Antal 1906–1988. US conductor, born in Hungary. He toured with ballet companies from 1933–45 and went on to conduct orchestras in the USA and Europe in a career spanning more than half a century. Dorati gave many first performances of Bartók's music and recorded all Haydn's symphonies with the Philharmonia Hungarica.

Dordogne /dɔːˈdɔɪn/ river in SW France, rising in Puy-de-Dôme *département* and flowing 490 km/300 mi to join the river Garonne, 23 km/14 mi N of Bordeaux. It gives its name to a *département* and is a major source of hydroelectric power.

Doré /'dɔːreɪ/ Gustave 1832–1883. French artist, chiefly known as a prolific illustrator, and also active as a painter, etcher, and sculptor. He produced closely worked engravings of scenes from, for example, Rabelais, Dante, Cervantes, the Bible, Milton, and Poe.

Dorian /'dɔːrɪən/ *n.* a people of ancient Greece. They entered Greece from the N and conquered most of the Peloponnese from the Achaeans, destroying the ◊Mycenaean civilization; this invasion appears to have been completed before 1000 BC. Their chief cities were Sparta, Argos, and Corinth.

Doric /'dɒrɪk/ *adj.* 1. (of a dialect) broad, rustic. 2. in architecture, of the oldest and simplest of the Greek orders. —*n.* rustic English or (especially) Scots. [from Latin from Greek (*Doris* in Greece)]

dormant /'dɔːmənt/ *adj.* sleeping, lying inactive as in a sleep; temporarily inactive; (of plants) alive but not actively growing. —**dormancy** *n.* [from participle of Old French *dormir* = sleep from Latin *dormire*]

dormer *n.* a projecting upright window in a sloping roof. [from Old French]

dormitory /'dɔːmɪtərɪ/ *n.* 1. a sleeping room with several beds, especially in a school or institution. 2. (in full **dormitory town**) a small town or suburb from which people travel to work in a city etc. [from Latin *dormire* = sleep]

dormouse *n.* (*plural* **dormice** /-maɪs/) a small rodent, of the family Gliridae, with a hairy tail. There are about ten species, living in Europe, Asia, and Africa. They are arboreal (live in trees) and nocturnal, and they hibernate during winter in cold regions. The common dormouse *Muscardinus avellanarius* lives all over Europe in thickets and forests with undergrowth. It is reddish fawn and 15 cm/6 in long, including tail. The fat or edible dormouse *Glis glis* lives in continental Europe, and is 30 cm/1 ft long including tail. It was a delicacy at Roman feasts, and was introduced to SE England.

dormy

Dostoievsky Russian novelist Fyodor Dostoievsky.

dormy /'dɔːmɪ/ *adj.* as many holes ahead in the score of golf as there are holes left to play.

dorsal /'dɔːsəl/ *adj.* of or on the back. —**dorsally** *adv.* [French, or from Latin *dorsum* = back]

Dorset /'dɔːsɪt/ county in SW England; **area** 2,650 sq km/1,023 sq mi; **administrative headquarters** Dorset; **physical** Chesil Bank, a shingle bank along the coast 19 km/11 mi long; Isle of Purbeck, a peninsula where china clay and Purbeck 'marble' are quarried; Dorset Downs; Cranborne Chase; rivers Frome and Stour; **products** Wytch Farm is the largest onshore oilfield in the UK; **population** (1987) 649,000

Dortmund /'dɔːtmund/ industrial centre in the ◊Ruhr, Germany, 58 km/36 mi NE of Düsseldorf; population (1988) 568,000. It is the largest mining town of the Westphalian coalfield and the S terminus of the Dortmund–Ems canal. Industries include iron, steel, construction machinery, engineering, and brewing.

dory /'dɔːrɪ/ *n.* or **John Dory** an edible sea-fish *Zeus faber* found in the Mediterranean and Atlantic. It grows up to 60 cm/2 ft, and has nine or ten long spines at the front of the dorsal fin, and four at the front of the anal fin. [from French *dorée* = gilded]

DOS acronym from *d*isc *o*perating *s*ystem in computing, an ◊operating system specifically designed for use with disc storage; also used as an alternative name for the ◊MS-DOS operating system.

dosage /'dəusɪdʒ/ *n.* the giving of a dose; the size of a dose.

dose *n.* **1.** the amount of medicine to be taken at one time; an amount of flattery, punishment etc.; an amount of radiation received by a person or thing. **2.** (*slang*) a venereal infection. —*v.t.* to give a dose or doses of medicine to; to treat (a person or animal) *with.* [French from Latin from Greek *dosis* = gift]

dosimeter /dəu'sɪmɪtə/ *n.* a device for measuring the amount of a dose; a recording device to measure ionizing radiation, especially one worn by a person exposed to potentially harmful radiation.

Dos Passos /dəus 'pæsəus/ John 1896–1970. US author, born in Chicago. He made a reputation with the war novels *One Man's Initiation* 1919 and *Three Soldiers* 1921. His greatest work is the *USA* trilogy 1930–36, which gives a panoramic view of US life through the device of placing fictitious characters against the real setting of newspaper headlines and contemporary events.

doss *v.i.* (*slang*) to sleep, especially in a dosshouse. —**doss down**, (*slang*) to sleep on a makeshift bed. —**dosshouse** *n.* (*slang*) a cheap lodging house. [probably = *doss* = ornamental cover for seatback, from Old French *dos* = back]

Dos Santos /dɒs sæntɒs/ Jose Eduardo 1942– . Angolan left-wing politician, president from 1979, a member of the People's Movement for the Liberation of Angola (MPLA).

dossier /'dɒsɪə, -ieɪ/ *n.* a set of documents containing information about a person or event. [French, from label on back (*dos* = back)]

Dostoievsky /dɒstɔɪ'efski/ Fyodor Mihailovich 1821–1881. Russian novelist. Remarkable for their profound psychological insight, Dostoievsky's novels have greatly influenced Russian writers, and since the beginning of the 20th century have been increasingly influential abroad. In 1849 he was sentenced to four years' hard labour in Siberia, followed by army service, for printing socialist propaganda. *The House of the Dead* 1861 recalls his prison experiences, followed by his major works *Crime and Punishment* 1866, *The Idiot* 1868–69, and *The Brothers Karamazov* 1880.

We degrade Providence too much by attributing our ideas to it out of annoyance at being unable to understand it.

Fyodor Mihailovich Dostoievsky
The Idiot

---

dot *n.* **1.** a small round mark or spot; this as part of *i* or *j* or as a decimal point. **2.** the shorter of the two signals used in the Morse code. —*v.t.* (**-tt-**) **1.** to mark with a dot or dots; to cover partly as with dots. **2.** (*slang*) to hit. —**dotted line**, a line of dots on a document to show the place for a signature. **dot the i's and cross the t's**, to be minutely accurate; to emphasize details. **on the dot**, exactly on time. **the year dot**, (*colloquial*) far in the past.

dotage /'dəutɪdʒ/ *n.* feeble-minded senility.

dotard /'dəutəd/ *n.* a person who is in his dotage.

dote *v.i.* to be silly or infatuated. —**dote on**, to be excessively fond of. [compare Middle Dutch *doten* = be silly]

dotterel /'dɒtər(ə)l/ *n.* a bird *Eudromias morinellus* of the plover family, nesting on high moors and tundra in Europe and Asia, migrating south for the winter. About 23 cm/9 in, it is clad in a pattern of black, brown, and white in summer, duller in winter, but always with white eyebrows and breastband. Females are larger than males, and the male incubates and rears the brood. [from *dote* named from the ease with which it is caught, a supposed sign of stupidity]

dottle *n.* the remnant of unburnt tobacco in a pipe.

dotty *adj.* (*colloquial*) feeble-minded, eccentric, silly. —**dottiness** *n.*

Douala /du:'ɑ:lə/ or **Duala** chief port and industrial centre (aluminium, chemicals, textiles, pulp) of Cameroon, on the Wouri river estuary; population (1981) 637,000. Known as Kamerunstadt until 1907, it was capital of German Cameroon 1885–1901.

double[1] /'dʌbəl/ *adj.* **1.** consisting of two parts or things. **2.** twofold, multiplied by two; twice as much or many. **3.** having twice the usual quantity, size, strength etc.; having some part double; (of a flower) having more than one circle of petals. **4.** folded, stooping. **5.** ambiguous, deceitful, hypocritical. **6.** (of a musical instrument) lower in pitch by an octave. —*adv.* at or to twice the amount etc.; two together. —*n.* **1.** a double quantity or thing; a double measure of spirits etc.; twice as much or many. **2.** the counterpart of a person or thing, a person who looks exactly like another. **3.** (in *plural*) a game between two pairs of players. **4.** a pair of victories over the same team or of championships at the same game etc.; a system of betting in which the winnings and stake from the first bet are transferred to a second; a doubling of an opponent's bid in bridge; a hit on the narrow ring between the outer circles in darts. —**at the double**, running, hurrying. **double agent**, one who spies simultaneously for two rival countries. **double-barrelled** *adj.* (of a gun) having two barrels; (of a name) having two parts with a hyphen. **double bass** /beɪs/ *n.* the largest and lowest-pitched instrument of the violin family, now possessing four strings (formerly three) and sounding an octave below the cello, with a range of nearly three octaves. **double-breasted** *adj.* (of a coat etc.) having fronts that overlap to fasten across the breast. **double-check** *v.t.* to verify twice or in two ways. **double chin**, a chin with a fold of loose flesh below it. **double cream**, thick cream with a high fat content. **double-cross** *v.t.* to deceive or betray (a person one is supposedly helping); (as *n.*) an act of doing this. **double-dealing** *n.* deceit, especially in business; (as *adj.*) practising deceit. **double-decker** *n.* a bus with two decks. **double Dutch**, gibberish. **double eagle**, a figure of a two-headed eagle. **double-edged** *adj.* having two cutting edges; (*figurative*) damaging to the user as well as his opponent. **double entry**, a system of book-keeping in which each transaction is entered as a debit in one account and a credit in another. **double figures**, the numbers from 10 to 99. **double glazing**, two layers of glass in a window to reduce loss of heat and exclude noise. **double helix**, a pair of parallel helices with a common axis, especially in the structure of the DNA molecule. **double-jointed** *adj.* having joints that allow unusual bending of the fingers etc. **double or quits**, a gamble to decide whether a player's loss or debt be doubled or cancelled. **double-park** *v.i.* to park a vehicle alongside one that is already parked at the roadside. **double pneumonia**, that affecting both lungs. **double-quick** *adj.* & *adv.* very quick(ly). **double standard**, a rule or principle applied more strictly to some than to others (or to oneself). **double star**, two stars that are actually or apparently very close together. **double-stopping** *n.* the sounding of two strings at once on a violin etc. **double take**, a delayed reaction to a situation etc. immediately after one's first reaction. **double-talk** *n.* verbal expression that is (usually deliberately) ambiguous or misleading. **doublethink** *n.* a mental capacity to accept contrary opinions at the same time. **double time**, payment of an employee at twice the normal rate. —**doubly** *adv.* [from Old French from Latin *duplus*]

double[2] *v.t./i.* 1. to make or become double, to increase twofold, to multiply by two; to amount to twice as much. 2. to fold or bend over on itself, to become folded. 3. to act (two parts) in the same play etc.; to be an understudy etc. (*for*); to play a twofold role (as). 4. to turn sharply in flight or pursuit; (of a ship) to sail round (a headland). 5. to make a call in bridge increasing the value of points to be won or lost on (an opponent's bid). —**double back**, to take a new direction opposite to the previous one. **double up**, to bend or curl up with pain or laughter, to cause to do this; to share or cause to share a room, quarters etc., with another or others.

double decomposition a reaction between two chemical substances (usually ◊salts in solution) that results in the exchange of a constituent from each compound to create two different compounds.

double entendre /duːbl ɑ̃tɑ̃dr/ a phrase affording two meanings, one usually indecent. [obsolete French = double understanding]

doublet /ˈdʌblɪt/ *n.* 1. a man's close-fitting jacket, with or without sleeves, worn in the 15th–17th centuries 2. either of a pair of similar things.

doubloon *n.* a former Spanish gold coin. [from French or Spanish]

doubt /daʊt/ *n.* a feeling of uncertainty about something, an undecided state of mind; an inclination to disbelieve; an uncertain state of things; a lack of full proof or clear indication. —*v.t./i.* to feel uncertain or undecided (about); to hesitate to believe; to call in question. —**no doubt**, certainly, probably, admittedly. **without (a) doubt**, certainly. —**doubter** *n.* [from Old French from Latin *dubitare*]

doubtful *adj.* feeling doubt; causing doubt, unreliable, undecided. —**doubtfully** *adv.*, **doubtfulness** *n.*

doubtless *adv.* certainly, probably.

douche /duːʃ/ *n.* a jet of liquid applied to a part of the body for cleansing or for a medicinal purpose; a device for producing such a jet. —*v.t./i.* to treat with a douche; to use a douche. [French from Italian *doccia* = pipe from Latin]

dough /dəʊ/ *n.* 1. a thick mixture of flour etc. and liquid, for baking. 2. (*slang*) money. —**doughy** *adj.* [Old English]

doughnut /ˈdəʊnʌt/ *n.* a small, sweetened, fried cake of dough.

doughty /ˈdaʊtɪ/ *adj.* (*archaic* or *jocular*) valiant, stout-hearted. —**doughtily** *adv.*, **doughtiness** *n.* [Old English]

Douglas /ˈdʌɡləs/ *n.* Douglas fir, pine, or spruce, a large conifer of the genus *Pseudotsuga*, originally of western North America. [from D *Douglas*, Scottish botanist (died 1834)]

Douglas capital of the Isle of Man in the Irish Sea; population (1981) 20,000. A holiday resort and terminus of shipping routes to and from Fleetwood and Liverpool.

Douglas Alfred (Bruce), 'Bosie', 1870–1945. British poet who became closely associated in London with Oscar ◊Wilde. Douglas's father, the 9th Marquess of Queensberry, strongly disapproved of the relationship and called Wilde a 'posing Somdomite' (sic). Wilde's action for libel ultimately resulted in his own imprisonment.

Douglas Gavin (or Gawain) 1475–1522. Scottish poet whose translation into Scots of Virgil's *Aeneid* in 1515 was the first translation from the classics into a vernacular of the British Isles.

Douglas Kirk. Stage name of Issur Danielovitch 1916– . US film actor, of Russian parents. Usually cast as a dynamic and intelligent hero, as in *Spartacus* 1960, he was a major star of the 1950s and 1960s in such films as *Ace in the Hole* 1951, *The Big Carnival* 1951, *Lust for Life* 1956, and *The War Wagon* 1967.

Douglas-Hamilton /ˈdʌɡləs ˈhæməltən/ the family name of the dukes of Hamilton, seated at Lennoxlove, East Lothian, Scotland.

Douglass /ˈdʌɡləs/ Frederick *c.*1817–1895. US antislavery campaigner. Born a slave in Maryland, he escaped in 1838. His autobiographical *Narrative of the Life of Frederick Douglass* 1845 aroused support in N states for the abolition of slavery. After the Civil War, he held several US government posts, including minister to Haiti.

Doulton /ˈdəʊltən/ Henry 1820–1897. English ceramicist. He developed special wares for the chemical, electrical, and building industries, and established the world's first stoneware drainpipe factory in 1846. From 1870 he created art pottery and domestic tableware in Lambeth, S London, and in Burslem, near Stoke-on-Trent.

Doumer /duːˈmeə/ Paul 1857–1932. French politician who was elected president of the Chamber in 1905, president of the Senate in 1927, and president of the republic in 1931. He was assassinated by Gorgulov, a White Russian emigré.

Dounreay /ˈduːnreɪ/ experimental nuclear reactor site on the N coast of Scotland, 12 km/7 mi W of Thurso. Development started in 1974 and continued until a decision was made in 1988 to decommission the site by 1994.

dour /dʊə/ *adj.* stern, severe, obstinate. —**dourly** *adv.*, **dourness** *n.* [probable from Gaelic *dúr* = dull, obstinate]

Douro /ˈdʊərəʊ/ (Spanish *Duero*) river rising in N central Spain and flowing through N Portugal to the Atlantic at Porto; length 800 km/500 mi. Navigation at the river mouth is hindered by sand bars. There are hydroelectric installations.

douse /daʊs/ *v.t.* 1. to plunge into water, to throw water over. 2. to extinguish (a light).

dove /dʌv/ *n.* 1. a bird of the family Columbidae, with short legs, small head, and large breast. 2. an advocate of peace or peaceful policy. 3. a gentle or innocent person. [from Old Norse]

dovecote /ˈdʌvkɒt/ *n.* a shelter with nesting-holes for domesticated pigeons.

Dover, Strait of /ˈdəʊvə/ (French *Pas-de-Calais*) stretch of water separating England from France, and connecting the English Channel with the North Sea. It is about 35 km/22 mi long and 34 km/21 mi wide at its narrowest part. It is one of the world's busiest sea lanes. By 1972 collisions, and shipwrecks had become so frequent that traffic-routeing schemes were enforced.

dovetail *n.* a joint formed by a mortise with a tenon shaped like a dove's spread tail. —*v.t./i.* 1. to fit together with dovetails. 2. to fit together or combine neatly.

dowager /ˈdaʊədʒə/ *n.* a woman with a title or property derived from her late husband; (*colloquial*) a dignified elderly woman. [from Old French *douage*]

dowdy /ˈdaʊdɪ/ *adj.* (of clothes) unattractively dull; (of a person) dressed in dowdy clothes. —**dowdily** *adv.*, **dowdiness** *n.*

dowel /ˈdaʊəl/ *n.* a headless wooden or metal pin for holding two pieces of wood or stone together. —*v.t.* (-ll-) to fasten with a dowel. [from Middle Low German *dovel*]

Dowell /ˈdaʊəl/ Anthony 1943– . British ballet dancer in the classical style who was principal dancer with the Royal Ballet 1966–86, and director 1986–89. Dowell joined the Royal Ballet in 1961. The choreographer Ashton chose him to create the role of Oberon in *The Dream* 1964 opposite Antoinette Sibley, the start of an outstanding partnership.

dowelling *n.* round rods for cutting into dowels.

dower /'daʊə/ *n.* 1. a widow's share for life of her husband's estate. 2. (*archaic*) a dowry. —*v.t.* 1. (*archaic*) to give a dowry to. 2. to endow *with* talent etc. —**dower house,** a smaller house near a big one, forming part of a widow's dower. [from Old French from Latin *dotarium* (*dos* = dowry)]

Dow—Jones index or **average** /daʊ'dʒəʊnz/ a figure indicating the relative price of American securities based on the current average rates of an agreed select list of industrial and other stocks. [from C H *Dow* (died 1902) and E D *Jones* (died 1920), American economists]

Dowland /'daʊlənd/ John 1563–1626. English composer remembered for his songs to lute accompaniment as well as music for lute alone, such as *Lachrymae* 1605.

down[1] /daʊn/ *adv.* 1. at, in, or towards a lower place, level, value, or condition, or a place etc. regarded as lower; to a finer consistency or smaller amount or size; southwards, further south; away from a central place or capital city or university; in or into a less strong or less active or losing position or condition; into quiescence; incapacitated *with* (an illness etc.). 2. from an erect or vertical position to a horizontal one. 3. so as to be deflated. 4. from an earlier to a later time. 5. in writing; in or into a recorded form. 6. to its source or place. 7. as a payment at the time of purchase. —*prep.* 1. downwards along, through, or into; from the top to the bottom of; along. 2. at or in a lower part of. —*adj.* directed downwards; (of travel) away from a capital or centre. —*v.t.* (*colloquial*) to knock or bring down; to swallow. —*n.* 1. an act of putting down. 2. a reverse of fortune (often in *ups and downs*). —**down and out,** penniless, destitute. **down-and-out** *n.* a destitute person. **downhearted** *adj.* dejected. **down in the mouth,** looking unhappy. **down on,** holding in disfavour. **down payment,** a partial payment made at the time of purchase. **down stage,** at or to the front of a theatre stage. **down-to-earth** *adj.* practical, realistic. **down tools,** to cease work; to go on strike. **down to the ground,** (*colloquial*) completely. **down under,** in the antipodes, especially Australia. **down with** interjection of disgust with or rejection of a stated person or thing. **have a down on,** to hold in disfavour. [from earlier *adown*]

down[2] *n.* the first covering of young birds, a bird's underplumage; fine, soft feathers or short hairs; a fluffy substance. [from Old Norse]

down[3] *n.* 1. or **downland** an area of high, open land. 2. (in *plural*) chalk uplands especially of S England. [Old English]

Down /daʊn/ county in SE Northern Ireland, facing the Irish Sea on the E; area 2,470 sq km/953 sq mi; population (1981) 53,000. In the S are the Mourne mountains, in the E Strangford sea lough. The county town is Downpatrick; the main industry is dairying.

downbeat *n.* an accented beat in music, when the conductor's baton moves downwards. —*adj.* 1. pessimistic, gloomy. 2. relaxed.

downcast *adj.* 1. (of the eyes) looking downwards. 2. (of a person) dejected.

downfall *n.* a fall from prosperity or power; a cause of this.

downgrade *v.t.* to lower in grade or rank.

downhill *adv.* down a slope; in a descending direction. —*adj.* sloping downwards, declining. —**go downhill,** to deteriorate.

Downing Street /'daʊnɪŋ/ street in Westminster, London, leading from Whitehall to St James's Park, named after Sir George Downing (died 1684), a diplomat under Cromwell and Charles II. **Number 10** is the official residence of the prime minister and **Number 11** is the residence of the chancellor of the Exchequer. **Number 12** is the office of the government whips.

downpipe *n.* a pipe for carrying rainwater from a roof to a drain.

downpour *n.* a heavy fall of rain.

downright *adj.* plain, straightforward; utter, complete. —*adv.* thoroughly, completely.

Down's syndrome /daʊnz/ a condition caused by a chromosomal abnormality (the presence of an extra chromosome) which in humans produces mental retardation; a flattened face; coarse, straight hair; and a fold of skin at the inner edge of the eye (hence the former name 'mongolism').

Doyle *Creator of the popular fictional duo of Sherlock Holmes and Dr Watson, Arthur Conan Doyle.*

Those afflicted are usually born to mothers over 40 (one in 100); they are good-natured and teachable with special education. [from J H *Down* physician (died 1896)]

downstairs *adv.* down the stairs; to or on a lower floor. —*adj.* situated downstairs. —*n.* a downstairs floor.

downstream *adj.* & *adv.* in the direction in which a stream flows; moving downstream.

downtown *adj.* (*US*) of a lower or more central part of a town or city. —*adv.* (*US*) in or into this part. —*n.* (*US*) a downtown area.

downtrodden *adj.* oppressed, badly treated.

downturn *n.* a decline, especially in an economic or business activity.

downward /'daʊnwəd/ *adv.* or **downwards** /-z/ towards what is lower, inferior, less important, or later. —*adj.* moving or extending downwards.

downwind *adj.* & *adv.* in the direction in which the wind is blowing.

downy *adj.* 1. of or like down, soft and fluffy. 2. (*slang*) aware, knowing.

dowry /'daʊərɪ/ *n.* property or money brought by a bride to her husband. [from Anglo-French and Old French = dower]

dowse[1] /daʊz/ *v.i.* to search for underground water or minerals by holding a Y-shaped stick or rod (*dowsing rod*) which dips abruptly when over the right spot. Unconscious muscular action by the dowser is thought to move the twig, usually held with one fork in each hand, possibly in response to a local change in the pattern of electrical forces. Dowsing has been known since at least the 16th century and, though not widely recognized by science, it has been used commercially. —**dowser** *n.*

dowse[2] /daʊs/ variant of **douse**.

Doxiadis /dɒksi'ɑ:di:s/ Constantinos 1913–1975. Greek architect and town planner; designer of ◊Islamabad.

doxology /dɒk'sɒlədʒɪ/ *n.* a liturgical formula of praise to God. [from Latin from Greek *doxa* = glory]

doyen /'dɔɪən/ *n.* a senior member of a body of colleagues. —**doyenne** /-'en/ *n. fem.* [French]

Doyle /dɔɪl/ Arthur Conan 1859–1930. British writer, creator of the detective Sherlock Holmes and his assistant Dr Watson, who feature in a number of stories, including *The Hound of the Baskervilles* 1902.

D'Oyly Carte /'dɔɪlɪ 'kɑːt/ Richard 1844–1901. British producer of the Gilbert and Sullivan operas at the Savoy Theatre, London, which he built. The old D'Oyly Carte Opera Company founded in 1876 was disbanded in 1982, but a new one opened its first season in 1988.

doz. abbreviation of dozen.

doze *v.i.* to be half asleep, to sleep lightly. —*n.* a short, light sleep. —**doze off,** to fall lightly asleep.

dozen /'dʌzən/ *n.* 1. (*singular* form is used, with plural verb, when qualified by a preceding word) twelve, a set of twelve. 2. (in *plural*) very many. —**talk nineteen to the dozen,** to talk incessantly. [from Old French, from Latin *duodecim* = twelve]

dozy /'dəʊzɪ/ *adj.* drowsy; (*colloquial*) stupid, lazy.

D.Phil. abbreviation of Doctor of Philosophy.

DPP abbreviation of Director of Public Prosecutions.

Dr abbreviation of Doctor.

drab *adj.* 1. dull, uninteresting. 2. of a dull brownish colour. —*n.* drab colour. —**drably** *adv.*, **drabness**

n. [from obsolete *drap* = cloth from Old French from Latin]

Drabble /'dræbəl/ Margaret 1939– . English writer whose novels include *The Millstone* 1966 (filmed as *The Touch of Love*), *The Middle Ground* 1980, *The Radiant Way* 1987, and *A Natural Curiosity* 1989. She edited the fifth edition of the *Oxford Companion to English Literature* 1985.

drachm /dræm/ *n.* a weight formerly used by apothecaries, one eighth of an ounce. [from Old French or Latin]

drachma /'drækmə/ *n.* (*plural* **drachmas**) 1. the unit of currency of Greece. 2. silver coin of ancient Greece. [Latin from Greek *drakhmē*]

Draco /'dreɪkəʊ/ 7th century BC. Athenian politician, the first to codify the laws of the Athenian city-state. These were notorious for their severity.

Draco *n.* in astronomy, a large but faint constellation, representing a dragon coiled around the north celestial pole. The star Alpha Draconis (Thuban) was the Pole Star 4,800 years ago.

Draconian /drə'kəʊnɪən/ *adj.* (of laws) very harsh, cruel. [from *Draco*]

Dracula /'drækjʊlə/ in the novel *Dracula* 1897 by Bram ◊Stoker, the caped count who, as a ◊vampire, drinks the blood of beautiful women.

draft /drɑːft/ *n.* 1. a rough preliminary outline of a scheme or written version of a speech, document etc. 2. a written order for the payment of money by a bank; drawing of money by this. 3. a detachment from a larger group for a special duty or purpose; selection of this; (*US*) conscription. —*v.t.* 1. to prepare a draft of (writing or a scheme). 2. to select for a special duty or purpose; (*US*) to conscript. [phonetic spelling of *draught*]

draftsman variant of **draughtsman**.

drag *v.t./i.* (-gg-) 1. to pull or pass along with effort, difficulty, or friction; to trail or allow to trail along the ground; (*colloquial*) to take (a person *to*, especially against his will). 2. to use a grapnel, to search (the bottom of a lake or river etc.) with grapnels, nets etc. 3. (*colloquial*) to draw *on* or *at* (a cigarette etc.). —*n.* 1. a hindrance to progress; a longitudinal retarding force exerted by air on aircraft etc. in flight. 2. a retarded motion. 3. (*colloquial*) a boring or tiresome person, duty etc. 4. a lure drawn before hounds as a substitute for a fox; a hunt using this; an apparatus for dredging etc.; a dragnet. 5. (*slang*) a draw on a cigarette etc. 6. (*slang*) women's clothes worn by men. —**drag one's feet**, to be deliberately slow or reluctant to act. **drag in**, to introduce (a subject) irrelevantly. **dragnet** *n.* a net drawn through a river or across ground to trap fish or game; a systematic hunt for criminals etc. **drag on**, to continue tediously. **drag out,** to prolong at length. **drag race**, an acceleration race between cars over a short distance. **drag up**, (*colloquial*) to introduce or revive (an unwelcome subject). [Old English or Old Norse]

draggle *v.t./i.* to make dirty, wet, or limp by trailing; to hang trailing.

dragon /'drægən/ *n.* 1. a mythical monster like a reptile, usually with wings and able to breathe out fire. 2. a fierce person. [from Old French from Latin from Greek *drakōn* = serpent]

dragonfly *n.* any of numerous insects of the order Odonata, including ◊damselflies. They all have a long narrow body, two pairs of almost equal-sized, glassy wings with a network of veins; short, bristle-like antennae; powerful, 'toothed' mouthparts; and very large compound eyes which may have up to 30,000 facets. They hunt other insects by sight, both as adults and as aquatic nymphs. The largest species have a wingspan of 18 cm/7 in, but fossils related to dragonflies, with wings up to 70 cm/2.3 ft across have been found.

dragoon /drə'guːn/ *n.* 1. a cavalryman (originally a mounted infantryman). 2. a fierce fellow. —*v.t.* to force *into* doing something. [originally = carbine, from French *dragon*]

drain *v.t./i.* 1. to draw off liquid from; to draw off (a liquid). 2. to flow or trickle away. 3. to dry or become dry as liquid flows away; to exhaust of strength or resources. 4. to drink (a liquid), to empty (a glass etc.) by drinking the contents. —*n.* 1. a channel, conduit, or pipe carrying off a liquid, sewage etc. 2. a constant outlet or expenditure. —**down the drain**, (*colloquial*) lost, wasted. **drainpipe** *n.* a pipe for

carrying off surplus water or liquid sewage from a building. **draining board**, a sloping grooved surface beside a sink on which washed dishes etc. are left to drain.

drainage *n.* 1. draining; a system of drains. 2. what is drained off.

drake *n.* a male duck.

Drake /dreɪk/ Francis *c.*1545–1596. English buccaneer and explorer. Having enriched himself as a pirate against Spanish interests in the Caribbean from 1567–72, he was sponsored by Elizabeth I for an expedition to the Pacific, sailing round the world from 1577–80 in the *Golden Hind*, robbing Spanish ships as he went. It was the second circumnavigation of the globe (the first was by the Portuguese explorer Magellan).

dram *n.* 1. a small drink of spirits. 2. = ◊drachm. [from Old French *drame* or Latin *drama*]

drama /'drɑːmə/ *n.* 1. a play for acting on stage or for broadcasting. 2. the art of writing and presenting plays. 3. a dramatic series of events; dramatic quality. [Latin from Greek *draō* = do]

dramatic /drə'mætɪk/ *adj.* of drama, sudden and exciting or unexpected; vividly striking; (of a gesture etc.) overdone or absurd. —**dramatically** *adv.* [from Latin from Greek]

dramatics *n.pl.* (often treated as *singular*) 1. the performance of plays. 2. exaggerated behaviour.

dramatis personae /'dræmətɪs pɜː'səʊnaɪ/ the characters in a play; a list of these. [Latin = persons of the drama]

dramatist /'dræmətɪst/ *n.* a writer of dramas.

dramatize /'dræmətaɪz/ *v.t./i.* 1. to make (a novel etc.) into a play. 2. to make a dramatic scene of; to behave dramatically. —**dramatization** /-'zeɪʃən/ *n.*

drank *n.* past of **drink**.

drape *v.t.* to cover loosely, hang, or adorn, with cloth etc.; to arrange (clothes, hangings) in graceful folds. —*n.* (in *plural*, *US*) curtains. [from Old French from Latin *drappus* = cloth]

draper *n.* a retailer of textile fabrics.

drapery *n.* 1. a draper's trade or fabrics. 2. fabric arranged in loose folds.

drastic /'dræstɪk/ *adj.* having a strong or far-reaching effect, severe. —**drastically** *adv.* [from Greek *drastikos* (*draō* = do)]

drat interjection of anger or annoyance, (*colloquial*) curse. —**dratted** *adj.* [for '*Od* (= God) *rot*]

draught /drɑːft/ *n.* 1. a current of air in a room etc., or in a chimney. 2. pulling, traction. 3. the depth of water needed to float a ship. 4. the drawing of liquor from a cask etc. 5. a single act of drinking; the amount so drunk. 6. the drawing in of a fishing-net; the fish caught in this. —**draught beer**, beer drawn from a cask, not bottled. **draught horse** *n.* a horse used for pulling heavy loads, a cart, plough etc. **feel the draught**, (*slang*) to feel the effect of financial or other difficulties.

draughts /drɑːfts/ *n.* a board game (known as **checkers** in the USA and Canada because of the chequered draught board of 64 squares) with elements of a simplified form of chess. Each of the two players has 12 men (disc-shaped pieces), and attempts either to capture all the opponent's men or to block their movements.

draughtsman *n.* (*plural* **draughtsmen**) or **draftsman** (*plural* **draftsmen**) 1. one who makes drawings, plans, or sketches. 2. a piece in the game of draughts. —**draughtsmanship** *n.*

draughty *adj.* (of a room etc.) letting in sharp currents of air.

Dravidian /drə'vɪdɪən/ *n.* 1. a member of a group of non-Indo-European peoples of the Deccan region of India and N Sri Lanka. 2. the group of languages spoken by them; the main ones are Tamil, which has a literary tradition two thousand years old; Kanarese; Telugu; Malayalam; and Tulu. —*adj.* of the Dravidians or their languages. [from Sanskrit *Dravida*, a province of S India]

draw *v.t./i.* (*past* **drew** /druː/; *past participle* **drawn**) 1. to pull or cause to move towards or after one; to pull up, over, or across; to pull (curtains etc.) open or shut. 2. to attract; to take in; to elicit or evoke; to induce. 3. to take out, to remove; to obtain by lot, to draw lots. 4. to take or get from a source; to obtain (water) from a well or tap; to bring out (liquid from a vessel, blood from the body); to disembowel. 5. to infer (a conclusion). 6. to trace (a line or mark); to produce (a picture) by lines and marks; to represent (a thing) thus. **7.** to formulate or perceive (a comparison, distinctions). **8.** to compose or write out (a document, cheque etc.). **9.** to finish (a contest or game) with neither side winning. **10.** to make one's way, to move. **11.** to make a call *on* a person, his skill etc. **12.** (of a ship) to require (a specified depth of water) to float in. **13.** to search (a cover) for game. —*n.* **1.** an act of drawing, a pull. **2.** a person or thing that draws custom, attention etc. **3.** a drawing of lots, a raffle. **4.** a drawn game. **5.** a suck on a cigarette etc. —**draw back,** to withdraw from an undertaking. **draw in,** (of days) to become shorter; to persuade to join. **draw in one's horns,** to become less assertive or ambitious. **draw the line at,** to set a limit (of tolerance etc.) at. **draw on,** to approach, to come near. **draw out,** to prolong; to elicit, to induce to talk; (of days) to become longer. **drawstring** *n.* one that can be pulled to tighten an opening. **draw up,** to compose or draft (a document etc.); to bring into order; to come to a halt; to make *oneself* stiffly erect, **quick on the draw,** quick to react. [Old English]

drawback *n.* a thing that impairs satisfaction, a disadvantage. ⸳

drawbridge *n.* a bridge, especially over a moat, hinged at one end for drawing up.

drawer /'drɔ:ə/ *n.* **1.** one who or that which draws, especially a person who draws a cheque etc. **2.** (also /drɔ:/) a boxlike storage compartment without a lid, for sliding in and out of a table etc. **3.** (in *plural*) an undergarment worn next to the body below the waist.

drawing *n.* **1.** the art of representing by line with a pencil etc. **2.** a picture etc. drawn thus. —**drawing board** a board on which paper is stretched while a drawing is made. **drawing pin** *n.* a flat-headed pin for fastening paper etc. to a surface.

drawing room a room for comfortable sitting or entertaining in a private house. [from earlier *withdrawing-room*]

drawl *v.t./i.* to speak with drawn-out vowel sounds. —*n.* a drawling utterance or way of speaking. [probably from Low German or Dutch *dralen* = linger]

drawn *n.* past participle of **draw.** —*adj.* looking strained from fear or anxiety.

dray *n.* a low cart without sides for heavy loads, especially beer barrels. —**drayman** *n.* (*plural* **draymen**) [Old English = drag-net]

dread /dred/ *v.t.* to fear greatly; to look forward to with great apprehension. —*n.* great fear or apprehension. —*adj.* dreaded; (*archaic*) dreadful, awe-inspiring. [Old English]

dreadful *adj.* terrible; (*colloquial*) troublesome, very bad. —**dreadfully** *adv.*

Dreadnought *n.* a class of battleships built for the British navy after 1905 and far superior in speed and armaments to anything then afloat. The first was launched on 18 Feb 1906, with armaments consisting entirely of big guns. The German Nassau class was begun in 1907, and by 1914, the USA, France, Japan, and Austria-Hungary had battleships of a similar class to the Dreadnought. German plans to build similar craft led to the naval race that contributed to Anglo-German antagonism and the origins of World War II.

dream *n.* **1.** a series of pictures or events in the mind of a sleeping person. **2.** a daydream, a fantasy; an ideal or aspiration. **3.** a beautiful or ideal person or thing. —*v.t./i.* (*past* and *past participle* **dreamt** /dremt/ or **dreamed**) **1.** to experience a dream; to imagine as in a dream. **2.** (with *negative*) to think of as a possibility. —**dreamland** *n.* ideal or imaginary land. **dream up,** to imagine, to invent. **like a dream,** (*colloquial*) easily, effortlessly. —**dreamer** *n.* [from Old English]

dreamless *adj.* without dreaming.

dreamtime *n.* or **dreaming** the complex system of religious beliefs surrounding stories of the creation of the Australian Aborigines. In dreamtime, spiritual beings shaped the land; the first people were created and placed in their proper territories; and laws and rituals were established.

dreamy *adj.* **1.** dreamlike. **2.** given to dreaming or fantasy, vague. —**dreamily** *adv.*, **dreaminess** *n.*

dreary *adj.* dismal, dull, gloomy. —**drearily** *adv.*, **dreariness** *n.* [Old English *drēor* = gore]

dredge[1] /dredʒ/ *n.* an apparatus for bringing up oysters etc. or clearing out mud etc. from a river or the sea bottom. —*v.t./i.* to bring *up* or clean out with a dredge; to use a dredge. [from Scottish *dreg*]

dredge[2] *v.t.* to sprinkle with flour, sugar etc. [from obsolete *dredge* = sweetmeat from Old French]

dredger[1] *n.* a dredge, a boat with a dredge.

dredger[2] *n.* a container with a perforated lid, used for sprinkling flour etc.

Drees /dreɪs/ Willem 1886–1988. Dutch socialist politician, prime minister 1948–58. Chair of the Socialist Democratic Workers' Party from 1911 until the German invasion of 1940, he returned to politics in 1947, after being active in the resistance movement. In 1947, as the responsible minister, he introduced a state pension scheme.

dregs *n.pl.* sediment, grounds, lees; the worst or most useless part.

Dreiser /'draɪsə/ Theodore 1871–1945. US novelist, formerly a Chicago journalist. He wrote the naturalistic novels *Sister Carrie* 1900 and *An American Tragedy* 1925, based on the real-life crime of a young man who in 'making good' kills a shop assistant he has made pregnant. It was filmed as *Splendor in the Grass* 1961.

drench *v.t.* **1.** to make thoroughly wet. **2.** to force (an animal) to take a dose of medicine. —*n.* a dose of medicine for an animal. [Old English]

Drenthe /'drentə/ low-lying N province of the Netherlands; **area** 2,660 sq km/1,027 sq mi; **population** (1988) 437,000; **capital** Assen; **physical** fenland and moors; well-drained clay and peat soils; **products** livestock, arable crops, horticulture, petroleum; **history** developed following land drainage initiated in the mid-18th century, and was established as a separate province of the Netherlands in 1796.

Dresden /'drezdən/ capital of the state of Saxony, Federal Republic of Germany; population (1990) 520,000. Industries include chemicals, machinery, glassware, and musical instruments. It was one of the most beautiful German cities prior to its devastation by Allied fire-bombing in 1945. Dresden county has an area of 6,740 sq km/2,602 sq mi and a population of 1,772,000.

Dresden *n.* **1.** or **Dresden china** etc. china of a kind made at Meissen near Dresden in Germany, with elaborate decoration and delicate colourings. **2.** (*attributive*) characterized by delicate or frail prettiness.

dress *v.t./i.* **1.** to put clothes upon; to provide oneself with and wear clothes; to put on one's clothes; to put on evening dress. **2.** to arrange or adorn (the hair, a shop window, etc.). **3.** to clean or treat (a wound etc.). **4.** to prepare (a bird, crab, or salad) for cooking or eating. **5.** to finish the surface of (a fabric, leather, stone). **6.** to apply manure to. **7.** to correct the alignment of (troops). —*n.* **1.** clothing, especially the visible part of it; formal or ceremonial costume. **2.** a woman's or girl's garment of bodice and skirt. **3.** an external covering, an outward form. —**dress circle** the first gallery in a theatre, where evening dress was formerly required. **dress down,** to scold, to reprimand. **dress rehearsal,** the final rehearsal in full costume. **dress up,** to put on special clothes; to make (a thing) more attractive or interesting. [from Old French from Latin *directus* = direct]

dressage /'dresɑːʒ/ *n.* the training of a horse in obedience and deportment; a display of this. [French *dresser* = train]

dresser[1] *n.* a kitchen sideboard with shelves for dishes etc. [from Old French *dresser* = prepare]

dresser[2] *n.* **1.** one who helps to dress actors or actresses. **2.** a surgeon's assistant in operations.

dressing *n.* **1.** putting clothes on. **2.** a sauce or stuffing etc. for food. **3.** a bandage, ointment etc., for a wound. **4.** manure etc. spread over the land. **5.** a substance used to stiffen textile fabrics during manufacture. —**dressing-down,** a scolding. **dressing gown** *n.* a loose gown worn when one is not fully dressed. **dressing room** *n.* a room for dressing or changing clothes, especially in a theatre etc., or attached to a bedroom. **dressing table** *n.* a piece of bedroom furniture with a mirror and usually drawers, for use while dressing, arranging the hair, applying make-up etc.

dressmaker *n.* a person who makes women's clothes. —**dressmaking** *n.*

dressy *adj.* smart, elegant, wearing stylish clothes. —**dressily** *adv.*

drew past of **draw.**

drey /dreɪ/ *n.* a squirrel's nest.

Dreyer /'draɪə/ Carl Theodor 1889–1968. Danish director. His wide range of films include the silent classic *La Passion de Jeanne d'Arc*/*The Passion of Joan of Arc* 1928 and the Expressionist horror film *Vampyr* 1932, after the failure of which Dreyer made no full-length films until *Vredens Dag*/*Day of Wrath* 1943.

Dreyfus /'dreɪfəs/ Alfred 1859–1935. French army officer, who became a victim of miscarriage of justice, anti-Semitism, and cover-up. In 1894, when employed in the War Ministry, he was accused of betraying military secrets to Germany. He was court-martialled and sent to the penal colony on ◊Devil's Island. When his innocence was discovered in 1896 the military establishment tried to conceal it, and the implications of the Dreyfus affair were passionately discussed in the press until he was exonerated in 1906.

dribble *v.t./i.* **1.** to allow saliva to flow from the mouth; to flow or cause to flow in drops. **2.** to move the ball forward in football or hockey with slight touches of the feet or stick. —*n.* **1.** an act of dribbling. **2.** a dribbling flow. [frequentative of *drib* obsolete variant of *drip*]

driblet /'drɪblɪt/ *n.* a small amount.

dribs and drabs small, scattered amounts.

drier /'draɪə/ *n.* a device for drying hair, laundry, etc.

drift *n.* **1.** being driven along, especially by a current; a slow movement or variation; a slow deviation of a ship, projectile etc. from a course. **2.** a mass of snow or sand driven along or heaped up by the wind; fragments of rock heaped up by wind, water etc. **3.** the policy of merely waiting on events, inaction. **4.** (in mining) a horizontal passage following a mineral vein. **5.** (*South African*) a ford. —*v.t./i.* **1.** to be carried by or as if by a current of air or water, (of a current) to cause to drift; to heap or be heaped in drifts. **2.** to move casually or aimlessly. —**drift mine**, a mine using a horizontal passage (see sense 4). **drift net** *n.* a net used in sea fishing and allowed to drift with the tide. [from Old Norse and Middle High German *trift* = movement of cattle]

drifter *n.* **1.** an aimless person. **2.** a boat used for fishing with a drift net.

driftwood *n.* wood floating on moving water or washed ashore by it.

drill[1] *n.* **1.** a tool or machine for boring holes or sinking wells. **2.** instruction in military exercises; thorough training, especially by a repeated routine; (*colloquial*) a recognized procedure. —*v.t./i.* **1.** to make (a hole) with a drill; to use a drill on. **2.** to train or be trained by means of drill. [from Middle Dutch *drillen* = bore]

drill[2] *n.* **1.** a small furrow for sowing seed in. **2.** a machine for making a furrow, sowing, and covering the seed. **3.** a row of seeds so sown. —*v.t.* to plant in drills.

drill[3] *n.* a strong twilled cotton or linen fabric. [from German *drilich* from Latin *trilix* = having three threads]

drill[4] *n.* a West African baboon *Mandrillus leucophaeus* related to the mandrill.

drily /'draɪlɪ/ *adv.* in a dry manner.

drink *v.t./i.* (*past* **drank**; *past participle* **drunk**) **1.** to swallow (a liquid); to swallow the contents of (a vessel); to take alcoholic liquor, especially to excess; to bring (*oneself*) to a specified state by drinking. **2.** (of a plant, sponge etc.) to absorb (moisture). —*n.* liquid for drinking; a glass etc. or portion of this, especially alcoholic; intoxicating liquor, the excessive use of it. —**the drink**, (*slang*) the sea. **drink a person's health**, to pledge good wishes to him or her by drinking. **drink in**, to listen to or understand eagerly. **drink to**, to drink a toast to, to wish success to. **drink up**, to drink all or the remainder (of). —**drinker** *n.* [Old English]

drinkable *adj.* suitable for drinking.

drinking water water that has been subjected to various treatments, including ◊filtration and ◊sterilization, to make it fit for human consumption; it is not pure water.

drip *v.t./i.* (**-pp-**) to fall or let fall in drops; to be so wet (*with* a liquid) as to shed drops. —*n.* **1.** a small falling drop of liquid; a liquid falling in drops, the sound of this; a drip-feed. **2.** (*slang*) a feeble or dull person. [from Middle Danish *drippe*]

drip-dry *v.t./i.* to dry easily when hung up; to leave to dry in this way. —*adj.* made of a fabric that will dry easily without creasing.

drip-feed *n.* feeding by liquid a drop at a time, especially intravenously; apparatus for this. —*v.t.* to apply a drip-feed to.

dripping *n.* fat melted from roasting meat.

dromedary

dripstone *n.* a projection above a wall or window etc., to divert water from the parts below.

drive *v.t./i.* (*past* **drove**; *past participle* **driven** /'drɪvən/) **1.** to urge in some direction by blows, threats, violence, etc. **2.** to cause to go in some direction; to direct and control (a vehicle or locomotive); to convey in a vehicle; to operate a motor vehicle, to be competent to do so; to travel in a private vehicle. **3.** to impel or carry along; to hit (a ball) forcibly; to force or hit (a nail or stake) *into*; to bore (a tunnel etc.); (of a power-source) to set or keep (machinery) going. **4.** to compel; to force into a state of being (*mad* etc.); to overwork. **5.** to be moved by wind, especially rapidly. **6.** to carry on, to conclude. **7.** to dash, to rush; to work hard *at.* —*n.* **1.** an excursion or journey in a vehicle. **2.** a street or road, especially a scenic one. **3.** a driveway. **4.** a forcible stroke of a ball. **5.** capacity or desire to achieve things; organized effort to some end. **6.** the transmission of power to machinery, the wheels of a motor vehicle etc.; the position of the steering-wheel of a motor vehicle. **7.** a social event of numerous simultaneous card-games etc. —**drive at**, to seek, to intend, to mean. **drive-in** *adj.* (of a cinema, bank etc.) for the use of passengers seated in cars; (*n.*) a cinema, bank etc., of this type. **driving licence**, a licence permitting one to drive a motor vehicle. **driving test**, an official test of competence to drive a motor vehicle. **driving wheel**, a wheel communicating motive power in machinery. [Old English]

drivel /'drɪvəl/ *n.* silly talk, nonsense. —*v.i.* (**-ll-**) **1.** to talk drivel. **2.** to run at the nose or mouth. [Old English]

driven past participle of **drive**.

driver *n.* **1.** a person who drives (especially a motor vehicle). **2.** a golf-club for driving from a tee.

driveway *n.* a road serving as an approach for vehicles, especially a private one to a house etc.

drizzle *n.* very fine rain. —*v.i.* (of rain) to fall in very fine drops. —**drizzly** *adj.* [perhaps related to Old English *drēosan* = fall]

drogue /drəʊg/ *n.* a truncated cone of fabric used as a brake for a landing aircraft or as a target, windsock etc.

droll /drəʊl/ *adj.* oddly or strangely amusing. —**drolly** /'drəʊl-lɪ/ *adv.* [from French *drôle*]

drollery /'drəʊlərɪ/ *n.* quaint humour.

dromedary /'drɒmɪdərɪ, 'drʌm-/ *n.* a light, one-humped camel, especially an Arabian, bred for riding. [from French or Latin from Greek *dromas* = runner]

drone *n.* **1.** a non-working male of the honey-bee; an idler. **2.** a deep humming sound; the bass-pipe of a bagpipe, its continuous note. —*v.t./i.* to make a deep humming sound; to speak or utter monotonously. [Old English]

drool /druːl/ *v.i.* to dribble, to slobber; to show unrestrained admiration (*over*).

droop /druːp/ *v.t./i.* to bend or hang downwards, especially through tiredness or weakness; to languish, to flag; to let (the eyes or head) drop. —*n.* a drooping attitude, a loss of spirit. —**droopy** *adj.* [from Old Norse]

drop *n.* **1.** a small, round portion of liquid such as hangs or falls separately or adheres to a surface; a thing in the shape of a drop, especially a sweet or a pendant; (in *plural*) a liquid medicine to be measured by drops; a minute quantity; a glass etc. of intoxicating liquor. **2.** an act of dropping, a fall of prices, temperature etc. **3.** a thing that drops or is dropped; a drop curtain. **4.** a steep or vertical descent; the distance of this. **5.** (*slang*) a hiding place for stolen or illicit goods etc.

6. (*slang*) a bribe. —*v.t./i.* **1.** to fall by the force of gravity from not being held; to allow to fall, to cease to hold. **2.** to fall or cause to fall in drops; to shed (tears, blood). **3.** to set down (a passenger, parcel etc.). **4.** to fell with a blow, bullet etc.; to sink to the ground, especially from exhaustion or injury. **5.** to fall naturally *asleep*, (*back*) *into* a habit etc. **6.** to fall in a direction, condition, amount, degree, or pitch. **7.** to lower, to direct downwards; to become lower; to perform (a curtsy). **8.** to move to or be left in a position further back. **9.** to cease to associate with, deal with, or discuss; to cease, to lapse. **10.** to utter or be uttered casually; to send casually; to come or go casually *by* or *in* as a visitor, or *into* a place. **11.** to lose (money, especially in gambling); to omit in speech. **12.** to send (the ball) or score (a goal) in football by a drop kick. **13.** to give birth to (especially a lamb). —**at the drop of a hat,** promptly, instantly. **drop curtain,** a painted curtain that can be lowered on to a theatre stage. **drop kick,** a kick at football made by dropping the ball and kicking it as it touches the ground. **drop off,** to fall asleep; to drop (a passenger). **drop on a person,** to be severe with him. **drop out,** to cease to take an active part. **dropout** *n.* one who withdraws from conventional society. **drop scone,** a scone made by dropping a spoonful of mixture on a cooking surface. [Old English]

droplet *n.* a small drop.

dropper *n.* a device for releasing a liquid in drops.

droppings *n.pl.* what falls or has fallen in drops, especially the dung of some animals and birds.

dropsy *n.* a disease in which watery fluid collects in the cavities or tissues of the body. —**dropsical** *adj.* [for earlier *hydropsy* from Old French from Latin from Greek *hudōr* = water]

Drosera /'drɒsərə/ *n.* Latin name for the ◊sundew plant.

drosophila /drə'sɒfilə/ *n.* a fruit-fly of the genus *Drosophila*, used extensively in genetic research. [from Greek *drosos* = dew, moisture and *philos* = loving]

dross /drɒs/ *n.* scum separated from metals in melting; impurities, rubbish. [Old English]

drought /draʊt/ *n.* an abnormally prolonged spell without rain. In the UK, drought is defined as the passing of 15 days with less than 0.5 mm/0.0078 in of rain. [Old English]

drove[1] *n.* a herd or flock being driven or moving together; a moving crowd. [Old English]

drove[2] past of **drive.**

drover *n.* a driver of cattle.

drown *v.t./i.* **1.** to suffocate by submersion in water or other liquid; to flood, to drench. **2.** to alleviate (a sorrow etc.) with drink. **3.** to overpower (a sound) with a louder noise. —**drowned valley,** a valley that has become submerged at its lower end by the sea or a lake. [related to Old Norse *drukna* = be drowned]

drowse /draʊz/ *v.i.* to be lightly asleep.

drowsy /'draʊzɪ/ *adj.* very sleepy, almost asleep. — **drowsily** *adv.,* **drowsiness** *n.* [related to Old English *drūsian* = be languid]

drub *v.t.* (-bb-) to beat, to thrash; to defeat thoroughly. —**drubbing** *n.* [ultimately from Arabic]

drudge *n.* one who does dull, laborious, or menial work. —*v.i.* to work hard or strenuously, to toil. —**drudgery** *n.*

drug *n.* a medicinal substance; a narcotic, hallucinogen, or stimulant, especially one causing addiction. —*v.t./i.* (-gg-) to add a drug to (food or drink); to give drugs to, to stupefy; to take drugs as an addict. —**drug on the market,** a commodity that is plentiful but no longer in demand. [from Old French *drogue*]

drug and alcohol dependence a physical or psychological craving for addictive drugs such as alcohol, nicotine (in cigarettes), tranquillizers, heroin, or stimulants (for example, amphetamines). Such substances can alter mood or behaviour. When dependence is established, sudden withdrawal from the drug can cause unpleasant physical and/or psychological reactions, which may be dangerous.

drug, generic any drug produced without a brand name that is identical to a branded product. Usually generic drugs are produced when the patent on a branded drug has expired, and are cheaper than their branded equivalents.

drugget /'drʌgɪt/ *n.* a coarse woven fabric used for floor coverings etc. [from French *droguet*]

druggist *n.* a pharmaceutical chemist. [from French]

drugstore *n.* (*US*) a chemist's shop also selling light refreshments and other articles.

Druid *n.* **1.** a priest of the ancient Celts in Gaul, Britain, and Ireland. **2.** a member of any of various movements attempting to revive Druid practices. The Druids regarded the oak as sacred; one of their chief rites was the cutting of mistletoe from it with a golden sickle. They taught the immortality of the soul and a reincarnation doctrine, were expert in astronomy, and are thought to have offered human sacrifices. Druidism was stamped out in Gaul after the Roman conquest. In Britain Druids were extirpated from their stronghold in Anglesey, Wales, by the Roman governor Agricola. They existed in Scotland and Ireland until the coming of the Christian missionaries. **3.** an officer of the Gorsedd. —**Druidism** *n.,* **Druidic** /-'ɪdɪk/ *adj.,* **Druidical** *adj.* [from French or Latin from Celtic]

drum *n.* **1.** a musical instrument or toy sounded by striking, made of a hollow cylinder or hemisphere with skin or parchment stretched over the opening(s); its player; the sound produced by striking it; (in *plural*) the percussion section of an orchestra or band. **2.** a cylindrical object, structure, or container. **3.** the eardrum. —*v.t./i.* (-mm-) **1.** to play a drum; to make the sound of a drum, to tap or beat continuously or rhythmically with the fingers etc. **2.** to drive facts or a lesson *into* a person by persistence. **3.** (of a bird or insect) to make a loud noise with the wings. —**drum brake,** a brake consisting of shoes acting on a revolving drum. **drum major,** the leader of a marching band. **drum majorette,** a female drum major. **drum out,** to dismiss with ignominy. **drum up,** to produce or obtain by vigorous effort. [from Low German *trommel*]

drumhead *n.* the part of a drum that is struck.

drumlin /'drʌmlɪn/ *n.* a long, oval mound of matter deposited by a glacier, flood etc., with its longer axis parallel to the direction of the flow. [from Gaelic and Irish *druim* = ridge]

drummer *n.* a player of a drum.

drumstick *n.* **1.** a stick for beating a drum. **2.** the lower joint of the leg of a cooked fowl.

drunk *adj.* lacking proper control of oneself from the effects of alcoholic drink; overcome *with* joy, success etc. —*n.* **1.** a drunken person. **2.** (*slang*) a bout of drinking. [past participle of *drink*]

drunkard /'drʌŋkəd/ *n.* a person who is habitually drunk.

drunken *adj.* drunk, often drunk; involving or caused by excessive alcoholic drinking. —**drunkenly** *adv.,* **drunkenness** /-kən-nɪs/ *n.*

drupe /druːp/ *n.* a fleshy ◊fruit containing one or more seeds which are surrounded by a hard, protective layer—for example cherry, almond, and plum. The wall of the fruit (◊pericarp) is differentiated into the outer skin (exocarp), the fleshy layer of tissues (mesocarp), and the hard layer surrounding the seed (endocarp). The coconut is a drupe, but here the pericarp becomes dry and fibrous at maturity. Blackberries are an aggregate fruit composed of a cluster of small drupes. [from Latin from Greek *druppa* = olive]

Drury Lane Theatre /'drʊərɪ/ a theatre first opened in 1663 on the site of earlier London playhouses. It was twice burned; the present building dates from 1812.

Druse /druːz/ *n.* or **Druze** a member of a religious sect in the Middle East of some 500,000 people. They are monotheists, preaching that the Fatimid caliph al-Hakim (996–1021) is God; their scriptures are drawn from the Christian gospels, the Torah (the first five books of the Old Testament), the Koran, and Sufi allegories. Druse militia groups form one of the three main factions involved in the Lebanese civil war (the others are Amal Shi'ite Muslims and Christian Maronites). The Druse military leader (from the time of his father's assassination 1977) is Walid Jumblatt. [French from Arabic, probably from their founder *al-Daraī* 11th century]

dry /draɪ/ *adj.* (**drier, driest**) **1.** without moisture, not wet; not rainy, deficient in rainfall; not yielding water, milk, etc.; parched, dried up; (*colloquial*) thirsty. **2.** prohibiting or opposed to the sale of alcoholic liquor at some or all times. **3.** unconnected with or not using liquid. **4.** solid, not liquid. **5.** without butter etc. **6.** (of a liquid) having disappeared by evaporation, draining, wiping etc. **7.** (of a wine) free from sweetness. **8.** plain, unelaborated, uninteresting; cold, impassive; (of wit) expressed with pretended seriousness. —*v.t./i.* to make or become dry; to preserve (food) by the removal of moisture. —**dry battery** *or* **cell,** a battery or

Dryden *English poet, satirist, dramatist, and biographer John Dryden, painted in 1693 by Kneller.*

cell in which the electrolyte is absorbed in a solid. **dry-clean** *v.t.* to clean (clothes etc.) with organic solvents that evaporate quickly, without using water. **dry dock,** a dry enclosure for building or repairing ships. **dry-fly** *adj.* (of fishing) using an artificial fly that floats. **dry ice** *n.* solid carbon dioxide used as a refrigerant. **dry land,** land as distinct from sea etc. **dry measure,** a measure for dry goods. **dry out,** to make or become fully dry; (of a drug addict etc.) to undergo treatment to cure an addiction. **dry point** *n.* a needle for engraving without acid on a bare copper plate; an engraving produced by this. **dry rot,** a decayed state of wood when not well ventilated; the fungi causing this; any moral or social decay. **dry run,** *(colloquial)* a rehearsal. **dry-shod** *adj. & adv.* without wetting one's shoes. **dry up,** to dry washed dishes; to make completely dry; to cease to yield liquid; to become unproductive; (of an actor) to forget one's lines; (in *imperative*) to cease to talk. —**dryness** *n.* [Old English]

dryad /ˈdraɪæd/ *n.* a wood-nymph. [from Old French from Latin from Greek *drus* = oak]

Dryden /ˈdraɪdn/ John 1631–1700. English poet and dramatist, noted for his satirical verse and for his use of the heroic couplet. His poetry includes the verse satire *Absalom and Achitophel* 1681, *Annus Mirabilis* 1667, and 'St Cecilia's Day' 1687. Plays include the comedy *Marriage à la Mode* 1671 and *All for Love* 1678, a reworking of Shakespeare's *Antony and Cleopatra.*

dryer variant of **drier.**

dryly variant of **drily.**

Drysdale /ˈdraɪzdeɪl/ George Russell 1912–1969. Australian artist, born in England whose drawings and paintings often depict the Australian outback, its drought, desolation, and poverty, and Aboriginal life.

drystone *adj.* (of a wall etc.) made of stones without mortar.

Dr Zhivago /ˈdɒktə ʒiˈvɑːgəʊ/ a novel by Boris Pasternak, published (in Italy) in 1957 which describes a scientist's disillusionment with the Russian revolution. It was banned in the USSR as a 'hostile act' and only published there in magazine form in 1988.

DSC abbreviation of Distinguished Service Cross.

D.Sc. abbreviation of Doctor of Science.

DSM abbreviation of Distinguished Service Medal.

DSO abbreviation of Distinguished Service Order.

d.t., d.t.'s abbreviation of delirium tremens.

DTI abbreviation of Department of Trade and Industry, UK government department.

dual /ˈdjuːəl/ *adj.* composed of two parts, twofold, double. —*n.* in grammar, a dual number or form. —**dual carriageway,** a road with a dividing strip between traffic flowing in opposite directions. **dual control,** two linked sets of controls, enabling either of two persons to operate a car or aircraft. —**duality** /djuːˈælɪtɪ/ *n.* [from Latin *dualis* (*duo* = two)]

Dual Entente an alliance between Russia and France that lasted from 1893 until the Bolshevik Revolution of 1917.

dualism *n.* in philosophy, the belief that reality is essentially dual in nature. ◊Descartes, for example, refers to thinking and material substance. These entities interact but are fundamentally separate and distinct. Dualism is contrasted with ◊monism.

Duarte /duːˈɑːteɪ/ José Napoleon 1925–1990. El Salvadorean politician, president 1980–82 and 1984–88. He was mayor of San Salvador from 1964–70, and was elected president in 1972, but exiled by the army in 1982. On becoming president again in 1984, he sought a negotiated settlement with the left-wing guerrillas in 1986, but resigned on health grounds.

dub[1] *v.t.* (**-bb-**) 1. to make (a person) a knight by touching his shoulders with a sword. 2. to give a specified name to. 3. to smear (leather) with grease. [from Old French *adober* = equip with armour, repair]

dub[2] *v.t.* (**-bb-**) to make an alternative sound-track of (a film) especially in a different language; to add (sound effects, music) to a film or broadcast.

Dubai /duːˈbaɪ/ one of the ◊United Arab Emirates.

Du Barry /djuː ˈbæri/ Marie Jeanne Bécu, Comtesse 1743–1793. Mistress of ◊Louis XV of France from 1768. At his death in 1774 she was banished to a convent, and during the Revolution fled to London. Returning to Paris in 1793, she was guillotined.

dubbin *n.* or **dubbing** a thick grease for softening and waterproofing leather.

Dubček /ˈdʊbtʃek/ Alexander 1921– . Czechoslovak politician, chair of the federal assembly from 1989. He was a member of the resistance movement and after World War II became first secretary of the Communist Party 1967–69. He launched a liberalization campaign (called the Prague Spring) that was opposed by the USSR and led to the Soviet invasion of Czechoslovakia in 1968. He was arrested by Soviet troops and expelled from the party in 1970. In 1989 he gave speeches at pro-democracy rallies, and in Dec, after the fall of the hardline regime, he was elected speaker of the Czechoslovak parliament.

dubiety /djuːˈbaɪətɪ/ *n.* a feeling of doubt. [from Latin]

dubious /ˈdjuːbɪəs/ *adj.* 1. hesitating, doubtful. 2. unreliable; of questionable or suspected character. —**dubiously** *adv.* [from Latin *dubiosus* (*dubium* = doubt)]

Dublin /ˈdʌblɪn/ county in Leinster province, Republic of Ireland, facing the Irish Sea; area 920 sq km/355 sq mi; population (1986) 1,021,000. It is mostly level and lowlying, but rises in the S to 753 m/2,471 ft in Kippure, part of the Wicklow mountains. The river Liffey enters Dublin Bay; Dún Laoghaire is the only other large town.

Dublin (Gaelic *Baile Atha Cliath*) capital and port on the E coast of the Republic of Ireland, at the mouth of the river Liffey, facing the Irish Sea; population (1981) 526,000, Greater Dublin (including Dún Laoghaire) 921,000. It is the site of one of the world's largest breweries (Guinness); other industries include textiles, pharmaceuticals, electrical goods, and machine tools. It was the centre of English rule from 1171 (exercised from Dublin Castle from 1220) until 1922.

Dubos /duːˈbəʊs/ René Jules 1901–1981. French–US microbiologist who studied soil microorganisms and became interested in their antibacterial properties.

Dubuffet /duːbuˈfeɪ/ Jean 1901–1985. French artist. He originated *l'art brut,* 'raw or brutal art', in the 1940s. He used a variety of materials in his paintings and sculptures – plaster, steel wool, straw, and so on—and was inspired by graffiti and children's drawings.

ducal /ˈdjuːkəl/ *adj.* of or like a duke. [from French]

ducat /ˈdʌkət/ *n.* a gold coin formerly current in most European countries. [from Italian or Latin = duchy]

Duccio di Buoninsegna /ˈduːtʃəʊ di bwɒnɪnˈseɪnjə/ *c.*1255–1319. Italian painter, a major figure in the Sienese school. His greatest work is his altarpiece for Siena Cathedral, the *Maestà* 1308–11; the figure of the Virgin is Byzantine in style, with much gold detail, but Duccio also created a graceful linear harmony in drapery hems, for example, and this proved a lasting characteristic of Sienese style.

Duce /ˈduːtʃeɪ/ *n.* the title bestowed on the fascist dictator Benito ◊Mussolini by his followers and later adopted as his official title. [Italian = leader]

Duchamp /djuːˈʃɒm/ Marcel 1887–1968. US artist, born in France. He achieved notoriety with his *Nude Descending a Staircase* 1912 (Philadelphia Museum of Art), influenced by Cubism and Futurism. An active exponent of ◊Dadaism, he invented 'ready-mades', everyday items like a bicycle wheel on a kitchen stool, which he displayed as works of art.

duchess /'dʌtʃɪs/ n. the wife or widow of a duke; a woman holding the rank of duke in her own right. [from Old French from Latin *ducissa*]

duchy /'dʌtʃɪ/ n. the territory of a duke or duchess; the royal dukedom of Cornwall or Lancaster. [from Old French from Latin *ducatus*]

duck[1] n. 1. a swimming bird of the genus *Anas* and kindred genera, especially the domesticated form of the mallard or wild duck; the female of this; its flesh as food. 2. the score of 0 in cricket. 3. (*colloquial*, especially as a form of address) dear. —*v.t./i.* 1. to bob down, especially to avoid being seen or hit; to dip the head under water and emerge; to plunge (a person) briefly in water. 2. (*colloquial*) to dodge or avoid (a task etc.). —**duckboards** *n.pl.* wooden slats forming a narrow path in a trench or over mud. **ducks and drakes,** the game of making a flat stone skim along the surface of water (*play ducks and drakes with,* to squander). **like water off a duck's back,** producing no effect. [Old English *dúcan* = dive]

duck[2] n. a strong linen or cotton cloth; (in *plural*) trousers made of this. [from Middle Dutch]

duckbill n. a platypus.

duckling n. a young duck.

duckweed n. any of a family of tiny plants Lemnaceae, especially of the genus *Lemna*, found floating on the surface of still water throughout most of the world, except the polar regions and tropics. Each plant consists of a flat, circular, leaflike structure 0.4 cm/0.15 in or less across, with a single thin root up to 15 cm/6 in long below.

ducky n. (*colloquial*, especially as a form of address) dear.

duct n. a channel or tube for conveying a fluid, cable etc.; a tube in the body conveying secretions etc. —*v.t.* to convey through a duct. [from Latin *ductus* = aqueduct (*ducere* = lead)]

ductile /'dʌktaɪl/ adj. 1. (of a metal) capable of being drawn into wire. 2. pliable, docile. —**ductility** /-'tɪlɪtɪ/ n. [from French or Latin]

ductless adj. without a duct. —**ductless gland,** a gland that passes its secretions directly into the bloodstream, not through a duct.

dud n. (*slang*) 1. a thing that fails to work, a useless thing. 2. (in *plural*) clothes, rags. —adj. (*slang*) defective, useless.

dude /dju:d/ n. (*US*) a dandy; a city man. [probably from German dialect *dude* = fool]

dudgeon /'dʌdʒən/ n. resentment, indignation, usually in *in high dudgeon*, very angry.

due /dju:/ adj. 1. owed as a debt or obligation; payable immediately. 2. merited, appropriate; that ought to be given *to* a person. 3. ascribable *to* a cause, agent etc. 4. under engagement *to* do something or arrive at a certain time; to be looked for or foreseen. —adv. (of a point of the compass) exactly, directly. —n. 1. what one owes; (usually in *plural*) a fee or amount payable. 2. a person's right, what is owed him or her. —**become** *or* **fall due,** to become payable. **due to,** (*disputed usage*) because of. [from Old French from Latin *debitus* (*debēre* = owe)]

duel /'dju:əl/ n. a formal fight with deadly weapons between two persons; a two-sided contest. —*v.i.* (-ll-) to fight a duel. —**duellist** n. [from Italian *duello* or Latin *duellum* = war]

duenna /dju'enə/ n. an older woman acting as a chaperon to girls, especially in a Spanish family. [Spanish from Latin *domina* = mistress]

due process of law a legal principle, dating back to the ◊Magna Carta 1215, and now enshrined in the Fifth and Fourteenth amendments of the US Constitution, that no person shall be deprived of life, liberty, or property without due process of law (a fair legal procedure). In the USA, the provisions have been given a wide interpretation, to include, for example, the right to representation by an attorney.

duet /dju:'et/ n. a musical composition for two performers; the performers. —**duettist** n. [from German or Italian from Latin *duo* = two]

Dufay /dju:'faɪ/ Guillaume 1400–1474. Flemish composer. He is recognized as the foremost composer of his time, of both secular songs and sacred music (including 84 songs and eight masses). His work marks a transition between the

music of the Middle Ages and that of the Renaissance and is characterized by expressive melodies and rich harmonies.

duff[1] adj. (*slang*) worthless, useless, counterfeit. —n. a boiled pudding. [northern pronunciation of *dough*]

duff[2] *v.t.* (*slang*) to bungle.

duffel variant of **duffle**.

duffer n. an inefficient or stupid person. [perhaps from Scottish *doufart* = stupid person]

duffle n. a heavy woollen cloth. —**duffle bag,** a cylindrical canvas bag closed by a drawstring. **duffle coat,** a hooded overcoat of duffle, fastened with toggles. [from *Duffel* town in Belgium]

Dufourspitze /du:'fuəʃpɪtsə/ second highest of the alpine peaks, 4,634 m/15,203 ft high. It is the highest peak in the Monte Rosa group of the Pennine alps on the Swiss–Italian frontier.

Du Fu another name for the Chinese poet ◊Tu Fu.

Dufy /'du:fi/ Raoul 1877–1953. French painter and designer. He originated a fluent, brightly coloured style in watercolour and oils, painting scenes of gaiety and leisure, such as horse racing, yachting, and life on the beach.

dug[1] past and past participle of **dig**.

dug[2] an udder, a teat.

dugong /'du:gɒŋ/ n. a marine mammal *Dugong dugong* of the order Sirenia (sea cows), found in the Red Sea, the Indian Ocean and W Pacific. It can grow to 3.6 m/11 ft long, and has a tapering body with a notched tail and two foreflippers. It is herbivorous, feeding on sea grasses and seaweeds. [from Malay]

dug-out n. 1. a canoe made by hollowing a tree trunk. 2. a roofed shelter, especially for troops in the trenches.

Dulker /'daɪkə/ Johannes 1890–1935. Dutch architect of the 1920s and 1930s avant-garde period. His works demonstrate great structural vigour, and include the Zonnestraal sanatorium 1926, Open Air School, Amsterdam, 1932, and the Cineac News Cinema, Amsterdam, 1933.

Duisburg /'dju:zbɜ:g/ river port and industrial city in North Rhine–Westphalia, Germany, at the confluence of the Rhine and Ruhr rivers; population (1987) 515,000. It is the largest inland river port in Europe. Heavy industries include oil refining and the production of steel, copper, zinc, plastics, and machinery.

Dukakis /du:'ka:kɪs/ Michael 1933– . US Democrat politician, governor of Massachusetts 1974–78 and from 1982, presiding over a high-tech economic boom, the 'Massachusetts miracle'. He was a presidential candidate in 1988.

Dukas /dju:'ka:s/ Paul (Abraham) 1865–1935. French composer. His orchestral scherzo *L'Apprenti Sorcier/The Sorcerer's Apprentice* 1897 is full of the colour and energy that characterizes much of his work.

duke /dju:k/ n. a person holding the highest hereditary title of nobility; a sovereign prince ruling a duchy or small state. —**dukedom** n. [from Old French from Latin *dux* = leader]

dulcet /'dʌlsɪt/ adj. sweet-sounding. [from Old French from Latin *dulcis* = sweet]

dulcimer /'dʌlsɪmə/ n. 1. a musical instrument consisting of a shallow closed box over which metal strings are stretched to be struck by wood, cane, or wire hammers; the prototype of the piano. 2. a musical instrument of the zither type, fretted and with steel strings which are stopped with one hand and plucked with a plectrum by the other, played in Kentucky and Alabama as an accompaniment to songs and dances. [from Old French perhaps from Latin *dulce melos* = sweet melody]

dull adj. 1. not bright, vivid, or clear; (of weather) overcast. 2. tedious, not interesting or exciting. 3. not sharp; (of pain) indistinctly felt; (of sound) not resonant. 4. slow in understanding, stupid; without keen perception. 5. listless, depressed; (of trade etc.) slow, sluggish. —*v.t./i.* to make or become dull. —**dully** /'dʌl-lɪ/ adv., **dullness** n. [from Middle Low German, Middle Dutch *dul* = Old English *dol* = stupid]

dullard /'dʌləd/ n. a mentally dull person.

Dulles /'dʌlɪs/ John Foster 1888–1959. US politician. Senior US adviser at the founding of the United Nations, he was largely responsible for drafting the Japanese peace treaty of 1951. As secretary of state from 1952–59, he secured US intervention in support of South Vietnam following the expulsion of the French in 1954 and was critical of Britain in the Suez Crisis of 1956.

Dulong /dju:'lɒŋ/ Pierre 1785–1838. French chemist and physicist who, along with ◊Petit, discovered in 1819 the law that, for many elements solid at room temperature, the product of the ◊atomic weight and ◊specific heat capacity is approximately constant. He had earlier, in 1811, and at the cost of an eye, discovered the explosive nitrogen trichloride.

duly /'dju:lɪ/ adv. in due time or manner; rightly, properly, sufficiently.

Duma n. in Russia, before 1917, an elected assembly that met four times following the short-lived 1905 revolution. With progressive demands that the government could not accept, the Duma was largely powerless. After the abdication of Nicholas II, the Duma directed the formation of a provisional government.

Dumas /'dju:mɑ:/ Alexandre 1802–1870. French author, known as Dumas *père* (the father). His play *Henri III et sa cour*/*Henry III and His Court* 1829 established French romantic historical drama, but today he is remembered for his romances, the reworked output of a 'fiction-factory' of collaborators. They include *Les trois mousquetaires*/*The Three Musketeers* 1844 and its sequels. Dumas *fils* was his illegitimate son.

Dumas Alexandre 1824–1895. French author, known as Dumas *fils* (the son), son of Dumas *père* and remembered for the play *La Dame aux camélias*/*The Lady of the Camellias* 1852, based on his own novel and source of Verdi's opera *La Traviata*.

Du Maurier /du:'mɒrieɪ/ Daphne 1907–1989. British novelist, whose romantic fiction includes *Jamaica Inn* 1936, *Rebecca* 1938, and *My Cousin Rachel* 1951. Her short story 'The Birds' was made into a film by Alfred Hitchcock in 1963. She was the granddaughter of George Du Maurier.

Du Maurier George (Louis Palmella Busson) 1834–1896. French-born British author of the novel *Trilby* 1894, the story of a natural singer able to perform only under the hypnosis of Svengali, her tutor.

dumb /dʌm/ adj. 1. unable to speak; silenced by surprise, shyness etc.; inarticulate; taciturn, reticent. 2. stupid, ignorant. 3. (of action) performed without speech. 4. giving no sound. —**dumb show,** gestures instead of speech. **dumb waiter,** a small movable set of shelves for serving food; a lift for food etc. —**dumbly** adv., **dumbness** n. [Old English]

dumbbell n. a short bar with a weight at each end used in pairs for exercising the muscles.

dumbfound /dʌm'faʊnd/ v.t. to nonplus, to make speechless with surprise.

dumdum bullet /'dʌmdʌm/ a soft-nosed bullet that expands on impact. [from *Dum-Dum* in India, where first produced]

Dumfries and Galloway /dʌm'fri:s, 'gæləweɪ/ region of Scotland; **area** 6,500 sq km/2,510 sq mi; **administrative headquarters** Dumfries; **physical** Solway Firth; Galloway Hills; Glen Trool National Park; Stranraer provides the shortest sea route to Ireland; **products** horses and cattle (for which the Galloway area was renowned), sheep, timber; **population** (1987) 147,000.

Dumfriesshire former county of S Scotland, merged in 1975 in the region of Dumfries and Galloway.

dummy n. 1. a model of the human form, especially as used to display clothes or by a ventriloquist; an imitation object, an object serving to replace a real or normal one. 2. a baby's rubber teat. 3. a stupid person; a person taking no real part, a figure-head. 4. a player or an imaginary player in some card games, whose cards are exposed and played by a partner. —adj. sham, imitation. —v.i. to use a feigned pass or swerve in football etc. —**dummy run,** a trial attempt, a rehearsal.

Dumont D'Urville /dju:'mɒn duə'vi:l/ Jean 1780–1842. French explorer in Australasia and the Pacific. In 1838–40 he sailed round Cape Horn on a voyage to study terrestial magnetism and reached Adélie Land in Antarctica.

dump v.t. 1. to deposit as rubbish; to put down firmly or clumsily; (colloquial) to abandon or get rid of. 2. to sell (excess goods) in a new market (especially abroad) at a lower price than in an original market. 3. in computing, the process of rapidly transferring data to external memory or a printer, usually done to help with debugging or as part of an error-recovery procedure. —n. 1. a place or heap for depositing rubbish; an accumulated pile of ore, earth,

Dumas French dramatist and novelist Alexandre Dumas.

etc.; a temporary store of ammunition etc. 2. (colloquial) an unpleasant or dreary place.

dumpling /'dʌmplɪŋ/ n. 1. a baked or boiled ball of dough, as part of a stew or containing apple etc. 2. a small, fat person. [perhaps from *dump* = small round object]

dumps n.pl. (colloquial) low spirits, depression, usually in *down in the dumps*. [probably from Middle Dutch *domp* = exhalation, mist]

dumpy adj. short and stout. —**dumpiness** n.

dun[1] adj. greyish-brown; (of a horse) having a golden sand-coloured body. —n. 1. dun colour. 2. a dun horse. [Old English]

dun[2] v.t. (-nn-) to ask persistently for payment of a debt. —n. a demand for payment. [abbreviation of obsolete *dunkirk* = privateer, from *Dunkirk* in France]

Dunaway /'dʌnəweɪ/ Faye 1941– . US actress whose first starring role was in *Bonnie and Clyde* 1967. Her subsequent films, including *Network* 1976 and *Mommie Dearest* 1981, received a varying critical reception. She also starred in Roman Polanski's celebrated *Chinatown* 1974, and *The Handmaid's Tale* 1990.

Dunbartonshire /dʌn'bɑ:tnʃə/ former county of Scotland, bordering the N bank of the Clyde estuary, on which stand Dunbarton (the former county town), Clydebank, and Helensburgh. It was merged in 1975 in the region of Strathclyde.

Duncan /'dʌŋkən/ Isadora 1878–1927. US dancer and teacher. An influential pioneer of modern dance, she adopted an expressive, free form, dancing barefoot and wearing a loose tunic, inspired by the ideal of Hellenic beauty. She toured extensively, often returning to Russia after her initial success there in 1905. She died in an accident when her long scarf caught in the wheel of the car in which she was travelling.

People do not live nowadays—they get about ten per cent out of life.

Isadora Duncan
This Quarter Autumn, 'Memoirs'

dunce n. one who is slow at learning, a dullard. [from *Duns Scotus* (died 1308), philosopher]

Dundee /dʌn'di:/ city and fishing port, administrative headquarters of Tayside, Scotland, on the N side of the Firth of Tay; population (1981) 175,000. Important shipping and rail centre with marine engineering, watch and clock, and textile industries.

Dundee cake /dʌn'di:/ a rich fruitcake usually decorated with split almonds. [from *Dundee* city in Scotland]

dunderhead /'dʌndəhed/ n. a stupid person.

dune /dju:n/ n. a mound or ridge of wind-drifted sand. Loose sand is blown and bounced along by the wind, up the windward side of a dune. The sand particles then fall to rest on the lee side, while more are blown up from the windward side. In this way a dune moves gradually downwind. [French, from Middle Dutch]

Dunedin /dʌn'i:dn/ port on Otago harbour, South Island, New Zealand; population (1986) 106,864. Also a road, rail and air centre, with engineering and textile industries. The city was founded in 1848 by members of the Free Church of Scotland and the university was established in 1869.

Dunfermline /dʌnˈfɜːmlɪn/ industrial town near the Firth of Forth in Fife region, Scotland; population (1981) 52,000. Site of the naval base of Rosyth; industries include engineering, shipbuilding, electronics, and textiles. Many Scottish kings, including Robert the Bruce, are buried in Dunfermline Abbey. Birthplace of the industrialist Andrew Carnegie.

dung *n.* the excrement of animals; manure. —*v.t.* to apply dung to, to manure (land). —**dung beetle** *n.* a beetle whose larvae develop in dung. [Old English]

dungaree /dʌŋɡəˈriː/ *n.* a strong, coarse cotton cloth; (in *plural*) overalls or trousers made of this. [from Hindi]

dungeon /ˈdʌndʒən/ *n.* an underground cell for prisoners. [from Old French from Latin *domnio* (*dominus* = lord)]

dunghill *n.* a heap of dung or refuse in a farmyard.

dunk *v.t.* to dip (bread etc.) into a soup or beverage before eating it; to immerse. [from German *tunken* = dip]

Dún Laoghaire /dʌnˈleərə/ (former name **Kingstown**) port and suburb of Dublin, Republic of Ireland. It is a terminal for ferries to Britain, and there are fishing industries.

dunlin /ˈdʌnlɪn/ *n.* the red-backed sandpiper *Calidris alpina*.

Dunlop /ˈdʌnlɒp/ John Boyd 1840–1921. Scottish inventor who founded the rubber company that bears his name. In 1887, to help his child win a tricycle race, he bound an inflated rubber hose to the wheels. The same year he developed commercially practical pneumatic tyres (first patented by R W Thomson in 1846) for bicycles and cars.

dunnock *n.* a European bird *Prunella modularis* similar in size and colouring to the sparrow, but with slate-grey head and breast, and more slender bill. It nests in bushes and hedges, and is often called 'hedge sparrow'.

dune

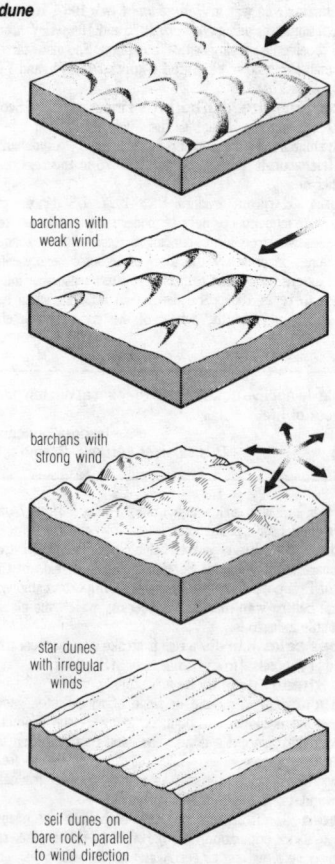

barchans with weak wind

barchans with strong wind

star dunes with irregular winds

seif dunes on bare rock, parallel to wind direction

Dunstable /ˈdʌnstəbəl/ John *c.* 1385–1453. English composer who wrote songs and anthems, and is generally considered one of the founders of Renaissance music.

duo /ˈdjuː:əʊ/ *n.* (*plural* **duos**) a pair of performers; a duet. [Latin = two]

duodecimal /djuːˈəʊdesɪml/ *adj.* of twelfths or twelve; proceeding or reckoning by twelves. This system was at one time considered superior to the decimal system in that 12 has more factors (2,3,4,6) than 10 (2, 5). [from Latin *duodecim* = twelve]

duodenum /djuːəʊˈdiːnəm/ *n.* in vertebrates, a short length of alimentary canal found between the stomach and the small intestine. Its role is in digesting carbohydrates, fats, and proteins. The smaller molecules formed are then absorbed, either by the duodenum or the ileum. —**duodenal** *adj.* [Latin from its length of 12 fingers' breadth]

duologue /ˈdjuː:əlɒɡ/ *n.* a dialogue between two persons. [from Latin or Greek *duo* = two]

dupe /djuː:p/ *n.* a victim of deception. —*v.t.* to deceive, to trick. [French, literally = hoopoe]

duple /ˈdjuː:pəl/ *adj.* of two parts. —**duple time,** in music, that with two beats to the bar. [from Latin *duo* = two]

duplex /ˈdjuː:pleks/ *adj.* having two parts; (of a set of rooms) on two floors. [Latin = double]

duplicate /ˈdjuː:plɪkət/ *adj.* exactly like another example; existing in two examples, having two corresponding parts; doubled, twice as large or as many; (of card games) with the same hand played by different players. —*n.* one of two things exactly alike, especially that made after the other; an exact copy of a letter or document. —/-keɪt/ *v.t.* to make or be an exact copy of; to double; to multiply by two; to repeat (an action etc.) especially unnecessarily. —**duplication** /-ˈkeɪʃən/ *n.* [from Latin]

duplicator *n.* a machine for producing documents in multiple copies.

duplicity /djuːˈplɪsɪtɪ/ *n.* double-dealing, deceitfulness. —**duplicitous** *adj.* [from Old French or Latin]

Du Pré /duːˈpreɪ/ Jacqueline 1945–1987. English cellist. Celebrated for her proficient technique and powerful interpretations of the Classical cello repertory, particularly of Edward ◊Elgar. She had an international concert career while still in her teens and made many recordings.

Dur. abbreviation of Durham (county).

durable /ˈdjuːrəbəl/ *adj.* likely to last; (of goods) remaining useful for a long period; resisting wear, decay etc. —**durability** /-ˈbɪlɪtɪ/ *n.* [from Old French from Latin *durare* = endure]

Duralumin trade name of a lightweight aluminium ◊alloy widely used in aircraft construction, containing copper, magnesium, and manganese.

Duras /djuːˈrɑː/ Marguerite 1914– . French writer whose works include short stories (*Des Journées entières dans les arbres*), plays (*La Musica*), film scripts (*Hiroshima mon amour* 1960), and novels such as *Le Vice-Consul* 1966, evoking an existentialist world from the actual setting of Calcutta.

duration /djuːˈreɪʃən/ *n.* the time during which a thing continues.

Durban /ˈdɜːbən/ principal port of Natal, South Africa, and second port of the republic; population (1985) 634,000, urban area 982,000. It exports coal, maize, and wool; imports heavy machinery and mining equipment; and is also a holiday resort.

Dürer /ˈdjuːrə/ Albrecht 1471–1528. German artist, the leading figure of the northern Renaissance. He was born in Nuremberg and travelled widely in Europe. Highly skilled in drawing and a keen student of nature, he perfected the technique of woodcut and engraving, producing woodcut series such as the *Apocalypse* 1498 and copperplate engravings such as *The Knight, Death, and the Devil* 1513, and *Melancholia* 1514; he may also have invented etching. His paintings include altarpieces and meticulously observed portraits (including many self-portraits).

duress /djuːˈres/ *n.* the use of force or threats, especially illegally; imprisonment. [from Old French from Latin *duritia* (*durus* = hard)]

Durga /ˈduːɡə/ a Hindu goddess; one of the many names for ◊Mahadevi.

Durham /'dʌrəm/ county in NE England; **area** 2,440 sq km/942 sq mi; **administrative headquarters** Durham; **products** sheep and dairy produce; site of one of Britain's richest coalfields; **population** (1987) 599,000.

Durham John George Lambton, 1st Earl of Durham 1792–1840. British politician. Appointed Lord Privy Seal in 1830, he drew up the first Reform Bill of 1832, and as governor general of Canada briefly in 1837 drafted the Durham Report which led to the union of Upper and Lower Canada.

during /'djuərɪŋ/ prep. throughout or at a point in the duration of. [from obsolete dure = continue from Old French]

Durkheim /'dɜ:khaɪm/ Emile 1858–1917. French sociologist, one of the founders of modern sociology, who also influenced social anthropology.

Durrell /'dʌrəl/ Gerald (Malcolm) 1925– . British naturalist. Director of Jersey Zoological Park, he is the author of travel and natural history books, and the humorous memoir *My Family and Other Animals* 1956. He is the brother of Lawrence Durrell.

Durrell Lawrence (George) 1912–1990. British novelist and poet. Born in India, he joined the foreign service and lived mainly in the E Mediterranean, the setting of his novels, including the Alexandria Quartet: *Justine, Balthazar, Mountolive*, and *Clea* 1957–60; he also wrote travel books. He is the brother of Gerald Durrell.

Shyness has laws: you can only give yourself, tragically, to those who least understand.
Lawrence Durrell
Justine

Dürrenmatt /'djuərənmæt/ Friedrich 1921– . Swiss dramatist, author of grotesquely farcical tragicomedies, for example *The Visit* 1956 and *The Physicists* 1962.

Durrës /'durəs/ chief port of Albania; population (1983) 72,000. It is a commercial and communications centre, with flour mills, soap and cigarette factories, distilleries, and an electronics plant. It was the capital of Albania from 1912–21.

Dushanbe /du:ʃæn'beɪ/ formerly (1929–69) **Stalinabad** capital of Tadzhik Republic, USSR, 160 km/100 mi N of the Afghan frontier; population (1987) 582,000. It is a road, rail, and air centre. Industries include cotton mills, tanneries, meat-packing factories, and printing works. It is the seat of Tadzhik state university.

dusk n. the darker stage of twilight. [from Old English dox = dark, swarthy]

dusky adj. shadowy, dim; dark-coloured. —**duskily** adv., **duskiness** n.

Düsseldorf /'dusəldɔ:f/ industrial city of Germany, on the right bank of the river Rhine, 26 km/16 mi NW of Cologne, capital of North Rhine–Westphalia; population (1988) 561,000. It is a river port and the commercial and financial centre of the Ruhr area, with food processing, brewing, agricultural machinery, textile, and chemical industries.

dust n. 1. finely powdered earth or other matter. 2. pollen; a fine powder of any material. 3. a dead person's remains. 4. confusion, turmoil. —v.t. 1. to clear of dust by wiping; to clear furniture etc. of dust. 2. to sprinkle (powder or dust) over, to sprinkle (an object) thus. —**bite the dust,** to be killed. **dustcart** n. a vehicle for collecting household refuse. **dust cover,** a sheet or cloth to keep the dust off furniture etc.; a dust jacket. **dust jacket,** a paper wrapper on a book. **dustsheet** n. a dust cover for furniture. **dust-up** n. (colloquial) a fight, a disturbance. **throw dust in (a person's) eyes,** to mislead him or her. [Old English]

dustbin n. a container for household refuse.

dust bowl an arid or unproductive dry region. —**the Dust Bowl,** an area in the Great Plains region of North America (Texas to Kansas) that suffered extensive wind erosion as the result of drought and poor farming practice in once fertile soil. Much of the topsoil was blown away in the droughts of the 1930s.

duster n. a cloth for dusting furniture etc.

dustman n. (plural **dustmen**) a man employed to empty dustbins.

dustpan n. a pan into which dust is brushed from a floor.

dusty adj. 1. covered with or full of dust. 2. like dust. 3. (of a colour) dull or vague. —**dusty answer,** a curt rejection of a request. **not so dusty,** (colloquial) fairly good. —**dustily** adv., **dustiness** n. [Old English]

dutch n. (slang) a costermonger's wife. [abbreviation of duchess]

Dutch adj. of the Netherlands or its people or language. —n. the Dutch language. —**the Dutch,** the people of the Netherlands. **Dutch auction,** one in which the price is reduced until a buyer is found. **Dutch barn,** a farm shelter for hay etc., consisting of a roof on poles. **Dutch cap,** a contraceptive diaphragm. **Dutch courage,** courage induced by alcoholic drink. **Dutch oven,** a metal box for cooking, of which the open side is turned towards an ordinary fire; a covered cooking-pot. **Dutch treat,** a party, outing etc., at which each participant pays for his or her own share. **go Dutch,** to share the expenses on an outing etc. **in Dutch,** (slang) in disgrace. **talk like a Dutch uncle,** to speak severely but kindly. [from Middle Dutch dutsch Old High German diutisc = national]

Dutch East India Company see ◊East India Company, Dutch.

Dutch East Indies former Dutch colony which in 1945 became independent as ◊Indonesia.

Dutch elm disease a disease of elm trees *Ulmus*, principally Dutch, English, and American elm, caused by the fungus *Certocystis ulmi*. The fungus is usually spread from tree to tree by the elm-bark beetle, which lays its eggs beneath the bark. The disease has no cure and control methods involve injecting insecticide into the trees annually to prevent infection, or the destruction of all elms in a broad band around an infected area, to keep the beetles out. In the 1970s, a new epidemic was caused by a much more virulent form of the fungus, probably brought to Britain from Canada.

Dutch Guiana /gi:'ɑnə/ former Dutch colony which in 1975 became independent as ◊Suriname.

Dutch language a member of the Germanic branch of the Indo-European language family, often referred to by scholars as Netherlandic and taken to include the standard language and dialects of the Netherlands (excluding Frisian) as well as Flemish (in Belgium and N France) and, more remotely, its offshoot Afrikaans in South Africa.

Dutchman n. (plural **Dutchmen**) a man of Dutch birth or nationality. —**I'm a Dutchman,** a phrase implying refusal or disbelief.

duteous /'dju:tɪəs/ adj. (literary) dutiful.

dutiable /'dju:tɪəbəl/ adj. requiring payment of duty.

dutiful /'dju:tɪfəl/ adj. doing or observant of one's duty, obedient. —**dutifully** adv.

duty /'dju:tɪ/ n. 1. a moral or legal obligation, what one is bound or ought to do; the binding force of what is right; a business, office, or function arising from these, an engagement in these. 2. deference, an expression of respect to a superior. 3. a tax levied on certain goods, imports, events, or services. —**do duty for,** to serve as or pass for (something else). **duty-bound** adj. obliged by duty. **duty-free shop,** a shop at an airport etc. at which goods can be bought free of duty. **on, off, duty,** actually engaged, not engaged, in one's regular work or some obligation. [from Anglo-French]

Duvalier /dju:'væliei/ François 1907–1971. Right-wing president of Haiti 1957–71. Known as **Papa Doc,** he ruled as a dictator, organizing the Tontons Macoutes ('bogeymen') as a private security force to intimidate and assassinate opponents of his regime. He rigged the 1961 elections in order to have his term of office extended until 1967, and in 1964 declared himself president for life. He was excommunicated by the Vatican for harassing the church, and was succeeded on his death by his son Jean-Claude Duvalier.

Duvalier Jean-Claude 1951– . Right-wing president of Haiti 1971–86. Known as **Baby Doc,** he succeeded his father François Duvalier, becoming, at the age of 19, the youngest president in the world. He continued to receive support from the USA but was pressured into moderating some elements of his father's regime, yet still tolerated no opposition. In 1986, with Haiti's economy stagnating and with increasing civil disorder, Duvalier fled to France, taking much of the Haitian treasury with him.

duvet /'du:veɪ/ n. a thick, soft quilt used instead of bedclothes. [French]

Duwez /'du:vəz/ Pol 1907– . US scientist, born in Belgium, who in 1959 developed metallic glasses (alloys rapidly cooled from the melt, which combine properties of glass and metal) with his team at the California Institute of Technology.

Dvořák /'dvɔ:ʒɑ:k/ Antonin (Leopold) 1841–1904. Czech composer. International recognition came with his series of *Slavonic Dances* 1877–86, and he was director of the National Conservatory, New York, 1892–95. Works such as his *New World Symphony* 1893 reflect his interest in American folk themes, including black and Native American. He wrote nine symphonies; tone poems; operas; including *Rusalka* 1901; large-scale choral works; the *Carnival* and other overtures; violin and cello concertos; chamber music; piano pieces; and songs. His Romantic music extends the classical tradition of Beethoven and Brahms and displays the influence of Czech folk music.

dwarf /dwɔ:f/ *n.* (*plural* **dwarfs**) 1. a person, animal, or plant much below normal size. 2. a small mythological being with magical powers. — *adj.* of a kind very small in size. —*v.t.* 1. to stunt in growth. 2. to make seem small by contrast or distance. [Old English]

dwarf star a main-sequence star as plotted on the ◊Hertzsprung–Russell diagram. Most of the stars, including the Sun, are within the main sequence, which runs diagonally from the top left of the diagram to the lower right. The most massive (and hence brightest) stars are at the top left, and the least massive (coolest) stars at the bottom right. A cool dwarf star is a ◊red dwarf and a hot one is a ◊white dwarf.

dwell *v.i.* (*past* and *past participle* **dwelt**) to live as an occupant or inhabitant. —**dwell on** *or* **upon**, to think or speak or write at length on. —**dweller** *n.* (Old English = lead astray]

dwelling *n.* a house, a residence.

dwindle *v.i.* to become gradually less or smaller; to lose importance. [from *dwine* = fade away from Old English]

Dy symbol for dysprosium.

Dyak /'daɪæk/ *n.* or Dayak 1. a member of any of several indigenous non-Muslim peoples inhabiting parts of Indonesia, including the Bahau of central and E Borneo, the Land Dyak of SW Borneo, and the Iban of Sarawak. 2. their language = ◊Iban, belonging to the Austronesian family. Some anthropologists now apply the term Iban to all Dyak peoples. [from Malay *dayak* = up-country]

dybbuk /'dɪbək/ *n.* (*plural* **dybukim**, **dybuks**) in Jewish folklore, the malevolent spirit of a dead person that enters and controls the body of a living person until exorcized. [from Hebrew *dābak* = cling]

Dyck /'daɪk/ Anthony van 1599–1641. Flemish painter. Born in Antwerp, van Dyck was an assistant to Rubens from 1618–20, then briefly worked in England at the court of James I, and moved to Italy in 1622. In 1626 he returned to Antwerp, where he continued to paint religious works and portraits. From 1632 he lived in England and produced numerous portraits of royalty and aristocrats, such as *Charles I on Horseback c.*1638 (National Gallery, London).

dye /daɪ/ *n.* a substance used to change the colour of hair, fabric, wood etc.; a colour produced by this. —*v.t.* (*participle* **dyeing**) to impregnate with dye; to make (a thing) a specified colour thus. —**dyed in the wool,** out-and-out, unchangeable. —**dyer** *n.* [Old English]

Dyfed /'dʌved/ county in SW Wales; **area** 5,770 sq km/ 2,227 sq mi; **administrative headquarters** Carmarthen; **physical** Pembrokeshire Coast National Park, part of the Brecon Beacons National Park, including the Black Mountain, and part of the Cambrian Mountains, including Plynlimon Fawr 752 m/2,468 ft; Anthracite mines produce about 50,000 tonnes a year; **population** (1987) 343,000.

dying participle of ◊die[1].

dyke variant of **dike**.

Dylan /'dɪlən/ Bob. Adopted name of Robert Allen Zimmerman 1941– . US singer and songwriter, whose work in the 1960s, with its emphasis on socially conscious lyrics, first in the folk music tradition and, beginning in 1965, in an individualistic rock style, had great influence on the development of Western popular music.

dynamic /daɪ'næmɪk/ *adj.* 1. of motive force (as opposed to *static*). 2. of force in actual operation (as opposed to *potential*). 3. of dynamics. 4. (of a person) active, energetic. —**dynamically** *adv.* [from French from Greek *dunamis* = force, power]

dynamics *n.* (usually treated as *singular*) 1. the mathematical study of motion and the forces causing it; the branch of any science in which forces or changes are considered. 2. motive forces, physical or moral, in any sphere. 3. in music, gradations or amount of volume of sound.

dynamism /'daɪnəmɪzəm/ *n.* energizing or dynamic action or power. [from Greek *dunamis* = power]

dynamite /'daɪnəmaɪt/ *n.* 1. a high explosive consisting of a mixture of nitroglycerine and diatomaceous earth (diatomite, an absorbent, chalklike material) first devised by Alfred Nobel. 2. a potentially dangerous person or thing. —*v.t.* to charge or blow up with dynamite.

dynamo /'daɪnəməʊ/ *n.* (*plural* **dynamos**) a simple generator or machine for transforming mechanical energy into electrical energy. A dynamo in basic form consists of a powerful field magnet, between the poles of which a suitable conductor, usually in the form of a coil (armature), is rotated. The mechanical energy of rotation is thus converted into an electric current in the armature. [abbreviation of *dynamo-electric machine*]

dynamometer /daɪnə'mɒmɪtə/ *n.* an instrument measuring the energy expended. [from French from Greek *dunamis* = force]

dynast /'dɪnæst/ *n.* a ruler; a member of a dynasty. [from Latin from Greek *dunamai* = be able]

dynasty /'dɪnəsti/ *n.* a line of hereditary rulers; a succession of leaders in any field. —**dynastic** /-'næstɪk/ *adj.* [from French or Latin from Greek]

dyne /daɪn/ *n.* c.g.s. unit (symbol dyn) of force. 10^5 dynes make one newton. The dyne is defined as the force that will accelerate a mass of 1 gram by 1 centimetre per second per second. [French, from Greek *dunamis* = force]

dys- prefix meaning bad, difficult. [from Greek *dus* -]

dyscalculus *n.* a disability demonstrated by a poor aptitude with figures.

dysentery /'dɪsəntri/ *n.* a disease with inflammation of the intestines, causing severe diarrhoea. [from Old French or Latin from Greek *entera* = bowels]

dyslexia /dɪs'leksiə/ *n.* abnormal difficulty in reading and spelling, caused by a condition of the brain. —**dyslexic** *adj.* & *n.* [from German from Greek *lexis* = speech]

dyspepsia /dɪs'pepsiə/ *n.* indigestion. —**dyspeptic** *adj.* & *n.* [Latin from Greek *peptos* = cooked, digested]

dysphagia *n.* difficulty in swallowing due to infection, obstruction, or spasm in the throat or oesophagus (gullet).

dysprosium /dɪs'prəʊziəm/ *n.* a silver-white, metallic element of the ◊lanthanide series, symbol Dy, atomic number 66, relative atomic mass 162.50. It is among the most magnetic of all known substances and has a great

Dvořák *Czech composer Antonin Dvořák.*

capacity to absorb neutrons. [from Greek *dusprositos* = hard to get]

dystopia *n.* an imaginary society whose evil qualities are meant to serve as a moral or political warning. The term was coined in the 19th century by John Stuart ◊Mill, and is the opposite of ◊Utopia. George Orwell's *1984* 1949 and Aldous Huxley's *Brave New World* 1932 are influential examples. Dystopias are common in science fiction.

dystrophy /'dɪstrəfɪ/ *n.* defective nutrition. —**muscular dystrophy**, hereditary progressive weakening and wasting of the muscles. [Latin from Greek *trophia* = nourishment]

e, E n. **1.** (*plural* **es, e's**) the fifth letter of the alphabet. **2.** in music, the third note in the scale of C major.

e symbol indicating conformity with EC standards for the indicated weights or volume of certain prepackaged products.

E abbreviation of east, eastern.

E- prefix (preceding a number) indicating conformity with an EC standard of quantities and capacities permitted for certain prepackaged products.

each *adj.* every one of (two or more persons or things) regarded separately. —*pron.* each person or thing. —**each other**, one another. **each way**, (of a bet) backing a horse etc. to win and to be placed. [Old English = ever alike]

eager /'iːgə/ *adj.* full of keen desire, enthusiastic. —**eager beaver**, (*colloquial*) a very or excessively diligent person. —**eagerly** *adv.*, **eagerness** n. [from Anglo-French from Latin *acer* = sharp]

eagle n. **1.** a large bird of prey of several genera of the family Accipitridae, with keen vision and powerful flight. The white-headed **bald eagle** *Haliaetus leucocephalus*, the symbol of the USA, rendered infertile through the ingestion of agricultural chemicals, is now very rare, except in Alaska. Another endangered species is the **Philippine eagle**, sometimes called the Philippine monkey-eating eagle. Loss of large tracts of forest, coupled with hunting by humans, have greatly reduced its numbers. The **golden eagle** *Aquila chrysaetos* of Eurasia and North America has a 2 m/6 ft wingspan and is dark brown. The **larger spotted eagle** *A. clanga* lives in Central Europe and Asia. The sea eagles *Haliaetus* include the **white-tailed sea eagle** *H. albicilla* which was renaturalized in Britain in the 1980s,

eagle

bald eagle

having died out in this country in 1916. **2.** the figure of an eagle, especially as (*historical*) a Roman or French ensign, or the symbol of the USA. **3.** in golf, a hole played in two under par or bogey. —**eagle eye**, keen sight or watchfulness. —**eagle-eyed** *adj.* [from Anglo-French from Latin *aquila*]

eaglet /'iːglɪt/ n. a young eagle.

Eagling /'iːglɪŋ/ Wayne 1950– . Canadian dancer. He joined the Royal Ballet in London, appearing in *Gloria* 1980, and other productions.

Eakins /'iːkɪnz/ Thomas 1844–1916. US painter. He studied in Europe and developed a realistic style with strong contrasts between light and shade, as in *The Gross Clinic* 1875 (Jefferson Medical College, Philadelphia), a group portrait of a surgeon, his assistants, and students. In his later years he painted distinguished, powerful portraits.

Ealing Studios /'iːlɪŋ/ film studios in W London headed by Michael Balcon. They produced a number of George Formby and Will Hay films in the 1940s, then a series of more genteel and occasionally satirical comedies, often written by T E B Clarke and starring Alec Guinness.

Eanes /eɪˈɑːneʃ/ Antonio dos Santos Ramalho 1935– . Portuguese politician. He helped plan the 1974 coup that ended the Caetano regime, and as army chief of staff put down a left-wing revolt in Nov 1975. He was president 1976–86.

ear[1] n. **1.** the organ of hearing in humans and animals. It responds to the vibrations that constitute sound, and these are translated into nerve signals and passed to the brain. A mammal's ear consists of three parts: outer ear, middle ear, and inner ear. The **outer ear** is a funnel that collects sound, directing it down a tube to the **ear drum** (tympanic membrane), which separates the outer and **middle ear**. Sounds vibrate this membrane, the mechanical movement of which is transferred to a smaller membrane leading to the **inner ear** by three small bones, the auditory ossicles. Vibrations of the inner ear membrane move fluid contained in the snail-shaped cochlea, which vibrates hair cells that stimulate the auditory nerve, connected to the brain. Three fluid-filled canals of the inner ear detect changes of position; this mechanism, with other sensory inputs, is responsible for the sense of balance. **2.** the faculty of discriminating sound. **3.** an ear-shaped thing. —**all ears**, listening attentively. **ear-piercing** *adj.* shrill. **earplug** n. a piece of wax etc. placed in the ear to protect against water, noise etc. **earring** n. an ornament worn on the lobe of the ear. **ear-splitting** *adj.* extremely loud. **ear trumpet**, a trumpet-shaped tube formerly used as an aid to hearing by the partially deaf. **give one's ears**, to make any sacrifice *for* a thing, *to* do, *if*. **have** *or* **keep an ear to the ground**, to be alert to rumours or the trend of opinion. **have a person's ear**, to have a person's favourable attention. **up to the ears**, (*colloquial*) deeply involved or occupied (*in*). [Old English]

ear[2] n. the seed-bearing head of a cereal plant. [Old English]

earache n. pain in the inner ear.

earful n. (*colloquial*) **1.** copious talk. **2.** a reprimand.

Earhart /'eəhɑːt/ Amelia 1898–1937. American aviator, born in Kansas. In 1932 she was the first woman to fly the Atlantic alone, and in 1937 disappeared without trace while

earthquake

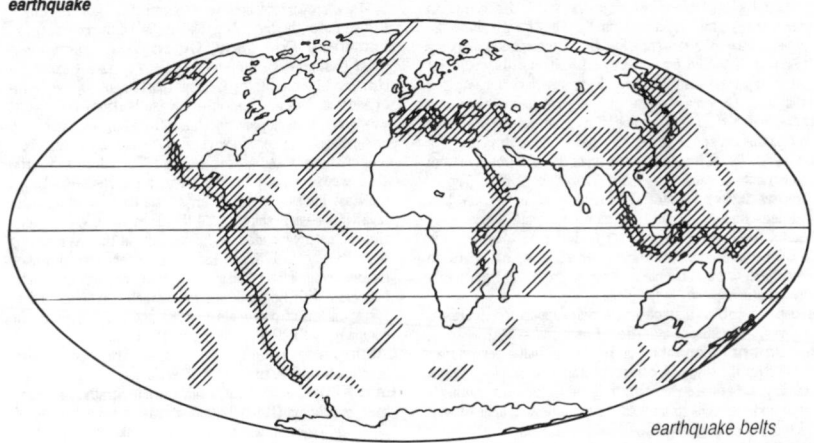

earthquake belts

making a Pacific flight. Clues found on Nikumuroro island in Kiribati in 1989 suggest that she and her navigator might have survived a crash only to die of thirst.

earl /ɜːl/ *n.* in the British peerage, the third title of a nobleman in order of rank, coming between marquess and viscount; it is the oldest of British titles, being of Scandinavian origin. The premier earldom is Arundel, now united with the dukedom of Norfolk. An earl's wife is a countess. —**Earl Marshal,** in the UK, the head of the ◊College of Arms, with ceremonial duties on royal occasions. [Old English]

earldom /ˈɜːldəm/ *n.* the position or domain of an earl.

early /ˈɜːlɪ/ *adj. & adv.* before the due, usual, or expected time; not far on in day, night, or time; not far on in a period, development, or process of evolution; forward in flowering, ripening etc. —**early bird,** (*colloquial*) one who arrives or gets up early. **early days,** early in time for something (to happen etc.). **early on,** at an early stage. [from Old English *aerlich*]

Early English[1] in architecture, the name given by Thomas Rickman (1776–1841) to the first of the three periods of the English Gothic style. It covers the period from about 1189 to about 1280, and is characterized by tall, elongated windows (lancets) without mullions (horizontal bars), often grouped in threes, fives, or sevens; the pointed arch; pillars of stone centres surrounded by shafts of black Purbeck marble; and dog-tooth (zig-zag) ornament. Salisbury Cathedral is almost entirely Early English.

Early English[1] the general name for the range of dialects spoken by Germanic settlers in England between the 5th and 11th centuries AD. The literature of the period includes *Beowulf*, an epic in West Saxon dialect, shorter poems of melancholic dignity such as *The Wanderer* and *The Seafarer*, and prose chronicles, Bible translations, spells, and charms.

earmark *n.* an identifying mark; an owner's mark on the ear of an animal. —*v.t.* 1. to set aside for a special purpose. 2. to mark (an animal) with an earmark.

earn /ɜːn/ *v.t.* 1. to bring in as income or interest. 2. (of a person, conduct etc.) to obtain or be entitled to as a reward of work or merit. [Old English]

earnest[1] /ˈɜːnɪst/ *adj.* ardently serious, showing intense feeling. —**in earnest,** serious, seriously, with determination. —**earnestly** *adv.,* **earnestness** *n.* [Old English]

earnest[2] *n.* money paid as an instalment, especially to confirm a contract; a token, a foretaste. [probably variant of *erles* from Latin *arrhula*, diminutive of *arr(h)a* = pledge]

earnings *n.pl.* money earned.

earphone *n.* a device worn over or put to the ear to receive radio, telephone etc. communication.

earshot *n.* hearing distance.

earth /ɜːθ/ *n.* 1. land and sea, as distinct from sky; dry land, the ground. 2. soil. 3. an electrical connection between an appliance and the ground. In the event of a fault in an electrical appliance, for example, involving connection between the live part of the circuit and the outer casing, the current flows to earth, causing no harm to the user. 4. the hole of a badger, fox etc. 5. (*colloquial*) a huge sum, a vast amount. —*v.t.* 1. to connect (an electrical circuit) to earth. 2. to cover (the roots of a plant) with earth. —**come back to earth,** to return to realities. **earthnut** *n.* any of various plants or their tubers, especially the peanut. **earth-shaking** *adj.* having a violent effect. **gone to earth,** in hiding. **on earth,** existing anywhere. **run to earth,** to find after a long search. [Old English]

Earth /ɜːθ/ *n.* the third planet from the Sun and the planet on which we live. It is almost spherical, flattened slightly at the poles, and is composed of three concentric layers: the ◊core, the ◊mantle, and the ◊crust; 70% of the surface (including the north and south polar icecaps) is covered with water. The Earth is surrounded by a life-supporting atmosphere and is the only planet on which life is known to exist.

earthbound *adj.* 1. attached (*literally* or *figuratively*) to the Earth or earthly things. 2. moving towards the Earth.

earthen *adj.* made of earth or baked clay.

earthenware *n.* pottery made of porous clay and fired. The term describes unglazed (flowerpots, winecoolers) and glazed (most tableware) pottery.

earthly *adj.* of the Earth or people's lives on it, terrestrial. —**no earthly,** (*colloquial*) absolutely no. **not an earthly,** (*slang*) no chance whatever. —**earthliness** *n.*

earthquake *n.* a shaking or convulsion of the Earth's surface, the scientific study of which is called seismology. Earthquakes result from a build-up of stresses within rocks until they are strained to fracturing point. Most occur along faults (fractures or breaks) in the Earth's crust. ◊Plate tectonic movements generate most earthquakes; as two plates move past each other, they can become jammed and deformed, and earthquakes occur when they spring free. Most earthquakes happen under the sea. Their force is measured on the ◊Richter scale.

earth sciences the scientific study of the planet Earth as a whole, a synthesis of several traditional subjects such as ◊geology, ◊meteorology, oceanography, ◊geophysics, ◊geochemistry, and ◊paleontology.

earthwork *n.* an artificial bank of earth in a fortification or in road building.

earthworm *n.* an ◊annelid worm of various genera of the class Oligochaeta. Earthworms are hermaphroditic. They deposit their eggs in cocoons. They live by burrowing in the soil, feeding on the organic matter it contains. They are vital to the formation of humus, aerating the soil and levelling it by transferring earth from the deeper levels to the surface as castings. The common British earthworms belong to the genera *Lumbricus* and *Allolobophora*. These are comparatively small, but some tropical forms reach over 1 m/3 ft. *Megascolides australis*, of Queensland, can be over 3 m/11 ft long.

earthy *adj.* 1. of or like earth or soil. 2. gross, coarse. 3. worldly. —**earthiness** *n.*

earwig *n.* a small insect of the order Dermaptera. The fore-wings ·are short and leathery and serve to protect the hind-wings, which are large and are folded like a fan when at rest; the insects seldom fly. They have a pincerlike appendage at the tail end. Earwigs are regarded as pests because they feed on flowers and fruit, but they also eat other insects, dead or alive. Eggs are laid beneath the soil, and the female cares for the young even after they have hatched. The common European earwig *Forficula auricularia* is one of several species found in Britain.

ease /iːz/ *n.* 1. freedom from pain or trouble; freedom from constraint. 2. facility. —*v.t./i.* 1. to relieve from pain or anxiety. 2. to relax, to slacken, to make or become less burdensome. 3. to cause to move by gentle force. —**at ease**, free from anxiety or constraint; (of soldiers etc.) in a relaxed attitude, with the feet apart. **ease off** *or* **up**, to become less burdensome or severe. [from Old French *aise* from Latin *adjacens* = lying near]

easel /ˈiːzəl/ *n.* a standing wooden support for an artist's canvas, a blackboard etc. [from Dutch *ezel* = ass]

easement /ˈiːzmənt/ *n.* in law, rights that a person may have over the land of another. A common example is a right of way; others are the right to bring water over another's land and the right to an uninterrupted flow of light to windows. [from Old French]

easily /ˈiːzɪlɪ/ *adv.* 1. in an easy manner, without difficulty. 2. by far. 3. very probably.

east /iːst/ *n.* 1. the point of the horizon where the Sun rises at the ♢equinoxes; the compass point corresponding to this; the direction in which this lies. 2. (usually **East**) the part of a country or town lying to the east; the regions or countries lying to the east of Europe. —*adj.* 1. towards, at, or facing the east. 2. (of wind) blowing from the east. —*adv.* towards, at, or near the east. —**East End**, the eastern part of London, including the docks. **east-northeast, east-southeast** *adjs.* & *advs.* midway between east and northeast, or southeast; (*ns.*) the compass point in this position. **East Side,** the eastern part of Manhattan. [Old English]

East Anglia /iːst ˈæŋglɪə/ region of E England, formerly a Saxon kingdom, including Norfolk, Suffolk, and parts of Essex and Cambridgeshire. Norwich is the principal city of East Anglia. The University of East Anglia was founded in Norwich in 1962, and includes the Sainsbury Centre for the Visual Arts, opened in 1978, which has a collection of ethnographic art and sculpture. East Anglian ports such as Harwich and Felixstowe have greatly developed as trade with the rest of Europe has increased.

Easter /ˈiːstə/ *n.* the Christian feast of the Resurrection of Christ, the greatest and oldest feast of the Christian church, celebrated on the first Sunday after the first full moon after the vernal equinox (21 March). —**Easter egg,** an edible artificial (usually chocolate) egg given as a gift at Easter. [Old English from *Eostre,* Anglo-Saxon goddess of spring who was honoured in April]

Easter Island or **Rapa Nui** Chilean island in the S Pacific Ocean, part of the Polynesian group, about 3,500 km/2,200 mi W of Chile; area about 166 sq km/64 sq mi; population (1985) 2,000. It was first reached by Europeans on Easter Sunday in 1722. On it stand huge carved statues and stone houses, the work of neolithic peoples of unknown origin. The chief centre is Hanga-Roa.

easterly /ˈiːstəlɪ/ *adj.* & *adv.* in an eastern position or direction; (of wind) blowing from the east (approximately).

eastern /ˈiːstən/ *adj.* of or in the east. —**Eastern Church,** the Orthodox Church. —**easternmost** *adj.*

easterner *n.* a native or inhabitant of the east.

Easter Rising or **Easter Rebellion** in Irish history, a republican insurrection that began on Easter Monday, April 1916, in Dublin. It was inspired by the Irish Republican Brotherhood (IRB) in an unsuccessful attempt to overthrow British rule in Ireland. It was led by Patrick Pearce of the IRB and James Conolly of Sinn Féin.

East Germany /ˈiːst ˈdʒɜːmənɪ/ see ♢Germany, East; ♢Germany, Federal Republic of.

East India Company, British a commercial company 1600–1858 chartered by Queen Elizabeth I and given a monopoly of trade between England and the Far East. In the 18th century it became, in effect, the ruler of a large part of India, and a form of dual control by the company and a committee responsible to Parliament in London was introduced by Pitt's India Act 1784. The end of the monopoly of China trade came 1834, and after the ♢Sepoy Rebellion

1857 the crown took complete control of the government of British India; the India Act 1858 abolished the company.

East India Company, Dutch (Dutch *Vereenigde Oost-Indische Compagnie (VOC)*) a trading company chartered by the States General (parliament) of the Netherlands, and established in the N Netherlands in 1602. It was given a monopoly on Dutch trade in the Indonesian archipelago, and certain sovereign rights such as the creation of an army and a fleet. In the 17th century some 100 ships were regularly trading between the Netherlands and the East Indies. The company's main base was Batavia in Java (Indonesia); ships sailed there via the Cape of Good Hope, a colony founded by the company in 1652 as a staging post. During the 17th and 18th centuries the company used its monopoly of East Indian trade to pay out high dividends, but wars with England and widespread corruption led to a suspension of payments in 1781 and a takeover of the company by the Dutch government in 1798.

easting *n.* (*nautical* etc.) 1. a distance travelled or measured eastward. 2. an easterly direction.

East Kilbride /ˈiːst kɪlˈbraɪd/ town in Strathclyde, Scotland; population (1985) 72,000. It was an old village developed as a new town from 1947 to take overspill from Glasgow, 11 km/6 mi to the NE. It is the site of the National Engineering Laboratory. There are various light industries and some engineering, including jet engines.

East London /ˈiːst ˈlʌndən/ port and resort on the SE coast of Cape Province, South Africa; population (1980) 160,582. Founded in 1846 as **Port Rex,** its name was changed to East London in 1848. It has a good harbour, is the terminus of a railway from the interior, and is a leading wool-exporting port.

East Lothian /ˈiːst ˈləʊðɪən/ former county of SE Scotland, merged with West Lothian and Midlothian in 1975 in the new region of ♢Lothian. Haddington was the county town.

Eastman /ˈiːstmən/ George 1854–1932. US entrepreneur and inventor who founded the Eastman Kodak photographic company in 1892. From 1888 he marketed his patented daylight-loading flexible roll films (to replace the glass plates used previously) and portable cameras. By 1900 his company was selling a pocket camera for as little as one dollar.

East River tidal strait 26 km/16 mi long, between Manhattan and the Bronx, and Long Island, in New York, USA. It links Long Island Sound with New York Bay and is also connected, via the Harlem River, with the Hudson. There are docks; most famous of its many bridges is the Brooklyn.

East Siberian Sea /ˈiːst saɪˈbɪərɪən/ part of the ♢Arctic Ocean, off the N coast of USSR, between the New Siberian Islands and Chukchi Sea. The world's widest continental shelf, with an average width of nearly 650 km/404 mi, lies in the East Siberian Sea.

East Sussex /ˈiːst ˈsʌsɪks/ county in SE England; **area** 1,800 sq km/695 sq mi; **administrative headquarters** Lewes; **physical** Beachy Head, highest headland on the S coast at 180 m/590 ft, the E end of the South ♢Downs; the Weald (including Ashdown Forest); Friston Forest; rivers: Ouse, Cuckmere, East Rother; Romney Marsh; **products** electronics, gypsum, timber; **population** (1987) 698,000.

East Timor /ˈiːst ˈtiːmɔː/ disputed territory on the island of ♢Timor in the Malay Archipelago; it was a Portuguese colony for almost 460 years, up to 1975; **area** 14,874 sq km/5,706 sq mi; **capital** Dili; **products** coffee; **population** (1980) 555,000; **recent history** following Portugal's withdrawal in 1975, the left-wing Revolutionary Front of Independent East Timor (Fretilin) occupied the capital, Dili, calling for independence. In opposition, troops from neighbouring Indonesia invaded the territory, declaring East Timor (**Loro Sae**) the 17th province of Indonesia in July 1976. This claim is not recognized by the United Nations.

eastward /ˈiːstwəd/ *adj.* & *adv.* or **eastwards** /-z/ towards the east. —*n.* an eastward direction or region.

Eastwood /ˈiːstwʊd/ Clint 1930– . US film actor and director. As the 'man with no name' in *A Fistful of Dollars* 1964, he started the vogue for 'spaghetti Westerns'. Later Westerns include *The Good, the Bad, and the Ugly* 1966 and *High Plains Drifter* 1973. He also starred in the 'Dirty Harry' police series, and directed *Bird* 1988.

easy /ˈiːzɪ/ *adj.* 1. not difficult, achieved without great effort. 2. free from pain, trouble, or anxiety. 3. free

from awkwardness, strictness etc., relaxed and pleasant.
4. compliant, obliging. —*adv.* with ease, in an effortless
or relaxed manner; (as *interjection*) go carefully. —**easy
chair**, a large comfortable chair. **easy on the eye**,
pleasant to look at. **Easy Street**, (*colloquial*) a state of
affluence. **go easy**, to be sparing or cautious (*with* or
on). **I'm easy**, (*colloquial*) I have no preference. **take it
easy**, to proceed gently, to relax. —**easiness** *n.* [from
Anglo-French]

easygoing *adj.* placid and tolerant, relaxed in manner.

eat *v.t./i.* (*past* **ate** /et, eɪt/, *past participle* **eaten**) 1.
to take into the mouth, to chew and swallow (food);
to consume food, to take a meal. 2. (often with *away*)
to destroy, to consume; (also with *at*) to trouble, to
vex. —**eat one's heart out**, to suffer greatly from
anxiety or longing. **eating apple** etc., one suitable for
eating raw. **eats** *n.pl.* (*colloquial*) food, a meal. **eat
up**, to eat or consume completely; to traverse (distance) rapidly. **eat one's words**, to retract them abjectly.
[Old English]

eatable *adj.* that may be eaten. —*n.* (usually in *plural*)
food.

eater *n.* 1. one who eats. 2. an eating apple etc.

eau de Cologne /əʊdəkə'ləʊn/ a refreshing toilet
water (weaker than perfume), made of alcohol and aromatic
oils, whose invention is ascribed to Giovanni Maria Farina
(1685–1766). He moved from Italy to Cologne in 1709 to
manufacture it. [French = water of Cologne]

eaves *n.pl.* the projecting lower edge of a roof. [Old English, related to *over*]

eavesdrop /'iːvzdrɒp/ *v.i.* (-**pp**-) to listen secretly to a
private conversation. —**eavesdropper** *n.*

ebb *n.* 1. the outward movement of the tide, away from
the land. 2. decline, poor condition. —*v.i.* to flow back; to
recede, to decline. [Old English]

Ebbw Vale /'ebu: 'veɪl/ town in Gwent, Wales; population
(1981) 21,100. The iron and steel industries ended in the
1970s, but tin-plate manufacture and engineering continues.
To the east is Blaenavon, where the Big Pit (no longer
working) is a tourist attraction.

EBCDIC   acronym from Extended Binary Coded
Decimal Interchange Code; in computing, a code used
for storing and communicating alphabetic and numeric
characters. It is an eight-bit code, capable of holding 256
different characters, although only 85 of these are defined
in the standard version. It is still used in many mainframe
computers, but almost all mini-and microcomputers now use
◊ASCII code.

ebonite /'ebənaɪt/ *n.* ◊vulcanite.

ebony /'ebənɪ/ *n.* a hardwood tree of the genus *Diospyros*,
mainly found in tropical regions. Their very heavy, hard
black timber polishes well and is used in cabinetmaking,
inlaying, for piano keys and knife handles. —*adj.* made of
ebony; black like ebony. [from Latin from Greek *ebenos* =
ebony tree]

Eboracum the Roman name for ◊York, English city. The
archbishop of York signs himself 'Ebor'.

Ebro /'iːbrəʊ/ river in NE Spain, which rises in the Cantabrian mountains and flows some 800 km/500 mi SE to
meet the Mediterranean sea SW of Barcelona. Zaragoza
is on its course, and ocean-going ships can sail as far as
Tortosa, 35 km/22 mi from its mouth. It is a major source
of hydroelectric power.

ebullient /ɪ'bʌlɪənt/ *adj.* exuberant, high-spirited. —**ebul-
lience** *n.*, **ebulliency** *n.* [from Latin *bullire* = boil]

ebullition /ebə'lɪʃən/ *n.* boiling; a sudden outburst of passion or emotion.

EC abbreviation of 1. East Central. 2. European Commission. 3. ◊European Community.

Ecce Homo the words of Pontius Pilate to the accusers of
Jesus; the title of paintings showing Jesus crowned with
thorns, presented to the people (New Testament, John
19:5). [Latin = behold the man]

eccentric /ɪk'sentrɪk/ *adj.* 1. odd or capricious in behaviour or appearance. 2. not placed centrally; not having its
axis placed centrally; (of a circle) not concentric (*to* another
circle); (of an orbit) not circular. —*n.* 1. an eccentric person. 2. a disc fixed eccentrically on a revolving shaft, for
changing rotatory to to-and-fro motion. —**eccentrically**
adv., **eccentricity** *n.* [from Latin from Greek *ek* = out of
and *kentron* = centre]

eccentricity /ɪksen'trɪsɪtɪ/ *n.* in geometry, a property of a
◊conic section (circle, ellipse, parabola, or hyperbola). It is
the distance of any point on the curve from a fixed point (the
focus) divided by the distance of that point from a fixed line
(the directrix). A circle has an eccentricity of zero; for an
ellipse it is less than one; for a parabola it is equal to one;
and for a hyperbola it is greater than one.

Eccles John Carew 1903– . Australian physiologist who
shared (with Alan ◊Hodgkin and Andrew ◊Huxley) the
1963 Nobel Prize for Physiology and Medicine for work
on conduction in the central nervous system. In some of
his later works, he argued that the mind has an existence
independent of the brain.

Eccles cake /'eklz/a round cake of pastry filled with currants. [from *Eccles* in Greater Manchester, England]

Ecclesiastes /ɪkliːzi'æstiːz/ *n.* also known as 'The
Preacher', a book of the Old Testament of the Bible,
traditionally attributed to ◊Solomon, on the theme of the
vanity of human life.

ecclesiastic /ɪkliːzi'æstɪk/ *n.* a clergyperson. [from
French or Latin from Greek *ekklēsia* = church]

ecclesiastical *adj.* of the church or clergy.

ecclesiastical law church law. In England, the Church
of England has special ecclesiastical courts to administer
church law. Each diocese has a consistory court with a
right of appeal to the Court of Arches (in the archbishop
of Canterbury's jurisdiction) or the Chancery Court of York
(in the archbishop of York's jurisdiction). They deal with the
constitution of the Church of England, church property, the
clergy, services, doctrine, and practice. These courts have
no influence on churches of other denominations, which are
governed by the usual laws of contract and trust.

ecclesiology /ɪkliːzi'ɒlədʒɪ/ *n.* the study of church building and decoration.

ECG abbreviation of ◊electrocardiogram.

echelon /'eʃəlɒn/ *n.* 1. a formation of troops or ships,
aircraft etc., in parallel rows with the end of each row
projecting further laterally than the one in front. 2. a grade
or rank in an organization. [French = rung of ladder]

echidna /ɪ'kɪdnə/ *n.* or **spiny anteater** any of several
species of toothless, egg-laying, spiny mammals of the genera *Tachyglossus* and *Zaglossus*, in the order Monotremata,
found in Australia and New Guinea. They feed entirely upon
ants and termites, which they dig out with their powerful
claws and lick up with their prehensile tongues. When
attacked, an echidna rolls itself into a ball, or tries to hide
by burrowing in the earth. [Latin from Greek = viper]

echinoderm /ɪ'kaɪnədɜːm, 'ekɪn-/ *n.* a group of marine
invertebrates of the phylum Echinodermata ('spiny-skin-
ned), including starfishes (or sea stars), brittlestars, sea-
lilies, sea-urchins, and sea-cucumbers. The basic body
structure is divided into five sectors; the skeleton is
external, made of a series of limy plates, and echinoderms
generally move by using tube-feet, small water-filled sacs
that can be protruded or pulled back to the body. [from
Greek *ekhinos* = hedgehog, sea urchin and *derma* = skin]

echo /'ekəʊ/ *n.* (*plural* **echoes**) 1. the repetition of sound
by the reflection of sound waves; a secondary sound so
produced. 2. a reflected radio, ◊radar, or ◊sonar beam.
3. a close imitation or imitator. —*v.t./i.* 1. (of a place) to
resound with an echo; to repeat (a sound) thus; (of a sound)
to be repeated, to resound. 2. to repeat (a person's words);
to imitate the opinions of. —**echo sounder**, a sounding
apparatus for determining the depth of sea beneath a ship
by measuring the time taken for an echo to be received.
echo sounding. [from Old French or Latin from Greek]

Echo in Greek mythology, a nymph who pined away
until only her voice remained, after being rejected by
◊Narcissus.

echoic /e'kəʊɪk/ *adj.* (of a word) imitating the sound it
represents, onomatopoeic. —**echoically** *adv.*

echolocation /ekəʊlə'keɪʃən/ *n.* the location of objects
by means of the echo reflected from them by a sound
signal, as with the ultrasonic sounds emitted by certain animals, notably bats and dolphins, or by man-made
devices.

Eckhart /'ekhaːt/ Johannes, called **Meister Eckhart**
*c.*1260–1327. German theologian and leader of a popular
mystical movement. In 1326 he was accused of heresy, and in 1329 a number of his doctrines were condemned by the pope as heretical. His theology stressed

eclipse

lunar eclipse

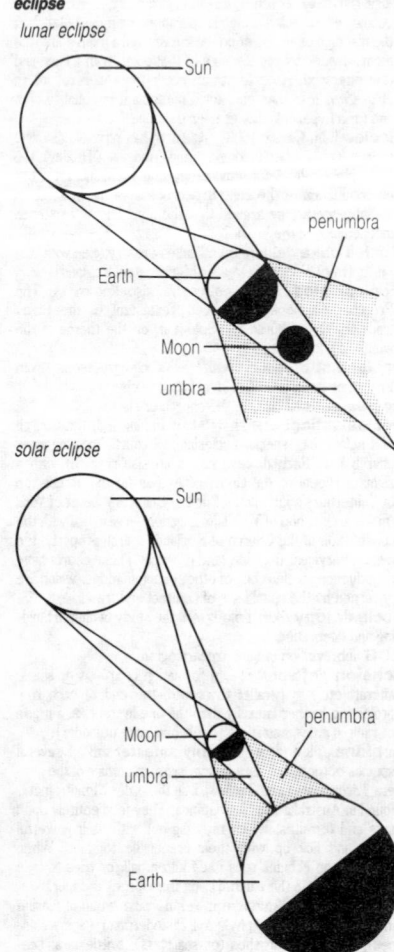

Sun
penumbra
Earth
Moon
umbra

solar eclipse

Sun
penumbra
Moon
umbra
Earth

the absolute transcendence of God, and the internal spiritual development through which union with the divine could be attained.

éclair /eɪ'kleə, ɪ-/ n. a finger-shaped cake of choux pastry filled with cream and iced. [French = lightning]

eclampsia n. a condition characterized by convulsions occurring due to ◊toxaemia of pregnancy.

éclat /'eɪklɑː/ n. brilliant success or display; renown, esteem. [French, literally = burst of light]

eclectic /ɪ'klektɪk/ adj. selecting ideas or beliefs from various sources. —n. an eclectic person. —**eclectically** adv., **eclecticism** /- sɪzəm/ n. [from Greek eklego = pick out]

eclipse /ɪ'klɪps/ n. 1. the obscuring of light from one heavenly body by another. 2. loss of light, brilliance, or importance. —v.t. 1. to cause an eclipse of; to intercept (light). 2. to outshine, to surpass. —**annular eclipse,** one leaving a complete ring of the solar surface open to view, occurring when the Moon passes before the Sun at a greater distance than average. **partial eclipse,** one that is not total. **total eclipse,** one where the entire surface of the luminous body is obscured. [from Old French, ultimately from Greek ekleiþō = fail to appear]

eclipsing binary a binary (double) star in which the two stars periodically pass in front of each other as seen from Earth.

ecliptic /ɪ'klɪptɪk/ n. the apparent path across the heavens of the Sun during the year, so called because lunar and solar eclipses will occur only when the Moon crosses this path. —adj. of an eclipse or the ecliptic.

eclogue /'eklɒg/ n. a short poem, especially a pastoral dialogue such as those of Theocritus and Virgil. [from Latin from Greek eklego = pick out]

Eco /'ekəʊ/ Umberto 1932– . Italian writer, semiologist, and literary critic. His works include The Role of the Reader 1979, the 'philosophical thriller' The Name of the Rose 1983, and Foucault's Pendulum 1988.

eco- prefix meaning ecology, ecological.

ecoclimate /'iːkəʊklaɪmət/ n. the climate as an ecological factor.

École Nationale d'Administration (ENA) the most prestigious of the French Grandes Écoles, higher education colleges that admit students only following a public competitive examination. The ENA was founded in 1945 to train civil servants; former pupils include Laurent Fabius, Valéry Giscard d'Estaing, and Jacques Chirac. [French = National School of Administration]

ecology /iː'kɒlədʒɪ/ n. the study of the relationship between an organism and the environment in which it lives, including other living organisms and the nonliving surroundings. The term was coined by the biologist Ernst Haeckel in 1866. —**ecological** /-'lɒdʒɪkəl/ adj., **ecologist** n. [from Greek oikos = home]

econometrics n. the application of mathematical and statistical analysis in the study of economic relationships, including testing economic theories and making quantitative predictions.

economic /iːkə'nɒmɪk, ek-/ adj. 1. of economics. 2. maintained for profit, on business lines; adequate to pay or recoup expenditure with some profit; practical, considered with regard to human needs. —**economically** adv.

economical adj. careful in the use of resources, avoiding waste; thrifty. —**economically** adv.

economic community or **common market** an organization of autonomous countries formed to promote trade. Examples include the Caribbean Community (Caricom) 1973, Central African Economic Community 1985, European Community (EC) 1957, and Latin American Economic System 1975.

economics n. 1. the science of the production and distribution of wealth; the application of this to a particular subject. Economics is usually divided into the disciplines of ◊microeconomics, the study of individual producers, consumers, or markets, and ◊macroeconomics, the study of whole economies or systems. 2. (as plural) the financial aspects of something.

economies of scale in economics, when production capacity is increased at a financial cost that is more than compensated for by the greater volume of output. In a dress factory, for example, a reduction in the unit cost may be possible only by the addition of new machinery, which would be worthwhile only if the volume of dresses produced were increased and there were sufficient market demand for them.

economist /iː'kɒnəmɪst/ n. an expert on or student of economics.

economize /iː'kɒnəmaɪz/ v.t./i. to be economical, to make economies, to reduce expenditure; (usually with on) to use sparingly.

economy /iː'kɒnəmɪ/ n. 1. the wealth and resources of a community; the administration or condition of these. 2. the careful management of (especially financial) resources, frugality; an instance of this. [from French or Latin from Greek oikonomia = stewardship]

ecosystem /'iːkəʊsɪstəm/ n. in ◊ecology, an integrated unit consisting of the ◊community of living organisms and the physical environment in a particular area. The relationships among species in an ecosystem are usually complex and finely balanced, and removal of any one species may be disastrous. The removal of a major predator, for example, can result in the destruction of the ecosystem through overgrazing by herbivores.

ecru /'eɪkruː/ n. a light fawn colour. [French = unbleached]

ECSC abbreviation of ◊European Coal and Steel Community.

ecstasy /'ekstəsɪ/ n. 1. an overwhelming feeling of joy, rapture. 2. or **MDMA** (3,4-methylenedioxymethamphetamine) an illegal drug in increasing use from the 1980s. It is a modified amphetamine with mild psychedelic effects, and works by depleting serotonin (a neurotransmitter) in the brain. —**ecstatic** /ek'stætɪk/ adj., **ecstatically** adv. [from Old French from Latin from Greek ekstasis = standing outside oneself]

Ecuador

ECT abbreviation of ◊electroconvulsive therapy.

ecto- prefix denoting outside. [from Greek *ektos*]

ectomorph /'ektəmɔ:f/ *n.* a person with a lean build of body, thought likely to be an introvert. [from Greek *morphē* = form]

-ectomy /-ektəmi/suffix forming nouns, denoting a surgical operation in which some part is removed (e.g. *tonsillectomy*). [from Greek *ektomē* = excision]

ectoparasite *n.* a ◊parasite that lives on the outer surface of its host.

ectopic /ek'tɒpɪk/ *adj.* in medicine, of or related to an anatomical feature that is displaced or found in an abnormal position. An **ectopic pregnancy** is one occurring outside the womb, usually in a Fallopian tube. [from Greek *ektopos* = out of place]

ectoplasm[1] /'ektəplæzəm/ *n.* the outer layer of a cell's ◊cytoplasm.

ectoplasm[2] *n.* a viscous substance supposed to emanate from the body of a spiritualist medium during a trance.

ectotherm *n.* a 'cold-blooded' animal (see ◊poikilotherm), such as a lizard, that relies on external warmth (ultimately from the Sun) to raise its body temperature so that it can become active. To cool the body, ectotherms seek out a cooler environment.

ECU /'eikju, 'i:-/ or **Ecu** or **ecu** acronym from European Currency Unit, the official monetary unit of the ◊European Community. It is based on the value of the different currencies used in the ◊European Monetary System.

Ecuador /'ekwədɔ:/ Republic of; country in South America, bounded to the N by Colombia, to the E and S by Peru, and to the W by the Pacific Ocean; **area** 270,670 sq km/ 104,479 sq mi; **capital** Quito; **physical** coastal plain rises charply to Andes Mountains which are divided into a series of cultivated valleys; flat, low-lying rainforest in the E; about 25,000 wildlife species became extinct 1965–90 as a result of environmental destruction; **head of state and government** Rodrigo Borja Cevallos from 1988; **political system** emergent democracy; **exports** bananas, cocoa, coffee, sugar, rice, balsa wood, fish, petroleum; **population** (1989 est) 10,490,000; **language** Spanish (official); Quechuan, Jivaroan; **recent history** independence was achieved from Spain in 1830. After a long period of instability, liberal and conservative governments alternated from 1948 until 1963 when the military junta came into power. In 1982, a state of emergency was declared after strikes and demonstrations, followed by austerity measures in 1983. Today Rodrigo Borja Cevallos leads the moderate left-wing coalition in power.

ecumenical /i:kju:'menɪkəl/ *adj.* of or representing the whole Christian world; seeking worldwide Christian unity.
—**ecumenicalism** *n.*, **ecumenism** /i:'kju:mənɪzəm/ *n.* [from Latin from Greek *oikoumenē* = the inhabited earth]

ecumenical council a meeting of church leaders worldwide to determine Christian doctrine; the decisions made are binding on all church members. Seven such councils are accepted as ecumenical by both Eastern and Western churches, while the Roman Catholic Church accepts a further 14 as ecumenical.

ecumenical movement a movement for reunification of the various branches of the Christian church. It began in the 19th century with the extension of missionary work to Africa and Asia, where the divisions created in Europe were incomprehensible; the movement gathered momentum from the need for unity in the face of growing secularism in Christian countries and of the challenge posed by such faiths as Islam. The ◊World Council of Churches was founded in 1948.

ecumenical patriarch the head of the Eastern Orthodox Church, the patriarch of Istanbul (Constantinople). The Bishop of Constantinople was recognized as having equal rights with the Bishop of Rome in 451, and first termed 'patriarch' in the 6th century. The office survives today but with only limited authority, mainly confined to the Greek and Turkish Orthodox churches.

eczema /'eksɪmə/ *n.* an inflammatory skin condition, a form of dermatitis, marked by dryness, rashes, itching, the formation of blisters, and the exudation of fluid. It may be allergic in origin and is sometimes complicated by infection. —**eczematous** /ek'zi:mətəs/ *adj.* [Latin from Greek *ek* = out and *zeō* = boil]

ed. abbreviation of **1.** edited (by); edition; editor. **2.** educated.

Edam /'i:dæm/ town in the Netherlands on the river IJ, North Holland province; population (1987) 24,200. It is famous for its spherical cheeses covered in red wax.

Edda /'edə/ the name given to two collections of early Icelandic literature, which together constitute the chief source of Old Norse mythology. The term strictly applies to the **Younger** or **Prose Edda**, compiled by Snorri Sturluson, a priest, about 1230. The **Elder** or **Poetic Edda** is a collection of poems discovered by Brynjólfr Sveinsson about 1643, written by unknown Norwegian poets of the 9th to 12th centuries.

Eddery /'edəri/ Pat(rick) 1952– . Irish-born flat-racing jockey who has won the jockey's championship eight times, including four in succession. He has won all the major races, including the Epsom Derby twice. He won the Prix de L'Arc de Triomphe four times, including three in succession 1985–87.

Eddington /'edɪŋtən/ Arthur Stanley 1882–1944. British astrophysicist, who studied the motions, equilibrium, luminosity, and atomic structure of the stars, and became a leading exponent of Einstein's relativity theory. In 1919 his observation of stars during an ◊eclipse confirmed Einstein's prediction that light is bent when passing near the Sun. His book *The Nature of the Physical World* 1928 is a popularization of science; in *The Expanding Universe* 1933 he expressed the theory that in the spherical universe the outer galaxies or spiral nebulae are receding from one another.

eddy /'edi/ *n.* an area of water swirling in a circular motion; smoke, fog etc., moving like this. —*v.t./i.* to move in eddies. [from Old English *ed-* = again, back]

Eddy Mary Baker 1821–1910. US founder of the ◊Christian Science movement. Her faith in divine healing was influenced by the work of a faith healer named Phineas Quimby and confirmed by her recovery from injuries caused by a fall.

eddy current an electric current induced, in accordance with ◊Faraday's laws, in a conductor located in a changing magnetic field. Eddy currents can cause much wasted energy in the cores of transformers and other electrical machines.

Eddystone Rocks /'edɪstən/ a group of rocks in the English Channel, 23 km/14 mi S of Plymouth. The lighthouse, built in 1882, is the fourth on this exposed site.

Edelman /'edlmən/ Gerald 1929– . US biochemist. The structure of the antibody gamma globulin (one of the body's defences) was worked out by Rodney ◊Porter by 1962. By 1969 Edelman had solved the related problem of working out the sequence of the 1330 amino acids from which the antibody is made up. He shared with Porter the 1972 Nobel Prize for Physiology and Medicine.

edelweiss *n.* a perennial alpine plant *Leontopodium alpinum*, family Compositae, with woolly white bracts round the flower heads. [German *edel* = noble and *weiss* = white]

Eden /ˈiːdn/ river in Cumbria, NW England; length 104 km/ 65 mi. From its source in the Pennines, it flows NW to enter the Solway Firth NW of Carlisle.

Eden Anthony, 1st Earl of Avon 1897–1977. British Conservative politician, foreign secretary 1935–38, 1940–45, and 1951–55; prime minister 1955–57. He resigned after the failure of the Anglo-French military intervention in the ◊Suez Crisis.

Eden, Garden of in the Old Testament book of Genesis and in the Koran, the 'garden' in which Adam and Eve lived after their creation, and from which they were expelled for disobedience. Its location has often been identified with the Fertile Crescent in Mesopotamia (now in Iraq). [from Hebrew = delight]

edentate /iˈdenteɪt/ adj. having few or no teeth. —n. an edentate animal, especially a mammal. [from Latin edentatus (dens = tooth)]

Edgar /ˈedɡə/ known as the **Atheling** ('of royal blood') c.1050–c.1130. English prince, born in Hungary. Grandson of Edmund Ironside, he was supplanted as heir to Edward the Confessor by William the Conqueror. He led two rebellions against William in 1068 and 1069, but made peace in 1074.

Edgar the Peaceful 944–975. King of all England from 959. He was the younger son of Edmund I, and strove successfully to unite English and Danes as fellow subjects.

edge /edʒ/ n. 1. the cutting side of a blade; the sharpness of this; (figurative) effectiveness. 2. an edge-shaped thing, especially the crest of a ridge. 3. the meeting line of surfaces; the boundary line of a region or surface; the brink of a precipice. —v.t./i. 1. to give or form a border to. 2. to insinuate (a thing or oneself, in etc.). 3. to advance (especially gradually and obliquely). 4. to give a sharp edge to. —have the edge on, (colloquial) to have an advantage over. on edge, tense and irritable. set one's teeth on edge, (of a taste or sound) to cause an unpleasant nervous sensation. take the edge off, to dull, to weaken, to make less intense. [Old English]

Edgehill, Battle of /edʒˈhɪl/ the first battle of the English ◊Civil War. It took place in 1642, on a ridge in S Warwickshire, between Royalists under Charles I and Parliamentarians under the Earl of Essex. The result was indecisive.

edgeways adv. or **edgewise** with the edge foremost or uppermost. —get a word in edgeways, to contribute to a conversation dominated by another or others.

Edgeworth /ˈedʒwɜːθ/ Maria 1767–1849. Irish novelist. Her first novel, Castle Rackrent 1800, dealt with Anglo-Irish country society and was followed by the similar The Absentee 1812 and Ormond 1817.

edging n. a thing forming an edge, a border.

edgy adj. irritable, anxious, on edge. —edgily adv., edginess n.

edible /ˈedɪbl/ adj. fit to be eaten. —n. an edible thing. —edibility /-ˈbɪlɪtɪ/ n. [from Latin edere = eat]

edict /ˈiːdɪkt/ n. an order proclaimed by authority. [from Latin edicere = proclaim]

edifice /ˈedɪfɪs/ n. a building, especially a large imposing one. [from Old French from Latin aedificium]

edify /ˈedɪfaɪ/ v.t. to benefit spiritually; to improve morally. —edification /-fɪˈkeɪʃən/ n. [from Old French from Latin aedificare = build]

Edinburgh /ˈedɪnbərə/ capital of Scotland and administrative centre of the region of Lothian, near the southern shores of the Firth of Forth; population (1985) 440,000. It is a cultural centre, and holds an annual festival of music and the arts; the university was established in 1583. Industries include printing, publishing, banking, insurance, chemical manufactures, distilling, brewing, and some shipbuilding.

Edirne /eˈdɪəneɪ/ town in European Turkey, on the river Maritsa, about 225 km/140 mi NW of Istanbul. Population (1985) 86,700. Founded on the site of ancient Uscadama, it was formerly known as **Adrianople**, named after the Emperor Hadrian in about AD 125.

Edison /ˈedɪsən/ Thomas Alva 1847–1931. US scientist and inventor, with over 1,000 patents. In Menlo Park, New Jersey, 1876–87, he produced his major inventions, including the electric lightbulb (1879). He constructed a system of electric power distribution for consumers, the telephone transmitter, and the phonograph.

Edison In his physics laboratory at West Orange, New Jersey, the inventor Thomas Edison holds one of his 'Edison Effect' lamps. By his discovery of this 'effect' in 1880 he revealed one of the fundamental principles on which modern electronics rests.

Genius is one per cent inspiration and ninety-nine per cent perspiration.

Thomas Alva Edison
Life

edit /ˈedɪt/ v.t. 1. to assemble or prepare (written material) for publication; to arrange or modify (another's work) for publication. 2. to act as editor of (a newspaper etc.). 3. to prepare (data) for processing by computer. 4. to take extracts from and collate (a film etc.) so as to form a unified sequence. 5. to reword for a purpose. [from French from Latin edere = publish]

edition /iˈdɪʃən/ n. 1. the edited or published form of a book etc. 2. the copies of a book, newspaper etc., issued at one time; the whole number of products of the same kind issued at one time. 3. a person etc. considered as resembling another.

editor /ˈedɪtə/ n. 1. one who edits. 2. one who directs the content and writing of a newspaper or a particular section of one. 3. the head of a department of a publishing house. —editorship n.

editorial /ediˈtɔːrɪəl/ adj. of an editor or editing. —n. a newspaper article commenting on a current topic, written or sanctioned by the editor. —editorially adv.

Edmonton /ˈedməntən/ capital of Alberta, Canada, on the North Saskatchewan River; population (1986) 576,249. It is the centre of an oil and mining area to the N and also an agricultural and dairying region. Petroleum pipelines link Edmonton with Superior, Wisconsin, USA, and Vancouver, British Columbia.

Edmund II /ˈedmənd/ known as **Edmund Ironside** c.989–1016. King of England in 1016, the son of Ethelred II the Unready. He led the resistance to ◊Canute's invasion in 1015, and on Ethelred's death in 1016 was chosen king by the citizens of London, whereas the Witan (the king's council) elected Canute. In the struggle for the throne, Edmund was defeated by Canute at Assandun (Ashington), Essex, and they divided the kingdom between them; when Edmund died the same year, Canute ruled the whole kingdom.

Edmund, St c.840–870. King of East Anglia from 855. In 870 he was defeated and captured by the Danes at Hoxne, Suffolk, and martyred on refusing to renounce Christianity. He was canonized and his shrine at Bury St Edmunds became a place of pilgrimage.

Edom /ˈiːdəm/ n. in the Old Testament, a mountainous area of S Palestine, which stretched from the Dead Sea to the Gulf of Aqaba. Its people, said to be descendants of Esau, were enemies of the Israelites.

EDP abbreviation of electronic data processing.

Edric the Forester /ˈedrɪtʃ/ or **Edric the Wild** 11th century. English chieftain on the Welsh border who revolted against William the Conqueror in 1067, around what is today Herefordshire, burning Shrewsbury. He was subsequently reconciled with William, and fought with him against the Scots in 1072. Later writings describe him as a legendary figure.

educable /'edjʊkəbəl/ *adj.* able to be educated.

educate /'edjuːkeɪt/ *v.t.* to train or instruct intellectually, morally, and socially; to provide schooling for. —**educated guess**, one based on experience. —**educative** *adj.*, **educator** *n.* [from Latin *educere* = draw out]

education *n.* the process, beginning at birth, of developing intellectual capacity, manual skill, and social awareness, especially by instruction. In its more restricted sense, the term refers to the process of imparting literacy, numeracy, and a generally accepted body of knowledge. —**educational** *adj.*, **educationally** *adv.*

educational psychology the work of psychologists, primarily in schools, including the assessment of children with achievement problems and advising on problem behaviour in the classroom.

educationist *n.* or **educationalist** an expert in educational methods.

educe /i'djuːs/ *v.t.* to bring out, to develop from latent or potential existence. —**eduction** /i'dʌkʃən/ *n.* [from Latin *educere* = draw out]

Edward /'edwəd/ **the Black Prince** 1330–1376. Prince of Wales, eldest son of Edward III of England. The epithet (probably posthumous) may refer to his black armour. During the Hundred Years' War he fought at the Battle of Crécy in 1346 and captured the French king at Poitiers in 1356. He ruled Aquitaine 1360–71; during the revolt that eventually ousted him, he caused the massacre of Limoges in 1370.

Edward (full name Edward Antony Richard Louis) 1964– . Prince of the UK, third son of Queen Elizabeth II. He is seventh in line to the throne after Charles, Charles's two sons, Andrew, and Andrew's two daughters.

Edward /'edwəd/ eight kings of England or the UK:

Edward I 1239–1307. King of England from 1272, son of Henry III. Edward led the royal forces against Simon de Montfort in the ◊Barons' War 1264–67, and was on a crusade when he succeeded to the throne. He established English rule over all Wales 1282–84, and secured recognition of his overlordship from the Scottish king, though the Scots fiercely resisted conquest. In his reign Parliament took its approximate modern form with the ◊Model Parliament of 1295. He was succeeded by his son Edward II.

Edward II 1284–1327. King of England from 1307. Son of Edward I and born at Caernarvon Castle, he was created the first Prince of Wales in 1301. His invasion of Scotland in 1314 to suppress revolt resulted in defeat at ◊Bannockburn. He was deposed in 1327 by his wife Isabella (1292–1358), daughter of Philip IV of France, and her lover Roger de ◊Mortimer, and murdered. He was succeeded by his son Edward III.

Edward III 1312–1377. King of England from 1327, son of Edward II. He assumed the government in 1330 from his mother, through whom in 1337 he laid claim to the French throne and thus began the ◊Hundred Years' War. He was succeeded by Richard II.

Edward IV 1442–1483. King of England 1461–70 and from 1471. He was the son of Richard, Duke of York, and succeeded Henry VI in the Wars of the ◊Roses, temporarily losing the throne to Henry when Edward fell out with his adviser ◊Warwick, but regaining it at the Battle of Barnet. He was succeeded by his son Edward V.

Edward V 1470–1483. King of England in 1483. Son of Edward IV, he was deposed three months after his accession in favour of his uncle Richard III, and is traditionally believed to have been murdered (with his brother) in the Tower of London on Richard's orders.

Edward VI 1537–1553. King of England from 1547, son of Henry VIII and Jane Seymour. The government was entrusted to his uncle the Duke of Somerset (who fell in 1549), and then to the Earl of Warwick, later created Duke of Northumberland. He was succeeded by his sister, Mary I.

Edward VII 1841–1910. King of Great Britain and Ireland from 1901. As Prince of Wales he was a prominent social figure, but his mother, Queen Victoria, considered him too frivolous to take part in political life. In 1860 he made the first tour of Canada and the USA ever undertaken by a British prince.

Edward the Confessor *A coin stamped with the head of the English king Edward the Confessor.*

Edward VIII 1894–1972. King of Great Britain and Northern Ireland Jan–Dec 1936, when he renounced the throne to marry Wallis Warfield ◊Simpson (see ◊abdication crisis). He was created Duke of Windsor and was governor of the Bahamas 1940–45, subsequently settling in France.

Edwardian /ed'wɔːdiən/ *adj.* belonging to or characteristic of the reign of Edward VII (1901–10). —*n.* a person of this period.

Edwards /'edwədz/ Blake. Adopted name of William Blake McEdwards 1922– . US film director and writer, formerly an actor. Specializing in comedies, he directed the series of *Pink Panther* films 1963–78, starring Peter Sellers. His other work includes *Breakfast at Tiffany's* 1961 and *Blind Date* 1986.

Edwards Gareth 1947– . Welsh Rugby Union player. He was appointed captain of his country when only 20 years old.

Edwards George 1908– . British civil and military aircraft designer, associated with the Viking, Viscount, Valiant V-bomber, VC-10, and Concorde.

Edwards Jonathan 1703–1758. US theologian who took a Calvinist view of predestination, and initiated a religious revival, the 'Great Awakening'; author of *The Freedom of the Will* (defending determinism) 1754.

Edward the Confessor *c.*1003–1066. King of England from 1042, the son of Ethelred II. He lived in Normandy until shortly before his accession. During his reign power was held by Earl ◊Godwin and his son ◊Harold, while the king devoted himself to religion, including the rebuilding of Westminster Abbey (consecrated in 1065), where he is buried. His childlessness led ultimately to the Norman Conquest in 1066. He was canonized in 1161.

Edward the Elder *c.*870–924. King of the West Saxons. He succeeded his father ◊Alfred the Great in 899. He reconquered SE England and the Midlands from the Danes, uniting Wessex and ◊Mercia with the help of his sister, Athelflad. By the time Edward died, his kingdom was the most powerful in the British Isles. He was succeeded by his son ◊Athelstan.

Edward the Martyr *c.*963–978. King of England from 975. Son of King Edgar, he was murdered at Corfe Castle, Dorset, probably at his stepmother Aelfthryth's instigation (she wished to secure the crown for her son, Ethelred). He was canonized in 1001.

Edwin /'edwin/ *c.*585–633. King of Northumbria from 617. He captured and fortified Edinburgh, which was named after him, and was killed in battle with ◊Penda of Mercia.

EEC abbreviation of European Economic Community; see ◊European Community.

EEG abbreviation of ◊electroencephalogram.

eel *n.* **1.** any fish of the order Anguilliformes. Eels are snakelike, with elongated dorsal and anal fins. They include the freshwater eels of Europe and North America (which breed in the Atlantic), the marine conger eels, and the morays of tropical coral reefs. **2.** an evasive person. [Old English]

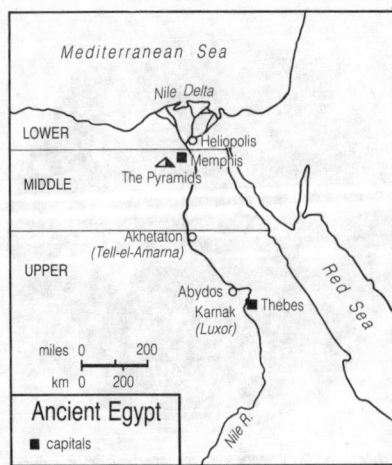

Egypt

eelgrass *n.* or **tape grass** or **glass wrack** a flowering plant *Zostera marina* of the pondweed family Zosteraceae, found in tidal mud flats. It is one of the few flowering plants to adapt to marine conditions, being completely submerged at high tide.

eerie /'ɪərɪ/ *adj.* gloomy and strange, weird. —**eerily** *adv.*, **eeriness** *n.* [Old English; originally = timid]

efface /ɪ'feɪs/ *v.t.* **1.** to rub or wipe out (a mark, recollection, or impression). **2.** to surpass, to eclipse. —**efface oneself**, to treat or regard oneself as unimportant. —**effacement** *n.* [from French]

effect /ɪ'fekt/ *n.* **1.** a result or consequence of an action etc. **2.** the state of being operative; efficacy. **3.** an impression produced on a spectator or hearer etc. **4.** (in *plural*) property. **5.** (in *plural*) sounds and visual features giving realism to a play, film etc. —*v.t.* to bring about, to accomplish, to cause to occur. —**bring** or **carry into effect**, to accomplish. **give effect to**, to make operative. **in effect**, for practical purposes, in reality. **take effect**, to become operative. **to that effect**, having that result or implication. **with effect from**, coming into operation at (a stated time). [from Old French or Latin *efficere* = accomplish]

effective /ɪ'fektɪv/ *adj.* **1.** having an effect, powerful in effect; striking, remarkable. **2.** actual, existing. **3.** operative. —**effectively** *adv.*, **effectiveness** *n.*

effectual /ɪ'fektʃuəl, -tjuəl/ *adj.* answering its purpose, sufficient to produce an effect; valid. —**effectually** *adv.* [from Latin]

effectuate /ɪ'fektʃueɪt, -tjueɪt/ *v.t.* to cause to happen.

effeminate /ɪ'femɪnət/ *adj.* (of a man) womanish in appearance or manner. —**effeminacy** *n.* [from Latin *femina* = woman]

effervesce /efə'ves/ *v.i.* **1.** to give off bubbles of gas. **2.** to show great liveliness. —**effervescence** *n.*, **effervescent** *adj.* [from Latin *fervescere* = begin to be hot]

effete /ɪ'fiːt/ *adj.* worn out, lacking vitality; feeble. —**effeteness** *n.* [from Latin *effetus* = worn out by bearing young]

efficacious /efɪ'keɪʃəs/ *adj.* producing or able to produce the desired effect. —**efficacy** /'efɪkəsɪ/ *n.* [from Latin *efficax* = powerful]

efficiency *n.* **1.** the attribute of being efficient. **2.** the output of a machine (work done by the machine) divided by the input (work put into the machine), usually expressed as a percentage. Because of losses caused by friction, efficiency is always less than 100%, although it can approach this for electrical machines with no moving parts (such as a transformer).

efficient /ɪ'fɪʃənt/ *adj.* **1.** productive with the minimum waste of effort. **2.** (of a person) capable, acting effectively. **3.** producing an effect. —**efficiently** *adv.* [from Latin *efficere* = accomplish]

effigy /'efɪdʒɪ/ *n.* a portrait or image of a person. [from Latin *fingere* = fashion]

effloresce /eflɔː'res/1. to burst into flower. **2.** (of a substance) to turn to fine powder on exposure to air; (of

salts) to come to the surface and crystallize; (of a surface) to become covered with such salt particles. —**efflorescence** *n.*, **efflorescent** *adj.* [from Latin *florescere* = begin to bloom]

effluence /'efluəns/ *n.* a flowing out of light or electricity etc.; that which flows out. [from Latin *effluere* = flow out]

effluent /'efluənt/ *adj.* flowing out. —*n.* a thing that flows out, especially a stream from a larger stream, or sewage.

effluvium /e'fluːvɪəm/ *n.* (*plural* **effluvia**) an outflow of a substance, especially an unpleasant or harmful one.

efflux /'eflʌks/ *n.* an outflow. [from Latin *effluxus*]

effort /'efət/ *n.* **1.** strenuous physical or mental exertion; the application of this, an attempt; the force exerted. **2.** (*colloquial*) something accomplished. [French from Old French *esforcier* from Latin *fortis* = strong]

effortless *adj.* done without effort, requiring no effort. —**effortlessly** *adv.*

effrontery /ɪ'frʌntərɪ/ *n.* shameless insolence, impudence. [from French from Latin *effrons* = shameless]

effulgent /ɪ'fʌldʒənt/ *adj.* radiant, bright. —**effulgence** *n.* [from Latin *fulgēre* = shine]

effuse /ɪ'fjuːz/ *v.t.* to pour forth, to send out (a liquid or light, or *figurative*). [from Latin *fundere* = pour]

effusion /ɪ'fjuːʒən/ *n.* an outpouring, especially (*derogatory*) of unrestrained literary work.

effusive /ɪ'fjuːsɪv/ *adj.* demonstrative, gushing. —**effusively** *adv.*, **effusiveness** *n.*

eft *n.* a newt. [Old English]

EFTA acronym from ◊European Free Trade Association.

EFTPOS acronym from Electronic Funds Transfer at Point Of Sale, the transfer of funds from one bank account to another by electronic means. For example, a bank customer inserts a plastic card in a point-of-sale computer terminal in a supermarket, and telephone lines are used to make an automatic debit from the customer's bank account to settle the bill. See also ◊credit card.

e.g. abbreviation of *exempli gratia*. [Latin = for the sake of example]

egalitarian /ɪgælɪ'teərɪən/ *adj.* of or advocating equal rights for all. —*n.* an egalitarian person. —**egalitarianism** *n.* [from French *égal* = equal]

Egbert /'egbɜːt/ King of the West Saxons from 802, the son of Ealhmund, an under-king of Kent. By 829 he had united England for the first time under one king.

Egerton /'edʒətən/ the family name of the dukes of Sutherland; seated at Mertoun, Roxburghshire, Scotland.

egg[1] *n.* **1.** a spheroidal body produced by the female of birds and reptiles etc. containing the germ of a new individual, especially that of the domestic fowl for eating. It is protected by a shell and well supplied with nutrients in the form of the yolk. **2.** the ovum or female ◊gamete (reproductive cell). **3.** (*colloquial*) a person (qualified in some way). —**egg cup**, a small cup for holding a boiled egg. **egg flip, eggnog**, a drink of alcoholic spirit with beaten egg, milk etc. **eggplant** *n.* a plant *Solanum melongena* with deep purple fruit used as a vegetable; its fruit, aubergine. **with egg on one's face**, (*colloquial*) made to look foolish. —**eggy** *adj.* [from Old Norse]

egg[2] *v.t.* to urge on. [from Old Norse]

egghead *n.* (*colloquial*) an intellectual person.

eggshell *n.* the shell of an egg. —*adj.* **1.** (of china) thin and fragile. **2.** (of paint) with a slight gloss.

eglantine /'egləntaɪn/ *n.* sweetbrier. [from French from Latin *acus* = needle]

Egmont, Mount /'egmɒnt/ (Maori *Taranaki*) symmetrical extinct volcano in North Island, New Zealand; situated S of New Plymouth; 2,517 m/8,260 ft high.

Egmont Lamoral, Graaf von 1522–1568. Flemish nobleman, born in Hainault. As a servant of the Spanish crown, he defeated the French at St Quentin in 1557 and Gravelines in 1558, and became *stadholder* (chief magistrate) of Flanders and Artois. From 1561 he opposed Philip II's religious policy in the Netherlands of persecuting Protestants, but in 1567 the duke of Alva was sent to crush the resistance, and Egmont was beheaded.

ego *n.* (*plural* **egos**) **1.** in psychology, a general term for the processes concerned with the self and one's conception of oneself, encompassing values and attitudes. In Freudian psychology, the term describes the element of the human mind that represents the conscious processes, concerned with reality, and is in conflict with the ◊id and

Egypt, ancient

5000 BC	Egyptian culture well established in the Nile Valley, with Neolithic farming villages.
3200 BC	Menes united Lower Egypt (the delta) with his own kingdom of Upper Egypt.
2800 BC	The architect Imhotep built the step pyramid at Sakkara.
c.2600 BC	Old Kingdom reached the height of its power and the kings of the 4th dynasty built the pyramids at Gîza.
c.2200–1800 BC	Middle Kingdom, under which the unity lost towards the end of the Old Kingdom was restored.
1730 BC	Invading Asian Hyksos people established their kingdom in the Nile Delta.
c.1580 BC	New Kingdom established by the 18th dynasty, following the eviction of the Hyksos, with its capital at Thebes. High point of ancient Egyptian civilization under pharaohs Thothmes, Hatshepsut, Amenhotep, Ikhnaton (who moved the capital to Akhetaton), and Tutankhamen.
c.1321 BC	19th dynasty: Ramses I built a temple at Karnak, Ramses II the temple at Abu Simbel.
1191 BC	Ramses III defeated the Indo-European Sea Peoples, but after him there was decline; power passed from the pharaohs to the priests of Ammon.
1090–663 BC	Late New Kingdom Egypt was often divided between two or more dynasties; the nobles became virtually independent.
8th–7th centuries BC	Brief interlude of rule by kings from Nubia.
666 BC	The Assyrians under Ashurbanipal occupied Thebes.
663–609 BC	Psammetichus I restored Egypt's independence and unity.
525 BC	Egypt was conquered by Cambyses and became a Persian province.
c.405–340 BC	A period of independence.
332 BC	Conquest by Alexander the Great. On the division of his empire, Egypt went to one of his generals, Ptolemy I, and his descendants, the Macedonian dynasty.
30 BC	Death of Cleopatra, last of the Macedonians, and conquest by the Roman emperor Augustus; Egypt became a province of the Roman and Byzantine empires.

the ◊superego. 2. self-esteem. —**ego trip**, (*colloquial*) an activity undertaken to boost one's self-esteem or feelings. [Latin = I]

egocentric /egəʊ'sentrɪk/ *adj.* self-centred. —**egocentricity** /-'trɪsɪtɪ/ *n.*

egoism /'egəʊɪzəm/ *n.* **1.** self-interest as the moral basis of behaviour; systematic selfishness. **2.** egotism. —**egoist** *n.*, **egoistic** /-'ɪstɪk/ *adj.*, **egoistically** *adv.*

egotism /'egəʊtɪzəm/ *n.* the practice of talking too much about oneself; self-conceit; selfishness. —**egotist** *n.*, **egotistic** /-'tɪstɪk/ *adj.*, **egotistically** *adv.*

egregious /i'gri:dʒəs/ *adj.* outstandingly bad; (*archaic*) remarkable. [from Latin = illustrious, literally 'standing out from the flock']

egress /'i:gres/ *n.* an exit; the right of going out. [from Latin *egredi* = walk out]

egret /'i:grɪt/ *n.* a kind of heron *Egretta alba* with long white feathers. [from French *aigrette*]

Egypt /'i:dʒɪpt/ Arab Republic of; country in NE Africa, bounded to the N by the Mediterranean, to the E by the Suez Canal and Red Sea, to the S by Sudan, and to the W by Libya; **area** 1,001,450 sq km/386,990 sq mi; **capital** Cairo; **physical** mostly desert; hills in E; fertile land along river Nile; cultivated and settled area is about 35,500 sq km/13,700 sq mi; **head of state and government** Hosni Mubarak from 1981; **political system** democratic republic; **exports** cotton and textiles, petroleum; **population** (1989 est) 54,779,000; **language** Arabic (official); **recent history** independence was achieved from Britain in 1936. President Gen Neguib declared Egypt a republic in 1953. In 1956, Nasser announced the nationalization of the Suez Canal, resulting in the Six Day War with Israel and the occupation of the Sinai and Gaza strip. The Camp David talks with Israel led to the exclusion of Egypt from the Arab League. President Sadat was assassinated and replaced by Hosni Mubarak in 1981. In 1987 Egypt was readmitted into the Arab League and diplomatic relations with Arab countries were restored.

Egyptian /ɪ'dʒɪpʃ(ə)n/ *adj.* of Egypt or its people or language. —*n.* **1.** a native or inhabitant of Egypt. **2.** the language of the ancient Egyptians.

Egyptian religion in the civilization of ancient Egypt, the worship of totemic animals believed to be the ancestors of the clan. Totems later developed into gods, represented as having animal heads. One of the main cults was that of ◊Osiris. Immortality, conferred by the magical rite of mummification, was originally the sole prerogative of the king, but was extended under the New Kingdom to all who could afford it; they were buried with the ◊Book of the Dead.

Egyptology /i:dʒɪp'tɒlədʒɪ/ *n.* the study of ancient Egypt. Interest in the subject was aroused by the Napoleonic expedition's discovery of the ◊Rosetta Stone in 1799. Various excavations continued throughout the 19th century and gradually assumed a more scientific character, largely as a result of the work of the British archaeologist Flinders ◊Petrie from 1880 onwards and the formation of

the Egyptian Exploration Fund in 1892. In 1922 another British archaeologist, Howard Carter, discovered the tomb of ◊Tutankhamen, the only royal tomb with all its treasures intact. —Egyptologist *n.*

eh /eɪ/(*colloquial*) interjection expressing inquiry or surprise, or inviting assent, or asking for repetition or explanation.

Ehrlich /'eəlɪk/ Paul 1854–1915. German bacteriologist and immunologist who developed the first cure for ◊syphilis. He developed the arsenic compounds, in particular Salvarsan, used in the treatment of syphilis before the discovery of antibiotics. He shared the 1908 Nobel Prize for Physiology and Medicine with Ilya Mechnikov (1845–1916) for his work on immunity.

Eichendorff /'aɪkəndɔːf/ Joseph Freiherr von 1788–1857. German lyric poet and romantic novelist, born in Upper Silesia, whose work was set to music by Schumann, Mendelssohn, and Wolf. He held various judicial posts.

Eichmann /'aɪkmən/ (Karl) Adolf 1906–1962. Austrian Nazi. As an ◊SS official during Hitler's regime (1933–45), he was responsible for atrocities against Jews and others, including the implementation of genocide. He managed to escape at the fall of Germany in 1945, but was discovered in Argentina in 1960, abducted by Israeli agents, tried in Israel in 1961 for ◊war crimes, and executed.

eider /'aɪdə(r)/ *n.* a large marine duck *Somateria mollissima* highly valued for its soft down, which is used in quilts and cushions for warmth. It is found on N coasts of the Atlantic and Pacific oceans. [from Icelandic]

eiderdown *n.* a quilt stuffed with feathers, down, or other soft material.

Eid ul-Adha /'i:d əl'ɑːdə/ a Muslim festival which takes place during the *hajj*, or pilgrimage to Mecca, and commemorates Abraham's willingness to sacrifice his son ◊Ishmael at the command of Allah.

Eid ul-Fitr /'i:d əl'fɪtə/ a Muslim festival celebrating the end of Ramadan, the month of fasting.

Eiffel /'aɪfəl/ (Alexandre) Gustave 1832–1923. French engineer who constructed the Eiffel Tower. In 1881 he provided the iron skeleton for the Statue of Liberty, USA.

Eiffel Tower an iron tower 320 m/1,050 ft high, designed by Gustave Eiffel for the Paris Exhibition in 1889. It stands in the Champ de Mars, Paris.

Eiger /'aɪgə/ mountain peak in the Swiss ◊Alps.

eight /eɪt/ *adj.* & *n.* **1.** one more than seven; the symbol for this (8, viii, VIII). **2.** a size etc. denoted by eight. **3.** an eight-oared rowing boat or its crew. —**have one over the eight**, (*slang*) to get slightly drunk. [Old English]

eighteen /eɪ'ti:n/ *adj.* & *n.* **1.** one more than seventeen; the symbol for this (18, xviii, XVIII). **2.** a size etc. denoted by eighteen. —**eighteenth** *adj.* & *n.*

eightfold *adj.* & *adv.* **1.** eight times as much or as many. **2.** consisting of eight parts.

eighth /eɪtθ/ *adj.* next after the seventh. —*n.* one of eight equal parts of a thing. —**eighthly** *adv.*

Eighth Route Army the Chinese **Red Army**, formed

in 1927 when the communists broke away from the ◊Guomindang (nationalists) and established a separate government in Jiangxi in SE China. When Japan invaded China in 1937 the Red Army was recognized as a section of the national forces under the name Eighth Route Army.

eightsome *adj.* for eight people. —**eightsome reel,** a lively Scottish dance for eight people.

eighty /'eɪtɪ/ *adj. & n.* **1.** eight times ten; the symbol for this (80, lxxx, LXXX). **2.** (in *plural*) the numbers, years, or degrees of temperature from 80 to 89. —**eightieth** *adj. & n.*

Eijkman /'aɪkmən/ Christiaan 1858–1930. Dutch bacteriologist. He identified vitamin B_1 deficiency as the cause of the disease beriberi, and pioneered the recognition of vitamins as essential to health. He shared the 1929 Nobel Prize for Physiology and Medicine with Frederick Hopkins.

Eindhoven /'aɪndhəʊvən/ town in North Brabant province, the Netherlands, on the river Dommel; population (1988) 381,000. Industries include electrical and electronic equipment.

Einstein /'aɪnstaɪn/ Albert 1879–1955. German-born US physicist, who formulated the theories of ◊relativity, and worked on radiation physics and thermodynamics. In 1905 he published the special theory of relativity, and in 1915 issued his general theory of relativity. His latest conception of the basic laws governing the universe was outlined in his ◊unified field theory, made public in 1953; his 'relativistic theory of the nonsymmetric field', was completed in 1955. Einstein wrote that this simplified the derivations as well as the form of the field equations and thus made the whole theory more transparent, without changing its content.

einsteinium *n.* a synthesized, radioactive, metallic element of the ◊actinide series, symbol Es, atomic number 99, relative atomic mass 254. It was first identified in 1955 and is now synthesized by bombarding lower-numbered ◊transuranics in particle accelerators. [named after Albert *Einstein*]

Einthoven /'aɪnthəʊvən/ Willem 1860–1927. Dutch physiologist and inventor of the electrocardiograph. He was able to show that certain disorders of the heart alter its electrical activity in characteristic ways.

Eire /'eərə/ Gaelic name for the Republic of ◊Ireland.

Eisai /'eɪsaɪ/ 1141–1215. Japanese Buddhist monk who introduced Zen and tea from China to Japan and founded the ◊Rinzai school.

Eisenach /'aɪzənæx/ industrial town in the state of Thuringia, Germany; products pottery, vehicles, machinery; population (1981) 50,700. Martin ◊Luther made the first translation of the Bible into German in Wartburg Castle and the composer J S Bach was born here.

Eisenhower /'aɪzənhaʊə/ Dwight David ('Ike') 1890–1969. 34th president of the USA 1953–60, a Republican. A general in World War II, he commanded the Allied forces in Italy in 1943, then the Allied invasion of Europe, and from Oct 1944 all the Allied armies in the West. As president he promoted business interests at home and conducted the ◊Cold War abroad. His vice president was Richard Nixon.

Your business is to put me out of business.
Dwight D. Eisenhower
Addressing a graduating class at a university.

Eisenstein /'aɪzənstaɪn/ Sergei Mikhailovich 1898–1948. Latvian film director who pioneered the use of film montage (a technique of deliberately juxtaposing shots to create a particular meaning) as a means of propaganda, as in *The Battleship Potemkin* 1925. His *Alexander Nevsky* 1938 was the first part of an uncompleted trilogy, the second part, *Ivan the Terrible* 1944, being banned in Russia.

eisteddfod /aɪˈsteðvɒd/ *n.* a Welsh gathering, lasting up to a week, of poets and musicians dedicated to the encouragement of music, poetry, and literature, which traditionally dates from pre-Christian times. [Welsh = sitting]

either /'aɪðə, 'iːðə/ *adj. & pron.* one or the other of two; each of two. — *adv. or conj.* **1.** as one possibility; as one choice or alternative, which way you will. **2.** (with negative or interrogative) any more than the other, moreover. [Old English]

ejaculate /iˈdʒækjʊleɪt/ *v.t./i.* **1.** to utter suddenly, to exclaim. **2.** to emit (especially semen) from the body. —**ejaculation** /-ˈleɪʃən/ *n.,* **ejaculatory** *adj.* [from Latin *ejaculari* = shoot out]

eject /iˈdʒekt/ *v.t.* **1.** to expel, to compel to leave; to dispossess (a tenant). **2.** to send out, to emit. —**ejection** *n.,* **ejectment** *n.* [from Latin *jacere* = throw]

ejector *n.* a device for ejecting something. —**ejector seat,** a device for the ejection of the pilot of an aircraft etc. in an emergency. The first seats of 1945 were powered by a compressed spring; later seats used an explosive charge.

Ekaterinburg /ekætəriːnˈbɜːg/ the prerevolutionary name of ◊Sverdlovsk, town in the western USSR, the site of the assassination of Tsar Nikolai II and his family in 1918.

Ekaterinodar /ekætəriːnəʊˈdɑː/ the prerevolutionary name of ◊Krasnodar, industrial town in the USSR.

Ekaterinoslav /ekætəriːnəʊˈslɑːv/ the prerevolutionary name of ◊Dnepropetrovsk, centre of an industrial region in Ukraine, USSR.

eke /iːk/ *v.t.* (with *out*) to make (a living) or support (an existence) with difficulty; to supplement (an income etc.). [Old English; cognate with Latin *augēre* = increase]

Ekman spiral effect an application of the ◊Coriolis effect to ocean currents, whereby the currents flow at an angle to the winds that drive them. [from the Swedish oceanographer Vagn *Ekman* (1874–1954)]

elaborate[1] /iˈlæbərət/ *adj.* minutely worked out; highly developed or complicated. —**elaborately** *adv.* [from Latin *laborare* = work]

elaborate[2] /iˈlæbəreɪt/ *v.t./i.* to work out or explain in detail. —**elaboration** /-ˈreɪʃən/ *n.*

élan /eɪˈlɑ̃/ *n.* vivacity, dash. [French *élancer* = launch]

eland *n.* the largest species of antelope *Taurotragus oryx.* It is pale fawn in colour and stands about 2 m/6 ft high; both sexes have spiral horns about 45 cm/18 in long. It is found in central and southern Africa. [Dutch = elk]

elapse /iˈlæps/ *v.i.* (of time) to pass away. [from Latin *labi* = glide]

elasmobranch /iˈlæzməbræŋk/ *n.* a fish of the class Chondrichthyes (shark, skate etc.). [from Greek *elasmos* = beaten metal and *bragkhia* = gills]

elastic /iˈlæstɪk/ *adj.* **1.** able to resume its normal length, bulk, or shape after being stretched or crushed; springy. **2.** (of the feelings or a person) buoyant; flexible, adaptable. —*n.* elastic cord or fabric, usually woven with strips of rubber. —**elastically** *adv.* [from Greek = propulsive (*elaunō* = drive)]

elasticated /iˈlæstɪkeɪtɪd/ *adj.* (of fabric) made elastic by weaving with rubber thread.

elasticity /iˈlæstɪsɪtɪ/ *n.* **1.** the quality or property of being elastic. **2.** in economics, the measure of response of one variable to changes in another. If the price of butter is reduced by 10% and the demand increases by 20%, the elasticity measure is 2. Such measures are used to test the effects of changes in prices, incomes, and supply and demand. Inelasticity may exist in the demand for necessities

Einstein *Albert Einstein received the Nobel Prize for Physics in 1921.*

such as water, the demand for which will remain the same even if the price changes considerably. **3.** in physics, the ability of a solid to recover its shape once deforming forces (stresses modifying its dimensions or shape) are removed. Metals are elastic up to a certain stress (the elastic limit), beyond which additional stress deforms them permanently as demonstrated by ◊Hooke's law.

elastomer /i'læstəmə/ *n.* a natural or synthetic rubber or rubberlike plastic. —**elastomeric** /-'merik/ *adj.*

Elat /ei'la:t/ or **Eilat** port at the head of the Gulf of Aqaba, Israel's only outlet to the Red Sea; population (1982) 19,500. It was founded in 1948, on the site of the Biblical Elath, and is linked by road with Beersheba. There are copper mines and granite quarries nearby, and a major geophysical observatory opened in 1968 is 16 km/10 mi to the N.

elate /i'leit/ *v.t.* to inspirit, to stimulate; (especially in *past participle*) to make pleased or proud. —**elation** *n.* [from Latin *efferre, elat-* = raise]

E layer (formerly called the Kennelly–Heaviside layer) the lower regions of the ◊ionosphere, which refract radio waves allowing their reception around the surface of the Earth. The E layer approaches the Earth by day and recedes from it at night.

Elba /'elbə/ island in the Mediterranean, 10 km/6 mi off the W coast of Italy; population (1981) 35,000; area 223 sq km/86 sq mi. Iron ore is exported from the capital, Portoferraio, to the Italian mainland, and there is a fishing industry. Elba was the place of exile of ◊Napoleon I 1814–15.

Elbe /elb/ one of the principal rivers of Germany, 1,166 km/725 mi long, rising on the southern slopes of the Riesengebirge, Czechoslovakia, and flowing NW across the German plain to the North Sea.

Elbląg /'elblɔŋk/ Polish port 11 km/7 mi from the mouth of the river Elbląg, which flows into the Vistula Lagoon, an inlet of the Baltic; population (1983) 115,900. It has shipyards, engineering works, and car and tractor factories.

elbow /'elbəu/ *n.* **1.** the joint between the forearm and upper arm; the corresponding part in an animal. **2.** the part of the sleeve of a garment covering this. **3.** an elbow-shaped bend etc. —*v.t.* to thrust or jostle (*oneself* or *one's way in, out,* etc.). —**elbow grease,** (*colloquial*) vigorous polishing; hard work. **elbowroom** *n.* plenty of room to move or work in. **out at (the) elbows,** worn, ragged, poor. [Old English]

Elbruz /el'bru:s/ or **Elbrus** highest mountain (5,642 m/18,517 ft) on the continent of Europe, in the Caucasus, Georgian Republic, USSR.

Elburz /el'buəz/ volcanic mountain range in NW Iran, close to the S shore of the Caspian Sea; the highest point is Mount Damavand at 5,670 m/18,602 ft.

Eldem /el'dem/ Sedad Hakki 1908– . Turkish architect whose work is inspired by the spatial harmony and regular rhythms of the traditional Turkish house. These qualities are reinterpreted in modern forms with great sensitivity to context, as in the Social Security Agency Complex, Zeyrek, Istanbul (1962–64), and the Ataturk Library, Istanbul (1973).

elder[1] *adj.* (of persons, especially related ones) senior, of greater age. —*n.* **1.** (in *plural*) persons of greater age or venerable because of age. **2.** an official in the early Christian church and some modern churches. —**elder statesman,** an influential experienced person (especially a politician) of advanced age. [Old English]

elder[2] *n.* a small tree or shrub of the genus *Sambucus,* family Caprifoliaceae. The common *S. nigra,* found in Europe, N Africa, and W Asia, has pinnate leaves and heavy heads of small, sweet-scented, white flowers in early summer. These are succeeded by clusters of small, black berries. The scarlet-berried *S. racemosa* is found in parts of Europe, Asia, and North America. [Old English]

elderberry *n.* the berry of the elder tree.

elderly *adj.* somewhat old, past middle age.

eldest *adj.* first-born, oldest surviving.

eldorado /eldə'ra:dəu/ *n.* (*plural* **eldorados**) a place of great abundance. [from Spanish *el dorado* = the gilded]

El Dorado /el də'ra:dəu/ a fabled city of gold believed by the Spanish and other Europeans in the 16th century to exist somewhere in the area of the Orinoco and Amazon rivers.

eldritch /'eldritʃ/ *adj.* (*Scottish*) weird; hideous. [perhaps related to *elf*]

Eleanor of Aquitaine /'elinər əv ækwi'tein/ *c.*1122–1204. Queen of France 1137–51 as wife of Louis VII, and of England from 1154 as wife of Henry II. She was the daughter of William X, Duke of Aquitaine, and was married 1137–52 to Louis VII of France, but the marriage was annulled. In 1152 she married Henry of Anjou, who became king of England in 1154. Henry imprisoned her in 1174–89 for supporting their sons, the future Richard I and King John, in revolt against him.

Eleanor of Castile /'elinər əv kæs'ti:l/ *c.*1245–1290. Queen of Edward I of England, the daughter of Ferdinand III of Castile. She married Prince Edward in 1254, and accompanied him on his crusade in 1270. She died at Harby, Nottinghamshire, and Edward erected stone crosses in towns where her body rested on the funeral journey to London. Several **Eleanor Crosses** are still standing, for example at Northampton.

elecampane /elikæm'pein/ *n.* a plant *Inula helenium* with bitter aromatic leaves and root. [corruption of medieval Latin name *Enula campana*]

elect /i'lekt/ *v.t.* to choose by voting; to choose (a thing, *to* do); in theology, of (God) to choose (a person) for salvation. —*adj.* chosen; select, choice; (after a noun) chosen but not yet in office. [from Latin *eligere* = pick out]

election /i'lekʃən/ *n.* **1.** electing, being elected; the process of electing, especially members of Parliament. **2.** in theology, God's choice of some people in preference to others.

electioneer /ilekʃə'niə/ *v.i.* to take part in an election campaign.

elective /i'lektiv/ *adj.* **1.** chosen or appointed by election. **2.** (of a body) having power to elect. **3.** optional, not urgently necessary.

elector /i'lektə/ *n.* **1.** one who has the right to elect or take part in an election. **2.** (*historical*) any of the German princes of the ◊Holy Roman Empire entitled to elect the emperor. The electors were the archbishops of Mainz, Trier, and Cologne, the count palatine of the Rhine, the Duke of Saxony, the Margrave of Brandenburg, and the king of Bohemia (in force to 1806). Their constitutional status was formalized in 1356 in the document known as the **Golden Bull,** which granted them extensive powers within their own domains, to act as judges, issue coins, and impose tolls.

electoral /i'lektərəl/ *adj.* of or ranking as electors. —**electoral college,** a body of people who cast votes for the election of a leader; in the USA, the body of electors, chosen by popular vote in each state, who elect the US president and vice president.

electoral system see ◊vote and ◊proportional representation.

electorate /i'lektərət/ *n.* **1.** the body of electors. **2.** the office or dominions of a German ◊elector.

Electra /i'lektrə/ *n.* in ancient Greek legend, the daughter of Clytemnestra and Agamemnon, king of Mycenae, and sister of Iphigenia and Orestes. Her story is the subject of two plays of the 5th century BC by Sophocles and Euripides.

electric /i'lektrik/ *adj.* **1.** of, worked by, or charged with electricity; producing or capable of generating electricity. **2.** causing sudden and dramatic excitement. —*n.* an electric light, vehicle etc.; (in *plural*) electrical equipment. —**electric blanket,** a blanket heated by an internal electric element. **electric chair,** a chair used to electrocute as a form of execution. **electric eel,** see ◊electric fish. **electric eye,** a photoelectric cell operating a relay when a beam of light is broken. **electric fire,** an appliance giving heat from an electrically charged wire coil or bar. **electric light,** a light produced by electricity in any of various devices (e.g. an incandescent lamp, fluorescent lamp, arc lamp). **electric shock,** the effect of a sudden discharge of electricity through the body of a person etc. [from Latin from Greek *ēlektron* = amber, from the static electricity found in it]

electrical /i'lektrikəl/ *adj.* **1.** of or concerned with electricity. **2.** suddenly exciting. —**electrically** *adv.*

electrical relay an electromagnetic switch.

electric arc a continuous discharge of high electric current between two electrodes, giving out a brilliant light and heat. The phenomenon is exploited in the carbon-arc lamp, once

electricity

coal-fired power station (highly simplified)

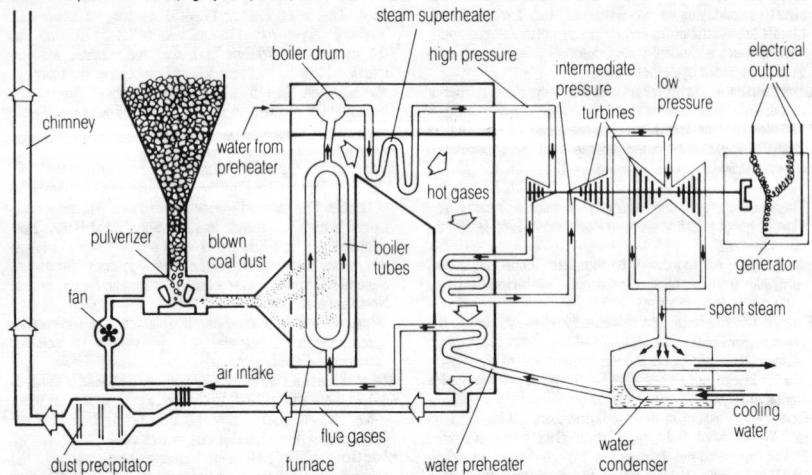

widely used in film projectors. In the electric-arc furnace an arc struck between very large carbon electrodes and the metal charge provides the heating. In arc welding (see ◊weld) an electric arc provides the heat to fuse the metal. The discharges in low-pressure gases, as in neon and sodium lights, can also be broadly considered as electric arcs.

electric charge the property of some bodies that causes them to exert forces on each other. Two bodies, both with positive or both with negative charges, repel each other, whereas bodies with opposite or 'unlike' charges attract each other, since each is in the ◊electric field of the other. In atoms, ◊electrons possess a negative charge, and ◊protons an equal positive charge. The unit of electric charge is the **coulomb** (symbol C).

electric current the rate of flow of electric charge. It is measured in amperes (coulombs per second).

electric energy in physics, the ◊energy of a body that is due to its position in an electric field (generated by an electric charge).

electric field in physics, a region in which an electric charge experiences a force owing to the presence of another electric charge. It is a type of ◊electromagnetic field.

electric fish any of several unrelated fishes that have electricity-producing powers. These include the South American 'electric eel' *Electrophorus electricus* (not a true eel), which has lateral tail muscles modified to form electric organs capable of generating 650 volts; the current passing from tail to head is strong enough to stun another animal. Not all electric fishes produce such strong discharges; most use weak electric fields to navigate and detect nearby objects.

electrician /ɪlekˈtrɪʃən/ *n.* a person whose profession is installing and maintaining electrical equipment.

electricity *n.* all phenomena caused by ◊electric charge, whether static or in motion. Electricity is the most useful and most convenient form of ◊energy, readily convertible into heat and light and used to power machines. It can be generated in one place and distributed anywhere because it readily flows through wires. Electricity is generated at power stations, where a suitable energy source is harnessed to drive the ◊turbines that spin electricity generators. Current energy sources are coal, oil, water power (hydroelectricity), natural gas, and ◊nuclear power. Research is under way to increase the contribution of wind, tidal, and geothermal power. Nuclear fuel has proved a more expensive source of electricity than initially anticipated and worldwide concern over radioactivity may limit its future development.

electric light bulb an ◊incandescent filament lamp, first demonstrated by Joseph Swan in the UK in 1878 and Thomas Edison in the USA in 1879. The present-day

light bulb is a thin glass bulb filled with an inert mixture of nitrogen and argon gas. It contains a filament made of fine tungsten wire. When electricity is passed through the wire, it glows white hot, producing light.

electric power the rate at which an electrical machine uses electrical ◊energy or converts it into other forms of energy, for example, light, heat, mechanical energy. Usually measured in watts (equivalent to joules per second), it is equal to the product of the voltage and the current flowing.

electrify /iˈlektrɪfaɪ/ *v.t.* **1.** to charge with electricity. **2.** to convert (a railway, factory etc.) to the use of electric power. **3.** to excite or startle suddenly. —**electrification** /-fɪˈkeɪʃən/ *n.*

electro- /ɪlektrəʊ-/ in combinations of, by, or caused by electricity.

electrocardiogram /ɪlektrəʊˈkɑːdɪəgræm/ *n.* (ECG or EKG) the record obtained by an electrocardiograph. [from Greek *cardia* = heart and *gramma* = thing written]

electrocardiograph /ɪlektrəʊˈkɑːdɪəgrɑːf/ *n.* an instrument used in the diagnosis of heart disease that receives electrical impulses from the heart muscle and transforms them into a graphic record.

electrochemical series a list of chemical elements arranged in descending order of the ease with which they can lose electrons to form cations (positive ions). An element can be displaced (◊displacement reaction) from a compound by any element above it in the series.

electrochemistry *n.* the branch of science that studies chemical reactions involving electricity. The use of electricity to produce chemical effects, ◊electrolysis, is employed in many industrial processes, such as the manufacture of chlorine and the extraction of aluminium. The use of chemical reactions to produce electricity is the basis of batteries, such as the dry cell and the ◊Leclanché cell.

electroconvulsive therapy (ECT) or **electroshock therapy** a treatment for ◊schizophrenia and ◊depression, given under anaesthesia and with a muscle relaxant. An electric current is passed through the brain to induce alterations in the brain's electrical activity. The treatment can cause distress and loss of concentration and memory, so there is much controversy about its use and effectiveness.

electrocute /iˈlektrəkjuːt/ *v.t.* to kill or execute by electric shock. —**electrocution** /-ˈkjuːʃ(ə)n/ *n.* death caused by electric current. It is used as a method of execution in some US states. The condemned person is strapped into a special chair and an electric shock of 1,800–2,000 volts is administered. See ◊capital punishment.

electrode /iˈlektrəʊd/ *n.* a conductor through which electricity enters or leaves an electrolyte, gas, vacuum etc. [from *electric* and Greek *hodos* = way]

electrodynamics *n.* the branch of physics dealing with the interaction between charged particles and their emission and absorption of electromagnetic ◊radiation. **Quantum**

electrodynamics (QED) combines quantum ◊mechanics and ◊relativity theory, making accurate predictions about subatomic processes involving charged particles such as electrons and protons.

electroencephalogram /ɪlektrəuen'sefələgræm/ *n.* (EEG) a record traced by an electroencephalograph.

electroencephalograph /ɪlektrəuen'sefələgrɑːf/ *n.* an instrument that records the electrical activity of the brain. The pattern of electrical activity revealed by electroencephalography is helpful in the diagnosis of some brain disorders, such as epilepsy. [from Greek *egkephalos* = brain]

electrolyse /i'lektrəlaɪz/ *v.t.* to subject to or treat by electrolysis.

electrolysis /ɪlek'trɒlɪsɪs/ *n.* 1. the production of chemical changes by passing an electric current through a solution (the electrolyte), resulting in the migration of the ions to the electrodes: positive ions (cations) to the negative electrode (cathode) and negative ions (anions) to the positive electrode (anode). 2. the breaking up of tumours, hair roots etc., by electric action. —**electrolytic** /-ə'lɪtɪk/ *adj.* [from Greek *lusis* = loosening]

electrolyte /i'lektrəlaɪt/ *n.* a solution (especially in an electric cell or battery) in which an electric current is made to flow by the movement and discharge of ions in accordance with ◊Faraday's laws of electrolysis; a substance that can dissolve to produce this.

electromagnet *n.* an iron bar with coils of wire around it, which acts as a magnet when an electric current flows through the wire. Electromagnets have many uses: in switches, electric bells, solenoids, and metal-lifting cranes.

electromagnetic /ɪlektrəumæg'netɪk/ *adj.* having both electrical and magnetic properties. —**electromagnetic radiation**, the kind of radiation that includes visible light, radio waves, gamma rays etc., in which electric and magnetic fields vary simultaneously. —**electromagnetically** *adv.*

electromagnetic field in physics, the agency by which a particle with an ◊electric charge experiences a force in a particular region of space. If it does so only when moving, it is in a pure **magnetic field**; if it does so when stationary, it is in an **electric field**. Both can be present simultaneously.

electromagnetic induction in physics, the production of an ◊electromotive force (emf) in a circuit by a change of ◊magnetic flux through the circuit. The emf so produced is known as an induced emf, and any current that may result is known as an induced current. The phenomenon is applied in the induction coil.

electromagnetic spectrum the complete range, over all wavelengths from the lowest to the highest, of ◊electromagnetic waves.

electromagnetic waves oscillating electric and magnetic fields travelling together through space at a speed of nearly 300,000 km/186,000 mi per second. The (limitless) range of possible wavelengths or ◊frequencies of electromagnetic waves, which can be thought of as making up the **electromagnetic spectrum**, includes radio waves, infrared radiation, visible light, ultraviolet radiation, X-rays, and gamma rays.

electromagnetism /ɪlektrəu'mægnətɪzəm/ *n.* magnetic forces produced by electricity; the study of these.

electromotive /ɪlektrəu'məutɪv/ *adj.* producing or tending to produce an electric current.

electromotive force (emf) the energy supplied by a source of electric power in driving a unit charge around an electrical circut. The unit is the ◊volt.

electron /i'lektrɒn/ *n.* a stable elementary particle with an indivisible charge of negative electricity, found in all atoms and acting as a carrier of electricity in solids, with mass of approximately 9×10^{-31} kg.

electronegativity *n.* the ease with which an atom can attract electrons to itself. Electronegative elements attract electrons, so forming negative ions.

electron gun a part in many electronic devices consisting of a series of ◊electrodes, including a cathode for producing an electron beam. It plays an essential role in cathode-ray tubes (television tubes) and ◊electron microscopes.

electronic /ɪlek'trɒnɪk/ *adj.* 1. produced by or involving a flow of electrons. 2. of electrons or electronics. —**electronically** *adv.*

electron microscope

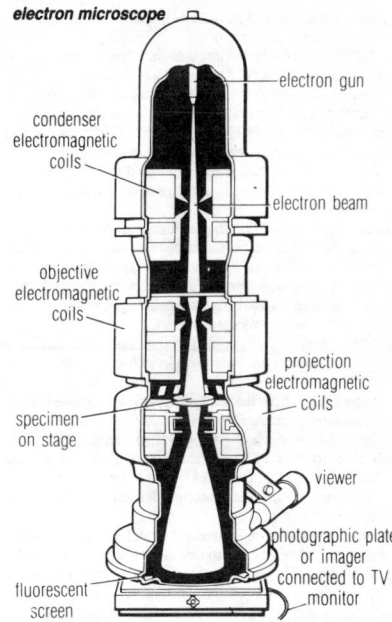

- electron gun
- electron beam
- projection electromagnetic coils
- viewer
- photographic plate or imager connected to TV monitor

condenser electromagnetic coils

objective electromagnetic coils

specimen on stage

fluorescent screen

electronic flash a discharge tube that produces a high-intensity flash of light, used for photography in dim conditions. The tube contains an inert gas such as krypton. The flash lasts only a few thousandths of a second.

electronic mail a ◊telecommunications system that sends messages to people or machines (such as computers) via computers and the telephone network rather than by letter.

electronic music a form of studio-based serial music composed entirely of electronically generated and modified tones, as opposed to **concrete music**, which arranges prerecorded sounds by intuition. The term was later broadened to include prerecorded vocal and instrumental sounds, although always implying a serial basis. ◊Maderna, ◊Stockhausen, and ◊Babbit were among the pioneers of electronic music in the 1950s.

electronics *n.* the branch of science that deals with the emission of ◊electrons from conductors and ◊semiconductors, with the subsequent manipulation of these electrons, and with the construction of electronic devices. The first electronic device was the ◊thermionic valve, or vacuum tube, in which electrons moved in a vacuum, and led to such inventions as ◊radio, ◊television, ◊radar, and the digital ◊computer. Replacement of valves with the comparatively tiny and reliable transistor in 1948 revolutionized electronic development. Modern electronic devices are based on minute integrated circuits and ◊silicon chips, wafer-thin crystal slices holding tens of thousands of electronic components.

electronic tagging or **electronic monitoring** a system for monitoring people on remand (charged with a crime but released on bail). Pioneered in the USA, electronic tagging was tested in the UK in 1989 in Nottingham. Volunteers were fitted with a tamper-proof anklet or 'tag', and their home with a special receiver-dialling unit. If the person moved out of the range of the unit, a signal would be transmitted to a central computer.

electron microscope a type of microscope that produces a magnified image by using a beam of ◊electrons instead of light rays, as in an optical ◊microscope. An **electron lens** is an arrangement of electromagnetic coils that control and focus the beam. Electrons are not visible to the eye, so instead of an eyepiece there is a fluorescent screen or a photographic plate on which the electrons form an image. The wavelength of the electron beam is much shorter than that of light, so much greater magnification and resolution (ability to distinguish detail) can be achieved.

electrons, delocalized ◊electrons that are not associated with individual atoms or identifiable chemical bonds, but are shared collectively by all the constituent atoms or ions of some chemical substances (such as metals, graphite, and ◊aromatic compounds).

electrons, localized a pair of electrons in a single covalent bond located between the nuclei of the two contributing atoms. Such electrons cannot move beyond this area.

electron volt a unit (symbol eV) for measuring the energy of a charged particle (◊ion or ◊electron) in terms of the energy of motion an electron would gain from a potential difference of one volt. Because it is so small, more usual units are mega-(million) and giga-(billion) electron volts (MeV and GeV).

electrophoresis n. the ◊diffusion of charged particles through a fluid under the influence of an electric field. It can be used in the biological sciences to separate ◊molecules of different sizes, which diffuse at different rates. In industry, electrophoresis is used in paint-dipping operations to ensure that paint reaches awkward corners.

electroplate /ɪˈlektrəupleɪt/ v.t. to coat with a thin layer of silver, chromium etc., by electrolysis for decorative and/or protective purposes. The commercial use of this process dates from the 19th century; it is employed in the preparation of printers' blocks, 'master' audio discs, and in many other processes. —n. objects so plated.

electropositivity n. a measure of the ability of elements (mainly metals) that donate electrons to form positive ions. The greater the metallic character, the more electropositive the element.

electroscope n. an instrument for detecting and measuring electricity, especially to indicate the ionization of air by radioactivity. The simple gold-leaf electroscope consists of a vertical conducting (metal) rod ending in a pair of rectangular pieces of gold foil, mounted inside and insulated from an earthed metal case. An electric charge applied to the end of the metal rod makes the gold leaves diverge, because each receives a similar charge (positive or negative) and so they repel each other.

electroshock /ɪlektrəuˈʃɒk/ n. electric shock. —**electroshock therapy,** ◊electroconvulsive therapy.

electrostatics n. the study of electric charges from stationary sources (not currents).

electrotechnology /ɪlektrəutekˈnɒlədʒɪ/ n. the science of the technological application of electricity.

electrotherapy /ɪlektrəuˈθerəpɪ/ n. the treatment of diseases by the use of electricity.

electrovalent bond a chemical ◊bond in which the combining atoms lose or gain electrons to form ions. It is also called an ionic bond.

electrum n. a naturally occurring alloy of gold and silver used by early civilizations to make the first coins, about the 6th century BC.

elegant adj. graceful in appearance or manner; tasteful, refined. —**elegance** n., **elegantly** adv. [from French or Latin, related to *eligere* = pick out]

elegiac adj. used for elegies; mournful. —n. (in *plural*) elegiac verses. —**elegiac couplet** or **metre**, a dactylic ◊hexameter and ◊pentameter. [from French or Latin]

elegy n. a sorrowful or serious poem or song; a lament for the dead; a poem in elegiac metre. [from French or Latin from Greek *elegos* = mournful poem]

element n. 1. a component part, a contributing factor. 2. a substance that cannot be split chemically into simpler substances. The atoms of a particular element all have the same number of protons in their nuclei (their atomic number). Elements are denoted by symbols, usually the first letter or letters of the English or Latinized name (for example, C for carbon, Ca for calcium, Fe for iron, *ferrum*). 3. any of the four substances (earth, water, air, and fire) in ancient and medieval philosophy. 4. a being's natural abode or environment. 5. a wire that gives out heat in an electric cooker, heater, etc. 6. (in *plural*) atmospheric agencies, especially wind and storm. 7. (in *plural*) the bread and wine of the ◊Eucharist. —**in one's element**, in one's accustomed or preferred surroundings, doing what one is skilled at and enjoys. [from Old French from Latin]

elemental adj. 1. of or like the elements or the forces of nature, powerful, tremendous. 2. basic, essential.

elementary adj. 1. dealing with the simplest facts of a subject, rudimentary. 2. in chemistry, not analysable. —**elementarily** adv., **elementariness** n.

elementary particle a subatomic particle that is not made up of smaller particles, and so can be considered

one of the fundamental units of matter. There are three groups of elementary particles: ◊quarks, ◊leptons, and gauge ◊bosons.

elephant n. a mammal of one of the two surviving species of the order Proboscidea: the **Asian elephant** *Elephas maximus* and the **African elephant** *Loxodonta africana*. Elephants can grow to 4 m/32 ft and weigh up to 8 tonnes; they have a thick, grey, wrinkled skin, a large head, a long trunk used to obtain food and water, and upper incisors or tusks, which grow to a considerable length. The African elephant has very large ears and a flattened forehead, and the Asian species has smaller ears and a convex forehead. In India, Myanmar (formerly Burma), and Thailand, Asiatic elephants are widely used for transport and logging. [from Old French from Latin from Greek *elephas*, originally = ivory]

Elephanta /eliˈfæntə/ island in Bombay harbour, Maharashtra, India, some 8 km/5 mi from Bombay. The Temple Caves (6th century), cut out of solid rock, have sculptures of many Hindu deities executed 450–740. There was formerly a large stone elephant near the island's landing place.

elephant bird another name for extinct members of the genus ◊Aepyornis.

elephantiasis n. in the human body, a condition of local enlargement and deformity, most often of a leg, the scrotum, a labium of the vulva, or a breast, caused by the blocking of lymph channels. The commonest form of elephantiasis is the tropical variety (filariasis) caused by infestation by parasitic roundworms (filaria); the enlargement is due to chronic blocking of the lymph channels by the worms and consequent overgrowth of the skin and tissues. [Latin from Greek]

elephantine adj. 1. of elephants. 2. huge, clumsy, unwieldy.

Eleusinian Mysteries /eljuˈsɪnɪən/ ceremonies held in ancient times in honour of the Greek deities ◊Demeter, ◊Persephone, and ◊Dionysus, celebrated at Eleusis, Greece. Worshippers saw visions in the darkened temple, supposedly connected with the underworld.

elevate v.t. to raise or lift up; to enhance morally or intellectually; (in *past participle*) exalted in rank or status. [from Latin *elevare* = lift]

elevation n. 1. elevating, being elevated. 2. the height above a given (especially sea) level; a high position; the angle (especially of a gun or the direction of a heavenly body) with the horizontal. 3. a flat drawing showing one side of a building.

elevation of boiling point a raising of the boiling point of a liquid above that of the pure solvent, caused by a substance being dissolved in it. The phenomenon is observed when salt is added to boiling water; the water ceases to boil because its boiling point has been elevated.

elevator n. 1. a person or thing that elevates; a hoisting machine. 2. the movable part of a tailplane, used for changing an aircraft's attitude to its flight path. 3. (*US*) ◊lift.

eleven adj. & n. 1. one more than ten; the symbol for this (11, xi, XI). 2. a size etc. denoted by eleven. 3. a team of eleven players at cricket, football, etc. —**eleven-plus** n. an examination taken in some districts of England and Wales at the age 11–12 before entering secondary school. [Old English, perhaps = one left over (ten)]

elevenfold adj. & adv. eleven times as much or as many; consisting of 11 parts.

elevenses n. light refreshment taken at about 11 a.m.

eleventh adj. next after the tenth. —n. one of 11 equal parts. —**eleventh hour**, the last possible moment.

elf n. (*plural* **elves** /elvz/) a supernatural being in Germanic mythology; a dwarf, a little creature. —**elfish** adj. [Old English]

El Faiyûm /el faɪˈjuːm/ city in N Egypt, 90 km/56 mi SW of Cairo; population (1985) 218,500. It was a centre of prehistoric culture; the crocodile god Sobek was worshipped nearby, and realistic mummy portraits dating from the 1st–4th centuries AD were found in the area.

El Ferrol /el feˈrɒl/ full name *El Ferrol del Caudillo* city and port in La Coruña province, on the NW coast of Spain; population (1986) 88,000. It is a naval base and has

Eliot Mary Ann Evans, otherwise known as the English novelist George Eliot.

a deep, sheltered harbour and shipbuilding industries. It is the birthplace of Francisco Franco.

elfin *adj.* of elves, elflike.

Elgar /'elgɑː/ Edward (William) 1857–1934. English composer. His *Enigma Variations* appeared in 1899, and although his celebrated choral work, the oratorio setting of Newman's *The Dream of Gerontius,* was initially a failure, it was well received at Düsseldorf in 1902. Many of his earlier works were then performed, including the *Pomp and Circumstance* marches.

Elgin marbles /'elgɪn/ a collection of ancient Greek sculptures mainly from the Parthenon at Athens, assembled by the 7th Earl of Elgin. Sent to England in 1812, and bought for the nation in 1816 for ˆ5,000, they are now in the British Museum. Greece has asked for them to be returned to Athens.

Eli /'iːlaɪ/ in the Old Testament, a priest and childhood teacher of the first prophet, Samuel.

elicit *v.t.* to draw out (a latent thing, especially a response etc.). [from Latin *lacere* = entice]

elide *v.t.* to omit (a vowel or syllable) in pronunciation. [from Latin *elidere* = crush out]

eligible *adj.* fit or entitled to be chosen (*for* an office, award etc.); desirable or suitable, especially for marriage. —**eligibility** /-'bɪltɪ/ *n.* [from French from Latin *eligere* = pick out]

Elijah /ɪ'laɪdʒə/ *c.* mid-9th century BC. In the Old Testament, a Hebrew prophet during the reigns of the Israelite kings Ahab and Ahaziah. He came from Gilead. He defeated the prophets of ◊Baal, and was said to have been carried up to heaven in a fiery chariot in a whirlwind. In Jewish belief, Elijah will return to Earth to herald the coming of the Messiah.

eliminate *v.i.* to remove, to get rid of; to exclude from consideration; to exclude from a further stage of competition through defeat etc. —**elimination** /-'neɪʃən/ *n.*, ·**eliminator** *n.* [from Latin *eliminare* (*limen* = threshold)]

Eliot /'eliət/ George. Pen name of Mary Ann Evans 1819–1880. English novelist who portrayed Victorian society, including its intellectual hypocrisy, with realism and irony. In 1857 she published the story 'Amos Barton', the first of the *Scenes of Clerical Life.* This was followed by the novels *Adam Bede* 1859, *The Mill on the Floss* 1860, and *Silas Marner* 1861. *Middlemarch* 1872 is now considered one of the greatest novels of the 19th century. Her final book *Daniel Deronda* 1876 was concerned with anti-Semitism. She also wrote poetry.

Eliot John 1592–1632. English politician, born in Cornwall. He became a member of Parliament in 1614, and with the Earl of Buckingham's patronage was made a vice-admiral in 1619. In 1626 he was imprisoned in the Tower of London for demanding Buckingham's impeachment. In 1628 he was a formidable supporter of the ◊Petition of Right opposing Charles I, and with other parliamentary leaders was again imprisoned in the Tower of London in 1629, where he died.

Eliot T(homas) S(tearns) 1888–1965. US poet, playwright, and critic, who lived in London from 1915. His first volume of poetry, *Prufrock and Other Observations* 1917, introduced new verse forms and rhythms; futher collections include *The Waste Land* 1922, *The Hollow Men* 1925, and *Old Possum's Book of Practical Cats* 1939 (the ◊Lloyd-Webber musical *Cats* was based on this). *Four Quartets* 1943 revealed his religious vision. His plays include *Murder in the Cathedral* 1935 and *The Cocktail Party* 1949. His critical works include *The Sacred Wood* 1920. He was awarded the Nobel Prize for Literature in 1948.

Elisabethville /i'lɪzəbəθvɪl/ the former name of ◊Lubumbashi, town in Zaïre.

Elisha /i'laɪʃə/ mid-9th century BC. In the Old Testament, a Hebrew prophet, successor to Elijah.

elision *n.* the omission of a vowel or syllable in pronouncing (as in *I'm, let's; e'en*) or of a passage in a book etc.

élite *n.* **1.** a select group or class; *the* best (of a group). An élite may be cultural, educational, religious, political, or social. **2.** a size of letters in typewriting (12 per inch). [from French]

élitism *n.* the recourse to or advocacy of leadership or dominance by a select group. —**élitist** *n.*

elixir *n.* **1.** an alchemist's preparation designed to change metal into gold or (*elixir of life*) to prolong life indefinitely; a remedy for all ills. **2.** an aromatic medicinal drug. [from Latin from Arabic, probably from Greek *xērion* = powder for wounds]

Elizabeth /i'lɪzəbəθ/ city in NE New Jersey, USA; population (1980) 106,000. Established 1664, it was the first English settlement in New Jersey. It has automobile, sewing machine, and tool factories; oil refineries, and chemical works.

Elizabeth in the New Testament, mother of John the Baptist. She was a cousin of Jesus' mother Mary, who came to see her shortly after the Annunciation; on this visit (called the Visitation), Mary sang the hymn of praise later to be known as 'the Magnificat'.

Elizabeth the **Queen Mother** 1900– . Wife of King George VI of England. She was born Lady Elizabeth Angela Marguerite Bowes-Lyon, and on 26 April 1923 she married Albert, Duke of York. Their children are Queen Elizabeth II and Princess Margaret.

Elizabeth two queens of England or the UK:

Elizabeth I 1533–1603. Queen of England 1558–1603, the daughter of Henry VIII and Anne Boleyn. Through her Religious Settlement of 1559 she enforced the Protestant religion by law and she had ◊Mary, Queen of Scots, executed in 1587. Her conflict with Catholic Spain led to the defeat of the ◊Spanish Armada in 1588. The Elizabethan age was expansionist in commerce and geographical exploration, and arts and literature flourished. The rulers of many European states made unsuccessful bids to marry Elizabeth, and she used these bids to strengthen her power. She was succeeded by James I.

Anger makes dull men witty, but it keeps them poor.
Queen Elizabeth I

Elizabeth II 1926– . Queen of Great Britain and Northern Ireland from 1952, the elder daughter of George VI. She married her third cousin, Philip, the Duke of Edinburgh, in 1947. They have four children: Charles, Anne, Andrew, and Edward.

Elizabeth 1709–1762. Empress of Russia from 1741, daughter of Peter the Great. She carried through a palace revolution and supplanted her cousin, the infant Ivan VI (1730–1764), on the throne. She continued the policy of westernization begun by Peter and allied herself with Austria against Prussia.

Elizabethan *adj.* belonging to or characteristic of the reign of Queen Elizabeth I (1558–1603). —*n.* a person of this period.

Elizavetpol /ɪlɪzə'vetpɒl/ the former name of ◊Kirovabad, industrial town in Azerbaijan Republic, USSR.

elk *n.* a large deer *Alces alces* inhabiting N Europe, Asia, Scandinavia, and North America, where it is known as the **moose**. It is brown in colour, stands about 2 m/6 ft at the shoulders, has very large palmate antlers, a fleshy muzzle, short neck, and long legs. It feeds on leaves and shoots. In North America, the ◊wapiti is called an elk. [probably Old English]

ell *n.* (*historical*) a measure of length, equal to 45 inches. [Old English = forearm (cognate with Latin *ulna*)]

Ellesmere Island /'elzmɪə/ second largest island of the Canadian Arctic archipelago, Northwest Territories; area 212,687 sq km/82,097 sq mi. It is for the most part barren or glacier-covered.

Ellesmere Port oil port and industrial town in Cheshire, England, on the river Mersey and the Manchester Ship Canal; population (1983) 81,900.

Ellice Islands /'elɪs/ the former name of ◊Tuvalu, group of islands in the W Pacific Ocean.

Ellington /'elɪŋtən/ Duke (Edward Kennedy) 1899–1974. US pianist, who had an outstanding career as a composer and arranger of jazz. He wrote numerous pieces for his own jazz orchestra, accentuating the strengths of individual virtuoso instrumentalists, and became one of the leading figures in jazz over a 55-year span. Some of his most popular compositions include 'Mood Indigo', 'Sophisticated Lady', 'Solitude', and 'Black and Tan Fantasy'. He was one of the founders of big band jazz.

ellipse /ɪ'lɪps/ *n.* a regular oval. An ellipse is one of a series of curves known as ◊conic sections. A slice across a cone that is not made parallel to, or does not pass through, the base will produce an ellipse. [from French from Latin from Greek *elleipsis* = deficit]

ellipsis *n.* (*plural* **ellipses** /-siːz/) the omission of words needed to complete a construction or sense; a set of three dots etc. indicating such an omission.

ellipsoid /ɪ'lɪpsɔɪd/ *n.* a solid of which all plane sections through one axis are ellipses and all other plane sections are ellipses or circles.

elliptical /ɪ'lɪptɪk(ə)l/ *adj.* 1. of or in the form of an ellipse. 2. of or containing an ellipsis. —**elliptically** *adv.*

Ellis /'elɪs/ (Henry) Havelock 1859–1939. English psychologist and writer of many works on the psychology of sex, including *Studies in the Psychology of Sex* (seven volumes) 1898–1928.

Ellis Island island in New York Harbour, USA; area 11 hectares/27 acres; former reception centre for steerage-class immigrants during the immigration waves between 1892–1943. It was later used as a detention centre for nonresidents without documentation, or for those who were being deported. No longer used, it was declared a National Historic Site in 1964 by President Lyndon Johnson.

Ellison /'elɪsən/ Ralph 1914– . US novelist. His *Invisible Man* 1952 portrays with humour and energy the plight of a black man whom postwar American society cannot acknowledge; it is regarded as one of the most impressive novels published in the USA in the 1950s.

elm *n.* any tree of the family Ulmaceae, found in temperate regions of the northern hemisphere and in mountainous parts of the tropics. The common English elm *Ulmus procera* is widely distributed throughout Europe. It reaches 35 m/115 ft, and has tufts of small, purplish-brown flowers, which appear before the rough, serrated leaves. See also ◊Dutch elm disease. [Old English]

El Niño /el 'niːnjəʊ/ a warm ocean surge of the ◊Peru (Humboldt) Current, so called because it tends to occur at Christmas, recurring about every ten years or so in the E Pacific off South America. [Spanish = the child]

El Obeid /el əʊ'beɪd/ capital of Kordofan province, Sudan; population (1984) 140,025. It is linked by rail with Khartoum, and is a market for cattle, gum arabic, and durra (Indian millet).

elocution *n.* the art or style of expressive speaking. —**elocutionary** *adj.*, **elocutionist** *n.* [from Latin]

elongate /'iːlɒŋɡeɪt/ *v.t.* to lengthen, to extend, to draw out. [from Latin *elongare*]

elongation /'iːlɒŋɡeɪʃən/ *n.* 1. the act or process of elongating; something that is elongated. 2. in astronomy, the angular distance between either a planet or the Moon and the Sun. This angle is 0° at either inferior ◊conjunction or superior conjunction. ◊Quadrature occurs when the elongation angle is 90° and ◊opposition (opposite the Sun in the sky) when the angle is 180°.

elope *v.i.* to run away secretly with a lover, especially in order to get married. —**elopement** *n.* [from Anglo-French]

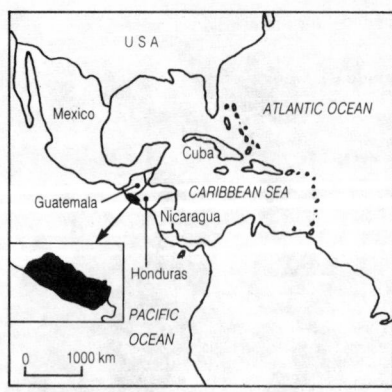

El Salvador

eloquence *n.* the fluent and effective use of language. [from Old French from Latin *loqui* = speak]

eloquent *adj.* having eloquence; expressive (*of*). —**eloquently** *adv.*

El Paso /el 'pæsəʊ/ city in Texas, USA, situated at the base of the Franklin mountains, on the Rio Grande, opposite the Mexican city of Ciudad Juárez; population (1980) 425,200. It is the centre of an agricultural and cattle-raising area, and there are electronics, food-processing, packing, and leather industries, as well as oil refineries and industries based on local iron and copper mines.

El Salvador /el 'sælvədɔː/ Republic of; country in Central America, bounded N and E by Honduras, S and SW by the Pacific Ocean, and NW by Guatemala; **area** 21,393 sq km/8,258 sq mi; **capital** San Salvador; **physical** narrow coastal plan, rising to mountains in N with central plateau; **head of state and government** Alfredo Cristiani from 1989; **political system** emergent democracy; **exports** coffee, cotton, sugar; **population** (1989 est) 5,900,000 (mainly of mixed Spanish and Indian ancestry; 10% Indian); **language** Spanish and Nahua; **recent history** independence was achieved from Spain in 1821. A right-wing government came into power in 1961, resulting in left-wing guerrilla activities. Following a coup, pacifist Archbishop Osca Romero was overthrown and replaced with a military–civilian junta. His assassination in 1980 brought the country to the verge of civil war. Jose Duarte became president in the same year, and a new constitution was written in 1983. In 1989 Alfredo Cristiani was elected; guerrilla activities are still continuing.

else *adv.* (with indefinite or interrogative pronoun) besides; instead; otherwise, if not. —**or else**, (*colloquial*) expressing threat or warning. [Old English, related to Latin *alius* = other]

elsewhere *adv.* in or to some other place.

Elsheimer /'elshaɪmə/ Adam 1578–1610. German painter and etcher, active in Rome from 1600. His small paintings, nearly all on copper, depict landscapes darkened by storm or night, with figures picked out by beams of light, as in *The Rest on the Flight into Egypt* 1609 (Alte Pinakothek, Munich).

Elsinore /'elsɪnɔː/ another form of ◊Helsingør, port on the NE coast of Denmark.

Elton /'eltən/ Charles 1900– . British ecologist, a pioneer of the study of animal and plant forms in their natural environments, and of animal behaviour as part of the complex pattern of life. Elton published *Animal Ecology and Evolution* 1930 and *The Pattern of Animal Communities* 1966.

Eluard /eɪlu'aː/ Paul. Pen name of Eugène Grindel 1895–1952. French poet, born in Paris. He expressed the suffering of poverty in his verse, and was a leader of the Surrealists. He fought in World War I, which inspired his *Poèmes pour la paix/Poems for Peace* 1918, and was a member of the Resistance in World War II. His books include *Poésie et vérité/Poetry and Truth* 1942 and *Au Rendezvous allemand/To the German Rendezvous* 1944.

elucidate *v.t.* to throw light on, to explain. —**elucidation** /-'deɪʃən/ *n.*, **elucidatory** *adj.* [from Latin *lucidus* = bright]

elude *v.t.* to escape adroitly from (danger etc.); to avoid compliance with or fulfilment of (a law, obligation etc.); to baffle (a person or the memory etc.). —**elusion** *n.*, **elusive** *adj.* [from Latin *ludere* = play]

elver *n.* a young eel. [variant of *eelfare*, a brood of young eels]

elves plural of elf.

elvish variant of elfish.

Ely city in Cambridgeshire, England, on the Great Ouse River 24 km/15 mi NE of Cambridge; population (1983) 11,030. It has sugar beet, paper, and engineering factories.

Elysée Palace /eɪliːzeɪ/ (French *Palais de l'Elysée*) a building in Paris erected in 1718 for Louis d'Auvergne, Count of Evreux. It was later the home of Mme de Pompadour, Napoleon I, and Napoleon III, and became the official residence of the presidents of France in 1870.

Elysium /ɪ'lɪʒɪəm/1. or **Elysian Fields** in Greek mythology, the abode of the blessed after death. 2. a place of ideal happiness. —**Elysian** *adj.* [from Latin from Greek *Elusion* (*pedion* = plain)]

Elytis /'eliːtiːs/ Odysseus. Pen name of Odysseus Alepoudelis 1911– . Greek poet, born in Crete. His work celebrates the importance of the people's attempts to shape an individual existence in freedom. His major work *To Axion Esti/Worthy It Is* 1959 is a lyric cycle, parts of which have been set to music by ◊Theodorakis. He was awarded the Nobel Prize for Literature in 1979.

Elzevir /'elzəviə/ Louis 1540–1617. Founder of the Dutch printing house Elzevir in the 17th century. Among the firm's publications were editions of Latin, Greek, and Hebrew works, as well as French and Italian classics.

em *n.* in printing, a unit of measurement equal to the space occupied by m. [name of letter *M*]

em- prefix, see ◊en-.

'em *pron.* (*colloquial*) them.

emaciate *v.t.* to make thin or feeble. —**emaciation** /-'eɪʃən/ *n.* [from Latin *emaciare* (*macies* = leanness)]

emanate *v.t./i.* to originate or proceed (*from* a source, person etc.); to cause to do this. —**emanation** /-'neɪʃən/ *n.* [from Latin *manare* = flow]

emancipate *v.t.* to free from slavery or from (especially political or social) restraint. —**emancipation** /-'peɪʃən/ *n.*, **emancipator** *n.*, **emancipatory** *adj.* [from Latin *mancipare* = transfer ownership of]

Emancipation Proclamation, The in US history, President Lincoln's Civil War announcement, on 22 Sept 1862, stating that from the beginning of 1863 all black slaves in states still engaged in rebellion against the federal government would be emancipated. Slaves in border states still remaining loyal to the Union were excluded.

emancipist /ɪ'mænsɪpɪst/ *n.* in Australian history, an ex-convict who had served his term.

emasculate /ɪ'mæskjʊleɪt/ *v.t.* 1. to castrate. 2. to deprive of strength or force. —/-t/ *adj.* 1. castrated; effeminate. 2. deprived of strength or force. —**emasculation** /-'leɪʃən/ *n.*, **emasculatory** *adj* [from Latin *masculus*, diminutive of *mas* = male]

embalm *v.t.* 1. to preserve (a corpse) from decay. 2. to preserve from decay or oblivion. 3. to make fragrant. —**embalmment** *n.* [from Old French]

embankment *n.* an earth or stone bank keeping back water or carrying a road, railway etc.

embargo *n.* (*plural* **embargoes**) an order forbidding foreign ships to enter, or any ships to leave, a country's ports; a prohibition or restraint, especially of commerce. —*v.t.* to place under an embargo. [Spanish, from *embargar* = arrest]

embark *v.t./i.* 1. to put or go on board ship (*for* a destination). 2. to engage *in* or *on* an enterprise. [from French]

embarkation *n.* embarking on a ship.

embarrass *v.t.* 1. to make (a person) feel awkward or ashamed. 2. to encumber; to perplex; to complicate (a question etc.). —**embarrassment** *n.* [from French from Spanish from Italian *imbarrare* = bar in]

embassy *n.* the offices or residence of an ambassador; an ambassador and his or her staff; a deputation to a foreign government. [from Old French]

embattled *adj.* 1. prepared or arrayed for battle. 2. fortified with battlements.

embed *v.t.* (**-dd-**) to fix firmly in a surrounding mass.

embellish *v.t.* to beautify, to adorn; to enhance (a narrative) with fictitious additions. —**embellishment** *n.* [from Old French *embellir* (*bel* = handsome)]

ember *n.* (usually in *plural*) a small piece of live coal etc. in a dying fire. [Old English]

ember days a group of three days in each season, observed as days of fasting and prayer in some churches. [Old English, perhaps from *ymbryne* = period]

embezzle *v.t.* to divert (money etc.) fraudulently to one's own use. —**embezzlement** *n.* in law, theft by an employee of property entrusted to him or her by an employer. **embezzler** *n.* [from Anglo-French *besiler*, Old French *besillier* = maltreat, ravage]

embitter *v.t.* to arouse bitter feelings in; to make bitter. —**embitterment** *n.*

emblazon *v.t.* to blazon. —**emblazonment** *n.*

emblem *n.* a symbol; a heraldic or representative device. —**emblematic** /-'mætik/ *adj.* [from Latin *emblēma* = inlaid work from Greek *emballō* = insert]

embody *v.t.* 1. to make (an idea etc.) actual or discernible; (of a thing) to be an expression of. 2. to include, to comprise. —**embodiment** *n.*

embolden *v.t.* to make bold, to encourage.

embolism *n.* an obstruction of a blood vessel by a clot of blood, an air bubble etc. [from Latin from Greek *emballō* = insert]

embolus *n.* (*plural* **emboli** /-laɪ/) a thing causing an embolism.

emboss *v.t.* to carve or decorate with a design in relief. —**embossment** *n.* [from Old French]

embrace *v.t.* 1. to hold closely in the arms, especially as a sign of affection; (of two people) to embrace each other; to clasp, to enclose. 2. to accept, to adopt (an idea, belief, etc.). 3. to take in with the eye or mind. —*n.* holding in the arms, a clasp. [from Old French from Latin *bracchium* = arm]

embrasure *n.* 1. the bevelling of a wall at the sides of a window 2. an opening between the merlons of an embattled parapet. [from French *embraser* = splay]

embrocation *n.* a liquid for rubbing on the body to relieve muscular pain. [from French or Latin from Greek *embrokhē* = lotion]

embroider *v.t.* 1. to decorate (cloth etc.) with needlework. 2. to embellish (a narrative). [from Anglo-French *enbrouder* from Germanic]

embroidery *n.* 1. embroidering; embroidered work. It includes ◊broderie anglaise, ◊gros point, and ◊petit point; all of which have been used for the adornment of costumes, gloves, book covers, curtains, and ecclesiastical vestments. 2. elaboration, as of a narrative by inessential detail.

embroil *v.t.* 1. to bring (affairs etc.) into confusion. 2. to involve (a person) in hostility (*with* another). —**embroilment** *n.* [from French *embrouiller* = entangle, mix]

embryo *n.* (*plural* **embryos**) an unborn or unhatched offspring; a human offspring in the first eight weeks from conception; a rudimentary plant in a seed; a thing in a rudimentary stage. —*adj.* undeveloped, immature. —**in embryo**, undeveloped. —**embryonic** /-'ɒnɪk/ *adj.* [Latin from Greek *bruō* = swell, grow]

embryology *n.* the science of the embryo. It is mainly concerned with the changes in cell organization in the embryo and the way in which these lead to the structures and organs of the adult (the process of ◊differentiation).

embryo research the study of human embryos at an early stage, in order to detect hereditary disease and genetic defects, and to investigate the problems of subfertility and infertility. The UK Medical Research Council laid down in 1982 that experiments on human embryos were acceptable for approved research purposes, provided both donors agreed. There must also be no intent to transfer the embryo to the uterus, or to culture it beyond the stage when implantation was possible. The Warnock Report 1984 proposed to limit experiment to up to 14 days after fertilization (the point at which it becomes possible to determine whether the embryo will become a single individual or a multiple birth). It also recommended strict controls on AID (artificial insemination by donor); IVF (*in vitro* fertilization), fertilization outside the body ('test-tube baby') when either the sperm or the egg (or both) do not necessarily come from the couple involved as eventual parents; and condemned surrogate motherhood, or 'womb leasing', in which a woman is artificially inseminated and bears a child for another couple. In 1990 the UK Parliament voted to continue experiments on embryos up to 14 days old.

embryo sac a large cell within the ovule of flowering plants that represents the female ◊gametophyte when fully developed. It typically contains eight nuclei. Fertilization occurs when one of these nuclei, the egg nucleus, fuses with a male ◊gamete.

Emden /'emdən/ port in Lower Saxony, Germany, at the mouth of the river Ems; population (1984) 51,000. It is a fishing port and an export outlet for the river ◊Ruhr, with which it is connected by the Dortmund–Ems canal. There are oil refineries here.

emend v.t. to correct or remove errors from (a text etc.), to seek to do this. —**emendation** /iːmen'deɪʃən/ n. [from Latin *menda* = fault]

emerald n. a clear, green gemstone variety of the mineral ◊beryl; the colour of this. —**Emerald Isle**, Ireland. [from Old French from Latin *smaragdus* from Greek]

emerge v.i. to come up or out into view; to become known or recognized, (of facts) to be revealed; (of a difficulty) to occur. – **emergence** n., **emergent** adj. [from Latin *emergere* (*mergere* = plunge)]

emergency n. a sudden state of danger, conflict etc., requiring immediate action; a condition needing immediate treatment, a patient with this. —*adj.* for use in an emergency.

emergent properties the features of a system that are due to the way in which its components are structured in relation to each other, rather than to the individual properties of those components. Thus the distinctive characteristics of chemical ◊compounds are emergent properties of the way in which the constituent elements are organized, and cannot be explained by the particular properties of those elements taken in isolation. In biology, ◊ecosystem stability is an emergent property of the interaction between the constituent species, and not a property of the species.

emeritus adj. retired and retaining a title as an honour. [Latin = that has earned his or her discharge by service]

Emerson /'eməsən/ Ralph Waldo 1803–1882. US philosopher, essayist, and poet. He settled in Concord, Massachusetts, which he made a centre of ◊transcendentalism, and wrote *Nature* 1836, which states the movement's main principles emphasizing the value of self-reliance and the God-like nature of human souls. His two volumes of *Essays* (1841, 1844) made his reputation. 'Self-Reliance' and 'Compensation' are among the best known of his essays.

emery /'eməri/ n. a greyish-black, opaque, metamorphic rock consisting of ◊corundum and magnetite, together with other minerals such as hematite. It is used for polishing metal etc. —**emery board**, emery-coated nailfile. [from French from Italian from Greek *smēris* = polishing powder]

Emery /'eməri/ Walter Bryan 1903–1971. British archaeologist, who in 1929–34 in ◊Nubia, N Africa, excavated the barrows at Ballana and Qustol, rich royal tombs of the mysterious X-group people (3rd to 6th centuries AD). He also surveyed the whole region 1963–64 before it was flooded as a result of the building of the Aswan High Dam.

emetic adj. that causes vomiting. —n. an emetic medicine. [from Greek *emeō* = vomit]

emf in physics, abbreviation of ◊electromotive force.

emigrant n. one who emigrates. —adj. emigrating.

emigrate v.i. to leave one's own country to settle in another. —**emigration** /-'greɪʃən/ n. [from Latin *emigrare*]

émigré n. an emigrant, especially a political exile.

Emi Koussi /emi'kuːsi/ highest point of the Tibesti massif in N Chad, rising to 3,415 m/11,204 ft.

Emilia-Romagna /e'miːljə rəu'mænjə/ region of N central Italy including much of the Po valley; area 22,100 sq km/8,531 sq mi; population (1988) 3,924,000. The capital is Bologna; other towns include Reggio, Rimini, Parma, Ferrara, and Ravenna. Agricultural produce includes fruit, wine, sugar beet, beef, and dairy products; oil and natural-gas resources have been developed in the Po valley.

eminence n. 1. distinction, recognized superiority. 2. a piece of rising ground. —**His, Your,** etc., **Eminence,**

Emerson *Ralph Waldo Emerson, poet and essayist. His lucid style and clarity of thought made his writings eminently quotable, although he claimed to hate quotations.*

a title used in addressing or referring to a cardinal. [from Latin]

éminence grise /'eminɒns 'griːz/ one who exercises power or influence without holding office. The nickname was originally applied (because of his grey cloak) to the French monk François Leclerc du Tremblay (1577–1638), also known as Père Joseph, who in 1612 became the close friend and behind-the-scenes adviser of Cardinal Richelieu. [French = grey eminence]

eminent adj. distinguished, notable, outstanding. —**eminently** adv. [from Latin, originally = jutting out]

eminent domain in the USA, the right of federal and state government and other authorized bodies to compulsorily purchase land that is needed for public purposes. The owner is entitled to receive a fair price for the land. In Britain, ◊compulsory purchase gives similar powers.

Emin Pasha /e'miːn/ Mehmed. Adopted name of Eduard Schnitzer 1849–1892. German explorer, doctor, and linguist. Appointed by General Gordon as chief medical officer and then governor of the Equatorial province of S Sudan, he carried out extensive research in anthropology, botany, zoology, and meteorology.

emir n. the title of various Muslim rulers. [from French]

emirate n. the rank, domain, or reign of an emir.

emissary n. a person sent on a special diplomatic mission. [from Latin = scout, spy]

emit v.t. (-tt-) to send out (light, heat etc.); to utter (a cry etc.). —**emission** n., **emissive** adj. [from Latin *mittere* = send]

Emmental /'eməntɑːl/ district in the valley of the Emme river, Berne, Switzerland, where a hard cheese of the same name has been made since the mid-15th century.

Emmet /'emɪt/ Robert 1778–1803. Irish nationalist leader. In 1803 he led an unsuccessful revolt in Dublin against British rule and was captured, tried, and hanged. His youth and courage made him an Irish hero.

emollient adj. softening or soothing the skin. —n. an emollient substance. [from Latin *mollis* = soft]

emolument n. a profit from employment, a salary. [from Old French or Latin, probably originally = payment for corn grinding (*molere* = grind)]

emote v.i. to act with a show of emotion.

emotion n. a strong mental or instinctive feeling such as love or fear. [from French *émouvoir* = excite]

emotional adj. of or expressing emotion(s); liable to excessive emotion. —**emotionalism** n., **emotionally** adv.

emotive *adj.* of or tending to excite emotion; arousing feeling. [from Latin *movere* = move]

emotivism *n.* a philosophical position in the theory of ethics. Emotivists deny that moral judgements can be true or false, maintaining that they merely express an attitude or an emotional response.

empanel *v.t.* (-ll-) to enter (a jury) on a panel. [from Anglo-French]

empathize *v.t./i.* to treat with empathy; to use empathy.

empathy *n.* the power of identifying oneself mentally with (and so fully comprehending) a person or object of contemplation. —**empathic** /-'pæθɪk/ *adj.* [translation of German *einfühlung* (*ein* = in, *fühlung* = feeling), after Greek *empatheia* (*pathos* = feeling)]

Empedocles /em'pedəkli:z/ *c.* 490–430 BC. Greek philosopher and scientist. He lived at Acragas (Agrigentum) in Sicily, and proposed that the universe is composed of four elements, fire, air, earth, and water, which through the action of love and discord are eternally constructed, destroyed, and constructed anew. According to tradition, he committed suicide by throwing himself into the crater of Mount Etna.

emperor *n.* the sovereign of an empire. —**emperor penguin**, the largest known species of penguin *Aptenodytes forsteri.* [from Old French from Latin *imperare* = command]

emphasis *n.* (*plural* **emphases** /-si:z/) **1.** special importance or prominence attached to a thing. **2.** the stress on a syllable or word(s) or on note(s) in music. **3.** vigour or intensity of expression, feeling etc. [Latin from Greek *emphainō* = exhibit]

emphasize *v.t.* to put emphasis on, to stress.

emphatic *adj.* full of emphasis, forcibly expressive; (of words) bearing stress, used to give emphasis. —**emphatically** *adv.*

emphysema *n.* an incurable lung disease characterized by disabling breathlessness. Progressive loss of the thin walls dividing the air spaces (alveoli) in the lungs reduces the area available for the exchange of oxygen and carbon dioxide, causing the lung tissue to swell. The term 'emphysema' can also refer to any abnormal swelling of body tissues caused by the accumulation of air. [Latin from Greek *emphusaō* = puff up]

empire *n.* **1.** an extensive group of countries or states under the supreme rule of one state or person. **2.** a large commercial organization etc. owned or directed by one person or group. **3.** supreme dominion (*over*). —**empire-building** *n.* deliberate accumulation of territory, authority etc. [from Old French from Latin *imperium*]

empirical *adj.* relying on observation and experiment, not on theory. —**empirically** *adv.*

empirical formula the simplest chemical formula for a compound. Quantitative analysis gives the proportion of each element present, and from this the empirical formula is calculated. It is related to the actual (molecular) formula by the relation (empirical formula)$_n$ = molecular formula where *n* is a small whole number (1,2,...).

empiricism *n.* **1.** the use of empirical methods. **2.** the theory that regards sense experience(s) as the only source of knowledge. —**empiricist** *n.* [from Greek *empeiria* = experience]

emplacement *n.* **1.** putting in position. **2.** a platform for guns.

employ *v.t.* to use the services of (a person) in return for payment; to use (a thing, time, energy etc.) to some effect; to keep occupied. —*n.* **in the employ of,** employed by. —**employer** *n.* [from Old French from Latin *implicari* = be involved]

employable *adj.* able to be employed.

employee *n.* a person employed for wages.

employers' association an organization of employers formed for purposes of collective action. In the UK there were formerly three main organizations, which in 1965 combined as the ◊Confederation of British Industry.

employment *n.* employing, being employed; one's regular trade or profession.

employment exchange an agency for bringing together employers requiring labour and workers seeking employment. Employment exchanges may be organized by central government or a local authority (known in the UK as Job Centres); or as private business ventures (employment agencies).

employment law a law covering the rights and duties of employers and employees. In the past, relations between employer and employee in the UK were covered mainly by the ◊common law, but during the 20th century statute law has increasingly been used to give new rights to employees.

emporium *n.* (*plural* **emporia, emporiums**) a centre of commerce, a market; a large shop, a store. [Latin from Greek *emporos* = merchant]

empower *v.t.* to give power or authority to.

empress *n.* a woman emperor; the wife or widow of an emperor.

Empson /'empsən/ William 1906–1984. English poet and critic, born in Yorkshire. He was professor of English literature at Tokyo and Beijing (Peking), and from 1953–71 at Sheffield University. His critical work examined the potential variety of meaning in poetry, as in *Seven Types of Ambiguity* 1930 and *The Structure of Complex Words* 1951. His verse was published in *Collected Poems* 1955.

empty *adj.* **1.** containing nothing; (of a house etc.) unoccupied or unfurnished. **2.** (*colloquial*) hungry. **3.** foolish, meaningless, vacuous. —*v.t./i.* to remove the contents of; to transfer (the contents of one thing *into* another); to become empty; (of a river) to discharge itself. —*n.* an empty bottle, box etc. —**empty-handed** *adj.* having or bringing nothing. **empty-headed** *adj.* foolish, lacking sense. —**emptily** *adv.*, **emptiness** *n.* [from Old English *æmetta* = leisure]

empyrean *n.* the highest heaven, as the sphere of fire in ancient cosmology or the abode of God. —*adj.* of this. —**empyreal** *adj.* [from Latin from Greek *pur* = fire]

EMS abbreviation of ◊European Monetary System.

emu *n.* a flightless bird *Dromaius novaehollandiae* native to Australia. It stands about 1.8 m/6 ft high and has coarse brown plumage, small rudimentary wings, short feathers on the head and neck, and powerful legs, well adapted for running and kicking. The female has a curious bag or pouch in the windpipe that enables her to emit the characteristic loud booming note. The emu is capable of running at speeds of up to 50 kph (30 mph). [from Portuguese *ema* = crane]

EMU abbreviation of economic and monetary union, the proposed European Community policy for a single currency and common economic policies.

emulate *v.t.* to try to equal or excel; to imitate. —**emulation** /-'leɪʃən/ *n.*, **emulative** *adj.*, **emulator** *n.* [from Latin *aemulari* = rival]

emulous *adj.* eagerly or jealously imitative (*of*); actuated by rivalry.

emulsifaction *n.* in mammals, the process in the small intestine by which bile, secreted from the liver, breaks down fat into microscopically small particles. These tiny droplets, less than 0.5 micrometres in diameter, are then attacked by the digestive enzyme lipase.

emulsifier *n.* a food ◊additive used to keep oils dispersed and in suspension, in products such as mayonnaise and peanut butter. Egg yolk is a naturally occurring emulsifier, but most of the emulsifiers in commercial use today are synthetic chemicals.

emulsify *v.t.* to convert into an emulsion.

emulsion *n.* **1.** a fine dispersion of one liquid in another, especially as paint, medicine etc. **2.** a mixture of a silver compound in gelatin etc. as a coating for a photographic plate or film. —**emulsive** *adj.* [from French from Latin *mulgēre* = milk]

en *n.* in printing, a unit of measurement equal to half an em. [name of letter *N*]

en- prefix (**em-** before *b, m, p*) **1.** = ◊in-[1], forming verbs (1) from nouns, in the sense 'put into or on' (e.g. *embed*), (2) from nouns or adjectives, in the sense 'bring into the condition of' (e.g. *enslave*), often with suffix *-en* (e.g. *enlighten*), (3) from verbs, in the sense 'in, into, on' (e.g. *enfold*) or intensively (e.g. *entangle*). [from French from Latin *in-*] **2.** in, inside (e.g. *energy, enthusiasm*). [from Greek *en-*]

enable *v.t.* to give the means or authority (*to do*); to make possible.

Enabling Act a legislative enactment enabling or empowering a person or corporation to take certain actions. Perhaps the best known example of an Enabling Law was that passed in Germany in March 1933 by the Reichstag and Reichsrat. It granted Adolf Hitler dictatorial powers until April 1937, and effectively terminated parliamentary government in Germany until 1950. The law firmly established the Nazi dictatorship by giving dictatorial powers to the government.

enact *v.t.* 1. to ordain, to decree. 2. to play (a part on the stage or in life). —**enactive** *adj.*

enactment *n.* a law enacted.

enamel *n.* 1. a glasslike (usually opaque) ornamental or preservative coating on metal. In ◊**cloisonné** the various sections of the design are separated by thin metal wires or strips. In **champlevé** the enamel is poured into engraved cavities in the metal surface. 2. a hard, smooth coating; a cosmetic simulating this; the hard coating of teeth. 3. a painting done in enamel. —*v.t.* (-**ll**-) to coat, inlay, or portray with enamel. [from Anglo-French from Germanic]

enamour *v.t.* (usually in *past participle*) to inspire with love or liking (*of*). [from Old French *enamourer* (*amour* = love)]

en bloc in a block, all at the same time. [French]

encamp *v.t./i.* to settle in a military or other camp. —**encampment** *n.*

encapsulate *v.t.* 1. to enclose (as) in a capsule. 2. to summarize; to isolate. —**encapsulation** /-'leɪʃən/ *n.* [from Latin *capsula* = capsule]

encase *v.t.* to confine (as) in a case. —**encasement** *n.*

encash *v.t.* to convert into cash. —**encashment** *n.*

encaustic *adj.* (of painting) using pigments mixed with hot wax, which are burned in as an inlay. —*n.* the art or product of this. [from Latin from Greek *kaustos* = burnt]

enceinte *adj.* pregnant. [French = ungirdled]

encephalin *n.* a naturally occurring chemical produced by nerve cells in the brain that has the same effect as morphine or other derivatives of opium, acting as a natural painkiller. Unlike morphine, encephalins are quickly degraded by the body, so there is no buildup of tolerance to them, and hence no 'addiction'. Encephalins are a variety of ◊**peptides**, as are ◊**endorphins**, which have similar effects.

encephalitis *n.* an inflammation of the brain, nearly always due to virus infection but also to parasites, fungi, or malaria. It varies widely in severity, from short-lived, relatively slight effects of headache, drowsiness, and fever to paralysis, coma, and death. One such type of viral infection is also sometimes called 'sleeping sickness'. [from Greek *egkephalos* = brain]

encephalogram *n.* an ◊**electroencephalogram**.

encephalograph *n.* an ◊**electroencephalograph**.

enchain *v.t.* 1. to chain up. 2. to hold (the attention or emotions) fast. [from French]

enchant *v.t.* to charm, to delight; to bewitch. —**enchanter**, **enchantment** *ns.*, **enchantress** *n.fem.* [from French from Latin *incantare* (*canere* = sing)]

encircle *v.t.* to surround; to form a circle round. —**encirclement** *n.*

Encke's comet /'eŋkə/ the comet with the shortest known orbital period, 3.3 years. It is named after German mathematician and astronomer, Johann Franz Encke (1791–1865) who in 1819 calculated the orbit from earlier sightings.

enclave *n.* the territory of one state surrounded by that of another. [from French *enclaver* = shut in, from Latin *clavis* = key]

enclitic *adj.* (of a word) pronounced with so little emphasis that it forms part of the preceding word. —*n.* such a word. [from Latin from Greek *klinō* = lean]

enclose *v.t.* 1. to shut in on all sides, to surround with a wall or fence etc.; to shut up in a receptacle (especially in an envelope besides a letter). 2. (in *past participle*, of a religious community) secluded from the outside world. [from Old French from Latin]

enclosure *n.* 1. the act of enclosing; the enclosing of common land to make it private property. This process began in Britain in the 14th century and became widespread in the 15th and 16th centuries. It caused poverty, homelessness, and rural depopulation, and resulted in revolts in 1536, 1569, and 1607. 2. an enclosed space or area. 3. a thing enclosed with a letter.

encode *v.t.* to put into code. —**encoder** *n.*

encomium *n.* (*plural* **encomiums**) formal or bombastic praise. [Latin from Greek]

encompass *v.t.* to surround; to contain.

encore *n.* an audience's demand for further performance or repetition of an item; such an item. —*v.t.* to call for an encore of (an item), to call back (a performer) for

this. —/also - 'kɔ:/ *int.* again, once more. [French = once more]

encounter *v.t.* 1. to meet by chance or unexpectedly. 2. to find oneself faced with (a problem etc.). 3. to meet as an adversary. —*n.* a meeting by chance or in conflict. [from Old French from Latin *contra* = against]

encourage *v.t.* 1. to give courage or confidence to. 2. to urge; to stimulate, to promote. —**encouragement** *n.* [from French]

encroach *v.i.* to intrude (*on* or *upon*); to advance gradually beyond due limits. —**encroachment** *n.* [from Old French *encrochier* (*croc* = hook)]

encrust *v.t./i.* to cover with or form a crust; to overlay with a crust of silver etc. [from French]

encumber *v.t.* to be a burden to; to hamper, to impede. [from Old French from Romanic]

encumbrance *n.* a burden, an impediment.

encyclical *adj.* for wide circulation. —*n.* a letter addressed by the pope to Roman Catholic bishops for the benefit of the people. The first was issued by Benedict XIV in 1740, but encyclicals became common only in the 19th century. They may be doctrinal (condemning errors), exhortative (recommending devotional activities), or commemorative. [from Latin from Greek *kuklos* = circle]

encyclopedia *n.* a work of reference covering either all fields of knowledge or one specific subject. Although most encyclopedias are alphabetical, with cross-references, some are organized thematically with indexes, to keep related subjects together. [Latin from Greek *egkuklios* = all-round and *paideia* = education]

encyclopedic *adj.* (of knowledge or information) comprehensive.

Encyclopédie *n.* an encyclopedia in 28 volumes written 1751–72 by a group of French scholars (*Encyclopédistes*) including D'Alembert and Diderot, inspired by the English encyclopedia produced by Ephraim Chambers in 1728. Religious scepticism and ◊**Enlightenment** social and political views were a feature of the work.

encyclopedist *n.* a writer of an encyclopedia.

end *n.* 1. the extreme limit, the furthest point; the extreme part or surface of a thing. 2. a finish or conclusion; the latter part; destruction, death. 3. a purpose, an object. 4. a result, an outcome. 5. a remnant, a piece left over. 6. the half of a sports pitch etc. occupied by one side. 7. the part or share with which a person is concerned. —*v.t./i.* to bring or come to an end, to finish; to result *in*. —**the end**, (*colloquial*) the limit of endurability. **end it all**, (*colloquial*) to commit suicide. **end on**, with the end facing one or adjoining the end of the next object. **end product**, the final product of manufacture, a transformation etc. **ends of the Earth**, the remotest regions. **end to end**, with the end of one adjoining the end of the next in a series. **end up**, to reach a certain state or action eventually. **in the end**, finally. **keep one's end up**, to do one's part despite difficulties. **make ends meet**, to live within one's income. **no end**, (*colloquial*) to a great extent. **no end of**, (*colloquial*) much or many of. **on end**, upright; continuously. **put an end to**, to stop, to abolish, to destroy. [Old English]

endanger *v.t.* to bring into danger.

endangered species a plant or animal species whose numbers are so few that it is at risk of becoming extinct. Officially designated endangered species are listed by the International Union for the Conservation of Nature (◊**IUCN**).

endear *v.t.* to make dear (*to*).

endearment *n.* 1. an act or words expressing affection. 2. liking, affection.

endeavour *v.t.* to try earnestly (*to do*). —*n.* an earnest attempt. [from French *devoir* = duty]

endemic *adj.* regularly or only found among a (specified) people or in a (specified) country. —*n.* an endemic disease or plant. —**endemically** *adv.* [from French or Latin from Greek *dēmos* = people]

Ender /'endə/ Kornelia 1958– . German swimmer. She won a record-tying four gold medals at the 1976 Olympics at freestyle, butterfly, and relay. She won a total of eight Olympic medals 1972–76. She also won a record ten world championship medals in 1973 and 1975.

Enders /'endəz/ John Franklin 1897–1985. US virologist. With Thomas Weller and Frederick Robbins, he discovered the ability of the polio virus to grow in cultures of various

endocrine

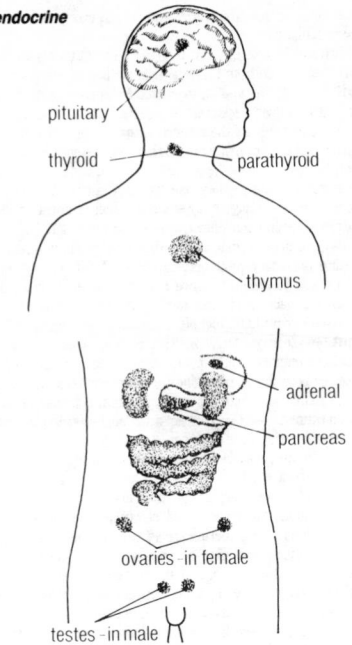

pituitary

thyroid — parathyroid

thymus

adrenal

pancreas

ovaries - in female

testes - in male

tissues, which led to the perfection of an effective vaccine. The three were awarded the Nobel Prize for Physiology and Medicine in 1954. Enders also succeeded in isolating the measles virus.

ending *n.* the end or final part, especially of a story; the inflected final part of a word.

endive /'endaɪv/ *n.* **1.** a curly leaved plant *Cichorium endivia*, family Compositae, used in salads. **2.** (*US*) a ◊chicory crown. [from Old French, ultimately from Latin *intibum*]

endless /'endlɪs/ *adj.* without end, infinite; incessant; continual; (*colloquial*) innumerable. —**endless belt** *or* **chain** etc., one with the ends joined for continuous action over wheels etc.

endmost *adj.* nearest the end.

endo- prefix denoting internal(ly). [from Greek *endon* = within]

endocrine /'endəʊkrəɪn/ *adj.* (of a gland) secreting directly into the blood. —**endocrine gland,** a gland that secretes hormones into the bloodstream to regulate body processes. Endocrine glands are most highly developed in vertebrates, but are also found in other animals, notably insects. In humans the main endocrine glands are the pituitary, thyroid, parathyroid, adrenal, pancreas, ovary, and testis. [from Greek *krinō* = sift]

endogenous /enəˈdɒdʒɪnəs/ *adj.* growing or originating from within.

endolymph *n.* a fluid found in the inner ◊ear, filling the central passage of the cochlea and the semicircular canals.

endometriosis *n.* a common gynaecological complaint in which patches of endometrium (the lining of the womb) are found outside the uterus.

endomorph /'endəʊmɔːf/ *n.* a person with a soft round build of the body, the type of physique said to be correlated with an extrovert personality. [from Greek *morphē* = form]

endoparasite *n.* a ◊parasite that lives inside the body of its host.

endoplasm *n.* the inner, liquid part of a cell's ◊cytoplasm.

endoplasmic reticulum (ER) a membranous structure in eukaryotic cells (see ◊eukaryot. It stores and transports proteins needed elsewhere in the cells and carries various enzymes needed for the synthesis of fats (see ◊lipid). The ◊ribosomes, which carry out protein synthesis, are attached to parts of the ER.

endorphin /en'dɔːfɪn/ *n.* a natural substance (a polypeptide) that modifies the action of nerve cells. Endorphins are produced by the pituitary gland and hypothalamus of

vertebrates. They have an effect similar to morphine, and lower the perception of pain by reducing the transmission of signals between nerve cells.

endorse /ɪn'dɔːs/ *v.t.* **1.** to confirm, to approve. **2.** to write a comment etc. on (a document); to sign the back of (a cheque). **3.** to enter the details of a conviction for an offence on (a licence). —**endorsement** *n.* [from Latin *indorsare* (*dorsum* = back)]

endoscope /'endəskəʊp/ *n.* an instrument used for viewing the internal parts of the body. An endoscope is equipped with an eyepiece, lenses, and its own light source to illuminate the field of vision. The endoscope used to examine the alimentary canal is a flexible fibreoptic instrument. It is swallowed by the patient. —**endoscopy** /'dɒskəpɪ/ *n.*

endoskeleton *n.* see ◊skeleton.

endosperm *n.* a nutritive tissue in the seeds of most flowering plants. It surrounds the embryo and is produced by an unusual process that parallels the ◊fertilization of the ovum by a male gamete. A second male gamete from the pollen grain fuses with two female nuclei within the ◊embryo sac. Thus endosperm cells are triploid (having three sets of chromosomes); they contain food reserves such as starch, fat, and protein, which are utilized by the developing seedling.

endotherm *n.* a 'warm-blooded', or homeothermic, animal. Endotherms have internal mechanisms for regulating their body temperatures to levels different from the environmental temperature. See ◊homeothermy.

endothermic reaction a physical or chemical change in which energy is absorbed by the reactants from the surroundings.

endow /ɪn'daʊ/ *v.t.* **1.** to bequeath or give a permanent income to (a person, institution etc.). **2.** (especially in *past participle*) to provide with talent or ability. [from Anglo-French]

endowment *n.* endowing; an endowed income.

endowment insurance a form of life insurance with payment of a fixed sum to the insured person on a specified date, or to his/her estate if he/she dies earlier. An endowment policy will run for a fixed number of years during which it accumulates a cash value; it provides a savings plan for a retirement fund, and may be used to help with a house purchase, linked to a building society mortgage.

endpaper *n.* a stout, blank leaf of paper fixed across the beginning or end of a book and the inside cover.

endue /ɪn'djuː/ *v.t.* to provide (a person *with* qualities etc.). [from Old French from Latin *inducere* = draw on, associated with *induere* = put on (clothes)]

endurable *adj.* able to be endured. [from Old French from Latin *durus* = hard]

endurance *n.* **1.** the power of enduring. **2.** the ability to withstand prolonged strain.

endure /ɪn'djuə/ *v.t./i.* **1.** to undergo (pain etc.); to tolerate, to bear. **2.** to last.

end user a user of a computer program, in particular someone who uses a program to perform a task (such as accounting or playing a computer game) rather than someone who writes programs (a programmer).

endways *adv.* or **endwise** **1.** with the end uppermost or foremost. **2.** end to end.

Endymion /en'dɪmɪən/ in Greek mythology, a beautiful young man loved by Selene, the moon goddess. He was granted eternal sleep in order to remain for ever young. *Endymion*, written in 1818 by the English poet, Keats, is an allegory of a search for perfection.

enema /'enɪmə/ *n.* the insertion of liquid through the anus into the rectum, especially to expel its contents; a liquid or syringe used for this. [Latin from Greek *eniēmi* = inject]

enemy /'enəmɪ/ *n.* a person actively hostile to another and seeking to defeat or harm him or her; a hostile nation or army, a member of this; an adversary, an opponent. —*adj.* of or belonging to the enemy. [from Old French from Latin *inimicus* (*amicus* = friend)]

energetic /enəˈdʒetɪk/ *adj.* full of energy; powerfully active. —**energetically** *adv.*

Energiya *n.* a Soviet shuttle booster, launched on 15 May 1987. When fully operational, the Energiya booster will be used to launch the Soviet shuttle Buran, and will be capable, with the use of strap-on boosters, of launching payloads of up to 230 tonnes/250 tons into Earth-orbit.

energize /'enədʒaɪz/ v.t. to give energy to; to provide (a device) with energy for operation.

energy /'enədʒɪ/ n. 1. the capacity for activity, force, vigour. 2. the ability of matter or radiation to do work. **Potential energy** (PE) is energy deriving from position; thus a stretched spring has elastic PE; an object raised to a height above the Earth's surface, or the water in an elevated reservoir, has gravitational PE; a lump of coal and a tank of petrol, together with the oxygen needed for their combustion, have chemical PE (due to relative positions of atoms). Other types of PE include electrical and nuclear. Moving bodies possess **kinetic energy** (KE). Energy can be converted from one form to another, but the total quantity stays the same (in accordance with the laws of conservation that govern many natural phenomena). For example, as an apple falls, it loses gravitational PE but gains KE. [from French or Latin from Greek *energeia* (*ergon* = work)]

energy of reaction the energy released or absorbed during a chemical reaction, also called **enthalpy of reaction** or **heat of reaction**; it has the symbol ΔH.

enervate /'enəveɪt/ v.t. to deprive of vigour or vitality. —**enervation** /-'veɪʃən/ n. [from Latin *enervare* (*nervus* = sinew)]

enfant terrible /ãfã te'riːbl/ one whose rash and unconventional behaviour shocks and embarrasses others; an unruly child. [French = terrible child]

enfeeble /ɪn'fiːbl/ v.t. to make feeble. —**enfeeblement** n. [from Old French]

enfilade /enfɪ'leɪd/ n. gunfire directed along a line from end to end. —v.t. to direct an enfilade at. [from French *fil* = thread]

enfold /ɪn'fəʊld/ v.t. to wrap (a person *in* or *with*); to clasp, to embrace.

enforce /ɪn'fɔːs/ v.t. to compel observance of (a law etc.); to impose (an action or one's will etc. *on* a person); to persist in (a demand etc.). —**enforceable** *adj.*, **enforcement** n. [from Old French *enforci(e)r* from Latin *fortis* = strong]

enfranchise /ɪn'fræntʃaɪz/ v.t. 1. to give (a person) the right to vote. 2. to give (a town) municipal rights, especially representation in parliament. 3. to free (a slave etc.). —**enfranchisement** /-ɪzmənt/ n. [from Old French *enfranchir* (*franc* = free)]

engage /ɪn'ɡeɪdʒ/ v.t./i. 1. to take into one's employment, to hire. 2. to arrange beforehand to occupy (a room, seat etc.). 3. to promise, to pledge. 4. to occupy the attention of; to occupy oneself. 5. to come or bring into battle (with). 6. to interlock (parts of a gear etc.) so as to transmit power; to become interlocked thus. [from French]

engaged *adj.* 1. having promised to marry. 2. occupied or reserved by a person etc.; occupied with business etc. 3. (of a telephone line) already in use.

engagement n. 1. engaging, being engaged. 2. an appointment made with another person. 3. a promise to marry a specified person. 4. a battle. —**engagement ring**, a finger ring given by a man to a woman when they promise to marry.

engaging *adj.* attractive, charming.

Engel /'eŋəl/ Carl Ludwig 1778–1840. German architect, who from 1815 worked in Finland. His great Neo-Classical achievement was the Senate Square in Helsinki, which is defined by his Senate House 1818–22 and University Building 1828–32, and crowned by the domed Lutheran cathedral 1830–40.

Engels /'eŋəlz/ Friedrich 1820–1895. German social and political philosopher, a friend of, and collaborator with, Karl ◊Marx on *The Communist Manifesto* 1848 and other key works. His later interpretations of Marxism, and his own philosophical and historical studies such as *Origins of the Family, Private Property, and the State* 1884 (which linked patriarchy with the development of private property), developed such concepts as historical materialism. His use of positivism and Darwinian ideas gave Marxism

a scientific and deterministic flavour which was to influence Soviet thinking.

engender /ɪn'dʒendə/ v.t. to give rise to (a feeling etc.). [from Old French from Latin *generare* = beget]

engine /'endʒɪn/ n. 1. a mechanical contrivance of parts working together, especially as a source of power. Most engines use a fuel as their energy store. The fuel is burnt to produce heat energy, which is then converted into movement, hence the name 'heat engine'. These can be classified according to the fuel they use (◊petrol or ◊diesel engine), or according to whether the fuel is burnt inside (◊internal-combustion engine) or outside (◊steam engine) the engine, or according to whether they produce a reciprocating or rotary motion (◊turbine or ◊Wankel engine). 2. a railway locomotive; a fire engine; a steam-engine. 3. (*archaic*) a machine of war; an instrument; a means. [from Old French from Latin *ingenium* = talent, device]

engineer /endʒɪ'nɪə(r)/ n. 1. a person skilled in some branch of engineering; a civil engineer. 2. a person who makes or is in charge of engines or other equipment. 3. one who designs and constructs military works, especially a soldier so trained. —v.t./i. 1. to act as an engineer; to plan and construct or control as engineer. 2. (*colloquial*) to contrive, to bring about. [from Old French from Latin *ingeniator*]

engineering n. the application of science for the control and use of power, especially in roads and other works of public utility, machines, and electrical apparatus. The main divisions of engineering are aerospace, chemical, civil, electrical, electronic, gas, marine, materials, mechanical, mining, production, radio, and structural engineering.

engineering drawing a technical drawing that forms the plans for the design and construction of engineering components and structures. Engineering drawings show different projections, or views of objects, with the relevant dimensions, and show how all the separate parts fit together.

England /'ɪŋɡlənd/ the largest division of the ◊United Kingdom; **area** 130,357 sq km/50,318 sq mi; **capital** London; **physical** variable climate and diverse landscape; **exports** agricultural produce (cereals, rape, sugar beet, potatoes); meat and meat products; electronic goods (software), and telecommunications equipment; scientific instruments; textiles and fashion goods; North Sea oil and gas, petrochemicals, pharmaceuticals; film and television programmes; sound recordings; tourism, banking and insurance are important industries; **population** (1986) 47,255,000; **language** English, plus more than 100 minority languages.

Engleheart /'eŋgəlhɑːt/ George 1752–1829. English miniature painter. Born in Kew, London, he studied under Joshua Reynolds and in 40 years painted nearly 5,000 miniatures including copies of many of Reynolds's portraits.

English /'ɪŋɡlɪʃ/ *adj.* of England or its people or language. —n. the language of England, a member of the Germanic branch of the Indo-European language family; its literary or standard form. The English language developed through four major stages over about 1,500 years: **Old English** or **Anglo-Saxon** (c.500–1050), rooted in the dialects of settling invaders (Jutes, Saxons, Angles, and Danes); **Middle English** (c.1050–1550), influenced by Norman French after the Conquest in 1066 and by ecclesiastical Latin; **Early Modern English** (c.1550–1700), standardization of the diverse influences of Middle English; and **Late Modern English** (c.1700 onwards), the development and spread of current Standard English. Through extensive exploration, colonization, and trade, English spread worldwide from the 17th century onwards and remains the most important international language of trade and technology. It is used in many variations, for example, British, US, Canadian, West Indian, Indian, Singaporean, and Nigerian English, and many pidgins and creoles. —**english** v.t. (*archaic*) to render into English. —**the English**, the people of England. **the King's** or **Queen's English**, the English language correctly spoken or written. [Old English]

English architecture Most of the building of the ◊Roman and ◊Saxon periods has disappeared, but is being rediscovered through archaeological excavations. The Anglo-Saxon stone church towers that remain, such as Earls Barton, appear to imitate timber techniques with features such as triangular arches. William the Conqueror initiated an extensive building programme in the ◊Norman style (the

England, history

5th–7th centuries	Anglo-Saxons overran all England except Cornwall and Cumberland, forming independent kingdoms including Northumbria, Mercia, Kent, and Wessex.
*c.*597	England converted to Christianity by St Augustine.
829	Egbert of Wessex accepted as overlord of all England.
878	Alfred ceded N and E England to the Danish invaders but kept them out of Wessex.
1066	Norman Conquest; England passed into French hands under William the Conqueror.
1172	Henry II became king of Ireland and established a colony there.
1215	King John forced to sign Magna Carta.
1284	Conquest of Wales, begun by the Normans, completed by Edward I.
1295	Model Parliament set up.
1338–1453	Hundred Years' War with France enabled Parliament to secure control of taxation and, by impeachment, of the king's choice of ministers.
1348–49	Black Death killed about 30% of the population.
1381	Social upheaval led to the ◊Peasants' Revolt, which was brutally repressed.
1399	Richard II deposed by Parliament for absolutism.
1414	Lollard revolt repressed.
1455–85	Wars of the Roses.
1497	Henry VII ended the power of the feudal nobility with the suppression of the Yorkist revolts.
1529	Henry VIII became head of the Church of England after breaking with Rome.
1536–43	Acts of Union united England and Wales after conquest.
1547	Edward VI adopted Protestant doctrines.
1553	Reversion to Roman Catholicism under Mary I.
1558	Elizabeth I adopted a religious compromise.
1588	Attempted invasion of England by the Spanish Armada.
1603	James I united the English and Scottish crowns; parliamentary dissidence increased.
1642–52	Civil War between royalists and parliamentarians, resulting in victory for Parliament.
1649	Charles I executed and the Commonwealth set up.
1653	Oliver Cromwell appointed Lord Protector.
1660	Restoration of Charles II.
1685	Monmouth rebellion.
1688	William of Orange invited to take the throne; flight of James II.
1707	Act of Union between England and Scotland under Queen Anne, after which the countries became known as Great Britain.
	For pre-Roman history, see ◊Britain, ancient; for further history, see ◊United Kingdom.

English form of Romanesque) 1066–1189. The ◊Gothic period followed three phases: the delicate ◊Early English style, exemplified by Salisbury Cathedral (late 12th–late 13th centuries); the ◊Decorated style spanning the 13th and early 14th centuries, of which Exeter Cathedral is a good example, and the ◊Perpendicular style (15th century), of which the King's College Chapel, Cambridge, is a fine example. ◊Tudor, a style of mainly domestic buildings of about 1485–1558, characterized by half-timbering and external decoration, was followed by the ◊Jacobean period, marked by the beginning of Italian Renaissance influence. The Stuart period saw the flowering of the English Renaissance, its apotheosis marked by Inigo ◊Jones's Queen's House, Greenwich, and Banqueting House, Whitehall, in London. After the Great Fire of London Christopher ◊Wren and his pupil Nicholas ◊Hawksmoor rebuilt 52 City churches and St Paul's Cathedral in ◊Neo-Classical style. Inigo Jones's Palladianism was revived in 18th-century ◊Georgian architecture, and Gothic architecture was evoked in the 19th-century neo-Gothic revival. Joseph ◊Paxton's Crystal Palace was the most spectacular example of Victorian iron and glass architecture. Recently English architects have achieved international recognition, especially Norman ◊Foster, and Richard ◊Rogers with the Lloyds Building (1979–84) in London.

English Channel stretch of water between England and France, leading in the west to the Atlantic Ocean, and in the east via the Strait of Dover to the North Sea; also known as *La Manche* (French 'the sleeve') from its shape. It is 450 km/280 mi long W–E; 35 km/22 mi wide at its narrowest (Cap Gris Nez–Dover) and 117 km/110 mi wide at its widest (Ushant–Land's End).

English horn the alternative name for ◊cor anglais, a musical instrument of the oboe family.

English law one of the major European legal systems; ◊Roman law is the other. English law has spread to many other countries, including former English colonies such as the USA, Canada, Australia, and New Zealand.

Englishman *n.* (*plural* **Englishmen**) one who is English by birth, descent, or naturalization. —**Englishwoman** *n.fem.* (*plural* **Englishwomen**)

English-Speaking Union a society for promoting the fellowship of the English-speaking peoples of the world, founded in 1918 by Evelyn Wrench.

engorged /ɪnˈgɔːdʒd/ *adj.* crammed full; congested with blood. [from French *gorge* = throat]

engraft /ɪnˈgrɑːft/ *v.t.* to graft (a shoot of one plant *on* or *into* another); to implant; to incorporate (a thing *into* another).

engrave /ɪnˈgreɪv/ *v.t.* **1.** to inscribe or cut (a design) on a hard surface; to inscribe (a surface) thus. **2.** to impress deeply *on* the memory.

engraving *n.* **1.** the art of creating a design by means of inscribing blocks of metal, wood, or some other hard material with a point. **2.** a print made from an engraved plate.

engross /ɪnˈgrʊs/ *v.t.* **1.** to absorb the attention of, to occupy fully. **2.** to write out in large letters or in legal form. —**engrossment** *n.* [from Anglo-French *engrosser* (*en gros* = wholesale); from *en* = in and *grosse* = large writing]

engulf /ɪnˈgʌlf/ *v.t.* to flow over and swamp, to overwhelm.

enhance /ɪnˈhɑːns/ *v.t.* to heighten or intensify (a quality or power etc.). —**enhancement** *n.* [from Anglo-French probably from Old French *enhaucier* from Latin *altus* = high]

enhanced radiation weapon another name for the ◊neutron bomb.

enharmonic *n.* in music, a harmony capable of different interpretations, or of leading into different keys.

enigma /ɪˈnɪgmə/ *n.* a puzzling thing or person; a riddle or paradox. —**enigmatic** /-ˈmætɪk/ *adj.*, **enigmatically** *adv.* [from Latin from Greek *ainigma*]

Eniwetok /eniˈwiːtɒk/ atoll in the ◊Marshall Islands, in the central Pacific Ocean; population (1980) 453. It was taken from Japan by the USA in 1944, which made the island a naval base; 43 atomic tests were conducted there from 1947. The inhabitants were resettled at Ujelang, but insisted on returning home in 1980. Despite the clearance of nuclear debris and radioactive soil to the islet of Runit, high radiation levels persisted.

enjoin /ɪnˈdʒɔɪn/ *v.t.* to command, to order; to impose (an action *on* a person); in law, to prohibit by injunction (*from* doing). [from Old French from Latin *injungere* = attach]

enjoy /ɪnˈdʒɔɪ/ *v.t.* to take pleasure in; to have the use or benefit of; to experience. —**enjoy oneself**, to experience pleasure. —**enjoyment** *n.* [from Old French]

enjoyable *adj.* pleasant, giving enjoyment. —**enjoyably** *adv.*

enkephalin /enˈkeflɪn/ *n.* either of two morphine-like peptides in the brain thought to be concerned with the perception of pain. [from Greek *egkephalos* = brain]

enkindle /ɪnˈkɪnd(ə)l/ *v.t.* to cause to blaze up; to arouse.

enlarge /ɪnˈlɑːdʒ/ *v.t./i.* 1. to make or become larger or wider; to reproduce (a photograph) on a larger scale. 2. to describe in greater detail. —**enlargement** *n.* [from Old French]

enlighten /ɪnˈlaɪt(ə)n/ *v.t.* to instruct or inform (a person *on* a subject); to free from superstition etc.

enlightenment *n.* in Buddhism, the term used to translate the Sanskrit *bodhi*, awakening: perceiving the reality of the world, or the unreality of the self, and becoming liberated from suffering (Sanskrit *duhkha*). It is the gateway to ◊nirvana.

Enlightenment *n.* a European intellectual movement that reached its high point in the 18th century. Enlightenment thinkers were believers in social progress and in the liberating possibilities of rational and scientific knowledge. They were often critical of existing society and were hostile to religion, which they saw as keeping the human mind chained down by superstition.

enlist *v.t./i.* 1. to enrol in the armed services. 2. to secure as a means of help or support. —**enlistment** *n.*

enliven *v.t.* to make lively or cheerful. —**enlivenment** *n.*

en masse as a group, in a body, all together. [French]

enmesh *v.t.* to entangle (as) in a net.

enmity *n.* the state or feeling of being an enemy, hostility. [from Old French]

Enniskillen /enɪsˈkɪlən/ county town of Fermanagh, Northern Ireland, between Upper and Lower Lough Erne; population (1981) 10,500. There is some light industry (engineering, food processing) and it has been designated for further industrial growth. A bomb exploded there at a Remembrance Day service in Nov 1987, causing many casualties.

ennoble *v.t.* to make (a person) a noble; to make noble. —**ennoblement** *n.* [from French]

ennui *n.* a state of mental weariness caused by idleness or lack of interest, a feeling of boredom. [French, from Latin *in odio* = hateful]

enormity *n.* 1. monstrous wickedness; a dreadful crime; a serious error. 2. great size. [from Latin *enormis* (*norma* = pattern, standard)]

enormous *adj.* extraordinarily large, vast, huge. —**enormously** *adv.*

enosis *n.* the movement, developed from 1930, for the union of ◊Cyprus with Greece. [Greek = union]

enough *adj.* as much or as many as required. —*n.* the amount or quantity that is enough. —*adv.* to the required degree, adequately; fairly; very, quite. —**have had enough of,** to want no more of; to be satiated with or tired of. **sure enough,** undeniably, as expected. [Old English]

enounce *v.t.* to enunciate, to pronounce. [from French *énoncer*]

en passant by the way. [French = in passing]

en plein air in the open air. [French]

enquire *v.t./i.* to ask to be told (a person's name, business etc.); to seek information (*about* etc.). —**enquiry** *n.*

enrage *v.t.* to make furious. [from French]

enrapture *v.t.* to delight intensely.

enrich *v.t.* to make rich or richer; to increase the strength or wealth or value of. —**enrichment** *n.* [from Old French]

enrol *v.t.* (-ll-) to write the name of (a person) on a list; to enlist; to incorporate as a member; to enrol oneself. —**enrolment** *n.* [from Old French]

en route on the way. [French]

ENSA (Entertainments National Service Association) an organization formed 1938–39 to provide entertainment for British and Allied forces during World War II. Directed by Basil Dean (1888–1978) from headquarters in the Drury Lane Theatre, it provided a variety of entertainment throughout the UK and also in all war zones.

ensconce *v.t.* to settle comfortably.

ensemble *n.* 1. a thing viewed as a sum of its parts. 2. a set of matching items of dress. 3. a group of actors, dancers, musicians etc., performing together; in music, a concerted passage for an ensemble. [French, from Latin *simul* = at the same time]

enshrine *v.t.* to enclose (as) in a shrine; to serve as a shrine for.

enshroud *v.t.* to cover completely (as) with a shroud; to hide from view.

ensign *n.* 1. a banner or flag, especially a nation's military or naval flag. 2. a standard-bearer. 3. (*historical*) the lowest commissioned infantry officer. 4. (*US*) the lowest commissioned officer in the navy. [from Old French from Latin *insignia*]

ensilage *n.* silage. [French]

enslave *v.t.* to make into a slave. —**enslavement** *n.*

ensnare *v.t.* to catch (as) in a snare.

Ensor /ˈensɔː/ James 1860–1949. Belgian painter and printmaker. His bold style uses strong colours to explore themes of human cruelty and the macabre, as in the *Entry of Christ into Brussels* 1888 (Musée Royale des Beaux-Arts, Brussels), and anticipated Expressionism.

ensue *v.i.* to happen later or as a result. [from Old French from Latin *sequi* = follow]

en suite forming a single unit. [French = in sequence]

ensure *v.t.* to make certain or secure; to make safe (*against* risks). [from Anglo-French]

ENT in medicine, abbreviation of ear, nose, and throat.

entablature *n.* in architecture, an upper part supported by columns, including the architrave, frieze, and cornice. [from Italian *intavolare* = board up (*tavola* = table)]

entail *v.t.* 1. to necessitate or involve unavoidably. 2. in law, to bequeath (an estate) inalienably to a named succession of beneficiaries. —*n.* an entailed estate or succession. An entail can be either **general**, in which case it simply descends to the heirs, or **special**, when it descends according to a specific arrangement—for example, to children by a named wife.

entangle *v.t.* to cause to get caught in a snare or tangle; to involve in difficulties; to complicate. —**entanglement** *n.*

Entebbe /enˈtebi/ town in Uganda, on the NW shore of Lake Victoria, 20 km/12 mi SW of Kampala, the capital; 1,136 m/3,728 ft above sea level; population (1983) 21,000. Founded 1893, it was the administrative centre of Uganda 1894–1962.

entente *n.* a friendly understanding or association, especially between States. —**entente cordiale** /kɔːˈdiːɑːl/, that between Britain and France in 1904 recognizing British interests in Egypt and French interests in Morocco. It formed the basis for Anglo-French cooperation before the outbreak of World War I in 1914. [French = understanding]

enter *v.t./i.* 1. to go or come in or into; to come on stage (especially as a direction); to penetrate. 2. to write (a name, details etc.) in a list, book etc.; to register as a competitor; to record (a plea etc.) formally. 3. to admit or obtain admission for (a pupil, a person as a member etc.). —**enter into,** to take part in (a conversation etc.); to subscribe to or become bound by (an agreement, contract etc.); to form part of (a calculation, plan etc.); to sympathize with (feelings). **enter on** *or* **upon,** to assume possession of (property) or the functions of (an office); to begin; to begin to deal with. [from Old French from Latin *intra* = within]

enteric *adj.* of the intestines. [from Greek *enteron* = intestine]

enteritis *n.* an inflammation of the intestines.

enterprise *n.* an undertaking, especially a bold or difficult one; readiness to be involved in such undertakings. [from Old French *entreprendre* variant of *emprendre* from Latin *prehendere* = take]

enterprise zone zones designated by government to encourage industrial and commercial activity, usually in economically depressed areas. Investment is attracted by means of tax reduction and other financial incentives.

enterprising *adj.* showing enterprise; energetic and resourceful.

entertain *v.t.* 1. to amuse, to occupy agreeably. 2. to receive as a guest; to receive guests. 3. to harbour, to cherish, to consider favourably (an idea etc.). [from French from Latin *tenēre* = hold]

entertainer *n.* one who provides entertainment, especially as a professional.

entertaining *adj.* amusing, diverting.

entertainment *n.* entertaining; a thing that entertains, especially before a public audience.

enthral *v.t.* (**-ll-**) to captivate, to please greatly. —**enthralment** *n.*

enthrone *v.t.* to place on a throne, especially ceremonially. —**enthronement** *n.*

enthuse *v.t./i.* (*colloquial*) to be or make enthusiastic. [from French from Latin from Greek *entheos* = possessed by a god]

enthusiasm *n.* an intensity of feeling or interest, great eagerness.

enthusiast *n.* a person full of enthusiasm for something.

enthusiastic *adj.* having or showing enthusiasm. —**enthusiastically** *adv.*

entice *v.t.* to persuade by an offer of pleasure or reward. —**enticement** *n.* [from Old French probably from Latin *titio* = firebrand]

entire *adj.* 1. whole, complete. 2. in one piece; continuous. 3. unqualified, absolute. [from Anglo-French from Latin *integer* (*tangere* = touch)]

entirely *adv.* wholly, solely.

entirety *n.* completeness; the sum total (*of*). —**in its entirety**, in its complete form.

entitle *v.t.* 1. to give a right or just claim *to*. 2. to give a title to (a book etc.). —**entitlement** *n.* [from Anglo-French from Latin *titulus* = title]

entity *n.* a thing with a distinct existence; a thing's existence in itself. [from French or Latin *ens* particle of *esse* = be]

entomb *v.t.* to place in a tomb; to serve as a tomb for. —**entombment** *n.*

entomology *n.* the study of insects. —**entomological** /-'lɒdʒɪkəl/ *adj.*, **entomologist** *n.* [from French or Latin from Greek *entomon* = insect]

entourage *n.* the people attending an important person. [French *entourer* = surround]

entr'acte an interval between the acts of a play; a dance or music etc. performed then. [French *entre* = between and *acte* = act]

entrails *n.pl.* 1. the bowels, the intestines. 2. the inner parts of a thing. [from Old French from Latin *intralia* (*inter* = among)]

entrance[1] *n.* 1. going or coming in; the coming of an actor on to a stage. 2. a door or passage etc. by which one enters. 3. the right of admission; the fee charged for this. [from Old French]

entrance[2] *v.t.* 1. to enchant, to delight. 2. to put into a trance. —**entrancement** *n.*

entrant *n.* one who enters an examination, profession etc.

entrap *v.t.* (**-pp-**) to catch (as) in a trap; to beguile. [from Old French]

entreat *v.t.* to ask earnestly, to beg. [from Old French]

entreaty *n.* an earnest request.

entrechat *n.* in ballet, criss-crossing of the legs while the dancer is in the air. There are two movements for each beat. Wayne ◊Sleep broke ◊Nijinsky's record of an *entrechat dix* (five beats) with an *entrechat douze* (six beats) in 1973. [French = cross-caper]

entrecôte *n.* a boned steak cut off a sirloin. [French = between-rib]

entrée *n.* 1. the right of admission. 2. a dish served between fish and meat courses; (*US*) the main dish of a meal. [French = entry]

entrench *v.t.* 1. to establish firmly (in a position, office etc.). 2. to surround with a trench as a fortification. —**entrenchment** *n.*

entrepôt *n.* a warehouse for temporary storage of goods in transit. [French *entreposer* = store]

entrepreneur *n.* one who undertakes a commercial enterprise with a chance of profit or loss; a contractor acting as an intermediary. —**entrepreneurial** *adj.* [French]

entropy *n.* in ◊thermodynamics, a parameter representing the state of disorder of a system at the atomic, ionic, or molecular level; the greater disorder, the higher the entropy. Thus the fast-moving disordered molecules in water vapour have higher entropy than those of more ordered liquid water, which in turn have more entropy than the molecules in solid crystalline ice. [from Greek *tropē* = transformation]

entrust *v.t.* to give (an object of care) with trust; to assign responsibility *to* (a person).

entry *n.* 1. entering; the liberty to do this. 2. a place of entrance, a door, gate etc. 3. a passage between buildings. 4. an item entered in a diary, list etc.; the recording of this. 5. a person or thing entered in a race, competition etc.; a list of such competitors. [from Old French]

entwine *v.t.* to twine round; to interweave.

E number a code number for additives that have been approved for use by the European Commission (EC). The E written before the number stands for European. E numbers do not have to be displayed on lists of ingredients, and the manufacturer may choose to list ◊additives by their name instead. E numbers cover all categories of additives apart from flavourings. Additives, other than flavourings, that are not approved by the EC, but are still used in Britain, are represented by a code number without an E.

enumerate *v.t.* to count; to specify (items). —**enumeration** /-'reɪʃən/ *n.*, **enumerative** *adj.* [from Latin *numerare* = number]

enumerator *n.* a person employed in census-taking.

enunciate /ɪ'nʌnsɪeɪt/ *v.t.* 1. to pronounce (words) clearly. 2. to state in definite terms. —**enunciation** /-'eɪʃən/ *n.* [from Latin *nuntiare* = announce]

enuresis /enjʊə'riːsɪs/ *n.* involuntary urination. [from Greek *enoureō* = urinate in (*ouron* = urine)]

envelop /ɪn'veləp/ *v.t.* to wrap up; to surround, to cover on all sides. —**envelopment** *n.* [from Old French]

envelope /'envələʊp, 'ɒn-/ *n.* 1. a folded paper container for a letter etc. 2. a wrapper, a covering. 3. the gas container of a balloon or airship. 4. in geometry, a curve that touches all the members of a family of lines or curves. For example, a family of three equal circles all touching each other and forming a triangular pattern (like a clover leaf) has two envelopes: a small circle that fits in the space in the middle, and a large circle that encompasses all three circles.

Enver Pasha /'envə 'pɑːʃə/ 1881–1922. Turkish politician and soldier. He led the military revolt in 1908 that resulted in the Young Turk's revolution (see ◊Turkey). He was killed fighting the Bolsheviks in Turkestan.

enviable /'envɪəbəl/ *adj.* such as to cause envy, desirable. —**enviably** *adv.*

envious /'envɪəs/ *adj. adj.* feeling or showing envy. —**enviously** *adv.*

environment /ɪn'vaɪərənmənt/ *n.* 1. surroundings, especially as affecting people's lives; conditions or circumstances of living. —**environmental** /-'mentəl/ *adj.* 2. in ecology, the sum of conditions affecting a particular organism, including physical surroundings, climate, and influences of other living organisms. See also ◊biosphere and ◊habitat. [from Old French *viron* = circuit, neighbourhood]

Environmentally Sensitive Area (ESA) a protected area under a scheme introduced by the UK Ministry of Agriculture in 1984 in an attempt to preserve some of the most beautiful areas of the British countryside from the loss and damage caused by agricultural change. The areas are in the Pennine Dales, the North Peak District, the Norfolk Broads, the Breckland, the Suffolk River Valleys, the Test Valley, the South Downs, the Somerset Levels and Moors, West Penw, Cornwall, the Shropshire Borders, the Cambrian Mountains, and the Lleyn Peninsular.

Environmental Protection Agency a US agency set up in 1970 to control water and air quality, industrial and commercial wastes, pesticides, noise, and radiation. It aims to protect 'the country from being degraded, and its health threatened, by a multitude of human activities initiated without regard to long-ranging effects upon the life-supporting properties, the economic uses, and the recreational value of air, land, and water'.

environment art large sculptural or spatial works creating environments the spectator may enter. The US artists Jim ◊Dine and Claes ◊Oldenburg were early exponents in the 1960s.

environment–heredity controversy see ◊nature–nurture controversy.

environs /ɪn'vaɪərənz/ *n.pl.* the district around a town etc.

envisage /ɪn'vɪzɪdʒ/ *v.t.* to have a mental picture of (a thing or conditions not yet existing); to conceive as possible or desirable. [from Old French]

envoy /'envɔɪ/ *n.* 1. a messenger or representative. 2. (in full **envoy extraordinary**) a diplomatic agent ranking below ambassador. [from French *envoyer* = send]

E number

a selection of food additives authorized by the European Commission

number	name	typical use	number	name	typical use
	COLOURS		E213	calcium benzoate	
E102	tartrazine	soft drinks	E214	ethyl para-hydroxy-benzoate	
E104	quinoline yellow				
E110	sunset yellow FCF	biscuits	E215	sodium ethyl para-hydroxy-benzoate	
E120	cochineal	alcoholic drinks			
E122	carmoisine	jams and preserves	E216	propyl para-hydroxy-benzoate	
E123	amaranth				
E124	ponceau 4R	dessert mixes	E217	sodium propyl para-hydroxy-benzoate	
E127	erythrosine	glacé cherries			
E131	patent blue V		E218	methyl para-hydroxy-benzoate	
E132	indigo carmine				
E142	green S	pastilles	E220	sulphur dioxide	
E150	caramel	beer, soft drinks, sauces, gravy browning	E221	sodium sulphate	dried fruit, dehydrated vegetables, fruit juices
E151	black PN		E222	sodium bisulphite	and syrups, sausages, fruit-based dairy
E160(b)	annatto; bixin; norbixin	crisps			desserts, cider, beer
E180	pigment rubine (lithol rubine BK)		E223	sodium metabisulphate	and wine; also used to prevent browning of raw
			E224	potassium metabisulphite	peeled potatoes and to condition biscuit doughs
	ANTIOXIDANTS				
E310	propyl gallate	vegetable oils; chewing gum	E226	calcium sulphite	
			E227	calcium bisulphite	
E311	octyl gallate		E249	potassium nitrite	
E312	dodecyl gallate		E250	sodium nitrite	bacon, ham, cured
E320	butylated hydroxynisole (BHA)	beef stock cubes; cheese spread			meats, corned beef and some cheeses
			E251	sodium nitrate	
E321	butylated hydroxytoluene (BHT)	chewing gum	E252	potassium nitrate	
	EMULSIFIERS AND STABILIZERS			OTHERS	
E407	carageenan	quick setting jelly mixes; milk shakes	E450(a)	disodium dihydrogen diphosphate;	
E413	tragacanth	salad dressings; processed cheese		trisodium diphosphate; tetrasodium diphosphate;	buffers, sequestrants, emulsifying salts, stabilizers, texturizers,
				tetrapotassium diphosphate	raising agents, used in whipping cream, fish
	PRESERVATIVES		E450(b)	pentasodium triphosphate;	and meat products, bread, processed
E210	benzoic acid			pentapotassium triphosphate	cheese, canned vegetables
E211	sodium benzoate	beer, jam, salad cream, soft drinks, fruit pulp	E450(c)	sodium polyphosphates; potassium polyphosphates	
E212	potassium benzoate	fruit-based pie fillings, marinated herring and mackere			

envy /'envɪ/ *n.* a feeling of discontented longing aroused by another's better fortune etc.; the object of this feeling. —*v.t.* to feel envy of. [from Old French from Latin *invidia*]

enwrap /ɪn'ræp/ *v.t.* (-pp-) to wrap or enfold.

enzyme /'enzaɪm/ *n.* any of a class of large molecules, consisting entirely or chiefly of protein, found in all cells and essential to life. Enzymes act as catalysts in biochemical reactions in all living organisms. They digest food, convert food energy into ◊ATP, help to manufacture all the molecular components of the body, produce copies of ◊DNA when the cell divides, and control the movement of substances into and out of cells. [from Greek *en* = in and *zumē* = leaven]

Eocene /'iːəʊsiːn/ *adj.* of the second epoch of the Tertiary period of geological time, 55–38 million years ago. —*n.* this epoch. Originally considered the earliest division of the Tertiary, the name means 'early recent', referring to the early forms of mammals evolving at the time, following the extinction of the dinosaurs. [from Greek *eos* = down and *kainos* = new]

E & O E abbreviation of errors and omissions excepted.

EOKA /i'əʊkə/ *n.* an underground organization formed by General George ◊Grivas in 1955 to fight for the independence of Cyprus from Britain and ultimately its union (◊enosis) with Greece. In 1971, 11 years after the independence of Cyprus, Grivas returned to the island to form EOKA B and to resume the fight for enosis, which had not been achieved by the Cypriot government. [acronym from Greek *Ethnikí Orgánosis Kipriakóu Agónos* = National Organization of Cypriot Struggle]

eolith /iːə'lɪθ/ *n.* a chipped stone, once thought to have been manufactured as a primitive tool during the Old Stone Age, but now generally believed to be the result of natural processes, for the most part. [from French from Greek *ēōs* = dawn and *lithos* = stone]

eolithic /iːə'lɪθɪk/ *adj.* of the earliest age of humankind that is represented by the use of worked flint implements.

Eos /'iːɒs/ in Greek mythology, the goddess of the dawn, equivalent to the Roman Aurora.

eotvos unit a unit (symbol E) for measuring small changes in the intensity of the Earth's ◊gravity with horizontal distance.

EP abbreviation of extended-play (record).

Epaminondas /epæmɪ'nɒndæs/ *c.*420–362 BC. The ban general and politician who won a decisive victory over the Spartans at Leuctra in 371. He was killed at the moment of victory at Mantinea.

epaulette /'epəlet/ *n.* an ornamental shoulder-piece worn on a uniform. [from French *épaule* = shoulder]

épée /eɪ'peɪ/ *n.* a sharp-pointed sword used (with the end blunted) in fencing. [French]

epergne /i'pɜːn/ *n.* an ornament for a dinner-table, with small bowls or vases on branched supports.

Epernay /epeə'neɪ/ town in Marne *département*, Champagne-Ardenne region, France; population (1986) 29,000. It is the centre of the champagne industry.

ephedrine /'efədrɪn/ *n.* a drug that acts like adrenaline on the sympathetic ◊nervous system (sympathomimetic). Ephedrine is an alkaloid, $C_{10}H_{15}NO_1$, derived from Asian gymnosperms (genus *Ephedra*) or synthesized. It was once used to relieve bronchospasm in ◊asthma, but has been superseded by safer, more specific drugs. It is contained in some cold remedies as a decongestant. Side effects include rapid heartbeat, tremor, dry mouth, and anxiety. [from *Ephedra*, genus of plants yielding it]

ephemera /i'femərə/ *n.pl.* things of only short-lived usefulness. [from Latin from Greek]

ephemeral /i'femərəl/ *adj.* lasting or living only a day or a few days; transitory. In botany, a plant with a very short life cycle, sometimes as little as six or eight weeks. It may complete several generations in one growing season. A number of common weeds are ephemerals, for example, many groundsels (ragworts and squaw-weeds) *Senecio*; many desert plants take advantage of short periods of rain to germinate and reproduce, passing the dry season as dormant seeds. [from Greek *ephēmeros* = lasting only a day (*epi* = on and *hēmera* = day)]

Ephesus /'efɪsəs/ ancient Greek seaport in Asia Minor, a centre of the ◊Ionian Greeks. St Paul visited the city, and is said to have addressed a letter (◊Epistle) to the Christians there, although it may have been written after his death. In the 2nd century AD Ephesus had a population of 300,000. Its temple of Artemis was destroyed by the Goths in AD 262. Now in Turkey, it is one of the world's largest archaeological sites.

ephod /'efəd/ *n.* a Jewish priestly vestment. [from Hebrew]

epi- /epɪ-/ prefix denoting upon, above, in addition. [from Greek]

epic /'epɪk/ *n.* a narrative poem or cycle of poems dealing with some great deed, often the founding of a nation or the forging of national unity, and frequently using religious or cosmological themes. The two major epic poems in the Western tradition are *The Iliad* and *The Odyssey*, attributed to Homer, and which were probably intended to be chanted in sections at feasts. —*adj.* of or like an epic; grand, heroic. [from Latin from Greek (*epos* = word, narrative song]

epicanthus /epɪ'kænθəs/ *n.* a downward fold of skin which sometimes covers the inner angle (*canthus*) of the eye, especially in Mongolian peoples. —**epicanthic** *adj.* [from Latin *canthus* = corner of the eye]

epicene /'epɪsiːn/ *adj.* of, for, or denoting both sexes; having the characteristics of both sexes or of neither sex. —*n.* an epicene person. [from Latin from Greek *koinos* = common]

epicentre *n.* **1.** the point on the Earth's surface immediately above the seismic focus of an ◊earthquake. Most damage usually takes place at an earthquake's epicentre. The term sometimes refers to a point directly above or below a nuclear explosion ('at ground zero'). **2.** the central point of a difficulty. [from Greek]

Epictetus /epɪk'tiːtəs/ *c.* AD 55–135. Greek Stoic philosopher who encouraged people to refrain from self-interest and to promote the common good of humanity. He believed that people were in the hands of an all-wise providence and that they should endeavour to do their duty in the position to which they were called.

epicure /'epɪkjuə/ *n.* a person of refined tastes in food and drink etc. —**epicurism** *n.* [from *Epicurus*, Greek philosopher]

epicurean /epɪkjuə'riːən/ *adj.* fond of refined sensuous pleasure and luxury. —*n.* a person with epicurean tastes.

Epicureanism /epɪkjuə'riːənɪzəm/ *n.* a system of philosophy that claims soundly based human happiness is the highest good, so that its rational pursuit should be adopted. It was named after the Greek philosopher Epicurus. The most distinguished Roman Epicurean was ◊Lucretius.

Epicurus /epɪ'kuərəs/341–270 BC. Greek philosopher, founder of Epicureanism, who taught at Athens from 306 BC.

epicyclic gear or **sun-and-planet gear** a gear system that consists of one or more gear wheels moving around another. Epicyclic gears are found in bicycle hub gears and in automatic gearboxes.

epicycloid *n.* in geometry, a curve resembling a series of arches traced out by a point on the circumference of a circle that rolls around another circle of a different diameter. If the two circles have the same diameter, the curve is a ◊cardioid.

Epidaurus /epɪ'dɔːrəs/ or **Epidavros** ancient Greek city and port on the E coast of Argolis, in the NE Peloponnese. The site contains a well-preserved ampitheatre of the 4th century BC; nearby are the ruins of the temple of Aesculapius, the god of healing.

epidemic /epɪ'demɪk/ *adj.* (especially of a disease) prevalent among a community at a particular time. —*n.* an epidemic disease. A widespread epidemic that sweeps across many countries (such as the ◊Black Death in the late Middle Ages) is known as a **pandemic.** [from French from Latin from Greek *epidēmia* = prevalence of disease (*dēmos* = the people)]

epidemiology /epɪdiːmi'ɒlədʒɪ/ *n.* the branch of medicine concerned with the control of epidemics.

epidermis /epɪ'dɜːmɪs/ *n.* the outermost layer of ◊cells on an organism's body. In plants and many invertebrates, especially insects, it consists of a single layer of cells,

epicycloid *a seven cusped epicycloid*

an outer noncellular ◊cuticle that protects the organism from dessication. In vertebrates such as reptiles, birds, and mammals, it consists of several layers of cells. The outermost layer of cells is dead and forms a tough, waterproof layer, the ◊skin, which is sloughed off continuously or shed periodically. —**epidermal** *adj.* [Latin from Greek *derma* = skin]

epidiascope /epɪ'daɪəskəup/ *n.* an optical projector giving images of both opaque and transparent objects.

epidural /epɪ'djuərəl/ *adj.* (of an anaesthetic) injected into the duramater round the spinal cord. —*n.* an epidural injection.

epigeal *n.* seed germination in which the ◊cotyledons are borne above the soil.

epiglottis /epɪ'glɒtɪs/ *n.* the cartilage at the root of the tongue. It is depressed to cover the wind-pipe in swallowing, a highly complex reflex process involving two phases. First, a mouthful of chewed food is lifted by the tongue towards the top and back of the mouth, the nasal areas are blocked from the mouth and breathing ceases. Second, the epiglottis moves over the larynx while the food passes down into the oesophagus. —**epiglottal** *adj.* [Greek *glōtta* = tongue]

epigram /'epɪgræm/ *n.* a short poem with a witty ending; a pointed saying. —**epigrammatic** /-grə'mætɪk/ *adj.* [from French or Latin from Greek]

epigraph /'epɪgrɑːf/ *n.* an inscription. —**epigraphic** /-'græfɪk/ *adj.* [from Greek]

epigraphy /e'pɪgrəfɪ/ *n.* the art of writing with a sharp instrument on hard, durable materials such as stone; also the scientific study of epigraphical writings or inscriptions. —**epigraphist** *n.* [Greek *epigráphein* = to write on]

epilepsy /'epɪlepsɪ/ *n.* a medical disorder characterized by a tendency to develop fits, which are convulsions or abnormal feelings caused by abnormal electrical discharges in the cerebral hemispheres of the ◊brain. Epilepsy can be controlled with a number of ◊anticonvulsant drugs. Epileptic fits can be classified into four categories. A *grand mal* seizure may be preceded by a vague feeling of uneasiness leading to loss of consciousness, during which there is a phase of generalized stiffening (the tonic phase), followed by a phase of generalized jerking (the clonic phase). The person may recover immediately, or remain unconscious for many minutes, and confused and drowsy on regaining consciousness. *Petit mal* episodes occur almost exclusively in school-age children; the child stops, stares, and pales slightly. The attack lasts only a few seconds. About 5% of children will have a fit at some time in their lives, but most of these are isolated instances caused by feverish illnesses. **Jacksonian** fits begin with jerking in a small area of the body, for example the angle of the mouth or the thumb. They may spread to involve the whole of one side of the body. After the fit, the affected limbs may be paralysed for several hours. **Temporal-lobe** fits result in hallucinations and feelings of unreality. They may also cause disordered speech and impaired consciousness. Epilepsy is common in the Third World, with up to 30 people per 1,000 affected in some areas; in industrialized countries the figure is 3–5 per 1,000.

epilogue /'epɪlɒg/ *n.* the concluding part of a book etc.; a speech or short poem addressed to an audience by an actor at the end of a play. [from French from Latin from Greek *logos* = speech]

Epiphany /ɪ'pɪfənɪ/ *n.* a festival of the Christian church, held 6 Jan, celebrating the coming of the Magi (the three Wise Men) to Bethlehem with gifts for the infant Jesus, and symbolizing the manifestation of Jesus to the world. It is the 12th day after Christmas, and marks the end of the Christmas festivities. [from Old French from Latin from Greek *phainō* = show]

epiphyte *n.* any plant that grows on another plant or object above the surface of the ground, and has no roots in the soil. An epiphyte does not parasitize the plant it grows on but merely uses it for support. Its nutrients are obtained from rainwater, organic debris such as leaf litter, or from the air. The greatest diversity of epiphytes is found in tropical areas and includes many orchids.

Epirus /ɪ'paɪrəs/ (Greek *Ipiros*) region of NW Greece; area 9,200 sq km/3,551 sq mi; population (1981) 325,000. Its capital is Yannina, and it consists of the provinces (nomes) of Arta, Thesprotia, Yannina, and Preveza. There is livestock farming.

episcopacy /e'pɪskəpəsɪ/ *n.* in the Christian church, a system of government in which administrative and spiritual power over a district (diocese) is held by a bishop. —**the episcopacy**, the bishops. [from French or Latin *episcopus* = bishop]

episcopal /e'pɪskəpəl/ *adj.* of a bishop or bishops; (of a Church) governed by bishops. —**episcopally** *adv.*

episcopalian /epɪskə'peɪlɪən/ *adj.* of episcopacy. —*n.* an adherent of episcopacy; a member of an episcopal Church. —**episcopalianism** *n.*

Episcopalianism /ɪpɪskə'peɪlɪənɪzəm/ *n.* US term for the ◊Anglican Communion.

episcopate /e'pɪskəpət/ *n.* the office or tenure of a bishop. —**the episcopate**, the bishops.

episiotomy /epɪsɪ'ɒtəmɪ/ *n.* an incision made in the perineum (the tissue bridging the vagina and rectum) during childbirth, to aid delivery. [from Greek *epision* = pubic region]

episode /'epɪsəud/ *n.* an incident in a narrative, one part of several in a serial story; an incident or event as part of a sequence; an incidental narrative or series of events. [from Greek *eisodos* = entrance]

episodic /epɪ'sɒdɪk/ *adj.* sporadic, occurring irregularly; incidental. —**episodically** *adv.*

epistemology /epɪstɪ'mɒlədʒɪ/ *n.* a branch of philosophy that examines the nature of knowledge and attempts to determine the limits of human understanding. Central issues include how knowledge is derived and how it is to be validated and tested. —**epistemological** /-ə'lɒdʒɪkəl/ *adj.* [from Greek *epistēmē* = knowledge]

epistle /ɪ'pɪsl/ *n.* in the New Testament, any of the 21 letters to individuals or to the members of various churches written by Christian leaders. The best known are the 13 written by St ◊Paul. The term is also used for a letter addressed to someone in the form of a poem, as in the epistles of ◊Horace and ◊Pope. More recently the word is also applied to letters with a suggestion of pomposity and literary affectation. The epistolary novel, a story told as a series of (fictitious) letters, was popularized by Samuel ◊Richardson in the 18th century. [from Old French from Latin from Greek *stellō* = send]

epistolary /ɪ'pɪstələrɪ/ *adj.* of or suitable for letters.

epitaph /'epɪtɑːf/ *n.* the words inscribed on a tomb or appropriate to a dead person. [from Old French from Latin from Greek *epitaphion* = funeral oration (*taphos* = tomb)]

epithalamium /epɪθə'leɪmɪəm/ *n.* (*plural* **epithalamia**) a nuptial song or poem. [from Latin from Greek *thalamos* = bridal chamber]

epithelium /epɪ'θiːlɪəm/ *n.* (*plural* **epithelia**) the tissue forming the outer layer of the body or lining an open cavity; the epidermis of young cells. —**epithelial** *adj.* [Latin (Greek *thēlē* = teat)]

epithet /'epɪθet/ *n.* an adjective expressing a quality or attribute, a descriptive word. —**epithetic** /-'θetɪk/ *adj.*, **epithetically** *adv.* [from French or Latin from Greek (*tithēmi* = place)]

epitome /e'pɪtəmɪ/ *n.* a person who embodies a quality etc.; a thing that represents another in miniature. [Latin from Greek = abridgement]

epitomize *v.t.* to be an epitome of.

EPLF abbreviation of **Eritrean People's Liberation Front**; see ◊Eritrea.

EPNS abbreviation of **electroplated nickel silver**; see ◊electroplating.

epoch /'iːpɒk/ *n.* a period of history etc. marked by notable events; the beginning of an era in history, life etc.; the division of a geological period, corresponding to a series in rocks. —**epoch-making** *adj.* very important or remarkable. —**epochal** *adj.* [from Latin from Greek = pause]

eponym /'epənɪm/ *n.* a person after whom a place etc. is named. —**eponymous** /ɪ'pɒnɪməs/ *adj.* [from Greek *onoma* = name]

epoxy /ɪ'pɒksɪ/ *adj.* of or derived from a compound in which an oxygen atom and two carbon atoms form a ring.

epoxy resin a synthetic ◊resin used as an ◊adhesive and as an ingredient in paints. Household epoxy resin adhesives come in component form as two separate tubes of chemical, one tube containing resin, the other a curing agent (hardener). The two chemicals are mixed just before application, and the mix soon sets hard.

EPROM /'iːprɒm/ an acronym from erasable programmable read-only memory); a computer memory device in the form of a chip that can record data and retain it indefinitely. The data can be erased by exposure to ultraviolet light and new data added. Other kinds of memory are ◊ROM, ◊PROM, and ◊RAM.

epsilon /ep'saɪlən/ *n.* the fifth letter of the Greek alphabet, = ε, Ε. [Greek = bare E (*psilos* = bare)]

Epsom salts /'epsəm/ hydrated magnesium sulphate, $MgSO_4 \cdot 7H_2O$, used as a relaxant and laxative and added to baths to soothe the skin. The name is derived from a bitter saline spring at Epsom, Surrey, England, which contains the salt in solution.

Epstein /'epstaɪn/ Jacob 1880–1959. British sculptor, born in New York. He experimented with abstract forms, but is chiefly known for muscular nude figures such as *Genesis* 1931 (Whitworth Art Gallery, Manchester).

equable /'ekwəbəl/ *adj.* even, not varying; (of climate) moderate; (of a person) not easily disturbed. —**equably** *adv.* [from Latin *aequabilis*]

equal /'iːkwəl/ *adj.* the same in number, size, degree, merit etc.; evenly balanced; having the same rights or status; uniform in operation. —*n.* a person or thing equal to another, especially a person equal in rank or status. —*v.t.* (**-ll-**) to be equal to; to achieve something that is equal to. —**be equal to**, to have the strength or capacity for. —**equally** *adv.* [from Latin *aequalis* (*aequus* = even, equal)]

equalitarian /ɪːkwɒlɪ'teərɪən/ a variant of **egalitarian**.

equality /ɪː'kwɒlɪtɪ/ *n.* the condition of being equal.

equalize /'iːkwəlaɪz/ *v.t./i.* to make or become equal; in games, to reach an opponent's score. —**equalization** /-'zeɪʃən/ *n.*

equalizer *n.* a goal etc. that equalizes a score.

equal opportunities the right to be employed or considered for employment without discrimination on the grounds of race, gender, physical, or mental handicap.

Equal Opportunities Commission a commission established by the UK government in 1975 to implement the Sex Discrimination Act of 1975. Its aim is to prevent discrimination, particularly on sexual or marital grounds.

equanimity /ekwə'nɪmɪtɪ, iːk-/ *n.* mental composure; acceptance of fate. [from Latin (*aequus* = even and *animus* = mind)]

equate /ɪ'kweɪt/ *v.t.* to regard as equal or equivalent (*to* or *with*). [from Latin *aequus* = equal]

equation /ɪ'kweɪʒən/ *n.* 1. the act of equating, making equal, balancing. 2. a statement of equality between two mathematical expressions involving constants and/or variables, and thus usually including an equals sign (=). For example, the equation $A = \pi r^2$ equates the area A of a circle of radius r to the product πr^2. The algebraic equation $y = mx + c$ is the general one in coordinate geometry for a straight line. 3. the chemical equation $2H_2O = 2H_2 + O_2$ represents the decomposition of water by electrolysis into its constituent elements. A chemical equation must 'balance'; that is, a given element must have the same total number of atoms on one side of the equation as on the other (thus there are four atoms of hydrogen on each side of the above equation). Chemical equations are often written with an arrow or arrows (instead of an equals sign) to indicate the direction of the reaction; thus $2H_2O = 2H_2 + O_2$. If a mathematical equation is true for all variables in a given domain, it is sometimes called an identity, and denoted by $\equiv$. Thus $(x + y)^2 \equiv x^2 + 2xy + y^2$ for all $x, y \in R$. 3. a formula indicating a chemical reaction by the use of symbols. [from Old French or Latin]

equations of motion mathematical equations that give the position and velocity of a moving object at any time. Given the mass of an object, the forces acting on it, and its initial position and velocity, the equations of motion are used to calculate its position and velocity at any later time. The equations must be based on ◊Newton's laws of motion or, if speeds near that of light are involved, on the theory of ◊relativity.

equator /ɪˈpkweɪtə/ n. an imaginary line round the Earth or other body, equidistant from the poles. The **terrestrial equator** is the ◊great circle whose plane is perpendicular to the Earth's axis (the line joining the poles). Its length is 40,092 km/24,901.8 mi, divided into 360 degrees of longitude. The **celestial equator** is the circle in which the plane of the Earth's equator intersects the ◊celestial sphere.

equatorial /ekwəˈtɔːrɪəl/ adj. of or near the equator.

Equatorial Guinea /ˈekwətɔːrɪəl ˈpˈɡɪni/ Republic of; country in W central Africa, bounded N by Cameroon, E and S by Gabon, and W by the Atlantic Ocean; also several small islands off the coast and the larger island of Bioko off the coast of Cameroon; **area** 28,051 sq km/10,828 sq mi; **capital** Malabo (Bioko); **physical** comprises mainland Rio Muni, the small islands of Corisco, Elobey Grande and Elobey Chico, and Bioko (formerly Fernando Po) together with Annobón (formerly Pagalu); **head of state and government** Teodoro Obiang Nguema Mbasogo from 1979; **political system** one-party military republic; **exports** cocoa, coffee, bananas, timber; **population** (1988 est) 336,000; **language** Spanish (official); pidgin English is widely spoken, and on Pagala a Portuguese dialect; **recent history** known as Spanish Guinea until 1968 when independence was achieved. In 1979 Teodoro Obiang Nguema Mbasogo overthrew his uncle, dictator Francisco Macias Nguema, establishing a military regime. Macias was tried and executed. 1982 saw a new constitution and 1989 the re-election of Obiang as president.

equerry /ˈekwərɪ/ n. an officer of the British royal household attending members of the royal family. [earlier *esquiry* from obsolete French *escurie* = stable]

equestrian /ɪˈkwestrɪən/ adj. of horse-riding; on horseback. —n. a rider or performer on a horse. [from Latin *equus* = horse]

equestrianism n. skill in horse riding, as practised under International Equestrian Federation rules. It is an Olympic sport, of which there are three main branches (1) **show jumping** over a course of fences; the winner is usually the competitor with fewest faults, or penalty marks; or, in timed events, the competitor who completes the course most quickly. (2) **three-day eventing**, which tests the all-round abilities of a horse and rider in dressage, a horse's response to control; cross-country, testing speed and endurance; and showjumping, in a final modified contest. (3) **dressage** tests the horse's obedience skills and the rider's control of the horse in a series of movements at walk, trot and canter.

equi- prefix denoting equal. [from Latin *aequus* = equal]

equiangular /iːkwɪˈæŋɡjulə/ adj. having equal angles.

Equiano /ekwɪˈɑːnəʊ/ Olaudah 1745–1797. African antislavery campaigner and writer. He travelled widely as a free man. His autobiography, *The Interesting Narrative of the Life of Olaudah Equiano, or Gustavus Vassa, the African* 1789, is one of the earliest significant works by an African written in English.

equidistant /iːkwɪˈdɪstənt/ adj. at equal distances.

equilateral /iːkwɪˈlætərl/ n. a geometrical figure having all sides of equal length. —adj. having all sides equal. [from Latin *latus* = side]

equilibrate /iːkwɪˈlaɪbreɪt/ v.t./i. to cause (two things) to balance; to balance. —**equilibration** /-ˈbreɪʃən/ n. [from Latin *aequilibrare* (*libra* = balance)]

equilibrium /iːkwɪˈlɪbrɪəm/ n.pl. (*plural* **equilibria**) a state of balance; composure. In physics, an unchanging condition in which forces on a particle or system of particles (a body) cancel out, or in which energy is distributed among the particles of a system in the most probable way; or the state in which a body is at rest or moving at constant velocity. A body is in **thermal equilibrium** if no heat enters or leaves it, so that all its parts are at the same temperature as its surroundings. See also ◊chemical equilibrium. [Latin]

equine /ˈekwaɪn/ adj. of or like a horse. [from Latin *equus* = horse]

equinoctial /iːkwɪˈnɒkʃəl, ek-/ adj. of, happening at or near, an equinox. —n. the celestial equator. —**equinoctial line**, the celestial equator. **equinoctial point**, see equinox.

equinox /ˈekwɪnɒks/ n. 1. the time or date at which the Sun crosses the equator, and day and night are everywhere of equal length. 2. the position of the Sun on the celestial sphere at either of these times (also called the *equinoctial point*). —**autumn** or **autumnal equinox**, about 22 Sept. **spring** or **vernal equinox**, about 20 March. [from Old French or Latin *nox* = night]

equip /ɪˈkwɪp/ v.t. (-pp-) to supply with what is needed. [from French, probably from Old Norse *skipa* = man (ship)]

equipage /ˈekwɪpɪdʒ/ n. equisites, an outfit; a carriage and horses with attendants.

equipment /ɪˈkwɪpmənt/ n. equipping; the necessary outfit, tools, apparatus etc.

equipoise /ˈekwɪpɔɪz, ˈiːk-/ n. 1. equilibrium. 2. a counterbalancing thing.

equitable /ˈekwɪtəbəl/ adj. fair, just; valid in equity rather than law. —**equitably** adv.

equitation /ekwɪˈteɪʃən/ n. riding on a horse; horsemanship. [from French or Latin *equitare* = ride horse]

equity /ˈekwɪtɪ/ n. 1. fairness; the principles of justice as supplementing the ordinary rules of law where the application of these would operate harshly in a particular case; sometimes it is regarded as an attempt to achieve 'natural justice'. So understood, equity appears as an element in most legal systems, and in a number of legal codes judges are instructed to apply both the rules of strict law and the principles of equity in reaching their decisions. 2. a company's assets, less its liabilities, which are the property of the owner or shareholders. Popularly, equities are stocks and shares which, unlike debentures and preference shares, do not pay interest at fixed rates but pay dividends based on the company's performance. The value of equities tends to rise over the long term, but in the short term they are a risk investment because of fluctuating values. [from Old French from Latin *aequus* = equal, fair]

Equity n. in the UK theatre, a shortened term for the British Actors' Equity Association, the trade union for professional actors in theatre, film, and television, founded in 1929. In the USA, its counterpart is the American Actors' Equity Association which, however, deals only with performers in the theatre.

equivalent /ɪˈkwɪvələnt/ adj. equal in value, amount, importance etc.; corresponding; meaning the same; having the same result. —n. an equivalent thing, amount etc. —**equivalence** n. [from Old French from Latin *valere* = be worth]

equivocal /ɪˈkwɪvəkəl/ adj. of double or doubtful meaning; of uncertain nature; questionable, dubious. —**equivocally** adv. [from Latin *aequivocus* (*vocare* = call)]

equivocate /ɪˈkwɪvəkeɪt/ v.i. to use equivocal terms to conceal the truth. —**equivocation** /-ˈkeɪʃən/ n., **equivocator** n.

ER abbreviation of 1. Queen Elizabeth (Latin *Elizabetha Regina*). 2. King Edward (Latin *Edwardus Rex*).

er /ɜː, ə/ interjection expressing hesitation. [imitative]

Er symbol for ◊erbium.

era /ˈɪərə/ n. a system of chronology starting from a noteworthy event; a historical or other period, the date beginning this; a major division of geological time. [Latin = number expressed in figures (originally plural of *aes* = money)]

eradicable /ɪˈrædɪkəbəl/ adj. able to be eradicated.

eradicate /ɪˈrædɪkeɪt/ v.t. to root out, to destroy completely. —**eradication** /-ˈkeɪʃən/ n., **eradicator** n. [from Latin *eradicare* (*radix* = root)]

Erasmus *An engraving by the German artist Dürer of Desiderius Erasmus, the Renaissance Dutch scholar and theologian.*

erase /ɪ'reɪz/ *v.t.* to rub out; to obliterate, to remove all traces of; to remove a recording from (magnetic tape). [from Latin *eradere* (*radere* = scrape)]

eraser *n.* a thing that erases, especially a piece of rubber etc. for removing pencil marks.

Erasmus /ɪ'ræzməs/ Desiderius *c.*1466–1536. Dutch scholar and leading humanist of the Renaissance era, he taught and studied all over Europe and was a prolific writer. His pioneer translation of the Greek New Testament in 1516 exposed the Vulgate as a second-hand document. Although opposed to dogmatism and abuse of church power, he remained impartial during Martin ◊Luther's conflict with the pope.

Erastianism /ɪ'ræstɪənɪzəm/ *n.* the belief that the church should be subordinated to the state. The name is derived from Thomas Erastus (1534–83), a German-Swiss theologian and opponent of Calvinism, who maintained in his writings that the church should not have the power of excluding people as a punishment for sin.

erasure /ɪ'reɪʒə/ *n.* 1. the act of erasing. 2. an erased word etc.

Eratosthenes /erə'tɒsθəniːz/ *c.*276–194 BC. Greek geographer and mathematician, whose map of the ancient world was the first to contain lines of latitude and longitude, and who calculated the Earth's circumference with an error of about 10%. His mathematical achievements include a method for duplicating the cube, and for finding ◊prime numbers (**Eratosthenes' sieve**).

erbium /'ɜːbɪəm/ *n.* a soft, lustrous, greyish, metallic element of the ◊lanthanide series, symbol Er, atomic number 68, relative atomic mass 167.26. It occurs with yttrium or as a minute part of various minerals. It is named after the town of Ytterby, Sweden, where the rare-earth elements were first discovered in 1843 by Carl Mosander (1797–1858).

ere /eə/ *prep. & conj.* (*archaic* or *poetic*) before. [Old English, originally a comparative]

Erebus, Mount /'erɪbəs/ the world's southernmost active volcano, 3,794 m/12,452 ft high, on Ross Island, Antarctica.

Erebus /'erɪbəs/ in Greek mythology, the god of darkness and the intermediate region between upper Earth and ◊Hades.

erect /ɪ'rekt/ *adj.* upright, vertical; (of hair) bristling; (of the penis etc.) enlarged and rigid from sexual excitement. —*v.t.* 1. to raise, to set upright, to build. 2. to establish. —**erection** *n.* [from Latin *erigere* = set up]

erectile /ɪ'rektaɪl/ *adj.* that can become erect (especially of body tissue by sexual excitement).

erector *n.* a person or thing that erects something; a muscle causing erection.

eremite /'erɪmaɪt/ a hermit, especially a Christian recluse. —**eremitic** /-'mɪtɪk/ *adj.*, **eremitical** *adj.* [from Old French]

Erfurt /'eəfʊət/ city in Federal Republic of Germany on the river Gera, capital of the state of Thuringia; popu-

lation (1990) 217,000. It is in a rich horticultural area, and its industries include textiles, typewriters, and electrical goods.

erg *n.* the c.g.s. unit of work or energy, replaced in the SI system by the ◊joule. One erg of work is done by a force of one ◊dyne moving through one centimetre. [from Greek *ergon* = work]

ergo /'ɜːgəʊ/ *adv.* therefore. [Latin]

ergonomics /ɜːgə'nɒmɪks/ *n.* the study of the efficiency of people in their working environment. The object is to improve work performance by removing sources of muscular stress and general fatigue; for example, by presenting data and control panels in easy-to-view form, making office furniture comfortable, and creating a generally pleasant environment. —**ergonomic** *adj.*, **ergonomically** *adv.*

ergot /'ɜːgət/ *n.* 1. certain parasitic fungi (especially of the genus *Claviceps*), whose brown or black grainlike masses replace the kernels of rye or other cereals. *C. purpurea* attacks the rye plant. Ergot poisoning is caused by eating infected bread, resulting in burning pains, gangrene, and convulsions. 2. a drug prepared from the fungus. 3. a horny protuberance on the inner side of a horse's fetlock. [French, from Old French *argot* = cock's spur (from the appearance of the diseased grain etc.)]

ergotamine *n.* an ◊alkaloid, $C_{33}H_{35}O_5N_5$, administered to treat migraine and to induce childbirth, isolated from ergot, a fungus that colonizes rye. It relieves symptoms by causing the cranial arteries to constrict. Its use is limited by severe side effects, including nausea and abdominal pain.

Erhard /'eəhɑːt/ Ludwig 1897–1977. West German Christian Democrat politician, chancellor of the Federal Republic 1963–66. The 'economic miracle' of West Germany's recovery after World War II is largely attributed to Erhard's policy of social free enterprise (German *Marktwirtschaft*), which he initiated during his period as federal economics minister (1949–63).

erica *n.* in botany, any plant of the genus *Erica*, family Ericaceae, including the heathers. There are about 500 species, distributed mainly in South Africa, with a few in Europe.

Ericsson /'erɪksən/ John 1803–1889. Swedish-born US engineer who took out a patent to produce screw-propeller powered paddle-wheel ships in 1836. He built a number of such ships, including the *Monitor*, which was successfully deployed during the Civil War.

Ericsson Leif *c.*AD 1000. Norse explorer, son of Eric the Red, who sailed west from Greenland about 1000 to find a country first sighted by Norsemen in 986. Landing with 35 companions in North America, he called it Vinland, because he discovered grape vines growing there.

Eric the Red /'erɪk/ 940–1010. Allegedly the first European to find Greenland. According to a 13th-century saga, he was the son of a Norwegian chieftain, who was banished from Iceland about 982 for murder and then sailed westward and discovered a land that he called Greenland.

Eridu /'eərɪduː/ ancient city of Mesopotamia about 5000 BC, according to tradition the cradle of Sumerian civilization. On its site is now the village of Tell Abu Shahrain, Iraq.

Erie, Lake /'ɪərɪ/ fourth largest of the Great Lakes of North America, connected to Lake Ontario by the Niagara river and bypassed by the Welland Canal; area 25,720 sq km/9,930 sq mi.

Erin /'ɪərɪn/ poetic name for Ireland derived from the dative case Érinn of the Gaelic name Ériu, possibly derived from Sanskrit 'western'.

Eritrea /eri'trɪə/ province of N Ethiopia: **area** 117,600 sq km/45,394 sq mi; **capital** Asmara; **towns** Assab and Massawa (Ethiopia's outlets to the sea); **physical** coastline on the Red Sea 1,000 km/620 mi; narrow coastal plain rising to an inland plateau; **products** coffee, salt, citrus fruits, grains, cotton; **currency** birr; **population** (1984) 2,615,000; **language** Amharic (official); **religion** Islam; **history** part of an ancient Ethiopian kingdom until the 7th century; under Ethiopian influence until it fell to the Turks mid-16th century; Italian colony 1889–1941, where it was the base for Italian invasion of Ethiopia; under British administration from 1941 to 1952, when it became an autonomous part of Ethiopia. Since 1962, when it became a region, various secessionist movements have risen. During the civil war 1970s, guerrillas held most of Eritrea; The

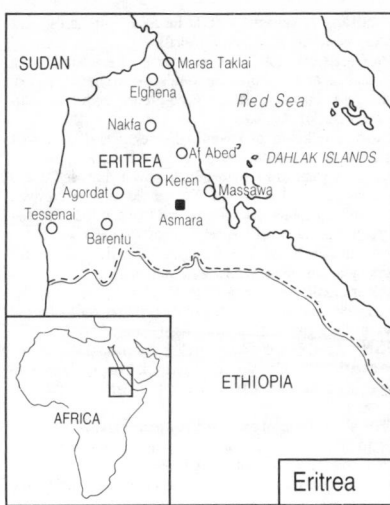

Eritrea

Ethiopian government, backed by Soviet and Cuban forces, recaptured most towns in 1978. Resistance continued throughout the 1980s, aided by conservative Gulf states, and some cooperation with guerrillas in Tigray province.

Erl-King /'ɜːlkɪŋ/ in Germanic folklore, the king of the elves. He inhabited the Black Forest and lured children to their death. The Romantic writer J W Goethe's poem 'Erlkönig' was set to music by Franz Schubert in 1816.

ERM abbreviation of ◊Exchange Rate Mechanism.

ermine /'ɜːmɪn/ *n.* **1.** the ◊stoat during winter, when its coat becomes white. In northern latitudes the coat becomes completely white, except for a black tip to the tail, but in warmer regions the back may remain brownish. **2.** its white fur, used in the robes of judges, peers etc. [from Old French]

erminois /'ɜːmɪˈnɔɪz/ *n.* a heraldic fur, or with sable 'spots' [from Old French = ermine]

erne /ɜːn/ *n.* the sea eagle *Haliaetus albicilla.* [Old English]

Ernie /'ɜːnɪ/ *n.* a device used (from 1956) for drawing the prize-winning numbers of Premium Bonds. [acronym from Electronic Random Number Indicator Equipment]

Ernst /eənst/ Max 1891–1976. German artist who worked in France 1922–38 and in the USA from 1941. He was an active Dadaist, experimenting with collage, photomontage, and surreal images, and helped found the Surrealist movement 1924. His paintings are highly diverse.

erode /ɪˈrəʊd/ *v.t.* to wear away or destroy gradually. —**erosion** *n.*, **erosional** *adj.*, **erosive** *adj.* [from French or Latin *rodere* = gnaw]

erogenous /ɪˈrɒdʒɪnəs/ *adj.* causing sexual desire, particularly sensitive to sexual stimulation. [from Greek *erōs* = sexual love]

Eros /'ɪərɒs/ **1.** in Greek mythology, boy-god of love, traditionally armed with bow and arrows. He was the son of Aphrodite, and fell in love with ◊Psyche. He is identified with the Roman Cupid. **2.** in astronomy, an asteroid, discovered 1898, 22 million km/14 million mi from the Earth at its nearest point. Eros was the first asteroid to be discovered that has an orbit coming within that of Mars. It is elongated, measures about 36 × 12 km/22 × 7 mi, rotates around its shortest axis every 5.3 hours, and orbits the Sun every 1.8 years.

erosion *n.* in geology, the processes whereby the rocks and soil of the Earth's surface are loosened, worn away, and transported (◊weathering does not involve transportation). **Chemical erosion** involves the alteration of the mineral component of the rock, by means of rainwater or the substances dissolved in it, and its subsequent movement. **Physical erosion** involves the breakdown and transportation of exposed rocks by physical forces. In practice the two work together.

erotic /ɪˈrɒtɪk/ *adj.* of or causing sexual excitement or desire. —**erotically** *adv.* [from French from Greek *erōs* = sexual love]

erotica /ɪˈrɒtɪkə/ *n.pl.* erotic literature or art.

eroticism /ɪˈrɒtɪsɪzəm/ *n.* erotic character, sexual excitement.

err /ɜː/ *v.i.* to be mistaken or incorrect; to do wrong, to sin. [from Old French from Latin *errare* = wander, stray]

errand /'erənd/ *n.* a short journey for taking a message, collecting goods etc.; the object of a journey. —**errand of mercy**, a journey to relieve distress etc. [Old English]

errant[1] /'erənt/ *n.* erring.

errant[2] *adj.* travelling in search of adventure. —**errantry** *n.* [from Old French from Latin *itinerare* (*iter* = journey)]

erratic /ɪˈrætɪk/ *adj.* uncertain in movement; irregular in conduct or opinion etc. —**erratic block**, a large rock brought from a distance by a glacier. —**erratically** *adv.* [from Old French from Latin *erraticus*]

erratum /eˈrɑːtəm/ *n.* (*plural* **errata**) an error in printing or writing. [Latin]

erroneous /ɪˈrəʊnɪəs/ *adj.* incorrect. —**erroneously** *adv.* [from Old French or Latin (*erro* = vagabond)]

error /'erə/ *n.* a mistake; the condition of being wrong in opinion or conduct; a wrong opinion; the amount of inaccuracy in a calculation or measurement.

error detection in computing, the techniques a program uses to detect incorrect data. A common method is to add a check digit to important codes, such as account numbers and product codes. The digit is chosen so that the code conforms to a rule that the program can verify. Another technique involves calculating the sum (called the ◊hash total) of each instance of a particular item of data and storing it at the end of the data.

ersatz /'eəzæts/ *n.* a substitute or imitation. —*adj.* synthetic, imitation. [German = replacement]

Erse /ɜːs/*adj.* & *n.* Irish Gaelic (see ◊Gaelic). [early Scottish form of *Irish*]

Ershad /'eəʃəd/ Hussain Mohammad 1930– . Military ruler of Bangladesh from 1982. He became chief of staff of the Bangladeshi army in 1979 and assumed power in a military coup in 1982. As president from 1983, Ershad introduced a successful rural-oriented economic programme. He was re-elected in 1986 and lifted martial law, but faced continuing political opposition.

Ershad Hussain Mohammad 1930– . Military leader of Bangladesh 1982–90. He became chief of staff in the Bangladesh army in 1979 and assumed power in a military coup in 1982. As president from 1983, Ershad introduced a successful rural-orientated economic programme. He was re-elected in 1986 and lifted martial law, but faced continuing political opposition.

erstwhile /'ɜːstwaɪl/ *adj.* former, previous. —*adv.* (*archaic*) formerly. [Old English superlative]

eructation /iːrʌkˈteɪʃən/ *n.* belching. [from Latin *ructare* = belch]

erudite /'eruːdaɪt/ *adj.* learned, showing great learning. —**erudition** /-'dɪʃən/ *n.* [from Latin *erudire* (*rudis* = untrained)]

erupt /ɪˈrʌpt/ *v.i.* **1.** to break out suddenly or dramatically. **2.** (of a volcano) to shoot out lava etc. **3.** (of a rash) to appear on the skin. —**eruption** *n.*, **eruptive** *adj.* [from Latin *rumpere* = break]

erysipelas /erɪˈsɪpɪləs/ *n.* an acute disease of the skin or mucous membranes due to infection by a streptococcus. Starting at some point where the skin is broken or injured, the infection spreads, producing a swollen red patch with small blisters and generalized fever. The condition is now rare.

erythrocyte /ɪˈrɪθrəʊsaɪt/ *n.* another name for a ◊red blood cell. [from Greek *eruthros* = red]

Es symbol for ◊einsteinium.

ESA abbreviation for ◊**European Space Agency.**

Esaki /ɪˈsɑːki/ Leo 1925– . Japanese physi~~~ in 1957 noticed that electrons could so~~~ through the barrier formed at th~ semiconductors. The effect ~ electronics industry. ~~~ the 1973 Nobel ~~~ and Ivar ~~~

Esarhaddon /ˈiːsɑːˈhædn/ King of Assyria from 680 BC, when he succeeded his father ◊Sennacherib. He conquered Egypt 674–71 BC.

Esau /ˈiːsɔː/ in the Old Testament, the son of Isaac and Rebekah, and the hirsute elder twin brother of Jacob. Jacob tricked the blind Isaac into giving him the blessing intended for Esau by putting on goatskins for Isaac to feel. Earlier Esau had sold his birthright to Jacob for a 'mess of red pottage'. Esau was the ancestor of the Edomites.

escalate /ˈeskəleɪt/ v.t./i. to increase or develop (usually rapidly) by stages; to become more intense, to cause to do so. —**escalation** /-ˈleɪʃən/ n. [from escalade = climb wall by ladder]

escalator /ˈeskəleɪtə/ n. an automatic moving staircase that carries people between floors or levels. It consists of treads linked in an endless belt arranged to form strips (steps), powered by an electric motor that moves both steps and handrails at the same speed. Towards the top and bottom the steps flatten out for ease of passage. The first escalator was exhibited in Paris in 1900.

escalope /ˈeskələup/ n. a slice of boneless meat, especially from a leg of veal. [French, originally = shell]

escapade /eskəˈpeɪd/ n. a piece of daring or reckless adventure. [French, from Provençal or Spanish]

escape /ɪˈskeɪp/ v.t./i. to get free of restriction or control, to get free from; (of gas etc.) to leak from a container etc.; to elude, to avoid (punishment, commitment etc.); to elude the notice or memory of; (of words etc.) to issue unawares from (a person, the lips). —n. the act of escaping; a means or the fact of escaping; a leakage of gas etc.; temporary relief from reality or worry. —**escape clause**, one specifying the conditions under which a party to a contract is free from obligations. **escape velocity**, the minimum velocity needed to escape from the gravitational field of a body. —**escaper** n. [from Anglo-French from Latin cappa = cloak]

escapee /eskeɪˈpiː/ n. one who has escaped.

escapement /ɪˈskeɪpmənt/ n. the part of a watch or clock mechanism connecting and regulating its motive power.

escape velocity the minimum velocity with which an object must be projected for it to escape from the gravitational pull of a planetary body. In the case of the Earth, the escape velocity is 11.2 kps/6.9 mps; the Moon, 2.4 kps/1.5 mps; Mars, 5 kps/3.1 mps; and Jupiter, 59.6 kps/37 mps.

escapism /ɪˈskeɪpɪzəm/ n. a tendency to seek distraction or relief from reality. —**escapist** n.

escapology /eskəˈpɒlədʒɪ/ n. the methods and technique of escaping from captivity or confinement. —**escapologist** n.

escarpment /ɪˈskɑːpmənt/ n. a long steep slope at the edge of a plateau. [from French from Italian scarpa]

eschatology /eskəˈtɒlədʒɪ/ n. a doctrine of death and the afterlife. —**eschatological** /-ˈlɒdʒɪkəl/ adj. [from Greek eskhatos = last]

escheat /ɪsˈtʃiːt/ n. (historical) the lapse of property to the government etc., on the owner's dying intestate without heirs; the property so lapsing. —v.t./i. to hand over or revert as an escheat; to confiscate. [from Old French from Latin excidere (cadere = fall)]

Escher /ˈeʃə/ Maurits Cornelis 1902–1972. Dutch graphic artist. His prints are often based on mathematical concepts and contain paradoxes and illusions. The lithograph Ascending and Descending 1960, with interlocking staircases creating a perspective puzzle, is typical.

eschew /ɪsˈtʃuː/ v.t. to avoid, to abstain from. [from Old French from Germanic]

escort /ˈeskɔːt/ n. a person or group of persons, vehicles, ships etc., accompanying a person or thing for protection or as a courtesy; a person accompanying another of the opposite sex socially. —/ɪˈskɔːt/ v.t. to act as an escort to. [from French from Italian scorgere = conduct]

escritoire /eskriˈtwɑː/ n. a writing-desk with drawers etc. [French, from Latin = scriptorium]

escrow n. in law, a document sealed and delivered to a third party and not released or coming into effect until some condition has been fulfilled or performed, whereupon the document takes full effect. [Old French escroe, 'scroll']

escudo /eˈskjuːdəu/ n. (plural escudos) the mon- ··· ··· ·unit of proprietary name of Portugal. [Spanish & ·· Latin scutum = shield]

esculent /ˈeskjulənt/ adj. fit for food. —n. an esculent substance. [from Latin esca = food]

escutcheon /ɪˈskʌtʃən/ n. a shield or emblem bearing a coat of arms. —**blot on one's escutcheon**, a stain on one's reputation. [from Anglo-French from Latin scutum = shield]

Esenin /jeˈsenin/ or **Yesenin**, Sergey 1895–1925. Soviet poet, born in Konstantinovo (renamed Esenino in his honour). He went to Petrograd 1915, attached himself to the Symbolists, welcomed the Russian Revolution, revived peasant traditions and folklore, and initiated the Imaginist group of poets in 1919. A selection of his poetry was translated in Confessions of a Hooligan 1973. He was married briefly to the US dancer Isadora Duncan 1922–23.

esker /ˈeskə/ n. a long ridge of gravel in a river valley, originally deposited by a stream formed from the melting of ice under a glacier. [from Irish eiscir]

ESN abbreviation of educationally subnormal.

esoteric /iːsəuˈterɪk/ adj. intelligible only to those with special knowledge. [from Greek (comparative of esō = within)]

ESP abbreviation of extra-sensory perception.

espadrille /ˈespəˈdrɪl/ n. a light canvas shoe with a plaited fibre sole. [French from Provençal]

espalier /ɪˈspælɪə/ n. a lattice-work along which the branches of a tree or shrub are trained; a tree or shrub so trained. [French from Italian spalla = shoulder]

esparto /eˈspɑːtəu/ n. a coarse grass Stipa tenacissima, native to S Spain, S Portugal, and the Balearics, but now widely grown in dry, sandy locations throughout the world. The plant is just over 1 m/3 ft high, producing greyish-green leaves, which are used for making paper, ropes, baskets, mats, and cables. [Spanish from Latin from Greek sparton = rope]

especial /ɪˈspeʃəl/ adj. special, exceptional. [from Old French from Latin specialis]

especially adv. particularly, more than in other cases.

Esperanto /espəˈræntəu/ n. an artificial language devised in 1887 by Ludwig L Zamenhof (1859–1917) as an international auxiliary language. For its structure and vocabulary it draws on Latin, the Romance languages, English, and German. [pen name (from Latin sperare = hope) of its inventor]

espionage /ˈespɪənɑːz/ n. the practice of spying; a way to gather ◊intelligence. [French espion = spy]

esplanade /espləˈneɪd/ n. a level open area, especially for walking on or separating a fortress from a town. [French from Spanish from Latin explanare = make level]

espousal /ɪˈspauzəl/ n. **1.** the espousing of a cause. **2.** (often in plural) betrothal, marriage. [from Old French from Latin sponsalia]

espouse /ɪˈspauz/ v.t. **1.** to adopt or support (a cause). **2.** to marry; to give (a woman) in marriage. [from Old French from Latin sponsare (spondēre = betroth)]

espresso /eˈspresəu/ n. (plural espressos) strong, concentrated coffee made under steam pressure; a machine for making this. [Italian = pressed out]

esprit /ˈespriː/ n. sprightliness; wit. —**esprit de corps** /də ˈkɔː/ devotion and loyalty to a body by its members. [French from Latin spiritus = breath]

Espronceda /espronˈθeɪðə/ José de 1808–1842. Spanish poet. Originally one of the Queen's guards, he lost his commission because of his political activities, and was involved in the Republican uprisings of 1835 and 1836. His lyric poetry and life style both owed much to Byron.

espy /ɪˈspaɪ/ v.t. to catch sight of. [from Old French espier = espy]

Esq. abbreviation of esquire.

-esque /-esk/ suffix forming adjectives in the sense 'after the style of' (romanesque). [French from Italian from Latin -iscus]

Esquipulas /eskiˈpʌləs/ a pilgrimage town in Chiquimula department, SE Guatemala; seat of the 'Black Christ' which is a symbol of peace throughout Central America. In May 1986 five Central American presidents met here to discuss a plan for peace in the region.

esquire /ɪˈskwaɪə/ n. **1.** a title added to a man's surname when no other title is used, especially as a form of address in letters. **2.** (archaic) a squire. [from Old French from Latin scutarius = shield-bearer (scutum = shield)]

Esquivel /eski'vel/ Adolfo 1932– . Argentine sculptor and architect. As leader of the Servicio de Paz y Justicia (Peace and Justice Service), a Catholic-Protestant human-rights organization, he was awarded the 1980 Nobel Peace Prize.

-ess /-ıs/ suffix forming nouns denoting females (*actress, goddess*). [from French, ultimately from Greek *-issa*]

essay /'eseı/ *n.* a short piece of nonfiction, often dealing with a particular subject from a personal point of view. The essay became a recognized genre with the French writer Montaigne's *Essais* 1580. Francis Bacon's *Essays* 1597 are among the most famous in English. From the 19th century the essay was increasingly used in Europe and the USA as a vehicle for literary criticism. —*v.t.* to attempt. [from French from Latin *exagium* = weighing]

essayist /'eseıist/ *n.* a writer of essays.

Essen /'esən/ city in North Rhine–Westphalia, West Germany; population (1988) 615,000. It is the administrative centre of the Ruhr, with textile, chemical, and electrical industries.

essence /'esəns/ *n.* 1. all that makes a thing what it is; an indispensable quality or element. 2. an extract got by distillation etc.; a perfume, a scent. —**in essence**, fundamentally. **of the essence**, indispensable. [from Old French from Latin *essentia* (*esse* = be)]

Essene /'esi:n/ *n.* a member of an ancient Jewish religious sect located in the area near the Dead Sea about 200 BC–AD 200, whose members lived a life of denial and asceticism, as they believed that the day of judgement was imminent.

essential /ı'senʃ(ə)l/ *adj.* necessary, indispensable; of or constituting a thing's essence. —*n.* an indispensable or fundamental element or thing. —**essential oil**, a volatile oil with an odour characteristic of the plant from which it is extract ed. —**essentiality** /-ʃı'ælıtı/ *n.*, **essentially** *adv.* [from Latin]

Essequibo /esi'kwi:bəu/ the longest river in Guyana, South America, rising in the Guiana highlands of S Guyana; length 1,014 km/630 mi. Part of the district of Essequibo, which lies to the west of the river, is claimed by Venezuela.

Essex /'esıks/ county in SE England: **area** 3,670 sq km/ 1,417 sq mi; **administrative headquarters** Chelmsford; **physical** former royal hunting ground of Epping Forest (controlled from 1882 by the City of London); the marshy coastal headland of the Naze. **products** dairy produce, cereals, fruit; **population** (1987) 1,522,000.

Essex Robert Devereux, 2nd Earl of Essex 1566–1601. English soldier and politician. He became a favourite with Elizabeth I from 1587, but was executed because of his policies in Ireland. Essex fought in the Netherlands 1585–86 and distinguished himself at the Battle of Zutphen. In 1596 he jointly commanded a force that seized and sacked Cádiz. In 1599 he became Lieutenant of Ireland and led an army against Irish rebels under the Earl of Tyrone in Ulster, but was unsuccessful, made an unauthorized truce with Tyrone, and returned without permission to England. He was forbidden to return to court, and when he marched into the City of London at the head of a body of supporters, he was promptly arrested, tried for treason, and beheaded on Tower Green.

est. abbreviation of estimate(d).

establish /ı'stæblıʃ/ *v.t.* 1. to set up (a system, business etc.) on a permanent basis; to settle (a person etc. *in* an office etc.). 2. to cause to be generally accepted, to prove, to place beyond dispute. —**Established Church**, the Church recognized by the State. [from Old French from Latin *stabilire* = make stable]

estate[1] /ı'steıt/ *n.* in law, a person's rights in relation to any property. **Real estate** is an interest in any land; **personal estate** is an interest in any other kind of property.

estate[2] *n.* in European history, an order of society that enjoyed a specified share in government. In medieval theory, there were usually three estates, the **nobility**, the **clergy**, and the **commons**, with the functions of, respectively, defending society from foreign aggression and internal disorder, attending to its spiritual needs, and working to produce the base with which to support the other two orders.

esteem /ı'sti:m/ *v.t.* to have a high regard for, to think favourably of; to consider to be. —*n.* high regard or favour. [from Old French from Latin *aestimare* = fix price of]

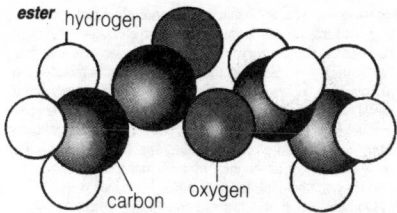

Model of the ester ethyl ethanoate, $CH_3 \, CO_2 \, CH_2 \, CH_3$

ester /'estə/ *n.* an organic compound formed by the reaction between an alcohol and an acid, with the elimination of water. Unlike ◊salts, esters are covalent compounds. [German, probably from *essig* = vinegar and *ather* = ether]

Esterházy, Schloss the palace of the princes Esterházy in the city of Eisenstadt, Austria. Originally a medieval stronghold, it was rebuilt in the Baroque style 1663–72. Under the patronage of the Esterházy's, the composer Josef Haydn was kappelmeister here for 30 years.

Esther /'estə/ in the Old Testament, the wife of the Persian king Ahasuerus (Xerxes I), who prevented the extermination of her people by the king's vizier Haman. Their deliverance is celebrated in the Jewish festival of Purim. Her story is told in the Old Testament Book.

estimable /'estıməbəl/ *adj.* worthy of esteem. [French from Latin]

estimate /'estımət/ *n.* an approximate judgement of number, amount, quality, character etc.; a price quoted for work etc. to be undertaken. —/-eıt/ *v.t.* 1. to form an estimate or opinion of; to form an estimate *that.* 2. to fix by estimate (*at*). —**estimator** *n.* [from Latin *aestimare* = fix price of]

estimation /esti'meıʃən/ *n.* estimating; a judgement of worth. [from Old French or Latin]

estoile /e'stɔıl/ *n.* in heraldry, a charge in the form of a star with wavy points or rays. [Old French = star]

Estonia /e'stəunıə/ constituent republic of the USSR from 1940: **area** 45,100 sq km/17,432 sq mi; **capital** Tallinn; **features** mild climate, lakes and marshes in a partly forested plain; **products** oil (from shale), wood products, flax, dairy and pig products; **population** (1987) 1,556,000; 61% Estonian, 28% Russian, 3% Ukrainian, 2% Byelorussian; **language** Estonian, allied to Finnish; **history** the workers' and soldiers' soviets took control in Nov 1917, were overthrown by German troops Mar in 1918, and were restored in Nov 1918. They were overthrown with the help of the British navy in May 1919, and Estonia was a democratic republic until overthrown by a fascist coup in 1934. It was incorporated into the the USSR in 1940. Nationalist dissent grew from 1980. In 1988 Estonia adopted its own constitution, with a power of veto on all Soviet legislation. The new constitution allowed private property and placed land and natural resources under Estonian control. In 1989 parliament passed a law replacing Russian with Estonian as the main language.

estradiol *n.* a type of ◊oestrogen (female sex hormone).

estrange /ı'streındʒ/ *v.t.* to cause (a person) to turn away in feeling or affection (*from* another). —**estrangement** *n.* [from Anglo-French from Latin *extraneare* = treat as a stranger]

estrogen *n.* an alternative spelling of ◊oestrogen.

estuary *n.* a river mouth widening into the sea, where fresh water mixes with salt water and tidal effects are felt. [from Latin *aestuarium* = tidal channel (*aestus* = tide)]

eta /'i:tə/ *n.* the seventh letter of the Greek alphabet, = η, H . [Greek]

ETA abbreviation of 1. estimated time of arrival. 2. /'etə/ (*Spanish*) a Basque separatist movement.

et al. abbreviation of et alii. [Latin = and others]

etc. abbreviation of et cetera. [Latin = and the rest, and so on]

et cetera /et 'setərə/and the rest, and so on. —**etceteras** *n.pl.* extras, sundries. [Latin]

etch *v.t./i.* 1. to reproduce (a picture etc.) by engraving a metal plate with acid, especially to print copies; to engrave (a plate) with acid; to practise this craft. 2. (*figurative*) to impress deeply (*on*). [from Dutch from German from Old High German *azzen* = cause to eat]

etching *n.* **1.** a print made from an etched plate; the art of producing etched prints. The first etchings date from the early 16th century, although the basic principle had been utilized earlier for the decoration of armour. **2.** a printmaking technique in which the design is made from a metal plate and the action of acid. The plate (usually copper or zinc) is covered with a waxy overlayer (ground) and then drawn on with an etching needle. The exposed areas are then 'etched', or bitten into, by a corrosive agent (acid), so that they will hold ink for printing.

ETD abbreviation of estimated time of departure.

eternal /i'tɜːnəl/ *adj.* existing always, without end or (usually) beginning; unchanging; constant, too frequentative —**the Eternal**, God. —**eternally** *adv.* [from Latin *aeternus* (*aevum* = age)]

eternity /i'tɜːnɪtɪ/ *n.* infinite (especially future) time; endless life after death; being eternal; (*colloquial*) a very long time. —**eternity ring**, a finger-ring with gems set all round it.

ethanal *n.* common name **acetaldehyde** one of the chief members, CH_3CHO, of the group of organic compounds known as ◊aldehydes. It is a colourless inflammable liquid boiling at $20.8°C/69.6°F$. Ethanal is formed by the oxidation of ethene and is used to make many other organic chemical compounds.

ethane *n.* a colourless, odourless gas, CH_3CH_3, the second member of the ◊alkane series of hydrocarbons (paraffins).

ethane-1,2-diol the technical name for ◊glycol.

ethanoate *n.* common name **acetate** a salt of ethanoic (acetic) acid, $CH_3CO_2^-$. In textiles, acetate rayon is a synthetic fabric made from modified cellulose (wood pulp) treated with ethanoic acid; in photography, acetate film is a non-flammable film made of cellulose ethanoate.

ethanoic acid common name **acetic acid** one of the simplest fatty acids (a series of organic acids), CH_3CO_2H. In the pure state it is a colourless liquid with an unpleasant pungent odour; it solidifies to an icelike mass of crystals at $16.7°C/62.4°F$, and hence is often called glacial ethanoic acid. Vinegar is 3–6% ethanoic acid.

ethanol *n.* common name **ethyl alcohol** an alcohol found in beer, wine, cider, spirits, and other alcoholic drinks, C_2H_5OH. When pure, it is a colourless liquid with a pleasant odour, miscible with water or ether, and which burns in air with a pale blue flame. The vapour forms an explosive mixture with air and may be used in high-compression internal combustion engines. It is produced naturally by the fermentation of carbohydrates by yeast cells. Industrially, it can be made by absorption of ethene and subsequent reaction with water, or by the reduction of ethanal in the presence of a catalyst; it is widely used as a solvent.

Ethelred II /'eθəlred/ **the Unready** *c.*968–1016. King of England from 978. The son of King Edgar, he became king after the murder of his half-brother, Edward the Martyr. He tried to buy off the Danish raiders by paying Danegeld. In 1002, he ordered the massacre of the Danish settlers, provoking an invasion by Sweyn I of Denmark. War with Sweyn and Sweyn's son, Canute, occupied the rest of Ethelred's reign. He was nicknamed the 'Unready' because of his apparent lack of foresight.

ethene *n.* common name **ethylene** a colourless, flammable gas, C_2H_4, the first member of the ◊alkene series of hydrocarbons. It is the most widely used synthetic organic chemical and is used to produce polyethylene (polythene), dichloroethane, and polyvinyl chloride (PVC). It is obtained from natural gas or coal gas, or by the dehydration of ethanol.

ether *n.* **1.** any of a series of organic compounds having an oxygen atom linking the carbon atoms of two hydrocarbon radical groups (general formula R-O-R`), for example dioxyethane $C_2H_5OC_2H_5$ (also called diethyl ether). Dioxyethane is a colourless, volatile, inflammable liquid, slightly soluble in water, miscible with ethanol. It is prepared by treatment of ethanol with excess concentrated sulphuric acid at $140°C/284°F$. It is used as an anaesthetic by vapour inhalation and as an external cleansing agent before surgical operations. It is also used as a solvent, and in the extraction of oils, fats, waxes, resins, and alkaloids. **2.** clear sky, the upper air. **3.** the medium formerly assumed to permeate space and transmit electromagnetic radiation. The concept originated with the Greeks, and has been revived on several occasions to explain the properties and propagation of light. It was abandoned with the acceptance of relativity. [from Old French or Latin from Greek *aithēr* (*aithō* = burn, shine)]

ethereal /i'θɪərɪəl/ *adj.* light, airy; delicate, especially in appearance; heavenly. —**ethereally** *adv.* [from Latin from Greek]

Etherege /'eθərɪdʒ/ George *c.*1635–*c.*1691. English Restoration dramatist whose play *Love in a Tub* 1664 was the first attempt at the comedy of manners (a genre further developed by Congreve and Sheridan). Later plays include *She Would if She Could* 1668 and *The Man of Mode, or Sir Fopling Flutter* 1676.

Writing, Madam, 's a mechanic part of wit! A gentleman should never go beyond a song or a billet.

George Etherege
The Man of Mode

---

ethic /'eθɪk/ *n.* a set of moral principles. —*adj.* ethical. [from Old French or Latin from Greek]

ethical *adj.* **1.** relating to morals, especially as concerning human conduct. **2.** morally correct. **3.** (of a medicine or drug) not advertised to the general public and usually available only on a doctor's prescription. —**ethically** *adv.*

ethics *n.* **1.** the area of philosophy concerned with moral values, which studies the meanings of moral terms and theories of conduct and goodness; also called **moral philosophy**. It is one of the three main branches of contemporary philosophy. **2.** (as *plural*) moral principles or code.

Ethiopia /iːθi'əupiə/ People's Democratic Republic of; country in E Africa, bounded NE by the Red Sea, E and SE by Somalia, S by Kenya, and W and NW by Sudan; **area** 1,221,900 sq km/471,653 sq mi; **capital** Addis Ababa; **physical** a high plateau with central mountain range divided by Rift Valley; plains in E; Blue Nile River; **head of state and government** Mengistu Haile Mariam from 1977; **exports** coffee, pulses, oilseeds, hides, skins; **population** (1989 est) 47,709,000 (Oromo 40%, Amhara 25%, Tigré 12% Sidama 9%; **language** Amharic (official); Tigrinya, Orominga, Arabic; **recent history** the annexation of Eritrea in 1962 by emperor Haile Selassie gave birth to a resistance movement. In 1974 a military government was put in place and a socialist state declared by Gen Teferi Benti. Killed in 1977, he was replaced by Colonel Mengisty Haile Mariam, who embarked on a 'Red Terror' reign killing thousands of people. 1985 saw widespread famine and Western aid was provided although food supplies were blocked by rebel guerillas. Today civil disorder and shortages continue.

ethnic /'eθnɪk/ *adj.* **1.** of a group of humankind distinguished from others by race or by having a common national or cultural tradition. **2.** (of clothes etc.) resembling the peasant clothes of an ethnic group or primitive people. —**ethnical** *adj.*, **ethnically** *adv.* [from Latin from Greek *ethnos* = nation]

ethnicity *n.* a people's own sense of cultural identity; a social term that overlaps with such concepts as race, nation, class, and religion. Social scientists use the term **ethnic group** to refer to groups or societies who feel a common sense of identity, often based on a traditional shared culture, language, religion, and customs. It may or may not include common territory, skin colour, or common descent. [from Greek *ethnos* = a people]

ethnology *n.* the study of contemporary peoples, concentrating on their geography and culture, as distinct from their social systems. —**ethnological** /-ə'lɒdʒɪkəl/ *adj.*, **ethnologist** *n.*

ethnomethodology *n.* the study of social order and routines used by people in their daily lives, to explain how everyday reality is created and perceived. Ethnomethodologists tend to use small-scale studies and experiments to examine the details of social life and structure (such as conversations) that people normally take for granted, rather than construct large-scale theories about society.

ethology *n.* the comparative study of animal behaviour in its natural setting. Ethology is concerned with the causal mechanisms (both the stimuli that elicit behaviour and the physiological mechanisms controlling it), the development

eucalyptus

of behaviour, its function, and its evolutionary history. —**ethologist** *n*. Ethology was pioneered during the 1930s by Konrad Lorenz and Karl von Frisch who, with Nikolaas Tinbergen, received the Nobel Prize for Pysiology or Medicine in 1973. Ethologists believe that the significance of an animal's behaviour can be understood only in its natural context, and emphasize the importance of field studies and an evolutionary perspective. A recent development within ethology is ◊sociobiology, the study of the evolutionary function of ◊social behaviour.

ethos /ˈiːθɒs/ *n*. the characteristic spirit or attitudes of a community etc. [Greek = character, disposition]

ethyl /ˈeθɪl/ *n*. a radical derived from ethane, present in alcohol and ether. [German]

ethyl alcohol common name for ◊ethanol.

ethylene common name for ◊ethene.

ethylene glycol alternative name for ◊glycol.

ethyne *n*. common name **acetylene** CHCH colourless inflammable gas produced by mixing calcium carbide and water. It is the simplest member of the ◊alkyne series of hydrocarbons. It is used in the manufacture of the synthetic rubber neoprene, and in oxyacetylene welding and cutting. Ethyne was discovered by Edmund Davy 1836. Its combustion provides more heat, relatively, than almost any other fuel known (its calorific value is five times that of hydrogen). This means that the gas gives an intensely hot flame; hence its use in oxyacetylene welding and cutting.

et in arcadia ego death exists even in Arcadia (a fabled land). [Latin = I also in Arcadia]

etiolate /ˈiːtɪəleɪt/ *v.t.* to make (a plant) pale by excluding light; to give a sickly hue to (a person). —**etiolation** /-ˈleɪʃən/ *n*. [from French from Norman *étieuler* = make into haulm from Latin *stipula* = straw]

etiolation *n*. in botany, a form of growth seen in plants receiving insufficient light. It is characterized by long, weak stems, small leaves, and a pale yellowish colour (◊chlorosis) owing to a lack of chlorophyll. The rapid increase in height enables a plant that is surrounded by others to reach a source of light quickly; when this is achieved.

etiquette /ˈetɪket/ *n*. conventional rules of social behaviour or professional conduct. [French = ticket]

Etna /ˈetnə/ volcano on the E coast of Sicily, 3,323 m/ 10,906 ft, the highest in Europe. Although about 90 eruptions have been recorded since 1800 BC, the cultivated zone on the lower slopes is densely populated, including the town of Catania, because of the rich soil. The most recent eruption was in Dec 1985.

Eton /ˈiːtn/ town in Berkshire, England, on the N bank of the Thames, opposite Windsor; population (1981) 3,500.

Etruscan /ɪˈtrʌskn/ *adj*. of ancient Etruria or its people or language. —*n*. 1. a native of ancient Etruria. 2. its language in Italy. The Etruscans appeared in the 8th century BC north and west of the river Tiber. [from Latin *Etruscus*]

Etruscan art the sculpture, painting, and design of the first known Italian civilization. Etruscan terracotta coffins (*sarcophagi*), carved with reliefs and topped with portraits of the dead reclining on one elbow, were to influence the later Romans and early Christians. Pottery, bronzeware, and mural paintings survive. Most examples

are from excavated tombs; bright colours and a vigorous style are typical and show influences of archaic Greece and the Middle East. The Etruscans appeared in the 8th century BC north and west of the river Tiber.

et seq. or *et seqq.* abbreviation of *et sequentia*. [Latin = and the following]

-ette /-et/ suffix forming nouns denoting smallness (*kitchenette*), imitation or substitution (*flannelette*), or female status (*suffragette*). [from French]

étude /eɪˈtjuːd/ *n*. a short musical composition (usually for one instrument), often intended to develop technique. [French = study]

etymology /etɪˈmɒlədʒɪ/ *n*. 1. the origin and development of a word's form and its meaning; an account of this. 2. the study of the origin of words. —**etymological** /-ˈlɒdʒɪkəl/ *adj*., **etymologist** *n*. [from Old French from Latin from Greek *etumon* = original form of word]

Eu symbol for ◊europium.

eu- prefix denoting well, easily. [Greek]

Euboea /juːˈbiːə/ (Greek **Evvoia**) mountainous island off the E coast of Greece, in the Aegean sea; area 3,755 sq km/ 1,450 sq mi; about 177 km/110 mi long; population (1981) 188,410. Mount Delphi reaches 1,743 m/5,721 ft. The chief town, Chalcis, is connected by a bridge to the mainland.

eucalyptus /juːkəˈlɪptəs/ *n*. or **eucalypt** 1. any tree of the genus *Eucalyptus*, family Myrtaceae; it is native to Australia and Tasmania, where it is commonly known as a gum tree. About 90% of Australian timber belongs to the eucalyptus genus, which comprises about 500 species. Although eucalyptus is a hardwood, it is fast-growing. 2. an oil obtained from it used as an antiseptic etc. [from Greek *kaluptos* = covered (the unopened flower being protected by a cap)]

Eucharist /ˈjuːkərɪst/ *n*. the chief Christian sacrament, in which bread is eaten and wine drunk in memory of the death of Jesus. Other names for it are the **Lord's Supper**, **Holy Communion**, and (among Roman Catholics, who believe that the bread and wine are transubstantiated, that is, converted to the body and blood of Christ) the **Mass**. The doctrine of transubstantiation was rejected by Protestant churches at the Reformation. 2. the consecrated elements, especially the bread. —**Eucharistic** /-ˈrɪstɪk/ *adj*. [from Old French from Latin from Greek = thanksgiving]

euchre /ˈjuːkə/ *n*. an American card-game for two, three, or four persons, played with a pack of 32 cards.

Euclid /ˈjuːklɪd/ *c*.330–*c*.260 BC. Greek mathematician, who lived in Alexandria and wrote the *Stoicheia/Elements* in 13 books, of which nine deal with plane and solid geometry and four with number theory. His great achievement lay in the systematic arrangement of previous discoveries, based on axioms, definitions, and theorems. —**Euclidean** /juːˈklɪdɪn/ *adj*. of Euclid. —**Euclidean geometry**, that of ordinary experience, based on the postulates used by Euclid (that parallel lines never meet, that the sum of the angles of a triangle is 180°). **Euclidean space**, that for which Euclidean geometry is valid.

There is no royal road to geometry.

Euclid

Eugène /juːˈdʒiːn/ Prince of Savoy 1663–1736. Austrian general, who had many victories against the Turkish invaders (whom he expelled from Hungary in 1697 in the Battle of Zenta) and against France in the War of the ◊Spanish Succession (battles of Blenheim, Oudenaarde, and Malplaquet).

Eugene Onegin /ˈjuːdʒiːn əʊˈnjeɪgɪn/ a novel in verse by Aleksandr Pushkin, published 1823–31. Eugene Onegin, bored with life but sensitive, rejects the love of Tatanya, a humble country girl; but she later rises in society and in turn rejects him. Onegin was the model for a number of Russian literary heroes.

eugenics /juːˈdʒenɪks/ *n*. the science of the production of fine (especially human) offspring by control of inherited qualities. The term was coined by Francis ◊Galton in 1883, and the concept was originally developed in the late 19th century with a view to improving human intelligence and behaviour. It was abused by the Nazi Party in Germany during the 1930s to justify the attempted extermination of entire groups of people. In 1986 Singapore became the first democratic country to adopt an openly eugenic policy by guaranteeing pay increases to female university graduates when they give birth to a child, while offering grants towards house purchases for nongraduate married women on condition that they are sterilized after the first or second child. Practitioners also try to control the spread of inherited genetic abnormalities by counselling prospective parents. —**eugenic** adj., **eugenically** adv. [from Greek gen = give birth to]

Eugénie /ɜːˈʒeɪˈniː/ Marie Ignace Augustine de Montijo 1826–1920. Empress of France, daughter of the Spanish count of Montijo. In 1853 she married Louis Napoleon, who had become emperor as ◊Napoleon III. She encouraged court extravagance and Napoleon III's intervention in Mexico, and urged him to fight the Prussians. After his surrender to the Germans at Sedan, NE France, 1870, she fled to England.

eukaryote n. one of the two major groupings into which all organisms are divided. The only organisms excluded from the category are bacteria and cyanobacteria, which belong to the ◊prokaryote grouping. The cells of eukaryotes, unlike those of prokaryotes, possess a clearly defined nucleus, bounded by a membrane, within which DNA is formed into distinct chromosomes. Eukaryotic cells also contain mitochondria, chloroplasts, and other structures (organelles). —**eukaryotic** adj.

Euler /ˈɔɪlə/ Leonhard 1707–1783. Swiss mathematician. He developed the theory of differential equations and the calculus of variations, and worked in astronomy and optics. He was a pupil of Johann ◊Bernoulli.

eulogize /ˈjuːlədʒaɪz/ v.t. to extol, to praise.

eulogy /ˈjuːlədʒɪ/ n. a speech or writing in praise of a person; an expression of praise. —**eulogistic** /-ˈdʒɪstɪk/ adj. [from Latin from Greek eulogia = praise]

Eumenides /juːˈmenɪdiːz/ in Greek mythology, an appeasing name for the ◊Furies. [Greek = kindly ones]

eunuch /ˈjuːnək/ n. a castrated man, especially one formerly employed in a harem or as a court official in the Orient or under the Roman Empire. Eunuchs were originally bedchamber attendants in harems in the East. They were usually castrated to discourage them from developing a sexual interest in their charges. The term became applied more generally. Eunuchs often filled high offices of state in China, India, and Persia. Italian castrati were singers castrated as boys to preserve their soprano voices, a practice that ended with the accession of Pope Leo XIII in 1878. [from Latin from Greek eunoukhos = one in charge of a bed]

euphemism /ˈjuːfɪmɪzəm/ n. the use of a mild or indirect expression instead of a blunt or direct one; such an expression. —**euphemistic** /-ˈmɪstɪk/ adj., **euphemistically** adv. [from Greek = speaking well (of something)]

euphonium /juːˈfəʊnɪəm/ n. a tenor tuba, a type of ◊brass instrument.

euphony /ˈjuːfənɪ/ n. the pleasantness of sounds, especially of words; a pleasing sound. —**euphonious** / ˈfəʊnɪəs/ adj. [from French from Latin from Greek phōnē = sound]

euphoria /juːˈfɔːrɪə/ n. a feeling of well-being or elation. —**euphoric** /-ˈfɒrɪk/ adj. [from Greek euphoros (pherō = bear)]

Euphrates /juːˈfreɪtiːz/ (Arabic Furat) river, rising in E Turkey, flowing through Syria and Iraq and joining the river Tigris above Basra to form the river Shatt-al-Arab, at the head of the Persian/Arabian Gulf. It is 3,600 km/2,240 mi long. The ancient cities of Babylon, Eridu, and Ur were situated along its course.

euphuism /ˈjuːfjuːɪzəm/ n. an affected or high-flown style of writing. —**euphuistic** /-ˈɪstɪk/ adj., **euphuistically** adv. [originally of writing in imitation of Lyly's Euphues (16th century)]

Eurasian /juˈreɪʒn/ adj. 1. of mixed European and Asian parentage. 2. of Europe and Asia. —n. a Eurasian person.

Euratom /juərˈætəm/ acronym from ◊European Atomic Energy Commission.

eureka[1] /juəˈriːkə/ an interjection (announcing a discovery etc.) I have found it. [Greek heurēka (heuriskō = find); attributed to Archimedes]

eureka[2] n. alternative name for the copper–nickel alloy ◊constantan, used in electrical equipment.

Eureka Stockade an incident at Ballarat, Australia, when about 150 goldminers, or 'diggers', rebelled against authority. They took refuge behind a wooden stockade, which was taken in a few minutes by the military on 3 Dec 1854. Some 30 diggers were killed, but the majority of the rebels were taken prisoner. Among those who escaped was Peter Lalor, their leader. Of the 13 tried for treason, all were acquitted, thus marking the emergence of Australian democracy.

eurhythmics /juːˈrɪðmɪks/ n.pl. harmony of bodily movement, especially as developed with music and dance into a system of education. The system was founded about 1900 by the Swiss musician Emil Jaques-Dalcroze, professor of harmony at the Geneva conservatoire. He devised a series of 'gesture' songs, to be sung simultaneously with certain bodily actions. [from Greek rhuthmos = proportion, rhythm]

Euripides /juːˈrɪpɪdiːz/ c.484–407 BC. Greek dramatist whose plays deal with ordinary people and social issues rather than the more grandiose themes used by his contemporaries. He wrote more than 80 plays, of which 18 survive, including Alcestis 438 BC, Medea 431 BC, Andromache 426 BC, Trojan Women 415 BC, Electra 417 BC, Iphigenia in Tauris 413 BC, Iphigenia in Aulis 405 BC, and Bacchae 405 BC. His influence on later drama was probably greater than that of the two tragedians Aeschylus and Sophocles. A realist, he was bitterly attacked for his unorthodox 'impiety' and sympathy for the despised: slaves, beggars, and women. He went into voluntary exile from Athens to Macedonia at the end of his life.

Euro- /juərəʊ/ prefix denoting Europe, European.

Eurobond n. a bond underwritten by an international syndicate and sold in countries other than the country of the currency in which the issue is denominated. They provide longer-term financing than is possible with loans in Eurodollars.

Eurocodes n. a series of codes giving design rules for all types of engineering structure, except certain specialized forms, such as nuclear reactors. The codes will be given the status of ENs (European standards) and will be administered by CEN (European Committee for Standardization). ENs will eventually replace national codes, in Britain currently maintained by the BSI (British Standards Institute), and will include parameters to reflect local requirements.

Eurocommunism n. a policy followed by communist parties in Western Europe to seek power within the framework of national political initiative rather than by revolutionary means.

Eurocrat /ˈjuərəʊkræt/ n. a bureaucrat of the European Communities.

Eurodollar n. US currency deposited outside the USA and held by individuals and institutions, not necessarily in Europe. Eurodollars originated in the 1960s when East European countries deposited their US dollars in West European banks. Banks holding Eurodollar deposits may lend in dollars, usually to finance trade, and often redeposit with other foreign banks. The practice is a means of avoiding credit controls and exploiting interest rate differentials.

Europa /juːˈrəʊpə/ in Greek mythology, the daughter of the king of Tyre, carried off by Zeus (in the form of a bull); she personifies the continent of Europe.

Europa n. 1. in astronomy, the fourth largest moon of the planet Jupiter, diameter 3,100 km/1,900 mi, orbiting 671,000 km/417,000 mi from the planet every 3.55 days. It is covered by ice and criss-crossed by thousands of thin cracks, each some 50,000 km/30,000 mi long.

Europa Nostra international federation established 1963 by representatives of 18 organizations (including Italia Nostra, National Trust, Irish Georgian Society, Vieilles Maisons Françaises) in 11 European countries for the preservation of historic sites, buildings, and monuments.

Europe /ˈjuərəp/ second smallest continent, comprising the land W of the Ural mountains; it comprises 8% of the Earth's surface, and 14.5% of world population; **area** 10,400,000 sq km/4,000,000 sq mi; **largest cities** (over 1.5 million inhabitants) Athens, Barcelona, Berlin, Birmingham, Budapest, Hamburg, Istanbul, Kiev, Leningrad, London, Madrid, Manchester, Milan, Moscow, Paris, Rome, Vienna, Warsaw; **physical** North European Plain on which stand London, Paris, Berlin, and Moscow; Central European Highlands (Sierra Nevada, Pyrenees, Alps, Apennines, Carpathians, Balkans); Scandinavian highland, which takes in the Scottish Highlands; highest point: Mount Elbruz in Caucasus mountains; rivers (over 1,600 km/ 1,000 mi): Volga, Don, Dnieper, Danube: lakes (over 5,100 sq km/2,000 sq mi): Ladoga, Onega, Vänern. The climate ranges from the variable NW, modified by the ◊Gulf Stream, through the central zone with warm summers and cold winters, becoming bitterly cold in E Europe, to the Mediterranean zone with comparatively mild winters and hot summers; **population** (1985) 492,000,000 (excluding Turkey and USSR); **language** mostly of Indo-European origin, with a few exceptions, including Finno-Ugrian (Finnish and Hungarian) and Altaic (such as Turkish), and Basque.

European /jʊrˈpiːn/ *adj.* 1. of the continent of Europe. 2. of the European (Economic) Community. —*n.* 1. a native or inhabitant of Europe; a descendant of such persons. 3. one who is concerned with European matters. [from French from Latin from Greek]

European Atomic Energy Commission (Euratom) an organization established by the second Treaty of Rome 1957, which seeks the cooperation of member states of the European Community in nuclear research and the rapid and large-scale development of non-military nuclear energy.

European Coal and Steel Community (ECSC) an organization established by the treaty of Paris in 1951 (ratified 1952) as a single authority for the coal and steel industries of France, West Germany, Italy, Belgium, Holland, and Luxembourg, eliminating tariffs and other restrictions; in 1967 it became part of the European Community. The ECSC arose out of the ◊Schuman plan 1950, which proposed a union of the French and German coal and steel industries so as to make future war between the two countries impossible. The ECSC was, in effect, a prototype institution for the European Community, and wass brought under EEC authority 1967. Subsequent members of the EC automatically became ECSC members also.

European Community (EC) a political and economic alliance consisting of the European Coal and Steel Community (ECSC) since 1952, European Economic Community (EEC), popularly called the Common Market) since 1957, and the European Atomic Energy Commission (Euratom) since 1957. The original six members—Belgium, France, West Germany, Italy, Luxembourg, and the Netherlands— were joined by the UK, Denmark, and the Republic of Ireland in 1974, Greece in 1981, and Spain and Portugal in 1985. Its aims include the expansion of trade, the reduction of competition, the abolition of restrictive trading practices, and the encouragement of the free movement of capital and labour within the community. From 1967 the EC has comprised the following institutions: the **Commission** of 13 members pledged to independence of national interests, who initiate Community action; the **Council of Ministers**, which makes decisions on the Commission's proposals; the ◊**European Parliament**, directly elected from 1979, which is mainly a consultative body but can dismiss the Commission; and the ◊**European Court of Justice**, to safeguard interpretation of the Rome Treaties (1957), which established the Community.

European Court of Justice the court of the European Community (EC), which is responsible for interpreting Community law and ruling on breaches of such law by member states and others. It sits in Luxembourg with judges from the member states. **The European Court of Human Rights** sits in Strasbourg to adjudicate on breaches of the European Convention on Human Rights.

European Democratic Group the group of British Conservative Party members of the European Parliament.

European Economic Community (EEC) one of the organizations of the ◊European Community (EC).

European Free Trade Association an organization established in 1960 and consisting since 1988 of Austria, Finland, Iceland, Norway, Sweden, and Switzerland. There are no import duties between members. Of the original members, Britain and Denmark left in 1972, and Portugal in 1985, to join the ◊European Community. In 1973 the EC signed agreements with EFTA members, setting up a free-trade area of over 300 million consumers. Trade between the two groups amounts to over half of total EFTA trade.

European Community *The signing of the Rome Treaties on 25 Mar 1957.*

European Monetary System (EMS) an attempt by the European Community to bring financial cooperation and monetary stability to Europe. It was established in 1979 in the wake of the 1974 oil crisis, which brought growing economic disruption to European economies because of floating exchange rates. Central to the EMS is the ◊**Exchange Rate Mechanism** (ERM), a voluntary system of semi-fixed exchange rates based on the European Currency Unit (ECU).

European Monetary Union (EMU) the proposed European Community policy for a single currency and common economic policies. The proposal was announced by a European Community committee headed by EC Commission president Jacques Delors in April 1989. Three stages are envisaged. In the first, all controls on member nations' capital flows would be ended, and the **European System of Central Banks** (ESCB) created. In stage two, the ESCB would begin to regulate money supply. Finally, exchange rates between member states would be fixed, and a single European currency created, and the ESCB would take over the function of members' central banks.

European Parliament the parliament of the European Community, which meets in Strasbourg to comment on the legislative proposals of the Commission of the European Communities. Members are elected for a five-year term. The European Parliament has 518 seats, apportioned on the basis of population, of which the UK, France, West Germany, and Italy each has 81, Spain 60, the Netherlands 25, Belgium, Greece, and Portugal 24 each, Denmark 16, the Republic of Ireland 15, and Luxembourg 6. Originally merely consultative, the European Parliament became directly elected in 1979, assuming increased powers. Though still not a true legislative body, it can dismiss the whole Commission and reject the Community budget. After the 1989 elections the Left held 260 seats (Socialist 180, Communist 41, Green 39) and the Right 242 (Christian Democrats 123, Liberals 44, European Democratic Group 34, European Right 21, European Democratic Alliance 20). Henry Plumb (UK) became president 1987.

European Space Agency (ESA) an organization of European countries (Belgium, Denmark, France, Ireland, Italy, the Netherlands, Spain, Sweden, Switzerland, the UK, and Germany) engaged in space research and technology. It was founded in 1975 and its headquarters are in Paris. It has developed scientific and communications satellites, the ◊*Giotto* space probe and the ◊Ariane rockets. ESA built ◊Spacelab, plans to build its own space station, *Columbus*, for attachment to the US space station, and is working on its own shuttle project, Hermes.

europium /jʊəˈrəʊpiəm/ *n.* a soft, greyish, metallic element of the ◊lanthanide series, symbol Eu, atomic number 63, relative atomic mass 151.96. It is used in lasers and as the red phosphor in colour televisions; its compounds are used to make control rods for nuclear reactors. It was named in 1901 by French chemist Eugène Demarçay (1852–1904) for the continent of Europe, where it was first found.

Eurydice /ju:'rɪdɪsɪ/ in Greek mythology, the wife of ◊Orpheus. She was a dryad, or forest nymph, and died of a snake bite. Orpheus attempted unsuccessfully to fetch her back from the realm of the dead.

Eusebio /ju:'seɪbiəu/ Adopted name of Eusebio Ferreira da Silva 1942– . Portuguese footballer, born in Lourenço Marques. He made his international debut in 1961 and played for his country 77 times. He spent most of his league career with Benfica, but also played in the USA. He was European Footballer of the Year in 1965.

Eusebius /ju:'si:biəs/ c.260–c.340. Bishop of Caesarea (modern Qisarya, Israel); author of a history of the Christian church to 324.

Euskadi /eɪu'skɑːdi/ the Basque name for the ◊Basque Country.

eusociality n. a form of social life found in insects such as honey bees and termites, in which the colony is made up of special castes (for example, workers, drones, and reproductives) whose membership is biologically determined. The worker castes do not usually reproduce. Only one mammal, the naked mole rat, has a social organization of this type. See also ◊social behaviour.

eustachian tube /ju:'steɪʃən/ the small air-filled canal connecting the middle ◊ear with the back of the throat. It is found in all land vertebrates and equalizes the pressure on both sides of the ear drum. [from B. *Eustachi* Italian anatomist]

Euston Road School /'ju:stən/ a British art school in Euston Road, London, 1937–39. William Coldstream (1908–87) and Victor Pasmore were teachers there. Despite its brief existence, the school influenced many British painters with its emphasis on careful, subdued naturalism.

Eutelsat /'ju:telsæt/ acronym from European Telecommunications Satellite Organization.

euthanasia /ju:θə'neɪzɪə/ n. the bringing about of a gentle and easy death in the case of incurable and painful disease; such a death. The Netherlands legalized voluntary euthanasia in 1983, but is the only country to have done so. [Greek *thanatos* = death]

eutrophication n. the excessive enrichment of lake waters, primarily by nitrate fertilizers, washed from the soil by rain, and by phosphates from detergents in municipal sewage. These encourage the growth of algae and bacteria which use up the oxygen in the water, thereby making it uninhabitable for fishes and other animal life.

Eutyches /ju:'taɪkiːz/ c.384–c.456. Christian theologian. An archimandrite (monastic head) in Constantinople, he held that Jesus had only one nature, the human nature being subsumed in the divine (a belief which became known as ◊Monophysitism). He was exiled after his ideas were condemned as heretical by the Council of ◊Chalcedon 451.

eV abbreviation of electron-volt(s).

evacuate /i'vækjueɪt/ v.t. 1. to send (people) away from a place of danger; to empty (a place) thus; to withdraw from. 2. to make empty; to empty the contents of. —**evacuation** /-'eɪʃən/ n. Large-scale evacuation took place during World War II in the UK when the government encouraged parents to send their children away from urban and industrial areas to places of greater safety. The term also has military applications, as in the evacuation of Allied troops from the beaches of ◊Dunkirk in 1940. [from Latin *vacuus* = empty]

evacuee /ɪvækju:'i:/ n. a person sent away from a place of danger.

evade /i'veɪd/ v.t. to avoid or escape from, especially by guile or trickery; to avoid doing or answering directly. [from French from Latin *vadere* = go]

evaluate /i'væljueɪt/ v.t. to find or state the number or amount of; to appraise, to assess. —**evaluation** /-'eɪʃən/ n. [from French]

evanesce /i:və'nes, e-/ v.i. to fade from sight, to disappear. [from Latin *evanescere* (*vanus* = empty)]

evanescent adj. (of an impression etc.) quickly fading. —**evanescence** n.

evangelical /i:væn'dʒelɪkəl/ adj. 1. of the Protestant Churches, as basing their claim pre-eminently on the gospel. 2. (formerly, in Germany and Switzerland) the Lutheran Churches as contrasted with the Calvinist (Reformed) Churches. 3. (in the Church of England) of the school (originating in the 18th century) that lays special stress on personal conversion and salvation by faith in the Atonement. —**evangelicalism** n. [from Latin from Greek]

Evangelical Movement in Britain, a 19th-century group that stressed basic protestant beliefs and the message of the four Gospels. The movement was associated with Rev Charles Simeon (1783–1836). It aimed to raise moral enthusiasm and ethical standards among Church of England clergy.

evangelism /i'vændʒəlɪzəm/ n. the preaching or promulgation of the gospel.

evangelist /i'vændʒəlɪst/ n. 1. the writer of any one of the four Gospels: Matthew, Mark, Luke, and John. 2. a preacher of the gospel. —**evangelistic** /-'lɪstɪk/ adj.

evangelize /i'vændʒəlaɪz/ v.t. to preach the gospel to; to convert to Christianity. —**evangelization** /-'zeɪʃən/ n. [from Latin from Greek *euaggelion* = good news]

Evans /'evənz/ Arthur John 1851–1941. English archaeologist. His excavation of ◊Knossos on Crete resulted in the discovery of pre-Phoenician Minoan script and proved the existence of the legendary Minoan civilization.

Evans Edith 1888–1976. English character actress, who performed on the London stage and on Broadway. Her many performances include the film role of Lady Bracknell in Oscar Wilde's comedy *The Importance of Being Earnest* 1952. Among her other films are *Tom Jones* 1963 and *Crooks and Coronets* 1969.

Evans Walker 1903–1975. US photographer. He specialized in documentary photographs of the people in the rural US south during the Great Depression of the 1930s. Many of his photographs appeared in James Agee's book *Let Us Now Praise Famous Men* 1941.

evaporable /i'væpərəbəl/ adj. able to be evaporated.

evaporate /i'væpəreɪt/ v.t./i. 1. to turn into vapour; to lose or cause to lose moisture as vapour. 2. to become lost or disappear; to cause to do this. —**evaporated milk**, unsweetened milk concentrated by partial evaporation and tinned. [from Latin *evaporare* (*vapor* = steam)]

evaporation /i'væp'reɪʃn/ n. the process by which a liquid turns to a vapour without its temperature reaching boiling point. A liquid left to stand in a saucer eventually evaporates because, at any time, a proportion of its molecules have sufficient energy to escape through the liquid surface into the atmosphere. The temperature of the liquid tends to fall because the evaporating molecules remove energy. The rate of evaporation rises with an increase in temperature.

evaporite n. a sedimentary deposit precipitated on evaporation of salt water. With a progressive evaporation of seawater, the most common salts are deposited in the following sequence: calcite (calcium carbonate), when the seawater is reduced to half its original volume; gypsum (hydrous calcium sulphate), when the seawater body is reduced to one-fifth; halite (sodium chloride), when the seawater is reduced to one-tenth; and, finally, salts of potassium and magnesium. Because of the concentrations of different dissolved salts in seawater, halite accounts for about 95% of the chlorides precipitated if evaporation is complete. More unusual evaporite minerals include borates (for example borax, hydrous sodium borate) and sulphates (for example glauberite, a combined sulphate of sodium and calcium).

evasion /i'veɪʒən/ n. 1. evading. 2. an evasive answer etc. [from Old French from Latin *vadere* = go]

evasive /i'veɪsɪv/ adj. seeking to evade; not direct in answer etc. —**evasively** adv., **evasiveness** n.

eve /i:v/ n. the evening or day before a festival etc.; the time just before an event; (*archaic*) evening.

Eve /i:v/ in the Old Testament, the first woman, wife of ◊Adam. She was tempted by Satan (in the form of a snake) to eat the fruit of the Tree of Knowledge of Good and Evil, thus bringing about their expulsion from the Garden of Eden. There are two versions of the creation myth in the Bible: in one of them, Eve was created simultaneously with Adam; in the other, she was created from his rib. In the Hebrew writings known as the 'Midrash', ◊Lilith was the first woman (and her children were the wives available to Eve's sons Cain and Abel).

Evelyn /'i:vlɪn/ John 1620–1706. English diarist and author. He was a friend of Samuel ◊Pepys, and like him remained in London during the Plague and the Great Fire. He wrote some 300 books, including his diary, first published in 1818, which covers the period 1640–1706. He was born in Surrey, enlisted for three years in the Royalist army 1624, but withdrew on finding his estate exposed to the enemy, and lived mostly away from England until 1652. He declined all office under the Commonwealth, but after the Restoration enjoyed great favour, received court appointments, and was one of the founders of the Royal Society.

I saw Hamlet Prince of Denmark played, but now the old plays began to disgust this refined age.
John Evelyn
26 Nov 1661

---

even[1] /'iːvən/ *adj.* 1. level, free from irregularities, smooth. 2. uniform in quality, constant. 3. equal in amount, value etc.; equally balanced. 4. in the same plane or line (with). 5. equable, calm. 6. (of a number such as 4 or 6) integrally divisible by 2; bearing such a number; not involving fractions. —*v.t./i.* (often with *up*) to make or become even or equal. —*adv.* (*a*) inviting comparison of the negation, assertion etc., with an implied one that is less strong or remarkable; (*b*) introducing an extreme case. —**be** *or* **get even with**, to have one's revenge on. **even chance**, an equal chance of success or failure. **even-handed** *adj.* impartial, fair. **even money**, **evens** *n.pl.* betting-odds offering gamblers the chance of winning the amount they staked. **even now**, now as well as previously, at this very moment. **even so**, despite some other consideration. —**evenly** *adv.*, **evenness** *n.* [Old English]

even[2] *n.* (*poetic*) evening. [Old English]

evening /'iːvnɪŋ/ *n.* 1. the end of the day, especially from about 6 p.m. (or earlier sunset) to bedtime. 2. the decline or last period (of life etc.). —**evening dress**, formal dress for evening wear. **evening star**, a planet, especially Venus, when seen in the west after sunset. [Old English]

evening primrose any plant of the genus *Oenothera*, family Onagraceae. Some 50 species are native to North America, several of which now also grow in Europe. Some are cultivated for their oil, which is used in treating eczema and premenstrual tension.

evensong *n.* the service of evening prayer in the Church of England.

event /i'vent/ *n.* a thing that happens or takes place, especially one of importance; the fact of a thing occurring; an item in an (especially sports) programme. —**at all events**, **in any** *or* **either event**, whatever happens. **in the event**, as it turned out. **in the event of**, if (the specified event) occurs. **in the event that**, if. [from Latin *evenire* = happen]

eventful *adj.* marked by noteworthy events. —**eventfully** *adv.*

eventide /'iːvəntaɪd/ *n.* (*archaic*) evening.

eventing *n.* see **three-day eventing** under ◊equestrianism.

eventual /i'ventʃuəl/ *adj.* occurring in due course or at last. —**eventually** *adv.*

eventuality /iventʃu'ælɪtɪ/ *n.* a possible event or result.

eventuate /i'ventʃueɪt/ *v.i.* to result, to be the outcome.

ever /'evə/ *adv.* 1. at all times, always; at any time. 2. (as an emphatic word) in any way, at all. —**did you ever?**, (*colloquial*) did you ever hear or see the like? **ever since**, throughout the period since (then). **ever so**, (*colloquial*) very; very much. **ever such a**, (*colloquial*) a very. [Old English]

Everest, Mount /'evərɪst/ the world's highest mountain, in the Himalayas, on the China–Nepál frontier; height 8,872 m/29,118 ft. It was first climbed by Edmund Hillary and Tenzing Norgay in 1953. Many expeditions have since scaled the peak. In 1987 a US expedition obtained measurements of ◊K2, which disputed Everest's claim to be the highest mountain, but recent satellite measurements have established Everest as taller. [Nepalese *Sagarmatha* = head of the earth; English from George Everest (1790–1866), surveyor-general of India.]

Everglades /'evəgleɪdz/ area of swamps and lakes in S ◊Florida, USA; area 12,950 sq km/5,000 sq mi.

evergreen *n.* a plant, such as pine, spruce, or holly, that bears its leaves all year round. Most ◊conifers are evergreen. Plants that shed their leaves in autumn or during a

dry season are described as ◊deciduous. —*adj.* retaining its leaves throughout the year.

everlasting /evə'lɑːstɪŋ/ *adj.* 1. lasting for ever; lasting a long time. 2. (of flowers) keeping their shape and colour when dried. Most are from the composite family, including some species of *Ammobium, Xeranthemum,* and *Helichrysum,* for example the strawflower of Australia, *H. bracteatum.* —*n.* eternity. —**everlastingly** *adv.*

evermore /evə'mɔː/ *adv.* for ever, always.

Evert /'evət/ Chris(tine) 1954– . US tennis player. She won her first Wimbledon title in 1974, and has since won 21 Grand Slam titles. She became the first woman tennis player to win $1 million in prize money. She has an outstanding two-handed backhand and is a great exponent of baseline technique. From 1974–89 at Wimbledon she never failed to reach the quarter-finals at least.

every /'evrɪ/ *adj.* 1. each single. 2. each at a specified interval in a series. 3. all possible; the utmost degree of. —**every bit as**, (*colloquial*) quite as. **every now and then**, from time to time. **every one**, each one. **every other**, each second in a series. **every so often**, at intervals, occasionally. [Old English = ever each]

everybody *pron.* every person.

everyday *adj.* occurring or used every day; ordinary, commonplace.

Everyman /'evrɪmæn/ *n.* an ordinary or typical person. [name of leading character in 15th-century morality play]

everyone *pron.* everybody.

everything *pron.* 1. all things. 2. the thing of chief importance.

everywhere *adv.* in every place; (*colloquial*) in many places.

evict /i'vɪkt/ *v.t.* to expel (a tenant) by legal process. —**eviction** *n.* [from Latin *vincere* = conquer]

evidence /'evɪdəns/ *n.* 1. an indication, a sign, the facts available as proving or supporting a notion etc. 2. in law, information given personally or drawn from a document etc. and tending to prove a fact; testimony admissible in court. Witnesses must swear or affirm that their evidence is true; in English law, giving false evidence is the crime of ◊perjury. Documentary evidence has a wide scope including maps, soundtracks, and films, in addition to documents in writing. Objects such as weapons used in crimes may serve as evidence. Evidence obtained illegally, such as a confession under duress, may be excluded from the court. —*v.t.* to indicate, to be evidence of. —**in evidence**, conspicuous. **turn King's** *or* **Queen's evidence**, said of an accused person who testifies for the prosecution against the person(s) associated with him or her in an alleged crime. [from Old French from Latin]

evident *adj.* obvious, plain, manifest. —**evidently** *adv.* [from Old French or Latin *vidēre* = see]

evidential /evi'denʃəl/ *adj.* of or providing evidence.

evil /'iːvəl, -ɪl/ *adj.* morally bad, wicked; harmful, tending to harm; disagreeable. —*n.* an evil thing; wickedness. —**evil eye**, a malicious look superstitiously believed to do material harm. —**evilly** *adv.* [Old English]

evildoer *n.* a sinner. —**evildoing** *n.*

evince /i'vɪns/ *v.t.* to indicate or exhibit (a quality). [from Latin *vincere* = conquer]

eviscerate /i'vɪsəreɪt/ *v.t.* to disembowel. —**evisceration** /-'reɪʃən/ *n.* [from Latin *viscera* = bowels]

evocative /i'vɒkətɪv/ *adj.* tending to evoke (especially feelings or memories).

evoke /i'vəuk/ *v.t.* to inspire or draw forth (memories, a response etc.). —**evocation** /evə'keɪʃən/ *n.* [from Latin *vocare* = call]

evolute /'iːvəljuːt, -luːt/ *n.* the locus of the centres of curvature of another curve that is its involute. [from Latin *volvere* = roll]

evolution /iːvə'luːʃən/ *n.* 1. evolving. 2. the origination of species by development from earlier forms, not by special creation; the gradual development of a phenomenon, organism etc.; for example, the evolution of life on Earth. This idea can be traced back to ◊Lucretius in the 1st century BC, but it gained wide acceptance only in the 19th century following the work of Charles ◊Lyell, Jean-Baptiste ◊Lamarck, Charles ◊Darwin, and Thomas ◊Huxley. Darwin assigned the major role in evolutionary change to ◊natural selection acting on randomly occurring variations (now known to be produced by spontaneous changes or ◊mutations in the genetic material of organisms). Natural selection occurs because those individuals better adapted to their environment reproduce more effectively, and contribute their characteristics (in the form of genes) to future generations. The current theory of evolution, called ◊Neo-Darwinism, combines Darwin's theory with Gregor ◊Mendel's theories on genetics. Besides natural selection and ◊sexual selection, it is now believed that chance may play a large part in deciding which genes become characteristic of a population, a phenomenon called 'genetic drift'; and that evolutionary change need not always occur at a constant rate. This has led to new theories, such as the ◊punctuated equilibrium model. See also ◊adaptive radiation. Some Christians and Muslims deny the theory of evolution as conflicting with the belief that God created all things (see ◊creationism) —**evolutionary** adj. [from Latin]

evolutionary stable strategy (ESS) in ◊sociobiology, an assemblage of behavioural or physical characters (collectively termed a 'strategy') of a population that is resistant to replacement by any forms bearing new traits, because the new traits will not be capable of successful reproduction. ESS analysis is based on ◊game theory and can be applied both to genetically determined physical characters (such as horn length), and to learned behavioural responses (for example, whether to fight or retreat from an opponent). An ESS may be conditional on the context, as in the rule 'fight if the opponent is smaller, but retreat if the opponent is larger'.

evolutionist n. one who upholds the theory that species developed by evolution rather than by special creation.

evolve /i'vɒlv/ v.t./i. 1. to develop gradually by a natural process; 2. to work out or devise (a theory, plan etc.). 3. to unfold, to open out. 4. to give off (gas, heat etc.). [from Latin volvere = roll]

Evvoia /'eviə/ Greek name for the island of ◊Euboea.

evzone n. member of a Greek infantry regiment whose soldiers wear distinctive white short-skirted uniform.

ewe /ju:/ n. a female sheep. [Old English]

ewer /'ju:ə/ n. a water-jug with a wide mouth. [from Old French from Latin aqua = water]

ex[1] prep. 1. (of goods) sold from. 2. outside, without, exclusive of. —**ex dividend,** (of stocks and shares) not including the next dividend. [Latin = out of]

ex[2] n. (colloquial) a former husband or wife.

ex-[1] (ef- before f; e- before some consonants) prefix forming a. verbs in the sense 'out', 'forth' (exclude, exit), 'upward' (extol), 'thoroughly' (excruciate), 'bring into a state' (exasperate). b. nouns from the titles of office, status etc., in the sense 'formerly' (ex-convict). [from Latin ex = out of]

ex-[2] prefix denoting out. [from Greek exodus]

exa- in combinations, denoting a factor of 10^{18}.

exacerbate /ek'sæsəbeit/ v.t. to make (pain, anger etc.) worse; to irritate. —**exacerbation** /-'beiʃən/ n. [from Latin exacerbare (acerbus = bitter)]

exact /ig'zækt/ adj. accurate, correct in all details; precise, (of a person) tending to precision. —v.t. to demand and enforce payment etc. of; to demand, to require urgently, to insist on. —**exact science,** one in which absolute precision is possible. —**exactness** n. , **exactor** n. [from Latin exigere (agere = drive)]

exacting adj. making great demands, calling for much effort.

exaction /ig'zækʃən/ n. 1. exacting (of money etc.). 2. the thing exacted. 3. an illegal or exorbitant demand, extortion.

exactitude /ig'zæktitju:d/ n. exactness, precision.

exactly adv. 1. accurately, precisely. 2. (said in reply) I quite agree.

exaggerate /ig'zædʒəreit/ v.t. to make (a thing, or absolute) seem larger or greater than it really is, in speech or writing; to enlarge or alter beyond normal or due proportions. —**exaggeration** /-'reiʃən/ n. [from Latin exaggerare = heap up (agger = heap)]

exalt /ig'zɔːlt/ v.t. 1. to raise in rank or power etc. 2. to praise highly. 3. to dignify, to ennoble. —**exaltation** /-'teiʃən/ n. [from Latin exaltare (altus = high)]

exam /ig'zæm/ (colloquial) abbreviation of examination.

examination /igzæmi'neiʃən/ n. examining, being examined; the testing of proficiency or knowledge by oral or written questions; the formal questioning of a witness etc. in a lawcourt.

examine /ig'zæmin/ v.t. 1. to inquire into the nature or condition etc. of. 2. to look closely at. 3. to test the proficiency of by a series of questions or exercises. 4. to question formally. —**examiner** n. [from Old French from Latin examen = tongue of balance]

examinee /igzæmi'niː/ n. one who is being examined, especially in a test of proficiency.

example /ig'zɑːmpəl/ n. 1. a thing characteristic of its kind or illustrating a general rule; a problem or exercise designed to do this. 2. a person or thing or conduct worthy of imitation. 3. a fact or thing seen as a warning to others. —**for example,** by way of illustration. [from Old French from Latin exemplum]

exasperate /ig'zæspəreit, -'zɑːs-/ v.t. to irritate intensely. —**exasperation** /-'reiʃən/ n. [from Latin exasperare (asper = rough)]

ex cathedra /eks kə'θiːdrə/ with full authority (especially of a papal pronouncement). [Latin = from the chair]

excavate /'ekskəveit/ v.t. to make (a hole or channel) by digging, to dig out (soil); to reveal or extract by digging. —**excavation** /-'veiʃən/ n. [from Latin excavare (cavus = hollow)]

excavator n. a machine designed for moving earth. Diggers using hydraulically powered digging arms and running on wheels or on ◊caterpillar tracks are widely used on building sites. The largest excavators are the draglines used in mining to strip away earth covering a coal or mineral deposit. They cast their digging bucket away like a fishing line being cast, and then drag it back along the ground, so filling it with earth. Britain's 'Big Geordie' walking dragline in the Northumberland coalfields has a bucket with a capacity of 50 cu m/65 cu yd.

exceed /ik'siːd/ v.t. 1. to be more or greater than, to surpass. 2. to go beyond (a limit etc.); to do more than is warranted by (instructions etc.). [from Old French from Latin excedere = go beyond]

exceedingly adv. very, extremely.

excel /ik'sel/ v.t./i. (-ll-) to be superior to; to be pre-eminent. [from Latin excellere (celsus = lofty)]

excellence /'eksələns/ n. great worth or quality.

Excellency n. His, Her, Your, etc., **Excellency,** a title used in addressing or referring to certain high officials.

excellent adj. extremely good. —**excellently** adv.

excentric variant (in technical senses) of ◊eccentric.

except /ik'sept/ v.t. to exclude from a general statement or condition etc. —prep. not including, other than. —conj. (archaic) unless. [from Latin excipere = take out]

excepting except.

exception /ik'sepʃən/ n. 1. excepting. 2. a thing or case excepted or apart, especially a thing not following a general rule. —**take exception,** to object (to). **with the exception of,** except.

exceptionable adj. open to objection.

exceptional adj. forming an exception, unusual; outstanding. —**exceptionally** adv.

excerpt /'eksɜːpt/ n. a short extract from a book, film etc. —/ik'sɜːpt/ v.t. to take excerpts from. —**excerption** /-'sɜːpʃən/ n. [from Latin excerpere (carpere = pluck)]

excess /ik'ses/ n. 1. the exceeding of due limits; (usually in plural) immoderate or outrageous behaviour. 2. the amount by which one number or quantity exceeds another. 3. an agreed amount subtracted by an insurer from the total payment to be made to an insured person who makes a claim. —/'ekses/ adj. that exceeds a limit or given amount; required as an excess. —**excess baggage,** that exceeding the weight allowance and liable to an extra charge. **in excess of,** more than. [from Old French from Latin excedere = go beyond]

excessive /ik'sesiv/ adj. too much, too great, more than is normal or necessary. —**excessively** adv.

exchange /iks'tʃeindʒ/ n. 1. the act or process of giving one thing and receiving another in its place; the giving of money for its equivalent in money of the same or another country. 2. the central telephone office of a district, where connections are effected. 3. the place where merchants, brokers etc., gather to transact business. 4. an office where certain information is given. 5. a system of settling debts between persons (especially in different countries) without the use of money, by bills of exchange (see ◊bill[1]). —v.t./i. to give or receive (a thing) in place of (or for) another; to give one and receive another of (things or persons); to make an exchange *with* someone else. **in exchange,** as a thing exchanged (*for*).

exchangeable *adj.* able to be exchanged.

exchange rate the price at which one currency is bought or sold in terms of other currencies, gold, or accounting units such as the special drawing right (SDR) of the ◊International Monetary Fund. Exchange rates may be fixed by international agreement or by government policy; or they may be wholly or partly allowed to 'float' (that is, find their own level) in world currency markets. Most major currencies have been allowed to float since the 1970s.

Exchange Rate Mechanism (ERM) a voluntary system for controlling exchange rates within the European Community's ◊European Monetary System.

exchequer /ɪks'tʃekə/ *n.* **1. Exchequer,** the former government department dealing with national revenue; a royal or national treasury. **2.** one's private funds. [from Old French from Latin *scaccarium* = chess-board, with reference to former keeping of accounts on chequered table-cloth]

excise[1] /'eksaɪz/ *n.* a duty or tax levied on goods produced or sold within a country, and on various licences etc.; it is collected by the government's ◊Customs and Excise department. —*v.t.* to charge excise on; to make (a person) pay excise.

excise[2] /ek'saɪz/ *v.t.* to remove by cutting out or away (a passage from a book, tissue from the body etc.). —**excision** /-'sɪʒən/ *n.* [from Latin *excidere* (*caedere* = cut)]

excitable /ɪk'saɪtəbəl/ *adj.* (especially of a person) easily excited. —**excitability** /-'bɪlɪtɪ/ *n.*

excite /ɪk'saɪt/ *v.t.* to rouse the feelings or emotion of (a person); to bring into play, to rouse up (feelings etc.); to provoke or bring about (an action etc.); to stimulate (a bodily organ etc.) to activity. [from Old French or Latin *excitare,* frequentative of *exciēre* = set in motion]

excitement *n.* **1.** a thing that excites. **2.** an excited state of mind.

exciting *adj.* arousing great interest or enthusiasm. —**excitingly** *adv.*

exclaim /ɪk'skleɪm/ *v.t./i.* to cry out, especially in anger, surprise, pain etc.; to utter or say in this manner. [from French or Latin *clamare* = shout]

exclamation /eksklə'meɪʃən/ *n.* **1.** exclaiming. **2.** a word or words etc. exclaimed. —**exclamation mark,** the punctuation mark (!) placed after and indicating an exclamation ('*That's terrible!*'). An exclamation mark is appropriate after interjections ('*Rats!*'), emphatic greetings ('*Ahoy there!*'), and orders ('*Shut up!*'), as well as those sentences beginning *How* or *What* that are not questions ('*How embarrassing!*', '*What a surprise!*').

exclamatory /ɪk'sklæmətərɪ/ *adj.* of or serving as an exclamation.

exclude /ɪk'sklu:d/ *v.i.* **1.** to shut or keep out from a place, group, or privilege etc. **2.** to remove from consideration. **3.** to make impossible, to preclude. —**exclusion** *n.* [from Latin *excludere* (*claudere* = shut)]

exclusion principle in physics, a principle of atomic structure originated by Wolfgang ◊Pauli. It states that no two electrons in a single atom may have the same set of ◊quantum numbers.

exclusive /ɪks'klu:sɪv/ *adj.* excluding, not inclusive; excluding all others; tending to exclude others, especially socially; (of shops or goods) high-class, catering for the wealthy; (of goods for sale, a newspaper article etc.) not available or appearing elsewhere. —**exclusive of,** not counting. —**exclusively** *adv.,* **exclusiveness** *n.,* **exclusivity** /-'sɪvɪtɪ/ *n.*

excommunicate /ekskə'mju:nɪkeɪt/ *v.t.* to deprive (a person) of membership and especially the sacraments of the Church. —/-ət/ *adj.* excommunicated. —/-ət/ *n.* an excommunicated person. —**excommunication** /-'keɪʃən/ *n.* [from Latin *excommunicare* = put out of the community]

excoriate /eks'kɔ:rɪeɪt/ *v.t.* **1.** to remove part of the skin of (a person etc.), as by abrasion; to strip off (skin). **2.** to censure severely. —**excoriation** /-'eɪʃən/ *n.* [from Latin *excoriare* (*corium* = hide)]

excrement /'ekskrɪmənt/ *n.* faeces. —**excremental** /-'mentəl/ *adj.* [from French or Latin]

excrescence /ɪk'skresəns/ *n.* an abnormal or morbid outgrowth on a body or plant; an ugly addition. —**excrescent** *adj.* [from Latin *crescere* = grow]

excreta /ek'skri:tə/ *n.pl.* faeces and urine. [Latin]

excrete /ɪk'skri:t/ *v.t.* to expel from the body as waste. —**excretory** *adj.* [from Latin *cernere* = sift]

excretion *n.* the removal of waste products from the cells of living organisms. In plants and simple animals, waste products are removed by diffusion, but in higher animals by specialized organs. In mammals, for example, carbon dioxide and water are removed via the lungs, and nitrogenous compounds and water via the liver, the kidneys, and the rest of the urinary system.

excruciating /ɪk'skru:ʃieɪtɪŋ/ *adj.* acutely painful; (*colloquial*) (of humour etc.) shocking, poor. [from Latin *excruciare* = torment (*crux* = cross)]

exculpate /'ekskʌlpeɪt/ *v.t.* to free from blame; to clear (a person *from* a charge). —**exculpation** /-'peɪʃən/ *n.,* **exculpatory** /-'kʌlpətərɪ/ *adj.* [from Latin *culpa* = blame]

excursion /ɪk'skɜ:ʃən/ *n.* a short journey or ramble for pleasure and returning to the starting-point. [from Latin *currere* = run]

excursive *adj.* digressive.

excusable *adj.* that may be excused.

excuse /ɪk'skju:z/ *v.t.* **1.** to try to lessen the blame attaching to (an act or fault or the person committing it); (of a fact or circumstance) to mitigate or justify thus; to overlook or forgive (a person or offence). **2.** to release from an obligation or duty; to gain exemption for. **3.** to allow to leave. —/ɪk'skju:s/ *n.* a reason put forward to mitigate or justify an offence; an apology. —**excuse me,** a polite apology for interrupting or disagreeing etc. **excuse oneself,** to ask permission or apologize for leaving. [from Old French from Latin *causa* = accusation]

ex-directory *adj.* (of a telephone number) omitted from the directory at the subscriber's request.

exeat /'eksɪæt/ *n.* leave of absence from college etc. [Latin = let him go out]

execrable /'eksɪkrəbəl/ *adj.* abominable. —**execrably** *adv.* [from Old French from Latin]

execrate /'eksɪkreɪt/ *v.t./i.* to express loathing for, to detest; to utter curses. —**execration** /-'kreɪʃən/ *n.* [from Latin *ex(s)ecrari* (*sacer* = sacred, accursed)]

executant /ɪg'zekjutənt/ *n.* a performer, especially of music. [from French]

execute /'eksɪkju:t/ *v.t.* **1.** to carry into effect, to perform (a plan, duty etc.). **2.** to produce (a work of art). **3.** to inflict capital punishment on. **4.** to make (a legal document) valid by signing, sealing etc. [from Old French from Latin *executare* (*sequi* = follow)]

execution /eksɪ'kju:ʃən/ *n.* **1.** carrying out, performance. **2.** an infliction of capital punishment. **3.** skill in or manner of a performance.

executioner *n.* one who carries out a death sentence.

executive /ɪg'zekjutɪv/ *adj.* concerned with executing laws, agreements etc., or with other administration or management. —*n.* a person or body having executive authority or in an executive position in a business organization etc.; the executive branch of government etc.

executor /ɪg'zekjutə/ *n.* a person appointed by a testator to carry out the terms of a will. A person so named has the right to refuse to act. The executor also has a duty to bury the deceased, prove the will, and obtain a grant of probate (that is, establish that the will is genuine and obtain official approval of his or her actions). —**executorial** /-'tɔ:rɪəl/ *adj.,* **executrix** *n. feminine*

exegesis /eksɪ'dʒi:sɪs/ *n.* (*plural* **exegeses** /-si:z/) an explanation, especially of a passage of Scripture. —**exegetic** /-'dʒetɪk/ *adj.* [from Greek, from *exēgeomai* = interpret]

exemplar /ɪg'zemplə/ *n.* a model, a type; an instance. [from Old French from Latin]

exemplary /ɪg'zemplərɪ/ *adj.* **1.** fit to be imitated, very good. **2.** serving as an example or as a warning. [from Latin]

exemplify /ɪg'zemplɪfaɪ/ *v.t.* to give or serve as an example of. —**exemplification** /-'keɪʃən/ *n.* [from Latin]

exempt /ɪg'zempt/ *adj.* freed (*from* an obligation or liability etc. imposed on others). —*v.t.* to make exempt (*from*). —**exemption** *n.* [from Latin *eximere* = take out]

exequies /'eksɪkwɪz/ *n.pl.* funeral rites. [from Old French from Latin *exsequiae*]

exercise /'eksəsaɪz/ *n.* **1.** an activity requiring physical effort, done to improve the health; (often in *plural*) a particular bodily task devised for this. **2.** the use or application (of a mental faculty, right etc.); the practice (of a virtue or function etc.). **3.** (often in *plural*) military drill or manœuvres. —*v.t.* **1.** to use or apply (a mental faculty, right etc.); to practise (a virtue or function etc.). **2.** to take or cause to take exercise; to give exercise to. **3.** to perplex, to worry. [from Old French from Latin *exercēre* = keep at work]

exert /ɪgˈzɜːt/ *v.t.* to bring into use, to bring (influence, pressure etc.) to bear. —**exert oneself**, to use efforts or endeavours. —**exertion** *n.* [from Latin *exserere* = put forth]

Exeter /ˈeksɪtə/ city, administrative headquarters of Devon, England, on the river Exe; population (1981) 96,000. It has medieval, Georgian, and Regency architecture, including a cathedral (1280–1369), a market centre, and a university (1955). It manufactures agricultural machinery, pharmaceuticals, and textiles.

exeunt /ˈeksɪʊnt/ (as a stage direction) they leave the stage. *exeunt omnes* /ˈɒmniːz/, all go off. [Latin = go out]

exfoliate /eksˈfəʊlɪeɪt/ *v.i.* to come off in scales or layers; (of a tree) to throw off bark thus. —**exfoliation** /-ˈeɪʃən/ *n.* [from Latin *exfoliare* (*folium* = leaf)]

ex gratia /eks ˈɡreɪʃə/ done or given as a concession, not from an (especially legal) obligation. [Latin = from kindness]

exhale /eksˈheɪl/ *v.t./i.* to breathe out; to give off or be given off in a vapour. —**exhalation** /-həˈleɪʃən/ *n.* [from Old French from Latin *halare* = breathe]

exhaust /ɪgˈzɔːst/ *v.t.* **1.** to consume or use up the whole of; to use up the strength or resources of, to tire out. **2.** to empty (a vessel etc. *of* its contents); to draw off (air). **3.** to study or expound on (a subject) completely. —*n.* **1.** the expulsion or exit of steam or waste gases from an engine etc.; such gases etc. **2.** the pipe or system through which they are expelled. [from Latin *exhaurire* = drain]

exhaustible *adj.* liable to be exhausted.

exhaustion /ɪgˈzɔːstʃən/ *n.* exhausting, being exhausted; complete loss of strength.

exhaustive *adj.* that exhausts a subject; thorough, comprehensive. —**exhaustively** *adv.*

exhibit /ɪgˈzɪbɪt/ *v.t.* to show or display, especially publicly; to manifest (a quality etc.). —*n.* a thing exhibited, especially in an exhibition or as evidence in a lawcourt. —**exhibitor** *n.* [from Latin *exhibēre* (*habēre* = hold)]

exhibition /eksɪˈbɪʃən/ *n.* **1.** exhibiting, being exhibited. **2.** a public display of works of art etc. **3.** a minor scholarship, especially from the funds of a school or college etc.

exhibitioner *n.* a student receiving an exhibition.

exhibitionism *n.* a tendency towards display or extravagant behaviour; a perverted mental condition characterized by indecent exposure of the genitals. —**exhibitionist** *n.*

exhilarate /ɪgˈzɪləreɪt/ *v.t.* to enliven or gladden. —**exhilaration** /-ˈreɪʃən/ *n.* [from Latin *hilaris* = cheerful]

exhort /ɪgˈzɔːt/ *v.t.* to urge or admonish earnestly. —**exhortation** /egzɔːˈteɪʃən/ *n.*, **exhortative** *adj.*, **exhortatory** *adj.* [from Latin *hortari* = exhort]

exhume /eksˈhjuːm/ *v.t.* to dig up or unearth (especially a buried corpse). —**exhumation** /-ˈmeɪʃən/ *n.* [from French from Latin *humare* = bury]

ex hypothesi /eks haɪˈpɒθəsɪ/ according to the hypothesis proposed. [Latin]

exigency /ˈeksɪdʒənsɪ/ *n.* or **exigence** an urgent need or demand; an emergency. —**exigent** *adj.* [from French and Latin *exigere*]

exiguous /egˈzɪgjuəs/ *adj.* scanty, small. —**exiguity** /-ˈɡjuːɪtɪ/ *n.*, **exiguousness** *n.* [from Latin *exiguus* = scanty (*exigere* = weigh exactly)]

exile /ˈeksaɪl, egˈz-/ *n.* **1.** being expelled from one's native country; a long absence abroad. **2.** a person in exile. —*v.t.* to send into exile. —**the Exile**, the Captivity of the Jews in Babylon. [from Old French from Latin *exilium* = banishment]

exist /ɪgˈzɪst/ *v.i.* **1.** to have a place in reality. **2.** (of circumstances etc.) to occur, to be found. **3.** to live, to sustain life; to continue in being.

existence /ɪgˈzɪstəns/ *n.* **1.** the fact or a manner of existing or living; continuance in life or being. **2.** all that exists. —**existent** *adj.* [from Old French or Latin *existentia* (*stare* = stand)]

existential /egzɪˈstenʃəl/ *adj.* of or relating to existence; concerned with human experience as viewed by existentialism. —**existentially** *adv.*

existentialism /egzɪˈstenʃlɪzm/ *n.* a branch of philosophy based on the concept of a universe in which people have free will. Existentialists argue that philosophy must begin with the concrete situation of the individual in such a world, and that people are responsible for and the sole judge of their actions as they affect others, (although to the individual, no one else's existence is real). The origin of existentialism is usually attributed to the Danish philosopher ◊Kierkegaard, and among its proponents were Martin Heidegger in Germany and Jean-Paul ◊Sartre in France. —**existentialist** *n.*

exit[1] /ˈeksɪt, ˈegz-/ *n.* **1.** the act or right of going out. **2.** a passage or door as the way out. **3.** an actor's departure from the stage. —*v.i.* to make one's exit. [from Latin *exitus* = going out]

exit[2] /ˈeksɪt, ˈegz-/ (as a stage direction) he or she leaves the stage. [Latin *exire* = go out]

ex lib. abbreviation of ex libris. [Latin = from the library of).

Exmoor /ˈeksmuə/ moorland in Devon and Somerset, England, forming (with the coast from Minehead to Combe Martin) a National Park since 1954.

exo- prefix denoting external(ly). [from Greek *exō* = outside]

exobiology *n.* the study of life forms elsewhere in the universe, and of the effects of extraterrestrial environments on Earth organisms.

exocrine gland /ˈeksəkraɪn, -krɪn/ a gland that discharges secretions, usually through a tube or a duct, onto a surface. Examples include sweat glands, which release sweat onto the skin, and digestive glands, which release digestive juices onto the walls of the intestine. Some animals also have ◊endocrine glands (ductless glands), which release hormones directly into the bloodstream. [from Greek *krinō* = sift]

exodus /ˈeksədəs/ *n.* a mass departure, especially (**Exodus**) that of the Israelites from Egypt. Exodus is also the name of the second book of the Old Testament, which relates the escape of the Israelites from slavery in Egypt, under the leadership of ◊Moses, for the Promised Land of Canaan. [Latin from Greek = way out]

ex officio /eks əˈfɪʃɪəʊ/ by virtue of one's office. —**ex-officio** *adj.* of a position held thus. [Latin]

exonerate /ɪgˈzɒnəreɪt/ *v.t.* to free or declare free from blame. —**exoneration** /-ˈreɪʃən/ *n.*, **exonerative** /ɪgˈzɒnərətɪv/ *adj.* [from Latin *exonerare* (*onus* = burden)]

exorbitant /ɪgˈzɔːbɪtənt/ *adj.* (of a price or demand etc.) grossly excessive. [from Latin]

exorcise /ˈeksɔːsaɪz/ *v.t.* to drive out (an evil spirit) by invocation etc.; to free (a person or place) thus. —**exorcism** *n.*, **exorcist** *n.* [from French or Latin from Greek *exorkizō* (*horkos* = oath)]

exordium /ekˈsɔːdɪəm/ *n.* (*plural* **exordiums**) the introductory part of a discourse or treatise. [from Latin *ordiri* = begin]

exoskeleton *n.* the hardened external skeleton of insects, spiders, crabs, and other arthropods. It provides attachment for muscles and protection for the internal organs, as well as support. To permit growth it is periodically shed in a process called ecdysis.

exosphere *n.* the uppermost layer of the ◊atmosphere. It is an ill-defined zone above the thermosphere, beginning at about 700 km/435 mi and fading off into the vacuum of space. It consists mainly of hydrogen and all its constituent gases are extremely thin.

exothermic reaction a chemical reaction during which heat is given out (see ◊energy of reaction).

exotic /ɪgˈzɒtɪk/ *adj.* introduced from abroad, not native; remarkably strange or unusual. —*n.* an exotic plant etc. —**exotically** *adv.* [from Latin from Greek]

exotica /ɪgˈzɒtɪkə/ *n.pl.* remarkably strange or rare objects. [Latin]

expand /ɪkˈspænd/ *v.t./i.* **1.** to increase in size, bulk, or importance. **2.** to unfold or spread out. **3.** to express at length (condensed notes, an algebraic expression etc.). **4.** to be genial or effusive. —**expander** *n.* [from Latin *expandere* = spread]

expanse /ɪk'spæns/ n. a wide area or extent of land, space etc.

expansible /ɪk'spænsɪbəl/ adj. that can be expanded. —**expansibility** /-'bɪlɪtɪ/ n.

expansion /ɪk'spænʃən/ n. 1. expanding; an enlargement, an increase. 2. in physics, the increase in size of a constant mass of substance (a body) caused by, for example, a rise in its temperature (thermal expansion) or its internal pressure. 3. in mechanics, the increase in volume of steam in the cylinder of a steam engine after cutoff, or of gas in the cylinder of an internal-combustion engine after explosion. **Expansivity**, or coefficient of cubical (or thermal) expansion, is the expansion per unit volume per degree rise in temperature.

expansionism n. advocacy of expansion, especially in territory. —**expansionist** n.

expansive /ɪk'spænsɪv/ adj. 1. able or tending to expand. 2. extensive. 3. effusive, genial. —**expansively** adv., **expansiveness** n.

expatiate /ɪk'speɪʃɪeɪt/ v.i. to speak or write at length (on). —**expatiation** /-'eɪʃən/ n., **expatiatory** adj. [from Latin exspatiari = walk about (spatium = space)]

expatriate /eks'pætrieɪt/ v.t. to expel, or to remove oneself, from one's native country. —/-ət/ adj. expatriated. —/-ət/ n. an expatriated person. —**expatriation** /-'eɪʃən/ n. [from Latin patria = native land]

expect /ɪk'spekt/ v.t. 1. to regard as likely, to assume as a future event or occurrence. 2. to look for as due. 3. (colloquial) to think, to suppose. —**be expecting**, (colloquial) to be pregnant. [from Latin ex(s)pectare (spectare = look)]

expectancy n. a state of expectation; a prospect or prospective chance.

expectant adj. expecting, having expectations. —**expectant mother**, a pregnant woman. —**expectantly** adv.

expectation /ekspek'teɪʃən/ n. 1. expecting, looking forward with hope or fear etc. 2. what one expects; the probability (of an event); the probable duration (of life); (in plural) prospects of inheritance.

expectorant /ek'spektərənt/ adj. that causes one to expectorate. —n. an expectorant medicine.

expectorate /ek'spektəreɪt/ v.t./i. to cough or spit out (phlegm etc.) from the chest or lungs; to spit. —**expectoration** /-'reɪʃən/ n. [from Latin expectorare (pectus = breast)]

expedient /ɪk'spiːdiənt/ adj. advantageous, advisable on practical rather than moral grounds; suitable, appropriate. —n. a means of achieving an end, a resource. —**expedience** n., **expediency** n., **expediently** adv.

expedite /'ekspɪdaɪt/ v.t. to assist the progress of, to hasten (an action, measure etc.); to accomplish (business) quickly. [from Latin expedire = free from difficulties, put in order]

expedition /ekspə'dɪʃən/ n. 1. a journey or voyage for a particular purpose especially exploration; the people or ships etc. undertaking this. 2. promptness, speed.

expeditionary adj. of or used in an expedition.

expeditious /ekspə'dɪʃəs/ adj. acting or done with speed and efficiency. —**expeditiously** adv.

expel /ɪk'spel/ v.t. (-ll-) to send or drive out by force; to compel (a person) by process of law to leave a school or country etc. [from Latin pellere = drive]

expend /ɪk'spend/ v.t. to spend or use up (money, time etc.). [from Latin expendere (pendere = weigh)]

expendable adj. that may be sacrificed or dispensed with; not worth preserving.

expenditure /ek'spendɪtʃə/ n. expending (especially of money); the amount expended.

expense /ɪk'spens/ n. a cost incurred; (in plural) the costs incurred in doing a job etc., reimbursement for these; the spending of money, a thing on which money is spent. —**at the expense of**, so as to cause loss or damage or discredit to. **expense account**, the record of an employee's expenses payable by an employer. [from Old French from Latin expensa]

expensive adj. costing much, of a high price. —**expensively** adv., **expensiveness** n.

experience /ɪk'spɪəriəns/ n. personal observation of or involvement with a fact, event etc.; knowledge or skill based on this; an event that affects one. —v.t. to have experience of, to undergo; to feel. [from Old French from Latin experiri = make trial of]

experienced adj. having had much experience; skilled from this.

experiential /ɪkspɪəri'enʃəl/ adj. involving or based on experience.

experiment /ɪk'sperɪmənt/ n. a procedure tried on the chance of success, or to test an hypothesis etc. or demonstrate a known fact. —/also -ent/ v.i. to make an experiment (on or with). —**experimentation** /-'teɪʃən/ n. [from Old French or Latin]

experimental /ɪksperi'mentəl/ adj. of, based on, or using an experiment; in the nature of an experiment. —**experimentalism** n., **experimentally** adv.

experimental psychology the application of scientific methods to the study of mental processes and behaviour. The term covers a wide range of fields of study including: **human and animal learning**, in which learning theories describe how new behaviours are acquired and modified; **cognition**, the study of a number of functions, such as perception, attention, memory, and language; **physiological psychology**, which relates the study of cognition to different regions of the brain. **Artificial intelligence** is the computer simulation of cognitive processes, such as language and problem-solving.

expert /'ekspɜːt/ adj. highly practised and skilful, or well informed, in a subject. —n. a person who is expert in a subject; (attributive) of or being an expert. —**expertly** adv. [from Old French from Latin]

expertise /ekspɜː'tiːz/ n. expert skill or knowledge or judgement. [French]

expert system a computer program that gives advice (such as diagnosing an illness or interpreting the law), incorporating knowledge derived from human expertise. It is a kind of ◊knowledge-based system containing rules that can be applied to find the solution to a problem. It is a form of ◊artificial intelligence.

expiate /'ekspieɪt/ v.t. to make amends for (a wrong); to pay the penalty of. —**expiable** adj., **expiation** /-'eɪʃən/ n., **expiatory** adj. [from Latin expiare = seek to appease]

expiratory /ɪk'spaɪrətərɪ/ adj. of breathing out.

expire /ɪk'spaɪə/ v.t./i. 1. (of a period, the validity of a thing etc.) to come to an end. 2. to breathe out (air, or absolute); to die. —**expiration** /ekspi'reɪʃən/ n. [from Old French from Latin exspirare (spirare = breathe)]

expiry /ɪk'spaɪrɪ/ n. the termination of a period of validity.

explain /ɪk'spleɪn, ɪk'spleɪn/ v.t. to make clear or intelligible, to give the meaning of; to make known in detail; to account for (conduct etc.). —**explain away**, to minimize the significance of. **explain oneself**, to justify one's conduct or attitude etc. [from Latin explanare (planus = flat, plain)]

explanation /eksplə'neɪʃən/ n. 1. explaining; a statement or circumstance that explains something. 2. in science, an attempt to make clear the cause of any natural event, by reference to physical laws and to observations.

explanatory /ɪk'splænətərɪ/ adj. serving or intended to explain.

expletive /ɪk'spliːtɪv/ n. an oath or meaningless exclamation; a word used to fill out a sentence etc. —adj. serving as an expletive. [from Latin explēre = fill out]

explicable /'eksplɪkəbəl, ɪk'splɪk-/ adj. that can be explained.

explicate /'eksplɪkeɪt/ v.t. to explain or develop (an idea etc.). —**explication** /-'keɪʃən/ n. [from Latin explicare = unfold]

explicit /ɪk'splɪsɪt/ adj. 1. expressly stated, not merely implied; stated in detail; definite. 2. outspoken. —**explicitly** adv., **explicitness** n.

explode /ɪk'spləʊd/ v.t./i. 1. to expand suddenly with a loud noise owing to the release of internal energy; to cause to do this. 2. to give vent suddenly to emotion or violence. 3. to increase suddenly or rapidly. 4. to expose or discredit (a theory etc.). 5. (usually in past participle) to show parts of (a diagram etc.) in relative positions but somewhat separated. [from Latin explodere = drive off the stage by clapping]

exploit /'eksplɔɪt/ n. a bold or daring feat. —/ɪk'splɔɪt/ v.t. to use or develop for one's own ends, to take advantage of. —**exploitation** /-'teɪʃən/ n. [from Old French]

explore /ɪk'splɔː/ v.t. 1. to travel extensively through (a country etc.) in order to learn or discover about it.

2. to inquire into. 3. to examine by touch. —**exploration** /ɛksplə'reɪʃən/ *n.*, **exploratory** /ɪk'splɒrətərɪ/ *adj.*, **explorer** *n.* from French from Latin *explorare*]

Explorer /ɪk'splɔːrə/ *n.* one of a series of US scientific satellites. *Explorer 1*, launched Jan 1958, was the first US satellite in orbit and discovered the Van Allen radiation belts around the Earth.

explosion /ɪk'spləʊʒən/ *n.* 1. exploding; a loud noise due to this. 2. a sudden outbreak of feeling etc. 3. a sudden or rapid increase. [from Latin]

explosive /ɪk'spləʊsɪv/ *adj.* 1. able to or tending or likely to explode. 2. likely to cause a violent outburst etc., dangerously tense. —*n.* an explosive substance. —**explosively** *adv.*

exponent /ɪk'spəʊnənt/ *n.* 1. a person who explains or interprets something. 2. a person who favours or promotes an idea etc. 3. a type or representative. 4. a raised symbol beside a numeral (e.g. 3 in 2^3) indicating how many times it is to be multiplied by itself; for example, $x^2 \times x^5 = x^7$. Division of such terms is achieved by subtracting the exponents; for example, $y^5 \div y^3 = y^2$. Any number with the exponent 0 is equal to 1; for example, $x^0 = 1$ and $99^0 = 1$. [from Latin *exponere* (*ponere* = put)]

exponential /ɛkspə'nɛnʃəl/ *n.* 1. of or indicated by a mathematical exponent. Exponential functions and series involve the constant $e = 2.71828....$ Napier devised natural ọlogarithms in 1614 with *e* as the base. They are basic mathematical functions, written as e^x or exp x. The expression e^x has five definitions, two of which are: **a.**e^x is the solution of the differential equation $dx/dt = x$ ($x = 1$ if $t = 0$); **b.**e^x is the limiting sum of the infinite series $1 + x + (x^2/2!) + (x^3/3!) + ... + (x^n/n!)$. 2. (of an increase etc.) more and more rapid. —**exponential curve**, one based on an exponential equation, increasing sharply in steepness. Curves of the form $y = Ae^{-ax}$, $a < 0$ are known as decay functions; those of the form $y = Be^{bx}$, $b < 0$ are growth functions. **Exponential growth** is not constant. It applies, for example, to population growth, where the population doubles in a short time period. A graph of population number against time produces a curve that is characteristically rather flat at first but then shoots almost directly upwards.

export /'ɛkspɔːt/ *v.t.* to send out goods or service produced in one country for sale in another. —*n.* 1. exporting. 2. an exported article; (usually in *plural*) the amount exported. Exports may be visible (goods physically exported) or invisible (services provided in the exporting country but paid for in another country). —**exportation** /-'teɪʃən/ *n.*, **exporter** /-'pɔːt-/ *n.* [from Latin *portare* = carry]

exportable /ɪk'spɔːtəbəl/ *adj.* that can be exported.

export credit a loan, finance, or guarantee provided by a government or a financial institution enabling companies to export goods and services when payment for them may be delayed or subject to risk.

expose /ɪk'spəʊz/ *v.t.* 1. to leave uncovered or unprotected, especially from the weather; to allow light to reach (a photographic film or plate); to leave (a baby) in the open to die. 2. to subject *to* (a risk etc.). 3. to reveal, to make known or visible; to show up in a true (usually unfavourable) light. —**expose oneself**, to expose one's body indecently. [from Old French from Latin]

exposé /ɛk'spəʊzeɪ/ *n.* an orderly statement of facts; a revealing of a discreditable thing. [French]

exposition /ɛkspə'zɪʃən/ *n.* 1. expounding, an explanatory account. 2. a large public exhibition. 3. in music, the part of a movement in which themes are presented. [from Old French or Latin]

ex post facto /ɛks pəʊst 'fæktəʊ/retrospective, retrospectively. [Latin = from what is done afterwards]

expostulate /ɪk'spɒstjʊleɪt/ *v.i.* to make a reasoned protest, to remonstrate. —**expostulation** /-'leɪʃən/ *n.*, **expostulatory** *adj.* [from Latin]

exposure /ɪk'spəʊʒə/ *n.* 1. exposing, being exposed. 2. the exposing of a photographic film or plate; the duration of this; the part of a film exposed for one picture.

exposure meter an instrument used in photography for indicating the correct exposure, or length of time the camera shutter should be open under given light conditions. Substances such as cadmium sulphide and selenium are used as light sensors in meters. These materials change electrically when light strikes them, the change being proportional to the intensity of the incident light. Many cameras have a built-in exposure meter that sets the camera controls automatically as the light conditions change.

expound /ɪk'spaʊnd/ *v.t.* to set forth in detail; to explain, to interpret. [from Old French]

express /ɪk'sprɛs/ *v.t.* 1. to represent or make known in words or by gestures, conduct etc. 2. to squeeze out (juice etc.). 3. to send by express service. —*adj.* 1. definitely stated, explicit. 2. sent or delivered by a specially fast service. 3. (of a train) travelling at high speed and with few stops. —*n.* 1. an express train etc. 2. (*US*) a service for the rapid transport of parcels etc. —*adv.* at high speed, by express. —**express oneself**, to say what one means or thinks. —**expressly** *adv.* [from Old French from Latin *exprimere*, originally = press out]

expressible /ɪk'sprɛsɪbəl/ *adj.* that can be expressed.

expression /ɪk'sprɛʃən/ *n.* 1. expressing; a word or phrase; a collection of symbols in mathematics expressing a quantity. 2. a look or facial aspect; the showing of feeling in the manner of speaking or of performing music; the representation of feeling in art.

Expressionism /ɪk'sprɛʃənɪzm/ *n.* 1.a style of painting, sculpture, and literature that expresses inner emotions; in particular, a movement in early 20th-century art in N and central Europe. Expressionists tended to distort or exaggerate natural appearance in order to create a reflection of an inner world; the Norwegian painter Edvard Munch's *Skriket/The Scream* 1893 (National Gallery, Oslo) is a notable example. Other leading Expressionist artists were James Ensor, Oskar Kokoschka, and Chaï m Soutine. The Blaue Reiter group was associated with this movement, and the Expressionist trend in German art emerged even more strongly after World War I in the work of Max Beckmann and Georg Grosz. Expressionist writers include August Strindberg and Frank Wedekind. 2.in music, atonal music that uses dissonance for disturbing effect. —**Expressionist** *n. & adj.*

expressionless *adj.* without positive expression, not revealing one's thoughts or feelings.

expressive *adj.* serving to express; full of expression. —**expressively** *adv.*, **expressiveness** *n.*

expressway *n.* (*US*) an urban motorway.

expropriate /ɛks'prəʊprɪeɪt/ *v.t.* to take away (property) from its owner; to dispossess (a person). —**expropriation** /-'eɪʃən/ *n.* [from Latin *proprium* [property]

expulsion /ɪk'spʌlʃən/ *n.* expelling, being expelled.

expulsive /ɪk'spʌlsɪv/ *adj.* expelling.

expunge /ɪk'spʌndʒ/ *v.t.* to erase or remove (a passage *from* a book etc.). [from Latin *expungere* = prick out (for deletion)]

expurgate /'ɛkspɜːgeɪt/ *v.t.* to remove matter thought to be objectionable from (a book etc.); to remove (such matter). —**expurgation** 'geɪʃən/ *n.*, **expurgator** *n.* [from Latin *purgare* = cleanse]

exquisite /'ɛkskwɪzɪt, ɛk'skwɪzɪt/*adj.* 1. extremely beautiful or delicate. 2. highly sensitive; acute, keen. —*n.* a person of refined (especially affected) tastes. —**exquisitely** *adv.* [from Latin *exquirere* = search out]

ex-serviceman /ɛks'sɜːvɪsmən/ *n.* or ex-servicewoman (*plural* **-men**, **-women**); a former member of the armed forces.

extant /ɛk'stænt, 'ɛk-/ *adj.* still existing. [from Latin *ex(s)tare* (*stare* = stand)]

extemporaneous /ɛkstɛmpə'reɪnɪəs/ *adj.* spoken or done without preparation. —**extemporaneously** *adv.*

extemporary /ɪk'stɛmpərərɪ/ *adj.* extemporaneous.

extempore /ɛk'stɛmpərɪ/ *adj. & adv.* without preparation, offhand. [from Latin *ex* = out of and *tempus* = time]

extemporize /ɪk'stɛmpəraɪz/ *v.t./i.* to speak, utter, or perform extempore. —**extemporization** /-'zeɪʃən/ *n.*

extend /ɪk'stɛnd/ *v.t./i.* 1. to lengthen in space or time; to increase in scope. 2. to stretch or lay out at full length; to reach or be continuous over a certain area; to have a certain scope. 3. to offer or accord a feeling, invitation etc., *to.* —**extended family**, one including relatives living near. **extended-play** *adj.* (of a gramophone record) playing for longer than most singles. **extend oneself** *or* **be extended**, to have one's abilities taxed to the utmost. —**extender** *n.* [from Latin *tendere* = stretch]

extensible /ɪkˈstensɪbəl/ *adj.* or **extendible** that can be extended.

extension /ɪkˈstenʃən/ *n.* 1. extending, being extended. 2. a part enlarging or added on to a main structure etc.; an additional period of time; a subsidiary telephone on the same line as the main one, its number. 3. extramural instruction by a university or college etc.

extensive *adj.* large; far-reaching. —**extensively** *adv.*, **extensiveness** *n.*

extensor *n.* a muscle that straightens a limb.

extent /ɪkˈstent/ *n.* the space over which a thing extends; a large area; range, scope, or degree.

extenuate /ɪkˈstenjueɪt/ *v.t.* to lessen the seeming seriousness of (an offence or guilt) by partial excuse. —**extenuation** /-ˈeɪʃən/ *n.* [from Latin *extenuare* (*tenuis* = thin)]

exterior /ɪkˈstɪəriə/ *adj.* outer, outward; coming from outside. —*n.* the exterior part or aspect; an outdoor scene in filming. [from Latin, comparative of *exterus* = outside]

exterminate /ɪkˈstɜːmɪneɪt/ *v.t.* to destroy (a disease, people etc.) utterly. —**extermination** /-ˈneɪʃən/ *n.*, **exterminator** *n.* [from Latin *terminare* = put an end to]

external /ekˈstɜːnəl/ *adj.* of or situated on the outside or visible part; coming from the outside or an outside source; of a country's foreign affairs; outside the conscious subject; (of medicine etc.) for use on the outside of the body; (of students) taking the examinations of, but not attending, a university. —*n.* (in *plural*) external features or circumstances; non-essentials. —**externality** /-ˈnælɪtɪ/ *n.*, **externally** *adv.* [from Latin *externus*]

externalize /ekˈstɜːnəlaɪz/ *v.t.* to give or attribute external existence to. —**externalization** /-ˈzeɪʃən/ *n.*

extinct /ɪkˈstɪŋkt/ *adj.* no longer existing, obsolete; no longer burning, (of a volcano) no longer active.

extinction *n.* making or becoming extinct, dying out. In biology, the complete disappearance of a species. In the past, extinctions are believed to have occurred because species were unable to adapt quickly enough to a naturally changing environment. Mass extinctions, episodes during which whole groups of species have become extinct, occurred about 65 million years ago, when the dinosaurs, other large reptiles, and various marine invertebrates died out; and about 10,000 million years ago, when many giant species of mammal died out. This is known as the 'Pleistocene overkill' because their disappearance was hastened by the hunting activities of prehistoric humans. In recent history, the dodo of Mauritius, the moas of New Zealand, and the passenger pigeon of North America, have all been exterminated by hunting. Today most extinctions are caused by human activity. See also ◊endangered species.

extinguish /ɪkˈstɪŋgwɪʃ/ *v.t.* 1. to cause (a fire or light etc.) to cease to burn or function. 2. to terminate, to make extinct, to destroy; to wipe out (a debt). [from Latin *exstinguere* (*stinguere* = quench)]

extinguisher *n.* a fire extinguisher.

extirpate /ˈekstɜːpeɪt/ *v.t.* to destroy, to root out. —**extirpation** /-ˈpeɪʃən/ *n.* [from Latin *exstirpare* (*stirps* = stem)]

extol /ɪkˈstəʊl/ *v.t.* (-ll -) to praise enthusiastically. [from Latin *extollere* (*tollere* = raise)]

extort /ɪkˈstɔːt/ *v.t.* to obtain (money, a secret etc.) by force, threats, or intimidation etc. [from Latin *torquere* = twist]

extortion /ɪkˈstɔːʃən/ *n.* extorting, especially of money; illegal exaction.

extortionate /ɪkˈstɔːʃənət/ *adj.* (of prices) excessively high; (of demands) excessive. —**extortionately** *adv.*

extortioner *n.* one who practises extortion.

extra /ˈekstrə/ *adj.* additional; more than is usual or necessary or expected. —*adv.* more than usually; additionally. —*n.* an extra thing; a thing charged extra; a person engaged temporarily for a minor part in a film etc.; a special issue of a newspaper etc.; a run in cricket not scored from a hit with the bat.

extra- prefix forming adjectives denoting 'outside', 'beyond the scope of'. [from Latin *extra* = outside]

extracellular matrix a strong material occurring naturally in animals and plants, made up of protein and long-chain sugars (polysaccharides) in which cells are embedded. It is often called a 'biological glue', forming part of ◊connective tissues such as bone and skin. The cell walls of plants and

bacteria, and the ◊exoskeletons of insects and other arthropods, are also formed by types of extracellular matrix.

extract /ɪkˈstrækt/ *v.t.* 1. to take out by effort or force (anything firmly rooted or fixed). 2. to obtain (money, an admission etc.) against a person's will. 3. to obtain (juice etc.) by pressure, distillation etc. 4. to derive (pleasure etc. *from*). 5. to quote or copy out (a passage from a book etc.). 6. to find (the root of a number). —/ˈekstrækt/ *n.* 1. a short passage from a book etc. 2. a substance got by distillation etc.; a concentrated preparation. [from Latin *extrahere* (*trahere* = draw)]

extraction /ɪkˈstrækʃən/ *n.* 1. extracting, especially of a tooth. 2. lineage.

extractive /ɪkˈstræktɪv/ *adj.* of or involving extraction. —**extractive industry,** one obtaining minerals etc. from the ground.

extractor /ɪkˈstræktə/ *n.* a person or thing that extracts. —**extractor fan,** a ventilating fan used to remove stale air.

extra-curricular /ekstrəkəˈrɪkjʊlə/ *adj.* not part of the normal curriculum.

extraditable /ˈekstrədaɪtəbəl/ *adj.* liable to or (of a crime) warranting extradition.

extradite /ˈekstrədaɪt/ *v.t.* to hand over (a person accused of a crime) to the state wishing to try him or her. When two nations are involved, a treaty is usually drawn up setting out the rules and conditions by which persons may be extradited. A country will not usually allow extradition for political offences or an offence it does not treat as a crime, even though it is a crime in the requesting country.—**extradition** /-ˈdɪʃən/ *n.* [from French]

extramarital /ekstrəˈmærɪtəl/ *adj.* (of sexual relationships) outside marriage.

extramural /ekstrəˈmjuərəl/ *adj.* (of university teaching) additional to normal degree courses. [from Latin *extra muros* = outside the walls]

extraneous /ɪkˈstreɪnɪəs/ *adj.* of external origin; not belonging (*to* the matter in hand). —**extraneously** *adv.* [from Latin *extra* = outside]

extraordinary /ɪkˈstrɔːdɪnərɪ, ekstrəˈɔːd-/ *adj.* unusual or remarkable; out of the usual course, additional; specially employed; unusually great. —**extraordinarily** *adv.* [from Latin *extra ordinem* = outside the usual order]

extrapolate /ekˈstræpəleɪt/ *v.t./i.* to estimate from known values, data etc. (others which lie outside the range of those known). —**extrapolation** /-ˈleɪʃən/ *n.*

extra-sensory /ekstrəˈsensərɪ/ *adj.* (of perception) derived by means other than the known senses.

extra-terrestrial /ekstrətɪˈrestrɪəl/ *adj.* outside the Earth or its atmosphere.

extravagant /ɪkˈstrævəgənt/ *adj.* 1. spending (especially money) excessively. 2. costing much. 3. passing the bounds of reason, absurd. —**extravagance** *n.*, **extravagantly** *adv.* [from Latin *vagari* = wander]

extravaganza /ekstrævəˈgænzə/ *adj.* a fanciful literary, musical, or dramatic composition; a spectacular theatrical production. [from Italian *estravaganza*]

extravasate /ekˈstrævəseɪt/ *v.t./i.* to force out (blood etc.) from its vessel; (of blood, lava etc.) to flow out. —**extravasation** /-ˈseɪʃən/ *n.* [from Latin *extra* = outside and *vas* = vessel]

extravert or **extraverted** alternative forms of ◊extrovert, extroverted.

Extremadura /estreɪməˈdʊərə/ autonomous region of W Spain including the provinces of Badajoz and Cáceres; area 41,600 sq km/16,058 sq mi; population (1986) 1,089,000. Irrigated land is used for growing wheat; the remainder is either oak forest or used for pig or sheep grazing.

extreme /ɪkˈstriːm/ *adj.* reaching a high or the highest degree; severe, going to great lengths; politically far to the left or right; outermost, furthest from the centre; utmost; last. —*n.* one or other of two things as remote or as different as possible, the thing at either end; an extreme degree; the first or last of a series. —**go to extremes,** to take an extreme course of action. **in the extreme,** to an extreme degree. [from Old French from Latin (superlative of *exterus* = outer)]

extremely *adv.* in an extreme degree, very.

extremist *n.* one who holds extreme (especially political) views. —**extremism** *n.*

eye

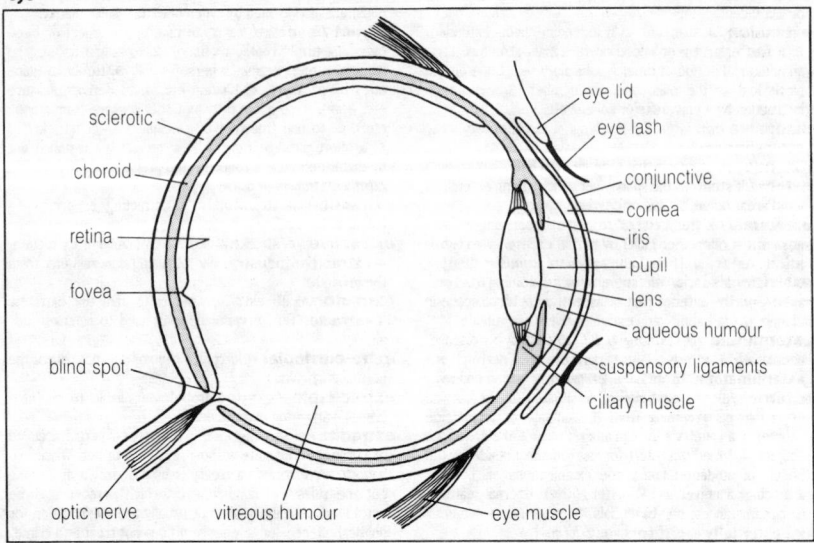

extremity /ɪkˈstremɪtɪ/ *n.* an extreme point, an end; extreme distress or difficulty; (in *plural*) the hands and feet.

extricable /ˈekstrɪkəbəl/ *adj.* that can be extricated.

extricate /ˈekstrɪkeɪt/ *v.t.* to free or disentangle (*from* a difficulty etc.). —**extrication** /-ˈkeɪʃən/ *n.* [from Latin *extricare* (*tricae* = entanglements)]

extrinsic /ek'strɪnsɪk/ *adj.* not inherent or intrinsic; extraneous, not belonging (*to*). —**extrinsically** *adv.* [from Latin *extrinsecus* = outwardly]

extrovert /ˈekstrəvɜːt/ *adj.* or **extroverted** or **extravert** or **extraverted** directing one's thoughts and interests to things outside oneself; socially unreserved. This personality dimension was first described by ◊Jung and later by ◊Eysenck. —*n.* an extrovert person.

extrude /ek'struːd/ *v.t.* to thrust or force out; to shape (metal, plastics etc.) by forcing through a die. —**extrusion** *n.*, **extrusive** *adj.* [from Latin *trudere* = thrust]

exuberant /ɪgˈzjuːbərənt/ *adj.* lively, effusive, high-spirited; (of a plant etc.) prolific, luxuriant; (of health, emotion etc.) overflowing, abundant. —**exuberance** *n.*, **exuberantly** *adv.* [from French from Latin *exuberare* (*uber* = fruitful)]

exude /ɪgˈzjuːd/ *v.t./i.* to ooze out; to give out (moisture); to emit (a smell); to show (pleasure etc.) freely. —**exudation** /eksjuˈdeɪʃən/ *n.* [from Latin *sudare* = sweat]

exult /ɪgˈzʌlt/ *v.i.* to rejoice greatly. —**exultation** /eksʌlˈteɪʃən/ *n.* [from Latin *saltare* = dance]

exultant *adj.* exulting, rejoicing.

Eyck /aɪk/ Jan van *c.* 1380–1441. Flemish painter of the early northern Renaissance, one of the first to work in oils. His paintings are technically brilliant and sumptuously rich in detail and colour. He is known to have worked in The Hague 1422–24 for John of Bavaria, Count of Holland. He served as court painter to Philip the Good, Duke of Burgundy, from 1425, and worked in Bruges from 1430. Philip the Good valued him not only as a painter but also as a diplomatic representative, sending him to Spain and Portugal in 1427 and 1428. Little is known of his brother, **Hubert van Eyck** (died 1426), who is supposed to have begun the massive and complex altarpiece in St Bavo's cathedral, Ghent, *The Adoration of the Mystical Lamb*, completed by Jan in 1432.

eye /aɪ/ *n.* **1.** the organ of sight in humans and animals; the iris of an eye; the region round an eye. The **human eye** is a roughly spherical structure contained in a bony socket. Light enters it through the **cornea**, and passes through the circular opening (**pupil**) in the **iris** (the coloured part of the eye). The light is focused by the combined action of the curved cornea, the internal fluids, and the **lens** (the rounded transparent structure behind the iris). The ciliary muscles act on the lens to change its shape, so that images of objects at different distances can be focused on the **retina**, at the back of the eye, which is packed with light-sensitive cells (rods and cones), connected to the brain by the optic nerve. The **insect eye** is compound, that is, made up of many separate facets, known as *ommatidia*, each of which collects light and directs it separately to a receptor to build up an image. Invertebrates, such as some worms and snails, and certain bivalves, have much simpler eyes, with no lens. **2.** a particular visual faculty. **3.** a thing like an eye, e.g. a spot on a peacock's tail or butterfly's wing, the leaf-bud of a potato; the hole of a needle; a calm region in the centre of a hurricane etc. —*v.t.* (*participle* **eyeing**) to look at, to observe (especially with curiosity or suspicion). —**all eyes**, watching intently. **all my eye**, (*slang*) nonsense. **cast** *or* **run an eye over**, to examine quickly. **catch a person's eye**, to succeed in attracting a person's attention. **close** *or* **shut one's eyes to**, to ignore, to disregard. **do in the eye**, to defraud or thwart. **an eye for an eye**, retaliation in kind. **eye-liner** *n.* a cosmetic applied as a line round the eye. **eye-opener** *n.* a surprising or revealing fact or circumstance. **eye-rhyme** *n.* correspondence of words in spelling but not in pronunciation (e.g. *dear* and *pear*). **eye-shade** *n.* a device to protect the eyes from strong light. **eye-shadow** *n.* a cosmetic applied to the skin round the eyes. **eye-strain** *n.* weariness of the eyes. **eye-tooth** *n.* a canine tooth in the upper jaw, below the eye. **get one's eye in**, to become accustomed to prevailing conditions especially in sport. **half an eye**, the slightest degree of perceptiveness. **have eyes for**, to be interested in, to wish to acquire. **in** *or* **through the eyes of**, from the point of view of, in the judgement of. **in the public eye**, receiving much publicity. **keep an eye on**, to watch carefully, to take care of. **keep an eye open** *or* **out for**, to watch for. **keep one's eyes open** *or* (*slang*) **peeled** *or* **skinned**, to be watchful. **make eyes at**, to look at amorously or flirtatiously. **one in the eye**, a setback or discomfiture (*for*). **see eye to eye**, to agree. **set eyes on**, to catch sight of. **up to the eyes**, deeply engaged or involved *in*.

eyeball *n.* the ball of the eye, within the lids and sockets. —**eyeball to eyeball**, (*colloquial*) confronting closely.

eyebath *n.* a small cup shaped to fit round the eye, for applying lotion to the eye.

eyebright *n.* any flower of the genus *Euphrasia*, family Scrophulariaceae. They are 2–30 cm/1–12 in high, bearing whitish flowers streaked with purple. The name indicates the plant's traditional use as a remedy for weak eyes.

eyebrow *n.* the fringe of hair growing on the ridge above the eye-socket. —**raise an eyebrow** *or* **one's eyebrows**, to show surprise or disbelief.

eyeful *n.* a thing thrown or blown into the eye; (*colloquial*) a thorough look; (*colloquial*) a visually striking person or thing.

eyeglass *n.* a lens for a defective eye.

eyehole *n.* 1. the socket containing the eye. 2. a hole to look through.

eyelash *n.* any of the fringe of hairs on the edge of the eyelid.

eyelet /'aɪlɪt/ *n.* a small hole for passing cord or rope through; a metal ring for strengthening this. [from Old French *oillet* diminutive of *oil* = eye]

eyelid *n.* either of the two folds of skin that can be moved together to cover the eye.

eyepiece *n.* the lens or lenses to which the eye is applied at the end of a microscope, telescope etc.

eyesight *n.* the faculty or power of seeing.

eyesore *n.* a thing that offends the sight; an ugly object etc.

eyewash *n.* 1. a lotion for the eye. 2. (*slang*) nonsense, insincere talk.

eyewitness *n.* a person who can give evidence of an incident from personal observation of it.

eyre in English history, one of the travelling courts set up by Henry II in 1176 to enforce conformity to the king's will; they continued into the 13th century. **Justices in eyre** were the judges who heard pleas at these courts.

Eyre /eə/ Edward John 1815–1901. English explorer who wrote *Expeditions into Central Australia* 1845. He was Governor of Jamaica 1864–65. *Lake Eyre* in South Australia is named after him.

Eyre Richard (Charles Hastings) 1943– . English stage and film director. He succeeded Peter Hall as artistic director of the National Theatre, London, 1988. His films include *The Ploughman's Lunch* 1983.

Eyre, Lake Australia's largest lake, in central South Australia, which frequently runs dry, becoming a salt marsh in dry seasons. It covers an area up to 9,000 sq km/ 3,500 sq mi. It is the continent's lowest point, 12 m/39 ft below sea level.

Eyre Peninsula peninsula in South Australia, which includes the iron and steel city of Whyalla. Over 50% of the iron used in Australia's steel industry is mined at Iron Knob; the only seal colony on mainland Australia is at Point Labatt.

eyrie /'aɪərɪ, 'ɪərɪ/ *n.* the nest of an eagle or other bird of prey built high up; a house etc. perched high up. [from Old French *aire* = lair from Latin *ager* = piece of ground]

Eysenck /'aɪsenk/ Hans Jurgen 1916– . English psychologist. He concentrated on personality theory and testing by developing ◊behaviour therapy. He is an outspoken critic of psychoanalysis as a therapeutic method.

Ezekiel /ɪ'zi:kɪəl/ lived c 600 BC. In the Old Testament, a Hebrew prophet. Carried into captivity in Babylon by ◊Nebuchadnezzar 597, he preached that Jerusalem's fall was due to the sins of Israel. The book of Ezekiel begins with a description of a vision of supernatural beings.

Ezra /'ezrə/ in the Old Testament, a Hebrew scribe who was allowed by Artaxerxes, king of Persia (probably Artaxerxes I, 464–423 BC), to lead his people back to Jerusalem from Babylon in 458 BC. He re-established the Mosaic law (laid down by Moses) and forbade intermarriage.

f, F *n.* (*plural* **fs, f's**) **1.** sixth letter of the English alphabet. **2.** in music, the fourth note in the scale of C major.

f in music, abbreviation of forte.

f. abbreviation of **1.** female; feminine. **2.** focal length. **3.** folio. **4.** following page etc.

F abbreviation of **1.** ◊Fahrenheit. **2.** farad(s). **3.** Fellow of. **4.** fine (pencil-lead).

F symbol for fluorine.

°F symbol for degrees Fahrenheit.

fa variant of ◊fah.

FA abbreviation of Football Association.

fab *adj.* (*colloquial*) marvellous. [abbreviation of *fabulous*]

Fabergé /ˈfæbəʒeɪ/ Peter Carl 1846–1920. Russian goldsmith and jeweller whose workshops in St Petersburg and Moscow were celebrated for the exquisite delicacy of their products, especially the use of gold in various shades. Among his masterpieces was a series of jewelled Easter eggs, the first of which was commissioned by Alexander III for the tsarina in 1884. Fabergé died in exile in Switzerland.

Fabian Society /ˈfeɪbɪən/ UK socialist organization for research, discussion, and publication, founded in London in 1884. Its name is derived from the Roman commander ◊Fabius Maximus, and refers to the fact that it hopes to attain socialism by a succession of gradual reforms rather than by violent revolutionary action. Early members included the playwright George Bernard Shaw and Beatrice and Sidney ◊Webb. —**Fabian** *n.* a member of the Fabian Society. **Fabianism** *n.*

Fabius /ˈfeɪbɪəs/ Laurent 1946– . French socialist politician, prime minister 1984–86. He introduced a liberal, free-market economic programme, but his career was damaged by the 1985 ◊Greenpeace sabotage scandal.

Fabius Maximus /ˈfeɪbɪəs ˈmæksɪməs/ name of an ancient Roman family of whom the best known is Quintus Fabius Maximus (died 203 BC), a general known as *Cunctator* or 'Delayer' because of his cautious tactics against Hannibal 217–214 BC, when he continually harassed Hannibal's armies but never risked a set battle.

fable /ˈfeɪbəl/ *n.* **1.** a story, especially a supernatural one, not based on fact; a short tale in which animals or inanimate objects are endowed with the mentality and speech of human beings in order to point out a moral; legendary tales. **2.** a lie, lies. **3.** a thing only supposed to exist. [from Old French from Latin *fabula* = discourse]

fabled *adj.* celebrated in fable, legendary.

Fabre /ˈfɑːbrə/ Jean Henri Casimir 1823–1915. French entomologist, celebrated for his vivid and intimate descriptions and paintings of the life of wasps, bees, and other insects.

fabric /ˈfæbrɪk/ *n.* **1.** woven, knitted, or felted material; a plastic resembling this. **2.** the walls, floors, and roof of a building. **3.** a structure (*literal* or *figurative*). [from French from Latin *faber* = metalworker]

fabricate /ˈfæbrɪkeɪt/ *v.t.* **1.** to construct, to manufacture. **2.** to invent (a story); to forge (a document). —**fabrication** /-ˈkeɪʃən/ *n.*, **fabricator** *n.* [from Latin]

Fabricius /fəˈbrɪsɪəs/ Geronimo 1537–1619. Italian anatomist and embryologist who made a detailed study of the veins and discovered the valves that direct the blood flow towards the heart. He also studied the development of chick embryos.

Fabritius /fəˈbriːtsɪəs/ Carel 1622–1654. Dutch painter, a pupil of Rembrandt. His own style, lighter and with more precise detail than his master's, is evident for example in *The Goldfinch* 1654. He painted religious scenes and portraits.

fabulous /ˈfæbjʊləs/ *adj.* **1.** famed in fable, legendary. **2.** incredible, absurd. **3.** (*colloquial*) marvellous. —**fabulously** *adv.* [from French or Latin]

façade /fəˈsɑːd/ *n.* **1.** the face or front of a building. **2.** an outward (especially deceptive) appearance. [French]

face *n.* **1.** the front of the head from the forehead to the chin; the expression of the facial features; a grimace. **2.** the surface of a thing, especially the functional surface of a tool etc.; the upper or forward-facing side, the front; the dial-plate of a clock. **3.** an outward appearance, an aspect. **4.** composure; effrontery, nerve. **5.** esteem. **6.** a typeface. —*v.t./i.* **1.** to have or turn the face towards; to be opposite to. **2.** to meet resolutely, not to shrink from; to meet (an opponent) in a contest; to present itself to. **3.** to cover the surface of (a wall etc.) with a facing; to put a facing on (a garment etc.). —**face card**, a court card. **facecloth** *n.* a face flannel; a smooth-surfaced woollen cloth. **faceflannel** *n.* a cloth for washing one's face. **face-lift** *n.* the operation of having one's face lifted; a procedure to improve a thing's appearance. **face to face**, facing, confronting each other. **face up to**, to face resolutely. **face value**, the value printed or stamped on money; what a thing seems to mean or imply. **have the face**, to be shameless enough. **in (the) face of**, despite. **lose face**, to be humiliated. **make** *or* **pull a face**, to grimace. **on the face of it**, to outward appearances. **put a bold** *or* **good face on**, to accept (a difficulty etc.) cheerfully. **save face**, to preserve esteem, to avoid humiliation. **set one's face against**, to resist determinedly. **show one's face**, to let oneself be seen. **to a person's face**, openly in his presence. [from Old French from Latin *facies*]

faceless /ˈfeɪslɪs/ *adj.* **1.** without identity, purposely not identifiable. **2.** lacking character.

facer *n.* a sudden unexpected difficulty.

facet /ˈfæsɪt/ *n.* **1.** one aspect of a problem etc. **2.** one side of a many-sided cut gem etc. —**faceted** *adj.* [from French]

facetious /fəˈsiːʃəs/ *adj.* intending or intended to be amusing —**facetiously** *adv.*, **facetiousness** *n.* [from French from Latin *facetiae* = wit]

facia /ˈfeɪʃə/ *n.* **1.** the instrument panel of a motor vehicle. **2.** the plate over a shop-front with the name etc. [variant of *fascia*]

facial /ˈfeɪʃəl/ *adj.* of or for the face. —*n.* a beauty treatment for the face. —**facially** *adv.*

facile /ˈfæsaɪl/ *adj.* **1.** easily achieved but of little value. **2.** easy, easily done; working easily, fluent. [from French or Latin *facilis* (*facere* = make, do)]

facilitate /fəˈsɪlɪteɪt/ *v.t.* to make easy or less difficult; to make (an action or result) more easily achieved. —**facilitation** /-ˈteɪʃən/ *n.* [from French from Italian]

facility /fəˈsɪlɪtɪ/ *n.* **1.** ease, absence of difficulty; fluency, dexterity. **2.** (especially in *plural*) the opportunity or equipment for doing something. [from French or Latin]

facing *n.* a layer of material over a part of a garment etc., for contrast or strength; an outer layer covering the surface of a wall etc.

facsimile /fæk'sɪmɪlɪ/ *n.* an exact copy of writing, a picture, etc. [Latin = make a likeness]

facsimile transmission full name for ◊**fax** or **telefax**.

fact *n.* a thing that is known to be true or to exist; truth, reality; a thing assumed as a basis for argument. —**facts and figures**, the precise details. **facts of life**, (*colloquial*) the realities of a situation; knowledge of human sexual functions. **in fact**, in reality, in short. [from Latin *factum*]

faction /'fækʃən/ *n.* a small group with special aims within a larger one. —**factional** *adj.* [from French from Latin]

factious /'fækʃəs/ *adj.* of a faction, characterized by factions. [from French or Latin]

factitious /fæk'tɪʃəs/ *adj.* made for a special purpose; artificial. —**factitiously** *adv.* [from Latin]

factor /'fæktər/ *n.* 1. a circumstance etc. contributing to a result. 2. a number that divides into another number exactly. For example, the factors of 64 are 1, 2, 4, 8, 16, 32, and 64. 3. a business agent; an agent or deputy; in Scotland, a land-steward. 4. a gene or other agent determining a hereditary character. [from French or Latin *facere* = make, do]

factorial /fæk'tɔːrɪ(ə)l/ *n.* of a positive number, the product of all the whole numbers (integers) inclusive between 1 and the number itself. A factorial is indicated by the symbol '!'. Thus 6! = $1 \times 2 \times 3 \times 4 \times 5 \times 6 = 720$. Factorial zero, 0!, is defined as 1. —*adj.* of a factor or factorial.

factorize /'fæktəraɪz/ *v.t.* to resolve into factors. —**factorization** /-'zeɪʃən/ *n.*

factory /'fæktərɪ/ *n.* a building or buildings in which goods are manufactured. —**factory ship**, one that processes and freezes its catch while still at sea. [from Portuguese or Latin]

factory act in Britain, an act of Parliament such as the Health and Safety at Work Act 1974, which governs conditions of work, hours of labour, safety, and sanitary provision in factories and workshops.

factory farming the intensive rearing of poultry or animals for food, usually on high-protein foodstuffs in confined quarters. For example, egg-laying hens are housed in 'batteries' of cages arranged in long rows; if caged singly, they lay fewer eggs, so there are often four to a cage. In some countries the use of antibiotics and growth hormones as aids to factory farming is restricted, because they can persist in the flesh of the animals after they are slaughtered. The European Commission banned steroid hormones for beef cattle at the end of 1985. Many consumers object to factory farming on the grounds of the cruelty to animals it involves, as well as to the health risks of eating factory-farmed produce.

factory system the basis of manufacturing in the modern world. In the factory system workers are employed at a place where they carry out specific tasks, which together result in a product. This is called the division of labour. Usually these workers will perform their tasks with the aid of machinery. Such mechanization is another feature of the modern factory system, which leads to ◊**mass production**.

factotum /fæk'təʊtəm/ *n.* an employee doing all kinds of work. [Latin = do the whole lot]

factual /'fæktjuəl/ *adj.* based on or concerning facts. —**factually** *adv.*

faculty /'fækəltɪ/ *n.* 1. an aptitude or ability for a particular activity; an inherent mental or physical power. 2. a department of a university teaching a particular subject; (*US*) the staff of a university or college. 3. authorization, especially by church authority. [from Old French from Latin *facultas* (*facilis* = easy)]

fad *n.* a craze; a peculiar notion. —**faddish** *adj.* **faddy** *adj.* having arbitrary likes and dislikes, especially about food. **faddiness** *n.* [probably from *fiddle-faddle*]

Fadden /'fædn/ Artie (Arthur) 1895–1973. Australian politician, born in Queensland. He was leader of the Country Party 1941–58 and prime minister Aug–Oct 1941.

fade *v.t./i.* to lose or cause to lose colour, freshness, or strength; to disappear gradually; to bring (a sound or picture) gradually *in* or *out* of perception. —*n.* an act of fading. —**fade away** *or* **out**, to become weaker or less distinct; to die away; to disappear. [from Old French *fade* = dull, insipid]

faeces /'fiːsiːz/ *n.pl.* waste matter discharged from the bowels. —**faecal** /'fiːkəl/ *adj.* [Latin]

Faerie Queene, The /'feərɪ 'kwiːn/ a poem by Edmund Spenser, published 1590–96, dedicated to Elizabeth I. The poem, in six books, describes the adventures of six knights. Spenser used a new stanza form, later adopted by Keats, Shelley, and Byron.

Faeroe Islands or **Faeroes** alternative spelling of the ◊Faroe Islands.

fag[1] *v.t./i.* (**-gg-**) 1. to tire (*out*), to exhaust. 2. to toil; (as a junior schoolboy) to run errands for a senior boy. —*n.* 1. (*colloquial*) drudgery. 2. (*slang*) a cigarette. 3. a schoolboy who fags. —**fag end** *n.* a cigarette end.

fag[2] *n.* (*US slang*) a homosexual. [abbreviation of *faggot*]

Fagatogo /'fɑːɡəˈtəʊɡəʊ/ capital of American ◊Samoa. Situated on Pago Pago Harbour, Tutuila Island.

faggot /'fæɡət/ *n.* 1. a ball or roll of seasoned chopped offal baked or fried. 2. a bundle of sticks, herbs, metal rods. 3. (*slang*) an unpleasant woman. 4. (*US slang*) a homosexual. [from Old French from Italian]

faggoting *n.* embroidery in which threads are fastened together like faggots.

fah /fɑː/ *n.* in music, the fourth note of the major scale in tonic ◊sol-fa.

Fahd /fɑːd/ 1921– . King of Saudi Arabia from 1982, when he succeeded his half-brother Khalid.

Fahrenheit /'færənhaɪt/ *adj.* of the scale of temperature on which water freezes at 32° and boils at 212°. [from G D *Fahrenheit*]

Fahrenheit /'fɑːrənhaɪt/ Gabriel Daniel 1686–1736. German physicist who lived mainly in England and Holland. He devised the Fahrenheit temperature scale.

faience /faɪˈɑːs/ *n.* decorated and glazed earthenware and porcelain. [from French from *Faenza* in Italy]

fail *v.t./i.* 1. not to succeed; to be unsuccessful in (an examination etc.); to grade (a candidate) as not having passed an examination. 2. to disappoint, to let down. 3. to neglect or forget, to be unable. 4. to be absent or deficient; (of crops) to produce a very poor harvest. 5. to become weak or ineffective, to cease functioning; to become bankrupt. —*n.* a failure in an examination. —**fail-safe** *adj.* reverting to a safe condition in the event of a breakdown etc. **without fail**, for certain, whatever happens. [from Old French from Latin *fallere* = deceive]

failed *adj.* unsuccessful.

failing *n.* a fault, a weakness. —*prep.* in default of, if not.

failure /'feɪljə/ *n.* 1. failing, non-performance, lack of success. 2. cessation of normal function through weakness etc. 3. deficiency, as through a poor harvest. 4. an unsuccessful person or thing.

fain *predic. adj.* willing or obliged (*to*). —*adv.* gladly. [Old English]

faint *adj.* 1. indistinct, pale, dim. 2. weak from hunger etc. 3. timid; feeble. —*v.i.* to lose consciousness, to become faint. —*n.* an act of fainting; a state of having fainted. —**faint-hearted** *adj.* cowardly, timid. —**faintly** *adv.*, **faintness** *n.* [from Old French, past participle of *feindre* = feign]

fair[1] *adj.* 1. just, unbiased, in accordance with the rules. 2. blond, not dark, pale. 3. of only moderate quality or amount. 4. favourable, satisfactory, promising; unobstructed. 5. (of a copied document) neat, without corrections. 6. beautiful. 7. (*slang*) complete, unquestionable. —*adv.* 1. in a fair manner. 2. exactly, completely. —**fair and square**, exactly; above-board, straightforward(ly). **fair game**, a thing one may reasonably or legitimately pursue etc. **fair play**, equitable conduct or conditions. **the fair sex**, women. **fair-weather friend**, a friend or ally who is unreliable in difficulties. **in a fair way to**, likely to. [Old English]

fair[2] *n.* 1. a periodical gathering for the sale of goods, often with entertainments. 2. a ◊funfair. —**fairground** *n.* an outdoor area where a fair is held. [from Old French from Latin *feriae* = holiday]

Fairbanks /'feəbæŋks/ Douglas, Sr. Stage name of Douglas Elton Ulman 1883–1939. US actor. He played acrobatic swashbuckling heroes in silent films such as *The Mark of Zorro* 1920, *The Three Musketeers* 1921, *Robin Hood* 1922, *The Thief of Baghdad* 1924, and *Don Quixote* 1925. He was married to the film star Mary Pickford ('America's Sweetheart') from 1920 to 1933. Together

Fairbanks US film actor Douglas Fairbanks Jr.

with Charlie Chaplin and D W Griffith they founded United Artists in 1919.

Fairbanks Douglas, Jr 1909– . US actor who appeared in the same type of swashbuckling film roles as his father, Douglas Fairbanks; for example in *Catherine the Great* 1934 and *The Prisoner of Zenda* 1937.

Fairfax family /'feəfæks/ an Australian publishing dynasty founded by John Fairfax (1804-1887). A British-born printer and bookbinder, he went to Australia in 1838 and became part-owner of the newspaper that became the *The Sydney Morning Herald*. John Fairfax and Sons, one of the last remaining business dynasties founded in the 19th century, had interests in journalism, yachting and art, and was noted for its philanthropy. In 1990, the John Fairfax Group went into receivership.

Fairfax Thomas, 3rd Baron Fairfax of Cameron 1612-1671. English general, commander in chief of the Parliamentary army in the English Civil War. With Oliver Cromwell he formed the ◊New Model Army and defeated Charles I at Naseby. He opposed the king's execution, resigned in protest in 1650 against the invasion of Scotland, and participated in the restoration of Charles II after Cromwell's death.

fairing[1] *n.* a streamlining structure added to a ship or aircraft.

fairing[2] *n.* an object bought at a fair.

Fair Isle island in N Scotland between the Orkneys and Shetlands, noted for its characteristic patterns on knitted articles. —*adj.* patterns of this kind.

fairly *adv.* 1. in a fair manner. 2. moderately. 3. to a noticeable degree.

Fair Trading, Office of a UK government department established in 1973 to keep commercial activities under review. It covers the areas of consumer affairs and credit, ◊monopolies and mergers, and anti-competitive and ◊restrictive practices in trading. The USA has a Bureau of Consumer Protection with similar scope.

fairway *n.* 1. a navigable channel. 2. a part of a golf course between a tee and the green, kept free of rough grass.

fairy *n.* 1. a small imaginary being with magical powers. 2. (*slang*) a male homosexual. —**fairy godmother**, a benefactress. **fairy lights**, small coloured lights especially for outdoor decorations. **fairy ring**, a ring of darker grass caused by fungi. **fairy story** *or* **tale** a tale about fairies; an incredible story, a falsehood. [from Old French]

fairyland /'feərɪlænd/ *n.* the home of the fairies; an enchanted place.

Faisal /'faɪsəl/ Ibn Abdul Aziz 1905–1975. King of Saudi Arabia from 1964, the younger brother of King Saud, on

whose accession in 1953 he was declared crown prince. He was prime minister from 1953 to 1960 and from 1962 until his assassination by a nephew. In 1964 he emerged victorious from a lengthy conflict with his brother and adopted a policy of steady modernization of his country.

Faisal I 1885–1933. Arab nationalist leader during World War I and king of Iraq 1921–33. Instrumental in liberating the Near East from Ottoman control, he was declared king of Syria in 1918 but deposed by the French in 1920. The British then installed him as king in Iraq, where he continued to foster pan-Arabism.

Faisalabad /'faɪsələbæd/ city in Punjab province, Pakistan; population (1981) 1,092,000. It trades in grain, cotton, and textiles.

fait accompli (French 'accomplished fact') something that has been done and cannot be undone.

faith *n.* 1. complete trust, unquestioning confidence. 2. strong belief, especially in a religious doctrine; a system of beliefs, a religion. 3. loyalty, trustworthiness. —**bad faith**, dishonest intention. **faith cure, healing**, etc., a cure etc. depending on faith rather than on medical treatment. **good faith**, sincere intention. [from Anglo-French from Latin *fides*]

faithful *adj.* 1. showing faith; loyal, trustworthy, constant. 2. accurate. 3. the Faithful, believers in a religion, followers. —**faithfulness** *n.*

faithfully *adv.* in a faithful manner. —**yours faithfully**, a formula for ending a business or formal letter.

faithless *adj.* 1. false, unreliable, disloyal. 2. without religious faith.

fake *n.* a thing or person that is not genuine. —*adj.* counterfeit, not genuine. —*v.t.* to make (a thing) so that it falsely appears genuine; to feign.

fakir /'feɪkɪə/ *n.* a Muslim or Hindu religious mendicant or ascetic. [Arabic = poor man]

Falange Española /fæ'læŋxe espæn'jəʊlə/ former Spanish Fascist Party, founded in 1933 by José Antonio de Rivera, son of the military ruler Miguel ◊Primo de Rivera. It was closely modelled in programme and organization on the Italian fascists and on the Nazis. In 1937, when ◊Franco assumed leadership, it was declared the only legal party, and altered its name to Traditionalist Spanish Phalanx. [Spanish = phalanx] [Spanish 'phalanx']

Falasha /fæ'lɑːʃə/ *n.* a member of a small group of people in Ethiopia holding the Jewish faith. They suffered discrimination, and, after being accorded Jewish status by Israel in 1975, began a gradual process of resettlement in Israel. In the early 1980s only about 30,000 Falashim remained in Ethiopia. [Amharic = exile, immigrant]

falchion /'fɔːltʃən/ *n.* a broad curved sword. [from Old French from Latin *falx* = scythe]

falcon /'fɔːlkən/ *n.* any bird of prey of the genus *Falco*, family Falconidae, order Falconiformes. Falcons are the smallest of the hawks (15–60 cm/6–24 in). They nest in high places and kill their prey by 'stooping' (swooping down at high speed). When stooping on its intended prey, the peregrine *F. peregrinus* is the fastest creature in the world, timed at 240 kph/150 mph. They include the worldwide merlin or pigeon hawk *F. columbarius* and the Eurasian kestrel *F. tinnunculus*. [from Old French from Latin *falco*]

falconry *n.* the use of specially bred and trained falcons and hawks to capture birds or small mammals. Falconry was practised in ancient times in the Middle East. The sport was introduced from continental Europe to Britain in Saxon times.

Faldo /'fældəʊ/ Nick 1957– . English golfer who is the only Briton to have won two British Open titles since World War II. In 1990 he won his second successive US Masters title. Since turning professional in 1976 he has won more than 25 tournaments worldwide.

Falkender /'fɔːlkəndə/ Marcia, Baroness Falkender (Marcia Williams) 1932– . British political secretary to Labour prime minister Harold Wilson from 1956. She was influential in the 'kitchen cabinet' of the 1964–70 government, as described in her book *Inside No 10* 1972.

Falkland /'fɔːklənd/ Lucius Cary, 2nd Viscount *c.*1610–1643. English soldier and politician who was elected to the ◊Long Parliament in 1640 and tried to secure a compromise peace between Royalists and Parliamentarians. He was killed at the Battle of Newbury in the Civil War.

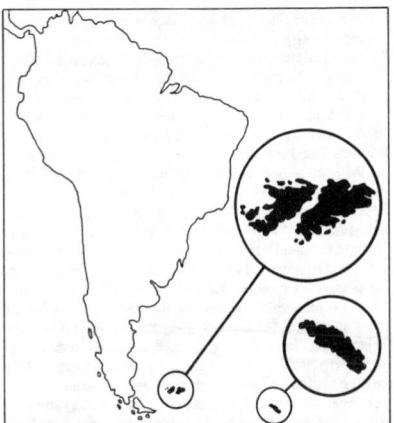

Falkland Islands

Falkland Islands /'fɔ:klənd/ British crown colony in the S Atlantic; **area** 12,173 sq km/4,700 sq mi; **capital** and chief port Stanley; **physical** made up of two main islands: East Falkland 6,760 sq km/2,610 sq mi, and West Falkland 5,413 sq km/2,090 sq mi; and about 200 small islands, all with wild scenery and rich bird life; **head of state** Elizabeth II represented by a governor-general (Gordon Jewkes from Oct 1985); **products** wool, alginates (used as dyes and as a food additive) from seaweed beds; **population** (1986) 1,916; **recent history** Argentina asserts its succession to the Spanish claim to the 'Islas Malvinas', but the inhabitants oppose cession. The islands were occupied by Argentina April 1982, and recaptured by British military forces in May–June of the same year.

Falkland Islands, Battle of the British naval victory (under Admiral Sturdee) 8 Dec 1914 over the German admiral von Spee.

fall /fɔ:l/ *v.i.* (*past* **fell**; *past participle* **fallen**) 1. to go or come down freely, to descend. 2. to cease to stand, to come suddenly to the ground from a loss of balance etc. 3. to become detached and descend, to slope or hang down; to become lower, to subside; to lose status or position; to yield to temptation; to succumb (*to*); to be overthrown or vanquished, to perish; (of the face) to show dismay or disappointment. 4. to take or have a particular direction or place; to come by chance or duty. 5. to occur. 6. to pass *in* or *into* a specified condition; to become. —*n.* 1. the act or manner of falling; succumbing to temptation. 2. the amount by which something falls; the amount that falls. 3. (especially in *plural*) a waterfall. 4. a wrestling-bout; a throw in this in which both shoulders touch the mat for one second. 5. (*US*) autumn; **fall away,** to become few or thin; to desert; to vanish. **fall back,** to retreat. **fall back on,** to have recourse to in an extremity. **fall down (on),** to fail (in). **fall flat,** to be a failure, to fail to win applause. **fall for,** (*colloquial*) to be captivated or deceived by. **fall foul of,** to collide or quarrel with. **fall guy,** (*slang*) an easy victim, a scapegoat. **fall in,** to take or cause to take one's place in a military formation; (of a building etc.) to collapse. **fall in with,** to meet (by chance); to agree or coincide with. **fall off,** to decrease; to deteriorate. **fall on** *or* **upon,** to assault; to meet. **fall on one's feet,** to get out of a difficulty successfully. **fall out,** to quarrel; to result, to occur; to leave or cause to leave one's place in a military formation. **fallout** *n.* radioactive debris in the air, from a nuclear explosion. **fall over,** to stumble and come to the ground. **fall over oneself,** (*colloquial*) to be eager or hasty; to be very confused. **fall short,** to be deficient or inadequate. **fall short of,** to fail to reach or obtain. **fall through,** to fail, (of a plan etc.) to come to nothing. **fall to,** to begin. [Old English]

Fall, the the Fall of Man, a myth that explains the existence of evil as the result of some primeval wrongdoing by humanity. It occurs independently in many cultures, and in the Bible is recorded in the Old Testament in Genesis 3 which provided the inspiration for the epic poem *Paradise Lost* 1667 by John ◊Milton.

Falla /'fæljə/ Manuel de 1876–1946. Spanish composer. Born in Cádiz, he lived in France, where he was influenced by the Impressionist composers Claude Debussy and Maurice Ravel. His opera *La vida breve*/*Brief Life* 1905 (performed 1913) was followed by the ballets *El amor brujo*/*Love the Magician* 1915 and *El sombrero de tres picos*/*The Three-Cornered Hat* 1919, and his most ambitious concert work, *Noches en los jardines de España*/*Nights in the Gardens of Spain* 1916. The folk idiom of southern Spain is an integral part of his compositions. He also wrote songs and pieces for piano and guitar.

fallacy /'fæləsɪ/ *n.* a mistaken belief; faulty reasoning or misleading argument; a tendency to mislead or delude. —**fallacious** /fə'leɪʃəs/ *adj.* [from Latin *fallere* = deceive]

fallible /'fælɪbəl/ *adj.* capable of making mistakes. —**fallibility** /-'bɪlɪtɪ/ *n.*, **fallibly** *adv.*

Fallopian tube /fə'ləʊpɪən/ or **oviduct** in mammals, one of two tubes that carry eggs from the ovary to the uterus. An egg is fertilized by sperm in a Fallopian tube, which is lined with cells bearing hair-like protruberances called cilia, which move the egg towards the ovary. [from *Fallopius*, Italian anatomist]

fallow[1] /'fæləʊ/ *adj.* (of land) ploughed but left unsown; uncultivated. —*n.* fallow land. [Old English]

fallow[2] *adj.* of a pale brownish or reddish yellow —**fallow deer,** a species (*Dama dama*) smaller than the red deer. [Old English]

false /fɔ:ls, fɒls/ *adj.* 1. wrong, incorrect. 2. deceitful, treacherous, unfaithful *to* ; deceptive. 3. spurious, sham, artificial. 4. improperly so called. —**false alarm,** an alarm needlessly given. **false pretences,** misrepresentation with intent to deceive. **false teeth,** artificial teeth. —**falsely** *adv.*, **falseness** *n.* [from Old English and Old French from Latin *falsus* (*fallere* = deceive)]

false-colour imagery a graphic technique that displays images in false (not true-to-life) colours so as to enhance certain features. It is widely used in displaying electronic images taken by spacecraft; for example, earth-survey satellites such as Landsat.

falsehood *n.* an untrue thing; a lie, lying.

falsetto /fɔ:l'setəʊ, fɒl-/ *n.* (*plural* **falsettos**) an artificial voice above the normal range, especially by a male tenor. [Italian, diminutive of *falso* = false]

falsies /'fɔ:lsɪz, 'fɒl-/ *n.pl* (*colloquial*) pads to make the breasts seem larger.

falsificationism *n.* in philosophy of science, the belief that a scientific theory must be under constant scrutiny and that its merit lies only in how well it stands up to rigorous testing. First expounded by the philosopher Karl ◊Popper in his *Logic of Scientific Discovery* 1934.

falsify /'fɔ:lsɪfaɪ, 'fɒl-/ *v.t.* to alter fraudulently; to misrepresent (facts etc.). —**falsification** /-fɪ'keɪʃən/ *n.* [from French or Latin *falsificus* = making false]

falsity *n.* being false.

falter /'fɔ:ltə/ *v.t./i.* to stumble; to move or function unsteadily; to say or speak hesitatingly; to lose strength.

Famagusta /fæmə'gʊstə/ seaport on the E coast of Cyprus, in the Turkish Republic of N Cyprus; population (1985) 19,500. It was the chief port of the island prior to the Turkish invasion in 1974.

fame *n.* renown; the state of being famous; (*archaic*) reputation. [from Old French from Latin *fama*]

famed *adj.* famous, much spoken of (*for*).

familiar /fə'mɪlɪə/ *adj.* 1. well acquainted *with*. 2. well known (*to*); often encountered or experienced. 3. informal, especially excessively so. —*n.* 1. an intimate friend. 2. a familiar spirit. —**familiar spirit,** a demon serving a witch etc. —**familiarity** /-'ærɪtɪ/ *n.*, **familiarly** *adv.* [from Old French from Latin]

familiarize /fə'mɪlɪəraɪz/ *v.t.* 1. to make well acquainted. 2. to make well known. —**familiarization** /-'zeɪʃən/ *n.* [from French]

family /'fæmɪlɪ/ *n.* 1. a set of parents and children or of relatives; a person's children; the members of a household. 2. all the descendants of a common ancestor; lineage; a race or group of peoples from a common stock; a group of languages derived from one early language. 3. a group of objects distinguished by common features. 4. a group of allied genera (◊genus) of animals or plants, usually a subdivision of an ◊order. —**family man,** one with a family; one who is fond of home life. **family name,**

family planning

386

a surname. **family tree**, a genealogical chart. **in the family way**, (*colloquial*) pregnant. [from Latin *familia* = household (*famulus* = servant)]

family planning or **birth control** spacing or preventing the birth of children. Access to family-planning services (see ◊contraceptive) is a significant factor in women's health as well as in limiting population growth. If all those women who wished to avoid further childbirth were able to do so, the number of births would be reduced by 27% in Africa, 33% in Asia, and 35% in Latin America; and the number of women who die during pregnancy or childbirth would be reduced by 50%.

famine /'fæmɪn/ *n.* extreme scarcity, especially of food. [from Old French from Latin *fames* = hunger]

famish /'fæmɪʃ/ *v.t./i.* to reduce or be reduced to extreme hunger. —**be famished** or **famishing**, (*colloquial*) to be very hungry. [from Old French]

famous /'feɪməs/ *adj.* 1. well known, celebrated. 2. (*colloquial*) excellent. —**famously** *adv.* [from Anglo-French and Old French from Latin]

fan¹ *n.* 1. a mechanical apparatus with rotating blades for ventilation. 2. a device (usually folding and sector-shaped when spread out) waved in the hand to cool the face etc.; anything spread out in this shape. —*v.t./i.* (**-nn-**) 1. to cool or kindle by agitating the air around; to blow gently upon. 2. to spread (*out*) in a fan shape. —**fan belt**, the belt transmitting the torque from a motor-vehicle engine to the fan which cools the radiator. **fanjet** *n.* a ◊turbofan. **fan tracery** or **vault(ing)**, ornamental vaulting with fanlike ribs. [Old English, from Latin *vannus* = winnowing-basket]

fan² *n.* a devotee of a specified amusement, performer etc. —**fan club**, one organized for a celebrity's admirers. **fan mail**, letters to a celebrity from fans. [abbreviation of *fanatic*]

fanatic /fə'nætɪk/ *n.* a person filled with excessive and often misguided enthusiasm for something. —*adj.* excessively enthusiastic. —**fanatical** *adj.*, **fanatically** *adv.*, **fanaticism** /-ɪsɪzəm/ *n.* [from French or Latin *fanum* = temple]

fancier /'fænsɪə/ *n.* a connoisseur, an enthusiast; an amateur breeder of some plant or animal.

fanciful /'fænsɪfəl/ *adj.* 1. existing only in imagination or fancy. 2. indulging in fancy. —**fancifully** *adv.*

fancy /'fænsɪ/ *n.* 1. the faculty of imagination; a mental image. 2. a supposition. 3. a caprice; a liking or whim. 4. those who have a certain hobby, fanciers. —*adj.* 1. elaborate, ornamental. 2. capricious, extravagant. —*v.t.* 1. to imagine. 2. (*colloquial*) to feel a desire for; to find sexually attractive; to have an unduly high opinion of (*oneself*, one's ability etc.). 3. to be inclined to think (*that*). 4. to breed or grow (animals or plants) with attention to certain points. —**fancy dress**, costume for masquerading as a different person etc. at a party etc. **fancy-free** *adj.* not in love. **fancy man**, (*slang*) a woman's lover, a pimp. **fancy that!** or **just fancy!** *int.* how strange! **fancy woman**, (*slang*) a mistress. [contraction of *fantasy*]

fandango /fæn'dæŋgəʊ/ *n.* (*plural* **fandagoes**) a lively Spanish dance; music for this. [Spanish]

fanfare /'fænfeə/ *n.* a short showy or ceremonious sounding of trumpets etc. [French]

fang *n.* 1. a canine tooth, especially of a dog or wolf. 2. a serpent's venom-tooth. 3. the root of a tooth or its prong. [Old English from Old Norse]

fanlight *n.* a small (originally semicircular) window over a door or other window.

fanny /'fænɪ/ *n.* (*slang*) the female genitals; the buttocks.

fantail *n.* a variety of domestic pigeon, often white, with a large, widely fanning tail.

fantasia /fæntə'zɪə, -'teɪzɪə/ *n.* fantasy or fancy a musical or other composition in which form is subordinate to imagination, or which is based on familiar tunes. [Italian = fantasy]

fantasize /'fæntəsaɪz/ *v.t./i.* to imagine, to create a fantasy (about); to daydream.

fantastic /fæn'tæstɪk/ *adj.* 1. extravagantly fanciful, fabulous; grotesque, quaint. 2. (*colloquial*) excellent, extraordinary. —**fantastically** *adv.*

fantasy /'fæntəsɪ/ *n.* 1. imagination, especially when extravagant; a mental image, a daydream. 2. a fanciful invention or composition, a book or film etc. relating fanciful

events. [from Old French from Latin from Greek *phantasia* = appearance]

Fantin-Latour /fɒn,tæn læ,tu/ Henri 1836–1904. French painter excelling in delicate still lifes, flower paintings, and portraits. *Homage à Delacroix* 1864 (Musée d'Orsay, Paris) is a portrait group with many poets, authors, and painters, including Charles Baudelaire and James Whistler.

Fao /faʊ/ or **Faw** an oil port on a peninsula at the mouth of the Shatt al-Arab in Iraq. Iran launched a major offensive against Iraq in 1986, capturing Fao for two years.

FAO abbreviation of ◊Food and Agriculture Organization.

far *adv.* (*comparative* **farther, further;** *superlative* **farthest, furthest**) 1. at, to, or by a great distance; a long way or a long way off in space or time. 2. to a great extent or degree, by much. —*adj.* distant, remote; more distant. —**as far as**, right to (a place); to the extent that. **by far**, by a great amount. **far and away**, by far. **far and wide**, over a large area. **far-away** *adj.* remote; (of a look) dreamy; (of a voice) sounding as if from a distance. **a far cry**, a long way. **Far East**, China, Japan, and other countries of E and SE Asia. **far-fetched** *adj.* (of an explanation etc.) strained, unconvincing. **far-flung** *adj.* extending far. **far-reaching** *adj.* of wide application or influence. **far-seeing** *adj.* showing foresight, prudent. **Far West**, the regions of North America in the Rocky Mountains and along the Pacific coast; (*formerly*) the area W of the earliest European settlements (now called the *Middle West*). **in so far as**, to the extent that. **so far**, to such an extent, to this point; until now **so far as**, as far as; in so far as. [Old English]

farad /'færəd/ *n.* a unit (symbol F) of electrical capacitance (how much electricity a ◊capacitor can store for a given voltage). One farad is a capacitance of one ◊coulomb per volt. For practical purposes the microfarad (one millionth of a farad) is more commonly used. [from M *Faraday*]

Faraday /'færədeɪ/ Michael 1791–1867. English chemist and physicist who in 1821 began experimenting with electromagnetism, and ten years later discovered the induction of electric currents and made the first dynamo. He subsequently found that a magnetic field will rotate the plane of polarization of light. Faraday also investigated electrolysis.

Faraday's laws three laws of electromagnetic induction, and two laws of electrolysis, all proposed originally by Michael Faraday:

induction (1) a changing magnetic field induces an electromagnetic force in a conductor; (2) the electromagnetic force is proportional to the rate of change of the field; (3) the direction of the induced electromagnetic force depends on the orientation of the field.

electrolysis (1) the amount of chemical change during electrolysis is proportional to the charge passing through the liquid; (2) the amount of chemical change produced in a substance by a given amount of electricity is proportional to the electrochemical equivalent of that substance.

farandole /'færən'dəʊl/ *n.* a lively Provençal dance; the music for this. [French from Provençal]

farce *n.* 1. a comedy based on ludicrously improbable events; this genre of theatre. 2. absurdly futile proceedings or pretence. —**farcical** *adj.*, **farcically** *adv.* [French from Old French from Latin *farcire* = to stuff]

fare /feə/ *n.* 1. the price charged to a passenger on public transport; a fare-paying passenger. 2. food provided. —*v.i.* to progress, to get on. [Old English]

farewell /feə'wel/ *interjection* meaning goodbye. —*n.* a leave-taking.

Fargo /'fɑːgəʊ/ William George 1818–1881. US long-distance transport pioneer. In 1844 he established with Henry Wells (1805–78) and Daniel Dunning the first express company to carry freight west of Buffalo. Its success led to his appointment in 1850 as secretary of the newly established American Express Company, of which he was president 1868–81. He also established **Wells Fargo & Company** 1851, carrying goods express between New York and San Francisco via Panama.

farina /fə'raɪnə, fə'riːnə/ *n.* flour or meal of corn, nuts, or starchy roots. [Latin]

farinaceous /færi'neɪʃəs/ *adj.* of or like farina, starchy.

farm *n.* an area of land and its buildings used under one management for growing crops, rearing animals etc.; any place for breeding animals; a farmhouse. —*v.t./i.* 1. to use (land) for growing crops, rearing animals etc.; to breed (fish etc.) commercially; to work as a farmer. 2.

Faraday *English chemist and physicist Michael Farady.*

to take the proceeds of (a tax) on payment of a fixed sum. —**farm hand** *n.* a worker on a farm. **farm out,** to delegate (work) to others. [from Old French from Latin *firma* = fixed payment; originally applied to leased land]
farmer *n.* an owner or manager of a farm.
farmhouse *n.* a dwelling-place attached to a farm.
farmost *adj.* furthest.
farmstead /'fɑːmsted/ *n.* a farm and its buildings.
farmyard *n.* the yard of a farmhouse.
Farnese /fɑːˈneɪseɪ/ an Italian family who held the duchy of Parma 1545–1731.
faro /'feərəʊ/ *n.* a gambling card-game. [from French *pharaon* = pharaoh (said to have been name of king of hearts)]
Faroe islands /'feərəʊ/ or **Faeroe islands** or **Faeroes** (Danish **Færøerne**, 'Sheep Islands') group of 22 islands, of which 18 are inhabited, in the N Atlantic, between the Shetland Islands and Iceland, forming an outlying part of ◊Denmark; **area** 1,399 sq km/540 sq mi; largest islands are Strømø, Østerø, Vagø, Suderø, Sandø, and Bordø; **capital** Thorshavn on Strømø, population (1986) 15,287; **products** fish, crafted goods; **population** (1986) 46,000; **language** Færøese, Danish; **recent history** since 1948 the islands have had full self-government; they withdrew from the European Free Trade Association in 1972; they do not belong to the EC.
Farouk /fəˈruːk/ 1920–1965. King of Egypt 1936–52. He succeeded his father ◊Fuad I. In 1952 a coup headed by General Muhammed Neguib and Colonel Gamal Nasser compelled him to abdicate, and his son Fuad II was temporarily proclaimed in his place.
Farquhar /'fɑːkə/ George 1677–1707. Irish dramatist. His plays *The Recruiting Officer* 1706 and *The Beaux' Stratagem* 1707 are in the tradition of the Restoration comedy of manners.

Charming women can true converts make,
We love the precepts for the teacher's sake.
George Farquhar
The Constant Couple

---

farrago /fəˈrɑːgəʊ/ *n.* (*plural* **farragos**) a hotchpotch, a medley. [Latin = mixed fodder (*far* = corn)]
Farragut /'færəgʌt/ David (Glasgow) 1801–1870. US admiral, born near Knoxville, Tennessee. During the US Civil War he took New Orleans in 1862, after destroying the Confederate fleet, and in 1864 effectively put an

end to blockade-running at Mobile. The ranks of vice-admiral (1864) and admiral (1866) were created for him by Congress.
Farrell /'færəl/ James T(homas) 1904–1979. US novelist and short-story writer. His naturalistic *Studs Lonigan* trilogy 1932–35, comprising *Young Lonigan, The Young Manhood of Studs Lonigan,* and *Judgment Day,* describes the development of a young Catholic man in Chicago after World War I, and was written from his own experience. *The Face of Time* 1953 is considered one of his finest works.
farrier /'færiə/ *n.* a smith who shoes horses. —**farriery** *n.* [from Old French from Latin *ferrarius* (*ferrum* = iron, horseshoe)]
farrow /'færəʊ/ *v.t./i.* (of a sow) to give birth, to give birth to (pigs). —*n.* farrowing; a litter of pigs. [Old English]
Farrow Mia 1945– . US film and television actress. Popular since the late 1960s, she has been associated with the director Woody Allen since 1982, both on and off screen. She starred in his films *Zelig* 1983, *Hannah and her Sisters* 1986, and *Crimes and Misdemeanors* 1990, as well as in Roman Polanski's *Rosemary's Baby* 1968.
Farsi /'fɑːsɪ/ *n.* the Persian language. [Persian]
fart *v.i.* (*vulgar*) to emit wind from the anus. —*n.* (*vulgar*) an emission of wind from the anus. [Old English]
farther /'fɑːðə/ *adv.* & *adj.* at or to a greater distance, more remote. [variant of *further*]
farthest /'fɑːðɪst/ *adv.* & *adj.* at or to the greatest distance, most remote. [variant of *furthest*]
farthing /'fɑːðɪŋ/ *n.* formerly the smallest English coin, a quarter of a penny. It was introduced as a silver coin in Edward I's reign. The copper farthing became widespread in Charles II's reign, and the bronze in 1860. It was legal tender until 1961. [Old English, from *fēortha* = fourth]
farthingale /'fɑːðɪŋgeɪl/ *n.* (*historical*) a hooped petticoat. [from French *verdugale* from Spanish (*verdugo* = rod)]
fasces /'fæsiːz/ *n.* a bundle of rods with a projecting axe-blade carried before an ancient Roman magistrate as a symbol of authority. The fasces were revived in the 20th century as the symbol of ◊Fascism. [Latin plural of *fascis* = bundle]
Fasching /'fæʃɪŋ/ *n.* the period preceding Lent in German-speaking towns, particularly Munich, Cologne, and Vienna, devoted to masquerades, formal balls, and street parades.
fascia /'feɪʃə/ *n.* 1. in architecture, a long, flat surface of wood or stone. 2. a stripe, a band. 3. = facia. [Latin = band, door-frame]
fascicle /'fæsɪkəl/ *n.* an instalment of a book. [from Latin *fasciculus* = diminutive of *fascis* = bundle]
fascinate /'fæsɪneɪt/ *v.t.* 1. to capture the interest of; to charm irresistibly. 2. (of a snake etc.) to paralyse (a victim) with fear. —**fascination** /-'neɪʃən/ *n.*, **fascinator** *n.* [from Latin *fascinare* = (*fascinum* = spell)]
Fascism /'fæʃɪzəm/ *n.* an extreme right-wing totalitarian political system or such views, specifically, the totalitarian nationalist movement founded in Italy 1919 by ◊Mussolini and followed by Hitler's Germany 1933. —**Fascist** *n.* & *adj.* [from Italian *fascio* = bundle, organized group, from Latin *fascis* = bundle]
fashion /'fæʃən/ *n.* 1. the current popular custom or style, especially in dress. 2. a manner of doing something. —*v.t.* to form or make (*into*). —**after a fashion,** to some extent, barely adequately. **in fashion,** fashionable at the present time. **out of fashion,** no longer fashionable. [from Anglo-French from Latin *factio* (*facere* = make)]
fashionable *adj.* following or in keeping with the current fashion; characteristic of or patronized by fashionable people. —**fashionably** *adv.*
Fashoda Incident /fəˈʃəʊdə/ a dispute in 1898 in the town of Fashoda (now Kodok), Sudan, in which a clash between French and British forces nearly led the two countries into war.
Fassbinder /'fæsbɪndə/ Rainer Werner 1946–1982. German film director, who began his career as a fringe actor and founded his own 'anti-theatre' before moving into films. His works are mainly stylized indictments of contemporary West German society. He made over 30 films, including *Die bitteren Tränen der Petra von Kant/The Bitter Tears of Petra von Kant* 1972 and *Die Ehe von Maria Braun/The Marriage of Maria Braun* 1979.
fast[1] /fɑːst/ *adj.* 1. moving or done quickly; enabling or causing quick motion; (of · clock etc.) showing a time

Fassbinder *German film director Rainer Werner Fassbinder.*

later than the correct time; (of photographic film) very sensitive to light and needing only a short exposure. 2. (of a person) immoral, dissipated. 3. firm, fixed, firmly attached; (of a colour) not fading when washed etc.; (of a friend) close. —*adv.* 1. quickly, in quick succession. 2. firmly, tightly. —**fast breeder (reactor)**, a reactor using mainly fast neutrons. **fast neutron**, a neutron with high kinetic energy. **fast one**, (*slang*) an unfair or deceitful action. [Old English]

fast[2] *v.i.* to abstain from food or certain food, especially as a religious observance. —*n.* fasting; a period of fasting. [Old English]

fasten /'fɑːsən/ *v.t./i.* 1. to fix firmly, to tie or join together; to join or close *up*. 2. to fix (one's glance or attention) intently. 3. to become fastened. —**fasten off**, to tie or secure the end of a thread etc. **fasten on** *or* **upon**, to seize on (as a victim etc.). [Old English]

fastener /'fɑːsnə/ *n.* (also **fastening**) a device that fastens something.

fastidious /fæ'stɪdɪəs/ *adj.* very careful in matters of choice or taste; easily disgusted, squeamish. —**fastidiously** *adv.*, **fastidiousness** *n.* [from Latin *fastidium* = aversion]

fastness /'fɑːstnɪs/ *n.* a stronghold. [Old English]

fast reactor or **fast breeder reactor** a ◊nuclear reactor that makes use of fast neutrons to bring about fission. Unlike other reactors used by the nuclear-power industry, it has little or no ◊moderator, to slow down neutrons. The reactor core is surrounded by a 'blanket' of uranium carbide. During operation, some of this uranium is converted into plutonium, which can be extracted and later used as fuel.

fat *adj.* 1. very plump; well-fed; (of an animal) made plump for slaughter. 2. containing much fat; covered with fat. 3. thick, substantial. 4. fertile. —*n.* 1. an oily or greasy substance found in animal bodies etc., another name for a ◊lipid. 2. the fat part of an animal's flesh (as opposed to *lean*). —*v.t.* (**-tt-**) to fatten. —**a fat chance**, (*slang*) very little chance. **fat-head** (*colloquial*) a stupid person. **the fat is in the fire**, there will be trouble. **a fat lot**, (*slang*) very little. **kill the fatted calf**, to celebrate, especially at a prodigal's return. **live off the fat of the land**, to live luxuriously. —**fatness** *n.* [Old English]

Fatah, al- /'fætə/ a Palestinian nationalist organization founded in 1956 to bring about an independent state of Palestine. Also called the Palestine National Liberation Movement, it is the main component of the ◊Palestine Liberation Organization. Its leader is Yasser ◊Arafat.

fatal /'feɪtəl/ *adj.* causing or ending in death; ruinous, disastrous, fateful. —**fatally** *adv.* [from Old French or Latin]

fatalism /'feɪtəlɪzəm/ *n.* the belief that all that happens is predetermined and therefore inevitable. —**fatalist** *n.*, **fatalistic** /-'lɪstɪk/ *adj.*

fatality /fə'tælɪtɪ/ *n.* 1. a death by accident or in war etc. 2. a fatal influence; a predestined liability to disaster.

fate *n.* 1. an irresistible power or force controlling all events. 2. what is destined; a person's destiny or fortune; death, destruction. —*v.t.* (especially in *passive*) to preordain. [from Italian and Latin *fatum*]

fateful *adj.* controlled by fate; decisive, important. —**fatefully** *adv.*

Fates in Greek mythology, the three goddesses, Atropos ('the inflexible'), Clotho ('she who spins'), and Lachesis ('getting by lot'), who decided the length of human life.

fat hen a plant *Chenopodium album* found on waste sites and in fields, up to 1 m/3 ft tall, with lance- or diamond-shaped leaves, and compact heads of small inconspicuous flowers. Now considered a weed, fat hen was once valued for its fatty seeds and edible leaves.

father /'fɑːðə/ *n.* 1. a male parent; a male guardian through adoption. 2. (usually in *plural*) a forefather; a founder or originator, an early leader; (in *plural*) elders, leading members. 3. **Father**, God, especially the first person of the Trinity. 4. a priest, especially of a religious order, or as a title or form of address. 5. venerable person, especially as a title in personifications. —*v.t.* 1. to beget; to originate (a scheme etc.). 2. to fix the paternity of (a child) or the responsibility for (a book, idea etc.) *on* or *upon*. —**father figure**, an older man who is respected like a father, a trusted leader. **father-in-law** *n.* (*plural* **fathers-in-law**) one's wife's or husband's father. **Father of the House**, the member of the House of Commons with the longest continuous service. **Fathers (of the Church)**, those early ecclesiastical writers, especially of the first five centuries, whose writings on Christian doctrines were regarded as especially authoritative. —**fatherhood** *n.* [Old English]

fatherland *n.* one's native country.

fatherly *adj.* of or like a father.

Father's Day a day set apart in many countries for honouring fathers, observed on the third Sunday in June in the USA, UK, and Canada. The idea for a father's day originated with Sonora Louise Smart Dodd of Spokane, Washington, USA, in 1909 (after hearing a sermon on Mother's Day), and through her efforts the first Father's Day was celebrated there in 1910.

fathom *n.* in seafaring especially in soundings, in mining, and in handling timber, a unit of depth measurement (6 ft/ 1.83 m) used before metrication; it approximates to the distance between an adult man's hands with arms outstretched. —*v.t.* 1. to understand. 2. to measure the depth of (water). [Old English = the outstretched arms] [Anglo-Saxon *faethm* 'to embrace']

Fathy /'fæθi/ Hassan 1900–1989. Egyptian architect. In his work at the village of New Gourna in Upper Egypt he demonstrated the value of native building technology and natural materials in solving contemporary housing problems. This, together with his book *The Architecture of the Poor* 1973, influenced the growth of community architecture, enabling people to work directly with architects in building their homes.

fatigue /fə'tiːg/ *n.* 1. extreme tiredness. 2. weakness in metals etc. from variations of stress. 3. a soldier's noncombatant duty; (in *plural*) clothing worn for this. —*v.t.* to cause fatigue in; to tire. [from French from Latin *fatigare* = exhaust]

Fatimid /'fætɪmɪd/ *n.* or **Fatimite** a dynasty of Muslim Shi'ite caliphs founded in 909 in N Africa by Obaidallah, who claimed to be a descendant of Fatima (the prophet Muhammad's daughter) and her husband Ali. In 969 the Fatimids conquered Egypt, and the dynasty continued until overthrown by Saladin in 1171.

fatstock *n.* livestock fattened for slaughter.

fatten *v.t./i.* to make or become fat.

fatty *adj.* like or containing fat. —**fatty acid**, a member of a series of acids occurring in or derived from natural fats.

fatty acid an organic compound consisting of a hydrocarbon chain, up to 24 carbon atoms long, with a carboxyl group (–COOH) at one end. The bonds may be single

fax

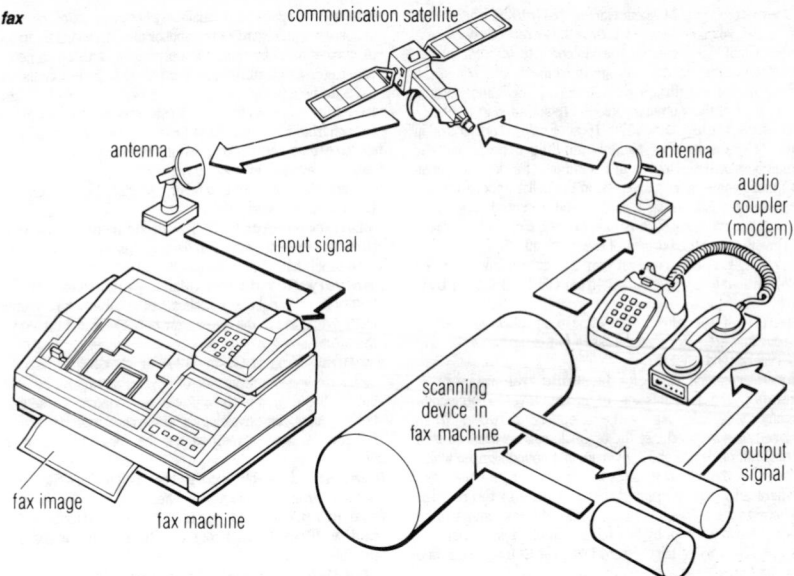

communication satellite

antenna   antenna

audio coupler (modem)

input signal

scanning device in fax machine

output signal

fax image

fax machine

or double; where a double bond occurs the carbon atoms concerned carry one instead of two hydrogen atoms. Chains with only single bonds have all the hydrogen they can carry, so they are said to to be **saturated** with hydrogen. Chains with one or more double bonds are said to be **unsaturated** (see ◊polyunsaturates). Saturated fatty acids include palmitic and stearic acids; unsaturated fatty acids include oleic (one double bond), linolenic (two double bonds) and linolenic (three double bonds). Fatty acids are generally found combined with glycerol in tryglycerides (see ◊fat).

fatuous /'fætjuəs/ *adj.* silly, purposeless. —**fatuity** /fə'tjuːɪtɪ/ *n.*, **fatuously** *adv.* [from Latin *fatuus*]

faucet /'fɔːsɪt/ *n.* a tap for a barrel etc.; (*US*) any tap. [from French *fausset* = vent-peg from Provençal *falsar* = bore]

Faulkner /'fɔːknə/ Brian 1921–1977. Northern Ireland Unionist politician. He was the last prime minister of Northern Ireland 1971–72 before the Stormont Parliament was suspended.

Faulkner William 1897–1962. US novelist who wrote in an experimental stream-of-consciousness style. His works include *The Sound and the Fury* 1929, dealing with a southern US family in decline; *As I Lay Dying* 1930; *Light in August* 1932, a study of segregation; *The Unvanquished* 1938, stories of the Civil War; and *The Hamlet* 1940, *The Town* 1957, and *The Mansion* 1959, a trilogy covering the rise of the materialist Snopes family. He was awarded the Nobel Prize for Literature in 1949.

fault[1] /fɔːlt, folt/ *n.* 1. a defect or blemish. 2. an offence or misdeed; the responsibility or blame for this; (in tennis etc.) an incorrect serve; (in show-jumping) a penalty for an error. —*v.t./i.* 1. to find fault with, to blame. 2. to cause a fault in (rock strata); (of rock) to have a fault —**at fault**, blameworthy. **find fault with**, to criticize unfavourably. **to a fault**, excessively. [from Old French from Latin *fallere* = deceive]

fault[2] *n.* in geology, a fracture in the Earth's crust along which the two sides have moved as a result of differing strains in the adjacent rock bodies. Displacement of rock masses horizontally or vertically along a fault may be microscopic, or it may be massive, causing an ◊earthquake. If the movement has a major vertical component, the fault is termed a **normal fault** when rocks on each side have moved apart, or a **reverse fault** when one side has overridden the other. A low angle reverse fault is called a **thrust**.

faultless *adj.* without faults. —**faultlessly** *adv.*

faulty *adj.* having a fault or faults, imperfect. —**faultily** *adv.*, **faultiness** *n.*

faun /fɔːn/ *n.* a Latin rural deity with a goat's horns, legs, and tail. [from Old French or Latin *Faunus*, Latin god identified with Greek Pan]

fauna /'fɔːnə/ *n.* (*plural* **faunas**) the animals of a particular region or period. [from name of Latin rural goddess]

Faust /faʊst/ a legendary magician who was said to have sold his soul to the Devil. The historical Georg Faust appears to have been a wandering scholar and conjurer in Germany at the start of the 16th century. In 1587 the first of a series of Faust books appeared. Marlowe's tragedy, *Dr Faustus*, was acted in 1594. In the 18th century the story was a subject for pantomime in England and puppet plays in Germany. In his play *Faust* Goethe made him a symbol of humanity's striving after the infinite. Heine, Thomas Mann, and Paul Valéry also used the legend, and it inspired musical works by Schumann, Berlioz, Gounod, Boito, and Busoni.

Faust a play by Goethe, completed in two parts 1808 and 1832, in which Mephistopheles attempts to win over the soul of world-weary Faust but ultimately fails after helping Faust in the pursuit of good.

faute de mieux /fəʊt də 'mjɜː/for want of any better alternative. [French]

Fauvism /'fəʊvɪzəm/ *n.* a style of painting with a bold use of vivid colours, a short-lived but influential art movement originating in Paris in 1905 with the founding of the Salon d'Automne by Henri ◊Matisse and others. Rouault, Dufy, Marquet, Derain, and Signac were early Fauves. The name originated in 1905 when the critic Louis Vauxcelles called their gallery '*une cage aux fauves*' (a cage of wild beasts).

faux pas /fəʊ 'pɑː/ (*plural* the same /'pɑːz/) a tactless mistake, a blunder. [French = false step]

favour /'feɪvə/ *n.* 1. liking, goodwill, approval. 2. a kind or helpful act. 3. partiality. 4. a badge or ornament worn as a mark of favour. —*v.t.* 1. to regard or treat with favour or partiality. 2. to support, to promote, to prefer; to oblige *with*; to be to the advantage of, to facilitate. 3. (*colloquial*) to resemble in features. 4. (in *past participle*) having special advantages; having specified looks. —**in** *or* **out of favour**, approved or disapproved of. **in favour of**, in support of; to the advantage of. [from Old French from Latin *favor* (*favēre* = show goodwill to)]

favourable *adj.* 1. well disposed, approving. 2. pleasing 3. satisfactory; helpful, suitable. —**favourably** *adv.*

favourite /'feɪvərɪt/ *adj.* preferred to all others. —*n.* a favourite person or thing, especially a person favoured by a monarch or superior; (in sport) a competitor thought most likely to win.

favouritism *n.* unfair favouring of one person or group at the expense of another.

Fawcett /'fɔːsɪt/ Millicent Garrett 1847–1929. English suffragette, younger sister of Elizabeth Garrett ◊Anderson. A nonmilitant, she rejected the violent acts of some of her contemporaries in the suffrage movement. She joined the first Women's Suffrage Committee in 1867 and became president of the Women's Unionist Association in 1889.

Fawkes /fɔːks/ Guy 1570–1606. English conspirator in the ◊Gunpowder Plot to blow up King James I and the members of both Houses of Parliament. Fawkes, a Roman Catholic convert, was arrested in the cellar underneath the House on 4 Nov 1605, tortured, and executed. The event is still commemorated in Britain every 5 Nov with bonfires, fireworks, and the burning of the 'guy', an effigy.

fawn[1] n. 1. a deer in its first year. 2. a light yellowish-brown colour. —adj. fawn-coloured. [from Old French from Latin *fetus* = offspring]

fawn[2] v.i. (especially of a dog etc.) to try to win affection by grovelling etc.; to lavish caresses (*on* or *upon*); to behave servilely. [Old English]

fax n. common name for **facsimile transmission** or **telefax**: the transmission of images over a ◊telecommunications link, usually the telephone network. When placed on a fax machine, the original image is scanned by a transmitting device and converted into coded signals, which travel via the telephone lines to the receiving fax machine, where an image is created that is a copy of the original. Photographs as well as printed text and drawings can be sent. —v.t. transmit by fax. [abbreviation of *facsimile*]

fay n. (*literary*) a fairy. [from Old French from Latin *fata* = the Fates]

FBI abbreviation of ◊Federal Bureau of Investigation.

Fe symbol for iron.

fealty /'fiːəltɪ/ n. the duty of a feudal tenant or vassal to his lord; allegiance. [from Old French from Latin]

fear n. 1. an unpleasant emotion caused by exposure to danger, the expectation of pain etc.; alarm. 2. awe and reverence. 3. a danger, a likelihood. —v.t./i. 1. to have fear, to expect with fear or anxiety; to be afraid of; to shrink from (*doing*). 2. to revere (God). —**no fear!**, (*colloquial*) certainly not! [Old English = sudden calamity, danger]

fearful adj. 1. afraid, reluctant through fear. 2. causing fear. 3. (*colloquial*) extreme, annoying. —**fearfully** adv.

fearless adj. without fear, brave. —**fearlessly** adv., **fearlessness** n.

fearsome adj. frightening, formidable.

feasible /'fiːzɪbəl/ adj. practicable, possible. —**feasibility** /-'bɪlɪtɪ/ n., **feasibly** adv. [from Old French from Latin *facere* = do]

feast n. 1. a large meal, a banquet. 2. a joyful religious festival. 3. something giving great pleasure. —v.t./i. 1. to partake of a feast, to eat and drink heartily (*on*). 2. to give a feast to. 3. to give pleasure to, to regale. [from Old French from Latin *festus* = festal]

feat n. a remarkable act or achievement. [from Old French from Latin *factum*]

feather /'feðə/ n. 1. a rigid outgrowth of the outer layer of the skin of birds, made of the protein keratin, with a horny stem and fine strands on both sides. Feathers provide insulation and facilitate flight. There are several types, including long quill feathers on the wings and tail, fluffy down feathers for retaining body heat, and contour feathers covering the body. The colouring of feathers is often important in camouflage or in courtship and other displays. Feathers are replaced at least once a year. a piece of this as a decoration etc. 2. (*collectively*) plumage; game birds. —v.t./i. 1. to cover or line with feathers. 2. to turn (an oar) so that it passes through the air edgeways; to make this movement. —**feather bed**, a mattress stuffed with feathers. **featherbed** v.t. to make things easy for, to pamper. **featherbrained, -headed** adjs. silly. **feather in one's cap**, an achievement to one's credit. **feather one's nest**, to enrich oneself. —**feathery** adj. [Old English]

feathering n. 1. plumage. 2. the feathers of an arrow 3. a feather-like structure or marking.

feather star any of an unattached, free-swimming group of sea lilies, order Comatulida. The arms are branched into numerous projections (hence 'feather' star), and grow from a small cup-shaped body.

featherweight n. 1. a ◊boxing-weight between bantamweight and lightweight. 2. a person or thing of very light weight.

feature /'fiːtʃə/ n. 1. (usually in *plural*) a part of the face, especially with regard to the appearance. 2. a characteristic or notable part of a thing. 3. a prominent article in a newspaper etc. 4. a feature film. —v.t./i. 1. to give prominence to. 2. to be a feature of. 3. to be a participant (*in*). —**feature film**, the main film in a cinema programme. [from Old French from Latin *factura* = formation (*facere* = make)]

featureless adj. lacking distinct features.

Feb. abbreviation of February.

febrile /'fiːbraɪl/ adj. of a fever, feverish. [from French or Latin *febris* = fever]

February /'februərɪ/ n. the second month of the year. [from Old French from Latin *februa* = purification feast held in this month]

February Revolution (March Western calendar) the first of the two political uprisings of the ◊Russian revolution in 1917 that led to the overthrow of the tsar and the end of the ◊Romanov dynasty.

Fechner /'fexnə/ Gustav 1801–1887. German psychologist. He became professor of physics at Leipzig in 1834, but in 1839 turned to the study of psychophysics (the relationship between physiology and psychology). He devised **Fechner's law**, a method for the exact measurement of sensation.

feckless adj. feeble, incompetent, helpless. —**fecklessness** n. [from Scottish *feck* = effect]

fecund /'fiːkənd/ adj. prolific, fertile; fertilizing. —**fecundity** /fɪ'kʌndɪtɪ/ n. [from French or Latin *fecundus* = fruitful]

fecundate /'fiːkəndeɪt/ v.t. to make fecund, to fertilize. —**fecundation** /-'deɪʃən/ n. [from Latin *fecundare*]

fecundity n. the rate at which an organism reproduces, as distinct from its ◊fertility (ability to reproduce). In vertebrates, it is usually measured as the number of offspring produced by a female each year.

fed past and past participle of ◊feed.

federal /'fedərəl/ adj. 1. of a system of government in which several states unite but remain independent in internal affairs; of such states or their central government. 2. relating to or favouring central as opposed to provincial government. 3. Federal, (*US*) of the northern states in the American Civil War. —**federalism** n., **federalist** n., **federally** adv. [from Latin *foedus* = covenant]

Federal Bureau of Investigation (FBI) an agency of the US Department of Justice that investigates violations of federal law not specifically assigned to other agencies, being particularly concerned with internal security. The FBI was established in 1908 and built up a position of powerful autonomy during the autocratic directorship of J Edgar Hoover 1924–72.

federalism n. system of government in which two or more separate states unite under a common central government while retaining a considerable degree of local autonomy. A federation should be distinguished from a **confederation**, a looser union of states for mutual assistance. Switzerland, the USSR, the USA, Canada, Australia, and Malaysia are all examples of countries with federal government, and many supporters of the European Community see it as the forerunner of a federal Europe.

Federalist n. in US history, one who advocated the ratification of the US Constitution 1787–88 in place of the Articles of Confederation. The Federalists became in effect the ruling political party during the presidencies of George Washington and John Adams 1789–1801, legislating to strengthen the authority of the newly created federal government.

federalize v.t. to make federal, to organize in a federal system. —**federalization** /-'zeɪʃən/ n.

Federal Reserve System ('Fed') the US central banking system and note-issue authority, established in 1913 to regulate the country's credit and monetary affairs. The Fed consists of the 12 federal reserve banks and their 25 branches and other facilities throughout the country; it is headed by a board of governors in Washington, appointed by the US president with Senate approval.

federate /'fedəreɪt/ v.t./i. to unite on a federal basis or for a common object. —/'fedərət/ adj. so united. [from Latin *foederare*]

federation /fedə'reɪʃən/ n. 1. an act of federating. 2. a federal group. —**federative** /'fedərətɪv/ adj. [from French from Latin]

fee *n.* **1.** the sum payable to an official or professional person for services; the charge for joining a society, taking an examination etc.; the money paid for the transfer to another employer of a footballer etc.; (in *plural*) regular payment for instruction at a school etc. **2.** an inherited estate of land, unlimited (**fee simple**) or limited (**fee tail**) as to the class of heir. —**in fee**, in absolute ownership. [from Anglo-French from Latin *feudum*, perhaps from Frankish *fehu-od* = cattle-property]

feeble *adj.* weak; lacking strength, energy, or effectiveness. —**feeble-minded** *adj.* mentally deficient. —**feebleness** *n.*, **feebly** *adv.* [from Old French from Latin *flebilis* = lamentable]

feed *v.t./i.* (*past* and *past participle* fed) **1.** to supply with food, to put food into the mouth of; to give as food to animals. **2.** (especially of animals or babies, or *colloquial*) to take food, to eat. **3.** to maintain a supply of (material required *into* a machine etc.), to keep (a machine, fire etc.) supplied thus. **4.** to gratify; to encourage *with*. **5.** to send passes to (a player) in football etc. —*n.* **1.** food for animals; a measured allowance of this. **2.** feeding. **3.** a meal (especially for babies, or *colloquial*). **4.** material supplied to machines etc. —**fed up**, (*colloquial*) discontented or bored (*with*). **feed on**, to consume; to be nourished or strengthened by. [Old English]

feedback *n.* **1.** return to the input of a part of the output of a system or process; a principle used in self-regulating control systems, from the simple ◊thermostat to automatic computer-controlled machine tools; In such systems the results produced in an ongoing reaction become factors in modifying or changing the reaction. Information about what *is* happening in a system (such as level of temperature, engine speed or size of workpiece) is fed back to a controlling device, which compares it with what *should* be happening. If the two are different, the device takes suitable action (such as switching on a heater, allowing more steam to the engine, or resetting the tools). Feedback is also the name given to the signal so returned. **2.** in music, a continuous tone, usually a high-pitched squeal, caused by the overloading of circuits between electric guitar and amplifier as the sound of the speakers is fed back through the guitar pickup. **3.** information about the result of an experiment etc.; response. See also ◊ biofeedback.

feeder *n.* **1.** one that feeds in a specified way. **2.** the feeding apparatus in a machine. **3.** a child's bib. **4.** a tributary, branch road, branch railway line etc., that links with the main system.

feel *v.t./i.* (*past* and *past participle* felt) **1.** to examine or search by touch; to perceive by touch, to have a sensation of. **2.** to be conscious of (an emotion etc.). **3.** to experience, to be affected by (an emotion or physical condition). **4.** to seem, to give an impression of being. **5.** to have a vague or emotional impression; to consider, to think; to be consciously, to consider oneself. **6.** to sympathize *with*, to have pity *for*. —*n.* **1.** an act of feeling; the sense of touch. **2.** the sensation characterizing a material, situation etc. —**feel like**, (*colloquial*) to have a wish for, to be inclined towards. **feel one's way**, to proceed cautiously (*literally* or *figuratively*). [Old English]

feeler *n.* **1.** an organ in certain animals for testing things by touch. **2.** a tentative proposal or suggestion. —**feeler gauge**, a gauge with blades that can be inserted to measure gaps.

feeling *n.* **1.** the capacity to feel, the sense of touch. **2.** an emotion; (in *plural*) emotional susceptibilities. **3.** an opinion or notion. **4.** sympathy with others. **5.** earnestness. —*adj.* sensitive, sympathetic; heartfelt.

feet plural of **foot**.

Fehling's test a chemical test to determine whether an organic substance is a reducing agent (a substance that donates electrons to other substances in a chemical reaction).

feign /feɪn/ *v.t.* to pretend; to simulate. [from Old French from Latin *fingere* = mould, fashion]

Feininger /ˈfaɪnɪŋə/ Lyonel 1871–1956. US abstract artist, an early Cubist. He worked at the Bauhaus, a key centre of design in Germany 1919–33 and later helped to found the Bauhaus in Chicago. In Germany, he formed the *Blaue Vier* (Blue Four) in 1924 with the painters Alexei von Jawlensky (1864–1941), Wassily Kandinsky and Paul Klee.

feint /feɪnt/ *n.* a sham attack, blow etc. to divert an opponent's attention from the main attack; a pretence. —*v.i.* to make a feint. —*adj.* (of paper etc.) having faintly ruled lines. [from French]

Feldman /ˈfeldmən/ Morton 1926–1988. US composer. An associate of John ◊Cage and Earle ◊Brown in the 1950s, he composed large-scale set pieces using the orchestra mainly as a source of colour and texture.

feldspar /ˈfeldspɑː/ *n.* or **felspar** any of a group of usually white or flesh-red rock-forming minerals which are aluminium silicates combined with various other metallic ions. Feldspars rank 6 on the ◊Mohs' scale of hardness. [from German *feldspat(h)* (*feld* = field and *spat(h)* = spar)]

feldspathoid *n.* a group of silicate minerals resembling feldspars but containing less silica. Examples are nepheline NaAlSiO$_4$ (with a little potassium) and leucite KAlSi$_{2}$O$_6$. Feldspathoids occur in igneous rocks that have relatively high proportions of sodium and potassium. Such rocks may also contain alkali feldspar, but they do not generally contain quartz because any free silica would have combined with the feldspathoid to produce more feldspar instead.

felicitate /fɪˈlɪsɪteɪt/ *v.t.* to congratulate. [from Latin *felicitare* = make very happy (*felix* = happy)]

felicitation /fɪlɪsɪˈteɪʃən/ *n.* (usually in *plural*) a congratulation.

felicitous /fɪˈlɪsɪtəs/ *adj.* well-chosen, apt. —**felicitously** *adv.*

felicity /fɪˈlɪsɪtɪ/ *n.* **1.** great happiness. **2.** a pleasing manner or style. [from Old French from Latin (*felix* = happy)]

feline /ˈfiːlaɪn/ *adj.* of cats; catlike. —*n.* an animal of the cat family. —**felinity** /fɪˈlɪnɪtɪ/ *n.* [from Latin *feles* = cat]

fell[1] *v.t.* **1.** to cut down (a tree); to strike down by a blow or cut. **2.** to stitch down (the edge of a seam). [Old English]

fell[2] *n.* a hill; a stretch of hills or moorland, especially in northern England. [Old Norse]

fell[3] *adj.* ruthless, destructive. —**at one fell swoop**, in a single (deadly) action. [from Old French]

fell[4] *n.* an animal's skin or hide with the hair. [Old English]

fell[5] past of **fall**.

fellah *n.* (*plural* **fellahin**) in Arab countries, a peasant farmer or farm labourer. [Arabic *falaha* = labour or till the soil]

fellatio /feˈlɑːtɪəʊ/ *n.* stimulation of the penis by sucking. [from Latin *fellare* = suck]

Fellini /feˈliːni/ Federico 1920–. Italian film director noted for his strongly subjective and dream imagery. His films include *I vitelloni/The Young and the Passionate* 1953, *La Strada/The Street* 1954 (Academy Award 1956), *Nights of Cabiria* 1956, *La dolce vita/The Sweet Life* 1960, *Otto e mezzo/8$\frac{1}{2}$* 1963, *Juliet of the Spirits* 1965, *Satyricon* 1969, *Roma/Fellini's Roma* 1972, *Amarcord* 1974, *Casanova* 1976, and *La città delle donne/City of Women* 1981.

fellow /ˈfeləʊ/ *n.* **1.** a comrade or associate. **2.** a counterpart, an equal. **3.** (*colloquial*) a man or boy. **4.** an incorporated senior member of a college; a research student receiving a fellowship. **5.** a member of a learned society. —*attributive* or *adj.* of the same class, associated in a joint action. —**fellow feeling**, sympathy with a person whose experience etc. one shares. **fellow traveller** *n.* a sympathizer with but not a member of a political (especially the Communist) party. [Old English from Old Norse]

fellowship *n.* **1.** friendly association with others, companionship. **2.** a body of associates. **3.** the position or income of a fellow of a college or learned society; the stipend granted to a graduate for a period of research.

felon /ˈfelən/ *n.* one who has committed a felony. [from Old French from Latin *fel(l)o*]

felony /ˈfelənɪ/ *n.* (*historical*) any of a class of crimes which may loosely be said to have been regarded by the law as of graver character than those called misdemeanours; in the USA, a crime generally punishable by imprisonment for a year or more. See also ◊criminal law. —**felonious** /fɪˈləʊnɪəs/ *adj.* , **feloniously** *adv.* [from Old French]

felspar variant of **feldspar**.

felt[1] *n.* a cloth of matted and pressed fibres of wool etc. —*v.t./i.* to make into felt; to cover with felt; to become matted. —**felt(-tip** *or* **-tipped) pen**, a pen with a felt point. [Old English]

felt[2] past and past participle of **feel**.

felucca /fɪˈlʌkə/ *n.* a small ship with lateen sails and/or oars, used on Mediterranean coasts. [from Italian from

Spanish from Arabic, perhaps from Greek *epholkion* = small boat towed after a ship]

fem. in grammar, abbreviation of feminine.

female /'fiːmeɪl/ *adj.* 1. of the sex that can bear offspring or produce eggs; (of plants) fruit-bearing; of women or female animals or plants. 2. (of a screw, socket etc.) made hollow to receive the corresponding inserted part. —*n.* a female person, animal, or plant. [from Old French from Latin *femella (femina* = woman)]

feminine /'femɪnɪn/ *adj.* 1. of a woman; having qualities associated with women. 2. in grammar, of or denoting the gender proper to women's names. 3. (of a rhyme or line-ending) having a stressed syllable followed by an unstressed one. —*n.* the feminine gender; a feminine word. —**femininity** /-'nɪnɪtɪ/ *n.* [from Old French or Latin *femina* = woman]

feminism /'femɪnɪzəm/ *n.* advocacy of women's rights on the basis of the equality of the sexes. —**feminist** *n.*

femme fatale /fæm fæ'taːl/a dangerously attractive woman. [French]

femto- /femtəʊ-/ in combinations, denoting a factor of 10⁻¹⁵ (*femtometre*). [from Danish or Norwegian *femten* = fifteen]

femur /'fiːmə(r)/ *n.* or **thigh-bone** the upper bone in the hind limb of a four-limbed vertebrate.

fen *n.* a low, marshy area of land. See the ◊**Fens**. [Old English]

fence *n.* 1. a barrier or railing enclosing a field, garden, etc.; a structure for a horse to jump over in a competition etc. 2. a guard or guide or gauge in a machine. 3. a dealer in stolen goods. —*v.t./i.* 1. to surround (as) with a fence; to enclose or separate with a fence. 2. to practise the sport of fencing; to be evasive, to parry. 3. to deal in (stolen goods).

fencing /'fensɪŋ/ *n.* 1. fences; material for fences. 2. the sport of fighting with swords including the **foil**, derived from the light weapon used in practice duels; the **épée**, a heavier weapon derived from the duelling sword proper; and the **sabre**, with a curved handle and narrow V-shaped blade. In sabre fighting, cuts count as well as thrusts. Masks and protective jackets are worn, and hits are registered electronically in competitions. Men's fencing has been part of every Olympic programme since 1896; women started to compete in 1924 but only using the foil.

fend *v.t./i.* 1. to ward *off*, to repel. 2. to provide *for*.

fender *n.* 1. a low frame bordering a fireplace to keep in falling coals etc. 2. a pad or bundle of rope etc. hung over a vessel's side to protect it against impact. 3. (*US*) the bumper of a motor vehicle.

Fender trade name of a pioneering series of electric guitars and bass guitars. The first solid-body electric guitar on the market was the 1948 Fender Broadcaster (renamed the Telecaster 1950), and the first electric bass guitar was the Fender Precision 1951. The Fender Stratocaster guitar dates from 1954. Their designer, Leo Fender, began manufacturing amplifiers in the USA in the 1940s.

Fénelon /feni'lɒn/ François de Salignac de la Mothe 1651–1715. French writer and ecclesiastic. He entered the priesthood in 1675 and in 1689 was appointed tutor to the Duke of Burgundy, grandson of Louis XIV. For him he wrote his *Fables* and *Dialogues des morts/Dialogues of the Dead* 1690, *Télémaque/Telemachus* 1699, and *Plans de gouvernement/Plans of Government.*

Fenian /'fiːnɪən/ *n.* a member of an Irish-American republican secret society, founded 1858 and named after the ancient Irish legendary warrior band of the Fianna. The collapse of the movement began when an attempt to establish an independent Irish republic by an uprising in Ireland in 1867 failed, as did raids into Canada in 1866 and 1870, and England in 1867.

fennec *n.* a small nocturnal desert ◊fox *Fennecus zerda* found in N Africa and Arabia. It has a head and body only 40 cm/1.3 ft long, and its enormous ears act as radiators to lose excess heat. It eats insects and small animals.

fennel /'fen(ə)l/ *n.* any of several varieties of a perennial plant *Foeniculum vulgare* with feathery green leaves, of the carrot family, Umbelliferae. Fennels have an aniseed flavour, and the leaves and seeds are used in seasoning. The thickened leafstalks of sweet fennel *F. vulgare dulce* are eaten. [Old English and from Old French from Latin *faeniculum*]

fenny *adj.* characterized by fens.

Fens /fenz/ level, low-lying tracts of land in E England, W and S of the Wash, about 115 km/70 mi N–S and 55 km/34 mi E–W. They fall within the counties of Lincolnshire, Cambridgeshire, and Norfolk, a huge area, formerly a bay of the North Sea. It is crossed by numerous drainage canals and forms some of the most productive agricultural land in Britain. The peat portion of the Fens is known as the **Bedford Level.**

Fenton /'fentən/ Roger 1819–1869. English photographer. The world's first war photographer, he went to the Crimea in 1855; he also founded the Royal Photographic Society in London.

fenugreek /'fenjuː griːk/ *n.* a leguminous plant *Trigonella foenum-graecum* with aromatic seeds. [from Old French from Latin = Greek hay]

feoff /fef/ *n.* a fief. [Anglo-French variant of **fief**]

feral /'fɪərəl/ *adj.* wild; uncultivated; in a wild state after escape from captivity; brutal. [from Latin *ferus* = wild]

Ferdinand /'fɜːdɪnænd/ 1861–1948. King of Bulgaria 1908–18. Son of Prince Augustus of Saxe-Coburg-Gotha, he was elected prince of Bulgaria in 1887 and, in 1908, proclaimed Bulgaria's independence of Turkey and assumed the title of tsar. In 1915 he entered World War I as Germany's ally, and in 1918 abdicated.

Ferdinand five kings of Castile, including:

Ferdinand I the Great *c.*1016–1065. King of Castile from 1035. He began the reconquest of Spain from the Moors and united all NW Spain under his and his brothers' rule.

Ferdinand V 1452–1516. King of Castile from 1474, **Ferdinand II** of Aragon from 1479, and **Ferdinand III** of Naples from 1504; first king of all Spain. In 1469 he married his cousin ◊Isabella I, who succeeded to the throne of Castile in 1474; together they were known as **the Catholic Monarchs** because, as a reaction to 700 years of rulle by the ◊Moors, they Catholicized Spain. When Ferdinand inherited the throne of Aragon in 1479, the two great Spanish kingdoms were brought under a single government for the first time. They introduced the ◊Inquisition in 1480; expelled the Jews, forced the final surrender of the Moors at Granada in 1492, and financed Columbus' expedition to the Americas, in 1492.

Ferdinand three Holy Roman emperors, including:

Ferdinand II 1578–1637. Holy Roman emperor from 1619, when he succeeded his uncle Matthias; king of Bohemia from 1617 and of Hungary from 1618. A zealous Catholic, he provoked the Bohemian revolt that led to the Thirty Years' War. He was a grandson of Ferdinand I.

Ferdinand III 1608–1657. Holy Roman emperor from 1637 when he succeeded his father Ferdinand II; king of Hungary from 1625. Although anxious to conclude the Thirty Years' War, he did not give religious liberty to Protestants.

Ferdinand 1865–1927. King of Romania from 1914, when he succeeded his uncle Charles I. In 1916 he declared war on Austria. After the Allied victory in World War I, Ferdinand acquired Transylvania and Bukovina from Austria-Hungary, and Bessarabia from Russia. In 1922 he became king of this Greater Romania. His reign saw agrarian reform and the introduction of universal suffrage.

Ferguson /'fɜːgəsən/ Harry 1884–1960. Irish engineer who pioneered the development of the tractor, joining forces with Henry Ford in 1938 to manufacture it in the USA. He experimented in automobile and aircraft development.

ferial /'fɪərɪəl/ *adj.* (of a day) not a festival or fast. [from Old French or Latin *ferialis (feriae* = holiday)]

Ferm. abbreviation of Fermanagh.

Fermanagh /fə'mænə/ county in the southern part of Northern Ireland; **area** 1,680 sq km/648 sq mi; **county town** Enniskillen; **physical** in the centre is a broad trough of low-lying land, in which lie Upper and Lower Lough Erne; **products** mainly agricultural; livestock, tweeds, clothing; **population** (1981) 52,000.

Fermat /feə'mɑː/ Pierre de 1601–1665. French mathematician, who with Blaise Pascal founded the theory of ◊probability and the modern theory of numbers and who made contributions to analytical geometry.

ferment /'fɜːment/ *n.* 1. fermentation; a fermenting agent. 2. excitement. —/fə'ment/ *v.t./i.* 1. to undergo or subject to fermentation. 2. to excite. [from Old French or Latin *fermentum (fervēre* = boil)]

fermentation /fɜ:men'teɪʃən/ *n.* **1.** a chemical change involving effervescence and the production of heat, induced by an organic substance such as yeast. In fermentation, sugars are broken down by bacteria and yeasts using a method of respiration without oxygen (◊anaerobic). These processes have long been utilized in baking bread, making beer and wine, and producing cheese, yoghurt, soy sauce, and many other foodstuffs. **2.** excitement. —**fermentative** /fə'mentətɪv/ *adj.* [from Latin]

Fermi /'fɜ:mi/ Enrico 1901–1954. Italian-born US physicist, who proved the existence of new radioactive elements produced by bombardment with neutrons, and discovered nuclear reactions produced by low-energy neutrons. He was awarded a Nobel prize in 1938.

Fermilab /'fɜ:milæb/ a US centre for ◊particle physics in Chicago, named after Enrico Fermi.

fermion /'fɜ:mɪɒn/ *n.* a particle obeying the relations stated by Fermi and Dirac, with half-integral spin. [from E *Fermi* 1954]

fermium /'fɜ:mɪəm/ *n.* a synthesized, radioactive, metallic element of the ◊actinide series, symbol Fm, atomic number 100, relative atomic mass 257. Ten isotopes are known, the longest-lived of which, Fe-257, has a half-life of 80 days. Fermium has been produced only in minute quantities in particle accelerators. It was discovered in 1952 in the debris of the first thermonuclear explosion.

fern *n.* a plant of the class Filicales, related to horsetails and clubmosses. Ferns are spore-bearing, not flowering, plants, and most are perennial, spreading by low-growing roots. The leaves, known as fronds, vary widely in size and shape. Some taller types, such as treeferns, grow in the tropics. There are over 7,000 species. —**ferny** *adj.* [Old English]

Fernández /fə'nændez/ Juan *c.*1536–*c.*1604. Spanish explorer and navigator. As a pilot on the Pacific coast of South America 1563, he reached the islands off the coast of Chile that now bear his name. Alexander ◊Selkirk was later marooned on one of these islands, and his story formed the basis of Daniel Defoe's *Robinson Crusoe.*

Fernandez de Quirós /fə'nændez də ki'rɒs/ Pedro 1565–1614. Spanish navigator, one of the first Europeans to search for the great southern continent that Ferdinand ◊Magellan believed lay to the south of the Magellan Strait. Despite a series of disastrous expeditions, he took part in the discovery of the Marquesas Islands and the main island of Espíritu Santo in the New Hebrides.

ferocious /fə'rəʊʃəs/ *adj.* fierce, savage. —**ferociously** *adv.*, **ferocity** /fə'rɒsɪtɪ/ *n.* [from Latin *ferox*]

Ferranti /fə'ræntɪ/ Sebastian de 1864–1930. British electrical engineer who electrified central London. He made and sold his first alternator in 1881.

Ferrari /fə'rɑ:ri/ Enzo 1898–1988. Italian founder of the Ferrari car empire, which specializes in Grand Prix racing cars and high-quality sports cars. He was a racing driver for Alfa Romeo in the 1920s, went on to become one of their designers and in 1929 took over their racing division. In 1947 the first 'true' Ferrari was seen. The Ferrari car has won more world championship Grands Prix than any other car.

Ferraro /fə'rɑ:rəʊ/ Geraldine 1935– . US Democrat politician, vice-presidential candidate in the 1984 election.

ferret /'ferɪt/ *n.* domesticated variety of the Old World ◊polecat. About 35 cm/1.2 ft long, it usually has yellowish-white fur and pink eyes, but may be the dark brown colour of a wild polecat. Ferrets may breed with wild polecats. They have been used since ancient times to hunt rabbits and rats. —*v.t./i.* **1.** to hunt with ferrets. **2.** to rummage, to search. —**ferret out**, to discover or produce by searching. [from Old French from Latin *fur* = thief]

ferric /'ferɪk/ *adj.* of iron; containing iron in trivalent form. [from Latin *ferrum* = iron]

Ferrier /'ferɪə/ Kathleen (Mary) 1912–1953. English contralto who sang oratorio and opera. In Benjamin Britten's *The Rape of Lucretia* 1946 she created the role of Lucretia, and she appeared in Gustav Mahler's *Das Lied von der Erde* 1947.

Ferris wheel /'ferɪs/a giant revolving vertical wheel with passenger cars on its periphery, used for rides at funfairs etc. [from name of inventor G W G *Ferris*, American engineer (died 1896)]

ferro- in combinations, containing iron; of iron.

fern

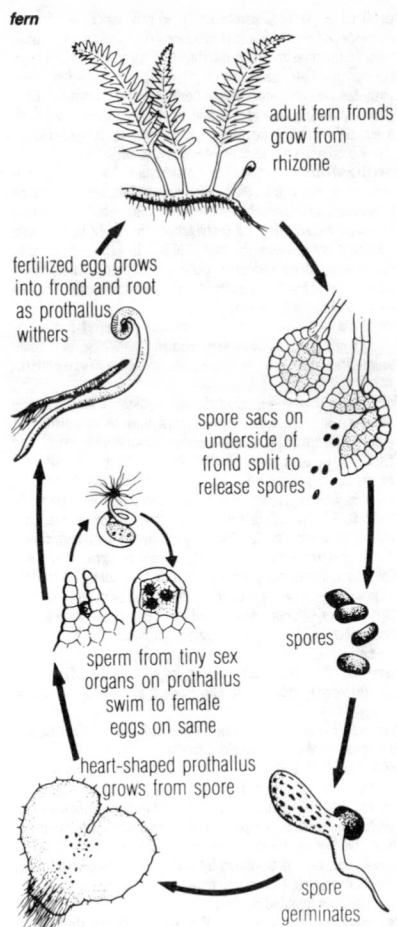

adult fern fronds grow from rhizome

fertilized egg grows into frond and root as prothallus withers

spore sacs on underside of frond split to release spores

spores

sperm from tiny sex organs on prothallus swim to female eggs on same

heart-shaped prothallus grows from spore

spore germinates

ferro-alloy *n.* alloy of iron with a high proportion of elements such as manganese, silicon, chromium, and molybdenum. Ferro-alloys are used in the manufacture of alloy steels. Each alloy is generally named after the added metal—for example, ferrochromium.

ferroconcrete /ferəu'kɒnkri:t/ *n.* reinforced concrete.

ferromagnetism /ferəu'mægnɪtɪzəm/ *n.* a form of magnetism found in substances (such as iron, cobalt, nickel, and their alloys) with high magnetic permeability and with some ability to retain their magnetization after the magnetizing field is removed. —**ferromagnetic** /-mæg'netɪk/ *adj.*

ferrous /'ferəs/ *adj.* containing iron; containing iron in divalent form. [from Latin *ferrum* = iron]

ferrous metal metal affected by magnetism. Iron, cobalt, and nickel are the three ferrous metals.

ferrule /'ferəl, -u:l/ *n.* a metal ring or cap strengthening the end of a stick etc. [from Old French *virelle* from Latin *viriae* = bracelet]

ferry /ˈferɪ/ *v.t./i.* **1.** to go or convey in a boat across water; (of a boat) to pass to and fro across water. **2.** to transport from one place to another, especially as a regular service. —*n.* a boat etc. used for ferrying; the place or service of ferrying. —**ferryman** *n.* [from Old Norse]

fertile /ˈfɜ:taɪl/ *adj.* **1.** (of soil) rich in the materials needed to support vegetation; fruitful (*literally* or *figuratively*). **2.** (of animals and plants) able to produce young or fruit. **3.** (of seeds or eggs) capable of developing into a new plant or animal. **4.** (of the mind) easily producing ideas, inventive. **5.** (of nuclear material) able to become fissile by the capture of neutrons. —**fertility** /fə'tɪlɪtɪ/ *n.* [from French from Latin *fertilis*]

fertility n. an organism's ability to reproduce, as distinct from the rate at which it reproduces (see ◊fecundity). Individuals become infertile (unable to reproduce) when they cannot generate gametes (eggs or sperm) or when their gametes cannot yield a viable ◊embryo after fertilization.

fertility drug any of a range of drugs taken to increase a female's fertility, developed in Sweden in the mid-1950s. They increase the chances of a multiple birth.

fertilization n. in ◊sexual reproduction, the union of two ◊gametes (sex cells, often called egg and sperm) to produce a ◊zygote, which combines the genetic material contributed by each parent. In self-fertilization the male and female gametes come from the same plant; in cross-fertilization they come from different plants. Self-fertilization rarely occurs in animals; usually even ◊hermaphrodite animals cross-fertilize each other.

fertilize /'fɜːtɪlaɪz/ v.t. 1. to make (soil etc.) fertile. 2. to introduce pollen or sperm into (a plant, egg, or female animal) so that seed or young develops. —**fertilization** /-'zeɪʃən/ n.

fertilizer n. a chemical or natural substance added to soil to make it more fertile. Fertilizers may be **organic**, for example farmyard manure, composts, bonemeal, blood, and fishmeal; or **inorganic**, in the form of compounds, mainly of nitrogen, phosphate, and potash, which have been used on a huge scale since 1945. Fertilizers applied externally tend to be applied in excess of plant requirements, and cause pollution by leaching away into lakes and rivers (see ◊eutrophication). For this reason agricultural science is concentrating on the search for other methods of maximizing to healthy plant growth, compensating for the deficiencies of poor or depleted soil, and increasing yields.

Fertö tó /'feətəʊtəʊ/ Hungarian name for the Neusiedler See.

fervent /'fɜːvənt/ adj. ardent, impassioned. —**fervency** n., **fervently** adv. [from Old French from Latin fervēre = boil)]

fervid /'fɜːvɪd/ adj. fervent. —**fervidly** adv. [from Latin]

fervour /'fɜːvə/ n. passion, zeal.

Fès /fez/ or **Fez** former capital of Morocco 808–1062, 1296–1548, and 1662–1912, in a valley N of the Great Atlas mountains, 160 km/100 mi E of Rabat; population (1982) 563,000. Textiles, carpets, and leather are manufactured, and the fez, a brimless hat worn in S and E Mediterranean countries, is traditionally said to have originated here. Kairwan Islamic University dates from 859; the second university was founded in 1961.

fescue n. any grass of the widely distributed genus *Festuca*. Many are used in temperate regions for ornament, lawns, pasture, and fodder. Two common species in W Europe are meadow fescue, up to 80 cm/2.6 ft high, and sheep's fescue, up to 50 cm/1.6 ft high. [from Old French from Latin *festuca* = stalk, straw]

fess n. in heraldry, a horizontal stripe across the middle of a shield, broader than a bar. [from Old French from Latin *fascia* = band]

Fessenden /'fesəndən/ Reginald Aubrey 1866–1932. Canadian physicist who worked in the USA, first for Thomas Edison and then for George Westinghouse. Fessenden patented the modulation of radio waves (transmission of a signal using a carrier wave), an essential technique for voice transmission. At the time of his death, he held 500 patents.

festal /'festəl/ adj. of a feast or festival; joyous. —**festally** adv. [from Old French from Latin]

fester v.t./i. 1. to make or become septic. 2. to cause continuing annoyance. 3. to rot or stagnate. [from Old French from Latin *fistula* = pipe, flute]

festival /'festɪvəl/ n. 1. a day or time of celebration. 2. a cultural event comprising a series of concerts, plays, films, etc., held regularly. [from Old French from Latin]

festive /'festɪv/ adj. of or characteristic of a festival; joyous. —**festively** adv. [from Latin *festum*]

festivity /fe'stɪvɪtɪ/ n. gaiety, festive celebration; (in plural) festive proceedings. [from Old French or Latin]

festoon /fe'stuːn/ n. a chain of flowers, ribbons etc., hung in a curve as a decoration; something arranged similarly. —v.t. to adorn with or form into festoons. [from French from Italian]

Festschrift /'festʃrɪft/ n. a published collection of writings in honour of a scholar. [German = festival writing]

fetal surgery any operation on the fetus to correct a congenital condition (for example, ◊hydrocephalus). Fetal surgery was pioneered in the USA in 1981. It leaves no scar tissue.

fetch /fetʃ/ v.t./i. 1. to go for and bring back. 2. to cause to come, to draw forth; to be sold for (a price). 3. (colloquial) to deal (a blow etc.). 4. (nautical) to arrive at; to sail close-hauled without tacking. —n. 1. an act of fetching. 2. a dodge, a trick. —**fetch up**, (colloquial) to arrive, to stop; to vomit. [Old English]

fetching adj. attractive.

fête /feɪt/ n. an outdoor function with a sale of goods, amusements etc., especially to raise funds for some purpose. —v.t. to honour or entertain lavishly. [French]

fetid /'fetɪd, 'fiːt-/ adj. stinking. [from Latin *fetēre* = stink]

fetish /'fetɪʃ/ n. 1. an object worshipped as magical by primitive peoples. 2. a thing evoking irrational devotion or respect. 3. a thing abnormally stimulating or attracting sexual desire. —**fetishism** n., **fetishist** n. [from French from Portuguese *feitiço* = charm]

fetlock n. the part of the back of a horse's leg above the hoof where a tuft of hair grows. [related to German *fessel* = pastern]

fetter /'fetə/ n. a shackle for holding a prisoner by the ankle; a bond, (in plural) captivity; a restraint. —v.t. to put into fetters; to restrict. [Old English]

fettle n. condition, trim. [Old English = girdle]

fetus /'fiːtəs/ n. or **foetus** a stage in the development of the mammalian ◊embryo. The human embryo is usually termed a fetus after the eighth week of development, when the limbs and external features of the head are recognizable. [from Latin *fetus* = young offspring]

feu /fjuː/ n. in Scotland a perpetual lease at a fixed rent; land so held. —v.t. to grant (land) on feu. [from Old French]

feud¹ /fjuːd/ n. a prolonged mutual hostility, especially between families or groups. —v.i. to conduct a feud. [from Old French from Middle Dutch]

feud² n. a fief. [from Latin *feudum*]

feudal /'fjuːdəl/ adj. of, resembling, or according to the feudal system. —**feudal system**, a medieval European politico-economic system based on the relation of vassal and superior arising from the holding of lands on condition of homage and military service or labour. The feudal system was reinforced by a complex legal system and supported by the Christian church. With the growth of commerce and industry from the 13th century, feudalism gradually gave way to the class system as the dominant form of social ranking. —**feudalism** n., **feudalist** n., **feudalistic** /-'lɪstɪk/ adj. [from Latin *feudalis*]

fever /'fiːvə/ n. 1. an abnormally high body temperature, often with delirium; a disease characterized by this. 2. nervous agitation or excitement. —v.t. to affect with fever or excitement. —**fever pitch**, a state of extreme excitement. [from Old English and Anglo-French from Latin *febris*]

feverfew /'fiːvəfjuː/ n. an aromatic herb *Chrysanthemum parthenium* with feathery leaves, formerly used to reduce fever. [Old English from Latin *febrifuga febris* = fever and *fugare* = put to flight)]

feverish adj. having the symptoms of fever; excited, restless. —**feverishly** adv., **feverishness** n.

few adj. not many. —n. a small number. —**a few**, some, several. **few and far between**, scarce. **a good** or **quite a few**, a fair number (of). **no fewer than**, as many as. —**fewness** n. [Old English]

fey /feɪ/ adj. strange, other-worldly; (Scottish) fated to die soon. —**feyness** n. [Old English]

Feynman /'faɪnmən/ Richard Phillips 1918–1988. US physicist whose work provided the foundations for quantum electrodynamics. For his work on the theory of radiation he was awarded a share of the Nobel Prize for Physics in 1965. As a member of the committee investigating the *Challenger* space-shuttle disaster in 1986, he demonstrated the lethal faults in the rubber seals on the shuttle's booster rocket.

fez n. (plural fezzes) a flat-topped, conical red cap with a tassel worn by men in some Muslim countries. [Turkish, perhaps from *Fez* in Morocco]

Fezzan /fe'zɑːn/ former province of Libya, a desert region, with many oases, and with rock paintings from about 3000 BC. It was captured from Italy in 1942, and placed under French control until 1951, when it became a province of the newly-independent United Kingdom of Libya. It was split into smaller divisions in 1963.

ff in music, abbreviation of fortissimo.

ff. abbreviation of following (pages etc).

fiancé /fiˈɑ̃seɪ/ *n.* a man or (**fiancée**) woman to whom a person is engaged to be married. [French *fiancer* = betroth]

Fianna Fáil /ˈfiənə ˈfɔɪl/ Republic of Ireland political party, founded by the Irish nationalist de Valera in 1926. It has been the governing party in the Republic of Ireland 1932–48, 1951–54, 1957–73, 1977–81, 1982, and 1987– . It aims at the establishment of a united and completely independent all-Ireland republic. [Gaelic = soldiers of destiny]

fiasco /fiˈæskəʊ/ *n.* (*plural* **fiascos**) a ludicrous or humiliating failure. [Italian, = bottle (with unexplained allusion)]

fiat /ˈfaɪæt/ *n.* an authorization; a decree. [Latin = let it be done]

fib *n.* a trivial lie. —*v.i.* (-bb-) to tell a fib. —**fibber** *n.* [perhaps from obsolete *fible-fable* = nonsense]

Fibonacci /fɪbəˈnɑːtʃi/ Leonardo, also known as **Leonardo of Pisa** *c.* 1175–*c.* 1250. Italian mathematician. He published *Liber abaci* in Pisa in 1202, which was instrumental in the introduction of Arabic notation into Europe. From 1960, interest increased in **Fibonacci numbers**, in their simplest form a sequence in which each number is the sum of its two predecessors (1, 1, 2, 3, 5, 8, 13, …). They have unusual characteristics with possible applications in botany, psychology, and astronomy (for example, a more exact correspondence than is given by ◊Bode's law to the distances between the planets and the Sun).

fibre /ˈfaɪbə/ *n.* **1.** any of the threads or filaments forming animal and vegetable tissue and textile substance. **2.** a piece of glass in the form of a thread. **3.** a substance formed of fibres. **4.** character. [from French from Latin *fibra*]

fibreboard *n.* flexible board made of compressed fibres of wood etc.

fibreglass *n.* glass that has been formed into fine fibres, either as long continuous filaments or as a fluffy, short-fibred glass wool. Fibreglass is heat-and fire-resistant and a good electrical insulator. It has applications in the field of fibre optics and as a strengthener for plastics in ◊GRP (glass-reinforced plastics).

fibre optics the branch of physics dealing with the transmission of light and images through glass or plastic fibres known as ◊optical fibres.

fibril /ˈfaɪbrɪl/ *n.* a small fibre.

fibrin *n.* an insoluble blood protein used by the body to stop bleeding. When an injury occurs fibrin is deposited around the wound in the form of a mesh, which dries and hardens, so that bleeding stops. Fibrin is developed in the blood from a soluble protein, fibrinogen.

fibroid /ˈfaɪbrɔɪd/ *adj.* of or like fibrous tissue. —*n.* a fibroid tumour in the uterus.

fibrosis /faɪˈbrəʊsɪs/ *n.* development of excessive fibrous tissue.

fibrositis /faɪbrəˈsaɪtɪs/ *n.* rheumatic inflammation of fibrous tissue.

fibrous /ˈfaɪbrəs/ *adj.* of or like fibre.

fibula /ˈfɪbjʊlə/ *n.* (*plural* **fibulae** /-iː/) **1.** the the rear lower bone in the hind leg of a vertebrate. It is paired and often fused with a smaller front bone, the tibia. **2.** an ancient brooch or clasp. [Latin = brooch]

fiche /fiː/ɕ/ *n.* (*plural* the same) a microfiche.

fickle *adj.* inconstant, changeable, especially in loyalty. —**fickleness** *n.*, **fickly** *adv.* [Old English]

fiction /ˈfɪkʃən/ *n.* **1.** an invented idea, statement, or narrative; literature describing imaginary events and people. In the 20th century the term is applied to imaginative works of narrative prose (such as the novel or the short story), and contrasted with nonfiction (such as history, biography, or works on practical subjects), and with poetry. **2.** a conventionally accepted falsehood. —**fictional** *adj.* [from Old French from Latin]

fictionalize *v.t.* to make into a fictional narrative.

fictitious /fɪkˈtɪʃəs/ *adj.* imagined or made up, not real or genuine. [from Latin]

fictive /ˈfɪktɪv/ *adj.* created or creating by imagination. [from French or Latin]

fiddle *n.* **1.** (*colloquial* or *derogatory*) a stringed instrument played with a bow, especially a violin. **2.** (*slang*) an instance of cheating or fraud. —*v.t./i.* **1.** to play restlessly (*with*), to move aimlessly. **2.** (*slang*) to cheat, to swindle, to falsify,

to get by cheating. **3.** to play (on) the fiddle. —**as fit as a fiddle**, in very good health. **play second fiddle,** to take a subordinate role. [Old English]

fiddle-faddle /ˈfɪdəlfædəl/ *n.* trivial matters. —*v.i.* to fuss, to trifle. —*int.* nonsense.

fiddler *n.* **1.** a player on the fiddle. **2.** (*slang*) a swindler. **3.** a small crab of the genus *Uca*, the male having one large claw held in a position like a violinist's arm.

fiddlesticks interjection meaning nonsense.

fiddling *adj.* petty, trivial.

fiddly *adj.* (*colloquial*) awkward to do or use.

Fidei Defensor /ˈfidɪə diˈfensɔː/ title of 'Defender of the Faith' (still retained by British sovereigns) conferred by Pope Leo X on Henry VIII of England to reward his writing of a treatise against the Protestant Martin Luther.

fidelity /fiˈdelɪtɪ/ *n.* **1.** faithfulness, loyalty. **2.** accuracy; precision in the reproduction of sound. [from French or Latin *fidelis* = faithful]

fidget /ˈfɪdʒɪt/ *v.t./i.* to move or act restlessly or nervously; to be or make uneasy. —*n.* **1.** one who fidgets. **2.** (in *plural*) fidgeting movements. —**fidgety** *adj.* [from obsolete or dialect *fidge* = twitch]

fiduciary /fiˈdjuːʃɪərɪ/ *adj.* of, held, or given in trust; (of a paper currency) depending for its value on public confidence or securities. —*n.* a trustee. [from Latin *fiducia* = trust]

fie /faɪ/ interjection expressing disgust or shame. [from Old French from Latin]

fief /fiːf/ *n.* **1.** land held under a feudal system or in fee. **2.** one's sphere of operation or control. [French]

field[1] /fiːld/ *n.* **1.** an area of open land, especially for pasture or crops; an area rich in some natural product, e. g. a coalfield, oilfield. **2.** a piece of land for a specified purpose, especially an area marked out for a game. **3.** the participants in a contest or sport; all the competitors or all but the one(s) specified; the fielding side in cricket. **4.** an expanse of ice, sea, snow etc. **5.** a place of battle or campaign. **6.** an area or sphere of operation, observation, intellectual activities etc. **7.** the background of a picture, coin, flag etc.; in heraldry, the surface of an escutcheon. **8.** in computing, a part of a record, representing a unit of information. —*attributive* **1.** (of an animal or plant) found in open country, wild. **2.** (of artillery etc.) light and mobile for use on campaign. **3.** carried out or working in the natural environment, not in the laboratory etc. —*v.t./i.* **1.** to act as a fielder in cricket etc.; to stop and return (a ball). **2.** to select (a team or individual) to play in a game. **3.** to deal with (a succession of questions etc.). —**field day** *n.* a military exercise or review, an important or successful occasion. **field events** *n.pl.* athletic sports other than races. **field glasses** *n.pl.* binoculars for outdoor use. **field officer,** an army officer of a rank above a captain and below a general. **field sports,** outdoor sports, especially hunting, shooting, and fishing. **hold the field,** not to be superseded. **take the field,** to begin a campaign. [Old English]

field[2] *n.* in physics, the region of space by which an object exerts a force on another separate object because of certain properties they both possess. For example, there is a force of attraction between any two objects that have mass, where one is in the gravitational field of the other. Other fields of force include ◊electric fields (caused by electric charges) and ◊magnetic fields (caused by magnetic poles), either of which can involve attractive or repulsive forces.

Field Sally 1946– . US film and television actress. She won an Academy Award for *Norma Rae* 1979 and again for *Places in the Heart* 1984. Her other films include *Hooper* 1978, *Absence of Malice* 1981, and *Murphy's Romance* 1985.

fielder *n.* a person who fields in a ball game such as cricket.

fieldfare *n.* a bird *Turdus pilaris* of the thrush family, a winter migrant in Britain, breeding in Scandinavia, N Russia, and Siberia. It has a pale-grey lower back and neck, and a dark tail.

Fielding /ˈfiːldɪŋ/ Henry 1707–1754. English novelist whose narrative power influenced the form and technique of the novel and helped to make it the most popular form of literature in England. In 1742 he parodied Richardson's novel *Pamela* in his *Joseph Andrews*, which was followed by *Jonathan Wild the Great* 1743; his masterpiece *Tom Jones* 1749, which he described as a 'comic epic in prose'; and *Amelia* 1751.

What is commonly called love, namely the desire of satisfying a voracious appetite with a certain quantity of delicate white human flesh.

Henry Fielding
Tom Jones

field marshal the highest rank in many European armies. A British field marshal is equivalent to a US ◊general.

Field of the Cloth of Gold the site between Guînes and Ardres near Calais, France, where a meeting took place between Henry VIII of England and Francis I of France June 1520, remarkable for the lavish clothes worn and tent pavilions erected. Francis hoped to gain England's support in opposing the Holy Roman emperor, Charles V, but failed.

Fields /fiːldz/ Gracie. Stage name of Grace Stansfield 1898–1979. English comedian and singer. Her humorously sentimental films include *Sally in our Alley* 1931 and *Sing as We Go* 1934.

Fields W C. Stage name of William Claude Dukenfield 1879–1946. US actor and screenwriter. His distinctive speech and professed attitudes such as hatred of children and dogs gained him enormous popularity in films such as *David Copperfield* 1935, *My Little Chickadee* (co-written with Mae West) and *The Bank Dick* both 1940, and *Never Give a Sucker an Even Break* 1941.

fieldsman *n.* (*plural* **fieldsmen**) a player (other than the bowler or pitcher) of the side deployed in the field while the opposing players are batting in cricket, baseball etc.

field studies the study of ecology, geography, geology, history, archaeology, and allied subjects, in the natural environment as opposed to the laboratory.

fieldwork *n.* **1.** practical work done outside libraries and laboratories by surveyors, scientists etc. **2.** a temporary fortification. —**fieldworker** *n.*

fiend /fiːnd/ *n.* **1.** an evil spirit, a devil; a very wicked or cruel person. **2.** (*slang*) a devotee or addict. —**fiendish** *adj.*, **fiendishly** *adv.* [Old English]

Fiennes /faɪnz/ Ranulph Twisleton-Wykeham 1944– . British explorer who made the first surface journey around the world's polar circumference between 1979 and 1982. Earlier expeditions included explorations of the White Nile 1969, Jostedalsbre Glacier, Norway, 1970, and the Headless Valley, Canada, 1971. Accounts of his adventures include *A Talent for Trouble* 1970, *Hell on Ice* 1979, and the autobiographical *Living Dangerously* 1987.

fierce *adj.* vehemently aggressive or frightening in temper or action, violent; eager, intense; strong or uncontrolled. —**fiercely** *adv.*, **fierceness** *n.* [from Old French from Latin *ferus* = savage]

fiery /ˈfaɪərɪ/ *adj.* **1.** consisting of fire, flaming; like fire in appearance, bright red; intensely hot. **2.** spirited, passionate, intense. —**fierily** *adv.*, **fieriness** *n.*]

fiesta /fiˈestə/ *n.* a festival, a holiday. [Spanish]

fife /faɪf/ *n.* a small shrill flute used in military music. Originally from Switzerland, it was known as the Swiss pipe and has long been played by military bands. [from German *pfeife* = pipe]

Fife region of E Scotland (formerly the county of Fife), facing the North Sea and Firth of Forth; **area** 1,300 sq km/502 sq mi; **administrative headquarters** Glenrothes; **physical** the only high land is the Lomond Hills, in the NW chief rivers Eden and Leven; **products** potatoes, cereals, electronics, petrochemicals (Mossmorran), light engineering; **population** (1987) 345,000.

fifteen /fɪfˈtiːn/ *adj.* & *n.* **1.** one more than fourteen; the symbol for this (15, xv, XV). **2.** the size etc. denoted by fifteen. **3.** a team of fifteen players, especially in rugby football. —**fifteenth** *adj.* & *n.* [Old English]

Fifteen, the the ◊Jacobite rebellion of 1715, led by the 'Old Pretender' ◊James Edward Stuart and the Earl of Mar, in order to place the former on the English throne. Mar was checked at Sheriffmuir, Scotland, and the revolt collapsed.

fifth *adj.* next after the fourth. —*n.* **1.** one of five equal parts of a thing. **2.** in music an interval or chord spanning five alphabetical notes (e.g. C to G). —**fifthly** *adv.* [Old English]

fifth column a group within a country secretly aiding an enemy attacking from without. The term originated in 1936 during the Spanish Civil War, when Gen Mola boasted that Franco supporters were attacking Madrid with four columns and that they had a 'fifth column' inside the city. **fifth columnist**, a member of this, a traitor.

fifth-generation computer an anticipated new type of computer based on emerging microelectronic technologies. The basis will be very fast computing machinery, with many processors working in parallel made possible by very large-scale integration (◊VLSI) which can put many more circuits onto a ◊silicon chip. Such computers will run advanced 'intelligent' programs. See also ◊computer generations.

fifty /ˈfɪftɪ/ *adj.* & *n.* **1.** five times ten; the symbol for this (50, l, L). **2.** (in *plural*) the numbers, years, or degrees of temperature from 50 to 59. —**fifty-fifty** *adj.* & *adv.* equal, equally. —**fiftieth** *adj.* & *n.* [Old English]

fig[1] *n.* **1.** any tree of the genus *Ficus* of the mulberry family Moraceae, including the many cultivated varieties of *F. carica*, originally from W Asia. They produce two or three crops of fruit a year. Eaten fresh or dried, figs have a high sugar content and laxative properties. **2.** a thing of little value. —**fig leaf** *n.* a device for concealing something, especially the genitals. [from Old French from Latin *ficus*]

fig[2] *n.* dress, equipment; condition. [from obsolete *feague*]

fig. abbreviation of figure.

fight /faɪt/ *v.t./i.* (*past* and *past participle* **fought** /fɔːt/) **1.** to contend or struggle (against) in physical combat or in war; to carry on (a battle). **2.** to contend or struggle in any way (about), to strive *for*; to strive to overcome. **3.** to make *one's way* by fighting or effort. —*n.* **1.** fighting, a battle or combat; a conflict or struggle, a vigorous effort. **2.** the power or inclination to fight. **3.** a boxing match. —**fighting chance**, an opportunity of succeeding by a great effort. **fighting fit**, fit and ready. **fight shy of**, to avoid. [Old English]

fighter *n.* **1.** one who fights; one who does not yield without a struggle. **2.** a fast military aircraft designed for attacking other aircraft.

fighting fish any of a SE Asian genus *Betta* of fishes of the gourami family, in particular *B. splendens*, about 6 cm/2 in long and a popular aquarium fish. It can breathe air, using an accessory breathing organ above the gill, and can live in poorly oxygenated water. The male has large fins and various colours, including shining greens, reds, and blues. The female is yellowish brown with short fins.

figment /ˈfɪgmənt/ *n.* a thing invented or existing only in the imagination. [from Latin *figmentum*]

figuration /fɪgjuˈreɪʃən/ *n.* an act or mode of formation; ornamentation. [from French or Latin]

figurative /ˈfɪgjʊrətɪv, -gə-/ *adj.* **1.** metaphorical, not literal; characterized by figures of speech. **2.** of pictorial or sculptural representation. —**figuratively** *adv.* [from Latin]

figure /ˈfɪgə/ *n.* **1.** external form, bodily shape; a geometrical space enclosed by lines or surfaces. **2.** a person as seen but not identified, or as contemplated mentally; an appearance as giving a certain impression. **3.** a representation of the human form etc.; an image or likeness. **4.** a diagram, an illustration; a decorative pattern; a series of movements forming a single unit in dancing etc.; a succession of notes forming a single idea in music. **5.** the symbol of a number, a numeral (especially 0–9); a value, an amount of money; (in *plural*) arithmetical calculations. —*v.t./i.* **1.** to appear or be mentioned, especially prominently. **2.** to represent in a diagram or picture. **3.** to imagine, to picture mentally. **4.** to embellish with a pattern. **5.** to mark with numbers or prices. **6.** to calculate, to do arithmetic. **7.** to be a symbol of. **8.** (*US*) to understand, to consider; (*colloquial*) to be likely or understandable. —**figure head** *n.* a carved image at a ship's prow; a person nominally at the head but with no real power. **figure out**, to work out by arithmetic or logic. [from Old French from Latin *figura* (*fingere* = fashion)]

figure of speech a poetic, imaginative, or ornamental expression used for purposes of comparison, emphasis, or stylistic effect; usually one of a list of such forms dating from discussions of literary and rhetorical style in Greece in the 5th century BC. These figures include euphemism, hyperbole, metaphor, metonymy, onomatopoeia, oxymoron, personification, the pun, simile, and synecdoche.

figurine /ˈfɪgjʊrɪn/ *n.* a statuette. [French from Italian]

figwort *n.* any Old World plant of the genus *Scrophularia* of the figwort family, which also includes foxgloves and snapdragons. Members of the genus have square stems, opposite leaves, and open two-lipped flowers in a cluster at the top of the stem.

Fiji Republic of; country comprising a group of 332 islands in the SW Pacific, about 100 of which are inhabited; **area** 18,333 sq km/7,078 sq mi; **capital** Suva; **physical** comprises 844 Melanesian and Polynesian islands and islets (about 110 inhabited), the largest being Viti Levu (10,429 sq km/4,028 sq mi) and Vanua Levu (5,550 sq km/ 2,146 sq mi); mountainous, volcanic, with tropical rainforest and grasslands; **head of state** Ratu Sir Penaia Ganilau from 1987; **head of government** Ratu Sir Kamisese Mara from 1987; **political system** democratic republic; **exports** sugar, coconut oil, ginger, timber, canned fish; tourism is important; **population** (1989 est) 758,000 (46% Fijian, holding 80% of the land communally, and 49% Indian, introduced in the 19th century to work the sugar crop); **language** English (official), Fijian, Hindi; **recent history** independence achieved from Britain in 1970; Ratu Sir Kamisese Mara elected as first prime minister. In 1987 a general election brought to power an Indian-dominated coalition led by Dr Timoci Bavadra, but two military coups followed in the same year, and Fiji was declared a republic and removed from the Commonwealth, and the constitution was suspended. In Dec civilian government was restored, with Rambuka retaining control of security as minister for home affairs.

filament /'fɪləmənt/ *n.* a threadlike strand or fibre; the conducting wire or thread in an electric bulb (now usually of tungsten). —**filamentary** /-'mentərɪ/ *adj.* [from French or Latin *filum* = thread]

filbert /'fɪlbət/ *n.* a nut of the cultivated hazel; the tree bearing it *Corylus maxima*. [from Anglo-French *philbert*, the nut being ripe about St Philibert's day (20 Aug.)]

filch *v.t.* to pilfer, to steal.

Filchner /'fɪlʃnə/ Wilhelm 1877–1957. German explorer who travelled extensively in Central Asia, but is remembered for his expedition into the Weddell Sea of Antarctica, where his ship became icebound for a whole winter. He landed a party and built a hut on the floating ice shelf, which eventually broke up and floated northwards.

file[1] *n.* **1.** a folder or box etc. for holding loose papers; its contents. **2.** a collection of (usually related) data stored under one reference in a computer. **3.** a line of people or things one behind the other. —*v.t./i.* **1.** to place in a file or among records; to submit (an application for divorce, a petition, etc.); (of a reporter) to send (a story etc.) to a newspaper. **2.** to walk in a line. [from French from Latin *filum* = thread]

file[2] *n.* a tool with a roughened steel surface for smoothing or shaping wood etc. —*v.t.* to smooth or shape with a file. [Old English]

file transfer in computing, the transmission of a file (data stored on disc, for example) from one machine to another. Both machines must be physically linked (for example, by a telephone line) and both must be running appropriate communications software.

filial /'fɪlɪəl/ *adj.* of or due from a son or daughter. —**filially** *adv.* [from Old French or Latin (*filius* = son, *filia* = daughter)]

filibuster /'fɪlɪbʌstə/ *n.* **1.** a person engaging in unauthorized warfare against a foreign state. **2.** one who obstructs progress in a legislative assembly; such obstruction. —*v.i.* to act as a filibuster. [ultimately from Dutch *vrijbuiter* (as *freebooter*)]

filigree /'fɪlɪgri/ *n.* fine ornamental work in gold etc. wire; similar delicate work. —**filigreed** *adj.* [from French *filigrane* from Italian (Latin *filum* = thread, *granum* = seed)]

filing *n.* (usually in *plural*) a particle rubbed off by a file.

Filipino /fɪlɪ'piːnəʊ/ *n.* (*plural* Filipinos) a native of the Philippine Islands. —*adj.* of Filipinos or the Philippine Islands. [Spanish = Philippine]

fill *v.t./i.* **1.** to make or become full (*with*); to occupy completely, to spread over or through; to block up (a cavity or hole); to drill and put a filling into (a decayed tooth); (of a sail) to be distended by the wind. **2.** to appoint a person to hold (a vacant post); to hold or discharge the duties of (an office etc.); to carry out or supply (an order, commission etc.); to occupy (vacant time). —*n.* as much as one wants or can bear of food etc.; enough to fill a thing. —**fill the bill**, to be suitable or adequate. **fill in**, to add information to complete (a form or document etc.); to complete (a drawing etc.) within the outline; to fill (a hole etc.) completely; to act as a substitute (*for*); to spend (time) in a temporary activity; (*colloquial*) to give the required information to. **fill out**, to enlarge to the required size; to become enlarged or plump. **fill up**, to make or become completely full; to fill in (a document); to fill the petrol tank of (a car etc.). [Old English]

filler *n.* material used to fill a cavity or increase the bulk; an item filling space in a newspaper etc.

fillet /'fɪlɪt/ *n.* **1.** a boneless piece of meat or fish. **2.** a headband, a hair ribbon; a narrow strip or ridge. **3.** in architecture, a narrow flat band between mouldings. —*v.t.* **1.** to remove the bones from; to divide (a fish etc.) into fillets. **2.** to bind or provide with a fillet or fillets. [from Old French from Latin *filum* = thread]

filling *n.* **1.** the material used to fill a cavity in a tooth. **2.** the material between the bread in a sandwich. —**filling station** *n.* an establishment selling petrol etc. to motorists.

fillip /'fɪlɪp/ *n.* **1.** a stimulus, an incentive. **2.** a flick with the finger or thumb. —*v.t.* to give a fillip to.

Fillmore /'fɪlmɔː/ Millard 1800–1874. the 13th president of the USA 1850–53, a Whig. Born into a poor farming family in New Cayuga County, New York State, he was Zachary Taylor's vice president from 1849, and succeeded him on Taylor's death, July 9 1850. Fillmore supported a compromise on slavery in 1850 to reconcile North and South.

filly /'fɪlɪ/ *n.* **1.** a young female horse. **2.** (*slang*) a lively young woman. [from Old Norse]

film *n.* **1.** a thin coating or covering layer. **2.** a photographic film. **3.** a motion picture; a story represented by this; (in *plural*) the cinema industry. **4.** a slight veil or haze etc.; a dimness or morbid growth affecting the eyes. —*v.t.* **1.** to make a film or motion picture of (a scene, story etc.). **2.** to cover or become covered with a film. —**film star**, a celebrated actor or actress in films. **film strip** *n.* a series of transparencies in a strip for projection. [Old English *filmen* = membrane]

film, art of see ◊cinema.

film noir (French 'dark film') a term originally used by French critics to describe any film characterized by pessimism, cynicism, and a dark, sombre tone. It has been used to describe black and white Hollywood films of the 1940s and 1950s that portrayed the seedy side of life.

film, photographic a strip of transparent material (usually cellulose acetate) coated with a light-sensitive emulsion, used in cameras to take pictures. The emulsion contains a mixture of light-sensitive silver halide salts (for example, bromide or iodide) in gelatin. Films differ in their sensitivities to light, this being indicated by their speeds. When the emulsion is exposed to light, the silver salts are invisibly altered, giving a latent image, which is then made visible by the process of ◊developing. Colour film consists of several layers of emulsion, each of which records a different colour in the light falling on it.

filmy *adj.* thin and transparent. —**filmily** *adv.*, **filminess** *n.*

filter *n.* a device for removing impurities from a liquid or gas passed through it; a screen for absorbing or modifying light, X-rays etc.; a device for suppressing electrical or sound waves of frequencies not required. **2.** an arrangement for filtering traffic. —*v.t./i.* **1.** to pass or cause to pass through a filter; to make a way gradually (*through, into* etc.), to leak out. **2.** (of traffic) to be allowed to pass in a certain direction while other traffic is held up (especially at traffic lights). —**filter paper** *n.* a porous paper for filtering. **filter tip** *n.* a cigarette with a filter for purifying smoke; the filter itself. [from French from Latin from Germanic (as *felt*[1], the earliest filters being of felt)]

filth *n.* repugnant or extreme dirt; obscenity. [Old English]

filthy *adj.* **1.** extremely or disgustingly dirty; obscene. **2.** (*colloquial*, of the weather) very unpleasant. —*adv.* in a filthy way; (*colloquial*) extremely. —**filthily** *adv.*, **filthiness** *n.*

filtrate /'fɪltreɪt/ *v.t.* to filter. —*n.* a filtered liquid. —**filtration** /-'treɪʃən/ *n.*

filtration *n.* a technique in which suspended solid particles in a fluid are removed by passing the mixture through a porous barrier, usually paper or cloth. The particles are retained by the paper or cloth to form a residue and the fluid passes through to make up the filtrate. Soot may be filtered from air, and suspended solids may be filtered from water.

fin *n.* **1.** a thin, flat organ for propelling and steering, growing on fish and cetaceans at various parts of the body; an underwater swimmer's flipper. **2.** a small projection on an aircraft or rocket for ensuring stability; any similar projection or attachment. [Old English]

finagle /fɪˈneɪgəl/ *v.t./i.* (*colloquial*) to act or obtain dishonestly. [from dialect *fainaigue* = cheat]

final /ˈfaɪnəl/ *adj.* situated at the end, coming last; conclusive, decisive. —*n.* **1.** the last or deciding heat or game in sports etc. **2.** the last edition of a day's newspaper. **3.** (usually in *plural*) a final examination. —**final cause,** an ultimate purpose. **final clause,** in grammar, a clause expressing purpose. —**finally** *adv.* [from Old French or Latin *finis* = end, goal]

finale /fɪˈnɑːlɪ/ *n.* the last movement or section of a piece of music or drama etc. [Italian]

finalist /ˈfaɪnəlɪst/ *n.* a competitor in the final of a competition etc.

finality /faɪˈnælɪtɪ/ *n.* the quality or fact of being final. [from French or Latin]

finalize /ˈfaɪnəlaɪz/ *v.t.* to put into a final form, to complete. —**finalization** /-ˈzeɪʃən/ *n.*

final solution a euphemism used by the Nazis to describe the extermination of Jews and other opponents of the regime during World War II. See ◊Holocaust [German *Endlosung der Judenfrage*) = final solution to the Jewish question]

finance /faɪˈnæns, fɪ-, ˈfaɪˈ/ *n.* **1.** the management of money; support in money for an enterprise. **2.** (in *plural*) money resources. —*v.t.* to provide the capital for (a person or enterprise). —**finance company** *or* **house,** a company concerned mainly with providing money for hire-purchase transactions. [from Old French *finer* = settle debt]

financial /faɪˈnænʃəl, fɪ-/ *adj.* of finance. —**financial year,** a year reckoned from 1 or 6 April for taxing and accounting. —**financially** *adv.*

Financial Times Index (FT Index) an indicator measuring the daily movement of 30 major industrial share prices on the London Stock Exchange (1935 = 100), issued by the UK *Financial Times* newspaper. Other FT indices cover government securities, fixed-interest securities, goldmine shares, and Stock Exchange activity.

financier /faɪˈnænsɪə, fɪ-/ *n.* a person engaged in large-scale finance. [French]

finch *n.* a bird of the family Fringillidae, in the order Passeriformes. They are seed-eaters with stout conical beaks, and include chaffinches, sparrows, and canaries.

Finch /fɪntʃ/ Peter 1916–1977. Australian-born English cinema actor who began his career in Australia before coming to London in 1949 to start on an international career with roles such as those in *A Town Like Alice* 1956; *The Trials of Oscar Wilde* 1960; *Sunday, Bloody Sunday* 1971; and *Network* 1976.

find /faɪnd/ *v.t.* (*past* and *past participle* **found** /faʊnd/) **1.** to discover or get possession of by chance or effort; to become aware of. **2.** to obtain, to succeed in obtaining. **3.** to seek out and obtain. **4.** to ascertain by inquiry, calculation etc. **5.** to perceive or experience; to regard or discover from experience. **6.** (of a jury, judge etc.) to decide and declare. **7.** to reach by a natural process. —*n.* a discovery; a thing or person discovered, especially when of value. —**find oneself,** to discover what one is, to discover one's vocation. **find one's feet,** to be able to walk; to develop one's independent ability. **find out,** to discover or detect (a wrongdoer etc.); to get information (about). [Old English]

finder *n.* **1.** one who finds. **2.** a small telescope attached to a large one to locate an object. **3.** a viewfinder.

finding *n.* (often in *plural*) a conclusion reached by an inquiry etc.

fine[1] *adj.* **1.** of high quality; excellent, of notable merit (also *ironically*); pure, refined; (of gold or silver) containing a specified proportion of pure metal. **2.** of handsome appearance or size, beautiful, imposing; in good health. **3.** (of the weather) bright; free from rain, fog etc. **4.** small, thin, or sharp of its kind; in small particles. **5.** (of speech) tritely complimentary, euphemistic. **6.** smart, showy, ornate. **7.**

fastidious, affectedly refined. **8.** (in cricket) behind and at a narrow angle to the wicket. —*n.* **1.** fine weather. **2.** (in *plural*) small particles in mining, milling etc. —*adv.* finely; (*colloquial*) very well. —*v.t./i.* (often with *away, down, off*) to make or become pure, clear, thinner etc. —**cut** *or* **run it fine,** to allow very little margin of time etc. **fine arts,** those appealing to the mind or the sense of beauty, especially painting, sculpture, and architecture. **finespun** *adj.* delicate; (of a theory) too subtle, unpractical. **fine-tooth comb,** a comb with narrow close-set teeth (*go over with a fine-tooth comb,* to search thoroughly). **not to put too fine a point on it,** to speak bluntly. —**finely** *adv.,* **fineness** *n.* [from Old French from Latin *finire* = finish]

fine[2] *n.* a sum of money (to be) paid as a penalty. —*v.t.* to punish by a fine. —**in fine,** in sum. [from Old French from Latin *finis* = end (in medieval times = sum paid on settling lawsuit)]

Fine Gael /ˈfɪnə ˈgeɪl/ Republic of Ireland political party founded by W J ◊Cosgrave and led by Alan Dukes from 1987. It is socially liberal but fiscally conservative. [Gaelic = 'United Ireland']

finery /ˈfaɪnərɪ/ *n.* showy dress or decoration.

fines herbes /fiːnz ˈeəb/ mixed herbs used in cooking. [French = fine herbs]

finesse /fɪˈnes/ *n.* **1.** refinement; subtle or delicate manipulation; artful tact in handling a difficulty. **2.** (in card-games) an attempt to win a trick by playing a card that is not the highest held. —*v.t./i.* **1.** to achieve by finesse. **2.** (in card-games) to make a finesse (with). [French]

finger /ˈfɪŋgə/ *n.* **1.** any of the five terminal members of the hand, any of these excluding the thumb. **2.** the part of a glove for a finger. **3.** a finger-like object or structure. **4.** a measure of liquor in a glass, based on the breadth of a finger. —*v.t.* to feel or turn about with the fingers; to play (music or an instrument) with the fingers. —**fingerboard** *n.* a flat strip at the top end of a stringed instrument, against which the strings are pressed to determine notes. **fingerbowl** *n.* a small bowl for rinsing the fingers during a meal. **fingermark** *n.* a mark left on a surface by a finger. **fingernail** *n.* the nail at the tip of a finger. **fingerplate** *n.* a plate fixed to a door above the handle to prevent finger-marks. **fingerstall** *n.* a sheath to cover an injured finger. **get** *or* **pull one's finger out,** (*slang*) to cease prevaricating and start to act. **put one's finger on,** to locate or identify exactly. [Old English]

fingering *n.* the manner or technique of using the fingers, especially to play an instrument; an indication of this in a musical score.

fingerprint *n.* an impression made on a surface by the fleshy pad at the end of a finger, especially as a means of identification. Fingerprinting was first used as a means of identifying crime suspects in India, and was adopted by the English police 1901; it is now widely employed in police and security work.

fingertip *n.* the tip of a finger. —**have at one's fingertips,** to be thoroughly familiar with (a subject etc.).

finial /ˈfɪnɪəl/ *n.* an ornamental top to a gable, canopy etc. [from Anglo-French from Latin *finis* = end]

finicky /ˈfɪnɪkɪ/ *adj.* (also **finical, finicking**) **1.** excessively detailed, fiddly. **2.** over-particular, fastidious. [probably slang extension of *fine*]

finis /ˈfɪnɪs, ˈfiːn-/ *n.* the end, especially of a book. [Latin]

finish /ˈfɪnɪʃ/ *v.t./i.* (often with *off* or *up*) to bring or come to an end, to come to the end of; to complete the manufacture of (cloth etc.) by surface treatment. —*n.* **1.** the end, the last stage; the point at which a race etc. ends. **2.** a method, material, or texture used for surface treatment of wood, cloth etc. —**finishing school,** a private school where girls are prepared for entry into fashionable society. **finish off,** to end, (*colloquial*) to kill. **finish with,** to have no more to do with. [from Old French from Latin *finis* = end]

finite /ˈfaɪnaɪt/ *adj.* limited, not infinite; (of a part of the verb) having a specific number and person. [from Latin *finire* = end, set limit to]

Finland /ˈfɪnlənd/ Republic of; country in Scandinavia, bounded N by Norway, E by the USSR, S and W by the Baltic Sea, and NW by Sweden; **area** 338,145 sq km/ 130,608 sq mi; **capital** Helsinki; **physical** most of the country is forest, with low hills and about 60,000 lakes; one-third is within the Arctic Circle; archipelago in S; **head of state** Mauno Koivisto from 1982; **head of government**

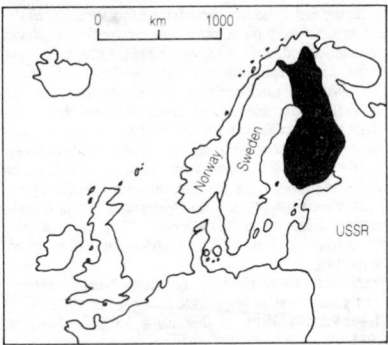

Finland

Esko Aho from 1991; **political system** democratic republic; **exports** metal, chemical and engineering products (ice-breakers and oil rigs), paper, timber, textiles, fine ceramics, glass, furniture; **population** (1989 est) 4,990,00; **language** Finnish 93%, Swedish 6% (both official), small Lapp- and Russian-speaking minorities **recent history** independence achieved from Russia in 1917, but defeated by USSR in Winter War, 1939 and later allowed Germany to station troops in Finland to attack USSR; USSR bombed Finland. In 1944 Finland a separate armistice was concluded with USSR. Finland joined the UN and the Nordic Council in 1955, signed treaties of trade with the EEC in 1973, and the USSR in 1977, and joined the Council of Europe in 1989.

Finland, Gulf of the eastern arm of the ◊Baltic Sea, separating Finland from Estonia.

Finn /fɪn/ n. a native of Finland. [Old English]

finnan /'fɪnən/ n. or **finnan haddock** haddock cured with the smoke of green wood, turf, or peat. [from *Findhorn* in Scotland]

Finney /'fɪni/ Albert 1936– . English stage and film actor, who created the title roles in Keith Waterhouse's stage play *Billy Liar* 1960 and John Osborne's *Luther* 1961, and was artistic director of the Royal Court Theatre from 1972 to 1975. His films include *Saturday Night and Sunday Morning* 1960, *Tom Jones* 1963, *Murder on the Orient Express* 1974, and *The Dresser* 1984.

Finnic /'fɪnɪk/ adj. 1. of the group of peoples allied to the Finns. 2. of the group of languages allied to Finnish.

Finnish /'fɪnɪʃ/ adj. of the Finns or their language. —n. the language of Finland.

Finnish language a language of the Finno-Ugric family, the national language of Finland, closely related to the neighbouring Estonian, Livonian, Karelian, and Ingrian languages. At the beginning of the 19th century Finnish had no official status, since Swedish was the language of education, government, and literature in Finland. The publication of the *Kalevala*, a national epic poem, in 1835, was influential in arousing Finnish national and linguistic feeling.

Finno-Ugric /fɪnəu'u:grɪk/ n. a group or family of more than 20 languages spoken by some 22 million people in scattered communities from Norway in the W to Siberia in the E and to the Carpathian mountains in the S. Members of the family include Finnish, Lapp, and Hungarian.

finsen unit a unit (symbol FU) for measuring the intensity of ultraviolet (UV) light; for instance, UV light of 2.5 FUs causes sunburn in 15 minutes. It is named after Niels Ryberg Finsen (1860—1904), the Danish physician, who first used ultraviolet light treatment for skin diseases.

fiord /fjɔ:d/ n. or **fjord** a long narrow inlet of the sea between high cliffs. Fiords are found in Norway and in other countries. **Fiordland** is the deeply indented SW coast of South Island, New Zealand; one of the most beautiful inlets is Milford Sound. [Norwegian from Old Norse]

fipple /'fɪpəl/ n. the plug at the mouth-end of a wind instrument. —**fipple flute**, a flute played by blowing endwise, e. g. a recorder. [compare Icelandic *flipi* = lip of horse]

fir n. an evergreen coniferous tree of the genus *Abies* in the pine family Pinaceae, with needles placed singly on the shoots. The true firs include the balsam fir of N North America and the Eurasian silver fir *Abies alba*. Douglas firs of the genus *Pseudotsuga* are native to W North America and the Far East; its wood. —**fir-cone** n. the fruit of a

fir. **noble fir,** a common fir *Abies procera* of fine and lofty appearance. [probably from Old Norse]

Firdausi /fɪə'dausi/ Abdul Qasim Mansur c. 935–c. 1020. Persian poet, whose epic *Shahnama/The Book of Kings* relates the history of Persia in 60,000 verses. In one episode it tells how Rustum unwittingly killed his son Sohrab in battle; this was used by Matthew ◊Arnold in his poem 'Sohrab and Rustum'.

fire n. **1.** the state or process of combustion causing heat and light, the active principle operative in this, flame or incandescence. **2.** destructive burning. **3.** burning fuel in a grate or furnace; an ◊electric or ◊gas fire. **4.** the firing of guns. **5.** angry or excited feeling, enthusiasm, vivacity. **6.** burning heat, fever. —v.t./i. **1.** to send (a missile) from a gun etc.; to detonate. **2.** to deliver or utter in rapid succession. **3.** to dismiss (an employee) from a job. **4.** to set fire to with the intention of destroying. **5.** to catch fire; (of an internal-combustion engine) to undergo ignition. **6.** to supply (a furnace etc.) with fuel. **7.** to stimulate (the imagination); to fill with enthusiasm. **8.** to bake or dry (pottery, bricks etc.). **9.** to become heated or excited. **10.** to cause to glow, to redden. —**catch fire,** to ignite, to start to burn. **fire alarm,** a device giving warning of a fire. **fireball** n. a large meteor; a ball of flame from a nuclear explosion; an energetic person. **firebomb** n. an incendiary bomb. **firebreak** n. an obstacle to the spread of fire in a forest etc. **firebrick** n. a fireproof brick used in a grate. **fire brigade,** an organized body of men trained and employed to extinguish fires. **fire-drill** n. a rehearsal of the procedure to be used in case of fire. **fire-eater** n. a conjuror who appears to swallow fire; a quarrelsome person. **fire engine,** a vehicle carrying the equipment for fighting large fires. **fire escape,** an emergency staircase or apparatus for escape from a building on fire. **fireguard** n. a protective screen or grid placed in front of a fire. **fireirons** n.pl. the tongs, poker, and shovel for tending a domestic fire. **firelighter** n. a piece of inflammable material used to help start a fire in a grate. **firepower** n. the destructive capacity of guns etc. **fire-practice** n. fire-drill. **fire-raising** n. arson. **fire station,** the headquarters of a fire-brigade. **firestorm** n. a high wind or storm following a fire caused by bombs. **firetrap** n. a building without proper provision for escape in case of fire. **firewatcher** n. a person keeping watch for fires, especially those caused by bombs. **firewater** n. (colloquial) strong alcoholic liquor. **on fire,** burning; excited. **open fire,** to start firing guns etc. **set fire to, set on fire,** to cause to burn or ignite. **set the world on fire,** to do something remarkable or sensational. **under fire,** being fired on (by the enemy etc.); being rigorously criticized or questioned. —**firer** n. [Old English]

firearm n. (usually in *plural*) a weapon from which projectiles are discharged by the combustion of an explosive. Firearms are generally divided into two main sections: ◊artillery (ordnance or cannon), with a bore greater than 2.54 cm/1 in, and ◊small arms, with a bore of less than 2.54 cm/1 in. Although gunpowder was known in Europe 60 years previously, the invention of guns dates from 1300–25, and is attributed to Berthold Schwartz, a German monk.

firebox n. the fuel chamber of a steam engine or boiler.

firebrand n. **1.** a piece of burning wood. **2.** a person who causes trouble.

fire clay a ◊clay with refractory characteristics (resistant to high temperatures), and hence suitable for making firebricks to line furnaces. Its chemical composition consists of a high percentage of silicon and aluminium oxides, and a low percentage of the oxides of sodium, potassium, iron, and calcium.

firecracker n. (US) an explosive firework.

firedamp n. a miners' name for a gas that occurs in coal mines and is explosive when mixed with air in certain proportions. It consists chiefly of methane (CH_4, natural gas or marsh gas) but always contains small quantities of other gases, such as nitrogen, carbon dioxide, and hydrogen, and sometimes ethane and carbon monoxide.

fire-danger rating unit an index used by the UK Forestry Commission to indicate the probability of a forest fire: 0 means a fire is improbable, 100 shows a serious fire hazard.

firedog n. an andiron.

fire-extinguisher *n.* a device for putting out a fire. Many domestic extinguishers contain liquid carbon dioxide under pressure. When the handle is pressed, carbon dioxide is released as a gas that blankets the burning material and prevents oxygen reaching it. Dry extinguishers spray powder, which then releases carbon dioxide gas. Wet extinguishers are often of the soda-acid type; when activated, sulphuric acid mixes with sodium bicarbonate, producing carbon dioxide. The gas pressure forces the solution out of a nozzle, and a foaming agent may be added to produce foam.

firefly *n.* a winged nocturnal beetle which emits light through the process of ◊bioluminescence. There are about 2,000 species.

firelight *n.* light from the fire in a fireplace.

fireman *n.* (*plural* -**men**) 1. a member of a fire brigade. 2. one who tends the furnace of a steam engine fire.

Firenze /fi'rentseɪ/ Italian form of ◊Florence.

fireplace *n.* an open recess for a domestic fire, at the base of a chimney; its surrounding structure.

fireproof *adj.* able to resist fire or great heat. —*v.t.* to make fireproof.

fire protection methods available for fighting fires. In the UK, a public fire-fighting service is maintained by local authorities, and similar services operate in other countries. Industrial and commercial buildings are often protected by an automatic sprinkler system: heat or smoke opens the sprinkler heads on a network of water pipes and immediately sprays the seat of the fire. In certain circumstances water is ineffective and may be dangerous; for example, for oil and petrol storage-tank fires, foam systems are used; for industrial plants containing flammable vapours, carbon dioxide is used; where electricity is involved, vaporizing liquids create a nonflammable barrier; and for some chemicals only various dry powders can be used.

fireside *n.* the area round a fireplace; one's home or home-life.

firewood *n.* wood for use as fuel.

firework *n.* 1. a pyrotechnic device, originating in China, for producing a display of coloured sparks and accompanying noises by burning chemicals. A firework consists of a container, usually cylindrical in shape and of rolled paper, enclosing a mixture capable of burning independently of the oxygen in the air. One of the ingredients holds a separate supply of oxygen that is readily given up to the other combustible ingredients. 2. (in *plural*) an outburst of passion, especially anger.

firing *n.* 1. the discharge of guns. 2. fuel. —**firing line**, the front line in a battle, the leading part in an activity etc.

firing-squad *n.* a group that fires the salute at a military funeral or shoots a condemned person.

firm[1] *adj.* solid, stable, steady, not fluctuating; resolute, determined; not easily shaken; (of an offer etc.) not liable to cancellation after acceptance. —*adv.* firmly. —*v.t./i.* to become or cause to become firm or secure. —**firmly** *adv.* [from Old French from Latin *firmus*]

firm[2] *n.* a business concern or its members. [earlier = signature, from Spanish and Italian from Latin *firmare* = ratify]

firmament /'fɜ:məmənt/ *n.* the sky regarded as a vault or arch. [from Old French from Latin]

firmware *n.* a computer program held permanently in the machine in ◊ROM (read-only memory) chips, as opposed to one that is read in from external memory as it is needed.

first *adj.* 1. foremost in time, order, or importance. 2. most willing or likely. 3. basic, evident. —*n.* 1. the person or thing that is first; the first day of a month; a first occurrence of something notable. 2. first-class honours in a university degree. —*adv.* 1. before anyone or anything else; before someone or something else. 2. for the first time. 3. in preference. —**at first**, at the beginning. **at first hand**, directly, from the original source. **first aid**, help given to the injured until medical treatment is available. **first blood**, the first success in a contest. **first-born** *adj.* eldest; (*n.*) the eldest child. **first class**, the best group or category; the best accommodation in a train, ship etc.; the class of mail to be most quickly delivered; the highest category of achievement in an examination. **first-class** *adj. & adv.* of or by the first class; excellent. **first-day cover**, an envelope with stamps postmarked on the first day of issue. **first finger**, that next to the thumb. **first-foot** *n.* (*Scottish*) the first person to cross the threshold in the New Year; (*v.i.*)

to be the first to do this. **first fruit**, (usually in *plural*) the first agricultural produce of the season; the first results of work etc. **First Lady**, (*US*) the wife of the President. **first light**, dawn. **first night**, the first public performance of a play etc. **first offender**, one against whom no previous conviction is recorded. **first officer**, the mate on a merchant ship. **first past the post**, winning an election by having most votes though not necessarily an absolute majority. **first-rate** *adj. & adv.* excellent; (*colloquial*) very well. **in the first place**, as the first consideration. [Old English]

First Fleet the 11 ships that transported the first white settlers from Britain to Australia. They set sail from Portsmouth in May 1787 and arrived at Sydney Cove in Jan 1788.

firsthand *adj. & adv.* from the original source, direct.

firstly *adv.* first, to begin with.

First World War another name for ◊World War I, 1914–18.

firth *n.* a narrow inlet of sea; an estuary. [from Old Norse]

fiscal /'fɪskəl/ *adj.* of the public revenue. —*n.* a legal official in some countries; (*Scottish*) a procurator fiscal. [from French or Latin *fiscus* = treasury]

fiscal policy that part of government policy devoted to achieving the desired level of revenue, notably through taxation, and deciding the priorities and purposes governing expenditure.

fiscal year the financial year, which does not necessarily coincide with the calendar year. In the UK, the fiscal year runs from 6 Apr in one year to 5 Apr in the following year. In the USA, the fiscal year runs from 1 July to 30 June.

Fischer /'fɪʃə/ Bobby (Robert James) 1943– . US chess champion. In 1958, after proving himself in international competition, he became the youngest grand master in history. He was the author of *Games of Chess* 1959, and was also celebrated for his unorthodox psychological tactics. He won the world title from Boris Spassky in Reykjavik, Iceland, in 1972.

Fischer Emil Hermann 1852–1919. German chemist who produced synthetic sugars and from these various enzymes. His descriptions of the chemistry of the carbohydrates and peptides laid the foundations for the science of biochemistry. He was awarded a Nobel Prize in 1902.

Fischer Hans 1881–1945. German chemist awarded a Nobel prize in 1930 for his discovery of haemoglobin in blood.

Fischer-Dieskau /'fɪʃə'di:skaʊ/ Dietrich 1925– . German baritone, renowned for his interpretation of Franz Schubert's songs.

fish[1] *n.* (*plural* usually the same) 1. a vertebrate cold-blooded animal with gills and fins living wholly in water; any animal living in water, e. g. a cuttlefish, a jellyfish. 2. the flesh of fish as food. 3. (*colloquial*) a person. 4. (in *plural*) **the Fish** or **Fishes**, the constellation or sign of the zodiac Pisces. —*v.t./i.* 1. to try to catch fish (in). 2. to search (for) in water or by reaching into something; (*colloquial*) to bring *out* thus. 3. to seek *for* (compliments, information etc.) by hinting or indirect questioning. —**fish cake**, a small fried cake of shredded fish and mashed potato. **fish-eye lens**, a wide-angled lens with a distorting effect. **fish finger**, a small oblong piece of fish in batter or bread-crumbs. **fish-hook** *n.* a barbed hook for catching fish. **fish-kettle** *n.* an oval pan for boiling fish. **fish-meal** *n.* ground dried fish as a fertilizer etc. **fishnet** *adj.* (of a fabric) made with an open mesh. **fish out of water**, a person not in his element. **fishtail** *n.* a thing shaped like a fish's tail. **other fish to fry**, more important things to do. [Old English]

fish[2] *n.* a piece of wood or iron etc. to strengthen a mast, beam etc. —*v.t.* to mend or strengthen with a fish. —**fishplate** *n.* a flat plate of iron etc. connecting railway rails. [from French *ficher* fix from Latin *figere*]

fisher *n.* 1. a fishing animal. 2. (*archaic*) a fisherman.

Fisher /'fɪʃə/ Andrew 1862–1928. Australian Labor politician. He was born in Scotland, and went to Australia in 1885. In 1901 he entered the Australian parliament. He was prime minister 1908–09, 1910–13, and 1914–15, and Australian high commissioner to the UK 1916–21.

Fisher John, St *c.*1469–1535. English bishop, created bishop of Rochester 1504. He was an enthusiastic supporter of the revival in the study of Greek, and a friend of the humanists Thomas More and Desiderius Erasmus. In 1535 he was tried on a charge of denying the royal supremacy of Henry VIII and beheaded.

Fisher John Fisher, bishop of Rochester, was beheaded in 1535 for denying the royal supremacy of Henry VIII.

Fisher Ronald Aylmer 1890–1962. English statistician and geneticist, who modernized Charles Darwin's theory of evolution, thus securing the key biological concept of genetic change by natural selection. Fisher developed several new statistical techniques and, applying his methods to genetics, published *The Genetical Theory of Natural Selection* in 1930.

fishery *n*. 1. a place where fish are caught. 2. the business of fishing.

fish farming or **aquaculture** raising fish under controlled conditions in tanks and ponds, sometimes in offshore pens. It has been practised for centuries in the Far East, where Japan alone produces some 100,000 tonnes of fish a year. In the 1980s one-tenth of the world's consumption of fish was farmed, notably trout, Atlantic salmon, turbot, eel, mussels, and oysters.

fishing *n*. the sport of trying to catch fish. —**fishing-line, -rod** *ns*. a line and rod with a fish-hook, used in this.

fishing and fisheries fisheries can be classified by (1) type of water: freshwater (lake, river, pond); marine (inshore, midwater, deep sea); (2) catch: for example salmon fishing, (3) fishing method: diving, stunning or poisoning, harpooning, trawling, drifting.

marine fishing The greatest proportion of the world's catch comes from the oceans. The primary production area is the photic zone, the relatively thin surface layer (50 m/164 ft) of water that can be penetrated by light, allowing photosynthesis by plant ◊plankton to take place. Plankton-eating fish include herrings and sardines. Demersal fishes, such as haddock, halibut, and cod, live primarily near the ocean floor, and feed on various invertebrate marine animals. Over 20 million tonnes of them are caught each year by trawling. Pelagic fish, such as tuna, live in the open sea, near the surface, and purse seine nets which close like a purse and may be as long as 30 nautical miles, are used to catch them; the annual catch is over 30 million tonnes a year.

freshwater fishing There is large demand for salmon, trout, carp, bass, pike, perch, and catfish. These inhabit ponds, lakes, rivers, or swamps, and some species have been successfully cultivated.

methods Lines, seine nets, drift nets (nets supported by floats and allowed to drift with the tide or current), and lift nets are the common commercial methods used.

history Until the introduction of refrigeration, fish was preserved by salting, smoking, and air-drying. Between 1950 and 1970, the global fish catch increased by an average of 7% each year. Japan evolved new techniques for locating shoals (by sonar and radar) and catching them (for example, with electrical charges and chemical baits). By the 1970s, indiscriminate overfishing had led to serious depletion of stocks. A United Nations resolution was passed 1989 to end drift-net fishing by June 1992.

ancillary industries These include the manufacture of nets, the processing of oil and fishmeal (nearly 25% of the fish caught annually are turned into meal for animal feed), pet food, glue, manure, and drugs such as insulin and other pharmaceutical products.

fishmonger *n*. a dealer in fish.

fish pond a pond used for fish farming. They were known in antiquity and were common from the 12th century. Many abbeys had fish ponds, for example, Glastonbury Abbey in Somerset, England.

fishwife *n*. a woman who sells fish.

fishy *adj*. 1. of or like a fish. 2. (*slang*) dubious, suspect. —**fishily** *adv*. , **fishiness** *n*.

fissile /'fɪsaɪl/ *adj*. capable of undergoing nuclear fission; tending to split. [from Latin]

fission /'fɪʃən/ *n*. 1. a method of biological reproduction by the division of a cell etc. 2. nuclear fission. —*v.t./i*. to undergo or cause to undergo fission. —**fission bomb**, an atomic bomb. [from Latin]

fissionable *adj*. capable of undergoing nuclear fission.

fissure /'fɪʃə/ *n*. a cleft made by splitting or separation of parts. —*v.t./i*. to split, to crack. [from Old French or Latin *findere fiss-* = cleave]

fist *n*. the tightly closed hand. [Old English]

fisticuffs /'fɪstɪkʌfs/ *n.pl* fighting with the fists.

fistula /'fɪstjʊlə/ *n*. 1. a long, pipelike ulcer. 2. an abnormal or surgically made passage in the body. —**fistular** *adj*., **fistulous** *adj*. [Latin = pipe]

fit[1] *adj*. 1. well suited or qualified. 2. competent, worthy; in a suitable condition, ready. 3. in good health or condition. 4. proper, befitting. —*v.t./i*. (**-tt-**) 1. to make or be of the right shape and size (for). 2. to put or go into position. 3. to adapt, to make or be suitable or competent. 4. to supply or equip *with*. —*n*. the way a thing fits. —**fit in**, to be or cause to be harmonious or in a suitable relationship; to find space or time for. **fit out** or **up**, to supply or equip *with*. **see** *or* **think fit**, to decide or choose (*to do*). —**fitly** *adv*., **fitness** *n*.

fit[2] *n*. 1. a sudden seizure of epilepsy, hysteria etc., usually with unconsciousness; a brief attack of an illness or its symptoms. 2. a sudden short bout or burst. —**by** *or* **in fits and starts**, spasmodically. **have a fit**, (*colloquial*) to be greatly surprised or outraged. **in fits**, laughing uncontrollably. [originally = position of danger]

fitful *adj*. active or occurring spasmodically or intermittently. —**fitfully** *adv*.

fitment *n*. a piece of fixed furniture.

fitness *n*. in genetic theory, a measure of the success with which a genetically determined character can spread in future generations. By convention, the normal character is assigned a fitness of one, and variants (determined by other ◊alleles) are then assigned fitness values relative to this. Those with fitness greater than one will spread more rapidly and will ultimately replace the normal allele; those with fitness less than one will gradually die out. See also ◊inclusive fitness.

fitter *n*. 1. a person concerned with the fitting of clothes etc. 2. a mechanic who fits together and adjusts machinery.

fitting *n*. 1. the process of having a garment etc. fitted. 2. (in *plural*) the fixtures and fitments of a building. —*adj*. proper, befitting.

Fitzalan-Howard /fɪts'ælən 'haʊəd/ the family name of the dukes of Norfolk; seated at Arundel Castle, Sussex.

Fitzgerald /fɪts'dʒerəld/ the family name of the dukes of Leinster.

Fitzgerald Edward 1809–1883. English poet and translator. In 1859 he published his poetic version of the *Rubaiyat of Omar Khayyam*, which is generally considered more an original creation than a translation.

Fitzgerald Ella 1918– . US jazz singer, recognized as one of the finest, most lyrical voices in jazz, both in solo work and with big bands. She is celebrated for her smooth interpretations of Gershwin and Cole Porter songs.

Fitzgerald F(rancis) Scott (Key) 1896–1940. US novelist and short-story writer. His early autobiographical novel *This Side of Paradise* 1920 made him known in the postwar society of the East Coast, and *The Great Gatsby* 1925 epitomizes the Jazz Age.

A big man has no time really to do anything but just sit
and be big.

Francis Scott (Key) Fitzgerald
This Side of Paradise

Fitzgerald George 1851–1901. Irish physicist known for
his work on electromagnetics. In 1895 he explained the
anomalous results of the ◊Michelson-Morley experiment
of 1887 by supposing that bodies moving through the
ether contracted as their velocity increased, an effect since
known as the **Fitzgerald-Lorentz contraction.**

FitzGerald Garret 1926– . Irish politician. As *Taoiseach*
(prime minister) 1981–82 and again 1982–86, he was noted
for his attempts to solve the Northern Ireland dispute,
ultimately by participating in the Anglo-Irish agreement in
1985. He tried to remove some of the overtly Catholic
features of the constitution to make the Republic more
attractive to Northern Protestants. He retired as leader
of the Fine Gael Party in 1987.

Fitzherbert /fɪtsˈhɜːbət/ Maria Anne 1756–1837. Wife
of the Prince of Wales, later George IV. She became Mrs
Fitzherbert by her second marriage in 1778 and, after her
husband's death in 1781, entered London society. She
secretly married the Prince of Wales in 1785 and finally
parted from him 1803.

Fitzroy /ˈfɪtsrɔɪ/ the family name of the dukes of Grafton;
descended from King Charles II by his mistress Barbara
Villiers; seated at Euston Hall, Norfolk.

five *adj. & n.* **1.** one more than four; the symbol for this (5,
v, V). **2.** the size etc. denoted by five. [Old English]

fivefold *adj. & adv.* **1.** five times as much or as many. **2.**
consisting of five parts.

five pillars of Islam the five duties required of every
Muslim: repeating the **creed**, which affirms that Allah is
the one God and Muhammad is his prophet; daily **prayer** or
◊salat; giving **alms**; **fasting** during the month of Ramadan;
and, if not prevented by ill health or poverty, the hajj, or
pilgrimage to Mecca, once in a lifetime.

fiver *n.* (*colloquial*) a £5 note.

fives /faɪvz/ *n.* a ball-game played with padded gloves in
a walled court, with three walls (**Eton fives**) or four
(**Rugby fives**).

Five-Year Plan a long-term strategic plan for the development of a country's economy. Five-year plans were from
1928 the basis of economic planning in the USSR, aimed
particularly at developing heavy and light industry in a primarily agricultural country. They have since been adopted
by many other countries.

fix *v.t./i.* **1.** to make firm or stable, to fasten, to secure;
to implant (an idea or memory) in the mind. **2.** to place
definitely or permanently. **3.** to decide, to settle, to specify
(a price, date etc.). **4.** to direct (the eyes or attention)
steadily. **5.** to determine the exact nature, position etc.,
of; to identify, to locate. **6.** to make (the eyes or features)
rigid; to become rigid; to congeal, to stiffen. **7.** to repair.
8. (*colloquial*) to punish or kill. **9.** (*colloquial*) to secure the
support of (a person) or result of (a race etc.) fraudulently.
10. (*slang*) to inject (*oneself*) with a narcotic. **11.** to make (a
colour, photographic image etc.) fast or permanent. **12.** (of
a plant) to assimilate (nitrogen, carbon dioxide) by forming
a non-gaseous compound. —*n.* **1.** a dilemma, a difficult
position. **2.** the act of finding a position, or a position found,
by bearings etc. **3.** (*slang*) a dose of a narcotic drug. —**be
fixed (for),** (*colloquial*) to be situated (as regards). **fixed
star,** a star so far from Earth as to appear motionless
except for the diurnal revolution of the heavens (as opposed
to *planet*, *comet* etc.). **fix on** or **upon,** to choose, to decide
on. **fix up,** to arrange, to organize; to accommodate. [ulti-
mately from Latin *figere fix*- = fix]

fixate /fɪkˈseɪt/ *v.t.* **1.** to direct one's gaze on. **2.** (chiefly
in *passive*) to cause to acquire an abnormal attachment to
persons or things. [from Latin]

fixation /fɪkˈseɪʃ(ə)n/ *n.* **1.** the act or process of being
fixated. **2.** an obsession, a concentration on one idea. **3.** the
process of fixing. [from Latin]

fixative /ˈfɪksətɪv/ *adj.* tending to fix or secure. — *n.* a
fixative substance.

fixedly /ˈfɪksɪdlɪ/ *adv.* in a fixed way, intently.

fixed point a temperature that can be accurately reproduced and used as the basis of a temperature scale. In
the Celsius scale, the fixed points are the temperature of
melting ice, which is 0°C (32°F), and the temperature of
boiling water (at standard atmospheric pressure), which is
100°C (212°F).

fixed-point notation a system of representing numbers
by a single set of digits with the decimal point in its correct
position (for example, 97.8, 0.978). For very large and
very small numbers this requires a lot of digits, and so in
computing the numbers that can be handled in this form will
be limited by the capacity of a computer; this means that
◊floating-point notation is often preferred.

fixer *n.* a person or thing that fixes; (*colloquial*) one who
makes (especially illicit) arrangements; a substance for fixing a photographic image etc.

fixings *n.pl.* (US) **1.** apparatus, equipment. **2.** the trimmings of a dress or dish.

fixity *n.* fixed state, stability, permanence.

fixture /ˈfɪkstʃə(r)/ *n.* **1.** a thing fixed in position; (in *plural*)
articles belonging to a house etc. **2.** a sporting event or date
fixed for it. [alteration of obsolete *fixure*]

fizz *v.i.* **1.** to effervesce. **2.** to hiss, to splutter. — *n.* **1.**
a hissing sound. **2.** effervescence; (*colloquial*) an effervescent drink.

fizzle *v.i.* to make a feeble hiss. —*n.* a fizzling sound.
—**fizzle out,** to end feebly.

fizzy *adj.* effervescent. —**fizziness** *n.*

fjord variant of fiord.

flab *n.* (*colloquial*) fat, flabbiness.

flabbergast /ˈflæbəɡɑːst/ *v.t.* (*colloquial*) to astound.

flabby *adj.* limp and hanging loose; feeble. —**flabbily** *adv.*,
flabbiness *n.*

flaccid /ˈflæksɪd/ *adj.* flabby; drooping. — **flaccidity**
/-ˈsɪdɪtɪ/ *n.*, in biology, the loss of rigidity (turgor) of
plant cells, caused by loss of water from the central
vacuole so that the cytoplasm no longer pushes against
the cellulose cell wall. If this condition occurs throughout
the plant, it wilts. **flaccidly** *adv.* [from French or Latin
flaccus = flabby]

flag[1] *n.* **1.** a piece of material, usually oblong or square and
attached by one edge to a pole, rope, etc., used as a country's emblem or as a standard, signal, etc. **2.** a small metal
plate showing that a taxi is for hire. **3.** a small paper etc.
device resembling a flag. **4.** in computing, a code indicating
whether or not a certain condition is true; for example, that
the end of a file has been reached. —*v.t.* (**-gg-**) **1.** to inform
or signal (as) with a flag, especially (often with *down*) to
signal (a vehicle or driver) to stop. **2.** to mark with a flag
or tag. —**flag day** *n.* a day on which money is raised from
passers-by etc. for a cause and small paper flags are given
as tokens. **flag of convenience,** a foreign flag under which
a ship is registered to avoid taxes etc. **flag-officer** *n.* an
admiral, vice-admiral, or rear- admiral; the commodore of a
yacht-club. **flag of truce,** a white flag, indicating a desire to
parley. **flagpole** *n.* a flagstaff. [perhaps from obsolete *flag*
= drooping]

flag[2] *v.i.* (**-gg-**) to lose momentum or vigour; to become
limp or feeble.

flag[3] *n.* a flagstone; (in *plural*) a pavement of these. —*v.t.*
(**-gg-**) to pave with flags. [compare Old Norse *flaga* =
slab of stone]

flag[4] *n.* a plant with a bladed leaf (especially *Iris pseuda-
corus*), usually growing on moist ground.

flagellant /ˈflædʒələnt/ *n.* one who flagellates him- or
herself or others. Flagellation was practised in many
religions from ancient times; notable outbreaks of this
type of extremist devotion occurred in Christian Europe
in the 11th–16th centuries. —*adj.* of flagellation. [from
Latin *flagellare* = whip

flagellate[1] /ˈflædʒəleɪt/ *v.t.* to whip, to flog, especially as
a religious discipline or sexual stimulus. —**flagellation**
/-ˈleɪʃ(ə)n/ *n.*

flagellate[2] /ˈflædʒələt/ *adj.* having flagella (see ◊flagel-
lum). —*n.* a protozoon having flagella.

flagellum /fləˈdʒeləm/ *n.* (*plural* **flagella**) **1.** in botany, a
runner, a creeping shoot. **2.** in biology, a lashlike appendage;
a small hairlike organ on the surface of certain cells. Flagella
are the motile organs of certain protozoa and single-celled
algae, and of the sperm cells of higher animals. Unlike
cilia (see ◊cilium, ◊ciliate, flagella usually occur singly or

in pairs; they are also longer and have a more complex whiplike action. A flagellum consists of contractile filaments producing snakelike movements that propel cells through fluids, or fluids past cells. Water movement inside sponges is also produced by flagella. [Latin = whip, diminutive of *flagrum* = scourge]

flageolet /flædʒəˈlet/ *n.* a fipple flute with two thumbholes. [French from Provençal]

flagon /ˈflægən/ *n.* a large, rounded vessel for holding liquids, usually with a handle and lid. [from Anglo-French from Latin]

flagrant /ˈfleɪgrənt/ *adj.* glaringly bad; notorious or scandalous. —**flagrancy** *n.*, **flagrantly** *adv.* [from French or Latin *flagrare* = blaze]

flagship *n.* a ship that carries an admiral and flies his flag; the principal vessel of a shipping line.

Flagstad /ˈflægstæd/ Kirsten (Malfrid) 1895–1962. Norwegian soprano who specialized in Wagnerian opera.

flagstaff *n.* a pole on which a flag is hoisted.

Flaherty /ˈflɑːəti/ Robert 1884–1951. US film director; the father of documentary film-making. He exerted great influence through his pioneer documentary of Inuit (Eskimo) life, *Nanook of the North* 1922, a critical and commercial success. Later films include *Moana* 1926, a South Seas documentary; *Man of Aran* 1934, *Elephant Boy* 1936, *The Lands* 1942, and the Standard Oil-sponsored *Louisiana Story* 1948.

flail *n.* a short, heavy stick swinging at the end of a wooden staff, used as an implement for threshing. — *v.t.i.* to wave or swing wildly; to beat (as) with a flail. [Old English, probably from Latin *flagellum* = whip]

flair *n.* a natural ability or talent for selecting or doing what is best, useful etc.; style, finesse. [French = power of scent]

flak *n.* 1. anti-aircraft fire. 2. a barrage of criticism. —**flak jacket,** a heavy protective jacket reinforced with metal. [German, abbreviation of *fliegerabwehrkanone* = pilot-defence-gun]

flake *n.* 1. a small, light piece, e. g. of snow; a thin broad piece shaved or split off. 2. dogfish as food. —*v.t.i.* to take or come *away* or *off* in flakes; to fall in or sprinkle with flakes. —**flake out,** (*colloquial*) to fall asleep or faint (as) with exhaustion. —**flaky** *adj.* [compare Old Norse *flakna* = flake off]

flambé /ˈflɑ̃beɪ/ *adj.* (of food) covered with spirit and served alight. [French = singed]

flamboyant /flæmˈbɔɪənt/ *adj.* showy or florid in appearance or manner. —**flamboyance** *n.*, **flamboyantly** *adv.* [French]

flame *n.* 1. ignited gas burning visibly; a tongue-shaped portion of this. 2. a bright light or bright red colour. 3. passion, especially of love. —*v.i.* 1. to burn with flames, to blaze. 2. (of a person or temper) to explode in anger. 3. to shine or glow like a flame. —**flame-thrower** *n.* a weapon throwing a jet of flame. [from Old French from Latin *flamma*]

flamenco /fləˈmeŋkəʊ/ *n.* (*plural* **flamencos**) a Spanish gypsy style of song or dance. [Spanish = Flemish]

flame test in chemistry, the use of a flame to identify metal ◊cations present in a solid.

flame tree any of various trees with brilliant red flowers, including the smooth-stemmed semi-deciduous tree *Sterculia acerifolia* with red or orange flowers, native to Australia, but spread throughout the tropics.

flaming *adj.* 1. burning with flames. 2. very hot or bright. 3. (*colloquial*) passionate. 4. (*colloquial*) damned.

flamingo *n.* (*plural* **flamingos**) a tall, long-necked wading-bird of the stork order Ciconiiformes. Largest of the family is the **greater** or **roseate flamingo** *Phoenicopterus ruber*, of both Africa and South America, with delicate pink plumage, and 1.25 m/4 ft high. They sift the mud for food with their downbent bills, and build colonies of high, conelike mud nests, with a little hollow for the eggs at the top. [from Portuguese from Provençal]

Flaminius /fləˈmɪniəs/ Gaius died 217 BC. Roman consul and general. He constructed the Flaminian Way northward from Rome to Rimini in 220 BC, and was killed at the battle of Lake Trasimene fighting ◊Hannibal.

flammable /ˈflæməbəl/ *adj.* that may be set on fire. —**flammability** /-ˈbɪlɪtɪ/ *n.* [from Latin]

flan *n.* an open sponge or pastry case filled or spread with a fruit or savoury filling. [French, originally = round cake]

Flanagan /ˈflænəgən/ Bud. Stage name of Robert Winthrop 1896–1968. British comedian, leader of the 'Crazy Gang' from 1931 to 1962. He played in variety theatre all over the world and, with his partner Chesney Allen, popularized such songs as 'Underneath the Arches'.

Flanders /ˈflɑːndəz/ a region of the Low Countries which, in the 8th and 9th centuries, extended from Calais to the Scheldt and is now covered by the Belgian provinces of Oost Vlaanderen and West Vlaanderen (East and West Flanders), the French *département* of Nord, and part of the Dutch province of Zeeland. The language is Flemish. East Flanders, capital Ghent, has an area of 3,000 sq km/1,158 sq mi and a population (1987) of 1,329,000. West Flanders, capital Bruges, has an area of 3,100 sq km/1,197 sq mi and a population (1987) of 1,035,000.

flange /flændʒ/ *n.* a rim or projection, especially for strengthening or attachment to another object. [perhaps from *flange, flanch* = widen outwards]

flank *n.* 1. the fleshy part of the side of the body between the ribs and the hip. 2. the side of a mountain etc. 3. the left or right side of a body of troops. —*v.t.* to be or be posted at or move along the flank or side of. [from Old French from Germanic]

flannel *n.* 1. a kind of woven, woollen, usually napless cloth; (in *plural*) flannel garments, especially trousers. 2. a cloth used for washing oneself. 3. (*slang*) nonsense, flattery. —*v.t.* (**-ll-**) 1. to wash with a flannel. 2. (*slang*) to flatter. —**flannelled** *adj.* [perhaps from Welsh *gwlanen* (*gwlan* = wool)]

flannelette /flænəˈlet/ *n.* a napped cotton fabric resembling flannel.

flap *v.t.i.* (**-pp-**) 1. to swing or sway about; to cause to do this, to move up and down. 2. to hit at (a fly etc.) with a flat object. 3. (*colloquial*, of ears) to listen intently. 4. (*colloquial*) to be agitated or panicky. —*n.* 1. a flat, broad piece attached at one edge, acting as a cover, extension, etc.; an aileron on an aircraft, a hinged or sliding section used to control lift. 2. the action or sound of flapping. 3. a light blow, usually with something flat. 4. (*colloquial*) a state of agitation or fuss. —**flappy** *adj.*

flapdoodle /ˈflæpduːdəl/ *n.* nonsense.

flapjack *n.* 1. a sweet oatcake. 2. a small pancake.

flapper *n.* 1. a broad, flat device, a flap. 2. (*colloquial*) a young (especially unconventional) woman in the 1920s.

flare /fleə/ *v.t.i.* 1. to blaze with a bright unsteady flame. 2. to burst into sudden activity or anger. 3. to widen gradually. —*n.* 1. a flame or bright light used as a signal or for illumination. 2. an outburst of flame. 3. a dazzling unsteady light; unwanted light resulting from reflection within a lens. 4. a flared shape, a gradual widening. —**flare path,** a line of lights to guide aircraft landing or taking off. **flare up,** to burst into flame; to become suddenly angry.

flare, solar a brilliant eruption on the Sun above a ◊sunspot, thought to be caused by release of magnetic energy. Flares reach maximum brightness within a few minutes, then fade away over about an hour. They eject a burst of atomic particles into space at up to 1,000 kps/600 mps. When these particles reach Earth they can cause radio blackouts, disruptions of the Earth's magnetic field, and ◊auroras.

flash *n.* 1. a sudden short blaze of flame or light. 2. a brief outburst of feeling, a transient display of wit etc.; an instant; a brief news item on the radio etc. 3. a photographic flashlight. 4. a coloured cloth patch as an emblem on military uniform. —*v.t.i.* 1. to give out a flash, to gleam. 2. to burst suddenly into view or perception. 3. to send or reflect like a flash or in flashes; to cause to shine briefly. 4. to rush past suddenly. 5. to send (news etc.) by radio or telegraph. 6. (*colloquial*) to show suddenly or ostentatiously; (*slang*) to display oneself indecently. —*adj.* (*colloquial*) gaudy, showy, smart. —**flashcube,** a set of four flashbulbs arranged as a cube and operated in turn. **flash in the pan,** a seemingly brilliant but fleeting success; a promising start followed by failure.

flashback *n.* a return to a past event, especially as a scene in a film.

flashbulb *n.* a bulb giving a bright light for flashlight photography.

flasher *n.* **1.** an automatic device for flashing lights intermittently. **2.** (*slang*) a person who exposes himself indecently.

flashing *n.* a strip of metal acting as waterproofing at a joint of roofing etc. [from dialect *flash* = seal with lead sheets, or obsolete *flash* = lightning]

flashlight *n.* **1.** a device producing a brief bright light for indoor etc. photography. **2.** an electric torch.

flashpoint *n.* **1.** in physics, the lowest temperature at which a liquid or volatile solid heated under standard conditions gives off sufficient vapour to ignite on the application of a small flame. The **fire point** of a material is the temperature at which full combustion occurs. For safe storage of materials such as fuel or oil, conditions must be well below the flash and fire points to reduce fire risks to a minimum. **2.** the point at which anger breaks out.

flashy *adj.* gaudy, showy, cheaply attractive. —**flashily** *adv.*, **flashiness** *n.*

flask /flɑːsk/ *n.* **1.** a vacuum flask. **2.** a narrow-necked bulbous bottle as used in chemistry. **3.** a small, flat bottle for spirits, carried in the pocket etc. [from French and Italian from Latin]

flat *adj.* **1.** horizontal, level; spread out, lying at full length. **2.** smooth, without bumps or indentations. **3.** absolute, downright; dull, uninteresting, monotonous; (of a drink) that has lost its effervescence; (of a battery etc.) no longer able to generate electric current. **4.** (of a tyre) deflated, especially from a puncture. **5.** in music, of a note, below the normal or correct pitch; a semitone lower than the corresponding note or key of natural pitch. —*adv.* **1.** in a flat manner. **2.** in music, below the correct pitch. **3.** (*colloquial*) absolutely, completely, exactly. —*n.* **1.** a group of rooms, usually on one floor, forming a residence. **2.** a flat thing or part, level ground; low land; (*colloquial*) a flat tyre; a section of stage scenery mounted on a frame. **3.** in music, a note that is a semitone lower than the corresponding one of natural pitch; the sign indicating this. —**the flat**, the season of flat races for horses. **flatfish** *n.* a type of fish with a flattened body (e. g. sole, plaice). **flatfeet**, feet with less than the normal arch beneath. **flat-footed** *adj.* having flat feet; (*colloquial*) resolute, uninspired, unprepared. **flatiron** *n.* a heavy iron for pressing linen etc., heated by external means. **flat out**, at top speed, using all one's strength or resources. **flat race**, a race over level ground, without jumps. **flat rate**, an unvarying rate or charge. **flat spin**, a nearly horizontal spin in an aircraft; (*colloquial*) agitation or panic. **that's flat**, (*colloquial*) that is definite. —**flatly** *adv.*, **flatness** *n.* [from Old Norse]

flatlet /ˈflætlɪt/ *n.* a small flat, usually of one or two rooms.

flatten *v.t./i.* **1.** to make or become flat. **2.** to defeat or refute decisively, to humiliate.

flatter *v.t.* to pay exaggerated or insincere compliments to, especially to win favour; to cause to feel honoured; (of a portrait etc.) to represent (a person) too favourably. —**flatter oneself**, to delude oneself smugly. —**flatterer** *n.*

flattery *n.* exaggerated or insincere praise.

flatulent /ˈflætjʊlənt/ *adj.* **1.** causing, caused by, or troubled with the formation of gas in the alimentary canal. **2.** inflated, pretentious. —**flatulence, flatulency** *ns.* [French from Latin *flatus* = wind in stomach]

flatworm *n.* an invertebrate of the phylum Platyhelminthes. Some are free-living, but many are parasitic (for example, tapeworms and flukes). The body is simple and bilaterally symmetrical, with one opening to the intestine. Many are hermaphroditic (with both male and female sex organs), and practise self-fertilization.

Flaubert /fləʊˈbeər/ Gustave 1821–1880. French novelist, author of *Madame Bovary* 1857. He entered Paris literary circles in 1840, but in 1846 moved to Rouen, where he remained for the rest of his life. *Salammbô* 1862 earned him the Legion of Honour in 1866, and was followed by *L'Education sentimentale*/*Sentimental Education* 1869, and *La Tentation de Saint Antoine*/*The Temptation of St Anthony* 1874. Flaubert also wrote the short stories *Trois contes*/*Three Tales* 1877.

flaunt *v.t./i.* to display proudly; to show off, to parade.

flautist /ˈflɔːtɪst/ *n.* a flute-player. [from Italian *flauto* = flute]

Flavian /ˈfleɪvɪən/ *adj.* of the dynasty of Roman emperors including Vespasian and his sons Titus and Domitian. —*n.* a member of this dynasty. [from Latin *Flavius* name of family]

flavour /ˈfleɪvə/ *n.* a distinctive taste; a mingled sensation of smell and taste; an indefinable characteristic quality. —*v.t.* to give a flavour to, to season. —**flavoursome** *adj.* [from Old French *flaor*, perhaps from Latin *flatus* = blowing and *foetor* = stench, assimilated to *savour*]

flavouring *n.* a thing used to flavour food or drink.

flaw¹ *n.* an imperfection, a blemish; a crack, a breach; an invalidating defect in a document etc. —*v.t.* to make a flaw in, to spoil. [perhaps from Old Norse *flaga* = slab]

flaw² *n.* a squall of wind. [from Middle Dutch *vlaghe*]

flax *n.* any plant of the genus *Linum*, family Linaceae. The species *L. usitatissimum* is the cultivated strain; linen is produced from the fibre in its stems. The seeds yield linseed oil, used in paints and varnishes. The plant, of almost worldwide distribution, has a stem up to 60 cm/24 in high, small leaves, and bright blue flowers. —**flaxseed** *n.* linseed. [Old English]

flaxen *adj.* of flax; pale yellow

flay *v.t.* **1.** to strip off the skin or hide of; to peel off. **2.** to criticize severely. [Old English]

F-layer *n.* the highest and most strongly ionized layer in the ionosphere.

flea *n.* a small, wingless jumping insect, order Siphonaptera, feeding on human and other blood. Some fleas can jump 130 times their own height. —**fleabite** *n.* a slight injury or inconvenience. **flea-bitten** *adj.* bitten by or infested with fleas; shabby. **a flea in one's ear**, a sharp reproof. **flea market**, (*colloquial*) a street market selling second-hand goods etc. [Old English]

fleabane *n.* a plant of the genera *Erigeron* or *Pulicaria*, family Compositae. Common fleabane *P. dysenterica* has golden-yellow flower heads and grows in wet and marshy places throughout Europe.

fleck *n.* a small spot of colour; a small particle, a speck. —*v.t.* to mark with flecks. [from Old Norse, or Middle Low German or Dutch]

fled past and past participle of **flee**.

fledge *v.t.* **1.** to provide (a bird, arrow etc.) with feathers or down. **2.** to rear (a young bird) until it can fly. **3.** (in *past participle*) able to fly; mature, independent, trained. [from obsolete *fledge* = fit to fly]

fledgeling /ˈfledʒlɪŋ/ *n.* **1.** a young bird. **2.** an inexperienced person.

flee *v.t./i.* (*past* and *past participle* **fled**) to run away (from), to leave hurriedly; to seek safety in flight; to vanish. [Old English]

fleece *n.* **1.** the woolly coat of a sheep etc.; the wool shorn from a sheep in one shearing. **2.** a soft fabric for lining etc. —*v.t.* **1.** to strip or rob of money, property etc. **2.** to remove the fleece from (a sheep). —**fleecy** *adj.* [Old English]

fleet *n.* **1.** a naval force, a navy; a group of ships under one commander. **2.** a number of vehicles under one proprietor. —*v.i.* to pass rapidly. —*adj.* swift, nimble. —**fleetly** *adv.*, **fleetness** *n.* [Old English]

fleeting *adj.* brief, passing rapidly. [Old English = float, swim]

Fleming /ˈflemɪŋ/ Alexander 1881–1955. Scottish bacteriologist who discovered the first antibiotic drug, Ϙpenicillin, in 1928 (it did not come into use until 1941). In 1922 he had discovered lysozyme, an antibacterial enzyme present in saliva, nasal secretions, and tears. While studying this, he found an unusual mould growing on a neglected culture dish, which he isolated and grew into a pure culture; this led to his discovery of penicillin. In 1945 he won the Nobel Prize for Physiology or Medicine with Howard W Florey and Ernst B Chain, whose research had brought widespread realization of the value of penicillin.

Fleming Ian 1908–1964. English author of suspense novels featuring the ruthless, laconic James Bond, British Secret Service agent No. 007. Most of the novels were made into successful films.

Fleming John Ambrose 1849–1945. English electrical physicist and engineer who invented the thermionic valve in 1904.

Fleming's rules memory aids for the directions of the magnetic field, current, and motion in an electric generator or motor, using one's fingers. The three directions are represented by the thumb (for motion), forefinger (for field) and second finger (current), all held at right angles to each other. The right hand is used for generators and the left

Fleming's rules

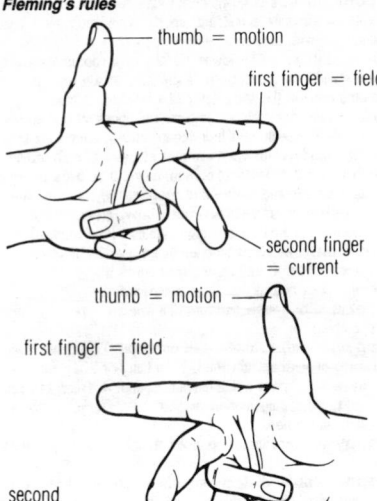

thumb = motion

first finger = field

second finger = current

thumb = motion

first finger = field

second finger = current

for motors. They were named after the English physicist John Fleming.

Flemish /'flemɪʃ/ *adj.* of Flanders or its people or their language. —*n.* this language, which is a member of the W Germanic branch of the Indo-European language family, spoken in N Belgium and the Nord *département* of France. It is closely related to Dutch. —**Flemish bond,** see ◊bond[1]. [from Dutch]

Flemish art the style of painting developed and practised in Flanders (a county in the Lowlands of NW Europe, largely coinciding with modern Belgium). A Flemish style emerged in the early 15th century, when Jan van Eyck made Bruges the first centre of Flemish art. Paintings are distinguished by keen observation, minute attention to detail, bright colours, and superb technique—oil painting was a Flemish invention. Apart from portraits, they depict religious scenes, often placed in contemporary Flemish landscapes, townscapes, and interiors. Flemish sculpture shows German and French influence.

flesh *n.* 1. the soft substance between the skin and bones. 2. the tissue of animal bodies (excluding fish and sometimes fowl) as food. 3. the body as opposed to the mind or soul. 4. the visible surface of the human body; the pulpy part of a fruit or plant; plumpness, fat. —*v.t./i.* (with *out*) to make or become substantial. —**the flesh,** the physical or sensual appetites. **flesh and blood,** the human body, human nature, mankind (*one's flesh and blood,* near relations). **flesh-coloured** *adj.* yellowish pink. **flesh wound** *n.* a wound not reaching a bone or vital organ. **in the flesh,** in bodily form, in person. [Old English]

fleshly *adj.* 1. mortal, worldly. 2. sensual. [Old English]

fleshpots *n.pl.* luxurious living.

fleshy *adj.* of or like flesh, plump, pulpy. —**fleshiness** *n.*

Fletcher /'fletʃə/ John 1579–1625. English dramatist who collaborated with ◊Beaumont, producing, most notably, *Philaster* 1609 and *The Maid's Tragedy* 1610–11. He is alleged to have collaborated with Shakespeare on *The Two Noble Kinsmen* and *Henry VIII* in 1612.

fleur-de-lis /flɜːdə'liː/ *n.* (also **-lys;** *plural* **fleurs**-*pronounced* the same) the heraldic lily of three petals; borne on coats of arms since the 12th century and the former royal arms of France, adopted by the French royal house of Bourbon. [from Old French = flower of lily]

Flevoland /'fleɪvəʊlænd/ formerly **IJsselmeerpolders** a low-lying province of the Netherlands established in 1986; **area** 1,410 sq km/544 sq mi; **population** (1988) 194,000; **capital** Lelystad; **history** created in 1986 out of land reclaimed from the Ijsselmeer 1950–68.

flew past of **fly**[1].

flex[1] *v.t.* to bend (a joint or limb); to move (a muscle) to bend a joint. [from Latin *flectere flex-* = bend]

flex[2] *n.* flexible insulated wire. [abbreviation *flexible*]

flexible /'fleksɪbəl/ *adj.* 1. that bends easily without breaking, pliable. 2. adaptable to circumstances. 3. easily persuaded, manageable. —**flexibility** /-'bɪlɪtɪ/ *n.*, **flexibly** *adv.* [from Old French or Latin]

flexion /'flekʃən/ *n.* bending; a bent state or part. [from Latin *flexio*]

flexitime /'fleksɪtaɪm/ *n.* a system of flexible working hours.

flexor *n.* any muscle that bends a limb. Flexors usually work in opposition to other muscles, the extensors, an arrangement known as antagonistic pairing.

flibbertigibbet /flɪbəti'dʒɪbɪt/ *n.* a gossiping or frivolous person.

flick *n.* 1. the sudden release of a bent finger or thumb. 2. a quick, light blow or stroke. 3. (*colloquial*) a cinema film; **the flicks,** a cinema performance. —*v.t.* to strike or knock or move with a flick. —**flick knife** *n.* a knife with a blade that springs out when a button etc. is pressed. **flick through,** to look cursorily through (a book etc.).

flicker *v.i.* 1. to burn or shine unsteadily or fitfully. 2. to quiver, to flutter. 3. (of hope etc.) to occur briefly. —*n.* 1. a flickering light or movement. 2. a brief spell (of hope, recognition etc.). [Old English]

flier variant of **flyer.**

flight[1] /flaɪt/ *n.* or **aviation** 1. an act or manner of flying; the movement or passage of a thing through the air; the distance flown. 2. a journey made by an aircraft or airline. 3. a group of birds etc. flying together; a volley (*of* arrows etc.). 4. a series (*of* stairs in a straight line, of hurdles etc. for racing). 5. an exceptional effort *of* fancy etc. 6. the tail of a dart. —**flight deck,** the cockpit of a large aircraft; the deck of an aircraft carrier. **flight lieutenant,** an RAF officer next below squadron leader. **flight recorder,** an electronic device in an aircraft, recording information about its flight. **flight sergeant,** the RAF rank next above sergeant. **in the first** *or* **top flight,** taking a leading place, excellent of its kind. [Old English].

flight[2] /flaɪt/ *n.* fleeing, an escape from danger etc. —**put to flight,** to cause to flee. **take (to) flight,** to flee. [Old English]

flightless /'flaɪtlɪs/ *adj.* (of a bird) lacking the power of flight.

flighty *adj.* (usually of a woman) frivolous, changeable. —**flightily** *adv.*, **flightiness** *n.*

flimsy /'flɪmzɪ/ *adj.* 1. lightly or carelessly assembled; easily damaged or knocked apart. 2. (of an excuse etc.) unconvincing. —**flimsily** *adv.*, **flimsiness** *n.*

flinch *v.i.* to draw back, to shrink (*from* an action); to wince. [from Old French *flenchir* from Germanic]

Flinders /'flɪndəz/ Matthew 1774–1814. English navigator who explored the Australian coasts in 1795–99 and 1801–03.

fling *v.t./i.* (*past* and *past participle* **flung**) 1. to throw, especially forcefully or hurriedly. 2. to put or send hurriedly or summarily. 3. to put *on* or take *off* (clothes) hurriedly or casually. 4. to rush, to go angrily or violently. —*n.* 1. the action of flinging. 2. a vigorous dance. 3. a short bout of self-indulgence. [perhaps from Old Norse]

flint *n.* 1. a compact, hard, brittle mineral (a variety of chert), brown, black, or grey in colour, found in fine nodules in limestone or shale deposits. It consists of fine-grained silica, SiO_2, in cryptocrystalline form (usually ◊quartz). A piece of this, especially as a prehistoric tool or weapon. 2. a piece of hard alloy used to produce a spark. 3. anything hard and unyielding. —**flinty** *adj.* [Old English]

flintlock *n.* an old type of gun fired by a spark from a flint.

flip[1] *v.t.* (-pp-) to turn over quickly, to flick; to toss (a thing) with a jerk so that it turns over in the air. —*n.* 1. the action of flipping. 2. (*colloquial*) a short trip. —**flip side,** the reverse side of a gramophone record. **flip through,** to look cursorily through (a book etc.).

flip[2] *n.* a drink of heated beer and spirit.

flip[3] *adj.* (*colloquial*) glib, flippant.

flippant /'flɪpənt/ *adj.* treating a serious matter lightly, disrespectful. —**flippancy** *n.*, **flippantly** *adv.*

flipper *n.* 1. a limb used by turtles, seals etc., in swimming. 2. a flat rubber etc. attachment worn on the foot in underwater swimming. 3. (*slang*) the hand.

flipping *adj. & adv.* (*slang*, expressing mild annoyance) damned.

flirt *v.t./i.* **1.** to behave lightheartedly in an amorous manner, to pretend courtship. **2.** to toy *with* an idea etc., to interest oneself superficially. **3.** to trifle *with* a danger etc. **4.** to wave or move briskly in short jerks. —*n.* one who flirts amorously. —**flirtation** /-'teɪʃən/ *n.*, **flirtatious** /-'teɪʃəs/ *adj.*, **flirtatiously** *adv.* [originally = move or throw with a jerk]

flit *v.i.* (**-tt-**) **1.** to move lightly and rapidly. **2.** to make short flights. **3.** to abscond, to disappear secretly (especially from one's abode to escape a creditor). —*n.* an act of flitting. [from Old Norse]

flitch *n.* a side of bacon. [Old English]

flitter *v.i.* to flit about. —**flittermouse** *n.* a bat.

float *v.t./i.* **1.** to rest or move on the surface of a liquid; to cause to do this; to move or be suspended *in* a liquid or gas. **2.** (*slang*) to move about in a leisurely way. **3.** to hover *before* the eyes or mind. **4.** (of a currency) to have a fluctuating exchange rate; to cause or allow (a currency) to have this. **5.** to start (a company, scheme etc.). —*n.* **1.** a raft. **2.** a floating device to control the flow of water, petrol etc. **3.** a structure enabling an aircraft to float on water. **4.** a cork or quill used on a fishing-line as an indicator; a cork supporting the edge of a fishing-net. **5.** a low-bodied lorry or cart, especially one used for display in a procession. **6.** a sum of money retained for minor expenditure or change-giving. **7.** a tool for smoothing plaster. **8.** (in *singular* or *plural*) the footlights in a theatre. —**floating dock**, a floating structure usable as a dry dock. **floating kidney**, one unusually movable. **floating population**, a population not settled in a definite place. **floating rib**, any of the ribs not joined to the breastbone. **floating voter**, a voter not permanently supporting any one political party. [Old English]

floatation variant of **flotation**.

floating-point notation a system of representing numbers as multiples of the appropriate base raised to some power; for example, the number 97.8 can be expressed as 0.0978×10^3 or 9780×10^{-2}. In computing, the number is expressed as a decimal fraction, so 97.8 becomes 0.978×10^2. See ◊fixed-point notation.

flocculation *n.* in soils, the artificially-induced coupling together of particles to improve aeration and drainage. Clay soils, which have very tiny particles and are difficult to work, are often treated in this way. The method involves adding lime to the soil.

flocculent /'flɒkjʊlənt/ *adj.* like tufts of wool; in or showing tufts. —**flocculence** *n.* [from Latin]

flock[1] *n.* **1.** a number of sheep, goats, or birds regarded as a group or unit. **2.** a large crowd of people; a number of people in the care of a priest or teacher etc. —*v.i.* to move or assemble in large numbers. [Old English]

flock[2] *n.* a lock or tuft of wool etc.; wool or cotton waste used as a stuffing. [from Old French from Latin *floccus*]

Flodden, Battle of /'flɒdn/ the defeat of the Scots by the English under the Earl of Surrey on 9 Sept 1513 on a site 5 km/3 mi SE of Coldstream, Northumberland, England; many Scots, including King James IV, were killed.

floe /fləʊ/ *n.* a sheet of floating ice. [from Norwegian]

flog /flɒg/ *v.t.* (**-gg-**) **1.** to beat with a whip, stick etc. **2.** (*slang*) to sell. —**flog a dead horse**, to waste one's efforts. **flog to death**, (*colloquial*) to talk about or promote at tedious length. —**flogging** *n.*

flood /flʌd/ *n.* **1.** an influx or the overflowing of water beyond its normal confines, especially over land; the water that overflows; an outpouring, an outburst of great quantity. **2.** the inflow of the tide. **3.** (*colloquial*) a floodlight. —*v.t./i.* **1.** to overflow; to cover or be covered with a flood. **2.** to come (*in*) in great quantities. **3.** to drive *out* (of a home etc.) by flood. **4.** to have a uterine haemorrhage. —**flood plain**, the level area over which a river spreads in flood. **flood-tide** *n.* a rising tide. [Old English]

Flood, the in the Old Testament, the Koran, and *The Epic of Gilgamesh* (an ancient Sumerian legend), a deluge lasting 40 days and nights, a disaster alleged to have obliterated all humanity except a chosen few (in the Old Testament, the survivors were the family of ◊Noah and the pairs of animals sheltered on his ark).

floodgate *n.* a gate that can be opened or closed to control the flow of water, especially the lower gate of a lock.

floodlight *n.* a large powerful light (usually one of several) to illuminate a building, sportsground etc. — *v.t.* to illuminate with this.

floor /flɔː/ *n.* **1.** the lower surface of a room, on which one stands. **2.** the bottom of the sea, a cave etc. **3.** the rooms etc. on the same level in a building. **4.** the part of a legislative assembly etc. where members sit and speak; the right to speak next in a debate etc. **5.** a level area. **6.** a minimum level for prices, wages etc. —*v.t.* **1.** to provide with a floor. **2.** to knock (a person) down. **3.** to baffle or nonplus; to overcome. —**floor manager**, the stage manager of a television production. **floor show**, an entertainment presented on the floor of a nightclub etc. [Old English]

floorboard *n.* a long wooden board used for flooring.

floorcloth *n.* a cloth for washing floors.

flooring *n.* boards etc. used as a floor.

floozie *n.* or **floosie** (*colloquial*) a woman, especially a disreputable one.

flop *v.i.* (**-pp-**) **1.** to fall or sit etc. (*down*) suddenly, awkwardly, or with a slight thud. **2.** to hang or sway limply or heavily. **3.** to make a dull flapping sound. **4.** (*slang*) to fail. —*n.* **1.** a flopping motion or sound. **2.** (*slang*) a failure. —*adv.* with a flop.

floppy *adj.* tending to flop, not firm or rigid. —**floppiness** *n.*

floppy disc or **disk** in computing, a storage device consisting of a light, flexible disk enclosed in a cardboard or plastic jacket. The disc is placed in a disc drive, where it rotates at high speed. Data are recorded magnetically on one or both surfaces.

flora /'flɔːrə/ *n.* (*plural* **floras**) the plants of a particular region or period. [Latin]

floral /'flɔːrəl, 'flɒ-/ *adj.* of or decorated with flowers. —**florally** *adv.* [from Latin]

floral diagram a diagram showing the arrangement and number of parts in a flower, drawn in cross section. An ovary is drawn in the centre, surrounded by representations of the other floral parts, indicating the position of each at its base. If any parts such as the petals or sepals are fused, this is also indicated. Floral diagrams allow the structure of different flowers to be compared, and are usually shown with the floral formula.

floral formula a symbolic representation of the structure of a flower. Each kind of floral part is represented by a letter (K for calyx, C for corolla, P for perianth, A for androecium, G for gynoecium) and a number to indicate the quantity of the part present, for example, C5 for a flower with five petals. The number is in brackets if the parts are fused. If the parts are arranged in distinct whorls within the flower, this is shown by two separate figures, such as A5 + 5, indicating two whorls of five stamens each.

Florence /'flɒrəns/ (Italian *Firenze*) capital of ◊Tuscany, N Italy, 88 km/55 mi from the mouth of the river Arno; population (1988) 421,000. It has printing, engineering, and optical industries; many crafts, including leather, gold and silver work, and embroidery; and its art and architecture attract large numbers of tourists. Notable Medieval and Renaissance citizens included the writers Dante and Boccaccio, and the artists Giotto, Leonardo da Vinci, and Michelangelo.

Florentine /'flɒrəntaɪn/ *adj.* of Florence in Italy. —*n.* a native of Florence. [from French or Latin]

florescence /flɔːˈresəns, flɒ-/ *n.* flowering time or state (*literal* or *figurative*). [from Latin *florescere* (*florēre* = bloom)]

floret /'flɔːrɪt/ *n.* a small flower, usually making up part of a larger, composite flower head. There are often two different types present on one flower head: disc florets in the central area, and ray florets around the edge which usually have a single petal known as the ligule. In the common daisy, for example, the disc florets are yellow, while the ligules are white. [from Latin *flos floris* = flower]

Florey /'flɔːri/ Howard Walter, Baron Florey 1898–1968. Australian pathologist whose research into lysozyme, an antibacterial enzyme discovered by Alexander ◊Fleming, led him to study penicillin (another of Fleming's discoveries), which he and Ernst ◊Chain isolated and prepared for widespread use. With Fleming, they were awarded the Nobel Prize for Physiology or Medicine in 1945.

floribunda /flɒri'bʌndə/ *n.* a rose or other plant bearing dense clusters of flowers. [Latin = freely flowering influenced by Latin *abundus* = copious]

florid /'flɒrɪd/ *adj.* 1. ornate, elaborate, showy. 2. ruddy, flushed. [from French or Latin *floridus* (*flos floris* = flower)]

Florida /'flɒrɪdə/ southeasterly state of the USA; mainly a peninsula jutting into the Atlantic, which it separates from the Gulf of Mexico; nickname Sunshine State; **area** 152,000 sq km/58,672 sq mi; **capital** Tallahassee; **physical** 50% forested; lakes (including Okeechobee 1,800 sq km/695 sq mi); Everglades National Park (5,000 sq km/1,930 sq mi, with birdlife, cypresses, alligators); **products** citrus fruit, melons, vegetables, cattle, fish, shellfish, phosphates (one third of world supply), chemicals, electrical and electronic equipment, aircraft, fabricated metals; **population** (1989) 13,000,000; one of the fastest-growing of the states; almost 15% nonwhite; almost 10% Hispanic, especially Cuban; **history** under Spanish rule from 1513 until its cession to England in 1763, Florida was returned to Spain in 1783, and purchased by the USA in 1819, becoming a state in 1845. It is a centre for drug trade with Latin America.

florin /'flɒrɪn/ *n.* a gold or silver coin, especially the former English two-shilling coin (10p). [from Old French from Italian *fiore* = flower, the original coin having the figure of a lily]

florist /'flɒrɪst/ *n.* one who deals in or grows flowers. [from Latin *flos floris* = flower]

floruit /'flɒruɪt/ *n.* the period or date at which a person lived or worked. [Latin = he or she flourished]

floss *n.* 1. the rough silk enveloping a silkworm's cocoon. 2. untwisted silk thread for embroidery. 3. dental floss (see ◊dental). —**flossy** *adj.* [from French *floche*]

flotation /flou'teɪʃən/ *n.* the launching of a commercial enterprise etc. [alteration of *floatation*]

flotation process a common method of preparing mineral ores for subsequent processing by making use of the different wetting properties of various components. The ore is finely ground and then mixed with water and a specially selected wetting agent. Air is bubbled through the mixture, forming a froth; the desired ore particles attach themselves to the bubbles and are skimmed off, while unwanted dirt or other ores remain behind.

flotilla /flɒ'tɪlə/ *n.* a small fleet; a fleet of small ships. [Spanish (*flota* = fleet)]

flotsam /'flɒtsəm/ *n.* wreckage found floating. —**flotsam and jetsam**, odds and ends; vagrants etc. —**flotsam, jetsam and lagan** in law, terminology referring to goods cast from ships at sea, due usually to the event or prevention of shipwreck: **flotsam** is the debris or cargo found floating; **jetsam** is what has been thrown overboard to lighten a sinking vessel; **lagan** is cargo secured, as to a buoy, for future recovery. Under English law all belong to the crown unless the owner is known. [from Anglo-French *floter* = float]

flounce[1] *v.i.* to go or move abruptly or angrily, with jerking movements. —*n.* a flouncing movement.

flounce[2] *n.* an ornamental frill round a woman's skirt etc. —*v.t.* to trim with flounces. [alteration of *frounce* = fold, pleat, from Old French]

flounder[1] *v.i.* to move or struggle helplessly or clumsily; to progress with great difficulty, to struggle. —*n.* an act of floundering.

flounder[2] *n.* a flatfish, especially a small edible species *Pleuronectes flesus*. [from Anglo-French, probably from Scandinavian]

flour /'flauə/ *n.* a fine meal or powder made by milling and usually sifting cereals, especially wheat; a fine, soft powder. —*v.t.* to sprinkle with flour. —**floury** *adj.*

flourish /'flʌrɪʃ/ *v.t./i.* 1. to grow vigorously and healthily; to prosper, to thrive, to be in one's prime. 2. to wave, to brandish. —*n.* 1. an ornamental curve in writing. 2. a dramatic gesture with the hand etc. 3. in music a florid passage, a fanfare. [from Old French from Latin *florēre*]

flout /flaut/ *v.t.* to disobey openly and scornfully. [perhaps from Dutch *fluiten* = whistle, hiss]

flow /flou/ *v.i.* 1. to glide along as a stream, to move freely like a liquid or gas. 2. (of blood, money, or electric current) to circulate. 3. to proceed steadily and continuously. 4. to hang easily, to undulate. 5. to be plentiful; to be plentifully

flow chart

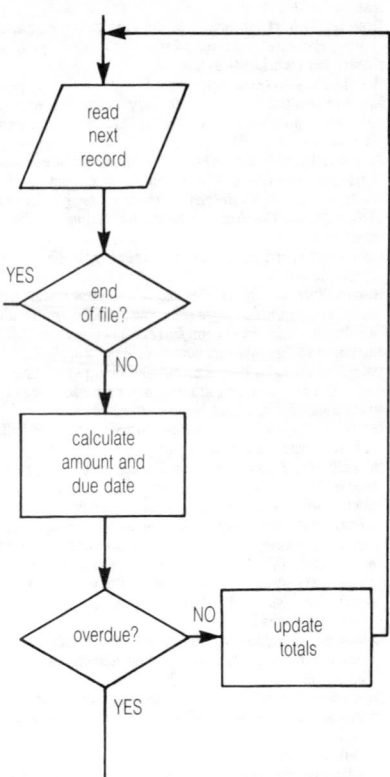

supplied *with*. 6. to gush out (*from*); to result from. 7. (of the tide) to rise. —*n.* 1. a flowing movement or mass; a flowing liquid, the amount of this. 2. an outpouring. 3. a rise of the tide. [Old English]

flow chart or **diagram** or **sheet** a diagram, often used in computing, to show the possible paths through a program. Different symbols are used to indicate processing, decision-making, input, and output. These are connected by arrows showing the flow of control through the program, that is, the paths the computer can take when executing the program. It is a way of visually representing an ◊algorithm.

flower /'flauə/ *n.* the part of a plant from which the fruit or seed is developed; typically consisting of four whorls of modified leaves: ◊sepals, ◊petals, ◊stamens, and ◊carpels. These are borne on a central axis or ◊receptacle. The many variations in size, colour, number and arrangement of parts are closely related to the method of pollination. Flowers adapted for wind pollination typically have reduced or absent petals and sepals and long, feathery ◊stigmas that hang outside the flower to trap airborne pollen. In contrast, the petals of insect-pollinated flowers are usually conspicuous and brightly coloured. a blossom (and its stem) used especially in groups for decoration; a plant cultivated or noted for its flowers. —*v.t./i.* 1. to bloom or blossom, to cause to do this. 2. to reach a peak. —**the flower of**, the best part of. **flowers of sulphur**, the fine powder produced when sulphur evaporates and condenses. **in flower**, with the flowers out. [from Old French from Latin *flos floris*]

flowering plant a term generally used for ◊angiosperms, which bear flowers with various parts, including sepals, petals, stamens and carpels. Sometimes the term is used more broadly, to include both angiosperms and ◊gymnosperms, in which case the ◊cones of conifers and cycads are referred to as 'flowers'. Usually, however, the angiosperms and gymnosperms are referred to collectively as ◊seed plants, or spermatophytes.

flowerpot *n.* a pot in which a plant may be grown.

flower power a youth movement of the 1960s; see ◊hip-pie.

flowery *adj.* 1. abounding in flowers. 2. (of language) ornate, elaborate. —**floweriness** *n.*

flown past participle of **fly**[1].

flu /flu:/ *n.* (*colloquial*) influenza.

fluctuate /'flʌktjueɪt/ *v.i.* to vary erratically, to rise and fall. —**fluctuation** /-'eɪʃən/ *n.* [from Latin *fluctuare* (*fluctus* = wave)]

Fludd /flʌd/ Robert 1574–1637. British physician who attempted to present a comprehensive account of the universe based on Hermetic principles (see ◊Hermes Trismegistus), *The History of the Macrocosm and the Microcosm* 1617.

flue /flu:/ *n.* the smoke-duct in a chimney; a channel for conveying heat.

fluent /'flu:ənt/ *adj.* (of a person) able to speak quickly and easily; (of speech) flowing easily, coming readily. —**fluency** *n.*, **fluently** *adv.* [from Latin *fluere* = flow]

fluff *n.* 1. a light, downy substance, e. g. that shed from fabric. 2. (*slang*) a bungle or mistake (in a performance). —*v.t./i.* 1. to shake or puff into a soft mass. 2. (*slang*) to make a mistake in, to bungle.

fluffy /'flʌfɪ/ *adj.* having or covered with a mass of fluff. —**fluffily** *adv.*, **fluffiness** *n.*

flugelhorn *n.* an alto brass instrument, similar in appearance to the ◊cornet.

fluid /'flu:ɪd/ *n.* a substance, as a gas or liquid, that is capable of flowing freely; a fluid part or secretion. —*adj.* able to flow freely; not solid or rigid, fluctuating. —**fluid mechanics**, the study of the mechanical properties of fluids. **fluid ounce**, one twentieth of a pint; (*US*) one sixteenth of a pint. —**fluidity** /-'ɪdɪtɪ/ *n.* [from French or Latin *fluere* = flow]

fluidics /flu:'ɪdɪks/ *n.* the technique of using small interacting flows and fluid jets for amplification, switching, etc.

fluidize /'flu:ɪdaɪz/ *v.t.* to cause (a mass of granular material, e. g. sand) to behave like a fluid by passing a current of gas, vapour, or liquid upwards through it. —**fluidization** /-'zeɪʃən/ *n.*

fluid, supercritical fluid brought by a combination of heat and pressure to the point at which, as a near vapour, it combines the properties of a gas and a liquid. Supercritical fluids are used as solvents in chemical processes, such as the extraction of lubricating oil from refinery residues or the decaffeination of coffee, because they avoid the energy-expensive need for phase changes (from liquid to gas and back again) required in conventional distillation processes.

fluke[1] /flu:k/ *n.* a thing that happens or succeeds by chance, a piece of luck. —*v.t.* to achieve, hit etc., by a fluke. —**fluky** *adj.* [perhaps from dialect *fluke* = guess]

fluke[2] /flu:k/ *n.* a flatfish, a flounder. [Old English]

fluke[3] *n.* a parasitic flatworm such as *Fasciola hepatica* that causes rot and dropsy of the liver in sheep, cattle, horses, dogs, and humans. Only the adult encysted stage of its life history is passed within the body, after ingestion by the host. The cyst dissolves in the stomach and the young fluke passes to the liver.

fluke[4] /flu:k/ *n.* 1. the triangular flat end of an anchor arm. 2. the lobe of a whale's tail.

flummery /'flʌmərɪ/ *n.* 1. a sweet milk dish. 2. nonsense, empty talk. [from Welsh *llymru*]

flummox /'flʌməks/ *v.t.* (*colloquial*) to bewilder, to disconcert.

flung past and past participle of **fling**.

flunk *v.t./i.* (*US colloquial*) to fail, especially in an examination. [compare *funk* and obsolete *flink* = be a coward]

flunkey /'flʌŋkɪ/ *n.* (usually *derogatory*) 1. a footman. 2. a toady, a snob. 3. (*US*) a cook, waiter etc. [perhaps from *flank*, with sense 'one who flanks']

fluoresce /fluə'res/ *v.i.* to be or become fluorescent.

fluorescence *n.* in scientific usage, very short-lived ◊luminescence (a glow not caused by high temperature). Generally, the term is used for any luminescence regardless of the persistence. See ◊phosphorescence.

fluorescent *adj.* (of a substance) absorbing radiation and emitting it in the form of light. —**fluorescent lamp**, one with such a substance.

fluoridate /'fluərɪdeɪt/ *v.t.* to add traces of fluoride to (drinking-water), especially to prevent tooth decay. In areas where fluoride ions are naturally present in the water, research found that the incidence of tooth decay in children from areas in which water authorities followed this practice was reduced by more than 50%. A concentration of one part per million of fluoride salts to drinking-water is sufficient to produce this beneficial effect. —**fluoridation** /-'deɪʃən/ *n.*

fluoride /'fluəraɪd/ *n.* a salt of hydrofluoric acid. Fluorides occur naturally in all water to a differing extent.

fluorinate /'fluərɪneɪt/ *v.t.* to fluoridate; to introduce fluorine into.

fluorine /'fluəri:n/ *n.* a chemical element, symbol F, atomic number 9, relative atomic mass 19. It occurs naturally as the minerals fluorspar (CaF_2) and cryolite (Na_3ALF_6), and is the first member of the halogen group of elements. At ordinary temperatures it is a pale yellow, highly poisonous, and reactive gas, and it unites directly with nearly all the elements. Hydrogen fluoride is used in etching glass, and the freons, which all contain fluorine, are widely used as refrigerants.

fluorite *n.* a glassy, brittle mineral, calcium fluoride CaF_2, forming cubes and octahedra; colourless when pure, otherwise violet.

fluorocarbon /fluərəu'ka:bən/ *n.* a compound formed by replacing the hydrogen atoms of a hydrocarbon with fluorine. Fluorocarbons are used as inert coatings, refrigerants, synthetic resins, and as propellants in aerosols.

fluorspar /'fluəspa:/ *n.* calcium fluoride as a mineral. [from *fluor* = mineral used as flux (Latin, from *fluere* = flow) + *spar*[3]]

flurry /'flʌrɪ/ *n.* a gust, a squall; a sudden burst of activity; nervous hurry, agitation. —*v.t.* to confuse or agitate.

flush[1] *v.t./i.* 1. to become or cause to become red in the face, to blush. 2. to cleanse (a drain, lavatory etc.) by the flow of water; to dispose of (a thing) thus. 3. (of water) to rush or spurt out. 4. to inflame with pride or passion. 5. to make level. —*n.* 1. a reddening of the face, a blush; a feeling of feverish heat. 2. a rush of excitement or elation. 3. a rush of water; cleansing by flushing. 4. freshness, vigour. —*adj.* 1. level, in the same plane. 2. (*colloquial*) having plenty of money etc.

flush[2] *v.t./i.* 1. to take wing and fly up or away, to cause to do this. 2. to reveal, to drive *out*.

flush[3] *n.* a hand of cards all of one suit. —**straight flush**, a flush that is also a sequence. **royal flush**, a straight flush headed by an ace. [from Old French from Latin]

Flushing Meadow lawn-tennis centre in the USA, officially the national tennis centre. It is situated in the Queens borough of New York, and replaced the West Side Club as the home of the US Open championships in 1978. The main court is the Stadium Court, one of the largest in the world.

fluster *v.t./i.* to confuse or agitate; to make nervous; to bustle. —*n.* a confused or agitated state.

flute /flu:t/ *n.* 1. an instrument of the woodwind family made in silver, stainless steel, or occasionally wood, having holes along it stopped by fingers or (since the 19th century) keys, and a blow-hole in the side near the end. 2. its player. 3. a semicylindrical vertical groove in a pillar; a similar groove elsewhere. —*v.t./i.* 1. to play (on) the flute. 2. to speak or utter in flute-like tones. 3. to make ornamental grooves in. [from Old French, probably from Provençal *flaut*]

fluting /'flu:tɪŋ/ *n.* a series of ornamental grooves.

flutter *v.t./i.* 1. to flap (the wings) in flying or trying to fly. 2. to wave or flap quickly and irregularly; to move about restlessly; (of the pulse) to beat feebly and irregularly. —*n.* 1. fluttering. 2. a state of nervous excitement. 3. a rapid fluctuation in pitch or loudness. 4. (*colloquial*) a small bet or speculation. [Old English]

fluvial /'flu:vɪəl/ *adj.* of or found in rivers. [from Latin *fluvius* = river]

flux[1] *n.* 1. in smelting, a substance that combines with the unwanted components of the ore to produce a fusible slag, which can be separated from the molten metal. For example, the mineral fluorite, CaF_2, is used as a flux in iron smelting; it has a low melting point and will form a fusible mixture with substances of higher melting point such as silicates and oxides. 2. in soldering, a substance that improves the bonding properties of solder by removing contamination from metal surfaces and preventing their oxidation, and by reducing the surface tension of the molten solder alloy. For example, with solder made of lead-tin alloys, the flux may be resin, borax, or zinc chloride.

flux[2] *n*. **1.** a continuous succession of changes. **2.** flowing; the inflow of the tide. [from Old French or Latin *fluxus* (*fluere* = flow)]

fly[1] /flaɪ/ *v.t./i.* (*past* **flew** /flu:/, *past participle* **flown** /floʊn/) **1.** to move through the air by means of wings. **2.** (of an aircraft etc. or its occupants) to travel through the air or space; to transport in an aircraft. **3.** (of a cloud etc.) to pass quickly through the air. **4.** to go or move quickly, to pass swiftly; to flee (from); (*colloquial*) to depart hastily. **5.** (of a flag, the hair etc.) to wave; to raise (a flag) so that it waves. **6.** to make (a kite) rise and stay aloft. **7.** to be driven or scattered; to come or be forced suddenly *off*, *open* etc. —*n*. **1.** flying. **2.** a flap on a garment to contain or cover a fastening, (usually in *plural*) this fastening on trousers; a flap at the entrance of a tent. **4.** (in *plural*) the space over the proscenium in a theatre. **5.** the part of a flag furthest from the staff. —**fly a kite**, (*colloquial*) to sound out public opinion. **fly-by-night** *adj.* unreliable, irresponsible; (*n*.) a person of this kind. **fly half**, the stand-off half in Rugby football. **fly in the face of**, to disregard or disobey openly. **fly off the handle**, (*colloquial*) to become uncontrollably angry. **fly-past** *n*. a ceremonial flight of aircraft past a person or place. [Old English]

fly[2] *n*. **1.** a two-winged insect, especially of the order Diptera. A fly has one pair of wings, antennae, and compound eyes; the hindwings have become modified into knoblike projections (halteres) used to maintain equilibrium in flight. There are over 90,000 species. **2.** some other winged insect, e. g. a firefly, mayfly. **3.** a disease of plants or animals caused by flies. **4.** a natural or artificial fly as a bait in fishing. —**flyblown** *adj.* (of meat etc.) tainted by flies' eggs. **fly-fish** *v.i.* to fish with a fly. **fly in the ointment**, a minor irritation that spoils enjoyment. **fly on the wall**, an unnoticed observer. **flypaper** *n*. a sticky treated paper for catching flies. **flyspray** *n*. a liquid sprayed from a canister to kill flies. **flytrap** *n*. a plant *Dionaea muscipula* able to catch flies. **there are no flies on him**, (*slang*) he is very astute. [Old English]

fly[3] *adj.* (*slang*) knowing, clever.

flycatcher *n*. a bird (especially of the genus *Muscicapa*) that catches insects in the air.

flyer *n*. **1.** an airman or airwoman. **2.** a fast-moving animal or vehicle. **3.** an ambitious or outstanding person.

flying *n*. flight. —*adj.* **1.** that flies. **2.** (of a flag etc.) fluttering, waving. **3.** hasty. **4.** (of an animal) able to make long leaps by the use of membranes etc. **5.** (of a vehicle etc.) designed for rapid movement. —**flying boat**, an aircraft that can land on and take off from water and whose main body is a hull which supports it in the water. **flying buttress**, a buttress formed from a separate column, usually forming an arch with the wall it supports. **flying lizard** another name for a ◊flying dragon; **flying fox**, a fruit-eating bat of the genus *Pteropus*. **flying lemur**, commonly used, but incorrect, name for ◊colugo. It cannot fly, and is not a lemur. **flying officer**, an RAF officer next below flight lieutenant. **flying picket**, a picket organized for moving from place to place. **flying saucer**, an unidentified saucer-shaped object reported as seen in the sky. **flying squad**, a police detachment or other body organized for rapid movement. **flying start**, a start in which the starting-point is passed at full speed; (*figurative*) a vigorous start giving an initial advantage. **with flying colours**, with great credit gained in a test etc.

flying dragon or **flying lizard** a lizard *Draco volans* of SE Asia, which can glide on flaps of skin spread and supported by its ribs. This small arboreal lizard (head and body measuring only 7.5 cm/3 in) can glide between trees for 6 m/20 ft or more.

flying fish an Atlantic fish *Exocoetus volitans*, family Exocoetidae, of order Beloniformes, which can glide for 100 m/325 ft over the surface of the sea on its winglike expanded pectoral fins.

flying squirrel any of many species of squirrel, not necessarily closely related. It is characterized by a membrane along the side of the body from forelimb to hindlimb, in some species running to neck and tail too, which allows it to glide through the air. Flying squirrels are found in the Old and New World, but most species are E Asian. The giant flying squirrel *Petaurista* grows up to 1.1 m/3.5 ft including tail, and can glide 65 m/210 ft.

flyleaf *n*. a blank leaf at the beginning or end of a book.

Flynn /flɪn/ Errol. Stage name of Leslie Thompson 1909–1959. Australian actor. He is renowned for his portrayal of swashbuckling heroes in such films as *Captain Blood* 1935, *The Sea Hawk* 1940, and *The Master of Ballantrae* 1953.

flyover *n*. a bridge that carries one road or railway over another.

flysheet *n*. a tract or circular of 2 or 4 pages.

flyweight *n*. the lightest professional ◊boxing weight.

flywheel *n*. a heavy wheel in an engine that helps keep it running and smooths its motion. The ◊crankshaft in a petrol engine has a flywheel at one end, which keeps the crankshaft turning in between the intermittent power strokes of the pistons. It also comes into contact with the ◊clutch, serving as the connection between the engine and the car's transmission system.

Fm symbol for ◊fermium.

FM 1. abbreviation of Field Marshal. **2.** in physics, abbreviation of frequency modulation. Used in radio, FM is constant in amplitude and varies the frequency of the carrier wave. Its advantage over ◊AM is its better signal-to-noise ratio.

FNLA abbreviation of *Front National de Libération de l'Angola* [French = National Front for the Liberation of Angola].

f-number *n*. the measure of the relative aperture of a telescope or camera lens; it indicates the light-gathering power of the lens. In photography, each successive f-number represents a halving of exposure speed. [from *focal number*]

Fo /foʊ/ Dario 1926– . Italian playwright. His plays are predominantly political satires combining black humour with slapstick. They include *Morte accidentale di un anarchico/Accidental Death of an Anarchist* 1970, and *Non si paga non si paga/Can't Pay! Won't Pay!* 1975/1981.

FO 1. abbreviation of Flying Officer. **2.** (*historical*) Foreign Office. (See ◊foreign relations).

foal *n*. the young of the horse or a related animal. —*v.t.* (of a mare etc.) to give birth to (a foal, or *absolute*). —**in** or **with foal**, (of a mare etc.) pregnant. [Old English]

foam *n*. **1.** a collection of small bubbles formed on or in a liquid by agitation, fermentation etc.; the froth of saliva or perspiration. **2.** a substance resembling foam, e. g. rubber or plastic in a cellular mass. —*v.i.* to emit foam, to froth; to run in a foam. —**foam at the mouth**, to be very angry. —**foamy** *adj.* [Old English]

fob[1] *n*. **1.** an ornamental attachment to a watch-chain, keyring etc. **2.** a small pocket for a watch etc. in the waistband of trousers. [probably from German]

fob[2] *v.t.* (**-bb-**) **fob off**, to deceive into accepting or being satisfied (*with* an inferior thing, excuse etc.); to palm or pass off (a thing) *on* (*to*) a person. [from obsolete *fop* = to dupe]

fob or **f.o.b.** abbreviation of free on board, used in commerce to describe a valuation of goods at point of embarkation, excluding transport and insurance costs. Export values are usually expressed fob for customs and excise purposes, while imports are usually valued ◊cif.

focal /'foʊkəl/ *adj.* of or at a focus. —**focally** *adv.* [from Latin *focus* = hearth]

focal distance or **focal length** the distance from the centre of a spherical mirror or lens to the focal point. For a concave mirror or convex lens, it is the distance at which parallel rays of light are brought to a focus to form a real image (for a mirror, this is half the radius of curvature). For a convex mirror or concave lens, it is the distance from the centre to the point at which a virtual image (an image produced by diverging rays of light) is formed.

Foch /fɒʃ/ Ferdinand 1851–1929. Marshal of France during World War I. He was largely responsible for the Allied victory at the first battle of the ◊Marne in Sept 1914, and commanded on the NW front from Oct 1914–Sep 1916. He was appointed Commander in Chief of the Allied armies in the spring of 1918, and launched the Allied counter-offensive in July that brought about the negotiation of an armistice to end the war.

focus /'foʊkəs/ *n*. (*plural* **focuses**, **foci** /'foʊsaɪ/) **1.** the point at which rays or waves meet after reflection or refraction; the point from which rays etc. appear to proceed; the point at which an object must be situated

focal distance

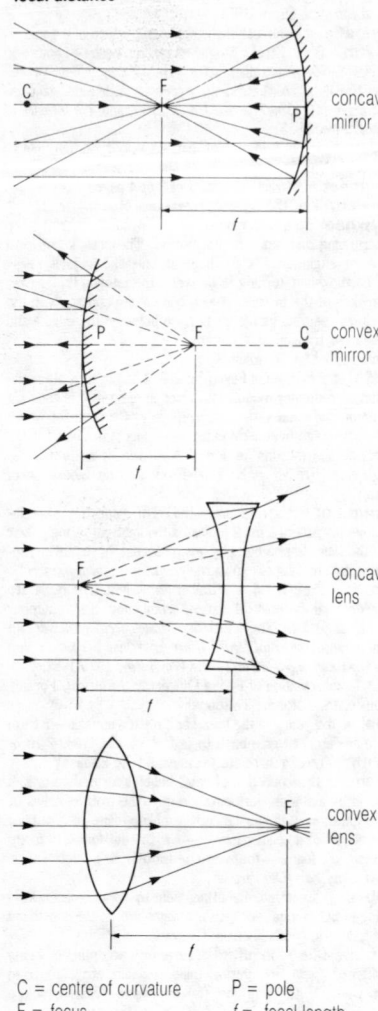

concave mirror

convex mirror

concave lens

convex lens

C = centre of curvature   P = pole
F = focus   *f* = focal length

for a lens or mirror to give a well-defined image; an adjustment of the eye or a lens to give a clear image; a state of clear definition. 2. a centre of interest or activity etc. —*v.t./i.* (*p.t.* **focused**) 1. to bring into focus; to adjust the focus of (a lens or the eye); to converge or cause to converge to a focus. 2. to concentrate or be concentrated *on.* [Latin = hearth]

fodder *n.* dried hay or straw etc. for animals. —*v.t.* to give fodder to. [Old English, related to *food*]

foe *n.* (chiefly *poetic*) an enemy. —**foeman** *n.* [Old English]

foetid /'fiːtɪd/ variant of **fetid**.

foetus variant of **fetus**.

fog *n.* 1. a thick cloud of fine water droplets suspended at or near the Earth's surface. Fog is caused when the air temperature falls below dew point (the temperature at which the air becomes saturated with water vapour). This usually occurs when warm and cold currents of air meet, or when warm air flows over a cold surface. The thickness of fog depends on the density of water droplets. 2. cloudiness obscuring the image on a photographic negative etc. —*v.t./i.* (**-gg-**) 1. to cover or become covered (as) with fog. 2. to perplex. —**fog bank,** a mass of fog at sea. **fogbound** *adj.* unable to leave because of fog. **foghorn** *n.* a horn sounding a warning to ships in fog. **foglamp** *n.* a powerful lamp for use in fog.

foggy *adj.* full of fog; of or like fog, indistinct. —**not have the foggiest,** (*colloquial*) to have no idea at all. —**fogginess** *n.*

fogy /'fəʊgɪ/ *n.* or **fogey** an old-fashioned person (usually *old fogy*).

foible /'fɔɪbəl/ *n.* a small weakness in a person's character. [French, obsolete form of *faible*]

foil[1] *v.t.* to baffle, to frustrate, to defeat. [perhaps from Old French *fouler* = to full cloth, to trample, from Latin *fullo*]

foil[2] *n.* 1. metal hammered or rolled into thin sheets. 2. a person or thing that enhances the qualities of another by contrast. [from Old French from Latin *folium* = leaf]

foil[3] *n.* a light blunt-edged sword used in fencing.

foist *v.t.* to force (an inferior, unwelcome, or undeserved thing) *on* (a person). [originally of palming false dice, from Dutch *vuisten* = take in the hand]

Fokine /'fɔːkiːn/ Mikhail 1880–1942. Russian dancer and choreographer, born in St Petersburg. He was chief choreographer to the Ballets Russes 1909–14, and with ◊Diaghilev revitalized and reformed the art of ballet, promoting the idea of artistic unity among dramatic, musical, and stylistic elements.

fold[1] /fəʊld/ *v.t./i.* 1. to bend or close (a flexible thing) over upon itself; to bend part of (a thing) *back* or *down*; to become or be able to be folded. 2. to embrace (*in* the arms or *to* the breast); to clasp (the arms etc.) *about* or *round*; to wrap, to envelop. 3. (in cookery) to mix (an ingredient) *in* lightly without stirring or beating. —*n.* 1. folding. 2. a folded part; a line made by folding. 3. a hollow among hills. —**fold one's arms,** to place them across the chest, together or entwined. **fold one's hands,** to clasp them. **fold up,** to collapse (*literally* or *figuratively*) ; to cease to function. [Old English]

fold[2] *n.* 1. a sheepfold. 2. the body of believers, the members of a church. —*v.t.* to enclose (sheep) in a fold. [Old English]

fold[3] *n.* in geology, a bend in a rock ◊bed. If the bend is arched up in the middle it is called an **anticline**; if it sags downwards in the middle it is called a **syncline**.

-fold /fəʊld/ suffix forming adjectives and adverbs from cardinal numbers, in sense 'in an amount multiplied by', 'with so many parts'. [Old English, originally = folded in so many layers]

folder *n.* 1. a folding cover or holder for loose papers. 2. a folded leaflet.

foliaceous /fəʊli'eɪʃəs/ *adj.* of or like leaves; laminated. [from Latin *folium* = leaf]

foliage /'fəʊliɪdʒ/ *n.* leaves, leafage. [from French *feuillage* (*feuille* = leaf)]

foliar /'fəʊliə/ *adj.* of leaves. —**foliar feed,** a feed supplied to the leaves of plants. [from Latin *folium* = leaf]

foliate /'fəʊliət/ *adj.* leaflike, having leaves. —/-eɪt/ *v.t./i.* to split or beat into thin layers. —**foliation** /-'eɪʃən/ *n.*

folic /'fɒlɪk, 'fəʊ-/ *adj.* **folic acid** a ◊vitamin of the B complex found in liver and green leafy vegetables, and synthesized by the intestinal bacteria. It is essential for growth, and plays many other roles in the body. Lack of folic acid causes anaemia. [from Latin *folium* = leaf (because found especially in green leaves)]

Folies-Bergère /fɒlibeə'ʒeə/ *n.* a music hall in Paris, France, built in 1869, named after its original proprietor and featuring lavish productions and striptease acts.

folio /'fəʊliəʊ/ *n.* (*plural* **folios**) 1. a leaf of paper etc., especially one numbered only on the front. 2. a sheet of paper folded once, making two leaves of a book; a book made of such sheets. —*adj.* (of a book etc.) made of folios, of the largest size. —**in folio,** made of folios. [Latin, ablative of *folium* = leaf]

foliot /'fəʊliət, 'fɒ-/ *n.* a type of clock escapement consisting of a bar with adjustable weights on the ends [from Old French, perhaps from *folier* = play the fool, dance about]

folk /fəʊk/ *n.* 1. a nation or people. 2. the people of a specified class; (often in *plural*) people in general; one's parents or relatives. 3. folk music. —*attrib.* of popular origin.

folk dance a dance characteristic of a particular people, nation, or region. Many European folk dances are derived from the dances accompanying the customs and ceremonies of pre-Christian times. Once an important part of many rituals, folk dance has tended to die out in industrialized countries.

folklore *n.* the oral traditions and culture of a people, expressed in legends, riddles, songs, tales, and proverbs. The term was coined in 1846 by W J Thoms (1803–85), but the founder of the systematic study of the subject was Jacob ◊Grimm; see also ◊oral literature. —**folklorist** *n.*

folk music a body of traditional music, originally transmitted orally. Many folk songs originated as a rhythmic accompaniment to manual work or to mark a specific ritual. Folk song is usually melodic, not harmonic, and the modes used are distinctive of the country of origin. See ◊roots music.

folksy /'fəʊksɪ/ *adj.* adopting the characteristics of ordinary people or of folk art; simple, unpretentious, friendly.

folk weave a rough, loosely woven fabric.

follicle *n.* **1.** in botany, a dry, usually many-seeded fruit that splits along one side only to release the seeds within. **2.** in zoology, a small group of cells that surround and nourish a structure such as a hair (hair follicle) or a cell such as an egg (Graafian follicle; see ◊menstrual cycle). —**follicular** /fɒ'lɪkjʊlə/ *adj.* [from Latin diminutive of *follis* = bellows]

follow /'fɒləʊ/ *v.t./i.* **1.** to go or come after (a person or thing proceeding ahead). **2.** to go along (a road etc.). **3.** to come next in order or time. **4.** to take as a guide or leader, to conform to; to practise (a trade or profession), to undertake (a course of study etc.). **5.** to understand the meaning or tendency of (an argument, speaker). **6.** to be aware of the present state or progress of (events etc.). **7.** to provide *with* a sequel or successor. **8.** to result *from*; to be necessarily true as a result of something else. —**follow on**, to continue; (of a cricket team) to have to bat again immediately after a first innings. **follow-on** *n.* an instance of this. **follow out**, to carry out, to adhere strictly to (instructions etc.). **follow suit**, to play a card of the suit led; to conform to another's actions. **follow through**, to continue (an action etc.) to its conclusion. **follow up**, to pursue; to develop; to supplement (one thing *with* another). **follow-up** *n.* a further or continued action, a measure etc. [Old English]

follower *n.* one who follows; a supporter or devotee.

following *n.* a body of supporters or devotees. —*adj.* that follows or comes after. —*prep.* after in time, as a sequel to. —**the following**, what follows; now to be given or named.

folly *n.* **1.** foolishness; a foolish act, behaviour, idea etc. **2.** a costly ornamental building that serves no practical purpose. [from Old French *folie* (*fol* = mad)]

Fomalhaut /'fɒmələʊt/ *n.* the brightest star in the southern constellation Pisces Austrinus and the 18th brightest star in the sky; known as 'the Solitary One' because it lies in a rather barren region of sky. It is a dwarf star 23 light years from Earth, with a true luminosity 14 times that of the Sun. Fomalhaut is one of a number of stars around which the Infra-Red Astronomy Satellite (see ◊infrared astronomy) detected excess infrared radiation, presumably from a region of solid particles around the star. This material may be a planetary system in the process of formation.

foment /fə'ment/ *v.t.* to instigate or stir up (trouble, discontent etc.). [from French from Latin *fomentum* = poultice (*fovēre* = warm, cherish)]

fomentation /fəʊmen'teɪʃən/ *n.* **1.** fomenting. **2.** a hot lotion applied to part of the body to relieve pain or inflammation.

fond *adj.* **1.** affectionate, loving; doting. **2.** (of hopes, beliefs, etc.) foolishly credulous or optimistic. —**fond of**, having a liking for. —**fondly** *adv.*, **fondness** *n.* [from obsolete *fon* = fool, be foolish]

Fonda /'fɒndə/ Henry 1905–1982. US actor whose engaging style made him ideal in the role of the American pioneer and honourable man. His many films include the Academy Award-winning *The Grapes of Wrath* 1940, *My Darling Clementine* 1946, and *On Golden Pond* 1981, for which he won the Academy Award for best actor. He was the father of the actress Jane Fonda and the actor and director Peter Fonda (1939–).

Fonda Jane 1937– . US actress. Her films include *Cat Ballou* 1965; *Barefoot in the Park* 1967; *Barbarella* 1968; *They Shoot Horses, Don't They?* 1969; *Julia* 1977; *The China Syndrome* 1979; *On Golden Pond* 1981, in which she appeared with her father, Henry Fonda; and *Agnes of God* 1985. She won Academy Awards for *Klute* 1971 and *Coming Home* 1979. She is also active in antiwar, pro-ecology politics and in promoting physical fitness.

***Fonteyn** One of the greatest partnerships in the history of ballet—Margot Fonteyn and Rudolf Nureyev in* Giselle.

fondant /'fɒndənt/ *n.* a soft sweet of flavoured sugar. [French = melting from Latin *fundere* = pour]

fondle *v.t.* to caress. [back-formation from *fondling* = fondled person]

fondue /'fɒndjuː, -duː/ *n.* a dish of flavoured melted cheese. [French, past participle of *fondre* = melt]

font[1] *n.* a receptacle in a church for baptismal water. —**fontal** *adj.* [Old English from Latin *fons* = fountain]

font[2] US variant of **fount**.

Fontainebleau school a French school of Mannerist painting and sculpture. It was established at the court of Francis I, who brought Italian artists to Fontainebleau near Paris to decorate his hunting lodge: Rosso Fiorentino (1494–1540) arrived in 1530, Francesco Primaticcio (1504/5–1570) came in 1532. They evolved a distinctive decorative style using a combination of stucco sculpture and painting.

Fontana /fɒn'taːn/ Domenico 1543–1607. Italian architect, employed by Pope Sixtus V. His principal works include the Vatican library and the completion of the dome of St Peter's in Rome, and the royal palace in Naples.

fontanelle /fɒntə'nel/ *n.* the membranous space in an infant's skull at the angles of the parietal bones. [from French *fontaine* = fountain]

Fontenoy, Battle of /'fɒntənwaː/ battle in the War of the ◊Austrian Succession 1745. Marshal Saxe and the French defeated the British, Dutch, and Hanoverians under the duke of Cumberland at a village in Hainaut province, Belgium, SE of Tournai.

Fonteyn /'fɒnteɪn/ Margot. Stage name of Margaret Hookham 1919–1991. English ballet dancer. She made her debut with the Vic-Wells Ballet in *Nutcracker* in 1934 and first appeared as Giselle in 1937, eventually becoming prima ballerina of the Royal Ballet, London. Renowned for her perfect physique, musicality, and interpretive powers, she created several roles in Frederick ◊Ashton's ballets and formed a successful partnership with Rudolf ◊Nureyev.

food *n.* anything eaten by human beings and other animals to sustain life and health. The building blocks of food are nutrients, utilized for both energy, measured in calories or kilojoules, and for building body tissues. Some nutrients, such as fat, carbohydrate, and alcohol, provide energy; others aid metabolism. Proteins provide energy and are necessary for cell structure. —**food for thought**, something that needs thinking about. **food-gatherer** *n.* a member of a people at a primitive stage of civilization obtaining food from

nutrients in food

type	sources
carbohydrate	as starch found in bread, potatoes, and pasta; as simple sugars in sucrose and honey; as fibres in cereals, fruit, and vegetables
protein	nuts, fish, meat, eggs, milk, and some vegetables
fat	most animal products, fish, butter, margarine, nuts, milk, oils, and lard
vitamins	found in a wide variety of foods, except for vitamin B12, which is mainly found in animal foodstuffs
minerals	found in a wide variety of foods; a good source of calcium is milk; of iodine is seafood; of iron is liver and green vegetables
water	ubiquitous in nature
alcohol	found in alcoholic beverages, from 40% in spirits to 0.01% in low-alcohol lagers and beers

natural sources not through agriculture. **food-gathering** *n.* this practice. **food processor,** an electrically driven device with blades for mixing or slicing food. **food value,** the nourishing power of a food. [Old English]

Food and Agriculture Organization (FAO) a United Nations agency that coordinates activities to improve food and timber production and levels of nutrition throughout the world. It is also concerned with investment in agriculture and dispersal of emergency food supplies. It has headquarters in Rome and was founded in 1945. The USA cut FAO funding in 1990 from $61.4 million to $18 million because of its alleged politicization.

food chain food pyramid or **food web** in ecology, the sequence of organisms through which energy and other nutrients are successively transferred. Since many organisms feed at several different levels (for example, omnivores feed on both fruit and meat), the relationships often form a complex web rather than a simple chain. See also ◊ecosystem and ◊heterotroph.

food irradiation a development in ◊food technology, whereby food is exposed to low-level radiation to kill microorganisms. Some vitamins, such as vitamin C, are partially destroyed, but this process does not make food any more radioactive than it is naturally. Irradiation is highly effective, and research carried out so far suggests that the process is relatively safe. However, it would be unwise to eat only irradiated fruit and vegetables, mainly because irradiation may be used by unscrupulous traders to 'clean up' – remove live bacteria – from consignments of food, particularly shellfish, with high bacterial counts. Bacterial toxins would remain in the food, so eating it could still cause illness. Other damaging changes may take place in the food, such as the creation of ◊free radicals.

food poisoning any acute illness characterized by vomiting and diarrhoea and caused by eating food contaminated with harmful bacteria (for example, ◊listeriosis), poisonous food (for example, certain mushrooms, puffer fish), or poisoned food (for example, lead or arsenic introduced accidentally during processing). A frequent cause of food poisoning is ◊salmonella bacteria. These come in many forms, and various strains are found in some cattle, pigs, poultry, and eggs.

foodstuff *n.* a substance used as a food.

food technology the application of science to the commercial processing of foodstuffs. Food is processed to render it more palatable and digestible, or to preserve it from spoilage. Food spoils because of the action of ◊enzymes within the food that change its chemical composition, or because of the growth of bacteria, moulds, yeasts, and other microorganisms. Fatty or oily foods also suffer oxidation of the fats, giving them a rancid flavour. Traditional forms of processing include boiling, frying, flour-milling, bread-making, yoghurt-and cheese-making, brewing, and various methods of **food preservation**, such as salting, smoking, pickling, drying, bottling, and preserving in sugar. Modern food technology still employs traditional methods but also uses many novel processes, such as freeze-drying, ultra-heat treatment, and ◊irradiation, and ◊additives, which allow a wider range of foodstuffs to be preserved.

fool[1] *n.* **1.** a person who acts or thinks unwisely or imprudently, a stupid person. **2.** (*historical*) a jester, a clown. **3.** a dupe. —*v.t./i.* to act in a joking or teasing way; to play or trifle (*about, around*); to cheat or deceive (a person) *out of* something or *into doing.* —**act** *or* **play the fool**, to behave in a silly way. **be no** *or* **nobody's fool**, to be shrewd or prudent. **fool's errand**, a fruitless errand. **fool's gold**, iron pyrites. **fool's paradise**, illusory happiness. **make a fool of**, to make (a person) look foolish; to trick or

deceive. [from Old French *fol* from Latin *follis* = bellows, empty-headed person]

fool[2] *n.* a dessert of fruit crushed and mixed with cream or custard.

foolery *n.* foolish acts or behaviour.

foolhardy *adj.* rashly or foolishly bold, reckless. —**foolhardiness** *n.* [from Old French]

foolish *adj.* (of a person or action) lacking good sense or judgement, unwise. —**foolishly** *adv.*, **foolishness** *n.*

foolproof *adj.* (of a procedure, machine etc.) so straightforward or simple as to be incapable of misuse or mistake.

foolscap /ˈfuːlskæp, -lz-/ *n.* a size of paper, about 330 ×200 (or 400) mm. [from use of fool's cap (jester's cap with bells) as watermark]

foot /fʊt/ *n.* (*plural* **feet**) **1.** the end part of the leg beyond the ankle. **2.** the lowest part of a page, table, hill etc.; the end of a bed where the feet are normally put. **3.** the part of a sock etc. covering the foot. **4.** (*plural* also **foot**) an imperial unit of length, a measure of 12 inches (30.48 cm) originally based on the measurement of a man's foot. **5.** a division of verse including one stressed syllable. **6.** step, pace, tread. **7.** (*historical*) infantry. —*v.t.* to pay (a bill). —**feet of clay**, a fundamental weakness in a person of supposed merit. **foot-and-mouth (disease)**, a contagious virus disease of cattle etc. **footbrake** *n.* a foot-operated brake on a vehicle. **footbridge** *n.* a bridge for pedestrians only. **footslog** *v.i.* (*colloquial*) to walk or march. **have one foot in the grave**, to be near death or very old. **my foot!** (*colloquial*) an exclamation of contemptuous contradiction. **on foot**, walking not riding. **put one's feet up**, to have a rest. **put one's foot down**, to be firm or insistent; to accelerate a motor vehicle. **put one's foot in it**, to blunder. **under one's feet**, in the way (*literally* and *figuratively*). **under foot**, on the ground. [Old English]

Foot Isaac 1880–1960. British Liberal politician. A staunch Nonconformist, he was minister of mines 1931–32. He was the father of Michael Foot.

Foot Michael 1913– . British Labour politician. A leader of the left-wing Tribune Group; he was secretary of state for employment 1974–76, Lord President of the Council and leader of the House 1976–79, and succeeded James Callaghan as Labour Party leader 1980–83.

Men of power have no time to read; yet men who do not read are unfit for power.

Michael Foot
Debts of Honour

footage *n.* a length in feet, especially of exposed cinema film.

foot-and-mouth disease contagious eruptive viral disease of cloven-hoofed mammals, characterized by blisters in the mouth and around the hooves. In cattle it causes deterioration of milk yield and abortions.

football *n.* **1.** a large inflated ball, usually of leather. **2.** a team ball game played in many different forms. See ◊football, American, ◊football, association, ◊football, Australian, ◊rugby football. —**football pool(s)**, a form of gambling on the results of football matches, the entry money being awarded in prizes. —**footballer** *n.*

football, American a contact sport similar to the English game of rugby. First match under Harvard rules was between Harvard University and McGill University, Montreal, Canada, in 1874.

football, association or **soccer** a form of football originating in the UK, popular in Europe and Latin America.

It is played between two teams each of 11 players, on a field 90–120 m/100–130 yd long and 45–90 m/50–100 yd wide, with a spherical, inflated (traditionally leather) ball, circumference 0.69 m/27 in. The object of the game is to send the ball with the feet or head into the opponents' goal, an area 7.31 m/8 yd wide and 2.44 m/8 ft high.

football, Australian an 18-a-side game that is a cross between Gaelic football, rugby, and soccer, and is unique to Australia, although association and rugby football are also played there.

foot-candle *n.* a unit of illuminance, now replaced by the lux. One foot-candle is the illumination received at a distance of one foot from an international candle. It is equal to 10.764 lux.

footfall *n.* the sound of a footstep.

foothill *n.* one of the low hills near the bottom of a mountain or range.

foothold *n.* a place where the foot can be supported securely; *(figurative)* a secure initial position.

footing *n.* 1. a foothold, a secure position. 2. the position or status of a person in relation to others.

footlights *n.pl.* a row of lights at the front of a stage at the level of the actors' feet.

footling /'fu:tlɪŋ/ *adj. (slang)* trivial, silly. [from *footle* = play the fool]

footloose *adj.* free to act as one pleases.

footman *n. (plural footmen)* a liveried servant for attending at the door or at table.

footnote *n.* a note printed at the foot of a page.

footpad *n. (historical)* an unmounted highwayman.

footpath *n.* a path for pedestrians, a pavement.

footplate *n.* a platform for the crew of a locomotive.

foot-pound *n.* an imperial unit of energy (ft-lb), defined as the work done when a force of one pound moves through a distance of one foot. It has been superseded for scientific work by the joule (one foot-pound equals 1.356 joule).

footprint *n.* an impression left by a foot or shoe.

footsore *adj.* with sore feet, especially from walking.

footstep *n.* a step taken in walking; the sound of this. —**follow in a person's footsteps** to do as he did.

footstool *n.* a stool for resting the feet on when sitting.

footway *n.* a path for pedestrians only.

footwear *n.* shoes, socks etc.

footwork *n.* the use or manner of using the feet in sports, dancing etc.

fop *n.* a dandy. —**foppery** *n.*, **foppish** *adj.* [perhaps from obsolete *fop* = fool]

for /fə, *emphatic* fɔ:/ *prep.* 1. in defence, support, or favour of; in the interest or to the benefit of. 2. suitable or appropriate to. 3. in respect or reference to, regarding, so far as concerns. 4. at the price of; in exchange with, corresponding to; as a penalty or reward resulting from. 5. with a view to, in hope or quest of, in order to get. 6. in the direction of, towards, to reach. 7. so as to have begun by (a specified time). 8. through or over (a distance or period), during. 9. in the character of, as being. 10. because of, on account of. 11. in spite of, notwithstanding. 12. considering or making due allowance in respect of. —*conj.* seeing that, since, because. —**be for it,** *(colloquial)* to be about to get punishment or other trouble. **for ever,** for all time (see also ◊forever). O *or* **oh for,** I wish I had. [Old English]

for- prefix forming verbs etc. meaning (1) away or off (*forget, forgive*); (2) prohibition (*forbid*); (3) abstention or neglect (*forgo, forsake*). [Old English]

f.o.r. abbreviation of free on rail.

forage /'fɒrɪdʒ/ *n.* 1. food for horses and cattle. 2. foraging. —*v.t./i.* to go searching, to rummage; to collect forage (from). —**forager** *n.* [from Old French from Germanic]

foraminifera *n.* single-celled marine animals, often classified as an order of Protozoa, which are enclosed by a thin shell. Some form part of ◊plankton, others live on the sea bottom.

forasmuch /fɒrəz'mʌtʃ/ *adv.* **forasmuch as,** *(archaic)* since, because. [= *for as much*]

foray /'fɒreɪ/ *n.* a sudden attack, a raid. —*v.i.* to make a foray. [from Old French *forrier* = forager]

forbade, forbad past of forbid.

forbear[1] /fɔ:'beə/ *v.t./i. (past forbore; past participle forborne)* to abstain (from) or refrain. [Old English]

forbear[2] variant of forebear.

forbearance *n.* patient self-control, tolerance.

Forbes /fɔ:bz/ Bryan (John Clarke) 1926– . British film producer, director, and screenwriter. After acting in films like *An Inspector Calls* 1954, he made his directorial debut with *Whistle Down the Wind* 1961; among his other films is *The L-Shaped Room* 1962.

forbid /fə'bɪd/ *v.t.* (-dd-; *past* forbade /-'bæd/, forbad; *past participle* forbidden) to order not *to do*; to refuse to allow (a thing, or a person to have a thing); to refuse a person entry to.

forbidding *adj.* uninviting, repellent, stern.

forbore past of forbear[1].

forborne past participle of forbear[1].

force[1] *n.* 1. strength, power, impetus, intense effort; coercion, compulsion; military strength. 2. an organized body of soldiers, police, workers etc. 3. binding power, validity, effect, precise significance. 4. influence, efficacy. 5. a measurable and determinable influence tending to cause the motion of a body; the intensity of this; a person or thing likened to this. —*v.t./i.* 1. to constrain (a person) by force or against his or her will. 2. to make (a way) into or through by force, to break open by force. 3. to drive or propel violently or against resistance. 4. to impose or press (a thing) *on* or *upon* a person. 5. to cause or produce by effort. 6. to strain or increase to the utmost, to overstrain. 7. to hasten the growth or maturity of (a plant, pupil etc.) artificially. —**forced labour,** compulsory labour, usually under harsh conditions. **forced landing,** an unavoidable landing of an aircraft in an emergency. **forced march,** a lengthy and vigorous march especially by troops. **force-feed** *v.t.* to feed (especially a prisoner) against his or her will. **force a person's hand,** to make someone act prematurely or unwillingly. **force the issue,** to make an immediate decision necessary. **in force,** valid, in great strength or numbers. [from Old French from Latin *fortis* = strong]

force[2] *n.* in physics, any influence that tends to change the state of rest or the uniform motion of a body in a straight line. It is measured by the rate of change of momentum of the body on which it acts, that is, the mass of the body multiplied by its acceleration: $F = ma$.

force[3] *n.* in the north of England, a waterfall. [from Old Norse *fors*]

forceful *adj.* powerful and vigorous; (of speech) impressive, compelling. —**forcefully** *adv.*, **forcefulness** *n.*

force majeure /fɔ:s mæ'ʒ:/ irresistible force; unforeseen circumstances excusing a person from the fulfilment of a contract. [French = superior strength]

forcemeat /'fɔ:smi:t/ *n.* meat etc. chopped and seasoned for a stuffing or garnish. [from Old French *farsir* = stuff]

forceps /'fɔ:seps/ *n. (plural the same)* surgical pincers. [Latin]

force ratio the magnification of a force by a machine; see ◊mechanical advantage.

forces, fundamental in physics, the four fundamental interactions believed to be at work in the physical universe. There are two long-range forces: **gravity,** which keeps the planets in orbit around the Sun, and acts between all ◊particles that have mass; and the **electromagnetic force,** which stops solids from falling apart, and acts between all particles with ◊electric charge. There are two very short-range forces: the **weak force,** responsible for the reactions that fuel the Sun and for the emission of ◊beta particles from certain nuclei; and the **strong force,** which binds together the protons and neutrons in the nuclei of atoms.

forcible /'fɔ:sɪbəl/ *adj.* done by or involving force; forceful. —**forcibly** *adv.* [from Old French]

ford *n.* a shallow place where a river or stream may be crossed by wading, in a motor vehicle etc. —*v.t.* to cross (water) thus. —**fordable** *adj.* [Old English]

Ford /fɔ:d/ Ford Madox. Adopted name of Ford Madox Hueffer 1873–1939. English writer of the novel *The Good Soldier* 1915 and editor of the *English Review* 1908, to which Thomas Hardy, D H Lawrence, and Joseph Conrad contributed. He was a grandson of the painter Ford Madox Brown.

Ford Gerald R(udolph) 1913– . the 38th president of the USA 1974–77, a Republican. He was elected to the House of Representatives in 1949, was nominated to the vice-presidency by Richard Nixon in 1973 following the resignation of Spiro ◊Agnew, and in 1974, when Nixon resigned, Ford became president. He pardoned Nixon, and gave amnesty to those who had resisted the draft for the Vietnam War.

Ford Glenn (Gwyllym Samuel Newton) 1916– . Canadian actor, active in Hollywood during the 1940s–1960s. Usually cast as the tough but good-natured hero, he was equally at home in Westerns, thrillers, and comedies. His films include *Gilda* 1946, *The Big Heat* 1953, and *Dear Heart* 1965.

Ford Henry 1863–1947. US automobile manufacturer, who built his first car in 1893 and founded the Ford Motor Company in 1903. His Model T (1908–27) was the first car to be constructed solely by mass-production methods, and 15 million of these cars were made.

Ford John 1586–*c*.1640. English poet and dramatist. His play *'Tis Pity She's a Whore* (performed about 1626, printed 1633) is a study of incest between brother and sister.

Ford John. Stage name of Sean O'Feeney 1895–1973. US film director. His films, especially his Westerns, were influential, and include *Stagecoach* 1939, *The Grapes of Wrath* 1940, and *The Man who Shot Liberty Valance* 1962.

fore *adj.* situated in front. —*n.* the front part, the bow of a ship. —*int.* (in golf) as a warning to a person likely to be hit by a ball. —**fore and aft**, at the bow and stern; all over the ship. **fore-and-aft** *adj.* (of a sail or rigging) lengthwise, not on yards. **to the fore**, in front, conspicuous. [Old English]

fore- prefix forming (1) verbs in senses 'in front' (*foreshorten*), 'beforehand' (*forewarn*); (2) nouns in senses 'situated in front' (*forecourt*), 'front part of' (*forehead*), 'of or near the bow of a ship' (*forecastle*), 'preceding' (*forerunner*).

forearm[1] /ˈfɔːrɑːm/ *n.* the arm between the elbow and the wrist or fingertips; the corresponding part in an animal.

forearm[2] /fɔːˈrɑːm/ *v.t.* to arm beforehand, to prepare.

forebear /ˈfɔːbeə/ *n.* (usually in *plural*) an ancestor.

forebode /fɔːˈbəud/ *v.t.* to be an advance sign of, to portend; to have a presentiment of (usually evil) or *that*.

foreboding *n.* an expectation of trouble.

forecast /ˈfɔːkɑːst/ *v.t.* (*past & past participle* forecast or forecasted) to predict or estimate beforehand. —*n.* forecasting; a prediction.

forecastle /ˈfəuksəl/ *n.* the forward part of a ship where formerly the crew were accommodated.

foreclose /fɔːˈkləuz/ *v.t.* **1.** to take possession of the mortgaged property of (a person) when the loan is not duly repaid; to stop (a mortgage) from being redeemable. **2.** to exclude, to prevent. —**foreclosure** *n.* [from Old French *forclore*]

forecourt *n.* an enclosed space in front of a building; the part of a filling station where petrol is dispensed.

foredoom /fɔːˈduːm/ *v.t.* to doom or condemn beforehand.

forefather *n.* (usually in *plural*) an ancestor, a member of a past generation of a family or people.

forefinger *n.* the finger next to the thumb.

forefoot *n.* (*plural* forefeet) a front foot of an animal.

forefront *n.* the foremost part; the leading position.

foregoing /fɔːˈgəuiŋ/ *adj.* preceding, previously mentioned.

foregone /fɔːgɒn/ *adj.* previous, preceding. —**foregone conclusion**, an easily foreseen or predictable result. [Old English]

foreground *n.* **1.** the part of a view or picture nearest the observer. **2.** the most conspicuous position.

forehand *n.* (in tennis etc.) a stroke made with the palm of the hand facing the opponent. —*adj.* (also **forehanded**) of or made with this stroke.

forehead /ˈfɒrɪd, ˈfɔːhed/ *n.* the part of the head above the eyebrows.

foreign /ˈfɒrən/ *adj.* **1.** of, from, situated in, or characteristic of a country or language other than one's own; dealing with other countries; of another district, society etc. **2.** unfamiliar, strange, uncharacteristic. **3.** coming from outside. —**foreign aid**, money etc. given or lent by one country to another. **Foreign and Commonwealth Office**, the UK government department dealing with foreign affairs. **Foreign Secretary**, the head of this. [from Old French from Latin *foris* = outside]

foreigner *n.* a person born in or coming from another country.

Foreign Legion a volunteer corps of foreigners within a country's army. The French *Légion Etrangère*, formed

in 1831, is one of a number of such forces. Enlisted volunteers are of any nationality (about half are now French), but the officers are usually French. Headquarters until 1962 was in Sidi Bel Abbés, Algeria; the main base is now Corsica, with reception headquarters at Aubagne, near Marseille, France.

foreign relations a country's dealings with other countries. Specialized diplomatic bodies first appeared in Europe during the 18th century. After 1818 diplomatic agents were divided into: **ambassadors**, papal legates, and nuncios; **envoys** extraordinary, **ministers** plenipotentiary, and other ministers accredited to the head of state; ministers resident; and **chargés d'affaires**, who may deputize for an ambassador or minister, or be themselves the representative accredited to a minor country. Other diplomatic staff may include counsellors and attachés (military, labour, cultural, press). **Consuls** are state agents with commercial and political responsibilities in foreign towns.

foreknow /fɔːˈnəu/ *v.t.* to know beforehand. —**foreknowledge** /fɔːˈnɒlɪdʒ/ *n.*

foreland *n.* a promontory, a cape.

foreleg *n.* a front leg of an animal.

forelimb *n.* a front limb of an animal.

forelock *n.* a lock of hair just above the forehead. —**take time by the forelock,** to seize an opportunity.

foreman *n.* (*plural* foremen) **1.** a workman supervising others. **2.** the president and spokesman of a jury.

foremast *n.* the mast nearest the bow of a ship.

foremost *adj.* most advanced in position; most notable, best. —*adv.* in the first place, most importantly. [from superlative of Old English *forma* = first]

forename *n.* a first or Christian name.

forenoon *n.* the day till noon, the morning.

forensic /fəˈrensik/ *adj.* of or used in courts of law. —**forensically** *adv.* [from Latin]

forensic science the use of scientific techniques to solve criminal cases. A multi-disciplinary field embracing chemistry, physics, botany, zoology, and medicine, forensic science includes the identification of human bodies or traces. Traditional methods such as ◊fingerprinting are still used, assisted by computers; in addition, blood analysis, forensic dentistry, voice and speech spectograms, and ◊genetic fingerprinting are increasingly applied. Ballistics (the study of projectiles, such as bullets), another traditional forensic field, today makes use of tools such as the comparison microscope and the ◊electron microscope. Chemicals, such as poisons and drugs, are analysed by ◊chromatography.

foreordain /fɔːrɔːˈdeɪn/ *v.t.* to destine beforehand. —**foreordination** /-dɪˈneɪʃən/ *n.*

forepaw *n.* a front paw of an animal.

foreplay *n.* stimulation preceding sexual intercourse.

forerunner *n.* a predecessor; an advance messenger.

foresail /ˈfɔːseɪl, -səl/ *n.* the principal sail on the foremast.

foresee /fɔːˈsiː/ *v.t.* (*past* foresaw ; *past participle* foreseen) to see or be aware of beforehand.

foreseeable /fɔːˈsiːəbəl/ *adj.* able to be foreseen. —**in the foreseeable future**, in the period ahead during which the general course of events can reasonably be predicted.

foreshadow /fɔːˈʃædəu/ *v.t.* to be a warning or indication of (a future event).

foreshore *n.* the shore between high-and low-water marks.

foreshorten /fɔːˈʃɔːtən/ *v.t.* to show or portray (an object) with apparent shortening due to visual perspective.

foresight *n.* **1.** regard or provision for the future. **2.** foreseeing. **3.** the front sight of a gun.

foreskin *n.* the loose skin covering the end of the penis.

forest /ˈfɒrɪst/ *n.* a large area of land covered chiefly with trees and undergrowth; the trees in this; a dense concentration (of things). —*v.t.* to plant with trees, to make into a forest. [from Old French from Latin *forestis*]

forestall /fɔːˈstɔːl/ *v.t.* to act in advance of in order to prevent; to deal with beforehand. [from Old English = an ambush, plot]

forestay *n.* a stay from the head of the foremast to a ship's deck to support the foremast.

forester *n.* **1.** an officer in charge of a forest. **2.** a dweller in a forest.

Forester /ˈfɒrɪstə/ C(ecil) S(cott) 1899–1966. English novelist, born in Egypt. He wrote a series of historical novels set in the Napoleonic era that, beginning with *The Happy Return* 1937, cover the career—from midshipman to admiral – of Horatio Hornblower.

forestry *n.* the science or management of forests.

foretaste *n.* a taste or experience of something in advance.

foretell /fɔː'tel/ *v.t.* (*past* and *past participle* **foretold**) to predict, to prophesy; to be a precursor of.

forethought *n.* care or provision for the future; deliberate intention.

forever /fə'revə/ *adv.* continually, persistently.

forewarn /fɔː'wɔːn/ *v.t.* to warn beforehand.

forewoman *n.* (*plural* **forewomen**) 1. a woman worker supervising others. 2. the woman foreman of a jury.

foreword *n.* the introductory remarks at the beginning of a book, often by a person other than the author.

forfeit /'fɔːfɪt/ *n.* a penalty, a thing surrendered as a penalty. —*v.t.* to lose or surrender as a penalty. —*adj.* lost or surrendered as a forfeit. —**forfeiture** *n.* [from Old French *forfaire* = transgress from Latin *foris* = outside and *facere* = do]

forgather /fɔː'gæðə/ *v.i.* to assemble, to associate. [from Dutch *vergaderen*]

forgave past of **forgive**.

forge[1] *v.t.* 1. to make or write in fraudulent imitation. 2. to shape (metal) by heating and hammering, ◊forging. —*n.* a furnace etc. for melting and refining metal; a workshop with this; a blacksmith's workshop. —**forger** *n.* [from Old French from Latin *fabrica*]

forge[2] *v.i.* to advance or move forward gradually or steadily.

forgery /'fɔːdʒəri/ *n.* 1. the act of forging. 2. a forged document etc. [from *forge*[1]]

forget /fə'get/ *v.t./i.* (**-tt-**; *past* **forgot** ; *past participle* **forgotten**, *US* **forgot**) to lose remembrance of or *about*, not to remember; to neglect or overlook; to cease to think of. —**forget oneself**, to put others' interests first; to behave without due dignity. [Old English]

forgetful *adj.* apt to forget, neglectful. —**forgetfully** *adv.*, **forgetfulness** *n.*

forget-me-not *n.* any plant of the genus *Myosotis*, family Boraginaceae, including *M. sylvatica* and *M. scorpioides*, with bright blue flowers.

forging *n.* one of the main methods of shaping metals, which involves hammering or a more gradual application of pressure. A blacksmith hammers red-hot metal into shape on an anvil. The blacksmith's mechanical equivalent is the drop forge. The metal is shaped by the blows from a falling hammer or ram, which is usually accelerated by steam or air pressure. Hydraulic presses forge by applying pressure gradually in a squeezing action.

forgive /fə'gɪv/ *v.t.* (*past* **forgave**; *past participle* **forgiven** /-'gɪvən/) 1. to cease to feel angry or resentful towards (a person) or about (an offence). 2. to pardon. 3. to remit (a debt). [Old English]

forgiveness *n.* the act of forgiving; the state of being forgiven.

forgiving *adj.* inclined readily to forgive.

forgo /fɔː'gəʊ/ *v.t.* (*past* **forwent** ; *past participle* **forgone**) to go without, to relinquish; to omit or decline to take or use (a pleasure, advantage etc.). [Old English]

forgot past and US past participle of **forget**.

forgotten past participle of **forget**.

fork *n.* 1. a pronged implement used in eating and cooking; a similar much larger implement used for digging, lifting etc. 2. a divergence of a stick, road, etc, into two parts; the place of this; one of the two parts. 3. the forked support for a bicycle wheel. 4. a pronged device pushed under a load to be lifted. —*v.t./i.* 1. to form a fork or branch by separating into two parts; to take one road at a fork. 2. to dig, lift, or throw with a fork. —**fork-lift truck**, a vehicle with a fork for lifting and carrying loads. **fork out**, (*slang*) to pay (usually reluctantly). [Old English from Latin *furca*]

forlorn /fə'lɔːn/ *adj.* sad and abandoned; in a pitiful state. —**forlorn hope**, a faint remaining hope or chance. —**forlornly** *adv.* [past participle of obsolete *forlese*; *forlorn hope* from Dutch *verloren hoop* = lost troop (originally of storming-party)]

form *n.* 1. shape, arrangement of parts, visible aspect. 2. a person or animal as visible or tangible. 3. the mode in which a thing exists or manifests itself. 4. a printed document

with blank spaces for information to be inserted. 5. a class in school. 6. a customary method; a set order of words. 7. a species, a kind. 8. behaviour according to rule or custom; correct procedure. 9. (of an athlete, horse etc.) condition of health and training; (in racing etc.) details of previous performances; (*slang*) a criminal record. 10. one of the ways in which a word may be spelt, pronounced, or inflected. 11. the arrangement and style in a literary or musical composition. 12. a bench. 13. a hare's lair. —*v.t./i.* 1. to fashion or shape. 2. to mould by discipline, to train or instruct. 3. to develop or establish as a concept, institution, or practice; to organize (*into* a company etc.) 4. to be the material of, to make up, to be. 5. to take shape, to come into existence. 6. to construct (a word) by inflexion etc. 7. (often with *up*) to bring or move into formation. —**on** *or* **off form**, performing or playing well or badly. [from Old French from Latin *forma*]

-form suffix forming adjectives (usually as **-iform**) in senses 'having the form of' (*cuneiform*), 'having such a number of forms' (*uniform*).

formal /'fɔːməl/ *adj.* 1. used or done or held in accordance with rules, convention, or ceremony; excessively stiff or methodical. 2. valid or correctly so called because of its form; explicit. 3. of or concerned with (outward) form, especially as distinct from content or matter. 4. perfunctory, following form only. 5. precise, symmetrical. —**formally** *adv.* [from Latin]

formaldehyde /fɔː'mældɪhaɪd/ *n.* common name for ◊methanal; the aldehyde of formic acid, used as a disinfectant and preservative.

formalin *n.* an aqueous solution of formaldehyde (methanal) used to preserve animal specimens.

formalism /'fɔːməlɪzəm/ *n.* 1. strict or excessive adherence to or concern with form or forms. 2. treatment of mathematics as the manipulation of meaningless symbols. 3. a symbolic and stylized manner of theatrical production. —**formalist** *n.*

formality /fɔː'mælɪtɪ/ *n.* a formal act, regulation, or custom (often lacking real significance); a thing done simply to comply with a rule; rigid observance of rules or convention. [from French or Latin]

formalize /'fɔːməlaɪz/ *v.t.* to make formal; to give a definite (especially legal) form to. —**formalization** /-'zeɪʃən/ *n.*

format /'fɔːmæt/ *n.* 1. the shape and size (of a book etc.). 2. style or manner of arrangement or procedure. 3. the arrangement of data etc. for a computer. —*v.t.* (**-tt-**) to arrange in a format, especially for a computer. [French from German, from Latin *formatus* (*liber*) = shaped (book)]

formation /fɔː'meɪʃən/ *n.* 1. forming. 2. a thing formed; a particular arrangement (e.g. of troops); a set of rocks or strata with a common characteristic. [from Old French or Latin *formare* = to shape]

formative /'fɔːmətɪv/ *adj.* serving to form or fashion; of formation. [from Old French or Latin]

Formby /'fɔːmbi/ George 1904–1961. English comedian. He established a stage and screen reputation as an apparently simple Lancashire working lad, and sang such songs as 'Mr Wu' and 'Cleaning Windows', accompanying himself on the ukulele. His father was a music-hall star of the same name.

forme /fɔːm/ *n.* a body of type secured in a chase for printing at one impression.

former *adj.* of the past, earlier. —**the former**, the first or first-mentioned of two. [comparative of Old English *forma* = first]

formerly *adv.* in former times.

Formica /fɔː'maɪkə/ *n.* the trade name for a heat-proof plastic laminate, widely used as a veneer on kitchen surfaces and children's furniture. It is made from formaldehyde resins similar to ◊Bakelite.

formic acid /'fɔːmɪk/ ◊methanoic acid; a colourless, irritant, volatile acid contained in the fluid emitted by ants. [from Latin *formica* = ant]

formidable /'fɔːmɪdəbəl/ -'mɪd-/ *adj.* 1. inspiring fear or dread. 2. likely to be difficult to overcome or deal with. —**formidably** *adv.* [French, or from Latin *formidare* = dread]

formless *adj.* without a definite or regular form.

formula /'fɔːmjʊlə/ *n.* (*plural* **formulas**, **formulae** /-iː/) 1. in chemistry, a representation of a molecule, radical, or ion, in which chemical elements are represented by their symbols. An **empirical formula** indicates the simplest ratio of the elements in a compound, without indicating how many of them there are or how they are combined. A **molecular formula** gives the number of each type of element present in one molecule. A **structural formula** shows the relative positions of the atoms and the bonds between them. For example, for ethanoic acid, the empirical formula is CH_2O, the molecular formula is $C_2H_4O_2$, and the structural formula is CH_3COOH. Formula is also another name for a chemical ◊equation. **2.** a mathematical rule expressed in figures. **3.** a fixed form of words, especially one used on social or ceremonious occasions; a form of words embodying or enabling an agreement. **4.** a list of ingredients. **5.** the classification of a racing car, especially by engine capacity. **6.** (*US*) an infant's food made according to a prescribed recipe. —**formulaic**/-'leɪɪk/ *adj.* [Latin, diminutive of *forma* = form]

formulary /'fɔːmjʊlərɪ/ *n.* a collection of formulas or set forms. [from French or Latin]

formulate /'fɔːmjʊleɪt/ *v.t.* to express in a formula; to express clearly and precisely. —**formulation**/-'leɪʃən/ *n.*

fornicate /'fɔːnɪkeɪt/ *v.i.* (of people not married to each other) to have sexual intercourse voluntarily. —**fornication** /-'keɪʃən/ *n.*, **fornicator** *n.* [from Latin *fornicare* (*fornix* = brothel)]

Forrest /'fɒrɪst/ John, 1st Baron Forrest 1847–1918. Australian explorer and politician. He crossed Western Australia W–E in 1870, when he went along the southern coast route, and in 1874, when he crossed much further north, exploring the Musgrave Ranges. He was born in Western Australia, and was its first premier 1890–1901.

forsake /fə'seɪk/ *v.t.* (*past* **forsook** /-'sʊk/; *past participle* **forsaken**) **1.** to give up, to renounce. **2.** to withdraw one's help or companionship from. [from Old English *sacan* = quarrel]

forsooth /fɔː'suːθ/ *adv.* (*archaic*, now usually *ironical.*) indeed, truly, no doubt. [from Old English *sōth* = true]

Forster /'fɔːstə/ E(dward) M(organ) 1879–1970. English novelist, concerned with the interplay of personality and the conflict between convention and instinct. His novels include *A Room with a View* 1908, *Howards End* 1910, and *A Passage to India* 1924. He also wrote short stories, for example 'The Eternal Omnibus' 1914; criticism, including *Aspects of the Novel* 1927; and essays, including *Abinger Harvest* 1936.

forswear /fɔː'sweə/ *v.t.* (*past* **forswore**; *past participle* **forsworn**) **1.** to abjure, to renounce. **2.** (in *past participle*) perjured. —**forswear oneself**, to perjure oneself. [Old English]

Forsyth /fɔː'saɪθ/ Frederick 1938– . English thriller writer. His books include *The Day of the Jackal* 1970, *The Dogs of War* 1974, and *The Fourth Protocol* 1984.

forsythia /fɔː'saɪθɪə/ *n.* any temperate E Asian shrub of the genus *Forsythia* of the olive family Oleaceae, which bear yellow flowers in early spring before the leaves appear. [from W. *Forsyth* English botanist (died 1804)]

fort *n.* a fortified military building or position. —**hold the fort**, to act as a temporary substitute, to cope with an emergency. [from French or Italian from Latin *fortis* = strong]

Fort-de-France /'fɔː də 'frɒns/ capital, chief commercial centre, and port of ◊Martinique, West Indies; population (1982) 99,844.

forte[1] /'fɔːteɪ/ *n.* one's strong point, a thing in which one excels. [from French *fort* = strong]

forte[2] *adj.* & *adv.* in music, loud, loudly. —*n.* loud playing; a passage played loudly. [Italian = strong, loud]

fortepiano /fɔːtɪpiæʊ/ *n.* (*plural* **fortepianos**) a pianoforte, especially an instrument of the 18th to early 19th century [Italian *forte* = loud and *piano* = soft]

forth /fɔːθ/ *adv.* (*archaic* except in set phrases) forward, into view; onwards in time; forwards; out from a starting-point. [Old English]

Forth river in SE Scotland, with its headstreams rising on the NE slopes of Ben Lomond. It flows approximately 72 km/45 mi to Kincardine where the **Firth of Forth** begins. The firth is approximately 80 km/50 mi long, and is 26 km/16 mi wide where it joins the North Sea.

forthcoming *adj.* **1.** approaching, coming or available soon. **2.** produced when wanted. **3.** (of a person) willing to give information, responsive.

forthright *adj.* straightforward; outspoken; decisive.

forthwith /fɔːθ'wɪð/ *adv.* at once, without delay. [from earlier *forthwithal*]

fortification /fɔːtɪfɪ'keɪʃən/ *n.* **1.** the act of fortifying. **2.** (usually in *plural*) defensive works, walls etc.

fortify /'fɔːtɪfaɪ/ *v.t./i.* **1.** to strengthen physically, mentally, morally etc. **2.** to provide with or erect fortifications. **3.** to strengthen (wine) with alcohol; to add extra nutrients, especially vitamins, to (food). [from Old French from Latin *fortificare* (*fortis* = strong)]

fortissimo /fɔː'tɪsɪməʊ/ *adj.* & *adv.* in music, very loud, very loudly. —*n.* (*plural* **fortissimos**) in music, very loud playing; a passage played very loudly. [Italian superlative of *forte*[2]]

fortitude /'fɔːtɪtjuːd/ *n.* courage in pain or adversity. [from French from Latin *fortis* = strong, brave]

Fort Knox /nɒks/ US army post and gold depository in Kentucky, established in 1917 as a training camp. The US Treasury gold-bullion vaults were built in 1937.

fortnight *n.* two weeks. [Old English = fourteen nights]

fortnightly *adj.* done, produced, or occurring once a fortnight. —*adv.* every fortnight. —*n.* a fortnightly magazine etc.

FORTRAN /'fɔːtræn/ acronym from **for**mula **tran**slation; a computer-programming language suited to mathematical and scientific computations. Developed in the mid-1950s, it is one of the earliest programming languages still in use.

fortress /'fɔːtrɪs/ *n.* a fortified building or town. [from Old French from Latin *fortis* = strong]

Fort Sumter /'sʌmtə/ fort in Charleston, South Carolina, USA, 6.5 km/4 mi SE of Charleston. The first shots of the US Civil War were fired here on 12 April 1861, after its commander had refused the call to surrender made by the Confederate general Beauregard.

Fort Ticonderoga /taɪcɒndə'rəʊgə/ fort in New York State, USA, near Lake Champlain. It was the site of battles between the British and the French 1758–59, and was captured from the British 10 May 1775 by Benedict ◊Arnold and Ethan Allen (leading the ◊Green Mountain Boys).

fortuitous /fɔː'tjuːɪtəs/ *adj.* happening by chance, accidental. —**fortuitously** *adv.*, **fortuitousness** *n.*, **fortuity** *n.* [from Latin *forte* = by chance]

fortunate /'fɔːtjʊnət, -tʃənət/ *adj.* lucky, auspicious. —**fortunately** *adv.*

fortune /'fɔːtjuːn, -tʃuːn/ *n.* **1.** chance or luck as a force in human affairs. **2.** the luck (good or bad) that befalls a person or enterprise. **3.** a person's destiny. **4.** good luck; prosperity, great wealth, a huge sum of money. —**fortune-teller** *n.* a person who claims to foretell one's destiny. **make a fortune**, to become very rich. [from Latin *fortuna* = luck, chance]

forty *adj.* & *n.* **1.** four times ten; the symbol for this (40, xl, XL). **2.** (in *plural*) the numbers, years, degrees of temperature etc., from 40 to 49. —**forty winks**, a short sleep. —**fortieth** *adj.* & *n.* [Old English]

Forty-Five, the the ◊Jacobite rebellion of 1745, led by Prince ◊Charles Edward Stuart. With his army of Highlanders 'Bonnie Prince Charlie' occupied Edinburgh and advanced into England as far as Derby, but then turned back. The rising was crushed by the Duke of Cumberland at Culloden in 1746.

forum /'fɔːrəm/ *n.* **1.** the public square or market-place in an ancient Roman city, used for judicial and other business. **2.** a place of or meeting for public discussion; a court, a tribunal. [Latin]

forward /'fɔːwəd/ *adj.* **1.** lying in one's line of motion, onward or towards the front. **2.** relating to the future. **3.** precocious, bold in manner, presumptuous. **4.** approaching maturity or completion; (of a plant etc.) well-advanced, early. —*n.* an attacking player near the front in football, hockey etc. —*adv.* **1.** to the front, into prominence; in advance, ahead. **2.** onward so as to make progress. **3.** towards the future. **4.** (also **forwards**) towards the front in the direction one is facing; in the normal direction of motion or of traversal; with a continuous forward motion. —*v.t.* **1.** to send (a letter etc.) on to a further destination; to dispatch (goods etc.). **2.** to help to advance; to promote. —**forwardness** *n.* [Old English]

Foss /fɒs/ Lukas 1922– . US composer and conductor. He wrote the cantata *The Prairie* 1942 and *Time Cycle* for soprano and orchestra 1960.

fosse /fɒs/ *n.* a long ditch or trench, especially in fortification. [from Old French from Latin *fossa* = ditch]

Fosse /fɒs/ Bob (Robert) 1927–1987. US film director who entered films as a dancer and choreographer from Broadway, making his directorial debut with *Sweet Charity* 1968. He received an Academy Award for his second film as director, *Cabaret* 1972. His other work includes *All That Jazz* 1979.

fossick /'fɒsɪk/ *v.i.* (*Australian* and *New Zealand slang*) to rummage, to search *about*; to search for gold etc. in abandoned workings. [perhaps from dialect *fossick* = bustle about]

fossil /'fɒsəl/ *n.* 1. the remains or impression of a (usually prehistoric) plant or animal hardened in a rock. Fossils may be formed by refrigeration (for example, Siberian ◊mammoths); carbonization (leaves in coal); formation of a cast (dinosaur or human footprints in mud); or mineralization of bones, more generally teeth or shells. The study of fossils is called ◊palaeontology. 2. an antiquated or unchanging person or thing. —*adj.* 1. of or like a fossil. 2. found buried, dug from the ground. [from French from Latin *fossilis* (*fodere* = dig)]

fossil fuel fuel, such as coal or oil, formed from the fossilized remains of plants that lived hundreds of millions of years ago. Fossil fuels are a ◊nonrenewable resource and will run out eventually.

fossilize /'fɒsɪlaɪz/ *v.t./i.* to become or cause to become a fossil. —**fossilization** /-'zeɪʃən/ *n.*

foster *v.t.* 1. to promote the growth or development of; to encourage or harbour (a feeling); (of circumstances) to be favourable to. 2. to bring up a child that is not one's own. —*adj.* (in combinations, as foster-brother, foster-mother) having a family connection by fostering not by birth. —**foster home,** a home in which a foster-child is brought up. [Old English = nourishment]

Foster Jodie 1962– . US film actress, who began as a child in a great variety of roles. Her work includes *Taxi Driver* 1976, *Bugsy Malone* 1976, and *The Accused* 1988, for which she won the Academy Award for best actress.

Foster Norman 1935– . British architect of the ◊high-tech school. His works include the Willis Faber office, Ipswich, 1978, the Sainsbury Centre for Visual Arts at the University of East Anglia 1979, and the headquarters of the Hongkong and Shanghai Bank, Hong Kong, 1986.

Foster Stephen Collins 1826–1864. US songwriter. He wrote sentimental popular songs including 'My Old Kentucky Home' 1853 and 'Beautiful Dreamer' 1864, and rhythmic minstrel songs such as 'Oh! Susanna' 1848 and 'Camptown Races' 1850.

Foucault /'fu:kəʊ/ Jean Bernard Léon 1819–1868. French physicist who used a pendulum to demonstrate the rotation of the Earth on its axis, and invented the gyroscope.

Foucault /'fu:kəʊ/ Michel 1926–1984. French philosopher who rejected phenomenology and existentialism. He was concerned with how forms of knowledge and forms of human subjectivity are constructed by specific institutions and practices.

Fouché /'fu:ʃeɪ/ Joseph, duke of Otranto 1759–1820. French politician. He was elected to the National Convention (the post-Revolutionary legislature), and organized the conspiracy that overthrew the ◊Jacobin leader ◊Robespierre. Napoleon employed him as police minister.

fouetté *n.* in ballet, a type of ◊pirouette in which one leg is extended to the side and then into the knee in a whiplike action, while the dancer spins on the supporting leg. Odile performs 32 fouettés in Act III of *Swan Lake*. [French = whipped]

fought past and past participle of **fight.**

foul *adj.* 1. offensive, loathsome, stinking; filthy, soiled; (*colloquial*) disgusting. 2. (of language etc.) obscene, disgustingly abusive. 3. (of weather) rough, stormy. 4. containing noxious matter; clogged, choked; overgrown with barnacles etc. 5. unfair, against the rules. 6. in collision; (of a rope etc.) entangled. —*n.* 1. a foul stroke or piece of play. 2. a collision, an entanglement. —*adv.* unfairly, contrary to the rules. —*v.t./i.* 1. to make or become foul. 2. to commit a foul against (a player). 3. to become or cause to become entangled; to collide with. —**foul-mouthed** *adj.* using abusive or offensive language. **foul play,** unfair play in sport; a treacherous or violent act, especially murder. **foul up,** to become or cause to

become blocked or entangled; to spoil or bungle. —**foully** *adv.* [Old English]

foulard /fu:'lɑ:d/ *n.* a thin, soft material of silk or silk and cotton. [French]

found[1] *v.t.* 1. to establish, especially with an endowment; to originate or initiate (an institution etc.), to be the original builder of (a town etc.). 2. to lay the base of (a building); to construct or base (a story, theory, rule etc.) *on* or *upon.* —**ill-founded** *adj.* unjustified. **well-founded** *adj.* justified, reasonable. —**founder**[1] *n.* [from Old French from Latin *fundare* (*fundus* = bottom)]

found[2] *v.t.* to melt and mould (metal); to fuse (the materials for glass); to make (a thing) thus. —**founder**[2] *n.* [from Old French from Latin *fundere* = pour]

found[3] past and past participle of **find.**

foundation /faʊn'deɪʃən/ *n.* 1. establishing, especially of an endowed institution; such an institution (e. g. a college, hospital, school) or its revenues. 2. the solid ground or base on which a building rests; (in *singular* or *plural*) the lowest part of a building usually below ground-level. 3. a basis, an underlying principle. 4. the material or part on which other parts are overlaid; (in full **foundation garment**) a woman's supporting undergarment, a corset. —**foundation stone** *n.* a stone laid ceremonially to celebrate the founding of a building; (*figurative*) a basis. [from Old French from Latin]

founder[1,2] see ◊found[1,2].

founder[3] *v.i.* (of a horse or rider) to fall to the ground, to fall from lameness, to stick in mud etc.; (of a plan etc.) to fail; (of a ship) to fill with water and sink. [from Old French from Latin *fundus* = bottom]

foundling *n.* an abandoned infant of unknown parents. [from past participle of *find*]

foundry *n.* a workshop for or the business of casting metal.

fount[1] /faʊnt, fɒnt/ *n.* a set of printing-type of the same face and size. [from French]

fount[2] *n.* a source; (*poetic*) a spring, a fountain.

fountain /'faʊntɪn/ *n.* 1. a jet or jets of water made to spout for ornamental purposes or for drinking; a structure provided for this. 2. a spring; the source (*of* wisdom etc.). —**fountainhead** *n.* the source. **fountain pen,** a pen with a reservoir holding ink. [from Old French from Latin *fontana* (*fons fontis* = spring)]

Fountains Abbey /'faʊntənz/ Cistercian abbey in North Yorkshire, England. It was founded about 1132, and suppressed in 1540. The ruins were incorporated into a Romantic landscape garden in 1720–40 with lake, formal water garden, temples, and a deer park.

Fouquet /fu:'keɪ/ Jean *c.*1420–1481. French painter. He became court painter to Charles VIII in 1448 and to Louis XI in 1475. His *Melun diptych* about 1450 (Musées Royaux, Antwerp, and Staatliche Museen, Berlin) shows Italian Renaissance influence.

Fouquet Nicolas 1615–1680. French politician, a rival to Louis XIV's minister ◊Colbert. Fouquet became *Procureur Général* of the Paris *parlement* in 1650 and *Surintendant des Finances* in 1651, responsible for raising funds for the long war against Spain, a post he held until arrested and imprisoned for embezzlement (at the instigation of Colbert, who succeeded him) from 1661 until his death.

four /'fɔ:/ *adj.* & *n.* 1. one more than three; the symbol for this (4, iv, IV). 2. the size etc. denoted by four. 3. a team of four; a four-oared boat or its crew. —**four-in-hand** *n.* a vehicle with four horses driven by one person. **the four last things,** death, judgement, heaven, and hell. **four-letter word,** a short word referring to the sexual or excretory functions and regarded as vulgar or obscene. **four-poster** *n.* a bed with four posts supporting a canopy. **foursquare, solidly based, steady;** (*adv.*) squarely, resolutely. **four-wheel drive,** drive acting on all four wheels of a vehicle. **on all fours,** on hands and knees. [Old English]

four-colour process colour ◊printing using four printing plates, based on the principle that any colour is made up of differing proportions of the primary colours blue, red, and green. The first stage in preparing a colour picture for printing is to produce separate films, one each for the blue, red, and green respectively in the picture (colour separations). From these separations three printing plates are made, with a fourth plate for black (for shading or outlines).

four-stroke cycle

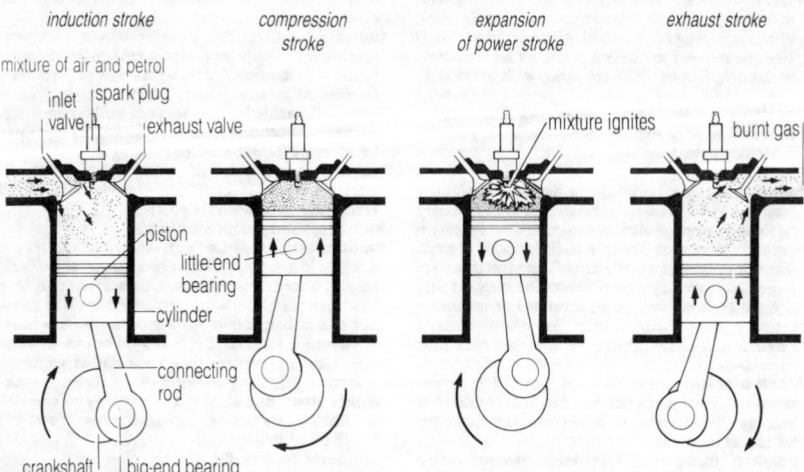

induction stroke   compression stroke   expansion of power stroke   exhaust stroke

mixture of air and petrol

inlet valve | spark plug | exhaust valve

mixture ignites   burnt gas

piston
little-end bearing
cylinder
connecting rod
crankshaft | big-end bearing

Fourdrinier machine /fuə'drɪnɪə/ a papermaking machine patented by the Fourdrinier brothers, Henry and Sealy, in England in 1803. On the machine, liquid pulp flows onto a moving wire-mesh belt, and water drains and is sucked away, leaving a damp paper web. This is passed first through a series of steam-heated rollers, which dry it, and then between heavy calendar rollers, which give it a smooth finish. The machine can measure up to 90 m/300 ft in length, and is still in use.

fourfold *adj.* & *adv.* four times as much or as many; consisting of four parts.

Fourier /'fʊrɪeɪ/ François Charles Marie 1772–1837. French socialist. In *Le Nouveau monde industriel/The New Industrial World* 1829–30, he advocated that society should be organized in self-sufficient cooperative units of about 1,500 people, marriage was to be abandoned.

Fourier Jean Baptiste Joseph 1768–1830. French applied mathematician whose formulation of heat flow 1807 contains the proposal that, with certain constraints, any mathematical function can be represented by trigonometrical series. This principle forms the basis of **Fourier analysis**, used today in many different fields of physics. His idea, not immediately well received, gained currency and is embodied in his *Théorie analytique de la chaleur/The Analytical Theory of Heat* 1822.

Four Noble Truths in Buddhism, a summary of the basic concepts: life is suffering (Sanskrit *duhkha*); suffering has its roots in desire (*tanha*, clinging or grasping); the cessation of desire is the end of suffering, *nirvana*; and this can be reached by the Noble Eightfold Path of *dharma* (truth).

foursome *n.* a group of four persons; a golf match between two pairs with partners playing the same ball.

four-stroke cycle the engine-operating cycle of most petrol and ◊diesel engines. The 'stroke' is an upward or downward movement of a piston in a cylinder. In a petrol engine the cycle begins with the induction of a fuel mixture as the piston goes down on its first stroke. On the second stroke (up) the piston compresses the mixture in the top of the cylinder. An electric spark then ignites the mixture, and the gases produced force the piston down on its third, power stroke. On the fourth stroke (up) the piston expels the burned gases from the cylinder into the exhaust.

fourteen /fɔː'tiːn/ *adj.* & *n.* **1.** one more than thirteen; the symbol for this (14, xiv, XIV). **2.** the size etc. denoted by fourteen. —**fourteenth** *adj.* & *n.* [Old English]

Fourteen Points the terms proposed by President Wilson of the USA in his address to Congress on 8 Jan 1918, as a basis for the settlement of World War I. The creation of the League of Nations was one of the points.

fourth *adj.* next after the third. —*n.* one of the four equal parts of a thing. —**fourthly** *adv.* [Old English]

fourth estate the press. The term was coined by the British politician Edmund Burke in analogy with the traditional three ◊estates.

fourth-generation language in computing, a type of programming language designed for the rapid programming of ◊applications but often lacking the ability to control the individual parts of the computer. Such a language typically provides easy ways of designing screens and reports, and of using databases. Other 'generations' (the term implies a class of language rather than a chronological sequence) are ◊machine code (first generation), ◊assembly language (second), and conventional high-level languages such as ◊BASIC and ◊PASCAL (third).

Fourth of July in the USA, the anniversary of the day in 1776 when the ◊Declaration of Independence was adopted by the Continental Congress. It is a public holiday, officially called **Independence Day**, commemorating independence from Britain.

Fourth Republic the French constitutional regime that was established between 1944 and 1946 and lasted until 4 Oct 1958: from liberation after Nazi occupation during World War II to the introduction of a new constitution by Gen de Gaulle.

fowl *n.* (*plural* **fowls** or *collectively* **fowl**) **1.** a domestic cock or hen kept for eggs and flesh; the flesh of birds as food. The **red jungle fowl** *Gallus gallus* is the ancestor of all domestic chickens. It is a forest bird of South Asia, without the size or egg-laying ability of many domestic strains. **2.** a bird (*archaic* except in combinations). —*v.i.* to hunt or shoot or snare wildfowl. —**fowler** *n.* [Old English]

Fowler /'faʊlə/ (Peter) Norman 1938– . British Conservative politician. He was a junior minister in the Heath government, transport secretary in the first Thatcher administration 1979, social services secretary 1981, and employment secretary 1987–89. He resigned in Jan 1990.

Fowler Henry Watson 1858–1933 and his brother Francis George 1870–1918. English scholars and authors of a number of English dictionaries. *Modern English Usage* 1926, the work of Henry Fowler, has become a classic reference work for advice on matters of style and disputed usage.

fox /fɒks/ *n.* **1.** member of the smaller species of wild dog of the family Canidae, which live in Europe, North America, Asia, and Africa. The fox feeds on a wide range of animals from worms to rabbits, scavenges for food, and also eats berries. It is largely nocturnal, and makes an underground den, or 'earth'. It is very adaptable, maintaining high populations in some urban areas. **2.** a cunning person. —*v.t.* **1.** to deceive, to baffle. **2.** (especially in *past participle*) to discolour (the pages of a book etc.) with brownish marks. —**fox terrier** *n.* a kind of short-haired terrier. [Old English]

Fox Charles James 1749–1806. English Whig politician, son of the 1st Baron Holland. He entered Parliament in 1769 as a supporter of the court, but went over to the opposition in 1774. As secretary of state 1782, leader of the opposition to Pitt, and foreign secretary 1806, he welcomed the French Revolution and brought about the abolition of the slave trade.

No man could be so wise as Thurlow looked.
Charles James Fox

Fox George 1624–1691. English founder of the Society of ◊Friends. After developing his belief in a mystical 'inner light', he became a travelling preacher in 1647, and in 1650 was imprisoned for blasphemy at Derby, where the name Quakers was first applied derogatorily to him and his followers, supposedly because he enjoined Judge Bennet to 'quake at the word of the Lord'.

Foxe /fɒks/ John 1516–1587. English Protestant propagandist. He became a canon of Salisbury in 1563. His *Book of Martyrs* 1563 luridly described persecutions under Queen Mary, reinforcing popular hatred of Roman Catholicism.

foxglove *n.* a flowering plant of the genus *Digitalis*, family Scrophulariaceae, found in Europe and the Mediterranean region. It bears purple or white flowers like glove-fingers, and grows up to 1.5 m/5 ft high.

foxhole *n.* a hole in the ground used as a shelter against missiles or as a firing-point.

foxhound *n.* a small, keen-nosed hound trained to hunt foxes. It is a combination of the old southern hound and other breeds, and has been bred in England for 300 years.

foxtrot *n.* a ballroom dance originating in the US about 1914. It has alternating long and short steps, supposedly like the movements of the fox; the music for this. —*v.i.* to dance the foxtrot.

foxy *adj.* 1. foxlike. 2. sly, cunning. 3. reddish-brown. —**foxily** *adv.*, **foxiness** *n.*

foyer /'fɔɪeɪ, 'fwæjeɪ/ *n.* the entrance hall or an open space in a theatre etc. for the audience's use during an interval; the entrance hall of a hotel. [French = hearth, home]

f.p.s. system a system of units based on the foot, pound, and second as units of length, mass, and time, respectively. It has now been replaced for scientific work by the ◊SI system.

fr. abbreviation of franc(s).

Fr symbol for francium.

Fr. abbreviation of 1. Father. 2. French.

fracas /'fræka:/ *n.* (*plural* the same /-ka:z/, (*US*) **fracases**) a noisy disturbance or quarrel. [French from Italian]

Fracastoro /fræka'stɔ:rəʊ/ Girolamo *c.* 1478–1553. Italian physician known for his two medical books. He was born and worked mainly in Verona. His first book, *Syphilis sive morbus gallicus/Syphilis or the French disease* 1530, was written in verse. It was one of the earliest texts on syphilis, a disease Fracastaro named. In his second work, *De contagione/ On contagion* 1546, he wrote, far ahead of his time, about 'seeds of contagion'.

fractal *n.* an irregular shape or surface produced by a procedure of repeated subdivision. Generated on a computer screen, fractals are used in creating models for geographical or biological processes (for example, the creation of a coastline by erosion or accretion, or the growth of plants). [from Latin *fractus* = broken]

fraction /'frækʃən/ *n.* 1. a numerical quantity that is not a whole number (e. g. $1/2$, 0.5). The number of equal parts into which the unit is divided (denominator) is usually written below a horizontal line, and the number of parts comprising the fraction (numerator) is written above; thus 2/3 or 3/4. Such fractions are called **vulgar** or **simple fractions** The denominator can never be zero. A **proper fraction** is one in which the numerator is less than the denominator. An **improper fraction** has a numerator larger than the denominator, for example 3/2. It can therefore be expressed as a mixed number, for example, 11/2. A **decimal fraction** has as its denominator a power of 10, and these are omitted by use of the decimal point and notation, for example 0.04, which is 4/100. The digits to the right of the decimal point indicate the numerators of vulgar

fractions whose denominators are 10, 100, 1,000, and so on. Most fractions can be expressed exactly as decimal fractions ($1/3 = 0.333...$). 2. a small part, piece, or amount. 3. a portion of a mixture obtained by distillation etc. [from Old French from Latin *frangere*= break]

fractional *adj.* 1. of fractions; being a fraction. 2. very slight. —**fractional distillation**, separation of parts of a mixture by making use of their different physical properties. —**fractionally** *adv.*

fractionate /'frækʃəneɪt/ *v.t.* to break up into parts; to separate (a mixture) by fractional distillation. **fractionator** *n.*

fractionating column device in which many separate ◊distillations can occur so that a liquid mixture can be separated into its components.

fractionation *n.* or **fractional distillation** process used to split complex mixtures (such as crude oil) into their components, usually by repeated heating, boiling, and condensation.

fractious /'frækʃəs/ *adj.* irritable, peevish. —**fractiously** *adv.*, **fractiousness** *n.*

fracture /'fræktʃə/ *n.* a breakage, especially of a bone or cartilage. —*v.t./i.* to cause a fracture in; to suffer a fracture. [from French or Latin]

fragile /'frædʒaɪl/ *adj.* easily broken, weak; of delicate constitution, not strong. —**fragilely** *adv.*, **fragility** /frə'dʒɪlɪtɪ/ *n.* [from French or Latin *fragilis*]

fragment /'frægmənt/ *n.* a part broken off; the remainder of an otherwise lost or destroyed whole; the extant remains or an unfinished portion of a book etc. —/also -'ment/ *v.t./i.* to break or separate into fragments. —**fragmentary** *adj.*, **fragmentation** /-'teɪʃən/ *n.* [from French or Latin *fragmentum*]

Fragonard /frægəʊ'nɑ:/ Jean Honoré 1732–1806. French painter, the leading exponent of the Rococo style (along with his master Boucher). His light-hearted subjects include *The Swing* about 1766 (Wallace Collection, London).

fragrance /'freɪgrəns/ *n.* sweetness of smell; a sweet scent. [from French or Latin *fragrare* = smell sweet]

fragrant /'freɪgrənt/ *adj.* sweet-smelling. —**fragrantly** *adv.*

frail *adj.* fragile, delicate; transient; morally weak. —**frailly** *adv.* [from Old French]

frailty *n.* frail quality; a weakness, a foible.

frame *v.t.* 1. to construct, to put together or devise (a complex thing, idea, theory etc.); to adapt or fit *to* or *into*. 2. to articulate (words). 3. to set in a frame; to serve as a frame for; (*slang*) to concoct a false charge or evidence against, to devise a plot against. —*n.* 1. the case or border enclosing a picture, window, door etc. 2. the human or animal body, especially with reference to its size. 3. the basic rigid supporting structure of a building, motor vehicle, aircraft, bicycle etc.; (in *plural*) the structure of spectacles holding the lenses. 4. construction, build, structure; the established order or system; a temporary state (*of mind*). 5. a single complete image or picture on a cinema film or transmitted in a series of lines by television. 6. a boxlike structure of glass etc. for protecting plants. 7. the triangular structure for positioning the balls in snooker etc.; a round of play in snooker etc. 8. (*US slang*) a frame-up. —**frame of reference**, a system of geometrical axes for defining position, a set of standards or principles governing behaviour, thought, etc. **frame-up** *n.* (*colloquial*) a conspiracy to make an innocent person appear guilty. [Old English = be helpful]

Frame /freɪm/ Janet. Pen name of Janet Paterson Frame Clutha 1924– . New Zealand novelist. After being wrongly diagnosed as schizophrenic, she reflected her experiences from 1945–54 in the novel *Faces in the Water* 1961 and the autobiographical *An Angel at My Table* 1984.

framework *n.* an essential supporting structure; a basic system.

franc *n.* the unit of currency in France, Belgium, Switzerland, etc. [from Old French from *Francorum Rex* = king of the Franks, legend on the earliest gold coins so called (14th century)]

France /frɑ:ns/ Republic of; country in W Europe, bounded NE by Belgium and Germany, E by Switzerland and Italy, S by the Mediterranean, SW by Spain and Andorra, and W by the Atlantic Ocean; **area** (including Corsica) 543,965 sq km/209,970 sq mi; **capital** Paris; **physical** rivers Seine, Loire, Garonne, Rhône, Rhine; mountain

France, history

5th century BC	France, then called Gaul (*Gallia* by the Romans) was invaded by Celtic peoples.
57–51 BC	Conquest by the Roman general Julius Caesar.
1st–5th centuries AD	During Roman rule the inhabitants of France accepted Roman civilization and the Latin language. As the empire declined, Germanic tribes overran the country and settled.
481–511	A Frankish chief, Clovis, brought the other tribes under his rule, accepted Christianity, and made Paris the capital.
511–751	Under Clovis' successors, the Merovingians, the country sank into anarchy.
741–68	Unity was restored by Pepin, founder of the Carolingian dynasty.
768–814	Charlemagne made France the centre of the Holy Roman empire.
912	The province of Normandy was granted as a duchy to the Viking leader Rollo, whose invading Norsemen had settled there.
987	The first king of the House of Capet assumed the crown. Under Charlemagne's weak successors the great nobles had become semi-independent. The Capets established rule in the district around Paris but were surrounded by vassals stronger than themselves.
11th–13th centuries	The power of the Capets was gradually extended, with the support of the church and the townspeople.
1337–1453	In the Hundred Years' War Charles VII expelled the English from France, aided by Joan of Arc.
1483	Burgundy and Brittany were annexed. Through the policies of Louis XI the restoration of the royal power was achieved.
1503–1697	Charles VIII's Italian wars initiated a struggle with Spain for supremacy in W Europe that lasted for two centuries.
1592–98	Protestantism (Huguenot) was adopted by a party of the nobles for political reasons; the result was a succession of civil wars, fought under religious slogans.
1589–1610	Henry IV restored peace, established religious toleration, and made the monarchy absolute.
1634–48	The ministers Richelieu and Mazarin, by their intervention in the Thirty Years' War, secured Alsace and made France the leading power in Europe.
1643–1763	Louis XIV embarked on an aggressive policy that united Europe against him; in his reign began the conflict with Britain that lost France its colonies in Canada and India in the War of the Spanish Succession (1701–14), War of the Austrian Succession (1756–58), and Seven Years' War (1756–63).
1789–99	The French Revolution abolished feudalism and absolute monarchy, but failed to establish democracy.
1799–1815	Napoleon's military dictatorship was aided by foreign wars (1792–1802, 1803–15). The Bourbon monarchy was restored 1814 with Louis XVIII.
1830	Charles X's attempt to substitute absolute for limited monarchy provoked a revolution, which placed his cousin, Louis Philippe, on the throne.
1848	In the Feb revolution Louis Philippe was overthrown and the Second Republic set up.
1852–70	The president of the republic, Louis Napoleon, Napoleon I's nephew, restored the empire 1852, with the title of Napoleon III. His expansionist foreign policy ended in defeat in the Franco-Prussian War and the foundation of the Third Republic.
1863–1946	France colonized Indochina, parts of N Africa, and the S Pacific.
1914	France entered World War I.
1936–38	A radical-socialist-communist alliance introduced many social reforms.
1939	France entered World War II.
1940	The German invasion allowed the extreme right to set up a puppet dictatorship under Pétain in Vichy, but resistance was maintained by the ◊maquis and the Free French under de Gaulle.
1944	Liberation from the Nazis.

For postwar history see ◊France.

ranges Alps, Massif Central, Pyrenees, Jura, Vosges, Cévennes; **territories** Guadeloupe, French Guiana, Martinique, Réunion, St Pierre and Miquelon, Southern and Antarctic Territories, New Caledonia, French Polynesia, Wallis and Futuna; **head of state** François Mitterrand from 1981; **head of government** Michel Rocard from 1988; **political system** liberal democracy; **exports** fruit (especially apples), wine, cheese, automobiles, aircraft, chemicals, jewellery, silk, lace; tourism is an important industry; **population** (1990 est.) 56,184,000 (including 4,500,000 immigrants); **language** French (regional dialects include Breton, Catalan, Provençal); **recent history** de Gaulle's provisional government of 1944–46 marked the start of the Fourth Republic; entry into the EEC took place in 1957; de Gaulle became president in 1957, resigned 1969. M. Mitterand, the first socialist president, was elected in 1981, and re-elected in 1988, when moderate socialist Michel Rocard became prime minister and continued in this post despite the Socialist Party failing to obtain a secure majority in the National Assembly elections. In Sept 1990, after Iraqi violation of the French ambassador's residence in Kuwait, the French government despatched 5,000 troops to Saudi Arabia, and took an important role in the ◊Gulf War and the liberation of Kuwait.

France Anatole. Pen name of Jacques Anatole Thibault 1844–1924. French writer, noted for the wit, urbanity, and style of his works. His first novel was *Le Crime de Sylvestre Bonnard/The Crime of Sylvester Bonnard* 1881; later books include the autobiographical series beginning with *Le Livre*

de mon ami/My Friend's Book 1885. He was awarded the Nobel Prize for Literature in 1921.

Francesca /fræn'tʃeskə/ Piero della see ◊Piero della Francesca, Italian painter.

Franche-Comté /'frɒnʃ kɒn'teɪ/ region of E France; **area** 16,200 sq km/6,253 sq mi; **population** (1987) 1,086,000. **capital** Besançon; and it includes the *départements* of Doubs, Jura, Haute Saône, and Territoire de Belfort; **products** in the mountainous Jura, there is farming and forestry, and elsewhere there are engineering and plastics industries; **history** once independent and ruled by its own count, it was disputed by France, Burgundy, Austria, and Spain from the 9th century until it became a French province under the Treaty of ◊Nijmegen 1678.

franchise /'fræntʃaɪz/ n. 1. the right to vote in a state election. 2. full membership of a corporation or state, citizenship. 3. a right or privilege granted to a person or corporation. 4. authorization to sell a company's goods etc. in a particular area. —*v.t.* to grant a franchise to. [from Old French *franc* = free]

Francis /'frɑːnsɪs/ or **François** two kings of France:

Francis I 1494–1547. King of France from 1515. He succeeded his cousin Louis XII, and from 1519 European politics turned on the rivalry between him and the Holy Roman emperor Charles V, which led to war in 1521–29, 1536–38, and 1542–44. In 1525 Francis was defeated and captured at Pavia and released only after signing a humiliating treaty. At home, he developed absolute monarchy.

Francis II 1544–1560. King of France from 1559 when he succeeded his father, Henry II. He married Mary Queen of

Scots in 1558. He was completely under the influence of his mother, ◊Catherine de' Medici.

Francis II 1768–1835. Holy Roman emperor 1792–1806. He became Francis I, Emperor of Austria in 1804, and abandoned the title of Holy Roman emperor in 1806. During his reign Austria was five times involved in war with France, 1792–97, 1798–1801, 1805, 1809, and 1813–14. He succeeded his father Leopold II.

Franciscan /fræn'sɪskən/ *adj.* of the order founded by St Francis of Assisi. —*n.* a monk or nun of the Franciscan order. [from French from Latin *Franciscus* = Francis]

Franciscan order Catholic order of friars, **Friars Minor** or **Grey Friars**, founded in 1209 by St Francis of Assisi. Subdivisions were the strict Observants; the Conventuals, who were allowed to own property corporately; and the ◊Capuchins, founded in 1529.

Francis of Assisi, St /ə'si:zi/ 1182–1226. Italian founder of the Roman Catholic Franciscan order of friars in 1209 and, with St Clare, of the Poor Clares in 1212. In 1224 he is said to have undergone a mystical experience during which he received the *stigmata* (five wounds of Jesus). Many stories are told of his ability to charm wild animals, and he is the patron saint of ecologists. His feast day is 4 Oct.

Francis of Sales, St /sæl/ 1567–1622. French bishop and theologian. He became bishop of Geneva in 1602, and in 1610 founded the order of the Visitation, an order of nuns. He is the patron saint of journalists and other writers. Feast day 24 Jan.

francium /'frænsiəm/ *n.* a metallic element, symbol Fr, atomic number 87, relative atomic mass 223. It is a highly radioactive metal; the most stable isotope has a half-life of only 21 minutes. Francium was discovered by Marguérite Perey (1909–   ) in 1939. [from *France*, country of its discoverer]

Franck /fræŋk/ César Auguste 1822–1890. Belgian composer. His music, mainly religious and Romantic in style, includes the Symphony in D minor 1866–68, *Symphonic Variations* 1885 for piano and orchestra, the Violin Sonata 1886, the oratorio *Les Béatitudes/The Beatitudes* 1879, and many organ pieces.

Franck James 1882–1964. US physicist influential in atom technology. He was awarded a Nobel prize in 1925 for his experiments of 1914 on the energy transferred by colliding electrons to mercury atoms, showing that the transfer was governed by the rules of ◊quantum theory.

Franco /'fræŋkəʊ/ Francisco (Paulino Hermenegildo Teódulo Bahamonde) 1892–1975. Spanish dictator from 1939. As a general, he led the insurgent Nationalists to victory in the Spanish ◊Civil War 1936–39, supported by Fascist Italy and Nazi Germany, and established a dictatorship. In 1942 Franco reinstated the Cortes (Spanish parliament), which in 1947 passed an act by which he became head of state for life.

Franco- in combinations, French and (*Franco-German*). [from Latin]

Franco-German entente a resumption of friendly relations between France and Germany, designed to erase the enmities of successive wars. It was initiated by the French president de Gaulle's visit to West Germany in 1962, followed by the Franco-German Treaty of Friendship and Cooperation 1963.

Franco-Prussian War 1870–71. The Prussian chancellor Bismarck put forward a German candidate for the vacant Spanish throne with the deliberate, and successful, intention of provoking the French emperor Napoleon III into declaring war. The Prussians defeated the French at ◊Sedan, then besieged Paris. The Treaty of Frankfurt, May 1871, gave Alsace, Lorraine, and a large French indemnity to Prussia. The war established Prussia, at the head of a newly established German empire, as Europe's leading power.

Franglais /'frɒŋgleɪ/ *n.* the French language when mixed with (usually unwelcome) elements of modern, especially American, English. *Le weekend*, *le drugstore*, and other such mixtures have prompted moves within France to protect the integrity of Standard French. [French *français* = French and *anglais* English]

frank /fræŋk/ *adj.* candid, open, outspoken, undisguised, unmistakable. —*v.t.* to mark (a letter etc.) to record the payment of postage. —*n.* a franking signature or mark. —**frankly** *adv.*, **frankness** *n.* [from Old French from

Latin *francus* = free (since only Franks had full freedom in Frankish Gaul)]

Frank *n.* a member of a group of Germanic peoples prominent in Europe in the 3rd–9th centuries. Believed to have originated in Pomerania on the Black Sea, they had settled on the Rhine by the 3rd century, spread into the Roman Empire by the 4th century, and gradually conquered most of Gaul, Italy, and Germany under the ◊Merovingian and ◊Carolingian dynasties. The kingdom of the W Franks became France, the kingdom of the E Franks became Germany. —**Frankish** *adj.* [Old English]

Frank Anne 1929–1945. German diarist who fled to the Netherlands with her family in 1933 to escape Nazi persecution. During the German occupation of Amsterdam, they and two other families remained in a sealed-off room, protected by Dutch sympathizers, from 1942–44, when betrayal resulted in their deportation and Anne's death in Belsen concentration camp. Her diary of her time in hiding was published in 1947 and has been made into a play and a film.

Frank Ilya 1908–. Russian physicist known for his work on radiation. In 1934 ◊Cherenkov had noted a peculiar blue radiation sometimes emitted as electrons passed through water. It was left to Frank and his colleague at Moscow University, Igor Tamm (1895–1971), to realize that this form of radiation was produced by charged particles travelling faster through the medium than the speed of light in the same medium. Frank shared the 1958 Nobel Prize for Physics with Cherenkov and Tamm.

Frankenstein /'fræŋkənstaɪn/ **or, The Modern Prometheus** a Gothic horror story by Mary Shelley, published in England in 1818. Frankenstein, a scientist, discovers how to bring inanimate matter to life, and creates a man-monster. When Frankenstein fails to provide a mate to satisfy the creature's human emotions, it seeks revenge by killing Frankenstein's brother and bride. Frankenstein dies in an attempt to destroy his creation.

Frankenthaler /'fræŋkənθɔːlə/ Helen 1928– . US Abstract Expressionist painter, inventor of the colour-staining technique whereby the unprimed, absorbent canvas is stained or soaked with thinned-out paint, creating deep, soft veils of translucent colour.

Frankfurt-am-Main /'fræŋkfɜːt æm 'maɪn/ city in Hessen, Germany, 72 km/45 mi NE of Mannheim; population (1988) 592,000. It is a commercial and banking centre, with electrical and machine industries, and an inland port on the river Main. An international book fair is held annually.

frankfurter /'fræŋkfɜːtə/ *n.* a seasoned smoked sausage. [from German *Frankfurter wurst* = Frankfurt sausage (*Frankfurt* in Germany)]

Frankfurt Parliament /'fræŋkfɜːt/ an assembly of liberal politicians and intellectuals who met for a few months in 1848 in the aftermath of the ◊revolutions of 1848 and the overthrow of monarchies in most of the German states. They discussed a constitution for a united Germany, but the restoration of the old order and the suppression of the revolutions ended the parliament.

frankincense /'fræŋkɪnsens/ *n.* the resin of various African and Asian trees of the genus *Boswellia*, family Burseraceae, burned as incense. Costly in ancient times, it is traditionally believed to be one of the three gifts brought by the Magi to the infant Jesus. [from Old French (as *frank* in obsolete sense 'of high quality', *incense*[2])]

Franklin /'fræŋklɪn/ Benjamin 1706–1790. US scientist and politician. He proved that lightning is a form of electricity by the experiment of flying a kite in a storm, distinguished between positive and negative electricity, and invented the lightning conductor.

Franklin John 1786–1847. English naval explorer who took part in expeditions to Australia, the Arctic, and N Canada, and in 1845 commanded an expedition to look for the North West Passage from the Atlantic to the Pacific, during which he and his crew perished.

Franklin Miles, (pseudonym 'Brent of Bin Bin') 1879–1954. Australian novelist. Her first novel, *My Brilliant Career* 1901 was made into a successful film. An Australian literary award bearing her name is made annually.

Franklin Rosalind 1920–1958. English biophysicist whose research on X-ray diffraction of DNA crystals helped Francis Crick and James D Watson to deduce the chemical structure of DNA.

Franz Joseph *Franz Joseph, Emperor of Austria, who precipitated World War I.*

frantic /'fræntɪk/ *adj.* wildly excited, frenzied; characterized by great hurry or anxiety, desperate, violent; (*colloquial*) extreme. —**frantically** *adv.* [from Old French from Latin]

Franz Ferdinand /'frænts 'fɜːdɪnænd/ or **Francis Ferdinand** 1863–1914. Archduke of Austria. He became heir to his uncle, Emperor Franz Joseph in 1884 but while visiting Sarajevo in 28 June 1914, he and his wife were assassinated by Serbian nationalists. Austria used the episode to make unreasonable demands on Serbia that ultimately precipitated World War I.

Franz Joseph /'frænts 'jəʊzef/ or **Francis Joseph** 1830–1916. Emperor of Austria-Hungary from 1848, when his uncle, Ferdinand I, abdicated. After the suppression of the 1848 revolution, Franz Joseph tried to establish an absolute monarchy but had to grant Austria a parliamentary constitution in 1861 and Hungary equality with Austria in 1867. He was defeated in the Italian War in 1859 and the Prussian War in 1866. In 1914 he made the assassination of his heir and nephew, Franz Ferdinand, the excuse for attacking Serbia, precipitating World War I.

frappé /'fræpeɪ/ (especially of wine) iced, chilled. [French, past participle of *frapper* = strike, ice (drinks)]

Frasch process /fræʃ/ a process used to extract underground deposits of sulphur. Superheated steam is piped to the sulphur deposit and melts it. Compressed air is then pumped down to force the molten sulphur to the surface. It was developed in the USA in 1891 by German-born Herman Frasch (1851–1914).

Fraser /'freɪzə/ Antonia 1932– . English author of biographies, including *Mary Queen of Scots* 1969; historical works, such as *The Weaker Vessel* 1984; and a series of detective novels featuring investigator Jemima Shore.

Fraser (John) Malcolm 1930– . Australian Liberal politician, prime minister 1975–83; nicknamed 'the Prefect' because of a supposed disregard of subordinates.

Fraser Peter 1884–1950. New Zealand Labour politician, born in Scotland. He held various cabinet posts from 1935–40, and was prime minister from 1940– 49.

fraternal /frə'tɜːnəl/ *adj.* of brothers, brotherly. —**fraternal twins**, twins developed from separate ova and not necessarily similar. —**fraternally** *adv.* [from Latin *frater* = brother]

fraternity /frə'tɜːnɪtɪ/ *n.* 1. a religious brotherhood. 2. a guild or group of people sharing interests or beliefs etc. 3. brotherliness.

fraternity and sorority student societies (fraternity for men; sorority for women) in some US and Canadian universities and colleges. Although mainly social and residential, some are purely honorary, membership being on the basis of scholastic distinction; for example Phi Beta Kappa, earliest of the fraternities, was founded at the College of William and Mary, Virginia in 1776.

fraternize /'frætənaɪz/ *v.i.* to associate or make friends (*with*); (of troops) to enter into friendly relations *with* enemy troops or inhabitants of an occupied country. —**fraternization** /-'zeɪʃən/ *n.*

fratricide /'frætrɪsaɪd/ *n.* 1. the crime of killing one's own brother or sister. 2. one who is guilty of this. —**fratricidal** *adj.*

Frau /fraʊ/ *n.* (*plural* **Frauen**) a German woman; the title of a German wife or widow, = Mrs.

fraud /frɔːd/ *n.* 1. in law, an act of deception resulting in injury to another. To establish fraud it has to be demonstrated that (1) a false representation has been made, with the intention that it should be acted upon; (2) the person making the representation knows it is false or does not attempt to find out whether it is true or not; and (3) the person to whom the representation is made acts upon it to his or her detriment. 2. a dishonest artifice or trick; an impostor. 3. a person or thing not fulfilling a claim or expectation. [from Old French from Latin]

fraudulent /'frɔːdjʊlənt/ *adj.* of, involving, or guilty of fraud. —**fraudulence** *n.*, **fraudulently** *adv.* [from Old French or Latin]

fraught /frɔːt/ *adj.* 1. filled or attended *with* (danger etc.). 2. (*colloquial*) causing or suffering anxiety or distress. [past participle of obsolete *fraught* = load with cargo, from Middle Dutch]

Fräulein /'frɔɪlaɪn/ *n.* an unmarried German woman; the title of a German spinster, = Miss.

Fraunhofer /'fraʊnhəʊfə/ Joseph von 1787–1826. German physicist who did important work in optics. The dark lines in the solar spectrum (**Fraunhofer lines**), which reveal the chemical composition of the Sun's atmosphere, were accurately mapped by him.

fray[1] *v.t./i.* to become or cause to become worn through by rubbing; to become ragged at the edge (*literal,* or *figurative* of nerves, temper etc.). [from French from Latin *fricare* = rub]

fray[2] *n.* a fight, a conflict; a brawl.

Fraze Ermai Cleon 1913–1989. US inventor of the ring-pull on drink cans. He created the device after having to resort to opening a can of beer on a car bumper while picnicking.

Frazer /'freɪzə/ James George 1854–1941. Scottish anthropologist, author of *The Golden Bough* 1890, a pioneer study of the origins of religion and sociology on a comparative basis. It exerted considerable influence on writers such as T S Eliot and D H Lawrence, but by the standards of modern anthropology many of its methods and findings are unsound.

frazzle *n.* a worn or exhausted state. [perhaps from *fray*[1] and dialect *fazzle* = tangle]

freak *n.* 1. a capricious or unusual idea, act etc. 2. a monstrosity, an abnormal person or thing. 3. an unconventional person; one who freaks out; a drug addict. —*v.t./i.* (with *out*) (*slang*) 1. to undergo or cause to undergo hallucinations through drug-taking etc. or a strong emotional experience. 2. to adopt an unconventional lifestyle. —**freak-out** *n.* (*slang*) the experience of freaking out. —**freakish** *adj.*

freckle *n.* a light brown spot on the skin. —*v.t./i.* to spot or be spotted with freckles. [from Old Norse]

Frederick V /'fredrɪk/ known as **the Winter King** 1596–1632. Elector palatine of the Rhine 1610–23 and king of Bohemia 1619–20 (for one winter, hence the name), having been chosen by the Protestant Bohemians as ruler after the deposition of Catholic emperor ◊Ferdinand II. His selection was the cause of the Thirty Years' War. Frederick was defeated at the Battle of the White Mountain, near Prague, in Nov 1620, by the army of the Catholic League and fled to Holland.

Frederick IX 1899–1972. King of Denmark from 1947. He was succeeded by his daughter who became Queen ◊Margrethe II.

Frederick the name of two Holy Roman emperors:

Frederick I Barbarossa ('red-beard') *c.*1123–1190. Holy Roman emperor from 1152. Originally Duke of Swabia, he was elected emperor in 1152, and was engaged in a struggle with Pope Alexander III from 1159–77, which ended in his submission; the Lombard cities, headed by Milan, took advantage of this to establish their independence of imperial control. Frederick joined the Third Crusade, and was drowned in Anatolia.

Frederick II 1194–1250. Holy Roman emperor from 1212, called 'the Wonder of the World'. He led a crusade 1228–29 that recovered Jerusalem by treaty, without fighting. He quarrelled with the pope, who excommunicated him three times, and a feud began that lasted at intervals until the end of his reign. Frederick, who was a religious sceptic, is often considered the most cultured man of his age. He was the son of Henry VI.

Frederick three kings of Prussia including:

Frederick II the Great 1712–1786. King of Prussia from 1740, when he succeeded his father Frederick William I. In that year he started the War of the ◊Austrian Succession by his attack on Austria. In the peace of 1745 he secured Silesia. The struggle was renewed in the ◊Seven Years' War 1756–63. He acquired West Prussia in the first partition of Poland 1772 and left Prussia as Germany's foremost state. He was an efficient and just ruler in the spirit of the Enlightenment and a patron of the arts.

> My people and I have come to an agreement which satisfies us both. They are to say what they please, and I am to do what I please.
>
> **Frederick II the Great**
> (attrib.)

Frederick III 1831–1888. King of Prussia and emperor of Germany 1888. The son of Wilhelm I, he married the eldest daughter (Victoria) of Queen Victoria of the UK in 1858 and, as a liberal, frequently opposed Chancellor Bismarck. He died three months after his accession.

Frederick William 1620–1688. Elector of Brandenburg from 1640, 'the Great Elector'. By successful wars against Sweden and Poland, he prepared the way for Prussian power in the 18th century.

Frederick William four kings of Prussia:

Frederick William I 1688–1740. King of Prussia from 1713, who developed Prussia's military might and commerce.

Frederick William II 1744–1797. King of Prussia from 1786. He was a nephew of Frederick II but had little of his relative's military skill. He was unsuccessful in waging war on the French from 1792–95 and lost all Prussia W of the Rhine.

Frederick William III 1770–1840. King of Prussia from 1797. He was defeated by Napoleon in 1806, but contributed to his final overthrow in 1813–15 and profited by being allotted territory at the Congress of Vienna.

Frederick William IV 1795–1861. King of Prussia from 1840. He upheld the principle of the ◊divine right of kings, but was forced to grant a constitution in 1850 after the Prussian revolution of 1848. He suffered two strokes in 1857 and became mentally debilitated. His brother William (later emperor) took over his duties.

Fredericton /ˈfredrɪktən/ capital of New Brunswick, Canada, on the St John River; population (1986) 44,000. It was known as **St Anne's Point** until 1785 when it was named after Prince Frederick, second son of George III.

free adj. (comparative **freer** /ˈfriːə/, superlative **freest** /ˈfriːɪst/ **1.** not a slave or under the control of another, having personal rights and social and political liberty; (of a state, citizens, or institutions) subject neither to foreign domination nor to despotic government. **2.** not fixed or held down, able to move without hindrance; permitted to do; unrestricted, not controlled by rules; (of a translation) not literal. **3.** (with of or from) without, not subject to or affected by. **4.** without payment, costing nothing to the recipient. **5.** not occupied or in use; without engagements; clear of obstructions. **6.** coming, given, or giving readily; impartial. **7.** in chemistry, not combined; in physics, not bound in an atom or molecule; (of power or energy) disengaged, available. —adv. freely; without cost or payment. —v.t. to make free, to set at liberty; to relieve from; to rid or ease of; to clear, to disentangle. —**free and easy,** informal. **free association,** association of ideas, by a person undergoing a psychological test, without suggestion or control by the tester. **freeborn** adj. born as a free citizen. **free enterprise,** freedom of private business from state control. **free fall,** movement under the force of gravity only. **free falling,** ◊skydiving. **free fight,** a general fight in which all present may join, without rules. **free-for-all** n. a free fight, an unrestricted discussion etc. **free hand,** freedom to act at one's own discretion. **freehand** adj. (of a drawing) done without instruments such as a ruler or compasses. **free-handed** adj. generous. **free house,** an inn or public

house not controlled by a brewery and therefore able to sell any brand of beer etc. **free kick,** a kick in football taken without interference from opponents, as a minor penalty. **freelance,** a person whose services are available to any would-be employer, not one only. **freelance** adj. of a freelance; (v.i.) to act as a freelance. **freeloader** n. (slang) a sponger. **free love,** sexual relations irrespective of marriage. **free market,** a market in which prices are determined by unrestricted competition. **free on board** (fob or f.o.b.) or **rail,** without charge for delivery to a ship, railway wagon, etc. **free port,** one open to all traders, or free from duty on goods in transit. **free-range** adj. (of hens etc.) given freedom of movement in seeking food etc. **free speech,** the freedom to express opinions of any kind. **free-spoken** adj. not concealing one's opinions. **freestanding** adj. not supported by another structure. **freestyle** adj. (of a swimming-race) in which any stroke may be used (of wrestling) with few restrictions on the holds permitted. **freethinker** n. one who rejects dogma or authority in religious belief. **free vote,** a parliamentary vote in which members are not bound by party policy. **freewheel,** the driving-wheel of a bicycle able to revolve with the pedals at rest. **freewheel** v.i. to ride a bicycle with the pedals at rest; to move or act without constraint. **free will,** the power of acting without the constraint of necessity or fate, the ability to act at one's own discretion. —**freely** adv. [Old English]

-free in combinations, free of or from (duty-free, fancy-free).

freeboard n. the part of a ship's side between the water line and the deck.

freebooter n. a pirate. [from Dutch vrijbuiter]

Free Church the Protestant denominations in England and Wales that are not part of the Church of England; for example, the Methodist Church, Baptist Union, and United Reformed Church (Congregational and Presbyterian). These churches joined for common action in the Free Church Federal Council 1940.

Free Church of Scotland the body of Scottish Presbyterians who seceded from the Established Church of Scotland in the Disruption of 1843. In 1900 all but a small section that retains the old name, and is known as the **Wee Frees,** combined with the United Presbyterian Church to form the United Free Church, which reunited with the Church of Scotland in 1929.

freedman n. (plural **freedmen**) an emancipated slave.

freedom /ˈfriːdəm/ n. **1.** the condition of being free or unrestricted; personal or civic liberty; liberty of action (to). **2.** frankness, undue familiarity. **3.** exemption (from); the unrestricted use (of a house etc.); honorary membership or citizenship. —**freedom of speech,** the right to express one's views freely.

freedom of the city (or borough) an honour bestowed on distinguished people by a city or borough in the UK and other countries. Historically, those granted freedom of a city or borough (called 'freemen') had the right of participating in its privileges.

Freedom, Presidential Medal of the highest peacetime civilian honour in the USA. Instituted by President Kennedy in 1963, it is awarded to those 'who contribute significantly to the quality of American life'. A list of recipients is published each Independence Day and often includes unknown individuals as well as artists, performers, and politicians.

Free French in World War II, a movement formed by General Charles ◊de Gaulle in the UK in June 1940, consisting of French soldiers who continued to fight against the Axis after the Franco-German armistice. They took the name **Fighting France** 1942 and served in many campaigns, among them General Leclerc's advance from Chad to Tripolitania 1942, the Syrian campaigns 1941, the campaigns in the Western Desert, the Italian campaign, the liberation of France, and the invasion of Germany. Their emblem was the Cross of Lorraine, a cross with two bars.

freehold n. in England and Wales, ownership of land which is for an indefinite period. It is contrasted with leasehold, which is always for a fixed period. In practical effect, a freehold is absolute ownership. —adj. owned thus. —**freeholder** n.

freeman n. (plural **freemen**) **1.** one who is not a slave or serf. **2.** one who has the ◊freedom of a city etc.

Freemasonry *n.* the beliefs and practices of the **Freemasons**, a group of linked national organizations open to men over the age of 21, united by a common code of morals and certain traditional 'secrets'. Freemasons do much charitable work, but have been criticized in recent years for their secrecy, their male exclusivity, and particularly their alleged use of influence within and between organizations (for example, the police or local government) to further each other's interests. There are approximately 6 million members. Freemasonry is descended from a medieval guild of itinerant masons, which existed in the 14th century and by the 16th was admitting men unconnected with the building trade. The term 'freemason' may have meant a full member of the guild or one working in free-stone, that is, a mason of the highest class.

free radical in chemistry, an atom or molecule that has an unpaired electron and is highly reactive.

freesia /'fri:zjə, -ʒə/ *n.* a bulbous African plant of the genus *Freesia*, with fragrant flowers. [from French. T H *Freese* German physician (died 1876)]

free thought post-Reformation movement opposed to Christian dogma.

Freetown /'fri:taʊn/ capital of Sierra Leone, W Africa; population (1988) 470,000. It has a naval station and a harbour. Industries include cement, plastics, footwear, and oil refining. Platinum, chromite, diamonds, and gold are traded. It was founded as a settlement for freed slaves in the 1790s.

Freetown /'fri:taʊn/ capital of Sierra Leone, W Africa; population (1988) 470,000. It has a naval station and a harbour. Industries include cement, plastics, footwear, and oil refining. Platinum, chromite, diamonds, and gold are traded. It was founded as a settlement for freed slaves in the 1790s.

free trade an economic system where governments do not interfere in the movement of goods between states; there are thus no taxes on imports. In the modern economy free trade tends to hold within economic groups such as the European Community or the Warsaw Pact, but not generally, despite such treaties such as ◊GATT (1948) and subsequent agreements to reduce tariffs. The opposite of free trade is ◊protectionism.

free verse poetry without metrical form. At the beginning of the 20th century, under the very different influences of Whitman and Mallarmé, many poets believed that the 19th century had accomplished most of what could be done with regular metre, and rejected it, in much the same spirit as Milton had rejected rhyme, preferring irregular metres that made it possible to express thought clearly and without distortion.

freeway *n.* an express highway, especially one with limited access.

freeze *v.t./i.* (*past* froze; *past participle* frozen) 1. to turn into ice or some other solid by cold; to cover or become covered with ice. 2. to be or feel very cold; to make or become rigid from cold; to adhere by frost. 3. to preserve (food) by refrigeration below freezing-point. 4. to become or cause to become motionless through fear, surprise etc. 5. to fix (prices, wages etc.) at a certain level; to make (assets) unavailable. —*n.* 1. a state or period of frost; the coming of a period of frost. 2. the fixing or stabilization of prices, wages, etc. —**freeze-dry** *v.t.* to freeze and dry by evaporation of ice in a high vacuum. **freeze on to,** (*slang*) to take or keep a tight hold of. **freeze up,** to freeze completely; to obstruct by the formation of ice etc. **freeze-up** *n.* a period or conditions of extreme cold. **freezingpoint** *n.* the temperature at which a liquid, especially water, freezes. [Old English]

freezer *n.* a refrigerated container or compartment in which food is preserved at a very low temperature.

freezing-point depression the lowering of a solution's freezing point below that of the pure solvent; it depends on the number of molecules of solute dissolved in it; for a single solvent, such as pure water, all substances in the same molecular concentration produce the same lowering of freezing point. The depression d for a molar concentration C is given by the equation $d = KC$, where K is a constant for the particular solvent (called the cryoscopic constant). Measurement of freezing-point depression is a useful method of determining molecular weights of solutes.

Frege /'freɪgə/ Friedrich Ludwig Gottlob 1848–1925. German philosopher, the founder of modern mathematical logic. He created symbols for concepts like 'or' and 'if ... then', which are now in standard use in mathematics. His *Die Grundlagen der Arithmetik/The Foundations of Arithmetic* 1884 influenced Bertrand ◊Russell and ◊Wittgenstein.

freight /freɪt/ *n.* 1. the transport of goods in containers or by water or air (or (*US*) by land). 2. the goods transported, a cargo, a load. 3. a charge for the transport of goods. —*v.t.* to transport (goods) by freight; to load with freight. [from Middle Low German or Middle Dutch *vrecht* variant of *vracht*]

freighter *n.* a ship or aircraft designed to carry freight; (*US*) a freight-wagon.

freightliner *n.* a train carrying goods in containers.

Frelimo /fre'li:məʊ/ acronym from Front for the Liberation of Mozambique, a nationalist group aimed at gaining independence for Mozambique from the occupying Portuguese. It began operating from S Tanzania in 1963 and continued until victory in 1975.

Frémont /'fri:mɒnt/ John Charles 1813–1890. US explorer and politician who travelled extensively throughout the western USA. He surveyed much of the territory between the Mississippi River and the coast of California with the aim of establishing an overland route E–W across the continent. In 1842 he crossed the the Rocky Mountains, climbing a peak that is named after him.

French *adj.* of France or its people or language; having French characteristics. —*n.* 1. the French language. 2. (*euphemism*) bad language. 3. dry vermouth. —**the French** (*plural*), the people of France. **French bean**, the kidney or haricot bean used as unripe sliced pods or as ripe seeds. **French bread**, bread in a long, crisp loaf. **French chalk**, finely powdered talc used as a marker, dry lubricant etc. **French dressing**, a salad dressing of seasoned oil and vinegar. **French fried potatoes** *or* **fries**, (*US*) potato chips. **French horn**, an instrument of the brass family, a coiled tube with a wide-flaring bell facing backwards. **French leave**, absence without permission. **French letter**, (*colloquial*) a condom. **French polish**, shellac polish for wood. **French window**, a glazed door in an outside wall. [Old English]

French art the painting and sculpture of France. A number of influential styles have emerged in France over the centuries, from Gothic in the Middle Ages. In the mid-19th century the ◊Barbizon school of landscape painting was followed by the ◊Impressionism. In the late 19th century Seurat developed ◊Pointillism, taking the Impressionists' ideas further. The individual styles of Cézanne and Gauguin heralded ◊Modernism. In the 1900s, ◊Fauvism was introduced by Matisse and others, and ◊Cubism was begun by Picasso and Braque. In the 1920s Paris was a centre of ◊Surrealism, and, in the 1930s, of the abstraction-création movement, form of abstract art constructed from nonfigurative, usually geometrical elements. After World War II the centre of the art world shifted from France to the USA.

French Community a former association consisting of France and those overseas territories joined with it by the constitution of the Fifth Republic, following the 1958 referendum. Many of the constituent states withdrew during the 1960s, and it no longer formally exists, but in practice all former French colonies have close economic and cultural as well as linguistic links with France.

French Guiana /gi:'ɑːnə/ (French *Guyane Française*) French overseas *département* from 1946, and administrative region from 1974, on the N coast of South America, bounded to the W by Suriname and to the E and S by Brazil; **area** 83,500 sq km/32,230 sq mi; **capital** Cayenne **population** (1987) 89,000; **language** 90% Creole, French, Amerindian; **history** first settled by France in 1604, the territory became a French possession in 1817; penal colonies, including ◊Devil's Island, were established from 1852; by 1945, the shipments of convicts from France ceased.

frenchify /'frentʃɪfaɪ/ *v.t.* (usually in *past participle*) to make French in form, manners etc.

French India former French possessions in India: Pondicherry, Chandernagore, Karikal, Mahé, and Yanam (Yanaon). They were all transferred to India by 1954.

French language a member of the Romance branch of the Indo-European language family, spoken in France, Belgium, Luxembourg, Monaco, and Switzerland in Europe,

425

Freud

Canada (especially the province of Québec) in North America, and various Caribbean and Pacific Islands (overseas territories such as Martinique and French Guiana), as well as certain N and W African countries (for example, Mali and Senegal).

Frenchman *n.* (*plural* **Frenchmen**) a man of French birth or nationality. —**Frenchwoman** *n.fem.* (*plural* **Frenchwomen**)

French Polynesia /pɒliˈniːziə/ French Overseas Territory in the S Pacific, consisting of five archipelagoes: Windward Islands, Leeward Islands (the two island groups comprising the ◊Society Islands), ◊Tuamotu Archipelago (including ◊Gambier Islands), ◊Tubuai Islands, and ◊Marquesas Islands; **total area** 3,940 sq km/1,521 sq mi; **capital** Papeete on Tahiti; **population** (1987) 185,000; **language** Tahitian (official), French; **government** a high commissioner (Alain Ohrel) and Council of Government; two deputies are returned to the National Assembly in France; **recent history** French protectorate from 1843; annexed to France 1880–82; became an Overseas Territory, changing its name from French Oceania 1958; self-governing 1977. Following demands for independence in ◊New Caledonia 1984–85, agitation increased also in Polynesia.

French Revolution the period 1789–1799 that saw the end of the monarchy and its claim to absolute rule, and the establishment of the First Republic. Although the revolution began as an attempt to create a constitutional monarchy, by late 1792 demands for long-overdue reforms resulted in the proclamation of the republic. The violence of the revolution, attacks by other nations, and bitter factional struggles, riots, and counterrevolutionary uprisings consumed the republic. This helped bring the extremists to power, and the bloody Reign of Terror followed. French armies then succeeded in holding off their foreign enemies and one of the generals, ◊Napoleon, seized power 1799.

French revolutionary calendar in the French Revolution 1789 was initially known as the 1st Year of Liberty. When the monarchy was abolished on 21 Sep 1792, the 4th Year of liberty became the 1st Year of the Republic. This calendar was formally adopted in Oct 1793 but its usage was backdated to 22 Sep 1793, which became 1 Vendémiaire. The calendar was discarded as from 1 Jan 1806.

French Sudan /suːˈdɑːn/ former name (1898–1959) of ◊Mali, NW Africa.

French West Africa a group of French colonies administered from Dakar 1895–1958. They are now Senegal, Mauritania, Sudan, Burkina Faso, Guinea, Niger, Ivory Coast, and Benin.

frenetic /frəˈnetɪk/ *adj.* frantic, frenzied; fanatic. —**frenetically** *adv.* [from Old French from Latin from Greek *phrēn* = mind]

frenzy /ˈfrenzɪ/ *n.* wild excitement or agitation; a delirious fury. —*v.t.* (usually in *past participle*) to drive to frenzy. —**frenziedly** *adv.* [from Old French from Latin *phrenesia* from Greek]

frequency /ˈfriːkwənsɪ/ *n.* **1.** commonness of occurrence; frequent occurrence. **2.** the rate of recurrence (of vibration etc.); the number of cycles of a carrier wave per second; a band or group of such values. The unit of frequency is the hertz (Hz), one hertz being equivalent to one cycle per second. Human beings can hear sounds from objects vibrating in the range 20–15,000 Hz. Ultrasonic frequencies well above 15,000 Hz can be detected by mammals such as bats. —**frequency modulation,** the varying of a carrier-wave frequency.

frequent /ˈfriːkwənt/ *adj.* occurring often or in close succession; habitual, constant. —/frɪˈkwent/ *v.t.* to attend or go to habitually. —**frequently** *adv.,* **frequentation** /-ˈteɪʃən/ *n.* [from French or Latin *frequens,* originally = crowded]

frequentative /frɪˈkwentətɪv/ *adj.* in grammar, of a verb etc., expressing frequent repetition or intensity of action. —*n.* a frequentative verb etc.

Frere /frɪə/ John 1740–1807. English archaeologist, a pioneering discoverer of Old Stone Age (Palaeolithic) tools in association with large extinct animals at Hoxne, Suffolk, in 1790. He suggested (long before Charles Darwin) that they predated the conventional biblical timescale. Frere was high sheriff of Suffolk and member of Parliament for Norwich.

fresco /ˈfreskəʊ/ *n.* (*plural* **frescoes**) a method of wall-painting, or a picture done, in which pure powdered pigments, mixed only in water, are applied to a wet, freshly laid lime-plaster ground. Some of the earliest frescoes (about 1750–1400 BC) were found in Knossos, Crete (now preserved in the Heraklion Museum). Fresco reached its finest expression in Italy from the 13th to the 17th centuries. Giotto, Masaccio, Michelangelo, and many other artists worked in the medium. [Italian = cool, fresh]

Frescobaldi /freskəˈbældi/ Girolamo 1583–1643. Italian composer of virtuoso pieces for the organ and harpsichord.

fresh *adj.* **1.** newly made or obtained; other, different, not previously known or used. **2.** lately arrived *from.* **3.** not stale or musty; not faded. **4.** (of food) not preserved by salting, tinning, freezing etc. **5.** not salty. **6.** pure, untainted; refreshing. **7.** not weary, vigorous; (of a wind) brisk. **8.** cheeky, amorously impudent; inexperienced. —*adv.* newly, recently (especially in combinations,: *fresh-baked, fresh-cut*). —**freshly** *adv.,* **freshness** *n.* [from Old French *freis fresche* from Germanic]

freshen *v.t./i.* to make or become fresh.

fresher *n.* (*slang*) a freshman.

freshet /ˈfreʃɪt/ *n.* a stream of fresh water flowing into the sea; a flood of a river. [from Old French]

freshman *n.* (*plural* **freshmen**) a first-year student at university or (*US*) high school.

freshwater *adj.* (of fish etc.) of fresh (not salt) water, not of the sea.

Fresnel /ˈfreɪnel/ Augustin 1788–1827. French physicist who refined the theory of ◊polarized light. Fresnel realized in 1821 that light waves do not vibrate like sound waves longitudinally, in the direction of their motion, but transversely, at right angles to the direction of the propagated wave.

fret¹ *v.t./i.* (**-tt-**) **1.** to worry, to vex; to be worried or distressed. **2.** to wear or consume by gnawing or rubbing. —*n.* worry, vexation. [Old English *fretan*]

fret² *n.* an ornamental pattern of continuous combinations of straight lines joined usually at right angles. —*v.t.* (**-tt-**) to adorn with a fret or with carved or embossed work. [from Old French *frete* = trellis-work]

fret³ *n.* a bar or ridge on the finger-board of a guitar etc. to guide fingering.

fretful *adj.* constantly fretting, querulous. —**fretfully** *adv.*

fretsaw *n.* a narrow saw stretched on a frame for cutting thin wood in patterns.

fretwork *n.* ornamental work in wood with a fretsaw.

Freud /frɔɪd/ Clement 1924– . British journalist, television personality, and until 1987 Liberal member of Parliament; a grandson of Sigmund Freud.

Freud Lucian 1922– . German-born British painter, whose realistic portraits with the subject staring intently from an almost masklike face include *Francis Bacon* 1952 (Tate Gallery, London). He is a grandson of Sigmund Freud.

Freud Sigmund 1865–1939. Austrian physician who pioneered the study of the unconscious mind. He developed the methods of free association and interpretation of dreams that are basic techniques of ◊psychoanalysis, and

Freud *Austrian pioneer of psychoanalysis Sigmund Freud.*

formulated the concepts of the ◊id, ◊ego, and ◊superego. His books include *Die Traumdeutung/The Interpretation of Dreams* 1900, *Totem and Taboo* 1913, and *Das Unbehagen in der Kultur/Civilization and its Discontents* 1930.

Freudian /'frɔɪdɪən/ *adj.* of Sigmund Freud or his theories or methods of psychoanalysis. —**Freudian slip**, an unintentional error that seems to reveal unconscious feelings.

Freya /'fraɪə/ or **Frigga** in Scandinavian mythology, wife of Odin and mother of Thor, goddess of married love and the hearth. Friday is named after her.

Freyberg /'fraɪbɜːg/ Bernard Cyril, Baron Freyberg 1889–1963. New Zealand soldier and administrator. He fought in World War I, and during World War II he commanded the New Zealand expeditionary force. He was governor-general of New Zealand 1946–52.

Fri. abbreviation of Friday.

friable /'fraɪəbəl/ *adj.* easily crumbled. —**friability** /-'bɪlɪtɪ/ *n.* [from French or Latin *friare* = crumble]

friar /'fraɪə/ *n.* a member of certain non-enclosed religious orders of men founded in the Middle Ages; originally the title of members of the mendicant (begging) orders, the chief of which were the Franciscans or Minors (Grey Friars), the Dominicans or Preachers (Black Friars), the Carmelites (White Friars), and Augustinians (Austin Friars). [from Old French from Latin *frater* = brother]

friar's balsam mixture containing ◊benzoin, used as an inhalant for relief from colds.

friary *n.* a monastery of friars.

fricassee /'frɪkəsiː, -'siː/ *n.* a dish of stewed or fried pieces of meat served in a thick sauce. —*v.t.* to make a fricassee of. [French *fricasser* = cut up and stew in sauce]

fricative /'frɪkətɪv/ *adj.* (of a consonant, e. g. *f*, *th*) sounded by the friction of the breath in a narrow opening. —*n.* a fricative consonant. [from Latin]

friction /'frɪkʃən/ *n.* 1. the rubbing of one object against another. 2. in physics, the force that opposes the relative motion of two bodies in contact. The **coefficient of friction** is the ratio of the force required to achieve this relative motion to the force pressing the two bodies together. 3. clash of wills, temperaments, opinions etc. —**frictional** *adj.* [from French from Latin *fricare* = rub]

Friday /'fraɪdeɪ, -dɪ/ *n.* the day of the week following Thursday. —*adv.* (*colloquial*) on Friday. —**girl** *or* **man Friday**, an assistant doing general duties in an office etc. [from Man Friday, character in Defoe's *Robinson Crusoe*]. [Old English = day of **Frigga**]

fridge *n.* (*colloquial*) a refrigerator.

Friedan /fri'dæn/ Betty 1921– . US liberal feminist. Her book *The Feminine Mystique* 1963 was one of the most influential books for the women's movement in both the USA and the UK. She founded the National Organization for Women (NOW) in 1966, the National Women's Political Caucus in 1971, and the First Women's Bank in 1973, and called the First International Feminist Congress in 1973.

Friedman /'friːdmən/ Milton 1912– . US economist. The foremost exponent of ◊monetarism, the argument that a country's economy, and hence inflation, can be controlled through its money supply, although most governments lack the 'political will' to control inflation by cutting government spending and thereby increasing unemployment.

Friedrich /'friːdrɪk/ Caspar David 1774–1840. German Romantic landscape painter, active mainly in Dresden. He imbued his subjects—mountain scenes and moonlit seas—with poetic melancholy and was later admired by Symbolist painters.

friend /frend/ *n.* 1. a person with whom one enjoys mutual affection and regard (usually exclusive of sexual or family bonds). 2. a sympathizer, a helper; a helpful thing or quality; one who is not an enemy. 3. some person already mentioned or under discussion. 4. (usually in *plural*) a regular contributor of money or other assistance to an institution. 5. **Friend**, a member of the Society of ◊Friends, a Quaker. [Old English]

friendless *adj.* without friends.

friendly *adj.* acting as or like a friend, well-disposed, kindly; on amicable terms (*with*); characteristic of friends, showing or prompted by kindness. —*n.* a friendly match. —*adv.* in a friendly manner. —**friendly match**, a match played for enjoyment and not in competition. —**friendliness** *n.*

Friendly Islands another name for ◊Tonga.

friendly society (*US* **benefit society**) an association designed to meet the needs of sickness and old age by money payments. There are some 6,500 registered societies in the UK, with funds totalling about £385 million: among the largest are the National Deposit, Odd Fellows, Foresters, and Hearts of Oak. In the USA there are similar 'fraternal insurance' bodies, including the Modern Woodmen of America 1883 and the Fraternal Order of Eagles 1898.

friendship *n.* a friendly relationship or feeling.

Friends of the Earth (**FoE** or **FOE**) an environmental pressure group, established in the UK in 1971, that aims to protect the environment and to promote rational and sustainable use of the Earth's resources. It campaigns on issues such as acid rain; air, sea, river, and land pollution; recycling; disposal of toxic wastes; nuclear power and renewable energy; the destruction of rainforests; pesticides; and agriculture. FoE has branches in 30 countries.

Friends, Society of or **Quakers** a Christian Protestant sect founded by George ◊Fox in England in the 17th century. They were persecuted for their nonviolent activism, and many emigrated to form communities elsewhere, for example in Pennsylvania and New England, USA. They now form a worldwide movement of about 200,000. Quakers believe the essence of Christianity to be the Inner Light, the revelation of truth to be found in each individual. Their worship stresses meditation and the freedom of all to take an active part in the service (called a meeting, held in a meeting house). They have no priests or ministers.

frier variant of **fryer**.

Friesian /'friːʒən/ *n.* one of a breed of large black-and-white dairy cattle, originally from Friesland, a northern province of the Netherlands. [variant of *Frisian*]

Friesland /'friːzlənd/ maritime province of the N Netherlands, which includes the Frisian Islands and land that is still being reclaimed from the former Zuyder Zee; the inhabitants of the province are called ◊Frisians; **area** 3,400 sq km/1,312 sq mi; **population** (1988) 599,000; **capital** Leeuwarden; **products** livestock (Friesian cattle originated here); dairy products, small boats.

frieze /friːz/ *n.* 1. the part of an entablature between the architrave and the cornice; a horizontal band of sculpture filling this. 2. a band of decoration, especially along a wall near the ceiling. [from French from Latin *Phrygium* (*opus*) = Phrygian work]

frigate /'frɪgɪt/ *n.* a naval escort-vessel like a large corvette; (*historical*) the warship next in size to ships of the line. [from French from Italian]

fright /fraɪt/ *n.* 1. sudden or extreme fear; an instance of this. 2. a person or thing looking grotesque or ridiculous. [Old English]

frighten *v.t.* to fill with fright; to force or drive (*away* or *off*) by fright.

frightful *adj.* dreadful, shocking, ugly; (*colloquial*) extreme, extremely bad. —**frightfully** *adv.*

frigid /'frɪdʒɪd/ *adj.* 1. lacking friendliness or enthusiasm, dull. 2. (of a woman) sexually unresponsive. 3. (especially of climate or air) cold. —**frigidity** /-'dʒɪdɪtɪ/ *n.*, **frigidly** *adv.* [from Latin *frigidus* (*frigēre* = be cold)]

frill *n.* 1. a strip of material gathered or pleated and fixed along one edge as a trimming. 2. (in *plural*) unnecessary embellishments or accomplishments. —*v.t.* to decorate with a frill. —**frilled** *adj.*, **frilly** *adj.*

fringe *n.* 1. a border or edging of tassels or loose threads. 2. the front hair hanging over the forehead. 3. the margin or outer limit of an area, population etc. 4. an area or part of minor importance. —*v.t.* to adorn with a fringe; to serve as a fringe to. —**fringe benefit**, an employee's benefit additional to the normal wage or salary. —**fringe medicine**, systems of treatment of diseases, injuries etc., that are not regarded by the medical profession as part of orthodox treatment. [from Old French from Latin *fimbria* = fibres, fringe]

fringe theatre plays that are anti-establishment or experimental, and performed in informal venues, in contrast to mainstream commercial theatre. In the UK, the term originated in the 1960s from the activities held on the 'fringe' of the Edinburgh Festival. The US equivalent is off-off-Broadway (off-Broadway is mainstream theatre that is not on Broadway).

fringing reef a ◊coral reef that is attached to the coast without an intervening lagoon.

Frink /frɪŋk/ Elisabeth 1930– . British sculptor of rugged, naturalistic bronzes, mainly based on animal forms.

frippery /'frɪpərɪ/ n. showy finery or ornament, especially in dress; empty display in speech, literary style etc. [from French *friperie* (Old French *frepe* = rag)]

Frisbee /'frɪzbɪ/ n. trade name for a concave plastic disc for skimming through the air as an outdoor game. [perhaps from *Frisbie* American baker whose pie-tins could be used similarly]

Frisch /frɪʃ/ Karl von 1886–1982. German zoologist, founder with Konrad Lorenz of ◊ethology, the study of animal behaviour. He specialized in bees, discovering how they communicate the location of sources of nectar by movements called 'dances'. He was awarded the Nobel Prize for Medicine in 1973 together with Konrad Lorenz and Nikolaas ◊Tinbergen.

Frisch Max 1911– . Swiss dramatist. Inspired by ◊Brecht, his early plays such as *Als der Krieg zu Ende war/When the War Is Over* 1949 are more romantic in tone than his later symbolic dramas, such as *Andorra* 1962, dealing with questions of identity. He wrote *Biedermann und die Brandstifter/The Fire Raisers* 1958.

Frisch–Peierls memorandum /frɪʃ 'paɪəlz/ a document revealing, for the first time, how small the critical mass (the minimum quantity of substance required for a nuclear chain reaction to begin) of uranium needed to be if the isotope uranium-235 was separated from naturally occurring uranium; the memo thus implied the feasibility of using this isotope to make an atom bomb. It was written by Otto Frisch (1904–1979) and Rudolf Peierls (1907–) at the University of Birmingham in 1940.

Frisian /'frɪzɪən/ adj. or **Friesian**, of Friesland, a northern province of the Netherlands, or its people or language. —n. 1. a native of Friesland. 2. the Germanic language spoken there. [from Latin *Frisii* (plural)]

frisk v.t./i. 1. to leap or skip playfully. 2. (*slang*) to feel over and search (a person) for a weapon etc. —n. 1. a playful leap or skip. 2. (*slang*) a search of a person. [from Old French *frisque* = lively]

frisky adj. lively, playful. —**friskily** adv., **friskiness** n.

frisson /'friːsɔ̃/ n. an emotional thrill. [French = shiver]

frith variant of **firth**.

fritillary n. 1. in botany, any plant of the genus *Fritillaria* of the lily family Liliaceae. Snake's head fritillary *F. meleagris* has bell-shaped flowers with purple-chequered markings. 2. a butterfly of the family Nymphalidae. There are many species, most with a chequered pattern of black on orange. [from Latin *fritillaria* from *fritillus* = dice box; probably with reference to the spotted markings]

fritter [1] v.t. (usually with *away*) to waste (money, time, energy, etc.) triflingly or indiscriminately. [from obsolete *fritters* = fragments]

fritter [2] n. a small, flat piece of fried batter containing meat or fruit etc. [from Old French *friture* from Latin *frigere* = fry]

Friuli-Venezia Giulia /fri'uːli viˈnetsiə 'dʒuːliə/ autonomous agricultural and wine-growing region of NE Italy, bordered on the E by Yugoslavia; area 7,800 sq km/ 3,011 sq mi; population (1988) 1,210,000. Cities includes Udine (the capital), Gorizia, Pordenone, and Trieste.

frivolous /'frɪvələs/ adj. paltry, trifling; lacking seriousness, silly. —**frivolity** /-'vɒlɪtɪ/ n., **frivolously** adv. [from Latin *frivolus* = silly, trifling]

frizz v.t. to form (hair) into a mass of small curls. —n. frizzed hair or a frizzed state. —**frizzy** adj. [from French *friser*]

frizzle [1] /'frɪzəl/ v.t./i. 1. to fry or cook with a sizzling noise. 2. to burn or shrivel (up). [from obsolete *frizz* = fry]

frizzle [2] v.t./i. to form into tight curls. —n. frizzled hair. —**frizzly** adj.

fro /frəʊ/ adv. **to and fro**, see ◊to. [from Old Norse = from]

Frobisher /'frəʊbɪʃə/ Martin 1535–1594. English navigator. He made his first voyage to Guinea, West Africa, in 1554. In 1576 he set out in search of the North West Passage, and visited Labrador, and Frobisher Bay, Baffin Island. Second and third expeditions sailed in 1577 and 1578.

frock n. 1. a woman's or girl's dress. 2. a monk's or priest's gown. 3. a smock. —v.t. to invest with priestly office. —**frockcoat** n. a man's long-skirted coat not cut away in front; a military coat of this shape. [from Old French *froc*]

Froebel /'frəʊbəl/ Friedrich August Wilhelm 1782–1852. German educationist. He evolved a new system of education using instructive play, described in *Education of Man* 1826 and other works. In 1836 he founded the first kindergarten (German 'garden for children') in Blankenburg.

frog [1] n. 1. a tailless, smooth-skinned, leaping amphibian of the order Anura, especially the common frog (genus *Rana*). Frogs vary in size from the *Sminthillus limbatus*, 12 mm/ 0.5 in long, to the giant frog *Telmatobius culeus* of Lake Titicaca, 50 cm/20 in. 2. Frog, (*derogatory*) a Frenchman (with reference to use of edible frogs' legs in French cooking). 3. the horny substance in the sole of a horse's foot. —**frog in one's throat,** (*colloquial*) hoarseness. [Old English]

frog [2] n. an ornamental coat-fastening of a spindle-shaped button and loop.

froghopper n. a type of leaping insect, family Cercopidae, which sucks the juice from plants. The larvae are pale green, and protect themselves (from drying out and from predators) by secreting froth ('cuckoo-spit') from the anus.

frogman n. (*plural* **frogmen**) a person equipped with a rubber suit and flippers etc. for underwater swimming.

frogmarch v.t. to hustle forward holding and pinning the arms from behind; to carry (a person) face downwards by means of four persons each holding a limb. —n. the process of frogmarching a person.

frogmouth n. a nocturnal bird, related to the nightjar, of which the commonest species, *Podargus strigoides*, is found throughout Australia, including Tasmania.

frolic /'frɒlɪk/ v.i. (-**ck**-) to play about cheerfully. —n. cheerful play; a prank; a merry party. [from Dutch *vrolijk* (*vro* = glad)]

frolicsome adj. merry, playful.

from /frəm, *emphatic* frɒm/ prep. expressing separation or origin, followed by: a person, place, time etc., that is the starting-point of a motion or action; a place, object etc., whose distance or remoteness is stated; a source, giver, sender; a thing or person avoided, deprived etc.; a reason, cause, motive; a thing distinguished or unlike; a lower limit; a state changed for another; adverbs or prepositions of time or place. [Old English]

Fromm /frɒm/ Erich 1900–1980. German psychoanalyst who moved to the USA in 1933. His *The Fear of Freedom* 1941 and *The Sane Society* 1955 were source books for alternative lifestyles.

frond n. a large leaf or leaflike structure; in ferns it is often pinnately divided. The term is also applied to the leaves of palms and less commonly to the plant bodies of certain seaweeds, liverworts, and lichens. [from Latin *frons frondis* = leaf]

Fronde /frɒnd/ n. French revolts in 1648–53 against the administration of the chief minister ◊Mazarin during Louis XIV's minority. In 1648–49 the Paris *parlement* attempted to limit the royal power, its leaders were arrested, Paris revolted, and the rising was suppressed by the royal army under Louis II Condé. In 1650 Condé led a new revolt of the nobility, but this was suppressed by 1653. The defeat of the Fronde enabled Louis to establish an absolutist monarchy in the later 17th century.

front /frʌnt/ n. 1. the side or part normally nearer or towards the spectator or direction of motion. 2. any face of a building, especially that of the main entrance. 3. the foremost part of an army, a line of battle, the ground towards the enemy, the scene of fighting; a sector of activity compared to a military front; an organized political group. 4. a forward or conspicuous position. 5. an outward appearance; a bluff, a pretext; a person etc. serving to cover subversive or illegal activities. 6. the promenade of a seaside resort. 7. the forward edge of an advancing mass of cold or warm air. 8. the auditorium of a theatre. —adj. of the front; situated in front; (of vowels) formed at the front of the mouth (as in *see*). —v.t./i. 1. to have the front facing or directed (*on, to, towards, upon*). 2. (*slang*) to act as a front or cover *for*. 3. to furnish with a front. —**frontbencher** n. a leading member of the government or opposition in Parliament. **front-runner,** the contestant most likely to succeed. **in front,** in an advanced or facing position. **in front of,** before, in advance of; in the presence of, confronting. [from Old French from Latin *frons frontis* = forehead]

frontage *n.* 1. the front of a building. 2. the land abutting on a street or water, or between the front of a building and a road. 3. the extent of a front. 4. the way a thing faces; an outlook.

frontal *adj.* 1. of or on the front; of the front as seen by an onlooker. 2. of the forehead. —*n.* 1. a covering for the front of an altar. 2. a façade.

frontal lobotomy See ◊lobotomy.

Frontenac et Palluau /frɒntə'næk eɪ pælju'əʊ/ Louis de Buade, Comte de Frontenac et Palluau 1622–1698. French colonial governor. He began his military career in 1635, and was appointed governor of the French possessions in North America in 1672. Although efficient, he quarrelled with the local bishop and his followers and was recalled in 1682. After the Iroqois, supported by the English, had won several military victories, Frontenac was reinstated in 1689. He defended Québec against the English in 1690 and defeated the Iroquois in 1696.

frontier /'frʌntiə/ *n.* 1. a border between two countries, the district on each side of it. 2. the limits of attainment or knowledge in a subject. [from Anglo-French from Latin]

frontier literature writing reflecting the US experience of frontier and pioneer life. It includes James Fenimore Cooper's *Leatherstocking Tales*; the humour writing of Artemus Ward, Bret Harte, and Mark Twain; dime novels; westerns; the travel records of Francis Parkman; and the pioneer romances of Willa Cather. The frontier theme has influenced much modern American writing.

frontispiece /'frʌntɪspiːs/ *n.* an illustration facing the title-page of a book. [from French or Latin = façade (*specere* = look)]

front-line states the black nations of southern Africa in the 'front line' of the struggle against the racist policies of South Africa: namely Mozambique, Tanzania, and Zambia. Botswana and Zimbabwe can also be included in this category.

frost *n.* 1. freezing; the prevalence of a temperature below the freezing point of water. 2. frozen dew or vapour. 3. a chilling influence, unfriendliness. —*v.t./i.* 1. to cover (as) with frost; to injure (a plant etc.) with frost. 2. to make (glass) non-transparent by giving it a rough frostlike surface. —**frostbite** *n.* injury to the tissue of the body due to freezing. **frostbitten** *adj.* affected with frost-bite. [Old English]

Frost /frɒst/ Robert (Lee) 1874–1963. US poet whose verse, in traditional form, is written with an individual voice and penetrating vision; his poems include 'Mending Wall' ('Something there is that does not love a wall'), 'The Road Not Taken', and 'Stopping by Woods on a Snowy Evening'.

frosting *n.* a sugar icing for cakes.

frosty *adj.* 1. cold with frost; covered (as) with frost. 2. unfriendly in manner. —**frostily** *adv.*, **frostiness** *n.*

froth /frɒθ/ *n.* 1. foam. 2. idle talk or ideas. —*v.t./i.* to emit or gather froth; to make (beer etc.) froth. —**frothy** *adj.* [from Old Norse]

froward /'frəʊəd/ *adj.* (*archaic*) perverse, difficult to deal with.

frown *v.i.* to wrinkle the brows, especially in displeasure or deep thought. —*n.* the action of frowning; a look of displeasure or deep thought. —**frown at** *or* **on**, to disapprove of. [from Old French *froigne* = surly look, from Celtic]

frowsty *adj.* stuffy, fusty.

frowzy *adj.* 1. fusty. 2. slatternly, dingy.

froze, frozen past and past participle of **freeze**.

FRS abbreviation of Fellow of the Royal Society.

fructify /'frʌktɪfaɪ/ *v.t./i.* to bear or cause to bear fruit. [from Old French from Latin]

fructose /'frʌktəʊz/ *n.* a fruit sugar, $C_6H_{12}O_6$, which occurs naturally in honey, the nectar of flowers, and many sweet fruits, and is commercially prepared from glucose.

frugal /'fruːgəl/ *adj.* 1. sparing or economical, especially as regards food. 2. meagre, costing little. —**frugality** /-'gælɪtɪ/ *n.*, **frugally** *adv.* [from Latin *frugi* = thrifty]

fruit /fruːt/ *n.* 1. in botany, the structure that develops from the carpel of a flower and encloses one or more seeds, except in cases of ◊parthenocarpy; this used as food; these products collectively. Fruits can be divided into **dry** (such as ◊capsule, ◊follicle, ◊schizocarp, ◊nut, ◊caryopsis, ◊pod or legume, ◊lomentum, and ◊achene), and those that become

fruit

pulp / exocarp (rind) / seed (pip) / orange (hesperidium)

mango (drupe) / exocarp (skin) / seed / endocarp / mesocarp (flesh) / seed (pip)

receptacle (flesh) / pericarp (core) / remains of flower / apple (pome)

fleshy (such as ◊drupe and ◊berry). 2. (usually in *plural*) vegetable products fit for food. 3. the product of action, the result; (in *plural*) profits. —*v.t./i.* to bear or cause to bear fruit. —**fruitcake** *n.* one containing dried fruit. **fruit machine**, a coin-operated gambling machine, often using symbols resembling fruit. **fruit sugar**, fructose. [from Old French from Latin *fructus* (*frui* = enjoy)]

fruiterer /'fruːtərə/ *n.* a dealer in fruit.

fruitful /'fruːtfəl/ *adj.* 1. producing much fruit. 2. producing good results, successful. —**fruitfully** *adv.*, **fruitfulness** *n.*

fruition /fruː'ɪʃən/ *n.* the bearing of fruit (literal or figurative); the realization of aims or hopes. [from Old French from Latin *frui* = enjoy]

fruitless /'fruːtlɪs/ *adj.* 1. not bearing fruit. 2. useless, unsuccessful. —**fruitlessly** *adv.*, **fruitlessness** *n.*

fruity /'fruːtɪ/ *adj.* 1. of fruit, tasting or smelling like fruit; full of fruit. 2. (of a voice etc.) of a full, rich quality. 3. (*colloquial*) full of rough humour or (usually scandalous) interest. —**fruitily** *adv.*, **fruitiness** *n.*

frump *n.* an unattractive, dowdy woman. —**frumpish** *adj.* [perhaps from dialect *frumple* = wrinkle from Middle Dutch]

frustrate /frʌ'streɪt/ *v.t.* to make (efforts) ineffective; to prevent (a person) from achieving a purpose; (in *past participle*) discontented because unable to achieve desires. —**frustration** *n.* [from Latin *frustra* = in vain]

frustum /'frʌstəm/ *n.* (*plural* **frustra**) in geometry, a 'slice' taken out of a solid figure by a pair of parallel planes. A conical frustum, for example, resembles a cone with the top cut off. The volume and area of a frustum are calculated by subtracting the volume or area of the 'missing' piece from those of the whole figure. [Latin = piece cut off]

fry[1] *v.t./i.* to cook or be cooked in hot fat. —*n.* 1. the internal parts of animals usually eaten fried. 2. fried food. —**frying pan**, a shallow pan used in frying (*out of the frying pan into the fire*, from a bad situation to a worse). **fry-up** *n.* miscellaneous fried food. [from Old French from Latin *frigere*]

fry[2] *n.* young or newly hatched fishes. —**small fry**, people of little importance; children. [from Old Norse = seed]

Fry /fraɪ/ Christopher 1907- . English dramatist. He was a leader of the revival of verse drama after World War II, notably *The Lady's Not for Burning* 1948. *Venus Observed* 1950, and *A Sleep of Prisoners* 1951. He has also written screen plays and made successful translations of Anouilh and Giraudoux.

Indulgences, not fulfillment, is what the world/Permits us.

Christopher Fry
A Phoenix Too Frequent

Fry Elizabeth (born Gurney) 1780–1845. English Quaker philanthropist. She formed an association for the improvement of conditions for female prisoners in 1817, and in 1819 worked with her brother, **Joseph Gurney** (1788–1847) on a report on prison reform.

Fry, Roger Eliot 1866–1934. British artist and art critic, a champion of Post-Impressionism and an admirer of Cézanne. He founded the Omega Workshops to improve design and to encourage young artists.

fryer *n.* 1. one who fries. 2. a vessel for frying food, especially fish.

FSH abbreviation of follicle-stimulating hormone.

f-stop *n.* variant of **f-number**.

ft abbreviation of ◊foot, feet.

FT Index abbreviation of Financial Times Industrial Ordinary Share Index, a list of leading share prices.

Fuad /fu'ɑ:d/ two kings of Egypt:

Fuad I 1868–1936. King of Egypt from 1922. Son of the Khedive Ismail, he succeeded his elder brother Hussein Kiamil as sultan of Egypt in 1917; when Egypt was declared independent in 1922 he assumed the title of king.

Fuad II 1952– . King of Egypt 1952–53, between the abdication of his father ◊Farouk and the establishment of the republic. He was a grandson of Fuad I.

Fuchs /fuks/ Klaus (Emil Julius) 1911–1988. German spy who worked on atom-bomb research in the UK in World War II. He was imprisoned 1950–59 for passing information to the USSR and resettled in East Germany.

Fuchs Vivian 1908– . British explorer and geologist. Before World War II, he accompanied several Cambridge University expeditions to Greenland, Africa, and Antarctica. In 1957-58, he led the Commonwealth Trans-Antarctic Expedition.

fuchsia /fju:ʃə/ *n.* any shrubs or herbaceous plants of the genus *Fuchsia* of the evening-primrose family Onagraceae. Species are native to South and Central America and New Zealand and bear red, purple, white or pink bell-shaped flowers that hang downwards. [from L *Fuchs*, German botanist (died 1566)]

fuck *v.t./i.* (*vulgar*) 1. to have sexual intercourse (*with*). 2. to make *off*; to idle *about* or *around*. 3. to mess *up*. —(*vulgar*) interjection expressing anger or annoyance. —*n.* (*vulgar*) 1. the act of or a partner in sexual intercourse. 2. the slightest amount. —**fucking** *adj. & adv.* (*vulgar*, often as a mere intensive).

fuddle *v.t.* to confuse or stupefy, especially with alcoholic liquor. —*n.* confusion; intoxication.

fuddy-duddy /'fʌdɪdʌdɪ/ *adj.* (*slang*) old-fashioned or quaintly fussy. —*n.* (*slang*) such a person.

fudge *n.* 1. a soft, toffee-like sweet made of milk, sugar, and butter. 2. nonsense. —*v.t.* to put together in a makeshift or dishonest way; to fake. [perhaps from obsolete *fadge* = fit]

fuel /'fju:əl/ *n.* 1. material for burning as a fire or as a source of heat or power; material used as a source of nuclear energy. 2. food as a source of energy. 3. a thing that sustains or inflames passion etc. —*v.t./i.* (**-ll-**) 1. to supply with fuel; to inflame (a feeling etc.). 2. to take in or get fuel. [from Anglo-French from Latin *focus* = hearth]

fuel cell a cell converting chemical energy directly to electrical energy. It works on the same principle as a ◊battery but is continually fed with fuel, usually hydrogen. Fuel cells are silent and reliable (no moving parts) but expensive to produce.

fuel injection injecting fuel directly into the cylinders of an internal combustion engine, instead of by way of a carburettor. It is the standard method used in ◊diesel engines, and is now becoming standard for ◊petrol engines. In the diesel engine oil is injected into the hot compressed air at the top of the second piston stroke and explodes to drive the piston down on its power stroke. In the petrol

engine, fuel is injected into the cylinder at the start of the first induction stroke of the ◊four-stroke cycle.

Fuentes /fu'entes/ Carlos 1928– . Mexican novelist, whose first novel *La región más transparente/Where the Air Is Clear* 1958 encompasses the history of the country from the Aztecs to the present day.

fug *n.* (*colloquial*) stuffiness of the air in a room. —**fuggy** *adj.*, **fugginess** *n.*

fugitive /'fju:dʒɪtɪv/ *adj.* 1. fleeing, that runs or has run away. 2. fleeting, transient; (of literature) of passing interest, ephemeral. —*n.* one who flees, e.g. from justice or an enemy. [from Old French from Latin *fugere* = flee]

fugue /fju:g/ *n.* a piece of music in which three or more parts or 'voices' (described thus whether vocal or instrumental) enter successively in imitation of each other. [French or from Italian, from Latin *fuga* = flight]

Führer /'fjuərə/ *n.* or **Fuehrer** title adopted by Adolf ◊Hitler as leader of the ◊Nazi Party. [German = leader]

Fujairah /fu'dʒaɪərə/ or **Fujayrah** one of the seven constituent member states of the ◊United Arab Emirates; area 1,150 sq km/450 sq mi; population (1985) 54,000.

Fujian /fu:dʒi'æn/ formerly **Fukien** province of SE China, bordering Taiwan Strait, opposite Taiwan; **area** 123,100 sq km/47,517 sq mi; **capital** Fuzhou **population** (1986) 27,490,000

Fujiyama /fu:dʒi'jɑ:mə/ or **Mount Fuji** Japanese volcano and highest peak, on Honshu Island; height 3,778 m/ 12,400 ft. Extinct since 1707, it has a ◊Shinto shrine and a weather station on its summit. Located near Tokyo, it has long been revered for its picturesque cone-shaped crater peak, and figures prominently in Japanese art, literature, and religion.

Fukuoka /fu:ku:'əukə/ formerly **Najime** Japanese industrial port on the NW coast of Kyushu island; population (1987) 1,142,000. It produces chemicals, textiles, paper, and metal goods.

-ful /-ful/ suffix forming (1) adjectives from nouns, in sense 'full of' (*beautiful*), 'having the qualities of' (*masterful*), or from adjectives (*direful*); or from verbs in sense 'apt to' (*forgetful*); (2) nouns (*plural* -**fuls**) in sense 'amount that fills' (*glassful*, *handful*, *spoonful*).

Fula /'fu:lə/ *n.* W African empire founded by people of predominantly Fulani extraction. The Fula conquered the Hausa states in the 19th century.

Fulani /fu:'lɑ:ni/ *n.* a member of a W African culture from the S Sahara and Sahel. Traditionally nomadic pastoralists and traders, Fulani groups are found in Senegal, Guinea, Mali, Burkina Faso, Niger, Nigeria, Chad, and Cameroon. The Fulani language is divided into four dialects, and belongs to the W Atlantic branch of the Niger-Congo family.

Fulbright /'fulbraɪt/ William 1905– . US Democratic politician. He was responsible for the **Fulbright Act** 1946 which provided grants for thousands of Americans to study overseas and for overseas students to enter the USA; he had studied at Oxford, UK, on a Rhodes scholarship. He chaired the Senate Foreign Relations Committee from 1959–1974, and was a strong internationalist and supporter of the United Nations.

fulcrum /'fulkrəm/ *n.* (*plural* **fulcra**) the point on which a lever is supported. [Latin = post of couch (*fulcire* = prop)]

fulfil /ful'fil/ *v.t.* (**-ll-**) to carry out (a task, prophecy, promise, command, or law); to satisfy (conditions, a desire, a prayer); to answer (a purpose). —**fulfil oneself,** to develop fully one's gifts and character. —**fulfilment** *n.* [Old English]

full[1] /ful/ *adj.* 1. holding all that its limits will allow; having eaten to one's limit or satisfaction. 2. abundant, copious, satisfying. 3. having an abundance *of*. 4. engrossed in thinking *of*. 5. complete, perfect, reaching the specified or usual or utmost limit. 6. (of a tone) clear and deep. 7. plump, rounded; (of clothes) made of much material hanging in folds. —*adv.* 1. very; quite, fully. 2. exactly. —**fullback** *n.* a defensive player near the goal in football, hockey, etc. **full-blooded** *adj.* vigorous, sensual; not hybrid. **full-blown** *adj.* fully developed. **full board,** the provision of bed and all meals at a hotel etc. **full-bodied** *adj.* rich in quality, tone etc. **full brother, sister,** a brother or sister with both parents the same. **full face,** with all the face visible to the spectator. **full house,** a large or full attendance at a theatre etc.; a hand in poker with three of a kind and a pair. **full-length** *adj.* not shortened or abbreviated; (of a mirror or portrait) showing the whole of the human figure. **full moon,** the Moon with the whole disc illuminated; the time when this occurs. **full pitch,** a full toss. **full-scale** *adj.* not reduced in size, complete. **full time,** the total normal duration of work etc. **full-time** *adj.* occupying or using the whole of the available working time. **full toss,** a ball pitched right up to the batsman in cricket. **in full,** without abridgement, to or for the full amount. **in full view,** entirely visible. **to the full,** to the utmost extent. [Old English]

full² *v.t.* to clean and thicken (cloth).

full employment in economics, a state in which the only unemployment is frictional (that share of the labour force which is in the process of looking for, or changing to, a new job), and when everyone wishing to work is able to find employment.

fuller /'fʊlə/ *n.* one who fulls cloth. —**fuller's earth,** a type of clay used in fulling. [Old English from Latin *fullo*]

Fuller (Richard) Buckminster 1895–1983. US architect and engineer. In 1947 he invented the lightweight **geodesic dome,** a half-sphere of triangular components independent of buttress or vault. It combined the maximum strength with the minimum structure. Within 30 years over 50,000 had been built.

I am a passenger on the spaceship, Earth.
Richard Buckminster Fuller
Operating Manual for Spaceship Earth.

Fuller Roy 1912– . English poet and novelist. His collections of poetry include *Poems* 1939, *Epitaphs and Occasions* 1951, *Brutus's Orchard* 1957, *Collected Poems* 1962, and *The Reign of Sparrows* 1980. Novels include *My Child, My Sister* 1965 and *The Carnal Island* 1970.

fullness *n.* being full. —**the fullness of time,** the appropriate or destined time.

full score in music, a complete transcript of a composition showing all parts individually, as opposed to a **short score** or **piano score** that is condensed into fewer lines of music.

full stop (or full point) 1. a punctuation mark (.). The full stop has two functions: to mark the end of a sentence and to indicate that a word has been abbreviated. It is also used in mathematics to indicate decimals and is then called a **point**. The term 'period' is the preferred usage in North America. 2. a complete cessation.

fully *adv.* completely, entirely; no less than. —**fully-fashioned** *adj.* (of women's clothing) shaped to fit the body.

fulmar /'fʊlmə(r)/ *n.* several species of petrels of the family Procellariidae, which are similar in size and colour to the common gull. The northern fulmar *Fulmarus glacialis* is found in the N Atlantic and visits land only to nest, laying a single egg. [from Old Norse *mar* = gull]

fulminant /'fʊlmɪnənt/ *adj.* 1. fulminating. 2. (of a disease) developing suddenly.

fulminate /'fʌlmɪneɪt, 'fʊ-/ *v.i.* 1. to express censure loudly and forcefully. 2. to explode violently, to flash like lightning. —**fulmination** /-'neɪʃən/ *n.*, **fulminator** *n.* [from Latin *fulmen* = lightning]

fulsome /'fʊlsəm/ *adj.* (of flattery etc.) cloying, disgustingly excessive.

Fulton /'fʊltən/ Robert 1765–1815. US engineer and inventor who designed the first successful steamships. He produced a submarine, the *Nautilus*, for Napoleon's government in France 1801, and experimented with steam navigation on the Seine, then returned to the USA. The first steam vessel of note, known as the *Clermont*, appeared on the Hudson in 1807, sailing between New York and Albany. The first steam warship was the USS *Fulton*, of 38 tonnes, built 1814–15.

fumble *v.t./i.* to use the hands awkwardly, to grope about; to handle clumsily or nervously. —*n.* an act of fumbling. [from Low German or Dutch]

fume /fju:m/ *n.* (usually in *plural*) exuded gas, smoke, or vapour, especially when harmful or unpleasant. —*v.t./i.* 1. to emit fumes; to issue in fumes. 2. to be very angry. 3. to subject to fumes, especially of ammonia to darken oak etc. [from Old French from Latin *fumus* = smoke]

fumigate /'fju:mɪgeɪt/ *v.t.* to disinfect or purify with the action of fumes. —**fumigation** /-'geɪʃən/ *n.*, **fumigator** *n.* [from Latin]

fumitory *n.* any plant of the genus *Fumeria,* family Fumariaceae, native to Europe and Asia. The common fumitory *F. officinalis* produces pink flowers tipped with blackish red; it was once used in medicine for stomach complaints.

fun *n.* lively or playful amusement; a source of this. —**for** *or* **in fun,** not seriously. **make fun of** *or* **poke fun at,** to tease, to ridicule. [from obsolete *fun* = befool]

function¹ /'fʌŋkʃən/ *n.* 1. the activity proper to a person or institution or by which a thing fulfils its purpose; an official or professional duty. 2. a public ceremony or occasion. 3. a social gathering, especially a large one. 4. a quantity whose value depends on varying values (of others). —*v.i.* to fulfil a function, to operate. [from French from Latin *fungi funct-* = perform]

function² in computing, a small part of a program that supplies a specific value; for example, the square root of a specified number, or the current date. Most programming languages incorporate a number of built-in functions; some allow programmers to write their own. A function may have one or more arguments (the values on which the function operates). A **function key** on a keyboard is one which, when pressed, performs a designated task, such as ending a program.

function³ in mathematics, a function f is a set of ordered pairs $(x, f(x))$ of which no two can have the same first element. Hence, if $f(x) = x^2$, two ordered pairs are $(-2, 4)$ and $(2, 4)$. In the algebraic expression $y = 4x^3 + 2$, the dependent variable y is a function of the independent variable x, generally written as $f(x)$.

functional *adj.* 1. of or serving a function; designed or intended to be practical rather than necessarily attractive or pleasing 2. affecting a function of a bodily organ but not its structure. —**functionally** *adv.*

functional group in chemistry, a small number of atoms in an arrangement that determines the chemical properties of the group and of the molecule to which it is attached (for example the carboxylic acid group, COOH, or the amine group, NH_2). Organic compounds can be considered as structural skeletons with functional groups attached.

functionalism *n.* belief in or stress on the practical application of a thing. —**functionalist** *n.*

Functionalism /'fʌŋkʃnəlɪzəm/ *n.* in architecture and design, a 20th-century school, also called Modernism or International Style, characterized by a desire to exclude everything that serves no practical purpose. It developed as a reaction against the 19th-century practice of imitating earlier styles, and its finest achievements are in the realm of industrial architecture and office furnishings. Its leading exponents were the German ◊Bauhaus school and the Dutch group de ◊Stijl; prominent architects in the field were Le Corbusier and Walter ◊Gropius.

functionary *n.* a person or official performing certain duties.

fund *n.* 1. a permanently available stock. 2. a stock of money, especially one set apart for a purpose; (in *plural*) money resources. —*v.t.* to provide with money; to make (a debt) permanent at a fixed interest. —**in funds,** having money to spend. [from Latin *fundus* = bottom]

fundamental /fʌndə'mentəl/ *adj.* of, affecting, or serving as a base or foundation, essential, primary. —*n.* 1. (usually in *plural*) a fundamental rule or principle. 2. (in full **fundamental note**) the lowest note of a chord. —**fundamental particle,** an elementary particle. —**fundamentally** *adv.* [from French or Latin *fundamentum* = foundation]

fundamental forces see ◊forces, fundamental.

fundamentalism *n.* in religion, an emphasis on basic principles or articles of faith. **Christian fundamentalism** emerged in the USA just after World War I (as a reaction to theological modernism and the historical criticism of the Bible) and insisted on belief in the literal truth of everything in the Bible. **Islamic fundamentalism** insists on strict observance of Muslim Shari'a law. —**fundamentalist** *n.*

fundamental particle variant of **elementary particle.**

funeral /'fju:nərəl/ *n.* 1. a burial or cremation of the dead with ceremonies. 2. (*slang*) one's (usually unpleasant) concern. —*attributive adj.* of or used at funerals. [from Old French from Latin *funus funer* = burial]

fungus

Structure of a fungus

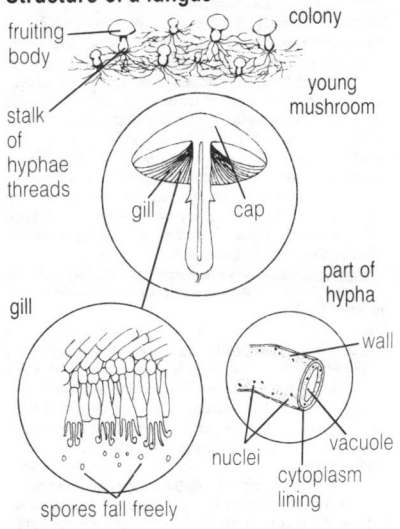

fruiting body

colony

young mushroom

stalk of hyphae threads

gill

cap

part of hypha

gill

wall

vacuole

nuclei

cytoplasm lining

spores fall freely

funerary /'fju:nərərɪ/ *adj.* of or used at a funeral or funerals. [from Latin]

funereal /fju:'nɪərɪəl/ *adj.* of or appropriate to a funeral, dismal, dark. —**funereally** *adv.*

funfair *n.* a fair consisting of amusements and sideshows.

fungicide /'fʌndʒɪsaɪd/ *n.* any chemical ◊pesticide used to prevent fungus diseases in plants and animals. Inorganic and organic compounds containing sulphur are widely used. —**fungicidal** /-saɪdəl/ *adj.*

fungoid /'fʌŋgɔɪd/ *adj.* fungus-like. —*n.* a fungoid plant.

fungus /'fʌŋgəs/ *n.* (*plural* **fungi** /-gaɪ/) any of a large group of organisms in the kingdom Fungi, including mushrooms, toadstools, moulds, yeasts, rusts, smuts and mildews. Fungi are not considered plants: they lack leaves and roots; they contain no chlorophyll and reproduce by spores. They must get food from organic substances and so are either ◊parasites, existing on living plants or animals, or ◊saprophytes, living on dead matter. Some 50,000 different species have been identified. Some are edible, but many are highly poisonous. 2. a spongy morbid growth. —**fungal** *adj.*, **fungous** *adj.* [Latin]

funicular /fju:'nɪkjʊlə/ *adj.* (of a railway especially on a mountain) operating by a cable with ascending and descending cars counterbalanced. —*n.* such a railway. [from Latin *funiculus* diminutive of *funis* = rope]

funk[1] /fʌŋk/ *n.* (*slang*) 1. fear, panic. 2. a coward. —*v.t./i.* (*slang*) to be afraid (of); to try to evade. —**blue funk**, (*slang*) extreme panic.

funk[2] *n.* a style of dance music of black US origin, relying on heavy percussion in polyrhythmic patterns. Leading exponents include James Brown (1928–) and George Clinton (1940–).

Funk Casimir 1884–1967. US biochemist, born in Poland, who pioneered research into vitamins. Funk proposed that certain diseases are caused by dietary deficiencies. In 1912 he demonstrated that rice extracts cure beriberi in pigeons. As the extract contains an ◊amine, he mistakenly concluded that he had discovered a class of 'vital amines', a phrase soon reduced to 'vitamins'.

funky /'fʌŋkɪ/ *adj.* (*slang*) 1. (especially of music) down-to-earth, emotional. 2. fashionable. 3. having a strong smell.

funnel /'fʌnəl/ *n.* 1. a narrow tube or pipe widening at the top, for pouring liquid etc. into a small opening. 2. a metal chimney on a steam engine or ship. —*v.t./i.* (-**ll**-) to move or cause to move (as) through a funnel. [from Provençal *fonilh* from Latin (*in*)*fundibulum* from *fundere* = pour]

funny *adj.* 1. amusing, comical. 2. strange, hard to account for; (*colloquial*) slightly unwell, eccentric etc. —**funny bone**, the part of the elbow over which a very sensitive nerve passes. —**funnily** *adv.*, **funniness** *n.*

fur *n.* 1. the short, fine, soft hair of certain animals. 2. an animal skin with the fur on it, used especially for making or trimming clothes etc.; a garment made or lined with this. 3. (in heraldry) a representation of tufts on a plain ground. 4. (*collectively*) furred animals. 5. the crust or coating formed on the tongue in sickness, in a kettle by hard water etc. —*v.t./i.* (-**rr**-) 1. (especially in *past participle*) to line or trim with fur. 2. (often with *up*) to make or become coated with a fur deposit. —**make the fur fly**, to cause trouble or dissension. [from Old French *forrer* (*forre, fuerre* = sheath)]

furbelow /'fɜ:bɪləʊ/ *n.* 1. a gathered strip or pleated border of a skirt or petticoat. 2. (in *plural*) showy ornaments. [from French *falbala*]

furbish /'fɜ:bɪʃ/ *v.t.* (often with *up*) to polish, to clean up or renovate. [from Old French *forbir*]

furcate /'fɜ:keɪt/ *adj.* forked, branched. —*v.i.* to fork, to divide. —**furcation** /-'keɪʃən/ *n.* [from Latin *furca* = fork]

Furies /'fjʊərɪz/ in Greek mythology, the **Erinyes**, appeasingly called the **Eumenides**, ('kindly ones'). They were the daughters of Earth or of Night, represented as winged maidens with serpents twisted in their hair. They punished such crimes as filial disobedience, murder, and inhospitality.

furious /'fjʊərɪəs/ *adj.* very angry, full of fury, raging, frantic. —**furiously** *adv.* [from Old French from Latin]

furl *v.t./i.* to roll up and bind (a sail etc.); to become furled. [from French *ferler* from Old French *ferm* = firm, *lier* = bind]

furlong /'fɜ:lɒŋ/ *n.* unit of measurement, equivalent to 220 yd (201.168 m), one-eighth of a mile. [Old English = furrow long]

furlough /'fɜ:ləʊ/ *n.* leave of absence, especially that granted to a serviceman or woman. —*v.t./i.* (*US*) to grant a furlough to; to spend a furlough. [from Dutch]

furnace /'fɜ:nɪs/ *n.* an enclosed structure for intense heating by fire, especially of metals or water; a very hot place. Furnaces are used in conjunction with ◊boilers for heating, to produce hot water, or steam for driving turbines—in ships for propulsion and in power stations for generating electricity. The largest furnaces are those used for smelting and refining metals, such as the ◊blast furnace, electric furnace, and ◊open-hearth furnace. [from Old French from Latin *fornax* (*fornus* = oven)]

furnish /'fɜ:nɪʃ/ *v.t.* 1. to provide (a house or room etc.) with furniture. 2. to supply *with* a thing. [from Old French *furnir*]

furnishings *n.pl.* the furniture and fitments in a house or room.

furniture /'fɜ:nɪtʃə/ *n.* 1. the movable equipment of a house or room etc., e. g. tables, chairs, and beds. 2. a ship's equipment. 3. accessories, e.g. the handles and lock on a door. [from French]

furore /fjʊə'rɔːrɪ/ *n.* an uproar of enthusiastic admiration or fury. [Italian, from Latin *furor* = madness]

furrier /'fʌrɪə/ *n.* a dealer in or dresser of furs. [from Old French]

furrow /'fʌrəʊ/ *n.* 1. a narrow cut in the ground made by a plough. 2. a rut, a groove, a wrinkle. 3. a ship's track. —*v.t.* 1. to plough. 2. to make furrows or grooves etc. in. [Old English]

furry /'fɜ:rɪ/ *adj.* like or covered with fur.

further /'fɜ:ðə/ *adv.* 1. more far in space or time. 2. more, to a greater extent. 3. in addition. —*adj.* 1. more distant or advanced. 2. more, additional. —*v.t.* to promote or favour (a scheme). —**further education**, that for persons above school age. [Old English comparative of *forth*]

furtherance *n.* the furthering of a scheme etc.

furthermore *adv.* in addition, besides.

furthermost *adj.* most distant.

furthest /'fɜ:ðɪst/ *adj.* most distant. —*adv.* to or at the greatest distance. [superlative from *further*]

furtive /'fɜ:tɪv/ *adj.* done by stealth; sly, stealthy. —**furtively** *adv.*, **furtiveness** *n.* [from French or Latin *furtum* = theft]

Furtwängler /'fʊətvɛŋglə/ (Gustav Heinrich Ernst Martin) Wilhelm 1886–1954. German conductor; leader of the Berlin Philharmonic Orchestra 1922–54. His interpretations of the German Romantic composers, such as Wagner, were regarded as classically definitive. He remained in Germany during the Nazi regime.

fury /'fjʊərɪ/ *n.* **1.** wild and passionate anger, rage. **2.** the violence of a storm, disease etc. **3. Fury,** each of the ◊Furies, avenging goddesses of Greek mythology. **4.** an angry or malignant woman. —**like fury,** (*colloquial*) with great force or effort. [from Old French from Latin *furia*]

furze *n.* a spiny evergreen shrub of the genus *Ulex* with yellow flowers, gorse. —**furzy** *adj.* [Old English]

fuse¹ /fju:z/ *v.t./i.* **1.** to melt with intense heat; to blend into a whole by melting. **2.** to mix or blend together. **3.** to provide (an electric circuit) with a fuse or fuses. **4.** (of an appliance) to fail owing to the melting of a fuse; to cause (an appliance) to do this. —*n.* a device with a strip or wire of easily melted metal placed in an electric circuit so as to interrupt an excessive current by melting. [from Latin *fundere fus-*= pour, melt]

fuse² *n.* a device or component of combustible matter for detonating a bomb etc. or an explosive charge. —*v.t.* to fit a fuse to. [from Italian from Latin *fusus* = spindle]

fuselage /'fju:zəlɑ:ʒ/ *n.* the body of an aeroplane. [French *fuseler* = cut in spindle form]

Fuseli /'fju:zəli/ Henry 1741–1825. British Romantic artist born in Switzerland. He painted macabre and dreamlike images, such as *The Nightmare* 1781 (Detroit Institute of Arts).

fusel oil a liquid with a characteristic unpleasant smell, obtained as a by-product of the distillation of the product of any alcoholic fermentation, and used in paints, varnishes, essential oils, and plastics. Fusel oil is a mixture of fatty acids, alcohols, and esters.

fusible /'fju:zɪbəl/ *adj.* that may be melted. —**fusibility** /-'bɪlɪtɪ/ *n.* [from Latin]

fusil /'fju:zɪl/ *n.* (*historical*) a light musket. [French from Latin *focus* = hearth]

fusilier /fju:zɪ'lɪə/ *n.* a member of any of several British regiments formerly armed with fusils. [French]

fusillade /fju:zɪ'leɪd/ *n.* **1.** a continuous discharge of firearms. **2.** a sustained outburst of criticism etc. [French from *fusiller* = shoot]

fusion /'fju:ʒən/ *n.* **1.** fusing or melting together; blending, coalition. **2.** ◊nuclear fusion. [from French or Latin]

fuss *n.* **1.** excited commotion, bustle. **2.** excessive concern about a trivial thing. **3.** a sustained protest or dispute. —*v.t./i.* to behave with nervous concern; to agitate, to worry. —**make a fuss,** to complain vigorously. **make a fuss of,** to treat with excessive attention etc.

fusspot *n.* (*colloquial*) a person given to fussing.

fussy *adj.* inclined to fuss; over-elaborate, fastidious. —**fussily** *adv.,* **fussiness** *n.*

fustian /'fʌstɪən/ *n.* **1.** a thick, twilled cotton cloth usually dyed dark. **2.** bombast. —*adj.* **1.** made of fustian. **2.** bombastic, worthless. [from Old French from Latin, originally referring to cloth from *Fostat,* suburb of Cairo]

fusty *adj.* musty, stuffy, stale-smelling; antiquated. —**fustiness** *adj.* [from Old French = smelling of the cask (*fust* = cask)]

futile /'fju:taɪl/ *adj.* useless, ineffectual, frivolous. —**futility** /-'tɪlɪtɪ/ *n.* [from Latin *futilis,* literally = leaky]

future¹ /'fju:tʃə/ *adj.* **1.** belonging to the time coming after the present; about to happen or be or become. **2.** in grammar, of a tense, describing an event yet to happen. —*n.* **1.** future time, events, or condition. **2.** a prospect of success etc. **3.** in grammar, a future tense. —**in future,** from this time onwards. [from Old French from Latin *futurus* future participle of *esse* = be]

future² *n.* in business, a contract to buy or sell a specific quantity of a particular commodity or currency at a particular date in the future. There is usually no physical exchange between buyer and seller. It is only the difference between the ground value and the market value that changes hands. The **futures market** trades in financial futures.

futures trading buying and selling commodities (usually cereals and metals) at an agreed price for delivery several months ahead.

Futurism /'fju:tʃərɪzəm/ *n.* a literary and artistic movement 1909–14, originating in Paris. The Italian poet ◊Marinetti published the **Futurist Manifesto** 1909 urging Italian artists to join him in Futurism. In their works they eulogized the modern world and the 'beauty of speed and energy', trying to capture the dynamism of a speeding car or train by combining the shifting geometric planes of ◊Cubism with vibrant colours. As a movement it died out during World War I, but the Futurists' exultation in war and violence was seen as an early manifestation of ◊Fascism. —**futurist** *n.*

futuristic /fju:tʃə'rɪstɪk/ *adj.* **1.** suitable for the future, ultra-modern. **2.** of futurism.

futurity /fju:'tjʊərɪtɪ/ *n.* future time; (in *singular* or *plural*) future events.

futurology /fju:tʃə'rɒlədʒɪ/ *n.* the forecasting of the future, especially from present trends in society.

Fuzhou /fu:'dʒəʊ/ formerly **Foochow** industrial port and capital of Fujian province, SE China; population (1986) 1,190,000. It is a centre for shipbuilding and steel production; rice, sugar, tea, and fruit pass through the port. There are joint foreign and Chinese factories.

fuzz¹ *n.* **1.** fluff; fluffy or frizzed hair. [probable from Low German or Dutch]

fuzz² *n.* (*slang*) the police; a policeman.

fuzzy *adj.* **1.** like fuzz. **2.** blurred, indistinct. —**fuzzily** *adv.,* **fuzziness** *n.*

Fylingdales /'faɪlɪŋdeɪlz/ site in the North Yorkshire Moors National Park, England, of an early-warning radar station, linked with similar stations in Greenland and Alaska, to give a four-minute warning of nuclear attack.

fyrd *n.* Anglo-Saxon local militia in Britain. All freemen were obliged to defend their shire but, by the 11th century, a distinction was drawn between the **great fyrd,** for local defence, and the **select fyrd,** drawn from better-equipped and experienced warriors who could serve farther afield.

g, G /dʒi:/ *n.* (*plural* **gs, g's**) **1.** seventh letter of the alphabet. **2.** in music, the fifth note in the scale of C major.

g. abbreviation of **1.** gram(s). **2.** gravity; acceleration due to gravity.

G abbreviation of **1.** gauss. **2.** giga-.

Ga symbol for gallium.

gab *n.* (*colloquial*) talk, chatter. —**gift of the gab,** eloquence, loquacity. [variant of *gob*²]

gabardine /ˈgæbədiːn/ variant of **gaberdine**

gabble *v. t. /i.* to talk or utter inarticulately or too fast. —*n.* fast unintelligible talk. —**gabbler** *n.* [from Middle Dutch]

gabbro *n.* a basic (low-silica) ◊igneous rock formed deep in the Earth's crust. It contains pyroxene and calcium-rich feldspar, and may contain small amounts of olivine and amphibole. Its coarse crystals of dull minerals give it a speckled appearance.

gabby /ˈgæbi/ *adj.* (*colloquial*) talkative. [from *gab*]

gaberdine /ˈgæbədiːn/ *n.* or **garbardine 1.** in history, a loose, long upper garment worn especially by Jews. **2.** a twill-woven cloth, especially of worsted. [from Old French *gauvardine*]

gable /ˈgeɪbəl/ *n.* **1.** the triangular upper part of a wall at the end of a ridged roof; an end wall with a gable. **2.** a gable-shaped canopy. —**gabled** *adj.* [from Old Norse and Old French]

Gable Clark 1901–1960. US film actor. A star for more than 30 years in 90 films, he was celebrated for his romantic, rakish nonchalance in roles such as Rhett Butler in *Gone with the Wind* 1939. Other films include *The Painted Desert* 1931 (his first), *It Happened One Night* 1934 (Academy Award), *Mutiny on the Bounty* 1935, and *The Misfits* 1960, after which he died of a heart attack. He was nicknamed the 'King' of Hollywood.

Gabo /ˈgɑːbəʊ/ Naum. The adopted name of Naum Neemia Pevsner 1890–1977. US abstract sculptor, born in Russia. One of the leading exponents of ◊Constructivism, he left the USSR in 1922 for Germany and taught at the Bauhaus in Berlin (a key centre of modern design). He lived in Paris and England in the 1930s, then settled in the USA in 1946. He was one of the first artists to make kinetic (moving) sculpture and often used transparent coloured plastics.

Gabon /gæˈbɒn/ (Gabonese Republic); country in central Africa, bounded N by Cameroon, E and S by the Congo, W by the Atlantic Ocean, and NW by Equatorial Guinea; **area** 267,667 sq km/103,319 sq mi; **capital** Libreville; **physical** virtually the whole country is tropical rainforest; narrow coastal plain rising to hilly interior with savanna in E and S; Ogooué River flows S–W; **head of state and government** Omar Bongo from 1967; **political system** authoritarian nationalism; **exports** petroleum, manganese, iron, uranium, timber; **population** (1988) 1,226,000 including 40 Bantu tribes; **language** French (official), Bantu; **recent history** part of the French Congo from 1889 until independence from France achieved in 1960. In 1967 an attempted coup against the first president, Léon M'ba foiled, but M'ba died and was succeeded by his protégé, Albert-Bernard Bongo. In 1968 he established a one-party state. Although his regime is authoritarian, Gabon's prosperity has diluted any serious opposition to President Bongo. He was re-elected in Nov 1986, and in 1989 an attempted coup against him was defeated by loyal troops. In September 1990 the first multiparty elections were held since 1964 amid claims of widespread frauds.

Gaborone /gæbəˈrəʊni/ capital of Botswana from 1965, mainly an administrative centre; population (1988) 111,000.

Gabriel /ˈgeɪbrɪəl/ in the New Testament, the archangel who foretold the birth of John the Baptist to Zacharias and of Jesus to the Virgin Mary. He is also mentioned in the Old Testament in the book of Daniel. In Muslim belief, Gabriel revealed the Koran to Muhammad and escorted him on his ◊Night Journey.

Gabrieli /gæbriˈeli/ Giovanni *c.*1555–1612. Italian composer and organist. Although he composed secular music and madrigals, he is best known for his motets, which are frequently dramatic and often use several choirs and groups of instruments. In 1585 he became organist at St Mark's, Venice.

gad¹ *v.i.* (**-dd-**) to go *about* idly or in search of pleasure. [from obsolete *gadling* = companion from Old English]

gad² or **by gad** or interjection expressing surprise or emphatic assertion. [= God]

gadabout /ˈgædəbaʊt/ *n.* one who gads about.

Gaddafi alternative spelling of ◊Khaddhafi, Libyan leader.

Gaddi /ˈgædi/ family of Italian painters in Florence: **Gaddo Gaddi** (*c.*1250–1330); his son **Taddeo Gaddi** (*c.*1300–1366), who was inspired by Giotto and painted the fresco cycle *Life of the Virgin* in Santa Croce, Florence; and grandson **Agnolo Gaddi** (active 1369–96), who also painted frescoes in Santa Croce, *The Story of the Cross* 1380s, and produced panel paintings in characteristic pale pastel colours.

gadfly *n.* **1.** a fly that bites cattle. **2.** an irritating person. [from obsolete *gad* = spike from Old Norse]

gadget /ˈgædʒɪt/ *n.* a small mechanical device or tool. —**gadgetry** *n.*

gadoid /ˈgeɪdɔɪd/ *adj.* of the cod family Gadidae. —*n.* a gadoid fish. [from Greek *gados* = cod]

gadolinium /gædəˈlɪnɪəm/ *n.* an element, symbol Gd, atomic number 64, relative atomic mass 157.25. It is a silvery-white metal, a member of the lanthanide series. It is found in the products of nuclear fission and used in electronic components, alloys, and products needing to withstand high temperatures. [from J *Gadolin*, Finnish mineralogist]

Gadsden Purchase, the /ˈgædzdən/ in US history, the purchase of approximately 77,700 sq km/30,000 sq mi in what is now New Mexico and Arizona by the USA in 1853. The land was bought from Mexico for $10 million in a treaty negotiated by James Gadsden (1788–1858) of South Carolina, to construct a transcontinental railroad route, the Southern Pacific, completed in the 1880s.

Gael /geɪl/ *n.* a Scottish Celt; a Gaelic-speaking Celtic [from Gaelic *Gaidheal*]

Gaelic /ˈgeɪlɪk, ˈgæ-/ *n.* a Celtic language spoken in Ireland and Scotland in two distinct varieties, referred to also as Irish (or Erse) and Scots Gaelic respectively. Until 1974 it was also spoken in the Isle of Man. —*adj.* of Gaelic or the Gaels.

Gaelic football a 15-a-side team game played mainly in Ireland. It is a kicking and catching game; goals are scored by kicking the ball into the net (as in association football) or over the crossbar (as in rugby). The game was first played in 1712 and is now one of the sports under the auspices of the Gaelic Athletic Association. The leading tournament is the All-Ireland Championship culminating in the final which is played in Dublin on the third Sunday in September each year, the winners receiving the Sam Maguire Trophy.

gaff[1] *n.* **1.** a stick with an iron hook for landing large fish; a barbed fishing-spear. **2.** a spar to which the head of a fore-and-aft sail is bent. —*v.t.* to seize (a fish) with a gaff. [from Provençal *gaf* = hook]

gaff[2] *n.* **blow the gaff,** (*slang*) to divulge a plot or secret.

gaffe /gæf/ *n.* a social blunder. [French]

gaffer *n.* **1.** an old fellow (also as a title or form of address). **2.** a foreman, a boss. [probable contraction of *godfather*]

gag *n.* **1.** a thing thrust into or tied across the mouth to prevent speech or hold the mouth open for an operation. **2.** a joke or comic scene in a play, film etc. **3.** a thing restricting free speech; a Parliamentary closure. —*v.t./i.* (**-gg-**) **1.** to apply a gag to. **2.** to silence, to deprive of free speech. **3.** to make gags in a play, film etc. **4.** to choke, to retch.

gaga /'gɑːgɑː/ *adj.* (*slang*) senile; fatuous, slightly crazy. [French]

Gagarin /gə'gɑːrɪn/ Yuri (Alexeyevich) 1934–1968. Soviet cosmonaut, who in 1961 became the first human in space aboard the spacecraft *Vostok 1*. He completed one orbit of the Earth, taking 108 minutes from launch to landing.

gage[1] *n.* **1.** a pledge, a thing deposited as security. **2.** the symbol of a challenge to fight, especially a glove thrown down. [from Old French]

gage[2] abbreviation of greengage.

gage[3] US and nautical variant of *gauge*.

gaggle *n.* **1.** a flock of geese. **2.** a disorderly group.

Gaia /'geɪə/ or **Ge** in Greek mythology, the goddess of the Earth. She sprang from primordial Chaos and herself produced Uranus, by whom she was the mother of the Cyclopes and Titans.

Gaia hypothesis the theory that the Earth's living and nonliving systems form an inseparable whole that is regulated and kept adapted for life by living organisms themselves. The Gaia hypothesis was elaborated by James Lovelock in the 1970s.

gaiety /'geɪətɪ/ *n.* being gay, mirth; merry-making, amusement; bright appearance. [from French]

gaily *adv.* in a gay manner.

gain *v.t./i.* **1.** to obtain or secure. **2.** to acquire as profit etc., to earn; to make a profit; to be benefited, improve, or advance *in* some respect. **3.** to obtain as an increment or addition. **4.** (of a clock etc.) to become fast, or fast by (a specified time). **5.** to come closer to something pursued, to catch up *on* or *upon*. **6.** to reach (a desired place). **7.** to win (land from the sea, a battle). —*n.* **1.** an increase of wealth or possessions. **2.** an improvement, an increase in amount or power. **3.** the acquisition of wealth. —**gain ground,** to make progress. **gain time,** to improve one's chances by causing or accepting a delay. —**gainer** *n.* [from Old French *gaigner* = till, acquire]

gainful *adj.* (of employment) paid; lucrative. —**gainfully** *adv.*

gainsay /geɪn'seɪ/ *v.t.* to deny, to contradict. [from obsolete *gain-* = against]

Gainsborough /'geɪnzbərə/ Thomas 1727–1788. English landscape and portrait painter. He was born in Sudbury, Suffolk; in 1760 he settled in Bath and painted society portraits. In 1774 he went to London and became one of the original members of the Royal Academy. He was one of the first British artists to follow the Dutch in painting realistic landscapes instead of imaginative Italianate scenery.

gait *n.* manner of walking; the manner of forward motion of a horse etc. [variant of dialect *gate* = road, going]

gaiter *n.* a covering of cloth, leather etc., for the leg below the knee, for the ankle, or for part of a machine etc. [from French *guêtre*]

Gaitskell /'geɪtskəl/ Hugh (Todd Naylor) 1906–1963. British Labour politician. In 1950 he became minister of economic affairs, and then chancellor of the Exchequer until Oct 1951. In 1955 he defeated Aneurin Bevan for the succession to Attlee as party leader, and tried to reconcile internal differences on nationalization and disarmament. He was re-elected leader in 1960.

gal *n.* (*colloquial*) a girl.

gal. abbreviation of gallon(s).

gala /'gɑːlə, 'geɪlə/ *n.* a festive occasion; a festive gathering for sports. [from French or Italian from Spanish from Arabic = presentation garment]

galactic /gə'læktɪk/ *adj.* of a galaxy or galaxies. [from Greek *galaktias*, variant of *galaxias* (*gala* = milk)]

Galahad /'gæləhæd/ in Arthurian legend, one of the knights of the Round Table. Galahad succeeded in the quest for the ◊Holy Grail because of his virtue. He was the son of ◊Lancelot of the Lake.

galantine /'gælənti:n/ *n.* white meat boned, spiced, etc., and served cold. [from Old French *galatine* = jellied meat]

Galápagos Islands /gə'læpəgɒs/ (official name **Archipeliégo de Colón**) a group of 15 islands in the Pacific, belonging to Ecuador; **area** 7,800 sq km/3,000 sq mi; **population** (1982) 6,120. The capital is San Cristóbal on the island of the same name. The islands are a nature reserve. Their unique fauna (including giant tortoises, iguanas, penguins, flightless cormorants, and Darwin's finches), which inspired Charles ◊Darwin to formulate the principle of evolution by natural selection, is under threat from introduced species.

galaxy /'gæləksɪ/ *n.* **1.** a congregation of millions or billions of stars, held together by gravity. **Spiral galaxies,** such as the ◊Milky Way, are flattened in shape, with a central bulge of old stars surrounded by a disc of younger stars, arranged in spiral arms like a Catherine wheel. They are classified from Sa to Sc depending on how tightly the arms are wound. **Barred spirals** are spiral galaxies that have a straight bar of stars across their centre, from the ends of which the spiral arms emerge. The arms of spiral galaxies contain gas and dust from which new stars are still forming. They are classified SBa to SBc. **Elliptical galaxies** contain old stars and very little gas. They include the most massive galaxies known, containing a trillion stars, classified from E0 to E7 depending on the degree of flatness. There are also irregular galaxies. Most galaxies occur in clusters, containing anything from a few to thousands of members. The largest galaxy ever discovered is an LSBG (low surface-brightness galaxy) measuring 300,000 light years across. **2. the Galaxy,** that which contains the Earth. Our own galaxy, the Milky Way, is about 100,000 light years in diameter, containing at least 100 billion stars. **3.** a brilliant company. [from Old French from Latin from Greek *galaxias* (*gala* = milk)]

Galbraith /gæl'breɪθ/ John Kenneth 1908–. Canadian economist of the Keynesian school whose major works include *The Affluent Society* 1958 and *Economics and the Public Purpose* 1974. In the former he argued that industrialized societies like the USA were suffering from private affluence accompanied by public squalor.

In the affluent society no useful distinction can be made between luxuries and necessaries.

J K Galbraith
The Affluent Society

---

gale[1] *n.* **1.** a very strong wind, especially (on the Beaufort scale) of 32–54 mph; a storm. **2.** an outburst, especially of laughter. **3.** (*poetic*) a breeze.

gale[2] *n.* (*usually in* **sweetgale**) bog myrtle, *Myrica gale*. [Old English]

Galen /'geɪlən/ *c.*130–*c.*200. Greek physician whose ideas dominated Western medicine for almost 1,500 years. Central to his thinking were the theories of ◊humours and the threefold circulation of the blood.

galena *n.* the chief ore of lead, consisting of lead sulphide, PbS. It is lead-grey in colour, has a high metallic lussstre and breaks into cubes due to its perfect cubic cleavage. It may contain up to 1% silver, and so the ore is sometimes mined for both metals.

Galicia /gə'lɪsɪə/ a mountainous but fertile autonomous region of NW Spain, formerly an independent kingdom; **area** 29,400 sq km/11,348 sq mi; **population** (1986) 2,785,000. It includes La Coruña, Lugo, Orense, and

Galileo *The Italian mathematician, astronomer and physicist, Galileo Galilei.*

Pontevedra. **Industries** include fishing and the mining of tungsten and tin. The **language** is similar to Portuguese.

Galilee /'gæltli:/ region of N Israel (once a Roman province in Palestine) which includes Nazareth and Tiberias, frequently mentioned in the Gospels of the New Testament. The **Sea of Galilee** is an alternative name for Lake Tiberias, into which the River Jordan flows.

galileo /gæli'leɪəʊ/ *n.* a unit (symbol gal) of acceleration, used in geological surveying. One galileo is 10⁻² metres per second per second. The Earth's gravitational field often differs by several milligals (thousandths of gals) in different places, because of the varying densities of the rocks beneath the surface. [from *Galileo* Galilei, Italian astronomer]

Galileo properly Galileo Galilei 1564–1642. Italian mathematician, astronomer, and physicist. He developed the astronomical telescope and was the first to see sunspots, the four main satellites of Jupiter, mountains and craters on the Moon, and the appearance of Venus going through 'phases', thus proving it was orbiting the Sun. In mechanics, Galileo discovered that freely falling bodies, heavy or light, had the same, constant acceleration, and that a body moving on a perfectly smooth horizontal surface would neither speed up nor slow down. He also discovered that each oscillation of a pendulum takes the same amount of time despite the difference in amplitude, invented a hydroscopic balance, and discovered that the path of a projectile is a parabola. Galileo's work was unwelcome to the church especially when it confirmed the theory of ◊Copernicus that the Earth orbits the Sun. He was forced to recant by the ◊Inquisition and spend his last years under house arrest.

Galileo a spacecraft launched from the Space Shuttle *Atlantis* in Oct 1989, on a six-year journey to Jupiter.

gall¹ /gɔːl/ *n.* **1.** the bile of animals. **2.** bitterness; asperity, rancour. **3.** (*slang*) impudence. —**gall bladder,** a small muscular sac attached to the underside of the liver and connected to the small intestine by the bile duct. It stores bile from the liver. [Old Norse]

gall² *n.* a sore made by chafing; mental soreness or its cause; a place rubbed bare. —*v.t.* **1.** to rub sore. **2.** to vex, to humiliate. [from Middle Low German or Middle Dutch]

gall³ *n.* an abnormal outgrowth on a plant which develops as a result of attack by insects or, less commonly, by bacteria, fungi, mites, or nematodes. The attack causes an increase in the number of cells or an enlargement of existing cells in the plant. Gall-forming insects generally pass the early stages of their life inside the gall. Gall wasps are responsible for the conspicuous bud galls forming on oak trees, 2.5 to 4 cm/1 to 1.5 in across, popularly known as 'oak apples'. [from Old French from Latin *galla*]

Gall /gæl/ Franz Joseph 1758–1828. Austrian anatomist, instigator of the discredited theory of ◊phrenology.

gallant /'gælənt/ *adj.* **1.** brave. **2.** fine, stately. **3.** /also gə'lænt/ very attentive to women. —*n.* /also gə'lænt/ a ladies' man. [from Old French *galer* = make merry]

gallantry /'gæləntrɪ/ *n.* **1.** bravery. **2.** devotion to women. **3.** a polite act or speech. [from French]

Galle /'gælə/ Johann Gottfried 1812–1910. German astronomer who located the planet Neptune 1846, close to the position predicted by French mathematician Urbain Leverrier, and one month later Triton, Neptune's largest moon.

Gallé /gælə/ Emile 1846–1904. French ◊Art Nouveau glassmaker. He produced glass in sinuous forms or rounded, solid-looking shapes almost as heavy as stone, typically decorated with flowers or leaves in colour on colour.

galleon /'gæljən/ *n.* a type of ship (especially Spanish used in the late 16th–17th century). [from Middle Dutch from French *galion*, or from Spanish *galeón*]

gallery /'gælərɪ/ *n.* **1.** a room or building for showing works of art. **2.** a balcony, especially in a hall or church; the highest tier of seats in a theatre; its occupants. **3.** a covered walk partly open at the side, a colonnade; a narrow passage in the thickness of a wall or on corbels, open towards the interior of a building. **4.** a long, narrow room or passage. **5.** a group of spectators at a golf match etc. **6.** a horizontal underground passage in a mine etc. —**play to the gallery,** to seek to win approval by appealing to unrefined taste. [from French from Italian from Latin *galeria*]

galley /'gælɪ/ *n.* **1.** (*historical*) a long, flat, one-decked vessel usually rowed by slaves or criminals. **2.** an ancient oared warship. **3.** a kitchen in a ship or aircraft. **4.** a long tray for set-up type in printing. **5.** (in full **galley proof**) a proof in a long, narrow form. [from Old French from Latin or Greek]

Gallic /'gælɪk/ *adj.* **1.** of Gaul or the Gauls. **2.** typically French. [from Latin *Gallus* = a Gaul]

Gallicism /'gælɪsɪzəm/ *n.* a French idiom.

gallinaceous /gælɪ'neɪʃəs/ *adj.* of the order including domestic poultry, pheasants etc. [from Latin *gallina* = hen]

Gallipoli /gə'lɪpəli/ port in European Turkey, giving its name to the peninsula (ancient name **Chersonesus**) on which it stands. In World War I, at the instigation of Winston Churchill, an unsuccessful attempt was made Feb 1915–Jan 1916 by Allied troops to force their way through the Dardanelles and link up with Russia. The campaign was fought mainly by Australian and New Zealand (◊ANZAC) forces, who suffered heavy losses. An estimated 36,000 Commonwealth troops died during the nine-month campaign.

gallium /'gælɪəm/ *n.* an element, symbol Ga, atomic number 31, relative atomic mass 69.75. It is a very scarce, grey metal, which liquefies at 30°C temperature. Gallium arsenide crystals are used in microelectronics, since electrons travel a thousand times faster through them than through silicon. It was discovered in 1875 by Lecoq de Boisbaudran. [from Latin *Gallia* = Gaul, in honour of France, country of its discoverer]

gallivant /gæli'vænt/ *v.i.* (*colloquial*) to gad about.

Gallo /'gæləʊ/ Robert Charles 1937– . US scientist who, with the French scientist Luc Montagnier (1932–), discovered the ◊AIDS virus at the Pasteur Institute, Paris. The Gallo virus, discovered in 1984, has been alleged to have been accidentally contaminated by samples of a virus discovered in 1983 by Montagnier, who gave them to Gallo for research at the National Cancer Institute near Washington DC, USA.

Gallo- /gæləʊ-/ in combinations French. [from Latin *Gallus* = a Gaul]

gallon /'gælən/ *n.* an imperial liquid or dry measure, equal to 4.546 litres, and subdivided into four quarts or eight pints. The US gallon is equivalent to 3.785 litres (usually in *plural, colloquial*) a large amount. [from Old French *jalon* from Romanic]

gallop /'gæləp/ *n.* the fastest pace of a horse etc., with all the feet off the ground together in each stride; a ride at this pace. —*v.t./i.* **1.** (of a horse etc. or its rider) to go at a gallop; to make (a horse) gallop. **2.** to read, talk etc., fast; to progress rapidly. [from Old French]

galloway /'gæləweɪ/ *n.* **1.** a horse of a small, strong breed from Galloway, an area in SW Scotland; a small horse. **2.** an animal of a breed of cattle from Galloway.

gallows /'gæləʊz/ *n.pl.* (usually treated as *singular*) a structure, usually of two uprights and a crosspiece, for the hanging of criminals. [from Old Norse]

gallstone /'gɔ:lstəun/ n. a pebblelike, insoluble accretion formed in the human gall bladder or bile ducts from cholesterol or calcium salts present in bile. Gallstones may be symptomless or they may cause pain, indigestion, or jaundice. They can be dissolved with medication or removed, along with the gall bladder, in an operation known as cholecystectomy.

Gallup /'gæləp/ George Horace 1901–1984. US journalist and statistician, who founded in 1935 the American Institute of Public Opinion and devised the **Gallup Poll**, in which public opinion is sampled by questioning a number of representative individuals.

Galois /gæl'wɑ:/ Evariste 1811–1832. French mathematician, who originated the theory of groups. His attempts to gain recognition for his work were largely thwarted by the French mathematical establishment, critical of his lack of formal qualifications. Galois was killed in a duel before he was 21. The night before, he had hurriedly written out his unpublished discoveries on group theory, the importance of which would come to be appreciated more and more as the 19th century progressed.

galop /'gæləp/ n. a lively dance in duple time; the music for this. [French = gallop]

galore /gə'lɔ:/ adv. in plenty. [from Irish]

galosh /gə'lɒʃ/ n. a waterproof overshoe. [from Old French from Latin *gallicula* = small Gallic shoe]

Galsworthy /'gɔ:lzwɜ:ði/ John 1867–1933. British novelist and dramatist whose work examines the social issues of the Victorian period. He is best known for *The Forsyte Saga* 1922 and its sequel *A Modern Comedy* 1929. Other novels include *The Country House* 1907 and *Fraternity* 1909; plays include *The Silver Box* 1906.

Galtieri /gæltiˈeəri/ Leopoldo 1926– . Argentine general, leading member of the right-wing military junta that ordered the seizure in 1982 of the Falkland Islands (Malvinas), a UK colony in the SW Atlantic claimed by Argentina. He and his fellow junta members were tried for abuse of human rights and court-martialled for their conduct of the war; he was sentenced to 12 years in prison in 1986.

Galton /'gɔ:ltən/ Francis 1822–1911. English scientist who studied the inheritance of physical and mental attributes in humans, with the aim of improving the human species. He discovered that no two sets of human fingerprints are the same, and is considered the founder of ◊eugenics.

galumph /gə'lʌmf/ v.i. (colloquial) to go prancing in triumph; to move noisily or clumsily. [coined by Lewis Carroll in *Through the Looking-glass* perhaps from *gallop* and *triumph*]

galvanic /gæl'vænɪk/ adj. **1.** producing an electric current by chemical action; (of electricity) produced by chemical action. **2.** stimulating, full of energy; sudden and remarkable. —**galvanically** adv. [from L *Galvani*, Italian anatomist (died 1798)]

galvanize /'gælvənaɪz/ v.t. **1.** to stimulate by or as by electricity *into* activity. **2.** to coat (iron) with zinc to protect from rust. —**galvanization** /-'zeɪʃən/ n.

galvanometer /gælvə'nɒmɪtə/ n. an instrument for measuring small electric currents.

Galway /'gɔ:lweɪ/ county on the W coast of the Republic of Ireland, in the province of Connacht; **area** 5,940 sq km/ 2,293 sq mi; **physical** the E is low-lying; in the S are the Slieve Aughty mountains and Galway Bay, and the Aran islands; W of Lough Corrib is Connemara, a wild area of moors, hills, lakes, and bogs; The Shannon is the principal river. **county town** Galway; **products** mining of lead, zinc, and copper; **population** (1986) 178,000.

Galway James 1939– . Irish flautist, born in Belfast. He was a member of the Berlin Philharmonic Orchestra 1969–75, before taking up a solo career.

Gama /'gɑ:mə/ Vasco da 1460–1524. Portuguese navigator, who commanded an expedition in 1497 to discover the route to India around the Cape of Good Hope in modern South Africa. He reached land, which he named Natal, on Christmas Day 1497. He then crossed the Indian Ocean, arriving at Calicut in May 1498, and returning to Portugal in Sept 1499.

Gambia /'gæmbiə/ Republic of; country in W Africa, surrounded to the N, E, and S by Senegal and bordered to the W by the Atlantic Ocean; **area** 10,402 sq km/ 4,018 sq mi; **capital** Banjul; **physical** banks of the river Gambia flanked by low hills; **head of state and government** Dawda Kairaba Jawara from 1970; **political system** liberal democracy; **exports** groundnuts, palm oil, fish; **population** (1990 est) 820,000; **language** English (official); Mandinka, Fula and other native tongues; **recent history** independence from UK as a constitutional monarchy within the Commonwealth achieved in 1965. The Gambia was declared a republic in 1970. The Confederation of Senegambia formed with Senegal in 1982; dissolved in 1989.

Gambier Islands /'gæmbiə/ island group, part of ◊French Polynesia, administered with the ◊Tuamotu Archipelago; **area** 36 sq km/14 sq mi; **population** (1983) 582. It includes four coral islands and many small islets. The main island is Mangareva, with its town Rikitea.

gambit /'gæmbɪt/ n. **1.** a chess opening in which a player sacrifices a pawn or piece for the sake of later advantage. **2.** an opening move in a discussion etc.; a trick, a device. [from Italian *gambetto* = tripping up]

gamble v.t./i. to play games of chance for money; to risk much in hope of great gain. —n. gambling; a risky undertaking. —**gamble away**, to lose by gambling. **gamble on,** to act in the hope of (an event). [from obsolete *gamel* = to sport]

gambler n. one who gambles, especially habitually.

gambling n. or **gaming** the staking of money or anything else of value on the outcome of a competition. Forms of gambling include betting on the outcome of sports results, casino games like blackjack and roulette, card games like poker, brag, and cribbage, fruit machines, or lotteries. Association football (via football pools) and horse racing attract gambling through either off-or on-course betting. Gambling is a multi-billion dollar operation worldwide. In the UK commercial gambling is restricted to premises licensed and registered under statute. These include gaming clubs and casinos, amusement arcades, and pubs. Gambling can be addictive. **Gamblers Anonymous** was set up in the USA in 1957 and in the UK in 1964 to help compulsive gamblers overcome their addiction. **Gam-anon** provides support for relatives of gamblers.

gamboge /gæm'bu:ʒ, -bəuʒ/ n. a gum resin used as a yellow pigment and as a purgative. [from *Cambodia*, where the substance is obtained]

gambol /'gæmbəl/ v.i. (-ll-) to jump about playfully. —n. a gambolling movement. [from *gambade* = leap from Italian (*gamba* = leg)]

game[1] n. **1.** a form of play or sport, especially a competitive one organized with rules, penalties etc. **2.** a portion of play forming a scoring unit e. g. in bridge or tennis; the winning score in a game; the state of the score. **3.** (in *plural*) a series of athletic etc. contests. **4.** a scheme, undertaking etc. **5.** wild animals or birds hunted for sport or food; their flesh as food. —adj. spirited, eager and willing. —v.i. to gamble for money stakes. —**the game is up**, the scheme is revealed or foiled. **game theory**, the branch of mathematics that deals with the selection of best strategies for participants. **give the game away**, to reveal intentions or a secret. **make game of,** to ridicule. **on the game,** (slang) involved in prostitution or thieving. —**gamely** adv., **gameness** n. [Old English]

game[2] adj. (of a leg, arm etc.) crippled.

gamecock n. a cock bred and trained for cock-fighting.

gamekeeper n. a person employed to breed and protect game.

gamelan /'gæmələn/ n. the standard instrumental ensemble of Indonesia, comprising sets of tuned gongs, gong-chimes, and other percussion instruments as well as string and woodwind instruments. [Javanese]

gamesmanship n. the art of winning games by gaining a psychological advantage over an opponent, first described by Stephen Potter in 1947.

gamesome /'geɪmsəm/ adj. playful, sportive.

gamester /'geɪmstə/ n. a gambler.

gamete /'gæmi:t/ n. a cell that functions in sexual reproduction by merging with another gamete to form a ◊zygote. Examples of gametes include sperm and ova cells. In most organisms, the gametes are ◊haploid (they contain half the number of chromosomes of the parent), owing to reduction division or ◊meiosis. —**gametic** /gə'metɪk/ adj. [from Greek = wife (*gamos* = marriage)]

gametophyte *n*. the ◊haploid generation in the life cycle of a plant that produces gametes; see ◊alternation of generations.

gamin /'gæmɪn/ *n*. a street urchin; an impudent child. [French]

gamine /gə'mi:n/ *n*. a girl with mischievous charm. [French feminine of *gamin*]

gamma /'gæmə/ *n*. 1. the third letter of the Greek alphabet, γ, Γ = g. 2. a third-class mark in an examination. 3. a designation of the third-brightest star in a constellation, or sometimes the star's position in a group. [Greek]

gamma radiation very high-frequency electromagnetic radiation emitted by the nuclei of radioactive substances during decay. It is used to kill bacteria and other microorganisms, sterilize medical devices, and change the molecular structure of plastics to modify their properties (for example, to improve heat and abrasion resistance for insulation purposes).

gamma-ray astronomy the study of gamma rays produced within our Galaxy, the Milky Way. They may be due to collisions between hydrogen gas and cosmic rays. Some sources have been identified, including the Crab nebula and the Vela pulsar (the most powerful gamma-ray source detected). Gamma rays are not plentiful and only about a million gamma-ray photons have been collected. This is equivalent to the number of photons of visible light received from a star such as Sirius in about a second. Gamma rays are difficult to detect and are generally studied by use of balloon-borne detectors and artificial satellites. The first gamma-ray satellites were SAS II (1972) and COS B (1975), although gamma-ray detectors were carried on the Apollo 15 and 16 missions. SAS II failed after only a few months, but COS B, carrying a single gamma-ray experiment, and intended to be operational for only two years, was finally switched off in 1982 after a mission in which it carried out a complete survey of the galactic disc.

gammon /'gæmən/ *n*. the bottom piece of a flitch of bacon including a hind leg; pig's ham cured like bacon. [from Old French *gambon* (*gambe* = leg)]

gammy *adj*. (*slang*) crippled. [from dialect form of *game*²]

Gamow /'geɪmaʊ/ George 1904–1968. Soviet cosmologist, nuclear physicist, and popularizer of science. His work in astrophysics included a study of the structure and evolution of stars and the creation of the elements. He also explained how the collision of nuclei in the solar interior could produce the nuclear reactions that power the Sun.

gamut /'gæmət/ *n*. 1. the lowest note in the medieval sequence of hexachords, = modern German on the lowest line of the bass stave. 2. the whole series of notes used in medieval or modern music; the major diatonic scale; the compass of a voice or instrument. 3. the entire series or range. [from Latin *gamma ut* (Gamma taken as name for note one tone lower than A of classical scale, *ut* first of six arbitrary names of notes forming hexachord, being italicized syllables of a 7th-century Latin hymn: *Ut* queant laxis *re*sonare fibris *Mi*ra gestorum *fa* muli tuorum, *Sol*ve polluti *la*bii reatum, Sancte Ioannes)]

gamy /'geɪmɪ/ *adj*. smelling or tasting like high ◊game⁵.

Gance /gɒns/ Abel 1889–1981. French film director, whose *Napoléon* 1927 was one of the most ambitious silent epic films. It features colour and triple-screen sequences, as well as multiple-exposure shots.

gander *n*. 1. a male goose. 2. (*slang*) a look, a glance. [Old English]

Gandhi /'gændi/ Indira (born Nehru) 1917–1984. Indian politician. Prime minister of India 1966–77 and 1980–84, and leader of the ◊Congress Party 1966–77 and subsequently of the Congress (I) party. Her father, Jawaharlal Nehru, was India's first prime minister. She married Feroze Gandhi in 1942 (died 1960, not related to Mahatma Gandhi) and had two sons. In 1975 the validity of her re-election to parliament was questioned, and she declared a state of emergency. During this time her son Sanjay was implementing a social and economic programme, which included an unpopular family-planning policy. This led to her defeat in 1977. Sanjay masterminded her return to power in 1980. She was assassinated in 1984 by members of her Sikh bodyguard, resentful of her use of troops to clear malcontents from the Sikh temple at ◊Amritsar.

Gandhi Mohandas Karamchand, called **Mahatma** ('Great Soul') 1869–1948. Indian Nationalist leader. A pacifist, he

Gandhi *Former Indian prime minister Rajiv Gandhi in New Delhi, 1984.*

led the struggle for Indian independence from the UK by advocating nonviolent noncooperation (*satyagraha*, defence of and by truth) from 1915. He was imprisoned several times by the British authorities and was influential in the Nationalist ◊Congress Party and in the independence negotiations 1947. He was assassinated by a Hindu nationalist in the violence that followed the partition of British India into India and Pakistan.

An unjust law is itself a species of violence. Arrest for its breach is more so.

Mahatma K. Gandhi
Non-Violence in Peace and War

Gandhi Rajiv 1944–1991. Indian politician, prime minister from 1984, following his mother Indira Gandhi's assassination, until Nov 1989. After the death in a plane crash of his brother **Sanjay** (1946–1980), he was elected to his brother's Amethi parliamentary seat 1981. In the Dec 1984 parliamentary elections he won a record majority. As prime minister in 1985 he reached a temporary settlement with the moderate Sikhs, but it failed to hold. He faced growing discontent with his party's elitism and lack of concern for social issues, and his reputation was tarnished by a scandal involving the Swedish munitions firm Bofors. Following his party's defeat in the general election of Nov 1989, Gandhi was forced to resign as premier. He was assassinated by a bomb blast during an election campaign in 1991.

Ganesh /gæ'neɪʃ/ Hindu god, son of Siva and Parvati; he is represented as elephant-headed and is worshipped as a remover of obstacles.

gang¹ *n*. 1. a band of persons associating for some (usually criminal) purpose. 2. a set of workers, slaves, or prisoners. 3. a set of tools working in coordination. —*v.t.* to arrange (tools etc.) to work in coordination. —**gang up**, to act in concert (*with*). **gang up on**, (*colloquial*) to combine against. [from Old Norse = going]

gang² *v.i.* (*Scottish*) to go. —**gang agley**, (of a plan, etc.) to go wrong. [Old English]

ganger *n*. the foreman of a gang of workers.

Ganges /'gændʒi:z/ (Hindi *Ganga*) the major river of India and Bangladesh; length 2,510 km/1,560 mi. It is the most sacred river for Hindus.

gangling /'gæŋglɪŋ/ *adj*. (of a person) loosely built, lanky.

ganglion /'gæŋglɪən/ *n*. (*plural* **ganglia**) 1. an enlargement or knot on a nerve forming a centre for the reception and transmission of impulses. 2. a centre of activity etc. —**ganglionic** /-'ɒnɪk/ *adj.* [Greek]

Gang of Four the chief members of the radical faction that tried to seize power in China after the death of Mao Zedong 1976. It included his widow, ◊Jiang Qing; the other members were Zhang Chunjao, Wang Hungwen, and Yao Wenyuan. The coup failed, and they were soon arrested. In the UK the name was subsequently applied to four members of the Labour Party who in 1981 resigned to form the Social Democratic Party (SDP): Roy Jenkins, David Owen, Shirley Williams, and William Rodgers.

gangplank *n.* a movable plank for walking into and out of a boat etc.

gangrene /'gæŋgriːn/ *n.* 1. the death and decay of body tissue (often of a limb) due to obstructed blood circulation or bacterial action; the affected part gradually turns black and causes blood poisoning. 2. moral corruption. —*v.t./i.* to affect or become affected with gangrene. —**gangrenous** /-grɪnəs/ *adj.* [from French from Latin from Greek]

gangster *n.* a member of a gang of violent criminals.

gangsterism *n.* a term popularized in relation to organized crime, particularly in the USA. One result of the 18th Amendment (Prohibition) in 1919 was an increase in organized crime. The prohibition law was difficult to enforce; illicit liquor could be brought into the USA over the long land borders or coastline, and illegal distilleries were soon established. Bootlegging activities (importing or making illegal liquor) and 'speakeasies' (where alcohol could be illegally purchased) gave rise to rivalry which resulted in hired gangs of criminals (gangsters) and gun battles. Social unrest and a widening gap between rich and poor also created a climate in which crime flourished. One of the most notorious gangsters was Al ◊Capone, who had his headquarters in Chicago. In 1933 the 21st Amendment was passed repealing Prohibition. This, and the actions of the Criminal Investigation Bureau (CIA) under J Edgar Hoover limited the opportunities for the 'gangster' and contributed to some reduction in crime.

gangue /gæŋ/ *n.* valueless earth etc. in which ore is found. [French, from German *gang* = lode]

gangway *n.* 1. a passage, especially between rows of seats. 2. the opening in a ship's bulwarks; a bridge from this to the shore.

gannet /'gænɪt/ *n.* or **solan goose** a sea bird *Sula bassana* found in the N Atlantic. When fully grown, it is white with black-tipped wings having a span of 1.7 m/5.6 ft. The young are speckled. It breeds on cliffs in nests made of grass and seaweed. Only one (white) egg is laid. [Old English, cognate with *gander*]

Gannet Peak the highest peak in Wyoming, USA, rising to 4,207 m/13,804 ft.

Gansu /gæn'suː/ or **Kansu** province of NW China; **area** 530,000 sq km/204,580 sq mi; **capital** Lanzhou; **products** coal, oil, hydroelectric power from the Huang He (Yellow) river; **population** (1986) 20,710,000, including many Muslims.

gantlet /'gæntlɪt/ *US* variant of gauntlet.

gantry /'gæntrɪ/ *n.* a structure supporting a travelling crane, railway signals, equipment for a rocket-launch etc.

Ganymede /'gænɪmiːd/ 1. in Greek mythology, a youth so beautiful he was chosen as cupbearer to Zeus. 2. in astronomy, the largest moon of the planet Jupiter, and the largest moon in the solar system, 5,300 km/3,300 mi in diameter (larger than the planet Mercury). It orbits Jupiter every 7.2 days at a distance of 1.1 million km/700,000 mi. Its surface is a mixture of cratered and grooved terrain.

gaol /dʒeɪl/ *n.* a public prison; confinement in this. —*v.t.* to put in gaol. [= *jail*; from Old French *jaiole* from Romanic diminutive of Latin *cavea* = cage]

gaolbird *n.* a habitual criminal; a prisoner.

gaolbreak *n.* an escape from gaol.

gaoler *n.* a person in charge of a gaol or the prisoners in it.

gap *n.* 1. a breach in a hedge, fence, or wall. 2. an empty space; an interval. 3. a deficiency. 4. a wide divergence in views etc. 5. a gorge or pass. —**gappy** *adj.* [from Old Norse = chasm]

gape *v.i.* to open the mouth wide; (of the mouth etc.) to open or be open wide; to stare *at*; to yawn. —*n.* an open-mouthed stare; a yawn; an open mouth. [from Old Norse]

gar *n.* a primitive bony fish of the order Semionotiformes, which also includes ◊sturgeons. Gar have long, beaklike snouts and elongated bodies covered in heavy, bony scales. All four species of gar inhabit freshwater rivers and lakes of the Mississippi drainage. See also ◊needlefish.

garage /'gærɑːdʒ, -ɑːʒ, -ɪdʒ/ *n.* 1. a building for housing a motor vehicle or vehicles. 2. an establishment repairing and selling motor vehicles. —*v.t.* to put or keep (a vehicle) in a garage. [from French (*garer* = shelter)]

garb *n.* clothing, especially of a distinctive kind. —*v.t.* (usually in *passive* or *reflexive*) to dress, especially in distinctive clothes. [from French from Italian from Germanic]

garbage /'gɑːbɪdʒ/ *n.* rubbish or refuse of any kind; domestic waste. [from Anglo-French]

garble *v.t.* to distort or confuse (facts, messages etc.). [from Italian from Arabic *garbala* = sift]

Garbo /'gɑːbəʊ/ Greta. Stage name of Greta Lovisa Gustafsson 1905–1990. Swedish film actress. She went to the USA in 1925, and her leading role in *The Torrent* 1926 made her one of Hollywood's first stars. Her later films include *Mata Hari* 1931, *Queen Christina* 1933, *Anna Karenina* 1935, and *Ninotchka* 1939.

García Lorca /gɑː'θiːə 'lɔːkə/ Federico, see ◊Lorca, Federico García.

García Márquez /gɑː'siːə 'mɑːkes/ Gabriel 1928– . Colombian novelist. His sweeping novel *Cien años de soledad/One Hundred Years of Solitude* 1967 (which tells the story of a family over a period of six generations) is an example of magic realism, a technique used to heighten the intensity of realistic portrayal of social and political issues by introducing grotesque or fanciful material. Other books include *El amor en los tiempos del cólera/Love in the Time of Cholera* 1985. He was awarded the Nobel Prize for Literature in 1982.

García Perez /gɑː'siːə 'peres/ Alan 1949– . Peruvian politician, leader of the moderate, left-wing APRA party; president 1985–90.

garden /'gɑːdən/ *n.* 1. a piece of ground for growing flowers, fruit, or vegetables. 2. (*attributive*) cultivated. 3. (especially in *plural*) grounds laid out for public enjoyment. —*v.i.* to cultivate a garden. —**garden centre**, an establishment selling garden plants and equipment. **garden party**, a party held in a garden. [from Old French *gardin* (French *jardin*)]

garden city in the UK, a town built in a rural area and designed to combine town and country advantages, with its own industries, controlled developments, private and public gardens, and cultural centre. The idea was proposed by Sir Ebenezer Howard (1850–1928), who in 1899 founded the Garden City Association, which established the first garden city, Letchworth (in Hertfordshire).

gardener /'gɑːdnə/ *n.* a person who gardens; a person employed to tend a garden.

gardenia /gɑː'diːniə/ *n.* a group of subtropical and tropical trees and shrubs of Africa and Asia, genus *Gardenia*, with evergreen foliage and flattened rosettes of fragrant, waxen-looking blooms, often white in colour. [from Dr A *Garden*, Scottish naturalist (died 1791)]

garderobe /gɑː'drəʊb/ *n.* (*historical*) 1. a storeroom or wardrobe. 2. a medieval lavatory often built into the thickness of a castle wall, with an open drop to the moat below. [from French *garder* = keep]

Gardner /'gɑːdnə/ Ava 1922–1990. US actress, who starred in the 1940s and 1950s in such films as *The Killers* 1946, *Pandora and the Flying Dutchman* 1951, and *The Barefoot Contessa* 1954. She remained active in films until the 1980s.

Garfield /'gɑːfiːld/ James A(bram) 1831–1881. the 20th president of the USA 1881, a Republican. He was born in a log cabin in Ohio, and served in the Civil War with the Union forces. He was elected president but held office for only four months before being assassinated in Washington DC railway station by a disappointed office-seeker.

garfish /'gɑːfɪʃ/ *n.* (*plural* the same) a fish with a long, spearlike snout. [from Old English *gar* = spear]

gargantuan /gɑː'gæntjuən/ *adj.* gigantic. [from *Gargantua* giant in book by Rabelais]

gargle *v.t.* to wash (the throat) with a liquid held there and kept in motion by the breath. —*n.* a liquid so used. [from French (Old French *gargouille* = throat)]

gargoyle /'gɑːgɔɪl/ *n.* a spout projecting from the roof gutter of a building with the purpose of directing water away from the wall. The term is usually applied to the ornamental forms found in Gothic architecture; these were carved in stone in the form of fantastic animals, angels, or human heads. They are often found on churches and cathedrals. [from Old French *gargouille* = throat]

garibaldi /gæri'bɔːldɪ/ *n.* a biscuit containing a layer of currants. [from *Garibaldi*, Italian patriot]

Garibaldi Giuseppe 1807–1882. Italian soldier who played a central role in the unification of Italy by conquering Sicily and Naples 1860. From 1834 a member of the Young Italy society founded by the nationalist ◊Mazzini, he was forced into exile until 1848 and again 1849–54. He fought against Austria 1848–49, 1859, and 1866, and led two unsuccessful expeditions to liberate Rome from papal rule in 1862 and 1867.

garish /'geərɪʃ/ *adj.* obtrusively bright, showy, gaudy. [apparently from obsolete *gaure* = stare]

garland /'gɑːlənd/ *n.* a wreath, usually of flowers, worn on the head or hung on an object as a decoration. —*v.t.* to deck with garlands; to crown with a garland. [from Old French]

Garland Judy. Stage name of Frances Gumm. 1922–1969. US singer and actress. Her films include *The Wizard of Oz* (which featured the tune that was to become her theme song, 'Over the Rainbow'), *Babes in Arms* 1939, *Strike Up the Band* 1940, *Meet Me in St Louis* 1944, *Easter Parade* 1948, *A Star is Born* 1954, and *Judgment at Nuremberg* 1961. Her unhappy personal life led to her early death from alcohol and drug addiction.

garlic /'gɑːlɪk/ *n.* a perennial plant *Allium sativum* of the lily family Liliaceae, with white flowers. The bulb, made of small segments, or cloves, is used in cookery, and its pungent essence has an active medical ingredient, allyl methyl trisulphide, which prevents blood clotting. —**garlicky** /'gɑːlɪkɪ/ *adj.* [Old English]

garment /'gɑːmənt/ *n.* an article of dress; an outward covering. [from Old French]

garner /'gɑːnə/ *v.t.* to store; to collect. —*n.* (*literary*) a storehouse, a granary (*literal* or *figurative*). [from Old French from Latin = granary]

garnet /'gɑːnɪt/ *n.* a group of silicate minerals with the formula $X_3Y_2(SiO_4)_3$, when X is calcium, magnesium, iron, or manganese, and Y is iron, aluminium, or chromium. They are used as semiprecious gems (usually pink to deep red) and as abrasives. Garnets occur in metamorphic rocks such as gneiss and schist. [from Old French from Latin *granatum* = pomegranate]

garnish /'gɑːnɪʃ/ *v.t.* to decorate (especially a dish for the table). —*n.* a decorative addition. —**garnishment** *n.* [from Old French *garnir*]

garotte variant of **garrotte**.

garret /'gærɪt/ *n.* an attic or room in the roof, especially a dismal one. [from Old French *garite* = watch-tower]

Garrick /'gærɪk/ David 1717–1779. British actor and theatre manager. He was a pupil of Samuel ◊Johnson. From 1747 he became joint licensee of the Drury Lane theatre with his own company, and instituted a number of significant theatrical conventions including concealed stage lighting and banishing spectators from the stage. He performed Shakespearean characters such as Richard III, King Lear, Hamlet, and Benedick, and collaborated with George Colman (1732–1794) in writing the play *The Clandestine Marriage* 1766. He retired from the stage in 1766, but continued as a manager.

A fellow-feeling makes one wond'rous kind.
David Garrick
An Occasional Prologue on Quitting the Theatre

garrison /'gærɪsən/ *n.* troops stationed in a town etc. to defend it. —*v.t.* to provide with or occupy as a garrison. [from Old French *garir* = defend]

garrotte /gə'rɒt/ *n.* 1. a Spanish method of capital punishment by strangulation with a metal collar; the apparatus for this. 2. a cord or wire used to strangle a victim. —*v.t.* to execute or strangle with a garrotte. [from French or Spanish *garrote* = cudgel]

Garvey *Jamaican-born Marcus Garvey, pictured here at a New York parade in 1922. He was the founder of the 'Back to Africa' movement.*

garrulous /'gærʊləs/ *adj.* talkative. —**garrulity** /gə'ruːlɪtɪ/ *n.*, **garrulously** *adv.*, **garrulousness** *n.* [from Latin *garrire* = chatter]

garter *n.* a band worn near the knee to keep up a sock etc. —**garter stitch,** rows of plain stitch in knitting. [from Old French *gartier* (*garet* = bend of knee)]

Garter, Order of the the senior British order of knighthood, founded by Edward III in about 1347. Its distinctive badge is a garter of dark blue velvet, with the motto of the order, *Honi soit qui mal y pense* ('Shame be to him who thinks evil of it') in gold letters.

garth *n.* 1. (*archaic*) a close or yard, a garden or paddock. 2. an open space within cloisters. [from Old Norse]

Garvey /'gɑːvi/ Marcus (Moziah) 1887–1940. Jamaican political thinker and activist, an early advocate of black nationalism. He founded the UNIA (Universal Negro Improvement Association) in 1914, and moved to the USA in 1916, where he established branches in New York and other northern cities. Aiming to achieve human rights and dignity for black people through black pride and economic self-sufficiency, he was considered one of the first militant black nationalists. He led a Back to Africa movement for black Americans to establish a black-governed country in Africa. ◊Rastafarianism is based largely on his ideas.

gas *n.* (*plural* **gases** /'gæsɪz/) 1. any substance which is compressible, expands to fill any space in which it is enclosed, and consists of molecules which are not bound together but move about relatively independently; a substance which is a gas at normal temperatures and pressures; a gas which at a given temperature cannot be liquefied by pressure alone (other gases generally being known as 'vapours' in this context). 2. such a substance (especially coal gas or natural gas) used for heating, lighting, or cooking. 3. nitrous oxide or other gas used as an anaesthetic. 4. a poisonous gas used to disable an enemy in war. 5. (*US colloquial*) petrol, gasoline. 6. (*colloquial*) idle talk, boasting. —*v.t./i.* (-ss-) 1. to expose to gas; to poison or injure by gas. 2. (*colloquial*) to talk idly or boastfully. —**gas chamber,** an enclosed space that can be filled with poisonous gas to kill animals or people. **gas fire,** a domestic heater burning gas. **gas-fired** *adj.* using gas as a fuel. **gas mask,** a device worn over the face as protection against poison gas. **gas ring,** a hollow perforated ring fed with gas for cooking etc. **gas turbine,** one driven by a flow of gas or by gas from combustion. **step on the gas,** (*colloquial*) to accelerate a motor vehicle. [word invented by J B van Helmont, Dutch chemist (died 1644), after Greek *khaos* = chaos]

gasbag *n.* 1. a container of gas. 2. (*slang*) an idle talker.

Gascoigne Paul. Nickname Gazza. 1967– . English footballer who has played for Tottenham Hotspur since July 1988. At the 1989 World Cup semi-final against West Germany, he was shown the yellow card, indicating that he would be denied a place on the Cup Final team, should England win. He reacted by crying and his lionization by the

British press for this incident, rather than for his prowess as a footballer, made his name..

Gascony /'gæskəni/ ancient province of SW France. With Guienne it formed the duchy of Aquitaine in the 12th century; Henry II of England gained possession of it through his marriage to Eleanor of Aquitaine in 1152, and it was often in English hands until 1451. It was then ruled by the king of France until it was united with the French royal domain in 1607 under Henry IV.

gas-cooled reactor a nuclear reactor; see ◊AGR (advanced gas-cooled reactor).

gas engine a type of internal-combustion engine in which a gas (coal gas, producer gas, natural gas, or gas from a blast furnace) is used as the fuel. The first practical gas engine was built in 1860 by Jean Etienne Lenoir, and the type was subsequently developed by Nikolaus August Otto, who introduced the ◊four-stroke cycle.

gaseous /'gæsiəs, 'geɪ-/ adj. of or like gas.

gash n. a long, deep cut, wound, or cleft. —v.t. to make a gash in, to cut. [variant of earlier garce from Old French garcer = wound]

gasholder /'gæshəʊldə/ n. a large receptacle for storing gas, a gasometer.

gasify /'gæsɪfaɪ/ v.t. to convert into a gas. —**gasification** /-fi'keɪʃən/ n.

Gaskell /'gæskəl/ 'Mrs' (Elizabeth Cleghorn) (born Stevenson) 1810–1865. British novelist. Her books include *Mary Barton* 1848 (set in industrial Manchester), *Cranford* (set in the town in which she was brought up, Knutsford, Cheshire) 1853, *North and South* 1855, *Sylvia's Lovers* 1863–64, the unfinished *Wives and Daughters* 1866, and a life of her friend, Charlotte ◊Brontë.

gasket /'gæskɪt/ n. **1.** a sheet or ring of rubber etc. to seal a junction of metal surfaces. **2.** a small cord securing a furled sail to a yard. [perhaps from French garcette = little girl, thin rope]

gaskin /'gæskɪn/ n. the hinder part of a horse's thigh.

gaslight n. the light given by burning gas.

gasohol n. a type of motor fuel that is 90% petrol and 10% ethanol (alcohol). The ethanol is usually obtained by fermentation, followed by distillation, using maize, wheat, potatoes, or sugar cane. It was used in early cars before petrol became economical, and its use was revived during the 1940s war shortage and the energy shortage of the 1970s, for example in Brazil.

gasoline /'gæsəli:n/ n. (US) petrol. A mixture of hydrocarbons derived from petroleum, whose main use is as a fuel for internal combustion engines. It is colourless and highly volatile.

gasometer /gæ'sɒmɪtə/ n. a large tank from which gas is distributed by pipes. [from French gazomètre]

gasp /gɑːsp/ v.t./i. to catch the breath with an open mouth as in exhaustion or surprise; to utter with gasps. —n. a convulsive catching of the breath. —**at one's last gasp**, at the point of death, exhausted. [from Old Norse]

Gasperi /'gæspəri/ Alcide de 1881–1954. Italian politician. A founder of the Christian Democrat Party, he was prime minister 1945–53 and worked for European unification.

gassy adj. **1.** of, like, or full of gas. **2.** verbose.

gas syringe a graduated piece of glass apparatus used to measure accurately volumes of gases produced or consumed in a chemical reaction.

gastric /'gæstrɪk/ adj. of the stomach. —**gastric flu**, (colloquial) sickness and diarrhoea of unknown cause. **gastric juice**, the digestive fluid secreted by the stomach glands. [from Greek gastēr = stomach]

gastro- /'gæstrəʊ-/ in combinations, stomach. [from Greek]

gastroenteritis /ˌgæstrəʊentə'raɪətiəs/ n. inflammation of the stomach and intestines, giving rise to abdominal pain, vomiting, and diarrhoea. It may be caused by food or other poisoning, allergy, or infection, and is dangerous in babies.

gastroenterology n. the medical speciality concerned with disorders of the ◊alimentary canal.

gastronome /'gæstrənəʊm/ n. a connoisseur of eating and drinking. [French]

gastronomy /gæ'strɒnəmi/ n. the science of good eating and drinking. —**gastronomic** /-'nɒmɪk/ adj. [from French from Greek gastēr = stomach and -nomia from nomos = law]

gastropod /'gæstrəpɒd/ n. a member of a very large class (Gastropoda) of ◊molluscs. Gastropods are single-shelled (in a spiral or modified spiral form), possess both tentacles and eyes, and move on a flattened, muscular ventral organ. They have well-developed heads and rough tongues. Some are marine, some freshwater, and others land creatures, but all tend to inhabit damp places. They include snails, slugs, limpets, and periwinkles. [from French from Greek gastér = stomach and pous podos = foot]

gastroscope /'gæstrəskəʊp/ n. an instrument that can be passed down the throat for looking inside the stomach.

gas turbine an engine in which burning fuel supplies hot gas to spin a ◊turbine. The most widespread application of gas turbines has been in aviation. All ◊jet engines are modified gas turbines, and some locomotives and ships also use gas turbines as a power source. They are also used in industry for generating and pumping purposes.

gas warfare the military use of gas to produce a toxic effect on the human body. See ◊chemical warfare.

gasworks n.pl. a place where gas for lighting and heating is manufactured.

gate n. **1.** a barrier, usually hinged, used to close an opening made for entrance and exit through a wall, fence etc. **2.** such an opening; a means of entrance or exit; a numbered place of access to an aircraft at an airport. **3.** a device regulating the passage of water in a lock etc. **4.** the number entering by payment at gates to see a football match etc.; the amount of money thus taken. —v.t. to confine to a college or school, especially after a fixed hour. —**gate-leg** adj., **gate-legged** adj. (of a table) with the legs in a gatelike frame which swings back to allow the top to fold down. [Old English]

gateau /'gætəʊ/ n. a large, rich cake often filled with cream, or cream and fruit, and highly decorated. [from French gâteau = cake]

gatecrash v.t./i. to go to (a private party etc.) without having been invited. —**gatecrasher** n.

gatehouse n. the lodge of a park etc.; the entrance building of a castle.

gateway n. an opening which can be closed with a gate; a means of access (literally or figuratively).

gather /'gæðə/ v.t./i. **1.** to bring or come together. **2.** to collect, to obtain gradually; to summon up (energy etc.). **3.** to infer or deduce. **4.** to pluck, to collect as harvest. **5.** to increase (speed etc.) gradually. **6.** to draw further in folds or wrinkles. **7.** to develop a purulent swelling. —n. (usually in plural) a fold or pleat. —**gather up**, to bring together; to pick up from the ground; to draw into a small compass. [Old English]

gathering n. **1.** an assembly. **2.** a purulent swelling. **3.** a group of leaves taken together in bookbinding.

Gatling /'gætlɪŋ/ Richard Jordan 1818–1903. US inventor of a rapid-fire gun. Patented in 1862, the Gatling gun had ten barrels arranged as a cylinder rotated by a hand crank. Cartridges from an overhead hopper or drum dropped into the breech mechanism, which loaded, fired and extracted them at a rate of 320 rounds per minute.

GATT /gæt/ acronym from General Agreement on Tariffs and Trade (a treaty to which more than 80 countries are parties, in operation since 1948, to promote trade and economic development).

gauche /gəʊʃ/ adj. lacking in ease and grace of manner, awkward and tactless. [French, literally = left(-handed)]

gaucherie /'gəʊʃəri/ n. gauche manners, a gauche act. [French]

gaucho /'gaʊtʃəʊ/ n. (plural gauchos) a mounted herdsman in the South American pampas. [Spanish, from Quechua]

Gaudí /gaʊ'di:/ Antonio 1852–1926. Spanish architect distinguished for his flamboyant Art Nouveau style. He designed both domestic and industrial buildings. His spectacular Church of the Holy Family, Barcelona, begun in 1883, is still under construction.

Gaudier-Brzeska /'gəʊdieɪ 'bʒeskə/ Henri (Henri Gaudier) 1891–1915. French artist, active in London from 1911; he is regarded as one of the outstanding sculptors of his generation. He studied art in Bristol, Nuremberg, and Munich, and became a member of the English Vorticist movement, which sought to reflect the industrial age by a sense of motion and angularity. From 1913 his sculptures showed the influence of Constantin Brancusi and Jacob Epstein. He died in World War I.

gentian /'dʒenʃən/ n. a plant of the genus *Gentiana* or *Gentianella*, especially one of the blue-flowered mountain kinds. —**gentian violet,** a purple dye with various uses, e. g. as an antiseptic. [Old English from Latin (according to Pliny, from *Gentius* king of Illyria)]

gentile adj. & n. not Jewish; heathen. —n. a non-Jewish person. [from Latin *gens* = race, family]

Gentile /dʒen'tileɪ/ da Fabriano c.1370–1427. Italian painter of frescoes and altarpieces in the International Gothic style. Gentile was active in Venice, Florence, Siena, Orvieto, and Rome and collaborated with the artists Pisanello and Jacopo Bellini. *The Adoration of the Magi* 1423 (Uffizi, Florence) is typically rich in detail and crammed with courtly figures.

Gentileschi /dʒenti'leski/ Artemisia 1593–c.1652. Italian painter, born in Rome. She trained under her father Orazio Gentileschi, but her work is more melodramatic than his. She settled in Naples from about 1630 and focused on macabre and grisly subjects, such as *Judith Decapitating Holofernes* (Museo di Capodimonte, Naples).

Gentileschi Orazio 1563–1637. Italian painter, born in Pisa. He was a follower and friend of Caravaggio, whose influence can be seen in the dramatic treatment of light and shade in *The Annunciation* 1623 (Galleria Sabauda, Turin). From 1626 he lived in London, painting for King Charles I.

Gentili /dʒen'tiːli/ Alberico 1552–1608. Italian jurist. He practised law in Italy but having adopted Protestantism was compelled to flee to England, where he lectured on Roman Law in Oxford. His publications, such as *De Jure Belli libri tres/On The Law Of War, Book Three* 1598, made him the first true international law writer and scholar.

gentility /dʒen'tɪlɪtɪ/ n. social superiority; good manners and elegance, upper-class habits. [from Old French *gentil*]

gentle adj. 1. not rough or severe; mild, moderate; quiet, requiring patience. 2. (of birth etc.) of good family. —**gently** adv., **gentleness** n. [from Old French *gentil*]

gentlefolk n.pl. people of good family.

gentleman n. (*plural* **gentlemen**) 1. (in polite or formal use) a man. 2. a chivalrous well-bred man; a man of good social position or of wealth and leisure. 3. a man of gentle birth attached to a royal household. —**gentleman-at-arms** n. one of the sovereign's bodyguard. **gentleman's** (*or* **-men's**) **agreement,** an agreement binding in honour but not enforceable. —**gentlemanly** adj.

Gentlemen-at-arms, Honourable Corps of in the British army, theoretically the main bodyguard of the sovereign; its functions are now ceremonial. Established in 1509, the corps is, next to the Yeomen of the Guard, the oldest in the army; it was reconstituted in 1862. It consists of army officers of distinction under a captain, a peer, whose appointment is political.

gentlewoman n. (*plural* **gentlewomen**) (*archaic*) a woman of good birth or breeding.

gentry /'dʒentrɪ/ n.pl. 1. people next below the nobility, particularly in England and Wales. By the later Middle Ages, the gentry included knights, esquires, and gentlemen, and after the 17th century, baronets. 2. (*derogatory*) people. [from Old French]

genuflect /'dʒenju:flekt/ v.i. to bend the knee, especially in worship. —**genuflexion** /-'flekʃən/ n. [from Latin *genu* = knee and *flectere* = bend]

genuine /'dʒenju:ɪn/ adj. 1. really coming from its reputed source etc.; not sham. 2. properly so called; pure-bred. —**genuinely** adv., **genuineness** n. [from Latin *genu* = knee, because a father acknowledged a new-born child by placing it on his knee]

genus /'dʒiː:nəs/ n. (*plural* **genera** /'dʒenərə/) 1. group of ◊species with many characteristics in common. Thus all doglike species (including dogs, wolves, and jackals) belong to the genus *Canis* (Latin 'dog'). Species of the same genus are thought to be descended from a common ancestor species. Related genera are grouped into families (see ◊family). 2. (in logic) kinds of things including subordinate kinds or species. 3. (*colloquial*) a kind, a class. [Latin = race, stock]

geo- /dʒiː:əʊ/ in combinations, Earth. [from Greek *gē* = Earth]

geocentric /dʒiː:əʊ'sentrɪk/ adj. 1. considered as viewed from the Earth's centre. 2. having the Earth as the centre. —**geocentrically** adv.

geochemistry /dʒi:əʊ'kemɪstrɪ/ n. the study of the chemistry of the Earth, especially the principles governing the geological distribution of the elements.

geochronology /dʒi:əʊkrə'nɒlədʒɪ/ n. the chronology of the Earth; the measurement of geological time and the ordering of past geological events.

geode /'dʒi:əʊd/ n. in geology, a subspherical cavity into which crystals have grown, from the outer wall into the centre. Geodes often contain very well-formed crystals of quartz (including amethyst), calcite, or other minerals. [from Greek *geōdēs* = earthy (*gē* = Earth)]

geodesic /dʒi:əʊ'di:sɪk, -desɪk/ adj. (*also* **geodetic**) of geodesy. —**geodesic** (*or* **geodetic**) **dome,** a dome built of short struts holding flat, triangular or polygonal pieces fitted together to form a rough hemisphere. **geodesic line,** the shortest possible line on a curved surface between two points. ·

geodesy /dʒi:'ɒdɪsɪ/ n. methods of surveying the Earth for making maps and correlating geological, gravitational, and magnetic measurements. Geodesic surveys, formerly carried out by means of various measuring techniques on the surface, are now commonly made by using radio signals and laser beams from orbiting satellites. [from Greek *geōdaisia* (*daiō* = divide)]

Geoffrey of Monmouth /'dʒefri, 'mɒnməθ/ c.1100–1154. Welsh writer and chronicler. While a canon at Oxford, he wrote *Historia Regum Britanniae/History of the Kings of Britain* c.1139, which included accounts of the semi-legendary kings Lear, Cymbeline, and Arthur. He was bishop-elect of St Asaph, N Wales, in 1151, and ordained a priest in 1152.

geographical /dʒi:ə'græfɪkəl/ adj. (*also* **geographic**) of geography. —**geographical mile,** 1 minute of latitude, about 1.85 km. —**geographically** adv.

geography /dʒi:'ɒgrəfɪ/ n. 1. the science of the Earth's form, physical features, climate, population etc. It is usually divided into **physical geography,** dealing with landforms and climates; **biogeography,** dealing with the conditions that affect the distribution of animals and plants; and **human geography,** dealing with the distribution and activities of peoples on Earth. 2. the features or arrangement of a place. —**geographer** n. [from French or Latin from Greek]

geological time the time scale embracing the history of the Earth from its physical origin to the present day. Geological time is divided into eras (Precambrian, Palaeozoic, Mesozoic, Cenozoic), which in turn are divided into periods, epochs, ages, and finally chrons.

geology /dʒi:'ɒlədʒɪ/ n. 1. the study of the composition, structure, and history of the Earth, and the processes occurring within it. It is divided into several branches: **mineralogy** (the minerals of Earth), **petrology** (rocks), **stratigraphy** (the deposition of successive beds of sedimentary rocks), **palaeontology** (fossils), and **tectonics** (the deformation and movement of the Earth's crust). The corresponding study of other planets. 2. the geological features of a district. —**geological** /-'lɒdʒɪkəl/ adj **geologically** adv., **geologist** n.

geomagnetism /dʒi:əʊ'mægnɪtɪzəm/ n. the study of the Earth's magnetic properties. —**geomagnetic** /-'netɪk/ adj.

geometric /dʒi:ə'metrɪk/ adj. (*also* **geometrical**) of geometry. —**geometrically** adv. [from French]

geometric mean in mathematics, the *n*th root of the product of *n* positive numbers. The geometric mean *m* of two numbers *p* and *q* is such that $m^2 = p \times q$, and hence *m*, *p*, and *q* are in a geometric progression.

geometric progression or **geometric sequence** in mathematics, a sequence of terms (progression) in which each term is a constant multiple (called the common ratio) of the one preceding it. For example, 3, 12, 48, 192, 768,... is a geometric sequence with a common ratio 4, since each term is equal to the previous term multiplied by 4.

geometry /dʒi:'ɒmɪtrɪ/ n. the branch of mathematics concerned with the properties of space, and the properties of such entities as points, lines, curves, planes, curved surfaces, usually in terms of plane (two-dimensional) and solid (three-dimensional) figures. The subject is usually divided into **pure geometry,** which embraces roughly the plane and solid geometry dealt with in Euclid's *Elements,* and **analytical** or ◊**coordinate geometry,** in which problems are solved using algebraic methods. A third, quite distinct, type includes the non-Euclidean geometries. —**geometer** *n.*, **geometrician** /-'trɪʃən/ *n.* [from Old French from Latin from Greek]

geomorphology /dʒiːəʊmɔː'fɒlədʒɪ/ *n.* the study of the physical features of the Earth's (or other planet's) surface and their relation to its geological structures.

geophysics /dʒiː əʊ'fɪzɪks/ *n.* the study of the physical properties of the Earth, especially of its crust; the application of the principles, methods, and techniques of physics to the study of the Earth. Geophysical studies also include winds, weather, tides, earthquakes, volcanoes, and their effects. —**geophysical** *adj.*, **geophysicist** *n.*

geopolitics /dʒiː əʊ'pɒlɪtɪks/ *n.* the influence of geographical features on the political character, history, and institutions etc. of states; the study of this.

Geordie /'dʒɔːdɪ/ *n.* a native of Tyneside. [from the name *George*]

George /geɪ'ɔːgə/ Stefan 1868–1933. German poet. His early poetry was influenced by French ◊Symbolism, but his concept of himself as regenerating the German spirit first appears in *Des Teppich des Lebens/The Tapestry of Life* 1899, and later in *Der siebente Ring/The Seventh Ring* 1907.

George /dʒɔːdʒ/ six kings of Great Britain:

George I 1660–1727. King of Great Britain and Ireland from 1714. He was the son of the first elector of Hanover, Ernest Augustus (1629–1698), and his wife ◊Sophia, and a great-grandson of James I. He succeeded to the electorate in 1698, and became king on the death of Queen Anne. He attached himself to the Whigs, and spent most of his reign in Hanover, never having learned English.

George II 1683–1760. King of Great Britain and Ireland from 1727, when he succeeded his father, George I. His victory at Dettingen 1743, in the War of the Austrian Succession, was the last battle commanded by a British king. He married Caroline of Anspach in 1705. He was succeeded by his grandson George III.

George III 1738–1820. King of Great Britain and Ireland from 1760, when he succeeded his grandfather George II. He supported his ministers in a hard line towards the American colonies, and opposed Catholic emancipation and other reforms. Possibly suffering from ◊porphyria, he had repeated attacks of insanity, permanent from 1811. He was succeeded by his son George IV.

George IV 1762–1830. King of Great Britain and Ireland from 1820, when he succeeded his father George III, for whom he had been regent during the king's insanity 1811–20. Strictly educated, he reacted by entering into a life of debauchery and in 1785 secretly married a Catholic widow, Maria ◊Fitzherbert, but in 1795 also married Princess ◊Caroline of Brunswick, in return for payment of his debts. His prestige was undermined by his treatment of Caroline (they separated in 1796), his dissipation and extravagance. His only child, Charlotte, died in childbirth in 1817. He was succeeded by his brother, the duke of Clarence, who became William IV.

George V 1865–1936. King of Great Britain from 1910, when he succeeded his father Edward VII. He was the second son, and became heir in 1892 on the death of his elder brother Albert, Duke of Clarence. In 1893, he married Princess Victoria Mary of Teck (Queen Mary), formerly engaged to his brother. During World War I he made several visits to the front. In 1917, he abandoned all German titles for himself and his family. The name of the royal house was changed from Saxe-Coburg-Gotha (popularly known as Brunswick or Hanover) to Windsor.

George VI 1895–1952. King of Great Britain from 1936, when he succeeded after the abdication of his brother Edward VIII, who had succeeded their father George V. Created Duke of York 1920, he married in 1923 Lady Elizabeth Bowes-Lyon (1900–), and their children are Elizabeth II and Princess Margaret. During World War II, he visited the Normandy and Italian battlefields.

George two kings of Greece:

George I 1845–1913. King of Greece 1863–1913. The son of King Christian IX of Denmark, he was nominated to the Greek throne and, in spite of early unpopularity, became a highly successful constitutional monarch. He was assassinated by a Greek, Schinas, at Salonika.

George II 1890–1947. King of Greece 1922–23 and 1935–47. He became king on the expulsion of his father

Constantine I in 1922 but was himself overthrown in 1923. Restored by the military in 1935, he set up a dictatorship under Joannis Metaxas, and went into exile during the German occupation 1941–45.

George Cross/Medal The **George Cross** is the highest civilian award in Britain for acts of courage in circumstances of extreme danger. It was instituted in 1940. It consists of a silver cross with a medallion in the centre bearing a design of St George and the Dragon, and is worn on the left breast. The **George Medal**, also instituted in 1940, is a civilian award for acts of great courage. The medal is silver and circular, bearing on one side a crowned effigy of the sovereign, and on the reverse St George and the Dragon. It is worn on the left breast.

George, St the patron saint of England. The story of St George rescuing a woman by slaying a dragon, evidently derived from the ◊Perseus legend, first appears in the 6th century. The cult of St George was introduced into W Europe by the Crusaders. His feast day is 23 Apr.

Georgetown¹ /'dʒɔːdʒtaʊn/ capital and port of Guyana; population (1983) 188,000.

Georgetown² /'dʒɔːdʒtaʊn/ or **Penang** chief port of the Federation of Malaysia, and capital of Penang, on the Island of Penang; population (1980) 250,600. It produces textiles and toys.

Georgetown, Declaration of the call in 1972, at a conference in Guyana of nonaligned countries, for a multipolar system to replace the two world power blocs, and for the Mediterranean Sea and Indian Ocean to be neutral.

georgette /dʒɔː'dʒet/ *n.* a thin dress material made from highly twisted yarn. [from *Georgette* de la Plante, French dressmaker]

Georgia /'dʒɔːdʒiə/ state in S USA; **area** 152,600 sq km/58,904 sq mi; **capital** Atlanta; **products** poultry, livestock, tobacco, maize, peanuts, cotton, soya beans, china clay, crushed granite, textiles, carpets, aircraft, paper products; **population** (1987) 6,222,000; **history** named after George II of England, it was founded 1733 and was one of the original Thirteen States of the USA.

Georgia constituent republic of the SW USSR from 1936; **area** 69,700 sq km/26,911 sq mi; **capital** Tbilisi; **products** tea, citrus and orchard fruits, tung oil, tobacco, vines, silk, hydroelectricity; **population** (1987) 5,266,000; 69% Georgian, 9% Armenian, 7% Russian, 5% Azeri, 3% Ossetian, 2% Abkhazian; **language** Georgian; **recent history** independent republic 1918–21; linked with Armenia and Azerbaijan as the Transcaucasian Republic within the SW USSR 1922–36. Increasing demands for autonomy from 1981, spearheaded from 1988 by a Georgian Popular Front, led to a clash with Soviet troops in Tbilisi 1989.

Georgian¹ /'dʒɔːdʒiən/ *adj.* **1.** a period of English architecture, furniture making, and decorative art between 1714 and 1830. The architecture is mainly Classical in style, although external details and interiors were often rich in rococo carving. Furniture designers include Thomas Chippendale, George Hepplewhite, and Thomas Sheraton. The silver of this period is particularly fine. **2.** the reigns of Kings George V and VI (1910–52), especially of the literature of 1910–20.

Georgian² *adj.* of Georgia in the USSR or its people or language. —*n.* **1.** a native or inhabitant of Georgia. **2.** the language of Georgia.

geostationary orbit or **geosynchronous orbit** the circular path 35,900 km/22,300 mi above the Earth's equator on which a ◊satellite takes 24 hours, moving from west to east, to complete an orbit, thus appearing to hang stationary over one place on the Earth's surface. Geostationary orbits are used for weather satellites and broadcasting and communications satellites. They were first thought of by the author Arthur C Clarke.

geothermal energy the energy produced by the use of natural steam, subterranean hot water, and hot dry rock for heating and electricity generation. Hot water is pumped to the surface and converted to steam or run through a heat exchanger; or dry steam is directed through turbines to produce electricity.

geotropism *n.* the movement of part of a plant in response to gravity. Roots are positively geotropic because they move towards a gravitational attraction.

geranium /dʒə'reɪnɪəm/ *n.* a herb or shrub of the genus *Geranium*, family Geraniaceae, having divided leaves and pink or purple flowers, bearing fruit shaped like a crane's bill; (*popular*) the cultivated pelargonium. [Latin from Greek *geranos* = crane]

gerbil /'dʒɜ:bıl/ *n.* a mouselike rodent of the family Cricetidae, (subfamily Gerbillinae) with long hind legs. Gerbils range from mouse-to rat-size, and have hairy tails. Many of the 13 genera live in dry, sandy, or sparsely vegetated areas of Africa and Asia. [from French]

gerenuk *n.* an antelope *Litocranius walleri* about 1 m/3 ft at the shoulder, with a greatly elongated neck. It browses on leaves, often balancing on its hind legs to do so. Sandy brown in colour, it is well camouflaged in its E African habitat of dry scrub.

Gerhard /'dʒɛrɑ:d/ Roberto 1896–1970. Spanish-born British composer. He studied with ◊Granados and ◊Schoenberg and settled in England in 1939, where he composed 12-tone works in Spanish style. He composed the *Symphony No 1* 1952–5, followed by three more symphonies and chamber music incorporating advanced techniques.

Gerhardie /dʒə'hɑ:di/ William 1895–. (born Gerhardi) British novelist, born in Russia. His novels include *Futility* and *The Polyglots*, which draws on his Russian upbringing.

geriatrics /dʒɛri'ætrıks/ *n.pl.* (usually treated as *singular*) the branch of medical science dealing with old age and its diseases. —**geriatric** *adj.*, **geriatrician** /-'trıʃən/ *n.* [from Greek *gēras* = old age and *iatros* = physician]

Géricault /ʒɛri'kəʊ/ Théodore (Jean Louis André) 1791–1824. French Romantic painter. *The Raft of the Medusa* 1819 (Louvre, Paris) was notorious for exposing a relatively recent scandal in which shipwrecked sailors had been cut adrift and left to drown.

germ *n.* **1.** a microorganism or microbe, especially one causing disease. **2.** a portion of an organism capable of becoming a new one; a rudiment of an animal or plant; the embryo of a seed. **3.** a thing that may develop, an elementary principle. —**germ warfare**, the use of germs to spread disease in war. [from French from Latin *germen* = sprout]

german /'dʒɜ:mən/ *adj.* (*placed after brother, sister, cousin*) having a full relationship, not a half-brother etc. [from Old French from Latin *germanus* = genuine, of same parents]

German /'dʒɜ:mən/ *adj.* of Germany or its people or language. —*n.* **1.** a native of Germany. **German shepherd dog**, an Alsatian. [from Latin *Germanus*]

German art painting and sculpture in the Germanic north of Europe from the early Middle Ages to the present. The arts were fostered by the emperor ◊Charlemagne in the early 9th century. In the 15th century the painter Stefan ◊Lochner, active in Cologne, excelled in the International ◊Gothic style. The incarnation of the ◊Renaissance in Germany was the 16th-century painter, Albrecht ◊Dürer. In the 19th century Caspar David ◊Friedrich was a pioneer of Romantic landscape painting; and at the turn of the century came Jugendstil (corresponding to French ◊Art Nouveau). In the 20th century the movement known as ◊*die Brücke* (the Bridge) was parallel with ◊Fauvism. It was followed by the Munich Expressionist group ◊*Blaue Reiter* (Blue Rider), and after World War I, Otto Dix, George Grosz, and Max Beckmann developed satirical Expressionist styles. The ◊Bauhaus school of design, emphasizing the dependence of form on function, had enormous impact abroad. The painter Max ◊Ernst moved to Paris and became a founding member of ◊Surrealism.

germander /dʒɜ:'mændə/ *n.* a plant of the genus *Teucrium*. —**germander speedwell**, a speedwell with leaves like a germander. [from Latin, ultimately from Greek *chamaedrys* = ground oak]

germane /dʒɜ:'meın/ *adj.* relevant *to* a subject. [variant of *german*]

Germanic /dʒɜ:'mænık/ *adj.* **1.** of the Germanic language. **2.** of the Scandinavians, Anglo-Saxons, or Germans. **3.** having German characteristics. **4.** (*historical*) of the Germans. —*n.* the primitive (unrecorded) language of the Germanic peoples. [from Latin]

Germanicus Caesar /dʒɜ:'mænıkəs 'si:zə/ 15 BC– AD 19. Roman general. He was the adopted son of the emperor ◊Tiberius and married Agrippina, granddaughter of the emperor ◊Augustus. Although he refused the suggestion of his troops that he claim the throne on the death of Augustus, his military victories in Germany made Tiberius

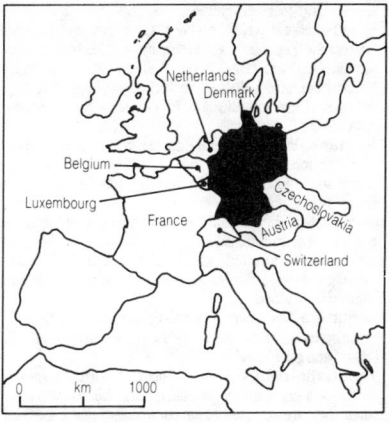

Germany, Federal Republic of

jealous. Sent to the East, he died near Antioch, possibly murdered at the instigation of Tiberius. He was the father of ◊Caligula, and of Agrippina, mother of ◊Nero.

germanium /dʒɜ:'meıniəm/ *n.* a metallic element, symbol Ge, atomic number 32, relative atomic mass 72.6. It is a grey-white, brittle, crystalline metal in the silicon group, with chemical and physical properties between those of silicon and tin. Germanium is a semiconductor material and is used in the manufacture of transistors and integrated circuits. The oxide is transparent to infrared radiation, and is used in military applications. It was discovered in 1886. [from Latin *Germanus* = German]

German language a member of the Germanic group of the Indo-European language family, the national language of Germany and Austria, and an official language of Switzerland. There are many spoken varieties of German. **High German** (*Hochdeutsch*), originally confined to 'High' or S Germany, is now accepted as the literary language of the whole country; **Low German** (*Plattdeutsch)* is the general name for the dialects of Germany which are not High German.

German measles or **rubella** a mild, communicable virus disease, usually caught by children. It is marked by a sore throat, a pinkish rash, and a slight fever, and has an incubation period of two to three weeks. If a woman contracts it in the first three months of pregnancy, serious damage may occur to the unborn child.

Germano- /dʒɜ:mənəʊ-/ in combinations, German.

German Ocean German name for the ◊North Sea.

German silver or **nickel silver** a silvery alloy of nickel, copper, and zinc. It is widely used for cheap jewellery and as the base metal for silver plating. The letters EPNS on silverware stand for electroplated nickel silver.

Germany, East /'dʒɜ:məni/ (German Democratic Republic) formerly the Soviet zone of occupation in the partition of Germany following World War II, East Germany was established in 1949, became a sovereign state in 1954, and was reunified with West Germany in Oct 1990.

Germany, Federal Republic of Federal Republic of; country in central Europe, bounded to the N by the North and Baltic Seas and Denmark, E by Poland and Czechoslovakia, S by Austria and Switzerland, and W by France, Belgium, Luxembourg, and the Netherlands. **area** 357,041 sq km/137,853 sq mi; **capital** Berlin; **physical** flat in N, mountainous in S with Alps; rivers Rhine, Weser, Elbe flow N, Danube flows SE, Oder, Neisse flow N along Polish frontier; many lakes, including Müritz; **head of state** Richard von Weizsäcker from 1984; **head of government** Helmut Kohl from 1982; **political system** democratic federal republic; **exports** machine tools, cars, commercial vehicles, electronics, industrial goods, textiles, chemicals, iron, steel, wine, lignite, uranium, cobalt, coal, iron, steel, fertilizers, plastics; **population** (1990 est.) 77,600,000 (including nearly 5,000,000 guest workers, *Gastarbeiter*, of whom 1,600,000 are Turks; the rest are Yugoslavs, Italians, Greeks, Spanish, and Portuguese); **languages** German, Serbian; **recent history** divided in 1945 into four occupation zones (US, French, British, Soviet). Federal Republic (West Germany) and German Democratic Republic (East Germany) established as independent states in 1949. Berlin Wall constructed in 1961. National borders, including the Wall, were opened in 1989 and the official reunification of Germany was declared in Oct 1990.

Germany, West (Federal Republic of Germany) country 1949–90, formed from the British, US, and French occupation zones following World War II; reunified with East Germany in Oct 1990.

germicide /'dʒɜːmɪsaɪd/ n. a substance that destroys germs. —**germicidal** adj.

germinal /'dʒɜːmɪnəl/ adj. 1. of germs. 2. in the earliest stage of development. 3. productive of new ideas etc. —**germinally** adv.

germinate /'dʒɜːmɪneɪt/ v.t./i. to sprout or bud (literally or figuratively); to cause to do this. n., **germinative** adj. [from Latin germinare]

germination /-'neɪʃən/ n. in botany, the initial stages of growth in a seed, spore, or pollen grain. Seeds germinate when they are exposed to favourable external conditions of moisture, light, and temperature, and when any factors causing dormancy have been removed.

germ layer in ◊embryology, a layer of cells that can be distinguished during the development of a fertilized egg. Most animals have three such layers: the inner, middle, and outer.

Geronimo /dʒə'rɒnɪməʊ/ 1829–1909. Chief of the Chiricahua Apache Indians and war leader. From 1875 to 1885, he fought US federal troops and settlers encroaching on tribal reservations in the SW, including SE Arizona and New Mexico. After surrendering to Gen George Crook in March 1886, and agreeing to go to Florida where their families were being held, Geronimo and his followers escaped. Captured again in Aug 1886, they were taken to Florida, then to Alabama. The climate proved unhealthy, and they were taken to Fort Sill, Oklahoma, where Geronimo became a farmer. He dictated Geronimo's Story of His Life 1906.

gerontology /dʒerɒn'tɒlədʒɪ/ n. the study of old age and the process of ageing. [from Greek gerōn = old man]

gerrymander /dʒeri'mændə/ v.t./i. to manipulate the boundaries of (a constituency etc.) so as to give undue influence to some party or class in an election. —n. this practice. [from Governor Gerry of Massachusetts (who rearranged boundaries for this purpose in 1812)]

Gershwin /'gɜːʃwɪn/ George 1898–1937. US composer, who wrote the tone poem An American in Paris 1928, Rhapsody in Blue 1924, and the opera Porgy and Bess 1935, in which he incorporated the essentials of jazz. He also wrote popular songs with his brother, the lyricist Ira Gershwin (1896–1983).

gerund /'dʒerənd/ n. in the grammar of certain languages, such as Latin, a noun formed from a verb and functioning as a noun to express an action or state. In English, gerunds end in -ing. —**gerundial** adj. [from Latin gerundum gerund of gerere = carry on]

gerundive /dʒə'rʌndɪv/ n. a Latin form of the verb functioning as an adjective with the sense 'that should be done' etc.

gesso /'dʒesəʊ/ n. (plural gessoes) gypsum as used in painting or sculpture. [Italian]

gestalt n. the concept of a unified whole that is greater than, or different from, the sum of its parts; that is, a complete structure whose nature is not explained simply by analysing its constituent elements. A chair, for example, will generally be recognized as a chair despite great variations between individual chairs in such attributes as size, shape, and colour. The term was first used in psychology in Germany about 1910. It has been adopted from German because there is no exact equivalent in English.

Gestapo /ge'stɑːpəʊ/ n. abbreviated form of **Geheime Staatspolizei**, Nazi Germany's secret police, formed in 1933, and under the direction of Heinrich Himmler from 1936; any comparable organization.

gestation /dʒe'steɪʃən/ n. 1. carrying in the womb; the period of this, between conception and birth; in humans the gestation period is about 266 days, in elephants 18–22 months, in cats about 60 days, and in some species of marsupial (such as opossum) as short as 12 days. 2. the development of an idea etc. [from Latin gestare = carry]

gesticulate /dʒe'stɪkjʊleɪt/ v.t./i. to use gestures instead of or to reinforce speech; to express thus. —**gesticulation** /-'leɪʃən/ n. [from Latin gesticulari (gesticulus diminutive of gestus from gerere = wield)]

gesture /'dʒestʃə/ n. 1. a movement of a limb or the body conveying meaning; the use of such movements. 2. an action to evoke a response or convey an intention. —v.t./i. to gesticulate. —**gestural** adj. [from Latin gerere = wield]

get /get/ v.t./i. (-tt-; past **got**; past participle **got** or (archaic and US) **gotten**) 1. to come into possession of, to obtain or receive. 2. to fetch or procure; to go to reach or catch (a train, bus etc.). 3. to prepare (a meal). 4. to receive (a broadcast signal); to establish communication by telephone etc. with. 5. to experience or suffer; to contract (an illness); to establish (an idea etc.) in one's mind. 6. to bring or come into a specified condition; to induce. 7. to come or go or arrive; to cause to do this. 8. (in perfect) to possess, to have, to be bound to do or be. 9. (colloquial) to understand. 10. (colloquial) to attract, obsess, or irritate. 11. (colloquial) to harm, injure, or kill, especially in retaliation. 12. to develop an inclination (with infinitive). 13. (usually of animals) to beget. —**get across**, (colloquial) to be or make effective or acceptable; (slang) to annoy. **get along**, to get on. **get at**, to reach; (colloquial) to mean, to imply; (slang) to imply a criticism of; (slang) to tamper with, to bribe. **get away**, to escape; to depart on a journey etc. **get away with**, to escape blame, punishment, or misfortune deserved for (an action). **get by**, (colloquial) to manage; to be acceptable. **get down**, to record in writing; to swallow; to make dejected. **get down to**, to begin working on. **get going**, (colloquial) to begin moving or acting. **get off**, to be or cause to be acquitted; to escape with little or no punishment; to start; to alight from (a bus etc.); (colloquial) to achieve an amorous or sexual relationship with. **get on**, to manage; to make progress; to be on friendly or harmonious terms. **get on!** (colloquial) an expression of incredulity. **get one's own back**, (colloquial) to have one's revenge. **get-out** n. a means of avoiding something. **get out of**, to avoid or escape (a duty etc.). **get over**, to get across; to recover from (an illness or shock etc.); **get round**, to evade (a rule or law); to coax or cajole (a person), especially to secure a favour. **get round to**, to deal with (a task etc.) in due course. **get somewhere**, to make progress, to be successful. **get there**, to reach one's goal; (slang) to succeed, to understand what is meant. **get through**, to pass (an examination etc.); to finish or use up; to make contact by telephone. **get through to**, (colloquial) to succeed in making (a person) understand. **get-together** n. (colloquial) a social gathering. **get up**, to rise from sitting etc., or from bed after sleeping; to prepare or organize; to work up (anger etc., a subject for an examination etc.); to dress or arrange elaborately. **get-up** n. (colloquial) a style or arrangement of dress etc. **get up to**, to become involved in (mischief etc.). [from Old Norse geta = obtain, beget, guess]

get-at-able /get'ætəbəl/ adj. accessible.

getaway n. an escape, especially after a crime.

Gethsemane /geθ'semənɪ/ site of the garden where Judas Iscariot, according to the New Testament, betrayed Jesus. It is on the Mount of Olives, E of Jerusalem. When Jerusalem was divided between Israel and Jordan 1948, Gethsemane fell within Jordanian territory.

Getty /'getɪ/ J(ean) Paul 1892–1976. US oil billionaire, president of the Getty Oil Company from 1947, and founder of the Getty Museum (housing the world's highest-funded art gallery) in Malibu, California.

The meek shall inherit the earth, but not the mineral rights.

Jean Paul Getty III (attrib.)

Gettysburg /'getɪzbɜːg/ site in Pennsylvania of a decisive battle of the American ◊Civil War in 1863, won by the North. The site is now a national cemetery, at the dedication of which President Lincoln delivered the **Gettysburg Address** 19 Nov 1863, a speech in which he reiterated the principles of freedom, equality, and democracy embodied in the US Constitution.

Getz /gets/ Stan(ley) 1927–1991. US tenor saxophonist of the 1950s 'cool jazz' school. He was the first US musician to be closely identified with the Latin American *bossa nova* sound.

geum /'dʒi:əm/ *n.* a perennial rosaceous plant of the genus *Geum* (which includes herb bennet), with red, orange, yellow, or white flowers. [variant of Latin *gaeum*]

gewgaw /'gju:gɔ:/ *n.* a gaudy plaything or ornament; a showy trifle.

geyser /'gaɪzə, 'gi:-, 'geɪ-/ *n.* **1.** an intermittently erupting hot spring. **2.** /'gi:zə/ an apparatus for heating water for use in baths, sinks etc. [from Icelandic *Geysir* name of a spring (*geysa* = gush)]

Gazira, El /gɪ'zɪərə/ plain in the Republic of Sudan, between the Blue and White Niles. The cultivation of cotton, sorghum, wheat and groundnuts is made possible by irrigation.

G-force *n.* the force pilots and astronauts experience when their craft accelerate or decelerate rapidly. One G is the ordinary pull of gravity. The first astronauts were subjected to launch and re-entry forces up to six Gs or more. Pilots and astronauts wear G-suits that prevent their blood from 'pooling' too much under severe G-forces, which can cause loss of consciousness.

Ghana /'gɑːnə/ Republic of; country in W Africa, bounded to the N by Burkina Faso, E by Togo, S by the Gulf of Guinea, and W by the Ivory Coast; **area** 238,305 sq km/ 91,986 sq mi; **capital** Accra; **physical** mostly plains; bisected by river Volta; **head of state and government** Jerry Rawlings from 1981; **political system** military republic; **exports** cocoa, coffee, timber, gold, diamonds, manganese, bauxite; **population** (1990 est) 15,310,000; **language** English (official) and African languages; **recent history** independence achieved from UK 1957; Kwame Nkrumah became president. Republic and one-party state formed 1960. Nkrumah deposed by military coup 1966. Return to civilian government in 1969–72, but ended 1979–1981 by further coups.

Ghana, Ancient a great trading empire that flourished in NW Africa between the 5th and 13th centuries. Founded by the Soninke people, the Ghana Empire was based, like the Mali Empire that superseded it, on the Saharan gold trade. Trade consisted mainly of the exchange of gold from inland deposits for salt from the coast. At its peak in the 11th century, it occupied an area that includes parts of present-day Mali, Senegal, and Mauritania. Wars with the Berber tribes of the Sahara led to its fragmentation and collapse in the 13th century, when much of its territory was absorbed into Mali.

ghastly /'gɑːstlɪ/ *adj.* **1.** horrible, frightful; (*colloquial*) objectionable. **2.** deathlike, pallid. **3.** (of a smile etc.) forced, grim. —*adv.* ghastlily (pale etc.). —**ghastlily** *adv.*, **ghastliness** *n.* [from obsolete *gast* = terrify]

ghat /gɔ:t/ *n.* or **ghaut** in India, steps leading to a river, a landing place. —**burning-ghat** *n.* a level area at the top of a river ghat where Hindus burn their dead. [from Hindi]

Ghats, Eastern and Western /gɔ:ts/ twin mountain ranges in S India, to the E and W of the central plateau; a few peaks reach about 3,000 m/9,800 ft. The name is a European misnomer, the Indian word *ghat* meaning 'pass'.

Ghazzali, al- /gæ'zɑ:li/ 1058–1111. Muslim philosopher and one of the most celebrated Sufis (Muslim mystics). He was responsible for easing the conflict between the Sufi and the Ulema, a body of Muslim religious and legal scholars.

ghee /gi:/ *n.* Indian clarified butter made from the milk of a buffalo or cow [from Hindi from Sanskrit = sprinkled]

Ghent /gent/ (Flemish *Gent*, French *Gand*) city and port in East Flanders, NW Belgium; population (1982) 237,500. Industries include textiles, chemicals, electronics, and metallurgy.

Gheorgiu-Dej /gɪɔ:dʒu:'deɪ/ Gheorge 1901–1965. Romanian communist politician. A member of the Romanian Communist Party from 1930, he played a leading part in establishing a communist regime in 1945. He was prime minister 1952–55 and state president 1961–65. Although retaining the support of Moscow, he adopted an increasingly independent line during his final years.

gherkin /'gɜ:kɪn/ *n.* a small cucumber for pickling. [from Dutch]

ghetto /'getəʊ/ *n.* (*plural* **ghettos**) a part of a city occupied by a minority group (*historically* the Jewish quarter in a city); a segregated group or area. [perhaps from Italian *getto* = foundry, as the first ghetto founded in Venice in 1516 was on the site of a foundry]

Ghiberti /gi'beəti/ Lorenzo 1378–1455. Italian sculptor and goldsmith. In 1401 he won the commission for a pair of gilded bronze doors for Florence's baptistry. He produced a second pair (1425–52), the *Gates of Paradise*, one of the masterpieces of the Early Italian Renaissance. They show sophisticated composition and use of perspective.

Ghirlandaio /giəlæn'daɪəʊ/ Domenico *c.*1449–1494. Italian fresco painter, head of a large and prosperous workshop in Florence. His fresco cycle 1486–90 in Sta Maria Novella, Florence, includes portraits of many Florentines and much contemporary domestic detail. He also worked in Pisa, Rome, and San Gimignano, and painted portraits.

ghost /gəʊst/ *n.* **1.** an apparition of a dead person or animal, a disembodied spirit. **2.** an emaciated or pale person. **3.** a shadow or semblance. **4.** a secondary or duplicated image in a defective telescope or television picture. —*v.t./i.* to act as a ghost writer (of). —**ghost town**, a town with few or no remaining inhabitants. **ghost writer**, a writer doing work for which the employer takes credit. **give up the ghost**, to die. —**ghostliness** *n.*, **ghostly** *adj.* [Old English]

Ghosts a play by Henrik Ibsen, first produced in 1881. Mrs Alving hides the profligacy of her late husband. The past catches up with her when her son inherits his father's syphilis and unwittingly plans to marry his half-sister.

ghoul /gu:l/ *n.* **1.** a person morbidly interested in death etc. **2.** (in Muslim folklore) a spirit preying on corpses. —**ghoulish** *adj.*, **ghoulishly** *adv.* [from Arabic = protean desert demon]

GHQ abbreviation of general headquarters.

ghyll variant of gill³.

GI /dʒi:'aɪ/ abbreviation of government, or general, issue; hence (in the USA) a common soldier. —*adj.* of or for US servicemen.

Giacometti /dʒækə'meti/ Alberto 1901–1966. Swiss sculptor and painter, who trained in Italy and Paris. In the 1930s, in his Surrealist period, he began to develop his characteristic spindly constructions. His mature style of emaciated single figures, based on wire frames, emerged in the 1940s.

Giambologna /dʒæmbə'lɒnjə/ (Giovanni da Bologna or Jean de Boulogne) 1529–1608. Flemish-born sculptor active mainly in Florence and Bologna. In 1583 he completed his public commission for the Loggia dei Lanzi in Florence, *The Rape of the Sabine Women*, a dynamic group of muscular figures and a prime example of Mannerist sculpture.

giant /'dʒaɪənt/ *n.* **1.** an imaginary or mythical being of human form but superhuman size. **2.** a person of great size, ability, strength etc.; an abnormally tall animal or plant. **3.** a star of relatively great luminosity arising from either high surface temperatures or very extended atmospheres. —*adj.* gigantic; of a very large kind. —**giantess** *n.fem.* [from Old French from Latin from Greek *gigas gigantos*]

Giant's Causeway a stretch of columnar basalt forming a promontory on the N coast of Antrim, Northern Ireland. It was formed by an outflow of lava in Tertiary times that solidified in polygonal columns.

gibber /'dʒɪbə/ *v.i.* to jabber inarticulately.

Gibberd /'gɪbəd/ Frederick 1908–1984. British architect and town planner. His works include the new towns of Harlow, England, and Santa Teresa, Venezuela; the Catholic Cathedral, Liverpool; and the Central London mosque in Regent's Park.

gibberellin *n.* the plant growth substance (see also ◊auxin) that mainly promotes stem growth but may also affect the breaking of dormancy in certain buds and seeds, and the induction of flowering. Application of gibberellin can stimulate the stems of dwarf plants to additional growth, delay the ageing process in leaves, and promote the production of seedless fruit (◊parthenocarpy).

gibberish /'dʒɪbərɪʃ/ *n.* unintelligible speech, meaningless sounds.

gibbet /'dʒɪbɪt/ *n.* (*historical*) a gallows, a post with an arm on which an executed criminal was hung. —*v.t.* **1.** to put to death by hanging; to expose or hang up on a gibbet. **2.** to hold up to contempt. [from Old French *gibet*, diminutive of *gibe* = club]

gibbon /'gɪbən/ n. a small ape genus *Hylobates* of which there are several species. The **common** or **black-handed gibbon** *Hylobates lar* is about 60 cm/2 ft tall, with a body that is hairy except for the buttocks, which distinguishes it from other types of apes. Gibbons have long arms, no tail, and are arboreal in habit, but when on the ground they walk upright. They are found from Assam through the Malay peninsula to Borneo. [French from aboriginal name]

Gibbon Edward 1737–1794. British historian, author of *The History of the Decline and Fall of the Roman Empire* 1776–88. The work was a continuous narrative from the 2nd century AD to the fall of Constantinople in 1453. He began work on it while in Rome in 1764.

Gibbon John Heysham 1903–1974. US surgeon who invented the heart–lung machine in 1953. It has become indispensable in heart surgery, maintaining the circulation while the heart is temporarily inactivated.

Gibbons /'gɪbənz/ Grinling 1648–1721. British woodcarver, born in Rotterdam. He produced carved wooden panels (largely of birds, flowers, and fruit) for St Paul's Cathedral, London, and for many large houses, including Petworth House, Sussex. He became master carver to George I in 1741.

Gibbons Orlando 1583–1625. English composer. A member of a family of musicians, he was appointed organist at Westminster Abbey, London in 1623. His finest works are his madrigals and motets.

gibbous /'gɪbəs/ adj. convex; (of the Moon or a planet) having the bright part greater than a semicircle but less than a circle; humpbacked. [from Latin *gibbus* = hump]

Gibbs /gɪbz/ James 1682–1754. Scottish Neo-Classical architect whose works include St Martin-in-the-Fields, London 1722–26, Radcliffe Camera, Oxford 1737–49, and Bank Hall, Warrington, Cheshire 1750.

Gibbs Josiah Willard 1839–1903. US theoretical physicist and chemist who developed a mathematical approach to thermodynamics. His book *Vector Analysis* 1881 established vector methods in physics.

gibe /dʒaɪb/ v.t./i. to jeer or mock (at). —n. a jeering remark, a taunt. [perhaps from Old French *giber* = handle roughly]

giblets /'dʒɪblɪts/ n.pl. the edible organs etc. of a bird, taken out and usually cooked separately. [from Old French *gibelet* = game stew (*gibier* = game)]

Gibraltar /dʒɪ'brɔːltə/ British dependency, situated on a narrow rocky promontory in S Spain; **area** 6.5 sq km/2.5 sq mi; **population** (1988) 30,000; **recent history** captured from Spain in 1970 by English admiral George Rooke (1650–1709), it was ceded to Britain under the Treaty of Utrecht 1713. A referendum in 1967 confirmed the wish of the people to remain in association with the UK, but Spain continues to claim sovereignty, and closed the border 1969–85. In 1989, the UK government announced it would reduce the military garrison by half.

Gibraltar, Strait of strait between N Africa and Spain, with the Rock of Gibraltar on the N side and Jebel Musa on the S, the so-called Pillars of Hercules.

Gibson Mel 1956– . Australian actor. His image as an international star and sex symbol is the result of his roles in George Miller's *Mad Max* films (1979, 1982, 1985), and in blockbusters such as *Lethal Weapon* 1987 and *Lethal Weapon 2* 1989. His other films include *The Year of Living Dangerously* 1983 and *Hamlet* 1991.

giddy /'gɪdɪ/ adj. 1. dizzy, tending to fall or stagger. 2. causing dizziness. 3. mentally intoxicated, frivolous; flighty. —**giddily** adv., **giddiness** n. [Old English = insane, literally 'possessed by a god']

Gide /ʒiːd/ André 1869–1951. French novelist, born in Paris. His work is largely autobiographical and concerned with the dual themes of self-fulfilment and renunciation. It includes *L'Immoraliste/The Immoralist* 1902, *La Porte étroite/Strait Is the Gate* 1909, *Les Caves*

du Vatican/The Vatican Cellars 1914, and *Les Faux-monnayeurs/The Counterfeiters* 1926; and an almost lifelong *Journal*. He was awarded the Nobel Prize for Literature in 1947.

Gideon /'gɪdɪən/ in the Old Testament, one of the Judges of Israel, who led a small band of Israelite warriors which succeeded in routing an invading Midianite army of overwhelming number in a surprise night attack.

Gielgud /'giːlgʊd/ John 1904– . English actor and director. He played many Shakespearean roles, including Hamlet in 1929. His film roles include Clarence in *Richard III* 1955 and the butler in *Arthur* 1981 (for which he won an Academy Award).

Gierek /'gɪərek/ Edward 1913– . Polish Communist politician. He entered the Politburo of the ruling Polish United Workers' Party (PUWP) in 1956 and was party leader 1970–80. His industrialization programme plunged the country heavily into debt and sparked a series of ◊Solidarity-led strikes.

Giffard /ʒɪˈfɑː/ Henri 1825–1882. French inventor of the first passenger-carrying powered and steerable airship, called a dirigible, built in 1852. The hydrogen-filled airship was 43 m/144 ft long, had a 3-hp steam engine which drove a propeller, and was steered using a saillike rudder. It flew at an average speed of 5 kph/3 mph.

gift /gɪft/ n. 1. a thing given, a present; a natural ability or talent. 2. giving. 3. (*colloquial*) an easy task. —v.t. to endow with gifts; to present *with* as a gift; to bestow as a gift. —**gift token** *or* **voucher**, a voucher used as a gift and exchangeable for goods. **giftwrap** v.t. to wrap attractively (as a gift). **in a person's gift**, his to bestow. [from Old Norse]

gifted adj. talented.

gig[1] /gɪg/ n. 1. a light, two-wheeled one-horse carriage. 2. a light ship's boat for rowing or sailing. 3. a rowing boat chiefly used for racing.

gig[2] /gɪg/ n. (*colloquial*) an engagement to play jazz etc., especially for one night.

giga- /gɪgə, gaɪgə-/ prefix signifying multiplication by 10^9 (1,000,000,000 or 1 billion), as in **gigahertz**, a unit of frequency equivalent to 1 billion hertz. [from Greek *gigas* = giant]

gigabyte n. in computing, a measure of the capacity of ◊memory or storage, equal to 1,024 ◊megabytes. It is also used, less precisely, to mean one thousand million bytes.

gigantic /dʒaɪ'gæntɪk/ adj. giant-like, huge. —**gigantically** adv. [from Latin *gigas gigantis* = giant]

giggle v.i. to laugh in small, half-suppressed bursts. —n. such a laugh; (*colloquial*) an amusing person or thing, a joke. —**giggly** adj.

gigolo /'ʒɪgəlaʊ/ n. (*plural* **gigolos**) a young man paid by an older woman to be an escort or lover. [French as masculine of *gigole* = dance-hall woman]

Gila /'hiːlə/ n. (in full **Gila monster**) a large lizard *Heloderma suspectum* found in the southwest US and Mexico. Belonging to the only venomous genus of lizards, it has poison glands in its lower jaw, but the bite is not usually fatal to humans. [from *Gila*, name of a river in New Mexico and Arizona]

Gilbert /'gɪlbət/ Cass 1859–1934. US architect, major developer of the ◊skyscraper. His most notable work is the Woolworth Building, New York 1913, the highest building in America (868 ft/265 m) when built and famous for its use of Gothic decorative detail. He was also architect of the US Supreme Court building in Washington DC, the Minnesota state capitol in St Paul, and the US Customs House in New York City.

Gilbert Humphrey c.1539–1583. English soldier and navigator who claimed Newfoundland (landing at St John's) for Elizabeth I in 1583. He died when his ship sank on the return voyage.

Gilbert Walter 1932– . US molecular biologist. Gilbert worked on the problem of genetic control, seeking the mechanisms which switch genes on and off. By 1966 he had established the existence of the *lac* repressor, the molecule which suppressed lactose production. Further work on the sequencing of ◊DNA nucleotides won for Gilbert a share of the 1980 Nobel Chemistry Prize with Frederick Sanger and Paul Berg.

Gilbert William 1544–1603. English scientist and physician to Elizabeth I and (briefly) James I. He studied magnetism

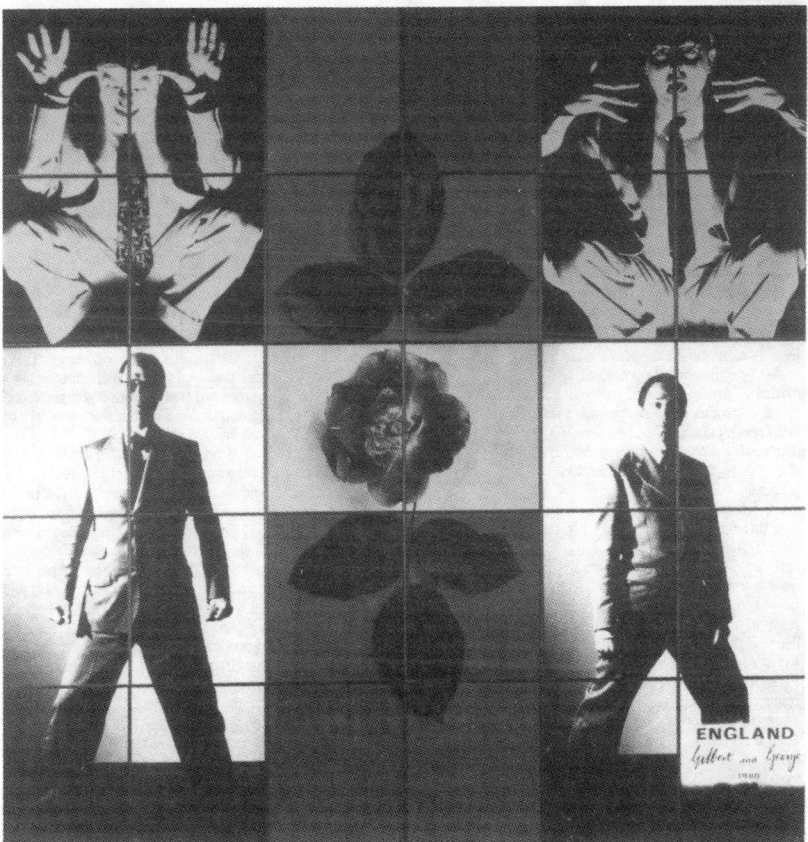

Gilbert and George English performance artists Gilbert and George first captured the public imagination in the 1960s when they offered themselves as works of art.

and static electricity, deducing that the Earth's magnetic field behaves as if a bar magnet joined the North and South poles. His book on magnets, published in 1600, is the first printed scientific book based wholly on experimentation and observation.

Gilbert W(illiam) S(chwenk) 1836–1911. British humorist and dramatist who collaborated with Arthur ◊Sullivan, providing the libretti for their series of light comic operas from 1871; they include *HMS Pinafore* 1878, *The Pirates of Penzance* 1879, and *The Mikado* 1885.

Gilbert and Ellice Islands /'gɪlbət, 'elɪs/ former British colony in the Pacific, known since independence 1978 as ◊Tuvalu and ◊Kiribati.

Gilbert and George /'gɪlbət, dʒɔː'dʒ/ Gilbert Proesch 1943– and George Passmore 1942– . English painters and performance artists who became known in the 1960s for their presentation of themselves as works of art – living sculpture.

gild[1] /gɪld/ *v.t.* (*past participle* sometimes **gilt** as adjective in literal sense, otherwise **gilded**) to cover thinly with gold; to tinge with golden colour. —**gild the lily**, to try to improve what is already satisfactory. [Old English]

gild[2] variant of **guild**.

Gilded Age, the in US history, a derogatory term referring to the opulence displayed in the post-Civil War decades. It borrows the title of an 1873 political satire by Mark Twain and Charles Dudley Warner (1829–1900), which highlights the respectable veneer of public life covering the many scandals of graft and corruption.

Gilgamesh /'gɪlgəmeʃ/ hero of Sumerian, Hittite, Akkadian, and Assyrian legend. The 12 verse 'books' of the *Epic of Gilgamesh* were recorded in a standard version on 12 cuneiform tablets by the Assyrian king Ashurbanipal's

scholars in the 7th century BC, and the epic itself is older than Homer's *Iliad* by at least 1,500 years. One-third mortal and two-thirds divine, Gilgamesh is lord of the Sumerian city of Uruk. The *Epic's* incident of the Flood is similar to the Old Testament account.

gill[1] /gɪl/ *n.* (usually in *plural*) **1.** a respiratory organ in a fish etc. **2.** a vertical radial plate on the underside of a mushroom etc. **3.** the flesh below a person's jaws and ears. [from Old Norse]

gill[2] /dʒɪl/ *n.* an imperial unit of volume for liquid measure, equal to a quarter of a pint or 4 fluid ounces (0.142 litre). It is used in selling alcoholic drinks. In many districts the gill is equal to half a pint, the quarter pint being called a jack. [from Old French from Latin *gillo* = water-pot]

gill[3] /gɪl/ *n.* **1.** a deep ravine, usually wooded. **2.** a narrow mountain torrent. [from Old Norse]

Gill Eric 1882–1940. English sculptor and engraver. He designed the typefaces Perpetua 1925 and Gill Sans (without serifs) 1927, and created monumental stone sculptures with clean, simplified outlines, such as *Prospero and Ariel* 1929–31 (on Broadcasting House, London).

Gillespie /gɪ'lespi/ Dizzy (John Birks) 1917– . US jazz trumpeter who, with Charlie ◊Parker, was the chief creator and exponent of the ◊bebop style.

gillie /'gɪli/ *n.* an attendant on a sportsman in Scotland. [from Gaelic *gille* = lad, servant]

gillyflower /'dʒɪliflaʊə/ *n.* a clove-scented flower, e. g. the wallflower; the clove-scented pink *Dianthus carophyllus*. [from Old French *gilofre, girofle* from Latin from Greek *karuophullon* = clove tree]

Gilmour Peter 1960– . Australian yachtsman. He is best known for three successive victories in the Congressional Cup, the world's foremost match-racing competition: in

1987 and 1988 he won the UK Congressional Cup, and in 1988 the US Congressional Cup. He has also won a number of other world yachting championships.

gilt[1] /gɪlt/ *adj.* covered thinly with gold; gold-coloured. —*n.* **1.** gilding. **2.** a gilt-edged security. —**gilt-edged** *adj.* (of securities, stocks etc.) having a high degree of reliability.

gilt[2] *n.* a young sow. [from Old Norse]

gilt-edged securities stocks and shares issued and guaranteed by the British government to raise funds and traded on the Stock Exchange. A relatively risk-free investment, gilts bear fixed interest and are usually redeemable on a specified date. According to the redemption date, they are described as short (up to five years), medium, or long (15 years or more).

gimbals /'dʒɪmbəlz/ *n.pl.* a contrivance of rings and pivots for keeping instruments horizontal at sea. [from Old French *gemel* = double finger-ring from Latin *gemellus* = twin]

gimcrack /'dʒɪmkræk/ *adj.* showy but flimsy and worthless. —*n.* a showy ornament etc., a knick-knack. [from earlier *gibecrake* = little ornament]

gimlet /'gɪmlɪt/ *n.* a small tool with a screw-tip for boring holes. —**gimlet eye**, an eye with a piercing glance. [from Old French *guimbelet*]

gimmick /'gɪmɪk/ *n.* a trick or device, especially to attract attention or publicity. —**gimmickry** *n.*, **gimmicky** *adj.* [originally US]

gimp /gɪmp/ *n.* a twist of silk etc. with a cord or wire running through it; a fishing line of silk etc. bound with wire. [from Dutch]

gin[1] /dʒɪn/ *n.* an alcoholic drink made by distilling a mash of maize, malt, or rye, with juniper flavouring. It was first produced in Holland. In Britain, the low price of corn led to a mania for gin during the 18th century, resulting in the Gin Acts of 1736 and 1751 which reduced gin consumption to a quarter of its previous level. —**gin rummy**, a form of the card game rummy. **gin sling**, (*US*) a cold drink of gin flavoured and sweetened. [abbreviation of *geneva* from Dutch from Old French *genevre* = juniper]

gin[2] *n.* **1.** a snare, a trap. **2.** a machine separating cotton from its seeds. **3.** a kind of crane and windlass. —*v.t.* (**-nn-**) **1.** to treat (cotton) in a gin. **2.** to trap. [from Old French *engin* = engine]

ginger /'dʒɪndʒə/ *n.* **1.** a hot, spicy root used in cooking and medicine and preserved in syrup or candied; the plant from which this comes *Zingiber officinale*. **2.** light reddish yellow. **3.** mettle, spirit; stimulation. —*v.t.* **1.** to flavour with ginger. **2.** to liven *up*. —**ginger ale, beer**, kinds of aerated, ginger-flavoured drink. **ginger group**, a group urging a party or movement to more decided action. **ginger nut**, a ginger-flavoured biscuit. **ginger snap**, a thin, brittle, ginger-flavoured biscuit. —**gingery** *adj.* [from Old English and Old French from Latin *zingiber* from Greek from Sanskrit]

gingerbread *n.* ginger-flavoured treacle cake. —*adj.* gaudy, tawdry.

gingerly /'dʒɪndʒəlɪ/ *adj.* showing great care or caution. —*adv.* in a gingerly manner. [perhaps from Old French *gensor* = delicate]

gingham /'gɪŋəm/ *n.* a plain-woven cotton cloth often striped or checked. [from Dutch from Malay = striped]

gingivitis /dʒɪndʒɪ'vaɪtɪs/ *n.* inflammation of the gums. [from Latin *gingiva* = gum]

ginkgo /'gɪŋkəʊ/ *n.* (*plural* **ginkgos**) a tree *Ginkgo biloba* of the gymnosperm (or naked-seed-bearing) division of plants, also known as the maidenhair tree because of the resemblance of its leaves to those of the maidenhair fern. It may reach a height of 30 m/100 ft by the time it is 200 years old. The only living member of its group (Ginkgophyta), widespread in Mesozoic times, it has been cultivated in China and Japan since ancient times, and is planted in many parts of the world. Its leaves are fan-shaped, and it bears fleshy, yellow, foul-smelling seeds enclosing edible kernels. [from Japanese from Chinese = silver apricot]

Ginsberg /'gɪnzbɜːg/ Allen 1926– . US poet. His 'Howl' 1956, the most influential poem of the ◊beat generation, criticizes the materialism of contemporary US society. In the 1960s Ginsberg travelled widely in Asia, and was a key figure in introducing Eastern thought to students of that decade.

ginseng /'dʒɪnseŋ/ *n.* a plant of the genus *Panax*, family Araliaceae, with a thick, forked aromatic root used in medicine in China and Korea, where it is thought to be a panacea, and is taken to promote longevity. It is found in eastern Asia and North America. [from Chinese perhaps = man-image alluding to forked root]

Giolitti /dʒəʊ'liːti/ Giovanni 1842–1928. Italian liberal politician, born in Mondovi. He was prime minister in 1892–93, 1903–05, 1906–09, 1911–14, and 1920–21. He opposed Italian intervention in World War I and pursued a policy of broad coalitions, which proved ineffective in controlling Fascism after 1921.

Giordano /dʒɔː'daːnəʊ/ Luca 1632–1705. Italian Baroque painter, born in Naples, active in Florence in the 1680s. In 1692 he was summoned to Spain by Charles II and painted ceilings in the Escorial palace for the next ten years.

Giorgione /dʒɔː'dʒəʊni/ del Castelfranco *c.*1475–1510. Italian Renaissance painter, active in Venice, probably trained by Giovanni Bellini. His work influenced Titian and other Venetian painters. His subjects are imbued with a sense of mystery and treated with a soft technique reminiscent of Leonardo da Vinci's later works, as in *The Tempest* 1504 (Accademia, Venice).

Giotto /'dʒɒtəʊ/ di Bondone 1267–1337. Italian painter and architect who broke away from the conventional Gothic style of the time, and introduced a naturalistic style, painting saints as real people. He painted cycles of frescoes in churches at Assisi, Florence, and Padua. He is said to have designed the campanile (bell tower) in Florence.

Giotto a space probe built by the European Space Agency to study ◊Halley's comet. Launched by an Ariane rocket in July 1985, *Giotto* passed within 600 km/375 mi of the comet's nucleus on 13 March 1986.

gippy tummy /'dʒɪpɪ/ (*colloquial*) diarrhoea affecting visitors to hot countries. [from *Egyptian*]

gipsy variant of gypsy.

giraffe /dʒɪ'rɑːf/ *n.* the tallest mammal *Giraffa camelopardalis*. It stands over 5.5 m/18 ft tall, the neck accounting for nearly half this amount. The giraffe has two small skin-covered horns on the head and a long tufted tail. The skin has a mottled appearance and is reddish brown and cream. Giraffes are now found only in Africa, S of the Sahara Desert. [from French ultimately from Arabic]

Giraldus Cambrensis /dʒɪ'rældəs kæm'brensɪs/ *c.*1146–1220. Welsh historian, born in Pembrokeshire, who was elected bishop of St David's in 1198. He wrote a history of the conquest of Ireland by Henry II, and *Itinerarium Cambriae* (Journey through Wales) 1191.

Giraudoux /ʒɪrəʊ'duː/ (Hippolyte) Jean 1882–1944. French playwright and novelist, who wrote the plays *Amphitryon 38* 1929 and *La Folle de Chaillot*/*The Madwoman of Chaillot* 1945, and the novel *Suzanne et la Pacifique*/*Suzanne and the Pacific* 1921. Other plays include *La Guerre de Troie n'aura pas lieu*/*Tiger at the Gates* 1935.

gird /gɜːd/ *v.t.* (*past* and *past participle* **girded** or **girt**) to encircle or attach or secure with a belt or band; to put (a cord) *round*; to enclose or encircle. —**gird up one's loins**, to prepare for action. [Old English]

girder *n.* an iron or steel beam or compound structure for a bridge-span etc.; a beam supporting joists.

girdle[1] /'gɜːdəl/ *n.* **1.** a belt or cord used to gird the waist. **2.** an elasticated corset not extending above the waist. **3.** a thing that surrounds. **4.** the bony support of a limb. —*v.t.* to surround with a girdle. [Old English]

girdle[2] *n.* (especially in Scotland) a round iron plate set over a fire or otherwise heated for baking etc. [variant of *griddle*]

girl /gɜːl/ *n.* **1.** a female child. **2.** a young woman. **3.** a female servant. **4.** a man's girlfriend. —**girl Friday**, see ◊Friday. **girlfriend** *n.* a regular female companion. —**girlhood** *n.*, **girlish** *adj.*, **girlishly** *adv.*, **girlishness** *n.* [perhaps cognate with Low German *gör* = child]

Girl Guides a ◊Scout organization founded in 1910 in the UK by Baden-Powell and his sister Agnes. There are three branches: Brownie Guides (age 7–11); Guides (10–16); Ranger Guides (14–20); and adult leaders – Guiders. The World Association of Girl Guides and Girl Scouts (as they are known in the USA) has over 6.5 million members.

girlie *n.* a little girl (as a term of endearment). —*adj.* (of a publication etc.) depicting young women in erotic poses.

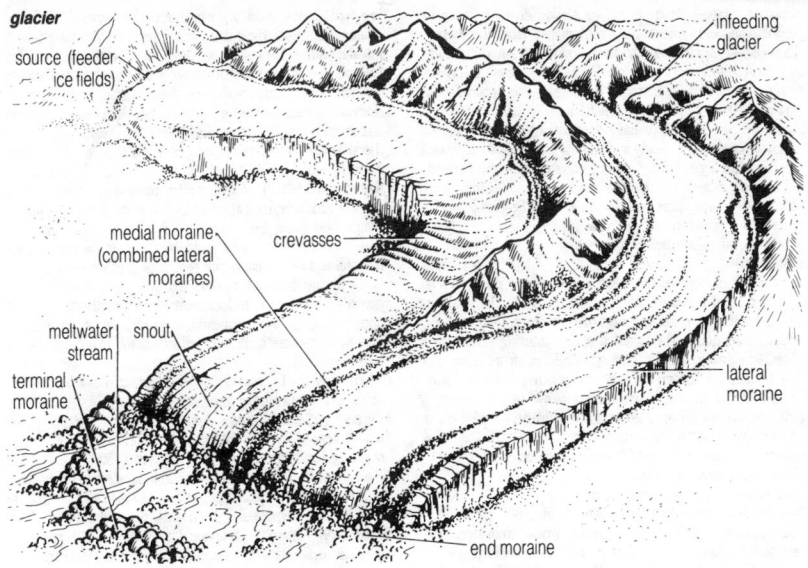

glacier
source (feeder ice fields)
infeeding glacier
medial moraine (combined lateral moraines)
crevasses
meltwater stream
snout
terminal moraine
lateral moraine
end moraine

giro /'dʒaɪrəʊ/ *n.* (*plural* **giros**) a system of credit transfer between banks, post offices etc. [German from Italian = circulation (of money)]

Girondin /dʒɪ'rɒndɪn/ a member of the right-wing republican party in the French Revolution, so called because a number of the leaders came from the Gironde region. The Girondins were driven from power by the ◊Jacobins in 1793.

girt see ◊gird.

girth /gɜːθ/ *n.* **1.** the distance round a thing. **2.** a strap round the body of a horse etc. securing the saddle etc. [from Old Norse]

Giscard d'Estaing /'ʒiːskɑː des'tæŋ/ Valéry 1926– . French conservative politician, president 1974–81. He was finance minister to de Gaulle 1962–66 and Pompidou 1969–74. As leader of the *Union pour la Démocratie Française*, which he formed in 1978, Giscard sought to project himself as leader of a 'new centre'. In 1989 he resigned from the National Assembly to play a leading role in the European Parliament.

Gish /gɪʃ/ Lillian. Stage name of Lillian de Guiche 1896– . US film actress, who began her career in silent films. Her most celebrated work was with the American director D W Griffith, including *Way Down East* 1920 and *Orphans of the Storm* 1922, playing virtuous heroines. She later made occasional appearances in character roles, and co-starred with Bette Davis in *The Whales of August* 1987.

Gissing /'gɪsɪŋ/ George (Robert) 1857–1903. English writer, dealing with social issues. Among his books are *New Grub Street* 1891 and the autobiographical *Private Papers of Henry Ryecroft* 1903.

gist /dʒɪst/ *n.* the main substance or essence of a matter. [Old French (*gesir* = lie from Latin *jacēre*)]

git /gɪt/ *n.* (*slang*) a silly or contemptible person. [variant of *get* = fool]

Giulini /dʒuː'liːni/ Carlo Maria 1914– . Italian conductor. Principal conductor at La Scala in Milan 1953–55, and musical director of the Los Angeles Philharmonic 1978–84, he is renowned as an interpreter of Verdi.

Giulio Romano /'dʒuːliəʊ/ *c.*1499–1546. Italian painter and architect. An assistant to Raphael, he developed a Mannerist style, creating effects of exaggerated movement and using rich colours in, for example, the frescoes in the Palazzo del Tè (1526, Mantua).

give /gɪv/ *v.t./i.* (*past* **gave**; *past participle* **given** /'gɪvən/) **1.** to transfer the possession of gratuitously; to cause to receive or have; to supply. **2.** to deliver (a message); to render (a benefit); to assign; to pledge (one's word etc.); to cause to undergo or experience. **3.** to make over in exchange or payment. **4.** to devote, to dedicate. **5.** to utter; to declare (judgement etc.) authoritatively; (*colloquial*) to

tell what one knows. **6.** to perform (an action or effort); to affect with this. **7.** to provide (a meal etc.) as host. **8.** to present or offer (news, a sign etc.); to perform (a play or lecture etc.) in public; (usually in *past participle*) to grant or specify. **9.** to yield as a product or result. **10.** to be the source of. **11.** (of a window or road etc.) to look or lead (*on to, into* etc.). **12.** to lose firmness, to be flexible, to yield when pressed or pulled. —**give and take,** exchange of talk or ideas; willingness to make concessions. **give away,** to transfer as a gift; to hand over (the bride) to the bridegroom at a wedding; to reveal (a secret etc.) unintentionally. **give-away** *n.* (*colloquial*) a thing given as a gift or at a low price; an unintentional disclosure. **give in,** to yield, to acknowledge defeat; to hand in (a document etc.) to the proper official. **give it to,** (*colloquial*) to scold or punish (a person). **give me,** (in *imperative*) I prefer or admire. **given name,** (*US*) a first or Christian name. **give off,** to emit (fumes etc.). **give or take,** (*colloquial*) to accept as a margin of error in estimating. **give out,** to distribute; to announce, to emit; to be exhausted, to run short. **give over,** to devote, to hand over; (*colloquial*) to stop or desist. **give tongue,** to speak one's thoughts; (of hounds) to bark, especially on tracing a scent. **give up,** to cease from effort or activity; to part with; to resign or surrender; to renounce hope (of); to pronounce incurable or insoluble; to deliver (a fugitive etc.) to pursuers etc.; to abandon or addict (*oneself to*). **give way,** to yield under pressure; to give precedence. —**giver** *n.* [Old English]

Giza, El /'giːzə/ or **al-Jizah** the site of the Great Pyramids and Sphinx; a suburb of ◊Cairo, Egypt; population (1983) 1,500,000. It has textile and film industries.

gizzard /'gɪzəd/ *n.* a muscular grinding organ of the digestive tract, below the ◊crop of birds, earthworms, and some insects, and forming part of the ◊stomach. The gizzard of birds is lined with a hardened horny layer of the protein keratin, preventing damage to the muscle layer during the grinding process. Most birds swallow sharp grit which aids maceration of food in the gizzard. [from Old French from Latin *gigeria* = cooked entrails of fowl]

glacé /'glæseɪ/ *adj.* **1.** (of fruit) iced or sugared. **2.** (of cloth etc.) smooth, polished. —**glacé icing,** icing made from icing sugar and water. [French = iced]

glacial /'gleɪʃəl/ *adj.* **1.** of ice; characterized or produced by ice. **2.** cold and forbidding. —**glacial period,** a period when an unusually large area was covered by an ice sheet. —**glacially** *adv.* [French or from Latin *glacies* = ice]

glaciated /'gleɪsɪeɪtɪd/ *adj.* covered with glaciers or an ice sheet; affected by the friction of moving ice. —**glaciation** /-'eɪʃən/ *n.* [from Latin *glaciare* = freeze]

glacier /'glæsɪə(r)/ *n.* a body of ice, originating in mountains in snowfields above the snowline, which traverses land surfaces (glacier flow). It moves slowly down a valley or depression, and is constantly replenished from its source. The scenery produced by the erosive action of glaciers is characteristic and includes U-shaped valleys, ◊corries, ◊arêtes, and various features formed by the deposition of ◊moraine (rocky debris). [French]

glad *adj.* **1.** pleased (usually *predicatively*); expressing or causing pleasure. **2.** ready and willing. **—be glad of,** to find useful. **glad eye,** (*slang*) an amorous glance. **glad hand,** (*colloquial*) a hearty welcome. **glad rags,** (*colloquial*) best clothes. **—gladly** *adv.*, **gladness** *n.* [Old English]

gladden /'glædən/ *v.t.* to make glad.

glade *n.* an open space in a forest.

gladiator /'glædɪeɪtə(r)/ *n.* in ancient Rome, a trained fighter. Gladiators were recruited mainly from slaves, criminals, and prisoners of war, and fought to the death in the arena for the entertainment of spectators. The custom, which originated in the practice of slaughtering slaves on a chieftain's grave, was introduced into Rome from Etruria in 264 BC and continued until the 5th century AD. **—gladiatorial** /-ə'tɔːriəl/ *adj.* [Latin *gladius* = sword]

gladiolus /glædi'əʊləs/ *n.* (*plural* **gladioli** /-laɪ/) a plant of the genus *Gladiolus*, family Iridaceae, with spikes of flowers and sword-shaped leaves springing from a corm. [Latin diminutive of *gladius* = sword]

gladsome *adj.* (*poetic*) cheerful, joyous.

Gladstone /'glædstən/ William Ewart 1809–1898. British Liberal politician, repeatedly prime minister. He entered Parliament as a Tory in 1833 and held ministerial office, but left the party in 1846 and after 1859 identified himself with the Liberals. He was chancellor of the Exchequer 1852–55 and 1859–66, and prime minister 1868–74, 1880–85, 1886, and 1892–94. He introduced elementary education in 1870, vote by secret ballot in 1872 and many reforms in Ireland, although he failed in his efforts to get a Home Rule Bill passed.

All the world over, I will back the masses against the classes.

William Ewart Gladstone

Gladstone bag a hinged bag which opens flat into two approximately equal compartments. [from W E Gladstone]

glair *n.* the white of an egg; a viscous substance made from or resembling this. [from Old French ultimately from Latin *clarus* = clear]

Glamorgan /glə'mɔːgən/ three counties of S Wales – ◊Mid Glamorgan, ◊South Glamorgan, and ◊West Glamorgan – created in 1974 from the former county of Glamorganshire. All are on the Bristol Channel, and the administrative headquarters of Mid and South Glamorgan is Cardiff; the headquarters of West Glamorgan is Swansea. **Mid Glamorgan,** which also takes in a small area of the former county of Monmouthshire to the E, contains the coalmining towns of Aberdare and Merthyr Tydfil, and the Rhondda in the valleys. The mountains are in the northern part of the county; **area** 1,019 sq km/394 sq mi; **population** (1983) 536,400. In **South Glamorgan,** there is mixed farming in the fertile Vale of Glamorgan, and towns include Cardiff, Penarth, and Barry; **area** 416 sq km/161 sq mi; **population** (1983) 391,700. **West Glamorgan** includes Swansea, with tin-plating and copper industries, Margam, with large steel rolling mills, Port Talbot, and Neath; **area** 815 sq km/315 sq mi; **population** (1983) 366,600.

glamorize /'glæməraɪz/ *v.t.* to make glamorous or attractive.

glamour /'glæmə/ *n.* **1.** alluring beauty. **2.** attractive and exciting qualities. **—glamorous** *adj.* [variant of *grammar* in obsolete sense 'magic']

glance /glɑːns/ *v.t./i.* **1.** to look briefly. **2.** to strike at an angle and glide *off* an object. **3.** (usually with *at*) to refer briefly or indirectly to (a subject). **4.** (of a light etc.) to flash or dart. **—n. 1.** a brief look. **2.** a flash or gleam. **3.** a glancing stroke in cricket. [probably from Old French *glacier* = to slip]

gland *n.* a specialized organ of the body that manufactures and secretes enzymes, hormones, or other chemicals. In animals, glands vary in size from small (for example, tear glands) to large (for example, the pancreas), but in plants they are always small, and may consist of a single cell. Some glands discharge their products internally like ◊endocrine glands, and others such as ◊exocrine glands, externally. Lymph nodes are sometimes wrongly called glands. [from French from Latin *glandulae* = throat glands]

glanders /'glændəz/ *n.pl.* a contagious disease of horses and related animals. [from Old French *glandre*]

glandular /'glændjʊlə/ *adj.* of a gland or glands. [from French]

glandular fever or **infectious mononucleosis** a viral disease characterized at onset by fever and painfully swollen lymph nodes (in the neck); there may also be digestive upset, sore throat, and skin rashes. Lassitude persists for months and even years, and recovery is often very slow. It is caused by the Epstein-Barr virus.

glare /gleə/ *v.i.* **1.** to look fiercely or fixedly. **2.** to shine oppressively. **—n. 1.** a fierce or fixed look. **2.** an oppressive light; tawdry brilliance. [from Middle Dutch or Middle Low German]

glaring *adj.* **1.** shining oppressively. **2.** obvious or conspicuous. **—glaringly** *adv.*

Glaser /'gleɪzə/ Donald Arthur 1926– . US physicist, who invented the ◊bubble chamber in 1952, for which he received the Nobel Prize for Physics in 1960.

Glasgow /'glæzgəʊ/ city and administrative headquarters of Strathclyde, Scotland; population (1985) 734,000. Industries include engineering, chemicals, printing, and distilling.

Glashow /'glæʃəʊ/ Sheldon Lee 1932– . US physicist who as an elementary particle physicist at Harvard, has made major contributions to the understanding of ◊quarks. In 1964 he proposed the existence of a fourth 'charmed' quark, and later argued that quarks must be coloured. Insights gained from these theoretical studies enabled Glashow to consider ways in which some of the fundamental forces of nature (the weak nuclear force and the electromagnetic force) could be unified as a single force now called **electroweak** force. For this work he shared the Nobel Prize for Physics with Abdus Salem and Steven Weinberg.

glasnost /'glæznɒst/ *n.* Soviet leader Mikhail ◊Gorbachev's policy of liberalizing various aspects of Soviet life, such as introducing greater freedom of expression and information, and opening up relations with Western countries. [Russian = openness]

glass /glɑːs/ *n.* **1.** a hard, usually brittle and transparent substance, physically neither a solid nor a liquid, made by fusing sand with soda or potash and other ingredients; a substance of similar properties, e. g. fibreglass. **2.** glass utensils, ornaments, windows, greenhouses etc. **3.** an object made (partly) of glass; a glass drinking vessel or its contents; a mirror; a lens; a barometer. **4.** (in *plural*) spectacles, binoculars. **—v.t.** to fit with glass. **glass-blowing** *n.* shaping semi-molten glass by blowing air into it through a tube. **glass-cloth** *n.* a cloth for drying glasses. **glass fibre,** a fabric made from or plastic reinforced by glass filaments. **glasspaper** *n.* paper coated with glass particles, for smoothing or polishing. **glass wool,** a mass of fine glass fibres for packing and insulation. **volcanic glass,** ◊obsidian. [Old English]

Glass Philip 1937– . US composer. As a student of Nadia ◊Boulanger, he was strongly influenced by Indian music; his work is characterized by repeated rhythmic figures that are continually expanded and modified. His compositions include the operas *Einstein on the Beach* 1975, *Akhnaten* 1984, and *The Making of the Representative for Planet 8* 1988.

Glasse /glɑːs/ Hannah 1708–1770. British cookery writer whose *The Art of Cookery made Plain and Easy* 1747 is regarded as the first classic recipe book in Britain.

glasshouse *n.* **1.** a greenhouse. **2.** (*slang*) a military prison.

glass lizard another name for ◊glass snake.

glass snake or **glass lizard** any of a worldwide genus *Ophisaurus* of legless lizards of the family Anguidae. Their tails are up to three times the head-body length and are easily broken off.

glassware *n.* articles made of glass.

glassy *adj.* **1.** like glass. **2.** (of the eye or expression) dull and fixed. **—glassily** *adv.*, **glassiness** *n.*

Glaswegian /glæz'wiːdʒən/ *adj.* of Glasgow, a city in western Scotland. **—n.** a native of Glasgow.

Glauber /'glaʊbə/ Johann 1604–1668. German chemist who made his living selling patent medicines, and is remembered for his discovery of the salt known variously as 'sal mirabile' and 'Glauber's salt'.

Glauber's salt /'glaʊbəz/ in chemistry, crystalline sodium sulphate decahydrate, $Na_2SO_4.10H_2O$, which melts at 31°C; the latent heat stored as it solidifies makes it a convenient thermal energy store. It is used in medicine.

glaucoma /glɔ:'kəʊmə/ n. a condition caused by increased pressure of the fluid within the eyeball, causing weakening or loss of sight. [Latin from Greek *glaukos* = greyish-blue]

glaucophane n. a blue amphibole, $Na_2(Mg,Fe,Al)_5 Si_8O_{22}(OH)_2$. Its typical occurrence is in glaucophane schists (blue schists), which are formed from the ocean floor basalt under metamorphic conditions of high pressure and low temperature; these conditions are believed to exist in subduction systems associated with destructive plate boundaries (see ◊plate tectonics), and so the occurrence of glaucophane schists can indicate the location of such boundaries in geological history.

glaze v.t./i. 1. to fit or cover with glass. 2. to coat with a glossy surface. 3. to cover (the eye) with a film. 4. to become glassy. —n. 1. a vitreous substance for glazing pottery. 2. a smooth, shiny coating on materials or food. 3. a coat of transparent paint to modify an underlying tone. 4. a surface formed by glazing.

glazier /'gleɪzɪə/ n. a person who glazes windows etc. professionally.

GLC abbreviation of Greater London Council (1963–86).

gleam n. 1. a subdued or transient light. 2. a faint or momentary show (*of* humour, hope etc.). —v.i. to emit gleams. [Old English]

glean v.t./i. 1. to acquire (facts etc.) in small amounts. 2. to gather (corn left by reapers). —**gleaner** n. [from Old French *glener*, probably from Celtic]

gleanings n.pl. things gleaned.

glebe /gli:b/ n. a portion of land going with a benefice and providing revenue. [from Latin *gl(a)eba* = clod, soil]

glee n. 1. lively or triumphant joy. 2. a part song for three or more (usually male) voices. —**glee club**, a society for singing part songs. [Old English]

gleeful adj. joyful. —**gleefully** adv.

glen n. a narrow valley. [from Gaelic and Irish]

Glendower /glen'daʊə/ Owen c.1359–c.1416. Welsh nationalist leader of a successful revolt against the English in N Wales, who defeated Henry IV in three campaigns 1400–02, although Wales was reconquered 1405–13. Glendower disappeared in 1416 after some years of guerrilla warfare.

Glendower, Sons of (*Meibion Glyndwr*) a Welsh guerrilla group, active from 1979, aiming for self-government and the compulsory introduction of the Welsh language. It is named after Owen Glendower.

glengarry /glen'gærɪ/ n. a kind of Highland cap with a pointed front. [from *Glengarry* in Scotland]

Glenn /glen/ John (Herschel) 1921– . US astronaut and politician. On 20 Feb 1962, he became the first American to orbit the Earth, three times in the Mercury spacecraft Friendship 7, in a flight lasting 4 hr 55 min. After retiring from ◊NASA, he was elected to the US Senate as a Democrat from Ohio 1974; re-elected 1980 and 1986. He unsuccessfully sought the Democratic presidential nomination in 1984.

glib adj. fluent but insincere. —**glibly** adv., **glibness** n. [related to obsolete *glibbery* = slippery]

glide v.t./i. 1. to move smoothly and continuously; to pass gradually or imperceptibly. 2. to fly in a glider or (of aircraft) without engine-power. —n. a gliding movement. —**glide path**, an aircraft's line of descent to land, especially as indicated by ground radar. [Old English]

glider /'glaɪdə/ n. a fixed-wing aircraft that is not power-driven when in flight.

gliding n. the art of using air currents to fly unpowered aircraft. Technically, gliding involves the gradual loss of altitude; gliders designed for soaring flight (utilizing air rising up a cliff face or hill, warm air rising as a 'thermal' above sun-heated ground, and so on) are known as sailplanes. The sport of ◊hang gliding was developed in the 1970s.

gliding tone a musical tone, continuously rising or falling in pitch between preset notes, produced by a synthesizer.

glimmer n. 1. a faint or intermittent light. 2. (also **glimmering**) a gleam (*of* hope etc.). —v.i. to shine faintly or intermittently. [probably from Scandinavian]

glimpse n. a brief view (*of*); a faint, transient appearance. —v.t. to have a brief view of. [corresponds to Middle High German *glimsen*]

Glinka /'glɪŋkə/ Mikhail Ivanovich 1804–1857. Russian composer. He broke away from the prevailing Italian influence and turned to Russian folk music as the inspiration for his opera *A Life for the Tsar* (originally *Ivan Susanin*) 1836. His later works include another opera, *Ruslan and Lyudmila* 1842, and the orchestral *Kamarinskaya* 1848.

glint v.i. to flash, to glitter. —n. a brief flash of light. [probably from Scandinavian]

glissade /gli'sɑ:d, -'seɪd/ v.i. 1. to make a controlled slide down a snow slope in mountaineering. 2. to make a gliding step in a dance. —n. a glissading movement or step. [French *glisser* = slide, slip]

glissando n. in music, a rapid, uninterrupted scale produced by sliding the finger across the keys or strings.

glisten /'glɪsən/ v.i. to shine like a wet or polished surface; to glitter, to sparkle. —n. glistening. [Old English]

glitter v.i. 1. to sparkle. 2. to be showy or splendid. —n. a sparkle. [from Old Norse]

gloaming n. the evening twilight. [Old English, related to *glow*]

gloat v.i. to look or ponder with greedy or malicious pleasure (*over* etc.). —n. the act of gloating. [perhaps related to Old Norse *glotta* = grin]

global /'gləʊbəl/ adj. 1. worldwide. 2. all-embracing. —**globally** adv. [French]

globe n. a spherical object, especially the Earth, or a representation of it with a map on its surface; a thing shaped like this, e. g. a lampshade or a fish bowl. —**globefish** n. or ◊puffer fish a fish of the family Tetraodontidae, that inflates itself into a globe form. **globeflower** n. a plant of the genus *Trollius*, with spherical, usually yellow, flowers. **globetrotter** n. one who travels widely. **globetrotting** n. such travel. [French or from Latin *globus*]

Globe Theatre a London theatre, octagonal and open to the sky, near Bankside, Southwark, where many of Shakespeare's plays were performed by Richard Burbage and his company. Built in 1599 by Cuthbert Burbage, it was burned down in 1613 after a cannon, fired during a performance of Henry VIII, set light to the thatch. It was rebuilt in 1614 but pulled down in 1644. The site was rediscovered in Oct 1989 near the remains of the contemporaneous Rose Theatre.

globular /'glɒbjʊlə/ adj. 1. globe-shaped. 2. composed of globules.

globular cluster a spherical ◊star cluster of between 10,000 and a million stars. More than a hundred globular clusters are distributed in a spherical halo around our Galaxy. They consist of old stars, formed early in our Galaxy's history. Globular clusters are also found around other galaxies.

globule /'glɒbju:l/ n. a small globe or round particle, a drop. [French or from Latin *globulus*]

globulin /'glɒbjʊlɪn/ n. a protein found usually associated with albumin in animal and plant tissues.

glockenspiel /'glɒkənspi:l/ n. a percussion instrument formed from a set of tuned metal bars each supported at two points but with both ends free and struck in the centre with small hand-held hammers. [German = bell-play]

glomerulus n. in the kidney, the blood capillaries responsible for forming the fluid that passes down the tubules and ultimately becomes urine. In the human kidney there are approximately one million tubules, each possessing its own glomerulus.

gloom n. 1. semi-darkness. 2. a feeling of sadness and depression. —v.t./i. to make, look, or be gloomy.

gloomy adj. 1. dark or dim. 2. depressed; depressing. —**gloomily** adv., **gloominess** n. [from obsolete *gloom* = a frown]

glorify /'glɔ:rɪfaɪ/ v.t. 1. to praise highly. 2. to worship with adoration and praise. 3. to make seem more splendid than it is. —**glorification** /-'keɪʃən/ n. [from Old French from Latin]

glorious /'glɔ:rɪəs/ adj. 1. possessing or conferring glory. 2. splendid, illustrious; excellent (often *ironic*). —**gloriously** adv. [from Anglo-French]

Glorious Revolution in British history the events surrounding the removal of James II from the throne and his replacement by Mary (daughter of Charles I) and William of Orange as joint sovereigns in 1689. James had become increasingly unpopular on account of his unconstitutional behaviour and Catholicism. Various elements in England, including seven prominent politicians, plotted to invite the Protestant William to invade. Arriving at Torbay on 5 Nov 1688, William rapidly gained support and James was allowed to flee to France after the army deserted him. William and Mary then accepted a new constitutional settlement, the Bill of Rights 1689, which assured the ascendency of parliamentary power over sovereign rule.

glory /'glɔːrɪ/ n. 1. fame and honour. 2. adoration and praise in worship. 3. resplendent beauty, magnificence etc.; an exalted or prosperous state. 4. a thing that brings renown, a special distinction. 5. the halo of a saint etc. —v.i. to take great pride (in). —**glory hole**, (slang) an untidy room or cupboard etc. **go to glory**, (slang) to die, to be destroyed. [from Old French from Latin gloria]

Glos. abbreviation of Gloucestershire.

gloss[1] n. 1. the lustre of a surface. 2. a deceptively attractive appearance. —v.t. to make glossy. —**gloss over**, to seek to conceal. **gloss paint**, paint giving a glossy finish.

gloss[2] n. an explanatory comment added to a text, e. g. in the margin; a comment or paraphrase. —v.t./i. to make such a comment; to add a comment to (a text or word etc.). [from Old French from Latin glossa = tongue from Greek]

glossary /'glɒsərɪ/ n. a dictionary or list of technical or special words; a collection of glosses. [from Latin]

glossy adj. having a gloss, shiny. —**glossily** adv., **glossiness** n.

glottal /'glɒtəl/ adj. of the glottis. —**glottal stop**, the sound produced by the sudden opening or shutting of the glottis.

glottis /'glɒtɪs/ n. the opening at the upper end of the windpipe between the vocal cords. [from Greek glōtta variant of glōssa = tongue]

Gloucester /'glɒstə/ n. a cheese made in Gloucestershire (now usually **double Gloucester**, originally a richer kind). [from Gloucester city in SW England]

Gloucester Richard Alexander Walter George, Duke of 1944– . Prince of the UK. Grandson of ◊George V, he succeeded his father to the dukedom owing to the death of his elder brother Prince William (1941–1972) in an air crash. In 1972 he married Birgitte van Deurs, daughter of a Danish lawyer. His heir is his son Alexander, Earl of Ulster (1974–).

Gloucestershire /'glɒstəʃə/ county in SW England; **area** 2,640 sq km/1,019 sq mi; **administrative headquarters** Gloucester; **products** cereals, fruit, dairy products; engineering, coal in the Forest of Dean; **population** (1987) 522,000.

glove /glʌv/ n. a hand covering, usually with separate fingers, for protection, warmth etc.; a boxing glove. v.t. to cover or provide with a glove or gloves. —**with the gloves off**, arguing or contending in earnest. [Old English]

glove box a protective device used when handling toxic, radioactive, or sterile materials within an enclosure containing a window for viewing. Gloves fixed to ports in the walls of a box allow manipulation of objects within the box. The risk that the operator might inhale fine airborne particles of poisonous materials is removed by maintaining a vacuum inside the box, so that any airflow is inwards.

glover /'glʌvə/ n. a glove-maker.

glow /gləʊ/ v.i. 1. to emit light and heat without flame. 2. to shine like a thing intensely heated; to show a warm colour. 3. to burn with or indicate bodily heat or fervour. —n. a glowing state; warmth of colour; ardour. [Old English]

glower /'glaʊə/ v.i. to look angrily (at).

glow-worm n. the wingless female of various luminous beetles in the family Lampyridae. The luminous organs situated under the abdomen usually serve to attract winged males for mating. There are about 2,000 species, distributed throughout the tropics, Europe, and N Asia.

gloxinia /glɒk'sɪnɪə/ n. an American tropical plant of the genus Gloxinia, with bell-shaped flowers. [from B P Gloxin, 18th-century German botanist]

Gluck /glʊk/ Christoph Willibald von 1714–1787. German composer who settled in Vienna as Kapellmeister to Maria Theresa in 1754. In 1762 his Orfeo ed Euridice/Orpheus and Eurydice revolutionized the 18th-century conception of opera by giving free scope to dramatic effect. Orfeo was followed by Alceste/Alcestis 1767 and Paride ed Elena/Paris and Helen 1770.

glucose /'glu:kəʊs, -əʊz/ n. $C_6H_{12}O_6$, a type of sugar or carbohydrate also known as **grape sugar** or **dextrose**. It is present in the blood, and is found in honey and fruit juices. It is a source of energy for the body, being produced from other sugars and starches to form the 'energy currency' of many biochemical reactions also involving ◊ATP. [French from Greek gleukos = sweet wine (glukus = sweet)]

glue /glu:/ n. a sticky substance used as an adhesive. —v.t. 1. to attach with glue. 2. to hold closely. —**gluey** adj. [from Old French from Latin gluten]

glue-sniffing n. or **solvent misuse** inhalation of the fumes from organic solvents of the type found in paints, lighter fuel, and glue, for their hallucinatory effects. Solvents are addictive and can damage the user's liver, heart, and lungs. It is believed that solvents produce hallucinations by dissolving the cell membrane of brain cells, thus altering the way the cells conduct electrical impulses.

glum adj. dejected, sullen. —**glumly** adv., **glumness** n. [related to dialect glum v. = frown, variant of gloom]

gluon n. a type of ◊elementary particle.

glut v.t. (-tt-) 1. to satisfy fully with food; to sate. 2. to overstock (a market). —n. an excessive supply. [probably from Old French gloutir = swallow from Latin]

glutamate /'glu:təmeɪt/ n. a salt or ester of glutamic acid, especially the sodium salt used to flavour food.

glutamic acid /glu:'tæmɪk/ an amino acid normally found in proteins.

gluten /'glu:tən/ n. 1. the viscous part of flour left when the starch is removed. 2. a viscous animal secretion. [French from Latin = glue]

glutinous /'glu:tɪnəs/ adj. sticky, gluelike, viscous. [from French or Latin]

glutton /'glʌtən/ n. 1. an excessive eater; a person insatiably eager (for work etc.). 2. the ◊wolverine. —**gluttonous** adj. [from Old French from Latin gluttire = swallow]

gluttony /'glʌtənɪ/ n. the character or conduct of a glutton.

glyceride /'glɪsəraɪd/ n. an ◊ester formed between one or more acids and glycerol (propan-1,2,3-triol). A glyceride is termed mono-, di-, or triglyceride, depending on the number of hydroxyl groups from the glycerol that have reacted with the acids. Glycerides, mainly triglycerides, occur naturally as esters of ◊fatty acids in animal and plant oils and fats.

glycerine /'glɪsərɪn/ n. common name for glycerol, or **trihydroxypropane**, $HOCH_2CH(OH)CH_2OH$, a thick, colourless, odourless, sweetish liquid. It is obtained from vegetable and animal oils and fats (by treatment with acid, alkali, superheated steam, or an enzyme), or by fermentation of glucose, and is used in the manufacture of high explosives, in antifreeze solutions, to maintain moist conditions in fruits and tobacco, and in cosmetics. [from French from Greek glukeros = sweet]

glycerol n. another name for ◊glycerine.

glycine n. $CH_2(NH_2)COOH$, the simplest amino acid, and one of the main components of proteins. When purified, it is a sweet, colourless, crystalline compound.

glycogen n. a polymer `(a polysaccharide) of the sugar ◊glucose made and retained in the liver as a carbohydrate store, for which reason it is sometimes called animal starch. It is a source of energy for muscles, where it is converted back into glucose by the hormone ◊insulin and metabolized.

glycol n. (technical name **dihydroxyethane**) thick, colourless, odourless, sweetish liquid also called ethylene glycol or ethanediol $(CH_2OH)_2$. Glycol is used in antifreeze solutions, in the preparation of ethers and esters (used for explosives), as a solvent, and as a substitute for glycerine.

Glyndebourne /'glaɪndbɔːn/ site of an opera house in East Sussex, England, established in 1934 by John Christie (1882–1962). Operas are staged at an annual summer festival and a touring company is also based there.

gm abbreviation of gram(s).

G-man /'dʒiː'mæn/ n. (US slang) a federal criminal investigation officer. [from Government and man]

GMT abbreviation of Greenwich Mean Time.

gnarled /nɑːld/ *adj.* (of a tree, hands etc.) knobbly, rugged, twisted.

gnash /næʃ/ *v.t./i.* to grind (one's teeth); (of the teeth) to strike together. [from Old Norse]

gnat /næt/ *n.* a small, biting fly of genus *Culex* and the family Culicidae, to which the mosquito also belongs. The eggs are laid in water, where they hatch into worm-like larvae, which pass through a pupal stage to emerge as adult insects. Species include **Culex pipiens**, abundant in England; **Anopheles maculipennis**, the carrier of malaria; and **Aedes aegypti**, which transmits yellow fever. [Old English]

gnaw /nɔː/ *v.t./i.* (*past tense* **gnawed** or **gnawn**) 1. to bite persistently. 2. (of a destructive agent) to corrode or consume. 3. (of pain etc.) to hurt continuously. [Old English]

gneiss /naɪs, gnaɪs/ *n.* a coarse-grained ◊metamorphic rock, formed under conditions of increasing temperature and pressure, and often occurring in association with schists and granites. It has a foliated, laminated structure, consisting of thin bands of micas and amphiboles alternating with granular bands of quartz and feldspar. Gneisses are formed during regional metamorphism; **paragneisses** are derived from sedimentary rocks and **orthogneisses** from igneous rocks. Garnets are often found in gneiss. [German]

gnome /nəʊm/ *n.* 1. a kind of dwarf in fairy tales, living underground and guarding the treasures of the Earth. 2. a figure of such, a dwarf as a garden ornament. 3. (in *plural*) persons (especially financiers) with secret influence. [French from Latin *gnomus* (word invented by Paracelsus)]

gnomic /'nəʊmɪk/ *adj.* of maxims, sententious. [from Greek *gnōmē* = opinion]

gnomon /'nəʊmən/ *n.* the rod or pin etc. of a sundial, showing the time by its shadow. [French or from Latin from Greek = indicator]

gnostic /'nɒstɪk/ *adj.* 1. of knowledge. 2. having special mystical knowledge. [from Latin from Greek *gnōsis* = knowledge]

Gnosticism *n.* an esoteric cult of divine knowledge (a synthesis of Christianity, Greek philosophy, Hinduism, Buddhism, and the mystery cults of the Mediterranean), which flourished during the second and third centuries and was a rival to, and influence on, early Christianity. The medieval French ◊Cathar heresy and the modern *Mandean* sect (in S Iraq) descend from Gnosticism. **Gnostic** adj. of the Gnostics or Gnosticism. —**Gnostic** *n.* an adherent of Gnosticism.

GNP abbreviation of Gross National Product.

gnu /nuː/ *n.* an oxlike antelope of the genus *Connochaetes*, also called a wildebeest, with a cow-like face, a beard, and mane, and heavy curved horns in both sexes. The body is up to 1.3 m/4.2 ft at the shoulder and slopes away to the hindquarters. [ultimately from Kaffir]

go[1] /gəʊ/ *v.i.* (*past* **went**; *past participle* **gone** /gɒn/; *participle* **going**) 1. to begin to move, to be moving from one position or point in time to another; (with *participle*) to make a trip for (a specified purpose). 2. to lie or extend in a certain direction. 3. to be functioning, moving etc. 4. to make a specified motion or sound. 5. to be in a specified state, habitually or for a time; to pass into a specified condition, to escape *free, unnoticed* etc. 6. (of time or a distance) to pass, to be traversed. 7. to be regularly kept or put, to belong; to fit, to be able to be put. 8. (of a number) to be contained in another, especially without a remainder. 9. to be current; to be on the average. 10. to fare, (of events) to turn out; to take a certain course or views. 11. to have a specified form or wording. 12. to be successful; (*colloquial*) to be acceptable or permitted, to be accepted without question. 13. to be sold. 14. (of money or supplies etc.) to be spent or used up. 15. to be relinquished or abolished. 16. to fail or decline; to give way, to collapse. 17. to die. 18. to be allotted or awarded. 19. to contribute, to tend, to extend, to reach. 20. to carry an action or commitment to a certain point. 21. (in *imperative, colloquial* or *US*) to proceed to. —*n.* 1. animation, dash. 2. a turn or try; an attack *of* an illness; a portion served at one time. 3. a success. 4. (*colloquial*) vigorous activity. 5. (*colloquial*) a state of affairs. —*adj.* (*colloquial*) functioning properly. —**go ahead,** to proceed immediately. **go-ahead** *n.* permission to proceed; (*adj.*) enterprising. **go along with,** to agree with. **go and,** (*colloquial*) to be so unwise etc. as to. **go back on,** to fail to keep (a promise etc.). **go-between**

n. an intermediary. **go by,** to be dependent on; to be guided by. **go-cart** *n.* a simple four-wheeled structure for a child to play on. **go down,** to descend or sink; to be swallowed; to be written down; to leave university; to find acceptance (*with*); to become ill (*with* a disease). **go for,** to like, to prefer, to choose; to pass or be accounted as (*little* etc.); (*slang*) to attack. **go-getter** *n.* (*colloquial*) a pushful enterprising person. **go-go** *adj.* (*colloquial*) very active or energetic. **go-go dancer,** a performer of lively erotic dances at a night-club, etc. **go in for,** to compete or engage in. **go into,** to become a member of (a profession etc.) or a patient in (a hospital, etc.); to investigate (a matter). **go a long way,** to have much effect *towards*; (of supplies) to last long; (of money) to buy much. **go off,** to explode; to deteriorate; to fall asleep; (of an event) to proceed *well* etc.; to begin to dislike. **go on,** to continue (*doing*); to persevere (*with*); to talk at great length; to proceed next *to do*; (*colloquial*) to nag (*at*). **go on** or **upon,** to judge by, to base conclusions on. **go out,** to be extinguished; to go to social functions; to be broadcast; to cease to be fashionable; (*US colloquial*) to lose consciousness; (of the heart etc.) to feel sympathy. **go round,** to be large enough or sufficient. **go slow,** to work at a deliberately slow pace as an industrial protest. **go-slow** *n.* such action. **go through,** to examine or revise; to perform or undergo; to spend or use up (money or supplies). **go through with,** to complete (an undertaking). **go to,** to attend (a school, church etc.). **go under,** to succumb, to fail. **go up,** to rise in price; to explode, to burn; to enter university. **go with,** to match or suit, to harmonize or belong with. **go without,** to abstain from, to tolerate the lack (of). **on the go,** (*colloquial*) in constant motion, active. [Old English; *went* originally past of *wend*]

go[2] *n.* a Japanese board game of territorial possession, played on a board of 18 × 18 squares, each player having about 200 pieces. [Japanese]

Goa /'gəʊə/ state of India; **area** 3,700 sq km/1,428 sq mi; **capital** Panaji; **population** (1981) 1,003,000; **history** captured by the Portuguese 1510; the inland area added in the 18th century. Goa was incorporated into India as a Union Territory with Daman and Diu in 1961 and became a state in 1987.

goad *n.* 1. a spiked stick for urging cattle. 2. a thing that torments or incites. —*v.t.* to urge with a goad. 2. to irritate; to drive or stimulate (*into* action etc.). [Old English]

goal *n.* 1. a structure into or through which a ball is to be driven in certain games. 2. a point or points scored thus. 3. an objective; a destination; the point where a race ends. —**goal line,** a line forming the end boundary of a field of play. **goal post,** either of the pair of posts marking the limits of a goal. [perhaps obsolete *gol* = boundary]

goalie /'gəʊlɪ/ *n.* (*colloquial*) a goalkeeper.

goalkeeper *n.* a player defending the goal.

goat *n.* 1. a ruminant mammal, genus *Capra*, family Bovidae, closely related to the sheep. Both males and females have horns and beards and are sure-footed. 2. the Goat, the constellation or sign of the zodiac Capricorn. 3. a licentious man. 4. (*colloquial*) a foolish person. —**get a person's goat,** (*slang*) to annoy him. [Old English]

goatee /gəʊ'tiː/ *n.* a small, pointed beard like a goat's.

goatherd *n.* one who tends goats.

goatsucker *n.* the ◊nightjar.

gob[1] *n.* (*slang*) the mouth. —**gobstopper** *n.* a large, hard sweet for sucking. [perhaps from Gaelic and Irish = beak, mouth]

gob[2] *n.* (*vulgar*) a clot of a slimy substance. [from Old French *go(u)be* = mouthful]

gobbet /'gɒbɪt/ *n.* an extract from a text, set for translation or comment. [from Old French *gobet*]

Gobbi /'gɒbi/ Tito 1913–1984. Italian baritone singer renowned for his opera characterizations of Figaro, Scarpia, and Iago.

gobble[1] *v.t./i.* to eat hurriedly and noisily.

gobble[2] *v.i.* 1. (of a turkey cock) to make a gurgling sound in the throat. 2. to speak thus.

gobbledegook /'gɒbəldɪguːk/ *n.* (*slang*) pompous or unintelligible official or professional jargon. [imitation of noise of turkey cock]

Gobelins /'gəʊbəlæŋ/ *n.* French tapestry factory, originally founded as a dyeworks in Paris by Gilles and Jean Gobelin about 1450. The firm began to produce tapestries in the 16th century, and in 1662 the establishment was bought by Colbert for Louis XIV. With the support of the French government, it continues to make tapestries.

Gobi /'gəubi/ Asian desert divided between the Mongolian People's Republic and Inner Mongolia, China; 800 km/500 mi N–S, and 1,600 km/1,000 mi E–W. It is rich in fossil remains of extinct species.

Gobind Singh /'gəubind 'sɪŋ/ 1666–1708. Indian religious leader, the tenth and last guru (teacher) of Sikhism, 1675–1708, and founder of the Sikh brotherhood known as the ◊Khalsa. On his death, the Sikh holy book, the *Guru Granth Sahib*, replaced the line of human gurus as the teacher and guide of the Sikh community.

goblet /'gɒblɪt/ *n.* a drinking vessel, especially of glass, with a foot and stem. [from Old French *gobel* = cup]

goblet cell a specialized ◊epithelial cell occurring in the alimentary canal. Goblet cells secrete mucus, a slimy material which covers the wall of the gut and prevents it from damage.

goblin /'gɒblɪn/ *n.* a mischievous, ugly demon in folklore. [from Latin *Gobelinus* name of spirit related to German *kobold* = demon in mines]

goby /'gəubi/ *n.* a small fish of the genus *Gobius*, with the ventral fins joined to form a disc or sucker. [from Latin *gōbius* from Greek *kōbios* = gudgeon]

god *n.* **1.** a superhuman being worshipped as having power over nature and human affairs. **2.** God, the supreme being, creator and ruler of the universe in the Christian and other monotheistic religions. **3.** an image of a god, an idol. **4.** a person or thing greatly admired or adored. —**the gods,** (*colloquial*) the gallery of a theatre. **God-fearing** *adj.* earnestly religious. **God forbid,** may it not be so. **Godforsaken** *adj.* dismal, wretched. **God knows,** we (or I) cannot know. **God Save the King** *or* **Queen,** the British national anthem. **God willing,** if circumstances allow. [Old English]

Godard /'gɒdɑː/ Jean-Luc 1930– . French film director, one of the leaders of ◊New Wave cinema, whose works are often characterized by experimental editing techniques, and an unconventional dramatic form. His films include *A bout de souffle* 1960, *Weekend* 1968, and *Je vous salue, Marie* 1985.

godchild *n.* a child or person in relation to a godparent or godparents.

Goddard /'gɒdəd/ Robert Hutchings 1882–1945. US rocket pioneer. His first liquid-fuelled rocket was launched at Auburn, Massachusetts, USA, in March 1926. By 1935 his rockets had gyroscopic control and carried cameras to record instrument readings. Two years later a Goddard rocket gained the world altitude record with an ascent of 3 km/1.9 mi.

goddaughter *n.* a female godchild.

goddess /'gɒdɪs/ *n. fem.* **1.** a female deity. **2.** an adored woman.

godetia /gə'diː ʃə/ *n.* a showy-flowered hardy annual of the genus *Godetia*. [from C H *Godet*, Swiss botanist (died 1879)]

godfather *n.* **1.** a male godparent. **2.** a person directing an illegal organization.

godhead *n.* **1.** divine nature, deity. **2. the Godhead,** God.

Godiva /gə'daɪvə/ Lady *c.*1040–1080. Wife of Leofric, Earl of Mercia (died 1057). Legend has it that her husband promised to reduce the heavy taxes on the people of Coventry if she rode naked through the streets at noon. The grateful citizens remained indoors as she did so, but 'Peeping Tom' bored a hole in his shutters and was struck blind. Leofric founded a Benedictine monastery at Coventry, England, where she is buried.

godless *adj.* not believing in God or a god; impious, wicked. —**godlessly** *adv.*, **godlessness** *n.*

godlike *adj.* like God or a god.

godly *adj.* pious, devout. —**godliness** *n.*

godmother *n.* a female godparent.

godown /gə'daʊn/ *n.* a warehouse in eastern Asia, especially in India. [from Portuguese from Malay]

godparent *n.* a person who sponsors another (especially a child) at baptism.

godsend *n.* a piece of unexpected good luck having a decisive effect, a useful or effective acquisition.

godson *n.* a male godchild.

Godspeed *n.* an expression of good wishes to a person starting a journey.

Godthaab /'gɒdhɔːb/ (Greenlandic *Nuuk*) capital and largest town of Greenland; population (1982) 9,700. It is a storage centre for oil and gas, and the chief industry is fish processing.

Godunov /'gɒdənɒv/ Boris 1552–1605. Tsar of Russia from 1598. He was assassinated by a pretender to the throne. The legend that has grown up around this forms the basis of Pushkin's play *Boris Godunov* 1831 and Mussorgsky's opera of the same name 1874.

Godwin /'gɒdwɪn/ Earl of Wessex from 1020. He secured the succession to the throne in 1042 of ◊Edward the Confessor, to whom he married his daughter Edith, and whose chief minister he became. King Harold II was his son.

Godwin William 1756–1836. English philosopher, novelist, and father of Mary Shelley. His *Enquiry concerning Political Justice* 1793 advocated an anarchic society based on a faith in people's essential rationality. At first a Nonconformist minister, he later became an atheist. His first wife was Mary ◊Wollstonecraft.

godwit *n.* a wading bird of the genus *Limosa*, like the curlew but with a straight or slightly upcurved bill.

Goebbels /'gɜːbəlz/ Paul Josef 1897–1945. German Nazi leader who was born in the Rhineland, became a journalist, joined the Nazi party in its early days, and was given control of its propaganda in 1929. As minister of propaganda from 1933, he brought all cultural and educational activities under Nazi control and built up sympathetic movements abroad to carry on the 'war of nerves' against Hitler's intended victims. On the capture of Berlin by the Allies, he poisoned himself.

Goehr /gɜː/ (Peter) Alexander 1932– . British composer, born in Berlin. A lyrical but often hard-edged serialist, he nevertheless usually remained within the forms of the symphony and traditional chamber works, and more recently turned to tonal and even Neo-Baroque models.

Goeppert-Mayer /'gəupətmaɪə/ Maria 1906–1972. German-born US physicist who worked mainly on the structure of the atomic nucleus. She shared the 1963 Nobel Prize for Physics with Eugene ◊Wigner and Hans Jensen (1907–1973).

goer /'gəuə/ *n.* **1.** a person or thing that goes. **2.** a lively or persevering person. **3.** in combinations a regular attender.

Goering /'gɜːrɪŋ/ (German *Göring* Hermann Wilhelm) 1893–1946. Nazi leader, German field marshal from 1938. He was part of Hitler's inner circle, and with Hitler's rise to power in 1933, he established the Gestapo and concentration camps. Appointed successor to Hitler in 1939, he built a vast economic empire in occupied Europe, but later lost favour and was expelled from the party in 1945. Tried at Nuremberg for war crimes, he poisoned himself before he could be executed.

Goes /xuːs/ Hugo van der, died 1482. Flemish painter, chiefly active in Ghent. His *Portinari altarpiece* about 1475 (Uffizi, Florence) is a huge oil painting of the Nativity, full of symbolism and naturalistic detail, and the *Death of the Virgin* about 1480 (Musée Communale des Beaux Arts, Bruges) is remarkable for the varied expressions on the faces of the apostles.

Goethe /'gɜːtə/ Johann Wolfgang von 1749–1832. German poet, novelist, and dramatist, generally considered the founder of modern German literature, and leader of the Romantic ◊Sturm und Drang movement. His works include the autobiographical *Die Leiden des Jungen Werthers/The Sorrows of the Young Werther* 1774 and *Faust* 1808, his masterpiece. A visit to Italy 1786–88 inspired the classical dramas *Iphigenie auf Tauris/Iphigenia in Tauris* 1787 and *Tasso* 1790.

goggle *v.t./i.* **1.** to look with wide-open eyes. **2.** (of the eyes) to be rolled, to project. **3.** to roll (the eyes). —*adj.* (of the eyes) protuberant, rolling. —*n.* (in *plural*) enclosed transparent shields for protecting the eyes from glare, dust etc.

Gogh /gɒx/ Vincent van 1853–1890. Dutch painter, a Post-Impressionist. He tried various careers, including preaching, and began painting in the 1880s. He met Paul ◊Gauguin in Paris, and when he settled in Arles, Provence, 1888, Gauguin joined him there. After a quarrel van Gogh cut off part of his own earlobe, and in 1889 he entered an asylum; the following year he committed suicide. The Arles paintings vividly testify to his intense emotional involvement in his art; among them are *The*

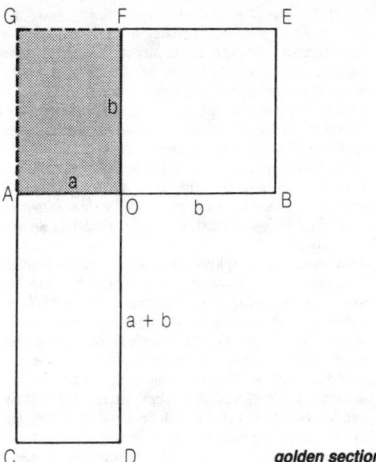

golden section

Yellow Chair and several *Sunflowers* 1888 (National Gallery, London).

Gogol /'gəʊgɒl/ Nicolai Vasilyevich 1809–1852. Russian writer. His first success was a collection of stories, *Evenings on a Farm near Dikanka* 1831–32, followed by *Mirgorod* 1835. Later works include *Arabesques* 1835, the comedy play *The Inspector General* 1836, and the picaresque novel *Dead Souls* 1842, which satirizes Russian provincial society.

Gambling is the great leveller. All men are equal—at cards.

Nikolai Vasilievich Gogol
Gamblers

---

going /'gəʊɪŋ/ *n.* **1.** the state of the ground for walking or riding on. **2.** rate of progress. —*adj.* in action; existing, functioning, available; currently valid. —**get going,** to begin, to start. **going on (for),** approaching (a time, age etc.). **going-over** *n.* (*colloquial*) an inspection or overhaul, (*slang*) a beating. **goings-on** *n.pl.* strange behaviour or events. **going to,** about to, intending or likely to. **to be going on with,** to start with, for present needs. **while the going is good,** while circumstances are favourable.

goitre /'gɔɪtə(r)/ *n.* an abnormal enlargement of the thyroid gland seen as a swelling on the neck. It is most pronounced in simple goitre, which is caused by iodine deficiency. Much more common is toxic goitre or thyrotoxicosis, caused by overactivity of the thyroid gland. [French, ultimately from Latin *guttur* = throat]

go-kart *n.* = ◊kart.

Golan Heights /'gəʊlæn/ (Arabic *Jawlan*) plateau on the Syrian border with Israel, bitterly contested in the ◊Arab-Israeli Wars and annexed by Israel on 14 Dec 1981.

gold /gəʊld/ *n.* **1.** a heavy, precious, yellow, malleable, ductile metallic element; symbol Au, atomic number 79, atomic weight 197.0. It is unaffected by temperature changes and is highly resistant to acids. For manufacture, gold is alloyed with another strengthening metal, its purity being measured in ◊carats on a scale of 24. In 1988 the three leading gold-producing countries were: South Africa, 621 tonnes; USA, 205 tonnes; and Australia, 152 tonnes. In 1989 gold deposits were found in Greenland with an estimated yield of 12 tonnes per year. **2.** its yellow colour. **3.** coins or articles made of gold, wealth; a gold medal, usually given as a first prize. **4.** the bull's-eye of an archery target; a shot that strikes this. **5.** something very good or precious. —*adj.* of or coloured like gold. —**gold-digger** *n.* (*slang*) a woman who uses her attractions to wheedle money out of men. **gold dust,** gold in fine particles as often found naturally. **gold field,** an area where gold is found. **gold mine,** a place where gold is mined; a source of wealth. **gold plate,** vessels of gold; material plated with

gold. **gold-plate** *v.t.* to plate with gold. **gold reserve,** gold held by a central bank to guarantee the value of a country's currency. [Old English]

goldcrest *n.* the smallest British bird *Regulus regulus* about 9 cm/3.5 in long. It is olive green, with a bright yellow streak across the crown.

golden *adj.* **1.** made of gold. **2.** yielding gold. **3.** coloured or shining like gold. **4.** precious, excellent. —**golden age,** a period of great prosperity or cultural achievement. **golden eagle,** a large eagle (*Aquila chrysaetos*) with yellow-tipped head-feathers. **golden handshake,** a gratuity as compensation for dismissal or early retirement. **golden jubilee,** a 50th anniversary. **golden mean,** neither too much nor too little. **goldenrod** *n.* a plant of the genus *Solidago*, with yellow flower spikes. **golden rule,** a basic principle of action. **golden syrup,** pale treacle. **golden wedding,** the 50th anniversary of a wedding.

Golden Ass, The or **Metamorphoses** a picaresque adventure by the Roman writer Lucius Apuleius, written in Latin about AD 160, sometimes called the world's first novel. Lucius, turned into an ass, describes his exploits with a band of robbers, weaving into the narrative several ancient legends, including that of Cupid and Psyche.

Golden Fleece in Greek mythology, the fleece of the winged ram Chrysomallus, which hung on an oak tree at Colchis and was guarded by a dragon. It was stolen by Jason and the Argonauts.

Golden Horde the invading Mongol-Tatar army that first terrorized Europe from 1237 under the leadership of Batu Khan, a grandson of Genghis Khan. ◊Tamerlane broke their power in 1395, and ◊Ivan III ended Russia's payment of tribute to them in 1480.

golden section a visually satisfying ratio, first constructed by the Greek mathematician ◊Euclid and used in art and architecture. It is found by dividing a line AB at a point O such that the rectangle produced by the whole line and one of the segments is equal to the square drawn on the other segment. The ratio of the two segments is about 8:13 or 1:1.168, and a rectangle whose sides are in this ratio is called a **golden rectangle**.

goldfinch *n.* a songbird *Carduelis carduelis* commonly found in Europe, W Asia, and N Africa. It is black, white, and red about the head, with gold and black wings.

goldfish *n.* a fish of the carp family *Carassius auratus* found in E Asia, often kept as an ornamental fish. Greenish-brown in its natural state, it has for centuries been bred by the Chinese, taking on highly coloured and freakishly shaped forms.

Golding /'gəʊldɪŋ/ William 1911– . English novelist. His first book, *Lord of the Flies* 1954, was about savagery taking over among a group of English schoolboys marooned on a Pacific island. Later novels include *The Spire* 1964, *Rites of Passage* 1980, *The Paper Men* 1984, and *Fire Down Below* 1989, about a ship in the Antarctic Ocean. He was awarded the Nobel Prize for Literature in 1983.

gold rush a large-scale influx of gold prospectors to an area where gold deposits have recently been discovered, especially the transcontinental journey to California after the discovery of gold there in 1848. The result is a dramatic increase in population. Cities such as Johannesburg, Melbourne, and San Francisco either originated or were considerably enlarged by gold rushes.

goldsmith *n.* one who works in gold.

Goldsmith /'gəʊldsmɪθ/ Jerry (Jerrald) 1930– . US composer of film music who originally worked in radio and television. His prolific output includes *Planet of the Apes* 1968, *The Wind and the Lion* 1975, *The Omen* 1976, and *Gremlins* 1984.

Goldsmith Oliver 1728–1774. Irish writer, whose works include the novel, *The Vicar of Wakefield* 1766; the poem, 'The Deserted Village' 1770; and the play, *She Stoops to Conquer* 1773.

gold standard a system under which a country's currency is exchangeable for a fixed weight of gold on demand at the central bank. It was almost universally applied 1870–1914, but by 1937 no single country was on the full gold standard. Britain abandoned the gold standard in 1931; the USA abandoned it in 1971. Holdings of gold are still retained because it is an internationally recognized commodity which cannot be legislated upon or manipulated by interested countries.

Goldwater /'gəuldwɔːtə/ Barry 1909–. US Republican politician; presidential candidate in the 1964 election, when he was overwhelmingly defeated by Lyndon ◊Johnson. As a US senator 1953–86, he voiced the views of his party's right-wing conservative faction. Many of Goldwater's conservative ideas were later adopted by the Republican right, especially the Reagan administration.

Goldwyn /'gəuldwin/ Samuel. Adopted name of Samuel Goldfish. 1882–1974. US film producer. Born in Warsaw, he emigrated to the USA in 1896. He founded the Goldwyn Pictures Corporation in 1917, which eventually merged into Metro-Goldwyn-Mayer (MGM) in 1924, although he was not part of the deal. He remained a producer for many years, making classics such as *Wuthering Heights* 1939, *The Little Foxes* 1941, *The Best Years of Our Lives* 1946, and *Guys and Dolls* 1955.

An oral contract is not worth the paper it's written on.
Samuel Goldwyn
(attrib.)

---

golf /gɒlf/ *n.* an outdoor game in which a small rubber-cored ball is hit with a wooden-or iron-faced club. The club faces have varying angles and are styled for different types of shot. On the first shot for each hole, the ball is hit from a tee, which elevates the ball slightly off the ground; subsequent strokes are played off the ground. The object of the game is to sink the ball in a hole than can be anywhere between 90 m/100 yd and 457 m/500 yd away, using the least number of strokes. Most courses consist of 18 holes and are approximately 5,500 m/6,000 yd in length. Each hole is made up of distinct areas: the **tee**, from where plays start at each hole; the **green**, a finely manicured area where the hole is located; the **fairway**, the grassed area between the tee and the green, not cut as finely as the green; and the **rough**, the perimeter of the fairway, which is left to grow naturally. Natural hazards such as trees, bushes, and streams make play more difficult, and there are additional artificial hazards in the form of sand-filled bunkers. —*v.i.* to play golf. —**golf ball**, a ball used in golf; a spherical unit carrying the type in some electric typewriters. —**golf course** *or* **links**, an area of land on which golf is played. —**golfer** *n.* [Scottish]

Golgi /'gɒldʒi/ Camillo 1843–1926. Italian cell biologist who with Santiago Ramon y Cajal produced the first detailed knowledge of the fine structure of the nervous system.

Golgi apparatus or **Golgi body** a membranous structure found in the cells of ◊eukaryotes. It produces the membranes that surround the cell vesicles or ◊lysosomes.

Goliath /gə'laiəθ/ in the Old Testament, the champion of the ◊Philistines, who was said to have been killed by a stone from a sling by the young ◊David in single combat in front of their opposing armies.

golliwog /'gɒliwɒg/ *n.* a black-faced, soft doll with bright clothes and fuzzy hair.

golly[1] an interjection expressing surprise. [euphemism for God]

golly[2] abbreviation of golliwog.

golosh variant of **galosh**.

Gomez /'gəumiʃ/ Diego 1440–1482. Portuguese navigator who discovered the coast of Liberia during a voyage sponsored by ◊Henry the Navigator 1458–60.

Gómez /'gəumes/ Juan Vicente 1864–1935. Venezuelan dictator 1908–35. The discovery of oil during his rule attracted US, British, and Dutch oil interests and made Venezuela one of the wealthiest countries in Latin America. Gómez amassed a considerable personal fortune and used his well-equipped army to dominate the civilian population.

Gompers /'gɒmpəz/ Samuel 1850–1924. US labour leader. His early career in the Cigarmakers' Union led him to found and lead the ◊American Federation of Labor 1882. Gompers advocated nonpolitical activity within the existing capitalist system to secure improved wages and working conditions for members.

Gomulka /gə'mulkɑ/ Wladyslaw 1905–1982. Polish Communist politician, party leader 1943–48 and 1956–70. He introduced moderate reforms, including private farming and tolerance for Roman Catholicism.

gonad /'gəunæd/ *n.* the part of an animal's body that produces the sperm or egg cells (ovules) required for sexual reproduction. The sperm-producing gonad is called a ◊testis, and the ovule-producing gonad is called an ◊ovary. [from Greek *gonē, gonos* = generation, seed]

gonadotrophin *n.* any hormone that supports and stimulates the function of the gonads (sex glands); some gonadotrophins are used as ◊fertility drugs.

Goncharov /gɒntʃə'rɒf/ Ivan Alexandrovitch 1812–1891. Russian novelist. His first novel, *A Common Story* 1847, was followed in 1858 by his humorous masterpiece *Oblomov*, which satirized the indolent Russian landed gentry.

Goncourt, de /gɒŋ'kuə/ the brothers Edmond 1822–1896 and Jules 1830–1870. French writers. They collaborated in producing a compendium, *L'Art du XVIIIème siècle/18th-Century Art* 1859–75, historical studies, and a *Journal* 1887–96 that depicts French literary life of their day. Edmond de Goncourt founded the *Académie Goncourt*, opened in 1903, which awards an annual prize, the Prix Goncourt, to the author of the best French novel of the year. It is equivalent to the British Booker Prize in prestige, but has a monetary value of only 50 francs.

Gond /gɒnd/ *n.* a member of a heterogenous people of central India, about half of whom speak unwritten languages belonging to the Dravidian family. There are over four million Gonds, most of whom live in Madhya Pradesh, E Maharashtra, and N Andra Pradesh, although some are found in Orissa.

gondola /'gɒndələ/ *n.* **1.** a light pleasure boat, much ornamented, with a high, rising and curving stem and sternpost, used on the canals of Venice and propelled by one man with a single oar, standing near the stern. **2.** an elongated car attached to the underside of a dirigible balloon or airship. [Italian from dialect = rock, roll]

gondolier /gɒndə'liə/ *n.* a rower of a gondola. [French from Italian]

Gondwanaland /gɒn'dwɑːnəlænd/ land mass, including the continents of South America, Africa, Australia, and Antarctica, that formed the southern half of ◊Pangaea, the 'supercontinent' or world continent that existed between 250 and 200 million years ago. The northern half was ◊Laurasia. The baobab tree of Africa and Australia is a relic of Gondwandaland.

gone past participle of **go**[1].

goner /'gɒnə/ *n.* (*slang*) a person or thing that is dead, ruined, or irretrievably lost.

gonfalon /'gɒnfələn/ *n.* a banner, often with streamers, hung from a crossbar. [from Italian from Germanic]

gong *n.* **1.** a large metal disc with a turned rim giving a resonant note when struck, especially one used as a signal for meals. **2.** a percussion instrument generally comprising a large, hanging, bronze disc with a bossed centre which is struck in the middle with a soft-headed drumstick. **3.** a saucer-shaped bell. **4.** (*slang*) a medal. [from Malay]

goniometer /gəuni'ɒmitə/ *n.* an instrument for measuring angles. [from French from Greek *gōnia* = angle]

gonorrhoea /gɒnə'riːə/ *n.* a common, sexually transmitted disease arising from infection with the bacterium *Neisseria gonorrhoeae*, which causes inflammation of the genito-urinary tract. After an incubation period of two to ten days, infected men experience pain while urinating and a discharge from the penis; infected women often have no external symptoms. [Latin from Greek *gonos* = semen and *rhoia* = flux]

González Márquez /gɒn'θɑːleθ 'mɑːkeθ/ Felipe 1942– . Spanish socialist politician, leader of the Socialist Workers' Party (PSOE), prime minister from 1982.

goo *n.* (*slang*) **1.** a viscous or sticky substance. **2.** sickly sentiment. [perhaps from slang *burgoo* = porridge]

Gooch /'guːtʃ/ Graham Alan 1953–. English cricketer who plays for Essex county and England. He made his first-class cricket debut in 1973 followed by his first appearance for the England team in 1975. Banned for three years for captaining a team for a tour of South Africa in 1982, he was later re-instated as England captain in 1989. He scored a world record 456 runs in a Test match against India in 1990. He became the fourth man to average 100 runs per innings in an English season and has appeared in more than 80 Test matches.

good /gʊd/ *adj.* (*comparative* **better**; *superlative* **best**) **1.** having the right or desirable qualities, satisfactory. **2.** right, proper, expedient. **3.** commendable, worthy (especially in *my good man* etc.). **4.** morally correct, virtuous; (of a child) well-behaved. **5.** agreeable, enjoyable. **6.** suitable, efficient, competent. **7.** thorough, considerable. **8.** valid, genuine; financially sound. **9.** not less than. **10.** used in exclamations (*good God!*, *gracious!* etc.). —*adv.* (*US colloquial*) well. —*n.* **1.** a good quality or circumstance, especially what is beneficial or morally right. **2.** (in *plural*) movable property or merchandise; things to be transported or supplied. —**the good,** (*plural*) good people. **all in good time,** in due course but without haste. **as good as,** practically. **for good (and all),** finally, permanently. **good afternoon, day,** etc., forms used in greeting or parting. **good faith,** an honest or sincere intention. **good for,** beneficial to, having a good effect on; able to undertake or pay. **good-for-nothing** *adj.* worthless; (*n.*) a worthless person. **good-looking** *adj.* having a pleasing appearance. **in good time,** with no risk of being late. **good will,** an intention that good shall result (see ◊goodwill). **to the good,** having as a profit or benefit. [Old English]

goodbye /gʊd'baɪ/ *interjection* meaning farewell (expressing good wishes on parting, ending a telephone conversation etc.). —*n.* a parting, a farewell. [contraction of *God be with you*]

Good Friday in the Christian church, the Friday before Easter, which is observed in memory of the Crucifixion (the death of Jesus on the cross). [probably a corruption of *God's Friday*]

Good King Henry a perennial plant *Chenopodium bonus henricus* growing to 50 cm/1.6 ft, with triangular leaves which are mealy when young. Spikes of tiny, greenish-yellow flowers appear above the leaves in midsummer.

goodly /'gʊdlɪ/ *adj.* **1.** handsome. **2.** of imposing size etc. —**goodliness** *n.* [Old English]

Goodman /'gʊdmən/ Benny (Benjamin David) 1909–1986. US clarinetist, nicknamed 'the King of Swing' for the new jazz idiom he introduced (with arranger Fletcher Henderson). Leader of his own swing band from 1934, he is celebrated for numbers such as 'Blue Skies' and 'Avalon'. In 1955 he organized a new band and continued touring with it throughout the world up until his death.

Goodman Paul 1911– . US writer and social critic, whose many works (novels, plays, essays) express his anarchist, anti-authoritarian ideas. He studied youth offenders in *Growing up Absurd* 1960.

goodness *n.* **1.** virtue, excellence; kindness. **2.** used instead of 'God' in exclamations. [Old English]

goodwill *n.* **1.** kindly feeling. **2.** the established reputation of a business etc. as enhancing its value.

goody *n.* **1.** something good or attractive, especially to eat. **2.** (*colloquial*) a good or favoured person. —*int.* expressing childish delight.

Goodyear /'gʊdjɪə/ Charles 1800–1860. US inventor who developed rubber coating in 1837 and vulcanized rubber in 1839, a method of curing raw rubber to make it strong and elastic. This led to many applications, especially the motor-vehicle tyre.

goody-goody *adj.* obtrusively or smugly virtuous. —*n.* a goody-goody person.

gooey *adj.* (*slang*) **1.** viscous or sticky. **2.** sentimental.

goof *n.* (*slang*) **1.** a foolish or stupid person. **2.** a mistake. —*v.t./i.* (*slang*) **1.** to blunder, to bungle. **2.** to idle. —**goofy** *adj.* [from French from Italian from Latin *gufus* = coarse]

googly /'gu:glɪ/ *n.* a ball in cricket bowled so as to bounce in an unexpected direction.

Goolagong Evonne maiden name of Australian tennis player Evonne ◊Cawley

goon *n.* (*slang*) **1.** a stupid person. **2.** a hired ruffian. [perhaps from dialect *gooney* = booby; influenced by subhuman cartoon character 'Alice the *Goon*']

Goonhilly /gun'hɪlɪ/ *n.* British Telecom satellite tracking station in Cornwall, England. It is equipped with a communications satellite transmitter-receiver in permanent contact with most parts of the world.

goosander /gu:'sændə/ *n.* a duck *Mergus merganser* with a sharp, serrated bill.

goose *n.* (*plural* **geese**) **1.** a web-footed bird of the genera *Anser* and *Branta* or subfamily Anserinae, between a duck and a swan in size; the female of this (compare **gander**);

Gorbachev President of the USSR and Communist Party leader Mikhail Gorbachev.

the flesh of the goose as food. **2.** a simpleton. **3.** (*plural* **gooses**) a tailor's smoothing-iron (with a handle like a goose's neck). —**goose flesh** *or* **pimples,** a bristling state of the skin due to cold or fright. **gooseneck** *n.* a thing shaped like the neck of a goose. **goose step,** a parade-step of marching soldiers with the legs kept straight. [Old English]

Goose Bay settlement at the head of Lake Melville on the Labrador coast of Newfoundland, Canada. In World War II it was used as a staging post by US and Canadian troops on their way to Europe. Until 1975 it was used by the US Air Force as a low-level-flying base.

gooseberry /'gʊzbərɪ/ *n.* the edible fruit of *Ribes grossularia*, a low-growing bush related to the currant. It is straggling in its growth, bearing straight sharp spines in groups of three, and rounded, lobed leaves. The flowers are green, and hang on short stalks. The fruits are generally globular, green, and hairy (the smooth-skinned variety is called *R. uva-crispa*), but there are reddish and white varieties. —**play gooseberry,** to be an unwanted extra person.

gopher /'gəʊfə/ *n.* **1.** an American burrowing rodent of the genus *Geomys* or *Thomomys*, family Geomyidae. **2.** a ground squirrel of the genus *Citellus*. **3.** a burrowing tortoise *Testudo carolina*. [perhaps from Canadian French *gaufre* = honeycomb]

Gorbachev /ɡɔːbə'tʃɒf/ Mikhail Sergeyevich 1931– . Soviet president, in power from 1985. He was a member of the Politburo from 1980 and, during the Chernenko administration 1984–85, was chair of the Foreign Affairs Commission. As general secretary of the Communist Party (CPSU) from 1985, and president of the Supreme Soviet from 1988, he introduced liberal reforms at home (◊perestroika and ◊glasnost), and attempted to halt the arms race abroad. He became head of state in 1989 and in March 1990 he was formally elected to a five-year term as executive president with greater powers. At home, his plans for economic reform failed to avert a food crisis in the winter of 1990–91 and his desire to preserve a single, centrally controlled USSR met with resistance from Soviet republics seeking more independent government systems. He was awarded the Nobel Peace Prize in 1990, but his international reputation suffered in the light of the harsh repression of nationalist demonstrations in the Baltic states early in 1991.

Gordian knot /'ɡɔːdɪən/ in Greek myth, the knot tied by King Gordius of Phrygia, to be unravelled only by the future conqueror of Asia. According to tradition, Alexander cut it with his sword in 334 BC. **—cut the Gordian knot,** to solve a problem forcefully.

Gordimer /'gɔːdɪmə/ Nadine 1923– . South African novelist, an opponent of apartheid. Her first novel, *The Lying Days*, appeared in 1953, and other works include *The Conservationist* 1974, the volume of short stories *A Soldier's Embrace* 1980, and *July's People* 1981. Her works are no longer banned in South Africa.

Gordon /'gɔːdn/ Charles (George) 1833–1885. British general who, after service against the Taiping rebels in China 1863–64, was sent to the Sudan in 1884 to rescue Egyptian garrisons that were under attack by the ◊Mahdi, Muhammad Ahmed. Gordon was besieged in Khartoum for ten months by the Mahdi's army. A relief expedition arrived on 28 Jan 1885 to find that Khartoum had been captured and Gordon killed two days earlier.

Gordon George 1751–1793. British organizer of the so-called **Gordon Riots** of 1778, a protest against removal of penalties imposed on Roman Catholics in the Catholic Relief Act of 1778; he was acquitted on a treason charge. Gordon and the 'No Popery' riots figure in Dickens's novel *Barnaby Rudge*.

gore[1] *n.* blood shed and clotted. [Old English = dirt]

gore[2] *v.t.* to pierce with a horn, tusk etc.

gore[3] *n.* a wedge-shaped piece in a garment; a triangular or tapering piece in an umbrella etc. —*v.t.* to shape with a gore. [Old English = triangle of land]

gorge *n.* 1. a narrow opening between hills. 2. gorging, a surfeit. 3. the contents of the stomach. —*v.t./i.* 1. to feed or devour greedily. 2. to satiate; to choke up. **—one's gorge rises at,** one is sickened by. [from Old French = throat]

gorgeous /'gɔːdʒəs/ *adj.* richly coloured, sumptuous; (*colloquial*) strikingly beautiful; (*colloquial*) very pleasant, splendid. **—gorgeously** *adv.*, **gorgeousness** *n.* [from Old French *gorgias* = elegant]

gorgon /'gɔːgən/ *n.* a frightening woman. [from Latin from Greek *Gorgō gorgos* = terrible]

Gorgon in Greek mythology, any of three sisters, Stheno, Euryale, and Medusa, who had wings, claws, enormous teeth, and snakes for hair. Medusa, the only one who was mortal, was killed by ◊Perseus, but even in death her head, which was fixed on Athene's shield, was so frightful that it turned the beholder to stone.

Gorgonzola /gɔːgən'zəʊlə/ *n.* a kind of rich blue-veined cheese. [from *Gorgonzola* in N Italy]

Goria /'gɔːrɪə/ Giovanni 1943– . Italian Christian Democrat (DC) politician, prime minister 1987–88. He entered the Chamber of Deputies 1976 and held a number of posts, including treasury minister, until he was asked to form a coalition government in 1987.

gorilla /gə'rɪlə/ *n.* the largest of the anthropoid apes, found in the dense forests of W Africa and mountains of Central Africa. The male stands about 2 m/6.5 ft, and weighs about 200 kg/450 lbs; females are about half the size. The body is covered with blackish hair, silvered on the back in the male. Gorillas live in family groups of a senior male, several females, some younger males, and a number of infants. They are vegetarian, highly intelligent, and will attack only in self-defence. They are dwindling in numbers, being shot for food by some local people, or by poachers taking young for zoos, but protective measures are having some effect. The breast-beating movement, once thought to indicate rage, actually signifies only nervous excitement. There are three races of one species, *Gorilla gorilla*: the Western lowland, Eastern lowland, and mountain gorillas. [perhaps African = wild man, in Greek account of Hanno's voyage (5th or 6th century BC), adapted as specific name in 1847]

Göring /'gɜːrɪŋ/ Hermann Nazi leader; see ◊Goering.

Gorky /'gɔːki/ (Russian *Gor'kiy*) former name until 1932 of **Nizhny-Novgorod** city in central USSR; population (1987) 1,425,000. Cars, locomotives, and aircraft are manufactured here.

Gorky Arshile 1904–1948. Armenian-born US painter, who lived in the USA from 1920. He painted Cubist abstracts before developing a more surreal Abstract-Expressionist style, using organic shapes and bold paint strokes.

Gorky Maxim. Pen name of Alexei Peshkov, 1868–1936. Russian writer. Born in Nizhny-Novgorod (renamed Gorky

in 1932 in his honour), he was exiled 1906–13 for his revolutionary principles. His works, which include the play *The Lower Depths* 1902 and the memoir *My Childhood* 1913, combine realism with optimistic faith in the potential of the industrial proletariat.

gormandize /'gɔːməndaɪz/ *v.t./i.* to eat greedily. **—gormandizer** *n.*

gormless /'gɔːmlɪs/ *adj.* (*colloquial*) foolish, lacking sense. [from dialect *gaum* = understanding]

gorse *n.* also known as **furze** or **whin** Eurasian genus of plants *Ulex*, family Leguminosae, consisting of thorny shrubs with spine-shaped leaves densely clustered along the stems, and bright yellow flowers. The gorse bush *U. europaeus* is an evergreen and grows on heaths and sandy areas throughout W Europe. **—gorsy** *adj.* [Old English]

Gorsedd /'gɔːseð/ *n.* a meeting of Welsh bards and druids (especially as the preliminary to an eisteddfod). [Welsh, literally 'throne']

Gorton /'gɔːtn/ John Grey 1911– . Australian Liberal politician. He was minister for education and science 1966–68, and prime minister 1968–71.

gory /'gɔːrɪ/ *adj.* covered with blood; involving bloodshed. **—gorily** *adv.*, **goriness** *n.*

gosh an interjection expressing surprise. [euphemism for *God*]

goshawk /'gɒshɔːk/ *n.* a large hawk *Accipiter gentilis* with short wings, used in falconry. [Old English]

gosling /'gɒzlɪŋ/ *n.* a young goose.

gospel /'gɒspəl/ *n.* 1. the tidings of redemption preached by Jesus Christ. 2. **Gospel**, each of the four books of the New Testament in which this was set forth, attributed to Matthew, Mark, Luke, and John. 3. a thing that may safely be believed; a principle one acts upon or advocates. [Old English *good* and *spell* = news]

gospel music a type of music developed in the 1920s in the black Baptist churches of the US South from spirituals, which were 18th-and 19th-century hymns joined to the old African pentatonic (five-note) scale. Outstanding among the early gospel singers was Mahalia Jackson (1911–1972), but from the 1930s to the mid-1950s male harmony groups predominated, among them the Dixie Hummingbirds, the Swan Silvertones, and the Five Blind Boys of Mississippi.

Gossaert /'gɒsɒt/ Jan, Flemish painter, known as ◊Mabuse.

gossamer /'gɒsəmə/ *n.* 1. the filmy substance of small spiders' webs. 2. delicate, flimsy material. —*adj.* light and flimsy as gossamer. [apparently *goose summer*, St Martin's summer, i.e. early November]

Gosse /gɒs/ Edmund William 1849–1928. English author. Son of a marine biologist, who was a member of the Plymouth Brethren, a Christian fundamentalist sect. Gosse's strict Victorian upbringing is reflected in his masterpiece of autobiographical work *Father and Son* (published anonymously in 1907).

gossip /'gɒsɪp/ *n.* 1. casual talk or writing, especially about persons or social incidents. 2. a person indulging in gossip. —*v.i.* to talk or write gossip. **—gossip column,** a section of a newspaper devoted to gossip about well-known people. **—gossipy** *adj.* [Old English, originally = godparent]

got *v.t./i.* past and past participle of **get**.

Göteborg /jɜːtə'bɔːrg/ (German *Gothenburg*) port and industrial (ships, vehicles, chemicals) city (Sweden's second largest) on the W coast of Sweden, on the Göta Canal (built 1832), which links it with Stockholm; population (1988) 432,000.

Goth /gɒθ/ *n.* a member of an E Germanic people who settled near the Black Sea around the 2nd century AD. There are two branches, the eastern Ostrogoths, and the western Visigoths. The **Ostrogoths** were conquered by the Huns in 372. They regained their independence in 454 and under ◊Theodoric the Great conquered Italy 488–93; they disappeared as a nation after the Byzantine emperor ◊Justinian I reconquered Italy 535–55. The **Visigoths** migrated to Thrace. Under ◊Alaric they raided Greece and Italy 395–410, sacked Rome, and established a kingdom in S France. Expelled from there by the Franks, they established a Spanish kingdom which lasted until the Moorish conquest of 711. [from Latin *Gothi* from Greek from Gothic]

Gothic /'gɒθɪk/ *adj.* 1. of the Goths. 2. in the style of architecture prevalent in western Europe in the 12th–16th century. **3.** in printing, of an old-fashioned German style of type, also known as 'black letter'. —*n.* **1.** Gothic architecture or type. **2.** the Gothic language. [from French or Latin]

Gothic architecture style of architecture that flourished in Europe from the mid-12th century to the end of the 15th century. It is characterized by vertical lines of tall pillars, spires, greater height in interior spaces, the pointed arch, rib vaulting, and the flying buttress. Gothic architecture originated in Normandy and Burgundy in the 12th century. The term became derisory, perhaps deriving from the 16th-century critic Vasari's attribution of medieval artistic styles to the Goths, who destroyed 'Classicism'. The style prevailed in W Europe until the 16th century when Classic architecture was revived.

Gothic art painting and sculpture in the style that dominated European art from the late 12th century until the early Renaissance. The great Gothic church façades held hundreds of sculpted figures and profuse ornamentation, and manuscripts were lavishly decorated. Stained glass replaced mural painting to some extent in N European churches. The **International Gothic** style in painting emerged in the 14th century, characterized by delicate and complex ornamentation and increasing realism.

Gothic novel the genre established by Horace Walpole's *The Castle of Otranto* 1765 and marked by mystery, violence, and horror; other exponents were Anne Radcliffe, Matthew 'Monk' Lewis, Bram Stoker, Mary Shelley, and Edgar Allan Poe.

Gothic revival the resurgence of interest in Gothic architecture, as displayed in 19th-century Britain and the USA. Gothic revival buildings include the Houses of Parliament, St Pancras Station, London, and the Town Hall, Vienna.

gotten see ◊get.

Götterdämmerung n. in Scandinavian mythology, the end of the world; the complete downfall of a regime. [German = twilight of the gods]

gouache /guːˈɑː∫/ *n.* painting with opaque pigments ground in water and thickened with gum and honey; these pigments. [French, from Italian *guazzo*]

Gouda /ˈgaʊdə/ *n.* a flat, round cheese with yellow rind, originally made at Gouda in Holland.

gouge /gaʊdʒ/ *n.* a chisel with a concave blade. —*v.t.* **1.** to cut with or as with a gouge. **2.** to scoop or force *out*. [French, from Latin *gubia*]

goulash /ˈguːlæ∫/ *n.* a stew of meat and vegetables highly seasoned with paprika. [from Magyar = herdsman's meat]

Gould /guːld/ Bryan Charles 1939– . British Labour politician, member of the shadow cabinet from 1986.

Gould Elliott. Stage name of Elliot Goldstein 1938– . US film actor. A successful child actor, his film debut, *The Night They Raided Minsky's* 1968, led rapidly to starring roles in such films as *M.A.S.H.* 1970, *The Long Goodbye* 1972, and *Capricorn One* 1978.

Gould Stephen Jay 1941– . US palaeontologist and author. In 1972 he proposed the theory of punctuated equilibrium, suggesting that the evolution of species did not occur at a steady rate but could suddenly accelerate, with rapid change occurring over a few hundred thousand years.

Gounod /ˈguːnəʊ/ Charles François 1818–1893. French composer. His operas include *Sappho* 1851, *Faust* 1859, *Philémon et Baucis* 1860, and *Roméo et Juliette* 1867. He also wrote sacred songs, masses, and an oratorio, *The Redemption* 1882. His music had great lyrical appeal and emotional power and it inspired many French composers of the later 19th century.

gourd /gʊəd/ *n.* **1.** the fleshy, usually large fruit of a trailing or climbing plant of the family Cucurbitaceae. **2.** a plant of the genus *Lagenaria*, of which the **bottle gourd** or ◊calabash *L. siceraria* is best known. **3.** the dried rind of this fruit used as a bottle or container. [from Anglo-French, ultimately from Latin *cucurbita*]

gourmand /ˈgʊəmənd/ *n.* **1.** a glutton. **2.** a gourmet. [from Old French]

gourmandise /ˈgʊəmãdiːz/ *n.* gluttony. [French]

gourmet /ˈgʊəmeɪ/ *n.* a connoisseur of good or delicate food. [French = wine-taster]

gout *n.* a hereditary form of ◊arthritis, marked by an excess of uric acid crystals in the tissues, causing pain and inflammation in one or more joints (usually of the

feet or hands). Acute attacks are treated with ◊anti-inflammatories. --**gouty** *adj.* [from Old French from Latin *gutta* = drop]

govern /ˈgʌvən/ *v.t.* **1.** to rule or control with authority, to conduct the policy and affairs of. **2.** to influence or determine (a person or course of action etc.). **3.** to restrain or control. **4.** in grammar, especially of a verb or preposition, to have (a noun or its case) depending on it. [from Old French from Latin *gubernare* from Greek *kubernaō* = steer]

governance /ˈgʌvənəns/ *n.* the act, manner, or function of governing. [from Old French]

governess /ˈgʌvənɪs/ *n.* a woman employed to teach children in a private household. [from Old French]

government /ˈgʌvənmənt/ *n.* **1.** governing; the system whereby political authority is exercised. Modern systems of government include liberal democracies, totalitarian (one-party) states, and autocracies (authoritarian, relying on force rather than ideology). The Greek philosopher Aristotle was the first to attempt a systematic classification of governments. His main distinctions were between government by one person, by few, and by many (monarchy, oligarchy, and democracy), each of which may degenerate into tyranny (rule by an oppressive élite in the case of oligarchy or by the mob in the case of democracy). **2.** the group of persons governing a state. **3.** the state as an agent. —**governmental** /-ˈmentəl/ *adj.* [from Old French]

Government Communications Headquarters the centre of the British government's electronic surveillance operations, see ◊GCHQ.

governor /ˈgʌvənə/ *n.* **1.** a ruler; an official governing a province, town etc., or representing the British monarchy in a colony. **2.** the executive head of each state of the USA. **3.** an officer commanding a fortress etc. **4.** the head, or a member of the governing body, of an institution; the official in charge of a prison; (*slang*) one's employer or father. **5.** an automatic regulator controlling the speed of an engine etc. —**Governor General**, a representative of the British monarchy in a Commonwealth country that regards the Queen as the head of state. [from Anglo-French from Latin *gubernator*]

Gower /ˈgaʊə/ David 1957– . English cricketer. A left-hander, since his debut for Leicestershire in 1975 he has scored over 20,000 first-class runs. He made his England debut in 1978, and was captain in 1984 and 1989. He now plays for Hampshire.

Gower John *c.*1330–1408. English poet remembered for his tales of love *Confessio Amantis* 1390, written in English, and other poems in French and Latin.

gown *n.* **1.** a loose, flowing garment, especially a long dress worn by a woman. **2.** the loose, flowing outer garment that is the official or uniform robe of a lawyer, judge, member of a university etc. **3.** a surgeon's overall. [from Old French from Latin *gunna* = fur garment]

Gowon /gaʊˈɒn/ Yakubu 1934– . Nigerian politician, head of state 1966–75. Educated at Sandhurst military college in the UK, he became chief of staff, and in the military coup of 1966 seized power. After the Biafran civil war 1967–70, he reunited the country with his policy of 'no victor, no vanquished'. In 1975 he was overthrown by a military coup.

goy *n.* (*plural* **goyim** or **goys**) the Jewish name for a non-Jew. [from Hebrew *goy* = people]

Goya /ˈgɔɪə/ Francisco José de Goya y Lucientes 1746–1828. Spanish painter and engraver. He painted portraits of four successive kings of Spain, and his etchings include *The Disasters of War*, depicting the French invasion of Spain 1810–14. Among his last works are the 'black paintings' (Prado, Madrid), with horrific images such as *Saturn Devouring One of His Sons* about 1822.

Goyen /ˈxɔɪən/ Jan van 1596–1656. Dutch landscape painter, active in Leiden, Haarlem, and from 1631 in The Hague. He was a pioneer of the Realist style of landscape with ◊Ruisdael, and he sketched from nature and studied clouds and light effects.

Gozzoli /ˈgɒtsəli/ Benozzo *c.*1421–1497. Florentine painter, a late exponent of the International Gothic style. He painted frescoes in 1459 in the chapel of the Palazzo Medici-Riccardi, Florence: the walls are crammed with figures, many of them portraits of the Medici family.

GP 1. in medicine, abbreviation of general practitioner. 2. in music, abbreviation of general pause, a moment when all players are silent.

GPO abbreviation of General Post Office.

GPU or **OGPU**; abbreviation of *Obedinyonnoye Gosudarstvennoye Polititcheskaye Upravleniye* (Unified State Political Administration), former name (1922–23) for ◊KGB, the Soviet security service.

gr. abbreviation of 1. gram(s). 2. grain(s). 3. gross.

Graaf /grɑːf/ Regnier de, 1641–1673. Dutch physician and anatomist who discovered the ovarian follicles, which were later named **Graafian follicles**. He named the ovaries and gave exact descriptions of the testicles. He was also the first to isolate and collect the secretions of the pancreas and gall bladder.

Graafian follicle /ˈgrɑːfiən/ or **vesicle** during the ◊menstrual cycle, a fluid-filled capsule that surrounds and protects the developing egg cell inside the mammalian ovary. After the egg cell has been released, the follicle remains and is known as a corpus luteum. [from R de *Graaf*]

grab *v.t./i.* (**-bb-**) 1. to grasp suddenly; to snatch *at.* 2. to take greedily; to appropriate. 3. (of brakes) to act harshly or jerkily. 4. (*slang*) to attract the attention of, to impress. —*n.* 1. a sudden clutch or attempt to seize. 2. a mechanical device for gripping things and lifting them. [from Middle Low German or Middle Dutch]

graben /ˈgrɑːbən/ *n.* a depression of the Earth's surface between faults. [German originally = ditch]

Grable /ˈgreɪbəl/ Betty (Elizabeth Ruth) 1916–1973. US film actress, singer and dancer, who starred in *Moon over Miami* 1941, *I Wake Up Screaming* 1941, and *How to Marry a Millionaire* 1953. As a publicity stunt, her legs were insured for a million dollars. Her popularity peaked during World War II when GIs voted her their number one 'pin-up' girl.

Gracchus /ˈgrækəs/ the brothers **Tiberius Sempronius** 163–133 BC and **Gaius Sempronius** 153–121 BC. Roman agrarian reformers. As ◊tribune (magistrate) 133 BC, Tiberius tried to prevent the ruin of small farmers by making large slave-labour farms illegal but was murdered. Gaius, tribune 123–122 BC, revived his brother's legislation, and introduced other reforms, but was outlawed by the Senate and committed suicide.

grace /greɪs/ *n.* 1. attractiveness, especially in design, manner, or movement. 2. becoming courtesy. 3. manner, bearing; an attractive feature, an accomplishment. 4. (in Christian theology) the supernatural assistance of God bestowed upon a rational being with a view to his salvation. 5. goodwill, favour; a delay granted as a favour. 6. a prayer of thanksgiving before or after a meal. —*v.t.* to add grace to; to bestow honour on. —**grace-and-favour house**, etc., a house etc. occupied by permission of a sovereign. **grace note**, a note embellishing a melody or harmony but not essential to it. **His, Her, Your,** etc., **Grace**, a title used in addressing or referring to a duke, duchess, or archbishop. **in a person's good graces**, in his or her favour. **with a good** (*or* **bad**) **grace**, as if willingly (or reluctantly). **year of grace**, a year of the Christian era. [from Old French from Latin *gratia* (*gratus* = pleasing)]

Grace W(illiam) G(ilbert) 1848–1915. English cricketer. By profession a doctor, he became the best batsman in England. He began playing first-class cricket at the age of 16, scored 152 runs in his first Test match, and in 1876 scored the first triple century.

graceful *adj.* having or showing grace or elegance. —**gracefully** *adv.*, **gracefulness.** *n.*

graceless *adj.* lacking grace, inelegant, ungracious.

Graces in Greek mythology, three goddesses (Aglaia, Euphrosyne, Thalia), daughters of Zeus and Hera, the personification of grace and beauty.

gracious /ˈgreɪʃəs/ *adj.* kind, indulgent and beneficent to inferiors; (of God) merciful, benign. —*int.* expressing surprise. —**gracious living**, an elegant way of life. —**graciously** *adv.*, **graciousness** *n.* [from Old French from Latin]

gradate /grəˈdeɪt/ *v.t./i.* to pass or cause to pass by gradations from one shade to another; to arrange in gradations.

gradation /grəˈdeɪʃən/ *n.* 1. (usually in *plural*) a stage of transition or advance. 2. a degree in rank, merit, intensity, etc.; arrangement in such degrees. 3. gradual passing from

grafting

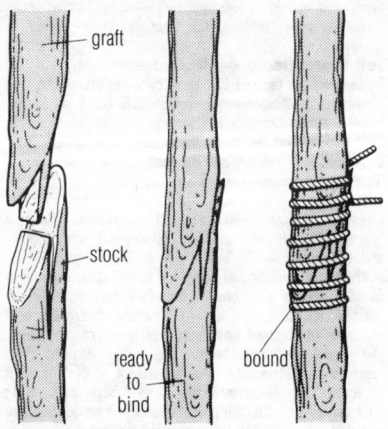

graft

stock

ready
to
bind

bound

one shade or tone etc. to another. —**gradational** *adj.* [from Latin *gradatio* (*gradus* = step)]

grade *n.* 1. a step, stage, or degree in rank, quality, proficiency etc. 2. a class of persons or things of the same grade. 3. a mark indicating the quality of a student's work. 4. a slope. 5. (*US*) a class or form in a school. —*v.t./i.* 1. to arrange in grades. 2. to give a grade to (a student). 3. to reduce (a road etc.) to easy gradients. 4. to pass gradually between grades or *into* a grade. —**grade school,** (*US*) an elementary school. **make the grade,** to succeed. [French, or from Latin *gradus* = step]

gradient /ˈgreɪdiənt/ *n.* the amount of slope in a road, railway etc.; a sloping road etc.

gradual /ˈgrædjuəl/ *adj.* occurring by degrees, not rapid or steep or abrupt. —**gradually** *adv.* [from Latin]

gradualism *n.* a policy of gradual change.

graduate /ˈgrædjuət/ *n.* the holder of an academic degree. —/-eɪt/ *v.t./i.* 1. to take an academic degree. 2. to move up *to* (a higher grade of activity etc.). 3. to mark out in degrees or parts; to arrange in gradations; to apportion (tax) according to a scale. —**graduation** /-ˈeɪʃən/ *n.* [from Latin *graduari* = take degree]

Graeco-Roman /griːkəʊˈrəʊmən/ *adj.* of the Greeks and Romans.

Graf /grɑːf/ Steffi 1969– . West German lawn tennis player, who brought Martina ◊Navratilova's long reign as the world's number one female player to an end. Graf reached the semifinal of the US Open 1985 at the age of 16, and won five consecutive Grand Slam singles titles 1988–89.

graffito /grəˈfiːtəʊ/ *n.* (*plural* **graffiti** /-tiː/) an inscription or drawing carved, scratched, or drawn on public surfaces such as walls, fences, or buildings. [from Italian *graffio* = scratching]

graft[1] /grɑːft/ *n.* 1. a shoot or scion from one plant or tree planted in a slit made in another. 2. a piece of living tissue transplanted surgically. 3. the process of grafting. 4. (*slang*) hard work. —*v.t./i.* 1. to insert (a graft) *in* or *on*; to transplant (living tissue). 2. to fix or join (a thing) permanently to another. 3. (*slang*) to work hard. [from Old French *grafe* from Latin from Greek *graphion* = stylus]

graft[2] *n.* (*colloquial*) practices, especially bribery, used to secure illicit gains in politics or business; such gains. —*v.i.* to seek or make such gains.

Grafton /ˈgrɑːftən/ Augustus Henry, 3rd Duke of, 1735–1811. British politician. Grandson of the first duke, who was the son of Charles II and Barbara Villiers (1641–1709), Duchess of Cleveland. He became First Lord of the Treasury in 1766 and an unsuccessful acting prime minister 1767–70.

Graham /ˈgreɪəm/ the family name of the dukes of Montrose.

Graham 'Billy' (William Franklin) 1918– . US Baptist evangelist. At 17 he was converted at an evangelistic meeting. His Evangelistic Association conducts worldwide 'crusades'.

Graham Martha 1894–1991. US dancer, choreographer, teacher and director. The leading exponent of modern dance in the USA, she has created over 150 works and developed a unique vocabulary of movement, *The Graham Technique* now taught worldwide.

Graham Thomas 1805–1869. Scottish chemist who laid the foundations of physical chemistry (the branch of chemistry concerned with changes in energy during a chemical transformation) by his work on the diffusion of gases and liquids. **Graham's Law** states that the diffusion rate of two gases varies inversely as the square root of their densities.

Grahame /ˈgreɪəm/ Kenneth 1859–1932. Scottish author. The early volumes of sketches of childhood, *The Golden Age* 1895 and *Dream Days* 1898, were followed by his masterpiece *The Wind in the Willows* 1908, an animal fantasy created for his young son, which was dramatized by A A Milne as *Toad of Toad Hall*.

Grail /greɪl/ *n.* **the Holy Grail,** in medieval legend, the cup or platter used by Jesus Christ at the Last Supper. [from French from Latin *gradalis* = dish]

grain *n.* 1. the fruit or a seed of a cereal; (*collectively*) wheat or an allied food-grass, its fruit, corn. 2. a small, hard particle of salt, sand etc. 3. the smallest unit of weight in some systems, 0.0648 gram; the least possible amount. 4. granular texture, roughness of a surface; the texture produced by the particles in skin, wood, stone etc.; the pattern of the lines of fibre in wood or paper, the lamination in stone etc. —*v.t./i.* 1. to paint in imitation of the grain of wood etc. 2. to give a granular surface to. 3. to dye in the grain. 4. to form into grains. —**against the grain,** contrary to one's natural inclination or feeling. —**grainy** *adj.* [from Old French from Latin *granum*]

Grainger /ˈgreɪndʒə/ Percy Aldridge 1882–1961. Australian-born US composer and concert pianist. He is remembered for a number of songs and short instrumental pieces drawing on folk idioms, including *Country Gardens* 1925, and for his settings of folk songs, such as *Molly on the Shore* 1921.

grallatorial /grælə'tɔːrɪəl/ *adj.* of the long-legged wading birds. [from Latin *grallator* = stilt-walker (*grallae* = stilts)]

gram *n.* the metric unit of mass, 0.001 kilogram, originally defined as the mass of 1 cc of pure water at its maximum density. [from French *gramme* from Greek *gramma* = small weight]

-gram suffix forming nouns denoting a thing (so) written or recorded (*diagram, monogram, telegram*); compare ◊-graph. [from Greek *gramma* = thing written]

graminaceous /græmi'neɪʃəs/ *adj.* of or like grass. [from Latin *gramen* = grass]

graminivorous /græmi'nɪvərəs/ *adj.* feeding on grass, cereals etc. [from Latin *gramen* = grass and *vorare* = devour]

grammar /ˈgræmə/ *n.* 1. the study of the main elements of a language, including its sounds, inflections or other means of showing the relation between words as used in speech or writing, and the established rules for using these. 2. the elements themselves. 3. a treatise or book on grammar. 4. a person's manner of using grammatical forms; speech or writing regarded as good or bad by the rules of grammar. 5. the elements of an art or science. [from Anglo-French from Latin from Greek *grammatikētekhnē* = art of letters]

grammarian /grə'meərɪən/ *n.* an expert in grammar or linguistics. [from Old French]

grammar school in the UK, a secondary school catering for children of high academic ability, usually measured by the Eleven Plus examination (originally a school for teaching Latin). Most grammar schools have now been replaced by ◊comprehensive schools.

grammatical /grə'mætɪkəl/ *adj.* of or according to grammar. —**grammatically** *adv.* [French, or from Latin from Greek]

gramme variant of **gram.**

gramophone /ˈgræməfəʊn/ *n.* an instrument for reproducing recorded sounds such as music or speech. [inversion of *phonogram*]

Grampian /ˈgræmpɪən/ region of Scotland; **area** 8,600 sq km/3,320 sq mi; **administrative headquarters** Aberdeen; **physical** part of the Grampian Mountains (the Cairngorms); valley of the river Spey; **products** beef cattle (Aberdeen Angus and Beef Shorthorn), fishing, North Sea

oil service industries, tourism (winter skiing); **population** (1987) 503,000.

grampus /ˈgræmpəs/ *n.* a sea animal *Grampus griseus* resembling the dolphin and famous for blowing. [from Old French from Latin *crassus piscis* = fat fish]

Gramsci /ˈgræmʃi/ Antonio 1891–1937. Italian Marxist who attempted to unify social theory and political practice. He helped to found the Italian Communist Party in 1921 and was elected to parliament in 1924, but was imprisoned by the Fascist leader Mussolini from 1926; his *Quaderni di carcere/Prison Notebooks* were published posthumously in 1947.

gran (*colloquial*) abbreviation of grandmother.

Granada /grə'nɑːdə/ city in the Sierra Nevada in Andalucia, S Spain; population (1986) 281,000. Founded by the Moors in the 8th century, it became the capital of an independent kingdom 1236–1492, when it was the last Moorish stronghold to surrender to the Spaniards. Ferdinand and Isabella, the first sovereigns of a united Spain, are buried in the cathedral (built 1529–1703). The **Alhambra,** a fortified hilltop palace, was built in the 13th and 14th centuries by the Moorish kings.

granadilla /grænə'dɪlə/ *n.* a passion fruit. [Spanish, diminutive of *granada* = pomegranate]

Granados /grə'nɑːdɒs/ Enrique 1867–1916. Spanish composer-pianist. His piano work *Goyescas* 1911, inspired by the art of ◊Goya, was converted to an opera in 1916.

granary /ˈgrænərɪ/ *n.* 1. a storehouse for threshed grain. 2. a region producing, and especially exporting, much corn. [from Latin *granarium*]

Gran Chaco /græn ˈtʃɑːkəʊ/ large, lowland plain in N Argentina, W Paraguay, and SE Bolivia; area 650,000 sq km/251,000 sq mi. It consists of swamps, forests (a source of quebracho timber), and grasslands, and there is cattle-raising.

grand *adj.* 1. splendid, magnificent, imposing, dignified. 2. main, of chief importance; of the highest rank. 3. (*colloquial*) excellent, enjoyable. —*n.* 1. a grand piano. 2. (*slang*) a thousand pounds, dollars etc. —**grand jury,** (*US*) a jury convened to decide whether the evidence against an accused justifies a trial. **grand piano,** a large full-toned piano with horizontal strings. **grand total,** the sum of other totals. **grand tour,** (*historical*) a tour of the chief cities etc. of Europe, completing a person's education; an extensive tour. —**grandly** *adv.,* **grandness** *n.* [from Old French from Latin *grandis* = full-grown]

grand- in combinations, denoting the second degree of ascent or descent in relationships.

grandad *n.* (*colloquial*) a grandfather; an elderly man.

grandam /ˈgrændæm/ *n.* (*archaic*) a grandmother; an elderly woman. [from Anglo-French]

Grand Banks /grænd ˈbæŋks/ continental shelf in the N Atlantic off SE Newfoundland, where the shallow waters are rich fisheries, especially for cod.

Grand Canal (Chinese *Da Yune*) the world's longest canal. It is 1,600 km/1,000 mi long and runs N from Hangzhou to Tianjin, China; it is 30–61 m/100–200 ft wide, and reaches depths of over 1.5 km/1 mi. The earliest section was completed in 486 BC, and the northern section was built in AD 1282–92, during the reign of Kublai Khan.

Grand Canyon /grænd ˈkænjən/ vast gorge containing the Colorado River, N Arizona, USA. It is 350 km/217 mi long, 6–29 km/4–18 mi wide, and reaches depths of over 1.7 km/1 mi. It was made a national park in 1919.

grandchild *n.* a person's child's child.

granddad variant of **grandad.**

granddaughter *n.* a female grandchild.

Grand Design in the early 17th century, a plan attributed by the French minister Sully to Henry IV of France (who was assassinated before he could carry it out) for a great Protestant union against the Holy Roman Empire; the term was also applied to President de Gaulle's vision of France's place in a united Europe.

Grande Dixence dam /grɒnd diːkˈsɒns/ the world's highest dam, located in Switzerland, which measures 285 m/935 ft from base to crest. Completed in 1961, it contains 6 million cu m/8 million cu yds of concrete.

grandee /græn'diː/ *n.* a Spanish or Portuguese noble of high rank; a great personage. [from Spanish and Portuguese *grande*]

grandeur /'grændjə, -ndʒə/ *n*. splendour, magnificence, grandness; high rank, eminence; nobility of character. [French]

grandfather *n*. a male grandparent. —**grandfather clock**, a clock in a tall, wooden case, worked by weights.

Grand Guignol /'grɒŋ 'giːnjɒl/ a genre of short horror play produced at the Grand Guignol theatre in Montmartre, Paris (named after the bloodthirsty character Guignol in late 18th-century marionette plays).

grandiloquent /græn'dɪləkwənt/ *adj*. pompous or inflated in language. —**grandiloquence** *n*., **grandiloquently** *adv*. [from Latin *grandiloquus* (*loqui* = speak)]

grandiose /'grændiəus/ *adj*. producing or meant to produce an imposing effect; planned on a large scale. —**grandiosity** /-'ɒsɪtɪ/ *n*. [French from Italian]

grandma /'grænmaː/ *n*. (*colloquial*) a grandmother.

grand mal /grɑ̃ mæl/ epilepsy with loss of consciousness. [French = great sickness]

grandmaster *n*. a chess player of the highest class.

grandmother *n*. a female grandparent.

Grand National in horseracing, the steeplechase run at Aintree, England, during the Liverpool meeting in March or April over 7 km 242 m/4.5 mi, with 30 formidable jumps. It was first run in 1839.

Grand Old Party (GOP) popular name for the US ◊Republican Party.

grand opera an opera characterized by high drama and no spoken dialogue (unlike the *opéra-comique*), as performed at the Paris *Opéra* 1820s–1880s. Using the enormous resources of the state-subsidized opera house, grand operas in Paris were extremely long (five acts), and included incidental music and a ballet.

Grand Prix /grɑ̃ 'priː/1. (in full **Grand Prix de Paris**) an international horse-race for three-year-olds, founded in 1863 and run annually in June at Longchamp near Paris. 2. any of various important motor-racing contests, governed by international rules. [French = great or chief prize]

Grand Remonstrance a petition passed by the British Parliament in Nov 1641 which listed all the alleged misdeeds of Charles I and demanded Parliamentary approval for the king's ministers and the reform of the church. Charles refused to accept the Grand Remonstrance and countered by trying to arrest five leading members of the House of Commons (Pym, Hampden, Holles, Hesilrige, and Strode). The worsening of relations between king and Parliament led to the outbreak of the English Civil War in 1642.

grandsire *n*. (*archaic*) a grandfather.

grand slam in tennis, the four major tournaments: the Australian Open, the French Open, Wimbledon, and the US Open. In golf, it is also the four major tournaments: the US Open, the British Open, the Masters, and the PGA. In baseball, a grand slam is a home run with runners on all the bases. A grand slam in bridge is when all 13 tricks are won by one team.

grandson *n*. a male grandchild.

grandstand *n*. the main stand for spectators at a racecourse etc. —**grandstand finish**, a close and exciting finish to a race.

Grand Teton /'grænd 'tiːtn/ the highest point of the spectacular Teton range, NW Wyoming, USA, rising to 4,197 m/13,770 ft. Grand Teton National Park was established in 1929.

grand unified theory (GUT) in physics, a sought-for theory that would combine the successful theory of the strong nuclear force (called quantum chromodynamics) with the theory of the weak and electromagnetic forces. The search for the GUT is part of a larger programme seeking a ◊unified field theory, which would combine all the forces of nature (including gravity) within one framework.

grange /greɪndʒ/ *n*. a country house with farm buildings. [from Anglo-French from Latin *granica*]

Grange Movement, the in US history, a farmers' protest in the South and Midwest states against economic hardship and exploitation. The National Grange of the Patrons of Husbandry, formed 1867, was a network of local organizations, employing cooperative practices and advocating 'granger' laws. The movement petered out in the late 1870s, to be superseded by the ◊Greenbackers.

Granger /'greɪndʒə/ (James) Stewart 1913– . British film actor. After several leading roles in British romantic films during World War II, he moved to Hollywood in 1950

Grant *General Ulysses S Grant, photographed in June 1864 at City Point, near Hopewell, Virginia, his headquarters during the American Civil War.*

and subsequently appeared in adventure films, for example, *Scaramouche* 1952, *The Prisoner of Zenda* 1952, and *The Wild Geese* 1978.

graniferous /grə'nɪfərəs/ *adj*. producing grain or grain-like seed. [Latin *ferre* = bear]

granite /'grænɪt/ *n*. a plutonic ◊igneous rock, acidic in composition (containing a high proportion of silica). The rock is coarse-grained, the characteristic minerals being quartz, feldspars (usually alkali), and micas. It may be pink or grey, depending on the composition of the feldspars. Granites are chiefly used as building materials. —**granitic** /-'nɪtɪk/ *adj*. [from Italian *granito* = grained (Latin *granum* = grain)]

granivorous /grə'nɪvərəs/ *adj*. feeding on grains. [Latin *vorare* = devour]

granny *n*. (*colloquial*) or **grannie** a grandmother. —**granny flat**, a part of a house, made into self-contained accommodation for a relative. **granny knot**, a reef knot crossed the wrong way and therefore insecure. [diminutive of obsolete *grannam* for *grandam*]

grant /graːnt/ *v.t*. 1. to consent to fulfil (a request etc.). 2. to give formally, to transfer (property) legally. 3. to admit as true; to concede, to allow. —*n*. 1. something granted, especially a sum of money. 2. granting; formal conferment. —**take for granted**, to assume to be true or valid; to cease to appreciate through familiarity. [from Old French *gr(e)anter* ultimately from Latin *credere* = entrust]

Grant Cary. Stage name of Archibald Leach. 1904–1986. British-born US film actor who became a US citizen in 1942. His witty, debonair screen personality made him a favourite for more than three decades. He made several movies for director Alfred ◊Hitchcock, including *Suspicion* 1941, *Notorious* 1946, *To Catch a Thief* 1955, and *North by Northwest* 1959. He received a 1970 Academy Award for general excellence.

Grant Duncan 1885–1978. British painter and designer, a member of the ◊Bloomsbury group and a pioneer of abstract art in the UK. He lived with Vanessa Bell from about 1914 and worked with her on decorative projects. Later works, such as *Snow Scene* 1921, showed the influence of the Post-Impressionists.

Grant Ulysses S(impson) 1822–1885. The 18th president of the USA 1869–77. He was a Union general in the American Civil War and commander in chief from 1864. As a Republican president, he carried through a liberal ◊Reconstruction policy in the South, although he failed to suppress extensive political corruption within his own party and cabinet, which tarnished the reputation of his presidency.

granthi *n.* in Sikhism, the man or woman who reads from the holy book, the *Guru Granth Sahib*, during the service.

grant-maintained school in the UK, a state school which has voluntarily withdrawn from local authority support (an action called **opting out**), and instead is maintained directly by central government. The first was Skegness Grammar School in 1989.

grantor /grɑːnˈtɔː/ *n.* a person by whom property etc. is legally transferred.

granular /ˈɡrænjʊlə/ *adj.* of or like grains or granules. —**granularity** /-ˈlærɪtɪ/ *n.* [from Latin]

granulate /ˈɡrænjʊleɪt/ *v.t./i.* **1.** to form into grains. **2.** to roughen the surface of. **3.** (of a wound etc.) to form small prominences as the beginning of healing or junction. —**granulation** /-ˈleɪʃən/ *n.*

granule /ˈɡrænjuːl/ *n.* a small grain. [from Latin *granulum* diminutive of *granum* = grain]

grape *n.* a berry (usually green or purple) growing in clusters on a vine, used as a fruit and in making wine. —**grape hyacinth**, a small plant of the genus *Muscari* with a cluster of flowers, usually blue. **grapeshot** (*historical*) small balls as a scattering charge for cannon. **grapevine** *n.* a vine; a means of transmission of rumour. [from Old French = bunch of grapes]

grapefruit *n.* (*plural* the same) a large, round, yellow citrus fruit (that of *Citrus paradisi*) with an acid, juicy pulp.

graph /grɑːf/ *n.* a diagram showing the relation of two variable quantities each measured along one of a pair of axes. —*v.t.* to plot or trace on a graph. —**graph paper**, paper ruled with a grid of lines as a help in drawing graphs. [abbreviation of graphic formula]

-graph /grɑːf/ suffix forming nouns denoting a thing written or drawn etc. in a specified way (*holograph*, *photograph*), an instrument that records (*telegraph*), or the corresponding verbs. [from French from Latin from Greek *graphō* = write]

graphic /ˈɡræfɪk/ *adj.* **1.** of writing, drawing, etching etc. **2.** vividly descriptive. —**graphically** *adv.* [from Latin from Greek *graphē* = writing]

-graphic /-ˈɡræfɪk/ also **-graphical** suffix forming adjectives from nouns in -*graph* or -*graphy*. [from Greek]

graphic equalizer a control used in hi-fi systems that allows the distortions introduced by unequal amplification of different frequencies to be corrected.

graphic notation in music, a sign language referring to unorthodox sound effects, such as electronic sounds, for which classical music notation is not suitable.

graphics /ˈɡræfɪks/ *n.pl.* **1.** the products of the graphic arts. **2.** (usually treated as *singular*) the use of diagrams in calculation and design.

graphics tablet or **bit pad** in computing, an input device in which a stylus or cursor is moved, by hand, over a flat surface. The computer can keep track of the position of the stylus, so enabling the operator to input drawings or diagrams into the computer.

graphite /ˈɡræfaɪt/ *n.* a crystalline, allotropic, electrically-conducting form of ◊carbon used in pencils, as a lubricant, in various electrical devices, as a moderator in nuclear reactors etc. —**graphitic** /-ˈɪtɪk/ *adj.* [from German from Greek *graphō* = write]

graphology /ɡrəˈfɒlədʒɪ/ *n.* the study of handwriting, especially as a guide to character. —**graphological** /-ˈlɒdʒɪkəl/ *adj.*, **graphologist** *n.*

-graphy suffix forming nouns denoting a descriptive science (*geography*) or a style or method of writing etc. (*calligraphy*, *stenography*). [ultimately from Greek *graphia* = writing]

grapnel /ˈɡræpnəl/ *n.* an instrument with iron claws, for dragging or grasping things; a small anchor with several flukes. [from Old French *grapon*]

grapple *v.t./i.* **1.** to seize or hold firmly. **2.** to struggle at close quarters (*with*). **3.** to try to deal *with* (a problem).

grass

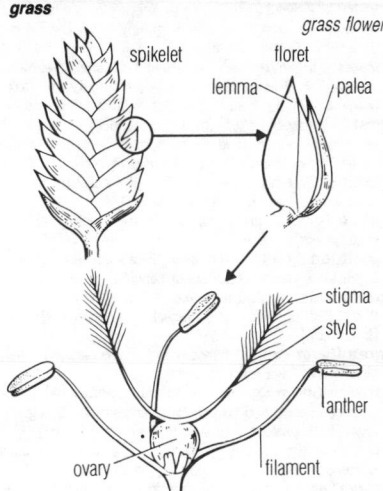

grass flower

spikelet · floret · lemma · palea · stigma · style · anther · ovary · filament

4. to seize (as) with a grapnel. —*n.* **1.** a hold (as) in wrestling. **2.** a close contest. **3.** a clutching instrument, a grapnel. —**grappling iron**, a grapnel. [from Old French from Provençal *grapa* = hook]

grasp /grɑːsp/ *v.t./i.* **1.** to seize or hold firmly, especially with the hands or arms; to seize eagerly or greedily. **2.** to understand or realize. —*n.* **1.** a firm hold, a grip. **2.** mastery, control. **3.** a mental hold, understanding. —**grasp at,** to try to seize; to accept eagerly. **grasp the nettle,** to tackle a difficulty boldly. [for earlier *grapse*]

grasping *adj.* greedy for money or possessions.

grass /grɑːs/ *n.* **1.** a plant of the large family Gramineae of monocotyledons, with about 9,000 species distributed worldwide except in the Arctic regions. The majority are perennial, with long, narrow leaves and jointed, hollow stems; hermaphroditic flowers are borne in spikelets; the fruits are grainlike. Included are bluegrass, wheat, rye, maize, sugarcane, and bamboo. **2.** pasture land; grass-covered ground, a lawn; grazing. **3.** (*slang*) marijuana. **4.** (*slang*) a person who 'grasses', an informer. —*v.t./i.* **1.** to cover with turf. **2.** (*US*) to provide with pasture. **3.** (*slang*) to betray, to inform the police. —**grass roots,** the fundamental level or source; ordinary people; the rank and file of a political party etc. **grass snake,** a small non-poisonous snake *Natrix natrix*. **grass widow,** a woman whose husband is away for a prolonged period. —**grassy** *adj.* [Old English]

Grass /grɑːs/ Günter 1927– . German writer. Born in Danzig, he studied at the art academies of Düsseldorf and Berlin, worked as a writer and sculptor (first in Paris and later in Berlin), and in 1958 won the coveted 'Group 47' prize. The grotesque humour and socialist feeling of his novels *Die Blechtrommel/The Tin Drum* 1959 and *Der Butt/The Flounder* 1977 are also characteristic of his poems.

grasshopper *n.* an insect of the order Orthoptera, suborder Saltatoria, usually with strongly developed hind legs which enable it to leap. Members of the order include ◊locusts and ◊crickets.

grassland *n.* a large, open area covered with grass, especially used for grazing.

grass of Parnassus a plant *Parnassia palustris*, unrelated to grasses, found growing in marshes and on wet moors in Europe and Asia. It is low-growing, with a rosette of heart-shaped, stalked leaves, and has five-petalled, white flowers with conspicuous veins growing singly on stem tips in late summer.

grass tree an Australian plant of the genus *Xanthorrhoea*. The tall, thick stems have a grasslike tuft at the top and are surmounted by a flower spike resembling a spear.

grate[1] *v.t./i.* **1.** to reduce to small particles by rubbing on a rough surface. **2.** to rub with a harsh noise; to grind (the teeth); to sound harshly. **3.** to have an irritating effect (*on* a person or the nerves). —**grater** *n.* [from Old French *grater*]

grate[2] *n.* a metal framework that keeps fuel in a fireplace; the fireplace itself. [originally = grating; from Old French from Latin *cratis* = hurdle]

grateful /'greɪtfʊl/ *adj.* 1. thankful, feeling or showing gratitude. 2. pleasant, acceptable. —**gratefully** *adv.* [from obsolete *grate* adj. from Latin *gratus* = thankful, pleasing]

gratify /'grætɪfaɪ/ *v.t.* to please, to delight; to please by compliance; to yield to (a desire). —**gratification** /-fɪ'keɪʃən/ *n.* [from French or Latin *gratificari*]

grating /'greɪtɪŋ/ *n.* a framework of parallel or crossed bars, wires, lines ruled on glass etc.

gratis /'greɪtɪs, 'grɑː-/ *adj. & adv.* free, without charge. [Latin *gratia* = thanks]

gratitude /'grætɪtjuːd/ *n.* being thankful, feeling or showing that one values a kindness or benefit received.

gratuitous /grə'tjuːɪtəs/ *adj.* 1. given or done gratis. 2. uncalled for, lacking good reason. —**gratuitously** *adv.* [from Latin]

gratuity /grə'tjuːɪtɪ/ *n.* money given in recognition of services. [from Old French or Latin]

gravamen /grə'veɪmen/ *n.* (*plural* **gravamens**) 1. the essence or most serious part (*of* an accusation). 2. a grievance. [Latin *gravare* = to load, from *gravis* = heavy]

grave[1] *n.* 1. a hole dug for the burial of a corpse; a mound or monument over this. 2. death. [Old English]

grave[2] *adj.* 1. serious, weighty, important; dignified, solemn; sombre. 2. (of a sound) low-pitched, not acute. —**gravely** *adv.* [French, or from Latin *gravis* = heavy]

grave[3] *v.t.* (*past participle* **graven, graved**) 1. to fix indelibly (*in* or *on* one's memory etc.). 2. (*archaic*) to engrave, to carve. —**graven image**, an idol. [Old English]

grave[4] /grɑːv, greɪv/ *n.* an accent ` over a vowel to show its quality or length.

grave[5] *v.t.* to clean (a ship's bottom) by burning and tarring. —**graving dock**, a dry dock. [perhaps from French *grave*, *grève* = shore]

gravel /'grævəl/ *n.* 1. a coarse ◊sediment consisting of pebbles or small fragments of rock, originating in the beds of lakes and streams or on beaches. Gravel is used for road building, railway ballast, and for an aggregate in concrete. It is obtained from quarries known as gravel pits, where it is often found mixed with sand or clay. Some gravel deposits also contain metal ores (particularly tin) or free metals (such as gold and silver). 2. crystals formed in the bladder. —*v.t.* (-ll-) 1. to lay with gravel. 2. to perplex. [from Old French, diminutive of *grave* = shore]

gravelly *adj.* 1. like gravel; consisting of gravel. 2. (of the voice) deep and rough-sounding.

graven *n.* see ◊grave[3].

Graves /grɑːv/ *n.* a wine (especially white) from the Graves district of the Bordeaux region in France.

In love as in sport, the amateur status must be strictly maintained.

Robert Graves
Occupation: Writer

Graves /greɪvz/ Robert (Ranke) 1895–1985. English poet and author. He was severely wounded on the Somme in World War I, and his frank autobiography *Goodbye to All That* 1929 is one of the outstanding war books. Other works include the poems *Over the Brazier* 1916; historical novels of imperial Rome, *I Claudius* and *Claudius the God* both 1934; and books on myth, for example *The White Goddess* 1948.

gravestone *n.* a stone (usually inscribed) marking a grave.

graveyard *n.* a burial ground.

gravid /'grævɪd/ *adj.* pregnant. [from Latin *gravidus*, *gravis* = heavy]

gravimeter /grə'vɪmɪtə/ *n.* an instrument measuring the difference in the force of gravity between two places.

gravimetry *n.* the study of the Earth's gravitational field. Small variations in the gravitational field can be caused by varying densities of rocks and structure beneath the surface, a phenomenon called the ◊Bouguer anomaly. These variations provide information about otherwise inaccessible subsurface conditions.

gravitate /'grævɪteɪt/ *v.t./i.* 1. to move or be attracted (*to*

or *towards*). 2. to move or tend by the force of gravity (*towards*); to sink by or as by gravity.

gravitation /grævɪ'teɪʃən/ *n.* 1. gravitating. 2. the attraction exercised by every particle of matter on every other; the movement or tendency produced by this; the falling of bodies to earth. —**gravitational** *adj.*

gravitational lens the gravitational field from a very large body, such as a star, which deflects light. It was predicted by Einstein's General Theory of Relativity and tested successfully during the solar eclipse of 1917 when the light from stars located beyond the sun was captured on photographs.

gravity /'grævɪtɪ/ *n.* 1. the force of attraction between objects because of their masses, gravity on Earth is the force of attraction between any object in the Earth's gravitational field and the Earth itself; the intensity of this. 2. weight. 3. importance, seriousness; solemnity. —**gravity feed**, the supply of material by its fall under gravity. [from French or Latin *gravitas* = heaviness]

gravure *n.* one of the three main ◊printing methods, in which printing is done from a plate etched with a pattern of recessed cells in which the ink is held. The greater the depth of a cell, the greater the strength of the printed ink. Gravure plates are expensive to make, but the process is economical for high-volume printing and reproduces illustrations well.

gravy /'greɪvɪ/ *n.* 1. the juices exuding from meat in and after cooking; a dressing for food, made of these. 2. (*slang*) unearned or unexpected money. —**gravy boat**, a boat-shaped vessel for gravy.

Gray /greɪ/ Eileen 1879–1976. Irish-born architect and furniture designer. She set up her own workshop and became known for her Art Deco designs which, in furniture, explored the use of tubular metal, glass, and new materials such as aluminium.

Gray Thomas 1716–1761. English poet, whose 'Elegy Written in a Country Churchyard' 1750 is one of the most quoted poems in English. Other poems include 'Ode on a Distant Prospect of Eton College', 'The Progress of Poesy', and 'The Bard'; these poems are now seen as the precursors of Romanticism.

grayling *n.* a freshwater fish, genus *Thymallus*, of the family Salmonidae. It has a long, multirayed dorsal fin, and a coloration shading from silver to purple. It is found in northern parts of N America, Europe, and Asia.

Graz /grɑːts/ capital of Styria province, and second largest city in Austria; population (1981) 243,400. Industries include engineering, chemicals, iron, and steel. It has a 15th-century cathedral and a university founded in 1573. Lippizaner horses are bred near here.

graze[1] *v.t./i.* to suffer or cause a slight abrasion of (a part of the body); to touch lightly in passing; to move (*against*, *along*, etc.) with such a contact. —*n.* an abrasion. [perhaps by transference from *graze*[2] 'take off the grass close to the ground']

graze[2] *v.t./i.* 1. (of cattle etc.) to eat growing grass; to feed on (grass). 2. to feed (cattle etc.) on growing grass; to pasture cattle. [Old English]

grazier /'greɪzɪə/ *n.* 1. one who feeds cattle for market. 2. (*Australian*) a sheep farmer.

grazing *n.* grassland suitable for pasturage.

grease /griːs/ *n.* oily or fatty matter, especially as a lubricant; the melted fat of a dead animal. also —/griːz/ *v.t.* to smear or lubricate with grease. —**greasepaint** *n.* the make-up used by actors etc. **grease the palm of**, (*colloquial*) to bribe. [from Old French *graisse* from Latin *crassus* = fat]

greasy *adj.* 1. of or like grease. 2. smeared or covered with grease; having much or too much grease; slippery. 3. (of a person or manner) too unctuous. —**greasily** *adv.*, **greasiness** *n.*

great /greɪt/ *adj.* 1. of a size, amount, extent, or intensity much above the normal or average (also *contemptuously*). 2. important, pre-eminent. 3. remarkable in ability, character, etc. 4. (also **greater**) the larger of the name. 5. fully deserving the name of; doing a thing much or on a large scale. 6. (*colloquial*) very enjoyable or satisfactory. 7. competent *at*; well-informed *on*. —*n.* a great person or thing. **Great Russian**, a member of the principal ethnic group in the USSR; their language. **Greats**, the Oxford BA course in classics and philosophy; the final examinations in this. **Great Seal**, the official seal used on important UK state

469

Great Trek

Ancient Greece

1600–1200 BC	Mycenean civilization, influenced by Minoan Crete, established in mainland Greece.
14th century BC	Achaeans invade Greece and Crete.
c. 1180 BC	Siege of Troy.
c. 1100 BC	Dorians settle in the Pelopponese and found Sparta.
750–550 BC	Greeks found colonies in Asia Minor, Sicily, S Italy, S France, Spain and N Africa.
594–507 BC	Development of democracy in Athens and other cities.
545 BC	Persia invades Ionian cities of Asia Minor.
499–449 BC	Persian Wars, ending in defeat of Persia at Salamis (480 BC) and Platea (479 BC). Confederacy of Delos established.
461–429 BC	Pericles attempts to establish Athenian empire.
431–404 BC	Peloponnesian War between Athens and Sparta destroys political power of Athens.
378–371 BC	Sparta rules until defeated by Thebes.
358–336 BC	Philip of Macedon establishes supremacy over Greece.
337–323 BC	Alexander of Macedon defeats Persia, conquers Syria and Egypt, and invades Punjab. After his death, the empire is divided between his generals.
324–212 BC	Achaean and Anatolian leagues attempt to maintain independence of Greek cities against Macedon, Egypt and Rome.
146 BC	Greece annexed by Rome.

papers. **Great War,** World War I (1914–18). —**greatness** *n.* [Old English]

great- in combinations (of family relationships) one degree more remote (*great-aunt, great-grandfather; great-great-grandfather*).

Great Artesian Basin the largest area of artesian water in the world, it underlies much of Queensland, New South Wales and South Australia, and in prehistoric times formed a sea. It has an area of 1,750,000 sq km/676,250 sq mi.

Great Australian Bight a broad bay in S Australia, notorious for storms. It was discovered by a Dutch navigator, Captain Thyssen in 1627. The coast was charted by the English explorer Captain Matthew Flinders in 1802.

Great Awakening, the a religious revival in the American colonies from the late 1730s to the 1760s, sparked off by George Whitefield (1714–1770), an itinerant English Methodist preacher whose evangelical fervour and eloquence made many converts.

Great Barrier Reef a chain of coral reefs and islands about 2,000 km/1,250 mi long, off the E coast of Queensland, Australia, at a distance of 15–45 km/10–30 mi. It is believed to be the world's largest living organism and forms an immense natural breakwater. The coral rock forms a structure larger than all human-made structures on Earth combined. Annually, a few nights after the full moon in Nov, 135 species of hard coral release their eggs and sperm for fertilization and the sea turns pink. This phenomenon, one of the wonders of the natural world, was discovered in 1983, and is triggered by a mechanism dependent on the Moon, the tides, and water temperatures.

Great Bear Lake lake on the Arctic Circle, in the Northwest Territories, Canada; area 31,800 sq km/12,275 sq mi.

Great Britain the official name for ◊England, ◊Scotland, and ◊Wales, and the adjacent islands (except the Channel Islands and the Isle of Man) from 1603, when the English and Scottish crowns were united under James I of England (James VI of Scotland). With Northern ◊Ireland it forms the ◊United Kingdom.

great circle a plane cutting through a sphere, and passing through the centre point of the sphere, cuts the surface along a great circle. Thus, on the Earth, all meridians of longitude are half great circles; among the parallels of latitude, only the equator is a great circle.

greatcoat *n.* a heavy overcoat.

Great Dane a large, short-haired dog, usually fawn in colour, standing up to 92 cm/36 in, and weighing up to 70 kg/154 lb, with a long head, a large nose, and small ears. It was formerly used for hunting boar and stags.

Great Dividing Range E Australian mountain range, extending 3,700 km/2,300 mi N–S from Cape York Peninsula, Queensland, to Victoria. It includes the Carnarvon Range, Queensland, which has many Aboriginal cave paintings, the Blue Mountains in New South Wales, and the Australian Alps.

Greater London Council (GLC) in the UK, the local authority that governed London 1965–86. When the GLC was abolished (see ◊local government) its powers either devolved back to the borough councils or were transferred to certain nonelected bodies.

Great Exhibition an exhibition held in Hyde Park, London, UK, in 1851, proclaimed by its originator Prince Albert as 'the Great Exhibition of the Industries of All Nations'. In practice, over half the 100,000 exhibits were from Britain or the British Empire. Over six million people attended the exhibition. The exhibition hall, popularly known as the ◊Crystal Palace, was constructed of glass with a cast-iron frame, and designed by Joseph ◊Paxton.

Great Lakes five freshwater lakes along the USA–Canada border: Lakes Superior, Michigan, Huron, Erie, and Ontario; total area 245,000 sq km/94,600 sq mi. Interconnecting canals make them navigable by large ships, and they are drained by the ◊St Lawrence River. They are said to contain 20% of the world's surface fresh water.

Great Leap Forward the change in the economic policy of the People's Republic of China introduced by ◊Mao Zedong under the second five-year plan of 1958–62. The aim was to convert China into an industrially based economy by transferring resources away from agriculture. This coincided with the creation of people's communes. The inefficient and poorly planned allocation of state resources led to the collapse of the strategy by 1960 and a return to more adequate support for agricultural production.

greatly *adv.* by a considerable amount, much.

Great Patriotic War a term used to describe the war of 1941–45 between the USSR and Germany. When Germany invaded the USSR in June 1941, advanced towards Leningrad and Moscow, but failed to take them, and were eventually forced to surrender at Stalingrad in Jan 1943. The Red Army, under the command of Marshal Zhukov, gradually forced the Germans back and by Feb 1945 the Russians had reached the German border. In April 1945 they entered Berlin, and in May the war ended officially. Some 20 million Russians were killed during the war, and millions more were wounded.

Great Plains a semiarid region E of the Rocky Mountains, USA, stretching as far as the 100th meridian of longitude through Oklahoma, Kansas, Nebraska and the Dakotas. The plains, which cover one-fifth of the USA, extend from Texas in the S over 2,400 km/1,500 mi N to Canada. Ranching and wheat farming have resulted in overexploitation of the water resources to such an extent that available farmland has been reduced by erosion.

Great Power any of the major European powers of the 19th century: Russia, Austria (Austria-Hungary), France, Britain, and Prussia.

Great Red Spot a prominent oval feature, 14,000 km/8,500 mi wide and over 30,000 km/20,000 mi long, in the atmosphere of the planet Jupiter, S of the equator. Observed for over a century, recent space probes showed it to be an anticlockwise vortex of cold clouds, coloured possibly by phosphorus.

Great Rift Valley the longest 'split' in the Earth's surface, 8,000 km/5,000 mi long, running S from the Dead Sea (Israel/Jordan) to Mozambique; see ◊Rift Valley, Great.

Great Schism in European history, the period 1378–1417 in which rival popes had seats at Rome and at Avignon; it was ended by the election of Martin V during the Council of Constance 1414–17.

Great Slave Lake lake in the Northwest Territories, Canada; area 28,450 sq km/10,980 sq mi. It is 615 m/2,020 ft, the deepest lake in North America.

Great Trek in South African history, the movement of 12,000–14,000 Boer (Dutch) settlers from Cape Colony in

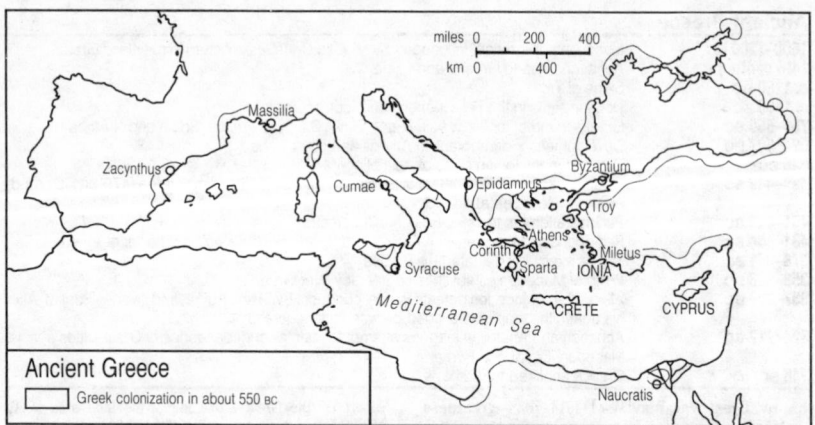

Ancient Greece

☐ Greek colonization in about 550 BC

1835–37 to escape British rule. They established republics in Natal and the Transvaal. It is seen by many white South Africans as the main event in the founding of the present republic and also as a justification for continuing whites-only rule.

Great Wall an array of galaxies arranged almost in a perfect plane, discovered by US astronomers in Cambridge, Massachusetts, in Nov 1989. It consists of some 2,000 galaxies (about 500 million × 200 million light years) and is thought to be the largest structure ever discovered.

Great Wall of China the continuous defensive wall stretching from W Gansu to the Gulf of Liaodong (2,250 km/ 1,450 mi). It was once even longer. It was built under the Qin dynasty from 214 BC to prevent incursions by the Turkish and Mongol peoples. Approximately 8 m/ 25 ft high, it consists of a brick-faced wall of earth and stone, has a series of square watchtowers, and has been carefully restored. It can be seen from space.

Great War another name for ◊World War I.

greave n. (usually in plural) armour for the shin. [from Old French = shin]

grebe n. any of 19 species of water birds belonging to the family Podicipedidae. The great crested grebe *Podiceps cristatus* is the largest of the Old World grebes. It lives in ponds and marshes in Eurasia, Africa, and Australia, feeding on fish. It grows to 50 cm/20 in long and has a white breast, with chestnut and black feathers on its back and head. The head and neck feathers form a crest, especially prominent during the breeding season. [from French]

Grecian /'gri:ʃən/ adj. (of architecture or facial outline) Greek. —**Grecian nose**, a straight nose that continues the line of the forehead without a dip. [from Old French or Latin *Graecia* = Greece]

Greco, El /'grekəʊ/ (Doménikos Theotokópoulos) 1541–1614. Spanish painter called 'the Greek' because he was born in Crete. He studied in Italy, worked in Rome from about 1570, and by 1577 had settled in Toledo. He painted elegant portraits and intensely emotional religious scenes with increasingly distorted figures and flickering light; for example, *The Burial of Count Orgaz* 1586 (Toledo).

Greece /gri:s/ Hellenic Republic; country in SE Europe, comprising the S Balkan peninsula, bounded N by Yugoslavia and Bulgaria, NE by Turkey, E by the Aegean Sea, S by the Mediterranean Sea, W by the Ionian Sea, NW by Albania, and numerous islands to the S and E; **area** 131,957 sq km/50,935 sq mi; **capital** Athens; **physical** mountainous; a large number of islands, notably Crete, Corfu, and Rhodes; **head of state** Christos Sartzetakis from 1985; **head of government** Xenophon Zolotas from 1989; **political system** democratic republic; **exports** tobacco, fruit, vegetables, olives, olive oil, textiles; **population** (1990 est) 10,066,000; **language** Greek; **recent history** civil war in 1946 followed the end of German occupation. The communists were defeated and the monarchy was re-established 1949, but overthrown by a military coup in 1967. Martial law and the ban on political parties were lifted in 1974 and a new constitution adopted in 1975. Greece became a member of the EEC in 1981.

greed n. an excessive desire, especially for food or wealth.

greedy adj. showing greed, wanting or taking in excess; gluttonous; very eager (to do a thing). —**greedily** adv., **greediness** n. [Old English]

Greek /'gri:k/ adj. of Greece or its people or language. —n. a native or the language of Greece. —**Greek cross**, a cross with four equal arms. **Greek fire**, a combustible composition for setting fire to an enemy's ships, works etc., emitted by a flame-throwing weapon, so called from being first used by the Greeks besieged in Constantinople (673–8). **Greek to me**, incomprehensible to me.

Greek art the sculpture, mosaic, and crafts of ancient Greece (no large-scale painting survives). It is usually divided into three periods: **Archaic** (late 8th century–480 BC), showing Egyptian influence; **Classical** (480–323 BC), characterized by dignified realism; and **Hellenistic** (323–27 BC), more exuberant or dramatic. Sculptures of human figures dominate all periods, and vase painting was a focus for artistic development for many centuries.

Greek language a member of the Indo-European language family. **Modern Greek**, which is principally divided into the general vernacular (**Demotic Greek**) and the language of education and literature (**Katharevousa**), has a long and well-documented history: **Ancient Greek** from the 14th to the 12th century BC; **Archaic Greek** including Homeric epic language, until 800 BC; **Classical Greek** until 400 BC; **Hellenistic Greek**, the common language of Greece, Asia Minor, W Asia, and Egypt, to 4th century AD, and **Byzantine Greek** used until the 15th century and still the ecclesiastical language of the Greek Orthodox Church.

green /gri:n/ adj. **1.** of a colour between blue and yellow. **2.** covered with leaves or grass. **3.** (of fruit etc. or wood) unripe or unseasoned; not dried, smoked, or tanned. **4.** inexperienced, gullible. **5.** sickly-hued; jealous, envious. **6.** young, flourishing; not withered or worn out. —n. **1.** green colour or pigment; green clothes or material. **2.** a piece of grassy public land; a grassy area for a special purpose. **3.** (in plural) green vegetables. **4.** vigour, youth. —v.t./i. to make or become green. —**green belt**, an area of open land for preservation round a city. **green card**, a motorist's international insurance document. **green-eyed** adj. jealous. **green fingers**, skill in growing plants. **green light**, a signal to proceed on a road etc., (colloquial) permission to go ahead with a project. **greenroom** n. a room behind the stage, probably so called because it was originally painted green, for the use of actors and actresses when not required on stage. **Greens** n.pl. (colloquial) Green Party. **greenstick fracture**, a fracture, especially in children, in which one side of a bone is broken and one only bent. **green tea**, tea made from steam-dried leaves. —**greenish** adj., **greenly** adv., **greenness** n. [Old English]

Green Henry. Pen name of Henry Vincent Yorke 1905–1974. British novelist, whose works (for example *Loving* 1945, and *Nothing* 1950) are characterized by an experimental colloquial prose style and extensive use of dialogue.

Greenaway /'gri:nəweɪ/ Kate 1846–1901. British illustrator, known for her drawings of children. In 1877 she first

Greene *English author Graham Greene by the Canadian photographer Karsh.*

exhibited at the Royal Academy, and began her collaboration with the colour-printer Edmund Evans, with whom she produced a number of children's books, including *Mother Goose.*

Greenbackers, the /ˈgriːbækəz/ in US history, a supporter of an alliance of agrarian and industrial organizations, known as the Greenback Labor Party, which campaigned for currency inflation by increasing the paper dollars 'greenbacks' in circulation. In 1880 the party's presidential nominee polled only 300,000 votes; the movement was later superseded by ◊Populism.

Greene /griːn/ (Henry) Graham 1904–1991. English writer, whose novels of guilt, despair, and penitence, include *The Man Within* 1929, *Brighton Rock* 1938, *The Power and the Glory* 1940, *The Heart of the Matter* 1948, *The Third Man* 1950, *The Honorary Consul* 1973, *Monsignor Quixote* 1982, and *The Captain and the Enemy* 1988.

greenery *n.* green foliage or growing plants.

greenfinch *n.* a bird *Carduelis chloris*, common in Europe and N Africa. The male is green with a yellow breast, and the female a greenish-brown.

greenfly *n.* a plant-sucking insect, a type of ◊aphid; such insects collectively.

greengage *n.* a round, green plum. [from Sir W *Gage* (*c.*1725)]

greengrocer *n.* a retailer of fruit and vegetables. —**greengrocery** *n.*

Greenham Common /ˈgriːnəm/ site of a continuous peace demonstration on common land near Newbury, Berkshire, UK, outside a US airbase. The women-only camp was established in Sept 1981 in protest against the siting of US cruise missiles in the UK. The demonstrations ended in 1990 with the closure of the base.

greenhorn *n.* an inexperienced person, a new recruit. [originally of animals with 'green' or young horns]

greenhouse *n.* a light structure with the sides and roof mainly of glass, for rearing plants.

greenhouse effect a phenomenon of the Earth's atmosphere by which solar radiation, absorbed by the Earth and re-emitted from the surface, is prevented from escaping by carbon dioxide in the air. The result is a rise in the Earth's temperature. The concentration of carbon dioxide in the atmosphere is estimated to have risen by 25% since the Industrial Revolution, and 10% since 1950; the rate of increase is now 0.5% a year. ◊Chlorofluorocarbon levels are rising by 5% a year, and nitrous oxide levels by 0.4% a year, resulting in a global warming effect of 0.5% since 1900, and a rise of about 0.1°C a year in the temperature of

the world's oceans during the 1980s. Arctic ice was 6–7 m, 20–23 ft thick in 1976 and had reduced to 4–5 m, 13–17 ft by 1987. The United Nations Environment Programme estimates an increase in average world temperatures of 1.5°C/2.7°F with a consequent rise of 20 cm/7.7 in in sea level by 2025.

Greenland /ˈgriːnlənd/ the world's largest island. It lies between the North Atlantic and Arctic Oceans; **area** 2,175,600 sq km/840,000 sq mi; **capital** Godthaab; **economy** fishing and fish-processing; **population** (1983) 51,903; Inuit, Danish and other European; **language** Greenlandic; **history** Greenland became a Danish colony in the 18th century, and obtained full internal self-government in 1981.

Green Mountain Boys in US history, irregular troops who fought to protect the Vermont part of what was then New Hampshire colony from land claims made by neighbouring New York. In the American Revolution they captured ◊Fort Ticonderoga from the British. Their leader was Ethan Allen (1738–89), who was later captured by the British. Vermont declared itself an independent republic, refusing to join the Union until 1791. It is popularly known as the Green Mountain State.

Green Paper a publication issued by a British government department setting out various aspects of a matter on which legislation is contemplated, and inviting public discussion and suggestions. In due course it may be followed by a ◊White Paper, giving details of proposed legislation. The first Green Paper was published in 1967.

Green Party a political party aiming to 'preserve the planet and its people', based on the premise that incessant economic growth is unsustainable. The leaderless party structure reflects a general commitment to decentralization. Green parties sprang up in W Europe in the 1970s and spread in the 1980s. Parties in different countries are linked to one another but unaffiliated to any pressure group. They had a number of parliamentary seats in 1989: Austria 8, Belgium 11, Finland 4, Italy 20, Luxembourg 2, Republic of Ireland 1, Sweden 20, Switzerland 9, West Germany 42; and 24 members of the European Parliament (Belgium 3, France 9, Italy 3, Portugal 1, West Germany 8).

Greenpeace *n.* an international environmental pressure group, founded in 1971, with a policy of nonviolent direct action backed by scientific research. During a protest against French atmospheric nuclear testing in the S Pacific in 1985, its ship *Rainbow Warrior* was sunk by French intelligence agents, killing a crew member.

green pound the exchange rate used by the European Community for the conversion of EC agricultural prices to sterling. The prices for all EC members are set in European Currency Units (ECUs) and are then converted into green currencies for each national currency.

green revolution in agriculture, a popular term (coined by ◊Borlaug) for the change in methods of arable farming in developing countries. The intention is to provide more and better food for their populations, albeit with a heavy reliance on chemicals and machinery. It was instigated in the 1940s and 1950s, but abandoned by some countries in the 1980s.

greensand *n.* a green sandstone.

greenshank *n.* a greyish bird *Tringa nebularia* of the sandpiper group. It has long olive-green legs and a slightly upturned bill. It breeds in Scotland and N Europe.

greenstone *n.* **1.** a green eruptive rock containing feldspar and hornblende. **2.** (*New Zealand*) a kind of jade.

Greenstreet /ˈgriːnstriːt/ Sidney 1879–1954. British character actor. He made an impressive film debut in *The Maltese Falcon* 1941 and became one of the cinema's best-known villains. His other films included *Casablanca* 1943 and *The Mask of Dimitrios* 1944.

greenstuff *n.* vegetation, green vegetables.

greensward *n.* an expanse of grassy turf.

Greenwich /ˈgrenɪdʒ/ inner borough of Greater London, England; population (1981) 212,001. Greenwich landmarks include the **Queen's House** 1637, designed by Inigo Jones, the first Palladian-style building in England; the **Royal Naval College**, designed by Christopher Wren in 1694; the **Royal Observatory** (founded here in 1675). The source of Greenwich Mean Time has been moved, but the Greenwich meridian (0°) remains unchanged. The *Cutty Sark*, one of the great tea clippers, is preserved as a museum of sail.

Greenwich Mean Time (GMT) local time on the zero

line of longitude (the **Greenwich meridian**), which passes through the Old Royal Observatory at Greenwich, London. It was replaced in 1986 by coordinated universal time (UTC); see ◊time.

Greenwich Village a section of New York's lower Manhattan. From the late 19th century it became the bohemian and artistic quarter of the city and, despite rising rentals, remains so.

greenwood /ˈgriːnwʊd/ n. woodlands in summer.

Greer /grɪə/ Germaine 1939–. Australian feminist, who became widely known on the publication of her book *The Female Eunuch* 1970. Later works include *The Obstacle Race* 1979, a study of contemporary women artists, and *Sex and Destiny: The Politics of Human Fertility* 1984. She is also a speaker and activist.

Probably the only place where a man can feel really secure is in a maximum security prison, except for the imminent threat of release.

Germaine Greer
The Female Eunuch

---

greet[1] v.t. 1. to address politely on meeting or arrival. 2. to salute, to receive (a person, news etc., *with* a reaction). 3. (of a sight, sound etc.) to meet (the eye, ear etc.). [Old English]

greet[2] v.i. (*Scottish*) to weep. [Old English]

greeting n. words, gestures etc., used to greet a person; (often in *plural*) an expression of goodwill. —**greetings card**, a decorative card sent to convey greetings.

gregarious /grɪˈgeərɪəs/ adj. 1. fond of company. 2. living in flocks or communities. —**gregariously** adv **gregariousness** n. [from Latin *grex* = flock]

Gregorian calendar /grɪˈɡɔːrɪən/the modified calendar, also known as the 'New Style', in which a century year is not a leap year unless it is divisible by 400, introduced by Pope Gregory XIII in 1582, adopted in Great Britain in 1752, and now in use throughout most of the Christian world.

Gregorian chant any of a body of plainsong choral chants associated with Pope Gregory the Great, which became standard in the Roman Catholic Church.

Gregory /ˈgregəri/ Isabella Augusta (born Persse) 1852–1932. Irish playwright, associated with W B Yeats in creating the ◊Abbey Theatre, Dublin 1904. Her plays include the comedy *Spreading the News* 1904 and the tragedy *Gaol Gate* 1906. Her journals covering the years 1916–30 were published in 1946.

Gregory name of 16 popes, including:

Gregory I St, **the Great** c.540–604. Pope from 590, who asserted Rome's supremacy and exercised almost imperial powers. In 596 he sent St ◊Augustine to England. He introduced the choral Gregorian chant into the liturgy. Feast day 12 Mar.

Gregory VII or **Hildebrand** c.1023–1085. Chief minister to several popes before his election to the papacy in 1073. In 1077 he forced the Holy Roman emperor Henry IV to wait in the snow at Canossa for four days, dressed as a penitent, before receiving pardon. He was driven from Rome and died in exile. Feast day 25 May.

Gregory XIII 1502–1585. Pope from 1572, who introduced the reformed Gregorian calendar, still in use.

Gregory of Tours, St /tuə/ 538–594. French Christian bishop of Tours from 573, author of a *History of the Franks*. Feast day 17 Nov.

gremlin /ˈgremlɪn/ n. (*slang*) a mischievous sprite said to interfere with machinery etc.

Grenada /grəˈneɪdə/ island country in the Caribbean, the southernmost of the Windward Islands. **area** (including the Grenadines) 340 sq km/131 sq mi; **capital** St George's; **physical** southernmost of the Windward Islands; **mountainous; head of state** Elizabeth II from 1974 represented by governor general; **head of government** Ben Jones from 1989; **political system** emergent democracy; **exports** coca, nutmeg, bananas, mace; **population** (1990 est) 84,000, 84% of black African descent; **language** English (official); some French patois spoken; **recent history** independence achieved from UK in 1974. Constitution suspended and people's revolutionary government

established 1979. Relations with USSR and Cuba strengthened. After a coup in 1983 the USA invaded and reinstated the 1974 constitution.

grenade /grɪˈneɪd/ n. a small bomb thrown by hand or shot from a rifle. [French, from Old French and Spanish = pomegranate]

grenadier /grenəˈdɪə/ n. (*historical*) a soldier armed with grenades. —**Grenadiers** or **Grenadier Guards**, the first regiment of the royal household infantry. [French]

Grenadines /ˈgrenədiːnz/ a chain of about 600 small islands in the Caribbean sea, part of the group known as the Windward Islands. They are divided between ◊St Vincent and ◊Grenada.

Grenville /ˈgrenvɪl/ George 1712–1770. British Whig politician, prime minister and chancellor of the Exchequer 1763–65. His government prosecuted the Radical John ◊Wilkes in 1763, and passed the Stamp Act 1765 that precipitated the American Revolution.

Grenville Richard 1542–1591. English naval commander and adventurer, renowned for his heroic death aboard his ship the *Revenge* when attacked by Spanish warships. Grenville fought in Hungary and Ireland 1566–69, and was knighted about 1577. In 1585 he commanded the expedition that founded Virginia, USA, for his cousin Walter ◊Raleigh. From 1586 to 1588 he organized the defence of England against the Spanish Armada.

Grenville William Wyndham, Baron 1759–1834. British Whig politician, son of George Grenville. He was foreign secretary in 1791 and resigned along with Pitt in 1801 over King George III's refusal to assent to Catholic emancipation. He headed the 'All the Talents' coalition of 1806–07, which abolished the slave trade.

Gretna Green /ˈgretnə ˈgriːn/ village in Dumfries and Galloway region, Scotland, where runaway marriages were legal after they were banned in England in 1754; all that was necessary was the couple's declaration, before witnesses, of their willingness to marry. From 1856 Scottish law required at least one of the parties to be resident in Scotland for a minimum of 21 days before the marriage, and marriage by declaration was abolished in 1940.

Greville /ˈgrevɪl/ Charles (Cavendish Fulke) 1794–1865. British diarist. He was Clerk of the Council in Ordinary 1821–59, an office which brought him into close contact with all the personalities of the court and of both political parties. They provided him with much of the material for his *Memoirs* 1817–60.

Greville Fulke, 1st Baron Brooke 1554–1628. Poet and courtier, friend and biographer of Philip Sidney. Greville's works, none of them published during his lifetime, include *Caelica*, a sequence of poems in different metres; *Mustapha* and *Alaham*, tragedies modelled on the Latin *Seneca* and the *Life of Sir Philip Sidney* 1652. He has been commended for his plain style and tough political thought.

grew past of **grow**.

grey /greɪ/ adj. 1. of a colour between black and white. 2. dull, dismal. 3. (of the hair) turning white; (of a person) with grey hair. 4. aged, experienced, mature, ancient. 5. anonymous, unidentifiable. —n. 1. grey colour or pigment; grey clothes or material. 2. a grey horse. —v.t./i. to become or make grey. —**grey area**, that part of a matter where there are no exact rules about right and wrong etc. **Grey Friars**, Franciscan friars, so called from their grey cloaks. **grey matter**, the parts of the brain, consisting of nerve-cell bodies, that are grey in appearance; (*colloquial*) intelligence. **grey squirrel**, a common squirrel of the USA *Sciurus carolinensis* which was introduced into Europe in the late 19th century —**greyish** adj., **greyness** n. [Old English]

Grey Beryl 1927– . British ballerina. Prima ballerina with the Sadler's Wells Company 1942–57, she then danced internationally, and was artistic director of the London Festival Ballet 1968–79.

Grey Charles, 2nd Earl 1764–1845. British Whig politician. He entered Parliament in 1786, and in 1806 became First Lord of the Admiralty, and foreign secretary soon afterwards. As prime minister 1830–34, he carried the Great Reform Bill that reshaped the Parliamentary representative system in 1832 and the act abolishing slavery throughout the British Empire in 1833.

Grey Edward, 1st Viscount Grey of Fallodon 1862–1933. British Liberal politician, nephew of Charles Grey. As foreign secretary 1905–16 he negotiated an entente with Russia in 1907, and backed France against Germany in the ◊Agadir Incident of 1911.

Grey Henry, 3rd Earl 1802–1894. British politician, son of Charles Grey. He served under his father as undersecretary for the colonies 1830–33, resigning because the cabinet would not back the immediate emancipation of slaves; he was secretary of war 1835–39 and colonial secretary 1846–52.

Grey Lady Jane 1537–1554. Queen of England for ten days, 9–19 July 1553, the great-granddaughter of Henry VII. She was married in 1553 to Lord Guildford Dudley (died 1554), son of the Duke of ◊Northumberland. Edward VI was persuaded by Northumberland to set aside the claims to the throne of his sisters Mary and Elizabeth. When Edward died on 6 July the same year, Jane reluctantly accepted the crown and was proclaimed queen four days later. Mary, although a Roman Catholic, had the support of the populace, and the Lord Mayor of London announced that she was queen on 19 July. Lady Jane Grey was executed on Tower Green.

Grey Zane 1875–1939. US author of westerns, such as *Riders of the Purple Sage* 1912.

greyhound *n.* an ancient breed of dog, with a long, narrow muzzle, slight build, and long legs, renowned for its swiftness and used in racing and coursing. It is up to 75 cm/2.5 ft tall, and can exceed 60 kph/40 mph. [Old English = bitch-hound]

greylag *n.* the European wild goose, *Anser anser*.

grid *n.* 1. a grating. 2. a system of numbered squares printed on a map and forming the basis of map references. 3. a network of lines, electric-power connections, gas-supply lines, etc. 4. a pattern of lines marking the starting places on a car-racing track. 5. a wire network between the filament and anode of a thermionic valve. 6. an arrangement of town streets in a rectangular pattern. 7. a gridiron.

griddle *n.* a girdle²; a round iron plate used in bakery. [from Old French from Latin *craticula* (*cratis* = hurdle)]

gridiron /'grɪdaɪən/ *n.* a cooking utensil of metal bars for broiling or grilling.

grief /griːf/ *n.* deep or intense sorrow; a cause of this. —**come to grief**, to meet with disaster. [from Old French]

Grieg /griːg/ Edvard Hagerup 1843–1907. Norwegian composer. Much of his music is small scale, particularly his songs, dances, sonatas, and piano works. Among his orchestral works are the *Piano Concerto* 1869 and the incidental music for Ibsen's *Peer Gynt* 1876.

grievance /'griːvəns/ *n.* a real or fancied ground of complaint. [from Old French]

grievance procedure formal arrangements with an employer, usually operating through a trade union, for settling employees' grievances.

grieve /griːv/ *v.t./i.* to cause grief to; to feel grief. [from Old French from Latin *gravare* (*gravis* = heavy)]

grievous /'griːvəs/ *adj.* (of pain etc.) severe; causing grief; injurious; flagrant, heinous. —**grievous bodily harm**, in law, serious injury. —**grievously** *adv.* [from Old French]

griffin a mythical monster, the supposed guardian of hidden treasure, with the body, tail, and hind legs of a lion, and the head, forelegs, and wings of an eagle. It is often found in heraldry, for example, the armorial crest of the City of London. [from Old French from Latin *gryphus* from Greek]

Griffith /'grɪfɪθ/ D(avid) W(ark) 1875–1948. US film director. He made hundreds of 'one reelers' (lasting 12 minutes) 1908–13, in which he pioneered the techniques of the flashback, crosscut, close-up, and longshot. After much experimentation with photography and new techniques came the epic *The Birth of a Nation* 1915, followed by *Intolerance* 1916. He was a cofounder of United Artists.

Griffith-Joyner /grɪfɪθ'dʒɔɪnə/ (born Griffith) Delorez Florence 1959– . US track athlete who won three gold medals at the 1988 Seoul Olympics, the 100 and 200 metres and the sprint relay. Her time in the 200 metres was a world record 21.34 seconds.

griffon /'grɪfən/ *n.* 1. a small breed of dog originating in Belgium, red, black, or black and tan in colour and weighing up to 5 kg/11 lb. Griffons are square-bodied and round-headed, and there are rough and smooth-coated varieties. 2. a griffin. [variant of *griffin*]

griffon vulture a bird *Gyps fulvus* found in S Europe, W and Central Asia, and parts of Africa. It has a bald head with

Grimaldi *Joseph Grimaldi, the clown who gave the name 'Joey' to all later clowns.*

a neck ruff, and is 1.1 m/3.5 ft long with a wingspan of up to 2.7 m/9 ft.

grill *n.* 1. a device on a cooker for radiating heat downwards. 2. a gridiron. 3. grilled food. 4. a grillroom. 5. a grille. —*v.t.* 1. to cook on a gridiron or under a grill. 2. to subject to or undergo torture or great heat; to subject to severe questioning, especially by the police. —**grillroom** *n.* a small restaurant serving grills etc. [variant of *grille*]

grille /grɪl/ *n.* 1. a grating or latticed screen, especially in a door. 2. a metal grid protecting the radiator of a motor vehicle. [French from Latin *cratis* = hurdle]

Grillparzer /'grɪlpɑːtsə/ Franz 1791–1872. Austrian poet and dramatist. His plays include the tragedy *Die Ahnfrau/The Ancestress* 1817, the classical *Sappho* 1818, and the trilogy *Das goldene Vliess/The Golden Fleece* 1821.

grilse *n.* a young salmon that has been only once to the sea.

grim *adj.* 1. of harsh or forbidding appearance; stern, merciless. 2. ghastly, joyless; unpleasant, unattractive. —**grimly** *adv.*, **grimness** *n.* [Old English]

grimace /grɪ'meɪs/ *n.* a distortion of the face in disgust etc., or to amuse. —*v.i.* to make a grimace. [French from Spanish *grimazo* (*grima* = fright)]

Grimaldi /grɪ'mɔːldi/ Joseph 1779–1837. British clown, born in London, the son of an Italian actor. He appeared on the stage at two years old. He gave his name 'Joey' to all later clowns, and excelled as 'Mother Goose' performed at Covent Garden in 1806.

grime *n.* soot or dirt ingrained in a surface, especially the skin. —*v.t.* to blacken with grime. —**grimy** *adj.*, **griminess** *n.* [from Middle Low German or Middle Dutch]

Grimm /grɪm/ Jakob Ludwig Karl 1785–1863. German philologist who formulated ◊Grimm's Law and collaborated with his brother **Wilhelm Karl** (1786–1859) in the *Fairy Tales* 1812–14, based on collected folk tales. Jakob's main work was his *Deutsche Grammatick/German Grammar* 1819, the first historical treatment of the ◊Germanic languages.

Grimm's law in linguistics, the rule (formulated in 1822 by Jacob Grimm) by which certain prehistoric sound changes have occurred in the consonants of Indo-European languages: for example Latin *p* became English and German *f*, as in *pater*—*father*, *Vater*.

Grimond /'grɪmənd/ Jo(seph), Baron Grimond 1913– . British Liberal politician. As leader of the party 1956–67, he aimed at making it 'a new radical party to take the place of the Socialist Party as an alternative to Conservatism'.

grin v.t./i. (-nn-) to smile broadly, showing the teeth; to make a forced, unrestrained or stupid smile; to express by grinning. —n. an act or the action of grinning. —**grin and bear it,** to take pain etc. stoically. [Old English]

grind /graɪnd/ v.t./i. (past and past participle ground) 1. to crush to small particles; to produce (flour) thus. 2. to oppress, to harass with exorbitant demands. 3. to sharpen or smooth by friction. 4. to rub together gratingly. 5. to study hard, to toil. 6. to produce or bring out with effort. 7. to turn the handle of (a barrel organ). —n. 1. grinding. 2. hard, dull work. 3. the size of ground particles. —**grind to a halt,** to stop laboriously with the sound of grating. **ground glass,** glass made opaque by grinding. [Old English]

grinder /ˈgraɪndə/ n. 1. a person or thing (especially a machine) that grinds. 2. a molar tooth.

grindstone n. a thick, revolving disc used for grinding, sharpening, and polishing; the kind of stone used for this. —**keep one's nose to the grindstone,** to work hard and continuously.

grip v.t./i. (-pp-) 1. to grasp tightly; to take a firm hold, especially by friction. 2. to compel the attention of. —n. 1. a firm hold, a grasp. 2. grasping power; way of clasping the hands or of grasping or holding. 3. mastery, intellectual hold. 4. a gripping part of a machine etc.; the part of a weapon etc. that is held. 5. a hairgrip. 6. (US) a suitcase, a travelling bag. —**come** or **get to grips with,** to approach purposefully, to begin to deal with. [Old English]

gripe v.t./i. 1. to cause colic; to affect with colic. 2. (slang) to complain. 3. to clutch, to grip. 4. to oppress. —n. 1. (usually in plural) colic. 2. (slang) a complaint. —**gripe water** n. a medicine to cure colic in babies. [Old English]

Gris /griːs/ Juan 1887–1927. Spanish abstract painter, one of the earliest Cubists. He developed a distinctive geometrical style, often strongly coloured. He experimented with paper collage and made designs for Diaghilev's Ballet Russes 1922–23.

grisaille /griˈzeɪl, -ˈzaɪ/ n. a method of decorative painting in grey monochrome representing figures and objects in relief; a stained-glass window of this kind. [French gris = grey]

grisly /ˈgrɪzlɪ/ adj. causing horror, disgust, or fear. —**grisliness** n. [Old English]

Grisons /griːˈsɒn/ French name for the Swiss canton of ◊Graubünden.

grist n. corn to grind. —**grist to the mill,** a source of profit or advantage. [Old English]

gristle /ˈgrɪsəl/ n. tough, flexible tissue, cartilage, especially in meat. —**gristly** adj. [Old English]

grit n. 1. particles of stone or sand, especially as causing discomfort, clogging machinery etc. 2. coarse sandstone. 3. (colloquial) courage, endurance. —v.t./i. (-tt-) 1. to spread grit on (icy roads etc.). 2. to clench (the teeth), especially in enduring pain or trouble. 3. to make a grating sound. —**gritty** adj., **grittiness** n. [Old English]

grits n.pl. coarsely ground grain, especially oatmeal; oats that have been husked but not ground. [Old English]

Grivas /ˈgriːvəs/ George 1898–1974. Greek Cypriot general who led the underground group EOKA's attempts to secure the union (Greek ◊enosis) of Cyprus with Greece.

grizzle v.i. (colloquial, especially of a child) to cry fretfully. —**grizzler** n.

grizzled /ˈgrɪzəld/ adj. grey-haired or partly so. [from grizzle = grey from Old French grisel (gris = grey)]

grizzly adj. grey, grey-haired. —n. a grizzly bear. —**grizzly bear,** a large, fierce bear Ursus horribilis of North America.

groan v.t./i. 1. to make a deep sound expressing pain, grief, or disapproval; to utter with groans. 2. to be loaded or oppressed. —n. the sound made in groaning. [Old English]

groat n. 1. a silver coin recognized from the 13th century in various countries of Europe; an English coin issued 1351–1662. 2. a fourpenny piece 1836–56. [from Middle Dutch = great]

groats n.pl. hulled or crushed grain, especially oats. [Old English]

grocer /ˈgrəusə/ n. a dealer in food and household provisions. [from Anglo-French grosser from Latin; originally one who sells in the gross]

grocery n. a grocer's trade or shop; (in plural) grocer's provisions.

grog n. a drink of spirit (originally rum) and water. [perhaps from Grogram, nickname of Admiral Vernon, who in 1740 first had grog served to sailors instead of neat rum]

groggy adj. unsteady, tottering. —**groggily** adv., **grogginess** n.

grogram /ˈgrɒgrəm/ n. a coarse fabric of silk, mohair etc. [from French gros grain = coarse grain]

groin n. 1. the depression between the belly and the thigh. 2. the edge formed by vaults intersecting in a roof; an arch supporting a vault. —v.t. to build with groins. [perhaps from Old English grynde = depression]

Gromyko /grəˈmiːkəu/ Andrei 1909–1989. President of the USSR 1985–88. As ambassador to the USA from 1943, he took part in the Tehran, Yalta, and Potsdam conferences; as United Nations representative 1946–49, he exercised the Soviet veto 26 times. He was foreign minister 1957–85. It was Gromyko who formally nominated Mikhail Gorbachev as Communist Party leader in 1985.

Groningen /ˈgrəunɪŋən/ most northerly province of the Netherlands; **area** 2,350 sq km/907 sq mi; **physical** Ems estuary, innermost W Friesian Islands; **capital** Groningen; **products** natural gas, arable crops, dairy produce, sheep, horses; **population** (1989) 555,200; **history** under the power of the bishops of Utrecht from 1040, Groningen became a member of the Hanseatic League in 1284. Taken by Spain in 1580, it was recaptured by Maurice of Nassau in 1594.

groom n. 1. a person employed to take care of horses. 2. a bridegroom. 3. any of certain officers of the Royal Household. —v.t. 1. to curry or tend (a horse). 2. to give a neat appearance to (a person etc.). 3. to prepare (a person) as a political candidate, for a career etc. [originally = boy]

grooming n. in biology, the use by an animal of teeth, tongue, feet, or beak to clean fur or feathers. Grooming also helps to spread essential oils for waterproofing. In many social species, notably monkeys and apes, grooming of other individuals is used to reinforce social relationships.

groove n. 1. a channel or hollow, especially one made to guide motion or receive a ridge; a spiral cut in a gramophone record for the stylus. 2. a piece of routine, a habit. 3. (slang) something excellent. —v.t./i. to make a groove or grooves in. [from Dutch]

groovy adj. 1. of or like a groove. 2. (slang) excellent.

grope v.t./i. to feel about as in the dark; to search blindly (literally or figuratively). —**grope one's way,** to proceed tentatively. [Old English]

Gropius /ˈgrəupiəs/ Walter Adolf 1883–1969. German architect who lived in the USA from 1937. A founder-director of the ◊Bauhaus school in Weimar 1919–28, he was an advocate of team architecture and artistic standards in industrial production. He was an early proponent of the international modern style defined by glass curtain walls, cubic blocks, and unsupported corners. His works include the Fagus-Werke (a shoe factory in Prussia), the Model Factory at the 1914 Werkbund exhibition in Cologne, and the Harvard Graduate Center 1949–50.

grosbeak n. the name of several thick-billed birds. The pine grosbeak Pinicola enucleator, also known as the **pinefinch,** breeds in Arctic forests. Its plumage is similar to that of the crossbill. [from French grosbec = large beak]

grosgrain /ˈgrəugreɪn/ n. a corded fabric of silk etc. [French = coarse grain]

gros point a type of embroidery, also known as cross-stitch, using wool to fill netting (see ◊petit point). It is normally used in colourful designs on widely spaced canvas. [French]

gross /grəus/ adj. 1. flagrant, outrageous. 2. total, without deductions, not net. 3. not refined, indecent, vulgar. 4. thick, solid. 5. overfed, bloated, repulsively fat; (of vegetation) luxuriant, rank. 6. (of the senses etc.) dull. —n. (plural the same) twelve dozen. —v.t. to produce as gross profit. —**grossly** adv. [from Old French from Latin grossus = big]

Gross Domestic Product (GDP) a measure (normally annual) of the total domestic output of a country, including exports but not imports; see also ◊Gross National Product.

Grossmith /ˈgrəusmɪθ/ George 1847–1912. British actor and singer. Turning from journalism to the stage, in 1877 he began a long association with the Gilbert and Sullivan operas, in which he created a number of parts. He collaborated with his brother **Weedon Grossmith** (1853–1919) on the comic novel *Diary of a Nobody* 1894.

Gross National Product the most commonly used measurement of the wealth of a country. GNP is the ◊Gross Domestic Product plus income from abroad, minus income earned during the same period by foreign investors within the country; see also ◊national income.

Grosz /grəus/ Georg 1893–1959. German Expressionist painter and illustrator, a founder of the Berlin group of the Dada movement 1918. Grosz excelled in savage satirical drawings criticizing the government and the military establishment. After numerous prosecutions he fled his native Berlin in 1932 and became a naturalized American in 1938.

Grosz Károly 1930– . Hungarian Communist politician, prime minister 1987–88. As leader of the ruling Hungarian Socialist Workers' Party (HSWP) 1988–89, he sought to establish a flexible system of 'socialist pluralism'.

Grotefend /ˈgrəutəfent/ George Frederick 1775–1853. German scholar who solved the riddle of the wedgelike ◊cuneiform script as used in ancient Persia: decipherment of Babylonian cuneiform followed from his work.

grotesque /grəuˈtesk/ *adj.* comically or repulsively distorted; incongruous, absurd. —*n.* 1. a decoration interweaving human and animal forms with foliage. 2. a comically distorted figure or design. —**grotesquely** *adv.*, **grotesqueness** *n.* [from French from Italian]

Grotius /ˈgrəutiəs/ Hugo 1583–1645. Dutch jurist and politician, born in Delft. He became a lawyer, and later received political appointments. In 1618 he was arrested as a republican and sentenced to imprisonment for life. His wife contrived his escape in 1620, and he settled in France, where he composed the *De Jure Belli et Pacis/On the Law of War and Peace* 1625, the foundation of international law. He was Swedish ambassador in Paris 1634–45.

grotto /ˈgrɒtəu/ *n.* (*plural* **grottoes**) a picturesque cave; an artificial or simulated cave. [from Italian *grotta* from Latin]

grotty *adj.* (*slang*) unpleasant, dirty, ugly, useless. [from *grotesque*]

grouch *v.i.* (*colloquial*) to grumble. —*n.* (*colloquial*) a discontented person; a fit of grumbling or the sulks. —**groucher** *n.*, **grouchy** *adj.*

ground[1] *n.* 1. the surface of the Earth, especially as contrasted with the air around it; a part of this specified in some way; a position or area on the earth's surface. 2. a foundation or motive. 3. an area of a special kind or use. 4. the surface worked upon in painting etc.; the predominant colour. 5. (in *plural*) enclosed land attached to a house. 6. (in *plural*) dregs, especially of coffee. 7. an electrical earth. 8. the bottom of the sea. 9. the floor of a room etc. —*attrib.* (in the names of birds) terrestrial; (of animals) burrowing, living on the ground; (of plants) dwarfish, trailing. —*v.t./i.* 1. to run aground, to strand. 2. to refuse authority for (an airman or aircraft) to fly. 3. to instruct thoroughly (*in* a subject). 4. to base (a principle or conclusion *on* a fact etc.). 5. to connect with the Earth as a conductor. 6. to alight on the ground. 7. to place or lay (especially weapons) on the ground. —**break new ground**, to treat a subject previously not dealt with. **cover the ground**, to deal adequately with a subject. **fall to the ground**, (of a plan etc.) to fail. **get off the ground**, to make a successful start. **give** *or* **lose ground**, to retreat, to decline. **go to ground**, (of a fox etc.) to enter an earth, etc.; (of a person) to withdraw from public notice. **ground bass**, a short theme constantly repeated in the bass with the upper parts of the music varied. **ground frost**, frost on the surface of the ground or in the top layer of soil. **ground plan**, a plan of a building at ground level, the general outline of a scheme. **ground rent**, the rent for land leased for building. **groundspeed** *n.* aircraft speed relative to the ground. **ground squirrel**, a burrowing rodent related to the squirrel. **ground swell**, a heavy sea due to a distant or past storm or earthquake. **ground water**, the water found in the surface soil. **hold one's ground**, not to retreat. [Old English]

ground[2] past and past participle of **grind**.

groundhog *n.* the North American marmot, the woodchuck.

grounding *n.* basic training or instruction in a subject.

groundless *adj.* without motive or foundation. —**groundlessly** *adv.*

groundnut *n.* another name for ◊peanut.

groundsel /ˈgraunsəl/ *n.* a plant of the genus *Senecio*, of which the commonest species, a garden weed, is used as a food for cagebirds. [Old English]

groundsheet *n.* a waterproof sheet for spreading on the ground.

groundsman *n.* (*plural* **groundsmen**) a person who maintains a sports ground.

groundwork *n.* preliminary or basic work.

group /gruːp/ *n.* 1. a number of persons or things close together, or belonging or classed together. 2. a number of commercial companies under a single ownership. 3. a pop group. 4. a division of an air force. 5. in mathematics, a set of elements with an operation for combining any pair to give another element in the set. —*v.t.* to form into a group; to place in a group or groups. —**group captain**, an RAF officer next below air commodore. **group theory**, in mathematics, the study of the structure and applications of sets that form groups. **group therapy**, therapy in which similarly affected patients are brought together to assist one another. [from French from Italian *gruppo*]

Group Areas Act in South Africa, an Act of 1950, under which the different races in South Africa were assigned to separate areas. Demonstrations and interracial riots resulted from such measures of segregation.

grouper *n.* a number of species of sea perch (family Serranidae), carnivorous fish found in warm waters. Some species grow to 2 m/6.5 ft long, and can weigh 300 kg/660 lbs.

grouse[1] /graus/ *n.* (*plural* the same) a fowl-like game bird of the family Tetraonidae, common in North America and N Europe. Grouse are mostly ground-living and are noted for their courtship displays, known as ◊leks.

grouse[2] *v.i.* (*colloquial*) to grumble, to complain. —*n.* (*colloquial*) a grumble. —**grouser** *n.*

grout *n.* thin, fluid mortar. —*v.t.* to apply grout to. [compare dialect French *grouter* = grout a wall]

grove *n.* a small wood, a group of trees. [Old English]

grovel /ˈgrɒvəl/ *v.i.* (-ll-) to lie prone in abject humility; to humble oneself.

grovelling *adj.* abject, base; prone. [from Old Norse from obsolete *grufe* = face down]

grow /grəu/ *v.t./i.* (*past* **grew**; *past participle* **grown**) 1. to increase in size, height, amount, intensity etc. 2. to develop or exist as a living plant or natural product. 3. to become gradually. 4. to produce by cultivation; to let (a beard etc.) develop; (in *passive*) to be covered (*over* etc.) with growth. —**growing pains**, neuralgic pain in children's legs due to fatigue etc.; early difficulties in the development of a project etc. **grown-up** *adj.* adult; (*n.*) an adult. **grow on**, to have an increasing charm etc. for. **grow out of**, to become too large to wear (a garment); to become too mature to retain (a habit etc.); to develop from. **grow up**, to advance to maturity; (of a custom) to arise. [Old English]

grower *n.* 1. a person growing produce, especially fruit. 2. a plant that grows in a specified way.

growl /graul/ *n.* a guttural sound of anger; a rumble; an angry murmur, a complaint. —*v.t./i.* to make a growl; to utter with a growl.

grown past participle of **grow**.

growth /grəuθ/ *n.* 1. growing, development. 2. increase in size or value. 3. what has grown or is growing. 4. a tumour. —**growth industry**, an industry developing faster than most others.

groyne /grɔin/ *n.* a structure of wood, stone, or concrete projecting towards the sea, preventing sand and pebbles from being washed away by the current. —*v.t.* to protect with groynes. [from dialect *groin* = snout from Old French from Latin *grunnire* = grunt]

GRP abbreviation of glass-reinforced plastic, plastic material strengthened by glass fibres, usually called, erroneously, ◊fibreglass. GRP is a favoured material for boat hulls and the bodies and some structural components of performance cars; it is also used in the manufacture of passenger cars.

grub *n.* 1. the larva of an insect; a maggot. 2. (*slang*) food. —*v.t./i.* (-bb-) 1. to dig superficially. 2. to clear (ground) of roots etc.; to clear away (roots etc.); to fetch *up* or *out* by digging (*literally* or *figuratively* in books etc.); to rummage. —**grub screw**, a headless screw.

grubby *adj.* 1. dirty. 2. full of grubs. —**grubbily** *adv.*, **grubbiness** *n.*

grudge *v.t.* to be resentfully unwilling to give or allow. —*n.* a feeling of resentment or ill will. —**grudging** *adj.*, **grudgingly** *adv.* [from Old French *grouc(h)ier* = murmur]

gruel /'gruəl/ *n.* a liquid food of oatmeal etc. boiled in milk or water. [from Old French]

gruelling /'gru:əlɪŋ/ *adj.* exhausting.

gruesome /'gru:səm/ *adj.* horrible, grisly, disgusting. [from Scottish *grue* = to shudder]

gruff *adj.* (of the voice) low and harsh; having a gruff voice; surly. —**gruffly** *adv.*, **gruffness** *n.* [from Dutch or Middle Low German *grof* = coarse]

grumble *v.t./i.* 1. to complain peevishly; to be discontented. 2. to make a rumbling sound. —*n.* an act or sound of grumbling. —**grumbler** *n.* [compare Middle Dutch *grommen*]

grummet /'grʌmɪt/ *n.* 1. an insulating washer placed round an electric conductor where it passes through a hole in metal. 2. (*nautical*) a ring usually of twisted rope as a fastening etc. [from French *gourmer* = to curb]

grumpy *adj.* morose and irritable, surly. —**grumpily** *adv.*, **grumpiness** *n.*

Grünewald /'gru:nəvælt/ (Mathias Gothardt/Neithardt) *c.*1475–1528. German painter, active in Mainz, Frankfurt, and Halle. He was court painter, architect, and engineer to the archbishop of Mainz 1508–14. His few surviving paintings show an intense involvement with religious subjects.

grunt *n.* the low, guttural sound characteristic of the pig. —*v.t./i.* 1. to utter a grunt. 2. to speak or say with a grunt. 3. to grumble. [Old English]

gruyère /'gru:jeə/ *n.* a kind of cheese, originally Swiss, with many holes. [from *Gruyère* in Switzerland]

gryphon variant of griffin.

g scale a scale for measuring force by comparing it with the force due to ◊gravity, *g.* Astronauts in the Space Shuttle experience over 3 *g* on liftoff.

G-string /'dʒi:strɪŋ/ *n.* 1. a narrow strip of cloth etc. covering the genitals, attached to a string round the waist. 2. the string on a violin etc. sounding the note G.

GT *n.* a high-performance car. [abbreviation of Italian *gran turismo* = great touring]

Guadalajara /gwɑ:dələ'hɑ:rə/ industrial (textiles, glass, soap, pottery) capital of Jalisco state, W Mexico; population (1986) 2,587,000. It is a key communications centre. It has a 16th–17th-century cathedral, the Governor's Palace, and an orphanage with murals by the Mexican painter José Orozco.

Guadalcanal /gwɑ:dlkə'næl/ the largest of the ◊Solomon Islands; area 6,500 sq km/2,510 sq mi; population (1987) 71,000. Gold, copra, and rubber are produced. During World War II it was the scene of a battle that was won by US forces after six months of fighting.

Guadeloupe /gwɑ:də'lu:p/ an island group in the Leeward Islands, West Indies, an overseas *département* of France; area 1,705 sq km/658 sq mi; population (1982) 328,400. The main islands are Basse-Terre, on which is the chief town of the same name, and Grande-Terre. Sugar refining and rum distilling are the main industries.

Guam /gwɑ:m/ the largest of the ◊Mariana Islands in the W Pacific, an unincorporated territory of the USA; area 540 sq km/208 sq mi; capital Agaña; government popularly elected governor (Ricardo Bordallo from 1985) and single-chamber legislature; products sweet potatoes, fish; tourism is important; population (1984) 116,000; language English, Chamorro (basically Malay-Polynesian); recent history ceded by Spain to the USA 1898; occupied by Japan 1941–44. It was granted full US citizenship and self-government from 1950. A referendum in 1982 favoured commonwealth status.

guan *n.* a type of large, pheasant-like bird which lives in the forests of South and Central America. It is olive-green or brown.

guanaco *n.* a wild member of the camel family *Lama guanacoe*, found in South America on pampas and mountain plateaux. It grows to 1.2 m/4 ft at the shoulder, with head and body about 1.5 m/5 ft long. It is sandy-brown in colour, with a blackish face, and has fine wool. It lives in small herds and is the ancestor of the domestic llama.

Guangdong /gwæŋ'dʊŋ/ formerly **Kwantung** province of S China; area 231,400 sq km/89,320 sq mi; capital ◊Guangzhou; physical tropical climate; products

rice, sugar, tobacco, minerals, fish; population (1986) 63,640,000.

Guangxi Zhuang /'gwæŋ ʃi:/ formerly **Kwangsi Chuang** autonomous region in S China; area 220,400 sq km/85,074 sq mi; capital Nanning; products rice, sugar, fruit; population (1986) 39,460,000; including the Zhuang people, allied to the Thai, who form China's largest ethnic minority.

Guangzhou /gwæŋ'dʒəu/ formerly **Kwangchow**/Canton, capital of Guangdong province, S China; population (1986) 3,290,000; products shipbuilding, engineering, chemicals, and textiles; history the first Chinese port opened to foreign trade, by the Portuguese visiting in 1516, and was a treaty port from 1842 until its occupation by Japan in 1938.

guano /'gwɑ:nəu/ *n.* (*plural* **guanos**) 1. excrement of sea fowl, used as manure. 2. artificial manure, especially that made from fish. [Spanish from Quechua]

Guanyin /ˌgwæn'jɪn/ in Chinese Buddhism, the goddess of mercy. In Japan she is **Kwannon** or Kannon, an attendant of the Amida Buddha (Amitābha). Her origins were in India as the male bodhisattva Avalokiteśvara.

guarana *n.* a Brazilian woody climbing plant *Paullinia cupana*, family Sapindaceae. A drink made from its roasted seeds has a high caffeine content, and it is the source of the drug known as zoom in the USA. Starch, gum, and several oils are extracted from it for commercial use.

Guarani /'gwɑ:rənɪ/ *n.* a member or the language of a South American ethnic group. —*adj.* of this group or their language. [Spanish]

guarantee /gærən'ti:/ *n.* 1. a formal promise or assurance, especially that a thing is of a specified quality and durability. 2. a guarantor. 3. a guaranty; a thing serving as a security. —*v.t.* to give or serve as a guarantee for; to provide with a guarantee; to give one's word; to secure (a thing *to* a person). [earlier *garante*, perhaps from Spanish and French]

guarantor /'gærəntə, -'tɔ:/ *n.* the giver of a guaranty or security.

guaranty /'gærəntɪ/ *n.* an undertaking, usually written, to answer for the payment of a debt or the performance of an obligation by the person primarily liable; the ground of a security. [from Anglo-French *guarantie*, variant of *warantie* = warranty]

guard /gɑ:d/ *v.t./i.* 1. to watch over and defend or protect. 2. to supervise (prisoners etc.) and prevent from escaping. 3. to keep (thoughts or speech) in check. 4. to take precautions (*against*). —*n.* 1. a state of vigilance or watchfulness. 2. a protector, a sentry; (*US*) a prison warder. 3. a railway official in charge of a train. 4. soldiers protecting a place or person; an escort; a separate portion of an army. 5. a device to prevent injury or accident. 6. a defensive posture or motion in boxing, fencing etc. 7. (in *plural*, usually **Guards**) the Household troops. —**on** (or **off**) **one's guard**, ready (or not ready) against an attack or challenge. **stand guard**, to act as a sentry or guard (*over*). [from Old French *garder*]

guardant /'gɑ:dənt/ *adj.* in heraldry, depicted with the body sideways but the face towards the spectator.

guard cell in plants, a specialized cell on the undersurface of leaves for controlling gas exchange and water loss. Guard cells occur in pairs and are shaped so that a pore, or ◊stomata, exists between them. They can change shape with the result that the pore disappears. During warm weather, when a plant is in danger of losing excessive water, the guard cells close, cutting down evaporation from the interior of the leaf.

guarded /'gɑ:dɪd/ *adj.* (of remarks) cautious.

guardhouse *n.* a building accommodating a military guard or securing prisoners.

Guardi /'gwɑ:di/ Francesco 1712–1793. Italian painter. He produced souvenir views of his native Venice that were commercially less successful than Canaletto's but are now considered more atmospheric, with subtler use of reflected light.

guardian /'gɑ:dɪən/ *n.* 1. a protector, a keeper. 2. a person having legal custody of one incapable of managing his or her own affairs, or of his or her property. —**guardianship** *n.* [from Anglo-French]

guardroom *n.* a room accommodating a military guard or securing prisoners.

guardsman *n.* (*plural* **guardsmen**) a soldier belonging to a guard or the Guards.

Guarneri /ˈgwɑːrneəri/ *n.* a celebrated family of stringed-instrument makers of Cremona, Italy. Giuseppe 'del Gesù' (1698–1744) produced the finest models.

Guatemala /gwɑːtəˈmɑːlə/ Republic of; country in Central America, bounded N and NW by Mexico, E by Belize and the Caribbean Sea, SE by Honduras and El Salvador, and SW by the Pacific Ocean. **area** 108,889 sq km/42,031 sq mi; **capital** Guatemala City; **physical** mountainous; narrow coastal plains; limestone plateau in N; frequent earthquakes; **head of state and government** Mario Vinicio Cerezo Arevalo from 1986; **political system** democratic republic; **exports** coffee, bananas, cotton; **population** (1990 est) 9,340,000 (Mayaquiche Indians 54%, mestizos 42%); **language** Spanish (official); 40% speak 18 Indian dialects; **recent history** independence achieved from Spain in 1839. A series of coups from 1954 led to widespread violence. A further coup in 1983 was followed by amnesty for the guerillas and the adoption of a new constitution.

Guatemala City /gwɑːtəˈmɑːlə/ capital of Guatemala; population (1983) 1,300,000. It produces textiles, tyres, footwear, and cement. It was founded in 1776 when its predecessor (Antigua) was destroyed in an earthquake. It was severely damaged by another earthquake in 1976.

guava /ˈgwɑːvə/ *n.* a tropical American tree *Psidium guajava*, family Myrtaceae; its edible, orange, acid fruit has a high vitamin C content. [from Spanish *guayaba*]

Guayaquil /gwaɪəˈkiːl/ largest city and chief Pacific port of Ecuador, at the mouth of the Guayas river; population (1982) 1,300,868.

gubernatorial /gjuːbənəˈtɔːriəl/ *adj.* (*US*) of a governor. [from Latin *gubernator* = governor]

Guderian /guˈdeəriən/ Heinz 1888–1954. German general in World War II. He created the Panzer (German 'armour') divisions that formed the ground spearhead of Hitler's *Blitzkrieg* attack strategy, achieving a significant breakthrough at Sedan in Ardennes, France in 1940, and leading the advance to Moscow in 1941.

gudgeon[1] /ˈgʌdʒən/ *n.* 1. a small freshwater fish *Gobio gobio* used as bait and found in Europe and N Asia on the gravel bottoms of streams. It is olive-brown, spotted with black, up to 20 cm/8 in long, and with a distinctive barbel (a sensory fleshy filament) at each side of the mouth. 2. a credulous person. [from Old French from Latin *gobio* = goby]

gudgeon[2] /ˈgʌdʒən/ *n.* a kind of pivot or metal pin; a socket for a rudder. [from Old French *goujon*]

guelder rose /ˈgeldə/ or **snowball tree** a shrub or small tree *Viburnum opulus*, with clusters of white flowers and shiny red berries, native to Europe and N Africa. [from Dutch *Gelderland* in Holland]

Guercino /gweəˈtʃiːnəu/ (Giovanni Francesco Barbieri) 1590–1666. Italian Baroque painter, active chiefly in Rome. In his ceiling painting of *Aurora* 1621–23 (Villa Ludovisi, Rome), the chariot-borne figure of dawn rides across the heavens, and the architectural framework is imitated in the painting, giving the illusion that the ceiling opens into the sky.

Guérin /geəræn/ Camille 1872–1961. French bacteriologist who, with ◊Calmette, developed the *bacille* Calmette-Guérin (◊BCG) vaccine for tuberculosis.

guernsey /ˈgɜːnzɪ/ 1. a thick, knitted, woollen (usually blue) outer tunic or jersey. 2. (*Australian*) a football shirt.

Guernsey /ˈgɜːnzɪ/ 1. the second largest of the ◊Channel Islands; **area** 63.5 sq km/24.5 sq mi; **population** (1986) 55,500. The **capital** is St Peter Port. Since 1975 it has been a major financial centre. 2. a breed of dairy cattle from Guernsey; an animal of this breed. —**Guernsey lily**, a kind of amaryllis *Nerine sarniensis*.

guerrilla /gəˈrɪlə/ *n.* an irregular soldier fighting in a small unofficial unit, typically against an established or occupying power, and engaging in sabotage, ambush, and the like, rather than pitched battles against an opposing army. Guerrilla tactics have been used both by resistance armies in wartime (for example, the Vietnam War) and in peacetime by national liberation groups and militant political extremists (for example, the ◊PLO; Tamil Tigers). [from Spanish (diminutive of *guerra* = war)]

Guesdes /ged/ Jules 1845–1922. French socialist leader from the 1880s who espoused Marxism and revolutionary change. His movement, the *Partie Ouvrier Français* (French Workers' Party), was eventually incorporated in the foundation of the SFIO (*Section Française de l'International Ouvrière*/French Section of International Labour) in 1905.

guess /ges/ *v.t./i.* 1. to estimate without measurement or detailed calculation. 2. to form an opinion; to form a hypothesis about; to think likely. 3. to conjecture (the answer to a riddle etc.) correctly. —*n.* a rough estimate; a conjecture. —**guess at**, to make a guess concerning. **I guess**, (*US*) I think it likely, I suppose. —**guesser** *n.*

guesswork *n.* guessing; procedure based on this.

guest /gest/ *n.* 1. a person invited to visit one's house or have a meal etc. at one's expense. 2. a person lodging at a hotel, etc. 3. a performer not belonging to the regular company. —**guesthouse** *n.* a superior boarding house. [from Old Norse]

Guevara /giˈvɑːrə/ 'Che' Ernesto 1928–1967. Latin American revolutionary. He was born in Argentina and trained there as a doctor, but in 1953 left his homeland because of his opposition to the right-wing president Perón. In effecting the Cuban revolution of 1959, he was second only to Castro and Castro's brother Raúl. In 1965 he went to the Congo to fight against white mercenaries, and then to Bolivia, where he was killed in an unsuccessful attempt to lead a peasant rising. He was an orthodox Marxist, and renowned for his guerrilla techniques.

guff *n.* (*slang*) empty talk.

guffaw /gʌˈfɔː/ *n.* a boisterous laugh. —*v.i.* to utter a guffaw.

Guiana /giːˈɑːnə/ the NE part of South America, which includes ◊French Guiana, ◊Guyana, and ◊Suriname.

guidance /ˈgaɪdəns/ *n.* guiding, being guided; advice on problems.

guide /gaɪd/ *n.* 1. one who shows the way. 2. a hired conductor for tourists. 3. a person or thing by which others regulate their movements. 4. Guide (formerly **Girl Guide**) a member of a girls' organization corresponding to the Scout Association. 5. an adviser; a directing principle. 6. a book of rudiments; a guidebook. 7. a rod etc. directing motion. 8. a thing marking a position or guiding the eye. —*v.t.* 1. to act as a guide to. 2. to be the principle or motive of. 3. to arrange the course of (events). —**guided missile**, a missile under remote control or directed by equipment within itself. **guide dog**, a dog trained to guide a blind person. **guided tour**, a tour accompanied by a guide. **guideline** *n.* a directing principle. [from Old French]

guidebook *n.* a book of information for tourists.

Guider *n.* an adult leader of Guides.

Guido /ˈgiːdəu/ Reni Italian painter, see ◊Reni.

Guienne /giːˈen/ the ancient province of SW France which formed the duchy of Aquitaine with Gascony in the 12th century. Its capital was Bordeaux. It became English in 1154 and passed to France in 1453.

guild /gɪld/ *n.* or **gild** an association formed for the mutual aid and protection of its members, or for some common purpose. Guilds, particularly of artisans and merchants, became politically powerful in Europe in the Middle Ages. After the 16th century the position of the guilds was undermined by the grow of capitalism. [probably from German and Dutch, related to Old English *gi(e)ld* = payment, guild]

guilder /ˈgɪldə/ *n.* 1. a currency unit of the Netherlands, a florin. 2. (*historical*) a gold coin of the Netherlands and Germany. [from Dutch *gulden*]

guildhall *n.* 1. a hall in which a medieval guild met. 2. a town hall. —**Guildhall**, the hall of the Corporation of the City of London, used for state banquets etc.

guile /gaɪl/ *n.* treachery, deceit; cunning, craftiness. —**guileful** *adj.*, **guileless** *adj.*, **guilelessness** *n.* [from Old French]

Guilin /gweɪˈlɪn/ formerly **Kweilin** principal tourist city of S China, on the Li river, Guangxi province. The dramatic limestone mountains are a major attraction.

Guillaume /giːˈəum/ Charles 1861–1938. Swiss physicist who studied measurement and alloy development. He discovered a nickel-steel alloy, invar, which showed negligible expansion with rising temperatures. He was awarded the Nobel Prize for Physics in 1920.

guillemot /ˈgɪlɪmɒt/ n. a diving sea bird of the auk family, genus *Uria* or *Capphus*, which breeds in large numbers on the rocky N Atlantic coasts. The **common guillemot** *Uria aalge* has a sharp bill and short tail, and sooty-brown and white plumage. Guillemots build no nest, but lay one large, almost conical egg on the rock. [French from *Guillaume* = William]

guillotine /ˈgɪlətiːn, -ˈtiːn/ n. 1. a machine with a blade sliding in grooves, used for beheading criminals. 2. a machine for cutting paper, metal etc. 3. a method of preventing a delay in Parliament by fixing the times for voting on parts of a bill. —*v.t.* to use a guillotine on. [French from J-I *Guillotin*, a physician who suggested its use in 1789]

guilt /gɪlt/ n. the fact of having committed a specified or implied offence; culpability; a feeling that one is to blame. [Old English]

guiltless adj. 1. innocent. 2. not having knowledge or possession *of*.

guilty adj. 1. having, showing, or due to guilt. 2. having committed the offence (of). —**guiltily** adv., **guiltiness** n.

guinea /ˈgɪnɪ/ n. 1. a former British gold coin worth 21 shillings (1.05), first coined for the African trade (whence its name). 2. this sum of money, used in stating professional fees etc. —**guinea fowl**, a domestic fowl of the genus *Numida* (especially *N. meleagris*) with grey plumage spotted with white. **guinea pig**, a South American rodent of the genus *Cavia* kept as a pet or for research in biology; a person used as a subject for experiment. [from *Guinea* in W Africa]

Guinea Republic of; country in W Africa, bounded to the N by Senegal, NE by Mali, SE by the Ivory Coast, SW by Liberia and Sierra Leone, W by the Atlantic, and NW by Guinea-Bissau; **area** 245,857 sq km/94,901 sq mi; **capital** Conakry; **physical** flat coastal plain with mountainous interior; sources of rivers Niger, Gambia, and Senegal; forest in SE; **head of state and government** Lansana Conté from 1984; **political system** military republic; **exports** coffee, rice, palm kernels, alumina, bauxite, diamonds; **population** (1990 est) 7,269,000 (chief peoples are Fulani, Malinke, Susu); **language** French (official), African languages spoken; **recent history** gained independence from France in 1958. Sekou Toure elected president; held office till his death in 1984, when a coup established a military government.

Guinea-Bissau /ˈgɪnɪ biˈsaʊ/ Republic of; country in W Africa, bounded to the N by Senegal, E and SE by Guinea, and SW by the Atlantic; **area** 36,125 sq km/13,944 sq mi; **capital** and chief port Bissau; **physical** flat coastal plain rising to savanna in E; **head of state and government** João Bernardo Vieira from 1980/1984; **political system** one-party Socialist republic; **exports** rice, coconuts, peanuts, fish, salt, timber; **population** (1989 est) 929,000; **language** Portuguese (official), Crioulo (Cape Verdean dialect of Portuguese), African languages; **recent history** formerly part of the Portuguese colony of Guinea and Cape Verde. Gained independence in 1974. Cape Verde decided against joining a unified state. In 1980, the president of the state council was deposed and a council of revolution set up.

Guinevere /ˈgwɪnɪvɪə(r)/ (Welsh *Gwenhwyfar*) in British legend, the wife of King ◊Arthur. Her adulterous love affair with the knight ◊Lancelot of the Lake led ultimately to Arthur's death.

Guinness /ˈgɪnɪs/ Alec 1914– . English actor whose many stage roles include Shakespeare's Hamlet 1938 and Lawrence of Arabia (in *Ross* 1960). In 1979 he gained a 'lifetime achievement' Academy Award. His films include *Kind Hearts and Coronets* 1949, *The Bridge on the River Kwai* 1957, and *Star Wars* 1977.

Guinness affair in British law, a case of alleged financial fraud during the attempted takeover by the brewing company Guinness, of Distillers in 1986. Those convicted of acting illegally to sustain Guinness share prices included Ernest Saunders, former chief executive. The trial, lasting from Feb to Aug 1990, was widely seen as the first major test of the government's legislation increasing control of financial dealings on London's Stock Exchange.

guipure /ˈgiːpʊə/ n. a heavy lace of linen pieces joined by embroidery. [French *guiper* = cover with silk etc.]

guise /gaɪz/ n. an assumed appearance, a pretence; external appearance. [from Old French]

Guise /gwiːz/ Francis, 2nd Duke of Guise 1519–1563. French soldier and politician. He led the French victory over Germany at Metz in 1552 and captured Calais from the English in 1558. Along with his brother **Charles** (1527–1574), he was powerful in the government of France during the reign of Francis II. He was assassinated attempting to crush the ◊Huguenots.

guitar /gɪˈtɑː/ n. a plucked string instrument with frets, played either with the fingers or with a plectrum or fingerpick. The **Hawaiian guitar**, laid across the lap, uses a metal bar to produce a distinctive gliding tone; the solid-bodied **electric guitar**, developed in the 1950s, mixes and amplifies vibrations from microphone contacts at different points to produce a range of tone qualities. —**guitarist** n. [from French or Spanish from Greek *kithara*]

Guiyang /gweɪˈjæŋ/ formerly **Kweiyang** capital and industrial city of Guizhou province, S China; population (1986) 1,380,000. Industries include metals and machinery.

Guizhou /gweɪˈdʒaʊ/ formerly **Kweichow** province of S China; **area** 174,000 sq km/67,164 sq mi; **capital** Guiyang; **products** rice, maize, nonferrous minerals; **population** (1986) 30,080,000; including many minority groups, which have often been in revolt.

Guizot /giːˈzəʊ/ François Pierre Guillaume 1787–1874. French politician and historian, professor of modern history at the Sorbonne, Paris, 1812–30. He wrote histories of French and European culture and became prime minister in 1847. His resistance to all reforms led to the ◊revolution of 1848.

Gujarat /gʊdʒəˈrɑːt/ state of W India; **area** 196,000 sq km/75,656 sq mi; **capital** Ahmedabad; **products** cotton, petrochemicals, oil, gas, rice, textiles; **population** (1984) 33,961,000; **language** Gujarati, Hindi.

Gujarati /gʊˈdʒəˈrɑːtɪ/ n. an inhabitant of Gujarat on the NW coast of India. The Gujaratis number approximately 30 million. They are predominantly Hindu (90%), with Muslim (8%) and Jain (2%) minorities.

Gujarati language or Gujerati language a member of the Indo-Iranian branch of the Indo-European language family, spoken in and around the state of Gujarat in W India. It is written in its own script, a variant of the Devanagari script used for Sanskrit and Hindi, and has a long literary tradition.

Gujranwala /gʊdʒrənˈwɑːlə/ city in Punjab province, Pakistan; population (1981) 597,000. It is a centre of grain trading, a former Sikh capital, and the birthplace of Sikh leader Ranjit Singh (1780–1839).

gulag n. a Russian term used to describe the forced labour camps, in particular during the Stalin era. In these remote camps thousands of prisoners, many of them dissidents and opponents of the regime, died from the harsh conditions.

gulch n. (*US*) a ravine, especially containing a torrent. [perhaps from dialect *gulch* = to swallow]

gules /gjuːlz/ n. & adj. in heraldry, red. [from Old French *go(u)les* (plural of *gole* = throat) red-dyed fur neck-ornaments]

gulf n. 1. a large area of sea partly surrounded by land. 2. a deep hollow, a chasm. 3. a wide difference of opinion etc. [from Old French from Italian from Greek *kolpos* = bosom, gulf]

Gulf States oil-rich countries sharing the coastline of the ◊Persian Gulf (Bahrain, Iran, Iraq, Kuwait, Oman, Qatar, Saudi Arabia, and the United Arab Emirates). In the USA, the term refers to those states bordering the Gulf of Mexico (Alabama, Florida, Louisiana, Mississippi, and Texas).

Gulf Stream an ocean ◊current branching from the warm waters of the equatorial current, which flows N from the Gulf of Mexico. It slows to a widening 'drift' off Newfoundland, splitting as it flows E across the Atlantic, and warms what would otherwise be a colder climate in the British Isles and Western Europe.

Gulf War 1. hostilities between the United Nations Security Forces and Iraq, culminating in war 15 Jan-28 Feb 1991. In Aug 1990 Saddam Hussein's Iraqi troops invaded and annexed neighbouring Kuwait. Resolutions made by the UN Security Council for his immediate withdrawal went unheeded and, in response to requests for help from King Fahd of Saudi Arabia, a large multi-national force was assembled near the Saudi-Kuwait border. Iraq's failure to withdraw by the UN deadline of 15 Jan 1991 signalled the beginning of the war. It ended six weeks later, when the United Nations forces successfully routed the Iraqi occupying forces from Kuwait. In the immediate aftermath of the war Iraq faced serious political uprisings from the Kurds and Shi'ites, who created a serious refugee problem in Jordan, Iran and other Middle Eastern countries. 2. the ◊Iran-Iraq war 1980–88.

gull[1] *n.* a large sea bird of the family Laridae, with webbed feet and long wings. Gulls are usually 25–75 cm/10–30 in long, white with grey or black on the back and wings, and with a large beak. [probably from Welsh *gwylan*]

gull[2] *n.* (*archaic*) a fool, a dupe. —*v.t.* (*archaic*) to cheat, to fool. [perhaps from obsolete *gull* = yellow from Old Norse]

gullet /'gʌlɪt/ *n.* the passage for food, extending from the mouth to the stomach. [from Old French diminutive (*goule* = throat from Latin *gula*)]

gullible /'gʌlɪbəl/ *adj.* easily persuaded or deceived. —**gullibility** /-'bɪlɪtɪ/ *n.*

Gullit /'gʊlɪt/ Ruud 1962– . Dutch international footballer, who was captain when Holland captured the European Championship in 1988. After playing in Holland with Haarlem, Feyenoord, and PSV Eindhoven, he moved to AC Milan in 1987 for a transfer fee of £5.5 million.

gully *n.* 1. a channel or ravine cut by water. 2. a gutter, a drain. 3. a fielding position in cricket between point and slips. [from French *goulet* = bottleneck]

gulp *v.t./i.* 1. to swallow (*down*) hastily, greedily, or with effort. 2. to keep (sobs etc.) *back* or *down* with difficulty. 3. to make a swallowing action with effort, to choke. —*n.* 1. the act of gulping. 2. a large mouthful of liquid. [from Middle Dutch *gulpen*]

gulper *n.* a deep-sea fish with a soft, tapered body, long tail, and greatly expandable stomach that can accommodate large prey.

gum[1] *n.* 1. complex polysaccharides (carbohydrates) formed by many plants and trees. There are four main groups: plant exudates (gum arabic; marine plant extracts (agar); seed extracts; and fruit and vegetable extracts. Some are made synthetically. Gums are tasteless and odourless, insoluble in alcohol and ether but generally soluble in water. They are used for adhesives, fabric sizing, in confectionery, medicine, and calico printing. 2. chewing gum. 3. a gumdrop. 4. gum arabic. 5. a gumtree. —*v.t.* (-mm-) to fasten with gum; to apply gum to. —**gum arabic,** a gum exuded by some kinds of acacia. **gumdrop** *n.* a hard, transparent sweet made of gelatine etc. **gumtree** *n.* a tree that exudes gum, especially a eucalyptus (*up a gumtree*, in great difficulty). **gum up,** (*colloquial*) to interfere with, to spoil. [from Old French from Latin *gummi, cummi* from Greek from Egyptian]

gum[2] *n.* (often in *plural*) the firm flesh around the roots of the teeth. [Old English]

gum[3] *n.* **by gum!,** (*slang*) by God!

gumboil *n.* a small abscess on the gum.

gumboot *n.* a rubber boot.

Gummer /'gʌmə/ John Selwyn 1939– . British Conservative politician. He was minister of state for employment 1983–84, paymaster general 1984–85, minister for agriculture 1985–88, chair of the party 1983–85, and minister for agriculture from 1989.

gummy[1] *adj.* sticky, exuding gum. —**gumminess** *n.*

gummy[2] *adj.* toothless.

gumption /'gʌmpʃən/ *n.* (*colloquial*) common sense; resource, initiative.

gun *n.* 1. any kind of weapon consisting of a metal tube for throwing missiles with an explosive propellant, see also ◊artillery, ◊machine gun, ◊pistol, and ◊small arms. 2. a starting pistol. 3. a device for discharging grease etc. on to a desired surface. 4. a person using a sporting gun as a member of a shooting party. 5. (*US*) a gunman. —*v.t.i.* (-**nn**-) 1. to shoot at or *down*. 2. (*colloquial*) to accelerate (an engine etc.). 3. to go shooting. —**at gunpoint,** threatened by a gun. **be gunning for,** to seek to attack or rebuke. **going great guns,** acting vigorously and near success. **gun carriage,** a wheeled support for a gun. **guncotton** *n.* an explosive of cellulose steeped in acid. **gun dog,** a dog trained to retrieve game in a shoot. **gunfight** *n.* (*US*) a fight with firearms. **gunmetal** *n.* an alloy of 88% copper with tin and zinc formerly used for guns; its bluish-grey colour. **gunrunner** *n.* a person involved in gunrunning. **gunrunning** *n.* the systematic smuggling of guns and

ammunition into a country. **stick to one's guns,** to maintain one's position. [perhaps from Scandinavian *Gunnhildr* woman's name]

gunboat *n.* a small warship with relatively heavy guns. —**gunboat diplomacy,** diplomacy backed by the threat of force.

gunfire *n.* the firing of guns.

gunman *n.* (*plural* **gunmen**) a man armed with a gun, especially in committing a crime.

gunnel variant of **gunwale.**

gunner *n.* 1. an artillery soldier especially as the official term for a private. 2. a naval warrant officer in charge of a battery, magazine etc. 3. an airman who operates a gun. 4. a game-shooter.

gunnery *n.* 1. the construction and management of large guns. 2. the firing of guns.

gunny *n.* a coarse sacking usually of jute fibre; a sack made of this. [from Hindi and Marathi from Sanskrit]

gunpowder *n.* or **black powder** the earliest known ◊explosive, a mixture of 75% potassium nitrate (saltpetre), 15% charcoal, and 10% sulphur. Sulphur ignites at a low temperature, charcoal burns readily, and the potassium nitrate provides oxygen for the explosion. Although progressively replaced since the late 19th century by high explosives, gunpowder is still widely used for quarry blasting, fuses, and fireworks.

Gunpowder Plot in British history, the Catholic conspiracy to blow up James I and his parliament on 5 Nov 1605. It was discovered through an anonymous letter. Guy ◊Fawkes was found in the cellar beneath the Palace of Westminster, ready to fire a store of explosives. Several of the conspirators were killed, and Fawkes and seven others were executed.

gunroom *n.* 1. a room in a warship for junior officers. 2. a room for sporting guns etc. in a house.

gunshot *n.* 1. a shot from a gun. 2. the range of a gun.

gunsmith *n.* a maker and repairer of small firearms.

Gunter /gʌntə(r)/ Edmund 1581–1626. English mathematician who became professor of astronomy at Gresham College, London, in 1619. He is reputed to have invented a number of surveying instruments as well as the trigonometrical terms 'cosine' and 'cotangent'.

gunwale /'gʌnəl/ *n.* the upper edge of a ship's or boat's side.

Guomindang /'gʌlɪvə/ *n.* the Chinese National People's Party, founded in 1894 by ◊Sun Yat-sen (Sun Zhong Shan), which overthrew the Manchu Empire in 1912. By 1927 the right wing, led by ◊Chiang Kai-shek (Jiang Jie Shi), was in conflict with the left, led by Mao Zedong until the Communist victory in 1949 (except for the period of the Japanese invasion 1937–45). It survives as the sole political party of Taiwan, where it is still spelled **Kuomintang.**

guppy /'gʌpɪ/ *n.* a small West Indian fish *Lebistes reticulatus.* [from R J L *Guppy*, who sent the first specimen to the British Museum]

gurdwara /gɜ:'dwɑ:rə/ *n.* Sikh place of worship and meeting. As well as a room housing the *Guru Granth Sahib,* the holy book, the gurdwara contains a kitchen and eating area for the *langar,* or communal meal. [Punjabi, from Sanskrit *guru* = teacher, *dvara* = door]

gurgle *n.* a bubbling sound as of water from a bottle. —*v.t./i.* to make gurgles; to utter with gurgles.

Gurkha /'gɜ:kə/ 1. a member of a people living in the mountains of Nepál, whose young men have been recruited since 1815 for the British army. They are predominantly Tibeto-Mongolians, but their language is Khas, a dialect of a N Indic language. 2. a member of one of the Gurkha regiments (originally specifically for Nepálese soldiers) in the British Army. [from Sanskrit *gāus* = cow, *raksh* = protect]

gurnard *n.* genus of coastal fish Trigla in the family Triglidae, with a large head and mailed cheeks, which creep along the sea bottom by means of three finger-like appendages detached from the pectoral fins. They are both tropic and temperate zone fish. [from Old French]

guru /'guru:/ *n.* 1. a Hindu or Sikh spiritual teacher or head of a religious sect. 2. an influential or revered teacher. [from Hindi, from Sanskrit = heavy]

gush *n.* 1. a sudden or copious stream. 2. effusiveness. —*v.t./i.* 1. to flow (*out* etc.) with a gush; to emit a gush of (water etc.). 2. to speak or behave effusively.

Gutenberg *The earliest illustration of a printing press, as invented by Johann Gutenberg. It is from the* Danse Macabre *printed by Mathias Lyons, 1499.*

Gush Emunim /ˈguʃ eˈmuːnɪm/ Israeli fundamentalist group, founded in 1973, that claims divine right to the West Bank, Gaza Strip, and Golan Heights as part of Israel through settlement, sometimes extending the claim to the Euphrates. [Hebrew = bloc of the faithful]

gusher *n.* **1.** an oil-well emitting unpumped oil. **2.** an effusive person.

gusset /ˈgʌsɪt/ *n.* **1.** a piece let into a garment etc. to strengthen or enlarge it. **2.** a strengthening iron bracket. [from Old French *gousset* = flexible piece filling up a joint in armour]

gust *n.* a sudden, violent rush of wind; a burst of rain, smoke, anger etc. —*v.i.* to blow in gusts. —**gusty** *adj.*, **gustily** *adv.* [from Old Norse]

Gustaf or Gustavus /ˈgustaf/ six kings of Sweden, including:

Gustavus Vasa /ˈvɑːsə/ 1496–1560. King of Sweden from 1523, when he was elected after leading the Swedish revolt against Danish rule. He united and pacified the country and established Lutheranism as the state religion.

Gustavus I king of Sweden, better known as ◊Gustavus Vasa.

Gustavus Adolphus /guˈstɑːvəs əˈdɒlfəs/ 1594–1632. King of Sweden from 1611, when he succeeded his father Charles IX. He waged successful wars with Denmark, Russia, and Poland, and in the ◊Thirty Years' War became a champion of the Protestant cause. Landing in Germany in 1630, he defeated the German general Wallenstein at Lützen, SW of Leipzig, on 6 Nov 1632, but was killed in the battle. He was known as the 'Lion of the North'.

Gustavus II king of Sweden, better known as ◊Gustavus Adolphus.

gustatory /ˈgʌstətərɪ/ *adj.* connected with the sense of taste. [from Latin *gustare* from *gustus* = taste]

gusto /ˈgʌstəʊ/ *n.* zest, enjoyment in doing a thing. [Italian from Latin *gustus* = taste]

gut *n.* or **alimentary canal 1.** in the ◊digestive system the part of an animal responsible for processing food and preparing it for entry into the blood, (in *plural*) the bowels or entrails. **2.** (in *plural*, *colloquial*) pluck, force of character; staying power. **3.** material for violin etc. strings or surgical use made from the intestines of animals; material for fishing-lines made from the intestines of the silk-worm. **4.** (in *plural*) the contents or fittings; a thing's essence. **5.** a narrow passage or water-passage. —*adj.* instinctive; fundamental. —*v.t.* (**-tt-**) **1.** to remove the guts of (a fish). **2.** to remove or destroy the internal fittings of (a building). **3.** to extract the essence of (a book

etc.). —**hate a person's guts,** to dislike him intensely. [Old English]

Gutenberg /ˈguːtnbɜːg/ Johann *c.*1400–1468. German printer, the inventor of printing from moveable metal type, based on the Chinese wood-block-type method (although Laurens Janszoon ◊Coster has a rival claim). Gutenberg began work on the process in the 1430s and in 1440 set up a printing business in Mainz with Johann Fust (*c.*1400–1466) as a backer. By 1455 he produced the first printed Bible (known as the Gutenberg Bible). Fust seized the press for nonpayment of the loan, but Gutenberg is believed to have printed the Mazarin and Bamberg bibles.

Guthrie /ˈgʌθri/ Woody (Woodrow Wilson) 1912–1967. US folk singer and songwriter, whose left-wing protest songs, 'dustbowl ballads', and 'talking blues' influenced, among others, Bob Dylan; they include 'Deportees', 'Hard Travelin'', and 'This Land Is Your Land'.

gutless *adj.* (*colloquial*.) lacking energy or courage.

gutsy *adj.* **1.** (*colloquial*) courageous. **2.** (*slang*) greedy.

gutta-percha /gʌtəˈpɜːtʃə/ *n.* a tough plastic substance from the latex of various Malayan trees. [from Malay]

guttation *n.* the secretion of water onto the surface of leaves through specialized pores, or ◊hydathodes. The process occurs most frequently during conditions of high humidity when the rate of transpiration is low. Drops of water found on grass in early morning are often the result of guttation, rather than dew. Sometimes the water contains minerals in solution, such as calcium, which leaves a white crust on the leaf surface as it dries.

gutter *n.* a shallow trough below the eaves, or a channel at the side of a street, for carrying off rain-water; a channel, a groove. —*v.i.* (of a candle) to burn unsteadily and melt away rapidly. —**the gutter,** a place of low breeding or vulgar behaviour. **gutter press,** sensational journalism. [from Anglo-French from Latin *gutta* = drop]

guttering *n.* material for gutters.

guttersnipe *n.* a street urchin.

guttural /ˈgʌtərəl/ *adj.* **1.** throaty, harsh-sounding. **2.** (of consonants) produced in the throat or by the back of the tongue and palate. **3.** of the throat. —*n.* a guttural consonant (as *g, k*). —**gutturally** *adv.* [French, or from Latin *guttur* = throat]

guv *n.* an informal form of address to a superior, abbreviation of *governor*.

guy[1] /gaɪ/ *n.* **1.** an effigy of Guy Fawkes burnt on 5 Nov. **2.** (*slang*) a man. **3.** a grotesquely-dressed person. —*v.t.* to ridicule. [from *Guy* Fawkes, conspirator in the Gunpowder Plot to blow up Parliament in 1605]

guy² *n.* a rope or chain to secure a tent or steady a crane-load etc. —*v.t.* to secure with guys.

Guyana /gaɪˈænə/ country in South America, bounded to the N by the Atlantic Ocean, E by Suriname, S and SW by Brazil, and NW by Venezuela.

Guzmán Blanco /guːsˈmæn ˈblæŋkəʊ/ Antonio 1829–1899. Venezuelan dictator and military leader (*caudillo*). He seized power in 1870 and remained absolute ruler until 1889. He modernized Caracas to become the political capital; committed resources to education, communications, and agriculture; and encouraged foreign trade.

guzzle *v.t./i.* to eat or drink greedily. [probable from Old French *gosiller* (*gosier* = throat)]

Gwalior /ˈgwɑːliɔː/ city in Madhya Pradesh, India; population (1981) 543,862. It was formerly a small princely state and has Jain and Hindu monuments.

Gwent /gwent/ county in S Wales; **area** 1,380 sq km/533 sq mi; **administrative headquarters** Cwmbran; **physical** Wye Valley; **products** salmon and trout on the Wye and Usk rivers; iron and steel at Llanwern; **population** (1987) 443,000; **language** 2.5% Welsh, English.

Gwyn /gwɪn/ 'Nell' (Eleanor) 1651–1687. English comedy actress from 1665, formerly an orange-seller at Drury Lane Theatre, London. The poet Dryden wrote parts for her, and from 1669 she was the mistress of Charles II.

Gwynedd /ˈgwɪnəθ/ county in NW Wales; **area** 3,870 sq km/1,494 sq mi; **administrative headquarters** Caernarvon; **physical** Snowdinia National Park including Snowdon, the highest mountain in Wales 1,085 m/3,561 ft, and the largest Welsh lake, Llyn Tegid (Bala); **products** cattle, sheep, gold (at Dolgellau), textiles, electronics, slate; **population** (1987) 236,000; **language** 61% Welsh, English.

gybe /dʒaɪb/ *v.t./i.* (of a fore-and-aft sail or boom) to swing to the other side; to make (a sail) gybe; (of a boat etc.) to change course thus. [from obsolete Dutch *gibjen*]

gym /dʒɪm/ *n.* (*colloquial*) 1. a gymnasium. 2. gymnastics. —**gym-slip** *n.* a sleeveless tunic, usually belted, worn by schoolgirls. [abbreviation]

gymkhana /dʒɪmˈkɑːnə/ *n.* a meeting for competition in a sport, especially horse-riding. [from Hindi *gendkhāna* = ball-house]

gymnasium /dʒɪmˈneɪzɪəm/ *n.* (*plural* **gymnasiums**) a room etc. equipped for gymnastics. [Latin from Greek *gumnos* = naked]

gymnast /ˈdʒɪmnæst/ *n.* an expert in gymnastics. [from French or Greek]

gymnastic /dʒɪmˈnæstɪk/ *adj.* of gymnastics. —**gymnastically** *adv.*

gymnastics *n.pl.* (occasionally treated as singular) physical exercises, originally for health and training (so-called from the fact that ancient Greeks trained naked). The *gymnasia* were schools for training competitors for public games. **Men's gynastics** includes high bar, parallel bars, horse vault, rings, pommel horse, and floor exercises. **Women's gymnastics** includes asymmetrical bars, side horse vault, balance beam, and floor exercises. Also popular are **sports acrobatics**, performed by gymnasts in pairs, trios, or fours to music, where the emphasis is on dance, balance, and timing, and **rhythmic gymnastics**,

choreographed to music and performed by individuals or six-girl teams, with small hand apparatus such as a ribbon, ball, or hoop.

gymnosperm /ˈdʒɪmnəspɜːm/ *n.* in botany, any plant whose seeds are exposed, as opposed to the structurally more advanced ◊angiosperms, where they are inside an ovary. The group includes conifers and related plants such as cycads and ginkgos, whose seeds develop in ◊cones. Fossil gymnosperms have been found in rocks about 350 million years old. [from Greek *gumnos* = naked]

gymp variant of *gimp*.

gynaecology /gaɪnɪˈkɒlədʒɪ/ *n.* the science of the physiological functions and diseases of women. —**gynaecological** /-kəˈlɒdʒɪkəl/ *adj.*, **gynaecologist** *n.* [from Greek *gunē* = woman]

gynoecium *n.* or **gynaecium** the collective term for the female reproductive organs of a flower, consisting of one or more ◊carpels, either free or fused together.

gyp /dʒɪp/ **to give a person gyp**, (*colloquial*) to punish severely or hurt him.

gypsum *n.* a common ◊mineral, composed of hydrous calcium sulphate, $CaSO_4 \cdot 2H_2O$. It ranks 2 on the Mohs' scale of hardness. Gypsum is used for making plaster of Paris for casts and moulds, for blackboard chalk, and as a fertilizer. —**gypseous** *adj.* [Latin from Greek *gupsos*]

gypsy /ˈdʒɪpsɪ/ *n.* a member of the travelling ◊Romany people usually living by seasonal work, itinerant trade, and fortune-telling. —**gypsy moth**, a kind of tussock-moth very destructive to foliage. **gypsy's warning**, a cryptic or sinister warning. [earlier *gipcyan*, *gipsen*, from Egyptian, reflecting their supposed origin when they appeared in England about the beginning of the 16th century]

gyrate /dʒaɪˈreɪt/ *v.i.* to move in a circle or spiral. —**gyration** *n.*, **gyratory** /ˈdʒaɪrətərɪ/ *adj.* [from Latin *gyrare*]

gyre *n.* the circular surface rotation of ocean water in each major sea (a type of ◊current). Gyres are large and permanent, and occupy the N and S halves of the three major oceans. Their movements are dictated by the prevailing winds and the ◊Coriolis effect. Gyres move clockwise in the northern hemisphere and anticlockwise in the southern hemisphere.

gyrfalcon /ˈdʒɜːfɔːlkən/ *n.* a large northern falcon (*Falco rusticolus*). [from Old French from Old Norse]

gyro- /gaɪrəʊ-/in combinations, rotation; gyroscopic. [from Greek *guros* = ring]

gyro /ˈdʒaɪrəʊ/ *n.* (*colloquial*) a gyroscope. [abbreviation]

gyrocompass *n.* a compass giving the true north and bearings from it relative to the Earth's rotation and depending on the properties of a gyroscope, independent of earth's magnetism.

gyroscope /ˈdʒaɪrəskəʊp/ *n.* mechanical instrument, used as a stabilizing device and consisting, in its simplest form, of a heavy wheel mounted on an axis fixed in a ring that can be rotated about another axis, which is also fixed in a ring capable of rotation about a third axis. Important applications of the gyroscope principle include the gyrocompass, the gyropilot for automatic steering, and gyro-directed torpedoes. —**gyroscopic** /-ˈskɒpɪk/ *adj.* [French]

Gysi /ˈgiːzɪ/ Gregor 1948–. German politician, elected leader of the Communist Party Dec 1989 following the resignation of Egon ◊Krenz. A lawyer, Gysi had acted as defence counsel for dissidents during the 1960s.

h, H /eɪtʃ/ *n.* (*plural* **hs, h's**) the eighth letter of the alphabet.

h. abbreviation of 1. hecto-. 2. hot. 3. hour(s).

H abbreviation of hard (pencil lead).

H symbol for hydrogen.

ha /hɑː/ interjection expressing surprise, suspicion, triumph etc.

ha. abbreviation of hectare(s).

Ha symbol for hahnium.

Haakon /ˈhɔːkɒn/ seven kings of Norway, including:

Haakon I the Good *c.*915–96i. King of Norway from about 935. The son of Harald Hárfagri ('Finehair') (*c.*850–930), king of Norway, he was raised in England. He seized the Norwegian throne and tried unsuccessfully to introduce Christianity there. His capital was at Trondheim.

Haakon IV 1204–1263. King of Norway from 1217, the son of Haakon III. Under his rule, Norway flourished both militarily and culturally; he took control of the Faroe Islands, Greenland in 1261, and Iceland 1262–64. His court was famed throughout N Europe.

Haakon VII 1872–1957. King of Norway from 1905. Born Prince Charles, the second son of Frederick VIII of Denmark, he was elected king of Norway on separation from Sweden, and in 1906 he took the name Haakon. In World War II he carried on the resistance from Britain during the Nazi occupation of his country. He returned in 1945.

Haarlem /ˈhɑːləm/ industrial city and capital of N Holland, the Netherlands, 20 km/12 mi W of Amsterdam; population (1988) 214,000. At Velsea to the N a road–rail tunnel runs under the North Sea Canal, linking N and S Holland. Industries include chemicals, pharmaceuticals, textiles, and printing.

habanera *n.* or **havanaise** a slow dance in two–four time, originating in Havana, Cuba, which was introduced into Spain during the 19th century. There is a celebrated example of this dance in Bizet's opera *Carmen.*

habeas corpus /ˈheɪbɪəs ˈkɔːpəs/ in law, a writ directed to someone who has custody of a prisoner, ordering him or her to bring the prisoner before the court issuing the writ and to justify why the prisoner is detained in custody. Traditional rights to habeas corpus were embodied in law mainly owing to Lord ◊Shaftesbury (1st Earl), in the English Habeas Corpus Act 1679. The main principles were adopted in the US Constitution. [Latin = you must have the body]

Haber /ˈhɑːbə/ Fritz 1868–1934. German chemist whose conversion of atmospheric nitrogen to ammonia opened the way for the synthetic fertilizer industry. His study of the combustion of hydrocarbons led to the commercial 'cracking' or fractionating of natural oil (petroleum) into its components (for example, diesel, petrol, and paraffin). In electrochemistry, he was the first to demonstrate that oxidation and reduction take place at the electrodes; from this he developed a general electrochemical theory.

haberdasher /ˈhæbədæʃə/ *n.* a dealer in accessories of dress and in sewing goods. —**haberdashery** *n.*

Haber process an industrial process in which ammonia is manufactured by direct combination of its elements, nitrogen and hydrogen. The reaction is carried out at 400–500°C and at 200 atmospheres pressure. The two gases, in the proportions of 1:3 by volume, are passed over a ◊catalyst of finely divided iron. Around 10% of the reactants combine, and the unused gases are recycled. The ammonia is separated by either dissolving in water or cooling to liquid.

habiliments /həˈbɪlɪmənts/ *n.pl.* clothing, attire. [from Old French *habiller* = fit out, from *habile* = able]

habit /ˈhæbɪt/ *n.* 1. a settled or regular tendency or practice; a practice that is hard to give up. 2. mental constitution. 3. dress, especially of a religious order. —**habitforming** *adj.* causing addiction. [from Old French from Latin *habitus* (*habēre* = have)]

habitable *adj.* suitable for living in. —**habitability** /-ˈbɪlɪtɪ/ *n.* [from Old French from Latin *habitare* = inhabit]

habitat /ˈhæbɪtæt/ *n.* in ecology, the localized ◊environment in which an organism lives. Habitats are often described by the dominant plant type or physical feature, such as a grassland habitat or rocky seashore habitat. [Latin = it inhabits]

habitation /hæbɪˈteɪʃən/ *n.* 1. a house or home. 2. inhabiting. [from Old French from Latin]

habitual /həˈbɪtjuəl/ *adj.* 1. done constantly or as a habit; regular, usual. 2. given to a habit. —**habitually** *adv.* [from Latin]

habituate /həˈbɪtjueɪt/ *v.t.* to accustom (to). —**habituation** /-ˈeɪʃən/ *n.* [from Latin]

habitué /həˈbɪtjueɪ/ *n.* a resident or frequent visitor (*of*). [French]

Habsburg /ˈhæbsbɜːg/ or **Hapsburg** European royal family, former imperial house of Austria–Hungary. The name comes from the family castle in Switzerland. The Habsburgs held the title Holy Roman emperor 1273–91, 1298–1308, 1438–1740, and 1745–1806. They ruled Austria from 1278, under the title emperor 1806–1918.

hachures /hæˈʃʊəz/ *n.pl.* parallel lines used on maps to indicate the degree of slope in hills. [French]

hacienda /hæsiˈendə/ *n.* in a Spanish-speaking country, a large estate etc. with a dwelling house. [Spanish, from Latin *facienda* = things to be done]

hack[1] *v.t./i.* 1. to cut or chop roughly. 2. to kick the shin of (an opponent at football); to deal chopping blows (*at*). 3. (*colloquial*) to gain unauthorized access to (computer files) either for fun or for malicious or fraudulent purposes; (in *participle*) to use a computer for the satisfaction that it gives. —*n.* 1. a kick with the toe of a boot etc.; a wound from this. 2. a mattock. 3. a miner's pick. —**hacking cough,** a short, dry, frequent cough. **hacksaw** *n.* a saw with a narrow blade set in a frame, for cutting metal. —**hacker** *n.* [Old English]

hack[2] *n.* 1. a horse for ordinary riding; a horse let out for hire. 2. a person hired to do dull routine work, especially as a writer. —*v.i.* to ride on horseback at an ordinary pace. —*adj.* used as a hack; commonplace. [abbreviation of *hackney*]

hackle *n.* 1. the long feather(s) on the neck of the domestic cock etc. 2. a steel comb for dressing flax etc. —**make a person's hackles rise,** to make him or her very angry. **with his/her hackles up,** angry, ready to fight.

Hackman /ˈhækmən/ Gene 1931– . US actor. He became a star as 'Popeye' Doyle in *The French Connection* 1971 and continued to play major roles in films such as *The Conversation* 1974, *French Connection II* 1975, and *Mississippi Burning* 1988.

hackney /'hæknɪ/ *n.* a horse for ordinary riding. —**hackney carriage**, a taxi. [perhaps from *Hackney* in London]

hackneyed /'hæknɪd/ *adj.* (of a phrase etc.) made commonplace or trite by long overuse.

had past and past participle of **have**.

haddock /'hædək/ *n.* (*plural* the same) a sea fish *Melanogrammus aeglefinus* of the cod family found off the N Atlantic coasts. It is brown with silvery underparts, and black markings above the pectoral fins. It can grow to a length of 1 m/3 ft.

Hades /'heɪdiːz/ in Greek mythology, the underworld where spirits went after death, usually depicted as a cavern or pit underneath the Earth. It was presided over by the god Hades or Pluto (Roman Dis). [Greek = unseen]

Hadith /'hædiθ/ *n.* a collection of the teachings of ◊Muhammad and stories about his life, regarded by Muslims as a guide to living second only to the ◊Koran.

hadj /hædʒ/ *n.* or **hajj** the pilgrimage to ◊Mecca that should be undertaken by every Muslim at least once in a lifetime, unless he or she is prevented by financial or health difficulties. Many of the pilgrims on hadj also visit Medina, where the prophet Muhammad is buried. [from Arabic = pilgrimage]

hadji /'hædʒɪ/ *n.* or **hajji** a Muslim who has been to Mecca as a pilgrim. [from Persian and Turkish = pilgrim]

Hadlee /'hædlɪ/ Richard John 1951– . New Zealand cricketer. In 1987 he surpassed Ian Botham's world record of 373 wickets in test cricket and went on to set the record at 431 wickets before retiring from international cricket in 1990.

hadn't (*colloquial*) had not.

Hadrian /'heɪdrɪən/ AD 76–138. Roman emperor from 117. He was born in Spain, and adopted by his relative, the emperor Trajan, whom he succeeded. He abandoned Trajan's conquests in Mesopotamia and adopted a defensive policy, which included the building of Hadrian's Wall in Britain.

Hadrian's Wall a Roman fortification built in AD 122–126 to mark England's northern boundary and abandoned in about 400; its ruins run 120 km/74 mi from the mouth of the river Tyne to the Solway Firth. In some parts, the wall was covered with a glistening, white coat of mortar. The fort at South Shields, Arbeia, built to defend the eastern end, is being reconstructed. In 1985 Roman letters (on paper-thin sheets of wood), the earliest and largest collection of Latin writing, were discovered at Vindolanda Fort.

hadron /'hædrɒn/ *n.* any strongly interacting subatomic particle. [from Greek *hadros* = thick, bulky]

Haeckel /'hekəl/ Ernst Heinrich 1834–1919. German scientist and philosopher. His theory of 'recapitulation', expressed as 'ontogeny repeats phylogeny' (or that embryonic stages represent past stages in the organism's evolution), has been superseded, but it stimulated research in ◊embryology.

haemal /'hiːməl/ *adj.* of the blood. [from Greek *haima* = blood]

haematic /hiː'mætɪk/ *adj.* of or containing blood.

hematite /'hiːmətaɪt/ variant of ◊hematite.

haematology /hiːmə'tɒlədʒɪ/ *n.* the study of the physiology of the blood.

haemoglobin /hiːmə'gləʊbɪn/ *n.* a protein that carries oxygen. In vertebrates it occurs in red blood cells, giving them their colour. Oxygen attaches to haemoglobin in the lungs or gills where the amount dissolved in the blood is high. This process effectively increases the amount of oxygen that can be carried in the bloodstream. The oxygen is later released in the body tissues where it is at low concentration. [from *haematin*, constituent of haemoglobin]

haemolymph *n.* the circulatory fluid of those molluscs and insects that have an 'open' circulatory system. Haemolymph contains water, amino acids, sugars, salts, and white cells like those of blood. Circulated by a pulsating heart, its main functions are to transport digestive and excretory products around the body. In molluscs, it also transports oxygen and carbon dioxide.

haemophilia /hiːmə'fɪlɪə/ *n.* a constitutional, usually hereditary, tendency to bleed severely from even a slight injury, through failure of the blood to clot normally. —**haemophilic** *adj.* [from Greek *haima* = blood and *philia* = loving]

haemophiliac /hiːmə'fɪliæk/ *n.* a person suffering from haemophilia.

haemorrhage /'hemərɪdʒ/ *n.* an escape of blood from a blood vessel, especially when profuse. —*v.i.* to undergo haemorrhage. [from French from Latin from Greek *haima* = blood and *rhēgnumi* = burst]

haemorrhoid /'hemərɔɪd/ *n.* (usually in *plural*) a swollen vein at or near the anus; popularly called piles. [from Old French or Latin from Greek *haima* = blood and *-rhoos* = -flowing]

haemostasis *n.* the natural or surgical stoppage of bleeding. In the natural mechanism, the damaged vessel contracts, restricting the flow, and blood ◊platelets plug the opening, releasing chemicals essential to clotting.

Hâfiz /'hɑːfɪz/ Shams al-Din Muhammad *c.*1326–1390. Persian lyric poet, who was born in Shiraz and taught in a Dervish college there. His *Diwan*, a collection of short odes, extols the pleasures of life and satirizes his fellow Dervishes.

hafnium /'hæfnɪəm/ *n.* a metallic element with a silver lustre, symbol Hf, atomic number 72, relative atomic mass 178.49. It occurs in nature in ores of zirconium, the properties of which it resembles. Hafnium absorbs neutrons better than most metals, so it is used for control rods in nuclear reactors; it is also used for light-bulb filaments. [from *Hafnia*, Latinized name of Copenhagen (Danish *havn* = harbour)]

haft /hɑːft/ *n.* a handle (of a dagger, knife etc.). —*v.t.* to furnish with a haft. [Old English]

hag *n.* an ugly old woman; a witch. —**haggish** *adj.* [Old English]

Haganah /hɑːgə'nɑː/ a Zionist military organization in Palestine. It originated under the Turkish rule of the Ottoman Empire before World War I to protect Jewish settlements, and many of its members served in the British forces in both world wars. After World War II it condemned guerrilla activity, opposing the British authorities only passively. It formed the basis of the Israeli army after Israel was established in 1948.

Haggadah /hə'gɑːdə/ *n.* in Judaism, the part of the Talmudic literature not concerned with religious law (the *Halakah*), but devoted to folklore and legends of heroes.

haggard /'hægəd/ *adj.* looking exhausted and distraught from prolonged worry etc. —*n.* a hawk caught when fullgrown. [from French]

Haggard H(enry) Rider 1856–1925. English novelist. He used his experience in the South African colonial service in his romantic adventure tales, including *King Solomon's Mines* 1885 and *She* 1887.

haggis /'hægɪs/ *n.* a Scottish dish made from a sheep's or calf's heart, liver, and lungs, minced up with onion, oatmeal, suet, spice, pepper, and salt, and traditionally boiled in the animal's stomach.

haggle *v.i.* to dispute or argue (especially *about* or *over* a price or terms). —*n.* haggling. [originally = to hack, from Old Norse]

hagio- /hægɪəʊ-/ in combinations, of saints. [from Greek *hagios* = holy]

hagiography /hægɪ'ɒgrəfɪ/ *n.* the writing of saints' lives. —**hagiographer** *n.*

hagiology /hægɪ'ɒlədʒɪ/ *n.* the literature of the lives and legends of saints.

hagridden *adj.* afflicted by nightmares or fears. [from *hag* and *ridden* = past participle of *ride*]

Hague, The /heɪg/ (Dutch *'s-Gravenhage* or *Den Haag*) capital of S Holland and seat of the Netherlands government, linked by canal with Rotterdam and Amsterdam; population (1988) 680,000. It is also the seat of the United Nations International Court of Justice.

ha ha /hɑː 'hɑː/ representing laughter. [Old English]

ha-ha /'hɑːhɑː/ *n.* a ditch with a wall on the inner side, forming the boundary to a park or garden without interrupting the view. [French, perhaps from cry of surprise at discovering the obstacle]

Hahn /hɑːn/ Otto 1879–1968. German physical chemist, who discovered nuclear fission (see ◊nuclear energy). In 1938, with Fritz Strassman (1902–1980), he discovered that uranium nuclei split when bombarded with neutrons,

Haile Selassie *Haile Selassie was emperor of Ethiopia until he was deposed in a military coup in 1974.*

which led to the development of the atom bomb. He was awarded the Nobel Prize for Chemistry in 1944.

hahnium /'hɑːnɪəm/ *n.* the name proposed by US scientists for the element currently known as ◊unnilpentium (atomic number 105), to honour German nuclear physicist Otto Hahn.

Haifa /'haɪfə/ port in NE Israel; population (1987) 223,000. Industries include oil refining and chemicals.

Haig /heɪg/ Alexander (Meigs) 1924–   . US general and Republican politician. He became President Nixon's White House chief of staff at the height of the ◊Watergate scandal, was NATO commander 1974–79, and secretary of state to President Reagan 1981–82.

Haig Douglas, 1st Earl Haig 1861–1928. British army officer, commander in chief in World War I. His Somme (France) offensive in the summer of 1916 made considerable advances only at enormous cost to human life, and his Passchendaele (Belgium) offensive (July–Nov 1917) achieved little at a similar huge loss. He was created field marshal in 1917.

haiku /'haɪkuː/ *n.* (*plural* the same) a Japanese lyric form of 17 syllables usually divided into three lines of five, seven, and five syllables. ◊Bashō popularized the form in the 17th century. It evolved from the 31-syllable *tanka* form dominant from the 8th century. [Japanese]

hail[1] *n.* **1.** pellets of frozen rain falling in a shower. **2.** a shower *of* blows, missiles, questions etc. —*v.t./i.* to fall or send down as or like hail. [Old English]

hail[2] interjection of greeting. —*v.t./i.* **1.** to salute; to greet *as.* **2.** to call to (a person or ship) in order to attract attention; to signal to (a taxi etc.) to stop. **3.** to originate, to have come. —*n.* hailing. —**be hail-fellow-well-met,** to be very friendly or too friendly (*with* strangers etc.). [from Old Norse *heill* = whole, sound]

Haile Selassie /'haɪli sɪ'læsi/ Ras (Prince) Tafari ('the Lion of Judah') 1892–1975. Emperor of Ethiopia 1930–74. He pleaded unsuccessfully to the League of Nations against the Italian conquest of his country 1935–36, and lived in the UK until his restoration in 1941. He was deposed by a military coup in 1974 and died in captivity the following year. Followers of the ◊Rastafarian religion believe that he was the Messiah, the incarnation of God (Jah).

Hailsham /'heɪlʃəm/ Quintin Hogg, Baron Hailsham of St Marylebone 1907–   . English lawyer and Conservative politician. The 2nd Viscount Hailsham, he renounced the title in 1963 to re-enter the House of Commons, and was then able to contest the Conservative Party leadership elections, but took a life peerage in 1970 on his appointment as Lord Chancellor 1970–74. He was Lord Chancellor again from 1979–87.

hailstone *n.* a pellet of hail.

hailstorm *n.* a prolonged period of heavy hail.

Hainan /haɪ'næn/ island in the South China Sea; **area** 34,000 sq km/13,124 sq mi; **population** (1986) 6,000,000; **capital** Haikou. In 1987 Hainan was designated a Special Economic Zone; in 1988 it was separated from Guangdong and made a new province. It is China's second largest island.

Haiphong /haɪ'fɒŋ/ industrial port in N Vietnam; population (1980) 1,305,000. Among its industries are shipbuilding and the making of cement, plastics, phosphates, and textiles.

hair *n.* **1.** any of the fine threadlike strands growing from the skin of animals, especially from the human head; these collectively; an elongated cell growing from the surface of a plant. **2.** a thing resembling a hair. **3.** a very small quantity. —**get in a person's hair,** to encumber or annoy him or her. **hairdo** *n.* (*plural* **hairdos**) (*colloquial*) a hairstyle; the process of a person's hairdressing. **hairgrip** *n.* a flat hairpin with the prongs closing tightly together. **hairline** *n.* the edge of a person's hair on the forehead etc.; a very narrow crack or line. **hairnet** *n.* a net worn to hold the hair in place. **hairpiece** *n.* a quantity of false hair worn to augment a person's natural hair. **hair-raising** *adj.* terrifying. **hair's breadth,** a minute distance. **hair shirt,** a shirt of haircloth worn by penitents or ascetics. **hair slide,** a clip for keeping the hair in position. **hairsplitting** *adj.* splitting hairs (see below). **hairstyle** *n.* a particular way of arranging the hair. **hair trigger,** a trigger set for release at the slightest pressure. **keep one's hair on,** (*slang*) to remain calm and not get angry. **let one's hair down,** (*colloquial*) to abandon restraint, to behave wildly; to become confidential. **make one's hair stand on end,** to horrify one. **not to turn a hair,** to remain unmoved or unaffected. **split hairs,** to make small and insignificant distinctions. [Old English]

hairbrush *n.* a brush for arranging the hair.

haircloth *n.* cloth woven from hair.

haircut *n.* cutting the hair; a style of doing this.

hairdresser *n.* one whose business is to arrange and cut hair.

hairpin *n.* a U-shaped pin for fastening the hair. —**hairpin bend,** a sharp U-shaped bend in a road.

hairspring *n.* a fine spring regulating the balance wheel in a watch.

hairstreak *n.* one of a group of butterflies, belonging to the Blues (Lycaenidae), which live in both temperate and tropical regions. Most are brownish in their adult form, and nearly all are tailed.

hairy *adj.* **1.** having much hair; made of hair. **2.** (*slang*) hair-raising, unpleasant, difficult. —**hairiness** *n.*

Haiti /'heɪti/ Republic of; country in the Caribbean, occupying part of Hispaniola, to the E is the Dominican Republic; **area** 27,750 sq km/10,712 sq mi; **capital** Port-au-Prince; **physical** mainly mountainous and tropical; occupies W third of Hispaniola Island in Caribbean Sea; **head of state and government** Jean Bertrand Aristide from 1991; **political system** transitional; **population** (1990 est) 6,409,000; **language** French (official, spoken by literate 10% minority), Creole (spoken by 90% black majority); **recent history** independence was achieved from France in 1804. Haiti was invaded by the USA in 1915 and remained under US control until 1934. François Duvalier was elected president in 1957; he was made president for life from 1964. He died in 1971 and was succeeded by his son, Jean-Claude, who was deposed in 1986. Military coups 1988–89; Aristide was elected president in 1991.

Haitink Bernard 1929–   . Dutch conductor of the Concertgebouw Orchestra, Amsterdam, from 1964, and music director of the Royal Opera House, Covent Garden, London, from 1987.

hajj variant of ◊hadj.

hake *n.* a sea fish *Merluccius merluccius* of the cod family, found in N European, African, and American waters. Its silvery, elongated body attains 1 m/3 ft. It has two dorsal fins and one long anal fin.

Haley *US pioneer of rock and roll music Bill Haley, remembered for his hit song 'Rock Around the Clock' 1954.*

Hakluyt /ˈhæklu:t/ Richard 1553–1616. English geographer whose chief work is *The Principal Navigations, Voyages and Discoveries of the English Nation* 1598–1600. He was assisted by Sir Walter Raleigh. The **Hakluyt Society**, established in 1846, published later accounts of exploration.

Halab /həˈlæb/ Arabic name of ◊Aleppo, a city in Syria.

Halabja /həˈlæbdʒə/ Kurdish town near the Iran border in Sulaymaniyah province, NE Iraq. In Aug 1988 international attention was focused on the town when Iraqi planes dropped poison gas, killing 5,000 of its inhabitants.

halal /hɑːˈlɑːl/ *v.t.* to kill (an animal for meat) as prescribed by Muslim law. —*n.* meat prepared thus. [from Arabic = lawful]

halberd /ˈhælbəd/ *n.* (*historical*) a combined spear and battle-axe. [from French from Italian from Middle High German *helmbarde*]

halcyon /ˈhælsiən/ *adj.* calm and peaceful; (of a period) happy, prosperous. [from Latin from Greek = kingfisher, reputed to calm the sea at midwinter]

Haldane /ˈhɔːldeɪn/ J(ohn) B(urdon) S(anderson) 1892–1964. English scientist and writer. A geneticist, Haldane was better known as a popular science writer of such books as *The Causes of Evolution* 1933 and *New Paths in Genetics* 1941.

hale[1] *adj.* strong and healthy. [northern variant of *whole*]

hale[2] *v.t.* (*archaic*) to drag or draw forcibly. [from Old French from Old Norse]

Hale /heɪl/ George Ellery 1868–1938. US astronomer, who made pioneer studies of the Sun and founded three major observatories. In 1889, he invented the spectroheliograph, a device for photographing the Sun at particular wavelengths.

Halévy /ˈæleɪˈviː/ Ludovic 1834–1908. French novelist and librettist. He collaborated with Hector Crémieux in the libretto for Offenbach's *Orpheus in the Underworld*; and with Henri Meilhac on librettos for Offenbach's *La Belle Hélène* and *La Vie Parisienne*, as well as for Bizet's *Carmen*.

Haley /ˈheɪli/ Bill 1927–1981. US pioneer of rock and roll who was originally a western-swing musician. His songs 'Rock Around the Clock' 1954 (recorded with his group the Comets and featured in the 1955 film *Blackboard Jungle*) and 'Shake, Rattle and Roll' 1955 became the anthems of the early rock-and-roll era.

half /hɑːf/ *n.* (*plural* **halves** /hɑːvz/) **1.** either of two equal or corresponding parts into which a thing is or might be divided; either of two equal periods of play in sports. **2.** a half-price ticket, especially for a child. **3.** a school term. **4.** (*colloquial*) a halfback. **5.** (*colloquial*) a half pint. —*adj.* amounting to half; forming a half. —*adv.* to the extent of half; (*loosely*) to some extent. —**at half cock**, when only half ready. **by half**, excessively. **by halves**, without complete commitment (usually after *negative*). **go halves**, to share equally (*with*). **half-and-half** *adj.* being half one thing and half another. **halfback** *n.* a player between the forwards and the fullback in football, hockey etc. **half-baked** *adj.* not thoroughly thought out, foolish. **half-binding** *n.* the binding of a book with leather on the spine and corners. **half-breed, half-caste** *ns.* a person of mixed race. **half-brother, half-sister** *ns.* a brother or sister with only one parent in common. **half-crown, half a crown**, (*historical*) a coin or amount of 2*s.* 6*d.* **half-hearted** *adj.* lacking enthusiasm. **half-hitch** *n.* a knot formed by passing the end of a rope round its standing part and then through the bight. **half landing**, a landing halfway up a flight of stairs. **half-mast** *n.* the position of a flag halfway up a mast, as a mark of respect for a dead person. **half measures**, measures lacking thoroughness. **half-moon** *n.* the Moon when only half its disc is illuminated; the time when this occurs; a semicircular object. **half-nelson** *n.* a hold in wrestling with the arm under an opponent's arm and behind his or her back. **half term**, the period about halfway through a school term, usually with a short holiday. **half-timbered** *adj.* having walls with a timber frame and brick or plaster filling, a structural style common in England in the 15th–16th centuries. **half-time** *n.* the time at which half of a game or contest is completed, the interval then occurring. **half-title** *n.* the title or short title of a book usually printed on the recto of the leaf preceding the title leaf. **half-track** *n.* a propulsion system with wheels at the front and an endless driven belt at the back; a vehicle having this. **half-truth** *n.* a statement conveying only part of the truth. **half volley**, a return of the ball in tennis as soon as it has touched the ground, a ball in cricket so pitched that the batsman may hit it as it bounces; a hit so made. **halfway** *adj.* & *adv.* at a point equidistant between two others (*halfway house*, a compromise). **not half**, by no means; (*colloquial*) not at all; (*slang*) extremely, violently. [Old English]

half-life *n.* the time taken for half of any sample of a particular radioactive isotope to decay into other materials.

halfpenny /ˈheɪpni/ *n.* (*plural* **halfpence**) (*historical*) half a penny, a coin of this value (legal tender until 1984). —**halfpennyworth** *n.*

halftone process a technique used in printing to reproduce the full range of tones in a photograph or other illustration. The intensity of the printed colour is varied from full strength to the lightest shades, even if one colour of ink is used. The picture to be reproduced is photographed through a screen ruled with a rectangular mesh of fine lines, which breaks up the tones of the original into areas of dots that vary in frequency according to the intensity of the tone. In the darker areas the dots run together; in the lighter areas they have more space between them.

halfwit *n.* a stupid or foolish person—**halfwitted** *adj.*

halibut /'hælɪbət/ *n.* a fish *Hippoglossus hippoglossus* of the family Pleuronectidae found in the N Atlantic. Largest of the flatfish, it may grow to 2 m/6 ft and weigh 90–135 kg/200–300 lb. It is very dark mottled brown or green above and pure white beneath. [from *haly* = holy and *butt* = flatfish, perhaps because eaten on holy days]

Halicarnassus /hælɪkɑː'næsəs/ ancient city in Asia Minor (now Bodrum in Turkey), where the tomb of Mausolus, built about 350 BC by widowed Queen Artemisia, was one of the Seven Wonders of the World. The Greek historian Herodotus was born there.

halide *n.* the family name for a compound produced by combination of a ◊halogen, such as chlorine or iodine, with a less electronegative element (see ◊electronegativity). Halides may be formed by ionic or ◊covalent bonds.

Halifax /'hælɪfæks/ 1. woollen textile town in West Yorkshire, England; population (1981) 87,500. 2. capital of Nova Scotia, E Canada's main port; population (1986) 296,000. Its industries include oil refining and food processing. There are six military bases in Halifax and it is a major centre of oceanography. It was founded by British settlers in 1749.

halite *n.* the mineral sodium chloride, NaCl, or common ◊salt. When pure it is colourless and transparent, but it is often pink, red or yellow. It is soft and has a low density.

halitosis /hæli'təʊsɪs/ *n.* unpleasant-smelling breath. [from Latin *halitus* = breath]

hall /hɔl/ *n.* 1. a space or passage into which the front entrance of a house etc. opens. 2. a large room or building for meetings, meals, concerts etc. 3. a large country house, especially with a landed estate; a university building used for the residence or instruction of students; in college etc., a common dining room. 4. a large public room in a palace etc.; the principal living room of a medieval house. 5. the building of a guild. [Old English]

Hall Charles 1863–1914. US chemist who developed a process for the commercial production of aluminium in 1886. He found that when mixed with cryolite (sodium aluminium fluoride), the melting point of aluminium was lowered and electrolysis became commercially viable. It had previously been as costly as gold.

Hall Peter (Reginald Frederick) 1930– . English theatre, opera, and film director. He was director of the Royal Shakespeare Theatre in Stratford-on-Avon 1960–68 and developed the Royal Shakespeare Company as director 1968–73 until appointed director of the National Theatre 1973–88, succeeding Laurence Olivier. His productions include *Waiting for Godot* 1955, *The Wars of the Roses* 1963, *The Homecoming* stage 1967 and film 1973, and *Amadeus* 1979. He was also appointed artistic director of opera at Glyndebourne in 1984, with productions of *Carmen* 1985 and *Albert Herring* 1985–86, but resigned in 1990.

Hall Radcliffe 1883–1943. English novelist. *The Well of Loneliness* 1928 brought her notoriety because of its lesbian theme. Its review in the *Sunday Express* newspaper stated: 'I had rather give a healthy boy or girl a phial of prussic acid than this novel'.

hallelujah variant of **alleluia.**

Haller /'hælə/ Albrecht von 1708–1777. Swiss physician and scientist, founder of ◊neurology. He studied the muscles and nerves, and concluded that nerves provide the stimulus that triggers muscle contraction. He also showed that it is the nerves, not muscle or skin, that receive sensation.

Halley /'hæli/ Edmund 1656–1742. English scientist. In 1682 he observed the comet named after him, predicting that it would return in 1759. Halley's other astronomical achievements include the discovery that stars have their own ◊proper motion. He was a pioneer geophysicist and meteorologist and worked in many other fields including

mathematics. He became the second Astronomer Royal in 1720. He was a friend of Isaac ◊Newton, whose *Principia* he financed.

Halley's comet a comet that orbits the Sun about every 76 years, named after Edmund Halley. It is the brightest and most conspicuous of the periodical comets. Recorded sightings go back over 2,000 years. It travels around the Sun in the opposite direction to the planets. Its orbit is inclined at almost 20° to the main plane of the solar system and ranges between the orbits of Venus and Neptune. It will next appear in 2061.

halliard variant of ◊halyard.

hallmark *n.* 1. an official mark stamped on British gold, silver, and (from 1973) platinum, instituted in 1327 (royal charter of London Goldsmiths) in order to prevent fraud. After 1363, personal marks of identification were added. Now tests of metal content are carried out at authorized assay offices in London, Birmingham, Sheffield, and Edinburgh; each assay office has its distinguishing mark, to which is added a maker's mark, date letter, and mark guaranteeing standard. 2. a distinctive feature. —*v.t.* to stamp with a hallmark.

hallo /hə'ləʊ/ interjection used in greeting, or to call attention or express surprise. —*n.* (*plural* **hallos**) the cry 'hallo'.

halloo /hə'luː/ *int.* & *n.* a cry used to urge on hounds, or to attract attention. —*v.t./i.* to shout 'halloo' (to).

hallow /'hæləʊ/ *v.t.* to make or honour as holy. [Old English]

Hallowe'en /hæləʊ'iːn/ the evening of 31 Oct, immediately preceding the Christian feast of Hallowmas or All Saints' Day. Customs associated with Hallowe'en in the USA and the UK include children wearing masks or costumes, and 'trick or treating' (going from house to house collecting sweets, fruit, or money). [from *hallow* = holy person and *even²*]

Hallstatt /'hælʃtæt/ archaeological site in Upper Austria, SW of Salzburg. The salt workings date from prehistoric times. In 1846 over 3,000 graves were discovered belonging to a 9th–5th century BC Celtic civilization transitional between the Bronze and Iron ages.

hallucinate /hə'luːsɪneɪt/ *v.t./i.* to experience or cause to experience hallucinations. —**hallucinant** *adj.* & *n.* [from Latin = wander in mind, from Greek *alussō* = be uneasy]

hallucination /həluːsɪ'neɪʃən/ *n.* an illusion of seeing or hearing an external object not actually present. —**hallucinatory** /hə'luːsɪnətərɪ/ *adj.*

hallucinogen /hə'luːsɪnədʒen/ *n.* any substance that acts on the ◊central nervous system to produce changes in perception and mood and often hallucinations. Hallucinogens include ◊LSD, ◊peyote, and ◊mescaline. Their effects are unpredictable and they are illegal in most countries. —**hallucinogenic** /-'dʒenɪk/ *adj.*

halma /'hælmə/ *n.* a game for two or four persons, played on a board of 256 squares, with figures that are moved by leaping over others into the vacant squares beyond, from one corner to the opposite corner. [Greek = leap]

halo /'heɪləʊ/ *n.* (*plural* **haloes**) 1. a disc or ring of light shown round the head of a sacred figure. 2. a glory round an idealized person etc. 3. a disc of light seen round a luminous body, especially the Sun or Moon, caused by the refraction of light through vapour. —*v.t.* to surround with a halo. [from Latin from Greek *halōs* = threshing floor, disc of Sun or Moon]

halogen /'hælədʒ(ə)n/ *n.* any of a group of five non-metallic elements with similar chemical bonding properties: fluorine, chlorine, bromine, iodine, and astatine. They form a linked group in the ◊periodic table of the elements, with fluorine the most reactive and descending to astatine, the least reactive. They combine directly with most metals to form salts, for example common salt (NaCl). Each halogen has seven electrons in its valence shell, which accounts for the chemical similarities displayed by the group. [from Greek *hals halos* = salt]

halon *n.* a compound containing one or two carbon atoms, together with ◊bromine and other ◊halogens. The most commonly used are halon 1211 (bromochlorodifluoromethane) and halon 1301 (bromotrifluoromethane). The halons are gases and are widely used in fire extinguishers. As destroyers of the ◊ozone layer, they are up to ten times more effective than ◊chlorofluorocarbons, to which they are chemically related.

halophyte *n.* a plant adapted to live where there is a high concentration of salt in the soil, for example, in salt marshes and mud flats. Halophytes contain a high percentage of salts in their root cells, so that, despite the salt in the soil, water can still be taken up by the process of ◊osmosis. Some species also have fleshy leaves for storing water, such as seablite *Suaeda maritima*, and sea rocket *Cakile maritima*.

halothane *n.* an anaesthetic agent (a liquid, CF₃CHBrCl) that produces a deep level of unconsciousness when inhaled.

Hals /hæls/ Frans *c.*1581–1666. Flemish-born painter of lively portraits, such as the *Laughing Cavalier* 1624 (Wallace Collection, London), and large groups of military companies, governors of charities, and others (many examples in the Frans Hals Museum, Haarlem, Holland). In the 1620s he experimented with genre (domestic) scenes.

halt¹ /hɔlt, hɒlt/ *n.* **1.** a stop (usually temporary); an interruption to progress. **2.** a railway stopping place for local services, without station buildings. —*v.t./i.* to come or bring to a halt. —**call a halt**, to decide to stop. [from German *halt* = hold]

halt² *v.i.* **1.** to walk hesitatingly; (*archaic*) to be lame. **2.** to waver. **3.** (especially of reasoning, verse etc.) to falter, to be defective. —**the halt**, (*archaic*) lame or crippled people. [Old English; originally in phrase *make halt* from German *halt* = hold]

halter /'hɔltə, 'hɒl-/ *n.* **1.** a rope or strap with a headstall, used for leading or tying up a horse. **2.** a style of dress top held up by a strap passing round the back of the neck. —*v.t.* to put a halter on (a horse). [Old English]

halve /ha:v/ *v.t.* **1.** to divide into two halves or parts. **2.** to reduce by half. **3.** in golf, to draw (a hole or match) with an opponent. **4.** to fit (crossing timbers) together by cutting out half the thickness of each.

halves plural of **half**.

halyard /'hæljəd/ *n.* a rope for raising or lowering a sail, yard etc.

ham *n.* **1.** the upper part of a pig's leg salted and dried or smoked for food; meat from this. **2.** the back of the thigh, the thigh and buttock. **3.** (*slang*) an inexpert performer or actor. **4.** (*colloquial*) the operator of an amateur radio station. —*v.t./i.* (**-mm-**) to overact, to exaggerate one's actions. —**ham-fisted** *adj.*, **ham-handed** *adj.* (*slang*) clumsy. [Old English]

Hamaguchi /hæmə'gu:tʃi/ Hamaguchi Osachi, also known as **Hamaguchi Yuko** 1870–1931. Japanese politician and prime minister 1929–30. His policies created social unrest and alienated military interests. His acceptance of the terms of the London Naval Agreement 1930 was also unpopular. Shot by an assassin in Nov 1930, he died of his wounds nine months later.

Hamburg /'hæmbɜːg/ largest port of Europe, in Germany, on the river Elbe; population (1988) 1,571,000. Industries include oil, chemicals, electronics, and cosmetics.

hamburger /'hæmbɜːgə/ *n.* a flat, round cake of minced beef served fried, often eaten in a soft bread roll. [German (from city of *Hamburg*)]

Hamilcar Barca /hæ'mɪlkaː 'baːkə/ *c.*270–228 BC. Carthaginian general, father of ◊Hannibal. From 247 to 241 he harassed the Romans in Italy and then led an expedition to Spain, where he died in battle.

Hamilton /'hæməltən/ industrial and university town on North Island, New Zealand, on the Waikato river; population (1986) 101,800. It trades in forestry, horticulture, and dairy-farming products. Waikato University was established here in 1964.

Hamilton capital (since 1815) of Bermuda, on Bermuda Island; population (1980) 1,617. It was founded in 1612.

Hamilton town in Strathclyde, Scotland; population (1981) 52,000. Industries include textiles, electronics, and engineering.

Hamilton port in Ontario, Canada; population (1986) 557,000. Linked with Lake Ontario by the Burlington Canal, it has a hydroelectric plant and steel, heavy machinery, electrical, chemical, and textile industries.

Hamilton Alexander 1757–1804. US politician who influenced the adoption of a constitution with a strong central government and was the first secretary of the treasury

1789–95. He led the Federalist Party, and incurred the bitter hatred of Aaron Burr (1756–1836) when he voted against Burr and in favour of Thomas Jefferson for the presidency in 1801.

Hamilton Emma (born Amy Lyon) 1765–1815. English courtesan. In 1782 she became the mistress of Charles ◊Greville and in 1786 of his uncle Sir William Hamilton, the British envoy to the court of Naples, who married her in 1791. After Admiral ◊Nelson's return from the Nile in 1798 during the Napoleonic Wars, she became his mistress and their daughter, Horatia, was born in 1801.

Hamilton James, 1st Duke of Hamilton 1606–1649. Scottish adviser to Charles I. He led an army against the ◊Covenanters in 1639 and subsequently took part in the negotiations between Charles and the Scots. In the second Civil War he led the Scottish invasion of England, but was captured at Preston and executed.

Hamilton Richard 1922– . English artist, a pioneer of pop art. His collage *Just what is it that makes today's homes so different, so appealing?* 1956 (Kunsthalle, Tübingen) is often cited as the first pop art work. Its 1950s interior, inhabited by the bodybuilder Charles Atlas and a pin-up, is typically humorous, concerned with popular culture and contemporary kitsch. His series *Swinging London 67* 1967 comments on the prosecution for drugs of his art dealer Robert Fraser and the singer Mick Jagger.

Hamilton William D 1936– . New Zealand biologist. By developing the concept of ◊inclusive fitness, he was able to solve the theoretical problem of explaining ◊altruism in animal behaviour in terms of ◊neo-Darwinism.

Hamite /'hæmaɪt/ *n.* a person regarded as a descendant of Ham, son of ◊Noah in the Bible; anthropologically a member of any of several dark-skinned Caucasoid peoples of N and E Africa, including the ancient Egyptians and the Berbers. Their languages belong to the Hamitic branch of the Hamito-Semitic (Afro-Asiatic) family.

Hamito-Semitic languages /hæmɪtəʊsɪ'mɪtɪk/ a family of languages spoken throughout the world but commonly associated with N Africa and W Asia. It has two main branches, the **Hamitic** languages of N Africa and the **Semitic** languages originating in Syria, Mesopotamia, Palestine, and Arabia, but now found from Morocco in the W to the Arabian or Persian Gulf in the E.

hamlet /'hæmlɪt/ *n.* a small village, especially one without a church. [from Anglo-French diminutive *hamelet*, ultimately from Middle Low German *hamm*]

Hamlet a tragedy by William ◊Shakespeare, first performed in 1602. Hamlet, after much hesitation, avenges the murder of his father, the king of Denmark, by the king's brother Claudius, who has married Hamlet's mother. The play ends with the death of all three.

Hammarskjöld /'hæmə ʃəʊld/ Dag 1905–1961. Swedish secretary general of the United Nations 1953–61. He opposed Britain over the ◊Suez Crisis in 1956. His attempts to solve the problem of the Congo (now Zaïre), where he was killed in a plane crash, were criticized by the USSR. He was awarded the Nobel Peace Prize in 1961.

hammer *n.* **1.** a tool with a heavy metal head at right angles to the handle, used for breaking, driving nails etc. **2.** a similar contrivance, as for exploding the charge in a gun, striking the strings of a piano etc.; an auctioneer's mallet indicating by a rap that an article is sold. —*v.t./i.* **1.** to hit or beat (as) with a hammer; to strike loudly. **2.** to defeat utterly. —**come under the hammer**, to be sold at an auction. **hammer and sickle**, the symbols of the industrial worker and the peasant, used as the emblem of the USSR. **hammer and tongs**, with great vigour and commotion. **hammer beam**, a beam that projects into a room etc. from the foot of one of the roof's principal rafters. **hammerhead** *n.* a shark of the family Sphyrnidae, with lateral extensions of the head bearing the eyes. **hammer out**, to devise (a plan) with great effort. **hammertoe** *n.* a toe bent permanently downwards. **throwing the hammer**, in track and field athletics, a throwing event in which only men compete. The hammer is a spherical weight attached to a chain with a handle. The competitor spins the hammer over his head to gain momentum and throws it as far as he can. The hammer weighs 7.26 kg/16 lb, and may originally have been a blacksmith's hammer. [Old English]

Hammett /'hæmɪt/ (Samuel) Dashiell 1894–1961. US crime novelist. His works, *The Maltese Falcon* 1930, *The*

Glass Key 1931, and the *The Thin Man* 1932, introduced the 'hard-boiled' detective character into fiction.

hammock /ˈhæmək/ *n.* a bed of canvas or rope network, suspended by cords at the ends, used especially on board ship. [from earlier *hamaca* from Spanish from Carib]

Hammond /ˈhæmənd/ Joan 1912– . Australian soprano, known in oratorio and opera, for example, *Madame Butterfly, Tosca,* and *Martha.*

Hammond organ an electric organ invented in the USA by Laurens Hammond in 1934 and widely used in gospel music. A precursor of the synthesizer.

Hampden /ˈhæmpdən/ John 1594–1643. English politician. His refusal in 1636 to pay ◊ship money, a compulsory tax levied to support the navy, made him a national figure. In the Short and Long Parliaments he proved himself a skilful debater and parliamentary strategist. King Charles's attempt to arrest him and four other leading MPs made the Civil War inevitable. He raised his own regiment on the outbreak of hostilities, and on 18 June 1643 was mortally wounded at the skirmish of Chalgrove Field in Oxfordshire.

Hampden Park /ˈhæmdən ˈpɑːk/ a Scottish football ground, opened in 1903, home of Queen's Park AFC and the national Scottish team. It plays host to the Scottish FA Cup and League Cup final each year as well as semifinal and other matches.

hamper[1] *n.* a large basket usually with a hinged lid, especially with contents of food. [from Old French *hanapier* = case for goblet (*hanap* = goblet)]

hamper[2] *v.t.* to prevent the free movement or activity of; to hinder.

Hampshire /ˈhæmpʃə/ county of S England; **area** 3,770 sq km/1,455 sq mi; **administrative headquarters** Winchester; **population** (1987) 1,537,000.

Hampstead /ˈhæmpstɪd/ district of N London, part of the borough of Camden.

Hampton Court Palace a former royal residence near Richmond, London, built in 1515 by Cardinal ◊Wolsey and presented by him to Henry VIII in 1525. Henry subsequently enlarged and improved it. In the 17th century William and Mary made it their main residence outside London, and the palace was further enlarged by Christopher Wren, although only part of his intended scheme was completed.

hamster *n.* a type of rodent of the family Cricetidae with a thickset body, short tail, and cheek pouches to carry food. A number of species are found across Asia and in SE Europe. Hamsters are often kept as pets. [German]

hamstring *n.* any of the five tendons at the back of the human knee; the great tendon at the back of the quadruped's hock. —*v.t.* (*past* and *past participle* **hamstringed** or **hamstrung**) 1. to cripple (a person, an animal) by cutting the hamstring or hamstrings. 2. to impair the activity or efficiency of.

Hamsun /ˈhæmsuːm/ Knut 1859–1952. Norwegian novelist, whose first novel *Sult/Hunger* 1890 was largely autobiographical. Other works include *Pan* 1894 and *The Growth of the Soil* 1917, which won him the Nobel Prize for Literature in 1920. His hatred of capitalism made him sympathize with Nazism, and he was fined in 1946 for collaboration.

Hanbury-Tenison /ˈhænbəri ˈtenɪsən/ (Airling) Robin 1936– . Irish adventurer, explorer, and writer, who made the first land crossing of South America at its widest point in 1958. He explored the southern Sahara intermittently during 1962–66, and in South America sailed in a small boat from the Orinoco River to Buenos Aires 1964–65. After expeditions to Ecuador, Brazil, and Venezuela, he rode across France in 1984 and along the Great Wall of China in 1986. In 1969 he became chair of Survival International, an organization campaigning for the rights of threatened tribal peoples.

Hancock /ˈhænkɒk/ John 1737–1793. US revolutionary politician. As president of the Continental Congress 1775–77, he was the first to sign the Declaration of Independence in 1776. Because he signed it in a large, bold hand (in popular belief, so that it would be big enough for George III to see), his name became a colloquial term for a signature in the USA. He coveted command of the Continental Army, deeply resenting the selection of George ◊Washington. He was governor of Massachusetts 1780–85 and 1787–93.

Hancock Tony (Anthony John) 1924–1968. British radio and television comedian. 'Hancock's Half Hour' from 1954 showed him always at odds with everyday life.

hand *n.* 1. the end part of the human arm beyond the wrist; the similar member of a monkey. 2. control, custody, disposal; a share in an action, active support; agency. 3. a thing like a hand, especially the pointer of a clock or watch. 4. the right or left side or direction relative to a person or thing. 5. a pledge of marriage. 6. skill; a person with reference to a skill. 7. style of writing; a signature. 8. a person who does or makes something; a person etc. as a source. 9. a manual worker in a factory, farm etc. 10. the playing cards dealt to a player; such a player; a round of play. 11. (*colloquial*) applause. 12. a forefoot of a quadruped; a forehock of pork. 13. the measure of a horse's height, 4 in. —*attrib.* operated by hand; held or carried by hand; done by hand not by machine. —*v.t.* to deliver, to transfer by hand or otherwise (*down, in, over* etc.); to serve or distribute *round.* —**all hands,** the entire crew of a ship. **at hand,** close by; about to happen. **by hand,** by a person not a machine; delivered by messenger not by post. **from hand to mouth,** with only one's immediate needs. **get** *or* **have** *or* **keep one's hand in,** to become or be in practice. **hand and** *or* **in glove,** in collusion or association (*with*). **handaxe** *n.* a prehistoric stone implement, normally oval or pear-shaped and bifacially worked, used for cutting and scraping things as well as for chopping. **hand down,** to transmit (a decision) from a higher court etc. **hand it to,** (*colloquial*) to award deserved praise to. **hand-me-down** *n.* clothing etc. passed on from someone else. **hand-out** *n.* something given free to a needy person; a statement given to the press etc. **hand-over-fist,** (*colloquial*) with rapid progress. **hand-picked** *adj.* carefully chosen. **hands down,** with no difficulty. **hand to hand,** (of fighting) at close quarters. **have one's hands full,** to be fully occupied. **in hand,** at one's disposal, under one's control, receiving attention. **off one's hands,** no longer one's responsibility. **on hand,** available. **on one's hands,** resting on one as a responsibility. **on the one (***or* **on the other) hand,** as one (or another) point of view. **out of hand,** out of control, peremptorily. **put** *or* **set** *or* **turn one's hand to,** to start work on, to engage in. **to hand,** within reach; available. [Old English]

handbag *n.* a small bag for holding a purse and small personal articles, carried especially by women.

handball *n.* 1. a ball for throwing with the hand. 2. a team ball game now played indoors, popularized in Germany in the late 19th century. It is similar to association football, but played with the hands instead of the feet. The indoor game has seven players in a team; the outdoor version has 11.

handbell *n.* a small bell rung by hand.

handbill *n.* a printed notice circulated by hand.

handbook *n.* a short manual or guidebook.

handbrake *n.* a brake operated by hand.

h. & c. abbreviation of hot and cold (water).

handcart *n.* a small cart pushed or drawn by hand.

handclap *n.* a clapping of the hands.

handcuff *v.t.* to put handcuffs on. —*n.* (in *plural*) a pair of lockable, linked metal rings for securing a prisoner's wrists.

Handel /ˈhændl/ Georg Friedrich (George Frederick) 1685–1759. German composer, who became a British subject in 1726. His first opera, *Almira,* was performed in Hamburg in 1705. In 1710 he was appointed Kapellmeister to the elector of Hanover (the future George I of England). In 1712 he settled in England, where he established his popularity with works such as the *Water Music* 1717 (written for George I). His great choral works include the *Messiah* 1742 and the later oratorios *Samson* 1743, *Belshazzar* 1745, *Judas Maccabaeus* 1747, and *Jephtha* 1752.

handful *n.* 1. a quantity that fills the hand. 2. a small number (*of* people or things). 3. (*colloquial*) a troublesome person or task.

handicap /ˈhændɪkæp/ *n.* 1. a disadvantage imposed on a superior competitor or competitors in order to make the chances more equal; a race or contest in which this is imposed. 2. the number of strokes by which a golfer normally exceeds par for the course. 3. a thing that makes progress or success difficult. 4. a physical or mental disability. —*v.t.* (**-pp-**) to impose a handicap on; to place (a person) at a disadvantage. [apparently from phrase *hand i'* (= in) *cap* describing a kind of sporting lottery]

handicapped *adj.* suffering from a physical or mental disability.

handicraft /'hændɪkrɑːft/ *n.* work that requires both manual and artistic skill. [from earlier *handcraft*]

handiwork /'hændɪwɜːk/ *n.* work done or a thing made by the hands, or by a particular person. [Old English *handgeweorc*]

Handke /'hæntkə/ Peter 1942– . Austrian novelist and playwright, whose first play *Insulting the Audience* 1966 was an example of 'anti-theatre writing'. His novels include *Die Hornissen/The Hornets* 1966 and *The Goalie's Anxiety at the Penalty Kick* 1970. He wrote and directed the film *The Left-handed Woman* 1979.

handkerchief /'hæŋkətʃɪf, -tʃiːf/ *n.* (*plural* **handkerchiefs, handkerchieves** /-tʃiːvz/) a square of linen, cotton etc., usually carried in a pocket for wiping the nose etc.

handle *n.* **1.** the part by which a thing is held, carried, or controlled. **2.** a fact that may be taken advantage of. **3.** (*colloquial*) a personal title. —*v.t./i.* **1.** to touch, to feel, or move with the hands. **2.** to manage or deal with; to deal in (goods); to discuss or write about (a subject). —**fly off the handle,** (*colloquial*) to lose one's self-control. [Old English]

handlebar *n.* (*often in plural*) the steering bar of a bicycle etc., with a handgrip at each end. —**handlebar moustache,** a thick moustache with curved ends.

handler *n.* a person who handles things; a person who handles animals, especially one in charge of a trained police dog etc.

handmade *adj.* made by hand not machine.

handmaid *n.* or **handmaiden** (*archaic*) a female servant.

handrail *n.* a narrow rail for holding as a support on stairs etc.

handset *n.* a telephone mouthpiece and earpiece as one unit.

handshake *n.* a shaking of a person's hand with one's own as a greeting etc.

handsome /'hænsəm/ *adj.* **1.** good-looking. **2.** generous; (of a price, fortune etc.) considerable. —**handsomely** *adv.*, **handsomeness** *n.* [originally = easily handled]

handspring *n.* a somersault in which one lands first on the hands and then on the feet.

handstand *n.* the acrobatic feat of supporting one's body on one's hands with feet in the air or against a wall.

handwriting *n.* writing with a pen, pencil etc.; a person's particular style of this. —**handwritten** *adj.*

handy *adj.* **1.** convenient to handle or use; ready to hand. **2.** clever with the hands. —**handily** *adj.*, **handiness** *n.*

handyman *n.* (*plural* **handymen**) a person who is good at doing household repairs etc. or who is employed to do odd jobs.

hang *v.t./i* (*past and past participle* **hung** except in sense 6) **1.** to cause a thing to be supported from above, especially with the lower part free. **2.** to set up (a door) on hinges. **3.** to place (a picture) on a wall or in an exhibition. **4.** to attach (wallpaper) to a wall. **5.** to decorate (a room etc.) *with* pictures, ornaments etc. **6.** (*past and past participle* **hanged**) to execute or kill by suspending from a rope round the neck. **7.** (*colloquial*, as an imprecation) damn, be damned. **8.** to let droop; to be or remain hung (in various senses); to be hanged. —*n.* the way a thing hangs. —**get the hang of,** (*colloquial*) to get the knack of, to understand. **hang about** *or* **around,** to loiter, not to move away. **hang back,** to show reluctance. **hang fire,** to be slow in taking action or in progressing. **hang heavily** *or* **heavy,** (of time) to pass slowly. **hang on,** to stick or hold closely (*to*); to depend on (a circumstance); to remain in office or doing one's duty etc.; to attend closely to; (*colloquial*) to not ring off in telephoning; (*slang*) to wait for a short time. **hang out,** to lean out (*of* a window etc.); to put on a clothesline etc. **hang over,** to threaten. **hang together,** to be coherent; to remain associated. **hang up,** to hang from a hook etc.; to put aside; to end a telephone conversation; to cause delay to. **hang-up** *n.* (*slang*) an emotional inhibition or problem. **hung parliament,** one in which no party has a clear majority. **not care** *or* **give a hang,** (*colloquial*) not to care at all. [Old English]

hangar /'hæŋə, -ŋgə/ *n.* a shed for housing aircraft etc. [French]

Hangchow /hæŋ'tʃau/ former name for ◊Hangzhou, port in Zhejiang province, China.

hangdog *adj.* shamefaced.

hanger *n.* **1.** a person or thing that hangs. **2.** a shaped piece of wood etc. from which clothes may be hung. **3.** a loop etc. by which a thing may be hung. —**hanger-on** *n.* (*plural* **hangers-on**) a follower or dependant, especially an unwelcome one.

hang-glider *n.* the frame used in hang-gliding.

hang-gliding *n.* a technique of unpowered flying using air currents, perfected by a US engineer named Rogallo in the 1970s. The aeronaut is strapped into a carrier, attached to a sail wing of nylon stretched on an aluminium frame like a paper dart, and jumps into the air from a high place.

hanging *n.* **1.** execution by suspension, usually with a drop of 0.6–2 m/2–6 ft, so that the powerful jerk of the tightened rope breaks the neck. This was once a common form of ◊capital punishment in Europe and is still practised in some states in the USA. It was abolished in the UK in 1965. **2.** (in *plural*) draperies hung on a wall etc. —*adj.* that hangs.

hanging participle a ◊participle that has nothing to relate to, e.g.: 'While driving along a country road there was a loud noise under the car.'. Such sentences need to be completely re-expressed, except in some well-established usages where the participle can stand alone (for example, 'Taking all things into consideration, your actions were justified.').

hangman *n.* (*plural* **hangmen**) an executioner who hangs condemned persons.

hangnail *n.* an ◊agnail. [corruption]

hangover *n.* **1.** a severe headache or other aftereffects caused by an excess of alcohol. **2.** something left over from an earlier time.

Hangzhou /hæŋ'dʒəu/ formerly **Hangchow** port and capital of Zhejiang province, China; population (1986) 1,250,000. It has jute, steel, chemical, tea, and silk industries.

hank *n.* a coil or length of wool or thread etc. [from Old Norse]

hanker *v.i.* to long *for*, to crave *after*.

hanky *n.* (*colloquial*) a handkerchief. [abbreviation]

hanky-panky *n.* (*slang*) dishonest dealing, trickery; naughtiness.

Hanley /'hænli/ Ellery 1961– . English rugby league player, a regular member of the Great Britain team since 1984 and the inspiration behind Wigan's domination of the sport in the 1980s.

Hannibal /'hænibəl/ 247–182 BC. Carthaginian general from 221 BC, son of Hamilcar Barca. His siege of Saguntum (now Sagunto, near Valencia) precipitated the Second ◊Punic War with Rome. Following a campaign in Italy (after crossing the Alps in 218 with 57 elephants), Hannibal was the victor at Trasimene in 217 and Cannae in 216, but he failed to take Rome. In 203 he returned to Carthage to meet a Roman invasion but was defeated at Zama in 202 and exiled in 196 at Rome's insistence.

Hanoi /hæˈnɔɪ/ capital of Vietnam, on the Red River; population (1979) 2,571,000. Industries include textiles, paper, and engineering.

Hanover /'hænəuvə/ industrial city, capital of Lower Saxony, Germany; population (1988) 506,000. Industries include machinery, vehicles, electrical goods, rubber, textiles, and oil refining.

Hanover the German royal dynasty that ruled Great Britain and Ireland 1714–1901. Under the Act of ◊Settlement 1701, the succession passed to the ruling family of Hanover, Germany, on the death of Queen Anne. On the death of Queen Victoria, the crown passed to Edward VII of the house of Saxe-Coburg.

Hanoverian /hænəu'viəriən/ *adj.* of British sovereigns from George I to Victoria. [from *Hanover*]

Hansard /'hænsɑːd/ *n.* the official report of the proceedings of the British Parliament, named after Luke Hansard (1752–1828), printer of the House of Commons *Journal* from 1774. The first official reports were published from 1803 by the political journalist Cobbett who, during his imprisonment 1810–12 sold the business to his printer, Thomas Curson Hansard, son of Luke Hansard. The publication of the debates remained in the hands of the family until 1889, and is now the responsibility of the Stationery Office. The name *Hansard* was officially adopted in 1943.

Hanseatic League /ˌhænsiˈætɪk/ a confederation of N European trading cities from the 12th century to 1669. At its height in the late 14th century the Hanseatic League included over 160 cities and towns, among them Lübeck, Hamburg, Cologne, Breslau, and Cracow. The basis of the league's power was its monopoly of the Baltic trade and its relations with Flanders and England. The decline of the Hanseatic League from the 15th century was caused by the closing and moving of trade routes and the development of nation states. [German *Hanse* = group, society]

Hansen's disease /ˈhænsənz/ ◊leprosy. [from G H A *Hansen*, Norwegian physician (1841–1912), discoverer of the leprosy bacillus]

hansom /ˈhænsəm/ n. (*historical*) (in full **hansom cab**) a two-wheeled horse-drawn cab for two inside, with the driver seated behind. [from J A *Hansom*]

Hansom Joseph Aloysius 1803–1882. British architect. His works include the Birmingham town hall 1831, but he is remembered as the designer of the hansom cab in 1834.

Hants abbreviation of Hampshire.

Hanukkah /ˈhaːnəkə/ n. or **Hanukah** or **Chanukah** in Judaism, an eight-day festival of lights which takes place at the beginning of Dec. It celebrates the recapture and rededication of the Temple in Jerusalem by Judas Maccabaeus in 165 BC. [from Hebrew = consecration]

Hanuman /hʌnuˈmɑːn/ in the Sanskrit epic ◊*Rāmāyana*, the Hindu monkey god and king of Hindustan (N India). He helped Rama (an incarnation of the god Vishnu) to retrieve his wife Sita, abducted by Ravana of Lanka (now Sri Lanka).

hap n. (*archaic*) chance, luck; a chance occurrence. —v.i. (–pp–) (*archaic*) to come about by chance. [from Old Norse]

haphazard /hæpˈhæzəd/ adj. done etc. by chance, random. —adv. at random. —**haphazardly** adv.

hapless adj. unlucky.

haploid /ˈhæplɔɪd/ adj. having a single set of ◊chromosomes in each cell. Most higher organisms are ◊diploid, that is they have two sets, but some plants, such as mosses, liverworts, and many seaweeds are haploid. Male honey bees are haploid because they develop from eggs that have not been fertilized. See also ◊meiosis. —n. a haploid cell or organism. [German, from Greek *haplous* = single and *eidos* = form]

ha'p'orth /ˈheɪpəθ/ a halfpennyworth. [contraction]

happen v.i. 1. to occur (by chance or otherwise). 2. to have the (good or bad) fortune (*to do* a thing). 3. to be the fate or experience of. —**happen on** or **upon**, to find by chance.

happening n. 1. an event. 2. an improvised or spontaneous theatrical etc. performance.

happy adj. 1. feeling or showing pleasure or contentment. 2. fortunate. 3. (of words or behaviour) apt, pleasing. —**happy event**, the birth of a child. **happy-go-lucky** adj. cheerfully casual. **happy medium**, a means of satisfactory avoidance of extremes. —**happily** adv., **happiness** n.

Hapsburg /ˈhæpsbɜːg/ English form of ◊Habsburg, former imperial house of Austria–Hungary.

Haq /hɑːk/ Fazlul 1873–1962. Leader of the Bengali Muslim peasantry. He was a member of the Viceroy's Defence Council, established in 1941, and was Bengal's first Indian prime minister 1937–43.

hara-kiri /ˌhærəˈkɪri/ n. ritual suicide involving disembowelment with the sword, formerly practised by samurai to avoid dishonour. [Japanese *hara* = belly and *kiri* = cutting]

harangue /həˈræŋ/ n. a lengthy and earnest speech. —v.t./i. to make a harangue to. [from Old French from Latin]

Harare /həˈrɑːri/ capital of Zimbabwe, on the Mashonaland plateau, about 1,525 m/5,000 ft above sea level; population (1982) 656,000. It is the centre of a rich farming area (tobacco and maize), with metallurgical and food processing industries.

harass /ˈhærəs/ v.t. to trouble and annoy continually; to make repeated attacks on (an enemy). —**harassment** /ˈhærəsmənt/ n. [from French from Old French *harer* = set dog on]

Harbin /hɑːˈbɪn/ formerly **Haerhpin** and **Pinkiang** port on the Songhua River, NE China; capital of Heilongjiang province; population (1986) 2,630,000. Industries include metallurgy, machinery, paper, food processing, and sugar refining, and it is a major rail junction.

harbinger /ˈhɑːbɪndʒə/ n. a person or thing that announces or signals the approach of another; a forerunner. [from Old French *herberge* = lodging, formerly = one sent on ahead to purvey lodgings for army etc.]

harbour /ˈhɑːbə/ n. a place of shelter for ships; shelter. —v.t. 1. to give shelter to (a criminal etc.). 2. to keep in one's mind (an unfriendly thought etc.). —**harbour master**, the officer in charge of a harbour. [Old English or from Old Norse = army shelter]

Harcourt /ˈhɑːkət/ William Vernon 1827–1904. British Liberal politician. Under Gladstone he was home secretary 1880–85 and chancellor of the Exchequer 1886 and 1892–95. He is remembered for his remark in 1892: 'We are all Socialists now.'

hard adj. 1. firm, not yielding to pressure; solid, not easily cut. 2. difficult to understand or do or answer. 3. causing unhappiness, difficult to bear; harsh, unpleasant; unsympathetic; (of a season or weather) severe, frosty; (of a bargain) without concessions. 4. strenuous, enthusiastic. 5. (of liquor) strongly alcoholic. 6. (of a drug) potent and addictive. 7. (of water) containing mineral salts that prevent soap from lathering freely and cause a hard coating to form inside kettles, water tanks etc. 8. (of facts etc.) established, not to be disputed. 9. (of currency or prices) not likely to fall suddenly in value. 10. (of pornography) highly obscene. 11. (of consonants) guttural (as *c* in *cat*, *g* in *go*). —adv. strenuously, intensively; copiously. —**hard and fast**, (of a rule or distinction) definite, unalterable. **hard-boiled** adj. (of an egg) boiled until the white and yolk are solid; (of a person) callous. **hard by**, close by. **hard case**, an intractable person; a case of hardship. **hard cash**, coins and banknotes, not cheques or credit. **hard copy**, printed material produced by computer, suitable for ordinary reading. **hard core**, an irreducible nucleus; heavy material as a road foundation. **hard-headed** adj. practical, not sentimental. **hardhearted** adj. unsympathetic. **hard labour**, heavy manual work (e.g. stone-breaking) formerly imposed on persons convicted of serious crimes. **hard line**, unyielding adherence to a firm policy. **hard of hearing**, somewhat deaf. **hard on** or **upon**, close to in pursuit or sequence. **hard pad**, a form of distemper in dogs etc. **hard palate**, the front part of the palate. **hard-pressed** adj. closely pursued; burdened with urgent business. **hard put to**, in difficulty. **hard sell**, aggressive salesmanship. **hard shoulder**, a hardened strip alongside a motorway for stopping on in an emergency. **hard up**, short of money; at a loss *for*. **hard-wearing** adj. able to stand much wear. [Old English]

hardback adj. bound in stiff covers. —n. a hardback book.

hard-bitten adj. tough and tenacious.

hardboard n. stiff board made of compressed and treated wood pulp.

hard disc in computing, a storage device consisting of a rigid magnetic disc permanently housed in a sealed case. Hard discs are the same sizes as ◊floppy discs but are much faster and have far greater memory capacities, typically between 20 and 600 ◊megabytes.

harden v.t./i. to make or become hard or harder, or (of an attitude etc.) unyielding.

hardening of oils transformation of liquid oils to solid products by ◊hydrogenation.

Hardicanute /ˈhɑːdɪkənuːt/ c.1019–1042. King of England from 1040. Son of Canute, he was king of Denmark from 1028. In England he was considered a harsh ruler.

Hardie /ˈhɑːdi/ (James) Keir 1856–1915. Scottish socialist, member of Parliament 1892–95 and 1900–15. He worked in the mines as a boy and in 1886 became secretary of the Scottish Miners' Federation. In 1888 he was the first Labour candidate to stand for Parliament; he entered Parliament independently as a Labour member in 1892 and was a chief founder of the ◊Independent Labour Party in 1893. Hardie was born in Lanarkshire but represented the parliamentary constituencies of West Ham, London, 1892–95 and Merthyr Tydfil, Wales, from 1900. A pacifist, he strongly opposed the Boer War, and his idealism in his work for socialism and the unemployed made him a popular hero.

hardihood /ˈhɑːdɪhʊd/ n. boldness, daring.

Harding /ˈhɑːdɪŋ/ Warren G(amaliel) 1865–1923. 29th president of the USA 1921–23, a Republican. He concluded the peace treaties of 1921 with Germany, Austria, and Hungary, and in the same year called the Washington Naval Conference to resolve conflicting British, Japanese, and US ambitions in the Pacific. He opposed US membership of the League of Nations. There were charges of corruption among members of his cabinet (the ◊Teapot Dome Scandal).

hardly adv. 1. only with difficulty. 2. scarcely, only just. 3. harshly.

hardness n. the physical property of materials that governs their use. Methods of heat treatment can increase the hardness of metals. A scale of hardness was devised by Friedrich ◊Mohs in the 1800s, based upon the hardness of certain minerals from soft talc (Mohs hardness 1) to diamond (10), the hardest of all materials. See also ◊Brinell hardness test.

Hardouin-Mansart /ɑːˈdwæn mænˈsɑː/ 1646–1708. French architect to Louis XIV from 1675. He designed the lavish Baroque extensions to the palace of Versailles (from 1678) and the Grand Trianon. Other works include the Invalides Chapel in Paris 1680–91, the Place de Vendome, and the Place des Victoires, in Paris.

hardship n. severe discomfort or lack of the necessaries of life; a circumstance causing this.

hardware n. 1. tools and household articles of metal etc. 2. heavy machinery or weaponry. 3. the mechanical, electrical, and electronic components of a computer system, as opposed to the various programs, which constitute ◊software.

hardwood n. the hard, heavy wood from deciduous trees; see ◊timber.

hardy /ˈhɑːdɪ/ adj. robust, capable of enduring difficult conditions; (of a plant) able to grow in the open air all the year. —**hardy annual**, an annual plant that may be sown in the open; a subject that comes up at regular intervals. —**hardiness** n. [from Old French hardi (hardir = become bold)]

Hardy Oliver 1892–1957. US film comedian, member of the duo ◊Laurel and Hardy.

Hardy Thomas 1840–1928. English novelist and poet. His novels, set in rural 'Wessex' (his native West Country), portray intense human relationships played out in a harshly indifferent natural world. They include Far From the Madding Crowd 1874, The Return of the Native 1878, The Mayor of Casterbridge 1886, The Woodlanders 1887, Tess of the D'Urbervilles 1891, and Jude the Obscure 1895. His poetry includes the Wessex Poems 1898, the blank-verse epic of the Napoleonic Wars The Dynasts 1904–08, and several volumes of lyrics.

My argument is that War makes rattling good history; but Peace is poor reading.

Thomas Hardy
The Dynasts

---

hare n. a field mammal of the genus Lepus like a rabbit, with long ears, a short tail, hind legs longer than the forelegs, and a divided upper lip. —v.i. to run rapidly. —**harebrained** adj. wild and foolish, rash. [Old English]

Hare David 1947– . British dramatist and director, whose plays include Slag 1970, Teeth 'n' Smiles 1975, Pravda 1985 (with Howard ◊Brenton), and Wrecked Eggs 1986.

harebell n. a perennial plant Campanula rotundifolia of the ◊bellflower family, with bell-shaped blue flowers, found on dry grassland and heaths. It is known in Scotland as the bluebell.

Hare Krishna /ˈhɑːreɪ ˈkrɪːʃnə/ the popular name for a member of the ◊International Society for Krishna Consciousness, derived from their chant.

harelip n. a congenital fissure of the upper lip.

harem /ˈhɑːriːm, -ˈriːm/ n. the women of a Muslim household, living in a separate part of the house; their quarters. [from Arabic = prohibited]

Hargobind /ˈhɑːɡəbɪnd/ 1595–1644. Indian religious leader, sixth guru (teacher) of Sikhism 1606–44. He

Harlow The American film star Jean Harlow, popularly known as the 'platinum blonde'.

encouraged Sikhs to develop military skills in response to growing persecution. At the festival of ◊Diwali, Sikhs celebrate his release from prison.

Hargraves /ˈhɑːɡreɪvz/ Edward Hammond 1816–1891. Australian prospector, born in England. In 1851 he found gold in the Blue Mountains of New South Wales, thus beginning the first Australian gold rush.

Hargreaves /ˈhɑːɡriːvz/ James died 1778. English inventor who co-invented a carding machine for combing wool in 1760. About 1764 he invented his 'spinning jenny', which enabled a number of threads to be spun simultaneously by one person.

haricot /ˈhærɪkəʊ/ n. (in full **haricot bean**) the white, dried seed of a variety of bean Phaseolus vulgaris. [French]

Harijan /ˈhɑːrɪdʒən/ n. a member of the Indian ◊caste of untouchables. The compassionate term was introduced by Mahatma Gandhi during the independence movement. [Hindi = children of god]

hark v.i. to listen attentively. —**hark back**, to revert to a subject.

Har Krishen /hɑː ˈkrɪʃən/ 1656–1664. Indian religious leader, eighth guru (teacher) of Sikhism 1661–64, who died at the age of eight.

Harlem Globetrotters a US touring basketball team that plays exhibition matches worldwide. Comedy routines as well as their great skills are features of the games. They were founded by Abraham Saperstein (1903–1966) in 1927.

Harlem Renaissance a movement in US literature in the 1920s that used Afro-American life and black culture as its subject matter; it was an early manifestation of black pride in the USA. The centre of the movement was the Harlem section of New York City.

harlequin /ˈhɑːlɪkwɪn/ adj. in varied colours. [French, from Harlequin, character in Italian comedy]

harlequinade /hɑːlɪkwɪˈneɪd/ n. 1. a play or section of a pantomime in which Harlequin plays the leading role. 2. a piece of buffoonery. [from French]

harlot /ˈhɑːlət/ n. (archaic) a prostitute. —**harlotry** n. [from Old French = lad, knave]

Harlow Jean. Stage name of Harlean Carpenter 1911–1937. US film actress, the first 'platinum blonde', and the wisecracking sex symbol of the 1930s. Her films include Hell's Angels 1930, Red Dust 1932, Platinum Blonde 1932, Dinner at Eight 1933, China Seas 1935, and Saratoga 1937, during the filming of which she died (her part was completed by a double, using rear and long shots).

harm n. damage, injury. —v.t. to cause harm to. —**out of harm's way**, in safety. [Old English]

harmattan /hɑːməˈtæn/ n. a dry, dusty NE wind that blows on the coast of Africa from Dec to Feb. [from African dialect haramata]

harmful adj. causing harm. —**harmfully** adv.

harmless adj. not able or likely to cause harm; inoffensive. —**harmlessly** adv., **harmlessness** n.

harmonic /hɑːˈmɒnɪk/ adj. 1. in music, of or relating to harmony; (of tones) produced by the vibration of a string etc. in any of certain fractions (half, third, quarter, fifth etc.) of its length. 2. harmonious. —n. a harmonic tone,

Harold II *After Edward the Confessor's death, Harold, Earl of Wessex, was crowned king in Jan 1066. Harold's short but eventful rule came to an abrupt end with his death at the Battle of Hastings in Oct 1066.*

an overtone. —**harmonic series,** in music, the series of overtones that make up the natural components of a single sound. —**harmonically** *adv.* [from Latin from Greek]

harmonica *n.* or **mouth organ** a pocket-sized reed organ blown directly from the mouth; it was invented by Charles Wheatstone in 1829. [Latin]

harmonious /hɑːˈməʊnɪəs/ *adj.* 1. sweet-sounding. 2. forming a pleasing or consistent whole. 3. free from disagreement or dissent. —**harmoniously** *adv.*

harmonium /hɑːˈməʊnɪəm/ *n.* a keyboard musical instrument in which the notes are produced by air driven through metal reeds by bellows operated by the feet. [French from Latin]

harmonize /ˈhɑːmənaɪz/ *v.t./i.* 1. to add notes to a melody to provide a harmonic accompaniment to it. 2. to bring into or be in harmony (*with*). —**harmonization** /-ˈzeɪʃən/ *n.* [from French]

harmony /ˈhɑːmənɪ/ *n.* 1. a combination of simultaneously sounded musical notes to form chords and chord progressions; the study of this. The term is applied to any combination of notes, whether consonant or dissonant. Harmony deals with the formation of chords and their interrelation and logical progression. 2. a pleasing effect of the apt arrangement of parts. 3. agreement, concord. —**in harmony (with)**, in agreement (with). [from Old French from Latin from Greek *harmonia* = joining (*harmos* = joint)]

harness /ˈhɑːnɪs/ *n.* the equipment of straps and fittings by which a horse is fastened to a cart etc. and controlled; a similar arrangement for fastening a thing to a person. —*v.t.* 1. to put a harness on (a horse); to attach by a harness (*to*). 2. to utilize (a river or other natural force) to produce electrical power etc. —**in harness**, in the routine of daily work. [from Old French = military equipment]

Harold /ˈhærəld/ two kings of England:

Harold I died 1040. King of England from 1035. The illegitimate son of Canute, known as **Harefoot,** he claimed the throne in 1035 when the legitimate heir, Hardicanute, was in Denmark. In 1037 he was elected king.

Harold II *c.*1020–1066. King of England from Jan 1066. He succeeded his father Earl ◊Godwin in 1053 as Earl of Wessex. In 1063 William of Normandy (◊William I) tricked him into swearing to support his claim to the English throne, and when the Witan (a council of high-ranking religious and secular men) elected Harold to succeed Edward the Confessor, William prepared to invade. Meanwhile, Harold's treacherous brother Tostig (died 1066) joined the king of Norway, Harald III Hardrada (1015–1066), in invading Northumbria. Harold routed and killed them at Stamford Bridge on 25 Sept. Three days later William landed at Pevensey, Sussex, and Harold was killed at the Battle of Hastings on 14 Oct 1066.

harp *n.* an instrument comprising a set of strings placed over an open frame so that they can be plucked or swept with the fingers from both sides. The **concert harp** is now

the largest musical instrument to be plucked by hand. It has up to 47 strings, and seven pedals set into the soundbox at the base to alter pitch. —*v.i.* to dwell tediously *on* (a subject). —**harpist** *n.* [Old English]

Harper's Ferry /ˈhɑːpəz ˈferɪ/ village in W Virginia, USA, where the Potomac meets the Shenandoah. It is famous for the incident in 1859 when antislavery leader John ◊Brown seized the government's arsenal here.

harpoon /hɑːˈpuːn/ *n.* a barbed, spearlike missile with a rope attached, for catching whales etc. —*v.t.* to spear with a harpoon. [from French *harpoon* from Latin from Greek *harpē* = sickle]

harp seal a Greenland seal with a dark, harp-shaped mark on its back.

harpsichord /ˈhɑːpsɪkɔːd/ *n.* a wing-shaped keyboard instrument common in the 16th–18th centuries, which differs from the clavichord and piano in that the strings are plucked by a small leather or quill plectrum. It was revived in the 20th century for the authentic performance of early music. —**harpsichordist** *n.* [from French from Latin *harpa* = harp and *chorda* = string]

harpy /ˈhɑːpɪ/ *n.* 1. a mythical monster with a woman's head and body and a bird's wings and claws. 2. a grasping, unscrupulous person. [from French or Latin from Greek *harpuiai* = snatchers (*harpazō* = snatch)]

Har Rai /hɒ ˈraɪ/ 1630–1661. Indian religious leader, seventh guru (teacher) of Sikhism 1644–61.

harridan /ˈhærɪdən/ *n.* a bad-tempered old woman. [perhaps from French *haridelle* = old horse]

harrier /ˈhærɪə/ *n.* 1. a hound used for hunting hares. 2. (in *plural*) cross-country runners. 3. a bird of prey of the genus *Circus* of the family Accipitridae. Harriers have long wings and legs, short beaks, and soft plumage. They are found throughout the world. Three species occur in Britain: the **hen harrier** *C. cyaneus,* **Montagu's harrier** *C. pygargus,* and the **marsh harrier** *C. aeruginosus.*

Harrier *n.* the only truly successful vertical takeoff and landing fixed-wing aircraft, often called the **jump jet.** It was built in Britain and made its first flight in 1966. It has a single jet engine and a set of swivelling nozzles. These deflect the jet exhaust vertically downwards for takeoff and landing, and to the rear for normal flight. Designed to fly from confined spaces with minimal ground support, the Harrier refuels in midair.

Harriman /ˈhærɪmən/ (William) Averell 1891–1986. US diplomat, administrator of ◊lend-lease in World War II, Democratic secretary of commerce in Truman's administration, 1946–48, negotiator of the Nuclear Test Ban Treaty with the USSR in 1963, and governor of New York 1955–58.

Harris /ˈhærɪs/ southern part of ◊Lewis with Harris, in the Outer ◊Hebrides; **area** 500 sq km/193 sq mi; **population** (1971) 2,900. It is joined to Lewis by a narrow isthmus. Harris tweeds are produced here.

Harris Frank 1856–1931. Irish journalist, who wrote colourful biographies of Oscar Wilde and and George Bernard Shaw, and an autobiography, *My Life and Loves* 1926, originally banned in the UK and the USA.

Harris Joel Chandler 1848–1908. US author, born in Georgia. He wrote tales narrated by the former slave 'Uncle Remus', based on black folklore, and involving the characters Br'er Rabbit and the Tar Baby.

Harris Paul P 1878–1947. US lawyer, who founded the first ◊Rotary Club in Chicago in 1905 (see under ◊Rotary).

Harris Richard 1932– . Irish film actor known for playing rebel characters in such films as *This Sporting Life* 1963. His other films include *Camelot* 1967, *A Man Called Horse* 1970, *Robin and Marian* 1976, and *Tarzan the Ape Man* 1981. He won the 1990 Evening Standard Award for best actor in Pirandello's *Henry IV.*

Harris Roy 1898–1979. US composer, born in Oklahoma, who used American folk tunes. Among his works are the 10th symphony 1965 (known as 'Abraham Lincoln') and the orchestral *When Johnny Comes Marching Home* 1935.

Harrison /ˈhærɪsən/ Benjamin 1833–1901. 23rd president of the USA 1889–93, a Republican. He called the first Pan-American Conference, which led to the establishment of the Pan American Union, to improve inter-American cooperation, and develop commercial ties. In 1948 this became the ◊Organization of American States.

Harrison Tony 1937– . British poet and translator. Born in Leeds, he became resident dramatist of the National Theatre but caused controversy with *v* 1987, dealing with the desecration of his parent's grave by Liverpool football supporters, and *The Blasphemers' Banquet* 1989 which attacked (in the name of Molière, Voltaire, Byron, and Omar Khayyam) the death sentence on Salman Rushdie. He has also translated and adapted Molière.

Harrison William Henry 1773–1841. 9th president of the USA in 1841. Elected in 1840 as a Whig, he died a month after taking office. Benjamin Harrison was his grandson.

Harrogate /ˈhærəgət/ resort and spa in N Yorkshire, England; population (1981) 66,500. There is a US communications station at Menw Hill.

harrow /ˈhærəʊ/ *n.* an agricultural implement used to break up the furrows left by the ◊plough and reduce the soil to a fine consistency or tilth, and to cover the seeds after sowing. The traditional harrow consists of spikes set in a frame; modern harrows use sets of discs. —*v.t.* **1.** to draw a harrow over (land). **2.** to distress greatly. [from Old Norse]

harry /ˈhærɪ/ *v.t.* to ravage or despoil; to harass. [Old English]

harsh *adj.* unpleasantly rough or sharp, especially to the senses; severe, cruel. —**harshly** *adv.*, **harshness** *n.* [from Middle Low German]

hart *n.* the male of the (red) deer, especially after the fifth year. [Old English]

Hart /hɑːt/ Gary 1936– . US Democrat politician, senator for Colorado from 1974. In 1980 he contested the Democratic nomination for the presidency, and stepped down from his Senate seat in 1986 to run, again unsuccessfully, in the 1988 presidential campaign.

hartebeest /ˈhɑːtɪbiːst/ *n.* a large African antelope *Alcelaphus buselaphus* with lyre-shaped horns set close on top of the head in both sexes. It may grow to 1.5 m/5 ft at the rather humped shoulders, and up to 2 m/6 ft long. They are clumsy-looking runners, but hartebeest can reach 65 kph/40 mph. [Afrikaans from Dutch]

Hartington Spencer Compton Cavendish, 8th Duke of Devonshire, Marquess of Hartington 1833–1908. British politician, first leader of the Liberal Unionists 1886–1903. As war minister he opposed devolution for Ireland in cabinet and later led the revolt of the Liberal Unionists that defeated Gladstone's Irish Home Rule bill in 1886. Hartington refused the premiership three times, in 1880, 1886, and 1887, and led the opposition to the Irish Home Rule bill in the House of Lords in 1893.

hart's-tongue a fern *Phyllitis scolopendrium* whose straplike, undivided fronds, up to 60 cm/24 in long, have prominent brown spore-bearing organs on the undersides. The plant is native to Eurasia and E North America. It is found on walls, in shady rocky places, and in woods.

Hartz Mountains /hɑːts/ range running N to S in Tasmania, Australia, with two remarkable peaks: Hartz Mountain (1,254 m/4,113 ft) and Adamsons Peak (1,224 m/4,017 ft).

harum-scarum /ˈheərəm ˈskeərəm/ *adj.* wild and reckless. —*n.* such a person.

Harvard University /ˈhɑːvəd/ the oldest educational institution in the USA, founded in 1636 at New Towne (later Cambridge), Massachusetts, and named after John Harvard (1607–1638), who bequeathed half his estate and his library to it. Women were first admitted in 1969; the women's college of the university is Radcliffe College.

harvest /ˈhɑːvɪst/ *n.* the gathering in of crops etc., the season of this; the season's yield; the product of any action. —*v.t./i.* to gather as a harvest, to reap. —**harvest festival**, a thanksgiving festival in church for the harvest. **harvest moon**, the full moon nearest to the autumn equinox (22 or 23 Sept). **harvest mouse**, a very small mouse *Micromys minutus* nesting in the stalks of standing corn. [Old English]

harvester *n.* **1.** a reaper. **2.** a reaping machine.

harvestman *n.* an arachnid of the order Opiliones. They are distinguished from true spiders by the absence of a waist or constriction in the oval body. They are carnivorous and found from the Arctic to the tropics. The long-legged harvestman *Phalangium opilio*, known as **daddy-long-legs** in the USA, is also called the **crane fly** in Britain.

Harvey /ˈhɑːvɪ/ Laurence. Adopted name of Lauruska Mischa Skikne 1928–1973. British film actor of Lithuanian descent who worked both in England (*Room at the Top* 1958) and in Hollywood (*The Alamo* 1960; *The Manchurian Candidate* 1962).

Harvey William 1578–1657. English physician who discovered the circulation of blood. In 1628 he published his great book *De Motu Cordis*/*On the Motion of the Heart*. He was court physician to James I and Charles I.

Harwich /ˈhærɪdʒ/ seaport in Essex, England; with ferry services to Scandinavia and the NW Europe; population (1981) 15,076. Reclamation of Bathside Bay mudflats is making it a rival, as a port, to Felixstowe.

Haryana /ˌhærɪˈɑːnə/ state of NW India; **area** 44,200 sq km/17,061 sq mi; **capital** Chandigarh; **products** sugar, cotton, oilseed, textiles, cement, iron ore; **population** (1981) 12,851,000; **language** Hindi.

has see ◊have¹. —**has-been** *n.* a person or thing that is no longer as famous or successful etc. as formerly.

Hasdrubal Barca /ˈhæzdrʊbəl ˈbɑːkə/ Carthaginian general, son of Hamilcar Barca and brother of Hannibal. He remained in command in Spain when Hannibal invaded Italy and, after fighting there against Scipio until 208, marched to Hannibal's relief. He was defeated and killed in the Metaurus valley, NE Italy.

Hašek /ˈhæʃek/ Jaroslav 1883–1923. Czech writer. His masterpiece is the anti-authoritarian comic satire on military life under Austro-Hungarian rule, *The Good Soldier Schweik* 1923. During World War I he deserted to Russia, and eventually joined the Bolsheviks.

hash¹ *n.* **1.** a dish of cooked meat cut into small pieces and recooked. **2.** a mixture, a jumble. **3.** reused material. —*v.t.* to make (meat) into a hash. —**make a hash of**, (*colloquial*) to make a mess of, to bungle. **settle a person's hash**, (*colloquial*) to deal with and subdue him or her. [from French *hacher* (*hache* = hatchet)]

hash² *n.* (*colloquial*) hashish. [abbreviation]

Hashemite /ˈhæʃmaɪt/ *adj.* of an Arab princely family related to Muhammad. [from *Hashim*, great-grandfather of Muhammad]

hashish /ˈhæʃiːʃ/ *n.* a drug made from the resin contained in the female flowering tops of hemp (◊cannabis). [from Arabic]

hash total in computing, an arithmetic total of a set of arbitrary numeric values, such as account numbers. Although the total itself is meaningless, it is stored along with the data to which it refers. On subsequent occasions, the program recalculates the hash total and compares it to the one stored to ensure that the original numbers are still correct.

Hasid /ˈhæsɪd/ *n.* or **Hassid** or **Chasid** (*plural* **Hasidin, Hassidin, Chasidim**) a member of a sect of Orthodox Jews, founded in 18th-century Poland, which stressed intense emotion as a part of worship. Many of their ideas are based on the ◊kabbala. —**Hasidic** *adj.* **Hasidism** *n.*

hasn't /ˈhæzənt/ (*colloquial*) has not.

hasp /hɑːsp/ *n.* a hinged metal clasp that fits over a staple and is secured by a padlock. [Old English]

Hassam /ˈhæsəm/ Childe 1859–1935. US Impressionist painter and printmaker. He studied in Paris 1886–89, and became one of the members of The Ten, a group of American Impressionists who exhibited together until World War I.

Hassan II /hæˈsɑːn/ 1930– . King of Morocco from 1961; from 1976 he undertook the occupation of the Western Sahara when it was ceded by Spain.

hassle *n.* (*colloquial*) a quarrel, a struggle; a difficulty. —*v.t./i.* (*colloquial*) to quarrel; to harass.

hassock /ˈhæsək/ *n.* **1.** a thick, firm cushion for kneeling on. **2.** a tuft of grass. [Old English]

haste /heɪst/ *n.* urgency of movement or action, hurry. —*v.i.* to hasten. —**in haste**, quickly, hurriedly. **make haste**, to be quick. [from Old French]

hasten /ˈheɪsən/ *v.t./i.* **1.** to make haste, to hurry. **2.** to cause to occur or be ready or be done sooner.

Hastings /ˈheɪstɪŋz/ resort in East Sussex, England; population (1981) 74,803. The chief of the ◊Cinque Ports, it has ruins of a Norman castle. The wreck of the Dutch East Indiaman *Amsterdam* (1749), is under excavation. It is adjoined by St Leonard's, developed in the 19th century.

Hastings Warren 1732–1818. British colonial administrator. A protégé of Lord Clive, who established British rule in India, Hastings carried out major reforms, and became governor of Bengal in 1772 and governor general of India in

1774. Impeached for corruption on his return to England in 1785, he was acquitted in 1795.

Hastings, Battle of the battle on 14 Oct 1066 at which William the Conqueror defeated Harold, king of England. The site is 10 km/6 mi inland of Hastings, at Senlac, Sussex; it is marked by Battle Abbey.

hasty /'heɪstɪ/ *adj.* 1. hurried, acting too quickly. 2. said, made, or done too quickly or too soon. —**hastily** *adv.*, **hastiness** *n.* [from Old French]

hat *n.* a covering for the head, especially worn out of doors. —**hat trick,** the taking of three wickets at cricket by the same bowler with three successive balls; the scoring of three goals or winning of three victories by one person. **keep it under one's hat,** to keep it secret. **out of a hat,** by random selection. **pass the hat round,** to collect contributions of money. **take off one's hat,** to applaud. **talk through one's hat,** (*slang*) to talk wildly or ignorantly. [Old English]

hatband *n.* a band of ribbon etc. round a hat above the brim.

hatch[1] *n.* 1. an opening in a floor or wall etc.; an opening or door in an aircraft etc. 2. a cover for a hatchway. [Old English]

hatch[2] *v.t./i.* 1. (of a young bird or fish etc.) to emerge from the egg; (of an egg) to produce a young animal; to incubate (an egg). 2. to devise (a plot etc.). — *n.* hatching; a brood hatched.

hatch[3] *v.t.* to mark with close parallel lines. —**hatching** *n.* [from French *hacher*]

hatchback *n.* a car with a sloping back hinged at the top to form a door.

hatchet /'hætʃɪt/ *n.* a light, short-handled axe. —**hatchet man,** a hired killer, a person employed to make personal attacks. [from Old French *hachette* (*hache* = axe)]

hatchway *n.* an opening in a ship's deck for lowering cargo.

hate *n.* 1. hatred. 2. (*colloquial*) a hated person or thing. —*v.t.* to feel hatred towards; to dislike greatly; (*colloquial*) to be reluctant. —**hater** *n.* [Old English]

hateful *adj.* arousing hatred.

Hathor /'hæθɔː/ in ancient Egyptian mythology, the sky goddess, identified with ◊Isis.

hatred /'heɪtrɪd/ *n.* intense dislike or ill will.

Hatshepsut /hæt'ʃepsut/ *c.*1540–*c.*1481 BC. Queen of Egypt during the 18th dynasty. She was the daughter of Thothmes I, with whom she ruled until the accession to the throne of her husband and half-brother Thotmes II. Throughout her reign real power lay with Hatshepsut, and she continued to rule after his death, as regent for her nephew Thotmes III.

hatter *n.* a maker or seller of hats.

Hatteras /'hætərəs/ cape on the coast of N Carolina, USA, noted for shipwrecks.

Hattersley /'hætəzlɪ/ Roy 1932– . British Labour politician. On the right wing of the Labour Party, he was prices secretary 1976–79, and in 1983 became deputy leader of the party.

Hatton /'hætn/ Derek 1948– . British left-wing politician, former deputy leader of Liverpool Council. A notorious member of the ◊Militant Tendency, Hatton was removed from office and expelled from the Labour Party in 1987.

Haughey /'hɔːhɪ/ Charles 1925– . Irish Fianna Fáil politician of Ulster descent. Dismissed in 1970 from Jack Lynch's cabinet for alleged complicity in IRA gunrunning, he was afterwards acquitted. Prime minister 1979–81, March–Nov 1982, and 1986– .

haughty /'hɔːtɪ/ *adj.* arrogantly proud of oneself and looking down on others. —**haughtily** *adv.*, **haughtiness** *n.* [from Old French *haut* = high from Latin *altus*]

haul /hɔːl/ *v.t./i.* 1. to pull or drag forcibly. 2. to transport by lorry or cart etc. 3. to turn a ship's course. 4. (*colloquial*) to bring (*up*) for reprimand or trial. —*n.* 1. hauling. 2. an amount gained or acquired. 3. a distance to be traversed.

haulage /'hɔːlɪdʒ/ *n.* transport of goods; the charge for this.

haulier /'hɔːlɪə/ *n.* a firm or person engaged in the transport of goods by road.

haulm /hɔːm/ *n.* a stalk or stem; (*collectively*) the stems of potatoes, peas, beans etc. [Old English]

Havel Czechoslovakia's 'playwright president' Vaclav Havel.

haunch /hɔːntʃ/ *n.* the fleshy part of the buttock and thigh; a leg and loin of deer etc. as food. [from Old French *hanche*]

haunt /hɔːnt/ *v.t.* 1. (of a ghost) to be frequently in (a place), especially with reputed manifestations of its presence. 2. to be persistently in (a place). 3. (of a memory etc.) to linger in the mind of. —*n.* a place frequented by a person. [from Old French *hanter*]

Hausa /'hausə/ *n.* (*plural* the same or **Hausas**) 1. a member of an agricultural Muslim people of the Sudan and N Nigeria, numbering 9 million. 2. their Afro-Asiatic language which is used as a trade language throughout W Africa.

Haussmann /ˈəʊsmæn/ Georges Eugène, Baron Haussmann 1809–1891. French administrator who replanned medieval Paris 1853–70 with wide boulevards and parks. The cost of his scheme and his authoritarianism caused opposition, and he was made to resign.

haustorium *n.* (*plural* **haustoria**) a specialized organ produced by a parasitic plant or fungus that penetrates the cells of its host to absorb nutrients. It may be either an outgrowth of hyphae (see ◊hypha), as in the case of parasitic fungi, or of the stems of flowering parasitic plants, as in dodders *Cuscuta*. The suckerlike haustoria of a dodder penetrate the vascular tissue of the host plant without killing the cells.

hautboy /'əʊbɔɪ/ obsolete name of the **oboe**. [from French = high wood]

haute couture /əʊt kuːˈtjuə/ high fashion; the leading fashion houses collectively, or their products. [French]

haute cuisine /əʊt kwiˈziːn/ high-class cookery. [French]

Haute-Normandie /'əʊt nɔːmənˈdiː/ or **Upper Normandy** coastal region of NW France lying between Basse-Normandie and Picardy and bisected by the Seine; area 12,300 sq km/4,757 sq mi; population (1986) 1,693,000. It comprises the *départements* of Eure and Seine-Maritime; its capital is Rouen. Major ports include Dieppe and Fécamp. The area has many beech forests.

hauteur /əʊˈtɜː/ *n.* haughtiness of manner. [French (*haut* = high)]

Havana /həˈvænə/ capital and port of Cuba; population (1986) 2,015,000. Products include cigars and tobacco.

have[1] /həv, *emphatic* hæv/ *v.t.* (*third person singular present* has /həz, *emphatic* hæz/; *past* and *past participle* had /had, *emphatic* hæd/; *participle* having) 1. to be in possession of; to possess in a certain relationship. 2. to contain as a part or quality. 3. to experience, to undergo. 4. to engage in (an activity). 5. to give birth to (a baby). 6. to form (an idea etc.) in the mind; to know (a language). 7. to receive; to eat or drink. 8. to be burdened with or committed to. 9. to be provided with. 10. to cause or instruct to be or do or be done etc.; to accept or tolerate; (usually *negative*) to permit to. **11.** to let (a feeling etc.) be present in the mind; to be influenced by (a quality, as mercy etc). **12.** (*colloquial*) to have sexual intercourse with. **13.** (*colloquial*) to deceive; to get the better of. —*v.aux.* with past participle of verbs forming past tenses (*I have, had, shall have, seen; had I known I would have gone*). **have had it,** (*colloquial*) to have missed one's chance, to have passed one's prime, to have been killed. **have it,** to express the view *that*; to win a discussion; (*colloquial*) to have found the answer; to possess an advantage. **have it in for,** (*colloquial*) to be hostile or ill-disposed to. **have it off,** (*slang*) to have sexual intercourse. **have it out,** to settle a dispute by argument (*with*). **have on,** to wear (clothes); to have (an engagement); to tease or hoax. **have to,** (*colloquial*) to have got to, to be obliged to, must. **have up,** to bring before a court of justice or to be interviewed. [Old English]

have[2] /hæv/ *n.* **1.** one who has (especially wealth or resources). **2.** (*slang*) a swindle. —**haves and have-nots,** the rich and the poor.

Havel /'hævel/ Vaclav 1936– . Czech playwright and politician, president from Dec 1989. His plays include *The Garden Party* 1963 and *Largo Desolato* 1985, about a dissident intellectual. Havel became widely known as a human-rights activist. He was imprisoned from 1979–83 and again in 1989 for support of Charter 77 (see ◊Czechoslovakia).

haven /'heɪvən/ *n.* a refuge; a harbour; a port. [Old English]

haven't /'hævənt/ (*colloquial*) have not.

haver /'heɪvə/ *v.i.* **1.** to hesitate, to vacillate. **2.** to talk foolishly.

Havers /'heɪvəz/ Robert Michael Oldfield, Baron Havers 1923– . British lawyer, Lord Chancellor 1987–88. After a successful legal career he became Conservative member of Parliament for Wimbledon in 1970 and was solicitor-general under Edward Heath and attorney-general under Margaret Thatcher. He was made a life peer in 1987 and served briefly, and unhappily, as Lord Chancellor before retiring in 1988.

haversack /'hævəsæk/ *n.* a strong canvas etc. bag carried on the back or over the shoulder. [from French from German = oats sack]

havoc /'hævək/ *n.* widespread destruction, great disorder. [from Anglo-French from Old French *havo*]

haw[1] *n.* a hawthorn berry [Old English]

haw[2] see ◊hum.

Hawaii /hɑ'waiɪ/ Pacific state of the USA; **area** 16,800 sq km/6,485 sq mi; **capital** Honolulu on Oahu; **physical** Hawaii consists of a chain of some 20 volcanic islands, of which the chief are (1) **Hawaii**, noted for Mauna Kea (4,201 m/13,788 ft) and Mauna Loa (4,170 m/13,686 ft); (2) **Maui** the second largest of the islands; (3) **Oahu** the third largest, with the greatest concentration of population and tourist attractions; (4) **Kauai**; and (5) **Molokai**, the site of a leper colony; **products** sugar, coffee, pineapples, flowers, ladies' garments; **population** (1987) 1,083,000; 34% European, 25% Japanese, 14% Filipino, 12% Hawaiian, 6% Chinese; **language** English; **history** a kingdom until 1893, Hawaii became a republic in 1894, ceded itself to the USA in 1898, and became a state in 1959.

Hawarden /'hɑ:dn/ town in Clwyd, N Wales; population 8,500. W E ◊Gladstone lived at Hawarden Castle for many years, and founded St Deiniol's theological library in Hawarden.

hawfinch *n.* a European finch *Coccothraustes coccothraustes* about 18 cm/7 in long. It is rather uncommon and spends most of its time in the treetops. It feeds on berries and seeds, and can crack cherry stones with its large and powerful bill.

hawk[1] *n.* **1.** any small to medium-sized bird of prey of the family Accipitridae. Hawks have an untoothed, hooked bill, short, broad wings, and keen eyesight. **2.** a person who advocates an aggressive policy. —*v.t./i.* to hunt with a hawk. —**hawk-eyed** *adj.* keen-sighted. [Old English]

hawk[2] *v.t./i.* to clear the throat of phlegm noisily; to bring up (phlegm) thus.

hawk[3] *v.t.* to carry (goods) about for sale.

Hawke /hɔ:k/ Bob (Robert) 1929– . Australian Labor politician, on the right wing of the party. He was president of the Australian Council of Trade Unions 1970–80 and became prime minister in 1983.

hawker *n.* one who hawks goods about. [probably from Low Dutch]

Hawkesbury /'hɔ:ksbəri/ river in New South Wales, Australia; length 480 km/300 mi. It is a major source of Sydney's water.

Hawking /'hɔ:kɪŋ/ Stephen 1942– . English physicist, who has researched ◊black holes and gravitational field theory. His books include *A Brief History of Time* 1988. Professor of gravitational physics at Cambridge from 1977, he discovered that the strong gravitational field around a black hole can radiate particles of matter. Confined to a wheelchair because of a muscular disease, he performs complex mathematical calculations entirely in his head.

Hawkins /'hɔ:kɪnz/ Coleman (Randolph) 1904–1969. US virtuoso tenor saxophonist. He was, until 1934, a soloist in the swing band led by Fletcher Henderson (1898–1952), and was an influential figure in bringing the jazz saxophone to prominence as a solo instrument.

Hawkins Jack 1910–1973. British film actor, usually cast in authoritarian roles. His films include *The Cruel Sea* 1953, *The League of Gentlemen* 1959, *Zulu* 1963, and *Waterloo* 1970. After 1966 his voice had to be dubbed following an operation for throat cancer that removed his vocal chords.

hawk moth a family of moths (Sphingidae) with more than 1,000 species distributed throughout the world, but found in mainly tropical regions.

Hawks /hɔ:ks/ Howard 1896–1977. US director and producer of a wide range of classic films, including *Scarface* 1932, *Bringing Up Baby* 1938, *The Big Sleep* 1946, and *Gentlemen Prefer Blondes* 1953.

Hawksmoor /'hɔ:ksmɔ:/ Nicholas 1661–1736. English architect, assistant to ◊Wren in designing London churches and St Paul's Cathedral; joint architect with ◊Vanbrugh of Castle Howard and Blenheim Palace. The original west towers of Westminster Abbey, long attributed to Wren, were designed by Hawksmoor.

Haworth /'hauəθ/ village in W Yorkshire, home of the ◊Brontë family. It is now part of Keighley.

Haworth Norman 1883–1950. English organic chemist who was the first to synthesize a vitamin (vitamin C), in 1933, for which he shared the 1937 Nobel Prize for Chemistry.

hawser /'hɔ:zə/ *n.* a thick rope or cable for mooring or towing a ship. [from Old French *haucier* = hoist from Latin *altus* = high]

hawthorn *n.* a shrub or tree of the genus *Crataegus* of the rose family Rosaceae. Species are most abundant in E North America, but many are also in Eurasia. All have alternate, toothed leaves and bear clusters of showy white, pink, or red flowers. Small applelike fruits can be red, orange, blue, or black. Hawthorns are popular as ornamentals. The common hawthorn, may, or whitethorn *C. monogyna*, a thorny shrub or small tree, bears clusters of white or pink flowers followed by groups of red berries. Native to Europe, N Africa, and W Asia, it has been naturalized in North America and Australia.

Hawthorne /'hɔ:θɔ:n/ Nathaniel 1804–1864. US writer of *The Scarlet Letter* 1850, a powerful novel of Puritan Boston. He wrote three other novels, including *The House of the Seven Gables* 1851, and many short stories, including *Tanglewood Tales* 1853, classic legends retold for children.

hay /heɪ/ *n.* grass mown and dried for fodder. —**hay fever,** an allergic disorder caused by pollen or dust. **hit the hay,** (*slang*) to go to bed. **make hay of,** to throw into confusion. **make hay while the sun shines,** to seize opportunities for profit. [Old English]

Hay Will 1888–1949. British comedy actor. Originally a music hall comedian, from the 1930s he made many films in which he usually played incompetents in positions of authority, including *Good Morning Boys* 1937; *Oh Mr Porter* 1938; *Ask a Policeman* 1939; *The Ghost of St Michaels* 1941; *My Learned Friend* 1944.

Hayden /'heɪdn/ Sterling. Stage name of John Hamilton 1916–1986. US film actor who played leading roles in Hollywood in the 1940s and early 1950s. Although later seen in some impressive character roles, his career as a whole failed to do justice to his talent. His work includes *The Asphalt Jungle* 1950, *Johnny Guitar* 1954, *Dr Strangelove* 1964, and *The Godfather* 1972.

Hayden William (Bill) 1933– . Australian Labor politician. He was leader of the Australian Labor Party and of the opposition 1977–83, and minister of foreign affairs in 1983. He became governor-general in 1989.

Haydn /'haɪdn/ Franz Joseph 1732–1809. Austrian composer. A teacher of Mozart and Beethoven, he was a major exponent of the classical sonata form in his numerous chamber and orchestral works (he wrote more than 100 symphonies). He also composed choral music, including the oratorios *The Creation* 1798 and *The Seasons* 1801. He was the first great master of the ◊string quartet.

Hayes /heɪz/ Rutherford Birchard 1822–1893. 19th president of the USA 1877–81, a Republican. He was a major general on the Union side in the Civil War. During his presidency federal troops (see ◊Reconstruction) were withdrawn from the Southern states and the Civil Service was reformed.

haymaking *n.* mowing grass and spreading it to dry. —**haymaker** *n.*

haystack *n.* or **hayrick** a packed pile of hay with a pointed or ridged top.

haywire *adj.* (*colloquial*) badly disorganized, out of control. [from use of hay-baling wire in makeshift repairs]

Hayworth /'heɪwɜːθ/ Rita. Stage name of Margarita Carmen Cansino 1918–1987. US film actress who gave vivacious performances in 1940s musicals and steamy, erotic roles in *Gilda* 1946 and *The Lady from Shanghai* 1948. She was known as Hollywood's 'Love Goddess' during the height of her career. Her later appearances were intermittent and she retired in 1972.

hazard /'hæzəd/ *n.* **1.** a danger or risk; a source of this. **2.** an obstacle on a golf course. —*v.t.* to risk; to venture (an action or suggestion etc.). [from French from Spanish from Arabic = chance, luck]

hazard labels a visual system of symbols for indicating the potential dangers of handling certain substances. The symbols used are recognized internationally.

hazardous *adj.* risky. —**hazardously** *adv.*

hazardous substances waste substances, usually generated by industry, which represent a hazard to the environment or to people living or working nearby. Examples include radioactive wastes, acidic resins, arsenic residues, residual hardening salts, lead, mercury, nonferrous sludges, organic solvents, and pesticides. Their economic disposal or recycling is the subject of research.

haze *n.* **1.** thin atmospheric vapour. **2.** mental confusion or obscurity.

haze factor the unit of visibility in mist or fog. It is the ratio of the brightness of the mist compared with that of the object.

hazel /'heɪz(ə)l/ *n.* **1.** a shrub or tree of the genus *Corylus*, family Corylaceae, including the European **common hazel** or **cob** *C. avellana*, of which the **filbert** is the cultivated variety. North American species include the **American hazel** *C. americana*. **2.** a light brown colour. —**hazelnut** *n.* [Old English]

Hazlitt /'hæzlɪt/ William 1778–1830. English essayist and critic, known for his invective, scathing irony and gift for epigram. His critical essays include *Characters of Shakespeare's Plays* 1817–18, *Lectures on the English Poets* 1818–19, *English Comic Writers* 1819, and *Dramatic Literature of the Age of Elizabeth* 1820. Other notable works are *Table Talk* 1821–22, *The Spirit of the Age* 1825, and *Liber Amoris* 1823.

hazy *adj.* **1.** misty; vague, indistinct. **2.** confused, uncertain. —**hazily** *adv.*, **haziness** *n.*

HB abbreviation of hard black (pencil lead).

H-bomb /'eɪtʃbɒm/ abbreviation of ◊hydrogen bomb.

HCF abbreviation of highest common factor.

HDTV abbreviation of high-definition ◊television.

he /hiː/ *pron. objective* **him**; *possessive* **his**; *plural* **they**) the man, boy, or male animal previously named or in question. —*n.* a male, a man. —*adj.* (usually with hyphen) male (e.g. *he-goat*). —**he-man** *n.* a masterful or virile man. [Old English]

He symbol for helium.

HE abbreviation of **1.** high explosive. **2.** His Eminence. **3.** His or Her Excellency.

head /hed/ *n.* **1.** the upper part of the human body, or the foremost part of an animal's body, containing the mouth, sense organs, and brain. **2.** the seat of the intellect and the imagination; mental aptitude. **3.** (*colloquial*) a headache. **4.** a person, an individual; an individual animal; (*collective*) animals. **5.** an image of the head on one side of a coin;

Hazlitt *A master of invective and irony, British essayist William Hazlitt was encouraged to take up journalism by S T Coleridge.*

(usually in *plural*) this side turning up in the toss of a coin. **6.** the height or length of the head as a measure. **7.** a thing like a head in form or position, e.g. the striking part of a tool, the flattened top of a nail, the mass of leaves or flowers at the top of a stem, the flat end of a drum; the foam on top of beer etc.; the closed end of the cylinder in a pump or engine; the component on a tape recorder that touches the moving tape in play and converts the signals. **8.** the upper end (of a table, occupied by the host; of a lake, at which a river enters; of a bed etc., for one's head); the front (of a procession etc.); the bows of a ship. **9.** the top or highest part (of stairs, a list, page, mast etc.). **10.** a chief person or ruler; a master etc. of a college; a headmaster or headmistress; (*attributive*) highest in authority. **11.** a position of command. **12.** a confined body of water or steam; the pressure exerted by this. **13.** a promontory (especially in place names). **14.** a division in a discourse; a category. **15.** a culmination, a climax or crisis. **16.** the fully developed top of a boil etc. —*v.t./i.* **1.** to be at the head of or in charge of. **2.** to strike (the ball) with the head in football. **3.** to provide with a head or heading. **4.** to face or move (in a specified direction). **5.** to direct the course (of). —**give a person his/her head,** to let him/her move or act freely. **go to one's head,** (of liquor) to make one dizzy or slightly drunk; (of success) to make one conceited. **headdress** *n.* an ornamental covering or band for the head. **head first,** (of a plunge etc.) with the head foremost; (*figurative*) precipitately. **head for,** to be moving towards (a place, or (*figuratively*) trouble). **head off,** to get ahead so as to intercept; to forestall. **head-on** *adj.* & *adv.* (of a collision etc.) head to head or front to front. **head over heels,** rolling the body over in a forward direction; topsy-turvy. **headshrinker** *n.* (*slang*) a psychiatrist. **head start,** an advantage granted or gained at an early stage. **headwind** *n.* a wind blowing from directly in front. **keep** (*or* **lose**) **one's head,** to keep (or lose) calm or self-control. **make head or tail of** (usually *negative*), to understand. **off one's head,** (*colloquial*) crazy. **off the top of one's head,** (*colloquial*) impromptu; at random. **on one's (own) head,** being one's responsibility. **over a person's head,** beyond his or her understanding; to a position or authority higher than his or hers. **put heads together,** to consult together. **turn a person's head,** to make him or her conceited. [Old English]

Head Bessie 1937– . South African writer living in exile in Botswana. Her novels include *When Rain Clouds Gather* 1969, *Maru* 1971, and *A Question of Power* 1973.

headache *n.* **1.** a continuous pain in the head. **2.** (*colloquial*) a worrying problem.

headboard *n.* an upright panel along the head of a bed.
header *n.* 1. a heading of the ball in football. 2. (*colloquial*) a dive or plunge with the head first. 3. a brick etc. laid at right angles to the face of a wall.
headgear *n.* a hat or headdress.
heading *n.* 1. a title at the head of a page or section of a book etc. 2. a horizontal passage in a mine.
Headingley/'hedɪŋli/ Leeds sports centre, home of the Yorkshire County Cricket Club and Leeds Rugby League Club. The two venues are separated by a large stand.
headlamp *n.* a headlight.
headland *n.* a promontory.
headlight *n.* a powerful light at the front of a motor vehicle or railway engine; the beam from this.
headline *n.* a heading at the top of an article or page, especially in a newspaper; (in *plural*) a summary of the most important items in a broadcast news bulletin.
headlong *adj.* & *adv.* with the head foremost; in a rush.
headman *n.* (*plural* **headmen**) the chief man of a tribe etc.
headmaster *n.* the principal master of a school, responsible for organizing it. —**headmistress** *n.fem.*
headphones *n.pl.* earphones held in position by a band fitting over the head.
headquarters *n.* (*as singular* or *plural*) the place where a military or other organization is centred.
headroom *n.* the space or clearance above a vehicle etc.
headship *n.* the position of chief or leader, especially of a headmaster or headmistress.
headstall *n.* the part of a bridle or halter fitting round a horse's head.
headstone *n.* a stone set up at the head of a grave.
headstrong *adj.* self-willed and obstinate.
headwaters *n.pl.* the streams formed from the sources of a river.
headway *n.* 1. progress; the rate of progress of a ship. 2. headroom.
headword *n.* a word forming a heading.
heady *adj.* 1. (of liquor) strong, likely to cause intoxication. 2. (of success etc.) likely to cause conceit. 3. impetuous. —**headily** *adv.*, **headiness** *n.*
heal /hi:l/ *v.t./i.* 1. (of sore or wounded parts) to form healthy flesh again; to unite after being cut or broken. 2. to cause to do this. 3. to put right (differences etc.); to alleviate (sorrow etc.). 4. (*archaic*) to cure. —**healer** *n.* [Old English]
Heal Ambrose 1872–1959. English cabinet-maker who took over the Heal's shop from his father and developed it into the renowned London store. He initially designed furniture in the Arts and Crafts style, often in oak, but in the 1930s he started using materials such as tubular steel. Heal was a founder member of the Design and Industries Association, which aimed to improve the quality of mass-produced items.
Healey /'hi:li/ Denis (Winston) 1917– . British Labour politician. While minister of defence 1964–70 he was in charge of the reduction of British forces east of Suez. He was chancellor of the Exchequer 1974–79. In 1976 he contested the party leadership, losing to James Callaghan, and again in 1980, losing to Michael Foot, to whom he was deputy leader 1980–83. In 1987 he resigned from the shadow cabinet.
health /helθ/ *n.* the state of being well in body or mind; a person's mental or physical condition. —**health centre**, the headquarters of a group of local medical services. **health food**, natural food thought to have health-giving qualities. **health visitor**, a trained person visiting babies or sick or elderly people at their homes. [Old English]
Health and Safety Commission in the UK, a government organization responsible for securing the health, safety, and welfare of people at work, and to protect the public against dangers to health and safety arising from work activities. It was established by the Health and Safety at Work Act 1974 and is responsible to the secretary of state for employment.
health education teaching and advice on healthy living, including hygiene, nutrition, sex education, and advice on alcohol and drug abuse, smoking, and other threats to health. Health education in most secondary schools is also included within a course of personal and social education, or integrated into subjects such as biology, home economics,

or physical education. School governors were given specific responsibility for the content of sex education lessons in the 1986 Education Act.
healthful *adj.* conducive to good health, beneficial. —**healthfully** *adv.*, **healthfulness** *n.*
health psychology a new development within ◊clinical psychology that applies psychological principles to promote physical wellbeing. For example, people with high blood pressure can learn methods such as relaxation, meditation, and lifestyle changes.
health service government provision of medical care on a national scale. In the UK, the National Health Service Act 1946 was largely the work of Aneurin ◊Bevan, Labour minister of health. It instituted a health service from July 1948 that sought to provide free medicine, dental, and optical treatment as a right. Successive governments, both Labour and Conservative, introduced charges for some services. The **National Health Service** (NHS) now includes hospital care, but nominal fees are made for ordinary doctors' prescriptions, eye tests and spectacles, and dental treatment, except for children and people on very low incomes. After a White Paper published in Jan 1989 by the Conservative government, legislation for decentralizing the control of hospitals and changes in general practice giving greater responsibilities to doctors to manage in general practice came into effect in April 1991.
healthy *adj.* 1. having, showing, or producing good health. 2. beneficial; functioning well. —**healthily** *adv.*, **healthiness** *n.*
Heaney /'hi:ni/ Seamus (Justin) 1939– . Irish poet, born in County Derry, who has written powerful verse about the political situation in Northern Ireland. Collections include *North* 1975, *Field Work* 1979, and *Station Island* 1984. He was elected professor of poetry at Oxford University in 1989.
heap *n.* 1. a number of things or particles lying irregularly upon one another. 2. (*colloquial*, especially in *plural*) a large number or amount. —*v.t./i.* 1. to pile or become piled (*up*) in a heap. 2. to load with large quantities; to give large numbers of. [Old English]
hear *v.t./i.* (*past* and *past participle* **heard** /hɜːd/) 1. to perceive with the ear. 2. to listen or pay attention to; to listen to and try (a case) in a lawcourt. 3. to be informed (*that*); to be told (*about*). 4. to grant (a prayer); to obey (an order). —**hear from**, to receive a letter etc. from. **hear! hear!** an expression of agreement or applause. **hear of**, to be told about; (with *negative*) to consider, to allow. [Old English]
hearer *n.* one who hears, especially as a member of an audience.
hearing *n.* 1. the faculty of perceiving sounds by the response of the brain to the action of sound upon the ear. 2. the range within which sounds may be heard; presence. 3. an opportunity to be heard; trial of a case in a lawcourt, especially before a judge without a jury. —**hearing aid**, a small sound amplifier worn by a deaf person.
hearken /'hɑːkən/ *v.i.* (*archaic*) to listen (*to*). [Old English]
hearsay *n.* rumour, gossip.
hearse /hɜːs/ *n.* a vehicle for conveying the coffin at a funeral. [from Old French *herse* = harrow from Latin (*h*)*irpex* = large rake]
Hearst /hɜːst/ William Randolph 1863–1951. US newspaper publisher, celebrated for his introduction of banner headlines, lavish illustration, and the sensationalist approach known as 'yellow journalism'.
heart /hɑːt/ *n.* 1. the hollow muscular organ maintaining the circulation of blood in the vascular system by rhythmic contraction and dilation. Annelid worms and some other invertebrates have simple hearts consisting of thickened sections of main blood vessels that pulse regularly. An earthworm has ten such hearts. Vertebrates have one heart. A fish heart has two chambers, the thin-walled **atrium** (once called the auricle) that expands to receive blood, and the thick-walled **ventricle** that pumps it out. Amphibians and most reptiles have two atria and one ventricle; birds and mammals have two atria and two ventricles. The beating of the heart is controlled by the autonomous nervous systems and an internal control centre or pacemaker, the sinoatrial node. 2. the region of the heart, the breast. 3. the centre of thought, feeling,

and emotion (especially love); capacity for feeling emotion; courage, enthusiasm. **4.** the central or innermost part, the essence; the compact head of a cabbage etc. **5.** a symmetrical figure conventionally representing a heart; a playing card of the suit (**hearts**) marked with red designs of this shape. —**at heart,** in one's innermost feelings; basically. **break a person's heart,** to distress him or her overwhelmingly. **by heart,** in or from memory. **change of heart,** a change in one's feeling about something. **give** (*or* **lose**) **one's heart to,** to fall in love with. **have the heart to,** (usually with *negative*) to be insensitive or hard-hearted enough *to do* a thing. **heart attack,** a sudden occurrence of heart failure. **heartbreak** *n.* overwhelming distress. **heartbreaking, heartbroken** *adjs.* causing or affected by this. **heart failure,** a failure of the heart to function properly. **heart–lung machine,** a machine which can temporarily take over the functions of the heart and lungs. **heart-rending** *adj.* very distressing. **heart-searching** *n.* an examination of one's own feelings and motives. **heartstrings** *n.* one's deepest feelings. **heart-throb** *n.* the beating of the heart; (*colloquial*) an object of romantic affections. **heart-to-heart** *adj.* frank and personal. **heart-warming** *adj.* emotionally rewarding or uplifting. **set one's heart on,** to want eagerly. **take to heart,** to be much affected by. **with all one's heart,** sincerely, with all goodwill. [Old English]

heartache *n.* mental anguish.

heartbeat *n.* the regular contraction and relaxation of the heart, and the accompanying sounds. As blood passes through the heart a double beat is heard. The first is produced by the sudden closure of the valves between the atria and the ventricles. The second, slightly delayed sound, is caused by the closure of the valves found at the entrance to the major arteries leaving the heart. Diseased valves may make unusual sounds, known as heart murmurs.

heartburn *n.* a burning sensation below the breastbone (sternum). It results from irritation of the lower oesophagus (gullet) by excessively acid stomach contents, as sometimes happens during pregnancy and in cases of duodenal ulcer or obesity. It is often due to a weak valve at the entrance to the stomach that allows its contents to well up into the oesophagus.

hearten *v.t./i.* to make or become more cheerful.

heartfelt *adj.* sincere, deeply felt.

hearth /hɑːθ/ *n.* **1.** the floor of a fireplace; the area in front of this. **2.** the fireside as the symbol of domestic comfort. **3.** the bottom of a blast furnace; a fire for heating metal for forging etc. [Old English]

heartland *n.* the central part of a homogeneous geographical, political, industrial etc., area.

heartless *adj.* unfeeling, pitiless. —**heartlessly** *adv.*, **heartlessness** *n.*

heartsick *adj.* despondent.

heartwood *n.* the dense inner part of a tree trunk, yielding the hardest timber.

hearty /hɑːtɪ/ *adj.* **1.** strong, vigorous. **2.** (of a meal or appetite) copious. **3.** showing warmth of feeling, enthusiastic. —**heartiness** *n.*

heat *n.* **1.** a form of internal energy of a substance due to the kinetic energy in the motion of its molecules or atoms. It is measured by ◊temperature. Heat energy is transferred by conduction, convection, and radiation. Heat always flows from a region of higher temperature to one of lower temperature. Its effect on a substance may be simply to raise its temperature, cause it to expand, melt it if a solid, vaporize it if a liquid, or increase its pressure if a confined gas. **2.** being hot; the sensation or perception of this; temperature; a high temperature. **3.** hot weather. **4.** an intense feeling, especially of anger; tension; the most vigorous stage of a discussion etc. **5.** a preliminary or trial round in a race or contest, of which winners take part in a further round or in the final. **6.** the receptive period of the sexual cycle, especially in female mammals. **7.** redness of the skin with a sensation of heat. —*v.t./i.* to make or become hot; to inflame. —**heat wave,** a period of very hot weather. [Old English]

heat capacity in physics, the quantity of heat required to raise the temperature of a substance by one degree. The **specific heat capacity** of a substance is the heat capacity per unit of mass, measured in joules per kilogram per kelvin (J kg^{-1} K^{-1}).

heated *adj.* (of a person or discussion etc.) angry, inflamed with passion or excitement. —**heatedly** *adj.*

heater *n.* a stove or other heating device.

heath /hiːθ/ *n.* **1.** an area of flat uncultivated land covered with heather and related plants. **2.** a plant growing on such land, especially of the genus *Erica* or *Calluna*. [Old English]

Heath Edward (Richard George) 1916– . British Conservative politician, party leader 1965–75. As prime minister 1970–74 he took the UK into the European Community but was brought down by economic and industrial relations crises at home.

He succeeded Home as Conservative leader in 1965, the first elected leader of his party. Defeated in the general election of 1966, he achieved a surprise victory in 1970, but his confrontation with the striking miners as part of his campaign to control inflation led to his defeat in Feb 1974 and again in Oct 1974. He was replaced as party leader by Margaret Thatcher in 1975.

heathen /ˈhiːðən/ *n.* one who is not a member of a widely held religion, especially not a Christian, Jew, or Muslim. —*adj.* of heathens; having no religion. —**the heathen,** heathen people. [Old English]

heather /ˈheðə(r)/ *n.* a low-growing evergreen shrub of the heath family, common on sandy or acid soil. The **common heather** or **ling** *Calluna vulgaris* is a carpet-forming shrub, growing up to 60 cm/24 in high, bearing pale pink-purple flowers. It is found over much of Europe and has been introduced to North America. It grows at altitudes of up to 750 m/2,400 ft above sea level. The **bell heather** *Erica cinerea* is found alongside common heather.

Heath Robinson /hiːθ ˈrɒbɪnsən/ absurdly ingenious and impracticable. [from W *Heath Robinson,* English cartoonist (1872–1944)]

heat pump a machine, run by electricity or other power source, that cools the interior of a building by removing heat from interior air and pumping it out or, conversely, heats the inside by extracting energy from the atmosphere or from a hot-water source and pumping it in.

heat shield any heat-protecting coating or system; especially the coating (for example, tiles) used in spacecraft to protect the astronauts and equipment inside from the heat of re-entry when returning to Earth. Air friction can generate temperatures of up to 1,500°C/2,700°F on re-entry into the atmosphere.

heat storage any means of storing heat for release later. It is usually achieved by using materials that undergo phase changes; for example, ◊Glauber's salt and sodium pyrophosphate, which melts at 70°C/158°F. The latter is used to store off-peak heat in the home: the salt is liquefied by cheap heat during the night and then freezes to give off heat during the day.

heatstroke *n.* or **sunstroke** a rise in body temperature caused by excessive exposure to heat. Mild heatstroke is experienced as feverish lassitude, sometimes with simple fainting; recovery is prompt following rest and replenishment of salt lost in sweat. Severe heatstroke causes collapse akin to that seen in acute shock (see ◊shock^1, sense 2), and is potentially lethal without prompt treatment of cooling the body carefully and giving fluids to relieve dehydration.

heat treatment in industry, the subjection of metals and alloys to controlled heating and cooling after fabrication to relieve internal stresses and improve their physical properties. Methods include annealing, quenching, and tempering.

heave *v.t./i.* (*past* **heaved** or (*nautical*) **hove**) **1.** to lift or haul (a heavy thing) with great effort. **2.** to utter with effort. **3.** (*colloquial*) to throw. **4.** (*nautical*) to haul by rope. **5.** to rise and fall alternately like waves at sea. **6.** to pant, to retch. —*n.* heaving. —**heave in sight,** to come into view. **heave to,** to bring (a ship) or come to a standstill with the ship's head to the wind. —**heaver** *n.* [Old English]

heaven /ˈhevən/ *n.* **1.** in Christian, Jewish, and Islamic theology, a place believed to be the abode of God and of the righteous after death. **2.** (usually **Heaven**) God, Providence. **3.** a place or state of supreme bliss; something delightful. —**the heavens,** the sky as seen from the Earth, in which the Sun, Moon, and stars appear. **heaven-sent** *adj.* providential. [Old English]

heavenly *adj.* **1.** of heaven, divine. **2.** of the heavens or sky. **3.** (*colloquial*) very pleasing. —**heavenly bodies,** the Sun, stars etc.

heavy /'hevɪ/ *adj.* **1.** of great weight or density, difficult to lift or carry or move; abundant; laden *with*; (of machinery, artillery etc.) very large of its kind, large in calibre etc. **2.** in physics, especially of isotopes and compounds containing them, having a greater-than-usual mass. **3.** severe, intense, extensive; doing a thing to excess; needing much physical effort. **4.** striking or falling with force; (*colloquial*) using brutal methods. **5.** (of ground) difficult to traverse, clinging; (of mist or fog) dense; (of bread etc.) dense from not having risen; (of food or *figuratively* of writings) stodgy, hard to digest. **6.** (of the sky) overcast, gloomy. **7.** clumsy or ungraceful in appearance or effect; unwieldy; tedious; serious or sombre in attitude or tone; stern. **8.** oppressive, hard to endure. —*n.* **1.** a villainous or tragic role or actor in a play etc. **2.** (usually in *plural*) a serious newspaper; a heavy vehicle. —*adv.* (especially in combinations) heavily. —**heavier-than-air** *adj.* (of an aircraft) weighing more than the air it displaces. **heavy-duty** *adj.* intended to withstand hard use. **heavy going,** slow or difficult progress. **heavy-handed** *adj.* clumsy, oppressive. **heavy-hearted** *adj.* sad, doleful. **heavy hydrogen,** deuterium. **heavy industry,** that producing metal, machinery etc. **heavy water,** deuterium oxide, water containing the isotope deuterium instead of hydrogen (relative molecular mass 20 as opposed to 18 for ordinary water) used as a moderator and coolant in some nuclear reactors. **make heavy weather of,** to exaggerate a difficulty or burden presented by a problem etc. —**heavily** *adv.*, **heaviness** *n.* [Old English]

heavy metal[1] a metallic element of high relative atomic mass, for instance platinum, gold, and lead. Heavy metals are poisonous and tend to accumulate and persist in living systems, causing, for example, high levels of mercury (from industrial waste and toxic dumping) in shellfish and fish, which are in turn eaten by humans.

heavy metal[2] in music, a style of rock characterized by loudness, sex-and-violence imagery, and guitar solos. Heavy metal developed out of the hard rock of the late 1960s and early 1970s, was performed by such groups as Led Zeppelin and Deep Purple, and enjoyed a resurgence in the late 1980s. Bands of recent years include Van Halen, Def Leppard, AC/DC, and Guns 'n' Roses. [term from *The Naked Lunch* by US author William Burroughs]

heavyweight *n.* **1.** the heaviest boxing-weight, with no upper limit (see ◊boxing under ◊boxing). **2.** a person of above average weight. **3.** a person of influence or importance —**light heavyweight,** the boxing-weight between middleweight and heavyweight.

hebdomadal /heb'dɒmədəl/ *adj.* weekly. [from Latin from Greek *hebdomas* = week (*hepta* = seven)]

Hebe /'hi:bi/ in Greek mythology, the goddess of youth, daughter of Zeus and Hera.

Hebei /hʌ'beɪ/ formerly **Hopei** province of N China; **area** 202,700 sq km/78,242 sq mi; **capital** Shijiazhuang; **products** cereals, textiles, iron, steel; **population** (1986) 56,170,000.

Hebraic /hiː'breɪɪk/ *adj.* of Hebrew or the Hebrews. [from Latin from Greek]

Hebraist /'hiːbreɪɪst/ *n.* an expert in Hebrew.

Hebrew /'hiː.bruː/ *n.* **1.** a member of a Semitic people living in ancient Palestine, an Israelite; a Jew. **2.** a member of the Hebrew-Semitic language family spoken in W Asia by the ancient Hebrews, sustained for many centuries in the Diaspora as the liturgical language of Judaism, and revived and developed in the 20th century as Israeli Hebrew, the national language of the state of Israel. It is the original language of the Old Testament of the Bible. —*adj.* **1.** of Hebrew. **2.** of the Hebrews or Jews. [from Old French, ultimately from Aramaic from Hebrew = one from the other side (of the river)]

Hebrew Bible the sacred writings of Judaism (some dating from as early as 1200 BC), called by Christians the Old Testament. It includes the Torah (the first five books, ascribed to Moses), historical and prophetical books, and psalms. Originally in Hebrew it was later translated into Greek.

Hebrides /'hebrɪdiːz/ a group of more than 500 islands (fewer than 100 inhabited) off W Scotland; total area 2,900 sq km/1,120 sq mi. The Hebrides were settled by Scandinavians during the 6th–9th centuries AD and passed under Norwegian rule from about 890 to 1266. The **Inner Hebrides** are divided between Highland and Strathclyde regions, and include Skye, Mull, Jura, Islay, Iona, Rum, Raasay, Coll, Tiree, Colonsay, Muck, and uninhabited Staffa. The **Outer Hebrides** form the islands area of the ◊Western Isles administrative area, separated from the Inner Hebrides by the Little Minch. They include Lewis with Harris, North Uist, South Uist, Barra, and St Kilda.

Hebron /'hebrən/ (Arabic *El Khalil*) town on the West Bank of the Jordan, occupied by Israel in 1967; population (1967) 43,000, including 4,000 Jews. It is a front-line position in the confrontation between Israelis and Arabs in the ◊Intifada. Within the mosque is the traditional site of the tombs of Abraham, Isaac, and Jacob.

Hecate /'hekətɪ/ in Greek mythology, the goddess of witchcraft and magic, sometimes identified with ◊Artemis and the Moon.

Hecht /hekt/ Ben 1893–1964. US screenwriter and occasional film director, who was formerly a journalist. His play *The Front Page* was adapted several times for the cinema by other writers. He wrote screenplays for such films as *Gunga Din* 1939, *Spellbound* 1945, and *Actors and Sin* 1952.

heck *n.* (*colloquial*) (in oaths) hell.

heckle *v.t.* to interrupt and harass (a public speaker). —**heckler** *n.*

hectare *n.* a metric unit of area equal to 100 acres or 10,000 square metres (2.47 acres). —**hectarage** *n.*

hectic *adj.* busy and confused, excited; feverish. —**hectically** *adv.* [from Old French from Latin from Greek *hexis* = habit]

hecto- /hektə-/ in combinations, one hundred. [French from Greek *hekaton* = a hundred]

hectogram /'hektəgræm/ *n.* a metric unit of mass, equal to 100 grams.

hector /'hektə/ *v.t.* to bully, to intimidate. —*n.* a bully. [from *Hector*]

Hector /'hektə/ in Greek mythology, a Trojan prince, son of King Priam who, in the siege of Troy, was the foremost warrior on the Trojan side until he was killed by ◊Achilles.

Hecuba /'hekjubə/ in Greek mythology, the wife of King Priam, and mother of ◊Hector and ◊Paris. She was captured by the Greeks after the fall of Troy.

hedge *n.* **1.** a fence or boundary formed by closely planted bushes or shrubs. **2.** a protection against possible loss. —*v.t./i.* **1.** to surround or bound with a hedge; to surround and restrict the movement of. **2.** to make or trim hedges. **3.** to reduce one's risk of loss on (a bet etc.) by compensating transactions on the other side. **4.** to avoid committing oneself. —**hedgehop** *v.i.* to fly at a very low altitude. **hedge sparrow,** a common brown-backed bird, the **dunnock** *Prunella modularis.* —**hedger** *n.* [Old English]

hedgehog *n.* a mammal of the genus *Erinaceus* common in Europe, W Asia, Africa, and India. The body, including the tail, is 30 cm/1 ft long. It is speckled-brown in colour, has a piglike snout, and is covered with sharp spines. When alarmed it can roll its body into a ball. Hedgehogs feed on insects, slugs, and carrion.

hedgerow *n.* a row of bushes etc. forming a hedge.

Hedin /he'diːn/ Sven Anders 1865–1952. Swedish archaeologist, geographer, and explorer in central Asia and China. Between 1891 and 1908 he explored routes across the Himalayas and produced the first maps of Tibet. During 1928–33 he travelled with a Sino-Swedish expedition which crossed the Gobi Desert. His publications include *My Life as Explorer* 1925 and *Across the Gobi Desert* 1928.

hedonic /hiː'dɒnɪk/ *adj.* of pleasure. [from Greek]

hedonism /'hiː.dənɪzəm/ *n.* the ethical theory that pleasure or happiness is, or should be, the main goal in life. Hedonist sects in ancient Greece were the ◊Cyrenaics, who held that the pleasure of the moment is the only human good, and the Epicureans (see ◊Epicureanism), who advocated the pursuit of pleasure under the direction of reason. Modern hedonistic philosophies, such as those of the British philosophers Jeremy Bentham and J S Mill, regard the happiness of society, rather than that of the individual, as the aim. —**hedonist** *n.*, **hedonistic** /-'nɪstɪk/ *adj.* [from Greek *hēdonē* = pleasure]

heebie-jeebies /'hiː bɪdʒiː bɪz/ *n.pl.* (*slang*) nervous depression or anxiety.

heed *v.t./i.* to attend to, to take notice of. —*n.* careful attention. [Old English]

heedless *adj.* not taking heed. —**heedlessly** *adv.*, **heedlessness** *n.*

hee-haw *n.* the bray of a donkey. —*v.i.* to bray like a donkey.

heel[1] *n.* 1. the back part of the human foot below the ankle; the corresponding part of the hind limb in a quadruped, often raised above the ground; the hinder part of a hoof; (in *plural*) hind feet. 2. the part of a stocking or sock covering the heel; the part of a shoe etc. supporting the heel. 3. a thing like a heel in form or position, e.g. the part of the palm next to the wrist, the handle end of a violin bow. 4. (*slang*) a dishonourable person. —*v.t./i.* 1. to fit or renew the heel on (a shoe etc.). 2. to touch the ground with the heel, as in dancing. 3. to pass the ball with the heel in rugby football. —**at** *or* **to heel,** (of a dog or *figurative*) close behind, under control. **at** *or* **on the heels of,** following closely after. **cool** *or* **kick one's heels,** to be kept waiting. **down at heel,** (of a shoe) with the heel worn down; (of a person) shabby. **take to one's heels,** to run away. **well-heeled** *adj.* wealthy. [Old English]

heel[2] *v.t./i.* (of a ship) to tilt temporarily to one side; to cause (a ship) to do this. —*n.* an act or the amount of heeling. [probably from obsolete *heeld* = incline, from Old English]

heel[3] variant of ◊hele.

heelball *n.* a mixture of hard wax and lampblack used by shoemakers for polishing; this or a similar mixture used in brass rubbing.

Hefei /hʌˈfeɪ/ formerly **Hofei** capital of Anhui province, China; population (1984) 853,000. Products include textiles, chemicals, and steel.

hefty *adj.* (of a person) big and strong; (of a thing) large, heavy, powerful. —**heftily** *adv.*, **heftiness** *n.* [from dialect *heft* = weight]

Hegel /ˈheɪɡəl/ Georg Wilhelm Friedrich 1770–1831. German philosopher who conceived of consciousness and the external object as forming a unity in which neither factor can exist independently, mind and nature being two abstractions of one indivisible whole. He believed development took place through dialectic: thesis and antithesis (contradiction) and synthesis, the resolution of contradiction. For Hegel, the task of philosophy was to comprehend the rationality of what already exists; leftist followers, including Karl Marx, used Hegel's dialectic to attempt to show the inevitability of radical change and to attack both religion and the social order of the European Industrial Revolution.

hegemony /hɪˈɡemənɪ/ *n.* the political dominance of one power over others in a group in which all are supposedly equal. The term was first used for the dominance of Athens over the other Greek city states, later applied to Prussia within Germany, and, in recent times, to the USA and USSR throughout the world. [from Greek *hēgemōn* = leader]

Hegira /ˈhedʒɪrə/ *n.* or **Hijra** Muhammad's flight from Mecca to Medina in AD 622. The Muslim calendar dates from this event, and the day of the Hegira is celebrated as the Muslim New Year. [Latin from Arabic = departure from one's country]

Heidegger /ˈhaɪdeɡə/ Martin 1889–1976. German philosopher. In *Being and Time* 1927, he used the methods of ◊Husserl's phenomenology to explore the structures of human existence. His later writings meditated on the fate of a world dominated by science and technology.

Heidi /ˈhaɪdi/ a novel for children by the Swiss writer, Johanna Spyri (1827–1901) published in 1881. Heidi, an orphan girl, shares a simple life with her grandfather high on a mountain, bringing happiness to those around her. Three years spent in Frankfurt as companion to a crippled girl, Clara, convince Heidi that city life is not for her and she returns to her mountain home.

heifer /ˈhefə/ *n.* a young cow, especially one that has not had a calf. [Old English]

heigh /heɪ/ *interjection* expressing surprise or curiosity.

height /haɪt/ *n.* 1. the measurement from the base to the top or (of a standing person) from the head to the foot. 2. the distance (of an object or position) above ground or sea level. 3. a high place or area. 4. the top; the highest point, the utmost degree. [Old English]

heighten *v.t./i.* to make or become higher or more intense.

Heike monogatari /ˈheɪki ˈmonəɡˌtɑːri/ a Japanese chronicle, written down in the 14th century but based on oral legend describing events that took place 200 years earlier, recounting the struggle for control of the country between the rival Genji (Minamoto) and Heike (Taira) dynasties. The conflict resulted in the end of the Heian period, and the introduction of the first shogunate (military dictatorship). Many subsequent Japanese dramas are based on material from the chronicle. [Japanese = tales of the Heike]

Heilongjiang /ˌheɪlʊŋdʒiˈæn/ formerly **Heilungkiang** province of NE China, in Manchuria; **area** 463,600 sq km/178,950 sq mi; **capital** Harbin; **products** cereals, gold, coal, copper, zinc, lead, cobalt; **population** (1986) 33,320,000.

Heilungkiang /ˌheɪlʊŋkiˈæn/ former name of ◊Heilongjiang, Chinese province.

Heine /ˈhaɪnə/ Heinrich 1797–1856. German Romantic poet and journalist, who wrote *Reisebilder* 1826 and *Das Buch der Lieder/The Book of Songs* 1827. From 1831 he lived mainly in Paris, working as a correspondent for German newspapers. Schubert and Schumann set many of his lyrics to music.

Heinkel /ˈhaɪŋkəl/ Ernst 1888–1958. German aircraft designer who pioneered jet aircraft. He founded his firm in 1922 and built the first jet aircraft in 1939. During World War II his company was Germany's biggest producer of warplanes, mostly propeller-driven.

Heinlein /ˈhaɪnlaɪn/ Robert A(nson) 1907–1988. US science-fiction writer, associated with the pulp magazines of the 1940s. He is best known for the militaristic novel *Starship Troopers* 1959 and the utopian cult novel *Stranger in a Strange Land* 1961. His work helped to increase the legitimacy of science fiction as a literary genre.

heinous /ˈheɪnəs/ *adj.* utterly odious or wicked. [from Old French *haine* = hatred]

heir /eə/ *n.* a person entitled to property or rank as the legal successor of its former owner. —**heir apparent,** an heir whose claim cannot be set aside by the birth of another heir. **heir presumptive,** one whose claim may be set aside thus. —**heiress** *n.fem.* [from Old French from Latin *heres*]

heirloom *n.* a piece of personal property that has been in a family for several generations; a piece of property as part of an inheritance.

Heisenberg /ˈhaɪzənbɜːɡ/ Werner Carl 1901–1976. German physicist. He was an originator of ◊quantum theory and the formulator of the ◊uncertainty principle (see under ◊uncertainty), which concerns matter, radiation and their reactions, and places absolute limits on the achievable accuracy of measurement. He was awarded the Nobel Prize for Physics in 1932.

Hejaz /hiːˈdʒæz/ former independent kingdom, merged in 1932 with Nejd to form ◊Saudi Arabia; population (1970) 2,000,000; the capital is Mecca.

Hekmatyar /ˈhekmətˈjɑː/ Gulbuddin 1949– . Afghani Islamic fundamentalist guerrilla leader. He became a mujaheddin guerrilla in the 1980s, leading the fundamentalist faction of the Hizb-i Islami (Islamic Party), dedicated to the overthrow of the Soviet-backed communist regime in Kabul. He has refused to countenance participation in any interim 'national unity' government which includes Afghani communists.

Hel /hel/ or **Hela** in Norse mythology, the goddess of the underworld.

held past and past participle of **hold.**

hele *v.t.* to set (a plant) in the ground and cover its roots in. [Old English]

Helen /ˈhelən/ in Greek mythology, the daughter of Zeus and Leda, and the most beautiful of women. She married Menelaus, king of Sparta, but during his absence was abducted by Paris, prince of Troy. This precipitated the Trojan War. Afterwards she returned to Sparta with her husband.

Helena, St /ˈhelɪnə/ c.248–328. Roman empress, mother of Constantine the Great, and a convert to Christianity. According to legend, she discovered the true cross of Jesus in Jerusalem. Her feast day is 18 Aug.

heliacal /hiˈlaɪəkəl/ *adj.* of or near the Sun. —**heliacal rising** (*or* **setting**), the first rising of a star after (or its last setting before) a period of invisibility due to its conjunction with the Sun. [from Latin from Greek *hēlios* = sun]

helical /ˈhelɪkəl/ *adj.* having the form of a helix.

helicopter

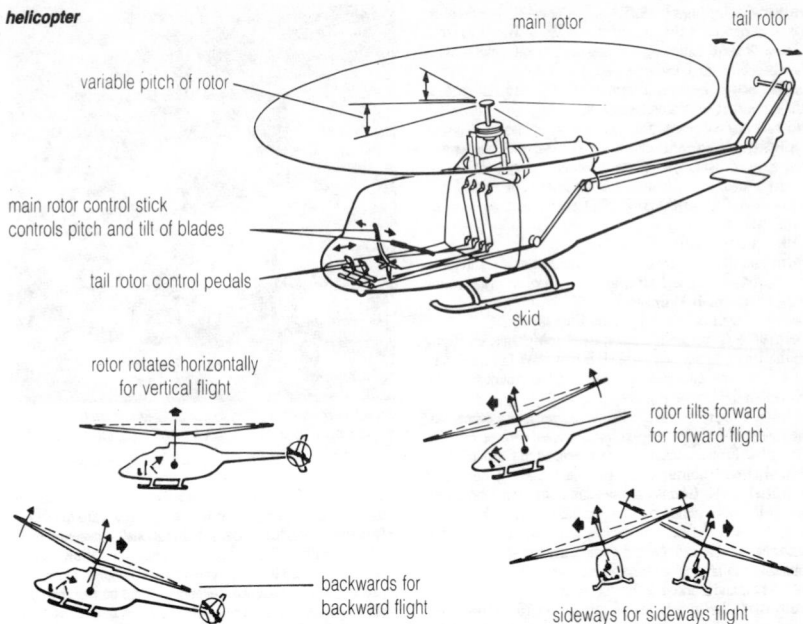

main rotor   tail rotor

variable pitch of rotor

main rotor control stick
controls pitch and tilt of blades

tail rotor control pedals

skid

rotor rotates horizontally
for vertical flight

rotor tilts forward
for forward flight

backwards for
backward flight

sideways for sideways flight

Helicon /'helɪkən/ a mountain in central Greece, on which was situated a spring and a sanctuary sacred to the ◊Muses.

helicopter /'helɪkɒptə/ *n.* an aircraft which derives both its lift and its control from one or more powered rotors which rotate about a vertical or near-vertical axis. It can take off and land vertically, move in any direction, or remain stationary in the air. Jet helicopters are also made. Naval carriers are increasingly being built, helicopters with depth charges and homing torpedoes being guided to submarine or surface targets beyond the ship's attack range. The helicopter may also use dunking sonar to find targets beyond the carrier's radar horizon. As many as 30 helicopters may be used on large carriers, in combination with V/STOL aircraft such as the Harrier. See also ◊autogiro, ◊convertiplane. [from French from Greek *helix* and *pteron* = wing]

helio- /hiːliə-/ in combinations, sun. [from Greek *hēlios* = sun]

heliocentric /hiːliə 'sentrɪk/ *adj.* 1. considered as viewed from the Sun's centre. 2. regarding the Sun as the centre.

heliograph /'hiːliəgrɑːf/ *n.* a signalling device reflecting the Sun's rays in flashes; a message sent by this. —*v.t.* to send (a message) thus.

Heliopolis /hiːli'ɒpəlɪs/ ancient Egyptian centre (the biblical **On**) of the worship of the sun god Ra, NE of Cairo and near the village of Matariah.

Helios /'hiːlios/ in Greek mythology, the sun god and father of ◊Phaethon, thought to make his daily journey across the sky in a chariot.

heliotrope /'hiːliətrəup/ *n.* 1. a decorative plant of the genus *Heliotropium* of the borage family Boraginaceae, with distinctive spikes of blue, lilac, or white flowers, including the **Peruvian** or **cherry pie heliotrope** *H. peruvianum*. 2. a light purple colour. [from Latin from Greek = plant turning its flowers to the Sun]

heliport /'helɪpɔt/ *n.* a place where helicopters take off and land.

helium /'hiːliəm/ *n.* a colourless, odourless, gaseous, nonmetallic element, symbol He, atomic number 2, relative atomic mass 4.0026. It is grouped with the ◊inert gases, is nonreactive, and forms no compounds. It is the second most abundant element (after hydrogen) in the universe, and has the lowest boiling point (−268.9°C/−452°F) and melting point (−272.2°C/−458°F) of all the elements. It is present in small quantities in the Earth's atmosphere from gases issuing from radioactive elements in the Earth's crust; after hydrogen it is the second lightest element. [from Greek *hēlios* = sun]

helix /'hiːlɪks/ *n.* (*plural* **helices** /-lisiːz/) in mathematics, a three-dimensional curve resembling a spring, corkscrew, or screw thread. It is generated by a line that encircles a cylinder or cone at a constant angle. —**double helix**, a pair of parallel helices with a common axis, especially in the structure of the DNA molecule. [Latin from Greek]

hell *n.* 1. the place or state of punishment for the wicked after death, the abode of devils. 2. a place or state of misery or wickedness. 3. (*colloquial*) an exclamation of surprise or annoyance. —**beat** *or* **knock hell out of,** to pound heavily. **come hell or high water,** no matter what the obstacles. **for the hell of it,** just for fun. **get hell,** (*colloquial*) to be scolded or punished. **give a person hell,** (*colloquial*) to scold or punish him or her. **hellbent** *adj.* recklessly determined (*on*). **hellfire** *n.* the fire(s) of hell. **hell for leather,** at full speed. **Hell's Angel,** a member of a gang of violent lawless youths, usually with motorcycles. [Old English from Germanic = cover, conceal]

hellebore /'helɪbɔ/ *n.* a poisonous European herbaceous plant of the genus *Helleborus* of the buttercup family Ranunculaceae. The **stinking hellebore** *H. foetidus* has greenish flowers early in the spring. The **Christmas rose** *H. niger* has white flowers from Dec onwards. [from Old French or Latin from Greek]

helleborine *n.* a temperate Old World orchid of the genera *Epipactis* and *Cephalanthera*, including the **marsh helleborine** *E. palustris* and the **hellebore orchid** *E. helleborine* introduced to North America.

Hellene /'heliːn/ *n.* a Greek person; an ancient Greek of genuine Greek descent. —**Hellenic** /-'liːnɪk/ *adj.* [from Greek *Hellēn* = eponymous ancestor, son or brother of Deucalion]

Hellenic period /'heliːnɪk/ the classical period of ancient Greek civilization, from the first Olympic Games in 776 BC until the death of Alexander the Great in 323 BC.

Hellenism /'helɪnɪzəm/ *n.* Greek character or culture (especially of ancient Greece). —**Hellenist** *n.* [from Greek]

Hellenistic /heli'nɪstɪk/ *adj.* of the Greek world from the death of Alexander the Great in 323 BC until the defeat of Mark Antony and Cleopatra by Roman forces under Octavian at the battle of Actium in 31 BC. Alexandria in Egypt was the centre of culture and commerce during this period, and Greek culture spread throughout the Mediterranean region.

Heller /'helə/ Joseph 1923– . US novelist. He drew on his experiences in the US airforce in World War II to write *Catch-22* 1961, satirizing war and bureaucratic methods. A film based on the book appeared in 1970.

Hellespont /'helɪspɒnt/ former name of the ◊Dardanelles, the strait that separates Europe from Asia.

hellish *adj.* of or like hell; extremely unpleasant.

Hellman /'helmən/ Lillian 1907–1984. US playwright, whose work is concerned with contemporary political and social issues. *The Children's Hour* 1934, *The Little Foxes* 1939, and *Toys in the Attic* 1960 are all examples of the 'well-made play'.

hello variant of **hallo**.

helm[1] *n.* the tiller or wheel by which a ship's rudder is controlled. —**at the helm,** at the head of an organization etc., in control. [Old English]

helm[2] *n.* (*archaic*) a helmet. [Old English]

Helmand /'helmənd/ longest river in Afghanistan. Rising in the Hindu Kush, W of Kabul, it flows SW for 1,125 km/703 mi before entering the marshland surrounding Lake Saberi on the Iranian frontier.

helmet *n.* a protective head covering worn by a policeman, fireman, diver, motorcyclist etc., or as part of armour. [from Old French, diminutive of *helme*, from Germanic]

Helmholtz /'helmhəʊlts/ Hermann Ludwig Ferdinand von 1821–1894. German physiologist, physicist, and inventor of the ophthalmoscope for examining the inside of the eye. He was the first to explain how the cochlea of the inner ear works, and the first to measure the speed of nerve impulses. In physics he formulated the law of conservation of energy, and worked in thermodynamics.

Helmont /'helmɒnt/ Jean Baptiste van 1577–1644. Belgian doctor who was the first to realize that there are gases other than air, and claimed to have coined the word 'gas'.

helmsman /'helmzmən/ *n.* or **helmswoman** (*plural* **helmsmen, helmswomen**) one who steers a ship.

Héloïse /'eləʊiːz/ 1101–1164. Abbess of Paraclete in Champagne, France, correspondent and lover of ◊Abelard. She became deeply interested in intellectual study in her youth and was impressed by the brilliance of Abelard, her teacher, whom she secretly married. After her affair with Abelard, and the birth of a son, Astrolabe, she became a nun in 1129, and with Abelard's assistance, founded a nunnery at Paraclete. Her letters show her strong and pious character and her devotion to Abelard.

helot /'helət/ *n.* a serf, especially in ancient Sparta. [from Latin from Greek]

help *v.t.* 1. to make it easier for (a person) to do something or for (a thing) to happen, to do part of the work of (a person) for him or her. 2. to be of use or service; to do something for the benefit of (one in need); to contribute to alleviating (a pain or difficulty). 3. to prevent, to remedy. 4. (with *negative*) to refrain from. —*n.* 1. the act of helping or being helped. 2. a person or thing that helps. 3. a domestic servant or servants; an employee or employees. 4. a remedy etc. —**cannot help oneself,** cannot avoid an undesired action. **help oneself (to),** to take without seeking help or permission. **help out,** to give help, especially in difficulty. **help a person to,** to serve him or her with (food at a meal). —**helper** *n.* [Old English]

helpful *adj.* giving help, useful. —**helpfully** *adv.,* **helpfulness** *n.*

helping *n.* a portion of food at a meal.

helpless *adj.* 1. lacking help, defenceless. 2. having or showing an inability to act without help; unable to help oneself. —**helplessly** *adv.,* **helplessness** *n.*

Helpmann /'helpmən/ Robert 1909–1986. Australian dancer, choreographer, and actor. The leading male dancer with the Sadler's Wells Ballet, London 1933–50, he partnered Margot ◊Fonteyn in the 1940s. His gift for mime and his dramatic sense are also apparent in his choreographic work, for example *Miracle in the Gorbals* 1944. He was knighted in 1968.

helpmate *n.* a helpful companion or partner.

Helsingør /'helsɪŋˈɜː/ (English **Elsinore**) port in NE Denmark; population (1987) 57,000. It is linked by ferry with Helsingborg across the Sound; Shakespeare made it the scene of *Hamlet.*

Helsinki /'helsɪŋki/ (Swedish **Helsingfors**) capital and port of Finland; population (1988) 490,000, metropolitan area 978,000. Industries include shipbuilding, engineering,

Helsingør Kronborg Castle about 45 km/28 mi N of Copenhagen, built by Frederick II 1574–85, the setting for Shakespeare's Hamlet.

and textiles. The homes of the architect Eliel Saarinen and the composer Jean Sibelius outside the town are museums.

Helsinki Conference an international conference held in 1975 at which 35 countries, including the USSR and the USA, attempted to reach agreement on cooperation in security, economics, science, technology, and human rights.

helter-skelter /heltə ˈskeltə/ *adv.* in disorderly haste. —*n.* a tall structure with an external spiral track for sliding down.

helve *n.* the handle of a weapon or tool. [Old English]

Helvetian /hel'viːʃən/ *adj.* Swiss. —*n.* a Swiss person. [from Latin *Helvetia* = Switzerland (*Helvetii* = Celtic tribe living there)]

Helvetius /elveɪˈsjuːs/ Claude Adrien 1715–1771. French philosopher. In *De l'Esprit* 1758 he argued, following David ◊Hume, that self-interest, however disguised, is the mainspring of all human action and that since conceptions of good and evil vary according to period and locality there is no absolute good or evil. He also believed that intellectual differences are only a matter of education.

hem[1] *n.* the border of cloth where the edge is turned under and sewn down. —*v.t.* (**-mm-**) to turn down and sew in the edge of (cloth etc.). —**hem in,** to surround and restrict the movement of. **hemstitch** *n.* an ornamental stitch; (*v.t.*) to hem with this. —**hemmer** *n.* [Old English]

hem[2] *interjection* calling attention or expressing hesitation by a slight cough. —*n.* an utterance of this. —*v.i.* (**-mm-**) to say *hem,* to hesitate in speech.

hematite /'hiːmətaɪt/ *n.* the principal ore of iron, consisting mainly of iron(III) (ferric) oxide, Fe_2O_3. It occurs as **specular hematite** (dark, metallic lustre), **kidney ore** (reddish radiating fibres terminating in smooth, rounded surfaces), and as a red earthy deposit. [from Latin from Greek = bloodlike stone]

hemi- /hemi-/ prefix meaning half. [from Greek *hēmi-* = Latin *semi-*]

Hemingway /'hemɪŋweɪ/ Ernest 1898–1961. US writer. War, bullfighting, and fishing were used symbolically in his writings to represent honour, dignity, and primitivism: prominent themes in his short stories and novels, which included *A Farewell to Arms* 1929, *For Whom the Bell Tolls* 1940, and *The Old Man and the Sea* 1952. His deceptively simple writing style attracted many imitators. He received the Nobel Prize for Literature in 1954.

hemipterous /he'mɪptərəs/ *adj.* of the insect order including aphids, bugs, and cicadas, with the base of the front wings thickened. [from Greek *pteron* = wing]

hemisphere /'hemɪsfɪə/ *n.* half a sphere; any half of the Earth, especially as divided by the equator or by a line passing through the poles. —**hemispherical** /-'sferɪkəl/ *adj.* [from Old French and Latin from Greek]

hemline *n.* the lower edge of a skirt or dress.

hemlock /'hemlɒk/ *n.* a plant *Conium maculatum* of the carrot family Umbelliferae, native to Europe, W Asia, and N Africa. Reaching up to 2 m/6 ft high, it bears umbels of small white flowers. The whole plant, especially the root and fruit, is poisonous, causing paralysis of the nervous system. The name hemlock is also applied to members of the genus *Tsuga* of North American and Asiatic conifers of the pine family. [Old English]

hemp *n.* **1.** an Asian herbaceous plant *Cannabis sativa*; its fibre, used to make rope and coarse fabrics. **2.** any of several narcotic drugs made from the hemp plant. —**hempen** *adj.* [Old English]

hen *n.* the female bird, especially of the common domestic fowl. —**hen party**, (*colloquial*) a social gathering of women only. [Old English]

Henan /hʌˈnæn/ or **Honan** province of east central China; **area** 167,000 sq km/64,462 sq mi; **capital** Zhengzhou; **products** cereals, cotton; **population** (1986) 78,080,000.

henbane *n.* a poisonous plant *Hyoscyamus niger* of the nightshade family Solanaceae, found on waste ground through most of Europe and W Asia. A branching plant, up to 80 cm/31 in high, it has hairy leaves and a nauseous smell. The yellow flowers are bell-shaped. Henbane is used in medicine as a source of hyoscyamine and scopolamine.

hence *adv.* **1.** from this time. **2.** for this reason. **3.** (*archaic*) from here. [Old English]

henceforth /hensˈfɔːθ/ *adv.* (*also* **henceforward**) from this time onwards.

henchman *n.* (*plural* **henchmen**) a trusty supporter. [from Old English *heng(e)st* = male horse]

Henderson /ˈhendəsən/ Arthur 1863–1935. British Labour politician, foreign secretary 1929–31, when he accorded the Soviet government full recognition. He was awarded the Nobel Peace Prize in 1934.

Hendrix /ˈhendrɪks/ Jimi (James Marshall) 1942–1970. US rock guitarist, songwriter, and singer, famous for his virtuoso experimental technique and flamboyance. He greatly expanded the vocabulary of the electric guitar and influenced both rock and jazz musicians.

Once you're dead, you're made for life.
                              Jimi Hendrix (attrib.)

Hendry /ˈhendri/ Stephen 1970– . Scottish snooker player who replaced Steve Davis as the top-ranking player during the 1989–90 season as well as becoming the youngest-ever world champion.

henge /hendʒ/ *n.* a monument of wood or stone resembling the circle of stones at Stonehenge in Wiltshire. [from *Stonehenge*]

Hengist /ˈhengɪst/ 5th century. Legendary leader, with his brother Horsa, of the Jutes, who originated in Jutland and settled in Kent about 450, the first Anglo-Saxon settlers in Britain.

Heng Samrin /heŋ/ 1934– . Cambodian politician. A former Khmer Rouge commander 1976–78, who had become disillusioned with its brutal tactics, he led an unsuccessful coup against ◊Pol Pot in 1978 and established the Kampuchean People's Revolutionary Party (KPRP) in Vietnam, before returning in 1979 to head the new Vietnamesebacked government.

Henlein /ˈhenlaɪn/ Konrad 1898–1945. Sudeten-German leader of the Sudeten Nazi Party in Czechoslovakia, and closely allied with Hitler's Nazis. He was partly responsible for the destabilization of the Czechoslovak state in 1938, which led to the ◊Munich Agreement and the secession of the Sudetenland to Germany.

Henley Royal Regatta /ˈhenli/ a UK rowing festival on the river Thames, inaugurated in 1839. It is as much a social as a sporting occasion. The principal events are the solo **Diamond Challenge Sculls**, and the **Grand Challenge Cup**, the leading event for eight-oared shells. The regatta is held in July.

henna *n.* **1.** a small shrub *Lawsonia inermis* of the loosestrife family Lythraceae, found in Iran, India, Egypt, and N Africa. **2.** the reddish dye made from it. The leaves and young twigs are ground to a powder, mixed to a paste with hot water, and applied to fingernails and hair. The colour may then be changed to black by applying a preparation of indigo. [from Arabic]

henpeck *v.t.* (of a wife) to domineer over (a husband).

Henri /ˈhenri/ Robert 1865–1929. US painter, a leading figure in the transition between 19th-century conventions

and Modern art in America. He was a principal member of the ◊Ashcan school.

Henrietta Maria /henriˈetə məˈriːə/ 1609–1669. Queen of England 1625–49. The daughter of Henry IV of France, she married Charles I of England in 1625. By encouraging him to aid Roman Catholics and make himself an absolute ruler, she became highly unpopular and was exiled during the period 1644–60. She returned to England at the Restoration but retired to France in 1665.

henry /ˈhenri/ *n.* (*plural* **henries**) the SI unit (symbol H) of ◊inductance (the reaction of an electric current against the magnetic field that surrounds it). One henry is the inductance of a circuit that produces an opposing voltage of one volt when the current changes at one ampere per second. [from J *Henry*]

Henry (Charles Albert David) known as **Harry** 1984– . Prince of the UK; second child of the Prince and Princess of Wales.

Henry Joseph 1797–1878. US physicist, inventor of the electromagnetic motor in 1829 and of a telegraphic apparatus. He also discovered the principle of electromagnetic induction, roughly at the same time as Michael ◊Faraday, and the phenomenon of self-induction. A unit of inductance (henry) is named after him.

Henry O. Pen name of William Sydney Porter 1862–1910. US short-story writer, whose collections include *Cabbages and Kings* 1904 and *The Four Million* 1906. His stories are written in a colloquial style and employ skilled construction with surprise endings.

Henry Patrick 1736–1799. US politician, who in 1775 supported the arming of the Virginia militia against the British by a speech ending, 'Give me liberty or give me death!'. He was governor of Virginia 1776–79 and 1784–86.

Henry /ˈhenri/ William 1774–1836. British chemist. In 1803 he formulated **Henry's law**: when a gas is dissolved in a liquid at a given temperature, the mass that dissolves is in direct proportion to the gas pressure.

Henry eight kings of England:

Henry I 1068–1135. King of England from 1100. Youngest son of William I, he succeeded his brother William II. He won the support of the Saxons by granting them a charter and marrying a Saxon princess. An able administrator, he established a professional bureaucracy and a system of travelling judges. He was succeeded by ◊Stephen.

Henry II 1133–1189. King of England from 1154, when he succeeded Stephen. He was the son of ◊Matilda and Geoffrey of Anjou (1113–1151). He curbed the power of the barons, but his attempt to bring the church courts under control had to be abandoned after the murder of Thomas à ◊Becket. During his reign the English conquest of Ireland began. He was succeeded by his son Richard I.

Henry III 1207–1272. King of England from 1216, when he succeeded John, but he did not rule until 1227. His financial commitments to the papacy and his foreign favourites led to de ◊Montfort's revolt in 1264. Henry was defeated at Lewes, Sussex, and imprisoned. He was restored to the throne after the royalist victory at Evesham in 1265. He was succeeded by his son Edward I.

Henry IV (Bolingbroke) 1367–1413. King of England from 1399, the son of ◊John of Gaunt. In 1398 he was banished by ◊Richard II for political activity but returned in 1399 to head a revolt and be accepted as king by Parliament. He was succeeded by his son Henry V. He had difficulty in keeping the support of Parliament and the clergy, and had to deal with baronial unrest and ◊Glendower's rising in Wales. In order to win support he had to conciliate the church by a law for the burning of heretics, and to make many concessions to Parliament.

Henry V 1387–1422. King of England from 1413, son of Henry IV. Invading Normandy in 1415 (during the Hundred Years' War), he captured Harfleur and defeated the French at ◊Agincourt. He invaded again 1417–19, capturing Rouen. He married ◊Catherine of Valois in 1420 to gain recognition as heir to the French throne by his father-in-law Charles VI. He was succeeded by his son Henry VI.

Henry VI 1421–1471. King of England from 1422, son of Henry V. He assumed royal power in 1442 and sided with the party opposed to the continuation of the Hundred Years' War with France. After his marriage in 1445, he was dominated by his wife, ◊Margaret of Anjou. The unpopularity of the government, especially after the loss of the English conquests in France, encouraged Richard, Duke of York, to claim the throne, and though York was killed in 1460, his son Edward IV proclaimed himself king in 1461 (see Wars of the ◊Roses). Henry was captured in 1465, temporarily restored in 1470, but again imprisoned in 1471 and then murdered.

Henry VII 1457–1509. King of England from 1485, son of Edmund Tudor, Earl of Richmond (*c.*1430–1456), and a descendant of ◊John of Gaunt. He spent his early life in Brittany until 1485, when he landed in Britain to lead the rebellion against Richard III which ended with Richard's defeat and death at ◊Bosworth. Yorkist revolts continued until 1497, but Henry restored order after the Wars of the ◊Roses by the ◊Star Chamber and achieved independence from Parliament by amassing a private fortune through confiscations. He was succeeded by his son Henry VIII.

Henry VIII 1491–1547. King of England from 1509, when he succeeded his father Henry VII and married Catherine of Aragon, the widow of his brother. His Lord Chancellor, Cardinal Wolsey, was replaced by Thomas More in 1529 for failing to persuade the pope to grant Henry a divorce. After 1532 Henry broke with papal authority, proclaimed himself head of the church, dissolved the monasteries, and divorced Catherine. His subsequent wives were Anne Boleyn, Jane Seymour, Anne of Cleves, Catherine Howard, and Catherine Parr. He was succeeded by his son Edward VI.

Henry four kings of France:
Henry I 1005–1060. King of France from 1031. He spent much of his reign in conflict with ◊William I the Conqueror, then duke of Normandy.

Henry II 1519–1559. King of France from 1547. He captured the fortresses of Metz and Verdun from the Holy Roman emperor Charles V and Calais from the English. He was killed in a tournament.

Henry III 1551–1589. King of France from 1574. He fought both the ◊Huguenots (headed by his successor, Henry of Navarre) and the Catholic League (headed by the Duke of Guise). Guise expelled Henry from Paris in 1588 but was assassinated. Henry allied with the Huguenots under Henry of Navarre to besiege the city, but was assassinated by a monk.

Henry IV 1553–1610. King of France from 1589. Son of Antoine de Bourbon and Jeanne, queen of Navarre, he was brought up as a Protestant and from 1576 led the ◊Huguenots. On his accession he settled the religious question by adopting Catholicism while tolerating Protestantism. He restored peace and strong government to France and brought back prosperity by measures for the promotion of industry and agriculture and the improvement of communications. He was assassinated by a Catholic extremist.

Henry seven Holy Roman emperors:
Henry I the Fowler *c.*876–936. King of Germany from 919, and duke of Saxony from 912. He secured the frontiers of Saxony, ruled in harmony with its nobles, and extended German influence over the Danes, the Hungarians, and the Slavonic tribes. He was about to claim the imperial crown when he died.

Henry II the Saint 973–1024. King of Germany from 1002, Holy Roman emperor from 1014, when he recognized Benedict VIII as pope. He was canonized in 1146.

Henry III the Black 1017–1056. King of Germany from 1028, Holy Roman emperor from 1039. He raised the empire to the height of its power, and extended its authority over Poland, Bohemia, and Hungary.

Henry IV 1050–1106. Holy Roman emperor from 1056, he was involved from 1075 in a struggle with the papacy (see ◊Gregory VII).

Henry V 1081–1125. Holy Roman emperor from 1106. He continued the struggle with the church until the settlement of the ◊investiture contest in 1122.

Henry VI 1165–1197. Holy Roman emperor from 1190. As part of his plan for making the empire universal, he captured and imprisoned Richard I of England and compelled him to do homage.

Henry VII 1269–1313. Holy Roman emperor from 1308. He attempted unsuccessfully to revive the imperial supremacy in Italy.

Henry the Navigator 1394–1460. Portuguese prince, the fourth son of John I. He set up a school for navigators in 1419 and under his patronage, Portuguese seamen explored and colonized Madeira, the Cape Verde Islands, and the Azores; they sailed down the African coast almost to Sierra Leone.

Henze /'hentsə/ Hans Werner 1926– . German composer whose large and varied output includes orchestral, vocal, and chamber music. He uses traditional symphony and concerto forms, and incorporates a wide range of styles including jazz. In 1953 he moved to Italy where his music became more expansive, as in the opera *The Bassarids* 1966.

hep *adj.* (*slang*) aware of the latest trends and styles.

hepatic /hi'pætik/ *adj.* of the liver. [from Latin from Greek *hēpar* = liver]

hepatitis /hepə'taitis/ *n.* any inflammatory disease of the liver, usually caused by a virus. Other causes include lupus erythematosus and amoebic dysentery. Symptoms include weakness, nausea, and jaundice.

Hepburn /'hepbə:n/ Audrey (Audrey Hepburn-Rushton) 1929– . British actress of Anglo-Dutch descent who often played innocent, childlike characters. Slender and doe-eyed, she set a different style from the pneumatic stars of the 1950s. After playing minor parts in British films in the early 1950s, she became a Hollywood star in such films as *Funny Face* 1957, *My Fair Lady* 1964, *Wait Until Dark* 1968, and *Robin and Marian* 1976.

Hepburn Katharine 1909– . US actress, who appeared in such films as *The African Queen* 1951, *Guess Who's Coming to Dinner* 1967, and *On Golden Pond* 1981. She won four Academy Awards.

Hephaestus /hi'fi:stəs/ in Greek mythology, the god of fire and metalcraft (Roman Vulcan), son of Zeus and Hera, husband of Aphrodite. He was lame.

Hepplewhite /'hepəlwait/ George died 1786. English furniture maker who developed a simple, elegant style, working mainly in mahogany or satinwood, adding delicately inlaid or painted decorations of feathers, shells, or wheat ears. His book of designs, *The Cabinetmaker and Upholsterer's Guide* 1788, was published posthumously.

hepta- in combinations, seven. [from Greek *hepta* = seven]

heptagon /'heptəgən/ *n.* a plane figure with seven sides and angles. —**heptagonal** /-'tægənəl/ *adj.* [from Greek *-gōnos* = -angled]

heptathlon *n.* a multi-event athletics discipline for women that consists of seven events over two days: 100 metres hurdles, high jump, shot put, 200 metres (day one); long jump, javelin, 800 metres (day two). Points are awarded for performances in each event in the same way as the ◊decathlon. It replaced the pentathlon in international competition in 1981.

Hepworth /'hepwə:θ/ Barbara 1903–1975. English sculptor who developed a distinctive abstract style, creating hollowed forms of stone or wood with spaces bridged by wires or strings; many later works are in bronze. In 1939 she moved to St Ives, Cornwall (where her studio is now a museum). She was created a Dame of the British Empire in 1965.

her *pron.* objective case of **she**; (*colloquial*) she. —*poss. adj.* 1. of or belonging to her. 2. (in titles) that she is (*Her Majesty*). [Old English dative and genitive of *she*]

Hera /'hiərə/ in Greek mythology, a goddess (Roman Juno), sister-consort of Zeus, mother of Hephaestus, Hebe, and Ares; protector of women and marriage.

Heracles /'herəkli:z/ in Greek mythology, a hero (Roman Hercules), son of Zeus and Alcmene, famed for strength. While serving Eurystheus, king of Argos, he performed 12 labours, including the cleansing of the Augean stables.

Heraclius /hiərə'klaiəs/ *c.*575–641. Byzantine emperor from 610. His reign marked a turning point in the empire's fortunes. Of Armenian descent, he recaptured Armenia in 622, and other provinces in 622–28 from the Persians, but lost them to the Muslims in 629–41.

Heraklion /hi'rækliən/ alternative name for ◊Iráklion.

herald /'herəld/ *n.* 1. a forerunner; a messenger, a bringer of news (often as the title of a newpaper). 2. an official concerned with pedigrees and coats of arms.

Hepworth English sculptor Barbara Hepworth before her 1930 exhibition, with her stone Mother and Child.

3. (*historical*) an officer who made state proclamations, bore messages between princes etc. **4.** an official of the Heralds' College. —*v.t.* to proclaim the approach of, to usher in. —**Heralds' College,** the ◊College of Arms —**heraldic** /-p'ræltkɪk/ *adj.* [from Old French from Germanic]

heraldry /'herəldrɪ/ *n.* the science or art of a herald, especially in blazoning armorial bearings and settling the right of persons to bear arms.

Herat /he'ræt/ capital of Herat province, and the largest city in W Afghanistan, on the N banks of the Hari Rud; population (1980) 160,000. A principal road junction, it was a great city in ancient and medieval times.

herb *n.* a plant whose stem is soft and dies to the ground after flowering; a plant whose leaves or seeds etc. are used for flavouring, food, medicine, scent etc. —**herby** *adj.* [from Old French from Latin *herba* = grass, herb]

herbaceous /hɜː'beɪʃəs/ *adj.* of or like herbs. —**herbaceous border,** a garden border containing especially perennial flowering plants. [from Latin]

herbage *n.* herbs collectively, especially as pasture. [from Old French from Latin]

herbal *adj.* of herbs in medicinal and culinary use. —*n.* a manual describing these. [from Latin]

herbalist *n.* a dealer in medicinal herbs; a writer on herbs.

herbarium /hɜː'beərɪəm/ *n.* (*plural* **herbaria**) a systematic collection of dried plants; a book, case, or room for these. [from Latin]

Herbert /'hɜːbət/ George 1593–1633. English poet. His volume of religious poems, *The Temple*, appeared in 1633, shortly before his death. His poems depict his intense religious feelings in clear, simple language. He became orator to Cambridge University in 1619, and a prebendary in Huntingdonshire in 1625. After ordination in 1630 he became vicar of Bemerton, Wiltshire. He died of tuberculosis.

Be calm in arguing; for fierceness makes Error a fault and truth discourtesy.

George Herbert
The Church Porch

Herbert Wally (Walter) 1934– . British surveyor and explorer. His first surface crossing by dog sledge of the Arctic Ocean 1968–69, from Alaska to Spitsbergen via the North Pole, was the longest sustained sledging journey (6,000 km/3,800 mi) in polar exploration.

herbicide /'hɜːbɪsaɪd/ *n.* a toxic substance used to destroy unwanted vegetation.

herbivore /'hɜːbɪvɔː/ *n.* an animal that feeds on green plants or their products, including seeds, fruit, and nectar, or on photosynthetic organisms in plankton (see ◊photosynthesis). Herbivores are more numerous than other animals because their food is the most abundant. They form a vital link in the food chain between plants and carnivores.

herbivorous /hɜː'bɪvərəs/ *adj.* feeding on plants. [from *herb* and Latin *vorare* = devour]

herb Robert a wild ◊geranium *Geranium robertianum* found throughout Europe and central Asia and naturalized in North America. About 30 cm/12 in high, it bears hairy leaves and small, pinkish to purplish flowers.

Herculaneum /hɜːkjuˈleɪnɪəm/ ancient city of Italy between Naples and Pompeii. Along with Pompeii, it was buried when Vesuvius erupted in AD 79. It was excavated from the 18th century onwards.

herculean /hɜːkjuˈliːən/ *adj.* **1.** extremely strong. **2.** (of a task) requiring great strength. [from *Hercules*]

Hercules /'hɜːkjuliːz/ Roman form of ◊Heracles.

Hercules *n.* in astronomy, the fifth largest constellation, visible in the northern hemisphere. Despite its size it contains no prominent stars. Its most important feature is a ◊globular cluster of stars 22,500 light years from Earth, one of the best examples in the sky.

herd *n.* **1.** a number of cattle or other animals feeding or staying together. **2.** a large number of people, a mob. —*v.t./i.* **1.** to collect, go, or drive in a herd. **2.** to tend (sheep or cattle). —**herd instinct,** the tendency to remain or conform with the majority. [Old English]

Herder /ˈheədə/ Johann Gottfried von 1744–1803. German poet, critic, and philosopher. Herder's critical writings indicated his intuitive rather than reasoning trend of thought. He collected folk songs of all nations in 1778, and in the *Ideen zur Philosophie der Geschichte der Menschheit/Outlines of a Philosophy of the History of Man* 1784–91 he outlined the stages of human cultural development.

herdsman *n.* (*plural* **herdsmen**) a person who tends a herd of animals.

here /hɪə/ *adv.* **1.** in, at, or to this place or position. **2.** at this point (in a speech, performance, writing etc.). —*interjection* calling attention or as a command; as a reply (= I am present) in a roll call. —*n.* this place. —**here and there,** in or to various places. **here goes,** I am ready to begin. **here's to,** I drink to the health of. **neither here nor there,** of no importance. [Old English]

hereabouts /hɪərəˈbaʊts/ *adv.* or **hereabout** near this place.

hereafter /hɪərˈɑːftə/ *adv.* in future, from now on. —*n.* the future; life after death.

hereby /hɪəˈbaɪ/ *adv.* by this means, as a result of this.

hereditable /hɪˈredɪtəbəl/ *adj.* that may be inherited. [from obsolete French or Latin *hereditare* = inherit from *heres* = heir]

hereditary /hɪˈredɪtərɪ/ *adj.* **1.** descending by inheritance. **2.** that may be transmitted from one generation to another. **3.** holding a hereditary office. [from Latin]

heredity /hɪˈredɪtɪ/ *n.* the property of organic beings by which offspring have the nature and characteristics of their parents or ancestors; the sum of these characteristics; genetic constitution. [from French or Latin *hereditas* = heirship]

Hereford /ˈherɪfəd/ a breed of red and white beef cattle; an animal of this breed. [from *Hereford* in England]

Hereford and Worcester /ˈherɪfəd, ˈwʊstə/ county in west central England; **area** 3,930 sq km/1,517 sq mi; **administrative headquarters** Worcester; **products** apples, pears, cider; hops, vegetables, Hereford cattle; carpets; porcelain; some chemicals and engineering; **population** (1987) 665,000.

herein /hɪərˈɪn/ *adv.* (*formal*) in this place, document etc.

hereinafter /hɪərɪnˈɑːftə/ *adv.* (*formal*) in a later part of this document etc.

hereof /hɪərˈɒv/ *adv.* (*archaic*) of this.

heresy /ˈherɪsɪ/ *n.* a doctrine opposed to orthodox belief, especially in religion. Those holding ideas considered heretical by the Christian church have included Gnostics, Arians, Pelagians, Montanists, Albigenses, Waldenses, Lollards, and Anabaptists. [from Old French from Latin *haeresis* = school of thought, from Greek *hairesis* = choice, sect (*haireomai* = choose)]

heretic /ˈherɪtɪk/ *n.* one advocating a heresy (especially in religion). —**heretical** /hɪˈretɪkəl/ *adj.* [from Old French from Latin from Greek *hairetikos* = able to choose]

hereto /hɪəˈtuː/ *adv.* (*archaic*) to this.

heretofore /hɪətuˈfɔː/ *adv.* (*formal*) formerly.

hereupon /hɪərəˈpɒn/ *adv.* after or in consequence of this.

Hereward /ˈherɪwəd/ **the Wake** 11th century. English leader of a revolt against the Normans in 1070. His stronghold in the Isle of Ely was captured by William the Conqueror in 1071. Hereward escaped, but his fate is unknown.

herewith /hɪəˈwɪð/ *adv.* with this (especially of an enclosure in a letter etc.).

Hergé /eəˈʒeɪ/ pen name of Georges Remi 1907–1983. Belgian artist, creator of the boy reporter Tintin, who first appeared in strip-cartoon form as *Tintin in the Land of the Soviets* 1929–30. [name taken from the pronunciation of the initial letters of his name]

heritable /ˈherɪtəbəl/ *adj.* **1.** that may be inherited; transmissible from parent to offspring. **2.** capable of inheriting. [from Old French *heriter*]

heritage /ˈherɪtɪdʒ/ *n.* what is or may be inherited; inherited circumstances or benefits etc.; one's portion or lot. [from Old French]

Herman /ˈhɜːmən/ Woody (Woodrow) 1913–1987. US band leader and clarinetist. A child prodigy, he was leader of his own orchestra at 23, and after 1945 formed his famous Thundering Herd band. Soloists in this or later versions of the band included Lester ◊Young and Stan ◊Getz.

hermaphrodite /hɜːˈmæfrədaɪt/ *n.* an organism that has both male and female sex organs. Hermaphroditism is the norm in species such as earthworms and snails, and is common in flowering plants. Cross-fertilization is the rule among hermaphrodites, with the parents functioning as male and female simultaneously, or as one or the other sex at different stages in their development. **Pseudo-hermaphrodites** have the internal sex organs of one sex, but the external appearance of the other. Their true sex becomes apparent at adolescence when the normal hormone activity appropriate to the internal organs begins to function. —*adj.* having such characteristics. —**hermaphroditic** /-ˈdɪtɪk/ *adj.* [from Latin from Greek *Hermaphroditus*]

Hermaphroditus /hɜːmæfrəˈdaɪtəs/ in Greek mythology, the son of Hermes and Aphrodite. He was loved by the nymph Salmacis, who prayed for eternal union with him, so that they became one body with dual sexual characteristics.

hermeneutics *n.* a philosophical tradition concerned with the nature of understanding and interpretation of human behaviour and social traditions.

Hermes /ˈhɜːmiːz/ in Greek mythology, a god, son of Zeus and ◊Maia; messenger of the gods; he wore winged sandals, a wide-rimmed hat, and a staff around which serpents coiled. Identified with the Roman Mercury and ancient Egyptian Thoth, and regarded as founder of alchemy, he protects thieves, travellers, and merchants.

hermetic /hɜːˈmetɪk/ *adj.* **1.** with an airtight closure. **2.** of alchemy or other occult science; esoteric. —**hermetically** *adv.* [from *Hermes*]

hermit /ˈhɜːmɪt/ *n.* a person (especially an early Christian) living in solitude. —**hermit crab,** a crab of the family Paguridae, that lives in a mollusc's cast-off shell. [from Old French or Latin from Greek *erēmitēs* (*erēmos* = solitary)]

hermitage /ˈhɜːmɪtɪdʒ/ *n.* the place of a hermit's retreat; a secluded dwelling.

hernia /ˈhɜːnɪə/ *n.* or **rupture** a protrusion of part of an internal organ through a weakness in the surrounding muscular wall, usually in the groin or navel. The appearance is that of a rounded soft lump or swelling. [Latin]

hero *n.* (*plural* **heroes**) **1.** a man admired for great deeds and noble qualities. **2.** the chief male character in a poem, play, or story. —**hero worship,** excessive devotion to an admired person. [from Latin from Greek *hērōs*]

Hero and Leander /ˈhɪərəʊ, liˈændə/ in Greek mythology, a pair of lovers. Hero was a priestess of Aphrodite at Sestos on the Hellespont, in love with Leander on the opposite shore at Abydos. When he was drowned while swimming across during a storm, she threw herself into the sea.

Herod /ˈherəd/ **the Great** 74–4 BC. King of the Roman province of Judaea, S Palestine, from 40 BC. With the aid of Mark Antony, he established his government in Jerusalem in 37 BC. He rebuilt the Temple in Jerusalem, but his Hellenizing tendencies made him suspect to orthodox Jewry. His last years were a reign of terror, and in the New Testament Matthew alleges that he ordered the slaughter of all the infants in Bethlehem to ensure the death of Jesus, whom he foresaw as a rival. He was the father of Herod Antipas.

Herod Agrippa I /əˈgrɪpə/ 10 BC–AD 44. Ruler of Palestine from AD 41. His real name was Marcus Julius Agrippa, erroneously called 'Herod' in the Bible. Grandson of Herod the Great, he was made tetrarch (governor) of Palestine by the Roman emperor Caligula and king by Emperor Claudius in AD 41. He put the apostle James to death and imprisoned the apostle Peter. His son was Herod Agrippa II.

Herod Agrippa II *c.* AD 40–93. King of Chalcis (now S Lebanon), son of Herod Agrippa I. He was appointed

Hertzsprung–Russell diagram

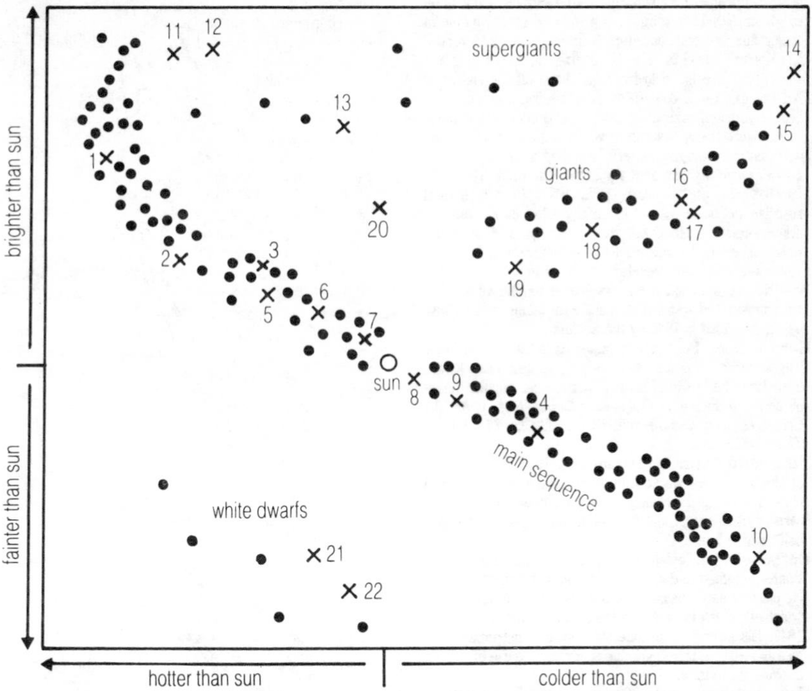

1	Spica	7	Procyon A
2	Regulus	8	Tau Ceti
3	Vega	9	61 Cygni A
4	61 Cygni B	10	Proxima Centauri
5	Sirius A	11	Rigel
6	Altair	12	Deneb
13	Polaris	18	Arcturus
14	Betelgeuse	19	Pollux
15	Antares	20	Capella
16	Mira	21	Sirius B
17	Aldebaran	22	Procyon B

by the Roman emperor Claudius about AD 50, and in 60 tried the apostle Paul. He helped the Roman emperor Titus take Jerusalem in 70, then went to Rome, where he died.

Herod Antipas /ˈæntɪpæs/ 21 BC–AD 39. Tetrarch (governor) of the Roman province of Galilee, N Palestine, 4 BC–AD 9, son of Herod the Great. He divorced his wife to marry his niece Herodias, who persuaded her daughter Salome to ask for John the Baptist's head when he reproved Herod's action. Jesus was brought before him on Pontius Pilate's discovery that he was a Galilean and hence of Herod's jurisdiction, but Herod returned him without giving any verdict. In AD 38 Herod Antipas went to Rome to try to get Emperor Caligula to give him the title of king, but was instead banished.

Herodotus /heˈrɒdətəs/ c.484–424 BC. Greek historian. After four years in Athens, he travelled widely in Egypt, Asia, and E Europe, before settling at Thurii in S Italy in 443 BC. He wrote a nine-book history of the Greek–Persian struggle that culminated in the defeat of the Persian invasion attempts in 490 and 480 BC. Herodotus was the first historian to apply critical evaluation to his material.

heroic /hɪˈrəʊɪk/ *adj.* having the characteristics of or suited to a hero, very brave. —*n.* (in *plural*) **1.** overdramatic talk or behaviour. **2.** heroic verse, a form used in epic poetry, e.g. the iambic pentameter. —**heroically** *adv.* [from French or Latin from Greek]

heroin /ˈherəʊɪn/ *n.* or **diamorphine** a powerful ◊opiate analgesic, an acetyl derivative of ◊morphine. It is more addictive than morphine but causes less nausea. It has an important place in the control of severe pain in terminal illness, severe injuries, and heart attacks, but is widely used illegally. In 1971 there were 3,000 registered heroin addicts in the UK; in 1989 there were over 100,000. [German, perhaps as *hero* (from its effects on the user's opinion of himself/herself)]

heroine /ˈherəʊɪn/ *n.fem.* a female hero. [from French or Latin from Greek]

heroism /ˈherəʊɪzəm/ *n.* heroic conduct or qualities. [from French]

heron /ˈherən/ *n.* a large wading bird of the family Ardeidae, which also includes bitterns, egrets, night herons, and boatbills. They have sharp bills, broad wings, long legs, and soft plumage. They are found mostly in tropical and subtropical regions, but also in temperate zones. [from Old French *hairon*]

heronry *n.* a place where herons breed.

herpes /ˈhɜːpiːz/ *n.* any of several infectious diseases caused by viruses of the herpes group. **Herpes simplex** I is the causative agent of a common inflammation, the cold sore. **Herpes simplex II** is responsible for genital herpes, a highly contagious, sexually transmitted disease characterized by painful blisters in the genital area. It can be transmitted in the birth canal from mother to newborn. **Herpes zoster** causes ◊shingles; another herpes virus causes chickenpox. The Epstein–Barr virus of ◊glandular fever also belongs to this group. [from Latin from Greek = shingles (*herpō* = creep)]

herpetology /hɜpɪˈtɒlədʒɪ/ *n.* the study of reptiles. —**herpetologist** *n.* [from Greek *herpeton* = reptile (*herpō* = creep)]

Herr /heə/ *n.* (*plural* **Herren**) a German man; the title of a German man = Mr. [German]

Herrick /ˈherɪk/ Robert 1591–1674. English poet and cleric, born in Cheapside, London. He published *Hesperides* in 1648, a collection of sacred and pastoral poetry admired for its lyric quality, including 'Gather ye rosebuds' and 'Cherry ripe'.

herring /'herɪŋ/ n. a salt-water fish *Clupea harengus*, of the family Clupeidae. It swims close to the surface, and may be 25–40 cm/10–16 in long. It is a silvered greenish-blue in colour and has only one dorsal fin and one short ventral fin. Herring travel in schools several kilometres long and wide. They are found in large quantities off the shores of NE Europe, the E coast of North America, and the White Sea. Overfishing and pollution have reduced their numbers. —**herringbone** n. a stitch or weave suggesting the bones of a herring; a zigzag pattern. **herring gull,** a large gull *Larus argentatus* with dark wing tips. [Old English]

Herriot /eri'əʊ/ Édouard 1872–1957. French Radical socialist politician. An opponent of Poincaré, who as prime minister carried out the French occupation of the Ruhr, Germany, he was briefly prime minister in 1924–25, 1926, and 1932. As president of the chamber of deputies in 1940, he opposed the policies of the right-wing Vichy government and was arrested and later taken to Germany; he was released in 1945 by the Soviets.

Herriot James. Pen name of James Alfred Wight 1916– . English writer. A practising veterinary surgeon in Yorkshire from 1940, he wrote of his experiences in a popular series of books including *If Only They Could Talk* 1970, *All Creatures Great and Small* 1972, and *The Lord God Made Them All* 1981.

Herrmann /'hɜːmən/ Bernard 1911–1975. US composer of film music. He worked for Alfred Hitchcock on several films, and wrote the chilling score for *Psycho* 1960.

hers /hɜːz/ *poss. pron.* of or belonging to her; the thing(s) belonging to her.

Herschel /'hɜːʃəl/ John Frederick William 1792–1871. English scientist and astronomer, son of William Herschel. He discovered thousands of close ◊double stars (see under ◊double¹), clusters, and nebulae (see ◊nebula), reported in 1847. His inventions include astronomical instruments, as well as sensitized photographic paper and the use of sodium thiosulphite to fix it.

Herschel William 1738–1822. German-born English astronomer. He was a skilled telescope maker, and pioneered the study of binary stars and nebulae. He discovered the planet Uranus in 1781 and infrared solar rays in 1801.

herself /hɜː'self/ *pron.* emphatic and reflexive form of **she** and **her**. —**be herself,** to behave in her normal manner, to be in her normal health and spirits. [Old English]

Hertfordshire /'hɑːfədʃə/ county in SE England; **area** 1,630 sq km/629 sq mi; **administrative headquarters** Hertford; **products** engineering, aircraft, electrical goods, paper and printing; general agricultural goods; **population** (1987) 987,000.

Herts. abbreviation of Hertfordshire.

hertz n. (*plural* the same) the SI unit (symbol Hz) of frequency (the number of repetitions of a regular occurrence in one second). Radio waves are often measured in megahertz (MHz), millions of hertz. [from Heinrich Rudolph *Hertz*, German physicist (1857–1894)]

Hertzog /'hɜːtsɒg/ James Barry Munnik 1866–1942. South African politician, prime minister 1924–39, founder of the Nationalist Party in 1913 (the **United South African National Party** from 1933). He opposed South Africa's entry into both world wars.

Hertzsprung–Russell diagram /'hɜːtsprʌŋ 'rʌsəl/ in astronomy, a graph on which the surface temperatures of stars are plotted against their luminosities. Most stars, including the Sun, fall into a narrow band called the ◊main sequence. When a star grows old it moves from the main sequence to the upper right part of the graph, into the area of the giants and supergiants. At the end of its life, as the star shrinks to become a white dwarf, it moves again, to the bottom left area. [the diagram is named after the Dane Ejnar *Hertzsprung* and the American Henry Norris *Russell*, who independently devised it in the years 1911–13]

Herzegovina /heətsəgə'viːnə/ or **Hercegovina** part of Yugoslavia; see ◊Bosnia and Herzegovina.

Herzl /'heətsəl/ Theodor 1860–1904. Austrian founder of the **Zionist** movement. He was born in Budapest and became a successful playwright and journalist, mainly in Vienna. The ◊Dreyfus case convinced him that the only solution to the problem of anti-Semitism was the resettlement of the Jews in a state of their own. His book *Jewish State* 1896 launched political Zionism, and he became the first president of the World Zionist Organization in 1897.

heterostyly

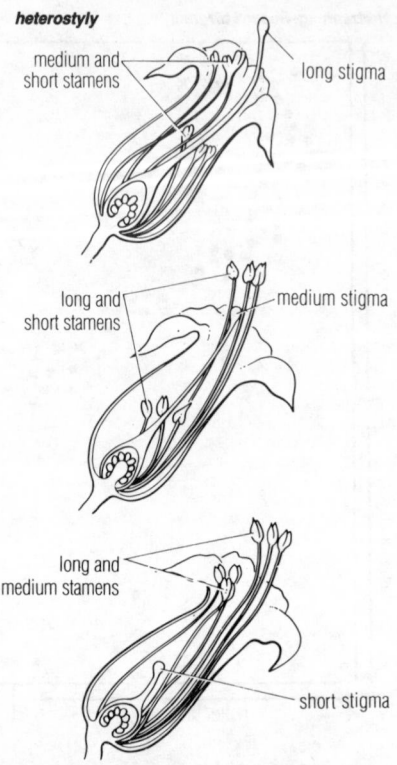

medium and short stamens — long stigma

long and short stamens — medium stigma

long and medium stamens — short stigma

Herzog /'heətsɒg/ Werner 1942– . German film director whose highly original and visually splendid films, often shot in exotic and impractical locations, include *Aguirre der Zom Gottes/Aguirre, Wrath of God* 1972, *Nosferatu Phantom der Nacht* 1979, and *Fitzcarraldo* 1982.

Heseltine /'hesəltaɪn/ Michael (Ray Dibdin) 1933– . English Conservative politician, member of Parliament for Henley, and secretary of state for the environment from 1990. He was minister of the environment 1979–83. He succeeded John Nott as minister of defence in Jan 1983 but resigned in Jan 1986 over the ◊Westland affair. On Nov 14 1990, Heseltine announced his decision to challenge Thatcher's leadership of the Conservative Party. Foreign secretary Douglas Hurd and chancellor of the Exchequer John Major joined the leadership contest and Major was elected on 27 Nov. Heseltine rejoined the cabinet as secretary of state for the environment from 1990.

Hesiod /'hiːsiəd/ lived c.700 BC. Greek poet. He is supposed to have lived a little later than Homer, and according to his own account he was born in Boeotia. He is the author of 'Works and Days', a poem that tells of the country life, and the 'Theogony', an account of the origin of the world and of the gods.

hesitant /'hezɪtənt/ adj. irresolute, hesitating. —**hesitancy** n., **hesitantly** adv.

hesitate /'hezɪteɪt/ v.i. to feel or show uncertainty or reluctance, to pause in doubt; to be reluctant. —**hesitation** /-'teɪʃən/ n., **hesitater** n. [from Latin *haesitare* (*haerēre* = stick fast)]

Hess /hes/ (Walter Richard) Rudolf 1894–1987. German Nazi leader. Imprisoned with Hitler 1923–25, he became his private secretary, taking down *Mein Kampf* from his dictation. In 1932 he was appointed deputy Führer to Hitler. On 10 May 1941 he landed by air in the UK with compromise peace proposals and was held a prisoner of war until 1945, when he was tried at Nuremberg as a war criminal and sentenced to life imprisonment. He died in ◊Spandau prison, Berlin.

Hess Victor 1883–1964. Austrian physicist, who emigrated to the USA shortly after sharing the Nobel Prize for Physics in 1936 for the discovery of cosmic radiation.

Hesse /'hesə/ Hermann 1877–1962. German writer who became a Swiss citizen in 1923. A conscientious objector in World War I and a pacifist opponent of Hitler, he published short stories, poetry, and novels, including *Peter Camenzind* 1904, *Siddhartha* 1922, and *Steppenwolf* 1927. Later works, such as *Das Glasperlenspiel*/*The Glass Bead Game* 1943, tend towards the mystical. He was awarded the Nobel Prize for Literature in 1946.

If you hate a person, you hate something in him that is part of yourself. What isn't part of ourselves doesn't disturb us.

Hermann Hesse
Demian

Hessen /'hesən/ administrative region (German *Land*) of Germany; **area** 21,100 sq km/8,145 sq mi; **capital** Wiesbaden; **products** wine, timber, chemicals, cars, electrical engineering, optical instruments; **population** (1988) 5,550,000; **history** until 1945, Hessen was divided in two by a strip of Prussian territory, the southern portion consisting of the valleys of the rivers Rhine and the Main, the northern being dominated by the Vogelsberg mountains. Its capital was Darmstadt.

hessian /'hesiən/ *n.* a strong, coarse fabric of hemp or jute, sackcloth. [from *Hesse* in Germany]

Hestia /'hestiə/ in Greek mythology, the goddess (Roman Vesta) of the hearth, daughter of Kronos (Roman Saturn) and Rhea.

Heston /'hestən/ Charlton. Stage name of Charles Carter 1924– . US film actor who often starred in biblical and historical epics (as Moses, for example, in *The Ten Commandments* 1956, and in the title role in *Ben-Hur* 1959).

het up, het up, (*slang*) excited, overwrought. [dialect *past participle* of *heat*]

hetaera /hi'tiərə/ *n.* (*plural* **hetaerae**) a courtesan, especially in ancient Greece. [Greek, literally = female companion]

hetero- /'hetərə-/ in combinations, other, different. [from Greek *heteros* = other]

heterodox /'hetərədɒks/ *adj.* not orthodox. —**heterodoxy** *n.* [from Greek *doxa* = opinion]

heterodyne /'hetərədaɪn/ *adj.* relating to the production of a lower radio frequency from a combination of two high frequencies.

heterogeneous /hetərə'dʒi:niəs/ *adj.* diverse in character; varied in content. —**heterogeneity** /-dʒi'ni:ɪtɪ/ *n.* [from Latin from Greek *genos* = kind]

heterogeneous reaction in chemistry, a reaction where there is an interface between the different components or reactants. Examples of heterogeneous systems are gas–solid, gas–liquid, two immiscible liquids, or different solids.

heteromorphic /hetərə'mɔ:fɪk/ *adj.* of dissimilar forms. —**heteromorphism** *n.* [from Greek *morphē* = form]

heterophony *n.* a form of choral melody singing and playing, found in folk music around the world, in which individual players have some freedom to improvise.

heterosexual /hetərə'seksjuəl/ *adj.* characterized by attraction to the opposite sex. —*n.* a heterosexual person. —**heterosexuality** /-'ælɪtɪ/ *n.*

heterostyly *n.* in botany, having styles of different lengths. Certain flowers, such as primroses *Primula vulgaris*, have different-sized anthers and styles to ensure cross-fertilization (through ◊pollination) by visiting insects.

heterotroph *n.* any living organism that obtains its energy from organic substances produced by other organisms. All animals and fungi are heterotrophs, and they include herbivores, carnivores, and saprotrophs (those that feed on dead animal and plant material).

heterozygous *adj.* in a living organism, having two different ◊alleles for a given trait. In ◊homozygous organisms, by contrast, both chromosomes carry the same allele. In an outbreeding population an individual organism will generally be heterozygous for some genes but homozygous for others.

heuristic /hjuə'rɪstɪk/ *adj.* serving or helping to find out or discover; proceeding by trial and error. [from Greek *heuriskō* = find]

heuristics *n.* (as *singular*) in computing, a process by which a program attempts to improve its performance by learning from its own experience.

hew *v.t./i.* (*past participle* **hewed** or **hewn**) to chop or cut with an axe, sword etc.; to cut into shape. [Old English]

Hewish /'hju:ɪʃ/ Antony 1924– . British radio astronomer, who was awarded, with Martin ◊Ryle, the 1974 Nobel Prize for Physics for his work on pulsars, rapidly rotating neutron stars which emit pulses of energy.

hexa- /heksə/ in combinations, six. [from Greek *hex* = six]

hexachlorophene *n.* $C_6HCl_3OH)_2CH_2$, a white, odourless bactericide, used in minute quantities in soaps and surgical disinfectants.

hexadecimal number system a number system to the base 16, used in computing. In hex (as it is commonly known) the decimal numbers 0–15 are represented by the characters 0, 1, 2, 3, 4, 5, 6, 7, 8, 9, A, B, C, D, E, F. Hexadecimal numbers are easy to convert to the computer's internal ◊binary code (see also ◊binary number system) and are more compact than binary numbers.

hexagon /'heksəgən/ *n.* a plane figure with six sides and angles. —**hexagonal** /-'ægənəl/ *adj.* [from Latin from Greek -*gōnos* = -angled]

hexagram /'heksəgræm/ *n.* a six-pointed star formed by two intersecting equilateral triangles.

hexameter /hek'sæmɪtə/ *n.* a line of six metrical feet, especially (**dactylic hexameter**) one with five dactyls and a trochee or spondee, any of the first four feet (and rarely the fifth) being replaceable by a spondee. [from Latin from Greek *metron* = measure]

hey /heɪ/ interjection calling attention or expressing surprise or inquiry. —**hey presto!** a conjuror's formula in performing a trick.

heyday /'heɪdeɪ/ *n.* the time of greatest success or prosperity. [from Low German *heidi, heida*, an exclamation of joy]

Heydrich /'haɪdrɪk/ Reinhard 1904–1942. German Nazi, head of the party's security service and ◊Himmler's deputy. He was instrumental in organizing the ◊final solution, the policy of genocide used against Jews and others. While deputy 'protector' of Bohemia and Moravia from 1941, he was ambushed and killed by three members of the Czechoslovak forces in Britain, who had landed by parachute. Reprisals followed, including several hundred executions and the massacre in ◊Lidice.

Heyerdahl /'haɪədɑːl/ Thor 1914– . Norwegian ethnologist. He sailed on the ancient-Peruvian-style raft *Kon Tiki* from Peru to the Tuamotu Islands along the Humboldt Current in 1947, and in 1969–70 used ancient-Egyptian-style papyrus reed boats to cross the Atlantic. His expeditions proved that ancient civilizations could have travelled the oceans in similar fashion.

Heywood /'heɪwʊd/ Thomas *c.* 1570–*c.* 1650. English actor and dramatist. He wrote or adapted over 220 plays, including the domestic tragedy *A Woman Kilde with Kindnesse* 1607.

Hezekiah /hezi'kaɪə/ in the Old Testament, king of Judah from 719 BC. Against the advice of the prophet Isaiah he rebelled against Assyrian suzerainty in alliance with Egypt, but was defeated by ◊Sennacherib and had to pay out large amounts in indemnities. He carried out religious reforms.

Hf symbol for ◊hafnium.

HF abbreviation of high frequency.

hg abbreviation of hectogram(s).

Hg symbol for mercury.

HGV abbreviation of heavy goods vehicle.

HH abbreviation of double-hard (pencil lead).

hi /haɪ/ interjection calling attention or as a greeting.

hiatus /haɪ'eɪtəs/ *n.* a break or gap in a sequence or series; a break between two vowels coming together but not in the same syllable. [Latin = gaping (*hiare* = gape)]

Hiawatha /haɪə'wɒθə/ 16th-century North American Indian teacher and Onondaga chieftain. He is said to have welded the Five Nations (later joined by a sixth) of the ◊Iroquois into the league of the **Long House**, as the confederacy was known in what is now upper New York State.

hibernate /'haɪbəneɪt/ *v.i.* (of an animal) to spend the winter in a dormant state, associated with a dramatic reduction in all metabolic processes, including body temperature, breathing, and heart rate. —**hibernation** /-'neɪʃən/ n. [from Latin *hibernare* (*hibernus* = of winter)]

Hibernian /haɪˈbɜːniən/ adj. of Ireland. —n. a native of Ireland. [from Latin *Hibernia* = Ireland from Greek *Iernē*]

hibiscus /hɪˈbɪskəs/ n. any plant of the genus *Hibiscus* of the mallow family. Hibiscuses range from large herbaceous plants to trees. Popular as ornamental plants because of their brilliantly coloured, red to white, bell-shaped flowers, they include *H. syriacus* and *H. rosa-sinensis* of Asia and the **rose mallow** *H. palustris* of North America. Some tropical species are also useful: *H. esculentus*, of which the edible fruit is **okra** or **ladies' fingers**; *H. tiliaceus*, which supplies timber and fibrous bark to South Pacific islanders; and *H. sabdariffa*, cultivated in the West Indies and elsewhere for its fruit. [Latin from Greek = marsh mallow]

hiccup /ˈhɪkʌp/ n. or **hiccough** an involuntary spasm of the respiratory organs with an abrupt coughlike sound. —v.i. to make a hiccup.

hic jacet an epitaph. [Latin = here lies]

hick n. (*US colloquial*) a country bumpkin. [familiar form of *Richard*]

Hick /hɪk/ Graeme 1966– . Rhodesian-born cricketer who became Zimbabwe's youngest professional cricketer at the age of 17. A prolific batsman, he joined Worcestershire, England, in 1984. He achieved the highest score in England in the 20th century in 1988 against Somerset with 405 not out.

Hickok /ˈhɪkɒk/ 'Wild Bill' (James Butler) 1837–1876. US pioneer and law enforcer, a legendary figure in the West. In the Civil War he was a sharpshooter and scout for the Union army. He then served as marshal in Kansas, killing as many as 27 men. He established his reputation as a gunfighter when he killed a fellow scout, turned traitor. He was a prodigious gambler and was fatally shot from behind while playing poker in Deadwood, South Dakota.

hickory /ˈhɪkərɪ/ n. a North American tree of the genus *Carya*, related to the walnut; its hard wood. It provides a valuable timber, and all species produce nuts, although some are inedible. The **pecan** *C. illinoensis* is widely cultivated in the southern USA, and the **shagbark** *C. ovata* in the northern USA. [from Virginian Indian *pohickery*]

hid past of ◊hide[1].

hidalgo /hɪˈdælɡʊ; Spanish iːˈdælɡʊ/ n. (*plural* **hidalgos**) a member of the lower nobility in Spain. [Spanish *hijo dalgo* = son of something]

Hidalgo y Costilla /iːˈdælɡəʊ iː kɒˈstiljə/ Miguel 1753–1811. Catholic priest, known as 'the Father of Mexican Independence'. A symbol of the opposition to Spain, he rang the church bell in Sept 1810 to announce to his parishioners in Dolores that the revolution against the Spanish had begun. He was captured and shot the following year.

hidden past participle of ◊hide[1].

hide[1] v.t./i. (*past* **hid**; *past participle* **hidden**) 1. to put or keep out of sight; to prevent from being seen. 2. to keep (a fact etc.) secret (*from*). 3. to conceal oneself. —n. a concealed place for observing wildlife. —**hide-and-seek** n. a children's game in which a player hides and is sought by others. **hide-out** n. (*colloquial*) a hiding place. [Old English]

hide[2] n. an animal's skin, raw or dressed; (*colloquial*) the human skin. [Old English]

hidebound adj. rigidly conventional, narrow-minded.

hideous /ˈhɪdɪəs/ adj. very ugly, revolting. —**hideously** adv., **hideousness** n. [from Anglo-French (Old French *hisde* = horror)]

hiding[1] /ˈhaɪdɪŋ/ n. the state of remaining hidden. —**hiding place**, a place in which one hides or where something is hidden.

hiding[2] n. (*colloquial*) a thrashing.

hie /haɪ/ v.i. & refl. (*archaic* or *poetic*) to go quickly. [Old English *higian* = strive, pant]

hierarchy /ˈhaɪərɑːkɪ/ n. a system in which grades of status or authority rank one above another. —**hierarchical** /-ˈrɑːkɪkəl/ adj. [from Old French from Latin from Greek *hieros* = sacred and *arkhō* = rule]

hieratic /haɪəˈrætɪk/ adj. of the priests, priestly. —n. hieratic script, a form of cursive hieroglyphs used from early times in ancient Egypt, originally for religious texts. [from Latin from Greek *hiereus* = priest]

hieroglyph /ˈhaɪərəɡlɪf/ n. 1. a picture of an object used to represent a word, sound, or syllable in any of the pictorial systems of writing, especially the ancient Egyptian. The Egyptian hieroglyphic writing system of the mid-4th millennium BC–3rd century AD, combined picture signs with those indicating letters. The direction of writing, though it can vary, is normally from right to left, the signs facing the beginning of the line. It was deciphered in 1822 by the French Egyptologist J F Champollion (1790–1832) with the aid of the ◊Rosetta Stone, which has the same inscription carved in hieroglyphic, demotic, and Greek. 2. a secret or enigmatic symbol. 3. (in *plural*, *jocular*) writing that is difficult to make out. [from French or Latin from Greek *hieros* = sacred and *gluphē* = carving]

hieroglyphic /haɪərəˈɡlɪfɪk/ adj. of or written in hieroglyphs. —n. (in *plural*) hieroglyphs, hieroglyphic writing.

hi-fi /ˈhaɪfaɪ/ adj. (*colloquial*) high-fidelity. —/also -ˈfaɪ/ n. (*colloquial*) high-fidelity equipment. A typical hi-fi system includes a turntable for playing vinyl records, a cassette tape deck to play magnetic tape recordings, a tuner to pick up radio broadcasts, an amplifier to serve all the equipment, possibly a compact disc player, and two or more loudspeakers. [abbreviation]

Higgins Jack. Pseudonym of British novelist Harry ◊Patterson.

higgledy-piggledy /ˈhɪɡəldɪˈpɪɡəldɪ/ adj. & adv. disordered, in confusion.

high /haɪ/ adj. 1. extending far upwards; extending above the normal or average level. 2. situated far above the ground or above sea level. 3. measuring a specified distance in upward extent. 4. ranking above others in importance or quality; luxurious. 5. extreme, intense, greater than the normal or average; (of opinion) very favourable. 6. (of time) far advanced; fully reached; (of a period) at its peak of development. 7. (of sound) having rapid vibrations, not deep or low. 8. (of meat etc.) beginning to go bad; (of game) hung until slightly decomposed and ready to cook. 9. (*colloquial*) intoxicated by or *on* alcohol or drugs. 10. (of animals or plants etc.) of complex structure, highly developed. —n. 1. a high or the highest level or number. 2. an area of high pressure. 3. (*slang*) a euphoric state caused by a drug. —adv. 1. far up, aloft. 2. in or to a high degree. 3. at a high price. 4. (of sound) at or to a high pitch. —**high and dry**, aground, stranded. **high and low**, everywhere. **high and mighty**, (*colloquial*) pompous, arrogant. **highchair** n. a young child's chair for meals, with long legs and usually an attached tray. **High Church**, the section of the Church of England which stresses historical continuity with Catholic Christianity and attaches 'high' importance to the authority of the episcopate and the saving grace of the Sacraments. **High Commission**, an embassy from one Commonwealth country to another. **high commissioner**, the head of this. **High Court (of Justice)**, the supreme court for civil cases. **higher education**, education at university etc. **high explosive**, an explosive with a violent shattering effect. **highfalutin(g)** adj. (*colloquial*) bombastic, pretentious. **high fidelity**, reproduction of sound with little distortion, giving a result very similar to the original. **high-flown** adj. (of language etc.) extravagant, bombastic. **high-flyer**, **high-flier** n. an ambitious person; a person or thing with the potential for great achievements. **high-flying** adj. ambitious. **high frequency**, (in radio) 3–30 megahertz. **high-handed** adj. overbearing. **high hat**, a tall hat; **high-hat** = ◊hi-hat. **high jump**, an athletic contest of jumping over a high horizontal bar; *be for the high jump*, to be likely to receive a severe punishment (the reference is to being hanged). **high-level** adj. (of discussions etc.) conducted by persons of the highest rank. **high-level language**, a computer language close to ordinary language and usually not machine-readable. **high-minded** adj. having high moral principles. **high-pitched** adj. (of a sound or voice) shrill; (of a roof) steep. **high-powered** adj. having or using great power, important or influential. **high pressure**, a high degree of activity or exertion; a condition of the atmosphere with the pressure above average. **high priest**, a chief priest, a head of a cult. **high-rise** adj. (of a building) having many storeys. **highroad** n. a main road. **high school**, a secondary (especially a grammar) school. **high seas**, the open seas not under any country's jurisdiction. **high season**, the regular period of the greatest number of visitors at a resort etc. **high-spirited** adj. in high spirits, cheerful. **high spot**, (*colloquial*) the most

Hill *Scottish photographers David Octavius Hill and Robert R Adamson produced some 2,500 calotypes between 1843 and 1848. The portrait by Hill and Adamson (c.1843) is an example of this early photography.*

important place or feature. **high street,** the principal street of a town etc. **high table,** an elevated table at a public dinner or in a college etc., for the most important guests or members. **high tea,** an evening meal of tea and cooked food. **high tech,** (*colloquial*) characterized by high technology; (of interior design etc.) imitating styles more usual in industry etc. **high technology,** a state of advanced technological development. **high tension,** high voltage. **high tide,** a tide at the highest level; the time of this. **high treason,** treason against one's ruler or country. **high-up** *n.* (*colloquial*) a person of high rank. **high water,** high tide. **high-water mark,** the level reached at high water; the highest recorded point or value. **high wire,** a high tightrope. **on high,** in or to a high place or heaven. [Old English]

highball *n.* (*US*) a drink of spirits and soda etc. served with ice in a tall glass.

highbrow *adj.* (*colloquial*) intellectual or highly cultural in interest or appeal. —*n.* (*colloquial*) a highbrow person.

higher education in most countries, education beyond the age of 18 leading to a university or college degree or similar qualification.

highland /ˈhaɪlənd/ *n.* (usually in *plural*) mountainous country, especially (**Highlands**) of northern Scotland. —*adj.* of the highland or the Scottish Highlands. —**Highland cattle,** a breed with shaggy hair and long curved horns.

Highland Clearances the forced removal of tenants from large estates in Scotland during the early 19th century, as landowners 'improved' their estates by switching from arable to sheep farming. It led ultimately to widespread emigration to North America.

highlander *n.* a native or inhabitant of highlands or (**Highlander**) of the Scottish Highlands.

Highland Games a traditional Scottish outdoor gathering that includes tossing the caber, putting the shot, running, dancing, and bagpipe playing. The most celebrated is the Braemar Gathering.

Highland Region administrative region of Scotland; **area** 26,100 sq km/10,077 sq mi; **administrative headquarters** Inverness; **products** oil services, winter sports,

timber, livestock, grouse and deer hunting, salmon fishing; **population** (1987) 201,000.

Highlands /ˈhaɪləndz/ one of the three geographical divisions of Scotland, lying to the N of a geological fault line that stretches from Stonehaven in the North Sea to Dumbarton on the Clyde. It is a mountainous region of hard rocks, shallow infertile soils, and high rainfall.

highlight *n.* **1.** a moment or detail of vivid interest; an outstanding feature. **2.** the bright part of a picture etc. —*v.t.* to bring into prominence.

highly *adv.* in a high degree; favourably. —**highly-strung** *adj.* very sensitive and nervous.

highness *n.* **1.** the title used in addressing or referring to a prince or princess. **2.** the state of being high (especially *figuratively*).

Highsmith /ˈhaɪsmɪθ/ Patricia 1921– . US crime novelist. Her first book, *Strangers on a Train* 1950, was filmed by Alfred Hitchcock. She excels in tension and psychological exploration of character, notably in her series dealing with the amoral Tom Ripley, including *The Talented Mr Ripley* 1956, *Ripley Under Ground* 1971, and *Ripley's Game* 1974.

high tech abbreviation of high technology; in architecture, buildings that display technical innovation of a high order and celebrate structure and services to create exciting forms and spaces. The Hong Kong and Shanghai Bank, Hong Kong, is a masterpiece of this approach.

highway *n.* **1.** a public road. **2.** a main route. **3.** a conductor transmitting signals in a computer. —**Highway Code,** the set of rules issued officially for the guidance of road users. **King's** *or* **Queen's highway,** a public road regarded as protected by royal power.

highwayman *n.* (*plural* **highwaymen**) (*historical*) a thief on horseback who robbed travellers on the highway (those who did so on foot were known as **footpads**). They continued to flourish well into the 19th century. Among the best-known highwaymen were Jonathan ◊Wild, Claude Duval, John Nevison (1639–1684), the original hero of the 'ride to York', Dick ◊Turpin and his partner Tom King, and Jerry Abershaw (*c.*1773–1795).

hi-hat /ˈhaɪhæt/ *n.* or **high-hat** a pair of cymbals worked by the foot.

hijack /ˈhaɪdʒæk/ *v.t.* to seize control of (a vehicle or aircraft), especially to force it to a new destination; to seize (goods in transit). —*n.* a hijacking. The term hijacking dates from 1923 and originally referred to the robbing of freight lorries. In recent times it (and its derivative, 'skyjacking') has been applied to the seizure of aircraft, usually in flight, by an individual or group, often with some political aim. International treaties (Tokyo 1963, The Hague 1970, and Montreal 1971) encourage international cooperation against hijackers and make severe penalties compulsory. —**hijacker** *n.*

Hijra /ˈhɪdʒrə/ variant of ◊Hegira.

hike *n.* a long walk, especially across country. —*v.i.* to go for a hike; to walk laboriously. —**hiker** *n.*

hilarious /hɪˈleəriəs/ *adj.* **1.** boisterously merry. **2.** extremely funny. —**hilariously** *adv.,* **hilarity** /hɪˈlærɪti/ *n.* [from Latin from Greek *hilaros* = cheerful]

Hilbert /ˈhɪlbət/ David 1862–1943. German mathematician who founded the formalist school with the publication of *Grundlagen der Geometrie*/*Foundations of Geometry* in 1899, which was based on his idea of postulates. He attempted to put mathematics on a logical foundation through defining it in terms of a number of basic principles, which ◊Gödel later showed to be impossible; none the less, his attempt greatly influenced 20th-century mathematicians.

hill /hɪl/ *n.* **1.** a natural elevation of the ground, not as high as a mountain. **2.** a sloping piece of road. **3.** a heap or mound. [Old English]

Hill David Octavius 1802–1870. Scottish photographer who, in collaboration with ◊Adamson, made extensive use of the ◊calotype process in their large collection of portraits taken in Edinburgh 1843–48.

Hill Rowland 1795–1879. British Post Office official who invented adhesive stamps and prompted the introduction of the penny prepaid post in 1840 (previously the addressee paid, according to distance, on receipt).

Hillary /ˈhɪləri/ Edmund 1919– . New Zealand mountaineer. In 1953, with Nepalese Sherpa mountaineer Tenzing Norgay, he was the first to reach the summit of Mount Everest, the world's highest peak. As a member of the

Commonwealth Transantarctic Expedition 1957–58, Hillary was the first person since Scott to reach the South Pole overland, on 3 Jan 1958. On the way to the South Pole he laid depots for ◊Fuchs's completion of the crossing of the continent.

hillbilly /'hɪlbɪlɪ/ n. 1. folk music like that of the southern USA. 2. (*US colloquial*, often *derogatory*) a person from a remote rural area in a southern state. [from *billy* = fellow]

hill figure in Britain, any of a number of ancient figures, usually of animals, cut from downland turf to show the underlying chalk. Examples include the ◊White Horses, the Long Man of Wilmington, East Sussex, and the Cerne Abbas Giant, Dorset. Their origins are variously attributed to Celts, Romans, Saxons, Druids, or Benedictine monks.

hillfort n. a European Iron Age site with massive banks and ditches for defence, used as both a military camp and a permanent settlement. An example is Maiden Castle, Dorset, England.

Hilliard /'hɪlɪəd/ Nicholas c.1547–1619. English miniaturist and goldsmith, court artist to Elizabeth I from about 1579. His sitters included the explorers Francis Drake and Walter Raleigh. The Victoria and Albert Museum, London, has a fine collection of his delicate portraits, set in gold cases. They include *Young Man Amid Roses* from about 1590.

hillock /'hɪlək/ n. a small hill, a mound.

Hillsborough Agreement /'hɪlzbərə/ another name for the ◊Anglo-Irish Agreement of 1985.

hillside n. the sloping side of a hill.

hilly adj. having many hills. —**hilliness** n.

hilt n. the handle of a sword, dagger etc. —**up to the hilt**, completely. [Old English]

him pron. objective case of *he*; (*colloquial*) he. [Old English, dative of *he*]

Himachal Pradesh /hɪ'mɑːtʃəl prə'deʃ/ state of NW India; **area** 55,700 sq km/21,500 sq mi; **capital** Simla; **products** timber, grain, rice, fruit; **population** (1981) 4,238,000; mainly Hindu; **language** Pahari; **history** created as a Union Territory in 1948, it became a full state in 1971.

Himalayas /hɪmə'leɪəz/ vast mountain system of central Asia, extending from the Indian states of Kashmir in the west to Assam in the east, covering the southern part of Tibet, Nepál, Sikkim, and Bhutan. It is the highest mountain range in the world. The two highest peaks are Mount ◊Everest and ◊Kangchenjunga. Other major peaks include Makalu, Annapurna, and Nanga Parbat, all over 8,000 m/26,000 ft.

Himmler /'hɪmlə/ Heinrich 1900–1945. German Nazi leader, head of the ◊SS (sense 3) élite corps from 1929, the police and the ◊Gestapo secret police from 1936, and supervisor of the extermination of the Jews in E Europe. During World War II he replaced Goering as Hitler's second-in-command. He was captured in May 1945 and committed suicide.

himself /hɪm'self/ pron. emphatic and reflexive form of *he* and *him*. [Old English]

Hīnayāna /'hɪnijɑːnə/ Mahāyāna Buddhist name for ◊Theravāda Buddhism. [Sanskrit = lesser vehicle]

hind[1] /haɪnd/ adj. situated at the back. [perhaps shortened from Old English *bihindan* = behind]

hind[2] /haɪnd/ n. the female of the (especially red) deer, especially in and after the third year. [Old English]

Hindemith /'hɪndəmɪt/ Paul 1895–1963. German composer. His Neo-Classical, contrapuntal works include chamber ensemble and orchestral pieces, such as the *Symphonic Metamorphosis on Themes of Carl Maria von Weber* 1944, and the operas *Cardillac* 1926, revised 1952, and *Mathis der Maler/Mathis the Painter* 1938.

Hindenburg /'hɪndənbɜːg/ Paul Ludwig Hans von Beneckendorf und Hindenburg 1847–1934. German field marshal and right-wing politician. During World War I he was supreme commander and, with Ludendorff, practically directed Germany's policy until the end of the war. He was president of Germany 1925–33.

Hindenburg Line the German western line of World War I fortifications built 1916–17.

hinder[1] /'hɪndə/ v.t. to keep (a person or thing) back by delaying progress. [Old English]

hinder[2] /haɪndə/ adj. = ◊hind[1].

Hindi /'hɪndɪ/ n. 1. a literary form of Hindustani. 2. a group of spoken dialects of N India, belonging to the

Indo-European family of languages and related to Urdu. —adj. of Hindi. [from Urdu (*Hind* = India)]

hindmost /'haɪndməʊst/ adj. furthest behind.

hindquarters /haɪnd'kwɔːtəz/ n.pl. the hind legs and adjoining parts of a quadruped.

hindrance /'hɪndrəns/ n. 1. a thing that hinders. 2. hindering, being hindered.

hindsight /'haɪndsaɪt/ n. wisdom after the event.

Hindu /hɪn'duː, 'hɪ-/ n. an adherent of Hinduism. —adj. of the Hindus. [Urdu, from Persian (*Hind* = India)]

Hinduism /'hɪnduːɪzəm/ n. a religion originating in N India about 4,000 years ago, which is superficially and in some of its forms polytheistic, but has a concept of the supreme spirit, ◊Brahman, above the many divine manifestations. These include the triad of chief gods (the Trimurti): Brahma, Vishnu, and Siva (creator, preserver, and destroyer). Central to Hinduism are the beliefs in reincarnation and ◊karma; the oldest scriptures are the *Vedas*. Temple worship is almost universally observed and there are many festivals. There are over 805 million Hindus worldwide. Women are not regarded as the equals of men but should be treated with kindness and respect. Muslim influence in N India led to the veiling of women and the restriction of their movements from about the end of the 12th century.

Hindu Kush /hɪndu: 'kuʃ/ mountain range in central Asia; length 800 km/500 mi; greatest height Tirich Mir 7,690 m/25,239 ft, in Pakistan. The narrow **Khyber Pass**, (53 km/33 mi long) separates Pakistan from Afghanistan and was used by ◊Zahir and other invaders of India. The present road was built by the British in the Afghan Wars.

Hindustan /hɪndu:'stɑːn/ the whole of India, but more specifically the plain of the Ganges and Jumna rivers, or that part of India N of the Deccan. [from *Hindu* and *-stan* = country]

Hindustani /hɪndə'stɑːnɪ/ n. a language of the Indo-Iranian branch of the Indo-European language family, closely related to Hindi and Urdu and originating in the bazaars of Delhi. It is a ◊lingua franca in many parts of the Republic of India. It was the contact language during the British Raj between many of the British in India and the native Indians and is sometimes known as Bazaar Hindi. —adj. of Hindustani.

Hine /haɪn/ Lewis 1874–1940. US sociologist. He recorded in photographs child labour conditions in US factories at the beginning of this century, leading to a change in the law.

hinge /hɪndʒ/ n. 1. a movable joint on which a door, lid etc. turns or swings. 2. a principle on which all depends. —v.t./i. 1. to attach or be attached by a hinge. 2. to depend *on*.

hinge joint in vertebrates, a joint where movement occurs in one plane only. Examples are the elbow and knee, which are controlled by pairs of muscles, the ◊flexors and ◊extensors.

Hinkler /'hɪŋklə/ Herbert John Louis 1892–1933. Australian pilot who in 1928 made the first solo flight from England to Australia. He was killed while making another attempt to fly to Australia.

hinny n. the offspring of a she-ass and a stallion. [from Latin *hinnus* from Greek]

Hinshelwood /'hɪnʃəlwʊd/ Cyril Norman 1897–1967. English chemist who shared the 1956 Nobel Prize for Chemistry with Nikolai Semenov for his work on chemical chain reactions. He also studied the chemistry of bacterial growth.

hint n. 1. a slight or indirect indication or suggestion. 2. a small piece of practical information. 3. a small amount, a trace. —v.t./i. to suggest slightly or indirectly. —**hint at**, to refer indirectly to. **take a hint**, to act upon a hint. [from obsolete *hent* = grasp]

hinterland /'hɪntəlænd/ n. the district behind a coast or a river's banks; an area served by a port or other centre. [German (*hinter* = behind)]

hip[1] n. 1. the projection formed by the pelvis and upper part of the thighbone. 2. the arris of a roof from ridge to eaves. —**hip bath**, a portable bath in which one sits immersed to the hips. **hipbone** n. the bone forming the hip. **hip flask**, a flattish flask for spirits, carried in the hip pocket. **hip pocket**, a trouser pocket just behind the hip. [Old English]

hip[2] n. the fruit of the (especially wild) rose. [Old English]

hip[3] interjection used in cheering (*hip, hip, hurray*).

hip[4] (*slang*) variant of **hep**.

Hiroshima *The total devastation caused by the atom bomb on Hiroshima towards the end of World War II.*

hip-hop *n.* a style of popular music originating in New York in the early 1980s. It uses scratching (a percussive effect obtained by manually rotating a vinyl record) and heavily accented electronic drums behind a rap vocal (see ◊rap music). The term 'hip-hop' also comprises break dancing and graffiti.

Hipparchos /hɪˈpɑːkɒs/ acronym from **high precision parallax** collecting satellite, the satellite launched by the European Space Agency in Aug 1989. It is the world's first astrometry satellite designed to provide the first measurements of the positions and apparent motions of stars from space. The accuracy of these measurements will be far greater than from ground-based telescopes. However, because of engine failure, *Hipparchos* is making more limited orbits than had been planned, which may restrict the data it is able to provide. [after the Greek astronomer *Hipparchus*]

Hipparchus /hɪˈpɑːkəs/ *c.* 190–*c.* 120 BC. Greek astronomer who invented trigonometry, calculated the lengths of the solar year and the lunar month, discovered the precession of the equinoxes, made a catalogue of 800 fixed stars, and advanced Eratosthenes' method of determining the situation of places on the Earth's surface by lines of latitude and longitude.

Hipparchus *c.* 555–514 BC. Greek tyrant. Son of ◊Pisistratus, he was associated with his elder brother Hippias as ruler of Athens 527–514 BC. His affection being spurned by Harmodius, he insulted her sister, and was assassinated by Harmodius and Aristogiton.

hippeastrum /hɪpiˈæstrəm/ *n.* a South American plant of the genus *Hippeastrum* with showy red or white flowers. [from Greek *hippeus* = horseman (the leaves appearing to ride on one another) and *astron* = star (from the flower shape)]

hippie /ˈhɪpi/ *n.* a member of a youth movement of the mid-1960s to mid-1970s, also known as **flower power**, which originated in San Francisco, California, and was characterized by nonviolent anarchy, concern for the environment, and rejection of Western materialism. The hippies formed a politically outspoken, antiwar, artistically prolific counterculture in North America and Europe. Their colourful psychedelic style, inspired by drugs such as ◊LSD, emerged in fabric design, graphic art, and music by bands such as Love (1965–71), the Grateful Dead (1965–   ), Jefferson Airplane (1965–74), and ◊Pink Floyd.

hippo /ˈhɪpəʊ/ *n.* (*plural* **hippos**) (*colloquial*) a hippopotamus. [abbreviation]

The life so short, the craft so long to learn.
Hippocrates
Aphorisms

Hippocrates /hɪˈpɒkrətiːz/ *c.* 460–*c.* 370 BC. Greek physician, often called the father of medicine. Impor-

tant Hippocratic ideas include cleanliness (for patients and physicians), moderation in eating and drinking, letting nature take its course, and living where the air is good.

Hippocratic oath /hɪpəˈkrætɪk/ an oath stating the obligations and proper conduct of physicians, formerly taken by those beginning medical practice. [from *Hippocrates*]

hippodrome /ˈhɪpədrəʊm/ *n.* **1.** a music hall or dance hall. **2.** in classical antiquity, a course for chariot races etc. [French, or from Latin from Greek *hippos* = horse and *dromos* = race course]

Hippolytus /hɪˈpɒlɪtəs/ in Greek mythology, the son of Theseus. When he rejected the love of his stepmother, Phaedra, she falsely accused him of making advances to her and turned Theseus against him. Killed by Poseidon at Theseus' request, he was restored to life when his innocence was proven.

hippopotamus /hɪpəˈpɒtəməs/ *n.* (*plural* **hippopotamuses**) a large, herbivorous, hoofed mammal of the family Hippopotamidae. The **common hippopotamus** *Hippopotamus amphibius* is found in Africa. It averages over 4 m/13 ft long, 1.5 m/5 ft high, weighs about 4,500 kg/5 tons, and has a brown or slate-grey skin. It is an endangered species. [from Latin from Greek *hippos* = horse and *potamos* = river]

hipster /ˈhɪpstə/ *adj.* (of a garment) hanging from the hips rather than the waist.

hire *v.t.* to obtain the use of (a thing) or the services of (a person) temporarily, for payment; (often with *out*) to grant the use of thus. —**for** *or* **on hire**, ready to be hired. —**hirer** *n.* [Old English]

hireable /ˈhaɪərəbəl/ *adj.* that may be hired.

hireling /ˈhaɪəlɪŋ/ *n.* (*usually derogatory*) a person who works for hire. [Old English]

hire-purchase *n.* (HP) a form of credit under which the buyer pays a deposit and makes instalment payments at fixed intervals over a certain period for a particular item. The buyer has immediate possession, but does not own the item until the final instalment has been paid.

Hirohito /hɪərəʊˈhiːtəʊ/ 1901–1989. Emperor of Japan from 1926. He succeeded his father Yoshihito. After the defeat of Japan in World War II in 1945, he was stripped of his divine powers and made constitutional monarch by the US-backed 1946 constitution. He was believed to have played a reluctant role in ◊Tōjō's prewar expansion plans. Hirohito ruled postwar occupied Japan with dignity. He was a scholar of botany and zoology and the author of books on marine biology. He was succeeded by his son ◊Akihito.

Hiroshige /hɪəˈrəʊʃigeɪ/ Andō 1797–1858. Japanese artist whose landscape prints, often using snow or rain to create atmosphere, include *Tōkaidōgojūsan-tsugi/Stations on the Tokaido Highway* 1833.

Hiroshima /hɪˈrɒʃɪmə/ industrial city and port on the S coast of Honshu, Japan, destroyed by the first wartime use of an atomic bomb on 6 Aug 1945. The city has largely been rebuilt since the war; population (1987) 1,034,000.

hirsute /'hɜːsjuːt/ adj. hairy, shaggy. [from Latin *hirsutus*]

his /hɪz/ poss. pron. & adj. 1. of or belonging to him, the thing(s) belonging to him. 2. (in titles) that he is (*His Majesty*). [Old English, genitive of *he*]

Hispanic /hɪs'pænɪk/ adj. of Spain (and Portugal); of Spain and other Spanish-speaking countries. —n. a Hispanic person. [from Latin *Hispania* = Spain]

Hispano-Suiza /hi'spænəu 'suːɪzə/ n. a car designed by a Swiss engineer Marc Birkigt (1878–1947) who emigrated to Barcelona, where he founded a factory which produced cars during the period 1900–38, legendary for their handling, elegance, and speed.

hiss /hɪs/ n. a sharp, sibilant sound, as of the letter *s*. —v.t./i. to make a hiss; to express disapproval (of) by hisses; to utter with an angry hiss. [Old English]

Hiss Alger 1904– . US diplomat and liberal Democrat, a former State Department official, controversially imprisoned in 1950 for allegedly having spied for the USSR.

histamine /'hɪstəmɪn, -iːn/ n. an inflammatory substance normally released in damaged tissues, which also accounts for many of the symptoms of ◊allergy. Substances that neutralize its activity are known as ◊antihistamines.

histochemistry n. the study of plant and animal tissue by visual examination, usually with a ◊microscope.

histogram /'hɪstəgræm/ n. a graph with the horizontal axis having discrete units or class boundaries with contiguous end points, and the vertical axis representing the frequency. Blocks are drawn such that their areas are proportional to the frequencies within a class or across several class boundaries. There are no spaces between blocks. [from Greek *histos* = mast]

histology /hɪs'tɒlədʒɪ/ n. the science of organic tissues. —**histological** /hɪstə'lɒdʒɪkəl/ adj. [from Greek *histos* = web]

historian /hi'stɔːrɪən/ n. a writer of history; a person learned in history. [from French from Latin]

historic /hi'stɒrɪk/ adj. 1. famous or important in history or potentially so. 2. in grammar, (of a tense) normally used of past events. [from Latin from Greek]

historical adj. 1. of or concerning history or facts in history; dealing with a past period. 2. having occurred in fact not legend or rumour. 3. (of the study of a subject) showing the development over a period of time. —**historically** adv.

historical novel a fictional prose narrative set in the past. Literature set in the historic rather than the immediate past has always abounded, but in the West Walter Scott began the modern tradition by setting imaginative romances of love, impersonation, and betrayal in a past based on known fact; his use of historical detail, and subsequent imitations of this technique by European writers such as Manzoni, gave rise to the genre.

historicism /hi'stɒrɪsɪzəm/ n. 1. the belief that historical events are governed by laws. 2. a tendency to stress historical development and the influence of the past etc.

historicity /hɪstə'rɪsɪtɪ/ n. historical truth or authenticity.

historiography /hɪstɒrɪ'ɒgrəfɪ/ n. the writing of history; the study of this. —**historiographer** n. [from Greek]

history /'hɪstərɪ/ n. 1. a continuous record of important or public events. 2. the study of past events, especially of human affairs. 3. past events; those connected with a person or thing. 4. an interesting or eventful past. —**history painting**, pictorial representation of an event or series of events. **make history**, to do something memorable; to be the first to do something. [from Latin from Greek *historia* = finding out by enquiry, narrative]

histrionic /hɪstrɪ'ɒnɪk/ adj. of acting; dramatic or theatrical in manner. —n. (in *plural*) theatricals; dramatic behaviour intended to impress others. [from Latin *histrio* = actor]

hit v.t./i. (-tt-; past and past participle **hit**) 1. to strike with a blow or missile; to aim a blow *at*; to come against (a thing) with force. 2. to have an effect on (a person), to cause to suffer. 3. to propel (a ball etc.) with a bat or club; to score runs or points thus. 4. (*colloquial*) to encounter, to reach. 5. (*slang*) to attack, to raid. —n. 1. a blow, a stroke. 2. a shot that reaches its target. 3. a success, especially in popularity. —**hit-and-run** adj. causing damage or injury and fleeing immediately. **hit back**, to retaliate. **hit in the eye**, to be glaringly obviously to. **hit it off**, to get on well (*with* a person). **hit list**, (*slang*) a list of people to be killed or eliminated etc. **hit man**, (*slang*) a hired assassin. **hit the nail on the head**, to guess or explain precisely. **hit on**, to find (a solution etc., especially by chance). **hit-or-miss** adj. aimed or done carelessly. **hit out**, to deal vigorous blows (*literally* or *figuratively*). **hit parade**, a list of the best-selling records of popular music. **hit the road**, (*slang*) to depart. [Old English from Old Norse = meet with]

hitch v.t./i. 1. to move (a thing) with a slight jerk. 2. to fasten or be fastened with a loop or hook etc. 3. to hitchhike; to obtain (a lift) in this way. —n. 1. a temporary difficulty, a snag. 2. a slight jerk. 3. any of various kinds of noose or knot. —**get hitched**, (*slang*) to get married.

Hitchcock /'hɪtʃkɒk/ Alfred 1899–1980. English director of suspense films, noted for his camera work, and for making 'walk-ons' (fleeting apearances) in his own films. His movies include *The Thirty-Nine Steps* 1935, *The Lady Vanishes* 1939, *Rebecca* 1940, *Strangers on a Train* 1951, *Psycho* 1960, and *The Birds* 1963.

hitchhike v.i. to travel by seeking free rides in passing vehicles. —**hitchhiker** n.

hither /'hɪðə/ adv. to or towards this place. —adj. situated on this side; the nearer (of two). —**hither and thither**, to and fro. [Old English]

hitherto /hɪðə'tuː/ adv. until this time, up to now.

Hitler /'hɪtlə/ Adolf 1889–1945. German Nazi dictator, born in Austria. Führer (leader) of the Nazi party from 1921, author of *Mein Kampf/My Struggle* 1925–27. As chancellor of Germany from 1933 and head of state from 1934, he created a dictatorship by playing party and state institutions against each other and continually creating new offices and appointments. His position was not seriously challenged until the 'Bomb Plot' of 20 July 1944 (see ◊July plot) to assassinate him. In foreign affairs, he reoccupied the Rhineland and formed an alliance with the Italian Fascist Mussolini in 1936, annexed Austria in 1938, and occupied the Sudetenland under the ◊Munich Agreement. The rest of Czechoslovakia was annexed in March 1939. The ◊Hitler–Stalin pact was followed in Sept by the invasion of Poland and the declaration of war by Britain and France (see ◊World War II). He committed suicide as Berlin fell.

Hitler–Stalin pact see ◊Nazi-Soviet pact.

Hittite /'hɪtaɪt/ n. 1. a member of a group of people who inhabited Anatolia and N Syria from the 3rd millennium to the 1st millennium BC. The city of Hattusas (now Boğazköy in central Turkey) became the capital of a strong kingdom which overthrew the Babylonian empire. After a period of eclipse the Hittite New Empire became a great power (about 1400–1200 BC), which successfully waged war with Egypt. 2. their Indo-European language. 3. in the Bible, a member of a Canaanite or Syrian tribe. [from Hebrew]

HIV abbreviation of human immunodeficiency virus, the infectious agent that causes ◊AIDS.

hive /haɪv/ n. 1. a box etc. for housing bees. 2. the bees occupying a hive. 3. a scene of busy activity. —v.t./i. place (bees) in a hive; to store (as) in a hive. —**hive off**, to separate from a larger group. [Old English]

hives n.pl. a skin eruption, especially nettle rash. [originally Scottish]

HM abbreviation of Her or His Majesty('s).

HMS abbreviation of Her or His Majesty's Ship.

HMSO abbreviation of Her or His Majesty's Stationery Office.

HNC abbreviation of Higher National Certificate.

HND abbreviation of Higher National Diploma.

ho /həu/ interjection expressing triumph or scorn, or calling attention.

Ho symbol for ◊holmium.

hoard n. a carefully kept store of money etc. —v.t./i. to amass and store in a hoard. —**hoarder** n. [Old English]

hoarding n. a temporary fence of light boards round a building; a structure erected to carry advertisements etc. [from obsolete *hoard* from Anglo-French]

hoarfrost n. frozen water vapour on lawns etc. [Old English *hār*]

hoarse adj. 1. (of the voice) rough and deep-sounding, husky, croaking. 2. having a hoarse voice. —**hoarsely** adv., **hoarseness** n. [from Old Norse and Old English]

hoary adj. 1. (of the hair) white or grey with age; having such hair, aged. 2. (of a joke etc.) old.

hoatzin *n.* a tropical bird *Opisthocomus hoatzin* found only in the Amazon, resembling a small pheasant in size and appearance. Adults are olive with white markings above and red-brown below.

hoax *v.t.* to deceive, especially by way of a joke. —*n.* a humorous or mischievous deception. —**hoaxer** *n.* [probably contraction of *hocus*]

hob *n.* a flat metal shelf at the side of a fireplace, where a kettle, pan etc., can be kept hot; a flat heating surface on a cooker.

Hoban /'həʊbən/ James C 1762–1831. Irish-born architect who emigrated to the USA. He designed the White House, Washington DC; he also worked on the Capitol and other public buildings.

Hobart /'həʊbɑːt/ capital and port of Tasmania, Australia; population (1986) 180,000. Products include zinc, textiles, and paper. Founded in 1804 as a penal colony, it was named after Lord Hobart, then secretary of state for the colonies.

Hobbema /'hɒbɪmə/ Meindert 1638–1709. Dutch landscape painter; a pupil of Ruisdael. His early work is derivative, but later works are characteristically realistic and unsentimental. He was popular with English collectors in the 18th and 19th centuries, and influenced English landscape painting.

Hobbes /hɒbz/ Thomas 1588–1679. English political philosopher and the first thinker since Aristotle to attempt to develop a comprehensive theory of nature, including human behaviour. In *The Leviathan* 1651, he advocates absolutist government as the only means of ensuring order and security; he saw this as deriving from the ◊social contract. He was tutor to the exiled Prince Charles.

hobbit /'hɒbɪt/ *n.* any of the imaginary dwarfish creatures in stories by J R R Tolkien. [invented by Tolkien and said by him to mean 'hole-builder']

Hobbit, The /'hɒbɪt/ or *There and Back Again* a fantasy for children by J R R ◊Tolkien, published in the UK in 1937. It describes the adventures of Bilbo Baggins, a 'hobbit' (small humanoid) in an ancient world, Middle-Earth, populated by dragons, dwarves, elves, and other mythical creatures, including the wizard Gandalf. *The Hobbit*, together with Tolkien's later trilogy *The Lord of the Rings* 1954–55, achieved cult status in the 1960s.

hobble *v.t./i.* **1.** to walk lamely; to cause to do this. **2.** to tie the legs of (a horse etc.) to limit its movement. —*n.* **1.** a hobbling walk. **2.** a rope etc. for hobbling a horse.

hobby[1] *n.* an occupation or activity pursued for pleasure, not as a livelihood.

hobby[2] *n.* a small falcon *Falco subbuteo* found across Europe and N Asia. It is about 30 cm/1 ft long, with a grey back, streaked front and chestnut thighs. It is found in open woods and heaths, and feeds on insects and small birds.

hobbyhorse *n.* **1.** a stick with a horse's head, used as a toy; a figure of a horse used in the morris dance etc. **2.** a favourite subject or idea. [from *Hobby*, pet form of name Robin]

hobgoblin /'hɒbgɒblɪn/ *n.* a mischievous or evil spirit; a bugbear. [from *Hob*, pet form of Robin (Goodfellow)]

hobnail *n.* a heavy-headed nail for boot soles.

hobnob *v.i.* (-bb-) to associate or spend time (*with*). [from *hob or nob* give or take, of alternate drinking]

hobo /'həʊbəʊ/ *n.* (*plural* **hobos**) (*US*) a wandering workman or tramp.

Hobson's choice /'hɒbsənz/ the option of taking what is offered or nothing. [from T *Hobson* (died 1631), Cambridge carrier who hired horses on this basis, customers being obliged to take the one nearest to the stable door]

Hochhuth /'hɒʊxhuːt/ Rolf 1931– . Swiss dramatist, whose controversial play *Soldaten/Soldiers* 1968 implied that the British politician Churchill was involved in a plot to assassinate the Polish general ◊Sikorski.

Ho Chi Minh /həʊ tʃi: 'mɪn/ adopted name of Nguyen That Tan 1890–1969. North Vietnamese Communist politician, premier and president 1954–69. Having trained in Moscow shortly after the ◊Russian Revolution, he headed the communist Vietminh from 1941 and fought against the French during the Indochina War 1946–54, becoming president and prime minister of the republic at the armistice. Aided by the communist bloc, he did much to develop industrial potential. He relinquished the premiership in 1955, but continued as president. In the years before his death, Ho successfully led his country's

fight against US-aided South Vietnam in the Vietnam War 1954–75.

Ho Chi Minh City /həʊ tʃi: 'mɪn/ (until 1976 **Saigon**) chief port and industrial city of S Vietnam; population (1985) 3,500,000. Industries include shipbuilding, textiles, rubber, and food products. Saigon was the capital of the Republic of Vietnam (South Vietnam) from 1954 to 1976, when it was renamed.

Ho Chi Minh Trails North Vietnamese troop and supply routes to South Vietnam via Laos during the Vietnam War, 1954–75.

hock[1] *n.* the joint of a quadruped's hind leg between the knee and the fetlock. [from obsolete *hockshin* from Old English]

hock[2] *n.* a German white wine, properly that of Hochheim on the River Main. [abbreviation of obsolete *hockamore* from *Hochheimer* (German name of the wine)]

hock[3] *v.t.* (*slang*) to pawn. —**in hock**, in pawn; in prison; in debt. [from Dutch *hok* = hutch, prison]

hockey[1] /'hɒkɪ/ *n.* a game played with hooked sticks and a ball, the object being to hit the ball into the goal. It is played between two teams, each of not more than 11 players. Hockey has been an Olympic sport since 1908 for men and since 1980 for women. In North America it is known as 'field hockey', to distinguish it from ◊ice hockey.

hockey[2] /'hɒkɪ/ *n.* in the game of darts, the line from which the player throws.

Hockney /'hɒkni/ David 1937– . English painter, printmaker, and designer, resident in California. He exhibited at the Young Contemporaries Show of 1961 and contributed to the Pop art movement. He developed an individual figurative style, as in his portrait *Mr and Mrs Clark and Percy* 1971, Tate Gallery, London, and has prolifically experimented with technique. His views of swimming pools reflect a preoccupation with surface pattern and effects of light. He has also produced drawings etchings, photo collages, and sets for opera.

hocus-pocus /həʊkəs 'pəʊkəs/ *n.* trickery.

hod *n.* **1.** a builder's light trough on a pole for carrying bricks etc. **2.** a container for shovelling and holding coal. [probably from Old French *hotte* = pannier]

Hodeida /hɒ'deɪdə/ or *Al Hudaydah* Red Sea port of Yemen; population (1986) 155,000. It trades in coffee and spices.

hodgepodge /'hɒdʒpɒdʒ/ variant of **hotchpotch**.

Hodgkin /'hɒdʒkɪn/ Alan Lloyd 1914– . British physiologist engaged in research with Andrew Huxley on the mechanism of conduction in peripheral nerves 1946–60. In 1963 they shared the Nobel Prize for Physiology and Medicine with John Eccles.

Hodgkin Dorothy Crowfoot 1910– . English biochemist who analysed the structure of penicillin, insulin, and vitamin B12. Hodgkin was the first to use a computer to analyse the molecular structure of complex chemicals, and this enabled her to produce three-dimensional models. She was awarded the Nobel Prize for Chemistry in 1964.

Hodgkin's disease a rare form of cancer (also known as **lymphoadenoma**), mainly affecting the lymph nodes and spleen. It undermines the immune system, leaving the sufferer susceptible to infection. However, it responds well to radiotherapy and ◊cytotoxic drugs, and long-term survival is usual.

Hodza /'hɒdʒə/ Milan 1878–1944. Czechoslovak politician, prime minister from Feb 1936. He and President Beneš were forced to agree to the secession of the Sudeten areas of Czechoslovakia to Germany before resigning on 22 Sept 1938 (see ◊Munich Agreement).

hoe *n.* a long-handled tool with a blade, used for loosening the soil or scraping up weeds etc. —*v.t./i.* (*participle* **hoeing**) to weed (crops), to loosen (ground), to dig up (weeds), with a hoe. [from Old French *houe*]

Hofei /həʊ'feɪ/ former name of ◊Hefei, city in China.

Hoffman /'hɒfmən/ Abbie (Abbot) 1936–1989. US leftwing political activist, founder of the Yippies (Youth International Party), a political offshoot of the ◊hippies. He was a member of the Chicago Seven, a radical group tried for attempting to disrupt the 1968 Democratic convention.

Hoffman Dustin 1937– . US actor, who won Academy Awards for his performances in *Kramer vs Kramer* 1979 and *Rain Man* 1988. His other films include *The Graduate* 1967 and *Midnight Cowboy* 1969.

Hodgkin *Nobel prizewinner in chemistry, Professor Dorothy Crowfoot Hodgkin is the first woman since Florence Nightingale to be awarded the Order of Merit.*

Hoffmann E(rnst) T(heodor) A(madeus) 1776–1822. German composer and writer. He composed the opera *Undine* 1816 and many fairy stories, including *Nüssknacker/Nutcracker* 1816. His stories inspired ◊Offenbach's *Tales of Hoffmann.*

Hoffmann Josef 1870–1956. Austrian architect, one of the founders of the Wiener Werkstätte, (a modern design cooperative of early 20th-century Vienna), and a pupil of Otto ◊Wagner.

Hofstadter /ˈhɒfstætə/ Robert 1915– . US high-energy physicist who revealed the structure of the atomic nucleus. He demonstrated that the nucleus is composed of a high-energy core and a surrounding area of decreasing density. He shared the 1961 Nobel Prize for Physics with Rudolf Mössbauer.

hog *n.* 1. a castrated male pig. 2. (*colloquial*) a greedy person. —*v.t./i.* (**-gg-**) to take greedily; to hoard selfishly. —**go the whole hog**, (*slang*) to do a thing thoroughly. **hog's back**, a steep-sided hill ridge. —**hoggish** *adj.* [Old English]

Hogan Paul 1940– . Australian TV comic, film actor and producer. He gained international fame after the success of the feature films *Crocodile Dundee* 1986 and *Crocodile Dundee 11* 1988, of which he was co-writer, star, and producer. *Crocodile Dundee* was the most profitable film in Australian history and set box office records in the USA.

Hogarth /ˈhəʊɡɑːθ/ William 1697–1764. English painter and engraver who produced portraits and moralizing genre scenes, such as the series *A Rake's Progress* 1735. His portraits are remarkably direct and full of character, for example *Heads of Six of Hogarth's Servants c.*1750–55 (Tate Gallery, London).

Hogg /hɒɡ/ James 1770–1835. Scottish novelist and poet, known as the 'Ettrick Shepherd'. He was born in Ettrick Forest, Selkirkshire, and worked as a shepherd at Yarrow 1790–99. Until the age of 30, he was illiterate. His novel *Confessions of a Justified Sinner* 1824 is a masterly portrayal of personified evil.

Hogg Quintin. British politician; see Lord ◊Hailsham.

hogmanay /ˈhɒɡməneɪ/ *n.* (*Scottish*) New Year's Eve. [compare Old French *aguillanneuf*]

hogshead *n.* a large cask; a liquid or dry measure, usually about 50 gallons.

hogwash *n.* nonsense, rubbish.

hogweed *n.* a tall plant of the genus *Heracleum*, with thick, hollow stems and umbrellalike clusters of white or pinkish flowers, liable to be eaten by animals.

Hohenlinden, Battle of /ˈhəʊən'lɪndən/ in the French ◊Revolutionary Wars, a defeat of the Austrians by the French in Dec 1800. Coming after the defeat at ◊Marengo,

it led the Austrians to make peace at the Treaty of Lunéville 1801.

Hohenstaufen /ˈhəʊən'ʃtaʊfən/ German family of princes, several members of which were Holy Roman emperors 1138–1208 and 1214–54. They were the first German emperors to make use of associations with Roman law and tradition to aggrandize their office, and included Conrad III; Frederick I (Barbarossa), the first to use the title Holy Roman emperor; Henry VI; and Frederick II. The last of the line, Conradin, was executed in 1268 with the approval of Pope Clement IV while attempting to gain his Sicilian inheritance.

Hohenzollern /ˈhəʊən'zɒlən/ German family, originating in Württemberg, the main branch of which held the titles of ◊elector of Brandenburg from 1415, king of Prussia from 1701, and German emperor from 1871. The last emperor, Wilhelm II, was dethroned in 1918 after the disastrous course of World War I. Another branch of the family were kings of Romania 1881–1947.

Hohhot /hɒˈhɒt/ formerly **Huhehot** city and capital of Inner Mongolia autonomous region, China; population (1984) 778,000. Industries include textiles, electronics, and dairy products. There are Lamaist monasteries and temples here.

ho-ho /həʊˈhəʊ/ interjection expressing surprise, triumph, or derision.

hoick *v.t.* (*slang*) to lift or bring (*out*), especially with a jerk.

hoi polloi /hɔɪ pəˈbɪ/ the masses, the common people. [Greek = the many]

hoist *v.t.* to raise or haul up; to lift with ropes and pulleys etc. —*n.* 1. an apparatus for hoisting things. 2. hoisting. —**hoist with one's own petard**, caught by one's own trick etc. [alteration of *hoise*, probably from Low German]

hoity-toity /ˈhɔɪtiˈtɔɪti/ *adj.* haughty. [from obsolete *hoit* = indulge in riotous mirth]

Hokkaido /hɒˈkaɪdəʊ/ northernmost of the four main islands of Japan, separated from Honshu to the S by Tsugaru Strait and from Sakhalin to the N by Soya Strait; **area** 83,500 sq km/32,231 sq mi; **capital** Sapporo; **population** (1986) 5,678,000, including 16,000 ◊Ainus. Natural resources include coal, mercury, manganese, oil and natural gas, timber, and fisheries. Coal mining and agriculture are the main industries.

hokum /ˈhəʊkəm/ *n.* (*slang*) 1. a speech, action, or properties etc. used in a play or film to make a sentimental or melodramatic appeal to an audience. 2. bunkum.

Hokusai /ˈhəʊkuˈsaɪ/ Katsushika 1760–1849. Japanese artist, the leading printmaker of his time. He published *Fugaku Sanjū-rokkei/Views of Mount Fuji* about 1823–29, and produced outstanding pictures of almost every kind of subject: birds, flowers, courtesans, and scenes from legend and everyday life.

Holbein /ˈhɒlbaɪn/ Hans, **the Elder** *c.*1464–1524. German painter, active in Augsburg. His works include altarpieces, such as that of *St Sebastian*, 1516 (Alte Pinakothek, Munich). He also painted portraits and designed stained glass.

Holbein Hans, **the Younger** 1497/98–1543. German painter and woodcut artist; the son and pupil of Hans Holbein the Elder. Holbein was born in Augsburg. In 1515 he went to Basel, where he became friendly with Erasmus; he painted three portraits of him in 1523, which were strongly influenced by Quentin ◊Matsys. He travelled widely in Europe and was court painter to England's Henry VIII from 1536. He also painted portraits of Thomas More and Thomas Cromwell; a notable woodcut series is *Dance of Death* about 1525. Pronounced Renaissance influence emerged in the *Meyer Madonna* 1526, a fine altarpiece in Darmstadt. During his time at the English court, he also painted miniature portraits, inspiring Nicholas ◊Hilliard.

hold[1] /həʊld/ *v.t./i.* (*past* and *past participle* **held**) 1. to take and keep in one's hand(s), arms, teeth etc.; to grasp. 2. to keep in a particular position or condition; to grasp so as to control; to detain in custody; to keep (a person) *to* (a promise etc.). 3. to be able to contain. 4. to have in one's possession; to have gained (a qualification or achievement); to have the position of, to occupy (a job or office). 5. to occupy militarily; to keep possession of (a place) against attack; to keep the attention of; to dominate (the stage etc.). 6. to conduct or celebrate (a conversation, meeting, festival etc.). **7.** to remain unbroken under pressure etc.; (of weather) to continue fine; (of a circumstance or condition) to remain. **8.** to believe, to consider; to assert. **9.** to restrain; (*colloquial*) to cause to cease action or movement. —*n.* **1.** the act or manner of holding something; grasp (*literal* or *figurative*). **2.** a means of exerting influence. —**hold back,** to restrain; to hesitate, to refrain *from*. **hold down,** to repress; (*colloquial*) to be competent enough to keep (one's job). **hold forth,** to speak at length or tediously. **hold it!** cease action etc. **hold the line,** not to ring off (on the telephone). **hold off,** to delay; to keep one's distance; not to begin. **hold on,** to maintain one's grasp; to wait a moment; not to ring off (on the telephone). **hold one's own,** to maintain one's position, not to be beaten. **hold out,** to offer (an inducement etc.); (of supplies etc.) to last; to maintain resistance; to continue to make a demand *for*. **hold out on,** (*colloquial*) to refuse something to (a person). **hold over,** to postpone. **hold up,** to hinder or obstruct; to support or sustain; to stop with force and rob. **hold-up** *n.* a stoppage or delay; a robbery by force. **hold water,** (of reasoning) to be sound, to bear examination. **hold with** (usually with *negative*), to approve of. **no holds barred,** with all restrictions on methods etc. relaxed. **take hold,** (of a custom or habit) to become established. —**holder** *n.* [Old English]

hold² *n.* a cavity below the deck of a ship for cargo. [Old English (related to *hollow*)]

holdall *n.* a large, soft travelling bag.

Holden /ˈhəʊldən/ William. Stage name of William Franklin Beedle 1918–1981. US film actor, a star in the late 1940s and 1950s. He played leading roles in *The Wild Bunch* 1969, *Sunset Boulevard* 1950, *Stalag 17* 1953, and *Network* 1976.

holdfast *n.* **1.** a clamp securing an object to a wall etc. **2.** an organ found at the base of many seaweeds, attaching them to the sea bed. It may be a flattened, suckerlike structure, or dissected and fingerlike, growing into rock crevices and firmly anchoring the plant.

holding *n.* the tenure of land; land or stocks held. —**holding company,** one formed to hold the shares of other companies, which it then controls.

hole *n.* **1.** an empty place in a solid body or mass; a sunken place on a surface; an opening through something. **2.** an animal's burrow. **3.** a small or gloomy place. **4.** (*slang*) an awkward situation. **5.** a hollow or cavity into which the ball etc. must be got in various games; in golf, a section of a course between the tee and the hole. —*v.t./i.* **1.** to make a hole or holes in; to pierce the side of (a ship). **2.** to put into a hole. —**hole-and-corner** *adj.* underhand. **hole in the heart,** a congenital defect in the heart membrane. **hole up,** (*US slang*) to hide oneself. **make a hole in,** to use a large amount of (one's supply). **pick holes in,** to find fault with. —**holey** *adj.* [Old English]

Holi /ˈhəʊli/ *n.* a Hindu spring festival celebrated in February or March in honour of Krishna the amorous cowherd. [Hindi from Sanskrit]

holiday /ˈhɒlɪdeɪ/ *n.* **1.** a day of break from one's normal work, especially for recreation or festivity; (also in *plural*) a period of this, a period of recreation away from home. **2.** a religious festival. —*v.i.* to spend a holiday. [Old English = *holy day*]

Holiday Billie. Stage name of Eleanora Gough McKay 1915–1959. US jazz singer, also known as 'Lady Day'. She made her debut in Harlem clubs and became known for her emotionally charged delivery and idiosyncratic phrasing; she brought a blues feel to performances with swing bands. Songs she made her own include 'Strange Fruit' and 'I Cover the Waterfront'.

holiday camp a site that provides an all-inclusive holiday, usually with entertainment, at an inclusive price. The first holiday camp on a permanent site was opened in 1894 near Douglas, Isle of Man, by Joseph Cunningham. Billy ◊Butlin's first camp (accommodating 3,000 people) opened at Skegness in 1935.

holiness /ˈhəʊlɪnɪs/ *n.* being holy or sacred. —**His Holiness,** the title of the pope. [Old English]

Holinshed /ˈhɒlɪnʃed/ Ralph *c.*1520–*c.*1580. English historian who published two volumes of the *Chronicles of England, Scotland and Ireland* 1578, on which Shakespeare based his history plays.

Holiday *Acknowledged as the supreme jazz singer of her day, Billie Holiday brought an individual blues sound to all her songs.*

holism *n.* **1.** in philosophy, the concept that the whole is greater than the sum of its parts. **2.** in medicine, the idea that physical and mental wellbeing are inextricably linked, so that all aspects of a patient's life must be taken into account. [from Greek *holos* = whole]

holistic /hɒˈlɪstɪk/ *adj.* of or involving the whole. —**holistic medicine,** a form of medical treatment that attempts to deal with the whole person and not merely with his or her physical condition.

Holkeri /ˈhɒlkəri/ Harri 1937– . Finnish politician, prime minister from 1987. Joining the centrist National Coalition Party (KOK) at an early age, he eventually became its national secretary.

holland /ˈhɒlənd/ *n.* a smooth, hard-wearing linen fabric. —**brown holland,** this fabric unbleached. [from *Holland* = Netherlands]

Holland Henry Richard Vassall Fox, 3rd Baron 1773–1840. British Whig politician. He was Lord Privy Seal 1806–07. His home, at Holland House, London, was for many years the centre of Whig political and literary society.

Holland John Philip 1840–1914. Irish engineer who developed some of the first submarines. He began work in Ireland in the late 1860s and emigrated to the USA in 1873. His first successful boat was launched in 1881 and, after several failures, he built the *Holland* in 1893, which was bought by the US Navy two years later.

Holland Sidney George 1893–1961. New Zealand politician, leader of the National Party 1940–57 and prime minister 1949–57.

holler *v.t./i.* (*US colloquial*) to shout. —*n.* a shout.

Hollerith /ˈhɒlərɪθ/ Herman 1860–1929. US inventor of a mechanical tabulating machine, the first device for data processing. Hollerith's tabulator was widely publicized after being successfully used in the 1890 census. The firm he established, the Tabulating Machine Company, was later one of the founding companies of International Business Machines (IBM).

hollow /ˈhɒləʊ/ *adj.* **1.** having a space or cavity inside, not solid. **2.** having a sunken area. **3.** hungry. **4.** (of a sound) echoing, as if made in or on a hollow container. **5.** without validity, worthless. **6.** cynical, insincere. —*n.* a hollow or sunken place, a hole; a valley. —*adv.* completely. —*v.t./i.* (often with *out*) to make or become hollow. —**hollowly** *adv.* [from Old English *holh* = cave]

holly *n.* a tree or shrub of the genus *Ilex*, family Aquifoliaceae, including the English **Christmas holly** *I. aquifolium*, an evergreen with spiny, glossy leaves, small white flowers, and poisonous scarlet berries on the female tree. Leaves of the **Brazilian holly** *I. paraguayensis* are used to make the tea **yerba maté**. [Old English]

Holly /'hɒli/ Buddy. Stage name of Charles Hardin Holley 1936–1959. US rock-and-roll singer, guitarist, and songwriter, born in Lubbock, Texas. Holly had a distinctive, hiccuping vocal style and was an early experimenter with recording techniques. Many of his hits with his band, the Crickets, such as 'That'll Be the Day' 1957, 'Peggy Sue' 1957, and 'Maybe Baby' 1958, have become classics. He died in a plane crash.

hollyhock /'hɒlɪhɒk/ n. a plant of the genus *Althaea* of the mallow family Malvaceae. *A. rosea*, originally a native of Asia, produces spikes of large white, yellow, or red flowers, growing up to 3 m/10 ft high when cultivated as a biennial. The hollyhock was introduced into Britain four centuries ago. [originally = marsh mallow, from *holy* and obsolete *hock* = mallow]

Hollywood /'hɒlɪwʊd/ a suburb of Los Angeles, California, USA; the centre of the American film industry from 1911.

holmium /'həʊlmɪəm/ n. a silvery, metallic element of the ◊lanthanide series, symbol Ho, atomic number 67, relative atomic mass 164.93. It occurs in combination with other rare-earths and in various minerals such as gadolinite. Its compounds are highly magnetic. [from *Holmia* = Stockholm, native city of its discoverer P T Cleve (1840–1905)]

holm oak /'həʊm ʊk/ an evergreen oak *Quercus ilex* with hollylike leaves, also known as the ilex. [from dialect *holm* = holly]

holocaust /'hɒləkɔːst/ n. large-scale destruction, especially by fire. [from Old French from Latin from Greek *holos* = whole and *kaustos* = burnt]

Holocaust, the the annihilation of more than 16 million people by the Hitler regime 1933–45 in the numerous extermination and ◊concentration camps, most notably Auschwitz, Sobibor, Treblinka, and Maidanek in Poland, and Belsen, Buchenwald, and Dachau in Germany. Of the victims, more than 6 million were Jews (over 67% of European Jewry); 10 million Ukrainian, Polish, and Russian civilians and prisoners of war; Romanies, socialists, homosexuals, and others (labelled 'defectives') were also imprisoned and/or exterminated. Victims were variously starved, tortured, experimented on, worked to death, and executed in gas chambers, or by shooting and hanging.

Holocene /'hɒləsiːn/ adj. of the epoch of geological time that began 10,000 years ago, the second epoch of the Quaternary period. —n. this period. During the Holocene, glaciers retreated, the climate became warmer, and humans developed significantly.

hologram /'hɒləgræm/ n. a photographic pattern that gives a three-dimensional image when illuminated with coherent light. [from Greek *holos* = whoie]

holograph¹ /'hɒləgrɑːf/ v.t. to record as a hologram. —**holographic** /-'græfɪk/ adj.

holograph² adj. wholly written by the person named as the author. —n. a holograph document. [from French or Latin from Greek *holos* = whole]

holography /hɒ'lɒgrəfɪ/ n. a method of producing three-dimensional (3-D) images by means of ◊laser light. Although the possibility of holography was suggested as early as 1947, it could not be demonstrated until a pure coherent light source, the laser, became available in 1963. Holography uses a photographic technique (involving the splitting of a laser beam into two beams) to produce a picture, or hologram, that contains 3-D information about the object photographed. Some holograms show meaningless patterns in ordinary light and produce a 3-D image only when laser light is projected through them, but reflection holograms produce images when ordinary light is reflected from them (as found on credit cards).

Holst /həʊlst/ Gustav(us Theodore von) 1874–1934. English composer. He wrote operas, including *Savitri* 1916 and *At the Boar's Head* 1925; ballets; choral works, including *Hymns from the Rig Veda* 1911 and *The Hymn of Jesus* 1920; orchestral suites, including *The Planets* 1918; and songs. He was a lifelong friend of Ralph ◊Vaughan Williams, with whom he shared an enthusiasm for English folk music. His musical style, although tonal and drawing on folk song, tends to be severe.

holster /'həʊlstə/ n. a leather case for a pistol or revolver, usually fixed to a saddle or belt.

Holt /həʊlt/ Harold Edward 1908–1967. Australian Liberal politician, prime minister 1966–67.

Holtby /'həʊltbi/ Winifred 1898–1935. English novelist, poet, and journalist. She was an ardent advocate of women's freedom and racial equality, and wrote the novel *South Riding* 1936, set in her native Yorkshire. Her other works include an analysis of women's position in contemporary society *Women and a Changing Civilization* 1934.

holy /'həʊli/ adj. 1. of God and therefore regarded with reverence; associated with God or religion. 2. consecrated, sacred. 3. devoted to the service of God. —**holier-than-thou** adj. (colloquial) self-righteous. **Holy Communion**, the ◊Eucharist, a Christian sacrament. **Holy Father**, the title of the pope. **Holy Ghost**, the Holy Spirit. **Holy Land**, W Palestine. **holy of holies**, the sacred inner chamber of a Jewish temple; any place or retreat regarded as most sacred. **Holy See**, papacy or papal court. **Holy Shroud**, the ◊Turin shroud. **Holy Spirit**, the third Person of the Trinity, God acting spiritually. **Holy Week**, the week before Easter Sunday. **Holy Writ**, holy writing, especially the Bible. [Old English]

Holy Alliance a 'Christian Union of Charity, Peace, and Love' initiated by Alexander I of Russia in 1815 and signed by every crowned head in Europe. The alliance became associated with Russian attempts to preserve autocratic monarchies at any price, and an excuse to meddle in the internal affairs of other states.

Holy Grail in Christian legend, the dish or cup used by Jesus at the Last Supper. Together with the spear with which he was wounded at the Crucifixion, it was an object of quest by King Arthur's knights in certain stories incorporated in the Arthurian legend.

Holyoake /'həʊliəʊk/ Keith Jacka 1904–1983. New Zealand National Party politician, prime minister in 1957 (for two months) and 1960–72.

Holy Office a tribunal of the Roman Catholic Church that deals with ecclesiastical discipline; see ◊Inquisition.

holy orders Christian priesthood, as conferred by the laying on of hands by a bishop. It is held by the Roman Catholic, Eastern Orthodox, and Anglican churches to have originated in Jesus' choosing of the apostles.

Holy Roman Empire the empire of ◊Charlemagne and his successors, and the German empire 962–1806, both being regarded as the Christian (hence 'holy') revival of the Roman Empire. At its height it comprised much of western and central Europe.

Holyrood House /'hɒlɪruːd/ a royal residence in Edinburgh, Scotland. The palace was built in 1498–1503 on the site of a 12th-century abbey by James IV. It has associations with Mary, Queen of Scots and Charles Edward, the Young Pretender.

holystone /'həʊlɪstəʊn/ n. a soft sandstone formerly used for scouring the decks of ships. —v.t. to scour with this. [probably from *holy* and *stone*; the stones were called *bibles*, perhaps because used while kneeling]

homage /'hɒmɪdʒ/ n. a tribute, an expression of reverence; in feudal law, a formal expression of allegiance. [from Old French from Latin *hominaticum* (*homo* = man)]

Homburg /'hɒmbɜːg/ n. a man's hat with a curled brim and a lengthwise dent in the crown. [from *Homburg* in Germany, where first worn]

home n. 1. the place where one lives; the fixed residence of a family or household. 2. one's native land; the district where one was born or has lived for a long time, or to which one feels attached. 3. a dwelling house or flat. 4. an institution where those needing care or rest etc. may live. 5. the place where a thing originates or is most common; the natural environment of a plant or animal. 6. the finishing point in a race etc. 7. in games, a home match or win. —adj. 1. of or connected with one's home or country; carried on, done, or produced there. 2. (of a game or team) played or playing on one's own ground etc. —adv. 1. to or at one's home. 2. to the point aimed at; as far as possible. —v.t./i. 1. (of a pigeon etc.) to make its way home. 2. (of a vessel, missile etc.) to be guided (in) to a destination or on a target. —**at home**, in one's own house etc.; at ease; familiar or well-informed (in, on, with, a subject); available to callers. **at-home** n. a reception of visitors within certain hours. **bring home to**, to cause to realize fully. **home and dry**, having achieved one's aim. **home-brew** n. beer brewed at home. **home economics**, the study of household management. **home farm**, a farm worked by the owner of an estate containing other farms. **home help**, a person who helps with housework etc., especially in a service organized by a local authority. **home-made** *adj.* made at home. **home truth,** a (usually unwelcome) truth about oneself heard from another. [Old English]

Home Counties the counties in close proximity to London, England: Hertfordshire, Essex, Kent, Surrey, and formerly Middlesex.

home front a term describing the organized sectors of domestic activity in wartime, mainly associated with World Wars I and II. Features of the home front in World War II included the organization of the black-out, evacuation, air raid shelters, ARP posts, the 'home guard', rationing, distribution of gas masks. With many men on active military service, women were called upon to carry out jobs previously only undertaken by men.

Home Guard an unpaid force formed in Britain in May 1940 to repel the expected German invasion, and known until July 1940 as the Local Defence Volunteers. It consisted of men aged 17–65 who had not been called up, formed part of the armed forces of the crown, and was subject to military law. Over 2 million strong in 1944, it was disbanded on 31 Dec 1945, but revived in 1951, then placed on a reserve basis in 1955, and ceased activities in 1957.

homeland *n.* 1. one's native land. 2. in the Republic of South Africa, an area reserved for African blacks, 1948– .

homeless *adj.* lacking a dwelling place.

homely *adj.* 1. simple and informal, unpretentious. 2. (*US*, of a person's appearance) plain, not beautiful. —**homeliness** *n.*

Home Office a British government department established in 1782 to deal with all the internal affairs of England except those specifically assigned to other departments. Responsibilities include the police, the prison service, immigration, race relations, and broadcasting. The **home secretary,** the head of the department, holds cabinet rank. There is a separate secretary of state for Scotland and another for Wales. The home secretary has certain duties in respect of the Channel Islands and the Isle of Man.

homeopathy alternative spelling of ◊homoeopathy.

homeothermy *n.* the maintenance of a constant body temperature in endothermic (warm-blooded) animals, by the use of chemical body processes to compensate for heat loss or gain when external temperatures change. Such processes include generation of heat by the breakdown of food and the contraction of muscles, and loss of heat by sweating, panting, and other means.

homer /'həʊmə/ *n.* a homing pigeon.

Homer lived *c.*8th century BC. Legendary Greek epic poet. According to tradition, he was a blind minstrel and the author of the ◊*Iliad* and the ◊*Odyssey.*

Homer Winslow 1836–1910. US painter and lithographer, known for his seascapes, both oils and watercolours, which date from the 1880s and 1890s.

Homeric /həʊ'merɪk/ *adj.* of the writings of Homer; of Bronze Age Greece as described in them. [from Latin from Greek]

Home Rule, Irish the movement to repeal the Act of ◊Union 1801 that joined Ireland to Britain and to establish an Irish parliament responsible for internal affairs. In 1870 Isaac Butt (1813–1879) formed the Home Rule Association and the movement was led in Parliament from 1880 by Charles ◊Parnell. After 1918 the demand for an independent Irish republic replaced that for home rule.

Homes à Court Michael Robert Hamilton 1937–1990. South Africa-born Australian businessman. He acquired interests in the media, the arts, mining. and energy, and acquired a reputation as a takeover specialist. He founded some charitable institutions in Australia.

home service force (HSF) a military unit established in the UK in 1982, linked to the ◊Territorial Army (see under ◊Territorial) and recruited from volunteers of ages 18–60 with previous army (TA or Regular) experience. It was introduced to guard key points and installations likely to be the target of enemy 'special forces' and saboteurs, so releasing other units for mobile defence roles.

homesick *adj.* depressed by absence from home. —**homesickness** *n.*

homespun *adj.* 1. made of yarn spun at home. 2. plain, simple. —*n.* a homespun fabric.

homestead /'həʊmsted/ *n.* 1. a house with its adjoining land and outbuildings, a farm. 2. (*Australian and New*

Zealand) the owner's residence on a sheep or cattle station. [Old English]

Homestead Act in US history, an act of Congress in 1862 to encourage settlement of land in the west by offering 65-hectare/160-acre plots cheaply or even free to those willing to cultivate and improve the land for a stipulated amount of time. By 1900 about 32,400,000 hectares/80,000,000 acres had been distributed. Homestead lands are available to this day.

homeward /'həʊmwəd/ *adv.* or **homewards** towards home. —*adj.* going towards home. [Old English]

homework *n.* work to be done at home by a school pupil; preparatory work or study.

homicide /'hɒmɪsaɪd/ *n.* 1. the killing of one person by another. This may be unlawful, lawful, or excusable, depending on the circumstances. Unlawful homicides include ◊murder, ◊manslaughter, ◊infanticide, and causing death by dangerous driving (vehicular homicide). Lawful homicide occurs where, for example, a police officer is justified in killing a criminal in the course of apprehension. Excusable homicide occurs when a person is killed in self-defence or by accident. 2. a person who kills another. —**homicidal** /-'saɪdəl/ *adj.* [from Old French from Latin *homo* = man]

homily /'hɒmɪlɪ/ *n.* a sermon, a moralizing lecture. —**homiletic** /-'letɪk/ *adj.* [from Latin from Greek *homilia* (*homilos* = crowd)]

homing *adj.* 1. (of a pigeon) trained to fly home from a distance. 2. (of a device) for guiding to a target etc.

hominid /'hɒmɪnɪd/ *adj.* of the zoological family Hominidae that includes existing and fossil man. —*n.* a member of this family. [from Latin *homo* = man]

hominoid /'hɒmɪnɔɪd/ *adj.* manlike. —*n.* an animal resembling man.

homo /'həʊməʊ/ *n.* (*plural* **homos**) (*colloquial*) a homosexual. [abbreviation]

homo- in combinations, same. [from Greek *homos* = same]

homoeopathy /həʊmɪ'ɒpəθɪ/ *n.* the treatment of disease by substances, usually in minute doses, that in a healthy person would produce symptoms like those of the disease. It was introduced by the German physician Samuel Hahnemann (1755–1843), and is contrasted with ◊allopathy. —**homoeopathic** /-'pæθɪk/ *adj.* **homoeopathist, homoeopath** *ns.* [from German from Greek *homoios* = like]

homogeneous /hɒmə'dʒiːnɪəs/ *adj.* of the same kind; consisting of parts all of the same kind. —**homogeneity** /-dʒi'niːɪtɪ/ *n.* [from Latin from Greek *genos* = kind]

homogeneous reaction in chemistry, a reaction where there is no interface between the components. The term applies to all reactions where only gases are involved or where all the components are in solution.

homogenize /hə'mɒdʒɪnaɪz/ *v.t.* 1. to make homogeneous. 2. to treat (milk) so that fat droplets are emulsified and cream does not separate. —**homogenization** /-'zeɪʃən/ *n.*

homograph /'hɒməɡrɑːf/ *n.* a word spelt like another, but of different meaning or origin, e.g. ◊bat[1], ◊bat[2].

homologous /hə'mɒləɡəs/ *adj.* having the same relation or relative position; corresponding; in biology, similar in position and structure but not necessarily in function; in chemistry, forming a series with constant successive differences of composition. [from Latin from Greek *logos* = ratio]

homologous series any of a number of series of organic chemicals whose members differ by a constant relative molecular mass.

homologue /'hɒməlɒɡ/ *n.* a homologous thing. [French from Greek]

homology /hə'mɒlədʒɪ/ *n.* a homologous state or relation. —**homological** /-'lɒdʒɪkəl/ *adj.*

homonym /'hɒmənɪm/ *n.* 1. a word of the same spelling or sound as another but with a different meaning, e.g. ◊pole[1], ◊pole[2]; their, there. 2. a namesake. [from Latin from Greek *onoma* = name]

homophone *n.* a word having the same sound as another, but of different meaning or origin, e.g. son, sun. [from Greek *phōnē* = sound]

homophony *n.* in music, a melody lead and accompanying harmony, as distinct from **heterophony** and **polyphony** in which different melody lines are combined.

Homo sapiens /ˈhəʊməʊ ˈsæpienz/ modern man regarded as a species. [Latin = wise man]

homosexual /ˌhəʊməʊˈseksjʊəl, hɒm-/ adj. feeling sexually attracted to people of the same sex. —n. a homosexual person. —**homosexuality** /-ˈælɪtɪ/ n.

homozygous /ˌhəʊməʊˈzaɪgəs/ adj. in a living organism, having two identical ◊alleles for a given trait. Individuals homozygous for a trait always breed true; that is, they produce offspring that resemble them in appearance when bred with a genetically similar individual; inbred varieties or species are homozygous for almost all traits. ◊Recessive alleles are only expressed in the homozygous condition. See also ◊heterozygous.

Homs /hɒms/ or **Hums** city, capital of Homs district, W Syria, near the Orontes River; population (1981) 355,000. Silk, cereals, and fruit are produced in the area, and industries include silk textiles, oil refining, and jewellery. ◊Zenobia, queen of Palmyra, was defeated at Homs by the Roman emperor ◊Aurelian in 272.

Hon. abbreviation of 1. Honorary. 2. Honourable.

Honan /həʊˈnæn/ former name of ◊Henan, Chinese province.

Honda /ˈhɒndə/ Japanese motorcycle and car manufacturers. They also make racing cars. Their racing motorcycles were first seen in Europe at the 1959 Isle of Man TT races, five years after setting their sights on grand prix racing. Mike Hailwood and Tom Phillis were their first world champions in 1961. They pulled out of motorcycle racing in 1967 but returned in 1979 to become one of the top teams.

Honduras /hɒnˈdjʊərəs/ Republic of; country in Central America, bounded to the N by the Caribbean, to the SE by Nicaragua, to the S by the Pacific, to the SW by El Salvador, and to the W and NW by Guatemala; **area** 112,100 sq km/43,282 sq mi; **capital** Tegucigalpa; **physical** narrow tropical coastal plain with mountainous interior; Bay Islands; **head of state and government** Rafael Leonardo Callejas from 1990; **political system** democratic republic; **exports** coffee, bananas, sugar, timber (including mahogany, rosewood); **population** (1989 est) 5,106,000 (90% mestizo, 10% Indians and Europeans); **language** Spanish, Indian dialects; **recent history** independence was achieved from Spain in 1838, followed by military rule. A civilian government was elected in 1980. Honduras was closely involved with the USA in providing naval and air bases for Nicaraguan 'Contras' in 1983; it declared support for the Central American peace plan to demobilize the Contras in 1989.

hone /həʊn/ n. a whetstone for sharpening razors and tools. —v.t. to sharpen (as) on a hone (literally and figuratively). [Old English = stone]

Honecker /ˈhɒnekə/ Erich 1912– . East German communist politician, in power 1973–89, elected chair of the council of state (head of state) in 1976. He governed in an outwardly austere and efficient manner and, while favouring East–West détente, was a loyal ally of the USSR. In Oct 1989, following a wave of pro-democracy demonstrations, he was replaced as leader of the Socialist Unity Party (SED) and head of state by Egon ◊Krenz, and in Dec expelled from the Communist Party.

Honegger /ˈhɒnegə/ Arthur 1892–1955. Swiss composer, one of ◊Les Six. His work was varied in form, for example, the opera Antigone 1927, the ballet Skating Rink 1922, the oratorio Le Roi David/King David 1921, programme music (Pacific 231 1923), and the Symphonie liturgique/Liturgical Symphony 1946.

Hōnen /ˈhəʊnen/ 1133–1212. Japanese Buddhist monk who founded the ◊Pure Land school of Buddhism.

honest /ˈɒnɪst/ adj. 1. truthful, trustworthy. 2. fairly earned. 3. sincere but undistinguished. [from Old French from Latin honestus (honos = honour)]

honestly adv. 1. in an honest way. 2. really.

honesty n. 1. being honest; truthfulness. 2. a plant of the genus Lunaria, with purple flowers and flat, round, semitransparent seed pods. [from Old French from Latin honestas]

honey /ˈhʌnɪ/ n. 1. the sweet, sticky fluid made by bees from nectar collected from flowers. Honey is made up of various sugars, mainly laevulose and dextrose, with enzymes, colouring matter, acids, and pollen grains. It has antibacterial properties, and was widely used in ancient Egypt, Greece, and Rome as a wound salve. 2. its yellowish

honeysuckle

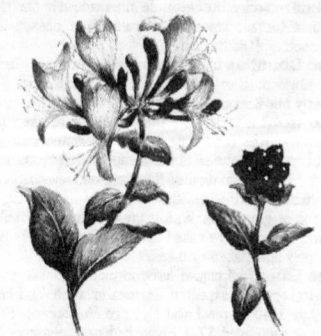

colour. 3. sweetness; a sweet thing. 4. an excellent person or thing; darling (especially as a form of address). —**honeybee** n. the common hive bee Apis mellifera (see ◊bee). —**honeyed** adj. [Old English]

honeycomb n. 1. the bees' wax structure of hexagonal cells for honey and eggs. 2. a pattern arranged hexagonally. —v.t. to fill with cavities or tunnels; to mark with a honeycomb pattern.

honeydew n. 1. a sweet, sticky substance found on leaves and stems, excreted by aphids. 2. a variety of melon with a smooth, pale skin and green flesh.

honey guide in botany, a line or spot on the petals of a flower that indicates to pollinating insects the position of the nectaries (see ◊nectar) within the flower. The orange dot on the lower lip of the toadflax flower Linaria vulgaris is an example. Sometimes the markings reflect only ultraviolet light, which can be seen by many insects although it is not visible to the human eye.

honeymoon n. 1. the holiday spent together by a newly-married couple. 2. an initial period of enthusiasm or goodwill. —v.i. to spend a honeymoon. [from honey and moon, originally with reference to waning affection, not to period of a month]

honeysuckle n. a vine or shrub of the genus Lonicera, family Caprifoliaceae. The **commmon honeysuckle** or **woodbine** L. periclymenum of Europe is a climbing plant with sweet- scented flowers, reddish and yellow-tinted outside and creamy-white inside; it now grows in the NE USA.

Hong Kong /ˈhɒŋ ˈkɒŋ/ British crown colony in SE Asia, comprising Hong Kong island, the Kowloon peninsula, and the mainland New Territories; **area** 1,070 sq km/413 sq mi; **capital** Victoria (Hong Kong City); **exports** textiles, clothing, electronic goods, clocks, watches, cameras, plastic products; a large proportion of the exports and imports of S China are transshipped here; tourism is important; **population** (1986) 5,431,000; 57% Hong Kong Chinese, most of the remainder refugees from the mainland; **languages** English, Chinese; **government** Hong Kong is a British dependency administered by a Crown-appointed governor who presides over an unelected executive council, and a legislative council; **history** formerly part of China, Hong Kong island was occupied by Britain in 1841, and ceded by China in 1842. The Kowloon Peninsula was acquired in 1860 and the New Territories secured on a 99-year lease from 1898. The colony was occupied by Japan 1941–45. Negotiations on Hong Kong's future in 1982 culminated in an agreement, signed in 1984, in which Britain agreed to transfer full sovereignty to China in 1997 in return for Chinese assurance that Hong Kong's social and economic freedom and capitalist lifestyle would be preserved for at least 50 years.

Honiara /hɒniˈɑːrə/ port and capital of the Solomon Islands, on the NW coast of Guadalcanal island; population (1985) 26,000.

honi soit qui mal y pense the motto of England's Order of the Garter. [French = shame on him or her who thinks evil of it]

honk n. 1. the hooting cry of the wild goose. 2. the sound of a vehicle's horn. —v.t./i. to make a honk; to sound (a horn).

honky-tonk /ˈhɒŋkɪtɒŋk/ n. (colloquial) 1. ragtime piano music. 2. a cheap or disreputable nightclub.

Honolulu /ˌhɒnəˈluːluː/ capital city and port of Hawaii, USA, on the S coast of Oahu; population (1980) 365,000. It is a holiday resort, known for its beauty and tropical vegetation, with some industry. Pearl Harbor is 11 km/7 mi to the SW, with naval and military installations. [Hawaiian = sheltered bay]

honorarium /ˌɒnəˈreəriəm/ n. (plural **honorariums**) a voluntary payment for services without the normal fee. [Latin]

honorary /ˈɒnərəri/ adj. 1. conferred as an honour. 2. (of an office or its holder) unpaid. [from Latin honorarius]

honorific /ˌɒnəˈrɪfɪk/ adj. conferring honour; implying respect. [from Latin honorificus (honor and -fic from facere = make)]

honour /ˈɒnə/ n. 1. great respect, high public regard. 2. a mark of this; an official award for bravery or achievement; a privilege given or received. 3. a person or thing that brings honour. 4. adherence to what is right or to an accepted standard of conduct; (of a woman) chastity, a reputation for this. 5. exalted position; a title of respect to certain judges and other important persons. 6. (in plural) a specialized degree course or special distinction in an examination. 7. in card games, the four or five highest-ranking cards. —v.t. 1. to respect highly; to confer honour on. 2. to accept or pay (a bill or cheque) when due; to observe the terms of (an agreement). —**do the honours**, to perform the duties of a host to guests etc. **on one's honour**, under a moral obligation (to do a thing). [from Old French from Latin honor]

honourable /ˈɒnərəbəl/ adj. 1. deserving, bringing, or showing honour. 2. **Honourable**, the courtesy title of certain high officials and judges, also of the children of viscounts and barons, the younger sons of earls, and used during debates by MPs to one another. —**Right Honourable**, see under ◊right. —**honourably** adv. [from Old French from Latin]

Honourable Company of Edinburgh Golfers the oldest golf club in the world, formed in 1744 as the Gentleman Golfers of Edinburgh and playing over the Leith links. The club drew up the first set of golf rules, which were later accepted by the ruling body of the Royal and Ancient Club of St Andrews.

honours list the military and civil awards approved by the sovereign Elizabeth II of the UK at New Year, and on her official birthday in June. Many Commonwealth countries, for example, Australia and Canada, have their own lists.

Honshu /ˈhɒnʃuː/ principal island of Japan. It lies between Hokkaido to the NE and Kyushu to the SW; **area** 231,100 sq km/89,205 sq mi, including 382 smaller islands; **population** (1986) 97,283,000. A chain of volcanic mountains runs along the island, which is subject to frequent earthquakes.

Honthorst /ˈhɒnthɔːst/ Gerrit van 1590–1656. Dutch painter who used extremes of light and shade, influenced by Caravaggio; with Terbrugghen he formed the **Utrecht school**.

hooch /huːtʃ/ n. (US colloquial) alcoholic liquor, especially inferior or illicit whisky. [abbreviation of Alaskan hoochinoo = liquor-making tribe]

Hooch /həʊx/ Pieter de 1629–1684. Dutch painter, active in Delft and, later, Amsterdam. The harmonious domestic interiors and courtyards of his Delft period were influenced by Vermeer.

hood[1] /hʊd/ n. 1. a covering for the head and neck, often forming part of a garment. 2. a separate hoodlike garment worn as a part of academic dress. 3. a thing resembling a hood, e.g. a folding soft roof over a car. 4. (US) the bonnet of a car. 5. a canopy to protect the user of machinery or to remove fumes etc. —v.t. to cover with a hood. [Old English]

hood[2] n. (US slang) a gangster, a gunman. [abbreviation of hoodlum]

-hood /hʊd/ suffix forming nouns of condition, quality, or grouping (e.g. childhood, falsehood, sisterhood). [Old English (originally a separate word hād = person, condition, quality)]

hooded adj. having a hood; (of an animal) having a hoodlike part.

hoodlum /ˈhuːdləm/ n. a hooligan, a young thug; a gangster.

hoodoo /ˈhuːduː/ n. (US) 1. bad luck; a thing that brings or causes this. 2. voodoo. —v.t. (US) to make unlucky, to bewitch.

hoodwink /ˈhʊdwɪŋk/ v.t. to deceive, to delude.

hooey /ˈhuːɪ/ n. & int. (slang) nonsense.

hoof /huːf/ n. (plural **hoofs**, **hooves**) the horny part of the foot of a horse etc. —v.i. (usually as **hoof it**) (slang) to go on foot. [Old English]

hoo-ha /ˈhuːhɑː/ n. (slang) a commotion.

hook /hʊk/ n. 1. a bent or curved piece of wire or metal etc. for catching hold of or for hanging things on. 2. a curved cutting instrument. 3. a hooklike thing or formation of land, a bend in a river etc. 4. a hooking stroke; a short swinging blow in boxing. —v.t./i. 1. to grasp or secure with a hook or hooks. 2. to catch with a hook or (figuratively) as if with a hook; (slang) to steal. 3. in sports, to send (the ball) in a curving or deviating path; in a rugby football scrum, to secure and pass (the ball) backward with the foot. —**be hooked on**, (slang) to be addicted to or captivated by. **by hook or by crook**, by one means or another. **hook and eye**, a small metal hook and loop as a dress fastener. **hook, line, and sinker**, entirely. **hook it**, (slang) to make off. **hook-up** n. a connection, especially an interconnection in a broadcast transmission. **off the hook**, (colloquial) out of difficulty or trouble. [Old English]

hookah /ˈhʊkə/ n. an oriental tobacco pipe with a long tube passing through water for cooling the smoke as it is drawn through. [Urdu from Arabic = casket]

Hooke /hʊk/ Robert 1635–1703. English scientist and inventor, originator of ◊Hooke's law, and considered the foremost mechanic of his time. His inventions included a telegraph system, the spirit level, marine barometer, and sea gauge. He coined the term 'cell' in biology.

hooked adj. in the shape of a hook.

hooker[1] /ˈhʊkə/ n. 1. a player in the front row of the scrum in rugby football, who tries to hook the ball. 2. (US slang) a prostitute.

hooker[2] n. a small Dutch or Irish fishing vessel. [from Dutch hoeker]

Hooker Joseph Dalton 1817–1911. English botanist who travelled to the Antarctic and made many botanical discoveries. His works include Flora Antarctica 1844–47, Genera Plantarum 1862–83, and Flora of British India 1875–97. In 1865 he succeeded his father, William Jackson Hooker (1785–1865), as director of the Royal Botanic Gardens, Kew, England.

Hooke's law in physics, a law stating that the tension in a lightly stretched spring is proportional to its extension from its natural length. It was discovered by Robert ◊Hooke.

hookey n. **play hookey** (US slang) to play truant.

hookworm n. a parasitic roundworm (see ◊worm) Necator which lives in tropic and subtropic regions, but also in humid sites in temperate climates. The eggs are hatched in damp soil, and the larvae bore into the human skin, usually through the feet. They make their way to the small intestine where they live by sucking blood. The eggs are expelled with faeces, and the cycle starts again.

hooligan /ˈhuːlɪgən/ n. a young ruffian. —**hooliganism** n. [perhaps originally name of Irish family of ruffians in SE London]

hoop /huːp/ n. 1. a circular band of metal or wood etc. for binding a cask etc., or forming part of a framework. 2. a large ring of wood etc., bowled along by a child, or for circus performers to jump through. 3. an iron etc. arch used in croquet. —v.t. to bind or encircle with a hoop or hoops. —**be put** or **go through the hoop**, to undergo an ordeal. [Old English]

Hooper /ˈhuːpə/ John c.1495–1555. English Protestant reformer and martyr. He adopted the views of ◊Zwingli and was appointed bishop of Gloucester in 1550. He was burned to death for heresy.

hoopla /ˈhuːplɑː/ n. a game in which rings are thrown in an attempt to encircle a prize.

hoopoe /ˈhuːpuː/ n. a bird Upupa epops in the order Coraciiformes. It is slightly larger than a thrush and has a long, thin bill and a bright, buff-coloured crest which expands into a fan shape. The wings are black and white, and the rest of the plumage is black, white, and buff. It is found in Europe, Asia, and Africa. [from Old French from Latin upupa, imitative of its cry]

hooray /huˈreɪ/ int. & n. variant of **hurrah**.

Hoover *As director of the FBI, J Edgar Hoover served under eight US presidents, and under his leadership the powers of the bureau were greatly extended.*

hoot /huːt/ n. 1. an owl's cry. 2. the sound made by a vehicle's horn or a steam whistle. 3. a shout expressing scorn or disapproval. 4. (*colloquial*) laughter; a cause of this. —*v.t./i.* to make a hoot or hoots; to sound (a horn). —**not care** or **give** etc. **a hoot**, (*slang*) not to care at all.

hooter /'huːtə/ n. 1. a siren, a steam whistle, especially as a signal for work to begin or cease. 2. a vehicle's horn. 3. (*slang*) the nose.

Hoover /'huːvə/ n. trade name of a type of vacuum cleaner. —**hoover** *v.t.* to clean with a vacuum cleaner. [from W H *Hoover*]

Hoover Herbert Clark 1874–1964. 31st president of the USA 1929–33, a Republican. Secretary of commerce 1921–28. He lost public confidence after the stock-market crash of 1929, when he opposed direct government aid for the unemployed in the Depression that followed.

Older men declare war. But it is youth that must fight and die.

Herbert Hoover
speech to Republican National Convention, Chicago,
27 June 1944

Hoover J(ohn) Edgar 1895–1972. US director of the Federal Bureau of Investigation (FBI) from 1924. He built up a powerful network for the detection of organized crime. His drive against alleged communist activities after World War II, and his opposition to the Kennedy administration and others brought much criticism over abuse of power.

Hoover William Henry 1849–1932. US manufacturer who developed the ◊vacuum cleaner.

Hoover Dam the highest concrete dam in the USA, 221 m/726 ft, on the Colorado River at the Arizona–Nevada border, built in 1931–36. Known as Boulder Dam from 1933–47, its name was restored by President Truman as the reputation of the former president, Herbert Hoover, was revived. It impounds Lake Meade, and has a hydroelectric power capacity of 1,300 megawatts.

Hooverville n. a colloquial term for any shantytown built by the unemployed and destitute in the USA during the Depression of 1929–40, named after US president Herbert ◊Hoover, whose policies were blamed for the plight of millions.

hooves plural of hoof.

hop[1] *v.t./i.* (-pp-) 1. (of a bird or animal) to spring with two or all feet at once. 2. (of a person) to jump on one foot. 3. to cross (a ditch etc.) —*n.* 1. a hopping movement. 2. an informal dance. 3. a short flight in an aircraft. —**hop in** (*or* out), (*colloquial*) to get into (or out of) a car. **hop it!** (*slang*) go away! **hopping**

mad, (*colloquial*) very angry. **on the hop,** unprepared. [Old English]

hop[2] *n.* a climbing plant *Humulus lupulus* bearing cones; (in *plural*) its ripe cones used to flavour beer. —*v.t.* (-pp-) to flavour with hops. —**hop-bind** *or* **hop-bine** *n.* the climbing stem of the hop. [from Middle Low German or Middle Dutch]

hope /həʊp/ *n.* 1. expectation and desire, e.g. for a certain event to occur. 2. a person, thing, or circumstance that encourages hope. 3. what is hoped for. — *v.t./i.* to feel hope; to expect and desire; to feel fairly confident. —**hope against hope,** to cling to a mere possibility. [Old English]

Hope Anthony. Pen name of Anthony Hope Hawkins 1863–1933. English novelist whose romance *The Prisoner of Zenda* 1894, and its sequel *Rupert of Hentzau* 1898, introduced the imaginary Balkan state of Ruritania.

Hope Bob. Stage name of Leslie Townes Hope 1904– . US comedian. His film appearances include a series of 'Road' films with Bing ◊Crosby, such as *Road to Morocco* 1942.

hopeful *adj.* feeling or causing hope; likely to succeed. —*n.* a person who hopes or seems likely to succeed.

hopefully *adv.* 1. in a hopeful manner. 2. (*disputed usage*) it is to be hoped.

Hopei /həʊ'peɪ/ former name of ◊Hebei, Chinese province.

hopeless *adj.* 1. feeling or admitting no hope. 2. inadequate, incompetent. —**hopelessly** *adv.*, **hopelessness** *n.*

Hope's apparatus an apparatus used to demonstrate the temperature at which water has its maximum density. [from Thomas Charles *Hope* (1766–1844)]

Hopewell /'həʊpwel/ *n.* a North American Indian agricultural culture of the central USA, dated about AD 200 and notable for burial mounds up to 12 m/40 ft high and structures such as Serpent Mound in Ohio; see also ◊moundbuilder.

Hopi /'həʊpi/ *n.* a member of a North American Indian people, presently numbering approximately 9,000, who live mainly in mountain villages in the the SW USA, especially NE Arizona. They live in houses of stone or of adobe (mud brick), and farm and herd sheep. Their language belongs to the Uto-Aztecan family.

Hopkins /'hɒpkɪnz/ Anthony 1937– . Welsh actor. Among his stage appearances are *Equus*, *Macbeth*, *Pravda*, and the title role in *King Lear*. His films include *The Lion in Winter* 1968, *A Bridge Too Far* 1977, *The Elephant Man* 1980, and *The Silence of the Lambs* 1991. He played television parts in *War and Peace* and *A Married Man.*

Hopkins Gerard Manley 1844–1889. English poet and Jesuit priest. His work, marked by its religious themes and use of natural imagery, includes 'The Wreck of the Deutschland' 1876 and 'The Windhover' 1877. His employment of 'sprung rhythm' greatly influenced later 20th-century poetry. His poetry was written in secret, and published 30 years after his death by his friend Robert Bridges.

Hopkins Harry Lloyd 1890–1946. US government official. Originally a social worker, in 1935 he became head of the WPA (Works Progress Administration), which was concerned with Depression relief work. After a period as secretary of commerce 1938–40, he was appointed supervisor of the ◊lend-lease programme in 1941, and undertook missions to Britain and the USSR during World War II.

hoplite /'hɒplaɪt/ *n.* a heavy-armed infantry soldier in ancient Greece. [from Greek *hoplon* = weapon]

hopper[1] *n.* 1. one who hops; a hopping insect. 2. a container tapering to the base, with an opening at the base for discharging the contents.

hopper[2] *n.* a hop-picker.

Hopper /'hɒpə/ Dennis 1936– . US film actor and director who caused a sensation with *Easy Rider* 1969, the archetypal 'road' film, but whose *The Last Movie* 1971 was poorly received by the critics. He made a comeback in the 1980s. His work as an actor includes *Rebel Without a Cause* 1955, *The American Friend/Der amerikanische Freund* 1977, and *Blue Velvet* 1986.

Hopper Edward 1882–1967. US painter and etcher. His views of New York in the 1930s and 1940s captured the loneliness and superficial glamour of city life, as in *Nighthawks* 1942 (Art Institute, Chicago).

hopsack *n.* a kind of loosely-woven fabric.

hopscotch *n.* a children's game of hopping over squares marked on the ground to retrieve a stone tossed into these.

Horace /'hɒrɪs/ 65–8 BC. Roman lyric poet and satirist who became a leading poet under the patronage of Emperor Augustus. His works include *Satires* 35–30 BC; the four books of *Odes* about 25–24 BC; *Epistles*, a series of verse letters; and a critical work, *Ars poetica.*

horde /hɔːd/ *n.* **1.** a large group, a gang. **2.** a troop of Tartar or other nomads. [from Polish from Turki *ordī, ordū* = camp]

Hordern /'hɔːdən/ Michael 1911– . English actor who appeared in stage roles such as Shakespeare's Lear and Prospero. His films include *The Man Who Never Was* 1956, *The Spy Who Came in From the Cold* 1965, *The Bed Sitting Room* 1969, and *Joseph Andrews* 1977.

Hore-Belisha /hɔː bə'liːʃə/ Leslie, Baron Hore-Belisha 1895–1957. British politician. A National Liberal, he was minister of transport 1934–37, introducing **Belisha beacons** to mark pedestrian crossings. As war minister from 1937, until removed by Chamberlain in 1940 on grounds of temperament, he introduced peacetime conscription in 1939.

horehound /'hɔːhaʊnd/ *n.* any plant of the genus *Marrubium* of the mint family Labiatae. The **white horehound** *M. vulgare*, found in Europe, N Africa, and W Asia and naturalized in N America, has a thick, hairy stem and clusters of dull white flowers; it has medicinal uses. [Old English]

horizon /hə'raɪzən/ *n.* **1.** the line at which earth and sky appear to meet; the limit to which one can see across the surface of the sea or a level plain, that is, about 5 km/3 mi at 1.5 m/5 ft above sea level, and about 65 km/40 mi at 300 m/1,000 ft. **2.** the limit of mental perception, experience, interest etc. —**on the horizon,** imminent, becoming apparent. [from Old French from Latin from Greek *horizō* = bound]

horizontal /hɒrɪ'zɒntəl/ *adj.* **1.** parallel to the plane of the horizon; at right angles to the vertical. **2.** at or concerned with the same status, work etc. —*n.* a horizontal line etc. —**horizontally** *adv.*

hormone /'hɔːməʊn/ *n.* any of numerous organic compounds secreted internally (especially into the bloodstream) by a specific group of cells, and regulating a specific physiological activity of other cells, or produced by plants whose growth and other physiological activities they regulate; a similar synthetic substance. Hormones bring about changes in the functions of various organs according to the body's requirements. The pituitary gland, at the base of the brain, is a centre for overall coordination of hormone secretion; the thyroid hormones determine the rate of general body chemistry; the adrenal hormones prepare the organism during stress for 'fight or flight'; and the sexual hormones such as oestrogen govern reproductive functions. —**hormonal** /-'məʊnəl/ *adj.* [from Greek *hormaō* = impel]

hormone-replacement therapy (HRT) the use of oral oestrogen to help limit the thinning of bone that occurs in women after menopause. The treatment was first used in the 1970s.

Hormuz /hɔː'muːz/ or **Ormuz** small island, 41 sq km/16 sq mi, in the Strait of Hormuz, belonging to Iran. It is strategically important because oil tankers leaving the Persian Gulf for Japan and the West have to pass through the strait to reach the Arabian Sea.

horn /hɔːn/ *n.* **1.** a hard outgrowth, often curved and pointed, from the head of an animal; each of the two branched appendages on the head of (especially male) deer. **2.** a hornlike projection on other animals, e.g. a snail's tentacle. **3.** the substance of which horns are made. **4.** a wind instrument, originally made of horn, now usually brass. See under ◊brass. **5.** an instrument for sounding a warning. **6.** a receptacle or instrument made of horn. **7.** a horn-shaped projection; an extremity of the Moon or other crescent, an arm of a river etc. **8.** either alternative of a dilemma. —*v.t.* **1.** to furnish with horns. **2.** to gore with the horns. —**the Horn,** Cape Horn. **horn in,** (*slang*) to intrude; to interfere. **Horn of Africa,** the peninsula of NE Africa which comprises Somalia and part of Ethiopia. **horn of plenty,** a cornucopia. [Old English, cognate with Latin *cornu*]

Horn Philip de Montmorency, Count of Horn 1518–1568. Flemish politician. He held high offices under the Holy Roman emperor Charles V and his son Philip II. From 1563 he was one of the leaders of the opposition to the rule of Cardinal Granvella (1517–1586) and to the introduction of the Inquisition. In 1567 he was arrested, together with the Resistance leader Egmont, and both were beheaded in Brussels.

hornbeam *n.* any tree of the genus *Carpinus* of the birch family Betulaceae. They have oval, serrated leaves and bear pendant clusters of flowers, each with a nutlike seed attached to the base. The trunk is usually twisted, with smooth grey bark. The **common hornbeam** *C. betulus* is found in woods throughout the temperate regions of Europe and Asia. The leaves are hairy on the undersurface.

hornbill *n.* a bird of the family of Bucerotidae, found in Africa, India, and Malaysia. It is omnivorous, about 1 m/3 ft long, and has a powerful bill surmounted by a bony growth or casque. During the breeding season, the female walls herself into a hole in a tree, and does not emerge until the young are hatched.

hornblende /'hɔːnblend/ *n.* a green or black rock-forming mineral, one of the ◊amphiboles; it is a hydrous silicate of calcium, iron, magnesium, and aluminium. Hornblende is found in both igneous and metamorphic rocks. [German]

hornet /'hɔːnɪt/ *n.* a large kind of wasp (especially *Vespa crabro*). —**hornet moth,** a kind of moth *Sesia apiformis* resembling the hornet. **stir up a hornet's nest,** to cause an angry outburst.

hornfels *n.* a ◊metamorphic rock formed by rocks heated by contact with a hot igneous body. It is fine-grained and brittle, without foliation.

Horniman /'hɔːnɪmən/ Annie Elizabeth Frederika 1860–1937. English pioneer of repertory theatre, who subsidized the Abbey Theatre, Dublin, and founded the Manchester company.

hornpipe *n.* a lively dance, usually for one person; the music for this. Its traditional association with British seamen seems to date from the late 18th century.

Hornung /'hɔːnəŋ/ E(rnest) W(illiam) 1866–1921. English novelist who, at the prompting of Conan ◊Doyle, created A J Raffles, the gentleman–burglar, and his assistant Bunny Manders in *The Amateur Cracksman* 1899.

hornwort *n.* an underwater aquatic plant, family Ceratophyllaceae. It has whorls of finely divided leaves and is found in slow-moving water. Hornwort may be up to 2 m/7 ft long.

horny *adj.* **1.** of or like horn; hard like horn, calloused. **2.** (*slang*) lecherous.

horology /hə'rɒlədʒɪ/ *n.* the art of measuring time or making clocks, watches etc. —**horological** /hɒrə'lɒdʒɪkəl/ *adj* [from Greek *hōra* = time]

horoscope /'hɒrəskəʊp/ *n.* a forecast of a person's future from a diagram showing the relative positions of the planets etc. at a particular time; this diagram. [French from Latin from Greek *skopos* = observer)]

Horowitz /'hɒrəwɪts/ Vladimir 1904–1989. US pianist, born in Kiev, Ukraine. He made his debut in the USA in 1928 with the New York Philharmonic Orchestra. Renowned for his commanding virtuoso style, he was a leading interpreter of Liszt, Schumann, and Rachmaninov.

horrendous /hə'rendəs/ *adj.* horrifying. [from gerundive of Latin *horrēre*]

horrible /'hɒrɪbəl/ *adj.* causing or exciting horror; (*colloquial*) unpleasant. —**horribly** *adv.* [from Latin *horribilis* (*horrēre* = bristle, shudder)]

horrid /'hɒrɪd/ *adj.* horrible, revolting; (*colloquial*) unpleasant. —**horridly** *adv.* [from Latin *horridus*]

horrific /hə'rɪfɪk/ *adj.* horrifying. —**horrifically** *adv.* [from French or Latin]

horrify /'hɒrɪfaɪ/ *v.t.* to arouse horror in, to shock. [from Latin]

horror /'hɒrə/ *n.* **1.** an intense feeling of loathing and fear; intense dislike or dismay. **2.** a person or thing causing horror; (*colloquial*) a bad or mischievous person etc. —**the horrors,** a fit of depression or nervousness etc. [from Old French from Latin]

horror fiction a genre of fiction and film, devoted primarily to scaring the reader, but often also aiming to be cathartic through the exaggeration of the bizarre and grotesque. Dominant figures in the horror tradition are Mary Shelley (*Frankenstein* 1818), Edgar Allan Poe, Bram Stoker, H P

horse

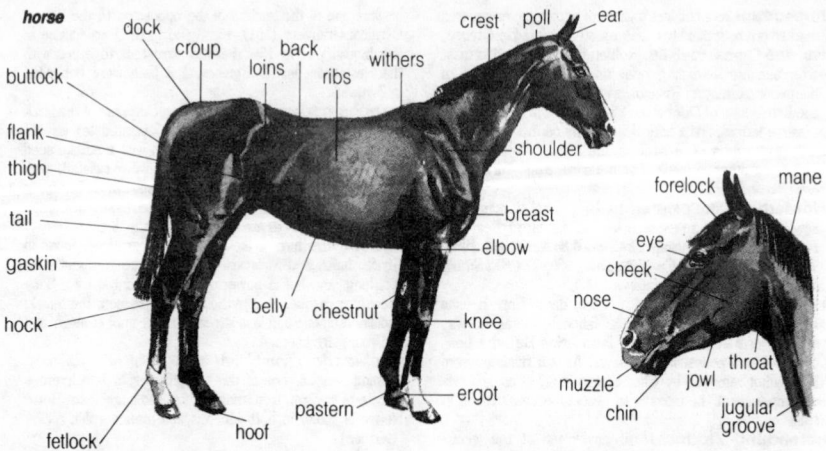

Lovecraft and, among contemporary writers, Stephen King and Clive Barker.

hors d'œuvre /ɔːrˈdɜːvr/ an appetizer served at the beginning of a meal. [French = outside the work]

hors de combat out of action. [French]

horse *n.* 1. a large four-legged animal *Equus caballus* with a long mane and tail, used for riding or to carry or pull loads; an adult male horse, a stallion. The family Equidae also includes zebras and asses. The many breeds of **domestic horse** of Euro-Asian derivation range in colour through grey, brown, and black. The yellow-brown **Mongolian wild horse** or **Przewalski's horse** *Equus przewalskii* is about the only surviving species of wild horse. 2. (*collective, as singular*) cavalry. 3. a gymnastic vaulting block. 4. a supporting frame. —*v.i.* (*colloquial*) to fool *around*. —**from the horse's mouth**, (of information etc.) from the original or an authoritative source. **horsebox** *n.* a closed vehicle for transporting a horse or horses. **horse latitudes**, a belt of calms at the northern edge of the NE trade winds. **horse laugh**, a loud, coarse laugh. **horse sense**, (*colloquial*) plain common sense. **horse trading** *n.* (*US*) dealing in horses; shrewd bargaining. on **one's high horse**, (*colloquial*) acting haughtily. on **horseback**, mounted on a horse. [Old English]

horse chestnut any tree of the genus *Aesculus* of the family Hippocastanaceae, especially *A. hippocastanum*, originally from SE Europe but widely planted elsewhere. They have large, showy spikes of bell-shaped flowers and bear large, shiny, inedible seeds in capsules (**conkers**). The horse chestnut is not related to the true chestnut. In North America it is called buckeye.

horseflesh *n.* 1. the flesh of the horse as food. 2. horses collectively.

horsefly *n.* or **gadfly** a fly of the family Tabanidae; there are over 2,500 species. The females suck blood from horses, cattle, and humans; males live on plants and suck nectar. The larvae are carnivorous.

Horse Guards in the UK, the Household Cavalry, or Royal Horse Guards, formed in 1661; their headquarters, in Whitehall, London, England, erected in 1753 by Vardy from a design by Kent, on the site of the Tilt Yard of Whitehall palace.

horsehair *n.* hair from the mane or tail of a horse, used for padding etc.

horseman *n.* or **horsewoman** (*plural* **horsemen**, **horsewomen**) a rider on horseback; a skilled rider. —**horsemanship** *n.*

Horse, Master of the the head of the department of the British royal household, responsible for the royal stables. The Earl of Westmorland became Master of the Horse in 1978.

horseplay *n.* boisterous play.

horsepower *n.* (*plural* the same) an imperial unit (symbol hp) of power, now replaced by the ◊watt. It was first used by the engineer James ◊Watt, who employed it to compare the power of steam engines with that of horses. Watt found a horse to be capable of 366 foot-pounds of work per second

but, in order to enable him to use the term 'horsepower' to cover the additional work done by the more efficient steam engine, he exaggerated the pulling power of the horse by 50%. Hence, one horsepower is equal to 550 foot-pounds per second/745.7 watts, which is more than any real horse could produce. The metric horsepower is 735.5 watts; the standard US horsepower is 746 watts.

horse racing the sport of racing mounted or driven horses. Two popular forms in Britain are **flat racing**, for thoroughbred horses over a flat course, and **National Hunt racing**, in which the horses have to clear obstacles.

horseradish *n.* a hardy perennial *Armoracia rusticana*, native to SE Europe but naturalized elsewhere, of the family Cruciferae. The thick, cream-coloured root is strong-tasting and is often made into a condiment.

horseshoe *n.* a U-shaped iron shoe for a horse; a thing of this shape.

horsetail *n.* a plant of the genus *Equisetum*, related to ferns and club mosses; some species are also called **scouring rush**. There are about 35 living species, bearing their spores on cones at the stem tip. The upright stems are ribbed and often have spaced whorls of branches. Today they are of modest size, but hundreds of millions of years ago giant treelike forms existed.

horsewhip *n.* a whip for driving horses. —*v.t.* (**-pp-**) to beat (a person) with a horsewhip.

horst *n.* a long plateau with a geological fault on each side. [German = heap]

Horst-Wessel-Lied /hɔːst ˈvesəl liːt/ *n.* a song introduced by the Nazis as a second German national anthem. The text was written to a traditional tune by Horst Wessel (1907–1930), a Nazi 'martyr'.

horsy *adj.* 1. of or like a horse. 2. concerned with or devoted to horses; showing this in dress, conversation etc.

hortative /ˈhɔːtətɪv/ *adj.* or **hortatory** /ˈhɔːtətərɪ/ tending or serving to exhort. [from Latin *hortari* = exhort]

Horthy de Nagybánya /ˈhɔːti də ˈnɒdʒbɑːnjə/ Nicholas 1868–1957. Hungarian politician and admiral. Leader of the counter-revolutionary White government, he became regent in 1920 on the overthrow of the communist Bela Kun regime by Romanian and Czechoslovak intervention. He represented the conservative and military class, and retained power until World War II, trying (although allied to Hitler) to retain independence of action. In 1944 he tried to negotiate a surrender to the USSR but Hungary was taken over by the Nazis and he was deported to Germany.

horticulture /ˈhɔːtɪkʌltʃə(r)/ *n.* the art and science of growing flowers, fruit, and vegetables. Horticulture is practised in gardens and orchards, along with millions of acres of land devoted to vegetable farming. Some areas, like California, have specialized in horticulture because they have the mild climate and light, fertile soil most suited to these crops. The growth of industrial towns in the 19th century led to the development of commercial horticulture in the form of nurseries and market gardens, pioneering methods such as glasshouses, artificial heat, herbicides, and pesticides, synthetic fertilizers, and machinery. In Britain, over half a million acres are devoted to professional horticulture, and vegetables account for almost three-quarters of the produce. —**horticultural** /-'kʌltʃərəl/ *adj.*, **horticulturist** *n.* [from Latin *hortus* = garden, after *agriculture*]

Horus /'hɔːrəs/ in ancient Egyptian mythology, the hawkheaded sun god, son of Isis and Osiris, of whom the pharaohs were declared to be the incarnation.

hosanna /həʊ'zænə/ *n.* a shout of adoration. [from Greek from Hebrew = save now]

hose /həʊz/ *n.* 1. or **hosepipe** a flexible tube for conveying water. 2. (*collective* as *plural*, especially in trade use) stockings and socks. 3. (*historical*) breeches. —*v.t.* to water or spray with a hose. [Old English]

hosier /'həʊziə/ *n.* a dealer in stockings and socks.

hosiery *n.* (especially in trade use) stockings and socks; knitted or woven underwear.

Hoskins /'hɒskɪnz/ Bob 1942– . British character actor who progressed to fame from a series of supporting roles. Films include *The Long Good Friday* 1980, *The Cotton Club* 1984, *Mona Lisa* 1985, *A Prayer for the Dying* 1987, and *Who Framed Roger Rabbit?* 1988.

hospice /'hɒspɪs/ *n.* 1. a lodging for travellers, especially one kept by a religious order. 2. a home for destitute or (especially terminally) ill people. [French, from Latin *hospitium*]

hospitable /hɒs'pɪtəbəl/ *adj.* giving or disposed to give hospitality. —**hospitably** *adv.* [French, from Latin *hospitare* = entertain]

hospital /'hɒspɪtəl/ *n.* 1. an institution providing medical and surgical treatment and nursing care for ill or injured people. 2. (*historical*) a charitable institution, a hospice. [from Old French from Latin *hospitale*]

hospitality /hɒspi'tælɪti/ *n.* friendly and generous reception and entertainment of guests or strangers.

hospitalize /'hɒspɪtəlaɪz/ *v.t.* to send or admit (a patient) to hospital. —**hospitalization** /-'zeɪʃən/ *n.*

hospitaller /'hɒspɪtələ/ *n.* a member of certain charitable religious orders.

host¹ /həʊst/ *n.* a large number of people or things; (*archaic*) an army. [from Old French from Latin *hostis* = enemy, army]

host² *n.* 1. one who receives or entertains another as his or her guest; the landlord of an inn. 2. an animal or plant having a parasite. —*v.t.* to act as host to (a person) or at (an event). [from Old French from Latin *hospes* = host, guest]

host³ *n.* in the Christian religion, the bread consecrated in the ◊Eucharist. [from Old French from Latin *hostia* = sacrificial victim]

hostage /'hɒstɪdʒ/ *n.* a person seized or held as security for the fulfilment of a condition or conditions. [from Old French from Latin *obses*]

hostel /'hɒstəl/ *n.* a house of residence or lodging for students or other special groups. [from Old French from Latin]

hostelry /'hɒstəlrɪ/ *n.* (*archaic*) an inn. [from Old French (h)*ostelier* = innkeeper]

hostess /'həʊstɪs/ *n.fem.* a woman host; a woman employed to entertain guests in a nightclub etc.

hostile /'hɒstaɪl/ *adj.* 1. of an enemy. 2. unfriendly, opposed (to). —**hostilely** *adv.* [French, or from Latin]

hostility /hɒ'stɪlɪti/ *n.* being hostile, enmity; a state of warfare; (in *plural*) acts of warfare. [from French or Latin]

hot *adj.* 1. having a relatively or noticeably high temperature; causing a sensation of heat; feeling heat. 2. (of pepper, spices etc.) producing a burning sensation to the taste. 3. eager, excited; having intense feeling, angry or upset. 4. (of news etc.) fresh, recent; (of a scent in hunting) strong. 5. (of a competitor, performer, feat) skilful, formidable. 6. (of music) strongly rhythmical and emotional. 7. (*slang*) (of goods) stolen, especially if difficult to dispose of. 8. (*slang*) radioactive. —*v.t./i.* (**-tt-**) (*colloquial*, often with *up*) 1. to make or become hot. 2. to become active or exciting. —**hot air**, (*slang*) empty or boastful talk. **hot-blooded** *adj.* ardent, passionate. **hot cross bun**, a bun marked with a cross and eaten on Good Friday. **hot dog**, (*colloquial*) a hot sausage sandwiched in a soft roll. **hot gospeller**, (*colloquial*) an eager preacher of the gospel. **hot line**, a direct exclusive line of communication especially for an emergency. **hot money**, capital frequently transferred. **hot potato**, (*colloquial*) a controversial or awkward matter or situation. **hot rod**, a motor vehicle modified to have extra power and speed. **hot seat**, (*slang*) a position of difficult responsibility; the electric chair. **hot stuff**, (*colloquial*) a formidably capable person; an important person or thing; a sexually attractive person. **hot-tempered** *adj.* impulsively angry. **hot water**, (*colloquial*) difficulty or trouble. **hot-water bottle**, a rubber, metal, or earthenware container filled with hot water to warm a bed etc. —**hotly** *adv.*, **hotness** *n.* [Old English]

hotbed *n.* 1. a bed of earth heated by fermenting manure. 2. a place promoting the growth of something (especially unwelcome).

hotchpotch /'hɒtʃpɒtʃ/ *n.* a confused mixture, a jumble; a mixed broth or stew. [from Old French *hochepot* (*hocher* = shake)]

hotel /həʊ'tel/ *n.* an establishment providing meals and accommodation for payment. [from French]

hotelier /həʊ'teliə/ *n.* a hotel keeper. [from French from Old French]

hotfoot *adv.* in eager haste. —*v.i.* (usually with *it*) to hurry eagerly.

hothead *n.* an impetuous person. —**hot-headed** *adj.*

hothouse *n.* a heated building, usually largely of glass, for rearing plants.

HOTOL /'həʊpɪl/ acronym from horizontal takeoff and landing, a British concept for a hypersonic transport and satellite launcher which could be operational before the end of the century. It will be a single-stage vehicle with no boosters and will take off and land on a runway. It will feature a revolutionary air-breathing rocket engine that will require it to carry much less oxygen than a conventional space plane. The USA has a similar development under way called the Orient Express.

hotplate *n.* a heated metal plate etc. (or a set of these) for cooking food or keeping it hot.

hotpot *n.* meat and vegetables cooked in an oven in a closed pot.

hot spot in geology, a hypothetical region of high thermal activity in the Earth's ◊mantle (sense 4). It is believed to be the origin of many chains of ocean islands, such as Polynesia and the Galàpagos.

Hottentot /'hɒtəntɒt/ *n.* (*plural* same or **Hottentots**) 1. a member of a South African nomadic, pastoral people inhabiting the SW corner of the continent when Europeans first settled there. 2. their Khoisan language which resembles that of the Kung (Bushmen), with mainly monosyllabic roots and explosive consonants that produce clicking sounds. [Afrikaans, perhaps = stutterer, from their mode of pronunciation]

Houdini /hu:'di:ni/ Harry. Stage name of Erich Weiss 1874–1926. US escapologist and conjurer. He was renowned for his escapes from ropes and handcuffs, from trunks under water, from straitjackets and prison cells.

Houdon /u:'dɒŋ/ Jean-Antoine 1741–1828. French sculptor, a portraitist who made characterful studies of Voltaire and a Neo-Classical statue of George Washington, commissioned in 1785.

hound *n.* 1. a dog used in hunting, a foxhound. 2. a contemptible man. —*v.t.* to harass or pursue; to urge or incite. [Old English]

Houphouët-Boigny /u:f'weɪ bwa:n'ji:/ Felix 1905– . Ivory Coast right-wing politician. He held posts in French ministries, and became president of the Republic of the Ivory Coast on independence in 1960. He was re-elected for a sixth term in 1985 representing the sole legal party.

hour /aʊə/ *n.* 1. a twenty-fourth part of a day and night, 60 minutes. 2. a time of day; a point in time; (in *plural* with preceding numerals in the form *18.00*, *20.30* etc.) this number of hours and minutes past midnight on the 24-hour clock. 3. a period set aside for some purpose; (in *plural*) a fixed period of time for work, the use of a building etc. 4. a short, indefinite period of time. 5. the present time; a time for action etc. 6. the distance traversed in an hour. 7. in the Roman Catholic Church, prayers said at one of seven fixed times of the day. —**the hour**, the time o'clock; the time of a whole number of hours. **after hours**, after normal business etc. hours. [from Anglo-French from Latin *hora* from Greek]

hourglass *n.* a sandglass that runs for an hour.

houri /'huərɪ/ *n.* a beautiful young woman of the Muslim paradise. [French from Persian from Arabic = gazellelike]

hourly /'auəlɪ/ *adj.* done or occurring every hour; frequentative. —*adv.* every hour; frequently.

Hours, Book of in medieval Europe, a collection of liturgical prayers for the use of the faithful. Books of Hours appeared in England in the 13th century, and contained short prayers and illustrations, with each prayer suitable for a different hour of the day, in honour of the Virgin Mary. The enormous demand for Books of Hours was a stimulus for the development of Gothic illumination. A notable example is the *Très Riches Heures du Duc de Berry*, illustrated in the early 15th century by the ◊Limbourg brothers.

house /haus/ *n.* (*plural* **houses** /'hauzɪz/) 1. a building for human habitation. 2. a building for a special purpose or for keeping animals or goods. 3. a residential establishment, especially of a religious order, university college, section of a boarding school etc. 4. a division of a day school for games, competitions etc. 5. a royal family or dynasty. 6. a firm or institution; its place of business. 7. a legislative etc. assembly; the building where it meets. 8. an audience or performance in a theatre etc. 9. a twelfth part of the heavens in astrology. —/haUz/ *v.t.* 1. to provide a house or accommodation for; to store (goods etc.). 2. to enclose or encase (a part or fitting). —**house agent,** an agent for the sale and letting of houses. **house arrest,** detention in one's own house, not prison. **housebound** *adj.* unable to leave one's house. **house dog,** a dog kept to guard a house. **house martin,** a bird *Delichon urbica* that builds a mud nest on house walls. **house of cards,** an insecure scheme etc. **House of Keys,** the elective branch of the legislature of the Isle of Man, with 24 members. **house party,** a group of guests staying at a country house etc. **house-proud** *adj.* attentive to the care and appearance of the home. **houseroom** *n.* space or provision in one's house (*would not give it houseroom,* would not have it in any circumstances). **house-trained** *adj.* (of animals) trained to be clean in the house; (*colloquial*) well-mannered. **house-warming** *n.* a party celebrating a move to a new home. **keep house,** to provide for a household. **like a house on fire,** vigorously, successfully. **on the house,** at the management's expense, free. **put** *or* **set one's house in order,** to make needed reforms. [Old English]

houseboat *n.* a boat fitted up for living in.

housebreaking *n.* the act of breaking into a building, especially in daytime, to commit a crime. (In 1968 the term was replaced, in English law, by *burglary*.)

housecoat *n.* a woman's long, dresslike garment for informal wear in the house.

housefly *n.* the most common type of fly of the family Muscidae. Houseflies are grey, and have mouthparts adapted for drinking liquids.

household *n.* 1. the occupants of a house regarded as a unit. 2. a house and its affairs. —**Household troops,** troops nominally employed to guard the sovereign. **household word,** a familiar saying or name.

householder *n.* 1. a person owning or renting a house. 2. the head of a household.

household, royal see ◊royal household.

housekeeper *n.* a person employed to manage a household.

housekeeping *n.* 1. management of household affairs. 2. money allowed for this.

houseleek *n.* a plant *Sempervivum tectorum* with pink flowers, growing on walls and roofs.

housemaid *n.* a woman servant in a house. —**housemaid's knee,** inflammation of the kneecap.

houseman *n.* (*plural* **housemen**) a resident doctor at a hospital etc.

housemaster *n.* or **housemistress** a teacher in charge of a house at a boarding school.

house music a type of dance music of the 1980s originating in the inner-city clubs of Chicago, USA, combining funk with European high-tech pop, and using dub, digital sampling, and cross-fading. **Acid house** has minimal vocals and melody, instead surrounding the mechanically emphasized 4/4 beat with found noises, stripped-down synthesizer riffs, and a wandering bass line.

House of Commons the lower chamber of the UK Parliament. It consists of 650 elected members of Parliament, each of whom represents a constituency. Its functions are to debate, legislate, and to scrutinize the activities of government. Constituencies are kept under continuous review by the Parliamentary Boundary Commissions. The House of Commons is presided over by the Speaker. Proceedings in the House of Commons have been televised from Nov 1989.

House of Lords the upper chamber of the UK Parliament. Its members are unelected and comprise the **temporal peers**: all hereditary peers of England created to 1707, all hereditary peers of Great Britain created 1707–1800, and all hereditary peers of the UK from 1801 onwards; all hereditary Scottish peers (under the Peerage Act 1963); all peeresses in their own right (under the same act); all life peers (both the ◊law lords and those created under the Life Peerages Act 1958); and the **spiritual peers**: the two archbishops and 24 of the bishops (London, Durham, and Winchester by right, and the rest by seniority). Since the Parliament Act of 1911 the powers of the Lords have been restricted in that they may delay a bill passed by the Commons but not reject it. The Lords are presided over by the Lord Chancellor.

housewife *n.* a woman managing a household. —**housewifely** *adj.*

housework *n.* the cleaning and cooking etc. done in housekeeping.

housing /'hauzɪŋ/ *n.* 1. dwelling houses collectively; provision of these; shelter, lodging. 2. a rigid casing enclosing machinery etc. 3. a shallow trench or groove cut across the grain in a piece of wood to receive an insertion. —**housing estate,** a residential area planned as a unit.

Housman /'hausmən/ A(lfred) E(dward) 1859–1936. English poet and classical scholar. His *A Shropshire Lad* 1896, a series of deceptively simple, nostalgic, balladlike poems, was popular during World War I. This was followed by *Last Poems* 1922 and *More Poems* 1936.

If a line of poetry strays into my memory, my skin bristles so that the razor ceases to act.

Alfred Edward Housman
lecture: *The Name and Nature of Poetry*
Cambridge, 9 May 1933

Houston /'hju:stən/ port in Texas, USA; population (1981) 2,891,000; linked by canal to the Gulf of Mexico. It is an agricultural centre, and industries include petrochemicals, chemicals, plastics, synthetic rubber, and electronics.

Houston Sam 1793–1863. US general who won the independence of Texas from Mexico in 1836 and was president of the Republic of Texas 1836–45. Houston, Texas, is named after him.

hove see ◊heave.

hovel /'hɒvəl/ *n.* a small, miserable dwelling.

Hovell /'hɒvəl/ William Hilton 1786–1875. Explorer of Australia with Hamilton ◊Hume.

hover /'hɒvə/ *v.i.* 1. (of a bird etc.) to remain in one place in the air. 2. to wait (*about, round*); to wait close at hand. —*n.* 1. hovering. 2. a state of suspense. [from obsolete *hove* = hover, linger]

hovercraft *n.* a vehicle that rides on a cushion of high-pressure air, free from all contact with the surface beneath, invented by British engineer Christopher Cockerell in 1959. Hovercraft need a smooth terrain when operating overland and are best adapted to use on waterways. They are useful in places where harbours have not been established.

how *adv.* 1. in what way, by what means. 2. in what condition (especially of health); to what extent. 3. in whatever way, as. 4. (*colloquial*) = that. —**how about,** what do you think of; would you like. **how do you do,** a formal greeting. **how-do-you-do** *n.* (*colloquial*) an awkward situation. **how many,** what number of. **how much,** what amount; what price. **how's that?** how do you regard or explain that?; (said to an umpire in cricket) is the batsman out or not? [Old English]

Howard /'hauəd/ Catherine *c.* 1520–1542. Queen consort of ◊Henry VIII of England from 1540. In 1541 the archbishop of Canterbury, Thomas Cranmer, accused her of being unchaste before marriage to Henry and she was beheaded in 1542 after Cranmer made further charges of adultery.

Howard Charles, 2nd Baron Howard of Effingham and 1st Earl of Nottingham 1536–1624. English admiral, a cousin of Queen Elizabeth I. He commanded the fleet against the Spanish Armada while lord high admiral from 1585–1618. He cooperated with the Earl of Essex in the attack on Cádiz in 1596.

Howard Ebenezer 1850–1928. English town planner and founder of the ideal of the ◊garden city, through his book *Tomorrow* 1898 (republished as *Garden Cities of Tomorrow* 1902).

Howard John 1726–1790. English philanthropist whose work to improve prison conditions is continued today by the Howard League for Penal Reform.

Howard Trevor (Wallace) 1916–1989. English actor, whose films include *Brief Encounter* 1945, *Sons and Lovers* 1960, *Mutiny on the Bounty* 1962, *Ryan's Daughter* 1970, and *Conduct Unbecoming* 1975.

howbeit /haʊˈbiːɪt/ *adv.* (*archaic*) nevertheless.

howdah /ˈhaʊdə/ *n.* a seat, usually with a canopy, for riding on the back of an elephant or camel. [from Urdu from Arabic = litter]

Howe /haʊ/ Elias 1819–1867. US inventor, in 1846, of a ◊sewing machine using double thread.

Howe Geoffrey 1926– . British Conservative politician, member of Parliament for Surrey East. Under Heath he was solicitor-general 1970–72 and minister for trade 1972–74; as chancellor of the Exchequer 1979–83 under Margaret Thatcher, he put into practice the monetarist policy which reduced inflation at the cost of a rise in unemployment. In 1983 he became foreign secretary, and in 1989 he unexpectedly became deputy prime minister and leader of the House of Commons. On Nov 1 1990 he resigned in protest against Thatcher's continued opposition to Britain's greater integration in Europe, precipitating the leadership election from which John Major emerged as prime minister.

Howe James Wong. Adopted name of Wong Tung Jim 1899–1976. Chinese-born director of film photography, who lived in the USA from childhood. One of Hollywood's best camera operators, he is credited with introducing the use of hand-held cameras and deep focus. His work ranges from *The Alaskan* 1924 to *Funny Lady* 1975.

Howe William, 5th Viscount Howe 1729–1814. British general. During the War of American Independence he won the Battle of Bunker Hill in 1775, and as commander in chief in America from 1776–78 captured New York and defeated Washington at Brandywine and Germantown. He resigned in protest at lack of home government support.

Howells /ˈhaʊəlz/ William Dean 1837–1920. US novelist and editor. The 'dean' of US letters in the post-Civil War era, and editor of *The Atlantic Monthly*, he championed the realist movement in fiction and encouraged many younger authors. He wrote 35 novels, 35 plays, and many books of poetry, essays, and commentary.

however /haʊˈevə/ *adv.* 1. in whatever way, to whatever extent. 2. nevertheless.

howitzer /ˈhaʊɪtsə(r)/ *n.* a cannon, in use since the 16th century, with a particularly steep angle of fire. It was much developed in World War I for demolishing the fortresses of the trench system. The multinational NATO FH70 field howitzer is mobile and fires, under computer control, three 43 kg/95 lb shells at 32 km/20 mi range in 15 seconds. [from Dutch from German from Czech = catapult]

howl *n.* 1. the long, doleful cry of a dog etc.; a similar noise, e.g. that made by a strong wind. 2. a loud cry of pain, rage, derision, or laughter. —*v.t./i.* 1. to make a howl. 2. to weep loudly. 3. to utter with a howl. —**howl down**, to prevent (a speaker) from being heard by howling derision. [= Middle Low German, Middle Dutch *hulen*]

howler *n.* 1. a South American monkey of the genus *Alouatta*, with a howling cry. 2. (*colloquial*) a glaring mistake.

howsoever /haʊsəʊˈevə/ *adv.* in whatsoever way, to whatever extent.

Hoxha /ˈhɒdʒə/ Enver 1908–1985. Albanian Communist politician, the country's leader from 1954. He founded the Albanian Communist Party in 1941, and headed the liberation movement from 1939–44. He was prime minister 1944–54, combining with foreign affairs 1946–53, and from 1954 was first secretary of the Albanian Party of Labour. In policy he was a Stalinist and independent of both Chinese and Soviet communism.

hoy interjection used to call attention.

hoyden /ˈhɔɪdən/ *n.* a girl who behaves boisterously. —**hoydenish** *adj.*

Hoyle /hɔɪl/ Fred(erick) 1915– . English astronomer and writer. In 1948 he joined with Hermann Bondi and Thomas Gold in developing the ◊steady-state theory. In 1957, with Geoffrey and Margaret Burbidge and William Fowler, he showed that chemical elements heavier than hydrogen and helium are built up by nuclear reactions inside stars. He has suggested that life originates in the gas clouds of space, and is delivered to the Earth by passing comets. His science fiction novels include *The Black Cloud* 1957. His work on the evolution of stars was published in *Frontiers of Astronomy* 1955.

HP abbreviation of 1. hire-purchase. 2. or **hp** horsepower. 3. or **h.p.** high pressure.

HQ abbreviation of headquarters.

HRH abbreviation of Her or His Royal Highness.

hr(s) abbreviation of hour(s).

Hsuan Tung /ˌʃwæn ˈtʊŋ/ the name adopted by Henry ◊P'u-i on becoming emperor of China in 1908.

HT abbreviation of high tension.

Hua Guofeng /ˈhwɑː gwəʊˈfʌŋ/ formerly **Hua Kuofeng** 1920– . Chinese politician, leader of the Chinese Communist Party (CCP) 1976–81, premier 1976–80. He dominated Chinese politics 1976–77, seeking economic modernization without major structural reform. From 1978 he was gradually eclipsed by Deng Xiaoping. Hua was ousted from the Politburo in Sept 1982 but remained a member of the CCP Central Committee.

Huallaga River /waɪˈɑɡə/ tributary of the Marayon in NE Peru. The upper reaches of the river valley are used for growing coca, a major source of the drug cocaine.

Huang He /ˈhwæŋ ˈhəʊ/ formerly **Hwang-Ho** river in China; length 5,464 km/3,395 mi. Formerly known as 'China's sorrow' because of disastrous floods, it is now largely controlled through hydroelectric works and flood barriers. [= yellow river, from its muddy waters]

Huáscar /ˈwɑːskə/ *c.*1495–1532. King of the Incas. He shared the throne with his half-brother Atahualpa from 1525, but the latter overthrew and murdered him during the Spanish conquest.

hub *n.* 1. the central part of a wheel, from which the spokes radiate. 2. a central point of interest, activity etc.

Hubbard /ˈhʌbəd/ L(afayette) Ron(ald) 1911–1986. US science-fiction writer of the 1930s and 40s, founder in 1954 of ◊Scientology.

Hubble /ˈhʌbəl/ Edwin Powell 1889–1953. US astronomer, who discovered the existence of other galaxies (see ◊galaxy) outside our own, and classified them according to their shape. His theory that the universe is expanding is now generally accepted.

hubble-bubble /ˈhʌbəl ˈbʌbəl/ *n.* 1. a simple form of ◊hookah. 2. a bubbling sound; confused talk.

Hubble Space Telescope (HST) a telescope placed into orbit around the Earth, at an altitude of 610 km/380 mi, by the Space Shuttle *Discovery* in April 1990. It has a main mirror 2.4 m/94 in wide, which suffers from spherical aberration and so cannot be focused properly. Yet, because it is above the atmosphere, the HST outperforms ground-based telescopes. Computer techniques are being used to improve the images from the telescope until the arrival of a maintenance mission to install corrective optics.

hubbub /ˈhʌbʌb/ *n.* a confused noise; a disturbance.

hubby *n.* (*colloquial*) a husband.

Hubei /huːˈbeɪ/ formerly **Hupei** province of central China, through which flow the river Chang Jiang and its tributary the Han Shui; **area** 187,500 sq km/72,375 sq mi; **capital** Wuhan; **products** beans, cereals, cotton, rice, vegetables, copper, gypsum, iron ore, phosphorus, salt; **population** (1986) 49,890,000.

hubris /ˈhjuːbrɪs/ *n.* arrogant pride or presumption. In ancient Greek tragedy, hubris was a defiance of the gods and invariably led to the downfall of the hubristic character. —**hubristic** /hjuːˈbrɪstɪk/ *adj.* [Greek]

huckaback /ˈhʌkəbæk/ *n.* a strong linen or cotton fabric with a rough surface, used for towels.

huckleberry /ˈhʌk(ə)lbərɪ/ *n.* a berry-bearing bush of the genus *Gaylussacia*; it is closely related to the genus *Vaccinium*, which includes the blueberry in the USA and the bilberry in Britain. Huckleberry bushes have edible dark-blue berries.

huckster *n.* 1. a hawker. 2. a mercenary person. —*v.i.* 1. to haggle. 2. to be a hawker.

huddle *v.t./i.* 1. to heap or crowd together. 2. to nestle closely; to curl one's body into a small space. —*n.* a confused mass. —**go into a huddle,** to hold a close or secret conference.

Hudson /ˈhʌdsən/ Henry *c.*1565–*c.*1611. English explorer. Under the auspices of the Muscovy Company 1607–08, he made two unsuccessful attempts to find the northeast passage to China. In Sept 1609, commissioned by the Dutch East India Company, he reached New York Bay and sailed 240 km/150 mi up the river that now bears his name, establishing Dutch claims to the area. In 1610, he sailed from London in the *Discovery* and entered what is now the Hudson Strait. After an icebound winter, he was turned adrift by a mutinous crew in what is now Hudson Bay.

Hudson Rock. Stage name of Roy Scherer Jr 1925–1985. US film actor, a star from the mid-1950s to the mid-1960s, who appeared in several melodramas directed by Douglas Sirk and in three comedies co-starring Doris Day (including *Pillow Talk* 1959).

Hudson William) H(enry) 1841–1922. British author, born of US parents in Argentina. He was inspired by recollections of early days in Argentina to write the romances *The Purple Land* 1885 and *Green Mansions* 1904, and his autobiographical *Far Away and Long Ago* 1918. He wrote several books on birds, and on the English countryside, for example, *Nature in Down-Land* 1900 and *A Shepherd's Life* 1910.

Hudson Bay inland sea of NE Canada, linked with the Atlantic by **Hudson Strait**, and with the Arctic by Foxe Channel; area 1,233,000 sq km/476,000 sq mi. [named after Henry *Hudson*]

Hudson River school a group of US landscape painters of the early 19th century, inspired by the dramatic scenery of the Hudson River valley and the Catskill Mountains in New York State.

Hudson's Bay Company a chartered company founded by Prince ◊Rupert in 1670 to trade in furs with North American Indians. In 1783 the rival North West Company was formed, but in 1851 this became amalgamated with the Hudson's Bay Company. It is still Canada's biggest fur company, but today also sells general merchandise through department stores and has oil and natural gas interests.

hue[1] /hjuː/ *n.* a colour, a tint; a variety or shade of a colour. —**hued** *adj.* [Old English]

hue[2] *n.* **hue and cry,** a loud outcry (*against*), a clamour. [from Old French = outcry. There is some ground for thinking that *hue* (as distinct from *cry*) originally meant inarticulate sound, including that of a horn or trumpet as well as of the voice.]

huff *n.* a fit of petty annoyance. —*v.t./i.* 1. to blow. 2. to remove (an opponent's piece) as a forfeit in draughts. —**in a huff,** annoyed and offended.

huffy *adj.* apt to take offence; offended.

Hudson River school A festival gathering of old sailing ships on the Hudson River, New York.

hug *v.t.* (-**gg**-) 1. to squeeze tightly in one's arms, usually with affection. 2. (of a bear) to squeeze between the forelegs. 3. to keep close to. —*n.* a strong clasp with the arms; a grip in wrestling.

huge /hjuːdʒ/ *adj.* extremely large, enormous; (of an abstract thing) very great. —**hugeness** *n.* [from Old French *ahuge*]

hugely *adv.* very much.

hugger-mugger /ˈhʌɡəmʌɡə/ *adj. & adv.* 1. secret(ly). 2. confused, in confusion. —*n.* 1. confusion. 2. secrecy. [perhaps related to obsolete *hoder* = huddle and *mokere* = conceal]

Hughes /hjuːz/ Howard 1905–1976. US tycoon. Inheriting wealth from his father, who had patented a successful oil-drilling bit, he created a legendary financial empire. A skilled pilot, he manufactured and designed aircraft. He formed a film company in Hollywood and made the classic film *Hell's Angels* 1930, about aviators of World War I; later successes included *Scarface* 1932 and *The Outlaw* 1943.

Hughes Richard (Arthur Warren) 1900–1976. English writer. His study of childhood, *A High Wind in Jamaica*, was published in 1929, and the trilogy *The Human Predicament* in 1961–73.

Hughes Ted 1930– . English poet, poet laureate from 1984. His work includes *The Hawk in the Rain* 1957, *Lupercal* 1960, *Wodwo* 1967, and *River* 1983, and is characterized by its harsh portrayal of the crueller aspects of nature. In 1956 he married the poet Sylvia Plath.

Hughes Thomas 1822–1896. English writer, author of the children's book *Tom Brown's School Days* 1857, a story of Rugby school under Thomas Arnold. It had a sequel, *Tom Brown at Oxford* 1861.

Hughes William Morris 1864–1952. Australian politician, prime minister 1915–23; originally Labor, he headed a national cabinet. After resigning as prime minister in 1923, he held many other cabinet posts from 1934–41. He was born in London, but emigrated to Australia in 1884. He represented Australia in the peace conference after World War I at Versailles.

Hugo /ˈhjuːɡəʊ/ Victor (Marie) 1802–1885. French poet, novelist, and dramatist. The *Odes et poésies diverses* appeared in 1822, and his verse play *Hernani* 1830 established him as the leader of French Romanticism. More volumes of verse followed between his series of dramatic novels, which included *The Hunchback of Notre Dame* 1831 and *Les Misérables* 1862.

The word is the verb and the verb is God.
Victor Hugo
Contemplations

Huguenot /ˈhjuːɡənəʊ/ *n.* (*historical*) a French Protestant in the 16th century; the term referred mainly to Calvinists. Severely persecuted under Francis I and Henry II, the Huguenots survived both an attempt to exterminate them (the **Massacre of ◊St Bartholomew** on 24 Aug 1572) and the religious wars of the next 30 years. In 1598 Henry IV (himself formerly a Huguenot) granted them toleration under the **Edict of ◊Nantes**. Louis XIV revoked the edict in 1685, attempting their forcible conversion, and 400,000 emigrated. Some of the nobles adopted Protestantism for political reasons, causing the civil wars of 1592–98. The Huguenots lost military power after the revolt at La Rochelle 1627–29, but were still tolerated by the chief ministers Richelieu and Mazarin. Provoked by Louis XIV they left, taking their industrial skills with them; 40,000 settled in Britain, where their descendants include the actor David Garrick and the textile manufacturer Samuel Courtauld. Many settled in North America, founding new towns. Only in 1802 was the Huguenot church again legalized in France. [French, assimilation of *eiguenot* (= confederate) to name of Geneva burgomaster Hugues]

huh /hʌ/ interjection expressing disgust, surprise etc.

Huhehot /huːhɜːˈhəʊt/ former name of ◊Hohhot, city in Inner Mongolia.

hula /ˈhuːlə/ *n.* a Hawaiian woman's dance with flowing movements of the arms. —**hula-hoop** *n.* a large hoop for spinning round the body. [Hawaiian]

hulk *n.* **1.** the body of a dismantled ship; (*historical*, in *plural*) this used as a prison. **2.** a large clumsy-looking person or thing. [Old English]

hulking *adj.* (*colloquial*) bulky, clumsy.

hull[1] *n.* the body of a ship, airship etc.

hull[2] *n.* the pod of peas or beans, the husk of certain seeds or fruits, the calyx of a ripe strawberry, raspberry etc. —*v.t.* to remove the hulls of (strawberries etc.). [Old English]

Hull /hʌl/ Cordell 1871–1955. US Democratic politician, born in Tennessee. He was a member of Congress 1907–33, and, as F D Roosevelt's secretary of state 1933–44, he opposed German and Japanese aggression. He was identified with the Good Neighbour Policy of nonintervention in Latin America. In his last months of office he paved the way for a system of collective security, for which he was called 'father' of the United Nations. He was awarded the Nobel Prize for Peace in 1945.

Hull officially **Kingston-upon-Hull** city and port on the river Humber, administrative headquarters of Humberside, England; population (1986) 258,000. It is linked with the S bank of the estuary by the Humber Bridge. Industries include fish processing, vegetable oils, flour milling, electricals, textiles, paint, pharmaceuticals, chemicals, caravans, and aircraft.

hullabaloo /hʌləbə'luː/ *n.* an uproar.

Hulme /hjuːm/ Keri 1947– . New Zealand novelist who won Britain's ◊Booker Prize with her first novel *The Bone People* 1985.

hum *v.t./i.* (-mm-) **1.** to make a low, steady, continuous sound like that of a bee. **2.** to sing with closed lips and without words. **3.** to utter a slight, inarticulate sound, especially of hesitation. **4.** (*colloquial*) to be in an active state. **5.** (*slang*) to smell unpleasantly. —*n.* **1.** a humming sound. **2.** an exclamation of hesitation. **3.** (*slang*) a bad smell. —**hum and ha** *or* **haw**, to hesitate.

hum, environmental a disturbing sound of frequency about 40 Hz, heard by individuals sensitive to this range, but inaudible to the rest of the population. It may be caused by industrial noise pollution or have a more exotic origin, such as the jet stream, a fast-flowing high-altitude (about 15,000 m/50,000 ft) mass of air.

human /'hjuːmən/ *adj.* **1.** of or belonging to mankind. **2.** having the qualities that distinguish mankind, not divine or animal or mechanical; showing mankind's better qualities (as kindness, pity etc.). —*n.* a human being. —**human being**, see ◊man! **/human rights**, the rights held to be claimable by any living person. [from Old French from Latin *humanus* (*homo* = man)]

human body the physical structure of the human being. It develops from the single cell of the fertilized ovum, is born at 40 weeks, and usually reaches sexual maturity between 11 and 18 years of age. The bony framework (skeleton) consists of more than 200 bones, over half of which are in the hands and feet. Bones are held together by joints, some of which allow movement. The circulatory system supplies muscles and organs with blood, which provides oxygen and food and removes carbon dioxide and other waste products. Body functions are controlled by the nervous system and hormones. In the upper part of the trunk is the thorax, which contains the lungs and heart. Below this is the abdomen, containing the digestive system (stomach and intestines); the liver, spleen, and pancreas; the urinary system (kidneys, ureters, and bladder); and in women, the reproductive organs (ovaries, uterus, and vagina). In men, the prostate gland and seminal vesicles only of the reproductive system are situated in the abdomen, the testes being in the scrotum, which, with the penis, is suspended in front of and below the abdomen. The bladder empties through a small channel (urethra); in the female this opens in the upper end of the vulval cleft, which also contains the opening of the vagina, or birth canal; in the male, the urethra is continued into the penis. In both sexes, the lower bowel terminates in the anus, a ring of strong muscle situated between the buttocks.

human–computer interaction the exchange of information between a person and a computer, through the medium of a ◊user interface, studied as a branch of ergonomics.

humane /hjuːˈmeɪn/ *adj.* benevolent, compassionate, merciful; (of learning), tending to civilize. —**humane killer**, an implement for the painless slaughter of animals. —**humanely** *adv.*

humanism /'hjuːmənɪzəm/ *n.* **1.** a belief or attitude emphasizing common human needs and seeking solely rational ways of solving human problems. **2.** literary culture, especially in the Renaissance. —**humanist** *n.*, **humanistic** /-'nɪstɪk/ *adj.* [from French from Italian]

humanitarian /hjuːˌmæniˈteəriən/ *adj.* concerned with promoting human welfare. —*n.* a humanitarian person. —**humanitarianism** *n.*

humanity /hjuːˈmænɪtɪ/ *n.* **1.** human nature or (in *plural*) qualities. **2.** the human race, people. **3.** being humane, kind-heartedness. **4.** (in *plural*) learning or literature concerned with human culture, formerly especially the Greek and Latin classics.

humanize /'hjuːmənaɪz/ *v.t.* to make human or humane. —**humanization** /-'zeɪʃən/ *n.* [from French]

humanly /'hjuːmənlɪ/ *adv.* in a human manner; by human means, within human limitations.

Human Rights, Universal Declaration of a charter of civil and political rights drawn up by the United Nations in 1948. They include the right to life, liberty, education, and equality before the law; to freedom of movement, religion, association, and information; and to a nationality. Under the European Convention of Human Rights of 1950, the Council of Europe established the **European Commission of Human Rights** (headquarters in Strasbourg, France), which investigates complaints by states or individuals, and its findings are examined by the **European Court of Human Rights** (established in 1959), whose compulsory jurisdiction has been recognized by a number of states, including the UK.

human species, origins of the evolution of humans from ancestral ◊primates (sense 2). The African apes (gorilla and chimpanzee) are shown by anatomical and molecular comparisons to be the closest living relatives of humans. Molecular studies put the date of the split between the human and African ape lines at 5–10 million years ago. There are no ape or **hominid** (of the human group) fossils from this period; the oldest known hominids, found in Ethiopia and Tanzania, date from 3.5 million years ago. These creatures are known as *Australopithecus afarensis*, and they walked upright. They were either direct ancestors or an offshoot of the line that led to modern humans. They might have been the ancestors of *Homo habilis* (considered by some to be a species of *Australopithecus*), who appeared about a million years later, had slightly larger bodies and brains, and were probably the first to use stone tools. *A. robustus* and *A. gracilis* also lived in Africa at the same time, but these are not generally considered to be our ancestors. Over 1.5 million years ago, *H. erectus*, believed by some to be descended from *H. habilis*, appeared in Africa. The *erectus* people had much larger brains, and were probably the first to use fire and the first to move out of Africa. Their remains are found as far afield as China, Spain, and S Britain. Modern humans, *H. sapiens sapiens*, and the Neanderthals, *H. sapiens neanderthalensis*, are probably descended from *H. erectus*. Neanderthals were large-brained and heavily built, probably adapted to the cold conditions of the ice ages. They lived in Europe and the Middle East, and died out about 40,000 years ago, leaving *H. sapiens sapiens* as the only remaining species of the hominid group. Creationists, however, believe that the origin of the human species is as written in the book of Genesis in the Old Testament of the Bible.

Humber Bridge /'hʌmbə/ a suspension bridge with twin towers 163 m/535 ft high, which spans the estuary of the river Humber in NE England. When completed in 1980, it was the world's longest bridge with a span of 1,410 m/4,628 ft.

Humberside /'hʌmbəsaɪd/ county of NE England; **area** 3,510 sq km/1,355 sq mi; **administrative headquarters** Hull; **products** petrochemicals, refined oil, processed fish, cereals, root crops, cattle; **population** (1987) 847,000.

humble *adj.* **1.** having or showing a low estimate of one's own importance. **2.** of a low social or political rank. **3.** (of a thing) not large or elaborate. —*v.t.* to make humble, to lower the rank or self-importance of. —**eat humble pie**, to make a humble apology. [from *umbles* = edible offal of deer] —**humbleness** *n.*, **humbly** *adv.* [from Old French from Latin *humilis* = lowly (*humus* = ground)]

Humboldt /'hʌmbəʊlt/ Friedrich Heinrich Alexander, Baron von 1769–1859. German botanist and geologist who, with the French botanist Aimé Bonpland (1773–1858), explored the regions of the Orinoco and the Amazon rivers in South America 1800–04, and gathered 60,000 plant specimens. On his return, Humboldt devoted 21 years to writing an account of his travels.

Humboldt Wilhelm von 1767–1835. German philologist, whose stress on the identity of thought and language influenced ◊Chomsky. He was the brother of Friedrich Humboldt.

humbug /'hʌmbʌg/ *n.* 1. deceptive or false talk or behaviour. 2. an impostor. 3. a hard-boiled sweet usually flavoured with peppermint. — *v.t./i.* (**-gg-**) to be or behave like an impostor; to deceive.

humdinger /'hʌmdɪŋə/ *n.* (*slang*) a remarkable person or thing.

humdrum /'hʌmdrʌm/ *adj.* dull, commonplace, monotonous.

Hume /hjuːm/ Basil 1923– . English Roman Catholic cardinal from 1976. A Benedictine monk, he was abbot of Ampleforth in Yorkshire 1963–76, and in 1976 became archbishop of Westminster, the first monk to hold the office.

Hume David 1711–1776. Scottish philosopher. *A Treatise of Human Nature* 1740 is a central text of British empiricism. Hume denies the possibility of going beyond the subjective experiences of 'ideas' and 'impressions'. The effect of this position is to invalidate metaphysics.

Hume Fergus 1859–1932. British writer. Educated in New Zealand, he returned to England in 1888; his *Mystery of a Hansom Cab* 1887 was one of the first detective stories.

Hume Hamilton 1797–1873. Australian explorer. In 1824, with William Hovell, he led an expedition from Sydney to the Murray River and Port Phillip. The Melbourne–Sydney **Hume Highway** is named after him.

Hume John 1937– . Northern Ireland Catholic politician, leader of the Social Democrat Party (SDLP) from 1979. Hume was a founder member of the Credit Union Party, which later became the SDLP.

humerus /'hjuːmərəs/ *n.* the upper bone of the forelimb of tetrapods. In humans the humerus is the bone above the elbow. —**humeral** *adj.* [Latin = shoulder]

humid /'hjuːmɪd/ *adj.* (of the air or a climate) damp. [from French or Latin ((*h*)*umēre* = be moist)]

humidifier /hjuː'mɪdɪfaɪə/ *n.* a device for keeping the air moist in a room etc.

humidify /hjuː'mɪdɪfaɪ/ *v.t.* to make humid.

humidity /hjuː'mɪdɪtɪ/ *n.* the quantity of water vapour in a given volume of the atmosphere (absolute humidity), or the ratio of the amount of water vapour in the atmosphere to the saturation value at the same temperature (relative humidity); at ◊dew point (see under ◊dew) the latter is 100%. Relative humidity is measured by various types of ◊hygrometer. [from Old French or Latin]

humiliate /hjuː'mɪlɪeɪt/ *v.t.* to harm the dignity or self-respect of. —**humiliation** /-'eɪʃən/ *n.* [from Latin *humiliare*]

humility /hjuː'mɪlɪtɪ/ *n.* a humble attitude of mind; humbleness. [from Old French from Latin]

hummingbird *n.* a small tropical bird of the family Trochilidae, found in the Americas. Hummingbirds are the only birds able to fly backwards. They are brilliantly coloured, and have long tongues to obtain nectar from flowers and capture insects. The Cuban **bee hummingbird** *Mellisuga helenae* is the world's smallest bird at 5.5 cm/2 in long, and weighs 2 g/less than 1/10 oz. [name derived from the sound produced by the rapid vibration of their wings]

hummock /'hʌmək/ *n.* a low hill or hump.

humoresque /hjuːmə'resk/ *n.* a light and lively musical composition. [from German *humoreske*]

humorist /'hjuːmərɪst/ *n.* a writer or speaker noted for humour.

humorous /'hjuːmərəs/ *adj.* full of humour, amusing. —**humorously** *adv.*

humour /'hjuːmə/ *n.* 1. the quality of being amusing. 2. the ability to enjoy what is comic or amusing. 3. a state of mind. 4. each of the four fluids (blood, phlegm, choler, and melancholy) formerly held to determine a person's physical and mental qualities. —*v.t.* to keep (a person) contented

by indulging his or her wishes. —**aqueous humour**, the transparent substance between the lens of the eye and the cornea. **vitreous humour**, that filling the eyeball. [from Old French from Latin (*h*)*umor* = moisture]

hump *n.* 1. the rounded protuberance on the back of a camel etc., or as an abnormality on a person's back. 2. a rounded, raised mass of earth etc. 3. (*slang*) a fit of depression or annoyance. —*v.t.* 1. to form into a hump. 2. to hoist or shoulder (one's pack etc.).

humpback *n.* a deformed back with a hump; a person with this. —**humpback bridge**, a small bridge with a steep ascent and descent. —**humpbacked** *adj.*

Humperdinck /'hʊmpədɪŋk/ Engelbert 1854–1921. German composer who studied music in Munich and in Italy and assisted Richard ◊Wagner at the Bayreuth Festival Theatre. He wrote the musical fairy operas *Hänsel und Gretel* 1893, and *Königskinder/King's Children* 1910.

humph /hʌmf/ *int.* & *n.* an inarticulate sound expressing doubt or dissatisfaction.

humus /'hjuːməs/ *n.* a rich, dark, organic material formed by the decay of dead leaves and plants etc., and essential to the fertility of soil. It has a higher carbon content than the original material and a lower nitrogen content, and is an important source of minerals in soil fertility. [Latin = ground]

Hun *n.* 1. (usually *derogatory*) a German. 2. a member of any of a number of nomad Mongol peoples who were first recorded historically in the 2nd century BC, raiding across the Great Wall into China. They entered Europe about AD 372, settled in the area that is now Hungary, and imposed their supremacy on the Ostrogoths and other Germanic peoples. Under the leadership of Attila they attacked the Byzantine Empire, invaded Gaul, and threatened Rome. After Attila's death in 453 their power was broken by a revolt of their subject peoples. The **White Huns**, or Ephthalites, a kindred people, raided Persia and N India in the 5th and 6th centuries. [Old English, ultimately from Turki *Hun-yü*]

Hunan /hu:'næn/ province of south central China; **area** 210,500 sq km/81,253 sq mi; **capital** Changsha; **products** rice, tea, tobacco, cotton; nonferrous minerals; **population** (1986) 56,960,000.

hunch *v.t./i.* to bend or arch into a hump. —*n.* 1. a hump, a hunk. 2. an intuitive feeling.

hunchback *n.* a humpback. —**hunchbacked** *adj.*

hundred /'hʌndrəd/ *adj.* & *n.* 1. (*singular* form is used, with plural verb, when qualified by a preceding word) ten times ten; the symbol for this (100, c, C). 2. (*in plural*) very many. 3. (*historical*) a subdivision of a county or shire with its own court. —**hundreds and thousands**, tiny coloured sweets for decorating a cake etc. —**hundredth** *adj.* & *n.* [Old English]

hundred days, the in European history, the period 20 March–28 June 1815, marking the French emperor Napoleon's escape from imprisonment on Elba to his departure from Paris after losing the battle of Waterloo on 18 June.

hundredfold *adj.* & *adv.* 1. a hundred times as much or as many. 2. consisting of a hundred parts.

hundredweight *n.* (*plural* the same) an imperial unit (symbol cwt) of mass, equal to 112 lb (50.8 kg). It is sometimes called the long hundredweight, to distinguish it from the short hundredweight or **cental**, equal to 100 lb (45.4 kg). —**metric hundredweight**, 50 kg.

Hundred Years' War the series of conflicts between England and France 1337–1453. Its origins lay with the English kings' possession of Gascony (SW France), which the French kings claimed as their ◊fief, and with trade rivalries over ◊Flanders.

hung see ◊hang.

Hungarian /hʌn'geərɪən/ *adj.* of Hungary or its people or language. —*n.* 1. a native or inhabitant of Hungary. 2. the language of Hungary, a member of the Finno-Ugric language group, spoken principally in Hungary but also in parts of Czechoslovakia, Romania, and Yugoslavia. Hungarian is known as *Magyar* among its speakers. It is written in a form of the Roman alphabet in which *s* corresponds to English *sh*, and *sz* to *s*. [from Latin *Hungari* = Magyar nation]

Hungary /'hʌŋgərɪ/ Republic of; country in central Europe, bordered to the N by Czechoslovakia, NE by the USSR, E by Romania, S by Yugoslavia, and W

Hungary

by Austria; **area** 93,032 sq km/35,910 sq mi; **capital** Budapest; **physical** Great Hungarian Plain covers E half of country; Bakony Forest; Transdanubian Highlands in W; rivers Danube, Tisza; Lake Balaton; **head of state** Matyas Szuros (acting) from 1989; **head of government** Károly Grosz from 1988; **political system** socialist pluralist republic; **exports** machinery, vehicles, chemicals; textiles; **population** (1990 est) 10,546,000 (Magyar 92%, Romany 3%, German 2.5%); **language** Hungarian (or Magyar); **recent history** a Stalinist regime was imposed in 1946 and a Soviet-style constitution was adopted in 1949. A national uprising in 1956 was quelled by the USSR. Reforms 1968–88 were followed by the opening of the border with Austria in May 1989.

hunger /'hʌŋgə/ *n.* 1. need for food, the discomfort felt when one has not eaten for some time. 2. strong desire. —*v.i.* to feel hunger. —**hunger strike**, refusal of food (especially by a prisoner) as a form of protest. [Old English]

hunger march a procession of the unemployed, a feature of social protest in interwar Britain. The first, from Glasgow to London, took place in 1922 and another in 1929. In 1932 the National Unemployed Workers' Movement organized the largest demonstration, with groups converging on London from all parts of the country, but the most emotive was probably the Jarrow Crusade of 1936, when 200 unemployed shipyard workers marched to the capital (see ◊unemployment).

hungry /'hʌŋgrɪ/ *adj.* feeling or showing hunger; inducing hunger. —**hungrily** *adv.* [Old English]

hunk *n.* a large piece cut off.

hunkers *n.pl.* the haunches. [originally Scottish (*hunker* = to squat)]

Hun Sen /'hʊn 'sen/ 1950–. Cambodian political leader, prime minister from 1985. Originally a member of the Khmer Rouge army, he defected in 1977 to join Vietnam-based anti-Khmer Cambodian forces.

hunt /hʌnt/ *v.t./i.* 1. to pursue (wild animals or game, or *absolute*) for sport or food; (of an animal) to pursue its prey. 2. to pursue with hostility. 3. to search for; to make a search (*for*); to search (a district) for game. 4. to use (a horse or hounds) for hunting. 5. (of an engine) to run alternately too fast and too slow. —*n.* 1. hunting. 2. an association of people hunting; the district where they hunt. [Old English *hentan* = seize]

Hunt William Holman 1827–1910. English painter, one of the founders of the ◊Pre-Raphaelite Brotherhood in 1848. Obsessed with realistic detail, he travelled from 1854 onwards to Syria and Palestine to paint biblical subjects. His works include *The Awakening Conscience* 1853 (Tate Gallery, London) and *The Light of the World* 1854 (Keble College, Oxford).

hunter /'hʌntə/ *n.* 1. one who hunts. 2. a horse ridden for hunting. 3. a watch with a hinged metal cover protecting the glass. —**hunter's moon**, the first full moon after the harvest moon.

Hunter John 1728–1793. Scottish surgeon, pathologist, and comparative anatomist. His main contribution to medicine was his insistence on rigorous scientific method. He was also the first to understand the nature of digestion.

Huntingdonshire /'hʌntɪŋdənʃə/ former English county, merged in 1974 in a much enlarged Cambridgeshire.

Huntington's chorea /'hʊntɪŋtənz kərɪə/ a rare hereditary disease that begins in middle age. It is characterized by involuntary movements and rapid mental degeneration progressing to ◊dementia. There is no known cure.

huntsman *n.* (*plural* **huntsmen**) a hunter; a person in charge of hounds.

Hunyadi /'hʊnjodi/ János Corvinus 1387–1456. Hungarian politician and general. Born in Transylvania, reputedly the son of the emperor ◊Sigismund, he won battles against the Turks from the 1440s. In 1456 he defeated them at Belgrade, but died shortly afterwards of the plague.

Hunza /'hʊnzə/ small state on the NW frontier of Kashmir, under the rule of Pakistan.

Hupei /hu:'peɪ/ former name of ◊Hubei, province of China.

Hurd /hɜ:d/ Douglas (Richard) 1930– . English Conservative politician, foreign secretary from 1989 and home secretary 1986–89. He entered the House of Commons in 1974, representing Witney from 1983. He was made a junior minister by Margaret Thatcher, and the sudden resignation of Leon Brittan projected Hurd into the home secretary's post in early 1986. In 1989 he was appointed foreign secretary in the reshuffle that followed Nigel Lawson's resignation as chancellor of the Exchequer. He was a candidate in the Tory leadership contest in Nov 1990 following Thatcher's unexpected resignation.

hurdle *n.* 1. a portable rectangular frame with bars, for a temporary fence etc. 2. each of a series of upright frames to be jumped over in a race; (in *plural*) a race with such jumps. 3. an obstacle; a difficulty. —*v.t./i.* 1. to fence off with hurdles. 2. to run in a hurdle race. [Old English]

hurdler *n.* 1. one who runs in hurdle races. 2. one who makes hurdles.

hurdy-gurdy /'hɜ:dɪgɜ:dɪ/ *n.* 1. a musical stringed instrument resembling a violin in tone but using a form of keyboard to play a melody and drone strings to provide a continuous harmony. An inbuilt wheel turned by a handle, acts as a bow. 2. (*colloquial*) a barrel organ.

hurl *v.t.* 1. to throw with great force. 2. to utter vehemently. —*n.* a forceful throw.

hurling *n.* or **hurley** a stick-and-ball team game played with 15 a side, popular in Ireland. It was first played over 3,000 years ago, and at one time it was outlawed. The rules were standardized in 1884, and are now under the control of the Gaelic Athletic Association.

hurly-burly /'hɜ:lɪbɜ:lɪ/ *n.* boisterous activity, a commotion.

Huron /'hjʊərən/ second largest of the Great Lakes of North America, on the US-Canadian border; area 60,000 sq km/23,160 sq mi. It includes Georgian Bay, Saginaw Bay, and Manitoulin Island.

hurrah /hʊ'rɑ:/ *int.* & *n.* or **hurray** /-'reɪ/ an exclamation of joy or approval.

hurricane /'hʌrɪkən/ *n.* a revolving storm in tropical regions, called **typhoon** in the N Pacific. It originates between 5° and 20° N or S of the equator, when the surface temperature of the ocean is above 27°C/80°F. A central calm area, called the eye, is surrounded by inwardly spiralling winds (counter-clockwise in the N hemisphere) of up to 320 kph/200 mph. A hurricane is accompanied by lightning and torrential rain, and can cause extensive damage. In meteorology, a hurricane is a wind of force 12 or more on the ◊Beaufort scale. The most intense hurricane recorded in the Caribbean/Atlantic sector was Hurricane Gilbert in 1988, with sustained winds of 280 kph/175 mph and gusts of over 320 kph/200 mph. —**hurricane lamp**, a lamp with the flame protected from violent wind. [from Spanish and Portuguese from Carib]

hurry /'hʌrɪ/ *n.* great haste; eagerness, urgency; the need for haste. —*v.t./i.* 1. to move or act with eager or excessive haste. 2. to cause to move or proceed in this way. 3. (in *past participle*) hasty, done rapidly. —**hurry up**, (*colloquial*) to make haste. **in a hurry**, hurrying; easily or readily.

hurry-scurry /hʌri'skʌrɪ/ *n.* disorderly haste. —*adj.* & *adv.* in confusion.

hurt *v.t./i.* (*past* and *past participle* **hurt**) 1. to cause pain, injury, or damage to; to cause pain or harm. 2. to cause mental pain or distress to. 3. to feel pain. —*n.* an injury, harm. [from Old French *hurter*]

hurtful *adj.* causing (especially mental) hurt. —**hurtfully** *adv.*

hurtle *v.t./i.* to move or hurl rapidly or with a clattering sound; to come with a crash. [from *hurt* in obsolete sense 'strike forcibly']

Husák /ˈhusɑːk/ Gustáv 1913– . Leader of the Communist Party of Czechoslovakia (CCP) 1969–87 and president 1975–89. After the 1968 Prague Spring of liberalization, his task was to restore control, purge the CCP, and oversee the implementation of a new, federalist constitution. He was deposed in the popular uprising of Nov-Dec 1989 and expelled from the Communist Party in Feb 1990.

husband /ˈhʌzbənd/ *n.* a married man in relation to his wife. —*v.t.* to use economically. [Old English from Old Norse = house dweller]

husbandry *n.* 1. farming. 2. the management of resources.

huscarl *n.* an Anglo-Danish warrior, in 10th-century Denmark and early 11th-century England. Huscarls formed the bulk of English royal armies until the Norman Conquest.

hush *v.t./i.* to make or become silent or quiet. —*n.* silence. —**hush-hush** *adj.* (*colloquial*) highly confidential, very secret. **hush money**, money paid to prevent the disclosure of a discreditable affair. **hush up**, to suppress public mention of (an affair).

husk *n.* 1. the dry outer covering of certain seeds and fruits. 2. the worthless outside part of anything. —*v.t.* to remove the husk(s) from. [from Low German = sheath]

husky[1] *adj.* 1. full of or dry as husks. 2. (of a person or voice) dry in the throat, hoarse. 3. big and strong. —**huskily** *adv.*, **huskiness** *n.*

husky[2] *n.* a sledge dog used in Arctic regions, growing to 70 cm/2 ft high, and weighing about 50 kg/110 lbs, with pricked ears, thick fur, and a bushy tail.

Huss /hʌs/ John *c.*1373–1415. Bohemian church reformer, rector of Prague University from 1402, who was excommunicated for attacks on ecclesiastical abuses. He was summoned before the Council of Constance in 1414, defended the English reformer Wycliffe, rejected the pope's authority, and was burned at the stake. His followers were called Hussites.

hussar /huˈzɑː/ *n.* a soldier of a light cavalry regiment. [from Magyar, ultimately from Italian]

Hussein /huˈseɪn/ ibn Ali *c.*1854–1931. Leader of the Arab revolt 1916–18 against the Turks. He proclaimed himself king of the Hejaz in 1916, accepted the caliphate in 1924, but was unable to retain it due to internal fighting. He was deposed in 1924 by Ibn Saud.

Hussein ibn Talal 1935– . King of Jordan from 1952. Great-grandson of Hussein ibn Ali, he became king after the mental incapacity of his father, Talal. By 1967 he had lost all his kingdom west of the river Jordan in the ◊Arab-Israeli Wars, and in 1970 suppressed the ◊Palestine Liberation Organization acting as a guerrilla force against his rule on the remaining East Bank territories. In recent years, he has become a moderating force in Middle Eastern politics. After Iraq's annexation of Kuwait in 1990 he attempted to mediate between the opposing sides.

Hussein Saddam 1937– . Iraqi left-wing politician, in power from 1968, president from 1979. Ruthless in the pursuit of his objectives, he fought a bitter war against Iran 1980–88 and dealt harshly with Kurdish rebels seeking a degree of independence. In 1990 he ordered the invasion and annexation of Kuwait, provoking an international crisis, a United Nations embargo, and the ◊Gulf War in 1991. He was forced to withdraw from Kuwait, but retained (controversially) the presidency in Iraq.

Husserl /ˈhusəl/ Edmund (Gustav Albrecht) 1859–1938. German philosopher, regarded as the founder of ◊phenomenology, a philosophy concentrating on what is consciously experienced.

Hussite /ˈhuːsaɪt/ *n.* a follower of John ◊Huss. Opposed to both German and papal influence in Bohemia, the Hussites waged successful war against the Holy Roman Empire from 1419, but Roman Catholicism was finally re-established in 1620.

hussy *n.* a saucy girl; an immoral woman. [contraction of *housewife*]

hustings *n.* 1. parliamentary election proceedings. 2. (*historical*) a platform from which (before 1872) candidates for Parliament were nominated and addressed electors. [plural of *husting*, Old English, from Old Norse = house of assembly (*house* and *thing*)]

hustle /ˈhʌsəl/ *v.t./i.* 1. to jostle, to push roughly. 2. to hurry. 3. to bustle; to cause to act quickly and without time to consider things. 4. (*slang*) to swindle; to obtain by force. —*n.* hustling, bustle. —**hustler**. *n.* [from Middle Dutch *husselen* = shake]

Huston /ˈhjuːstən/ John 1906–1987. US film director, screenwriter, and actor. An impulsive and individualistic filmmaker, he often dealt with the themes of greed, treachery in human relationships, and the loner. His works as a director include *The Maltese Falcon* 1941 (his debut), *The Treasure of the Sierra Madre* 1948 (in which his father Walter Huston starred and for which both won Academy Awards), *The African Queen* 1951, and *The Dead* 1987.

hut *n.* a small, simple or crude house or shelter; a temporary housing for troops. —*v.t.* (**-tt-**) 1. to place (troops etc.) in huts. 2. to furnish with huts. [from French *hutte* from Middle High German]

hutch *n.* a boxlike pen for rabbits etc. [originally = coffer, from Old French *huche* from Latin]

Hutton /ˈhʌtn/ James 1726–1797. Scottish geologist, known as the 'founder of geology', who formulated the concept of ◊uniformitarianism. In 1785 he developed a theory of the igneous origin of many rocks.

Hutton Leonard 1916–1990. English cricketer, born in Pudsey, West Yorkshire. He captained England in 23 test matches 1952–56 and was England's first professional captain. In 1938 at the Oval he scored 364 against Australia, a world record test score until beaten by Gary ◊Sobers in 1958.

Huxley /ˈhʌksli/ Aldous (Leonard) 1894–1963. English writer. The satirical disillusionment of his first novel, *Crome Yellow* 1921, continued throughout *Antic Hay* 1923, *Those Barren Leaves* 1925, *Point Counter Point* 1928, and *Brave New World* 1932, in which human beings are mass produced in the laboratory under the control of the omnipotent 'Big Brother'.

Happiness is like coke – something you get as a by-product in the process of making something else.

Aldous Huxley
Point Counter Point

Huxley Andrew 1917– . English physiologist, awarded the Nobel Prize for Medicine in 1963 with Allan Hodgkin and John Eccles, for work on nerve impulses.

Huxley Julian 1887–1975. English biologist, first director-general of UNESCO, and a founder of the World Wildlife Fund (now the World Wide Fund for Nature).

Huxley Thomas Henry 1825–1895. English scientist and humanist. Following the publication of Charles Darwin's *On the Origin of Species* 1859, he became known as 'Darwin's bulldog', and for many years was a prominent champion of evolution. In 1869, he coined the word 'agnostic' to express his own religious attitude. His grandsons include Aldous, Andrew, and Julian Huxley.

Hu Yaobang /ˈhuː jaʊˈbæŋ/ 1915–1989. Chinese politician, Communist Party (CCP) chair 1981–87. A protégé of the communist leader Deng Xiaoping, Hu presided over a radical overhaul of the party structure and personnel 1982–86. His death ignited the prodemocracy movement, which was eventually crushed in Tiananmen Square, Beijing, in June 1989.

Huygens /ˈhaɪɡənz/ Christiaan 1629–1695. Dutch mathematical physicist and astronomer, who proposed the wave theory of light. He developed the pendulum clock, discovered polarization, and observed Saturn's rings.

Huysmans /wiːsˈmɒns/J(oris) K(arl) 1848–1907. French novelist of Dutch ancestry. His novel *Marthe* 1876, the story of a courtesan, was followed by other realistic novels, including *À rebours*/*Against Nature* 1884, a novel of self-absorbed aestheticism that symbolized the 'decadent' movement.

Hwang-Ho /hwæŋ ˈhəʊ/ former name of the ◊Huang He, river in China.

hyacinth /ˈhaɪəsɪnθ/ *n.* **1.** any bulb-producing plant of the genus *Hyacinthus* of the lily family Liliaceae, native to the E Mediterranean and Africa. The **cultivated hyacinth** *H. orientalis* has large, scented, cylindrical heads of pink, white, or blue flowers. The ◊**water hyacinth**, genus *Eichhornia*, a floating plant from South America, is unrelated. **2.** purplish-blue. —**wild hyacinth**, the bluebell. [from French from Latin from Greek *huakinthos* = flower and gem, also name of youth loved by Apollo]

Hyades /ˈhaɪədiːz/ *n.* a V-shaped cluster of stars that forms the face of the bull in the constellation Taurus. It is 130 light years away and contains over 200 stars, although only about 12 are visible to the naked eye.

hybrid /ˈhaɪbrɪd/ *n.* **1.** the offspring of two animals or plants of different species or varieties. In most cases, hybrids between species are infertile and unable to reproduce sexually. In plants, however, doubling of the chromosomes (see ◊polyploid) can restore the fertility of such hybrids. **2.** a thing composed of diverse elements; a word with parts from different languages. —*adj.* bred or produced as a hybrid; cross-bred. —**hybridism** *n.*, **hybridity** /-ˈbɪdɪtɪ/ *n.* [from Latin *hybrida* originally = offspring of tame sow and wild boar]

hybridize *v.t./i.* to subject (a species etc.) to cross-breeding; to produce hybrids; (of an animal or plant) to interbreed. —**hybridization** /-ˈzeɪʃən/ *n.*

hydathode *n.* a specialized pore, or less commonly, a hair, through which water is secreted by hydrostatic pressure from the interior of a plant leaf on to the surface. Hydathodes are found on many different plants and are usually situated around the leaf margin at vein endings. Each pore is surrounded by two crescent-shaped cells and resembles an open ◊stoma, but the size of the opening cannot be varied as in a stoma. The process of water secretion through hydathodes is known as ◊guttation.

Hyderabad /ˈhaɪdərəbæd/ **1.** capital city of the S central Indian state of Andhra Pradesh, on the river Musi; population (1981) 2,528,000. Products include carpets, silks, and metal inlay work. It was formerly the capital of the state of Hyderabad. Buildings include the Jama Masjid mosque and Golconda fort. **2.** city in Sind province, SE Pakistan; population (1981) 795,000. It produces gold, pottery, glass, and furniture. It is the third largest city of Pakistan and was founded in 1768.

Hyder Ali /ˈhaɪdər ˈɑːliː/ *c.*1722–1782. Indian general, sultan of Mysore from 1759. In command of the army in Mysore from 1749, he became the ruler of the state in 1759, and rivalled British power in the area until his triple defeat by Sir Eyre Coote in 1781 during the Anglo-French wars. He was the father of Tippu Sultan.

hydra /ˈhaɪdrə/ *n.* **1.** a thing hard to extirpate. **2.** a water snake. **3.** a freshwater polyp of the genus *Hydra*, with a tubular body and tentacles around the mouth. [Greek = water snake]

Hydra 1. in Greek mythology, a huge monster with nine heads. If one were cut off, two would grow in its place. One of the 12 labours of Heracles was to kill it. **2.** in astronomy, the longest constellation, winding across more than a quarter of the sky between Cancer and Libra in the southern hemisphere. Hydra represents the multiheaded monster slain by Heracles. Despite its size, it is not prominent; its brightest star is second-magnitude Alphard, about 85 light years from Earth.

hydrangea /haɪˈdreɪndʒə/ *n.* any flowering shrub of the genus *Hydrangea* of the saxifrage family Hydrangeaceae, native to Japan. Cultivated varieties of *H. macrophylla* normally produce round heads of pink flowers, but these may be blue if certain chemicals, such as alum or iron, are in the soil. [from Greek *hudōr* = water and *aggos* = vessel (from shape of seed capsules)]

hydrant /ˈhaɪdrənt/ *n.* a pipe (especially in a street) with a nozzle for a hose, for drawing water from a main.

hydrate /ˈhaɪdreɪt/ *n.* a chemical compound of water with another compound or an element. The water is known as **water of crystallization** and the number of water molecules associated with one molecule of the compound is denoted in both its name and chemical formula: for example, $CuSO_4 \cdot 5H_2O$ is copper(II) sulphate pentahydrate. —also -ˈdreɪt/ *v.t.* to combine chemically with water; to cause to absorb water. —**hydration** /-ˈdreɪʃən/ *n.* [French]

hydraulic /haɪˈdrɔːlɪk/ *adj.* **1.** (of water etc.) conveyed through pipes or channels. **2.** operated by the movement of liquid. —**hydraulically** *adv.* [from Latin from Greek *hudōr* = water and *aulos* = pipe]

hydraulics *n.pl.* (usually treated as *singular*) the field of study concerned with utilizing the properties of water and other liquids, in particular the way they flow and transmit pressure, and with the application of these properties in engineering. It applies the principles of ◊hydrostatics and hydrodynamics. The oldest type of hydraulic machine is the hydraulic press, invented by Joseph ◊Bramah in England in 1795. The hydraulic principle of pressurized liquid increasing mechanical efficiency is commonly used on vehicle braking systems, the forging press, and the hydraulic systems of aircraft and excavators.

hydride /ˈhaɪdraɪd/ *n.* a chemical compound containing hydrogen and one other element only, in which the hydrogen is the more electronegative element (see ◊electronegativity).

hydro /ˈhaɪdrəʊ/ *n.* (*plural* **hydros**) (*colloquial*) **1.** a hotel etc. providing hydropathic treatment. **2.** a hydroelectric power plant.

hydro- /ˈhaɪdrə(ʊ)-/ in combinations **1.** water, liquid. **2.** combined with hydrogen. [from Greek *hudōr* = water]

hydrocarbon /haɪdrəʊˈkɑːbən/ *n.* a compound consisting only of hydrogen and carbon (e.g. methane, benzene). Hydrocarbons are obtained industrially principally from petroleum and coal tar.

hydrocephalus /haɪdrəʊˈsefələs/ *n.* a condition (especially in young children) with an accumulation of fluid in the cavity of the cranium, which can impair the mental faculties. —**hydrocephalic** /-siˈfælɪk/ *adj.* [from Greek *kephalē* = head]

hydrochloric /haɪdrəʊˈklɒrɪk/ *adj.* containing hydrogen and chlorine.

hydrochloric acid HCl, a solution of hydrogen chloride (a colourless, acidic gas) in water. The concentrated acid is about 35% HCl and is corrosive. The acid is a typical strong, monobasic acid forming only one series of salts, the chlorides. When oxidized, for example by manganese(IV) oxide, it releases chlorine. It has many industrial uses, including recovery of zinc from galvanized scrap iron and the production of chlorides and chlorine. It is also produced in the stomachs of animals for the purposes of digestion.

hydrochloride /haɪdrəʊˈklɔːraɪd/ *n.* a compound of an organic base with hydrochloric acid.

hydrocyanic /haɪdrəʊsaɪˈænɪk/ *adj.* containing hydrogen and cyanogen.

hydrocyanic acid or **prussic acid** a solution of hydrogen cyanide gas (HCN) in water. It is a colourless, highly poisonous, volatile liquid, smelling of bitter almonds.

hydrodynamics /haɪdrəʊdaɪˈnæmɪks/ *n.pl.* (usually treated as *singular*) the science of the forces acting on or exerted by liquids (especially water). —**hydrodynamic** *adj.*

hydroelectric /haɪdrəʊiˈlektrɪk/ *adj.* developing electricity by the utilization of water power; (of electricity) produced thus. In a typical hydroelectric power (HEP) scheme, water stored in a reservoir, often created by damming a river, is piped into water ◊turbines, coupled to electricity generators. In pumped storage plants, water flowing through the turbines is recycled. A ◊tidal power station (see under ◊tidal) exploits the rise and fall of the tides. About one-fifth of the world's electricity comes from hydroelectric power. —**hydroelectricity** /-ˈtrɪsɪtɪ/ *n.*

hydrofoil /ˈhaɪdrəfɔɪl/ *n.* a boat equipped with a device for raising the hull out of the water to enable rapid motion; this device, a wing that develops lift in the water in much the same way that an aeroplane wing develops lift in the air. The first hydrofoil was fitted to a boat in 1906. The first commercial hydrofoil went into operation in 1956. One of the most advanced hydrofoil boats is the Boeing ◊jetfoil.

hydrogen /ˈhaɪdrədʒən/ *n.* a colourless, odourless, gaseous, nonmetallic element, symbol H, atomic number 1, relative atomic mass 1.00797. It is the lightest of all the elements and occurs on Earth chiefly in combination with oxygen as water. Hydrogen is the most abundant element in the universe, where it accounts for 93% of the total number of atoms and 76% total mass. It is a component of most stars, including the Sun, whose heat and light are produced through the nuclear-fusion process, which converts hydrogen into helium. When subjected to a pressure 500,000 times greater than that of the Earth's atmosphere, hydrogen becomes a solid metal. Its common and industrial uses include the hardening of fats and oils by hydrogenation and the creation of high-temperature flames for welding. —**hydrogen sulphide,** an unpleasant-smelling poisonous gas formed by rotting animal matter. —**hydrogenous** /-'drɒdʒɪnəs/ *adj.* [from French]

hydrogenate /haɪ'drɒdʒɪneɪt/ *v.t.* to charge with or cause to combine with hydrogen. —**hydrogenation** /-'neɪʃən/ *n.*

hydrogen bomb a bomb that works on the principle of nuclear fusion (see under ◊nuclear energy). A large-scale explosion results from the thermonuclear release of energy when hydrogen nuclei are condensed to helium nuclei. The first hydrogen bomb was exploded at Eniwetok Atoll by the USA in 1952.

hydrogen carbonate or **bicarbonate** a salt containing the HCO_3^- ion, derived from carbonic acid (solution of carbon dioxide in water) in which only one of the hydrogen atoms has been replaced by a ◊cation (negative ion). Because carbonic acid is a weak acid, hydrogen carbonates behave more as bases than acids (see ◊acid salt). When heated or treated with dilute acids, they evolve carbon dioxide. The presence of calcium and magnesium hydrogen carbonates in water causes temporary hardness.

hydrogen cyanide HCN, a poisonous gas formed by the reaction of sodium cyanide with dilute sulphuric acid, used for fumigation.

hydrography /haɪ'drɒgrəfɪ/ *n.* the scientific study of seas, lakes, rivers etc. —**hydrographer** *n.*, **hydrographic** /-'græfɪk/ *adj.*

hydrology /haɪ'drɒlədʒɪ/ *n.* the science of the properties of water, especially of its movement in relation to the land. —**hydrological** /haɪdrə'lɒdʒɪkəl/ *adj.*

hydrolyse /'haɪdrəlaɪz/ *v.t.* to decompose by hydrolysis.

hydrolysis /haɪ'drɒlɪsɪs/ *n.* a chemical reaction in which the action of water or its ions breaks down a substance into smaller molecules. Hydrolysis occurs in certain inorganic salts in solution, in nearly all nonmetallic chlorides, in esters, and in other organic substances. It is one of the mechanisms for the breakdown of food by the body, as in the conversion of starch to glucose. [from Greek *lusis* = dissolving]

hydrometer /haɪ'drɒmɪtə(r)/ *n.* an instrument used to measure the density of liquids compared with that of water, usually expressed in grams per cubic centimetre. It consists of a thin glass tube ending in a sphere that leads into a smaller sphere, the latter being weighted so that the hydrometer floats upright, sinking deeper into lighter liquids than into heavier liquids. It is used in brewing.

hydropathy /haɪ'drɒpəθɪ/ *n.* medical treatment by external and internal application of water. —**hydropathic** /-'pæθɪk/ *adj.*

hydrophilic /haɪdrə'fɪlɪk/ *adj.* having an affinity for water; able to be wetted by water. [from Greek *philos* = loving]

hydrophily *n.* a form of ◊pollination in which the pollen is carried by water. Hydrophily is very rare but occurs in a few aquatic species. In Canadian pondweed *Elodea* and tape grass *Vallisneria*, the male flowers break off whole and rise to the water surface where they encounter the female flowers, which are borne on long stalks. In eel grasses *Zostera*, which are coastal plants growing totally submerged, the filamentous pollen grains are released into the water and carried by currents to the female flowers where they become wrapped around the stigmas.

hydrophobia /haɪdrə'fəʊbɪə/ *n.* aversion to water, especially as a symptom of ◊rabies in man; rabies, especially in man. —**hydrophobic** *adj.* [from Latin from Greek]

hydrophone *n.* an underwater ◊microphone and ancillary equipment capable of picking up waterborne sounds. It was originally developed to detect enemy submarines but is now also used, for example, for listening to the sounds made by whales.

hydrophyte *n.* a plant adapted to live in water, or in waterlogged soil.

hydroplane /'haɪdrəpleɪn/ *n.* **1.** a light, fast motor boat designed to skim over the surface of the water. **2.** a finlike device on a submarine enabling it to rise or descend.

hydroponics /haɪdrə'pɒnɪks/ *n.* the cultivation of plants without soil, using specially prepared solutions of mineral salts. Beginning in the 1930s, large crops were grown by hydroponic methods, at first in California, but since then, in many other parts of the world. [from Greek *ponos* = labour]

hydrosphere /'haɪdrəsfɪə/ *n.* the water component of the Earth, usually encompassing the oceans, seas, rivers, streams, swamps, lakes, groundwater, and atmospheric water vapour.

hydrostatic /haɪdrəʊ'stætɪk/ *adj.* of the equilibrium of liquids and the pressure exerted by liquids at rest. [from Greek *hudrostatēs* = hydrostatic balance]

hydrostatics *n.pl.* (usually treated as *singular*) the branch of mechanics concerned with the hydrostatic properties of liquids.

hydrothermal *adj.* in geology, pertaining to a fluid whose principal component is hot water, or to a mineral deposit believed to be precipitated from such a fluid.

hydrous /'haɪdrəs/ *adj.* (of substances) containing water.

hydroxide /haɪ'drɒksaɪd/ *n.* an inorganic compound containing one or more hydroxyl (OH) groups and generally combined with a metal. Hydroxides include caustic soda (sodium hydroxide, NaOH), caustic potash (potassium hydroxide, KOH), and slaked lime (calcium hydroxide, $Ca(OH)_2$).

hydroxyl /haɪ'drɒksɪl/ *n.* a radical containing hydrogen and oxygen.

hydroxyl group an atom of hydrogen and an atom of oxygen bonded together and covalently bonded to an organic molecule. Common compounds containing hydroxyl groups are alcohols and phenols.

hyena /haɪ'iːnə/ *n.* a carnivorous mammal of the order Hyaenidae of Africa and Asia, with a shrill cry resembling laughter. It has very strong limbs and jaws. It is a scavenger although it will also attack and kill live prey. [from Old French and Latin from Greek *huaina*]

hygiene /'haɪdʒiːn/ *n.* the principles of maintaining health, especially by cleanliness; sanitary science. —**hygienic** /-'dʒiːnɪk/ *adj.*, **hygienically** *adv.*, **hygienist** *n.* [from French from Greek *hugieinē(tekhnē)* (*hugiēs* = healthy)]

hygrometer /haɪ'grɒmɪtə/ *n.* an instrument for measuring the humidity of the air or a gas. A wet and dry bulb hygrometer consists of two vertical thermometers, with one of the bulbs covered in absorbent cloth dipped into water. As the water evaporates, the bulb cools producing a temperature difference between the two thermometers. The amount of evaporation, and hence cooling of the wet bulb, depends on the relative humidity of the air. [from Greek *hugros* = wet]

hygroscope /'haɪgrəskəʊp/ *n.* an instrument indicating but not measuring the humidity of the air.

hygroscopic /haɪgrə'skɒpɪk/ *adj.* **1.** of the hygroscope. **2.** (of a substance) tending to absorb moisture from the air.

hymen /'haɪmen/ *n.* the membrane partially closing the external opening of the vagina of a virgin. [Latin from Greek *humēn* = membrane]

Hymen /'haɪmen/ in Greek mythology, either the son of Apollo and one of the Muses, or of Dionysus and Aphrodite. He was the god of marriage, and in painting is represented as a youth carrying a bridal torch.

hymenopterous /haɪmə'nɒptərəs/ *adj.* of the order of insects including the ant, bee, wasp etc., with four membranous wings. [from Greek *humēn* = membrane and *pteron* = wing]

hymn /hɪm/ *n.* a song in praise of a deity. Examples include Ikhnaton's hymn to the Aton in ancient Egypt, the ancient Greek Orphic hymns, Old Testament psalms, extracts from the New Testament (such as 'Ave Maria'), and hymns by the British writers John Bunyan ('Who would true valour see') and Charles Wesley ('Hark the herald angels sing'). ◊Gospel music is a form of Christian hymn singing. —*v.t.* to praise or celebrate in hymns. [from Old French from Latin from Greek *humnos*]

hymnal /'hɪmnəl/ *n.* a book of hymns. [from Latin]

hymnology /hɪm'nɒlədʒɪ/ *n.* the composition or study of hymns. —**hymnologist** *n.*

hyoscine /'haɪəsiːn/ *n.* or **scopolamine** a drug that acts on the autonomic nervous system and is frequently included in ◊premedication to dry up lung secretions and as a postoperative sedative. It is an alkaloid, $C_{17}H_{21}NO_2$,

hyperbola

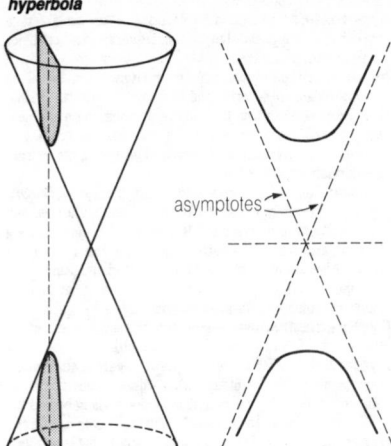

asymptotes

obtained from various plants of the nightshade family (such as ◊belladonna).

hyoscyamine /haɪə'saɪəmiːn/ *n.* a poisonous alkaloid used as a sedative, got from henbane. [from Greek *huoskuamos* = henbane (*hus* = pig and *kuamos* = bean)]

hyper- /haɪpə-/ *prefix* in the senses 'over', 'above', 'too'. [from Greek *huper* = over]

hyperactive /haɪpə'ræktɪv/ *adj.* (of a person) abnormally active.

hyperactivity *n.* a condition of excessive activity in young children, combined with inability to concentrate and difficulty in learning. The cause is not known, although some food ◊additives have come under suspicion. In the majority of cases there is improvement at puberty.

hyperbola /haɪ'pɜːbələ/ *n.* in geometry, a curve formed by cutting a right circular cone with a plane so that the angle between the plane and the base is greater than the angle between the base and the side of the cone. All hyperbolas are bounded by two ◊asymptotes. —**hyperbolic** /-'bɒlɪk/ *adj.*

hyperbole /haɪ'pɜːbəlɪ/ *n.* a statement exaggerated for special effect. —**hyperbolical** /-'bɒlɪkəl/ *adj.* [Latin from Greek = excess (*ballō* = throw)]

hypercharge *n.* in physics, a property of certain ◊elementary particles, analogous to electric charge, that accounts for the absence of some expected behaviour (such as decay) in terms of the short-range strong interaction force, which holds atomic nuclei together.

hypercritical /haɪpə'krɪtɪkəl/ *adj.* excessively critical. —**hypercritically** *adv.*

hyperinflation *n.* rapid and uncontrolled ◊inflation, or increases in prices, usually associated with political and/or social instability (as in Germany in the 1920s).

hypermarket /haɪpəmɑːkɪt/ *n.* a very large self-service store usually outside a town. [from French *hypermarché*]

hyperon *n.* an unstable baryon (elementary particle); all baryons that are not nucleons are known as hyperons.

hypersensitive /haɪpə'sensɪtɪv/ *adj.* excessively sensitive. —**hypersensitivity** /-'tɪvɪtɪ/ *n.*

hypersonic /haɪpə'sɒnɪk/ *adj.* **1.** of speeds more than about five times that of sound. **2.** of sound frequencies above about 1,000 megahertz.

hypertension /haɪpə'tenʃən/ *n.* **1.** abnormally high ◊blood pressure due to a variety of causes, leading to excessive contraction of the smooth muscle cells of the walls of the arteries; it increases the risk of kidney disease, stroke, and heart attack. **2.** great emotional tension.

hyperthyroidism *n.* or **thyrotoxicosis** overactivity of the thyroid gland due to enlargement or tumour. Symptoms include accelerated heart rate, sweating, anxiety, tremor, and weight loss. Treatment is by drugs or surgery.

hypertrophy /haɪpɜːtrəfɪ/ *n.* enlargement of an organ etc. due to excessive nutrition. —**hypertrophic** /-pə'trɒːfɪk/ *adj.* [from Greek *trophē* = nourishment]

hypha (*plural* **hyphae**) a delicate, usually branching filament, many of which collectively form the mycelium and fruiting bodies of a ◊fungus. Food molecules and other substances are transported along hyphae by the movement of the cytoplasm, known as 'cytoplasmic streaming'.

hyphen /haɪf(ə)n/ *n.* a punctuation mark (-) with two functions: to join words, parts of words, syllables, and so on, as an aid to sense; and to mark a word break at the end of a line. Adjectival compounds (see ◊adjective) are hyphenated because they modify the noun jointly rather than separately ('a small-town boy' is a boy from a small town; 'a small town boy' is a small boy from a town). The use of hyphens with adverbs is redundant unless an identical adjective exists (e.g. *well, late, long*). The rules for hyphenation of compound nouns in English are by no means generally agreed. —*v.t.* to join (words) with a hyphen; to write (a word or words) with a hyphen. [Latin from Greek *huphen* = together]

hyphenate /haɪfəneɪt/ *v.t.* to hyphen. —**hyphenation** /-'neɪʃən/ *n.*

hypnosis /hɪp'nəʊsɪs/ *n.* (*plural* **hypnoses** /-əʊsiːz/) a state like sleep in which the subject acts only on external suggestion; an artificially produced sleep. The subject may carry out orders after being awakened, and may be made insensitive to pain. Hypnosis is sometimes used to treat addictions to tobacco or overeating, or to assist amnesia victims. Discovered by Friedrich ◊Mesmer, it was used by charlatans and entertainers until laws such as the Hypnosis Act 1952 in the UK controlled exploitation of hypnosis as entertainment. [from Greek *hupnos* = sleep]

hypnotic /hɪp'nɒtɪk/ *adj.* of or producing hypnosis. —*n.* a hypnotic drug or influence. —**hypnotically** *adv.* [from French from Latin from Greek *hupnoō* = put to sleep]

hypnotism /hɪpnətɪzəm/ *n.* the production or process of hypnosis. —**hypnotist** *n.*

hypnotize *v.t.* to produce hypnosis in; to fascinate, to capture the mind of (a person).

hypo[1] /haɪpəʊ/ *n.* sodium thiosulphate (incorrectly called hyposulphite), discovered in 1819 by John ◊Herschel and used as a fixative for photographic images since 1837.

hypo[2] /haɪpəʊ/ *n.* (*plural* **hypos**) (*slang*) a hypodermic. [abbreviation]

hypo- /haɪpə(ʊ)-/ *prefix* in the senses 'under', 'below', 'slightly'. [from Greek *hupo* = under]

hypocaust /haɪpəkɔːst/ *n.* a hollow space under a floor into which hot air from a furnace was sent for heating an ancient Roman house or baths. [from Latin from Greek *kaiō* = burn]

hypochondria /haɪpə'kɒndrɪə/ *n.* abnormal anxiety about one's health. [Latin from Greek = parts of body below ribs (whence melancholy was thought to arise)]

hypochondriac *n.* a person suffering from hypochondria. —*adj.* of hypochondria.

hypocrisy /hɪ'pɒkrɪsɪ/ *n.* simulation of virtue or goodness, insincerity. [from Old French from Latin from Greek = acting of a part]

hypocrite /hɪpəkrɪt/ *n.* a person guilty of hypocrisy. —**hypocritical** /-'krɪtɪkəl/ *adj.*, **hypocritically** *adv.*

hypocycloid *n.* in geometry, a cusped curve traced by a point on the circumference of a circle that rolls around the inside of another larger circle.

hypodermic /haɪpə'dɜːmɪk/ *adj.* **1.** of the area beneath the skin. **2.** injected there; used for such injection. —*n.* a hypodermic injection or syringe. —**hypodermic syringe**, a syringe with a hollow needle for injection beneath the skin. —**hypodermically** *adv.* [from Greek *derma* = skin]

hypogeal *adj.* germinating or developing below the ground. The term can refer to fruits that develop underground, such as peanuts *Arachis hypogea*. [from Greek *gē* = earth]

hypoglycaemia *n.* a condition of abnormally low level of sugar (glucose) in the blood, which starves the brain. It causes weakness, the shakes, and perspiration, sometimes fainting. Untreated victims have suffered paranoia and extreme anxiety. Treatment is by special diet. —**hypoglycaemic**, *n.* a drug that lowers the level of glucose sugar in the blood.

hyponymy *n.* in semantics, a relationship in meaning between two words such that one (for example, *sport*) includes the other (for example, *football*), but not vice versa.

hypostasis

hypostasis /haɪˈpɒstəsɪs/ *n.* (*plural* **hypostases** /-siːz/)
1. the underlying substance of a thing as distinct from its
attributes. 2. any of the three persons of the Trinity. [Latin
from Greek *stasis* = standing]

hypostatic /haɪpəˈstætɪk/ *adj.* of or involving hypostasis. —**hypostatic union**, the union of divine and human
natures in Christ, a doctrine formally accepted by the
church in 451.

hypotension /haɪpəˈtenʃən/ *n.* abnormally low blood
pressure.

hypotenuse /haɪˈpɒtənjuːz/ *n.* the side opposite the right
angle of a right-angled triangle. [from Latin from Greek =
subtending line]

hypothalamus /haɪpəʊˈθæləməs/ *n.* the region of the
brain below the ◊cerebrum which regulates rhythmic activity and physiological stability within the body, including
water balance and temperature. It regulates the production
of the pituitary gland's hormones and controls that part of
the ◊nervous system regulating the involuntary muscles.
[from Greek *thalamos* = room]

hypothecate /haɪˈpɒθɪkeɪt/ *v.t.* to pledge, to mortgage.
—**hypothecation** /-ˈkeɪʃən/ *n.* [from Latin from Greek
hupothēcē = deposit (*tithēmi* = place)]

hypothermia /haɪpəˈθɜːmiə/ *n.* the condition of having
an abnormally low body temperature. If it is not discovered,
coma and death ensue. Most at risk are the aged and babies
(particularly if premature). [from Greek *thermē* = heat]

hypothesis /haɪˈpɒθɪsɪs/ *n.* (*plural* **hypotheses** /-siːz/) a
proposition or supposition made from known facts as the
basis for reasoning or investigation. [Latin from Greek
= foundation]

hypothesize /haɪˈpɒθɪsaɪz/ *v.t./i.* to form a hypothesis; to
assume as a hypothesis.

hypothetical /haɪpəˈθetɪkəl/ *adj.* of or based on a
hypothesis; supposed but not necessarily real or true.
—**hypothetically** *adv.*

hyrax *n.* a type of mammal, order Hyracoidea, that lives
among rocks, in deserts, and in forests in Africa, Arabia,
and Syria. It is about the size of a rabbit, with a plump
body, short legs, short ears, long, curved front teeth, and
brownish fur. Hyraxes are believed to be among the nearest
living relatives of elephants.

hyssop /ˈhɪsəp/ *n.* 1. an aromatic herb *Hyssopus officinalis*
of the mint family Labiatae, found in Asia, S Europe, and
around the Mediterranean. It has blue flowers, oblong
leaves, and stems that are woody near the ground but
herbaceous above. It was formerly used medicinally. 2.
a plant used for sprinkling in ancient Jewish rites. [Old
English, ultimately from Greek from Semitic]

hysterectomy /hɪstəˈrektəmɪ/ *n.* the surgical removal of
the womb. [from Greek *hustera* = womb]

hysteresis /hɪstəˈriːsɪs/ *n.* (*plural* **hystereses** /-siːz/)
the lagging of an effect when the cause varies in
amount, especially of magnetic induction lagging behind the
magnetizing force. [from Greek *husteros* = coming after]

hysteria /hɪˈstɪərɪə/ *n.* 1. wild, uncontrollable emotion
or excitement. 2. a functional disturbance of the nervous
system, of psychoneurotic origin.

hysteric /hɪˈsterɪk/ *n.* 1. a hysterical person. 2. (in *plural*)
a fit of hysteria. [from Latin from Greek *hustera* = womb,
hysteria being thought to affect women more than men]

hysterical *adj.* of or caused by hysteria; suffering from
hysteria. —**hysterically** *adv.*

Hz abbreviation of hertz.

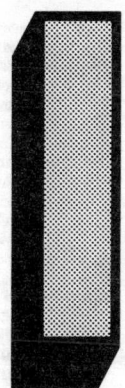

i, I /aɪ/ *n.* (*plural* **is, i's**) **1.** the ninth letter of the alphabet. **2.** (as a Roman numeral) one.

I symbol for ◊iodine.

I /aɪ/ *pron.* (*objective* me[1]; *possessive* my, mine[1]; *plural* we etc.) the person who is speaking and referring to himself or herself. [Old English]

I. abbreviation of Island(s); Isle(s).

iambic /aɪˈæmbɪk/ *adj.* of or using iambuses. —*n.* (usually in *plural*) iambic verse.

iambus /aɪˈæmbəs/ *n.* (*plural* **iambuses**) a metrical foot with one short or unstressed syllable followed by one long or stressed syllable. [Latin from Greek *iaptō* = assail in words]

Iaşi /ˈjæʃi/ (German *Jassy*) city in NE Romania, former capital of Moldova (1565–1859); population (1985) 314,000. It has chemical, machinery, electronic and textile industries.

iatrogenic *adj.* caused by medical treatment; the term 'iatrogenic disease' may be applied to any pathological condition or complication that is caused by the treatment, the facility, or the staff.

IBA abbreviation of Independent Broadcasting Authority, (now ◊Independent Television Commission) UK regulatory body for commercial television and radio.

Ibadan /iˈbædn/ city in SW Nigeria and capital of Oyo state; population (1981) 2,100,000. Industries include chemicals, electronics, plastics, and vehicles.

Iban /ˈiːbæn/ *n.* a Dayak people of central Borneo. Approximately 250,000 Iban live in the interior uplands of Sarawak, while another 10,000 live in the border area of W Kalimantan. The Iban speak languages belonging to the Austronesian family.

Ibáñez /iːˈbɑːnjeθ/ Vincente Blasco 1867–1928. Spanish novelist and revolutionary politician, born in Valencia. His novels include *La barraca/The Cabin* 1898, the best of his regional works; *Sangre y arena/Blood and Sand* 1908, the story of a famous bullfighter; and *Los cuatro jinetes del Apocalipsis/The Four Horsemen of the Apocalypse* 1916, a product of the effects of World War I.

Ibarruri /iːˈbæruri/ Dolores, known as *La Pasionaria* ('the passion flower') 1895–1989. Spanish Basque politician, journalist, and orator; she was first elected to the Cortes in 1936. She helped to establish the Popular Front government and was a Loyalist leader in the Civil War. When Franco came to power in 1939 she left Spain for the USSR, where she was active in the Communist Party. She returned to Spain in 1977 after Franco's death and was re-elected to the Cortes (at the age of 81) in the first parliamentary elections for 40 years.

Iberian /aɪˈbɪərɪən/ *adj.* of Iberia, the peninsula comprising Spain and Portugal. —*n.* a native or the language of ancient Iberia. [from Latin *Iberia* from Greek]

ibex /ˈaɪbeks/ *n.* a type of wild goat, genus *Capra*, found in mountainous areas of Europe, NE Africa, and Central Asia. They grow to 100 cm/3.5 ft, and have brown or grey coats and heavy horns. They are herbivorous and live in small groups. [Latin]

ibid. abbreviation of ibidem used with the meaning in the same book or passage etc. [Latin = in the same place]

ibis /ˈaɪbɪs/ *n.* a type of wading bird, about 60 cm/2 ft tall, related to the storks and herons, with long legs and neck, and a long curved beak. Various species occur in the warmer regions of the world. [from Latin from Greek]

Ibiza /iˈbiːθə/ one of the ◊Balearic Islands, a popular tourist resort; area 596 sq km/230 sq mi; population (1986) 45,000. The capital and port, also called Ibiza, has a cathedral.

-ible suffix forming adjectives as a variant of -able (*terrible, defensible, forcible, possible*). [French or from Latin *-ibilis*]

Iblis /ˈɪblɪs/ the Muslim name for the ◊devil.

IBM abbreviation of International Business Machines the largest manufacturer of computers in the world. The company is a descendant of the Tabulating Machine Company, formed in 1896 by Herman ◊Hollerith to exploit his punched card machines. It adopted its present name in 1924. It now has an annual turnover (1988–89) of $60 billion and employs (1988) about 387,000 people.

Ibn Battuta /ˈɪbən bəˈtuːtə/ or **Ibn Batuta** *c.* 1304–1368. Arab traveller born in Tangiers. In 1325, he went on an extraordinary 120,675 km/75,000 mi journey via Mecca to Egypt, E Africa, India, and China, returning some 30 years later. During this journey he also visited Spain and crossed the Sahara to Timbuktu. He wrote about his travels in a book called the Rihlah. Another narrative of his travels, *Travels with Ibn Battuta*, was written with an assistant, Ibn Juzayy.

Ibn Saud /ˈɪbən ˈsaʊd/ 1880–1953. First king of Saudi Arabia from 1932. His father was the son of the sultan of Nejd, at whose capital, Riyadh, Ibn Saud was born. In 1891 a rival group seized Riyadh, and Ibn Saud went into exile with his father, who resigned his claim to the throne in his son's favour. In 1902 Ibn Saud recaptured Riyadh and recovered the kingdom, and by 1921 he had brought all central Arabia under his rule. In 1924 he invaded the Hejaz, of which he was proclaimed king in 1926.

Ibn Sina /ˈɪbən ˈsiːnə/ Arabic name of ◊Avicenna, scholar and translator.

Ibo /ˈiːbəʊ/ *n.* or **Ebo** (*plural* the same or **Ibos**), a member of the W African Ibo culture group occupying SE Nigeria. Primarily cultivators, they inhabit the richly forested tableland, bound by the river Niger to the W and the Cross River to the E. They are divided into five main divisions, and their languages belong to the Kwa branch of the Niger-Congo family.

Ibsen /ˈɪbsən/ Henrik (Johan) 1828–1906. Norwegian playwright and poet, whose realistic and often controversial plays revolutionized European theatre. Driven into exile 1864–91 by opposition to the satirical *Love's Comedy* 1862, he wrote the verse dramas *Brand* 1866 and *Peer Gynt* 1867, followed by realistic plays dealing with social issues, including *Pillars of Society* 1877, *The Doll's House* 1879, *Ghosts* 1881, *An Enemy of the People* 1882, and *Hedda Gabler* 1891.

Icarus /ˈɪkərəs/ in Greek mythology, the son of ◊Daedalus, who with his father, escaped from the labyrinth in Crete using wings made from feathers fastened with wax. Icarus plunged to his death when he flew too near the Sun, and the wax melted.

Icarus *n.* in astronomy, an ◊Apollo asteroid 1.5 km/1 mi in diameter, discovered in 1949. It orbits the Sun every

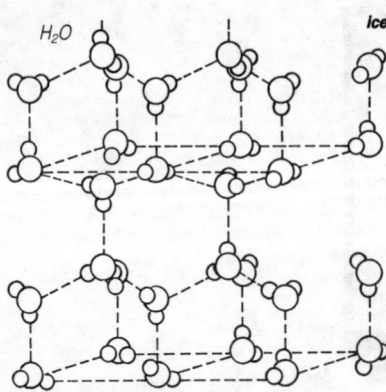

H_2O

ice

the crystal structure of ice in which water molecules are held together by hydrogen bonds

409 days at a distance of 28 million–186 million km/28 million–300 million mi (0.19–2.0 astronomical units). It is the only asteroid known to approach the Sun closer than does the planet Mercury. In 1968 it passed 6 million km/4 million mi from the Earth.

ICBM abbreviation of intercontinental ballistic missile; see ◊nuclear warfare.

ice /ais/ *n.* **1.** frozen water; a sheet of this on the surface of water. **2.** a portion of ice cream or water ice. **3.** a form of methamphetamine that is smoked to give a high; in illegal use in the USA from 1989. —*v.t./i.* **1.** to become covered with ice; to freeze. **2.** to cover or mix with ice; to cool in ice. **3.** to cover (a cake etc.) with icing. —**break the ice**, to make a start; to overcome formality. **ice-blue** *adj.* very pale blue. **icebreaker** *n.* a ship designed to break through ice. **icecap** *n.* a permanent covering of ice, e. g. in polar lands. **ice field**, a large expanse of floating ice. **ice lolly**, a kind of water ice on a stick. **on ice**, (*colloquial*) held in a state of temporary suspension, or in reserve; quite certain. **on thin ice**, in a risky situation. [Old English]

Ice Age any period of glaciation occurring in the Earth's history, but particularly that in the Pleistocene epoch, immediately preceding historic times. On the North American continent, ◊glaciers reached as far south as the Great Lakes, and an ice sheet spread over N Europe, leaving its remains as far south as Switzerland. There were several glacial advances separated by interglacial stages during which the ice melted and temperatures were higher than today.

iceberg /'aisbɜːg/ *n.* a floating mass of ice, about 80% of which is submerged, rising sometimes to 100 m/300 ft above sea level. Glaciers that reach the coast become extended into a broad foot; as this enters the sea, masses break off and drift towards temperate latitudes, becoming a danger to shipping. [probably from Dutch]

icebox *n.* a compartment in a refrigerator for making or storing ice; (*US*) a refrigerator.

ice cream a frozen liquid confectionery, commercially made from the early 20th century from various milk products and sugar, and today also with 'non-milk' (animal or vegetable) fat, with usually artificial additives to give colour and flavour, and improve its keeping qualities and ease of serving. Ice cream was made in China before 1000 BC and probably introduced to Europe by Marco Polo; water ices were known in ancient Greece and Persia. Italy and Russia were noted for ice cream even before it became a mechanized industry, first in the USA and in the 1920s in Britain.

ice hockey a game played on ice between two teams of six, developed in Canada from field hockey or bandy, with a puck (a rubber disc) in place of a ball. Players wear skates and protective clothing.

Iceland /'aisland/ Republic of; island in the N Atlantic, situated S of the Arctic Circle, between Greenland and Norway; **area** 103,000 sq km/39,758 sq mi; **capital** Reykjavik; **physical** warmed by the Gulf Stream; glaciers and lava fields cover 75% of the country; active volcanoes, geysers, hot springs and new islands created offshore (Surtsey in 1963); subterranean hot water heats Iceland's

homes; **head of state** Vigdís Finnbogadóttir from 1980; **head of government** Steingrimur Hermannsson from 1988; **political system** democratic republic; **exports** cod and other fish products, aluminium, diatomite; **language** Icelandic; **population** (1990 est) 251,000; **recent history** declared independence from Denmark in 1944; 1976 'Cod War' with UK.

Icelandic /ais'lændik/ *adj.* of Iceland or its language. —*n.* the language of Iceland, a member of the N Germanic branch of the Indo-European language family, spoken only in Iceland and the most conservative in form of the Scandinavian languages. Despite seven centuries of Danish rule, lasting until 1918, Icelandic has remained virtually unchanged since the 12th century.

Iceni /ai'siːnai/ *n.* an ancient people of E England, who revolted against occupying Romans under ◊Boudicca.

ice-skating see ◊skate[1].

I Ching or **Book of Changes** an ancient Chinese book of divination based on 64 hexagrams, or patterns of six lines. The lines may be 'broken' or 'whole' (yin or yang) and are generated by tossing yarrow stalks or coins. The enquirer formulates a question before throwing, and the book gives interpretations of the meaning of the hexagrams.

ichneumon /ik'njuːmən/ *n.* **1.** a mongoose (*Herpestes ichneumon*) of North Africa etc., noted for destroying crocodiles' eggs. **2.** an ichneumon fly, an insect of the family Ichneumonidae, that deposits its eggs in or on the eggs, larvae, or pupae of other insects, usually butterflies or moths. [Latin from Greek *ikhneuō* = track]

ichthyology /ikpθi'ɒlədʒi/ *n.* the study of fishes. [from Greek *ikhthus* = fish]

ichthyosaurus /ikpθiə'sɔːrəs/ *n.* (*plural* **ichthyosauruses**) an extinct marine animal of the order Ichthyosauria, with a long head, tapering body, four paddles, and a large tail. [from Greek *ikhthus* = fish and *sauros* = lizard]

ICI abbreviation of Imperial Chemical Industries.

icicle /'aisikəl/ *n.* a tapering, hanging spike of ice formed from dripping water. [from ice and dialect *ickle* = icicle]

icing /'aisiŋ/ *n.* **1.** a coating of sugar etc. on a cake or biscuit. **2.** the formation of ice on an aircraft. —**icing sugar**, finely powdered sugar used for making icing.

icon /'aikɒn/ *n.* **1.** an image or statue; (in the Orthodox Church) a painting or mosaic of a sacred person, itself regarded as sacred. **2.** in computing, a small picture on the screen representing an object or function that the user may manipulate or otherwise use. [Latin from Greek *eikōn* = image]

iconoclast /ai'kɒnəklæst/ *n.* **1.** a breaker of images, especially one who took part in a movement in the 8th–9th century against the use of images in religious worship in churches in the Eastern Roman Empire, or a Puritan of the 16th–17th century. **2.** one who attacks cherished beliefs. —**iconoclasm** *n.*, **iconoclastic** /-'klæstik/ *adj.* [from Latin from Greek *eikōn* = image and *klaō* = break]

iconography /aikə'nɒgrəfi/ *n.* **1.** the illustration of a subject by drawings etc. **2.** the study of portraits especially of one person. **3.** in art history, significance attached to symbols that can help to identify subject matter (e.g. a saint holding keys usually represents St Peter) and place a work of art in its historical context. [from Greek = sketch]

icosahedron /aikɒsə'hiːdrən/ *n.* a solid figure with twenty faces. [from Latin from Greek *eikosi* = twenty and *hedra* = base]

ictus /'iktəs/ *n.* a rhythmical or metrical stress. [Latin = a blow (*icere* = strike)]

icy /'aisi/ *adj.* **1.** very cold. **2.** covered with or abounding in ice. **3.** (of tone or manner) unfriendly, hostile. —**icily** *adv.*, **iciness** *n.*

id *n.* in Freudian psychology, the instinctual element of the human mind, concerned with pleasure, which demands immediate satisfaction. It is regarded as the unconscious element of the human psyche, and is said to be in conflict with the ◊ego and the ◊superego. [Latin = that]

Id. abbreviation of idem. [Latin = the same]

IDA abbreviation of International Development Association.

Idaho /'aidəhəu/ state of NW USA; nickname Gem State; **area** 216,500 sq km/ 83,569 sq mi; **capital** Boise; **products** potatoes, wheat, livestock, timber, silver, lead, zinc, antimony; **population** (1984) 1,001,000; **history** first permanently settled in 1860 after the discovery of gold, Idaho became a state in 1890.

idea /aɪ'diə/ *n.* 1. a plan or scheme formed in the mind by thinking. 2. a mental impression or conception. 3. an opinion or belief; a vague notion, a fancy. 4. an ambition or aspiration. 5. an archetype, a pattern. —**have no idea,** (*colloquial*) to be ignorant or incompetent. [Latin from Greek = look, form, kind]

ideal /aɪ'diəl/ *adj.* 1. satisfying one's idea of what is perfect. 2. existing only in an idea, visionary. —*n.* a person or thing regarded as perfect or as a standard for attainment or imitation; a conception of this. [from French from Latin]

idealism /aɪ'diəlɪzəm/ *n.* (usually as opposed to realism) 1. the representation of things in an ideal or idealized form; imaginative treatment; the practice of forming or following after ideals. 2. a system of thought in which the object of external perception is held to consist of ideas. —**idealist** *n.,* **idealistic** /-'lɪstɪk/ *adj.*

idealize /aɪ'diəlaɪz/ *v.t.* to regard or represent as ideal or perfect. —**idealization** /-'zeɪʃən/ *n.*

ideally /aɪ'diəlɪ/ *adv.* according to an ideal; in ideal circumstances.

idée fixe /i:deɪ 'fi:ks/ a recurrent or dominating idea. [French = fixed idea]

identical /aɪ'dentɪkəl/ *adj.* 1. one and the same. 2. agreeing in all details. 3. (of twins) developed from a single fertilized ovum and thus of the same sex and very similar in appearance. —**identically** *adv.* [from Latin]

identifiable /aɪ'dentɪfaɪəbəl/ *adj.* that may be identified.

identification /aɪdentɪfɪ'keɪʃən/ *n.* identifying; a means of identifying. —**identification parade,** an assembly of persons from whom a suspect is to be identified.

identify /aɪ'dentɪfaɪ/ *v.t.i.* 1. to establish the identity of, to recognize. 2. to treat as identical (*with*). 3. to associate (a person, *oneself*) closely (*with* a party, policy etc.); to associate oneself *with;* to regard oneself as sharing characteristics *with* another person. 4. to select by consideration. [from Latin *identificare*]

identikit /aɪ'dentɪkɪt/ *n.* a set of drawings of different parts of the face used to compose a likeness of a person for identification. It was evolved by Hugh C McDonald (1913–) in the USA. It has largely been replaced by ◊photofit, based on photographs, which produces a more realistic likeness. Identikit was first used by the police in Britain in 1961.

identity /aɪ'dentɪtɪ/ *n.* 1. the condition of being a specified person or thing. 2. the state of being identical, absolute sameness. 3. individuality, personality. 4. equality of two algebraic expressions for all values of quantities, the expression of this. [from Latin *idem* = same]

ideogram /'ɪdiəgræm/ *n.* a character or symbol indicating the idea of a thing without expressing the sounds in its name.

ideograph /'ɪdiəgrɑ:f/ *n.* an ideogram. —**ideographic** /-'græfɪk/ *adj.,* **ideography** /-'ɒgrəfɪ/ *n.*

ideologue /'aɪdiəlɒg/ *n.* an adherent of an ideology.

ideology /aɪdi'ɒlədʒɪ/ *n.* the ideas at the basis of an economic or political theory or system, or characteristic of some class etc. —**ideological** /-'lɒdʒɪkəl/ *adj.,* **ideologist** *n.* [from French]

ides /aɪdz/ *n. pl.* the 15th day of March, May, July, Oct, the 13th of other months, in the ancient Roman calendar. [from Old French from Latin *idus*]

idiocy /'ɪdiəsɪ/ *n.* 1. the state of being an idiot. 2. extreme stupidity; stupid behaviour or action.

idiom /'ɪdiəm/ *n.* 1. a form of expression or usage peculiar to a language, especially one whose meaning is not given by those of its separate words. 2. the language of a people. 3. a characteristic mode of expression in art etc. [from French or Latin from Greek *idiōma* (*idios* = own, private)]

idiomatic /ɪdiə'mætɪk/ *adj.* relating or conforming to an idiom; characteristic of a language. —**idiomatically** *adv.*

idiosyncrasy /ɪdiə'sɪŋkrəsɪ/ *n.* an attitude, form of behaviour, or mental or physical constitution, peculiar to a person. —**idiosyncratic** /-'krætɪk/ *adj.* [from Greek (*idios* = own, *sun* = together, and *krasis* = mixture)]

idiot /'ɪdiət/ *n.* 1. a mentally deficient person who is permanently incapable of rational conduct. 2.(*colloquial*) a stupid person. —**idiotic** /-'ɒtɪk/ *adj.,* **idiotically** /-'ɒtɪkəl/ *adv.* [from Old French from Latin from Greek = private citizen, layman]

idle /'aɪdəl/ *adj.* 1. doing no work, not employed; not active or in use. 2. avoiding work, lazy. 3. (of time) unoccupied. 4. useless; having no special purpose; groundless. —*v.t./i.* 1.

(of an engine) to run slowly without doing work. 2. to pass (time etc.) in idleness. —**idleness** *n.,* **idler** *n.,* **idly** *adv.* [Old English]

idol /'aɪdəl/ *n.* 1. an image of a deity as an object of worship. 2. an object of excessive or supreme devotion. [from Old French from Latin from Greek *eidōlon* (*eidos* = form)]

idolater /aɪ'dɒlətə/ *n.* one who worships idols; a devout admirer. —**idolatrous** *adj.,* **idolatry** *n.* [from Old French from Latin from Greek *eidos* = form and *latreuō*= worship]

idolize /'aɪdəlaɪz/ *v.t.* to venerate or love excessively; to treat as an idol. —**idolization** /-'zeɪʃən/ *n.*

idyll /'ɪdɪl/ *n.* a short description, usually in verse, of a picturesque scene or incident especially in rustic life; such a scene or incident. [from Latin from Greek *eidullion* (*eidos* = form)]

idyllic /ɪ'dɪlɪk/ *adj.* of or like an idyll; peaceful and happy. —**idyllically** *adv.*

i.e. abbreviation of id est. [Latin = that is to say]

if *conj.* 1. on the condition or supposition that; in the event that; supposing or granting that. 2. even though. 3.whenever. 4. whether. 5. expressing a wish or surprise. —*n.* a condition or supposition. —**as if,** as the case would be if. [Old English]

Ifugao /i:fu:'gaʊ/ *n.* a member of an indigenous people of N Luzon in the Philippines, numbering approximately 70,000. Their language belongs to the Austronesian family.

igloo /'ɪglu:/ *n.* an Inuit dome-shaped hut, especially one built of snow. [Inuit = house]

Ignatius Loyola, St /ɪg'neɪʃəs lɔɪ'əʊlə/ 1491–1556. Spanish noble who founded the ◊Jesuit order in 1540.

Ignatius of Antioch, St /'æntɪpɒk/ 1st–2nd century AD. Christian martyr. Traditionally a disciple of St John, he was bishop of Antioch, and was thrown to the wild beasts in Rome. He wrote seven epistles, important documents of the early Christian church. Feast day 1 Feb.

igneous /'ɪgniəs/ *adj.* 1. of fire, fiery. 2. (of rocks) formed by solidification of magma. [from Latin *igneus* = fire]

ignite /ɪg'naɪt/ *v.t./i.* to set fire to; to catch fire; to make intensely hot. [from Latin *ignire*]

ignition /ɪg'nɪʃən/ *n.* 1. igniting. 2. the mechanism for or act of starting combustion in the cylinder of an internal combustion engine. [French or from Latin]

ignition coil a ◊transformer that is an essential part of a petrol engine's ignition system. It consists of two wire coils wound around an iron core. The primary coil, which is connected to the car battery, has only a few turns. The secondary coil, connected via the ◊distributor to the ◊spark plugs, has many turns. The coil takes in a low voltage (usually 12 volts) from the battery and transforms it to a high voltage (about 20,000 volts) to ignite the engine.

ignition temperature or **fire point** the minimum temperature to which a substance must be heated before it will spontaneously burn independently of the source of heat; for example, ethanol has an ignition temperature of 425°C, and a ◊flash point of 12°C.

ignoble /ɪg'nəʊbəl/ *adj.* 1. dishonourable, not noble in character, aims, or purpose. 2. of lowly birth or position. —**ignobly** *adv.* [French or from Latin]

ignominious /ɪgnə'mɪniəs/ *adj.* bringing contempt or disgrace, humiliating. —**ignominiously** *adv.* [from French or Latin]

ignominy /'ɪgnəmɪnɪ/ *n.* disgrace, humiliation. [from French or Latin *nomen*= name]

ignoramus *n.* an ignorant person. [Latin = we do not know]

ignorant *adj.* lacking knowledge; uninformed; uncouth through lack of knowledge. —**ignorance** *n.,* **ignorantly** *adv.* [from Old French from Latin]

ignore /ɪg'nɔ:/ *v.t.* to refuse to take notice of; to disregard intentionally. [from French or Latin *ignorare* = not know]

Iguaçu Falls /i:gwæ'su:/ or **Iguassú Falls,** a waterfall in South America, on the border between Brazil and Argentina. The falls lie 19 km/12 mi above the junction of the river Iguaç with the Paraná, are divided by forested, rocky islands and form a spectacular tourist attraction. The water plunges in 275 falls, many of which have separate names. They have a height of 82 m/269 ft and a width about 4 km/2.5 mi.

ignition coil

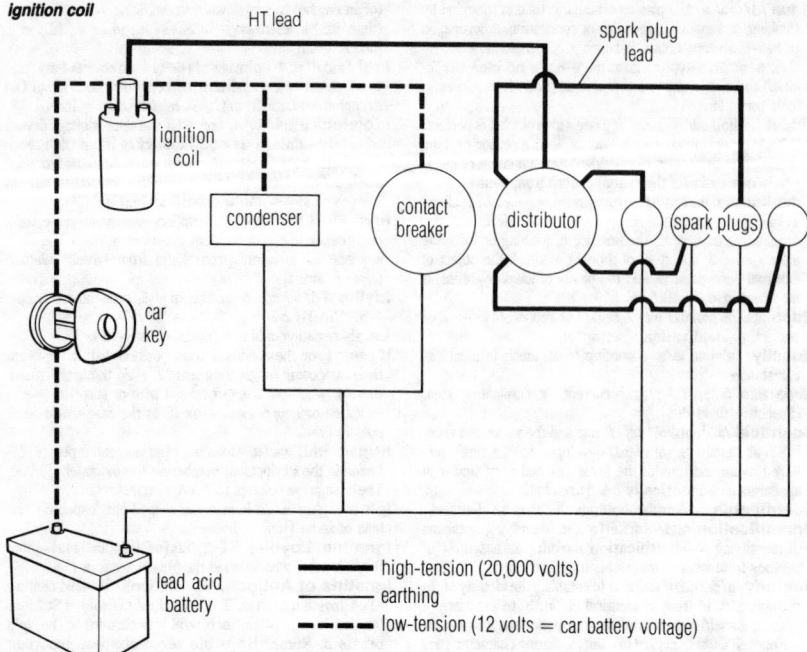

HT lead

spark plug lead

ignition coil

condenser

contact breaker

distributor

spark plugs

car key

lead acid battery

high-tension (20,000 volts)
earthing
low-tension (12 volts = car battery voltage)

iguana /ɪgˈwɑːnə/ n. a large tree lizard (of the family Iguanidae) of the West Indies and South America. [Spanish from Carib]

iguanodon /ɪgˈwɑːnədɒn/ n. a large herbivorous dinosaur. [from iguana]

Ijsselmeer /ˈaɪsəlmɪə/ a lake in the Netherlands, formed in 1932 after the Zuider Zee was cut off by a dyke from the North Sea; freshwater since 1944. Area 1,217 sq km/ 470 sq mi.

ikat n. the Indonesian term for a textile which is produced by resist-printing the warp or weft before weaving.

ikebana n. the Japanese art of flower arrangement dating from the 6th–7th century when arrangements of flowers were placed as offerings in Buddhist temples, a practice learned from China. In the 15th century, ikebana became a favourite pastime of the nobility.

Ikhnaton /ɪkˈnɑːtn/ or **Akhenaton** 14th century BC. King of Egypt of the 18th dynasty (c.1379–1362 BC), who may have ruled jointly for a time with his father Amenhotep III. He developed the cult of the Sun, ◊Aton, rather than the rival cult of ◊Ammon. Some historians believe that his attention to religious reforms rather than imperial defence led to the loss of most of Egypt's possessions in Asia. His favourite wife was Nefertiti, and two of their six daughters were married to his successors Smenkhare and Tutankaton (later known as Tutankhamen).

il-[1,2] prefix. See ◊in-[1,2].

ILEA /ˈiːliə ˈiːliə/ abbreviation of Inner London Education Authority, the former UK educational body which administered education in London. It was abolished in 1990 and replaced by smaller, borough-based education authorities.

Île-de-France /ˈiːl də ˈfrɒns/ region of N France; area 12,000 sq km/4,632 sq mi; population (1986) 10,251,000. It includes the French capital, Paris, and the towns of Versailles, Sèvres, and St-Cloud and comprises the *départements* of Essonne, Val-de-Marne, Val d'Oise, Ville de Paris, Seine-et-Marne, Hauts-de-Seine, Seine-Saint-Denis, and Yvelines. From here the early French kings extended their authority over the whole country.

ileum /ˈiliəm/ n. (plural **ilea**) part of the small intestine of the digestive system, between the duodenum and the colon, that absorbs digested food. Its wall is muscular so that waves of contraction (peristalsis) can mix the food and push it forward. Numerous finger-like projections (see ◊villus) point inwards from the wall, increasing the surface area available for absorption. The ileum has an excellent blood supply, which receives the food molecules passing through the wall and transports them to the liver via the hepatic portal vein. [variant of Latin *ilium*]

ilex /ˈaɪleks/ n. 1. the holm-oak. 2. a plant of the genus *Ilex*, including holly. [from Latin]

iliac /ˈɪliæk/ adj. of the flank. [from Latin *ilia* = flanks]

Iliad /ˈɪliəd/ a Greek epic poem in 24 books, probably written before 700 BC, attributed to ◊Homer. Its title is derived from Ilion, the Greek name for Troy. Its subject is the wrath of Achilles, an incident during the tenth year of the Trojan War, when Achilles kills Hector to avenge the death of his friend Patroclus.

ilk n. of that ilk, (Scottish) of the ancestral estate with the same name as a family; (colloquial) of that kind. [Old English = same]

ill adj. 1. physically or mentally unwell; (of health) unsound, not good. 2. harmful. 3. wretched, disastrous; hostile, unfavourable. 4. irritable. 5. improper, deficient. —adv. 1. badly, wrongly. 2. unfavourably. 3. imperfectly, scarcely. —n. injury, harm, evil; (in plural) misfortunes. —ill-advised adj. (of an action) unwise. ill at ease, embarrassed, uncomfortable. ill-bred adj. badly brought up, rude. ill-fated adj. unlucky. ill-favoured adj. unattractive. ill-gotten adj. acquired by evil or unlawful means. ill-mannered adj. having bad manners. ill-natured adj. churlish, unkind. ill-starred adj. unlucky. ill-tempered adj. morose, irritable. ill-timed adj. done or occurring at an unsuitable time. ill-treat v.t., ill-use v.t. to treat badly or cruelly. ill will, hostility, unkind feeling. [from Old Norse]

illegal /ɪˈliːgəl/ adj. not legal, contrary to the law —**illegality** /ɪliˈgælɪti/ n., **illegally** adv. [from French or Latin]

illegible /ɪˈledʒɪbəl/ adj. not legible. —**illegibility** /-ˈbɪlɪti/ n., **illegibly** adv. [from Latin *legere* = to read]

illegitimate /ɪliˈdʒɪtɪmət/ adj. 1. (of a child) born of parents who are not married to each other. 2. not authorized by the law or by rules. 3. illogical, wrongly inferred. —**illegitimacy** n., **illegitimately** adv. [from Latin *legitimus* = lawful]

illiberal /ɪˈlɪbərəl/ adj. 1. intolerant, narrow-minded. 2. without liberal culture, sordid. 3. stingy. —**illiberality** /-ˈrælɪti/ n., **illiberally** adv. [from French from Latin *liber* = free]

Illich /'ɪlɪtʃ/ Ivan 1926– . US radical philosopher and activist, born in Austria. His works, which include *Deschooling Society* 1971, *Towards a History of Need* 1978, and *Gender* 1983, are a critique against contemporary economic development, especially in the Third World.

In a consumer society there are inevitably two kinds of slaves: the prisoners of addiction and the prisoners of envy.

Ivan Illich
Tools for Conviviality

---

illicit /i'lɪsɪt/ *adj.* unlawful, forbidden. —**illicitly** *adv.* [from French or Latin *licere* = to be lawful]

Illinois /ɪlə'nɔɪ/ midwest state of the USA; nickname Inland Empire/Prairie State; **area** 146,100 sq km/56,395 sq mi; **capital** Springfield; **population** (1987) 11,582,000; **history** originally explored by the French in the 17th century, ceded to Britain by the French in 1763, Illinois passed to American control in 1783, and became a state in 1818.

illiterate /i'lɪtərət/ *adj.* unable to read; uneducated. —*n.* an illiterate person. —**illiteracy** *n.* [from Latin *litera* = letter]

illness *n.* 1. ill health, the state of being ill. 2. a disease.

illogical /i'lɒdʒɪkəl/ *adj.* contrary to or devoid of logic. —**illogicality** /-kælɪtɪ/ *n.*, **illogically** *adv.*

illuminant /i'lu:mɪnənt/ *n.* a means of illumination. —*adj.* serving to illuminate.

illuminate /i'lu:mɪneɪt/ *v.t.* 1. to light up, to make bright. 2. to enlighten spiritually or intellectually; to help to explain (a subject); to shed lustre on. 3. to decorate with lights as a sign of festivity. 4. to decorate (a manuscript, initial letter, etc.) with gold or other bright colours. —**illumination** /-'neɪʃən/ *n.*, **illuminative** *adj.* [from Latin *lumen* = light]

illumine /i'lju:mɪn/ *v.t.* (*literary*) to light up; to enlighten spiritually.

illusion /i'lu:ʒən, i'lju:-/ *n.* 1. a false belief; something wrongly believed to exist. 2. deceptive appearances. —**illusive** *adj.*, **illusory** *adj.* [from French from Latin *illudere* = mock]

illusionist *n.* a producer of illusions, a conjuror.

illustrate /'ɪləstreɪt/ *v.t.* 1. to provide (a book, newspaper, etc.) with pictures. 2. to make clear, especially by examples or drawings. 3. to serve as an example of. —**illustrator** *n.* [from Latin *illustrare* = light up]

illustration /ɪlə'streɪʃən/ *n.* 1. illustrating. 2. a picture or drawing in a book etc. 3. an explanatory example.

illustrative /'ɪləstrətɪv/ *adj.* illustrating, explanatory (*of*).

illustrious /i'lʌstrɪəs/ *adj.* distinguished, renowned. [from Latin *illustris*]

Illyria /i'lɪrɪə/ the ancient name for the eastern coastal region on the Adriatic, N of the Gulf of Corinth, conquered by Philip of Macedon. It became a Roman province in AD 9. The Albanians are the survivors of its ancient peoples. —**Illyrian** *adj.* & *n.*

im-[1,2] see ◊in-[1,2].

image /'ɪmɪdʒ/ *n.* 1. a representation of an object's external form, e. g. a statue (especially as an object of worship). 2. reputation, the general impression of a person or thing as perceived by the public. 3. a simile, a metaphor. 4. a mental representation. 5. an optical counterpart produced by rays of light reflected from a mirror etc. 6. a counterpart in appearance. 7. an idea, a conception. —*v.t.* 1. to describe or imagine vividly. 2. to make an image of, to portray. 3. to reflect, to mirror. [from Old French from Latin *imago*]

imagery *n.* 1. figurative illustration; use of images in literature etc. 2. images, statuary; carving.

imaginable /i'mædʒɪnəbəl/ *adj.* able to be imagined.

imaginary /i'mædʒɪnərɪ/ *adj.* existing only in the imagination. [from Latin]

imaginary number a term often used to describe the non-real element of a ◊complex number. For the complex number $(a + ib)$, ib is the imaginary number where $i = \sqrt{-1}$, and b any real number.

imagination /ɪmædʒi'neɪʃən/ *n.* the mental faculty forming images or concepts of objects not existent or present, the creative faculty of the mind. [from Old French from Latin]

imaginative /i'mædʒɪnətɪv/ *adj.* having or showing a high degree of imagination. —**imaginatively** *adv.*

imagine /i'mædʒɪn/ *v.t.* 1. to form a mental image of, to picture in one's mind. 2. to think or believe; to guess; (*colloquial*) to suppose. [from Old French from Latin]

Imagism *n.* a movement in Anglo-American poetry which flourished 1912–14 and affected much US and British poetry and critical thinking thereafter. A central figure was Ezra Pound, who asserted the principles of free verse, hard imagery, and poetic impersonality.

imago /i'meɪgəʊ/ *n.* (*plural* **imagines** /-dʒɪni:z/) the fully developed stage of an insect, e. g. a butterfly. [Latin]

imam /i'mɑ:m/ *n.* 1. the leader of prayers in a mosque. 2. the title of various Muslim leaders, especially of one succeeding Muhammad as leader of Islam. —**imamate** *n.* [from Arabic = leader]

imbalance /ɪm'bæləns/ *n.* lack of balance; disproportion.

imbecile /'ɪmbisi:l/ *n.* 1. a mentally deficient person; an adult whose intelligence is equal to that of an average five-year-old child. 2. a stupid person. —*adj.* idiotic. —**imbecility** /-'sɪlɪtɪ/ *n.* [from French from Latin *imbecillus* = weak]

imbibe /ɪm'baɪb/ *v.t.* 1. to drink (especially alcoholic liquor). 2. to absorb (ideas, moisture etc.). 3. to inhale (air etc.). [from Latin *bibere* = drink]

imbroglio /ɪm'brəʊljəʊ/ *n.* (*plural* **imbroglios**) 1. a complicated or confused situation. 2. a confused heap. [Italian]

imbue /ɪm'bju:/ *v.t.* 1. to inspire or permeate (*with* feelings, opinions, or qualities). 2. to saturate or dye (*with*). [from French or Latin *imbuere* = moisten]

IMF abbreviation of ◊International Monetary Fund.

Imhotep /ɪm'həʊtep/ *c.*2800 BC. Egyptian physician and architect, adviser to King Zoser (3rd dynasty). He is thought to have designed the step pyramid at Sakkara, and his tomb (believed to be in the N Sakkara cemetery) became a centre of healing. He was deified as the son of Ptah and was identified with Aesculapius, the Greek god of medicine.

imitable /'ɪmɪtəbəl/ *adj.* able to be imitated.

imitate /'ɪmɪteɪt/ *v.t.* to follow the example of; to mimic; to make a copy of; to be like. —**imitator** *n.* [from Latin]

imitation /ɪmɪ'teɪʃən/ *n.* 1. imitating. 2. a copy, a counterfeit (often *attributive*). [French or from Latin]

imitative /'ɪmɪtətɪv/ *adj.* imitating.

immaculate /i'mækjʊlət/ *adj.* pure, spotless; faultless, innocent. —**Immaculate Conception,** the doctrine that the Virgin Mary was conceived, and remained, free from all stain of original sin. —**immaculacy** *n.*, **immaculately** *adv.* [from Latin *macula* = spot]

immanent /'ɪmənənt/ *adj.* inherent; (of God) permanently pervading the universe. —**immanence** *n.* [from Latin *manēre* = remain]

immaterial /ɪmə'tɪərɪəl/ *adj.* not material, not corporeal; unimportant, irrelevant. —**immateriality** /-'ælɪtɪ/ *n.* [from Latin]

immature /ɪmə'tjʊə/ *adj.* not mature; unripe. —**immaturity** *n.* [from Latin]

immeasurable /i'meʒərəbəl/ *adj.* not measurable; immense. —**immeasurably** *adv.*

immediate /i'mi:dɪət/ *adj.* 1. occurring at once. 2. without an intervening medium; direct, nearest; not separated by others. —**immediacy** *n.* [from French or Latin *medius* = middle]

immediately *adv.* 1. without pause or delay. 2. without an intermediary. —*conj.* (*colloquial*) as soon as.

immemorial /ɪmi'mɔ:rɪəl/ *adj.* ancient beyond memory or record; very old.

immense /i'mens/ *adj.* exceedingly large; (*colloquial*) great. —**immensely** *adv.*, **immensity** *n.* [from French from Latin *mensus*, past participle of *metiri* = measure]

immerse /i'mɜ:s/ *v.t.* 1. to put completely in water or other liquid. 2. to absorb or involve deeply in thought, business, etc. 3. to embed. [from Latin *immergere* (*mergere mers-* = dip)]

immersion /i'mɜ:ʃən/ *n.* immersing, being immersed. —**immersion heater,** an electric heater designed to be immersed in the liquid to be heated, especially as a fixture in a hot-water tank.

immigrant /'ɪmɪgrənt/ *n.* one who immigrates; a descendant of recent immigrants. —*adj.* immigrating; of immigrants.

immigrate /'ɪmɪgreɪt/ *v.i.* to come into a foreign country as a settler. —**immigration** /-'greɪʃən/ *n.* [from Latin *immigrare*]

imminent /'ɪmɪnənt/ *adj.* of an event, especially danger about to happen. —**imminence** *n.* [from Latin *imminēre* = overhang]

immiscible /i'mɪsɪbəl/ *adj.* that cannot be mixed (*with* another substance). —**immiscibility** /-'bɪlɪtɪ/ *n.* [from Latin]

immobile /i'məʊbaɪl/ *adj.* immovable; not mobile; motionless. —**immobility** /ɪmə'bɪlɪtɪ/ *n.* [from Old French from Latin]

immobilize /i'məʊbɪlaɪz/ *v.t.* to make or keep immobile; to keep (a limb or patient) still for healing purposes. —**immobilization** /-'zeɪʃən/ *n.*

immoderate /i'mɒdərət/ *adj.* excessive, lacking moderation. —**immoderately** *adv.* [from Latin]

immodest /i'mɒdɪst/ *adj.* 1. lacking in modesty, indecent. 2. conceited. —**immodestly** *adv.*, **immodesty** *n.* [from French or Latin]

immolate /'ɪməleɪt/ *v.t.* to kill as a sacrifice. —**immolation** /-'leɪʃən/ *n.* [from Latin *immolare*, originally = sprinkle with meal (*mola*)]

immoral /i'mɒrəl/ *adj.* not conforming to the accepted rules of morality, morally wrong (especially in sexual matters). —**immorality** /ɪmə'rælɪtɪ/ *n.*, **immorally** *adv.*

immortal /i'mɔ:təl/ *adj.* 1. not mortal, living for ever. 2. famous for all time. —*n.* an immortal being or person. —**immortality** /-'tælɪtɪ/ *n.*, **immortally** *adv.* [from Latin]

immortalize /i'mɔ:təlaɪz/ *v.t.* to make immortal.

immovable /i'mu:vəbəl/ *adj.* 1. unable to be moved; motionless. 2. steadfast, unyielding, not changing in one's purpose; not moved emotionally. 3. (of property) consisting of land, houses etc. —**immovability** /-'bɪlɪtɪ/ *n.*, **immovably** *adv.*

immune /i'mju:n/ *adj.* having immunity (*from* punishment or taxation; *against* infection or poison; *to* criticism). [from Latin *immunis* = exempt from public service]

immunity /i'mju:nɪtɪ/ *n.* 1. the ability of an organism to resist and overcome infection. 2. freedom or exemption (*from*).

immunize /'ɪmjʊnaɪz/ *v.t.* to make immune, especially against infection. —**immunization** /-'zeɪʃən/ *n.* conferring immunity to infectious disease by artificial methods, the most widely used technique being vaccination (see ◊vaccine).

immunodeficient *n.* lacking one or more elements of a working immune system. Immune deficiency is the term generally used for patients who are born with such a defect, while those who acquire such a deficiency later in life are referred to as **immunocompromised** or immunosuppressed.

immunoglobulin *n.* human globulin ◊protein that can be separated from blood and administered to confer immediate immunity on the recipient.

immunology /ɪmju'nɒlədʒɪ/ *n.* the study of resistance to infection.

immunosuppressive *n.* any drug that suppresses the body's normal immune responses to infection or foreign tissue. It is used in the treatment of autoimmune disease (see ◊autoimmunity); as part of chemotherapy for leukaemias, lymphomas, and other cancers; and to help prevent rejection following organ transplantation.

immure /i'mjʊə/ *v.t.* to imprison; to shut in. [from French or Latin *immurare* (*murus* = wall)]

immutable /i'mju:təbəl/ *adj.* unchangeable. —**immutability** /-'bɪlɪtɪ/ *n.*, **immutably** *adv.* [from Latin]

imp *n.* 1. a small devil. 2. a mischievous child. [Old English = young shoot]

impact /'ɪmpækt/ *n.* 1. a collision; the force of a collision. 2. strong effect or influence, especially of something new —/ɪm'pækt/ *v.t.* 1. to press or fix firmly. 2. (in past participle, of a tooth) wedged between another tooth and the jaw, (of a fractured bone) with the parts pushed together. —**impaction** /-'pækʃən/ *n.* [from Latin]

impair /ɪm'peə/ *v.t.* to damage, to weaken. —**impairment** *n.* [from Old French from Latin *pejor* = worse]

impala /ɪm'pɑ:lə/ *n.* (*plural* the same) African antelope *Aepyceros melampus* found from Kenya to South Africa in savannas and open woodlands. The body is sandy brown. The males have lyre-shaped horns up to 75 cm/2.5 ft long.

Impala grow up to 1.5 m/5 ft long and 90 cm/3 ft tall. They live in herds and spring high in the air when alarmed. [Zulu]

impale /ɪm'peɪl/ *v.t.* 1. to fix or pierce with a pointed stake etc. 2. in heraldry, to combine (two coats of arms) by placing side by side on one shield separated by a vertical line down the middle. —**impalement** *n.* [from French or Latin *palus* = stake]

impalpable /ɪm'pælpəbəl/ *adj.* 1. not palpable. 2. not easily grasped by the mind, intangible. 3. (of a powder) very fine. —**impalpability** /-'bɪlɪtɪ/ *n.*, **impalpably** *adv.* [French or from Latin]

impart *v.t.* 1. to give a share of. 2. to communicate (news etc. *to*). [from Old French from Latin *pars* = part]

impartial /ɪm'pɑ:ʃəl/ *adj.* not favouring one side more than another. —**impartiality** /-ʃɪ'ælɪtɪ/ *n.*, **impartially** *adv.*

impassable /ɪm'pɑ:səbəl/ *adj.* that cannot be traversed. —**impassability** /-'bɪlɪtɪ/ *n.*, **impassably** *adv.*

impasse /'æmpɑ:s/ *n.* deadlock; a position from which there is no escape.

impassible /ɪm'pæsɪbəl/ *adj.* not liable to pain or injury; impassive. —**impassibility** /-'bɪlɪtɪ/ *n.*, **impassibly** *adv.* [from Old French from Latin *passibilis* = capable of suffering]

impassioned /ɪm'pæʃənd/ *adj.* deeply moved, ardent [from Italian *impassionato*]

impassive /ɪm'pæsɪv/ *adj.* not feeling or showing emotion; serene. —**impassively** *adv.*, **impassivity** /-'sɪvɪtɪ/ *n.*

impasto /ɪm'pæstəʊ/ *n.* the laying on of paint thickly so that it projects from the picture surface and gives a textured quality, catching and reflecting light and throwing its own shadow. [Italian *pasta* = paste]

impatient /ɪm'peɪʃənt/ *adj.* 1. unable to wait patiently; eager. 2. showing a lack of patience. 3. intolerant (*of*). —**impatience** *n.*, **impatiently** *adv.* [from Old French from Latin]

impeach /ɪm'pi:tʃ/ *v.t.* 1. to accuse of treason or other serious crime before a competent tribunal. 2. to call in question, to disparage. —**impeachment** *n.* [from Old French *empecher* from Latin *pedica* = fetter]

impeccable /ɪm'pekəbəl/ *adj.* faultless; not liable to sin. —**impeccability** /-'bɪlɪtɪ/ *n.*, **impeccably** *adv.* [from Latin *peccare* = sin]

impecunious /ɪmpɪ'kju:nɪəs/ *adj.* having little or no money. —**impecuniosity** /-'ɒsɪtɪ/ *n.* [from Latin *pecuniosus* (*pecunia* = money)]

impedance /ɪm'pi:dəns/ *n.* 1. the total effective resistance of an electric circuit etc. to the flow of alternating current. 2. a similar mechanical property.

impede /ɪm'pi:d/ *v.t.* to retard by obstructing, to hinder. [from Latin *impedire* = shackle the feet of (*pes* = foot)]

impediment /ɪm'pedɪmənt/ *n.* 1. a hindrance. 2. a defect in speech, especially a lisp or stammer.

impedimenta /ɪmpedɪ'mentə/ *n. pl.* encumbrances; baggage, especially of the army.

impel /ɪm'pel/ *v.t.* (-ll-) 1. to urge or drive to do something. 2. to send or drive forward, to propel. [from Latin *impellere* (*pellere puls-* = drive)]

impend /ɪm'pend/ *v.i.* of an event or danger to be imminent; to hang (*over*). [from Latin *pendēre* = hang]

impenetrable /ɪm'penɪtrəbəl/ *adj.* 1. not penetrable. 2. inscrutable. 3. impervious (*to* or *by* ideas etc.). —**impenetrability** /-'bɪlɪtɪ/ *n.*, **impenetrably** *adv.* [from French from Latin]

impenitent /ɪm'penɪtənt/ *adj.* not penitent. —**impenitence** *n.* [from Latin]

imperative /ɪm'perətɪv/ *adj.* 1. essential, urgently needed. 2. in grammar, of the mood expressing command. 3. peremptory. —*n.* in grammar, the imperative mood. [from Latin *imperare* = command]

imperceptible /ɪmpə'septɪbəl/ *adj.* not perceptible, very slight or gradual. —**imperceptibly** *adv.* [from French or Latin]

imperfect /ɪm'pɜ:fɪkt/ *adj.* 1. not perfect, incomplete, faulty. 2. in grammar, of a tense denoting action going on but not completed (especially in the past, e. g. *was doing*). —*n.* in grammar, the imperfect tense. —**imperfectly** *adv.* [from Old French from Latin]

imperfection /ɪmpə'fekʃən/ *n.* 1. being imperfect. 2. a fault, a blemish.

imperial /ɪm'pɪərɪəl/ *adj.* **1.** of or characteristic of an empire or similar sovereign state; of an emperor or empress. **2.** majestic. **3.** of weights and measures used (now or formerly) by statute in the UK. —**imperially** *adv.* [from Old French from Latin *imperium* = supreme power]

imperialism *n.* **1.** imperial rule; an imperial system. **2.** (usually *derogatory*) the policy of extending a country's influence over less powerful, less developed countries by acquiring dependencies or through trade, diplomacy etc. —**imperialist** *n.*, **imperialistic** /-'lɪstɪk/ *adj.*

Imperial War Museum a British military museum, founded in 1917 which includes records of all operations fought by British forces since 1914. Its present building (formerly the Royal Bethlehem, or Bedlam, Hospital) in Lambeth Road, London, was opened in 1936. It was rebuilt and enlarged in 1989.

imperil /ɪm'perɪl/ *v.t.* (-ll-) to endanger.

imperious /ɪm'pɪərɪəs/ *adj.* **1.** domineering. **2.** urgent. —**imperiously** *adv.* [from Latin]

imperishable /ɪm'perɪʃəbəl/ *adj.* that cannot perish.

impermanent /ɪm'pɜːmənənt/ *adj.* not permanent. —**impermanence** *n.*, **impermanency** *n.*

impermeable /ɪm'pɜːmɪəbəl/ *adj.* not permeable. —**impermeability** /-'bɪlɪtɪ/ *n.* [from French or Latin]

impersonal /ɪm'pɜːsənəl/ *adj.* **1.** not influenced by personal feeling; showing no emotion. **2.** not referring to any particular person. **3.** having no existence as a person. **4.** (of a verb) used without a definite subject (e. g. *it is raining*); (of a pronoun) indefinite. —**impersonality** /-'nælɪtɪ/ *n.*, **impersonally** *adv.* [from Latin]

impersonate /ɪm'pɜːsəneɪt/ *v.t.* to pretend to be (another person); to play the part of. —**impersonation** /-'neɪʃən/ *n.*, **impersonator** *n.*

impertinent /ɪm'pɜːtɪnənt/ *adj.* **1.** insolent, not showing proper respect. **2.** irrelevant. —**impertinence** *n.*, **impertinently** *adv.* [from Old French from Latin]

imperturbable /ɪmpə'tɜːbəbəl/ *adj.* not excitable, calm. —**imperturbability** /-'bɪlɪtɪ/ *n.*, **imperturbably** *adv.* [from Latin]

impervious /ɪm'pɜːvɪəs/ *adj.* **1.** not able to be penetrated, not affording passage *to* water etc. **2.** not responsive (*to* an argument etc.). [from Latin]

impetigo /ɪmpɪ'taɪɡəʊ/ *n.* any of various skin diseases marked by the eruption of pustules, such as *Staphylococcus aureus*, a contagious bacterial infection of the skin that forms yellowish crusts; it is curable with antibiotics. [from Latin *impetere* = assail]

impetuous /ɪm'petjuːəs/ *adj.* acting or done rashly or on impulse or with sudden energy; moving violently or fast. —**impetuosity** /-'ɒsɪtɪ/ *n.*, **impetuously** *adv.* [from Old French from Latin *impetus* = assault]

impetus /'ɪmpɪtəs/ *n.* the force or energy with which a body moves; an impulse, a driving force. [Latin = assault]

impiety /ɪm'paɪətɪ/ *n.* lack of piety or reverence. [from Old French or Latin]

impinge /ɪm'pɪndʒ/ *v.i.* to make an impact; to encroach. —**impingement** *n.* [from Latin *impingere (pangere* = fix, drive)]

impious /'ɪmpɪəs/ *adj.* not pious; wicked. —**impiously** *adv.* [from Latin]

impish *adj.* of or like an imp; mischievous. —**impishly** *adv.*, **impishness** *n.*

implacable /ɪm'plækəbəl/ *adj.* not able to be placated, relentless. —**implacability** /-'bɪlɪtɪ/ *n.*, **implacably** *adv.* [from French or Latin]

implant /ɪm'plɑːnt/ *v.t.* **1.** to plant, to insert or fix (*in*). **2.** to instil (an idea etc.) *in* a person's mind. **3.** to insert (tissue etc.) in a living body. —/'ɪmplɑːnt/ *n.* a thing implanted, especially a piece of tissue. —**implantation** /-'teɪʃən/ *n.* [from French or Latin]

implausible /ɪm'plɔːzɪbəl/ *adj.* not plausible. —**implausibility** /-'bɪlɪtɪ/ *n.*, **implausibly** *adv.*

implement /'ɪmplɪmənt/ *n.* a tool, an instrument, a utensil. —/also -ment/ *v.t.* to put (a contract, decision, promise, etc.) into effect. —**implementation** /-'teɪʃən/ *n.* [from Latin *implēre* = fill up]

implicate /'ɪmplɪkeɪt/ *v.t.* **1.** to show (a person) to be concerned (*in* a charge, crime etc.). **2.** to lead to as a consequence or inference. [from Latin *plicare* = fold]

implication /ɪmplɪ'keɪʃən/ *n.* **1.** implying; implicating. **2.** a thing implied.

implicit /ɪm'plɪsɪt/ *adj.* **1.** implied though not expressed. **2.** absolute, unquestioning. —**implicitly** *adv.* [from French or Latin]

implode /ɪm'pləʊd/ *v.t./i.* to burst or cause to burst inwards. —**implosion** /-'pləʊʒən/ *n.* [from Latin]

implore /ɪm'plɔː/ *v.t.* to entreat, to request earnestly. —**imploringly** *adv.* [from French or Latin *plorare* = lament]

imply /ɪm'plaɪ/ *v.t.* **1.** to indicate or suggest without stating directly. **2.** to involve the truth or existence of. **3.** to mean. [from Old French from Latin = implicate]

impolite /ɪmpə'laɪt/ *adj.* not polite. —**impolitely** *adv.* [from Latin]

impolitic /ɪm'pɒlɪtɪk/ *adj.* inexpedient, unwise.

imponderable /ɪm'pɒndərəbəl/ *adj.* **1.** that cannot be estimated. **2.** weightless, very light. —*n.* an imponderable thing. —**imponderably** *adv.*

import /ɪm'pɔːt/ *v.t.* **1.** to bring (goods etc.) into a country from abroad; to bring in from an outside source. **2.** to imply, to indicate. —/'ɪmpɔːt/ *n.* **1.** the importing of goods etc. **2.** something imported. **3.** meaning. **4.** importance. —**importation** /-'teɪʃən/ *n.*, **importer** *n.* [from Latin *portare* = carry]

important /ɪm'pɔːtənt/ *adj.* **1.** having or able to have a great effect. **2.** (of a person) having high rank or great authority or influence. **3.** pompous. —**importance** *n.*, **importantly** *adv.* [French from Latin]

importunate /ɪm'pɔːtʊnət/ *adj.* making persistent or pressing requests. —**importunity** /ɪmpɔː'tjuːnɪtɪ/ *n.* [from Latin *importunus* = inconvenient, originally = harbourless]

importune /ɪm'pɔːtjuːn, -'tjuːn/ *v.t.* **1.** to make insistent requests (to). **2.** to solicit for an immoral purpose. [from French or Latin]

impose /ɪm'pəʊz/ *v.t./i.* **1.** to lay (a tax, duty, etc., *on* or *upon*). **2.** to enforce compliance with. **3.** to inflict; to palm off (a thing *upon* a person). **4.** to lay (pages of type) in proper order. —**impose on** *or* **upon**, to take advantage of (a person, his good nature etc.), to deceive, to impress, to overawe. [from French from Latin *ponere* = put]

imposing *adj.* impressive, formidable, especially in appearance.

imposition /ɪmpə'zɪʃən/ *n.* **1.** an unfair demand or burden. **2.** a tax, a duty. **3.** work set as a punishment at school. **4.** the laying on of hands in blessing etc. **5.** an act of deception or taking advantage. [from Old French from Latin]

impossible /ɪm'pɒsɪbəl/ *adj.* **1.** not possible, unable to be done or to exist; (*loosely*) not easy, inconvenient, incredible. **2.** (*colloquial*) outrageous, intolerable. —**impossibility** /-'bɪlɪtɪ/ *n.*, **impossibly** *adv.* [from Old French or Latin]

impost[1] /'ɪmpəʊst/ *n.* a tax or duty. [French from Latin]

impost[2] *n.* the upper course of a pillar, carrying the arch. [from French or Italian *imposta* from Latin]

impostor or **imposter** /ɪm'pɒstə/ *n.* one who assumes a false character or personality; a swindler. [from French from Latin]

imposture /ɪm'pɒstʃə/ *n.* a deception, a sham. [French from Latin]

impotent /'ɪmpətənt/ *adj.* **1.** powerless, unable to take action. **2.** (of a male) unable to copulate or reach orgasm; unable to procreate. —**impotence** *n.*, **impotently** *adv.* [from Old French from Latin]

impound /ɪm'paʊnd/ *v.t.* **1.** to confiscate; to take legal possession of. **2.** to shut up (cattle etc.) in a pound.

impoverish /ɪm'pɒvərɪʃ/ *v.t.* **1.** to make poor. **2.** to exhaust the vitality or fertility of. —**impoverishment** *n.* [from Old French *poverir* from *povre* = poor]

impracticable /ɪm'præktɪkəbəl/ *adj.* not practicable. —**impracticability** /-'bɪlɪtɪ/ *n.*, **impracticably** *adv.*

impractical /ɪm'præktɪkəl/ *adj.* **1.** not practical. **2.** not practicable. —**impracticality** /-'kælɪtɪ/ *n.*

imprecate /'ɪmprɪkeɪt/ *v.t.* to invoke (evil *upon*). —**imprecation** /-'keɪʃən/ *n.* [from Latin *precari* = pray]

imprecatory /'ɪmprɪkeɪtərɪ/ *adj.* making an imprecation.

imprecise /ɪmprɪ'saɪs/ *adj.* not precise. —**imprecision** /-'sɪʒən/ *n.*

impregnable /ɪm'pregnəbəl/ *adj.* (of a fortress etc. or *figuratively*) proof against attack. —**impregnability** /-'bɪlɪtɪ/ *n.*, **impregnably** *adv.* [from Old French *imprenable (prendre* = take)]

impregnate /'ɪmpregneɪt/ v.t. 1. to fill or saturate (with). 2. to imbue (with). 3. to make (a female) pregnant; to fertilize (an ovum). —**impregnatable** adj., **impregnation** /-'neɪʃən/ n. [from Latin praegnare = be pregnant]

impresario /ɪmprɪ'sɑːrɪəʊ/ n. (plural **impresarios**) an organizer of public entertainment, especially an opera or concert. [Italian impresa = undertaking]

impress[1] /ɪm'pres/ v.t. 1. to cause to form a strong (usually favourable) opinion. 2. to fix or imprint (an idea etc. on a person). 3. to imprint or stamp (a mark etc. on a thing, a thing with a mark). —/'ɪmpres/ n. 1. a mark impressed. 2. a characteristic quality. —**impressible** adj. [from Old French]

impress[2] v.t. (historical) to force to serve in the army or navy. —**impressment** n.

impression /ɪm'preʃən/ n. 1. an effect, especially on the mind or feelings. 2. an uncertain idea, belief, or remembrance. 3. an imitation of a person or sound, done to entertain. 4. impressing; a mark impressed. 5. an unaltered reprint from standing type or plates; the copies forming one issue of a book, newspaper etc. 6. a print made from type or from an engraving. [from Old French from Latin]

impressionable adj. easily influenced. —**impressionability** /-'bɪlɪtɪ/ n., **impressionably** adv. [from French]

Impressionism n. 1. movement in painting that originated in France in the 1860s. The Impressionists wanted to depict real life, to paint straight from nature, and to capture the changing effects of light. The term was first used abusively to describe Monet's painting Impression, Sunrise 1872; other Impressionists were Renoir, Sisley, Cézanne, Manet, and Degas. 2. in music, a style of composition emphasizing instrumental colour and texture. The term was first applied to the music of Debussy. —**impressionist** n., **impressionistic** /-'nɪstɪk/ adj. [from French]

impressive /ɪm'presɪv/ adj. able to excite deep feeling, especially of approval or admiration. —**impressively** adv.

imprimatur /ɪmprɪ'meɪtə/ n. a licence to print, usually from the Roman Catholic Church; authoritative permission. [Latin = let it be printed]

imprint /ɪm'prɪnt/ v.t. 1. to set firmly (a mark on, an idea etc. on or in the mind). 2. to stamp (with a figure). 3. to make or become recognized by (a young bird or animal in the first hours of its life) as an object of trust etc. —/'ɪmprɪnt/ n. 1. a mark made by pressing or stamping a surface. 2. a publisher's name etc. on the title-page of a book. [from Old French from Latin]

imprison /ɪm'prɪzən/ v.t. to put into prison; to confine. —**imprisonment** n. [from Old French]

improbable /ɪm'prɒbəbəl/ adj. not likely. —**improbability** /-'bɪlɪtɪ/ n., **improbably** adv. [French or from Latin]

improbity /ɪm'prəʊbɪtɪ/ n. wickedness, dishonesty. [from Latin]

impromptu /ɪm'prɒmptjuː/ adj. & adv. unrehearsed. —n. 1. a musical composition resembling an improvisation. 2. an extempore performance. [French from Latin in promptu = in readiness]

improper /ɪm'prɒpə/ adj. 1. not conforming to the rules of social or lawful conduct; indecent. 2. wrong, incorrect. —**improper fraction**, a fraction with the numerator greater than the denominator. —**improperly** adv. [from French or Latin]

impropriety /ɪmprə'praɪɪtɪ/ n. being improper; an improper act or remark etc.

improvable /ɪm'pruːvəbəl/ adj. able to be improved.

improve /ɪm'pruːv/ v.t./i. 1. to make or become better. 2. to make good use of (an occasion, opportunities). —**improve on** or **upon**, to produce something better than. —**improvement** n. [from Anglo-French emprower from Old French prou = profit]

improver n. 1. a person who works at a trade for little or no payment in order to improve his skill. 2. a substance added to food by a manufacturer or processor in order to improve its texture, keeping quality etc.

improvident /ɪm'prɒvɪdənt/ adj. lacking foresight or care for the future, wasting one's resources. —**improvidence** n., **improvidently** adv. [from French]

improvise /'ɪmprəvaɪz/ v.t. 1. to compose (verse, music, etc.) extempore. 2. to construct from materials not intended for the purpose. —**improvisation** /-'zeɪʃən/

n., **improviser** n. [from French or Italian improvviso = extempore]

imprudent /ɪm'pruːdənt/ adj. unwise, rash. —**imprudence** n., **imprudently** adv. [from Latin]

impudent adj. impertinent, cheeky. —**impudence** n., **impudently** adv. [from Latin pudēre = be ashamed]

impugn /ɪm'pjuːn/ v.t. to express doubts about the truth or honesty of, to try to discredit. —**impugnment** n. [from Latin impugnare = assail (pugnare = fight)]

impulse /'ɪmpʌls/ n. 1. impelling; a push or thrust, impetus; a sharp force producing change of momentum; this change. 2. a stimulating force in a nerve. 3. a sudden inclination to act, without thought for the consequences. [from Latin]

impulsion /ɪm'pʌlʃən/ n. 1. impelling, a push; impetus. 2. a mental impulse. [from Old French from Latin]

impulsive /ɪm'pʌlsɪv/ adj. 1. tending to act on impulse; done on impulse. 2. tending to impel. —**impulsively** adv., **impulsiveness** n. [from French or Latin]

impunity /ɪm'pjuːnɪtɪ/ n. exemption from punishment or injurious consequences. [from Latin poena = penalty]

impure /ɪm'pjuə/ adj. not pure. [from Latin purus = pure]

impurity /ɪm'pjuərɪtɪ/ n. 1. being impure. 2. a substance that makes another impure by being present in it.

impute /ɪm'pjuːt/ v.t. to attribute (a fault etc.) to. —**imputation** /-'teɪʃən/ n. [from Old French from Latin imputare, originally = enter in an account]

in prep. 1. expressing inclusion or a position within the limits of space, time, circumstances, surroundings etc. 2. expressing quantity, proportion (packed in tens), form or arrangement (written in French; hanging in folds), material, dress, or colour (in shades of blue), influence or respect (spoke in anger, lacking in courage). 3. expressing activity, occupation, or membership (he or she is in the army). 4. within the ability of. 5. (of a female animal) pregnant with (in calf). 6. (with verbs of motion or change) into (put it in your pocket). 7. introducing an indirect object after a verb (believe in; share in). 8. forming adverbial phrases (in any case; in vain). —adv. 1. expressing position bounded by certain limits, or to a point enclosed by these. 2. into a room, house, etc. 3. at home. 4. on or towards the inside. 5. in fashion, season, or office; elected; in effective or favourable action; (of the tide) high; (in cricket and baseball) batting. 6. (of a domestic fire) burning. 7. having arrived or been gathered or received. —adj. 1. internal; living etc. in, inside. 2. fashionable. —**in for**, about to undergo; competing in or for. **in on**, sharing in, privy to. **ins and outs**, all the details of an activity or procedure. **in shore**, on the water near or nearer to the shore. **in that**, because; in so far as. **in with**, on good terms with; sharing or co-operating with. **nothing** (or **not much**) **in it**, no (or little) advantage to be seen in one possibility over another. [Old English]

in. abbreviation of inch(es).

in-[1] (il- before l; im- before b, m, p; ir- before r) prefix in, on, into, towards, within. [from Old English or Latin in = in, into]

in-[2] (il- etc. as 'in') prefix added to adjectives in sense 'not', and to nouns in sense 'without', 'lacking'. [Latin]

In symbol for indium.

inability /ɪnə'bɪlɪtɪ/ n. being unable.

in absentia /ɪn æb'sentɪə/ in (his or her or their) absence. [Latin]

inaccessible /ɪnæk'sesɪbəl/ adj. not accessible; (of a person) unapproachable. —**inaccessibility** /-'bɪlɪtɪ/ n., **inaccessibly** adv. [from French or Latin]

inaccurate /ɪn'ækjʊrət/ adj. not accurate. —**inaccuracy** n., **inaccurately** adv.

inaction /ɪn'ækʃən/ n. lack of action, doing nothing.

inactive /ɪn'æktɪv/ adj. not active, showing no activity. —**inactively** adv., **inactivity** /-'tɪvɪtɪ/ n.

inadequate /ɪn'ædɪkwət/ adj. not adequate. —**inadequately** adv., **inadequacy** n.

inadmissible /ɪnəd'mɪsɪbəl/ adj. not allowable. —**inadmissibility** /-'bɪlɪtɪ/ n., **inadmissibly** adv.

inadvertent /ɪnəd'vɜːtənt/ adj. 1. unintentional. 2. negligent, inattentive. —**inadvertence** n., **inadvertency** n., **inadvertently** adv.

inadvisable /ɪnəd'vaɪzəbəl/ adj. not advisable.

inalienable /ɪn'eɪlɪənəbəl/ adj. not able to be given or taken away. —**inalienability** /-'bɪlɪtɪ/ n., **inalienably** adv.

545   inch

inamorato /ɪnæməˈrɑːtəʊ/ n. (*feminine* **inamorata** /-tə/) a lover. [Italian]

inane /ɪˈneɪn/ adj. silly, senseless; empty, void. —**inanely** adv., **inanity** /ɪˈnænɪtɪ/ n. [from Latin *inanis* = empty]

inanimate /ɪnˈænɪmət/ adj. 1. not endowed with life; lacking animal life. 2. showing no sign of life. 3. spiritless, dull. —**inanimation** /-ˈmeɪʃən/ n. [from Latin]

inanition /ɪnəˈnɪʃən/ n. emptiness, especially from lack of nourishment. [from Latin *inanire* = make empty]

inapplicable /ɪnˈæplɪkəbəl/ adj. not applicable.

inapposite /ɪnˈæpəzɪt/ adj. not apposite, out of place.

inapprehensible /ɪnæprɪˈhensɪbəl/ adj. that cannot be grasped by the mind or perceived by the senses.

inappropriate /ɪnəˈprəʊprɪət/ adj. unsuitable. —**inappropriately** adv.

inapt /ɪnˈæpt/ adj. 1. unsuitable. 2. unskilful. —**inaptitude** n., **inaptly** adv., **inaptness** n.

inarticulate /ɪnɑːˈtɪkjʊlət/ adj. 1. unable to speak distinctly or express oneself clearly. 2. not expressed in words; indistinctly pronounced. 3. dumb. 4. not jointed. —**inarticulately** adv. [from Latin]

inartistic /ɪnɑːˈtɪstɪk/ adj. not artistic. —**inartistically** adv.

inasmuch /ɪnəzˈmʌtʃ/ adv. inasmuch as, since, because; (*archaic*) in so far as.

inattention /ɪnəˈtenʃən/ n. lack of attention; neglect.

inattentive /ɪnəˈtentɪv/ adj. not paying attention; neglecting to show courtesy. —**inattentively** adv., **inattentiveness** n.

inaudible /ɪnˈɔːdɪbəl/ adj. not audible, unable to be heard. —**inaudibility** /-ˈbɪlɪtɪ/ n., **inaudibly** adv.

inaugural /ɪˈnɔːɡjʊrəl/ adj. of an inauguration. —n. an inaugural speech or lecture. [French]

inaugurate /ɪˈnɔːɡjʊreɪt/ v.t. 1. to admit formally to office. 2. to begin (an undertaking) ceremonially; to initiate the public use of (a building etc.) with a ceremony. 3. to begin, to introduce. —**inauguration** /-ˈreɪʃən/ n., **inaugurator** n. [from Latin]

inauspicious /ɪnɔːˈspɪʃəs/ adj. not auspicious. —**inauspiciously** adv., **inauspiciousness** n.

inboard /ˈɪnbɔːd/ adv. within the sides or towards the centre of a ship, aircraft, or vehicle. —adj. situated inboard.

inborn adj. naturally inherent, innate.

inbred adj. 1. inborn. 2. produced by inbreeding.

inbreeding n. breeding from closely related animals or persons.

in-built adj. built-in.

Inc. abbreviation of Incorporated.

Inca /ˈɪŋkə/ n. (*plural* the same or **Incas**) former ruling class of South American Indian people of Peru. The first emperor or 'Inca' (believed to be a descendant of the Sun) was Manco Capac about AD 1200. Inca rule eventually extended from Quito in Ecuador to beyond Santiago in S Chile, but the civilization was destroyed by the Spanish conquest in the 1530s. The descendants of the Incas are the ◊Quechua.

incalculable /ɪnˈkælkjʊləbəl/ adj. too great for calculation; not calculable beforehand, uncertain. —**incalculability** /-ˈbɪlɪtɪ/ n., **incalculably** adv.

incandesce /ɪnkænˈdes/ v.t./i. to glow with heat; to cause to do this.

incandescent /ɪnkænˈdesənt/ adj. glowing with heat; shining; (of artificial light) produced by a glowing filament etc. —**incandescence** n. [French from Latin *incandescere* (*candēre* = be white)]

incantation /ɪnkænˈteɪʃən/ n. a magical formula, a spell or charm. —**incantatory** adj. [from Old French from Latin *cantare* = sing]

incapable /ɪnˈkeɪpəbəl/ adj. not capable; not capable of rational conduct. —**incapability** /-ˈbɪlɪtɪ/ n., **incapably** adv. [French or from Latin]

incapacitate /ɪnkəˈpæsɪteɪt/ v.t. to make incapable or unfit. —**incapacitation** /-ˈteɪʃən/ n.

incapacity /ɪnkəˈpæsɪtɪ/ n. inability, lack of power; legal disqualification. [from French or Latin]

incarcerate /ɪnˈkɑːsəreɪt/ v.t. to imprison. —**incarceration** /-ˈreɪʃən/ n. [from Latin *carcer* = prison]

incarnate /ɪnˈkɑːneɪt/ adj. /*also* -ət/ embodied in flesh, especially in human form. —v.t. 1. to embody in flesh. 2. to put (an idea etc.) into concrete form. 3. to be a

living embodiment of (a quality etc.). [from Latin *incarnare* (*caro* = flesh)]

incarnation /ɪnkɑːˈneɪʃən/ n. 1. embodiment in flesh, especially in human form. 2. a living type (*of* a quality). —**the Incarnation**, the embodiment of God in human form as Jesus Christ. [from Old French from Latin]

incautious /ɪnˈkɔːʃəs/ adj. not cautious, rash. —**incautiously** adv., **incautiousness** n.

incendiarism /ɪnˈsendɪərɪzəm/ n. an act or acts of arson.

incendiary /ɪnˈsendɪərɪ/ adj. 1. (of a bomb) filled with material for causing fires. 2. tending to stir up strife, inflammatory. 3. of arson; guilty of arson. —n. 1. an incendiary bomb. 2. an arsonist. 3. a person who stirs up strife. [from Latin *incendere* = set fire to]

incense[1] /ˈɪnsens/ n. a gum or spice giving a sweet smell when burning; the smoke of this, especially in religious ceremonial. —v.t. to burn incense to; to perfume or fumigate (as) with incense. [from Old French from Latin *incensum*]

incense[2] /ɪnˈsens/ v.t. to make angry. [from Old French from Latin *incendere*]

incentive /ɪnˈsentɪv/ n. a motive or incitement; a payment or concession encouraging an effort in work. —adj. inciting. [from Latin = setting the tune (*canere* = sing)]

inception /ɪnˈsepʃən/ n. beginning. [from Old French or Latin *incipere* = begin]

inceptive /ɪnˈseptɪv/ adj. beginning; initial; (of a verb) denoting the beginning of action. [from Latin]

incertitude /ɪnˈsɜːtɪtjuːd/ n. uncertainty. [French or from Latin]

incessant /ɪnˈsesənt/ adj. continual, repeated; unceasing. —**incessantly** adv. [French or from Latin]

incest /ˈɪnsest/ n. sexual intercourse between persons thought to be too closely related to marry; the exact relationships which fall under the incest taboo vary widely from society to society. A biological explanation for the incest taboo is based on the necessity to avoid ◊inbreeding. [from Latin *castus* = chaste]

incestuous /ɪnˈsestjuːəs/ adj. of incest; guilty of incest.

inch n. 1. a twelfth of a (linear) foot, 2.54 cm; this used as a unit of rainfall (= 1 inch depth of water) or as a unit of

Inca Civilization
◻ Inca Empire in 11th century
◻ Inca Empire in 1533

map-scale (= 1 inch to 1 mile). 2. a small amount. —*v.t./i.* to move gradually. —**every inch,** thoroughly. **within an inch of his life,** almost to death. [Old English from Latin *uncia* = twelfth part]

inchoate /'ɪnkəuət/ *adj.* undeveloped; just begun. —**inchoation** /-'eɪʃən/ *n.* [from Latin *inchoare, incohare* = begin]

Inchon /ɪn'tʃɒn/ formerly **Chemulpo** chief port of Seoul, South Korea; population (1985) 1,387,000. It produces steel and textiles.

incidence /'ɪnsɪdəns/ *n.* 1. falling on or contact with a thing. 2. the range, scope, extent, or rate of occurrence or influence (*of* a disease, tax etc.). 3. the falling of a line, ray, particles etc., on a surface. [from Old French or Latin]

incident /'ɪnsɪdənt/ *n.* 1. an event or occurrence, especially a minor one. 2. a clash of armed forces. 3. a public disturbance. 4. a distinct piece of action in a film, play etc. —*adj.* 1. apt to occur; naturally attaching (*to*). 2. (of rays etc.) falling (*on* or *upon*). [from French or Latin *incidere* = fall on (*cadere* = fall)]

incidental /ɪnsɪ'dentəl/ *adj.* having a minor role in relation to a more important thing or event etc., not essential. —**incidental music,** music played during or between the scenes of a play, film etc.

incidentally *adv.* 1. as an unconnected remark. 2. in an incidental way.

incinerate /ɪn'sɪnəreɪt/ *v.t.* to consume by fire. —**incineration** /-'reɪʃən/ *n.* [from Latin *cinis* = ashes]

incinerator /ɪn'sɪnəreɪtə/ *n.* a furnace or device for incinerating things.

incipient /ɪn'sɪpiənt/ *adj.* beginning, in its early stages. [from Latin]

incise /ɪn'saɪz/ *v.t.* to make a cut in; to engrave. —**incision** /ɪn'sɪʒən/ *n.* [from French from Latin *incidere* (*caedere* = cut)]

incisive /ɪn'saɪsɪv/ *adj.* sharp; clear and effective. —**incisively** *adv.,* **incisiveness** *n.* [from Latin]

incisor /ɪn'saɪzə/ *n.* sharp tooth at the front of the mammalian mouth. Incisors are used for biting or nibbling, as when a rabbit or a sheep eats grass. Rodents, such as rats and squirrels, have large continually-growing incisors, adapted for gnawing. The elephant tusk is a greatly enlarged incisor. [Latin = cutter]

incite /ɪn'saɪt/ *v.t.* to urge or stir up (*to* action). —**incitement** *n.* [from French from Latin *citare* = rouse]

incivility /ɪnsɪ'vɪlɪtɪ/ *n.* rudeness; an impolite act. [from French or Latin]

inclement /ɪn'klemənt/ *adj.* (of weather) severe or stormy. —**inclemency** *n.* [from French or Latin]

inclination /ɪnklɪ'neɪʃən/ *n.* 1. a tendency. 2. a liking or preference. 3. the slope or slant (*of* a line from the vertical, *to* another line); the angle between the lines; the angle between the ◊ecliptic and the plane of the orbit of a planet, asteroid, or comet. 4. a leaning or bending movement; the dip of a magnetic needle. [from Old French or Latin]

incline /ɪn'klaɪn/ *v.t./i.* 1. to lean or cause to lean, usually from the vertical; to bend forward or downward. 2. to dispose or influence. 3. to have a certain tendency. —/'ɪnklaɪn/ *n.* a slope; an inclined plane. —**inclined plane,** a sloping plane used e. g. to raise a load with less force. **incline one's ear,** to listen favourably. [from Old French from Latin *inclinare* = bend]

include /ɪn'kluːd/ *v.t.* 1. to have, regard, or treat as part of a whole. 2. to put into a certain category etc. —**inclusion** *n.* [from Latin *includere* = enclose]

inclusive /ɪn'kluːsɪv/ *adj.* including (with *of*); including the limits stated; including all or much. —**inclusively** *adv.* [from Latin]

inclusive fitness in ◊genetics, the success with which a given variant (or allele) of a ◊gene is passed on to future generations by a particular individual, after additional copies of the allele in the individual's relatives and their offspring have been taken into account.

incognito /ɪnkɒg'niːtəu, ɪn'kɒgnɪtəu/ *adv.* under a false name, with one's identity concealed. —*adj.* acting incognito. —*n.* (*plural* incognitos) a pretended identity; a person who is incognito. [Italian]

incognizant /ɪn'kɒgnɪzənt/ *adj.* unaware. —**incognizance** *n.*

incoherent *adj.* rambling in speech or reasoning. —**incoherence** *n.,* **incoherently** *adv.*

incombustible /ɪnkəm'bʌstɪbəl/ *adj.* not able to be burnt by fire. [from Latin]

income /'ɪnkʌm/ *n.* money received, especially periodically or in a year, from one's work, lands, investments etc. —**income tax,** a tax levied on income. —**incomes policy,** a government-initiated exercise to curb ◊inflation by restraining rises in incomes, on either a voluntary or a compulsory basis; often linked with action to control prices, in which case it becomes a prices and incomes policy.

incoming /'ɪnkʌmɪŋ/ *adj.* coming in; succeeding another person or thing.

incommensurable /ɪnkə'menʃərəbəl/ *adj.* not commensurable; having no common measure integral or fractional (*with*). —**incommensurability** /-'bɪlɪtɪ/. [from Latin]

incommensurate *adj.* disproportionate, inadequate (*to*); incommensurable.

incommode /ɪnkə'məud/ *v.t.* to inconvenience; to annoy; to impede. [from French or Latin *commodus* = convenient]

incommodious /ɪnkə'məudiəs/ *adj.* not providing comfort, inconvenient.

incommunicable /ɪnkə'mjuːnɪkəbəl/ *adj.* that cannot be shared or told. [from Latin]

incommunicado /ɪnkə'mjuːnɪkɑːdəu/ *adj.* without means of communication; (of a prisoner) in solitary confinement. [from Spanish *incomunicar* = deprive of communication]

incommunicative /ɪnkə'mjuːnɪkətɪv/ *adj.* not communicative, taciturn.

incomparable /ɪn'kɒmpərəbəl/ *adj.* without an equal, matchless. —**incomparability** /-'bɪlɪtɪ/ *n.,* **incomparably** *adv.* [from Old French from Latin]

incompatible /ɪnkəm'pætɪbəl/ *adj.* not compatible; inconsistent. —**incompatibility** /-'bɪlɪtɪ/ *n.,* **incompatibly** *adv.* [from Latin]

incompetent /ɪn'kɒmpɪtənt/ *adj.* not qualified or able; not able to function; not legally qualified. —*n.* an incompetent person. —**incompetence** *n.,* **incompetently** *adv.* [from French or Latin]

incomplete /ɪnkəm'pliːt/ *adj.* not complete. —**incompletely** *adv.,* **incompleteness** *n.* [from Latin]

incomplete dominance in genetics, a condition in which a pair of alleles are both expressed in the ◊phenotype because neither can completely mask the other. For example, a red flower crossed with a white flower may produce a pink offspring.

incomprehensible /ɪnkɒmpri'hensɪbəl/ *adj.* not able to be understood. —**incomprehensibility** /-'bɪlɪtɪ/ *n.,* **incomprehensibly** *adv.* [from Latin]

incomprehension /ɪnkɒmpri'henʃən/ *n.* failure to understand.

inconceivable /ɪnkən'siːvəbəl/ *adj.* that cannot be imagined; (*colloquial*) most unlikely. —**inconceivably** *adv.*

inconclusive /ɪnkən'kluːsɪv/ *adj.* (of evidence or an argument etc.) not fully convincing, not decisive. —**inconclusively** *adv.*

incongruous /ɪn'kɒŋgruəs/ *adj.* out of place, absurd; out of keeping (*with*). —**incongruity** /-'uːɪtɪ/ *n.,* **incongruously** *adv.* [from Latin]

inconsequent /ɪn'kɒnsɪkwənt/ *adj.* irrelevant; disconnected; not following logically. —**inconsequence** *n.,* **inconsequently** *adv.* [from Latin]

inconsequential /ɪnkɒnsɪ'kwenʃəl/ *adj.* unimportant; inconsequent. —**inconsequentially** *adv.*

inconsiderable /ɪnkən'sɪdərəbəl/ *adj.* not worth considering; of small size, amount, or value. —**inconsiderably** *adv.* [from obsolete French or Latin]

inconsiderate /ɪnkən'sɪdərət/ *adj.* (of a person or action) lacking in regard for others' feelings, thoughtless. —**inconsiderately** *adv.* [from Latin]

inconsistent /ɪnkən'sɪstənt/ *adj.* not consistent. —**inconsistency** *n.,* **inconsistently** *adv.*

inconsolable /ɪnkən'səuləbəl/ *adj.* unable to be consoled. —**inconsolability** /-'bɪlɪtɪ/ *n.,* **inconsolably** *adv.* [French or from Latin]

inconsonant /ɪn'kɒnsənənt/ *adj.* not consistent, not harmonious.

inconspicuous /ɪnkən'spɪkjuəs/ *adj.* not conspicuous. —**inconspicuously** *adv.,* **inconspicuousness** *n.* [from Latin]

inconstant /ɪnˈkɒnstənt/ adj. fickle; variable. —**inconstancy** n. [from Old French from Latin]

incontestable /ɪnkənˈtestəbəl/ adj. that cannot be disputed. —**incontestably** adv. [French or from Latin]

incontinent /ɪnˈkɒntɪnənt/ adj. unable to control excretions voluntarily; lacking self-restraint (especially in sexual desire). —**incontinence** n. [from Old French or Latin]

incontrovertible /ɪnkɒntrəˈvɜːtɪbəl/ adj. indisputable, undeniable. —**incontrovertibility** /-ˈbɪlɪtɪ/ n., **incontrovertibly** adv.

inconvenience /ɪnkənˈviːnɪəns/ n. being inconvenient; a cause or instance of this. —v.t. to cause inconvenience to. [from Old French from Latin]

inconvenient /ɪnkənˈviːnɪənt/ adj. not convenient, not suiting one's needs or requirements; slightly troublesome. —**inconveniently** adv. [from Old French from Latin]

incorporate /ɪnˈkɔːpəreɪt/ v.t./i. 1. to include as a part or ingredient; to unite. 2. to form into a corporation; to admit as a member of a company etc. —/-ət/ adj. incorporated. —**incorporation** /-ˈreɪʃən/ n. [from Latin corpus = body]

incorporeal /ɪnkɔːˈpɔːrɪəl/ adj. without substance or material existence. —**incorporeally** adv., **incorporeity** /-ˈriːɪtɪ/ n. [from Latin incorporeus]

incorrect /ɪnkəˈrekt/ adj. not correct. —**incorrectly** adv., **incorrectness** n. [from Old French from Latin]

incorrigible /ɪnˈkɒrɪdʒɪbəl/ adj. (of a person or habit) incurably bad. —**incorrigibility** /-ˈbɪlɪtɪ/ n., **incorrigibly** adv. [from Old French or Latin]

incorruptible /ɪnkəˈrʌptɪbəl/ adj. that cannot decay or be corrupted (especially by bribery). —**incorruptibility** /-ˈbɪlɪtɪ/ n., **incorruptibly** adv. [from Old French or Latin]

increase /ɪnˈkriːs/ v.t./i. 1. to make or become greater or more numerous. 2. to advance (in power etc.). —/ˈɪnkriːs/ n. 1. growth, enlargement; the amount of this. 2. (of people, animals, or plants) multiplication. —**on the increase**, increasing. —**increasingly** adv. [from Old French from Latin crescere = grow]

incredible /ɪnˈkredɪbəl/ adj. that cannot be believed; (colloquial) surprising. —**incredibility** /-ˈbɪlɪtɪ/ n., **incredibly** adv.

incredulous /ɪnˈkredjʊləs/ adj. unwilling to believe. —**incredulity** /ɪnkrɪˈdjuːlɪtɪ/ n., **incredulously** adv. [from Latin]

increment /ˈɪnkrɪmənt/ n. an increase, an added amount; profit. —**incremental** /-ˈmentəl/ adj. [from Latin incrementum]

incriminate /ɪnˈkrɪmɪneɪt/ v.t. to indicate as involved in a crime. —**incrimination** /-ˈneɪʃən/ n., **incriminatory** adj. [from Latin crimen = accusation]

incrustation /ɪnkrʌsˈteɪʃən/ n. 1. encrusting. 2. a crust, a hard coating; a deposit on a surface. [French or from Latin]

incubate /ˈɪnkjʊbeɪt/ v.t./i. 1. to hatch (eggs) by sitting on them or by artificial heat; to sit on eggs. 2. to cause (bacteria etc.) to develop. [from Latin cubare = lie]

incubation /ɪnkjʊˈbeɪʃən/ n. incubating; the development of disease germs before the first symptoms appear.

incubator /ˈɪnkjʊbeɪtə/ n. 1. an apparatus with artificial warmth for hatching eggs or developing bacteria. 2. an apparatus in which babies born prematurely can be kept in a constant controlled heat and supplied with oxygen etc.

incubus /ˈɪŋkjʊbəs/ n. (plural incubuses) 1. an oppressive person or thing. 2. a male demon who in the popular belief of the Middle Ages had sexual intercourse with women in their sleep; a nightmare. [Latin = nightmare]

inculcate /ˈɪnkʌlkeɪt/ v.t. to implant (a habit or idea) by persistent urging. —**inculcation** /-ˈkeɪʃən/ n. [from Latin calcare = tread]

inculpate /ˈɪnkʌlpeɪt/ v.t. to incriminate; to accuse, to blame. —**inculpation** /-ˈpeɪʃən/ n., **inculpatory** /ɪnˈkʌlpətərɪ/ adj. [from Latin culpare = blame]

incumbency /ɪnˈkʌmbənsɪ/ n. the office or tenure of an incumbent.

incumbent /ɪnˈkʌmbənt/ adj. 1. forming an obligation or duty. 2. lying or resting (on). —n. the holder of an office, especially a benefice. [from Latin incumbere = lie on]

incunabulum /ɪnkjuːˈnæbjʊləm/ n. (plural incunabula) 1. an early printed book, especially from before 1501. 2. (in plural) the early stages of a thing. [Latin (in plural) = swaddling-clothes]

incur /ɪnˈkɜː/ v.t. (-rr-) to bring on oneself (danger, blame, loss etc.). [from Latin currere = run]

incurable /ɪnˈkjʊərəbəl/ adj. that cannot be cured. —n. an incurable person. —**incurability** /-ˈbɪlɪtɪ/ n., **incurably** adv. [from Old French or Latin]

incurious /ɪnˈkjʊərɪəs/ adj. feeling or showing no curiosity about something. —**incuriously** adv. [from Latin]

incursion /ɪnˈkɜːʃən/ n. an invasion or attack, especially sudden or brief. —**incursive** adj. [from Latin]

incurve /ɪnˈkɜːv/ v.t. to bend into a curve; (especially in past participle) to curve inwards. —**incurvation** /-ˈveɪʃən/ n. [from Latin incurvare]

indebted /ɪnˈdetɪd/ adj. under a debt or obligation (to). —**indebtedness** n. [from Old French endetté]

indecent /ɪnˈdiːsənt/ adj. offending against decency; unseemly. —**indecent assault**, a sexual attack not involving rape. —**indecency** n., **indecently** adv. [from French or Latin]

indecipherable /ɪndɪˈsaɪfərəbəl/ adj. that cannot be deciphered.

indecision /ɪndɪˈsɪʒən/ n. lack of decision, hesitation. [from French]

indecisive /ɪndɪˈsaɪsɪv/ adj. not decisive. —**indecisively** adv., **indecisiveness** n.

indeclinable /ɪndɪˈklaɪnəbəl/ adj. (of words) having no inflexions. [from French from Latin]

indecorous /ɪnˈdekərəs/ adj. improper, not in good taste. —**indecorously** adv. [from Latin]

indeed /ɪnˈdiːd/ adv. 1. in truth, really. 2. admittedly. —int. expressing incredulity, surprise etc.

indefatigable /ɪndɪˈfætɪgəbəl/ adj. not becoming tired; unremitting. —**indefatigably** adv. [from obsolete French or Latin defatigare = tire out]

indefeasible /ɪndɪˈfiːzɪbəl/ adj. (of a right, possession, etc.) that cannot be forfeited or annulled. —**indefeasibly** adv. [Anglo-French from Old French defaire = undo]

indefensible /ɪndɪˈfensɪbəl/ adj. that cannot be defended or justified. —**indefensibility** /-ˈbɪlɪtɪ/ n., **indefensibly** adv.

indefinable /ɪndɪˈfaɪnəbəl/ adj. that cannot be defined or described clearly. —**indefinably** adv.

indefinite /ɪnˈdefɪnɪt/ adj. 1. not clearly defined, stated, or decided; unlimited. 2. (of adjectives, adverbs, and pronouns) not determining the person etc. referred to (e. g. some, someone, anyhow). —**indefinite article**, see Þarticle. —**indefinitely** adv.

indelible /ɪnˈdelɪbəl/ adj. that cannot be rubbed out; that makes indelible marks. —**indelibly** adv. [from French or Latin delēre = efface]

indelicate /ɪnˈdelɪkət/ adj. 1. slightly indecent; not refined. 2. tactless. —**indelicacy** n., **indelicately** adv.

indemnify /ɪnˈdemnɪfaɪ/ v.t. 1. to protect or insure (a person from or against loss); to exempt from a penalty (for actions). 2. to compensate. —**indemnification** /-ˈkeɪʃən/ n. [from Latin indemnis = free from loss]

indemnity /ɪnˈdemnɪtɪ/ n. 1. protection or insurance against damage or loss; exemption from a penalty. 2. compensation for damage. [from French from Latin]

indent /ɪnˈdent/ v.t./i. 1. to make notches, dents, or recesses in. 2. to start (a line of print or writing) further from the margin than the others. 3. to place an indent for goods; to order (goods) by an indent. 4. to draw up (a document) in duplicate. —/ˈɪndent/ n. 1. an official order for goods. 2. an indentation. 3. an indenture. [from Anglo-French from Latin dens = tooth]

indentation /ɪndenˈteɪʃən/ n. 1. indenting. 2. a notch; a deep recess.

indention /ɪnˈdenʃən/ n. indenting, especially in printing; a notch.

indenture /ɪnˈdentʃə/ n. 1. a formal, sealed agreement, especially (usually in plural) one binding an apprentice to a master. The term derives from the practice of writing the agreement twice on paper or parchment and then cutting it with a jagged edge so that both pieces fit together, proving the authenticity of each half. 2. a formal list, certificate etc. —v.t. to bind by indentures. [from Anglo-French]

independence /ɪndɪˈpendəns/ n. being independent. —**Independence Day**, 4 July, celebrated in the USA as the anniversary of the date in 1776 when the American colonies formally declared themselves free and independent of Britain; a similar festival elsewhere.

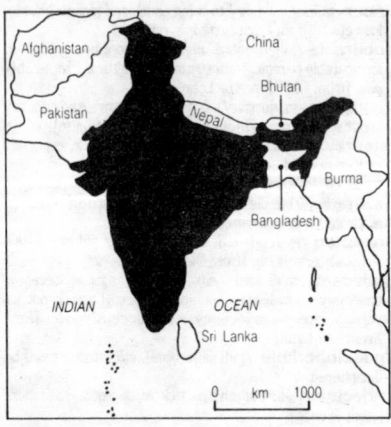

India

independent /ˌɪndɪˈpendənt/ *adj.* **1.** not depending on the authority or control (*of*, or absolute); self-governing. **2.** not depending on another thing for validity etc., or on another person for one's opinion or livelihood. **3.** (of broadcasting, a school etc.) not supported from public funds. **4.** (of an income or resources) making it unnecessary to earn one's living. **5.** unwilling to be under obligation to others. **6.** acting independently of any political party. —*n.* a person who is politically independent. —**independently** *adv.*

Independent Labour Party (ILP) British socialist party, founded in Bradford in 1893 by the Scottish member of Parliament Keir Hardie. In 1900 it joined with trades unions and Fabians in founding the Labour Representation Committee, the nucleus of the ◊Labour Party. Many members left the ILP to join the Communist Party in 1921, and in 1932 all connections with the Labour Party were severed. After World War II the ILP dwindled, eventually becoming extinct.

Independent Television Commission (ITC; formerly the Independent Broadcasting Authority) in the UK, the corporate body established by legislation to provide commercially funded television (ITV from 1955) and local radio (ILR from 1973) services. During the 1980s this role was expanded to include the setting-up of Channel 4 (launched in 1982) and the provision of services broadcast directly by satellite into homes (DBS).

indescribable /ˌɪndɪˈskraɪbəbəl/ *adj.* too unusual to be described; vague. —**indescribably** *adv.*

indestructible /ˌɪndɪˈstrʌktɪbəl/ *adj.* that cannot be destroyed. —**indestructibility** /-ˈbɪlɪtɪ/ *n.*, **indestructibly** *adv.*

indeterminable /ˌɪndɪˈtɜːmɪnəbəl/ *adj.* that cannot be ascertained or settled. —**indeterminably** *adv.* [from Latin]

indeterminate /ˌɪndɪˈtɜːmɪnət/ *adj.* not fixed in extent, character etc.; left doubtful. —**indeterminate vowel,** the vowel /ə/ heard in 'a moment ago'. —**indeterminacy** *n.*, **indeterminately** *adv.*, **indeterminateness** *n.* [from Latin]

indetermination /ˌɪndɪtɜːmiˈneɪʃən/ *n.* lack of determination.

index /ˈɪndeks/ *n.* (*plural* **indexes** or **indices** /-ɪsiːz/) **1.** an alphabetical list of subjects etc. with references, usually at the end of a book. **2.** a number indicating the level of prices or wages as compared with some standard value; for example, the ◊retail price index (RPI) and the *Financial Times* Industrial Ordinary Share Index (FT). **3.** the exponent of a number. **4.** a pointer (*literally* or *figuratively*). —*v.t.* **1.** to furnish (a book) with an index; to enter in an index. **2.** to relate (wages etc.) to the value of a price index. —**index finger,** the forefinger. **index-linked** *adj.* related to the value of a price index. [Latin = forefinger, informer]

indexation /ˌɪndekˈseɪʃən/ *n.* making wages etc. index-linked.

Index Librorum Prohibitorum the list of books formerly officially forbidden to members of the Roman Catholic church. The process of condemning books and bringing the Index up to date was carried out by a congregation of cardinals, consultors, and examiners from the 16th century until its abolition in 1966. [Latin = Index of Prohibited Books]

India /ˈɪndɪə/ country in S Asia, having borders to the N with Afghanistan, China, Nepál, and Bhutan; to the E with Myanmar; and to the NW with Pakistan. Situated within the NE corner of India, N of the Bay of Bengal, is Bangladesh, and India is surrounded to the SE, S, and SW by the Indian Ocean. **area** 3,166,829 sq km/1,222,396 sq mi; **capital** New Delhi; **physical** Himalaya mountains on N border; plains around rivers Ganges, Indus, Brahmaputra; Deccan peninsular S of the Narmada River forms plateau between W and E Ghats mountain ranges; desert in W; Andaman and Nicobar Islands, Lakshadweep Islands; **head of government** Chandra Shekar from 1990; **political system** federal democratic republic; **exports** tea, coffee, fish, iron ore, leather, textiles, polished diamonds; **population** (1989 est) 833,422,000; **language** Hindi, English, 14 other official languages; **recent history** 1947 independence achieved from Britain; 1971 war with Pakistan leads to the creation of Bangladesh; central rule imposed in Jammu and Kashmir following Muslim separatist violence in 1990; Rajiv Gandhi, leader of the Congress I party and Indira Gandhi's son, assassinated during the 1991 elections.

India ink (*US*) Indian ink.

Indiaman /ˈɪndɪəmən/ *n.* (*plural* **Indiamen**) (*historical*) a ship engaged in trade with India or the East Indies.

Indian /ˈɪndɪən/ *adj.* **1.** of India; of the subcontinent comprising India, Pakistan, and Bangladesh. **2.** of the original inhabitants (other than Inuit) of America and the West Indies. —*n.* **1.** a native of India. **2.** an original inhabitant (other than an Inuit) of America or the West Indies; a Red Indian. —**Indian clubs,** a pair of bottle-shaped clubs swung to exercise the arms. **Indian corn,** maize. **Indian file,** single file. **Indian ink,** a black pigment. **Indian summer,** a calm, dry period in late autumn; (*figuratively*) a tranquil late period.

Indiana /ˌɪndɪˈænə/ state of the midwest USA; nickname Hoosier State; **area** 93,700 sq km/36,168 sq mi; **capital** Indianapolis; **population** (1988) 5,575,000; **history** first white settlements established 1731–35 by French traders; ceded to Britain by the French in 1763; passed to American control in 1783; became a state in 1816.

Indian art the painting, sculpture, and architecture of India. Indian art dates back to the ancient Indus Valley civilization of about 3000 BC. Sophisticated artistic styles emerged from the 1st century AD. Buddhist art includes sculptures and murals. Hindu artists created sculptural schemes in caves and huge temple complexes; the Hindu style is lively, with voluptuous nude figures. The Islamic Mogul Empire of the 16th–17th centuries created an exquisite style of miniature painting, inspired by Persian examples.

Indian languages traditionally, the languages of the subcontinent of India; since 1947, the languages of the Republic of India. These number some 200, depending on whether a variety is classified as a language or a dialect. They fall into five main groups, the two most widespread of which are the Indo-European languages (mainly in the north) and the Dravidian languages (mainly in the south).

Indian Mutiny see ◊Sepoy Rebellion.

Indian National Congress Indian political party founded by the British colonialist Allan Hume (1829–1912) in 1885. It was a moderate body until World war I when, under the leadership of Mahatma Gandhi, the party began a campaign of non-violent non-cooperation with the British colonizers. It was declared illegal 1932–34, but was recognized as the paramount power in India at the granting of independence in 1947. Dominated in the early years of Indian independence by Nehru, the party won the elections of 1952, 1957 and 1962. Under the leadership of Indira Gandhi from 1966, it went on to win the elections of 1967 and 1971, but was defeated for the first time in 1977. Heading a splinter group, known as **Congress I,** she won an overwhelming victory in the 1980 elections, reducing the main **Congress Party** to a minority,

Indian Ocean ocean between Africa and Australia, with India to the N, and the S boundary being an arbitrary line from Cape Agulhas to S Tasmania; area 73,500,000 sq km/28,371,000 sq mi; average depth 3,872 m/12,708 ft. The greatest depth is the Java Trench 7,725 m/25,353 ft.

indiarubber /ındıə'rʌbə/ *n.* a rubber, especially for rubbing out pencil marks etc.

Indic /'ındık/ *adj.* Indo-Aryan. [from Latin from Greek *Indikos* = Indian]

indicate /'ındıkeɪt/ *v.t.* 1. to point out, to make known. 2. to be a sign of, to show the presence of. 3. to show the need of, to require. 4. to state briefly. —**indication** /-'keɪʃən/ *n.* [from Latin *indicare* = point out]

indicative /ın'dıkətıv/ *adj.* 1. suggestive *of*, giving an indication. 2. in grammar, of a mood, expressing a statement not a command, wish etc. —*n.* in grammar, the indicative mood or form. [from French from Latin]

indicator *n.* 1. a person or thing that indicates or points to something; chemical compound that changes its structure and colour in response to its environment. 2. a device indicating the condition of a machine etc. 3. a board giving current information. 4. a device to show the direction of an intended turn by a vehicle.

indicator species a plant or animal whose presence or absence in an area indicates certain environmental conditions. For example, some lichens are sensitive to sulphur dioxide in the air, and absence of these species indicates atmospheric pollution. Many plants show a preference for either alkaline or acid soil conditions, while certain plants, mostly trees, require aluminium, and are found only in soils where it is present.

indicatory /ın'dıkətərı/ *adj.* indicative (*of*).

indices *n.* plural of ◊index.

indict /ın'daıt/ *v.t.* to accuse formally by legal process. [from Anglo-French]

indictable /ın'daıtəbəl/ *adj.* (of an offence) making the doer liable to be charged with a crime; (of a person) so liable.

indictment /ın'daıtmənt/ *n.* a document stating alleged crimes; an accusation. [from Anglo-French]

indifference /ın'dıfərəns/ *n.* 1. lack of interest or attention. 2. unimportance. [from Latin]

indifferent /ın'dıfərənt/ *adj.* 1. showing indifference or lack of interest. 2. neither good nor bad. 3. of poor quality or ability. 4. unimportant. —**indifferently** *adv.* [from Old French or Latin]

indigenous /ın'dıdʒınəs/ *adj.* native or belonging naturally (*to* a place). [from Latin *indigena*]

indigent /'ındıdʒənt/ *adj.* needy, poor. —**indigence** *n.* [from Old French from Latin *indigēre*]

indigestible /ındı'dʒestıbəl/ *adj.* difficult or impossible to digest. —**indigestibility** /-'bılıtı/ *n.* [French or from Latin]

indigestion /ındı'dʒestʃən/ *n.* difficulty in digesting food; pain caused by this. [from Old French or Latin]

indignant /ın'dıgnənt/ *adj.* feeling or showing indignation. —**indignantly** *adv.* [from Latin *indignari* = regard as unworthy]

indignation /ındıg'neıʃən/ *n.* scornful anger at supposed injustice, wickedness etc. [from Old French or Latin]

indignity /ın'dıgnıtı/ *n.* humiliating treatment, an insult; humiliating quality. [from French or Latin *indignitas*]

indigo /'ındıgəʊ/ *n.* (*plural* indigos) deep violet-blue; a dye of this colour. [Spanish or Portuguese from Latin from Greek = Indian dye]

indirect /ındı'rekt, -daı-/ *adj.* not direct. —**indirect object**, a person or thing affected by verbal action but not primarily acted on (e. g. *him or her* in *give him or her the book*). **indirect question**, a question in indirect speech. **indirect speech**, reported speech. **indirect tax**, a tax paid in the form of an increased price for taxed goods. —**indirectly** *adv.* [from Old French or Latin]

indiscernible /ındı'sɜ:nıbəl/ *adj.* that cannot be discerned. —**indiscernibly** *adv.*

indiscipline /ın'dısıplın/ *n.* lack of discipline.

indiscreet /ındıs'kri:t/ *adj.* 1. not discreet, revealing secrets. 2. incautious, unwary. —**indiscreetly** *adv.* [from Latin *indiscretus*]

indiscretion /ındıs'kreʃən/ *n.* indiscreet conduct or action. [from Old French or Latin]

indiscriminate /ındıs'krımınət/ *adj.* done or acting without judgement or discrimination. —**indiscriminately** *adv.*, **indiscrimination** /-'neıʃən/ *n.*

indispensable /ındı'spensəbəl/ *adj.* that cannot be dispensed with, necessary *to* or *for*. —**indispensability** /-'bılıtı/ *n.*, **indispensably** *adv.* [from Latin]

indisposed /ındı'spəʊzd/ *adj.* 1. slightly unwell. 2. averse or unwilling. —**indisposition** /-spə'zıʃən/ *n.*

indisputable /ındı'spju:təbəl/ *adj.* not able to be disputed, undeniable. —**indisputability** /-'bılıtı/ *n.*, **indisputably** *adv.* [from Latin]

indissoluble /ındı'sɒljubəl/ *adj.* that cannot be dissolved or destroyed, firm and lasting. —**indissolubly** *adv.* [from Latin]

indistinct /ındı'stıŋkt/ *adj.* not distinct; confused, obscure. —**indistinctness** *n.* [from Latin]

indistinguishable /ındı'stıŋgwıʃəbəl/ *adj.* that cannot be distinguished. —**indistinguishably** *adv.*

indite /ın'daıt/ *v.t.* to put into words; to write (a letter etc.). [from Old French]

indium /'ındıəm/ *n.* soft, ductile, silver-white, metallic element, symbol In, atomic number 49, relative atomic mass 114.82. It occurs in nature in some zinc ores, is resistant to abrasion, and is used as a coating on metal parts. It was discovered and named in 1863 by German metallurgists Ferdinand Reich (1799–1882) and H T Richter (1824–1898). [from Latin *indicum* = indigo]

individual /ındı'vıdjuəl/ *adj.* 1. single, separate; of or for one person. 2. having a distinct character; characteristic of a particular person or thing. —*n.* a single member of a class; a single human being; (*colloquial*) a person. —**individually** *adv.* [originally = indivisible, from Latin *individuus*]

individualism *n.* 1. self-reliant action by an individual. 2. a social theory favouring free action by individuals. 3. egotism. —**individualist** *n.*, **individualistic** /-'lıstık/ *adj.*

individuality /ındıvıdju'ælıtı/ *n.* 1. separate existence. 2. individual character, especially when strongly marked.

individualize *v.t.* to give an individual character to.

indivisible /ındı'vızıbəl/ *adj.* not divisible. —**indivisibility** /-'bılıtı/ *n.*, **indivisibly** *adv.* [from Latin]

Indo- /ındəʊ-/ in combinations, Indian (and).

Indo-Aryan /ındəʊ 'ərɪən/ *adj.* of the group of Indo-European languages comprising Sanskrit and the modern Indian languages which are its descendants. —*n.* 1. this language group. 2. its speakers.

Indo-China /'ındəʊ'tʃaınə/ former French dependency of Kampuchea, Laos, and Vietnam, which became independent after World War II. —**Indo-Chinese** *adj.* & *n.*

Indo-China War successful war of independence 1946–1954 between the Nationalist forces of what was to become Vietnam and France, the occupying colonial power.

indoctrinate /ın'dɒktrıneıt/ *v.t.* to imbue with a doctrine or opinion; to teach, to instruct. —**indoctrination** /-'neıʃən/ *n.*

Indo-European /'ındʊ'jʊr'pi:n/ *adj.* of the family of languages (also called **Indo-Germanic** or **Aryan**) spoken over the greater part of Europe and extending into Asia as far as northern India. —*n.* 1. this family of languages. 2. a speaker of any of these.

indolent /'ındələnt/ *adj.* lazy, averse to exertion. —**indolence** *n.*, **indolently** *adv.* [from Latin *dolere* = suffer pain]

indomitable /ın'dɒmıtəbəl/ *adj.* unyielding, stubbornly persistent. —**indomitably** *adv.* [from Latin *domitare* = tame]

Indonesia /ındəʊ'ni:zıə/ Republic of; country in SE Asia, consisting of many island groups, situated on the equator, between the Indian and Pacific oceans; **area** 1,919,443 sq km/740,905 sq mi; **capital** Jakata; **physical** comprises 13,677 tropical islands of the Greater Sunde group (including Java and Madura, part of Kalimantan/Borneo, Sumatra, Sulawesi and Belitung) and the Lesser Sundes/Nusa Tenggara (including Bali, Lombok, Sumba, Timor), Malaku/ Moluccas and part of New Guinea; **head of state and government** T N J Suharto from 1967; **political system** authoritarian nationalist republic; **exports** coffee, rubber, palm oil, cocnuts, tin, tea, tobacco, oil, liquid natural gas; **population** (1989 est) 187,726,000; **language** Indonesian; **recent history** 1950 unitary constitution established after the formal transfer of Dutch sovereignty the year before.

indoor *adj.* of or done or for use in a building or under cover. [for earlier within-door]

indoors /ın'dɔ:z/ *adv.* in(to) a building; under a roof.

Indra /'ındrə/ the Hindu god of the sky, shown as a four-armed man on a white elephant, carrying a thunderbolt. The intoxicating drink ◊soma is associated with him.

indrawn /'ındrɔːn/ adj. 1. drawn in. 2. aloof.

indubitable /ın'djuːbıtəbəl/ adj. that cannot be doubted. —**indubitably** adv. [French or from Latin dubitare = doubt]

induce /ın'djuːs/ v.t. 1. to persuade. 2. to produce or cause; to bring on (labour in childbirth) artificially. 3. to produce by induction; to infer as an induction. [from Latin inducere = lead]

inducement n. a thing that induces; an attraction, a motive.

inducible adj. that may be induced.

induct /ın'dʌkt/ v.t. to install or initiate (into a benefice or office etc.).

inductor n. an element possessing the characteristic of inductance (electromagnetic property).

inductance /ın'dʌktəns/ n. in physics, the measure of the capability of an electronic circuit or circuit component to form a magnetic field or store magnetic energy when carrying a current. Its symbol is L, and its unit of measure is the ◊henry.

induction /ın'dʌkʃən/ n. 1. inducting. 2. inducing. 3. the inferring of a general law from particular instances. 4. the production of an electric or magnetic state by the proximity (without contact) of an electrified or magnetized body; the quantity giving the measure of such an influence; the production of an electric current by a change of magnetic field. 5. the drawing of a fuel mixture into the cylinder(s) of an internal-combustion engine. [from Old French or Latin]

induction coil a type of electrical transformer, similar to an ◊ignition coil, that produces an intermittent high voltage from a low-voltage supply.

inductive /ın'dʌktıv/ adj. 1. (of reasoning etc.) based on or using induction. 2. of electric or magnetic induction. [from Latin]

indulge /ın'dʌldʒ/ v.t./i. 1. to take pleasure freely (in an activity etc.). 2. to yield freely to (a desire etc.). 3. to gratify by compliance with wishes. [from Latin indulgēre]

indulgence /ın'dʌldʒəns/ n. 1. indulging. 2. a privilege granted. 3. remission of the temporal punishment still due for sins even after sacramental absolution. The doctrine of indulgence began as the commutation of church penances in exchange for suitable works of charity or money gifts to the church, and became a great source of church revenue. This trade in indulgences roused Luther in 1517 to initiate the Reformation. The Council of Trent in 1563 recommended moderate retention of indulgences, and they continue, notably in 'Holy Years'. [from Old French from Latin]

indulgent adj. indulging; lenient, willing to overlook faults etc.; too lenient. —**indulgently** adv. [French or from Latin]

indurate /'ındjuəreıt/ v.t./i. to make or become hard; to make callous. —**induration** /-'reıʃən/ n., **indurative** adj. [from Latin indurare = hard]

Indus /'ındəs/ river in Asia, rising in Tibet and flowing 3,180 km/1,975 mi to the Arabian Sea. In 1960 the use of its waters, including those of its five tributaries, was divided between India (rivers Ravi, Beas, Sutlej) and Pakistan (rivers Indus, Jhelum, Chenab).

industrial /ın'dʌstriəl/ adj. of, engaged in, for use in, or serving the needs of industries; (of a nation etc.) having highly developed industries. —**industrial action**, a strike or other disruptive action used in an industrial dispute. —**industrially** adv.

industrialism n. a system involving the prevalence of industries.

industrialist n. a person engaged in the management of industry.

industrialize v.t. to make (a nation or area etc.) industrial. —**industrialization** /-'zeıʃən/ n.

industrial relations the relationship between employers and employees, and their dealings with each other. In most industries, wages and conditions are determined by **free collective bargaining** between employers and ◊trades unions. Some European and American countries have **worker participation** through profit-sharing and industrial democracy. Another solution is **co-ownership**, in which a company is entirely owned by its employees.

Industrial Revolution the sudden acceleration of technical and economic development that began in Britain in the second half of the 18th century. The traditional agrarian economy was replaced by one dominated by machinery and manufacturing, made possible through technical advances such as the steam engine. This transferred the balance of political power from the landowner to the industrial capitalist and created an urban working class. From 1830 to the early 20th century, the Industrial Revolution spread throughout Europe and the USA and to Japan and the various colonial empires.

industrious /ın'dʌstriəs/ adj. hard-working. —**industriously** adv. [from French or Latin]

industry /'ındəstri/ n. 1. the extraction and conversion of raw materials, the manufacture of goods, and the provision of services. Industry can be either low technology, unspecialized and labour-intensive as in the less developed countries, or highly automated, mechanized, and specialized, using advanced technology, as in the 'industrialized' countries. Major trends in industrial activity 1960–90 were the growth of electronic, robotic, and microelectronic technologies, the expansion of the offshore oil industry, and the prominence of Japan and the Pacific region countries in manufacturing and distributing electronics, computers, and motor vehicles. 2. diligence. [from French or Latin industria]

Indus Valley Civilization a prehistoric culture existing in the NW Indian subcontinent about 2500–1600 BC. Remains include soapstone seals with engravings of elephants and snakes.

indwelling adj. permanently present in something.

inebriate /ı'niːbrıət/ adj. drunken. —n. a drunkard. —/-eıt/ v.t. to make drunk. —**inebriation** /-'eıʃən/ n., **inebriet** /-'braıətı/ n. [from Latin inebriare = drunk]

inedible /ın'edıbəl/ adj. not edible (because of its nature).

ineducable /ın'edjukəbəl/ adj. incapable of being educated, especially through mental retardation.

ineffable /ın'efəbəl/ adj. 1. too great for description in words. 2. that must not be uttered. —**ineffably** adv. [from Old French or Latin effari = speak out]

ineffaceable /ını'feısəbəl/ adj. not able to be effaced.

ineffective /ını'fektıv/ adj. not effective; (of a person) inefficient. —**ineffectively** adv.

ineffectual /ını'fektjuəl/ adj. not effectual. —**ineffectually** adv. [from Latin]

inefficacious /ınefı'keıʃəs/ adj. (of a remedy etc.) not efficacious.

inefficient /ını'fıʃənt/ adj. not efficient. —**inefficiency** n., **inefficiently** adv.

inelastic /ını'læstık/ adj. not elastic, not adaptable.

inelegant /ın'eləgənt/ adj. not elegant. —**inelegance** n., **inelegantly** adv. [from French from Latin]

ineluctable /ını'lʌktəbəl/ adj. against which it is useless to struggle. [from Latin eluctari = struggle clear]

inept /ı'nept/ adj. 1. unskilful. 2. unsuitable, absurd. —**ineptitude** n., **ineptly** adv. [from Latin ineptus]

inequable /ın'ekwəbəl/ adj. 1. unfair. 2. not uniform. [from Latin]

inequality /ını'kwɒlıtı/ n. lack of equality in any respect, variableness; unevenness of surface. [from Old French or Latin]

inequitable /ın'ekwıtəbəl/ adj. unfair, unjust.

inequity /ın'ekwıtı/ n. unfairness, bias.

ineradicable /ını'rædıkəbəl/ adj. that cannot be eradicated.

inert /ı'nɜːt/ adj. 1. without an inherent power of action, reaction, motion, or resistance. 2. sluggish, slow —**inertly** adv., **inertness** n. [from Latin iners]

inert gas or **noble gas** member of group 0 in the ◊periodic table of the elements. There are six inert gases: helium, neon, argon, krypton, xenon, and radon. They are so named because originally they were thought not to enter into any chemical reactions. The term inert is no longer strictly applicable, since it is possible to form compounds with four of the group: argon, krypton, xeno, and radon.

inertia /ı'nɜːʃə/ n. 1. inertness. 2. the property by which matter continues in its existing state of rest or uniform motion in a straight line unless that state is changed by an external force. —**inertia reel**, a reel allowing the automatic adjustment of a safety-belt rolled round it. **inertia selling**, the sending of goods not ordered in the hope that they will not be refused. [Latin]

inertial /ı'nɜːʃəl/ adj. of or involving inertia; (of navigation) in which the course of a vehicle or vessel is calculated or controlled automatically, by a computer, from its acceleration at each successive moment.

inescapable *adj.* that cannot be escaped or avoided. —**inescapably** *adv.*

inescutcheon /ˌɪnɪˈskʌtʃən/ *n.* in heraldry, a small escutcheon placed on a larger one.

inessential /ˌɪnɪˈsenʃəl/ *adj.* not essential. —*n.* an inessential thing.

inestimable /ɪnˈestɪməbəl/ *adj.* too good, great etc. to be estimated. —**inestimably** *adv.* [from Old French from Latin]

inevitable /ɪnˈevɪtəbəl/ *adj.* unavoidable, bound to happen or appear; (*colloquial*) tiresomely familiar. —**inevitability** /-ˈbɪlɪtɪ/ *n.*, **inevitably** *adv.* [from Latin *evitare* = avoid]

inexact *adj.* not exact. —**inexactitude** *n.*, **inexactly** *adv.*

inexcusable /ˌɪnɪkˈskjuːzəbəl/ *adj.* that cannot be excused or justified. —**inexcusably** *adv.* [from Latin]

inexhaustible /ˌɪnɪɡˈzɔːstɪbəl/ *adj.* that cannot be totally used up, available in unlimited quantity.

inexorable /ɪnˈeksərəbəl/ *adj.* relentless; that cannot be persuaded by entreaty. —**inexorably** *adv.* [French or from Latin *exorare* = move by entreaty]

inexpedient /ˌɪnɪkˈspiːdɪənt/ *adj.* not expedient. —**inexpediency** *n.*

inexpensive /ˌɪnɪkˈspensɪv/ *adj.* not expensive, offering good value for the price. —**inexpensively** *adv.*

inexperience /ˌɪnɪkˈspɪərɪəns/ *n.* lack of experience or of knowledge or skill arising from experience. —**inexperienced** *adj.* [from French from Latin]

inexpert /ɪnˈekspɜːt/ *adj.* unskilful, lacking expertise. —**inexpertly** *adv.* [from Old French from Latin]

inexpiable /ɪnˈekspɪəbəl/ *adj.* that cannot be expiated or appeased. [from Latin]

inexplicable /ɪnˈeksplɪkəbəl, ɪnɪkˈsplɪk-/ *adj.* that cannot be explained. —**inexplicably** *adv.* [French or from Latin]

inexpressible /ˌɪnɪkˈspresɪbəl/ *adj.* that cannot be expressed in words. —**inexpressibly** *adv.*

in extenso /ɪn eksˈtensəʊ/ at full length. [Latin]

in extremis /ɪn eksˈtriːmɪs/ **1.** at the point of death. **2.** in great difficulties. [Latin]

inextricable /ɪnˈekstrɪkəbəl/ *adj.* **1.** cannot be resolved or escaped from. **2.** cannot be loosened. —**inextricably** *adv.* [from Latin]

INF abbreviation of intermediate nuclear forces, as in the ◊Intermediate Nuclear Forces Treaty.

infallible /ɪnˈfælɪbəl/ *adj.* **1.** incapable of making a mistake or being wrong. **2.** never failing in its effect. —**infallibility** /-ˈbɪlɪtɪ/ *n.*, **infallibly** *adv.* [from French or Latin]

infamous /ˈɪnfəməs/ *adj.* having or deserving a very bad reputation, abominable. —**infamy** /ˈɪnfəmɪ/ *n.* [from Latin]

infant /ˈɪnfənt/ *n.* **1.** a child during the earliest period of life; (in law a person under the age of 18. **2.** a thing in an early stage of development. —**infancy** *n.* [from Old French from Latin *fari* = speak, literally one unable to speak]

infanta /ɪnˈfæntə/ *n.* a daughter of the Spanish or (*historical*) Portuguese sovereign. [Spanish and Portuguese from Latin]

infante /ɪnˈfænteɪ/ *n.* the title given in Spain and (*historical*) Portugal to the sons (other than the heir apparent) of the sovereign.

infanticide /ɪnˈfæntɪsaɪd/ *n.* the killing of an infant soon after birth; one who is guilty of this. [French from Latin]

infantile /ˈɪnfəntaɪl/ *adj.* of or like infants. —**infantile paralysis**, poliomyelitis. [French or from Latin]

infant mortality rate measure of the number of infants dying under one year of age. Improved sanitation, nutrition, and medical care have considerably lowered figures throughout much of the world.

infantry /ˈɪnfəntrɪ/ *n.* soldiers marching and fighting on foot. [from French from Italian *infante* = youth]

infarct *n.* or **infarction** death and scarring of a portion of the tissue in an organ, as a result of congestion or blockage of a vessel serving it. Myocardial infarct is the technical term for a heart attack.

infatuate /ɪnˈfætjʊeɪt/ *v.t.* to inspire with intense fondness and admiration. —**infatuation** /-ˈeɪʃən/ *n.* [from Latin *infatuare* = foolish]

infect /ɪnˈfekt/ *v.t.* **1.** to affect or contaminate with a germ or virus or the consequent disease. **2.** to imbue with an opinion or feeling etc. [from Latin *inficere* = taint]

infection /ɪnˈfekʃən/ *n.* infecting, being infected; an instance of this; a disease; the communication of disease, especially by the agency of air, water etc. [from Old French or Latin]

infectious /ɪnˈfekʃəs/ *adj.* **1.** infecting others. **2.** able to be transmitted by infection. —**infectiousness** *n.*

infelicitous /ˌɪnfɪˈlɪsɪtəs/ *adj.* not felicitous, unfortunate. —**infelicitously** *adv.*

infelicity /ˌɪnfɪˈlɪsɪtɪ/ *n.* **1.** unhappiness. **2.** an infelicitous expression or detail. [from Latin]

infer /ɪnˈfɜː/ *v.t.* (**-rr-**) **1.** to deduce or conclude. **2.** (*disputed usage*) to imply, to suggest. [Latin *ferre* = bring]

inferable *adj.* that may be inferred.

inference /ˈɪnfərəns/ *n.* **1.** inferring. **2.** a thing inferred. —**inferential** /-ˈrenʃəl/ *adj.* [from Latin]

inferior /ɪnˈfɪərɪə/ *adj.* **1.** lower in rank or quality etc. (*to*); of poor quality. **2.** situated below; written or printed below the line. —*n.* a person inferior to another especially in rank. [from comparative of Latin *inferus* = that is below]

inferiority /ɪnˌfɪərɪˈɒrɪtɪ/ *n.* being inferior.

inferiority complex in psychology, a ◊complex described by Arthur ◊Adler based on physical inferiority; the term has been popularly used to describe general feelings of inferiority and the overcompensation that often ensues.

inferior planet a planet (Mercury or Venus) whose orbit lies within that of the Earth, best observed when at its greatest elongation from the Sun, either at eastern elongation in the evening (setting after the Sun) or at western elongation in the morning (rising before the Sun).

infernal /ɪnˈfɜːnəl/ *adj.* **1.** of hell; hellish. **2.** (*colloquial*) detestable, annoying. —**infernally** *adv.* [from Old French from Latin *infernus* = situated below]

inferno /ɪnˈfɜːnəʊ/ *n.* (*plural* **infernos**) a raging fire; a scene of horror or distress; hell. [Italian = hell]

infertile /ɪnˈfɜːtaɪl/ *adj.* not fertile. —**infertility** /-ˈtɪlɪtɪ/ *n.* [from French or Latin]

infest /ɪnˈfest/ *v.t.* (of harmful persons or things, especially vermin) to overrun (a place) in large numbers. —**infestation** /-ˈeɪʃən/ *n.* [from French or Latin *infestare* = assail (*infestus* = hostile)]

infibulation /ɪnˌfɪbjuˈleɪʃən/ *n.* fastening with a clasp; fastening of the genitals thus or surgically to prevent sexual intercourse. [from Latin *infibulare*]

infidel /ˈɪnfɪdəl/ *n.* a disbeliever in religion or in a specified religion. —*adj.* unbelieving; of infidels. [from French or Latin *fidelis* = faithful]

infidelity /ˌɪnfɪˈdelɪtɪ/ *n.* disloyalty, especially to one's husband or wife. [from French or Latin]

infield *n.* in cricket, the part of the ground near the wicket.

infighting *n.* **1.** hidden conflict in an organization. **2.** boxing within arm's length.

infilling *n.* the placing of buildings in the gaps between others.

infiltrate /ˈɪnfɪltreɪt/ *v.t./i.* **1.** to enter (a territory, political party etc.) gradually and imperceptibly; to cause (troops etc.) to do this. **2.** to pass (fluid) by filtration (*into*); to permeate by filtration. —**infiltration** /-ˈtreɪʃən/ *n.*, **infiltrator** *n.*

infinite /ˈɪnfɪnɪt/ *adj.* **1.** having no limit, endless. **2.** very great; very many. **3.** in mathematics, greater than any assignable quantity or countable number; (of a series) that may be continued indefinitely. —**the Infinite**, God. **the infinite**, infinite space. —**infinitely** *adv.* [from Latin]

infinite series in mathematics, a series of numbers consisting of a denumerably infinite sequence of terms. The sequence n, n^2, n^3, ... gives the series $n + n^2 + n^3 + ...$ For example, $1 + 2 + 3 + ...$ is a divergent infinite arithmetic series, and $8 + 4 + 2 + 1 + 1/2 + ...$ is a convergent infinite geometric series whose sum to infinity is 16.

infinitesimal /ˌɪnfɪnɪˈtesɪməl/ *adj.* infinitely or very small. —**infinitesimal calculus**, that dealing with very small quantities. —**infinitesimally** *adv.*

infinitive /ɪnˈfɪnɪtɪv/ *n.* a verb form expressing the verbal notion without a particular subject, tense etc. (often with *to*; e.g. *see* in *we came to see, let him or her see*). —*adj.* having this form. —**infinitival** /-ˈtaɪvəl/ *adj.* [from Latin *finitivus* = definite]

infinitude /ɪnˈfɪnɪtjuːd/ *n.* infinity, being infinite.

infinity /ɪnˈfɪnɪtɪ/ *n.* **1.** an infinite number, extent, or time; a mathematical quantity that is larger than any fixed

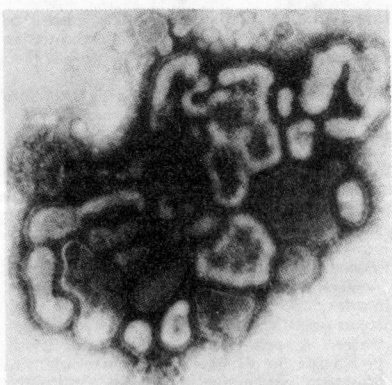

influenza An influenza virus, magnified under an electron microscope × 132,000.

assignable quantity; symbol ∞. By convention, the result of dividing any number by zero is regarded as infinity. 2. being infinite. [from Old French from Latin]

infirm /ɪnˈfɜːm/ *adj.* 1. physically weak, especially from age. 2. weak, irresolute. [from Latin]

infirmary *n.* a hospital; the sick-quarters in a monastery, school etc.

infirmity *n.* 1. being infirm. 2. a particular physical weakness.

infix /ɪnˈfɪks/ *v.t.* to fasten or fix in.

in flagrante delicto /ɪn flæˈgrænti deˈlɪktəʊ/ in the very act of committing an offence. [Latin = in blazing crime]

inflame /ɪnˈfleɪm/ *v.t./i.* 1. to provoke to strong feeling; to arouse anger in. 2. to cause inflammation in. 3. to catch fire, to cause to do this; to light up with or as with a flame; to make hot. [from Old French from Latin *inflammare*]

inflammable /ɪnˈflæməbəl/ *adj.* easily set on fire or excited. —**inflammably** *adv.*

inflammation /ɪnfləˈmeɪʃən/ *n.* 1. inflaming (*literally* or *figuratively*). 2. a condition of a part of the body with heat, swelling, redness, and usually pain. [from Latin]

inflammatory /ɪnˈflæmətərɪ/ *adj.* 1. tending to arouse anger or strong feeling. 2. of inflammation.

inflatable /ɪnˈfleɪtəbəl/ *adj.* that may be inflated.

inflate /ɪnˈfleɪt/ *v.t.* 1. to distend or become distended with air or gas. 2. to puff up (*with* pride etc.). 3. to increase (a price etc.) artificially. 4. to resort to the inflation of (currency). [from Latin *flare* = blow]

inflation /ɪnˈfleɪʃən/ *n.* 1. inflating, being inflated. 2. a general rise in prices and fall in the purchasing power of money; an increase in the supply of money, regarded as the cause of such a rise.

inflationary *adj.* causing inflation.

inflation tax a tax imposed on companies that increase wages by more than an amount fixed by law (except to take account of increased profits or because of a profit-sharing scheme).

inflect /ɪnˈflekt/ *v.t.* 1. to change the pitch of (the voice). 2. to modify (a word) to express grammatical relation. 3. to bend, to curve. [from Latin *flectere* = bend]

inflective /ɪnˈflektɪv/ *adj.* of grammatical inflexion.

inflexible /ɪnˈfleksɪbəl/ *adj.* 1. not flexible, that cannot be bent. 2. that cannot be altered. 3. refusing to alter one's demands etc., unyielding. —**inflexibility** /-ˈbɪlɪtɪ/ *n.*, **inflexibly** *adv.*

inflexion /ɪnˈflekʃən/ *n.* 1. a modulation of the voice. 2. an inflected word; a suffix etc. used to inflect. 3. inflecting. —**inflexional** *adj.* [French or from Latin]

inflict /ɪnˈflɪkt/ *v.t.* 1. to deal (a blow etc.) *on.* 2. to impose or deliver forcibly. —**infliction** *n.*, **inflictor** *n.* [from Latin *fligere* = strike]

inflorescence /ɪnfləˈresəns/ *n.* 1. the arrangement of the flowers of a plant in relation to the axis and to each other. Inflorescences can be divided into two main types: **cymose** and **racemose**. In a cymose inflorescence, the terminal growing point produces a single flower and subsequent flowers arise on lower lateral branches. A **racemose inflorescence** consists of a main axis, bearing flowers

along its length, with an active growing region at the apex. 2. the flower(s) of a plant. 3. flowering (*literal* or *figurative*). [from Latin *inflorescere*]

inflow *n.* 1. flowing in. 2. that which flows in.

influence /ˈɪnfluəns/ *n.* 1. the power to produce an effect. 2. the ability to affect a person's character, beliefs, or actions. 3. a thing or person with this ability. —*v.t.* to exert an influence on, to affect. —**under the influence**, (*colloquial*) drunk. [from Old French or Latin *influentia* = inflow]

influential /ɪnfluˈenʃəl/ *adj.* having great influence. —**influentially** *adv.* [from Latin]

influenza /ɪnfluˈenzə/ *n.* an acute virus disease usually with fever and severe aching and catarrh, occurring in epidemics. [Italian from Latin]

influx /ˈɪnflʌks/ *n.* a flowing in, especially of persons or things into a place. [French or from Latin *influxus*]

inform /ɪnˈfɔːm/ *v.t./i.* 1. to give information to. 2. to bring a charge or complaint (*against* or *on*). 3. (in *past participle*) knowing the facts, enlightened. [from Old French from Latin originally, give shape to]

informal /ɪnˈfɔːməl/ *adj.* not formal; without formality. —**informality** /-ˈmælɪtɪ/ *n.*, **informally** *adv.*

informant /ɪnˈfɔːmənt/ *n.* a giver of information. [from Latin]

information /ɪnfəˈmeɪʃən/ *n.* 1. facts told, heard, or discovered. 2. a charge or complaint lodged with a court etc. 3. facts fed into a computer etc. 4. the process of informing. —**information technology**, a wide range of modern technologies based on the widespread availability of computing power for recording, transmitting and disseminating information, and including computing science, telecommunications, printing, and broadcasting. [from Old French from Latin]

informative /ɪnˈfɔːmətɪv/ *adj.* giving information, instructive. [from Latin]

informer *n.* one who informs against others.

infra /ˈɪnfrə/ *adv.* below or further on in a book etc. [Latin = below]

infra- /ɪnfrə-/ *prefix* giving meaning of below [Latin]

infraction /ɪnˈfrækʃən/ *n.* infringement. [from Latin]

infra dig (*colloquial*) beneath one's dignity. [abbreviation of Latin *infra dignitatem*]

infrared /ɪnfrəˈred/ *adj.* of or using rays with a wavelength just below the red end of the visible spectrum.

infrared astronomy the study of infrared radiation produced by relatively cool gas and dust in space, such as in the areas around forming stars. In 1983, the Infrared Astronomy Satellite (IRAS) surveyed the entire sky at infrared wavelengths. It found five new comets, thousands of galaxies undergoing bursts of star formation, and the possibility of planetary systems forming around several dozen stars.

infrared radiation invisible electromagnetic radiation of wavelength between about 0.75 micrometres and 1 millimetre, that is, between the limit of the red end of the visible spectrum and the shortest microwaves. All bodies above the ◊absolute zero of temperature absorb and radiate infrared radiation. Infrared radiation is used in medical photography and treatment, and in industry, astronomy, and criminology.

infrastructure *n.* the subordinate parts of an undertaking, especially permanent installations forming a basis of defence. [French]

infrequent /ɪnˈfriːkwənt/ *adj.* not frequentative —**infrequency** *n.*, **infrequently** *adv.* [from Latin]

infringe /ɪnˈfrɪndʒ/ *v.t./i.* 1. to act contrary to (a law, another's rights etc.). 2. to encroach or trespass (*on*). —**infringement** *n.* [from Latin *infringere* (*frangere* = break)]

infuriate /ɪnˈfjʊərɪeɪt/ *v.t.* to make furious. [from Latin *infuriare*]

infuse /ɪnˈfjuːz/ *v.t./i.* 1. to cause to be saturated or filled *with* a quality. 2. to instil (life, a quality etc., *into*). 3. to steep (tea etc.) in a liquid to extract the constituents; (of tea etc.) to be steeped thus. [from Latin *fundere* = pour]

infusible /ɪnˈfjuːzɪbəl/ *adj.* that cannot be melted. —**infusibility** /-ˈbɪlɪtɪ/ *n.*

infusion /ɪnˈfjuːʒən/ *n.* 1. infusing. 2. a liquid extract so obtained. 3. an infused element. [from French or Latin]

Ingenious *adj.* 1. clever at inventing things or methods. 2. cleverly contrived. —**ingeniously** *adv.* [from French or Latin *ingenium* = cleverness]

Ingénue /ˈæʒeɪnjuː/ *n.* an artless young woman, especially as a stage role. [French]

Ingenuity /ɪndʒɪˈnjuːɪtɪ/ *n.* ingeniousness.

Ingenuous /ɪnˈdʒenjuəs/ *adj.* artless; frank. —**ingenuously** *adv.*, **ingenuousness** *n.* [from Latin *ingenuus* = free-born, frank]

Ingest /ɪnˈdʒest/ *v.t.* to take in by swallowing or absorbing. —**ingestion** *n.* [from Latin *gerere* = carry]

Ingestion *n.* the process of taking food into the mouth. The method of food capture varies but may involve biting, sucking, or filtering. Many single-celled organisms have a region of their cell wall that acts as a mouth. In these cases surrounding tiny hairs (cilia) sweep food particles together, ready for ingestion.

Inglenook /ˈɪŋɡəlnʊk/ *n.* a nook providing a seat beside a recessed fireplace. [from *ingle* = fire in hearth (originally Scottish, perhaps from Gaelic)]

Inglorious /ɪnˈglɔːrɪəs/ *adj.* 1. ignominious. 2. not famous. [from Latin]

Ingoing *adj.* going in.

Ingot /ˈɪŋgət/ *n.* a mass, usually oblong, of cast metal, especially gold, silver, or steel.

Ingrained /ɪnˈgreɪnd/, *attrib.* ˈɪn-/ *adj.* 1. (of habits, feelings, or tendencies) deeply rooted, inveterate. 2. (of dirt etc.) deeply embedded. [from Old French *engrainer* = dye thoroughly]

Ingratiate /ɪnˈgreɪʃɪeɪt/ *v.t.* to bring *oneself* into favour (*with*). [from Latin *in gratiam* = into favour]

Ingratitude /ɪnˈgrætɪtjuːd/ *n.* lack of due gratitude. [from Old French or Latin]

Ingredient /ɪnˈgriːdɪənt/ *n.* a component part in a mixture. [from Latin *ingredi* = enter into]

Ingres /ˈæ̃ŋgrə/ Jean Auguste Dominique 1780–1867. French painter, a student of David and leading exponent of the Neo-Classical style. He studied and worked in Rome about 1807–20, where he began the *Odalisque* series of sensuous female nudes, then went to Florence, and returned to France in 1824. His portraits painted in the 1840s–50s are meticulously detailed and highly polished.

Drawing is the true test of art.
                Jean Auguste Dominique Ingres
                            Pensées d'Ingres

Ingress /ˈɪngres/ *n.* going in; the right to go in. [from Latin *ingressus*]

Ingrowing *adj.* (of a nail) growing into the flesh.

Inguinal /ˈɪŋgwɪnəl/ *adj.* of the groin. [from Latin *inguen* = groin]

Inhabit /ɪnˈhæbɪt/ *v.t.* to live in (a place) as one's home or dwelling-place. [from Old French or Latin *habitare* = dwell]

Inhabitable *adj.* suitable for inhabiting.

Inhabitant *n.* a person etc. who inhabits a place. [from Old French from Latin]

Inhalant /ɪnˈheɪlənt/ *n.* a medicinal substance for inhaling. [from Latin]

Inhale /ɪnˈheɪl/ *v.t./i.* to breathe in (air, gas, etc.); to take (tobacco-smoke etc.) into the lungs. —**inhalation** /ɪnhəˈleɪʃən/ *n.* [from Latin *halare* = breathe]

Inhaler *n.* an inhaling-apparatus, especially a device for sending out vapour for inhaling.

Inharmonious /ɪnhɑːˈməʊnɪəs/ *adj.* not harmonious.

Inhere /ɪnˈhɪə/ *v.i.* to be inherent. [from Latin *haerēre* = stick]

Inherent /ɪnˈhɪərənt/ *adj.* existing or abiding in something as an essential quality or characteristic. —**inherence** *n.*, **inherently** *adv.* [from Latin]

Inherit /ɪnˈherɪt/ *v.t.* to receive (property or rank) as an heir; to derive (qualities, problems etc.) from parents, a predecessor etc. —**inheritor** *n.* [from Old French from Latin *inheredilare* (*heres* = heir)]

Inheritance *n.* 1. what is inherited. 2. inheriting. [from Anglo-French]

Inhibit /ɪnˈhɪbɪt/ *v.t.* 1. to restrain, to prevent. 2. to hinder the impulses of; to cause inhibitions in. —**inhibitory** *adj.* [from Latin *inhibēre* (*habēre* = hold)]

Inhibition /ɪnhɪˈbɪʃən/ *n.* 1. inhibiting, being inhibited. 2. the restraint of a direct expression of instinct; (*colloquial*) an emotional resistance to a thought or action. [from Old French or Latin]

Inhibition, neural in biology, the process in which activity in one nerve cell suppresses activity in another. Neural inhibition in networks of nerve cells leading from sensory organs, or to muscles, plays an important role in allowing an animal to make fine sensory discriminations and to exercise fine control over movements.

Inhibitor *n.* or **negative catalyst** catalyst that reduces the rate of a reaction. Inhibitors are widely used in foods, medicines, and toiletries.

Inhospitable /ɪnˈhɒspɪtəbəl, -ˈpɪt-/ *adj.* not hospitable; (of a place or climate) not giving shelter or favourable conditions. —**inhospitably** *adv.* [from obsolete French]

In-house *adv.* within an institution. —*adj.* done or existing in-house.

Inhuman /ɪnˈhjuːmən/ *adj.* brutal, lacking the human qualities of kindness, pity etc. —**inhumanity** /-ˈmænɪtɪ/ *n.* [from Latin]

Inhumane /ɪnhjuːˈmeɪn/ *adj.* not humane.

Inimical /ɪˈnɪmɪkəl/ *adj.* hostile, harmful. —**inimically** *adv.* [from Latin *inimicus* = enemy]

Inimitable /ɪˈnɪmɪtəbəl/ *adj.* that cannot be imitated. —**inimitably** *adv.* [French or from Latin]

Iniquity /ɪˈnɪkwɪtɪ/ *n.* 1. wickedness. 2. gross injustice. —**iniquitous** *adj.* [from Old French from Latin]

Initial /ɪˈnɪʃəl/ *adj.* of or at the beginning; (of a letter) at the beginning of a word. —*n.* an initial letter, especially (in *plural*) those of a person's names. —*v.t.* (**-ll-**) to mark or sign with initials. —**initially** *adv.* [from Latin *initium* = beginning]

Initiate /ɪˈnɪʃɪeɪt/ *v.t.* 1. to originate, to begin, to set going. 2. to admit (a person) into a society, office etc. 3. to instruct, especially in rites or forms. —/-ət/ *n.* an initiated person. —**initiation** /-ˈeɪʃən/ *n.*, **initiator** *n.*, **initiatory** *adj.* [from Latin *initiare*]

Initiative /ɪˈnɪʃɪətɪv/ *n.* 1. the ability to initiate things, enterprise. 2. the first step. 3. the power or right to begin. 4. device whereby the voters may play a direct part in making laws. A proposed law is drawn up and signed by petitioners, and submitted to the legislature. [French]

Inject /ɪnˈdʒekt/ *v.t.* 1. to force (a fluid, medicine etc., *into* a cavity etc.) by or as by a syringe; to fill with fluid etc. thus; to administer medicine etc. to (a person) thus. 2. to introduce (a new element or quality etc.). —**injection** *n.*, **injector** *n.* [from Latin *injicere* (*jacere* = throw)]

Injudicious /ɪndʒuːˈdɪʃəs/ *adj.* unwise, ill-judged. —**injudiciously** *adv.*, **injudiciousness** *n.*

Injunction /ɪnˈdʒʌŋkʃən/ *n.* an authoritative order; a judicial process restraining a person from a specified act, compelling restitution etc. [from Latin]

Injure /ˈɪndʒə/ *v.t.* to cause harm, damage, or hurt to; to do wrong to.

Injurious /ɪnˈdʒʊərɪəs/ *adj.* causing or likely to cause injury. [from French or Latin]

Injury /ˈɪndʒərɪ/ *n.* 1. harm, damage; a particular form of this. 2. an unjust action. [from Anglo-French from Latin *injuria*]

Injustice /ɪnˈdʒʌstɪs/ *n.* lack of justice, unfairness; an unjust action. —**do a person an injustice,** to judge him unfairly. [from Old French from Latin]

Ink *n.* 1. a black or coloured fluid used for writing, printing, etc. 2. a black liquid ejected by cuttlefish etc. —*v.t.* to mark (*in*, *over* etc.) with ink. —**ink out,** to obliterate with ink. **inkwell** *n.* a pot for holding ink, fitted into a hole in a desk. [from Old French from Latin from Greek *egkauston* = Roman emperors' purple ink]

Inkatha /ɪŋˈkɑːtə/ *n.* South African political organization formed 1975 by Chief Gatsha ◊Buthelezi, leader of six million Zulus, the country's biggest ethnic group. Inkatha aims to create a nonracial democratic political situation. Because Inkatha has tried to work with the white regime, Buthelezi has been regarded as a collaborator by blacks and the United Democratic Front. Fighting between Inkatha and African National Congress members cost more than 1,000 lives in the first five months of 1990. [from the grass coil worn by Zulu women for carrying head loads; its many strands give it strength]

Inkerman, Battle of /'ɪŋkəmən/ a battle of the Crimean War, fought on 5 Nov 1854, during which an attack by the Russians on Inkerman Ridge, occupied by the British army besieging Sevastopol, was repulsed.

inkling /'ɪŋklɪŋ/ n. a hint, slight knowledge or suspicion (of). [from obsolete *inkle* = utter in an undertone]

inkstand n. a stand for one or more ink-bottles.

inky adj. 1. of ink; stained with ink. 2. very black. —**inkiness** n.

INLA abbreviation of ◊Irish National Liberation Army.

inland /'ɪnlənd, -lænd/ adj. 1. in the interior of a country, remote from the sea or a border. 2. within a country. —usually -'lænd/ adv. in or towards the interior of a country. —n. the interior of a country. —**inland revenue**, revenue from taxes and inland duties.

in-laws n. pl. (colloquial) relatives by marriage.

inlay /ɪn'leɪ/ v.t. (past and past participle **inlaid**) to set or embed (pieces of wood or metal etc.) in another material so that the surfaces are level, forming a design; to decorate thus. —/'ɪnleɪ/ n. 1. inlaid material or work. 2. a filling shaped to fit a tooth-cavity.

inlet /'ɪnlet/ n. 1. a small arm of a sea, lake, or river. 2. a piece inserted. 3. a way in.

in loco parentis /ɪn ləʊkəʊ pə'rentɪs/ in a parental capacity. [Latin = in place of a parent]

inmate /'ɪnmeɪt/ n. any of the occupants of a house, hospital, prison etc.

in memoriam /ɪn mi'mɔːriæm/ in memory of. [Latin]

inmost adj. most inward. [Old English]

inn /ɪn/ n. a house providing lodgings etc. for payment, especially for travellers; a house providing alcoholic liquor. [Old English]

innards /'ɪnədz/ n. pl. (colloquial) inner parts, especially entrails. [from dialect pronunciation of inward]

innate /ɪ'neɪt, 'ɪn-/ adj. inborn, natural. [from Latin *innatus* (*nasci* = be born)]

inner adj. nearer to the centre or inside, interior, internal. —n. the division of a target next outside the bull's-eye; a shot striking this. —**inner city**, the central area of a city, usually with overcrowding and poverty. **inner man** or **woman,** the soul, the mind; the stomach. **inner tube,** a separate inflatable tube in a pneumatic tyre. —**innermost** adj. [Old English]

innings /'ɪnɪŋz/ n. (plural the same) 1. the part of a game of cricket etc. in which one side or player is batting. 2. the time of power etc. of a political party etc.; the period of a person's chance to achieve something.

innkeeper n. the keeper of an inn.

innocent /'ɪnəsənt/ adj. 1. not guilty of a particular crime etc. 2. free of all evil or wrongdoing. 3. harmless, without guile; affectedly so. —n. an innocent person, especially a child. —**innocence** n., **innocently** adv. [from Old French or Latin *nocēre* = do harm]

Innocent thirteen popes including:

Innocent III 1161–1216. Pope from 1198 who asserted papal power over secular princes, especially over the succession of Holy Roman Emperors. He also made King John of England his vassal, compelling him to accept ◊Langton as archbishop of Canterbury. He promoted the fourth Crusade and crusades against the non-Christian Livonians and Letts, and Albigensian heretics of S France.

Greediness closed Paradise; it beheaded John the Baptist.

Pope Innocent III
De Contemptu Mundi

Innocents' Day or **Childermas** a festival of the Roman Catholic Church, celebrated on 28 Dec in memory of the **Massacre of the Innocents**, the children of Bethlehem who were allegedly slaughtered by King ◊Herod the Great after the birth of Jesus.

innocuous /ɪ'nɒkjuəs/ adj. harmless. [from Latin *innocuus*]

innovate /'ɪnəveɪt/ v.i. to bring in new methods, ideas, etc.; to make changes *in*. —**innovation** /-'veɪʃən/ n., **innovative** adj., **innovator** n., **innovatory** adj. [from Latin *novus* = new]

Innsbruck /'ɪnzbrʊk/ capital of Tyrol state, W Austria; population (1981) 117,000. It is a tourist and winter sports centre and a route junction for the Brenner Pass. The 1964 and 1976 Winter Olympics were held here.

Inns of Court four private societies in London, England: Lincoln's Inn, Gray's Inn, Inner Temple, and Middle Temple. All barristers must belong to one of the Inns of Court. The main function of each Inn is the education, government, and protection of its members. Each is under the administration of a body of Benchers (judges and senior barristers).

innuendo /ɪnjuː'endəʊ/ n. (plural **innuendoes**) an allusive remark or hint, usually disparaging. [Latin = by nodding at (nuere= nod)]

innumerable /ɪ'njuːmərəbəl/ adj. too many to be counted. —**innumerably** adv. [from Latin *numerare* = count]

innumerate /ɪ'njuːmərət/ adj. not knowing basic mathematics and science. —**innumeracy** n.

inoculate /ɪ'nɒkjuleɪt/ v.t. to treat (a person or animal) with a vaccine or serum, especially as a protection against disease. —**inoculation** /-'leɪʃən/ n. [from Latin *inoculare* = engraft]

inoffensive /ɪnə'fensɪv/ adj. not offensive, harmless, not objectionable.

inoperable /ɪn'ɒpərəbəl/ adj. that cannot be cured by surgical operation. [from French]

inoperative /ɪn'ɒpərətɪv/ adj. not working or taking effect.

inopportune /ɪn'ɒpətjuːn/ adj. not opportune, coming or happening at an unsuitable time. —**inopportunely** adv. [from Latin]

inordinate /ɪ'nɔːdɪnət/ adj. excessive. —**inordinately** adv. [from Latin]

inorganic /ɪnɔː'gænɪk/ adj. 1. (of a chemical compound etc.) mineral not organic. 2. without an organized physical structure. 3. extraneous.

inorganic chemistry the branch of chemistry dealing with the elements and their compounds, excluding the more complex carbon compounds which are considered in ◊organic chemistry.

in-patient n. a patient residing in hospital during treatment.

input /'ɪnpʊt/ n. 1. what is put in. 2. the place of entry of energy, information etc. —v.t. (-tt-; past and past participle **input, inputted**) to put in or *into*; to supply (data, programs etc., *to* a computer).

input device a device for entering information into a computer. Input devices include keyboards, joysticks, touch-sensitive screens, ◊graphics tablets, speech recognition devices, and vision systems.

inquest n. 1. an inquiry held by a coroner into the cause of death. 2. a prolonged discussion after misfortune, failure etc.

inquietude /ɪn'kwaɪɪtjuːd/ n. uneasiness. [from Old French or Latin]

inquire /ɪn'kwaɪə/ v.i. to undertake a formal investigation (*into*). [from Old French from Latin *inquirere* (*quaerere* = seek)]

inquiry /ɪn'kwaɪərɪ/ n. an investigation, especially an official one.

inquisition /ɪnkwi'zɪʃən/ n. an intensive investigation or inquiry. —**inquisitional** adj.

Inquisition n. the tribunal of the Roman Catholic church established in 1233 to suppress heresy (dissenting views), originally by excommunication. Sentence was pronounced during a religious ceremony, the ◊auto-da-fé. The Inquisition operated in France, Italy, Spain, and the Holy Roman empire, and was especially active following the ◊Reformation; it was later extended to the Americas. Its trials were conducted in secret, under torture, and penalties ranged from fines, through flogging and imprisonment, to death by burning.

inquisitive /ɪn'kwɪzɪtɪv/ adj. seeking knowledge; unduly curious, prying. —**inquisitively** adv.

inquisitor n. one who questions searchingly; an official investigator; an officer of the Inquisition. [from French from Latin]

inquisitorial /ɪnkwɪzɪ'tɔːriəl/ adj. of or like an inquisitor; prying. —**inquisitorially** adv. [from Latin]

in re /ɪn riː/ =**re**[1]. [Latin = in the matter (of)]

insect classification

Class Insecta Subclass	Order	Number of species	Common names
Apterytgota (wingless insects)	Thysanura	350	Three-pronged bristletails, silverfish
	Diplura	400	Two-pronged bristletails, campodeids, japygids
	Protura	50	Minute insects living in soil
	Collembola	1500	Springtails
Pterygota (winged insects or forms secondarily wingless)			
Exopterygota (young resemble adults but have externally developing wings)	Ephemeroptera	1,000	Mayflies
	Odonata	5,000	Dragonflies, damselflies
	Plecoptera	3,000	Stoneflies
	Grylloblattodea	12	Wingless soil-living insects of North America
	Orthoptera	20,000	Crickets, grasshoppers, locusts, mantids, roaches
	Phasmida	2,000	Stick insects, leaf insects
	Dermaptera	1,000	Earwigs
	Embioptera	150	Web-spinners
	Dictyoptera	5,000	Cockroaches, praying mantises
	Isoptera	2,000	Termites
	Zoraptera	16	Tiny insects living in decaying plants
	Psocoptera	1,600	Booklice, barklice, psocids
	Mallophaga	2,500	Biting lice, mainly parasitic on birds
	Anoplura	250	Sucking lice, mainly parasitic on mammals
	Hemiptera	55,000	True bugs, including aphids, shield- and bedbugs, froghoppers, pond skaters, water boatmen
	Thysanoptera	5,000	Thrips
Endopterygota (young unlike adults, undergo sudden metamorphosis)	Neuroptera	4,500	Lacewings, alder flies, snake flies, ant lions
	Mecoptera	300	Scorpion flies
	Lepidoptera	165,000	Butterflies, moths
	Trichoptera	3,000	Caddis flies
	Diptera	70,000	True flies, including bluebeetles, mosquitoes, leather jackets, midges
	Siphonaptera	1,400	Fleas
	Hymenoptera	100,000	Bees, wasps, ants, sawflies
	Coloeoptera	350,000	Beetles, including weevils, ladybirds, glow-worms, wood–worms, chafers

INRI abbreviation of Latin *Iesus Nazarenus Rex Iudaeorum* Jesus of Nazareth, king of the Jews.

inroad *n.* 1. a hostile incursion. 2. (often in *plural*) an encroachment; the using up of resources etc.

inrush *n.* a violent influx.

insalubrious /ɪnsə'luːbrɪəs/ *adj.* (of a place or climate etc.) unhealthy. [from Latin]

insane /ɪn'seɪn/ *adj.* 1. not sane, mad. 2. very foolish. —**insanely** *adv.*, **insanity** /-'sænɪtɪ/ *n.* [from Latin]

insanitary /ɪn'sænɪtərɪ/ *adj.* unclean and likely to be harmful to health.

insatiable /ɪn'seɪʃəbəl/ *adj.* that cannot be satisfied, very greedy. —**insatiability** /-'bɪlɪtɪ/ *n.*, **insatiably** *adv.* [from Old French or Latin]

insatiate /ɪn'seɪʃɪət/ *adj.* never satisfied. [from Latin]

inscribe /ɪn'skraɪb/ *v.t.* 1. to write (words etc. *in* or *on* a surface); to mark (a surface *with* characters). 2. to draw (a geometrical figure) within another so that points of it lie on the other's boundary. 3. to enter (a name) on a list or in a book. 4. to place an informal dedication in or on (a book etc.). [from Latin *scribere* = write]

inscription /ɪn'skrɪpʃən/ *n.* 1. words inscribed. 2. inscribing. —**inscriptional** *adj.* [from Latin]

inscrutable /ɪn'skruːtəbəl/ *adj.* baffling, impossible to understand or interpret. —**inscrutability** /-'bɪlɪtɪ/ *n.*, **inscrutably** *adv.* [from Latin *scrutari* = search]

insect /'ɪnsekt/ *n.* any of a class of small invertebrate animals of the phylum Arthropoda, typically having six legs, two or four wings, and a body divided into three sections: head, thorax, and abdomen. [from Latin *insectum* = notched]

insecticide /ɪn'sektɪsaɪd/ *n.* any chemical pesticide used to kill insects. Among the most effective insecticides are synthetic organic chemicals such as ◊DDT and dieldrin, which are chlorinated hydrocarbons. These chemicals have proved persistent in the environment and are poisonous to all animal life, including humans. Other synthetic insecticides include organic phosphorus compounds such as malathion. Insecticides prepared from plants, such as derris and pyrethrum are safer to use but need to be applied frequently and carefully.

insectivore /ɪn'sektɪvɔː/ *n.* an animal that feeds on insects and other small creatures —**insectivorous** /-'tɪvərəs/ *adj.* [French from Latin *vorare* = devour]

insectivorous plant a plant that can capture and digest animals. Some are passive traps, for example, pitcher plants *Nepenthes*. Others, for example, sundews *Drosera*, butterworts *Pinguicula*, and Venus's-flytrap *Dionaea muscipula*, have an active trapping mechanism.

insecure /ɪnsi'kjuə/ *adj.* 1. not secure or safe or dependable. 2. feeling a lack of security, constantly anxious. —**insecurely** *adv.*, **insecurity** *n.* [from Latin]

inselberg /'ɪnzəlbɜːg/ *n.* a prominent steep-sided hill of resistant, solid rock, such as granite, rising out of a plain, usually in a tropical area. Its rounded appearance is caused by so-called onion-skin weathering, in which the surface is eroded in successive layers.

inseminate /ɪn'semɪneɪt/ *v.t.* 1. to impregnate with semen. 2. to sow (a seed etc., *literally* and *figuratively*, *in*). —**insemination** /-'neɪʃən/ *n.* [from Latin *inseminare*]

insemination, artificial the introduction by instrument of semen from a sperm bank or donor into the female reproductive tract to bring about fertilization. Originally used by animal breeders to improve stock with sperm from high-quality males, in the 20th century it has been developed for use in humans, to help the infertile. In ◊in vitro fertilization, the egg is fertilized in a test-tube and then implanted in the womb.

insensate /ɪn'senseɪt/ *adj.* 1. without sensibility, unfeeling. 2. stupid. 3. without physical sensation. [from Latin]

insensible /ɪnˈsɛnsɪbəl/ *adj.* **1.** unconscious. **2.** unaware (*of, to, how*). **3.** callous. **4.** too small or gradual to be perceived. —**insensibility** /-ˈbɪlɪtɪ/ *n.*, **insensibly** *adv.* [from Old French or Latin]

insensitive /ɪnˈsɛnsɪtɪv/ *adj.* not sensitive. —**insensitively** *adv.*, **insensitivity** /-ˈtɪvɪtɪ/ *n.*

insentient /ɪnˈsɛnʃənt/ *adj.* not sentient.

inseparable /ɪnˈsɛpərəbəl/ *adj.* **1.** that cannot be separated. **2.** liking to be constantly together. —*n.* (usually in *plural*) an inseparable person or thing, especially a friend. —**inseparability** /-ˈbɪlɪtɪ/ *n.*, **inseparably** *adv.* [from Latin]

insert /ɪnˈsɜːt/ *v.t.* to place or put (one thing into another). —/ˈɪnsɜːt/ *n.* the thing inserted. [from Latin *serere*= join]

insertion /ɪnˈsɜːʃən/ *n.* **1.** inserting. **2.** a thing inserted. [from Latin]

inset /ˈɪnsɛt/ *n.* an extra piece inserted in a book, garment etc.; a small map etc. within the border of a larger one. —/ɪnˈsɛt/ *v.t.* (-tt-; *past* and *past participle* **inset** or **insetted**) to put in as an inset; to decorate with an inset.

inshore *adj. & adv* near the shore.

inside *n.* **1.** the inner side, surface, or part. **2.** a position on the inner side. **3.** (in *singular* or *plural*, *colloquial*) the stomach and bowels. **4.** (of a path) the side away from the road. —*adj.* of or on or in the inside; nearer to the centre of a games field. —*adv.* **1.** on, to, or in the inside. **2.** (*slang*) in prison. —*prep.* **1.** within, on the inside of. **2.** in less than. —**inside information**, information not accessible to outsiders. **inside job**, (*colloquial*) a burglary etc. by one living or working on the premises. **inside out**, turned so that the inner side becomes the outer.

insider *n.* a person within a group or a society etc.; one who is in the secret.

insider trading or **insider dealing** the illegal use of privileged information in dealing on the stock exchanges, for example when a company takeover bid is imminent. Insider trading is in theory detected by the **Securities and Exchange Commission** (SEC) in the USA, and by the **Securities and Investment Board** (SIB) in the UK. Neither agency has any legal powers other than public disclosure and they do not bring prosecution themselves.

insidious /ɪnˈsɪdɪəs/ *adj.* **1.** proceeding inconspicuously but harmfully. **2.** crafty. —**insidiously** *adv.*, **insidiousness** *n.* [from Latin = cunning (*insidiae* = ambush)]

insight *n.* **1.** the ability to perceive and understand a thing's true nature; mental penetration. **2.** a piece of knowledge obtained by this.

insignia /ɪnˈsɪgnɪə/ *n.pl.* badges or emblems of rank, office, etc. [from Latin *insignis* = distinguished]

insignificant /ɪnsɪgˈnɪfɪkənt/ *adj.* of no importance or meaning; worthless, trivial. —**insignificance** *n.*, **insignificantly** *adv.*

insincere /ɪnsɪnˈsɪə/ *adj.* not sincere or candid. —**insincerely** *adv.*, **insincerity** /-ˈsɛrɪtɪ/ *n.* [from Latin]

insinuate /ɪnˈsɪnjʊeɪt/ *v.t.* **1.** to hint obliquely or unpleasantly. **2.** to insert gradually or stealthily. —**insinuation** /-ˈeɪʃən/ *n.* [from Latin *sinuare* = curve]

insipid /ɪnˈsɪpɪd/ *adj.* **1.** lacking in flavour. **2.** dull, without liveliness. —**insipidity** /-ˈpɪdɪtɪ/ *n.*, **insipidly** *adv.* [from French or Latin]

insist /ɪnˈsɪst/ *v.t./i.* to demand or declare emphatically. [from Latin *sistere* = stand]

insistent *adj.* **1.** insisting. **2.** forcing itself upon the attention. —**insistence** *n.*, **insistently** *adv.*

in situ /ɪn ˈsɪtjuː/in its original place. [Latin]

insobriety /ɪnsəˈbraɪətɪ/ *n.* intemperance, especially in drinking.

insofar /ɪnsəʊˈfɑː/ *adv.* in so far.

insolation /ɪnsəˈleɪʃən/ *n.* exposure to the Sun's rays. [from Latin *sol* = sun]

insole /ˈɪnsəʊl/ *n.* the inner sole of a boot or shoe; a removable inner sole for use in a shoe.

insolent /ˈɪnsələnt/ *adj.* impertinently insulting. —**insolence** *n.*, **insolently** *adv.* [from Latin unaccustomed, immoderate (*solēre* = be accustomed)]

insoluble /ɪnˈsɒljʊbəl/ *adj.* that cannot be dissolved or solved. —**insolubility** /-ˈbɪlɪtɪ/ *n.*, **insolubly** *adv.* [from Old French or Latin]

insolvent /ɪnˈsɒlvənt/ *adj.* unable to pay debts. —*n.* an insolvent debtor. —**insolvency** *n.*

insomnia /ɪnˈsɒmnɪə/ *n.* habitual sleeplessness. [Latin *somnus* = sleep]

insomniac /ɪnˈsɒmnɪæk/ *n.* a person suffering from insomnia.

insomuch /ɪnsəʊˈmʌtʃ/ *adv.* to such an extent *that*; inasmuch *as*.

insouciant /ɪnˈsuːsɪənt/ *adj.* carefree, unconcerned. —**insouciance** *n.* [French *soucier* = care]

inspan /ɪnˈspæn/ *v.t.* (-nn-) (*South African*) to yoke (oxen etc.) in a team to a vehicle; to harness animals to (a wagon). [from Dutch]

inspect /ɪnˈspɛkt/ *v.t.* to examine carefully and critically, especially looking for faults; to examine officially; to visit in order to see that rules and standards are being observed. —**inspection** *n.* [from Latin *specere* = look at]

inspector *n.* **1.** a person employed to inspect or supervise. **2.** a police officer next above sergeant. —**inspector of taxes**, an official assessing income tax payable.

inspiration /ɪnspɪˈreɪʃən/ *n.* **1.** inspiring. **2.** a sudden brilliant idea. **3.** a source of inspiring influence.

inspire /ɪnˈspaɪə/ *v.t.* **1.** to stimulate (a person) to creative or other activity. **2.** to animate (a person etc. *with* a feeling); to instil thought or feeling into (a person). **3.** to breathe (air etc.) in. [from Old French from Latin *spirare* = breathe]

inspirit /ɪnˈspɪrɪt/ *v.t.* to put life into, to animate; to encourage. —**inspiriting** *adj.*

inst. abbreviation of instant (= of the current month).

instability /ɪnstəˈbɪlɪtɪ/ *n.* lack of stability or firmness. [from French from Latin]

install /ɪnˈstɔːl/ *v.t.* **1.** to place (a person) formally or ceremonially in office. **2.** to fix or establish (a person, equipment etc.). —**installation** /ɪnstəˈleɪʃən/ *n.* [from Latin *installare*]

instalment /ɪnˈstɔːlmənt/ *n.* any of the successive parts in which a sum is (to be) paid; any of the parts of a whole successively delivered, published etc. [from Anglo-French *estaler* = fix]

instalment credit a form of þhire purchase.

instance /ˈɪnstəns/ *n.* an example, an illustration of a general truth; a particular case. —*v.t.* to cite as an instance. —**in the first instance**, as the first stage (in a process). [from Old French from Latin]

instant /ˈɪnstənt/ *adj.* **1.** immediate. **2.** (of food) that can be prepared easily for immediate use. **3.** of the current month. —*n.* **1.** a precise moment. **2.** a short time, a moment. [from French from Latin *instare* = be urgent]

instantaneous /ɪnstənˈteɪnɪəs/ *adj.* occurring or done in an instant. —**instantaneously** *adv.* [from Latin]

instantly *adv.* immediately.

instead /ɪnˈstɛd/ *adv.* as an alternative or substitute.

instep /ˈɪnstɛp/ *n.* the top of the foot between the toes and the ankle; the part of a shoe etc. over or under this.

instigate /ˈɪnstɪgeɪt/ *v.t.* to incite or persuade; to bring about thus. —**instigation** /-ˈgeɪʃən/ *n.*, **instigator** *n.* [from Latin *stigare* = prick]

instil /ɪnˈstɪl/ *v.t.* (-ll-) **1.** to put (ideas etc. *into* the mind etc.) gradually. **2.** to put *into* by drops. —**instillation** /-ˈleɪʃən/ *n.*, **instilment** *n.* [from Latin *stilla* = drop]

instinct /ˈɪnstɪŋkt/ *n.* an innate propensity, especially in lower animals, to seemingly rational acts; an innate impulse or behaviour; intuition. —/ɪnˈstɪŋkt/ *adj.* filled or charged (*with* life, energy etc.). —**instinctive** /ɪnˈstɪŋktɪv/ *adj.*, **instinctively** *adv.*, **instinctual** /ɪnˈstɪŋktjʊəl/ *adj.*, **instinctually** *adv.* [from Latin *instinctus*]

institute *n.* **1.** an organized body for the promotion of an educational, scientific, or similar object. **2.** its building. —*v.t.* **1.** to establish, to found. **2.** to initiate (an inquiry etc.). **3.** to appoint (a person *to* or *into* a benefice). —**institutor** *n.* [from Latin *statuere* = set up]

Institute for Advanced Study a department of Princeton University in New Jersey, USA, established in 1933, to encourage gifted scientists to further their research uninterrupted by teaching duties or an imposed research scheme. Its first professor was Albert Einstein.

Institute of Directors an organization formed in 1903, and incorporated by royal charter in 1906, to represent directors of companies in Britain.

Institute of Personnel Management (IPM) founded in 1913 as the professional personnel management organization in Britain. An independent and non-political body, it aims to promote the exchange of knowledge and experience of its members, improve their standards of competence and represent their views.

institution /ɪnstɪ'tjuːʃən/ *n.* **1.** instituting, being instituted. **2.** an organized body, especially with a charitable purpose. **3.** an established law, custom, or practice. **4.** (*colloquial*) a person who has become a familiar figure in some activity. [from Old French from Latin]

institutional *adj.* of or like an institution; typical of charitable institutions. —**institutionally** *adv.*

institutionalize *v.t.* to make institutional; to place or keep (a person needing care) in an institution.

instruct /ɪn'strʌkt/ *v.t.* **1.** to give instruction to (a person *in* a subject or skill). **2.** to inform. **3.** to give instructions to. **4.** to authorize (a solicitor or counsel) to act on one's behalf. —**instructor** *n.*, **instructress** *n.fem.* [from Latin *instruere* = furnish, teach]

instruction /ɪn'strʌkʃən/ *n.* **1.** the process of teaching. **2.** knowledge or teaching imparted. **3.** (usually in *plural*) statements making known to a person what he is required to do; orders. —**instructional** *adj.* [from Old French from Latin]

instructive /ɪn'strʌktɪv/ *adj.* tending to instruct, enlightening.

instrument /'ɪnstrʊmənt/ *n.* **1.** a tool or implement, especially for delicate or scientific work. **2.** a device for measuring or controlling the function of a machine or aircraft etc. **3.** a device for giving controlled musical sounds. **4.** a thing used in an action; a person used and controlled by another to perform an action. **5.** a formal or legal document. [from Old French or Latin]

instrumental /ɪnstrʊ'mentəl/ *adj.* **1.** serving as an instrument or means. **2.** (of music) performed on instruments. **3.** of or due to an instrument. **4.** (in grammar, of a case) denoting the means. [from French from Latin]

instrumentalist *n.* a performer on a musical instrument.

instrumentality /ɪnstrʊmen'tælɪtɪ/ *n.* agency or means.

instrumentation /ɪnstrʊmen'teɪʃən/ *n.* **1.** the arrangement of music for instruments. **2.** the provision or use of mechanical or scientific instruments. [French]

instrument landing system a landing aid for aircraft that uses ◊radio beacons on the ground and instruments on the flight deck. One beacon (localizer) sends out a vertical radio beam along the centre line of the runway. Another beacon (glide slope) transmits a beam in the plane at right angles to the localizer beam at the ideal approach-path angle. The pilot can tell from the instruments how to manoeuvre to attain the correct approach path.

insubordinate /ɪnsə'bɔːdɪnət/ *adj.* disobedient, rebellious. —**insubordination** /-'neɪʃən/ *n.*

insubstantial /ɪnsəb'stænʃəl/ *adj.* **1.** not existing in reality. **2.** not strongly made, lacking solidity. [from Latin]

insufferable *adj.* **1.** intolerable. **2.** unbearably conceited or arrogant. —**insufferably** *adv.*

insufficient /ɪnsə'fɪʃənt/ *adj.* not sufficient. —**insufficiency** *n.*, **insufficiently** *adv.* [from Old French from Latin]

insufflate /'ɪnsʌfleɪt/ *v.t.* to blow or breathe (air, gas, powder etc.) into a cavity of the body; to treat thus. —**insufflation** /-'fleɪʃən/ *n.*, **insufflator** *n.* [from Latin *sufflare* = blow upon]

insular /'ɪnsjʊlə/ *adj.* **1.** of or on an island; forming an island. **2.** of or like islanders; unable or unwilling to take a broad mental view —**insularity** /-'lærɪtɪ/ *n.*

insulate /'ɪnsjʊleɪt/ *v.t.* to isolate, especially with a substance or device preventing the passage of electricity, heat, or sound. —**insulation** /-'leɪʃən/ *n.*, **insulator** *n.* [from Latin *insula* = island]

insulator *n.* any poor ◊conductor of heat, sound, or electricity. Most substances lacking free (mobile) ◊electrons, such as nonmetals, are electrical or thermal insulators.

insulin /'ɪnsjʊlɪn/ *n.* protein hormone, produced by specialized cells in the islets of Langerhans in the pancreas, that regulates the metabolism (rate of activity) of glucose, fats, and proteins. Insulin was discovered by Canadian physician Frederick Banting, who pioneered its use in treating ◊diabetes. [from Latin *insula* = island (because it is produced by the islets of Langerhans)]

insult *v.t.* **1.** to abuse scornfully. **2.** to offend the self-respect or modesty of. **3.** to affect and damage (an organ etc. of the body). —/'ɪnsʌlt/ *n.* **1.** an insulting remark or

action. **2.** damage to the body; a substance causing this. [from Latin *insultare* = leap upon, assail]

insuperable /ɪn'suːpərəbəl/ *adj.* (of a barrier, difficulty, etc.) that cannot be surmounted or overcome. —**insuperability** /-'bɪlɪtɪ/ *n.*, **insuperably** *adv.* [from Old French or Latin *superare* = overcome]

insupportable /ɪnsə'pɔːtəbəl/ *adj.* unbearable; unjustifiable. —**insupportably** *adv.* [French]

insurable /ɪn'ʃʊərəbəl/ *adj.* that may be insured.

insurance /ɪn'ʃʊərəns/ *n.* **1.** a procedure or contract securing compensation for loss, damage, or injury etc., especially in return for a premium paid in advance. **2.** the business of providing this. **3.** the sum paid to effect such a contract, a premium. **4.** the amount paid in compensation. [from Old French]

insure /ɪn'ʃʊə/ *v.t.* to effect insurance *against* or with respect to. —**insurer** *n.* [variant of ensure]

insurgent /ɪn'sɜːdʒənt/ *n.* a rebel. —*adj.* in revolt, rebellious. —**insurgence** *n.*, **insurgency** *n.* [French from Latin *surgere* = rise]

insurmountable /ɪnsə'maʊntəbəl/ *adj.* unable to be surmounted, insuperable.

insurrection /ɪnsə'rekʃən/ *n.* a rising in open resistance to established authority, an incipient rebellion. —**insurrectionist** *n.* [from Old French from Latin]

insusceptible /ɪnsə'septɪbəl/ *adj.* not susceptible.

intact /ɪn'tækt/ *adj.* **1.** undamaged, unimpaired. **2.** entire. **3.** untouched. [from Latin *tangere* = touch]

intaglio /ɪn'tɑːlɪəʊ/ *n.* (*plural* **intaglios**) an engraved design; a gem with an incised design. [Italian *tagliare* = cut]

intake /'ɪnteɪk/ *n.* **1.** the action of taking in. **2.** the place where water is taken into a pipe, fuel or air into an engine etc. **3.** the persons, things, or quantity taken in or received.

intangible /ɪn'tændʒɪbəl/ *adj.* that cannot be touched or mentally grasped. —**intangibly** *adv.* [French or from Latin]

integer /'ɪntɪdʒə/ *n.* a whole number, for example, 3. Integers may be positive or negative; 0 is an integer, and is often considered positive. Formally, integers are members of the set $Z = \{... -3, -2, -1, 0, 1, 2, 3,...\}$. Fractions, such as $1/2$ and 0.35, are known as non-integral numbers (not integers). [Latin = untouched, whole]

integral /'ɪntɪgrəl/ *adj.* **1.** of or necessary to a whole. **2.** complete, forming a whole. **3.** of or denoted by an integer. —*n.* in mathematics, a quantity of which a given function is a derivative. —**integrally** *adv.* [from Latin]

integral calculus the branch of mathematics using the process of ◊integration. It is concerned with finding volumes and areas and summing infinitesimally small quantities.

integrate /'ɪntɪgreɪt/ *v.t./i.* **1.** to combine (parts) into a whole. **2.** to bring or come into equal membership of a community; to end racial segregation (of or at). **3.** to complete by the addition of parts. **4.** in mathematics, to find the integral of. —**integration** /-'reɪʃən/ *n.* [from Latin *integrare* = make whole]

integrated circuit a complete electronic circuit produced on a single crystal of a semiconductor (intermediate between an insulator and a conductor of electricity) such as silicon. The circuit might contain more than a million transistors, resistors, and capacitors and yet measure only 8 mm/0.3 in across. See also ◊silicon chip.

integration *n.* in mathematics, a method in ◊calculus of evaluating definite or indefinite integrals. An example of a definite integral can be thought of as finding the area under a curve (as represented by an algebraic expression or function) between particular values of the function's variable.

integrity /ɪn'tegrɪtɪ/ *n.* **1.** honesty. **2.** wholeness; soundness. [from French or Latin]

integument /ɪn'tegjʊmənt/ *n.* a skin, husk, rind, or other covering. [from Latin *integere* = cover]

intellect /'ɪntɪlekt/ *n.* **1.** the faculty of knowing and reasoning. **2.** ability to use this well; a person with such ability. [from Old French from Latin]

intellectual /ɪntɪ'lektjʊəl/ *adj.* of, requiring, or using the intellect; having a highly developed intellect. —*n.* an intellectual person. —**intellectuality** /-'ælɪtɪ/ *n.*, **intellectually** *adv.* [from Latin]

intellectualism n. 1. (especially excessive) exercise of the intellect alone. 2. the theory that knowledge is wholly or mainly derived from pure intellect. —**intellectualist** n.

intelligence /ɪn'telɪdʒəns/ n. 1. mental ability, the power of learning; quickness of understanding. 2. information, news; the collection of this, especially for military purposes; persons engaged in such collection. —**intelligence quotient**, the ratio of a given person's intelligence to the normal or average. [from Old French from Latin]

intelligence test a test that attempts to measure innate intellectual ability, rather than acquired ability.

intelligent /ɪn'telɪdʒənt/ adj. having or showing great intelligence, clever. —**intelligently** adv. [from Latin intellegere = understand]

intelligentsia /ɪnteli'dʒentsɪə/ n. intellectuals as a class, especially those regarded as cultured and politically enterprising. [Russian from Polish from Latin]

intelligible /ɪn'telɪdʒɪbəl/ adj. that can be understood. —**intelligibility** /-'bɪlɪtɪ/ n., **intelligibly** adv.

intemperate /ɪn'tempərət/ adj. 1. lacking moderation. 2. excessive in indulging the appetite; addicted to drinking. —**intemperance** n., **intemperately** adv. [from Latin]

intend /ɪn'tend/ v.t. 1. to have as one's purpose or wish. 2. to plan or destine (a person or thing for a purpose, as something, to do). [from Latin tendere = stretch, tend]

intendant n. official appointed by the French crown under Louis XIV to administer a territorial département. Their powers were extensive but counteracted to some extent by other local officials. The term was also used for certain administrators in Spain, Portugal, and Latin America.

intended adj. done on purpose. —n. (colloquial) a fiancé(e).

intense /ɪn'tens/ adj. 1. strong in quality or degree, violent, vehement; having a quality strongly. 2. eager, ardent, strenuous. 3. feeling or apt to feel emotion strongly. —**intensely** adv., **intenseness** n. [from Old French or Latin]

intensify /ɪn'tensɪfaɪ/ v.t./i. to make or become intense or more intense. —**intensification** /-ɪ'keɪʃən/ n.

intensity /ɪn'tensɪtɪ/ n. 1. intenseness. 2. the concentration of a force or energy over a given area or time. For example, the intensity or loudness of a sound is related to the energy per unit area carried by the sound wave; the intensity or brightness of a light source is measured by the energy per unit area carried by the light.

intensive /ɪn'tensɪv/ adj. 1. employing much effort, concentrated. 2. (of words) giving emphasis. 3. (as suffix) making much use of (labour-intensive). —**intensive care**, medical treatment with constant supervision of the patient. —**intensively** adv. [from French or Latin]

intent /ɪn'tent/ n. intention. —adj. 1. with one's mind or intention fixed on a purpose. 2. with one's attention concentrated (on); earnest, eager. —**to all intents and purposes**, virtually, practically. —**intently** adv., **intentness** n. [from Old French or Latin]

intention /ɪn'tenʃən/ n. 1. a thing intended, a purpose. 2. intending. [from Old French from Latin]

intentional adj. done on purpose, intended. —**intentionally** adv.

inter /ɪn'tɜː/ v.t. (-rr-) to place (a corpse etc.) in the Earth or a tomb, to bury. [from Old French enterrer from Latin terra = earth]

inter- prefix with the meaning of between, among, mutually, reciprocally. [from Old French entre- or Latin inter-]

interact /ɪntər'ækt/ v.i. to act on each other. —**interaction** n., **interactive** adj.

inter alia /ɪntə 'eɪlɪə/ among other things. [Latin]

interbreed /ɪntə'briːd/ v.t./i. to breed with each other; to cause animals to do this; to produce (a hybrid individual).

intercalary /ɪntə'kælərɪ/ adj. (of a day or days or month) inserted to harmonize the calendar with the solar year; (of a year) having such additions; interpolated. [from Latin]

intercalate /ɪn'tɜːkəleɪt/ v.t. to interpose; to insert (an intercalary day etc.). —**intercalation** /-'leɪʃən/ n. [from Latin calare = proclaim]

intercede /ɪntə'siːd/ v.i. to interpose on another's behalf, to mediate; to plead (with a person for another). [from French or Latin cedere = go]

intercept /ɪntə'sept/ v.t. to seize, catch, or stop in transit or progress; to cut off (light etc. from). —/'ɪntəsept/ n. 1. a message or conversation picked up by intercepting a letter or a telephone or radio conversation. 2. a device for performing such interception. —**interception** n., **interceptive** adj., **interceptor** n. [from Latin intercipere (capere = catch)]

intercession /ɪntə'seʃən/ n. interceding. —**intercessor** n. [French or from Latin]

interchange /ɪntə'tʃeɪndʒ/ v.t. 1. to put (things) in each other's place. 2. (of two persons) to exchange (things) with each other. 3. to alternate. —/'ɪntətʃeɪndʒ/ n. 1. an exchange (of things) between persons etc. 2. alternation. 3. a junction of roads on different levels. —**interchangeability** /-ə'bɪlɪtɪ/ n., **interchangeable** adj.

inter-city /ɪntə'sɪtɪ/ adj. existing or travelling between cities.

intercom /'ɪntəkɒm/ n. (colloquial) a system of intercommunication operating like a telephone. [abbreviation]

intercommunicate /ɪntəkə'mjuːnɪkeɪt/ v.i. to communicate mutually; to have free passage into each other. —**intercommunication** /-'keɪʃən/ n.

intercommunion /ɪntəkə'mjuːnɪən/ n. mutual communion, especially between Christian denominations.

interconnect /ɪntəkə'nekt/ v.t./i. to connect with each other. —**interconnection** n.

intercontinental /ɪntəkɒntɪ'nentəl/ adj. connecting or travelling between continents.

intercostal muscle muscle found between the ribs, responsible for producing the rib cage movements involved in some types of breathing.

intercourse /'ɪntəkɔːs/ n. 1. social communication between individuals. 2. communication between countries etc., especially in trade. 3. sexual intercourse.

interdenominational adj. of or involving more than one Christian denomination.

interdepartmental /ɪntədiːpɑːt'mentəl/ adj. of more than one department.

interdependent /ɪntədi'pendənt/ adj. dependent on each other. —**interdependence** n., **interdependency** n.

interdict /ɪntə'dɪkt/ v.t. to prohibit or forbid authoritatively. —/'ɪntədɪkt/ n. an authoritative prohibition; in the Roman Catholic church, a sentence debarring a person or place from ecclesiastical functions etc. —**interdiction** /-'dɪkʃən/ n., **interdictory** /-'dɪktərɪ/ adj. [from Old French from Latin dicere = say]

interdisciplinary /ɪntədɪsɪ'plɪnərɪ/ adj. of or involving different branches of learning.

interest /'ɪntrəst/ n. 1. a feeling of curiosity or concern; a quality causing this; the thing towards which one feels it. 2. advantage, benefit. 3. money paid for the use of a loan of money. 4. a legal concern, title, or right (in property); a money stake (in a business); a thing in which one has a stake or concern. —v.t. to arouse the interest of; to cause to be interested or involved (in). —**compound interest**, interest (on a loan) reckoned on the principal and accumulations of interest. **simple interest**, interest reckoned on the principal only and paid at fixed intervals. [from Anglo-French from Latin = it matters]

interested adj. 1. feeling interest or curiosity. 2. having a private interest, not impartial.

interesting n. adj. causing curiosity, holding the attention.

interface n. 1. a surface forming the common boundary of two regions. 2. a place or piece of equipment where interaction occurs between two systems; in computing, the point of contact between two programs or pieces of equipment. The term is most often used for the physical connection between the computer and a peripheral device, such as a printer or a mouse.

interfere /ɪntə'fɪə/ v.i. 1. to take part in dealing with others' affairs without right or invitation. 2. to obstruct wholly or partially. [from Old French = strike one another from Latin ferire = strike]

interference n. 1. interfering. 2. the fading of received radio signals because of atmospherics or unwanted signals. 3. in physics, the phenomenon of two or more wave motions interacting and combining to produce a resultant wave of larger or smaller amplitude (depending on whether the combining waves are in or out of ɸphase with each other).

interferon /ɪntə'fɪərɒn/ n. a protein released by an animal cell, usually in response to the entry of a virus, which has the property of inhibiting further development of viruses of any kind in the animal or in others of the same species.

intermediate technology
windpump

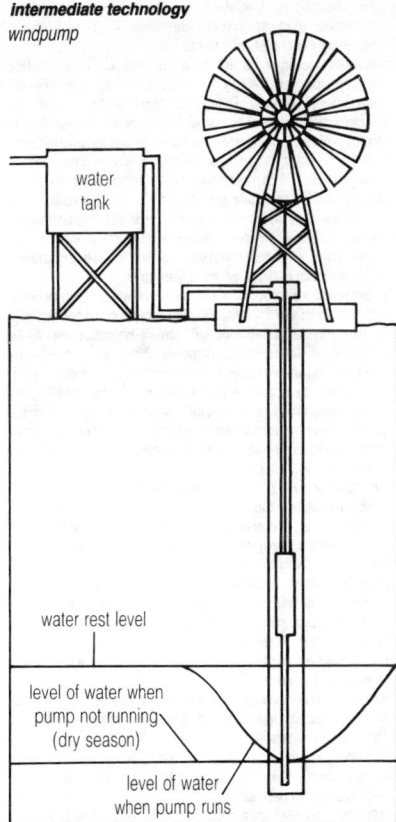

water
tank

water rest level

level of water when
pump not running
(dry season)

level of water
when pump runs

interfuse /ɪntəˈfjuːz/ v.t./i. to intersperse; to blend. —**interfusion** n. [from Latin *fundere* = pour]

interglacial /ɪntəˈgleɪʃəl/ n. a period of milder climate between glacial periods.

interim /ˈɪntərɪm/ n. the intervening time. —adj. temporary, provisional. [Latin = meanwhile]

interior /ɪnˈtɪərɪə/ n. 1. the inner part, the inside. 2. an inland region. 3. the inside of a room etc.; a picture of this. 4. the home affairs of a country. —adj. 1. situated or coming from within. 2. further in. 3. inland. 4. internal, domestic. 5. existing in the mind. [Latin comparative of *inter* = among]

interject /ɪntəˈdʒekt/ v.t. to put in (words) abruptly or parenthetically. [from Latin *interjicere* (*jacere* = throw)]

interjection /ɪntəˈdʒekʃən/ n. an exclamation, especially as a part of speech (e. g. *ah, whew*). [from Old French from Latin]

interlace /ɪntəˈleɪs/ v.t./i. to bind intricately together, to interweave; to cross each other intricately. —**interlacement** n.

interlard /ɪntəˈlɑːd/ v.t. to mix (writing or speech *with* unusual words or phrases).

interleave /ɪntəˈliːv/ v.t. to insert leaves, usually blank, between the leaves of (a book).

interlinear /ɪntəˈlɪnɪə/ adj. written or printed between the lines of a text.

interlink /ɪntəˈlɪŋk/ v.t./i. to link together.

interlock /ɪntəˈlɒk/ v.t./i. to engage with each other by overlapping; to lock or clasp in each other. —adj. (of a fabric) knitted with closely interlocking stitches. —n. such a fabric.

interlocutor /ɪntəˈlɒkjʊtə/ n. one who takes part in a conversation. [from Latin *loqui* = speak]

interlocutory /ɪntəˈlɒkʊtərɪ/ adj. 1. of dialogue. 2. (of a decree etc.) given in the course of a legal action. [from Latin]

interloper /ˈɪntələʊpə/ n. an intruder, one who thrusts himself into others' affairs, especially for profit. [from Dutch *loper* as in *landloper* = vagabond]

interlude /ˈɪntəluːd/ n. 1. a pause between the parts of a play etc.; something performed during this. 2. an intervening time or event of a different character. 3. a piece of music played between the verses of a hymn etc. [from Latin *ludus* = play]

intermarry /ɪntəˈmærɪ/ v.i. (of tribes, nations, families etc.) to become connected by marriage. —**intermarriage** n.

intermediary /ɪntəˈmiːdɪərɪ/ n. 1. a mediator. 2. an intermediate thing. —adj. 1. acting as a mediator. 2. intermediate. [from French from Latin *medius* = middle]

intermediate /ɪntəˈmiːdɪət/ adj. coming between two things in time, place, character etc. —n. 1. an intermediate thing. 2. a chemical compound formed by one reaction and then taking part in another. [from Latin]

Intermediate Nuclear Forces Treaty the agreement signed on 8 Dec 1987 between the USA and the USSR to eliminate all ground-based nuclear missiles in Europe that were capable of hitting only European targets (including European Russia). It reduced the countries' nuclear arsenals by some 2,000 (4% of the total). The treaty included provisions for each country to inspect the other's bases. A total of 1,269 weapons (945 Soviet, 234 US) was destroyed in the first year of the treaty.

intermediate technology the application of mechanics, electrical engineering, and other technologies, based on inventions and designs developed in scientifically sophisticated cultures, but utilizing materials, assembly, and maintenance methods found in technologically less advanced regions.

interment /ɪnˈtɜːmənt/ n. a burial.

intermezzo /ɪntəˈmetsəʊ/ n. (plural **intermezzi** /-tsiː/) 1. a short connecting movement in a musical work, or a similar but independent piece. 2. a short, light dramatic or other performance between the acts of a play or opera. [Italian]

interminable /ɪnˈtɜːmɪnəbəl/ adj. tediously long; endless. —**interminably** adv. [from Latin]

intermingle /ɪntəˈmɪŋgəl/ v.t./i. to mix together, to mingle.

intermission /ɪntəˈmɪʃən/ n. an interval, a pause in work or action. [French or from Latin]

intermittent /ɪntəˈmɪtənt/ adj. occurring at intervals, not continuous. —**intermittently** adv. [from Latin *mittere* = let go]

intermix /ɪntəˈmɪks/ v.t./i. to mix together.

intermolecular force or **van der Waals' force** force of attraction between molecules. Intermolecular forces are relatively weak, hence simple molecular compounds are gases, liquids, or low-melting-point solids.

intern /ɪnˈtɜːn/ v.t. to oblige (a prisoner, alien etc.) to live within prescribed limits. —/ˈɪntɜːn/ n. (US) a recent graduate or advanced student living in a hospital and acting as an assistant physician or surgeon. —**internment** n. [from French]

internal /ɪnˈtɜːnəl/ adj. 1. of or in the inside or invisible part. 2. relating or applied to the interior of the body. 3. of a country's domestic affairs. 4. of students attending a university as well as taking its examinations. 5. used or applying within an organization. 6. intrinsic. 7. of the mind or soul. —**internal evidence**, evidence derived from the contents of the thing discussed. —**internality** /-ˈnælɪtɪ/ n., **internally** adv. [from Latin *internus*]

internal-combustion engine a heat engine in which fuel is burned inside the engine, contrasting with an external combustion engine (such as the steam engine) in which fuel is burned in a separate unit. The diesel and petrol engine are both internal-combustion engines. Gas turbines and jet and rocket engines are sometimes also considered to be internal-combustion engines because they burn their fuel inside their combustion chambers.

International, the a coordinating body established by labour and socialist organizations, including: **First International** or **International Working Men's Association** 1864–72, formed in London under Karl ◊Marx. **Second International** 1889–1940, founded in Paris. **Third (Socialist) International** or **Comintern** 1919–43, formed in Moscow by the Soviet leader Lenin, advocating from 1933 a popular front (communist, socialist, liberal) against the German dictator Hitler. **Fourth International** or **Trotskyist International** 1936, somewhat indeterminate, anti-Stalinist. **Revived Socialist International** 1951, formed in Frankfurt, West Germany, a largely anti-communist association of social democrats.

international /ɪntəˈnæʃənəl/ *adj.* existing or carried on between nations; agreed on or used by all or many nations. —*n.* 1. a contest, usually in sport, between representatives of different nations. 2. such a representative. /-ˈnælɪtɪ/ *n.*, **internationally** *adv.*

International Brigade the international volunteer force on the Republican side in the Spanish Civil War 1936–39, (see ◊Civil War, Spanish).

International Civil Aviation Organization an agency of the ◊United Nations, established in 1947 to regulate safety and efficiency and air law; headquarters Montreal, Canada.

International Court of Justice the main judicial organ of the United Nations, at The Hague, the Netherlands.

International Date Line (IDL) a modification of the 180th meridian that marks the difference in time between east and west. The date is put forward a day when crossing the line going west, and back a day when going east. The IDL was chosen at the International Meridian Conference in 1884.

Internationale *n.* the international revolutionary socialist anthem; composed in 1870 and first sung in 1888. The words by Eugène Pottier (1816–1887) were written shortly after Napoleon III's surrender to Prussia; the music is by Pierre Degeyter. It was the Soviet national anthem 1917–44.

International Fund for Agricultural Development an agency of the United Nations, established in 1977, to provide funds for benefiting the poor in developing countries.

internationalism *n.* 1. advocacy of the community of interests among nations. 2. support of an International. —**internationalist** *n.*

internationalize *v.t.* to make international; to bring under the protection or control of two or more nations.

international law a body of rules generally accepted as governing the relations between countries, pioneered by Hugo ◊Grotius, especially in matters of human rights, territory, and war. Neither the League of Nations nor the United Nations proved able to enforce it, successes being achieved only when the law coincided with the aims of a predominant major power, e. g., the Korean War. The scope of the law is now extended to space, e. g., the 1967 treaty that (among other things) banned nuclear weapons from space.

International Maritime Organization the agency of the United Nations concerned with world shipping. Established in 1958; headquarters in London, England.

International Monetary Fund (IMF) specialized agency of the United Nations, headquarters Washington DC, established under the 1944 ◊Bretton Woods agreement and operational since 1947. It seeks to promote international monetary cooperation and the growth of world trade, and to smooth multilateral payment arrangements among member states. IMF stand-by loans are available to members in balance of payments difficulties (the amount being governed by the member's quota), usually on the basis of acceptance of instruction on stipulated corrective measures.

International Society for Krishna Consciousness (ISKCON) a Hindu sect based on the demonstration of intense love for Krishna (an incarnation of the god Vishnu), especially by chanting the mantra 'Hare Krishna'. Members wear distinctive yellow robes, and men often have their heads partly shaven. Their holy books are the Hindu scriptures and particularly the *Bhagavad-Gītā*, which they study daily.

internecine /ɪntəˈniːsaɪn/ *adj.* mutually destructive. [originally = deadly, murderous; from Latin *necare* = kill]

internee /ɪntɜːˈniː/ *n.* a person interned.

internist /ɪnˈtɜːnɪst/ *n.* a specialist in internal diseases; (*US*) a general practitioner.

interpenetrate /ɪntəˈpenɪtreɪt/ *v.t./i.* to penetrate each other; to pervade. —**interpenetration** /-ˈtreɪʃən/ *n.*

interpersonal /ɪntəˈpɜːsənəl/ *adj.* between persons.

interplanetary /ɪntəˈplænɪtərɪ/ *adj.* between planets; of travel between planets.

interplanetary matter gas and dust thinly spread through the solar system. The gas flows outwards from the Sun as the ◊solar wind. Fine dust lies in the plane of the solar system, scattering sunlight to cause zodiacal light. Swarms of dust shed by comets enter the Earth's atmosphere to cause ◊meteor showers.

interplay /ˈɪntəpleɪ/ *n.* interaction.

Interpol acronym from International Criminal Police Organization, an agency founded following the Second International Judicial Police Conference 1923 with its headquarters in Vienna, and reconstituted after World War II with its headquarters in Paris. It has an international criminal register, fingerprint file, and methods index.

interpolate /ɪnˈtɜːpəleɪt/ *v.t.* 1. to interject. 2. to insert (new material) misleadingly into a book etc.; to make such insertions in (a book). 3. to insert (terms) in a mathematical series; to estimate (values) from known ones in the same range. —**interpolation** /-ˈleɪʃən/ *n.*, **interpolator** *n.* [from Latin *interpolare* = furbish up]

interpose /ɪntəˈpəʊz/ *v.t./i.* 1. to insert (a thing *between* others). 2. to say (words) as an interruption; to speak thus. 3. to exercise or advance (a veto or objection) so as to interfere. 4. to intervene (*between* parties). —**interposition** /-pəˈzɪʃən/ *n.* [from French from Latin *ponere* = put]

interpret /ɪnˈtɜːprɪt/ *v.t./i.* 1. to explain the meaning of. 2. to understand in a specified way. 3. to act as interpreter. —**interpretation** /-ˈteɪʃən/ *n.*, **interpretative** *adj.*, **interpretive** *adj.* [from Old French or Latin *interpres* = one who explains]

interpreter *n.* 1. one who interprets, especially one who orally translates the words of persons speaking different languages. 2. a computer program that translates statements from a ◊programming language into ◊machine code and causes them to be executed.

interregnum /ɪntəˈregnəm/ *n.* (*plural* **interregnums**) 1. an interval when usual government is suspended, especially between successive reigns. 2. an interval, a pause. [Latin *regnum* = reign]

interrelated /ɪntərɪˈleɪtɪd/ *adj.* related to each other. —**interrelation** *n.*

interrogate /ɪnˈterəgeɪt/ *v.t.* to question closely or formally. —**interrogation** /-ˈgeɪʃən/ *n.*, **interrogator** *n.* [from Latin *rogare* = ask]

interrogative /ɪntəˈrɒgətɪv/ *adj.* of or like or used in questions. —*n.* an interrogative word (e. g. *who?*). —**interrogatively** *adv.*

interrogatory /ɪntəˈrɒgətərɪ/ *adj.* questioning. —*n.* a formal set of questions.

interrupt /ɪntəˈrʌpt/ *v.t.* 1. to break the continuity of. 2. to break the flow of (a speech or speaker etc.) by inserting a remark. 3. to obstruct (a view etc.). —**interrupter** *n.*, **interruption** *n.* [from Latin *rumpere* = break]

intersect /ɪntəˈsekt/ *v.t./i.* 1. to divide (a thing) by passing or lying across it. 2. (of lines, roads etc.) to cross each other. [from Latin *secare* = cut]

intersection *n.* 1. a place where two roads intersect. 2. the point or line common to lines or planes that intersect. 3. intersecting.

interspace /ˈɪntəspeɪs/ *n.* an intervening space. —/ɪntəˈspeɪs/ *v.t.* to put a space or spaces between.

intersperse /ɪntəˈspɜːs/ *v.t.* to insert contrasting material here and there in (a thing); to scatter (material) thus. [from Latin *interspergere* (*spargere* = scatter)]

interstate /ˈɪntəsteɪt/ *adj.* existing or carried on between States especially of the USA.

interstellar /ɪntəˈstelə/ *adj.* between stars. [from Latin *stella* = star]

interstellar molecules over 50 different types of molecules existing in gas clouds in our Galaxy. Most have been detected by their radio emissions, but some have been found by the absorption lines they produce in the spectra of starlight. The most complex molecules, many of them based on ◊carbon, are found in the dense clouds where stars are forming. They may be significant for the origin of life elsewhere in space.

interstice /ɪnˈtɜːstɪs/ *n.* an intervening space; a chink, a crevice. [from Latin *interstitium* (*sistere* = stand)]

interstitial /ɪntəˈstɪʃəl/ *adj.* of or in or forming interstices. —**interstitially** *adv.*

intertwine /ɪntəˈtwaɪn/ *v.t./i.* to twine closely together.

interval /ˈɪntəvəl/ *n.* 1. an intervening time or space. 2. a pause, a break, especially between parts of a performance. 3. the difference of pitch between two sounds. —**at intervals**, here and there, now and then. [from Latin = space between ramparts (*vallum* = rampart)]

intervene /ɪntəˈviːn/ v.i. 1. to occur in time between events. 2. to cause hindrance by occurring; to enter a discussion or dispute etc. in order to change its course or resolve it. 3. to come in as an extraneous thing. 4. to be situated *between* others. [from Latin *venire* = come]

intervention /ɪntəˈvenʃən/ n. intervening, interference, especially by the State; mediation.

interventionist n. one who favours intervention.

interview /ˈɪntəvjuː/ n. 1. a conversation between a reporter and a person whose views he wishes to publish or broadcast. 2. an oral examination of an applicant. 3. a meeting of persons face to face, especially for consultation. —v.t. to have an interview with. —**interviewee** /-vjuːˈiː/ n., **interviewer** n. [from French *entrevue*]

interwar /ɪntəˈwɔː/ adj. existing in the period between two wars.

interweave /ɪntəˈwiːv/ v.t. to weave together; to blend intimately.

intestacy n. the absence of a will at a person's death. In law, special legal rules apply on intestacy for appointing administrators to deal with the deceased person's affairs, and for disposing of the deceased person's property in accordance with statutory provisions.

intestate /ɪnˈtesteɪt/ adj. not having made a will before death. —n. a person who has died intestate. n. [from Latin *testari* = make a will]

intestine n. (*in singular* or *plural*) in vertebrates, the digestive tract from the stomach outlet to the anus. The human **small intestine** is 6 m/20 ft long, 4 cm/1.5 in in diameter, and consists of the duodenum, jejunum, and ileum; the **large intestine** is 1.5 m/5 ft long, 6 cm/2.5 in in diameter, and includes the caecum, colon, and rectum. Both are muscular tubes comprising an inner lining that secretes alkaline digestive juice, a submucous coat containing fine blood vessels and nerves, a muscular coat, and a serous coat covering all, supported by a strong peritoneum, which carries the blood and lymph vessels, and the nerves. The contents are passed along slowly by ◊peristalsis. The term intestine is also applied to the lower digestive tract of invertebrates. —**intestinal** adj. [from Latin *intestinus* = internal]

Intifada /ɪntiˈfɑːdə/ n. a Palestinian uprising; also the title of the involved **Liberation Army of Palestine**, a loosely organized group of Palestinians active since 1987 in attacks on Israeli troops in the occupied territories of Palestine. [Arabic = resurgence, throwing off]

intimacy /ˈɪntɪməsɪ/ n. 1. being intimate. 2. an intimate act; sexual intercourse.

intimate /ˈɪntɪmət/ adj. 1. closely acquainted, familiar. 2. private and personal. 3. having sexual relations (*with*). 4. (of knowledge) detailed, thorough. 5. (of relations between things) close. —n. an intimate friend. —/-eɪt/ v.t. to state or make known; to imply, to hint. —**intimately** adv., **intimation** /-ˈmeɪʃən/ n. [from Latin *intimus* = inmost]

intimidate /ɪnˈtɪmɪdeɪt/ v.t. to frighten, especially in order to subdue or influence. —**intimidation** /-ˈdeɪʃən/ n., **intimidator** n. [from Latin *timidus* = timid]

into /ˈɪntu, -tə/ prep. 1. expressing motion or direction to a point on or within. 2. expressing a change of state. 3. (*colloquial*) interested and involved in. [Old English]

intolerable /ɪnˈtɒlərəbəl/ adj. that cannot be endured. —**intolerableness** n., **intolerably** adv. [from Old French or Latin]

intolerant /ɪnˈtɒlərənt/ adj. not tolerant, especially of views or beliefs differing from one's own. —**intolerance** n., **intolerantly** adv. [from Latin]

intonation /ɪntəˈneɪʃən/ n. 1. intoning. 2. a modulation of the voice, a slight accent. [from Latin]

intone /ɪnˈtəʊn/ v.t. 1. to recite (prayers etc.) with prolonged sounds, especially in a monotone. 2. to utter with a particular tone. [from Latin *tonus* = tone]

in toto /ɪn ˈtəʊtəʊ/ completely. [Latin]

intoxicant /ɪnˈtɒksɪkənt/ adj. intoxicating. —n. an intoxicant drink or substance.

intoxicate /ɪnˈtɒksɪkeɪt/ v.t. to make drunk; to excite or elate beyond self-control. —**intoxication** /-ˈkeɪʃən/ n. [from Latin *intoxicare* = poison]

intra- prefix with the meaning within, on the inside. [from Latin *intra* = inside]

intractable /ɪnˈtræktəbəl/ adj. hard to control or deal with; difficult, stubborn. —**intractability** /-ˈbɪlɪtɪ/ n., **intractably** adv. [from Latin]

intramural /ɪntrəˈmjuərəl/ adj. 1. situated or done within walls. 2. forming part of ordinary university work. —**intramurally** adv. [from Latin *murus* = wall]

intransigent /ɪnˈtrænsɪdʒənt/ adj. uncompromising, stubborn. —n. an intransigent person. —**intransigence** n. [from French from Spanish *los intransigentes* = extreme republicans]

intransitive /ɪnˈtrænsɪtɪv/ adj. (of a verb) not taking a direct object. —**intransitively** adv. [from Latin]

intra-uterine /ɪntrəˈjuːtəraɪn, -rɪn/ adj. within the womb.

intra-uterine device IUD or coil, a contraceptive device that is inserted into the womb (uterus). It is a tiny plastic object, sometimes containing copper. By causing a mild inflammation of the lining of the uterus it prevents fertilized eggs from becoming implanted.

intravenous /ɪntrəˈviːnəs/ adj. in or into a vein or veins. —**intravenously** adv. [from Latin *vena* = vein]

in-tray n. a tray for incoming documents.

intrepid /ɪnˈtrepɪd/ adj. fearless, brave. —**intrepidity** /ɪntrɪˈpɪdɪtɪ/ n., **intrepidly** adv. [from French or Latin *trepidus* = alarmed]

intricate /ˈɪntrɪkət/ adj. very complicated. —**intricacy** /ˈɪntrɪkəsɪ/ n., **intricately** adv. [from Latin *tricae* = tricks, perplexities]

intrigue /ɪnˈtriːg/ v.t./i. 1. to plot in an underhand way; to use secret influence. 2. to rouse the interest or curiosity of. —/also ˈɪn-/ n. 1. underhand plotting or plot. 2. (*archaic*) a secret love affair. [from French from Italian]

intrinsic /ɪnˈtrɪnsɪk/ adj. inherent, essential. —**intrinsically** adv. [from French from Latin *intrinsecus* = inwardly]

intro- prefix with the meaning into, inwards. [from Latin = to the inside]

introduce /ɪntrəˈdjuːs/ v.t. 1. to make known by name *to* another. 2. to announce or present to an audience. 3. to bring (a bill) before Parliament. 4. to cause to become acquainted with a subject. 5. to bring (a custom or idea etc.) into use or into a system. 6. to bring or put in. [from Latin *ducere* = lead]

introduction /ɪntrəˈdʌkʃən/ n. 1. introducing. 2. a formal presentation of a person to another. 3. an explanatory section at the beginning of a book etc. 4. an introductory treatise. 5. a thing introduced. [from Old French or Latin]

introductory /ɪntrəˈdʌktərɪ/ adj. that introduces; preliminary. [from Latin]

introit /ˈɪntrɔɪt/ n. a psalm or antiphon sung or said while a priest approaches the altar for Eucharist. [from Old French from Latin *introitus* = entrance]

introspection /ɪntrəˈspekʃən/ n. examining one's own thoughts. —**introspective** adj. [from Latin *specere* = look]

introvert /ˈɪntrəvɜːt/ n. an introverted person.

introverted /ˈɪntrəvɜːtɪd/ adj. principally interested in one's own thoughts; reserved, shy. —**introversion** /-ˈvɜːʃən/ n. [from Latin *vertere* = turn]

intrude /ɪnˈtruːd/ v.t./i. to force or come uninvited or unwanted. [from Latin *trudere* = thrust]

intruder n. one who intrudes; a burglar; a raiding aircraft.

intrusion n. 1. intruding. 2. a mass of ◊igneous rock that has formed by 'injection' of molten rock into existing cracks beneath the surface of the Earth, as distinct from a volcanic rock mass which has erupted from the surface. —**intrusive** adj. [from Old French or Latin]

intuition /ɪntjuːˈɪʃən/ n. a rapid, unconscious thought process. In philosophy, intuition is that knowledge of a concept which does not derive directly from the senses. Thus, we may be said to have an intuitive idea of God, beauty, or justice. The concept of intuition is similar to Bertrand ◊Russell's theory of knowledge by acquaintance. In both cases, it is contrasted with ◊empirical knowledge. —**intuitional** adj. [from Latin *tueri* = look]

intuitive /ɪnˈtjuːɪtɪv/ adj. of, having, or perceived by intuition. —**intuitively** adv. [from Latin]

Inuit /ˈɪnuɪt/ n. or **Eskimo** a people inhabiting the Arctic coasts of North America, the E coasts of the Canadian Arctic, and the ice-free coasts of Greenland. They were first called Eskimos (foul eaters of raw meat) by the Algonquin Indians. Their language, Inuktitut, belongs to the Eskimo-Aleut group.

inundate /'mʌndeɪt/ v.t. to flood or overwhelm (with). —**inundation** /-'deɪʃən/ n. [from Latin *unda* = wave]

inure /ɪ'njuə/ v.t./i. 1. to accustom (to a difficulty etc.). 2. in law, to take effect. —**inurement** n. [from Old French *euvre* = work from Latin *opera*]

in vacuo /ɪn 'vækjuːəu/ in a vacuum. [Latin]

invade /ɪn'veɪd/ v.t. 1. to enter (a country) with armed forces to control or subdue it. 2. to swarm into. 3. (of a disease etc.) to attack. 4. to encroach on (rights, especially privacy). —**invader** n. [from Latin *vadere* = go]

invalid[1] /'ɪnvəliːd/ n. a person enfeebled or disabled by illness or injury. —*adj.* of or for invalids; being an invalid. —v.t. 1. to remove from active service or send away (*home* etc.) as an invalid. 2. to disable by illness. —**invalidism** n. [from Latin *validus* = strong]

invalid[2] /ɪn'vælɪd/ adj. not valid. [from Latin]

invalidate /ɪn'vælɪdeɪt/ v.t. to make (an argument, contract, etc.) invalid. —**invalidation** /-'deɪʃən/ n. [from Latin]

Invalides, Hôtel des /ɪnvə'liːd/ a building in Paris, S of the Seine, founded in 1670 as a home for disabled soldiers. The church, Dôme des Invalides, contains the tomb of Napoleon I.

invalidity /ɪnvə'lɪdɪtɪ/ n. 1. lack of validity. 2. being an invalid. [from French or Latin]

invaluable /ɪn'væljuːəbəl/ adj. having a value that is too great to be measured. —**invaluably** adv.

Invar trade name for an alloy of iron containing 36% nickel, which expands or contracts very little when the temperature changes. It is used to make precision instruments (such as pendulums and tuning forks) whose dimensions must not alter.

invariable /ɪn'veərɪəbəl/ adj. not variable, always the same. —**invariably** adv. [French or from Latin]

invasion /ɪn'veɪʒən/ n. invading, being invaded. —**invasive** adj. [French or from Latin]

invected /ɪn'vektɪd/ adj. in heraldry, bordered by or consisting of a series of small convex lobes.

invective /ɪn'vektɪv/ n. a strong verbal attack; abusive language. [from Old French from Latin]

inveigh /ɪn'veɪ/ v.i. to speak or write with strong hostility (*against*). [from Latin *invehi* = ride into, assail]

inveigle /ɪn'veɪgəl/ v.t. to entice, to persuade by guile (*into*). —**inveiglement** n. [from Old French *aveugler* = to blind]

invent /ɪn'vent/ v.t. 1. to create by thought, to make or design (something that did not exist before). 2. to concoct (a false or fictional story). —**inventor** n. [from Latin *invenire* = discover]

invention /ɪn'venʃən/ n. 1. inventing. 2. a thing invented; a fictitious story. 3. inventiveness. [from Latin]

inventive /ɪn'ventɪv/ adj. able to invent. —**inventiveness** n. [from French or Latin]

inventory /'ɪnvəntərɪ/ n. a detailed list (of goods etc.); goods in this. —v.t. to make an inventory of; to enter (goods) in an inventory. [from Latin *inventorium*]

Invergordon Mutiny /ɪnvə'gɔːdn/ an incident in the British Atlantic Fleet, Cromarty Firth, Scotland, 15 Sept 1931. Ratings refused to prepare the ships for sea following the government's cuts in their pay; the cuts were consequently modified.

Inverness /ɪnvə'nes/ town in Highland region, Scotland, lying in a sheltered site at the mouth of the river Ness; population (1985) 58,000. It is a tourist centre with tweed, tanning, engineering, and distilling industries.

Inverness-shire /ɪnvə'nesʃə/ the largest of the former Scottish counties, it was merged with the Highland region in 1975.

inverse /ɪn'vɜːs, 'ɪn-/ adj. 1. inverted in position or order or relation. 2. (of a proportion or ratio) between two quantities one of which increases in proportion as the other decreases. —n. 1. an inverted state. 2. a thing that is the direct opposite (*of* another). —**inversely** adv. [from Latin]

inverse square law in physics, the statement that the magnitude of an effect (usually a force) at a point is inversely proportional to the square of the distance between that point and the point location of its cause.

inversion /ɪn'vɜːʃən/ n. 1. turning upside down; reversal of normal order, position, or relation. 2. in music, the

mirror-image of a melody used in counterpoint; alternatively a chord whose natural order of notes is rearranged. —**inversive** adj.

invert /ɪn'vɜːt/ v.t. to turn upside down; to reverse the position, order, or relation of. —/'ɪnvɜːt/ n. a homosexual. —**inverted commas**, quotation marks. [from Latin *vertere* = turn]

invertebrate /ɪn'vɜːtɪbrət/ adj. without a backbone or spinal column. —n. an invertebrate animal. The invertebrates comprise over 95% of the million or so existing animal species and include the sponges, coelenterates, flatworms, nematodes, annelid worms, arthropods, molluscs, echinoderms, and primitive aquatic chordates such as sea-squirts and lancelets.

invest /ɪn'vest/ v.t./i. 1. to use (money) to buy stocks, shares, or property etc. so as to earn interest or bring profit; to spend money, time, or effort *in* obtaining stocks etc. or something useful. 2. to endow *with* qualities, insignia, or rank. 3. to clothe, to cover (as) with a garment. 4. to lay siege to. [from French or Latin *vestire* = clothe]

investigate /ɪn'vestɪgeɪt/ v.t./i. to make a careful study of (a thing) in order to discover the facts about it; to make a systematic inquiry. —**investigation** /-'geɪʃən/ n., **investigative** adj., **investigator** n., **investigatory** adj. [from Latin *vestigare* = track]

investiture /ɪn'vestɪtʃə/ n. the process of investing a person with rank or office etc.; a ceremony at which the sovereign confers honours. [from Latin]

investiture contest the conflict between the papacy and the Holy Roman Empire 1075–1122, which centred on the right of lay rulers to appoint prelates (investiture).

investment n. 1. investing. 2. money invested. 3. something in which money, time, or effort is invested.

investment trust a public company that makes investments in other companies on behalf of its shareholders. It may issue shares to raise capital and issue fixed interest securities. See ◊mutual fund.

investor n. one who invests money.

inveterate /ɪn'vetərət/ adj. (of a habit etc.) deep-rooted; (of a person) confirmed in a habit etc. —**inveteracy** n. [from Latin *vetus* = old]

invidious /ɪn'vɪdɪəs/ adj. likely to excite ill-will or indignation against the performer, possessor etc. —**invidiously** adv. [from Latin *invidia* = envy]

invigilate /ɪn'vɪdʒɪleɪt/ v.i. to supervise candidates at an examination. —**invigilation** /-'leɪʃən/ n., **invigilator** n. [from Latin *vigilare* = keep watch]

invigorate /ɪn'vɪgəreɪt/ v.t. to give vigour or strength to. [from Latin *vigorare* = make strong]

invincible /ɪn'vɪnsɪbəl/ adj. unconquerable. —**invincibility** /-'bɪlɪtɪ/ n., **invincibly** adv. [from Old French from Latin *vincere* = conquer]

inviolable /ɪn'vaɪələbəl/ adj. not to be violated or profaned. —**inviolability** /-'bɪlɪtɪ/ n., **inviolably** adv. [French or from Latin]

inviolate /ɪn'vaɪələt/ adj. not violated. —**inviolacy** n. [from Latin]

invisible /ɪn'vɪzɪbəl/ adj. that cannot be seen. —**invisible exports, imports**, items for which payment is made by or to another country but which are not goods. —**invisibility** /-'bɪlɪtɪ/ n., **invisibly** adv. [from Old French or Latin]

invitation /ɪnvɪ'teɪʃən/ n. 1. inviting, being invited. 2. a letter or card etc. used to invite someone. 3. a thing that invites (unintentional) consequences.

invite /ɪn'vaɪt/ v.t. 1. to ask courteously to come to one's house or to a function etc., or to do something). 2. to ask for (suggestions etc.). 3. to tend to call forth (criticism etc.), to act so as to be likely to cause (a thing) unintentionally. 4. to attract, to tempt. —/'ɪnvaɪt/ n. (*colloquial*) an invitation. [from French or Latin *invitare*]

inviting adj. attractive, tempting.

in vitro fertilization (IVF) a method of artificial insemination in which eggs and sperm are allowed to unite in a laboratory to form embryos. The embryos produced may then either be implanted into the womb of the otherwise infertile mother. The first baby to be produced by this method, Louise Brown, was born in 1978 in the UK. [from Latin *vitro* = glass]

invocation /ɪnvə'keɪʃən/ n. 1. invoking. 2. an appeal to a Muse for inspiration. 3. a preacher's prefatory words 'In the name of the Father' etc. —**invocatory** /ɪn'vɒkətərɪ/ adj. [from Old French from Latin]

invoice /'ɪnvɔɪs/ n. a list of goods shipped or sent, or services rendered, with prices. —v.t. to make an invoice of; to send an invoice to. [apparently from Old French envoy = dispatch of goods (envoyer = send)]

invoke /ɪn'vəʊk/ v.t. 1. to call on (a deity etc.) in prayer or as a witness. 2. to appeal to (a law, authority etc.) for protection or help. 3. to summon (a spirit) by charms. 4. to ask earnestly for (vengeance etc.). [from French from Latin vocare = call]

involuntary /ɪn'vɒləntərɪ/ adj. done without exercise of the will; not controlled by the will. —**involuntarily** adv., **involuntariness** n. [from Latin]

involute /'ɪnvəluːt, -ljuːt/ adj. 1. involved, intricate. 2. spirally curved. —n. the locus of a point fixed on a straight line that rolls without sliding on a curve and is in the plane of that curve. [from Latin]

involuted /'ɪnvəluːtɪd/ adj. complicated, abstruse.

involution /ɪnvə'luːʃən/ n. 1. involving; intricacy; entanglement. 2. curling inwards; a part so curled.

involve /ɪn'vɒlv/ v.t. 1. to cause to share (in) an experience or effect; to include or affect in its operation. 2. to contain within itself, to make necessary as a condition or result. 3. to implicate. 4. (in past participle) concerned (in); complicated in thought or form. —**involvement** n. [from Latin volvere = roll]

invulnerable /ɪn'vʌlnərəbəl/ adj. that cannot be wounded or hurt (especially figuratively). —**invulnerability** /-'bɪlɪtɪ/ n., **invulnerably** adv. [from Latin]

inward /'ɪnwəd/ adj. 1. directed towards the inside, going in. 2. situated within. 3. mental, spiritual. —adv. (also **inwards**) 1. towards the inside. 2. within the mind or spirit. [Old English]

inwardly adv. 1. on the inside. 2. not aloud. 3. in the mind or spirit. [Old English]

inwardness n. inner nature; spirituality.

inwrought /ɪn'rɔːt, attrib. 'ɪn-/ adj. (of fabric) decorated (with a pattern); (of a pattern) wrought (in or on fabric).

INXS n. internationally-acclaimed Australian rock band, formed in Sydney in the late 1970s around lead singer Michael Hutchence. Their first worldwide hit album Kick was released in 1988.

Io /'aɪəʊ/ n. in astronomy, the third largest moon of the planet Jupiter, 3,600 km/2,240 mi in diameter, orbiting in 1.77 days at a distance of 413,000 km/257,000 mi. It is the most volcanically active body in the solar system, covered by hundreds of vents that erupt not lava but sulphur, giving Io an orange-coloured surface.

iodide /'aɪədaɪd/ n. a compound formed between iodine and another element in which the iodine is the more electronegative element (see ◊electro-negativity, ◊halide).

iodine /'aɪədiːn, -ɪn/ n. a greyish-black nonmetallic element, symbol I, atomic number 53, relative atomic mass 126.9044. It is a member of the ◊halogen group. Its crystals give off, when heated, a violet vapour with an irritating odour resembling that of chlorine. It only occurs in combination with other elements. As a mineral nutrient it is vital to the proper functioning of the thyroid gland, where it occurs in trace amounts as part of the hormone thyroxine. Iodine is used in photography, in medicine as an antiseptic, and in making dyes. [from French from Greek iōdēs = violet-like (ion = violet)]

iodize /'aɪədaɪz/ v.t. to impregnate with iodine.

iodoform n. (technical name **triiodomethane**) CHI_3, an antiseptic that crystallizes into yellow hexagonal plates. It is soluble in ether, alcohol, and chloroform, but not in water.

IOM abbreviation of Isle of Man.

ion /'aɪən/ n. an atom, or group of atoms, which is either positively charged (**cation**) or negatively charged (**anion**), as a result of the loss or gain of electrons during chemical reactions or exposure to certain forms of radiant energy. [Greek, participle of eimi = go]

Iona /aɪ'əʊnə/ an island in the Inner Hebrides; area 2,100 acres/850 hectares. A centre of early Christianity, it is the site of a monastery founded in 563 by St ◊Columba. It later became a burial ground for Irish, Scottish, and Norwegian kings. It has a 13th-century abbey.

ion engine a rocket engine that uses ions (charged particles) rather than hot gas for propulsion. Ion engines have been successfully tested in space, where they will

eventually be used for gradual rather than sudden velocity changes. In an ion engine, atoms of mercury, for example, are ionized (given an electric charge by an electric field) and then accelerated at high speed by a more powerful electric field.

Ionesco /iːə'neskəʊ/ Eugène 1912– . Romanian-born French dramatist, a leading exponent of the Theatre of the ◊Absurd. Most of his plays are in one act and concern the futility of language as a means of communication. These include La Cantatrice chauve/The Bald Prima Donna 1950 and La Leçon/The Lesson 1951.

I am in the position of someone who hopes to win first prize in a lottery without having bought a ticket.

Eugène Ionesco
Fragments of a Journal

---

ion exchange the process whereby the ions in one compound replace the ions in another. The exchange occurs because one of the products is insoluble in water. For example, when hard water is passed over an ion-exchange resin, the dissolved calcium and magnesium ions are replaced by either sodium or hydrogen ions, so the hardness is removed. Commercial water softeners use ion-exchange resins. The addition of ◊washing-soda crystals to hard water is also an example of ion exchange:
$$Na_2CO_{3\,(aq)} + CaSO_{4\,(aq)} \rightarrow CaCO_{3\,(s)} + Na_2SO_{4\,(aq)}.$$

ion half equation equation that describes the reactions occurring at the electrodes of a chemical cell or in electrolysis. It indicates which ion is losing electrons (oxidation) or gaining electrons (reduction). Examples are given from the electrolysis of dilute hydrochloric acid (HCl):
$$2Cl^- - 2e^- \rightarrow Cl_2 \text{ (positive electrode)}$$
$$2H^+ + 2e^- \rightarrow H_2 \text{ (negative electrode)}$$

Ionia /aɪ'əʊnɪə/ in classical times the W coast of Asia Minor, settled about 1000 BC by a Hellenic people from beyond the Black Sea who crossed the Balkans around 1980 BC and invaded Asia Minor. Driven back by the ◊Hittites, they settled all over mainland Greece, later being supplanted by the ◊Achaeans. Ionia included the cities of Ephesus, Miletus, and later Smyrna. **Ionian** adj. & n.

Ionic /aɪ'ɒnɪk/ adj. of an order of Greek architecture characterized by columns with scroll-shapes on either side of the capital. [from Latin from Greek]

ionic /aɪ'ɒnɪk/ adj. of or using ions. —**ionically** adv.

ionic bond the bond produced when atoms of one element donate electrons to another element that accepts the electrons, forming positively and negatively charged ◊ions respectively. The electrostatic attraction between the oppositely charged ions constitutes the bond.

ionic compound a substance composed of oppositely charged ions. All salts, most bases, and some acids are examples of ionic compounds. They possess the following general properties: they are crystalline solids with a high melting point; are soluble in water and insoluble in organic solvents; and always conduct electricity when molten or in aqueous solution. A typical ionic compound is sodium chloride (Na^+Cl^-).

ionic equation an equation showing only those ions in a chemical reaction that actually undergo a change, either by combining together to form an insoluble salt or by combining together to form one or more molecular compounds. Examples are the precipitation of insoluble barium sulphate when barium and sulphate ions are combined in solution, and the production of ammonia and water from ammonium hydroxide:
$$Ba^{2+}_{(aq)} + SO_4{}^{2-}_{(aq)} \rightarrow BaSO_{4(s)}$$
$$NH_4{}^+_{(aq)} + OH^-_{(aq)} \rightarrow NH_{3(g)} + H_2O_{(l)}$$
The other ions in the mixtures do not take part and are called ◊spectator ions.

ionization n. the process of ion formation. It can be achieved in two ways. The first way is by the loss or gain of electrons by atoms to form positive or negative ions:
$$Na - e^- \rightarrow Na^+ \quad 1/2Cl_2 + e^- \rightarrow Cl^-$$
In the second mechanism, ions are formed when a covalent bond breaks, as when hydrogen chloride gas is dissolved in water. One portion of the the molecule retains both electrons, forming a negative ion, and the other portion

becomes positively charged. This bond-fission process is sometimes called disassociation:

$$HCl_{(g)} + aq \rightarrow H^+_{(aq>} + Cl^-_{(aq)}$$

ionize /'aɪənaɪz/ *v.t.* to convert or be converted into an ion or ions. **—ionization** /-'zeɪʃən/ *n.*

ionizing radiation radiation that knocks electrons from atoms during its passage, thereby leaving ions in its path. Electrons and alpha particles are much more ionizing than are neutrons or ◊gamma radiation.

ionosphere /aɪ'ɒnəsfɪə/ *n.* an ionized layer of Earth's outer atmosphere (60–1,000 km/38–620 mi) that contains sufficient free electrons to modify the way in which radio waves are propagated, for instance by reflecting them back to Earth. **—ionospheric** /-'ferik/ *adj.*

ion plating a method of applying corrosion-resistant metal coatings.

iota /aɪ'əʊtə/ *n.* **1.** the ninth letter of the Greek alphabet (ι, I) = i. **2.** the smallest possible amount, a jot. [Greek *iōta*]

IOU /aɪəu'ju:/ *n.* a signed document acknowledging a debt. [= I owe you]

IOW abbreviation of Isle of Wight.

Iowa /'aɪəwə/ state of the midwest USA; nickname Hawkeye State; **area** 145,800 sq km/56,279 sq mi; **capital** Des Moines; **population** (1984) 2,837,000; **history** part of the ◊Louisiana Purchase in 1803, it remains an area of small farms; it became a state 1846.

IPA abbreviation of International Phonetic Alphabet.

ipecacuanha /ɪpɪkæku'ɑ:nə/ *n.* or **ipecac** the root of a South American plant (*Cephaëlis ipecacuanha*), used as an emetic or purgative. [from Portuguese from Tupi-Guarani = emetic creeper]

ipso facto /'ɪpsəu 'fæktəu/ by that very fact. [Latin]

IQ abbreviation of intelligence quotient, the ratio between a subject's mental and chronological ages, multiplied by 100. A score of 100 ± 10 is considered average. See ◊intelligence test.

Iqbāl /'ɪkbɑ:l/ Muhammad 1875–1938. Islamic poet and thinker. His literary works, in Urdu and Persian, were mostly verse in the classical style, suitable for public recitation. His most celebrated work, the Persian *Asrā-e khūdi/Secrets of the Self* 1915, put forward a theory of the self that was opposite to the traditional abnegation found in Islam. He was an influence on the movement that led to the creation of Pakistan.

Ir symbol for iridium.

ir-[1,2] see ◊in[1,2].

IRA abbreviation of ◊Irish Republican Army.

Iráklion /i'ræklɪən/ or **Heraklion** largest city and capital (since 1971) of Crete, Greece; population (1981) 102,000.

Iran /i'rɑ:n/ Islamic Republic of; country in SW Asia, bounded to the N by the USSR and the Caspian Sea, to the E by Afghanistan and Pakistan, to the S and SW by the Gulf of Oman, to the W by Iraq, and to the NW by Turkey; **area** 1,648,000 sq km/636,128 sq mi; **capital** Tehran; **physical** plateau surrounded by mountains, including Elburz and Zagros; Lake Rezayeh; Dasht-Ekhavir desert; occupies islands of Abu Musa, Greater Tunb and Lesser Tunb in the Gulf; **leader of the Revolution** Ali Khamenei from 1989; **head of government** Ali Akbar Rafsanjani from 1989; **political system** authoritarian Islamic republic; **exports** carpets, cotton textiles, metalwork, leather goods, oil, petrochemicals, fruit; **population** (1989 est) 51,005,000; **language** Farsi; **recent history** British, US and Soviet forces left Iran in 1946. In 1951 Prime Minister Mossadeq nationalized the oilfields, but was deposed in 1953; the shah took control of the government and introduced a single-party system. From 1978 Ayatollah Khomeini organized opposition to the shah from France; in 1979 the shah left Iran and Khomeini returned to create an Islamic state. Students seized US hostages at the embassy in Tehran. In 1980 the first Gulf War against Iraq began, and lasted until 1988. In 1981 the US hostages were released. Before his death in 1989, Khomeini called for the murder of British writer Salman Rushdie. In June Ali Khamenei was elected interim Leader of the Revoluion and the Speaker of the Iranian parliament, Ali Akbar Rafsanjani, was elected president. A secret oil deal with Israel was discovered.

Irangate /i'rɑ:ngeɪt Iɪ'rɑ:ngeɪt/ *n.* a US political scandal involving senior members of the Reagan administration (called this to echo the Nixon administration's ◊Watergate). Arms, including Hawk missiles, were sold to Iran via Israel (at a time when the USA was publicly calling for a worldwide ban on sending arms to Iran), violating the law prohibiting the sale of US weapons for resale to a third country listed as a 'terrorist nation', as well as the law requiring sales above $14 million to be reported to Congress.

Iranian language the main language of Iran, more commonly known as ◊Persian or Farsi.

Iran-Iraq War 1. the war between Iran and Iraq 1980–88, claimed by the former to have begun with the Iraq offensive on 21 Sept 1980, and by the latter with the Iranian shelling of border posts on 4 Sept 1980. Occasioned by a boundary dispute over the ◊Shatt-al-Arab waterway, it fundamentally arose because of Iran's encouragement of the Shi'ite majority in Iraq to rise against the Sunni government of Saddam Hussein. An estimated 1 million people died in the war. **2.** see ◊Gulf War.

Iraq /i'rɑ:k/ Republic of; country in SW Asia, bounded to the N by Turkey, to the E by Iran; to the S by the Persian Gulf, Kuwait, and Saudi Arabia; to the SW by Jordan; and to the W by Syria; **area** 434,924 sq km/167,881 sq mi; **capital** Baghdad; **physical** mountains in N, desert in W; wide valley of rivers Tigris and Euphrates NW-SE; **head of state and government** Saddam Hussein At-Takriti from 1979; **political system** one-party Socialist republic; **exports** dates, wool, oil; **population** (1989 est) 27,610,000; **language** Arabic; **recent history** became a League of Nations protectorate in 1920; in 1921 the Hashemite dynasty, with Faisal I as king, was established. Independence achieved in 1932. The monarchy was overthrown and Iraq became a republic in 1958. In 1968 a military coup put Gen al-Bakr in power; replaced by Saddam Hussein in 1979. The Gulf War with Iran broke out in 1980, lasting until 1988. General peace terms were agreed in 1990. In August 1990 Iraq invaded and annexed Kuwait. US forces massed in Saudi Arabia at the request of King Fahd. A UN resolution ordered Iraqi withdrawal and imposed a total trade ban; a UN resolution sanctioning force was approved. Saddam Hussein released all foreign hostages. In Jan 1991 an aerial assault by allied forces began, destroying the Iraqi infrastructure. Land-sea-air offensives were successful. As the Gulf war ended, Saddam Hussein brutally suppressed uprisings by the Kurds and Shias.

irascible /i'ræsɪbəl/ *adj.* irritable, hot-tempered. **—irascibility** /-'bɪlɪtɪ/ *n.*, **irascibly** *adv.* [from Latin *irasci* = grow angry]

irate /aɪ'reɪt/ *adj.* angry, enraged. [from Latin *iratus*]

ire /'aɪə/ *n.* (*literary*) anger. [from Old French from Latin *ira* = anger]

Ireland, Northern constituent part of the UK; **area** 13,460 sq km/5,196 sq mi; **capital** Belfast; **physical** Mourne mountains, Belfast Lough and Lough Neagh; Giant's Causeway; comprises the six counties (Antrim, Armagh, Down, Fermanagh, Londonderry, and Tyrone) that form part of Ireland's northernmost province of Ulster; **exports** engineering, especially shipbuilding, textile machinery, aircraft components; linen and synthetic textiles; processed foods, especially dairy and poultry products—all affected by the 1980s depression and political unrest; **population** (1986) 1,567,000; **language** English; **recent history** the creation of Northern Ireland dates from 1921 when the mainly Protestant counties of Ulster withdrew from the newly established Irish Free State. Spasmodic outbreaks of violence by the IRA continued, but only in 1968–69 were there serious disturbances arising from Protestant political dominance and discrimination against the Roman Catholic minority in employment and housing. British troops were sent to restore peace and protect Catholics, but disturbances continued and in 1972 the parliament at Stormont was prorogued, and superseded by direct rule from Westminster.

Ireland, Republic of; country occupying the main part of the island of Ireland, off the NW coast of Europe. It is bounded to the E by the Irish Sea, to the S and W by the Atlantic, and to the NE by Northern Ireland; **area** 70,282 sq km/27,146 sq mi; **capital** Dublin; **physical** central plateau surrounded by hills; rivers Shannon, Liffey, Boyne; **head of state** Mary Robinson from 1990; **head of government** Charles Haughey from 1987; **political system** democratic republic; **exports** livestock, dairy products, Irish whiskey, microelectronic components and assemblies, mining and engineering products, chemicals, tobacco. clothing; tourism is important; **population** (1989 est) 3,734,00; **language** Irish and English; **recent history** 1937 independence achieved from Britain; Eire left the Commonwealth in 1949 and became the Republic of Ireland.

Irene /aɪˈriːni/ in Greek mythology, the goddess of peace (Roman **Pax**).

Irene, St /aɪˈriːni/ c.752–c.803. Byzantine emperor 797–802. The wife of Leo IV (750–80), she became regent for their son Constantine (771–805) on Leo's death. In 797 she deposed her son, had his eyes put out, and assumed full title of *basileus* (emperor), ruling in her own right until deposed and exiled to Lesvos by a revolt in 802. She was made a saint by the Greek Orthodox church for her attacks on iconoclasts.

Irian Jaya /ˈɪriən ˈdʒaɪə/ the western portion of the island of New Guinea, part of Indonesia; **area** 420,000 sq km/162,000 sq mi; **capital** Jayapura; **population** (1980) 1,174,000; **history** part of the Dutch East Indies in 1828 as Western New Guinea; retained by the Netherlands after Indonesian independence in 1949 but ceded to Indonesia in 1963 by the United Nations and remained part of Indonesia by an Act of Free Choice 1969. In the 1980s, 283,500 hectares/700,000 acres were given over to Indonesia's controversial transmigration programme for the resettlement of farming families from overcrowded Java, causing destruction of rain forests and displacing indigenous people.

iridaceous /ɪrɪˈdeɪʃəs/ *adj.* of the iris family (Iridaceae).

iridescent /ɪrɪˈdesənt/ *adj.* showing rainbow-like colours; changing colour with position. —**iridescence** *n.* [from Latin *iris* = rainbow]

iridium /ɪˈrɪdiəm/ *n.* hard, brittle, silver-white, metallic element, symbol Ir, atomic number 77, relative atomic mass 192.2. It is twice as heavy as lead and is resistant to tarnish and corrosion. It is one of the so-called platinum group of metals; it occurs in platinum ores and as a free metal with osmium in osmiridium, a natural alloy that includes platinum, ruthenium, and rhodium. [Latin *iridis* = rainbow]

iris /ˈaɪərɪs/ *n.* 1. the circular coloured membrane behind the cornea of the eye, with a circular opening (the pupil) in the centre. 2. a perennial herbaceous plant of the genus *Iris* usually with tuberous roots, sword-shaped leaves, and showy flowers. 3. a diaphragm with a hole of variable size. [from Latin from Greek = rainbow]

Irish /ˈaɪərɪʃ/ *adj.* of Ireland; of or like its people. —*n.* the Celtic language of Ireland. **the Irish**, the people of Ireland. **Irish stew**, a stew of mutton, potato, and onion. [from Old English]

Irish Gaelic first official language of the Irish Republic, but much less widely used than the second official language, English. See ◊Gaelic language.

Irishman *n.* (*plural* **Irishmen**) a man of Irish birth or descent. —**Irishwoman** *n.fem.* (*plural* **Irishwomen**)

Irish National Liberation Army (INLA) a guerrilla organization committed to the end of British rule in Northern Ireland and the incorporation of Ulster into the Irish Republic. The INLA was a 1974 offshoot of the Irish Republican Army. Among the INLA's activities was the killing of British politician Airey Neave in 1979.

Irish Republican Army (IRA) a militant Irish nationalist organization whose aim is to create a united Irish socialist republic including Ulster. The paramilitary wing of ◊Sinn Féin, it was founded in 1919 by Michael ◊Collins and fought a successful war against Britain 1919–21. It came to the fore again in 1939 with a bombing campaign in Britain, and was declared illegal in Eire. Its activities intensified from 1968 onwards, as the civil-rights disorders (the Troubles) in Northern Ireland developed. In 1970 a group in the north broke away to become the **Provisional IRA**; their commitment is to the expulsion of the British from Northern Ireland.

irk *v.t.* to annoy, to be tiresome to.

irksome /ˈɜːksəm/ *adj.* tiresome, annoying.

Irkutsk /ɪəˈkutsk/ city in S USSR; population (1987) 609,000. It produces coal, iron, steel, and machine tools. Founded in 1652, it began to grow after the Trans-Siberian railway reached it in 1898.

iron /ˈaɪən/ *n.* 1. hard, malleable and ductile, silver-grey, metallic element, symbol Fe (from Latin *ferrum*), atomic number 26, relative atomic mass 55.847. It is the fourth most abundant element (the second most abundant metal, after aluminium) in the Earth's crust. 2. a tool or implement made of iron; an implement (originally of iron) with a flat base that is heated for smoothing cloth or clothes etc.; a golf club with an iron or steel head and a sloping face; (in *plural*) fetters, stirrups; (often in *plural*) a leg support to rectify malformations etc. 3. a preparation of iron as a tonic. —*adj.* 1. of iron. 2. very robust. 3. unyielding, merciless. —*v.t.* to smooth (cloth or clothes etc.) with an iron. **iron grey**, grey like the colour of freshly broken iron. **ironing board**, a narrow flat stand on which clothes etc. are ironed. **iron lung**, a rigid case over a patient's body for prolonged artificial respiration. **iron out**, to remove (difficulties etc.). **iron ration**, a small supply of tinned food etc. for use in an emergency. **many irons in the fire**, many undertakings or resources. **strike while the iron is hot**, to act promptly at a good opportunity. [Old English]

Iron Age the developmental stage of human technology when weapons and tools were made from iron. Iron was produced in Thailand by about 1600 BC but was considered inferior in strength to bronze until about 1000 when metallurgical techniques improved and the alloy steel was produced by adding carbon during the smelting process.

ironclad *adj.* covered in or protected with iron. —*n.* (*historical*) a wooden warship covered with armour plate. The first to be constructed was the French *Gloire* 1858, but the first to be launched was the British HMS *Warrior* 1859. The design was replaced by battleships of all-metal construction in the 1890s.

Iron Cross a medal awarded for valour in the German armed forces. Instituted in Prussia in 1813, it consists of a Maltese cross of iron, edged with silver.

Iron Curtain in Europe after World War II, the symbolic boundary between capitalist West and communist East. The term was popularized by the UK prime minister Winston Churchill from 1945.

Iron Guard a pro-fascist group controlling Romania in the 1930s. To counter its influence, King Carol II established a dictatorship in 1938 but the Iron Guard forced him to abdicate in 1940.

ironic /aɪˈrɒnɪk/ *adj.* (*also* **ironical**) using or displaying irony. —**ironically** *adv.* [from French or Latin from Greek *eirōnikos* = dissembling]

ironmaster *n.* a manufacturer of iron.

ironmonger /ˈaɪənmʌŋgə/ *n.* a dealer in hardware etc. —**ironmongery** *n.*

iron ore any mineral from which iron is extracted. The chief iron ores are ◊**magnetite**, a black oxide; ◊**hematite**, or kidney ore, a reddish oxide; **limonite**, a black hydroxide; and **siderite**, a brownish carbonate.

iron pyrites or **pyrite** FeS$_2$, a common iron ore. Brassy yellow, and occurring in cubic crystals, it is often called 'fool's gold'.

Ironsides /ˈaɪənsaɪdz/ *n.* 1. a man of great bravery. 2. (as *plural*) Cromwell's cavalry troopers during the English Civil War, so called by their Royalist opponents in allusion to their hardiness in battle.

ironstone *n.* 1. hard iron ore. 2. a kind of hard, white pottery.

ironware *n.* things made of iron.

ironwork *n.* work in iron; things made of iron.

ironworks *n. pl.* (often treated as *singular*) a place where iron is smelted or where heavy iron goods are made.

irony /ˈaɪərəni/ *n.* 1. the expression of one's meaning by language of the opposite or a different tendency, e. g. adoption of a laudatory tone for the purpose of ridicule. 2. the ill-timed or perverse occurrence of an event or circumstance that would in itself be desirable. —**dramatic** *or* **tragic irony**, (originally in Greek tragedy) the use of statements etc. whose implications are understood by the audience but not by the person(s) addressed or concerned (occasional including the speaker). **Socratic irony**, a pose of ignorance assumed in order to confute others by enticing them into a display of supposed knowledge. [from Latin from Greek = simulated ignorance (*eirōn* = dissembler)]

Iroquois /ˈɪrəkwɔɪ/ *n.* a member of a confederation of NE North American Indians, the Six Nations (Cayuga, Mohawk, Oneida, Onondaga, and Seneca, with the Tuscarora after 1723), traditionally formed by Hiawatha (actually a priestly title) in 1570.

irradiate /ɪˈreɪdieɪt/ *v.t.* 1. to subject to radiation; to shine upon, to light up. 2. to throw light on (a subject). —**irradiation** /-ˈeɪʃən/ *n.* in technology, subjecting anything to radiation, including cancer tumours. Food can be sterilized by bombarding it with low-strength gamma rays. Although the process is now legal in several countries, uncertainty remains about possible long-term effects on consumers from irradiated food. [from Latin *radius* = ray]

irrational /ɪ'ræʃənəl/ *adj.* 1. unreasonable, illogical. 2. not endowed with reason. 3. not commensurable with natural numbers. **irrationality** /-'nælɪtɪ/ *n.*, **irrationally** *adv.* [from Latin]

irrationalism *n.* a feature of many philosophies rather than a philosophical movement. Irrationalists deny that the world can be comprehended by conceptual thought, and often see the human mind as determined by unconscious forces.

irrational number a number that cannot be expressed as an exact ◊fraction. Irrational numbers include some square roots (for example, $\sqrt{2}$, $\sqrt{3}$ and $\sqrt{5}$ are irrational) and numbers such as π (the ratio of the circumference of a circle to its diameter, which is approximately equal to 3.14159) and e (the base of ◊natural logarithms, approximately 2.71828).

Irrawaddy /ɪrə'wɒdi/ (Myanmar *Ayeyarwady*) chief river of Myanmar, flowing roughly N to S for 2,090 km/1,300 mi across the centre of the country into the Bay of Bengal. Its sources are the Mali and N'mai rivers; its chief tributaries are the Chindwin and the Shweli.

irreconcilable /ɪ'rekənsaɪləbəl/ *adj.* 1. implacably hostile. 2. incompatible. —**irreconcilability** /-'bɪlɪtɪ/ *n.*, **irreconcilably** *adv.*

irrecoverable /ɪrɪ'kʌvərəbəl/ *adj.* that cannot be recovered or remedied. —**irrecoverably** *adv.*

irredeemable /ɪrɪ'diːməbəl/ *adj.* that cannot be redeemed; hopeless. —**irredeemably** *adv.*

irredentist /ɪrɪ'dentɪst/ *n.* person who wishes to reclaim the lost territories of a state. The term derives from an Italian political party founded about 1878 intending to incorporate Italian-speaking areas into the newly formed state.

irreducible /ɪrɪ'djuːsɪbəl/ *adj.* that cannot be reduced or simplified. —**irreducibly** *adv.*

irrefutable /ɪ'refjʊtəbəl, ɪrɪ'fjuː-/ *adj.* that cannot be refuted. —**irrefutably** *adv.* [from Latin]

irregular /ɪ'regjʊlə/ *adj.* 1. not regular; unsymmetrical, uneven, varying. 2. contrary to a rule, principle, or custom. 3. (of troops) not in the regular army. 4. abnormal. 5. (of a verb, noun etc.) not inflected normally. 6. disorderly. —*n.* (in *plural*) irregular troops. —**irregularity** /-'lærɪtɪ/ *n.*, **irregularly** *adv.* [from Old French from Latin]

irrelevant /ɪ'relɪvənt/ *adj.* not relevant. —**irrelevance** *n.*, **irrelevancy** *n.*, **irrelevantly** *adv.*

irreligious /ɪrɪ'lɪdʒəs/ *adj.* lacking or hostile to religion. [from Latin]

irremediable /ɪrɪ'miːdiəbəl/ *adj.* that cannot be remedied. —**irremediably** *adv.* [from Latin]

irremovable /ɪrɪ'muːvəbəl/ *adj.* that cannot be removed, especially from office. —**irremovably** *adv.*

irreparable /ɪ'repərəbəl/ *adj.* that cannot be rectified or made good. —**irreparably** *adv.* [from Old French from Latin]

irreplaceable /ɪrɪ'pleɪsəbəl/ *adj.* that cannot be replaced. —**irreplaceability** /-'bɪlɪtɪ/ *n.*, **irreplaceably** *adv.*

irrepressible /ɪrɪ'presɪbəl/ *adj.* that cannot be repressed or restrained. —**irrepressibly** *adv.*

irreproachable /ɪrɪ'prəʊtʃəbəl/ *adj.* faultless, blameless. —**irreproachably** *adv.* [from French]

irresistible /ɪrɪ'zɪstɪbəl/ *adj.* too strong or delightful or convincing to be resisted. —**irresistibly** *adv.* [from Latin]

irresolute /ɪ'rezəluːt/ *adj.* feeling or showing uncertainty, hesitating. —**irresolutely** *adv.*, **irresoluteness** *n.*, **irresolution** /-'luːʃən/ *n.*

irrespective /ɪrɪ'spektɪv/ *adj.* not taking account *of*, regardless *of*.

irresponsible /ɪrɪ'spɒnsɪbəl/ *adj.* acting or done without due sense of responsibility; not responsible for one's conduct. —**irresponsibility** /-'bɪlɪtɪ/ *n.*, **irresponsibly** *adv.*

irretrievable /ɪrɪ'triːvəbəl/ *adj.* that cannot be retrieved or recovered. —**irretrievably** *adv.*

irreverent /ɪ'revərənt/ *adj.* lacking reverence. —**irreverence** *n.*, **irreverently** *adv.* [from Latin]

irreversible /ɪrɪ'vɜːsɪbəl/ *adj.* not reversible or alterable. —**irreversibly** *adv.*

irrevocable /ɪ'revəkəbəl/ *adj.* unable to be revoked, unalterable; gone beyond recall. —**irrevocably** *adv.* [from Latin]

irrigate /'ɪrɪgeɪt/ *v.t.* 1. to supply (land or crops) with water by means of streams, channels, pipes etc. 2. to wash (a wound) with a constant flow of liquid. —**irrigation** /-'geɪʃən/ *n.*, **irrigator** *n.* [from Latin *rigare* = moisten]

irritable /'ɪrɪtəbəl/ *adj.* 1. easily annoyed, bad-tempered. 2. (of an organ etc.) sensitive. —**irritability** /-'bɪlɪtɪ/ *n.*, **irritably** *adv.* [from Latin]

irritant /'ɪrɪtənt/ *adj.* causing irritation. —*n.* an irritant substance.

irritate /'ɪrɪteɪt/ *v.t.* 1. to annoy, to rouse slight anger or impatience in. 2. to cause itching in (a part of the body). 3. to stimulate (an organ) to action. —**irritation** /-'teɪʃən/ *n.*, **irritative** *adj.* [from Latin *irritare*]

irrupt /ɪ'rʌpt/ *v.i.* to enter forcibly or violently (*into*). —**irruption** *n.* [from Latin *rumpere* = break]

Irving /'ɜːvɪŋ/ Henry. Stage name of John Brodribb 1838–1905. English actor who established his reputation from 1871, chiefly at the Lyceum Theatre in London, where he became manager in 1878. He staged a series of successful Shakespearean productions, including *Romeo and Juliet* 1882, with himself and Ellen ◊Terry playing the leading roles. He was the first actor to be knighted, in 1895.

Irving Washington 1783–1859. US essayist and short-story writer. He published a mock-heroic *History of New York* in 1809, supposedly written by the Dutchman 'Diedrich Knickerbocker'. In 1815 he went to England where he published *The Sketch Book of Geoffrey Crayon, Gent.* 1820, which contained such stories as 'Rip van Winkle' and 'The Legend of Sleepy Hollow'.

Whenever a man's friends begin to compliment him about looking young, he may be sure that they think he is growing old.

Washington Irving
Bracebridge Hall 'Batchelors'

---

is *v.i.* see ◊be.

Isaac /'aɪzək/ in the Old Testament, a Hebrew patriarch, son of Abraham and Sarah, and father of Esau and Jacob.

Isaacs /'aɪzəks/ Alick 1921–1967. Scottish virologist who, with Jean Lindemann, in 1957 discovered ◊interferon.

Isabella /ɪzə'belə/ two Spanish queens:

Whosoever hath a good presence and a good fashion, carries continual letters of recommendation.

Isabella I of Spain
as reported by Francis Bacon in *Apothegms*

Isabella I the Catholic 1451–1504. Queen of Castile from 1474, after the death of her brother Henry IV. By her marriage with Ferdinand of Aragon 1469, the crowns of two of the Christian states in the Moorish-held Spanish peninsula were united. In her reign, during 1492, the Moors were driven out of Spain; she introduced the ◊Inquisition into Castile, expelled the Jews, and gave financial encouragement to ◊Columbus. Her youngest daughter was Catherine of Aragon, first wife of Henry VIII of England.

Isabella II 1830–1904. Queen of Spain from 1833, when she succeeded her father Ferdinand VII (1784–1833). The Salic Law banning a female sovereign had been repealed by the Cortes (parliament), but her succession was disputed by her uncle Don Carlos de Bourbon (1788–1855). After seven years of civil war, the ◊Carlists were defeated. She abdicated in favour of her son Alfonso XII in 1868.

Isaiah /aɪ'zaɪə/ 8th century BC. In the Old Testament, the first major Hebrew prophet. The son of Amos, he was probably of high rank, and lived largely in Jerusalem.

-isation, -ise variants of -ization, -ize.

ISBN abbreviation of international standard book number.

ischaemia *n.* reduction of blood supply to any part of the body.

Isfahan /ɪsfə'hɑːn/ or **Eşfahan** industrial (steel, textiles, carpets) city in central Iran; population (1986) 1,001,000. It was the ancient capital (1598–1722) of ◊Abbas I and its

Isherwood Lifelong friend of W H Auden, English novelist Christopher Isherwood was a leading intellectual of the 1930s.

features include the Great Square, the Grand Mosque, and the Hall of Forty Pillars.

-ish suffix forming adjectives **a.** from nouns, in the senses 'having the qualities of' (*knavish*), 'of the nationality of' (*Danish*); **b.** from adjectives, in the sense of 'somewhat' (*thickish*); **c.** (*colloquial*) of an approximate age or time (*fortyish*). [Old English]

Isherwood /'ɪʃəwʊd/ Christopher (William Bradshaw) 1904–1986. English novelist. Educated at Cambridge, he lived in Germany 1929–33 just before Hitler's rise to power, a period that inspired *Mr Norris Changes Trains* 1935 and *Goodbye to Berlin* 1939, creating the character of Sally Bowles (the basis of the musical *Cabaret* 1968).

We live in stirring times—tea-stirring times.
Christopher Isherwood
Mr Norris Changes Trains

Ishiguro /ɪʃi'gʊrəʊ/ Kazuo 1954– . Japanese-born British novelist. His novel *An Artist of the Floating World* won the 1986 Whitbread Prize, and *The Remains of the Day* won the Booker Prize 1989.

Ishmael /'ɪʃmeɪəl/ in the Old Testament, the son of Abraham and his wife Sarah's Egyptian maid Hagar; traditional ancestor of Muhammad and the Arab people. He and his mother were driven away by Sarah's jealousy. Muslims believe that it was Ishmael, not Isaac, whom God commanded Abraham to sacrifice, and that Ishmael helped Abraham build the ◊Kaaba in Mecca.

Ishtar /'ɪʃtɑ:/ a goddess of love and war worshipped by the Babylonians and Assyrians, and personified as the legendary queen Semiramis.

Isidore of Seville /'ɪzədɔ:/ c.560–636. Bishop of Seville, writer and missionary. His *Ethymologiae* was the model for later medieval encyclopedias and helped to preserve classical thought during the Middle Ages; his *Chronica Maiora* remains an important source for the history of Visigothic Spain.

isinglass /'aɪzɪŋglɑ:s/ n. **1.** a kind of gelatin obtained from fish, especially the sturgeon, and used for jellies, glue etc. **2.** mica. [from obsolete Dutch *huisenblas* = sturgeon's bladder]

Isis /'aɪsɪs/ the principal goddess of ancient Egypt. She was the daughter of Geb and Nut (earth and sky), and as the sister-wife of Osiris searched for his body after his death at the hands of his brother, Set. Her son Horus then defeated and captured Set, but cut off his mother's head because she

would not allow Set to be killed. The cult of Isis ultimately spread to Greece and Rome.

Islam /'ɪzlɑ:m, -'lɑ:m/ n. the religion of Muslims, founded in the Arabian peninsula in the early 7th century AD. It emphasizes the oneness of God, his omnipotence, benificence, and inscrutability. The sacred book is the **Koran** of the prophet ◊Muhammad, the Prophet or Messenger of Allah. There are two main sects: ◊**Sunni** and ◊**Shi'ite**. Other schools include **Sufism**, a mystical movement originating in the 8th century. —**Islamic** /-'læmɪk/ *adj.* [from Arabic = submission (to God), from *aslama* = resign oneself]

Islamabad /ɪz'læməbæd/ capital of Pakistan from 1967, in the Potwar district, at the foot of the Margala Hills and immediately NW of Rawalpindi; population (1981) 201,000. The city was designed by Constantinos Doxiadis in the 1960s. The Federal Capital Territory of Islamabad has an area of 907 sq km/350 sq mi and a population (1985) of 379,000.

Islamic art the art, architecture, and design of Muslim nations and territories. Because the Koran forbids representation in art, Islamic artistry was channelled into calligraphy and ornament. Despite this, there was naturalistic Persian painting, which inspired painters in the Mogul and Ottoman empires. Ceramic tiles decorated mosques and palaces from Spain (Alhambra, Granada) to S Russia and Mogul India (Taj Mahal, Agra). Wood, stone, and stucco sculpture ornamented buildings. Islamic artists produced intricate metalwork and woven textiles and carpets.

island /'aɪlənd/ n. **1.** a piece of land surrounded by water. **2.** a detached or isolated thing; a traffic island. —**islands area**, an administrative area in Scotland, consisting of a number of islands. [Old English, originally *igland*]

islander n. an inhabitant of an island.

isle /aɪl/ n. (*chiefly poetic* and in names) an island, especially a small one. [from Old French from Latin *insula*]

Isle of Man see ◊Man, Isle of.

Isle of Wight see ◊Wight, Isle of.

islet /'aɪlɪt/ n. **1.** a small island. **2.** a detached portion of tissue. [Old French, diminutive of *isle*]

islets of Langerhans /'læŋəhæns/ group of cells within the pancreas responsible for the secretion of the hormone insulin. They are sensitive to the blood sugar, producing more hormone when glucose levels rise.

ism /ɪzəm/ n. (*usually derogative*) any distinctive doctrine or practice.

-ism suffix forming nouns, especially a system or principle (*Conservatism*, *jingoism*), a state or quality (*barbarism*, *heroism*), or a peculiarity in language (*Americanism*). [from French from Latin from Greek]

Ismail /ɪzmɑː'iːl/ 1830–1895. Khedive (governor) of Egypt 1866–79. A grandson of Mehemet Ali, he became viceroy of Egypt in 1863 and in 1866 received the title of khedive from the Ottoman sultan. He amassed huge foreign debts and in 1875 Britain, on Prime Minister Disraeli's suggestion, bought the khedive's Suez Canal shares for nearly £4 million, establishing Anglo-French control of Egypt's finances. In 1879 the UK and France persuaded the sultan to appoint Tewfik, his son, khedive in his place.

Ismail I /ɪzmɑː'iːl/ 1486–1524. Shah of Persia from 1501, founder of the **Safavi dynasty**, who established the first national government since the Arab conquest and Shi'ite Islam as the national religion.

Ismaili /ɪz'maɪlɪ/ n. a sect of ◊Shi'ite Muslims.

isn't /'ɪzənt/ (*colloquial*) is not.

iso- /aɪsʊ-/ in combinations, equal. [from Greek *isos* = equal]

isobar n. a line drawn on maps and weather charts linking all places with the same atmospheric pressure (usually measured in millibars). When used in weather forecasting, the distance between the isobars is an indication of the barometric gradient. —**isobaric** /-'bærɪk/ *adj.* [from Greek *baros* = weight]

isochronous /aɪ'sɒkrənəs/ *adj.* **1.** occupying an equal time. **2.** occurring at the same time. [from Greek *khronos* = time]

isoclinal /aɪsəʊ'klaɪnəl/ *adj.* **1.** corresponding to equal values of magnetic dip. **2.** (in geology, of a fold) with the parts of each side parallel to each other. [from Greek *klinō* = slope]

isolate 568

isolate /'aɪsəleɪt/ *v.t.* **1.** to place apart or alone. **2.** to separate (a patient with a contagious or infectious disease) from others. **3.** to separate (a substance) from a compound. **4.** to insulate (electrical apparatus). —**isolation** /-'leɪʃən/ *n.* [from French from Italian from Latin *insulatus*]

isolationism *n.* in politics, concentration on internal rather than foreign affairs; a foreign policy having no interest in international affairs that do not affect the country's own interests. In the USA, isolationism is usually associated with the Republican Party, especially politicians of the Midwest (for example, the Neutrality Acts 1935–39). Intervention by the USA in both World Wars was initially resisted. In the 1960s some Republicans demanded the removal of the United Nations from American soil. —**isolationist** *n.*

isomer /'aɪsəmə:/ *n.* any of two or more substances whose molecules have the same atoms in different arrangements. —**isomeric** /-'merɪk/ *adj.*, **isomerism** /aɪ'somərɪzəm/ *n.* [German from Greek *meros*= portion]

isometric /aɪsə'metrɪk/ *adj.* **1.** (of muscle action) developing tension while the muscle is prevented from contracting. **2.** (of a drawing or projection) with the plane of projection at equal angles to the three principal axes of the object shown. **3.** of equal measure. [from Greek *isometria* = equality of measure]

isometrics *n. pl.* a system of physical exercises in which muscles are caused to act against each other or against a fixed object.

isomorph /'aɪsəmɔ:f/ *n.* a substance having the same form as another. —**isomorphic** *adj.*, **isomorphous** *adj.* [from Greek *morphē* = form]

isoprene *n.* $CH_2CHC(CH_3)CH_2$ (technical name **methylbutadiene**), colourless, volatile fluid obtained from petroleum and coal, used to make synthetic rubber.

isosceles /aɪ'sɒsɪliːz/ *adj.* (of a triangle) having two sides equal. [Latin from Greek *skelos* = leg]

isotherm /'aɪsəθɜ:m/ *n.* a line on a map connecting places with the same temperature. —**isothermal** /-'θɜ:məl/ *adj.* [from French from Greek *thermē*= heat]

isotope /'aɪsətəʊp/ *n.* any of two or more types of atom of the same element that contain equal numbers of protons but different numbers of neutrons in their nuclei, and hence differ in atomic weight but not in chemical properties. —**isotopic** /-'tɒpɪk/ *adj.* [from Greek *topos* = place (i.e. in the periodic table of elements]

isotropic /aɪsə'trɒpɪk/ *adj.* having the same physical properties in all directions. —**isotropy** /aɪ'sɒtrəpɪ/ *n.* [from Greek *tropos* = turn]

Israel /'ɪzreɪəl/ State of; country in SW Asia, bounded N by Lebanon, E by Syria and Jordan, S by the Gulf of Aqaba, and W by Egypt and the Mediterranean; **area** 20,800 sq km/8,029 sq mi (as at 1949 armistice); **capital** Jerusalem; **physical** coastal plain of Sharon between Haifa and Telo Aviv noted since ancient times for fertility; central mountains of Galilee, Samariq and Judea; river Jordan Rift Vallley along the E is below sea level; Negev desert in the S occupies Golan Heights, West Bank and Gaza; **head of state** Chaim Herzog from 1983; **head of government** Itzhak Shamir from 1986; **political systems** democratic republic; **exports** citrus and other fruit, avocados, chinese leaves, fertilizers, plastics, petrochemicals, textiles, electronics (military, medical, scientific, industrial), electro-optics, precision instruments, aircraft and missiles; **population** (1989 est) 4,477,000; **language** Hebrew and Arabic; **recent history** 1948 state of Israel proclaimed in 1948; 1967 victorious in the Six-Day War with Egypt gaining the West Bank area of Jordan, the Sinai peninsula in Egypt and the Golan Heights in Syria but withdrew from Sinai in 1982; 1974 another Israeli-Arab war called the ◊Yom Kippur War; attacked by Iran during the ◊Gulf War in 1991.

Israeli /ɪz'reɪlɪ/ *adj.* of the modern State of Israel. —*n.* an Israeli person.

Israelite /'ɪzrəlaɪt/ *adj.* of ancient Israel. —*n.* an Israelite person.

Issigonis /ɪsɪ'gəʊnɪs/ Alec 1906–1988. British engineer who designed the Morris Minor 1948 and the Mini-Minor 1959 cars.

issue /'ɪʃuː, 'ɪsjuː/ *n.* **1.** an outgoing or outflow **2.** the issuing of things for use or for sale; the number or quantity issued. **3.** any set of publications in a series issued regularly. **4.** a result, an outcome. **5.** the point in question, an

important topic of discussion or litigation. **6.** a way out; a place of emergence of a stream etc. **7.** (in law, progeny, children. —*v.t./i.* **1.** to go or come or flow out. **2.** to put out for sale or as information etc., to publish; to send out (orders etc.). **3.** to supply or distribute for use. **4.** to result; to originate. —**at issue**, in dispute, under discussion. **join** or **take issue**, to proceed to argue. [from Old French from Latin *exitus*]

-ist suffix forming personal nouns expressing an adherent of a creed etc. in *-ism* (*Marxist, fatalist*), a person concerned with something (*pathologist, tobacconist*), a person who uses a thing (*violinist, motorist*), or a person who does a thing expressed by a verb in *-ize* (*plagiarist*). [French and Latin from Greek]

Istanbul /ɪstæn'buːl/ city and chief seaport of Turkey; population (1985) 5,495,000. It produces textiles, tobacco, cement, glass, and leather. Founded as **Byzantium** about 660 BC, it was renamed **Constantinople** in AD 330 and was the capital of the ◊Byzantine Empire until captured by the Turks in 1453. As **Istamboul** it was capital of the Ottoman Empire until 1922.

isthmus /'ɪsməs/ *n.* a narrow piece of land connecting two larger bodies of land; a narrow connecting part. —**isthmian** *adj.* [Latin from Greek]

it[1] *pron.* (*plural* **they**) **1.** the thing (or occasionally animal or child) previously named or in question; the person in question. **2.** as the subject of an impersonal verb making a general statement about the weather or about circumstances etc., or as an indefinite object. **3.** as a substitute for a deferred subject or object; as the antecedent to a relative pronoun. **4.** exactly what is needed. **5.** the extreme limit of achievement etc. **6.** (*colloquial*) sexual intercourse; sex appeal. **7.** (in children's games) the player who has to catch others. [Old English]

it[2] (*colloquial*) abbreviation of Italian vermouth.

Italian /ɪ'tæliən/ *adj.* of Italy or its people or language. —*n.* **1.** a native or inhabitant of Italy. **2.** the language of Italy. —**Italian vermouth**, sweet vermouth. [from Italian *Italia* = Italy]

Italian art the painting and sculpture of Italy from the early Middle Ages to the present. By the 13th century there was a strong tradition of ◊fresco painting, and a type of Gothic classicism was developed by the sculptors Nicola and Giovanni ◊Pisano. Schools of painting arose in many of the city-states. The early artists of the ◊Renaissance such as ◊Ghiberti, ◊Donatello, ◊Masaccio, and ◊Uccello were based in Florence; by the middle and later part of the century dozens of sculptors and painters were at work there, among them ◊Botticelli, ◊Fra Angelico and Fra Filippo and Filippino ◊Lippi. In Venice the ◊Bellini family of painters influenced their successors ◊Giorgione and ◊Titian, and his most notable pupil, ◊Tintoretto. The High Renaissance was dominated by ◊Leonardo da Vinci, ◊Michelangelo, and ◊Raphael. ◊Bernini and ◊Caravaggio were influential in developing the dramatic 17th-century ◊Baroque style. The rediscovery of classical Roman works inspired Neo-Classicism in the 18th and early 19th centuries, led by ◊Canova and ◊Piranesi.

Italianate /ɪ'tæliəneɪt/ *adj.* of Italian style or appearance. [from Italian *Italianato*]

Italian language a member of the Romance branch of the Indo-European language family, the most direct descendant of the Roman form of Latin. Broadcasting and films have standardized the Italian national tongue, but most Italians speak a regional dialect as well as Standard Italian. The Italian language is also spoken in Switzerland and by people of Italian descent, especially in the USA, Canada, Australia, the UK, and Argentina.

italic /ɪ'tælɪk/ *adj.* **1.** (of printed letters) of a sloping kind now used especially for emphasis and in foreign words. **2.** (of handwriting) compact and pointed like early Italian handwriting. —*n.* **1.** a letter in italic type; such type. **2.** of a form of handwriting (developed in Italy) somewhat resembling this, or a modern adaptation of such a form.

Italic *adj.* of ancient Italy. [from Latin from Greek]

italicize /ɪ'tælɪsaɪz/ *v.t.* to print in italics.

Italy /'ɪtəlɪ/ Republic of; country in S Europe, bounded N by Switzerland and Austria, E by Yugoslavia and the Adriatic Sea, S by the Ionian and Mediterranean seas, and W by the Tyrrhenian Sea and France; **area** 301,300 sq km/ 116,332 sq mi; **capital** Rome; **physical** mountainous

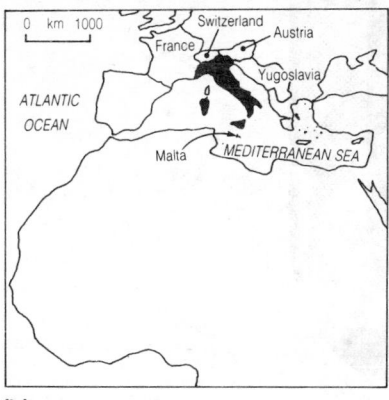

Italy

(Maritime Alps, Dolomites, Apennines); rivers Po, Adige, Arno, Tiber, Rubicon; islands of Sicily, Sardinia, Elba, Capri, Ischia, Lipari, Pantelleria; lakes Como, Maggiore, Garda; **exports** wine, fruit, vegetables, textiles, leather goods, motor vehicles, electrical goods, chemicals, marble (Carrara), sulfur, mercury, iron, steel; **head of state** Francesco Cossiga from 1985; **head of government** Giuilio Andreotti from 1989; **political system** democratic republic; **population** (1990 est) 57,657,000; **language** Italian; **recent history** monarchy replaced by republic in 1946; 1988 Christian Democrats established a five-party coalition including the Socialists; 1989 Communists formed 'shadow government'.

itch *n.* 1. an irritation in the skin; a contagious disease accompanied by this. 2. an impatient desire. —*v.i.* to feel an itch. —**itching palm**, avarice. [Old English]

itchy *adj.* having or causing an itch. —**itchiness** *n.*

item /'aɪtəm/ *n.* any one of enumerated things; a detached piece of news etc. [Latin = in like manner, also]

itemize /'aɪtəmaɪz/ *v.t.* to state by items. —**itemization** /-'zeɪʃən/ *n.*

iterate /'ɪtəreɪt/ *v.t.* to repeat, to state repeatedly. —**iteration** /-'reɪʃən/ *n.*, **iterative** /-rətɪv/ *adj.* [from Latin *iterum* = again]

iteroparity *n.* in biology, the repeated production of offspring at intervals throughout the life cycle. It is usually contrasted with ◊semelparity, where each individual reproduces only once during its life. Most vertebrates are iteroparous.

itinerant /aɪ'tɪnərənt, ɪ-/ *adj.* travelling from place to place. —*n.* an itinerant person. [from Latin *itinerare* (*iter* = journey)]

itinerary /aɪ'tɪnərərɪ, ɪ-/ *n.* a route, a list of places to be visited on a journey. [from Latin]

-itis /-aɪtɪs/ suffix forming nouns, especially names of inflammatory diseases (*appendicitis*) or (*colloquial*) of mental states fancifully regarded as diseases (*electionitis*). [Greek]

Ito /'iːtəʊ/ Hirobumi, Prince 1841–1909. Japanese politician, prime minister 1892–96, 1898, 1900–01. He was a key figure in the modernization of Japan and was involved in the Meiji restoration under ◊Mutsuhito 1866–68 and in government missions to the USA and Europe in the 1870s. As minister for home affairs, he helped draft the Meiji constitution in 1889 and oversaw its implementation as prime minister the following year. While resident-general in Korea, he was assassinated by a Korean Nationalist, which led to Japan's annexation of that country.

its *poss. pron. & adj.* of it, of itself.

it's (*colloquial*) it has, it is.

itself /ɪt'self/ *pron.* emphatic and reflexive form of it. —**by itself**, apart from its surroundings, automatically. **in itself**, viewed in its essential qualities. [Old English]

ITV abbreviation of independent television.

IUCN abbreviation of International Union for the Conservation of Nature, an organization established by the United Nations to promote the conservation of wildlife and habitats as part of the national policies of member states.

IUD abbreviation of intra-uterine (contraceptive) device.

IUPAC abbreviation of International Union of Pure and Applied Chemistry; an organization that recommends the nomenclature to be used for naming substances, the units to be used, and which conventions are to be adopted when describing particular changes.

Ivan /'aɪvən/ six rulers of Russia, including:

Ivan III the Great 1440–1505. Grand duke of Muscovy from 1462, who revolted against Tatar overlordship by refusing tribute to Grand Khan Ahmed 1480. He claimed the title of tsar, and used the double-headed eagle as the Russian state emblem.

Ivan IV the Terrible 1530–1584. Grand duke of Muscovy from 1533; he assumed power in 1544 and was crowned as first tsar of Russia in 1547. He conquered Kazan 1552, Astrakhan 1556, and Siberia 1581. He reformed the legal code and local administration in 1555 and established trade relations with England. In his last years he alternated between debauchery and religious austerities, executing thousands and, in rage, his own son.

Ives /aɪvz/ Charles (Edward) 1874–1954. US composer who experimented with ◊atonal forms, quarter tones, clashing time signatures, and quotations from popular music of the time. He wrote five symphonies, including *Holidays Symphony* 1904–13, chamber music, including the *Concord Sonata*, and the orchestral *Three Places in New England* 1903–14 and *The Unanswered Question* 1908.

Ives Frederic Eugene 1856–1937. US inventor who developed the ◊halftone process of printing photographs in 1878.

IVF abbreviation of ◊in vitro fertilization.

ivory /'aɪvərɪ/ *n.* 1. the hard substance of the tusks of the elephant etc. 2. the creamy-white colour of this. 3. (usually in *plural*) an article made of ivory. 4. (usually in *plural*, *slang*) a dice; a billiard-ball; a piano key; a tooth. —**ivory tower**, seclusion or withdrawal from harsh realities. [from Old French from Latin *ebur*]

Ivory Coast Republic of; country in W Africa, bounded to the N by Mali and Burkina Faso, E by Ghana, S by the Gulf of Guinea, and W by Liberia and Guinea; **area** 322,463 sq km/124,471 sq mi; **capital** Abidjan; capital designate Yamoussoukro; **physical** tropical rainforest in S; savanna and low mountains in N; **head of state and government** Félix Houphouët-Boigny from 1960 **political system** one-party presidential republic since 1960; **exports** coffee, cocoa, timber, petroleum products; **population** (19909 est) 12,070,000; **language** French; **recent history** part of French West Africa 1904 until independence achieved from France in 1960. The name was changed officially to Côte d'Ivoire in 1986.

ivy /'aɪvɪ/ *n.* any tree or shrub of the genus *Hedera* of the ginseng family Araliaceae. English or European ivy *H. helix* has shiny, evergreen, triangular or oval-shaped leaves, and clusters of small, yellowish-green flowers, followed by black berries. It climbs by means of rootlike suckers put out from its stem, and is injurious to trees. [Old English]

Ivy League a collective term for eight long-established universities in the USA. The term arose from the pronunciation of IV, the Roman numeral for four—being the first four East Coast private universities: Harvard, Yale, Columbia, and Brown. The universities of Princeton, Pennsylvania, Dartmouth, and Cornell joined the league later to compete in intercollegiate athletics.

IWW abbreviation of Industrial Workers of the World.

ixia /'ɪksɪə/ *n.* a South African iridaceous plant of the genus *Ixia* with large, showy flowers. [Latin from Greek = kind of thistle]

Ixion /ɪk'saɪən/ in Greek mythology, a king whom Zeus punished for his crimes by binding him to a fiery wheel rolling endlessly through the underworld.

Izmir formerly **Smyrna** port and naval base in Turkey; population (1985) 1,490,000. Products include steel, electronics, and plastics. The largest annual trade fair in the Middle East is held here. It is the headquarters of ◊North Atlantic Treaty Organization SE Command.

j, J /dʒeɪ/ n. (pl. **js, j's**) the 10th letter of the English alphabet. The English value of *j* is that of a compound consonant, *d* followed by the sound *zh* (as in pleasure, pronounced pleʒ'ur).

J abbreviation of joule(s).

jab v.t. (-bb-) to poke roughly; to thrust abruptly (a thing *into*). —n. 1. an abrupt blow with a pointed thing or with the fist. 2. (*colloquial*) a hypodermic injection. [variant of *job* = prod]

jabber v.t./i. to chatter volubly; to utter (words) fast and indistinctly. —n. chatter, gabble.

jabiru n. a species of stork *Jabiru mycteria* found in Central and South America. It is 1.5 m/5 ft high with white plumage. The head is black and red.

jabot /'ʒæbəʊ/ n. an ornamental frill or ruffle of lace etc. worn on the front of a shirt or blouse. [French, originally = crop of bird]

jacamar n. a bird of the family Galbulidae of Central and South America. Jacamars have long sharp-pointed bills, long tails, and paired toes. The plumage is brilliantly coloured. The largest species grows to 30 cm/12 in.

jacana n. one of seven species of wading birds, family Jacanidae, with very long toes and claws, enabling it to walk on the flat leaves of river plants, hence the name 'lily trotter'. It is found in South America, Africa, South Asia, and Australia.

jacaranda /dʒækə'rændə/ n. a tropical American tree of the genus *Dalbergia* etc. with hard scented wood, or one of the genus *Jacaranda* with blue flowers. [Tupi-Guarani]

jacinth /'dʒæsɪnθ/ n. a reddish-orange gem, a variety of zircon. [from Old French or Latin]

jack n. 1. a device for lifting heavy objects, especially one for raising the axle of a motor vehicle so that a wheel may be changed. A **screw jack** uses the principle of the screw to magnify an applied effort; in a car jack, for example, turning the handle many times causes the lifting screw to rise slightly, and the effort is magnified to lift heavy weights. A **hydraulic jack** uses a succession of piston strokes to increase pressure in a liquid and force up a lifting ram. 2. a court-card with a picture of a soldier or page. 3. a ship's flag, especially one flown from the bow and showing nationality. 4. a device using a single plug to connect an electrical circuit. 5. a device for turning a spit. 6. a type of the common man. 7. (*slang*) a policeman, a detective. 8. a small white ball in bowls for the players to aim at. 9. a pike, especially a young one. 10. the male of various animals. —v.t. (often with *up*) to raise with or as with a jack. —**Jack Frost**, frost personified. **jack in** *or* **up**, (*slang*) to abandon (an attempt etc.). **jack-in-the-box** n. a toy figure that springs out of a box when the lid is lifted. **jack-in-office** n. a self-important official. **jack of all trades,** a person who can do many different kinds of work. **jack rabbit,** (*US*) a large prairie hare (*Lepus townsendii* etc.) with very long ears. **Jack tar,** a sailor. [from *Jack*, pet-name for John]

jackal /'dʒækɔl, -əl/ n. 1. any of several members of the dog family found wild in S Europe, Asia, and Africa, living on carrion and small animals. Jackals can grow to 80 cm/2.7 ft long, have greyish-brown fur, and a bushy tail. 2. one who does the preliminary drudgery etc. for another. [from Turkish from Persian]

jackanapes /'dʒækəneɪps/ n. a pert or insolent fellow [from *Jack Napes*, nickname (1450) of Duke of Suffolk whose badge was an ape's clog and chain]

jackass /'dʒækæs/ n. 1. a male ass. 2. a stupid person. —**laughing jackass**, the kookaburra.

jackboot n. 1. a large boot reaching above the knee. 2. military oppression, bullying behaviour.

jackdaw n. a bird *Corvus monedula* of the crow family, found in Europe and W Asia. It is mainly black, but greyish on the sides and back of the head, and is about 33 cm/1.1 ft long. It nests in tree holes or on buildings, and has a chuckling call.

jacket /'dʒækɪt/ n. 1. a short coat, usually reaching to the hips. 2. a thing worn similarly. 3. an outer covering round a boiler etc. to reduce loss of heat. 4. a dust jacket. 5. the skin of a potato. 6. an animal's coat. —**jacketed** adj. [from Old French *ja(c)quet*]

jackknife n. 1. a large clasp-knife. 2. a dive in which the body is first bent at the waist and then straightened. —v.i. (of an articulated vehicle) to fold against itself in an accidental skidding movement.

jackpot n. the accumulated prize or stakes in a lottery, the game of poker etc. —**hit the jackpot**, to win remarkable luck or success.

Jackson /'dʒæksən/ Alexander Young 1882–1974. Canadian landscape painter, a leading member of the **Group of Seven**, who aimed to create a specifically Canadian school of landscape art.

Jackson Andrew 1767–1845. 7th president of the USA 1829–37, a Democrat. Born in South Carolina, he spent his early life in poverty. He defeated a British force during the War of 1812 at New Orleans in 1815 (after the official end of the war in 1814) and was involved in the war which led to the purchase of Florida in 1819. After an unsuccessful attempt in 1824, he was elected president in 1828. This was the first election in which electors (see ◊electoral college) were chosen directly by voters rather than state legislators. The political organization he built, with Martin ◊Van Buren, served as the basis for the modern ◊Democratic party. He demanded and received absolute loyalty from his cabinet members and made wide use of his executive powers. In 1832 he vetoed the renewal of the US bank charter and was reelected, whereupon he continued his struggle against the power of finance.

Jackson Glenda 1936– . English actress. She has made many stage appearances, including *Marat/ Sade* 1966, and her films include the Oscar-winning *Women in Love* 1971. On television she played Queen Elizabeth I in *Elizabeth R* 1971. In 1990 she was chosen as the Labour candidate for Highgate, N London.

Jackson Jesse 1941– . US Democrat politician, campaigner for minority rights. He contested his party's 1984 and 1988 presidential nominations in an effort to increase voter registration and to put black issues on the national agenda. He is a notable public speaker.

Jackson John Hughlings 1835–1911. English neurologist and neurophysiologist. As a result of his studies of ◊epilepsy, Jackson demonstrated that specific areas of the cerebral cortex (outer mantle of the brain) control the functioning of particular organs and limbs.

Jackson Michael 1958– . US rock singer and song-writer, known for his androgynous appearance and his single sequinned glove used during his meticulously cho-reographed performances. His first solo hit was 'Got to Be There' 1971, but worldwide popularity was achieved with the albums *Thriller* 1982 and *Bad* 1987.

Jackson Stonewall (Thomas Jonathan) 1824–1863. US Confederate general in the American Civil War. He acquired his nickname and his reputation at the Battle of Bull Run, from the firmness with which his brigade resisted the Northern attack. In 1862 he organized the Shenandoah Valley campaign and assisted Robert E ◊Lee's invasion of Maryland. He helped to defeat Gen Joseph E Hooker's Union army at the battle of Chancellorsville, Virginia, but was fatally wounded by one of his own men in the confusion of battle.

Jacksonian Democracy /dʒæk'səʊnɪən/ in US history, the populist, egalitarian spirit pervading the presidencies of Andrew Jackson and Martin Van Buren 1829–1841, which encouraged greater participation in the democratic process. Recent studies have questioned the professed commitment to popular control, emphasizing Jackson's alleged cult of personality.

Jacksonville /'dʒæksənvɪl/ port, resort, and commercial centre in Florida, USA; population (1980) 541,000. The port has naval installations and ship repair yards. To the N the Cross-Florida Barge Canal links the Atlantic with the Gulf of Mexico.

Jack the Ripper /dʒæk/ popular name for the unidentified mutilator and murderer of at least five women prostitutes in the Whitechapel area of London in 1888.

Jacob /dʒeɪkəb/ in the Old Testament, Hebrew patriarch, son of Isaac and Rebecca, who obtained the rights of seniority from his twin brother Esau by trickery. He married his cousins Leah and Rachel, serving their father Laban seven years for each, and at the time of famine in Canaan joined his son Joseph in Egypt. His 12 sons were the traditional ancestors of the 12 tribes of Israel.

Jacob François 1920– . French biochemist who, with Jacques Monod, pioneered research into molecular genetics and showed how the production of proteins from ◊DNA is controlled. He shared the Nobel Prize for Medicine in 1965.

Jacob Joseph 1854–1916. Australian-born US folklorist and collector of fairy tales. He published collections of vividly re-told fairy stories such as *English Fairy Tales* 1890, *Celtic Fairy Tales* 1892 and 1894, and *Indian Fairy Tales* 1892.

Jacobean /dʒækə'biːən/ *adj.* 1. of James I's reign of England (1603–1625). 2. a style in the arts, particularly in architecture and furniture, during the reign of James I. Following the general lines of Elizabethan design, but using classical features more widely, it adopted many motifs from

Italian ◊Renaissance design. [from Latin *Jacobus* = James from Greek *Iakōbos* = Jacob]

Jacobin /'dʒækəbɪn/ *n.* a member of an extremist republican club of the French Revolution founded at Versailles in 1789, which later used a former Jacobin (Dominican) friary as its headquarters in Paris. Helped by ◊Danton's speeches, they proclaimed the French republic, had the king executed, and overthrew the moderate ◊Girondins 1792–93. Through the Committee of Public Safety, they began the Reign of Terror, led by ◊Robespierre. After his execution in 1794, the club was abandoned and the name 'Jacobin' passed into general use for any left-wing extremist.

Jacobite /'dʒækəbaɪt/ *n.* an adherent of the deposed James II, or of his descendants, or of the Stuarts after the Revolution of 1688, in their claim to the British throne. The Jacobites included the Scottish Highlanders, who rose unsuccessfully in 1689; and those who rose in Scotland and N England under the leadership of ◊James Edward Stuart, the Old Pretender, in 1715, and followed his son ◊Charles Edward Stuart in an invasion of England that reached Derby in 1745–46. After the defeat at ◊Culloden, Jacobitism disappeared as a political force. [from Latin *Jacobus* = James from Greek *Iakōbos* = Jacob]

Jacquard /'dʒækɑːd/ *n.* 1. an apparatus with perforated cards, fitted to a loom to facilitate the weaving of figured fabrics. 2. a fabric made thus. [from J M *Jacquard*]

Jacquard Joseph Marie 1752–1834. French textile manufacturer who invented a punched-card system for programming designs on a carpet-making loom. In 1804 he constructed looms that used a series of punched cards to control the pattern of longitudinal warp threads depressed before each sideways passage of the shuttle. On later machines the punched cards were joined to form an endless loop that represented the 'program' for the repeating pattern of a carpet.

Jacquerie /ʒækə'riː/ *n.* a French peasant uprising in 1358, caused by the ravages of the English army and French nobility during the Hundred Years' War, which reduced the rural population to destitution. [from the nickname for French peasants, *Jacques Bonhomme*]

Jacuzzi /dʒə'kuːzɪ/ *n.* trade name for a large bath with underwater jets of water to massage the body. [from C *Jacuzzi*]

Jacuzzi Candido 1903–1986. Italian-born US inventor and engineer who invented the Jacuzzi, a pump that produces a whirlpool effect in a bathtub. He developed it for his 15-month-old son, a sufferer from rheumatoid arthritis.

jade[1] *n.* 1. a hard green, blue, or white semiprecious stone, a silicate of calcium and magnesium. 2. its green colour. [French, from Spanish (*piedra de*) *ijada* = (stone of) the colic from Latin *ilia* = flanks]

jade[2] *n.* 1. a poor worn-out horse. 2. a hussy.

jaded /'dʒeɪdɪd/ *adj.* tired and bored; (of the appetite) dulled, lacking zest for food.

Jade Emperor in Chinese religion, the supreme god, Yu Huang, of pantheistic Taoism, who watches over human actions and is the ruler of life and death.

jadeite /'dʒeɪdaɪt/ *n.* a jadelike silicate of sodium and aluminium.

Jaffa /'dʒæfə/ 1. (biblical name **Joppa**), port in W Israel, part of ◊Tel Aviv from 1950. 2. (*also* **Jaffa orange**) a large, oval, thick-skinned variety of orange.

Jaffna /'dʒæfnə/ capital of Jaffna district, Northern Province, Sri Lanka. The focal point of Hindu Tamil nationalism and the scene of recurring riots during the 1980s.

jag[1] *n.* a sharp projection of rock etc. —*v.t.* (**-gg-**) to cut or tear unevenly; to make indentations in.

jag[2] *n.* (*slang*) a drinking bout; a period of indulgence in an activity, emotion etc. [originally = load for one horse]

Jagan /'dʒeɪgən/ Cheddi Berrat 1918– . Guyanese left-wing politician. Educated in British Guiana (former name of Guyana) and the USA, he led the People's Progressive Party from 1950, and in 1961 he became the first prime minister of British Guiana.

Jagan Janet 1920– . Guyanese left-wing politician, wife of Cheddi Jagan. She was general secretary of the People's Progressive Party 1950–70.

jagged /'dʒægɪd/ *adj.* with an unevenly cut or torn edge.

jaguar *n.* the largest species of cat *Panthera onca* in the Americas. It can grow up to 2.5 m/8 ft long including the

Jackson *English stage and film actress Glenda Jackson.*

tail. The ground colour of the fur varies from creamy white
to brown or black, and is covered with black spots. The
jaguar is usually solitary. [from Tupi-Guarani]

Jaguar *n.* a British car manufacturer, one of the most
successful companies in the 1950s. Jaguar has a long association with motor racing, and won the Le Mans 24 Hour
race five times 1951–58.

jaguarundi *n.* a wild cat *Felis yaguoaroundi* found in forests in Central and South America. Up to 1.1 m/3.5 ft long,
it is very slim, with rather short legs and short rounded
ears. It is uniformly coloured dark brown or chestnut. A
good climber, it feeds on birds and small mammals, and,
unusually for a cat, has been reported to eat fruit.

Jahangir /dʒəˈhɑːngiə/ 'Conqueror of the World'. Adopted name of Salim, 1569–1627. Mogul emperor of India
1605–27, succeeding his father ◊Akbar the Great. In 1622
he lost Kandahar province in Afghanistan to Persia. He
designed the Shalimar Gardens in Kashmir and buildings and
gardens in Lahore. His rule was marked by the influence of
his wife, Nur Jahan, and her conflict with Prince Khurran
(later Shah Jahan). His addiction to alcohol and opium weakened his power.

Jahweh /ˈjɑːweɪ/ variant of ◊Jehovah.

jai alai another name for the ball-game ◊pelota.

jail, jailer variant of ◊gaol, ◊gaoler.

Jain /dʒaɪn/ *adj.* of an Indian religion with doctrines like
those of Buddhism. —*n.* an adherent of Jainism. [Hindi from
Sanskrit *jainas* = of the conquerors (*ji* = conquer)]

Jainism /ˈdʒaɪnɪzəm/ *n.* an Indian religion, sometimes
regarded as an offshoot of Hinduism. Jains believe that
non-injury to living beings is the highest religion, and
their code of ethics is based on sympathy and compassion. They also believe in ◊karma. In Jainism there is no
deity and, like Buddhism, it is a monastic, ascetic religion.
Jains number about 3.3 million. There are two main sects:
the Digambaras, who originally went about naked, and the
Swetambaras. Jainism practises ahimsā, the most extreme
form of non-violence of all Indian sects, and influenced the
philosophy of MahātmāGāndhī.

Jaipur /dʒaɪˈpuə/ capital of Rajasthan, India; population
(1981) 1,005,000. Formerly the capital of the state of Jaipur,
which was merged with Rajasthan in 1949. Products include
textiles and metal products.

Jakarta /dʒəˈkɑːtə/ or **Djakarta** capital of Indonesia
on the NW coast of Java; population (1980) 6,504,000.
Industries include textiles, chemicals, and plastics; a canal
links it with its port of Tanjung Priok where rubber, oil,
tin, coffee, tea, and palm oil are among its exports; also
a tourist centre.

Jakeš /ˈjɑːkeʃ/ Miloš 1922– . Czech communist politician, a member of the Politburo from 1981 and party leader
1987–89. A conservative, he supported the Soviet invasion
of Czechoslovakia in 1968. He was forced to resign in Nov
1989 following a series of pro-democracy mass rallies.

Jalalabad /dʒəˈlɑːləbɑːd/ capital of Nangarhar province, E Afghanistan, on the road from Kabul to Peshawar
in Pakistan. The city was beseiged by mujaheddin rebels
in 1989 after the withdrawal of Soviet troops from Afghanistan.

jalap /ˈdʒæləp/ *n.* a purgative drug from the tubers of
a Mexican plant *Exogonium purga*. [French from Spanish
Jalapa, Xalapa Mexican city]

jalopy /dʒəˈlɒpɪ/ *n.* (*colloquial*) a dilapidated old motor
vehicle.

jalousie /ˈʒæluːziː/ *n.* a slatted blind or shutter to admit
air and light but not rain etc. [French = jealousy]

jam[1] *v.t./i* (-**mm**-) **1.** to squeeze or wedge (*into* a space);
to become wedged. **2.** to cause (machinery) to become
wedged etc. so that it cannot work; to become thus
wedged. **3.** to force or thrust violently. **4.** to push or
cram together in a compact mass; to block (a passage,
road etc.) by crowding. **5.** to make (a radio transmission) unintelligible by causing interference. **6.** (*colloquial*,
in jazz etc.) to extemporize with other musicians. —*n.*
1. a squeeze, a crush; a stoppage (of a machine etc.)
due to jamming. **2.** a crowded mass. **3.** (*colloquial*) an
awkward position, a fix. **4.** (*colloquial*) improvised playing
by a group of jazz musicians. —**jam-packed** *adj.* (*colloquial*) very full.

jam[2] *n.* **1.** a sweet substance made of fruit and sugar boiled
until thick. **2.** (*colloquial*) something easy or pleasant.

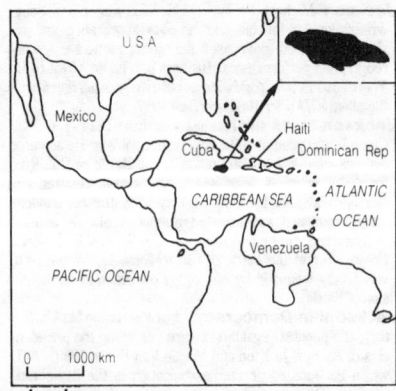

Jamaica

—**jam tomorrow**, a pleasant thing continually promised
but usually never produced.

Jamaica /dʒəˈmeɪkə/ island in the Caribbean, S of Cuba
and W of Haiti; **area** 10,957 sq km/4,230 sq mi; **capital**
Kingston; **physical** mountainous tropical island; **head of
state** Elizabeth II from 1962 represented by governor-
general; **head of government** Michael Manley from 1989;
political system constitutional monarchy; **exports** sugar,
bananas, bauxite, rum, coffee, coconuts, liqueurs, cigars,
citrus; **population** (1990 est) 2,513,000 (African 76%,
mixed 15%, Chinese, Caucasian, East Indian); **language**
English, Jamaican Creole; **recent history** discovered by
Columbus in 1494, it remained a Spanish possession until
1655 when it was conquered by the British. Mass violence
broke out in the mid-19th century against the British
which resulted in suppression of representative government for twenty years, granted internal self-government
in 1944; achieved independence from Britain within the
Commonwealth in 1962, with Alexander Bustamente, of
the Jamaica Labour Party, as prime minister. The PNP
(People's National Party) held power during the 1970s,
but economic decline led to a decisive victory for the JLP in
the 1980 elections, an end to the JLP's policies of economic
self-reliance, and closer relations with the USA. In 1989
Manley and the PNP were elected, promising moderate
economic policies.

jamb /dʒæm/ *n.* a side post or side of a doorway, window,
or fireplace. [from Old French *jambe* = leg from Latin]

jamboree /dʒæmbəˈriː/ *n.* **1.** a celebration, merry-
making. **2.** a large rally of Scouts.

James /dʒeɪmz/ Henry 1843–1916. US novelist, who lived
in Europe from 1875 and became a naturalized British subject in 1915. His novels deal with the impact of sophisticated
European culture on the innocent American. They include
The Portrait of a Lady 1881, *Washington Square* 1881, *The
Bostonians* 1886, *The Ambassadors* 1903, and *The Golden
Bowl* 1904. He also wrote more than a hundred shorter
works of fiction, notably the supernatural tale *The Turn of
the Screw* 1898.

James Jesse 1847–1882. US bank and train robber, born
in Missouri and a leader (with his brother Frank) of the
Quantrill raiders, a Confederate guerilla band in the Civil
War. Frank later led his own gang. Jesse was killed by
Bob Ford, an accomplice; Frank remained unconvicted and
became a farmer.

James M(ontague) R(hodes) 1862–1936. British writer,
theologian, linguist, and medievalist. He wrote *Ghost Stories
of an Antiquary* 1904 and other supernatural tales.

James William 1842–1910. US psychologist and philosopher, brother of the novelist Henry James. He turned from
medicine to psychology and taught at Harvard 1872–1907.
His books include *Principles of Psychology* 1890, *The Will
to Believe* 1897, and *Varieties of Religious Experience*
1902, one of the most important works on the psychology of religion.

James I the Conqueror 1208–1276. King of Aragon
from 1213, when he succeeded his father. He conquered
the Balearic Islands and took Valencia from the ◊Moors,
dividing it with Alfonso X of Castile by a treaty of 1244. Both
these exploits are recorded in his autobiography *Llibre dels*

feyts. He largely established Aragon as the dominant power in the Mediterranean.

James two kings of Britain:

James I 1566–1625. King of England from 1603 and Scotland (as **James VI**) from 1567. The son of Mary Queen of Scots and Lord Darnley, he succeeded on his mother's abdication from the Scottish throne, assumed power in 1583, established a strong centralized authority, and in 1589 married Anne of Denmark (1574–1619). As successor to Elizabeth I in England, he alienated the Puritans by his High Church views and Parliament by his assertion of ◊divine right, and was generally unpopular because of his favourites, such as ◊Buckingham, and because of his schemes for an alliance with Spain. He was succeeded by his son Charles I.

James II 1633–1701. King of England and Scotland (as **James VII**) from 1685, second son of Charles I. He succeeded Charles II. James married Anne Hyde in 1659 (1637–1671, mother of Mary II and Anne) and ◊Mary of Modena in 1673 (mother of James Edward Stuart). He became a Catholic in 1671, which led first to attempts to exclude him from the succession, then to the rebellions of ◊Monmouth and Argyll, and finally to the Whig and Tory leaders' invitation to William of Orange to take the throne in 1688. James fled to France, then led an uprising in Ireland in 1689, but after defeat at the Battle of the ◊Boyne in 1690 remained in exile in France.

James seven kings of Scotland:

James I 1394–1437. King of Scotland 1406–37, who assumed power in 1424. He was a cultured and strong monarch whose improvements in the administration of justice brought him popularity among the common people. He was assassinated by a group of conspirators led by the Earl of Atholl.

James II 1430–1460. King of Scotland from 1437, who assumed power in 1449. The only surviving son of James I, he was supported by most of the nobles and parliament. He sympathized with the Lancastrians during the Wars of the ◊Roses, and attacked English possessions in the south of Scotland. He was killed while besieging Roxburgh Castle.

James III 1451–1488. King of Scotland from 1460, who assumed power in 1469. His reign was marked by rebellions by the nobles, including his brother Alexander, duke of Albany. He was murdered during a rebellion.

James IV 1473–1513. King of Scotland from 1488, who married Margaret (1489–1541, daughter of Henry VII) in 1503. His reign was internally peaceful, but he allied himself with France against England, invaded in 1513 and was defeated and killed at the Battle of ◊Flodden.

James V 1512–1542. King of Scotland from 1513, who assumed power in 1528. During the long period of James's minority, he was caught in a struggle between pro-French and pro-English factions. When he assumed power, he allied himself with France and upheld Catholicism against the Protestants. Following an attack on Scottish territory by Henry VIII's forces, he was defeated near the border at Solway Moss in 1542.

James VI of Scotland. See ◊James I of England.

James VII of Scotland. See ◊James II of England.

James Edward Stuart 1688–1766. British prince, known as the **Old Pretender** (for the ◊Jacobites, he was James III). Son of James II, he was born at St James's Palace and after the revolution of 1688 was taken to France. He landed in Scotland in 1715 to head a Jacobite rebellion but withdrew for lack of support. In his later years he settled in Rome.

Jameson /'dʒɛmɪsən/ Leander Starr 1853–1917. British colonial administrator. In South Africa, early in 1896, he led the **Jameson Raid** from Mafeking into Transvaal to support the non-Boer colonists there, in an attempt to overthrow the government, for which he served some months in prison. Returning to South Africa, he succeeded Cecil ◊Rhodes as leader of the Progressive Party of Cape Colony, where he was prime minister 1904–08.

James, St several Christian saints, incuding:

James, St the Great died AD 44. A New Testament apostle, originally a Galilean fisherman, he was the son of Zebedee and brother of the apostle John. He was put to death by ◊Herod Agrippa. Patron saint of Spain. Feast day 25 July.

James, St the Just 1st century AD. The New Testament brother of Jesus, to whom Jesus appeared after the Resurrection. Leader of the Christian church in Jerusalem, he was the author of the biblical Epistle of James.

Jammu and Kashmir /'dʒʌmuː, kæʃˈmɪə/ state of N India; **area** 101,300 sq km/39,102 sq mi; another 78,900 sq km/30,455 sq mi is occupied by Pakistan, 42,700 sq km/16,482 sq mi by China; **capital** Jammu (winter); Srinagar (summer); **towns** Leh; **population** (1981) 5,982,000 (Indian-occupied territory); **recent history** in 1947 Jammu was attacked by Pakistan and chose to become part of the new state of India. Dispute over the area caused further hostilities in 1971 between India and Pakistan. This was ended by the Simla agreement of 1972.

jammy *adj.* 1. covered with jam. 2. (*colloquial*) lucky, profitable.

Jan. abbreviation of January.

Janácvek /'jænətʃek/ Leoš 1854–1928. Czech composer. He became director of the Conservatoire at Brno in 1919 and professor at the Prague Conservatoire in 1920. His music, highly original and influenced by Moravian folk music, includes arrangements of folk songs, operas (*Jenůfa* 1904, *The Cunning Little Vixen* 1924), and the choral *Glagolitic Mass* 1927.

Janam Sakhis /'dʒʌnəm 'saːkiz/ a collection of stories about the life of Nanak, the first guru (teacher) of ◊Sikhism.

Janata /'dʒʌnəta:/ *n.* an alliance of political parties in India formed in 1971 to oppose Indira Gandhi's Congress Party. Victory in the election brought Morarji Desai to power as prime minister but he was unable to control the various groups within the alliance and resigned in 1979. His successors fared little better, and the elections of 1980 overwhelmingly returned Indira Gandhi to office.

Janata Dal /'dʒʌnəta: 'dʌl/ (People's Party) Indian centre-left coalition, formed Oct 1988 under the leadership of V P ◊Singh and comprising the Janata, Lok Dal (B), Congress (S), and Jan Morcha parties. In a loose alliance with the Hindu fundamentalist Bharatiya Janata Party and the Communist Party of India, the Janata Dal was victorious in the Nov 1989 general election, taking power out of the hands of the Congress (I) Party for the first time since 1947. Its minority government fell in Nov 1990.

jangle *v.t./i* 1. to make or cause to make a harsh metallic sound. 2. to cause irritation to (nerves etc.). —*n.* a jangling sound. [Old French *jangler*]

janissary /'dʒænɪsərɪ/ *n.* a Turkish soldier; (*historical*) the bodyguard of the Ottoman sultan, the Turkish standing army 1330–1826. Until the 16th century janissaries were Christian boys forcibly converted to Islam; after this time they were allowed to marry and recruit their own children. The bodyguard ceased to exist when it revolted against the decision of the sultan in 1826 to raise a regular force. [Turkish *yeniçeri* = new force]

janitor /'dʒænɪtə/ *n.* a door-keeper; the caretaker of a building. —**janitorial** /-'tɔːrɪəl/ *adj.* [Latin *janua* = door]

Jannequin /ʒænˈkæn/ Clament *c.*1472–*c.*1560. French composer. He studied with Josquin ◊Desprez and is remembered for choral works that incorporate images from real life, such as birdsong and the cries of street vendors.

Jannings /'jænɪŋs/ Emil. Stage name of Theodor Emil Jarenz. 1882–1950. German actor in silent films of the 1920s, such as *The Last Command* 1928. In *Der Blaue Engel/The Blue Angel* 1930 he played a schoolteacher who becomes infatuated with Marlene Dietrich.

Jansen /'dʒænsən/ Cornelius 1585–1638. Dutch Roman Catholic theologian, founder of **Jansenism** with his book *Augustinus* 1640.

Jansenism /'dʒænsənɪzəm/ *n.* the Christian teaching of Cornelius Jansen, which divided the Roman Catholic Church in France in the mid-17th century. He emphasized the more predestinatory approach of Augustine's teaching, as opposed to that of the Jesuits. Jansenism was supported by the philosopher Pascal. In 1713 a Jansenist work by Pasquier Quesnel (1634–1719), the leader of the Jansenist party, was condemned by Pope Clement XI as heretical, and Jansenists were excommunicated in 1719.

jansky /'dʒænski/ *n.* a unit of radiation received from outer space, used in radio astronomy, named after K G Jansky.

Jansky Karl Guthe 1905–1950. US radio engineer, who discovered that the Milky Way galaxy emanates radio

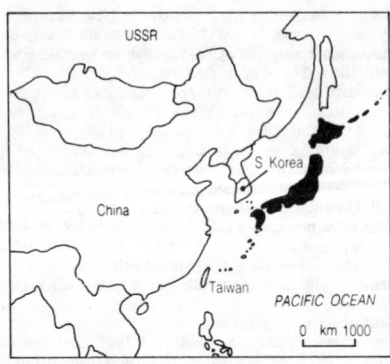

Japan

waves; he did not follow up his discovery, but it marked the birth of radioastronomy.

January /'dʒænjuəri/ *n.* the first month of the year. [Latin (*mensis*) *Januarius* = (month) of Janus]

Janus /'dʒeɪnəs/ in Roman mythology, the god of doorways and passageways, patron of the beginning of the day, month, and year, after whom January is named; he is represented as having two faces looking both forwards and backwards.

Jap (*colloquial*) abbreviation of Japanese.

japan /dʒə'pæn/ *n.* a hard usually black varnish, especially a kind brought originally from Japan. —*v.t.* (**-nn-**) to coat with japan.

Japan country in E Asia, occupying a group of islands of which the four main ones are Hokkaido, Honshu, Kyushu, and Shikoku. Japan is situated in the N Pacific, E of North and South Korea. **area** 377,535 sq km/145,822 sq mi; **capital** Tokyo; **physical** mountainous, volcanic; comprises over 1,000 islands, including Hokkaido, Honshu, Shikoku, Kyushu, Ryukyu; **head of state** (figurehead) Emperor Akihito from 1989; **head of government** Toshiki Kaifu from 1989; **exports** televisions, cassette and video recorders, radios, cameras, computers, robots, other electronic and electrical equipment, motor vehicles, ships, iron, steel, chemicals, textiles; **population** (1990) 123,778,000; **language** Japanese; **recent history** World War II ended wih Japanese surrender; an allied control commission took power and, in 1946, a Peace Constitution was framed. Full sovereignty was regained in 1958. The postwar period has been marked by rapid economic growth and the opening of extensive foreign markets. in 1989 Emperor Hirohito died and was succeeded by his son Akihito. In 1989 the Recruit corporation insider-trading scandal, and other revelations, led to a number of ministerial resignations.

Japan Current or **Kuroshio** a warm ocean ◊current flowing from Japan to North America.

Japanese /dʒæpə'niːz/ *adj.* of Japan or its people or language. —*n.* 1. a Japanese person. 2. the language of Japan.

Japanese language the language of E Asia, spoken almost exclusively in the islands of Japan. Traditionally isolated, but possibly related to Korean, Japanese was influenced by Mandarin Chinese in the 6th–9th centuries and is written in Chinese-derived ideograms supplemented by two syllabic alphabets.

japonica /dʒə'pɒnɪkə/ *n.* an ornamental variety of quince bearing red flowers in spring. [Latin *Japonicus* = Japanese]

jar[1] *v.t./i* (**-rr-**) 1. to jolt. 2. to sound with a harsh or unpleasant effect. 3. to shock. —*n.* a jarring movement or effect.

jar[2] *n.* 1. a glass or ceramic container with or without handle(s) and usually cylindrical. 2. its contents. 3. (*colloquial*) a glass (of beer etc.). [from French from Arabic *jarra*]

jardinière /ʒɑːdi'njeə/ *n.* a large ornamental pot for holding indoor plants. [French]

jargon /'dʒɑːgən/ *n.* words or expressions developed for use within a particular group or profession. In writing, jargon may be highly formal, whereas in speech it often contains ◊slang expressions, sounding ugly and unintelligible to outsiders. [Old French = chatter]

Jarrett /'dʒærət/ Keith 1945– . US jazz pianist and composer, an eccentric innovator who performs both alone and with small groups. Jarrett was a member of the rock-influenced Charles Lloyd Quartet 1966–67, and played with Miles Davis 1970–71. *The Köln Concert* 1975 is a characteristic solo live recording.

Jarry /'ʒæri/ Alfred 1873–1907. French satiric dramatist, whose *Ubu Roi* 1896 foreshadowed the Theatre of the ◊Absurd and the French ◊Surrealist movement.

Jaruzelski /jæruː'zelski/ Wojciech 1923– . Polish general, communist leader from 1981, president 1985–1990. He imposed martial law for the first year of his rule, suppressed the opposition, and banned trade-union activity, but later released many political prisoners. In 1989, elections in favour of the free trade union Solidarity forced Jaruzelski to speed up democratic reforms, overseeing a transition to a new form of 'socialist pluralist' democracy, and stepping down as president in 1990.

Jarvik 7 /'dʒɑːvɪk/ the first successful artificial heart intended for permanent implantation in a human being. Made from polyurethane plastic and aluminium, it is powered by compressed air. Barney Clark became the first person to receive a Jarvik 7, in Salt Lake City, Utah, USA, in Dec 1982; it kept him alive for 112 days.

jasmine /'dʒæzmɪn/ *n.* any subtropical plant of the genus *Jasminium* of the olive family Oleaceae, with fragrant white or yellow flowers, and yielding jasmine oil, used in perfumes. The **common jasmine** *J. officinale* has pure white flowers; the **red jasmine** is a red-flowered frangipani *Plumeria rubra*; the Chinese **winter jasmine** *J. nudiflorum* has bright yellow flowers that appear before the leaves. [from French, ultimately from Persian *yāsamin*]

Jason /'dʒeɪsən/ in Greek mythology, leader of the **Argonauts** who sailed in the *Argo* to Colchis in search of the ◊Golden Fleece.

jasper /'dʒæspə/ *n.* an opaque variety of quartz, usually red, yellow, or brown. [from Old French from Latin from Greek *iaspis*, of oriental origin]

Jataka /'dzɑːtəkə/ *n. pl.* collections of Buddhist legends compiled at various dates in several countries; the oldest and most complete has 547 stories. They were collected before AD 400. [Sanskrit, from *jata* = born]

jaundice /'dʒɔːndɪs/ *n.* 1. a condition caused by obstruction of the bile or by infective hepatitis and other diseases, and marked by yellowness of the skin, fluids, and tissues and occasionally by disordered vision. 2. disordered mental vision; resentment, jealousy. —*v.t.* 1. to affect with jaundice. 2. to fill with resentment or jealousy. [from Old French *jaunice* = yellowness (*jaune* = yellow)]

jaunt *n.* an excursion or journey, especially for pleasure. —*v.i.* to take a jaunt. —**jaunting car,** a two-wheeled horse-drawn vehicle formerly common in Ireland.

jaunty *adj.* 1. cheerful and self-confident. 2. (of clothes) stylish and cheerful. —**jauntily** *adv.*, **jauntiness** *n.* [from French *gentil*]

Jaurès /'ʒɔʊres/ Jean Léon 1859–1914. French socialist politician and advocate of international peace. He was a lecturer in philosophy at Toulouse until his election in 1885 as a deputy (member of parliament). In 1893 he joined the Socialist Party, established a united party, and in 1904 founded the newspaper *L'Humanité*, becoming its editor until his assassination.

Java /'dʒɑːvə/ or **Jawa** the most important island of Indonesia, situated between Sumatra and Bali; **area** (with the island of Madura) 132,000 sq km/51,000 sq mi; **capital** Jakarta (also capital of Indonesia); **towns** ports include Surabaja and Semarang; **population** (with Madura; 1980) 91,270,000; including people of Javanese, Sundanese, and Madurese origin, with differing languages; **religion** predominantly Muslim; **history** fossilized early human remains (*Homo erectus*) were discovered 1891–92. In central Java there are ruins of magnificent Buddhist monuments and of the Sivaite temple in Prambanan. The island's last Hindu kingdom, Majapahit, was destroyed about 1520 and followed by a number of short-lived Javanese kingdoms. The Dutch East India company founded a factory in 1610. Britain took over during the Napoleonic period, 1811–16, and Java then reverted to Dutch control. The island was occupied by Japan 1942–45 while under Dutch control, and then became part of the republic of ◊Indonesia.

javelin /'dʒævəlɪn/ *n.* a light spear thrown by hand as a weapon or in athletics. In athletics events, the men's javelin is about 260 cm/8.5 ft long, weighing 800 g/28 oz;

the women's 230 cm/7.5 ft long, weighing 600 g/21 oz. It is thrown from a scratch line at the end of a run-up. The centre of gravity on the men's javelin was altered in 1986 to reduce the vast distances (90 m/100 yd) that were being thrown. [from French]

jaw *n.* 1. the bone(s) forming the framework of the mouth and (in vertebrates) carrying the teeth; the lower of these, the part of the face covering it; (in *plural*) the mouth, its bones and teeth. 2. (in *plural*) something resembling or gripping like jaws. 3. (*colloquial*) talkativeness, a lecture, a gossiping talk. —*v.t./i.* (*slang*) to talk long and boringly, to gossip. —**jawbone** *n.* a bone of the jaws, especially the lower jaw. **jawbreaker** *n.* a word that is very long, or hard to pronounce. [from Old French *joe* = cheek, jaw]

jay *n.* a bird of the crow family, especially the noisy chattering European bird *Garrulus glandarius* which has pinkish-brown plumage, a black tail, and a small blue barred patch on each wing. [from Old French from Latin *gaius*, perhaps from name *Gaius*]

Jayawardene /dʒaɪə'wɑːdɪnə/ Junius Richard 1906– . Sri Lankan politician. Leader of the United Nationalist Party from 1973, he became prime minister in 1977 and was the country's first president 1978–88.

jay-walk *v.i.* to cross or walk in a road carelessly without regard for traffic or signals. —**jay-walker** *n.* [from *jay* = stupid person]

jazz *n.* 1. a type of polyphonic, syncopated music characterized by solo virtuosic improvisation and strong rhythm which developed in the USA at the turn of the 20th century. It had its roots in black, American, and other indigenous popular music and evolved various distinct vocal and instrumental forms. 2. pretentious talk or behaviour. —*adj.* of, in or like jazz. —*v.t./i.* 1. to play or arrange as jazz. 2. to brighten or liven *up*.

jazz dance a type of dance that combines African and US techniques and rhythms and was introduced into modern dance by choreographers such as Jerome ◊Robbins and Alvin Ailey.

jazzy *adj.* 1. of or like jazz. 2. vividly coloured, showy.

J-curve *n.* in economics, a graphic illustration of the likely effect of a currency devaluation on the balance of payments. Initially, there will be a deterioration as import prices increase and export prices decline, followed by a decline in import volume and upsurge of export volume.

jealous /'dʒeləs/ *adj.* 1. resentful of a rival or a person's advantages etc. 2. watchfully tenacious (*of* rights etc.). 3. (of God) intolerant of disloyalty. —**jealously** *adv.*, **jealousy** *n.* [from Old French from Latin *zelosus*]

jean /dʒiːn/ *n.* 1. a kind of twilled cotton cloth. 2. (in *plural*) trousers, traditionally blue, originally cut from jean cloth ('jene fustian'), a heavy canvas made in Genoa, Italy. Levi Strauss (1830–1902), a Bavarian immigrant to the USA, made sturdy trousers for goldminers in San Francisco from jean material intended for wagon covers, hence the name 'Levis'. Later a French fabric, serge de Nîmes (corrupted to 'denim'), was used. [from Old French from Latin *Janua* = Genoa]

Jeans /dʒiːnz/ James Hopwood 1877–1946. British mathematician and scientist. In physics he worked on the kinetic theory of gases, and on forms of energy radiation; in astronomy, his work focused on giant and dwarf stars, the nature of spiral nebulae, and the origin of the cosmos. He did much to popularize astronomy.

Jedda /'dʒedə/ alternative spelling for the Saudi Arabian port ◊Jiddah.

Jeep *n.* trade name of a small, sturdy motor vehicle with four-wheel drive. [from *GP* = general purposes, influenced by 'Eugene the *Jeep*', animal in a comic strip]

jeer *v.t./i* to laugh or shout (*at*) rudely or scornfully. —*n.* a jeering remark or shout.

Jefferson /'dʒefəsən/ Thomas 1743–1826. 3rd president of the USA 1801–09, founder of the Democratic Republican party. He was born in Virginia into a wealthy family. He published *A Summary View of the Rights of America* 1774 and as a member of the Continental Congresses of 1775–76 was largely responsible for the drafting of the ◊Declaration of Independence. He was governor of Virginia 1779–81, ambassador to Paris 1785–89, secretary of state 1789–93, and vice president 1797–1801.

No government ought to be without censors, and where the press is free, no one ever will.

Thomas Jefferson
letter to George Washington 9 Sept 1792

Jeffreys /'dʒefrɪz/ Alec John 1950– . British geneticist, who discovered the DNA probes necessary for accurate ◊genetic fingerprinting so that a murderer or rapist could be identified by, for example, traces of blood, tissue, or semen.

Jeffreys George, 1st Baron 1648–1689. Welsh judge. Born in Denbighshire, he became Chief Justice of the King's Bench in 1683, and presided over many political trials, notably those of Sidney, Oates, and Baxter, becoming notorious for his brutality.

Jehosophat /dʒi'hɒsəfæt/ 4th king of Judah *c.*873–849 BC; he allied himself with Ahab, king of Israel, in the war against Syria.

Jehovah /dʒi'həʊvə/ or **Jahweh** in the Old Testament the name of God, revealed to Moses; in Hebrew texts of the Old Testament the name was represented by the letters YHVH (without the vowels 'a o a') as it was regarded as too sacred to be pronounced. [from Hebrew *yahveh*]

Jehovah's Witness a member of a religious organization originating in the USA in 1872 under Charles Taze Russell (1852–1916). Jehovah's Witnesses attach great importance to Christ's second coming, which Russell predicted would occur in 1914, and which Witnesses still believe is imminent. All Witnesses are expected to take part in house-to-house preaching; there are no clergy.

Jehu /'dʒiːhjuː/ king of Israel *c.*842–815 BC. He led a successful rebellion against the family of ◊Ahab and was responsible for the death of Jezebel.

jejune /dʒi'dʒuːn/ *adj.* 1. insipid, unsatisfying to the mind. 2. deficient in nourishing qualities, barren. [Latin *jejunus* = fasting]

jejunum /dʒi'dʒuːnəm/ *n.* the part of the small intestine between the duodenum and the ileum. [Latin]

Jekyll /'dʒiːkl/ Gertrude 1843–1932. English landscape gardener and writer. She created over 200 gardens, many in collaboration with the architect Edwin ◊Lutyens. Her own home at Munstead Wood, Surrey was designed for her by Lutyens.

Jekyll and Hyde /'haɪd/ the two conflicting sides of a personality, as in the novel by the Scottish writer R L Stevenson, *The Strange Case of Dr Jekyll and Mr Hyde* 1886, where the good Jekyll by means of a potion periodically transforms himself into the evil Hyde.

jell *v.i.* (*colloquial*) 1. to set as jelly. 2. to take definite form.

jellaba /'dʒeləbə/ *n.* a loose, hooded cloak worn by Arab men in some countries. [Arabic]

jelly[1] *n.* 1. a soft, solid, semitransparent food made of or with gelatine. 2. a substance of similar consistency. 3. a kind of jam made of strained fruit-juice and sugar. —*v.t./i.* 1. to set or cause to set as jelly, to congeal. 2. to set (food) in jelly. —**jelly baby**, a gelatinous sweet in the shape of a baby. [from Old French *gelee* = frost, from Latin *gelare* = freeze (*gelu* = frost)]

jelly[2] *n.* (*slang*) gelignite.

jellyfish *n.* (*plural* **jellyfish**) a coelenterate (usually marine) animal with a saucer-shaped gelatinous body and stinging tentacles. Most jellyfish move freely, but some are attached by a stalk to rocks or seaweed. They feed on small animals which are paralysed by their sting. See also ◊medusa.

jemmy *n.* a burglar's crowbar for forcing doors, windows, etc. [pet-form of *James*]

je ne sais quoi a certain indescribable quality. [French = I don't know what]

Jenkins /'dʒeŋkɪnz/ Roy (Harris) 1920– . British politician. He became a Labour minister in 1964, was home secretary 1965–67 and 1974–76, and chancellor of the Exchequer 1967–70. He was president of the European Commission 1977–81. In 1981 he became one of the founders of the Social Democratic Party and was elected in 1982, but lost his seat in 1987. In the same year, he was elected chancellor of Oxford University and made a life peer.

Jenner /'dʒenə/ Edward 1749–1823. English physician who pioneered vaccination. In Jenner's day, smallpox was a major killer. His discovery that inoculation with cowpox gives immunity to smallpox was a great medical breakthrough. He coined the word 'vaccination' from the Latin word for cowpox, *vaccina*.

jeopardize /'dʒepədaɪz/ *v.t.* to endanger.

jeopardy /'dʒepədɪ/ *n.* danger. [from Old French *ieu parti* = divided (i.e. even) game from Latin *jocus* = game and *partiri* = divide]

Jerablus /'dʒerəbləs/ ancient Syrian city, adjacent to Carchemish on the river Euphrates.

jerboa /dʒɜː'bəuə/ *n.* 1. several genera of rodents, about 15–20 cm/6–8 in long, found in Africa, Asia, and E Europe. They are mainly herbivorous and nocturnal. 2. any of various Australian genera resembling these. [Latin, from Arabic *yarbū* = flesh of loins, jerboa]

jeremiad /dʒeri'maɪəd/ *n.* a long, mournful complaint about one's troubles. [from French]

Jeremiah /dʒeri'maɪə/ 7th–6th century BC. Old Testament Hebrew prophet, whose ministry continued 626–586 BC. He was imprisoned during ◊Nebuchadnezzar's siege of Jerusalem on suspicion of intending to desert to the enemy. On the city's fall, he retired to Egypt.

Jericho /'dʒerɪkəu/ Israeli-administered town in Jordan, north of the Dead Sea. It was settled by 8000 BC, and by 6000 BC had become a walled city with 2,000 inhabitants. In the Old Testament it was the first Canaanite stronghold captured by the Israelites, and its walls, according to the Book of ◊Joshua, fell to the blast of Joshua's trumpets. Successive archaeological excavations since 1907 show that the walls of the city were destroyed many times.

jerk[1] *n.* 1. a sudden sharp pull, push, twist, start etc. 2. a movement caused by involuntary contraction of a muscle. —*v.t./i.* to move with a jerk; to throw with suddenly arrested motion. —**jerky** *adj.*, **jerkily** *adv.*, **jerkiness** *n.*

jerk[2] *v.t.* to cure (beef etc.) by cutting it into long slices and drying it in the sun. [from American Spanish from Quechua *echarqui* = dried flesh]

jerkin *n.* 1. a sleeveless jacket. 2. (*historical*) a man's close-fitting jacket, often of leather.

jeroboam /dʒerə'bəuəm/ *n.* a wine-bottle of 4 times the ordinary size. [named after *Jeroboam*]

Jeroboam 10th century BC. First king of Israel *c.* 922–901 BC after it split from the kingdom of Judah. He was described as a 'mighty man of valour' (1 Kings 11:28).

Jerome /dʒə'rəum/ Jerome K(lapka) 1859–1927. English journalist and writer. His works include the humorous essays *Idle Thoughts of an Idle Fellow* 1889, the novel *Three Men in a Boat* 1889, and the play *The Passing of the Third Floor Back* 1907.

Jekyll English horticulturalist Gertrude Jekyll introduced the wild garden style to Britain in the early years of this century. This portrait was painted by William Nicholson in 1920.

I like work; it fascinates me. I can sit and look at it for hours.

> Jerome K. Jerome
> *Three Men in a Boat*

Jerome, St *c.* 340–420. One of the early Christian leaders and scholars known as the Fathers of the Church. His Latin versions of the Old and New Testaments form the basis of the Roman Catholic Vulgate. He is usually depicted with a lion. Feast day 30 Sept.

Jerry *n.* (*colloquial*) a German; Germans collectively. [from German]

jerry *n.* (*slang*) a chamber-pot.

jerry-built *adj.* built badly and with poor materials —**jerry-builder** *n.*, **jerry-building** *n.*

jerrycan /'dʒerɪkæn/ *n.* a kind of five-gallon can for petrol or water, used by the Germans and named and later adopted by the Allied forces in World War II.

jersey /'dʒɜːzɪ/ *n.* 1. a pullover with sleeves. 2. machine-knitted fabric used for making clothes. [from *Jersey* in the Channel Islands]

Jersey largest of the ◊Channel Islands; **area** 117 sq km/45 sq mi; **capital** St Helier; **population** (1986) 80,000. It is governed by a lieutenant-governor, representing the English crown, and an assembly.

Jersey *n.* a breed of light-brown dairy cattle that originated in Jersey, producing milk with a high fat content; an animal of this breed.

Jerusalem /dʒə'ruːsələm/ ancient city of Palestine, divided in 1948 between Jordan and the new republic of Israel; area (pre-1967) 37.5 sq km/14.5 sq mi, (post-1967) 108 sq km/42 sq mi, including areas of the West Bank; population (1989) 500,000, about 350,000 Israelis and 150,000 Palestinians. In 1950 the western New City was proclaimed as the Israeli capital, and, having captured from Jordan the eastern Old City in 1967, Israel affirmed in 1980 that the united city was the country's capital; the United Nations does not recognize the claim.

Jerusalem artichoke a variety of ◊artichoke.

Jervis /'dʒɜːvɪs/ John, Earl of St Vincent 1735–1823. English admiral who secured the blockage of Toulon, France, in 1795 in the Revolutionary Wars, and the defeat of the Spanish fleet off Cape St Vincent in 1797, in which Admiral ◊Nelson played a key part. Jervis was a rigid disciplinarian.

jess *n.* a short strap put round the leg of a hawk used in falconry. [from Old French *ges*, from Latin *jactus* = throw]

jessamine /'dʒesəmɪn/ *n.* = ◊jasmine.

Jessop /'dʒesəp/ William 1745–1814. British canal engineer, who built the first canal in England entirely dependent on reservoirs for its water supply (the Grantham Canal 1793–97), and who designed (with Thomas ◊Telford) the 300 m/1,000 ft long Pontcysyllte aqueduct over the river Dee.

jest *n.* a joke. —*v.i.* to joke. —**in jest**, jokingly. [originally = exploit, from Old French *geste* from Latin *gesta* (*gerere* = do)]

jester *n.* 1. a professional entertainer employed at a king's court or in a noble household in the Middle Ages. 2. a person who makes jests.

Jesuit /'dʒezjuɪt/ *n.* a member of the largest and most influential Roman Catholic religious order (also known as the **Society of Jesus**) founded by Ignatius ◊Loyola in Paris in 1534, with the aims of protecting Catholicism against the Reformation and carrying out missionary work. During the 16th and 17th centuries Jesuits were missionaries in Japan, China, Paraguay, and among the North American Indians. The order now has about 29,000 members (15,000 priests plus students and lay members), and their schools and universities are renowned. [from *Jesus*]

Jesuitical /dʒezju'ɪtɪkəl/ *adj.* 1. of or like Jesuits. 2. (*derogatory*) dissembling, equivocating.

Jesus /'dʒiːzəs/ *c.* 4 BC–AD 29 or 30. Hebrew preacher on whose teachings ◊Christianity was founded. According to the accounts of his life in the four Gospels, he was born in Bethlehem, Palestine, son of God and the Virgin Mary, and brought up by Mary and her husband Joseph as a carpenter in Nazareth. After adult baptism, he gathered

12 disciples, but his preaching antagonized the Roman authorities and he was executed by crucifixion. Three days later there came reports of his resurrection and, later, his ascension to heaven.

jet[1] *n.* **1.** a stream of water, gas(es), or flame etc. ejected, usually from a small opening. **2.** a spout or opening from which this comes; a burner on a gas cooker. **3.** a jet-propelled aircraft; a jet engine. —*v.t./i.* (**-tt-**) **1.** to spurt in jets. **2.** to travel or convey by jet-propelled aircraft. **3.** to jut. —**jet engine,** an engine utilizing jet propulsion to provide forward thrust. See ◊ramjet, ◊turbofan, ◊turbojet and ◊turboprop. [from French *jeter* = throw from Latin *jactare* frequentative of *jacere* = throw]

jet[2] *n.* **1.** hard black lignite that takes a brilliant polish. It is cut and polished for use in jewellery and ornaments. Articles made of jet have been found in Bronze Age tombs. **2.** its colour, deep glossy black. —*adj.* of this colour. —**jet-black** *adj. & n.* [from Greek *Gagai,* town in Asia Minor]

JET acronym from Joint European Torus, a ◊tokamak machine built in England to conduct experiments on nuclear fusion. It is the focus of the European effort to produce a practical fusion-power reactor.

jeté n. in dance, a jump from one foot to the other. A **grand jeté** is a big jump in which the dancer pushes off on one foot, holds a brief pose in mid-air, and lands lightly on the other foot. [French = thrown]

jetfoil *n.* an advanced type of ◊hydrofoil boat built by Boeing, propelled by water jets. It features horizontal, fully submerged hydrofoils fore and aft and has a sophisticated computerized control system to maintain its stability in all waters.

jet lag the effect of a sudden switch of time zones in air travel, resulting in tiredness and feeling 'out of step' with day and night. In 1989 it was suggested that use of the hormone melatonin helped to lessen the effect of jet lag by re-setting the body clock. See also ◊circadian rhythm.

jet propulsion a method of propulsion in which an object is propelled in one direction by a jet, or stream of gases, moving in the other. This follows from ◊Newton's celebrated third law of motion 'to every action, there is an equal and opposite reaction'. The most widespread application of the jet principle is in the jet engine, the most common kind of aircraft engine. —**jet-propelled** *adj.* using jet propulsion.

jetsam *n.* goods thrown overboard from a ship in distress to lighten it, especially those that are washed ashore. See ◊flotsam, jetsam, and lagan.

jet set the wealthy élite making frequent air journeys between social or business events.

jet stream a narrow band of very fast wind (velocities of over 150 kph/95 mph) found at altitudes of 10–16 km/6–10 mi in the upper troposphere or lower stratosphere. Jet streams usually occur about the latitudes of the Westerlies (35°–60°).

jettison /'dʒetɪsən/ *v.t.* **1.** to throw (goods) overboard; to release or drop from an aircraft or spacecraft in flight. **2.** to discard as unwanted. [from Anglo-French and Old French from Latin *jactare,* frequentative of *jacere* = throw]

jetty *n.* a breakwater or landing-stage. [from Old French]

Jew /dʒuː/ *n.* a follower of ◊Judaism, the Jewish religion. The term is also used to refer to those who claim descent from the ancient Hebrews, a Semitic people of the Near East. Today, some may recognize their ethnic heritage but not practise the religious or cultural traditions. The term came into use in medieval Europe, based on the Latin name for Judeans, the people of Judah. Prejudice against Jews is termed ◊anti-Semitism. —**Jew's harp,** a musical instrument consisting of a small U-shaped metal frame held in the teeth while a springy metal clip joining its ends is twanged with a finger. The resulting drone excites resonances in the mouth that can be varied in pitch to produce a melody. [from French, ultimately from Hebrew *yehudi,* member of the tribe of Judah]

jewel /'dʒuː.əl/ *n.* **1.** a precious stone worn as an ornament, a jewelled ornament. **2.** a highly valued person or thing. [from Anglo-French]

jewelled /'dʒuː.əld/ *adj.* **1.** set with jewels. **2.** (of a watch) fitted with jewels for the pivot-holes on account of their resistance to wear.

jeweller /'dʒuː.ələ/ *n.* a person who deals in or makes jewellery or jewels.

jet propulsion

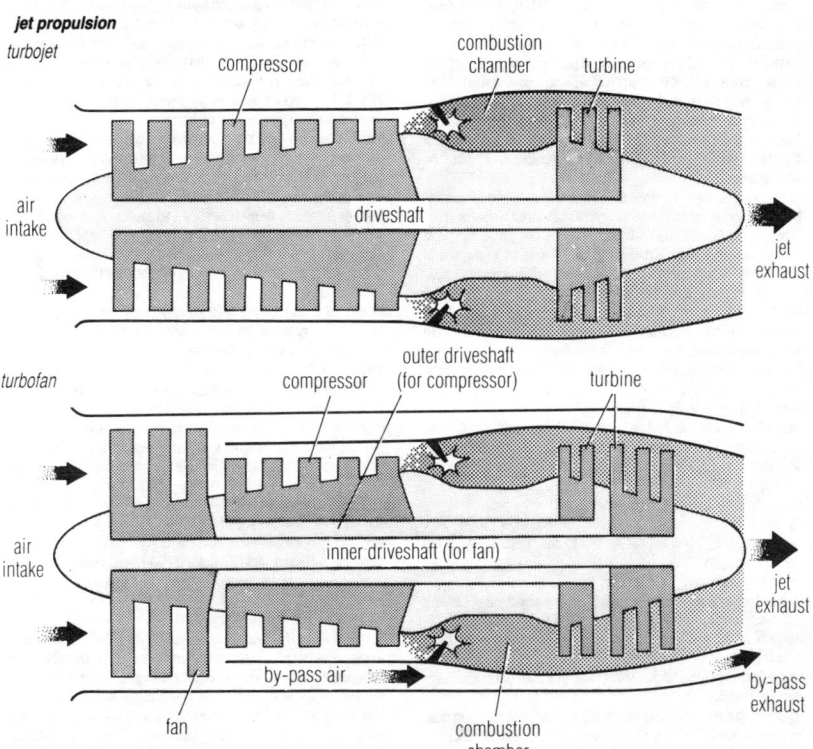

turbojet

compressor
combustion chamber
turbine
air intake
driveshaft
jet exhaust

turbofan

compressor
outer driveshaft (for compressor)
turbine
air intake
inner driveshaft (for fan)
jet exhaust
by-pass air
by-pass exhaust
fan
combustion chamber

jewellery /'dʒuːəlrɪ/ *n.* jewels or similar ornaments to be worn.

Jewess /'dʒuːes/ *n.* a female Jew.

Jewish /'dʒuːɪʃ/ *adj.* of Jews.

Jewish Agency an administrative body created by the British mandate power in Palestine in 1929 to oversee the Jewish population and immigration. In 1948 it took over as the government of an independent Israel.

Jewish calendar a complex combination of lunar and solar cycles, varied by consideration of religious observance. A year may have 12 or 13 months, which normally alternate between 29 and 30 days; New Year (Rosh Hashonah) falls between 5 Sept and 5 Oct. The calendar dates from the hypothetical creation of the world (taken as 7 Oct 3761 BC).

Jewry /'dʒuri/ *n.* the Jewish people.

Jezebel /'dʒezəbel/ in the Old Testament, daughter of the king of Sidon. She married King Ahab of Israel, and was brought into conflict with the prophet Elijah by her introduction of the worship of Baal.

Jiang /dʒi'æŋ/ Zemin 1926– . Chinese political leader. The son-in-law of ◊Li Xiannian, he joined the Chinese Communist Party's politburo in 1967 after serving in the Moscow embassy and as mayor of Shanghai. He succeeded ◊Zhao Ziyang as party leader after the Tiananmen Square massacre of 1989. A cautious proponent of economic reform coupled with unswerving adherence to the party's 'political line', he subsequently replaced ◊Deng Xiaoping as head of the influential central military commission.

Jiang Jie Shi /dʒizæŋ dʒeɪ 'ʃiː/ alternative transcription of ◊Chiang Kai-shek.

Jiang Qing /dʒi'æŋ 'tʃɪŋ/ formerly **Chiang Ching** 1913– . Chinese communist politician, wife of the party leader Mao Zedong. In 1960 she became minister for culture, and played a key role in the 1966–69 Cultural Revolution as the leading member of the Shanghai-based Gang of Four, who attempted to seize power in 1976. Jiang was imprisoned.

Jiangsu /dʒiæŋ'suː/ formerly **Kiangsu**, province on the coast of E China; **area** 102,200 sq km/39,449 sq mi; **capital** Nanjing; **physical** the swampy mouth of the Chang Jiang; **products** cereals, rice, tea, cotton, soya beans, fish, silk, ceramics, textiles, coal, iron, copper, cement; **population** (1986) 62,130,000.

Jiangxi /dʒiæŋ'ʃiː/ formerly **Kiangsi**, province of SE China; **area** 164,800 sq km/63,613 sq mi; **capital** Nanchang; **population** (1986) 35,090,000; **products** rice, tea, cotton, tobacco, porcelain, coal, tungsten, uranium; **history** the province was Mao Zedong's original base in the first phase of the Communist struggle against the Nationalists.

jib[1] *n.* 1. a triangular stay-sail from the outer end of the jib-boom to the head of the fore-topmast in large ships or from bowsprit to masthead in smaller ones. 2. the projecting arm of a crane. —*v.t./i.* (-bb-) = gybe. —**cut of a person's jib**, his general appearance or manner. **jib-boom** *n.* a spar run out from the end of a bowsprit.

jib[2] *v.i.* (-bb-) 1. to refuse to proceed in some action. 2. (of a horse) to stop suddenly and refuse to go forwards. —**jib at,** to show unwillingness or dislike for.

jibbah /'dʒɪbə/ *n.* a long coat worn by Muslim men in some countries. [Arabic]

jibe /dʒaɪb/ *v.t./i. & n.* = gibe.

Jiddah /'dʒɪdə/ or **Jedda**; port in Hejaz, Saudi Arabia, on the E shore of the Red Sea; population (1986) 1,000,000. Industries include cement, steel, and oil refining. Pilgrims pass through here on their way to Mecca.

jiff *n.* or **jiffy** (*colloquial*) a short time.

jig *n.* 1. a lively jumping dance; the music for this. 2. a device that holds a piece of work and guides the tools operating upon it. 3. a template. —*v.t./i.* (-gg-) to move up and down rapidly and jerkily.

jigger[1] *n.* 1. a measure of spirits etc.; a small glass holding this amount. 2. (*slang*) a cue-rest used in billiards.

jigger[2] *n.* 1. = chigger. 2. = chigoe. [corruption of these words]

jiggered /'dʒɪgəd/ *adj.* (*colloquial*, in a mild oath) euphemism for damned.

jiggery-pokery /'dʒɪgərɪ 'pəʊkərɪ/ *n.* (*colloquial*) trickery, underhand dealing. [Scottish *jouk* = dodge, skulk]

jiggle *v.t./i.* to rock or jerk lightly.

Jiangsu Massed silkworm cocoons are gathered from the cut branches by a member of a commune which is striving to diversify the local economy.

jigsaw /'dʒɪgsɔː/ *n.* 1. a mechanically operated fretsaw. 2. (also **jigsaw puzzle**) a picture on wood or cardboard etc. cut into irregular pieces which can be shuffled and reassembled for amusement.

jihad /dʒi'hɑːd/ *n.* a holy war undertaken by Muslims against non-believers. In the **Mecca Declaration** of 1981, the Islamic powers pledged a jihad against Israel, though not necessarily a military attack. [Arabic = fight, struggle]

Jilin /dʒiː'lɪn/ formerly **Kirin**, province of NE China in central ◊Manchuria; **area** 187,000 sq km/72,182 sq mi; **capital** Changchun; **population** (1986) 23,150,000.

jilt *v.t.* to reject or abandon (a person) after having courted or promised to marry him or her.

Jim Crow /'dʒɪm 'krəʊ/ originally a derogatory term used by Americans for a black person, it refers to the systematic practice of segregating black Americans, which was common in the South until the 1960s. **Jim Crow laws** are laws designed to deny civil rights to blacks or to enforce the policy of segregation, which existed until Supreme Court decisions and civil-rights legislation of the 1950s and 1960s (Civil Rights Act 1964, Voting Rights Act 1965) denied their legality.

Jinan /dʒiː'næn/ or **Tsinan** city and capital of Shandong province, China; population (1986) 1,430,000. It has food-processing and textile industries.

jingle *v.t./i.* to make or cause to make a metallic ringing or clinking sound. —*n.* 1. a jingling sound. 2. verse or words with simple catchy rhymes or repetitive sounds.

jingo *n.* (*plural* **jingoes**) an aggressive, fanatical patriot. —**jingoism** *n.*, **jingoist** *n.*, **jingoistic** *adj.* [The term originated in 1878, when the British prime minister Disraeli developed a pro-Turkish policy, which nearly involved the UK in war with Russia. His supporters' war song included the line 'We don't want to fight, but by jingo if we do … '.]

jink *v.i.* to move with sudden quick turns, especially in dodging —*n.* an act of jinking. —**high jinks**, boisterous fun. [originally Scottish, probably imitation of nimble motion]

jinn /dʒɪn/ see **jinnee**

Jinnah /'dʒɪnə/ Muhammad Ali 1876–1948. Indian politician, Pakistan's first governor general from 1947. He was president of the ◊Muslim League from 1934, and by 1940 was advocating the need for a separate state of Pakistan; at the 1946 conferences in London he insisted on the partition of British India into Hindu and Muslim states.

jinnee /dʒɪ'niː/ *n.* (*plural* **jinn** also used as *singular*) in Islamic mythology, any of the supernatural beings, similar to but distinguished from angels, able to appear in human and animal form. [Arabic]

Jinsha Jiang /dʒɪn'ʃɑ: dʒɪ'æn/ river of China, which rises in SW China and forms the Chang Jiang (Yangtze) at Yibin.

jinx *n.* (*colloquial*) a person or thing that seems to bring bad luck. [perhaps variant of *jynx* = the wryneck, a bird used in witchcraft]

Jiricna /'jɪrɪtʃnə/ Eva 1939–. Czech architect who has worked in the UK since 1968. Her striking fashion shops, bars, and cafés for Joseph Ettedgui (1900–) are built in a highly refined Modernist style.

jitter *v.i.* (*colloquial*) to be nervous, to behave nervously. —*n.* (*in plural, colloquial*) nervousness. —**jittery** *adj.*

jitterbug *n.* 1. a nervous person. 2. a dance performed chiefly to boogie-woogie and swing music, popular in the early 1940s. —*v.i.* (-**gg**-) to dance the jitterbug.

Jivaro /hiː'vɑːrəʊ/ *n.* a member of a South American Indian peoples of the tropical forests of SE Ecuador and NE Peru. They live by farming, hunting, fishing, and weaving; the Jivaro language belongs to the Andean-Equatorial family. They were formerly famous for preserving the hair and shrunken skin of the heads of their enemies as battle trophies.

jive *n.* a type of fast lively jazz music, a forerunner of rock and roll; an energetic American dance popular in the 1940s and 1950s. —*v.i.* to dance to or play jive.

jnr, Jnr. abbreviation of junior.

Joan of Arc, St /dʒəʊn, ɑ:k/ 1412–1431. French military leader. In 1429 at Chinon, NW France, she persuaded Charles VII that she had a divine mission to expel the occupying English from N France (see ◊Hundred Years' War) and secure his coronation. She raised the siege of Orléans, defeated the English at Patay, north of Orléans, and Charles was crowned in Reims. However, she failed to take Paris and was captured in May 1430 by the Burgundians, who sold her to the English. She was found guilty of witchcraft and heresy by a tribunal of French ecclesiastics who supported the English. She was burned to death at the stake in Rouen on 30 May 1431. In 1920 she was canonized.

job *n.* 1. a piece of work. 2. a position in paid employment. 3. a difficult task. —*v.t./i.* (-**bb**-) 1. to do jobs, to do piecework. 2. to hire or let out for a definite time or job. 3. to buy and sell (stock or goods) as a middleman. —**bad** (*or* **good**) **job**, an unsatisfactory (or satisfactory) state of affairs. **job lot**, a collection of miscellaneous articles. **just the job**, (*slang*) precisely what is wanted. **make a** (**good**) **job of**, to do thoroughly or successfully.

Job /dʒəʊb/ *c.*5th century BC. In the Old Testament, Hebrew leader who in the *Book of Job* questioned God's infliction of suffering on the righteous while enduring great sufferings himself.

jobber *n.* 1. name until Oct 1986 for a dealer on the London stock exchange who negotiated with a broker who, in turn, dealt with the general public. The jobber's role is now combined with that of the broker, and is known as a ◊market-maker. 2. one who jobs.

jobbery /'dʒɒbərɪ/ *n.* corrupt dealing.

jobless *adj.* unemployed.

Jock /dʒɒk/ *n.* a nickname for a Scotsman. [Scottish form of *Jack*]

jockey *n.* a person who rides in horse-races, especially a professional. —*v.t./i.* to manœuvre in order to gain an advantage. [from Scottish *Jock* = Jack]

jock-strap *n.* a support or protection for the male genitals, worn especially by sportsmen. [from vulgar *jock* = genitals]

jocose /dʒə'kəʊs/ *adj.* joking. —**jocosely** *adv.*, **jocoseness** *n.*, **jocosity** /-'kɒsɪtɪ/ *n.* [from Latin *jocus* = jest]

jocular /'dʒɒkjʊlə/ *adj.* joking, humorous. **jocularly** *adv.*, **jocularity** /-'lærɪtɪ/ *n.*

jocund /'dʒɒkənd/ *adj.* (*literary*) merry, cheerful. —**jocundity** /dʒə'kʌndɪtɪ/ *n.* [from Old French from Latin *jocundus* = pleasant]

jodhpurs /'dʒɒdpəz/ *n.pl.* riding-breeches reaching to the ankle, fitting closely below the knee and loosely above it. [from *Jodhpur*, city and former State of India]

Jodl /'jəʊdl/ Alfred 1892–1946. German general. In World War II he drew up the Nazi government's plan for the attack on Yugoslavia, Greece, and the USSR. In Jan 1945 he became Chief of Staff and headed the delegation that signed Germany's surrender in Reims on 7 May 1945. He was tried for war crimes in Nuremberg 1945–46 and hanged.

Jodrell Bank /'dʒɒdrəl 'bæŋk/ site in Cheshire, England, of the Nuffield Radio Astronomy Laboratories of the University of Manchester. Its largest instrument is the 76 m/250 ft radio dish, completed in 1957 and modified in 1970. A 38 m × 25 m/125 ft × 82 ft elliptical radio dish was introduced in 1964, capable of working at shorter wavelengths. These radio telescopes are used in conjunction with other smaller dishes to produce detailed maps of radio sources.

joey *n.* (*Australian*) 1. a young kangaroo. 2. a young animal. [Aboriginal *joë*]

Joffre /'ʒɒfrə/ Joseph Jacques Césaire 1852–1931. Marshal of France during World War I. He was chief of general staff in 1911. The German invasion of Belgium in 1914 took him by surprise, but his stand at the Battle of the ◊Marne resulted in his appointment as supreme commander of all the French armies in 1915. His failure to make adequate preparations at Verdun in 1916 and the military disasters on the ◊Somme led to his replacement by Nivelle in Dec 1916.

jog *v.t./i.* (-**gg**-) 1. to shake with a push or jerk, to nudge. 2. to rouse or stimulate (memory). 3. to move up and down with an unsteady motion. 4. to move at a jogtrot, to run at a leisurely pace with short strides as a form of exercise. —*n.* 1. a slight shake or push, a nudge. 2. a slow walk, run, or trot. —**jog on** *or* **along,** to proceed slowly or laboriously. —**jogger** *n.*

joggle *v.t./i.* to shake slightly, to move by slight jerks. —*n.* a slight shake, a joggling movement.

jogtrot *n.* a slow regular trot.

Johannesburg /dʒəʊ'hænɪsbɜːg/ largest city of South Africa, situated on the Witwatersrand River in Transvaal; population (1985) 1,609,000. It is the centre of a large gold-mining industry; other industries include engineering works, meat-chilling plants, and clothing factories.

John /dʒɒn/ *Augustus* (Edwin) 1878–1961. British painter of landscapes and portraits, including *The Smiling Woman* 1910 (Tate Gallery, London) of his second wife, Dorelia.

John Elton. Stage name of Reginald Kenneth Dwight 1947– . English pop singer, pianist, and composer, noted for his melodies and elaborate costumes and glasses.

John known as **John Lackland** 1167–1216. King of England from 1199 and acting king from 1189 during his brother Richard I (the Lion-Hearted)'s absence on the third Crusade. He lost Normandy and almost all the other English possessions in France to Philip II of France by 1205. His repressive policies and excessive taxation brought him into conflict with his barons, and he was forced to seal the ◊Magna Carta in 1215. Later repudiation of it led to the first Barons' War 1215–17, during which he died.

John two kings of France, including:

John II 1319–1364. King of France from 1350. He was defeated and captured by the Black Prince at Poitiers in 1356 and imprisoned in England. Released in 1360, he failed to raise the money for his ransom and returned to England in 1364, where he died.

John name of 23 popes, including:

John XXII 1249–1334. Pope 1316–34. He spent his papacy in Avignon, France, engaged in a long conflict with the Holy Roman emperor, Louis of Bavaria, and the Spiritual Franciscans, a monastic order who preached the absolute poverty of the clergy.

John XXIII Angelo Giuseppe Roncalli 1881–1963. Pope from 1958. He improved relations with the USSR in line with his encyclical *Pacem in Terris*/*Peace on Earth* 1963, established Roman Catholic hierarchies in newly emergent states, and summoned the Second Vatican Council, which reformed church liturgy and backed the ecumenical movement.

'John XXIII' Baldassare Costa died 1419. Anti-pope 1410–15. In an attempt to end the ◊Great Schism he was elected pope by a council of cardinals in Bologna, but was deposed by the Council of Constance in 1415, together with the popes of Avignon and Rome. His papacy is not recognized by the church.

John three kings of Poland, including:

John III Sobieski 1624–1696. King of Poland from 1674. He became commander-in-chief of the army in 1668 after victories over the Cossacks and Tatars. A victory over the Turks in 1673 helped to get him elected to the Polish throne, and he saved Vienna from the besieging Turks in 1683.

John six kings of Portugal, including:

John I 1357–1433. King of Portugal from 1385. An illegitimate son of Pedro I, he was elected by the Cortes (parliament). His claim was supported by an English army against the rival king of Castile, thus establishing the Anglo-Portuguese Alliance in 1386. He married Philippa of Lancaster, daughter of ◊John of Gaunt.

John IV 1603–1656. King of Portugal from 1640. Originally Duke of Braganza, he was elected king when the Portuguese rebelled against Spanish rule. His reign was marked by a long war against Spain, which did not end until 1668.

John VI 1769–1826. King of Portugal and regent for his insane mother **Maria I** from 1799 until her death in 1816. He fled to Brazil when the French invaded Portugal in 1807 and did not return until 1822. On his return Brazil declared its independence, with John's elder son Pedro as emperor.

John Bull /bʊl/ an imaginary figure who is a personification of the English nation, similar to the American Uncle Sam. The name was popularized by Dr ◊Arbuthnot's *History of John Bull* 1712. He is represented as a prosperous farmer of the 18th century. [originally character in satire (1712)]

johnny /'dʒɒnɪ/ *n. (colloquial)* a fellow, a man. —**johnny-come-lately** *n.* a newcomer, an upstart. [diminutive of forename *John*]

John of Damascus, St /dʒɒn/ *c.*676–*c.*754. Eastern Orthodox theologian and hymn writer, a defender of image worship against the iconoclasts (image-breakers). Contained in his *The Fountain of Knowledge* is *An Accurate Exposition of the Orthodox Faith*, an important chronicle of theology from the 4th–7th centuries. He was born in Damascus, Syria. Feast day 4 Dec.

John of Gaunt 1340–1399. English politician, born in Ghent, fourth son of Edward III, duke of Lancaster from 1362. He distinguished himself during the Hundred Years' War. During Edward's last years, and the years before Richard II attained the age of majority, he acted as head of government, and Parliament protested against his corrupt rule.

John of Salisbury *c.*1115–1180. English philosopher and historian. His *Policraticus* portrayed the church as the guarantee of liberty against the unjust claims of secular authority.

John of the Cross, St 1542–1591. Spanish Roman Catholic Carmelite friar from 1564, who was imprisoned several times for attempting to impose the reforms laid down by St Teresa. His verse describes spiritual ecstasy. Feast day 24 Nov.

John Paul /dʒɒn pɔːl/ the name of two popes:

John Paul I Albino Luciani 1912–1978. Pope 26 Aug–28 Sept 1978. His name was chosen as the combination of his two immediate predecessors.

John Paul II Karol Wojtyla 1920– . Pope 1978– , the first non-Italian to be elected pope since 1522. He was born near Kraków, Poland. He has upheld the tradition of papal infallibility, condemned artificial contraception, women priests, married priests, and modern dress for monks and nuns, measures which have aroused criticism from liberalizing elements in the Church. He has warned against involvement of priests in political activity.

Johns Jasper 1930– . US painter and printmaker who rejected the abstract in favour of such simple subjects as flags, maps, and numbers. He uses pigments mixed with wax (encaustic) to create a rich surface with unexpected delicacies of colour. He has also created collages and lithographs.

John, St 1st century AD. New Testament apostle. Traditionally, he wrote the fourth Gospel and the Johannine Epistles (when he was bishop of Ephesus), and the Book of Revelation (while exiled to the Greek island of Patmos). His emblem is an eagle; his feast day 27 Dec.

Johnson /'dʒɒnsən/ Amy 1904–1941. British aviator. She made a solo flight from England to Australia in 1930, in 19 1/2 days, and in 1932 made the fastest ever solo flight from England to Cape Town, South Africa. Her plane disappeared over the English Channel in World War II while she was serving with the Air Transport Auxiliary.

John Paul II The first Polish pope, John Paul II is an author and an accomplished linguist.

Johnson Andrew 1808–1875. 17th president of the USA 1865–69, a Democrat. He was born in Raleigh, North Carolina, and was a congressman from Tennessee 1843–53, governor of Tennessee 1853–57, senator 1857–62, and vice president in 1865. He succeeded to the presidency on Lincoln's assassination (15 April 1865). His conciliatory policy to the defeated South after the Civil War involved him in a feud with the Radical Republicans. When he tried to dismiss Edwin Stanton, a cabinet secretary, his political opponents seized on the opportunity to charge him with 'high crimes and misdemeanours' and attempted to remove him from office. This battle culminated with his impeachment before the Senate in 1868, which failed to convict him by one vote.

Johnson Ben 1961– . Canadian sprinter. In 1987, he broke the world record for the 100 metres, running it in 9.83 seconds. At the Olympic Games in 1988, he again broke the record, but was disqualified and suspended for using anabolic steroids to enhance his performance.

Johnson Jack 1878–1968. US heavyweight boxer. He overcame severe racial prejudice to become the first black heavyweight champion of the world in 1908 when he travelled to Australia to challenge Tommy Burns. The US authorities wanted Johnson 'dethroned' because of his colour but could not find suitable challengers until 1915, when he lost the title in a dubious fight decision to the giant Jess Willard.

Johnson Lyndon Baines 1908–1973. 36th president of the USA 1963–69, a Democrat. He was born in Stonewall, Texas, elected to Congress 1937–49 and the Senate 1949–60. His persuasive powers and hard work on domestic issues led J F Kennedy to ask him to be his vice presidential running mate in 1960. Johnson brought critical Southern support which won a narrow victory.

You never want to give a man a present when he's feeling good. You want to do it when he's down.

Lyndon B. Johnson (attrib.)

Johnson Philip Cortelyou 1906– . US architect who coined the term 'international style'. He originally designed in the style of ◊Mies van der Rohe, and later became an exponent of ◊Post-Modernism. He designed the giant AT&T building in New York in 1978, a pink skyscraper with a Chippendale-style cabinet top.

Johnson Samuel, known as 'Dr Johnson', 1709–1784. English lexicographer, author, and critic, also a brilliant conversationalist and the dominant figure in 18th-century London literary society. His *Dictionary*, published in 1755, remained authoritative for over a century, and is still remarkable for the vigour of its definitions. In 1764 he founded the 'Literary Club', whose members included Reynolds, Burke, Goldsmith, Garrick, and ◊Boswell, Johnson's biographer.

John the Baptist, St /dʒɒn/ *c.*12 BC–*c.*AD 27. In the New Testament, an itinerant preacher. After preparation in the wilderness, he proclaimed the coming of the Messiah and baptized Jesus in the River Jordan. He was later executed by ◊Herod Antipas at the request of Salome, who demanded that his head be brought to her on a platter.

joie de vivre /ʒwɑː də ˈviːvr/ a feeling of exuberant enjoyment of life; high spirits. [French, = joy of living]

join *v.t./i.* **1.** to put together, to fasten, to unite. **2.** to connect (points) by a line etc. **3.** to become a member of (a club, army etc.); to take one's place with or in (a company, procession etc.); to take part with others (*in* an activity etc.). **4.** to unite (persons, or one *with* or *to* another); to be united in marriage, an alliance etc. **5.** (of a river, road etc.) to become continuous or connected with (another). —*n.* the point, line, or surface where things join. —**join battle,** to begin fighting. **join forces,** to combine efforts. **join up,** to enlist in an army etc. [from Old French *joindre* from Latin *jungere*]

joiner *n.* a maker of furniture and light woodwork. —**joinery** *n.* [from Anglo-French and Old French]

joint *n.* **1.** a place where two things are joined. **2.** in any animal with a skeleton, a point of movement or articulation. In invertebrates with an ◊exoskeleton, the joints are places where the exoskeleton is replaced by a more flexible outer covering, the arthrodial membrane, which allows the limb to bend at that point. In vertebrates, it is the point where two bones meet. **3.** a section of an animal's carcass used for food. **4.** a fissure in a mass of rock. **5.** (*slang*) a place of meeting for drinking etc. **6.** (*slang*) a marijuana cigarette. —*adj.* belonging to or done by two or more persons etc. in common; sharing in possession etc. —*v.t.* **1.** to connect by a joint or joints. **2.** to divide (a carcass) into joints or at a joint. —**joint-stock company,** a company with the capital held jointly by the shareholders. **out of joint,** dislocated; (*figuratively*) out of order. —**jointly** *adv.* [from Old French]

joint consultation the process of involving employees, through their representatives, in discussions with representatives of their employers, with the object of influencing management decisions relating to their employment before those decisions are actually taken.

Joint European Torus an experimental nuclear-fusion machine, known as ◊JET.

jointure /ˈdʒɔɪntʃə/ *n.* an estate settled on a wife for the period during which she survives her husband. —*v.t.* to provide with a jointure. [from Old French from Latin]

joint venture in business, an undertaking in which an individual or legal entity of one country forms a company with those of another country, with risks being shared.

Joinville /ʒwænˈviːl/ Jean, Sire de Joinville 1224–1317. French historian, born in Champagne. He accompanied Louis IX on the crusade of 1248–54, which he described in his *History of St Louis.*

joist *n.* one of the parallel timbers stretched from wall to wall to carry floorboards or a ceiling. [from Old French *giste* from Latin *jacēre* = lie]

joke *n.* **1.** a thing said or done to excite laughter. **2.** a ridiculous circumstance, person etc. —*v.i.* to make jokes. —**no joke,** a serious matter. [perhaps from Latin *jocus* = jest]

joker *n.* **1.** one who jokes. **2.** an extra playing-card used in some games. **3.** (*slang*) a person.

jokey /ˈdʒəʊkɪ/ *adj.* joking, not serious.

Joliot-Curie /ˈʒɒliəu ˈkjuəri/ Irène 1897–1956. and Frédéric (born Frédéric Joliot) 1900–1958. French physicists who made the discovery of artificial radioactivity for which they were jointly awarded the 1935 Nobel Prize for Chemistry.

jollify /ˈdʒɒlɪfaɪ/ *v.t./i.* to make or be merry. —**jollification** /-fɪˈkeɪʃən/ *n.*

jollity /ˈdʒɒlɪtɪ/ *n.* being jolly; merry-making. [from Old French *joliveté*]

jolly *adj.* **1.** full of high spirits, cheerful, merry. **2.** slightly drunk. **3.** (*colloquial,* of a person or thing) pleasant, delightful (also *ironic*). —*adv.* (*colloquial*) very. —*v.t.* to coax or humour (a person) in a friendly way. [from Old French *jolif* = gay, pretty]

jolly-boat *n.* a clinker-built ship's boat, smaller than a cutter.

Jolson /ˈdʒəʊlsən/ Al. Stage name of Asa Yoelson

1886–1950. Russian-born US singer and entertainer. Formerly a Broadway and vaudeville star, he gained instant cinema immortality as the star of the first talking picture, *The Jazz Singer* 1927.

jolt /dʒəʊlt/ *v.t./i.* **1.** to shake or dislodge with a jerk. **2.** to move along jerkily, as on a rough road. **3.** to give a mental shock to. —*n.* **1.** a jolting movement. **2.** a surprise or shock.

Jonah /ˈdʒəʊnə/ 7th century BC. Hebrew prophet whose name is given to a book in the Old Testament. According to this, he fled by ship to evade his mission to prophesy the destruction of Nineveh. The crew threw him overboard in a storm, as a bringer of ill fortune, and he spent three days and nights in the belly of a whale before coming to land.

Jonathan /ˈdʒɒnəθən/ Chief (Joseph) Leabua 1914–1987. Lesotho politician. A leader in the drive for independence, Jonathan became prime minister of Lesotho in 1965. His rule was ended by a coup in 1986.

Jones /dʒəʊnz/ Bobby (Robert Tyre) 1902–1971. US golfer. He was the game's greatest amateur player, who never turned professional but won 13 major amateur and professional tournaments, including the Grand Slam of both the amateur and professional opens of both the USA and Britain in 1930.

Jones Charles Martin (Chuck) 1912– . US film animator and cartoon director who worked at Warner Brothers with characters such as Bugs Bunny, Daffy Duck, Wile E Coyote, and Elmer Fudd.

Jones Inigo 1573–*c.*1652. English architect. Born in London, he studied in Italy and was influenced by the works of Palladio. He was employed by James I to design scenery for Ben Jonson's masques. In 1619 he designed his English Renaissance masterpiece, the banqueting room at Whitehall, London.

Jones John Paul 1747–1792. Scottish-born American naval officer in the War of Independence in 1775. Heading a small French-sponsored squadron in the *Bonhomme Richard,* he captured the British warship *Serapis* in a bloody battle off Scarborough, England, in 1799.

Jonestown /ˈdʒəʊnztaʊn/ *n.* commune of the **People's Temple Sect,** NW of Georgetown, Guyana, established in 1974 by the American Jim Jones (1933–78), who originally founded the sect among San Francisco's black community. After a visiting US congressman was shot dead, Jones enforced mass suicide on his followers by instructing them to drink cyanide; 914 died, including over 240 children.

jonquil /ˈdʒɒŋkwɪl/ *n.* a species of narcissus *Narcissus jonquilla,* family Amaryllidaceae, with white or yellow fragrant flowers. Native to Spain and Portugal, it is cultivated elsewhere. [from French from Spanish from Latin *juncus* = rush; so called from its rushlike leaves]

Jonson /ˈdʒɒnsən/ Ben(jamin) 1572–1637. English dramatist, poet, and critic. *Every Man in his Humour* 1598 established the English 'comedy of humours', in which each character embodies a 'humour', or vice, such as greed, lust, or avarice. This was followed by *Cynthia's Revels* 1600 and *Poetaster* 1601. His first extant tragedy is *Sejanus* 1603, with Burbage and Shakespeare as members of the original cast. The plays of his middle years include *Volpone, or The Fox* 1606, *The Alchemist* 1610, and *Bartholomew Fair* 1614.

Joplin /ˈdʒɒplɪn/ Janis 1943–1970. US blues and rock singer, born in Texas. She was lead singer with the San Francisco group Big Brother and the Holding Company 1966–68. Her biggest hit, Kris Kristofferson's 'Me and Bobby McGee', was released on the posthumous *Pearl* LP in 1971.

Joplin Scott 1868–1917. US ◊ragtime pianist and composer active in Chicago. His 'Maple Leaf Rag' 1899 was the first instrumental sheet music to sell a million copies, and 'The Entertainer', as the theme tune of the film *The Sting* 1973, revived his popularity. He was an influence on Jelly Roll Morton and other early jazz musicians.

Jordaens /jɔːˈdɑːns/ Jacob 1593–1678. Flemish painter, born in Antwerp. His style follows Rubens, whom he assisted in various commissions. Much of his work is exuberant and on a large scale, including scenes of peasant life, altarpieces, portraits, and mythological subjects.

Jordan /ˈdʒɔːdn/ Hashemite Kingdom of; country in SW Asia, bordered to the N by Syria, NE by Iraq, E and SE by Saudi Arabia, S by the Gulf of Aqaba, and W by Israel. **area** 89,206 sq km/34,434 sq mi (West Bank, incorporated into Jordan in 1950 but occupied by Israel since 1967, area 5,879 sq km/2,269 sq mi); **capital** Amman; **physical** desert plateau in E; rift valley separates E and W banks of the Jordan; **head of state and government** King Hussein ibn Talai from 1952; **political system** absolute monarchy; **exports** potash, phosphates, citrus; **population** (1990 est) 3,065,000 (including Palestinian refugees); West Bank (1988) 866,000; **language** Arabic (official); English; **recent history** independence achieved from Britain as Transjordan in 1946; new state of Jordan declared in 1949. In 1958 Jordan and Iraq formed Arab Federation, which ended when the Iraqi monarchy was deposed. Since assuming power in 1952, and despite the fact that three of Jordan's eight administrative provinces have been occupied by Israel since 1967, King Hussein has tried to act as a mediating influence in Middle Eastern politics; in 1985 he proposed a framework for a Middle East peace settlement; and in 1988 ceased administering the West Bank as part of Jordan, passing responsibility to the Palestine Liberation Organization. In 1989 an 80-member parliament was elected and Mudar Baḍran appointed prime minister. In 1990 Hussein unsuccessfully tried to mediate after Iraq's invasion of Kuwait, and accepted thousands of refugees who fled to Jordan from Kuwait and Iraq.

Jordan river rising on Mount Hermon, Syria at 550 m/1,800 ft above sea level and flowing S for about 320 km/200 mi via the Sea of Galilee to the Dead Sea. 390 m/1,290 ft below sea level. It occupies th northern part of the Great Rift Valley; its upper course forms the boundary of Israel with Syria and the kingdom of Jordan; its lower course runs through Jordan; the West Bank has been occupied by Israel since 1967.

Jörgensen Jörgen 1779–1845. Danish sailor who in 1809 seized control of Iceland, announcing it was under the protection of England. His brief reign of corruption ended later the same year when he was captured by an English naval ship and taken to London, where he was imprisoned.

Joseph /'dʒəʊzɪf/ in the New Testament, the husband of the Virgin Mary, a descendant of King David of the Tribe of Judah, and a carpenter by trade. Although Jesus was not the son of Joseph, Joseph was his legal father. According to Roman Catholic tradition, he had a family by a previous wife, and was an elderly man when he married Mary.

Joseph in the Old Testament, the 11th and favourite son of ◊Jacob, sold into Egypt by his jealous half-brothers. After he had risen to power there, they and his father joined him to escape from famine in Canaan.

Joseph Keith (Sinjohn), Baron 1918– . British Conservative politician. A barrister, he entered Parliament in 1956. He held ministerial posts 1962–64, 1970–74, 1979–81, and was secretary of state for education and science 1981–86. He was made a life peer in 1987.

Joseph two Holy Roman emperors:

Joseph I 1678–1711. Holy Roman emperor from 1705 and king of Austria, of the house of Habsburg. He spent most of his reign involved in fighting the War of the ◊Spanish Succession.

Joseph II 1741–1790. Holy Roman emperor from 1765, son of Francis I (1708–65). The reforms he carried out after the death of his mother, ◊Maria Theresa, in 1780, provoked revolts from those who lost privileges.

Josephine /'dʒəʊzɪfiːn/ Marie Josèphe Rose Tascher de la Pagerie 1763–1814. As wife of ◊Napoleon Bonaparte, she was empress of France 1796–1809. Born on Martinique, she married in 1779 Alexandre de Beauharnais, who played a part in the French Revolution, and in 1796 Napoleon, who divorced her in 1809 because she had not produced children.

Joseph of Arimathaea, St /ˌærɪmə'θiːə/ 1st century AD. In the New Testament, a wealthy Hebrew, member of the Sanhedrin (supreme court), and secret supporter of Jesus. On the evening of the Crucifixion he asked the Roman procurator Pilate for Jesus's body and buried it in his own tomb. Feast day 17 March.

Josephson /'dʒəʊzɪfsən/ Brian 1940– . British physicist, a leading authority on superconductivity. In 1973 he shared a Nobel prize for his theoretical predictions of the properties of a supercurrent through a tunnel barrier.

Josephson junction a device used in 'superchips' (large and complex integrated circuits) to speed the passage of signals by a phenomenon called 'electron tunnelling'. Although these superchips respond a thousand times faster than the ◊silicon chip, they have the disadvantage that the components of the Josephson junctions operate only at temperatures close to ◊absolute zero. They are named after Brian Josephson.

Josephus /dʒəʊ'siːfəs/ Flavius AD 37–c.100. Jewish historian and general, born in Jerusalem. He became a Pharisee and commanded the Jewish forces in Galilee in their revolt against Rome from AD 66 (which ended with the mass suicide at Masada). When captured, he gained the favour of the Roman emperor Vespasian and settled in Rome as a citizen. He wrote *Antiquities of the Jews*, an early history to AD 66; *The Jewish War*, and an autobiography.

josh v.t./i. (*US slang*) to make fun of; to hoax; to indulge in ridicule. —n. (*US slang*) a good-natured joke.

Joshua /'dʒɒʃuə/ 13th century BC. In the Old Testament, successor of Moses, who led the Jews in their return to and conquest of the land of Canaan. The city of Jericho was the first to fall: according to the Book of Joshua, the walls crumbled to the blast of his trumpets.

Josiah /dʒəʊ'saɪə/ c.647–609 BC. King of Judah. Grandson of Manasseh and son of Amon, he succeeded to the throne at the age of eight. The discovery of a Book of Instruction (probably Deuteronomy, a book of the Old Testament) during repairs of the Temple in 621 BC stimulated thorough reform, which included the removal of all sanctuaries except that of Jerusalem. He was killed in a clash at ◊Megiddo with Pharaoh-nechoh, king of Egypt.

Josquin Desprez /ʒɒ'skæŋ deɪ'preɪ/ or **des Prés** 1440–1521. Franco-Flemish composer. His music combines a technical mastery with the feeling for words that became a hallmark of Renaissance vocal music. His works, which include 18 masses, over 100 motets, and secular vocal works, are characterized by their vitality and depth of feeling.

joss n. a Chinese idol. —**joss-house** n. a temple. **joss-stick** n. a stick of fragrant tinder and clay for incense. [perhaps ultimately from Portuguese *deos* from Latin *deus* = god]

jostle v.t./i. to push roughly, especially when in a crowd; to struggle. —n. jostling.

jot n. a small amount, a whit. —v.t. (-tt-) to write (usually *down*) briefly. [from Latin from Greek *iota*]

jotter n. a small notebook or note-pad.

jottings n.pl. jotted notes.

Joubert /ʒuː'beə/ Petrus Jacobus 1831–1900. Boer general in South Africa. He opposed British annexation of the Transvaal in 1877, proclaimed its independence in 1880, led the Boer forces in the First ◊South African War against the British 1880–81, defeated ◊Jameson in 1896, and fought in the Second South African War.

joule /dʒuːl/ n. the SI unit (symbol J) of work and energy, replacing the ◊calorie (one joule equals 4.2 calories). A joule represents the work done by a force of 1 newton when its point of application moves 1 metre in the direction of action of the force, work done or heat generated by a current of 1 ampere flowing for 1 second against a resistance of 1 ohm. [from J *Joule*]

Joule James Prescott 1818–1889. British physicist whose work on the relations among electrical, mechanical, and chemical effects led to the discovery of the first law of ◊thermodynamics.

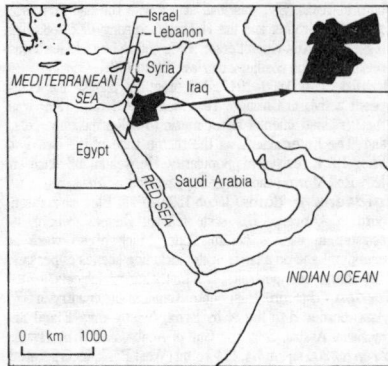

Jordan

Joyce Irish writer, James Joyce.

Joule-Thomson effect /dʒuːlˈtɒmpsən/ in physics, the fall in temperature of a gas as it expands adiabatically (without loss or gain of heat to the system) through a narrow jet. It can be felt when, for example, compressed air escapes through the valve of an inflated bicycle tyre. Only hydrogen does not exhibit the effect. It is the basic principle of most refrigerators. [from J P *Joule* and Sir William *Thomson*]

jounce *v.t./i.* to bump, to bounce, to jolt.

Jounieh /ˈdʒuːniə/ a port on the Mediterranean coast of Lebanon, 15 km/9 mi N of Beirut. The centre of an anti-Syrian Christian enclave.

journal /ˈdʒɜːnəl/ *n.* 1. a daily record of events or of business transactions and accounts. 2. a periodical (originally a daily newspaper). 3. the part of a shaft or axle that rests on the bearings. [from Old French from Latin]

journalese /dʒɜːnəˈliːz/ *n.* a hackneyed style of language characteristic of some newspaper writing.

journalism *n.* the profession of reporting, photographing, or editing news events for newspapers, magazines, radio, television, documentary films and newsreels.

journalist /ˈdʒɜːnəlist/ *n.* a person employed to write for a journal or newspaper. —**journalistic** /-ˈlɪstɪk/ *adj.*

journey /ˈdʒɜːnɪ/ *n.* an act of going from one place to another, especially at a long distance; the distance travelled in a specified time. —*v.i.* to make a journey. [from Old French = day's work or travel, from Latin *diurnus* = daily]

journeyman *n.* (*plural* **journeymen**) 1. in Britain, a man who served his apprenticeship in a trade and worked as a fully-qualified employee; a qualified mechanic or artisan working for another. 2. a sound but undistinguished workman. [from French *journée* = a day, because in the past journeymen were paid daily]

joust /dʒaʊst/ *n.* a combat with lances between two mounted knights or men-at-arms. —*v.i.* to engage in a joust. [from Old French *juster* = bring together from Latin *juxta* = beside]

Jove /dʒəʊv/ *n.* Jupiter. —**by Jove!**, an exclamation of surprise or approval. —**Jovian** *adj.* [from Latin *Jovis* used as genitive of *Jupiter*]

jovial /ˈdʒəʊviəl/ *adj.* full of cheerful good humour. —**joviality** /-ˈælɪtɪ/ *n.*, **jovially** *adv.* [French from Latin; originally referring to influence of planet Jupiter]

Jovian 331–364. Roman emperor from 363. Captain of the imperial bodyguard, he was chosen as emperor by the troops after ◊Julian's death in battle with the Persians. He concluded an unpopular peace and restored Christianity as the state religion.

Jowett /ˈdʒaʊɪt/ Benjamin 1817–1893. English scholar. He promoted university reform, including the abolition of the theological test for degrees, and translated Plato, Aristotle, and Thucydides.

jowl *n.* 1. the jaw or jawbone; the cheek. 2. loose skin on the throat, a dewlap. [Old English]

joy *n.* gladness, deep pleasure; a cause of this. —**no joy**, (*colloquial*) no satisfaction or success. —**joyous** *adj.*, **joyously** *adv.* [from Old French *joie* from Latin *gaudia* (*gaudēre* = rejoice)]

Joyce /dʒɔɪs/ James (Augustine Aloysius) 1882–1941. Irish writer, born in Dublin, who revolutionized the form of the English novel with his 'stream of consciousness' technique. His works include *Dubliners* 1914 (short stories), *Portrait of the Artist as a Young Man* 1916, *Ulysses* 1922, and *Finnegans Wake* 1939.

Always see a fellow's weak point in his wife.
James Joyce
Ulysses

joyful *adj.* full of joy. —**joyfully** *adv.*, **joyfulness** *n.*
joyless *adj.* without joy.
joy ride a ride taken for pleasure in a car etc., usually unauthorized. —**joy-rider** *n.*, **joy-riding** *n.*
joystick *n.* 1. the control-lever of an aeroplane. 2. in computing, an input device which signals to a computer the direction and extent of displacement of a hand-held lever.
JP abbreviation of Justice of the Peace.
jr, Jr abbreviation of junior.

Juan Carlos /ˈhwæn ˈkɑːlɒs/ 1938– . King of Spain. The son of Don Juan, pretender to the Spanish throne, he married in 1962 Princess Sofia, eldest daughter of King Paul of Greece. In 1969 he was nominated by ◊Franco to succeed on the restoration of the monarchy intended to follow Franco's death; his father was excluded because of his known liberal views. Juan Carlos became king in 1975 and has sought to steer his country from dictatorship to democracy.

Juárez /ˈxwɑːreθ/ Benito 1806–1872. Mexican politician, president 1861–64 and 1867–72. In 1861 he suspended repayments of Mexico's foreign debts, which prompted a joint French, British, and Spanish expedition to exert pressure. French forces invaded and created an empire for ◊Maximilian, brother of the Austrian emperor. After their withdrawal in 1867, Maximilian was executed, and Juárez returned to the presidency.

jubilant /ˈdʒuːbɪlənt/ *adj.* exultant, rejoicing. —**jubilance** *n.*, **jubilantly** *adv.* [from Latin *jubilare* = shout for joy]

jubilation /dʒuːbɪˈleɪʃən/ *n.* exultation, rejoicing.

jubilee /ˈdʒuːbɪliː/ *n.* 1. an anniversary (especially the 50th). 2. a time of rejoicing. [from Old French from Latin ultimately from Hebrew *yobel* = ram's-horn trumpet; associated with Latin *jubilare*]

Judaea /dʒuːˈdiːə/ (or **Judea**) southern division of ancient Palestine, see ◊Judah.

Judah /ˈdʒuːdə/ or **Judaea** district of S Palestine. After the death of King Solomon in 937 BC, Judah adhered to his son Rehoboam and the Davidic line, whereas the rest of Israel elected Jeroboam as ruler of the northern kingdom. In New Testament times, Judah was the Roman province of Judaea, and in current Israeli usage it refers to the southern area of the West Bank.

Judah Ha-Nasi /hɑːnɑːˈsiː/ 'the Prince' *c.* AD 135–*c.* 220. Jewish scholar who with a number of colleagues edited the collection of writings known as the *Mishna*, which formed the basis of the ◊*Talmud*, in the 2nd century AD.

Judaic /dʒuːˈdeɪɪk/ *adj.* of or characteristic of the Jews. [from Latin from Greek]

Judaism /ˈdʒuːdeɪɪzəm/ *n.* the religion of the ancient Hebrews and their descendants the Jews, based, according to the Old Testament, on a covenant between God and Abraham about 2000 BC, and the renewal of the covenant with Moses about 1200 BC. It rests on the concept of one eternal invisible God, whose will is revealed in the ◊Torah and who has a special relationship with the Jewish people. The Torah comprises the first five books of the Bible (the Pentateuch), which contains the history, laws, and guide to life for correct behaviour. Besides those living in Israel, there are large Jewish populations today in the USA, USSR, the UK and Commonwealth nations, and in Jewish communities throughout the world. There are approximately 18 million Jews, with about 9 million in the Americas, 5 million in Europe, and 4 million in Asia, Africa, and the Pacific.

Judaize /ˈdʒuːdeɪaɪz/ *v.t.* to make Jewish; to follow Jewish customs.

Judas Iscariot /ˈdʒuːdəs ɪsˈkæriət/ 1st century AD. In the New Testament, the disciple who betrayed Jesus

Christ. Judas was the treasurer of the group. At the last Passover supper, he arranged, for 30 pieces of silver, to point out Jesus to the chief priests so that they could arrest him. Afterwards Judas was overcome with remorse and committed suicide.

judder v.i. to shake noisily or violently. —n. a juddering movement or sound.

Jude, St /dʒuːd/ 1st century AD. Supposed half-brother of Jesus and writer of the Epistle of Jude in the New Testament; patron saint of lost causes. Feast day 28 Oct.

judge /dʒʌdʒ/ n. 1. a public officer appointed to try causes in a court of justice. 2. a person appointed to decide a dispute or contest. 3. a person fit to decide on the merits of a thing or question. 4. (in ancient Israel) any of the leaders with temporary authority in the period between Joshua and the kings (c.13th–11th centuries BC). —v.t./i. 1. to try (a cause) in a court of justice. 2. to pronounce sentence on. 3. to decide (a contest or question). 4. to form an opinion about; to estimate; to conclude or consider. 5. to act as judge (of). —**Judges' Rules**, a set of rules about the mode of questioning of suspects by police. [from Old French from Latin judex]

judgement /'dʒʌdʒmənt/ n. (in law also **judgment**) 1. judging, being judged. 2. ability to judge; good sense. 3. the decision of a judge etc. in a court of justice. 4. the judging of mankind by God. 5. a misfortune as a sign of divine displeasure. —**Judgement Day** or **Day of Judgement**, the day of the Last Judgement when God will judge all mankind.

judicature /'dʒuːdɪkətʃə/ n. 1. the administration of justice. 2. a judge's office. 3. a body of judges. [from Latin judicare = to judge]

judicial /dʒuː'dɪʃəl/ adj. 1. of or by a court of law 2. having the function of judgement. 3. of or proper to a judge. 4. expressing a judgement. 5. able to judge wisely, impartial. —**judicially** adv. [from Latin judicium = court, judgement]

judicial review in English law, action in the High Court to review the decisions of lower courts, tribunals, and administrative bodies. Various court orders can be made: **certiorari** (which quashes the decision); **mandamus** (which commands a duty to be performed); **prohibition** (which commands that an action should not be performed because it is unauthorized); a **declaration** (which sets out the legal rights or obligations); or an ◊**injunction**.

judicial separation an action in a court by either husband or wife, in which it is not necessary to prove an irreconcilable breakdown of a marriage, but in which the grounds are otherwise the same as for divorce. It does not end a marriage, but a declaration may be obtained that the complainant need no longer cohabit with the defendant. The court can make similar orders to a divorce court in relation to custody and support of children and maintenance.

judiciary /dʒuː'dɪʃɪərɪ/ n. the judges of a state collectively.

judicious /dʒuː'dɪʃəs/ adj. judging wisely, showing good sense. —**judiciously** adv. [from French from Latin]

Judith /'dʒuːdɪθ/ in Christian legend, a woman who saved her community from a Babylonian siege by killing the enemy general, Holofernes. The Book of Judith is part of the Apocrypha, a section of the Old Testament.

judo /'dʒuːdəʊ/ n. a sport of unarmed combat that developed from ◊ju-jitsu primarily in Japan. The two combatants wear loose-fitting, belted jackets and trousers to facilitate holds, and falls are broken by a square mat; when one has established a painful hold that the other cannot break, the latter signifies surrender by slapping the ground with a free hand. Degrees of proficiency are indicated by the colour of the belt: for novices white; after examination brown (three degrees); and finally black (nine degrees). [Japanese jū = gentle and dō = way]

judoist /'dʒuːdəʊɪst/ n. a student of or an expert in judo.

jug n. 1. a deep vessel for liquids, with a handle and often a shaped lip. 2. (slang) prison. —v.t. (-gg-) to stew (a hare) in a covered vessel.

juggernaut /'dʒʌgənɔːt/ n. 1. a large heavy vehicle. 2. an overpowering force or object.

Juggernaut or **Jagannath** a name for Vishnu, the Hindu god. His temple is in Puri, Orissa, India. A statue of the god, dating from about 318, is annually carried in procession on a large vehicle. Devotees formerly threw themselves beneath its wheels. [from Hindi Jagannath = lord of the world]

juggins /'dʒʌgɪnz/ n. (slang) a simpleton.

juggle v.t./i. 1. to perform feats of dexterity (with objects), especially by tossing and catching them, keeping several in the air at once. 2. to manipulate or arrange (facts, figures, etc.) to suit a purpose. —n. a trick, a deception. [from Old French jogler from Latin joculari = jest]

juggler n. one who juggles, especially to entertain. [from Old French from Latin joculator]

Jugoslavia /juːgəʊ'slɑːvɪə/ alternative spelling of ◊Yugoslavia.

jugular /'dʒʌgjʊlə/ adj. of the neck or throat. —n. the jugular vein. —**jugular vein**, either of the two large veins in the neck, returning blood from the head to the superior (or anterior) vena cava and thence to the heart. [from Latin jugulum = collar-bone, throat]

Jugurtha /dʒuː'gɜːθə/ died 104 BC. King of Numidia, N Africa, who, after a long resistance, was betrayed to the Romans in 107 BC, and put to death.

juice /dʒuːs/ n. 1. the liquid content of fruits, vegetables, or meat. 2. a liquid bodily secretion. 3. (slang) electricity. 4. (slang) petrol used in an engine etc. [from Old French from Latin jus = broth]

juicy adj. 1. full of juice. 2. (colloquial) interesting, especially because scandalous. —**juicily** adv., **juiciness** n.

ju-jitsu /dʒuː'dʒɪtsuː/ n. a Japanese method of self-defence using throws, punches, kicks, arm-locks etc. [from Japanese jū = gentle and jutsu = skill]

ju-ju /'dʒuːdʒuː/ n. an object venerated in W Africa as a charm or fetish; the magic attributed to this.

jujube /'dʒuːdʒuːb/ n. 1. a tree of the genus Zizyphus of the buckthorn family Thamnaceae, with berrylike fruits. 2. a sweet fruit-flavoured lozenge of gelatin etc. [French or from Latin ultimately from Greek zizuphon = edible fruit of the jujube tree]

jukebox /'dʒuːkbɒks/ n. a machine that automatically plays a selected gramophone record when a coin is inserted. [juke = cheap roadhouse providing music for dancing, from Negro dialect (of W African origin) in the SW USA]

Jul. abbreviation of July.

julep /'dʒuːlep/ n. 1. a sweet drink, especially as a vehicle for medicine; a medicated drink. 2. (US) iced and flavoured spirit and water, especially **mint julep**. [from Old French from Arabic from Persian = rose-water]

Julian /'dʒuːlɪən/ adj. of Julius ◊Caesar. —**Julian calendar**, the calendar introduced by him in 46 BC in which the ordinary year has 365 days, and every fourth year is a leap year of 366 days. [from Latin Julianus]

Julian /'dʒuːlɪən/ **the Apostate** c.331–363. Roman emperor. Born in Constantinople, the nephew of Constantine the Great, he was brought up as a Christian but early in life became a convert to paganism. Sent by Constantius to govern Gaul in 355, he was proclaimed emperor by his troops in 360, and in 361 was marching on Constantinople when Constantius' death allowed a peaceful succession. He revived pagan worship and refused to persecute heretics. He was killed in battle against the Persians.

Juliana /dʒuːli'ɑːnə/ 1909– . Queen of the Netherlands. The daughter of Queen Wilhelmina (1880–1962), she married Prince Bernhard of Lippe-Biesterfeld in 1937 and ruled 1948–80, when she abdicated and was succeeded by her daughter ◊Beatrix.

julienne /dʒuːli'en/ n. a clear meat soup containing vegetables cut into thin strips; such vegetables. —adj. cut into thin strips. [French, from names Jules or Julien]

Juliet cap /'dʒuːljət/ a small network skull-cap, usually ornamented with pearls. [from name of heroine of Shakespeare's romantic tragedy Romeo and Juliet]

Julius II /'dʒuːlɪəs/ 1443–1513. Pope 1503–13. A politician who wanted to make the Papal States the leading power in Italy. He formed international alliances first against Venice and then against France. He began the building of St Peter's Church, Rome, in 1506, and was the patron of the artists Michelangelo and Raphael.

July /dʒuː'laɪ/ n. the seventh month of the year. [from Anglo-French from Latin Julius (mensis), named after Julius Caesar]

July Plot or **July Conspiracy** an unsuccessful attempt to assassinate the German dictator Adolph Hitler and to overthrow the Nazi regime 20 July 1944. Colonel von Stauffenberg planted a bomb under the conference table at Hitler's headquarters at Rastenburg, East Prussia.

Jung *Swiss psychiatrist and pioneer psychoanalyst Carl Jung.*

Believing that Hitler had been killed, Stauffenberg flew to Berlin to proclaim a new government. Hitler was only injured and reprisals were savage: 150 alleged conspirators were executed, while 15 prominent personalities, including Field Marshall Rommel, committed suicide.

July Revolution revolution of 27–29 July 1830 in France that overthrew the restored Bourbon monarchy of Charles X and substituted the constitutional monarchy of Louis Philippe, whose rule (1830–48) is sometimes referred to as the July Monarchy.

jumble *v.t.* to mix *up*, to confuse. —*n.* 1. a confused pile etc., a muddle. 2. articles for a jumble sale. —**jumble sale**, a sale of miscellaneous articles, usually second-hand, to raise funds for charity etc.

jumbo /ˈdʒʌmbəu/ *n.* (*plural* **jumbos**) 1. a person, animal, or thing that is very large of its kind. 2. an elephant. 3. a jumbo jet. —*adj.* very large of its kind. —**jumbo jet**, the popular name for a generation of huge wide-bodied airliners such as the **Boeing 747**, which is 71 m/232 ft long, has a wingspan of 60 m/196 ft, a maximum takeoff weight of nearly 380 tonnes/400 tons, and can carry more than 400 passengers.

jump *v.t./i.* 1. to move up off the ground etc. by bending and then extending the legs or (of fish) by a movement of the tail. 2. to move suddenly with a jump or bound; to rise suddenly from a seat etc.; to give a sudden movement from shock or excitement etc. 3. to pass over by jumping; to cause (a horse etc.) to jump. 4. to pass over (a thing) to a point beyond; to skip (part of a book etc.) in reading or studying. 5. to come *to* (a conclusion) hastily. 6. (of a train etc.) to leave (the rails). 7. to ignore and pass (a red traffic-light etc.). 8. to abscond from. 9. to pounce upon or attack (a person etc.). 10. to take summary possession of (a claim allegedly forfeit etc.). —*n.* 1. an act of jumping. 2. an abrupt rise in a price etc. 3. an obstacle to be jumped, especially by a horse. 4. a sudden transition. 5. a sudden movement caused by shock, excitement etc. —**have the jump on**, (*slang*) to have an advantage over. **jump at**, to accept eagerly. **jump down a person's throat**, to reprimand or contradict him severely. **jumped-up** *adj.* upstart. **jump the gun**, (*colloquial*) to begin before the signal is given, or prematurely. **jump-jet** *n.* a jet aircraft that can take off and land vertically. **jump-lead** *n.* a cable for conveying current from one battery through another. **jump-off** *n.* a deciding round in show-jumping. **jump on**, to attack or criticize crushingly. **jump the queue**, to take unfair precedence. **jump suit**, a one-piece garment for the whole body. **jump to it**, to act promptly and energetically. **one jump ahead**, one stage ahead of a rival etc.

jumper[1] *n.* 1. a person or animal that jumps. 2. a short wire used to make or break an electrical circuit.

jumper[2] *n.* 1. a woman's knitted garment for the upper part of the body. 2. a loose outer jacket worn by sailors. [perhaps from dialect *jump* = short coat]

jumping hare a long-eared S African rodent *Pedetes capensis*, similar in appearance and habits to the ◊jerboa, but with head and body about 40 cm/1.3 ft long, and a

bushy tail about the same length. It is nocturnal and herbivorous.

jumpy *adj.* nervous, easily startled; making sudden movements. —**jumpily** *adv.*, **jumpiness** *n.*

Jun. abbreviation of 1. Junior. 2. June.

junction /ˈdʒʌŋkʃən/ *n.* 1. joining. 2. a place where things join. 3. a place where railway lines or roads meet. —**junction box**, a box containing a junction of electric cables etc. [from Latin *jungere*]

juncture /ˈdʒʌŋktʃə/ *n.* 1. a critical convergence of events; a point of time. 2. joining. 3. a place where things join. [from Latin]

June /dʒuːn/ *n.* the sixth month of the year. [from Old French and Latin *Junius* (goddess *Juno*)]

Jung /juŋ/ Carl Gustav 1875–1961. Swiss psychiatrist who collaborated with Sigmund ◊Freud until their disagreement in 1912 over the importance of sexuality in causing psychological problems. Jung studied religion and dream symbolism, saw the unconscious as a source of spiritual insight, and distinguished between introversion and extroversion. His books include *Modern Man in Search of a Soul* 1933.

Show me a sane man and I will cure him for you.
Carl Gustav Jung
The Observer

---

jungle *n.* 1. land overgrown with tangled vegetation, especially in the tropics; an area of such land. 2. a tangled mass. 3. a place of bewildering complexity or confusion, or of ruthless struggle. 4. a popular name for ◊rainforest. —**jungly** *adj.* [from Hindi from Sanskrit]

junior /ˈdʒuːniə/ *adj.* 1. the younger (especially appended to a name for distinction between two persons of the same name). 2. younger in age; lower in rank or authority. 3. of a low or the lowest position. 4. for younger children. —*n.* 1. a junior person. 2. a person acting or working in a junior capacity. [Latin, comparative of *juvenis* = young]

juniper /ˈdʒuːnɪpə/ *n.* an aromatic evergreen shrub or tree of the genus *Juniperus*, family Cupressaceae, especially one with purple berrylike cones yielding an oil used for flavouring gin and in medicine. Junipers are found throughout temperate regions. [from Latin *juniperus*]

junk[1] *n.* 1. discarded articles, rubbish; anything regarded as of little value. 2. (slang) a narcotic drug, especially heroin. —**junk food**, food which is not nutritious. **junk shop**, a shop selling miscellaneous cheap second-hand goods.

junk[2] *n.* a flat-bottomed sailing vessel in the China seas. [from French, Portuguese or Dutch, from Javanese]

junk bond a derogatory term for a security officially rated as 'below investment grade'. It is issued in order to raise capital quickly, typically to finance a takeover to be paid for by the sale of assets once the company is acquired. Junk bonds have a high yield, but are a high-risk investment.

Junkers /ˈjuŋkəs/ Hugo 1859–1935. German aeroplane designer. In 1919 he founded in Dessau the aircraft works named after him. Junkers planes, including dive bombers, night fighters, and troop carriers, were used by the Germans in World War II.

junket /ˈdʒʌŋkɪt/ *n.* 1. a dish of milk curdled by rennet and sweetened and flavoured. 2. a feast. 3. (*US*) a pleasure outing. 4. (*US*) an official's tour at public expense. —*v.i.* 1. to feast, to make merry. 2. (*US*) to hold a picnic or outing. —**junketing** *n.* [from Old French *jonquette* = rush-basket (used for junket) from Latin *juncus* = rush]

junkie /ˈdʒʌŋkɪ/ *n.* (*slang*) a drug addict.

Juno /ˈdʒuːnəu/ a principal goddess in Roman mythology (identified with the Greek Hera). The wife of Jupiter and the queen of heaven, she was concerned with all aspects of women's lives.

junta /ˈdʒʌntə/ *n.* a political clique or faction, especially one holding power after a revolution. [Spanish and Portuguese from Latin *jungere*]

Jupiter /ˈdʒuːpɪtə/ *n.* the fifth planet from the Sun, and the largest in the solar system (equatorial diameter 142,800 km/88,700 mi), with a mass more than twice that of all the other planets combined, 318 times that of the Earth's. It takes 11.86 years to orbit the Sun, at an average distance of 778 million km/484 million mi, and has at least 16 moons. It is largely composed of hydrogen and helium, liquefied by pressure in its interior, and probably with a rocky core larger than the Earth. Its main feature is the Great Red Spot, a cloud of rising gases, revolving anticlockwise, 14,000 km/8,500 mi wide and some 30,000 km/20,000 mi long.

Jupiter or **Jove** in mythology, chief god of the Romans, identified with the Greek ◊Zeus. He was god of the sky, associated with lightning and thunderbolt; protector in battle; and bestower of victory. The son of Saturn, he married his sister Juno, and reigned on Mount Olympus as lord of heaven.

jural /'dʒuərəl/ *adj.* of the law; of (moral) rights and obligations. [from Latin *jus* = law, right]

Jura mountains /'dʒuərə/ a series of parallel mountain ranges running SW–NE along the French-Swiss frontier between the rivers Rhône and Rhine, a distance of 250 km/156 mi. The highest peak is *Crête de la Neige*, 1,723 m/5,650 ft.

Jurassic /dʒuə'ræsɪk/ *n.* a period of geological time 213–144 million years ago; the middle period of the Mesozoic era. Climates worldwide were equable, creating forests of conifers and ferns, dinosaurs were abundant, birds evolved, and limestones and iron ores were deposited. —*adj.* of this period. [from French *jurassique* from *Jura*]

juridical /dʒuə'rɪdɪkəl/ *adj.* of judicial proceedings; relating to the law —**juridically** *adv.* [from Latin *juridicus* (*jus* = law and *dicere* = say)]

jurisdiction /dʒuərɪs'dɪkʃən/ *n.* 1. authority to interpret and apply the law 2. official power exercised within a particular sphere of activity. 3. the extent or territory over which legal or other power extends. [from Old French and Latin]

jurisprudence /dʒuərɪs'pruːdəns/ *n.* the science or philosophy of law in the abstract—that is, not the study of any particular laws or legal system, but of the principles upon which legal systems are founded. —**jurisprudential** /-'denʃəl/ *adj.* [from Latin]

jurist /'dʒuərɪst/ *n.* one who is skilled in the law —**juristic** /-'rɪstɪk/ *adj.*, **juristical** *adj.*, **juristically** *adv.* [from French or Latin *jus* = law]

juror /'dʒuərə/ *n.* 1. a member of a jury. 2. a person taking an oath. [from Anglo-French from Latin *jurare* = swear]

jury /'dʒuərɪ/ *n.* 1. a body of lay people (usually 12, sometimes 6) sworn to render a verdict in a court of justice or a coroner's court. Juries, used mainly in English speaking countries, are implemented primarily in criminal cases, but also sometimes in civil cases. 2. a body of persons selected to award the prizes in a competition. —**jury box**, an enclosure for the jury in a court. **grand jury**, see ◊grand. **petty** *or* **trial jury**, a jury of 12 persons who try the final issue of fact in civil or criminal cases and pronounce the verdict. —**juryman** *n.* (*plural* **jurymen**), **jurywoman** *n.fem.* (*plural* **jurywomen**) [from Anglo-French *jurée* = oath, inquiry]

jury-mast /'dʒuərɪmɑːst/ *n.* a temporary mast replacing one broken or lost.

jury-rigged /'dʒuərɪɡd/ *adj.* makeshift.

just *adj.* 1. giving proper consideration to the claims of everyone concerned. 2. deserved, right in amount etc. 3. well-grounded in fact. —*adv.* 1. exactly. 2. barely, no more than; by only a short distance etc. 3. at this or that moment, only a little time ago. 4. (*colloquial*) simply, merely. 5. positively, quite. 6. (*slang*) really, indeed. —**just about**, (*colloquial*) almost exactly; almost completely. **just in case**, as a precaution. **just now**, at this moment; only a little time ago. **just so**, exactly arranged; exactly as you say. —**justly** *adv.*, **justness** *n.* [from Old French from Latin *justus* (*jus* = law, right)]

justice /'dʒʌstɪs/ *n.* 1. justness, fairness; the exercise of authority in the maintenance of right. 2. judicial proceedings. 3. a judge or magistrate. —**do justice to**, to treat fairly; to appreciate duly. **do oneself justice**, to perform in a manner worthy of one's abilities. **Mr** (*or* **Mrs**) **Justice** —, the title of a High Court judge. [from Old French from Latin *justitia*]

Justice of the Peace (JP) in England, an unpaid magistrate appointed by the Lord Chancellor after consulting local advisory committees. Two or more sit to dispose of minor charges (formerly their jurisdiction was much wider), to commit more serious cases for trial by a higher court, and to grant licences for the sale of alcohol. In the USA, where

they receive fees and are usually elected, their courts are the lowest in the States, and deal only with minor offences, such as traffic violations; they may also conduct marriages. See also ◊magistrates court.

justiciar *n.* the chief justice minister of Norman and early Angevin kings, second in power only to the king. By 1265, the government had been divided into various departments, such as the Exchequer and Chancery, which meant that it was no longer desirable to have one official in charge of all.

justiciary /dʒʌ'stɪʃərɪ/ *n.* an administrator of justice. —**Court of Justiciary**, the supreme criminal court in Scotland. [from Latin]

justifiable /'dʒʌstɪfaɪəbəl/ *adj.* that can be justified or defended. —**justifiably** *adv.* [French]

justify /'dʒʌstɪfaɪ/ *v.t.* 1. to show the justice or truth of. 2. (of circumstances) to be an adequate ground for, to warrant. 3. to adjust (a line of type) to fill the space evenly. —**justification** /-fɪ'keɪʃən/ *n.*, **justificatory** /-fɪ'keɪtərɪ/ *adj.* [from French from Latin *justificare* (*jus* = law, right)]

Justinian I /dʒʌ'stɪnɪən/ 483–565. Byzantine emperor from 527. He recovered N Africa from the Vandals, SE Spain from the Visigoths, and Italy from the Ostrogoths, largely owing to his great general Belisarius. He ordered the codification of Roman law, which has influenced European jurisprudence.

Justin, St /'dʒʌstɪn/ *c.*100–*c.*163. One of the early Christian leaders and writers known as the Fathers of the Church. Born in Palestine of a Greek family, he was converted to Christianity and wrote two *Apologies* in its defence. He spent the rest of his life as an itinerant missionary, and was martyred in Rome. Feast day 1 June.

just price a traditional economic belief that everything bought and sold has a 'natural' price, which is the price unaffected by adverse conditions, or by individual or monopoly influence. The belief dates from the scholastic philosophers and resurfaced early in the 20th century in the writings of Major Douglas and his Social Credit theory.

jut *v.i.* (-tt-) to project. —*n.* a projection. [variant of *jet*¹]

jute /dʒuːt/ *n.* fibre obtained from the bark of two tropical plants of the genus *Corchorus* of the linden family: *C. capsularis* and *C. olitorius*. Jute is used for sacks and sacking, upholstery, webbing, twine, and stage canvas. [from Bengali from Sanskrit]

Jute /dʒuːt/ *n.* a member of a Germanic people who originated in Jutland but later settled in Frankish territory. They occupied Kent, SE England, about 450, according to tradition under Hengist and Horsa, and conquered the Isle of Wight and the opposite coast of Hampshire in the early 6th century. [Old English (compare Icelandic *Iatar* = people of Jutland in Denmark)]

Jutland /'dʒʌtlənd/ (Danish *Jylland*) a peninsula of N Europe; area 29,500 sq km/11,400 sq mi. It is separated from Norway by the Skagerrak and from Sweden by the Kattegat, with the North Sea to the W. The larger northern part belongs to Denmark, the southern part to Germany.

Jutland, Battle of /'dʒʌtlənd/ a naval battle of World War I, fought between England and Germany on 31 May 1916, off the W coast of Jutland. Its outcome was indecisive, but the German fleet remained in port for the rest of the war.

Juvenal /'dʒuːvənl/ *c.* AD 60–140. Roman satirist and poet. His genius for satire brought him to the unfavourable notice of the emperor Domitian. Juvenal's 16 extant satires give an explicit and sometimes brutal picture of the decadent Roman society of his time.

juvenile /'dʒuːvənaɪl/ *adj.* youthful; of or for young persons. —*n.* a young person; an actor playing such a part. —**juvenile delinquency**, violation of the law by persons below the age of legal responsibility. **juvenile delinquent**, such an offender. [from Latin *juvenis* = young person]

juvenilia /dʒuːvə'nɪlɪə/ *n.pl.* the works produced by an author or artist in his youth. [Latin]

juvenility /dʒuːvə'nɪlɪtɪ/ *n.* youthfulness; a youthful manner etc.

juxtapose *v.t.* to put side by side. —**juxtaposition** /-pə'zɪʃən/ *n.* [from French from Latin *juxta* = next and *ponere* = put]

k, K (*plural* ks, k's) the 11th letter of the English alphabet, derived from the Greek ◊*kappa* (κ, K) and representing the voiceless velar stop. In English, it is silent before *n* at the beginning of a word (for example, in *knee*), a change accomplished, probably, in the 17th century.

k symbol for kilo-, as in kg (kilogram) and km (kilometre).

K abbreviation of 1. kelvin, a scale of temperature (see ◊kelvin scale). 2. king (in chess). 3. the unit of core-memory size in computers = 1,024 (often taken as 1,000) words; by extension, a thousand, as in a salary of £30K.

K symbol for ◊potassium. [from modern Latin *kalium* from Arabic]

K. abbreviation of 1. ◊carat. 2. King('s). 3. Köchel (catalogue of Mozart's works).

K2 the second highest mountain in the world, about 8,900 m/29,210 ft, in the Karakoram range, Kashmir, N India; it is also known as *Dapsang* (Hidden Peak) and formerly as **Mount Godwin-Austen** (after the son of a British geologist). It was first climbed in 1954 by an Italian expedition.

Kaaba /'kɑ:bə/ in Mecca, Saudi Arabia, the oblong building in the quadrangle of the Great Mosque, into the NE corner of which is built the Black Stone, declared by the prophet Muhammad to have been given to Abraham by the archangel Gabriel, and revered by Muslims. [Arabic = chamber]

kabbala /kə'bɑ:lə/ *n.* or **cabbala** an ancient esoteric Jewish mystical tradition of philosophy, containing strong elements of pantheism, yet akin to neo-Platonism. Kabbalistic writing reached its peak between the 13th and 16th centuries. It is largely rejected by current Judaic thought as medieval superstition, but is basic to the Hassid sect. [Hebrew = tradition]

Kabinda a part of Angola. See ◊Cabinda.

kabuki /kə'bu:kı/ *n.* a form of drama originating in late 16th-century Japan, drawing on ◊Nō, puppet plays, and folk dance. Kabuki actors specialize in particular characters, female impersonators being the biggest stars. [Japanese = music, dance, skill]

Kabul /'kɑ:bʊl/ the capital of Afghanistan, 2,100 m/6,900 ft above sea level, on the river Kabul; population (1984) 1,179,300. Products include textiles, plastics, leather, and glass. It commands the strategic routes to Pakistan via the ◊Khyber Pass.

Kádár /'kɑ:dɑ:/ János 1912–1989. Hungarian communist leader, in power 1956–88, after suppressing the national rising. As Hungarian Socialist Workers' Party (HSWP) leader and prime minister 1956–58 and 1961–65, Kádár introduced a series of market-socialist economic reforms, while retaining cordial political relations with the USSR.

Kaddish /'kædıʃ/ *n.* a Jewish prayer recited as a doxology in the synagogue service and as a prayer of mourning. [from Aramaic = holy]

Kaffir /'kæfə/ *n.* 1. former term for a member of any of various people of the Bantu family. 2. (*offensive South African*) a black person. [from Arabic = infidel]

Kafka /'kæfkə/ Franz 1883–1924. Czechoslovak novelist, born in Prague, who wrote in German. His three unfinished allegorical novels *Der Prozess/The Trial* 1925, *Der Schloss/The Castle* 1926, and *Amerika/America* 1927 were published posthumously despite his instructions that they should be destroyed. His short stories include 'Die Verwandlung/'The Metamorphosis' 1915, in which a man turns into a beetle.

> Guilt is always beyond doubt.
>
> **Franz Kafka**
> *In the Penal Colony*

Kahn /kɑ:n/ Louis 1901–1974. US architect, born in Estonia. He developed a classically romantic style, in which functional 'servant' areas, such as stairwells and air ducts, featured prominently, often as towerlike structures surrounding the main living and working, or 'served', areas. His works are characterized by an imaginative use of concrete and brick and include the Salk Institute for Biological Studies, La Jolla, California, and the British Art Center at Yale University.

Kaifu /'kaifu/ Toshiki 1932– . Japanese conservative politician, prime minister from 1989. A protégé of former premier Takeo Miki, he was selected as a compromise choice as Liberal Democratic Party president and prime minister in Aug 1989.

Kairouan /kaiə'wɑ:n/ a Muslim holy city in Tunisia, N Africa, S of Tunis; population (1984) 72,200. It is a centre of carpet production. The city, said to have been founded in AD 617, ranks after Mecca and Medina as a place of pilgrimage.

Kaiser /'kaizə/ *n.* (*historical*) a title used by the Holy Roman emperors, Austrian emperors 1806–1918, and German emperors 1871–1918. [from German from Latin = *Caesar*]

Kaiser Georg 1878–1945. German playwright, the principal exponent of German ◊Expressionism. His large output includes *Die Bürger von Calais/The Burghers of Calais* 1914 and *Gas* 1918–20.

Kakadu a national park E of Darwin in the Alligator Rivers region of Arnhem Land, Northern Territory, Australia. Established in 1979, it overlies one of the richest uranium deposits in the world.

kakapo /'kɑ:kəpəʊ/ *n.* (*plural* kakapos) a flightless parrot *Strigops habroptilus* that lives in burrows in New Zealand. It is green, yellow, and brown, and is nocturnal. It is in danger of extinction.

kakemono /kæki'məʊnəʊ/ *n.* (*plural* kakemonos) a Japanese wall picture, usually painted or inscribed on paper or silk and mounted on rollers. [Japanese *kake* = hang and *mono* = thing]

Kalahari Desert /kælə'hɑ:ri/ a semi-desert area forming most of Botswana and extending into Namibia, Zimbabwe, and South Africa; area about 900,000 sq km/ 347,400 sq mi. The only permanent river, the Okavango, flows into a delta in the NW forming marshes rich in wildlife. Its inhabitants are the nomadic Kung.

kale *n.* a hardy variety of ◊cabbage with wrinkled leaves. [northern form of *cole* from Latin *caulis*]

kaleidoscope /kə'laidəskəʊp/ *n.* a tube containing mirrors and pieces of coloured glass whose reflections produce patterns when the tube is rotated. —**kaleido-scopic** /-'skɒpɪk/ *adj.*, **kaleidoscopically** /-'skɒpɪkɒlɪ/ *adv.* [from Greek *kalos* = beautiful, *eidos* = form, and *skopeō* = look at]

Kalevala /kɑ:lə'vɑ:lə/ the Finnish national epic poem compiled from legends and ballads by Elias Lönnrot (died 1884) in 1835; its hero is Väinämöinen, god of music and poetry.

kaleyard /'keɪljɑ:d/ *n.* (*Scottish*) a kitchen garden.

Kalf /kɑ:lf/ Willem 1619–1693. Dutch painter, active in Amsterdam from 1653. He specialized in still lifes set off against a dark background.

Kalgan /kɑ:l'gɑ:n/ a city in NE China, now known as ◊Zhangjiakou.

Kali /'kɑ:li/ in Hindu mythology, the goddess of destruction and death. She is the wife of ◊Siva.

Kālidāsa /kɑ:li'dɑ:sə/ lived 5th century AD. Indian epic poet and dramatist. His works, in Sanskrit, include the classic drama *Sakuntala*, the love story of King Dushyanta and the nymph Sakuntala.

Kalimantan /kæli'mæntən/ a province of the republic of Indonesia occupying part of the island of Borneo; **area** 543,900 sq km/210,000 sq mi; **towns** Banjermasin and Balikpapan; **physical** mostly low-lying, with mountains in the north; **products** petroleum, rubber, coffee, copra, pepper, timber; **population** (1980) 6,723,086.

Kalinin /kə'li:nɪn/ Mikhail Ivanovich 1875–1946. Soviet politician, founder of the newspaper *Pravda*. He was prominent in the 1917 October Revolution, and in 1919 became head of state (president of the Central Executive Committee of the Soviet government until 1937, then president of the Presidium of the Supreme Soviet until 1946).

Kaliyuga /kɑ:li'ju:gə/ *n.* in Hinduism, the last of the four *yugas* (ages) that make up one cycle of creation. The Kaliyuga, in which Hindus believe we are now living, is characterized by wickedness and disaster, and leads up to the destruction of this world in preparation for a new creation and a new cycle of *yugas*.

Kalki in Hinduism, the last avatar (manifestation) of Vishnu, who will appear at the end of the Kaliyuga, or final age of the world, to destroy it in readiness for a new creation.

Kaltenbrunner /'kæltənbrʊnə/ Ernst 1901–1946. Austrian Nazi leader. After the annexation of Austria in 1938 he joined police chief Himmler's staff, and as head of the Security Police (SS) from 1943 was responsible for the murder of millions of Jews (see ◊Holocaust) and Allied soldiers in World War II. After the war, he was tried in Nuremberg and hanged.

Kamchatka /kæm'tʃætkə/ a mountainous peninsula separating the Bering Sea and Sea of Okhotsk forming (together with the Chukchi and Koryak national districts) a region of the USSR. Its capital, Petropavlovsk, is the only town.

Kamenev /'kæmənev/ Lev Borisovich 1883–1936. Russian leader of the Bolshevik movement after 1917 who, with Stalin and Zinoviev, formed a ruling triumvirate in the USSR after Lenin's death in 1924. His alignment with the Trotskyists led to his dismissal from office and from the Communist Party by Stalin in 1926. Tried for plotting to murder Stalin, he was condemned and shot in 1936.

kamikaze /kæmi'kɑ:zi/ *n.* in World War II, a Japanese aircraft laden with explosives and suicidally crashed on a target by the pilot; the pilot of this. [Japanese *kami* = divinity and *kaze* = wind]

Kampala /kæm'pɑ:lə/ the capital of Uganda; population (1983) 455,000. It is linked by rail with Mombasa. Products include tea, coffee, textiles, fruit, and vegetables.

Kampuchea see ◊Cambodia.

Kananga /kə'næŋgə/ the chief city of Kasai Occidental region, W central Zaïre, on the Lulua river; population (1984) 291,000. It was known as **Luluabourg** until 1966.

Kanchenjunga /kæntʃən'dʒʊŋgə/ a variant spelling of ◊Kangchenjunga, a Himalayan mountain.

Kandinsky /kæn'dɪnski/ Wassily 1866–1944. a Russian painter, a pioneer of abstract art. Born in Moscow, he travelled widely, settling in Munich, Germany, in 1896. He was an originator of the ◊*Blaue Reiter* movement 1911–12. From 1921 he taught at the ◊Bauhaus school of design. He moved to Paris in 1933, becoming a French citizen in 1939.

Kandy /'kændi/ a city in central Sri Lanka, former capital of the kingdom of Kandy 1480–1815; population (1985)

kangaroo

140,000. Products include tea. It is the site of one of the most sacred Buddhist temples.

kangaroo /kæŋgə'ru:/ *n.* a marsupial mammal of the family Macropodidae found in Australia, Tasmania, and New Guinea. Kangaroos are plant-eaters and live in herds. They are adapted to hopping, most species having very large back legs and feet compared with the small forelimbs. The larger types can jump 9 m/30 ft at a single bound. Species range from the small rat kangaroos, only 30 cm/ 1 ft long, to the large red and great grey kangaroos, the largest living marsupials, which may be 1.6 m/5.2 ft long with 1.1 m/3.5 ft tails. —**kangaroo court**, an illegal court held by strikers, prisoners, etc. **kangaroo paw**, a bulbous plant *Anigozanthos manglesii*, family Hameodoraceae, with a row of small white flowers emerging from velvety green tubes with red bases. It is the floral emblem of Western Australia.

Kangchenjunga /kæntʃən'dʒʊŋgə/ a Himalayan mountain on the Nepál–Sikkim border, 8,598 m/20,208 ft high, 120 km/75 mi SE of Everest. Kangchenjunga was first climbed by a British expedition in 1955 and is the third highest peak in the world. [= five treasure houses of the great snows]

Ka Ngwane /kæŋ'gwɑ:neɪ/ a ◊Black National State in Natal province, South Africa; it achieved self-governing status in 1971; population (1985) 392,800.

Kannon or **Kwannon** in Japanese Buddhism, a female form (known to the West as 'goddess of mercy') of the bodhisattva ◊Avalokiteśvara. Sometimes depicted with many arms extending compassion.

Kano /'kɑ:nəʊ/ the capital of Kano state in N Nigeria, trade centre of an irrigated area; population (1983) 487,100. Products include bicycles, glass, furniture, textiles, and chemicals. Founded about 1000 BC, Kano is a walled city, with New Kano extending beyond the walls.

Kanpur /kɑ:n'pʊə/ formerly **Cawnpore** the capital of Kanpur district, Uttar Pradesh, India, SW of Lucknow, on the river Ganges; a commercial and industrial centre. Products include cotton, wool, jute, chemicals, plastics, iron, steel; population (1981) 1,688,000.

Kansas /'kænzəs/ a state of central USA; nickname Sunflower State; **area** 213,200 sq km/82,295 sq mi; **capital** Topeka; **towns** Kansas City, Wichita, Overland Park; **physical** undulating prairie; rivers Missouri, Kansas, and Arkansas; **products** wheat, cattle, coal, petroleum, natural gas, aircraft; **population** (1985) 2,450,000.

Kansas City a twin city in the USA at the confluence of the Missouri and Kansas rivers, partly in Kansas and partly in Missouri; a market and agricultural distribution centre and one of the chief livestock centres of the USA. Population (1980) of Kansas City (Kansas) 161,087, Kansas City (Missouri) 448,159, metropolitan area 1,327,000.

Kansu alternative spelling for the Chinese province ◊Gansu.

Kant /kænt/ Immanuel 1724–1804. German philosopher who believed that knowledge is not merely an aggregate of sense impressions but is dependent on the conceptual apparatus of the human understanding, which is itself not derived from experience. In ethics, Kant argued that right action cannot be based on feelings or inclinations but conforms to a law given by reason, the **categorical imperative.**

Kanto /'kæntəʊ/ a flat, densely populated region of E Honshu island, Japan; population (1986) 37,156,000; area 32,377 sq km/12,505 sq mi. The chief city is Tokyo.

KANU acronym from Kenya African National Union a political party founded in 1944 and led by Jomo ◊Kenyatta from 1947, when it was the Kenya African Union; it became KANU on independence.

kaoliang /'keɪəʊli'æŋ/ n. a variety of ◊sorghum.

kaolin /'keɪəlɪn/ n. a fine white clay used for porcelain and in medicine. [French from Chinese *kao-ling*, name of mountain]

kapok /'keɪpɒk/ n. the silky hairs produced round the seeds of certain trees, particularly the kapok tree *Bombax ceiba* of India and Malaysia and the silk-cotton tree *Ceiba pentandra*, a native of tropical America. Kapok is used for stuffing cushions and mattresses and for sound insulation; oil obtained from the seeds is used in food and soap preparation. [from Malay]

kappa /'kæpə/ n. the tenth letter of the Greek alphabet, (κ, K) = k. [Greek]

kaput /kæ'pʊt/ adj. (slang) broken, ruined, done for. [from German]

Karachi /kə'rɑːtʃi/ the largest city and chief seaport of Pakistan, and capital of Sind province, NW of the Indus delta; population (1981) 5,208,000. Industries include engineering, chemicals, plastics, and textiles. It was the capital of Pakistan 1947–59.

Karajan /'kærəjæn/ Herbert von 1908–1989. Austrian musician, conductor of the Berlin Philharmonic Orchestra 1955–89. He directed the Salzburg Festival from 1964 and became director of the Vienna State Opera in 1976. He is associated with the Classical and Romantic repertoire—Beethoven, Brahms, Mahler, and Richard Strauss.

Karakoram /kærə'kɔːrəm/ a mountain range in central Asia, divided among China, Pakistan, and India. Peaks include K2, Masharbrum, Gasharbrum, and Mustagh Tower. The **Ladakh** subsidiary range is in NE Kashmir on the Tibetan border.

karakul /'kærəkʊl/ n. 1. an Asian sheep whose lambs have a dark curled fleece. 2. a fur made from or resembling this. [Russian]

Karamanlis /kærəmæn'liːs/ Constantinos 1907– . Greek politician of the New Democracy Party. A lawyer and an anti-communist, he was prime minister Oct 1955–March 1958, May 1958–Sept 1961, and Nov 1961–June 1963 (when he went into self-imposed exile). He was recalled as prime minister on the fall of the regime of the 'colonels' in July 1974, and was president 1980–85.

karaoke n. a form of entertainment in which people sing into a microphone to the accompaniment of taped backing tracks of standard songs without the vocals. A popular afterwork entertainment for male office executives in Japanese city bars, karaoke was imported to the UK and other western countries during the 1980s by Japanese restaurateurs. [Japanese = empty orchestra]

karate /kə'rɑːtɪ/ n. one of the ◊martial arts, a type of unarmed combat derived from kempo, a form of Chinese Shaolin boxing. It became popular in the 1930s. [Japanese *kara* = empty and *te* = hand]

Karelia /kə'riːlɪə/ an autonomous republic of the Russian Soviet Republic (RSFSR), in NW USSR; **area** 66,550 sq mi/172,400 sq km; **capital** Petrozavodsk; **physical** mainly forested; **products** fishing, timber, chemicals, coal; **population** (1986) 787,000; **recent history** Karelia was annexed to Russia by Peter the Great in 1721 as part of Finland. Part of Karelia was retained by Finland when it gained its independence from Russia in 1917; the remainder became an autonomous region in 1920, an autonomous republic of the USSR from 1923, and in 1946 the Karelo-Finnish Soviet Socialist Republic was set up. In 1956 the greater part of the republic returned to its former status as an autonomous Soviet socialist republic.

Karelian bear dog a medium-sized dog, rather like a husky, formerly used to protect Russian settlements from bears. In 1989 some were sent to Yellowstone National Park, USA, to keep bears away from tourists.

Karen /kə'ren/ n. 1. a member of a group of SE Asian peoples, inhabiting E Myanmar (formerly Burma), Thailand and the Irrawaddy delta and numbering 1.9 million. In 1984 the Burmese government began a large-scale military campaign against the Karen National Liberation Army, the armed wing of the Karen National Union. 2. the language of the Karen, which belongs to the Thai division of the Sino-Tibetan family.

Karg-Elert /kɑː'gelət/ Sigfrid 1877–1933. German composer. After studying at Leipzig he devoted himself to the European harmonium. His numerous concert pieces and graded studies exploit a range of impressionistic effects such as the 'endless chord'.

Karl-Marx-Stadt /'kɑːl 'mɑːks ʃtæt/ former name (1954–90) of ◊Chemnitz, town in Germany.

Karloff /'kɑːlɒf/ Boris. Stage name of William Henry Pratt 1887–1969. British actor who worked almost entirely in the USA. He is chiefly known for his role as the monster in *Frankenstein* 1931. His other films include *Scarface* 1932, *The Lost Patrol* 1934, and *The Body Snatcher* 1945.

karma /'kɑːmə/ n. 1. in Hinduism, the sum of a human being's actions, carried forward from one life to the next, resulting in an improved or worsened fate. 2. in Buddhism, physical and mental elements carried on from birth to birth, until the power holding them together disperses in the attainment of ◊nirvana. [Sanskrit = action, fate]

Karmal /'kɑːməl/ Babrak 1929– . Afghani communist politician. In 1965 he formed what became the banned People's Democratic Party of Afghanistan (PDPA) in 1977. As president 1979–86, with Soviet backing, he sought to broaden the appeal of the PDPA but encountered wide resistance from the ◊Mujaheddin Muslim guerrillas.

Karnataka /kə'nɑːtəkə/ formerly (until 1973) **Mysore** a state in SW India; **area** 191,800 sq km/74,035 sq mi; **capital** Bangalore; **products** mainly agricultural; minerals include manganese, chromite, and India's only sources of gold and silver; **language** Kannada; **population** (1981) 37,043,000.

Karoo /kə'ruː/ another spelling of ◊Karroo, a high plateau in South Africa.

Karpov /'kɑːpɒf/ Anatoly 1951– . Soviet chess player. He succeeded Bobby Fischer of the USA as world champion in 1975, and held the title until losing to Gary ◊Kasparov in 1985.

karri /'kɑːri/ n. a giant eucalyptus tree *Eucalyptus diversifolia* found in the extreme SW of Australia. It can grow to a height of 120 m/400 ft or more. Its exceptionally strong timber is used for girders.

Karroo /kə'ruː/ two areas of semidesert in Cape Province, South Africa, divided into the **Great Karroo** and **Little Karroo** by the Swartberg mountains. The two Karroos together have an area of about 260,000 sq km/100,000 sq mi. [Hottentot]

karst n. a limestone region with underground streams and many cavities caused by dissolution of the rock. The most dramatic is found near the city of Guilin in the Guangxi province of China. [name of such a region in Yugoslavia]

kart n. a miniature wheeled vehicle usually consisting of a tubular frame with a small rear-mounted engine and a seat for the driver, used for a motor-racing sport (**karting**).

karyotype /'kæriətaɪp/ n. in biology, the set of ◊chromosomes characteristic of a given species. It is described as the number, shape, and size of the chromosomes in a single cell of an organism. In humans, for example, the karyotype consists of 46 chromosomes, in mice 40, in crayfish 200, and in fruit flies 8.

kasbah /'kæzbɑː/ n. 1. the citadel of an Arab city in North Africa. 2. the old crowded part near this, especially in Algiers. [from French from Arabic = citadel]

Kashmir /kæʃ'mɪə/ a Pakistan-occupied region in the NW of the former state of Kashmir, now ◊Jammu and Kashmir; **area** 78,900 sq km/30,445 sq mi; **towns** Gilgit, Skardu; **physical** W Himalayan peak Nanga Parbat 8,126 m/26,660 ft, Karakoram Pass, Indus River, Baltoro Glacier; **population** 1,500,000. Azad ('free') Kashmir in the W has its own legislative assembly based in Muzaffarabad, while Gilgit and Baltistan regions to the N and E are governed directly by Pakistan. The ◊Northern Areas are claimed by India and Pakistan.

Kasparov Gary 1963– . Soviet chess player. When he beat his compatriot Anatoly ◊Karpov to win the world title in 1985, he was the youngest ever champion at 22 years 210 days.

karyotype

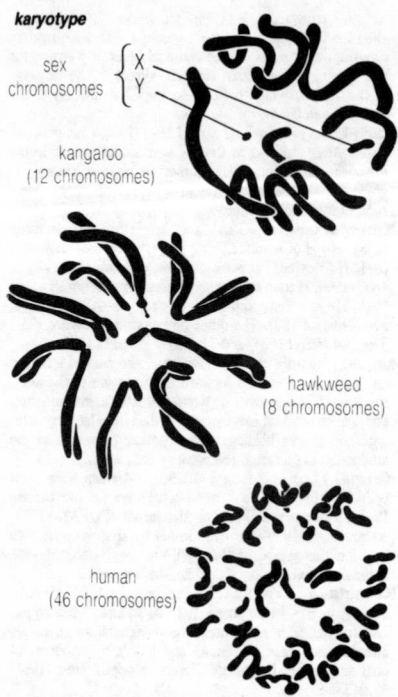

sex chromosomes { X
Y

kangaroo
(12 chromosomes)

hawkweed
(8 chromosomes)

human
(46 chromosomes)

Kassem /kæ'sem/ Abdul Karim 1914–1963. Iraqi politician, prime minister from 1958; he adopted a pro-Soviet policy. He pardoned the leaders of the pro-Egyptian party who tried to assassinate him in 1959, but was executed after the 1963 coup.

Katmandu /kætmən'duː/ or **Kathmandu** the capital of Nepál; population (1981) 235,000. Founded in the 8th century on an ancient pilgrim and trade route from India to Tibet and China, it has a royal palace, Buddhist temples, and monasteries.

Katō /kʌ'tɔː/ Kiyomasa 1562–1611. Japanese warrior and politician, who was instrumental in the unification of Japan and the banning of Christianity in the country. He led the invasion of Korea in 1592.

Katō Taka-akira 1860–1926. Japanese politician and prime minister 1924–26. After a long political career with several terms as foreign minister, Katō led probably the most democratic and liberal regime of the Japanese Empire.

Katowice /kætəu'viːtseɪ/ an industrial city in Upper Silesia, S Poland. Products include anthracite, iron and coal mining, iron foundries, smelting works, and machine shops; population (1985) 363,000.

Katsura /kæt'suərə/ Tarō 1847–1913. Prince of Japan, army officer, politician, and prime minister. He was responsible for the Anglo-Japanese treaty of 1902, the successful prosecution of the Russo-Japanese war 1904–05, and the annexation of Korea in 1910.

katydid /'keɪtɪdɪd/ n. a large green grasshopper, family Tettigoniidae, of the USA. [imitative of its sound]

Katyn Forest /kæ'tɪn/ a forest near Smolensk, USSR, where 4,500 Polish officer prisoners of war (captured in the German-Soviet partition of Poland in 1940) were shot; 10,000 others were killed elsewhere. In 1989 the USSR accepted responsibility for the massacre.

Kauffmann /'kaufmən/ Angelica 1741–1807. Swiss Neo-Classical painter who worked extensively in England. She was in great demand as a portraitist, but also painted mythological scenes for large country houses.

Kaunda /kɑ:'undə/ Kenneth (David) 1924– . Zambian politician. Imprisoned 1958–60 as founder of the Zambia African National Congress, in 1964 he became first prime minister of Northern Rhodesia, then first president of Zambia. In 1973 he introduced one-party rule. A supporter of the nationalist movement in Southern Rhodesia,

now Zimbabwe, he survived a coup attempt in 1980 thought to have been promoted by South Africa. In 1987, he was elected chair of the Organization of African Unity. In 1990 his popularity fell and he was faced with wide anti-government demonstrations.

kauri pine /'kauri/ a New Zealand timber conifer *Agathis australis*, family Araucariaceae, whose fossilized gum deposits are valued in varnishes; the wood is used for carving and handicrafts. [Maori]

Kautsky /'kautski/ Karl 1854–1938. German socialist theoretician, who opposed the reformist ideas of Edouard ◊Bernstein from within the Social Democratic Party. In spite of his Marxist ideas, he remained in the party when its left wing broke away to form the German Communist Party (KPD).

Kawabata /kauə'batə/ Yasunari 1899–1972. Japanese novelist, translator of Lady ◊Murasaki, and author of *Snow Country* 1947 and *A Thousand Cranes* 1952. His novels are characterized by melancholy and loneliness. He was the first Japanese to win the Nobel Prize for Literature, in 1968.

Kawasaki /kauə'saki/ an industrial city (iron, steel, shipbuilding, chemicals, textiles) on Honshu island, Japan; population (1987) 1,096,000.

Kay /keɪ/ John 1704–c.1764. English inventor who developed the flying shuttle, a machine to speed up the work of hand-loom weaving. In 1733 he patented his invention but was ruined by the litigation necessary for its defence.

kayak /'kaɪæk/ n. **1.** a light, covered-in, canoe-type boat, employed by the ◊Inuit for fishing, consisting of a wooden framework covered with sealskins, in which the paddler sits facing forward and using a double-bladed paddle. **2.** a boat developed from this, used for touring and sport. [Inuit]

Kaye /keɪ/ Danny. Stage name of David Daniel Kaminski 1913–1987. US actor, comedian, and singer. He appeared in many films, including *Wonder Man* 1944, *The Secret Life of Walter Mitty* 1946, and *Hans Christian Andersen* 1952.

kayser n. a unit of wave number (number of waves in a unit length), used in spectroscopy. It is expressed as waves per centimetre, and is the reciprocal of the wavelength. A wavelength of 0.1 cm has a wave number of 10 kaysers.

Kayseri /'kaɪsəri/ (ancient name **Caesarea Mazaca**) the capital of Kayseri province, central Turkey; population (1985) 378,000. It produces textiles, carpets, and tiles. In Roman times it was the capital of the province of Cappadocia.

Kazakh /kə'zɑːk/ n. a member of a nomadic pastoral Kirghiz people of Kazakhstan, now a republic of the USSR. The Kazakhs speak a Turkic language belonging to the Altaic family and are predominantly Muslim.

Kazakhstan /kæzæk'stɑːn/ a constituent republic of the USSR from 1936, part of Soviet Central Asia; **area** 2,717,300 sq km/1,049,150 sq mi; **capital** Alma-Ata; **towns** Karaganda, Semipalatinsk, Petropavlovsk; **physical** second largest republic in the USSR; Caspian and Aral seas, Lake Balkhash; Steppe region; **products** grain (second only to Ukraine in production), copper, lead, zinc, manganese, coal, oil; **language** Russian; Kazakh, related to Turkish; **population** (1987) 16,244,000; 41% Russian, 36% Kazakh, 6% Ukrainian; **recent history** the region first came under Russian control in the 18th century. In 1936 it joined the USSR and became a full union republic in 1936; there were nationalist and inter-ethnic riots in 1986 and 1989.

Kazan /kə'zæn/ the capital of the Tatar autonomous republic in central USSR, on the river Volga; population (1987) 1,068,000. It is a transport, commercial, and industrial centre (engineering, oil refining, petrochemicals, textiles, large fur trade). Formerly the capital of a Tatar khanate, Kazan was captured by Ivan IV 'the Terrible' in 1552.

Kazan Elia 1909– . US stage and film director, a founder of the ◊Actors Studio 1947. Plays he directed include *The Skin of Our Teeth* 1942, *A Streetcar Named Desire* 1947, and *Cat on a Hot Tin Roof* 1955; films include *Gentleman's Agreement* 1948, *East of Eden* 1954, and *The Visitors* 1972.

Kazantzakis /kæzænd'zɑːkɪs/ Nikos 1885–1957. Greek writer, whose works include the poem *I Odysseia/The Odyssey* 1938 (which continues Homer's *Odyssey*), and the novel *Zorba the Greek* 1946.

591 kelson

kazoo /kə'zu:/ *n.* (*plural* **kazoos**) a simple wind instrument adding a buzzing quality to the singing voice on the principle of 'comb and paper' music.

KBE abbreviation of Knight (Commander of the Order) of the British Empire.

kcal symbol for kilocalorie (see ◊calorie).

KCB abbreviation of Knight Commander of the Order of the Bath.

KCMG abbreviation of Knight Commander of the Order of St Michael and St George.

kc/s abbreviation of kilocycles per second.

kea /'keɪə/ *n.* a hawklike, greenish parrot *Nestor notabilis* found in New Zealand, which eats insects, fruits, and sheep offal. [Maori, imitative]

Kean /ki:n/ Edmund 1787–1833. English tragic actor, noted for his portrayal of villainy in the Shakespearean roles of Shylock, Richard III, and Iago.

Keane /ki:n/ Molly (Mary Nesta) 1905– . Irish novelist, whose comic novels of Anglo-Irish life include *Good Behaviour* 1981, *Time After Time* 1983, and *Loving and Giving* 1988. She also writes under the name M J Farrell.

Keaton /'ki:tn/ Buster. Stage name of Joseph Frank Keaton 1896–1966. US comedian, actor and film director. He was one of the great comedians of the silent film era, his deadpan expression masking a sophisticated acting ability. His films include *One Week* 1920, *The Navigator* 1924, *The General* 1927, and *The Cameraman* 1928.

Keats /ki:ts/ John 1795–1821. English poet, a leading figure of the Romantic movement. He published his first volume of poetry in 1817; this was followed by *Endymion*, *Isabella*, and *Hyperion* 1818, 'The Eve of St Agnes', his odes 'To Autumn', 'On a Grecian Urn', and 'To a Nightingale', and 'Lamia' 1819. His final volume of poems appeared in 1820.

kebab /kɪ'bæb/ *n.* a collection of small pieces of meat, vegetables, etc., grilled on a skewer. [from Urdu from Arabic]

kedge *v.t./i.* to move (a ship) by a hawser attached to a small anchor. —*n.* a small anchor for this purpose.

kedgeree /'kedʒərɪ, -'ri:/ *n.* **1.** a European dish of fish, rice, hard-boiled eggs, etc. **2.** an Indian dish of rice, pulse, onions, eggs, etc. [from Hindi]

keel *n.* **1.** the lengthwise timber or steel structure along the base of a ship, from which the framework is built up. **2.** a structure resembling this; a ridge along the breastbone of many birds. —*v.t./i.* to turn keel upwards. —**keel over**, to overturn; to fall or collapse. **on an even keel,** level, steady. [from Old Norse]

Keeler /'ki:lə/ Christine 1942– . English model of the 1960s. She became notorious in 1963 after revelations of affairs with both a Soviet attaché and the war minister John ◊Profumo, who resigned after admitting lying to the House of Commons about their relationship. Her patron, the osteopath Stephen Ward, convicted of living on immoral earnings, committed suicide and Keeler was subsequently imprisoned for related offences.

keelhaul *v.t.* **1.** to haul (a person) under a keel as a punishment. **2.** to rebuke severely.

keelson variant of ◊kelson.

keen[1] **1.** showing or feeling intense interest or desire; (of desire etc.) intense. **2.** perceiving things very distinctly; intellectually acute. **3.** sharp, having a sharp edge or point. **4.** (of sound or light etc.) acute, penetrating; (of wind etc.) piercingly cold; (of pain) acute. **5.** (of a price) competitively low. —**keen on,** (*colloquial*) much attracted by. —**keenly** *adv.*, **keenness** *n.* [Old English]

keen[2] an Irish funeral song accompanied by wailing. —*v.t./i.* to utter the keen; to bewail (a person) thus. [from Irish *caoine*]

keep *v.t./i.* (*past* and *past participle* **kept**) **1.** to have continuous charge of; to retain possession of; to reserve (*for* a future time etc.). **2.** to remain or cause to remain in a specified condition, position, course, etc. **3.** to restrain, to hold back *from*; to detain. **4.** to observe; to pay due regard to (a law, promise, appointment, etc.). **5.** to refrain from disclosing (a secret etc.). **6.** to own and look after (animals etc.); to maintain in return for sexual favours. **7.** to guard or protect (a person, place, goal at football, etc.). **8.** to maintain (a house etc.) in proper order; to manage (a shop etc.); to maintain (a diary, account books, etc.) by making the requisite entries. **9.** to preserve in being; to continue to have or do. **10.** (of food etc.) to remain in good condition; to

be able to be put aside until later. **11.** to have (a commodity) regularly on sale. **12.** to celebrate (a feast or ceremony). —*n.* **1.** maintenance, food. **2.** the central tower or other strongly fortified structure in a castle etc. —**for keeps,** (*colloquial*) permanently. **keep on,** to continue; to nag *at*. **keep to oneself,** to avoid contact with others; to keep (a thing) a secret. **keep under,** to repress. **keep up,** to maintain; to prevent from sinking (especially one's spirits etc.). **keep up with,** to achieve the same pace as. **keep up with the Joneses,** to strive to remain on terms of obvious social equality with one's neighbours. [Old English]

keeper *n.* a person who keeps or looks after something; a custodian of a museum or art gallery or forest; a wicketkeeper.

Keeper of the Great Seal in the Middle Ages, an officer who had charge of the Great Seal of England (the official seal authenticating state documents).

keeping *n.* **1.** custody, charge. **2.** harmony, conformity.

keepsake *n.* a thing kept in memory of its giver.

keg *n.* a small cask or barrel. —**keg beer,** beer supplied from a sealed metal container. [from Old Norse]

Keillor /'ki:lə/ Garrison 1942– . US writer and humorist. His hometown in the American Midwest inspired his Lake Wobegon stories, including *Lake Wobegon Days* 1985 and *Leaving Home* 1987, which were often originally radio monologues.

Keitel /'kaɪtl/ Wilhelm 1882–1946. German field marshal in World War II, chief of the supreme command from 1938. He signed Germany's unconditional surrender in Berlin on 8 May 1945. He was tried in Nuremberg for war crimes and was hanged.

Kekulé von Stradonitz /'kekjuleɪ/ Friedrich August 1829–1896. German chemist whose 1858 theory of molecular structure revolutionized organic chemistry. He proposed two resonant forms of the ◊benzene ring.

Kellogg–Briand pact /'kelɒg, brɪɑ/ an agreement made in 1927 between the USA and France to renounce war and seek settlement of disputes by peaceful means. Other powers signed in Aug 1928, making a total of 67 signatories. Some successes were achieved in settling South American disputes, but the pact made no provision for measures against aggressors and became ineffective in the 1930s, with Japan in Manchuria, Italy in Ethiopia, and Hitler in central Europe. [from the US secretary of state Frank B Kellogg (1856–1937) and the French foreign minister Aristide Briand]

Kells, Book of /kelz/ the 8th-century illuminated manuscript of the Gospels produced at the monastery of Kells in County Meath, Ireland. It is now in Trinity College library, Dublin.

Kelly /'keli/ Gene (Eugene Curran) 1912– . US film actor, dancer, choreographer, and director, a star of the 1940s and 1950s in a series of MGM musicals, including *Singin' in the Rain* 1952. His subsequent attempts at straight direction were less well received.

Kelly Grace (Patricia) 1928–1982. US film actress, who retired from acting after marrying Prince Rainier III of Monaco in 1956. She starred in *High Noon* 1952, *The Country Girl* 1954, for which she received an Academy Award, and *High Society* 1955. She also starred in three Hitchcock classics – *Dial M for Murder* 1954, *Rear Window* 1954, and *To Catch a Thief* 1955.

Kelly Ned (Edward) 1855–1880. Australian ◊bushranger. The son of an Irish convict, he wounded a police officer in 1878 while resisting the arrest of his brother Daniel for horse stealing. The two brothers escaped and carried out bank robberies. Kelly wore a distinctive home-made armour. In 1880 he was captured and hanged.

keloid /'ki:lɔɪd/ *n.* in medicine, an overgrowth of fibrous tissue, usually produced at the site of a scar. Black skin produces more keloid than does white skin; it has a puckered appearance caused by clawlike offshoots. Surgical removal is often unsuccessful because the keloid returns.

kelp *n.* any large brown seaweed, such as those of the Fucaceae and Laminariaceae families; the powdery ash of burned seaweeds, a source of iodine.

kelpie *n.* (*Scottish*) **1.** a malevolent water spirit usually in the form of a horse. **2.** an Australian sheepdog of Scottish origin.

kelson /'kelsən/ *n.* the line of timber fixing a ship's floor timbers to the keel.

Kelvin *Irish physicist William Kelvin pioneered the Kelvin scale of temperature used by scientists.*

kelt *n.* a salmon or sea trout after spawning.

Kelvin /'kelvɪn/ William Thomson, 1st Baron Kelvin 1824–1907. Irish physicist, who introduced the **kelvin scale**, the absolute scale of temperature. His work on the conservation of energy in 1851 led to the second law of ◊thermodynamics.

kelvin scale a temperature scale used by scientists. It begins at ◊absolute zero (-273.16°C) and increases by the same degree intervals as the Celsius scale; that is, 0°C is the same as 273 K and 100°C is 373 K.

Kemal Atatürk Mustafa. Turkish politician; see ◊Atatürk.

Kemble /'kembəl/ Charles 1775–1854. English actor and theatre manager, younger brother of Philip Kemble. His greatest successes were in romantic roles with his daughter Fanny Kemble.

Kemble Fanny (Frances Anne) 1809–1893. English actress, daughter of Charles Kemble. She first appeared as Shakespeare's Juliet in 1829.

Kemble (John) Philip 1757–1823. English actor and theatre manager. He excelled in tragedy, including the Shakespearean roles of Hamlet and Coriolanus. As manager of Drury Lane 1788–1803 and Covent Garden 1803–17 in London, he introduced many innovations in theatrical management, costume, and scenery.

Kempe /kemp/ Margery *c.*1373–*c.*1439. English Christian mystic. She converted to religious life after a period of mental derangement, and travelled widely as a pilgrim. Her *Boke of Margery Kempe* of about 1420 describes her life and experiences, both religious and worldly. It has been called the first autobiography in English.

Kempis Thomas à. Medieval German monk and religious writer; see ◊Thomas à Kempis.

ken *v.t.* (**-nn-**) (*Scottish*) to know. —*n.* the range of knowledge or sight. [Old English]

kendo /'kendəʊ/ *n.* the Japanese armed ◊martial art in which combatants fence with bamboo replicas of samurai swords. Masks and padding are worn for protection. The earliest recorded reference to kendo is AD 789. [Japanese = sword way]

Keneally /kɪ'niːli/ Thomas (Michael) 1935– . Australian novelist who won the ◊Booker Prize with *Schindler's Ark* 1982, a novel based on the true account of Polish Jews saved from the gas chambers in World War II by a German industrialist.

Kennedy /'kenədi/ Edward (Moore) 1932– . US Democratic politician. He aided his brothers John and Robert Kennedy in the presidential campaign of 1960, and entered politics as a senator from Massachusetts in 1962. He failed to gain the presidential nomination in 1980, largely because of questions about his delay in reporting a car crash at Chappaquiddick Island, near Cape Cod, Massachusetts, in 1969, in which his passenger, Mary Jo Kopechne, was drowned.

Kennedy John F(itzgerald) 1917–1963. The 35th president of the USA 1961–63, a Democrat. Kennedy was the first Roman Catholic and the youngest person to be elected president. In foreign policy he carried through the unsuccessful ◊Bay of Pigs invasion of Cuba, and in 1963 secured the withdrawal of Soviet missiles from the island. His programme for reforms at home, called the **New Frontier**, was posthumously executed by Lyndon Johnson. Kennedy was assassinated while on a state visit to Dallas, Texas, on 22 Nov 1963 by Lee Harvey Oswald (1939–1963), who was in turn shot dead by Jack Ruby.

> Do you realize the responsibility I carry? I'm the only person standing between Nixon and the White House.
> **John Fitzgerald Kennedy**
> October 1960

Kennedy Joseph Patrick 1888–1969. US industrialist and diplomat; ambassador to the UK 1937–40. A self-made millionaire, he groomed each of his four sons – Joseph Patrick Kennedy Jr (1915–1944), John ◊Kennedy, Robert ◊Kennedy, Edward ◊Kennedy – for a career in politics. His eldest son, Joseph, was killed in action in World War II.

Kennedy Robert (Francis) 1925–1968. US Democratic politician and lawyer. He was presidential campaign manager for his brother John F ◊Kennedy in 1960, and as attorney general 1961–64 pursued a racket-busting policy and promoted the Civil Rights Act of 1964. He was also a key aide to his brother. When John Kennedy's successor, Lyndon Johnson, preferred Hubert H Humphrey for the 1964 vice presidential nomination, Kennedy resigned and was elected senator for New York. In 1968 he campaigned for the Democratic Party's presidential nomination, but during a campaign stop in California was assassinated by Sirhan Bissara Sirhan (1944–), a Jordanian.

Kennedy Space Center the ◊NASA launch site on Merritt Island, near Cape Canaveral, Florida, from where the Apollo and Space Shuttle missions were launched.

kennel /'kenəl/ *n.* **1.** a small shelter for a dog. **2.** (in *plural*) a place where dogs are bred or boarded. **3.** a pack of dogs. —*v.t.* (**-ll-**) to put or keep in a kennel. [from Old French *chenil* from Latin *canis* = dog]

Kennelly–Heaviside layer /kenəli 'hevɪsaɪd/ former term for the ◊E layer.

Kenneth /'kenəθ/ two kings of Scotland including:

Kenneth I MacAlpin died 858. King of Scotland from about 844. Traditionally, he is regarded as the founder of the Scottish kingdom (Alba) by virtue of his final defeat of the Picts about 844. He invaded Northumbria six times, and drove the Angles and the Britons over the river Tweed.

Kent /kent/ county in SE England, nicknamed the 'garden of England'; **area** 3,730 sq km/1,440 sq mi; **principal town** Maidstone; **physical** Romney Marsh; the Isles of Grain, Sheppey and Thanet; rivers: Darent, Medway, Stour; **products** hops, apples, soft fruit, coal, cement, paper; **population** (1987) 1,511,000.

Kent Bruce 1929– . British peace campaigner who acted as general secretary for the Campaign for Nuclear Disarmament 1980–85. He has published numerous articles on disarmament, Christianity, and peace. He was a Catholic priest until 1987.

> Preparing for suicide is not a very intelligent means of defence.
> **Bruce Kent**
> August 1986

Kent Edward George Alexander Edmund, 2nd Duke of Kent 1935– . British prince, grandson of George V. His father, **George** (1902–1942), was created Duke of Kent just before his marriage in 1934 to Princess Marina of Greece and Denmark (1906–1968). The second duke succeeded when his father was killed in an air crash on active service with the RAF.

Kent William 1685–1748. British architect, landscape gardener, and interior designer. In architecture he was foremost in introducing the Palladian style into Britain from Italy.

Kent and Strathearn /stræθ'ɜːn/ Edward, Duke of Kent and Strathearn 1767–1820. British general. The fourth son of George III, he married Victoria Mary Louisa (1786–1861), widow of the Prince of Leiningen, in 1818, and had one child, the future Queen Victoria.

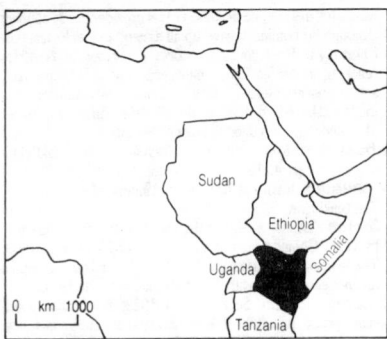

Kenya

Kentucky /ken'tʌki/ state of S central USA; nickname Bluegrass State; **area** 104,700 sq km/40,414 sq mi; **capital** Frankfort; **products** tobacco, cereals, steel goods, textiles, transport vehicles; **population** (1987) 3,727,000; **history** Kentucky's first permanent settlements were established after Daniel Boone had blazed his Wilderness Trail. Originally part of Virginia, it became a state in 1792.

Kenya /'kenjə/ Republic of; country in E Africa, bordered to the N by Sudan and Ethiopia, E by Somalia, SE by the Indian Ocean, SW by Tanzania, and W by Uganda; **area** 582,600 sq km/224,884 sq mi; **physical** mountains and highlands in W and centre; coastal plain in S; N arid; Great Rift Valley, Mount Kenya, Lake Nakuru, Lake Turkana, Olduvai Gorge; **head of state and government** Daniel arap Moi from 1978; **political system** authoritarian nationalism; **exports** coffee, tea, pineapples, petroleum products; **language** Kiswahili; **recent history** Kenya achieved independence from Britain in 1964. Kenyatta, the then leader of the Kenya African National Union (KANU), became prime minister and then president after full independence in 1964. On his death in 1978, he was succeeded by Vice-President Daniel arap Moi.

Kenyatta /ken'jætə/ Jomo. Assumed name of Kamau Ngengi c.1894–1978. Kenyan nationalist politician, prime minister from 1963, as well as first president of Kenya from 1964 until his death. He led the Kenya African Union from 1947 (◊KANU from 1963) and was active in liberating Kenya from British rule.

kepi /'kepɪ, 'keɪpɪ/ n. a French military cap with a horizontal peak. [from French from Swiss German]

Kepler /'keplə/ Johann 1571–1630. German mathematician and astronomer. He formulated what are now called **Kepler's laws** of planetary motion: the orbit of each planet is an ellipse with the Sun at one of the foci; the radius vector of each planet sweeps out equal areas in equal times; the squares of the periods of the planets are proportional to the cubes of their mean distances from the Sun.

kept past and past participle of **keep**.

Kerala /'kerələ/ a state of SW India, formed in 1956 from the former princely states of Travancore and Cochin; **area** 38,900 sq km/15,015 sq mi; **capital** Trivandrum; **products** tea, coffee, rice, oilseed, rubber, textiles, chemicals, electrical goods; **language** Kannada, Malayalam, Tamil; **population** (1981) 25,403,000.

keratin /'kerətɪn/ n. a fibrous protein found in the ◊skin of vertebrates and also in hair, nails, claws, hooves, feathers, and the outer coating of horns in animals, such as cows and sheep.

kerb n. a stone edging to a pavement or raised path. [variant of *curb*]

kerbstone n. each of the stones forming a kerb.

kerchief /'kɜːtʃɪf/ n. 1. a square cloth used to cover the head. 2. a handkerchief. [from Old French *couvre* = cover and *chief* = head]

Kerekou /kerə'kuː/ Mathieu (Ahmed) 1933– . Benin socialist politician and soldier, president from 1980. In 1972, when deputy head of the Dahomey army, he led a coup to oust the ruling president and establish his own military government. He changed his country's name to Benin. Re-elected president in 1984, he resigned from the army in 1987 and confirmed a civilian administration.

Kerensky /'kerənski/ Alexander Feodorovich 1881–1970. Russian revolutionary politician, prime minister of the second provisional government before its collapse in Nov 1917, during the ◊Russian Revolution. He fled to France in 1918 and lived in the USA from 1940.

kerfuffle /kə'fʌfəl/ n. (*colloquial*) a fuss, a commotion. [originally Scottish]

Kerkira /'keəkɪrə/ Greek form of ◊Corfu, an island in the Ionian Sea.

kermes /'kɜːmɪz/ n. the female of an insect *Kermes ilicis*, formerly taken to be a berry, which feeds on an evergreen oak *Quercus coccinea*; a red dye made from the dried bodies of these. [from French from Arabic and Persian]

Kern /kɜːn/ Jerome (David) 1885–1945. US composer. He wrote the operetta *Show Boat* 1927, which includes the song 'Ol' Man River'.

kernel /'kɜːnəl/ n. 1. the softer part within the hard shell of a ◊nut or stone fruit. 2. a seed within a husk etc., e. g. a grain of wheat. 3. the central or essential part of a thing. [Old English]

kerosene /'kerəsiːn/ n. a thin oil obtained from the distillation of petroleum or from coal or bituminous shale; a highly refined form is used in jet aircraft fuel. Kerosene is a mixture of hydrocarbons of the ◊paraffin series. [from Greek *kēros* = wax]

Kerouac /'keruæk/ Jack 1923–1969. US novelist, who named and epitomized the ◊Beat Generation of the 1950s. His books, all autobiographical, include *On the Road* 1957, *Big Sur* 1963, and *Desolation Angel* 1965.

Kerr /kɑː/ Deborah 1921– . English actress, who often played genteel, ladylike roles. Her performance in British films such as *Major Barbara* 1940 and *Black Narcissus* 1946 led to starring parts in Hollywood films such as *Quo Vadis* 1951, *From Here to Eternity* 1953, and *The King and I* 1956.

Kerry /'keri/ a county of Munster province, Republic of Ireland, east of Cork; **area** 4,700 sq km/1,814 sq mi; **county town** Tralee; **physical** western coastline deeply indented; northern part low-lying, but in the south are the highest mountains in Ireland including Carrantuohill 1,041 m/ 3,417 ft, the highest peak in Ireland; many rivers and lakes; **products** engineering, woollens, shoes, cutlery; tourism is important; **population** (1986) 124,000.

Kertesz /'kɜːtes/ André 1894–1986. Hungarian-born US photographer. A master of the 35-mm camera, he recorded his immediate environment (Paris, New York) with wit and style.

Kesselring /'kesəlrɪŋ/ Albert 1885–1960. German field marshal in World War II, commander of the Luftwaffe (air force) 1939–40, during the invasions of Poland and the Low Countries and the early stages of the Battle of Britain. He later served under Field Marshal Rommel in N Africa, took command in Italy in 1943, and was commander in chief on the western front in March 1945. His death sentence for war crimes at the Nuremberg trials of 1947 was commuted to life imprisonment, but he was released in 1952.

kestrel /'kestr(ə)l/ n. a kind of small falcon (especially *Falco tinnunculus*), which breeds in Europe, Asia, and Africa. About 30 cm/1 ft long, the male has a head and tail of bluish-grey, and its back is a light chestnut-brown with black spots. The female is slightly larger and reddish-brown above, with bars. The kestrel hunts mainly by hovering in mid-air while searching for prey.

ketch n. a small sailing vessel with two masts.

ketchup /'ketʃəp/ n. a thick spicy sauce made from tomatoes, mushrooms, etc. [from Chinese = pickled-fish brine]

ketone /'kiːtəʊn/ n. a member of the group of organic compounds containing the carbonyl group (CO) bonded to two atoms of carbon (instead of one carbon and one hydrogen as in ◊aldehydes). Ketones are liquids or low-melting-point solids, slightly soluble in water. [from German *keton* alteration of *aketon* = acetone]

kettle n. a vessel, usually of metal with a spout and handle, for boiling water. —**a fine** or **pretty** etc. **kettle of fish**, an awkward state of affairs. [from Old Norse ultimately from Latin]

kettledrum n. 1. a large drum consisting of an inverted metal bowl over which an adjustable membrane is stretched, enabling it to be tuned to a definite note. 2. (**in** *plural*) the timpani of an orchestra.

Kew Gardens /kju:/ the popular name for the Royal Botanic Gardens, Kew, Surrey. They were founded in 1759 by the mother of King George III as a small garden and passed to the nation by Queen Victoria in 1840. By then they were almost their present size of 149 hectares/368 acres and since 1841 have been open daily to the public. They contain a collection of over 25,000 living plant species and are a centre for botanical research. There are many fine buildings, among them the majestic Palm House 1848 designed by Decimus Burton. Many trees were destroyed by a gale in 1987.

key[1] /ki:/ **1.** an instrument, usually of metal, for moving the bolt of a lock so that it locks or unlocks. **2.** a similar implement for operating a switch in the form of a lock, winding a clock etc., or grasping a screw, nut, etc. **3.** each of a set of levers or buttons pressed by the finger in a musical instrument, typewriter, etc. **4.** in music, a system of notes based on material in a particular scale; (*figurative*) the general tone or style of thought or expression. **5.** a solution to a problem, an explanation, a word or system for solving a cipher or code. **6.** a thing or factor governing an opportunity for or access to something; (*attributive*) essential, of vital importance. **7.** a piece of wood or metal inserted between others to secure them. **8.** a mechanical device for making or breaking an electric circuit. **9.** the winged fruit of the sycamore, ash, etc. **10.** roughness of surface to help adhesion of plaster etc. —*v.t./i.* **1.** to fasten with a pin, wedge, bolt, etc. **2.** to roughen (a surface), to help the adhesion of plaster etc. **3.** to align or link (*to*). **key in**, to enter (data) by means of a keyboard. **key money**, a payment required from an incoming tenant nominally for the provision of the key to a premises. **keypad** *n.* a miniature keyboard for holding in the hand. **key-ring** *n.* a ring for keeping keys on. **key up**, to stimulate or excite (a person). [Old English]

key[2] /ki:/ a reef, a low island. [from Spanish *cayo*]

keyboard *n.* **1.** a set of keys on a typewriter, piano, etc. **2.** in computing; an input device resembling a typewriter keyboard, used to enter instructions and data. There are many variations on the layout and labelling of keys for different purposes. Extra numeric keys may be added, as can special-purpose function keys, such as LOAD, SAVE, PRINT, whose effect can be defined by programs in the computer.

keyhole *n.* the hole by which a key is put into a lock.

Keynes /keɪnz/ John Maynard, 1st Baron Keynes 1883–1946. English economist whose *General Theory of Employment, Interest, and Money* 1936 proposed the prevention of financial crises and unemployment by adjusting demand through government control of credit and currency. He is responsible for that part of economics now known as ◊macroeconomics.

Keynesian economics /keɪnzɪən/ the economic theory of J M Keynes, which argues that a fall in national income, lack of demand for goods, and rising unemployment should be countered by increased government expenditure to stimulate the economy. It is opposed by monetarists (see ◊monetarism).

keynote *n.* **1.** the prevailing idea or tone in a speech etc. **2.** the lowest note in a scale on which a musical key is based.

keystone *n.* **1.** the central locking stone in an arch. **2.** a central principle.

keyword *n.* the key to a cipher.

kg abbreviation of ◊kilogram(s).

KG abbreviation of Knight of the Order of the Garter.

KGB the Soviet secret police, the *Komitet Gosudarstvennoye Bezhopaznosti*/Committee of State Security, in control of frontier and general security and the forced-labour system. KGB officers hold key appointments in all fields of daily life, reporting to administration offices in every major town. [Russian abbreviation]

Khabarovsk /xa'barəfsk/ a territory of the SE USSR bordering the Sea of Okhotsk and drained by the Amur; area 824,600 sq km/318,501 sq mi; population (1985) 1,728,000. The capital is Khabarovsk. Mineral resources include gold, coal, and iron ore.

Khachaturian /kætʃə'tuəriən/ Aram Il'yich 1903–1978. Armenian composer. His use of folk themes is shown in the ballets *Gayaneh* 1942, which includes the 'Sabre Dance', and *Spartacus* 1956.

Khaddhafi /kə'dæfi/ or **Gaddafi** or **Qaddafi**, Moamer al 1942– . Libyan revolutionary leader. After overthrowing King Idris in 1969, he became virtual president of a republic, although he nominally gave up all except an ideological role from 1974. He favours territorial expansion in N Africa reaching as far as Zaïre, has supported rebels in Chad, and proposed mergers with a number of countries. His theories, based on those of the Chinese communist leader Mao Zedong, are contained in a *Green Book*.

khaki /'kɑːkɪ/ *adj.* dull brownish-yellow. —*n.* khaki cloth or uniform. [from Urdu = dust coloured]

Khalistan /kɑːli'stɑːn/ projected independent Sikh state. See ◊Sikhism.

Khalsa /'kɑːlsə/ *n.* the brotherhood of the Sikhs, created by Guru Gobind Singh at the festival of Baisakhi in 1699. The Khalsa was originally founded as a militant group, a distinct community with direct allegiance to the Guru.

Khama /'kɑːmə/ Seretse 1921–1980. Botswanan politician, prime minister of Bechuanaland in 1965, and first president of Botswana from 1966 until his death.

khan /kɑːn/ *n.* **1.** a title given to rulers and officials in Central Asia, Afghanistan, etc. **2.** *Historical* the supreme ruler of Turkish, Tartar, and Mongol tribes, and emperor of China, in the Middle Ages [from Turki = lord]

Khan Imran 1952– . Pakistani cricketer. He played county cricket for Worcestershire and Sussex in the UK, and made his Test debut for Pakistan in 1971, subsequently playing for his country 82 times.

Khan Jahangir 1963– . Pakistani squash player who won the world open championship a record six times, from 1981 to 1985 and in 1988.

Khan Liaquat Ali 1895–1951. Indian politician, deputy leader of the ◊Muslim League 1941–47, first prime minister of Pakistan from 1947. He was assassinated by a Muslim fanatic.

Khardung La Pass a road linking the Indian town of Leh with the high-altitude military outpost on the Siachen Glacier at 5,662 m/1,744 ft in the Karakoram range, Kashmir. It is thought to be the highest road in the world.

Kharg Island /kɑːg/ a small island in the Persian Gulf used by Iran as a deepwater oil terminal. Between 1982 and 1988 Kharg Island came under frequent attack during the Iran/Iraq War.

Kharkov /'kɑːkɒf/ the capital of the Kharkov region, Ukraine, USSR, 400 km/250 mi E of Kiev; population (1987) 1,587,000. It is a railway junction and an industrial city notable for engineering and tractors, close to the Donets Basin coalfield and the Krivoy Rog iron mines. Kharkov was founded in 1654 as a fortress town.

Khartoum /kɑː'tuːm/ the capital and trading centre of Sudan, at the junction of the Blue and White Nile; population (1983) 476,000, and of Khartoum North, across the Blue Nile, 341,000. ◊Omdurman, a suburb of Khartoum, gives the urban area a population of over 1.3 million.

khedive /ki'diːv/ *n.* the title granted by the Turkish sultan to his Egyptian viceroy 1867, retained by succeeding rulers until 1914.

Khe Sanh /'keɪ 'sæn/ in the Vietnam War, US Marine outpost near the Laotian border and just south of the demilitarized zone between North and South Vietnam. Garrisoned by 4,000 Marines, it was attacked unsuccessfully by 20,000 North Vietnamese troops from 21 Jan to 7 Apr 1968.

Khirbet Qumran /'kiəbet 'kumrɑːn/ an archaeological site in Jordan; see ◊Qumran.

Khmer /kmeə/ *n.* or **Kmer** a member of the largest ethnic group in Cambodia (formerly Kampuchea) living mainly in agricultural and fishing villages. Khmer minorities also live in E Thailand and S Vietnam. The Khmer language belongs to the Mon-Khmer family of Austro-Asiatic languages.

Khmer Republic the former name of ◊Cambodia, a country in SE Asia.

Khmer Rouge /ruːʒ/ the communist movement in ◊Cambodia (formerly called Kampuchea). It formed the largest opposition group to the US-backed regime led by Lon Nol 1970–75. By 1975 the Khmer Rouge controlled the countryside and had captured the capital, Phnom Penh, and Prince ◊Sihanouk was installed as head of state. Internal disagreements led to the creation of the Pol Pot government in 1976 and mass deportations and executions. Several million people died. Since 1978, when Vietnam invaded Kampuchea, the Khmer Rouge has conducted a guerrilla campaign, first against the Vietnamese forces, then against the Vietnamese-backed government.

Khomeini /kɒˈmeɪni/ Ayatollah Ruhollah 1900–1989. Iranian Shi'ite Muslim leader, born in Khomein, central Iran. Exiled for opposition to the Shah from 1964, he returned when the Shah left the country 1979, and established a fundamentalist Islamic republic. His rule was marked by a protracted war with Iraq and suppression of opposition within Iran, involving the execution of thousands.

Khorana /kɔːˈrɑːnə/ Har Gobind 1922– . Indian biochemist who in 1976 led the team that first synthesized a biologically active gene.

Khrushchev /kruʃˈtʃɒf/ Nikita Sergeyevich 1894–1971. Soviet politician, secretary general of the Communist Party 1953–64, premier 1958–64. He emerged as leader from the power struggle following Stalin's death and was the first official to denounce Stalin in 1956. His destalinization programme gave rise to revolts in Poland and Hungary in 1956.

Khufu /ˈkuːfuː/ c.3000 BC. Egyptian king of Memphis, who built the largest of the pyramids, known to the Greeks as the pyramid of Cheops (the Greek form of Khufu).

Khulna /ˈkʊlnə/ the capital of Khulna region, SW Bangladesh, situated close to the Ganges delta; population (1981) 646,000. Industry includes shipbuilding and textiles; it trades in jute, rice, salt, sugar, and oilseed.

Khwārizmī, al- /ˈkwɑːrɪzmi/ Muhammad ibn-Mūsā c.780–c.850. Persian mathematician from Khwarizm (now Khiva, USSR), who lived and worked in Baghdad. He wrote a book on algebra, from part of whose title (al-jabr) comes the word 'algebra', and a book in which he introduced to the West the Hindu-Arabic decimal number system. The word 'algorithm' is a corruption of his name.

Khyber Pass /ˈkaɪbə/ a pass 53 km/33 mi long, reaching heights of 1,280 m/3,518 ft through the mountain range that separates Pakistan from Afghanistan. The Khyber Pass was used by invaders of India. The present road was constructed by the British during the Afghan Wars.

kHz abbreviation of kilohertz (see ◊hertz).

Kiangsi former spelling of ◊Jiangxi, province of China.

Kiangsu former spelling of ◊Jiangsu, province of China.

kibbutz /kɪˈbuːts/ n. (plural **kibbutzim** /-ˈtsiːm/) Israeli communal collective settlement with collective ownership of all property and earnings, collective organization of work and decision making, and communal housing for children. A modified version, the Moshav Shitufi, is similar to the ◊collective farms of the USSR. Other Israeli cooperative rural settlements include the Moshav Ovdim, which has equal opportunity, and the similar but less strict Moshav settlement. [from Hebrew = gathering]

kibosh /ˈkaɪbɒʃ/ n. (slang) nonsense. —**put the kibosh on,** (slang) to put an end to.

kick v.t./i. 1. to thrust, strike, or propel forcibly with the foot or hoof. 2. to score (a goal) by a kick. 3. to protest, to show dislike. 4. (slang) to abandon (a habit). —n. 1. a kicking action or blow. 2. the recoil of a gun when fired. 3. (colloquial) resilience. 4. (colloquial) a temporary interest or enthusiasm; a sharp, stimulant effect, (usually in plural) a thrill. —**kick about** or **around,** to treat roughly; to move idly from place to place; to be unused or unwanted. **kick off,** to begin a football game; (colloquial) to make a start. **kick off** a start, especially of a football match. **kick out,** (colloquial) to expel forcibly, to dismiss. **kick up,** (colloquial) to create or cause (a fuss, trouble, etc.). **kick upstairs,** to promote (a person) to an ostensibly higher position, to remove him or her from the scene of real influence. —**kicker** n.

kickback n. 1. a recoil. 2. (colloquial) a payment for help in making a profit or for showing favour etc.

kick-start n. or **kick-starter** a device to start the engine of a motorcycle etc. by a downward thrust of a pedal. —v.t. to start (a motorcycle etc.) thus.

kid n. 1. a young goat. 2. the leather made from its skin. 3. (slang) a child. —v.t./i (-dd-) 1. to give birth to a young goat. 2. (slang) to deceive or hoax. —**handle** or **treat** etc. **with kid gloves,** to treat tactfully. [from Old Norse]

Kidd /kɪd/ 'Captain' (William) c.1645–1701. Scottish pirate. He spent his youth privateering for the British against the French off the North American coast, and in 1695 was given a royal commission to suppress piracy in the Indian Ocean. Instead, he joined a group of pirates in Madagascar. On his

way to Boston, Massachusetts, he was arrested in 1699, taken to England, and hanged.

kidnap /ˈkɪdnæp/ v.t. (-pp-) to carry off (a person) illegally especially to obtain a ransom; to steal (a child). —**kidnapper** n.

kidney /ˈkɪdni/ n. 1. either of the pair of glandular organs of mammals, birds, and reptiles, responsible for water regulation, excretion of waste products, and maintaining the ionic composition of the blood; an animal's kidney as food. The kidneys are situated on the rear wall of the abdomen. Each one consists of a number of long tubules; the outer parts filter the aqueous components of blood, and the inner parts selectively reabsorb vital salts, leaving waste products in the remaining fluid (urine), which is passed through the ureter to the bladder. 2. nature, kind, temperament. —**kidney bean,** a kidney-shaped dwarf French bean, a scarlet runner bean. **kidney dish,** an oval dish indented at one side. **kidney machine,** a machine able to take over the functions of a kidney.

Kiefer /ˈkiːfə/ Anselm 1945– . German painter. He studied under Joseph ◊Beuys, and his works include monumental landscapes on varied surfaces, often with the paint built up into relief with other substances. Much of his highly Expressionist work deals with recent German history.

Kierkegaard /ˈkɪəkəgɔːd/ Søren (Aabye) 1813–1855. Danish philosopher considered to be the founder of ◊existentialism. Disagreeing with the German dialectical philosopher ◊Hegel, he argued that no system of thought could explain the unique experience of the individual. He defended Christianity, suggesting that God cannot be known through reason, but only through a 'leap of faith'. He believed that God and exceptional individuals were above moral laws.

Job endured everything—until his friends came to comfort him, then he grew impatient.
Søren Kierkegaard
Journal

Kiev /ˈkiːef/ the capital of Ukraine, industrial centre (chemicals, clothing, leatherwork) and third largest city of the USSR, on the confluence of the Desna and Dnieper rivers; population (1987) 2,554,000.

Kigali /kiˈgɑːli/ the capital of Rwanda, central Africa; population (1981) 157,000. Products include coffee and minerals.

Kikuyu /kiˈkuːjuː/ n. a member of an E African agricultural people. They are Kenya's dominant ethnic group. Their language belongs to the Bantu branch of the Niger-Congo family.

Kildare /kɪlˈdeə/ county of Leinster province, Republic of Ireland, south of Meath; **area** 1,690 sq km/652 sq mi; **county town** Naas; **physical** wet and boggy in the N; **products** oats, barley, potatoes, cattle; **population** (1986) 116,000.

Kilimanjaro /kɪlɪmənˈdʒɑːrəʊ/ a volcano in Tanzania, the highest mountain in Africa, 5,900 m/19,364 ft.

Kilkenny /kɪlˈkeni/ county of Leinster province, Republic of Ireland, east of Tipperary; **area** 2,060 sq km/795 sq mi; **county town** Kilkenny; **products** agricultural, coal; **population** (1986) 73,000.

kill v.t. 1. to deprive of life or vitality, to cause the death of. 2. to put an end to; to render ineffective; to switch off (a light, engine, etc.). 3. (colloquial) to cause severe pain to; to overwhelm with amusement. 4. to spend (time) unprofitably while waiting for something. —n. 1. the act of killing. 2. the animal(s) killed, especially in sport. —**dressed to kill,** dressed extrovertly or alluringly. **in at the kill,** present at the time of victory. **kill off,** to get rid of by killing. **make a killing,** to have a great financial success. —**killer** n.

killer whale a whale Orcinus orca found in all seas of the world. It is black on top, white below, and grows up to 9 m/30 ft long. It has been observed to prey on other whales, as well as on seals and sea birds.

killjoy n. a person who spoils or questions others' enjoyment.

kiln n. a high-temperature furnace used commercially for drying timber, roasting metal ores, or for making cement, bricks, and pottery. Oil- or gas-fired kilns are used to bake ceramics at up to 1,760°C/3,200°F; electric kilns do not generally reach such high temperatures. [Old English from Latin *culina* = kitchen]

kilo /'ki:ləʊ/ *n.* (*plural* **kilos**) 1. a kilogram. 2. a kilometre. [French, abbreviation]

kilo- /'kɪlə-/ in combinations, thousand. [French from Greek *khilioi*]

kilobyte *n.* in computing, a unit of memory equal to 1,024 ◊bytes.

kilocycle /'kɪləsaɪkəl/ *n.* a kilohertz.

kilogram /'kɪləgræm/ *n.* an SI unit (symbol kg) of mass equal to 1,000 grams (2.2 lb).

kilohertz /'kɪləhɜ:ts/ *n.* a unit of frequency of electromagnetic waves, = 1,000 cycles per second.

kilolitre /'kɪləli:tə/ *n.* a metric unit of capacity, 1,000 litres or approximately 35.31 cubic feet.

kilometre /'kɪləmi:tə, kɪ'lɒmɪtə/ *n.* a metric unit of length (symbol km), 1,000 metres (3,280.89 ft) or approximately 0.62 mile.

kiloton /'kɪlətʌn/ *n.* a unit of explosive force equal to 1,000 tons of TNT.

kilotonne /'kɪlətʌn/ *n.* 1. 1,000 tonnes. 2. a metric unit equivalent to the kiloton.

kilowatt /'kɪləwɒt/ *n.* a unit of electrical power (symbol kW), equal to 1,000 watts or about 1.34 horsepower. —**kilowatt-hour** *n.* (symbol kWh) the energy equal to one kilowatt working for one hour.

kilt *n.* a pleated, usually tartan, skirt reaching from the waist to the knee, especially worn by a Highland man. —*v.t.* 1. to tuck up (skirts) round the body. 2. to gather in vertical pleats. [from Scandinavian]

kilted *adj.* wearing a kilt.

Kilvert /'kɪlvət/ Francis 1840–1879. British cleric who wrote a diary recording social life on the Welsh border 1870–79, published in 1938–39.

kimberlite *n.* an igneous rock that is ultrabasic (containing very little silica). It is a type of alkaline ◊peridotite containing mica in addition to olivine and other minerals. Kimberlite represents the world's principal source of diamonds. It is found in carrot-shaped pipelike ◊intrusions called **diatremes**, where mobile material from very deep in the Earth's crust has forced itself upwards, expanding in its ascent. Diatremes are found principally near Kimberley, South Africa, from which the name of the rock is derived, and in the Yakut area of Siberia, USSR.

Kim Dae Jung /kɪm deɪ 'dʒʊŋ/ 1924– . South Korean social democratic politician. As a committed opponent of the regime of General Park Chung Hee, he suffered imprisonment and exile. He was a presidential candidate in 1971 and 1987.

Kim Il Sung /kɪm i:l 'sʊŋ/ 1912– . North Korean communist politician and marshal. He became prime minister in 1948 and president in 1972, retaining the presidency of the Communist Workers' Party. He likes to be known as the 'Great Leader' and has campaigned constantly for the reunification of Korea. His son **Kim Jong Il** (1942–), known as the 'Dear Leader', has been named as his successor.

kimono /kɪ'məʊnəʊ/ *n.* (*plural* **kimonos**) 1. a long, loose Japanese robe with wide sleeves, secured with a sash called an *obi*). For the finest kimonos a rectangular piece of silk (about 11 m/36 ft × 0.5 m/1.5 ft) is cut into seven pieces for tailoring. The design (which must match perfectly over the seams) is then painted by hand and enhanced by embroidery or gilding. Worn as early as the Han period (1,000 years ago), it is still used by women for formal wear and informally by men. 2. a European dressing gown modelled on this. [Japanese]

Kim Young Sam /kɪm jʌŋ 'sæm/ 1927– . South Korean democratic politician. A member of the National Assembly from 1954 and president of the New Democratic Party (NDP) from 1974, he lost his seat and was later placed under house arrest because of his opposition to President Park Chung Hee. In 1983 he led a pro-democracy hunger strike but in 1987 failed to defeat Roh Tae-Woo in the presidential election. In 1990 he merged the NDP with the ruling party to form the new Democratic Liberal Party (DLP).

kin *n.* one's relatives or family. —*predic. adj.* related. —**kinship** *n.* in anthropology, human relationship based on blood or marriage, and sanctified by law and custom. Kinship forms the basis for most human societies and

for such social groupings as the family, clan, or tribe. [Old English]

-kin suffix forming diminutive nouns (*catkin*, *lambkin*). [from Middle Dutch -*kijn*, -*ken*, Old High German - *chin*]

Kincardineshire /kɪn'ka:dɪnʃə/ a former county of E Scotland, merged in 1975 into the Grampian region. The county town was Stonehaven.

kind[1] /kaɪnd/ a class of similar or related things or animals. —**a kind of**, something resembling or belonging approximately to (the class named). **in kind**, (of payment) in goods or produce, not money; (of repayment, especially *figuratively*) in the same form as that received. **kind of**, (*colloquial*) somewhat. [Old English]

kind[2] gentle or considerate in conduct or manner towards others. —**kind-hearted** *adj.*, **kindness** *n.* [originally = natural, native]

kindergarten /'kɪndəga:tən/ *n.* a school for very young children. [German = children's garden]

kindle *v.t./i.* 1. to set on fire; to cause (a fire) to begin burning. 2. to arouse or stimulate (a feeling etc.). 3. to become kindled. [from Old Norse, relative to *kindill* = candle, torch]

kindling /'kɪndlɪŋ/ *n.* small sticks etc. for lighting a fire.

kindly /'kaɪndlɪ/ *adj.* 1. kind. 2. (of a climate) pleasant, genial. —*adv.* 1. in a kind way. 2. (in a polite request or ironically command) please. —**not take kindly to**, to be displeased by. —**kindliness** *n.*

kindred /'kɪndrɪd/ *n.* 1. blood relationship. 2. one's relatives. 3. resemblance in character. —*adj.* related, of similar kind. —**kindred spirit**, a person whose tastes are similar to one's own. [from Old English *ræden* = condition]

kine /kaɪn/ *archaic plural of* **cow**[1].

kinematic /kɪnɪ'mætɪk/ *adj.* of motion considered abstractly without reference to force or mass. [from Greek *kinēma* = motion]

kinematics /kɪnɪ'mætɪks/ *n.* the science of pure motion.

kinetic /kɪ'netɪk, kaɪ-/ *adj.* of or due to motion. —**kinetic art**, a form of visual art depending on moving components for its effect. **kinetic energy**, a body's ability to do work by virtue of its motion; see ◊energy. **kinetic theory**, a theory describing the physical properties of matter in terms of the behaviour—principally movement—of its component atoms or molecules. A gas consists of rapidly moving atoms or molecules and, according to kinetic theory, it is their continual impact on the walls of the containing vessel that accounts for the pressure of the gas. [from Greek *kinētikos* (*kineō* = move)]

kinetics /kɪ'netɪks, kaɪ-/ *n. plural* (usually treated as *singular*) 1. the science of the relations between the motions of bodies and the forces acting upon them; it is a branch of dynamics. 2. the study of the mechanisms and rates of chemical reactions or other processes.

king /kɪŋ/ *n.* 1. a male sovereign (especially hereditary) ruler of an independent state. 2. a male person or a thing regarded as pre-eminent in a specified field or class. 3. (*attributive*) the large or largest kind of. 4. the piece in chess that has to be protected from checkmate. 5. a crowned piece in draughts. 6. a court-card with a picture of a king. —**King of Arms**, a chief herald (at the College of Arms, Garter, Clarenceaux, and Norroy & Ulster; in Scotland, Lyon). **king of beasts**, the lion. **king of birds**, the eagle. **king post** an upright post from a tie-beam to the top of a rafter. **king's evil**, scrofula, formerly held to be curable by the royal touch. **king-size, king-sized** *adjs.* larger than normal, very large. —**kingly** *adj.*, **kingship** *n.* [Old English]

King Billie Jean (born Moffitt) 1943– . US lawn-tennis player. She won a record 20 Wimbledon titles 1961–79 and 39 Grand Slam titles.

He who passively accepts evil is as much involved in it as he who helps to perpetrate it.

Martin Luther King Jr
Stride Towards Freedom

King Martin Luther, Jr 1929–1968. US civil-rights campaigner, black leader, and Baptist minister. He first came to national attention as leader of the ◊Montgomery, Alabama, bus boycott of 1955, and was one of the organizers of the massive (200,000 people) march on Washington DC in 1963 to demand racial equality. An advocate of ◊nonviolence, he was awarded the Nobel Peace Prize 1964. He was assassinated by James Earl Ray, in Memphis, Tennessee. King's birthday (15 Jan) is observed on the third Monday in Jan as a public holiday in the USA.

King William Lyon Mackenzie 1874–1950. Canadian Liberal prime minister 1921–26, 1926–30, and 1935–48. He maintained the unity of the English- and French-speaking populations, and was instrumental in establishing equal status for Canada with Britain.

king crab or **horseshoe crab** a marine arthropod, class Arachnida, subclass Xiphosura, which lives on the Atlantic coast of North America, and the coasts of Asia. The upper side of the body is entirely covered with a rounded shell, and it has a long spinelike tail. It is up to 60 cm/2 ft long. It is unable to swim, and lays its eggs in the sand at the high-water mark.

kingcup *n.* the marsh marigold.

kingdom /'kɪŋdəm/ *n.* **1.** a territory or state ruled by a king or queen; a domain. **2.** the primary division in biological ◊classification. At one time, only two kingdoms were recognized: animals and plants. Today most biologists prefer a five- kingdom system, even though it still involves grouping together organisms that are probably unrelated. One widely accepted scheme is as follows: **Kingdom Animalia** (all multicellular animals); **Kingdom Plantae** (all plants, all seaweeds and other algae, including unicellular algae); **Kingdom Fungi** (all fungi, including the unicellular yeasts, but not slime moulds); **Kingdom Protista** or **Protoctista** (protozoa, diatoms, dinoflagellates, slime moulds, and various other lower organisms with eukaryotic cells); and **Kingdom Monera** (all prokaryotes—the bacteria and cyanobacteria). The first four of these kingdoms make up the eukaryotes. —**kingdom come** *n.* (*slang*) the next world. [Old English]

kingfisher *n.* a small bird of the family Alcedinidae, especially *Alcedo atthis*, found in parts of Europe, Africa, and Asia. The plumage is brilliant blue green on the back and chestnut beneath. Kingfishers feed on fish and aquatic insects, and make nests of fishbones in a hole in the river bank.

King Lear /lɪə/ a tragedy by William Shakespeare, first performed 1605–06. Lear, king of Britain, favours his grasping daughters Goneril and Regan with shares of his kingdom but refuses his third, honest daughter, Cordelia, a share. Rejected by Goneril and Regan, the old and unbalanced Lear is reunited with Cordelia but dies of grief when she is murdered.

kingpin *n.* **1.** a vertical bolt used as a pivot. **2.** an essential person or thing.

King/Queen's Champion in English history, a ceremonial office held by virtue of possessing the lordship of Scrivelsby, Lincolnshire. Sir John Dymoke established his right to champion the monarch on coronation day 1377 and it is still held by his descendant.

King's Counsel in England, a ◊barrister of senior rank; the term is used when a king is on the throne and ◊Queen's Counsel when the monarch is a queen.

Kingsley /'kɪŋzli/ Ben (Krishna Banji) 1944– . British film actor who usually plays character parts. He played the title role of *Gandhi* 1982 and appeared in *Betrayal* 1982, *Testimony* 1987, and *Pascali's Island* 1988.

Kingsley Charles 1819–1875. English author. A rector, he was known as the 'Chartist clergyman' because of such social novels as *Alton Locke* 1850. His historical novels include *Westward Ho!* 1855. He also wrote *The Water-Babies* 1863.

King's proctor in England, the official representing the crown in certain court cases; the term is used when a king is on the throne, and Queen's proctor when the monarch is a queen.

Kingston /'kɪŋstən/ the capital and principal port of Jamaica, West Indies, the cultural and commercial centre of the island; population (1983) 101,000, metropolitan area 525,000. Founded in 1693, Kingston became the capital of Jamaica in 1872.

Kingston-upon-Hull /'kɪŋstən əpɒn 'hʌl/ the official name of ◊Hull, city in Humberside in NE England.

Kinnock *British Labour Party leader since 1983, Neil Kinnock.*

Kingstown /'kɪŋztaʊn/ the capital and principal port of St Vincent and the Grenadines, West Indies, in the SW of the island of St Vincent; population (1987) 29,000.

kink *n.* **1.** a sudden bend or twist in something straight or smoothly curved. **2.** a mental peculiarity or twist. —*v.t./i.* to form or cause to form a kink. [from Middle Low German]

kinkajou /'kɪŋkədʒuː/ *n.* a Central and South American mammal *Potos flavus* of the raccoon family. Yellowish-brown, with a rounded face and slim body, the kinkajou grows to 55 cm/1.8 ft long with a 50 cm/1.6 ft tail, and has short legs with sharp claws. It spends its time in the trees and has a prehensile tail. It feeds largely on fruit.

Kinki /'kɪŋki/ a region of S Honshu island, Japan; population (1986) 21,932,000; area 33,070 sq km/12,773 sq mi. The chief city is Osaka.

kinky *adj.* **1.** having kinks. **2.** (*colloquial*) bizarre, perverted (especially sexually). —**kinkily** *adv.*, **kinkiness** *n.*

Kinnock /'kɪnək/ Neil 1942–. British Labour politician, party leader from 1983. Born and educated in Wales, he was elected to represent a Welsh constituency in Parliament from 1970 (Islwyn from 1983). He was further left than prime ministers Wilson and Callaghan, but as party leader (in succession to Michael Foot) adopted a moderate position, initiating a major policy review 1988–89.

Political renegades always start their career of treachery as 'the best men of all parties' and end up in the Tory knackery.

Neil Kinnock
Welsh Labour Party Conference 1985

Kinross-shire /kɪn'rɒs/ a former county of E central Scotland, merged in 1975 in Tayside region. Kinross was the county town.

Kinsey /'kɪnzi/ Alfred 1894–1956. US researcher whose studies of male and female sexual behaviour 1948–53, based on questionnaires, were the first serious published research on this topic.

kinsfolk /'kɪnzfəʊk/ *n.* one's blood relations.

Kinshasa /kɪn'ʃɑːsə/ formerly **Léopoldville** the capital of Zaïre on the river Zaïre, 400 km/250 mi inland from Matadi; population (1984) 2,654,000. Industries include chemicals, textiles, engineering, food processing, and furniture. It was founded by the explorer Henry Stanley in 1887.

Kinski /'kɪnski/ Klaus 1926– . German actor who has appeared in several Werner Herzog films, such as *Aguirre der Zorn Gottes/Aguirre Wrath of God* 1972, *Nosferatu* 1978, and *Fitzcarraldo* 1982.

kinsman /'kɪnzmən/ n. (plural **kinsmen**) a (male) blood relation. —**kinswoman** n.fem. (plural **kinswomen**).

kiosk /'ki:ɒsk/ n. 1. a light usually outdoor structure for the sale of newspapers, food, etc. 2. a boxlike structure in the street etc. for a public telephone. [from French from Turkish from Persian = pavilion]

kip n. (slang) 1. a sleep. 2. a place to sleep, a bed. —v.i. (-pp-) (slang) to sleep.

Kipling /'kɪplɪŋ/ (Joseph) Rudyard 1865–1936. English writer, born in India. His stories for children include the Jungle Books 1894–1895, Stalky and Co 1899, and the Just So Stories 1902. Other works include the novel Kim 1901, the short story 'His Gift', poetry, and the unfinished autobiography Something of Myself 1937. In his heyday he enjoyed enormous popularity, and although subsequently denigrated for alleged 'jingoist imperialism', his work is increasingly valued for its complex characterization and subtle moral viewpoints. Nobel prize 1907.

kipper n. 1. a kippered fish, especially a herring. 2. a male salmon in the spawning season. —v.t. to cure (a herring etc.) by splitting open, salting, drying, and smoking.

Kirchner /'kiəknə/ Ernst Ludwig 1880–1938. German Expressionist artist, a leading member of the group Die ◊Brücke in Dresden from 1905 and in Berlin from 1911. He suffered a breakdown during World War I and settled in Switzerland, where he committed suicide.

Kirghiz /'kɜ:gɪz/ n. (plural the same) a member of a pastoral people who inhabit the Central Asian region bounded by the Hindu Kush, the Himalayas, and the Tian Shan mountains; their language. The Kirghiz are Sunni Muslims, and their Turkic language belongs to the Altaic family.

Kirghizia /kɜ:'gɪziə/ constituent republic of the USSR from 1936, part of Soviet Central Asia; **area** 198,500 sq km/ 76,641 sq mi; **capital** Frunze; **physical** mountainous, an extension of the Tian Shan range; **products** cereals, sugar, cotton, coal, oil, sheep, yaks, horses; **population** (1987) 4,143,000; 48% Kirghiz of Mongol-Tatar origin (and related to the Kazakhs), 26% Russian, 12% Uzbek, 3% Ukrainian, 2% Tatar; **language** Kirghiz; **recent history** annexed by Russia in 1864, Khirghizia was part of an independent Turkestan republic from 1917 until 1924, when it was reincorporated in the USSR.

Kiribati /'kɪrɪbæs/ Republic of; a republic in the central Pacific, consisting of three groups of coral atolls and a volcanic island; **area** 717 sq km/277 sq mi; **capital** and port Bairiki (on Tarawa Atoll); **physical** comprises 33 Pacific coral islands: the Gilbert, Phoenix, and Line Islands, and Banaba (Ocean Island); **head of state and government** Ieremia Tabai from 1979; **political system** liberal democracy; **exports** copra, fish; **language** English, Gilbertese (official); **recent history** achieved independence from Britain and became a Republic in 1979.

Kirin /ki:'rɪn/ alternative name for ◊Jilin, Chinese province.

kirk n. (Scottish and north of England.) a church. —**kirk session** the lowest court in the Church of Scotland and (historical) other Presbyterian churches, composed of ministers and elders. [from Old Norse from Old English = church]

Kirk /kɜ:k/ Norman 1923–1974. New Zealand Labour politician, prime minister 1972–74.

Kirkcudbright /kə'ku:bri/ former county of S Scotland, merged 1975 in Dumfries and Galloway region. The county town was Kirkcudbright.

Kirov /'kiərɒf/ Sergei Mironovich 1886–1934. Russian Bolshevik leader, who joined the party in 1904 and played a prominent part in the 1917–20 civil war. As one of ◊Stalin's closest associates, he became first secretary of the Leningrad Communist Party. His assassination in 1934, possibly engineered by Stalin, led to the political trials held during the next four years as part of the ◊purge.

Kishi /'kɪʃi/ Nobusuke 1896–1987. Japanese politician and prime minister 1957–60. A government minister during World War II and imprisoned 1945, he was never put on trial and returned to politics 1953. During his premiership, Japan began a substantial rearmament programme and signed a new treaty with the USA that gave greater equality in the relationship between the two states.

Kishinev /kɪʃiˈnjɒf/ capital of Moldavian republic, USSR; population (1987) 663,000. Industries include cement, food processing, tobacco, and textiles.

kismet /'kɪsmet, 'kɪz-/ n. destiny, fate. [Turkish, from Arabic]

kiss n. a touch given with the lips. —v.t. 1. to touch with the lips, especially as a sign of love, affection, greeting, or reverence; (absolute, of two persons) to touch each other's lips thus. 2. to kiss gently. —**kiss curl** n. a small curl of hair arranged on the face or at the nape. **kiss hands**, to greet a sovereign thus. **kiss of death**, an apparently friendly act causing ruin. **kiss of life**, the mouth-to-mouth method of artificial respiration. [Old English]

kisser n. (slang) the mouth or face.

Kissinger /'kɪsɪndʒə/ Henry 1923– . German-born US diplomat. Following a brilliant academic career at Harvard University, he was appointed assistant for National Security Affairs in 1969 by President Nixon, and was secretary of state 1973–77. His missions to the USSR and China improved US relations with both countries, and he took part in negotiating US withdrawal from Vietnam 1973 and in Arab-Israeli peace negotiations 1973–75. He was awarded the Nobel Peace Prize in 1973.

kit n. 1. the equipment or clothing required for a particular activity or situation. 2. a soldier's or traveller's pack or equipment. 3. a set of parts sold together from which a whole thing can be made. —v.t./i. (-tt-) to equip, to fit out or up with a kit. [from Middle Dutch = wooden vessel]

Kitaj /ki'taɪ/ Ron B 1932– . US painter and printmaker, active in Britain. His work is mainly figurative, and his distinctive decorative pale palette was in part inspired by studies of the Impressionist Degas.

Kitakyushu /kɪtə'kju:ʃu:/ industrial (coal, steel, chemicals, cotton thread, plate glass, alcohol) port city in Japan, on the Hibiki Sea, N Kyushu, formed in 1963 by the amalgamation of Moji, Kokura, Tobata, Yawata, and Wakamatsu; population (1987) 1,042,000. A tunnel built in 1942 links it with Honshu.

Kitasato /kɪtə'satəʊ/ Shibasaburo 1852–1931. Japanese bacteriologist who discovered the ◊plague bacillus while investigating an outbreak of plague in Hong Kong. Kitasato was the first to grow the tetanus bacillus in pure culture. He and the German bacteriologist Behring discovered that increasing nonlethal doses of tetanus toxin give immunity to the disease.

kitbag n. a large, usually cylindrical, bag for a soldier's or traveller's kit.

kitchen /'kɪtʃɪn/ n. a place where food is prepared and cooked. —**kitchen cabinet**, a group of unofficial advisers (originally of the president of the USA) popularly believed to have greater influence than the official cabinet or other elected group. **kitchen garden**, a garden for growing fruit and vegetables. [Old English, ultimately from Latin coquina (coquere = cook)]

Kitchener /'kɪtʃɪnə/ Horatio Herbert, Earl Kitchener of Khartoum 1850–1916. British soldier and administrator. He defeated the Sudanese dervishes at Omdurman 1898 and reoccupied Khartoum. In South Africa, he was chief of staff 1900–02 during the Boer War, and commanded the forces in India 1902–09. He was appointed war minister on the outbreak of World War I, and drowned when his ship was sunk on the way to Russia.

kitchenette /kɪtʃi'net/ n. a small room or alcove used as a kitchen.

kite n. 1. a toy consisting of a light framework with paper etc. stretched over it and flown in the wind at the end of a long string. 2. one of several birds of prey in the family Accipitridae, found in all parts of the world except the Americas. The red kite Milvus milvus, found in Europe, has a forked tail and narrow wings, and is about 60 cm/2 ft long. The darker and slightly smaller black kite M. migrans is found over most of the Old World. It scavenges in addition to hunting. —**fly a kite**, (colloquial) to sound out public opinion. [Old English]

Kitemark n. the official kite-shaped mark on goods approved by the British Standards Institution.

kith /kɪθ/ n. **kith and kin**, friends and relations. [Old English, originally = knowledge (from cuth past participle of cunnan = know)]

kitsch /kɪtʃ/ n. worthless pretentiousness or bad taste in art; art of this type. —**kitschy** adj. [German]

kitten /'kɪtən/ n. the young of a cat, ferret, etc. —v.t./i. to give birth to (kittens). —**have kittens**, (colloquial) to be

599   knightly

very upset or nervous. —**kittenish** adj. [from Old French *chitoun* diminutive of *chat* = cat]

kittiwake /'kɪtɪweɪk/ n. a kind of small seagull *Rissa tridactyla*. [imitative of its cry]

kitty n. a fund of money for communal use; the pool in some card games.

kiwi /'ki:wi:/ n. 1. a flightless New Zealand bird of the genus *Apteryx*, with rudimentary wings and no tail. Kiwis have long and hairlike brown plumage, a very long beak with nostrils at the tip, and are nocturnal and insectivorous. 2. **Kiwi**, (*colloquial*) a New Zealander. —**kiwi fruit**, the fruit of a deciduous fruiting vine *Actinidia chinensis*, also called Chinese gooseberry, commercially grown on a large scale in New Zealand. Kiwi fruit is egg-sized, oval, and of similar flavour to a gooseberry, with a fuzzy brown skin. [Maori]

kl symbol for kilolitre(s).

Klammer /'klæmə/ Franz 1953– . Austrian skier who won a record 35 World Cup downhill races between 1974 and 1985. Olympic gold medallist 1976.

Klaproth /'klæprəʊt/ Martin Heinrich 1743–1817. German chemist who first identified the elements uranium, zirconium, cerium, and titanium.

klaxon /'klæksən/ n. trade name of a powerful electric horn. [from name of manufacturer]

Klee /kleɪ/ Paul 1879–1940. Swiss painter. He settled in Munich, Germany, 1906, joined the ◊*Blaue Reiter* group 1912, and worked at the Bauhaus school of art and design 1920–31, returning to Switzerland 1933. His style in the 1920s and 1930s was dominated by humorous linear fantasies.

Klein /klaɪn/ Melanie 1882–1960. Austrian child psychoanalyst. She pioneered child psychoanalysis and play studies, and was influenced by Sigmund ◊Freud's theories. She published *The Psychoanalysis of Children* in 1960.

kleptomania /kleptə'meɪnɪə/ n. a behavioural disorder characterized by an overpowering desire to steal, without regard for need or profit. —**kleptomaniac** n. and adj. [from Greek *kleptēs*= thief]

Klimt /klɪmt/ Gustav 1862–1918. Austrian painter, influenced by Jugendstil ('youth style', a form of Art Nouveau); a founding member of the Vienna ◊Sezession group 1897. His paintings have a jewelled effect similar to mosaics, for example *The Kiss* 1909 (Musée des Beaux-Arts, Strasbourg). His many portraits include *Judith I* 1901 (Österreichische Galerie, Vienna).

Klondike /'klɒndaɪk/ a former gold-mining area in ◊Yukon, Canada, named after the river valley where gold was found in 1896. About 30,000 people moved there during the following 15 years. Silver is still mined there.

kloof n. (*South African*) a ravine or valley. [Dutch = cleft]

Klopstock /'klɒpstɒk/ Friedrich Gottlieb 1724–1803. German poet, whose religious epic *Der Messias/The Messiah* 1748–73 and *Oden/Odes* 1771 anticipated Romanticism.

God and I both knew what it meant once; now God alone knows.

Friedrich Klopstock
C Lombroso, The Man of Genius

Klosters /'kləʊstəz/ an alpine skiing resort northeast of Davos in E Switzerland.

km symbol for ◊kilometre(s).

knack /næk/ n. 1. an acquired or intuitive ability to do something skilfully. 2. a habit.

knacker /'nækə/ n. a buyer of useless horses for slaughter, or of old houses etc. for their materials. —v.t. (especially in *past participle*) (*slang*) to exhaust, to wear out.

knapsack /'næpsæk/ n. a soldier's or traveller's bag, usually of canvas, strapped to the back. [Middle Low German]

knapweed /'næpwi:d/ n. a plant of the genus *Centaurea*, with purple flowers in a globular head.

knave /neɪv/ n. 1. an unprincipled or dishonest person, a rogue. 2. the jack in playing-cards. —**knavish** adj. [Old English = boy, servant]

knavery n. the conduct of a knave.

knead /ni:d/ v.t. 1. to work (moist flour, clay, etc.) into dough by pressing with the hands; to make (bread, pottery)

thus. 2. to operate on using such motions (in massaging etc.). [Old English]

knee /ni:/ n. 1. the joint between the thigh and the lower leg in humans. 2. the corresponding joint in an animal. 3. the upper surface of the thigh of a sitting person. 4. the part of a garment covering the knee. —v.t. to touch or strike with the knee. —**bring a person to the knees**, to reduce a person to submission. **knee-breeches** n.pl. breeches reaching to or just below the knee. **knee-deep** adj. immersed up to the knees; deeply involved; so deep as to reach the knees. **knee-high** adj. so high as to reach the knees. **kneehole** n. a space for the knees, especially between columns of drawers at each side of a desk etc. **knee jerk** a sudden involuntary kick caused by a blow on the tendon below the knee. **knees-up** n. (*colloquial*) a lively party with dancing. [Old English]

kneecap n. 1. the convex bone in the front of the knee joint. 2. a protective covering for the knee.

kneecapping n. shooting in the legs to lame a person as a punishment.

kneel /ni:l/ v.i. (*past* and *past participle* knelt or (*US*) kneeled) to take or be in a position where the body is supported on the knee(s) with the lower part of the leg(s) bent back, especially in prayer or reverence.

kneeler n. a hassock etc. for kneeling on.

knell /nel/ n. 1. the sound of a bell, especially after a death or at a funeral. 2. an omen of death or extinction. [Old English]

Kneller /'nelə/ Godfrey 1646–1723. German-born portrait painter, who lived in England from 1674. He was court painter to Charles II, James II, William III, and George I.

knelt past and past participle of **kneel**.

Knesset /'knesɪt/ n. the Israeli parliament, consisting of a single chamber of 120 deputies elected for a period of four years. [Hebrew = gathering]

knew past of **know**.

knickerbockers /'nɪkəbɒkəz/ n.pl. loose-fitting breeches gathered in at the knee. [from Diedrich *Knickerbocker*, pretended author of Washington Irving's *History of New York* 1809]

knickers /'nɪkəz/ n.pl. a woman's undergarment covering the body below the waist and having separate legs or leg holes.

knick-knack /'nɪknæk/ n. a trinket or small ornament. [reduplication of *knack* in obsolete sense 'trinket']

knife /naɪf/ n. (*plural* knives) a cutting instrument or weapon consisting of a metal blade with a long sharpened edge fixed in a handle; a cutting blade in a machine. —v.t. to cut or stab with a knife. —**at knife-point**, threatened by a knife. **the knife**, (*colloquial*) surgery. **have got one's knife into**, to be persistently malicious or vindictive towards. **knife edge** the sharp edge of a knife, a position of tense uncertainty about an outcome. **knife pleat** n. a narrow flat pleat in an overlapping series. [Old English from Old Norse]

knight /naɪt/ n. 1. a man raised to the rank below the baronetcy as a reward for personal merit or services to crown or country, entitling the holder to the prefix *Sir*. 2. (*historical*) a man raised to an honourable military rank by a king etc. 3. (*historical*) a military follower, especially one devoted to the service of a lady as her attendant or champion in a war or tournament. 4. a chess piece usually with the shape of a horse's head. —v.t. to confer a knighthood on. —**knight errant**, a medieval knight wandering in search of chivalrous adventures; a man of such a spirit. **knight-errantry** n. [Old English = boy, youth]

knighthood n. the rank or dignity of a knight.

knighthood, order of a fraternity carrying with it the rank of knight, admission to which is granted as a mark of royal favour or as a reward for public services. During the Middle Ages such fraternities fell into two classes, religious and secular. The first class, including the ◊Templars and the **Knights of** ◊St John, consisted of knights who had taken religious vows and devoted themselves to military service against the Saracens (Arabs) or other non- Christians. The secular orders probably arose from bands of knights engaged in the service of a prince or great noble. A **knight bachelor** belongs to the lowest stage of knighthood, not being a member of any specially named order.

knightly adj. of or like a knight; chivalrous.

knit /nɪt/ v.t./i. (-tt-; past and past participle **knitted** or (especially figuratively) **knit**) 1. to make (a garment etc. or absolute) by interlocking loops of yarn or thread. Knitting uses two needles and may have developed from ◊crochet, which uses a single hooked needle, or from netting (see ◊net[1]), which uses a shuttle. 2. to form (yarn) into a fabric etc. in this way. 3. to make (a plain stitch) in knitting. 4. to wrinkle (the brow). 5. to make or become close or compact, to grow together. —**knitter** n. [Old English]

knitting n. work being knitted. —**knitting needle** each of a pair of slender pointed rods used in knitting by hand.

knitwear n. knitted garments.

knob /nɒb/ n. 1. a rounded protuberance, especially at an end or on a surface of a thing, e. g. a handle of a door, drawer, etc. or for adjusting a radio etc. 2. a small lump (of butter etc.). —**with knobs on**, (slang) that and more (often as an emphatic or ironical agreement). —**knobbly** adj. [from Middle Low German]

knobbly /ˈnɒblɪ/ adj. hard and lumpy. [from knobble diminutive of knob]

knobkerrie /ˈnɒbkerɪ/ n. in South Africa, a short stick with a knob at the end as a weapon. [from Afrikaans knopkierie]

knock /nɒk/ v.t./i. 1. to strike with an audible, sharp blow. 2. to make a noise by striking a door etc. to summon a person or gain admittance. 3. to drive or make by striking. 4. (of an engine) to make a thumping or rattling noise, to pink. 5. to criticize or insult. —n. an act or sound of knocking; a sharp blow. —**knock about or around**, to treat roughly, to strike repeatedly; to wander about aimlessly. **knock back**, (slang) to eat or drink, especially hastily; to disconcert. **knock down**, to strike (a person) to the ground; to demolish; to dispose of (an article to a bidder) by the knock of the hammer at an auction. **knock-down** adj. (of a price) very low; (of furniture etc.) easily dismantled and reassembled; overwhelming. **knock-for-knock** adj. (of insurance terms) with each company paying its policy holder in a claim, regardless of liability. **knocking shop** (slang) a brothel. **knock knees**, an abnormal inward curving of the legs at the knees. **knock-kneed** adj having this. **knock off**, (colloquial) to cease work; to complete (a piece of work etc.) quickly; to deduct (a sum from a total); (slang) to steal or kill. **knock-on effect**, the effect of an alteration that causes similar alterations elsewhere. **knock out**, to render unconscious, especially by a blow to the head; to disable (a boxer) so that he is unable to recover in the required time; to defeat in a knock-out competition; to exhaust or disable. **knock spots off**, (colloquial) to surpass easily. **knock up**, to make or arrange hastily; to arouse by knocking at the door; to score (runs) at cricket, (US slang) to make pregnant. **knock-up** n. a practice game etc. [Old English]

knockabout adj. rough, boisterous.

knocker n. a hinged metal device on a door for knocking to call attention.

knocking n. in a spark-ignition petrol engine, unburned fuel-air mixture exploding in the combustion chamber before being ignited by the spark. The resulting shock waves produce a metallic knocking sound.

knock-out adj. 1. that knocks a boxer etc. out. 2. (of a competition) in which the loser of each round is eliminated. —n. 1. a knock-out blow. 2. (slang) an outstanding person or thing.

knoll /nəʊl/ n. a hillock, a mound. [Old English]

knop /nɒp/ n. 1. an ornamental knob. 2. a loop, a tuft in a yarn. [from Middle Low German or Middle Dutch]

Knossos /ˈknɒsɒs/ n. the chief city of ◊Minoan Crete, near present-day Iráklion, 6 km/4 mi SE of Candia. The archaeological site excavated by Arthur ◊Evans 1899–1935 dates from about 2000 BC, and includes the palace throne room and a labyrinth, legendary home of the ◊Minotaur.

knot[1] /nɒt/ 1. an intertwining of one or more pieces of rope, string, etc., to fasten them together. 2. a tangle. 3. a ribbon etc. tied with a knot for ornament etc. 4. a group or cluster. 5. a hard mass formed in a tree trunk where a branch once grew out; a corresponding cross-grained piece in a board. 6. a difficulty or problem. 7. that which forms or maintains a union, especially a marriage. 8. the unit of a ship's or aircraft's speed equal to one ◊nautical mile per hour (1 knot = 1.85 kph = 1.15 mph). —v.t./i. (-tt-) 1. to tie in or with a knot or knots. 2. to make (a fringe) by knotting threads. 3. to entangle. 4. to unite closely or intricately. —**at a rate of knots**, (colloquial) very fast. **knotgrass** n. a weed Polygonum aviculare with intricate creeping stems and pink flowers. **knothole** n. a hole in a wooden board, where a knot has fallen out. **tie in knots**, to make (a person) confused or baffled. [Old English]

knot[2] a small wading bird Calidris canutus of the sandpiper family. In the winter it is grey above and white below, but in the breeding season it is brick red on the head and chest, and black on the wings and back. It feeds on insects and molluscs. Breeding in arctic regions, knots travel widely in winter, to be found as far south as South Africa, Australasia, and southern parts of South America.

knotty adj. 1. full of knots. 2. puzzling, difficult.

know /nəʊ/ v.t./i. (past **knew** /njuː/, past participle **known** /nəʊn/) 1. to have in the mind or memory as the result of experience, learning, or information. 2. to feel certain. 3. to be acquainted or have regular social contact with (a person). 4. to recognize or identify. 5. to understand and be able to use (a language, subject, or skill). 6. to have personal experience of (fear etc.). 7. to be subject to (limits etc.). —n. (colloquial) **in the know**, knowing secret or inside information. —**know-all** n. (derogatory) a person who claims to know much. **know-how** n. practical knowledge or skill. **know one's own mind**, to know one's intentions firmly. **you never know**, it is always possible. [Old English]

knowable adj. that may be known.

knowing adj. having or showing knowledge or awareness; shrewd, clever. —**knowingly** adv.

knot

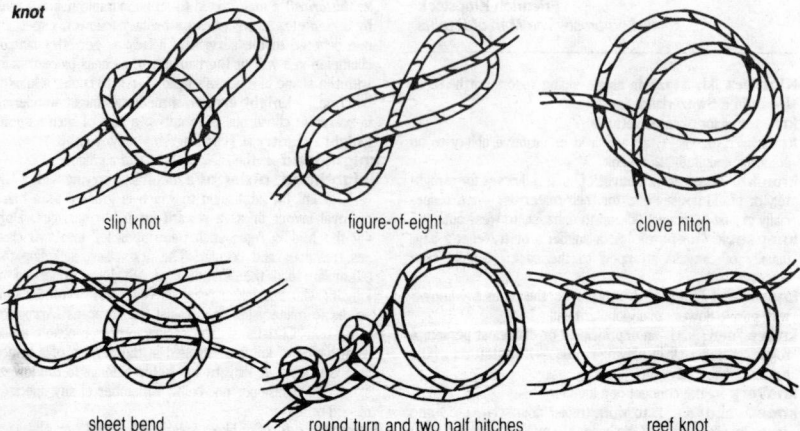

slip knot figure-of-eight clove hitch

sheet bend round turn and two half hitches reef knot

knowledge /ˈnɒlɪdʒ/ *n.* 1. knowing. 2. all that a person knows. 3. the sum of what is known to humankind. —**to my knowledge**, as far as I know.

knowledgeable /ˈnɒlɪdʒəbəl/ *adj.* having much knowledge, well-informed.

knowledge-based system a computer program that uses an encoding of human knowledge to help solve problems. It was first discovered in research into ◊artificial intelligence, in which heuristics (rules of thumb) were added to enable programs to tackle problems that were otherwise difficult to solve by the usual techniques of computer science.

known past participle of **know**.

Knox /nɒks/ John *c.*1505–1572. Scottish Protestant reformer, founder of the Church of Scotland. He spent several years in exile for his beliefs, including a period in Geneva where he met John ◊Calvin. He returned to Scotland 1559 to promote Presbyterianism.

A man with God is always in the majority.
John Knox
Inscription on the Reformation Monument,
Geneva, Switzerland

---

knuckle /ˈnʌkəl/ *n.* 1. the bone at the finger-joint, especially at the root of the finger. 2. the knee- or ankle-joint of an animal, especially with the adjacent parts as a joint of meat. —*v.t./i.* to strike, press, or rub with the knuckles. —**knuckle down**, to apply oneself earnestly (*to* work etc.). **knuckle-duster** *n.* a metal guard worn over the knuckles in fist-fighting especially to increase the violence of a blow. **knuckle under**, to give in, to submit. **near the knuckle**, (*colloquial*) verging on indecency. [from Middle Low German or Middle Dutch (diminutive of *knoke* = bone)]

knurl /nɜːl/ *n.* a small projecting ridge etc. [from Middle Dutch or Middle Low German]

KO abbreviation of knock-out.

koala /kəʊˈɑːlə/ *n.* an Australian arboreal marsupial *Phascolarctos cinereus* of the family Phalangeridae, found only in E Australia. It feeds almost entirely on eucalyptus shoots. It is about 60 cm/2 ft long and resembles a bear. The popularity of its greyish fur led to its almost complete extermination by hunters, but under protection from 1936, it has rapidly increased in numbers. [from Aboriginal *kül(l)a*]

kōan /ˈkəʊæn/ *n.* in Zen Buddhism, a superficially nonsensical question or riddle used by a Zen master to help a pupil achieve satori (◊enlightenment). It is used in the Rinzai school of Zen.

Kobe /ˈkəʊbeɪ/ a deep-water port in S Honshu, Japan; population (1987) 1,413,000. **Port Island**, created 1960–68 from the rock of nearby mountains, area 5 sq km/2 sq mi, is one of the world's largest construction projects.

København /kɜːbənˈhaʊn/ the Danish name for ◊Copenhagen, capital of Denmark.

Koch /kɒx/ Robert 1843–1910. German bacteriologist. Koch and his assistants devised the techniques to culture bacteria outside the body, and formulated the rules for showing whether or not a bacterium is the cause of a disease. His techniques enabled him to identify the bacteria responsible for diseases like anthrax, cholera, and tuberculosis. He was awarded the Nobel Prize for Medicine in 1905.

Kodály /ˈkəʊdaɪ/ Zoltán 1882–1967. Hungarian composer. With ◊Bartók, he recorded and transcribed Magyar folk music, the scales and rhythm of which he incorporated in a deliberately nationalist style. His works include the cantata *Psalmus Hungaricus* 1923, a comic opera *Háry János* 1925–27, and orchestral dances and variations.

Koestler /ˈkɜːstlə/ Arthur 1905–1983. Hungarian author. Imprisoned by the Nazis in France in 1940, he escaped to England. His novel *Darkness at Noon* 1941, regarded as his masterpiece, is a fictional account of the Stalinist purges, and draws on his experiences as a prisoner under sentence of death during the Spanish Civil War. He also wrote extensively about creativity, parapsychology, politics, and culture.

One may not regard the world as a sort of metaphysical brothel for emotions.
Arthur Koestler
Darkness at Noon

Koh-i-noor /ˌkəʊɪˈnʊə/ *n.* a fabulous diamond, originally part of the Aurangzeb treasure, seized in 1739 by the shah of Iran from the Moguls in India, taken back by Sikhs, and acquired by Britain in 1849 when the Punjab was annexed. [Persian = mountain of light]

kohl /kəʊl/ *n.* a powdered form of antimony sulphide, used in Asia and the Middle East to darken the area around the eyes. [from Arabic]

Kohl Helmut 1930– . German conservative politician, leader of the Christian Democratic Union from 1976, West German chancellor 1982–90, and chancellor of the newly united Germany from 1990. He skilfully managed the negotiations for the reunification of East and West Germany and was elected leader of a single German coalition government in Dec 1990.

kohlrabi /kəʊlˈrɑːbɪ/ *n.* a cabbage *Brassica oleracea* with a turnip-like edible stem. [German from Italian from Latin *caulorapa*]

koine /ˈkɔɪnɪ/ *n.* a common language shared by various peoples, a lingua franca. [from Greek = common (language)]

Kokoschka /kəˈkɒʃkə/ Oskar 1886–1980. Austrian Expressionist painter and writer, who lived in England from 1938. Initially influenced by the Vienna ◊Sezession painters, he developed a disturbingly expressive portrait style. His writings include several plays.

kola alternative spelling of ◊cola, a genus of tropical tree.

Kolchak /kɒlˈtʃæk/ Alexander Vasilievich 1875–1920. Russian admiral, commander of the White forces in Siberia after the Russian Revolution. He proclaimed himself Supreme Ruler of Russia in 1918, but was later handed over to the Bolsheviks by his own troops and shot.

kolinsky /kɒˈlɪnskɪ/ *n.* the Siberian mink *Mustela sibirica*; its fur. [from Russian (*Kola* in NW Russia)]

kolkhoz /ˈkɒlkɒz/ *n.* a collective farm in the USSR. [Russian]

Koller /ˈkɒlə/ Carl 1857–1944. Austrian ophthalmologist who introduced local anaesthesia in 1884.

Kollontai /kɒlənˈtaɪ/ Alexandra 1872–1952. Russian revolutionary, politician, and writer. In 1905 she published *On the Question of the Class Struggle*, and, as commissar for public welfare, was the only female member of the first Bolshevik government. She campaigned for domestic reforms such as acceptance of free love, simplification of divorce laws, and collective childcare.

Kollwitz /ˈkəʊvɪts/ Kathe 1867–1945. German sculptor and printmaker. Her early series of etchings of workers and their environment are realistic and harshly expressive. Later themes include war, death, and maternal love.

Komi /ˈkəʊmɪ/ autonomous Soviet Republic in the NW Urals, USSR; **area** 415,900 sq km/160,540 sq mi; **population** (1986) 1,200,000.

Komsomol *n.* the youth section of the Communist Party in the USSR, officially the All-Union Leninist Communist Youth League, founded in 1918. [Russian]

Kongur Shan /ˈkʊŋɡʊə ʃɑːn/ a mountain peak in China, 7,719 m/25,325 ft high, part of the Pamir range (see ◊Pamirs). The expedition that first reached the summit in 1981 was led by British climber Chris Bonington.

Kong Zi Pinyin form of ◊Confucius, Chinese philosopher.

Koniev /ˈkɒnjef/ Ivan Stepanovich 1898–1973. Soviet marshal who in World War II liberated Ukraine from the invading German forces in 1943 and advanced from the south on Berlin to link up with the British-US forces.

Konoe Fumimaro, Prince 1891–1946. Japanese politician and prime minister 1937–39 and 1940–41. Entering politics in the 1920s, Konoe was active in trying to curb the power of the army in government and preventing an escalation of the war with China. He helped to engineer the fall of the ◊Tojo government in 1944 but committed suicide after being suspected of war crimes.

Kon-Tiki /ˈkɒn ˈtiːki/ *n.* **1.** a legendary sun king who ruled the country later occupied by the ◊Incas, and was supposed to have migrated out into the Pacific. **2.** a raft sailed by explorer Thor Heyerdahl in 1947 on the Humboldt current from Peru to the Tuamotu Islands, near Tahiti in the Pacific, in an attempt to show that ancient South Americans might have reached Polynesia.

koodoo variant of ◊kudu.

kook /kuːk/ *n.* (*US slang*) a crazy or eccentric person. —**kooky** *adj.*

kookaburra /ˈkʊkəbʌrə/ *n.* or **laughing jackass** an Australian bird, the largest of the world's kingfishers *Dacelo novaeguineae*, with a discordant laughing call. It feeds on insects and other small creatures. The body and tail measure 45 cm/18 in, the head is greyish with a dark eye stripe, and the back and wings are flecked brown with grey underparts. [Aboriginal]

kopje /ˈkɒpɪ/ *n.* or **koppie** (*South African*) a small hill. [Dutch and Afrikaans, diminutive of *kop* = head]

kora /ˈkɔːrə/ *n.* a 21-string instrument of W African origin made from gourds, with a harp-like sound.

Koran /kɔːˈrɑːn, kə-/ *n.* (alternatively transliterated as **Quran**) the sacred book of Islam. Written in the purest Arabic, it contains 114 **suras** (chapters), and is stated to have been divinely revealed to the prophet Muhammad about 616. —**Koranic** /-ˈrɑːnɪk, -ˈræ-/ *adj.* [from Arabic = recitation (*kara'a* = read)]

Korda /ˈkɔːdə/ Alexander 1893–1956. Hungarian-born British film producer and director, a dominant figure during the 1930s and 1940s. His films include *The Private Life of Henry VIII* 1933, *The Third Man* 1950, and *Richard III* 1956.

Korean language the language of Korea, written from the 5th century AD in Chinese characters until the invention of an alphabet by King Sejong in 1443. The linguistic affiliations of Korean are unclear, but it may be distantly related to Japanese.

Korea, North /kəˈrɪə/ Democratic People's Republic of; a country in E Asia, bounded N by China, E by the Sea of Japan, S by South Korea, and W by the Yellow Sea; **area** 120,538 sq km/46,528 sq mi; **capital** Pyongyang; **physical** wide coastal plain in W rising to mountains cut by deep valleys in the interior; **head of state** Kim Il Sung from 1972 (also head of communist party); **head of government** Yon Hyong Muk from 1988; **political system** communism; **exports** coal, iron, copper, textiles, chemicals; **language** Korean; **recent history** North Korea was formed from the zone north of the 38th parallel of latitude, occupied by Soviet troops after Japan's surrender in 1945. Declared a Democratic People's Republic in 1948, it invaded South Korea in 1950 in an attempt at reunification, initiating the three-year ◊Korean War which, after intervention by UN forces supported by the USA (on the side of the South) and by China (on the side of the North), ended in stalemate. A United Nations–patrolled demilitarized buffer zone was created. North Korea has never accepted this agreement and remains committed to reunification.

Korea, South /kəˈrɪə/ Republic of; country in E Asia, bordered N by North Korea, E by the Sea of Japan, S by the E China Sea, and W by the Yellow Sea; **area** 98,799 sq km/38,161 sq mi; **capital** Seoul; **physical** S end of a mountainous peninsula separating the Sea of Japan from the Yellow Sea; **head of state** Roh Tae-Woo from 1988; **head of government** Kang Young Hoon from 1988; **political system** emergent democracy; **exports** steel, ships, chemicals, electronics, textiles, plastics; **language** Korean; **recent history** proclaimed a Republic in 1948, it was invaded by, and at war with, North Korea from 1950 until 1953 when an armistice was signed. In 1990 two minor opposition parties united with the ruling Democratic Justice Party to form the Democratic Liberal Party.

Kornberg /ˈkɔːnbɜːg/ Arthur 1918– . US biochemist. In 1956, while working on enzymes at Washington University, Kornberg discovered the enzyme DNA-polymerase, which enabled molecules of ◊DNA to be synthesized for the first time. For this work Kornberg shared the 1959 Novel Prize for Medicine with Severo ◊Ochoa.

Korngold /ˈkɔːngəʊld/ Erich Wolfgang 1897–1957. Austrian-born composer. He began composing operas while still in his teens and in 1934 moved to Hollywood to become a composer for Warner Brothers. His film scores combine a richly orchestrated and romantic style, reflecting the rapid changes of mood characteristic of screen action.

Korolev /kəˈrɒljef/ Sergei Pavlovich 1906–1966. Soviet designer of the first Soviet intercontinental missile, used in 1957 to launch the first ◊Sputnik satellite and in 1961 to launch the ◊Vostok crewed Earth-orbiting spacecraft (also designed by Korolev).

Kosciusko /kɒsɪˈʌskəʊ/ the highest mountain in Australia (2,229 m/7,316 ft), in New South Wales.

Kościuszko /kɒsˈtʃʊʃkəʊ/ Tadeusz 1746–1817. Polish general and nationalist who served with George Washington in the American Revolution (1776–83). He returned to Poland in 1784, fought against the Russian invasion that ended in the partition of Poland, and withdrew to Saxony. He returned in 1794 to lead the revolt against the occupation, but was defeated by combined Russian and Prussian forces and imprisoned until 1796.

kosher /ˈkəʊʃə/ *adj.* **1.** (of food or a foodshop) fulfilling the requirements of Jewish religious law. For example, only animals that chew the cud and have cloven hooves (cows and sheep, but not pigs) may be eaten. There are rules governing their humane slaughter and their preparation (such as complete draining of blood) which also apply to fowl. Only fish with scales and fins may be eaten; shellfish may not. Milk products must not be cooked or eaten with meat or poultry. Utensils for meat must be kept separate from those for milk. **2.** (*colloquial*) correct, genuine, legitimate. —*n.* kosher food; a kosher shop. [from Hebrew = proper]

Kosovo /ˈkɒsəvəʊ/ an autonomous region (since 1974) in S Serbia, Yugoslavia; **area** 10,900 sq km/4,207 sq mi; **capital** Priština; **products** wine, nickel, lead, zinc; **population** (1986) 1,900,000 consisting of about 200,000 Serbs and about 1.7 million Albanians; **history** since Kosovo is largely inhabited by Albanians and bordering on Albania, there have been recurring demands for unification with that country, while in the late 1980s Serbians were agitating for Kosovo to be merged with the rest of Serbia. A state of emergency was declared in Feb 1990 after fighting broke out between ethnic Albanians, police, and the Slavic minority.

Kossuth /ˈkɒʃuːt/ Lajos 1802–1894. Hungarian nationalist and leader of the revolution of 1848. He proclaimed Hungary independent of Habsburg rule in 1849 but shortly after, when the Hungarians were defeated by Austria and Russia, fled to Turkey and then to exile in Britain and Italy.

Kosygin /kɒˈsiːgɪn/ 22 Alexei Nikolaievich 1904–1980. Soviet politician, prime minister 1964–80. He was elected to the Supreme Soviet in 1938, became a member of the Politburo from 1946, deputy prime minister from 1960, and succeeded Khrushchev as premier.

koto /ˈkɒtəʊ/ *n.* (*plural* **kotos**) a Japanese musical instrument; a long zither of ancient Chinese origin, having 13 silk strings supported by movable bridges. It rests on the floor and the strings are plucked with an ivory plectra, producing a brittle sound.

kouprey *n.* a type of wild cattle *Bos sauveli* native to the forest of N Cambodia. It has been known to science only since 1937, and is in great danger of extinction.

Kourou /kuˈruː/ *n.* a river and the second largest town of French Guiana, NW of Cayenne, site of the Guiana Space Centre of the European Space Agency. Situated near the equator, it is an ideal site for launches of satellites into ◊geostationary, or geosynchronous, orbit.

Kowloon /kaʊˈluːn/ a peninsula on the Chinese coast forming part of the British crown colony of Hong Kong; the town of Kowloon is a residential area.

kowtow /kaʊˈtaʊ/ *v.i.* **1.** to behave obsequiously. **2.** to perform the kowtow. —*n.* the Chinese custom of touching the ground with the head as a sign of worship or submission. [from Chinese = knock the head]

kph or **km/h** symbol for kilometres per hour.

Kr symbol for ◊krypton.

kraal /krɑːl/ *n.* (*South African*) **1.** a village of huts enclosed by a fence. **2.** an enclosure for sheep or cattle. [Afrikaans from Portuguese *curral* , of Hottentot origin]

kraken /ˈkrɑːkən/ *n.* a mythical sea monster said to appear off the coast of Norway. [Norwegian]

Kraków /ˈkrækaʊ/ or **Cracow** a city in Poland, on the river Vistula; population (1985) 716,000. It is an industrial centre producing railway wagons, paper, chemicals, and tobacco. It was capital of Poland from about 1300 to 1595.

Krasnodar /krəsnaˈdar/ a territory of the Russian Soviet Federal Socialist Republic in the N Caucasus, adjacent to the Black Sea; area 83,600 sq km/32,290 sq mi; population (1985) 4,992,000. The capital is Krasnodar. In addition to stock rearing and the production of grain, rice, fruit, and tobacco, oil is refined.

Krasnoyarsk /krəsnaˈjarsk/ a territory of the USSR in central Siberia stretching north to the Arctic Ocean; area 2,401,600 sq km/927,617 sq mi; population (1985) 3,430,000. The capital is Krasnoyarsk. It is drained by the Yenisei river. Mineral resources include gold, graphite, coal, iron ore, and uranium.

Kraut /kraʊt/ n. (slang, derogatory) a German. [from sauerkraut]

Krebs /krebz/ Hans 1900–1981. German-born British biochemist who discovered the citric acid cycle, also known as the **Krebs cycle**, by which food is converted into energy in living tissues. For this work he shared with Fritz Lipmann the 1953 Nobel Prize for Medicine.

Krebs cycle or citric acid cycle a part of the chain of biochemical reactions through which organisms break down food using oxygen (respiration) to release energy. It breaks down food molecules in a series of small steps, producing energy-rich molecules of ◊ATP.

Kreisler /ˈkraɪslə/ Fritz 1875–1962. Austrian violinist and composer, renowned as an interpreter of Brahms and Beethoven. From 1911 he was one of the earliest recording artists of classical music, including records of his own compositions.

kremlin /ˈkremlɪn/ n. a citadel within a Russian town, especially that of Moscow, traditionally the centre of administration as well as the last bastion of defence. The Moscow Kremlin dates from the 12th century. —**the Kremlin**, the government of the USSR. [French from Russian]

Krenz /krents/ Egon 1937– . German communist politician. A member of the East German Socialist Unity Party (SED) from 1955, he was a hardline protégé of Erich ◊Honecker, succeeding him as party leader and head of state in 1989 after widespread pro-democracy demonstrations. Krenz opened the country's western border but in the face of continued popular protests he resigned after a few weeks in Dec 1989.

krill n. any small shrimplike crustacean of the order Euphausiacea, which form food for fishes and whales. The most common species, Euphausia superba, is about 6 cm/2.5 in long, with two antennae, five pairs of legs, seven pairs of light organs along the body, and is coloured orange above and green beneath. [from Norwegian krill = tiny fish]

kris /kriːs, krɪs/ n. a Malay dagger with a wavy blade. [ultimately from Malay]

Krishna /ˈkrɪʃnə/ the incarnation of the Hindu god ◊Vishnu. The devotion of the ◊bhakti movement is usually directed towards Krishna; an example of this is the ◊International Society for Krishna Consciousness. Many stories are told of Krishna's mischievous youth, and he is the charioteer of Arjuna in the Bhagavad-Gītā.

Krishna Consciousness Movement the popular name for the ◊International Society for Krishna Consciousness.

Kristallnacht /krɪˈstaːlnaːxt/ n. the night of 9–10 Nov 1938 when the Nazi Sturmabteilung (SA) militia in Germany and Austria mounted a concerted attack on Jews, their synagogues, homes, and shops. It followed the assassination of a German embassy official in Paris by a Polish-Jewish youth. Subsequent measures included German legislation against Jews owning businesses or property, and restrictions on their going to school or leaving Germany. It was part of the ◊Holocaust. [German = night of (broken) glass]

Kristiansen /ˈkrɪstjənsən/ Ingrid 1956– . Norwegian athlete, an outstanding long-distance runner at 5,000 metres, 10,000 metres, marathon, and cross-country running. She has won all the world's leading marathons. In 1986 she knocked 45.68 seconds off the world 10,000-metres record. She was the world cross-country champion in 1988 and won the London marathon in 1984–1985 and 1987–1988.

krona /ˈkrəʊnə/ n. the currency unit of Sweden (plural kronor) and of Iceland (plural kronur). [Swedish and Icelandic = crown]

krone /ˈkrəʊnə/ n. (plural kroner) the currency unit of Denmark and of Norway. [Danish and Norwegian = crown]

Kronos /ˈkrɒnɒs/ or **Cronus** in Greek mythology, ruler of the world and one of the ◊Titans. He was the father of Zeus, who overthrew him.

Kronstadt uprising /kranˈʃtat/ in Soviet history, a revolt in March 1921 by sailors of the Russian Baltic Fleet at their headquarters in Kronstadt, outside Petrograd (now Leningrad). On the orders of the leading Bolshevik Trotsky, Red Army troops, dressed in white camouflage, crossed the ice to the naval base and captured it on 18 March. The leaders were subsequently shot.

Kropotkin /krɒˈpɒtkɪn/ Peter Alexeivich, Prince Kropotkin 1842–1921. Russian anarchist. Imprisoned for revolutionary activities in 1874, he escaped to the UK in 1876 and later moved to Switzerland. Expelled from Switzerland, he went to France, where he was imprisoned 1883–86. He lived in Britain until 1917, when he returned to Moscow, but, unsympathetic to the Bolsheviks, he retired from politics. Among his works are Memoirs of a Revolutionist 1899, Mutual Aid 1902, and Modern Science and Anarchism 1903.

The word state is identical with the word war.
Peter Alexeivich Kropotkin

Kruger /ˈkruːgə/ Stephanus Johannes Paulus 1825–1904. President of the Transvaal 1883–1900. He refused to remedy the grievances of the uitlanders (English and other non-Boer white residents) and so precipitated the Second ◊South African War.

krugerrand /ˈkruːgərɑːnt/ n. a South African gold coin bearing a portrait of Kruger.

Kruger telegram a message sent by Kaiser Wilhelm II of Germany to President Kruger of the Transvaal on 3 Jan 1896 congratulating him on defeating the ◊Jameson raid of 1895. The text of the telegram provoked indignation in Britain and elsewhere, representing a worsening of Anglo-German relations, in spite of a German government retraction.

Krupp /krʊp/ n. a German steelmaking armaments firm founded 1811 by **Friedrich Krupp** (1787–1826) and developed by **Alfred Krupp** (1812–1887) by pioneering the Bessemer steelmaking process. Krupp developed the long-distance artillery used in World War I, and supported Hitler's regime in preparation for World War II, after which the head of the firm, another Alfred Krupp (1907–1967), was imprisoned and his property confiscated until 1951 when he was granted an amnesty.

krypton /ˈkrɪptɒn/ n. a colourless, odourless, gaseous, nonmetallic element, symbol Kr, atomic number 36, relative atomic mass 83.80. It is grouped with the inert gases and was long believed not to enter into reactions, but it is now known to combine with fluorine under certain conditions; it remains inert to all other reagents. It is present in very small quantities in the air (about 114 parts per million). It is used chiefly in fluorescent lamps, lasers, and gas-filled electronic valves. [from Greek kryptos = hidden]

Kt abbreviation of Knight.

Kuala Lumpur /ˈkwɑːlə ˈlʊmpʊə/ the capital of the Federation of Malaysia; area 240 sq km/93 sq mi; population (1980) 938,000. The city developed after 1873 with the expansion of tin and rubber trading; these are now its major industries. Formerly within the state of Selangor, of which it was also the capital, it was created a federal territory in 1974.

Kuanyin /kwænˈjɪn/ transliteration of ◊Guanyin, goddess of mercy in Chinese Buddhism.

Kublai Khan /ˈkuːblaɪ ˈkɑːn/ 1216–1294. Mongol emperor of China from 1259. He completed his grandfather ◊Genghis Khan's conquest of N China from 1240, and on his brother Mungo's death in 1259 established himself as emperor of China. He moved the capital to Beijing and founded the Yuan dynasty, successfully expanding his empire into Indochina, but was defeated in an attempt to conquer Japan in 1281.

Kubrick /ˈkuːbrɪk/ Stanley 1928– . US-born British director, producer, and screenwriter. His films include Paths

kurd

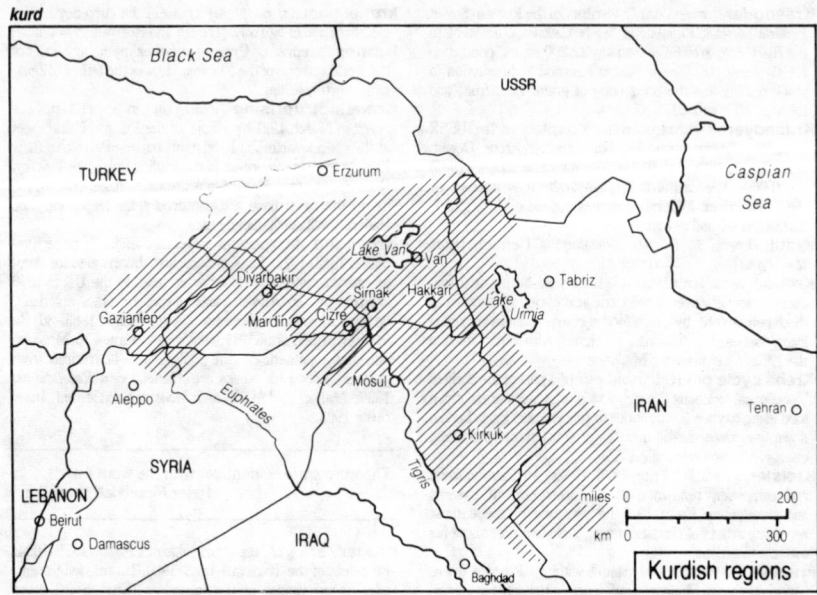

Kurdish regions

of Glory 1957, *Dr Strangelove* 1964, *2001: A Space Odyssey* 1968, *A Clockwork Orange* 1971, and *The Shining* 1979.

The great nations have always acted like gangsters, and the small nations like prostitutes.

Stanley Kubrick
The Guardian 5 June 1963

---

kudos /'kju:dɒs/ *n.* (*colloquial*) renown, glory. [Greek]

kudu /'ku:du:/ *n.* an African antelope, especially *Tragelaphus strepsiceros*. It is fawn coloured with thin, white vertical stripes, and stands 1.3 m/4.2 ft at the shoulder, with head and body 2.4 m/8 ft long. Males have long spiral horns. The kudu is found in bush country from Angola to Ethiopia. [from Xhosa]

kudzu *n.* a Japanese creeper *Pueraria lobata*, family Leguminosae, which helps fix nitrogen (see ◊nitrogen cycle) and can be used as fodder, but became a pest in the southern USA when introduced to check soil erosion.

Kuhn /ku:n/ Thomas S 1922– . US historian and philosopher of science, who showed that social and cultural conditions affect the directions of science. *The Structure of Scientific Revolutions* 1962 argued that even scientific knowledge is relative, dependent on the paradigm (theoretical framework) that dominates a scientific field at the time.

Kuibyshev /'ku:ibiʃev/ or **Kuybyshev** the capital of Kuibyshev region, USSR, and port at the junction of the rivers Samara and Volga, situated in the centre of the fertile middle Volga plain; population (1987) 1,280,000. Industries include aircraft, locomotives, cables, synthetic rubber, textiles, fertilizers, petroleum refining, and quarrying.

Ku Klux Klan /'ku: 'klʊks 'klæn/ a US secret society dedicated to white supremacy, founded in 1866 in the southern states of the USA to oppose ◊Reconstruction after the Civil War and to deny political rights to the black population. Members wore hooded white robes to hide their identity, and burned crosses as a rite of intimidation. It was active in the 1960s in terrorizing civil-rights activists and organizing racist demonstrations.

kukri /'kʊkrɪ/ *n.* a heavy curved knife, broadening towards the point, used by ◊Gurkhas as a weapon. [from Hindi]

kulak *n.* (*historical*) in Russia, a peasant who could afford to hire labour and often acted as village usurer. The kulaks resisted the Soviet government's policy of collectivization, and in 1930 they were 'liquidated as a class', with up to 5 million being either killed or deported to Siberia. [Russian]

Kulturkampf *n.* in German history, a policy introduced by Chancellor Bismarck in 1873 that isolated the Catholic interest and attempted to reduce its power to create a political coalition of liberals and agrarian conservatives. The alienation of such a large section of the German population as the Catholics could not be sustained, and the policy was abandoned after 1876 to be replaced by an anti-socialist policy. [German = culture struggle]

Kumasi /ku:'mɑ:si/ the second largest city in Ghana, W Africa, capital of Ashanti region, with trade in cocoa, rubber, and cattle; population (1984) 376,200.

kümmel /'kʊməl/ *n.* a liqueur flavoured with caraway and cumin seeds. [German = cumin]

kumquat /'kʌmkwɒt/ *n.* a plum-sized orange-like fruit of the genus *Fortunella* used in preserves. [dialect form of Chinese *kin kü = golden orange*]

Kun /ku:n/ Béla 1885–1938. Hungarian politician who created a Soviet republic in Hungary in March 1919, which was overthrown Aug 1919 by a Western blockade and Romanian military actions.

Kundera /'kʊndərə/ Milan 1929– . Czech writer. His first novel *The Joke* 1967 brought him into official disfavour in Prague, and, unable to publish further works, he moved to France. His novels include *The Book of Laughter and Forgetting* 1979 and *The Unbearable Lightness of Being* 1984.

Kung /kʊŋ/ *n.* a member of an aboriginal people of southern Africa, formerly known as **Bushmen**. They still live nomadically, mainly in the Kalahari Desert. Although formerly numerous, only some 26,000 now remain. They are traditionally hunters and gatherers, and speak a Khoisan language. Their early art survives in cave paintings.

kung fu /kʌŋ 'fu:/ Chinese martial art of unarmed combat. It is practised in many forms, the most popular being *wing chun*, 'beautiful springtime'. The basic principle is to use attack as a form of defence. [Mandarin *ch'üan fa*]

Kunming /kʊn'mɪŋ/ formerly **Yunnan** the capital of Yunnan province, China, on Lake Dian Chi, about 2,000 m/6,500 ft above sea level; population (1986) 1,490,000. Industries include chemicals, textiles, and copper smelted with nearby hydroelectric power.

Kuomintang /kwəʊmɪn'tæŋ/ *n.* the original name of the Chinese nationalist party, now known (outside Taiwan) as ◊Guomindang.

kurchatovium /kɜ:ʃə'təʊviəm/ *n.* the element now known as ◊rutherfordium, atomic number 104. It was originally assigned temporary identification as unnilquadium by the International Union of Pure and Applied Chemistry. [name proposed by Soviet scientists to honour Soviet nuclear physicist Igor Kurchatov (1903–1960)]

Kurd /kɜ:d/ *n.* a member of a pastoral people, living mostly in the region called Kurdistan. Although divided among more powerful states, the Kurds have nationalist aspirations; there are approximately 8 million in Turkey, 5 million in Iran, 4 million in Iraq, 500,000 in Syria, and 100,000 in the USSR. Some 1 million Kurds were made homeless and 25,000 killed as a result of chemical weapon attacks by Iraq 1984–89; and millions were again made homeless as a result of Iraqi government reprisals after the ◊Gulf War of 1991. The Kurdish language is a member of the Iranian branch of the Indo-European family and the Kurds are a non-Arab ethnic group. —**Kurdish** *adj.* and *n.*

Kurdistan /kɜ:diˈstɑːn/ or **Kordestan** a hilly region in SW Asia near Mount Ararat, where the borders of Iran, Iraq, Syria, Turkey, and the USSR meet; area 193,000 sq km/74,600 sq mi; total population around 18 million.

Kuril Islands /kuˈriːl/ a chain of about 50 small islands stretching from the NE of Hokkaido, Japan, to the S of Kamchatka, USSR; area 14,765 sq km/5,700 sq mi; population (1970) 15,000. Some of them are of volcanic origin. Two of the Kurils are claimed by both Japan and the USSR.

Kuropatkin /kuərəˈpætkɪn/ Alexei Nikolaievich 1848–1921. Russian general. He distinguished himself as chief of staff during the Russo-Turkish War 1877–78, was commander in chief in Manchuria 1903, and resigned after his defeat at Mukden in the ◊Russo-Japanese War. During World War I he commanded the armies on the northern front until 1916.

Kurosawa /kuərəˈsɑːwə/ Akira 1929– . Japanese director whose film *Rashomon* 1950 introduced Western audiences to Japanese cinema. Epics such as *Seven Samurai* 1954 combine spectacle with intimate human drama. His other films include *Drunken Angel* 1948, *Yojimbo* 1961, *Kagemusha* 1981, and *Ran* 1985.

Kutuzov /kuːˈtuːzɒf/ Mikhail Larionovich, Prince of Smolensk 1745–1813. Commander of the Russian forces in the Napoleonic Wars. He commanded an army corps at ◊Austerlitz and the retreating army in 1812. After the burning of Moscow, he harried the French throughout their retreat and later took command of the united Prussian armies.

Kuwait /kuˈweɪt/ State of; country in SW Asia, bordered N and NW by Iraq, E by the Persian Gulf, and S and SW by Saudi Arabia; **capital** Kuwait (also chief port); **physical** hot desert and islands of Bubiyan and Warba at NE corner of Arabian Peninsula; **head of state and government** Jabir al-Ahmad al-Sabah from 1977; **political system** absolute monarchy; **exports** oil; **language** Arabic 78%, Kurdish 10%, Farsi 4%; **recent history** recognized as an independent sovereign state from 1914, Kuwait achieved full independence from Britain in 1961. On 2 Aug 1990 President Saddam Hussain of Iraq, reactivating a longstanding territorial dispute, annexed Kuwait. The emir and his family escaped to Saudi Arabia. By March 1991 UN coalition forces had liberated Kuwait (see ◊Gulf War), but by flooding the Gulf with crude oil and firing the oil wells around Kuwait city, the occupying forces had left the country an ecological disaster area.

Kuwait City (Arabic *Al Kuwayt*) formerly **Qurein** the chief port and capital of the state of Kuwait, on the southern shore of Kuwait Bay; population (1985) 44,300, plus the suburbs of Hawalli, population (1985) 145,100, Jahra, population (1985) 111,200, and as-Salimiya, population (1985) 153,400. Kuwait was a banking and investment centre before the Iraqi invasion of 1990. During the ◊Gulf War it was destroyed and looted by the occupying troops.

Kuznetsk Basin /kʊzˈnetsk/ an industrial area in Kemorovo region, S USSR. It is abbreviated to Kuzbas.

Kuznetsov /kʊznɪtˈsɒf/ Anatoli 1930–1979. Russian writer. His novels *Babi Yar* 1966, describing the wartime execution of Jews at Babi Yar, near Kiev, and *The Fire* 1969, about workers in a large metallurgical factory, were seen as anti-Soviet. He lived in Britain from 1969 until his death.

kV abbreviation of kilovolt(s).

kW abbreviation of ◊kilowatt.

Kwa Ndebele /kwɑːˈndəˈbeɪli/ a black homeland in Transvaal province, South Africa; achieved self-governing status 1981; population (1985) 235,800.

Kwangchow alternative name of ◊Guangzhou, city in China.

Kwangchu /kwæŋˈdʒuː/ or **Kwangju** the capital of South Cholla province, SW South Korea; population (1985) 906,000. It is at the centre of a rice-growing region.

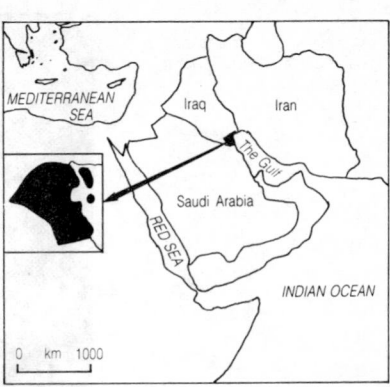

Kuwait

Kwangsi-Chuang alternative name of ◊Guanxi Zhuang, region of China.

Kwangtung alternative name of ◊Guangdong, province of China.

kwashiorkor *n.* a severe protein deficiency in children under five years, resulting in retarded growth and a swollen abdomen.

Kwa Zulu a black homeland in Natal province, South Africa; population (1985) 3,747,000. It achieved self-governing status in 1971.

Kweilin alternative name of ◊Guilin in China.

kWh symbol for kilowatt-hour(s).

kyanite *n.* a pale blue mineral, alluminium silicate, Al_2SiO_5, occurring as blade-shaped crystals. It is an indicator of high pressure conditions in metamorphic rocks formed from clay sediments. Andalusite, kyanite, and sillimanite are all polymorphs.

Kyd /kɪd/ Thomas *c.* 1557–1595. English dramatist, author in about 1588 of a bloody revenge tragedy, *The Spanish Tragedy*, which anticipated elements present in Shakespeare's *Hamlet*.

Thus must we toil in other men's extremes,
That know not how to remedy our own.

Thomas Kyd
The Spanish Tragedy

---

kyle /kaɪl/ *n.* a narrow channel between an island and the mainland (or another island) in western Scotland. [from Gaelic]

Kyoto the former capital of Japan 794–1868 (when the capital was changed to Tokyo) on Honshu island, linked by canal with Biwa Lake; population (1987) 1,469,000. Industries include electrical, chemical, and machinery plants; silk weaving; and the manufacture of porcelain, bronze, and lacquerware.

kyphosis /kaɪˈfəʊsɪs/ *n.* an exaggerated outward curve of the upper spine, resulting in a lump. It is usually due to spinal disease, arthritis, or bad posture.

Kyprianou /kɪpriəˈnuː/ Spyros 1932– . Cypriot politician. Foreign minister 1961–72, he founded the Democratic Front (DIKO) in 1976. He was president 1977–88.

Kyrie eleison (Greek 'Lord have mercy') the words spoken or sung at the beginning of the mass in the Catholic, Orthodox, and Anglican churches.

Kyushu /ˈkjuːʃuː/ the southernmost of the main islands of Japan, separated from Shikoku and Honshu by Bungo Channel and Suo Bay, but connected to Honshu by bridge and rail tunnel; **area** 42,150 sq km/16,270 sq mi, including about 370 small islands; **capital** Nagasaki; **physical** mountainous, volcanic, with subtropical climate; the active volcano Aso-take (1,592 m/5,225 ft), with the world's largest crater; **products** coal, gold, silver, iron, tin, rice, tea, timber; **population** (1986) 13,295,000.

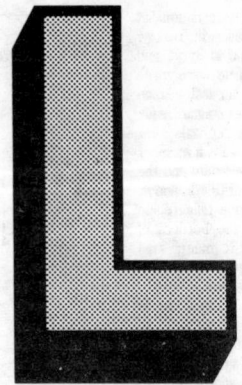

I,L /el/ *n.* (*plural* **Is, I's**) 1. the 12th letter of the alphabet. 2. an L-shaped thing. 3. (as a Roman numeral) 50.

l. abbreviation of 1. left. 2. line. 3. litre(s).

L abbreviation of learner (driver).

L. abbreviation of 1. Lake. 2. Liberal. 3. Licentiate of.

£ abbreviation of pound (money). [from Latin *libra*]

la variant of ◊lah.

La symbol for ◊lanthanum.

LA abbreviation of Los Angeles.

lab *n.* (*colloquial*) ◊laboratory. [abbreviation]

Lab. abbreviation of 1. Labour. 2. ◊Labrador, Canada.

Labanotation *n.* a comprehensive system of accurate dance notation (*Kinetographie Laban*) devised in 1928 by Rudolf von Laban (1879–1958), dancer, choreographer, and dance theorist.

label /'leɪbəl/ *n.* 1. a slip of paper etc. attached to an object to give some information about it. 2. a general classifying phrase applied to persons etc. —*v.t.* (-ll-) 1. to attach a label to. 2. to assign to a category. 3. to make (a substance, molecule, or constituent atom) recognizable, for identification in an experiment. [from Old French = ribbon]

labelled compound or **tagged compound** a chemical compound in which a radioactive isotope is substituted for a stable one. Thus labelled, the path taken by the compound through a system can be followed, for example by measuring the radiation emitted.

labelling *n.* in sociology, a method of defining a person in terms of his or her behaviour, for example, describing someone who has broken a law as a criminal. Labelling theory deals with human interaction, behaviour, and control, particularly in the field of deviance.

labellum *n.* the lower petal of an orchid flower, which is a different shape from the two other lateral petals and gives the orchid its characteristic appearance.

labial /'leɪbɪəl/ *adj.* 1. of the lips. 2. of the nature of a lip. 3. pronounced with partially or completely closed lips. —*n.* a labial sound (e.g. *p, m, v*). [from Latin *labia* = lips]

labium /'leɪbɪəm/ *n.* (*plural* **labia**) 1. (usually in *plural*) the lip of the female genitals. 2. the lower part of the mouth of an insect, crustacean etc. —**labia majora**, the outer folds of the genital labia. **labia minora**, the inner folds. [Latin = lip]

laboratory /lə'bɒrətərɪ/ *n.* a room or building used for scientific experiments and research. [from Latin *laborare* = toil]

laborious /lə'bɔːrɪəs/ *adj.* 1. needing much work or perseverance. 2. showing signs of effort. 3. hard-working. —**laboriously** *adv.* [from Old French from Latin]

Labor, Knights of in US history, a national labour organization founded by Philadelphia tailor, Uriah Stephens, in 1869 and committed to cooperative enterprise, equal pay for both sexes, and an eight-hour day. The Knights grew rapidly in the mid-1880s under Terence V Powderly (1849–1924) but gave way to the ◊American Federation of Labor after 1886.

Labor Party in Australia, a political party based on socialist principles. It was founded in 1891 and first held office in 1904. It formed governments 1929–31 and 1939–49, but in the intervening periods internal discord provoked splits, and reduced its effectiveness. It returned to power

under Gough Whitlam 1972–75, and again under Bob Hawke from 1983.

labour /'leɪbə/ *n.* 1. bodily or mental work, exertion. 2. a task. 3. the body of those doing (especially manual or nonmanagerial) work; such a body as a political force. 4. **Labour**, the Labour Party. 5. the pains of childbirth; the process of giving birth. —*v.t./i.* 1. to exert oneself, to work hard. 2. to have to make a great effort, to operate or progress only with difficulty. 3. to treat (a point etc.) at great length or in excessive detail. 4. to suffer *under* (a delusion etc.). —**labour camp**, a place where prisoners must work as labourers. **Labour Exchange**, (*colloquial* or *historical*) an employment exchange. **labour-saving** *adj.* designed to reduce or eliminate work. [from Old French from Latin]

Labour Day a legal holiday in honour of workers. In Canada and the USA, **Labor day** is celebrated on the first Monday in September. In many countries it coincides with ◊May Day.

laboured *adj.* showing signs of great effort, not spontaneous.

labourer *n.* a person who labours, especially one employed to do unskilled manual work.

labour market the market that determines the cost and conditions of the work force. This will depend on the demand of employers, the levels and availability of skills, and social conditions.

Labour Party the UK political party based on socialist principles, originally formed to represent workers. It was founded in 1900 and first held office in 1924. The first majority Labour government 1945–51 introduced nationalization (see ◊nationalize) and the National Health Service, and expanded ◊social security. Labour was again in power 1964–70 and 1974–79. The party leader is elected by Labour members of Parliament. Neil ◊Kinnock became leader in 1983.

labour theory of value in classical economics, the theory that the price (value) of a product directly reflects the amount of labour it involves. According to theory, if the price of a product falls, either the share of labour in that product has declined or that expended in the production of other goods has risen.

Labrador /'læbrədɔː/ area of NE Canada, part of the province of Newfoundland, lying between Ungava Bay on the NW, the Atlantic Ocean on the E, and the Strait of Belle Isle on the SE; area 266,060 sq km/102,699 sq mi; population (1986) 28,741.

Labrador *n.* a retriever dog of a breed with a smooth black or golden coat. [from *Labrador* in Canada]

labrum /'leɪbrəm/ *n.* (*plural* **labria**) the upper lip of an insect. [Latin = lip]

The pleasure of criticizing robs us of the pleasure of being moved by some very fine things.

Jean de La Bruyère
Les Caractères: 'des ouvrages de l'esprit'.

La Bruyère /læbru:'jeə/ Jean de 1645–1696. French essayist. He was born in Paris, studied law, took a post in the revenue office, and in 1684 entered the service of the house of Condé. His *Caractères* 1688, satirical portraits of his contemporaries, made him many enemies.

laburnum /lə'bɜ:nəm/ *n.* any ornamental tree of the genus *Laburnum*, family Leguminosae, especially *L. anagyroides*, which has drooping yellow pealike flowers. [Latin]

labyrinth /'læbərɪnθ/ *n.* 1. a complicated or confusing network of passages. 2. a tangled or intricate arrangement. 3. the complex cavity of the inner ear. —**labyrinthine** /læbə'rɪnθaɪn/ *adj.* [from French or Latin from Greek]

lac /læk/ *n.* a resinous substance secreted by a SE Asian insect as a protective covering. See also ◊lacquer. [ultimately from Hindi from Sanskrit]

Laccadive, Minicoy, and Amindivi Islands /'lækə dɪv, 'mɪnɪkɔɪ, æmɪn'diːvi/ former name of Indian island group ◊Lakshadweep.

lace *n.* 1. a cord or narrow strip threaded through holes or hooks for fastening or tightening shoes etc. 2. a fabric or trimming of ornamental, openwork design. —*v.t.* 1. to fasten or tighten with a lace or laces; to pass (a cord etc.) *through*. 2. to trim with lace. 3. to add a dash of spirits etc. to (a drink). 4. to beat, to lash. [from Old French from Latin *laqueus* = noose]

lacerate /'læsəreɪt/ *v.t.* to tear (flesh etc.) roughly; to wound (the feelings). —**laceration** /-'reɪʃən/ *n.* [from Latin *lacer* = torn]

lacewing *n.* a neuropterous insect of the families Hemerobiidae (the brown lacewings) and Chrysopidae (the green lacewings), order Neuroptera. They have narrow bodies, long thin antennae, and two pairs of delicately veined, semitransparent wings. Lacewings are predators, especially of aphids.

Lachish /'leɪkɪʃ/ ancient city SW of Jerusalem, destroyed in 589 BC. Inscribed pottery fragments found there have thrown light on Hebrew manuscripts and the early development of the alphabet.

lachrymal /'lækrɪməl/ *adj.* of tears. [from Latin *lacrima* = tear]

lachrymose /'lækrɪməʊs/ *adj.* tearful, given to weeping.

lack *n.* the state or fact of not having something. —*v.t.* not to have when needed, to be without. —**be lacking**, to be undesirably absent or deficient. [related to Middle Dutch, Middle Low German *lak* = deficiency]

lackadaisical /lækə'deɪzɪkəl/ *adj.* lacking vigour or determination, unenthusiastic. —**lackadaisically** *adv.* [from archaic *lackaday*, *lackadaisy* (interjection)]

lackey /'lækɪ/ *n.* an obsequious follower; a humble servant. —*v.t.* to play lackey to. [from French from Catalan]

lacklustre /'læklʌstə/ *adj.* without lustre, dull.

Laclos /læ'kləʊ/ Pierre Choderlos de 1741–1803. French author. He was an army officer who wrote a single novel in letter form, *Les Liaisons dangereuses/Dangerous Liaisons* 1782, an analysis of moral corruption.

laconic /lə'kɒnɪk/ *adj.* terse, using few words. —**laconically** *adv.* [from Latin from Greek *Lakōn* = Spartan, the Spartans being proverbially terse]

lacquer /'lækə/ *n.* 1. a hard, shiny shellac or synthetic varnish. 2. a resinous substance obtained from Oriental trees (especially *Toxicodendron verniciflua*) and used for decorating furniture and art objects. 3. a substance sprayed on the hair to keep it in place. —*v.t.* to coat with lacquer. [from obsolete French *lacre* = sealing wax from Portuguese]

lacrosse /lə'krɒs/ *n.* a field game, adopted from the North American Indians; it is played with a netted stick with which a ball is driven or thrown, caught, and carried. [French *la* = the and *crosse* = crozier]

lactate /læk'teɪt/ *v.i.* to secrete milk. —/'lækteɪt/ *n.* a salt or ester of lactic acid. [from Latin *lactare* = suckle (*lac* = milk)]

lactation /læk'teɪʃən/ *n.* 1. suckling. 2. the secretion of milk from the mammary glands of mammals.

lacteal *adj.* of, like, or related to milk. —*n.* a small vessel responsible for absorbing fat in the small intestine. Occurring in the fingerlike villi (see ◊villus) of the ileum, lacteals drain into the lymphatic system.

lactic *adj.* of milk.

lactic acid a colourless, almost odourless, syrupy organic acid, $CH_3CHOHCOOH$, produced by certain bacteria during fermentation; technical name **hydroxypropanoic acid**.

It occurs in yoghurt, buttermilk, sour cream, wine, and certain plant extracts; it is present in muscles when they are exercised hard, and also in the stomach.

lactose /'læktəʊs/ *n.* a sugar present in milk.

lacuna /lə'kjuːnə/ *n.* (*plural* **lacunas**, **lacunae** /-iː/) a gap or missing part, especially in a manuscript. [Latin, originally = pool]

lacy /'leɪsɪ/ *adj.* like lace fabrics, especially in fineness.

lad /læd/ *n.* a boy, a young fellow; (*colloquial*) a man.

Ladd Alan 1913–1964. US actor whose first leading role, as the professional killer in *This Gun for Hire* 1942, made him a star. His career declined after the mid-1950s although his last role, in *The Carpetbaggers* 1964, was one of his best. His other films include *The Blue Dahlia* 1946 and *Shane* 1953.

ladder *n.* 1. a series of horizontal bars fixed between a pair of long uprights, used for climbing up or down. 2. a vertical ladderlike flaw in stockings etc. 3. a means of progress in a career etc. —*v.t./i.* to cause a ladder in (a stocking etc.); to develop a ladder. —**ladder back**, a chair with the back made of horizontal bars between uprights. [Old English]

lade *v.t.* (*past participle* **laden**) to load (a ship), to ship (goods); (in *past participle*) loaded or burdened (*with*). —**bill of lading**, a detailed list of a ship's cargo. [Old English]

la-di-da /lɑːdɪ'dɑː/ *adj.* (*colloquial*) pretentious or affected in manner or speech. [imitative of pronunciation used]

Ladin /læ'diːn/ *n.* 1. a member of an ethnic community (about 16,000) in the Dolomites, S Tyrol; they may be descended from the Etruscans and other early Italian tribes, and have links with the speakers of ◊Romansch in Switzerland. 2. the language of this community, derived directly from Latin.

ladle /'leɪdəl/ *n.* a deep long-handled spoon for transferring liquids. —*v.t.* to transfer with a ladle. [Old English]

Ladoga /'lædəgə/ (Russian *Ladozhskoye*) the largest lake on the continent of Europe, in the USSR, just NE of Leningrad; area 18,400 sq km/7,100 sq mi. It receives the waters of several rivers, including the Svir, which drains Lake Onega and runs to the Gulf of Finland by the river Neva.

lady /'leɪdɪ/ *n.* 1. a woman of good social standing; (as a polite term) any woman; a woman of polite or refined disposition. 2. **Lady**, the titled used as a less formal prefix to the name of a peeress below a duchess, or to the Christian name of a daughter of a duke, marquis, or earl, or to the surname of the wife or widow of a baronet or knight. 3. the woman with the authority in a household. 4. (*archaic*) a wife. 5. (*attributive*) female. —**the Ladies**, (as *singular*) a women's public lavatory. **ladies' man**, a man fond of women's company. **Lady Chapel**, a chapel dedicated to the Virgin Mary. **Lady Day**, the feast of the Annunciation of the Virgin Mary, 25 March. **lady-in-waiting** *n.* a lady attending a royal lady. **lady-killer** *n.* a man given to making amorous conquests of women. **lady's maid**, the personal maidservant of a lady. **lady's slipper**, a flower of the genus *Cypripedium* of the orchid family, with flowers shaped like a slipper or pouch. **Our Lady**, the Virgin Mary. [Old English = loaf kneader]

ladybird *n.* a small round beetle of the family Coccinellidae, usually reddish brown with black spots. Both adults and larvae feed on aphids and scale insect pests.

ladylike *adj.* like or appropriate to a lady.

ladyship *n.* the title used in addressing or referring to a woman with the rank of Lady.

lady's smock an alternative name for the ◊cuckoo flower *Cardamine pratensis*.

Laënnec /leɪ'nek/ René Théophile Hyacinthe 1781–1826. French physician, inventor of the ◊stethoscope in 1814. He introduced the new diagnostic technique of auscultation (evaluating internal organs by listening with a stethoscope) in his book *Traité de l'auscultation médiaté* 1819, which quickly became a medical classic.

Lafayette /læfeɪ'et/ Marie Joseph Gilbert de Motier, Marquis de Lafayette 1757–1834. French soldier and politician. He fought against Britain in the American Revolution 1777–79 and 1780–82. During the French Revolution he sat in the National Assembly as a constitutional royalist and in 1789 presented the Declaration of the Rights of Man. After the storming of the ◊Bastille, he was given command of the National Guard. In 1792 he fled the country after attempting to restore the monarchy and was imprisoned by the Austrians until 1797. He supported Napoleon in 1815, sat in the chamber of deputies as a Liberal from 1818, and played a leading part in the revolution of 1830.

Lafayette Marie-Madeleine, Comtesse de Lafayette 1634–1693. French author. Her *Mémoires* of the French court are keenly observed, and *La Princesse de Clèves* 1678 is the first French psychological novel and *roman à clef* ('novel with a key'), in that real-life characters (including ◊La Rochefoucauld, who was for many years her lover) are presented under fictitious names.

La Fontaine /læ fon'teɪn/ Jean de 1621–1695. French poet. He was born at Château-Thierry, and from 1656 lived largely in Paris, the friend of Molière, Racine, and Boileau. His works include *Fables* 1668–94, and *Contes* 1665–74, a series of witty and bawdy tales in verse.

Better a living beggar than a dead emperor.
Jean de La Fontaine
La Matrone d'Ephèse

Lafontaine Oskar 1943– . German socialist politician, federal deputy chair of the Social Democrat Party (SPD) from 1987. Leader of the Saar regional branch of the SPD from 1977 and former mayor of Saarbrucken, Germany, he was dubbed 'Red Oskar' because of his radical views on military and environmental issues. His attitude became more conservative once he had become minister–president of Saarland in 1985.

Laforgue /læ'fɔːg/ Jules 1860–1887. French poet, who pioneered ◊free verse and who inspired later French and English writers.

lag[1] *v.i.* (**-gg-**) to go too slow, to fail to keep up with the others. —*n.* lagging, a delay. —**lagger** *n.* [originally = hindmost person]

lag[2] *v.t.* (**-gg-**) to enclose (a boiler etc.) with a heat-insulating material. —*n.* such a material; an insulating cover. —**lagger** *n.*

lag[3] *n.* a convict (especially in *old lag*).

Lagash /'lɑːgəʃ/ Sumerian city to the N of Shatra, Iraq, under independent and semi-independent rulers from about 3000–2700 BC. Besides objects of high artistic value, it has provided about 30,000 clay tablets giving detailed information on temple administration. It was discovered in 1877 and excavated by Ernest de Sarzec, then French consul in Basra.

lager /'lɑːgə/ *n.* a kind of light beer. [from German *lager-bier* = beer brewed for keeping (*lager* = store)]

Lagerkvist /'lɑːgəkvɪst/ Pär 1891–1974. Swedish author of lyric poetry, dramas (including *The Hangman* 1935), and novels, such as *Barabbas* 1950. He was awarded the Nobel Prize for Literature in 1951.

Lagerlöf /'lɑːgələːf/ Selma 1858–1940. Swedish novelist. She was originally a schoolteacher, and in 1891 published a collection of stories of peasant life, *Gösta Berling's Saga*. She was awarded the Nobel Prize for Literature in 1909 and was the first woman to receive a Nobel prize in any category.

laggard /'lægəd/ *n.* a person who lags behind, a procrastinator.

lagging[1] *n.* a material used to lag a boiler etc.

lagging[2] *n.* a term of imprisonment.

lagoon /lə'guːn/ *n.* a body of salt water separated from the sea by a sandbank or coral reef etc. [from French or Italian and Spanish from Latin]

Lagos /'leɪgɒs/ chief port and former capital of Nigeria, located at the W end of an island in a lagoon and linked by bridges with the mainland via Iddo Island; population (1983) 1,097,000. Industries include chemicals, metal products, and fish. ◊Abuja was established as the new capital in 1982.

Lagrange /læ'grɒnʒ/ Joseph Louis 1736–1813. French mathematician. His *Mécanique analytique* 1788 applied mathematical analysis, using principles established by Newton, to such problems as the movements of planets when affected by each other's gravitational force. He presided over the commission that introduced the metric system in 1793.

Lagrangian points /lə'grɑːnʒiən/ the five locations in space where the centrifugal and gravitational forces of two bodies neutralize each other; a third, less massive body located at any one of these points will be held in equilibrium with respect to the other two.

La Guardia /lə 'gwɑːdiə/ Fiorello (Henrico) 1882–1947. US Republican politician; congressman in 1917, 1919, 1923–33; mayor of New York 1933–45. Elected against the opposition of the powerful Tammany Hall Democratic Party organization, he cleaned up the administration, suppressed racketeering; and organized unemployment relief, slum-clearance schemes, and social services.

lah /lɑː/ *n.* in music, the sixth note of the major scale in ◊tonic sol-fa.

Lahore /lə'hɔː/ capital of the province of Punjab and second city of Pakistan; population (1981) 2,920,000. Industries include engineering, textiles, carpets, and chemicals. It is associated with Mogul rulers Akbar, Jahangir, and Aurangzeb, whose capital it was in the 16th and 17th centuries.

laicize /'leɪɪsaɪz/ *v.t.* to make secular. —**laicization** /-'zeɪʃən/ *n.* [from *laic* = lay]

laid past and past participle of **lay**[1].

Lailat ul-Barah /laɪ'lɑːt əl'bɑːrə/ a Muslim festival, the **Night of Forgiveness**, which takes place two weeks before the beginning of the fast of Ramadan (the ninth month of the Islamic year) and is a time for asking and granting forgiveness.

Lailat-al-Isra Wal Mi'raj /laɪ'lɑːt əl'ɪsrə wɑːl mi'rɑːdʒ/ a Muslim festival that celebrates the prophet Muhammad's ◊Night Journey.

Lailat ul-Qadr /laɪlɑːt əl'kɑːdə/ a Muslim festival, the **Night of Power**, which celebrates the giving of the Koran to Muhammad. It usually falls at the end of Ramadan.

lain past participle of **lie**[1].

Laing /læŋ/ R(onald) D(avid) 1927–1989. Scottish psychoanalyst, originator of the 'social theory' of mental illness, for example that ◊schizophrenia is promoted by family pressure for its members to conform to standards alien to themselves. His books include *The Divided Self* 1960 and *The Politics of the Family* 1971.

We are effectively destroying ourselves by violence masquerading as love.
Ronald David Laing
The Politics of Experience

---

lair *n.* 1. a sheltered place where a wild animal habitually rests or eats. 2. a person's hiding place.

laird *n.* a landowner in Scotland. [Scottish form of *lord*]

laissez-faire /leɪseɪ'fe ə(r)/ *n.* or **laisser-faire** the theory that the state should not intervene in economic affairs, except to break up a monopoly. The phrase originated with the Physiocrats, 18th-century French economists, whose maxim was *laissez-faire et laissez-passer* (leave the individual alone and let commodities circulate freely). [French = let act]

laity /'leɪtɪ/ *n.* a body of laymen, especially in a church.

lake[1] *n.* a large expanse of still water lying in depressed ground without direct communication with the sea. Lakes are common in formerly glaciated regions, along the courses of slow rivers, and in low land near the sea. —**Lake District** *or* **the Lakes**, the region round the lakes in Cumbria in NW England. **lake dwelling**, a prehistoric dwelling built on piles driven into the bed or shore of a lake. [from Old French from Latin *lacus*]

lake[2] *n.* a pigment made from a dye and a mordant; a reddish pigment, originally made from ◊lac.

Lake /leɪk/ Veronica. Stage name of Constance Frances Marie Ockelman 1919–1973. US film actress who was almost as celebrated for her much imitated 'peekaboo' hairstyle as her acting. She co-starred with Alan Ladd in several films during the 1940s, including *The Blue Dahlia* 1946. She also appeared in *Sullivan's Travels* 1942 and *I Married a Witch* 1942.

lakh /læk/ *n.* in India, 100,000 (especially in *a lakh of rupees*). [from Hindustani from Sanskrit]

Lakshadweep /læk'ʃædwiːp/ group of 36 coral islands, 10 inhabited, in the Indian Ocean, 320 km/200 mi off the Malabar coast; area 32 sq km/12 sq mi; population (1981) 40,000.

Lakshmi /ˈlækʃmi/ the Hindu goddess of wealth and beauty, consort of Vishnu; her festival is ◊Diwali.

Lalande /læˈlɑːnd/ Michel de 1657–1726. French organist and composer of church music for the court at Versailles.

Lalique /læˈliːk/ René 1860–1945. French designer and manufacturer of ◊Art Nouveau glass, jewellery, and house interiors.

Lallan /ˈlæln/ adj. (Scottish) of the Lowlands of Scotland. —n. (Scottish; also **Lallans**) Lowland Scots dialect, especially as a literary language. [variant of lowland]

Lalo /ˈlɑːləʊ/ (Victor Antoine) Edouard 1823–1892. French composer. His Spanish ancestry and violin training are evident in the Symphonie Espagnole 1873 for violin and orchestra, and Concerto for cello and orchestra 1877. He also wrote an opera, Le Roi d'Ys 1887.

lam /læm/ v.t. (-mm-) (slang) to hit hard, to thrash.

Lam Wilfredo 1902–1982. Cuban abstract painter. Influenced by Surrealism in the 1930s (he lived in Paris 1937–41), he created a semi-abstract style using mysterious and sometimes menacing images and symbols, mainly taken from Caribbean tradition. His Jungle series, for example, contains voodoo elements.

lama /ˈlɑːmə/ n. an honorific applied to a spiritual leader in Tibetan Buddhism; any Tibetan Buddhist monk. [from Tibetan blama = superior one]

lamaism /ˈlɑːməɪzəm/ n. a common but (strictly) incorrect term for Tibetan Buddhism.

Lamarck /læˈmɑːk/ Jean Baptiste de 1744–1829. French naturalist, who proposed the theory of evolution known as ◊Lamarckism. His works include Philosophie Zoologique/ Zoological Philosophy 1809 and Histoire naturelle des animaux sans vertèbres/Natural History of Invertebrate Animals 1815–22.

Lamarckism n. a theory of evolution, advocated during the early 19th century by Lamarck. It differed from the Darwinian theory of evolution in that it was based on the idea that ◊acquired characteristics (see ◊acquired character) are inheritable: Lamarck argued that particular use of an organ or limb strengthens it, and that this development may be 'preserved by reproduction'.

Lamartine /læmɑːˈtiːn/ Alphonse de 1790–1869. French poet. He wrote romantic poems, including Méditations 1820, followed by Nouvelles méditations/New Meditations 1823, and Harmonies 1830. His Histoire des Girondins/History of the Girondins 1847 helped to inspire the revolution of 1848.

lamasery /ləˈmɑːsərɪ/ n. a common but (strictly) incorrect term for a Tibetan Buddhist monastery.

lamb /læm/ n. 1. a young sheep. 2. its flesh as food. 3. a gentle, endearing, or vulnerable person. —v.t.i. 1. to give birth to a lamb; (in passive, of a lamb) to be born. 2. to tend (lambing ewes). —**Lamb (of God)**, Christ. **lamb's wool**, soft fine wool. [Old English]

Lamb Charles 1775–1834. English essayist and critic. He collaborated with his sister Mary Lamb (1764–1847) on Tales from Shakespeare 1807, and his Specimens of English Dramatic Poets 1808 helped to revive interest in Elizabethan plays. As 'Elia' he contributed essays to the London Magazine from 1820 (collected 1823 and 1833).

Lamb Willis 1913– . US physicist who revised the quantum theory of Paul ◊Dirac. The hydrogen atom was thought to exist in either of two distinct states carrying equal energies. More sophisticated measurements by Lamb in 1947 demonstrated that the two energy levels were not equal. This discrepancy, since known as the **Lamb shift**, won for him the 1955 Nobel Prize for Physics.

lambaste /læmˈbeɪst/ v.t. (colloquial) to thrash, to beat.

lambda /ˈlæmdə/ n. the 11th letter of the Greek alphabet (λ, Λ) = l. [Greek]

lambent /ˈlæmbənt/ adj. (of a flame or light) playing about a surface; (of the eyes, wit etc.) gently brilliant. —**lambency** n. [from Latin lambere = lick]

lambert n. a unit of luminance (the light shining from a surface), equal to one ◊lumen per square centimetre. In scientific work the ◊candela per square metre is preferred.

Lambeth Conference a meeting of bishops of the Anglican Communion every ten years, presided over by the archbishop of Canterbury; its decisions on doctrinal matters are not binding.

Lamburn /ˈlæmbɜːn/ Richmal Crompton. Full name of British writer Richmal ◊Crompton.

lame adj. 1. (of a person or limb) disabled or unable to walk normally, especially by an injury or defect in the foot or leg. 2. (of an excuse etc.) unconvincing. 3. (of a metre) halting. —v.t. to make lame, to disable. —**lame duck**, a person or firm unable to cope without help. —**lamely** adv., **lameness** n. [Old English]

lamé /ˈlɑːmeɪ/ n. a fabric with gold or silver thread interwoven. [French]

lament /ləˈment/ n. a passionate expression of grief; an elegy. —v.t.i. to feel or express grief for or about; to utter a lament; (in past participle) mourned for. [from Latin lamentum, French or Latin lamentari]

lamentable /ˈlæməntəbəl/ adj. deplorable, regrettable. —**lamentably** adv.

lamentation /læmənˈteɪʃən/ n. 1. a lament. 2. lamenting.

lamina /ˈlæmɪnə/ n. (plural laminae /-iː/) 1. a thin plate, scale, or layer. 2. in botany, the blade of the ◊leaf on either side of the midrib. —**laminar** adj. [Latin]

laminate /ˈlæmɪneɪt/ v.t./i. 1. to beat or roll into laminae; to split into layers. 2. to overlay with metal plates, a plastic layer etc. —/-ət/ n. a laminated structure, especially of layers fixed together. —/-ət/ adj. in the form of a lamina or laminae. —**lamination** /-ˈneɪʃən/ n.

Lammas /ˈlæməs/ n. a medieval harvest festival, celebrated on 1 August. At one time it was an English ◊quarter day (date for payment of quarterly rates or dues), and is still a quarter day in Scotland. [from Old English hlafmæsse = loaf mass]

lammergeier n. a bird of prey Gypaetus barbatus, also known as the bearded vulture, with a wingspan of 2.7 m/ 9 ft. It ranges over S Europe, N Africa, and Asia, in wild mountainous areas.

Lamming /ˈlæmɪŋ/ George 1927– . Barbadian novelist, author of the autobiographical In the Castle of my Skin 1953, describing his upbringing in the small village where he was born. He later moved to London, England.

lamp n. a device or vessel for giving light or rays by the use of electricity or gas or by burning oil or spirit. [from Old French from Latin from Greek lampas = torch]

lampblack n. a pigment made from soot.

Lampedusa /læmpiˈduːzə/ Giuseppe Tomasi di 1896– 1957. Italian aristocrat, author of The Leopard 1958, a novel set in his native Sicily during the period following its annexation by Garibaldi in 1860. It chronicles the reactions of an aristocratic family to social and political upheavals.

lamplight n. the light given by a lamp.

lamplighter n. (usually historical) a person who lights street lamps.

lampoon /læmˈpuːn/ n. a piece of virulent or scurrilous satire on a person. —v.t. to write a lampoon against. —**lampoonist** n. [from French lampon]

lamppost n. a tall post supporting a street lamp.

lamprey /ˈlæmprɪ/ n. an eel-shaped, jawless fish, with a sucker mouth, belonging to the family Petromyzonidae. Lampreys feed on other fish by fixing their round mouths to their hosts and boring into the flesh with their toothed tongues. [from Old French from Latin lampetra]

lampshade n. a shade placed over a lamp.

Lanarkshire /ˈlænəkʃə/ former inland county of Scotland, merged in the region of Strathclyde in 1975. The county town was Lanark.

Lancashire /ˈlæŋkəʃə/ county in NW England; **area** 3,040 sq km/1,173 sq mi; **administrative headquarters** Preston; **physical** river Ribble; the Pennines; Forest of Bowland (moors and farming valleys); Pendle Hill; **products** formerly a world centre of cotton manufacture, now replaced with high-technology aerospace and electronics industries; **population** (1987) 1,381,000.

Lancaster, Duchy and County Palatine of /ˈlæŋkəstə/ created in 1351, and attached to the crown since 1399. The office of Chancellor of the Duchy is a sinecure without any responsibilities, usually held by a member of the Cabinet with a special role outside that of the regular ministries, for example, Harold Lever as financial adviser to the Wilson–Callaghan governments from 1974.

Lancaster Burt (Burton Stephen) 1913– . US film actor who was formerly an acrobat. A star from his first film, The Killers 1946, he proved himself adept both at action roles and more complex character parts in such films as The Flame and the Arrow 1950, Elmer Gantry 1960, and The Leopard/Il Gattopardo 1963.

Lancaster Osbert 1908–1986. English cartoonist and writer. In 1939 he began producing daily 'pocket cartoons' for the *Daily Express*, in which he satirized current social mores through such characters as Maudie Littlehampton.

Lancaster, House of the English royal house that reigned from 1399 to 1461, a branch of the ◊Plantagenets.

Lancastrian /læn'kæstriən/ *adj.* **1.** of Lancashire or Lancaster. **2.** of the family descended from John of Gaunt, Duke of Lancaster, or of the Red Rose party supporting it in the Wars of the Roses (compare ◊Yorkist). —*n.* **1.** a native or inhabitant of Lancashire or Lancaster. **2.** a member or adherent of the Lancastrian family.

lance /lɑːns/ *n.* a long spear, especially one used by a horseman. —*v.t.* **1.** to pierce with a lance. **2.** to prick or cut open with a surgical lancet. —**lance corporal**, in the British army, a noncommissioned officer below a corporal. [from Old French from Latin *lancea* = lance]

lancelet *n.* a marine animal, genus *Amphioxus*, included in the ◊chordates, about 2.5 cm/1 in long. It has no skull, brain, eyes, heart, vertebral column, centralized brain, nor paired limbs, but there is a notochord (a supportive rod) which runs from end to end of the body, a tail, and a number of gill slits. It burrows in the sand but when disturbed swims freely.

Lancelot of the Lake /ˈlɑːnslɒt/ in British legend, the most celebrated of King Arthur's knights, the lover of Queen Guinevere. Originally a folk hero, he first appeared in the Arthurian cycle of tales in the 12th century.

lanceolate /ˈlænsiələt/ *adj.* shaped like a spearhead, tapering to each end. [from Latin *lanceola*, diminutive of *lancea* = lance]

lancer /ˈlɑːnsə/ *n.* **1.** a soldier of a cavalry regiment originally armed with lances. **2.** (in *plural*) a kind of quadrille; the music for this.

lancet /ˈlɑːnsɪt/ *n.* **1.** a surgical instrument with a point and two edges for small incisions. **2.** a narrow pointed arch or window.

Lancs. abbreviation of Lancashire.

land /lænd/ *n.* **1.** the solid part of the Earth's surface, not covered by water. **2.** the ground, the soil, an expanse of country; this as a basis for agriculture, building etc. **3.** landed property; (in *plural*) estates. **4.** a country or state. —*v.t./i.* **1.** to set or go ashore from a ship etc. **2.** to bring (an aircraft) to the ground or other surface; to come down thus. **3.** to alight after a jump etc. **4.** to reach or find oneself in a certain place or situation; to cause to do this. **5.** to deliver (a person a blow etc.). **6.** to present (a person *with* a problem etc.). **7.** to bring (a fish) to land; to win (a prize); to secure (an appointment etc.). —**how the land lies**, what is the state of affairs. **land agent**, a steward of an estate; a dealer in estates. **land girl**, a woman doing farm work, especially in wartime. **land line**, a means of telegraphic communication over land. **land-locked** *adj.* almost or entirely surrounded by land. **land mass**, a large area of land. **land mine**, an explosive mine laid in or on the ground. [Old English]

Land Edwin 1909– . US inventor in 1947 of the Polaroid camera, which develops the film inside the camera and produces an instant photograph.

landau /ˈlændɔː/ *n.* a four-wheeled horse-drawn carriage with a top of which the front and back halves can be raised and lowered independently. [from *Landau* near Karlsruhe in Germany, where first made]

Landau /ˈlændaʊ/ Lev Davidovich 1908–1968. Russian theoretical physicist. He was awarded the 1962 Nobel Prize for Physics for his work on liquid helium.

landed *adj.* **1.** owning much land. **2.** consisting of land.

landfall *n.* viewing or nearing land after a sea or air journey.

landing *n.* **1.** the process of coming or bringing to land. **2.** a place for disembarking. **3.** the area at the top of a flight of stairs or between flights. —**landing craft**, a naval craft for putting ashore troops and equipment. **landing gear**, the undercarriage of an aircraft. **landing stage**, a platform for disembarking passengers and goods.

landlady *n.* a female ◊lessor.

Land League an Irish peasant-rights organization, formed by Michael ◊Davitt and Charles ◊Parnell in 1879 to fight against tenant evictions. Through its skilful use of the boycott against anyone who took a farm from which another had been evicted, it forced Gladstone's government to introduce a law in 1881 restricting rents and granting tenants security of tenure.

landless *adj.* holding no land.

landlord *n.* a person who lets rooms or keeps a boarding house, a public house etc.

landlubber *n.* a person with little or no experience of ships and the sea.

landmark *n.* **1.** a conspicuous and easily recognized feature of the landscape. **2.** an event marking an important stage in a process or history.

Landor /ˈlændɔː/ Walter Savage 1775–1864. English poet and essayist. He lived much of his life abroad, dying in Florence, where he had fled after a libel suit in 1858. His works include the epic *Gebir* 1798 and *Imaginary Conversations of Literary Men and Statesmen* 1824–29.

landowner *n.* one who owns land, especially a large area.

Landowska /læn'dɒfskə/ Wanda 1877–1959. Polish harpsichordist and scholar. She founded a school near Paris for the study of early music, and was for many years one of the few artists regularly performing on the harpsichord. She moved to the USA in 1941.

Land Registry, HM in England and Wales, the official body set up in 1925 to register legal rights to land.

Landsat *n.* a series of satellites used for monitoring Earth resources. The first was launched in 1972.

landscape /ˈlændskeɪp/ *n.* **1.** the features of a land area as seen in broad view. **2.** a picture of this. —*v.t./i.* to lay out or enhance (an area of land) with natural features. —**landscape gardening**, the laying-out of grounds to imitate natural scenery. [from Dutch]

Landseer /ˈlændsiə/ Edwin Henry 1802–1873. English painter, sculptor, and engraver of animal studies. Much of his work reflects the Victorian taste for sentimental and moralistic pictures, for example *Dignity and Impudence* 1839 (Tate Gallery, London).

landslide
mudflow landslide

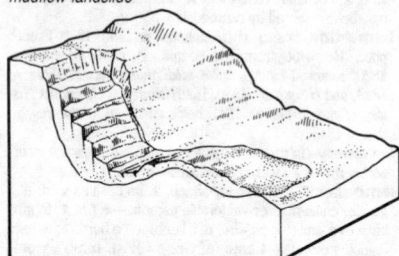

slump landslide

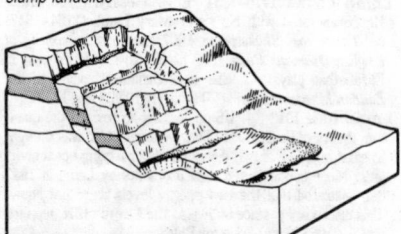

landslip landslide

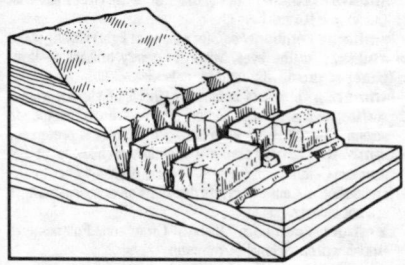

Land's End /lændz 'end/ a promontory of W Cornwall, 15 km/9 mi WSW of Penzance, the westernmost point of England.

landslide *n.* 1. a sudden downward movement of a mass of soil or rocks from a cliff or steep slope. 2. an overwhelming majority of votes for one side in an election.

landslip *n.* the sliding down of a mass of land on a slope or mountain.

Landsteiner /'lændstaɪnə/ Karl 1868–1943. Austrian immunologist who discovered the ABO ◊blood group system 1900–02, and aided in the discovery of the Rhesus blood factors in 1940. He also discovered the polio virus. He was awarded the Nobel Prize for Physiology and Medicine in 1930.

landward /'lændwəd/ *adv.* or **landwards** toward the land. —*adj.* going or facing towards the land.

lane *n.* 1. a narrow road or street. 2. a passage between rows of people. 3. a strip of road for one line of traffic. 4. a strip of track or water for a competitor in a race. 5. a regular course followed by or prescribed for ships or aircraft. [Old English]

Lanfranc /'lænfræŋk/ *c.*1010–1089. Italian archbishop of Canterbury from 1070; he rebuilt the cathedral, replaced English clergy by Normans, enforced clerical celibacy, and separated the ecclesiastical from the secular courts.

Lang /læŋ/ Andrew 1844–1912. Scottish historian and folklore scholar. His writings include historical works; anthropological essays, such as *Myth, Ritual and Religion* 1887 and *The Making of Religion* 1898, which involved him in controversy with the anthropologist James ◊Frazer; novels; and a series of children's books, beginning with *The Blue Fairy Tale Book* 1889.

Lang Fritz 1890–1976. Austrian film director whose films are characterized by a strong sense of social realism. His German movies include *Metropolis* 1927, the sensational *M* 1931 in which Peter Lorre starred as a child killer, and the series of Dr Mabuse films, after which he fled from the Nazis to Hollywood in 1936. His US films include *Fury* 1936, *You Only Live Once* 1937, *Scarlet Street* 1945 and *Rancho Notorious* 1952, and *The Big Heat* 1953. He returned to Germany and directed a third picture in the *Dr Mabuse* series in 1960.

Lange /'lɒŋi/ David (Russell) 1942– . New Zealand Labour Party prime minister 1983–89. Lange, a barrister, was elected to the House of Representatives in 1977. Labour had a decisive win in the 1984 general election on a non-nuclear military policy, which Lange immediately put into effect, despite criticism from the USA. He introduced a free-market economic policy and was re-elected in 1987. He resigned in Aug 1989 over a disagreement with his finance minister.

Langland /'læŋlənd/ William *c.*1332–*c.*1400. English poet. His alliterative *Vision Concerning Piers Plowman* appeared in three versions between about 1362 and 1398, but some critics believe he was only responsible for the first of these. The poem forms a series of allegorical visions, in which Piers develops from the typical poor peasant to a symbol of Jesus, and condemns the social and moral evils of 14th-century England.

Langobard /'læŋgəʊbɑːd/ alternative name for ◊Lombard, a member of a Germanic people.

Langton /'læŋtən/ Stephen *c.*1150–1228. English priest. He studied in Paris, where he became chancellor of the university, and in 1206 was created a cardinal. When in 1207 Pope Innocent III secured Langton's election as archbishop of Canterbury, King John refused to recognize him, and he was not allowed to enter England until 1213. He supported the barons in their struggle against John and was mainly responsible for drafting the charter of rights, the ◊Magna Carta.

Langtry /'læŋtri/ Lillie. Stage name of Emilie Charlotte le Breton 1853–1929. English actress, mistress of the future Edward VII. She was known as the 'Jersey Lily' from her birthplace and considered to be one of the most beautiful women of her time.

language /'læŋgwɪdʒ/ *n.* 1. words and their use; the faculty of speech. 2. a system of words prevalent in one or more countries or communities or in a profession etc. 3. a method or style of expression. See also ◊sign language (see under ◊sign). 4. a system of symbols and rules for computer programs. —**language laboratory,** a room with

tape recorders etc. for learning foreign languages. [from Old French from Latin *lingua* = tongue]

Languedoc /lɑːŋgə'dɒk/ former province of S France, bounded by the Rhône river, the Mediterranean sea, and the regions of Guienne and Gascony.

Languedoc-Roussillon /ruːsiː'jɒn/ region of S France, comprising the *départements* of Aude, Gard, Hérault, Lozère, and Pyrénées-Orientales; area 27,400 sq km/ 10,576 sq mi; population (1986) 2,012,000. Its capital is Montpellier, and products include fruit, vegetables, wine, and cheese.

languid /'læŋgwɪd/ *adj.* 1. lacking vigour, not inclined to exert oneself. 2. (of a stream etc., or *figurative*) slowmoving, slack. —**languidly** *adv.* [from French or Latin]

languish /'læŋgwɪʃ/ *v.i.* 1. to lose or lack vitality. 2. to live *under* depressing conditions; to be neglected. 3. to pine (*for*). [from Old French from Latin *languēre*]

languor /'læŋgə/ *n.* 1. a languid state, listlessness. 2. a soft or tender mood or effect. 3. an oppressive stillness of the air. —**languorous** *adj.*

langur *n.* a type of leaf-eating monkey that lives in trees in S Asia. It is related to the colobus monkey of Africa.

lank *adj.* 1. tall and lean. 2. (of grass, hair etc.) long and limp. [Old English]

lanky *adj.* ungracefully lean and tall or long. —**lankiness** *n.*

lanolin /'lænəlɪn/ *n.* a sticky, purified wax obtained from sheep's wool and used in cosmetics, soap, and leather preparation. [from German from Latin *lana* = wool and *oleum* = oil]

Lansbury /'lænzbəri/ George 1859–1940. British Labour politician. In 1921, while mayor of the London borough of Poplar, he went to prison with most of the council rather than modify their policy of more generous unemployment relief. He was a member of Parliament 1910–12 and 1922–40; he was leader of the parliamentary Labour party 1931–35, but resigned (as a pacifist) in opposition to the party's militant response to the Italian invasion of Abyssinia (present-day Ethiopia).

lantern /'læntən/ *n.* 1. a transparent case holding a light and shielding it from wind etc. 2. the light chamber of a lighthouse. 3. an erection on top of a dome or room, with glazed sides. —**lantern jaws,** long thin jaws giving the face a hollow look. [from Old French from Latin]

lanthanide /'lænθənaɪd/ *n.* any of a series of 15 rare earth elements from lanthanum to lutetium (atomic numbers 57–71); the same series excluding lanthanum itself. [from German]

lanthanum *n.* a soft, silvery, ductile and malleable, metallic element, symbol La, atomic number 57, relative atomic mass 138.91, the first of the ◊lanthanide series. It is used in making alloys. [from Greek *lanthanein* = to be hidden]

lanyard /'lænjəd/ *n.* 1. a short rope used on a ship for securing or fastening. 2. a cord worn round the neck or on the shoulder to which a knife etc. may be attached. [from Old French]

Lanzhou /læn'dʒəʊ/ formerly **Lanchow** capital of Gansu province, China, on the river Huang He, 190 km/120 mi S of the Great Wall; population (1986) 1,350,000. Industries include oil refining, chemicals, fertilizers, and synthetic rubber.

Lao /laʊ/ *n.* 1. a member of a predominantly Buddhist people living along the Mekong river system. There are approximately 9 million Lao in Thailand and 2 million in Laos. 2. the language of this people, a member of the Sino-Tibetan family.

Laois /liːʃ/ or **Laoighis** a county in Leinster province, Republic of Ireland; **area** 1,720 sq km/664 sq mi; **county town** Portlaoise; **physical** flat except for the Slieve Bloom mountains in the NW; **products** sugarbeets, dairy products, woollens, agricultural machinery; **population** (1986) 53,000.

Laos /laʊs/ Lao People's Democratic Republic; landlocked country in SE Asia, bordered to the N by China, E by Vietnam, S by Cambodia, and W by Thailand; **area** 236,790 sq km/91,400 sq mi; **capital** Vientiane; **physical** high mountains in E; Mekong River in W; jungle; **head of state** Prince Souphanouvong from 1975; Phoumi Vongvichit acting president from 1986; **head of government** Kaysone Phomvihane from 1975; **political system**

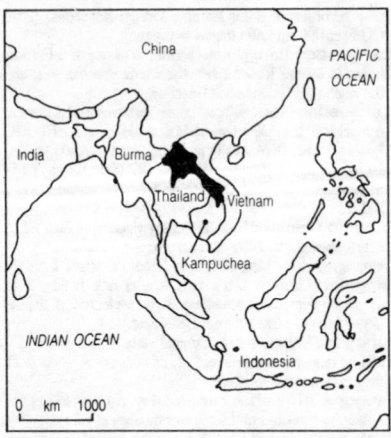

Laos

communism, one-party state; **exports** tin, teak, coffee, electricity; **population** (1990 est) 4,024,000 (Lao 48%, Thai 14%, Khmer 25%, Chinese 13%); **recent history** independence was achieved from France in 1954. In 1960 civil war followed a right-wing coup. In 1975 a communist-dominated republic was proclaimed. In 1988 the withdrawal was announced of 40% of Vietnamese forces stationed in Laos. The first assembly elections since the communist takeover were held in 1989, and a draft constitution was published in 1990.

Lao Zi /laʊˈdziː/ *c.* 604–531 BC. Chinese philosopher, commonly regarded as the founder of ◊Taoism. Nothing certain is known of his life, and he is variously said to have lived in the 6th or the 4th century BC. The *Tao Tê Ching,* the Taoist scripture, is attributed to him but apparently dates from the 3rd century BC.

lap[1] *n.* **1.** the flat area formed by the front of the thighs of a seated person; the part of a dress etc. covering this. **2.** one circuit of a racetrack etc. **3.** a section of a journey etc. **4.** the amount of overlap; an overlapping part. **5.** a single turn of thread etc. round a reel etc. —*v.t./i.* (**-pp-**) **1.** to be ahead of (a competitor in a race) by one or more laps. **2.** to fold or wrap (*about* or *round*); to enfold (*in* wraps); (especially in *passive*) to enfold caressingly. **3.** to cause to overlap. —**in the lap of the gods,** beyond human control. **in the lap of luxury,** in great luxury. **in a person's lap,** as his or her responsibility. **lapdog** *n.* a small pet dog. **lap of honour,** a ceremonial circuit of a racetrack etc. by the winner(s). **lap over,** to extend beyond (a limit). [Old English]

lap[2] *v.t./i.* (**-pp-**) **1.** to drink by scooping liquid with movements of the tongue. **2.** (usually with *up*) to take in (facts etc.) eagerly. **3.** to flow (against) in ripples making a gentle splashing sound. —*n.* an act or sound of lapping. [Old English]

laparotomy /læpəˈrɒtəmɪ/ *n.* an exploratory surgical cutting through the abdominal wall for access to the internal organs etc. in the abdomen. [from Greek *lapara* = flank]

La Paz /læ ˈpæz/ capital city of Bolivia, in Murillo province, 3,800 m/12,400 ft above sea level; population (1985) 992,600. Products include textiles and copper. La Paz was founded by the Spanish in 1548, and has been the seat of government since 1900.

lapel /ləˈpel/ *n.* the part of either side of a coat front etc. folded back against the outer surface. —**lapelled** *adj.*

lapidary /ˈlæpɪdərɪ/ *adj.* **1.** concerned with stones. **2.** engraved on stone. —*n.* a cutter, polisher, or engraver of gems. [from Latin *lapis* = stone]

lapis lazuli a deep blue mineral, made up of lazurite in a matrix of white calcite with small amounts of other minerals. It is a gemstone and a source of the pigment ultramarine. It occurs in silica-poor igneous rocks and metamorphic limestones in Afghanistan, Siberia, Iran, and Chile. [from Latin *lapis* = stone]

Laplace /læˈplæs/ Pierre Simon, Marquis de Laplace 1749–1827. French astronomer and mathematician. In 1796, he theorized that the solar system originated from a

cloud of gas (the nebular hypothesis). He studied the motion of the Moon and planets, and published a five-volume survey of ◊celestial mechanics, *Traité de méchanique céleste* 1799–1825. Among his mathematical achievements was the development of probability theory.

Lapland /ˈlæplænd/ region of Europe within the Arctic Circle in Norway, Sweden, Finland, and the USSR, without political definition. Its chief resources are chromium, copper, iron, timber, hydroelectric power, and tourism. There are about 20,000 Lapps, who live by hunting, fishing, reindeer herding, and handicrafts.

La Plata /læ ˈplɑːtə/ capital of Buenos Aires province, Argentina; population (1980) 560,300. Industries include meat packing and petroleum refining. It was founded in 1882.

la Plata, Río de or **River Plate** estuary in South America into which the rivers Paraná and Uruguay flow; length 320 km/200 mi and width up to 240 km/150 mi. The basin drains much of Argentina, Bolivia, Brazil, Uruguay, and Paraguay, who all cooperate in its development.

Lapp /læp/ *n.* **1.** a member of the indigenous population of the extreme north of Scandinavia. See also ◊Lapland. **2.** their language. —*adj.* of the Lapps or their language. —**Lappish** *adj.* [from Swedish]

lappet /ˈlæpɪt/ *n.* **1.** a flap or fold of a garment etc. or of flesh. **2.** a kind of large moth whose caterpillars have side lobes.

lapse *n.* **1.** a slight mistake, a slip of the memory etc. **2.** a weak or careless decline to an inferior state. **3.** the passage *of* time. —*v.i.* **1.** to fail to maintain a position or standard; to fall back (*into* an inferior or previous state). **2.** (of a right etc.) to become no longer valid because not used or claimed or renewed. **3.** (in *past participle*) that has lapsed. [from Latin *lapsus* (*labi* = slip, fall)]

laptop computer a portable ◊microcomputer, small enough to be used on the operator's lap. It consists of a single unit, incorporating a keyboard, ◊floppy disc or ◊hard disc drives, and a screen, the latter often forming a lid which folds back in use.

lapwing /ˈlæpwɪŋ/ *n.* a bird *Vanellus vanellus* of the plover family, also known as the **green plover** and, from its call, the **peewit**. It is bottle-green above and white below, with a long thin crest and rounded wings, and is about 30 cm/1 ft long. It inhabits moorland in Europe and Asia, making a nest scratched out of the ground.

larboard /ˈlɑːbəd/ *n.* & *adj.* ◊port[3].

larceny /ˈlɑːsənɪ/ *n.* the theft of personal goods. —**larcenous** *adj.* [from Old French from Latin *latro* = robber]

larch *n.* any deciduous coniferous tree of the genus *Larix,* family Pinaceae; its wood. [from Middle High German from Latin *larix*]

lard *n.* pig fat prepared for use in cooking etc. —*v.t.* **1.** to insert strips of bacon in (meat etc.) before cooking. **2.** to garnish (talk etc.) *with* strange terms etc. [from Old French = bacon, from Latin *lardum, lāridum*]

larder *n.* a room or cupboard for storing food. [from Anglo-French]

lardy *adj.* like lard. —**lardy cake,** *n.* cake made with lard, currants etc.

lares and penates in Roman mythology, spirits of the farm and of the store cupboard, often identified with the family ancestors, whose shrine was the centre of family worship in Roman homes.

large /lɑːdʒ/ *adj.* **1.** of considerable or relatively great size or extent. **2.** of the larger kind. **3.** of wide range, comprehensive. **4.** doing a thing on a large scale. —**at large,** at liberty; as a body or whole; with all details; without a specific aim. —**large-scale** *adj.* made or occurring on a large scale or in large amounts. —**largeness** *n.* [from Old French from Latin *largus* = copious]

Large Electron–Positron Collider (LEP) the world's largest particle ◊accelerator (sense 2), in operation from 1989 at the CERN laboratories near Geneva. It occupies a tunnel 3.8 m/12.5 ft wide and 27 km/16.7 mi long, which is buried 180 m/590 ft underground and forms a ring consisting of eight curved and eight straight sections.

large intestine in the ◊digestive system, the lower gut or bowels, made up of the colon, the caecum, and the rectum.

largely *adv.* to a great or preponderating extent.

largess /lɑːˈdʒes/ n. or **largesse** money or gifts freely given, especially on an occasion of rejoicing. [from Old French from Latin]

largo /ˈlɑːgəʊ/ adv. in music, in a slow tempo with a broad dignified treatment. —n. (*plural* **largos**) a movement to be played in this way. [Italian = broad]

Largo Caballero /kæbəˈjeərəʊ/ Francisco 1869–1946. Spanish socialist and leader of the Spanish Socialist Party (PSOE). He became prime minister of the Popular Front government elected in Feb 1936 and remained in office for the first ten months of the Civil War before being replaced by Juan Negrin (1887–1956) in May 1937.

lariat /ˈlæriət/ n. a lasso, a rope used to catch or tether a horse etc. [from Spanish *la reata* (*reatar* = tie again)]

La Rioja /læ riˈɒxə/ region of N Spain; area 5,000 sq km/ 1,930 sq mi; population (1986) 263,000.

lark[1] n. any small songbird of the family Alaudidae, especially the skylark. —**get up with the lark**, to get up early. [Old English]

lark[2] n. (*colloquial*) 1. a frolic or spree; an amusing incident. 2. an affair, a type of activity etc. —v.i. (*colloquial*) to play (*about*).

Larkin /ˈlɑːkɪn/ Philip 1922–1985. English poet. His perfectionist, pessimistic verse includes *The North Ship* 1945, *The Whitsun Weddings* 1964, and *High Windows* 1974. He edited *The Oxford Book of 20th-Century English Verse* 1973.

larkspur n. a plant of the genus *Delphinium*, with a spur-shaped ◊calyx.

larn v.t./i. jocular or vulgar variant of learn; (*colloquial*) to teach.

La Rochefoucauld /læ rɒʃfuːˈkəʊ/ François, duc de La Rochefoucauld 1613–1680. French writer. His *Réflexions, ou sentences et maximes morales/Reflections, or Moral Maxims* 1665 is a collection of brief, epigrammatic, and cynical observations on life and society, with the epigraph 'Our virtues are mostly our vices in disguise'. He was a lover of Mme de ◊Lafayette.

Larousse /læˈruːs/ Pierre 1817–1875. French grammarian and lexicographer. His encyclopedic dictionary, the *Grand dictionnaire universel du XIXème siècle/Great Universal 19th-Century Dictionary* 1865–76, was an influential work and continues in publications in revised form.

larrikin /ˈlærɪkɪn/ n. (*Australian*) a hooligan.

Lartigue /lɑːˈtiːg/ Jacques-Henri 1894–1986. French photographer. He began taking photographs of his family at the age of seven, and went on to make ◊autochrome colour prints of women. During his lifetime he took over 40,000 photographs, documenting everyday people and situations.

larva n. (*plural* **larvae** /-viː/) the immature form, between hatching and adulthood, of those species of animal in which the young have a different appearance and way of life from the adults. —**larval** adj. [Latin = ghost, mask]

laryngeal /ləˈrɪndʒiəl/ adj. of the larynx.

laryngitis /lærɪnˈdʒaɪtɪs/ n. an inflammation of the larynx, causing soreness of the throat, a dry cough, and hoarseness.

larynx /ˈlærɪŋks/ n. in mammals, a cavity at the upper end of the trachea (windpipe), containing the vocal cords. It is stiffened with cartilage and lined with mucous membrane. Amphibians and reptiles have much simpler larynxes, with no vocal cords. [from Greek]

lasagne /ləˈsænje/ n. pasta in a wide ribbon form, especially as served with minced meat and a sauce. [Italian plural, from Latin *lasanum* = cooking pot]

la Salle /lə ˈsæl/ René Robert Cavelier, Sieur de la Salle 1643–1687. French explorer. He made an epic voyage through North America, exploring the Mississippi River down to its mouth, and in 1682 founded Louisiana.

Lascar /ˈlæskə/ n. an East Indian seaman. [ultimately from Urdu and Persian]

Las Casas /læs ˈkɑːsəs/ Bartolomé de 1474–1566. Spanish missionary, historian, and colonial reformer, known as the **Apostle of the Indies**. He was the first European to call for the abolition of Indian slavery in Latin America. *Apologetica historia de las Indias* (first published 1875–76) is his account of Indian traditions and his witnessing of Spanish oppression of the Indians.

Lascaux /læsˈkəʊ/ a cave system in SW France, richly decorated with prehistoric wall paintings of buffaloes, horses, and red deer of the Upper Palaeolithic period,

Las Casas *Las Casas, Spanish missionary in the Americas who called for the abolition of Indian slavery.*

about 18,000 BC. The caves are closed to prevent deterioration of the pigments but the public are admitted to replicas nearby.

lascivious /ləˈsɪviəs/ adj. lustful; inciting to lust. —**lasciviously** adv., **lasciviousness** n. [from Latin *lascivus* = sportive, wanton]

laser /ˈleɪzə/ n. acronym from light amplification by stimulated emission of radiation, any device that is capable of producing a very intense, narrow, parallel beam of highly monochromatic and coherent light (or other electromagnetic radiation), either continuously or in pulses. Lasers operate by using light to stimulate the emission of more light of the same wavelength and phase by atoms or molecules that have been excited by some means. Their uses include communications, cutting, drilling, welding, satellite tracking, medical and biological research, and surgery.

laser printer a computer printer in which an image is formed by the action of a laser on a light-sensitive drum, then transferred to paper by means of an electrostatic charge. The image, which can be text or pictures, is made up of tiny dots, usually at a density of 120 per cm/300 per in.

laser surgery the use of intense light from a laser to cut, coagulate, and vaporize tissue. Less invasive than normal surgery, it destroys diseased tissue gently and allows quicker, more natural healing.

lash v.t./i. 1. to move in a sudden whiplike movement. 2. to strike with a whip; to beat or strike violently. 3. to attack violently in words. 4. to urge as with a lash. 5. to fasten or secure with cord etc. —n. 1. a stroke with a whip etc. (*literal* or *figurative*). 2. the flexible part of a whip. 3. an eyelash. —**lash out**, to hit or speak out angrily; to spend lavishly.

lashings n.pl. (*slang*) a lot (*of*).

Las Palmas /læs ˈpælməs/ or **Las Palmas de Gran Canaria** tourist resort on the NE coast of Gran Canaria, Canary Islands; population (1986) 372,000. Products include sugar and bananas.

lass /læs/ n. (also diminutive **lassie**) (especially *Scottish, N English*, or *poetic*) a girl. [from Old Norse = unmarried]

Lassa fever /ˈlæsə/ an acute disease caused by a virus, first detected in 1969, and spread by a species of rat found only in W Africa. It is characterized by high fever and inflammation of various organs. There is no known cure, the survival rate being less than 50%. [from *Lassa* in Nigeria]

Lassalle /læˈsæl/ Ferdinand 1825–1864. German socialist. He was imprisoned for his part in the ◊revolutions of 1848, during which he met ◊Marx, and in 1863 founded the General Association of German Workers (later the Social-Democratic Party). His publications include *The Working Man's Programme* 1862 and *The Open Letter* 1863. He was killed in a duel arising from a love affair.

lassitude /'læsɪtjuːd/ n. tiredness, listlessness. [French or from Latin *lassus* = tired]

lasso /læ'suː/ n. (*plural* **lassos**) a rope with a running noose, especially for catching cattle. —v.t. to catch with a lasso. [from Spanish]

Lassus /'læsəs/ Roland de. Also known as **Orlando di Lasso** c.1532–1594. Franco-Flemish composer. His works include polyphonic sacred music, songs, and madrigals, including settings of poems by his friend ◊Ronsard.

last[1] /lɑːst/ adj. **1.** after all the others in position or time, coming or belonging at the end. **2.** most recent; next before a specified time. **3.** only remaining. **4.** least likely, least suitable. —adv. **1.** (especially in combinations) after all the others. **2.** on the last occasion before the present. **3.** lastly. —n. **1.** a person or thing that is last. **2.** the last mention or sight. **3.** the last performance of certain actions; the end or last moment, death. —**at (long) last**, in the end, after much delay. **have the last laugh**, to be ultimately the victor. **last ditch**, a place of final desperate defence. **last minute** *or* **moment**, the time just before a decisive event. **last name**, a surname. **last rites**, rites for a dying person. **last straw**, an addition to a burden or difficulty that makes it finally unbearable. **last word**, a final or definitive statement; the latest fashion. [Old English = *latest*]

last[2] v.t./i. to remain unexhausted, adequate, or alive for a specified or long time; to continue for a specified time. —**last out**, to be strong enough or sufficient to last. [Old English]

last[3] n. a shoemaker's model for shaping a shoe etc. on. [Old English]

lasting adj. permanent, durable.

lastly adv. finally, in the last place.

Las Vegas /læs 'veɪgəs/ a city in Nevada, USA, known for its nightclubs and gambling casinos; population (1986) 202,000.

lat. abbreviation of latitude.

latch n. **1.** a bar with a catch and lever as the fastening of a gate etc. **2.** a spring lock preventing a door from being opened from the outside without the key after being shut. —v.t./i. to fasten with a latch. —**latch on to**, (*colloquial*) to attach oneself to; to understand. **on the latch**, fastened by the latch only. [from Old English]

latchkey n. a key of an outer door.

late adj. (*comparative* **later** *or* ◊**latter**; *superlative* **latest**, ◊**last**[1]) **1.** after the due or usual time; occurring or done etc. thus. **2.** far on in the day or night or in a time, period, or development. **3.** flowering or ripening towards the end of the season. **4.** no longer alive or having a specified status. **5.** of recent date. —adv. **1.** after the due or usual time. **2.** far on in time, at or until a late hour. **3.** at a late stage of development. **4.** formerly but not now. —**late in the day**, (*colloquial*) at a late stage in the proceedings. **of late**, recently. —**lateness** n. [Old English]

lateen /lə'tiːn/ adj. (of a sail) triangular and on a long yard at an angle of 45° to the mast. —**lateen-rigged** adj. rigged with such a sail. [from French *voile latine* = Latin sail (because common in the Mediterranean)]

lately adv. in recent times, not long ago. [Old English]

La Tène a prehistoric settlement near the E end of Lake Neuchâtel, Switzerland. It has given its name to an Iron Age culture which lasted from the 5th century BC to the Roman conquest; sites include Glastonbury Lake village, England.

latent /'leɪtənt/ adj. concealed, dormant, existing but not developed or manifest. —**latent heat**, the amount of heat lost or gained by a substance changing from a solid to a liquid or from a liquid to a vapour, without change of temperature. —**latency** n. [from Latin *latère* = be hidden]

lateral adj. **1.** of, at, towards, or from the side(s). **2.** descended from a brother or sister of a person in the direct line. —n. a lateral shoot or branch. —**lateral thinking**, seeking to solve problems by indirect or unexpected methods. —**laterally** adv. [from Latin *latus* = side]

lateral line system a system of sense organs in fishes and larval amphibians that detects water movement. It usually consists of a row of interconnected pores on either side of the body that divide into a system of canals across the head.

Lateran Treaties /'lætərən/ a series of agreements that marked the reconciliation of the Italian state with the papacy in 1929.

laterite n. a red residual soil characteristic of tropical rainforests. It is formed by the weathering of basalts, granites, and shales and contains a high percentage of aluminium and iron hydroxides.

latex /'leɪteks/ n. **1.** a milky fluid, containing proteins and other organic substances, exuded from the cut surface of certain plants, such as the rubber tree. **2.** a synthetic substance resembling this. [Latin = liquid]

lath /lɑː θ/ n. (*plural* **laths** /lɑːðz/) a thin, narrow strip of wood. [Old English]

lathe /leɪð/ n. a machine for shaping wood, metal etc., by rotating the article against cutting tools.

lather /'lɑːðə/ n. **1.** the froth produced by soap etc. mixed with water. **2.** frothy sweat, especially of a horse. **3.** a state of agitation. —v.t./i. **1.** to form a lather. **2.** to cover with a lather. **3.** to thrash. [Old English]

latifundium n. in ancient Rome, a large agricultural estate designed to make maximum use of cheap labour, of both free workmen or slaves.

Latimer /'lætɪmə/ Hugh 1490–1555. English Christian church reformer and bishop. After his conversion to Protestantism in 1524 he was imprisoned several times but was protected by Cardinal Wolsey and Henry VIII. He was burned for heresy.

Latin /'lætɪn/ n. the language of ancient Rome and its empire. —adj. **1.** of or in Latin. **2.** of W European culture, science, philosophy, and law during the Middle Ages and the Renaissance. **3.** of the countries or peoples (e.g. France, Spain) using the languages developed from Latin. **4.** of the Roman Catholic Church. —**Latin America**, the parts of Central and South America where Spanish or Portuguese is the main language. [from Old French or Latin *Latinus* (*Latium* = district of Italy including Rome)]

Latinate /'lætɪneɪt/ adj. like or having the character of Latin.

latish /'leɪtɪʃ/ adj. fairly late.

latitude /'lætɪtjuːd/ n. **1.** angular distance on a meridian; a place's angular distance north or south of the equator; (usually in plural) regions with reference to their distance from the equator. See also ◊longitude. **2.** freedom from restriction in action or opinion. [from Latin *latus* = broad]

latitudinarian /lætɪtjuːdiˈneərɪən/ adj. liberal, especially in religion. —n. a latitudinarian person.

La Tour /læ'tuə/ Georges de 1593–1652. French painter active in Lorraine. He was patronized by the duke of Lorraine and perhaps also by Louis XIII. Many of his pictures are illuminated by a single source of light, with deep contrasts of light and shade. They range from religious paintings to domestic genre scenes.

latrine /lə'triːn/ n. a lavatory in a camp or barracks etc.; a trench or pit for human excreta where there are no sewers. [French from Latin *lavare* = wash]

La Trobe /lə 'trəub/ Charles Joseph 1801–1875. Australian administrator. He was superintendent of Port Phillip district 1839–51 and first lieutenant-governor of Victoria 1851–54. The Latrobe River in Victoria is named after him.

latter adj. **1.** second-mentioned of two; last-mentioned of three or more. **2.** nearer to the end; recent; belonging to the end of a period, the world etc. —**the latter**, the latter person or thing. **latter-day** adj. modern, newfangled. **Latter-day Saints**, the Mormons' name for themselves. [Old English = *later*]

latterly adv. in the later part of life or of a period; of late.

lattice /'lætɪs/ n. **1.** a structure of crossed laths or bars with spaces between, used as a screen, fence etc. **2.** a regular arrangement of atoms or molecules. —**lattice window**, a window with small panes set in diagonally crossing strips of lead. [from Old French *lattis* (*latte* = lath)]

Latvia /'lætvɪə/ a constituent republic of W USSR from 1940, on the Baltic Sea; **area** 63,700 sq km/24,595 sq mi; **capital** Riga; **physical** lakes, marshes, wooded lowland; **products** meat and dairy products, communications equipment, consumer durables, motorcycles, locomotives; **population** (1987) 2,647,000; 54% Lett, 33% Russian; **language** Latvian; **recent history** there has been nationalist dissent since 1980. A Latvian popular front was established in Oct 1988 to campaign for independence, and a multiparty system is in place, with, following the republic's elections of Dec 1989, a coalition government set to be formed. In Oct 1988 the prewar flag was readopted and offical status given to the Latvian language. In Jan 1990

latitude and longitude

Point X lies on longitude 60°W

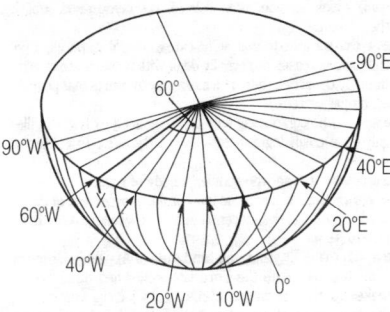

Point X lies on latitude 20°S

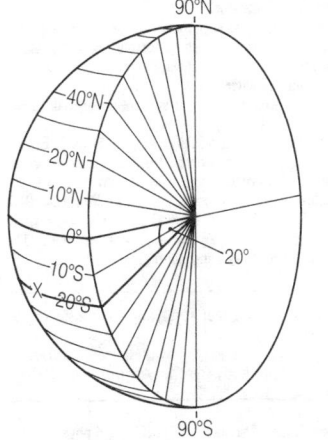

Together longitude 60°W latitude 20°S places point X on a precise position on the globe.

the Latvian Communist Party broke its links with Moscow and in May of the same year Latvia unilaterally declared its independence from the Soviet Union, subject to a 'transition period' for negotiation.

Latvian /'lætvɪən/ *adj.* of Latvia or its people or language. —*n.* 1. a native or inhabitant of Latvia. 2. (also *Lettish*) the language of Latvia.

Latynina /læ'tɪnɪnə/ Larissa Semyonovna 1935– . Soviet gymnast, winner of more Olympic medals than any other person in any sport. She won 18 between 1956 and 1964, including nine gold medals. She won a total of 12 individual Olympic and world championship gold medals.

laud /lɔːd/ *v.t.* to praise. —*n.* 1. praise, a hymn of praise. 2. (in *plural*) the first religious service of the day in the Western (Roman Catholic) Church. In the Book of Common Prayer parts of Lauds and Matins were combined to form the service of Morning Prayer. [from Latin *laudare* (*laus* = praise)]

Laud William 1573–1645. English priest. As archbishop of Canterbury from 1633, his High Church policy, support for Charles I's unparliamentary rule, censorship of the press, and persecution of the Puritans all aroused bitter opposition, while his strict enforcement of the statutes against ◊enclosures and of laws regulating wages and prices alienated the propertied classes. His attempt to impose the use of the Prayer Book on the Scots precipitated the English ◊Civil War. He was impeached by Parliament in 1640 and beheaded.

Lauda /'laʊdə/ Niki 1949– . Austrian motor racing driver, who won the world championship in 1975, 1977, and 1984. He was also runner-up in 1976 just six weeks after a horrific

accident at Nurburgring, Germany, which left him badly burned and permanently scarred.

laudable *adj.* commendable. —**laudability** /-'bɪlɪtɪ/ *n.*, **laudably** *adv.* .

laudanum /'lɔːdnəm, 'lɒd-/ *n.* tincture of opium, used formerly as a narcotic and painkiller. [originally name of a costly medicament prescribed by Paracelsus]

laudatory /'lɔːdətərɪ/ *adj.* praising.

Lauderdale /'lɔːdədeɪl/ John Maitland, Duke of Lauderdale 1616–1682. Scottish politician. Formerly a zealous ◊Covenanter, he joined the Royalists in 1647, and as High Commissioner for Scotland 1667–79 persecuted the Covenanters. He was created Duke of Lauderdale in 1672, and was a member of the so-called ◊Cabal ministry 1667–73.

laugh /lɑːf/ *v.t./i.* to make the sounds and movements usual in expressing lively amusement, scorn etc.; to utter with a laugh. —*n.* 1. a sound, act, or manner of laughing. 2. (*colloquial*) a comical thing. —**laugh at**, to ridicule. **laugh in** *or* **up one's sleeve**, to laugh secretly. **laugh off**, to get rid of (embarrassment or humiliation) with a jest. [Old English (imitative)]

laughable *adj.* ridiculous, causing amusement. —**laughably** *adv.*

laughing *n.* laughter. —**laughing gas**, nitrous oxide as an anaesthetic, with an exhilarating effect when inhaled. **laughing stock**, a person or thing generally ridiculed. **no laughing matter**, a serious thing.

laughter /'lɑːftə/ *n.* the act or sound of laughing.

Laughton /'lɔːtn/ Charles 1899–1962. English actor, who became a US citizen in 1950. Initially a classical stage actor, his dramatic film roles included the king in *The Private Life of Henry VIII* 1933 (for which he won an Academy Award), Captain Bligh in *Mutiny on the Bounty* 1935, Quasimodo in *The Hunchback of Notre Dame* 1939, and Gracchus in *Spartacus* 1960.

launch[1] /lɔːntʃ/ *v.t./i.* 1. to cause (a ship) to move or slide from land into the water. 2. to send forth by hurling or thrusting; to send on its course. 3. to put into action; to enter boldly or freely on a course of action. —*n.* the launching of a ship or spacecraft etc., or of an enterprise. —**launch out**, to spend money freely; to burst out into strong language; to start on an ambitious enterprise. —**launcher** *n.* [from Anglo-French]

launch[2] *n.* 1. a large motor boat. 2. a warship's largest boat. [from Spanish]

launder /'lɔːndə/ *v.t.* 1. to wash and iron (clothes etc.). 2. to transfer (funds) so as to conceal their illegal origin. [from Old French *lavandier* = washer of linen from Latin *lavare* = to wash]

launderette *n.* or **laundrette** a premises containing coin-operated washing machines for public use.

laundress /'lɔːndrɪs/ *n.* a woman whose job is to launder clothes, sheets etc.

laundry *n.* 1. a place for washing clothes. 2. a batch of clothes to be laundered.

Laurasia /lɔːˈreɪʃə/ a former land mass or supercontinent, formed by the fusion of North America, Greenland, Europe, and Asia. It made up the northern half of ◊Pangaea, the 'world continent' that is thought to have existed between 250 and 200 million years ago. The southern half was ◊Gondwanaland.

laureate /'lɒrɪət, 'lɔː-/ *adj.* wreathed with laurel as an honour. —*n.* a poet laureate. —**laureateship** *n.* [from Latin *laureatus* (*laurea* = laurel wreath)]

laurel /'lɒrəl/ *n.* 1. an evergreen shrub *Prunus laurocerasus* with dark, glossy leaves. 2. (in *singular* or *plural*) a wreath of bay leaves *Laurus nobilis* as an emblem of victory or poetic merit. —**look to one's laurels**, to take care not to lose pre-eminence. **rest on one's laurels**, not to seek further success. [from Old French from Provençal from Latin *laurus* = bay tree]

Laurel and Hardy /'hɑːdɪ/ Stan Laurel, stage name of Arthur Stanley Jefferson (1890–1965), and Oliver Hardy (1892–1957). US film comedians who were the most successful comedy team in film history (Stan was slim; Oliver, rotund). Their unique partnership began in 1927, survived the transition from silent films to sound, and resulted in more than 200 short and feature-length films.

Laurence /'lɒrəns/ Margaret 1926–1987. Canadian writer, whose novels include *A Jest of God* 1966 and *The Diviners*

1974. She also wrote short stories set in Africa, where she lived for a time.

Laurier /ˈlɒrieɪ/ Wilfrid 1841–1919. Canadian politician, leader of the Liberal Party 1887–1919 and prime minister 1896–1911. The first French-Canadian to hold the office, he encouraged immigration into Canada from Europe and the USA, established a separate Canadian navy, and sent troops to help Britain in the Boer War.

laurustinus *n.* an evergreen shrub *Viburnum tinus* of the family Caprifoliaceae, of Mediterranean origin. It has clusters of white or pink flowers in winter.

Lausanne /loʊˈzæn/ resort and capital of Vaud canton, W Switzerland, above the N shore of Lake Geneva; population (1987) 262,000. Industries include chocolate, scientific instruments, and publishing.

lav *n.* (*colloquial*) a lavatory. [abbreviation]

lava /ˈlɑːvə/ *n.* a molten material that erupts from a ◊volcano and cools to form extrusive ◊igneous rock. [Italian from Latin *lavare* = to wash]

Laval /ləˈvæl/ Pierre 1883–1945. French right-wing politician. He was prime minister and foreign secretary 1931–32, and again 1935–36. In World War II he joined Pétain's ◊Vichy government as vice-premier in June 1940; dismissed in Dec 1940, he was reinstated by Hitler's orders as head of the government and foreign minister in 1942. After the war he was executed.

La Vallière /læ væliˈeə/ Louise de la Baume le Blance, Duchesse de La Vallière 1644–1710. Mistress of the French king Louis XIV; she gave birth to four children 1661–74. She retired to a convent when superseded in his affections by the Marquise de Montespan.

lavatory /ˈlævətəri, -tri/ *n.* a pan (usually a fixture) into which urine and faeces may be discharged for hygienic disposal; a room, building, or compartment containing this. [from Latin *lavare* = wash]

lave *v.t.* (*literary*) to wash or bathe; (of water) to wash against, to flow along. [from Old French from Latin *lavare* = wash]

lavender /ˈlævɪndə/ *n.* 1. a sweet-smelling herb of the genus *Lavandula*, family Labiatae, native to W Mediterranean countries. 2. a light purple colour. —**lavender water,** a light perfume made from lavender. [from Anglo-French from Latin]

laver /ˈleɪvə, ˈlɑː-/ *n.* edible seaweed. [Latin]

lavish /ˈlævɪʃ/ *v.t.* to bestow or spend (money, effort, praise etc.) abundantly. —*adj.* giving or producing in large quantities. —**lavishly** *adv.*, **lavishness** *n.* [originally = profusion, from Old French *lavasse* = deluge of rain]

Lavoisier /læˈvwæzieɪ/ Antoine Laurent 1743–1794. French chemist. He proved that combustion needed only a part of the air, which he called oxygen, thereby destroying the theory of phlogiston (an imaginary 'fire element' released during combustion). With Pierre Laplace (1749–1827), he showed that water was a compound of oxygen and hydrogen. In this way he established the basic rules of chemical combination.

Lavrentiev /læˈvrentief/ Mikhail 1900– . Soviet scientist who developed the Akademgorodok ('Science City') in Novosibirsk, Russia, from 1957.

law /lɔː/ *n.* 1. a rule established in a community by authority or custom; a body of such rules; the controlling influence of or obedience to this; the subject or study of such rules. In western Europe there are two main systems: ◊Roman law and ◊English law. 2. the legal profession. 3. (*colloquial*) the police. 4. a judicial remedy; the lawcourts providing it. 5. a divine commandment; **the Law,** the Jewish name for the Pentateuch. 6. something that must be obeyed. 7. a factual statement of what always happens in certain circumstances; a regularity in natural occurrences. —**be a law unto oneself,** to disregard custom. **law-abiding** *adj.* obedient to the laws. **take the law into one's own hands,** to redress a grievance by one's own means, especially by force. [Old English from Old Norse *lag* = something 'laid down' or fixed]

Law Andrew Bonar 1858–1923. British Conservative politician, born in New Brunswick, Canada. He made a fortune in Scotland as a banker and iron merchant, and entered Parliament in 1900. Elected leader of the opposition in 1911, he became colonial secretary in Asquith's coalition government 1915–16, chancellor of the Exchequer 1916–19, and Lord Privy Seal 1919–21 in Lloyd George's coalition. He

formed a Conservative Cabinet in 1922, but resigned on health grounds.

Law Commissions in Britain, statutory bodies established in 1965 (one for England and Wales and one for Scotland) which consider proposals for law reform and publish their findings.

law court a body that adjudicates in legal disputes. Civil and criminal cases are usually dealt with by separate courts. In many countries there is a hierarchy of courts that provide an appeal system.

lawful *adj.* conforming with or recognized by law; not illegal; (of a child) legitimate. —**lawfully** *adv.*, **lawfulness** *n.*

lawgiver *n.* one who codifies a body of laws.

lawless *adj.* 1. having no laws or no enforcement of them. 2. disregarding laws, uncontrolled. —**lawlessly** *adv.*, **lawlessness** *n.*

law lords in England, the ten Lords of Appeal in Ordinary who, together with the Lord Chancellor and other peers, make up the House of Lords in its judicial capacity as the final court of appeal in both criminal and civil cases. Law Lords rank as life peers. Their total number must not exeed 11.

lawmaker *n.* a legislator.

lawn[1] *n.* a piece of grass kept mown and smooth in a garden etc. —**lawn mower,** a machine for cutting the grass of lawns. **lawn tennis,** see ◊tennis. [from obsolete *laund* = glade from Old French]

lawn[2] *n.* a fine woven cotton or synthetic material. [probably from *Laon* in France]

Lawrence /ˈlɒrəns/ D(avid) H(erbert) 1885–1930. English writer whose work expresses his belief in emotion and the sexual impulse as creative and true to human nature. His novels include *Sons and Lovers* 1913, *The Rainbow* 1915, *Women in Love* 1921, and *Lady Chatterley's Lover* 1928. Lawrence also wrote short stories (for example 'The Woman Who Rode Away') and poetry.

> I like to write when I feel spiteful: it's like having a good sneeze.
>
> **David Herbert Lawrence**
> letter to Lady Cynthia Asquith Nov 1913

Lawrence Ernest O(rlando) 1901–1958. US physicist. His invention of the cyclotron pioneered the production of artificial radioisotopes. He was awarded the Nobel Prize for Physics in 1939.

Lawrence T(homas) E(dward), known as **Lawrence of Arabia** 1888–1935. British soldier and writer. Appointed to the military intelligence department in Cairo, Egypt, during World War I, he took part in negotiations for an Arab revolt against the Ottoman Turks, and in 1916 attached himself to the emir Faisal. He became a guerrilla leader of genius, combining raids on Turkish communications with the organization of a joint Arab revolt, described in *The Seven Pillars of Wisdom* 1935.

Lawrence Thomas 1769–1830. British painter, the leading portraitist of his day. He became painter to George III in 1792 and president of the Royal Academy in 1820.

lawrencium /ləˈrensiəm/ *n.* a synthesized, radioactive, metallic element, the last of the ◊actinide series, symbol Lr, atomic number 103, relative atomic mass 262. It has a half-life of about a minute and was originally synthesized at the University of California at Berkeley in 1961 by bombarding californium with boron nuclei. [from E O *Lawrence*]

Lawson /ˈlɔːsən/ Nigel 1932– . British Conservative politician. A former financial journalist, he was financial secretary to the Treasury 1979–81, secretary of state for energy 1981–83, and chancellor of the Exchequer from 1983. He resigned in 1989 after criticism of his policy of British membership of the ◊European Monetary System by government adviser Alan Walters.

lawsuit *n.* a prosecution of a claim in a lawcourt.

law, rule of the principle that law (as administered by the ordinary courts) is supreme and that all citizens (including members of the government) are equally subject to it and equally entitled to its protection.

lawyer /ˈlɔːjə/ *n.* a person pursuing law as a profession; a solicitor; an expert at law.

lax *adj.* not strict, careless, slack. —**laxity** *n.*, **laxly** *adv.* [from Latin]

laxative /'læksətɪv/ *adj.* tending to cause or facilitate evacuation of the bowels. —*n.* a medicine for this. [from Old French or Latin *laxare* = loosen]

lay[1] *v.t./i.* (*past* and *past participle* **laid**) 1. to place on a surface or in a certain position; to place or arrange in a horizontal position, to put into place; to locate (a scene). 2. to apply or impose; to assign. 3. to present or put forward for consideration. 4. (of a hen bird) to produce (an egg, or *absolute*). 5. to cause to subside or lie flat. 6. to stake as a wager, to bet. 7. to prepare (a plan or trap). 8. to prepare (a table) for a meal; to arrange fuel for (a fire). 9. to coat or strew *with*. 10. (*slang*) to have sexual intercourse with. —*n.* 1. the way, position, or direction in which something lies. 2. (*slang*) a partner in sexual intercourse. —**in lay**, (of a hen) laying eggs regularly. **laid paper**, paper with the surface marked in fine ribs. **lay about one**, to hit out on all sides. **lay bare**, to reveal. **lay down**, to put on the ground etc.; to give up (office); to establish as a rule or instruction; to store (wine) in a cellar for future use; to sacrifice (one's life). **lay down the law**, to talk authoritatively or as if sure of being right. **lay hands on**, to seize or attack. **lay one's hands on**, to obtain; to be able to find. **lay hold of**, to seize or grasp. **lay in**, to provide oneself with a stock of. **lay into**, (*slang*) to punish or scold harshly. **lay it on thick** *or* **with a trowel**, (*slang*) to exaggerate greatly. **lay low**, to overthrow; to humble; to incapacitate. **lay off**, to discharge (workers) temporarily through shortage of work; (*colloquial*) to cease, especially from causing trouble or annoyance. **lay-off** *n.* a temporary discharge of workers. **lay on**, to inflict blows forcibly; to provide; to spread (paint etc.). **lay open**, to break the skin of; to expose *oneself* (to criticism etc.). **lay out**, to arrange according to a plan; to prepare (a body) for burial; to spend (money) for a purpose; (*colloquial*) to knock unconscious; to cause (oneself) to make every effort. **lay up**, to store or save; to cause (a person) to be confined to bed or unfit for work etc. **lay waste**, to destroy the crops and buildings of. [Old English]

lay[2] *adj.* 1. nonclerical; not ordained into the clergy. 2. not professionally qualified, especially in law or medicine; of or done by such persons. —**lay reader**, a layman licensed to conduct some religious services. [from French from Latin from Greek *laïkos* (*laos* = people)]

lay[3] *n.* a minstrel's song, a ballad. [from Old French or Provençal]

lay[4] past of **lie**[1].

layabout *n.* a habitual loafer or idler.

Layamon /'laɪəmən/ lived about 1200. English poet, author of the *Brut*, a chronicle of about 30,000 alliterative lines on the history of Britain from the legendary Brutus onwards, which gives the earliest version of the Arthurian story in English.

Layard /'leɪəd/ Austen Henry 1817–1894. British archaeologist. He travelled to the Middle East in 1839, conducted two expeditions to Nineveh and Babylon 1845–51, and sent to the UK the specimens forming the greater part of the Assyrian collection in the British Museum.

lay-by *n.* (*plural* **lay-bys**) an extra strip at the side of the open road for vehicles to stop temporarily.

layer *n.* 1. a thickness of matter, especially one of several, spread over a surface. 2. a person etc. that lays. 3. a shoot fastened down to take root while attached to the parent plant. —*v.t.* 1. to arrange or cut (hair) in layers. 2. to propagate (a plant) by fastening down an attached shoot to take root.

layette /leɪ'et/ *n.* the clothes etc. prepared for a new-born child. [French, diminutive of Old French *laie* = drawer from Middle Dutch]

lay figure 1. a jointed figure of the human body used by artists for arranging drapery on etc. 2. an unreal character in a novel etc. 3. a person lacking in individuality.

layman *n.* or **laywoman** (*plural* **laymen, laywomen**) 1. a person not in holy orders. 2. a person without professional or special knowledge.

layout *n.* the disposing or arrangement of ground, printed matter etc.; a thing arranged thus.

layshaft *n.* a second or intermediate transmission shaft in a machine.

Lazarus /'læzərəs/ in the New Testament, the brother of Martha, a friend of Jesus, raised by him from the dead. Lazarus is also the name of a beggar in a parable told by Jesus (Luke 16).

Lazarus Emma 1849–1887. US poet, author of the poem on the base of the Statue of Liberty which includes the words: 'Give me your tired, your poor/Your huddled masses yearning to breathe free.'

laze *v.i.* (*colloquial*) to spend time doing nothing or relaxing. —*n.* a spell of lazing.

Lazio /'lætsɪəʊ/ (Roman Latium) a region of W central Italy; **area** 17,200 sq km/6,639 sq mi; **capital** Rome; **population** (1988) 5,137,000. Products include olives, wine, chemicals, pharmaceuticals, and textiles. Home of the Latins from the 10th century BC, it was dominated by the Romans from the 4th century BC.

lazy *adj.* 1. disinclined to work, doing little work. 2. of or inducing idleness. —**lazybones** *n.* a lazy person. —**lazily** *adv.*, **laziness** *n.*

lb symbol for pound(s) weight. [from Latin *libra*]

l.b.w. abbreviation of ◊leg before wicket (see ◊leg).

l.c. abbreviation of 1. in the passage etc. cited. [from Latin *loco citato*] 2. lower case, or 'small' letters, as opposed to capitals.

LCD abbreviation of ◊liquid crystal display.

LCM abbreviation of lowest common multiple.

L-dopa /el'dəʊpə/ *n.* a chemical, normally produced by the body, which is converted by an enzyme in the bloodstream to dopamine in the brain. It is essential for integrated movement of localized muscle groups.

LDR abbreviation of light-dependent resistor, a resistor which conducts electricity better when light falls on it. LDRs are made from ◊semiconductors, such as cadmium sulphide, and are used in electric eye burglar alarms and light meters.

lea *n.* (*poetic*) a piece of meadow or pasture or arable land. [Old English]

LEA in the UK, abbreviation of local education authority.

leach *v.t.* to make (liquid) percolate through some material; to subject (bark, ore, ash, soil) to the action of a percolating fluid; (with *away* or *out*) to remove or be removed thus. [probably from Old English *leccan* = to water]

Leach /li:tʃ/ Bernard 1887–1979. British potter. His simple designs, inspired by a period of study in Japan, pioneered a revival of the art. He established the Leach Pottery at St Ives, Cornwall, in 1920.

leaching *n.* a process by which substances are washed out of the ◊soil[1]. Fertilizers leached out of the soil find their way into rivers and cause water pollution. In tropical areas, leaching of the soil after ◊deforestation removes scarce nutrients and leads to a dramatic loss of soil fertility.

Leacock /'li:kɒk/ Stephen Butler 1869–1944. Canadian humorist, whose writings include *Literary Lapses* 1910, *Sunshine Sketches of a Little Town* 1912, and *Frenzied Fiction* 1918.

lead[1] /li:d/ *v.t./i.* (*past* and *past participle* **led**) 1. to cause to go with one, to guide or help to go, especially by going in front or by taking a person's hand or an animal's halter etc. 2. to influence the actions or opinions of, to guide by persuasion, example, or argument. 3. to provide access; (with *to*) to have as its result. 4. to make (a rope, water etc.) go in a certain course. 5. to live or go through (a life etc. of a specified kind). 6. to have the first place in; to go first; to be first in a race or game. 7. to be in charge of; to be pre-eminent in some field. 8. in card games, to play as one's first card; to be the first player in a trick. —*n.* 1. guidance given by going in front; an example; a clue. 2. the leader's place; the amount by which a competitor is ahead of the others. 3. a strip of leather or cord for leading a dog etc. 4. a conductor (usually a wire) conveying an electric current to the place of use. 5. the chief part in a play etc.; its player. 6. in card games, the act or right of playing first; a card so played. —**lead by the nose**, to control the actions of (a person) completely. **lead off**, to begin. **lead on**, to entice. **lead up the garden path**, to mislead. **lead up to**, to form the preparation for or introduction to; to direct a conversation towards. [Old English]

lead[2] /led/ *n.* 1. a heavy, soft grey metallic element, symbol Pb, (Latin *plumbum*) atomic number 82, relative atomic mass 207.19. It is bluish-grey, and the heaviest, softest, and weakest of the common metals. Lead is used as a shield for radioactive sources, and in ammunition, batteries, glass, ceramics, and alloys such as pewter and solder. Lead is a cumulative poison within the body, and lead water pipes and lead-based paints are a health hazard, as is the use of lead in 'anti-knock' petrol additives. 2. (also called 'black lead') the graphite used in pencils; a stick of this. 3. a lump of lead used for taking soundings in water. 4. (in *plural*) strips of lead covering a roof; a piece of lead-covered roof; the lead frames holding the glass of a lattice etc. 5. a metal strip in printing to give a space between lines. 6. (*attributive*) made of lead. —*v.t.* to cover, weight, frame, or space with lead(s). —**lead pencil,** a pencil of graphite enclosed in wood. —**leaded** *adj.* [Old English]

lead—acid cell a type of ◊accumulator (storage battery).

leaded petrol a type of petrol containing the lead compound tetraethyllead, $(C_2H_5)_4Pb$, an anti-knock agent. It improves the combustion of petrol and the performance of a car engine. The lead from the exhaust fumes enters the atmosphere, mostly as simple lead compounds.

leaden /'ledən/ *adj.* 1. of or like lead, heavy or slow. 2. lead-coloured.

leader /'li:də/ *n.* 1. a person or thing that leads; a person followed by others. 2. the principal first violin in an orchestra, or the first violin in a quartet etc. 3. a leading article. —**Leader of the House,** a member of the government in the House of Commons or Lords who arranges and announces the business of the House. —**leadership** *n.*

leading[1] /'li:dɪŋ/ *adj.* direct, most important. —**leading aircraftman,** one ranking above aircraftman. **leading article,** a newspaper article giving the editorial opinion. **leading light,** a prominent and influential person. **leading note,** the seventh note of the diatonic scale. **leading question,** one prompting the desired answer.

leading[2] /'ledɪŋ/ *n.* a covering or framework of lead.

leaf *n.* (*plural* **leaves**) 1. a lateral outgrowth of a plant, usually on a stem, and in most species the primary organ of ◊photosynthesis; (*collectively*) leaves. 2. the state of having leaves out. 3. a single thickness of paper, especially in a book with each side forming a page. 4. a very thin sheet of metal etc. 5. a hinged flap of a table etc.; an extra section inserted to extend a table. —*v.i.* to put forth leaves. —**leaf mould,** soil, chiefly composed of decaying leaves. **leaf through,** to turn over the pages of (a book etc.). —**leafy** *adj.* [Old English]

leafage *n.* the leaves of plants.

leaf-hopper *n.* any of numerous species of ◊bug of the family Cicadellidae. They feed on the sap of leaves. Each species is associated with only a limited range of plants.

leaf insect an insect of the order Phasmida, about 10 cm/ 4 in long, with a green, flattened body, remarkable for closely resembling the foliage on which it lives. It is most common in SE Asia.

leaflet *n.* 1. a division of a compound leaf; a young leaf. 2. a sheet of paper (sometimes folded but not stitched) giving information, especially for free distribution.

league[1] /li:g/ *n.* 1. a group of people or countries etc. combining for a particular purpose. 2. an agreement to combine in this way. 3. a group of sports clubs which compete against each other for a championship. 4. a class of contestants. —*v.t./i.* to join in a league. —**in league,** allied, conspiring. **league table,** a list of contestants etc. in order of merit. [from French or Italian *legare* = bind from Latin]

league[2] *n.* (*archaic*) a varying measure of travelling distance, usually about 3 miles. [ultimately from Latin]

League of Nations an international organization formed after World War I to solve international disputes by arbitration. It was dissolved in 1946. Its subsidiaries included the **International Labour Organization** and the **Permanent Court of International Justice** in The Hague, Netherlands, both now under the auspices of the ◊United Nations.

leak *n.* 1. a hole or crack etc. through which liquid or gas passes wrongly in or out. 2. the liquid or gas passing through this. 3. a similar escape of an electric charge; the charge that escapes. 4. a disclosure of secret information. —*v.t./i.* 1. to escape wrongly through an opening. 2. (of a container) to allow such escape; to let out (liquid or gas) wrongly. 3. to disclose (a secret). —**leak out,** (of a secret) to become known. —**leaky** *adj.*

leakage *n.* 1. leaking. 2. that which has leaked out.

Leakey /'li:ki/ Louis (Seymour Bazett) 1903–1972. British archaeologist, born in Kenya. In 1958, with his wife Mary Leakey, he discovered fossils of gigantic extinct animals in ◊Olduvai Gorge, as well as many remains of an early human type.

Leakey Mary 1913– . British archaeologist. In 1948, she discovered, on Rusinga Island, Lake Victoria, E Africa, the prehistoric ape skull known as *Proconsul*, about 20 million years old; and human remains at Laetolil, to the south, about 3,750,000 years old.

Leakey Richard 1944– . British archaeologist, son of Louis and Mary Leakey. In 1972 he discovered at Lake Turkana, Kenya, an apelike skull, estimated to be about 2.9 million years old; it had some human characteristics and a brain capacity of 800 cu cm. In 1984 his team found an almost complete skeleton of *Homo erectus*, some 1.6 million years old.

lean[1] *v.t.* (*past* and *past participle* **leaned** or **leant** /lent/) 1. to be or put in a sloping position; to incline from the perpendicular. 2. to rest *against, on,* or *upon* for support. 3. to rely *on* or *upon* for help. 4. to be inclined or have a leaning *to* or *towards.* —*n.* a deviation from the perpendicular, an inclination. —**lean on,** (*slang*) to put pressure on (a person) to make him or her cooperate. **lean-to** *n.* a building with the roof resting against a larger building or wall. [Old English]

lean[2] *adj.* 1. (of a person or animal) without much flesh, having no superfluous fat. 2. (of meat) containing little fat. 3. meagre. —*n.* the lean part of meat (as opposed to *fat*). —**lean years,** a period of scarcity. —**leanness** *n.* [Old English]

Lean /li:n/ David 1908–1991. English film director. His atmospheric films include *Brief Encounter* 1946, *The Bridge on the River Kwai* 1957, *Lawrence of Arabia* 1962 (Academy Award), a revamped version released in 1990, and *A Passage to India* 1985.

leaning *n.* a tendency or partiality.

leap *v.t./i.* (*past* and *past participle* **leaped** /li:pt, lept/ or **leapt** /lept/) to jump or spring vigorously. —*n.* a vigorous jump. —**by leaps and bounds,** with startlingly rapid progress. **leap in the dark,** a rash step or enterprise. **leap year,** a year with 366 days (including 29 Feb as an intercalary day). [Old English]

leapfrog *n.* a game in which the players in turn vault with parted legs over another who is bending down. —*v.t./i.* (-gg-) 1. to perform such a vault (over). 2. to overtake alternately.

Lear /liə/ Edward 1812–1888. English artist and humorist. His *Book of Nonsense* 1846 popularized the limerick. He first attracted attention by his paintings of birds, and later turned to landscapes. He travelled to Italy, Greece, Egypt, and India, publishing books on his travels with his own illustrations, and spent most of his later life in Italy.

learn /lɜ:n/ *v.t./i.* (*past* and *past participle* **learned** /lɜ:nt, learnt) 1. to gain knowledge of or skill in by study, experience, or being taught. 2. to commit to memory. 3. to receive instruction; to become aware *of* by information or observation. 4. (*archaic, vulgar,* or *jocular*) to teach. [Old English]

learned /'lɜ:nɪd/ *adj.* 1. having much knowledge acquired by study; showing or requiring learning. 2. concerned with the interests of learned persons. —**learnedly** *adv.*

learner *n.* one who is learning a subject or skill. —**learner driver,** one who is learning to drive a motor vehicle but has not yet passed a driving test.

learning *n.* knowledge acquired by study.

learning theory in psychology, a theory about how an organism acquires new behaviours. Two main theories are classical and operant ◊conditioning.

lease /li:s/ *n.* a contract by which the owner of a building or land allows another to use it for a specified time, usually in return for payment. —*v.t.* to grant or take on lease. —**a new lease of** or (*US*) **on life,** an improved prospect of living or of use after repair. [from Anglo-French *lesser* = let]

leasehold *n.* the holding of property by lease; property held thus. —**leaseholder** *n.* See also ◊lessee; ◊lessor.

leash *n.* a thong for holding hounds etc. under restraint; a dog's lead. —*v.t.* to put a leash on; to hold in a leash. —**straining at the leash,** eager to begin. [from Old French *laisser* = let run on slack lead]

least *adj.* 1. smallest in amount or degree; of a very small species etc. 2. lowest in rank or importance. —*n.* the least amount. —*adv.* in the least degree. —**at least,** at all events, anyway; not less than. **(in) the least,** at all. **to say the least (of it),** putting the case moderately. [Old English]

leather /'leðə/ *n.* 1. material made from animal skins by tanning or a similar process. 2. the leather part(s) of something. 3. a piece of leather for polishing with. 4. (in *plural*) leggings, breeches. —*v.t.* 1. to cover with leather. 2. to polish or wipe with a leather. 3. to beat, to thrash. —**leatherback** *n.* the largest existing turtle *Sphargis coriacea* with a flexible shell. **leatherjacket** *n.* a crane-fly grub, which has a tough skin. [Old English]

leatherette /leðə'ret/ *n.* an imitation leather.

leathery *adj.* like leather; tough. —**leatheriness** *n.*

leave[1] *v.t./i.* (*past* and *past participle* **left**) 1. to go away (from); to go away finally or permanently; to abandon, to desert. 2. to cease to reside at or belong to or work for. 3. to cause or allow to remain; to depart without taking. 4. to have remaining after one's death. 5. to give as a legacy. 6. to allow to stay or proceed without interference. 7. to commit or refer *to* another person; to depute (a person) to perform a function in one's absence. 8. to refrain from consuming or dealing with. 9. to deposit for collection or transmission. —**leave alone,** to refrain from disturbing; not to interfere with. **leave off,** to discontinue; to come to or make an end. **leave out,** to omit. **left luggage,** luggage deposited for later retrieval. **leftovers** *n.pl.* items (especially food) remaining after the rest has been used. [Old English]

leave[2] *n.* 1. permission. 2. permission to be absent from duty; the period for which this lasts. —**on leave,** legitimately absent from duty. **take (one's) leave (of),** to bid farewell (to). **take leave of one's senses,** to go mad. [Old English]

leaved *adj.* having leaves; having a specified number of leaves.

leaven /'levən/ *n.* 1. a substance (especially yeast) used to make dough ferment and rise. 2. a pervasive transforming influence; an admixture *of* some quality. —*v.t.* 1. to ferment (dough) with leaven. 2. to permeate and transform; to modify *with* a tempering element. [from Old French from Latin *levamen* (*levare* = lift)]

leaves plural of **leaf.**

leavings *n.pl.* things left over, especially as worthless.

Leavis /'liːvɪs/ F(rank) R(aymond) 1895–1978. English literary critic. He was the cofounder with his wife Q D Leavis (1906–1981) and editor of the controversial review *Scrutiny* 1932–53. He championed the work of D H Lawrence and James Joyce and in 1962 attacked C P Snow's theory of 'The Two Cultures' (the natural alienation of the arts and sciences in intellectual life).

Lebanon /'lebənən/ Republic of; country in W Asia, bordered to the N and E by Syria, S by Israel, and W by the Mediterranean; **area** 10,452 sq km/4,034 sq mi; **capital** and port Beirut; **physical** narrow coastal plain; Bekka valley N–S between Antilebanon mountain ranges; **head of state** Elias Hrawi from 1989; **head of government** Selim El-Hoss from 1989; **political system** emergent democratic republic; **exports** citrus and other fruit; industrial products to Arab neighbours; **population** (1990 est) 3,340,000 (Lebanese 82%, Palestinian 9%, Armenian 5%); **language** Arabic, French (both official); Armenian, English; **recent history** independence was achieved from France in 1944. In 1964 the Palestine Liberation Organization (PLO) was founded in Beirut. Civil War between Christians and Muslims broke out in 1975–76 and resumed in 1978 after Israel invaded S Lebanon in search of PLO fighters. By 1985 Lebanon neared chaos. Foreigners were taken hostage. Successive attempts to establish a government failed until 1990, when the government of Elias Hrawi and Selim El-Hoss regained control of Beirut and proposals for a new constitution for a Second Republic were discussed.

Lebedev /'lebɪdjef/ Peter Nikolaievich 1866–1912. Russian physicist. He proved by experiment, and then measured, the minute pressure that light exerts upon a physical body.

Lebensraum *n.* a theory developed by Hitler for the expansion of Germany into E Europe, and in the 1930s used by the Nazis to justify their annexation of neighbouring states

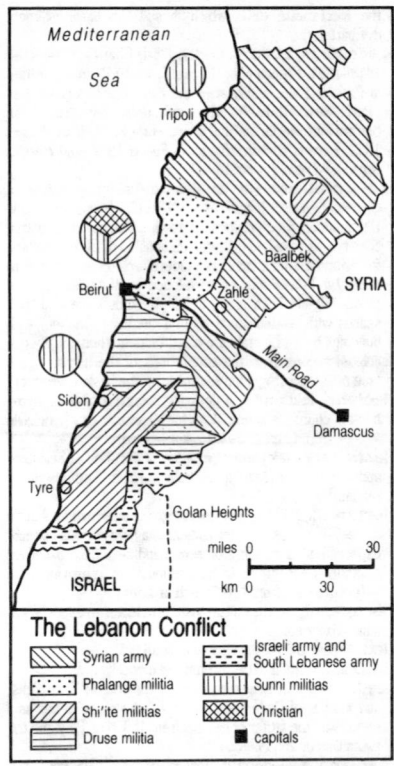

Mediterranean Sea

Tripoli

Baalbek

Beirut   Zahlé   **SYRIA**

Sidon

Damascus

Tyre

Golan Heights

miles 0   30

ISRAEL   km 0   30

The Lebanon Conflict

Syrian army	Israeli army and South Lebanese army
Phalange militia	Sunni militias
Shi'ite militias	Christian
Druse militia	capitals

on the grounds that Germany was overpopulated. [German = living space]

Lebowa /lə'bəuə/ a black homeland in Transvaal province, South Africa; it achieved self-governing status in 1972; population (1985) 1,836,000.

Le Brun /lə'brɜːŋ/ Charles 1619–1690. French artist, painter to Louis XIV from 1662. In 1663 he became director of the French Academy and of the Gobelin factory, which produced art, tapestries, and furnishings for the new palace of Versailles.

Le Carré /lə 'kæreɪ/ John. Pseudonym of David John Cornwell 1931– . English writer of thrillers. His low-key realistic accounts of complex espionage include *The Spy Who Came in from the Cold* 1963, *Tinker Tailor Soldier Spy* 1974, *Smiley's People* 1980, and *The Russia House* 1989. He was a member of the Foreign Service 1960–64.

A committee is an animal with four back legs.
                       John Le Carré
           Tinker, Tailor, Soldier, Spy

Le Chatelier's principle /lə ʃætəl'jeɪ/ or **Le Chatelier-Braun principle** in science, the principle that if a change in conditions is imposed on a system in equilibrium, the system will react to counteract that change and restore the equilibrium. [from H-L *Le Chatelier* (1850–1936)]

lecher /'letʃə/ *n.* a lecherous man, a debauchee. [from Old French *lechier* = live in debauchery or gluttony]

lecherous /'letʃərəs/ *adj.* lustful, having strong or excessive sexual desire.

lechery /'letʃərɪ/ *n.* unrestrained indulgence of sexual desire.

lecithin *n.* a type of lipid, containing nitrogen and phosphorus, that forms a vital part of the cell membranes of plant and animal cells. [from Greek *lekithos* = egg yolk, eggs being a major source of lecithin]

Leclanché /lə'klɒnʃeɪ/ Georges 1839–1882. French engineer. In 1866 he invented a primary electrical cell, the **Leclanché cell**, which is still the basis of most dry batteries.

Leconte de Lisle /lə'kɒnt də 'li:l/ Charles Marie René 1818–1894. French poet. He was born on Réunion, settled in Paris in 1846, and headed the anti-Romantic group Les Parnassiens 1866–76. His work drew inspiration from the ancient world, as in *Poèmes antiques/Antique Poems* 1852, *Poèmes barbares/Barbaric Poems* 1862, and *Poèmes tragiques/Tragic Poems* 1884.

Le Corbusier /lə kɔ:'bju:ziei/ assumed name of Charles-Édouard Jeanneret 1887–1965. Swiss architect. His functionalist approach to town planning in industrial society was based on the interrelationship between machine forms and the techniques of modern architecture. His concept, *La Ville Radieuse*, developed in Marseille, France (1945–50) and Chandigarh, India, placed buildings and open spaces with related functions in a circular formation, with buildings based on standard-sized units mathematically calculated according to the proportions of the human figure (see ◊Fibonacci, ◊golden section). [= the basket weaver]

lectern /'lektɜ:n/ *n.* a desk for holding a bible or hymn book in church; a similar desk for a lecturer etc. [from Old French from Latin *lectrum* (*legere* = read)]

lectionary /'lekʃənərɪ/ *n.* a list of portions of Scripture appointed to be read in churches. [from Latin *lectio* = reading]

lecture /'lektʃə/ *n.* a discourse giving information about a subject to a class or other audience; a long serious speech, especially as a scolding or reprimand. —*v.t./i.* to deliver a lecture or lectures; to talk seriously or reprovingly to. —**lecturer** *n.* [from Old French or Latin]

lectureship *n.* the official position of lecturer, especially at a university etc.

led past and past participle of **lead**[1].

LED abbreviation of ◊light-emitting diode.

Leda /'li:də/ in Greek mythology, the wife of Tyndareus, and mother of Clytemnestra. Zeus, who came to her as a swan, was the father of her children, Helen of Troy and the twins Castor and Pollux.

Lederberg /'ledəbɜ:g/ Joshua 1925– . US geneticist who showed that bacteria can reproduce sexually, combining genetic material so that offspring possess characteristics of both parent organisms.

ledge *n.* a narrow horizontal projection or shelf.

ledger *n.* a tall narrow book in which a firm's accounts are kept.

Ledru-Rollin /lə'dru: rɒ'læŋ/ Alexandre Auguste 1807–1874. French politician and contributor to the radical and socialist journal *La Réforme*. He became minister for home affairs in the provisional government formed in 1848 after the overthrow of Louis Philippe and the creation of the Second Republic, but he opposed the elected president Louis Napoleon.

Le Duc Tho /'lei dʊk 'təʊ/ 1911– . North Vietnamese diplomat, who was joint winner (with US secretary of state, Kissinger) of the Nobel Peace Prize in 1973 for his part in the negotiations to end the Vietnam War. He indefinitely postponed receiving the award.

lee /li:/ *n.* 1. the shelter given by a neighbouring object. 2. (in full **lee side**) the sheltered side, the side away from the wind. —**lee shore**, the shore to leeward of a ship. [Old English]

Lee Bruce. Stage name of Lee Yuen Kam 1941–1973. US 'Chinese Western' film actor, an expert in ◊kung fu, who popularized the oriental martial arts in the West with pictures made in Hong Kong, such as *Fists of Fury* 1972 and *Enter the Dragon* 1973, his last film.

Lee Christopher 1922– . English film actor, whose tall, gaunt figure was memorable in the title role of *Dracula* 1958 and its sequels. He has not lost his sinister image in subsequent Hollywood productions. His other films include *Hamlet* 1948, *The Mummy* 1959, *Julius Caesar* 1970, and *The Man with the Golden Gun* 1974.

Lee Laurie 1914– . English writer, born near Stroud, Gloucestershire. His works include the autobiographical novel *Cider with Rosie* 1959, a classic evocation of childhood; nature poetry such as *The Bloom of Candles* 1947; and travel writing including *A Rose for Winter* 1955.

Lee Robert E(dward) 1807–1870. US Confederate general in the ◊American Civil War, a military strategist. As military adviser to Jefferson ◊Davis, president of the Confederacy,

and as commander of the army of N Virginia, he made several raids into Northern territory, but was defeated at Gettysburg and surrendered in 1865 at Appomattox.

> It is well that war is so terrible, else we would grow too fond of it.
>
> **Robert E. Lee**
> to a fellow general during the
> battle of Fredericksburg

Lee and Yang /jæŋ/ Lee Tsung Dao (1926–) and Yang Chen Ning (1922–) Chinese physicists who studied how parity operates at the nuclear level. They found no proof for the claim, made by ◊Wigner, that nuclear processes were indistinguishable from their mirror images, and that elementary particles made no distinction between left and right. In 1956 they predicted that parity was not conserved in weak interactions. They shared the Nobel Prize for Physics in 1957.

leech[1] *n.* a worm in the class Hirudinea that inhabits fresh water, and in tropical countries infest damp forests. Leeches are injurious to people and animals, to whom they attach themselves by means of a strong mouth adapted to sucking blood. 2. a person who sponges on another. [Old English]

leech[2] *n.* a vertical side of a square sail; the after side of a fore-and-aft sail. [perhaps related to Old Norse *lik*, nautical term of uncertain meaning]

Leeds /li:dz/ city in West Yorkshire, England, on the river Aire; population (1984) 712,200. Industries include engineering, printing, chemicals, glass, and woollens.

leek *n.* a vegetable *Allium porrum* of the onion family with a cylindrical white bulb; this as the Welsh national emblem. [Old English]

Lee Kuan Yew /'li: kwɑ:n 'ju:/ 1923– . Singapore politician, prime minister from 1959. Lee founded the anticommunist Socialist People's Action Party in 1954 and entered the Singapore legislative assembly in 1955. He was elected the country's first prime minister in 1959, and took Singapore out of the Malaysian federation in 1965.

leer *v.i.* to look slyly or lasciviously or maliciously. —*n.* a leering look. [perhaps from obsolete *leer* = cheek from Old English, as though 'to glance over one's cheek']

leery *adj.* knowing, sly, wary *of*.

lees /li:z/ *n.pl.* the sediment of wine etc.; the dregs. [from Old French *lie*]

Lee Teng-hui /'li: tɑŋ 'hu:i/ 1923– . Taiwanese right-wing politician, vice president 1984–88, president and Kuomintang (see ◊Guomindang) party leader from 1988. Lee, the country's first island-born leader, is viewed as a reforming technocrat.

Leeuwenhoek /'leɪwənhu:k/ Anton van 1632–1723. Dutch pioneer of microscopic research. He ground his own lenses, some of which magnified up to 200 times. With these he was able to see individual red blood cells, sperm, and bacteria, achievements not repeated for more than a century.

leeward /'li:wəd, (*nautical*) 'lu:əd/ *adj.* & *adv.* on or towards the sheltered side. —*n.* the leeward side or region.

Leeward Islands 1. a group of islands, part of the ◊Society Islands, in ◊French Polynesia, S Pacific. 2. a general term for the northern half of the Lesser ◊Antilles in the West Indies. 3. former British colony in the West Indies (1871–1956) comprising Antigua, Montserrat, St Christopher/St Kitts-Nevis, Anguilla, and the Virgin Islands.

leeway *n.* 1. a ship's sideways drift leeward of a desired course. 2. an allowable deviation or freedom of action.

Lefebvre /lə'fevrə/ Marcel 1905–1991. French Catholic priest in open conflict with the Roman Catholic Church. In 1976, he was suspended by Pope Paul VI for the unauthorized ordination of priests at his Swiss headquarters. He continued and in June 1988 he was excommunicated by Pope John Paul II, in the first formal schism within the church since 1870.

left[1] *adj.* 1. on or towards the side of the human body which in the majority of persons has the less-used hand and on which the heart lies; on or towards the analogous part of a thing. 2. politically to the left (see sense 3 below). —*adv.* on or to the left side. —*n.* 1. the left-hand part, region, or direction. 2. the left hand; a blow with this; in marching, the left foot. 3. (often **Left**) a political group or section favouring radical socialism; such radicals collectively; the more advanced or innovative section of any group. —**have two left feet,** to be clumsy. **left bank,** the bank of a river on the left as one faces downstream. **left-hand** *adj.* of, on, or towards the left side of a person or thing. **left-handed** *adj.* using the left hand by preference as more serviceable; made by or for the left hand; turning to the left; awkward or clumsy; (of a compliment) ambiguous, of doubtful sincerity. **left-hander** *n.* a left-handed person or blow. **left wing,** the left side of a football etc. team on the field; a player in this position; the left section of a political party (see sense 3 above). **left-winger** *n.* a person on the left wing. —**left-handedness** *n.* [originally = weak, worthless; compare Old English *lyft-adl* = paralysis]

left[2] past and past participle of **leave**[1].

left-hand rule a rule used to recall which way a wire connected to a source of electricity will move when near a magnet. The thumb and first two fingers of the left hand are placed at right angles to each other. If the first finger is pointed in the direction of the magnetic field (from the N to the S pole of the magnet) and the second finger is pointed in the direction of the electric current (from the positive terminal to the negative terminal of the electric source), the thumb will point in the direction in which the wire will move.

leftism *n.* radical socialism. —**leftist** *n.*

leftward /'leftwəd/ *adv.* or **leftwards** toward the left. —*adj.* going toward or facing the left.

lefty *n.* (*colloquial*) 1. a left-winger in politics. 2. a left-handed person.

leg *n.* 1. each of the projecting parts of an animal's body, on which it stands or moves; either of the two lower limbs of the human body; an artificial replacement of this. 2. the part of a garment covering the leg. 3. any of the projecting supports beneath a chair or other piece of furniture. 4. the part of a cricket field on the side where the batsman places his feet. 5. one section of a journey. 6. each of several stages in a competition etc. 7. one branch of a forked object. 8. (*nautical*) a run made on a single tack. —**give a person a leg up,** to help him or her to mount a horse etc. or get over an obstacle or difficulty. **leg before wicket,** (of a batsman) out because of an illegal obstruction of the ball with a part of the body other than the hand. **leg it,** to walk or run hard. **leg-pull** *n.* a hoax. **not have a leg to stand on,** to be unable to support an argument by facts or sound reasons. **on one's last legs,** near death or the end of usefulness etc. —**legged** /legd, 'legɪd/ *adj.* [from Old Norse]

legacy /'legəsɪ/ *n.* 1. money or a chattel bequeathed to a survivor. 2. something handed down by a predecessor. [from Old French from Latin *legare* = bequeath, commit]

legal /'liːgəl/ *adj.* of or based on law; concerned with, appointed, required, or permitted by law. —**legal aid,** a payment from public funds for legal advice or proceedings. **legal tender,** currency that cannot legally be refused in payment of a debt. —**legality** /lɪ'gælɪtɪ/ *n.*, **legally** /'liːgəlɪ/ *adv.* [from French or Latin *lex* = law]

legalism *n.* excessive adherence to a law or formula. —**legalist** *n.*, **legalistic** /-'lɪstɪk/ *adj.*

legalize *v.t.* to make lawful; to bring into harmony with the law. —**legalization** /-'zeɪʃən/ *n.*

legate /'legət/ *n.* an ambassador (now only one representing the pope). [from Old French from Latin *legare* = commission]

legatee /legə'tiː/ *n.* a recipient of a legacy.

legation /lɪ'geɪʃən/ *n.* 1. a body of deputies. 2. a diplomatic minister (especially below ambassadorial rank) and his or her staff. 3. a diplomatic minister's residence. 4. a legateship.

legato /lɪ'gɑːtəʊ/ *adv* & *adj.* in music, in a smooth manner. —*n.* (*plural* **legatos**) in music, smooth playing; a passage played smoothly. [Italian = bound, from Latin *ligare* = bind]

legend /'ledʒənd/ *n.* 1. a story (true or invented) handed down from the past; such stories collectively. 2. an inscription on a coin or medal. 3. a caption. 4. an explanation on a map etc. of the symbols used. [from Old French from Latin *legenda* = what is to be read (*legere* = read)]

legendary /'ledʒəndərɪ/ *adj.* 1. of or based on legends, described in a legend. 2. (*colloquial*) famous, often talked about.

Léger /le'ʒeɪ/ Fernand 1881–1955. French painter, associated with ◊Cubism. From around 1909 he evolved a characteristic style, composing abstract and semi-abstract works with cylindrical forms, reducing the human figure to constructions of pure shape.

legerdemain /ledʒədə'meɪn/ *n.* sleight of hand, juggling; trickery, sophistry. [from French = light of hand]

leger line /'ledʒə/ a short line added in a musical score for notes above or below the range of the staff. [variant of *ledger*]

legging *n.* (usually in plural) a protective outer covering of leather etc. for the leg from the knee to the ankle.

leggy *adj.* long-legged. —**legginess** *n.*

leghorn /'leghɔːn, lɪ'gɔːn/ *n.* 1. fine plaited straw; a hat of this. 2. **Leghorn,** one of a small hardy breed of domestic fowl. [from *Leghorn* (*Livorno*) in Italy]

legible /'ledʒɪbəl/ *adj.* clear enough to be deciphered, readable. —**legibility** /-'bɪlɪtɪ/ *n.*, **legibly** *adv.* [from Latin *legere* = read]

legion /'liːdʒən/ *n.* 1. a division of 3,000–6,000 men in the ancient Roman army. 2. a vast group, a multitude. [from Old French from Latin *legere* = choose]

legionary *adj.* of a legion or legions. —*n.* a member of a legion; a legionary soldier in the ancient Roman army. [from Latin]

legionnaire /liːdʒə'neə/ *n.* a member of the foreign legion or of the American or Royal British Legion. —**legionnaires' disease,** a form of bacterial pneumonia first identified after an outbreak at an American Legion meeting in 1976. [from French]

legislate /'ledʒɪsleɪt/ *v.i.* to make laws. —**legislator** *n.*

legislation /ledʒɪs'leɪʃən/ *n.* law-making; the laws made. [from Latin *lex legis* = law and *latio* = proposing]

legislative /'ledʒɪslətɪv/ *adj.* of or empowered to make legislation.

legislature /'ledʒɪsleɪtʃə/ *n.* the legislative body of a state.

legitimate /lɪ'dʒɪtɪmət/ *adj.* 1. in accordance with the law or rules. 2. (of a child) born of parents married to each other. 3. logically acceptable, justifiable. —**legitimate drama** *or* **theatre,** plays of recognized merit, normal comedy and tragedy as distinct from musical comedy, farce, revue etc. The term arose in the 18th century. —**legitimacy** *n.*, **legitimately** *adv.* [from Latin *legitimus* = lawful]

legitimatize /lɪ'dʒɪtɪmətaɪz/ *v.t.* to legitimize.

Legitimist *n.* the party in France that continued to support the claims of the house of ◊Bourbon after the revolution of 1830. When the direct line became extinct in 1883, the majority of the party transferred their allegiance to the house of Orléans.

legitimize /lɪ'dʒɪtɪmaɪz/ *v.t.* to make legitimate; to serve as a justification for. —**legitimization** /-'zeɪʃən/ *n.*

Legnano, Battle of /len'jɑːnəʊ/ the defeat of Holy Roman emperor Frederick I Barbarossa by members of the Lombard League in 1176 at Legnano, NW of Milan. It was a major setback to the emperor's plans for imperial domination over Italy and showed for the first time the power of infantry against feudal cavalry.

legume /'legjuːm/ *n.* a leguminous plant; a fruit or edible part or pod of this. [from French from Latin *legere* = pick]

leguminous /lɪ'gjuːmɪnəs/ *adj.* of the family of plants Leguminosae, with seeds in pods (e.g. peas, beans).

Leh /leɪ/ capital of Ladakh region, E Kashmir, India, situated E of the Indus, 240 km/150 mi E of Srinagar. Leh is the nearest supply base to the Indian army outpost on the Siachen Glacier.

Lehár /leɪ'hɑː/ Franz 1870–1948. Hungarian composer. He wrote many operettas, among them *The Merry Widow* 1905, *The Count of Luxembourg* 1909, *Gypsy Love* 1910, and *The Land of Smiles* 1929. He also composed songs, marches, and a violin concerto.

Le Havre /lə 'hɑːvrə/ industrial port (engineering, chemicals, oil refining) in Normandy, NW France, on the river Seine; population (1982) 255,000. It is the largest port in Europe, and has transatlantic passenger links.

lei /'leɪiː/ *n.* a Polynesian garland of flowers. [Hawaiian]

Leibniz /'laɪbnɪts/ Gottfried Wilhelm 1646–1716. German mathematician and philosopher. Independently of, but concurrently with, the British scientist Isaac Newton he developed ◊calculus. In his metaphysical works, such as *The Monadology* 1714, he argued that everything consisted of innumerable units, **monads**, whose individual properties determined each thing's past, present, and future.

Leicester /'lestə/ an industrial city and the administrative headquarters of Leicestershire, England, on the river Soar; population (1983) 282,300. Its products include food processing, hosiery, footwear, engineering, electronics, printing, and plastics.

Leicester Robert Dudley, Earl of Leicester *c.*1532–1588. English courtier. Son of the Duke of Northumberland, he was created earl of Leicester in 1564. Queen Elizabeth I gave him command of the army sent to the Netherlands in 1585–87 and of the forces prepared to resist the threat of Spanish invasion in 1588.

Leicestershire /'lestəʃə/ county in central England; **area** 2,550 sq km/984 sq mi; **administrative headquarters** Leicester; **physical** Rutland Water, one of Europe's largest reservoirs; Charnwood Forest; Vale of Belvoir (under which are large coal deposits); **products** horses, cattle, sheep, dairy products, coal; **population** (1987) 879,000.

Leichhardt /'laɪkhɑːt/ Friedrich 1813–1848. Prussian-born Australian explorer. In 1843, he walked 965 km/ 600 mi from Sydney to Moreton Bay, Queensland, and in 1844 walked from Brisbane to Arnhem Land; he disappeared during a further expedition from Queensland in 1848.

Leics abbreviation of ◊Leicestershire.

Leigh /liː/ Mike 1943– . English playwright and director. He directs his own plays, which evolve through improvisation before they are scripted; they include the comedies *Abigail's Party* 1977 and *Goose-Pimples* 1981. He wrote and directed the films *High Hopes* 1989 and *Life is Sweet* 1991.

Leigh Vivien. Stage name of Vivien Mary Hartley 1913–1967. English actress, born in Darjeeling, India. She appeared on the stage in London and New York, and won Academy Awards for her performances as Scarlett O'Hara in *Gone With the Wind* 1939 and as Blanche du Bois in *A Streetcar Named Desire* 1951. She was married to Laurence Olivier 1940–60, and starred with him in the play *Antony and Cleopatra* in 1951.

Leinster /'lenstə/ the SE province of the Republic of Ireland, comprising the counties of Carlow, Dublin, Kildare, Kilkenny, Laois, Longford, Louth, Meath, Offaly, Westmeath, Wexford, and Wicklow; **area** 19,630 sq km/7,577 sq mi; **capital** Dublin; **population** (1986) 1,850,000.

Leipzig /'laɪpzɪg/ the capital of Leipzig county, Germany, 145 km/90 mi SW of Berlin; population (1986) 552,000. Products include furs, leather goods, cloth, glass, cars, and musical instruments. The county of Leipzig has an area of 4,970 sq km/1,918 sq mi and a population of 1,374,000.

leishmaniasis *n.* any of several parasitic diseases, prevalent in NE Africa and S Asia, caused by microscopic protozoans of the genus *Leishmania* and transmitted by sandflies. Either localized infection or fever can be a symptom. [from William *Leishman* (1865–1926) who first identified the disease]

leisure /'leʒə/ *n.* free time, time at one's disposal; the enjoyment of this. —**at leisure**, not occupied; in an unhurried manner. **at one's leisure**, when one has time. [from Anglo-French from Latin *licēre* = be allowed]

leisured *adj.* having ample leisure.

leisurely *adj.* unhurried, relaxed. —*adv.* without hurry. —**leisureliness** *n.*

leitmotiv /'laɪtməʊtiːf/ *n.* or **leitmotif** a theme associated throughout a musical etc. composition with a particular person or idea. [German]

Leitrim /'liːtrɪm/ county in Connacht province, Republic of Ireland, bounded on the NW by Donegal Bay; **area** 1,530 sq km/591 sq mi; **county town** Carrick-on-Shannon; **physical** rivers: Shannon, Bonet, Drowes and Duff; **products** potatoes, cattle, linen, woollens, pottery, coal, iron, lead; **population** (1986) 27,000.

lek *n.* in biology, a closely spaced set of very small territories (see ◊territory, sense 5) each occupied by a single male during the mating season. Leks are found in the mating systems of several ground-dwelling birds, such as grouse, and a few antelopes.

Lely /'liːli/ Peter. Adopted name of Pieter van der Faes 1618–1680. Dutch painter, active in England from 1641, who painted fashionable portraits in Baroque style. His subjects included Charles I, Cromwell, and Charles II.

Lemaître /lə'meɪtrə/ Georges Edouard 1894–1966. Belgian cosmologist who proposed the ◊Big Bang theory of the origin of the universe in 1927.

Le Mans /lə 'mɒn/ industrial town in Sarthe *département*, France; population (1982) 150,000, conurbation 191,000. It has a motor-racing circuit where the annual endurance 24-hour race (established in 1923) for sports cars and their prototypes is held.

lemming /'lemɪŋ/ *n.* any small rodent of the genus *Lemmus* found in northern and arctic areas. One species undertakes mass migrations when its population exceeds available food supply, and has been reputed to continue headlong into the sea and drown. [Norwegian]

Lemmon /'lemən/ Jack (John Uhler III) 1925– . US character actor, often cast as the lead in comedy films, such as *Some Like it Hot* 1959 but equally skilled at straight drama, as in *The China Syndrome* 1979 and *Dad* 1990.

lemon[1] /'lemən/ *n.* 1. a pale-yellow oval fruit with acid juice; the tree bearing it *Citrus limon*. 2. pale yellow colour. 3. (*slang*) a simpleton; something disappointing or unsuccessful. —**lemon cheese** *or* **curd**, a thick, creamy spread made from lemons. —**lemony** *adj.* [from Old French from Arabic]

lemon[2] *n.* (in full **lemon sole**) a kind of plaice *Microstomus kitt*. [from French *limande*]

lemonade /lemə'neɪd/ *n.* a drink made from lemon juice or a synthetic substitute with similar flavour.

lemon balm a perennial herb *Melissa officinalis* of the Labiatae family, with lemon-scented leaves. It is widely used in teas, liqueurs, and medicines.

LeMond /lə'mɒnd/ Greg 1961– . US racing cyclist, the first American to win the Tour de France, in 1986. He regained his title in 1989 by seven seconds, the smallest margin ever, and won it again in 1990. He also won the World Professional Road Race in 1983 and 1989.

lemur /'liːmə(r)/ *n.* any of various species of ◊primate (sense 2) of the family Lemuridae inhabiting Madagascar and the Comoro Islands. They are arboreal animals, and some species are nocturnal. They can grow to 1.2 m/4 ft long, have large eyes, and long, bushy tails. They feed on fruit, insects, and small animals. Many are threatened with extinction owing to loss of their forest habitat and, in some cases, from hunting. [from Latin *lemures* = spirits of the dead, from its spectrelike face]

Lena /'liːnə, Russian 'ljenə/ the longest river in Asiatic Russia, 4,400 km/2,730 mi, with numerous tributaries. Its source is near Lake Baikal, and it empties into the Arctic Ocean through a delta 400 km/240 mi wide. It is ice-covered for half the year.

Lenard /'leɪnɑːt/ Phillip 1862–1947. German physicist who investigated the photoelectric effect (light causes metals to emit electrons) and cathode rays (the stream of electrodes emitted from the cathode in a vacuum tube). He was awarded the Nobel prize for Physics in 1905.

Lenclos /lɒn'kləʊ/ Ninon de 1615–1705. French courtesan. As the recognized leader of Parisian society, she was the mistress of many highly placed men, including General Condé and the writer La Rochefoucauld.

lend *v.t.* (*past* and *past participle* **lent**) 1. to give or allow the use of (a thing) temporarily on the understanding that it or its equivalent will be returned. 2. to provide (money) temporarily in return for payment of interest. 3. to contribute as a temporary help or effect etc. —**lend an ear**, to listen. **lend a hand**, to help. **lend itself to**, to be suitable for. **lend oneself to**, to accommodate oneself to. —**lender** *n.* [Old English]

Lendl /'lendl/ Ivan 1960– . Czech lawn tennis player. He has won seven Grand Slam singles titles, including the US and French titles three times each. He has won more than $15 million in prize money.

Lend-Lease *n.* an act of the US congress in March 1941 that gave the president power to order 'any defense article for the government of any country whose defence the president deemed vital to the defense of the USA'. During World War II, the USA negotiated many lend-lease agreements, most notably with Britain and the Soviet Union.

Leng /leŋ/ Virginia 1955– . British three-day eventer, born in Malta. She has won world, European, and most major British championships.

Lenglen /'lɒŋglen/ Suzanne 1899–1938. French tennis player, Wimbledon singles and doubles champion in 1919–23 and 1925, and Olympic champion in 1921. She became professional in 1926. She also popularised sports clothes designed by French designer Jean Patou (1880–1936).

length /leŋθ/ *n.* **1.** the measurement or extent from end to end, especially along a thing's greatest dimension. **2.** the amount of time occupied by something. **3.** the distance a thing extends as a unit of measurement; the length of a horse, boat etc., as a measure of the lead in a race. **4.** the degree of thoroughness in an action. **5.** a piece of cloth etc. cut from a longer one; a piece of a certain length. **6.** the quantity of a vowel or syllable. **7.** in cricket, the distance from the batsman at which the ball pitches; the proper amount of this. —**at length**, after a long time; taking a long time, in detail. [Old English]

lengthen /'leŋθən/ *v.t./i.* to make or become longer.

lengthways *adv.* or **lengthwise** in a direction parallel with a thing's length.

lengthy *adj.* of unusual length; long and tedious. —**lengthily** *adv.*, **lengthiness** *n.*

lenient /'li:niənt/ *adj.* merciful, not severe, mild. —**lenience** *n.* **leniency** *n.*, **leniently** *adv.* [from Latin *lenis* = gentle]

Lenin /'lenin/ Vladimir Ilyich. Adopted name of Vladimir Ilyich Ulyanov 1870–1924. Russian revolutionary, first leader of the USSR, and communist theoretician. Active in the 1905 Revolution, Lenin had to leave Russia when it failed, settling in Switzerland in 1914. He returned to Russia after the February revolution of 1917 (see ◊Russian Revolution). He led the Bolshevik revolution in Nov 1917 and became leader of a Soviet government, concluded peace with Germany, and organized a successful resistance to White Russian (pro-tsarist) uprisings and foreign intervention 1918–20. His modification of traditional Marxist doctrine to fit conditions prevailing in Russia became known as **Marxism–Leninism**, the basis of communist ideology.

Leningrad /'leningræd/ capital of the Leningrad region, at the head of the Gulf of Finland; population (1987) 4,948,000. Industries include shipbuilding, machinery, chemicals, and textiles. Originally called **St Petersburg**, it was renamed **Petrograd** in 1914 and **Leningrad** in 1924.

Lennon /'lenən/ John 1940–1980. English rock singer and songwriter, a former member of the ◊Beatles.

Le Nôtre /lə 'nəutrə/ André 1613–1700. French landscape gardener, creator of the gardens at Versailles and Les Tuileries, Paris.

lens /lenz/ *n.* **1.** a piece of transparent material, such as glass, with one or both sides curved to concentrate or disperse light rays in optical instruments. **2.** a combination of lenses in photography. **3.** the transparent substance behind the iris of the eye. [Latin = lentil (from its shape)]

lens, gravitational see ◊gravitational lens.

lent past and past participle of **lend**.

Lent *n.* in the Christian church, the period from Ash Wednesday to Easter Eve of which the 40 weekdays are devoted to fasting and penitence in commemoration of Christ's fasting in the wilderness. —**Lenten** *adj.*

lenticel *n.* a small pore on the stems of woody plants or the trunks of trees, which provides a means of gas exchange between the stem interior and the atmosphere.

lentil /'lentil/ *n.* an annual leguminous plant *Lens culinaris* with white, blue, or purplish flowers; its edible seed. [from Old French from Latin]

lento /'lentəu/ *adj. & adv.* in music, slow, slowly. [Italian]

Lenz's law /lents/ in physics, a law stating that the direction of an electromagnetically induced current (generated by moving a magnet near a wire, or a wire in a magnetic field) will oppose the motion producing it. [from German physicist Heinrich Friedrich Lenz (1804–1865) who announced it in 1833]

Leo /'li:əu/ *n.* a zodiac constellation in the northern hemisphere between Cancer and Virgo and near Ursa Major; it is represented as a lion. In astrology, the dates for Leo are between about 23 July and 22 Aug (see ◊precession).

Leo III the Isaurian *c.*680–740. Byzantine emperor and soldier. He seized the throne in 717, successfully defended Constantinople against the Saracens 717–18, and attempted to suppress the use of images in church worship (see ◊iconoclast).

Leo 13 popes, including:

Leo I St **the Great** *c.*390–461. Pope from 440 who helped to establish the Christian liturgy. Leo summoned the Council of Chalcedon where his **Dogmatical Letter** was accepted as the voice of St Peter. Acting as ambassador for the emperor Valentinian III (425–455), Leo saved Rome from devastation by the Huns by buying off their king, Attila.

Leo III *c.*750–816. Pope from 795. After the withdrawal of the Byzantine emperors, the popes had become the real rulers of Rome. Leo III was forced to flee because of a conspiracy in Rome and took refuge at the court of ◊Charlemagne. He returned to Rome in 799 and crowned Charlemagne emperor on Christmas Day in 800, establishing the secular sovereignty of the pope over Rome under the suzerainty of the emperor (who became the Holy Roman emperor).

Leo X Giovanni de' Medici 1475–1521. Pope from 1513. The son of Lorenzo the Magnificent of Florence, he was created a cardinal at 13. He bestowed on Henry VIII of England the title of Defender of the Faith. A patron of the arts, he sponsored the rebuilding of St Peter's Church, Rome. He raised funds for this by selling indulgences (remissions of punishment for sin), a sale that led the religious reformer Martin Luther to rebel against papal authority. Leo X condemned Luther in the bull *Exsurge domine* in 1520 and excommunicated him in 1521.

León /lei'ron/ city in W Nicaragua; population (1985) 101,000. Industries include textiles and food processing. It was founded in 1524, and was the capital of Nicaragua until 1855.

Leonard /'lenəd/ Elmore 1925– . US author of westerns and thrillers, marked by vivid dialogue, for example *Stick* 1983 and *Freaky Deaky* 1988.

Leonard Sugar Ray 1956– . US boxer. In 1988 he became the first man to have won world titles at five officially recognized weights. In 1976 he was Olympic

lens

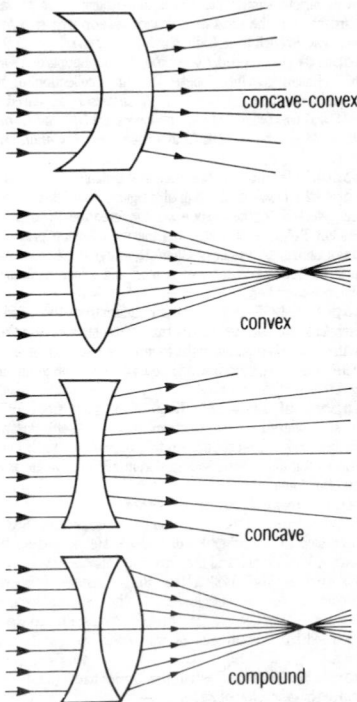

concave-convex

convex

concave

compound

light-welterweight champion; he won his first professional title in 1979 when he beat Wilfred Benitez for the WBC welterweight title. He later won titles at junior-middleweight (WBA version) 1981, middleweight (WBC) 1987, light-heavyweight (WBC) 1988, and super-middleweight (WBC) 1988. In 1989 he drew with Thomas Hearns.

Leonardo da Vinci /liːəˈnɑːdəʊ də ˈvɪntʃi/ 1452–1519. Italian painter, sculptor, architect, engineer, and scientist, one of the greatest figures of the Italian Renaissance, active in Florence, Milan, and from 1516 in France. As state engineer and court painter to the duke of Milan, he painted the *Last Supper* mural about 1495 (Sta Maria delle Grazie, Milan), and on his return to Florence painted the *Mona Lisa* about 1503–06 (Louvre, Paris). His notebooks and drawings show an immensely inventive and enquiring mind, studying aspects of the natural world from anatomy to aerodynamics.

Leoncavallo /leɪɒnkəˈvæləʊ/ Ruggiero 1857–1919. Italian operatic composer, born in Naples. He played in restaurants, composing in his spare time, until the success of *Il Pagliacci* in 1892. His other operas include *La Bohème* 1897 (contemporary with Puccini's version) and *Zaza* 1900.

León de los Aldamas industrial city in central Mexico; population (1986) 947,000. Products include leather goods and footwear.

Leone /leɪˈəʊni/ Sergio 1928–1989. Italian film director, responsible for popularizing 'spaghetti' Westerns (Westerns made in Italy and Spain, usually with a US leading actor and a European supporting cast and film crew) and making a world star of Clint Eastwood. His films include *A Fistful of Dollars* 1964, *Once upon a Time in the West* 1968, and *Once Upon a Time in America* 1984.

Leonidas /liːˈɒnɪdæs/ died 480 BC. King of Sparta. He was killed while defending the pass of ◊Thermopylae with 300 Spartans, 700 Thespians, and 400 Thebans against a huge Persian army.

leonine /ˈliːənaɪn/ *adj.* of or like a lion. [from Old French or Latin *leo* = lion]

Leonov /ljeˈɔːnɒf/ Aleksei Arkhipovich 1934– . Soviet cosmonaut. In 1965 he was the first person to walk in space, from the spacecraft *Voskhod 2*.

leopard /ˈlepəd/ *n.* 1. a large African and South Asian carnivorous animal *Panthera pardus* of the cat family, with a dark-spotted, yellowish fawn or black coat, a panther. 2. any of various similar animals. 3. in heraldry, a lion passant guardant as in the arms of England. —**leopardess** *n.fem.* [from Old French from Latin *pardus* = panther]

Leopardi /leɪəʊˈpɑːdi/ Giacomo, Count Leopardi 1798–1837. Italian romantic poet. The first collection of his uniquely pessimistic poems, *I Versi/Verses*, appeared in 1824, and was followed by his philosophical *Operette Morali/Minor Moral Works* 1827, in prose, and *I Canti/Lyrics* 1831.

Leopold /ˈleɪəpəʊld/ three kings of Belgium:

Leopold I 1790–1865. King of Belgium from 1831, having been elected to the throne on the creation of an independent Belgium. Through his marriage, when prince of Saxe-Coburg, to Princess Charlotte Augusta, he was the uncle of Queen ◊Victoria of Britain and had considerable influence over her.

Leopold II 1835–1909. King of Belgium from 1865, son of Leopold I. He financed the journalist Stanley's explorations in Africa, which resulted in the foundation of the Congo Free State (now Zaïre), from which he extracted a huge fortune by ruthless exploitation.

Leopold III 1901–1983. King of Belgium from 1934. He surrendered to the German army in 1940. Postwar charges against his conduct led to a regency by his brother Charles and his eventual abdication in 1951 in favour of his son ◊Baudouin.

Leopold two Holy Roman emperors:

Leopold I 1640–1705. Holy Roman emperor from 1658, in succession to his father Ferdinand III. He warred against Louis XIV of France and the Ottoman Empire.

Leopold II 1747–1792. Holy Roman emperor in succession to his brother Joseph II, he was the son of Empress Maria Theresa. His hostility to the French Revolution led to the outbreak of war a few weeks after his death.

Léopoldville /ˈliːəpəʊldvɪl/ the former name (until 1966) of ◊Kinshasa, capital of Zaïre.

Leopardi 19th-century Italian poet Giacomo Leopardi suffered from physical deformity, ill health, and unhappy love affairs. His work is pessimistic, but of great lyrical beauty.

leotard /ˈliːətɑːd/ *n.* a close-fitting one-piece garment worn by dancers etc. [from Jules *Léotard*, French trapeze artist (died 1870)]

Lepanto, Battle of /lɪˈpæntəʊ/ a sea battle on 7 Oct 1571, fought in the Mediterranean Gulf of Corinth off Lepanto (Italian name of the Greek port of **Naupaktos**), then in Turkish possession, between the Ottoman Empire and forces from Spain, Venice, Genoa, and the Papal States, jointly commanded by Don John of Austria. The combined western fleets delivered a crushing blow to Muslim sea power.

Le Pen /lə ˈpen/ Jean-Marie 1928– . French extreme right-wing politician. In 1972 he formed the French National Front, supporting immigrant repatriation and capital punishment; the party gained 14% of the national vote in the 1986 election. Le Pen was elected to the European Parliament in 1984.

Lepenski Vir /lepənski ˈvɪə/ the site of Europe's oldest urban settlement (6th millennium BC), now submerged by an artificial lake on the river Danube.

leper /ˈlepə/ *n.* 1. a person with leprosy. 2. a person shunned on moral grounds. [originally = leprosy, from Old French from Latin from Greek *lepros* = scaly]

Lepidoptera /lepɪˈdɒptərə/ *n.* an order of insects consisting of some 165,000 species, including ◊butterflies and ◊moths, which both have overlapping scales on their wings. —**lepidopterist**, a student or collector of moths and butterflies. —*adj.* [from Greek *lepis* = scale and *pteron* = wing]

leprechaun /ˈleprəkɔːn/ *n.* a small mischievous sprite in Irish folklore.

leprosy /ˈleprəsi/ *n.* or **Hansen's disease** a chronic, progressive disease, caused by a bacterium *Mycobacterium leprae*. It affects the nerves, skin, and certain other tissues of the human body, resulting in mutilations and deformities. Once common in many countries, leprosy is now confined almost entirely to the tropics. It is controlled with drugs.

leprous /ˈleprəs/ *adj.* of leprosy; having or resembling leprosy. [from Old French from Latin]

Leptis Magna /ˈleptɪs ˈmægnə/ a ruined city in Libya, 120 km/75 mi E of Tripoli. It was founded by the Phoenicians, then came under Carthage, and in 47 BC under Rome.

leptospirosis infectious disease of domestic animals, especially cattle, causing abortion; transmitted to humans, it causes meningitis and jaundice.

lepton *n.* a type of ◊elementary particle.

Lermontov /ˈleəməntɒf/ Mikhail Yurevich 1814–1841. Russian Romantic poet and novelist. In 1837 he was sent into active military service in the Caucasus for writing a revolutionary poem on the death of Pushkin, which criticized Court values, and for participating in a duel. Among his works are the psychological novel *A Hero of Our Time* 1840 and a volume of poems *October* 1840.

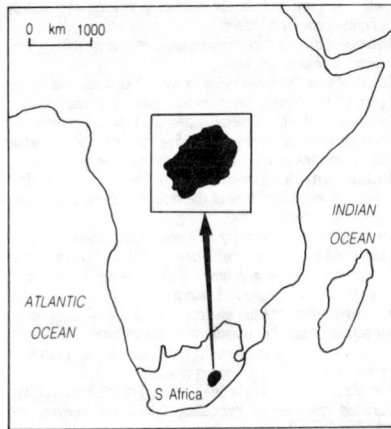

Lesotho

Le Sage /lə ˈsɑːʒ/ Alan René 1668–1747. French novelist and dramatist. Born in Brittany, he abandoned law for literature. His novels include *Le Diable boîteux/The Devil upon Two Sticks* 1707 and his picaresque masterpiece *Gil Blas* 1715–1735, much indebted to Spanish originals.

lesbian /ˈlezbiən/ *n.* a homosexual woman. —*adj.* of lesbians; of homosexuality in women. —**lesbianism** *n.* [from *Lesbos*, Greek island, home of the reputedly homosexual Sappho]

Lesbos /ˈlezbɒs/ alternative spelling of ◊Lesvos.

lèse-majesté /leɪzˈmæʒesteɪ/ *n.* or **lese-majesty** /liːz ˈmædʒɪstɪ/ 1. treason; an insult to a sovereign or ruler. 2. presumptuous conduct. [French from Latin]

lesion /ˈliːʒən/ *n.* 1. damage, injury. 2. a change in the functioning or texture of an organ of the body as a result of disease or injury. [from Old French from Latin *laesio* (*laedere* = injure)]

Lesotho /liˈsuːtuː/ Kingdom of; landlocked country in southern Africa, an enclave within South Africa; **area** 30,355 sq km/11,717 sq mi; **physical** mountainous with plateau; **political system** military-controlled monarchy; **head of state** King Letsie I from 1990; **head of government** Justin Lekhanya from 1986; **exports** wool, mohair, diamonds; **population** (1990 est) 1,757,000; **language** Sesotho, English (official), Zulu, Xhosa; **recent history** in 1966 Basutoland, a British protectorate, achieved independence as the Kingdom of Lesotho, within the Commonwealth. A state of emergency was imposed 1970–73; in 1975 members of the ruling party were attacked by South-Africa-backed guerrillas; and in 1986 South Africa imposed a border blockade, forcing deportation of 60 ANC members. Gen Lekhanya gained power in a coup and abolished the National Assembly. In 1990 King Moshoeshoe II was dethroned by military council and replaced by his son Mohato.

less *adj.* 1. smaller in size, degree, duration, number etc. 2. of smaller quantity, not so much. 3. (*disputed usage*) fewer. —*adv.* to a smaller extent, in a lower degree. —*n.* a smaller amount, quantity, or number. —*prep.* minus, deducting. [Old English]

-less /-lɪs/ suffix forming adjectives and adverbs from nouns, in the sense 'not having, without, free from' (e.g. *doubtless, powerless*), and from verbs, in the sense 'unable to be —ed', 'not —ing' (e.g. *fathomless, tireless*). [Old English]

lessee /leˈsiː/ *n.* a person holding property by lease, a tenant. [from Anglo-French]

lessen *v.t./i.* to make or become less, to diminish.

Lesseps /ˈlesəps/ Ferdinand, Vicomte de Lesseps 1805–1894. French engineer, constructor of the ◊Suez Canal 1859–69; he began the ◊Panama Canal in 1879, but withdrew after failing to construct it without locks.

lesser *adj.* (usually *attributive*) not so great as the other or the rest.

Lessing /ˈlesɪŋ/ Doris (May) (née Taylor) 1919– . British novelist, born in Iran and brought up in Rhodesia. Concerned with social and political themes, particularly the place of women in society, her work includes *The Grass is Singing* 1950, *The Golden Notebook* 1962, the five-novel series *Children of Violence* 1952–69, *The Good Terrorist* 1985, and *The Fifth Child* 1988. She has also written an 'inner space fiction' series *Canopus in Argus Archives* 1979–83, and, under the pen name 'Jane Somers', *The Diary of a Good Neighbour* 1981.

Lessing Gotthold Ephraim 1729–1781. German dramatist and critic. His plays include *Miss Sara Sampson* 1755, *Minna von Barnhelm* 1767, *Emilia Galotti* 1772, and the verse play *Nathan der Weise* 1779. His works of criticism *Laokoon* 1766 and *Hamburgische Dramaturgie* 1767–68 influenced German literature. He also produced many theological and philosophical writings.

A man who does not lose his reason over certain things has none to lose.

Gotthold Ephraim Lessing
Emilia Galotti

Les Six a group of French composers: Georges ◊Auric, Louis Durey (1888–1979), Arthur ◊Honegger, Darius Milhaud (1892–1974), Francis ◊Poulenc, and Germaine Tailleferre (1892–1983). Formed in 1917, they were dedicated to producing works free from foreign influences and reflecting the contemporary world. They split up in the early 1920s. [French = the six]

lesson /ˈlesən/ *n.* 1. a spell of teaching. 2. (in *plural*) systematic instruction in a subject. 3. a thing to be learnt by a pupil. 4. an experience that serves to warn or encourage. 5. a passage from the Bible read aloud during a church service. [from Old French from Latin *legere* = read]

lessor /leˈsɔː/ *n.* a person who lets a property by lease.

lest *conj.* 1. in order that not, for fear that. 2. that. [Old English = whereby less that]

Lesvos /ˈlezvɒs/ Greek island in the Aegean Sea, near the coast of Turkey; **area** 2,154 sq km/831 sq mi; **capital** Mytilene; **products** olives, wine, grain; **population** (1981) 104,620; **history** ancient name Lesbos; an Aeolian settlement, the home of the poets ◊Alcaeus and ◊Sappho; conquered by the Turks from Genoa in 1462 (see ◊Genoa); annexed to Greece in 1913.

let[1] *v.t./i.* (-tt-; *past* and *past participle* let) 1. to allow, enable, or cause to, not to prevent or forbid. 2. to allow or cause to come, go, or passive 3. to grant the use of (rooms, land etc.) for rent or hire. 4. as an auxiliary verb (with 1st and 3rd persons) expressing commands, appeals etc. —*n.* the letting of rooms, land etc. —**let alone**, to refrain from interfering with or doing; apart from, far less or more than, let be, to refrain from interfering with or doing. **let down**, to lower; to let out air from (an inflated tyre etc.); to fail to support or satisfy, to disappoint; to lengthen (a garment); to treat (gently etc.). **let-down** *n.* a disappointment. **let go**, to release, to loose one's hold (*of*). **let oneself go**, to abandon self-restraint. **let in for**, to involve in (loss or difficulty). **let loose**, to release. **let off**, to fire (a gun), to explode (a bomb); to ignite (a firework); to excuse from (duties etc.); to give little or no punishment to. **let off steam**, to allow steam to escape; to release pent-up energy or feeling. **let on**, (*colloquial*) to reveal a secret. **let out**, to release from restraint or obligation; to reveal (a secret etc.), to make (a garment) looser; to put out to rent or to contract. **let-out** *n.* an opportunity to escape. **let up**, (*colloquial*) to become less intense or severe, to relax one's efforts. **let-up** *n.* a reduction in intensity, a relaxation of effort. **to let**, available to rent. [Old English]

let[2] *n.* an obstruction of the ball or a player in tennis etc., requiring the ball to be served again. —*v.t.* (-tt-; *past* and *past participle* **letted** or **let**) (*archaic*) to hinder, to obstruct. —**without let or hindrance**, unimpeded. [Old English]

-let /-lɪt/ suffix forming nouns usually diminutive (e.g. *flatlet*) or denoting articles of ornament or dress (e.g. *anklet*).

lethal /ˈliːθəl/ *adj.* causing or sufficient to cause death. —**lethality** /-ˈælɪtɪ/ *n.*, **lethally** *adv.* [from Latin *letum* = death]

lethargy /ˈleθədʒɪ/ *n.* lack of energy or vitality; abnormal drowsiness. —**lethargic** /lɪˈθɑːdʒɪk/ *adj.*, **lethargically**

lever

first-order lever

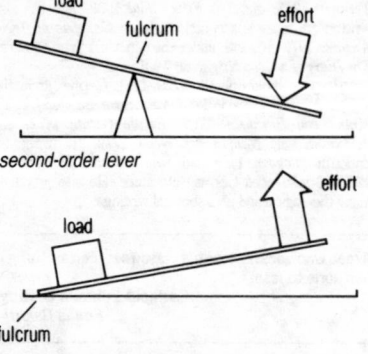

second-order lever

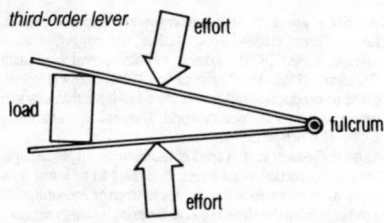

third-order lever

adv. [from Old French from Latin from Greek *lēthargos* = forgetful]

Lethe /ˈliːθiː/ in Greek mythology, a river of the underworld whose waters, when drunk, brought forgetfulness of the past.

Lett *n.* a member of a people living near the Baltic, mainly in Latvia. [from German from Lettish *Latvi*]

letter /ˈletə/ *n.* 1. any of the characters, representing one or more of the simple or compound sounds used in speech, of which written words are composed; an alphabetic symbol. 2. a written or printed communication, usually sent by post or messenger; (in *plural*) an addressed legal or formal document. 3. the precise terms of a statement, strict verbal interpretation. 4. (in *plural*) literature; acquaintance with books; erudition. —*v.t.* 1. to inscribe letters on. 2. to classify with letters. —**letter bomb,** a terrorist explosive device in the form of a letter sent through the post. **letter box,** a slit in a door, with a hinged flap, through which letters are delivered; a postbox. **letter of credit,** a letter from a bank authorizing the bearer to draw money from another bank. **man of letters,** a scholar or author. **to the letter,** with adherence to every detail. [from Old French from Latin *littera*]

lettered *adj.* well-read, well-educated.

letterhead *n.* a printed heading on stationery; stationery with this.

letterpress *n.* 1. the printed words in an illustrated book. 2. printing from raised type, a method pioneered by Johann ◊Gutenberg in Europe in the 1450s.

Lettish /ˈletɪʃ/ *adj.* of the Letts. —*n.* the language of the Letts, Latvian.

lettre de cachet /letrə də ˈkæʃeɪ/ (*plural* **lettres de cachet**) in French history, an order signed by the king and closed with his seal, especially an order under which persons might be imprisoned or banished without trial. They were used as a means of disposing of political opponents or criminals of high birth, and abolished during the French Revolution. [French = letter with a seal]

lettuce /ˈletɪs/ *n.* an annual edible plant *Lactuca sativa*, family Compositae, believed to have been derived from the wild species *L. serriola*. There are many varieties, including the **cabbage lettuce,** with round or loose heads, and the **Cos lettuce,** with long, upright heads. [from Old French from Latin *lactuca* (*lac* = milk, from its milky juice)]

leucite *n.* a silicate mineral, $KAlSi_2O_6$, occurring frequently in some potassium-rich volcanic rocks. It is dull white to grey, and usually opaque. It is used as a source of potassium for fertilizer.

leuco- /ˈluːkəʊ-/ in combinations, denoting white. [from Greek *leukos* = white]

leucocyte /ˈluːkəʊsaɪt/ *n.* a white blood cell that forms part of the body's defences and gives immunity against disease. Of the several different types, ◊phagocytes and ◊macrophages engulf invading microorganisms, while ◊lymphocytes produce more specific immune responses.

leucotomy /luːˈkɒtəmɪ/ *n.* surgical incision into the white tissue of the frontal lobe of the brain to relieve some cases of mental disorder.

leukaemia /luːˈkiːmɪə/ *n.* a progressive disease with an abnormal accumulation of white corpuscles, which crowd the bone marrow and other blood-forming tissue. [from Greek *leukos* = white and *haima* = blood]

Levant /lɪˈvænt/ the eastern part of the Mediterranean together with its islands and neighbouring countries. —**Levantine** /lɪˈvæntaɪn, ˈlevən-/ *adj. & n.* [French = point of sunrise, east (*lever* = rise)]

Le Vau /lə ˈvəʊ/ Louis 1612–1670. French architect who drafted the plan of Versailles, rebuilt the Louvre, and designed Les Tuileries in Paris.

levee[1] /ˈlevɪ/ *n.* (*archaic*) an assembly of visitors or guests, especially at a formal reception; (*historical*) a sovereign's assembly for men only. [from French *levé*, variant of *lever* = rising]

levee[2] *n.* 1. an embankment against river floods; a river's natural embankment. 2. a landing place. [from French *levée* (*lever* = raise)]

level /ˈlevəl/ *n.* 1. a horizontal line or plane, one joining points of equal height. 2. a measured height or value etc., a position on a scale; a social, moral, or intellectual standard. 3. a plane of rank or authority. 4. an instrument for giving or testing a horizontal line or plane. 5. a more or less flat surface or area. —*adj.* 1. horizontal. 2. on a level or equality (with); at the same height, rank, or position on a scale. 3. (of ground) flat, without hills or hollows. 4. steady, even, uniform. 5. equable or well-balanced in quality, style, temper, judgement etc. —*v.t./i.* (**-ll-**) 1. to make or become level, even, or uniform. 2. to place on the same level; to bring *up* or *down* to a standard. 3. to raze or demolish. 4. to aim (a missile or gun). 5. to direct (an accusation etc., or *absolute, at* or *against*). —**do one's level best,** (*colloquial*) to do one's utmost. **find one's level,** to reach the social or intellectual level etc. that is most suitable for oneself. **level crossing,** a crossing of a railway and road, or two railways, at the same level. **level-headed** *adj.* mentally well-balanced, sensible. **level pegging,** equality of scores or achievements. **on the level,** (*colloquial*) honest, honestly, without deception. **on a level with,** in the same horizontal plane, as, equal with. —**leveller** *n.* [from Old French from Latin *libella* (*libra* = scales, balance)]

Leveller *n.* a member of the democratic party in the English Civil War. They found wide support among Cromwell's New Model Army and the yeoman farmers, artisans, and small traders, and proved a powerful political force 1647–49. Their programme included the establishment of a republic, government by a parliament of one house elected by male suffrage, religious toleration, and sweeping social reforms.

lever /ˈliːvə/ *n.* 1. a bar resting on a pivot and used to raise a heavy or firmly fixed object. 2. a device consisting of a straight bar or other rigid structure of which one point (the *fulcrum*) is fixed, another is connected with the force (*weight*) to be resisted or acted upon, and a third is connected with the force (*power*) applied. 3. a projecting handle moved to operate mechanism. 4. a means of exerting moral pressure. —*v.t./i.* to use a lever; to lift or move etc. by means of a lever. [from Anglo-French *lever* = raise from Latin *levare*]

leverage /ˈliːvərɪdʒ/ *n.* 1. the action or power of a lever. 2. the means of accomplishing a purpose; power, influence.

leveraged buyout in business, the purchase of a controlling proportion of the shares of a company by its own management, financed almost exclusively by borrowing. It is so called because the ratio of a company's long-term debt to its equity (capital assets) is known as its 'leverage'.

leveret /ˈlevərɪt/ *n.* a young hare, especially in the first year. [from Anglo-French diminutive of *levre* = hare from Latin *lepus*]

Leverrier /ləveri'eɪ/ Urbain Jean Joseph 1811–1877. French astronomer, who predicted the existence and position of the planet Neptune, discovered in 1846.

Lévesque /le'vek/ René 1922–1987. French-Canadian politician. In 1968 he founded the *Parti Québecois*, with the aim of an independent Québec, but a referendum rejected the proposal in 1980. He was premier of Québec 1976–85.

Levi /'levi/ Primo 1919–1987. Italian novelist. He joined the anti-Fascist resistance during World War II, was captured and sent to the concentration camp at Auschwitz. He wrote of these experiences in *Se questo è un uomo/If This Is a Man* 1947.

leviathan /li'vaɪəθən/ *n.* 1. in the Bible, a sea monster. 2. anything very large or powerful. [from Latin from Hebrew]

Levi-Montalcini /mɒntæl't ʃiːni/ Rita 1909– . Italian neurologist who discovered nerve-growth factor, a substance that controls how many cells make up the adult nervous system. She was awarded the Nobel Prize for Physiology and Medicine in 1986.

Levis /'liː vaɪz/ *n.pl.* the trade name of a type of (usually blue) denim jeans or overalls reinforced with rivets. [from *Levi* Strauss, original US manufacturer in 1860s]

Lévi-Strauss /'levi 'straʊs/ Claude 1908–1990. French anthropologist, who sought to find a universal structure governing all societies, as reflected in the way their myths are constructed. His works include *Tristes Tropiques* 1955, and *Mythologiques/Mythologies* 1964–71.

levitate /'levɪteɪt/ *v.t./i.* to rise and float in the air, to cause to do this (especially with reference to spiritualism). —**levitation** /-'teɪʃən/ *n.* [from Latin *levis* = light]

Levite /'liː vaɪt/ *n.* a member of the Hebrew tribe of Levi, from which priests were drawn until after the Exile, when Levites were allotted only inferior duties in the Temple. [from Latin from Greek from *Levi*, son of Jacob]

levity *n.* a disposition to make light of weighty matters, frivolity, lack of serious thought. [from Latin *levis* = light]

levy /'levɪ/ *v.t.* 1. to impose or collect (a payment etc.) compulsorily. 2. to enrol (troops etc.). 3. to wage (war). —*n.* 1. levying. 2. a payment etc. levied. 3. (in *plural*) troops levied. [from Old French *lever* = raise from Latin *levare*]

lewd /ljuː d/ *adj.* lascivious; indecent, treating sexual matters in a vulgar way. —**lewdly** *adv.*, **lewdness** *n.* [Old English = lay]

Lewes /'luː ɪs/ George Henry 1817–1878. English philosopher and critic. From acting he turned to literature and philosophy; his works include a *Biographical History of Philosophy* 1845–46, and *Life and Works of Goethe* 1855. He married in 1840, but left his wife in 1854 to form a life-long union with the writer Mary Ann Evans (George ◊Eliot), whom he had met in 1851.

Lewes, Battle of a battle in 1264 caused by the baronial opposition to England's Henry III, led by Simon de Montfort, earl of Leicester (1208–1265). The king was defeated and captured at the battle.

Lewis /'luː ɪs/ Carl (Frederick Carleton) 1961– . US track and field athlete. At the 1984 Olympic Games he equalled the performance of Jesse ◊Owens, winning gold medals in the 100 and 200 metres, sprint relay, and long jump. In the 1988 Olympics, he repeated his golds in the 100 metres and long jump, and won a silver in the 200 metres.

Lewis Cecil Day; see ◊Day Lewis.

Lewis C(live) S(taples) 1898–1963. British academic and writer, born in Belfast. His books include the medieval study, *The Allegory of Love* 1936, and the space fiction, *Out of the Silent Planet* 1938. He was a committed Christian and wrote essays in popular theology such as *The Screwtape Letters* 1942 and *Mere Christianity* 1952; the autobiographical *Surprised by Joy* 1955; and a series of books of Christian allegory for children, set in the magic land of Narnia, including *The Lion, the Witch, and the Wardrobe* 1950.

Lewis Jerry. Stage name of Joseph Levitch 1926– . US comic actor, formerly in partnership with Dean Martin (1946–1956). He enjoyed great commercial success as a solo performer and was revered by French critics, but his later films, such as *The Nutty Professor* 1963, were less well received in the USA. He appeared with Robert de Niro in *King of Comedy* 1982.

Lewis Jerry Lee 1935– . US rock-and-roll and country singer and pianist. His trademark was the 'pumping piano' style in hits such as 'Whole Lotta Shakin' Going On' and 'Great Balls of Fire' 1957; later recordings include 'What Made Milwaukee Famous' 1968.

Lewis Meriwether 1774–1809. US explorer. He was commissioned by president Thomas Jefferson to find a land route to the Pacific with William Clark (1770–1838). They followed the Missouri River to its source, crossed the Rocky Mountains (aided by an Indian girl, Sacajawea), and followed the Columbia River to the Pacific, then returned overland to St Louis 1804–06.

Lewis (Harry) Sinclair 1885–1951. US novelist. He made a reputation with *Main Street* 1920, depicting American small-town life; *Babbitt* 1922, the story of a real-estate dealer of the Midwest caught in the conventions of his milieu; and *Arrowsmith* 1925, a study of a scientist. He was awarded the Nobel Prize for Literature in 1930.

Lewis (Percy) Wyndham 1886–1957. English writer and artist who pioneered ◊Vorticism, which with its feeling of movement sought to reflect the age of industry. He had a hard and aggressive style in both his writing and his painting. His literary works include the novels *Tarr* 1918 and *The Childermass* 1928, the essay *Time and Western Man* 1927, and autobiographies.

Lewis with Harris /'luː ɪs, 'hærɪs/ largest island in the Outer Hebrides; area 2,220 sq km/857 sq mi; population (1981) 23,400. Its main town is Stornoway. It is separated from NW Scotland by the Minch. There are many lakes and peat moors.

lexical /'leksɪkəl/ *adj.* 1. of the words of a language. 2. of a lexicon or dictionary. [from Greek]

lexicography /leksi'kɒgrəfɪ/ *n.* the compilation of dictionaries. —**lexicographer** *n.*, **lexicographical** /-'græfɪkəl/ *adj.*

lexicology /leksi'kɒlədʒɪ/ *n.* the study of words and their form, history, and meaning.

lexicon /'leksɪkən/ *n.* 1. a dictionary, especially of Greek, Hebrew, Syriac, or Arabic. 2. the vocabulary of a person, language, branch of knowledge etc. [from Greek *lexicon* (*biblion* = book), from *lexis* = word (*legō* = speak)]

lexis /'leksɪs/ *n.* words, vocabulary; a total stock of words.

ley[1] /leɪ/ *n.* land temporarily under grass. [from *ley*, *lea* adj. = fallow]

ley[2] /liː , leɪ/ *n.* the supposed straight line of a prehistoric track, usually between hilltops, with identifying points such as ponds, mounds etc., marking its route.

Leyden /'laɪdn/ Lucas van; see ◊Lucas van Leyden, Dutch painter.

Leyden jar /'leɪdən/ a type of electrical condenser with a glass jar as a dielectric between sheets of tin foil, invented in 1745 at Leyden University. [from *Leyden* (now *Leiden*) in the Netherlands]

LF abbreviation of low frequency.

l.h. abbreviation of left hand.

LH abbreviation of ◊luteinizing hormone.

Lhasa /'lɑː sə/ ('the Forbidden City') capital of the autonomous region of Tibet, China, at 5,000 m/16,400 ft; population (1982) 105,000. Products include handicrafts and light industry.

Li symbol for lithium.

liability /laɪə'bɪlɪt/ *n.* 1. being liable. 2. a troublesome person, a handicap. 3. (in *plural*) debts etc. for which one is liable. 4. in accounting, a financial obligation.

liable /'laɪəbəl/ *adj.* 1. legally obliged; subject or under an obligation *to*. 2. exposed or open *to* (something undesirable); apt or likely *to*. 3. answerable (*for*). [perhaps from Old French *lier* = bind]

liaise /li'eɪz/ *v.i.* (*colloquial*) to act as a liaison or go-between.

liaison /li'eɪzən/ *n.* 1. communication and co-operation between units of an organization; a person effecting this. 2. an illicit sexual relationship. [French *lier* = bind] helen

liana /li'ɑː nə/ *n.* a woody, perennial, climbing plant in tropical forests. [from French *liane*, *lierne* = clematis]

Liaoning /liaʊ'nɪŋ/ province of NE China; **area** 151,000 sq km/58,300 sq mi; **capital** Shenyang; **products** cereals, coal, iron, salt, oil; **population** (1986) 37,260,000; **history** developed by Japan 1905–45, including the **Liaodong Peninsula**, whose ports had been conquered from the Russians. Liaoning is one of China's most heavily industrialized areas.

liar /'laɪə/ n. a person who tells lies.
lias /'laɪəs/ n. a blue limestone rich in fossils. —**liassic** /li'æsɪk/ adj. [from Old French]
Lib. abbreviation of 1. Liberal. 2. (colloquial) liberation.
libation /laɪ'beɪʃən/ n. the pouring of a drink offering to a god; such a drink offering. [from Latin libare = pour as an offering]
libel /'laɪbəl/ n. 1. a published false statement that is damaging to a person's reputation; the act of publishing it. 2. a false defamatory statement or representation. —v.t. (-ll-) to utter or publish a libel against. —**be a libel on**, do injustice to. —**libellous** adj. [from Old French from Latin libellus, diminutive of liber = book]
liberal /'lɪbərəl/ adj. 1. given or giving freely; abundant. 2. open-minded, not prejudiced; not strict or rigorous; (of studies etc.) for general broadening of the mind. 3. favouring moderate political and social reform; **Liberal**, of the Liberal Party. —n. 1. a person of liberal views. 2. **Liberal**, a member or supporter of the Liberal Party. —**liberalism** n., **liberality** /-'rælɪtɪ/ n., **liberally** adv. [originally = befitting a free man, from Old French from Latin (liber = free)]
Liberal Democrats in UK politics, the common name for the ◊Social and Liberal Democrats.
liberalism n. a political and social theory that favours representative government, freedom of the press, speech, and worship, the abolition of class privileges, the use of state resources to protect the welfare of the individual, and international ◊free trade. It is historically associated with the Liberal Party in the UK and the Democratic Party in the USA.
liberalize /'lɪbərəlaɪz/ v.t. to make more liberal or less strict. —**liberalization** /-'zeɪʃən/ n.
Liberal Party 1. in the UK, a former political party, the successor to the ◊Whig Party, with an ideology of liberalism. In 1988, it merged with the Social Democratic Party (SDP) to form the Social and ◊Liberal Democrats. 2. in Australia, a political party with an ideology of conservatism, established in 1944 and derived from the former United Australia Party. 3. any political party favouring moderate reform.
liberate /'lɪbəreɪt/ v.t. 1. to set free. 2. to free (a country) from an oppressor or enemy occupation. 3. to free from rigid social conventions. —**liberation** /-'reɪʃən/ n., **liberator** n. [from Latin]
liberation theology a Christian theory of Jesus' primary importance as the 'Liberator', personifying the poor and devoted to freeing them from oppression (Matthew 19:21, 35:35, 40). Initiated by the Peruvian priest Gustavo Gutierrez in The Theology of Liberation 1969, and enthusiastically (and sometimes violently) adopted in Latin America, it embodies a Marxist interpretation of the class struggle, especially by Third World nations. It has been criticized by some Roman Catholic authorities including Pope John Paul II.
Liberia /laɪ'bɪərɪə/ Republic of; country in W Africa, bounded N and NE by Guinea, E by the Ivory Coast, S and SW by the Atlantic, and NW by Sierra Leone; **area** 111,370 sq km/42,989 sq mi; **capital** and port Monrovia; **physical** forested highlands; swampy coast where six rivers enter the sea; **head of state and government** Amos Sawyer from 1990; **political system** emergent democratic republic; **exports** iron ore, rubber, diamonds, coffee, cocoa, palm oil; **population** (1990 est) 2,644,000 (95% indigenous); **language** English (official); over 20 Niger-Congo languages; **recent history** Liberia was founded in 1847 as an independent republic. In 1980 President Tolbert, in power since 1971, was assassinated in a coup led by Samuel Doe, who suspended the constitution. A new constitution was approved in 1984, when the National Democratic Party of Liberia (NDPL) was founded. In 1985 it won the general election. In 1990 Doe was killed in a civil war between rival rebel factions and an interim government was formed.
libertine /'lɪbəti:n/ n. a dissolute or licentious man. —adj. licentious. [from Latin = freedman (liber = free)] helen
liberty /'lɪbətɪ/ n. 1. freedom from captivity, slavery, imprisonment, or despotic control. 2. the right or power to do as one pleases. 3. a right or privilege granted by authority. —**at liberty**, free, not imprisoned; allowed. **take liberties**, to behave in an unduly familiar manner;

Libya

to interpret facts etc. too freely. [from Old French from Latin liber = free]
liberty, equality, fraternity (liberté, egalité, fraternité) motto of the French republic from 1793.
libidinous /li'bɪdɪnəs/ adj. lustful. [from Latin]
libido /li'bi:dəʊ/ n. (plural libidos) a psychic impulse or drive, especially that associated with sexual desire. —**libidinal** /li'bɪdɪnəl/ adj. [Latin = lust]
LIBOR acronym from London Interbank Offered Rates; in the UK, loan rates for a specified period which are offered to first-class banks in the London interbank market. Banks link their lending to LIBOR as an alternative to the base lending rate when setting the rate for a fixed term, after which the rate may be adjusted.
Libra /'lɪbrə/ n. a constellation and the seventh sign of the zodiac, the Scales, which the Sun enters at the autumnal equinox. [Latin = scales, balance]
librarian /laɪ'breərɪən/ n. a person in charge of or assisting in a library. —**librarianship** n. [from Latin]
library /'laɪbrərɪ/ n. 1. a collection of books for reading or borrowing. 2. a room or building where these are kept. 3. a similar collection of films, records, computer routines etc.; the place where they are kept. 4. a series of books issued in similar bindings as a set. [from Old French from Latin liber = book]
libretto /li'bretəʊ/ n. (plural libretti /-tɪ/, librettos) the text of an opera or other long musical vocal work. —**librettist** n. [Italian, diminutive of libro = book]
Libreville /'li:brəvi:l/ capital of Gabon, on the estuary of the river Gabon; population (1985) 350,000. Products include timber, oil, and minerals. It was founded in 1849 as a refuge for slaves freed by the French.
Libya /'lɪbɪə/ Great Socialist People's Libyan Arab Jamahiriya; country in N Africa, bordered to the N by the Mediterranean, E by Egypt, SE by Sudan, S by Chad and Niger, and W by Algeria and Tunisia; **area** 1,759,540 sq km/679,182 sq mi; **capital** Tripoli; **physical** desert with plateaus and depressions; mountains in N and S; **political system** one-party socialist state; **head of state and government** Moamer Khaddhafi from 1969; **exports** oil, natural gas; **population** (1990 est) 4,280,000 (including 500,000 foreign workers); **language** Arabic; **recent history** an Italian colony until 1942, when it was under British and French control. In 1951 Libya achieved independence as the United Kingdom of Libya, under King Idris. Col Khaddhafi deposed the king in a coup in 1969, set up a Revolution Command Council and proclaimed the Arab Socialist Union the only legal party. In 1972–81 federations and mergers with Syria, Egypt, and Chad were proposed and abandoned. In 1986, the USA accused Khaddafi of complicity in terrorist activities and bombed his headquarters; in 1989 it accused him of building a chemical-weapons factory and shot down two Libyan planes.
lice plural of louse.
licence /'laɪsəns/ n. 1. a permit from the government etc. to own or do something or carry on some trade. 2. leave, permission. 3. excessive liberty of action. 4. disregard of law, rules, or custom; a writer's or artist's transgression

of established rules for effect. [from Old French from Latin *licēre* = be allowed]

license /'laɪsəns/ *v.t.* 1. to grant a licence to or for. 2. to authorize the use of (premises) for a certain purpose, especially the sale of alcoholic liquor.

licensee /laɪsən'siː/ *n.* a holder of a licence, especially to sell alcoholic liquor.

licensing laws laws governing the sale of alcoholic drinks.

licentiate /laɪ'senʃɪət/ *n.* a holder of a certificate of competence to practise a certain profession. [from Latin]

licentious /laɪ'senʃəs/ *adj.* disregarding the rules of conduct, especially in sexual matters. —**licentiousness** *n.* [from Latin]

lichee variant of ◊litchi.

lichen /'laɪkən, 'lɪtʃən/ *n.* a plant organism of the group Lichenes, composed of a fungus and an alga in association, usually of grey green, or yellow tint growing on and colouring rocks, tree trunks, walls, roofs etc. —**lichenous** *adj.* [Latin, from Greek]

Lichfield /'lɪtʃfiːld/ Patrick Anson, 5th Earl of Lichfield 1939– . British portrait photographer.

lich gate a roofed gateway to a churchyard, where a coffin awaits the clergyman's arrival. [Old English *lic* = corpse]

Lichtenstein /'lɪktənstaɪn/ Roy 1923– . US Pop artist. He uses advertising imagery and comic-strip techniques, often focusing on popular ideals of romance and heroism, as in *Whaam!* 1963 (Tate Gallery, London). He has also produced sculptures in brass, plastic, and enamelled metal.

licit /'lɪsɪt/ *adj.* not forbidden. —**licitly** *adv.* [from Latin]

lick *v.t./i.* 1. to pass the tongue over; to take *up* or *off* or make *clean* by doing this. 2. (of a flame or waves etc.) to move like a tongue, to touch lightly. 3. (*slang*) to thrash. 4. (*slang*) defeat; to excel. —*n.* 1. an act of licking with the tongue. 2. a blow with a stick etc. 3. (*slang*) a (fast) pace. —**a lick and a promise**, (*colloquial*) a slight and hasty wash. **lick into shape**, to make presentable or efficient. **lick one's chops** *or* **lips**, to look forward with relish. **lick one's wounds**, to be in retirement trying to recover after a defeat. **lick a person's boots**, to be servile towards him or her. [Old English]

lid *n.* 1. a hinged or removable cover, especially at the top of a container. 2. an eyelid. 3. (*slang*) a hat. —**put the lid on**, (*slang*) to be the culmination of; to put a stop to. —**lidded** *adj.* [Old English]

Liddell Hart /'lɪdl 'hɑːt/ Basil 1895–1970. British military scientist. He was an exponent of mechanized warfare, and his ideas were adopted in Germany in 1935 in creating the 1st Panzer Division, combining motorized infantry and tanks. From 1937 he advised the UK War Office on army reorganization.

Lidice /'liːdɪtseɪ/ Czechoslovak mining village, replacing one destroyed by the Nazis on 10 June 1942 as a reprisal for the assassination of ◊Heydrich. The men were shot, women sent to concentration camps, and the children taken to Germany. The officer responsible was hanged in 1946.

lido /'liːdəʊ/ *n.* (*plural* lidos) a public open-air swimming pool or bathing beach. [Italian, name of beach near Venice]

lie[1] /laɪ/ *v.i.* (*past* lay; *past participle* lain; *participle* lying) 1. to be in or assume a horizontal position on a supporting surface. 2. to be resting on a surface. 3. to be or be kept or remain in a specified state or place; to be situated; (of troops) to be encamped. 4. (of an abstract thing) to exist or be found. 5. to be spread out to view. 6. in law, to be admissible or able to be upheld. —*n.* the way, direction, or position in which a thing lies. —**lie down**, to assume a lying position; to have a short rest. **lie-down** *n.* a short rest. **lie down under**, to accept (an insult etc.) without protest. **lie in**, to remain in bed in the morning; to be brought to bed in childbirth. **lie-in** *n.* remaining in bed in the morning. **lie low**, to keep quiet or unseen; to be discreet about one's intentions. **lie of the land**, the state of affairs. **lie with**, to be the responsibility of. **take lying down**, to accept (an insult etc.) without protest. [Old English]

lie[2] *n.* 1. an intentionally false statement. 2. an imposture, a thing that deceives. —*v.i.* (*participle* lying) to tell lies; (of a thing) to be deceptive. —**give the lie to**, to serve to show the falsity of (a supposition etc.).

Liebig /'liːbɪg/ Justus, Baron von 1803–1873. German chemist, a major contributor to agricultural chemistry. He introduced the theory of radicals and discovered chloroform and chloral.

Liebknecht /'liːpknext/ Karl 1871–1919. German socialist, son of Wilhelm Liebknecht. A founder of the German Communist Party, originally known as the Spartacus League (see ◊Spartacist), in 1918 he was one of the few socialists who refused to support World War I. He led an unsuccessful revolt with Rosa ◊Luxemburg in Berlin in 1919 and both were murdered by army officers.

Liebknecht Wilhelm 1826–1900. German socialist. A friend of the communist theoretician Marx, with whom he took part in the ◊revolutions of 1848, he was imprisoned for opposition to the Franco-Prussian War 1870–71. He was one of the founders of the Social Democratic Party in 1875. He was the father of Karl Liebknecht.

Liechtenstein /'lɪktənstaɪn/ Principality of; landlocked country in W central Europe, situated between Austria to the E and Switzerland to the W; **area** 160 sq km/ 62 sq mi; **capital** Vaduz; **physical** Alpine; includes part of Rhine Valley in the W; **head of state** Prince Hans Adam II from 1989; **head of government** Hans Brunhart from 1978; **political system** constitutional monarchy; **exports** microchips, dental products, processed foods, postage stamps; **population** (1990 est) 30,000 (33% foreign); **language** German (official), Alemannic dialect; **recent history** a sovereign state since 1342; the present boundaries were established in 1434; former counties of Schellenberg and Vaduz incorporated from 1719. In 1921, Swiss currency was adopted and in 1923 Liechtenstein united in a customs union with Switzerland. Prince Franz Josef II ruled 1938–1989, the year Liechtenstein sought admission to the UN.

Lied /liːd/ *n.* (*plural* Lieder /'liːdə/) a musical setting of a poem, usually for solo voice and piano; referring to the Romantic songs of Schubert, Schumann, Brahms, and Hugo Wolf. [German = song]

lie detector the popular name for a ◊polygraph.

lief /liːf/ *adv.* (*archaic*) gladly, willingly (usually *had* or *would lief*). [originally adj., from Old English = dear]

liege /liːdʒ/ *adj.* (usually *historical*) entitled to receive or bound to give feudal service or allegiance. —*n.* 1. a liege lord. 2. (usually in *plural*) a vassal, a subject. —**liege lord**, a feudal superior, a sovereign. [from Old French from Latin]

Liège /li'eɪʒ/ (German *Luik*) industrial city and capital of Liège province in Belgium, SE of Brussels, on the river Meuse; population (1988) 200,000. Products include weapons, textiles, paper, and chemicals. The province of Liège has an area of 3,900 sq km/1,505 sq mi and a population (1987) of 992,000.

lien /'liːən/ *n.* the right to hold another's property until a debt on it is paid. [from Old French from Latin *ligamen* = bond]

lieu /lju:/ *n.* **in lieu**, instead or in the place (*of*). [from French from Latin *locus* = place]

Lieut. abbreviation of Lieutenant.

lieutenant /lef'tenənt/ *n.* 1. a deputy or substitute acting for a superior. 2. (*British*) an army officer of the rank next below captain. 3. (*British*) a naval officer of the rank next below lieutenant commander. —**lieutenant colonel, lieutenant commander, lieutenant general** *ns.* (*British*) an officer ranking next below colonel etc. —**lieutenancy** *n.* [from Old French]

Lifar /li'fɑː/ Serge 1905–1986. Russian dancer and choreographer. Born in Kiev, he studied under ◊Nijinsky, joined the Diaghilev company in 1923, and was *maître de ballet* at the Paris Opéra 1930–44 and 1947–59.

life *n.* (*plural* lives) 1. being alive, the functional activity and continual change that is peculiar to animals and plants (before their death) and is not found in rocks and synthetic substances; state of existence as a living individual. 2. a living person; living things and their activity. 3. the period during which life lasts; the period from birth to the present time or from the present time to death. 4. an individual's actions and fortunes; a manner of existence or a particular aspect etc. of this. 5. energy, liveliness, animation. 6. the active part of existence; the business, pleasures, and social activities of the world. 7. a biography. 8. the time for which a thing exists or continues to function. 9. spiritual salvation, regenerate condition. 10. (*colloquial*) a sentence of imprisonment for life. —**as large as life**, life-size; (*jocular*) in

life table

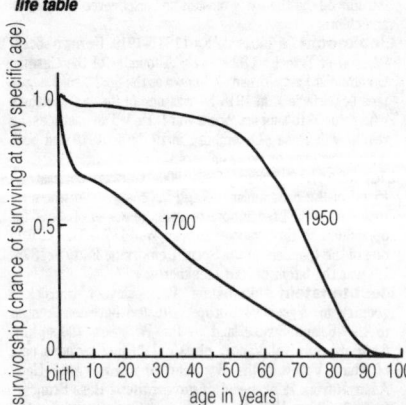

y-axis: survivorship (chance of surviving at any specific age)

1.0

0.5

1700   1950

0

birth 10 20 30 40 50 60 70 80 90 100

age in years

person. **for dear life,** to escape death or as if to do this. **for life,** for the rest of one's life. **lifeblood** *n.* the blood necessary to life; a vital factor or influence. **life expectancy,** the average number of years of life remaining at any given age, derived form statistical information. **lifeguard** *n.* an expert swimmer employed to rescue bathers from drowning; a bodyguard of soldiers. **Life Guards,** a regiment of the Household cavalry. **life insurance** an insurance policy that pays money on the death of the holder. **life jacket,** a jacket of buoyant material for supporting a person in the water. **life peer,** a peer whose title lapses on his or her death. **life preserver,** a short stick with a heavily leaded end; a life jacket etc. **life-size(d)** *adj.* of the same size as the person or thing represented. **life style,** an individual's way of life. **life table,** the probability that an individual will give birth or die during a given period of life. **matter of life and death,** an issue on which a person's living or dying depends; a matter of great importance. **this life,** earthly life. [Old English]

lifebelt *n.* a belt of buoyant or inflatable material for supporting a person in the water.

lifeboat *n.* a specially constructed boat for rescuing those in distress at sea, launched from the land; a ship's small boat for use in an emergency.

lifebuoy *n.* a buoyant support for a person in the water.

life cycle in biology, the sequence of developmental stages through which members of a given species pass. Most vertebrates have a simple life cycle consisting of ◊fertilization of sex cells or ◊gametes, a period of development as an ◊embryo, a period of juvenile growth after hatching or birth, an adulthood including ◊sexual reproduction, and finally death. Invertebrate life cycles are generally more complex and may involve major reconstitution of the individual's appearance (◊metamorphosis) and completely different styles of life. Plants have a special type of life cycle with two distinct phases, known as ◊alternation of generations.

lifeless *adj.* 1. lacking life, dead. 2. lacking movement or vitality. —**lifelessness** *n.*

lifelike *adj.* closely resembling the person or thing represented.

lifeline *n.* 1. a rope used for life-saving, e.g. that attached to a lifebuoy. 2. a diver's signalling line. 3. a sole means of communication or transport.

lifelong *adj.* lasting a lifetime.

lifer *n.* (*slang*) 1. a person sentenced to imprisonment for life. 2. such a sentence.

life sciences the scientific study of the living world as a whole, a new synthesis of several traditional scientific disciplines including ◊biology, ◊zoology, and ◊botany, and newer, more specialized areas of study such as ◊biophysics and ◊sociobiology.

lifetime *n.* the duration of a person's life.

LIFFE acronym from London International Financial Futures Exchange; an exchange in London, UK, where futures contracts are traded (see ◊future²).

Liffey /'lɪfi/ river in E Ireland, flowing from the Wicklow mountains to Dublin Bay; length 80 km/50 mi.

lift *v.t./i.* 1. to raise to a higher level or position; to give an upward direction to (the eyes or face). 2. to take up from

the ground or from its resting place; to dig up (potatoes at harvest, plants for storing etc.). 3. to go up, to rise; (of fog etc.) to disperse. 4. to steal; to copy from another source. 5. to remove (a barrier or restriction). —*n.* 1. lifting, being lifted. 2. a ride as a passenger in a vehicle without payment. 3. (*US* **elevator**) an apparatus for raising and lowering people or things from one floor to another in a building; an apparatus for carrying people up or down a mountain etc. 4. the upward pressure that air exerts on an aircraft in flight. 5. an airlift of goods etc.; the quantity thus transported. 6. a supporting or elating influence; a feeling of elation. —**liftoff** *n.* the vertical takeoff of a spacecraft or rocket. [from Old Norse]

Ligachev /'lɪɡətʃef/ Egor (Kuzmich) 1920– . Soviet politician. He joined the Communist Party in 1944, and became a member of the Politburo in 1985. He was replaced as the party ideologist in 1988 by Vadim Medvedev.

ligament /'lɪɡəmənt/ *n.* a band of tough fibrous connective tissue binding bones together. [from Latin *ligare* = bind]

ligature /'lɪɡətʃə/ *n.* 1. a thing used in tying, especially a band or cord used in surgery. 2. the process of tying. 3. in music, a slur, a tie. 4. two or more letters joined (as *æ*). 5. a bond, a thing that unites. —*v.t.* to bind with a ligature. [from Latin]

Ligeti /'lɪɡəti/ György (Sándor) 1923– . Hungarian-born Austrian composer who developed a dense, highly chromatic, polyphonic style in which melody and rhythm are sometimes lost in shifting blocks of sound. He achieved international prominence with *Atmosphères* 1961 and *Requiem* 1965, which were used for Kubrick's film epic *2001: A Space Odyssey*. Other works include an opera *Le Grand Macabre* 1978, and *Poème symphonique* 1962, for 100 metronomes.

light¹ /laɪt/ *n.* 1. the natural agent that stimulates the sense of sight; visible or other electromagnetic radiation from the Sun, a fire, a lamp etc. 2. the medium or condition of space in which this is present and therefore sight is possible (as opposed to *darkness*). 3. an appearance of brightness; the amount of this. 4. an object from which brightness emanates; a lamp lighthouse, traffic light etc. 5. a flame or spark serving to ignite something; a device producing this. 6. a thing's aspect, the way it appears to the mind. 7. enlightenment, elucidation. 8. spiritual illumination by divine truth. 9. vivacity, enthusiasm, or inspiration in a person's face, especially in the eyes. 10. (in *plural*) one's mental attitude. 11. an eminent person. 12. the bright parts of a picture etc. 13. a window or opening in a wall to let in light. 14. (in a crossword etc.) a word to be deduced from clues. —*adj.* 1. well provided with light, not dark. 2. pale. —*v.t./i.* (*past* lit; *past participle* lit or (especially as *attributive adj.*) lighted) 1. to set burning; to begin to burn. 2. (often with *up*) to provide (a room etc.) with light; to show (a person) the way or the surroundings with a light. 3. to brighten with animation. —**bring** (*or* come) **to light,** to reveal (or be revealed). **in a good** (*or* bad) **light,** easily (or barely) visible; giving a favourable (or unfavourable) impression. **in the light of,** drawing information from; with the help given by. **lighting-up time,** the time after which vehicles on the road must show prescribed lights. **light meter,** an instrument for measuring the intensity of light, especially to assess the correct photographic exposure. **light pen,** a penlike photosensitive device held to the screen of a computer terminal for passing information on to it, or for sending barcodes. **light up,** to begin to smoke a cigarette etc.; to switch on lights. **lit up,** (*slang*) drunk. **strike alight,** to produce a spark or flame with matches etc. [Old English]

light² /laɪt/ *adj.* 1. of little weight, not heavy; easy to lift, carry, or move. 2. relatively low in weight, amount, density, strength etc.; deficient in weight. 3. carrying or suitable for small loads; (of a ship) unladen; carrying only light arms, armaments etc. 4. (of food) easy to digest. 5. easily borne or done. 6. intended only as entertainment, not profound. 7. (of sleep) easily disturbed. 8. free from sorrow, cheerful. 9. giddy. 10. nimble, quick-moving. 11. unchaste, wanton. 12. (of a building) elegant, graceful. —*adv.* 1. in a light manner. 2. with a minimum load. —*v.i.* (*past* and *past participle* lit or lighted) to come by chance *on* or *upon*. —**lighter-than-air** *adj.* (of an aircraft) weighing less than the air it displaces. **light-fingered** *adj.* given to stealing. **light-headed** *adj.* giddy; frivolous; delirious. **light-hearted** *adj.* cheerful; (unduly) casual. **light industry,** that producing small or light articles. **light into**, to attack. **light out**, to depart. **make light of**, to treat as unimportant. —**lightly** *adv.*, **lightness** *n.* [Old English]

light-emitting diode (LED) a means of displaying symbols in electronic instruments and devices. An LED is made of ◊semiconductor material, such as gallium arsenide phosphide, that glows when electricity is passed through it. The first digital watches and calculators had LED displays, but many later models use ◊liquid crystal displays.

lighten[1] /'laɪtən/ *v.t./i.* **1.** to shed light on; to make or become brighter. **2.** to emit lightning.

lighten[2] *v.t./i.* **1.** to make or become lighter in weight. **2.** to reduce the weight or load of. **3.** to bring relief to (the heart, mind etc.). **4.** to mitigate (a penalty).

lighter[1] *n.* a device for lighting cigarettes etc.

lighter[2] *n.* a boat, usually flat-bottomed, for transporting goods between a ship and a wharf etc. [from Middle Dutch]

lighthouse *n.* a tower or other structure containing a powerful light to warn or guide ships at sea.

lighting *n.* the equipment in a room or street etc. for producing light; an arrangement or effect of lights.

lightning /'laɪtnɪŋ/ *n.* a flash of bright light produced by an electric discharge between clouds or between a cloud and the ground. —*adj.* very quick. —**lightning conductor** *or* (*US*) **rod**, a metal rod or wire fixed to an exposed part of a building or to a mast to divert lightning into the Earth or sea. **like (greased) lightning**, (*colloquial*) with great speed.

light reaction the first stage of ◊photosynthesis, in which light energy splits water into oxygen and hydrogen ions. The second stage does not require light and results in the formation of carbohydrates.

lights *n.pl.* the lungs of sheep, pigs etc., used as food especially for pets.

light second a unit of length, equal to the distance travelled by light in one second. It is equal to $2.997,925 \times 10^8$ m/$9.835,592 \times 10^8$ ft. See ◊light year.

lightship *n.* a moored or anchored ship with a beacon light.

lightsome /'laɪtsəm/ *adj.* gracefully light, agile, merry.

light watt a unit of radiant power (brightness of light). One light watt is the power required to produce a perceived brightness equal to that of light at a wavelength of 550 nanometres and 680 lumens.

lightweight *adj.* **1.** below average weight. **2.** of little importance or influence. —*n.* **1.** a lightweight person or thing. **2.** a boxing weight between featherweight and welterweight.

light year in astronomy, the distance travelled by a beam of light in a vacuum in one year, approximately 9.45 trillion (million million) km/5.88 trillion miles.

ligneous /'lɪgnɪəs/ *adj.* of the nature of wood; (of plants) woody. [from Latin *lignum* = wood]

lignin *n.* a naturally occurring substance produced by plants to strengthen their tissues.

lignite /'lɪgnaɪt/ *n.* a type of ◊coal that is brown and fibrous, with a relatively low carbon content.

lignocaine *n.* a short-term local anaesthetic injected into tissues or applied to skin.

lignum vitae /'lɪgnəm 'vaɪti:, 'vi:taɪ/ a hard-wooded tree of the genus *Guaiacum.* [Latin = wood of life]

Liguria /lɪ'gjuərɪə/ coastal region of NW Italy, which includes the resorts of the Italian Riviera, lying between the western Alps and the Mediterranean Gulf of Genoa. The region comprises the provinces of Genova, La Spezia, Imperia, and Savona, with a population (1988) of 1,750,000 and an area of 5,418 sq km/2,093 sq mi. Genoa is the chief town and port.

like[1] *adj.* **1.** having some or all of the qualities or appearance etc. of; similar. **2.** characteristic of. **3.** such as, for example. **4.** in a suitable state or mood for. **5.** (*archaic* or *colloquial*) likely.—*prep.* in the manner of, to the same degree as. —*adv.* **1.** (*archaic*) in the same manner *as.* **2.** (*vulgar*) so to speak. —*conj.* **1.** (*colloquial, disputed usage*) as. **2.** (*US*) as if. —*n.* one that is like another, a similar thing. —**like anything** *or* **blazes** etc., (*colloquial*) very much; vigorously. **like hell**, recklessly; (*ironically*) not at all. **like-minded** *adj.* having the same tastes, opinions etc. **what is he/she** (*or it* etc.) **like?** what sort of person is he/she (or thing is it etc.)? [Old English]

like[2] *v.t.* **1.** to find agreeable or pleasant (also *ironic*). **2.** to choose to have, to prefer; to wish or be inclined *to.* —*n.* (usually in *plural*) a thing one likes or prefers. [Old English]

-like /-laɪk/ suffix forming adjectives from nouns in the sense 'similar to', 'characteristic of'.

likeable *adj.* pleasant, easy to like. —**likeably** *adv.*

likelihood /'laɪklɪhʊd/ *n.* probability. —**in all likelihood**, very probably.

likely /'laɪklɪ/ *adj.* **1.** such as may reasonably be expected to happen or be true etc. **2.** apparently suitable. **3.** showing promise of being successful. —*adv.* probably. —**not likely**, (*colloquial*) certainly not, I refuse. [from Old Norse]

liken *v.t.* to indicate or find a resemblance of (one person or thing to another).

likeness *n.* **1.** being like, a resemblance. **2.** a semblance or guise. **3.** a portrait, a representation.

likewise *adv.* **1.** also, moreover. **2.** similarly.

liking *n.* **1.** what one likes, one's taste. **2.** one's feeling that one likes something. [Old English]

Likud /lɪ'ku:d/ *n.* an alliance of right-wing Israeli political parties that defeated the Labour Party coalition in the May 1977 election and brought Menachem Begin to power. In 1987 Likud became part of an uneasy national coalition with Labour, formed to solve Israel's economic crisis. In 1989, another coalition was formed under Yitzhak Shamir.

lilac /'laɪlək/ *n.* **1.** a shrub of the genus *Syringa*, family Oleaceae, (especially *S. vulgaris*), with fragrant pale pinkish-violet or white blossoms. **2.** a pale pinkish-violet colour. —*adj.* of lilac colour. [obsolete French, ultimately from Persian *nil* = blue]

Lilburne /'lɪlbɜ:n/ John 1614–1657. English republican agitator. He was imprisoned 1638–40 for circulating Puritan pamphlets, fought in the Parliamentary army in the Civil War, and by his advocacy of a democratic republic won the leadership of the ◊Levellers.

liliaceous /lɪlɪ'eɪʃəs/ *adj.* of the lily family. [from Latin]

Lilienthal /'li:lɪənta:l/ Otto 1848–1896. German aviation pioneer who inspired the ◊Wright brothers. He made and successfully flew many gliders before he was killed in a glider crash.

Lilith /'lɪlɪθ/ in the Old Testament, an Assyrian female demon of the night. According to the ◊Talmud, she was the wife of Adam before Eve's creation.

Lille /li:l/ (Flemish *Ryssel*) industrial city (textiles, chemicals, engineering, distilling), capital of Nord-Pas-de-Calais, France; population (1982) 174,000, metropolitan area 936,000. The world's first entirely automatic underground system was opened here in 1982.

lilliputian /lɪlɪ'pju:ʃən/ *n.* a diminutive person or thing. —*adj.* diminutive. [from *Lilliput*, place in Swift's 'Gulliver's Travels', inhabited by people six inches high]

Lilongwe /lɪ'lɒŋgweɪ/ capital of Malawi since 1975; population (1985) 187,000. Products include tobacco and textiles.

lilt *n.* a light, pleasant rhythm; a song or tune with this. —*v.t./i.* to move or utter with a lilt.

lily /'lɪlɪ/ *n.* a plant of the genus *Lilium*, growing from a bulb, with white, yellow, orange, or purple, trumpet-shaped flowers on a tall, slender stem; its flowers; a heraldic figure of a lily. —*attrib.* delicately white. —**lily-livered** *adj.* cowardly. **lily of the valley**, a spring plant *Convallaria majalis* with fragrant white bell-shaped flowers. [Old English from Latin]

Lima /'li:mə/ capital of Peru, an industrial city with its port at Callao; population (1988) 418,000, metropolitan area 4,605,000. Products include textiles, chemicals, glass, and cement. Lima was founded by the conquistador Pizarro in 1535, and rebuilt after destruction by an earthquake in 1746.

limb[1] /lɪm/ *n.* **1.** a projecting part of an animal body, used in movement or in grasping things. **2.** a main branch of a tree. **3.** an arm of a cross. —**out on a limb**, isolated, stranded, at a disadvantage. [Old English]

limb[2] *n.* in astronomy, a specified edge of the Sun etc. [from French or Latin *limbus* = border]

limber[1] /'lɪmbə/ *adj.* flexible; lithe, agile. —*v.t./i.* to make limber. —**limber up**, to exercise in preparation for athletic activity etc.

limber[2] *n.* the detachable front part of a gun carriage. —*v.t.* to attach a limber to (a gun). [apparently related to Latin *limonarius* (*limo* = shaft)]

limbo¹ /'lɪmbəʊ/ *n.* **1.** in medieval Christian theology, a region on the border of hell, the supposed abode of pre-Christian righteous persons and of unbaptized infants. **2.** an intermediate state or condition (e.g. of a plan awaiting decision); a condition of being neglected and forgotten. [from Latin phrase *in limbo* (*limbus* = border)]

limbo² *n.* (*plural* **limbos**) a West Indian dance in which the dancer bends backwards to pass under a horizontal bar which is progressively lowered.

Limbourg brothers Franco-Flemish painters, Pol, Herman, and Jan (Hennequin, Janneken), active in the late 14th and early 15th centuries, first in Paris, then at the ducal court of Burgundy. They produced richly detailed manuscript illuminations, including two Books of ◊Hours.

Limburg /'lɪmbɜːg/ southernmost province of the Netherlands in the plain of the Maas (Meuse); area 2,170 sq km/838 sq mi; population (1988) 1,095,000. Its capital is Maastricht, the oldest city in the Netherlands.

lime¹ *n.* or **quicklime** a white substance (calcium oxide) obtained by heating limestone and used for making mortar, as a fertilizer etc. —*v.t.* to treat with lime. —**limekiln** *n.* a kiln for heating limestone. [Old English]

lime² *n.* the round fruit of the tree *Citrus aurantifolia*, like a lemon but smaller and more acid. —**lime green**, the pale green colour of the lime. [French from Provençal or Spanish from Arabic]

lime³ *n.* or **linden** an ornamental tree of the genus *Tilia*, family Tiliaceae, bearing fragrant yellow blossom on a winged stalk.

limelight *n.* an intense white light obtained by heating a cylinder of lime in an oxyhydrogen flame, formerly used to illuminate the stages of theatres. —**the limelight**, the full glare of publicity.

limerick /'lɪmərɪk/ *n.* a five-line humorous verse, often nonsensical, which first appeared in England about 1820 and was popularized by Edward ◊Lear. [from *Limerick* in Ireland]

Limerick county in SW Republic of Ireland, in Munster province; **area** 2,690 sq km/1,038 sq mi; **county town** Limerick; **physical** fertile, with hills in the S; **products** dairy products; **population** (1986) 164,000.

Limerick county town of Limerick, Republic of Ireland, the main port of W Ireland, on the Shannon estuary; population (1986) 77,000. It was founded in the 12th century.

limestone *n.* a sedimentary rock composed mainly of calcium carbonate.

limewater *n.* common name for a dilute solution of slaked lime (calcium hydroxide, $Ca(OH)_2$). In chemistry, it is used to detect the presence of carbon dioxide.

Limey /'laɪmɪ/ *n.* (*US slang*) a British person (originally a sailor) or ship. [from *lime²*, from the former issue of lime juice on British ships as a drink to prevent scurvy]

limit /'lɪmɪt/ *n.* **1.** the point, line, or level beyond which something does not or may not extend or pass. **2.** the greatest or smallest amount permitted. —*v.t.* to set or serve as a limit to; to restrict. —**be the limit**, (*slang*) to be intolerable. **within limits**, with some degree of freedom. [from Latin *limes* = boundary]

limitation /lɪmɪ'teɪʃən/ *n.* **1.** limiting, being limited. **2.** a lack of ability. **3.** a limiting rule or circumstance.

Limitation, Statutes of in English law, acts of Parliament limiting the time within which legal action may be inaugurated.

limited *adj.* **1.** confined within limits. **2.** not great in scope or talents. **3.** (of a monarch etc.) subject to constitutional restrictions. —**limited edition**, the production of a limited number of copies.

limited company or **joint stock company** in the UK, the usual type of company formation, with capital divided into small units, and profits distributed according to shareholding. The members of a limited company are legally responsible only to a limited degree for its debts.

Limited Liability Acts UK acts of Parliament of 1855 and 1862, which provided a legal framework for the consolidation of large companies that existed as legal entities in perpetuity; they restricted the maximum loss for individual shareholders to the purchase price of their shares.

limiting factor any factor affecting the rate of a metabolic reaction. Levels of light or of carbon dioxide are limiting factors in ◊photosynthesis because both are necessary for the production of carbohydrates.

Limits, Territorial and Fishing see ◊maritime law.

limn /lɪm/ *v.t.* to paint (a picture), to portray. [from obsolete *lumine* = illuminate]

limnology /lɪm'nɒlədʒɪ/ *n.* the study of fresh waters and their inhabitants. —**limnological** /-'lɒdʒɪkəl/ *adj.*, **limnologist** *n.* [from Greek *limnē* = lake]

limonite *n.* or **brown iron ore** an iron ore, mostly poorly crystalline iron oxyhydroxide, but usually mixed with ◊hematite and other iron oxides. It is often found in bog deposits.

Limousin /lɪmuː'zæn/ former province and modern region of central France; area 16,900 sq km/6,544 sq mi; population (1986) 736,000. It consists of the *départements* of Corrèze, Creuse, and Haute-Vienne. The chief town is Limoges. A thinly populated and largely unfertile region, it is crossed by the mountains of the Massif Central. Fruit and vegetables are produced in the more fertile lowlands. Kaolin is mined.

limousine /lɪmu'ziːn/ *n.* a motorcar with a closed body and a partition behind the driver; a luxurious motorcar. [French, originally = caped cloak worn in province of *Limousin*]

limp¹ *v.i.* **1.** to walk lamely. **2.** (of a damaged ship etc.) to proceed with difficulty. **3.** (of verse) to be defective. —*n.* a lame walk. [related to Old English *lemphealt* = lame]

limp² *adj.* **1.** not stiff or firm, easily bent. **2.** without will or energy. —**limply** *adv.*, **limpness** *n.*

limpet /'lɪmpɪt/ *n.* a type of mollusc. It has a conical shell, and adheres firmly to rocks by a disclike foot. —**limpet mine**, a mine attached to a ship's hull that explodes after a set time. [Old English]

limpid /'lɪmpɪd/ *adj.* clear, transparent. —**limpidity** /-'pɪdɪtɪ/ *n.* [from French or Latin]

Limpopo /lɪm'pəʊpəʊ/ river in SE Africa, rising in the Transvaal and reaching the Indian Ocean in Mozambique; length 1,600 km/1,000 mi.

Lin Biao /lɪn'bjaʊ/ 1907–1971. Chinese politician and general. He joined the Communists in 1927, became a commander of ◊Mao Zedong's Red Army, and led the Northeast People's Liberation Army in the civil war after 1945. He became defence minister in 1959, and as vice chairman of the party in 1969 he was expected to be Mao's successor. But in 1972 the government announced that Lin had been killed in an aeroplane crash in Mongolia on the 17 Sept 1971 while fleeing to the USSR following an abortive coup attempt.

linchpin *n.* **1.** a pin passed through the axle end to keep a wheel in position. **2.** a person or thing vital to an organization etc. [from Old English]

Lincoln /'lɪŋkən/ Abraham 1809–1865. 16th president of the USA 1861–65. In the US Civil War, his chief concern was the preservation of the Union from which the Confederate (Southern) slave states had seceded on his election. In 1863 he announced the freedom of the slaves with the **Emancipation Proclamation**. He was re-elected in 1864 with victory for the North in sight, but assassinated at the end of the war.

No man is good enough to govern another man without that other's consent.

Abraham Lincoln
speech 1854

Lincolnshire /'lɪŋkənʃə/ county in E England; **area** 5,890 sq km/2,274 sq mi; **administrative headquarters** Lincoln; **physical** Lincoln Wolds; marshy coastline; the Fens in the SE; rivers: Witham, Welland; **products** cattle, sheep, horses, cereals, flower bulbs, oil; **population** (1987) 575,000.

Lincs. abbreviation of Lincolnshire.

linctus *n.* a medicine, especially a soothing syrupy cough mixture. [Latin *lingere* = lick]

Lindbergh /'lɪndbɜːg/ Charles (Augustus) 1902–1974. US aviator who made the first solo nonstop flight across the Atlantic (New York–Paris) in 1927 in the *Spirit of St Louis*.

linden /'lɪndən/ another name for ◊lime³.

Lindow Man /'lɪndəʊ/ the remains of an Iron Age man discovered in a peat bog at Lindow Marsh, Cheshire, UK, in 1984. The chemicals in the bog had kept the body in an excellent state of preservation.

line[1] *n.* **1.** a long, narrow mark traced on a surface; its use in art; a thing resembling such a traced mark, a band of colour, a furrow or wrinkle. **2.** a straight or curved continuous extent of length without breadth, the track of a moving point. **3.** a curve connecting all points having a specified common property. **4.** a straight line. **5.** a limit, a boundary; a mark limiting the area of play in sports; the starting point in a race. **6.** a row of persons or things; a direction as indicated by them, a trend; (*US*) a queue. **7.** a piece of cord, rope etc., serving a specified purpose. **8.** a wire or cable for a telephone or telegraph; a connection by this. **9.** a contour, outline, or lineament; the shape to which a garment is designed. **10.** a course of procedure, conduct, thought etc.; (in *plural*) a plan, a draft, a manner of procedure. **11.** a row of printed or written words, a verse; (in *plural*) a piece of poetry, the words of an actor's part, a specified amount of text etc. to be written out as a school punishment. **12.** a single track of a railway; one branch of a railway system; the whole system under one management. **13.** a regular succession of buses, ships, aircraft etc., plying between certain places; a company conducting this. **14.** a connected series of persons following one another in time (especially several generations of a family); lineage, stock. **15.** a direction, a course, a track. **16.** a department of activity, a province, a branch of business; a class of commercial goods. **17.** a connected series of military fieldworks; an arrangement of soldiers side by side, ships etc. drawn up in battle array. **18.** each of the very narrow horizontal sections forming a television picture. —*v.t.* **1.** to mark with lines. **2.** to position or stand at intervals along. —**the line,** the equator. **all along the line,** at every point. **bring** (*or* **come**) **into line,** to make conform, to conform. **drop a person a line,** to send him or her a short letter etc. **get a line on,** (*colloquial*) to learn something about. **in line for,** likely to receive. **in line with,** in accordance with. **lay** *or* **put it on the line,** to speak frankly. **line drawing,** one done with pen or pencil. **line of fire,** the path of a bullet etc. about to be shot. **line of vision,** the straight line along which an observer looks. **line-out** *n.* (in Rugby football) parallel lines of opposing forwards at right angles to the touchline for the throwing in of the ball. **line printer,** a machine that prints the output from a computer a line at a time. **line up,** to arrange or be arranged in line(s). **line-up** *n.* a line of people for inspection; an arrangement of persons in a team etc. **out of line,** not in alignment; discordant. [Old English and from Old French from Latin *linea* (*linum* = flax)]

line[2] *v.t.* **1.** to cover the inside surface of (a garment, box etc.) with a layer of material. **2.** to serve as a lining for. **3.** to fill (a purse, stomach, etc.). [from obsolete *line* = fine linen (used for linings), from Latin *linum* = flax]

lineage /'lɪniɪdʒ/ *n.* lineal descent, ancestry. [from Old French]

lineal /'lɪnɪəl/ *adj.* **1.** in the direct line of descent or ancestry. **2.** linear. —**lineally** *adv.*

lineament /'lɪnɪəmənt/ *n.* (usually in *plural*) a distinctive feature or characteristic, especially of the face.

line and staff management those managers whose responsibilities cover those aspects of a firm directly involved in the production of a good or service, e.g. production or sales.

linear /'lɪnɪə/ *adj.* **1.** of or in lines. **2.** long and narrow and of uniform breadth. —**linearity** /-'ærɪtɪ/ *n.*

linear accelerator in physics, a machine in which charged ◊particles are accelerated (as in an ◊accelerator) to high speed in passing down a straight evacuated tube, or waveguide, by electromagnetic waves in the tube or by electric fields.

linear equation in mathematics, an equation involving two variables (x, y) of the general form $y = mx + b$, where m is the slope of the line represented by the equation and b is the y-intercept, or the value of y where the line crosses the y-axis in the Cartesian coordinate system (see ◊Cartesian). Linear equations are used to describe the behaviour of buildings, bridges, trusses, and other static structures.

linear motor a type of electric induction motor, in which the fixed stator and moving armature are straight and parallel to each other (rather than being circular and one inside the other as in an ordinary induction motor). Linear motors are used, for example, to power sliding doors. There is a magnetic force between the stator and armature; this force has been used to support

vehicles, as in the experimental ◊maglev linear motor train.

lineation /lɪni'eɪʃən/ *n.* marking with or an arrangement of lines.

linen /'lɪnɪn/ *n.* **1.** cloth woven from ◊flax. **2.** (*collectively*) articles made (or originally made) of linen, e.g. sheets, shirts, undergarments. —*adj.* made of linen. [Old English]

liner[1] /'laɪnə/ *n.* a ship or aircraft etc. carrying passengers on a regular route. —**liner train,** a fast freight train with detachable containers on permanently coupled wagons.

liner[2] *n.* a removable lining.

linesman *n.* (*plural* **linesmen**) an umpire's or referee's assistant who decides whether a ball falls within the playing area or not.

ling[1] *n.* a long, slender sea fish *Molva molva.*

ling[2] *n.* a kind of heather, especially *Calluna vulgaris.* [from Old Norse]

-ling suffix forming nouns denoting a person or thing connected with (e.g. *hireling*) or having the property of being (e.g. *weakling*) or undergoing (e.g. *starveling*), or denoting a diminutive (e.g. *duckling*), often derogatory (e.g. *lordling*). [Old English]

linga /'lɪŋɡə/ *n.* or **lingam** a phallus, especially as the symbol of the Hindu god Siva. [Sanskrit = mark, symbol]

linger /'lɪŋɡə/ *v.i.* **1.** to stay a long time, especially as if reluctant to leave; to dawdle. **2.** to remain alive although becoming weaker, to be slow in dying. [frequentative of obsolete *long* = remain]

lingerie /'læʒərɪ/ *n.* women's underwear and nightclothes. [French (*linge* = linen)]

lingo /'lɪŋɡəʊ/ *n.* (*plural* **lingos**) (*colloquial*) **1.** a foreign language. **2.** the vocabulary of a special subject or class of people. [probably from Portuguese *lingoa* from Latin *lingua* = tongue]

lingua franca /lɪŋɡwə 'fræŋkə/ any language that is used as a means of communication by groups who do not themselves normally speak that language. For example, English is a lingua franca used by Japanese doing business in Finland, or by Swedes in Saudi Arabia. [Italian = Frankish tongue]

lingual /'lɪŋɡwəl/ *adj.* **1.** of or formed by the tongue. **2.** of speech or languages. —**lingually** *adv.* [from Latin *lingua* = tongue, language]

linguist /'lɪŋɡwɪst/ *n.* a person skilled in languages or linguistics. [from Latin *lingua* = language]

linguistic /lɪŋ'ɡwɪstɪk/ *adj.* of language or linguistics. —**linguistically** *adv.*

linguistics *n.* the scientific study of language, covering its origins (historical linguistics), the changing way it is pronounced (phonetics), the derivation of words through various languages (etymology), the development of meanings (semantics), and the arrangement and modifications of words to convey a message (grammar).

liniment /'lɪnɪmənt/ *n.* an embrocation, usually made with an oil. [from Latin *linere* = smear]

lining /'laɪnɪŋ/ *n.* a layer of material used to line a surface.

link *n.* **1.** one loop or ring of a chain etc. **2.** a connecting part; a thing or person that unites or provides continuity, one in a series; the state or a means of connection. **3.** a cuff link. —*v.t./i.* **1.** to make or be a connection between. **2.** to be joined (to a system, company etc.). [from Old Norse]

linkage *n.* **1.** a system of links; linking; a link. **2.** in genetics, the association between two or more genes that tend to be inherited together because they are on the same chromosome.

linkman *n.* (*plural* **linkmen**) a person providing continuity in a broadcast programme.

links *n.* (treated as *singular* or *plural*) a golf course. [plural of *link* = rising ground]

Linlithgowshire /lɪn'lɪθɡəʊʃə/ former name of West Lothian, now included in Lothian region, Scotland.

Linnaeus /lɪ'niːəs/ Carolus 1707–1778. Swedish naturalist and physician. His botanical work *Systema naturae* 1758 contained his system for classifying plants into groups depending on shared characteristics (such as the number of stamens in flowers), providing a much-needed framework for identification. He also devised the concise and precise system for naming plants and animals, using one Latin (or Latinized) word to represent the genus and a second to distinguish the species. For example, in the Latin name of the daisy *Bellis perennis, Bellis* is the name of the genus

liquid crystal display

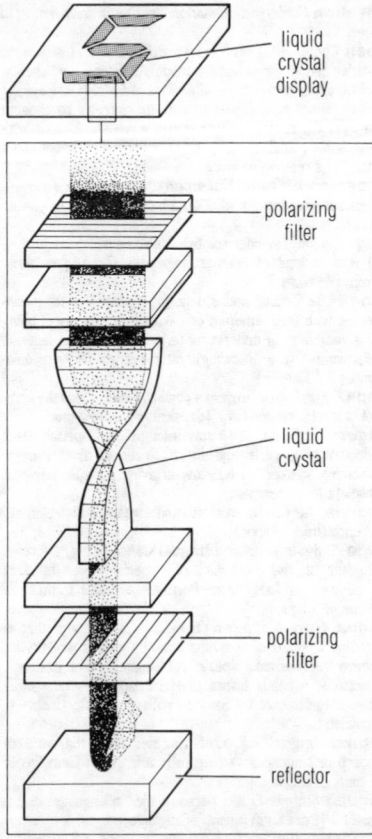

liquid crystal display

polarizing filter

liquid crystal

polarizing filter

reflector

to which the plant belongs and *perennis* distinguishes the species from others of the same genus. See also ◊binomial system of nomenclature (under ◊binomial), ◊taxonomy. [Latinized form of Carl von Linné]

linnet /'lınıt/ *n.* a bird of the finch family *Acanthis cannabina* common in Asia, NW Africa, and Europe. Linnets are mainly brown, but the males have a crimson crown and breast in summer. They nest in low bushes and feed on weed seeds and some insects. They are about 13 cm/5 in long, and are noted for their song. [from Old French *linette* (*lin* = flax, from its food)]

lino /'laınəʊ/ *n.* (*plural* **linos**) linoleum. [abbreviation]

linocut /'laınəʊkʌt/ *n.* a design cut in relief on a block of linoleum; a print made from this.

linoleum /lɪ'nəʊlɪəm/ *n.* a floor covering of canvas backing thickly coated with a preparation of linseed oil and powdered cork etc. [from Latin *linum* = flax and *oleum* = oil]

Linotype /'laınəʊtaıp/ *n.* the trade name of a composing machine which sets lines of hot metal type (slugs) as operators type the copy at a keyboard, formerly in universal use for newspapers.

Lin Piao /'lın pi'aʊ/ alternative form of ◊Lin Biao.

linsang *n.* a nocturnal, arboreal, and carnivorous mammal of the mongoose family, about 75 cm/2.5 ft long. It is native to Africa and SE Asia.

linseed /'lɪnsi:d/ *n.* **1.** the seed of ◊flax. **2.** an oil extracted from it and used in paint and varnish. [Old English *line* = flax]

linsey-woolsey /ˌlɪnzi'wʊlzɪ/ *n.* a fabric of coarse wool woven on a cotton warp. [probably from *Lindsey* in Suffolk]

lint *n.* **1.** linen with one side made fluffy by scraping, used for dressing wounds. **2.** fluff. [perhaps from Old French *linette* = linseed (*lin* = flax)]

lintel /'lɪntəl/ *n.* a horizontal timber or stone across the top of a door or window. [from Old French]

Linz /lɪnts/ industrial port on the river Danube in N Austria; population (1981) 199,900. Industries include iron, steel, and metalworking.

lion /'laıən/ *n.* **1.** a large, powerful member of the cat family *Panthera leo* now found only in Africa and parts of India. **2.** a brave or celebrated person. **3. the Lion,** the sign or constellation Leo. **4. Lions,** the Rugby Union team representing Britain, so called from the symbol on their official tie. —**lion-heart** *n.* a courageous person. **lion-hearted** *adj.* courageous. **lion's share,** the largest or best portion. —**lioness** *n.fem.* [from Anglo-French from Latin from Greek]

lionize *v.t.* to treat as a celebrity.

lip *n.* **1.** either of the fleshy parts forming the edges of the mouth opening. **2.** the edge of a cup etc.; the edge of a vessel shaped for pouring from. **3.** (*slang*) impudent speech. —*v.t.* (**-pp-**) **1.** to touch with the lips; to apply the lips to. **2.** to touch lightly. —**bite one's lip,** to repress emotion, laughter etc. **curl one's lip,** to express scorn. **lip-read** *v.t./i.* (especially of a deaf person) to understand speech (of) entirely from observing the speaker's lip movements. **lip service** *n.* an insincere expression of support. **smack one's lips,** to part the lips noisily in relish or anticipation, especially of food. —**lipped, -lipped** *adj.* [Old English]

lipase *n.* the enzyme responsible for breaking down fats into fatty acids and glycerol. It is produced by the ◊pancreas and requires a slightly alkaline environment. The products of fat digestion are absorbed by the intestinal wall.

Lipatti /lɪ'pæti/ Dinu 1917–1950. Romanian pianist, who perfected a small repertoire, notably Chopin. He died of leukaemia at 33.

Li Peng /'li: 'pʌn/ 1928– . Chinese communist politician, a member of the Politburo from 1985, and head of government from 1987. During the prodemocracy demonstrations in 1989 he supported the massacre of students by Chinese troops and the subsequent executions of others. He favours maintaining firm central and party control over the economy, and seeks improved relations with the USSR.

lipid /'lɪpɪd/ *n.* any of a group of compounds that are esters of fatty acids or fatlike substances. [from French from Greek *lipos* = fat]

Li Po /li:'bəʊ/ 705–762. Chinese poet. He used traditional literary forms, but his exuberance, the boldness of his imagination, and the intensity of his feeling have won him recognition as perhaps the greatest of all Chinese poets. Although he was mostly concerned with higher themes, he is also remembered for his celebratory verses on drinking.

lipophilic *adj.* in chemistry, with an affinity for fats and oils. [Greek = fat-loving]

lipophobic *adj.* in chemistry, tending to repel fats and oils. [Greek = fat-hating]

Lippershey /'lɪpəʃaɪ/ Hans *c.*1570–1619. Dutch lens maker, credited with inventing the telescope in 1608.

Lippi /'lɪpi/ Filippino 1457–1504. Italian painter of the Florentine school, trained by Botticelli. He produced altarpieces and several fresco cycles, full of detail and drama, elegant and finely drawn. He was the son of Fra Filippo Lippi.

Lippi Fra Filippo 1406–1469. Italian painter, born in Florence and patronized by the Medici family. His works include frescoes depicting the lives of St Stephen and St John the Baptist in Prato Cathedral 1452–66. He also painted many altarpieces of Madonnas and groups of saints.

Lippizaner /lɪpi'tsɑ:nə/ *n.* a horse of a fine white breed used especially in displays of dressage. [German, from *Lippiza* in Yugoslavia, the home of the former Austrian Imperial Stud where such a strain of horses was originally bred]

Lippmann /'lɪpmən/ Gabriel 1845–1921. French doctor, who invented the direct colour process in photography. He won the Nobel Prize for Physics in 1908.

lipsalve *n.* an ointment for sore lips.

lipstick *n.* a small stick of cosmetic for colouring the lips.

liquefied petroleum gas (LPG) any liquid form of butane, propane, or pentane, produced by the distillation of petroleum during oil refining.

liquefy /'lɪkwɪfaɪ/ *v.t./i.* to make or become liquid. —**liquefaction** /-'fækʃən/ *n.* [from French from Latin]

liqueur /li'kjʊə/ *n.* any of several strong, sweet alcoholic spirits, variously flavoured.

liquid /'lɪkwɪd/ *adj.* 1. having a consistency like that of water or oil, flowing freely but not gaseous; having the qualities of water in appearance. 2. (of sounds) clear and pure. 3. (of assets) easily converted into cash. —*n.* 1. a liquid substance. 2. the sound of *l* or *r*. [from Latin *liquere* = be liquid]

liquid air air that has been cooled so much that it has liquefied. This happens at temperatures below about –196°C.

liquidate /'lɪkwɪdeɪt/ *v.t./i.* 1. to wind up the affairs of (a company or firm) by ascertaining liabilities and apportioning its assets. 2. to undergo liquidation. 3. to pay off (a debt). 4. to put an end to or get rid of (especially by violent means). —**liquidator** *n.* [from Latin]

liquidation /lɪkwɪ'deɪʃən/ *n.* the liquidating of a company etc. —**go into liquidation**, (of a company etc.) to be wound up and have the assets apportioned.

liquid crystal display (LCD) a display of numbers (for example, in a calculator) or picture (such as on a pocket television screen) produced by molecules of a substance in a semiliquid state with some crystalline properties, in that clusters of molecules align in parallel formations. The display is a blank until the application of an electric field, which 'twists' the molecules so that they reflect or transmit light falling on them.

liquidity /lɪ'kwɪdɪtɪ/ *n.* the state of being liquid or having liquid assets. [from French or Latin]

liquidize /'lɪkwɪdaɪz/ *v.t.* to reduce to a liquid state.

liquidizer *n.* a machine for making purées etc.

liquor /'lɪkə/ *n.* 1. alcoholic drink. 2. juice or other liquid (especially produced in cooking). [from Old French from Latin]

liquorice /'lɪkərɪs, -ɪʃ/ *n.* 1. a black substance used as a sweet and in medicine. 2. the plant *Glycyrrhiza glabra* from whose root it is obtained. [from Anglo-French from Latin from Greek *glukurrhiza* (*glukus* = sweet and *rhiza* = root]

lira /'lɪərə/ *n.* (*plural* **lire** /-reɪ/, **liras**) the currency unit in Italy and in Turkey. [Italian from Provençal from Latin *libra* = pound]

Lisbon /'lɪzbən/ (Portuguese *Lisboa*) city and capital of Portugal, in the SW on the tidal lake and estuary formed by the river Tagus; population (1984) 808,000. Industries include steel, textiles, chemicals, pottery, shipbuilding, and fishing.

lisle /laɪl/ *n.* a fine smooth cotton thread for stockings etc. [from *Lille* in France]

lisp *n.* a speech defect in which /s/ is pronounced /θ/ and /z/ is pronounced /ð/. —*v.t./i.* to speak or say with a lisp. [Old English (imitative)]

Lisp *n.* a computer-programming language for list processing used primarily in artificial-intelligence (AI) research.

lissom /'lɪsəm/ *adj.* lithe, agile. —**lissomness** *n.*

list[1] *n.* 1. a number of connected items, names etc., written or printed together as a record or to aid the memory. 2. (in *plural*) palisades enclosing a tiltyard; the scene of a contest. —*v.t.* 1. to make a list of, to enter in a list. 2. to include (a building) in a list of those considered to be of special architectural or historic interest, having official protection from demolition or from alteration or extension affecting its character. —**enter the lists**, to issue or accept a challenge. [Old English, originally = edging, strip]

list[2] *v.i.* (of a ship etc.) to lean over to one side. —*n.* a listing position, a tilt.

listed building in Britain, a building officially recognised as having historical or architectural interest and therefore legally protected from uncontrolled alteration or demolition.

listen /'lɪsən/ *v.i.* 1. to make an effort to hear something, to wait alertly for a sound. 2. to hear with attention as a person speaks; to pay attention. 3. to allow oneself to be persuaded by a suggestion or request. —**listen in**, to tap a communication made by telephone; to listen to a radio broadcast. [Old English]

listener /'lɪsnə/ *n.* one who listens; a person listening to a radio broadcast.

Lister /'lɪstə/ Joseph, 1st Baron Lister 1827–1912. English surgeon and founder of antiseptic surgery, influenced by Louis dʒPasteur's work on bacteria. He introduced dressings soaked in carbolic acid and strict rules of hygiene to combat wound sepsis in hospitals.

listeriosis *n.* a disease of animals that may occasionally infect humans, caused by the bacterium *Listeria*

monocytogenes. The bacteria multiply at temperatures close to 0°C/32F, which means they may flourish in precooked frozen meals if the cooking has not been thorough. Listeriosis causes inflammation of the brain and its surrounding membranes, but can be treated with penicillin.

listless *adj.* without energy or enthusiasm. —**listlessly** *adv.*, **listlessness** *n.* [from obsolete *list* = inclination]

Liszt /lɪst/ Franz 1811–1886. Hungarian pianist and composer. An outstanding virtuoso of the piano, he was an established concert artist by the age of 12. His expressive, romantic, and frequently chromatic works include piano music (*Transcendental Studies* 1851), symphonies, piano concertos, and organ music. Much of his music is programmatic; he also originated the symphonic poem.

lit past and past participle of dʒlight[1] and dʒlight[2].

Litani /lɪ'tɑnɪ/ river rising near Baalbek in the Anti-Lebanon mountains of E Lebanon. It flows NE–SW through the Beqa'a Valley then E to the Mediterranean 8 km/5 mi N of Tyre. The Israelis invaded Lebanon as far as the Litani River in 1978.

litany /'lɪtənɪ/ *n.* a series of supplications to God recited by a priest etc. with set responses by the congregation; **the Litany**, that in the Book of Common Prayer. [from Old French from Latin from Greek *litē* = supplication]

litchi /'li:tʃi:/ *n.* or **lychee** a sweetish, pulpy, ovate fruit in a thin brown shell; the tree *Litchi chinensis* (originally Chinese) bearing this. [from Chinese]

literacy /'lɪtərəsɪ/ *n.* the ability to read and write.

literal *adj.* 1. taking words in their usual sense without metaphor or allegory. 2. exactly corresponding to the original words. 3. (of a person) tending to interpret things in a literal way, unimaginative. 4. so called without exaggeration. 5. of a letter or letters of the alphabet. —*n.* a misprint of a letter. —**literally** *adv.*, **literalness** *n.* [from Old French or Latin]

literalism *n.* insistence on literal interpretation, adherence to the letter. —**literalist** *n.*

literary /'lɪtərərɪ/ *adj.* 1. of, concerned with, or interested in literature or books or written composition. 2. (of a word or idiom) used chiefly by writers, not in ordinary speech. —**literariness** *n.* [from Latin]

literary criticism the establishment of principles governing literary composition, and the assessment and interpretation of literary works.

literate /'lɪtərət/ *adj.* able to read and write. —*n.* a literate person. [from Latin]

literati /lɪtə'rɑːtiː/ *n.pl.* people of letters, the learned class. [Latin]

literature /'lɪtərətʃə/ *n.* 1. written works, especially those valued for their beauty of form and style. 2. the writings of a country, period, or particular subject. 3. a literary production. 4. (*colloquial*) printed matter, leaflets etc. [from Latin]

lithe /laɪð/ *adj.* flexible, supple. [Old English]

lithification another term for dʒdiagenesis.

lithium /'lɪθɪəm/ *n.* a soft silver-white element of the alkali-metal group, symbol Li, atomic number 3, relative atomic mass 6.941. Lithium is the lightest metallic element; it is soft and ductile and burns in air at 200°C. It is used as a reducing agent, in batteries, to harden alloys, and in producing tritium. Lithium compounds are used in medicine to treat depression. [from Greek *lithos* = stone]

litho /'laɪθəʊ/ *n.* (*colloquial*) (*plural* **lithos**) the lithographic process. —*adj.* lithographic. —*v.t.* (*colloquial*) to lithograph. [abbreviation of *lithograph*]

lithograph /'lɪθəgrɑːf/ *n.* a print produced by lithography. —*v.t.* to produce a lithographic print of.

lithography *n.* a printmaking technique originated by Aloys Senefelder in 1798, based on the antipathy of grease and water. A drawing is made with greasy crayon on an absorbent stone, which is then wetted. The wet stone repels ink (which is greasy) applied to the surface and the crayon attracts it, so that the drawing can be printed. Modern lithographic printing using complex photographic techniques is now the usual printing process for books, newspapers, etc. —**lithographer** *n.* **lithographic** /-'græfɪk/ *adj.*, **lithographically** *adv.* [from German from Greek *lithos* = stone]

lithosphere *n.* the topmost layer of the Earth's structure, forming the jigsaw of plates that take part in the movements of dʒplate tectonics. The lithosphere comprises the dʒcrust (sense 2) and a portion of the upper ◊mantle (sense 4). It is regarded as being rigid and moves about on the semimolten ◊asthenosphere. The lithosphere is about 75 km/47 mi thick.

Lithuania /lɪθjuːˈeɪnɪə/ constituent republic of the W USSR from 1940; **area** 65,200 sq km/25,174 sq mi; **capital** Vilnius; **physical** river Niemen; 25% forested; lakes, marshes, and complex sandy coastline; **products** bacon, dairy products, cereals, potatoes, heavy engineering, electrical goods, cement; **population** (1987) 3,641,000; 80% Lithuanian, 9% Russian, 8% Polish; **language** Lithuanian; **recent history** the independent Soviet republic created in 1918 was overthrown by the Germans, Poles, and nationalist Lithuanians in 1919, and a democratic republic was established. This was overthrown by a fascist coup in 1926. In 1939 the USSR demanded military bases and in 1940 incorporated Lithuania as a constituent republic. There has been nationalist dissent since 1980. A popular front, the Lithuanian Restructuring Movement (Sajudis), was formed in Oct 1988 to campaign for increased autonomy, and in Nov 1989 the republic's Supreme Soviet (state assembly) decreed Lithuanian the state language and readopted the flag of the independent interwar republic. A month later, the republic's Communist Party split into two, with the majority wing formally breaking away from the Communist Party of the Soviet Union and establishing itself as a social-democratic, Lithuanian-nationalist body. A multiparty system is effectively in place in the republic. In March 1990 Lithuania unilaterally declared its independence.

Lithuanian *adj.* of or relating to Lithuania. —*n.* **1.** a native or inhabitant of Lithuania. **2.** the Indo-European language spoken by the people of Lithuania, which through its geographical isolation has retained many ancient features of the Indo-European language family. It acquired a written form in the 16th century, using the Latin alphabet, and is currently spoken by some 3–4 million people.

litigant /ˈlɪtɪɡənt/ *n.* a party to a lawsuit. —*adj.* engaged in a lawsuit.

litigate /ˈlɪtɪɡeɪt/ *v.t./i.* to go to law; to contest (a point) at law. —**litigation** /-ˈɡeɪʃən/ *n.* [from Latin *litigare* (*lis* = lawsuit)]

litigious /lɪˈtɪdʒəs/ *adj.* fond of litigation, contentious. —**litigiousness** *n.* [from Old French or Latin]

litmus /ˈlɪtməs/ *n.* a dye obtained from various lichens and used as an indicator to test the acidic or alkaline nature of aqueous solutions; it turns red in the presence of acid, and blue in the presence of alkali. —**litmus paper,** paper stained with litmus and used as a test for acids or alkalis. [from Old Norwegian = dye moss]

litotes /laɪˈtəʊtiːz/ *n.* an ironic understatement, especially using a negative of its contrary (e.g. *I shan't be sorry* = I shall be glad). [Latin from Greek *litos* = meagre]

litre /ˈliːtə/ *n.* a metric unit of capacity, equal to 1 cubic decilitre or about 1.76 pints. [French (*litron* = obsolete measure of capacity from Latin from Greek *litra* = Sicilian monetary unit)]

Lit. D. abbreviation of Doctor of Letters. [from Latin *Litterarum Doctor*]

litter *n.* **1.** refuse, especially paper, discarded on streets etc.; odds and ends lying about. **2.** a vehicle containing a couch and carried on people's shoulders or by beasts of burden. **3.** a kind of stretcher for the sick and wounded. **4.** the young animals brought forth at a birth. **5.** straw etc. as bedding for animals. **6.** straw and dung, of a farmyard etc. —*v.t.* **1.** to make (a place) untidy by discarding rubbish. **2.** to give birth to (whelps etc., or *absolute*). **3.** to provide (a horse etc.) with litter as bedding; to spread straw etc. on (a stable floor etc.). [from Anglo-French from Latin *lectus* = bed]

litterbug *n.* or **litter lout** a person who carelessly strews litter in a street etc.

little *adj.* (*comparative* **less, lesser, littler;** *superlative* **least, littlest**) **1.** small in size, amount, degree etc., not great or big; short in stature; of short distance or duration. **2.** relatively unimportant; operating on a small scale. **3.** young or younger. **4.** smaller or smallest of the name. **5.** trivial, paltry, mean. **6.** not much; a certain though small amount of. —*n.* not much, only a small amount; a certain but no great amount; a short time or distance. —*adv.* (*comparative* **less;** *superlative* **least**) **1.** to a small extent only. **2.** not at all. —**little by little,** gradually, by a small amount

at a time. **little end,** the smaller end of a connecting rod, attached to a piston. **Little Englander,** (*historical*) one desiring to restrict the dimensions of the British Empire and Britain's responsibilities. **the little people,** the fairies. **Little Russian,** Ukrainian. **little theatre,** a small playhouse, especially one used for experimental productions. **the little woman,** (*colloquial*) one's wife. [Old English]

Little Bighorn /ˈlɪtl ˈbɪɡhɔːn/ site in Montana, USA, of Gen George ◊Custer's defeat by the ◊Sioux Indians on 25 June 1876 under chiefs ◊Crazy Horse and Sitting Bull, known as **Custer's last stand.**

Little Dipper another name for ◊Ursa Minor, the Little Bear. The name has also been applied to the stars in the ◊Pleiades open star cluster, the overall shape of the cluster being similar to that of the Plough, or Big Dipper.

Little Entente a series of alliances between Czechoslovakia, Romania, and Yugoslavia 1920–21 for mutual security and the maintenance of existing frontiers. Reinforced by the Treaty of Belgrade in 1929, the entente collapsed upon Yugoslav cooperation with Germany 1935–38 and the Anglo-French abandonment of Czechoslovakia in 1938.

Littlewood /ˈlɪtlwʊd/ Joan 1914– . English theatre director. She was responsible for many vigorous productions at the Theatre Royal, Stratford (London) 1953–75, such as *A Taste of Honey* 1959, *The Hostage* 1959–60, and *Oh, What a Lovely War* 1963.

littoral /ˈlɪtərəl/ *adj.* of or on the shore. —*n.* a region lying along the shore. [from Latin *litus* = shore]

liturgy /ˈlɪtədʒɪ/ *n.* the fixed form of public worship used in churches; the Book of Common Prayer. —**liturgical** /lɪˈtɜːdʒɪkəl/ *adj.*, **liturgically** *adv.* [from French or Latin from Greek *leitourgia* = public worship]

Liu Shaoqi /lju: ʃaʊˈtʃiː/ formerly **Liu Shao-chi** 1898–1969. Chinese communist politician, in effective control of government 1960–65. A labour organizer, he was a firm proponent of the Soviet style of government based around disciplined one-party control, the use of incentive gradings, and priority for industry over agriculture. This was opposed by Mao Zedong, but began to be implemented by Liu while he was state president 1960–65. Liu was brought down during the ◊Cultural Revolution.

live¹ /lɪv/ *v.t./i.* **1.** to have life, to be or remain alive. **2.** to subsist or feed *on*; to depend for livelihood, subsistence, or position. **3.** to have one's home. **4.** to lead (one's life) or arrange one's habits in a specified way; to express in one's life. **5.** to enjoy life to the full. **6.** (of a thing) to survive or endure. —**live down,** to cause (past guilt or scandal etc.) to be forgotten by blameless conduct thereafter. **live it up,** (*colloquial*) to live gaily and extravagantly. **live off,** to derive support or sustenance from. **live together,** (especially of a couple not married to each other) to share a home and have a sexual relationship. **live up to,** to live or behave in accordance with (principles etc.). [Old English]

live² /laɪv/ *attrib. adj.* **1.** that is alive, living. **2.** actual, not pretended or toy. **3.** burning or glowing. **4.** (of a match, bomb etc.) ready for use, not yet exploded or kindled. **5.** (of a wire etc.) charged with or carrying electricity. **6.** (also *predicative*, of a performance, broadcast etc.) transmitted during the occurrence or undertaken with an audience present. **7.** of current or intense interest or importance; moving or imparting motion. —**live wire,** a highly energetic and forceful person.

liveable /ˈlɪvəbəl/ *adj.* **1.** (of life) worth living. **2.** (of a house, person etc.) fit to live in or *with*.

livelihood /ˈlaɪvlɪhʊd/ *n.* a means of living, sustenance.

livelong /ˈlɪvlɒŋ/ *adj.* in its entire length.

lively /ˈlaɪvlɪ/ *adj.* full of life, vigorous, energetic; cheerful; keen. —**liveliness** *n.*

liven /ˈlaɪvən/ *v.t./i.* to make or become lively, to cheer.

liver¹ /ˈlɪvə/ *n.* **1.** a large glandular organ in vertebrates. It receives the products of digestion, converts glucose to glycogen (a long-chain carbohydrate used for storage), breaks down fats, and removes excess amino acids from the blood, converting them to urea for excretion by the kidneys. The liver also synthesizes vitamins, produces bile and blood-clotting factors, and removes damaged red cells and toxins from the blood. **2.** the flesh of some animals' liver as food. **3.** dark reddish-brown. —**liver salts,** salts for curing dyspepsia or biliousness. **liver sausage,** sausage of cooked liver etc. [Old English]

liver² *n.* a person who lives in a specified way.

liveried /'lɪvərɪd/ *adj.* wearing livery.

liverish /'lɪvərɪʃ/ *adj.* suffering from a disorder of the liver; peevish, glum.

Livermore Valley /'lɪvəmɔː/ valley in California, USA, site of the **Lawrence Livermore Laboratory**. Part of the University of California, it shares with Los Alamos Laboratory, New Mexico, all US military research into nuclear warheads and atomic explosives. It also conducts research into nuclear fusion, using high-integrity lasers.

Liverpool /'lɪvəpuːl/ city, seaport, and administrative headquarters of Merseyside, NW England; population (1984) 497,300. In the 19th and early 20th centuries it exported the textiles of Lancashire and Yorkshire. It is the UK's chief Atlantic port with miles of specialized, mechanized quays on the river Mersey.

Liverpool Robert Banks Jenkinson, 2nd Earl Liverpool 1770–1825. British Tory politician. He entered Parliament in 1790 and was foreign secretary 1801–03, home secretary 1804–06 and 1807–09, war minister 1809–12, and prime minister 1812–27. His government conducted the Napoleonic Wars to a successful conclusion, but its ruthless suppression of freedom of speech and of the press aroused such opposition that during 1815–20 revolution frequently seemed imminent.

Liverpudlian /lɪvə'pʌdliən/ *n.* a native of Liverpool. —*adj.* of Liverpool. [from *Liverpool* in NW England]

liverwort /'lɪvəwɜːt/ *n.* a round, flat bryophyte of the class Hepaticae, without stems or leaves and sometimes with a lobed body; a mosslike plant of the same group.

livery /'lɪvərɪ/ *n.* **1.** a distinctive uniform worn by a male servant or by a member of a City Company. **2.** a distinctive guise or marking. **3.** an allowance of fodder for horses. —**at livery**, (of a horse) kept for the owner for a fixed charge. **livery company**, any of the London City Companies or ◊guilds that formerly had a distinctive costume. **livery stable**, a stable where horses are kept at livery or let out for hire. [from Anglo-French *livrer* = deliver]

lives plural of **life**.

livestock /'laɪvstɒk/ *n.* animals kept or dealt in for use or profit.

Livia Drusilla /'lɪvɪə druː'sɪlə/ 58 BC–AD 29. Roman empress, wife of ◊Augustus from 39 BC. She was the mother by her first husband of ◊Tiberius and engaged in intrigue to secure his succession to the imperial crown. She remained politically active to the end of her life.

livid /'lɪvɪd/ *adj.* **1.** of a bluish leaden colour. **2.** (*colloquial*) very angry. [from French or Latin *livēre* = be bluish]

living /'lɪvɪŋ/ *n.* **1.** being alive. **2.** a means of earning or providing enough food etc. to sustain life. **3.** a position held by a member of the clergy, providing an income. —*adj.* **1.** having life; now alive. **2.** contemporary. **3.** (of a likeness) lifelike, exact. **4.** (of a language) still in vernacular use. —**living room**, a room for general use during the day. **living wage**, a wage on which one can live without privation. **within living memory**, within the memory of people still alive.

Livingston /'lɪvɪŋstən/ industrial new town in West Lothian, Scotland, established in 1962; population (1985) 40,000. Industries include electronics and engineering.

Livingstone /'lɪvɪŋstən/ David 1813–1873. Scottish missionary explorer. In 1841 he went to Africa, reached Lake Ngami in 1849, followed the Zambezi to its mouth, saw the Victoria Falls in 1855, and went to East and Central Africa 1858–64, reaching Lakes Shirwa and Malawi. From 1866, he tried to find the source of the river Nile, and reached Ujiji in Oct 1871.

Men are immortal until their work is done.

David Livingstone
letter describing the death of Bishop Mackenzie,
March 1862

Livingstone Ken(neth) 1945– . British left-wing Labour politician. He was leader of the Greater London Council (GLC) 1981–86 and a member of Parliament from 1987.

Livonia /lɪ'vəuniə/ former region in Europe on the E coast of the Baltic Sea comprising most of present-day Latvia and Estonia. Conquered and converted to Christianity in the early 13th century by the Livonian Knights, a crusading order, Livonia was independent until 1583, when it was

lizard

divided between Poland and Sweden. In 1710 it was occupied by Russia, and in 1721 was ceded to Peter the Great, Tsar of Russia.

Livy /'lɪvɪ/ Titus Livius 59 BC–AD 17. Roman historian, author of a *History of Rome* from the city's foundation to 9 BC, based partly on legend. It was composed of 142 books, of which 35 survive, covering the periods from the arrival of Aeneas in Italy to 293 BC and from 218 to 167 BC.

Li Xiannian /li: iæn ni'æn/ 1905– . Chinese politician, member of the Chinese Communist Party (CCP) Politburo from 1956. He fell from favour during the 1966–69 Cultural Revolution, but was rehabilitated as finance minister in 1973, supporting cautious economic reform. He was state president 1983–88.

lizard /'lɪzəd/ *n.* any reptile of the suborder Lacertilia, belonging with the snakes in the order Squamata. Lizards are normally distinguishable from snakes by having four legs, movable eyelids, eardrums, and a fleshy tongue, but some lizards are legless and very snakelike in appearance. There are over 3,000 species of lizard worldwide. [from Old French from Latin]

Lizard Point southernmost point of England in Cornwall. The coast is broken into small bays overlooked by two cliff lighthouses.

LJ (*plural* **LJJ**) abbreviation of Lord Justice.

Ljubljana /luːb'ljɑːnə/ (German **Laibach**) capital and industrial city of Slovenia, Yugoslavia; population (1981) 305,200. Products include textiles, chemicals, paper, and leather goods. It has a nuclear research centre and is linked with S Austria by the Karawanken road tunnel under the Alps (1979–83).

'll *v.* (*colloquial*, usually after pronouns) abbreviation of shall, will.

llama /'lɑːmə/ *n.* a South American ruminant *Lama glama* or *L. peruana* kept as a beast of burden and for its soft, woolly, white or brown hair, a member of the camel family. Llamas spit profusely when annoyed.

Llewellyn /luˈwelɪn/ Richard. Pen name of Richard Vivian Llewellyn Lloyd 1907–1983. Welsh writer. His novel about a S Wales mining family, *How Green Was My Valley* 1939, was made into a play and a film.

Llewelyn /luˈwelɪn/ Welsh, ʃəˈwelɪn/ two kings of Wales:

Llewelyn I 1173–1240. King of Wales from 1194, who extended his rule to all Wales not in Norman hands, driving the English from N Wales in 1212, and taking Shrewsbury in 1215. During the early part of Henry III's reign, he was several times attacked by English armies. He was married to Joanna, illegitimate daughter of King John.

Llewelyn II *c.*1225–1282. King of Wales from 1246, grandson of Llewelyn I. In 1277 Edward I of England compelled Llewelyn to acknowledge him as overlord and to surrender S Wales. His death while leading a national uprising ended Welsh independence.

Lloyd /lɔɪd/ Harold 1893–1971. US film comedian, noted for his 'trademark' of thick horn-rimmed glasses and straw hat and his extraordinary acrobatic ability. He appeared from 1913 in silent and talking films. His silent films include *Grandma's Boy* 1922, *Safety Last* 1923, and *The Freshman* 1925. His first talkie was *Movie Crazy* 1932. He produced films after 1938, including the reissued *Harold Lloyd's World of Comedy* 1962 and *Funny Side of Life* 1964.

Lloyd John lived 15th century. Welsh sailor, known as John Scoluus, 'the skilful', who carried out an illegal trade with Greenland and is claimed to have reached North America, sailing as far south as Maryland, in 1477 (15 years before the voyage of Columbus).

Lloyd Selwyn. See ◊Selwyn Lloyd, British Conservative politician.

Lloyd George /ˈlɔɪd ˈdʒɔːdʒ/ David 1863–1945. Welsh Liberal politician, prime minister 1916–22. A pioneer of social reform, as chancellor of the Exchequer 1908–15 he introduced old-age pensions in 1908 and health and unemployment insurance in 1911. High unemployment, intervention in the Russian Civil War, and use of the military police force, the ◊Black and Tans, in Ireland eroded his support as prime minister, and creation of the Irish Free State in 1921 and his pro-Greek policy against the Turks caused the collapse of his coalition government.

Lloyd's Register of Shipping an international society for the survey and classification of merchant shipping, which provides rules for the construction and maintenance of ships and their machinery. It was founded in 1760.

Lloyd Webber /ˈlɔɪd ˈwebə/ Andrew 1948– . English composer. His early musicals, with lyrics by Tim Rice, include *Joseph and the Amazing Technicolor Dreamcoat* 1968; *Jesus Christ Superstar* 1970; and *Evita* 1978, based on the life of the Argentinian leader Eva Perón. He also wrote *Cats* 1981 and *The Phantom of the Opera* 1986.

Llull /ljuːl/ Ramon 1232–1315. Spanish scientist and theologian. His encyclopedic *Ars Magna* was a mechanical device, a kind of prototype computer, by which all problems could be solved through manipulation of fundamental Aristotelian categories.

lm abbreviation of lumen.

lo /ləʊ/ (*archaic*) look. —**lo and behold,** an introduction to the mentioning of a surprising fact. [Old English = interjection of surprise]

loa *n*. a spirit in voodoo. Loas may be male or female, and include Maman Brigitte, the loa of death and cemeteries, and Aida-Wedo, the rainbow snake. Believers may be under the protection of one particular loa.

loach *n*. a carplike freshwater fish, family Cobitidae, with a long narrow body, and no teeth in the small downward pointing mouth, which is surrounded by barbels. They are native to Asian and European waters. [from Old French]

load *n*. **1.** what is carried or to be carried; the debris carried along by a river. **2.** an amount usually or actually carried; this as a weight or measure of some substances. **3.** a weight of care, responsibility etc. **4.** the amount of power carried by an electric circuit or supplied by a generating station. **5.** a material object or force acting as a weight etc. **6.** (in *plural, colloquial*) plenty. —*v.t./i.* **1.** to put a load on or aboard; to place (a load) aboard ship, on a vehicle etc.; (of a ship, vehicle, or person) to take a load aboard. **2.** to burden, to strain. **3.** to supply or assail overwhelmingly. **4.** to put ammunition in (a gun), a film in (a camera), a cassette in (a tape recorder) etc.; to put (a program or data etc.) in a computer. —**get a load of,** (*slang*) to take note of. **loaded question,** one put in such a way as to evoke a required answer. **load line,** a Plimsoll line. —**loader** *n*., **-loading** *adj*. (of a gun or machine). [Old English = way]

loaded *adj*. (*slang*) **1.** rich. **2.** drunk. **3.** (*US*) drugged.

loadstone *n*. **1.** a magnetic oxide of iron. **2.** a piece of it used as a magnet. **3.** a thing that attracts.

loaf¹ *n*. (*plural* **loaves**) **1.** a quantity of bread baked alone or as a separate or separable part of a batch, usually of a standard weight. **2.** minced or chopped meat made in the shape of a loaf and cooked. **3.** (*slang*) the head. [Old English]

loaf² *v.i.* to spend time idly, to hang about. —**loafer** *n*. [perhaps from German *landläufer* = vagabond]

loam *n*. a rich soil of clay, sand, and decayed vegetable matter. —**loamy** *adj*., **loaminess** *n*. [Old English]

loan *n*. **1.** a thing lent, especially a sum of money to be returned with or without interest. **2.** lending, being lent. —*v.t.* (*disputed usage*) to lend. —**loan word,** a word adopted by one language from another in a more or less modified form (e.g. *morale, naïve*). **on loan,** being lent. [from Old Norse]

loath /ləʊθ/ *predic. adj*. averse, disinclined. [Old English]

loathe /ləʊð/ *v.t.* to regard with hatred and disgust. —**loathing** *n*. [Old English]

loathsome /ˈləʊðsəm/ *adj*. arousing hatred and disgust; repulsive.

loaves plural of loaf.

lob *v.t./i.* (**-bb-**) to send or strike (a ball) slowly or in a high arc in cricket or tennis etc. —*n*. a lobbed ball; a slow underarm delivery in cricket.

lobar /ˈləʊbə/ *adj*. of a lobe, especially of the lung.

lobate /ˈləʊbeɪt/ *adj*. having a lobe or lobes.

lobby *n*. **1.** an entrance hall, a porch; an anteroom, a corridor. **2.** in the UK, in the House of Commons, a large hall open to the public used especially for interviews between MPs and others; (in full **division lobby**) each of two corridors to which members retire to vote. **3.** a body of lobbyists. —*v.t./i.* **1.** to seek to influence (an MP etc.) to support one's cause; to get (a bill etc.) through by interviews etc. in a lobby. [from Latin *lobia, lobium* = lodge]

lobbyist *n*. a person who lobbies an MP etc.

lobe *n*. a rounded flattish part or projection, especially of an organ of the body; the lower, soft, pendulous part of the outer ear. [from Latin from Greek *lobos* = lobe, pod]

lobelia /ləˈbiːliə/ *n*. any temperate and tropical plant of the genus *Lobelia* with brightly coloured flowers. [from M de *Lobel*, Flemish botanist in England (1538–1616)]

lobotomy /ləˈbɒtəmi/ *n*. the surgical cutting of a lobe, in particular the operation of frontal lobotomy, or ◊leucotomy, in which the frontal lobes are disconnected from the rest of the brain by cutting the white matter that joins them.

lobscouse /ˈlɒbskaʊs/ *n*. a sailor's dish of meat stewed with vegetables and ship's biscuit.

lobster *n*. a large edible sea crustacean of the family Homaridae, with stalked eyes and heavy pincerlike claws, that turns from bluish-black to scarlet when boiled; its flesh as food. —**lobster pot,** a basket for trapping lobsters. [Old English, corruption of Latin *locusta* = crustacean]

lobworm /ˈlɒbwɜːm/ *n*. a large earthworm used as a fishing bait.

local /ˈləʊkəl/ *adj*. **1.** in regard to place. **2.** belonging to or affecting a particular place or a small area; of one's own neighbourhood. **3.** (of a train or bus etc.) of the neighbourhood, not long-distance; stopping at all points on a route. —*n*. **1.** an inhabitant of a particular district. **2.** a local train, bus etc. **3.** (*colloquial*) the local public house. —**local authority,** a body charged with the administration of local government. **local colour,** details characteristic of the place in which a story etc. is set, added to make it seem more real. **local government,** a system of administration of a county or district etc. by elected representatives of those living there. —**locally** *adv*. [from Old French from Latin *locus* = place]

locale /ləʊˈkɑːl/ *n*. the scene or locality of operations or events. [from French]

Local Group in astronomy, a cluster of about 36 galaxies that includes our own, the Milky Way.

locality /ləʊˈkælɪti/ *n*. **1.** a thing's position; the site or scene of something, especially in relation to the surroundings. **2.** a district. [from French or Latin]

localize /ˈləʊkəlaɪz/ *v.t.* **1.** to assign or confine to a particular place. **2.** to invest with the characteristics of a particular place. **3.** to decentralize.

local option the right granted by a government to the electors of each particular area to decide whether the sale of intoxicants shall be permitted. Such a system has been tried in certain states of the USA, in certain Canadian provinces, and in Norway and Sweden.

Locarno, Pact of a series of diplomatic documents initialled in Locarno on 16 Oct 1925 and formally signed in London on 1 Dec 1925. The pact settled the question of French security, and the signatories (Britain, France, Belgium, Italy, and Germany) guaranteed Germany's existing frontiers with France and Belgium. Following the signing of the pact, Germany was admitted to the League of Nations.

locate /ləʊˈkeɪt/ *v.t.* **1.** to discover the place where something is. **2.** to establish in a place; to state the locality of. [from Latin]

location /ləʊˈkeɪʃən/ *n*. **1.** a particular place. **2.** locating. —**on location,** (of filming) in a natural setting rather than in a studio.

locative /ˈlɒkətɪv/ *n*. in grammar, the case expressing location. —*adj*. in grammar, of or in the locative.

loc. cit. abbreviation of loco citato. [Latin = at the place cited]

loch /lɒx, lɒk/ *n*. a Scottish lake or land-locked arm of the sea. [from Gaelic]

639 locust

Lochner /ˈlɒxnə/ Stephan died 1451. German painter, active in Cologne from 1442, a master of the International Gothic style (see ◊Gothic art). Most of his work is still in Cologne: for example, the *Virgin in the Rose Garden* (Wallraf-Richartz Museum) and *Adoration of the Magi* (Cologne Cathedral).

Loch Ness /lɒx ˈnes/ lake in Highland region, Scotland, forming part of the Caledonian Canal; 36 km/22.5 mi long, 229 m/754 ft deep. There have been unconfirmed reports of a **Loch Ness monster** since the 15th century.

loci plural of ◊locus.

lock[1] *n.* **1.** a mechanism for fastening a door, lid etc., with a bolt that requires a key of a particular shape to work it. **2.** a section of a canal or river confined within sluiced gates for moving boats from one level to another. **3.** a mechanism for exploding the charge of a gun. **4.** the turning of the front wheels of a vehicle; the maximum extent of this. **5.** an interlocked or jammed state. **6.** a wrestling hold that keeps the opponent's arm etc. fixed. **7.** (in full **lock forward**) a player in the second row of the scrum in Rugby football. —*v.t./i.* **1.** to fasten with a lock. **2.** to shut into or out of a place by locking. **3.** to store away securely or inaccessibly. **4.** to bring or come into a rigidly fixed position, to jam. —**lock keeper,** a person in charge of a lock on a canal or river. **lock-knit** *adj.* knitted with an interlocking stitch. **lock-out** *n.* an employer's procedure of refusing the entry of workers to their place of work until certain terms are agreed to. **lock, stock, and barrel,** the whole of a thing, completely. **lock-up** *n.* premises that can be locked up; the time or process of locking up; a house or room for the temporary detention of prisoners; (*adj.*) able to be locked up. [Old English]

lock[2] *n.* a portion of hair that hangs together; (in *plural*) the hair of the head. [Old English]

lock and key a security device, usually fitted to a door of some kind.

Locke /lɒk/ John 1632–1704. English philosopher. His *Essay Concerning Human Understanding* 1690 maintained that experience was the only source of knowledge (empiricism), and that 'we can have knowlege no farther than we have ideas' prompted by such experience. *Two Treatises on Government* 1690 helped to form contemporary ideas of liberal democracy.

locker *n.* a small lockable cupboard or compartment.

locket /ˈlɒkɪt/ *n.* a small ornamental case containing a portrait or lock of hair and usually hung from the neck. [from Old French diminutive of *loc* = latch]

lockjaw *n.* a form of tetanus in which the jaws become rigidly closed.

locksmith *n.* a maker and mender of locks.

loco[1] /ˈləʊkəʊ/ *n.* (*plural* **locos**) (*colloquial*) a locomotive engine. [abbreviation]

loco[2] *adj.* (*US slang*) crazy. [Spanish]

locomotion /ləʊkəˈməʊʃən/ *n.* **1.** motion or the power of motion from place to place. **2.** travel, a way (especially artificial) of travelling. [from Latin *locus* = place]

locomotive /ˈləʊkəməʊtɪv/ *n.* (in full **locomotive engine**) an engine for drawing trains. —*adj.* of, having, or effecting locomotion, not stationary.

locum tenens /ləʊkəm ˈtiːnenz/ or (*colloquial*) **locum** a deputy, especially one acting for a doctor or cleric in his or her absence. [Latin = (one) holding place]

locus /ˈləʊkəs/ *n.* (*plural* **loci** /ˈləʊsaɪ/) the line or curve etc. made by all points satisfying certain conditions, or by the defined motion of a point or line or surface. [Latin = place]

locus classicus /ləʊkəs ˈklæsɪkəs/ the best known or most authoritative passage on a subject. [Latin = classic place]

locust /ˈləʊkəst/ *n.* **1.** an African or Asian grasshopper of the family Acrididae, migrating in swarms and consuming

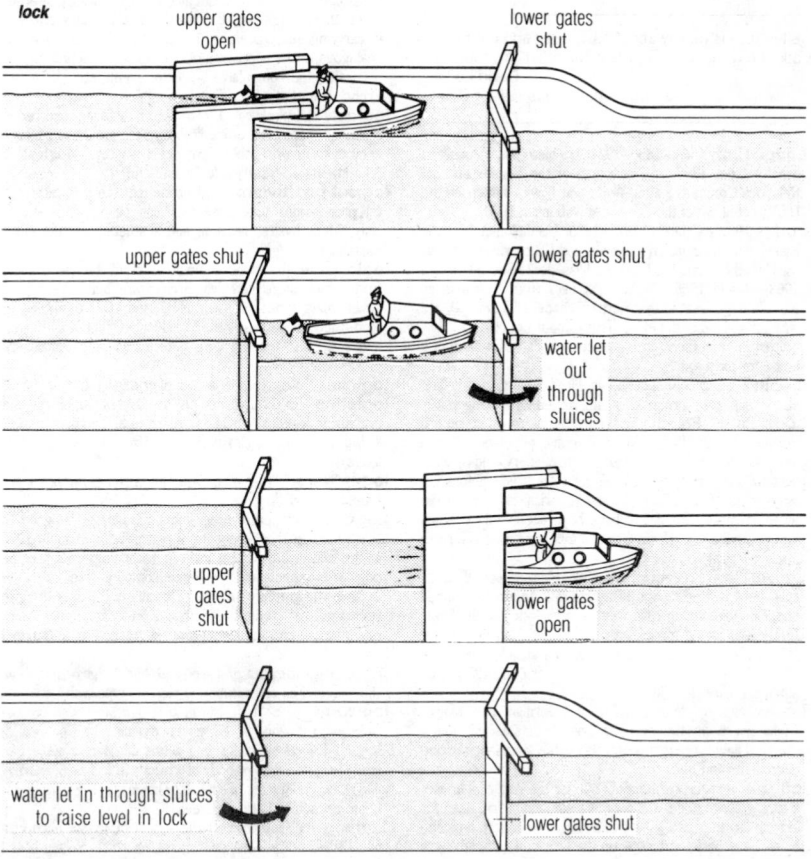

lock

upper gates open / lower gates shut

upper gates shut / lower gates shut / water let out through sluices

upper gates shut / lower gates open

water let in through sluices to raise level in lock / lower gates shut

all vegetation. 2. a person of devouring or destructive propensities. [from Old French from Latin *locusta* = lobster, locust]

locust tree an alternative name for the ◊carob, a small tree of the Mediterranean region. It is also the name of several North American trees of the family Leguminosae, especially the false acacia *Robinia pseudoacaia*.

locution /lə'kju:ʃən/ *n.* 1. a word, phrase, or idiom. 2. style of speech. [from Old French or Latin *loqui* = speak]

lode *n.* a vein of metal ore.

lodestar *n.* or **loadstar** 1. a star used as a guide in navigation, especially the pole star. 2. a guiding principle; an object of pursuit.

lodge /lɒdʒ/ *n.* 1. a small house at the entrance to a park or the grounds of a large house, occupied by a gatekeeper or other employee. 2. a small house used in sporting seasons. 3. a porter's room at the entrance or gateway of a factory, college etc. 4. the members or meeting place (originally a mason's hut or workshop on a building site) of a branch of the Freemasons or other society. 5. a beaver's or otter's lair. —*v.t./i.* 1. to provide with temporary accommodation. 2. to live as a lodger. 3. to deposit (money etc.) for security. 4. to submit (a complaint etc.) for attention. 5. to place (power etc.) in or with a person. 6. to stick or become embedded in; to cause to do this. [from Old French from Latin]

Lodge David (John) 1935– . British novelist, short-story writer, playwright, and critic. Much of his fiction concerns the role of Catholicism in mid-20th-century England, exploring the situation both through broad comedy and parody, as in *The British Museum is Falling Down* 1967, and realistically, as in *How Far Can You Go?* 1980. His other works include *Changing Places* 1975 and its sequel *Small World* 1984, both satirical 'campus' novels; *Nice Work* 1988, which was short-listed for the Booker prize; and the play *The Writing Game* 1990.

Literature is mostly about having sex and not much about having children; life is the other way round.

David Lodge
The British Museum is Falling Down

Lodge Henry Cabot 1850–1924. US historian, Republican senator from 1893, and chairman of the Senate Foreign Relations Committee after World War I, who influenced the USA to stay out of the League of Nations in 1920.

Lodge Henry Cabot, Jr 1902–1985. US diplomat. He was Eisenhower's campaign manager, and US representative at the United Nations 1953–60. Ambassador to South Vietnam 1963–64 and 1965–67, he took over from Harriman as Nixon's negotiator in the Vietnam peace talks in 1969. He was a grandson of the elder Henry Cabot Lodge.

lodger *n.* a person receiving accommodation in another's house for payment.

lodging *n.* accommodation in hired rooms, a dwelling place; (in *plural*) a room or rooms rented for lodging in.

Łódź /lodz, Polish wu:tʃ/ industrial town in central Poland, 120 km/75 mi SW of Warsaw; population (1984) 849,000. Products include textiles, machinery, and dyes.

loess /'ləuɪs/ *n.* a layer of fine, light-coloured soil found in large areas of Asia, Europe, and America and very fertile when irrigated, thought to have been deposited by winds during the ice age. [from German *löss* from Swiss German *lösch* = loose]

Loewe /'ləui/ Frederick 1901–1988. US composer of musicals, born in Berlin. Son of an operatic tenor, he studied under Busoni, and in 1924 went with his father to the USA. In 1942 he joined forces with the lyricist Alan Jay Lerner (1918–1986), and their joint successes include *Brigadoon* 1947, *Paint Your Wagon* 1951, *My Fair Lady* 1956, *Gigi* 1958, and *Camelot* 1960.

Loewi /'lɜ:vi/ Otto 1873–1961. German physiologist whose work on the nervous system established that a chemical substance is responsible for the stimulation of one neurone by another.

loft *n.* 1. a space (with a floor) under the roof of a house; a similar space under the roof of a stable or barn, used for storing hay etc. 2. a gallery in a church or hall. 3. a pigeon house. 4. a backward slope on the face of a golf club. 5. a lofting stroke. —*v.t.* to send (a ball) in a high arc. [from Old Norse = air, upper room]

Lofting /'lɒftɪŋ/ Hugh 1886–1947. English-born US writer and illustrator of children's books, especially the 'Dr Dolittle' series, in which the hero can talk to animals.

lofty *adj.* 1. towering, of imposing height. 2. haughty, keeping aloof. 3. exalted, noble. —**loftily** *adv.*, **loftiness** *n.*

log[1] *n.* 1. an unhewn piece of a felled tree; any large rough piece of wood, especially one cut for firewood. 2. a floating device used to ascertain a ship's speed. 3. a logbook. —*v.t.* (-gg-) 1. to enter in a ship's logbook. 2. to enter (data etc.) in a regular record; to attain (a cumulative total thus recorded). 3. to cut into logs. —**logbook** *n.* a book in which details of a voyage or journey or the registration of a vehicle are recorded. **log cabin,** a hut built of logs. **log in** (*or* **out**), to begin (or finish) operations at a terminal of a multi-access computer. **log line,** a line to which the float of a ship's log is attached.

log[2] abbreviation of ◊logarithm.

logan /'ləugən/ *n.* or **logan-stone** a poised heavy stone rocking at a touch. [= *logging* (*log* = to rock)]

loganberry /'ləugənberi/ *n.* a dark-red fruit, a hybrid of the raspberry and an American blackberry. [from J H *Logan*, American horticulturist (1841–1928)]

logarithm /'lɒgərɪðəm/ *n.* any of a series of arithmetic exponents tabulated to simplify computation by making it possible to use addition and subtraction instead of multiplication and division. —**logarithmic** /-'rɪðmɪk/ *adj.*, **logarithmically** *adv.* [from Greek *logos* = reckoning, ratio and *arithmos* = number]

loggerhead /'lɒgəhed/ *n.* **at loggerheads,** disagreeing, disputing. [from dialect *logger* = block of wood]

loggia /'lɒudʒə/ *n.* an open-sided gallery or arcade; an open-sided extension to a house. [Italian]

logic /'lɒdʒɪk/ *n.* 1. the science of reasoning; a particular system or method of reasoning; a chain of reasoning (regarded as sound or unsound); use of or ability in argument. 2. in computing, the principles or circuitry involved in carrying out processes, on electrical or other signals, analogous to the processes of reasoning, deduction etc. 3. necessity, the compulsive power of events etc. [from Old French from Latin from Greek]

logical /'lɒdʒɪkəl/ *adj.* 1. of or according to logic; correctly reasoned; defensible or explicable on the ground of consistency. 2. using or capable of correct reasoning. —**logicality** /-'kælɪtɪ/ *n.*, **logically** *adv.* [from Latin]

logical positivism the doctrine that the only meaningful propositions are those that can be verified empirically. Metaphysics, religion, and aesthetics are therefore meaningless.

logic gate the basic component of digital electronics, from which more complex circuits are built. There are seven main types of gate: Not, And, Or, Equivalence, Non-Equivalence (also called Exclusive Or, or Xor), Nand, and Nor. The type of gate determines how signals are processed.

logician /lɒ'dʒɪʃən/ *n.* a user of or expert in logic.

logistics /lɒ'dʒɪstɪks/ *n.pl.* the art of supplying and organizing (originally military) services and equipment etc. —**logistic** *adj.*, **logistically** *adv.* [from French (*loger* = lodge)]

logo /'ləugəu, 'lɒ-/ *n.* (*plural* **logos**) (*colloquial*) a logotype. [abbreviation]

Logo *n.* a computer-programming language designed to teach mathematical concepts. It was developed about 1970 at the Massachusetts Institute of Technology, and became popular in schools and with home computer users because of its 'turtle graphics' feature. This allows the user to write programs that create line drawings on a computer screen, or drive a small mobile robot (a 'turtle' or a 'buggy') around the floor.

logotype /'lɒgəutaɪp/ *n.* a nonheraldic design or symbol as the badge of an organization; a piece of type with this.

logwood *n.* a West Indian tree *Haematoxylon campechianum*; the wood of this used in dyeing.

-logy /-lədʒɪ/ suffix forming nouns denoting a subject of study (e.g. *biology*), or body of writings (e.g. *trilogy, martyrology*), or a character of speech or language (e.g. *tautology*). [from French or Latin or Greek]

Lohengrin /'ləuəngrɪn/ the son of ◊Parsifal, hero of a late 13th-century Germanic legend, on which Wagner based his German opera *Lohengrin* 1847. Lohengrin married Princess Elsa, who broke his condition that she never ask his origin, and he returned to the temple of the ◊Holy Grail.

loin *n.* 1. (in *plural*) the side and back of the body between the ribs and hipbones. 2. (in *singular*) a joint of meat that includes the loin vertebrae. [from Old French from Latin]

loincloth *n.* a cloth worn round the hips, especially as the sole garment.

Loire /lwɑː/ longest river in France, rising in the Cévennes mountain, at 1,350 m/4,430 ft and flowing for 1,050 km/650 mi first N then W until it reaches the Bay of Biscay at St Nazaire, passing Nevers, Orléans, Tours, and Nantes. It gives its name to the *départements* of Loire, Haute-Loire, Loire-Atlantique, Indre-et-Loire, Maine-et-Loire, and Saône-et-Loire. There are many chateaux and vineyards along its banks.

loiter *v.i.* to stand about idly, to linger; to move or proceed indolently with frequent pauses. —**loiterer** *n.* [from Middle Dutch *loteren* = wag about]

Loki /'ləʊki/ in Norse mythology, one of the ◊Aesir, but the cause of dissension among the gods, and the slayer of ◊Balder. His children are the Midgard serpent Jörmungander, which girdles the Earth, the wolf Fenris, and Hela, goddess of death.

loll *v.t./i.* 1. to recline, sit, or stand in a lazy attitude. 2. to rest (one's head or limbs) lazily on something. 3. to hang (one's tongue) out; (of the tongue) to hang out. [probably imitative]

Lollard /'lɒləd/ *n.* a follower of the English religious reformer John ◊Wycliffe in the 14th century. The Lollards condemned ◊transubstantiation, advocated the diversion of ecclesiastical property to charitable uses, and denounced war and capital punishment.

lollipop /'lɒlɪpɒp/ *n.* a large, round, usually flat boiled sweet on a small stick. —**lollipop lady** *or* **man,** (*colloquial*) an official using a circular sign on a stick to stop traffic for children to cross a road. [perhaps from dialect *lolly* = tongue]

lollop *v.i.* (*colloquial*) to move in ungainly bounds; to flop about.

lolly *n.* 1. (*colloquial*) a lollipop; an ice lolly. 2. (*slang*) money.

Lombard /'lɒmbɑːd/ Carole. Stage name of Jane Alice Peters 1908–1942. US comedy film actress. Her successful career, which included starring roles in some of the best comedies of the 1930s, was cut short by her death in a plane crash; her films include *Twentieth Century* 1934, *My Man Godfrey* 1936, and *To Be or Not To Be* 1942. She was married to Clark Gable in 1939.

Lombard *n.* or **Langobard** a member of a Germanic people who invaded Italy in 568 and occupied Lombardy (named after them) and central Italy. Their capital was Monza. They were conquered by the Frankish ruler Charlemagne in 774.

Lombard league an association of N Italian communes established in 1164 to maintain their independence against the Holy Roman emperors' claims of sovereignty (Lombardy had been conquered by ◊Charlemagne in 774).

Lombardy /'lɒmbədi/ (Italian *Lombardia*) region of N Italy, including Lake Como; **area** 23,900 sq km/9,225 sq mi; **capital** Milan; **population** (1988) 8,886,000. It is the country's chief industrial area (chemicals, pharmaceuticals, engineering, textiles).

Lomé /'ləʊmeɪ/ capital and port of Togo; population (1983) 366,000. It is a centre for gold, silver, and marble crafts; major industries include steel production and oil refining.

Lomé Convention a convention in 1975 that established economic cooperation between the European Community and African, Caribbean, and Pacific countries. It was renewed in 1979 and in 1985.

lomentum *n.* a type of ◊fruit, similar to a pod but constricted between the seeds. When ripe, it splits into one-seeded units, as seen, for example, in the fruit of sainfoin *Onobrychis viciifolia* and radish *Raphanus raphanistrum*. It is a type of ◊schizocarp.

Lomond, Loch /'ləʊmənd/ largest freshwater Scottish lake, 37 km/21 mi long, area 70 sq km/27 sq mi, divided between Strathclyde and Central regions. It is overlooked by the mountain **Ben Lomond** (973 m/3,154 ft) and linked to the Clyde estuary.

London /'lʌndən/ capital of England and the UK, on the river Thames; area 1,580 sq km/610 sq mi; population (1987) 6,770,000, larger metropolitan area about 9 million. The **City of London**, known as the 'square mile', area 677 acres/274 hectares, is the financial and commercial centre of the UK. **Greater London** comprises the City of London and 32 boroughs. Popular tourist attractions include the Tower of London, St Paul's Cathedral, Buckingham Palace, and Westminster Abbey. Roman *Londinium* was established soon after the Roman invasion in AD 43; in the 2nd century London became a walled city; by the 11th century, it was the main city of England and gradually extended beyond the walls to link with the originally separate Westminster.

London Jack (John Griffith) 1876–1916. US novelist, born in San Francisco. His adventure stories include *The Call of the Wild* 1903, *The Sea Wolf* 1904, and *White Fang* 1906.

Londonderry /lʌndən'deri/ former name (until 1984) of the county and city of ◊Derry in Northern Ireland.

London Working Men's Association (LWMA) a campaigning organization for political reform, founded in June 1836 by William Lovett and others, who in 1837 drew up the first version of the People's Charter (see ◊Chartism). It was founded in the belief that popular education, achieved through discussion and access to a cheap and honest press, was a means of obtaining political reform. By 1837 the LWMA had 100 members.

lone *attrib. adj.* 1. solitary, without companions. 2. uninhabited, lonely. —**lone hand,** a hand played or a player playing against the rest at cards; a person or action without allies. **lone wolf,** a loner.

lonely *adj.* 1. lacking friends or companions; despondent because of this. 2. isolated, unfrequented, uninhabited. —**loneliness** *n.*

lone pair in chemistry, a pair of electrons in a bonding atomic orbital that both belong to the atom itself, rather than having been paired by the sharing of electrons from different atoms. Such pairs can be involved in bonding with atoms that are deficient in electrons, forming **dative bonds,** in which both electrons in a bond are donated by one atom.

loner /'ləʊnə/ *n.* a person or animal preferring to act alone or not to associate with others.

lonesome /'ləʊnsəm/ *adj.* lonely, causing loneliness.

long[1] *adj.* 1. having great length in space or time. 2. having a specified length or duration. 3. seeming to be longer than it really is, tedious. 4. lasting, reaching far into the past or future. 5. far-reaching, acting at a distance; involving a great interval or distance. 6. of elongated shape. 7. (of a vowel sound or a syllable) having the greater of two recognized durations. 8. (of stocks etc.) bought in large quantities in advance, with the expectation of a rise in price. —*n.* 1. a long interval or period. 2. a long syllable or vowel. —*adv.* for a long time; by a long time; throughout a specified duration; (in *comparative*) after an implied point of time. —**as** *or* **so long as,** provided that. **in the long run,** over a long period, eventually. **the long and the short of it,** all that need be said, the eventual outcome. **long-distance** *adj.* travelling or operating between distant places. **long division,** division of numbers with the details of the calculation written down. **long-drawn (-out)** *adj.* prolonged. **long face,** a dismal expression. **long-haired** *adj.* intellectual; hippie. **long-headed** *adj.* shrewd, far-seeing; sagacious. **long house** a large communal village house in certain parts of Malaysia and Indonesia. **long in the tooth,** rather old. **long johns,** (*colloquial*) long underpants. **long jump,** an athletic contest of jumping as far as possible along the ground in one leap. **long leg,** the position of a fieldsman in cricket far behind the batsman on the leg side. **long-life** *adj.* (of milk etc) treated to prolong the period of usability. **long-lived** *adj.* having a long life, durable. **long odds,** very uneven odds. **long off, long on,** the position of fieldsmen in cricket far behind the bowler and towards the off (or on) side. **long on,** (*colloquial*) well supplied with. **long-playing** *adj.* (of a gramophone record) playing for 15–30 minutes on each side. **long-range** *adj.* having a long range; relating to a long period of future time. **long shot,** a wild guess or venture; a bet at long odds (*not by a long shot,* by no means). **long-sighted** *adj.* able to see clearly only what is at a distance; having imagination or foresight. **long-standing** *adj.* that has long existed. **long-suffering** *adj.* bearing provocation patiently. **long suit,** many cards of one suit in a hand; one's strong point. **long-term** *adj.* occurring in or relating to a long period of time. **long wave** a radio wave of frequency less than 300 kHz. **long-winded** adj. (of a speech or writing) tediously lengthy. [Old English]

long[2] v.i. to feel a strong desire; to wish ardently. [Old French = seem long to]

long. abbreviation of longitude.

longboat n. the largest boat carried by a sailing ship.

longbow n. a large bow drawn by hand and shooting a long feathered arrow. —**longbowman** n. (plural **longbowmen**)

Longchamp a French horseracing course situated at the Bois de Boulogne, near Paris. Most of the major races in France are run at Longchamp including the most prestigious open-age-group race in Europe, the Prix de L'Arc de Triomphe, which attracts a top-quality field every October.

longeron /'lɒndʒərən/ n. (usually in plural) a longitudinal member of an aeroplane's fuselage. [French = girder]

longevity /lɒn'dʒevɪtɪ/ n. long life. [from Latin longaevus = aged]

Longfellow /'lɒŋfeləʊ/ Henry Wadsworth 1807–1882. US poet, born in Portland, Maine. He is remembered for ballads ('Excelsior' and 'The Wreck of the Hesperus'), the narrative Evangeline 1847, and his metrically haunting The Song of ◊Hiawatha 1855.

Longford /'lɒŋfəd/ county of Leinster province, Republic of Ireland; **area** 1,040 sq km/401 sq mi; **county town** Longford; **physical** rivers: Camlin, Inny, Shannon (the W boundary); several lakes; **population** (1986) 31,000.

longhand n. ordinary writing as distinct from typing, shorthand etc.

longhorn n. one of a breed of cattle with long horns.

longing /'lɒŋɪŋ/ n. an intense desire.

Longinus /lɒn'dʒaɪnəs/ Dionysius lived 1st century AD. Greek critic, author of the treatise On the Sublime, which influenced the English poets John Dryden and Alexander Pope.

Long Island /lɒŋ 'aɪlənd/ island off the coast of Connecticut and New York, USA, separated from the mainland by Long Island Sound; area 3,627 sq km/1,400 sq mi. It includes two boroughs of New York City (Queens and Brooklyn), John F Kennedy airport, suburbs, and resorts.

longitude /'lɒŋgɪtjuːd, 'lɒndʒ-/ n. **1.** the angular distance east or west from the meridian of Greenwich or other standard meridian to that of any place. See ◊latitude. **2.** in astronomy, a body's or point's angular distance especially along an ecliptic. [from Latin longitudo (longus = long)]

longitudinal /lɒŋgi'tjuːdɪnəl, lɒndʒ-/ adj. **1.** of longitude. **2.** of or in length. **3.** lying longways. —**longitudinally** adv.

Long March in Chinese history, the 10,000 km/6,000 mi trek undertaken 1934–35 by ◊Mao Zedong and his Communist forces from SE to NW China, under harassment from the Nationalist army.

Long Parliament the English Parliament 1640–53 and 1659–60, which continued through the Civil War.

longshore adj. **1.** found on the shore. **2.** employed along the shore, especially near a port. —**longshore drift**, the gradual movement of beach materials (such as sand and shingle) along a shore.

longshoreman n. (plural **longshoremen**) a person employed in loading and unloading ships from the shore.

long sight or hypermetropia or presbyopia an eyesight defect where a person is able to focus on objects in the distance, but not on close objects. It is caused by the failure of the lens to return to its normal rounded shape, or by the eyeball being too short, with the result that the image is focussed on a point behind the retina. Long sightedness can be corrected by convex spectacles.

longways adv. or longwise lengthways.

Lonsdale /'lɒnzdeɪl/ Hugh Cecil Lowther, 5th Earl of Lonsdale 1857–1944. British sporting enthusiast. **Lonsdale Belts** in boxing, first presented in 1909, are named after him. Any fighter who wins three British title fights in one weight division retains a Lonsdale Belt.

loo n. (colloquial) a lavatory. [perhaps from Waterloo, but there are a number of other possible derivations]

loofah /'luːfə/ n. the dried pod of a kind of gourd Luffa aegyptiaca used as a rough sponge while bathing. [from Egyptian Arabic]

look /lʊk/ v.t./i. **1.** to use or direct one's eyes in order to see, search, or examine. **2.** to direct one's attention, to consider. **3.** to have a specified appearance, to seem. **4.**

(of a thing) to face in a certain direction. **5.** to indicate (an emotion etc.) by one's looks. —n. **1.** the act of looking, a gaze or glance. **2.** an inspection or search. **3.** (in singular or plural) the appearance of the face, the expression, the personal aspect. **4.** (of a thing) appearance. —int. (also **look here!**) of protest or demanding attention. —**look after**, to attend to, to take charge of. **look-alike** n. a person or thing closely resembling another. **look down on** or **down one's nose at**, to regard with contempt or a feeling of superiority. **look for**, to expect; to try to find. **look forward to**, to await (an expected event) eagerly or with specified feelings. **look in**, to make a short visit or call. **look-in** n. a brief visit; a chance of participation or success. **look into**, to investigate. **look on**, to regard (as); to be a spectator. **look out**, to be vigilant or prepared; to search for and produce; to have an outlook on or over. **look over**, to inspect. **look-see** n. (slang) an inspection. **look sharp**, to make haste. **look to**, to consider; to be careful about; to rely on. **look up**, to seek information about in a reference book etc.; to improve in prospect; (colloquial) to go to visit. **look up to**, to respect or admire (a senior or superior person). **not like the look of**, to find alarming or suspicious. [Old English]

looker n. **1.** a person of specified appearance. **2.** (colloquial) an attractive person, especially a woman. —**looker-on** n. a spectator.

looking glass a glass mirror.

lookout n. **1.** a careful watch. **2.** an observation post. **3.** a person etc. stationed to keep watch. **4.** a prospect. **5.** a person's own concern.

loom[1] n. an apparatus for weaving cloth. [Old English = tool]

loom[2] v.i. to appear dimly, to be seen in vague and often magnified or threatening form (literally or figuratively). [probably from Low Dutch]

loon n. **1.** a kind of diving bird with a wild cry, especially a grebe or large diver. **2.** (slang) a crazy person (compare following entry). [alteration from loom from Old Norse]

loony n. (slang) a lunatic. —adj. (slang) crazy. —**loony bin**, (slang) a mental home or mental hospital. [abbreviation]

loop[1] n. **1.** the figure produced by a curve or doubled thread etc. that crosses itself. **2.** a thing, path, or pattern forming roughly this figure; a length of cord or wire etc. that crosses itself and is fastened at the crossing; a fastening shaped thus. **3.** a curved piece of metal serving as a handle etc. **4.** a contraceptive coil. **5.** a complete circuit for an electrical current. **6.** an endless strip of tape or film allowing continuous repetition. **7.** a sequence of computer operations repeated until some condition is satisfied. —v.t./i. **1.** to form (into) a loop or loops. **2.** to enclose with or as with a loop. **3.** to fasten or join with a loop or loops. —**loop line**, a railway or telegraph line that diverges from the main line and joins it again. **loop the loop**, to perform an aerobatic loop, with the aircraft turning upside down between climb and dive.

loop[2] n. a loophole in a fort etc.

looper n. a caterpillar (of a kind of moth) that progresses by arching itself into loops.

loophole n. **1.** a means of evading a rule etc. without infringing the letter of it. **2.** a narrow vertical slit in the wall of a fort etc. for shooting or looking through or to admit light or air.

loopy adj. (slang) crazy.

Loos /ləʊs/ Adolf 1870–1933. Austrian architect and author of the article Ornament and Crime 1908, in which he rejected the ornamentation and curved lines of the Viennese Jugendstil movement (see ◊Art Nouveau). His buildings include private houses on Lake Geneva 1904 and the Steiner House in Vienna 1910.

Loos /luːz/ Anita 1888–1981. US writer, author of the humorous fictitious diary Gentlemen Prefer Blondes 1925.

loose adj. **1.** not or no longer held by bonds or a restraint. **2.** detached or detachable from its place, not held together or contained or fixed. **3.** slack, relaxed. **4.** inexact, indefinite, vague or incorrect. **5.** not compact or dense. **6.** morally lax. —v.t. **1.** to free, untie, or detach. **2.** to release. **3.** to discharge (a missile). **4.** to loosen, to relax. —**at a loose end**, without definite occupation. **loose box**, a stall in which a horse can move about. **loose cover**, a removable cover for an armchair etc. **loose-leaf** adj. (of a notebook etc.) with each leaf separately removable. **on the**

loose, enjoying oneself freely. —**loosely** *adv.*, **looseness** *n.* [from Old Norse]

loosen /'lu:sən/ *v.t./i.* to make or become loose or looser. —**loosen a person's tongue,** to make him or her talk freely.

loosestrife *n.* **1.** any of several plants of the family Primulaceae, including the **yellow loosestrife** *Lysimachia vulgaris.* **2.** the striking **purple loosestrife** *Lythrum saclicaria* of the family Lythraceae.

loot *n.* goods taken from an enemy or by theft. —*v.t./i.* to plunder, to take as loot; to steal from shops or houses left unprotected after a violent event. —**looter** *n.* [from Hindi]

lop[1] *v.t.* (**-pp-**) to cut away the branches or twigs of; to cut off. [compare obsolete *lip* = to prune]

lop[2] *v.i.* (**-pp-**) to hang limply. —**lop-eared** *adj.* having drooping ears.

lope *v.i.* to run with a long, bounding stride. —*n.* a long, bounding stride. [from Old Norse]

Lope de Vega (Carpio) /'ləupeɪ də 'veɪgə/ Felix 1562–1635. Spanish poet and dramatist, one of the founders of modern Spanish drama. He was born in Madrid, served with the Armada in 1588, and in 1613 took holy orders. He wrote epics, pastorals, odes, sonnets, novels, and, reputedly, over 1,500 plays (of which 426 are still in existence), mostly tragicomedies. He set out his views on drama in *Arte nuevo de hacer comedias/The New Art of Writing Plays* 1609, while reaffirming the classical form. *Fuenteovejuna* 1614 has been acclaimed as the first proletarian drama.

López /'ləupes/ Carlos Antonio 1790–1862. Paraguayan dictator (in succession to his uncle José Francia) from 1840. He achieved some economic improvement; he was succeeded by his son Francisco López.

López Francisco Solano 1827–1870. Paraguayan dictator in succession to his father Carlos López. He involved the country in a war with Brazil, Uruguay, and Argentina, during which approximately 80% of the population died.

Lopez Nancy 1957– . US golfer, who turned professional in 1977 and in 1979 became the first woman to win $200,000 in a season. She has won the US LPGA title three times and has won over 35 tour events, and $3 million in prize money.

lopsided /lɒp'saɪdɪd/ *adj.* with one side lower etc., unbalanced.

loquacious /lɒ'kweɪʃəs/ *adj.* talkative. —**loquaciously** *adv.*, **loquacity** /-'kwæsɪtɪ/ *n.* [from Latin *loqui* = speak]

Lorca /'lɔːkə/ Federico García 1898–1936. Spanish poet and playwright, born in Granada. *Romancero gitano/Gipsy Ballad-book* 1928 shows the influence of the Andalusian songs of the area. In 1929–30 Lorca visited New York, and his experiences are reflected in *Poeta en Nuevo York* 1940. He returned to Spain, founded a touring theatrical company, and wrote plays such as *Bodas de sangre/Blood Wedding* 1933 and *La casa de Bernarda Alba/The House of Bernarda Alba* 1936. His poems include *Lament*, written for the bullfighter Mejías. He was shot by the Falangists during the Spanish Civil War.

lord *n.* **1.** a master or ruler; (*historical*) a feudal superior, especially of a manor. **2.** a nobleman; **Lord**, the title of a marquis, earl, viscount, baron, or (before a Christian name) of the younger son of a duke or marquis, or in the titles of certain high officials. —*int.* expressing surprise or dismay etc. —*v.t.* (with *it*) to domineer. —**the Lord,** God or Christ. **the Lords,** the House of Lords. **Lord Advocate,** in Scotland, the chief law officer of the Crown who has ultimate responsibility for criminal prosecutions. **Lord Chamberlain,** the head of management in the royal household. **Lord Chief Justice,** the president of the Queen's Bench Division. **Lord (High) Chancellor,** the highest officer of the Crown, presiding in the House of Lords etc. **Lord Lieutenant,** the chief executive authority and head of magistrates in each county; (*historical*) the viceroy of Ireland. **Lord Mayor,** the title of the mayor in some large cities. **Lord President of the Council,** the cabinet minister presiding at the Privy Council. **Lord Privy Seal,** a senior cabinet minister without official duties. **Lord's day,** Sunday. **Lord's Prayer,** the prayer taught by Christ to his disciples (Matthew 6: 9–13), beginning 'Our Father'. **Lords Spiritual,** the bishops in the House of Lords. **Lord's Supper,** the ◊Eucharist. **Lords Temporal,** the members of the House of Lords who are not bishops. **Our Lord,** Christ. [Old English, originally = bread keeper]

Lorenz Austrian zoologist and biologist Konrad Lorenz, 1969.

lordly *adj.* **1.** haughty, imperious. **2.** suitable for a lord. —**lordliness** *n.*

Lord's one of England's cricket test match grounds, St John's Wood, London, and the headquarters of cricket's governing body, the Marylebone Cricket Club (MCC), since 1788 when the MCC was formed following the folding of the White Conduit Club. [from Yorkshireman Thomas Lord (1757–1832) who developed the first site at Dorset Square, London]

lordship *n.* the title used in addressing or referring to a man with the rank of Lord.

lore[1] *n.* the body of traditions and facts on a subject. [Old English]

lore[2] *n.* a straplike surface between the eye and upper mandible of birds or between the eye and nostril of snakes. [from Latin *lorum* = strap]

Lorelei /'lɔːrəlaɪ/ in Germanic folklore, a river nymph of the Rhine who lures sailors on to the rock where she sits combing her hair; a ◊siren. She features in several poems, including 'Die Lorelei' by the Romantic writer Heine. The *Lurlei* rock S of Koblenz is 130 m/430 ft high.

Loren /'lɔːrən/ Sophia. Stage name of Sofia Scicolone 1934– . Italian film actress who achieved fame under the guidance of her husband, producer Carlo Ponti. Her work includes *Aida* 1953, *The Key* 1958, *La ciociara/Two Women* 1961, *Judith* 1965, and *Firepower* 1979.

Lorentz /'lɔːrənts/ Hendrik Antoon 1853–1928. Dutch physicist, winner (with his pupil Pieter ◊Zeeman) of the Nobel Prize for Physics in 1902 for his work on the Zeeman effect.

Lorenz Konrad 1903–1989. Austrian ethologist. Director of the Max Planck Institute for the Physiology of Behaviour in Bavaria 1955–73, he wrote the studies of ethology (animal behaviour) *King Solomon's Ring* 1952 and *On Aggression* 1966. In 1973 he shared the Nobel Prize for Medicine with Nikolaas Tinbergen and Karl von Frisch.

Lorenz Ludwig Valentine 1829–1891. Danish mathematician and physicist. He developed mathematical formulae to describe phenomena such as the relation between the refraction of light and the density of a pure transparent substance, and the relation between a metal's electrical and thermal conductivity and temperature.

Lorenzetti /lɔːrən'zeti/ Ambrogio *c.*1319–1347. Italian painter active in Siena and Florence. His allegorical frescoes *Good and Bad Government* 1337–39 (Town Hall, Siena) include a detailed panoramic landscape and a view of the city of Siena that shows an unusual mastery of spatial effects.

Lorenzetti Pietro *c.*1306–1345. Italian painter of the Sienese school, active in Assisi. His frescoes in the Franciscan basilica, Assisi, reflect ◊Giotto's concern with mass and weight. He was the brother of Ambrogio Lorenzetti.

lorgnette /lɔː'njet/ *n.* a pair of eyeglasses or opera glasses held to the eyes on a long handle. [French *lorgner* = squint]

lorikeet *n.* a small, brightly coloured parrot, found in SE Asia and Australasia.

loris /'lɔːrɪs/ *n.* a small, slender, tailless lemur, with very large dark eyes, especially the **slender loris** *Loris gracilis* of S India and the **slow loris** *Bradicebus tardigradus* of S and SE Asia. Lorises are slow-moving, arboreal, and nocturnal. They have no tails. They climb without leaping, gripping branches tightly and moving on or hanging below them. [French, perhaps from obsolete Dutch *loeris* = clown]

lorn *adj.* (*archaic*) desolate, forlorn. [Old English, past participle of obsolete *leese* = lose]

Lorrain /lɒˈræn/ Claude French painter; see ◊Claude Lorrain.

Lorraine /lɒˈreɪn/ region of NE France in the upper reaches of the Meuse and Moselle rivers; bounded to the N by Belgium, Luxembourg, and Germany and to the E by Alsace; area 23,600 sq km/9,095 sq mi; population (1986) 2,313,000. It comprises the *départements* of Meurthe-et-Moselle, Meuse, Moselle, and Vosges, and its capital is Nancy. There are deposits of coal, iron ore, and salt; grain, fruit, and livestock are farmed. In 1871 the region was ceded to Germany as part of Alsace-Lorraine until 1919.

Lorraine, Cross of /lɒˈreɪn/ a heraldic cross with double crossbars, emblem of the medieval French nationalist Joan of Arc. It was adopted by the ◊Free French forces in World War II.

Lorre /ˈlɒri/ Peter. Stage name of Lazlo Löwenstein 1904–1964. Hungarian character actor, whose bulging eyes and sinister voice made him one of cinema's most memorable performers. He made several films in Germany before moving to Hollywood in 1935. He appeared in *M* 1931, *Mad Love* 1935, *The Maltese Falcon* 1941, *Casablanca* 1942, *Beat the Devil* 1953, and *The Raven* 1963.

lorry *n.* a large, strong motor vehicle for transporting goods etc. [originally N English, perhaps from name *Laurie*]

Los Alamos /lɒs ˈæləmɒs/ town in New Mexico, USA, which has had a centre for atomic and space research since 1942. In World War II the first atom (nuclear fission) bomb was designed there (under Robert ◊Oppenheimer), based on data from other research stations; the ◊hydrogen bomb was also developed there.

Los Angeles /lɒs ˈændzəliːz/ city and port in SW California, USA; population of urban area (1980) 2,967,000, the metropolitan area of Los Angeles–Long Beach 9,478,000. Industries include aerospace, electronics, chemicals, clothing, printing, and food processing.

lose /luːz/ *v.t./i.* (*past* and *past participle* lost) **1.** to be deprived of; to cease to have or maintain. **2.** to become unable to find; to fail to keep in sight or follow or grasp mentally. **3.** to let or have pass from one's control or reach. **4.** to get rid of. **5.** to fail to obtain or catch or perceive. **6.** to be defeated in (a contest, lawsuit, argument etc.). **7.** to have to forfeit. **8.** to spend (time, efforts etc.) to no purpose. **9.** to suffer loss or detriment; to be the worse off. **10.** to cause a person the loss of. **11.** (of a clock etc.) to become slow (by a specified time). **12.** (in *passive*) to disappear, to perish, to die or be dead. —**be lost** *or* **lose oneself in**, to be engrossed in. **be lost on**, to be wasted on, not to be noticed or appreciated by. **be lost to**, to be no longer affected by or accessible to. **get lost**, (*slang*, usually in *imperative*) to go away. **lose out**, (*colloquial*) to be unsuccessful, not to get a full chance or advantage. **losing battle**, (especially *figurative*) a battle in which defeat seems certain. [Old English = perish]

loser /ˈluːzə/ *n.* a person who loses, especially a contest or game; (*colloquial*) one who regularly fails.

Losey /ˈləʊsi/ Joseph 1909–1984. US film director. Blacklisted as a former communist in the ◊McCarthy era, he settled in England, where his films included *The Servant* 1963 and *The Go-Between* 1971.

loss *n.* **1.** losing, being lost. **2.** a thing or amount lost. **3.** detriment resulting from losing. —**at a loss**, (sold etc.) for less than was paid for it. **be at a loss**, to be puzzled or uncertain. **loss leader**, an article sold at a loss so as to attract customers.

lost past and past participle of **lose**.

Lost Generation, the the disillusioned US literary generation of the 1920s who went to live in Paris. The phrase is attributed to the writer Gertrude Stein in Ernest Hemingway's early novel of 1920s Paris, *The Sun Also Rises* 1926.

lot /lɒt/ *n.* **1.** (*colloquial* often in *plural*) a large number or amount; much. **2.** each of a set of objects used in making a chance selection; this method of deciding; a share or office resulting from it. **3.** a person's destiny or appointed task etc. **4.** a piece of land; (*US*) an area for a particular purpose.

5. an article or set of articles for sale at an auction etc. **6.** a number or quantity of associated persons or things. —**bad lot**, a person of bad character. **cast** *or* **draw lots**, to decide with lots. **throw in one's lot with**, to decide to share the fortunes of. **the (whole) lot**, the total number or quantity. [Old English]

Lot in the Old Testament, Abraham's nephew, who escaped the destruction of Sodom. Lot's wife disobeyed the condition of not looking back at Sodom and was punished by being turned into a pillar of salt.

loth variant of **loath**.

Lothair /ləʊˈθeə/ 825–869. King of Lotharingia (called after him, and later corrupted to Lorraine, now part of Alsace-Lorraine) from 855, when he inherited from his father, the Holy Roman emperor Lothair I, a district W of the Rhine, between the Jura mountains and the North Sea.

Lothair two Holy Roman emperors:

Lothair I 795–855. Holy Roman emperor from 817 in association with his father Louis I. On Louis's death in 840, the empire was divided between Lothair and his brothers; Lothair took N Italy and the valleys of the rivers Rhône and Rhine.

Lothair II *c.*1070–1137. Holy Roman emperor from 1133 and German king from 1125. His election as emperor, opposed by the ◊Hohenstaufens, was the start of the feud between the ◊Guelph and Ghibelline factions, who supported the papal party and the Hohenstaufens' claim to the imperial throne respectively.

Lothario /lə'θeəriəʊ/ *n.* (*plural* **lotharios**) a libertine. [character in Rowe's *Fair Penitent* 1703]

Lothian /ˈləʊðiən/ region of Scotland; area 1,800 sq km/695 sq mi; administrative headquarters Edinburgh; physical hills: Lammermuir, Moorfoot, Pentland; Bass Rock in the Firth of Forth, noted for seabirds; products bacon, vegetables, coal, whisky, engineering, electronics; population (1987) 744,000.

lotion /ˈləʊʃən/ *n.* a medicinal or cosmetic liquid preparation applied to the skin. [from Old French or Latin *lavare* = wash]

lottery /ˈlɒtəri/ *n.* **1.** a means of raising money by selling numbered tickets and giving prizes to the holders of numbers drawn at random. **2.** a thing whose outcome is governed by chance. [probably from Dutch]

lotto /ˈlɒtəʊ/ *n.* a game of chance similar to bingo but with the numbers drawn instead of called. [Italian]

Lotto Lorenzo *c.*1480–1556. Italian painter, born in Venice, active in Bergamo, Treviso, Venice, Ancona, and Rome. His early works were influenced by Giovanni Bellini; his mature style belongs to the High Renaissance. He painted dignified portraits, altarpieces, and frescoes.

lotus /ˈləʊtəs/ *n.* **1.** a legendary plant, whose fruit induced a luxurious languor when eaten. **2.** the ◊jujube shrub *Zizyphus lotus*, believed to be the bearer of this. **3.** the white lotus *Nymphaea lotus*, frequent in Egyptian art. **4.** the pink Asiatic lotus *Nelumbo nucifera*, a sacred symbol in Hinduism and Buddhism, which floats its flowerhead erect above the water. **5.** the American lotus *Nelumbo lutea*, a pale yellow water lily of the southern USA. **6.** any plant of the genus *Lotus*, family Leguminosae. —**lotus-eater** *n.* a person given to indolent enjoyment. **lotus position**, a cross-legged position of meditation with the feet resting on the thighs. [Latin from Greek]

Lotus a motorcar company founded by Colin Chapman (1928–1982), who built his first racing car in 1948, and also developed high-powered production saloons and sports cars, such as the Lotus-Cortina and Lotus Elan. Lotus has been one of the leading Grand Prix manufacturers since its first Grand Prix in 1960. Jim ◊Clark, twice world champion, had all his Grand Prix wins in a Lotus. The last Lotus world champion was Mario Andretti in 1978.

Lotus 1–2–3 a popular ◊spreadsheet computer program, produced by Lotus Development Corporation. It first appeared in 1982, and is credited with being one of the main reasons for the widespread acceptance of the IBM Personal Computer in businesses.

Lotus Sūtra a scripture of Mahāyāna Buddhism. It is Buddha Śākyamuni's final teaching, emphasizing that everyone can attain Buddhahood with the help of bodhisattvas. The original is in Sanskrit (*Saddharmapundarīka Sūtra*) and is thought to date to some time after 100 BC.

loud *adj.* 1. strongly audible, producing much noise. 2. (of colours etc.) gaudy, obtrusive. —*adv.* loudly. —**loud hailer**, an electronic device for amplifying the sound of the voice so that it can be heard at a distance. **out loud**, aloud. —**loudly** *adv.*, **loudness** *n.* [Old English]

loudspeaker /ˈlaʊdˈspiːkə/ *n.* an apparatus that converts electrical impulses into sound.

lough /lɒk, -x/ *n.* (*Irish*) a lake, an arm of the sea. [from Gaelic]

Louis /ˈluːɪs/ Joe. Assumed name of Joseph Louis Barrow 1914–1981. US boxer, nicknamed 'the Brown Bomber'. He was world heavyweight champion between 1937 and 1949 and made a record 25 successful defences (a record for any weight).

Louis Morris 1912–1962. US abstract painter. From Abstract Expressionism he turned to the colour-staining technique developed by Helen ◊Frankenthaler, using thinned-out acrylic paints poured on rough canvas to create the illusion of vaporous layers of colour. The *Veil* paintings of the 1950s are examples.

Louis /ˈluːi/ 18 kings of France, including:

Louis I the Pious 788–840. Holy Roman emperor from 814, when he succeeded his father Charlemagne.

Louis II the Stammerer 846–879. King of France from 877, son of Charles II the Bald. He was dominated by the clergy and nobility, who exacted many concessions from him.

Louis III 863–882. King of N France from 879, while his brother Carloman (866–884) ruled S France. He was the son of Louis II. Louis countered a revolt of the nobility at the beginning of his reign, and his resistance to the Normans made him a hero of epic poems.

Louis IV (*d'Outremer*) 921–954. King of France from 936. His reign was marked by the rebellion of nobles who refused to recognize his authority. As a result of his liberality they were able to build powerful feudal lordships.

Louis VII *c.*1120–1180. King of France from 1137, who led the Second ◊Crusade.

Louis X the Stubborn 1289–1316. King of France who succeeded his father Philip IV in 1314. His reign saw widespread discontent among the nobles that he countered by granting charters guaranteeing seignorial rights, although some historians claim that by using evasive tactics, he gave up nothing.

Louis XI 1423–1483. King of France from 1461. He broke the power of the nobility (headed by ◊Charles the Bold) by intrigue and military power.

Louis XII 1462–1515. King of France from 1499. He was duke of Orléans until he succeeded his cousin Charles VIII to the throne. His reign was devoted to Italian wars.

Louis XIII 1601–1643. King of France from 1610 (in succession to his father Henry IV), he assumed royal power in 1617. He was under the political control of ◊Richelieu 1624–42.

Louis XIV the Sun King 1638–1715. King of France from 1643, when he succeeded his father Louis XIII; his mother was Anne of Austria. Until 1661 France was ruled by the chief minister, Mazarin, but later Louis took absolute power, summed up in his saying *L'Etat c'est moi* ('I am the State'). Throughout his reign he was engaged in unsuccessful expansionist wars 1667–68, 1672–78, 1688–97, and 1701–13 (the War of the ◊Spanish Succession) against various European alliances, always including Britain and the Netherlands. He was a patron of the arts.

Louis XV 1710–1774. King of France from 1715, with the Duke of Orléans as regent until 1723. He was the great-grandson of Louis XIV. Indolent and frivolous, Louis left government in the hands of his ministers, the Duke of Bourbon and Cardinal Fleury (1653–1743). On the latter's death he attempted to rule alone but became entirely dominated by his mistresses, Madame de ◊Pompadour and Madame ◊Du Barry. His foreign policy led to Canada and India being lost to England.

Louis XVI 1754–1793. King of France from 1774, grandson of Louis XV, and son of Louis the Dauphin. He was dominated by his queen, ◊Marie Antoinette, and the finances fell into such confusion that in 1789 the ◊States General (parliament) had to be summoned, and the ◊French Revolution began. Louis lost his personal popularity in June 1791 when he attempted to flee the country (the Flight to Varennes), and in Aug 1792 the Parisians stormed the

Louis XIV *A marble bust of the 'Sun King' Louis XIV of France, by Italian sculptor Bernini.*

Tuileries palace and took the royal family prisoner. Deposed in Sept 1792, Louis was tried in Dec, sentenced for treason in Jan 1793, and guillotined.

Louis XVII 1785–1795. Nominal king of France, the son of Louis XVI. During the French Revolution he was imprisoned with his parents in 1792 and probably died in prison.

Louis XVIII 1755–1824. King of France 1814–24, the younger brother of Louis XVI. He assumed the title of king in 1795, having fled into exile in 1791 during the French Revolution, but became king only on the fall of Napoleon I in April 1814. Expelled during Napoleon's brief return (the 'hundred days') in 1815, he resumed power after Napoleon's final defeat at Waterloo, pursuing a policy of calculated liberalism until ultra-royalist pressure became dominant after 1820.

Louisiana /luːiːziˈænə/ state of the S USA; nickname Pelican State; **area** 135,900 sq km/52,457 sq mi; **capital** Baton Rouge; **physical** Mississippi delta; **products** rice, cotton, sugar, maize, oil, natural gas, sulphur, salt, processed foods, petroleum products, lumber, paper; **population** (1987) 4,461,000, which includes the Cajuns, descendants of 18th-century religious exiles from Canada, who speak a French dialect; **history** explored by La Salle; named after Louis XIV and claimed for France in 1682; became Spanish 1762–1800; passed to the USA under the ◊Louisiana Purchase of 1803; admitted to the Union as a state in 1812.

Louisiana Purchase the sale by France in 1803 to the USA of an area covering about 2,144,000 sq km/ 828,000 sq mi, including the present-day states of Louisiana, Missouri, Arkansas, Iowa, Nebraska, North Dakota, South Dakota, and Oklahoma.

Louis Philippe /luːi fiˈliːp/ 1773–1850. King of France 1830–48. Son of Louis Philippe Joseph, Duke of Orléans 1747–93; both were known as *Philippe Egalité* from their support of the 1792 Revolution. He fled into exile 1793–1814, but became king after the 1830 revolution with the backing of the rich bourgeoisie. Corruption discredited his regime, and after his overthrow he escaped to the UK, where he died.

Louis, Prince of Battenberg /ˈluːi/ 1854–1921. German-born British admiral, who took British nationality in 1917 and translated his name to Mountbatten.

lounge /laʊndʒ/ *v.i.* to recline casually and comfortably; to loll; to stand or move about idly. —*n.* 1. a public room (e.g. in a hotel) for sitting in. 2. a waiting room at an airport etc. with seats for waiting passengers. 3. a sitting room in a house. 4. a spell of lounging. —**lounge suit**, a man's suit for ordinary wear. —**lounger** *n.* [perhaps from obsolete *lungis* = lout, laggard]

lour /lauə/ v.i. to frown, to look sullen or (of the sky etc.) dark and threatening.

Lourdes /luəd/ town in SW France, population (1982) 18,000. Its Christian shrine to St ◊Bernadette has a reputation for miraculous cures.

Lourenço Marques /lə'rensəu 'mɑːks/ former name of ◊Maputo, capital of Mozambique.

louse /laus/ n. 1. (plural **lice**) any of various insects of the orders Anoplura (sucking lice) and Mallophaga (biting lice), parasitic on mammals, birds, fish, or plants; a parasitic insect Pediculus humanus, order Anoplura, infesting human hair and skin and transmitting many diseases. 2. (slang, plural **louses**) a contemptible person. — v.t. to remove lice from. —**louse up,** (slang) to spoil, to mess up. [Old English]

lousy /'lauzɪ/ adj. 1. infected with lice. 2. (slang) disgusting, very bad. 3. (slang) swarming, well supplied. —**lousily** adv., **lousiness** n.

lout n. a hulking or rough-mannered fellow. —**loutish** adj.

Louth /lauð/ smallest county of the Republic of Ireland, in Leinster province; county town Dundalk; area 820 sq km/ 317 sq mi; population (1986) 92,000.

louvre /'luːvə/ n. 1. any of a set of overlapping slats arranged to admit air and exclude light or rain. 2. a domed erection on a roof with side openings for ventilation etc. [from Old French lov(i)er = skylight]

Louvre /'luːvrə/ n. French art gallery, former palace of the French kings, in Paris. It was converted to an art gallery in 1793 and houses the sculpture Venus de Milo and Leonardo da Vinci's painting Mona Lisa.

lovable /'lʌvəbəl/ adj. inspiring love or affection.

lovage /'lʌvɪdʒ/ n. a herb Levisticum officinale used for flavouring. [from Old French from Latin]

love /lʌv/ n. 1. warm liking or affection for a person or thing. 2. sexual passion; sexual relations. 3. a beloved one, a sweetheart (often as a form of address); (colloquial) a person of whom one is fond. 4. affectionate greetings. 5. (often **Love**) a representation of Cupid. 6. in games, no score, nil. — v.t./i. 1. to feel love for. 2. to like greatly, to delight in. 3. to be inclined, especially as a habit. —**for love,** because of affection; without receiving payment. **in love (with),** feeling (especially sexual) love (for). **love affair,** a romantic or sexual relationship between two people who are in love. **lovebird** n. a parakeet (especially of the genus Agapornis) seeming to show great affection for its mate. **love child,** an illegitimate child. **love game,** a game in which the loser makes no score. **love-hate relationship,** an intense emotional response involving ambivalent feelings of love and hate towards the same object. **love-in-a-mist** n. a perennial plant of S Europe Nigella damascena of the buttercup family Ranunculaceae, with fernlike leaves and delicate blue or white flowers. **love letter,** a letter between sweethearts, expressing their love. **love-lies-bleeding** n. a garden plant Amaranthus caudatus with drooping spikes of purple-red bloom. **love match,** a marriage between two people who are in love with each other. **love song,** a song expressing love. **love story,** a story in which the theme is romantic love. **make love,** to have sexual intercourse; to pay amorous attentions to. **not for love or money,** not in any circumstances. [Old English]

Lovecraft /'lʌvkrɑːft/ H(oward) P(hillips) 1890–1937. US writer of horror fiction, whose stories of hostile, supernatural forces have lent names and material to many other writers in the genre. Much of his work on this theme was collected in The Outsider and Others 1939.

Lovelace /'lʌvleɪs/ Richard 1618–1658. English poet. Imprisoned in 1642 for petitioning for the restoration of royal rule, he wrote 'To Althea from Prison', and in a second term in jail in 1648 revised his collection Lucasta 1649.

loveless adj. unloving or unloved or both.

lovelorn adj. pining from unrequited love.

lovely adj. exquisitely beautiful; (colloquial) pleasing, delightful. —n. (colloquial) a pretty woman. —**loveliness** n. [Old English]

lover n. 1. a person in love with another; a person with whom one is having sexual relations; (in plural) a pair in love. 2. one who likes or enjoys something.

lovesick adj. languishing with love.

lovey-dovey /lʌvi'dʌvi/ adj. (colloquial) fondly affectionate and sentimental.

loving /'lʌvɪŋ/ adj. feeling or showing love. —**loving cup,** a large drinking vessel with two or more handles, passed from hand to hand at a banquet etc. so that each person may drink from its contents. —**lovingly** adv.

low[1] /ləu/ adj. 1. not high or tall, not extending far upwards; coming below the normal or average level. 2. not elevated in position. 3. ranking below others in importance or quality. 4. of a small or less than normal amount, extent, intensity etc.; (of opinion) unfavourable. 5. dejected, lacking vigour. 6. unfavourable. 7. ignoble, vulgar. 8. (of a sound or voice) deep not shrill, having slow vibrations; not loud. 9. (in comparative) situated on less high land or to the south; (of a geological period) earlier (called 'lower' because of the position of the corresponding rock formations); (of animals or plants etc.) of relatively simple structure, not highly developed. —n. 1. a low or the lowest level or number. 2. an area of low pressure. —adv. 1. in or to a low position (literally or figuratively). 2. in a low tone; (of a sound) at or to a low pitch. **Low Church,** the section of the Church of England which gives a relatively unimportant or 'low' place to the claims of the episcopate, priesthood, and sacraments. **low comedy,** that in which the subject and its treatment border on farce. **Low Countries,** the district now forming the Netherlands, Belgium, and Luxemburg. **low-down** adj. ignoble, dishonourable. **low-down** n. (slang) the relevant information (on). **low frequency,** (in radio) 30–300 kilohertz. **low-key** adj. restrained, lacking intensity. **low-level language,** a computer language close in form to a machine-readable code. **low-pitched** adj. (of a sound) low; (of a roof) having only a slight slope. **low pressure,** a low degree of activity or exertion; a condition of the atmosphere with the pressure below average. **low season,** the period of fewest visitors at a resort etc. **Low Sunday,** the Sunday after Easter. **low tide,** a tide of the lowest level; the time of this. **low water,** low tide; in low water, short of money. [from Old Norse]

low[2] /ləu/ n. the deep sound made by cows, a moo. —v.i. to make this sound. [Old English]

lowbrow adj. (colloquial) not intellectual or cultured. —n. (colloquial) a lowbrow person.

Lowell /'ləuəl/ Amy (Lawrence) 1874–1925. US poet, who began her career by publishing the conventional A Dome of Many-Colored Glass 1912 but eventually succeeded Ezra Pound as leader of the Imagists (see ◊Imagism). Her works, in free verse, include Sword Blades and Poppy Seed 1916.

Lowell Robert (Traill Spence) 1917–1977. US poet whose work includes Lord Weary's Castle 1946 and For the Union Dead 1964. He converted to Roman Catholicism in 1940 and was imprisoned in 1943 as a conscientious objector.

lower[1] /'ləuə/ adj. 1. less high in place or position. 2. situated on lower ground or to the south. 3. ranking below others. 4. (of a geological or archaeological period) earlier (compare ◊upper, sense 4). —v.t. 1. to let or haul down. 2. to make or become lower; to reduce in amount or quantity etc. 3. to direct (one's gaze) downwards. —**lower case,** see ◊case[2]. **Lower Chamber** or **House,** the lower and usually elected body in a legislature, especially the UK House of Commons.

lower[2] variant of ◊lour.

lowermost adj. lowest.

Lower Saxony /'sæksənɪ/ (German Niedersachsen) administrative region (German Land) of NW Germany; **area** 47,400 sq km/18,296 sq mi; **capital** Hanover; **physical** Lüneburg Heath; **products** cereals, cars, machinery, electrical engineering; **population** (1988) 7,190,000; **recent history** formed in 1946 from Hanover, Oldenburg, Brunswick, and Schaumburg-Lippe.

lowland n. a low-lying country. —adj. of or in a lowland. —**lowlander** n.

lowly /'ləulɪ/ adj. of humble rank or condition. —**lowliness** n.

Lowry /'lauri/ L(aurence) S(tephen) 1887–1976. English painter. Born in Manchester, he lived mainly in nearby Salford and painted northern industrial townscapes. His characteristic style of matchstick figures and almost monochrome palette emerged in the 1920s.

Loy /lɔɪ/ Myrna. Stage name of Myrna Williams 1905– . US film actress who played Nora Charles in the Thin Man series (1943–47) co-starring William Powell. Her other films include *The Mask of Fu Manchu* 1932 and *The Rains Came* 1939.

loyal /'lɔɪəl/ *adj.* faithful; steadfast in allegiance, devoted to the legitimate sovereign etc. —**loyal toast,** a toast to the sovereign. —**loyally** *adv.*, **loyalty** *n.* [from Old French from Latin]

loyalist *n.* **1.** one who remains loyal to the legitimate sovereign etc., especially in the face of rebellion or usurpation. **2. Loyalist,** in Northern Ireland, one who favours retaining Ulster's link with Britain; in US history, members of the population remaining loyal to Britain during the ◊American Revolution. —**loyalism** *n.*

Loyola /lɔɪ'əʊlə/ founder of the Jesuits. See ◊Ignatius Loyola.

lozenge /'lɒzɪndʒ/ *n.* **1.** a small sweet or medicinal etc. tablet to be dissolved in the mouth. **2.** a rhombus, a diamond figure. **3.** a lozenge-shaped object. [from Old French]

LP abbreviation of long-playing (record).

L-plate /'elpleɪt/ *n.* a sign bearing the letter L, attached to the front and rear of a motor vehicle to indicate that it is being driven by a learner.

Lr symbol for ◊lawrencium.

LSD abbreviation of lysergic acid diethylamide, a powerful hallucinogenic drug. It is colourless, odourless, and easily synthesized. LSD is nonaddictive and nontoxic, but its effects are unpredictable. Its use is illegal in most countries.

£.s.d. /eles'diː/ pounds, shillings, and pence (in former British currency); money, riches. [from Latin *librae, solidi, denarii*]

LSI abbreviation of large-scale integration, the technology by which whole electrical circuits can be etched into a piece of semiconducting material just a few millimetres square. Most of today's electronics industry is based on LSI.

Lt. abbreviation of **1.** Lieutenant. **2.** light.

LT abbreviation of low tension.

Ltd abbreviation of limited; see ◊limited company; ◊private limited company.

Lu symbol for ◊lutetium.

Luanda /luː'ændə/ formerly **Loanda** capital and industrial port of Angola; population (1988) 1,200,000. Products include cotton, sugar, tobacco, timber, paper, and oil. It was founded in 1575 and became a Portuguese colonial administrative centre as well as an outlet for slaves transported to Brazil.

lubber *n.* a clumsy fellow, a lout. —**lubberly** *adj.* [perhaps from Old French = swindler]

Lubbers /'lʌbəs/ Rudolph (Frans Marie) 1939– . Netherlands politician. He became minister for economic affairs in 1973 and prime minister in 1983.

Lubitsch /'luːbɪtʃ/ Ernst 1892–1947. German film director known for his stylish comedies, who worked in the USA from 1921. Starting as an actor in silent films in Berlin, he turned to writing and directing, including *Die Augen der Mummie Ma/The Eyes of the Mummy* 1918 and *Die Austernprinzessin/The Oyster Princess* 1919. In the USA he directed *The Marriage Circle* 1924 and *The Student Prince* 1927. His sound films include *Trouble in Paradise* 1932, *Design for Living* 1933, *Ninotchka* 1939, and *To Be or Not to Be* 1942.

lubricant /'luːbrɪkənt/ *n.* an oil or grease etc. used to reduce friction in machinery etc.

lubricate /'luːbrɪkeɪt/ *v.t.* to apply a lubricant to; to make slippery. —**lubrication** /-'keɪʃən/ *n.*, **lubricator** *n.* [from Latin *lubricus* = slippery]

lubricity /luː'brɪsɪtɪ/ *n.* **1.** slipperiness. **2.** skill in evasion. **3.** lewdness. [from French or Latin]

Lucan /'luːkən/ Marcus Annaeus Lucanus AD 39–65. Latin poet, born in Cordova, a nephew of ◊Seneca and favourite of ◊Nero until the emperor became jealous of his verse. He then joined a republican conspiracy and committed suicide on its failure. His epic *Pharsalia* deals with the civil wars of the Roman rulers in Caesar and Pompey.

Lucas /'luːkəs/ George 1944– . US director and producer. His films, often with science-fiction themes and using special effects, include *THX 1138* 1971, *American Graffiti* 1973, the *Star Wars* trilogy 1977–83, *Raiders of the Lost Ark* 1981, *Indiana Jones and the Temple of Doom* 1984, *Willow* 1988, and *Indiana Jones and the Last Crusade* 1989, most of which were box-office hits.

Lucas van Leyden /'luːkəs væn 'laɪdn/ 1494–1533. Dutch painter and engraver, active in Leiden and Antwerp. He was a pioneer of Netherlandish genre scenes, for example *The Chess Players* (Staatliche Museen, Berlin). His woodcuts and engravings were inspired by Albrecht Dürer, whom he met in Antwerp in 1521.

Luce /luːs/ Clare Boothe 1903–1987. US journalist, playwright, and politician. She was managing editor of *Vanity Fair* magazine 1933–34, and wrote several successful plays, including *The Women* 1936 and *Margin for Error* 1939, both made into films.

Luce Henry Robinson 1898–1967. US publisher, founder of the magazine *Time* 1923, and of the pictorial weekly *Life* 1936. He married Clare Boothe Luce.

lucerne /luː'sɜːn/ another name for the plant ◊alfalfa.

Lucerne (German *Luzern*) capital and tourist centre of Lucerne canton, Switzerland, on the river Reuss where it flows out of Lake Lucerne; population (1987) 161,000. It developed around the Benedictine monastery, established in about 750, and owes its prosperity to its position on the St Gotthard road and railway.

Lucian /'luːsɪən/ *c.*125–*c.*190. Greek writer of satirical dialogues, in which he pours scorn on all religions. He was born at Samosata in Syria, and for a time was an advocate at Antioch, but later travelled before settling in Athens in about 165. He occupied an official post in Egypt, where he died.

All that belongs to mortals is mortal; all things pass us by, or if not, we pass them by.
Lucian
Greek Anthology

lucid /'luːsɪd/ *adj.* **1.** expressed or expressing things clearly. **2.** sane. —**lucidity** /-'sɪdɪtɪ/ *n.*, **lucidly** *adv.* [from French or Italian or Latin *lucidus* = bright]

Lucifer 1. in Christian theology, the leader of the angels that rebelled against God, the ◊devil. **2.** the morning star (the planet ◊Venus). [Latin = bearer of light]

luck *n.* chance regarded as a bringer of good or bad fortune; the circumstances of life (beneficial or not) brought by this; good fortune, success due to chance. —**down on one's luck,** in a period of bad fortune. **hard luck,** worse fortune than one deserves. **push one's luck,** to take undue risks. **try one's luck,** to make a venture. **worse luck,** unfortunately. [from Low German]

luckless *adj.* **1.** invariably having bad luck. **2.** ending in failure.

Lucknow /'lʌknaʊ/ capital and industrial city of the state of Uttar Pradesh, India; population (1981) 1,007,000. Industries include engineering, chemicals, textiles, and many handicrafts. During the Indian Mutiny against British rule, it was besieged 2 July–16 Nov 1857.

lucky *adj.* having or resulting from good luck, especially as distinct from skill or design or merit; bringing good luck. —**lucky dip,** a tub etc. containing articles of different value into which one may dip at random on payment of a small sum. —**luckily** *adv.*

lucrative *adj.* profitable, producing much money. —**lucrativeness** *n.* [from Latin *lucrari* = to gain]

lucre /'luːkə/ *n.* (*derogatory*) money, money-making as a motive for action. [from French or Latin *lucrum* = profit]

Lucretia /luː'kriːʃɪə/ Roman woman, the wife of Collatinus, said to have committed suicide after being raped by Sextus, son of ◊Tarquinius Superbus. According to tradition, this incident led to the dethronement of Tarquinius and the establishment of the Roman Republic in 509 BC.

Lucretius /luː'kriːʃɪəs/ (Titus Lucretius Carus) *c.*99–55 BC. Roman poet and Epicurean philosopher (see ◊Epicureanism), whose *De Rerum natura/On the Nature of Things* envisaged the whole universe as a combination of atoms, and had some concept of evolutionary theory.

What is food to one man is bitter poison to others.
Lucretius
On the Nature of the Universe

Lucullan /lu'kʌlən, lu:-/ *adj.* (especially of a feast) very sumptuous or luxurious. [from *Lucullus*]

Lucullus /lu:'kʌləs/ Lucius Licinius 110–56 BC. Roman general and consul. As commander against ◊Mithridates of Pontus 74–66 BC he proved to be one of Rome's ablest generals and administrators, until superseded by Pompey. He then retired from politics. His wealth enabled him to live a life of luxury and Lucullan feasts became legendary.

Lüda formerly **Hüta** industrial port in Liaoning, China, on Liaodong Peninsula, facing the Yellow Sea; population (1986) 4,500,000. Industries include engineering, chemicals, textiles, oil refining, ship building, and food processing. It comprises the naval base of Lüshun (known under 19th-century Russian occupation as Port Arthur) and the commercial port of Dalien (formerly Talien/Dairen).

Luddite /'lʌdaɪt/ *n.* 1. a member of the bands of English craftsmen who, when their jobs were threatened by the progressive introduction of machinery into their trades in the early 19th century, attempted to reverse the trend towards mechanization by wrecking the offending machines. 2. a person similarly seeking to obstruct progress. —*adj.* of Luddites. [perhaps from Ned *Lud*, an insane person said to have destroyed two stocking frames *c.* 1779]

Ludendorff /'lu:dndɔ:f/ Erich von 1865–1937. German general, chief of staff to ◊Hindenburg in World War I, and responsible for the eastern-front victory at the Battle of ◊Tannenberg in 1914. After Hindenburg's appointment as chief of general staff and Ludendorff's as quartermaster-general in 1916, he was also politically influential. He took part in the Nazi rising in Munich in 1923 and sat in the Reichstag (parliament) as a right-wing Nationalist.

ludicrous /'lu:dɪkrəs/ *adj.* absurd, ridiculous, laughable. —**ludicrously** *adv.* [from Latin *ludicrum* = stage play]

ludo /'lu:dəʊ/ *n.* a simple game played with dice and counters on a special board. [Latin = I play]

Ludwig /'lʊdvɪg/ three kings of Bavaria:

Ludwig I 1786–1868. King of Bavaria 1825–48, succeeding his father Maximilian Joseph I. He made Munich an international cultural centre, but his association with the Irish actress and dancer Lola Montez (1818– 1861), who dictated his policies for a year, led to his abdication in 1848.

Ludwig II 1845–1886. King of Bavaria from 1864, when he succeeded his father Maximilian II. He supported Austria during the Austro-Prussian War of 1866, but brought Bavaria into the Franco-Prussian War as Prussia's ally and in 1871 offered the German crown to the king of Prussia. He was the composer Wagner's patron and built the Bayreuth theatre for him. Declared insane in 1886, he drowned himself soon after.

Ludwig III 1845–1921. King of Bavaria 1913–1918, when he abdicated upon the formation of a republic.

Luening /'lu:nɪŋ/ Otto 1900– . US composer. He studied in Zurich, and privately with Busoni. In 1949 he joined the staff at Columbia University, and in 1951 began a series of pioneering compositions for instruments and tape, some in partnership with Vladimir Ussachevsky (*Incantation* 1952, *Poem in Cycles and Bells* 1954). In 1959 he became codirector, with Milton ◊Babbitt and Vladimir Ussachevsky, of the Columbia–Princeton Electronic Music Center.

luff *n.* the side of a fore-and-aft sail next to the mast or stay. —*v.t./i.* 1. to bring a ship's head nearer the wind; to bring the head of (a ship) thus. 2. to raise or lower (a crane's jib). [from Old French]

Luftwaffe /'lʊftvɑ:fə/ *n.* the German air force. In World War I and, as reorganized by the Nazi leader Goering in 1933, in World War II, it also covered anti-aircraft defence and the launching of the flying bombs ◊V1, V2. [German = air weapon]

lug *v.t./i.* (-gg-) to drag or carry with great effort; to pull hard. —*n.* 1. a hard or rough pull. 2. a projection on an object by which it may be carried, fixed in place etc. 3. (*colloquial*) an ear. [probably from Scandinavian]

luge /lu:ʒ/ *n.* a short, raised toboggan for one person seated. —*v.i.* to ride on a luge. [Swiss French]

luggage /'lʌgɪdʒ/ *n.* suitcases, bags etc., for containing a traveller's belongings.

lugger *n.* a small ship with four-cornered sails.

Lugosi /lu:'gəʊsi/ Bela. Stage name of Bela Ferenc Blasko 1882–1956. Hungarian film actor who appeared in Hungarian and German films before going to Hollywood in 1921. His most famous role was Count Dracula in *Dracula*

1930, followed by horror roles in *Son of Frankenstein* 1939, *The Body Snatcher* 1945, and *Bride of the Monster* 1956.

lugsail *n.* a four-cornered sail on a yard.

lugubrious /lu:'gu:brɪəs/ *adj.* doleful. —**lugubriously** *adv.* [from Latin *lugēre* = mourn]

lugworm *n.* or **lobworm** a marine worm of the genus *Arenicola* that grows up to 25 cm/10 in long, and is common between tidemarks. Lugworms are useful for their cleansing and powdering of the sand, of which they may annually bring to the surface about 5,000 tonnes per hectare/1,900 tons per acre.

Lu Hsün   former transcription of Chinese writer ◊Lu Xun.

Lukács /'lu:kɑ:tʃ/ Georg 1885–1971. Hungarian philosopher, one of the founders of 'Western' or 'Hegelian' Marxism, a philosophy opposed to the Marxism of the official communist movement.

Luke, St /lu:k/ 1st century AD. Traditionally the compiler of the third Gospel and of the Acts of the Apostles in the New Testament. Luke is supposed to have been a Greek physician born in Antioch (Antakiyah, Turkey) and to have accompanied Paul after the ascension of Jesus. He is the patron saint of painters; his emblem is a winged ox, and his feast day is 18 Oct.

lukewarm /'lu:kwɔ:m/ *adj.* 1. moderately warm, tepid. 2. not enthusiastic, indifferent. [from dialect *luke* = tepid]

Luks /lʌks/ George 1867–1933. US painter and graphic artist, a member of the ◊Ashcan school.

lull *v.t./i.* 1. to soothe or send to sleep. 2. to calm (suspicions etc.), usually by deception. 3. (of a storm or noise) to lessen, to become quiet. — *n.* an intermission in a storm etc.; a temporary period of inactivity or quiet. [imitative of sounds used in lulling a child]

lullaby /'lʌləbaɪ/ *n.* a soothing song to send a child to sleep.

Lully /lu:'li/ Jean-Baptiste. Adopted name of Giovanni Battista Lulli 1632–1687. French composer of Italian origin who was court composer to Louis XIV. He composed music for the ballet, for Molière's plays, and established French opera with such works as *Alceste* 1674 and *Armide et Renaud* 1686. He was also a ballet dancer.

lumbago /lʌm'beɪgəʊ/ *n.* pain in the lower region of the back, usually due to strain or faulty posture. If it occurs with ◊sciatica, it may be due to pressure on spinal nerves by a displaced vertebra. [Latin *lumbus* = loin]

lumbar /'lʌmbə/ *adj.* of the loins. [from Latin]

lumbar puncture or **spinal tap** the insertion of a hollow needle between two lumbar (lower back) vertebrae to withdraw a sample of cerebrospinal fluid (CSF) for testing. Normally clear and colourless, the CSF acts as a fluid buffer around the brain and spinal cord. Changes in its quantity, colour, or composition may indicate neurological damage or disease.

lumber *n.* 1. disused and cumbersome articles; useless stuff. 2. partly prepared timber. —*v.t./i.* 1. to encumber. 2. to fill up space inconveniently; to obstruct (a place). 3. to move in a blundering noisy way. 4. to cut and prepare forest timber. —**lumberjacket** *n.* a jacket of the kind worn by lumberjacks. **lumber room**, a room in which disused articles are kept.

lumberjack *n.* one who fells and removes lumber (timber).

Lumbini /lʊm'bi:ni/ the birthplace of ◊Buddha in the foothills of the Himalayas near the Nepalese-Indian frontier. A sacred garden and shrine were established in 1970 by the Nepalese government.

lumen *n.* 1. the SI unit (symbol lm) of luminous flux (the amount of light passing through an area per second). 2. the hollow interior of the alimentary canal, and the site of digestion in many invertebrates and all vertebrates. [Latin = light, opening]

Lumet /'lu:meɪ/ Sidney 1924– . US film director. His films, sometimes marked by a heavy-handed seriousness, have met with varying critical and commercial success. They include *Twelve Angry Men* 1957, *Fail Safe* 1964, *The Deadly Affair* 1967, *Network* 1976, and *Equus* 1977.

Lumière /lu:mi'eə/ Auguste Marie 1862–1954 and Louis Jean 1864–1948. French brothers who pioneered cinematography. In 1895 they patented their cinematograph, a combined camera and projector operating at 16 frames

lung

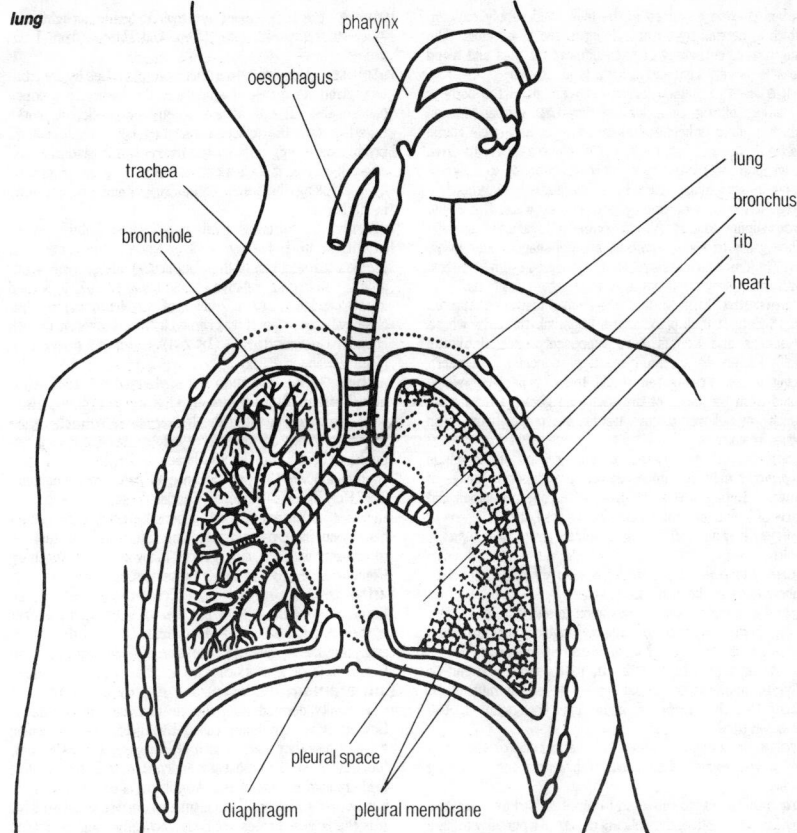

pharynx
oesophagus
trachea
bronchiole
lung
bronchus
rib
heart
pleural space
diaphragm
pleural membrane

per second, and opened the world's first cinema in Paris to show their films.

luminary /'luːmɪnərɪ/ *n.* **1.** a natural light-giving body, especially the Sun or Moon. **2.** a person as a source of intellectual or spiritual light. [from Old French or Latin *lumen* = light]

luminescence *n.* the emission of light from a body when its atoms are excited to incandescence by means other than raising its temperature.

luminescent /luːmɪˈnesənt/ *adj.* emitting light without heat.

luminism *n.* a method of painting, associated with the ◊Hudson River school in the 19th century, that emphasized the effects of light on water.

luminous /'luːmɪnəs/ *adj.* shedding light, phosphorescent and so visible in darkness. —**luminosity** /-ˈnɒsɪtɪ/ *n.* [from Old French or Latin]

luminous paint a preparation containing a mixture of pigment, oil, and a phosphorescent sulphide, usually calcium or barium. After exposure to light it appears luminous in the dark. The luminous paint used on watch faces contains radium, is radioactive and therefore does not require exposure to light.

lump[1] *n.* **1.** a hard or compact mass of no particular or regular shape. **2.** a protuberance or swelling on a surface. **3.** (*slang*) a great quantity, a lot. **4.** a heavy, dull, or ungainly person. —*v.t.* to put or consider together; to treat as all alike. —**the lump,** casual workers especially in the building trade who are paid in lump sums. **in the lump,** generally, taking things as a whole. **lump in one's throat,** a feeling of discomfort there due to anxiety or emotion. **lump sugar,** sugar in small lumps or cubes. **lump sum,** a sum covering a number of items; money paid down all at once. [perhaps from Scandinavian]

lump[2] *v.t.* (*colloquial*) to put up with ungraciously.

lumpish *adj.* **1.** heavy and clumsy. **2.** stupid, lethargic.

lumpy *adj.* full of or covered with lumps; (of water) choppy. —**lumpily** *adv.*, **lumpiness** *n.*

Lumumba /luˈmʊmbə/ Patrice 1926–1961. Congolese politician, prime minister of Zaïre in 1960. Imprisoned by the Belgians, but released in time to attend the conference giving the Congo independence in 1960, he led the National Congolese Movement to victory in the subsequent general election. He was deposed in a coup d'état, and murdered some months later.

lunacy /'luːnəsɪ/ *n.* **1.** insanity. **2.** great folly.

lunar /'luːnə/ *adj.* of, like, or concerned with the Moon. —**lunar (excursion) module,** a module for making a journey from an orbiting spacecraft to the Moon's surface and back. **lunar month,** the period of the Moon's revolution, especially a lunation; (*popularly*) a period of four weeks. [from Latin *luna* = moon]

lunate /'luːneɪt/ *adj.* crescent-shaped.

lunatic /'luːnətɪk/ *adj.* insane; extremely reckless or foolish. —*n.* a lunatic person. —**lunatic asylum,** (*historical*) a mental home or mental hospital. **lunatic fringe,** a fanatical or eccentric or visionary minority of a party etc. [from Old French from Latin, because formerly believed to be affected by changes of the Moon]

lunation /luːˈneɪʃən/ *n.* the interval between new moons, about 29½ days. [from Latin]

lunch *n.* **1.** the midday meal. **2.** a light refreshment at midmorning. —*v.t./i.* **1.** to take lunch. **2.** to provide lunch for.

luncheon /'lʌntʃən/ *n.* (*formal*) the midday meal. —**luncheon meat,** tinned meat loaf of pork etc. **luncheon voucher,** a voucher given to an employee as part of his or her pay and exchangeable for food at certain restaurants and shops.

lung *n.* a large cavity of the body, used for gas exchange. Lungs are found in some slugs and snails, particularly those that live on land, some fishes, and most ◊tetrapod vertebrates, which have a pair of lungs that occupy the thorax (the upper part of the trunk). Their function is to remove carbon dioxide dissolved in the blood and supply oxygen, which is carried by ◊haemoglobin in red blood cells. The lung tissue, consisting of multitudes of air sacs and blood vessels, is very light and spongy. [Old English]

lunge n. 1. a sudden forward movement of the body in thrusting, hitting, or kicking; a thrust. 2. a long rope on which a horse is held and made to move in a circle round its trainer. —v.t./i. 1. to deliver or make a lunge; to drive (a weapon etc.) violently in some direction. 2. to exercise (a horse) on a lunge. [from French *allonger* = lengthen]

lungfish n. any of three genera of freshwater fish of the order Dipnoi, found in Africa, South America, and Australia. They grow to about 2 m/6 ft, are eel-shaped, long-lived, and in addition to gills have 'lungs' (modified swim bladders) with which they can breathe air in drought conditions.

Lupercalia /lu:pə'keɪlɪə/ n. a Roman festival celebrated on 15 Feb. It took place at the Lupercal, the cave where ◊Romulus and Remus were supposedly suckled by the wolf. Lupercalia included feasting, dancing, and sacrificing goats. Priests ran round the city carrying whips made from the hides of the sacrificed goats, a blow from which was believed to cure sterility in women. [from Latin *lupus* = wolf]

lupin /'lu:pɪn/ n. a garden or fodder plant of the genus *Lupinus*, family Leguminosae, with long tapering spikes of flowers. Lupins are native to Mediterranean regions and parts of North and South America. [from Latin]

lupine /'lu:paɪn/ adj. of or like wolves. [from Latin *lupus* = wolf]

lupus /'lu:pəs/ n. an ulcerous skin disease, especially tuberculosis of the skin. [Latin = wolf]

lurch[1] n. a sudden lean or deviation to one side, a stagger. —v.i. to make a lurch, to stagger. [originally nautical, from *lee-lurch*, alteration of *lee-latch* = drifting to leeward]

lurch[2] n. **leave in the lurch**, to abandon (a friend or ally) to an awkward situation; to desert in difficulties. [from French *lourche* = game like backgammon, bad defeat in this]

lurcher n. a dog cross-bred between a collie or sheepdog and a greyhound, often used by poachers for retrieving game.

lure /ljuə/ v.t. 1. to entice. 2. to recall with a lure. —n. 1. a thing used to entice; the enticing quality of a pursuit etc. 2. a falconer's apparatus for recalling a hawk. [from Old French]

lurid /'ljuərɪd/ adj. 1. strong and glaring in colour. 2. sensational, showy. 3. horrifying. 4. ghastly, wan. —**luridly** adv., **luridness** n. [from Latin *luror* = wan or yellow colour]

lurk v.i. 1. to linger furtively or unobtrusively. 2. to lie hidden while waiting to attack. 3. to be latent.

Lusaka /lu:'sɑ:kə/ capital of Zambia from 1964 (of Northern Rhodesia 1935–64), 370 km/230 mi NE of Livingstone; commercial and agricultural centre (flour mills, tobacco factories, vehicle assembly, plastics, printing); population (1987) 819,000.

luscious /'lʌʃəs/ adj. 1. richly sweet in taste or smell. 2. (of style) over-rich. 3. voluptuously attractive. —**lusciously** adv., **lusciousness** n.

lush adj. 1. (of grass etc.) luxuriant and succulent. 2. luxurious. —**lushly** adv., **lushness** n.

Lusitania /lu:sɪ'teɪnɪə/ an ocean liner sunk by a German submarine on 7 May 1915 with the loss of 1,200 lives, including some Americans; its destruction helped bring the USA into World War I.

lusophone adj. of or related to the countries in which the Portuguese language is spoken, or which were formerly ruled by Portugal.

lust n. 1. strong sexual desire. 2. any passionate desire or enjoyment. 3. sensuous appetite regarded as sinful. —v.i. to have a strong or excessive (especially sexual) desire. —**lustful** adj., **lustfully** adv. [Old English]

lustre /'lʌstə/ n. 1. the soft brightness of a smooth or shining surface. 2. glory, distinction. 3. an iridescent metallic glaze on pottery and porcelain; pottery and porcelain with this. —**lustrous** adj. [French from Italian (Latin *lustrare* = illuminate)]

lusty adj. healthy and strong; vigorous, lively. —**lustily** adv., **lustiness** n.

lute[1] /lu:t/ n. a plucked stringed instrument with frets and a round body, resembling a halved pear. [from French, ultimately from Arabic]

lute[2] n. clay or cement for making joints airtight etc. —v.t. to treat with lute. [from Old French from Latin *lutum* = mud]

luteinizing hormone a ◊hormone produced by the pituitary gland. In males, it stimulates the testes to produce ◊androgens. In the female ◊menstrual cycle, it works together with the follicle stimulating hormone to initiate production of egg cells by the ovary. If fertilization of the egg cell occurs, it plays a part in maintaining the pregnancy by controlling the levels of oestrogen and progesterone in the body.

lutenist /'lu:tənɪst/ n. a lute player. [from Latin]

lutetium /lu:'ti:ʃəm/ n. a silver-white, metallic element, the heaviest and last of the ◊lanthanide series, symbol Lu, atomic number 71, relative atomic mass 174.97. It is used in the 'cracking', or breakdown, of petroleum and in other chemical processes. It was named by its discoverer, French chemist Georges Urbain (1872–1938) for his native city. [Latin *Lutetia* = Paris]

Luther /'lu:θə, German 'lʊtə/ Martin 1483–1546. German Christian church reformer, a founder of Protestantism. While he was a priest at the University of Wittenberg, he wrote an attack on the sale of indulgences (remissions of punishment for sin) in 95 theses which he nailed to a church door in 1517, in defiance of papal condemnation. The Holy Roman Emperor Charles V summoned him to the Diet of Worms in 1521, where he refused to retract his objections. Originally intending reform, his protest led to schism, with the emergence, following the ◊Augsburg Confession of 1530, of a new Protestant church.

Lutheran /'lu:θərən/ adj. of Martin Luther or the Lutheran Church. —n. a follower of Luther; a member of the Lutheran Church. —**Lutheran Church,** the church accepting the Augsburg Confession of 1530, with justification by faith alone as its cardinal doctrine. [from M *Luther*]

Lutheranism /lu:θərənɪzəm/ n. a form of Protestant Christianity derived from the life and teaching of Martin Luther; it is sometimes called Evangelical to distinguish it from the other main branch of European Protestantism, the Reformed. The most generally accepted statement of Lutheranism is that of the **Augsburg Confession** 1530 but Luther's Shorter Catechism also carries great weight. It is the largest Protestant body, including some 80 million persons, of whom 40 million are in Germany, 19 million in Scandinavia, 8.5 million in the USA and Canada, with most of the remainder in central Europe.

Luthuli /lu:'tu:li/ or **Lutuli** Albert 1899–1967. South African politician, president of the African National Congress from 1952. Luthuli, a Zulu tribal chief, preached nonviolence and multiracialism.

Lutoslawski /lu:təu'swæfski/ Witold 1913– . Polish composer and conductor, born in Warsaw. His early music, dissonant and powerful (*First Symphony* 1947), was criticized by the communist government, so he adopted a more popular style. With the lifting of artistic repression, he quickly adopted avant-garde techniques, including improvisatory and aleatoric forms. He has written chamber, vocal, and orchestral music, including three symphonies, *Livre pour orchestre* 1968 and *Mi-parti* 1976.

Lutyens /'lʌtjənz/ Edwin Landseer 1869–1944. English architect. His designs ranged from picturesque to Renaissance style country houses and ultimately evolved into a Classical style as in the Cenotaph, London, and the Viceroy's House, New Delhi.

lux /lʌks/ n. the SI unit (symbol lx) of illuminance or illumination (the light falling on an object). It is equivalent to one lumen per square metre or to the illuminance of a surface one metre distant from a point source of one candela. [Latin = light]

luxe /lʌks, lʊks/ n. luxury. Compare ◊de luxe. [French from Latin]

Luxembourg /'lʌksəmbɜ:g, French lʊksæm'buəg/ capital of Luxembourg; population (1985) 76,000. The 16th-century Grand Ducal Palace, European Court of Justice, and European Parliament secretariat are situated here, but plenary sessions of the parliament are now held only in ◊Strasbourg. Products include steel, chemicals, textiles, and processed food.

Luxembourg Grand Duchy of; landlocked country in W Europe, bordered to the N and W by Belgium, E by Germany, and S by France; **area** 2,586 sq km/998 sq mi;

651 lymphokines

Luxor *The temple of Queen Hatshepsut in Luxor, Egypt, showing a bust of the queen on one of the columns.*

capital Luxembourg; **physical** on the river Moselle; part of the Ardennes (Oesling) forest in N; **head of state** Grand Duke Jean from 1964; **head of government** Jacques Santer from 1984; **political system** liberal democracy; **exports** pharmaceuticals, synthetic textiles; **population** (1990 est) 369,000; **language** French (official), local Letzeburgesch, German; **recent history** a duchy since 1354, under Hapsburg control 1482–1797; under French control 1797–1815; a grand duchy under Dutch rule from 1815 until the accession of grand Duke Adolphe of Nassau-Weilburg in 1830. Luxembourg formed the Benelux customs union with Belgium and the Netherlands in 1948. In 1964 Grand Duchess Charlotte abdicated in favour of her son.

Luxembourg Accord a French-initiated agreement of 1966 that a decision of the Council of Ministers of the European Community may be vetoed by a member whose national interests are at stake.

Luxembourg, Palais du a palace in Paris, France, in which the Senate sits. It was built in 1615 for Marie de' Medici by Salomon de Brosse.

Luxemburg /'luksəmbuək/ Rosa 1870–1919. Polish-born German communist, a leader of the left wing of the German Social Democratic Party from 1898 and collaborator with Karl Liebknecht in founding the communist Spartacus League in 1918 (see ◊Spartacist). She was murdered with him by army officers during the Jan 1919 Berlin workers' revolt.

Luxor /'lʌksɔː/ (Arabic *al-Uqsur*) small town in Egypt on the E bank of the Nile near the ruins of ◊Thebes.

Lu Xun /luː 'ʃuːn/ pen name of Chou Shu-jêu 1881–1936. Chinese short-story writer. His three volumes of satirically realistic stories, *Call to Arms*, *Wandering*, and *Old Tales Retold*, reveal the influence of Gogol. He is one of the most popular of modern Chinese writers.

luxuriant /lʌg'zjuəriənt/ *adj.* growing profusely; exuberant, florid. —**luxuriance** *n.* [from Latin *luxuriare* = grow rank]

luxuriate /lʌg'zjuərieɪt/ *v.i.* to revel or feel keen delight; to abandon oneself to enjoyment or ease.

luxurious /lʌg'zjuəriəs/ *adj.* 1. supplied with luxuries, extremely comfortable. 2. fond of luxury. —**luxuriously** *adv.*, **luxuriousness** *n.* [from Old French from Latin]

luxury /'lʌkʃərɪ/ *n.* 1. choice or costly surroundings, possessions, food etc.; the habitual use or enjoyment of these. 2. a thing desirable for comfort or enjoyment but not

essential. 3. (*attributive*) comfortable and expensive. [from Old French from Latin *luxus* = abundance]

Luzern /luː't'seən/ German name of ◊Lucerne, town and lake in Switzerland.

Luzon /luː'zɒn/ largest island of the ◊Philippines; **area** 108,130 sq km/41,750 sq mi; **capital** Quezon City; **population** (1970) 18,001,270. The chief city is Manila, capital of the Philippines. Products include rice, timber, and minerals. It has US military bases.

LV abbreviation of luncheon voucher.

LW abbreviation of long wave, a radio wave with a wavelength of over 1,000 m/3,300 ft. LW is one of the main wavebands into which radio frequency transmissions are divided.

LWM abbreviation of low water mark.

lx abbreviation of ◊lux.

LXX abbreviation of the ◊Septuagint. [Latin numeral = 70]

lycanthropy 1. in folk belief, the transformation of a human being into a ◊werewolf. 2. in psychology, a delusion involving this belief.

Lyceum /laɪ'siːəm/ *n.* 1. an ancient Athenian gymnasium and garden, with covered walks, where Aristotle taught. 2. his followers, his philosophy. [Latin from Greek *Lukeios* = epithet of Apollo, whose temple stood near by]

lychee /'laɪtʃiː/ variant of ◊litchi.

lych gate variant of ◊lich gate.

Lycurgus /laɪ'kɜːgəs/ Spartan lawgiver. He is said to have been a member of the royal house, who, while acting as regent, gave the Spartans their constitution and system of education. Many scholars believe him to be purely mythical.

Lydgate /'lɪdgeɪt/ John *c.*1370–*c.*1450. English poet. He was a Benedictine monk and later prior. His numerous works were often translations or adaptations, such as *Troy Book* and *The Fall of Princes*.

Lydia /'lɪdɪə/ ancient kingdom in Anatolia (7th–6th centuries BC), with its capital at Sardis. The Lydians were the first Western people to use standard coinage. Their last king, Croesus, was conquered by the Persians in 546 BC.

lye /laɪ/ *n.* water made alkaline with wood ashes; any alkaline solution for washing things. [Old English]

Lyell /'laɪəl/ Charles 1797–1875. Scottish geologist. In his book *The Principles of Geology* 1830–33, he opposed ◊Cuvier's theory that the features of the Earth were formed by a series of catastrophes, and expounded ◊Hutton's view, known as ◊uniformitarianism, that past events were brought about by the same processes that occur today. He implied that the Earth was much older than the 6,000 years of prevalent contemporary theory, and provided the first detailed description of the ◊Tertiary period. Although it was only in old age that he accepted that species had changed through evolution, he nevertheless provided Darwin with a geological framework within which evolutionary theories could be placed.

lying participle of ◊lie[1], ◊lie[2].

Lyly /'lɪlɪ/ John *c.*1553–1606. English playwright and author of the romance *Euphues, or the Anatomy of Wit* 1578. Its elaborate stylistic devices gave rise to the word 'euphuism' for an affected rhetorical style.

lymph /lɪmf/ *n.* the fluid found in the lymphatic system of vertebrates, which carries nutrients, oxygen, and white blood cells to the tissues, and waste matter away from them. [from French or Latin *lympha* = water]

lymphatic /lɪm'fætɪk/ *adj.* 1. of, secreting, or conveying lymph. 2. (of a person) flabby, pale, sluggish.

lymph nodes small masses of lymphatic tissue in the body that occur at various points along the major lymphatic vessels. Tonsils and adenoids are large lymph nodes. As the lymph passes through them it is filtered, and bacteria and other microorganisms are engulfed by cells known as macrophages.

lymphocyte *n.* a type of white blood cell with a large nucleus, produced in the bone marrow. Most occur in the ◊lymph and blood, and around sites of infection. B-lymphocytes or ◊B cells are responsible for producing ◊antibodies. T-lymphocytes or ◊T cells have several roles in forming ◊immunity.

lymphokines *n.pl.* chemical messengers produced by ◊lymphocytes that carry messages between the cells of the immune system (see ◊immunity). Examples include

Lynn British singer Vera Lynn captured the hearts of the troops in World War II through her renditions of songs such as 'White Cliffs of Dover'.

interferon, which initiates defensive reactions to viruses, and the interleukins, which activate specific immune cells.

lynch /lɪntʃ/ *v.t.* (of a mob) to execute or punish violently without lawful trial. —**lynch law**, such a procedure by a self-constituted illegal court. [apparently from Capt W *Lynch*, judge in Virginia *c.* 1780]

Lynch /lɪntʃ/ 'Jack' (John) 1917– . Irish politician, prime minister 1966–73 and 1977–79. A Gaelic footballer and a barrister, in 1948 he entered the parliament of the republic as a Fianna Fáil member.

lynchet /'lɪntʃɪt/ *n.* a ridge or ledge formed by prehistoric ploughing on a slope. [from Old English]

Lynn /lɪn/ Vera 1917– . British singer, the 'Forces' Sweetheart' of World War II with 'We'll Meet Again' and 'White Cliffs of Dover', and in 1952 'Auf Wiederseh'n, Sweetheart'.

lynx /lɪŋks/ *n.* a cat *Felis lynx* found in rocky and forested regions of North America and Europe. Larger than a wild cat, it has a short tail, tufted ears, and long, silky fur, which is reddish brown or grey with dark spots. The US **bobcat** or **bay lynx** *Felix rufus* is a smaller relative. —**lynx-eyed** *adj.* keen-sighted. [from Latin from Greek]

Lyon /'liːɒn/ (English **Lyons**) industrial city and capital of Rhône *département*, Rhône-Alpes region, and third largest city of France, at the confluence of the rivers Rhône and Saône rivers, 275 km/170 mi NNW of Marseille; population (1982) 418,476, conurbation 1,221,000. Products include textiles, chemicals, machinery, and printing. Formerly a chief fortress of France, it was the ancient **Lugdunum**, taken by the Romans in 43 BC.

Lyons /'laɪənz/ Joseph 1848–1917. British entrepreneur, founder of the catering firm of J Lyons in 1894. He popularized 'tea shops', and the 'Corner Houses', incorporating several restaurants of varying types, were long a feature of London life.

lyophilization *n.* the technical term for the freeze-drying process (see ◊freeze) used for foods and drugs and in the preservation of organic archaeological remains.

Lyra /'laɪrə/ *n.* a small but prominent constellation of the northern hemisphere, representing the lyre of Orpheus. Its brightest star is Vega, 27 light years from Earth.

lyre /laɪə/ *n.* a plucked stringed instrument in which strings are fixed to a crossbar supported by two arms. It is played with a plectrum or with the fingers. The lyre is a musical instrument of great antiquity. —**lyrebird** *n.* an Australian bird of the genus *Menura*, the male of which has a lyre-shaped tail display. [from Old French from Latin from Greek]

lyric /'lɪrɪk/ *adj.* **1.** (of poetry) expressing the writer's emotions, usually briefly and in stanzas or groups of lines; (of a poet) writing in this manner. **2.** of or for the lyre; meant to be sung; fit to be expressed in song; of the nature of song. —*n.* **1.** a lyric poem. **2.** (especially in *plural*) the words of a song. **3.** (in *plural*) lyric verses. [from French from Latin from Greek]

lyrical /'lɪrɪkəl/ *adj.* **1.** resembling or using language appropriate to lyric poetry. **2.** (*colloquial*) highly enthusiastic. —**lyrically** *adv.*

lyricist /'lɪrɪsɪst/ *n.* a writer of lyrics.

Lysander /laɪ'sændə/ Spartan general. He brought the Peloponnesian War to a successful conclusion by capturing the Athenian fleet at Aegospotami in 405 BC, and by starving Athens into surrender in the following year. He then aspired to make Sparta supreme in Greece and himself supreme in Sparta; he set up puppet governments in Athens and her former allies, and tried to secure for himself the Spartan kingship, but he was killed in battle with the Thebans.

Lysenko /lɪ'sɛŋkəʊ/ Trofim Denisovich 1898–1976. Soviet biologist who believed in the inheritance of acquired characteristics (changes acquired in an individual's lifetime) and used his position under Stalin officially to exclude ◊Mendel's theory of inheritance. He was removed from office after the fall of Khrushchev in 1964.

Lysippus /laɪ'sɪpəs/ 4th century BC. Greek sculptor. He made a series of portraits of Alexander the Great (Roman copies survive, including examples in the British Museum and the Louvre) and also sculpted the *Apoxyomenos*, an athlete (copy in the Vatican), and a colossal *Hercules* (lost).

lysis *n.* in biology, any process that destroys a cell by rupturing its membrane (see ◊lysosome).

-lysis /-lɪsɪs/ suffix forming nouns denoting disintegration or decomposition (e.g. *electrolysis*). [Latin from Greek *lusis* = loosening (*luō* = loosen)]

Lysistrata /laɪ'sɪstrətə/ a Greek comedy by Aristophanes, produced in 411 BC. The women of Athens, tired of war, refuse to make love to their husbands and occupy the Acropolis to force a peace between the Athenians and the Spartans.

lysosome *n.* a membrane-enclosed structure, or organelle, inside a ◊cell (sense 3), principally found in animal cells. Lysosomes contain enzymes that can break down proteins and other biological substances. They play a part in digestion, and in the white blood cells known as phagocytes the lysosyme enzymes attack ingested bacteria.

-lyte suffix forming nouns denoting substances that can be decomposed (e.g. *electrolyte*). [Latin from Greek *lutos* = loosed]

m, M /em/ *n.* (*plural* **ms, m's**) the 13th letter of the alphabet.

m abbreviation of 1. metre(s). 2. mile(s). 3. million(s). 4. milli-. 5. minute(s). 6. (also **m.**) masculine; married; male.

M abbreviation of 1. mega-. 2. motorway.

M *n.* Roman numeral for 1,000.

M. abbreviation of 1. Master. 2. *Monsieur.*

'm (*colloquial*) = *am* in *I'm.*

ma /maː/ *n.* (*colloquial*) mother. [abbreviation of mamma]

MA in education, abbreviation of Master of Arts degree.

ma'am /mæm, maːm, məm/ abbreviation of madam (used especially in addressing a royal lady or an officer in the WRAC etc.).

Mabinogion, the /mæbi'nəugiən/ a collection of medieval Welsh myths and folk tales put together in the mid-19th century and drawn from two manuscripts: *The White Book of Rhydderch* 1300–25 and *The Red Book of Hergest* 1375–1425. [Welsh *mabinogi* = instruction for young poets]

Mabuse /mə'bjuːz/ Jan. Adopted name of Jan Gossaert *c.*1478–*c.*1533. Flemish painter, active chiefly in Antwerp. His common name derives from his birthplace, Maubeuge. His visit to Italy in 1508 with Philip of Burgundy started a new vogue in Flanders for Italianate ornament and Classical detail in painting, including sculptural nude figures. His works include *The Adoration of the Magi* (National Gallery, London).

mac (*colloquial*) abbreviation of mackintosh.

macabre /mə'kaːbr/ *adj.* grim, gruesome. [from Old French, perhaps from *Macabé* = Maccabee, with reference to play containing slaughter of the Maccabees]

macadam /mə'kædəm/ *n.* a material for road-making with successive layers of broken stone compacted; tar macadam (see ◊tar[1]). [from J *McAdam*]

McAdam /mə'kædəm/ John Loudon 1756–1836. Scottish engineer, inventor of the macadam road surface. It consisted of broken granite bound together with slag or gravel, raised for drainage. Today, it is bound with tar or asphalt.

macadamia *n.* an edible nut from the tree *Macadamia ternifolia*, family Proteaceae, native to Australia and cultivated in Hawaii.

macadamize /mə'kædəmaiz/ *v.t.* to surface with macadam.

Macao /mə'kau/ Portuguese possession on the S coast of China, about 65 km/40 mi W of Hong Kong, from which it is separated by the estuary of the Canton River; it consists of a peninsula and the islands of Taipa and Colôane; **area** 17 sq km/7 sq mi; **capital** Macao; **population** (1986) 426,000; **language** Cantonese; Portuguese (official); **recent history** recognized as a Portuguese colony by the Chinese government in a treaty 1887. In April 1987 Portugal and China signed the Macao Pact, under which Portugal agreed to hand over sovereignty to the People's Republic in Dec 1999, and China agreed in return to guarantee to maintain the port's capitalist economic and social system for at least 50 years. The colony concentrates on local trade and is a centre for gambling and tourism.

macaque /mə'kaːk/ *n.* a type of monkey of the genus *Macaca*. Various species of these medium-sized monkeys live in forests from the Far East to N Africa. The ◊rhesus and the ◊Barbary ape are part of this group. [French from Portuguese = monkey]

macaroni /mækə'rəuni/ (*plural* **macaronies**) *n.* 1. pasta formed into tubes. 2. an 18th-century dandy. [from Italian from Greek *makaria* = barley food]

macaronic /mækə'rɒnik/ *adj.* (of verse) of burlesque form containing Latin or other foreign words and vernacular words with Latin etc. terminations. [from obsolete Italian, jocular]

macaroon /mækə'ruːn/ *n.* a small cake or biscuit made with ground almonds or coconut. [from French from Italian]

MacArthur /mə'kaːθə/ Douglas 1880–1964. US general in World War II, commander of US forces in the Far East and, from March 1942, of the Allied forces in the SW Pacific. After the surrender of Japan he commanded the Allied occupation forces there.

Macaulay /mə'kɔːli/ Thomas Babington, Baron Macaulay 1800–1859. English historian, essayist, poet, and politician, secretary of war 1839–41. His *History of England* in five volumes 1849–61 celebrates the Glorious Revolution of 1668 as the crowning achievement of the Whig party.

macaw /mə'kɔː/ *n.* a large, brilliantly coloured, long-tailed tropical American ◊parrot of the genus *Ara* etc. [from Portuguese *Macao*]

Macbeth /mək'beθ/ died 1057. King of Scotland from 1040. The son of Findlaech, hereditary ruler of Moray, he was commander of the forces of Duncan I, King of Scotia, whom he killed in battle in 1040. His reign was prosperous until Duncan's son Malcolm III led an invasion and killed him at Lumphanan. Shakespeare's tragedy *Macbeth* was based on the 16th-century historian ◊Holinshed's *Chronicles*.

Macbeth a tragedy by William Shakespeare, first performed 1605–06. Acting on a prophecy by three witches that he will be king of Scotland, Macbeth, egged on by Lady Macbeth, murders King Duncan and becomes king but is eventually killed by Macduff.

Maccabees /'mækəbiːz/ Hebrew family, sometimes known as the **Hasmonaeans**. It was founded by the priest Mattathias (died 166 BC) who, with his sons, led the struggle for independence against the Syrians in the 2nd century BC. Judas (died 161 BC) reconquered Jerusalem in 164 BC, and Simon (died 142 BC) established its independence in 142 BC. The revolt of the Maccabees lasted until the capture of Jerusalem by the Romans in 63 BC. The story is told in four books of the ◊Apocrypha.

McCarthy /mə'kɒːθi/ Joe (Joseph Raymond) 1909–1957. US right-wing Republican politician, whose unsubstantiated claim in 1950 that the State Department and US army had been infiltrated by Communists started a wave of anticommunist hysteria, wild accusations, and blacklists, which continued until he was discredited in 1954. He was censured by the US senate for misconduct.

McCarthy Mary (Therese) 1912–1989. US novelist and critic. Much of her work looks probingly at US society, for example the novels *The Groves of Academe* 1952, which describes the anticommunist witch-hunts of the time (see J ◊McCarthy), and *The Group* 1963, which follows the post-college careers of eight women.

McCarthy US senator Joe McCarthy exhibiting 'evidence' to the House of Representatives Un-American Activities Committee.

McCartney /məˈkɑːtnɪ/ Paul 1942– . English rock singer, songwriter, and bass guitarist; former member of the ◊Beatles, and leader of the pop group Wings 1971–81. His subsequent solo hits have included collaborations with Michael Jackson and Elvis Costello.

McClellan /məˈklelən/ George Brinton 1826–1885. US Civil War general, commander in chief of the Union forces 1861–62. He was dismissed by President Lincoln when he delayed five weeks in following up his victory over the Confederate general Lee at Antietam (see under ◊Civil War, American). He was the unsuccessful Democrat presidential candidate against Lincoln in 1864.

McClure /məˈkluə/ Robert John le Mesurier 1807–1873. Irish-born British admiral and explorer. While on an expedition 1850–54 searching for John ◊Franklin, he was the first to pass through the North West Passage.

McCowen /məˈkaʊən/ Alec 1925– . British actor. His Shakespearean roles include Richard II and the Fool in *King Lear*; he is also known for his dramatic one-man shows.

McCoy /məˈkɔɪ/ n. **the real McCoy**, (*colloquial*) the real thing, the genuine article. [origin unknown]

MacCready /məˈkriːdɪ/ Paul 1925– . US designer of the *Gossamer Condor* aircraft, which made the first controlled flight by human power alone in 1977. His *Solar Challenger* flew from Paris to London under solar power; and in 1985 he constructed a powered model of a giant pterosaur, an extinct flying animal.

McCullers /məˈkʌləz/ Carson (Smith) 1917–1967. US novelist. Most of her writing (including her most popular novels *The Heart is a Lonely Hunter* 1940 and *Reflections in a Golden Eye* 1941) is set in the South, where she was born, and deals with spiritual isolation, containing elements of sometimes macabre violence.

McDiarmid /məkˈdɜːmɪd/ Hugh. Pen name of Christopher Murray Grieve 1892–1978. Scottish nationalist and Marxist poet. His works include *A Drunk Man looks at the Thistle* 1926 and two *Hymns to Lenin* 1930, 1935.

Macdonald /məkˈdɒnld/ Flora 1722–1790. Scottish heroine who rescued Prince Charles Edward Stuart, the Young Pretender, after his defeat at Culloden in 1746. Disguising him as her maid, she escorted him from her home in the Hebrides to France. She was arrested, but released in 1747.

Macdonald George 1824–1905. Scottish novelist and children's writer. Mystical imagination pervades all his books and this inspired later writers including G K Chesterton, C S Lewis, and J R R Tolkien. *David Elginbrod* 1863 and *Robert Falconer* 1868 are characteristic novels and his children's stories include *At the Back of the North Wind* 1871 and *The Princess and the Goblin* 1872.

Macdonald John Alexander 1815–1891. Canadian Conservative politician, prime minister 1867–73 and 1878–91. He was born in Glasgow but taken to Ontario as a child. In 1857 he became prime minister of Upper Canada. He took the leading part in the movement for federation, and in 1867 became the first prime minister of Canada. He was defeated in 1873 but returned to office in 1878 and retained it until his death.

MacDonald (James) Ramsay 1866–1937. British politician, first Labour prime minister Jan–Oct 1924 and 1929–31. He joined the ◊Independent Labour Party in 1894, and became first secretary of the new Labour Party in 1900. In Parliament he led the party 1906–14 and 1922–31 and was prime minister of the first two Labour governments. Failing to deal with worsening economic conditions, he left the party to form a coalition government in 1931, which was increasingly dominated by Conservatives, until he was replaced by Stanley Baldwin in 1935.

McDowell /məkˈdaʊəl/ Malcolm 1943– . English actor who played the rebellious hero in Lindsay Anderson's film *If* 1969 and confirmed his acting abilities in Stanley Kubrick's *A Clockwork Orange* 1971.

mace[1] *n.* **1.** a staff of office, especially the symbol of the Speaker's authority in the House of Commons. **2.** (*historical*) a heavy club usually having a metal head and spikes. [from Old French]

mace[2] *n.* the dried outer covering of the nutmeg as a spice. [from Old French from Latin *macir* = spicy bark]

macédoine /ˈmæsɪdwɑːn/ *n.* mixed fruit or vegetables, especially cut up small or in jelly. [French]

Macedonia /mæsɪˈdəʊnɪə/ ancient region of Greece, forming parts of modern Greece, Bulgaria, and Yugoslavia. Macedonia gained control of Greece after Philip II's victory at Chaeronea in 338 BC. His son, ◊Alexander the Great, conquered a vast empire. Macedonia became a Roman province in 146 BC; was settled by Slavs in the 6th century; conquered by Bulgars in the 7th century; by Byzantium in 1014, by Serbia in the 14th century, and by the Ottoman Empire 1355; and was divided between Serbia, Bulgaria, and Greece after the Balkan Wars of 1912–13.

Macedonia (Greek *Makedhonia*) mountainous region of N Greece, bounded to the W and N by Albania and Yugoslavia; **area** 34,177 km2/13,200 sq mi; **chief city** Thessaloniki; **population** (1981) 2,122,000; **features** Mt Olympus (2,918 m/9,570 ft).

Macedonia (Serbo-Croat *Makedonija*) a federal republic of Yugoslavia; **area** 25,700 sq km/9,920 sq mi; **capital** Skopje; **physical** mountainous; **population** (1981) 2,040,000, 63% Macedonians, 19% Albanians, 4% Turks; **language** Macedonian, closely allied to Bulgarian and written in Cyrillic.

macerate /ˈmæsəreɪt/ *v.t./i.* **1.** to make or become soft by soaking. **2.** to waste away by fasting. —**maceration** /-ˈreɪʃən/ *n.* [from Latin *macerare*]

McEwan /məˈkjuːən/ Ian 1948– . English novelist and short story writer. His tightly written works often have sinister or macabre undertones and contain elements of violence and bizarre sexuality, as in the short stories in *First Love, Last Rites* 1975. His novels include *The Comfort of Strangers* 1981 and *The Child in Time* 1987.

Machel /mæˈʃel/ Samora 1933–1986. Mozambican nationalist leader, president 1975–86. Machel was active in the liberation front ◊Frelimo from its conception in 1962, fighting for independence from Portugal. He became Frelimo leader in 1966, and Mozambique's first president from independence in 1975 until his death in a plane crash near the South African border.

machete /məˈtʃetɪ, -ˈtʃeɪtɪ/ *n.* a broad heavy knife used in Central America and the West Indies. [Spanish *macho* = hammer, from Latin]

Machiavelli /mækɪəveli/ Niccolò 1469–1527. Italian politician and author, whose name is now synonymous with cunning and cynical statecraft. In his most celebrated political writings, *Il principe*/*The Prince* 1513 and *Discorsi*/*Discourses* 1531, he discusses ways in which rulers can advance the interests of their states (and themselves) through an often amoral and opportunistic manipulation of other people.

machiavellian /mækɪəˈvelɪən/ *adj.* elaborately cunning; deceitful, perfidious. [from N *Machiavelli*]

machicolation /məʃɪkəˈleɪʃən/ *n.* an opening between the corbels of a projecting parapet, through which missiles etc. could be hurled down on attackers; a structure with such openings. [from Old French, ultimately from Provençal *macar* = crush and *col* = neck]

machinate /ˈmækɪneɪt, ˈmæʃ-/ *v.i.* to lay plots, to intrigue. —**machination** /-ˈneɪʃən/ *n.*, **machinator** *n.* [from Latin *machinari* = contrive]

machine /məˈʃiːn/ *n.* 1. an apparatus for applying mechanical power, having several parts each with a definite function; a device which allows a small force (the effort) to overcome a larger one (the load). There are three basic machines: the sloping or inclined plane, the lever, and wheel and axle. All other machines are combinations of these three basic types. Simple machines derived from the inclined plane include the wedge and the screw; the spanner is derived from the lever; the pulley from the wheel. 2. a bicycle, motorcycle, etc., an aircraft; a computer. 3. the controlling system of an organization. 4. a person who acts mechanically. —*v.t.* to make or operate on with a machine (especially of sewing or printing). —**machine-readable** *adj.* in a form that a computer can process. [from French from Latin *machina* from Greek *mekhanē* = contrivance]

machine code in computing, the 'language' the computer understands. In machine-code programs, instructions and storage locations are represented as binary numbers. A programmer writes programs in a high-level (easy-to-use) language, and this is converted to machine code by a ◊compiler or ◊interpreter program within the computer.

machine-gun *n.* a mounted automatic gun giving continuous fire. —*v.t.* (**-nn-**) to shoot at with a machine-gun.

machine politics the organization of a local political party to ensure its own election by influencing the electorate, and then to retain power through control of key committees and offices. The idea of machine politics was epitomized in the USA in the late 19th century, where it was used to control individual cities, most notably Chicago and New York.

machinery *n.* 1. machines; a mechanism. 2. an organized system; a means arranged.

machine tool for an automatic or semi-automatic power-driven machine for cutting and shaping metals. Machine tools have powerful electric motors to force cutting tools into the metal. They are made from hardened steel containing heat-resistant metals such as tungsten and chromium. The use of precision machine tools in ◊mass-production assembly methods ensures that all duplicate parts produced are virtually identical.

machinist *n.* 1. one who operates a machine, especially a sewing-machine or a machine tool. 2. one who makes machinery. [from French and from Latin]

machismo /məˈtʃɪzməʊ/ *n.* assertive manliness, masculine pride. [Spanish]

Mach number /mɑːk, mæk/ the ratio of the speed of a body to the speed of sound in the undisturbed medium through which the body travels. Mach 1 is reached when a body (such as an aircraft) has a velocity greater than that of sound ('passes the sound barrier'), namely 331 m/1,087 ft per second at sea level. [from E *Mach*, Austrian physicist (died 1916)]

macho /ˈmætʃəʊ/ *adj.* manly, virile. —*n.* (*plural* **machos**) 1. a macho man. 2. machismo. [Spanish = male, from Latin *masculus*]

Machtpolitik *n.* (German) power politics.

Machu Picchu /mɑːtʃuː ˈpiːktʃuː/ a ruined Inca city in Peru, built *c.* AD 1500, NW of Cuzco, discovered in 1911 by Hiram Bingham. It stands at the top of 300 m/1,000 ft cliffs, and contains the well-preserved remains of houses and temples.

Macias Nguema /məˈsiːəs əŋˈgweɪmə/ former name (until 1979) of ◊Bioko, an island of Equatorial Guinea in the Bight of Bonny, W Africa.

McIndoe /ˈmækɪndəʊ/ Archibald 1900–1960. New Zealand plastic surgeon. He became known in the UK during World War II for his remodelling of the faces of badly burned pilots.

MacInnes /məˈkɪnɪs/ Colin 1914–1976. English novelist, son of the novelist Angela Thirkell. He made a reputation with sharp depictions of London youth and subcultures of the 1950s, as in *City of Spades* 1957 and *Absolute Beginners* 1959.

Macintosh /ˈmækɪntɒʃ/ Charles 1766–1843. Scottish manufacturing chemist who invented a waterproof fabric lined with rubber that was used for raincoats—hence **mackintosh**. Other waterproofing processes have now largely superseded this method.

mack variant of ◊mac.

McKay /məˈkaɪ/ Heather Pamela (born Blundell) 1941– . Australian squash player. She won the British Open title for an unprecedented 16 years in succession 1962–1977.

Mackay of Clashfern /məˈkaɪ, klæʃˈfɜːn/ Baron James Peter Hymers 1927–. Scottish lawyer and Conservative politician. He became Lord Chancellor 1987 and in 1989 announced a reform package to end legal restrictive practices. This included ending the barristers' monopoly of advocacy in the higher courts; promoting the combination of the work of barristers and solicitors in 'mixed' practices; and allowing building societies and banks to do property conveyancing, formerly limited to solicitors. The plans met with fierce opposition.

Macke /ˈmækə/ August 1887–1914. German Expressionist painter, a founding member of the ◊Blaue Reiter group in Munich. With Franz Marc he developed a semi-abstract style comprising Cubist and Fauve characteristics. He was killed in World War I.

McKellen /məˈkelən/ Ian 1939– . British actor, whose stage roles include Richard II and Edward II, and Mozart in the stage version of *Amadeus*. His films include *Priest of Love* 1982 and *Plenty* 1985.

Mackendrick /məˈkendrɪk/ Alexander 1912– . US-born Scottish film director responsible for some of ◊Ealing studios' finest comedies, including *Whisky Galore* 1949 and *The Man in the White Suit* 1951. He made *Mandy* 1952 before leaving to work in Hollywood, where his films included *Sweet Smell of Success* 1957.

Mackensen /ˈmækənzən/ August von 1849–1945. German field marshal. During ◊World War I he achieved the breakthrough at Gorlice and the conquest of Serbia in 1915, and in 1916 played a major role in the overthrow of Romania.

Mackenzie /məˈkenzɪ/ Alexander *c.*1755–1820. British explorer and fur trader. In 1789, he was the first European to see the river, now part of N Canada, named after him. In 1792–93 he crossed the Rocky Mountains to the Pacific.

Mackenzie Compton 1883–1972. Scottish author. His parents were actors. He was educated at Oxford University and published his first novel *The Passionate Elopement* in 1911. Later works were *Carnival* 1912, *Sinister Street* 1913–14 (an autobiographical novel), and the comic *Whisky Galore* 1947. He published his autobiography in ten 'octaves' (volumes) 1963–71.

Mackenzie William Lyon 1795–1861. Canadian politician, born in Scotland. He emigrated to Canada in 1820, and led the rebellion of 1837–38, an unsuccessful attempt to limit British rule and establish more democratic institutions in Canada. After its failure he lived in the USA until 1849, and in 1851–58 sat on the Canadian legislature as a Radical. He was grandfather of W L Mackenzie King, the Liberal prime minister.

Mackenzie River a river in the Northwest Territories, Canada, flowing from Great Slave Lake NW to the Arctic Ocean; about 1,800 km/1,120 mi long. It is the main channel of the Finlay-Peace-Mackenzie system, 4,241 km/2,635 mi long.

mackerel /ˈmækərəl/ *n.* (*plural* the same) a sea-fish *Scomber scombrus*, found in the N Atlantic and Mediterranean, used as food. It is blue with irregular black bands down its sides, the latter and the under surface showing a metallic sheen. —**mackerel sky**, a sky dappled with rows of small, white, fleecy clouds (cirrocumulus). [from Anglo-French]

McKinley /məˈkɪnlɪ/ William 1843–1901. 25th president of the USA 1897–1901, a Republican. He was born in Ohio, and elected to Congress in 1876. His period as president was marked by the USA's adoption of an imperialist policy, as exemplified by the Spanish-American War of 1898 and the annexation of the Philippines. He was assassinated in Buffalo, New York.

McKinley, Mount peak in Alaska, USA, the highest in North America, 6,194 m/20,320 ft; named after US president William McKinley. See ◊Rocky Mountains.

mackintosh /ˈmækɪntɒʃ/ *n.* 1. a waterproof coat or cloak. 2. cloth waterproofed with rubber. [from C *Macintosh*]

Mackintosh Charles Rennie 1868–1928. Scottish ◊Art Nouveau architect, designer, and painter, who exercised considerable influence on European design. His chief work includes the Glasgow School of Art 1896.

Mackmurdo /məkˈmɜːdəʊ/ Arthur H 1851–1942. English designer and architect. He founded the Century Guild in 1882, a group of architects, artists, and designers inspired

Macmillan *British Conservative prime minister 1957–53, Harold Macmillan.*

by William ◊Morris and John ◊Ruskin. His book and textile designs are forerunners of ◊Art Nouveau.

MacLaine /məˈkleɪn/ Shirley. Stage name of Shirley MacLean Beaty 1934– . US actress, sister of Warren Beatty. She has played both comedy and dramatic roles. Her many offscreen interests have limited her film appearances, which include *The Trouble with Harry* 1955, *The Apartment* 1960, and *Terms of Endearment* 1983.

Maclean /məˈkleɪn/ Donald 1913–1983. British spy, who worked for the USSR while in the UK civil service. He defected to the USSR in 1951 together with Guy ◊Burgess.

MacLennan /məˈklenən/ Robert (Adam Ross) 1936– . Scottish centrist politician. Member of Parliament for Caithness and Sutherland from 1966. He left the Labour Party for the Social Democrats (SDP) in 1981, and was SDP leader in 1988 during merger negotiations with the Liberals. He then became a member of the new Social and Liberal Democrats.

McLuhan /məˈkluːən/ (Herbert) Marshall 1911–1980. Canadian theorist of communication, famed for his views on the effects of technology on modern society. He coined the phrase 'the medium is the message', meaning that the form rather than the content of information has become crucial. His works include *The Gutenberg Galaxy* 1962 (in which he coined the phrase 'the global village' for the worldwide electronic society then emerging), *Understanding Media* 1964, and *The Medium is the Massage* (sic) 1967.

> It is the weak and confused who worship the pseudosimplicities of brutal directness.
>
> **Marshal McLuhan**
> 'The Tough as Narcissus', *The Mechanical Bride*

MacMahon /məkˈmɑːn/ Marie Edmé Patrice Maurice, Comte de 1808–1893. Marshal of France. Captured at Sedan in 1870 during the Franco-Prussian War, he suppressed the ◊Paris Commune after his release, and as president of the republic 1873–79 worked for a royalist restoration until forced to resign.

Macmillan /məkˈmɪlən/ (Maurice) Harold, 1st Earl of Stockton 1894–1986. British prime minister 1957–63. Conservative MP for Stockton 1924–29 and 1931–45; and for Bromley 1945–64. As minister of housing 1951–54 he achieved the construction of 300,000 new houses a year. He

became foreign secretary in 1955 and was chancellor of the Exchequer from 1955 to 1957. He became prime minister on the resignation of Anthony ◊Eden after the Suez crisis. Macmillan led the Conservative Party to victory in the 1959 elections on the slogan 'You've never had it so good' (the phrase was borrowed from a US election campaign). Internationally, his realization of the 'wind of change' in Africa advanced the independence of former colonies. In 1963 he attempted to negotiate British entry to the European Economic Community, but was blocked by the French president Charles de Gaulle. Much of his career as prime minister was spent trying to maintain a UK nuclear weapon, and he was responsible for the purchase of US Polaris missiles in 1962. Macmillan's nickname Supermac was coined by the cartoonist Vicky. He was awarded an earldom in 1984.

MacMillan Kenneth 1929– . Scottish choreographer. After studying at the Sadler's Wells Ballet School he was director of the Royal Ballet 1970–77 and then principal choreographer.

MacMillan Kirkpatrick died 1878. Scottish blacksmith, who invented the bicycle in 1839. His invention consisted of a 'hobby-horse' that was fitted with treadles and propelled by pedalling.

MacNeice /məkˈniːs/ Louis 1907–1963. British poet, born in Belfast. He made his debut with *Blind Fireworks* 1929 and developed a polished ease of expression, reflecting his classical training, as in *Autumn Journal* 1939. Unlike many of his contemporaries, he was politically uncommitted. Later works include the play *The Dark Tower* 1947, written for radio, for which he also wrote features 1941–49; a verse translation of Goethe's *Faust*, and the radio play *The Administrator* 1961. He also translated the Greek classics.

McPhee /məkˈfiː/ Colin 1900–1964. US composer. His studies of Balinese music 1934–36 produced two works, *Tabuh-tabuhan* for two pianos and orchestra 1936 and *Balinese Ceremonial Music* for two pianos 1940, which influenced John ◊Cage and later generations of US composers.

Macpherson /məkˈfɜːsən/ James 1736–1796. Scottish writer and forger, author of *Fragments of Ancient Poetry collected in the Highlands of Scotland* 1760, followed by the epics *Fingal* 1761 and *Temora* 1763, which he claimed as the work of the 3rd-century bard ◊Ossian. After his death they were shown to be forgeries.

Macquarie /məˈkwɒri/ Lachlan 1762–1834. Scottish administrator in Australia. He succeeded ◊Bligh as governor of New South Wales in 1808, raised the demoralized settlement to prosperity, and did much to rehabilitate ex-convicts. He opened the first school for aborigines. In 1821 he returned to Britain in poor health, exhausted by struggles with his opponents. Lachlan River, Macquarie River and Island, and Macquarie University in Sydney are named after him.

Macquarie Island outlying Australian territorial possession, a Tasmanian dependency, some 1,370 km/850 mi SE of Hobart; area 170 sq km/65 sq mi; it is uninhabited except for an Australian government research station.

McQueen /məˈkwiːn/ Steve (Terrence Steven) 1930–1980. US actor. He was one of the most popular film stars of the 1960s and 1970s, admired for his portrayals of the strong, silent loner, and noted for performing his own stunt work. After television success in the 1950s he became a film star with *The Magnificent Seven* 1960. His films include *The Great Escape* 1963, *Bullitt* 1968, *Papillon* 1973 and *The Hunter* 1980.

macramé /məˈkrɑːmɪ/ *n.* the art of knotting cord or string in patterns to make decorative articles; work so made. [from Turkish *makrama* = bedspread, from Arabic]

Macready /məˈkriːdi/ William Charles 1793–1873. British actor. He made his debut at Covent Garden, London, in 1816. Noted for his roles as Shakespeare's tragic heroes (Macbeth, Lear, and Hamlet), he was partly responsible for persuading the theatre to return to the original texts of Shakespeare and abandon the earlier, bowdlerized versions.

macro *n.* in computer programming, a new command created by combining a number of existing ones. For example, if the language has separate commands for obtaining data from the keyboard and for displaying data on the screen, the programmer might create a macro that performs both these tasks with one command. A **macro key**

is a key on the keyboard that combines the effects of several individual key presses.

macro- in combinations, long, large, large-scale. [from Greek *makros* = long]

macrobiotics *n.* a dietary system of organically grown wholefoods. It originates in Zen Buddhism, and attempts to balance the principles of ◊yin and yang, which are regarded as present in various foods in different proportions. —**macrobiotic** *adj.* of or following this dietary system. [from Greek *macro* and *biotos* = life]

macrocosm /'mækrəʊkɒzəm/ *n.* the Universe; any great whole. [from French from Latin Greek *kosmos* = world]

macroeconomics /mækrəʊi:kə'nɒmɪks/ *n.* the division of economics concerned with the study of whole (aggregate) economies or systems, including such aspects as government income and expenditure, the balance of payments, fiscal policy, investment, inflation, and unemployment. It seeks to understand the influence of all relevant economic factors on each other and thus to quantify and predict aggregate national income.

macromolecule /'mækrəʊmɒlɪkju:l/ *n.* a molecule containing a very large number of atoms.

macron /'mækrɒn/ *n.* the written or printed mark (¯) over a long or stressed vowel. [Greek, neuter of *makros* = long]

macrophage *n.* a type of white blood cell, or ◊leucocyte, found in all vertebrate animals. Macrophages specialize in the removal of bacteria and other micro-organisms, or of cell debris after injury. Like phagocytes, they engulf foreign matter, but they are larger than phagocytes and have a longer life span. They are found throughout the body, but mainly in the lymph and connective tissues, and especially the lungs, where they ingest dust, fibres, and other inhaled particles.

macroscopic /mækrəʊ'skɒpɪk/ *adj.* 1. visible to the naked eye. 2. regarded in terms of large units. —**macroscopically** *adv.*

macula /'mækjʊlə/ *n.* (*plural* **maculae** /-li:/) a dark spot; a spot, especially a permanent one, in the skin. —**maculation** /-'leɪʃən/ *n.* [Latin]

mad *adj.* 1. having a disordered mind, insane. 2. extremely foolish. 3. wildly enthusiastic or infatuated. 4. frenzied. 5. (*colloquial*) angry. 6. wildly light-hearted. —**like mad,** (*colloquial*) with great energy or enthusiasm. **mad cow disease,** see ◊BSE. —**madness** *n.* [Old English]

MAD acronym from mutual assured destruction; the basis of the theory of ◊deterrence by possession of nuclear weapons.

Madagascar /mædə'gæskə/ Democratic Republic of; island in the Indian Ocean, off the coast of E Africa, about 400 km/280 mi from Mozambique; **area** 587,041 sq km/ 226,598 sq mi; **capital** Antananarivo; **physical** central highlands; humid valleys and coastal plains; arid in S; **head of state and government** Didier Ratsiraka from 1975; **political system** one-party socialist republic; **population** (1990 est) 11,802,000; **language** Malagasy (official); French, English; **recent history** independence from France achieved in 1960. In 1972 the army took control of the government, with Didier Ratsiraka as president; in 1977 the National Front for the Defence of Malagasy Socialist Revolution (FNDR) became the sole legal political organization.

madam /'mædəm/ *n.* 1. a polite or respectful formal address or mode of reference to a woman. 2. (*colloquial*) a conceited or precocious young woman. 3. a woman brothel-keeper. [from Old French]

Madame /'mædəm, mæ'dɑ:m/ *n.* (*plural* **Mesdames** /meɪ'dɑ:m, -'dæm/) the title used of or to a French-speaking woman, corresponding to Mrs or madam. [French = my lady]

Madame Bovary /bəʊvə'ri:/ a novel by Flaubert, published in France 1857. It aroused controversy by its portrayal of a country doctor's wife driven to suicide by a series of unhappy love affairs.

madcap *n.* a wildly impulsive person. —*adj.* wildly impulsive.

madden *v.t./i.* to make or become mad; to irritate.

madder *n.* 1. a herbaceous plant *Rubia tinctoria* with yellowish flowers. 2. the red dye obtained from its root; a synthetic substitute for this. [Old English]

made *past* and *past participle* of ◊make. —*adj.* (of a person) 1. built or formed (*well-made; loosely-made*). 2. successful. —**have it made,** (*slang*) to be sure of success. **made for,** ideally suited to. **made of,** consisting of. **made of money,** (*colloquial*) very rich.

Madeira /mə'dɪərə/ group of islands forming an autonomous region of Portugal off the NW coast of Africa, about 420 km/260 mi N of the Canary Islands. Madeira, the largest, and Porto Santo are the only inhabited islands. The Desertas and Selvagens are uninhabited islets. Their mild climate makes them year-round resorts; **area** 796 sq km/ 308 sq mi; **capital** Funchal, on Madeira; **population** (1986) 269,500; **recent history** Portuguese from the 15th century; occupied by Britain in 1801 and 1807–14. In 1980 Madeira gained partial autonomy but remains a Portuguese overseas territory.

Madeira *n.* a fortified white wine from Madeira. —**Madeira cake,** a rich cake containing no fruit.

Madeira River river of W Brazil; length 3,250 km/ 2,020 mi. It is formed by the rivers Beni and Mamoré, and flows NE to join the Amazon.

Mademoiselle /mædəmwə'zel/ *n.* (*plural* **Mesdemoiselles** /meɪdm-/) 1. the title used of or to an unmarried French-speaking woman, corresponding to Miss or madam. 2. **mademoiselle,** a young Frenchwoman; a French governess. [French *ma* = my and *demoiselle* from Latin *domina* = lady]

Maderna /mə'deənə/ Bruno 1920–1973. Italian composer and conductor. He studied with Malapiero and ◊Scherchen, and collaborated with ◊Berio in setting up an electronic studio in Milan. His compositions combine advanced techniques with an elegance of sound, and include a pioneering work for live and pre-recorded flute, *Musica su due dimensioni* 1952, numerous concertos, and the aleatoric *Aura* for orchestra 1974.

madhouse *n.* 1. (*colloquial*) a mental home or mental hospital. 2. a scene of confused uproar.

Madhya Pradesh /'mʌdjə prə'deʃ/ state of central India; the largest of the Indian states; **area** 442,700 sq km/170,921 sq mi; **capital** Bhopal; **population** (1981) 52,132,000; **language** Hindi; **recent history** formed in 1950 from the former British province of Central Provinces and Berar and the princely states of Makrai and Chattisgarh; lost some SW districts in 1956, including ◊Nagpur, and absorbed Bhopal, Madhya Bharat, and Vindhya Pradesh.

Madison /'mædɪsn/ James 1751–1836. 4th president of the USA 1809–17. In 1787 he became a member of the Philadelphia Constitutional Convention and took a leading part in drawing up the US constitution and the Bill of Rights. As secretary of state in Jefferson's government 1801–09, his main achievement was the ◊Louisiana Purchase. He was elected president in 1808 and re-elected in 1812. During his period of office the War of 1812 with Britain took place.

Madison Square Garden venue in New York, built as a boxing arena and also used for concerts. The current 'Garden' is the fourth to bear the name and staged its first boxing match in 1968. It is situated over Pennsylvania Station on 7th Avenue, New York City.

madly *adv.* in a mad manner; (*colloquial*) passionately, extremely.

madman *n.* or **madwoman** (*plural* **madmen** or **madwomen**) a person who is mad.

Madoc, Prince /'mædək/ legendary prince of Gwynedd, Wales, supposed to have discovered the Americas and been an ancestor of a group of light-skinned, Welsh-speaking Indians in the American West.

madonna /mə'dɒnə/ *n.* a picture or statue of the Virgin Mary. —**madonna lily,** a tall white lily *Lilium candidum* often depicted in pictures of the Annunciation. [Italian = my lady]

Madonna Italian name for the Virgin ◊Mary, meaning 'my lady'.

Madonna stage name of Madonna Louise Ciccone 1958– . US pop singer and actress who presents herself on stage and in videos with exaggerated sexuality and Catholic trappings. Her first hit was 'Like a Virgin' 1984; others include 'Material Girl' 1985 and 'Like a Prayer' 1989. Her films include *Desperately Seeking Susan* 1985 and *Dick Tracy* 1990.

Madonna US pop singer and film actress.

Madras /mə'drɑːs/ industrial port (cotton, cement, chemicals, iron, and steel) and capital of Tamil Nadu, India, on the Bay of Bengal; population (1981) 4,277,000. Fort St George 1639 remains from the East India Company when Madras was the chief port on the E coast. Madras was occupied by the French during 1746–48 and shelled by the German ship *Emden* in 1914, the only place in India attacked in World War I.

Madrid /mə'drɪd/ industrial city (leather, chemicals, furniture, tobacco, paper) and capital of Spain and of Madrid province; population (1986) 3,124,000. Built on an elevated plateau in the centre of the country, at 655 m/2,183 ft it is the highest capital city in Europe and has excesses of heat and cold. **Madrid province** has an area of 8,000 sq km/3,088 sq mi and a population of 4,855,000. Madrid began as a Moorish citadel captured by Castile in 1083, became important in the times of Charles V and Philip II, and was designated capital in 1561.

madrigal /'mædrɪɡəl/ *n.* 1. a form of secular song in four or five parts, usually sung without instrumental accompaniment. It originated in 14th-century Italy. 2. a short amatory poem. The form was developed and perfected by Petrarch. [from Italian from Latin *matricalis* = mother]

Madurai /'mædjʊraɪ/ city in Tamil Nadu, India; site of the 16th–17th-century Hindu temple of Sundareswara, and of Madurai University 1966; cotton industry; population (1981) 904,000.

Maecenas /maɪ'siːnəs/ Gaius Cilnius 69–8 BC. Roman patron of the arts who encouraged the work of ◊Horace and ◊Virgil.

maelstrom /'meɪlstrɒm/ *n.* 1. a great whirlpool. 2. a confused state. [Dutch from *whirlpool off* the Lofoten Islands, Norway, also known as the Moskenesstraumen]

maenad /'miːnæd/ *n.* in Greek mythology, one of the women participants in the orgiastic rites of ◊Dionysus; maenads were also known as **Bacchae**, or bacchantes. [from Latin from Greek *mainomai* = rave]

maestro /'maɪstrəʊ/ *n.* (*plural* **maestri** /-riː/) 1. a great conductor, composer, or teacher of music. 2. a masterly performer in any sphere. [Italian = master]

Maeterlinck /'meɪtəlɪŋk/ Maurice, Count Maeterlinck 1862–1949. Belgian poet and dramatist. His plays include *Pelléas et Mélisande* 1892, *L'Oiseau bleu/The Blue Bird* 1908, and *Le Bourgmestre de Stilmonde/The Burgomaster of Stilemonde* 1918. The latter celebrates Belgian resistance in World War I, a subject that led to his exile in the USA from 1940. He won the Nobel Prize for Literature in 1911.

We possess only the happiness we are able to understand.
Count Maurice Maeterlinck
Wisdom and Destiny

Mafia /'mæfiə/ *n.* 1. secret society reputed to control organized crime such as gambling, loansharking, drug traffic, prostitution, and protection. It originated in the 1600s in Sicily (although some sources claim that it originated as early as the 13th century) and now operates chiefly there and in US cities; connected with the ◊Camorra of Naples and also known in the USA and **La Cosa Nostra** ('our affair') or the Mob. 2. **mafia**, a network of persons regarded as exerting hidden influence. [Italian dialect = bragging]

Mafikeng /'mæfɪkeŋ/ town (until 1980 Mafeking) in Bophuthatswana, South Africa; it was the capital of Bechuanaland, and the British officer Baden-Powell held it under Boer siege 12 Oct 1899–17 May 1900.

Mafioso /mæfi'əʊsəʊ, mɑː-/ *n.* (*plural* **Mafiosi** /-siː/) a member of the Mafia. [Italian]

Magadha /'mʌɡədə/ a kingdom of ancient NE India, roughly corresponding to the middle and southern parts of modern ◊Bihar. It was the scene of many incidents in the life of Buddha and was the seat of the Maurya dynasty, founded by Chandragupta in the 3rd century BC. Its capital Pataliputra was a great cultural and political centre.

magazine /mæɡə'ziːn/ *n.* 1. a periodical publication (now usually illustrated) containing contributions by various writers. 2. a store for arms, ammunition, and provisions, for use in war; a store for explosives. 3. a chamber for holding the supply of cartridges to be fed automatically to the breech of a gun; a similar device in a camera, slide-projector, etc. [from French from Italian from Arabic = store-house]

Magdeburg /'mæɡdəbɜːɡ/ industrial city (vehicles, paper, textiles, machinery), former capital of Saxony and since German reunification in 1990 capital of Saxony-Anhalt, population (1990) 290,000. In 1938 the city was linked by canal with the Rhine and Ruhr rivers.

Magellan /mə'ɡelən/ Ferdinand 1480–1521. Portuguese navigator. In 1519 he set sail in the *Victoria* from Seville with the intention of reaching the East Indies by a westerly route. He sailed through the **Magellan Strait** at the tip of South America, crossed an ocean he named the Pacific, and in 1521 reached the Philippines, where he was killed in a battle with the islanders. His companions returned to Seville in 1522, completing the voyage under the ◊Cano. Magellan and his Malay slave, Enrique de Malacca, are considered the first circumnavigators of the globe.

Magellanic clouds /mædʒɪ'lænɪk/ in astronomy, the two galaxies nearest to the Earth. They are irregularly shaped, and appear as detached parts of the ◊Milky Way, in the southern constellations Dorado and Tucana.

maggot /'mæɡət/ *n.* the footless larva of an insect, especially of the bluebottle or cheese-fly. —**maggoty** *adj.*

Maghreb /'mʌɡrəb/ name for NW Africa. The Maghreb powers—Algeria, Libya, Morocco, Tunisia, and Western Sahara—agreed on economic coordination 1964–65, with Mauritania cooperating from 1970. Chad and Mali are sometimes included. See also ◊Mashraq. [Arabic = far west, sunset]

magi /'meɪdʒaɪ/ *n.* plural of ◊magus. Magi were priests of the Zoroastrian religion of ancient Persia, noted for their knowledge of astrology. The term is used in the New Testament of the Latin Vulgate Bible where the Authorized Version gives 'wise men'. The magi who came to visit the infant Jesus with gifts of gold, frankincense, and myrrh (the **Adoration of the Magi**) were in later tradition described as 'the three kings' – Caspar, Melchior, and Balthazar. [from Latin from Greek from Persian]

magic /'mædʒɪk/ *n.* 1. the supposed art of influencing the course of events by the occult control of nature or of spirits, witchcraft. The central ideas are that like produces like (**sympathetic magic**) and that influence carries by **contagion** or association; for example, by the former principle an enemy could be destroyed through an effigy, by the latter principle through personal items such as hair or nail clippings. 2. conjuring tricks. 3. an inexplicable or remarkable influence; an enchanting quality or phenomenon. —*adj.* of magic; producing surprising results. —*v.t.* (-ck-) to change or make by or as if by magic. —**magic carpet,** a mythical carpet able to transport the person on it to any place. **magic eye,** a photoelectric device for automatic control. **magic lantern,** a simple form of image-projector using slides. —**magical** *adj.,* **magically** *adv.* [from Old French from Latin from Greek]

magic bullet a term sometimes used for drugs that are specifically targeted on certain cells or tissues in the body, such as a small collection of cancerous cells (see ◊cancer) or cells that have been invaded by a virus.

magician /mə'dʒɪʃən/ *n.* 1. one skilled in magic. 2. a conjuror.

Magic Mountain, The a novel by Thomas Mann, published in Germany 1924. It is an ironic portrayal of the lives of a group of patients in a Swiss sanatorium, showing the futility of their sheltered existence.

magic realism in literature, a fantastic situation realistically treated, as in the works of many Latin American writers such as Isabel Allende, Borges, García Márquez.

magic square in mathematics, a square array of different numbers in which the rows, columns, and diagonals add up to the same total. A simple example employing the numbers 1 to 9, with a total of 15, is:

6	7	2
1	5	9
8	3	4.

Maginot Line /'mæʒɪnəʊ/ French fortification system along the German frontier from Switzerland to Luxembourg built 1929–36 under the direction of the war minister, André Maginot. It consisted of semi-underground forts joined by underground passages, and protected by antitank defences; lighter fortifications continued the line to the sea. In 1940 German forces pierced the Belgian frontier line and outflanked the Maginot Line.

magisterial /mædʒɪ'stɪərɪəl/ *adj.* 1. imperious; having authority. 2. of a magistrate. —**magisterially** *adv.* [from Latin *magister*]

magistracy /'mædʒɪstrəsɪ/ *n.* magisterial office; magistrates collectively.

magistrate /'mædʒɪstreɪt/ *n.* in English law, a person who presides in a magistrates' court: either a ◊justice of the peace (with no legal qualifications, and unpaid) or a stipendiary magistrate. Stipendiary magistrates are paid, qualified lawyers largely used in London and major cities. [from Latin *magistratus*]

magistrates' court in England and Wales, a local law court that mainly deals with minor criminal cases, but also decides, in ◊committal proceedings, whether more serious criminal cases should be referred to the crown court. It also deals with some civil matters, such as certain matrimonial proceedings. A magistrates' court consists of between two and seven lay justices of the peace (who are advised on the law by a clerk to the justices), or one stipendiary magistrate.

maglev acronym from **mag**netic **lev**itation, high-speed surface transport using the repellent force of superconductive magnets (see ◊superconductivity) to propel and support, for example, a train above a track. Maglev trains have been developed in Japan and in Germany. A ship launched in Japan in 1990 has been fitted with superconducting thrusters instead of propellers for sea trials in 1991.

magma *n.* (*plural* **magmas** or **magmata**) a molten material made up of solids and gases beneath the Earth's surface from which ◊igneous rock is formed by cooling. Magma released by volcanoes is called ◊lava. [Latin from Greek *massō* = knead]

Magna Carta /'mægnə'kɑːtə/ in English history, the charter granted by King John in 1215, traditionally seen as guaranteeing human rights against the excessive use of royal power. As a reply to the king's demands for excessive feudal dues and attacks on the privileges of the church, Archbishop Langton proposed to the barons the drawing-up of a binding document in 1213. John was forced to accept this at Runnymede (now in Surrey) on 15 June 1215. As feudalism declined Magna Carta lost its significance, and under the Tudors was almost forgotten. During the 17th century it was rediscovered and reinterpreted by the parliamentary party as a democratic document. Four original copies exist, one each in Salisbury

magnetic field   *the earth's magnetic field*

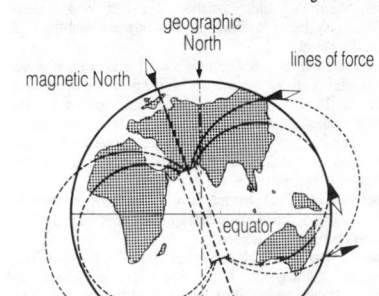

and Lincoln cathedrals and two in the British Library. [Latin 'great charter']

magnanimous /mæg'nænɪməs/ *adj.* noble and generous in feelings or conduct, not petty.   —**magnanimity** /-nə'nɪmɪtɪ/*n.,* **magnanimously** *adv.* [from Latin *magnus* = great and *animus* = mind]

magnate /'mægneɪt/ *n.* a wealthy and influential person, especially in business. [from Latin *magnus* = great]

magnesia /mæg'niːʃə/ *n.* magnesium oxide, symbol MgO, white powder or colourless crystals formed when magnesium is burned in air or oxygen; a typical basic oxide. It is used to treat acidity of the stomach, and in some industrial processes – for example as a lining brick in furnaces, as it is very stable when heated (refractory oxide). [from *Magnesia* in Asia Minor]

magnesium *n.* lightweight, very ductile and malleable, silver-white, metallic element, symbol Mg, atomic number 12, relative atomic mass 24.305. It is one of the ◊alkaline-earth elements, the lightest of the commonly used metals. Magnesium silicate, carbonate, and chloride are widely distributed in nature. The metal is used in alloys and flash photography. It is a necessary trace element in the human diet, and green plants cannot grow without it since it is an essential constituent of chlorophyll.

magnet /'mægnɪt/ *n.* 1. a piece of iron, steel, alloy, ore, etc., having the properties of attracting iron and of pointing approximately north and south when suspended; a lodestone. 2. a person or thing that attracts. [from Latin from Greek = stone of Magnesia]

magnetic /mæg'netɪk/ *adj.* 1. having the properties of a magnet. 2. produced or acting by magnetism; capable of acquiring the properties of or of being attracted by a magnet. 3. strongly attractive. —**magnetic compass,** one using a magnetic needle. **magnetic needle,** an indicator made of magnetized steel, pointing north and south on the dial of a compass. **magnetic north,** the direction indicated by a magnetic needle, close to the geographical north but not identical with it. **magnetic pole,** the point near the north or south pole where a magnetic needle dips vertically. **magnetic storm,** in meteorology, a sudden disturbance affecting the Earth's magnetic field, causing anomalies in radio transmissions and magnetic compasses; it is probably caused by ◊sunspot activity. —**magnetically** *adv.*

magnetic field the physical field or region around a permanent magnet, or around a conductor carrying an electric current, in which a force acts on a moving charge or on a magnet placed in the field. The field can be represented by lines of force, which by convention link north and south poles and are parallel to the directions of a small compass needle placed on them. Its magnitude and direction are given by the magnetic flux density.

magnetic flux a measurement of the strength of the magnetic field around electric currents and magnets. It is measured in ◊webers; one weber per square metre is equal to one ◊tesla. The amount of magnetic flux through an area equals the product of the area and the magnetic field strength at a point within that area.

magnetic resonance imaging (MRI) diagnostic scanning system based on the principles of nuclear magnetic resonance. MRI yields finely detailed three-dimensional images of structures within the body without exposing the patient to harmful radiation. The technique is useful for imaging the soft tissues of the body, such as the brain and the spinal cord.

magnetic tape a plastic strip coated or impregnated with magnetic particles for the recording and reproduction of signals. It is used in sound recording, audiovisual systems (videotape), and computing. For mass storage on commercial mainframe computers, large reel-to-reel tapes are used, but for the smaller mini-and microcomputers, tape cassettes and cartridges are more usual.

magnetism /'mægnɪtɪzəm/ n. 1. magnetic phenomena; the science of these; the natural agency producing them. 2. great charm and attraction.

magnetite n. a black iron ore, iron oxide, Fe_3O_4. Widely distributed, magnetite is found in nearly all igneous and metamorphic rocks. It is strongly magnetic and some deposits, called **lodestone**, are permanently magnetized. Lodestone has been used as a compass since the first millenium BC.

magnetize /'mægnɪtaɪz/ v.t. 1. to give magnetic properties to; to make into a magnet. 2. to attract (*literal* or *figurative*) as a magnet does. —**magnetization** /-'zeɪʃən/ n.

magneto n. (*plural* **magnetos**) a simple electric generator, often used to provide the electricity for the ignition system of motorcycles and used in early automobiles. It consists of a rotating magnet that sets up an electric current in a coil, providing the spark. [from *magneto-electric* (combined from *magnet* and *electric*)]

magnetohydrodynamics n. (MHD) the field of science concerned with the behaviour of ionized gases or liquid in a magnetic field. Systems have been developed that use MHD to generate electrical power.

magnetosphere n. the volume of space, surrounding a planet, controlled by the planet's magnetic field, and acting as a magnetic 'shell'. The Earth's extends 64,000 km/ 40,000 mi towards the Sun, but many times this distance on the side away from the Sun.

magnetron n. a ◊thermionic valve (electron tube) for generating very high-frequency oscillations, used in radar and to produce microwaves in a microwave oven. The flow of electrons from the tube's cathode to one or more anodes is controlled by an applied magnetic field.

Magnificat /mæg'nɪfɪkæt/ n. a canticle, the song of praise (so called from the first word of the Latin text) in Luke 1:46–55 sung by the Virgin Mary when she was greeted by her cousin Elizabeth as the mother of the Lord. [Latin = magnifies (extols)]

magnification n. measure of the enlargement or reduction of an object in an imaging optical system. **Linear magnification** is the ratio of the size (height) of the image to that of the object. **Angular magnification** is the ratio of the angle subtended at the observer's eye by the image to the angle subtended by the object when viewed directly.

magnificent /mæg'nɪfɪsənt/ adj. 1. splendid in appearance etc.; sumptuously constructed or adorned; splendidly lavish. 2. (*colloquial*) excellent. —**magnificence** n., **magnificently** adv. [French or from Latin *magnificus* (*magnus* = great and *facere* = make)]

magnify /'mægnɪfaɪ/ v.t. 1. to make (a thing) appear larger than it is, as with a lens. 2. to exaggerate; to intensify. 3. (*archaic*) to extol. —**magnifying glass**, a lens used to magnify things. —**magnifier** n. [from Old French or Latin *magnificare*]

magnitude /'mægnɪtjuːd/ n. 1. largeness; size. 2. importance. 3. in astronomy, a measure of the brightness of a star or other celestial object. The larger the number denoting the magnitude, the fainter the object. Zero or first magnitude indicates some of the brightest stars. Still brighter are those of negative magnitude, such as Sirius, whose magnitude is –1.42. —**absolute magnitude**, the magnitude that a star would seem to have if at a distance of 10 parsecs or 32.6 light-years. **apparent magnitude**, as seen from the Earth. [from Latin *magnitudo* (*magnus* = great)]

magnolia n. any tree or shrub of the genus *Magnolia*, family Magnoliaceae, native to North America and E Asia. Magnolias vary in height from 60 cm/2 ft to 30 m/150 ft. They have dark-green foliage and the large, waxlike fragrant single flowers are white, rose, or purple. The Southern magnolia *M. grandiflora* of the USA grows up to 24m/80 ft tall and has white flowers 23 cm/9 in across. [from *Magnol*, French botanist (died 1715)]

Magnox n. an early type of nuclear reactor used in the UK, for example in Calder Hall, the world's first commercial nuclear power station. This type of reactor uses uranium fuel encased in tubes of magnesium alloy called Magnox. Carbon dioxide gas is used as a coolant to extract heat from the reactor core. See also ◊nuclear energy.

magnum /'mægnəm/ n. a bottle containing two reputed quarts of wine or spirits. [Latin, neuter of *magnus* = great]

magnum opus /mægnəm 'əupəs/ a great work of literature etc.; an author's greatest work. [Latin]

magpie /'mægpaɪ/ n. 1. genus of birds *Pica* in the crow family. They feed on insects, snails, young birds, and carrion, and are found in Europe, Asia, N Africa, and W North America. The common magpie *Pica pica* has black and white plumage, the long tail having a metallic gloss. It is reputed to collect objects. 2. a random collector. 3. a chatterer. [from *Mag*, abbreviation of woman's name *Margaret*, and Latin *pica*]

Magritte /mə'griːt/ René 1898–1967. Belgian Surrealist painter. His paintings focus on visual paradoxes and everyday objects taken out of context. Recurring motifs include bowler hats, apples, and windows.

magus /'meigəs/ n. (*plural* **magi** /-dʒaɪ/) a poet of ancient Persia; a sorcerer. [from Latin from Greek from Persian]

Magyar /'mægjɑː/ n. a member of the largest ethnic group in Hungary, comprising 92% of the population. Magyars are of mixed Ugric and Turkic origin, and they arrived in Hungary towards the end of the 9th century. The Magyar language (Hungarian) belongs to the Uralic group. —adj. of this people or their language. [native name]

Mahabad /'mʌhəbʌd/ Kurdish town in Azerbaijan, W Iran, population (1983) 63,000. Occupied by Russian troops in 1941, it formed the centre of a short-lived Kurdish republic (1945–46) before being reoccupied by the Iranians. In the 1980s Mahabad was the focal point of resistance by Iranian Kurds against the Islamic republic.

Mahābhārata /məhɑː'bɑːrətə/ Sanskrit Hindu epic consisting of 18 books probably composed in its present form about 300 BC. It forms with the *Rāmāyana* the two great epics of the Hindus. It deals with the fortunes of the rival families of the Kauravas and the Pandavas, and contains the ◊*Bhagavad-Gītā*, or *Song of the Blessed*, an episode in the sixth book. [Sanskrit = great poem of the Bharatas]

Mahādeva /məhɑː'deɪvə/ a title given to the Hindu god ◊Siva. [Sanskrit = great god]

Mahādevī /məhɑː'deɪvi/ a title given to Sakti, the consort of the Hindu god Siva. She is worshipped in many forms, including her more active manifestations as Kali or Durga and her peaceful form as Parvati. [Sanskrit = great goddess]

Mahan Alfred Thayer 1840–1914. US naval officer and military historian, author of *The Influence of Sea Power upon History* 1890, in which he propounded a global strategy based on the importance of sea power.

maharaja /mɑːhə'rɑːdʒə/ n. (also **maharajah**) (*historical*) the title of some Indian princes. [from Hindi = great rajah]

maharanee /mɑːhə'rɑːnɪ/ n. (also **maharani**) (*historical*) a maharaja's wife or widow. [from Hindi = great ranee]

Maharashtra /mɑːhə'ræʃtrə/ state in W central India; area 307,800 sq km/118,811 sq mi; **capital** Bombay; **features** cave temples of Ajanta, containing 200 BC–7th century AD Buddhist murals and sculptures; Ellora cave temples 6th–9th century with Buddhist, Hindu, and Jain sculptures; **population** (1981) 62,694,000; **language** Marathi 50%; **recent history** formed in 1960 from the southern part of the former Bombay state.

maharishi /mɑːhə'riːʃi/ n. a Hindu guru (teacher), or spiritual leader. [from Sanskrit = great sage]

mahatma /mə'hætmə/ n. (in India etc.) 1. a title of respect for a person regarded with reverence; the title was conferred on Mohandas K ◊Gandhi by his followers as the first great national Indian leader. 2. a member of a class of persons supposed by some Buddhists to have preternatural powers. [from Sanskrit = great soul]

Mahāyāna /mɑːhə'jɑːnə/ n. one of the two major forms of ◊Buddhism, common in N Asia (China, Korea, Japan,

Mahler Austrian composer and conductor Gustav Mahler.

and Tibet). Veneration of bodhisattvas (those who achieve enlightenment but remain on the human plane in order to help other living beings) is a fundamental belief in Mahāyāna, as is the idea that everyone has within them the seeds of Buddhahood. [Sanskrit = greater vehicle]

Mahdi /ˈmɑːdi/ *n.* in Islam, the title of a coming messiah who will establish the reign of justice on Earth. The title has been assumed by many Muslim leaders, notably the Sudanese sheik Muhammad Ahmed (1848–85), who headed a revolt in 1881 against Egypt and in 1885 captured Khartoum. [Arabic = he who is guided aright]

Mahfouz /mɑːˈfuːz/ Naguib 1911– . Egyptian novelist and playwright. His novels, which deal with the urban working class, include a semi-autobiographical trilogy 1957, *Children of Gebelawi* 1959 (banned in Egypt because of its treatment of religious themes), and *Respected Sir* 1988. He was awarded the Nobel Prize for Literature in 1988.

mah-jong /mɑːˈdʒɒŋ/ *n.* or **mah-jongg** originally an ancient Chinese card game, dating from the Song dynasty 960–1279. It is now usually played by four people with 136 or 144 small ivory tiles, divided into six suits. [from Chinese dialect *ma-tsiang* = sparrows]

Mahler /ˈmɑːlə/ Gustav 1860–1911. Austrian composer and conductor. His ten symphonies, the moving *Das Lied von der Erde/Song of the Earth* 1909, and his song cycles display a synthesis of Romanticism and new uses of chromatic harmonies and musical forms.

mahlstick /ˈmɑːlstɪk/ variant of ◊maulstick.

Mahmud /mɑːˈmuːd/ two sultans of the Ottoman Empire:

Mahmud I /mɑːˈmuːd/ 1696–1754. Ottoman sultan from 1730. After restoring order to the empire in Istanbul 1730, he suppressed the ◊Janissary rebellion 1731 and waged war against Persia 1731–46. He led successful wars against Austria and Russia, concluded by the Treaty of Belgrade in 1739. He was a patron of the arts and also carried out reform of the army.

Mahmud II 1785–1839. Ottoman sultan from 1808 who attempted to westernize the declining empire, carrying out a series of far-reaching reforms in the civil service and army. In 1826 he destroyed the ◊Janissaries. Wars against Russia 1807–12 led to losses of territory. The pressure for Greek independence after 1821 led to conflict with Britain, France, and Russia, leading to the destruction of the Ottoman fleet at the Battle of Navarino in 1829 and defeat in the Russo-Turkish war 1828–29. He was forced to recognize Greek independence in 1830.

mahogany /məˈhɒgəni/ *n.* 1. a reddish-brown timber from several genera of trees found in the Americas and Africa and especially from the Aerican *Swietenia majogani*, used for furniture. Mahogany is a tropical hardwood obtained chiefly by rainforest logging. 2. its colour. 3. a tree yielding mahogany.

mahout /məˈhaʊt/ *n.* (in India etc.) an elephant-driver. [from Hindi from Sanskrit]

Maia in Greek mythology, daughter of Atlas and mother of Hermes.

maid *n.* 1. a female servant. 2. (*archaic*) a girl; a young woman. —**maid of all work**, a female servant doing general housework; a person doing many jobs.

maiden /ˈmeɪdən/ *n.* 1. a girl, a young unmarried woman. 2. a maiden over. 3. a maiden horse. —*adj.* 1. unmarried. 2. (of a female animal) unmated. 3. (of a horse) that has never won a prize; (of a race) open only to such horses. 4. (of a speech, voyage, etc.) first. —**maiden name**, a woman's surname before marriage. **maiden over**, an over in cricket in which no runs are scored. —**maidenhood** *n.*, **maidenly** *adj.* [Old English]

maidenhair *n.* any fern of the genus *Adiantum*, especially *A. capillus-veneris* with hairlike fronds terminating in small kidney-shaped, spore-bearing pinnules. It is widely distributed in the Americas, and is sometimes found in the British Isles.

maidenhair tree another name for ◊ginkgo, a surviving member of an ancient group of gymnosperms.

maidenhead /ˈmeɪdnhed/ *n.* virginity; the hymen.

maid of honour 1. in Britain, the closest attendant on a queen. They are chosen generally from the daughters and granddaughters of peers, but in the absence of another title bear that of Honourable. 2. an unmarried lady attending a queen or princess. 3. a kind of small custard tart. 4. (*US*) a principal bridesmaid.

maidservant *n.* a female servant.

mail[1] *n.* 1. matter conveyed by post; this system of conveyance; letters, parcels, etc., sent, collected, or delivered at one place on one occasion. 2. a vehicle carrying post. —*v.t.* to send by post. —**mail-bag** *n.* a large bag for carrying mail. **mailing list**, a list of persons to whom mail (especially advertising matter) is to be posted. **mail order**, purchase of goods by post. [from Old French *male* = wallet]

mail[2] *n.* armour composed of metal rings or plates. —**coat of mail**, a jacket or tunic covered with mail. [from Old French from Latin *macula* = spot, mesh]

Mailer /ˈmeɪlə/ Norman 1923– . US writer and journalist. He gained wide attention with his novel of World War II *The Naked and the Dead* 1948.

Once a newspaper touches a story, the facts are lost forever, even to the protagonists.

Norman Mailer
The Presidential Papers

---

maim *v.t.* to cripple, to disable, to mutilate. [from Old French *mahaignier*]

Maimonides /maɪˈmɒnɪdiːz/ Moses (Moses Ben Maimon) 1135–1204. Jewish rabbi and philosopher, born in Córdoba, Spain. Known as one of the greatest Hebrew scholars, he attempted to reconcile faith and reason.

main *adj.* 1. principal, most important. 2. greatest in size or extent; exerted to the full. —*n.* 1. a principal channel, duct, etc., for water or sewage etc.; (usually in *plural*) a principal cable for the supply of electricity. 2. (*archaic*) the mainland; the high seas. —**have an eye to the main chance**, to consider one's own interests. **in the main**, for the most part. **main brace**, a brace attached to the main yard. **main line**, an important railway line linking large cities. **main-topmast** *n.* the mast above the maintop. **main yard**, the yard on which the mainsail is extended. [from Old Norse and Old English]

Maine /meɪn/ NE state of the USA, largest of the New England states; nickname Pine Tree State; **area** 86,200 sq km/33,273 sq mi; **capital** Augusta; **population** (1986) 1,174,000; **history** settlement took place from 1623; became a state in 1820.

mainframe *n.* 1. the central processing unit of a computer. 2. (often *attributive*) a large computer as distinct from a microcomputer etc.

mainland /ˈmeɪnlənd/ *n.* a large continuous extent of land, excluding neighbouring islands etc.

mainly *adv.* for the most part, chiefly.

mainmast *n.* the principal mast of a ship.

mainsail /ˈmeɪnseɪl, -səl/ *n.* (in a square-rigged vessel) the lowest sail on a mainmast; (in a fore-and-aft rigged vessel) a sail set on the after part of a mainmast.

main sequence in astronomy, the part of the ◊Hertzsprung-
Russell diagram that contains most of the stars, including
the Sun. It runs diagonally from the top left of the diagram
to the lower right. The most massive (and hence brightest)
stars are at the top left, with the least massive (coolest)
stars at the bottom right.

mainspring *n.* 1. the principal spring of a watch, clock,
etc. 2. a chief motivating force or initiative.

mainstay *n.* 1. the chief support. 2. the stay from the
maintop to the foot of the foremast.

mainstream *n.* 1. the principal current of a river etc. 2.
the prevailing trend of opinion, fashion, etc.

maintain /meɪn'teɪn/ *v.t.* 1. to cause to continue; to continue one's action in; to keep in existence. 2. to take action
to preserve (a machine, house, etc.) in good order. 3. to
support, to provide sustenance for; to provide means for.
4. to assert as true. —**maintained school**, a school supported from public funds. [from Old French *maintenir* from
Latin *manu tenēre* = hold in the hand]

maintenance /'meɪntɪnəns/ *n.* 1. maintaining, being
maintained. 2. keeping equipment etc. in repair. 3. provision
of the means to support life; in law, payments to support
children or a spouse, under the terms of an agreement, or
by a court order.

Maintenon /mæntə'nɒŋ/ Françoise d'Aubigné, Marquise
de 1635–1719. Second wife of Louis XIV of France from
1684, and widow of the writer Paul Scarron (1610–60).
Her political influence was considerable, and, as a Catholic convert from Protestantism, her religious opinions
were zealous.

maintop *n.* a platform above the head of the lower mainmast.

maiolica variant of ◊majolica.

maisonette /meɪzə'net/ *n.* 1. part of a house let or used
separately (usually not all one one floor). 2. a small house.
[from French, diminutive of *maison* = house]

Maitland John, see Lauderdale, Duke of

Maitreya /maɪ'treɪə/ *n.* the Buddha to come, 'the kindly
one', a principal figure in all forms of Buddhism; he
is known as **Mi-lo-fo** in China and **Miroku** in Japan.
Buddhists believe that a Buddha appears from time to
time to maintain knowledge of the true path; Maitreya is
the next future Buddha.

maize *n.* 1. (North American **corn**) a cereal plant *Zea
mays* of North American origin. Grown extensively in all
subtropical and warm temperate regions, its range has been
extended to colder zones by hardy varieties developed in
the 1960s. It is widely used as animal feed. 2. the grain of
this. 3. the yellow colour of its ripe cobs. [from French or
Spanish, of Carib origin]

Maiziere /mez'jeə/ Lothar de 1940– . German conservative politician, leader of the former East German
Christian Democratic Union. He became premier after
East Germany's first democratic elections in April 1990,
until German reunification in Oct 1990.

majestic /mə'dʒestɪk/ *adj.* stately and dignified, imposing. —**majestically** *adj.*

majesty /'mædʒɪstɪ/ *n.* 1. impressive stateliness. 2. sovereign power. —**Christ in Majesty**, a representation of
Christ enthroned within an aureole. **His, Her, Your**, etc.,
Majesty, a title used in addressing or referring to a king or
queen or a sovereign's spouse or widow. [from Old French
from Latin *majestas*]

majolica /mə'jɒlɪkə, -'dʒɒl-/ *n.* Italian earthenware of the
Renaissance period with coloured ornamentation on white
enamel; a modern imitation of this. [from Italian, from
former name of *Majorca*, ships of which brought Spanish
wares to Italy]

major /'meɪdʒə/ *adj.* 1. greater or relatively great in size
or importance. 2. of full legal age. 3. (in music, of a scale)
having intervals of a semitone above its third and seventh
notes; (of an interval) normal or perfect (compare ◊minor);
(of a key) based on a major scale. —*n.* 1. an army officer
next below lieutenant-colonel. 2. an officer in charge of
a section of band instruments. 3. a person of full legal
age. 4. (*US*) a student's special course or subject. —*v.i.*
(*US*) to specialize (in a subject). —**major-general** *n.* an
army officer next below lieutenant-general. [from Latin,
comparative of *magnus* = great]

Major /'meɪdʒə/ John 1943– . British Conservative politician, foreign secretary 1989, chancellor of the Exchequer

*Major John Major, the unexpected victor in the 1990
Conservative leadership election following the resignation of
Margaret Thatcher.*

1989–90, and elected prime minister in the Conservative
party leadership election in November of that year. As
chancellor he led Britain into the European Exchange Rate
Mechanism (ERM) in Oct 1990. He was elected prime
minister in a leadership contest with Michael Heseltine and
Douglas Hurd after the resignation of Margaret Thatcher
the following month.

Majorca /mə'jɔːkə/ (Spanish *Mallorca*) largest of the
◊Balearic Islands, belonging to Spain, in the W Mediterranean; **area** 3,640 sq km/1,405 sq mi; **capital** Palma;
population (1981) 561,215.

major-domo /meɪdʒə'dəʊməʊ/ *n.* (*plural* **major-domos**)
the chief steward of a great household; a house-steward, a
butler. [from Spanish and Italian from Latin *major domus* =
highest official of household]

majority /mə'dʒɒrɪtɪ/ *n.* 1. the greater number or part of
a group etc. 2. the number by which votes for the winning
party etc. exceed those for the next or for all others
combined; the party etc. receiving a majority of votes. 3.
full legal age (in Britain, since 1970 the age of 18 years,
formerly 21 years). 4. the rank of major. —**majority rule**,
the principle that the greater number should exercise the
greater power. [from French from Latin]

majuscule /'mædʒəskjuːl/ *adj.* (of lettering) large; written in large lettering. —*n.* large lettering, a large letter,
whether capital or uncial. [French from Latin *majuscula*
(*littera* = letter), diminutive of *major*]

Makarios III /mə'kɑːrɪɒs/ 1913–1977. Cypriot politician,
Greek Orthodox archbishop 1950–77. A leader of the
Resistance organization ◊EOKA, he was exiled by the
British to the Seychelles 1956–57 for supporting armed
action to achieve union with Greece (*enosis*). He was president of the republic of Cyprus 1960–77 (briefly deposed by
a Greek military coup July–Dec 1974).

Makarova /mə'kɑːrəvə/ Natalia 1940– . Russian ballerina. She danced with the Kirov Ballet 1959–70, then
sought political asylum in the West. Her roles include the
title role in *Giselle*, and Aurora in *The Sleeping Beauty*.

make *v.t./i* (*past* and *past participle* **made**) 1. to construct,
create, or prepare from parts or other substances. 2. to
bring about, to cause to exist, to give rise to. 3. to frame
in the mind. 4. to draw up as a legal document etc. 5. to
establish (a distinction, rule, or law). 6. to gain or acquire.
7. to secure the advancement or success of. 8. to cause
to be or become or seem. 9. to cause or compel (to). 10.
to proceed, to act as if intending (to). 11. to perform (an
action etc.). 12. to consider to be, to estimate as. 13. to

constitute, to amount to. **14.** to serve for, to be adequate as; to form or be reckoned as; to bring to (a chosen value etc.). **15.** to accomplish or achieve (a distance, speed, score, etc.); to achieve a place in (a team, prize-list, etc.); to arrive at, to come in sight of; (*slang*) to catch (a train etc.). —*n.* **1.** the way a thing is made. **2.** the origin of manufacture, a brand. **make away with,** to get rid of; to kill; to squander. **make believe,** to pretend. **make-believe** *adj.* pretended; (*n.*) pretence. **make a day** *or* **night** etc. **of it,** to devote a whole day etc. to an activity or relaxation. **make do,** to manage with the limited or inadequate means available. **make for,** to conduce to; to proceed towards (a place); to attack. **make good,** to repay, repair, or compensate for; to achieve (a purpose), to be successful. **make the grade,** to succeed. **make it,** to achieve one's purpose, to be successful. **make much** (*or little*) **of,** to treat as important (or unimportant). **make nothing of,** to treat as trifling; to be unable to understand or use or deal with. **make off,** to depart hastily. **make off with,** to carry away, to steal. **make or break,** to cause the success or ruin of; to be crucial for. **make out,** to discern or understand; to fare or progress; to write out (a document etc.) or fill in (a form); to prove or try to prove to be; to pretend or claim. **make over,** to transfer possession of; to refashion or convert to a new purpose. **make time,** to contrive to find time to do something. **make up,** to put or get together; to prepare, to invent (a story etc.); to compensate (for); to complete (an amount originally deficient); to form or constitute; to apply cosmetics (to). **make (it) up,** to be reconciled. **make-up** *n.* cosmetics; the way a thing is made or composed; character or temperament. **make up to,** to court, to curry favour with. **on the make,** (*slang*) intent on gain. [Old English]

maker *n.* **1.** one who makes something. **2. our Maker,** God.

makeshift *n.* a temporary substitute or device. —*adj.* serving as this.

makeweight *n.* **1.** a small quantity added to make up the weight. **2.** a person or thing supplying a deficiency.

making *n.* **1.** (in *plural*) earnings, profits. **2.** (in *plural*) the essential qualities for becoming. —**be the making of,** to be the main factor in the success or favourable development of. **in the making,** in the course of being made or formed. [Old English]

mal- /mæl-/ prefix with the meaning, bad (*malpractice*); badly (*maltreat*); faulty (*malfunction*); not (*maladroit*). [from French *mal* = badly from Latin *male*]

Malabo /mə'lɑːbəʊ/ port and capital of Equatorial Guinea, on the island of Bioko; population (1983) 15,253. It was founded in the 1820s by the British as Port Clarence. Under Spanish rule it was known as Santa Isabel (until 1973).

Malacca /mə'lækə/ or *Malaka* state of W Peninsular Malaysia: **capital** Malacca; **area** 1,700 sq km/656 sq mi; **population** (1980) 465,000 (about 70% Chinese); **products** rubber, tin, and wire; **history** a trading port, Portuguese from 1511, then Dutch from 1641, it was ceded to Britain 1824, becoming part of the Straits Settlements.

Malacca cane a rich-brown cane from the stem of the palm-tree *Calamus rotang*, used for walking-sticks etc. [from *Malacca* state and city of Malaysia]

malachite /'mæləkaɪt/ *n.* a common copper ore, basic copper carbonate, $Cu_2CO_3(OH)_2$. It is a source of green pigment and is polished for use in jewellery, ornaments, and art objects. [from Old French from Latin from Greek *molokhitis* (*molokhē* = mallow)]

maladjusted /mælə'dʒʌstɪd/ *adj.* (of a person) not satisfactorily adjusted to his or her environment and conditions of life. —**maladjustment** *n.*

maladminister /mæləd'mɪnɪstə/ *v.t.* to manage badly or improperly. —**maladministration** /-'streɪʃən/ *n.*

maladroit /mælə'drɔɪt, 'mæ-/ *adj.* clumsy, bungling. —**maladroitly** *adv.*, **maladroitness** *n.* [French]

malady /'mælədɪ/ *n.* a disease or ailment (*literal* or *figurative*). [from Old French *malade* = sick]

Málaga /'mæləgə/ industrial seaport (sugar refining, distilling, brewing, olive-oil pressing, shipbuilding) and holiday resort in Andalusia, Spain; capital of Málaga province on the Mediterranean; population (1986) 595,000. Founded by the Phoenicians and taken by the Moors in 711, Málaga was capital of the Moorish kingdom of Malaga from the 13th

century until captured in 1487 by the Catholic Monarchs Ferdinand and Isabella.

Malagasy /mælə'gæsɪ/ *adj.* of Madagascar or its people or language. —*n.* **1.** a native or inhabitant of Madagascar. **2.** the language of Madagascar. [originally *Malegass*, from *Madagascar*]

malaise /mæ'leɪz/ *n.* bodily discomfort, especially without the development of a specific disease; an uneasy feeling. [French]

Malamud /'mæləmʌd/ Bernard 1914–1986. US novelist and short-story writer. He first attracted attention with *The Natural* 1952, making a professional baseball player his hero. Later novels, often dealing with the Jewish immigrant tradition, include *The Assistant* 1957, *The Fixer* 1966, *Dubin's Lives* 1979, and *God's Grace* 1982.

malapropism /'mæləprɒpɪzəm/ *n.* a ludicrous misuse of a word especially in mistake for one resembling it (e.g. *it will percussion the blow* for *cushion the blow*). [from Mrs *Malaprop* in Sheridan's *The Rivals*]

malapropos /mælæprə'pəʊ/ *adv.* & *adj.* inopportunely said, done, or happening. [from French *mal à propos* (*mal* = ill and *à propos* = to the purpose)]

malaria /mə'leərɪə/ *n.* an infectious parasitic disease of the tropics transmitted by mosquitoes, marked by periodic fever and an enlarged spleen. The disease, caused by a protozoan parasite of the genus *Plasmodium*, is transmitted from infected persons by the bite of a female *Anopheles* mosquito after developing in the body of this insect. —**malarial** *adj.* [from Italian *mala aria* = bad air, the unwholesome condition of the atmosphere which results from the exhalations of marshy districts, to which the disease was formerly attributed]

malarkey /mə'lɑːkɪ/ *n.* (*slang*) humbug, nonsense.

malathion /mælə'θaɪən/ *n.* an insecticide containing phosphorous and relatively harmless to plants and animals.

Malatya /mælət'jɑː/ capital of a province of the same name in E central Turkey, lying W of the river Euphrates; population (1985) 251,000.

Malawi /mə'lɑːwɪ/ Republic of; country in SE Africa, bordered N and NE by Tanzania; E, S and W by Mozambique; and W by Zambia; **area** 118,000 sq km/45,560 sq mi; **capital** Lilongwe; **physical** rolling plains; mountainous W of Lake Malawi; **head of state and government** Hastings Kamusu Banda from 1966 for life; **population** (1990 est) 9,080,000 (nearly 1 million refugees from Mozambique); **language** English, Chichewa (both official); **recent history** achieved independence from Britain in 1964, and became a one-party republic, with Hastings Banda as president, in 1966.

Malawi, Lake formerly Lake Nyasa African lake, bordered by Malawi, Tanzania, and Mozambique, formed in a section of the Great ◊Rift Valley. It is about 500 m/ 1,650 ft above sea level and 560 km/350 mi long, with an area of 37,000 sq km/14,280 sq mi. It is intermittently drained to the south by the river Shiré into the Zambezi.

Malay /mə'leɪ/ *n.* a member of a large group of peoples, comprising the majority population of the Malay Peninsula and Archipelago, and also found in S Thailand and coastal Sumatra and Borneo.

Malay language a member of the Western or Indonesian branch of the Malayo-Polynesian language family, used in the Malay peninsula and many of the islands of Malaysia and Indonesia. The Malay language can be written with either Arabic or Roman scripts.

Malayo-Polynesian /məleɪəʊpɒli'niːzɪən/ *n.* or ◊Austronesian, a family of languages spoken in Malaysia, the Indonesian archipelago, parts of the region that was formerly Indochina, Taiwan, Madagascar, Melanesia, and Polynesia (excluding Australia and most of New Guinea). The group contains some 500 distinct languages, including Malay in Malaysia, Bahasa in Indonesia, Fijian, Hawaiian, and Maori.

Malaysia /mə'leɪzɪə/ country in SE Asia, comprising the Malay Peninsula, (bordered to the N by Thailand, and surrounded E, S, and W by the South China Sea); and the states of Sabah and Sarawak in the northern part of the island of Borneo (S Borneo is part of Indonesia); **area** 329,759 sq km/127,287 sq mi; **capital** Kuala Lumpur; **physical** comprises Peninsular Malaysia (the nine Malay states—Perlis, Kedah, Johore, Selangor,

Perak, Negri Sembilan, Kelantan, Trengganu, Pahang—plus Penang and Malacca); and E Malaysia (Sarawak and Sabah); 75% tropical jungle; central mountain range; swamps in E; **head of state** Rajah Azlan Muhibuddin Shah (sultan of Perak) from 1989; **head of government** Mahathir bin Mohamad form 1981; **language** Bahasa Malaysia (official); English, Chinese, Indian languages; **recent history** the area was under British control since 1867. In 1963 the Federation of Malaysia was formed, including Malaya, Singapore, Sabah and Sarawak; Singapore seceded from the federation in 1965.

Malcolm /'mælkəm/ four kings of Scotland, including:

Malcolm III called **Canmore** c. 1031–1093. King of Scotland from 1054, the son of Duncan I (murdered by ◊Macbeth in 1040). He was killed at Alnwick while invading Northumberland, England.

Malcolm X assumed name of Malcolm Little 1926–1965. US black nationalist leader. While serving a prison sentence for burglary from 1946 to 1953, he joined the ◊Black Muslims sect. On his release he campaigned for black separatism, condoning violence in self-defence, but in 1964 modified his views to found the Islamic-socialist Organization of Afro-American Unity, preaching racial solidarity. A year later he was assassinated by Black Muslim opponents while addressing a rally in Harlem, New York. His *Autobiography of Malcolm X* was published 1964.

malcontent /'mælkəntent/ n. a discontented person. —adj. discontented. [French]

Maldives /'mɔ:ldi:vz/ Republic of; group of 1,196 islands in the N Indian Ocean, about 640 km/400 mi SW of Sri Lanka, only 203 of which are inhabited; **area** 298 sq km/115 sq mi; **capital** Malé; **physical** comprises almost 1,200 coral islands, grouped into 12 clusters of atolls, largely flat, none bigger than 13 sq km/5 sq mi; **head of state and government** Maumoon Abdul Gayoom from 1978; **political system** authoritarian nationalism; **population** (1990 est) 219,000; **language** Divehi (Sinhalese dialect), English; **recent history** a British protectorate from 1887, the Maldives achieved full independence outside the Commonwealth in 1965. In 1968 the sultan was deposed and a republic installed. The Maldives rejoined the Commonwealth in 1985. A coup attempt in 1988 was foiled by Indian paratroops.

male adj. **1.** of the sex that can beget offspring by performing the fertilizing function; (of plants or flowers) containing stamens but no pistil; of men or male animals or plants. **2.** (of parts of machinery etc.) designed to enter or fill a corresponding hollow part. —n. a male person or animal. [from Old French *ma(s)le* from Latin *masculus*]

Malé /'mɑːleɪ/ capital of the Maldives in the Indian Ocean; population (1985) 38,000. It trades in copra, breadfruit, and palm products.

malediction /mæli'dɪkʃən/ n. a curse; the uttering of a curse. —**maledictory** adj. [from Latin *male* = ill and *dicere* = speak]

malefactor /'mælɪfæktə/ n. a criminal; an evil-doer. —**malefaction** /-'fækʃən/ n. [from Latin *male* = ill and *facere* = do]

malevolent /mə'levələnt/ adj. wishing ill to others. —**malevolence** adj. [from Old French or Latin *male* = ill and *volens* = willing]

malfeasance /mæl'fi:zəns/ n. misconduct, especially in an official capacity. [from Anglo-French (*faire* = do)]

malformation /mælfɔ:'meɪʃən/ n. faulty formation. —**malformed** /-'fɔ:md/ adj.

malfunction /mæl'fʌŋkʃən/ n. a failure to function in the normal manner. —v. i. to function faultily.

Malherbe /mæ'leəb/ François de 1555–1628. French poet and grammarian, born in Caen. He became court poet about 1605 under Henry IV and Louis XIII. He advocated reform of language and versification, and established the 12-syllable Alexandrine as the standard form of French verse.

Mali /'mɑːli/ Republic of; landlocked country in NW Africa, bordered to the NE by Algeria, E by Niger, SE by Burkina Faso, S by the Ivory Coast, SW by Senegal and Guinea, and W and N by Mauritania; **area** 1,240,142 sq km/478 695 sq mi; **capital** Bamako; **physical** river Niger and savanna in S; part of the Sahara in N; hills in NE; **head of state and government** Moussa Traoré from 1968; **political system** one-party republic; **population** (1990 est) 9,182,000; **language** French (official), Bambara; **recent**

history came under French rule in 1898, and became the independent Republic of Mali in 1969. Moussa Traoré took power through an army coup in 1968, and brought in a new constitution making Mali a one-party state in 1974.

malic acid an organic crystalline acid, $COOHCH_2$ $CH(OH)COOH$, that can be extracted from apples, plums, cherries, grapes, and other fruits, but occurs in all living cells in smaller amounts, being one of the intermediates of ◊Krebs's cycle.

malice /'mælɪs/ n. desire to harm or cause difficulty to others, ill-will; (in law) harmful intent. [from Old French from Latin *malitia* (*malus* = bad)]

malicious /mə'lɪʃəs/ adj. feeling, showing, or arising from malice. —**maliciously** adv., **maliciousness** n.

Mali Empire a Muslim state in NW Africa during the 7th–15th centuries. Thriving on its trade in gold, it reached its peak in the 14th century under Mansa Musa (reigned 1312–37), when it occupied an area covering present-day Senegal, Gambia, Mali, and S Mauritania. Mali's territory was similar to (though larger than) that of the ◊Ghana Empire, and gave way in turn to the ◊Songhai Empire.

malign /mə'laɪn/ adj. **1.** harmful; (of a disease) malignant. **2.** malevolent. —v.t. to slander, to speak ill of. —**malignity** /-'lɪgnɪti/ n. [from Old French or Latin *malignus* (*malus* = bad)]

malignant /mə'lɪgnənt/ adj. **1.** (of a tumour) tending to spread and to recur after removal, cancerous. **2.** (of a disease) very virulent. **3.** feeling or showing intense ill-will. **4.** harmful. —**malignancy** n., **malignantly** adv. [from Latin *malignare*]

malinger /mə'lɪŋgə/ v.i. to pretend to be ill to escape a duty. —**malingerer** n. [from French *malingre* = sickly]

Malinowski /mæli'nɒfski/ Bronislaw 1884–1942. Polish-born British anthropologist, one of the founders of the theory of ◊functionalism in the social sciences. His study of the peoples of the Trobriand Islands led him to see customs and practices in terms of their function in creating and maintaining social order.

mall /mæl, mɔ:l/ n. a sheltered walk or promenade. [variant of maul, used of the hammer in the croquet-like game of pall-mall; applied to *The Mall* in London, originally an alley where this game was played]

mallard /'mælɑ:d/ n. (*plural* the same) a kind of wild duck *Anas platyrhynchos* of which the male has a green head. [from Old French]

Mallarmé /mælɑ:'meɪ/ Stéphane 1842–1898. French poet who founded the Symbolist school with Paul Verlaine. His belief that poetry should be evocative and suggestive was reflected in *L'Après-midi d'un faune/Afternoon of a Faun* 1876, which inspired the composer Debussy. Later works are *Poésies complètes/Complete Poems* 1887, *Vers et prose/Verse and Prose* 1893, and the prose *Divagations/Digressions* 1897.

Malle /mæl/ Louis 1932– . French film director. After a period as assistant to Robert Bresson, he directed *Les Amants/The Lovers* 1958, audacious for its time in its explicitness. His subsequent films, made in France and the USA, include *Zazie dans le métro* 1961, *Viva Maria* 1965, *Pretty Baby* 1978, *Atlantic City* 1980, and *Au Revoir les Enfants* 1988.

malleable /'mæliəbəl/ adj. **1.** (of a metal etc.) that can be shaped by hammering. **2.** adaptable, pliable. —**malleability** /-'bɪlɪti/ n. [from Old French from Latin *malleare* = to hammer]

mallet /'mælɪt/ n. **1.** a hammer, usually of wood. **2.** a similarly shaped implement with a long handle, for striking the ball in croquet or polo. [from Old French *maillet* (*mail* = hammer from Latin *malleus*)]

Mallorca Spanish form of ◊Majorca, an island in the Mediterranean.

mallow /'mæləʊ/ n. any flowering plant of the family Malvaceae, especially of the genus *Malva*, including the European common mallow *M. sylvestris*; the tree mallow *Lavatera arborea*; and the marsh mallow *Althaea officinalis*. The ◊hollyhock is of the mallow family. Most have pink or purple flowers. [Old English from Latin *malva*]

Malmö /'mælməʊ/ industrial port (shipbuilding, engineering, textiles) in SW Sweden; population (1988) 231,000.

malmsey /'mɑːmzi/ n. a sweet fortified wine made in Madeira, Cyprus, the Canary Islands, etc., from a kind of grape which came originally from the eastern Mediterranean. [from Middle Dutch or Middle Low German from *Monemvasia* in Greece]

malnutrition /mæl'nju:'trɪʃən/ *n.* the physical condition resulting from a poor or unbalanced diet. The high global death toll linked to malnutrition arises mostly through diseases killing people weakened by poor diet and an impure water supply.

malodorous /mæl'ɔʊdərəs/ *adj.* evil-smelling.

Malory /'mæləri/ Thomas 15th century. English author of the prose romance *Le Morte d'Arthur* about 1470. It is a translation from French, modified by material from other sources, and deals with the exploits of King Arthur's knights of the Round Table and the quest for the Grail.

Malpighi /mæl'pi:gi/ Marcello 1628–1694. Italian physiologist who made many anatomical discoveries (still known by his name) in his microscope studies of animal and plant tissues.

malpractice /mæl'præktɪs/ *n.* 1. wrong-doing; an illegal action for one's own benefit while in a position of trust. 2. the improper or negligent treatment of a patient by a physician. In US law, ◊negligence by a professional person, usually a doctor, that may lead to an action for damages by the client.

Malraux /mæl'rəʊ/ André 1901–1976. French writer. An active anti-fascist, he gained international renown for his novel *La Condition humaine/Man's Estate* 1933, set during the Nationalist/Communist Revolution in China in the 1920s. *L'Espoir/Days of Hope* 1937 is set in Civil War Spain, where he was a bomber pilot in the International Brigade. In World War II he supported the Gaullist resistance, and was minister of cultural affairs 1960–69.

malt /mɔːlt, mɒlt/ *n.* 1. in brewing, grain (barley, oats, or wheat) artificially germinated by soaking in water and then dried in a kiln. Malts are fermented to make beers or lagers, or fermented and then distilled to produce spirits such as whisky. 2. (*colloquial*) malt liquor; malt whisky. —*v.t.* to convert (grain) into malt. —**malted milk,** a drink made from dried milk and extract of malt. **malt whisky,** whisky made entirely of malted barley. [Old English]

Malta /'mɔːltə/ Republic of; island in the Mediterranean, S of Sicily, E of Tunisia, and N of Libya; **area** 320 sq km/124 sq mi; **capital** and port Valletta; **physical** includes islands of Gozo 67 sq km/26 sq mi and Comino 2.5 sq km/1 sq mi; **head of state** Vincent Tabone from 1989; of government Edward Fench Adami from 1987; **political system** liberal democracy; **recent history** annexed to Britain in 1814, Malta achieved self-government in 1947; full independence was achieved in 1964. Malta applied for European Community membership in 1990.

Malta, Knights of another name for members of the military-religious order of the Hospital of ◊St John of Jerusalem.

maltase *n.* an enzyme found in plants and animals that breaks down the disaccharide maltose into glucose.

Maltese /mɔː'li:z, mɒl-/ *adj.* of Malta or its people or language. —*n.* 1. a native or inhabitant of Malta. 2. the Semitic language of Malta. —**Maltese cross,** a cross with the arms broadening outwards, often indented at the ends.

Malthus /'mælθəs/ Thomas Robert 1766–1834. English economist and cleric, whose *Essay on the Principle of Population* 1798 (revised 1803) argued for population control, since populations increase in geometric ratio and food only in arithmetic ratio.

Population, when unchecked, increases in a geometrical ratio. Subsistence only increases in an arithmetical ratio.

Thomas Robert Malthus
Essays on the Principle of Population

---

maltose *n.* a ◊disaccharide sugar in which both monosaccharide units are glucose, symbol $C_{12}H_{22}O_{11}$.

maltreat /mæl'tri:t/ *v.t.* to ill-treat. —**maltreatment** *n.*

malt tax in Britain, a tax on malt was first introduced in 1697 on the use of malt in brewing. It supplemented the existing beer duty when a hop duty was imposed between 1711 and 1862. The malt tax was abolished in 1880 when replaced by a tax on drinking beer.

Maluku /mə'lu:ku:/ or **Moluccas** group of Indonesian islands; **area** 74,500 sq km/28,764 sq mi; **capital** Ambon, on Amboina; **population** (1980) 1,411,000; **history** as the Spice Islands, they were formerly part of the Netherlands East Indies, and the S Moluccas attempted secession from the newly created Indonesian republic from 1949; exiles continue agitation in the Netherlands.

malversation /mælvə'seɪʃən/ *n.* corrupt behaviour in a position of trust; corrupt administration of public money etc. [French (*malverser* from Latin *male* = badly and *versari* = behave)]

Malvinas /mæl'vi:nəs/ Argentine name for the ◊Falkland Islands.

mama variant of ◊mamma.

mamba /'mæmbə/ *n.* a kind of venomous African snake of the genus *Dendroaspis*. [from Zulu *m'namba*]

Mameluke /'mæmɔlu:k/ *n.* a member of a powerful political class which dominated Egypt from the 13th century until their massacre in 1811 by Mehmet Ali.

Mamet /'mæmɪt/ David 1947– . US playwright. His plays, with their vivid, freewheeling language and sense of ordinary US life, include *American Buffalo* 1977, *Sexual Perversity in Chicago* 1978, and *Glengarry Glen Ross* 1984.

mamma *n.* (*archaic*) mother. [imitative of child's *ma, ma*]

mammal /'mæməl/ *n.* any vertebrate of the class Mammalia, characterized by the secretion of milk to feed its young and the possession of hair, lungs, and a four-chambered heart. Mammals maintain a constant body temperature in varied surroundings. Most mammals give birth to live young, but the platypus and echidna lay eggs. There are over 4,000 species, adapted to almost every way of life. The smallest shrew weighs only 2 g/0.07 oz, the largest whale up to 150 tonnes. —**mammalian** /mə'meɪliən/ *adj. & n.* [from Latin *mammalis* (*mamma* = breast)]

mammary /'mæməri/ *adj.* of the breasts.

mammary gland in female mammals, milk-producing gland derived from epithelial cells underlying the skin, active only after the production of young. In all but monotremes (egg-laying mammals), the mammary glands terminate in teats which aid infant suckling. The number of glands and their position vary between species. In humans there are two, in cows four, and in pigs between ten and fourteen.

mammography *n.* an X-ray procedure used to detect breast cancer at an early stage, before the tumours can be seen or felt.

Mammon /'mæmən/ an evil personification of wealth and greed; originally a Syrian god of riches, cited in the New Testament as opposed to the Christian god.

mammoth /'mæməθ/ *n.* a large extinct elephant of the genus *Mammuthus*, with a hairy coat and curved tusks. —*adj.* huge. [from Russian]

Mamoullian /mə'mu:liən/ Rouben 1898–1987. Armenian film director who lived in the USA from 1923. After several years on Broadway he turned to films, making the first sound version of *Dr Jekyll and Mr Hyde* 1932 and *Queen Christina* 1933. His later work includes *The Mark of Zorro* 1940 and *Silk Stockings* 1957.

man *n.* (*plural* **men**) 1. a creature of the genus *Homo*, distinguished from other animals by superior mental development, power of articulate speech, and upright stance; (*collectively*) the human race, mankind. 2. an adult human male. 3. a person of a particular type or historical period. 4. (in indefinite or general application, without specification of sex) a person. 5. an individual person, especially in the role of assistant, opponent, or expert, or considered in terms of suitability. 6. a husband. 7. (usually in *plural*) an employee, a workman. 8. (usually in *plural*) a member of the armed forces, especially of those not officers. 9. (*colloquial*) as a form of address. 10. one of a set of objects used in playing chess, draughts, etc. —*v.t.* (**-nn-**) to supply with a man or manpower for service or to operate something. —**as one man,** in unison. **be one's own man,** to be independent. **man about town,** a fashionable socializer. **man-at-arms** *n.* (*plural* **men-at-arms**) (*archaic*) a soldier. **man-hour** *n.* the work done by one person in one hour. **man-hunt** *n.* an organized search for a person (especially a criminal). **man in the street,** an ordinary average man. **man-made** *adj.* artificially made. **man-of-war** *n.* (*plural* **men-of-war**) an armed ship of a country's navy. **man of the world,** see ◊world. **man-sized** *adj.* of the size of a man; adequate to a man, large. **man to man**, candidly. **to a man,** without exception. —**mannish** *adj.* [Old English]

-man /-mən/ (*plural* **-men**) suffix denoting a man concerned with (*clergyman*), or skilful with (*oarsman*), or describable as (*Welshman*).

manacle /'mænəkəl/ *n.* (usually in *plural*) 1. a fetter for the hand, a handcuff. 2. a restraint. —*v.t.* to fetter with manacles. [from Old French from Latin *manicula* (*manus* = hand)]

manage /'mænɪdʒ/ *v.t./i.* 1. to organize or regulate; to be the manager of (a business etc.). 2. to succeed in achieving, to contrive; to succeed with limited resources or means, to be able to cope (with). 3. to secure the co-operation of (a person) by tact, flattery, etc. 4. to have under effective control. 5. to use or wield (a tool etc.) effectively. [from Italian *maneggiare* from Latin *manus* = hand]

manageable /'mænɪdʒəbəl/ *adj.* that may be managed.

management *n.* 1. managing, being managed. 2. the administration of business concerns or public undertakings; persons engaged in this.

manager *n.* 1. a person conducting a business, institution, etc.; a person controlling the activities of a person or team in sport, entertainment, etc. 2. a person who manages money, household affairs, etc., in a specified way. —**manageress** /-'res/ *n.fem.*, **managerial** /mænə'dʒɪərɪəl/ *adj.*

Managua /mə'nɑːgwə/ capital and chief industrial city of Nicaragua, on the lake of the same name; population (1985) 682,000. It has twice been destroyed by earthquake and rebuilt, in 1931 and 1972; it was also badly damaged during the civil war in the late 1970s.

Manama /mə'nɑːmə/ (Arabic *Al Manamah*) capital and free trade port of Bahrain, on Bahrain Island; handles oil and entrepôt trade; population (1988) 152,000.

mañana /mən'jɑːnə/ *n.* & *adv.* tomorrow (as a symbol of easy-going procrastination); the indefinite future. [Spanish]

manatee /mænə'tiː/ *n.* a plant-eating aquatic mammal of the genus *Trichechus* belonging to the order Sirenia (sea cows). Manatees are found on the E coasts of tropical North and South America, and around West Africa. They are in danger of becoming extinct. [from Spanish from Caribbean]

Manaus /mə'naʊs/ capital of Amazonas, Brazil, on the Rio Negro, near its confluence with the Amazon; population (1980) 612,000. It can be reached by sea-going vessels, although 1,600 km/1,000 mi from the Atlantic. Formerly a centre of the rubber trade, it developed as a tourist centre in the 1970s.

Manchester /'mæntʃɪstə/ city in NW England, on the river Irwell, 50 km/31 mi E of Liverpool. It is a manufacturing (textile machinery, chemicals, rubber, processed foods) and financial centre; population (1985) 451,000. It is linked by the Manchester Ship Canal, built 1894, to the river Mersey and the sea.

Manchester, Greater former (1974–86) metropolitan county of NW England, replaced by a residuary body in 1986 which covers some of its former functions; **area** 1,290 sq km/498 sq mi; **administrative headquarters** Manchester; **population** (1987) 2,580,000.

Manchu /mæn'tʃuː/ *n.* last ruling dynasty in China, from 1644 until their overthrow in 1912; their last emperor was the infant ◊P'u-i. Originally a nomadic people from Manchuria, they established power through a series of successful invasions from the N, then granted trading rights to the USA and Europeans, which eventually brought strife and the ◊Boxer Rebellion.

Manchukuo /mæntʃuː'kwəʊ/ former Japanese puppet state in Manchuria and Jehol 1932–45.

Manchuria /mæn'tʃʊərɪə/ European name for the NE region of China, comprising the provinces of Heilongjiang, Jilin, and Liaoning. It was united with China by the Manchu dynasty 1644, but as the Chinese Empire declined, Japan and Russia were rivals for its control. The Russians were expelled after the ◊Russo-Japanese War 1904–05, and in 1932 Japan consolidated its position by creating a puppet state, Manchukuo, which disintegrated on the defeat of Japan in World War II.

Mancunian /mæn'kjuːnɪən/ *adj.* of Manchester. —*n.* a native or inhabitant of Manchester. [from Latin *Mancunium* Roman settlement on site of Manchester]

mandala /'mændələ/ *n.* a circular figure as a Hindu and Buddhist religious symbol of the universe. [from Sanskrit]

Mandela *Deputy leader of the African National Congress, Nelson Mandela, pictured shortly after his release from prison in 1990.*

Mandalay /mændə'leɪ/ chief town of upper Myanmar (formerly Burma), on the river Irrawaddy, about 495 km/370 mi N of Yangon; population (1983) 533,000.

mandamus /mæn'deɪməs/ *n.* a judicial writ issued as a command to an inferior court, or ordering a person to perform a public or statutory duty. [Latin = we command]

mandarin /'mændərɪn/ *n.* 1. an influential person, especially a reactionary or secretive bureaucrat. 2. (*historical*) a Chinese official. 3. a small flat ◊orange with a loose skin, a variety of the tangerine orange *Citrus reticulata*. [from Portuguese from Malay ultimately from Sanskrit *mantrin* = counsellor]

Mandarin *n.* the standard form of the ◊Chinese language. Historically it derives from the language spoken by mandarins, Chinese imperial officials, from the 7th century onwards. It is used by 70% of the population.

mandatary /'mændətərɪ/ *n.* a holder or receiver of a mandate. [from Latin]

mandate /'mændeɪt/ *n.* 1. authority to act for another; the political authority supposed to be given by the electors to a government. 2. a judicial or legal command from a superior. 3. in history, a territory whose administration was entrusted to Allied states by the League of Nations under the Treaty of Versailles after World War I. Mandated territories were former German and Turkish possessions (including Iraq, Syria, Lebanon, and Palestine). When the United Nations replaced the League of Nations in 1945, mandates that had not achieved independence became known as ◊trust territories. —/mæn'deɪt/ *v.t.* 1. to give authority to (a delegate). 2. to commit (a territory) to a mandatary. [from Latin *mandatum* (*mandare* = command, entrust)]

mandatory /'mændətərɪ/ *adj.* compulsory; of or conveying a command. —**mandatorily** *adv.* [from Latin]

Mandela /mæn'delə/ Nelson (Rolihlahla) 1918– . South African politician and lawyer. As organizer of the banned ◊African National Congress (ANC), he was acquitted of treason in 1961, but was given a life sentence in 1964 on charges of sabotage and plotting to overthrow the government. In prison he became a symbol of unity for the worldwide anti-apartheid movement. In Feb 1990 he was released, the ban on the ANC having been lifted.

Mandela Winnie (Nomzamo) 1934– . Civil-rights activist in South Africa and wife of Nelson Mandela. A leading spokesperson for the African National Congress during her husband's imprisonment 1964–90, she has been jailed for a year and put under house arrest several times. In 1991 she was convicted of being involved in the abduction of four youths, one of whom was later murdered. She was subsequently sentenced to six years imprisonment, but was later released on bail pending an appeal.

Mandelbrot /'mændəlbrɒt/ Benoit B 1924– . Polish-born US scientist who coined the term **fractal geometry** to describe 'self-similar' shape, a motif that repeats indefinitely, each time smaller. This is associated with chaos theory.

Mandelshtam /'mændlʃtæm/ Osip Emilevich 1891–1938. Russian poet. Son of a Jewish merchant, he was sent to a concentration camp by the communist authorities in the 1930s, and died there. His posthumously published work, with its classic brevity, established his reputation as one of the greatest 20th-century Russian poets. His wife Nadezhda's memoirs of her life with her husband, *Hope Against Hope*, were published in the West in 1970, but not until 1988 in the USSR.

mandible /'mændɪbəl/ *n.* a jaw, especially the lower jaw in mammals and fishes; the upper or lower part of a bird's beak; either half of the crushing organ in the mouth-parts of an insect etc. [from Old French or Latin *mandibula* (*mandere* = chew)]

mandolin /'mændəlɪn/ *n.* a plucked stringed instrument of the lute family with metal strings tuned in pairs and a characteristic tremolo when sustaining long notes. [French from Italian *mandorla* = almond]

mandorla /mæn'dɔːlə/ *n.* = ◊vesica. [Italian = almond]

mandragora /mæn'drægərə/ *n.* the mandrake, especially as a narcotic (Shakespeare *Othello* III. iii. 330). [from Greek *mandragoras*]

mandrake /'mændreɪk/ *n.* a plant of the genus *Mandragora*, with white or purple flowers and large yellow fruit, having emetic and narcotic properties. [probably from Middle Dutch, ultimately from Greek *mandragoras*, associated with *man* and *drake* = dragon]

mandrel /'mændrəl/ *n.* 1. a lathe-shaft to which work is fixed while being turned. 2. a cylindrical rod round which metal or other material is forged or shaped.

mandrill /'mændrɪl/ *n.* a kind of large baboon *Mandrillus sphinx* of West Africa, with highly coloured patches and callosities on its face and hindquarters.

mane *n.* 1. the long hair on the neck of an animal, especially a horse or lion. 2. the long hair of a person. [Old English]

manège /mə'neɪʒ/ *n.* 1. a riding-school. 2. horsemanship. 3. the movements of a trained horse. [French from Italian]

Manet /mæ'neɪ/ Edouard 1832–1883. French painter, active in Paris. Rebelling against the academic tradition, he developed a clear and unaffected Realist style. His subjects were mainly contemporary, such as *Un Bar aux Folies-Bergère*/*A Bar at the Folies-Bergère* 1882 (Courtauld Art Gallery, London).

manful *adj.* brave, resolute. —**manfully** *adv.*

manganese /'mæŋgəniːz/ *n.* 1. a hard, brittle, grey-white metallic element, symbol Mn, atomic number 25, relative atomic mass 54.9380. It resembles iron (and rusts), but it is not magnetic and is softer. It is used chiefly in making steel alloys, also alloys with aluminium and copper. 2. an oxide of this, a black mineral used in glass-making etc. [from French from Italian]

manganese ore any mineral from which manganese is produced. The main ores are the oxides, such as **pyrolusite**, MnO_2; **hausmannite**, Mn_3O_4; and **manganite**, $MnO(OH)$.

mange /meɪndʒ/ *n.* a skin disease in hairy and woolly animals. [from Old French *mangeue* = itch (*mangier* = eat from Latin *manducare* = chew)]

mangel-wurzel /'mæŋgəl wɜːzəl/ *n.* or **mangold** variety of the common beet *Beta vulgaris* used chiefly as feed for cattle and sheep. [German *mangold* = beet and *wurzel* = root]

manger /'meɪndʒə/ *n.* a long, open box or trough for horses or cattle to eat from. [from Old French *mangeoire* from Latin]

mangle[1] /'mæŋgəl/ *v.t.* 1. to hack or mutilate by blows; to cut roughly so as to disfigure. 2. to spoil (a text etc.) by gross blunders. [from Anglo-French *ma(ha)ngler*]

mangle[2] *n.* a machine of two or more cylinders for squeezing water from and pressing washed clothes etc. —*v.t.* to press (clothes) in a mangle. [from Dutch, ultimately from Greek *magganon* = pulley]

mango /'mæŋgəʊ/ *n.* (*plural* **mangoes**) a tropical fruit with yellowish flesh; the tree *Mangifera indica* bearing this, native to India but now widely cultivated in other tropical and subtropical areas. [from Portuguese from Malay from Tamil]

mangold /'mæŋgəld/ *n.* = ◊mangel-wurzel.

mangrove /'mæŋgrəʊv/ *n.* any tropical tree or shrub of the genus *Rhizophora*, growing in shore-mud with many tangled aerial roots. [origin unknown]

mangy /'meɪndʒɪ/ *adj.* 1. having mange. 2. squalid, shabby.

manhandle *v.t.* 1. to move by human effort alone. 2. to treat roughly.

Manhattan /mæn'hætn/ an island 20 km/12.5 mi long and 4 km/2.5 mi wide, lying between the Hudson and East rivers and forming a borough of the city of New York, USA; population (1980) 1,428,000. It includes the Wall Street business centre and Broadway theatres.

Manhattan Project code name for the development of the ◊atom bomb in the USA in World War II, to which the physicists Enrico Fermi and J Robert Oppenheimer contributed.

manhole *n.* an opening (usually with a lid) through which a person can enter a sewer, conduit, etc., to inspect or repair it.

manhood *n.* 1. the state of being a man. 2. manliness, courage. 3. the men of a country.

mania /'meɪnɪə/ *n.* 1. violent madness. 2. extreme enthusiasm. [from Latin from Greek, = madness (*mainomai* = be mad)]

-mania suffix forming nouns denoting a special type of mental disorder (*megalomania*), or enthusiasm or admiration.

maniac /'meɪnɪæk/ *n.* a person affected with mania. —*adj.* of or affected with mania.

-maniac suffix forming nouns with the sense 'a person affected with -mania' and adjectives with the sense 'affected with -mania'.

maniacal /mə'naɪəkəl/ *adj.* of or like a mania or a maniac. —**maniacally** *adv.*

manic /'mænɪk/ *adj.* of or affected with mania. —**manic depression** a mental disorder characterized by recurring periods of ◊depression which may or may not alternate with periods of inappropriate elation (mania) or overactivity. Sufferers may be genetically predisposed to the condition. **manic-depressive** *adj.* relating to manic depression; (*n.*) a person having such a disorder.

Manichaeism *n.* religion founded by the prophet Mani (Latinized as Manichaeus, *c.*216–276). Despite persecution it spread and flourished until about the 10th century. It held that the material world is an invasion of the realm of light by the powers of darkness: particles of goodness imprisoned in matter were to be rescued by messengers such as Jesus, and finally by Mani himself.

manicure /'mænɪkjuə/ *n.* cosmetic treatment of the hands and finger-nails. —*v.t.* to apply such treatment to. —**manicurist** *n.* [French from Latin *manus* = hand and *cura* = care]

manifest /'mænɪfest/ *adj.* clear and unmistakable. —*v.t./i.* 1. to show clearly, to give signs of; to make or become apparent or visible. 2. to be evidence of, to prove. 3. to record in a manifest. —*n.* a list of cargo or passengers carried by a ship or aircraft etc. —**manifestation** /-'steɪʃən/ *n.*, **manifestly** *adv.* [from Old French or Latin *manifestus*]

manifesto /mænɪ'festəʊ/ *n.* (*plural* **manifestos**) a public declaration of policy, especially by a political party. [Italian]

manifold /'mænɪfəʊld/ *adj.* 1. many and various. 2. having various forms, applications, component parts, etc. —*n.* 1. a pipe or chamber (in a piece of a mechanism) with several openings. 2. a manifold thing. [Old English]

manikin /'mænɪkɪn/ *n.* a little man, a dwarf. [from Dutch diminutive of *man*]

manila /mə'nɪlə/ *n.* (also **manilla**) 1. the strong fibre of a Philippine tree *Musa textilis*. 2. a brown paper originally made from this, used especially for envelopes. [from *Manila*, capital of the Philippines]

Manila industrial port (textiles, tobacco, distilling, chemicals, shipbuilding) and capital of the Philippines, on the island of Luzon; population (1980) 1,630,000, metropolitan area (including ◊Quezon City) 5,926,000.

manioc /'mæniɒk/ n. another name for the plant ◊cassava; flour made from this. [from Tupi *mandioca*]

maniple /'mænɪpəl/ n. 1. a strip of material worn over the left arm by a priest celebrating the Eucharist. 2. a subdivision of a legion in the army of ancient Rome. [Old French, or from Latin *manipulus* = handful, troop (*manus* = hand)]

manipulable /mə'nɪpjʊləbəl/ adj. that may be manipulated.

manipulate /mə'nɪpjʊleɪt/ v.t. 1. to handle, manage, or use (a thing) skilfully. 2. to examine manually and treat (a part of the body) for a fracture etc. 3. to arrange or influence cleverly or unfairly. —**manipulation** /-'leɪʃən/ n., **manipulator** n. [from French *manipuler* from Latin *manipulus*]

Manipur /mʌni'pʊə/ state of NE India; area 22,400 sq km/8,646 sq mi; capital Imphal; population (1981) 1,434,000; language Hindi; religion Hindu 70%; recent history administered from the state of Assam until 1947 when it became a Union Territory. It became a state in 1972.

Man, Isle of /mæn/ island in the Irish Sea, a dependency of the British crown, but not part of the UK; area 570 sq km/220 sq mi; capital Douglas; population (1986) 64,000; language English (Manx, nearer to Scottish than Irish Gaelic, has been almost extinct since the 1970s); government crown-appointed lieutenant-governor, a legislative council, and the representative House of Keys, which together make up the Court of Tynwald, passing laws subject to the royal assent. Laws passed at Westminster only affect the island if specifically so provided; history Norwegian until 1266, when the island was ceded to Scotland; it came under UK administration 1765. It was Britain's first free port and is a tax haven.

Manitoba /mæni'təubə/ prairie province of Canada; area 650,000 sq km/250,900 sq mi; capital Winnipeg; population (1986) 1,071,000; history known as Red River settlement until it joined Canada 1870. It was the site of the Riel Rebellion 1885. The area of the province was extended in 1881 and 1912.

mankind /mæn'kaɪnd/ n. 1. human beings in general, the human species. 2. /'mæn-/ men in general.

Manley /'mænli/ Michael 1924– . Jamaican politician, prime minister 1972–80 and from 1989, adopting more moderate socialist policies. His father, Norman Manley (1893–1969), was founder of the People's National Party and prime minister 1959–62.

manly adj. having the qualities associated with a man (e. g. strength and courage); befitting a man. —**manliness** n.

Mann /mæn/ Anthony. Stage name of Emil Anton Bundmann 1906–1967. US film director who made a series of violent but intelligent 1950s Westerns starring James Stewart, such as *Winchester '73* 1950. He also directed one of the best film epics, *El Cid* 1961. His other films include *The Glenn Miller Story* 1954 and *A Dandy in Aspic* 1968.

Mann Thomas 1875–1955. German novelist and critic, concerned with the theme of the artist's relation to society. His first novel was *Buddenbrooks* 1901, which, followed by *Der Zauberberg/The Magic Mountain* 1924, led to the Nobel Prize for Literature in 1929. Later works include *Dr Faustus* 1947 and *Die Bekenntnisse des Hochstaplers Felix Krull/Confessions of Felix Krull* 1954. Notable among his works of short fiction is *Der Tod in Venedig/Death in Venice* 1913.

If you are possessed by an idea, you find it expressed everywhere, you even *smell* it.

Thomas Mann
Death in Venice

---

manna /'mænə/ n. 1. a sweetish exudation obtained from many trees such as the ash and larch, and used in medicine. 2. a substance miraculously supplied as food to the Israelites in the wilderness (Exod. 16). 3. something unexpected and delightful. [Old English ultimately from Hebrew, probably from Arabic *mann* = exudation of tamarisk]

manned adj. (of a spacecraft etc.) having a human crew.

mannequin /'mænɪkɪn/ n. 1. a person, usually a woman, employed by a dress designer etc. to model clothes. 2. a dummy for the display of clothes in a shop. [French = manikin]

manner /'mænə/ n. 1. the way a thing is done or happens. 2. a person's bearing or way of behaving towards others, style of speaking, etc. 3. (in *plural*) modes of life, conditions of society. 4. (in *plural*) social behaviour; polite social behaviour. 5. style in literature or art. 6. kind, sort. —**all manner of**, every kind of. **comedy of manners**, a comedy with satirical portrayal of the manners of society. **in a manner of speaking**, in some sense, to some extent, so to speak. [from Anglo-French from Latin *manuarius* (*manus* = hand)]

mannered adj. 1. behaving in a specified way (*ill-*, *well-mannered*). 2. full of mannerisms.

Mannerheim /'mænəheɪm/ Carl Gustav Emil von 1867–1951. Finnish general and politician, leader of the conservative forces in the civil war 1917–18 and regent 1918–19. He commanded the Finnish army 1939–40 and 1941–44, and was president of Finland 1944–46.

mannerism /'mænərɪzəm/ n. 1. a distinctive gesture or feature of style; excessive use of these in art etc. —**mannerist** n.

Mannerism n. in painting and architecture, a style characterized by a subtle but conscious breaking of the 'rules' of classical composition, for example, displaying the human body in an off-centre, distorted pose, and using harsh, non-blending colours. The term was coined by Giorgio ◊Vasari and used to describe the 16th-century reaction to the peak of Renaissance Classicism as achieved by Raphael, Leonardo da Vinci, and early Michelangelo.

mannerly adj. well-behaved, polite.

Mannheim /'mænhaɪm/ Karl 1893–1947. Hungarian sociologist, who settled in the UK in 1933. In *Ideology and Utopia* 1929 he argued that all knowledge, except in mathematics and physics, is ideological, a reflection of class interests and values; that there is therefore no such thing as objective knowledge or absolute truth.

Manning /'mænɪŋ/ Henry Edward 1808–1892. English priest, one of the leaders of the Oxford Movement. In 1851 he was converted to Roman Catholicism, and in 1865 became archbishop of Westminster. He was created a cardinal in 1875.

Manoel /mən'wel/ two kings of Portugal, including:

Manoel I 1469–1521. King of Portugal from 1495, when he succeeded his uncle John II (1455–95). He was known as 'the Fortunate', because his reign was distinguished by the discoveries made by Portuguese navigators and the expansion of the Portuguese empire.

manœuvre /mə'nu:və/ n. 1. a planned and controlled movement of a vehicle or body of troops etc.; (in *plural*) large-scale exercises of troops or ships. 2. a deceptive or elusive movement; a skilful plan. —v.t./i. 1. to move (a thing, especially a vehicle) carefully. 2. to perform manœuvres; to cause (troops or ships) to do this. 3. to guide skilfully or craftily. [from French from Latin *man(u)operari* = work by hand (*manus* = hand and *operari* = to work)]

manometer /mə'nɒmɪtə/ n. an instrument for measuring the pressure of liquids (including human blood pressure) or gases. In its basic form, it is a U-tube partly filled with coloured liquid; pressure of a gas entering at one side is measured by the level to which the liquid rises at the other. [from French from Greek *manos* = thin]

manor /'mænə/ n. 1. a large landed estate or its house (also **manor-house**). 2. (*historical*) a territorial unit under the feudal control of a lord. 3. (*slang*) an area for which a police unit is responsible. —**manorial** /mə'nɔ:riəl/ adj. [from Anglo-French from Latin *manēre* = remain]

manpower n. the number of persons available for work or military service.

manqué /'mɑːkeɪ/ adj. (placed after a noun) that might have been but is not. [French *manquer* = lack]

Man Ray /reɪ/ adopted name of Emmanuel Rudnitsky 1890–1977. US photographer, painter, and sculptor, active mainly in France; associated with the Dada movement. His pictures often showed Surrealist images like the photograph *Le Violon d'Ingres* 1924.

mansard /'mænsɑːd/ n. a roof with each face having two slopes, with the steeper one below [from F *Mansart*, French architect (died 1666)]

mantis

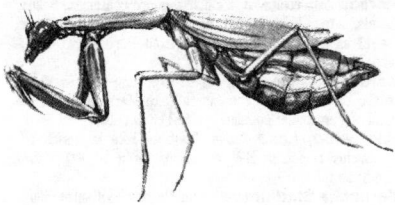

manse *n.* an ecclesiastical residence, especially a Scottish Presbyterian minister's house. [from Latin]

Mansell /'mænsəl/ Nigel 1954– . English motor-racing driver. Runner-up in the world championship on two occasions.

manservant *n.* (*plural* **menservants**) a male servant.

Mansfield /'mænzfiːld/ Jayne. Stage name of Vera Jayne Palmer 1933–1967. US actress who had a short career as a kind of living parody of Marilyn Monroe in films including *The Girl Can't Help It* 1956 and *Will Success Spoil Rock Hunter?* 1957.

Mansfield Katherine. Pen name of Kathleen Beauchamp 1888–1923. New Zealand writer who lived most of her life in England. Her delicate artistry emerges not only in her volumes of short stories—such as *In a German Pension* 1911, *Bliss* 1920, and *The Garden Party* 1923 – but also in her *Letters* and *Journal.*

mansion /'mænʃən/ *n.* a large grand house. —**the Mansion House**, the official residence of the Lord Mayor in the City of London. [from Old French from Latin]

manslaughter *n.* the unlawful killing of a human being in circumstances less culpable than ◊murder – for example, when the killer suffers extreme provocation, is in some way mentally ill (diminished responsibility), did not intend to kill but did so accidentally in the course of another crime or by behaving with criminal recklessness, or is the survivor of a genuine suicide pact that involved killing the other person. **Corporate manslaughter** is manslaughter in which the accused is alleged to be responsible for the deaths of many people.

Manson /'mænsən/ Patrick 1844–1922. Scottish physician who showed that insects are responsible for the spread of diseases like elephantiasis and malaria.

manta *n.* another name for the ◊devil ray, a large fish.

Mantegna /mæn'tenjə/ Andrea *c.*1431–1506. Italian Renaissance painter and engraver, active chiefly in Padua and Mantua, where some of his frescoes remain. Paintings such as *The Agony in the Garden* about 1455 (National Gallery, London) reveal a dramatic linear style, mastery of perspective, and strongly Classical architectural detail.

mantel /'mæntəl/ *n.* 1. a structure of wood or marble etc. above and around a fireplace. 2. a mantelpiece. [variant of *mantle*]

mantelpiece *n.* a shelf over a fireplace.

mantilla /mæn'tilə/ *n.* a lace scarf worn especially by Spanish women over the hair and shoulders. [Spanish]

mantis /'mæntis/ *n.* one of many insects of the family Mantidae, related to cockroaches. Some species can reach a length of 20 cm/8 in. There are about 2,000 species of mantis, mainly tropical. —**praying mantis** a predacious insect *Mantis religiosa* that holds its forelegs in a position suggesting hands folded in prayer. [Greek = prophet]

mantissa *n.* in mathematics, the decimal part of a ◊logarithm. For example, the logarithm of 347.6 is 2.5411; in this case, the 0.5411 is the mantissa, and the integral (whole number) part of the logarithm, the 2, is the ◊characteristic.

mantle *n.* 1. a loose sleeveless cloak; a covering. 2. a fragile tube fixed round a gas-jet to give an incandescent light. 3. a bird's back, scapulars, and wing-coverts, especially when these are of a distinctive colour. 4. the intermediate zone of the Earth between the ◊crust and the ◊core. It is thought to consist of silicate minerals such as olivine and spinel. —*v.t.* to clothe in or as in a mantle; to conceal, to envelop. [from Old French from Latin *mantellum*]

mantra /'mæntrə/ *n.* 1. a sacred syllable, word, or phrase (especially in Buddhism and Hinduism) believed to possess supernatural powers. 2. a Vedic hymn. [Sanskrit = instrument of thought (*man* = think)]

mantrap *n.* a trap for catching trespassers etc.

Manu /'maːnuː/ in Hindu mythology, the founder of the human race, who was saved by ◊Brahma from a deluge.

manual /'mænjuəl/ *adj.* of or done with the hands; worked by hand, not by automatic equipment. —*n.* 1. a handbook; a reference book. 2. an organ keyboard played with the hands not the feet. —**manually** *adv.* [from Old French from Latin *manualis* (*manus* = hand)]

Manuel II 1889–1932. King of Portugal 1908–10. He ascended the throne on the assassination of his father, Carlos I, but was driven out by a revolution in 1910, and lived in England.

manufacture /mænju'fæktʃə/ *v.t.* 1. to produce (articles) by labour, especially by machinery on a large scale. 2. to invent or fabricate (evidence or a story etc.). —*n.* the manufacturing of articles; a branch of such an industry. —**manufacturer** *n.* [French from Italian and Latin (*manu facere* = make by hand)]

manure /mə'njuə/ *n.* a fertilizer, especially dung. —*v.t.* to apply manure to (land). [from Anglo-French]

manuscript /'mænjuskrɪpt/ *n.* 1. a book or document written by hand. 2. an author's copy, written by hand or typed (not printed). 3. manuscript state. —*adj.* written by hand. [from Latin *manu scribere* = write by hand]

Manutius /mə'njuːʃiəs/ Aldus 1450–1515. Italian printer, established in Venice (which he made the publishing centre of Europe) from 1490; he introduced ◊italic type and was the first to print books in Greek.

Manx /mæŋks/ *adj.* of the Isle of Man or its people or language. —*n.* the Celtic language of the Isle of Man, a dialect of Gaelic. —**the Manx**, the Manx people. **Manx cat**, a cat of a tailless variety. **Manxman** *n.* (*plural* **Manxmen**), **Manxwoman** *n. fem.* (*plural* **Manxwomen**) [from Old Norse from Old Irish *Manu* = Isle of Man]

many /'meni/ *adj.* (*comparative* **more**, *superlative* **most**) great in number, numerous. —*n.pl.* many people or things. —**the many**, the multitude of people. **a good many**, a fair number. **a great many**, a large number. [Old English]

Manzoni /mænd'zəuni/ Alessandro, Count Manzoni 1785–1873. Italian poet and novelist, famed for his historical romance, *I promessi sposi/The Betrothed* 1825–27, set in Spanish-occupied Milan during the 17th century. Verdi's *Requiem* commemorates him.

Maoism /'mauɪzəm/ *n.* form of communism based on the ideas and teachings of the Chinese communist leader ◊Mao Zedong. It involves an adaptation of ◊Marxism to suit conditions in China and apportions a much greater role to agriculture and the peasantry in the building of socialism, thus effectively bypassing the capitalist (industrial) stage envisaged by Marx. —**Maoist** *n.* [from *Mao Zedong*]

Maori /'mauri/ *n.* 1. a member of the indigenous Polynesian people of New Zealand, who numbered 294,200 in 1986, about 10% of the total population. In recent years there has been increased Maori consciousness, and a demand for official status for the Maori language and review of the Waitangi Treaty of 1840 (under which the Maoris surrendered their lands to British sovereignty). The **Maori Unity Movement/Kotahitanga** was founded in 1983 by Eva Rickard. The Maoris claim 70% of the country's land, and have secured a ruling that the fishing grounds of the far north belong solely to local tribes. 2. their Polynesian language. —*adj.* of the Maoris or their language.

Mao Zedong /'mau dzi'dʌŋ/ or **Mao Tsetung** 1893–1976. Chinese political leader and Marxist theoretician. A founder of the Chinese Communist Party (CCP) 1921, Mao soon emerged as its leader. He organized the ◊Long March 1934–36 and the war of liberation 1937–49, following which he established a People's Republic and Communist rule in China; he headed the CCP and government until his death. His influence diminished with the failure of his 1958–60 ◊Great Leap Forward, but he emerged dominant again during the 1966–69 ◊Cultural Revolution. Mao adapted communism to Chinese conditions, as set out in the *Little Red Book.*

map *n.* 1. a representation (usually on a flat surface) of the Earth's surface or a part of it; a similar representation of the sky (showing the positions of stars etc.) or of the Moon etc. 2. a diagram showing an arrangement or the components of a thing. —*v.t.* (**-pp-**) to represent on a map. —**map out,** to plan in detail. [from Latin *mappa* = napkin]

Mapai /mæːˈpaɪ/ *n.* (Miphlegeth Poale Israel) the Israeli Workers' Party or Labour Party, founded 1930. Its leading figure until 1965 was David Ben-Gurion. In 1968, the party allied with two other democratic socialist parties to form the Israeli Labour Party, led initially by Levi Eshkol and later by Golda Meir.

maple /ˈmeɪpəl/ *n.* **1.** any deciduous tree of the genus *Acer*, family Aceraceae, with lobed leaves and green flowers, followed by two-winged fruits, or samaras. There are over 200 species, chiefly in northern temperate regions. **2.** its wood. —**maple-leaf** *n.* the emblem of Canada. **maple sugar,** a sugar obtained by evaporating the sap of some kinds of maple. **maple syrup,** a syrup made by evaporating maple sap or dissolving maple sugar. [from Old English]

Mappa Mundi /ˈmæpə ˈmʊndi/ 13th-century symbolic map of the world. It is circular and shows Asia at the top, with Europe and Africa below and Jerusalem at the centre (reflecting Christian religious rather than geographical belief). It was drawn by David de Bello, a canon at Hereford Cathedral, England, who left the map to the cathedral, where it was used as an altarpiece. In 1988 there were plans, later abandoned, to sell the map to raise money for repairs.

map projection ways of depicting the spherical surface of the Earth on a flat piece of paper. Traditional projections include the **conic, azimuthal,** and **cylindrical.** The weakness of these systems is that countries in different latitudes are disproportionately large, and lines of longitude and latitude appear distorted. In 1973 the German historian Arno Peters devised the **Peters projection** in which the countries of the world retain their relative areas.

Maputo /məˈpuːtəʊ/ formerly (until 1975) **Lourenço Marques** capital of Mozambique, and Africa's second largest port, on Delagoa Bay; population (1986) 883,000. Linked by rail with Zimbabwe and South Africa, it is a major outlet for minerals, steel, textiles, processed foods, and furniture.

maquette /məˈket/ *n.* a preliminary model or sketch. [French from Italian *macchia* = spot]

maquis *n.* mostly evergreen vegetation common in many Mediterranean countries, consisting of scrub woodland with many low-growing tangled bushes and shrubs, typically including species of broom, gorse, and heather.

Maquis /mækiː, ˈmɑː-/ *n.* French ◊Resistance movement that fought against the German occupation during World War II; a member of this. [French = brushwood, scrub (traditionally used as a refuge by fugitives)]

mar *v.t.* (-rr-) to spoil, to disfigure, to impair the perfection of. [Old English]

Mar. abbreviation of March.

Mara /ˈmɑːrə/ **1.** in Buddhism, a supernatural being who attempted to distract the Buddha from the meditations that led to his enlightenment. **2.** In Hinduism, a goddess of death. [Sanskrit = killing]

marabou /ˈmærəbuː/ *n.* **1.** a kind of stork *Leptoptilus crumeniferus.* It is about 120 cm/4 ft tall, has a bald head, and eats snakes, lizards, insects, and carrion. It is largely dark grey and white and has an inflatable throat pouch. **2.**

maple

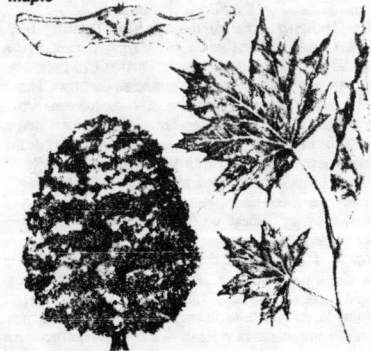

its down as a trimming etc. [French, from Arabic = holy man (the stork being regarded as holy)]

maraca /məˈrækə/ *n.* a clublike gourd containing beans, beads, etc., held in the hand and shaken (usually in pairs) as a musical instrument. [from Portuguese, probably from Tupi]

Maracaibo /mærəˈkaɪbəʊ/ oil-exporting port in Venezuela, on the channel connecting Lake Maracaibo with the Gulf of Venezuela; population (1981) 889,000.

Maracaibo, Lake /mærəˈkaɪbəʊ/ lake in a rich oil-producing region in NW Venezuela; area 14,000 sq km/ 5,400 sq mi.

Maracaña Stadium the world's largest football stadium, in Rio de Janeiro, Brazil, built 1950. It has a crowd capacity of 175,000 but held a world record 199,854 spectators for the 1950 World Cup final between Brazil and Uruguay.

Maradona /mærəˈdɒnə/ Diego 1960– . Argentine footballer who helped his country to win the ◊World Cup 1986.

maraschino /mærəˈskiːnəʊ/ *n.* (*plural* **maraschinos**) a sweet liqueur made from cherries. —**maraschino cherry,** a cherry preserved in this. [Italian *marasca* = small black cherry from *amaro* =bitter]

Marat /ˈmærɑː/ Jean Paul 1743–1793. French Revolutionary leader and journalist. He was elected in 1792 to the National Convention, where he carried on a long struggle with the ◊Girondins, ending in their overthrow in May 1793. In July he was murdered by Charlotte ◊Corday.

marathon /ˈmærəθən/ *n.* **1.** a long-distance foot-race over roads, especially of 42.195 km/26 mi 385 yd. It was first included in the Olympic Games at Athens 1896. The distance varied until it was standardized in 1924. More recently, races have been opened to wider participation. **2.** a feat of endurance; an undertaking of long duration. [from *Marathon* in Greece]

Marathon, Battle of 490 BC. Fought between the Greeks, who were ultimately victorious, and invading Persians on the plain of Marathon, NE of Athens. News of the victory was announced in Athens by an unnamed courier who ran the 42 km/26 mi from the field of battle.

maraud /məˈrɔːd/ *v.t./i.* to make a plundering raid (on); to go about pilfering. —**marauder** *n.* [from French *marauder* (*maraud* = rogue)]

marble *n.* **1.** metamorphosed ◊limestone that takes and retains a good polish; it is used in building and sculpture. In its pure form it is white and consists almost entirely of calcite, $CaCO_3$. Mineral impurities give it various colours and patterns. **2.** this as a type of hardness or durability or smoothness (often *attributive*). **3.** (in *plural*) a collection of sculptures. **4.** a small ball of glass etc. as a toy; (in *plural*) a game using these. —*v.t.* to stain or colour to look like variegated marble. [from Old French from Latin *marmor* from Greek]

Marble Arch a triumphal arch in London designed by John ◊Nash to commemorate Nelson's victories. Intended as a ceremonial entry to Buckingham Palace, it was moved in 1851 to Hyde Park at the end of Oxford Street.

marbled *adj.* **1.** looking like variegated marble. **2.** (of meat) streaked with fat.

Marburg disease or **green monkey disease** a viral disease of central Africa, first occurring in Europe in 1967 among research workers in Germany working with African green monkeys. It is characterized by haemorrhage of the mucous membranes, fever, vomiting, and diarrhoea; mortality is high.

Marc /mɑːk/ Franz 1880–1916. German Expressionist painter, associated with Wassily Kandinsky in founding the ◊Blaue Reiter movement. Animals played an essential part in his view of the world, and bold semi-abstracts of red and blue horses are characteristic of his work.

marcasite /ˈmɑːkəsaɪt/ *n.* crystalline iron sulphide; a piece of this as an ornament. [from Latin from Arabic from Persian]

Marceau /mɑːˈsəʊ/ Marcel 1923– . French mime artist. He is the creator of the clown-harlequin Bip and mime sequences such as 'Youth, Maturity, Old Age, and Death'.

march[1] *v.t./i.* **1.** to walk in a military manner with a regular and measured tread; to advance thus. **2.** to walk purposefully. **3.** (of events) to proceed steadily. **4.** to cause to march or walk. —*n.* **1.** the marching of troops; the uniform step of troops etc.; the distance covered by marching troops etc.

Marconi *Italian inventor Guglielmo Marconi whose pioneering work on radio ('wireless telegraphy') won him a Nobel prize in 1909.*

2. a long toilsome walk. 3. a procession as a protest or demonstration. 4. a piece of music meant to accompany a march. —**marching orders,** a command to troops to depart for war etc.; a dismissal. **march past,** the marching of troops in line past a saluting-point at a review —**marcher** *n.* [from French *marcher* from Latin *marcus* = hammer]

march[2] *n.* (*historical*) 1. a boundary or frontier (often in *plural,* especially of the ◊marches between England and Scotland or Wales). 2. a tract of land, often disputed, between two countries. —*v.i.* (of countries, estates, etc.) to have a common frontier, to border. [from Old French]

March *n.* the third month of the year. —**mad as a March hare,** a proverb referring to the seemingly insane antics of male hares in the breeding season (March), when they are seen bucking on stiff legs, boxing each other standing on hind legs, etc. [from Old French from Latin *Martius* (*mensis* = month) of Mars]

Marchais /mɑːˈʃeɪ/ Georges 1920– . Leader of the French Communist Party (PCF) from 1972. Under his leadership, the party committed itself to a 'transition to socialism' by democratic means and entered into a union of the left with the Socialist Party (PS). This was severed in 1977, and the PCF returned to a more orthodox pro-Moscow line, since when its share of the vote has decreased.

Marche /ˈmɑːkeɪ/ region of E central Italy consisting of the provinces of Ancona, Ascoli Piceno, Macerata, and Pesaro e Urbino; **area** 9,700 sq km/3,744 sq mi; **capital** Ancona; **population** (1988) 1,429,000.

marches /ˈmɑːtʃɪz/ the boundary areas of England with Wales, and England with Scotland. In the Middle Ages these troubled frontier regions were held by lords of the marches, sometimes called *marchiones* and later earls of March.

marchioness /ˈmɑːʃənɪs, -ˈnes/ *n.* a marquis's wife or widow; a woman holding the rank of a marquis in her own right. [from Latin *marchio* = captain of the marches]

Marciano /mɑːsiˈɑːnəʊ/ Rocky (Rocco Francis Marchegiano) 1923–1969. US boxer, world heavyweight champion 1952–56. He retired after 49 professional fights, the only heavyweight champion to retire undefeated.

Marconi /mɑːˈkəʊni/ Guglielmo 1874–1937. Italian electrical engineer and pioneer in the invention and development of radio. In 1895 he achieved radio communication over more than a mile, and in England in 1896 he conducted successful experiments that led to the formation of the company that became Marconi's Wireless Telegraph Company Ltd. He shared the Nobel Prize for Physics 1909.

Marconi Scandal a scandal in 1912 in which UK chancellor Lloyd George and two other government ministers were found by a French newspaper to have dealt in shares of the US Marconi company shortly before it was announced

that the Post Office had accepted the British Marconi company's bid to construct an imperial wireless chain. A parliamentary select committee, biased towards the Liberal government's interests, found that the other four wireless systems were technically inadequate and therefore the decision to adopt Marconi's tender was not the result of ministerial corruption. The scandal did irreparable harm to Lloyd George's reputation.

Marcos /ˈmɑːkɒs/ Ferdinand 1917–1989. Filipino rightwing politician, president from 1965 to 1986, when he was forced into exile in Hawaii. He was backed by the USA when in power, but in 1988 US authorities indicted him and his wife **Imelda Marcos** (1931–   ) for racketeering, embezzlement, and defrauding US banks; she was acquitted after his death.

Marcus Aurelius Antoninus /ˈmɑːkəs ɔːˈriːliəs æntəˈnaɪnəs/ AD 121–180. Roman emperor from 161 and Stoic philosopher. Although considered one of the best of the Roman emperors, he persecuted the Christians for political reasons. He wrote the philosophical *Meditations.*

Waste no more time arguing what a good man should be. Be one.

Marcus Aurelius
Meditations

Mardi Gras /mɑːdi ˈɡrɑː/ the French term for ◊Shrove Tuesday. A festival was traditionally held on this day in Paris, and there are carnivals in many parts of the world, including New Orleans, Louisiana; Italy; and Brazil. [French = fat Tuesday, from the custom of using up all the fat in the household before the beginning of ◊Lent]

mare[1] /meə/ *n.* the female of a horse or related animal. —**mare's nest,** an illusory discovery. **mare's tail,** a slender, perennial marsh plant *Hippuris vulgaris;* (in *plural*) long straight streaks of cirrus cloud. [Old English]

mare[2] /ˈmɑːri/ *n.* (*plural* **maria** /ˈmɑːriə/) a large flat area on the Moon, once thought to be a sea. [Latin = sea]

Marengo, Battle of /məˈreŋɡəʊ/ defeat of the Austrians by the French emperor Napoleon on 14 June 1800, as part of his Italian campaign, near the village of Marengo in Piedmont, Italy.

Margaret /ˈmɑːɡrət/ the Maid of Norway 1282–1290. Queen of Scotland from 1285, the daughter of Eric II, king of Norway, and Princess Margaret of Scotland. When only two years old, she became queen of Scotland on the death of her grandfather, Alexander III, but died in the Orkneys on the voyage from Norway to her kingdom.

Margaret (Rose) 1930– . Princess of the UK, younger daughter of George VI and sister of Elizabeth II. In 1960 she married Anthony Armstrong-Jones, later created Lord Snowdon, but they were divorced in 1978. Their children are **David, Viscount Linley** (1961–) and **Lady Sarah Armstrong-Jones** (1964–).

Margaret of Anjou /ɒnˈʒuː/ 1430–1482. Queen of England from 1445, wife of ◊Henry VI of England. After the outbreak of the Wars of the ◊Roses in 1455, she acted as the leader of the Lancastrians, but was defeated and captured at the battle of Tewkesbury 1471 by Edward IV.

Margaret, St 1045–1093. Queen of Scotland, the granddaughter of King Edmund Ironside of England. She went to Scotland after the Norman Conquest, and soon after married Malcolm III. The marriage of her daughter Matilda to Henry I united the Norman and English royal houses.

margarine /mɑːˈdʒəriːn, mɑːgˈ-/ *n.* a butter substitute, made from animal fats and vegetable oils. The French chemist Hippolyte Mège-Mouries invented margarine in 1889. Modern margarines are usually made with vegetable oils, such as sunflower oil, giving a product that is low in saturated fats; see ◊polyunsaturate. [French, ultimately from Greek *margaron* pearl]

margay *n.* a small wild cat *Felis wiedi* found from southern USA to South America in forested areas, where it hunts birds and small mammals. It is about 60 cm/2 ft long with a 40 cm/1.3 ft tail, has a rather rounded head, and black spots and blotches on a yellowish-brown coat.

marge *n.* (*colloquial*) margarine. [abbreviation]

margin /ˈmɑːdʒɪn/ *n.* **1.** an edge or border of a surface. **2.** a plain space beside the main body of print etc. on a page. **3.** an extra amount (of time, money, etc.) over and above the necessary or minimum; a sum deposited with a stockbroker to cover the risk of loss on a transaction. **4.** a condition near the limit below or beyond which a thing ceases to be possible. —*v.t.* to furnish with a margin or with marginal notes. —**margin of error**, the difference allowed for miscalculation or mischance. [from Latin *margo*]

marginal /ˈmɑːdʒɪnəl/ *adj.* **1.** written in a margin. **2.** of or at an edge. **3.** (of a constituency) having an elected MP with only a small majority that may be lost at the next election. **4.** close to the limit, especially of no profit, barely adequate or provided for. —**marginal cost**, the cost of producing one extra item of output. —**marginally** *adv.* [from Latin]

marginalia /mɑːdʒɪˈneɪliə/ *n.pl.* marginal notes. [Latin]

marginal utility in economics, the measure of additional satisfaction (utility) gained by a consumer who receives one additional unit of a product or service. The concept is used to explain why consumers buy more of a product when the price falls.

margrave *n.* German title (equivalent of marquess) for the 'counts of the march', who guarded the frontier regions of the Holy Roman Empire from Charlemagne's time. Later the title was used by other territorial princes. Chief among these were the margraves of Austria and of Brandenburg.

Margrethe II /mɑːˈɡreɪdə/ 1940– . Queen of Denmark from 1972, when she succeeded her father Frederick IX. In 1967, she married the French diplomat Count Henri de Laborde de Monpezat, who took the title Prince Hendrik. Her heir is Crown Prince Frederick (1968–).

marguerite /mɑːɡəˈriːt/ *n.* an ox-eye daisy or similar flower. [French, from Latin *margarita* pearl from Greek]

Marguerite of Navarre /mɑːɡəˈriːt, naˈvɑː/ also known as **Margaret d'Angoulême** /dɒŋuːˈleɪm/ 1492–1549. Queen of Navarre from 1527, French poet, and author of the *Heptaméron* 1558, a collection of stories in imitation of Boccaccio's *Decameron*. The sister of Francis I of France, she was born in Angoulême. Her second husband from 1527 was Henri d'Albret, king of Navarre.

maria plural of ◊mare².

Mariana Islands /mæriˈɑːnəz/ or **Marianas** archipelago in the NW Pacific, divided politically into ◊Guam (an unincorporated territory of the USA) and the **Northern Marianas** (a commonwealth in union with the USA of 16 mountainous islands, extending 560 km/350 mi north from Guam; **area** 480 sq km/185 sq mi; **capital** Garapan on Saipan; **population** (1988) 21,000, mainly Micronesian; **language** Chamorro 55%, English; **government** own constitutionally elected government; **recent history** sold

to Germany by Spain in 1899. The islands were mandated by the League of Nations to Japan in 1918, and taken by US Marines 1944–45 in World War II. The islands were under US trusteeship from 1947 and voted to become a Commonwealth of the USA in 1975.

Mariana Trench the lowest region on the Earth's surface; the deepest part of the sea floor. The trench is 2,400 km/1,500 mi long and is situated 300 km/200 mi E of the Mariana Islands, in the NW Pacific Ocean. Its deepest part is the gorge known as the Challenger Deep, which extends 11,034 m/36,201 ft below sea level.

Marianne /mæriˈæn/ symbolic figure of the French republic, dating from the Revolution. Statues of her adorn public buildings in France. Her name combines those of the Virgin Mary and St Anne.

Maria Theresa /məˈriːə təˈreɪzə/ 1717–1780. Empress of Austria from 1740, when she succeeded her father, the Holy Roman Emperor Charles VI; her claim to the throne was challenged and she became embroiled, first in the War of the ◊Austrian Succession 1740–48, then in the ◊Seven Years' War 1756–63; she remained in possession of Austria but lost Silesia. The rest of her reign was peaceful and, with her son Joseph II, she introduced social reforms.

Marie Antoinette /məˈriː æntwəˈnet/ 1755–1793. Queen of France from 1774. She was the daughter of Empress Maria Theresa of Austria, and married ◊Louis XVI of France in 1770. Her reputation for extravagance helped provoke the ◊French Revolution of 1789. She was tried for treason in Oct 1793 and guillotined.

Marie de France /də ˈfrɒns/ *c.*1150–1215. French poet, thought to have been the half-sister of Henry II of England, and abbess of Shaftesbury 1181–1215. She wrote *Lais* (verse tales that dealt with Celtic and Arthurian themes) and *Ysopet*, a collection of fables.

Marie de' Medici /deɪ ˈmedɪtʃɪ/ 1573–1642. Queen of France, wife of Henry IV from 1600, and regent (after his murder) for their son Louis XIII. She left the government to her favourites, the Concinis, until in 1617 Louis XIII seized power and executed them. She was banished, but after she led a revolt in 1619, ◊Richelieu effected her reconciliation with her son. When she attempted to oust him again in 1630, she was exiled.

Marie Louise /luːˈiːz/ 1791–1847. Queen consort of Napoleon I from 1810 (after his divorce from Josephine), mother of Napoleon II. She was the daughter of Francis I of Austria (see Emperor ◊Francis II) and on Napoleon's fall returned with their son to Austria, where she was granted the duchy of Parma 1815.

Mariette /mæriˈet/ Auguste Ferdinand François 1821–1881. French Egyptologist, whose discoveries from 1850 included the 'temple' between the paws of the Sphinx. He founded the Egyptian Museum in Cairo.

marigold /ˈmærɪɡəʊld/ *n.* any of various plants, especially of the genus *Calendula* or *Tagetes*, with golden or bright yellow flowers. [from *Mary* (probably the Virgin) and *gold*]

marijuana /mæriˈhwɑːnə/ *n.* or **marihuana** the dried leaves and flowers and stems of the hemp plant ◊cannabis, used as a narcotic. [American Spanish]

marimba /məˈrɪmbə/ *n.* **1.** a type of base xylophone of Africa and Central America. **2.** a modern orchestral instrument evolved from this. [of Congolese origin]

marina /məˈriːnə/ *n.* a place with moorings for pleasure-yachts etc. [Italian and Spanish from Latin *mare* = sea]

marinade /mæriˈneɪd/ *n.* a mixture of wine, vinegar, oil, herbs, etc., for steeping meat or fish; meat or fish so steeped. —*v.t.* to steep in a marinade. [French from Spanish (*marinar* = pickle in brine]

marinate /ˈmærɪneɪt/ *v.t.* to ˌmarinade. [from Italian or French]

marine /məˈriːn/ *adj.* **1.** of, found in, or produced by the sea. **2.** of shipping or naval matters. **3.** for use at sea. —*n.* **1.** a member of a corps trained to serve on land or sea. **2.** a country's shipping, fleet, or navy. [from Old French from Latin *marinus* (*mare* = sea)]

mariner /ˈmærɪnə/ *n.* a seaman. [from Anglo-French from Latin *marinarius* (*mare* = sea)]

Mariner spacecraft a series of US space probes that explored the planets Mercury, Venus, and Mars 1962–75.

marines *n.* a fighting force that operates both on land and at sea.

Marinetti /mæri'neti/ Filippo Tommaso 1876–1944. Italian author, who in 1909 published the first manifesto of ◊Futurism, which called for a break with tradition in art, poetry, and the novel, and glorified the machine age.

Marini /mə'ri:ni/ Marino 1901–1980. Italian sculptor. Inspired by ancient art, he developed a distinctive horse-and-rider theme and a dancers series, reducing the forms to an elemental simplicity. He also produced fine portraits in bronze.

marionette /mæriə'net/ *n.* a type of ◊puppet, a jointed figure controlled from above by wires or strings. Intricately crafted marionettes were used in Burma (now Myanmar) and Ceylon (now Sri Lanka) and later at the courts of Italian princes in the 16th–18th centuries. [from French (*Marion* diminutive of *Marie* = Mary)]

Mariotte Edme 1620–1684. French physicist and priest known for his recognition in 1676 of ◊Boyle's law about the inverse relationship of volume and pressure in gases, formulated in 1672. He had earlier, in 1660, discovered the eye's blind spot.

marital /'mærɪtəl/ *adj.* of marriage; of or between a husband and wife. —**maritally** *adv.* [from Latin (*maritus* = husband)]

maritime /'mærɪtaɪm/ *adj.* 1. situated or living or found near the sea. 2. connected with the sea or seafaring. [from Latin *maritimus* (*mare* = sea)]

maritime law that part of the law dealing with the sea: in particular, fishing areas, ships, and navigation. Seas are divided into **internal waters** governed by a state's internal laws (such as harbours, inlets); ◊territorial waters (the area of sea adjoining the coast over which a state claims rights); the **continental shelf** (the seabed and subsoil that the coastal state is entitled to exploit beyond the territorial waters); and the **high seas**, where international law applies.

Marivaux /mæri'vəʊ/ Pierre Carlet de Chamblain de 1688–1763. French novelist and dramatist. His sophisticated comedies include *Le Jeu de l'amour et du hasard/The Game of Love and Chance* 1730 and *Les Fausses confidences/False Confidences* 1737; his novel *La Vie de Marianne/The Life of Marianne* 1731–41 has autobiographical elements. Marivaux gave the word *marivaudage* (overly-subtle lovers' conversation) to the French language.

marjoram /'mɑːdʒərəm/ *n.* an aromatic herb of the genus *Origanum* or *Majorana*, used in cookery. Wild marjoram *Origanum vulgare* is found both in Europe and Asia and has become naturalized in the Americas; the culinary sweet marjoram *Origanum majorana* is widely cultivated. [from Old French from Latin *majorana*]

mark¹ *n.* 1. a line or area that visibly breaks the uniformity of a surface, especially one that spoils its appearance. 2. a written or printed symbol; this as an assessment of conduct or proficiency; a numerical unit awarded for merit in an examination etc. 3. something that indicates the presence of a quality or feeling. 4. a sign or symbol placed on a thing to identify it or indicate its origin. 5. a cross etc. made in place of a signature by an illiterate person. 6. a lasting effect or influence. 7. a target or other object to be aimed at; a desired object. 8. a line etc. serving to indicate a position; a standard; a runner's starting-point in a race. 9. (followed by a numeral) a particular type or design of equipment etc. —*v.t.* 1. to make a mark on. 2. to distinguish with a mark; to characterize. 3. to assign marks of merit to (a student's work etc.). 4. to attach figures indicating prices to (goods). 5. to notice, to watch carefully. 6. to keep close to (an opposing player) in football etc. so as to hamper him or her if he or she receives the ball. —**make one's mark,** to attain distinction. **mark down,** to make a written note of; to mark at a lower price. **mark-down** *n.* a reduction in price. **mark off,** to separate, to mark the limits of. **mark out,** to mark the boundaries of; to trace (a course); to destine; to single out. **mark time,** to move the feet as in marching but without advancing; to occupy time routinely while awaiting events or an opportunity. **mark up,** to mark at a higher price. **mark-up** *n.* an amount the seller adds to the cost-price of an article to cover the profit margin etc. **off the mark,** having made a start; irrelevant. **on the mark,** ready to start; relevant. [Old English]

mark² *n.* the currency unit of Germany (Deutschmark) and of Finland. [German]

Mark Antony *A great orator and soldier, Mark Antony committed suicide after his defeat at the battle of Actium in 31 BC.*

Mark Antony /'mɑːk 'æntəni/ Antonius, Marcus 83–30 BC. Roman politician and soldier. He was tribune and later consul under Julius Caesar, serving under him in Gaul. In 44 BC he tried to secure for Caesar the title of king. After Caesar's assassination, he formed the Second Triumvirate with Octavian (◊Augustus) and Lepidus. In 42 BC he defeated Brutus and Cassius at Philippi. He took Egypt as his share of the empire and formed a liaison with ◊Cleopatra. In 40 BC he returned to Rome to marry Octavia, the sister of Augustus. In 32 BC the Senate declared war on Cleopatra. Antony was defeated by Augustus at the battle of Actium 31 BC. He returned to Egypt and committed suicide.

marked *adj.* clearly noticeable or evident. —**marked man,** one singled out, especially as an object of attack etc. —**markedly** /-ɪdlɪ/ *adv.*

marker *n.* 1. a thing marking a position. 2. a person or thing that marks. 3. a scorer in a game etc.

market /'mɑːkɪt/ *n.* 1. a gathering for the purchase and sale of provisions, livestock, etc.; a space or building used for this. 2. a demand for a commodity or service; a place or group providing such a demand; the conditions as regards buying or selling; the opportunity for this. 3. the rate of purchase and sale. —*v.t./i.* to sell; to offer for sale; to buy or sell goods in a market. —**in the market for,** wishing to buy. **market-day** *n.* a day on which markets are regularly held. **market garden,** a place where vegetables are grown for market. **market-place** *n.* an open space where a market is held in a town; the scene of actual dealings. **market price,** the price in current dealings. **market research,** study of consumers' needs and preferences. **market town,** a town where a market is held. **market value,** the value as a saleable thing. **on the market,** offered for sale. [from Old Saxon from Latin *mercatus* (*mercari* = buy)]

marketable *adj.* able or fit to be sold.

marketing *n.* promoting goods and services to consumers. In the 20th century marketing has played an increasingly larger role in determining company policy, influencing product development, pricing, methods of distribution, advertising, and promotion techniques. Marketing skills are beginning to appear on the curriculum of some schools and colleges.

market maker in the UK, a stockbroker entitled to deal directly on the stock exchange. The role was created in Oct 1986, when the jobber (intermediary) disappeared from the stock exchange. Market makers trade in the dual capacity of broker and jobber.

Markevich /mɑːˈkjevɪtʃ/ Igor 1912–1983. Russian-born composer and conductor, who settled in Paris in 1927. He composed the ballet *L'Envol d'Icare* 1932, and the cantata *Le Paradis Perdu* 1933–35 to words by Milton. After World War II he concentrated on conducting.

Markievicz /ˈmɑːkjɪvɪtʃ/ Constance Georgina, Countess Markievicz (born Gore Booth) 1868–1927. Irish nationalist, who married the Polish count Markievicz in 1900. Her death sentence for taking part in the Easter Rising of 1916 was commuted, and after her release from prison in 1917 she was elected to the Westminster Parliament as a Sinn Féin candidate in 1918 (technically the first British woman member of Parliament), but did not take her seat.

marking *n.* 1. an indentification mark. 2. the colouring of an animal's fur or feathers etc.

Markov Georgi 1929–1978. Bulgarian playwright and novelist who fled to the UK in 1971; he was assassinated by being jabbed with a poisoned umbrella.

Markova /mɑːˈkəʊvə/ Alicia. Adopted name of Lilian Alicia Marks 1910– . British ballet dancer. Trained by ◊Pavlova, she was ballerina with ◊Diaghilev's company 1925–29, was the first resident ballerina of the Vic-Wells Ballet 1933–35, partnered Anton ◊Dolin in their own Markova-Dolin Company 1935–37, and danced with the Ballets Russes de Monte Carlo 1938–41 and Ballet Theatre, USA, 1941–46. She is associated with the great classical ballets, such as *Giselle*.

Marks /mɑːks/ Simon, 1st Baron of Broughton 1888–1964. English chain-store magnate. His father, Polish immigrant Michael Marks, had started a number of 'penny bazaars' with Yorkshireman Tom Spencer in 1887; Simon Marks entered the business in 1907 and built up a national chain of Marks and Spencer stores.

Mark, St /mɑːk/ 1st century AD. In the New Testament, Christian apostle and evangelist, whose name is given to the second Gospel. It was probably written AD 65–70, and used by the authors of the first and third Gospels. He is the patron saint of Venice, and his emblem is a winged lion; feast day 25 April.

marksman *n.* (*plural* **marksmen**) a skilled shot, especially with a rifle. —**marksmanship** *n.*

marl *n.* a soil consisting of clay and lime, used as a fertilizer. —*v.t.* to apply marl to. —**marly** *adj.* [from Old French from Latin *margila*]

Marlborough /ˈmɔːlbrə/ John Churchill, 1st Duke of Marlborough 1650–1722. English soldier, created a duke in 1702 by Queen Anne. He was granted the Blenheim mansion in Oxfordshire in recognition of his services, which included defeating the French army outside Vienna in the Battle of ◊Blenheim 1704, during the War of the ◊Spanish Succession.

Marley /ˈmɑːli/ Bob (Robert Nesta) 1945–1981. Jamaican reggae singer, a Rastafarian whose songs, many of which were topical and political, popularized reggae in the 1970s. One of his greatest hit songs is 'No Woman No Cry'; his albums include *Natty Dread* 1975 and *Exodus* 1977.

marlin *n.* or **spearfish** several genera of fish, family Istiophoridae, order Perciformes. Some 2.5 m/7 ft long, they are found in warmer waters, have elongated snouts, and high-standing dorsal fins.

marlinspike /ˈmɑːlɪnspaɪk/ *n.* a pointed tool used to separate strands of rope or wire. [from *marline* = line of two strands, from Dutch]

Marlowe /ˈmɑːləʊ/ Christopher 1564–1593. English poet and dramatist. His work includes the blank-verse plays *Tamburlaine the Great* about 1587, *The Jew of Malta* about 1589, *Edward II* and *Dr Faustus*, both about 1592, the poem *Hero and Leander* 1598, and a translation of Ovid's *Amores*.

Excess of wealth is cause of covetousness.
Christopher Marlowe
The Jew of Malta

---

marmalade /ˈmɑːməleɪd/ *n.* a preserve of citrus fruit (usually oranges) made like jam. [from French from Portuguese *marmelada* (*marmelo* = quince)]

Marmara /ˈmɑːmərə/ small inland sea separating Turkey in Europe from Turkey in Asia, connected through the Bosporus with the Black Sea, and through the Dardanelles with the Aegean; length 275 km/170 mi, breadth up to 80 km/50 mi.

Marmontel /ˈmɑːmɒnˈtel/ Jean François 1723–1799. French novelist and dramatist. He wrote tragedies and libretti, and contributed to the *Encyclopédie* (see ◊encyclopedia). In 1758 he obtained control of the journal *Le Mercure/The Mercury*, in which his *Contes moraux/Moral Studies* 1761 appeared. Other works include *Bélisaire/Belisarius* 1767 and *Les Incas/The Incas* 1777.

marmoreal /mɑːˈmɔːriəl/ *adj.* of or like marble. [from Latin]

marmoset /ˈmɑːməzet/ *n.* a small monkey of the family Callithricidae, found in South and Central America. Most species have characteristic tufted ears, bearlike claws, and a handsome tail, and some are fully grown when the body is only 18 cm/7 in. The tail is not prehensile. [from Old French *marmouset* = grotesque image]

marmot /ˈmɑːmət/ *n.* a large burrowing rodent of the genus *Marmota* which eats plants and insects. Marmots are found from the Alps to the Himalayas, and also in North America. They live in colonies, make burrows, one to each family, and hibernate. In North America they are called woodchucks or groundhogs. [from French probably from Romansch *murmont* from Latin = mouse of the mountain]

Marne, Battles of the /mɑːn/ in World War I, two unsuccessful German offensives along the Marne River to the east of Paris in France: **First Battle** 6–9 Sept 1914, von Moltke's advance was halted by the British Expeditionary Force and the French under Foch; **Second Battle** 15 July–4 Aug 1918, Ludendorff's advance was defeated by British, French, and US troops under the French general Pétain, and German morale crumbled.

marocain /ˈmærəkeɪn/ *n.* a kind of crêpe dress-fabric. [French = Moroccan]

Maronite /ˈmærənaɪt/ *n.* a member of a Christian sect deriving from refugee Monothelites (Christian heretics) of the 7th century. They were subsequently united with the Roman Catholic Church and number about 400,000 in Lebanon and Syria, with an equal number scattered in S Europe and the Americas.

maroon[1] /məˈruːn/ *adj.* brownish-crimson. —*n.* 1. brownish-crimson colour. 2. a kind of firework that explodes with a sound like a cannon, used as a warning signal. [from French *marron* = a chestnut]

maroon[2] *v.t.* 1. to put (a person) ashore in a desolate place and abandon him or her there. 2. to make unable to leave a place safely. [originally = fugitive slave living rough, from French from Spanish *cimarrón* = wild (*cima* = peak)]

Maroon *n.* in the West Indies and Suriname, a freed or escaped African slave. They were organized and armed by the Spanish in Jamaica in the late 17th century and early 18th century. They harried the British with guerrilla tactics.

marque /mɑːk/ *n.* a make of motor car, as opposed to a specific model. [French]

marquee /mɑːˈkiː/ *n.* a large tent used for a party or exhibition etc.

Marquesas Islands /mɑːˈkeɪzəz/ (French *Îles Marquises*) island group in ◊French Polynesia, lying N of the Tuamotu Archipelago; **area** 1,270 sq km/490 sq mi; **administrative headquarters** Atuona, on Hiva Oa **population** (1983) 6,500. The group was annexed by France in 1842.

marquess variant of **marquis**.

marquetry /ˈmɑːkɪtri/ *n.* the inlaying of various woods, bone, or ivory, usually on furniture, to create ornate patterns and pictures. **Parquetry** is the term used for geometrical inlaid patterns. [French *marqueter* = variegate]

Márquez Gabriel García see ◊García Márquez, Colombian novelist.

marquis /ˈmɑːkwɪs/ *n.* a nobleman ranking between a duke and (in the UK) an earl or (elsewhere) a count. [from Old French *marchis*]

marquise /mɑːˈkiːz/ *n.* (in foreign nobility) a marchioness. [French]

Marrakesh /ˈmærəˈkeʃ/ historic town in Morocco in the foothills of the Atlas mountains, about 210 km/130 mi S of Casablanca; population (1982) 549,000. It is a tourist centre, and has textile, leather, and food processing industries. Founded 1062, it has a medieval palace and mosques, and was formerly the capital of Morocco.

marram /'mærəm/ n. a coarse perennial grass *Ammophila arenaria*, flourishing on sandy areas. Because of its tough, creeping rootstocks, it is widely used to hold coastal dunes in place. [from Old Norse = sea-haulm]

Marrano /məˈrɑːnəʊ/ n. a Spanish or Portuguese Jew who, during the 14th and 15th centuries, converted to Christianity to escape death or persecution at the hands of the ◊Inquisition. Many continued to adhere secretly to Judaism and carry out Jewish rites. During the Spanish Inquisition thousands were burned at the stake as 'heretics'. [Spanish *marrano* = pig]

marriage /'mærɪdʒ/ n. 1. the legally or culturally sanctioned union of one man and one woman (monogamy); one man and two or more women (polygamy); one woman and two or more men (polyandry). There is generally an expectation that children will be born of the union to continue the family line. 2. an act or ceremony etc. establishing this condition. 3. a particular matrimonial union. —**marriage bureau,** an establishment arranging introductions between persons wishing to marry. **marriage certificate,** a certificate stating that a marriage ceremony has taken place. **marriage guidance,** the counselling of married couples who have problems in living together harmoniously. **marriage lines,** a marriage certificate. **marriage of convenience,** a marriage not made primarily for love. **marriage settlement,** an arrangement securing property to either party in a marriage. [from Old French]

marriageable adj. old enough to marry; (of an age) fit for marriage.

marron glacé /ˌmærɒn ˈɡlæseɪ/ a chestnut preserved in sugar as a sweet. [French = iced chestnut]

marrow /'mærəʊ/ n. 1. a gourd (the fruit of *Cucurbita pepo*) with whitish flesh, cooked as a vegetable. 2. the fatty substance in the cavities of bones. —**to the marrow,** right through. [Old English]

marrowbone n. a bone containing edible marrow.

marrowfat n. a kind of large pea.

marry /'mærɪ/ v.t./i. 1. to take, give, or join in marriage; to enter into a marriage. 2. to unite intimately, to correlate as a pair. [from Old French *marier* from Latin *maritus* = husband]

Mars /mɑːz/ 1. in Roman mythology, the god of war, after whom the month of March is named. He is equivalent to the Greek Ares. 2. the fourth planet from the Sun, average distance 227.8 million km/141.5 million mi. It revolves around the Sun in 687 Earth days, and has a rotation period of 24 hr 37 min. It is much smaller than Venus or Earth, with diameter 6,780 km/4,210 mi, and mass 0.11 that of Earth. Mars is slightly pear-shaped, with a low, level N hemisphere, which is comparatively uncratered and geologically 'young', and a heavily cratered 'ancient' S hemisphere.

Marsala /mɑːˈsɑːlə/ n. a dark, usually sweet, fortified wine. [from *Marsala* in Sicily]

Marseillaise, La /mɑːseɪˈeɪz/ the French national anthem; the words and music were composed in 1792 as a revolutionary song by the army officer Rouget de Lisle.

Marseille /mɑːˈseɪ/ the chief seaport of France, industrial centre (chemicals, oil refining, metallurgy, shipbuilding, food processing), and capital of the *département* of Bouches-du-Rhône, on the Golfe du Lion, Mediterranean Sea; population (1982) 1,111,000.

marsh /mɑːʃ/ n. low-lying watery land. —**marsh gas,** a gas consisting mostly of ◊methane, produced in swamps and marshes by the action of bacteria on dead vegetation. **marsh mallow,** a shrubby herb *Althaea officinalis*. **marsh marigold,** a plant *Caltha palustris* with golden flowers, growing in moist meadows. —**marshy** adj. [Old English]

Marsh Ngaio 1899–1982. New Zealand writer of detective fiction. Her first detective novel *A Man Lay Dead* 1934 introduced her protagonist Chief Inspector Roderick Alleyn.

marshal /'mɑːʃəl/ n. 1. a high-ranking officer of state or in the armed forces. 2. an official arranging ceremonies, controlling the procedure at races, etc. —v.t. (-ll-) 1. to arrange in due order. 2. to conduct (a person) ceremoniously. —**marshalling yard,** a railway yard in which goods trains etc. are assembled. **Marshal of the RAF,** the highest rank in the Royal Air Force. [from Old French *mareschal* from Latin]

Marshall /'mɑːʃəl/ George Catlett 1880–1959. US general and diplomat. He was army chief of staff in World War II, secretary of state 1947–49, and secretary of defence Sept 1950–Sept 1951. He initiated the **Marshall Plan** 1947 and received the Nobel Peace Prize 1953,

Marshall John Ross 1912–1988. New Zealand National Party politician, notable for his negotiations of a free-trade agreement with Australia. He was deputy to K J Holyoake as prime minister and succeeded him Feb–Nov 1972.

Marshall Islands the Radak (13 islands) and Ralik (11 islands) chains in the W Pacific; **area** 180 sq km/69 sq mi; **capital** Majuro; **features** include two atolls used for US atom-bomb tests 1946–63, Eniwetok and Bikini; and Kwajalein atoll (the largest) which has a US intercontinental missile range; **population** (1988) 41,000; **recent history** administered by Japan from 1919 until 1946, passed to the USA as part of the Pacific Islands Trust Territory in 1947. They were used for many atomic bomb tests during 1946–63, and the islanders are demanding compensation. In 1986 a compact of Free Association with the USA was signed, under which the islands manage their own internal and external affairs but the USA controls military activities in exchange for financial support.

Marshall Plan a programme of US financial aid to Europe, set up at the end of World War II, totalling $13,000 billion 1948–52. Officially known as the European Recovery Programme, it was announced by Secretary of State George Marshall in a speech at Harvard in June 1947, but it was in fact the work of a State Department group led by Dean ◊Acheson.

marshmallow n. a soft sweet made from sugar, albumen, gelatine, etc.

marsh marigold a plant *Caltha palustris* of the buttercup family Ranunculaceae, known as the kingcup in the UK and as the cowslip in the USA. It grows in moist sheltered spots and has five-sepalled flowers of a brilliant yellow.

Marston Moor, Battle of /'mɑːstən 'mʊə/ battle fought in the English Civil War on 2 July 1644 on Marston Moor, 11 km/7 mi W of York. The Royalists were completely defeated by the Parliamentarians and Scots.

marsupial /mɑːˈsuːpɪəl/ n. a mammal of the order Marsupialia, which includes the kangaroo and opossum. The young are born in a very undeveloped state and usually nourished in an external pouch on the mother's abdomen. —adj. of marsupials. [from Latin from Greek *marsupion* = pouch]

mart n. a trade centre; an auction-room, a market. [from obsolete Dutch = market]

marten /'mɑːtɪn/ n. a small carnivorous mammal belonging to the weasel family Mustelidae, genus *Martes*. Martens live in North America, Europe, and Asia. The **pine marten** (*Martes martes*) has long brown fur and is about 75 cm/2.5 ft long. It is found in Britain. [from Middle Dutch from Old French]

Martens /'mɑːtəns/ Wilfried 1936– . Prime minister of Belgium from 1979, member of the Social Christian Party. He was president of the Dutch-speaking CVP 1972–79 and, as prime minister, headed several coalition governments in the period from 1979.

martial /'mɑːʃəl/ adj. of or appropriate to warfare; warlike, brave, fond of fighting. —**martial arts,** styles of armed and unarmed combat developed in the East from ancient techniques and arts. Common martial arts include aikido, judo, jujitsu, karate, kendo, and kung fu. **martial law,** the replacement of civilian by military authorities in the maintenance of order, by which ordinary law is suspended. [from Old French or Latin *martialis* = of Mars, god of war]

Martial /'mɑːʃəl/ (Marcus Valerius Martialis) AD 41–104. Latin epigrammatist. His poetry, often bawdy, reflects contemporary Roman life.

Gifts are like hooks.

Marcus Valerius Martialis (Martial)
Epigrams

Martian /'mɑːʃən/ adj. of the planet Mars. —n. a hypothetical inhabitant of Mars. [from Old French or Latin]

martin /'mɑ:tɪn/ n. several genera of birds, related to the swallow, in the family Hirundinidae. The European house martin *Delichon urbica*, a summer migrant from Africa, is blue-black above and white below, distinguished from the swallow by its shorter, less forked tail.

Martin /'mɒ:tɪn/ five popes, including:

Martin V 1368–1431. Pope from 1417. A member of the Roman family of Colonna, he was elected during the Council of Constance, and ended the Great Schism between the rival popes of Rome and Avignon.

martinet /mɑ:ti'net/ n. a strict disciplinarian. [from J *Martinet*]

Martinet Jean died 1672. French inspector-general of infantry under Louis XIV, whose constant drilling brought the army to a high degree of efficiency.

martingale /'mɑ:tɪŋgeɪl/ n. a strap, or set of straps, fastened at one end to the nose-band and at the other end to the girth, to prevent a horse from rearing etc. [French]

Martini /mɑ:'ti:ni:/ n. trade name of a vermouth; a cocktail made of gin and vermouth. [from *Martini* & Rossi, firm selling vermouth]

Martinique /mɑ:ti'ni:k/ French island in the West Indies (Lesser Antilles); **area** 1,079 sq km/417 sq mi; **capital** Fort-de-France; **features** several active volcanoes; **population** (1984) 327,000; **history** Martinique was reached by Spanish navigators in 1493, and became a French colony in 1635; since 1972 it has been a French overseas region.

Martinmas n. in the Christian calendar, the feast of St Martin, 11 Nov.

Martins /'mɑ:tɪnz 'mɑ:tɪnz/ Peter 1946– . Danish-born US dancer, choreographer, and director, principal dancer with the New York City Ballet from 1965 and its joint director from 1983.

Martin, St /'mɑ:tɪn/ 316–400. Bishop of Tours, France, from about 371, and founder of the first monastery in Gaul. He is usually represented as tearing his cloak to share it with a beggar. His feast day is Martinmas, 11 Nov.

Martinu /'mɑ:tɪnu:/ Bohuslav (Jan) 1890–1959. Czech composer, who studied in Paris. He left Czechoslovakia after the Nazi occupation of 1939. The quality of his music varies but at its best it is richly expressive and has great vitality. His works include the operas *Julietta* 1937 and *The Greek Passion* 1959, symphonies, and chamber music.

martyr /'mɑ:tə/ n. one who voluntarily suffers death for refusing to renounce a religious faith; one who undergoes death or suffering for any great cause. —v.t. 1. to put to death as a martyr. 2. to torment. —**martyr to,** a constant sufferer from (an ailment). [Old English from Latin from Greek, originally = witness]

martyrdom n. the sufferings and death of a martyr; torment.

martyrology /mɑ:tə'rɒlədʒɪ/ n. a list or history of martyrs. —**martyrologist** n. [from Latin from Greek]

marvel /'mɑ:vəl/ n. a wonderful thing; a wonderful example. —v.i. (-ll-) to feel surprise or wonder. [from Old French *merveille* from Latin *mirabilis* (*mirari* = wonder at)]

Marvell /'mɑ:vəl/ Andrew 1621–1678. English metaphysical poet and satirist. His poems include 'To His Coy Mistress' and 'Horatian Ode upon Cromwell's Return from Ireland'. He was committed to the parliamentary cause, and was member of Parliament for Hull from 1659. He devoted his last years mainly to verse satire and prose works attacking repressive aspects of government.

marvellous /'mɑ:vələs/ adj. astonishing; excellent. —**marvellously** adv. [from Old French]

Marvin /'mɑ:vɪn/ Lee 1924–1987. US film actor who began his career playing violent, often psychotic villains and progressed to playing violent, occasionally psychotic heroes. His work includes *The Big Heat* 1953, *The Killers* 1964, and *Cat Ballou* 1965.

Marx /mɑ:ks/ Karl (Heinrich) 1818–1883. German philosopher, economist, and social theorist whose account of change through conflict is known as historical, or dialectical, materialism (see ◊Marxism). His ◊*Das Kapital/Capital* 1867–95 is the fundamental text of Marxist economics, and his systematic theses on class struggle, history, and the importance of economic factors in politics have exercised an enormous influence on later thinkers and political activists.

Marx Brothers US film comedians Leonard '**Chico**' (from the 'chicks' (girls) he chased) 1891–1961; Arthur (**Adolph**) '**Harpo**' (from the harp he played) 1893–1964;

Mary Portrait of Mary, Queen of Scots, after Nicholas Hilliard (c.1610) National Portrait Gallery, London.

Julius '**Groucho**' 1890–1977; Milton '**Gummo**' (from his gumshoes or galoshes) 1894–1977, who left the team early on; and Herbert '**Zeppo**' (born at the time of the first zeppelins) 1901–1979, part of the team until 1934. Their films include *Animal Crackers* 1932, *Duck Soup* 1933, *A Night at the Opera* 1935, and *Go West* 1937.

Marxism /'mɑ:ksɪzəm/ n. the political and economic theory of the German socialist philosopher Karl Marx, predicting the violent overthrow of the capitalist class and the taking over of the means of production by the proletariat. —**Marxist** n. [from K *Marx*]

Mary /'meəri/ in the New Testament, the mother of Jesus through divine intervention (see ◊Annunciation), wife of ◊Joseph. The Roman Catholic Church maintains belief in her ◊Immaculate Conception and bodily assumption into heaven, and venerates her as a mediator. Feast day of the Assumption 15 Aug.

Mary Queen of Scots 1542–1587. Queen of Scotland 1542–67. Also known as **Mary Stuart**, she was the daughter of James V. Mary's connection with the English royal line from Henry VII made her a threat to Elizabeth I's hold on the English throne, especially as she represented a champion of the Catholic cause. She was married three times. After her forced abdication she was imprisoned but escaped in 1568 to England. Elizabeth I held her prisoner, while the Roman Catholics, who regarded Mary as rightful queen of England, formed many conspiracies to place her on the throne, and for complicity in one of these she was executed.

Mary Duchess of Burgundy 1457–1482. Daughter of Charles the Bold. She married Maximilian of Austria in 1477, thus bringing the Low Countries into the possession of the Habsburgs and, ultimately, of Spain.

Mary Queen 1867–1953. Consort of George V of the UK. The daughter of the Duke and Duchess of Teck, the latter a grand-daughter of George II, in 1891 she became engaged to the Duke of Clarence, eldest son of the Prince of Wales (later Edward VII). After his death in 1892, she married in 1893 his brother George, Duke of York, who succeeded to the throne in 1910.

Mary two queens of England:

Mary I Bloody Mary 1516–1558. Queen of England from 1553. She was the eldest daughter of Henry VIII by Catherine of Aragon. When Edward VI died, Mary secured the crown without difficulty in spite of the conspiracy to substitute Lady Jane ◊Grey. In 1554 Mary married Philip II of Spain, and as a devout Roman Catholic obtained the restoration of papal supremacy and sanctioned the persecution of Protestants. She was succeeded by her half-sister Elizabeth I.

Mary II 1662–1694. Queen of England, Scotland, and Ireland from 1688. She was the Protestant elder daughter of the Catholic ◊James II, and in 1677 was married to her cousin ◊William III of Orange. After the 1688 revolution she accepted the crown jointly with William.

Maryland /'meərɪlænd/ state of the E USA; nickname Old Line State or Free State; **area** 31,600 sq km/12,198 sq mi; **capital** Annapolis; **population** (1986) 4,463,000; **history** one of the original Thirteen Colonies, first settled in 1634; it became a state 1788.

Mary Magdalene, St /mægdə'li:ni/ 1st century AD. In the New Testament, woman whom Jesus cured of possession by evil spirits, was present at the Crucifixion and burial, and was the first to meet the risen Jesus. She is often identified with the woman of St Luke's gospel who anointed Jesus' feet, and her symbol is a jar of ointment; feast day 22 July.

Mary of Modena /'mɒdɪnə/ 1658–1718. Queen consort of England and Scotland. She was the daughter of the Duke of Modena, Italy, and married James, Duke of York, later James II, in 1673. The birth of their son James Francis Edward Stuart was the signal for the revolution of 1688 that overthrew James II. Mary fled to France.

Mary Poppins /'pɒpɪnz/ a collection of children's stories by P(amela) L Travers (1906–   ), published in the UK 1934. They feature the eccentric Mary Poppins who looks after the children of the Banks family and entertains her charges by using her magical powers. Sequels include *Mary Poppins Comes Back* 1935.

Mary Rose greatest warship of Henry VIII of England, which sank off Southsea, Hampshire, on 19 July 1545. The wreck was located in 1971, and raised in 1982 for preservation in dry dock in Portsmouth harbour.

marzipan /'mɑːzɪpæn/ n. a paste of ground almonds, sugar, etc. [German from Italian]

Masaccio /mə'zætʃəʊ/ (Tomaso di Giovanni di Simone Guidi) 1401–1428. Florentine painter, a leader of the early Italian Renaissance. His frescoes in Sta Maria del Carmine, Florence, 1425–28, which he painted with Masolino da Panicale (about 1384–1447), show a decisive break with Gothic conventions. He was the first painter to apply the scientific laws of perspective, newly discovered by the architect Brunelleschi.

Masaryk /'mæsərɪk/ Jan (Garrigue) 1886–1948. Czechoslovak politician, son of Tomáš Masaryk. He was foreign minister from 1940, when the Czechoslovak government was exiled in London in World War II. He returned in 1945, retaining the post, but as a result of political pressure by the communists committed suicide.

Masaryk Tomáš (Garrigue) 1850–1937. Czechoslovak nationalist politician. He directed the revolutionary movement against the Austrian Empire, founding with Eduard Beneš and Stefanik the Czechoslovak National Council, and in 1918 was elected first president of the newly formed Czechoslovak Republic. Three times re-elected, he resigned in 1935 in favour of Beneš.

Mascagni /mæs'kuːnji/ Pietro 1863-1945. Italian composer of the one-act opera *Cavalleria rusticana/Rustic Chivalry*, first produced in Rome in 1890.

mascara /mæ'skaːrə/ n. a cosmetic for darkening the eyelashes etc. [Italian = mask]

mascot /'mæskɒt/ n. a person or animal or thing supposed to bring luck. [from French from Provençal *masco* = witch]

masculine /'mæskjʊlɪn/ adj. 1. of men; having the qualities appropriate to a man. 2. in grammar, of the gender proper to men's names. 3. (of a rhyme or line-ending) having a final stressed syllable. —n. in grammar, the masculine gender; a masculine word. —**masculinity** /-'lɪnɪtɪ/ n. [from Old French from Latin]

Masefield /'meɪsfiːld/ John 1878–1967. English poet and novelist. Early volumes of poetry such as *Salt Water Ballads* 1902 were followed by *The Everlasting Mercy* 1911, a long verse narrative characterized by its forcefully colloquial language, and *Reynard the Fox* 1919. His other works include the novel *Sard Harker* 1924, the critical work *Badon Parchments* 1947, the children's book *The Box of Delights* 1935, and plays. He was poet laureate from 1930.

maser /'meɪzə(r)/ acronym from microwave amplification by stimulated emission of radiation. In physics, a device for amplifying microwaves in which the signal to be amplified is used to stimulate unstable atoms into emitting energy at the same frequency. Atoms or molecules are raised to a higher energy level and then allowed to lose this energy

by radiation emitted at a precise frequency. The principle has been extended to other parts of the electromagnetic spectrum as, for example, in the ◊laser.

Maserati /mæzə'rɑːti/ n. Italian racing-car company, founded 1926 by the six Maserati brothers. The most outstanding Maserati was the 250F Grand Prix car, which the Argentine Juan Manuel Fangio drove during his world championship-winning year 1957. The company withdrew from Grand Prix racing at the end of 1957.

Maseru /mə'seəru:/ capital of Lesotho, South Africa, on the Caledon river; population (1986) 289,000. It is a centre for trade and diamond processing.

mash n. 1. a soft or confused mixture; a mixture of boiled grain, bran, etc., used as animal food. 2. (colloquial) mashed potatoes. 3. a mixture of malt and hot water used in brewing. —v.t. 1. to reduce (potatoes etc.) to a uniform mass by crushing; to crush to a pulp. 2. to mix (malt) with hot water. [Old English]

Mashraq /mæʃ'rɑːk/ the Arab countries of the E Mediterranean: Egypt, Sudan, Jordan, Syria, and Lebanon. The term is contrasted with ◊Maghreb, comprising the Arab countries of NW Africa. [Arabic = east]

Masire /mæ'siərei/ Quett Ketumile Joni 1925–   . President of Botswana from 1980. In 1962, with Seretse ◊Khama, he founded the Botswana Democratic Party (BDP) and in 1965 was made deputy prime minister. After independence, in 1966, he became vice president and, on Khama's death in 1980, president, continuing a policy of nonalignment.

mask /mɑːsk/ n. 1. a covering for all or part of the face, worn as a disguise, for protection, or (by a surgeon etc.) to prevent infection of the patient. 2. a respirator used to filter inhaled air or to supply gas for inhalation. 3. a likeness of a person's face, especially (as *death-mask*) one made by taking a mould from the face. 4. a disguise or pretence. —v.t. to cover or disguise with a mask; to conceal or protect. —**masking tape,** adhesive tape used in painting to cover areas on which paint is not wanted. [from French *masque* from Italian from Arabic = buffoon]

Maskelyne /'mæskəlɪn/ Nevil 1732–1811. English astronomer, who accurately measured the distance from the Earth to the Sun by observing a transit of Venus across the Sun's face 1769. In 1774 he measured the mass of the Earth by noting the deflection of a plumb line near Mount Schiehallion in Scotland.

masochism /'mæsəkɪzəm/ n. 1. a desire to subject oneself to physical or mental pain, humiliation, or punishment, for erotic pleasure, to alleviate guilt, or out of destructive impulses turned inwards. 2. (colloquial) enjoyment of what appears to be painful or tiresome. —**masochist** n., **masochistic** /-'kɪstɪk/ adj. [from L von Sacher-*Masoch*, Austrian novelist (died 1895)]

mason /'meɪsən/ n. 1. one who builds with stone. 2. **Mason,** a Freemason. [from Old French *masson*]

Mason James 1909–1984. English actor who portrayed romantic villains in British films of the 1940s. After *Odd Man Out* 1947 he worked in the USA, notably in *A Star is Born* 1954. Other films include *The Wicked Lady* 1946, *Lolita* 1962, and *Cross of Iron* 1977.

Mason–Dixon Line /'meɪsən 'dɪksən/ in the USA, the boundary line between Maryland and Pennsylvania (latitude 39° 43′ 26.3μ N), named after Charles Mason (1730–87) and Jeremiah Dixon (died 1777), English astronomers and surveyors who surveyed it 1763–67. It was popularly seen as dividing the North from the South.

Masonic /mə'sɒnɪk/ adj. of Freemasons.

masonry /'meɪsənrɪ/ n. 1. a mason's work; stonework. 2. **Masonry,** Freemasonry.

masque /mɑːsk/ n. an amateur dramatic and musical entertainment especially in the 16th–17th century, with scenery and elaborate costumes, originally in dumb show but later with metrical dialogue; a dramatic composition for this.

masquerade /mɑːskə'reɪd/ n. 1. a false show, a pretence. 2. a ball at which the guests wear masks. —v.i. to appear in disguise, to assume a false appearance. [from Spanish *mascara* = mask]

mass[1] /mæs/ n. 1. a coherent body of matter of indefinite shape. 2. a dense aggregation of objects. 3. (in *singular* or *plural*) a large number or amount. 4. an unbroken expanse of colour etc. 5. the quantity of matter a body contains, measured in terms of resistance to acceleration by a force (i.e., its inertia). —*v.t./i.* to gather into a mass; to assemble into one body. —*adj.* of or relating to large numbers of persons or things, large-scale. —**the mass**, the majority. **the masses**, the ordinary people. **in the mass**, in the aggregate. **mass media**, means of communication (e.g. newspapers or broadcasting) to large numbers of people. **mass meeting**, a large assembly of people. [from Old French from Latin *massa* from Greek *maza* = barley-cake]

mass[2] /mæs, mɑːs/ *n.* a celebration of the Eucharist, now especially in the Roman Catholic and High Church; the liturgy used in this; a musical setting for parts of it. [Old English from Latin *missa* (*mittere* = dismiss), perhaps from the concluding words *Ite, missa est*]

Massachusetts /mæsə'tʃuːsɪts/ New England state of the USA; nickname Bay State or Old Colony; **area** 21,500 sq km/8,299 sq mi; **capital** Boston; **population** (1985) 5,819,000; **history** one of the original ◊Thirteen Colonies, it was first settled in 1620 by the Pilgrims at Plymouth, and became a state 1788.

massacre /'mæsəkə/ *n.* 1. a general slaughter (of persons, occasionally of animals). 2. utter defeat or destruction. —*v.t.* to make a massacre of; to murder (a large number of people) cruelly or violently. [French]

massage /'mæsɑːʒ/ *n.* the rubbing, kneading, etc., of the muscles and joints of the body with the hands, to stimulate their action, cure strains, etc. —*v.t.* 1. to treat (a part or person) thus. 2. to manipulate the presentation of (figures, data, etc.) so as to give a more acceptable result. [French]

mass–energy equation ◊Einstein's equation $E = mc^2$, denoting the equivalence of mass and energy, where E is the energy in joules, m is the mass in kilograms, and c is the speed of light, in a vacuum, in metres per second.

Massenet /mæsə'neɪ/ Jules Emile Frédéric 1842–1912. French composer of opera, ballets, oratorios, and orchestral suites.

masseur /mæ'sɜː/ *n.* one who provides massage professionally. —**masseuse** /-'sɜːz/ *n. fem.* [French]

Massey /'mæsi/ Vincent 1887–1967. Canadian Liberal Party politician. He was the first Canadian to become governor general of Canada (1952–59).

massif /'mæsiːf, -'siːf/ *n.* mountain heights forming a compact group. [French]

Massif Central /sɒn'trɑːl/ mountainous plateau region of S central France; area 93,000 sq km/36,000 sq mi, highest peak Puy de Sancy 1,886 m/6,188 ft. It is a source of hydroelectricity.

Massine /mæ'siːn/ Léonide 1895–1979. Russian choreographer and dancer with the Ballets Russes. He was a creator of comedy in ballet and also symphonic ballet using concert music.

massive /'mæsɪv/ *adj.* 1. large and heavy or solid. 2. substantial, unusually large. —**massiveness** *n.* [from French *massif*]

mass number = ◊nucleon number.

Masson /'mæsɒ/ André 1896–1987. French artist and writer, a leader of Surrealism until 1929. His interest in the unconscious led him to experiment with 'automatic' drawing—simple pen and ink work, and later multi-textured accretions of pigment, glue, and sand.

Massorah /mə'sɔːrə/ *n.* a collection of philological notes on the Hebrew text of the Old Testament. It was at first an oral tradition, but was committed to writing in the Aramaic language at Tiberias, Palestine, between the 6th and 9th centuries.

mass production the manufacture of goods on a large scale, a technique that aims for low unit cost and high output. In factories mass production is achieved by a variety of means, such as division and specialization of labour and mechanization. These speed up production and allow the manufacture of near-identical, interchangeable parts. Such parts can then be assembled quickly into a finished product on an ◊assembly line.

mass spectrometer in physics, an apparatus for analysing chemical composition. Positive ions (charged particles) of a substance are separated by an electromagnetic system, which permits accurate measurement of the relative concentrations of the various ionic masses present, particularly isotopes.

mast[1] /mɑːst/ *n.* 1. a long, upright post set up on a ship's keel to support the sails. 2. a post or lattice-work upright to support a radio or television aerial. 3. a flag-pole. —**before the mast**, as an ordinary sailor. —**masted** *adj.* [Old English]

mast[2] *n.* the fruit of the beech, oak, etc., especially as food for pigs. [Old English]

mastectomy /mæ'stektəmɪ/ *n.* surgical removal of a breast. [from Greek *mastos* = breast]

master /'mɑːstə/ *n.* 1. a person having control of people or things, especially an employer; the male head of a household or of a college etc.; the male owner of an animal or slave; (in full **master mariner**) the captain of a merchant ship. 2. a male teacher or tutor, a schoolmaster. 3. one who has or gets the upper hand. 4. a skilled workman, or one in business on his own account. 5. a holder of a master's degree from a university, originally giving the holder authority to teach in a university; a revered teacher in philosophy etc. 6. a great artist; a picture by one. 7. a chess player of proved ability at international level. 8. a thing from which a series of copies (e.g. of a film or gramophone record) is made. 9. **Master**, a title prefixed to the name of a boy not old enough to be called *Mr.* —*adj.* 1. commanding, superior. 2. main, principal. 3. controlling others. —*v.t.* 1. to overcome, to bring under control. 2. to acquire knowledge or skill in. —**master key** a key that opens several locks, each also having its own key. **Master of Ceremonies**, a person in charge of a ceremonial or social occasion, a person introducing the speakers at a banquet or the performers at a variety show. Record Office. **master stroke** *n.* an outstandingly skilful act of policy etc. **master switch** *n.* a switch controlling the electricity etc. supply to an entire system. [Old English from Latin *magister*]

masterful *adj.* 1. imperious, domineering. 2. masterly. —**masterfully** *adv.*

masterly *adj.* worthy of a master; very skilful.

mastermind *n.* 1. a person with an outstanding intellect. 2. a person directing an intricate operation. —*v.t.* to plan and direct (a scheme).

Master of the King's/Queen's Musick appointment to the British royal household, the holder composing appropriate music for state occasions. The first was Nicholas Lanier, appointed by Charles I in 1626; the composer Malcolm ◊Williamson was appointed in 1975.

Master of the Rolls title of an English judge ranking immediately below the Lord Chief Justice. The Master of the Rolls presides over the Court of Appeal, besides being responsible for ◊Chancery records and for the admission of solicitors.

masterpiece *n.* an outstanding piece of artistry; one's best work. [probably from Dutch or German, originally denoting the piece of work by which a craftsman gained from his guild the recognized rank of 'master']

Masters /'mɑːstəz/ Edgar Lee 1869–1950. US poet. In his *Spoon River Anthology* 1915, a collection of free-verse epitaphs, the people of a small town tell of their frustrated lives.

mastery /'mɑːstərɪ/ *n.* 1. complete control, supremacy. 2. masterly skill or knowledge. [from Old French]

masthead *n.* 1. the highest part of a ship's mast. 2. the title details of a newspaper at the head of its front or editorial page.

mastic /'mæstɪk/ *n.* 1. a gum or resin exuded from certain trees (especially *Pistacia lentiscus*). 2. a type of cement. [from Old French from Latin from Greek]

masticate /'mæstɪkeɪt/ *v.t.* to grind (food) with the teeth, to chew. —**mastication** /-'keɪʃən/ *n.*, **masticatory** *adj.* [from Latin from Greek *mastikhaō* = gnash the teeth]

mastiff /'mæstɪf/ *n.* a British dog, usually fawn in colour, originally bred for sporting purposes. It has a large head, wide-set eyes, and broad muzzle. It can grow up to 90 cm/ 3 ft at the shoulder, and weigh 100 kg/220 lb. [ultimately from Old French *mastin* from Latin *mansuetus* = tame]

mastodon /'mæstədɒn/ *n.* a large extinct animal of the genus *Mammut*, whose fossil remains have been discovered in all the continents except Australia, chiefly in deposits from the Pleistocene Age in the USA and Canada. It resembled the modern elephant, but was lower and longer; its teeth suggest that it ate leaves in the primeval swamps and forests. [from Greek *mastos* = breast and *odous* = tooth, from the nipple-shaped tubercles on its molars]

mastoid /'mæstɔɪd/ *adj.* shaped like a woman's breast.

—*n.* the conical prominence on the temporal bone behind the ear (also **mastoid process**); (*colloquial*, usually in *plural*) inflammation of this. [from French from Greek *mastos* = breast]

Mastroianni /mæstrɔɪ'aːni/ Marcello 1924– . Italian film actor, most popular for his carefully understated roles as an unhappy romantic lover in such films as Antonioni's *La Notte/The Night* 1961. He starred in several films with Sophia Loren such as *A Special Day* 1977 and worked with Fellini in *La dolce vita* 1960, *8½* 1963, *Roma* 1971, and *Ginger and Fred* 1985.

masturbate /'mæstəbeɪt/ *v.t./i.* to produce sexual orgasm or arousal (of) by stimulation of the genitals other than by sexual intercourse. —**masturbation** /-'beɪʃən/ *n.*, **masturbatory** *adj.* [from Latin]

mat[1] *n.* **1.** a piece of coarse material as a floor-covering or for wiping shoes on, especially a doormat. **2.** a piece of cork, rubber, plastic, etc., to protect a surface from the heat or moisture of an object placed on it. **3.** a piece of resilient material for landing on in gymnastics or wrestling. —*v.t./i.* (-tt-) **1.** to make or become entangled in a thick mass. **2.** to cover or furnish with mats. —**on the mat**, (*slang*) being reprimanded. [Old English, from Latin *matta*]

mat[2] variant of ◊**matt**.

matador /'mætədɔː/ *n.* a bullfighter whose task is to kill the bull. [Spanish *matar* = kill, from Persian]

Mata Hari /'maːtə 'haːri/ stage name of Gertrud Margarete Zelle 1876–1917. Dutch courtesan, dancer, and probable spy. In World War I she had affairs with highly placed military and government officials on both sides and told Allied secrets to the Germans. She may have been a double agent, in the pay of both France and Germany. She was shot by the French on espionage charges.

matamata *n.* a South American freshwater turtle or terrapin *Chelys fimbriata* with a shell up to 40 cm/15 in long.

match[1] *n.* **1.** a contest or game of skill etc. in which persons or teams compete against each other. **2.** a competitor able to contend with another as an equal; a person equal to another in some quality. **3.** a person or thing exactly like or corresponding to another. **4.** a marriage. **5.** a person viewed in regard to eligibility for marriage. —*v.t./i.* **1.** to be equal; to correspond in some essential respect. **2.** to place in competition or conflict. **3.** to find a material etc. that matches (another). **4.** to find a person or thing suitable for another. —**match point**, the state of a game when one side needs only one more point to win the match; this point. [Old English = companion]

match[2] *n.* **1.** a short thin piece of wood etc. tipped with a composition that bursts into flame when rubbed on a rough or specially prepared surface. **2.** a fuse for firing a cannon etc. [from Old French *mesche*]

matchboard *n.* a board with a tongue cut along one edge and a groove along the other, so as to fit with similar boards.

matchbox *n.* a box for holding matches.

matchless *adj.* incomparable.

matchmaker *n.* a person fond of scheming to bring about marriages. —**matchmaking** *adj.* & *n.*

matchstick *n.* the stem of a match.

matchwood *n.* **1.** wood suitable for making matches. **2.** wood reduced to minute splinters.

mate[1] *n.* **1.** a companion, a fellow worker; (*colloquial*) a general form of address to an equal. **2.** one of a pair, especially of birds; (*colloquial*) a partner in marriage. **3.** a subordinate officer on a merchant ship. **4.** an assistant to a worker. —*in combinations*, a fellow member or joint occupant of (*team-mate, room-mate*). —*v.t./i.* **1.** to bring or come together in marriage or for breeding. **2.** to put or come together as a pair or as corresponding. [from Middle Low German]

mate[2] *n.* a ◊**checkmate**. —*v.t.* to checkmate. [from French *mat(er)*]

maté *n.* dried leaves of the Brazilian ◊**holly** *Ilex paraguensis*, an evergreen shrub that grows in Paraguay and Brazil. The roasted, powdered leaves are made into a tea.

mater /'meɪtə/ *n.* (*archaic slang*) mother. [Latin]

material /mə'tɪərɪəl/ *n.* **1.** the substance or things from which something is or can be made; (in *plural*) the things needed for an activity. **2.** a person or thing suitable for a specified purpose. **3.** cloth, fabric. **4.** information etc. to be used in writing a book etc. —*adj.* **1.** of matter; consisting of

matter; of the physical (as opposed to spiritual) world. **2.** of bodily comfort etc. **3.** important, significant, relevant. [from Old French from Latin]

materialism *n.* **1.** the tendency to prefer material possessions and physical comfort to spiritual values. **2.** the theory that nothing exists but matter and its movements and modifications. Such a theory excludes the possibility of deities. It also sees mind as an attribute of the physical, denying idealist theories that see mind as something independent of body; for example, Descartes' theory of 'thinking substance'. —**materialist** *n.*, **materialistic** /-'lɪstɪk/ *adj.*

materialize *v.t./i.* **1.** to become a fact, to happen. **2.** to appear, to become visible. **3.** to represent in or assume bodily form. —**materialization** /-'zeɪʃən/ *n.*

materially *adv.* substantially, considerably.

maternal /mə'tɜːnəl/ *adj.* **1.** of or like a mother, motherly. **2.** related through one's mother. **3.** of the mother in pregnancy and childbirth. —**maternally** *adv.* [from Old French or Latin *maternus* (*mater* = mother)]

maternity /mə'tɜːnɪti/ *n.* **1.** motherhood. **2.** motherliness. **3.** (*attributive*) for women in pregnancy or childbirth. [from French from Latin]

matey /'meɪti/ *adj.* sociable, familiar and friendly. —*n.* (*colloquial*, as a form of address) mate. —**matily** *adv.*, **matiness** *n.*

mathematical /mæθɪ'mætɪkəl/ *adj.* of or involving mathematics. —**mathematically** *adv.*

mathematical induction a formal method of proof in which the proposition $P(n + 1)$ is proved true on the hypothesis that the proposition $P(n)$ is true. The proposition is then shown to be true for a particular value of n, say k, and therefore by induction the proposition must be true for $n = k + 1, k + 2, k + 3, \ldots$. In many cases $k = 1$, so then the proposition is true for all positive integers.

mathematician /mæθɪmə'tɪʃən/ *n.* one who is skilled in mathematics.

mathematics /mæθɪ'mætɪks/ *n.pl.* (also treated as *singular*) **1.** the science of spatial and numerical relationships. The main divisions of **pure mathematics** include geometry, arithmetic, algebra, calculus, and trigonometry. Mechanics, statistics, numerical analysis, computing, the mathematical theories of astronomy, electricity, optics, thermodynamics, and atomic studies come under the heading of **applied mathematics**. **2.** (as *plural*) the use of this in calculation etc. [from French from Latin from Greek *mathēma* = science from *manthanō* = learn]

Mather /'meɪθə/ Cotton 1663–1728. US theologian and writer. He was a Puritan minister in Boston, and wrote over 400 works of history, science, annals, and theology, including *Magnalia Christi American/The Great Works of Christ in America* 1702, a vast compendium of early New England history and experience. Mather appears to have supported the Salem witch-hunts.

maths /mæθs/ (*colloquial*) abbreviation of mathematics.

Matilda /mə'tɪldə/ 1102–1167. Claimant to the throne of England. On the death of her father, Henry I, in 1135, the barons elected her cousin Stephen to be king. Matilda invaded England 1139, and was crowned by her supporters 1141. Civil war ensued until in 1153 Stephen was finally recognized as king, with Henry II (Matilda's son) as his successor.

matinée /'mætɪneɪ/ *n.* an afternoon performance at a theatre or cinema. —**matinée coat**, a baby's short coat. [French = what occupies a morning]

matins /'mætɪnz/ *n.pl.* the service of morning prayer, especially in the Church of England. [from Old French from Latin *matutinus* = of morning]

Matisse /mæ'tiːs/ Henri 1869–1954. French painter, sculptor, illustrator, and designer; one of the most original creative forces in early 20th-century art. His work concentrates on designs that emphasize curvaceous surface patterns, linear arabesques, and brilliant colour. Subjects include odalisques (women of the harem), bathers, and dancers; later, purely abstract works include collages of coloured paper shapes and the designs 1949–51 for the decoration of a chapel for the Dominican convent in Vence, near Nice.

mathematics

$a \rightarrow b$	a implies b
∞	infinity
lim	limiting value
$a \sim b$	numerical difference between a and b
$a \approx b$	a approximately equal to b
$a = b$	a equal to b
$a \equiv b$	a identical with b (for formulae only)
$a > b$	a greater than b
$a < b$	a smaller than b
$a \neq b$	a not equal to b
$b < a < c$	a greater than b and smaller than c, that is a lies between the values b & c but cannot equal either.
$a \geq b$	a equal to or greater than b, that is, a at least as great as b
$a \leq b$	a equal to or less than b, that is, a at most as great as b
$b \leq a < c$	a lies between the values b & c and could take the values b and c.
$\|a\|$	absolute value of a; this is always positive, for example $\|-5\| = 5$
$+$	addition sign, positive
$-$	subtraction sign, negative
$\times$ or $\odot$	multiplication sign, times
: or $\div$ or /	division sign, divided by
$a + b = c$	$a+b$, read as 'a plus b', denotes the addition of a and b. The result of the addition, c, is also known as the sum.
$\int$	indefinite integral
$\int_a^b f(x)dx$	definite integral, or integral between $x=a$ and $x=b$
$a - b = c$	$a-b$, read as 'a minus b', denotes subtraction of b from a. $a-b$, or c, is the difference. Subtraction is the opposite of addition.
$a \times b = c$ $ab = c$ $a.b = c$	$a \times b$, read as 'a multiplied by b', denotes multiplication of a by b. $a \times b$, or c, is the product, a and b are factors of c.
$a : b = c$ $a \div b = c$	$a:c$, read as 'a divided by b', denotes division. a is the dividend, b is the divisor; $a:b$, or c, is the quotient. One aspect of division – repeated subtraction, is the opposite of multiplication – repeated addition.
$a/b = c$	In fractions, or a/b, a is the numerator (= dividend), b the denominator (= divisor).
$a^b = c$	a^b, read as 'a to the power b'; a is the base, b the exponent.
$^b\sqrt{a} = c$	$^b\sqrt{a}$, is the bth root of a, b being known as the root exponent. In the special case of $^2\sqrt{a}=c$, $^2\sqrt{a}$ or c is known as the square root of a, and the root exponent is usually omitted, that is, $^2\sqrt{a} = \sqrt{a}$.
e	exponential constant and is the base of natural (napierian) logarithms = 2.7182818284.......
π	ratio of the circumference of a circle to its diameter = 3.1415925535........

There is nothing more difficult for a truly creative painter than to paint a rose, because before he can do so he has first to forget all the roses that were ever painted..

Henri Matisse

Mato Grosso /ˈmætəu ˈɡrɒsəu/ area of SW Brazil, now forming two states, with their capitals at Cuiaba and Campo Grande. The forests, now depleted, supplied rubber and rare timbers; diamonds and silver are mined. [Portuguese = dense forest]

matriarch /ˈmeɪtriɑːk/ *n.* a woman who is head of a family or tribe. —**matriarchal** /-ˈɑːkəl/ *adj.* [from Latin *mater* = mother]

matriarchy /ˈmeɪtriɑːkɪ/ *n.* a form of social organization in which women head the family, and descent and relationship are reckoned through the female line. Matriarchy, often associated with polyandry (one wife with several husbands), occurs in certain parts of India, in the South Pacific, Central Africa, and among some North American Indian peoples. In matrilineal societies, powerful positions are usually held by men but acceded to through female kin.

matricide /ˈmeɪtrɪsaɪd/ *n.* 1. the crime of killing one's own mother. 2. one who is guilty of this. —**matricidal** *adj.* [from Latin *mater* = mother]

matriculate /məˈtrɪkjʊleɪt/ *v.t./i.* to admit (a student) to membership of a university; to be thus admitted. [from Latin *matricula* = register]

matriculation /mətrɪkjuˈleɪʃən/ *n.* matriculating; an examination to qualify for this.

matrilineal /mætriˈlɪnɪəl/ *adj.* of or based on kinship with the mother or the female line of ancestors. [from Latin *mater* = mother]

matrimony /ˈmætrɪmənɪ/ *n.* 1. the rite of marriage. 2. the state of being married. —**matrimonial** /-ˈməunɪəl/ *adj.*, **matrimonially** *adv.* [from Anglo-French from Latin *matrimonium*]

matrix /ˈmeɪtrɪks/ *n.* (*plural* **matrices** /-ɪsiːz/) 1. a mould in which a thing is cast or shaped. 2. a place in which a thing is developed. 3. a mass of rock enclosing gems etc. 4. a rectangular array of mathematical quantities treated as a single quantity. 5. in biology, usually refers to the ◇extracellular matrix. [Latin = womb]

matron /ˈmeɪtrən/ *n.* 1. a married woman, especially one who is middle-aged or elderly and dignified. 2. a woman managing the domestic arrangements of a school etc. 3. a woman in charge of nurses in a hospital (now usually called **senior nursing officer**). —**matron of honour**, a married woman attending the bride at a wedding. —**matronly** *adj.* [from Old French from Latin *matrona*]

Matsudaira /mɑːtsudaɪra/ Tsuneo 1877–1949. Japanese diplomat and politician who became the first chair of the Japanese Diet (parliament) after World War II.

Matsukata /mɑːtsukata/ Masayoshi, Prince 1835–1924. Japanese politician, premier 1891–92 and 1896–98. As minister of finance 1881–91 and 1898–1900, he paved the way for the modernization of the Japanese economy.

Matsuoka /mɑːtsuɔka/ Yosuke 1880–1946. Japanese politician, foreign minister 1940–41. A fervent nationalist,

Matsuoka led Japan out of the League of Nations when it condemned Japan for the seizure of Manchuria. As foreign minister, he allied Japan with Germany and Italy. At the end of World War II, he was arrested as a war criminal but died before his trial.

Matsys /'mætsaɪs/ **Massys** or **Metsys** Quentin *c.*1464–1530. Flemish painter, born in Louvain, active in Antwerp. He painted religious subjects such as the *Lamentation* 1511 (Musées Royaux, Antwerp) and portraits set against landscapes or realistic interiors.

matt *adj.* (of a colour etc.) dull, not lustrous. [from French]

matter *n.* **1.** that which occupies space and possesses rest mass, including atoms, their major constituents, and substances made of atoms, but not light and other electromagnetic radiation; physical substance in general, as distinct from mind and spirit. **2.** a particular substance or material. **3.** a discharge from the body, pus. **4.** material for thought or expression; the content of a book, speech, etc. **5.** a thing or things of a specified kind. **6.** a situation or business being considered. **7.** (with *of*) a quantity or extent of; a thing that depends on. —*v.i.* to be important. —**the matter**, the thing that is amiss, the trouble or difficulty. **as a matter of fact**, in reality (especially to correct a falsehood or misunderstanding). **for that matter**, as far as that is concerned; and indeed also. **a matter of course**, a thing to be expected. **matter-of-fact** *adj.* strictly factual and not imaginative or emotional. **no matter**, it is of no importance. [from Anglo-French from Latin *materia*]

Matterhorn /'mætəhɔ:n/ (French **le Cervin**, Italian **il Cervino**) mountain peak in the Alps on the Swiss-Italian border; 4,478 m/14,690 ft.

Matthau /'mæθaʊ/ Walter. Stage name of Walter Matuschanskavasky 1922– . US character actor, impressive in both comedy and dramatic roles. He gained film stardom in the 1960s after his stage success in *The Odd Couple* 1965. His many films include *Kotch* 1971 and *Charley Varrick* 1973.

Matthews /'mæθju:z/ Stanley 1915– . English footballer who played for Stoke City, Blackpool, and England. He played nearly 700 Football League games, and won 54 international caps. He was the first European Footballer of the Year 1956.

Matthew, St /'mæθju:/ 1st century AD. Christian apostle and evangelist, the traditional author of the first Gospel. He is usually identified with Levi, who was a tax collector in the service of Herod Antipas, and was called by Jesus to be a disciple as he sat by the Lake of Galilee receiving customs dues. His emblem is a man with wings; feast day 21 Sept.

Matthias Corvinus /mə'θaɪəs kɔ:'vaɪnəs/ 1440–1490. King of Hungary from 1458. His aim of uniting Hungary, Austria, and Bohemia involved him in long wars with the Holy Roman emperor and the kings of Bohemia and Poland, during which he captured Vienna (1485) and made it his capital. His father was János ◊Hunyadi.

matting *n.* fabric for mats.

mattock /'mætək/ *n.* an agricultural tool like a pickaxe with an adze and a chisel edge as the ends of its head. [Old English]

mattress /'mætrɪs/ *n.* a pad of soft or firm or springy material enclosed in a fabric case, used on or as a bed. [from Old French *materas* from Italian from Arabic]

maturate /'mætjʊreɪt/ *v.i.* (of a boil etc.) to come to maturation. [from Latin]

maturation /mætju'reɪʃən/ *n.* maturing, development; (of a boil etc.) the formation of purulent matter. [from French or Latin]

mature /mə'tjʊə/ *adj.* **1.** with fully developed powers of body and mind, adult. **2.** complete in natural development, ripe. **3.** (of thought, intentions, etc.) duly careful and adequate. **4.** (of a bill etc.) due for payment. —*v.t./i.* to make or become mature. —**maturely** *adv.*, **maturity** *n.* [from Latin *maturus*]

Mature /mə'tjʊə/ Victor 1915– . US actor, film star of the 1940s and early 1950s. He gave memorable performances in, among others, *My Darling Clementine* 1946, *Kiss of Death* 1947, and *Samson and Delilah* 1949.

matutinal /mætju:'taɪnəl/ *adj.* of or occurring in the morning; early. [from Latin *matutinus*]

Mauchly John William 1907–1980. US physicist and engineer. He constructed in 1946 the first general-purpose computer, the ENIAC, in collaboration with John Eckert (1919–). Their company was bought by Remington Rand in 1950, and they built the Univac 1 computer in 1951 for the US census. The idea for ENIAC grew out of the pair's work in World War II on ways of automating the calculation of artillery firing tables for the US Army.

maudlin /'mɔ:dlɪn/ *adj.* weakly or tearfully sentimental, especially from drunkenness. [originally = St Mary Magdalen, from Old French *Madeleine* from Latin]

Maugham /mɔ:m/ (William) Somerset 1874–1965. English writer. His work includes the novels *Of Human Bondage* 1915, *The Moon and Sixpence* 1919, and *Cakes and Ale* 1930; the short-story collections *The Trembling of a Leaf* 1921 and *Ashenden* 1928; and the plays *Lady Frederick* 1907 and *Our Betters* 1923.

> No married man's ever made up his mind till he's heard what his wife has got to say about it.
> **William Somerset Maugham**
> *Lady Frederick*

maul /mɔ:l/ *v.t.* **1.** to treat roughly; to injure by rough handling or clawing. **2.** to make damaging criticisms of. —*n.* **1.** a loose scrum in Rugby football. **2.** a brawl. **3.** a heavy hammer. [from Old French from Latin *malleus* = hammer]

maulstick /'mɔ:lstɪk/ *n.* a stick used to support the hand in painting. [from Dutch *maalstok* (*malen* = to paint)]

Mau Mau /'maʊmaʊ/ a Kenyan secret guerrilla movement 1952–60, an offshoot of the Kikuyu Central Association banned in World War II. Its aim was to end British colonial rule. This was achieved in 1960 with the granting of Kenyan independence and the election of Jomo Kenyatta as Kenya's first prime minister.

Mauna Kea /'maʊnə 'keɪə/ astronomical observatory in Hawaii, USA, built on a dormant volcano at 4,200 m/13,784 ft above sea level. Because of its elevation high above clouds, atmospheric moisture, and artificial lighting, Mauna Kea is ideal for infrared astronomy. The first telescope on the site was installed in 1970.

Mauna Loa /maʊnə'ləʊə/ active volcano rising to a height of 4,169 m/13,678 ft on the Pacific island of Hawaii. It has numerous craters, including the second largest active crater in the world.

maunder /'mɔ:ndə/ *v.i.* **1.** to talk in a dreamy or rambling manner. **2.** to move or act listlessly or idly. [perhaps from obsolete *maunder* = beggar, to beg]

Maundy /'mɔ:ndɪ/ *n.* the ceremony of washing the feet of a number of poor people, performed by royal or other eminent persons, or by ecclesiastics, on the Thursday before Easter, and commonly followed by the distribution of clothing, food, or money. —**Maundy Thursday**, the Thursday before Easter, celebrated in memory of the Last Supper. [from Old French *mandé* from Latin = commandment, reference to John 13: 34]

Maupassant /məʊpæ'sɒŋ/ Guy de 1850–1893. French author who established a reputation with the short story 'Boule de Suif/Ball of Fat' 1880 and wrote some 300 short stories in all. His novels include *Une Vie/A Woman's Life* 1883 and *Bel-Ami* 1885. He was encouraged as a writer by ◊Flaubert.

Mauriac /mɔ:ri'æk/ François 1885–1970. French novelist. His novel *Le Baiser au lépreux/A Kiss for the Leper* 1922 describes the conflict of an unhappy marriage. The irreconcilability of Christian practice and human nature are examined in *Fleuve de feu/River of Fire* 1923, *Le Désert de l'amour/The Desert of Love* 1925, and *Thérèse Desqueyroux* 1927. He won the Nobel Prize for Literature in 1952.

Mauritania /mɒri'teɪnɪə/ Islamic Republic of; country in NW Africa, bordered NE by Algeria, E and S by Mali, SW by Senegal, W by the Atlantic Ocean, and NW by Western Sahara; **area** 1,030,700 sq km/397,850 sq mi; **capital** Nouakchott; **physical** valley river of Senegal in S; remainder flat and arid; **head of state and government** Moaouia Ould Sidi Mohamed Taya from 1984; **political system** military republic; **population** (1990 est) 2,038,000 (30% Arab-Berber, 30% black Africans, 30% Haratine—descendants of black slaves, who remained slaves until 1980); **language** French (official), Hasaniya Arabic; **recent history** independence achieved

from France in 1960, and Western Sahara ceded by
Spain in 1975.

Mauritius /mə'rɪʃəs/ State of; island in the Indian Ocean,
E of Madagascar; **area** 1,865 sq km/720 sq mi; the island
of Rodrigues is part of Mauritius; there are several small
island dependencies; **capital** Port Louis; **physical** mountainous, volcanic island surrounded by coral reefs; **head of
state** Elizabeth II represented by governor-general; **head
of government** Aneerood Jugnauth from 1982; **political
system** constitutional monarchy; **population** (1990 est)
1,141,900; **language** English (official); French, Creole;
recent history independence was achieved from Britain
within the Commonwealth in 1968. An attempt in 1990 to
create a republic failed.

Maurois /mɔː'wɑː/ André. Pen name of Emile Herzog
1885–1967. French novelist and writer, whose works
include the semi-autobiographical *Bernard Quesnay* 1926
and fictionalized biographies, such as *Ariel* 1923, a life of
Shelley.

Mauroy /mɔː'wɑː/ Pierre 1928– . French socialist politician, prime minister 1981–84. He oversaw the introduction
of a radical reflationary programme.

Maurya dynasty /'maurɪə/ Indian dynasty *c.*321–*c.*185
BC, founded by **Chandragupta Maurya** (321–*c.*279 BC).
Under Emperor ◊Asoka most of India was united for the
first time, but after his death in 232 the empire was riven
by dynastic disputes.

mausoleum /mɔː:sə'li:əm/ *n.* a large magnificent tomb.
[from *Mausolos*, King of Caria (died 353 BC), for whom a
great tomb was built]

mauve /məʊv/ *adj.* pale purple. —*n.* mauve colour or dye.
[French = mallow, from Latin *malva*]

maverick /'mævərɪk/ *n.* 1. an unorthodox or independent
person. 2. an unbranded calf or yearling. [from S A *Maverick*, Texan who did not brand his cattle (*c.*1850)]

maw *n.* 1. the stomach, especially of an animal. 2. the jaws
or throat of a voracious animal. [Old English]

mawkish *adj.* sentimental in a feeble or sickly way.
—**mawkishly** *adv.*, **mawkishness** *n.* [from obsolete
mawk = maggot]

Mawson /'mɔːsən/ Douglas 1882–1958. Australian explorer, born in Britain, who reached the magnetic South
Pole on ◊Shackleton's expedition of 1907–09.

max. abbreviation of maximum.

maxi- /'mæksɪ-/ in combinations, very large or long (*maxi-
coat*). [abbreviation of maximum; compare *mini-*]

maxilla /mæk'sɪlə/ *n.* (*plural* **maxillae** /-liː/) 1. the jaw,
especially (in vertebrates) the upper one. 2. a masticatory mouth-part of insects and other arthropods. —**maxillary** *n.* [Latin]

maxim /'mæksɪm/ *n.* the succinct expression of a general
truth or rule of conduct. [from French or Latin *maxima*
(*propositio*)]

Maxim /'mæksɪm/ Hiram Stevens 1840–1916. US-born
(naturalized British) inventor of the first automatic machine
gun, in 1884.

maximal /'mæksɪməl/ *adj.* being or related to a maximum. —**maximally** *adv.*

Maximilian /mæksi'mɪliən/ 1832–1867. Emperor of
Mexico 1864–67. He accepted that title when the French
emperor Napoleon III's troops occupied the country, but
encountered resistance from the deposed president Benito
◊Juárez. In 1866, after the French troops withdrew on the
insistence of the USA, Maximilian was captured by Mexican
republicans and shot.

Maximilian I /mæksi'mɪliən/ 1459–1519. Holy Roman
emperor from 1493, the son of Emperor Frederick III.
He had acquired the Low Countries through his marriage
to Mary of Burgundy in 1477.

maximize /'mæksɪmaɪz/ *v.t.* to increase or enhance to the
utmost. —**maximization** /-'zeɪʃən/ *n.* [from Latin]

maximum /'mæksɪməm/ *n.* (*plural* **maxima**) the highest
amount possible, attained, usual, etc. —*adj.* that is a maximum. [neuter of Latin *maximus* = greatest]

maximum and minimum in mathematics, points at
which the slope of a curve representing a ◊function in ◊coor-
dinate geometry changes from positive to negative (maximum), or from negative to positive (minimum). A tangent
to the curve at a maximum or minimum has zero gradient.

maxwell /'mækswəl/ *n.* c.g.s. unit (symbol Mx) of magnetic flux (the strength of a ◊magnetic field in an area

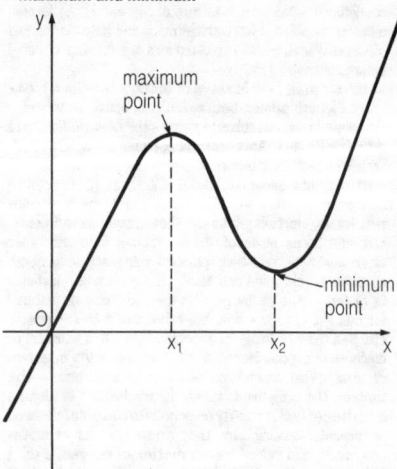

multiplied by the area). It is now replaced by the SI
unit, the ◊weber (one maxwell equals 10^{-8} weber). [from
J C *Maxwell*]

Maxwell James Clerk 1831–1879. Scottish physicist. His
major achievement was in the understanding of electromagnetic waves: **Maxwell's equations** bring together
electicity, magnetism, and light in one set of relations. He
contributed to every branch of physical science—gases,
optics, and colour sensation. His theoretical work in magnetism prepared the way for wireless telegraphy and
telephony.

Maxwell (Ian) Robert 1923– . Czech-born British publishing and newspaper proprietor, owner of several UK
national newspapers, including the *Daily Mirror*. He was
Labour Member of Parliament for Buckingham 1964–70.

Maxwell–Boltzmann distribution /'mækswel
'bəʊltsmən/ a basic equation concerning the distribution of
velocities of the molecules of a gas.

May *n.* the fifth month of the year. —**May Day,** 1 May
especially as a festival or (since 1889) as an international
holiday in honour of workers. **May Queen** *or* **Queen of
the May,** a girl chosen to be queen of the games on
May Day. [from Old French from Latin *Maius* (*mensis*) =
(month) of goddess Maia]

may[1] *n.* the hawthorn; its blossom.

may[2] *v.aux.* (*third person singular present* **may;** *past*
might[1]) expressing possibility, permission, wish, uncertainty. [Old English]

maya /'mɑːjə/ *n.* in Hindu philosophy, illusion, magic, the
supernatural power wielded by gods and demons; (in Hindu
and Buddhist philosophy) the power by which the universe
becomes manifest, the illusion or appearance of the phenomenal world. [from Sanskrit *mā*= create]

Maya /'maɪə/ *n.* member of an American Indian civilization
originating in the Yucatán Peninsula in Central America in
about 2600 BC, with later sites in Mexico, Guatemala,
and Belize, and enjoying a classical period AD 325–925,
after which it declined. The Maya constructed stone
buildings and stepped pyramids without metal tools; used
hieroglyphic writing in manuscripts, of which only three
survive; were skilled potters, weavers, and farmers; and
regulated their rituals and warfare by observations of the
planet Venus.

Mayan art /'maɪən/ art of the Central American civilization of the Maya, between about AD 300 and 900. Mayan
figures have distinctive squat proportions and squared-off
composition. Large, steeply inclined pyramids were built,
such as those at ◊Chichén Itzá , decorated with sculpture
and inscription.

maybe /'meɪbi:/ *adv.* perhaps, possibly. [from *it may be*]

mayday /'meɪdeɪ/ *n.* an international radio distress-signal
used by ships and aircraft. [representing pronunciation of
French *m'aider* = help me]

Mayer /'maɪə/ Julius Robert von 1814–1878. German
physicist who in 1842 anticipated ◊Joule in deriving the

mechanical equivalent of heat, and ◊Helmholtz in the principle of conservation of energy.

Mayer /'meɪə/ Louis B(urt). Adopted name of Eliezer Mayer 1885–1957. Russian-born US film producer. Attracted to the entertainment industry, he became a successful theatre owner in New England and in 1914 began to buy the distribution rights to feature films. Mayer soon became involved in film production, moving to Los Angeles in 1918 and becoming one of the founders of Metro-Goldwyn-Mayer (MGM) studios in 1924. In charge of production, Mayer instituted the Hollywood 'star' system. He retired from MGM in 1951.

mayflower *n.* any of various flowers that bloom in May.

Mayflower *n.* the ship in which, in 1620, the ◊Pilgrim Fathers sailed from Plymouth, England, to found Plymouth in present-day Massachusetts, USA.

mayfly *n.* insect of the order Ephemeroptera (Greek *ephemeros* 'lasting for a day', an allusion to the very brief life of the adult). The larval stage is passed in water. The adult has transparent, net-veined wings.

mayhem /'meɪhem/ *n.* 1. violent or damaging action. 2. (*historical*) the crime of injuring a person so as to render him wholly or partly defenceless. [from Anglo-French and Old French]

mayn't /meɪnt/ (*colloquial*) may not.

Mayo /'meɪəʊ/ county in Connacht province, Republic of Ireland; **area** 5,400 sq km/2,084 sq mi; **administrative town** Castlebar; **population** (1986) 115,000.

mayonnaise /meɪə'neɪz/ *n.* a dressing made of egg-yolks, oil, vinegar, etc.; a dish dressed with this. [French, perhaps = of Port *Mahon* in Minorca]

mayor /meə/ *n.* the head of the municipal corporation of a city or borough; the head of a district council with the status of a borough. In certain cases the chair of a city council may have the right to be called **Lord Mayor** (a usage also followed by Australian cities). In the USA a mayor is the elected head of a city or town. —**mayoral** *adj.* [from Old French *maire* from Latin]

mayoralty /'meərəltɪ/ *n.* the office of mayor; the period of this.

mayoress /'meərɪs/ *n.* a female mayor; a woman fulfilling the ceremonial duties of a mayor's wife; a mayor's wife.

maypole *n.* a pole decked with ribbons, for dancing round in celebrations on May Day.

mayweed *n.* several species of the daisy family Compositae, including the European dog fennel or stinking daisy *Anthemis cotula*, naturalized in North America, and Eurasian pineapple mayweed *Matricaria matricarioides*. All have finely divided leaves.

Mazarin /mæzə'ræŋ/ Jules 1602–1661. French politician, who succeeded Richelieu as chief minister of France in 1642. His attack on the power of the nobility led to the ◊Fronde and his temporary exile, but his diplomacy achieved a successful conclusion to the Thirty Years' War, and, in alliance with Oliver Cromwell during the British protectorate, he gained victory over Spain.

maze *n.* 1. a complicated network of paths, a labyrinth; a network of paths and hedges designed as a puzzle in which to try and find one's way. 2. a state of bewilderment; a confused mass etc.

Mazowiecki /mæzor'jetski/ Tadeusz 1927– . Polish politician, founder member of ◊Solidarity, and Poland's first postwar noncommunist prime minister 1989–1990. Forced to introduce unpopular economic reforms, he was knocked out in the first round of the Nov 1990 presidential elections, resigning in favour of his former colleague, Lech Walesa.

mazurka /mə'zɜːkə/ *n.* a lively national dance of Poland from the 16th century, in triple time, and characterized by foot-stamping and heel-clicking, together with a turning movement; the music for this. [French or from German from Polish = woman of province *Mazovia*]

Mazzini /mæt'siːni/ Giuseppe 1805–1872. Italian nationalist. He was a member of the revolutionary society, the ◊Carbonari, and founded in exile the nationalist movement Giovane Italia (Young Italy) 1832. Returning to Italy on the outbreak of the 1848 revolution, he headed a republican government established in Rome, but was forced into exile again on its overthrow in 1849. He acted as a focus for the movement for Italian unity (see ◊Risorgimento).

MB abbreviation of Bachelor of Medicine. [from Latin *Medicinae Baccalaureus*]

Mbabane /əmbɑː'bɑːneɪ/ capital (since 1902) of Swaziland, 160 km/100 mi W of Maputo, in the Dalgeni Hills; population (1986) 38,000.

MBE abbreviation of Member of the Order of the British Empire.

Mboya /əm'bɔɪə/ Tom 1930–1969. Kenyan politician, a founder of the Kenya African National Union (◊KANU), and minister of economic affairs from 1964 until his assassination.

MC abbreviation of 1. Master of Ceremonies. 2. Military Cross.

MCC abbreviation of Marylebone Cricket Club.

MD abbreviation of Doctor of Medicine. [from Latin *Medicinae Doctor*]

Md symbol for mendelevium.

MDMA *n.* psychedelic drug, also known as ◊ecstasy.

me¹ /miː, mɪ/ *pron.* objective case of I; (*colloquial*) = I. [Old English]

me² /miː/ *n.* in music, the third note of the major scale in tonic sol-fa.

ME abbreviation of 1. myalgic encephalitis, a debilitating condition still not universally accepted as a genuine disease. The condition occurs after a flulike attack and has a diffuse range of symptoms. These strike and recur for years and include extreme fatigue, muscular pain, weakness, and depression. 2. Middle English, the period of the English language 1050–1550;

mead *n.* an alcoholic drink made from fermented honey and water. [Old English]

meadow /'medəʊ/ *n.* a piece of grassland, especially one used for hay; low, well-watered ground, especially near a river. —**meadowy** *adj.* [Old English]

meadowsweet *n.* a plant *Filipendula ulmaria* with masses of fragrant creamy-white flowers, often growing in profusion in damp meadows.

meagre /'miːgə/ *adj.* of poor quality and scanty in amount; (of a person) lean. [from Old French *maigre* from Latin *macer*]

meal¹ *n.* 1. an occasion when food is eaten. 2. the food eaten on one occasion. —**make a meal of,** to treat (a task etc.) too laboriously or fussily. **meals-on-wheels** *n.* a public service whereby meals are delivered to old people, invalids, etc. **meal ticket,** a source of food or income. [Old English]

meal² *n.* 1. coarsely ground grain or pulse. 2. (*Scottish*) oatmeal. 3. (*US*) maize flour. [Old English]

mealie /'miːlɪ/ *n.* (in southern Africa) maize, a cob with the corn on it. [from Afrikaans from Portuguese from Latin *milium* = millet]

mealtime *n.* the (usual) time of eating.

mealy *adj.* of, like, or containing meal; dry and powdery. —**mealy-mouthed** *adj.* trying excessively to avoid offending people. [from **meal²**]

mean¹ *v.t.* (*past* and *past participle* meant /ment/) 1. to have as one's purpose or intention. 2. to design or destine for a purpose. 3. to intend to convey (a specified sense) or indicate or refer to (a thing). 4. to signify; (of words) to have as an equivalent in the same or another language. 5. to entail, to involve; to be likely or certain to result in. 6. to be of specified importance to. —**mean it,** not to be joking or exaggerating. **mean well,** to have good intentions. [Old English]

mean² *adj.* 1. miserly, niggardly, not generous. 2. poor in quality or capacity; poor in appearance, not imposing. 3. malicious, ill-tempered; (*US*) vicious, nastily behaved. 4. (*US slang*) skilful. —**no mean,** very good. —**meanly** *adv.,* **meanness** *n.* [Old English]

mean³ *n.* 1. a condition, quality, or course of action equally removed from two opposite extremes. 2. the quotient of the sum of several quantities and their number. 3. a term between the first and last of an arithmetical etc. progression, especially of three terms. —*adj.* (of a point or quantity) equally far from two extremes. —**in the mean time,** meanwhile. **mean sea level,** the level half-way between high and low water. [from Old French *meien, moien* from Latin]

meander /miː'ændə/ *v.i.* 1. (of a stream) to wind about. 2. to wander at random. —*n.* 1. (in *plural*) the sinuous windings of a river. 2. a circuitous journey. [from Latin from Greek *Maiandros*, winding river in W Turkey]

mean deviation in statistics, a measure of the spread of a population from the ◊mean³.

mean free path in physics, the average distance travelled by a particle, atom, or molecule between successive collisions. It is of importance in the ◊kinetic theory of gases.

meaning *n.* what is meant, the significance. —*adj.* expressive, significant. —**meaningful** *adj.*, **meaningfully** *adv.*, **meaningless** *adj.*, **meaninglessly** *adv.* [from *mean¹*]

means *n.pl* 1. (usually treated as *singular*) that by which a result is brought about. 2. money resources, wealth. —**by all means**, certainly. **by no means**, not at all; far from it; certainly not. **means test**, an official inquiry to establish need before financial assistance is given. [as *mean³*]

meant past and past participle of **mean¹**.

meantime *adv.* meanwhile.

meanwhile *adv.* 1. in the intervening period of time. 2. at the same time.

meany *n.* (*colloquial*) a niggardly or small-minded person.

measles /'mi:zəlz/ *n.* an acute virus disease (rubeola), spread by airborne infection. Symptoms are fever, severe catarrh, small spots inside the mouth, and a raised, blotchy red rash appearing for about a week after two weeks' incubation. Prevention is by vaccination. [from Middle Low German *masele* or Middle Dutch *masel* = pustule]

measly /'mi:zlı/ *adj.* 1. of or affected with measles. 2. (*slang*) meagre; inferior, contemptible.

measure /'meʒə/ *n.* 1. the size or quantity of something, found by measuring. 2. a unit, standard, or system used in measuring. 3. a device used in measuring, especially a rod, tape, or vessel marked with standard units. 4. degree or extent. 5. (often in *plural*) suitable action taken to achieve some end; a law or proposed law 6. that by which a thing is computed. 7. a prescribed quantity or extent. 8. a poetical rhythm, a metre; the metrical group of a dactyl or two disyllabic feet; (*archaic*) a dance. 9. a stratum containing a mineral. —*v.t./i.* 1. to find the extent or quantity of (a thing) by comparison with a fixed unit or with an object of known size; to ascertain the size and proportions of (a person etc.) for fitting clothing etc. 2. to be of a specified size. 3. to mark out (a given length) or deal out as a specified quantity. 4. to estimate (a quality etc.) by comparing it with some standard. 5. to bring into competition. —**beyond measure**, very great, very much. **for good measure**, in addition to what is necessary. **in some measure**, partly, to some extent. **made to measure**, made from measurements specially taken. **measure up (to)**, to reach the necessary standard (for). [from Old French from Latin *mensura* (*metiri* = to measure)]

measured *adj.* 1. rhythmical, regular in movement. 2. (of language) carefully considered.

measurement *n.* an act or the result of measuring; (in *plural*) detailed dimensions.

meat *n.* 1. animal flesh as food (usually excluding fish and poultry). 2. the essence or chief part. —**meat and drink**, a source of great pleasure *to*. **meat-safe** *n.* a ventilated cupboard for storing meat. [Old English = food]

meatball *n.* a small ball of minced meat.

Meath /mi:ð/ county in the province of Leinster, Republic of Ireland; **area** 2,340 sq km/903 sq mi; **county town** Trim; **population** (1986) 104,000.

meatus /mɪ'eɪtəs/ *n.* (*plural* the same or **meatuses**) a channel or passage in the body; its opening. —**auditory meatus**, a channel of the ear. [Latin = passage (*meare* = flow, run)]

meaty *adj.* 1. like meat. 2. full of meat, fleshy. 3. full of informative matter. —**meatiness** *n.*

Mecca /'mekə/ Arabic **Makkah** city in Saudi Arabia and, as birthplace of Muhammad, the holiest city of the Islamic world; population (1974) 367,000. In the centre of Mecca is the Great Mosque, in whose courtyard is the ◊Kaaba.

Meccano /mɪ'kɑ:nəu/ *n.* toy metal construction sets launched in 1901 by British inventor Frank Hornby (1863–1936) (also the creator of Hornby train sets and Dinky toys), which continued in production until 1979.

mechanic /mɪ'kænɪk/ *n.* a skilled worker, especially one who makes or uses or repairs machinery. [from Old French or Latin from Greek *mekhanē*= contrivance]

mechanical /mɪ'kænɪkəl/ *adj.* 1. of machines or a mechanism. 2. working or produced by machinery. 3. (of a person or action) like a machine, acting or done without conscious thought; lacking originality; (of work) needing little or no

thought. 4. of or belonging to the science of mechanics. —**mechanically** *adv.*

mechanical advantage the amount by which a machine can magnify a force. It is the load (the weight lifted or moved by the machine) divided by the effort (the force used by the operator).

mechanical equivalent of heat in physics, a constant factor relating the calorie (the c.g.s. unit of heat) to the joule (the unit of mechanical energy), equal to 4.1868 joules per calorie. It is redundant in the SI system of units, which measures heat and all forms of energy in joules (so that the mechanical equivalent of heat is 1).

mechanics /mɪ'kænɪks/ *n.pl.* (usually treated as *singular*) 1. the branch of applied mathematics dealing with motion and tendencies to motion. 2. the science of machinery. 3. (as *plural*) the processes by which something is done or functions.

mechanism /'mekənɪzəm/ *n.* 1. the structure or parts of a machine or other set of mutually adapted parts. 2. the mode of operation of a process or machine. [from Greek]

mechanize /'mekənaɪz/ *v.t.* 1. to introduce or use machines in; to equip with machines. 2. to give a mechanical character to. —**mechanization**/-'zeɪʃən/ *n.*

Mechnikov /'metʃnɪkɒf/ Elie 1845–1916. Russian scientist who discovered the function of white blood cells and ◊phagocytes. After leaving Russia and joining ◊Pasteur in Paris, he described how these 'scavenger cells' can attack the body itself (autoimmune disease).

Mecklenburg–West Pomerania /'meklənbɜːg/ (German *Mecklenburg-Vorpommern*) administrative *Land* (state) of Germany; **area** 22,887 sqkm/8,840 sq mi; **capital** Schwerin; **population** (1990) 2,100,000; **recent history** the state was formerly the two grand duchies of Mecklenburg-Schwerin and Mecklenburg-Strelitz, which became free states of the Weimar Republic 1918–34, and were joined in 1946 with part of Pomerania to form a region of East Germany. In 1952 it was split into the districts of Rostock, Schwerin, and Neubrandenburg. Following German reunification in 1990, the districts were abolished and Mecklenburg–West Pomerania was reconstructed as one of the five new states of the Federal Republic.

Med (*colloquial*) abbreviation of the Mediterranean Sea.

medal /'medəl/ *n.* a piece of metal, usually in the form of a coin, struck or cast with an inscription and device to commemorate an event etc., or awarded as a distinction. [from French from Italian from Latin *metallum*]

medallion /mɪ'dæljən/ *n.* 1. a large medal. 2. a thing so shaped, e. g. a decorative panel, a portrait. [from French from Italian]

medallist /'medəlɪst/ *n.* a winner of a medal.

Medan /mə'dɑ:n/ seaport and economic centre of the island of Sumatra, Indonesia; population (1980) 1,379,000. It trades in rubber, tobacco, and palm oil.

Medawar /'medəwə/ Peter (Brian) 1915–1987. Brazilian-born British immunologist who, with Macfarlane ◊Burnet, discovered that the body's resistance to grafted tissue is undeveloped in the newborn child, and studied the way it is acquired. He and Burnet shared the Nobel Prize for Medicine 1960.

meddle *v.i.* 1. to interfere in people's affairs. 2. to tinker. —**meddler** *n.* [from Old French variant of *mesler*, ultimately from Latin *miscēre* = mix]

meddlesome *adj.* fond of meddling.

Mede /mi:d/ *n.* a member of a people of NW Iran who in the 9th century BC were tributaries to Assyria, with their capital at Ecbatana (now Hamadán). Allying themselves with Babylon, they destroyed the Assyrian capital of ◊Nineveh in 612 BC, and extended their conquests into central Anatolia. In 550 BC they were overthrown by the Persians, with whom they rapidly merged.

Medea /mɪ'dɪə/ in Greek mythology, the sorceress daughter of the king of Colchis. When ◊Jason reached the court, she fell in love with him, helped him acquire the Golden Fleece, and they fled together. When Jason married Creusa, Medea killed his bride with the gift of a poisoned garment, and also killed her own two children by Jason.

Medea Greek tragedy by Euripides, produced 431 BC. It deals with the later part of the legend of Medea: her murder of Jason's bride and of her own children.

Medellín /meðe'i:n/ industrial town (textiles, chemicals, engineering, coffee) in the Central Cordillera, Colombia,

1,538 m/5,048 ft above sea level; population (1985) 2,069,000. It is a centre of the Colombian drug trade, and there has been considerable violence in the late 1980s.

media plural of medium. (See also ◊mass¹)

mediaeval variant of medieval.

medial /'mi:diəl/ *adj.* situated in the middle. —**medially** *adv.* [from Latin *medius* = middle]

median /'mi:diən/ *adj.* medial —*n.* **1.** the straight line drawn from any vertex of a triangle to the middle of the opposite side. **2.** a medial number or point in a series. **3.** (in statistics) the value of a quantity such that exactly half of a given population have greater values of that quantity. [from French or Latin]

mediate /'mi:dieɪt/ *v.t./i.* **1.** to act as negotiator or peacemaker between the two sides in a dispute. **2.** to bring about (a result) thus. —/'mi:diət/ *adj.* connected not directly but through some other person or thing. —**mediation** /-'eɪʃən/ *n.*, **mediator** *n.* [from Latin *mediare*]

medic /'medɪk/ *n.* (*colloquial*) a medical practitioner or student. [from Latin *medicus* = physician (*medēri* = heal)]

medical /'medɪkəl/ *adj.* of the science of medicine in general or as distinct from surgery. —*n.* (*colloquial*) a medical examination. —**medical certificate**, a certificate of fitness or unfitness to work etc. **medical examination**, an examination to determine a person's physical fitness. **medical officer**, a person in charge of the health services of a local authority or other organization. —**medically** *adv.* [from French or Latin]

medicament /mi'dɪkəmənt/ *n.* a substance used in curative treatment. [from French or Latin]

medicate /'medɪkeɪt/ *v.t.* **1.** to treat medically. **2.** to impregnate with a medicinal substance. —**medication** /-'keɪʃən/ *n.*, **medicative** *adj.* [from Latin *medicare*]

Medici /'medɪtʃi/ noble family of Florence, the city's rulers from 1434 until they died out in 1737. Family members included ◊Catherine de' Medici, Pope ◊Leo X, Pope ◊Clement VII, ◊Marie de' Medici.

Medici Cosimo de' 1389–1464. Italian politician and banker. Regarded as the model for Machiavelli's *The Prince*, he dominated the government of Florence from 1434 and was a patron of the arts. He was succeeded by his inept son **Piero de' Medici** (1416–69).

Medici Lorenzo de' the **Magnificent** 1449–1492. Italian politician, ruler of Florence from 1469. He was also a poet and a generous patron of the arts.

medicinal /mi'dɪsɪnəl/ *adj.* of medicine; having healing properties. —**medicinally** *adv.* [from Old French from Latin]

medicine /'medsɪn, -ɪsɪn/ *n.* **1.** the art of restoring and preserving health, especially by means of remedial substances etc. as distinct from surgery. **2.** a substance used in this, especially one taken internally. —**medicine-man** *n.* a witch-doctor. **take one's medicine,** to submit to rebuke or punishment etc. [from Old French from Latin *medicina*]

medicine, alternative forms of medical treatment that do not use synthetic drugs or surgery in response to the symptoms of a disease, but aim to treat the patient as a whole (◊holism). The emphasis is on maintaining health (with diet and exercise) and on dealing with the underlying causes rather than just the symptoms of illness. It may involve the use of herbal remedies and techniques like ◊acupuncture, ◊homeopathy, and ◊chiropractic.

medico /'medɪkəʊ/ *n.* (*plural* **medicos**) (*colloquial*) a medical practitioner or student. [Italian from Latin]

medieval /medɪ'i:vəl/ *adj.* of or imitating the Middle Ages. [from Latin *medius* = middle and *aevum* = age]

medieval art painting and sculpture of the Middle Ages in Europe and parts of the Middle East, dating roughly from the 4th century to the emergence of the Renaissance in Italy in the 1400s. This includes early Christian, Byzantine, Celtic, Anglo-Saxon, and Carolingian art. The Romanesque style was the first truly international style of medieval times, superseded by Gothic in the late 12th century. Religious sculpture, frescoes, and manuscript illumination proliferated; panel painting came only towards the end of the period.

Medina /me'di:nə/ (Arabic *Madinah*) Saudi Arabian city, about 355 km/220 mi N of Mecca; population (1974) 198,000. It is the second holiest city in the Islamic world, containing the tomb of Muhammad. It produces grain and fruit.

mediocre /mi:di'əʊkə/ *adj.* of middling quality; secondrate. [from French or Latin *mediocris*]

mediocrity /mi:di'ɒkrɪtɪ/ *n.* **1.** mediocre quality. **2.** a mediocre person. [from French from Latin]

meditate /'medɪteɪt/ *v.t./i.* **1.** to think deeply and quietly; to do this in religious contemplation. **2.** to plan in one's mind. —**meditation** /-'teɪʃən/ *n.* act of spiritual contemplation, practised by members of many religions or as a secular exercise. It is a central practice in Buddhism. The Sanskrit term is *dhyāna*. See also ◊transcendental meditation (TM). **meditator** *n.* [from Latin *meditari*]

meditative /'medɪtətɪv/ *adj.* inclined to meditate; indicative of meditation. —**meditatively** *adv.*

Mediterranean /medɪtə'reɪnɪən/ *adj.* of or characteristic of the Mediterranean Sea or the countries in and round it. —**Mediterranean Sea,** inland sea separating Europe from N Africa, with Asia to the E; extreme length 3,700 km/ 2,300 mi; area 2,966,000 sq km/1,145,000 sq mi. It is linked to the Atlantic (at the Strait of Gibraltar), Red Sea, and Indian Ocean (by the Suez Canal), Black Sea (at the Dardanelles and Sea of Marmara). The main subdivisions are the Adriatic, Aegean, Ionian, and Tyrrhenian seas. [from Latin = inland (*medius* = middle and *terra* = land)]

medium /'mi:diəm/ *n.* (*plural* **media,** in sense 6 **mediums**) **1.** a middle quality or degree of intensiveness etc. **2.** a substance or surroundings in which something exists, moves, or is transmitted; an environment. **3.** an agency or means by which something is done. **4.** (in *plural,* sometimes treated erroneously as *singular*) the mass media (see ◊mass¹). **5.** the material or form used by an artist or composer etc. **6.** (*plural* **mediums**) a person claiming to be able to communicate with the spirits of the dead etc. —*adj.* intermediate between two degrees or amounts; average, moderate. —**medium wave,** a radio wave of frequency between 300 kHz and 3 MHz. [Latin, neuter of *medius* = middle]

mediumistic /mi:diə'mɪstɪk/ *adj.* of a spiritualist medium.

medlar /'medlə/ *n.* a fruit like a small apple, palatable when decay has set in; the tree or shrub bearing this, *Mespilus germanica* of the rose family Rosaceae. [from Old French from Latin from Greek *mespilē*]

medley /'medlɪ/ *n.* a varied mixture, a miscellany; a collection of musical items from various sources. [from Old French from Latin]

medulla /mi'dʌlə/ *n.* **1.** the marrow within a bone; the substance of the spinal cord. **2.** the hindmost section of the brain. **3.** the central part of some organs, e.g. that of the kidneys. **4.** the soft internal tissue of plants. —**medullary** *adj.* [Latin]

medusa /mi'dju:zə/ *n.* (*plural* **medusae** or **medusas**) a jellyfish. [from *Medusa,* snake-haired Gorgon]

Medusa /mə'dju:zə/ in Greek mythology, a mortal woman who was transformed into a ◊Gorgon. The winged horse ◊Pegasus was supposed to have sprung from her blood.

Medvedev /mɪd'vjedef/ Vadim 1929– . Soviet communist politician. He was deputy chief of propaganda 1970–78, was in charge of party relations with communist countries 1986–88, and in 1988 was appointed by the Soviet leader Gorbachev to succeed the conservative Ligachev as head of ideology. He adheres to a firm Leninist line.

meek *adj.* quiet and obedient, making no protest. —**meekly** *adv.*, **meekness** *n.* [from Old Norse]

meerschaum /'mɪəʃəm/ *n.* a white substance resembling clay; a tobacco-pipe with the bowl made of this. [German = sea-foam]

meet¹ *v.t./i.* (*past* and *past participle* **met**) **1.** to come by accident or design into the company of, to come face to face (with). **2.** to go to a place to be present at the arrival of (a person, train, etc.). **3.** to come together or into contact (with). **4.** to make the acquaintance of, to be introduced (to). **5.** (of people or a group) to assemble. **6.** to deal with or answer (a demand, objection, etc.) effectively; to satisfy or conform with (a person's wishes). **7.** to pay (the cost, a bill at maturity). **8.** to experience or receive (one's death, fate, etc.). **9.** to oppose or be in opposition in a contest etc. —*n.* a meeting of persons and hounds for a hunt. —**meet the case,** to be adequate. **meet the eye** (*or* **ear**), to be visible (or audible) (*more in it than meets the eye,* hidden qualities or complications). **meet a person's eye,** to look into the eyes of a person looking at one. **meet a person half-way,** to

Western medicine: chronology

c. 400 BC	Hippocrates recognized that disease had natural causes.
c. AD 200	Galen, the authority of the Middle Ages, consolidated the work of the Alexandrian doctors.
1543	Andreas Versalius gave the first accurate account of the human body.
1628	William Harvey discovered the circulation of the blood.
1768	John Hunter began the foundation of experimental and surgical pathology.
1785	Digitalis was used to treat heart disease; the active ingredient was isolated 1904.
1798	Edward Jenner published his work on vaccination.
1882	Robert Koch isolated the tuberculosis bacillus.
1884	Edwin Klebs, German pathologist, isolated the diptheria bacillus.
1885	Louis Pasteur produced the rabies vaccine.
1890	Joseph Lister demonstrated antiseptic surgery.
1897	Martinus Beijerinck, Dutch botanist, discovered viruses.
1899	German doctor Felix Hoffman developed aspirin; Sigmund Freud founded psychoanalysis.
1910	Paul Ehrlich synthesized the first specific bacterial agent, salvarsan (cure for syphilis).
1922	Insulin was first used to treat diabetes.
1928	Alexander Fleming discovered the antibiotic penicillin.
1930s	Electro-convulsive therapy (ECT) was developed.
1932	Gerhard Domagk, German bacteriologist and pathologist, began work on the sulphonamide drugs, a kind of antibiotic.
1940s	Lithium treatment for depression was developed.
1950s	Major development of antidepressant drugs and beta blockers for heart disease; Medawar's work on the immune system.
1950–75	Manipulation of the molecules of synthetic chemicals, the main source of new drugs.
1953	Vaccine for polio developed by Jonas Salk.
1960s	Heart-transplant surgery began with the work of Christiaan Barnard; new generation of minor tranquillizers called benzodiazepenes developed.
1971	Viroids, disease-causing organisms smaller than viruses, were isolated outside the living body.
1975	Nuclear medicine, for example positron-emission tomography (Hounsfield), came into use.
1978	Birth of the first 'test-tube baby', Louise Brown, in England.
1980s	AIDS (acquired immune-deficiency syndrome) first recognized in the USA; recognition of the discovery of the transposable gene by Barbara McClintock, US geneticist.
1980	Smallpox eradicated by the World Health Organization.
1984	Vaccine for leprosy developed; discovery of the human immuno-deficiency virus (HIV), responsible for AIDS, at the Institut Pasteur in Paris and in the USA.
1987	World's longest-surviving heart-transplant patient died in France, 18 years after his operation.
1989	Patient with Parkinson's disease first treated by graft of fetal brain tissue.

respond to a person's advances, to make a compromise with him or he. **meet up with,** (*colloquial*) to happen to meet (a person). [Old English]

meet² *adj.* (*archaic*) fitting, proper. [Old English]

meeting *n.* 1. coming together. 2. an assembly of people, e. g. for discussion or (especially of Quakers) worship. 3. a race-meeting.

mega- /'megə-/ in combinations 1. large. 2. one million. [Greek *megas* = great]

megabyte *n.* in computing, a measure of the capacity of ◊memory or storage, equal to 1024 ◊kilobytes. It is also used, less precisely, to mean one million bytes.

megadeath /'megədeθ/ *n.* the death of one million people (especially as a unit in estimating casualties of war).

megahertz /'megəhɜːts/ *n.* a unit of frequency, equal to one million cycles per second.

megalith /'megəlɪθ/ *n.* a large stone, especially one forming (part of) a prehistoric monument of the late Neolithic or early Bronze Age. Monuments include single, large uprights (**menhirs,** for example the Five Kings, Northumberland, England); **rows** (for example, Carnac, Brittany, France); **circles,** generally with a central 'altar stone' (for example Stonehenge, Wiltshire, England); and the remains of burial chambers with the covering earth removed, looking like a hut (**dolmens,** for example Kits Coty, Kent, England). —**megalithic** /-'lɪθɪk/ *adj.* [from Greek *lithos* = stone]

megalomania /megələ'meɪnɪə/ *n.* a mental disorder involving an exaggerated idea of one's own importance; a passion for grandiose schemes etc. —**megalomaniac** *n.*

megamouth *n.* a filter-feeding deep-sea shark *Megachasma pelagios,* first discovered in 1976. It has a bulbous head with protruding jaws and blubbery lips, is 4.5 m/15 ft long, and weighs 750 kg/1,650 lb.

megaphone /'megəfəʊn/ *n.* a large funnel-shaped device for sending the sound of the voice to a distance. [from Greek *phōnē* = voice, sound]

megapode *n.* a large (70 cm/2.3 ft long) ground-living bird of the family Megapodidae, found mainly in Australia, but also in SE Asia. They lay their eggs in a pile of rotting vegetation 4 m/13 ft across, and the warmth from this provides the heat for incubation. The male bird feels the mound with his tongue and adjusts it to provide the correct temperature.

megaton /'megətʌn/ *n.* one million (10⁶) tons. Used with reference to the explosive power of a nuclear weapon, it is equivalent to the explosive force of one million tons of trinitrotoluene (TNT).

megavolt /'megəvəʊlt/ *n.* a unit of electromotive force equal to one million volts.

megawatt /'megəwɒt/ *n.* a unit of electrical power equal to one million watts.

Meghalaya /megə'leɪə/ state of NE India; **area** 22,500 sq km/8,685 sq mi; **capital** Shillong; **population** (1981) 1,328,000, mainly Khasi, Jaintia, and Garo; **language** various.

Megiddo /mə'gɪdəʊ/ *n.* site of a fortress town in N Israel, where Thothmes III defeated the Canaanites about 1469 BC; the Old Testament figure Josiah was killed in battle about 609 BC; and in World War I the British field marshal Allenby broke the Turkish front 1918. It is identified with ◊Armageddon.

megohm /'megəʊm/ *n.* a unit of electrical resistance equal to one million ohms.

Mehemet Ali /mi'hemɪt 'ɑːli/ 1769–1849. Pasha (governor) of Egypt from 1805, and founder of the dynasty that ruled until 1953. An Albanian in the Ottoman service, he had originally been sent to Egypt to fight the French. As pasha, he established a European-style army and navy, fought his Turkish overlord 1831 and 1839, and conquered Sudan.

Meier /'meɪə/ Richard 1934– . US architect whose white designs spring from the poetic modernism of the ◊Le Corbusier villas of the 1920s. His abstract style is at its most mature in the Museum für Kunsthandwerk (Museum of Arts and Crafts), Frankfurt, Germany, which was completed 1984.

Meiji /'meɪdʒi/ Mutsuhito 1852–1912. Emperor of Japan from 1867, when he took the title *meiji tennō* ('enlightened sovereign'). During his reign Japan became a world industrial and naval power. He abolished the feudal system and discrimination against the lowest caste, established state schools, and introduced conscription, the Western calendar, and other measures in an attempt to modernize Japan, including a constitution in 1889.

Meiji era in Japanese history, the reign of Emperor Meiji 1867–1912.

Meikle /'miːkəl/ Andrew 1719–1811. Scottish millwright who in 1785 designed and built the first practical threshing machine for separating cereal grains from the husks.

Meinhof /'maɪnhɒf/ Ulrike 1934–1976. A 1970s West German urban guerrilla, member of the ◊Baader–Meinhof gang. As the faction's chief ideologist, Meinhof was arrested in 1972 and, in 1974, sentenced to eight years' imprisonment. She committed suicide in 1976 in the Stammheim high-security prison.

Mein Kampf /maɪn 'kæmpf/ book written by Adolf ◊Hitler 1924 during his jail sentence for his part in the abortive 1923 Munich beer-hall putsch. Part autobiography, part political philosophy, the book presents Hitler's ideas of German expansion, anticommunism, and anti-Semitism. [German = my struggle]

meiosis /maɪ'əʊsɪs/ n. (plural meioses /-siːz/) 1. litotes. 2. the process of division of cell nuclei forming gametes (sex cells, sperm and egg), each containing half the normal number of chromosomes. It occurs only in ◊eukaryotic cells, and is part of a life cycle that involves sexual reproduction. [from Greek meioō = make less]

Meir /meɪ'ɪə/ Golda 1898–1978. Israeli Labour (Mapai) politician. Born in Russia, she emigrated to the USA in 1906, and in 1921 went to Palestine. She was foreign minister 1956–66 and prime minister 1969–74. Criticism of the Israelis' lack of preparation for the 1973 Arab-Israeli War led to election losses for Labour and, unable to form a government, she resigned.

Meistersinger /'maɪstəsɪŋə(r)/ n. one of a group of German lyric poets, singers, and musicians of the 14th–16th centuries, who formed guilds for the revival of minstrelsy. Hans ◊Sachs was a Meistersinger, and Richard Wagner's opera, Die Meistersinger von Nürnberg 1868, depicts the tradition. [German = master singer]

Mekele /'meɪkəleɪ/ capital of Tigray region, N Ethiopia. Population (1984) 62,000.

Mekong /miː'kɒŋ/ river rising as the Za Qu in Tibet and flowing into the South China Sea, through a vast delta (about 200,000 sq km/77,000 sq mi); length 4,425 km/2,750 mi. It is being developed for irrigation and hydroelectricity by Cambodia, Laos, Thailand, and Vietnam.

Melaka /mə'lækə/ Malaysian form of ◊Malacca, state of peninsular Malaysia.

melaleuca tree tropical tree, also known as the paperbark Melaleuca leucadendron, family Myrtaceae. The leaves produce **cajuput oil**, which has medicinal uses.

melamine n. a tough, resilient plastic, symbol $C_3N_6H_6$, a ◊thermosetting ◊polymer based on urea–formaldehyde. It is extremely resistant to heat and is also scratch-resistant. Its uses include synthetic resins. [from melam (arbitrary) and amine]

melancholia /melən'kəʊliə/ n. a mental disorder marked by depression and ill-founded fears.

melancholic /melən'kɒlɪk/ adj. melancholy; liable to melancholy.

melancholy /'melənkəlɪ/ n. pensive sadness; mental depression; a habitual or constitutional tendency to this. —adj. 1. sad, gloomy. 2. saddening, depressing. 3. (of words etc.) expressing sadness. [from Old French from Latin from Greek (melas = black and kholē = bile)]

Melanchthon /mə'læŋkθən/ Philip. Assumed name of Philip Schwarzerd 1497–1560. German theologian who helped Luther prepare a German translation of the New Testament. In 1521 he issued the first systematic formulation of Protestant theology, reiterated in the Confession of ◊Augsburg 1530.

Melanesia /melə'niːziə/ islands in the SW Pacific between Micronesia to the N and Polynesia to the E, embracing all the islands from the New Britain archipelago to Fiji.

mélange /meɪ'lɑːʒ/ n. a medley. [French mêler = mix]

melanin /'melənɪn/ n. a dark pigment in the hair, skin, etc. [from Greek melas = black]

melanoma n. a mole or growth containing the dark pigment melanin. Malignant melanoma is a type of skin cancer developing in association with a pre-existing mole. Once rare, this disease is now frequent, possibly due to depletion

meiosis

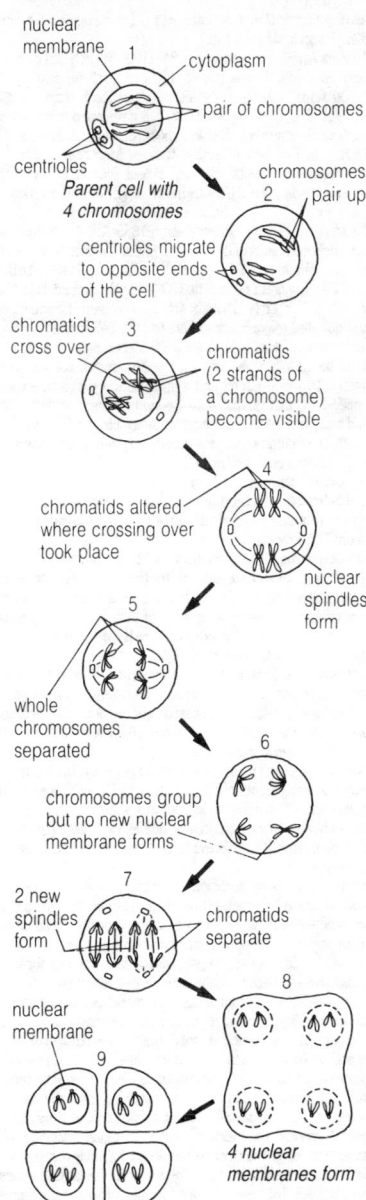

nuclear membrane 1
cytoplasm
pair of chromosomes
centrioles
Parent cell with 4 chromosomes
chromosomes pair up 2
centrioles migrate to opposite ends of the cell
chromatids cross over 3
chromatids (2 strands of a chromosome) become visible
chromatids altered where crossing over took place 4
nuclear spindles form
whole chromosomes separated 5
chromosomes group but no new nuclear membrane forms 6
2 new spindles form 7
chromatids separate
nuclear membrane 8
9
4 nuclear membranes form

4 daughter cells with 2 chromosomes each. None of the new chromosomes are exactly like the original chromosomes

of the ozone layer, which provides some protection against ultraviolet radiation from the Sun. Most at risk are those with fair hair and light skin.

Melba toast thin crisp toast. [from Nellie Melba, Australian soprano (died 1931)]

Melbourne /'melbən/ capital of Victoria, Australia, near the mouth of the river Yarra; population (1986) 2,943,000. Industries include engineering, shipbuilding, electronics, chemicals, food processing, clothing, and textiles.

Melchite /'melkaɪt/ n. or **Melkite** a member of a Christian church in Syria, Egypt, Lebanon, and Israel. The Melchite Church was founded in Syria in the 6th–7th centuries and is now part of the Eastern Orthodox Church. [Syriac = royalist]

mêlée /'meleɪ/ n. 1. a confused fight or struggle. 2. a muddle. [French *mêler* = mix]

Méliès /mel'jes/ Georges 1861–1938. French film pioneer, born in Paris. In the period 1896 to 1912 he made over 1,000 films, mostly fantasies, such as *Le Voyage dans la Lune/A Trip to the Moon* 1902. He developed trick effects such as slow motion, double exposure, and dissolves, and in 1897 built Europe's first film studio at Montreuil.

mellifluous /me'lɪfluəs/ adj. sweet-sounding. —**mellifluously** adv., **mellifluousness** n. [from Old French or Latin *mel* = honey and *fluere* = flow]

Mellon /'melən/ Andrew William 1855–1937. US financier who donated his art collection to found the National Gallery of Art, Washington DC in 1937. His son, **Paul Mellon** (1907–) was its president 1963–79. He funded Yale University's Center for British Art, New Haven, Connecticut, and donated major works of art to both collections.

mellow /'meləʊ/ adj. 1. (of fruit) sweet and rich in flavour from being fully ripe; (of wine) well-matured; (of soil) rich, loamy. 2. made kindly and sympathetic by age or experience. 3. genial, jovial. 4. (of sound, colour, or light) soft and rich, free from harshness or sharp contrast. —v.t./i. to make or become mellow. —**mellowly** adv., **mellowness** n. [perhaps related to *meal*²]

melodic /mɪ'lɒdɪk/ adj. of melody.

melodious /mɪ'ləʊdɪəs/ adj. of or producing melody; sweet-sounding. —**melodiously** adv., **melodiousness** n. [from Old French]

melodrama /'melədrɑːmə/ n. 1. a play with a sensational plot and crude appeal to the emotions, originally accompanied by music; such plays as a genre. 2. behaviour or an occurrence suggestive of this. —**melodramatic** /-drə'mætɪk/ adj., **melodramatically** adv. [from French from Greek *melos* = music]

melody /'melədɪ/ n. 1. sweet music. 2. a musical arrangement of words, a song or tune. 3. an arrangement of single notes in a musically expressive succession; the principal part in harmonized music. [from Old French from Latin from Greek *melōidia* = ode]

melon /'melən/ n. any of several large, juicy, thick-skinned fruit of trailing plants of the gourd family Cucurbitaceae. The muskmelon *Cucumis melo* and the watermelon *Citrullus vulgaris* are two of the many edible varieties. [from Old French from Latin, abbreviation of *melopepo* from Greek = apple-gourd]

melt v.t./i. (*past participle* melted, or (as adj., of substances not easily melted) molten) 1. to change from solid to liquid by heat. 2. to become softened or dissolved easily. 3. to make or become gentler through pity or love. 4. to dwindle or fade away; to pass slowly into another form. 5. (*colloquial*) to depart unobtrusively. —**melt down**, to melt (metal articles) in order to use the metal as a raw material; to become liquid and lose structure. **melting-point** n. the temperature at which a solid melts. **melting-pot** n. a container (e.g. a crucible) in which substances are melted; a place or situation where ideas etc. are being fused or reconstructed. **melt-water** n. water resulting from the melting of ice or snow, especially that of a glacier. [Old English]

meltdown n. the melting of (and consequent damage to) a structure, e. g. the overheated core of a nuclear reactor.

Melville /'melvɪl/ Herman 1819–1891. US writer, whose ◊*Moby Dick* 1851 was inspired by his whaling experiences in the South Seas. These experiences were also the basis for earlier fiction, such as *Typee* 1846 and *Omoo* 1847. He published several volumes of verse, as well as short stories (*The Piazza Tales* 1856). *Billy Budd* was completed just before his death and published 1924. Although most of his works were unappreciated during his lifetime, today he is one of the most highly regarded of US authors.

Old age is always wakeful; as if, the longer linked with life, the less man has to do with aught that looks like death.

Herman Melville
Moby Dick

---

member n. 1. a person or thing belonging to a particular society or group. 2. **Member**, (in full **member of Parliament** or (*US*) **of Congress**) a person formally elected to take part in the proceedings of a parliament (in the UK the House of Commons; in the USA Congress). 3. a part of a complex structure. 4. a part or organ of the body. [from Old French from Latin *membrum* = limb]

membership n. 1. being a member. 2. the number of members; the body of members.

membrane /'membreɪn/ n. a pliable sheetlike tissue connecting or lining structures in an animal or vegetable body. —**membranous** /'membreɪnəs/ adj. [from Latin *membrana*]

memento /mɪ'mentəʊ/ n. (*plural* -oes) an object serving as a reminder or souvenir. [Latin, imperative of *meminisse* = remember]

Memling /'memlɪŋ, -lɪŋk/ (or **Memlinc**) Hans c.1430–1494. Flemish painter, born near Frankfurt-am-Main, Germany, but active in Bruges. He painted religious subjects and portraits. Some of his works are in the Hospital of St John, Bruges, including the *Adoration of the Magi* 1479.

memo /'meməʊ/ (*plural* memos) (*colloquial*) abbreviation of memorandum.

memoir /'memwɑː/ n. 1. a record of events, written from personal knowledge or special sources of information. 2. (usually in *plural*) an autobiography; a biography. 3. an essay on a learned subject specially studied by the writer. [from French *mémoire* from Latin *memor* = mindful]

memorabilia /memərə'bɪlɪə/ n.pl. noteworthy things. [Latin]

memorable /'memərəbəl/ adj. 1. worth remembering. 2. easily remembered. —**memorability** /-'bɪlɪtɪ/ n. **memorably** adv. [from French or Latin *memorabilis* (*memorare* = bring to mind)]

memorandum /memə'rændəm/ n. (*plural* memoranda or memorandums) 1. a note or record made for future use. 2. an informal written message, especially in business etc. [Latin = to be remembered]

memorial n. an object, institution, or custom established in memory of a person or event. —adj. serving as a memorial. [from Old French or Latin]

Memorial Day in the USA, a day of remembrance (formerly Decoration Day) instituted in 1868 for those killed in the US Civil War. Since World War I it has been observed as a public holiday on the last Monday in May, traditionally falling on May 30, in remembrance of all Americans killed in war.

memorize /'meməraɪz/ v.t. to learn by heart.

memory /'memərɪ/ n. 1. the faculty by which things are recalled to or kept in the mind; this in an individual. Memory does not seem to be based in any particular part of the brain; it may depend on changes to the pathways followed by nerve impulses as they move through the brain. Memory can be improved by regular use as the connections between ◊nerve-cells (neurons) become 'well-worn paths' in the brain. Events stored in **short-term memory** are forgotten quickly, whereas those in **long-term memory** can last for many years, enabling recall of information and recognition of people and places over long periods of time. Research is just beginning to uncover the biochemical and electrical bases of the human memory. 2. remembering; a person or thing remembered. 3. posthumous repute. 4. the length of time over which memory extends. 5. in computing, the part of a system used to store data and programs either permanently or temporarily. There are two main types: internal memory and external memory. Memory capacity is measured in ◊kilobytes or ◊megabytes. —**from memory**, without verification. **in memory of**, to keep alive the remembrance of. [from Old French from Latin *memoria* (*memor* = mindful)]

Memphis /'memfɪs/ ruined city beside the Nile, 19 km/12 mi S of Cairo, Egypt. Once the centre of the worship of Ptah, it was the earliest capital of a united Egypt under King Menes about 3200 BC, but was superseded by Thebes under the new empire 1570 BC. It was later used as a stone quarry, but the 'cemetery city' of Sakkara survives, with the step pyramid built for King Zoser by ◊Imhotep, probably the world's oldest stone building.

Memphis industrial city (pharmaceuticals, food processing, cotton, timber, tobacco) on the Mississippi River, in Tennessee, USA; population (1986) 960,000.

Mendelssohn (-Bartholdy) *German composer and pianist Felix Mendelssohn.*

memsahib /ˈmemsɑːɪb, -sɑːb/ *n.* (*historical*) a European married woman as spoken of or to by Indians. [from *ma'am* and *sahib*]

men plural of man.

menace /ˈmenɪs/ *n.* 1. a threat. 2. a dangerous or obnoxious person or thing. —*v.t.* to threaten. —**menacing** *adj.*, **menacingly** *adv.* [from Anglo-French from Latin *minaciae* (*minax* = threatening)]

ménage /meɪˈnɑː/ *n.* a domestic establishment. —**ménage à trois** /ɑː trwɑː/ a household consisting of a husband, wife, and the lover of one of these. [from Old French from Latin]

menagerie /mɪˈnædʒərɪ/ *n.* a collection of wild animals in captivity for exhibition etc. [from French]

Menander /meˈnændə/ *c.*342–291 BC. Greek comic dramatist, born in Athens. Of his 105 plays only fragments (many used as papier-mâché for Egyptian mummy cases) and Latin adaptations were known prior to the discovery in 1957 of the *Dyscholos/The Bad-Tempered Man*.

Mencken /ˈmeŋkən/ H(enry) L(ouis) 1880–1956. US essayist and critic, known as 'the sage of Baltimore'. His unconventionally phrased, satiric contributions to the periodicals *The Smart Set* and *American Mercury* (both of which he edited) aroused controversy.

mend *v.t./i.* 1. to make whole (something that is damaged), to repair. 2. to regain health. 3. to improve. —*n.* a place where a material etc. has been repaired. —**mend one's fences**, to make peace with a person. **on the mend**, improving in health or condition. [from Anglo-French]

mendacious /menˈdeɪʃəs/ *adj.* untruthful, lying. —**mendaciously** *adv.*, **mendacity** /-ˈdæsɪtɪ/ *n.* [from Latin *mendax*]

Mendel /ˈmendl/ Gregor Johann 1822–1884. Austrian biologist, founder of ◊genetics. His experiments with successive generations of peas gave the basis for his theory of particulate inheritance rather than blending, involving dominant and recessive characters. His results, published 1865–69, remained unrecognized until early this century.

mendelevium /mendəˈliːvɪəm/ *n.* a synthesized, radioactive metallic element of the ◊actinide series, symbol Md, atomic number 101, relative atomic mass 258. It was first produced by bombardment of Es-253 with helium nuclei. Its longest-lived isotope, Md-258, has a half-life of about two months. The element is chemically similar to thulium. It was first synthesized by US physicists at the University of California at Berkeley in 1955. [from D I *Mendeleyev*]

Mendeleyev /mendəˈleɪef/ Dmitri Ivanovich 1834–1907. Russian chemist who in 1869 framed the periodic law in chemistry, which states that the chemical properties of the elements depend on their relative atomic masses. This law is the basis of the ◊periodic table of elements.

Mendelian /menˈdiːlɪən/ *adj.* of Mendel's theory of heredity by genes. [from G J *Mendel*]

Mendelism /ˈmendəlɪzəm/ *n.* that part of genetics concerned with the manner in which hereditary factors (genes) and the characteristics they control are inherited during the course of sexual reproduction. The main principles were first outlined by Mendel, although they have been modified by later discoveries.

Mendelssohn (-Bartholdy) /ˈmendlsən/ (Jakob Ludwig) Felix 1809–1847. German composer, also a pianist and conductor. Among his many works are *A Midsummer Night's Dream* 1827; the *Fingal's Cave* overture 1832; and five symphonies, which include the Reformation 1830, the Italian 1833, and the Scottish 1842.

Mendes /ˈmendɪs/ Chico (Filho Francisco) 1944–1988. Brazilian environmentalist and labour leader. Opposed to the destruction of Brazil's rainforests, he organized itinerant rubber tappers into the Workers' Party (PT) and was assassinated by Darci Alves, a cattle rancher's son.

Mendès-France /mɒndesˈfrɒns/ Pierre 1907–1982. French prime minister and foreign minister 1954–55. He extricated France from the war in Indochina, and prepared the way for Tunisian independence.

mendicant /ˈmendɪkənt/ *adj.* begging; (of a friar) living solely on alms. —*n.* a beggar; a mendicant friar. [from Latin *mendicare* (*mendicus* = beggar)]

mendicant order a religious order dependent on alms. In the Roman Catholic Church there are four orders of mendicant friars: Franciscans, Dominicans, Carmelites, and Augustinians. Hinduism has similar orders.

Mendoza /menˈdəʊsə/ Antonio de *c.*1490–1552. First Spanish viceroy of New Spain (Mexico) 1535–51. He attempted to develop agriculture and mining and supported the church in its attempts to convert the Indians. The system he established lasted until the 19th century. He was subsequently viceroy of Peru 1551–52.

Menem /ˈmenem/ Carlos Saul 1935– . Argentine politician, president from 1989; leader of the Peronist (Justice Party) movement. As president, he improved relations with the UK.

Menes /ˈmiːniːz/ *c.*3200 BC. Traditionally, the first king of the first dynasty of ancient Egypt. He is said to have founded Memphis and organized worship of the gods.

menfolk *n.* 1. men in general. 2. the men in a family.

Mengistu /menˈgɪstu/ Haile Mariam 1937– . Ethiopian soldier and socialist politician, head of state from 1977 (president from 1987). As an officer in the Ethiopian army, he took part in the overthrow in 1974 of Emperor ◊Haile Selassie and in 1977 led another coup, becoming head of state. He was confronted with severe problems of drought and secessionist uprisings, but survived with help from the USSR and the West. In 1987 civilian rule was formally reintroduced, but with the Marxist-Leninist Workers' Party of Ethiopia the only legally permitted party.

menhir /ˈmenhɪə/ *n.* a tall, upright, prehistoric monumental stone. [from Breton *men* = stone and *hir* = long]

menial /ˈmiːnɪəl/ *adj.* (of work) lowly, degrading. —*n.* a lowly domestic servant; a person who does humble tasks. —**menially** *adv.* [from Anglo-French *meinie* = retinue]

meninges /mɪˈnɪndʒiːz/ *n.pl.* the membranes enclosing the brain and spinal cord. [from Greek *mēnigx-iggos* = membrane]

meningitis /menɪnˈdʒaɪtɪs/ *n.* inflammation of the meninges caused by bacterial or viral infection. The severity of the disease varies from mild to rapidly lethal, and symptoms include fever, headache, nausea, neck stiffness, delirium, and (rarely) convulsions. Many common viruses can cause the occasional case of meningitis, although not usually in its more severe form. The treatment for viral meningitis is rest. Bacterial meningitis, though treatable by antibiotics, is a much more serious threat. Diagnosis is by ◊lumbar puncture.

meniscus /mɪˈnɪskəs/ *n.* (*plural* menisci /-saɪ/) 1. the curved upper surface of a liquid in a tube, usually concave upwards when the walls are wetted and convex when they are dry, because of the effects of surface tension. 2. a lens that is convex on one side and concave on the other. [from Greek = crescent (*mēnē* = moon)]

Mennonite /ˈmenənaɪt/ *n.* a member of a Protestant Christian sect, originating in Zürich in 1523. Members refuse to hold civil office or do military service, and reject infant baptism. [from *Menno* Simons (1496–1561), leader of a group in Holland]

menopause /ˈmenəpɔːz/ *n.* in women, the cessation of reproductive ability, characterized by menstruation (see ◊menstrual cycle) becoming irregular and eventually ceasing. The onset is at about the age of 50, but often varies greatly. Menopause is usually uneventful, but some women suffer from complications such as flushing, excessive bleeding, and nervous disorders. Since the 1950s, hormone replacement therapy (HRT), using ◊oestrogen alone

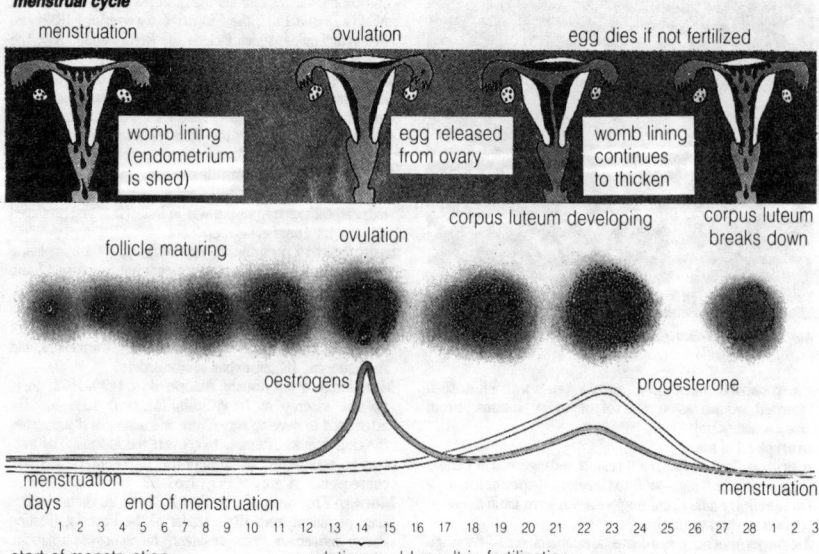

menstrual cycle

menstruation — ovulation — egg dies if not fertilized

womb lining (endometrium is shed)

egg released from ovary

womb lining continues to thicken

corpus luteum developing — corpus luteum breaks down

follicle maturing — ovulation

oestrogens — progesterone

menstruation — menstruation

days — end of menstruation

1 2 3 4 5 6 7 8 9 10 11 12 13 14 15 16 17 18 19 20 21 22 23 24 25 26 27 28 1 2 3

start of menstruation — copulation could result in fertilization

or with ◊progesterone, has been developed to counteract such effects. —**menopausal** *adj.* [from Greek *mēn* = month and *pause*]

menorah /məˈnɔːrə/ *n.* a holy seven-branched candelabrum used in the ancient Temple in Jerusalem; a candelabrum with any number of branches used in modern synagogues. [Hebrew = candlestick]

Mensa International /ˈmensə/ organization founded in the UK 1945 with membership limited to those passing an 'intelligence' test. It has been criticized by many who believe that intelligence is not satisfactorily measured by IQ tests alone.

menses /ˈmensiːz/ *n.pl.* the flow of blood etc. from the mucous lining of the human or primate womb, occurring in women at monthly intervals from puberty until middle age. [Latin plural of *mensis* = month]

Menshevik /ˈmenʃəvɪk/ *n.* a member of the minority (Russian *menshinstvo* 'minority') of the Russian Social Democratic Party, who split from the ◊Bolsheviks 1903. The Mensheviks believed in a large, loosely organized party and that, before socialist revolution could occur in Russia, capitalist society had to develop further. During the Russian Revolution they had limited power and set up a government in Georgia, but were suppressed in 1922.

menstrual /ˈmenstruəl/ *adj.* of menstruation. [from Latin *menstruus* = monthly from *mensis* = month]

menstrual cycle the cycle that occurs in female mammals of reproductive age, in which the body is prepared for pregnancy. At the beginning of the cycle, a Graafian (egg) follicle develops in the ovary, and the inner wall of the uterus forms a soft, spongy lining. The egg is released from the ovary, and the lining of the uterus becomes vascularized (filled with blood vessels). If fertilization does not occur, the corpus luteum (remains of the Graafian follicle) degenerates, and the uterine lining breaks down, and is shed. This is what causes the loss of blood that marks menstruation. The cycle then begins again. Human menstruation takes place from puberty to menopause, occurring about every 28 days.

menstruate /ˈmenstrueɪt/ *v.i.* to discharge the menses. —**menstruation** /-ˈeɪʃən/ *n.* [from Latin *menstruare*]

mensurable /ˈmensjurəbəl/ *adj.* measurable; having fixed limits.

mensuration /mensjuəˈreɪʃən/ *n.* measuring; the mathematical rules for finding lengths, areas, and volumes. [French or from Latin *mensurare* = to measure]

menswear *n.* clothes for men.

-ment /-mənt/ suffix forming nouns expressing the result or means of a verbal action (*fragment, ornament, treatment*); also forming nouns from adjectives (*merriment, oddment*). [from French from Latin *-mentum*]

mental /ˈmentəl/ *adj.* 1. of the mind; done by the mind. 2. caring for mental patients. 3. (*colloquial*) affected with mental disorder. —**mental age**, the degree of a person's mental development expressed as the age at which the same degree is attained by the average child. **mental deficiency**, imperfect mental development leading to abnormally low intelligence. **mental patient**, a sufferer from mental illness. —**mentally** *adv.* [from Old French or Latin *mens* = mind]

mental handicap impairment of intelligence. It can be very mild, but in more severe cases, it is associated with social problems and difficulties in living independently. A person may be born with a mental handicap or may acquire it through brain damage. There are between 90 and 130 million people in the world suffering such disabilities.

mental illness abnormal working of the mind. Since normal working cannot be defined, the borderline between mild mental illness and normality is a matter of opinion (not to be confused with normative behaviour; see ◊norm). Mild forms are known as **neuroses**, affecting the emotions, whereas more severe forms, **psychoses**, distort conscious reasoning.

mentality /menˈtælɪtɪ/ *n.* mental character or outlook; mental ability.

menthol /ˈmenθɒl/ *n.* a camphor-like substance, $C_{10}H_{19}OH$, obtained from oil of peppermint etc., used as a flavouring or to relieve local pain etc. [German, from Latin *mentha* = mint]

mentholated /ˈmenθəleɪtɪd/ *adj.* treated with or containing menthol.

mention /ˈmenʃən/ *v.t.* to refer to briefly or by name. —*n.* 1. mentioning. 2. a formal acknowledgement of merit. —**don't mention it**, a polite reply to thanks or an apology. **not to mention**, and also. [from Old French from Latin]

mentor /ˈmentɔː/ *n.* an experienced and trusted adviser. [French, from *Mentor* adviser of young Telemachus, son of Odysseus]

menu /ˈmenjuː/ *n.* 1. a list of the dishes available in a restaurant etc. or to be served at a meal. 2. a list of options, displayed on a screen, from which a user selects what he requires a computer to do. [French = detailed list]

Menuhin /ˈmenjuɪn/ Yehudi 1916– . US violinist. A child prodigy, he achieved great depth of interpretation, and was often accompanied on the piano by his sister **Hephzibah** (1921–81). He conducted his own chamber orchestra and in 1963 founded a school in Surrey, England, for training young musicians.

Menzies /ˈmenzɪz/ Robert Gordon 1894–1978. Australian politician, leader of the United Australia (now Liberal) Party and prime minister 1939–41 and 1949–66.

Menzies William Cameron 1896–1957. US art director of films, later a film director and producer, who was one of Hollywood's most imaginative and talented designers. He was responsible for the sets of such classics as *Gone With the Wind* (Academy Award for best art direction) 1939 and *Foreign Correspondent* 1940. His films as director include *Things to Come* 1936 and *Invaders from Mars* 1953.

MEP abbreviation of Member of the European Parliament.

Mephistopheles /mefiˈstɒfɪliˈz/ or **Mephisto** another name for the ◊devil, or an agent of the devil, associated with the ◊Faust legend.

mercantile /ˈmɜːkəntaɪl/ *adj.* of trade, commercial; trading. —**mercantile marine**, the merchant navy. [French from Italian]

mercantilism /ˈmɜːkəntɪlɪzəm/ *n.* economic theory, held in the 16th–18th centuries, that a nation's wealth (in the form of bullion or treasure) was the key to its prosperity. To this end, foreign trade should be regulated to create a surplus of exports over imports, and the state should intervene where necessary (for example, subsidizing exports and taxing imports). The bullion theory of wealth was demolished by Adam ◊Smith in Book IV of *The Wealth of Nations* 1776.

Mercator /mɜːˈkeɪtə/ Gerardus 1512–1594. Latinized form of the name of the Flemish map-maker Gerhard Kremer. He devised the first modern atlas, showing **Mercator's projection** in which the parallels and meridians on maps are drawn uniformly at 90°. It is often used for navigational charts, because compass courses can be drawn as straight lines, but the true area of countries is increasingly distorted the further N or S they are from the equator.

Mercedes-Benz /məˈseɪdɪz ˈbenz/ *n.* German car-manufacturing company created by a merger of the Daimler and Benz factories 1926. The first cars to carry the Mercedes name were those built by Gottlieb ◊Daimler 1901.

mercenary /ˈmɜːsɪnərɪ/ *adj.* working merely for money or other reward; hired. —*n.* a hired soldier in foreign service or in a private army. —**mercenarily** *adv.* [from Latin *mercenarius* (*merces* = reward)]

mercer *n.* a dealer in textile fabrics. [from Anglo-French from Latin *merx* = goods]

mercerize /ˈmɜːsəraɪz/ *v.t.* to treat (cotton fabric or thread) with caustic alkali to give greater strength and lustre. [from *J Mercer*, alleged inventor of the process]

merchandise /ˈmɜːtʃəndaɪz/ *n.* the commodities of commerce; goods for sale. —*v.t./i.* to promote the sales of (goods etc.); to trade. [from Old French *marchandise*]

merchant /ˈmɜːtʃənt/ *n.* 1. a wholesale trader, especially with foreign countries. 2. (*US & Scottish*) a retail trader. 3. (*slang*) a person fond of an activity etc. —**merchant bank**, a bank whose main business is the providing of long-term credit and the financing of trading enterprises. **merchant navy**, shipping engaged in commerce. **merchant prince**, a wealthy merchant. **merchant ship**, a ship carrying merchandise. [from Old French *marchand* from Latin *mercari* = trade]

Merchant Ismail 1936– . Indian film producer, known for his stylish collaborations with James Ivory on films including *Shakespeare Wallah* 1965, *The Europeans* 1979, *Heat and Dust* 1983, *A Room with a View* 1986, and *Maurice* 1987.

merchantable *adj.* saleable.

merchantman *n.* (*plural* **merchantmen**) a merchant ship.

Merchant of Venice, The a comedy by William Shakespeare, first performed 1596–97. Antonio, a rich merchant, borrows money from Shylock, a Jewish moneylender, promising a pound of flesh if the sum is not repaid; when Shylock presses his claim, the heroine, Portia, disguised as a lawyer, saves Antonio's life.

Merchants Adventurers English trading company founded in 1407, which controlled the export of cloth to continental Europe. It comprised guilds and traders in many N European ports. In direct opposition to the Hanseatic League, it came to control 75% of English overseas trade by 1550. In 1689 it lost its charter for furthering the traders' own interests at the expense of the English economy. The company was finally dissolved in 1806.

Mercia /ˈmɜːsiə/ Anglo-Saxon kingdom that emerged in the 6th century. By the late 8th century it dominated all

England S of the Humber, but from about 825 came under the power of ◊Wessex. Mercia eventually came to denote an area bounded by the Welsh border, the river Humber, East Anglia, and the river Thames.

merciful /ˈmɜːsɪfʊl/ *adj.* 1. having, showing, or feeling mercy. 2. giving relief from pain etc. —**mercifully** *adv.*, **mercifulness** *n.*

merciless /ˈmɜːsɪlɪs/ *adj.* showing no mercy. —**mercilessly** *adv.*, **mercilessness** *n.*

Merckx /merks/ Eddie 1945– . Belgian cyclist known as 'the Cannibal'. He won the Tour de France a joint record five times 1969–74. He retired in 1977.

mercurial /mɜːˈkjʊəriəl/ *adj.* 1. (of a person) volatile, ready-witted. 2. of or containing mercury. [from Old French or Latin]

mercury /ˈmɜːkjʊrɪ/ *n.* or **quicksilver** heavy, silver-grey, metallic element, symbol Hg (from Latin *hydrargyrum*), atomic number 80, relative atomic mass 200.59. It is a dense, mobile liquid with a low melting point (–38.87°C/–37.96°F). The chief source is the mineral cinnabar, HgS. Mercury sometimes occurs as a free metal. Its alloys with other metals are called amalgams. Industrial uses include drugs and chemicals, mercury-vapour lamps, arc rectifiers, power-control switches, barometers and thermometers. —**mercuric** /-ˈkjʊərɪk/ *adj.*, **mercurous** *adj.* [from *Mercury*, the planet]

Mercury 1. Roman god, identified with the Greek Hermes, and like him represented with winged sandals and a winged staff entwined with snakes. He was the messenger of the gods. 2. in astronomy, the closest planet to the Sun, at an average distance of 58 million km/36 million mi. Its diameter is 4,880 km/3,030 mi, its mass 0.056 that of Earth. Mercury orbits the Sun every 88 days, and spins on its axis every 59 days. On its sunward side the surface temperature reaches over 400°C/752°F, but on the 'night' side it falls to –170°C/–274°F. Mercury has an atmosphere with minute traces of argon and helium. In 1974 the US space probe *Mariner 10* discovered that its surface is cratered by meteorite impacts. Mercury has no moons.

mercury fulminate highly explosive compound used in detonators and percussion caps. It is a grey, sandy powder and extremely poisonous.

Mercury project the US project to put a human in space in the one-seat Mercury spacecraft 1961–63.

mercy /ˈmɜːsɪ/ *n.* 1. refraining from inflicting punishment or pain on an offender or enemy etc. who is in one's power. 2. a tendency to behave in this way. 3. a merciful act; a thing to be thankful for. —**at the mercy of**, wholly in the power of; liable to danger or harm from. **mercy killing**, euthanasia. [from Old French from Latin *merces* = reward, later = pity, thanks]

mere[1] /mɪə/ *attributive adj.* that is solely or no more or better than what is specified. [from Anglo-French from Latin *merus* = unmixed]

mere[2] *n.* (*poetic*) a lake. [Old English]

Meredith George 1828–1909. English novelist and poet. He published the first realistic psychological novel *The Ordeal of Richard Feverel* 1859. Later works include *Evan Harrington* 1861. *The Egoist* 1879, *Diana of the Crossways* 1885, and *The Amazing Marriage* 1895. His best verse is in *Modern Love* 1862.

merely *adv.* only, just.

merengue *n.* a type of Latin American dance music with a lively 2/4 beat. Accordion and saxophone are prominent instruments, with ethnic percussion. It originated in the Dominican Republic and became popular in New York in the 1980s.

meretricious /merɪˈtrɪʃəs/ *adj.* showily attractive but cheap or insincere. —**meretriciously** *adv.*, **meretriciousness** *n.* [from Latin *meretrix* = prostitute]

merganser /mɜːˈgænsə/ *n.* a type of diving duck with a sawbill for catching fish. It is widely distributed in the N hemisphere. [from Latin *mergus* = diver and *anser* = goose]

merge /mɜːdʒ/ *v.t./i.* 1. to unite or combine into a whole. 2. to pass (one) into something else; to blend or become blended. [from Latin *mergere* = dip]

Mergenthaler /ˈmɜːgəntɑːlə/ Ottmar 1854–1899. German-born American who invented a typesetting method. He went to the USA in 1872 and developed the first linotype machine (for casting hot-metal type in complete lines) 1876–86.

merger /'mɜːdʒə/ *n.* the linking of two or more companies, either by creating a new organization by consolidating the original companies or by absorption by one of the others. Unlike a takeover, which is not always a voluntary fusion of the parties, a merger is the result of an agreement. [from Anglo-French]

Mérida /'meriðə/ capital of Yucatán state, Mexico, a centre of the sisal industry; population (1986) 580,000. It was founded in 1542, and has a cathedral built in 1598. Its port on the Gulf of Mexico is Progreso.

meridian /mə'ridiən/ *n.* 1. a circle of constant longitude, passing through a given place and the terrestrial poles; a corresponding line on a map or the sky. 2. prime, full splendour. [from Old French or Latin *meridies* = midday]

meridional /mə'ridiənəl/ *adj.* 1. of the south, especially of Europe, or its inhabitants. 2. of a meridian. [from Old French from Latin]

Mérimée /meri'mei/ Prosper 1803–1870. French author. Among his works are the short novels *Colomba* 1841, *Carmen* 1846, and the *Lettres à une inconnue/Letters to an Unknown Girl* 1873.

meringue /mə'ræŋ/ *n.* a mixture of white of egg, sugar, etc., baked crisp. [French]

merino /mə'riːnəʊ/ *n.* (*plural* **merinos**) 1. a variety of sheep with fine wool. 2. a soft woollen yarn or fabric originally of merino wool. [Spanish]

merit /'merit/ *n.* 1. the quality of deserving to be praised, excellence. 2. a feature or quality that deserves praise. —*v.t.* to deserve. —**Order of Merit**, an order, founded in 1902, for distinguished achievement. [from Latin *meritum* (*merēri* = deserve)]

meritocracy /meri'tɒkrəsi/ *n.* government by persons selected for their merit.

meritorious /meri'tɔːriəs/ *adj.* having merit, praiseworthy. —**meritoriously** *adv.*, **meritoriousness** *n.* [from Latin]

merlin /'mɜːlin/ *n.* a kind of small falcon *Falco columbarius*. [from Anglo-French]

Merlin /'mɜːlin/ legendary magician and counsellor to King ◊Arthur. Welsh bardic literature has a cycle of poems attributed to him, and he may have been a real person.

merlon /'mɜːlən/ *n.* the solid part of an embattled parapet, between two embrasures. [French, from Italian *merlone* (*merlo* = battlement)]

mermaid /'mɜːmeid/ *n.* a legendary sea-creature with a woman's head and trunk and a fish's tail. [from *mere²* in obsolete sense 'sea' and *maid*]

Meroe /'merəʊi/ ancient city in Sudan, on the Nile near Khartoum, capital of Nubia from about 600 BC to AD 350. Tombs and inscriptions have been excavated, and iron-smelting slag heaps have been found.

Merovingian dynasty /merə'vindʒiən/ a Frankish dynasty, named after its founder, Clovis I **Merovaeus** (5th century AD). His descendants ruled France from the time of Clovis (481–511) to 751.

merry *adj.* joyous, full of laughter or gaiety; (*colloquial*) slightly tipsy. —**make merry**, to be festive. **merry-go-round** *n.* a revolving machine with horses, cars, etc., for riding on at a fair etc., a revolving device in a playground, a cycle of bustling activities. **merry-making** *n.* festivity. —**merrily** *adv.*, **merriment** *n.* [Old English]

Mersey /'mɜːzi/ river in NW England; length 112 km/ 70 mi. Formed by the confluence of the Goyt and Etherow rivers, it flows W to join the Irish Sea at Liverpool Bay. It is linked to the Manchester Ship Canal.

Mersey beat a type of pop music of the mid-1960s that originated in the NW of England. It was also known as the Liverpool sound or beat music in the UK or the British Invasion in the US. The beat groups characteristically had a simple, guitar-dominated line-up, vocal harmonies and catchy tunes. It was almost exclusively performed by all-male groups, of whom the most celebrated was the Beatles.

Merseyside /'mɜːzisaid/ former (1974–86) metropolitan county of NW England, replaced by a residuary body in 1986 which covers some of its former functions; **area** 650 sq km/251 sq mi; **administrative headquarters** Liverpool; **population** (1987) 1,457,000.

Merv /meəf/ oasis in Soviet Turkmenistan, a centre of civilization from at least 1200 BC, and site of a town founded by Alexander the Great. Old Merv was destroyed by the emir of Bokhara 1787, and the modern town of Mary, founded by the Russians in 1885, lies 29 km/18 mi to its west.

mesa /'meisə/ *n.* (*US*) a flat-topped steep-sided plateau, consisting of horizontal weak layers of rock topped by a resistant formation; in particular, those found in the desert areas of the USA and Mexico. A small mesa is called a butte. [Spanish = table]

mésalliance /mei'zæliɑ̃s/ *n.* marriage with a social inferior. [French]

mescal /'meskæl/ *n.* the peyote cactus. —**mescal buttons**, its disc-shaped dried tops. [from Spanish from Nahuatl]

mescaline /'meskəliːn/ *n.* a hallucinogenic crystalline alkaloid, $C_{11}H_{17}NO_3$, present in mescal buttons.

Mesdames plural of *Madame*; also used as plural of **Mrs**.

Mesdemoiselles plural of *Mademoiselle*.

mesembryanthemum /mizembri'ænθiməm/ *n.* a plant of the genus *Mesembryanthemum*, with flowers that are open in the middle of the day. [from Greek *mesēmbria* = noon and *anthemon* = flower]

mesh *n.* 1. the open spaces between the threads or wires in a net, sieve, wire screen, etc. 2. network fabric. 3. (in *plural*) a network; a trap or snare. —*v.t./i.* 1. (of toothed wheels) to engage with another or others. 2. to be harmonious. 3. to catch in a net (*literal* or *figurative*). —**in mesh**, (of the teeth of wheels) engaged. [from Middle Dutch]

Meskhetian /me'sketiən/ *n.* a member of a community of Turkish descent who formerly inhabited Meskhetia, USSR, on the Turkish-Soviet border. They were deported by Stalin in 1944 to Kazakhstan and Uzbekistan, and have campaigned since then for a return to their homeland. In June 1989 at least 70 were killed in pogroms directed against their community in the Ferghana Valley of Uzbekistan by the native Uzbeks.

Mesmer /'mesmə/ Friedrich Anton 1733–1815. Austrian physician, an early experimenter in ◊hypnosis.

mesmerize /'mezməraiz/ *v.t.* to hypnotize; to fascinate, to dominate the attention or will of. —**mesmeric** /-'merik/ *adj.*, **mesmerism** *n.* [from F A *Mesmer*]

meso- /'mesəʊ-/ in combinations, middle, intermediate. [from Greek *mesos* = middle]

mesolithic /mesə'liθik/ *adj.* of the transitional period of prehistory between the palaeolithic and neolithic, especially in Europe. [from Greek *lithos* = stone]

mesomorph /'mesəmɔːf/ *n.* a person with a compact muscular build of body. [from Greek *morphē* = form]

meson /'miːzɒn/ *n.* an unstable fundamental particle with mass intermediate between those of the electron and the proton, found in cosmic radiation and emitted by nuclei under bombardment by very high-energy particles. [alteration of earlier *mesotron*]

mesopause /'mesəpɔːz/ *n.* the boundary between the mesosphere and the thermosphere, where the temperature stops decreasing with height and starts to increase.

mesophyll *n.* the tissue between the upper and lower epidermis of a leaf blade (◊lamina), consisting of parenchyma-like cells containing numerous ◊chloroplasts.

Mesopotamia /mesəpə'teimiə/ the land between the Tigris and Euphrates rivers, now part of Iraq where the civilizations of Sumer and Babylon flourished. Sumer (3500 BC) may have been the earliest civilization. —**Mesopotamian** *adj.* & *n.* [from Greek *mesos* = middle and *potamos* = river]

mesosphere /'mesəsfiə(r)/ *n.* layer in the Earth's ◊atmosphere above the stratosphere and below the thermosphere. It extends between about 50 km/31 mi and 80 km/50 mi above the ground.

Mesozoic /mesə'zəʊik/ *adj.* of an era of geological time 248–65 million years ago, consisting of the Triassic, Jurassic, and Cretaceous periods. At the beginning of the era, the continents were joined together as Pangaea, dinosaurs and other giant reptiles dominated the sea and air; and ferns, horsetails, and cycads thrived in a warm climate worldwide. By the end of the Mesozoic era, the continents had begun to assume their present positions, flowering plants were dominant and many of the large reptiles and marine fauna were becoming extinct. —*n.* this era. [from Greek *zōion* = animal]

mess *n.* **1.** a dirty or untidy state of things; an untidy collection of things; something spilt. **2.** a difficult or confused situation, trouble. **3.** a disagreeable substance or concoction; excreta. **4.** (*colloquial*) a person who looks untidy, dirty, or slovenly. **5.** a group of people who take meals together, especially in the armed services; the room where such meals are taken; a meal so taken. **6.** a portion of liquid or pulpy food. —*v.t./i.* **1.** to make untidy or dirty. **2.** to muddle or bungle (often with *up*). **3.** to potter or fool *about* or *around*; to tinker. **4.** to take one's meals with a military or other group. —**make a mess of,** to bungle. **mess-jacket** *n.* a short close-fitting coat worn at mess. **mess-kit** *n.* a soldier's cooking and eating utensils. [from Old French from Latin *missus* = course at dinner (*mittere* = send)]

message /'mesɪdʒ/ *n.* **1.** a spoken or written communication sent or transmitted from one person to another. **2.** an inspired or significant communication from a prophet, writer, preacher, etc. —**get the message,** (*colloquial*) to understand what is meant. [from Old French, ultimately from Latin *mittere* = send]

Messalina /mesə'li:nə/ Valeria c. AD 22–48. Third wife of the Roman emperor ◊Claudius, whom she dominated. She was notorious for her immorality, forcing a noble to marry her in AD 48, although still married to Claudius, who then had her executed.

messenger /'mesɪndʒə/ *n.* one who carries a message.

Messerschmitt /'mesəʃmɪt/ Willy 1898–1978. German aeroplane designer whose Me-109 was a standard Luftwaffe fighter in World War II, and whose Me-262 (1942) was the first mass-produced jet fighter.

Messiaen /mesi'ɒŋ/ Olivier 1908– . French composer and organist. His music is mystical in character, vividly coloured, and incorporates transcriptions of birdsong. Among his works are the *Quartet for the End of Time* 1941, the large-scale *Turangalîla Symphony* 1949, and solo organ and piano pieces.

Messiah /mi'saɪə/ *n.* **1.** the expected deliverer and ruler of the Jewish people, whose coming was prophesied in the Old Testament. **2.** Christ, regarded by Christians as this. **3.** a liberator of oppressed people. [from Old French, ultimately from Hebrew = anointed]

Messianic /mesi'ænɪk/ *adj.* of the Messiah; inspired by hope or belief in a Messiah. [from French]

Messier /mesi'eɪ/ Charles 1730–1817. French astronomer, who discovered 15 comets and in 1781 published a list of 103 star clusters and nebulae. Objects on this list are given M (for Messier) numbers, which astronomers still use today, such as M1 (the Crab nebula) and M31 (the Andromeda galaxy).

Messieurs plural of *Monsieur*.

Messina, Strait of /me'si:nə/ channel in the central Mediterranean separating Sicily from mainland Italy; in Greek legend a monster (Charybdis), who devoured ships, lived in the whirlpool on the Sicilian side, and another (Scylla), who devoured sailors, in the rock on the Italian side. The classical hero Odysseus passed safely between them.

Messrs /'mesəz/ *n.* used as plural of **Mr**, especially as a prefix to the name of a firm or to a list of men's names. [abbreviation of *Messieurs*]

messuage /'meswɪdʒ/ *n.* in law, a dwelling-house with outbuildings and land. [from Anglo-French, perhaps alteration of *mesnage* = dwelling]

messy *adj.* **1.** untidy or dirty. **2.** causing or accompanied by a mess. **3.** difficult to deal with. —**messily** *adv.,* **messiness** *n.*

met[1] (*colloquial*) abbreviation of **1.** meteorological. **2.** metropolitan. —**the Met,** the Meteorological Office; the Metropolitan Opera House (New York).

met[2] past and past participle of **meet**[1].

meta- /metə/ prefix denoting a position or condition behind, after, beyond or transcending (*metacarpus*), or a change of position or condition (*metabolism*). [Greek *meta* = with, after]

metabolism /mi'tæbəlɪzəm/ *n.* the chemical processes of living organisms: a constant alternation of building up (**anabolism**) and breaking down (**catabolism**). For example, green plants build up complex organic substances from water, carbon dioxide, and mineral salts (photosynthesis); by digestion animals partially break down complex organic substances, ingested as food, and subsequently resynthesize them in their own bodies. —**metabolic** /metə'bɒlɪk/ *adj.* [from Greek *metabolē* = change]

metabolize /mi'tæbəlaɪz/ *v.t.* to process (food) in metabolism.

metacarpus /metə'kɑːpəs/ *n.* (*plural* **metacarpi** /-paɪ/) the part of the hand between the wrist and the fingers; the set of bones in this. —**metacarpal** *adj.* [from Greek]

metal /metəl/ *n.* **1.** any of a large class of elements which in general can take the form of opaque solids having a characteristic lustre; an alloy of these. **2.** (in *plural*) the rails of a railway-line; road-metal (see ◊road). —*adj.* made of metal. —*v.t.* (**-ll-**) **1.** to furnish or fit with metal. **2.** to make or mend (a road) with road-metal. [from Old French or Latin from Greek *metallon* = mine]

metal detector electronic device for detecting metal, usually below ground, developed from the wartime mine detector. In the head of the metal detector is a coil, which is part of an electronic circuit. The presence of metal causes the frequency of the signal in the circuit to change, setting up an audible note in the headphones worn by the user. They are used to survey areas for buried metallic objects, especially in archaeology.

metal fatigue condition in which metals fail or fracture under relatively light loads, when these loads are applied repeatedly. Structures that are subject to flexing, such as the airframes of aircraft, are prone to metal fatigue.

metallic /mi'tælɪk/ *adj.* **1.** of metal; characteristic of metals. **2.** sounding like struck metal. —**metallically** *adv.* [from French from Latin from Greek]

metallic bond the force of attraction operating in a metal that holds the atoms together. In the metal the ◊valency electrons are able to move within the crystal and these electrons are said to be delocalized (see ◊electrons, delocalized). Their movement creates short-lived, positively charged ions. The electrostatic attraction between the delocalized electrons and the ceaselessly forming ions constitutes the metallic bond.

metallic character chemical properties associated with those elements classed as metals. These properties, which arise from the element's ability to lose electrons, are: the displacement of hydrogen from dilute acids; the formation of ◊basic oxides; the formation of ionic chlorides; and their reducing reaction, as in the ◊thermite process (see ◊reduction).

metalliferous /metə'lɪfərəs/ *adj.* (of rocks etc.) containing metal. [from Latin]

metallize /'metəlaɪz/ *v.t.* **1.** to render metallic. **2.** to coat with a thin layer of metal. —**metallization** /-'zeɪʃən/ *n.*

metallography /metə'lɒgrəfɪ/ *n.* the descriptive science of metals.

metalloid *n.* or **semimetal** a chemical element having some of but not all the properties of metals; metalloids are thus usually electrically semiconducting. They comprise the elements germanium, arsenic, antimony, and tellurium.

metallurgy /mi'tælədʒɪ, 'metələdʒɪ/ *n.* the science and technology of producing metals, which includes extraction, alloying, and hardening. **Extractive,** or **process, metallurgy** is concerned with the extraction of metals from their ◊ores and refining and adapting them for use. **Physical metallurgy** is concerned with their properties and application. **Metallography** establishes the microscopic structures that contribute to hardness, ductility, and strength. —**metallurgical** /metə'lɜːdʒɪkəl/ *adj.,* **metallurgist** *n.* [from Greek (*-ourgia* = working)]

metamorphic /metə'mɔːfɪk/ *adj.* **1.** of or characterized by metamorphism. **2.** (of rock) that has undergone structural, chemical, or mineralogical change by natural agencies, especially heat and pressure (see ◊igneous, ◊sedimentary), as in the transformation of limestone into marble. [from Greek *morphē* = form]

metamorphism /metə'mɔːfɪzəm/ *n.* the process of metamorphic change in rock.

metamorphose /metə'mɔːfəuz/ *v.t.* to change into a new form; to change the nature of. [from French]

metamorphosis /metə'mɔːfəsɪs, -'fəusɪs/ *n.* (*plural* **metamorphoses** /-siːz/) **1.** a change of form, especially by magic or natural development. **2.** a change of character, conditions, etc. **3.** a period during the life cycle of many invertebrates, most amphibians, and some fish, during which the individual's body changes from one form to another through a major reconstitution of its tissues. For example, adult frogs are produced by metamorphosis from tadpoles, and butterflies are produced from caterpillars following metamorphosis within a pupa. [Latin from Greek]

metaphor /'metəfə/ n. an application of a name or descriptive term or phrase to an object or action where it is not literally applicable (e. g. *a glaring error*). —**metaphorical** /-'forɪkəl/ *adj.* , **metaphorically** *adv.* [from French or Latin from Greek *metapherō* = transfer]

metaphysical /metə'fɪzɪkəl/ *adj.* 1. of or involving metaphysics. 2. based on abstract reasoning, over-subtle. 3. in English literature, a term applied to a group of 17th-century poets whose work is characterized by conciseness, ingenious, often highly intricate wordplay, and striking imagery. Some of the best exponents of this genre are John ◊Donne, George ◊Herbert, and Abraham ◊Cowley.

metaphysics /metə'fɪzɪks/ *n.pl.* (usually treated as *singular*) 1. the branch of speculative inquiry that deals with such concepts as being, knowing, substance, cause, identity, time, space, etc. 2. (*popularly*) abstract or subtle talk, mere theory. [from Old French ultimately from Greek *ta meta ta phusica*, the title applied, at least from the 1st century AD, to the 13 books of Aristotle dealing with questions of ontology]

metastasis /me'tæstəsɪs/ n. (*plural* **metastases** /-əsiːz/) the transfer of disease etc. from one part of the body to another. [Latin from Greek = removal, change]

metatarsus /metə'taːsəs/ n. (*plural* **metatarsi** /-saɪ/) the part of the foot between the ankle and the toes; the set of bones in this. —**metatarsal** *adj.*

mete /miːt/ *v.t.* to allot or deal (a punishment, reward, etc.). [Old English]

metempsychosis n. = ◊reincarnation.

meteor /'miːtiə/ n. a bright moving body popularly known as a **shooting** or **falling star** formed by a small mass of matter from outer space rendered incandescent by friction with the air as it passes through the Earth's atmosphere. [from Greek *meteōros* = high in the air]

meteor-burst communications technique for sending messages by bouncing radio waves off the fiery tails of ◊meteors. High-speed computer-controlled equipment is used to sense the presence of a meteor and to broadcast a signal during the short time that the meteor races across the sky.

meteoric /miːti'ɒrɪk/ *adj.* 1. of meteors. 2. like a meteor in brilliance, sudden appearance, or transience. —**meteorically** *adv.*

meteorite /'miːtiəraɪt/ n. a piece of rock or metal from space that reaches the surface of the Earth, Moon, or other body. Meteorites are thought to be fragments from asteroids, although some may be pieces from the heads of comets. Most are stony, although some are made of iron and a few have a mixed rock-iron composition. Meteorites provide evidence for the nature of the solar system and may be similar to the Earth's core and mantle, neither of which can be observed directly. Thousands of meteorites hit the Earth each year, but most fall in the sea or in remote areas and are never recovered.

meteoroid /'miːtiərɔɪd/ n. a body moving through space, of the same nature as those which become visible as meteors.

meteorological /miːtiərə'lɒdʒɪkəl/ *adj.* of meteorology. —**Meteorological Office**, a government department providing weather forecasts etc.

meteorology /miːtiə'rɒlədʒɪ/ n. the scientific observation and study of the atmosphere, so that weather can be accurately forecasted. Data from meteorological stations and weather satellites is collated by computer at central agencies such as the UK Meteorological Office in Bracknell, near London, and a forecast and weather maps based on current readings are issued at regular intervals. —**meteorologist** n. [from Greek]

meter /'miːtə/ n. an instrument for recording the amount of a substance supplied or used, time spent, distance travelled, etc. —*v.t.* to measure by a meter.

-meter /-mɪtə/ suffix forming names of automatic measuring instruments (*thermometer, voltmeter*) or of lines of verse with a specified number of measures (*pentameter*). [from Greek *metron* = measure]

methanal n. (common name **formaldehyde**) HCHO gas at ordinary temperatures, condensing to a liquid at −21°C/ −5.8°F. It has a powerful penetrating smell. Dissolved in

water, it is used as a biological preservative. It is used in the manufacture of plastics, dyes, foam (for example urea-formaldehyde foam, used in insulation), and in medicine.

methane /'miːθeɪn/ n. CH_4 the simplest hydrocarbon of the paraffin series. Colourless, odourless, and lighter than air, it burns with a bluish flame and explodes when mixed with air or oxygen. It is the chief constituent of natural gas and also occurs in the explosive firedamp of coal mines. In marsh gas methane forms from rotting vegetation by spontaneous combustion resulting in the pale flame seen over marshland and known as ◊will-o'-the-wisp.

methanogenic bacteria one of a group of primitive bacteria (◊archaebacteria). They give off methane gas as a by-product of their metabolism, and are common in sewage treatment plants and hot springs, where the temperature is high and oxygen is absent.

methanoic acid (common name **formic acid**) HCOOH a colourless, slightly fuming liquid that melts at 8°C/46.4°F and boils at 101°C/213.8°F. It occurs in stinging ants, nettles, sweat, and pine needles, and is used in dyeing, tanning, and electroplating.

methanol n. (common name **methyl alcohol**) CH_3OH the simplest of the alcohols. It can be made by the dry distillation of wood (hence it is also known as wood alcohol), but is usually made from coal or natural gas. When pure, it is a colourless, flammable liquid with a pleasant odour, and is highly poisonous.

methinks /mi'θɪŋks/ *v.i.* (*impersonal*) (*past* **methought** /mi'θɔːt/) (*archaic*) it seems to me. [Old English]

method /'meθəd/ n. 1. a procedure or way of doing something. 2. orderliness; the orderly arrangement of ideas. [from French or Latin from Greek *methodos* = pursuit of knowledge (**meta**-and *hodos* = way)]

Method n. the US adaptation of ◊Stanislavsky's teachings on acting and direction, in which importance is attached to the psychological building of a role rather than the technical side of its presentation. Emphasis is placed on improvisation, aiming for a spontaneous and realistic style of acting. One of the principal exponents of the Method was the US actor and director Lee Strasberg, who taught at the ◊Actors Studio in New York.

methodical /mi'θɒdɪkəl/ *adj.* characterized by method or order. —**methodically** *adv.* [from Latin from Greek]

Methodism n. evangelical Protestant Christian movement that was founded by John ◊Wesley 1739 within the Church of England, but became a separate body 1795. The Methodist Episcopal Church was founded in the USA 1784. In 1988 there were over 50 million Methodists worldwide.

Methodist /'meθədɪst/ n. a member of a Protestant denomination originating in an 18th-century evangelistic movement which grew out of a religious society established within the Church of England (from which it formally separated in 1791) by John and Charles Wesley at Oxford. —**Methodism** n.

methodology /meθə'dɒlədʒɪ/ n. 1. the science of method. 2. the body of methods used in an activity.

methought past of **methinks**.

meths (*colloquial*) abbreviation of methylated spirit.

Methuselah /mə'θjuːzələ/ n. in the Old Testament, a Hebrew patriarch who lived before the Flood; his lifespan of 969 years makes him a byword for longevity.

methyl /'meθɪl, 'miː'θaɪl/ n. the chemical radical present in methane etc. [German or French, ultimately from Greek *methu* = wine and *hulē* = wood]

methyl alcohol common name for methanol.

methylated /'meθɪleɪtɪd/ *adj.* mixed or impregnated with methyl alcohol. —**methylated spirit(s)**, alcohol so treated to make it unfit for drinking and so exempt from duty.

meticulous /mi'tɪkjʊləs/ *adj.* giving great or excessive attention to details, very careful and precise. —**meticulously** *adv.*, **meticulousness** n. [from Latin *metus* = fear]

métier /'meɪtjeɪ/ n. one's trade, profession, or field of activity; one's forte. [French]

metonymy /mi'tɒnɪmɪ/ n. figure of speech that works by association, naming something closely connected with what is meant; for example, calling the theatrical profession 'the stage', horse racing 'the turf', or journalists 'the press'. See also ◊synecdoche. [from Latin from Greek *onoma* = name]

metope n. a square space between triglyphs in a Doric frieze. [from Latin from Greek *opē* = hole for beam-end]

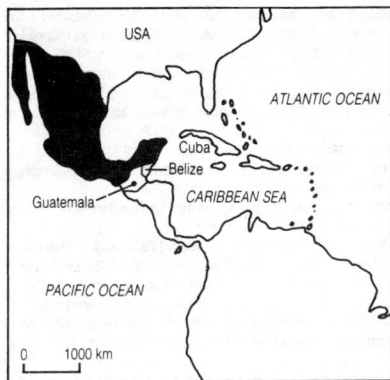

Mexico

metre[1] /'mi:tə/ *n.* any form of poetic rhythm, determined by the character and number of feet; a metrical group. [Old English, ultimately from Greek *metron* = measure]

metre[2]   *n.* an   SI unit (symbol m) of length, equivalent to 1.093 yards. It is defined by scientists as the length of the path travelled by light in a vacuum during a time interval of 1/299,792,458 of a second. [from French *mètre*]

metric /'metrɪk/ *adj.* 1. of or based on the metre as a unit. 2. metrical. —**metric system**, a decimal measuring-system with the metre, litre, and gram as the units of length, capacity, and weight or mass. —**metrically** *adv.* [from French *métrique*]

-metric or **-metrical** suffix forming adjectives from nouns in *-meter* or *-metry*. [from French from Latin]

metrical /'metrɪkəl/ *adj.* 1. of or composed in metre. 2. of or involving measurement. —**metrically** *adv.* [from Latin from Greek]

metricate /'metrɪkeɪt/ *v.t./i.* to change or adapt to the metric system. —**metrication** /-'keɪʃən/ *n.*

Metro-Goldwyn-Mayer /'metrəʊ 'gəʊldwɪn 'meɪə/ *n.* (MGM) US film-production company 1924–1970s. MGM was formed by the amalgamation of the Metro Picture Corporation, the Goldwyn Picture Corporation, and Louis B Mayer Pictures. One of the most powerful Hollywood studios of the 1930s to the 1950s, it produced such prestige films as *David Copperfield* 1935 and *The Wizard of Oz* 1939. Among its stars were Greta Garbo, James Stewart, and Elizabeth Taylor.

metronome /'metrənəʊm/ *n.* a clockwork device, invented by Johann Maelzel in 1814, with a sliding weight to regulate the speed of a pendulum, used to indicate tempo while practising music. [from Greek *metron* = measure and *nomos* = law]

metropolis /mɪ'trɒpəlɪs/ *n.* the chief city of a county or region, a capital. [Latin from Greek *mētēr* = mother and *polis* = city]

metropolitan /metrə'pɒlɪtən/ *adj.* 1. of a metropolis. 2. of or forming the mother country as distinct from colonies etc. —*n.* 1. a bishop with authority over the bishops of a province. 2. an inhabitant of a metropolis. —**metropolitan county**, in England, a group of six counties (1974–86) established under the Local Government Act 1972 in the major urban areas outside London: Tyne and Wear, South Yorkshire, Merseyside, West Midlands, Greater Manchester, and West Yorkshire. Their elected assemblies were abolished 1986 when their areas of responsibility reverted to district councils. **metropolitan district**, each of the areas into which a metropolitan county is divided.

Metropolitan Opera Company the foremost opera company in the USA, founded in 1883 in New York. The Metropolitan Opera House (opened in 1883) was demolished in 1966, and the company transferred to the Lincoln Center.

-metry /-mɪtrɪ/ suffix forming names of procedures and systems involving measurement (*geometry*). [from Greek]

Metternich /'metənɪk/ Klemens (Wenzel Lothar), Prince von Metternich 1773–1859. Austrian politician, the leading figure in European diplomacy after the fall of Napoleon. As foreign minister 1809–48 (as well as chancellor from

1821), he tried to maintain the balance of power in Europe, supporting monarchy and repressing liberalism. At the Congress of Vienna 1815 he advocated cooperation by the great powers to suppress democratic movements. The ◊revolution of 1848 forced him to flee to the UK; he returned in 1851 as a power behind the scenes.

mettle *n.* quality or strength of character, courage. —**on one's mettle**, incited to do one's best. [variant of *metal*]

mettlesome *adj.* spirited.

Meuse /mɜ:z/ (Dutch *Maas*) river flowing through France, Belgium, and the Netherlands; length 900 km/560 mi. It was a line of battle in both World Wars.

mew[1] *n.* the characteristic cry of a cat. —*v.i.* to utter a mew.

mew[2] *n.* a gull. [Old English]

mews /mju:z/ *n.pl.* (treated as *singular*) a set of stables round an open yard or lane, now often converted into dwellings. [originally singular *mew* = cage for hawks while moulting, from Old French from Latin *mutare* = change; originally of royal stables on site of hawks' cages at Charing Cross in London]

Mexican Empire /'meksɪkən/ short-lived empire 1822–23 following the liberation of Mexico from Spain. The empire lasted only eight months, under the revolutionary leader Agustín de ◊Iturbide.

Mexican War war between the USA and Mexico 1846–48, begun when General Zachary Taylor invaded New Mexico. Mexico City was taken in 1847, and under the Treaty of Guadaloupe-Hidalgo, Mexico lost Texas, New Mexico, and California (half its territory) to the USA for $15 million compensation.

Mexico /'meksɪkəʊ/ United States of; country in Central America, bordered N by the USA, E by the Gulf of Mexico, SE by Belize and Guatemala, and SW and W by the Pacific Ocean; **area** 1,958,201 sq km/756 198 sq mi; **capital** Mexico City; **physical** partly arid central highlands; Sierra Madre mountain ranges E and W; tropical coastal plains; **head of state and government** Carlos Salinas de Gortari from 1988; **political system** federal democratic republic; **population** (1990 est) 88,335,000 (10% Spanish descent, 30% Indian, 60% mixed descent; 50% under 20 years of age); **language** Spanish (official) 92%; Nahuatl, Maya, Mixtec; **recent history** independence achieved from Spain in 1821. Loses territory in wars with the USA 1846–48. In 1917 a new constitution was introduced, designed to establish permanent democracy.

Mexico City (Spanish *Ciudad de México*) capital, and industrial (iron, steel, chemicals, textiles) and cultural centre of Mexico, 2,255 m/7,400 ft above sea level on the southern edge of the central plateau; population (1986) 18,748,000. It is thought to be the most polluted city in the world.

Meyerbeer /'maɪəbeə/ Giacomo. Adopted name of Jakob Liebmann Beer 1791–1864. German composer. He is renowned for his spectacular operas, including *Robert le Diable* 1831 and *Les Huguenots* 1836.

mezuzah *n.* in Judaism, a small box containing a parchment scroll inscribed with a prayer, the Shema (from Deuteronomy 6:4–9; 11:13–21), which is found on the doorpost of every room in a traditional Jewish home except the bathroom.

mezzanine /'metsəni:n/ *n.* an extra storey between two others, usually between the ground and first floors. [French from Italian *mezzano* = middle]

mezzo /'metsəʊ/ *adv.* (especially in music) half, moderately. —*mezzo forte*, fairly loud. *mezzo piano*, fairly soft. *mezzo-soprano*, a voice between soprano and contralto; a singer with this voice. [Italian from Latin *medius* = middle]

mezzotint /'metsəʊtɪnt/ *n.* 1. a method of engraving using a uniformly roughened plate, on which the rough areas give shaded parts and the areas scraped smooth give light. 2. a print produced by this. [from Italian]

mf abbreviation of *mezzo forte*.

Mfecane /əmfe'ta:neɪ/ *n.* in African history, a series of disturbances in the early 19th century among communities in what is today the eastern part of South Africa. They arose when chief ◊Shaka conquered the Nguni peoples between the Tugela and Pongola rivers, then created by conquest a centralized, militaristic Zulu kingdom from several communities, resulting in large-scale displacement of people.

mg symbol for milligram(s).

Mg symbol for magnesium.

Mgr. abbreviation of 1. Monsignor; 2. Monseigneur.

MHD abbreviation of ◊magnetohydrodynamics.

mho *n.* SI unit of electrical conductance, now called the ◊siemens; equivalent to a reciprocal ohm.

MHz abbreviation of megahertz.

ml symbol for ◊mile.

ml variant of ◊me².

Miami /maɪˈæmi/ city and port in Florida, USA: population (1984) 383,000. It is the hub of finance, trade, and air transport for Latin America and the Caribbean.

Miandad /miˈændæd/ Javed 1957– . Pakistani test cricketer, his country's leading run-maker. He scored a century on his test debut in 1976 and has since become one of a handful of players to make 100 test appearances. He has captained his country. His highest score of 311 was made when he was aged 17.

miaow /miˈaʊ/ *n.* the cry of a cat, a mew. —*v.i.* to make this cry.

miasma /miˈæzmə, maɪ–/ *n.* (*plural* **miasmata**) an infectious or noxious escape of air etc. [Greek = defilement (*miainō* = pollute)]

mica /ˈmaɪkə/ *n.* a group of silicate minerals that split easily into thin flakes along lines of weakness in their crystal structure (perfect basal cleavage). They are glossy, have a pearly lustre, and are found in many igneous and metamorphic rocks. Their good thermal and electrical insulation qualities make them valuable in industry. [Latin = crumb]

Micawber /miˈkɔːbə/ *n.* a person who is perpetually hoping that something good will turn up while making no positive effort. —**Micawberish** *adj.*, **Micawberism** *n.* [character in Dickens's novel *David Copperfield*, for whom the model was Dickens's father]

mice plural of **mouse**.

Michael /ˈmaɪkəl/ in the Old Testament, an archangel, referred to as the guardian angel of Israel. In the New Testament Book of Revelation he leads the hosts of heaven to battle against Satan. In paintings, he is depicted with a flaming sword and sometimes a pair of scales. Feast day 29 Sept (Michaelmas).

Michael Mikhail Fyodorovich Romanov 1596-1645. Tsar of Russia from 1613. He was elected tsar by a national assembly, at a time of chaos and foreign invasion, and was the first of the Romanov dynasty, which ruled until 1917.

Michael 1921– . King of Romania 1927–30 and 1940–47. The son of Carol II, he succeeded his grandfather as king in 1927 but was displaced when his father returned from exile in 1930. In 1940 he was proclaimed king again on his father's abdication, overthrew in 1944 the fascist dictatorship of Ion Antonescu (1882–1946), and enabled Romania to share in the victory of the Allies at the end of World War II. He abdicated and left Romania in 1947.

Michaelmas /ˈmɪkəlməs/ *n.* the feast of St Michael, 29 Sept. —**Michaelmas term**, the university and law term beginning near Michaelmas.

michaelmas daisy popular name for species of ◊aster, family Compositae, and also for the sea aster or starwort.

Michelangelo /maɪkəlˈændʒələu/ Buonarroti /bwɒnəˈrɔti/ 1475–1564. Italian sculptor, painter, architect, and poet, active in his native Florence and in Rome. His giant talent dominated the High Renaissance. The marble *David* 1501–04 (Accademia, Florence) set a new standard in nude sculpture. His massive figure style was translated into fresco in the Sistine Chapel 1508–12 and 1536–41 (Vatican). Other works in Rome include the dome of St Peter's basilica.

Michelet /miːˈʃleɪ/ Jules 1798–1874. French historian, author of a 17-volume *Histoire de France*/*History of France* 1833–67, in which he immersed himself in the narrative and stressed the development of France as a nation. He also produced a number of books on nature, including *L'Oiseau*/*The Bird* 1856 and *La Montagne*/*The Mountain* 1868.

Michelson /ˈmaɪkəlsən/ Albert Abraham 1852–1931. German-born US physicist. In conjunction with Edward Morley, he performed in 1887 the **Michelson–Morley experiment** to detect the motion of the Earth through the postulated ether (a medium believed to be necessary for the propagation of light). The failure of the experiment indicated the nonexistence of the ether, and led ◊Einstein to his theory of ◊relativity. Michelson was the first American to be awarded a Nobel prize, in 1907.

Michigan /ˈmɪʃɪgən/ state of the USA, bordered by the Great Lakes, Ohio, Indiana, Wisconsin, and Canada; nickname Great Lake State or Wolverine State; **area** 151,600 sq km/58,518 sq mi; **capital** Lansing; **population** (1986) 9,145,000; **history** explored by the French from 1618, it became British in 1763, and a US state in 1837.

Michigan, Lake lake in north central USA, one of the Great Lakes; area 58,000 sq km/22,390 sq mi. Chicago and Milwaukee are its main ports.

mickey /ˈmɪki/ *n.* (*slang*) **take the mickey (out of)**, to tease or mock.

Mickiewicz /mɪtskiˈevɪtʃ/ Adam 1798–1855. Polish revolutionary poet, whose *Pan Tadeusz* 1832–34 is Poland's national epic. He died at Constantinople while raising a Polish corps to fight against Russia in the Crimean War.

mickle *adj.* much, great. —*n.* a large amount. (The proverb *many a mickle makes a muckle* is an error for *many a little* (or *pickle*) *makes a mickle*.) [from Old Norse]

micro– /ˈmaɪkrəʊ–/ in combinations, 1. small. 2. (symbol μ) one millionth of (*microgram*, *microsecond*). [from Greek *mikros* = small]

microbe /ˈmaɪkrəʊb/ *n.* another name for ◊micro-organism, especially a bacterium causing disease or fermentation. —**microbial** /-ˈrəʊbiəl/ *adj.*, **microbially** *adv.* [French from Greek *bios* = life]

microbiological warfare the use of harmful micro-organisms as a weapon. See ◊biological warfare.

microbiology /maɪkrəʊbaɪˈɒlədʒi/ *n.* the study of micro-organisms. The practical applications of microbiology are in medicine (since many micro-organisms cause disease); in brewing, baking, and other food and beverage processes, where the micro-organisms carry out fermentation; and in genetic engineering, which is creating increasing interest in the field of microbiology.

microchip /ˈmaɪkrəʊtʃɪp/ *n.* a tiny piece of semiconductor carrying many electrical circuits.

microcircuit /ˈmaɪkrəʊsɜːkɪt/ *n.* an integrated circuit or other very small electrical circuit.

microclimate /ˈmaɪkrəʊklaɪmət/ *n.* the particular climate found in a small area or locality.

microcomputer /maɪkrəʊkəmˈpjuːtə(r)/ *n.* or **micro** a small desktop or portable computer, typically designed to be used by one person at a time. Since the appearance in 1975 of the first commercially available microcomputer, the Altair 8800, micros have become widely accepted in commerce and industry.

microcosm /ˈmaɪkrəkɒzəm/ *n.* 1. a complex thing, especially man, viewed as an epitome of the universe. 2. a miniature representation. —**microcosmic** /-ˈkɒzmɪk/ *adj.* [from French or Latin from Greek *mikros kosmos* = little world]

microdot *n.* a photograph of a document etc. reduced to the size of a dot.

microeconomics *n.* the division of economics concerned with the study of individual decision-making units within an economy: a consumer, a firm, or an industry. Unlike macroeconomics, it looks at how individual markets work; how individual producers and consumers make their choices, and with what consequences. This is done by analysing how relevant prices of goods are determined and the quantities that will be bought and sold.

microelectronics /maɪkrəʊiˌlekˈtrɒnɪks/ *n.* the design, manufacture, and use of microcircuits.

microfiche /ˈmaɪkrəʊfiːʃ/ *n.* (*plural* the same) a small sheet of film generally 105 mm × 148 mm, bearing tiny photographs of pages of documents etc. [from French *fiche* = slip of paper]

microfilm /ˈmaɪkrəʊfɪlm/ *n.* a length of film similar to the film in an ordinary camera, bearing a microphotograph of a document etc. —*v.t.* to record on this.

microform *n.* generic name for media on which text or images are photographically reduced. The main examples are **microfilm** and **microfiche**. Microform has the advantages of low reproduction and storage costs, but it requires special devices for reading the text. It is widely used for archiving and for storing large volumes of text such as library catalogues.

microlight /ˈmaɪkrəʊlaɪt/ *n.* a kind of motorized hang-glider.

microlith /ˈmaɪkrəlɪθ/ *n.* a very small worked flint, usually mounted on a piece of bone, wood, or horn as part of

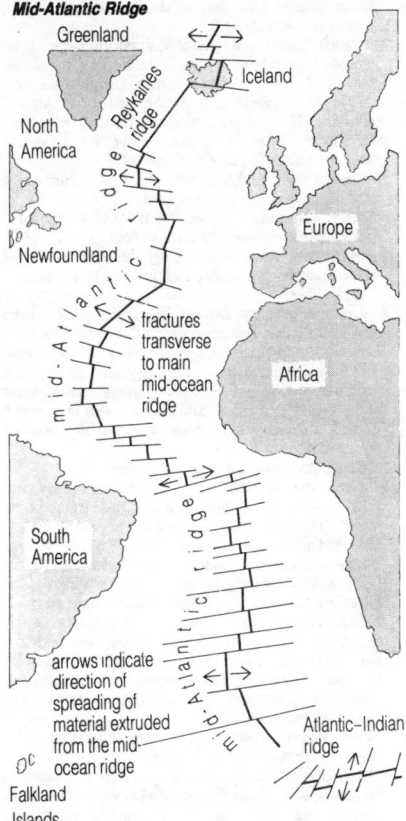

Mid-Atlantic Ridge

Greenland

Iceland

North America

Reykjanes ridge

Europe

Newfoundland

fractures transverse to main mid-ocean ridge

Africa

South America

Atlantic–Indian ridge

arrows indicate direction of spreading of material extruded from the mid-ocean ridge

Falkland Islands

a composite tool, characteristic especially of mesolithic industries in Europe. —**microlithic** *adj.* [from Greek *lithos* = stone]

micrometer /maɪˈkrɒmɪtə(r)/ *n.* instrument for measuring minute lengths or angles with great accuracy; different types of micrometer are used in astronomical and engineering work.

micrometre *n.* (former name **micron**) one millionth of a ◊metre (symbol μm) [from Greek *mikros* = small].

microminiaturization *n.* the reduction in size and weight of electronic components. The first size reduction in electronics was brought about by the introduction of the ◊transistor. Further reductions were achieved with ◊integrated circuits and the ◊silicon chip.

micron /ˈmaɪkrɒn/ *n.* former name for **micrometre**.

Micronesia /maɪkrəʊˈniːziə/ islands in the Pacific Ocean lying N of ◊Melanesia, including the Federated States of Micronesia, Belau, Kiribati, the Mariana and Marshall Islands, Nauru, and Tuvalu.

Micronesia Federated States of; self-governing island group (Kosrae, Ponape, Truk, and Yap) in the W Pacific; **area** 700 sq km/270 sq mi; **capital** Kolonia, on Ponape; **population** (1988) 86,000. It is part of the US Trust Territory.

micro-organism /maɪkrəʊˈɔːgənɪzəm/ *n.* or **microbe** a living organism invisible to the naked eye but visible under a microscope. Micro-organisms include viruses and single-celled organisms such as bacteria, protozoa, yeasts, and some algae. The term has no taxonomic significance in biology. The study of micro-organisms is known as microbiology.

microphone /ˈmaɪkrəfəʊn/ *n.* an instrument for converting sound-waves into electrical energy which may be reconverted into sound elsewhere. [from Greek *phōnē* = sound]

microprocessor /ˈmaɪkrəʊprəʊsesə(r)/ *n.* a computer's central processing unit (◊CPU) contained on a single ◊integrated circuit. The appearance of the first

microprocessors in 1971 heralded the introduction of the microcomputer. The microprocessor has led to a dramatic fall in the size and cost of computers.

micropyle *n.* in flowering plants, a small hole towards one end of the ovule. At pollination the pollen tube growing down from the ◊stigma eventually passes through this pore. The male gamete is contained within the tube and is able to travel to the egg in the interior of the ovule. Fertilization can then take place, with subsequent seed formation and dispersal.

microscope /ˈmaɪkrəskəʊp/ *n.* an instrument for magnification with high resolution for detail. Optical and electron microscopes are the ones chiefly in use; other types include acoustic and X-ray. In 1988 a scanning tunnelling microscope was used to photograph a single protein molecule for the first time. Laser microscopy is under development.

microscopic /maɪkrəˈskɒpɪk/ *adj.* 1. too small to be visible without a microscope. 2. extremely small. 3. of or by means of a microscope. —**microscopically** *adv.*

microscopy /maɪˈkrɒskəpɪ/ *n.* use of the microscope.

microsurgery /ˈmaɪkrəʊsɜːdʒərɪ/ *n.* surgery using a microscope to see the tissue and instruments involved.

microtubules *n.* tiny tubes found in almost all cells with a nucleus. They help to define the shape of a cell by forming scaffolding for cilia and form fibres of mitotic spindle.

microwave /ˈmaɪkrəʊweɪv/ *n.* 1. an ◊electromagnetic wave with a wavelength in the range 0.3 to 30 cm/0.1 in to 12 in, or 300–300,000 megahertz (between radio waves and ◊infrared radiation). They are used in radar, as carrier waves in radio broadcasting, and in microwave heating and cooking. 2. an oven using microwaves.

microwave heating heating by means of microwaves. Microwave ovens use this form of heating for the rapid cooking or reheating of foods, where the moisture present in food selectively absorbs microwaves and converts the energy into heat generated throughout the food simultaneously. If food is not heated completely, there is a danger of bacterial growth that may lead to food poisoning. Industrially, microwave heating is used for destroying insects in grain and enzymes in processed food, pasteurizing and sterilizing liquids, and drying timber and paper.

micturition /mɪktjʊəˈrɪʃən/ *n.* urination. [from Latin = desire to urinate (*mingere* = urinate)]

mid *adj.* 1. in the middle of (usually as a combination: *mid-air*, *mid-week*). 2. that is in the middle, medium, half. —**mid-off**, **mid-on** *ns.* the positions of fieldsmen in cricket near the bowler on the off or on side. [Old English]

MIDAS /ˈmaɪdæs/ acronym from Missile Defence Alarm System.

Midas in Greek legend, a king of Phrygia who was granted the gift of converting all he touched to gold, and who, for preferring the music of Pan to that of Apollo, was given ass's ears by the latter.

Mid-Atlantic Ridge the ◊ocean ridge, formed by the movement of plates described by ◊plate tectonics, that runs along the centre of the Atlantic Ocean, parallel to its edges, for some 14,000 km/8,800 mi—almost from the Arctic to the Antarctic.

midday /ˈmɪdeɪ/ *n.* noon; the time near noon.

midden /ˈmɪdən/ *n.* a dunghill, a refuse-heap. [compare Danish *mødding* (as *muck* and *dynge* = heap)]

middle *attributive adj.* 1. at an equal distance from extremities. 2. (of a member of a group) so placed as to have the same number of members on each side. 3. intermediate in rank, quality, etc.; average. —*n.* 1. a middle point, position, or part. 2. the waist. —**in the middle of**, during or half-way through (an activity or process). **middle age**, the middle part of normal life. **middle-aged** *adj.* of middle age. **middle C**, the C note at the centre of the piano keyboard, the note between the treble and bass staves. **middle class**, the social class between the upper and lower, including professional and business people. **middle ear**, the cavity behind the ear-drum. **middle name**, a given name between the first name and the surname; a person's most characteristic quality. **middle-of-the-road** *adj.* (of a person or action) moderate, avoiding extremes. **middle school**, a school for children from about 9 to 13. **middle-sized** *adj.* of medium size.

Middle Ages the period of European history between the fall of the Roman Empire in the 5th century and the Renaissance in the 15th. Among the period's distinctive features were the unity of W Europe within the Roman Catholic church, the feudal organization of political, social, and economic relations, and the use of art for largely religious purposes.

Middle East an indeterminate area now usually taken to include the Balkan States, Egypt, and SW Asia. Until the 1940s, this area was generally called the Near East, and the term Middle East referred to the area from Iran to Burma (now Myanmar).

Middle English the period of the ◊English language from about 1050 to 1550.

Middle Kingdom Egyptian: a period of Egyptian history extending from the late 11th to the 13th dynasty (roughly 2040–1670 BC); **Chinese**: Chinese term for China and its empire until 1912, describing its central position in the Far East.

middleman n. (plural **middlemen**) 1. any of the traders who handle a commodity between its producer and its customer. 2. an intermediary.

Middlemarch: A Study of Provincial Life /ˈmɪdlmɑːtʃ/ a novel by George Eliot, published in England 1871–72. Set in the fictitious provincial town of Middlemarch, the novel has several interwoven plots played out against a background of social and political upheaval.

Middlesex /ˈmɪdlseks/ former English county, absorbed by Greater London in 1965. Contained within the Thames basin, it provided good agricultural land before it was built over. It was settled in the 6th century by Saxons, and its name comes from its position between the kingdoms of the East and West Saxons.

Middleton /ˈmɪdltən/ Thomas c.1570–1627. English dramatist. He produced numerous romantic plays, tragedies, and realistic comedies, both alone and in collaboration, including A Fair Quarrel and The Changeling 1622 with Rowley; The Roaring Girl with Dekker; and Women Beware Women 1621.

Middle Way the path to enlightenment, taught by Buddha, which avoids the extremes of indulgence and asceticism.

middleweight n. the boxing-weight between welterweight and heavyweight.

middling adj. moderately good; fairly well in health. —adv. fairly, moderately.

Middx abbreviation of Middlesex, former county of England.

midfield n. the part of a football pitch away from the goals.

midge n. popular name for many insects resembling ◊gnats, generally divided into biting midges (family Ceratopogonidae) that suck blood, and non-biting midges (family Chironomidae). [Old English]

midget /ˈmɪdʒɪt/ n. an extremely small person or thing. —adj. extremely small.

Mid Glamorgan /ˈmɪd ɡləˈmɔːɡən/ county in S Wales; area 1,020 sq km/394 sq mi; **administrative headquarters** Cardiff; **population** (1987) 535,000; **language** 8% Welsh, English.

MIDI acronym from Musical Instrument Digital Interface, a manufacturer's standard allowing different pieces of digital music equipment used in composing and recording to be freely connected.

Midi-Pyrénées /ˈmiːdiː piːrəˈneɪ/ region of SW France, comprising the départements of Ariège, Aveyron, Haute-Garonne, Gers, Lot, Haute-Pyrénées, Tarn, and Tarn-et-Garonne; **area** 45,300 sq km/17,486 sq mi; **capital** Toulouse; **population** (1986) 2,355,000; **history** occupied by the Basques since prehistoric times, this region once formed part of the prehistoric province of Gascony that was taken by the English in 1154, recaptured by the French in 1453, inherited by Henry of Navarre, and reunited with France in 1607.

midland /ˈmɪdlənd/ adj. of the middle part of a country.

Midlands /ˈmɪdləndz/ an area of England corresponding roughly to the Anglo-Saxon kingdom of ◊Mercia. **E Midlands** Derbyshire, Leicestershire, Northamptonshire, Nottinghamshire. **W Midlands** the former metropolitan county of ◊West Midlands created from parts of Staffordshire, Warwickshire, and Worcestershire; and (often included) **S Midlands** Bedfordshire, Buckinghamshire, and Oxfordshire.

midnight /ˈmɪdnaɪt/ n. 12 o'clock at night; the time near this; the middle of the night. —**midnight blue**, very dark blue. **midnight sun**, the sun visible at midnight during summer in polar regions.

Midrash /ˈmɪdræʃ/ n. (plural **Midrashim**) the medieval Hebrew commentaries on the Bible, in the form of sermons, in which allegory and legendary illustration are used. They were compiled mainly in Palestine between AD 400 and 1200. [Hebrew = commentary (darash = study)]

midriff /ˈmɪdrɪf/ n. the region of the front of the body just above the waist. [Old English = mid-belly]

midshipman /ˈmɪdʃɪpmən/ n. (plural **midshipmen**) a naval officer ranking next above cadet.

midst n. the middle part. —**in the midst of**, among; in the middle of. [earlier middest from in middes]

midsummer /ˈmɪdsʌmə, ˈmɪd-/ n. the period of or near the summer ◊solstice, about 21 June. —**Midsummer's Day**, 24 June.

Midsummer Night's Dream, A a comedy by William Shakespeare, first performed 1595–96. Hermia, Lysander, Demetrius, and Helena in their various romantic endeavours are subjected to the playful manipulations of the fairies Puck and Oberon in a wood near Athens. Titania, queen of the fairies, is similarly bewitched and falls in love with Bottom, a stupid weaver, whose head has been replaced with that of an ass.

midway /ˈmɪdweɪ/ adv. half-way between.

Midway Islands two islands in the Pacific, 1,800 km/1,120 mi NW of Honolulu; **area** 5 sq km/2 sq mi; **population** (1980) 500. They were annexed by the USA in 1867, and are now administered by the US Navy. The naval **Battle of Midway** 3–6 June 1942, between the USA and Japan, was the turning point in the Pacific in World War II.

Midwest /ˈmɪdwest/ or **Middle West** a large area of N central USA. It is loosely defined, but is generally taken to comprise the states of Ohio, Indiana, Illinois, Michigan, Iowa, Wisconsin, Minnesota, and sometimes Nebraska. It tends to be conservative socially and politically, and isolationist. Traditionally its economy is divided between agriculture and heavy industry.

midwicket /ˈmɪdˈwɪkɪt/ n. a position in cricket on the leg side opposite the middle of the pitch.

midwife n. (plural **midwives** /-vz/) a person trained to assist women in childbirth. —**midwifery** /-wɪfrɪ/ n. [from obsolete mid= with and wife, in sense 'one who is with the mother']

midwinter /ˈmɪdˈwɪntə/ n. the period of or near the winter ◊solstice, about 22 Dec.

mien /miːn/ n. a person's bearing or look. [from obsolete demean = behave]

Mies van der Rohe /ˈmiːs væn də ˈrəʊə/ Ludwig 1886–1969. German architect who practised in the USA from 1937. He succeeded ◊Gropius as director of the ◊Bauhaus 1929–33. He became professor at the Illinois Technical Institute 1938–58, for which he designed new buildings on characteristically functional lines from 1941. He also designed the bronze-and-glass Seagram building in New York City 1956–59 and numerous apartment blocks. He designed the National Gallery, Berlin 1963–68.

Mifune /mɪˈfuːne/ Toshiro 1920– . Japanese actor who appeared in many films directed by Akira ◊Kurosawa, including Rashomon 1950, Seven Samurai 1954 and Throne of Blood 1957. He has also appeared in European and American films.

might[1] /maɪt/ v.aux. used as past tense of may[1] especially (1) in reported speech, (2) with a perfect infinitive expressing possibility based on a condition not fulfilled, or based on an obligation not fulfilled; also used (loosely) as = may[2]. —**might-have-been** n. an event etc. that might have happened but did not.

might[2] /maɪt/ n. great strength or power. —**with might and main**, with all one's power. [Old English]

mightn't /ˈmaɪtənt/ (colloquial) might not.

mighty /ˈmaɪtɪ/ adj. 1. powerful, strong. 2. massive, bulky; (colloquial) great, considerable. —adv. (colloquial) very. —**mightily** adv., **mightiness** n.

mignonette /ˈmɪnjəˈnet/ n. an annual plant of the genus Reseda with small, yellowish-green fragrant flowers in racemes. [from French diminutive of mignon = small]

migraine /ˈmiːɡreɪn/ n. a severe recurring form of headache, often with nausea and disturbance of the vision. [French, from Latin from Greek hēmikrania]

migrant /'maɪgrənt/ *adj.* that migrates. —*n.* a migrant person or animal, especially a bird.

migrant labour people who leave their homelands to work elsewhere, usually because of economic or political pressures.

migrate /maɪ'greɪt/ *v.i.* **1.** to leave one place and settle in another. **2.** (of animals) to go periodically from one area to another, living in each place for part of a year. —**migration** *n.*, **migratory** /'maɪgrətərɪ/ *adj.* [from Latin *migrare*]

Mihailović /mi'haɪləvitʃ/ Draza 1893–1946. Yugoslav soldier, leader of the guerrilla ◊Chetniks of World War II against the German occupation. His feud with Tito's communists led to the withdrawal of Allied support and that of his own exiled government from 1943. He turned for help to the Italians and Germans, and was eventually shot for treason.

mihrab /'miːrɑːb/ *n.* a niche or slab in a mosque, used to show the direction of Mecca. [from Arabic = praying-place]

mikado /mi'kɑːdəʊ/ *n.* (*plural* **mikados**) the title of the Japanese emperor until 1867, when it was replaced by the term *tennō* (heavenly sovereign). [Japanese = august door]

mike (*colloquial*) abbreviation of microphone.

milady /mi'leɪdɪ/ *n.* an English noblewoman. [French, from *my lady*]

Milan /mi'læn/ (Italian *Milano*) industrial city (aircraft, cars, locomotives, textiles), financial and cultural centre, capital of Lombardy, Italy; population (1988) 1,479,000.

milch /miltʃ/ *adj.* giving milk. —**milch cow**, a cow kept for milk; a source of regular or easy profit.

mild /maɪld/ *adj.* **1.** moderate in intensity, character, or effect, not severe or harsh or drastic; (of climate etc.) moderately warm. **2.** gentle in manner. **3.** not strongly flavoured, not sharp or bitter in taste. —*n.* mild ale. —**mild steel**, steel that is tough but not easily tempered. —**mildly** *adv.*, **mildness** *n.* [Old English]

mildew /'mɪldjuː/ *n.* a growth of minute fungi forming on surfaces exposed to damp. —*v.t./i.* to taint or be tainted with mildew. —**mildewed** *adj.*, **mildewy** *adj.* [Old English = honey dew]

mile *n.* **1.** an imperial unit of linear measure, equal to 1,760 yds. (1.609 km). The nautical mile, used in navigation, is a unit of 2,026 yds. (1.852 km). **2.** a great distance or amount. **3.** a race extending over a mile. [Old English, ultimately from Latin *mille* = thousand]

mileage *n.* **1.** the number of miles travelled. **2.** the advantage to be derived from something.

miler /'maɪlə/ *n.* a person or horse specializing in races of one mile.

Miles /maɪlz/ Bernard (Baron Miles) 1907– . English actor and producer. He appeared on stage as Briggs in *Thunder Rock* 1940 and Iago in *Othello* 1942, and his films include *Great Expectations* 1947. He founded a trust that in 1959 built the City of London's first new theatre for 300 years, the Mermaid.

milestone *n.* **1.** a stone set up beside a road to mark the distance in miles. **2.** a significant event or stage in life or history.

milfoil /'mɪlfɔɪl/ *n.* a plant *Achillea millefolium* with small white flowers and finely divided leaves; yarrow. [from Old French from Latin *millefolium* (*mille* = thousand and *folium* = leaf)]

milieu /'miːljɜː/ *n.* (*plural* **milieux** /-jɜːz/) an environment; a state of life; social surroundings. [French *mi* = mid and *lieu* = place]

militant /'mɪlɪtənt/ *adj.* **1.** prepared to take aggressive action in support of a cause. **2.** engaged in warfare. —*n.* a militant person. —**militancy** *n.*, **militantly** *adv.* [from Old French from Latin]

Militant Tendency in British politics, a left-wing faction originally within the Labour Party, aligned with the publication *Militant*. It became active in the 1970s, with radical socialist policies based on Trotskyism, and gained some success in local government. In the mid-1980s the Labour Party considered it to be an organization within the party and banned it.

militarism /'mɪlɪtərɪzəm/ *n.* military spirit; an aggressive policy of reliance on military strength and means. —**militarist** *n.*, **militaristic** /-'rɪstɪk/ *adj.* [from French]

militarize /'mɪlɪtəraɪz/ *v.t.* **1.** to make military or warlike. **2.** to equip with military resources. **3.** to imbue with militarism. —**militarization** /-'zeɪʃən/ *n.*

Mill *Educated by his father, John Stuart Mill was reading Plato and Demosthenes with ease at the age of ten. His Autobiography gives a painful account of the teaching methods that turned him against Utilitarianism.*

military /'mɪlɪtərɪ/ *adj.* of or for or done by soldiers or the armed forces. —**the military** (as *singular* or *plural*), the army (as distinct from the police or civilians). —**militarily** *adv.* [from French or Latin *militaris* (*miles* = soldier)]

military-industrial complex the conjunction of the military establishment and the arms industry, both inflated by Cold War demands. The phrase was first used by US president and former general Dwight D Eisenhower in 1961 to warn Americans of the potential misplacement of power.

militate /'mɪlɪteɪt/ *v.i.* (of facts or evidence) to tell or serve as a strong influence (*against*, rarely *in favour of*, a conclusion etc.). [from Latin *militare*]

militia /mi'lɪʃə/ *n.* a military force, especially one raised from the civil population and supplementing the regular army in an emergency. [Latin = military service]

milk *n.* **1.** an opaque white fluid secreted by female mammals for the nourishment of their young; milk, especially of the cow, as a food. **2.** a milklike liquid, e. g. in a coconut. —*v.t.* **1.** to draw milk from (an animal). **2.** to exploit or extract money etc. from (a person). —**milk and honey**, abundant means of prosperity. **milk and water**, a feeble or insipid or mawkish discourse or sentiment. **milk float**, a light, low vehicle used in delivering milk. **milk run**, a routine expedition or mission. **milk shake**, a drink of milk and a flavouring mixed or shaken until frothy. [Old English]

milking machine a machine that uses suction to milk cows. The first milking machine was invented in the USA by L O Colvin in 1860. Later it was improved so that the suction was regularly released by a pulsating device, since it was found that continuous suction is harmful to cows.

milkmaid *n.* a woman who milks or works in a dairy.

milkman /'mɪlkmən/ *n.* (*plural* **milkmen**) a man who sells or delivers milk.

milksop *n.* a weak or timid man or youth.

milk tooth any of the first temporary teeth in young mammals.

milkweed *n.* any of various wild plants with a milky juice, especially sowthistle *Sonchus oleraceus.*

milky *adj.* of, like, or containing milk; (of a liquid) cloudy, unclear. —**milkiness** *n.*

Milky Way the faint band of light crossing the night sky, consisting of stars in the plane of our Galaxy. The name Milky Way is often used for the Galaxy itself. It is a spiral ◊galaxy, about 100,000 light years in diameter, containing at least 100 billion stars. The Sun is in one of its spiral arms, about 25,000 light years from the centre.

mill /mɪl/ *n.* **1.** a building fitted with mechanical apparatus for grinding corn; such apparatus. **2.** an apparatus for grinding any solid substance to a powder or pulp. **3.** a building fitted with machinery for manufacturing-processes etc.; such machinery. —*v.t./i.* **1.** to grind (corn) in a mill; to produce (flour) in a mill. **2.** to produce regular markings on the edge of (a coin). **3.** to cut or shape (metal) with a rotating tool. **4.** (of people or animals) to move in an aimless manner. —**go** (*or* **put**) **through the mill,** to undergo (or cause to undergo) training or experience or suffering. **mill-pond** *n.* a pond formed by damming a stream to use the water in a mill. **mill-race** *n.* a current of water that works a mill-wheel. **mill-wheel** *n.* a wheel used to drive a watermill. [Old English ultimately from Latin *mola* = millstone (*molere* = grind)]

Mill James 1773–1836. Scottish philosopher and political thinker who developed the theory of ◊utilitarianism. He is remembered for his political articles, and for the rigorous education he gave his son John Stuart Mill.

Mill John Stuart 1806–1873. English philosopher and economist who wrote *On Liberty* 1859, the classic philosophical defence of liberalism, and *Utilitarianism* 1863, a version of the 'greatest happiness for the greatest number' principle in ethics.

Millais /'mɪleɪ/ John Everett 1829–1896. British painter, a founder member of the ◊Pre-Raphaelite Brotherhood (PRB) in 1848. By the late 1850s he had dropped out of the PRB, and his style became more fluent and less detailed.

millennium /mɪ'leniəm/ *n.* (*plural* **milleniums** or **millenia**) **1.** a period of 1,000 years. **2.** Christ's prophesied reign of 1,000 years on earth (Revelation 20). **3.** a coming time of justice and happiness. —**millennial** *adj.* [from Latin *mille* = thousand and *annus* = year]

millepede /'mɪlɪpiːd/ *n.* a many-legged arthropod of the class Diplopoda, having two pairs of legs to each segment. [from Latin = wood-louse (*mille* = thousand and *pes pedis* = foot)]

miller *n.* one who works or owns a mill, usually a cornmill. —**miller's thumb,** a kind of small fish of the genus *Cottus.*

Miller /'mɪlə/ Arthur 1915– . US playwright. His plays deal with family relationships and contemporary American values, and include *Death of a Salesman* 1949 and *The Crucible* 1953, based on the Salem witch trials and reflecting the communist witch-hunts of Senator Joe ◊McCarthy. He was married 1956–61 to the film star Marilyn Monroe, for whom he wrote the film *The Misfits* 1960.

A good newspaper, I suppose, is a nation talking to itself.

Arthur Miller
The Observer 1961

Miller Glenn 1904–1944. US trombonist and, as bandleader, exponent of the big-band swing sound from 1938. He composed his signature tune 'Moonlight Serenade'. Miller disappeared without trace on a flight between England and France during World War II.

Miller Stanley 1930– . US chemist. In the early 1950s, under laboratory conditions, he tried to imitate the original conditions of the Earth's atmosphere (a mixture of methane, ammonia, and hydrogen), added an electrical discharge, and waited. After a few days he found that amino acids, the ingredients of protein, had been formed.

millesimal /mɪ'lesɪməl/ *adj.* **1.** thousandth. **2.** consisting of thousandths. —*n.* a thousandth part. [from Latin *millesimus* (*mille* = thousand)]

millet /'mɪlɪt/ *n.* any of several grasses, family Gramineae, of which the grains are used as a cereal food and the stems as fodder; these grains [from French diminutive from Latin *milium*]

Millet /miː'leɪ/ Jean François 1814–1875. French artist, a leading member of the ◊Barbizon school, who painted scenes of peasant life and landscapes. *The Angelus* 1859 (Musée d'Orsay, Paris) was widely reproduced in his day.

Millett /'mɪlɪt/ Kate 1934– . US radical feminist lecturer, writer, and sculptor whose book *Sexual Politics* 1970 was a landmark in feminist thinking. She was a founding member of the **National Organization of Women** (NOW). Later

Milton *The 17th-century English poet John Milton.*

books include *Flying* 1974, *The Prostitution Papers* 1976, and *Sita* 1977.

milli- /mɪlɪ-/ in combinations, **1.** thousand. **2.** one thousandth. [from Latin *mille* = thousand]

milliard /'mɪljəd/ *n.* one thousand million.

millibar /'mɪlɪbɑː/ *n.* a unit of pressure equal to one thousandth of a bar.

milligram /'mɪlɪgræm/ *n.* a metric unit of mass, equal to 0.001 gram, symbol mg.

Millikan /'mɪlɪkən/ Robert Andrews 1868–1953. US physicist, awarded a Nobel prize 1923 for his determination of the ◊electric charge on an electron 1913.

millilitre /'mɪlɪliːtə/ *n.* a metric unit of capacity (symbol ml), equal to 0.001 litre, equivalent to one cubic centimetre.

millimetre /'mɪlɪmiːtə/ *n.* a metric unit of length (symbol mm), equal to 0.001 metre or about 0.04 in.

millimetre of mercury unit (symbol mmHg) of pressure, used in medicine for measuring blood pressure, defined as the pressure exerted by a column of mercury one millimetre high, under the action of gravity.

milliner /'mɪlɪnə/ *n.* a person who makes or sells women's hats. —**millinery** *n.* [from *Milan* in Italy; originally = vendor of goods from Milan]

million /'mɪljən/ *adj. & n.* (for plural usage, see ◊hundred). **1.** one thousand thousand. **2.** a million pounds or dollars. **3.** (in *plural*) very many. —**millionth** *adj. n.* [from Old French probably from Italian *mille* = thousand]

millionaire /mɪljə'neə/ *n.* a person possessing a million pounds, dollars, etc.; a very rich person. [from French]

millipede variant of ◊millepede.

Mills /mɪlz/ John 1908– . English actor who appeared in films such as *In Which We Serve* 1942, *The Rocking Horse Winner* 1949, *The Wrong Box* 1966, and *Oh, What a Lovely War* 1969. He received an Academy Award for *Ryan's Daughter* 1971. He is the father of the actresses Hayley Mills and Juliet Mills.

millstone *n.* **1.** either of two circular stones for grinding corn. **2.** a heavy burden or responsibility.

millwright /'mɪlraɪt/ *n.* one who designs or erects mills.

Milne /mɪln/ A(lan) A(lexander) 1882–1956. English writer. His books for children were based on the teddy bear and other toys of his son Christopher Robin (*Winnie-the-Pooh* 1926 and *The House at Pooh Corner* 1928). He also wrote children's verse (*When We Were Very Young* 1924 and *Now We Are Six* 1927) and plays, including an adaptation of Kenneth Grahame's *The Wind in the Willows* as *Toad of Toad Hall* 1929.

milometer /maɪ'lɒmɪtə/ *n.* an instrument for measuring the number of miles travelled by a vehicle.

Miłosz /'mi:wɒʃ/ Czesław 1911– . Polish writer, born in Lithuania. He became a diplomat before defecting and becoming a US citizen. His poetry in English translation, classical in style, includes *Selected Poems* 1973 and *Bells in Winter* 1978. His best-known work is a collection of essays *The Captive Mind* 1953, concerning the impact of communism on Polish intellectuals. Among his novels are *The Seizure of Power* 1955, *The Issa Valley* 1981, and *The Land of Ulro* 1984. He was awarded the Nobel Prize for Literature in 1980.

Milstein /'mɪlstaɪn/ César 1927– . Argentine molecular biologist who developed monoclonal antibodies, giving immunity against specific diseases. He shared the Nobel Prize for Medicine 1984.

milt *n.* 1. the reproductive gland or sperm of a male fish. 2. the spleen of mammals. [Old English]

Our torments also may in length of time
Become our elements.

                              John Milton
                              Paradise Lost

Milton /'mɪltən/ John 1608–1674. English poet. His early poems include the pastoral *L'allegro* and *Il penseroso* 1632, the masque *Comus* 1633, and the elegy *Lycidas* 1637. His later works include *Paradise Lost* 1667, *Paradise Regained* 1677, and the classic drama *Samson Agonistes* 1677.

Milwaukee /mɪl'wɔːki/ industrial (meatpacking, brewing, engineering, textiles) port in Wisconsin, USA, on Lake Michigan; population (1980) 1,207,000.

mimbar /'mɪmbɑː/ *n.* a pulpit in a mosque. [from Arabic]

mime *n.* acting with gestures and without words; a performance involving this. —*v.t./i.* to perform in the form of a mime. [from Latin from Greek *mimos*]

mimeograph /'mɪmɪəɡrɑːf/ *n.* an apparatus for making copies from stencils. —*v.t.* to reproduce by means of this. [from Greek *mimeomai* = imitate]

mimetic /mɪ'metɪk/ *adj.* of or given to imitation or mimicry. [from Greek *mimētikos*]

mimic /'mɪmɪk/ *v.t.* (**-ck-**) 1. to copy the appearance or ways of (a person etc.) playfully or for entertainment. 2. to copy minutely or servilely. 3. (of a thing) to resemble closely. —*n.* a person skilled in imitation, especially for entertainment. —**mimicry** *n.* [from Latin from Greek]

mimosa *n.* any of several usually tropical or subtropical trees, shrubs, or herbs of the genus *Mimosa* of the family Leguminosae. All bear small, fluffy, golden, ball-like flowers.

min. abbreviation of 1. minute(s). 2. minimum. 3. minim.

Min. abbreviation of 1. Minister. 2. Ministry.

mina /'maɪnə/ *n.* a talking bird *Gracula religiosa* of the starling family. [from Hindi]

minaret /mɪnə'ret, 'mɪ-/ *n.* a slender turret connected with a mosque, from which a muezzin calls at the hours of prayer. [French or Spanish from Turkish from Arabic]

minatory /'mɪnətərɪ/ *adj.* threatening, menacing. [from Latin *minari* = threaten]

mince *v.t./i.* 1. to cut into very small pieces, especially in a machine. 2. to walk or speak in an affected way. —*n.* minced meat. —**mince pie,** a pie containing mincemeat. **not to mince matters** *or* **one's words,** to speak plainly. [from Old French from Latin]

mincemeat *n.* a mixture of currants, sugar, spices, suet, etc. —**make mincemeat of,** to defeat or refute utterly.

mind /maɪnd/ *n.* 1. the seat of consciousness, thought, volition, and feeling. 2. intellectual powers as distinct from the will and emotions. 3. remembrance. 4. opinion; this as expressed. 5. a way of thinking or feeling; a direction of thought or desires. 6. the normal condition of the mental faculties. 7. a person as embodying mental faculties. —*v.t./i.* 1. to object to (usually with negative or interrogative). 2. to remember and take care (about). 3. to have charge of for a while. 4. to apply oneself to; to concern oneself about. —**be in two minds,** to be undecided. **change one's mind,** to adopt a different opinion etc. in favour of another. **do you mind?** (*ironically*) please stop that. **have a mind of one's own,** to be capable of an independent opinion. **have a (good) mind to,** to feel (much) inclined or tempted to. **have in mind,** to think

of; to intend. **in one's mind's eye,** in one's imagination. **make up one's mind,** to decide, to resolve. **mind one's P's and Q's,** to be careful in speech or conduct. **mind out,** to be careful; (in *imperative*) let me pass. **mind-reader** *n.* one who claims to be able to become aware of another's thoughts. **mind (you),** please take note. **never mind,** do not be troubled (about); I prefer not to answer; you may ignore. **on one's mind,** in one's thoughts; worrying one. [Old English]

Mindanao /mɪndə'naʊ/ the second-largest island of the Philippines; **area** 94,627 sq km/36,526 sq mi; **towns** Davao, Zamboanga; **physical** mountainous rainforest; **population** (1980) 10,905,250.

minded *adj.* 1. inclined to think in a specified way or concern oneself with a specified thing. 2. having a mind of a specified kind. 3. inclined or disposed (to do something).

minder *n.* 1. a person whose business it is to attend to something, especially a child or machinery. 2. a bodyguard.

mindful *adj.* taking thought or care (of something). —**mindfully** *adv.*, **mindfulness** *n.*

mindless *adj.* 1. lacking intelligence, stupid. 2. heedless (of). —**mindlessly** *adv.*, **mindlessness** *n.*

mine[1] possessive pronoun of or belonging to me; the thing(s) belonging to me. [Old English]

mine[2] *n.* 1. an excavation in the Earth for extracting metal, coal, salt, etc. 2. an abundant source (*of* information etc.). 3. a receptacle filled with explosive placed in or on the ground or in the water for destroying enemy personnel, material, or ships. —*v.t./i.* 1. to obtain (metal, coal, etc.) from a mine; to dig in the Earth etc. for ore etc. 2. to lay explosive mines under or in. [from Old French]

minefield *n.* 1. an area where explosive mines have been laid. 2. a subject etc. presenting many unseen hazards.

minelayer *n.* a ship or aircraft for laying explosive mines.

miner *n.* one who works in a mine.

mineral /'mɪnərəl/ *n.* 1. a substance obtained by mining, including coal and oil, despite their organic origins. 2. a natural inorganic substance having a definite chemical composition and usually a characteristic crystalline structure. Either in their perfect crystalline form or otherwise, minerals are the constituents of ◊rocks. —*adj.* 1. obtained by mining. 2. inorganic, not animal or vegetable. —**mineral water,** water with mineral constituents gathered from the rocks over which it flows, and classified by these into earthy, brine, and oil mineral waters; or water with artificially added minerals and, sometimes, carbon dioxide. [from Old French from Latin *minera* = ore]

mineral extraction the recovery of valuable ores from the Earth's crust. The processes used include open-cast mining, shaft mining, and quarrying, as well as more specialized processes such as those used for oil and sulphur (see, for example, ◊Frasch process).

mineralogy /mɪnə'rælədʒɪ/ *n.* the science of minerals. —**mineralogical** /-rə'lɒdʒɪkəl/ *adj.*, **mineralogist** *n.*

mineral salt in nutrition, a simple inorganic chemical that is required by living organisms. Plants usually obtain their mineral salts from the soil, while animals get theirs from their food. Important mineral salts include iron salts (needed by both plants and animals), magnesium salts (needed mainly by plants, to make chlorophyll), and calcium salts (needed by animals to make bone or shell).

Minerva /mɪ'nɜːvə/ in Roman mythology, the goddess of intelligence, and of the handicrafts and arts, counterpart of the Greek ◊Athena. From the earliest days of ancient Rome, there was a temple to her on the Capitoline Hill, near the Temple of Jupiter.

minestrone /mɪnɪ'strəʊnɪ/ *n.* an Italian soup containing vegetables and pasta or rice.

minesweeper *n.* a ship for clearing explosive mines from the sea.

mineworker *n.* a miner.

mingle /'mɪŋɡəl/ *v.t./i.* to mix, to blend. —**mingle with,** to go about among.

Mingus /'mɪŋɡəs/ Charles 1922–1979. US jazz bassist and composer. His experimentation with atonality and dissonant effects opened the way for the new style of free collective jazz improvisation of the 1960s.

mingy /'mɪndʒɪ/ *adj.* (*colloquial*) mean, stingy. —**mingily** *adv.*

mini- /mɪnɪ-/ in combinations, miniature, small of its kind (*minicar; mini-budget*).

mini /'mɪnɪ/ (*colloquial*) abbreviation of miniskirt.

Mini /'mɪnɪ/ *n.* trade name; abbreviation of Mini-minor, a type of small car.

miniature /'mɪnɪtʃə/ *adj.* 1. much smaller than normal. 2. represented on a small scale. —*n.* 1. a small, minutely finished portrait. 2. miniature thing. —**in miniature**, on a small scale. [from Italian from Latin *miniare* (*minium* = red lead)]

miniaturist /'mɪnɪtʃərɪst/ *n.* a painter of miniatures.

miniaturize /'mɪnɪtʃəraɪz/ *v.t.* 1. to make miniature. 2. to produce in a smaller version.

minibus /'mɪnɪbʌs/ *n.* a small bus for about twelve passengers.

minicab /'mɪnɪkæb/ *n.* a small car like a taxi, that can be booked but does not ply for hire.

minicomputer /mɪnɪkəm'pju:tə/ *n.* a computer that is smaller than a mainframe but larger than a microcomputer.

minim /'mɪnɪm/ *n.* 1. in music, a note half as long as a semibreve. 2. (*historical*) one sixtieth of a fluid drachm, about 1 drop. [from Latin]

minimal /'mɪnɪməl/ *adj.* being or related to a minimum; very small or slight. —**minimally** *adv.*

Minimalism *n.* a movement beginning in the late 1960s in abstract and music towards a severely simplified composition. In painting, it emphasized geometrical and elemental shapes. In sculpture, Carl André focused on industrial materials. In music, large-scale statements are based on layers of imperceptibly shifting repetitive patterns; its major exponents are Steve ◊Reich and Philip ◊Glass.

minimize /'mɪnɪmaɪz/ *v.t.* 1. to reduce to a minimum. 2. to estimate at the smallest possible amount or degree; to estimate or represent at less than the true value or importance. —**minimization** /-'zeɪʃən/ *n.*

minimum /'mɪnɪməm/ *n.* (*plural* **minima**) the least amount possible, attained, usual, etc. [Latin, neuter of *minimus* = least]

mining *n.* the extraction of minerals from under the land or sea for industrial or domestic uses. Exhaustion of traditionally accessible resources has led to development of new mining techniques; for example, extraction of oil from offshore deposits and from land shale reserves. Technology is also under development for the exploitation of minerals from entirely new sources such as mud deposits and mineral nodules from the sea bed.

minion /'mɪnjən/ *n.* (*derogatory*) a subordinate, an assistant. [originally = favourite child etc., from French *mignon* = dainty]

miniskirt /'mɪnɪskɜ:t/ *n.* a skirt ending well above the knees.

minister /'mɪnɪstə/ *n.* 1. a person at the head of a government department or a main branch of this. 2. a clergyman, especially in the Presbyterian and Nonconformist Churches. 3. a diplomatic agent, usually ranking below ambassador. 4. a person employed in the execution of one's purpose, will, etc. —*v.t./i.* to render aid or service (to a person, cause, etc.). —**Minister of State**, a departmental senior minister between departmental head and junior minister. —**ministerial** /-'stɪərɪəl/ *adj.* [from Old French from Latin *minister* = servant]

ministration /mɪnɪ'streɪʃən/ *n.* giving aid or service; ministering, especially in religious matters. —**ministrant** /'mɪnɪstrənt/ *adj.* & *n.* [from Old French or Latin]

ministry /'mɪnɪstrɪ/ *n.* 1. a government department; the building occupied by it. 2. the body of ministers of the government; a period of government under one Prime Minister. 3. office as a minister in the Christian Church; the period of this. 4. ministering; ministration. —**the ministry**, the clerical profession. [from Latin *ministerium*]

mink *n.* 1. a small stoatlike animal of the family Mustelidae, especially *Mustela vison*. 2. its fur. 3. a coat made from this. [compare Swedish *mänk*]

Minneapolis /mɪnɪ'æpəlɪs/ city in Minnesota, USA, forming with St Paul the Twin Cities area; population (1980) 371,000, metropolitan area 2,114,000.

Minnelli /mɪ'neli/ Liza 1946– . US actress and singer, daughter of Judy ◊Garland and the director Vincente Minnelli. She achieved stardom in the musical *Cabaret* 1972. Her subsequent films include *New York New York* 1977 and *Arthur* 1981.

Minnelli Vincente 1910–1986. US film director who specialized in musicals and occasional melodramas. His best

films, such as *Meet Me in St Louis* 1944 and *The Band Wagon* 1953, display a powerful visual flair.

minnesinger /'mɪnɪsɪŋə(r)/ *n.* (*plural* the same) any of a group of German lyric poets of the 12th and 13th centuries who, in their songs, dealt mainly with the theme of courtly love without revealing the identity of the object of their affections. Minnesingers included Dietmar von Aist, Friedrich von Hausen, Heinrich von Morungen, Reinmar, and Walther von der Vogelweide.

Minnesota /mɪnɪ'səʊtə/ state of the northern midwest USA; nickname North Star or Gopher State; **area** 218,700 sq km/84,418 sq mi; **capital** St Paul; **population** (1987) 4,246,000; **history** the first Europeans to explore were French fur traders in the 17th century; part was ceded to Britain in 1763, and part passed to the USA under the Louisiana Purchase 1803; it became a territory in 1849 and a state in 1858.

minnow /'mɪnəʊ/ *n.* a small freshwater fish (especially *Phoxinus phoxinus*). [Old English, probably influenced by French *menu* (*poisson*) = small fish]

Minoan /mɪ'nəʊən/ *adj.* of the Bronze Age civilization of Crete *c.*3000–1100 BC or its people, culture, or language. —*n.* 1. an inhabitant of Minoan Crete or other parts of the Minoan world. 2. the language or scripts associated with the Minoan civilization. [from *Minos*, legendary king of Crete]

minor /'maɪnə/ *adj.* 1. lesser or relatively less in size or importance. 2. under full legal age. 3. in music, (of a scale) having intervals of a semitone above its second and seventh notes; (of an interval) less by a semitone than a major interval; (of a key) based on a minor scale. —*n.* 1. a person under full legal age. 2. (*US*) a student's subsidiary subject or course. —*v.i.* (*US*) to undertake study (in a subject) as a subsidiary course. —**minor planets**, (also called **asteroids**) the small rocky bodies (less than a few kilometres across) orbiting the Sun. [Latin = smaller, lesser]

Minorca /mɪ'nɔ:kə/ (Spanish **Menorca**) second largest of the ◊Balearic Islands in the Mediterranean; **area** 689 sq km/266 sq mi; **towns** Mahon, Ciudadela; **population** (1985) 55,500.

Minorite /'maɪnəraɪt/ *n.* a Franciscan friar, so called because the Franciscans regarded themselves as of humbler rank than members of other orders.

minority /maɪ'nɒrɪtɪ, mɪ-/ *n.* 1. the smaller number or part of a group etc. 2. the state of having fewer than half the votes. 3. a small group of persons differing from others in race, religion, language, opinion on a topic, etc. 4. the state or period of being under full legal age (see ◊majority). [from French or Latin]

Minos /'maɪnɒs/ in Greek mythology, a king of Crete (son of ◊Zeus and ◊Europe).

Minotaur /'maɪnətɔ:/ in Greek mythology, a monster, half man and half bull, offspring of Pasiphaë, wife of King Minos of Crete, and a bull. It lived in the Labyrinth at Knossos, and its victims were seven girls and seven youths, sent in annual tribute by Athens, until ◊Theseus killed it, with the aid of Ariadne, the daughter of Minos.

Minsk /mɪnsk/ industrial city (machinery, textiles, leather; centre of the Soviet computer industry) and capital of Byelorussia, USSR; population (1987) 1,543,000.

minster /'mɪnstə/ *n.* in the UK, a church formerly attached to a monastery, for example, York Minster. Originally the term meant a monastery, and in this sense it is often preserved in place names, such as Westminster.

minstrel /'mɪnstrəl/ *n.* 1. a medieval singer or musician, who sang or recited (often his own) poetry; (in earlier use) an entertainer of any kind. 2. (usually in *plural*) a member of a band of public entertainers, with blackened faces etc., performing songs and music ostensibly of Black origin. [from Old French *menestral* = attendant from Latin]

minstrelsy /'mɪnstrəlsɪ/ *n.* a minstrel's art or poetry.

mint[1] *n.* 1. an aromatic herb of the genus *Mentha*, used in cooking. 2. peppermint; a small sweet flavoured with this. —**minty** *adj.* [Old English from Latin *ment(h)a* from Greek]

mint[2] *n.* 1. a place where money is coined, usually under state authority. 2. a vast sum or amount. —*v.t.* 1. to make (a coin) by stamping metal. 2. to coin (a word or phrase). —**in mint condition**, as new, unsoiled. [Old English from Latin *moneta*]

Minto /'mɪntəʊ/ Gilbert, 4th Earl of 1845–1914. British colonial administrator who succeeded Curzon as viceroy of

India, 1905–10. With John Morley, secretary of state for India, he co-sponsored the Morley Minto reforms of 1909. The reforms increased Indian representation in government at provincial level, but also created separate Muslim and Hindu electorates which, it was believed, helped the British Raj in the policy of divide and rule.

Mintoff /'mɪntɒf/ Dom(inic) 1916– . Labour prime minister of Malta 1971–84 who negotiated the removal of British and other foreign military bases 1971–79 and made treaties with Libya.

Minton /'mɪntən/ Thomas 1765–1836. English potter. He first worked under the potter Josiah Spode, but in 1789 established himself at Stoke-on-Trent as an engraver of designs (he originated the 'willow pattern') and in the 1790s founded a pottery there, producing high-quality bone china, including tableware.

minuet /mɪnju'et/ n. a slow, stately dance in triple measure; music for this, or in the same rhythm and style (often as a movement in a suite, sonata, or symphony). [from French *menuet*]

minus /'maɪnəs/ prep. 1. with the subtraction of (symbol –). 2. below zero. 3. (*colloquial*) deprived of. —*adj.* 1. (of a number) less than zero, negative. 2. having a negative electrical charge. 3. (in evaluating) rather worse or lower than. —*n.* 1. a minus sign. 2. a disadvantage. 3. a negative quantity. —**minus sign**, the symbol –. [Latin, neuter of *minor*]

minuscule /'mɪnəskju:l/ adj. 1. extremely small. 2. lower-case. 3. (of a kind of cursive script developed in the 7th century) small. —*n.* 1. a lower-case letter. 2. a letter in minuscule script. [French, from Latin *minusculus* (diminutive of *minor*)]

minute[1] /'mɪnɪt/ n. 1. a period of 60 seconds, a sixtieth part of an hour; the distance traversed in this. 2. a very brief portion of time. 3. a particular point of time. 4. a sixtieth part of a degree of measurement of angles. 5. (in *plural*) a brief summary of the proceedings of an assembly, committee, etc. 6. an official memorandum authorizing or recommending a course of action. 7. a rough draft, a memorandum. —*v.t.* 1. to record in minutes; to make a note of. 2. to send a minute to (a person). —**in a minute**, very soon. **minute steak**, a thin slice of steak that can be cooked quickly. **up to the minute**, having the latest information; in the latest fashion. [from Old French from Latin *minutus*]

minute[2] /maɪ'nju:t/ adj. 1. very small. 2. precise, detailed. —**minutely** adv., **minuteness** n. [from Latin *minutus* (*minuere* = lessen)]

Minuteman n. in weaponry, a US three-stage intercontinental ballistic missile (ICBM) with a range of about 8,000 km/5,000 mi. In US history the term was applied to members of the citizens' militia in the 1770s. These citizen-soldiers had pledged to be available for battle at a 'minute's notice' during the ◊American Revolution.

minutiae /maɪ'nju:ʃiː, mɪ-/ n.pl. very small or unimportant details. [Latin]

minx /mɪŋks/ n. a pert or mischievous or sly girl.

Miocene /'maɪəsi:n/ adj. the fourth epoch of the Tertiary period of geological time, 25–5 million years ago. At this time grasslands spread over the interior of continents, and hoofed mammals rapidly evolved. [from Greek *meiōn* = less and *kainos* = new]

mips n. (million instructions per second) in computing, a measure of the speed of a processor.

mir /mɪə/ n. in Russia before the 1917 Revolution, a self-governing village community in which the peasants distributed land and collected taxes. [Russian = world]

Mir n. Soviet space station, the core of which was launched 20 Feb 1986. *Mir* is intended to be a permanently occupied space station. [Russian = peace]

Mira /'maɪrə/ n. or **Omicron Ceti** the brightest long-period pulsating ◊variable star, located in the constellation ◊Cetus. Mira was the first star discovered to vary in brightness over a regular period.

Mirabeau /'mɪrəbəu/ Honoré Gabriel Riqueti, Comte de 1749–1791. French politician, leader of the National Assembly in the French Revolution. He wanted to establish a parliamentary monarchy on the English model. From May 1790 he secretly acted as political adviser to the king.

miracle /'mɪrəkəl/ n. 1. a marvellous and welcome event that seems impossible to explain by means of the known laws of nature and is therefore attributed to a supernatural

agency; a remarkable occurrence. 2. a remarkable specimen. [from Old French from Latin *miraculum* = object of wonder (*mirari* = wonder at)]

miracle play another name for ◊mystery play.

miraculous /mɪ'rækjuləs/ adj. 1. that is a miracle, supernatural. 2. remarkable. —**miraculously** adv. [from French or Latin]

mirage /mi'rɑːʒ/ n. 1. an optical illusion caused by atmospheric conditions, especially the appearance of a sheet of water in the desert or on a hot road. 2. an illusory thing. [French *se mirer* = be reflected]

Miranda /mi'rændə/ Carmen. Stage name of Maria de Carmo Miranda da Cunha 1909–1955. Portuguese dancer and singer who lived in Brazil from her childhood. Successful in Brazilian films, she went to Hollywood in 1939 via Broadway and appeared in over a dozen musicals, including *Down Argentine Way* 1940 and *The Gang's All Here* 1943. Her hallmarks were extravagant costumes and exotic headgear adorned by an array of tropical fruits as well as a staccato singing voice and fiery temperament.

mire n. 1. swampy ground, a bog. 2. mud. —*v.t.* 1. to plunge in mire. 2. to involve in difficulties. 3. to defile, to bespatter (*literal* or *figurative*). —**in the mire**, in difficulties. —**miry** adj. [from Old Norse]

Miró /mi'rəu/ Joan 1893–1983. Spanish Surrealist painter, born in Barcelona. In the mid-1920s he developed a distinctive abstract style with amoeba shapes, some linear, some highly coloured, generally floating on a plain background.

mirror /'mɪrə/ n. 1. a polished surface (usually of amalgam-coated glass) reflecting an image. 2. what gives a faithful reflection or true description of a thing. —*v.t.* to reflect as in a mirror. —**mirror image**, a reflection or copy in which the left and right sides are reversed. [from Old French from Latin *mirare* = look at]

mirth n. merriment; laughter. —**mirthful** adj., **mirthless** adj. [Old English]

MIRV acronym from multiple independently targeted re-entry vehicle, used in ◊nuclear warfare.

mis- prefix 1. to verbs and verbal derivatives, in the sense 'amiss', 'badly', 'wrongly', 'unfavourably' (*mislead*, *misshapen*, *mistrust*). 2. to verbs, adjectives, and nouns, in the sense 'amiss', 'badly', 'wrongly', or negative (*misadventure*, *mischief*). [sense 1 Old English; sense 2 from Old French *mes*-from Latin]

misadventure /mɪsəd'ventʃə/ n. 1. a piece of bad luck. 2. the killing of a person by a lawful act without negligence or any intention of hurt, for which there is no criminal responsibility.

misalliance /mɪsə'laɪəns/ n. an unsuitable alliance, especially a marriage with a social inferior.

misanthrope /'mɪsənθrəup, 'mɪz-/ n. a hater of mankind; one who avoids human society. —**misanthropic** /-'θrɒpɪk/ adj., **misanthropically** /-'θrɒpɪkəli/ adv. [French from Greek *misos* = hatred and *anthrōpos* = man]

Misanthrope, The a comedy by Molière, first produced in France 1666. The play contrasts the noble ideals of Alceste with the worldliness of his lover Celimene.

misanthropy /mi'sænθrəpi, mi'z-/ n. the condition or habits of a misanthrope.

misapply /mɪsə'plaɪ/ v.t. to apply (especially funds) wrongly. —**misapplication** /-æpli'keɪʃən/ n.

misapprehend /mɪsæpri'hend/ v.t. to misunderstand. —**misapprehension** /-ʃən/ n.

misappropriate /mɪsə'prəuprieɪt/ v.t. to take wrongly; to apply (another's money) wrongly to one's own use. —**misappropriation** /-ʃən/ n.

misbegotten /mɪsbi'gɒtən/ adj. 1. contemptible, disreputable. 2. bastard.

misbehave /mɪsbi'heɪv/ v.i. to behave improperly. —**misbehaviour** n.

miscalculate /mɪs'kælkjuleɪt/ v.t./i. to calculate wrongly. —**miscalculation** /-'leɪʃən/ n.

miscall /mɪs'kɔːl/ v.t. to misname.

miscarriage /mɪs'kærɪdʒ, 'mɪs-/ n. 1. a spontaneous abortion; a delivery of the fetus in the 12th–28th week of pregnancy. 2. the miscarrying of a plan etc. —**miscarriage of justice**, the failure of a legal procedure to achieve justice.

miscarry /mɪs'kæri/ v.i. 1. (of a woman) to have a miscarriage. 2. (of a scheme etc.) to go wrong, to fail. 3. (of a letter etc.) to fail to reach its destination.

miscast /mɪsˈkɑːst/ *v.t.* (*past* and *past participle* **miscast**) to allot an unsuitable part to (an actor).

miscegenation /mɪsɪdʒɪˈneɪʃən/ *n.* interbreeding of races, especially of Whites with non-Whites. [from Latin *miscēre* = mix and *genus* = race]

miscellaneous /mɪsəˈleɪnɪəs/ *adj.* 1. of various kinds. 2. of mixed composition or character. [from Latin *miscellus* = mixed]

miscellany /mɪˈselənɪ/ *n.* 1. a mixture, a medley. 2. a book containing various literary compositions etc. [from French]

mischance /mɪsˈtʃɑːns/ *n.* misfortune.

mischief /ˈmɪstʃɪf/ *n.* 1. troublesome but not malicious conduct, especially of children; playful malice or archness. 2. harm or injury, especially caused by a person. —**make mischief**, to create discord. [from Old French *chever* = come to an end]

mischievous /ˈmɪstʃɪvəs/ *adj.* (of a person) disposed to mischief; (of conduct) playfully malicious, mildly troublesome; (of a thing) having harmful effects. —**mischievously** *adv.*, **mischievousness** *n.* [from Anglo-French]

miscible /ˈmɪsɪbəl/ *adj.* that can be mixed. —**miscibility** /-ˈbɪlɪtɪ/ *n.* [from Latin *miscēre* = mix]

misconceive /mɪskənˈsiːv/ *v.t./i.* to have a wrong idea or conception (of). —**misconception** /-ˈsepʃən/ *n.*

misconduct /mɪsˈkɒndʌkt/ *n.* 1. improper conduct, especially adultery. 2. bad management.

misconstrue /mɪskənˈstruː/ *v.t.* to misinterpret. —**misconstruction** *n.*

miscopy /mɪsˈkɒpɪ/ *v.t.* to copy wrongly.

miscount /mɪsˈkaʊnt/ *v.t./i.* to make a wrong count; to count (things) wrongly. —*n.* a wrong count, especially of votes.

miscreant /ˈmɪskrɪənt/ *n.* a wrongdoer, a villain. [from Old French *creant* = believer]

misdeal /mɪsˈdiːl/ *v.t./i.* (*past* and *past participle* **misdealt** /-ˈdelt/) to make a mistake in dealing (cards). —*n.* such a mistake; a misdealt hand.

misdeed /mɪsˈdiːd/ *n.* a wrong or improper act, a crime.

misdemeanour /mɪsdɪˈmiːnə/ *n.* a misdeed; in law, an indictable offence, formerly (in the UK) one less heinous than a felony.

misdirect /mɪsdɪˈrekt, -daɪ-/ *v.t.* to direct wrongly. —**misdirection** *n.*

misdoing /mɪsˈduːɪŋ/ *n.* a misdeed.

mise en scène /miːz ɑ̃ ˈseɪn/ 1. the scenery and properties of an acted play. 2. the surroundings of an event. [French, past participle of *mettre* = put from Latin *mittere miss-* = send, put]

miser /ˈmaɪzə/ *n.* a person who hoards wealth, especially one who lives miserably. —**miserliness** *n.*, **miserly** *adj.* [Latin = wretched]

miserable /ˈmɪzərəbəl/ *adj.* 1. full of misery, wretchedly unhappy or uncomfortable. 2. wretchedly poor in quality etc., contemptible. 3. causing wretchedness. —**miserably** *adv.* [from French from Latin = pitiable (*miserari* = pity)]

misericord /mɪˈzerɪkɔːd/ *n.* a projection under a hinged seat in a choir stall serving (when the seat is turned up) to support a person standing. [from Old French from Latin *misericordia* = compassion]

misery /ˈmɪzərɪ/ *n.* 1. a condition or feeling of extreme unhappiness or discomfort. 2. a cause of this. 3. (*colloquial*) a constantly grumbling or doleful person. [from Old French or Latin *miseria*]

misfire /mɪsˈfaɪə/ *v.i.* 1. (of a gun, motor, engine, etc.) to fail to go off or start its action or function regularly. 2. (of a plan etc.) to fail to have the intended effect. —*n.* such a failure.

misfit /ˈmɪsfɪt/ *n.* 1. a person unsuited to his environment or work. 2. a garment etc. that does not fit properly.

misfortune /mɪsˈfɔːtʃuːn/ *n.* bad luck; an instance of this.

misgive /mɪsˈgɪv/ *v.t.* (*past* **-gave**, *past participle* **-given**) (of a person's mind, heart, etc.) to fill (him or her) with misgivings.

misgiving *n.* a feeling of doubt, mistrust, or apprehension.

misgovern /mɪsˈgʌvən/ *v.t.* to govern badly. —**misgovernment** *n.*

misguided /mɪsˈgaɪdɪd/ *adj.* mistaken in thought or action. —**misguidedly** *adv.*

Mishima *Japanese novelist Yukio Mishima 1970.*

mishandle /mɪsˈhændəl/ *v.t.* 1. to deal with incorrectly or ineffectively. 2. to handle (a person or thing) roughly or rudely.

mishap /ˈmɪshæp/ *n.* an unlucky accident.

mishear /mɪsˈhɪə/ *v.t.* (*past* and *past participle* **-heard** /-hɜːd/) to hear incorrectly or imperfectly.

Mishima /ˈmɪʃmə/ Yukio 1925–1970. Japanese novelist, whose work often deals with sexual desire and perversion, as in *Confessions of a Mask* 1949 and *The Temple of the Golden Pavilion* 1956. He committed hara-kiri (ritual suicide) as a protest against what he saw as the corruption of the nation and the loss of the samurai warrior tradition.

mishit *v.t.* (**-tt-**; *past* and *past participle* **-hit**) to hit (a ball) faultily or badly. —/ˈmɪshɪt/ *n.* a faulty or bad hit.

mishmash /ˈmɪʃmæʃ/ *n.* a confused mixture.

Mishna /ˈmɪʃnə/ *n.* a collection of commentaries on written Hebrew law, consisting of discussions between rabbis, handed down orally from their inception in AD 70 until about 200, when, with the Gemara (the main body of rabbinical debate on interpretations of the Mishna) it was committed to writing to form the Talmud. —**Mishnaic** /ˈneɪk/ *adj.* [Hebrew = (teaching by) repetition]

misinform /mɪsɪnˈfɔːm/ *v.t.* to give wrong information to. —**misinformation** /-fəˈmeɪʃən/ *n.*

misinterpret /mɪsɪnˈtɜːprɪt/ *v.t.* to give a wrong interpretation to; to make a wrong inference from. —**misinterpretation** /-ˈteɪʃən/ *n.*

misjudge /mɪsˈdʒʌdʒ/ *v.t./i.* 1. to have a wrong opinion of. 2. to judge wrongly. —**misjudgement** *n.*

mislay /mɪsˈleɪ/ *v.t.* (*past* and *past participle* **-laid**) to put (a thing) in a place and be unable to remember where it is; to lose temporarily.

mislead /mɪsˈliːd/ *v.t.* (*past* and *past participle* **-led**) to lead astray, to cause to go wrong in conduct or belief.

mismanage /mɪsˈmænɪdʒ/ *v.t.* to manage badly or wrongly. —**mismanagement** *n.*

mismatch /mɪsˈmætʃ/ *v.t.* to match unsuitably or incorrectly. —/ˈmɪsmætʃ/ *n.* a bad match.

misname /mɪsˈneɪm/ *v.t.* to name wrongly or unsuitably.

misnomer /mɪsˈnəʊmə/ *n.* a name or term used wrongly; the use of a wrong name. [from Anglo-French *nommer* = name from Latin *nominare*]

misogynist /mɪˈsɒdʒɪnɪst/ *n.* one who hates all women. —**misogyny** *n.* [from Greek *misos* = hatred and *gunē* = woman]

misplace /mɪsˈpleɪs/ *v.t.* 1. to put in the wrong place. 2. to bestow (affections or confidence) on the wrong object. 3. to time (words or an action) badly. —**misplacement** *n.*

misprint /ˈmɪsprɪnt/ *n.* a mistake in printing. —/mɪsˈprɪnt/ *v.t.* to print wrongly.

misprision /mɪsˈprɪʒən/ *n.* in law, a wrong act or an omission. —**misprision of treason** *or* **of felony**, concealment of one's knowledge of a treasonable or felonious intent. [from Anglo-French *prendre* = take]

mispronounce /mɪsprəˈnaʊns/ *v.t.* to pronounce (a word etc.) wrongly. —**mispronunciation** /-nʌnsɪˈeɪʃən/ *n.*

misquote /mɪs'kwəʊt/ v.t. to quote inaccurately. —**misquotation** /-'teɪʃən/ n.

misread /mɪs'riːd/ v.t. (past and past participle -**read** /-'red/) to read or interpret wrongly.

misrepresent /mɪsreprɪ'zent/ v.t. to give a false account of, to represent wrongly. —**misrepresentation** /-'teɪʃən/ n.

misrule /mɪs'ruːl/ n. 1. bad government. 2. disorder. —v.t. to govern badly.

miss[1] v.t./i. 1. to fail to hit, reach, or catch (an object). 2. to fail to catch (a train etc.) or see (an event) or meet (a person); to fail to keep (an appointment) or seize (an opportunity). 3. to fail to hear or understand. 4. to notice or regret the loss or absence of. 5. to avoid. 6. (of an engine) to misfire; to fail. —n. a failure to hit or attain what is aimed at. —**miss out**, to omit, to leave out. **miss out (on)**, (colloquial) to fail to get benefit or enjoyment (from). [Old English]

miss[2] n. 1. a girl or unmarried woman. 2. **Miss**, the title of an unmarried woman or girl; the title of a beauty queen from a specified region etc. [abbreviation of *mistress*]

missal /'mɪsəl/ n. in the Roman Catholic Church, a service book containing the complete office of Mass for the entire year. A simplified missal in the vernacular was introduced in 1969 (obligatory from 1971): the first major reform since 1570. [from Latin *missa* = mass]

missel-thrush /'mɪsəlθrʌʃ/ n. a large thrush *Turdus viscivorus* that feeds on mistletoe etc. berries. [from Old English *mistel* = mistletoe]

misshapen /mɪs'ʃeɪpən/ adj. ill-shaped, deformed; distorted. [from *shapen*, old past participle of *shape*]

missile /'mɪsaɪl/ n. 1. an object or weapon suitable for throwing at a target or for discharge from a machine. 2. a weapon directed by remote control or automatically. Modern missiles are classified according to range into **intercontinental ballistic missiles** (ICBMs, capable of reaching targets over 5,500 km/3,400 mi), **intermediate-range** (1,100 km/680 mi–2,750 km/1,700 mi), and **short-range** (under 1,100 km/680 mi) missiles. The first long-range ballistic missiles used in warfare were the ◊V1 and V2 launched by Germany against Britain in World War II. [from Latin *missilis* (*mittere* = send)]

missing adj. 1. not in its place, lost. 2. (of a person) not yet traced or confirmed as alive but not known to be dead. 3. not present. —**missing link**, a thing lacking to complete a series; a hypothetical creature called upon to bridge the gap between man and his evolutionary non-human ancestors.

mission /'mɪʃən/ n. 1. a body of persons sent to conduct negotiations or propagate a religious faith. 2. a missionary post. 3. a task to be performed; a journey for such a purpose; an operational sortie; the dispatch of an aircraft or spacecraft. 4. a person's vocation. [French or from Latin]

missionary adj. of religious etc. missions. —n. a person doing missionary work.

missis /'mɪsɪz/ (vulgar) as a form of address to a woman. —**the missis**, my or your wife. [corruption of *mistress*]

Mississippi /mɪsɪ'sɪpɪ/ river in the USA, the main arm of the great river system draining the USA between the Appalachian and the Rocky mountains. The length of the Mississippi is 3,780 km/2,350 mi; with its tributary Missouri 6,020 km/3,740 mi.

Mississippi state of the S USA; nickname Magnolia State; **area** 123,600 sq km/47,710 sq mi; **capital** Jackson; **population** (1985) 2,657,000; **history** settled in turn by the French, English, and Spanish until passing under US control in 1798; statehood achieved in 1817. After secession from the Union during the Civil War, it was readmitted in 1870.

Mississippian /mɪsɪ'sɪpɪən/ n. US term for the lower ◊Carboniferous period of geological time, named after the state of Mississippi.

missive /'mɪsɪv/ n. an official or long and serious letter. [from Latin]

Missouri /mɪ'zʊərɪ/ state of the central USA; nickname Show Me State; **area** 180,600 sq km/69,712 sq mi; **capital** Jefferson City; **population** (1986) 5,066,000; **history** explored by de Soto in 1541; acquired under the ◊Louisiana Purchase; achieved statehood in 1821.

Missouri Compromise in US history, the solution by Congress (1820–21) of a sectional crisis caused by the 1819 request from Missouri for admission to the union as a slave state, despite its proximity to existing nonslave states. The compromise was the simultaneous admission of Maine as a nonslave state to keep the same ratio.

Missouri River river in central USA, a tributary of the Mississippi, which it joins at St Louis; length 3,725 km/2,328 mi.

misspell /mɪs'spel/ v.t. (past and past participle –**spelt**, –**spelled**) to spell wrongly.

misspend /mɪs'spend/ v.t. (past and past participle -**spent**) to spend amiss or wastefully.

misstate /mɪs'steɪt/ v.t. to state wrongly. —**misstatement** n.

mist n. 1. water vapour near the ground in droplets smaller than raindrops and obscuring the atmosphere. 2. a condensed vapour obscuring windscreens etc. 3. a dimness or blurring of sight caused by tears etc. —v.t./i. to cover or become covered with or as with mist. [Old English]

mistake /mɪ'steɪk/ n. an incorrect idea or opinion; a thing incorrectly done or thought. —v.t./i. (past **mistook** /-'stʊk/, past participle **mistaken**) 1. to misunderstand the meaning or intention of. 2. to choose or identify wrongly.

mistaken /mɪ'steɪkən/ adj. wrong in opinion; ill-judged. —**mistakenly** adv.

mister n. 1. a person without a title of nobility etc. 2. (vulgar) as a form of address to a man. [variant of *master*; compare *Mr*]

mistime /mɪs'taɪm/ v.t. to say or do (a thing) at the wrong time.

mistletoe /'mɪsəltəʊ/ n. a parasitic plant *Viscum album* growing on apple and other trees and bearing white berries. [Old English *misteltan*]

mistook past of **mistake**.

mistral /'mɪstrəl, -'trɑːl/ n. a cold, dry, northerly wind that occasionally blows during the winter on the Mediterranean coast of France. It has been known to reach a velocity of 145 kph/90 mph. [French from Provençal from Latin *magistralis*]

Mistral /mɪs'trɑːl/ Gabriela. Pen name of Lucila Godoy de Alcayaga 1889–1957. Chilean poet, who wrote *Sonnets of Death* 1915. Nobel Prize for Literature 1945.

mistreat /mɪs'triːt/ v.t. to treat badly. —**mistreatment** n.

mistress /'mɪstrɪs/ n. 1. a woman in authority or with power; the female head of a household or of a college etc.; the female owner of an animal or slave. 2. a female teacher or tutor, a schoolmistress. 3. a woman having an illicit sexual relationship with a (usually married) man. [from Old French *maistresse* (*maistre* = master)]

mistrial /mɪs'traɪəl/ n. a trial vitiated by an error.

mistrust /mɪs'trʌst/ v.t. to feel no confidence in; to be suspicious of. —n. lack of confidence, suspicion. —**mistrustful** adj., **mistrustfully** adv.

misty adj. 1. of or covered with mist. 2. of dim outline; (figurative) obscure, vague. —**mistily** adv., **mistiness** n. [Old English]

misunderstand /mɪsʌndə'stænd/ v.t. (past and past participle -**stood** /-'stʊd/) to understand in a wrong sense; (especially in past participle) to misinterpret the words or action of.

misunderstanding n. 1. failure to understand correctly. 2. a slight disagreement or quarrel.

misusage /mɪs'juːsɪdʒ/ n. 1. a wrong or improper usage. 2. ill-treatment.

misuse /mɪs'juːz/ v.t. 1. to use wrongly, to apply to a wrong purpose. 2. to ill-treat. —/mɪs'juːs/ n. wrong or improper use or application.

Mitchell /'mɪtʃəl/ Arthur 1934– . US dancer, director of the Dance Theater of Harlem, which he founded with Karel Shook in 1968. Mitchell was a principal dancer with the New York City Ballet 1956–68, creating many roles in Balanchine's ballets.

Mitchell /'mɪtʃəl/ Margaret 1900–1949. US novelist, born in Atlanta, Georgia, which is the setting for her one book, the bestseller *Gone With the Wind* 1936, a story of the US Civil War.

> After all, tomorrow is another day.
> **Margaret Mitchell**
> closing words of *Gone with the Wind*

Mitchell /'mɪtʃəl/ R(eginald) J(oseph) 1895–1937. British aircraft designer whose Spitfire fighter was a major factor in winning the Battle of Britain during World War II.

Mitchum /'mɪtʃəm/ Robert 1917– . US film actor, a star for over 30 years. His films include *Out of the Past* 1947, *The Night of the Hunter* 1955, and *Farewell My Lovely* 1975.

mite *n.* 1. a small arachnid of the order Acari, especially of a kind found in cheese etc. 2. a modest contribution. 3. a small object or child. [Old English]

Mithraism /'mɪθreɪɪzəm/ *n.* the ancient Persian worship of Mithras. His cult was introduced into the Roman Empire in 68 BC and spread rapidly, gaining converts especially among soldiers; by about AD 250 it rivalled Christianity in strength.

Mithras /'mɪθræs/ in Persian mythology, the god of light. Mithras represented the power of goodness, and promised his followers compensation after death for present evil. He was said to have captured and killed the sacred bull, from whose blood all life sprang.

Mithridates VI Eupator /mɪθri'deɪtiːz/ known as **the Great** 132–63 BC. King of Pontus (NE Asia Minor, on the Black Sea) from 120 BC. He massacred 80,000 Romans in overrunning the rest of Asia Minor and went on to invade Greece. He was defeated by ◊Sulla in the First Mithridatic War 88–84 BC; by ◊Lucullus in the Second 83–81 BC; and by ◊Pompey in the Third 74–64 BC. He was killed by a soldier at his own order rather than surrender.

mitigate /'mɪtɪgeɪt/ *v.t.* to make milder or less intense or severe; (of circumstances) to excuse (wrongdoing) partially. —**mitigation** /-'geɪʃən/ *n.* [from Latin *mitigare* (*mitis* = mild)]

mitochondria *n.* (singular **mitochondrion**) membrane-enclosed organelles in ◊eukaryotic cells, containing enzymes responsible for energy production during aerobic respiration. These rodlike or spherical bodies are thought to be derived from free-living bacteria that, at a very early stage in the history of life, invaded larger cells and took up a symbiotic way of life inside. Each still contains its own small loop of DNA, and new mitochondria arise by division of existing ones.

mitosis /maɪ'təʊsɪs, mɪt-/ *n.* (*plural* **mitoses** /-siːz/) a process of division of cell nuclei in which two new nuclei each with the full number of chromosomes are formed. —**mitotic** /-'tɒtɪk/ *adj.* [from Greek *mitos* = thread]

mitre /'maɪtə/ *n.* 1. a head-dress forming part of the insignia of a bishop in the Western Church, and worn also by abbots and other ecclesiastics as a mark of exceptional dignity. 2. a joint of two pieces of wood or other material at an angle of 90°, such that the line of junction bisects this angle. —*v.t.* 1. to bestow a mitre on. 2. to join with a mitre. [from Old French from Latin from Greek *mitra* = turban]

Mitre /'mɪtreɪ/ Bartólome 1821–1906. Argentine president 1862–68. In 1852 he helped overthrow the dictatorial regime of Juan Manuel de Rosas, and in 1861 he helped unify Argentina. Mitre encouraged immigration and favoured growing commercial links with Europe. He is seen as a symbol of national unity.

mitt *n.* 1. a mitten. 2. a baseball-player's glove. 3. (*slang*) a hand.

mitten /'mɪtən/ *n.* a kind of glove that leaves the fingers and thumb-tip bare, or that has no partitions between the fingers. [from Old French *mitaine* from Latin *medietas* = half]

Mitterrand /mi:tə'rɒŋ/ François 1916– . French socialist politician, president from 1981. He held ministerial posts in 11 governments 1947–1958. He founded the French Socialist Party (PS) 1971. In 1985 he introduced proportional representation, allegedly to weaken the growing opposition from left and right.

mix *v.t./i.* 1. to combine or put together (two or more substances or things) so that the constituents of each are diffused among those of the other(s). 2. to prepare (a compound, cocktail, etc.) by mixing the ingredients. 3. to be capable of being blended. 4. to combine; (of things) to be compatible. 5. (of a person) to be harmonious or sociable; to have dealings. —*n.* a mixture; the proportion of materials in this; a mixture prepared commercially from suitable ingredients for making something. —**be mixed up in** *or* **with**, to be involved in or with. **mix it**, (*colloquial*) to start fighting. **mix up**, to mix thoroughly, to confuse. **mix-up** *n.* a confusion; a misunderstanding.

Mix /mɪks/ Tom (Thomas) 1880–1940. US actor who was a cowboy star of silent films. At their best his films, such as *The Range Riders* 1910 and *King Cowboy* 1928, were fast-moving and full of impressive stunts.

mixed /mɪkst/ *adj.* 1. of diverse qualities or elements. 2. (of a group of persons) containing persons from various races or social classes. 3. for persons of both sexes. —**mixed bag**, a diverse assortment. **mixed blessing**, a thing having advantages but also disadvantages. **mixed doubles**, (in tennis) a doubles game with a man and woman as partners on each side. **mixed farming**, farming of both crops and livestock. **mixed feelings**, a mixture of pleasure and dismay. **mixed grill**, a dish of various grilled meats and vegetables. **mixed marriage**, a marriage between persons of different race or religion. **mixed metaphor**, a combination of inconsistent metaphors. **mixed-up** *adj.* (*colloquial*) mentally or emotionally confused, socially illadjusted. [from earlier *mixt* from Old French from Latin *mixtus*, past participle of *miscēre* = mix]

mixer *n.* 1. a device for mixing or blending foods etc. 2. a person who manages socially in a specified way. 3. a drink to be mixed with another.

mixture /'mɪkstʃə/ *n.* 1. the process or result of mixing; a thing made by mixing; a combination of ingredients, qualities, characteristics, etc. 2. in chemistry, a substance containing two or more compounds that still retain their separate physical and chemical properties. There is no chemical bonding between them and they can be separated from each other by physical means. —**the mixture as before**, the same treatment repeated. [from French or Latin *mixtura*]

mizen *n.* (also **mizen-sail**) the lowest fore-and-aft sail of a full-rigged ship's mizen-mast. —**mizen-mast** *n.* the mast next aft of the mainmast. [from French *misaine* from Italian]

Mizoguchi /mɪzɒ'gutʃi/ Kenji 1898–1956. Japanese film director whose *Ugetsu Monogatari* 1953 confirmed his international reputation. He also directed *Blood and Soul* 1923, *The Poppies* 1935, and *Street of Shame* 1956.

Mizoram /maɪzə'ræm/ state of NE India; **area** 21,100 sq km/8,145 sq mi; **capital** Aizawl; **population** (1981) 488,000; **religion** 84% Christian; **recent history** made a Union Territory in 1972 from the Mizo Hills District of Assam. Rebels carried on a guerrilla war 1966–76, but in 1976 acknowledged Mizoram as an integral part of India. It became a state in 1986.

m.k.s. system system of units in which the base units metre, kilogram, and second replace the centimetre, gram, and second of the ◊c.g.s. system. From it developed the SI system (see ◊SI units).

ml symbol for millilitre(s).

Mladenov /mlæ'deɪnɒf/ Petar 1936– . Bulgarian Communist politician, secretary general of the Bulgarian Communist Party from Nov 1989, after the resignation of ◊Zhivkov, until Feb 1990. He was elected state president in April 1990 but replaced four months later.

Mlle(s) abbreviation of *Mademoiselle, Mesdemoiselles.*

MLR abbreviation of minimum lending rate.

mm symbol for millimetre(s).

MM abbreviation of 1. *Messieurs.* 2. Military Medal.

Mme(s) abbreviation of *Madame, Mesdames.*

Mn symbol for manganese.

mnemonic /ni'mɒnɪk/ *adj.* of or designed to aid the memory. —*n.* 1. a mnemonic device. 2. (in *plural*) the art of or a system for improving the memory. —**mnemonically** *adv.* [from Greek *mnēmōn* = mindful]

mo /məʊ/ (*slang*) (*plural* **mos**) abbreviation of moment.

Mo symbol for molybdenum.

MO abbreviation of 1. Medical Officer. 2. money order.

moa /'məʊə/ *n.* an extinct kiwi-like bird, order Dinornithoformes, 19 species of which lived in New Zealand. They varied from 0.5 to 3.5 m/2 to 12 ft, with strong limbs, a long neck, and no wings. The last moa was killed in the 1800s. [Maori]

Moab /'məʊæb/ ancient country in Jordan E of the S part of the river Jordan and the Dead Sea. The inhabitants were closely akin to the Hebrews in culture, language, and religion, but were often at war with them, as recorded in the Old Testament. Moab eventually fell to Arab invaders. The **Moabite Stone**, discovered in 1868 at Dhiban, dates from the 9th century BC and records the rising of Mesha, king of Moab, against Israel.

moan *n.* 1. a long murmur expressing physical or mental suffering; the low plaintive sound of wind etc. 2. a complaint, a grievance. —*v.t./i.* to make a moan or moans; to utter with moans. [Old English]

moat *n.* a defensive ditch round a castle, town, etc., usually filled with water. —**moated** *adj.* [from Old French *mot(t)e* = mound]

mob *n.* 1. a disorderly crowd, a rabble. 2. the common people. 3. (*slang*) a gang; an associated group of persons. —*v.t.* (**-bb-**) to crowd round in order to attack or admire. [abbreviation of *mobile* from Latin *mobile vulgus* = excitable crowd]

mob-cap *n.* (*historical*) a woman's large indoor cap covering all the hair. [from obsolete *mob* = slut]

mobile /'məʊbaɪl/ *adj.* 1. movable, not fixed; able to move or be moved easily. 2. (of the face etc.) readily changing its expression. 3. (of a shop etc.) accommodated in a vehicle so as to serve various places. 4. (of a person) able to change social status. —*n.* a light, decorative structure that may be hung so as to turn freely. —**mobile home**, a caravan. —**mobility** /məˈbɪlɪtɪ/ *n.* [from French from Latin *mobilis* (*movēre* = move)]

mobile ion ion that is free to move; mobile ions are only found in aqueous solutions or a ◊melt of an ◊electrolyte. The mobility of the ions in an electrolyte is what allows it to conduct electricity.

mobilize /'məʊbɪlaɪz/ *v.t./i.* 1. to assemble (troops etc.) for service; to prepare for war or other emergency. 2. to assemble for a particular purpose. —**mobilization** /- ˈzeɪʃən/ *n.*

Möbius /'mɜːbɪəs/ August Ferdinand 1790–1868. German mathematician, discoverer of the Möbius strip and considered one of the founders of ◊topology.

Möbius strip a surface with only one side and one edge, formed by joining the ends of a rectangular strip after twisting one end through 180°. [from A F *Möbius*]

mobster *n.* (*slang*) a gangster.

Mobutu /məˈbuːtuː/ Sese-Seko-Kuku-Ngbeandu-Wa-Za-Banga 1930– . Zaïrean president from 1965. He assumed the presidency by coup, and created a unitary state under his centralized government. He abolished secret voting in elections in 1976 in favour of a system of acclamation at mass rallies.

Moby Dick /məʊbi ˈdɪk/ US novel by Herman Melville, published 1851. Its story of the conflict between the monomaniac Captain Ahab and the great white whale explores the mystery and the destructiveness of both man and nature's power.

moccasin /'mɒkəsɪn/ *n.* a soft heelless shoe as originally worn by North American Indians. [from American Indian]

mocha /'mɒkə, 'məʊ-/ *n.* a kind of coffee; flavouring made with this. [from *Mocha*, port on Red Sea]

mock *v.t./i.* 1. to make fun of by imitating, to mimic. 2. to scoff or jeer; to defy contemptuously. —*attributive adj.* sham, imitation (especially without intent to deceive). **mock orange**, a shrub *Philadelphus coronarius* with fragrant white flowers. **mock turtle soup**, a soup made from a calf's head etc., to resemble turtle soup. **mock-up** *n.* an experimental model or replica of a proposed structure etc. [from Old French *mo(c)quer*]

mockery /'mɒkərɪ/ *n.* 1. derision; the subject or occasion of this. 2. a counterfeit or absurdly inadequate representation. 3. a ludicrously or insultingly futile action etc.

mockingbird *n.* American bird *Mimus polyglottus*, related to the thrushes, brownish grey with white markings on the black wings and tail. It is remarkable for its ability to mimic.

mod 1. (*colloquial*) abbreviation of modification. 2. British youth subculture that originated in London and Brighton in the early 1960s around the French view of the English; revived in the late 1970s. Mods were fashion-conscious, speedy, and upwardly mobile; they favoured scooters and soul music. —*adj.* modern. —**mod cons**, modern conveniences.

mod *n.* 1. (*colloquial*) abbreviation of modification. 2. British youth subcultre that originated in London and Brighton in the early 1960s around the French view of the English; revived in the late 1970s. Mods were fashion-conscious, speedy, and upwardly mobile; they favoured scooters and soul music. —*adj.* modern. —**mod cons**, modern conveniences.

MOD abbreviation of Ministry of ◊Defence.

modal /'məʊdəl/ *adj.* 1. of mode or form as opposed to substance. 2. in grammar, of the mood of a verb; (of a verb, e. g. *would*) used to express the mood of another verb. [from Latin]

mode *n.* 1. the way or manner in which a thing is done; a method of procedure. 2. the prevailing fashion or custom. 3. in music, any of the scale systems or types of melody that make up the characteristic sound of the music of a country or tradition. 4. in mathematics, the element that appears most frequently in a given group. For example, the mode of the group 0,0,9,9,9,12,87,87 is 9. (Not all groups have modes.) [French and from Latin *modus*]

model /'mɒdəl/ *n.* 1. a representation in three dimensions of an existing person or thing or of a proposed structure, especially on a smaller scale. 2. a simplified description of a system for calculations etc. 3. a figure in clay, wax, etc., to be reproduced in another material. 4. a particular design or style of structure, especially of a motor vehicle. 5. a person or thing regarded as excellent of its kind and proposed for imitation. 6. a person employed to pose for an artist, or to display clothes etc. by wearing them. 7. a garment etc. by a well-known designer; a copy of this. —*adj.* exemplary, ideally perfect. —*v.t./i.* (**-ll-**) 1. to fashion or shape (a figure) in clay, wax, etc. 2. to design or plan on or after the model of. 3. to act or pose as an artist's or fashion model; to display (clothes) thus. [from French from Italian *modello* from Latin]

Model Parliament English parliament set up in 1295 by Edward I; it was the first to include representatives from outside the clergy and aristocracy, and was established because Edward needed the support of the whole country against his opponents: Wales, France, and Scotland. His sole aim was to raise money for military purposes, and the parliament did not pass any legislation.

modem /'məʊdem/ acronym from **mo**dulator-**dem**odulator a device for transmitting data over telephone lines. The modem converts digital signals to analogue, and back again. Modems are used for linking remote terminals to central computers, and enable computers to communicate with each other anywhere in the world.

moderate /'mɒdərət/ *adj.* 1. medium in amount, intensity, or quality etc.; avoiding extremes. 2. temperate in conduct or expression; not holding extremist views. 3. fairly large and good, tolerably so. 4. (of prices) fairly low. —*n.* one who holds moderate views in politics etc. —/-eɪt/ *v.t./i.* to make or become moderate or less intense etc.; to act as a moderator of. —**moderately** *adv.*, **moderateness** *n.* [from Latin *moderare* = reduce, control]

moderation /mɒdəˈreɪʃən/ *n.* 1. moderating. 2. moderateness. —**in moderation**, in moderate amounts or degree. [from Old French from Latin]

moderator *n.* 1. an arbitrator, a mediator. 2. a presiding officer; a Presbyterian minister presiding over a church court or assembly. 3. a substance used in nuclear reactors to retard neutrons. [from Latin]

modern /'mɒdən/ *adj.* of present and recent times; in current fashion, not antiquated. —*n.* a person living in modern times. —**modernity** /-'dɜːnɪtɪ/ *n.* [from French or Latin *modo* = just now]

modernism *n.* 1. modern views or methods. 2. a tendency in matters of religious belief to subordinate tradition to harmony with modern thought. 3. a modern term or usage. —**modernist** *n.*, **modernistic** /-'nɪstɪk/ *adj.*

Modernism *n.* in the arts, a general term used to describe the 20th century's conscious attempt to break with the artistic traditions of the 19th century; it is based on a concern with form and the exploration of technique as opposed to content and narrative.

modernize *v.t./i.* to make modern, to adapt to modern needs or habits; to adopt modern ways or views. —**modernization** /-'zeɪʃən/ *n.*

modest /'mɒdɪst/ *adj.* 1. having a humble or moderate estimate of one's own merits. 2. diffident, not putting oneself forward. **3.** decorous in manner and conduct. **4.** (of a demand, statement, etc.) not excessive or exaggerated. **5.** unpretentious in appearance, amount, etc. —**modestly** *adv.*, **modesty** *n.* [from French from Latin = keeping due measure]

modicum /'mɒdɪkəm/ *n.* a small quantity. [Latin, neuter of *modicus* = moderate]

modification /ˌmɒdɪfɪ'keɪʃən/ *n.* **1.** modifying, being modified. **2.** a change made. —**modificatory** *adj.* [French or from Latin]

modify /'mɒdɪfaɪ/ *v.t.* **1.** to make less severe or decided, to tone down. **2.** to make partial changes in. **3.** in grammar, to qualify the sense of (a word etc.). [from Old French from Latin *modificare*]

Modigliani /mɒdɪl'jɑːni/ Amedeo 1884–1920. Italian artist, active in Paris from 1906. He painted and sculpted graceful nudes and portrait studies. His paintings have a distinctive elongated, linear style. The portrait of *Jeanne Hebuterne* 1919 (Guggenheim Museum, New York) is typical.

modish /'məʊdɪʃ/ *adj.* fashionable. —**modishly** *adv.*, **modishness** *n.*

modiste /mɒ'diːst/ *n.* a milliner, a dressmaker. [French]

modular /'mɒdjʊlə/ *adj.* consisting of modules or moduli. —**modular course** in education, a course, usually leading to a recognized qualification, which is divided into short and often optional units that are assessed as they are completed. [from Latin *modulus*]

modulate /'mɒdjʊleɪt/ *v.t./i.* **1.** to regulate or adjust; to moderate. **2.** to adjust or vary the tone or pitch of (the speaking voice); to alter the amplitude or frequency of (a wave) by a wave of lower frequency to convey a signal; in music, to pass from one key to another. —**modulation** /ˈleɪʃən/ *n.* [from Latin *modulari*]

module /'mɒdjuːl/ *n.* a standardized part or independent unit in construction (especially of furniture), buildings, spacecraft, etc., or in an academic course. [French or from Latin]

modulus /'mɒdjʊləs/ *n.* (*plural* **moduli** /-laɪ/) a constant factor or ratio; in mathematics, the positive value of a ◊real number, irrespective of its sign, indicated by a pair of vertical lines. Thus |3| is 3; and |–5| is 5. [Latin = measure]

modus operandi /'məʊdəs ɒpə'rændɪ/ the way a person goes about a task; the way a thing operates. [Latin = mode of working]

modus vivendi /'məʊdəs vɪ'vendɪ/ a way of living or coping; an arrangement whereby those in dispute can carry on pending a settlement. [Latin = mode of living]

mog *n.* or **moggie** (*slang*) a cat.

Mogadishu /mɒgə'dɪʃuː/ or **Mugdisho** capital and chief port of Somalia; population (1988) 1,000,000. It is a centre for oil refining, food processing, and uranium mining.

mogul /'məʊgəl/ *n.* (*colloquial*) an important or influential person.

Mogul /'məʊgəl/ *adj.* Mongolian; of the Moguls. —*n.* a Mongolian; a member of a Mongolian (Muslim) dynasty in India in the 16th–19th century —**the (Great** *or* **Grand) Mogul**, the Mogul emperor. [from Persian and Arabic]

Mohács, Battle of /'məʊhɑːtʃ/ Austro-Hungarian defeat of the Turks in 1687, which effectively marked the end of Turkish expansion into Europe. Mohács is also the site of a Turkish victory in 1526. It is now a river port on the Danube in Hungary.

mohair /'məʊheə/ *n.* the hair of the Angora goat; a yarn or fabric from this. [ultimately from Arabic = choice]

Mohamad /mə'hæməd/ Mahathir bin 1925– . Prime minister of Malaysia from 1981 and leader of the United Malays' National Organization (UMNO). His 'look east' economic policy emulates Japanese industrialization.

Mohammed /məʊ'hæmɪd/ *n.* alternative form of ◊Muhammad, founder of Islam.

Mohammedanism *n.* misnomer for ◊Islam, the religion founded by Muhammad.

Mohawk *n.* member of a North American Indian people, part of the ◊Iroquois confederation, who lived in the Mohawk Valley, New York, and now live on reservations in Ontario, Québec, and New York State, as well as among the general population.

Mohenjo Daro /mə'hendʒəʊ 'dɑːrəʊ/ site of a city about 2500–1600 BC on the lower Indus River, Pakistan,

Number	Defining mineral	Other substances compared
1	talc	
2	gypsum	2½ fingernail
3	calcite	3½ copper coin
4	fluorite	
5	apatite	5½ steel blade
6	orthoclase	5¾ glass
7	quartz	7 steel file
8	topaz	
9	corundum	
10	diamond	

The scale is not regular; diamond, at number 10, the hardest natural substance, is 90 times harder in absolute terms than corundum, number 9.

Mohs' scale

where excavations from the 1920s have revealed the ◊Indus Valley civilization.

Mohican and Mohegan or **Mahican** two closely related North American Indian peoples, speaking an Algonquian language, who formerly occupied the Hudson Valley and parts of Connecticut respectively. The novelist James Fenimore ◊Cooper confused the two peoples in his fictional account *The Last of the Mohicans* 1826.

Moholy-Nagy /'məʊhɔɪ 'nɒdʒ/ Laszlo 1895–1946. US photographer, born in Hungary. He lived in Germany 1923–29, where he was a member of the Bauhaus school, and fled from the Nazis in 1935. Through the publication of his illuminating theories and practical experiments, he had great influence on 20th-century photography and design.

Mohorovičić discontinuity /məʊhə'rəʊvɪtʃɪtʃ/ or **Moho** or **M-discontinuity** boundary that separates the Earth's crust and mantle, marked by a rapid increase in the speed of earthquake waves. It follows the variations in the thickness of the crust and is found approximately 32 km/20 mi below the continents and about 10 km/6 mi below the oceans. [from A Mohorovičić, Yugoslav geophysicist (died 1936)].

Mohs /məʊz/ Friedrich 1773–1839. German mineralogist, who in 1812 devised **Mohs' scale** of minerals, classified in order of relative hardness.

Moi /mɔɪ/ Daniel arap 1924– . Kenyan politician, president from 1978. Originally a teacher, he became minister of home affairs in 1964, vice president in 1967, and succeeded Jomo Kenyatta as president.

moiety /'mɔɪtɪ/ *n.* in law or literature, a half; either of the two parts of a thing. [from Old French from Latin *medietas* (*medius* = middle)]

moil *v.i.* to drudge. [from Old French *moillier* = paddle in mud]

moire /mwɑː/ *n.* or **moire antique** a watered fabric, usually silk. [French]

moiré /'mwɑːreɪ/ *adj.* **1.** (of silk) watered. **2.** (of metal) having a clouded appearance like watered silk. [French]

Moissan /mwæ'sʌn/ Henri 1852–1907. French chemist. For his preparation of pure fluorine in 1886, Moissan was awarded the 1906 Nobel Prize for Chemistry. He also attempted to create artificial diamonds by rapidly cooling carbon heated to high temperatures. His claims of success were treated with suspicion.

moist *adj.* slightly wet, damp; (of a season) rainy. —**moistness** *n.* [from Old French, perhaps from Latin *mucidus*]

moisten /'mɔɪsən/ *v.t./i.* to make or become moist.

moisture /'mɔɪstʃə/ *n.* liquid diffused in a small quantity as a vapour, within a solid, or condensed on a surface. [from Old French]

moisturize *v.t.* to make less dry (especially the skin by use of a cosmetic). —**moisturization** /-'zeɪʃən/ *n.*, **moisturizer** *n.*

Mojave Desert /məʊ'hɑːvi/ arid region in S California, USA, part of the Great Basin; area 38,500 sq km/15,000 sq mi.

moke *n.* (*slang*) a donkey.

moksha /'mɒkʃə/ *n.* in Hinduism and Jainism, liberation from the chain of births impelled by the law of karma; the bliss attained by this liberation. [Sanskrit = release (*muc* = to release)]

molecule

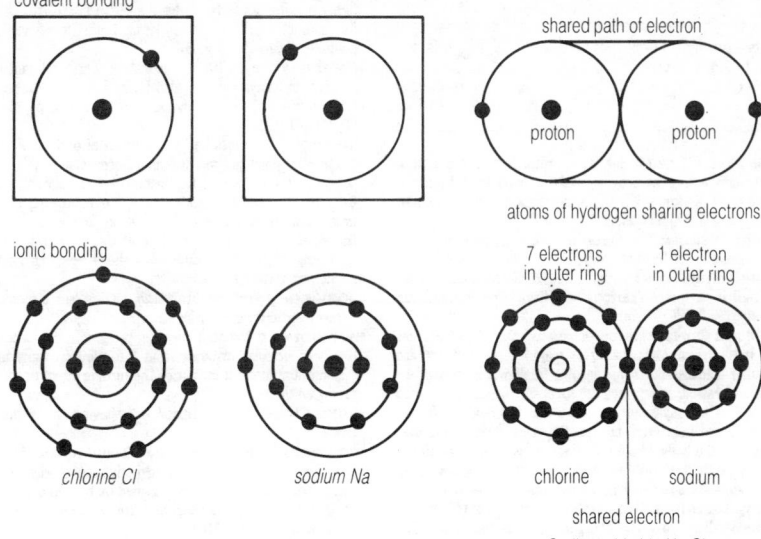

covalent bonding

shared path of electron

proton   proton

atoms of hydrogen sharing electrons

ionic bonding

chlorine Cl   *sodium Na*

7 electrons   1 electron
in outer ring   in outer ring

chlorine   sodium

shared electron

Sodium chloride Na Cl

molar /'məulə/ *adj.* (especially of a mammal's back teeth) serving to grind. —*n.* a molar tooth. [from Latin *molaris* (*mola* = millstone)]

molarity *n.* the ◊concentration of a solution expressed as the number of ◊moles in grams of solute per cubic decimetre of solution.

molar volume volume occupied by one ◊mole (the molecular mass in grams) of any gas at standard temperature and pressure, equal to 2.24136×10^{-2} cu m.

molasses /mə'læsız/ *n.* uncrystallized syrup drained from raw sugar; (*US*) treacle. [from Portuguese from Latin *mellaceum* = must (*mel* = honey)]

Moldavia /mɒl'deıvıə/ see ◊Moldova.

Moldova constituent republic of the USSR; **area** 33,700 sq km/13,012 sq mi; **capital** Kishinev; **population** (1987) 4,185,000; Moldavian (a branch of the Romanian people) 64%, Ukrainian 14%, Russian 13%, Gagauzi 4%, Jewish 2%; **language** Moldavian, allied to Romanian; **religion** Russian Orthodox; **recent history** former principality in Eastern Europe, on the river Danube, occupying an area divided today between the Soviet republic of Moldova and Romania. It was independent between the 14th and 16th centuries, when it became part of the Ottoman Empire. In 1940 the E part, Bessarabia, became part of the USSR, whereas the W part remained in Romania. In 1988 a popular front, the Democratic Movement for Perestroika, was formed, campaigning for accelerated political reform.

mole[1] *n.* **1.** a small burrowing mammal of the genus *Talpa*, with usually blackish velvety fur and very small eyes. Moles grow to 18 cm/7 in, and have acute senses of hearing, smell, and touch, but poor vision. They have strong, clawed front feet, and eat insects, grubs, and worms. **2.** a person who secretly leaks confidential information, especially when placed in an organization etc. as a spy. **3.** in construction, a mechanical device for boring horizontal holes underground without the need for digging trenches, used for laying pipes and cables.

mole[2] *n.* a small permanent dark spot on the human skin. [Old English]

mole[3] *n.* a massive structure usually of stone, as a pier, breakwater, or causeway; an artificial harbour. [from French from Latin *moles* = mass]

mole[4] *n.* the base unit of amount of substance (symbol mol), the amount of substance of a system which contains as many elementary entities as there are atoms in 0.012 kilogram of carbon 12. [from German *mol* (*molekül*)]

molecular /mə'lekjulə/ *adj.* of, relating to, or consisting of molecules. —**molecularity** /-'lærıtı/ *n.*

molecular biology the study of the molecular basis of life, including the biochemistry of molecules such as DNA, RNA, and proteins, and the molecular structure and function of the various parts of living cells.

molecular clock the use of rates of ◊mutation in genetic material to calculate the length of time elapsed since two related species diverged from each other during evolution. The method can be based on comparisons of the DNA or of widely occurring proteins, such as haemoglobin.

molecular formula formula indicating the actual number of atoms of each element present in a single molecule of a chemical compound. This is determined by two pieces of information: the ◊empirical formula and the ◊relative molecular mass, which is determined experimentally.

molecular solid solid composed of molecules that are held together by relatively weak ◊intermolecular forces. Such solids are low-melting and tend to dissolve in organic solvents. Examples of molecular solids are sulphur, ice, sucrose, and solid carbon dioxide.

molecular weight (also known as ◊relative molecular mass) the mass of a molecule, calculated relative to one-twelfth the mass of an atom of carbon 12. It is found by adding the relative atomic masses of the atoms that make up the molecule.

molecule /'mɒlıkju:l/ *n.* the smallest unit of an ◊element or ◊compound that can exist and still retain the characteristics of the element or compound. A molecule of an element consists of one or more like ◊atoms; a molecule of a compound consists of two or more different atoms bonded together. They vary in size and complexity from the hydrogen molecule (H_2) to the large ◊macromolecules found in polymers. They are held together by electrovalent bonds, in which the atoms gain or lose electrons to form ◊ions, or covalent bonds, where electrons from each atom are shared in a new molecular orbital. [from French]

molehill *n.* a small mound thrown up by a mole in burrowing. —**make a mountain out of a molehill**, to over-react to a small difficulty.

molest /mə'lest/ *v.t.* to annoy or pester (a person) in a hostile or injurious way. —**molestation** /-'steıʃən/ *n.* [from Old French or Latin *molestare* (*molestus* = troublesome)]

Molière /'mɒlıeə/ pen-name of Jean Baptiste Poquelin 1622–1673. French satirical playwright from whose work modern French comedy developed. One of the founders of the Illustre Théâtre 1643, he was later its leading actor. In 1655 he wrote his first play, *L'Etourdi*, followed by *Les Précieuses ridicules* 1659. His satires include *L'Ecole des femmes* 1662, ◊*Le Misanthrope* 1666,

Le Bourgeois gentilhomme 1670, and *Le Malade imaginaire* 1673.

It is a public scandal that gives offence, and it is no sin to sin in secret.

Molière
Tartuffe

Molise /mɒˈliːzeɪ/ mainly agricultural region of S central Italy, comprising the provinces of Campobasso and Isernia; area 4,400 sq km/1,698 sq mi; population (1988) 335,000. Its capital is Campobasso.

moll *n.* (*colloquial*) 1. a prostitute. 2. a gangster's female companion. [pet-form of *Mary*]

mollify /ˈmɒlɪfaɪ/ *v.t.* to appease; to soothe the anger of. —**mollification** /-fɪˈkeɪʃən/ *n.* [from French or Latin *mollificare* (*mollis* = soft)]

mollusc /ˈmɒləsk/ *n.* any of various invertebrate animals of the phylum Mollusca. The majority of molluscs are marine animals, but some inhabit fresh water, and a few are terrestrial. They include shellfish, snails, slugs, and cuttles. The body is soft, limbless, and cold-blooded. There is no internal skeleton, but most species have a hard shell covering the body. [from Latin *molluscus* (*mollis* = soft)]

mollycoddle /ˈmɒlɪkɒdəl/ *v.t.* to coddle excessively, to pamper. —*n.* an effeminate man or boy, a milksop.

Molly Maguires, the /ˈmɒli məˈgwaɪəz/ in US history, a secret Irish coalminers' organization in the 1870s that staged strikes and used violence against coal-company officials and property in the anthracite fields of Pennsylvania, prefiguring a long period of turbulence in industrial relations. The movement was infiltrated by ◊Pinkerton agents (detectives), and in 1876 trials led to convictions and executions.

Moloch /ˈməʊlɒk/ or **Molech** in the Old Testament, a Phoenician deity worshipped in Jerusalem in the 7th century BC, to whom live children were sacrificed by fire.

Molotov /ˈmɒlətɒf/ Vyacheslav Mikhailovich. Assumed name of V M Skriabin 1890–1986. Soviet communist politician. He was chair of the Council of People's Commissars (prime minister) 1930–41 and foreign minister 1939– 49 and 1953–56. He negotiated the 1939 nonaggression treaty with Germany (the ◊Hitler–Stalin pact), and, after the German invasion of 1941, the Soviet partnership with the Allies. His postwar stance prolonged the Cold War and in 1957 he was expelled from the government for Stalinist activities.

Molotov cocktail or **petrol bomb** a home-made weapon consisting of a bottle filled with petrol, plugged with a rag as a wick, ignited, and thrown as a grenade. Resistance groups during World War II named them after the Soviet foreign minister Molotov.

molten /ˈməʊltən/ *adj.* melted, especially made liquid by heat.

Moltke /ˈmɒltkə/ Helmuth Carl Bernhard, Count von 1800–1891. Prussian general. He became chief of the general staff in 1857, and was responsible for the Prussian strategy in the wars with Denmark 1863–64, Austria 1866, and France 1870–71.

Moltke Helmuth Johannes Ludwig von 1848–1916. German general (nephew of Count von Moltke, the Prussian general), chief of the German general staff 1906–14. His use of General Alfred von Schlieffen's (1833–1913) plan for a rapid victory on two fronts failed and he was relieved of command after the defeat at the Marne.

Moluccas /məʊˈlʌkəz/ another name for ◊Maluku, Indonesia.

moly /ˈməʊlɪ/ *n.* in Greek legend, a magical plant with a white flower and black root, given by Hermes to Odysseus as a charm against the sorceries of Circe. [from Greek *mōlu*]

molybdenite *n.* molybdenum sulphide, symbol MoS$_2$, the chief ore mineral of molybdenum. It possesses a hexagonal crystal structure similar to graphite, has a blue metallic lustre, and is very soft (1–1.5 on Mohs' scale).

molybdenum /məˈlɪbdɪnəm/ *n.* heavy, hard, lustrous, silver-white, metallic element, symbol Mo, atomic number 42, relative atomic mass 95.94. The chief ore is the mineral molybdenite. The element is highly resistant to heat and conducts electricity easily. It is used in alloys, often to harden steels. It is a necessary trace element in human nutrition. It was named in 1781 by Swedish chemist Karl Scheele, after its isolation by P J Helm (1746–1813), for its resemblance to lead ore. [from Latin from Greek = plummet (*molubdos* = lead)]

Mombasa /mɒmˈbæsə/ industrial port (oil refining, cement) in Kenya (serving also Uganda and NE Tanzania), built on Mombasa Island and adjacent mainland; population (1984) 481,000.

moment /ˈməʊmənt/ *n.* 1. a very brief portion of time. 2. an exact point of time. 3. importance. 4. in physics, the product of a force and the distance of its line of action from the centre of rotation. —**at the moment**, at this time, now. **in a moment**, very soon. **may etc.** **of the moment**, the one of importance at the time in question. **moment of truth**, a time of crisis or test. [from Old French from Latin]

momentary /ˈməʊməntərɪ/ *adj.* lasting only a moment. —**momentarily** *adv.* [from Latin]

moment of a force in physics, product of the force and the perpendicular distance from the point to the line of action of the force; it measures the turning effect or torque produced by the force.

momentous /məˈmentəs/ *adj.* having great importance.

momentum /məˈmentəm/ *n.* (*plural* **momenta**) the quantity of motion of a moving body, the product of its mass and its velocity; impetus gained by movement (*literal* or *figurative*). [Latin *movimentum* from *movēre* = move]

Mon. abbreviation of Monday.

Monaco /ˈmɒnəkəʊ/ Principality of; small sovereign state forming an enclave in S France, with the Mediterranean to the S; **area** 1.95 sq km/0.75 sq mi; **capital** Monaco-Ville; **physical** steep and rugged; surrounded landward by French territory, being expanded by filling in the sea; **head of state** Prince Rainier III from 1949; **head of government** Jean Ausseil from 1986; **political system** constitutional monarchy under French protectorate; **population** (1989) 29,000; **language** French; **recent history** became an independent state under French protection in 1861. In 1918 France was given a veto over the succession to the throne.

Monaghan /ˈmɒnəhən/ (Irish *Mhuineachain*) county in the NE of the Republic of Ireland, province of Ulster; area 1,290 sq km/498 sq mi; population (1986) 52,000. The county town is Monaghan. The county is low and rolling, and includes the rivers Finn and Blackwater. Products include cereals, linen, potatoes, and cattle.

monarch /ˈmɒnək/ *n.* a sovereign with the title of king, queen, emperor, empress, or the equivalent; a supreme ruler (*literal* or *figurative*). —**monarchic** /məˈnɑːkɪk/ *adj.*, **monarchical** /məˈnɑːkɪkəl/ *adj.* [from French or Latin from Greek *monos* = alone and *arkhō* = rule]

monarchism /ˈmɒnəkɪzəm/ *n.* the advocacy of or principles of monarchy. —**monarchist** *n.* [from French]

monarchy /ˈmɒnəkɪ/ *n.* a form of government with a monarch at the head; a state governed in this way. [from Old French from Latin from Greek]

monastery /ˈmɒnəstərɪ/ *n.* the residence of a community of monks. [from Latin from Greek *monazō* = live alone]

monastic /məˈnæstɪk/ *adj.* 1. of or like monks, nuns, friars, etc. 2. of monasteries. —**monastically** *adv.*, **monasticism** /məˈnæstɪsɪzəm/ *n.* [from French from Latin from Greek]

Monastir /mɒnəstɪ/ resort town on the Mediterranean coast of Tunisia, 18 km/11 mi S of Sousse. Birthplace of the former president, Habib Bourguiba, and summer residence of the president of Tunisia.

Monck /mʌŋk/ or **Monk** George, 1st Duke of Albemarle 1608–1669. English soldier. During the Civil War he fought for King Charles I, but after being captured changed sides and took command of the Parliamentary forces in Ireland. Under the Commonwealth he became commander in chief in Scotland, and in 1660 he led his army into England and brought about the restoration of Charles II.

Mond /mɒnd/ Ludwig 1839–1909. German chemist who perfected a process for recovering sulphur during the manufacture of alkali.

Monday /ˈmʌndeɪ, -dɪ/ *n.* the day of the week following Sunday. —*adv.* (*colloquial*) on Monday. [Old English = day of the Moon]

Mondrian /'mɒndriɑ:n/ Piet (Pieter Mondriaan) 1872–1944. Dutch painter, a pioneer of abstract art. He lived in Paris 1919–38, then in London, and from 1940 in New York. He was a founder member of the de ◊Stijl movement and chief exponent of Neo-Plasticism, a rigorous abstract style based on the use of simple geometric forms and pure colours.

Monet /'mɒneɪ/ Claude 1840–1926. French painter, a pioneer of Impressionism and a lifelong exponent of its ideals; his painting *Impression, Sunrise* 1872 gave the movement its name. In the 1870s he began painting the same subjects at different times of day to explore the effects of light on colour and form; the *Haystacks* and *Rouen Cathedral* series followed in the 1890s, and from 1899 he painted a series of *Water Lilies* in the garden of his house at Giverny, Normandy (now a museum).

monetarism /'mʌnɪtərɪzəm/ n. an economic policy, that proposes control of a country's money supply to keep it in step with the country's ability to produce goods, with the aim of curbing inflation. —**monetarist** n.

monetary /'mʌnɪtərɪ/ adj. of the currency in use; of or consisting of money. —**monetarily** adv. [from French or Latin]

monetary policy an economic policy that sees control of both the money supply and liquidity as important determinants of the level of employment and inflation. By influencing interest rates, the policy aims to ease balance of payment problems.

money /'mʌnɪ/ n. 1. the current medium of exchange in the form of coins and banknotes. 2. (in *plural* **moneys** or **monies**) sums of money. 3. wealth, property viewed as convertible into money. 4. a rich person or rich people. —**in the money**, having or winning plenty of money. **make money**, to acquire wealth. **money-bag** n. a bag for money; (in *plural* treated as *singular, colloquial*) a wealthy person. **money-box** n. a closed box for holding money dropped in through a slit. **money-changer** n. one whose business it is to change money, especially at an official rate. **money for jam**, (*slang*) a profit for little or no trouble. **money-grabber** n. a person greedily intent on amassing money. **money-grabbing** adj. given to this practice; (n.) this practice. **money-lender** n. one whose business it is to lend money at interest. **money-making** adj. producing wealth; (n.) the acquisition of wealth. **money-market** n. the sphere of operation of dealers in short-dated loans, stocks, etc. **money of account**, a unit of money used in accounting but not current as a coin or note. **money order**, an order for the payment of a specified sum, issued by a bank or the Post Office. **money-spider** n. a small spider supposed to bring good luck in money or other matters to the person over whom it crawls. **money-spinner** n. a thing that brings in much profit. **money's-worth** n. good value for one's money. **put money into**, to make an investment in. [from Old French from Latin *moneta* = mint]

moneyed /'mʌnɪd/ adj. wealthy; consisting of money.

money supply the quantity of money present in an economy at a given moment. Monetarists hold that a rapid increase in money supply inevitably provokes a rise in the rate of inflation.

monger /'mʌŋgə/ n. (chiefly *in combinations*) 1. a dealer or trader (*fishmonger*). 2. (usually *derogatory*) a spreader (*scandalmonger, scaremonger*). [Old English from Latin *mango*]

Mongol /'mɒŋgəl/ adj. 1. a member of any of the various Mongol (or Mongolian) ethnic groups of Central Asia. Mongols live in the Mongolian People's Republic, the USSR, Inner Mongolia, Tibet, and Nepál. The Mongol language belongs to the Altaic family; some groups of Mongol descent speak languages in the Sino-Tibetan family however. 2. having Mongoloid characteristics. —n. a Mongol person.

Mongol Empire empire established by Genghis Khan, who extended his domains from Russia to N China and became khan of the Mongol tribes in 1206. His grandson Kublai Khan conquered China and used foreigners such as Marco Polo as well as subjects to administer his empire. The Mongols lost China in 1367 and suffered defeats in the West in 1380; the empire broke up soon afterwards.

Mongolia /mɒŋ'gəʊliə/ People's Republic of (formerly **Outer Mongolia**); country in E Central Asia, bounded N by the USSR and S by China; **area** 1,565,000 sq km/

604,480 sq mi; **capital** Ulaanbaatar; **physical** a high plateau with steppe (grasslands); **head of state** Punsalmaagiyn Ochirbat from 1990; **head of government** Dashiyn Byambasuren from 1990; **political system** communism; **population** (1990 est) 2,185,000; **language** Khalkha Mongolian (official), Chinese, Russian; **recent history** Chinese rule overthrown with Soviet help in 1921, and in 1924 Mongolia was proclaimed a People's Republic. A democratization campaign was launched by the Mongolian Democratic Union in 1990; Ochirbat's Mongolian People's Revolutionary Party was elected in free multiparty elections.

Mongolia, Inner /mɒŋ'gəʊliə/ (Chinese *Nei Mongol*) autonomous region of NE China from 1947; **area** 450,000 sq km/173,700 sq mi; **capital** Hohhot; **physical** grassland and desert; **population** (1986) 20,290,000.

Mongolian /mɒŋ'gəʊliən/ adj. of Mongolia or its people or language. —n. 1. a native or inhabitant of Mongolia. 2. Mongol, Mongoloid. 3. the language of Mongolia.

mongolism n. former name (now considered offensive) for ◊Down's syndrome.

Mongoloid /'mɒŋgələɪd/ n. a former racial classification, based on physical features, used to describe people of E Asian and North American origin; see ◊race. —n. a Mongoloid person.

mongoose /'mɒŋgu:s/ n. (*plural* **mongooses**) a carnivorous mammal of the family Viverridae. The Indian mongoose *Herpestes mungo* is greyish in colour, about 50 cm/1.5 ft long, with a long tail. It may be tamed, and is often kept for its ability to kill snakes. The Egyptian mongoose or ichneumon is larger. [from Marathi]

mongrel /'mʌŋgrəl/ n. 1. a dog of no definable breed. 2. an animal or plant resulting from the crossing of different breeds or types. —adj. of mixed origin, nature, or character.

moniker /'mɒnɪkə/ n. (*slang*) a name, a nickname.

monism /'mɒnɪzəm/ n. the theory that there is only a single ultimate principle or kind of being, not two or more (as opposed to **dualism** and **pluralism**); any of the theories that deny the duality of matter and mind. —**monist** n., **monistic** /-'nɪstɪk/ adj. [from Greek *monos* = single]

monitor /'mɒnɪtə/ n. 1. a pupil in a school with disciplinary or other duties. 2. a television receiver used in selecting or verifying the broadcast picture; a highly definitive screen used with a computer. 3. one who listens to and reports on foreign broadcasts etc. 4. a detector of radioactive contamination. —v.t./i. 1. to act as a monitor (of); to maintain regular surveillance (over). 2. to regulate the strength of (a recorded or transmitted signal). —**monitor lizard**, a lizard of the family Varanidae, found in tropical and subtropical regions. —**monitorial** /-'tɔ:rɪəl/ adj., **monitress** n.fem. [Latin *monēre* = warn]

monitory /'mɒnɪtərɪ/ adj. giving or serving as a warning. [from Latin *monitorius*]

monk /mʌŋk/ n. a member of a community of men living apart under religious vows. —**monkish** adj. [Old English, ultimately from Greek *monakhos* = solitary]

Monk Thelonious 1917–1982. US jazz pianist and composer. Working in Harlem, New York, during the Depression, he took part in the development of the jazz style known as **bebop** or **bop**. He became popular in the 1950s, and is remembered for numbers such as 'Round Midnight', 'Blue Monk', and 'Hackensack'.

monkey /'mʌŋkɪ/ n. 1. a mammal of a group closely allied to and resembling man, especially a small long-tailed member of the order Primates. 2. a mischievous person, especially a child. 3. (*slang*) £500; (*US*) $500. —v.i. 1. to play mischievously. 2. to tamper or play mischievous tricks. —**monkey business**, (*slang*) mischief. **monkey-nut** n. a peanut. **monkey-tricks** n.pl. (*slang*) mischief. **monkey-wrench** n. a wrench with an adjustable jaw.

monkey puzzle or **Chilean pine** a coniferous evergreen tree *Araucaria araucana* (see ◊araucaria), native to Chile; it has whorled branches covered in prickly leaves of a leathery texture.

monkshood /'mʌŋkshʊd/ n. a poisonous plant *Aconitum napellus* with hood-shaped flowers.

Monmouth /'mʌnməθ/ James Scott, Duke of Monmouth 1649–1685. Claimant to the English crown, the

monkey puzzle tree

illegitimate son of Charles II and Lucy Walter. After James II's accession in 1685, Monmouth landed in England at Lyme Regis, Dorset, claimed the crown, and raised a rebellion, which was crushed at ◊Sedgemoor in Somerset. He was executed with 320 of his accomplices.

Monmouthshire /'mʌnməʃə/ former county of Wales, which in 1974 became, minus a small strip on the border with Mid Glamorgan, the new county of **Gwent**.

mono /'mɒnəʊ/ abbreviation of monophonic. —*n. (plural* **monos***)* a monophonic record, reproduction, etc.

mono- in combinations, (before a vowel usually **mon-**) one, alone, single. [Greek *monos* = alone]

monocarpic *adj.* or **hapaxanthic** describing plants that flower and produce fruit only once during their life cycle, after which they die. Most ◊annual plants and ◊biennial plants are monocarpic, but there are also a small number of monocarpic ◊perennial plants for example, century plant *Agave* and some species of bamboo *Bambusa*. The general biological term for organisms that reproduce only once during their lifetime is ◊semelparity.

monochromatic /mɒnəkrə'mætɪk/ *adj.* 1. (of light or other radiation) containing only one colour or wavelength. 2. executed in monochrome. —**monochromatically** *adv.*

monochrome /'mɒnəkrəʊm/ *n.* a picture done in one colour or different tints of this, or in black and white only. —*adj.* having or using only one colour. [from Greek *khrōma* = colour]

monocle /'mɒnəkəl/ *n.* a single eyeglass. [French, originally from Latin *monoculus* = one-eyed]

monoclonal antibodies (MABs) antibodies produced by fusing an antibody-producing lymphocyte with a cancerous myeloma (bone-marrow) cell. The resulting fused cell, called a hybridoma, is immortal and can be used to produce large quantities of a single, specific antibody. By choosing antibodies that are directed against antigens found on cancer cells, and combining them with cytotoxic drugs, it is hoped to make so-called magic bullets that will be able to pick out and kill cancers.

monocotyledon /mɒnəkɒtɪ'liːdən/ *n.* a flowering plant with a single cotyledon. Monocotyledons usually have narrow leaves with parallel veins and smooth edges, and hollow or soft stems. Their flower parts are arranged in threes. Most are small plants such as orchids, grasses, and lilies, but some are trees such as palms. —**monocotyledonous** *adj.*

monocular /mə'nɒkjʊlə/ *adj.* with or for one eye.

monodrama /'mɒnədrɑːmə/ *n.* a dramatic piece for one performer.

monody /'mɒnədɪ/ *n.* 1. an ode sung by a single actor in a Greek play. 2. a poem in which a mourner bewails someone's death. —**monodist** *n.* [from Latin from Greek *monōidia*]

monoecious *n.* having separate male and female flowers on the same plant.

monogamy /mə'nɒgəmɪ/ *n.* the practice or state of being married to one person at a time. —**monogamist** *n.*, **monogamous** *adj.* [from French from Latin from Greek *gamos* = marriage]

monogram /'mɒnəgræm/ *n.* two or more letters, especially a person's initials, interwoven as a device. —**monogrammed** *adj.* [from French from Latin]

monograph /'mɒnəgrɑːf/ *n.* a separate treatise on a single subject or aspect of it.

monohybrid inheritance a pattern of inheritance seen in simple ◊genetics experiments, where the two animals (or two plants) being crossed are genetically identical except for one gene.

monolith /'mɒnəlɪθ/ *n.* 1. a single block of stone, especially shaped into a pillar etc. 2. a person or thing like a monolith in being massive, immovable, or solidly uniform. —**monolithic** /-'lɪθɪk/ *adj.* [from French from Greek *lithos* = stone]

monologue /'mɒnəlɒg/ *n.* 1. a scene in a drama where a person speaks alone; a dramatic composition for one performer. 2. a long speech by one person in a company. [French from Greek *monologos* = speaking alone]

monomania /mɒnə'meɪnɪə/ *n.* an obsession of the mind by one idea or interest. —**monomaniac** /-iæk/ *adj. & n.* [from French]

monomer *n.* chemical compound composed of simple molecules from which ◊polymers can be made. Under certain conditions the simple molecules (of the monomer) join together (polymerize) to form a very long chain molecule (macromolecule) called a polymer. For example, the polymerization of ethene monomers produces the polymer polyethene.

monophonic /mɒnə'fɒnɪk/ *adj.* (of reproduction of sound) using only one channel of transmission. [from Greek *phōnē* = sound]

Monophysite /mə'nɒfɪzaɪt/ *n.* an adherent of the doctrine that there was in the person of Christ only a single nature, part divine and part human, the human element being totally subordinate to the divine. [from Latin from Greek *monos* = one and *phusis* = nature]

monoplane /'mɒnəpleɪn/ *n.* an aeroplane with one pair of wings.

Monopolies and Mergers Commission (MMC) UK government body re-established in 1973 under the Fair Trading Act and, since 1980, embracing the Competition Act. Its role is to investigate and report when there is a risk of creating a monopoly following a company merger or takeover, or when a newspaper or newspaper assets are transferred. It also investigates companies, nationalized industries, or local authorities which are suspected of operating in a non-competitive way. The US equivalent is the **Federal Trade Commission** (FTC).

monopolist /mə'nɒpəlɪst/ *n.* one who has or advocates a monopoly. —**monopolistic** /-'lɪstɪk/ *adj.*

monopolize /mə'nɒpəlaɪz/ *v.t.* 1. to obtain exclusive possession or control of (a trade or commodity). 2. to dominate or prevent others from sharing in (a conversation etc.). —**monopolization** /-'zeɪʃən/ *n.*

monopoly /mə'nɒpəlɪ/ *n.* 1. exclusive possession of the trade in some commodity. 2. exclusive possession, control, or exercise (*of*, (*US*) *on*). 3. a thing of which one person or firm etc. has a monopoly. [from Latin from Greek *pōleō* = sell]

monorail /'mɒnəʊreɪl/ *n.* a railway that runs on a single rail; the cars can be balanced on it or suspended from it. It was invented in 1882 to carry light loads, and when run by electricity was called a **telpher**.

monosaccharide *n.* or **simple sugar** a ◊carbohydrate that cannot be hydrolysed (split) into smaller carbohydrate units. Examples are glucose and fructose, both of which have the molecular formula $C_6H_{12}O_6$.

monosodium glutamate (MSG) $NaC_5H_8NO_4$ a white, crystalline powder, the sodium salt of glutamic acid (an ◊amino acid found in proteins that plays a role in the metabolism of plants and animals). It is used to enhance the flavour of many packaged and 'fast foods', and in Chinese cooking. Ill effects may arise from its overconsumption.

monosyllable *n.* a word of one syllable. —**monosyllabic** /-'læbɪk/ *adj.*

monotheism /'mɒnəθiːɪzəm/ *n.* the doctrine that there is only one god. —**monotheist** *n.*, **monotheistic** /-'ɪstɪk/ *adj.* [from Greek *theos* = god]

monotone /'mɒnətəʊn/ *n.* 1. a sound or utterance continuing or repeated on one note without change of pitch. 2.

Monroe *The film star Marilyn Monroe dancing with Truman Capote, 1955.*

sameness in style of writing. —*adj.* without change of pitch. [from Greek]

monotonous /mə'nɒtənəs/ *adj.* lacking in variety, wearisome through sameness. —**monotonously** *adv.*, **monotony** *n.*

monotreme /'mɒnətri:m/ *n.* a mammal of the subclass Monotremata of primitive egg-laying Australasian animals with a single vent. [from Greek *trēma* = hole]

Monotype /'mɒnətaɪp/ *n.* (trade name) a composing-machine that casts and sets up pieces of type singly.

monovalent /'mɒnəveɪlənt/ *adj.* univalent.

monoxide /mə'nɒksaɪd/ *n.* an oxide containing one oxygen atom.

Monroe /mən'rəʊ/ James 1758–1831. 5th president of the USA 1817–25, born in Virginia. He served in the War of Independence, was minister to France 1794–96, and in 1803 negotiated the ◊Louisiana Purchase. He was secretary of state 1811–17. His name is associated with the Monroe Doctrine.

Monroe Marilyn. Stage name of Norma Jean Mortenson or Baker 1926–1962. US film actress who made comedies such as Gentlemen Prefer Blondes, *How To Marry a Millionaire* 1953, *The Seven Year Itch* 1955, *Bus Stop* 1956, and *Some Like It Hot* 1959. Her second husband was baseball star Joe di Maggio, and her third was playwright Arthur ◊Miller who wrote her last film *The Misfits* 1961. Combining a vibrant sex appeal with a fragile vulnerability, she has become the ultimate Hollywood sex symbol.

Monroe Doctrine the declaration by President Monroe in 1823 that any further European colonial ambitions in the western hemisphere would be threats to US peace and security, made in response to proposed European intervention against newly independent former Spanish colonies in South America. In return the USA would not interfere in European affairs. The doctrine, subsequently broadened, has been a recurrent theme in US foreign policy, although it has no basis in US or international law.

Monrovia /mɒn'rəʊviə/ capital and port of Liberia; population (1985) 500,000. Industries include rubber, cement, and petrol processing.

Monseigneur /mɒnsen'jɜ:/ *n.* the title given to an eminent Frenchman, especially a prince, cardinal, archbishop, or bishop. [French *mon* = my and *seigneur*]

Monsieur /mə'sjɜ:/ *n.* (*plural* **Messieurs** /me'sjɜ:/) the title used of or to a French-speaking man, corresponding to Mr or sir. [French *mon* = my and *sieur* = lord]

Monsignor /mɒn'si:njə/ *n.* the title of various Roman Catholic prelates. [Italian]

monsoon /mɒn'su:n/ *n.* a wind in S Asia, especially in the Indian Ocean, blowing from the SW in summer and from the NE in winter; the rainy season accompanying the SW monsoon. [from obsolete Dutch from Portuguese from Arabic = fixed season]

monster *n.* 1. an imaginary creature, usually large and frightening, compounded of incongruous elements. 2. a misshapen animal or plant. 3. an inhumanly cruel or wicked person. 4. an animal or thing of huge size. —*adj.* huge. [from Old French from Latin = portent (*monēre* = warn)]

monstera *n.* or **Swiss cheese plant** evergreen climbing plant, genus *Monstera*, of the arum family Araceae, native to tropical America. *M. deliciosa* is cultivated as a house plant. Areas between the veins of the leaves dry up, creating deep marginal notches and ultimately holes.

monstrance /'mɒnstrəns/ *n.* (in the Roman Catholic Church) a vessel in which the Host is exposed for veneration. [from Latin *monstrantia* (*monstrare* = show)]

monstrosity /mɒn'strɒsɪtɪ/ *n.* 1. a misshapen animal or plant; an outrageous thing. 2. monstrousness. [from Latin]

monstrous /'mɒnstrəs/ *adj.* 1. like a monster; huge. 2. abnormally formed. 3. outrageously wrong or absurd, atrocious. —**monstrously** *adv.* [from Old French or Latin]

montage /mɒn'tɑ:ʒ/ *n.* 1. a composite picture or piece of music etc. made of heterogeneous juxtaposed items, a pastiche; production of this. 2. (in cinematography) combination of images in quick succession to compress background information or provide atmosphere; a system of editing in which the narrative is modified or interrupted to include images that are not necessarily related to the dramatic development. [from French *monter* = to mount]

Montaigne /mɒn'teɪn/ Michel Eyquem de 1533–1592. French writer, regarded as the creator of the essay form. In 1580 he published the first two volumes of his *Essais*, the third volume appeared in 1588. Montaigne deals with all aspects of life from an urbanely sceptical viewpoint. Through the translation by John Florio in 1603, he influenced Shakespeare and other English writers.

One should always have one's boots on, and be ready to leave.

Michel de Montaigne
Essais

Montana /mɒn'tænə/ state of the W USA on the Canadian border; nickname Treasure State **area** 381,200 sq km/147,143 sq mi; **capital** Helena; **population** (1986) 819,000; **history** first settled in 1809; influx of immigrants pursuing gold in the mid-19th century; became a state in 1889.

Montana Joe 1956– . US footballer player. As quarterback for San Francisco 49ers he appeared in four winning Super Bowls 1982, 1985, 1989, and 1990, winning the most valuable player award in all but 1989, and setting a record for passing yardage 1989 and the most touchdown passes 1990.

Montand /mɒn'tɒn/ Yves 1921– . French actor and singer who achieved fame in the thriller *Le Salaire de la peur/The Wages of Fear* 1953 and continued to be popular in French and American films, including *Let's Make Love* 1960 (with Marilyn Monroe), *Grand Prix* 1966, *Le Sauvage/The Savage* 1976, *Jean de Florette* 1986, and *Manon des sources* 1986.

Montanism movement within the early Christian church that strove to return to the purity of primitive Christianity. It originated in Phrygia in about 156 with the teaching of a prophet named Montanus. The theologian ◊Tertulian was a noted Montanist.

Mont Blanc /mɒm 'blɒŋ/ (Italian **Monte Bianco**) the highest mountain in the ◊Alps, between France and Italy; height 4,807 m/15,772 ft. It was first climbed in 1786.

montbretia /mɒn'bri:ʃə/ *n.* a hybrid plant of the iris family (genus *Crocosmia*) with bright orange-coloured flowers. [from A F E Coquebert de *Montbret*, French botanist (died 1801)]

Montcalm /mɒnt'kɑ:m/ Louis-Joseph de Montcalm-Gozon, Marquis de 1712–1759. French general, appointed military commander in Canada in 1756. He won a succession

Monteverdi *One of the great composers of operas, Claudio Monteverdi.*

of victories over the British during the French and Indian War, but was defeated in 1759 by James ◊Wolfe at Québec, where both he and Wolfe were killed; this battle marked the end of French rule in Canada.

Monte Carlo /'mɒnti 'kɑːləʊ/ a town and resort in ◊Monaco, known for its gambling; population (1982) 12,000.

Montenegro /mɒnti'niːgrəʊ/ (Serbo-Croat *Crna Gora*) constituent republic of Yugoslavia; **area** 13,800 sq km/ 5,327 sq mi; **capital** Titograd; **physical** mountainous; **population** (1986) 620,000, including 400,000 Montenegrins, 80,000 Muslims, and 40,000 Albanians *language* Serbian variant of Serbo-Croat; **history** part of ◊Serbia from the late 12th century, it became independent (under Venetian protection) after Serbia was defeated by the Turks in 1389. It was overrun by Austria in World War I, and in 1918 voted after the deposition of King Nicholas to become part of Serbia. In 1946 it became a republic of Yugoslavia. In Jan 1989 the entire Communist Party leadership resigned after mass protests.

Monterrey /mɒntə'reɪ/ industrial city (iron, steel, textiles, chemicals, food processing) in NE Mexico; population (1986) 2,335,000.

Montessori /mɒntə'sɔːri/ Maria 1870–1952. Italian educationalist. From her experience with mentally handicapped children, she developed the **Montessori method**, an educational system for all children based on an informal approach, incorporating instructive play and allowing children to develop at their own pace.

We teachers can only help the work going on, as servants wait upon a master.

Maria Montessori
The Absorbent Mind

Monteverdi /mɒnti'veɑdi/ Claudio (Giovanni Antonio) 1567–1643. Italian composer. He contributed to the development of the opera with *Orfeo* 1607 and *The Coronation of Poppea* 1642. He also wrote madrigals, ◊motets, and sacred music, notably the *Vespers* 1610.

Montevideo /mɒntɪvɪ'deɪəʊ/ capital and chief port (grain, meat products, hides) of Uruguay, on Río de la Plata; population (1985) 1,250,000. It was founded in 1726.

Montezuma II /mɒnti'zuːmə/ 1466–1520. Aztec emperor 1502–20. When the Spanish conquistador Cortés invaded Mexico, Montezuma was imprisoned and killed during the Aztec attack on Cortés' force as it tried to leave Tenochtitlán, the Aztec capital city.

Montfort /'mɒntfət/ Simon de Montfort, Earl of Leicester *c.*1208–1265. English politician and soldier. From 1258 he led the baronial opposition to Henry III's misrule during the second ◊Barons' War and in 1264 defeated and captured the king at Lewes, Sussex. In 1265, as head of government, he summoned the first parliament in which the towns were represented; he was killed at the Battle of Evesham during the last of the Barons' Wars.

Montgolfier /mɒŋ'gɒlfieɪ/ Joseph Michel 1740–1810 and Étienne Jacques 1745–1799. French brothers whose hot-air balloon was used for the first successful human flight 21 Nov 1783.

Montgomery /mənt'gʌməri/ Robert (Henry) 1904–1981. US film actor of the 1930s and 1940s. He directed some of his later films, such as *Lady in the Lake* 1947, before leaving the cinema for television and Republican politics. His other films include *Night Must Fall* 1937 and *Mr and Mrs Smith* 1941.

Montgomery Bernard Law, 1st Viscount Montgomery of Alamein 1887–1976. British field marshal. In World War II he commanded the 8th Army in N Africa in the Second Battle of El ◊Alamein 1942. As commander of British troops in N Europe from 1944, he received the German surrender in 1945.

Montgomeryshire /mənt'gʌmrɪʃə/ former county of N Wales, included in Powys in 1974.

month /mʌnθ/ *n.* **1.** unit of time based on the motion of the Moon around the Earth. The time from one new or full Moon to the next (the **synodic** or **lunar month**) is 29.53 days. The time for the Moon to complete one orbit around the Earth relative to the stars (the **sidereal month**) is 27.32 days. The **solar month** equals 30.44 days, and is exactly one-twelfth of the solar or tropical year, the time taken for the Earth to orbit the Sun. The **calendar month** is a human invention, devised to fit the calendar year. **2.** a period of 28 days. —**month of Sundays**, a very long period. [Old English]

monthly *adj.* produced or occurring once every month. —*adv.* every month. —*n.* a monthly periodical.

Montréal /mɒntrɪ'ɔːl/ inland port, industrial city (aircraft, chemicals, oil and petrochemicals, flour, sugar, brewing, meat packing) of Québec, Canada, on Montreal island at the junction of the Ottawa and St Lawrence rivers; population (1986) 2,921,000.

Montrose /mɒn'trəʊz/ James Graham, 1st Marquess of Montrose 1612–1650. Scottish soldier, son of the 4th earl of Montrose. He supported the ◊Covenanters against Charles I, but after 1640 changed sides. Defeated in 1645 at Philiphaugh, he escaped to Norway. Returning in 1650 to raise a revolt, he survived shipwreck only to have his weakened forces defeated, and (having been betrayed to the Covenanters) was hanged in Edinburgh.

Montserrat /'mɒntsəræt/ volcanic island in the West Indies, one of the Leeward group, a British crown colony; **area** 110 sq km/42 sq mi; **capital** Plymouth; **population** (1985) 12,000. Practically all buildings were destroyed by Hurricane Hugo in Sept 1989.

Monty Python's Flying Circus /'mɒnti 'paɪθən/ English satirical TV comedy series 1969–74, written and performed by John Cleese, Terry Jones, Michael Palin, Eric Idle, Graham Chapman, and the US animator Terry Gilliam. The series achieved cult status and the group made several films: *And Now for Something Completely Different* 1971, *Monty Python and the Holy Grail* 1975, *The Life of Brian* 1979, *The Meaning of Life* 1983. Individual members of the team have written, directed, and appeared in separate projects.

monument /'mɒnjumənt/ *n.* **1.** anything enduring (especially a structure or building) designed or serving to celebrate or commemorate a person or event etc. **2.** a structure preserved because of its historical importance. [from French from Latin *monēre* = remind]

monumental /mɒnju'mentəl/ *adj.* **1.** of or serving as a monument. **2.** (of a literary work) massive and of permanent importance. **3.** extremely great. —**monumental mason**, a maker of tombstones etc. —**monumentally** *adv.*

moo *n.* the characteristic vocal sound of the cow, a low. —*v.i.* to make this sound.

mooch *v.t./i.* (*slang*) **1.** to loiter, to walk slowly. **2.** to steal. [probably from Old French *muchier* = skulk]

mood[1] *n.* **1.** a state of mind or feeling. **2.** (in *plural*) fits of melancholy or bad temper. **—in the mood,** disposed or inclined. [Old English]

mood[2] *n.* in grammar, a form or forms of a verb serving to indicate whether it is to express a fact, command, wish, etc.; a group of such forms, a distinction of meaning expressed by this.

moody *adj.* gloomy, sullen, subject to moods. **—moodily** *adv.*, **moodiness** *n.*

moon *n.* **1.** = ◊Moon. **2.** (*poetic*) a month. **3.** any rocky or icy body orbiting a planet as a satellite. **4.** something regarded as unlikely to be attained. *—v.i.* to move or look dreamily or listlessly. **—moon-daisy** *n.* an ox-eye daisy. **over the Moon,** (*colloquial*) in raptures; highly excited. [Old English]

Moon *n.* the natural satellite of Earth, 3,476 km/2,160 mi in diameter, with a mass 0.012 (approximately one-eightieth) that of Earth. Its average distance from Earth is 384,404 km/238,857 mi, and it orbits in a west-to-east direction every 27.32 days (the **sidereal month**). It spins on its axis with one side permanently turned towards Earth. The Moon is thought to have no atmosphere or water.

Moon /'muːn/ Sun Myung 1920– . Korean industrialist and founder of the ◊Unification Church (**Moonies**) 1954. From 1973 he launched a major mission in the USA and elsewhere. The church has been criticized for its manipulative methods of recruiting and keeping members. He was convicted of tax fraud in the USA in 1982.

Moon William 1818–1894. English inventor of the **Moon** alphabet for the blind. Devised in 1847, it uses only nine symbols in different orientations. From 1983 it has been possible to write it with a miniature typewriter.

moonbeam *n.* a ray of moonlight.

Moonie /'muːnɪ/ *n.* popular name for a follower of the ◊Unification Church, a religious sect founded by Sun Myung Moon.

moonlight *n.* the light of the Moon. *—adj.* lighted by the Moon. *—v.i.* (*colloquial*) to have two paid occupations, especially one by day and one by night. **—moonlight flit,** a hurried removal by night to avoid paying rent. [Old English]

moonlit *adj.* lighted by the Moon.

Moon probe a crewless spacecraft used to investigate the Moon. Early probes flew past the Moon or crash-landed on it, but later ones achieved soft landings or went into orbit. Soviet probes included the long Lunik/Luna series. US probes (Ranger, Surveyor, Lunar Orbiter) prepared the way for the Apollo project crewed flights.

moonshine *n.* **1.** visionary talk or ideas. **2.** illicitly distilled or smuggled alcoholic liquor.

moonstone *n.* a feldspar with a pearly appearance.

moonstruck *adj.* deranged in mind.

moony *adj.* **1.** of or like the Moon. **2.** foolishly dreamy. **—moonily** *adv.*

moor[1] /'muə/ *n.* a stretch of open uncultivated land with low shrubs (e. g. heather); this used for preserving game for shooting. [Old English]

moor[2] *v.t.* to attach (a boat etc.) to a fixed object.

Moor *n.* a member of a Muslim people of mixed Berber and Arab descent, inhabiting NW Africa. **Moorish** *adj.* [from Old French from Latin from Greek *Mauros* = inhabitant of Mauretania]

moorage *n.* a place or charge made for mooring.

Moorcock /'muəkɒk/ Michael 1939– . English writer, associated with the 1960s new wave in science fiction, editor of the magazine *New Worlds* 1964–69. He wrote the Jerry Cornelius novels, collected as *The Cornelius Chronicles* 1977, and *Gloriana* 1978.

Moore /muə/ Dudley 1935– . English actor and comedian, formerly teamed with comedian Peter Cook, who became a Hollywood star after appearing in *10* 1979. His other films, mostly comedies, include *Bedazzled* 1968, *Arthur* 1981, and *Santa Claus* 1985.

Moore Henry 1898–1986. British sculptor. His subjects include the reclining nude, mother and child groups, the warrior, and interlocking abstract forms. Many of his post-World War II works are in bronze or marble, including monumental semi-abstracts such as *Reclining Figure* 1957–58 (outside the UNESCO building, Paris), and often designed to be placed in landscape settings.

Moore (John) Jeremy 1928– . British major general of the Commando Forces, Royal Marines, 1979–82. He commanded the land forces in the UK's conflict with Argentina over the Falklands in 1982.

Moore John 1761-1809 . British general born in Glasgow. In 1808 he commanded the British army sent to Portugal in the Peninsular War. After advancing into Spain he had to retreat to Corunna in the NW, and was killed in the battle fought to cover the embarkation.

Moore Marianne 1887–1972. US poet. She edited the literary magazine *The Dial* 1925–29, and published several volumes of witty and intellectual verse, including *Observations* 1924, *What are Years* 1941, and *A Marianne Moore Reader* 1961.

Moore Roger 1928– . English actor who starred in the television series *The Saint* 1962–70, and assumed the title role of James Bond in 1973 in *Live and Let Die*. His films include *Diane* 1955, *Gold* 1974, *The Wild Geese* 1978, and *Octopussy* 1983.

moorhen *n.* a bird *Gallinula chloropus* of the rail family, common in water of swamps, lakes, and ponds in Eurasia, Africa, and North and South America. It is about 33 cm/13 in long, mainly brown and grey, but with a red bill and forehead, and a vivid white underside to the tail. The big feet are not webbed or lobed, but the moorhen can swim well.

Moorhouse /'muəhaus/ Adrian 1964– . English swimmer who won the 100 metres breaststroke at the 1988 Seoul Olympics.

mooring *n.* (usually in *plural*) **1.** permanent anchors and chains laid down for ships to be moored to. **2.** a place where a vessel is moored.

moorland *n.* an area of moor.

moose *n.* (*plural* the same) a North American animal *Alces americana* closely allied to or the same as the European elk. [from N American Indian *moos*]

moot *adj.* debatable. *—v.t.* to raise (a question) for discussion. *—n.* (*historical*) an assembly. [Old English]

mop *n.* **1.** a bundle of coarse yarn or cloth fastened at the end of a stick, for cleaning floors etc., a similarly shaped instrument for various purposes. **2.** a thick head of hair like a mop. *—v.t.* (**-pp-**) **1.** to wipe or clean (as) with a mop. **2.** to wipe tears, sweat, etc., from (the face etc.); to wipe (tears etc.) thus. **—mop up,** to wipe up (as) with a mop; (*slang*) to absorb; (*slang*) to dispatch or make an end of; to complete the military occupation of (a district etc.) by capturing or killing the troops left there; to capture or kill (stragglers).

mope *v.i.* to be depressed and listless. *—n.* **1.** one who mopes. **2.** (in *plural*) low spirits. **—mopy** *adj.*

moped /'məuped/ *n.* a motorized bicycle. [Swedish (*motor* and *pedal*er = pedals)]

moppet /'mɒpɪt/ *n.* (as a term of endearment) a baby or small child. [from obsolete *moppe* = baby, doll]

moquette /mɒ'ket/ *n.* a material of wool on cotton with a looped pile, used for upholstery etc. [French]

moraine /mɒ'reɪn/ *n.* debris carried down and deposited by a glacier. Material eroded from the side of a glaciated valley and carried along the glacier's edge is called **lateral moraine**; that worn from the valley floor and carried along the base of the glacier is called **ground moraine**. Rubble dropped at the foot of a melting glacier is called **terminal moraine**. **—morainic** *adj.* [French]

moral /'mɒrəl/ *adj.* **1.** concerned with goodness or badness of character or disposition or with the principles of what is right and what is wrong. **2.** virtuous in general conduct. **3.** (of rights or duties etc.) founded on moral law **4.** capable of moral action. *—n.* **1.** the moral lesson of a fable, story, event, etc. **2.** (in *plural*) moral habits, e. g. sexual conduct. **—moral certainty,** a probability so great as to leave no reasonable doubt. **moral courage,** the courage to face disapproval rather than abandon the right course of action. **moral law,** the conditions to be fulfilled by any right course of action. **moral philosophy,** that concerned with ethics. **moral support,** that giving psychological rather than physical help. **moral victory,** a defeat that has some of the satisfactory elements of a victory. **—morally** *adv.* [from Latin *moralis* (*mos* = custom)]

morale /mɒ'rɑːl/ *n.* the mental attitude or bearing of a person or group, especially as regards confidence, discipline, etc. [respelling of French *moral*]

Moravia *Italian writer, journalist, and critic Alberto Moravia. He was a leading figure in Italian intellectual and cultural life until his death in 1990.*

moralist /'mɒrəlɪst/ *n.* one who practises or teaches morality; one who follows a natural system of ethics. —**moralistic** /-'lɪstɪk/ *adj.*

morality /mɒ'rælɪtɪ/ *n.* **1.** degree of conformity to moral principles. **2.** (especially good) moral conduct. **3.** moralizing. **4.** the science of morals; a particular system of morals. [from Old French or Latin]

morality play a didactic medieval verse drama, in part a development of the ◊mystery play (or miracle play), in which human characters are replaced by personified virtues and vices, the limited humorous elements being provided by the Devil. Morality plays, such as *Everyman*, flourished in the 15th century. They exerted an influence on the development of Elizabethan drama and comedy.

moralize /'mɒrəlaɪz/ *v.t./i.* **1.** to indulge in moral reflection or talk. **2.** to interpret morally. **3.** to make (more) moral. —**moralization** /-'zeɪʃən/ *n.* [from French or Latin]

Moral Rearmament (MRA) an international movement calling for 'moral and spiritual renewal'. Founded by the Christian evangelist F N D Buchman in the 1920s, it called itself the 'Oxford Group', and based its teachings on the 'Four Absolutes' (honesty, purity, unselfishness, love).

morass /mə'ræs/ *n.* **1.** a marsh or bog. **2.** an entanglement or confusion. [from Dutch from Old French]

moratorium /mɒrə'tɔːrɪəm/ *n.* (*plural* **moratoriums**) **1.** a legal authorization to debtors to postpone payment; the period of this. **2.** a temporary prohibition or suspension on an activity. [from Latin *moratorius* (*morari* = to delay)]

Moravia /mə'reɪvɪə/ (Czech *Morava*) district of central Europe, from 1960 two regions of Czechoslovakia: **South Moravia** (Czech *Jihomoravský*) **area** 15,030 sq km/5,802 sq mi; **capital** Brno; **population** (1986) 2,075,000. **North Moravia** (Czech *Severomoravský*) **area** 11,070 sq km/4,273 sq mi; **capital** Ostrava; **population** (1986) 1,957,000; **recent history** fief of Bohemia since 1029, it was passed to the Habsburgs in 1526, and became an Austrian crown land in 1849. It was incorporated in the new republic of Czechoslovakia in 1918, forming a province until 1949.

Moravia Alberto. Pen-name of Alberto Pincherle 1907–1990. Italian novelist. His first successful novel was *Gli indifferenti/The Time of Indifference* 1929. Its criticism of Mussolini's regime led to the government censoring his work until after World War II. Later books include *La romana/Woman of Rome* 1947, *La ciociara/Two Women* 1957, and *La noia/The Empty Canvas* 1961, a study of an artist's obsession with his model.

Moravian /mə'reɪvɪən/ *adj.* **1.** of Moravia, a region of Czechoslovakia round the River Morava. **2.** of a Protestant sect holding Hussite doctrines and a simple unworldly form of Christianity with the Bible as the only source of faith, founded in Saxony in 1722 by emigrants from Moravia. —*n.* **1.** a native or inhabitant of Moravia. **2.** a member of the Moravian Church. [from *Moravia*]

Moray Earl of Moray another spelling of ◊Murray, regent of Scotland 1567–70.

Morazán /mɒrə'sɑːn/ Francisco 1792–1842. Central American politician, born in Honduras. He was elected president of the United Provinces of Central America in 1830. In the face of secessions he attempted to hold the union together by force but was driven out by the Guatemalan dictator Rafael Carrera. Morazán was eventually captured and executed in 1842.

morbid /'mɔːbɪd/ *adj.* **1.** (of the mind, ideas, etc.) unwholesome, sickly. **2.** given to morbid feelings; (*colloquial*) melancholy. **3.** of the nature of or indicative of disease. —**morbidity** /-'bɪdɪtɪ/ *n.*, **morbidly** *adv.*, **morbidness** *n.* [from Latin *morbidus* (*morbus* = disease)]

mordant /'mɔːdənt/ *adj.* **1.** (of sarcasm etc.) caustic, biting, pungent. **2.** corrosive or cleansing. **3.** serving to fix colouring matter. —*n.* a mordant acid or substance. —**mordancy** *n.* [from French from Latin *mordēre* = bite]

more /mɔː/ *adj.* **1.** greater in quantity or degree. **2.** additional, further. —*n.* a greater quantity or number. —*adv.* **1.** in a greater degree. **2.** again. **3.** moreover. **4.** forming the comparative of adjectives and adverbs (e. g. *more absurd, more easily*), especially those of more than one syllable. —**more or less**, in a greater or less degree, approximately. **what is more**, as an additional point, moreover. [Old English]

More /mɔː/ Kenneth 1914–1982. British actor, a film star of the 1950s, cast as leading man in adventure films and light comedies such as *Genevieve* 1953, *Doctor in the House* 1954, and *Northwest Frontier*. His film career declined in the 1960s, although he played occasional character parts.

More (St) Thomas 1478–1535. English politician and author. From 1509 he was favoured by ◊Henry VIII and employed on foreign embassies. He was a member of the privy council from 1518 and Lord Chancellor from 1529 but resigned over Henry's break with the pope. For refusing to accept the king as head of the church, he was executed. The title of his political book *Utopia* 1516 has come to mean any supposedly perfect society. More was canonized in 1935.

Moreau /mɔː'rəʊ/ Gustave 1826–1898. French Symbolist painter. His works are atmospheric biblical, mythological, and literary scenes, richly coloured and detailed, for example *Salome Dancing Before Herod* 1876.

Moreau Jeanne 1928– . French actress who has appeared in international films, often in passionate roles. Her work includes *Les Amants/The Lovers* 1958, *Jules et Jim/Jules and Jim* 1961, *Chimes at Midnight* 1966, and *Querelle* 1982.

moreish /'mɔːrɪʃ/ *adj.* (*colloquial*) pleasant to eat, causing a desire for more.

morel *n.* any edible mushroom of the genus *Morchella*. The common morel, *M. esculenta*, grows in Europe and North America. The yellowish-brown cap is pitted like a sponge and about 2.5 cm/1 in long. It is used for seasoning gravies, soups, and sauces.

morello /mə'reləʊ/ *n.* (plural **morellos**) a bitter kind of dark cherry. [from Italian = blackish, from Latin]

moreover /mɔː'rəʊvə/ *adv.* besides, in addition to that already said.

mores /'mɔːriːz/ *n.pl.* the customs or conventions regarded as characteristic of or essential to a community. [Latin, plural of *mos* = custom]

Morgagni /mɔː'gænji/ Giovanni Battista 1682–1771. Italian anatomist. As professor of anatomy at Padua, Morgagni carried out more than 400 autopsies, and developed the view that disease was not an imbalance of the body's humours but a result of alterations in the organs. His work *On the Seats and Causes of Diseases as Investigated by Anatomy* 1761 formed the basis of ◊pathology.

Morgan /'mɔːgən/ Henry *c.*1635–1688. Welsh buccaneer in the Caribbean who made war against Spain, capturing and sacking Panama in 1671. In 1674 he was knighted and appointed lieutenant-governor of Jamaica.

Morgan J(ohn) P(ierpont) 1837–1913. US financier and investment banker whose company (sometimes criticized as 'the money trust') became after the Civil War the most influential private banking house, being instrumental in the formation of many trusts to stifle competition. He set up the US Steel Corporation in 1901, and International Harvester in 1902.

Morgan Thomas Hunt 1866–1945. US geneticist, awarded the 1933 Nobel Prize for Medicine for his pioneering studies in classical genetics. He was the first to work on the fruit fly, *Drosophila*, which has since become a major subject of genetic studies. He helped establish that the genes were located on the chromosomes, discovered sex chromosomes, and invented the techniques of genetic mapping.

morganatic /mɔːgə'nætɪk/ *adj.* (of a marriage) between a man of high rank and a woman of lower rank, the wife and children having no claim to the possessions or title of the father; (of a wife) so married. —**morganatically** *adv.* [from French or German from Latin, probably from Germanic = morning gift, with reference to husband's gift to wife on the morning after consummation (her sole claim on his possessions)]

Morgan horse breed of riding and driving show horse originating in the USA in the 1780s from a single stallion named *Justin Morgan* after his owner. They were introduced to the UK in 1975, and are marked by high, curved necks and high stepping action. The breed is renowned for its strength, endurance, and speed.

Morgan le Fay /'mɔːgən lə 'feɪ/ in the romance and legend of the English king ◊Arthur, an enchantress and healer, ruler of ◊Avalon and sister of the king, whom she tended after his final battle. In some versions of the legend she is responsible for the suspicions held by the king of his wife ◊Guinevere.

morgue /mɔːg/ *n.* 1. a mortuary. 2. (in journalism) the repository where miscellaneous material for reference is kept. [French, originally = building in Paris where those found dead were exposed for identification]

moribund /'mɒrɪbʌnd/ *adj.* at the point of death (*literal* or *figurative*). [from Latin *mori* = die]

Morisot /mɒri'səʊ/ Berthe 1841–1895. French Impressionist painter who specialized in pictures of women and children.

Morley /'mɔːli/ Edward 1838–1923. US physicist who collaborated with Albert ◊Michelson on the **Michelson–Morley experiment** 1887. In 1895 he established precise and accurate measurements of the densities of oxygen and hydrogen.

Morley Robert 1908– . English actor and playwright, active in both Britain and the US. His film work has been mainly character roles, in movies such as *Marie Antoinette* 1938, *The African Queen* 1952, and *Oscar Wilde* 1960.

Morley Thomas 1557–1602. English composer. A student of William ◊Byrd, he became organist at St Paul's Cathedral, London, and obtained a monopoly on music printing. A composer of the English madrigal school, he also wrote sacred music, songs for Shakespeare's plays, and a musical textbook.

Mormon /'mɔːmən/ *n.* or **Latter-day Saint** member of a Christian sect, the **Church of Jesus Christ of Latter-day Saints**, founded at Fayette, New York, in 1830 by Joseph ◊Smith. According to Smith, Mormon was an ancient prophet in North America whose *Book of Mormon*, of which Smith claimed divine revelation, is accepted by Mormons as part of the Christian scriptures. In the 19th century the faction led by Brigham ◊Young was polygamous. It is a missionary church with headquarters in Utah and a worldwide membership of about 6 million.

morn *n.* (*poetic*) morning. [Old English]

mornay /'mɔːneɪ/ *n.* a cheese-flavoured white sauce.

morning *n.* the early part of the day, ending at noon or at the hour of the midday meal. —**morning after**, (*colloquial*) a time of hangover. **morning-after pill**, a contraceptive pill effective when taken some hours after intercourse. **morning coat**, a coat with the front cut away to form tails. **morning dress**, formal dress for a man of a morning coat and striped trousers. **morning glory**, a twining plant of the genus *Ipomoea* with trumpet-shaped flowers. **morning star**, a planet, especially Venus, seen in the E before sunrise.

Moro /'mɔːrəʊ/ Aldo 1916–1978. Italian Christian Democrat politician. Prime minister 1963–68 and 1974–76, he was expected to become Italy's president, but he

was kidnapped and shot by Red Brigade urban guerrillas.

Moroccan Crises /mə'rɒkən/ two periods of international tension in 1905 and 1911 following German objections to French expansion in Morocco. Their wider purpose was to break up the Anglo-French entente of 1904, but both crises served to reinforce the entente and isolate Germany.

morocco /mə'rɒkəʊ/ *n.* (*plural* **moroccos**) a fine, flexible leather of goatskin tanned with sumac. [from *Morocco*]

Morocco The Kingdom of; country in N Africa, bordered N and NW by the Mediterranean, E and SE by Algeria, and S by Western Sahara; **area** 458,730 sq km/177,070 sq mi; **capital** Rabat; **physical** mountain ranges NE-SW; fertile coastal plains in W; **head of state** Hassan II from 1961; **head of government** Mohamed Karim Lamrani from 1984; **political system** constitutional monarchy; **population** (1990 est) 26,249,000; **language** Arabic (official) 75%, Berber 25%, French, Spanish; **recent history** established as a French and Spanish protectorate in 1912; independence achieved from France in 1956, and former Spanish province of Ifni returned to Morocco in 1969.

moron /'mɔːrɒn/ *n.* 1. an adult with an intelligence equal to that of an average child of 8–12 years. 2. (*colloquial*) a very stupid person. —**moronic** /mə'rɒnɪk/ *adj.* [from Greek, neuter of *mōros* = foolish]

Moroni /mə'rəʊni/ capital of the Comoros Republic, on Njazídja (Grand Comore); population (1980) 20,000.

morose /mə'rəʊs/ *adj.* sullen, gloomy, and unsociable. —**morosely** *adv.*, **moroseness** *n.* [from Latin *mos* = manner]

morpheme /'mɔːfiːm/ *n.* a morphological element considered in respect of its functions in a linguistic system; the smallest morphological unit of a language (*farmer* consists of two morphemes, *farm* and *-er*; *farmers* of three, *farm*, *-er*, *-s*). [from French (after *phoneme*), from Greek *morphē* = form]

Morpheus /'mɔːfjuːs/ in Greek and Roman mythology, the god of dreams, son of Hypnos or Somnus, god of sleep.

morphia /'mɔːfɪə/ *n.* morphine.

morphine /'mɔːfiːn/ *n.* narcotic alkaloid, $C_{17}H_{19}NO_3$, derived from ◊opium and prescribed only to alleviate severe pain. Its use produces serious side effects, including nausea, constipation, tolerance, and addiction, but it is highly valued for the relief of the terminally ill. [from German from Latin *Morpheus*]

morphogen *n.* in medicine, one of a class of substances believed to be present in the growing embryo, controlling its growth pattern. It is thought that variations in the concentration of morphogens in different parts of the embryo cause them to grow at different rates.

morphology /mɔː'fɒlədʒɪ/ *n.* the study of the forms of things, especially of plants and animals; the study of the forms of words, the system of forms in a language. —**morphological** /-ə'lɒdʒɪkəl/ *adj.* [from Greek *morphē* = form]

Morrigan /'mɒrɪgən/ in Celtic mythology, a goddess of war and death who could take the shape of a crow.

Morris /'mɒrɪs/ Henry 1889–1961. British educationalist who inspired and oversaw the introduction of the 'village college' and ◊community school education, which he saw as regenerating rural life. His ideas were also adopted in urban areas.

Morris William 1834–1896. English designer, socialist, and poet who shared the Pre-Raphaelite painters' fascination with medieval settings. His first book of verse was *The Defence of Guenevere* 1858. In 1862 he founded a firm for the manufacture of furniture, wallpapers, and the like, and in 1890 he set up the Kelmscott Press to print beautifully decorated books. The prose romances *A Dream of John Ball* 1888 and *News from Nowhere* 1891 reflect his socialist ideology. He also lectured on socialism.

Have nothing in ycur houses that you do not know to be useful, or believe to be beautiful.

William Morris
Hopes and Fears for Art

---

morris dance an English folk dance. In early times it was usually performed by six men, one of whom wore girl's

Morse code

A	B	C	D	E	F
G	H	I	J	K	L
M	N	O	P	Q	R
S	T	U	V	W	X
	Y	Z			
1	2	3	4	5	
6	7	8	9	0	

clothing while another portrayed a horse. The others wore costumes decorated with bells. Morris dancing probably originated in pre-Christian ritual dances and is still popular in the UK and USA. [from *morys* variant of Morrish (dance)]

Morrison /'mɒrɪsən/ Herbert Stanley, Baron Morrison of Lambeth 1888–1965. British Labour politician. He was secretary of the London Labour Party 1915–45, and a member of the London County Council 1922–45. He entered Parliament in 1923, and in 1955 was defeated by Hugh Gaitskell in the contest for leadership of the party.

Morrison Toni 1931– . US novelist, whose fiction records black life in the South. Her works include *Song of Solomon* 1978, *Tar Baby* 1981, and *Beloved* 1987, based on a true story about infanticide in Kentucky, which won the Pulitzer Prize in 1988.

morrow /'mɒrəʊ/ *n.* (*poetic*) the following day.

morse /mɔːs/ *n.* the clasp, often jewelled or ornamented, of a cope. [from Old French from Latin *morsus* = bite, catch (*mordēre* = bite)]

Morse *n.* or **Morse code** an international signalling code in which letters are represented by various combinations of two signs, e.g. dot and dash, long and short flash. —*adj.* of this code. —*v.t./i.* to signal by Morse code. [from S F B *Morse*]

Morse Samuel (Finley Breese) 1791–1872. US inventor. In 1835 he produced the first adequate electric ◊telegraph, and in 1843 was granted $30,000 by Congress for an experimental line between Washington and Baltimore. With his assistant Alexander Bain he invented the Morse code. He was also a respected portrait painter.

morsel /'mɔːsəl/ *n.* a small piece or quantity; a mouthful; a fragment. [from Old French *mors* = a bite]

mortal /'mɔːtəl/ *adj.* 1. subject to death. 2. causing death, fatal; (of a combat) fought to the death. 3. accompanying death. 4. (of an enemy) implacable. 5. (of a pain, fear, affront, etc.) intense, very serious. 6. (*colloquial*) whatsoever. 7. (*colloquial*) long and tedious. —*n.* a mortal being; a human being. —**mortal sin,** a sin that causes the death of the soul or is fatal to salvation. —**mortally** *adv.* [from Old French or Latin *mors* = death]

mortality /mɔː'tælɪtɪ/ *n.* 1. being subject to death. 2. loss of life on a large scale. 3. the number of deaths in a given period etc. —**mortality rate,** the death rate. [from Old French from Latin]

mortar /'mɔːtə/ *n.* 1. a mixture of lime or cement, sand, and water, for joining stones or bricks in building. 2. a short large-bore cannon for throwing shells at high angles. 3. a vessel in which ingredients are pounded with a pestle. —*v.t.* 1. to plaster or join with mortar. 2. to attack or bombard with mortars. —**mortar-board** *n.* a board for holding mortar; an academic cap with a stiff square top. [from Anglo-French from Latin *mortarium*]

Morte D'Arthur, Le /'mɔːt 'dɑːθə/ a series of episodes from the legendary life of King Arthur by Thomas Malory, completed 1470, regarded as the first great prose work in English literature. Only the last of the eight books composing the series is titled *Le Morte D'Arthur*.

mortgage /'mɔːgɪdʒ/ *n.* conveyance of a property by a debtor to a creditor as security for a debt (especially one incurred by the purchase of the property), with the proviso that it shall be returned on payment of the debt within a certain period; the deed effecting this; a sum of money lent by this. —*v.t.* to convey (property) by a mortgage. [from Old French = dead pledge]

mortgagee /mɔːgɪ'dʒiː/ *n.* the creditor in a mortgage.

mortgager /'mɔːgɪdʒə/ *n.* in law, **mortgagor** the debtor in a mortgage.

mortician /mɔː'tɪʃən/ *n.* (*US*) an undertaker. [from Latin *mors* = death]

mortify /'mɔːtɪfaɪ/ *v.t./i.* 1. to humiliate greatly; to wound (feelings). 2. to subdue by discipline or self-denial. 3. (of flesh) to be affected by gangrene or necrosis. —**mortification** /-fɪ'keɪʃən/ *n.* [from Old French from Latin *mortificare* = kill]

Mortimer /'mɔːtɪmə/ John 1923– . English barrister and writer. His works include the plays *The Dock Brief* 1958 and *A Voyage Round My Father* 1970, the novel *Paradise Postponed* 1985, and the television series 'Rumpole of the Bailey', from 1978, centred on a fictional barrister.

Mortimer Roger de, 8th Baron of Wigmore and 1st Earl of March *c.*1287–1330. English politician and adventurer. He opposed Edward II and with Edward's queen, Isabella, led a rebellion against him in 1326, bringing about his abdication. From 1327 Mortimer ruled England as the queen's lover, until Edward III had him executed.

mortise /'mɔːtɪs/ *n.* a hole in a framework to receive the end of another part, especially a tenon. —*v.t.* to join securely, especially by a mortise and tenon; to cut a mortise in. —**mortise lock,** a lock recessed in the edge of a door etc. [from Old French from Arabic = fixed in]

Morton /'mɔːtn/ Jelly Roll. Stage name of Ferdinand Joseph La Menthe 1885–1941. US New Orleans-style jazz pianist, singer, and composer. Influenced by Scott Joplin, he was a pioneer in the development of jazz from ragtime to swing by improvising and imposing his own personality on the music. His 1920s band was called the Red Hot Peppers.

mortuary /'mɔːtjʊərɪ/ *n.* a building in which dead bodies may be kept for a time. —*adj.* of death or burial. [from Anglo-French from Latin *mortuus* = dead]

mosaic /məʊ'zeɪɪk/ *n.* 1. a picture or pattern produced by juxtaposing small pieces of glass, stone, etc., of different colours; this form of art. 2. a thing consisting of diverse elements in juxtaposition. [from French, ultimately from Greek *mous(e)ion*]

Mosaic *adj.* of Moses. [from French (*Moses* from Hebrew)]

Moscow /'mɒskəʊ/ (Russian **Moskva**) capital of the USSR and of the Moskva region, on the Moskva river 640 km/400 mi SE of Leningrad; population (1987) 8,815,000. Its industries include machinery, electrical equipment, textiles, chemicals, and many food products.

Moseley /'məʊzlɪ/ Henry Gwyn-Jeffreys 1887–1915. English physicist who in 1913–14 devised the series of atomic numbers that led to the ◊periodic table of the elements. He did valuable work on atomic structure.

moselle /məʊ'zel/ *n.* a white wine produced in the valley of the Moselle and its tributaries in Germany.

Moses /'məʊzɪz/ *c.*13th century BC. Hebrew lawgiver and judge who led the Israelites out of Egypt to the promised land of Canaan. On Mount Sinai he claimed to have received from Jehovah the **Ten Commandments** engraved on tablets of stone. The first five books of the Old Testament—in Judaism, the *Torah* – are ascribed to him.

Moses Ed(win Corley) 1955– . US track athlete and 400 metres hurdler. Between 1977 and 1987 he ran 122 races without defeat.

Moses 'Grandma' (born Anna Mary Robertson) 1860– 1961. US painter. She was self-taught, and began full-time painting in about 1927, after many years as a farmer's wife. She painted naive and colourful scenes from rural American life.

Moslem *n.* alternative spelling of **Muslim,** a follower of ◊Islam.

Mosley /'məʊzlɪ/ Oswald (Ernald) 1896–1980. British politician, founder of the British Union of Fascists (BUF). He was a member of Parliament 1918–31, then led the BUF until his internment 1940–43, when he was released on health grounds. In 1946 Mosley was denounced when it became known that Italy had funded his prewar efforts to establish ◊fascism in Britain, but in 1948 he resumed fascist propaganda with his Union Movement, the revived BUF.

mosque /mɒsk/ n. a Muslim place of worship. [from French, ultimately from Arabic *masjid*]

mosquito /mɒs'kiːtəʊ/ n. (*plural* **mosquitoes**) a gnat especially of the genus *Culex* or *Anopheles*, of which the female punctures the skin of man and animals and sucks their blood. Some mosquitoes carry diseases such as ◊malaria. —**mosquito-net** n. a net to keep mosquitoes from a bed, room, etc. [Spanish and Portuguese, diminutive of *mosca* = fly]

Mosquito Coast the Caribbean coast of Honduras and Nicaragua, characterized by swamp, lagoons and tropical rainforest. It is a largely undeveloped territory occupied by Miskito Indians, Garifunas and Zambos, many of whom speak English. Between 1823 and 1860 Britain maintained a protectorate over the Mosquito Coast which was ruled by a succession of 'Mosquito Kings'.

moss n. a small non-flowering plant of the class Musci (10,000 species), forming with the ◊liverworts and the ◊hornworts the order Bryophyta. The stem of each plant bears ◊rhizoids that anchor it; there are no true roots. Leaves spirally arranged on its lower portion have sexual organs at their tips. Most mosses flourish best in damp conditions where other vegetation is thin. —**moss-rose** n. a variety of rose with a mosslike growth on the calyx and stalk. —**mossy** adj. [Old English]

Moss Stirling 1929– . Despite being one of the best known names in British motor racing, Moss never won the world championship. He was runner-up on four occasions, losing to Juan Manuel ◊Fangio in 1955, 1956 and 1957 and to fellow Briton Mike Hawthorn (1929–1959) in 1958.

Mössbauer /'mɜːsbaʊə/ Rudolf 1929– . German physicist who discovered in 1958 that in certain conditions a nucleus can be stimulated to emit very sharply defined beams of gamma rays. This became known as the **Mössbauer effect**. Such a beam was used in 1960 to provide the first laboratory test of ◊Einstein's general theory of relativity. For his work on gamma rays Mössbauer shared the 1961 Nobel Prize for Physics with Robert ◊Hofstadter.

most /məʊst/ adj. greatest in quantity or degree; the majority of. —n. the greatest quantity or degree; the majority. —adv. 1. in the highest degree. 2. forming the superlative of adjectives and adverbs (as *most absurd*, *most easily*), especially those of more than one syllable. —**at (the) most**, as the greatest amount. **for the most part**, in the main; usually. **make the most of**, to use or enjoy to the best advantage. **Most Reverend**, see ◊Reverend. [Old English]

-most suffix forming adjectives with a superlative sense from prepositions and other words indicating relative position (*foremost*, *inmost*, *topmost*, *uttermost*). [Old English]

Mostel /mɒ'stell/ Zero (Samuel Joel) 1915–1977. US comedian and actor, active mainly in the theatre. His films include *Panic in the Streets* 1950, *A Funny Thing Happened on the Way to the Forum* 1966, *The Producers* 1967, and *The Front* 1976.

mostly adv. for the most part.

mot /məʊ/ n. a witty saying. —**mot juste** /ʒuːst/ an exactly appropriate expression. [French = word]

MOT (*historical*) abbreviation of 1. Ministry of Transport. 2. (in full **MOT test**) (*colloquial*) a compulsory annual test of motor vehicles of more than a specified age.

mote n. a particle of dust. [Old English]

motel /məʊ'tel/ n. a roadside hotel often consisting of a group of furnished cabins accommodating motorists and their vehicles. [acronym from *motor* and *hotel*]

motet /məʊ'tet/ n. a short, usually unaccompanied, anthem in the Roman Catholic or Lutheran church. [from Old French]

moth n. a lepidopterous mainly nocturnal insect resembling a butterfly; an insect of this kind (of the family Tineidae) breeding in cloth etc., on which its larvae feed. —**moth-eaten** adj. damaged or destroyed by moths, antiquated, time-worn. [Old English]

mothball n. a small ball of naphthalene etc. placed in stored clothes to keep away moths. —**in mothballs**, stored out of use for a considerable time.

mother /'mʌðə/ n. 1. a female parent. 2. a quality or condition etc. that gives rise to something else. 3. the head of a female religious community. 4. (*colloquial*) a title used to or of an elderly woman. —v.t. 1. to give birth to; to be the origin of. 2. to look after in a motherly way. —**Mother**

Carey's chickens, stormy petrels. **mother country**, a country in relation to its colonies. **mother earth**, the Earth as the mother of its inhabitants. **Mother Goose rhyme**, (*US*) a nursery rhyme. **Mothering Sunday**, the fourth Sunday in Lent, with the old custom of giving one's mother a gift. **mother-in-law** n. (*plural* **mothers-in-law**) a wife's or husband's mother. **mother-of-pearl** n. a smooth shining iridescent substance forming the inner layer of the oyster etc. shell. **Mother's Day**, Mothering Sunday. **mother tongue**, one's native language. —**motherhood** n. [Old English]

mothercraft n. skill in looking after one's children as a mother.

motherland n. one's native land.

motherly adj. having or showing the good qualities of a mother. —**motherliness** n. [Old English]

Motherwell /'mʌðəwel/ Robert 1915– . US painter associated with the New York school of ◊action painting. Borrowing from Picasso, Matisse, and the Surrealists, Motherwell's style of Abstract Expressionism retained some suggestion of the figurative. His works include the 'Elegies to the Spanish Republic' 1949–76, a series of over 100 paintings devoted to the Spanish Revolution.

mothproof adj. (of clothes) treated so as to repel moths. —v.t. to treat (clothes) thus.

mothy /'mɒθɪ/ adj. infested with moths.

motif /məʊ'tiːf/ n. 1. a distinctive feature or dominant idea in an artistic, literary, or musical composition. 2. an ornament sewn separately on to a garment. 3. an ornament on a vehicle identifying the maker etc. [French]

motion /'məʊʃən/ n. 1. moving, change of position. 2. manner of movement. 3. change of posture; a particular movement; a gesture. 4. a formal proposal that is to be discussed and voted on at a meeting; an application for an order from a judge. 5. an evacuation of the bowels; (in *singular* or *plural*) faeces. —v.t./i. to direct by a gesture etc.; to make such a gesture. —**go through the motions**, to do a thing perfunctorily or superficially. **in motion**, not at rest, moving. **motion picture**, a film recording a story or events with movement as in real life. [from Old French from Latin]

motionless adj. not moving. —**motionlessly** adv.

motivate /'məʊtɪveɪt/ v.t. 1. to supply a motive to, to be the motive of; to cause (a person) to act in a particular way. 2. to stimulate the interest of (a person) in an activity. —**motivation** /-'veɪʃən/ n.

motive /'məʊtɪv/ n. 1. what induces a person to act in a particular way. 2. a motif. —adj. tending to initiate movement; concerned with movement. —**motive power**, moving or impelling power, especially the source of energy used to drive machinery. [from Old French from Latin *motivus*]

motley /'mɒtlɪ/ adj. 1. diversified in colour. 2. of varied character. —n. (*historical*) a jester's particoloured dress.

moto-cross /'məʊtəʊkrɒs/ n. (also called **scrambling**) a form of motorcycle racing held on a closed circuit consisting of a variety of cross-country terrain and natural obstacles.

motor n. 1. a machine (especially an internal-combustion engine) supplying the motive power for a vehicle etc. or for some other device with moving parts. 2. a motor car. —adj. 1. giving, imparting, or producing motion. 2. driven by a motor. 3. of or for motor vehicles. —v.t./i. to go or convey in a motorcar. —**motor bicycle**, a motor cycle; a moped. **motorbike** n. (*colloquial*) a motorcycle. **motorcar** n. a short-bodied motor-driven vehicle that can carry a driver and usually passengers. **motorcycle** n. a two-wheeled motor-driven road vehicle. **motorcyclist** n. the rider of a motorcycle. **motor vehicle**, a vehicle driven by a motor (especially an internal-combustion engine). [Latin = mover]

motorboat n. small, waterborne craft for pleasure cruising or racing, powered by a petrol, diesel, or gas-turbine engine.

motorcade /'məʊtəkeɪd/ n. a procession or parade of motorcars.

motorcar n. another term for ◊car.

motorcycle racing speed contests on motorcycles. It has many different forms: **road racing** over open roads; **circuit racing** over purpose-built tracks; **speedway** over oval-shaped dirt tracks; **motocross** over natural terrain, incorporating hill climbs; and **trials**, also over natural terrain, but with the addition of artificial hazards.

motor effect the tendency of a wire carrying an electric current in a magnetic field to move. The direction of the movement is given by the ◊left-hand rule. This effect is used in the ◊electric motor. It also explains why streams of electrons produced, for instance, in a television tube can be directed by electromagnets.

motorist *n.* the driver of a motorcar.

motorize *v.t./i.* 1. to equip with motor transport. 2. to equip (a device etc.) with a motor. —**motorization** /-'zeıʃən/ *n.*

motor nerve in anatomy, a nerve which transmits impulses from the central nervous system to muscles or body organs. Motor nerves cause voluntary and involuntary muscles contractions, and stimulate glands to secrete hormones.

motor neurone disease incurable wasting disease in which the nerve cells controlling muscle action gradually die, causing progressive weakness and paralysis. It usually occurs in later life and may be caused by an abnormal protein retained within the nerve cells.

motor racing competitive racing of motor vehicles. It has forms as diverse as hill-climbing, stock-car racing, rallying, sports-car racing, and Formula One Grand Prix racing. The first organized race was from Paris to Rouen in 1894.

motorway *n.* a road designed for fast traffic, with two or more lanes in each direction, and with special access points (junctions) fed by 'slip' roads.

Motown /'məʊtaʊn/ *n.* the first black-owned US record company, founded in Detroit (Mo[tor] Town) in 1959 by Berry Gordy, Jr (1929–). Its distinctive, upbeat sound (exemplified by the Four Tops and the ◊Supremes) was a major element in 1960s pop music.

Mott /mɒt/ Nevill Francis 1905– . British physicist, who researched the electronic properties of metals, semiconductors, and noncrystalline materials. He shared the Nobel Prize for Physics 1977.

motte /mɒt/ *n.* a mound forming the site of an ancient castle, camp, etc., found in Britain and parts of N France, dating from the Norman period onwards. [from French]

mottle *v.t.* (especially in *past participle*) to mark with spots or smears of colour.

motto /'mɒtəʊ/ *n.* (*plural* **mottoes**) 1. a maxim adopted as a rule of conduct or as expressing the aims and ideals of a family, country, institution, etc. 2. a sentence inscribed on an object. 3. a maxim, verse, or riddle etc. inside a paper cracker. [Italian]

mould[1] /məʊld/ *n.* 1. a hollow container into which molten metal etc. is poured or soft material is pressed to harden in a required shape. 2. a vessel used to give a shape to puddings etc.; a pudding etc. so shaped. 3. form, shape. 4. a pattern or shape used in making mouldings. —*v.t.* 1. to bring into a particular shape or form. 2. to influence or control the development of. [from Old French *modle* from Latin]

mould[2] *n.* any mainly saprophytic ◊fungi living on foodstuffs and other organic matter, a few being parasitic on plants, animals, or each other. Many are of medical or industrial importance, for example penicillin.

mould[3] *n.* loose earth; the upper soil of cultivated land, especially when rich in organic matter. [Old English]

moulder /'məʊldə/ *v.i.* to decay to dust, to rot or decline.

moulding *n.* 1. a moulded object, especially an ornamental strip of wood. 2. an ornamental variety of outline in the cornices etc. of a building; a similar shape in woodwork etc. 3. the use of a pattern, hollow form, or matrix to give a specific shape to something in a plastic or molten state. It is commonly used for shaping plastics, clays, and glass. In **injection moulding**, molten plastic, for example, is injected into a water-cooled mould and takes the shape of the mould when it solidifies. In **blow moulding**, air is blown into a blob of molten plastic inside a hollow mould. In **compression moulding**, synthetic resin powder is simultaneously heated and pressed into a mould.

mouldy *adj.* 1. covered with mould. 2. out-of-date, stale. 3. (*slang*) dull, miserable. —**mouldiness** *n.*

moult /məʊlt/ *v.t./i.* to shed feathers, hair, skin, etc., before a new growth; to shed (feathers etc.) thus. —*n.* the process of moulting. [earlier *moute* ultimately from Latin *mutare* = change]

mound *n.* 1. a mass of piled-up earth or stones. 2. a small hill. 3. a heap or pile.

Moundbuilder a member of various North American Indian peoples who built earth mounds, linear and conical in shape, for tombs, platforms for chiefs' houses, and temples, from about 300 BC. A major site is Monk's Mound in Mississippi. They were in decline by the time of the Spanish invasion, but traces of their culture live on in the folklore of the Choctaw and Cherokee Indians.

mount[1] *v.t./i.* 1. to ascend; to go upwards; to rise to a higher level or rank etc. 2. to get or put on (a horse etc.) in order to ride; to provide with a horse for riding. 3. to increase in amount or intensity. 4. to put into place on a support; to fix in position for use, display, or study. 5. to arrange and carry out (a programme, campaign, etc.). 6. to place on guard. 7. to put (a play) on the stage. —*n.* 1. a horse for riding. 2. something on which a thing is mounted for support or display etc. [from Old French from Latin]

mount[2] *n.* a mountain or hill (*archaic* except before a name, as in *Mount Everest*). [Old English and from Old French from Latin *mons*]

mountain /'maʊntın/ *n.* 1. a mass of land that rises to a great height, especially of over 1,000 ft. The process of mountain building (orogenesis) consists of volcanism, folding, faulting, and thrusting, resulting from the collision and welding together of two tectonic plates. 2. a large heap or pile; a huge quantity. 3. a large surplus stock. —**mountain ash,** a tree (*Sorbus aucuparia*) bearing scarlet berries, rowan. **mountain bike,** bicycle with a toughened frame, ten or 15 gears, and wider treads on the tyres than an ordinary cycle. **mountain dew,** (*colloquial*) whisky, especially that illicitly distilled. **mountain goat,** a white goatlike animal, *Oreamnos montanus*, of the Rocky Mountains etc. **mountain lion,** the puma. [from Old French *montaigne*]

mountaineer /maʊntı'nıə/ *n.* one skilled in mountain-climbing. —*v.i.* to climb mountains as a recreation.

mountainous /'maʊntınəs/ *adj.* 1. having many mountains. 2. huge.

mountainside *n.* the sloping side of a mountain.

Mountbatten /maʊnt'bætn/ Louis, 1st Earl Mountbatten of Burma 1900–1979. British admiral and administrator. In World War II he became chief of combined operations in 1942 and commander in chief in SE Asia in 1943. As last viceroy of India in 1947 and first governor general of India until 1948, he oversaw that country's transition to independence. He was killed by an Irish Republican Army bomb aboard his yacht in the Republic of Ireland.

I can't think of a more wonderful thanksgiving for the life I have had than that everyone should be jolly at my funeral.

Louis, 1st Earl Mountbatten of Burma
television interview, shown shortly after his death in August 1979

---

mountebank /'maʊntıbæŋk/ *n.* 1. a swindler, a charlatan. 2. (*historical*) an itinerant quack. [from Italian = mount on bench]

mounted *adj.* serving on horseback etc.

Mountie /'maʊntı/ *n.* (*colloquial*) a member of the Royal Canadian Mounted Police.

mourn /mɔːn/ *v.t./i.* to feel or show deep sorrow or regret for (a dead person, a lost or regretted thing); to grieve. [Old English]

mourner *n.* one who mourns; one who attends a funeral.

mournful *adj.* sorrowful, showing grief. —**mournfully** *adv.*, **mournfulness** *n.*

mourning *n.* 1. expression of sorrow at a death etc. 2. black or dark clothes worn as a conventional sign of bereavement.

mouse *n.* (*plural* **mice**) 1. a small rodent, especially of the genus *Mus*; a species of this, *M. musculus*, infesting houses etc. 2. a shy or timid person. 3. a small hand-held device for controlling the position of the cursor on the visual display unit of a computer. —*v.i.* to hunt mice. —**mouser** *n.* [Old English]

mousetrap *n.* 1. a trap for catching mice. 2. (*colloquial*) cheese of poor quality.

moussaka /muˈsɑːkə/ n. a Greek dish of minced meat, aubergines, eggs, etc. [Greek or Turkish]

mousse /muːs/ n. 1. a dish of cold whipped cream or a similar substance flavoured with fruit, chocolate, or meat or fish purée. 2. a substance of similar texture. [French = moss, froth]

moustache /məˈstɑːʃ/ n. hair left to grow on a man's upper lip. [French, from Italian *mostaccio* from Greek]

Moustier, Le /ˈmuːstieɪ/ cave in the Dordogne, SW France, with prehistoric remains, giving the name **Mousterian** to the flint-tool culture of Neanderthal peoples; the earliest ritual burials are linked with Mousterian settlements (150,000 years ago).

mousy /ˈmaʊsɪ/ adj. 1. greyish-brown. 2. shy, timid; quiet.

mouth /maʊθ/ n.ʹ (plural **mouths** /maʊðz/) 1. the external opening in the head, with a cavity behind it, through which food is taken in and from which the voice is emitted; this cavity. 2. the opening of a bag, cave, cannon, trumpet, etc. 3. the place where a river enters the sea. 4. an individual as needing sustenance. —/maʊð/ v.t./i. 1. to utter or speak with affectation, to declaim. 2. to grimace; to move the lips silently. —**mouth-organ** n. a thin rectangular musical instrument played by blowing and sucking air through it, a harmonica. **keep one's mouth shut,** (slang) to refrain from revealing a secret. **mouth-watering** adj. making one's mouth water, appetizing. **put words into a person's mouth,** to tell a person what to say; to represent him or her as having said such words. **take the words out of a person's mouth,** to say what he or she was about to say. [Old English]

mouthful n. 1. an amount that fills the mouth. 2. a small quantity of food etc. 3. a lengthy word or phrase; something difficult to utter.

mouthpiece n. 1. the part of a pipe, musical instrument, telephone, etc., placed between or near the lips. 2. a person who speaks for another or others.

mouthwash n. a liquid for rinsing the mouth or gargling.

movable /ˈmuːvəbəl/ adj. that can be moved; varying in date from year to year.

move /muːv/ v.t./i. 1. to change or cause to change position, place, or posture. 2. to be or cause to be in motion. 3. to change one's place of residence or business. 4. to live or be active in a specified group. 5. to provoke a reaction or emotion in, to stimulate; to prompt or incline, to motivate. 6. to cause (bowels) to empty; to be emptied thus. 7. (of goods etc.) to be sold. 8. to propose (a resolution) formally at a meeting. 9. to initiate action. —n. 1. the act or process of moving. 2. a change of residence, business premises, etc. 3. the moving of a piece in chess etc.; a player's turn to do this. 4. a calculated action done to achieve some purpose. —**get a move on,** (colloquial) to hurry. **move house,** to change one's place of residence. **move in,** to take possession of a new residence etc. **move over** or **up,** to adjust one's position to make room for another. **on the move,** progressing, moving about. —**mover** n. [from Anglo-French from Latin *movēre*]

movement n. 1. moving, being moved. 2. action, activity. 3. the moving parts of a mechanism, especially of a clock or watch. 4. a campaign to achieve some purpose; a group undertaking this. 5. a trend. 6. market activity in some commodity. 7. any of the principal divisions in a long musical work. [from Old French from Latin]

movie /ˈmuːvɪ/ n. (US slang) a motion picture.

moving adj. emotionally affecting. —**movingly** adv.

mow /maʊ/ v.t. (past participle **mowed** or **mown**) to cut (grass etc.) with a scythe or machine; to cut down the grass of (a lawn) or the produce of (a field) thus. —**mow down,** to kill or destroy randomly or in great numbers. [Old English]

Mow Cop /ˈmaʊ ˈkɒp/ the site in England of an open-air religious gathering on 31 May 1807 that is considered to be the start of ◊Primitive Methodism. Mow Cop is a hill at the S end of the Pennines on the Cheshire–Staffordshire border and dominates the surrounding countryside. It remained a popular location for revivalist meetings.

mower /ˈmaʊə/ n. 1. a mowing machine, especially a lawn-mower. 2. a person who mows.

Mozambique /məʊzəmˈbiːk/ People's Republic of; country in SE Africa, bordered N by Zambia, Malawi, and Tanzania; E by the Indian Ocean; S by South Africa; and E by Swaziland and Zimbabwe; **area** 799,380 sq km/ 308,561 sq mi; **capital** and chief port Maputo; **physical** mostly flat; mountains in W; **head of state and government** Joaquim Alberto Chissano from 1986; **political system** one-party socialist republic; **population** (1990 est) 14,718,000 (mainly indigenous Bantu peoples; Portuguese 50,000); **language** Portuguese (official), 16 African languages; **recent history** overseas province of Portugal (Portuguese East Africa) from 1951. Independence achieved as a Socialist republic in 1975. One-party rule was ended in 1990.

Mozart /ˈmɔʊtsɑːt/ Wolfgang Amadeus 1756–1791. Austrian composer and performer who showed astonishing precocity as a child and was an adult virtuoso. He was trained by his father, **Leopold Mozart** (1719–1787). From an early age he composed prolifically, his works including 27 piano concertos, 23 string quartets, 35 violin sonatas, and more than 50 symphonies. His operas include *Idomeneo* 1781, *Le Nozze di Figaro*/*The Marriage of Figaro* 1786, *Don Giovanni* 1787, *Così fan tutte*/*Thus Do All Women* 1790, and *Die Zauberflöte*/*The Magic Flute* 1791. Strongly influenced by ◊Haydn, Mozart's music marks the height of the Classical age in its purity of melody and form.

mp abbreviation of mezzo piano.

MP abbreviation of member of Parliament.

m.p.g. abbreviation of miles per gallon.

m.p.h. abbreviation of miles per hour.

MPLA acronym from Popular Movement for the Liberation of Angola, Portuguese *Movimento Popular de Libertaçaõ de Angola* socialist organization founded in the early 1950s that sought to free Angola from Portuguese rule 1961–75 before being involved in the civil war against its former allies ◊UNITA and ◊FNLA 1975–76. The MPLA took control of the country, but UNITA guerrilla activity continues, supported by South Africa.

Mr /ˈmɪstə/ (plural **Messrs**) abbreviation of Mister. The title of a man without a higher title, or prefixed to a designation of an office etc. (*Mr Jones*; *Mr Speaker*).

MRBM abbreviation of medium-range ballistic missile.

Mrs /ˈmɪsɪz/ (plural the same or **Mesdames**) abbreviation of Mistress, the title of a married woman without a higher title.

Ms /mɪz/ n. the title of a woman without a higher title, whether or not married. [combination of Mrs and Miss]

MS abbreviation of 1. manuscript. 2. multiple sclerosis.

M.Sc abbreviation of Master of Science.

MS-DOS acronym from Microsoft Disc Operating System, an ◊operating system produced by the Microsoft Corporation, which is widely used on ◊microcomputers. A version called PC-DOS is sold by IBM specifically for their range of personal computers. MS-DOS and PC-DOS are usually referred to as DOS.

MSS /emˈesɪz/ abbreviation of manuscripts.

Mt abbreviation of Mount.

mu /mjuː/ n. the twelfth letter of the Greek alphabet, (μ, Μ;) = m. [Greek]

Mubarak /muːˈbɑːræk/ Hosni 1928– . Egyptian politician, president from 1981. He commanded the air force 1972–75 (and was responsible for the initial victories in the Egyptian campaign of 1973 against Israel), when he became an active vice president to Anwar Sadat, and succeeded him on his assassination. He has continued to pursue Sadat's moderate policies, and has significantly increased the freedom of the press and of political association.

much adj. existing in great quantity. —n. a great quantity. —adv. 1. in a great degree. 2. often; for a large part of one's time. 3. approximately. —**as much,** that amount etc. **much of a muchness,** very alike, very nearly the same. **not much,** (colloquial) certainly not. **not much of a,** (colloquial) not a great or good example of. [from *muchel* = mickle]

mucilage /ˈmjuːsɪlɪdʒ/ n. a viscous substance extracted from plants; an adhesive gum. [from French from Latin *mucilago* = musty juice]

muck n. farmyard manure; (colloquial) dirt, filth; (colloquial) mess. —v.t./i. 1. to manure. 2. to make dirty. —**make a muck of,** (slang) to bungle. **muck about** or **around,** (slang) to potter or fool about; to interfere. **muck in,** (colloquial) to share tasks etc. equally. **muck out,** to remove the manure from. **muck-raking** n. (colloquial) searching out and revealing scandal. **muck**

sweat, (*colloquial*) a profuse sweat. **muck up,** (*slang*) to bungle, to spoil.

muckle *adj. & n.* ◊mickle.

mucky *adj.* covered with muck, dirty.

mucous /'mju:kəs/ *adj.* of or covered with mucus. —**mucous membrane,** the thin skin lining all animal body cavities and canals that come into contact with the air (for example, eyelids, breathing and digestive passages, genital tract). It secretes mucus, a moistening, lubricating, and protective fluid.—**mucosity** /-'kɒsɪtɪ/ *n.* [from Latin *mucosus*]

mucus /'mju:kəs/ *n.* the slimy substance secreted by the mucous membrane. [Latin]

mud *n.* 1. wet soft earth. 2. a liquid (commonly a suspension of clay and other substances in water) used as a lubricant and sealant etc. of the drill pipe in the drilling of an oil or gas well. —**mud-flat** *n.* a stretch of muddy land uncovered at low tide. **mud pack,** a cosmetic paste applied thickly to the face. **one's name is mud,** one is in disgrace. **sling** *or* **throw mud,** to speak slanderously.

muddle *v.t./i.* 1. to bring into disorder. 2. to confuse (a person) mentally. 3. to confuse (one thing etc.) with another. 4. to act in a confused way. —*n.* disorder, a muddled condition. —**muddle-headed** *adj.* confused, stupid. **muddle through,** to succeed despite one's inefficiency etc. —**muddler** *n.*

muddy *adj.* 1. like mud. 2. covered in or full of mud. 3. confused, obscure. —*v.t.* to make muddy. —**muddiness** *n.*

mudguard *n.* a curved strip or cover over the upper part of a wheel to protect a rider or another road-user from spray thrown up by the wheel.

mudpuppy *n.* a brownish amphibian *Necturus maculosus* about 20 cm/8 in long, with large external gills. It lives in streams in North America and eats fish, snails, and other invertebrates.

mudskipper *n.* a fish, genus *Periophthalmus*, found in brackish water and shores in the tropics, except for the Americas. It can walk or climb over mudflats, using its strong pectoral fins as legs, and has eyes set close together on top of the head. It grows up to 30 cm/12 in long.

muesli /'mju:zlɪ/ *n.* a food of crushed cereals, dried fruit, nuts etc. [Swiss German]

muezzin /mu:'ezɪn/ *n.* a Muslim crier who proclaims the hours of prayer, usually from a minaret. [from Arabic]

muff¹ *n.* a tubular covering, especially of fur, in which the hands are put to keep them warm. [from Dutch *mof* from Latin]

muff² *v.t.* to bungle; to miss (a catch, ball, etc.); to blunder in (a theatrical part etc.).

muffin /'mʌfɪn/ *n.* a light, flat, round, spongy cake eaten toasted and buttered.

muffle *v.t.* 1. to wrap or cover for warmth or protection, or to deaden sound. 2. (usually in *past participle*) to repress, to deaden the sound of. [perhaps from Old French *enmoufler* (*moufle* = thick glove]

muffler *n.* 1. a scarf or wrap worn for warmth. 2. a thing used to deaden sound.

mufti /'mʌftɪ/ *n.* plain clothes worn by one who normally wears uniform (especially *in mufti*). [from Arabic, originally = Muslim priest]

mug¹ *n.* 1. a drinking-vessel, usually cylindrical, with a handle, and used without a saucer; its contents. 2. (*slang*) the face or mouth. 3. (*slang*) a gullible person, a simpleton. —*v.t.* (**-gg-**) to attack and rob, especially in a public place. —**a mug's game,** an unprofitable or senseless occupation. —**mugger** *n.*

mug² *v.t./i.* (**-gg-**) (with *up*) to learn (a subject) by concentrated study.

Mugabe /mu:'ga:bi/ Robert (Gabriel) 1925–   . Zimbabwean politician, prime minister from 1980 and president from 1987. He was in detention in Rhodesia for nationalist activities 1964–74, then carried on guerrilla warfare from

mudskipper

Mozambique. As leader of ◊ZANU he was in an uneasy alliance with Joshua ◊Nkomo of ZAPU (Zimbabwe African People's Union) from 1976. The two parties merged in 1987.

muggins /'mʌgɪnz/ *n.* (*plural* **mugginses** or the same) (*colloquial*) a person who allows himself to be outwitted.

muggy *adj.* (of the weather etc.) oppressively humid and warm. —**mugginess** *n.* [from dialect *mug* = mist, from Old Norse]

Muhammad /mə'hæmməd/ or **Mohammed, Mahomet** *c.*570–632. Founder of Islam, born in Mecca on the Arabian peninsula. In about 616 he claimed to be a prophet and that the *Koran* was revealed to him by God (it was later written down by his followers). He fled from persecution to the town now known as Medina in 622: this flight, the **Hegira**, marks the beginning of the Islamic era.

Muhammadan /mə'hæmmɪdən/ *adj.* of Muhammad; Muslim. —*n.* a Muslim. [from *Muhammad*]

Mujaheddin *n.* Islamic fundamentalist guerrillas of contemporary Afghanistan and Iran. [Arabic *mujahid* = fighters, from *jihad* = holy war]

Mukalla /mu'kælə/ seaport capital of the Hadhramaut coastal region of Yemen; on the Gulf of Aden 480 km/299 mi E of Aden; population (1984) 158,000.

Mukden, Battle of /'mukdən/ the taking of Mukden (now Shenyang), NE China, from Russian occupation by the Japanese in 1905, during the ◊Russo-Japanese War. Mukden was later the scene of a surprise attack on 18 Sept 1931 by the Japanese on the Chinese garrison, which marked the beginning of their invasion of China.

mulatto /mju:'lætəu/ *n.* (*plural* **mulattos**) a person of mixed White and Black parentage. [from Spanish]

mulberry /'mʌlbərɪ/ *n.* 1. a tree of the genus *Morus*, bearing purple or white edible berries and with leaves which are used to feed silkworms. 2. its fruit. 3. dull purplish-red. [earlier *murberie*, from Latin *morum* = mulberry]

Mulberry Harbour a prefabricated floating harbour, used on D-day in World War II, to assist in the assault on the German-held French coast of Normandy.

mulch *n.* a mixture of wet organic material spread to protect the roots of newly planted trees etc. —*v.t.* to treat with mulch. [probably from obsolete *mulsh* = soft]

mulct *v.t.* to extract money from by fine, taxation, or fraudulent means. [from French from Latin *mulctare* = to fine]

Muldoon /mʌl'du:n/ Robert David 1921–   . New Zealand National Party politician, prime minister 1975–84.

mule¹ /mju:l/ *n.* 1. an animal that is the offspring of a mare and a male ass, or (*loosely*) of a she-ass and a stallion (*properly* **hinny**), known for its stubbornness. 2. a kind of spinning-machine invented in 1779 by Samuel Crompton (died 1827) so called because it was a cross between Arkwright's 'water frame' and Hargreaves's spinning jenny. [from Old French from Latin *mulus*]

mule² /mju:l/ *n.* a backless slipper. [French]

muleteer /mju:li'tɪə/ *n.* a mule-driver. [from French *muletier*]

mulish *adj.* obstinate.

mull¹ *v.t./i.* to think (over), to ponder.

mull² *v.t.* to make (wine or beer) into a hot drink with sugar, spices, etc.

mull³ *n.* (*Scottish*) a promontory. [compare Gaelic *maol*]

mullah *n.* a Muslim learned in Islamic theology and sacred law. [from Persian, Turkish and Urdu from Arabic]

Müller /'mju:lə/ Johannes Peter 1801–1858. German comparative anatomist whose studies of nerves and sense organs opened a new chapter in physiology by demonstrating the physical nature of sensory perception. His name is associated with a number of discoveries, including the **Müllerian ducts** in the mammalian fetus and the lymph heart in frogs.

mullet¹ /'mʌlɪt/ *n.* two species of fish. The **red mullet** *Mullus surmuletus* is found in the Mediterranean and warm Atlantic as far N as the English Channel. It is about 40 cm/16 in long, red with yellow stripes, and has long barbels round the mouth. The **grey mullet** *Crenimugil labrosus* lives in ponds and estuaries. It is greyish above, with longitudinal dark stripes, and grows to 60 cm/24 in. [from Old French from Latin *mullus* from Greek]

mullet² /'mʌlɪt/ *n.* in heraldry; a star-shaped figure, usually with five points, given as a mark of cadency for a third son. [from Old French = rowel]

mulligatawny /ˌmʌlɪɡəˈtɔːnɪ/ *n.* a highly seasoned soup, originally from India. [from Tamil = pepper-water]

Mulliken /ˈmʌlɪkən/ Robert Sanderson 1896–1986. US chemist and physicist, who received the 1966 Nobel Prize for Chemistry for his development of the molecular orbital theory.

mullion /ˈmʌljən/ *n.* a vertical bar dividing the panes in a window.

Mulroney /mʌlˈrəʊni/ Brian 1939– . Canadian politician. A former business executive, he replaced Joe Clark as Progressive Conservative party leader in 1983, and achieved a landslide in the 1984 election to become prime minister. He won the 1988 election on a platform of free trade with the USA, but with a reduced majority.

multi- /ˈmʌltɪ-/ prefix with the meaning 'many'. [Latin (*multus* = much, many)]

multi-access /mʌltɪˈækses/ *adj.* (of a computer system) allowing access to the central processor from several terminals at the same time.

multicoloured /ˈmʌltɪkʌləd/ *adj.* of many colours.

multicultural education education aimed at preparing children to live in a multiracial society by giving them an understanding of the culture and history of different ethnic groups.

multifarious /mʌltɪˈfeərɪəs/ *adj.* many and various; having a great variety. —**multifariously** *adv.* [from Latin *multifarius*]

multiform /ˈmʌltɪfɔːm/ *adj.* having many forms, of many kinds.

multilateral /mʌltɪˈlætərəl/ *adj.* 1. (of an agreement, treaty, etc.) in which three or more parties participate. 2. having many sides.

multilateralism *n.* trade among more than two countries without discrimination over origin or destination and regardless of whether a large trade gap is involved.

multilingual /mʌltɪˈlɪŋɡwəl/ *adj.* in, using, or speaking many languages.

multimillionaire /mʌltɪmɪljəˈneə/ *n.* a person possessing several million pounds, dollars etc.

multinational /mʌltɪˈnæʃənəl/ *adj.* operating in several countries. —*n.* a multinational company.

multinational corporation company or enterprise operating in several countries, usually defined as one that has 25% or more of its output capacity located outside its country of origin.

multiple /ˈmʌltɪpəl/ *adj.* 1. having several parts, elements, or components. 2. many and various. —*n.* a quantity that contains another some number of times without a remainder. —**least** *or* **lowest common multiple**, the least quantity that is a multiple of two or more given quantities.

multiple-choice *adj.* (of a question in an examination) accompanied by several possible answers from which the correct one is to be selected. [French from Latin *multiplus*]

multiple birth in humans, the production of more than two babies from one pregnancy. Multiple births can be caused by more than two eggs being produced and fertilized (often as the result of hormone therapy to assist pregnancy), or by a single fertilized egg dividing more than once before implantation.

multiple proportions, law of in chemistry, the principle that states that if two elements combine with each other to form more than one compound, then the ratio of the masses of one of them that combine with a particular mass of the other is a small whole number.

multiple sclerosis (MS) incurable chronic disease of the central nervous system, occurring in young or middle adulthood. It is characterized by degeneration of the myelin sheath that surrounds nerves in the brain and spinal cord. It is also known as disseminated sclerosis. Its cause is unknown.

multiplex /ˈmʌltɪpleks/ *adj.* of many elements, manifold. [Latin *-plex* = -fold]

multiplicand /mʌltɪplɪˈkænd/ *n.* a quantity to be multiplied by another. [from Latin, gerundive of *multiplicare*]

multiplication /mʌltɪplɪˈkeɪʃən/ *n.* multiplying, especially the arithmetical process. —**multiplication sign**, ×, as in 2×3. **multiplication table**, a table of the products of pairs of factors, especially 1 to 12. [from Old French or Latin]

multiplicity /mʌltɪˈplɪsɪtɪ/ *n.* a great variety or number. [from Latin]

multiplier /ˈmʌltɪplaɪə/ *n.* the quantity by which a multiplicand is multiplied; in economics, the theoretical concept, formulated by John Maynard Keynes, of the effect on national income or employment by an adjustment in overall demand.

multiply /ˈmʌltɪplaɪ/ *v.t./i.* 1. to obtain from (a number) another that is a specified number of times its value. 2. to increase in number, as by breeding. 3. to produce a large number of (instances). 4. to breed (animals); to propagate (plants). [from Old French from Latin *multiplicare*]

multi-purpose /mʌltɪˈpɜːpəs/ *adj.* serving many purposes.

multiracial /mʌltɪˈreɪʃəl/ *adj.* composed of or concerning people of several races.

multistage rocket a rocket launch vehicle made up of several rocket stages (often three) joined end to end.

multi-storey /ˈmʌltɪstɔːrɪ/ *adj.* having several storeys.

multitasking *n.* or **multiprogramming** in computing, a system in which one processor appears to run several different programs (or different parts of the same program) at the same time. All the programs are held in memory together, and each is allowed to run for a certain period, for example while other programs are waiting for a ◊peripheral device to work or for input from an operator. The ability to multitask depends on the ◊operating system rather than the type of computer.

multitude /ˈmʌltɪtjuːd/ *n.* 1. a crowd of people. 2. a great number. —**the multitude**, the common people. [from Old French from Latin *multitudo* (*multus* = many)]

multitudinous /mʌltɪˈtjuːdɪnəs/ *adj.* very numerous; consisting of many individuals. [from Latin]

mum[1] *adj.* (*colloquial*) silent. —**mum's the word**, say nothing.

mum[2] *v.i.* (**-mm-**) to act in a mime.

mum[3] (*colloquial*) abbreviation of mummy[1].

mumble *v.t./i.* to speak or utter indistinctly. —*n.* an indistinct utterance. —**mumbler** *n.*

mumbo-jumbo /mʌmbəʊˈdʒʌmbəʊ/ *n.* 1. meaningless ritual. 2. language or action intended to mystify or confuse. 3. an object of senseless veneration. [from *Mumbo Jumbo*, a supposed African idol]

mummer /ˈmʌmə/ *n.* an actor in a traditional mime. [from Old French *momeur*]

mummers' play or **St George play** British folk drama enacted in dumb show by a masked cast, performed on Christmas Day to celebrate the death of the old year and its rebirth as the new year. The plot usually consists of a duel between St George and an infidel knight, in which one of them is killed but later revived by a doctor. Mummers' plays are still performed in some parts of Britain.

mummery /ˈmʌmərɪ/ *n.* 1. a performance by mummers. 2. a ridiculous (especially religious) ceremonial. [from Old French *momerie*]

mummify /ˈmʌmɪfaɪ/ *v.t.* to preserve (a body) as a mummy. —**mummification** /-fɪˈkeɪʃən/ *n.*

mummy[1] *n.* (*colloquial*) mother. [imitative of child's pronunciation]

mummy[2] /ˈmʌmɪ/ *n.* the body of a person or animal embalmed for burial, especially in ancient Egypt. [from French, ultimately from Persian *mū m* = wax]

mumps *n.* a virus infection marked by fever and swelling of the parotid salivary glands (such as those under the ears). It is usually minor in children, although meningitis is a possible complication. In adults the symptoms are severe and it may cause sterility in adult men. [from obsolete *mump* = grimace]

munch *v.t./i.* to eat steadily with marked action of the jaws.

Munch /mʊŋk/ Edvard 1863–1944. Norwegian painter and printmaker. He studied in Paris and Berlin, and his major works date from the period 1892–1908, when he lived mainly in Germany. His paintings often focus on neurotic emotional states. The *Frieze of Life* 1890s, a sequence of highly charged, symbolic paintings, includes some of his most characteristic images, such as *Skriket/The Scream* 1893.

Münchhausen /mʊnˈtʃaʊzən/ Karl Friedrich, Freiherr (Baron) von 1720–1797. German soldier, born in Hanover. He served with the Russian army against the Turks, and after his retirement in 1760 told exaggerated stories of his adventures. This idiosyncrasy was utilized by the

Murdoch *Winner of many awards including the Booker Prize in 1978 for* The Sea, The Sea, *Iris Murdoch was again shortlisted for the award in 1987 for* The Book and the Brotherhood.

German writer Rudolph Erich Raspe (1737–1794) in his extravagantly fictitious *Adventures of Baron Munchhausen* 1785, which he wrote in English while living in London.

Münchhausen's syndrome an emotional disorder in which a patient feigns or invents symptoms to secure medical treatment. In some cases the patient will secretly ingest substances to produce real symptoms. [from Baron *Münchhausen*]

mundane /mʌn'deɪn/ *adj.* 1. dull or routine. 2. of this world, worldly. [from Old French from Latin (*mundus* = world)]

Munich /'mjuːnɪk/ (German *München*) industrial city (brewing, printing, precision instruments, machinery, electrical goods, textiles), capital of Bavaria, Germany, on the river Isar; population (1986) 1,269,400.

Munich Agreement a pact signed on 29 Sept 1938 by the leaders of the UK (Neville ◊Chamberlain), France (Edouard ◊Daladier), Germany (Hitler), and Italy (Mussolini), under which Czechoslovakia was compelled to surrender its Sudeten-German districts (the **Sudetenland**) to Germany. Chamberlain claimed it would guarantee 'peace in our time', but it did not prevent Hitler from seizing the rest of Czechoslovakia in March 1939.

Munich Putsch an unsuccessful uprising led by Adolf Hitler, attempting to overthrow the government of Bavaria in Nov 1923. More than 2,000 Nazi demonstrators were met by armed police, who opened fire killing 16 of Hitler's supporters. At the subsequent trial for treason, General Ludendorff, who had supported Hitler, was acquitted. Hitler was sentenced to prison, during which time he wrote ◊*Mein Kampf*.

municipal /mju:'nɪsɪpəl/ *adj.* of or concerning a municipality or its self-government. —**municipally** *adv.* [from Latin *municipium* = self-governing town of Italy or a Roman province]

municipality /mju:nɪsɪ'pælɪtɪ/ *n.* 1. a town or district having local self-government. 2. the governing body of this. [from French]

munificent /mju:'nɪfɪsənt/ *adj.* splendidly generous. —**munificence** *n.*, **munificently** *adv.* [from Latin *munificus* (*munus* = gift)]

muniment /mju:'nɪmənt/ *n.* (usually in *plural*) a document kept as evidence of rights or privileges. [from Old French from Latin *munimentum* = title-deed, originally = defence]

munition /mju:'nɪʃən/ *n.pl* military weapons, ammunition, equipment, and stores. [French from Latin *munire* = fortify]

Munro /mən'rəʊ/ H(ugh) H(ector). British author who wrote under the pen name ◊Saki.

Munster /'mʌnstə/ southern province of the Republic of Ireland, comprising the counties of Clare, Cork, Kerry, Limerick, North and South Tipperary, and Waterford; **area** 24,140 sq km/9,318 sq mi; **population** (1986) 1,019,000.

muntjac /'mʌntdʒæk/ *n.* or **muntjak** small deer, genus *Muntiacus*, found in SE Asia. The buck has short spiked antlers and two sharp canine teeth forming tusks. They are sometimes called 'barking deer' because of their voices.

mural /'mjʊərəl/ *adj.* of or like a wall; on a wall. —*n.* a mural painting etc. [French from Latin *muralis* (*murus* = wall)]

Murasaki /muərə'sɑki/ Shikibu *c.*978–*c.*1015. Japanese writer, a lady at the court. Her masterpiece of fiction, *The Tale of Genji*, is one of the classic works of Japanese literature, and may be the world's first novel.

Murat /mjuə'rɑː/ Joachim 1767–1815. King of Naples from 1808. An officer in the French army, he was made king by Napoleon, but deserted him in 1813 in the vain hope that Austria and Great Britain would recognize him. In 1815 he attempted unsuccessfully to make himself king of all Italy, but when he landed in Calabria in an attempt to gain the throne he was captured and shot.

Murcia /'muəθiə/ autonomous region of SE Spain; **area** 11,300 sq km/4,362 sq mi; **population** (1986) 1,014,000. It includes the cities Murcia and Cartagena, and produces esparto grass, lead, zinc, iron, and fruit.

murder *n.* 1. the intentional and unlawful killing of one person by another. 2. (*colloquial*) a highly troublesome or dangerous state of affairs. —*v.t.* 1. to kill (a person) unlawfully with malice aforethought; to kill wickedly or inhumanly. 2. (*colloquial*) to spoil by bad performance, mispronunciation, etc. 3. (*colloquial*) to defeat utterly. —**cry blue murder**, (*slang*) to make an extravagant outcry. **get away with murder**, (*colloquial*) to do whatever one wishes. —**murderer** *n.*, **murderess** *n.fem.* [Old English]

murderous /'mɜːdərəs/ *adj.* capable of, intent on, or involving murder or great harm.

Murdoch /'mɜːdɒk/ Iris 1919– . British novelist, born in Dublin. Her novels combine philosophical speculation with often outrageous situations and tangled human relationships. They include *The Sandcastle* 1957, *The Sea, The Sea* 1978, and *The Message to the Planet* 1989.

Writing is like getting married. One should never commit oneself until one is amazed at one's luck.

    Iris Murdoch
    The Black Prince

Murdoch Rupert 1931– . Australian entrepreneur and owner of media-oriented businesses, with interests in Australia, the UK, the USA, and other countries. Among his Australian interests are the *Australian*, the *Daily Telegraph* and the *Daily Mirror*; among his UK newspapers are the *Sun*, the *News of the World*, and *The Times*; in the USA, he has a 50% stake in 20th Century Fox, and he also owns publishing companies.

Murillo /mjuə'rɪləʊ/ Bartolomé Esteban *c.*1617–1682. Spanish painter, active mainly in Seville. He painted sentimental pictures of the Immaculate Conception; he also specialized in studies of street urchins.

murk *n.* darkness, poor visibility.

murky *adj.* 1. dark, gloomy; (of liquid etc.) thick and dirty. 2. suspiciously obscure. —**murkily** *adv.*, **murkiness** *n.*

Murmansk /muə'mænsk/ seaport in NW USSR, on the Barents Sea; population (1987) 432,000. It is the largest city in the Arctic, the USSR's most important fishing port, and base of the icebreakers that keep the North East Passage open.

murmur /'mɜːmə/ *n.* 1. a subdued continuous sound. 2. softly spoken or nearly inarticulate speech. 3. a subdued expression of discontent. —*v.t./i.* to make a murmur; to utter (words) softly; to complain in low tones. —**murmurous** *adj.* [from Old French or Latin]

Murnau /'muənau/ F W 1889–1931. Adopted name of Friedrich Wilhelm Plumpe. German silent-film director, known for his expressive images and 'subjective' use of a moving camera in *Der letzte Mumm/The Last Laugh* 1924. Other films include *Nosferatu* 1922, a version of the Dracula story, and *Sunrise* 1927.

muscle

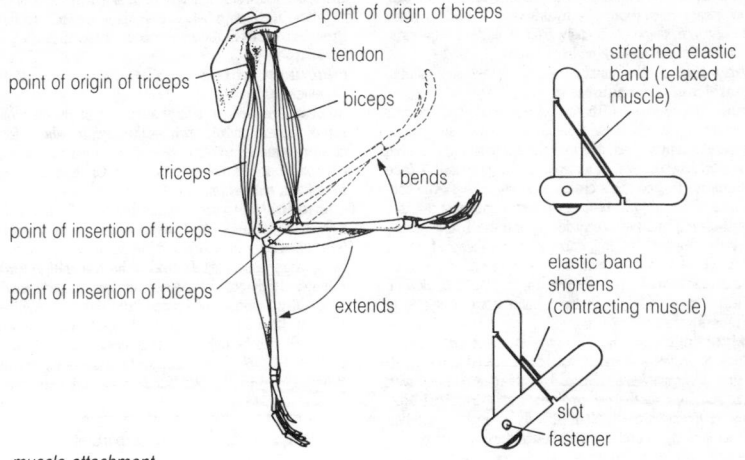

point of origin of biceps
tendon
point of origin of triceps
biceps
triceps
bends
point of insertion of triceps
point of insertion of biceps
extends

stretched elastic band (relaxed muscle)

elastic band shortens (contracting muscle)

slot
fastener

muscle attachment

murphy /'mɜːfɪ/ *n.* (*slang*) a potato. [Irish surname, from the potato being regarded as the staple food of Ireland]

Murphy Audie 1924–1971. US actor and war hero who starred mainly in low-budget Western films. His work includes *The Red Badge of Courage* 1951, *The Quiet American* 1958, and *The Unforgiven* 1960.

Murphy's law a name humorously given to various expressions of the apparent perverseness of things (roughly, 'anything that can go wrong will go wrong'). [Irish surname; origin of phrase uncertain]

murrain /'mʌrɪn/ *n.* an infectious disease in cattle. [from Anglo-French *moryn*]

Murray /'mʌrɪ/ principal river of Australia, 2,575 km/ 1,600 mi long. It rises in the Australian Alps near Mount Kosciusko and flows W, forming the boundary between New South Wales and Victoria, and reaches the sea at Encounter Bay, South Australia. With its main tributary, the Darling, it is 3,750 km/2,330 mi long.

Murray James Augustus Henry 1837–1915. Scottish philologist. He was the first editor of the *Oxford English Dictionary* (originally the *New English Dictionary*) from 1878 until his death; the first volume was published in 1884.

Murray James Stuart, Earl of Murray, or Moray 1531–1570. Regent of Scotland from 1567, an illegitimate son of James V. He was one of the leaders of the Scottish Reformation, and after the deposition of his half-sister ◊Mary Queen of Scots, he became regent. He was assassinated by one of her supporters.

murray cod Australian freshwater fish *Maccullochella macquariensis* which grows to about 2 m/6 ft. It is is named after the river in which it is found.

Murrayfield /'mʌrɪfiːld/ *n.* Scottish rugby ground and home of the national team. It staged its first international in 1925 when Scotland beat England 14–11. The crowd capacity is approximately 70,000.

muscadine /'mʌskədiːn, -daɪn/ *n.* a musk-flavoured kind of grape.

muscat /'mʌskət/ *n.* **1.** a muscadine. **2.** wine made from muscadines. [French from Provençal]

Muscat /'mʌskæt/ or **Masqat** capital of Oman, E Arabia, adjoining the port of Matrah, which has a deepwater harbour; combined population (1982) 80,000. It produces natural gas and chemicals.

muscatel /mʌskə'tel/ *n.* **1.** a muscadine. **2.** wine or a raisin made from this. [from Old French]

muscle /'mʌsəl/ *n.* **1.** the contractile tissue that produces movement in an animal's body; a structure composed of such tissue, especially a skeletal muscle of a vertebrate. **2.** that part of the animal body which is composed of muscles, the chief constituent of flesh. **3.** power, strength. —*v.i.* (*slang*) to force one's way. —**muscle-bound** *adj.* with

the muscles stiff and inelastic through excessive exercise or training. **muscle-man** *n.* a man with highly-developed muscles, especially as an intimidator. [French from Latin *musculus*]

muscovite *n.* white mica, $KAl_2(Al, Si_3O_{10}(OH, F)_2$, a common silicate. It is colourless to silvery white with shiny surfaces, and like all micas it splits into thin flakes along its one perfect cleavage. Muscovite is a metamorphic mineral occurring mainly in schists; it is also found in some granites, and appears as shiny flakes on bedding planes of some sandstones.

Muscovite /'mʌskəvaɪt/ *adj.* of Moscow. —*n.* a citizen of Moscow. [from Russian *Moskva* = Moscow]

muscular /'mʌskjʊlə/ *adj.* **1.** of or affecting the muscles. **2.** having well-developed muscles. —**muscularity** /-'lærɪtɪ/ *n.*

muscular dystrophy any of a group of inherited chronic muscle disorders marked by weakening and wasting of muscle. Muscle fibres degenerate, to be replaced by fatty tissue, although the nerve supply remains unimpaired.

muse /mjuːz/ *v.t./i.* to ponder, to meditate; to say meditatively. [from Old French perhaps from Latin *musum* = muzzle]

Muse /mjuːz/ *n.* **1.** in Greek and Roman mythology, any of the goddesses who presided over the arts and sciences; the nine daughters of Zeus and Mnemosyne (goddess of memory); **Calliope** epic poetry; **Clio** history; **Erato** love poetry; **Euterpe** lyric poetry; **Melpomene** tragedy; **Polyhymnia** hymns; **Terpsichore** dance; **Thalia** comedy; **Urania** astronomy. **2.** muse, a poet's inspiring genius. [from Old French or Latin from Greek *mousa*]

museum /mjuː'ziːəm/ *n.* a building used for the exhibition and storage of objects illustrating antiquities, natural history, the arts etc. —**museum piece**, a specimen of art, manufacture etc., fit for a museum; an old-fashioned person or machine etc. [Latin from Greek = seat of the Muses]

Museveni /muː'sevəni/ Yoweri Kaguta 1945– . Ugandan general and politician, president from 1986. He led the opposition to Idi Amin's regime 1971–78 and was minister of defence 1979–80 but, unhappy with Milton Obote's autocratic leadership, formed the National Resistance Army (NRA), which helped to remove him. Museveni leads a broad-based coalition government.

mush[1] *n.* **1.** soft pulp. **2.** feeble sentimentality. **3.** (*US*) maize porridge.

mush[2] *v.i.* (*N American*) **1.** to travel across snow with a dog-sledge. **2.** (as a command to sledge-dogs) get moving. [probably corruption from French *marchons* = let us advance]

mushroom /'mʌʃrʊm/ *n.* the fruiting body of certain fungi, consisting of an upright stem and a spore-producing cap with radiating gills on the undersurface. There are many edible species belonging to the genus *Agaricus*.

See also ◊fungus and ◊toadstool. —*v.i.* 1. to spring up rapidly. 2. to expand and flatten like a mushroom cap. 3. to gather mushrooms. —**mushroom cloud,** a cloud of mushroom shape, especially from a nuclear explosion. [from Old French *mousseron* from Latin]

mushy *adj.* 1. like mush, soft. 2. feebly sentimental. —**mushily** *adv.,* **mushiness** *n.*

music /'mju:zɪk/ *n.* 1. the art of combining vocal and/or instrumental sounds in harmonious and expressive ways; the sounds so produced. 2. a musical composition; a printed or written score of this. 3. a pleasant natural sound. —**face the music,** to face one's critics etc., not to shirk the consequences. **music centre,** equipment combining a radio, record-player, and tape-recorder. **music-hall** *n.* a variety entertainment with singing, dancing etc.; a theatre for this. **music-stool** *n.* a stool with adjustable height of the seat, for a pianist. **music to one's ears,** what one is pleased to hear. [from Old French from Latin from Greek = of the Muses]

musical /'mju:zɪkəl/ *adj.* 1. of music. 2. (of a sound etc.) melodious or harmonious. 3. fond of or skilled in music. 4. set to or accompanied by music. —*n.* a film or play etc. with music and song as the principal feature. —**musical box,** a box containing a mechanism (usually a revolving toothed cylinder striking a comblike metal plate) for playing a certain tune when set in motion. **musical chairs,** a party game in which players walk round chairs (one fewer than the number of players) until the music stops, when the player who finds no chair is eliminated and a chair is removed before the next round. **musical comedy,** an entertainment in which a story is told by a combination of spoken dialogue and songs. —**musicality** /-'kælɪtɪ/ *n.,* **musically** *adv.*

musician /mju:'zɪʃən/ *n.* a person skilled in music, especially one practising it professionally. —**musicianship** *n.* [from Old French]

musicology /mju:zɪ'kɒlədʒɪ/ *n.* the study of the history and forms of music as distinct from study to perform or compose it. —**musicologist** *n.* [from French]

musique concrète /mju:zi:k kɔ̃'kret/ concrete music (see ◊concrete). [French]

musk *n.* 1. a substance secreted by the male musk deer, used as the basis of perfumes. 2. a plant (especially *Mimulus moschatus*) which has or used to have a musky smell. **musk-melon** *n.* the common yellow melon melo. **musk-rose,** *n.* a rambling rose *Rosa moschata* etc. with a musky fragrance. [from Latin from Persian]

musk deer a small deer *Moschus moschiferus* native to mountains of central Asia. It is about 50 cm/20 in high, sure-footed, with large ears, no antlers or horns, and is solitary. It is hunted and farmed for the musk secreted by an abdominal gland, which is used as medicine or perfume.

musket /'mʌskɪt/ *n.* (*historical*) an infantryman's (especially smooth-bored) light gun. [from French from Italian *moschetto* = crossbow bolt]

musketeer /mʌskɪ'tɪə/ *n.* a soldier armed with a musket.

musk ox a hoofed mammal *Ovibos moschatus* native to the Arctic regions of North America. It displays characteristics of sheep and oxen, is about the size of a small domestic cow, and has long brown hair. At certain seasons it exhales a musky odour.

muskrat *n.* an aquatic rodent *Ondatra zibethicus* about 30 cm/12 in long, living in watery regions of North America. It has webbed feet, a flattened tail, and shiny light-brown fur. It builds up a store of food, plastering it over with mud, for winter consumption. It is hunted for its fur (**musquash**).

musky *adj.* smelling like musk. —**muskiness** *n.*

Muslim /'mʊslɪm, -z-/ *n.* a believer in Islam. —*adj.* of Muslims. [from Arabic = one who submits]

Muslim Brotherhood a movement founded by members of the Sunni branch of Islam in Egypt in 1928. It aims at the establishment of a theocratic Islamic state and is headed by a 'supreme guide'. It is also active in Jordan, Sudan, and Syria.

Muslim League Indian political organization. The All India Muslim League was founded 1906 under the leadership of the Aga Khan. In 1940 the League demanded an independent Muslim state. The Congress Party and the Muslim League won most seats in the 1945 elections for an Indian Central Legislative Assembly. In 1946 the Indian Constituent Assembly League was boycotted by the Muslim League. It was partly the activities of the League that led to the establishment of ◊Pakistan.

muslin /'mʌzlɪn/ *n.* a fine, delicately woven, cotton fabric. [from French from Italian (*Mussolo* = Mosul in Iraq, where it was made)]

musquash /'mʌskwɒʃ/ *n.* 1. the muskrat. 2. its fur. [Algonquian]

mussel /'mʌsəl/ *n.* one of a number of bivalve molluscs, some of them edible, such as the *Mytilus edulis*, found in clusters attached to rocks around the N Atlantic and American coasts. It has a blue-black shell. [Old English ultimately from Latin *musculus*]

Mussolini /mʊsə'li:ni/ Benito 1883–1945. Italian dictator from 1925 to 1943. As founder of the Fascist Movement (see ◊fascism) in 1919 and prime minister from 1922, he became known as *Il Duce* ('the leader'). He invaded Ethiopia 1935–36, intervened in the Spanish Civil War 1936–39 in support of Franco, and conquered Albania in 1939. In June 1940 Italy entered World War II supporting Hitler. Forced by military and domestic setbacks to resign in 1943, Mussolini established a breakaway government in N Italy 1944–45, but was killed trying to flee the country.

Fascism is not an article for export.

Benito Mussolini
report in the German press, 1932

Mussorgsky /mu'sɔ:gski/ Modest Petrovich 1839–1881. Russian composer, who was largely self-taught. His opera *Boris Godunov* was completed in 1869, although not produced in St Petersburg until 1874. Some of his works were 'revised' by ◊Rimsky-Korsakov, and only recently has their harsh and primitive beauty been recognized.

must[1] *v.aux.* (*present* and *past* **must**; no other parts used) expressing obligation, insistence, rightness or advisability, certainty or likelihood. —*n.* (*colloquial*) a thing that must be done, seen etc. [Old English]

must[2] *n.* grape-juice before the end of fermentation; new wine. [Old English from Latin *mustum*]

Mustafa Kemal /'mʊstəfə kə'mɑ:l/ Turkish leader who assumed the name of ◊Atatürk.

mustang /'mʌstæŋ/ *n.* a half-wild domestic horse of Mexico and California. [from Spanish *mestengo* and *mostrenco*]

mustard /'mʌstəd/ *n.* 1. a plant *Brassica nigra* with yellow flowers. 2. a condiment made by grinding the seeds of this and making them into a paste with water or vinegar. 3. a fodder plant *Sinapis alba* the seed-leaves of which form part of 'mustard and cress'. 4. a brownish-yellow colour. —**mustard gas,** a colourless oily liquid or its vapour, a powerful irritant. **mustard plaster,** a plaster containing mustard, applied to the skin as a poultice. [from Old French from Latin *mustum* the condiment being originally prepared with must]

muster *v.t./i.* 1. to assemble or cause to assemble (originally of soldiers assembled to check numbers etc. or for inspection). 2. to summon (courage, strength etc.). —*n.* an assembly or gathering. —**pass muster,** to be accepted as adequate. [from Old French *mo(u)strer* from Latin *monstrare* = show]

mustn't /'mʌsənt/ (*colloquial*) must not.

musty *adj.* 1. mouldy, stale. 2. antiquated. —**mustily** *adv.,* **mustiness** *n.*

mutable /'mju:təbəl/ *adj.* liable to change; fickle. —**mutability** /-'bɪlɪtɪ/ *n.* [from Latin *mutabilis* (*mutare* = change)]

mutagen *n.* any substance that makes ◊mutation of genes more likely. A mutagen is likely to also act as a ◊carcinogen.

mutant /'mju:tənt/ *adj.* resulting from mutation. —*n.* a mutant form. [from Latin]

mutate /mju:'teɪt/ *v.t./i.* to undergo mutation; to cause to do this.

mutation /mju:'teɪʃən/ *n.* 1. a change, an alteration. 2. a genetic change which when transmitted to an offspring gives rise to heritable variation. 3. a mutant. 4. umlaut. [from Latin (*mutare* = change)]

mutatis mutandis /mu:'tɑ:tɪs mu:'tændɪs/ with due alteration of details (in comparing cases). [Latin]

mute /mju:t/ *adj.* 1. silent, refraining from speech. 2. not emitting articulate sound; (of a person or animal) dumb. 3. (of a letter) not pronounced. 4. not expressed in speech. —*n.* 1. a dumb person. 2. an actor whose part is in dumb show. 3. a device to deaden the sound of a musical instrument. 4. a mute consonant. —*v.t.* to deaden or soften the sound of (especially a musical instrument). 2. to tone down, to make less intense. —**mute swan**, the common white swan *Cygnus olor*. —**mutely** *adv.*, **muteness** *n.* [from Old French from Latin *mutus*]

mutilate /'mju:tɪleɪt/ *v.t.* 1. to injure or disfigure by cutting off an important part. 2. to render (a book etc.) imperfect by excision etc. —**mutilation** /-'leɪʃən/ *n.*, **mutilator** *n.* [from Latin *mutilare* (*mutilus* = maimed)]

mutineer /mju:tɪ'nɪə/ *n.* one who mutinies. [from French *mutin* = rebellious from *muete* = movement from Latin *movere* = move]

mutinous /'mju:tɪnəs/ *adj.* rebellious, ready to mutiny. —**mutinously**, *adv.* [from obsolete *mutine* = rebellion]

mutiny *n.* an open revolt against authority, especially by servicemen against officers. —*v.i.* to engage in a mutiny, to revolt.

Mutsuhito /mu:tsu:'hi:təʊ/ personal name of the Japanese emperor ◊Meiji.

mutt (*slang*) abbreviation of mutton-head, a stupid person.

mutter /'mʌtə/ *v.t./i.* 1. to speak or utter in a low, unclear tone. 2. to utter subdued grumbles. —*n.* muttering; muttered words.

mutton *n.* the flesh of the sheep as food. —**mutton dressed as lamb**, a middle-aged or elderly woman dressed to look young. **mutton-head** *n.* (*colloquial*) a stupid person. —**muttony** *adj.* [from Old French from Latin *multo* = sheep]

mutton bird any of a group of shearwaters and petrels that breed in burrows on Australasian islands. The young are very fat, and are killed for food and oil.

mutual /'mju:tjuəl/ *adj.* 1. (of feeling, action, etc.) felt or done by each to or towards the other. 2. standing in (a specified) relation to each other. 3. (*colloquial*) (disputed usage) common to two or more persons. —**mutuality** /-'ælɪtɪ/ *n.*, **mutually** *adv.* [from Old French from Latin *mutuus*]

mutual fund another name for ◊unit trust, used in the USA.

mutual induction in physics, the production of an electromotive force (emf) or voltage in an electric circuit caused by a changing ◊magnetic flux in a neighbouring circuit. The two circuits are often coils of wire, as in a ◊transformer, and the size of the induced emf depends largely on the numbers of turns of wire in each of the coils.

mutualism /'mju:p:tjuəlɪzəm/ *n.* or ◊symbiosis an association between two organisms of different species whereby both profit from the relationship.

Muybridge /'maɪbrɪdʒ/ Eadweard. Adopted name of Edward James Muggeridge 1830–1904. British photographer. He made a series of animal locomotion photographs in the USA in the 1870s and proved that, when a horse trots, there are times when all its feet are off the ground. He also explored motion in birds and humans.

Muzak /'mju:zæk/ *n.* trade name of a system of music transmission for playing in shops, factories, etc.; recorded light music as a background.

Muzorewa /mu:zə'reɪwə/ Abel (Tendekayi) 1925– . Zimbabwean politician and Methodist bishop. He was president of the African National Council 1971–85 and prime minister of Rhodesia/Zimbabwe 1979. He was detained for a year in 1983–84. He is leader of the minority United Africa National Council.

muzzle *n.* 1. the projecting part of an animal's head including the nose and mouth. 2. the open end of a firearm. 3. a contrivance of strap or wire etc. put over an animal's head to prevent it from biting or feeding. —*v.t.* 1. to put a muzzle on. 2. to impose silence on. [from Old French from Latin *musum*]

muzzy *adj.* 1. dazed, feeling stupefied. 2. indistinct. —**muzzily** *adv.*, **muzziness** *n.*

MVD Soviet Ministry of Internal Affairs, name of the secret police 1946–53; now the ◊KGB.

MW abbreviation of megawatt(s).

Mwiiny /mwi:'i:ni/ Ali Hassan 1925– . Tanzanian socialist politician, president from 1985, when he succeeded

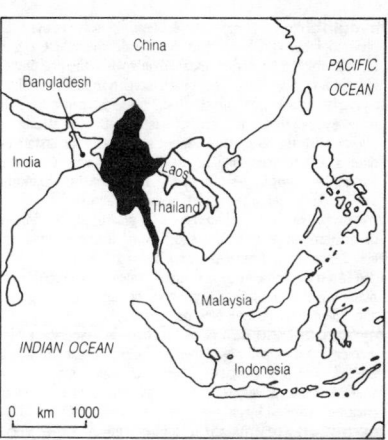

Myanmar

Julius Nyerere. He began a revival of private enterprise and control of state involvement and spending.

my /maɪ/ *poss adj.* 1. of or belonging to me. 2. used in affectionate collocations and as an exclamation of surprise.

myalgia /maɪ'ældʒɪə/ *n.* pain in muscle(s). [from Greek *mus* = muscle and *algos* = pain]

myall /'maɪəl/ *n.* an Australian acacia with hard scented wood used for fences etc. [from Aboriginal *maiāl*]

Myanmar Union of; formerly (until 1989) **Burma** country in SE Asia, bordered NW by India, NE by China, SE by Laos and Thailand, and SW by the Bay of Bengal; **area** 676,577 sq km/261,228 sq mi; **capital** and chief port Yangon (formerly Rangoon); **physical** over half is rainforest; mountains in N, W, and E; **head of state and government** Gen Saw Maung from 1988; **political system** military republic; **population** (1990 est) 41,279,000; **language** Burmese; **recent history** a crown colony in the British Commonwealth from 1937, Burma achieved independence in 1948 and left the Commonwealth. Gen Saw Maung seized power in a military coup in Sept 1988.

myasthenia gravis in medicine, an uncommon condition characterized by loss of muscle power, especially in the face and neck. The muscles tire rapidly and fail to respond to repeated nervous stimulation. ◊Autoimmunity is the cause.

mycelium *n.* an interwoven mass of threadlike filaments or ◊hyphae, forming the main body of most fungi. The reproductive structures, or fruiting bodies, grow from the mycelium.

Mycenae /maɪ'si:ni:/ ancient Greek city in the E Peloponnese, which gave its name to the Mycenaean (Bronze Age) civilization. Its peak was 1400–1200 BC, when the Cyclopean walls (using close-fitting stones) were erected. The city ceased to be inhabited after about 1120 BC.

Mycenaean /maɪsi'ni:ən/ *adj.* of the culture developed in mainland Greece in the late Bronze Age, *c.*1580–1100 BC, illustrated by remains at Mycenae and other ancient cities of the Peloponnese. —*n.* a Mycenaean person. [from Latin *Mycenaeus*]

mycology /maɪ'kɒlədʒɪ/ *n.* the study of fungi. —**mycologist** *n.* [from Greek *mukēs* = mushroom]

mycorrhiza *n.* a mutually beneficial (mutualistic) association occurring between plant roots and a soil fungus. Mycorrhizal roots take up nutrients more efficiently than non-mycorrhizal roots, and the fungus benefits by obtaining carbohydrates from the tree.

myelin sheath the insulating layer that surrounds nerve cells in vertebrate animals. It acts to speed up the passage of nerve impulses. Myelin is made up of fats and proteins and is formed from up to a hundred layers, laid down by special cells, the **Schwann cells**.

My Lai massacre /mi: 'laɪ/ the killing of 109 civilians in My Lai, a village in South Vietnam, by US troops in March 1968. An investigation in 1969 was followed by the conviction of Lt William Calley, commander of the platoon.

myna, mynah variant of ◊mina.

myoglobin *n.* a globular protein, closely related to ◊haemoglobin and located in vertebrate muscle. Oxygen binds to myoglobin and is released only when the haemoglobin can no longer supply adequate oxygen to muscle cells.

myopia /maɪˈəʊpiə/ *n.* short-sightedness, caused either by an eyeball that is too long or a lens that is too strong. A person with this complaint cannot see clearly for distances over a few metres, and needs spectacles with diverging lenses. —**myopic** /-ˈɒpɪk/ *adj.*, **myopically** /-ˈɒpɪkəlɪ/ *adv.* [from Greek *muō* = shut and *ōps* = eye]

myriad /ˈmɪriəd/ *n.* (*literary*) 1. (in *plural*) an indefinitely great number. 2. ten thousand. —*adj.* (*literary*) innumerable. [from Latin from Greek *murioi* = 10,000]

myriapod /ˈmɪriəpɒd/ *n.* a small crawling arthropod with many legs, of the group Myriapoda comprising centipedes and millepedes. [Greek *pous podos* = foot]

myrmecophyte *n.* a plant that lives in association with a colony of ants and possesses specialized organs in which the ants live. For example, *Myrmecodia*, an epiphytic plant from Malaysia, develops root tubers containing a network of cavities inhabited by ants.

myrmidon /ˈmɜːmɪdən/ *n.* a hired ruffian, a base servant. [from *Myrmidons*, Thessalians who followed Achilles to Troy]

Myron /ˈmaɪrən/ *c.*500–440 BC. Greek sculptor. His *Discobolus/Discus-Thrower* and *Athene and Marsyas*, much admired in his time, are known through Roman copies. They confirm his ancient reputation for brilliant composition and naturalism.

myrrh /mɜː/ *n.* a gum resin from trees of the genus *Commiphora*, used in perfumes, medicine, and incense. [Old English from Latin from Greek *murra*]

myrtle /ˈmɜːtəl/ *n.* an evergreen shrub of the genus *Myrtus*, with shiny leaves and fragrant white flowers. [from Latin diminutive (*myrta, myrtus* from Greek)]

myself /maɪˈself/ *pron.* emphatic and reflexive form of I, me[1].

mysterious /mɪˈstɪəriəs/ *adj.* 1. full of or wrapped in mystery. 2. (of a person) enjoying mystery. —**mysteriously** *adv.* [from French]

mystery /ˈmɪstərɪ/ *n.* 1. an inexplicable or secret matter. 2. secrecy, obscurity. 3. the practice of making a secret of things. 4. a fictional work dealing with a puzzling event, especially a crime. 5. a religious truth that is beyond human powers to understand. 6. (in *plural*) any of various cults of the ancient world, open only to the initiated, which generally included mystic ideas. —**mystery tour** *or* **trip,** a pleasure excursion to an unspecified destination. [from Old French or Latin from Greek *mustērion*]

mystery play or **miracle play** a vernacular medieval religious drama based on stories from the Bible. Mystery plays were performed around the time of church festivals, reaching their height in Europe during the 15th and 16th centuries. A whole cycle running from the Creation to the Last Judgement was performed in separate scenes on mobile wagons by various town guilds.

mystic /ˈmɪstɪk/ *n.* one who seeks by contemplation and self-surrender to obtain union with or absorption into the Deity, or who believes in the spiritual apprehension of truths beyond the understanding. —*adj.* 1. mysterious and awe-inspiring. 2. spiritually allegorical or symbolic. 3. occult, esoteric; of hidden meaning. [from Old French orLatin from Greek *mustēs* = initiated person]

mystical *adj.* 1. of mystics or mysticism. 2. having direct spiritual significance. —**mystically** *adv.*

mysticism /ˈmɪstɪsɪzəm/ *n.* 1. religious belief or spiritual experience based on direct, intuitive communion with the divine. Mysticism is a widespread experience in Christianity and in many non-Christian religions, e.g. Buddhism, Taoism, Hinduism, and Islam. 2. being a mystic.

mystify /ˈmɪstɪfaɪ/ *v.t.* to cause to feel puzzled. —**mystification** /-fɪˈkeɪʃən/ *n.* [from French]

mystique /mɪˈstiːk/ *n.* an atmosphere of mystery and veneration attending some activity or person; a skill or technique impressive to the layman. [French]

myth /mɪθ/ *n.* 1. a traditional narrative usually involving supernatural or imaginary persons etc. and embodying popular ideas on natural or social phenomena etc.; such narratives collectively. 2. an imaginary person or thing. 3. a widely held but false notion. 4. an allegory. —**mythical** *adj.*, **mythically** *adv.* [from Latin from Greek *muthos*]

mythology /mɪˈθɒlədʒɪ/ *n.* 1. a body of myths. 2. the study of myths. —**mythological** /mɪθəˈlɒdʒɪkəl/ *adj.*, **mythologically** *adv.*, **mythologist** *n.* [from French or Latin from Greek]

myxoedema *n.* thyroid-deficiency disease developing in adult life, most commonly in middle-aged women. The symptoms are loss of energy and appetite, inability to keep warm, mental dullness, and dry, puffy skin. It is completely reversed by giving the thyroid hormone known as thyroxine.

myxomatosis *n.* a virus disease in rabbits, with tumours in mucous tissue. [from Greek *muxa* = mucus]

n, N /en/ (*plural* **ns, n's**) *n.* **1.** the 14th letter of the alphabet. **2.** an indefinite number. —**to the nth degree**, to the utmost.

n. abbreviation of **1.** name. **2.** neuter. **3.** note.

N abbreviation of **1.** ◊newton(s); **2.**in chess, knight.

N symbol for nitrogen.

N. abbreviation of **1.** New **2.** north, northern.

Na symbol for sodium. [from Latin *natrium*]

NAACP abbreviation of ◊National Association for the Advancement of Colored People.

NAAFI /ˈnæfɪ/ acronym from Navy, Army, and Air Force Institutes a non-profit-making association providing canteens for HM British Forces in the UK and abroad.

nab *v.t.* (**-bb-**) (*slang*) **1.** to catch (a wrongdoer) in the act; to arrest. **2.** to seize, to grab. [also *nap*, as in *kidnap*]

Nabis, les /ˈnɑːbiː/ a group of French artists, active in the 1890s in Paris, united in their admiration of Gauguin – the mystic content of his work, the surface pattern and intense colour. In practice their work was decorative. ◊Bonnard and ◊Vuillard were members. [Hebrew = prophets]

nabob /ˈneɪbɒb/ *n.* **1.** (*historical*) a Muslim official or governor under the Mogul empire. **2.** (*archaic*) a wealthy, luxury-loving person, especially one who has returned from India with a fortune. [from Portuguese or Spanish from Urdu from Arabic = deputy]

Nabokov /nəˈbəʊkɒf/ Vladimir 1899–1977. US writer who left his native Russia in 1917 and began writing in English in the 1940s. His most widely known book is *Lolita* 1955, the story of the middle-aged Humbert Humbert's infatuation with a precocious child of 12. His other books include *Laughter in the Dark* 1938, *The Real Life of Sebastian Knight* 1945, *Pnin* 1957, and his memoirs *Speak, Memory* 1947.

Life is a great surprise. I do not see why death should not be an even greater one.

Vladimir Nabokov
'Commentary', *Pale Fire*

Nachingwea /nəˈtʃɪŋɡweɪə/ *n.* military training base in Tanzania, about 360 km/225 mi S of Dar-es-Salaam. It was used by the guerrillas of Frelimo (Mozambique) 1964–75 and the African National Congress 1975–80.

nacre /ˈneɪkə/ *n.* mother-of-pearl; the shellfish yielding this. —**nacreous** /-krɪəs/ *adj.* [French]

Nadar /nəˈdɑː/ adopted name of Gaspard-Félix Tournachon 1820–1910. French portrait photographer and caricaturist. He took the first aerial photographs (from a balloon in 1858) and was the first to use artificial light in photography.

nadir /ˈneɪdɪə/ *n.* **1.** the point of the heavens directly under the observer (as opposed to **zenith**). **2.** the lowest point, the state or time of greatest depression etc. [from Old French through Arabic = opposite (to zenith)]

Nadir Shah (Khan) *c.*1880–1933. King of Afghanistan from 1929. Nadir played a key role in the 1919 Afghan War, but was subsequently forced into exile in France. He returned to Kabul in 1929 to seize the throne and embarked on an ambitious modernization programme. This alienated the Muslim clergy and in 1933 he was assassinated by fundamentalists. His successor as king was his son ◊Zahir Shah.

naevus /ˈniːvəs/ *n.* (*plural* **naevi** /-vaɪ/) a birthmark in the form of a sharply defined red mark in the skin; a mole. [Latin]

Nafud /næˈfuːd/ desert area in Saudi Arabia to the S of the Syrian Desert.

nag[1] *v.t./i.* (**-gg-**) **1.** to find fault or scold persistently. **2.** (of pain etc.) to be persistent. —**nagger** *n.*

nag[2] *n.* (*colloquial*) a horse.

Nagaland /ˈnɑːɡəlænd/ state of NE India, bordering Myanmar (Burma) on the E; **area** 16,721 sq km/6,456 sq mi; **capital** Kohima; **population** (1981) 775,000; **history** formerly part of Assam, it was seized by Britain from Burma (now Myanmar) in 1826. The British sent 18 expeditions against the Naga peoples in the north 1832–87. After India attained independence in 1947, there was Naga guerrilla activity against the Indian government; the state of Nagaland was established in 1963 in response to demands for self-government, but fighting continued sporadically.

Nagasaki /ˌnæɡəˈsɑːki/ industrial port on Kyushu island, Japan; **products** coal, iron, shipbuilding; **population** (1987) 447,000. An atom bomb was dropped on it on 9 Aug 1945.

Nagorno-Karabakh /nəˈɡɔːnəʊ kærəbæx/ autonomous region (*oblast*) of the Soviet republic of ◊Azerbaijan; **area** 4,400 sq km/1,700 sq mi; **capital** Stepanakert; **population** (1987) 180,000 (76% Armenian, 23% Azeri), the Christian Armenians forming an enclave within the predominantly Shi'ite Muslim Azerbaijan. Since Feb 1988 the region has been the site of ethnic conflicts between the two groups and the subject of violent disputes between Azerbaijan and the neighbouring republic of Armenia.

Nagoya /nəˈɡɔɪə/ industrial seaport (cars, textiles, clocks) on Honshu island, Japan; population (1987) 2,091,000. It has a shogun fortress of 1610 and a notable Shinto shrine, Atsuta Jingu.

Nagpur /næɡˈpʊə/ industrial city in Maharashtra, India; population (1981) 1,298,000; **products** textiles, metals.

Nagy /nɒdʒ/ Imre 1895–1958. Hungarian politician, prime minister 1953–55 and in 1956. He led the Hungarian revolt against Soviet domination in 1956, for which he was executed.

Nahayan /nɑːhəˈjɑːn/ Sheik Zayed bin Sultan al- 1918– . Emir of Abu Dhabi from 1969, when he deposed his brother, Sheik Shakhbut. He was elected president of the supreme council of the United Arab Emirates in 1971. Before 1969 he was governor of the E province of Abu Dhabi, one of seven ◊Trucial States in the Persian Gulf and Gulf of Oman, then under British protection. He was unanimously re-elected emir in 1986.

Nahua /ˈnɑːwɑː/ *n.* **1.** a member of an indigenous people of central Mexico. **2.** The Nahua language, in the Uto-Aztecan family, spoken by over 1 million people today. —*adj.* of the Nahua people or language.

naiad /ˈnaɪæd/ *n.* in classical mythology, a water-nymph. [from Latin from Greek]

nail *n.* **1.** the horny covering of the upper surface of the tip of a finger or toe of primates (humans, monkeys, and apes).

Nails are derived from the ◊claws of ancestral primates. 2. a small metal spike hammered in to hold things together or serve as a peg or ornament. —*v.t.* 1. to fasten with a nail or nails. 2. to secure, catch, or arrest (a person, thing, attention etc.). 3. to identify precisely. —**nail down,** to bind to a promise etc.; to define precisely. **nail in a person's coffin,** a thing hastening a person's death. **nail-punch** *n.* a driving punch for nails. **on the nail,** (especially of payment) without delay. [Old English]

nainsook /'neɪnsʊk/ *n.* a fine soft cotton fabric, originally from India. [from Hindi]

Naipaul /'naɪpɔːl/ V(idiadhar) S(urajprasad) 1932– . British writer, born in Trinidad. His novels include *A House for Mr Biswas* 1961, *The Mimic Men* 1967, *A Bend in the River* 1979, and *Finding the Centre* 1984.

I'm the kind of writer that people think other people are reading.

V S Naipaul
Radio Times 1979.

Nairobi /naɪ'rəʊbi/ capital of Kenya, in the central highlands at 1,660 m/5,450 ft; population (1985) 1,100,000. It has light industry and food processing and is the headquarters of the United Nations Environment Programme. Nairobi was founded 1899.

naïve /naː'iːv/ *adj.* 1. simple, unaffected, unconsciously artless. 2. (of art etc.) straightforward in style, eschewing subtlety or conventional technique. —**naïvely** *adv.*, **naïveté** /-'iːvteɪ/ *n.*, **naïvety** /-'iːvtɪ/ *n.* [French, feminine of *naïf* from Latin *nativus* = native]

Najaf /'nædʒxf/ holy city near the Euphrates in Iraq, 144 km/90 mi S of Baghdad.

Najibullah /nædʒi'bʊlə/ Ahmadzai 1947– . Afghan communist politician, a member of the Politburo from 1981 and leader of the ruling People's Democratic Party of Afghanistan (PDPA) from 1986, later state president. His attempts to broaden the support of the PDPA regime had little success, but his government survived the withdrawal of Soviet troops in Feb 1989.

Nakasone /næka'səʊneɪ/ Yasuhiro 1917– . Japanese conservative politician, leader of the Liberal Democratic Party and prime minister 1982–87. He stepped up military spending and increased Japanese participation in international affairs, with closer ties to the USA. He was forced to resign his party post in May 1989 as a result of having profited from insider trading in the ◊Recruit scandal.

naked /'neɪkɪd/ *adj.* 1. unclothed, nude. 2. without the usual covering or furnishings; unsheathed or unprotected. 3. undisguised. 4. (of the eye) unassisted by a telescope or microscope etc. —**nakedly** *adv.*, **nakedness** *n.* [Old English]

Nakhichevan /næxɪtʃə'væn/ autonomous republic forming part of Azerbaijan Republic, USSR, even though it is entirely outside Azerbaijan, separated from it by the Armenian Republic; **area** 5,500 sq km/2,120 sq mi; **capital** Nakhichevan; **population** (1986) 278,000; 85% are Muslim Azeris who maintain strong links with Iran to the south. Taken by Russia in 1828, it was annexed to the Azerbaijan Republic in 1924. It has been affected by the Armenia–Azerbaijan conflict; many Azeris have fled to Azerbaijan, and in Jan 1990 frontier posts and fences with Iran were destroyed and Nakhichevan declared itself independent of the USSR.

Nakuru, Lake /nə'kuəruː/ salt lake in the Great Rift Valley, Kenya.

namby-pamby /næmbi 'pæmbɪ/ *adj.* insipid, feeble, spineless. —*n.* a person of this kind. [from *Ambrose* Philips, English pastoral writer (died 1749)]

name *n.* 1. the word by which an individual person, animal, place, or thing is spoken of or to. 2. the word denoting an object of thought, especially one applicable to many individuals. 3. a reputation. 4. a person as known, famed etc. 5. a family, a clan. —*v.t.* 1. to give a name to. 2. to state the name of. 3. to mention, to specify, to cite. 4. to nominate or appoint. —**call a person names,** to address or speak of him or her abusively. **have to one's name,** to possess. **in the name of,** invoking; as representing. **in name only,** not in reality. **name-dropping** *n.* familiar mention

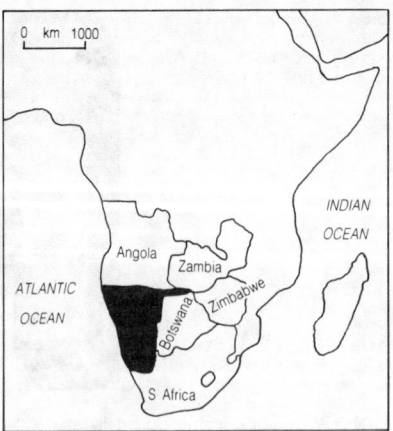

Namibia

of famous names as a form of boasting. **name-plate** *n.* a plate with a name inscribed on it, identifying the occupant etc. [Old English, related to Latin *nomen*]

nameable *adj.* that may be named.

nameless *adj.* 1. having no name or no known name. 2. left unnamed. 3. unmentionable, loathsome.

namely *adv.* that is to say, in other words, specifically.

namesake *n.* a person or thing with the same name as another.

Namib Desert /'nɑːmɪb/ coastal desert region in Namibia between the Kalahari Desert and the Atlantic Ocean. Its sand dunes are among the tallest in the world, reaching heights of 370 m/1,200 ft.

Namibia /nə'mɪbɪə/ formerly **South West Africa** (to 1968) country in SW Africa, bounded N by Angola and Zambia, E by Botswana and South Africa, and W by the Atlantic Ocean; **area** 824,300 sq km/318,262 sq mi; **capital** Windhoek; **physical** mainly desert; includes the enclave of Walvis Bay (area 1,120 sq km/432 sq mi); **head of state and government** Sam Nujoma from 1990; **political system** democratic republic; **exports** diamonds, uranium; **population** (1990 est) 1,372,000; **language** Afrikaans, German, English (all official); **recent history** administered by South Africa, under League of Nations mandate, as British South Africa 1920–1946. South Africa did not accept the termination of the mandate in 1966 by the UN and extended apartheid laws to the country. The UN redesignated it Namibia in 1968; in 1978 Security Council Resolution 435 granting full sovereignty was accepted by South Africa, then rescinded. SWAPO, formed in 1958 to seek full independence and racial equality, pursued an armed resistance campaign for independence until 1989, when a UN peacekeeping force was stationed in Namibia to oversee multi-party elections. These were won by SWAPO. In 1990 Liberal multi-party 'independence' constitution adopted and independence achieved from South Africa.

Nanak /'nɑːnək/ 1469–*c.*1539. Indian guru and founder of Sikhism, a religion based on the unity of God and the equality of all human beings. He was strongly opposed to caste divisions.

Nana Sahib /'nɑːni 'sɑːb/ popular name for Dandhu Panth 1820–*c.*1859. The adopted son of a former peshwa (chief minister) of the Mahratta people of central India, he joined the rebels in the ◊Indian Mutiny 1857–58, and was responsible for the massacre at Kanpur when safe conducts given to British civilians were broken and many women and children massacred.

Nancarrow /næn'kærəʊ/ Conlon 1912– . US composer who settled in Mexico from 1940. Using a player-piano as a form of synthesizer, punching the rolls by hand, he experimented with complicated combinations of rhythm and tempo, producing a series of studies that anticipated minimalism and brought him recognition in the 1970s.

Nanchang /næn'tʃæŋ/ industrial capital of Jiangxi province, China, about 260 km/160 mi SE of Wuhan; **population** (1986) 1,120,000; **products** textiles, glass, porcelain, soap.

nancy /'nænsɪ/ *n.* (*slang*) an effeminate or homosexual man or boy. [from *Nancy*, pet-form of woman's name *Ann*]

Nanjing /næn'dʒɪŋ/ formerly **Nanking** capital of Jiangsu province, China, 270 km/165 mi NW of Shanghai; centre of industry (engineering, shipbuilding, oil refining), commerce, and communications; population (1986) 2,250,000. The bridge of 1968 over the Chang Jiang river is the longest in China at 6,705 m/22,000 ft.

nankeen /næn'ki:n/ *n.* **1.** a yellow cotton cloth. **2.** the colour of this. [from *Nankin(g)* former name of Nanjing in China]

Nanning /næn'nɪŋ/ industrial river port, capital of Guangxi Zhuang autonomous region, China, on the river You Jiang; population (1982) 866,000. It was a supply town during the Vietnam War and the Sino-Vietnamese confrontation 1979.

nanny *n.* **1.** a child's nurse or nurse. **2.** (*colloquial*) grandma. —**nanny-goat** *n.* a female goat. [from *Nancy*, pet form of woman's name *Ann*]

nano- /nænəʊ-, neɪnəʊ-/ prefix used in SI units of measurement, equivalent to a one-billionth part (10^{-9}, one thousand millionth). For example, a nanosecond is one-billionth of a second. [from Latin from Greek *nanos* = dwarf]

Nansen /'nænsən/ Fridtjof 1861–1930. Norwegian explorer and scientist. In 1893, he sailed to the Arctic in the *Fram*, which was deliberately allowed to drift north with an iceflow. Nansen, accompanied by F Hjalmar Johansen (1867–1923), continued north on foot and reached 86° 14| | N, the highest latitude then attained. After World War I, Nansen became League of Nations high commissioner for refugees. He was awarded the Nobel Peace Prize in 1923.

Nantes, Edict of a decree by which Henry IV of France granted religious freedom to the ◊Huguenots in 1598. It was revoked in 1685 by Louis XIV.

nap[1] *n.* a short period of light sleep, especially during the day. —*v.i.* (**-pp-**) to have a nap. —**catch a person napping**, to take him or her unawares; to find him or her remiss. [Old English]

nap[2] *n.* a surface of cloth consisting of fibre-ends raised, cut even, and smoothed. [from Middle Dutch or Middle Low German]

nap[3] *n.* **1.** a card-game like whist, with bidding. **2.** a racing tip claimed to be almost a certainty. —*v.t.* (**-pp-**) to name (a horse) as an almost certain winner. —**go nap**, to make the highest bid in nap; to risk everything. [abbreviation of *Napoleon*]

napalm /'neɪpɑːm/ *n.* a fuel used in flamethrowers and incendiary bombs; jellied petrol, made from naphthalene and coconut oil. Napalm causes extensive burns because it sticks to the skin even when aflame. It was widely used by the US Army during the Vietnam War. —*v.t.* to attack with napalm bombs. [from *naph*thenic acid (in petroleum) and *palm*itic acid (in coconut oil)]

nape *n.* the back of the neck.

naphtha /'næfpθəə/ *n.* a flammable oil obtained by destructive distillation of petroleum, coal tar, and shale oil. It is raw material for the petrochemical and plastics industries. The term originally applied to naturally occurring liquid hydrocarbons. [Latin from Greek]

naphthalene /'næfpθəliːn/ *n.* a solid, white, shiny, aromatic hydrocarbon $C_{10}H_8$ obtained from coal tar. The smell of moth-balls is due to their napthalene content. Naphthalene is used in making indigo and certain azo dyes, as a mild disinfectant, and an insecticide.

Napier /'neɪpɪə/ John 1550–1617. Scottish mathematician who invented ◊logarithms in 1614 and 'Napier's bones', an early mechanical calculating device for multiplication and division.

napkin *n.* **1.** a piece of cloth or paper used at meals for wiping the lips and fingers or protecting the clothes. **2.** a nappy. [from Old French *nappe* from Latin *mappa*]

Naples /'neɪpəlz/ (Italian *Napoli*) industrial port and capital of Campania, Italy, on the Tyrrhenian Sea; **population** (1988) 1,201,000; **products** shipbuilding, cars, textiles, paper, food processing. To the S is the Isle of Capri, and behind the city is Mount Vesuvius, with the ruins of Pompeii at its foot.

Naples, Kingdom of the southern part of Italy, alternately independent and united with ◊Sicily in the Kingdom of the Two Sicilies.

Napoleon I /nə'pəʊlɪən/ Bonaparte 1769–1821. Emperor of the French 1804–14 and 1814–15. A general from

1796 in the ◊Revolutionary Wars, in 1799 he overthrew the ruling Directory (see ◊French Revolution) and made himself dictator. From 1803 he conquered most of Europe (the **Napoleonic Wars**) and installed his brothers as puppet kings (see ◊Bonaparte). After the Peninsular War and retreat from Moscow in 1812, he was forced to abdicate in 1814 and was banished to the island of Elba. In March 1815 he reassumed power but was defeated by British forces at the Battle of ◊Waterloo and exiled to the island of St Helena. His internal administrative reforms and laws are still evident in France.

Napoleon II 1811–1832. Title given by the Bonapartists to the son of Napoleon I and ◊Marie Louise; until 1814 he was known as the king of Rome and after 1818 as the duke of Reichstadt. After his father's abdication in 1814 he was taken to the Austrian court, where he spent the rest of his life.

Napoleon III 1808–1873. Emperor of the French 1852–70, known as **Louis-Napoleon**. After two attempted coups (1836 and 1840) he was jailed, then went into exile, returning for the revolution of 1848, when he became president of the Second Republic but soon turned authoritarian. In 1870 he was manoeuvred by the German chancellor Bismarck into war with Prussia (see ◊Franco-Prussian war); he was forced to surrender at Sedan, NE France, and the empire collapsed.

Napoleonic Wars /nəpəʊlɪ'nɒɪk/ 1803–15 a series of European wars conducted by Napoleon I following the ◊Revolutionary Wars, aiming for a French conquest of Europe.

nappy *n.* a piece of material wrapped round the lower part of a baby's body and between its legs to hold or absorb excreta. [abbreviation of **napkin**]

narcissism /nɑː'sɪsɪzəm/ *n.* an exaggeration of normal self-respect and self-involvement which may amount to mental disorder when it precludes relationships with other people. —**narcissistic** /-'sɪstɪk/ *adj.* [from *Narkissos* or *Narcissus*]

narcissus /nɑː'sɪsəs/ *n.* (*plural* **narcissi** /-saɪ/) a flowering bulb of the genus *Narcissus* (which includes the daffodil), especially the white-flowered *N. poeticus*.

Narcissus in Greek mythology, a beautiful youth who rejected the love of the nymph ◊Echo, and was condemned to fall in love with his own reflection in a pool. He pined away and in the place where he died a flower sprang up that was named after him.

narcolepsy *n.* a rare disorder characterized by bouts of overwhelming sleepiness and loss of muscle power. It is controlled by drugs.

narcosis /nɑː'kəʊsɪs/ *n.* an insensible state; the induction of this. [from Greek *narkoō* = benumb]

narcotic /nɑː'kɒtɪk/ *adj.* (of a substance) pain-relieving and inducing sleep, drowsiness, or stupor etc. —*n.* a

Napoleon I Napoleon Crossing the Alps *(1800) by Jacques Louis David, Charlottenburg Castle, Berlin.*

Napoleonic wars

1803	Britain renewed the war against France after an appeal from Malta against Napoleon's 1798 seizure of the island.
1805	Napoleon's planned invasion of Britain from Boulogne ended with Nelson's victory at ◊Trafalgar. Britain, Austria, Russia, and Sweden formed coalition against France. Austria defeated at Ulm; Austria and Russia at ◊Austerlitz.
1806	Prussia joined coalition. Defeated at Jena. Napoleon instituted the ◊Continental System, a blockade, to isolate Britain.
1807	Russia defeated at Eylau and Friedland, signed the peace Treaty of Tilsit with Napoleon, changed sides, agreeing to attack Sweden, but was forced to retreat.
1808	Napoleon's invasion of Portugal and installation of his relatives as puppet kings led to the ◊Peninsular War.
1809	Revived Austrian opposition to Napoleon was ended by defeat at ◊Wagram.
1812	Continental System rejected by Russia and collapsed. Napoleon invaded Russia and reached Moscow, but was defeated by the Russian resistance and by the bitter winter as he retreated through a countryside laid waste by the retreating Russians; 380,000 French soldiers died.
1813	Britain, Prussia, Russia, Austria, and Sweden formed a new coalition, which defeated Napoleon at the Battle of the Nations, Leipzig, Germany. He abdicated and was exiled to Elba.
1814	Louis XVIII became king of France, and the Congress of Vienna met to conclude peace.
1815	Napoleon returned to Paris. 16 June the British commander Wellington defeated the French Marshal Ney at Quatre Bras (SE of Brussels, Belgium), and Napoleon was finally defeated at Waterloo, S of Brussels, 18 June.

narcotic substance, drug, or influence. The chief narcotics induce dependency, and include opium, its derivatives and synthetic modifications (such as morphine and heroin); alcohols (for example paraldehyde and ethyl alcohol); and barbiturates. [from Old French or Latin from Greek]

nard *n.* spikenard; the plant (probably *Nardostachys jatamansi*) yielding this. [from Latin from Greek]

nark *v.t.* (*slang*) to annoy. —*n.* (*slang*) a police informer or spy. [from Romany *năk* = nose]

Narmada River /nɑ'mɑːdə/ river that rises in the Maikala range in Madhya Pradesh state, central India, and flows 1,245 km/778 mi WSW to the Gulf of Khambat, an inlet of the Arabian Sea. Forming the traditional boundary between Hindustan and Deccan, the Narmada is a holy river of the Hindus. India's **Narmada Valley Project** is one of the largest and most controversial river development projects in the world. Between 1990 and 2040 it is planned to build 30 major dams, 135 medium-sized dams and 3,000 smaller dams in a scheme that will involve moving 1 million of the valley's population of 20 million people.

Narodnik /nə'rɒdnɪk/ *n.* a member of a secret Russian political movement, active 1873–76 before its suppression by the tsarist authorities. Narodniks were largely university students, and their main purpose was to convert the peasantry to socialism.

narrate /nə'reɪt/ *v.t./i.* to tell (a story), to give an account of; to write or speak a narrative. —**narration** *n.*, **narrator** *n.* [from Latin *narrare*]

narrative /'nærətɪv/ *n.* a spoken or written account of connected events in order of happening. —*adj.* of or by narration. [from French from Latin]

narrow /'nærəʊ/ *adj.* 1. of small width in proportion to length, not broad. 2. with little scope or variety. 3. with little margin. 4. narrow-minded. —*n.* (usually in *plural*) the narrow part of a sound, strait, river, pass, or street. —*v.t./i.* to make or become narrower; to lessen, to contract. —**narrow boat**, a canal boat. **narrow-minded** *adj.* intolerant; rigid or restricted in one's views. **narrow seas**, the English Channel and the Irish Sea. —**narrowly** *adv.*, **narrowness** *n.* [Old English]

Narses /'nɑːsiːz/ *c.*478–*c.*573. Byzantine general. Originally a eunuch slave, he later became an official in the imperial treasury. He was joint commander with the Roman general Belisarius in Italy 538–39, and in 552 destroyed the Ostrogoths at Taginae in the Apennines.

narwhal /'nɑːwəl/ *n.* a whale (*Monodon monoceros*), found only in the Arctic Ocean. It grows to 5 m/16 ft long, has a grey and black body, a small head, and short flippers. The male has a single spirally fluted tusk which may be up to 2.7 m/9 ft long. [Dutch from Danish]

NASA /'næsə/ acronym from National Aeronautics and Space Administration, the US government agency, founded 1958, for spaceflight and aeronautical research. Its headquarters are in Washington DC and its main installation is at the ◊Kennedy Space Center.

nasal /'neɪzəl/ *adj.* 1. of the nose. 2. (of a letter or sound) pronounced with the nose passage open (e.g. *m*, *n*, *ng*). 3. (of a voice or speech) having many nasal sounds. —*n.* a nasal letter or sound. —**nasally** *adv.* [French or from Latin *nasus* = nose]

nasalize /'neɪzəlaɪz/ *v.t./i.* to speak nasally; to give a nasal sound to.

nascent /'næsənt, 'neɪ-/ *adj.* in the process of birth, incipient, not mature. —**nascence** *n.*, **nascency** *n.* [from Latin *nasci* = be born]

Naseby, Battle of /'neɪzbi/ the decisive battle of the English Civil War on 14 June 1645, when the Royalists, led by Prince Rupert, were defeated by Oliver Cromwell and General Fairfax. It is named after the nearby village of Naseby, 32 km/20 mi S of Leicester.

Nash /næʃ/ (Richard) 'Beau' 1674–1762. British dandy. As master of ceremonies at Bath from 1705, he made the town a fashionable spa resort, and introduced a polished code of manners into polite society.

Nash John 1752–1835. English architect. He laid out Regent's Park, London, and its approaches. Between 1813 and 1820 he planned Regent Street (later rebuilt), repaired and enlarged Buckingham Palace (for which he designed Marble Arch), and rebuilt Brighton Pavilion in flamboyant oriental style.

Nash Ogden 1902–1971. US poet. He published numerous volumes of humorous verse characterized by puns, light epigrams, and unorthodox rhymes.

The best way to give a party Is to leave town the night before.

Ogden Nash
You Can't Get There From Here

Nash Paul 1889–1946. English painter, an official war artist in World Wars I and II. In the 1930s he was one of a group of artists promoting avant-garde styles in the UK. Two of his most celebrated works are *Totes Meer/Dead Sea* (Tate Gallery, London) and *The Battle of Britain* (Imperial War Museum, London).

narwhal

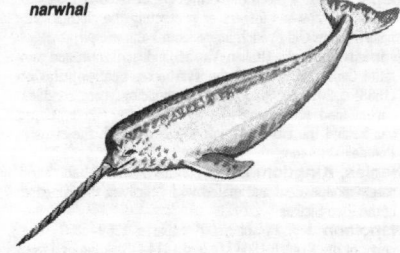

Nasser Egyptian politician and prime minister Gamal Abdel Nasser, Oct 1964.

Nash(e) Thomas 1567–1601. English poet, satirist, and anti-Puritan pamphleteer. Born in Suffolk, he settled in London about 1588, where he was rapidly drawn into the Martin Marprelate controversy (a pamphleteering attack on the clergy of the Church of England by Puritans), and wrote at least three attacks on the Martinists. Among his later works are the satirical *Pierce Pennilesse* 1592 and the religious *Christes Teares over Jerusalem* 1593; his *The Unfortunate Traveller* 1594 is a picaresque narrative mingling literary parody and mock-historical fantasy.

Nash Walter 1882–1968. New Zealand Labour politician. He was born in England, and emigrated to New Zealand 1909. He held ministerial posts 1935–49, was prime minister 1957–60, and leader of the Labour Party until 1963.

Nashville /'næʃvɪl/ port on the Cumberland river and capital of Tennessee, USA; population (1986) 931,000. It is a banking and commercial centre and has large printing, music-publishing, and recording industries.

Nassau /'næsɔː/ capital and port of the Bahamas, on New Providence island; population (1980) 135,000. English settlers founded it in 1629.

Nassau agreement a treaty signed on 18 Dec 1962 whereby the USA provided Britain with Polaris missiles, marking a strengthening in Anglo-American relations.

Nasser /'næsə/ Gamal Abdel 1918–1970. Egyptian politician, prime minister 1954–56 and from 1956 president of Egypt (the United Arab Republic 1958–71). In 1952 he was the driving power behind the Neguib coup, which ended the monarchy. His nationalization of the Suez Canal 1956 led to an Anglo-French invasion, and the ◊Suez Crisis, and his ambitions for an Egyptian-led union of Arab states led to disquiet in the Middle East (and in the West). Nasser was also an early and influential leader of the non-aligned movement.

nastic movement a plant movement caused by an external stimulus, such as light or temperature, but directionally independent of its source, unlike a ◊tropism. Nastic movements are due to changes in water pressure within specialized cells or differing rates of growth in parts of the plant. Examples include the opening and closing of crocus flowers, following an increase or decrease in temperature (**thermonasty**), and of evening-primrose (*Oenothera*) flowers on exposure to dark and light (**photonasty**).

nasturtium /nə'stɜːʃəm/ n. 1. a trailing garden plant of the Mexican and South American genus *Tropaeolum*, family Tropaeolaceae, with bright orange, yellow, or red flowers. 2. any plant of the genus *Nasturtium*, family Cruciferae,

including watercress *N. officinale*, a perennial aquatic plant of Europe and Asia, grown as a salad crop. [Latin = a kind of cress]

nasty /'nɑːstɪ/ adj. 1. unpleasant. 2. unkind, malicious. 3. difficult to deal with. —**nasty piece of work**, (*colloquial*) an unpleasant or undesirable person. —**nastily** adv., **nastiness** n.

Nat. or **nat.** abbreviation of 1. National; Nationalist. 2. Natural.

natal /'neɪtəl/ adj. of or concerning birth. [from Latin *natalis* (*nasci* = be born)]

Natal /nə'tæl/ province of South Africa, NE of Cape Province, bounded on the E by the Indian Ocean; **area** 91,785 sq km/35,429 sq mi; **capital** Pietermaritzburg; **physical** slopes from the Drakensberg to a fertile subtropical coastal plain; **population** (1985) 2,145,000; **history** called Natal ('of [Christ's] birth') because Vasco da Gama reached it Christmas Day 1497; part of the British Cape Colony from 1843 until 1856, when it was made into a separate colony. Zululand was annexed to Natal in 1897, and the districts of Vrijheid, Utrecht, and part of Wakkerstroom were transferred from the Transvaal to Natal in 1903; the colony joined the Union of South Africa in 1910.

Nataraja /nɑːtəˈrɑːdʒə/ in Hinduism, a title of ◊Siva. [Lord of the Dance]

Natchez /'nætʃɪz/ n. a member of a North American Indian people of the Mississippi area, one of the ◊Moundbuilder peoples. They had a highly developed caste system, unusual in North America, headed by a ruler priest (the 'Great Sun'). Members of the highest caste always married members of the lowest caste. The system lasted until the French colonized the area. Only a few Natchez now survive in Oklahoma. Their Muskogean language is extinct.

nation /'neɪʃən/ n. a community of people of mainly common descent, language, history, or political institutions and usually sharing one territory and government. —**nationwide** adj. extending over the whole nation. [from Old French from Latin *natio* (*nasci* = be born)]

national /'næʃənəl/ adj. of a nation; affecting or concerning a whole nation. —n. a citizen or subject of a specified country; one's fellow countryman. —**the National**, the ◊Grand National, a UK horse race. **national anthem**, a song of patriotism or loyalty adopted by a nation. **national grid**, a network of high-voltage electric power-lines between major power-stations; a metric system of geographical co-ordinates used in maps of the British Isles. **national park**, an area of countryside under state supervision to preserve it for public enjoyment. —**nationally** adv.

national accounts the organization of a country's finances. In the UK the economy is divided into the **public sector** (central government, local authorities, and public corporations), the **private sector** (the personal and company sector), and the **overseas sector** (transactions between residents and non-residents of the UK).

national assistance in the UK, the term used 1948–66 for a weekly allowance paid by the state to ensure a minimum income.

National Association for the Advancement of Colored People (NAACP) a US civil-rights organization, dedicated to ending inequality and segregation for African-Americans through nonviolent protest. It was founded in 1910 and its first aim was to eradicate lynching. The NAACP campaigned to end segregation in state schools; it funded test cases that eventually led to the Supreme Court decision of 1954 outlawing school segregation, although it was only through the ◊civil rights movement of the 1960s that desegregation was achieved. In 1987 the NAACP had about 500,000 members, black and white.

National Country Party former name for the Australian ◊National Party.

National Curriculum a scheme set up by the UK government in 1987 to establish a single course of study in ten subjects common to all primary and secondary state schools. The national curriculum is divided into three core subjects, English, maths, and science, and seven foundation subjects, geography, history, technology, a foreign language (for secondary-school pupils), art, music, and physical education. There are four key stages, on completion of which the pupil's work is assessed. The stages are for ages 5–7, 7–11, 11–14, and 14–16.

national debt the debt incurred by the central government of a country to its own people and institutions and to overseas creditors. As an alternative to raising taxes to finance its activities or support an ailing currency, a government can borrow from the public by means of selling interest-bearing bonds, for example, or from abroad. On 31 Mar 1988 the UK national debt was £197,295 million, or £3,465 per head of population.

National Dock Labour Scheme in the UK, a scheme that guaranteed continued employment and pay for dock workers, even if there was no work to be done; some 9,000 dockers were registered under the scheme, which operated from 1947 until its abolition by the Thatcher government in 1989.

National Economic Development Council (NEDC) known as **Neddy**, the UK forum for economic consultation between government, management, and trade unions, established in 1962. It examines the country's economic and industrial performance, in both the public and private sectors, and seeks agreement on ways to improve efficiency. Its role diminished during the 1980s.

National Endowment for Democracy (NED) a US political agency founded in 1983 with government backing. It has funded a range of political organizations abroad. Since 1984 more than 95% of its $114 million annual income has come from the US government.

National Front in the UK, an extreme right-wing political party founded in 1967. It was formed from a merger of the League of Empire Loyalists and the British National Party. Some of its members had links with the National Socialist Movement of the 1960s (see ◊Nazism).

National Government (1931) in British politics, a government of Labour, Liberal and Conservative MPs formed in 1931, consequent upon a rapidly declining financial situation which had led to a split in the Labour government. The Labour leader, Ramsay Macdonald, was prime minister of the National Government but the majority of his own party refused to support him. Thus the National Government was mainly Conservative, and Macdonald (who resigned in 1935) was succeeded as prime minister by the Conservative leader Stanley ◊Baldwin.

National Guard a ◊militia force recruited by each state of the USA. The volunteer National Guard units are under federal orders in emergencies, and under the control of the governor in peacetime, and are now an integral part of the US Army. The National Guard has been used against demonstrators; in May 1970 at Kent State University, Ohio, they killed four students who were protesting against the bombing of Cambodia by the USA.

National Health Service (NHS) the UK government medical scheme; see ◊health service.

national income the total income of a state in one year, comprising both the wages of individuals and the profits of companies. It is equal to the value of the output of all goods and services during the same period. National income is equal to gross national product (the value of a country's total output) minus an allowance for replacement of ageing capital stock.

national insurance in the UK, a state social security scheme which provides child allowances, maternity benefits, and payments to the unemployed, sick, and retired, and also covers medical treatment. It is paid for by weekly contributions from employees and employers.

National Insurance Act the 1911 UK act of Parliament, introduced by Lloyd George, Liberal chancellor, which first provided insurance for workers against ill health and unemployment.

nationalism *n.* 1. patriotic feeling, principles, or efforts. 1. in music, a 19th-century movement in which composers (such as Smetana and Grieg) included the folk material of their country in their works, projecting the national spirit and its expression. 3. a policy of national independence that aims to unify a nation, create a state, or liberate it from foreign rule. Nationalist movements became a potent factor in European politics during the 19th century; since 1900 nationalism has become a strong force in Asia and Africa and in the late 1980s revived strongly in E Europe. —**nationalist** *n.*

nationality /ˌnæʃəˈnælɪtɪ/ *n.* 1. the status of belonging to a particular nation. 2. distinctive national quality, being

national. 3. an ethnic group forming part of one or more political nations.

nationalize /ˈnæʃənəlaɪz/ *v.t.* to make national; to convert (an industry, institution etc.) to public ownership. —**nationalization** /-ˈzeɪʃən/ *n.* In recent years the trend towards nationalization has slowed and in many countries (the UK, France, and Japan) reversed (see ◊privatization). Assets in the hands of foreign governments or companies may also be nationalized; for example, Iran's oil industry (see ◊Abadan), the ◊Suez Canal, and US-owned fruit plantations in Guatemala were all nationalized in the 1950s.

National Liberal Foundation the central organization of the British ◊Liberal Party, established in 1877 in Birmingham. The first president was Joseph Chamberlain.

National Party, Australian an Australian political party representing the interests of the farmers and people of the smaller towns. It developed from about 1860 as the **National Country Party**, and holds the balance of power between Liberals and Labor. It gained strength following the introduction of proportional representation in 1918, and has been in coalition with the Liberals since 1949.

National Portrait Gallery a London art gallery containing the national collection of portraits of distinguished British men and women. It was founded in 1856.

National Rivers Authority the UK environmental agency responsible for managing water resources, investigating pollution controls, and taking over flood controls and land drainage from the former ten regional water authorities of England and Wales; it was launched in 1989.

national security directive in the USA, a secret decree issued by the president which can establish national policy and commit federal funds without the knowledge of Congress, under the National Security Act 1947. The National Security Council alone decides whether these directives may be made public; most are not. The directives have been criticized as unconstitutional, since they enable the executive branch of government to make laws.

national service conscription into the armed services in peacetime.

National Socialism official name for the ◊Nazi movement in Germany; see also ◊fascism.

National Sound Archive a department of the British Library. It has over 750,000 discs and over 40,000 hours of tapes, ranging from birdsong to grand opera.

National Theatre the Royal National Theatre of Great Britain, established in 1963, and the complex, opened in 1976, that houses it on London's South Bank. The national theatre of France is the ◊Comédie Française, founded in 1680.

National Trust a British trust founded in 1895 for the preservation of land and buildings of historic interest or beauty, incorporated by act of Parliament in 1907. It is the largest private landowner in Britain. The National Trust for Scotland was established in 1931.

native /ˈneɪtɪv/ *adj.* 1. inborn, innate, natural. 2. of one's birth; belonging to one by right of birth. 3. born in a particular place, indigenous; of the natives of a place. 4. (of metal etc.) found in a pure or uncombined state. Copper and silver can be found as native metals. Examples of native nonmetals are carbon and sulphur. —*n.* 1. one born in a particular place. 2. a local inhabitant. 3. a member of an indigenous people, especially non-European. 4. an indigenous animal or plant. [from Old French or Latin *nativus* (*nasci* = be born)]

nativity *n.* a birth; a Christian festival celebrating a birth: the nativity, or **Christmas** has been celebrated on 25 Dec since AD 336 in memory of the birth of Jesus in Bethlehem; the **Nativity of the Virgin Mary** is celebrated on 8 Sept by the Catholic and Eastern Orthodox churches; the **Nativity of John the Baptist** is celebrated on 24 June by the Catholic, Eastern Orthodox, and Anglican churches.

nativity /nəˈtɪvɪtɪ/ *n.* birth; a Christian festival celebrating a birth: **Christmas** is celebrated on 25 Dec from AD 336 in memory of the birth of Jesus in Bethlehem; **Nativity of the Virgin Mary** is celebrated on 8 Sept by the Catholic and Eastern Orthodox churches; **Nativity of John the Baptist** is celebrated on 24 June by the Catholic, Eastern Orthodox, and Anglican churches.

NATO /ˈneɪtəʊ/ or **Nato** acronym from ◊North Atlantic Treaty Organization.

Natron, Lake /'neɪtrən/ salt and soda lake in the Great Rift Valley, Tanzania; length 56 km/35 mi, width 24 km/15 mi.

natter *v. i.* (*colloquial*) to chat, to chatter idly. —*n.* (*colloquial*) a chat, idle chatter. [originally Scottish, imitative]

natterjack /'nætədʒæk/ *n.* a kind of small toad (*Bufo calamita*), with a yellow stripe down its back, which runs instead of hopping.

natty *adj.* neat and trim, dapper. —**nattily** *adv.*

natural /'nætʃərəl/ *adj.* 1. of, existing in, or produced by nature. 2. conforming to the ordinary course of nature, normal. 3. suited to be such by nature. 4. not affected in manner etc. 5. not surprising, to be expected. 6. (of a child) illegitimate. 7. in music, a note that is neither a sharp nor a flat. A natural trumpet or horn is an instrument without valves. —*n.* 1. a person or thing that seems naturally suited (for a role, purpose etc.). 2. in music, a natural note; a sign denoting this. 3. pale fawn colour. **natural history,** the study of animal and vegetable life. **natural law,** a correct statement of the invariable sequence between specified conditions and a specified phenomenon. **natural number,** any whole number greater than 0. **natural religion,** religion based on reason without accepting revelation (◊deism). **natural science,** science dealing with natural or material phenomena. **natural theology,** knowledge of God gained by reason and without the aid of revelation. —**naturalness** *n.* [from Old French from Latin]

Natural Environment Research Council (NERC) a UK organization established by royal charter in 1965 to undertake and support research in the earth sciences, to give advice both on exploiting natural resources and on protecting the environment, and to support education and training of scientists in these fields of study. Research areas include geothermal energy, industrial pollution, waste disposal, satellite surveying, acid rain, biotechnology, atmospheric circulation, and climate. Research is carried out principally within the UK but also in Antarctica and in many countries outside Europe. It comprises 13 research bodies.

natural frequency the frequency at which a mechanical system will vibrate freely. A pendulum, for example, always oscillates at the same frequency when set in motion. This natural frequency depends upon the weight and tension of the cord or rod suspending it.

natural gas mixture of flammable gases found in the Earth's crust (often in association with petroleum), now one of the world's three main fossil fuels (with coal and oil). Natural gas is a mixture of ◊hydrocarbons, chiefly methane, with ethane, butane, and propane.

naturalism /'nætʃərəlɪzəm/ *n.* 1. a realistic method or adherence to nature in literature and art. 2. action based on natural instincts. 3. a theory of the world, and of the relationship to it of human beings, in which only the operation of natural laws and forces (as opposed to to supernatural or spiritual ones) is assumed; the theory that moral concepts can be explained wholly in terms of concepts applicable to natural phenomena. —**naturalistic** /-'lɪstɪk/ *adj.*

naturalist *n.* 1. an expert in natural history. 2. an adherent of naturalism.

naturalize *v. t.* 1. to admit (an alien) to citizenship. 2. to introduce and acclimatize (an animal or plant) into a country where it is not native. 3. to adopt (a foreign word or custom). 4. to cause to appear natural. —**naturalization** /-'zeɪʃən/ *n.*

natural logarithm in mathematics, the exponent of a number expressed to base *e*, where *e* represents the ◊irrational number 2.71828.... .

naturally *adv.* 1. in a natural manner. 2. of course, as might be expected.

natural radioactivity radioactivity generated by those radioactive elements that exist in the Earth's crust. All the elements from polonium (atomic number 84) to uranium (atomic number 92) are radioactive. Radioisotopes of some lighter elements are also found in nature (for example potassium-40).

natural selection the process whereby gene frequencies in a population change as a result of certain individuals producing more descendants than others, because they are better able to reproduce. The accumulated effect of natural selection is to produce ◊adaptations such as the insulating coat of a polar bear or the spadelike forelimbs of a mole. It was recognized by Charles Darwin and Alfred Russel Wallace as the main process driving ◊evolution.

nature /'neɪtʃə/ *n.* 1. the phenomena of the physical world as a whole, the physical power causing these; especially the living world, including plants, animals, fungi, and all microorganisms, and naturally formed features of the landscape, such as mountains and rivers; **Nature,** these personified. 2. a thing's essential qualities; a person's or animal's innate character. 3. a kind or class. 4. vital force, functions, or needs. —**by nature,** innately. **by or in the nature of things,** inevitable, inevitably. **call of nature,** the need to urinate or defecate. **in a state of nature,** in an uncivilized or uncultivated state; totally naked. **nature trail,** a path through the countryside planned to show interesting natural objects. —**natured** *adj.* (*good-natured*). [from Old French from Latin *natura* (*nasci nat-* = be born)]

Nature Conservancy Council (NCC) a UK government agency established by Act of Parliament in 1973 (Nature Conservancy created by royal charter 1949). It is responsible for designating and managing national nature reserves and other conservation areas, advising government ministers on policies, providing advice and information, and commissioning or undertaking relevant scientific research. A Bill before Parliament in 1991 called for its division into three separate bodies with responsibility for England, Scotland and Wales respectively.

nature–nurture controversy or **environment–heredity controversy** a long-standing dispute among philosophers and psychologists over the relative importance of environment, that is, upbringing, experience and learning ('nurture'), and heredity, that is, genetic inheritance ('nature') in determining the make-up of an organism, as related to human personality and intelligence.

nature reserve (*US* preserve) an area set aside to protect a habitat and the wildlife living within it, with only restricted admission for the public. A nature reserve often provides a sanctuary for rare species. The world's largest is Etosha Reserve, Namibia; area 99,520 sq km/38,415 sq mi.

naturist *n.* a nudist. —**naturism** *n.*

naught /nɔːt/ *n.* (*archaic*) nothing, nought. —*predic. adj.* (*archaic*) worthless, useless. —**come to naught,** not to succeed; to come to nothing. **set at naught,** to despise. [Old English *none* and *wight* = thing, creature]

naughty /'nɔːtɪ/ *adj.* 1. badly behaved, disobedient. 2. mildly indecent. —**naughtily** *adv.*, **naughtiness** *n.*

Naukratis /'nɔːkrətɪs/ city of Greek traders in ancient Egypt, in the Nile delta, rediscovered by the British archaeologist Flinders ◊Petrie 1884.

Nauru /nau'ruː/ Republic of; island country in the SW Pacific, in ◊Polynesia, W of Kiribati; **area** 21 sq km/8 sq mi; **seat of government** Yaren District; **physical** tropical island country in W Pacific; plateau circled by coral cliffs and sandy beaches; **head of state and government** Hammer DeRoburt from 1987; **political system** liberal democracy; **exports** phosphates; **population** (1990 est) 8,100; **language** Nauruan (official), English; **recent history** administered by Australia, New Zealand, and UK from 1920 until independence, except 1942–45, when it was occupied by Japan. In 1968 independence achieved from Australia, New Zealand, and Britain with 'special member' Commonwealth status.

nausea /'nɔːzɪə/ *n.* 1. inclination to vomit (originally = seasickness). 2. loathing. —**nauseous** *adj.* [Latin from Greek *naus* = ship]

nauseate /'nɔːzɪeɪt/ *v. t./i.* 1. to affect with nausea, to disgust. 2. to loathe. 3. to feel nausea.

nautch /nɔːtʃ/ *n.* a performance of traditional Indian female dancers. [from Urdu from Sanskrit]

nautical /'nɔːtɪkəl/ *adj.* of sailors or navigation. —**nautical mile,** a unit of distance used in navigation. In the UK it was formerly defined as 6,082 ft; the international nautical mile is now defined as 1,852 m. —**nautically** *adv.* [from French or Latin from Greek *nautikos* (*nautēs* = sailor)]

nautilus /'nɔːtɪləs/ *n.* (*plural* **nautiluses**, **nautili** /-laɪ/) a mollusc of the genus *Nautilus*, with a spiral shell divided into compartments. The nautilus is a ◊cephalopod many short, grasping tentacles surrounding a sharp beak, found in the Indian and Pacific oceans. The pearly nautilus (*N. Pompilius*) has a shell about 20 cm/8 in in diameter. [Latin from Greek]

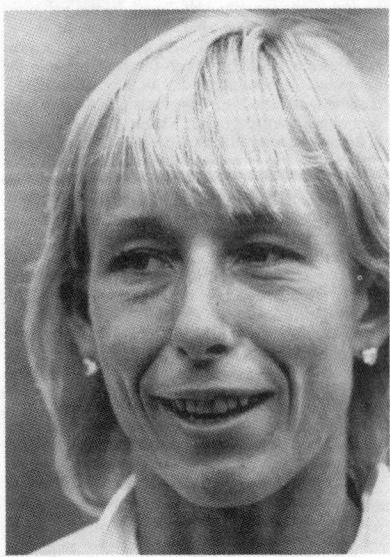

Navratilova *Martina Navratilova reached the zenith of her career in women's tennis in 1987, by winning her sixth successive Wimbledon singles title, and equalling the record held by Helen Wills Moody.*

Navajo /'nævəhəu/ or **Navaho** (*plural* **Navajos**) a member of a peaceable agricultural North American Indian people, related to the ◊Apache; population about 200,000. They were attacked by Kit ◊Carson and US troops in 1864 and were rounded up and exiled. Their reservation, created in 1868, is the largest in the USA (65,000 sq km/ 25,000 sq mi), and is mainly in NE Arizona but extends into NW New Mexico and SE Utah. Many Navajo now herd sheep and earn an income from crafts and tourism. Like the Apache, they speak an Athabaskan language. —*adj.* of or concerning the Navajo.

naval /'neɪvəl/ *adj.* of the or a navy; of ships. [from Latin *navis* = ship]

Navarino, Battle of /nævə'riːnəu/ a decisive naval action on 20 Oct 1827 off Pylos in the Greek war of liberation, which was won by the combined fleets of the English, French, and Russians under Vice-Admiral Edward Codrington (1770–1851) over the Turkish and Egyptian fleets. Navarino is the Italian and historic name of Pylos Bay, Greece, on the SW coast of the Peloponnese.

Navarre /nə'vaː/ (Spanish *Navarra*) autonomous mountain region of N Spain; **area** 10,400 sq km/4,014 sq mi; **capital** Pamplona; **population** (1986) 513,000; **history** part of the medieval kingdom of ◊Navarre. Estella, to the SW, where Don Carlos was proclaimed king 1833, was a centre of agitation by the ◊Carlists.

Navarre, Kingdom of /nə'vaː/ a former kingdom comprising the Spanish province of Navarre and part of what is now the French *département* of Basses-Pyrénées. It resisted the conquest of the ◊Moors and was independent until it became French in 1284 on the marriage of Philip IV to the heiress of Navarre. In 1479 Ferdinand of Aragon annexed Spanish Navarre; French Navarre went to Catherine of Foix (1483–1512), who kept the royal title. Her grandson became Henry IV of France, and Navarre was absorbed in the French crown lands in 1620.

nave[1] *n.* in architecture the body of a church (apart from the choir or chancel, aisles, and transepts). [French from Latin *navis* = ship]

nave[2] *n.* the hub of a wheel. [Old English]

navel /'neɪvəl/ *n.* 1. the hollow in the belly left by the detachment of the umbilical cord. 2. the central point of anything. —**navel orange**, an orange with a navel-like formation on the top. [Old English]

navigable /'nævɪgəbəl/ *adj.* 1. (of a river etc.) suitable for ships to sail in. 2. (of a ship etc.) seaworthy. 3. (of a balloon) steerable. —**navigability** /-'bɪlɪtɪ/ *n.*, **navigably** *adv.* [French or from Latin]

navigate /'nævɪgeɪt/ *v.t./i.* 1. to sail in or through (a sea or river etc.). 2. to direct the course of (a ship, aircraft, or vehicle etc.). —**navigator** *n.* [from Latin *navigare* (*navis* = ship and *agere* = drive)]

navigation /nævi'geɪʃən/ *n.* navigating; methods of determining the position and course of a ship or an aircraft by geometry and astronomy or radio signals. Traditional methods include the magnetic ◊compass and the ◊sextant. In **satellite navigation** time and position signals are broadcast by satellites. —**navigation, biological**, the ability of animals or insects to navigate, following established routes or known landmarks, or navigating without such aids; for example, birds fly several thousand miles back to their nest site, over unknown terrain. Such feats may be based on compass information derived from the position of the Sun, Moon, or stars, or on the characteristic patterns of the Earth's magnetic field. —**navigational** *adj.*

Navigation Acts in British history, acts of Parliament passed from 1381 to protect English shipping from foreign competition and to ensure monopoly trading between Britain and its colonies. The last was repealed in 1849. They helped to establish England as a major sea power, but led to higher prices. They ruined the Dutch merchant fleet in the 17th century, and were among the causes of the ◊American Revolution.

Navratilova /nævræti'ləuvə/ Martina 1956– . Czechoslovak tennis player, a naturalized US citizen from 1981. The most outstanding woman player of the 1980s, she has 52 Grand Slam victories, including 18 singles titles. She has won the Wimbledon singles title nine times, including six in succession 1982–87.

navvy /'nævɪ/ *n.* a labourer employed in excavating for roads, railways, canals etc. —*v.i.* to work as a navvy. [abbreviation of *navigator*]

navy /'neɪvɪ/ *n.* 1. a state's ◊warships with their crews and organization. 2. the officers and non-commissioned members of the navy. 3. (*poetic*) a fleet. —**navy (blue)**, dark blue as of naval uniforms. [from Old French *navie* from Latin]

nawab /nə'waːb/ *n.* 1. the title of a distinguished Muslim in Pakistan. 2. (*historical*) the title of a governor or nobleman in India. [from Urdu from Arabic = deputy]

Naxalite /'næksəlaɪt/ a member of an Indian extremist communist movement named after the town of Naxalbari, W Bengal, where a peasant uprising was suppressed in 1967. The movement was founded by Charu Mazumdar (1915–1972).

nay *adv.* 1. (*archaic*) no. 2. or rather, and even, and more than that. —*n.* the word 'nay'. —**say nay**, to refuse, to contradict. [from Old Norse *ne* = not]

Nazarene /næzə'riːn, 'næ-/ *adj.* of Nazareth or the Nazarenes. —*n.* 1. a person of Nazareth, especially Jesus. 2. (in Jewish or Muslim use) a Christian. [from Latin from Greek *Nazaret* = Nazareth]

Nazareth /'næzərəθ/ town in Galilee, N Israel, SE of Haifa; population (1981) 64,000. According to the New Testament, it was the boyhood home of Jesus.

Nazarite /'næzəraɪt/ *n.* (more correctly **Nazirite**) any of the Israelites specially consecrated to the service of God who were under vows to abstain from wine, let their hair grow, and avoid the defilement of contact with a dead body. [from Latin from Hebrew *nazar* = consecrate oneself]

Nazi /'naːtsɪ/ *n.* a member of the Nazi Party; a person of similar ideology. —*adj.* of this party. —**Nazism** *n.* [representing pronunciation of *Nati* in German *Nationalsozialist*]

Nazism /'naːtsɪzəm/ *n.* an ideology based on racism, nationalism, and the supremacy of the state over the individual. The German Nazi party, the *Nationalsozialistiche Deutsche Arbeiterpartei* (National Socialist German Workers' Party), was formed from the German Workers' Party (founded in 1919) and led by Adolph ◊Hitler 1921–45.

Nazi-Soviet pact a non-aggression treaty signed by Germany and the USSR on 23 Aug 1939. Under the terms of the treaty both countries agreed to remain neutral and to refrain from acts of aggression against each other if either went to war. Secret clauses allowed for the partition of Poland – Hitler was to acquire W Poland, Stalin the E part. On 1 Sept 1939 Hitler invaded Poland. The Pact ended when Hitler invaded Russia on 22 June 1941. See also ◊World War II.

NB abbreviation of note well. [from Latin *nota bene*]

Nb symbol for niobium.

NCO abbreviation of non-commissioned officer.

Nd symbol for neodymium.

n.d. abbreviation of no date.

N'djamena /əndʒəˈmeɪnə/ capital of Chad, at the confluence of the Chari and Logone rivers, on the Cameroon border; population (1985) 511,700.

Ndola /ənˈdəʊlə/ mining centre and chief city of the Copperbelt province of central Zambia; population (1987) 418,000.

NE abbreviation of northeast, northeastern.

Ne symbol for neon.

Neagh, Lough /neɪ/ lake in Northern Ireland, 25 km/15 mi W of Belfast; area 396 sq km/153 sq mi. It is the largest lake in the British Isles.

Neanderthal /niˈændətɑːl/ *n.* a hominid of the Mid-Late Palaeolithic, named from a skeleton found in the Neander Thal (valley) near Düsseldorf, Germany, in 1856. *Homo sapiens neanderthalensis* lived from about 100,000 to 40,000 years ago and was similar in build to people today, but slightly smaller, stockier, and heavier-featured, with a strong jaw and prominent brow ridges on a sloping forehead.

neap *n.* (in full **neap tide**) the tide at times of the month when there is least difference between high and low water. [Old English *nēpflōd*]

Neapolitan /niəˈpɒlɪtən/ *adj.* of Naples. —*n.* a native of Naples. [from Latin *Neapolis* = Naples, from Greek]

near *adv.* 1. to, at, or within a short distance in space or time. 2. closely, nearly. —*prep.* 1. near to in space, time, condition, or semblance. 2. in combinations, resembling, intended as a substitute for (*near-silk*), that is almost (*near-hysterical*). —*adj.* 1. with only a short distance or interval between. 2. closely related. 3. (of part of a vehicle, horse, or road) nearer to the side of the road when facing forward, usually left. 4. with little margin. 5. niggardly. —*v.t./i.* to draw near (to), to approach. —**near by**, not far off. **Near East**, the region comprising the countries of the eastern Mediterranean, sometimes also including those of the Balkan peninsula, SW Asia, or north Africa. **near miss**, something that misses its objective only narrowly; a narrowly avoided collision. **near-sighted** *adj.* short-sighted. **near thing**, a narrow escape. —**nearness** *n.* [from Old Norse, originally = *nigher*]

nearby *adj.* close in position.

nearly *adv.* 1. almost. 2. closely. —**not nearly**, nothing like, far from.

neat *adj.* 1. simple, clean, and orderly in appearance. 2. done or doing things in a precise and skilful way. 3. (of alcoholic drink) undiluted. —**neatly** *adv.*, **neatness** *n.* [from French]

neaten *v.t.* to make neat.

neath *prep.* (*poetic*) beneath.

Nebraska /nəˈbræskə/ plains state of the central USA; nickname Cornhusker State; **area** 200,400 sq km/77,354 sq mi; **capital** Lincoln; **population** (1987) 1,594,000; **history** ceded to Spain by France in 1763, retroceded to France in 1801, and part of the ◊Louisiana Purchase in 1803. It was first settled in 1847, became a territory in 1854, and a state in 1867.

Nebuchadnezzar /nebjʊkədˈnezə/ or **Nebuchadrezzar** II king of Babylonia from 60 BC. Shortly before his accession he defeated the Egyptians at Carchemish and brought Palestine and Syria into his empire. Judah revolted, with Egyptian assistance, in 596 and 587–586 BC; on both occasions he captured Jerusalem and took many Hebrews into captivity. He largely rebuilt Babylon and constructed the hanging gardens.

nebula /ˈnebjʊlə/ *n.* (*plural* **nebulae** /-iː/) a cloud of gas and dust in space. An **emission nebula**, such as the ◊Orion nebula, glows brightly because its gas is energized by stars that have formed within it. In a **reflection nebula**, like the one surrounding the ◊Pleiades cluster, starlight reflects off grains of dust in the nebula. A **dark nebula** is a dense cloud, composed of molecular hydrogen, which partially or completely absorbs light behind it. Examples include the Coalsack nebula in ◊Crux and the Horsehead nebula in Orion. Some nebulae are produced

by gas thrown off from dying stars (see ◊planetary nebula; ◊supernova). [Latin = mist]

nebular /ˈnebjʊlə/ *adj.* of a nebula or nebulae. —**nebular theory** or **hypothesis**, the theory that the solar and stellar systems were developed from nebulae.

nebulous /ˈnebjʊləs/ *adj.* cloudlike, indistinct, having no definite form.

necessary /ˈnesəsərɪ/ *adj.* 1. indispensable, required in order to achieve something. 2. inevitable, determined by natural laws or predestination and not by free will. —*n.* (usually *plural*) a thing without which life cannot be maintained or is unduly harsh. —**the necessary**, (*slang*) the money or action needed for a purpose. —**necessarily** *adv.* [from Old French from Latin *necessarius* (*necesse* = needful)]

necessitarianism /nɪsesɪˈteərɪənɪzəm/ *n.* the denial of free will and the belief that all action is determined by causes. —**necessitarian** *adj.* & *n.*

necessitate /nɪˈsesɪteɪt/ *v.t.* to make necessary, to involve as a condition, accompaniment, or result.

necessitous /nɪˈsesɪtəs/ *adj.* needy.

necessity /nɪˈsesɪtɪ/ *n.* 1. constraint or compulsion regarded as a law governing all human action. 2. the constraining power of circumstances. 3. an imperative need. 4. an indispensable thing. 5. poverty, hardship. —**of necessity**, unavoidably.

neck *n.* 1. the narrow part of the body connecting the head with the shoulders. In the back of the neck are the upper seven vertebrae and the many powerful muscles that support and move the head. In the front are the pharynx and trachea, and behind these is the oesophagus. The large arteries (carotid, temporal, maxillary) and veins (jugular) that supply the brain and head are also located in the neck. 2. a narrow part, piece, or channel; the lower part of a capital, above the astragal terminating the shaft of a column. 3. the part of a garment around the neck. 4. the length of a horse's head and neck as a measure of its lead in a race. 5. the flesh of an animal's neck as food. 6. (*slang*) impudence. —*v.i.* (*slang*) to kiss and caress amorously. —**get it in the neck**, (*colloquial*) to suffer a heavy blow, to be severely reprimanded or punished. **neck and neck**, running level in a race. **risk** (*or* **save**) **one's neck**, to risk (*or* save) one's own life. **up to one's neck**, (*colloquial*) very deeply involved; very busy. [Old English]

neckband *n.* a strip of material round the neck of a garment.

neckerchief /ˈnekətʃɪf/ *n.* a square of cloth worn round the neck. [from *kerchief*]

necklace /ˈneklɪs/ *n.* an ornament of beads, precious stones etc., worn round the neck.

necklet /ˈneklɪt/ *n.* an ornament or fur garment for the neck.

neckline *n.* the outline of a garment-opening at the neck.

necktie *n.* a band of material tied round a shirt-collar.

necro- /nekrəʊ-/ in combinations, corpse. [from Greek *nekros* = corpse]

necromancy /ˈnekrəʊmænsɪ/ *n.* dealings with the dead as a means of divination; magic. —**necromancer** *n.* [from Old French from Latin from Greek *mantis* = seer]

necrophilia /nekrəʊˈfɪlɪə/ *n.* abnormal (especially erotic) attraction to corpses. [Greek *-philia* = loving]

necropolis /neˈkrɒpəlɪs/ *n.* a cemetery, especially an ancient one. [Greek *polis* = city]

necrosis /neˈkrəʊsɪs/ *n.* (*plural* **necroses** /-siːz/) the death of a piece of bone or body tissue, usually due to bacterial poisoning or loss of blood supply. —**necrotic** /-ˈkrɒtɪk/ *adj.* [from Greek *nekroō* = kill]

nectar /ˈnektə/ *n.* 1. a sweet fluid secreted by some plants from a nectary, a specialized gland usually situated near the base of the flower. In many plants it accumulates in pouches or spurs, not always in the same location as the nectary. Nectar attracts insects, birds, bats, and other animals to flowers for ◊pollination and is the raw material used by bees in the production of honey. 2. (*Greek and Roman mythology*) the drink of the gods. 3. any delicious drink. —**nectarous** *adj.* [from Latin from Greek]

nectarine /ˈnektərɪn, -iːn/ *n.* a smooth, shiny-skinned variety of ◊peach, usually smaller than other peaches and with firmer flesh. It arose from a natural mutation.

nectary /ˈnektərɪ/ *n.* a plant's nectar-secreting organ.

NEDC (*colloquial* **Neddy**) abbreviation of ◊National Economic Development Council.

neddy *n.* (*colloquial*) a donkey. [pet-form of man's name *Edward*]

née /neɪ/ *adj.* born (used followed by a surname to indicate the name of a woman before marriage: *Anne Hall, née Browne*). [French, feminine past participle of *naître* = be born]

need *n.* **1.** circumstances requiring some course of action. **2.** a requirement or want. **3.** a time of difficulty or crisis. **4.** destitution or poverty. —*v.t./i.* (in negative interrogative *to* can be omitted, and *third person singular present* is **need**) **1.** to be in need of, to require. **2.** to be under a necessity or obligation. —**have need of,** to require. **need not have done,** did not need to do (but did). [Old English]

needful *adj.* necessary. —**the needful,** (*slang*) money or action needed for a purpose. —**needfully** *adv.*

Needham /'niːdəm/ Joseph 1900– . British biochemist and sinologist known for his work on the history of Chinese science. He worked first as a biochemist concentrating mainly on problems in embryology. In the 1930s he learnt Chinese and began to collect material. The first volume of his *Science and Civilization in China* was published in 1954 and by 1989 15 volumes had appeared.

needle *n.* **1.** a long slender piece of polished steel pointed at one end and with an eye for thread at the other, used in sewing. **2.** a similar larger instrument of bone or plastic etc., without an eye, used in knitting or crocheting etc. **3.** a piece of metal etc., transmitting the vibrations from a revolving gramophone record, a stylus. **4.** the pointer of a compass or other instrument. **5.** the pointed end of a hypodermic syringe. **6.** the slender pointed leaf of a fir or pine. **7.** a sharp rock or peak. **8.** an obelisk. —*v.t.* (*colloquial*) to annoy or provoke. —**needle game** or **match,** a game or match closely contested or arousing exceptional personal feeling. **needle-point** *n.* embroidery on canvas; lace made with needles, not bobbins. [Old English]

needlecord *n.* a finely ribbed corduroy fabric.

needlefish *n.* a long thin-bodied fish of the ◊garfish type with needle teeth.

needless *adj.* unnecessary, uncalled for. —**needlessly** *adv.*

needlewoman *n.* (*plural* **needlewomen**) a seamstress; a woman or girl who sews.

needlework *n.* sewing or embroidery.

needn't (*colloquial*) need not.

needs *adv.* (*archaic*) of necessity (especially in **must needs** or **needs must**).

needy *adj.* lacking the necessaries of life, extremely poor. —**neediness** *n.*

ne'er /neə/ (*poetic*) never. [contraction]

ne'er-do-well a good-for-nothing person. —*adj.* good-for-nothing.

nefarious /nɪ'feəriəs/ *adj.* wicked. —**nefariously** *adv.* [from Latin *nefarius* (*nefas* = wrong)]

Nefertiti /nefə'tiːtiː/ or **Nofretète** queen of Egypt, who ruled *c.*1372–1350 BC; wife of the pharoah ◊Ikhnaton.

neg. abbreviation of negative.

negate /nɪ'geɪt/ *v.t.* to nullify; to imply or involve the non-existence of. —**negation** *n.* [from Latin *negare* = deny]

negative /'negətɪv/ *adj.* **1.** expressing or implying denial, prohibition, or refusal. **2.** not positive, lacking positive attributes; marked by an absence of qualities. **3.** (of a quantity in algebra) less than zero; to be subtracted from others or from zero. **4.** in the direction opposite that regarded as positive. **5.** of or containing or producing the kind of electrical charge carried by electrons. **6.** (of a photograph) having the lights and shades of the objects or scene reversed, or the colours replaced by complementary ones. —*n.* **1.** a negative statement or word. **2.** a developed photographic film etc. bearing a negative image from which positive pictures are obtained (see Fox ◊Talbot). —*v.t.* **1.** to veto; to refuse consent to. **2.** to serve to disprove. **3.** to contradict (a statement). **4.** to neutralize (an effect). —**in the negative,** with a refusal; with a negative statement or reply. —**negative sign,** the minus sign -. —**negatively** *adv.* [from Old French or Latin]

negative/positive in photography, a reverse image, which when printed is again reversed, restoring the original scene. It was invented by ◊Talbot about 1834.

Negev /'negev/ desert in S Israel that tapers to the port of Eilat. It is fertile under irrigation, and it yields minerals, including oil and copper.

neglect /nɪ'glekt/ *v.t.* **1.** to pay too little or no attention to. **2.** to fail to take proper care of. **3.** to omit to do, to be remiss about. —*n.* neglecting, being neglected; disregard. —**neglectful** *adj.* [from Latin *neglegere* (*neg-*= not and *legere* = choose, pick up)]

negligé /'neglɪʒeɪ/ *n.* a woman's light flimsy dressing-gown. [French, past participle of *négliger* = neglect]

negligence /'neglɪdʒəns/ *n.* lack of proper care or attention, carelessness. In law, negligence consists in committing some act that a 'prudent and reasonable' person would not do, or omitting to carry out some action that such a person would do. **Contributory negligence** is a defence sometimes raised when the defendant to an action for negligence claims that the plaintiff by his or her own negligence contributed to the cause of the action. —**negligent** *adj.,* **negligently** *adv.*

negligible /'neglɪdʒɪbəl/ *adj.* too small or unimportant to be considered.

negotiable /nɪ'gəʊʃəbəl/ *adj.* **1.** that can be modified after discussion. **2.** (of a cheque etc.) that can be converted into cash or transferred to another person.

negotiate /nɪ'gəʊʃieɪt/ *v.t./i.* **1.** to try to reach agreement by discussion; to arrange (an affair) or bring about (a result) thus. **2.** to get or give the money value for (a cheque or bonds etc.). **3.** to get over or through (an obstacle or difficulty). —**negotiation** /-'eɪʃən/ *n.,* **negotiator** *n.* [from Latin *negotiari* (*negotium* = business)]

Negro /'niːgrəʊ/ *n.* (*plural* **Negroes**) a member of the indigenous people of Africa south of the Sahara, today distributed around the world. The term generally preferred today is ◊black. —*adj.* of Negroes, black-or dark-skinned. —**Negress** *n.fem.* [Spanish and Portuguese, from Latin *niger* = black]

Negroid /'niːgrɔɪd/ *adj.* of the group having physical characteristics resembling those of black people. —*n.* a Negroid person.

negus /'niːgəs/ *n.* hot sweetened wine with water. [from Col. F. *Negus,* its inventor]

Nehemiah /niːə'maɪə/ Hebrew governor of Judaea under Persian rule. He rebuilt Jerusalem's walls in 444 BC, and made religious and social reforms.

Nehru /'neəruː/ Jawaharlal 1889–1964. Indian nationalist politician, prime minister from 1947. Before the partition (the division of British India into India and Pakistan) he led the socialist wing of the Congress Party (see ◊Indian National Congress Party, and was second in influence only to Mahatma ◊Gandhi. He was imprisoned nine times by the British 1921–45 for political activities. As prime minister from the creation of the dominion (later republic) of India in Aug 1947, he originated the idea of a ◊non-aligned policy (neutrality towards major powers).

Democracy is good. I say this because other systems are worse.

Jawaharlal Nehru
The New York Times 1961

---

neigh /neɪ/ *n.* the cry of a horse. —*v.i.* to utter a neigh. [Old English (imitative)]

neighbour /'neɪbə/ *n.* **1.** a person who lives next door or near by. **2.** a person or thing near or next to another. **3.** a fellow human being. **4.** (*attributive*) neighbouring. —*v.t./i.* to adjoin, to border (on). [Old English]

neighbourhood *n.* **1.** a district. **2.** the people of a district. **3.** nearness, vicinity. —**in the neighbourhood of,** approximately. **neighbourhood watch,** a local crime-prevention scheme in the UK.

neighbourly *adj.* like a good neighbour, friendly, helpful. —**neighbourliness** *n.*

neither /'naɪðə, 'niːðə/ *adv.* not either, not on the one hand (introducing one of two negative statements, the other often introduced by *nor*). —*adj. & pron.* not either, not the one nor the other. —*conj.* (*archaic*) nor, not yet. [Old English]

Nekrasov /nɪ'krɑːsɒf/ Nikolai Alekseevich 1821–1877. Russian poet and publisher. He espoused the cause of the freeing of the serfs and identified himself with the peasants in such poems as 'Who Can Live Happy in Russia?' 1876.

nelly *n.* not on your nelly, (*slang*) certainly not.

nelson /'nelsən/ *n.* a wrestling hold in which the arm is passed under the opponent's arm from behind and the hand applied to his neck.

Nelson Azumah 1958– . Ghanaian featherweight boxer, world champion 1984–1987.

Nelson Horatio, Viscount Nelson 1758–1805. English admiral. He joined the navy in 1770. In the Revolutionary Wars against France he lost the sight in his right eye in 1794 and lost his right arm in 1797. He became a national hero, and rear admiral, after the victory off Cape St Vincent, Portugal. In 1798 he tracked the French fleet to Aboukir Bay and almost entirely destroyed it in the Battle of the Nile. In 1801 he won a decisive victory over Denmark at the Battle of ◊Copenhagen, and in 1805, after two years of blockading Toulon, he won another over the Franco-Spanish fleet at the Battle of ◊Trafalgar, near Gibraltar.

England expects every man will do his duty
Horatio Nelson
Battle of Trafalgar

---

nematode *n.* a slender unsegmented worm of the phylum Aschelminthes. Nematodes are pointed at both ends, with a tough, smooth outer skin. They include some soil and water forms, but a large number are parasites, for example the roundworms and pinworms that live in humans, and the eelworms that attack plant roots. [from Greek *nēma* = thread]

nem. con. abbreviation of with no one dissenting. [from Latin *nemine contradicente*]

Nemerov /'nemərɒv/ Howard 1920– . US poet, critic, and novelist. He published his poetry collection *Guide to the Ruins* 1950, a short-story collection *A Commodity of Dreams* 1959, and in 1977 his *Collected Poems* won both the National Book Award and the Pulitzer Prize.

nemesia /ni'mi:ʒə/ *n.* a South African plant of the genus *Nemesia*, cultivated for its variously coloured irregular flowers. [from Greek *nemesion* name of a similar plant]

nemesis /'neməsɪs/ *n.* inevitable retribution. [Greek]

Nemesis in Greek mythology, the goddess of retribution, who especially punished hubris (Greek *hybris*), the arrogant defiance of the gods.

nemo me impune lacessit 'no one injures me with impunity': the motto of Scotland. [Latin]

Nennius /'neniəs/ *c.*800. Welsh historian, believed to be the author of a Latin *Historia Britonum*, which contains the earliest reference to King Arthur's wars against the Saxons.

neo- /ni:əʊ-/ in combinations, new, modern; a new development of an older form, often in a different spirit. Examples include **neo-Marxism** *and* **Neo-Classicism**. [*Greek neos* = new]

neoclassic /ni:əʊ'klæsɪk/ *adj.* Neo-Classical.

Neo-Classical /ni:əʊ'klæsɪkəl/ *adj.* or **neoclassical** of a revival of classical style or treatment in the arts.

neo-classical economics a school of economic thought based on the work of 19th-century economists, such as Alfred Marshall, using ◊marginal theory to modify classical economic theories. Mathematics and microeconomic theoretical systems both play important parts. Neo-classicists believed competition to be the regulator of economic activity, in that it could establish equilibrium between output and consumption. Neo-classical economics was largely superseded from the 1930s by the work of ◊Keynes.

Neo-Classicism /ni:əʊ'klæsɪsɪzəm/ *n.* a movement in art and architecture in Europe and North America about 1750–1850, a revival of classical art, which superseded the rococo style. It was partly inspired by the excavation of the Roman cities of Pompeii and Herculaneum. The architect Piranesi was an early Neo-Classicist; in sculpture ◊Canova and in painting ◊David were exponents.

neocolonialism *n.* a disguised form of ◊imperialism, by which a country may grant independence to another, but continue to dominate it by control of markets for goods or raw materials.

neo-Darwinism /ni:əʊ'dɑ:wɪnɪzəm/ *n.* the modern theory of ◊evolution, built up since the 1930s by integrating ◊Darwin's theory of evolution through natural selection with the theory of genetic inheritance founded on the work of ◊Mendel.

néo-Destour /neɪəude'stuə/ *n.* (New Socialist Destour Party) the sole political party of Tunisia; it has held power since independence from France in 1956. Founded in 1934, néo-Destour rose to prominence under the leadership of Habib ◊Bourguiba after 1937 and led the rebellion of 1953 which resulted in independence three years later.

neodymium /ni:ə'dɪmiəm/ *n.* a yellowish metallic element of the ◊lanthanide series, symbol Nd, atomic number 60, atomic weight 144.24. Its rose-coloured salts are used in colouring glass, and neodymium is used in lasers.

Neo-Impressionism /ni:əʊɪm'preʃənɪzəm/ *n.* a movement in French painting in the 1880s, an extension of the Impressionists' technique of placing small strokes of different colour side by side. Seurat was the chief exponent; his minute technique became known as 'pointillism'. Signac and Pissarro practised the same style for a few years.

Neolithic /niə'lɪpθɪk/ *n.* of the last period of the ◊Stone Age. —*n.* this period, characterized by developed communities based on agriculture and domesticated animals, and identified by sophisticated, finely honed stone tools. The earliest Neolithic communities appeared about 9,000 BC in the Middle East, followed by Egypt, India, and China, the four regions of the Old World where civilization first developed. In Europe farming began in about 6,500 BC in the Balkans and Aegean, spreading north and east by 1,000 BC. [from Greek *lithos* = stone]

neologism /ni:'ɒlədʒɪzəm/ *n.* 1. a newly coined word. 2. the coining of words. [from French from Greek *logos* = word]

neon /'ni:ɒn/ *n.* a colourless, odourless, nonmetallic gaseous element, symbol Ne, atomic number 10, relative atomic mass 20.183. It is grouped with the inert gases, is nonreactive, and forms no compounds. It occurs in small quantities in the Earth's atmosphere. [Greek, neuter of *neos* = new]

neophyte /'ni:əʊfaɪt/ *n.* 1. a new convert. 2. a religious novice. 3. a beginner. [from Latin from Greek (*phuton* = plant)]

neoplasm *n.* any lump or tumour, which may be benign or malignant (cancerous). [Greek 'new growth']

Neo-Platonism /niəʊ'pleɪtənɪzəm/ *n.* the revived Platonism that was the dominant philosophy of the Mediterranean region from the mid-3rd century AD until the closing of the Athenian schools of philosophy by the emperor Justinian in 529. It strongly influenced medieval and Renaissance thought. —**Neo-Platonist** *n.*

neoprene *n.* synthetic rubber, developed in the USA in 1931 from the polymerization of chloroprene. It is much more resistant to heat, light, oxidation, and petroleum than is ordinary rubber.

Neo-Realism /ni:əʊ'rɪəlɪzəm/ *n.* a movement in Italian cinema that emerged in the 1940s. It is characterized by its naturalism, social themes, and the visual authenticity achieved through location filming. Exponents included the directors De Sica, Visconti, and Rossellini.

neoteny *n.* in biology, the retention of some juvenile characteristics in an animal that seems otherwise mature. An example is provided by the ◊axolotl, a salamander that can reproduce sexually although still in its larval form.

Nepál /ni'pɔ:l/ landlocked country in the Himalayan mountain range, bounded N by Tibet, E by Sikkim, and S and W by India; **area** 147,181 sq km/56,850 sq mi; **capital** Kátmándu; **physical** descends from the Himalayan mountain range in N through foothills to the river Ganges plain in S; **head of state** King Birendra Bir Bikram Sháh Dev from 1972; **head of government** Marich Man Singh Shrestha from 1986; **political system** constitutional monarchy; **exports** jute, rice, timber; **population** (1990 est) 19,158,000; **language** Nepáli (official); 20 dialects spoken; **recent history** independence achieved from Britain in 1923; restoration of the monarchy in 1951. In 1960 parliament was dissolved by the king, and political parties were banned. A series of popular agitations for greater democracy, followed by referendums and elections, took place throughout the 1980s. Eventually, in 1990, the

Panchayat system of partyless government collapsed, a new constitution was introducted; and elections were set for 1991. In 1989 a border blockad was imposed by India in a treaty dispute.

neper *n.* a unit used in telecommunications to express a ratio of powers and currents; symbol Np. It gives the attenuation of amplitudes as the natural logarithm of the ratio.

nephew /'nefjuː, -v-/ *n.* one's brother's or sister's son. [from Old French from Latin *nepos*]

nephritic /ne'frɪtɪk/ *adj.* of or in the kidneys. [from Latin from Greek *nephros* = kidney]

nephritis /ne'fraɪtɪs/ *n.* inflammation of the kidneys, caused by bacterial infection or, sometimes, by a body disorder that affects the kidneys, such as streptococcal infection of the throat. The degree of illness varies, and it may be acute or chronic, requiring a range of treatments from antibiotics to ◊dialysis.

nephron *n.* a microscopic unit in vertebrate kidneys that forms **urine**. A human kidney is composed of over a million nephrons. Each nephron consists of a filter cup surrounding a knot of blood capillaries and a long narrow collecting tubule in close association with yet more capillaries. Waste materials and water pass from the bloodstream into the filter cup, and essential minerals and some water are reabsorbed from the tubule back into the blood. The urine that is left eventually passes out from the body.

ne plus ultra /neɪ plʊs 'ʊltrɑː/ **1.** the furthest attainable point. **2.** the acme, perfection. [Latin = not further beyond (supposed inscription on Straits of Gibraltar)]

nepotism /'nepətɪzəm/ *n.* favouritism shown to relatives in conferring offices (originally by popes for their illegitimate sons, euphemistically called nephews). [from French from Italian *nepote* = nephew]

Neptune /'neptjuːn/ in mythology, the Roman god of the sea, the equivalent of the Greek ◊Poseidon.

Neptune *n.* in astronomy, the eighth planet in average distance from the Sun. Neptune orbits the Sun every 164.8 years at an average distance of 4.497 billion km/2.794 billion mi. It is a giant gas planet of hydrogen, helium and methane, with a diameter of 48,600 km/30,200 mi and a mass 17.2 times that of Earth. It has three narrow orbital rings enclosed in a disc of dust that may reach down to the Neptunian cloudtops. Its rotation period is 16 hours 3 minutes. Neptune has two named moons (Triton and Nereid), and six more discovered by the *Voyager 2* probe in 1989, of which one, with a diameter of 418 km/260 mi is larger than Nereid.

neptunium *n.* a silvery, radioactive metallic element of the ◊actinide series, symbol Np, atomic number 93, relative atomic mass 237.048. It occurs in nature in minute amounts in ◊pitchblende and other uranium ores; it is produced from the decay of the neutron-bombarded uranium they contain. The longest-lived isotope, Np-237, has a half-life of 2.2 million years. The element can be produced by bombardment of U-238 with neutrons and is chemically highly reactive. [from *Neptune* (planet)]

NERC abbreviation of ◊Natural Environment Research Council.

nereid /'nɪəriɪd/ *n.* a long sea-worm or centipede.

Nereid *n.* any of the sea-nymphs, daughters of the Greek sea-god Nereus.

Nergal /'nɜːgæl/ Babylonian god of the sun, war, and pestilence, ruler of the underworld, symbolized by a winged lion.

Nernst /neənst/ (Walther) Hermann 1864–1941. German physical chemist. His investigations, for which he won the 1920 Nobel Prize for Chemistry, were concerned with heat changes in chemical reactions. He proposed in 1906 the principle known as the **Nernst heat theorem** or the third law of thermodynamics: the law states that chemical changes at the temperature of ◊absolute zero involve no change of ◊entropy (disorder).

Nero /'nɪərəʊ/ AD 37–68. Roman emperor from AD 54. Son of Domitius Ahenobarbus and Agrippina, he was adopted by Claudius and succeeded him as emperor. He was a poet and connoisseur of art, and performed publicly as an actor and singer. He is said to have murdered Britannicus, son of his stepfather ◊Claudius, his own mother, his wives Octavia and Poppaea, and many others. After the great fire of Rome in 64, he persecuted the Christians, who were suspected of causing it. Military revolt followed in 68; the Senate condemned Nero to death, and he committed suicide.

Neruda /ne'ruːdə/ Pablo. Pen name of Neftalí Ricardo Reyes y Basualto 1904–1973. Chilean poet and diplomat, considered one of the greatest Chilean poets. His work includes lyrics and the epic poem of the American continent *Canto General* 1950. He was awarded the Nobel Prize for Literature in 1971. He served as consul and ambassador to many countries.

Nerva /'nɜːvə/ Marcus Cocceius Nerva AD *c.*35–98. Roman emperor. He was proclaimed emperor in AD 96 on Domitian's death, and introduced state loans for farmers, family allowances, and allotments of land to poor citizens.

Nerval /neə'væl/ Gérard de. Pen name of Gérard Labrunie 1808–1855. French writer and poet, precursor of French ◊Symbolism and ◊Surrealism. His writings include the travelogue *Voyage en Orient* 1851; short stories, including the collection *Les Filles du feu* 1854; poetry; a novel *Aurélia* 1855, containing episodes of visionary psychosis; and drama. He lived a wandering life and suffered from periodic insanity, finally committing suicide.

nerve *n.* **1.** a strand of nerve-cells enclosed in a sheath of connective tissue joining the ◊central and the ◊autonomic nervous systems with receptor and effector organs, conveying impulses of sensation or of movement between the brain or spinal cord and other parts of the body. A single nerve may contain both ◊motor and sensory nerve cells, but they act independently. **2.** courage, coolness in danger. **3.** (*colloquial*) impudent boldness. **4.** (*plural*) nervousness; a condition of mental and physical stress. **5.** in botany, the rib of a leaf. —*v.t.* to give strength, courage, or vigour to; to brace (oneself) to face danger etc. —**bundle of nerves,** a very nervous person. **get on a person's nerves,** to irritate him or her. **lose one's nerve,** to become timid or irresolute. **nerve-centre** *n.* **a.** a group of closely connected ganglion-cells; **b.** a centre of control. **nerve gas,** a poison gas that affects the nervous system. **nerve impulse,** a travelling wave of chemical and electrical changes that affects the surface membrane of the nerve fibre. **nerve-racking** *adj.* greatly taxing the nerves. **strain every nerve,** to do one's utmost. [from Latin *nervus* = sinew]

nerve cell or **neuron** an elongated cell, part of the ◊nervous system, which transmits electrical impulses. A nerve impulse is a travelling wave of chemical and electrical changes that affects the surface membrane of the *nerve* fibre. Sequential changes in the permeability of the membrane to positive sodium (Na^+) ions and potassium (K^+) ions, produce electrical signals called action potentials. Impulses are received by the cell body and passed, as a pulse of electric charge, along the ◊axon. At the far end of the axon, the impulse triggers the release of chemical ◊neurotransmitters across a ◊synapse (junction), thereby stimulating another nerve cell or the action of an effector organ (for example, a muscle). Nerve impulses travel quickly, in humans as fast as 160 m/525 ft per second along a nerve cell.

nerveless *adj.* lacking vigour or spirit; incapable of effort.

Nervi /'neəvi:/ Pier Luigi 1891–1979. Italian architect who used soft steel mesh within concrete to give it flowing form. For example, the Turin exhibition hall 1949; the UNESCO building in Paris 1952; and the cathedral at New Norcia, near Perth, Australia, 1960.

nervous /'nɜːvəs/ *adj.* **1.** timid and anxious, easily agitated; fearful. **2.** of or affecting the nerves or nervous system; full of nerves. —**nervous breakdown,** loss of emotional and mental stability. —**nervously** *adv.*, **nervousness** *n.* [from Latin *nervosus* = sinewy]

nervous system the system of interconnected ◊nerve cells of most invertebrates and all vertebrates. It is composed of the ◊central and ◊autonomic nervous systems. It may be as simple as the nerve net of coelenterates (for example, jellyfishes) or as complex as the mammalian nervous system, with a central nervous system comprising brain and spinal cord, and a peripheral nervous system connecting up with sensory organs, muscles, and glands.

nervure /'nɜːvjə/ *n.* **1.** any of the tubes forming the framework of an insect's wing. **2.** the principal vein of a leaf. [French *nerf* = nerve]

nervy *adj.* nervous, easily excited.

Netherlands, the

nescient /'nesiənt/ *adj.* not having knowledge (of). —**nescience** *n.* [from Latin *nescire* = not know]

ness *n.* a headland. [Old English]

-ness /-nɪs/ suffix forming nouns from adjectives, expressing a state or condition (*happiness*) or an instance of this (*a kindness*). [Old English]

nest *n.* 1. a structure or place where a bird lays eggs and shelters its young; an animal's or insect's building-place or lair. 2. a snug retreat or shelter. 3. a brood or swarm. 4. a group or set of similar objects, often of different sizes. —*v.t./i.* 1. to have or build a nest. 2. to take wild birds' nests or eggs. 3. (of objects) to fit together or one inside another. —**nest-egg** *n.* a sum of money saved for the future. [Old English]

nestle /'nesəl/ *v.t./i.* 1. to curl oneself up or press comfortably into a soft place. 2. to lie half-hidden or sheltered or embedded. [Old English]

nestling /'nestlɪŋ/ *n.* a bird too young to leave the nest.

Nestorianism /nes'tɔːriənɪzəm/ *n.* Christian doctrine held by the Syrian ecclesiastic Nestorius (died *c.*457), patriarch of Constantinople 428–431. He asserted that Jesus had two natures, human and divine. He was banished for maintaining that Mary was the mother of the man Jesus only, and therefore should not be called the Mother of God. His followers survived as the Assyrian church in Syria, Iraq, Iran, and as the Christians of St Thomas in S India.

net[1] *n.* 1. open-work material of thread, cord, or wire etc. woven or jointed at intervals. 2. a piece of this for a particular purpose, e.g. catching fish, covering or protecting something, or enclosing a goal-space. —*v.t./i.* (-tt-) 1. to catch or procure (as) with a net. 2. to cover or confine with nets. 3. to put (a ball) into a net, especially of the goal. 4. to make cord etc. into a net. [Old English]

net[2] *adj.* 1. remaining after necessary deductions. 2. (of a price) off which a discount is not allowed. 3. (of an effect, result etc.) ultimate; excluding unimportant effects or those that cancel each other out. —*v.t.* (-tt-) to gain or yield (a sum) as net profit. —**net profit,** the actual profit after working expenses have been paid. **net weight,** that excluding the weight of wrappings etc. [French]

netball *n.* a seven-a-side game in which a ball has to be thrown so as to fall through an elevated horizontal ring from which a net hangs. It is a variant of basketball.

nether /'neðə/ *adj.* lower. —**nether regions** or **world,** hell, the underworld. —**nethermost** *adj.* [Old English]

Netherlands, the /'neðələndz/ Kingdom of the; country in W Europe on the North Sea, bounded E by West Germany and S by Belgium; popularly referred to as Holland. **area** 41,863 sq km/16,169 sq mi; **capital** Amsterdam; **physical** flat; rivers Rhine, Schelde (*Scheldt*), Maas; Frisian Islands; **territories** Aruba, Netherlands Antilles (Caribbean); **head of state** Queen Beatrix Wilhelmina Armgard from 1980; **head of government** Ruud Lubbers; **political system** constitutional monarchy; **exports** dairy products, flowers, bulbs, vegetables, petrochemicals, electronics; **population** (1990 est) 14,864,000; **language** Dutch; **recent history** occupied by Germany during World

War II; joined ◊Benelux Union in 1947; founding member of ◊NATO in 1949; joined EC in 1958; In 1980 Queen Juliana abdicated in favour of her daughter Beatrix; In the 1980s opposition to cruise missiles prevented their being sited on Dutch soil.

Netherlands Antilles /'neðələndz æn'tɪliːz/ two groups of Caribbean islands, part of the Netherlands with full internal autonomy, comprising ◊Curaçao and Bonaire off the coast of Venezuela (◊Aruba is considered separately), and St Eustatius, Saba, and the S part of St Maarten in the Leeward Islands, 800 km/500 mi NE; **area** 797 sq km/ 308 sq mi; **capital** Willemstad on Curaçao; **language** Dutch (official), Papiamento, English; **population** (1983) 193,000.

netsuke /'netsukeɪ/ *n.* a carved button-like ornament formerly worn with Japanese dress to hang articles from a girdle. [Japanese]

nett variant of **net**[2].

netting *n.* netted fabric; a piece of this.

nettle *n.* a plant of the genus *Urtica* covered with stinging hairs; a plant resembling this. The **common nettle** *U. dioica* grows on waste ground in Europe and North America. —*v.t.* to irritate or provoke. —**nettle-rash** *n.* a skin eruption like nettle-stings. [Old English]

network *n.* 1. an arrangement or pattern with intersecting lines and interstices; a complex system of railways etc. 2. a chain of interconnected persons, operations, electrical conductors etc.; a group of broadcasting stations connected for simultaneous broadcasts of the same programme. 3. a method of connecting computers so that they can share data and ◊peripheral devices such as printers. The main types are classified by the pattern of the connections, for example, star or ring network; or by the degree of geographical spread. —*v.t.* to broadcast or associate by network.

Neumann /'nɔɪmæn/ Balthasar 1687–1753. German rococo architect and military engineer, whose work includes the bishop's palace in Würzburg.

neural /'njuərəl/ *adj.* of the nerves. —**neurally** *adv.* [from Greek *neuron*]

neuralgia /njuə'rældʒə/ *n.* an intense intermittent pain originating in a nerve, especially of the face and head. —**neuralgic** *adj.* [Greek *algos* = pain]

neural network an artificial network of processors that attempts to mimic the structure of neurons in the human brain. Neural networks may be electronic, optical, or simulated by computer software. A basic network has three layers of processors: an input layer, an output layer, and a 'hidden' layer in between. Each processor is connected to every other in the network by a system of 'synapses'; every processor in the top layer connects to every one in the hidden layer, and each of these connects to every processor in the output layer. Thus, each processor in the middle and bottom layers receives input from several different sources; only when the amount of input exceeds a critical level does it fire an output signal.

neurasthenia /njuərəs'θiːniə/ *n.* debility of the nerves causing fatigue etc. —**neurasthenic** *adj.* [Greek *astheneia* = weakness]

neuration /njuə'reɪʃən/ *n.* the distribution of nervures.

neuritis /njuə'rɪtɪs/ *n.* inflammation of a nerve or the nerves.

neuro- /njuərəu-/ in combinations nerve, nerves. [from Greek *neuron* = nerve]

neurology /njuə'rɒlədʒɪ/ *n.* the scientific study of nerve systems; the branch of medicine concerned with the study and treatment of the brain, spinal cord, and peripheral nerves. —**neurological** /-'lɒdʒɪkəl/ *adj.*, **neurologist** *n.*

neuron /'njuərɒn/ *n.* (also **neurone** /-rɒn/) a nerve-cell (see ◊nerve.

neuropterous /njuə'rɒptərəs/ *adj.* of the Neuroptera, an order of insects having four membranous transparent wings with a network of nervures. [Greek *pterux* = wing]

neurosis /njuə'rəusɪs/ *n.* (*plural* **neuroses** /-siːz/) in psychology, a general term referring to emotional disorders, such as anxiety, depression, and obsessions. The main disturbance tends to be one of mood; contact with reality is relatively unaffected, in contrast to the effects of ◊psychosis.

neurotic /njuə'rɒtɪk/ *adj.* caused by or suffering from neurosis; (*colloquial*) anxious or obsessive. —*n.* a neurotic person. —**neurotically** *adv.*

neuron

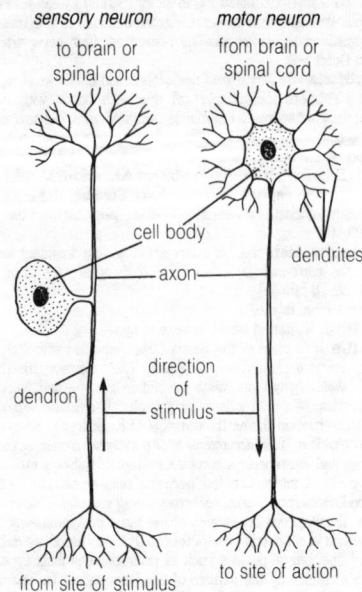

sensory neuron   motor neuron
to brain or   from brain or
spinal cord   spinal cord

cell body
dendrites
axon
direction
of
stimulus
dendron
from site of stimulus   to site of action

intermediate neuron

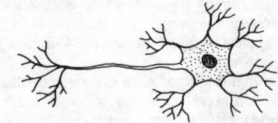

neurotransmitter *n.* a chemical that diffuses across a ◊synapse, and thus transmits impulses between ◊nerve-cells, or between nerve-cells and effector organs (for example, muscles). Common neurotransmitters are nore-pinephrine (which also acts as a hormone) and acetylcholine, the latter occurring most frequently at junctions between nerve and muscle. Nearly 50 different neurotransmitters have been identified.

neuter /'nju:tə/ *adj.* 1. (of a noun etc.) neither masculine nor feminine. 2. (of plants) having neither pistils nor sta-mens. 3. (of insects) sexually undeveloped, sterile. —*n.* 1. a neuter word; the neuter gender. 2. a sexually undeveloped female insect, especially a bee or ant. 3. a castrated animal. —*v.t.* to castrate. [from Old French or Latin = neither]

Neutra /'nɔɪtrɑ:/ Richard Joseph 1892–1970. Austrian-born architect, a US citizen from 1929. His works, often in impressive landscape settings, include Lovell Health House, Los Angeles in 1929, and Mathematics Park, Princeton, New Jersey.

neutral /'nju:trəl/ *adj.* 1. not helping or supporting either of two opposing sides, impartial; belonging to a neutral state etc. 2. having no positive or distinctive characteristics, indeterminate; (of colours) not strong or positive, grey or fawn. 3. (of a gear) in which the engine is disconnected from the driven parts. 4. in chemistry, neither acid nor alkaline. 5. of electricity, neither positive nor negative. 6. in biology, sexually undeveloped, asexual. —*n.* 1. a neutral state or person; a subject of a neutral state. 2. a neutral gear. —**neutrality** /-'trælɪtɪ/ *n.*, the legal status of a country that decides not to choose sides in a war. Certain states, notably Switzerland and Austria, have opted for permanent neutrality. Neutrality always has a legal connotation. In peacetime, neutrality towards the big power alliances is called **non-alignment** (see ◊non-aligned movement). **neutrally** *adv.*

neutralize *v.t.* 1. to make neutral, to make ineffective by an opposite force or effect. 2. to exempt or exclude (a place) from the sphere of hostilities. —**neutralization** /-'zeɪʃən/

n. in chemistry, a process that takes place when the excess acid (or excess base) in a substance is reacted with added base (or added acid) in an amount such that the resulting substance is neither acidic nor basic.

neutral solution a solution of pH 7.0, in which the con-centrations of H+$_{(aq)}$ and OH-$_{(aq)}$ ions are equal.

neutrino /nju:'tri:nəʊ/ *n.* (*plural* **neutrinos**) an elemen-tary particle with zero electric charge and probably zero mass, very difficult to detect and of great penetrating power, emitted in all radioactive disintegrations that give rise to beta rays (see ◊beta particle). Nuclear reactors emit neutrinos. [Italian diminutive of *neutro* = neutral]

neutron /'nju:trɒn/ *n.* an elementary particle of about the same mass as a proton but without electric charge, present in all atomic nuclei except the common ◊isotope of hydro-gen. They contribute to the mass of atoms but do not affect their chemistry, which depends on the proton or electron numbers. For instance, isotopes of a single element (with different masses) differ only in the number of neutrons in their nuclei and have identical chemical properties. —**neu-tron beam machine**, a nuclear reactor or accelerator producing a stream of neutrons, which can 'see' through metals. It is used in industry to check molecular changes in metal under stress. —**neutron bomb**, a small hydrogen bomb that kills by intense radiation but does little damage to buildings and other structures. —**neutron star**, a very small, 'superdense' star composed mostly of ◊neutrons. They are thought to form when massive stars explode as ◊supernovae, during which the protons and electrons of the star's atoms merge, due to intense gravitational collapse, to make neutrons. A neutron star may have the mass of up to three Suns, compressed into a globe only 20 km/12 mi in diameter. If its mass is any greater, its gravity will be so strong that it will shrink even further to become a ◊black hole. Being so small, neutron stars can spin very quickly. The rapidly flashing radio stars called ◊pulsars are believed to be neutron stars.

Nevada /ni'vɑ:də/ state of the W USA; nickname Sage-brush, Silver, or Battleborn State; **area** 286,400 sq km/110,550 sq mi; **capital** Carson City; **physical** Mojave Desert, Lake Tahoe, mountains and plateaux alternating with valleys; **population** (1987) 1,053,000; **history** ceded to the USA after the Mexican War in 1848; first permanent settlement from 1858; discovery of silver the same year led to rapid population growth; became a state in 1864; water projects and military installations in the 20th century.

névé /'neveɪ/ *n.* an expanse of granular snow not yet com-pressed into ice at the head of a glacier. [Swiss French = glacier from Latin *nix nivis* = snow]

never /'nevə/ *adv.* 1. at no time, on no occasion, not ever. 2. not at all. 3. (*colloquial*) surely not. —**never-never** *n.* (*colloquial*) hire-purchase. **well I never**, an exclamation of surprise. [Old English (*ne* not and *ever*)]

nevermore *adv.* at no future time.

nevertheless /nevəðə'les/ *adv.* for all that, notwith-standing.

new /nju:/ *adj.* 1. not existing before; of recent origin or arrival; made, invented, discovered, acquired, or experi-enced recently or now for the first time. 2. in the original condition, not worn or used. 3. renewed or reformed; now invigorated. 4. changed or different from a previous one; additional to another or others already existing. 5. unfamiliar or strange. 6. later, modern; (*derogatory*) new-fangled; advanced in method or doctrine; (in place-names) discovered or founded later than and named after. —*adv.* newly, recently (*new-born, new-found, new-laid*). —**New Age**, *adj.* relating to the field of alternative medicine, parapsychology and esoteric religions. —*n.* in music, instru-mental ambient music of the 1980s, often semi-acoustic or electronic. **the new mathematics**, the system using set theory (see ◊set[2]) in elementary teaching. **new moon**, the Moon when first seen as a crescent after conjunction with the Sun; the time of such an appearance. **new potatoes**, the earliest potatoes of the new crop. **new star**, a ◊nova. **New Style**, (of a date) reckoned by the reformed or Gregorian calendar. **new town**, a town established as a completely new settlement with government sponsorship. **New World**, North and South America, so called by the first Europeans who reached them. —*adj.* of animals and plants that live in the western hemisphere. **new year**, the year about to begin or just begun; the first few days of the

year. **New Year's Day**, 1 Jan. **New Year's Eve**, 31 Dec.
—newness *n.* [Old English]

New Brunswick /nju:ˈbrʌnzwɪk/ maritime province of E Canada; **area** 73,400 sq km/28,332 sq mi; **capital** Fredericton; **population** (1986) 710,000; 37% French-speaking; **history** first reached by Europeans (Cartier) in 1534; explored by Champlain in 1604; remained a French colony as part of Nova Scotia until ceded to England in 1713. After the American Revolution many United Empire Loyalists settled there, and it became a province of the Dominion of Canada in 1867.

New Caledonia /nju: kæliˈdəʊniə/ island group in the S Pacific, a French overseas territory between Australia and the Fiji Islands; **area** 18,576 sq km/7,170 sq mi; **capital** Nouméa; **physical** fertile, surrounded by a barrier reef; **population** (1983) 145,300; **language** French (official); **history** visited by Captain Cook in 1774 and became French in 1853. A general strike to gain local control of nickel mines in 1974 was defeated. The 1985 elections resulted in control of most regions by Kanaks, but not the majority of seats. In 1986 the French conservative government reversed earlier reforms. A 1987 referendum on remaining a French dependency was boycotted by the Kanaks. In 1989 the leader of the Socialist National Liberation front (the most prominent separatist group), Jean-Marie Tjibaou, was murdered.

Newcastle-upon-Tyne /nju:kɑ:səl əpɒn ˈtaɪn/ industrial port, commercial and cultural centre, in Tyne and Wear, NE England, administrative headquarters of Tyne and Wear and Northumberland; **products** coal, shipbuilding, marine and electrical engineering, chemicals, metals; **population** (1981) 278,000. **history** Newcastle first began to trade in coal in the 13th century. In 1826 ironworks were established by George ◊Stephenson, and the first engine used on the Stockton and Darlington railway was made in Newcastle.

Newcomen /nju:kʌmən/ Thomas 1663–1729. English inventor of an early steam engine. He patented his 'fire engine' 1705, which was used for pumping water from mines, until James ◊Watt invented one with a separate condenser.

newcomer *n.* a person recently arrived.

New Deal in US history, a programme introduced by President F D Roosevelt in 1933 to counter the depression of 1929, including employment on public works, farm loans at low rates, and social reforms such as old-age and unemployment insurance, prevention of child labour, protection of employees against unfair practices by employers, and loans to local authorities for slum clearance.

New Delhi /nju: ˈdeli/ city in the Union Territory of Delhi, designed by Lutyens; capital of India since 1912; population (1981) 273,000.

New Democratic Party (NDP) a Canadian political party, moderately socialist, formed in 1961 by a merger of the Labour Congress and the Cooperative Commonwealth Federation.

New Economic Policy (NEP) the economic policy of the USSR 1921–29 devised by the Soviet leader, Lenin. Rather than requisition all agricultural produce above a stated subsistence allowance, the state requisitioned only a fixed proportion of the surplus; the rest could be traded freely by the peasants. The NEP thus reinstated a limited form of free-market trading, although the state retained complete control of major industries.

newel /ˈnju:əl/ *n.* the supporting central pillar of a winding stair; a post supporting a stair-handrail at the top or bottom of a flight of stairs. [from Old French *no(u)el* knob from Latin *nodus* = knot]

New England region of NE USA, comprising the states of Maine, New Hampshire, Vermont, Massachusetts, Rhode Island, and Connecticut, originally settled by Pilgrims and Puritans from England.

newfangled /nju:ˈfæŋgəld/ *adj.* objectionably new in method or style. [originally = fond of novelty, from Old English]

Newfoundland a breed of dog, said to have originated in Newfoundland. Males can grow to 70 cm/2.3 ft tall, and weigh 65 kg/145 lbs; the females are slightly smaller. They are gentle in temperament, and their fur is dense, flat, and usually dull black. Dogs that are black and white or brown and white are called **Landseers**.

Newfoundland and Labrador /nju:fənlənd, ˈlæbrə dɔ:/ Canadian province on the Atlantic Ocean; **area** 405,700 sq km/156,600 sq mi; **capital** St John's; **physical** Newfoundland island and ◊Labrador on the mainland on the other side of the Straits of Belle Isle; rocky; **population** (1986) 568,000; **history** colonized by Vikings about AD 1000; Newfoundland was reached by the English, under the Italian navigator Giovanni ◊Caboto, in 1497. It was the first English colony, established in 1583. French settlements also made and when British sovereignty was recognized in 1713, France retained the offshore islands of St Pierre and Miquelon. Internal self-government was achieved in 1855. In 1934, as Newfoundland had fallen into financial difficulties, administration was vested in a governor and a special commission. After a referendum the province joined Canada in 1949.

New Guinea /nju: ˈgɪni/ island in the SW Pacific, N of Australia, comprising Papua New Guinea and the Indonesian province of West Irian (◊Irian Jaya); area 306,000 sq mi/792,000 sq km; population (1980) 1,174,000. Part of the Dutch East Indies from 1828, it was ceded by the United Nations to Indonesia in 1963.

New Hampshire /nju: ˈhæmpʃə/ state of the NE USA; nickname Granite State; **area** 24,000 sq km/9,264 sq mi; **capital** Concord; **population** (1987) 1,057,000; **history** settled in 1623, it was the first colony to declare its independence from Britain. It became a state in 1788, one of the original Thirteen States.

New Hebrides /nju: ˈhebrɪdi:z/ former name (until 1980) of ◊Vanuatu.

Ne Win /neɪ ˈwɪn/ adopted name of Maung Shu Maung 1911– . Myanmar (Burmese) politician, prime minister 1958–60, ruler from 1962 to 1974, president 1984–81. He was active in the Nationalist movement in the 1930s, joined the Allied forces in the war against Japan in 1945 and held senior military posts until 1958. After leading a coup in 1962, he ruled the country as chair of the revolutionary council until 1974, and state president until 1981, when he continued to dominate political affairs as chair of the ruling Burma Socialist Programme Party (BSPP). His domestic 'Burmese Way to Socialism' programme caused economic and he gave up the BSPP leadership in 1988 after riots in Rangoon (now Yangon). [Burmese = brilliant sun]

New Ireland Forum a meeting between politicians of the Irish Republic and Northern Ireland in May 1983. It offered three potential solutions to the Northern Irish problem, but all were rejected by the UK the following year.

New Jersey /nju: ˈdʒɜ:zi/ state of NE USA; nickname Garden State; **area** 20,200 sq km/7,797 sq mi; **capital** Trenton; **population** (1985) 7,562,000; **history** colonized in the 17th century by the Dutch, it was ceded to England in 1664, and became a state in 1787, one of the original Thirteen States.

newly *adv.* recently, afresh, new-; **—newly-weds** *n.pl.* a recently married couple (or couples).

Newman /ˈnju:mən/ Barnett 1905–1970. US painter, sculptor, and theorist. His paintings are solid-coloured canvases with a few sparse vertical stripes. They represent a mystical pursuit of simple or elemental art. His sculptures, such as *Broken Obelisk* 1963–67, consist of geometric shapes on top of each other.

Newman John Henry 1801–1890. English Roman Catholic theologian. While still an Anglican, he wrote a series of *Tracts for the Times* 1833–41, which gave their name to the Tractarian Movement (subsequently called the ◊Oxford Movement) for the revival of Catholicism. He became a Catholic in 1845 and was made a cardinal in 1879. In 1864 his autobiography, *Apologia pro vita sua*, was published.

Ten thousand difficulties do not make one doubt.
John Henry Newman
Position of My Mind Since 1845

Newman Paul 1925– . US actor and director, Hollywood's leading male star of the 1960s and 1970s. His films include *The Hustler* 1962, *Butch Cassidy and the Sundance Kid* 1969, *The Sting* 1973, and *The Color of Money* 1986 (for which he won an Academy Award).

Newmarket /'nju:mɑ:kɪt/ a British racecourse in Cambridgeshire. It has been the home of horse racing since the days of Charles II. The straight mile is nicknamed Rowley Mile. Newmarket stages two classics each year, the 1,000 and 2,000 Guineas, and the Autumn Double of the Cambridgeshire and Cesarwitch. The national stud is situated in Newmarket.

New Mexico /nju: 'meksɪkəʊ/ state of the SW USA; nickname Land of Enchantment; **area** 315,000 sq km/ 121,590 sq mi; **capital** Santa Fé; **physical** more than 75% of the area is over 1,200 m/3,900 ft above sea level; plains, mountains, caverns; **population** (1987) 1,500,000; **history** explored by Spain in the 16th century; most of it was ceded to the USA by Mexico in 1848, and it became a state in 1912.

New Model Army an army created 1645 by Oliver Cromwell to support the cause of Parliament during the English ◊Civil War. It was characterized by organization and discipline. Thomas Fairfax was its first commander.

New Orleans /nju: 'ɔ:lInz/ commercial and industrial city and Mississippi river port in Louisiana, USA; **products** banking, oil refining, rockets; **population** (1980) 557,500. It is the traditional birthplace of jazz.

Newport Riots violent demonstrations in Newport, Wales, in support of the Peoples' Charter by the Chartists (see ◊Chartism) in 1839. It was suppressed with the loss of 20 lives.

New Rochelle /nju: rə'ʃel/ residential suburb of New York on Long Island Sound; population (1980) 70,800.

news /nju:z/ *n.pl.* (usually treated as *singular*) information about recent events, especially when published or broadcast; a broadcast report of news; new or interesting information. —**news-stand** *n.* a stall for the sale of newspapers. **news-vendor** *n.* a newspaper-seller.

news agency an agency handling news stories and photographs that are then sold to newspapers and magazines. Major world agencies include Associated Press (AP), Agence France-Presse (AFP), United Press International (UPI), Telegraphic Agency of the Soviet Union (TASS), and Reuters.

newsagent *n.* a dealer in newspapers.

newscast *n.* a radio or television broadcast of news reports.

newscaster *n.* a person who reads a newscast.

newsletter *n.* an informal printed report issued to members of a club or some other group.

New South Wales /'nju: saʊθ 'weɪlz/ state of SE Australia; **area** 801,600 sq km/309,418 sq mi; **capital** Sydney; **physical** Great Dividing Range (including Blue Mountains) and part of the Australian Alps (including Snowy Mountains and Mount Kosciusko); Riverina district, irrigated by the Murray-Darling-Murrumbidgee river system; **population** (1987) 5,570,000; **history** convict settlement 1788–1850; opened to free settlement by 1819; self-government from 1856; became a state of the Commonwealth of Australia in 1901. Since 1973 decentralization has counteracted the pull of Sydney, and the New England and Riverina districts have separatist movements. It was called New Wales by James ◊Cook, who landed at Botany Bay in 1770 and thought that the coastline resembled that of Wales.

newspaper *n.* a printed publication (usually daily or weekly) containing news, advertisements, correspondence etc.; the sheets of paper forming this. News-sheets became commercial undertakings after the invention of printing and were introduced in 1609 in Germany and in 1616 in the Netherlands. In 1622 the first newspaper appeared in English, the *Weekly News*; in 1645 there were 14 news weeklies on sale in London. Improved ◊printing (steam printing from 1814, the rotary press from 1846) and a higher literacy rate led to the growth of newspapers. In recent years, production costs have fallen with the introduction of computer technology. The oldest national newspaper in the UK is the *Observer* 1791; the highest circulation UK newspaper is the Sunday *News of the World* (over 5 million copies weekly).

Newspeak /'nju:spi:k/ *n.* ambiguous euphemistic language used especially in political propaganda. [name of artificial official language in Orwell's novel *Nineteen Eighty-Four*]

newsprint *n.* the type of paper on which newspapers are printed. It is made from woodpulp; used in the UK from the 1880s.

Newton Portrait of Isaac Newton by Godfrey Kneller (1702) National Portrait Gallery, London.

newsreel *n.* a cinema film giving recent news; these preceded feature films until the spread of television.

newsworthy *adj.* topical, noteworthy as news.

newsy /'nju:zɪ/ *adj.* (*colloquial*) full of news.

newt /nju:t/ *n.* a small, tailed amphibian especially of the genus *Triturus*, allied to the salamander found in Europe, Asia, and North America. [*a newt* from *an ewt* (variant of Old English *eft*)]

New Testament the second part of the ◊Bible, recognized by the Christian church from the 4th century as sacred doctrine. The New Testament includes the Gospels, which tell of the life and teachings of Jesus, the history of the early church, the teachings of St Paul, and mystical writings. It was written in Greek during the 1st and 2nd centuries AD, and its divisions have been ascribed to various authors by biblical scholars.

newton /'nju:tən/ *n.* the SI unit (symbol N) of ◊force. One newton is the force needed to accelerate an object with mass of one kilogram by one metre per second per second. [from Sir Isaac *Newton*, English physicist]

Newton Isaac 1642–1727. English physicist and mathematician, who laid the foundations of physics as a modern discipline. He discovered the law of gravity, created calculus, discovered that white light is composed of many colours, and developed the three standard laws of motion still in use today. During 1665–66, he discovered the binomial theorem and differential and integral calculus, and began to investigate the phenomenon of gravitation. In 1685, he expounded his universal law of gravitation. His *Philosophiae naturalis principia mathematica*, usually referred to as *Principia*, was published in three volumes 1686–87, with the aid of Edmund ◊Halley.

Newton's laws of motion in physics, three laws that form the basis of Newtonian mechanics. (1) Unless acted upon by a net force, a body at rest stays at rest, and a moving body continues moving at the same speed in the same straight line. (2) A net force applied to a body gives it a rate of change of ◊momentum proportional to the force and in the direction of the force. (3) When a body A exerts a force on a body B, B exerts an equal and opposite force on A; that is, to every action there is an equal and opposite reaction.

Newton's rings (in optics) an ◊interference phenomenon seen (using white light) as concentric rings of spectral colours where light passes through a thin film of transparent medium, such as the wedge of air between a large-radius convex lens and a flat glass plate. With monochromatic light (light of a single wavelength), the rings take the form of alternate light and dark bands. They are caused by interference (interaction) between light rays reflected from the plate and those reflected from the curved surface of the lens.

New Wave a French literary movement of the 1950s, a cross-fertilization of the novel (Marguerite Duras, Alain Robbe-Grillet, Nathalie Sarraute) and film (directors Jean-Luc Godard, Alain Resnais, and François Truffaut). [French *nouvelle vague*]

New Wave in music, a style of rock that evolved parallel to punk in the second half of the 1970s. It shared the urban aggressive spirit of punk but was musically and lyrically more sophisticated; examples are the early work of Elvis Costello and the Talking Heads.

New York /nju: 'jɔ:k/ state of the NE USA; nickname Empire State; **area** 127,200 sq km/49,099 sq mi; **capital** Albany; **physical** Adirondack and Catskill mountains; Lake Placid; bordering on lakes Erie and Ontario; Hudson River; Niagara Falls; ◊Long Island; **population** (1985) 17,783,000; **history** explored by Champlain and Hudson in 1609, colonized by the Dutch from 1614, and annexed by the English in 1664. The first constitution was adopted in 1777, when New York became one of the original Thirteen States.

New York /nju: 'jɔ:k/ largest city in the USA, industrial port, cultural and commercial centre in New York State, at the junction of the Hudson and East rivers; comprises the boroughs of the Bronx, Brooklyn, Manhattan, Queens, and Staten Island; **products** printing, publishing, clothing; **population** (1980) 9,081,000.

New Zealand /nju: 'zi:lənd/ or *Aotearoa* country in the S Pacific, SE of Australia; **area** 268,680 sq km/103,777 sq mi; **capital** Wellington; **physical** comprises North Island, South Island, Stewart Island, Chatham Islands, and minor islands; mainly mountainous; on North Island are Ruapehu, at 2,797 m/9,180 ft the highest of three active volcanoes, the geysers and hot springs of the Rotorua district, Lake Taupo (616 sq km/238 sq mi) source of Waikato River, and NE of the lake, Kaingaroa state forest, one of the world's largest planted forests. On South Island are the Southern Alps and Canterbury Plains, extensively used as sheep pasture. **head of state** Elizabeth II from 1952 represented by Governor-General Catherine Iizard from 1990; **head of government** Prime Minister Jim Bolger from 1990; **political system** constitutional monarchy; **exports** lamb, beef, wool, leather, dairy products, processed foods, kiwi fruit; seeds and breeding stock; timber, paper, pulp, light aircraft; **population** (1990 est) 3,397,000; **language** English (official); Maori; **recent history** achieved independence from Britain in 1931; independence within the Commonwealth confirmed 1947. In 1985 a non-nuclear military policy created disagreements with France and the USA; in 1987 the National Party declared support for the Labour government's non-nuclear policy. New Zealand officially became a 'friendly' rather than 'allied' country to the USA because of its non-nuclear military policy. A free-trade agreement was signed with Australia in 1988. In 1990 Labour Party defeated by National Party in general election. [Maori 'Land of the long white cloud']

next *adj.* **1.** being, lying, or living nearest (*to*). **2.** nearest in order or time, soonest come to. —*adv.* **1.** in the next place or degree. **2.** on the next occasion. —*n.* the next person or thing. —*prep.* next to. —**next-best** *adj.* second-best. **next door**, in the next room or house. **next of kin**, one's closest living relative. **next to**, almost. **the next world**, life after death. [Old English, superlative of *nigh*]

nexus /'neksəs/ *n.* a connected group or series. [Latin (*nectere* = bind)]

Ney /neɪ/ Michael, Duke of Elchingen, Prince of Ney 1769–1815. Marshal of France under ◊Napoleon I, who commanded the rearguard of the French army during the retreat from Moscow. When Napoleon returned from Elba, Ney was sent to arrest him, but instead deserted to him and fought at Waterloo. He was subsequently shot for treason.

Ngorongoro Crater /əŋgɒrəŋ'gɒrəʊ/ crater in the Tanzanian section of the African Great ◊Rift Valley notable for its large numbers of wildebeest, gazelle, and zebra.

Ngugi wa Thiong'o /əŋ'gu:gi wɑ: θi'ɒŋgəʊ/ 1938– . Kenyan writer of essays, plays, short stories, and novels. He was imprisoned after the first performance of the play *Ngaahika Ndeenda/I Will Marry When I Want* in 1977 and lived in exile from 1982. His novels, written in English and Gikuyu, include *The River Between, Petals of Blood,* and *Caitaani Mutharaba-ini/Devil on the Cross,* and deal with colonial and post-independence oppression.

New Zealand: Territories

Area in sq km	
North Island	114,700
South Island	149,800
Chatham Islands	960
Stewart Island	1,750
minor islands	823
	268,033
Island Territories	
Cook Islands	290
Niue	260
Ross Dependency	450,000
Tokelau	10

Nguyen Van Linh /'nu:jən væn 'lɪn/ 1914– . Vietnamese communist politician, member of the Politburo 1976–81 and from 1985; party leader from 1986. He began economic liberalization and troop withdrawal from Cambodia and Laos.

NHS abbreviation of National ◊Health Service.

NI abbreviation of **1.** National Insurance. **2.** Northern Ireland.

Ni symbol for nickel.

niacin /'naɪəsɪn/ another name for ◊nicotinic acid. [from *nicotinic acid*]

Niagara Falls /naɪ'ægərə/ two waterfalls on the Niagara River, on the Canada–USA border, separated by Goat Island. The **American Falls** are 51 m/167 ft high, 330 m/1,080 ft wide; **Horseshoe Falls**, in Canada, are 49 m/160 ft high, 790 m/2,600 ft across.

Niamey /niə'meɪ/ river port and capital of Niger; population (1983) 399,000. It produces textiles, chemicals, pharmaceuticals, and foodstuffs.

nib *n.* **1.** a pen-point. **2.** (in *plural*) crushed coffee- or cocoa-beans. **3.** a small projection on a tile.

nibble *v.t./i.* **1.** to take small quick or gentle bites at. **2.** to eat in small amounts. **3.** (with *at*) to show a cautious interest in (an offer etc.). —*n.* **1.** an act of nibbling. **2.** a very small amount of food.

Nibelungenlied /'ni:bəlʊŋənli:d/ *Song of the Nibelungs,* an anonymous 12th-century German epic poem, derived from older sources. The composer Richard ◊Wagner made use of the legends in his *Ring* cycle.

nibs /nɪbz/ *n.* (*slang*) **his nibs,** a burlesque title of an important or self-important person.

Nicaea, Council of /naɪ'si:ə/ a Christian church assembly held in Nicaea (now Iznik, Turkey) in 325, called by the Roman emperor Constantine. It condemned ◊Arianism as heretical and upheld the doctrine of the Trinity in the Nicene ◊Creed.

Nicaragua /nɪkə'rægjuə, Spanish nɪkə'rɑ:gwə/ Republic of; country in Central America, between the Pacific Ocean and the Caribbean, bounded N by Honduras and S by Costa Rica; **area** 127,849 sq km/49,363 sq mi; **capital** Managua; **physical** narrow Pacific coastal plain separated from broad Atlantic coastal plain by volcanic mountains and lakes Managua and Nicaragua; **head of state and government** Violeta Barrios de Chamorro from April 1990; **political system** emergent democracy; **exports** coffee,

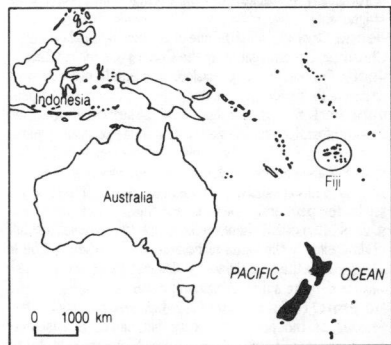

New Zealand

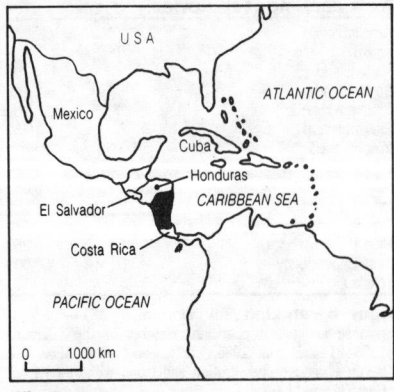

Nicaragua

cotton, sugar, bananas; **population** (1990) 3,606,000; **language** Spanish (official), Indian, English; **recent history** US military bases established at government's request in 1912; guerrilla group under Augusto Sandino opposed their presence. In 1933 US forces withdrew, leaving Gen. Somoza in charge of national guard. Sandinista National Liberation Front (FSLN) formed in 1962 to fight Somoza regime; ousted Somoza in 1979. USA promoted subversive activity against the government in 1982, and actively supported the counter-revolutionary forces (◊Contras); state of emergency declared; USA mined Nicaraguan harbours. US president Reagan denounced Sandinista government, but FSLN won assembly elections. In 1987 a Central American peace agreement was co-signed by Nicaraguan leaders, but the agreement failed in 1988. Nicaragua held talks with Contra rebel leaders. Hurricane left 180,000 people homeless. Demobilization of rebels and release of former Somozan supporters took place in 1989; the cease-fire ended. In 1990 the FSLN was defeated by UNO (National Opposition Union), a US-backed coalition; Violeta Chamorro elected president. Anti-government riots.

Nicaraguan Revolution /nɪkəˈrægjuən/ the revolt 1978–79 in Nicaragua, led by the socialist **Sandinistas** against the US-supported right-wing dictatorship established by Anastasio ◊Somoza. His son, President Anastasio (Debayle) ◊Somoza (1925–80), was forced into exile in 1979 and assassinated in Paraguay. The Sandinista National Liberation Front (FSLN) is named after Augusto César Sandino, a guerrilla leader killed by the US-trained National Guard in 1934.

Nice /niːs/ city on the French Riviera; population (1982) 449,500. Founded in the 3rd century BC, it repeatedly changed hands between France and the Duchy of Savoy from the 14th to the 19th century. In 1860 it was finally transferred to France.

nice *adj.* 1. pleasant, satisfactory, (of a person) kind, good-natured. 2. (*ironically*) bad, difficult, awkward. 3. needing precision and care; subtle. 4. fastidious, delicately sensitive. —**nice and**, satisfactorily. —**nicely** *adv.*, **niceness** *n.* [originally = stupid, from Old French from Latin *nescius* = ignorant]

Nicene Creed /ˈnaɪsiːn/ one of the fundamental creeds of Christianity, promulgated by the Council of ◊Nicaea 325.

nicety /ˈnaɪsɪtɪ/ *n.* 1. precision. 2. a subtle distinction or detail. —**to a nicety**, exactly.

niche /nɪtʃ, niːʃ/ *n.* 1. a shallow recess, especially in a wall. 2. a comfortable or suitable position in life or employment. 3. in ecology, the 'place' occupied by a species in its habitat, including all chemical, physical, and biological components, such as the food supply, the time of day at which the species feeds, temperature, moisture, and the parts of the habitat it uses. Ecological theory holds that two species cannot occupy exactly the same niche and coexist; they will be in direct competition, and one will displace the other. [French (*nicher* = make a nest from Latin *nidus* = nest)]

Nichiren /ˈnɪtʃɪren/ 1222–1282. Japanese Buddhist monk, founder of the sect that bears his name. It bases its beliefs on the *Lotus Sūtra*, which Nichiren held to be the only true revelation of the teachings of Buddha, and

stresses the need for personal effort to attain enlightenment.

Nicholas /ˈnɪkələs/ two tsars of Russia:

Nicholas I 1796–1855. Tsar of Russia from 1825. His Balkan ambitions led to war with Turkey 1827–29 and the Crimean War 1853–56.

Nicholas II 1868–1918. Tsar of Russia 1894–1917. He was dominated by his wife, Princess Alix of Hessen (Tsarina ◊Alexandra), who was under the influence of ◊Rasputin. His mismanagement of the Russo-Japanese War and of internal affairs led to the revolution of 1905, which he suppressed, although he was forced to grant limited constitutional reforms. He took Russia into World War I in 1914, was forced to abdicate in 1917 (see ◊Russian Revolution) and was executed with his family.

Nicholas, St /ˈnɪkələs/ also known as **Santa Claus** 4th century AD. In the Christian church, patron saint of Russia, children, merchants, sailors, and pawnbrokers; bishop of Myra (now in Turkey). His legendary gifts of dowries to poor girls led to the custom of giving gifts to children on the eve of his feast day, 6 Dec, still retained in some countries, such as the Netherlands; elsewhere the custom has been transferred to Christmas Day. His emblem is three balls.

Nicholson /ˈnɪkəlsən/ Ben 1894–1982. English abstract artist. After early experiments influenced by Cubism and de Stijl (see ◊Mondrian), Nicholson developed a style of geometrical reliefs, notably a series of white reliefs (from 1933).

Nicholson Jack 1937– . US film actor who captured the mood of non-conformist, uncertain young Americans in such films as *Easy Rider* 1969 and *Five Easy Pieces* 1970. He subsequently became a mainstream Hollywood star, appearing in *Chinatown* 1974, *One Flew over the Cuckoo's Nest* (Academy Award) 1975, *The Shining* 1979, *Terms of Endearment* (Academy Award) 1983, and *Batman* 1989.

nick *n.* 1. a small cut or notch. 2. (*slang*) prison; a police station. 3. (*slang*) condition. —*v.t.* 1. to make a nick or nicks in. 2. (*slang*) to steal. 3. (*slang*) to catch, to arrest. —**in the nick of time**, only just in time.

nickel /ˈnɪkəl/ /ˈnɪkəˈlɔːdɪən/ *n.* 1. a hard, malleable and ductile, silver-white metallic element, symbol Ni, atomic number 28, relative atomic mass 58.71. It occurs in igneous rocks and as a free or native metal (one that is found in its natural state), occasionally occurring in fragments of iron-nickel meteorite. It is a component of the Earth's core, which is held to consist principally of iron with some nickel. It has a high melting point, low electrical and thermal conductivity, and can be magnetized. It does not tarnish and therefore is much used for alloys, electroplating, and for coinage. 2. (*US*) a five-cent piece. —**nickel silver**, an alloy of nickel, zinc, and copper. **nickel steel**, an alloy of nickel with steel. [abbreviation of German *kupfernickel*, the ore from which it was first obtained]

nickelodeon /nɪkəˈlɔːdɪən/ *n.* (*US colloquial*) a juke-box.

nicker *n.* (*plural* the same) (*slang*) £1 sterling.

Nicklaus /ˈnɪkləs/ Jack (William) 1940– . US golfer, nicknamed 'the Golden Bear'. He won a record 20 major titles, including 18 professional majors between 1962 and 1986.

nickname *n.* a familiar or humorous name given to a person or thing instead of or as well as the real name. —*v.t.* to give a nickname to. [*a nickname* from *an eke-name* (*eke* = addition)]

Nicobar Islands /ˈnɪkəbɑː/ group of Indian islands, part of the Union Territory of ◊Andaman and Nicobar Islands.

Nicolle /niːˈkɒl/ Charles 1866–1936. French bacteriologist whose discovery in 1909 that typhus is transmitted by the body louse made the armies of World War I introduce delousing as a compulsory part of military routine.

Nicosia /nɪkəˈsiːə/ capital of Cyprus, with leather, textile, and pottery industries; population (1987) 165,000. Nicosia was the residence of Lusignan kings of Cyprus 1192–1475. The Venetians, who took Cyprus in 1489, surrounded Nicosia with a high wall, which still exists; it fell to the Turks in 1571. It was again partly taken by the Turks in the invasion of 1974.

nicotine /ˈnɪkətiːn/ *n.* a poisonous ◊alkaloid extracted as an oily liquid from the dried leaves of the tobacco plant and used as an insecticide. A colourless oil, soluble in water, it turns brown on exposure to the air. [French, from generic name (*nicotiana herba*) of tobacco, from J. *Nicot*, French diplomat who introduced tobacco into France in 1560]

nicotinic acid /nɪkə'tɪnɪk/a vitamin of the B group, formed by oxidation of nicotine and acting to prevent pellagra.

nictitate /'nɪktɪteɪt/ *v.i.* to blink, to wink. —**nictitating membrane**, the third or inner eyelid of many animals (including birds and fishes). —**nictitation** /-'teɪʃən/ *n.* [from Latin *nictare* = blink]

niece /niːs/ *n.* one's brother's or sister's daughter. [from Old French from Latin *neptis* = grand-daughter]

nielsbohrium *n.* name proposed by Soviet scientists for the element currently known as ◊unnilpentium (atomic number 105), to honour Danish physicist Niels Bohr.

Nielsen /'niːlsən/ Carl (August) 1865–1931. Danish composer. His works show a progressive tonality, especially his opera *Saul and David* 1902 and six symphonies.

Niemeyer /'niːmaɪə/ Oscar 1907– . Brazilian architect, joint designer of the United Nations headquarters in New York, and of many buildings in Brasilia.

Niemöller /'niːmɜːlə/ Martin 1892–1984. German Christian Protestant pastor. He was imprisoned in a concentration camp 1938–45 for campaigning against Nazism in the German church. He was president of the World Council of Churches 1961–68.

Nietzsche /'niːtʃə/ Friedrich Wilhelm 1844–1900. German philosopher who rejected the accepted absolute moral values and the 'slave morality' of Christianity. He argued that 'God is dead' and therefore people were free to create their own values. His ideal was the *Übermensch*, or 'Superman', who would impose his will on the weak and worthless. Nietzsche claimed that knowledge is never objective but always serves some interest or unconscious purpose.

Morality is the herd instinct in the individual.

Friedrich Wilhelm Nietzsche
Die Fröhliche Wissenschaft

---

niff *n.* (*slang*) a smell, a stink. —*v.i.* (*slang*) to smell, to stink. —**niffy** *adj.* [*originally dialect*]

nifty *adj.* (*slang*) 1. smart, stylish. 2. excellent, clever.

Niger /'naɪdzə/ third longest river in Africa, 4,185 km/2,600 mi from the highlands bordering Sierra Leone and Guinea NE through Mali, then SE through Niger and Nigeria to an inland delta on the Gulf of Guinea. Its flow has been badly affected by the expansion of the Sahara Desert. It is sluggish and frequently floods its banks. It was explored by Mungo Park 1795–96.

Niger /niː'ʒeə/ Republic of; landlocked country in W Africa, bounded N by Nigeria and Libya, E by Chad, S by Nigeria and Benin, and W by Burkina Faso and Mali; **area** 1,186,408 sq km/457,953 sq mi; **physical** desert plains between hills in N and savanna in S; River Niger in SW, Lake Chad in SE; **head of state and government** Ali Seybou from 1987; **political system** military republic; **exports** peanuts, livestock, gum arabic, tin, uranium; **population** (1990 est) 7,691,000; **language** French (official), Hausa, Djerma; **recent history** full independence from France achieved 1960; Hamani Diori elected president, but ousted in army coup led by Seyni Kountché. Cooperation agreement signed with France in 1977. In 1987 Kountché died and was replaced by Col Ali Seybou. Multi-party politics promised for 1990.

Nigeria /naɪ'dʒɪərɪə/ Federal Republic of; country in W Africa on the Gulf of Guinea, bounded N by Niger, E by Chad and Cameroon, and W by Benin; **area** 923,773 sq km/356,576 sq mi; **capital** and chief port Lagos; Abuja (capital-designate) **physical** arid in N; savanna; tropical rain-forest in S, with mangrove swamps along the coast; river Niger forms wide delta; **head of state and government** Ibrahim Babangida from 1985; **political system** military republic pending promised elections; **exports** petroleum (largest oil resources in Africa), cocoa, peanuts, palm oil, cotton, rubber, tin; **population** (1990 est) 118,865,000 (Yoruba in W, Ibo in

E, and Hausa-Fulani in N); **language** English (official), Hausa, Ibo, Yoruba; Independence achieved from Britain within the Commonwealth in 1960; became a republic in 1963. A military coup in 1966 was followed by a counter-coup and the slaughter of many members of the Ibo tribe in N. Conflict over oil revenues led to declaration of an independent state of Biafra and civil war 1966–70, followed by a series of political coups and counter-coups. In 1989 two new parties were approved. Babangida promised a return to pluralist politics by 1992.

niggard /'nɪgəd/ *n.* a stingy person.

niggardly *adj.* stingy. —**niggardliness** *n.*

nigger *n.* (*offensive*) a black, a dark-skinned person. —**nigger in the woodpile**, a hidden cause of trouble or inconvenience. [from French *nègre* from Spanish from Latin *niger* = black]

niggle *v.t./i.* 1. to fuss over details, to find fault in a petty way. 2. to irritate, to nag.

niggling *adj.* petty, troublesome; nagging.

nigh /naɪ/ *adv., prep.,* and *adj.* (*archaic and dialect*) near. [Old English]

night /naɪt/ *n.* 1. the period of darkness between one day and the next, the time from sunset to sunrise. 2. nightfall. 3. the darkness of night. 4. a night or evening appointed for some activity. —**make a night of it,** to spend most or all of the night enjoying oneself. **night-club** *n.* a club that is open at night and provides refreshment and entertainment. **night-dress** *n.* a woman's or girl's loose garment worn in bed. **night-gown** *n.* a night-dress or night-shirt. **night-life** *n.* the entertainment available at night in a town. **night-light** *n.* a short thick candle or dim bulb kept burning in a bedroom at night. **night-long** *adj. & adv.* throughout the night. **night safe,** a safe with an opening in the outer wall of a bank for the deposit of money etc., when the bank is closed. **night school,** a school providing evening classes for those working by day. **night-shirt** *n.* a man's or boy's long shirt for sleeping in. **night-time** *n.* the time of darkness. **night-watchman** *n.* a person employed to look after unoccupied premises at night; (in cricket) an inferior batsman sent in near the close of play to avoid the dismissal of a better one in adverse conditions. [Old English]

nightcap *n.* 1. a cap worn in bed. 2. a hot or alcoholic drink taken at bedtime.

nightfall *n.* the end of daylight.

nightie *n.* (*colloquial*) a night-dress. [abbreviation]

nightingale /'naɪtɪŋgeɪl/ *n.* a small bird of the genus *Luscinia* of the thrush family, of which the male sings melodiously both by day and by night. About 16.5 cm/6.5 in long, it is dull brown, lighter below, with a reddish-brown tail. It migrates to Europe and winters in Africa. It feeds on insects and small animals. [Old English = night-singer]

Nightingale Florence 1820–1910. English nurse, the founder of nursing as a profession. She took a team of nurses to Scutari (now Üsküdar, Turkey) in 1854 and reduced the ◊Crimean War hospital death rate from 42% to 2%. In 1856 she founded the Nightingale School and Home for Nurses in London.

nightjar *n.* a nocturnal bird of the family Caprimulgidae with a harsh cry. *Caprimulgus europaeus* has a large bristle-fringed gape that catches moths and other flying insects in the air. About 28 cm/11 in long, it is patterned in shades of brown, and well camouflaged. It is a summer visitor to Europe, and migrates to Africa for the European winter. [from **night** and **jar**[1]]

Night Journey or *al-Miraj* (Arabic = the ascent) in Islam, the journey of the prophet Muhammad, guided by the archangel Gabriel, from Mecca to Jerusalem, where he met the earlier prophets, including Adam, Moses, and Jesus; he then ascended to paradise, where he experienced the majesty of Allah, and was also shown hell.

nightly *adj.* 1. happening, done, or existing in the night. 2. recurring every night. —*adv.* every night.

nightmare *n.* 1. a terrifying dream. 2. (*colloquial*) a terrifying or very unpleasant experience or situation; a haunting fear. —**nightmarish** *adj.* [originally = monster supposed to sit on and suffocate sleepers, from obsolete *mare* = goblin]

Night of the Long Knives in World War II, a purge of the German Nazi party to root out possible opposition to Adolph Hitler. On the night of 29–30 June 1934 (and the following two days) the SS units under Heinrich ◊Himmler were used by Hitler to exterminate the Nazi private army Sturm Abteilung (SA or the Brownshirts) under Captain Ernst Roehm. Others were also executed for alleged conspiracy against Hitler (including Kurt von Schleicher). The Nazi purge enabled Hitler to gain the acceptance of the German Officer Corps and, when President Hindenburg died five weeks later, to become head of state.

nightshade *n.* a plant of the genus *Solanum* with poisonous berries. —**deadly nightshade**, ◊belladonna.

nihilism /ˈnaɪɪlɪzəm/ *n.* **1.** negative doctrines or total rejection of current beliefs in religion or morals, often involving a general sense of despair coupled with the belief that life is devoid of meaning. **2.** philosophical scepticism that denies all existence. **3.** the doctrine of a Russian extreme-revolutionary group in the 19th–20th century, finding nothing to approve of in the established order or social and political institutions. In 1878 the nihilists launched a guerrilla campaign leading to the murder of Tsar Alexander II in 1881. —**nihilist** *n.*, **nihilistic** /-ˈlɪstɪk/ *adj.* [from Latin *nihil* = nothing]

Nijinsky /nɪˈdʒɪnski/ Vaslav 1890–1950. Russian dancer and choreographer. Noted for his powerful but graceful technique, he was a member of ◊Diaghilev's Ballets Russes, for whom he choreographed Debussy's *Prélude à l'Après-midi d'un faune* 1912 and *Jeux* 1913, and Stravinsky's *The Rite of Spring* 1913. He also took lead roles in ballets such as *Petrushka* 1911. He rejected conventional forms of classical ballet in favour of free expression. His sister was the choreographer **Bronislava Nijinska** (1891–1972).

Nijmegen, Treaties of /ˈnaɪmeɪɡən/ peace treaties 1678–79 between France on the one hand and the Netherlands, Spain, and the Holy Roman Empire on the other, ending the Third Dutch War.

nil *n.* nothing, no number or amount, especially as a score in games. [Latin *nihil* = nothing]

nil desperandum never despair. [Latin]

Nile /naɪl/ river in Africa, the world's longest, 6,695 km/4,160 mi. The **Blue Nile** rises in Lake Tana, Ethiopia, the **White Nile** at Lake Victoria, and they join at Khartoum, Sudan. It enters the Mediterranean at a vast delta in N Egypt.

nilgai *n.* a large antelope, *Boselaphus tragocamelus*, native to India. The bull has short conical horns and is bluish-grey. The female is brown.

nimble *adj.* quick and light in movement or action, agile; (of the mind) quick, clever. —**nimbleness** *n.*, **nimbly** *adv.* [Old English = quick to seize]

nimbo-stratus /nɪmbəʊˈstreɪtəs, -ˈstrɑː-/ *n.* a low dark-grey layer of cloud. [Latin *stratum* = something spread or laid down]

nimbus /ˈnɪmbəs/ *n.* (*plural* nimbi /-baɪ/, nimbuses) **1.** a halo, an aureole. **2.** a storm-cloud. [Latin]

nincompoop /ˈnɪnkəmpuːp/ *n.* a foolish person.

nine *adj.* & *n.* **1.** one more than eight; the symbol for this (9, ix, IX). **2.** the size etc. denoted by nine. —**nine days' wonder**, a thing attracting interest for a short time. [Old English]

ninefold *adj.* & *n.* **1.** nine times as much or as many. **2.** consisting of nine parts.

ninepins *n.pl.* a kind of skittles.

nineteen /naɪnˈtiːn/ *adj.* & *n.* **1.** one more than 18; the symbol for this (19, xix, XIX). **2.** the size etc. denoted by nineteen. —**nineteenth** *adj.* & *n.* [Old English]

1992 *n.* popular name for the European Commission's aim to achieve a single market, without import tariffs or frontier controls, within Europe by 1992.

Nineteen Propositions a set of demands presented by the English Parliament to Charles I in 1642. They were designed to limit the powers of the crown, and their rejection represented the beginning of the Civil War.

ninety *adj.* & *n.* **1.** nine times ten; the symbol for this (90, xc, XC). **2.** (in *plural*) the numbers, years, or degrees of temperature from 90 to 99. —**ninetieth** *adj.* & *n.* [Old English]

Nineveh /ˈnɪnɪvə/ capital of the Assyrian Empire from the 8th century BC until its destruction by the Medes under King Cyaxares in 612 BC, as forecast by the Old Testament prophet Nahum. It was situated on the river Tigris (opposite the present city of Mosul, Iraq) and was adorned with palaces.

Ningxia /ˈnɪŋʃiɑː/ or **Ningxia Hui** autonomous region of NW China (formerly **Ninghsia-Hui**); **area** 170,000 sq km/65,620 sq mi; **capital** Yinchuan; **physical** desert plateau; **population** (1986) 4,240,000; including many Muslims and nomadic herders.

ninny *n.* a foolish person.

ninth /naɪnθ/ *adj.* next after the eighth. —*n.* each of nine equal parts into which a thing may be divided. —**ninthly** *adv.*

niobium /naɪˈəʊbiəm/ *n.* a soft, grey-white, somewhat ductile and malleable, metallic element, symbol Nb, atomic number 41, relative atomic mass 92.906. It occurs in nature with tantalum, which it resembles in chemical properties. It is used in making stainless steel and other alloys for jet engines and rockets and for making superconductor magnets. [from *Niobe* in Greek mythology]

nip[1] *v.t./i.* (-pp-) **1.** to pinch or squeeze sharply; to bite quickly with the front teeth. **2.** to pinch *off*. **3.** to pain or harm with biting cold. **4.** (*colloquial*) to go quickly or nimbly. —*n.* **1.** a sharp pinch, squeeze, or bite. **2.** biting coldness. —**nip in the bud**, to destroy at an early stage of development.

nip[2] *n.* a small quantity of spirits. [abbreviation of *nipperkin* = small measure]

nipper *n.* **1.** a crustacean's claw. **2.** (in *plural*) pincers or forceps for gripping things or cutting things off. **3.** (*colloquial*) a young child.

nipple *n.* **1.** a small projection in which the mammary ducts of either sex of mammals terminate and from which in females milk is secreted for the young. **2.** the teat of a feeding-bottle. **3.** a nipple-like protuberance.

Nippon /ˈnɪpɒn/ English transliteration of the Japanese name for ◊Japan.

Nipponese /nɪpɒˈniːz/ *adj.* & *n.* (*plural* the same) Japanese.

nippy *adj.* (*colloquial*) **1.** nimble, quick. **2.** chilly, cold. [from *nip*[1]]

nirvana /nɜːˈvɑːnə/ *n.* the final goal of Buddhism, a transcendent state in which there is neither suffering, desire, nor sense of self (*atman*), with release from the effects of karma. [from Sanskrit = extinction (i.e. the extinction of illusion, since suffering, desire, and self are all illusions)]

Nissen hut /ˈnɪsən/ a tunnel-shaped hut of corrugated iron with a cement floor. [from N *Nissen*, British engineer]

nit *n.* **1.** a louse or other parasite; its egg. **2.** (*slang*) a stupid person. —**nit-picking** *n.* & *adj.* (*colloquial*) fault-finding in a petty way. [Old English]

Niterói /niːtəˈrɔɪ/ or **Nictheroy** port and resort city in Brazil on the E shore of Guanabara Bay, linked by bridge with Rio de Janeiro; population (1980) 382,700.

nitrate[1] /ˈnaɪtreɪt/ *n.* **1.** a salt or ester of nitric acid, containing the NO_3^- ion. **2.** potassium or sodium nitrate used as a fertilizer. [French]

nitrate[2] /ˈnaɪtreɪt/ *v.t.* to treat, combine, or impregnate with nitric acid.

nitre /ˈnaɪtə(r)/ *n.* or **saltpetre**, potassium nitrate, KNO_3, a mineral found on and just under the ground in desert regions; used in explosives. [from Old French from Latin from Greek *nitron*]

nitre /ˈnaɪtə/ *n.* saltpetre. [from Old French from Latin from Greek *nitron*]

nitric /ˈnaɪtrɪk/ *adj.* of or containing nitrogen. —**nitric acid**, or **aqua fortis**, HNO_3, a pungent corrosive caustic liquid obtained by the oxidation of ammonia or the action of sulphuric acid on potassium nitrate. It is a strong oxidizing agent, dissolves most metals, and is used for nitration and esterification of organic substances; for explosives, plastics, and dyes; and in making sulphuric acid and nitrates.

nitric acid or **aqua fortis** HNO_3 fuming acid obtained by the oxidation of ammonia or the action of sulphuric acid on potassium nitrate. It is a strong oxidizing agent, dissolves most metals, and is used for nitration and esterification of organic substances; for explosives, plastics, and dyes; and in making sulphuric acid and nitrates.

nitride /ˈnaɪtraɪd/ *n.* a binary compound of nitrogen.

nitrify /ˈnaɪtrɪfaɪ/ *v.t.* to turn into a nitrite or nitrate. —**nitrification** /-fɪˈkeɪʃən/ *n.* a process that takes place in soil when bacteria oxidize ammonia, turning it into nitrates. Nitrates can be absorbed by the roots of plants, so this is a stage in the ◊nitrogen cycle.

nitrite /'naɪtraɪt/ *n.* any salt or ester of nitrous acid, containing the nitrite ion (NO_2^-). Nitrites are used as preservatives (for example, to prevent the growth of botulism spores) and as colouring agents in cured meats such as bacon and sausages.

nitro- /naɪtrəʊ-/ in combinations of or made with nitric acid, nitre, or nitrogen. —**nitro-glycerine** *n.* a yellowish oily highly explosive liquid made by adding glycerine to nitric and sulphuric acids. Although it is poisonous, it is used in cardiac medicine. It explodes with great violence if heated in a confined space and is used in the preparation of dynamite, cordite, and other high explosives. [Greek *nitron*]

nitrogen *n.* a colourless, odourless, tasteless, gaseous, non-metallic element, symbol N, atomic number 7, relative atomic mass 14.0067. It forms almost 80% of the Earth's atmosphere by volume and is a necessary part of all plant and animal tissues (in proteins and nucleic acids). For industrial uses it is obtained by liquifaction and fractional distillation of air. —**nitrogenous** /-'trɒdʒɪnəs/*adj.* [from French] [Greek *nitron* 'native soda', sodium or potassium nitrate]

nitrogen cycle in ecology, the process through which nitrogen passes through the ecosystem. In the form of inorganic compounds (such as nitrates) in the soil, it is absorbed by plants and turned into organic compounds (such as proteins) in plant tissue. A proportion of this nitrogen is eaten by ◊herbivores and utilized by their own biological processes; some of this is passed on to the carnivores that feed on the herbivores. The nitrogen is ultimately returned to the soil as excrement, and by the decomposition and reconversion to inorganic form of dead organisms by bacterial ◊decomposers.

nitrogen fixation the process by which nitrogen in the atmosphere is converted into nitrogenous compounds by the action of microorganisms, such as cyanobacteria and bacteria, in conjunction with certain ◊legumes. These organisms can extract nitrogen directly from the atmosphere and convert it to compounds such as nitrates that other organisms can use. Some live mutually with leguminous plants (peas and beans) or other plants (for example, alder), forming characteristic nodules on the roots. The presence of such plants increases the nitrate content, and hence the fertility, of the soil. Several chemical processes reproduce nitrogen fixation to produce fertilizers.

nitroglycerine *n.* $C_3H_5(ONO_2)_3$, a flammable, explosive oil produced by the action of nitric and sulphuric acids on glycerol. Although poisonous, it is used in cardiac medicine. It explodes with great violence if heated in a confined space and is used in the preparation of dynamite, cordite, and other high explosives.

nitrous /'naɪtrəs/ *adj.* of, like, or impregnated with nitre. —**nitrous acid**, HNO_2. a liquid resembling nitric acid but containing less oxygen. In solution with water it decomposes quickly to form nitric acid and nitrogen dioxide. **nitrous oxide**, N_2O, a colourless, nonflammable gas, laughing gas, that reduces sensitivity to pain. In higher doses it is an anaesthetic. It is less potent than some other anaesthetic gases, and is often combined with other drugs to allow lower doses to be used. It may be self-administered; for example, in childbirth. [from Latin]

nitty-gritty *n.* (*slang*) the realities or basic facts of a matter.

nitwit *n.* (*colloquial*) a stupid person.

Niven /'nɪvən/ David 1909–1983. Scottish-born US film actor. He went to Hollywood in the 1930s, where he made *The Charge of the Light Brigade* 1936, *Bachelor Mother* 1939, and *Wuthering Heights* 1939 before serving as a British officer in World War II. He returned to Hollywood and starred in *Around the World in Eighty Days* 1956, *Separate Tables* 1958 (Academy Award), *The Guns of Navarone* 1961, and *The Pink Panther* 1964.

nix *n.* (*slang*) nothing. [German, colloquial form of *nichts* = nothing]

Nixon /'nɪksən/ Richard (Milhous) 1913– . 37th president of the USA 1969–74, a Republican. He attracted attention as a member of the Un-American Activities Committee in 1948, and was vice president to Eisenhower 1953–61. As president he was responsible for US withdrawal from Vietnam, and forged new links with China, but at home his culpability in the cover-up of the ◊Watergate scandal and the existence of a 'slush fund' for political machinations during his 1972 re-election campaign led

Nkrumah *The first president of Ghana, Kwame Nkrumah.*

to his resignation in 1974 after being threatened with impeachment.

Nkomati Accord /əŋkəʊ'mɑːti/ a non-aggression treaty between South Africa and Mozambique concluded in 1984, under which they agreed not to give material aid to opposition movements in each other's countries. In effect, South Africa pledged itself not to support the Mozambique National Resistance (Renamo), while Mozambique was committed not to help the then outlawed African National Congress.

Nkomo /əŋ'kəʊməʊ/ Joshua 1917– . Zimbabwean politician, president of ZAPU (Zimbabwe African People's Union) from 1961 and a leader of the black nationalist movement against the white Rhodesian regime. He was a member of Robert ◊Mugabe's cabinet in 1980–82 and from 1987.

Nkrumah /əŋ'kruːmə/ Kwame 1909–1972. Ghanaian nationalist politician, prime minister of the Gold Coast (Ghana's former name) 1952–57 and of newly independent Ghana 1957–60. He became Ghana's first president in 1960 but was overthrown in a coup in 1966. His policy of 'African socialism' led to links with the Communist bloc.

NKVD the Soviet secret police 1934–38, replaced by the ◊KGB. The NKVD was responsible for Stalin's infamous ◊purges. [Russian = People's Commissariat of Internal Affairs]

NNE abbreviation of north-north-east.

NNW abbreviation of north-north-west.

No symbol for nobelium.

No. abbreviation of number. [from Latin *numero* (*numerus* = number)]

no /nəʊ/ *adj.* 1. not any. 2. not a, quite other than. 3. hardly any. —*adv.* 1. (as a negative answer to a question, etc.) it is not so, I do not agree, I shall not etc. 2. (with *comparative*) by no amount, not at all. 3. (after *or*) not. —*n.* (*plural* noes) 1. the word or answer 'no'. 2. a denial or refusal; a negative vote. —**no-ball** *n.* an unlawfully delivered ball in cricket etc. **no-claim bonus,** a reduction of an insurance premium for a person who has not claimed payment under the insurance since a previous renewal. **no go,** it is hopeless or impossible. **no-go area,** one to which entry is forbidden or restricted. **no man's land,** the space between two opposing enemies; an area not assigned to any owner. **no one,** no person, nobody. **no way,** (*colloquial*) it is impossible; not at all. [from Old English *none* = not one, originally before consonants]

Nō /nəʊ/ *n.* or **Noh** the classical, aristocratic Japanese drama, which developed from the 14th to the 16th century and is still performed. There is a repertory of some 250 pieces, of which five, one from each of the several classes devoted to different subjects, may be put on in a performance lasting a whole day. Dance, mime, music, and chanting develop the mythical or historical themes. All the actors are men, some of whom wear masks and elaborate costumes; scenery is limited. Nō influenced ◊kabuki drama.

Noah /'nəʊə/ in the Old Testament, the son of Lamech and father of Shem, Ham, and Japheth, who, according to God's instructions, built an ark so that he and his family and specimens of all existing animals might survive the ◊Flood.

There is also a Babylonian version of the tale, *The Epic of Gilgamesh*.

nob[1] *n.* (*slang*) a person of wealth or high social standing. —**nobby** *adj.*

nob[2] *n.* (*slang*) the head.

nobble *v.t.* (*slang*) 1. to tamper with (a racehorse) to prevent its winning. 2. to influence (a person) by underhand means; to get possession of dishonestly. 3. to catch (a criminal).

Nobel /nəu'bel/ Alfred Bernhard 1833–1896. Swedish chemist and engineer. He invented ◊dynamite in 1867 and ballistite, a smokeless gunpowder, in 1889. He amassed a large fortune from the manufacture of explosives and the exploitation of the Baku oilfields in Azerbaijan, near the Caspian Sea. He left this fortune in trust for the endowment of five ◊Nobel prizes.

nobelium /nəu'bi:liəm/ *n.* a synthesized, radioactive, metallic element of the ◊actinide series, symbol No, atomic number 102, relative atomic mass 259. It is synthesized bombarding curium with carbon nuclei. [from Alfred *Nobel*]

Nobel Prize /nəu'bel/ an annual international prize, first awarded 1901 under the will of Alfred ◊Nobel. The interest on the Nobel fund is divided each year among the persons who have made the greatest contributions in the fields of physics, chemistry, medicine, literature, world peace, and, from 1969, economics.

nobility /nəu'bɪlɪtɪ/ *n.* nobleness of character, mind, birth, or rank. —**the nobility**, the aristocracy, the ranks of society who originally enjoyed certain hereditary privileges. Their wealth was mainly derived from land. In many societies until the 20th century, they provided the elite personnel of government and the military. [from Old French or Latin *nobilitas*]

noble /'nəubəl/ *adj.* 1. belonging to the aristocracy by birth or rank. 2. of excellent character, free from pettiness or meanness, magnanimous. 3. of imposing appearance, excellent. —*n.* a nobleman or noblewoman. —**noble gas**, any of the chemically similar ◊inert gases (helium, neon, argon, krypton, xenon, and radon). **noble metal**, a metal (e.g. gold) that resists chemical attack. —**nobleness** *n.*, **nobly** *adv.* [from Old French from Latin *nobilis*]

nobleman *n.* (*plural* **noblemen**) a peer.

Noble Savage, the an Enlightenment idea of the virtuous innocence of 'savage' peoples, often embodied in the American Indian, celebrated by the writers J J Rousseau, Chateaubriand (in *Atala* 1801), and James Fenimore Cooper.

noblesse oblige /nəu'bles ɒ'bli:ʒ/ the aristocracy ought to behave honourably. [French = nobility obliges]

noblewoman *n.* (*plural* **noblewomen**) a peeress.

nobody /'nəubədɪ/ *pron.* 1. no person. 2. a person of no importance.

nock *n.* a notch on a bow or arrow for the bowstring.

nocturnal /nɒk'tɜ:nəl/ *adj.* 1. of or in the night. 2. done or active by night. —**nocturnally** *adv.* [from Latin *nocturnus* = of night, from *nox* = night]

nocturne /'nɒktɜ:n/ *n.* 1. a dreamy musical piece, often for piano; the form was introduced by John Field (1782–1837) and adopted by Chopin. 2. a picture of a night scene. [French]

nod *v.t./i.* (**-dd-**) 1. to incline the head slightly and briefly in greeting, assent, or command. 2. to let the head droop in drowsiness; to be drowsy. 3. to incline (the head); to signify (assent etc.) by a nod. 4. (of flowers etc.) to bend downwards and sway. 5. to make a mistake due to a momentary lack of alertness or attention. —*n.* a nodding of the head. —**nod off**, to fall asleep.

noddle *n.* (*colloquial*) the head.

noddy *n.* 1. a simpleton. 2. a tropical sea-bird of the genus *Anous*, resembling the tern.

node *n.* 1. a knob-like swelling. 2. the point on the stem of a plant where a leaf or bud grows out. 3. a point at which a curve crosses itself. 4. the intersecting point of a planet's orbit and the ecliptic or of two great circles of the celestial sphere. 5. a position in a ◊standing wave pattern at which there is no vibration. Points at which there is maximum vibration are called **antinodes**. Stretched strings, for example, can show nodes when they vibrate. —**nodal** *adj.* [from Latin *nodus* = knot]

nodule /'nɒdju:l/ *n.* a small rounded lump; a small node; (in geology, a lump of mineral or other matter found within rocks or formed on the seabed. —**nodular** *adj.* [from Latin *nodulus* diminutive of *nodus* = knot]

Noel /nəu'el/ *n.* (in carols etc.) Christmas. [French from Latin *natalis* (*nasci* = be born)]

nog[1] *n.* a small block or peg of wood.

nog[2] *n.* 1. strong beer. 2. an egg-nog.

noggin /'nɒgɪn/ *n.* 1. a small mug. 2. a small (usually 1/4-pint) measure. 3. (*slang*) the head.

nogging *n.* brickwork in a wooden frame.

Noh /nəu/ a variant of ◊Nō, traditional Japanese drama.

noise /nɔɪz/ *n.* 1. a sound, especially a loud or unpleasant one; a series of loud sounds. 2. irregular fluctuations accompanying a transmitted signal. 3. (in *plural*) utterances, especially conventional remarks. —*v.t.* to make public, to make generally known. [from Old French = outcry, from Latin]

noiseless *adj.* without a sound. —**noiselessly** *adv.*

noisome /'nɔɪsəm/ *adj.* (*literary*) noxious, disgusting, especially to the smell. [from obsolete *noy* (from *annoy*)]

noisy /'nɔɪzɪ/ *adj.* full of, making, or attended with noise; given to making a noise. —**noisily** *adv.*, **noisiness** *n.*

Nolan /'nəulən/ Sidney 1917– . Australian artist. He created atmospheric paintings of the outback, exploring themes from Australian history such as the life of the outlaw Ned Kelly and the folk heroine Mrs Fraser.

Noland /'nəulənd/ Kenneth 1924– . US painter, associated with ◊Abstract Expressionism. In the 1950s and early 1960s his work centred on geometry, colour, and symmetry. His later 1960s paintings experimented with the manipulation of colour vision and afterimages, pioneering the field of ◊Op art.

Nolde /'nɒldə/ Emil. Adopted name of Emil Hansen 1867–1956. German Expressionist painter. Nolde studied in Paris and Dachau, joined the group of artists known as Die Brücke 1906–07, and visited Polynesia in 1913; he then became almost a recluse in NE Germany. Many of his themes were religious.

Nollekens /'nɒlɪkənz/ Joseph 1737–1823. English sculptor, specializing in portrait busts and memorials.

Nom *n.* Chinese-style characters used in writing the Vietnamese language. Nom characters were used from the 13th century for Vietnamese literature, but were replaced in the 19th century by a romanized script known as **Quoc Ngu**. The greatest Nom writer was the poet Nguyen Du.

nomad /'nəumæd/ *n.* a member of a people roaming from place to place for pasture; a wanderer. —**nomadic** /-'mædɪk/ *adj.*, **nomadism** *n.* [from French from Latin from Greek (*nemō* = to pasture)]

nom de plume /nɒm də 'plu:m/ (*plural* **noms de plume** *pronounced* the same) a writer's assumed name. [sham French = pen-name]

nomen /'nəumen/ *n.* (in ancient Rome) the second or family name, e.g. Marcus *Tullius* Cicero. [Latin = name]

nomenclature /nəu'menklətʃə/ *n.* a system of names or naming, terminology. [French from Latin *calare* = call)]

nominal /'nɒmɪnəl/ *adj.* 1. of, as, or like a noun. 2. of or in names. 3. existing in name only, not real or actual. 4. (of a sum of money etc.) virtually nothing, much below the actual value. —**nominal value**, face value. —**nominally** *adv.*

nominalism /'nɒmɪnəlɪzəm/ *n.* the theory that universals or general ideas (abstract concepts) are mere names (as opposed to ◊realism). —**nominalist** *n.*, **nominalistic** /-'lɪstɪk/ *adj.*

nominate /'nɒmɪneɪt/ *v.t.* to appoint to or propose for election to an office; to name or appoint (a date etc.). —**nominator** *n.* [from Latin *nominare*]

nomination /nɒmɪ'neɪʃən/ *n.* 1. nominating, being nominated. 2. the right of nominating.

nominative /'nɒmɪnətɪv/ *n.* in the grammar of some inflected languages, such as Latin, Russian, and Sanskrit, the form of a word used to indicate that a noun or pronoun is the subject of a finite verb. —*adj.* (*Grammar*) of or in the nominative.

nominee /nɒmɪ'ni:/ *n.* a person who is nominated.

non- prefix meaning not; (with *v.* to form *adj.*) not doing (*non-skid*), not behaving in a specified way (*non-stick*), not to be treated in a specified way (*non-iron*). [from Old French from Latin *non* = not]

nonage /'nəunɪdʒ, 'nɒn-/ *n.* being under full legal age, minority; immaturity. [from Anglo-French]

nonagenarian /nəʊnədʒɪˈneərɪən, ˈnɒn-/ *n.* a person from 90 to 99 years old. [from Latin (*nonageni* = ninety each)]

nonagon /ˈnɒnəgɒn/ *n.* a plane figure with nine sides and angles. [Latin (*nonus* = ninth and Greek *-gōnos* = angled)]

non-aligned *adj.* (of a state) not in alliance with any major bloc. —**non-aligned movement** the states adopting the strategic and political position of neutrality towards the USA and USSR. The 1989 non-aligned summit meeting was attended by 102 member states.

non-belligerent *adj.* taking no active or open part in a war. —*n.* a non-belligerent state.

nonce *n.* the time being, the present, especially in **for the nonce**, for the occasion only. —**nonce-word** *n.* a word coined for one occasion. [from obsolete *than anes* = the one (occasion), alteration by wrong division]

nonchalant /ˈnɒnʃələnt/ *adj.* not feeling or showing anxiety or excitement, calm and casual. —**nonchalance** *n.*, **nonchalantly** *adv.* [French (*chaloir* = be concerned)]

non-com abbreviation of non-commissioned (officer).

non-combatant *adj.* not fighting (especially in war, as being a civilian, army chaplain etc.). —*n.* such a person.

non-commissioned *adj.* (especially of an officer) of a grade below those with commissions.

non-committal *adj.* not committing oneself to a definite opinion, course of action etc. —**non-committally** *adv.*

non compos mentis /nɒn ˈkɒmpɒs ˈmentɪs/ not in one's right mind, insane. [Latin, = not in control of one's mind]

non-conductor *n.* a substance that does not conduct heat or electricity.

nonconformist /nɒnkənˈfɔːmɪst/ *n.* 1. one who does not conform to the doctrine or discipline of an established church; **Nonconformist**, a member of a (usually Protestant) sect dissenting from the Church of England. 2. one who does not conform to a prevailing principle.

nonconformity /nɒnkənˈfɔːmɪtɪ/ *n.* 1. nonconformists or their principles etc. 2. failure to conform. 3. lack of correspondence between things.

non-contributory *adj.* not involving contributions.

non-co-operation *n.* failure or refusal to co-operate, especially as a protest.

nondescript /ˈnɒndɪskrɪpt/ *adj.* indeterminate, lacking distinctive characteristics. —*n.* a nondescript person or thing. [from *descript* = described (Latin *scribere* = write)]

none /nʌn/ *pron.* not any, no one; no person(s). —*adj.* not any (usually with the reference supplied by an earlier or later noun). —*adv.* by no amount. —**none the less** nevertheless. [Old English = not one]

nonentity /nɒˈnentɪtɪ/ *n.* 1. a person or thing of no importance. 2. non-existence; a non-existent thing. [from Latin (*ens* participle of *esse* = be)]

nones /nəʊnz/ *n.pl.* the 7th day of Mar, May, July, Oct, the 5th of the other months, in the ancient Roman calendar. [from Old French from Latin *nonae* (*nonus* = ninth)]

nonesuch variant of nonsuch.

non-event *n.* an event that turns out to be insignificant (usually contrary to hopes or expectations).

non-existent *adj.* not existing.

non-ferrous *adj.* (of a metal) not iron or steel.

non-fiction *n.* a classification of literature that includes books in all subjects other than fiction.

non-intervention *n.* the principle or practice of not interfering in others' disputes.

Nonjuror *n.* a priest of the Church of England who, after the revolution of 1688, refused to take the oaths of allegiance to William and Mary. The Nonjurors continued to exist as a rival church for over a century, and consecrated their own bishops, the last of whom died in 1805.

non-metal *n.* one of a set of elements (around 20 in total) with certain physical and chemical properties opposite to those of metals. Non-metals accept electrons (see ◊electronegativity) and are sometimes called electronegative elements.

non-moral *adj.* not concerned with morality.

non-nuclear *adj.* not involving nuclei or nuclear energy.

Nono /ˈnəʊnəʊ/ Luigi 1924–1990. Italian composer. After the opera *Intolleranza* 1960 his style moved away from ◊serialism to become increasingly expressionistic. His music is frequently polemical in subject matter, and a number of works incorporate tape-recorded elements.

nonpareil /ˈnɒnpərəl/ *adj.* unrivalled, unique. —*n.* such a person or thing. [French (*pareil* = equal)]

non-party /nɒnˈpɑːtɪ/ *adj.* independent of political parties.

nonplus /nɒnˈplʌs/ *v.t.* (-ss-) to perplex completely. [from Latin *non plus* = not more]

non-profit-making *adj.* (of an enterprise) not conducted primarily with a view to making profits.

non-proliferation *n.* limitation of the number especially of nuclear weapons.

nonrenewable resource a natural resource, such as coal or oil, that takes thousands or millions of years to form naturally and can therefore not be replaced once it is consumed.

nonsense /ˈnɒnsəns/ *n.* 1. words put together in a way that does not make sense. 2. absurd or foolish talk, ideas, or behaviour. —*interjection* you are talking nonsense. —**nonsensical** /-ˈsensɪkəl/ *adj.*, **nonsensically** *adv.*

non sequitur /nɒn ˈsekwɪtə(r)/ 1. a statement that has little or no relevance to the one that preceded it. 2. a conclusion that does not logically follow from the premises. [Latin = it does not follow]

non-skid *adj.* that does not, or is designed not to, skid.

non-smoker *n.* 1. a person who does not smoke. 2. a compartment in a train etc., where smoking is forbidden.

non-starter *n.* (*colloquial*) an idea or person not worth consideration.

non-stick *adj.* (of a saucepan etc.) to which food will not stick during cooking.

nonstop *adj.* 1. (of a train etc.) not stopping at intermediate stations. 2. not ceasing, done without pausing. —*adv.* without stopping.

nonsuch /ˈnʌnsʌtʃ/ *n.* 1. an unrivalled person or thing, a paragon. 2. a plant (*Medicago lupulina*) resembling lucerne with black pods.

non-U *adj.* (*colloquial*) not characteristic of upper-class speech or behaviour.

non-union *adj.* not belonging to or not made by members of a trade union.

non-voting *adj.* (of shares) not entitling the holder to a vote.

non-white *adj.* belonging to a race other than the white race. —*n.* a non-white person.

noodle *n.* 1. a simpleton. 2. (*slang*) the head.

noodles /ˈnuːdlz/ *n.pl.* narrow strips of pasta used in soups etc. [from German *nudel*]

nook /nʊk/ *n.* a secluded corner or recess.

noon *n.* 12 o'clock in the day, midday. [Old English, from Latin *nona* (*hora*) = ninth hour]

noonday *n.* midday.

noose *n.* a loop in a rope etc. with a running knot; a snare, a bond. —*v.t.* to catch with or enclose in a noose.

nor *conj.* and not; and not either. [contraction from obsolete *nother*.

nor' abbreviation of north, especially in compounds (*nor'-ward, nor'wester*).

Nordenskjöld /ˈnɔːdnʃəʊld/ Nils Adolf Erik 1832–1901. Swedish explorer. He made voyages to the Arctic with the geologist Torell and in 1878–79 discovered the Northeast Passage. He published the results of his voyages in a series of books, including *Voyage of the Vega round Asia and Europe* 1881.

Nordic /ˈnɔːdɪk/ *adj.* 1. of or belonging to an extremely artificial, unscientific sub-racial grouping of people who, as a population, are tall, fair-coloured, and long-headed. 2. of Scandinavia, Finland, or Iceland. —*n.* a Nordic person. [from French *nordique* (*nord* = north)]

Nord-Pas-de-Calais /ˈnɔː pɑː də kæˈleɪ/ region of N France; **area** 12,400 sq km/4,786 sq mi; **capital** Lille; **départements** Nord and Pas-de-Calais; **population** (1986) 3,923,000.

Norfolk /ˈnɔːfək/ county on E coast of England; **area** 5,360 sq km/2,069 sq mi; **administrative headquarters** Norwich; **physical rivers**: Ouse, Yare, Bure, Waveney; the Broads; Halvergate Marshes wildlife area; **population** (1987) 736,000.

Norfolk Broads area of some 12 interlinked freshwater lakes in E England, created about 600 years ago by the digging out of peat deposits; they are used for boating and fishing.

North America: early history

*c.*35,000 BC	American Indians entered North America from Asia.
*c.*9000 BC	Marmes man, earliest human remains.
*c.*300 BC	Earliest Moundbuilder sites.
*c.*AD 1000	Leif Ericsson reached North America.
12th–14th centuries	Height of the Moundbuilder and Pueblo cultures.
1492	12 Oct Columbus first sighted land in the Caribbean.
1497	Giovanni Caboto reached Canada.
1565	First Spanish settlements in Florida.
1585	First attempted English settlement in North Carolina.
1607	First permanent English settlement, Jamestown, Virginia.

Noriega /nɒri'eɪgə/ Manuel (Antonio Morena) 1940– . Panamanian soldier and politician, effective ruler of Panama 1982–1989. He was commissioned in the National Guard in 1962, became intelligence chief in 1970 and chief of staff in 1982. He wielded considerable political power behind the scenes, which led to his enlistment by the US Central Intelligence Agency until charges of drug trafficking discredited him. Relations with the USA deteriorated and in Dec 1989 President Bush ordered an invasion of Panama by 24,000 US troops. This eventually resulted in Noriega's arrest and detention, pending trial, in the USA.

norm *n.* a standard, pattern, or type; a standard amount of work etc.; customary behaviour. [from Latin *norma*, literally = carpenter's square]

normal /'nɔːməl/ *adj.* 1. conforming to what is standard or usual; typical. 2. free from mental or emotional disorder. 3. (of a line) at right angles, perpendicular. —*n.* 1. the normal value of a temperature etc.; the usual state, level etc. 2. a line at right angles. —**normalcy** *n.*, **normality** /-'mælɪtɪ/ *n.* [French or from Latin *normalis*]

normalize *v.t./i.* to make or become normal; to cause to conform. —**normalization** /-'zeɪʃən/ *n.*

normally *adv.* 1. in a normal manner. 2. usually.

Norman /'nɔːmən/ *n.* 1. a native or inhabitant of Normandy. 2. in the Middle Ages, any of the descendants of the Norsemen (to whose chief, Rollo, Normandy was granted by Charles III of France in 911) who adopted French language and culture. During the 11th and 12th centuries they conquered England in 1066 (under William the Conqueror), Scotland in 1072, parts of Wales and Ireland, S Italy, Sicily, and Malta, and took a prominent part in the Crusades. 3. any of the kings of England from William I to Stephen. 4. ◊Norman architecture —*adj.* of the Normans or their style of architecture, the English term for ◊Romanesque. —**Norman French,** the form of medieval French spoken by the Normans; the later form of this in English legal use. It remained the language of the English court until the 15th century, the official language of the law courts until the 17th century, and is still used in the Channel Islands. [from Old French from Old Norse = north man]

Norman /'nɔːmən/ Greg 1955– . Australian golfer, nicknamed 'the Great White Shark'. After many wins in his home country, he enjoyed success on the European PGA Tour before joining the US Tour. He has won the world match-play title three times.

Norman architecture English term for ◊Romanesque, the style of architecture used in England in the 11th–12th centuries. Norman buildings are massive, with round arches (although trefoil arches are sometimes used for small openings). Buttresses are of slight projection, and vaults are barrel-roofed. Examples in England include the Keep of the Tower of London and parts of the cathedrals of Chichester, Gloucester, and Ely.

Normandy /'nɔːməndɪ/ two regions of NW France: ◊Haute-Normandie and ◊Basse-Normandie; **principal towns** Alençon, Bayeux, Caen, Cherbourg, Dieppe, Deauville, Lisieux, Le Havre, and Rouen. It was named after the Viking Northmen (Normans), the people who conquered and settled the area in the 9th century. As a French duchy it reached its peak under William the Conqueror and was renowned for its centres of learning established by Lanfranc and St Anselm. Normandy was united with England 1100–35. England and France fought over it during the Hundred Years' War, England finally losing it in 1449 to Charles VII. In World War II the Normandy beaches were the site of the Allied invasion on D-day, 6 June 1944.

Normandy landings alternative name for ◊D-Day.

normative /'nɔːmətɪv/ *adj.* of or establishing a norm. [from French from Latin *norma*]

Norn /nɔːn/ in Scandinavian mythology, any of three goddesses of fate – the goddess of the past (Urd), the goddess of the present (Verdandi), and the goddess of the future (Skuld).

Norris /'nɒrɪs/ Frank 1870–1902. US novelist. A naturalist writer, he completed only two parts of his projected trilogy, the *Epic of Wheat: The Octopus* 1901, dealing with the struggles between wheat farmers, and *The Pit* 1903, describing the Chicago wheat exchange.

Norse /nɔːs/ *n.* 1. the Norwegian language. 2. the Scandinavian language group. —*adj.* of ancient Scandinavia, especially Norway. —**the Norse,** the Norwegians. **Old Norse,** the Germanic language of Norway and its colonies, or of Scandinavia, down to the 14th century [from Dutch (*noord* = north)]

Norseman /'nɔːsmæn/ *n.* (*plural* **Norsemen**) an early inhabitant of Norway. The term Norsemen is also applied to Scandinavian ◊Vikings who during the 8th–11th centuries raided and settled in Britain, Ireland, France, Russia, Iceland, and Greenland.

north /nɔːθ/ *n.* 1. the point of the horizon corresponding to the compass point 90° anticlockwise from east; the direction in which this lies. 2. (usually **North**) the part of a country or town lying to the north. —*adj.* 1. towards, at, near, or facing the north. 2. (of wind) blowing from the north. —*adv.* towards, at, or near the north. —**north country,** the northern part of England. **north-north-east** *n.*, *adj.*, & *adv.* midway between north and north-east. **north-north-west** *n.*, *adj.*, & *adv.* midway between north and north-west. **North Pole,** the northern end of the Earth's axis of rotation. **North Star,** the Pole Star (see ◊Polaris). [Old English]

North Oliver 1943– . US Marine lieutenant colonel. In 1981 he was inducted into the National Security Council, where he supervised the mining of Nicaraguan harbours 1983, an air-force bombing raid on Libya 1986, and an arms-for-hostages deal with Iran 1985 which, when uncovered in 1986 (◊Irangate), forced his dismissal and conviction on felony charges.

North Thomas 1535–1601. English translator, whose version of ◊Plutarch's *Lives* 1579 was the source for Shakespeare's Roman plays.

North America the third largest of the continents (including Central America), and over twice the size of Europe; **area** 24,000,000 sq km/9,500,000 sq mi; **largest cities** (population over 1 million) Mexico City, New York, Chicago, Toronto, Los Angeles, Montreal, Guadalajara, Monterrey, Philadelphia, Houston, Guatemala City, Vancouver, Detroit; **physical** mountain belts to the east (Appalachians) and west (see ◊Cordilleras), the latter including the Rocky Mountains and the Sierra Madre; coastal plain on the Gulf of Mexico, into which the Mississippi River system drains from the central Great Plains; the St Lawrence and the Great Lakes form a rough crescent (with the Great Bear and Great Slave lakes, and lakes Athabasca and Winnipeg) around the exposed rock of the great Canadian/Laurentian Shield, into which Hudson Bay breaks from the north; **exports** the immensity of the US home market makes it less dependent on exports, and the USA's industrial and technological strength automatically tends to exert a pull on Canada, Mexico, and Central America. The continent is unique in being dominated in this way by a single power, which also exerts great influence over the general world economy; **population** (1981) 345 million; the native American Indian, Inuit, and Aleut peoples are now a minority within a population predominantly of European immigrant origin. Many Africans were brought in as part of the slave trade; **language** predominantly English, Spanish, French.

North American Indian an indigenous inhabitant of North America (see ◊American Indians). Many prefer to describe themselves as 'Native Americans' rather than 'American Indians', the latter term having arisen because Columbus believed he had reached the East Indies.

Northamptonshire /nɔː'θæmptənʃə/ county in central England; **area** 2,370 sq km/915 sq mi; **administrative headquarters** Northampton; **population** (1987) 562,000.

Northants abbreviation of Northamptonshire.

North Atlantic Drift a warm ocean ◊current in the N Atlantic Ocean; the continuation of the ◊Gulf Stream. It flows east across the Atlantic and has a mellowing effect on the climate of W Europe, particularly the British Isles and Scandinavia.

North Atlantic Treaty an agreement signed in 1949 by Belgium, Canada, Denmark, France, Iceland, Italy, Luxembourg, the Netherlands, Norway, Portugal, the UK, the USA; Greece, Turkey in 1952; West Germany in 1955; and Spain in 1982. They agreed that 'an armed attack against one or more of them in Europe or North America shall be considered an attack against them all'. The North Atlantic Treaty Organization (NATO) is based on this agreement.

North Atlantic Treaty Organization (NATO) an association set up 1949 to provide for the collective defence of the major W European and North American states against the perceived threat from the USSR. Its chief body is the Council of Foreign Ministers (who have representatives in permanent session), and there is an international secretariat in Brussels, Belgium, and also the Military Committee consisting of the Chiefs of Staff. The military headquarters SHAPE (Supreme Headquarters Allied Powers, Europe) is in Chièvres, near Mons, Belgium.

North Brabant /'nɔːθ brə'bænt/ (Dutch *Noordbrabant*) southern province of the Netherlands, lying between the Maas (Meuse) and Belgium; **area** 4,940 sq km/1,907 sq mi; **population** (1988) 2,156,000. The capital is 's Hertogenbosch. Former heathland is now under mixed farming. Towns such as Breda, Tilburg, and Eindhoven are centres of brewing, engineering, microelectronics, and textile manufacture.

North Cape (Norwegian *Nordkapp*) cape in the Norwegian county of Finnmark; the most northerly point of Europe.

North Carolina /'nɔːθ kærə'laɪnə/ state of the USA; nickname Tar Heel or Old North State; **area** 136,400 sq km/52,650 sq mi; **capital** Raleigh; **population** (1986) 6,331,000; **history** the first permanent settlement was made in 1663; it became one of the original Thirteen States in 1789.

Northcliffe /'nɔːθklɪf/ Alfred Charles William Harmsworth, 1st Viscount Northcliffe 1865–1922. British newspaper proprietor, born in Dublin. Founding the *Daily Mail* in 1896, he revolutionized popular journalism, and with the *Daily Mirror* from 1903 originated the picture paper. In 1908 he also obtained control of *The Times*.

North Dakota /'nɔːθ də'kəʊtə/ prairie state of the N USA; nickname Sioux or Flickertail State; **area** 183,100 sq km/70,677 sq mi; **capital** Bismarck; **towns** Fargo, Grand Forks, Minot; **population** (1984) 686,000; **history** acquired by the USA partly in the ◊Louisiana Purchase of 1803, and partly by treaty with Britain in 1813; it became a state in 1889.

north-east *n.* **1.** the point midway between north and east; the direction in which this lies. **2.** (usually **North-East**) the part of a country or town lying to the north-east. —*adj.* of, towards, or coming from the north-east. —*adv.* towards, at, or near the north-east.

northeaster /nɔː'θiːstə/ *n.* a north-east wind.

North-East India an area of India comprising Meghalaya, Assam, Mizoram, Tripura, Manipur, Nagaland, and Arunachal Pradesh, linked with the rest of India only by a narrow corridor. There is opposition to immigration from Bangladesh and the rest of India, and demand for secession.

North East Passage sea route from the N Atlantic, around Asia, to the N Pacific, pioneered by ◊Nordenskjöld 1878–79 and developed by the USSR in settling N Siberia from 1935. The USSR owns offshore islands and claims it as an internal waterway; the USA claims that it is international.

northerly /'nɔː'ðəlɪ/ *adj.* & *adv.* **1.** in a northern position or direction. **2.** (of wind) blowing from the north (approximately).

northern /'nɔː'ðən/ *adj.* of or in the north. —**northern lights**, the ◊aurora borealis. —**northernmost** *adj.* [Old English]

northerner *n.* a native or inhabitant of the north.

Northern Ireland see ◊Ireland, Northern.

northern lights common name for the ◊aurora borealis.

Northern Rhodesia /'nɔː'ðən rəʊ'diː ʃə/ former name (until 1964) of ◊Zambia.

Northern Territory territory of Australia; **area** 1,346,200 sq km/519,633 sq mi; **capital** and chief port Darwin; **population** (1987) 157,000; **history** originally part of New South Wales, it was annexed in 1863 to South Australia but from 1911 until 1978 (when self-government was achieved) was under the control of the Commonwealth of Australia government. Mineral discoveries on land occupied by Aborigines led to a royalty agreement in 1979.

North Holland (Dutch *Noord-Holland*) low-lying coastal province of the Netherlands occupying the peninsula jutting northwards between the North Sea and the IJsselmeer; **area** 2,670 sq km/1,031 sq mi; **population** (1988) 2,353,000. Most of it is below sea level, protected by sand dunes and artificial dykes. The capital is Haarlem. The province is famous for its bulbfields, and produces grain and vegetables.

northing /'nɔː'θɪŋ/ *n.* (*Nautical*, etc.) **1.** a distance travelled or measured northward. **2.** a northerly direction.

North Korea see ◊Korea, North.

Northman *n.* (*plural* **Northmen**) **1.** a ◊Viking. **2.** a native of Scandinavia, especially of Norway.

North Pole the northern point where an imaginary line penetrates the Earth's surface by the axis about which it revolves; see also ◊Poles and ◊Arctic.

North Rhine–Westphalia /'nɔː'θ 'raɪn west'feɪlɪə/ (German *Nordrhein-Westfalen*) administrative region of Germany (German *Land*); **area** 34,100 sq km/13,163 sq mi; **capital** Düsseldorf; **population** (1988) 16,700,000; **history** see ◊Westphalia.

Northrop /'nɔː'θrəp/ John 1891–1987. US chemist. In the 1930s he crystallized a number of enzymes, including pepsin and trypsin, showing conclusively that they were proteins. He shared the 1946 Nobel Prize for Chemistry with Wendell ◊Stanley and James ◊Sumner.

North Sea sea to the E of Britain and bounded by the coasts of Belgium, the Netherlands, Germany, Denmark, and Norway; area 523,000 sq km/202,000 sq mi; average depth 55 m/180 ft, greatest depth 660 m/2,165 ft. In the NE it joins the Norwegian Sea, and in the S it meets the Straits of Dover. It has fisheries, oil, and gas. Pollution from Britain's sewage disposal is a problem.

Northumb. abbreviation of Northumberland.

Northumberland /nɔː'θʌmbələnd/ county in N England; **area** 5,030 sq km/1,942 sq mi; **administrative headquarters** Newcastle-upon-Tyne; **population** (1986) 301,000.

Northumberland /nɔː'θʌmbələnd/ John Dudley, Duke of Northumberland *c.*1502–1553. English politician, son of the privy councillor Edmund Dudley (beheaded in 1510), and chief minister until Edward VI's death in 1553. He tried to place his daughter-in-law Lady Jane ◊Grey on the throne, and was executed on Mary I's accession.

Northumbria /nɔː'θʌmbrɪə/ Anglo-Saxon kingdom that covered NE England and SE Scotland, comprising the 6th-century kingdoms of Bernicia (Forth–Tees) and Deira (Tees–Humber), united in the 7th century. It accepted the supremacy of Wessex in 827 and was conquered by the Danes in the late 9th century.

northward /'nɔː'θwəd/ *adj.* & *adv.* northwards towards the north. —*n.* a northward direction or region.

north-west *n.* **1.** the point midway between north and west; the direction in which this lies. **2.** (usually **North-West**) the part of a country or town lying to the north-west. —*adj.* of, towards, or coming from the north-west. —*adv.* towards, at, or near the north-west. —**north-westerly** *adj.* & *adv.*, **north-western** *adj.*

northwester /nɔː'θ'westə/ *n.* a north-west wind.

North West Passage Atlantic–Pacific sea route around the N of Canada. Early explorers included the Englishmen Martin ◊Frobisher and, later, John Franklin, whose failure to return 1847 led to the organization of 39 expeditions in the next 10 years. The polar explorer ◊Amundsen was the first European to sail through. Canada, which owns offshore islands, claims it as an internal waterway; the USA insists that it is an international waterway and sent an icebreaker through without permission in 1985.

Northwest Territories /'nɔːθwest 'terɪtəriz/ territory of Canada; **area** 3,426,300 sq km/1,322,552 sq mi; **capital** Yellowknife; **physical** extends to the North Pole, to Hudson's Bay in the E, and in the W to the edge of the Canadian Shield; **population** (1986) 52,000; over 50% native peoples (Indian, Inuit); **history** the area was the northern part of Rupert's Land, bought by the Canadian government from the Hudson's Bay Company in 1869. An act of 1952 placed the Northwest Territories under a commissioner acting in Ottawa under the Ministry of Northern Affairs and Natural Resources. In 1990 territorial control of over 350,000 sq km/135,000 sq mi of the Northwest Territories was given to the ◊Inuit.

North Yorkshire /'jɔːkʃə/ county in NE England; **area** 8,320 sq km/3,212 sq mi; **administrative headquarters** Northallerton; **population** (1987) 706,000.

Norway /'nɔːweɪ/ Kingdom of; country in NW Europe, on the Scandinavian peninsula, bounded E by Sweden and NE by Finland and the USSR; **area** 387,000 sq km/149,421 sq mi (includes Svalbard and Jan Mayen); **capital** Oslo; **physical** fjords; glaciers in north; midnight sun and northern lights; mountainous; forests cover 25%; extends N of Arctic Circle; **territories** dependencies in the Arctic (Svalbard and Jan Mayen) and in Antarctica (Bouvet and Peter I Island, and Queen Maud Land); **head of state** Harald V from 1991; **head of government** Prime Minister Gro Harlem Brundtland from 1990; **political system** constitutional monarchy; **exports** petrochemicals from North Sea oil and gas, paper, wood pulp, furniture, iron ore and other minerals, high-tech goods, sports goods, fish **population** (1990 est) 4,214,000; **language** Norwegian (official); Lapp; **recent history** 1940–45 occupied by Germany; joined NATO 1949, Nordic Council 1952, EFTA 1960; accepted into EC 1972, but application withdrawn after a referendum. In 1988 Gro Harlem Brundtland awarded Third World Prize. In 1991 King Olaf V succeeded by his son Harald V.

Norwegian /nɔː'wiːdʒən/ adj. of Norway or its people or language. —n. **1.** a native or inhabitant of Norway. **2.** the language of Norway. [from Latin *Norvegia* = Norway]

Norwich /'nɒrɪdʒ/ cathedral city in Norfolk, E England; population (1986) 121,600. Industries include shoes, clothing, chemicals, confectionery, engineering, and printing.

Nos. abbreviation of numbers.

nose /nəuz/ n. **1.** the organ above the mouth on the face or head of a human or animal, used for smelling and breathing. The external part is divided down the middle by a septum of ◊cartilage. The nostrils contain plates of cartilage that can be moved by muscles and have a growth of stiff hairs at the margin to prevent foreign objects from entering. The whole nasal cavity is lined with a ◊mucous membrane that warms and moistens the air and ejects dirt. In the upper parts of the cavity the membrane contains 50 million olfactory receptor cells (cells sensitive to smell). **2.** the sense of smell. **3.** the ability to detect a particular thing. **4.** an odour or perfume, e.g. of a wine. **5.** the open end of a tube, pipe etc.; the front end or projecting part of a thing, e.g. of a car or aircraft. **6.** (slang) a police informer. —v.t./i. **1.** to perceive a smell or; to discover by smell; to detect. **2.** to thrust one's nose against or into. **3.** to pry or search. **4.** to make one's way cautiously forward. —**by a nose**, by a very narrow margin. **keep one's nose clean**, to stay out of trouble. **pay through the nose**, to have to pay an exorbitant price. **put a person's nose out of joint**, to embarrass or disconcert him or her. **rub a person's nose in it**, to remind him or her humiliatingly of an error etc. **turn up one's nose**, to show disdain. **under one's nose**, right before one. **with one's nose in the air**, haughtily. [Old English]

nosebag n. a bag containing fodder, hung on a horse's head.

noseband n. the lower band of a bridle passing over the horse's nose and attached to the cheek-straps.

nosebleed n. bleeding from the nose. Although usually minor and easily controlled, the loss of blood may occasionally be so rapid as to be life-threatening, particularly in small children. Most nosebleeds can be stopped by simply squeezing the nose for a few minutes with the head tilted back, but in cases of severe bleeding the nose may need to

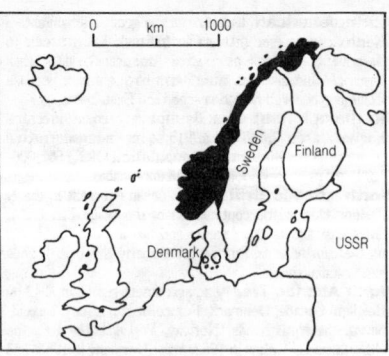

Norway

be packed with ribbon gauze or cauterized, and in exceptional cases transfusion may be required.

nose-cone n. the cone-shaped nose of a rocket etc.

nosedive n. a steep downward plunge by an aeroplane; a sudden plunge or drop. —v.i. to make a nosedive.

nosegay /'nəuzgeɪ/ n. a small bunch of flowers. [from *nose* and obsolete *gay* = ornament]

nosh v.t./i. (slang) to eat. —n. (slang) food, especially a snack. —**nosh-up** n. (slang) a large meal. [Yiddish]

nosocomial adj. of any infection acquired in a hospital or other medical facility, whether its effects are seen during the patient's stay or following discharge. Widely prevalent in some hospitals, nosocomial infections threaten patients who are seriously ill or whose immune systems have been suppressed. The threat is compounded by the prevalence of drug-resistant ◊pathogens endemic to the hospital environment.

nostalgia /nɒ'stældʒiə/ n. **1.** sentimental yearning for the past. **2.** homesickness. —**nostalgic** adj., nostalgically adv. [from Greek *nostos* = return home and *algos* = pain]

Nostradamus /nɒstrə'dɑːməs/ Latinized name of Michel de Nôtredame 1503–1566. French physician and astrologer who was consulted by Catherine de' Medici and was physician to Charles IX. His book of prophecies in rhyme, *Centuries* 1555, has had a number of interpretations.

nostril /'nɒstrɪl/ n. either of the openings in the nose. [Old English = nose-hole]

nostrum /'nɒstrəm/ n. **1.** a quack remedy, a patent medicine. **2.** a pet scheme, especially for political or social reform. [Latin = of our own make]

nosy /'nəuzɪ/ adj. inquisitive, prying. —**Nosy Parker**, a busybody. —**nosily** adv., noosiness n.

not adv. expressing negation (also colloquial -n't as in *don't, haven't*); expressing denial or refusal, or used elliptically for a negative phrase etc. —**not at all**, (in a polite reply to thanks) there is no need to thank me. [contraction of *nought*]

notable /'nəutəbəl/ adj. worthy of notice, remarkable, eminent. —n. an eminent person. —**notability** /-'bɪlɪtɪ/ n., **notably** adv. [from Old French from Latin *notabilis* (*nota* = mark)]

notary /'nəutərɪ/ n. (in full **notary public**) a person with the authority to draw up deeds and perform other legal formalities. —**notarial** /-'teəriəl/ adj. [from Latin = secretary]

notate /nəu'teɪt/ v.t. to write in notation. [back-formation]

notation /nəu'teɪʃən/ n. the representing of numbers, quantities, sounds (in music), dance movements etc., by symbols; any set of such symbols. [French or from Latin]

notch n. **1.** a V-shaped cut or indentation. **2.** a step in a graded system. —v.t. **1.** to make a notch or notches in. **2.** (often with *up*) to score (as) with notches. [from Anglo-French]

note n. **1.** a brief record of facts, topics etc., written down to aid the memory. **2.** a short or informal letter; a memorandum; a formal diplomatic communication. **3.** a short comment on or explanation of a word or passage in a book etc. **4.** a banknote. **5.** a written promise of payment. **6.** notice, attention; eminence. **7.** a written sign representing the pitch and duration of a musical sound; a single tone of definite pitch made by a musical instrument, a voice etc.; a key of a piano etc. **8.** a significant sound or feature of expression. **9.** a characteristic, a distinguishing feature. —*v.t.* **1.** to notice, to give attention to. **2.** (often with *down*) to record as a thing to be remembered or observed. **3.** (in *past participle*) celebrated, well known *for.* —**hit** or **strike the right note,** to speak or act in exactly the right manner. [from Old French from Latin *nota* = mark or *notare* = to mark]

notebook *n.* a small book with blank pages in which to write memoranda.

notecase *n.* a wallet for holding bank-notes.

notelet /'nəʊtlɪt/ *n.* a small folded card or sheet for an informal letter.

notepaper *n.* paper for writing letters.

noteworthy *adj.* worthy of attention, remarkable.

nothing /'nʌθɪŋ/ *n.* **1.** no thing; not anything. **2.** a person or thing of no importance. **3.** non-existence, what does not exist. **4.** no amount, nought. —*adv.* not at all, in no way. —**for nothing,** at no cost, without payment; to no purpose. **have nothing on,** to be naked. **have nothing on (a person),** to possess no advantage over; to be much inferior to. **nothing doing,** (*colloquial*) no prospect of success or agreement. [Old English]

nothingness *n.* **1.** non-existence. **2.** worthlessness, triviality.

notice /'nəʊtɪs/ *n.* **1.** attention, observation; heed. **2.** news or information of what has happened or is about to happen; a warning. **3.** written or printed information or instructions displayed publicly. **4.** formal declaration of one's intention to end an agreement or leave employment at a specified time. **5.** an account or review in a newspaper or magazine. —*v.t.* **1.** to perceive, to become aware of. **2.** to remark upon. —**at short notice,** with little warning. **notice-board** *n.* a board for displaying notices. **take (no) notice,** to show (no) signs of interest. **take notice of,** to observe; to act upon. [from Old French from Latin *notitia* = being known (*notus* = known)]

noticeable *adj.* **1.** noteworthy. **2.** perceptible. —**noticeably** *adv.*

notifiable /'nəʊtɪfaɪəbəl/ *adj.* (of a disease or pest etc.) that must be notified to a public authority.

notify /'nəʊtɪfaɪ/ *v.t.* **1.** to inform. **2.** to report; to make (a thing) known. —**notification** /-fɪ'keɪʃən/ *n.* [from Old French from Latin *notificare*]

notion /'nəʊʃən/ *n.* **1.** a concept or idea, a conception; a vague view or opinion. **2.** an understanding, an inclination; an intention. **3.** (in *plural*, *US*) small items used in sewing, haberdashery. [from Latin *notio* (*notus* = known)]

notional *adj.* hypothetical; imaginary. —**notionally** *adv.*

notochord /'nəʊtəʊkɔːd/ *n.* a flexible longitudinal rod found at some stage of the life cycle of all ◊chordates. [from Greek *nōton* = back and *chord*²]

notorious /nəʊ'tɔːrɪəs/ *adj.* well known, especially for an unfavourable reason. —**notoriety** /-tə'raɪtɪ/ *n.*, **notoriously** *adv.* [from Latin *notitia* = being known (*notus* = known)]

Nottingham /'nɒtɪŋəm/ industrial city and administrative headquarters of Nottinghamshire, England; products include engineering, coalmining, bicycles, textiles, knitwear, pharmaceuticals, tobacco, lace, electronics; population (1981) 217,080.

Nottinghamshire /'nɒtɪŋəmʃə/ county in central England; **area** 2,160 sq km/834 sq mi; **administrative headquarters** Nottingham; **population** (1987) 1,008,000.

Notts. abbreviation of Nottinghamshire.

notwithstanding /nɒtwɪθ'stændɪŋ, -wɪð-/ *prep.* in spite of, without prevention by. —*adv.* nevertheless.

Nouakchott /nu:æk'ʃɒt/ capital of Mauritania; population (1985) 500,000. Products include salt, cement, and insecticides.

nougat /'nu:gɑː/ *n.* a sweet made from sugar or honey, nuts, and egg-white. [French from Provençal *noga* = nut]

nought /nɔːt/ *n.* **1.** the figure 0. **2.** (*poetic* or *archaic*) nothing. —**noughts and crosses,** a game in which two players seek to complete a row of three of either kind in a square array of usually nine spaces. [Old English (*ne* = not and *aught* = anything)]

Nouméa /nu:'meɪə/ port on the SW coast of New Caledonia; population (1983) 60,100.

noun /naʊn/ *n.* in grammar, a word used as the name of a person, animal, place, object, idea, quality, or time. **Concrete nouns** name objects, for example *house, tree;* **proper nouns** name persons and places, for example *John Alden,* the *White House;* **abstract nouns** name ideas, for example *love, anger.* [from Anglo-French from Latin *nomen* = name]

nourish /'nʌrɪʃ/ *v.t.* **1.** to sustain with food (*literal* or *figurative*). **2.** to foster or cherish (a feeling etc.). [from Old French from Latin (as *nutrire*)]

nourishing *adj.* containing much nourishment.

nourishment *n.* **1.** sustenance, food. **2.** nourishing.

nous /naʊs/ *n.* **1.** in philosophy, the mind or intellect. **2.** (*colloquial*) common sense. [Greek]

nouveau riche /nu:vəʊ 'ri:ʃ/ (*plural* **nouveaux riches,** pronounced the same) one who has acquired wealth only recently, especially one who displays this ostentatiously. [French = new rich]

nouvelle cuisine a style of French cooking that avoids rich sauces, emphasizing fresh ingredients and attractive presentation. [French = new cooking]

Nov or **Nov.** abbreviation of November.

nova /'nəʊvə/ *n.* (*plural* **novae, novas**) a faint star that suddenly erupts in brightness and then subsides. Novae are believed to occur in close ◊double star systems, when gas from one star flows to a companion ◊white dwarf. The gas ignites and is thrown off in an explosion, the star increasing in brightness by 10,000 times or more. Unlike a ◊supernova, the star is not completely disrupted by the outburst. [Latin, femine of *novus* -new]

Novak /'nəʊvæk/ Kim (Marilyn Pauline) 1933– . US film actress who starred in such films as *Pal Joey* 1957, *Bell, Book and Candle* 1958, *Vertigo* 1958, *Kiss Me Stupid* 1964, and *The Legend of Lyla Clare* 1968.

Novalis /nəʊ'vɑːlɪs/ pen name of Friedrich Leopold von Hardenberg 1772–1801. Pioneer German Romantic poet, who wrote *Hymnen an die Nacht/Hymns to the Night* 1800, prompted by the death of his fiancée. He left two unfinished romances, *Die Lehrlinge zu Sais/The Novices of Sais* and *Heinrich von Ofterdingen.*

Nova Scotia /'nəʊvə 'skəʊʃə/ province of E Canada; **area** 55,500 sq km/21,423 sq mi; **capital** and chief port Halifax; **population** (1986) 873,000; **history** a French settlement was established in 1604, but the settlers were expelled in 1613 by English colonists from Virginia. The name of the colony was changed from **Acadia** to Nova Scotia in 1621. England and France contended for possession of the territory until Nova Scotia (which then included present-day New Brunswick and Prince Edward Island) was ceded to Britain in 1713; Cape Breton Island remained French until 1763. Nova Scotia was one of the four original provinces of the dominion of Canada.

novel /'nɒvəl/ *adj.* of a new kind, strange, hitherto unknown. —*n.* a fictitious prose story published as a complete book. As the main form of narrative fiction in the 20th century, the novel is frequently classified according to genres and subgenres such as the ◊historical novel, ◊detective fiction, ◊fantasy, and ◊science fiction. [from Old French from Latin *novellus* (*novus* = new)]

novelette /nɒvə'let/ *n.* **1.** a short novel. **2.** (*derogatory*) a romantic novel.

novelist /'nɒvəlɪst/ *n.* a writer of novels.

novella /nə'velə/ *n.* a short novel or narrative story. [Italian]

Novello /nə'veləʊ/ Ivor. Stage name of Ivor Novello Davies 1893–1951. Welsh composer and actor-manager. He wrote popular songs, such as 'Keep the Home Fires Burning', in World War I, and musicals in which he often appeared as the romantic lead, including *Glamorous Night* 1925, *The Dancing Years* 1939, and *Gay's the Word* 1951.

novelty /'nɒvəltɪ/ *n.* **1.** the quality of being novel. **2.** a novel thing or occurrence. **3.** a small unusual object. [from Old French]

November /nəʊ'vembə/ *n.* the 11th month of the year. [from Old French from Latin (*novem* = nine, because originally the ninth month in the Roman calendar)]

novena /nə'viːnə/ *n.* a Roman Catholic devotion consisting of special prayers or services on nine successive days. [Latin (*novem* = nine)]

Noverre /nɒˈveə/ Jean-Georges 1727–1810. French choreographer, writer, and ballet reformer. He promoted ◊*ballet d'action* (with a plot) and simple, free movement, and is often considered the creator of modern Classical ballet. *Les Petits Riens* 1778 was one of his works.

Novgorod /ˈnɒvgərɒd/ industrial city on the Volkhov river, NW USSR; products include chemicals, engineering, clothing, and brewing; population (1987) 228,000. It was a major trading city in medieval times.

Novgorod school a Russian school of icon and mural painters, active in Novgorod from the late 14th to the 16th centuries. The artists were inspired by the work of the refugee Byzantine artist ◊Theophanes the Greek. Russian artists imitated his linear style, but this became increasingly stilted and mannered.

novice /ˈnɒvɪs/ *n.* 1. a probationary member of a religious order. 2. a new convert. 3. an inexperienced person, a beginner. [from Old French from Latin *novicius* (*novus* = new)]

noviciate /nəˈvɪʃɪət/ *n.* or **novitiate** 1. the period of being a novice. 2. a religious novice. 3. novices' quarters. [from French or Latin]

Novi Sad /ˈnɒvi ˈsɑː/ industrial and commercial city, capital of the autonomous province of Vojvodina, Yugoslavia, on the river Danube; products include pottery, cotton, leather, textiles, and tobacco; population (1981) 257,700.

Novocaine *n.* trade name of *procaine*, the first synthetic local anaesthetic, invented 1905. It has now been replaced by agents such as ◊lignocaine.

Novosibirsk /nɒvəsiˈbiəsk/ industrial city in W Siberia, USSR, on the river Ob; products include engineering, textiles, chemicals, and food processing; population (1987) 1,423,000.

now *adv.* 1. at the present or mentioned time. 2. by this time. 3. immediately. 4. on this further occasion. 5. in the present circumstances. 6. (without reference to time, giving various tones to a sentence) surely, I insist, I wonder etc. —*conj.* (also with *that*) as a consequence of the fact. —*n.* this time, the present. —**for now**, until a later time. **now and again** or **then**, from time to time, intermittently. [Old English]

nowadays /ˈnaʊədeɪz/ *adv.* at the present time or age, in these times. —*n.* the present time.

Nowa Huta /ˈnəʊvə ˈhuːtə/ an industrial suburb of Kraków, on the Vistula River. It is the centre of Poland's steel industry.

nowhere /ˈnəʊweə/ *adv.* in or to no place. —*pron.* no place. —**get nowhere**, to make no progress. **nowhere near**, not nearly. [Old English]

nowt *n.* (*colloquial* or *dialect*) nothing. [variant of *nought*]

noxious /ˈnɒkʃəs/ *adj.* harmful, unwholesome. [from Latin *noxius* (*noxa* = harm)]

nozzle *n.* the spout of a hose etc., for a jet to issue from. [diminutive of *nose*]

Np symbol for neptunium.

NPA abbreviation of the Philippine New People's Army.

npn in electronics, when a ◊p-type layer occurs between two ◊n-type layers in a semiconductor device or a region in this.

nr or **nr.** abbreviation of near.

NS abbreviation of 1. New Style. 2. new series. 3. Nova Scotia.

NSAID abbreviation for *nonsteroidal anti-inflammatory drug*. There are several and they are effective in the long-term treatment of rheumatoid ◊arthritis and osteoarthritis, by reducing swelling and pain in soft tissues. Bleeding into the digestive tract is a serious side effect: NSAIDs should not be taken by persons with peptic ulcers.

NSPCC abbreviation of National Society for the Prevention of Cruelty to Children, a British charity.

NSW abbreviation of New South Wales.

n't see ◊not

NT abbreviation of 1. New Testament. 2. (*Australian*) Northern Territory. 3. (Royal) National Theatre.

NTP abbreviation of 1. normal temperature and pressure, now called **standard temperature and pressure** (see ◊STP).

nu /njuː/ *n.* the 13th letter of the Greek alphabet, (ν, N) = n.

Nu /nuː/ (Thakin) 1907– . Myanmar politician, prime minister of Burma (now Myanmar) for most of the period from

Novgorod The theatre, the monument to the thousandth anniversary of the foundation of the Russian state (862), and the cathedral of St Sophia (11th century) inside the Novgorod kremlin.

1948 to the military coup of 1962. Exiled from 1966, U Nu returned to the country in 1980 and, in 1988, helped found the National League for Democracy opposition movement.

nuance /ˈnjuːɑ̃s/ *n.* a subtle difference in or shade of meaning, feeling, colour etc. [French (*nuer* = to shade)]

nub *n.* 1. or **nubble** a small lump, especially of coal. 2. the central point or core of a matter or problem etc. —**nubbly** *adj.*

Nuba /ˈnjuːbə/ *n.* a member of the peoples of the Nuba mountains, west of the White Nile, Sudan. Their languages belong to the Nubian branch of the Chari-Nile family.

nubile /ˈnjuːbaɪl/ *adj.* (of a woman) marriageable, sexually attractive. —**nubility** /-ˈbɪlɪtɪ/ *n.* [from Latin (*nubere* = become wife of)]

nuclear /ˈnjuːklɪə/ *adj.* 1. of or constituting a nucleus. 2. using nuclear energy. **nuclear accident**, an explosion or the accidental release of radioactive materials. (see ◊Chernobyl; ◊nuclear energy; ◊nuclear reactor). **nuclear family**, a father, mother, and their child or children. **nuclear fission**, see ◊nuclear energy; **nuclear fuel**, a source of nuclear energy. **nuclear fusion** see ◊nuclear energy. **nuclear physics**, physics dealing with atomic nuclei and their reactions (see ◊nuclear reaction, nuclear forces, and ◊radioactive decay. **nuclear power** ◊nuclear energy; a country possessing nuclear weapons. **nuclear waste** see separate entry. **nuclear weapon**, see ◊nuclear warfare. **nuclear winter**, a conjectural period of changed climatic conditions following a nuclear war, characterized by extreme cold temperatures and other effects catastrophic to animal and vegetable life, caused by an atmospheric layer of smoke and dust particles blocking the Sun's rays.

nuclear arms verification the process of checking the number and types of nuclear weapons held by a country in accordance with negotiated limits. Techniques used include reconnaissance satellites, which use angled cameras to detect submarines or weapon silos; ◊telemetry, or radio transmission of instrument readings; **interception** to gain information on the performance of weapons under test; **on-site inspection** by experts visiting bases, launch sites, storage facilities, and test sites in another country; **radar tracking** of missiles in flight; **seismic monitoring** of underground tests.

nuclear energy energy from the inner core or ◊nucleus of the atom, as opposed to energy released in chemical processes, which is derived from the electrons surrounding the nucleus. **Nuclear fission**, as in an atom bomb, is achieved by allowing a ◊neutron to strike the nucleus of an atom of uranium-235, which then splits apart to release two or three other neutrons. If the uranium-235 is pure, a ◊chain reaction is set up when these neutrons in turn strike other nuclei. This happens very quickly, resulting in the burst of energy seen in the atomic bomb. However, the process can be controlled by absorbing excess neutrons in 'control rods' (which may be made of steel alloyed with boron), which is the method used in a ◊nuclear reactor. **Nuclear fusion** is the process that occurs in the hydrogen bomb, and in the sun and other stars, whereby hydrogen nuclei fuse to form helium nuclei with an accompanying release of energy. Attempts to harness fusion for commercial power production have so far been unsuccessful, although machines such as the Joint European Torus (or ◊JET) have demonstrated that fusion power is theoretically feasible. In 1989 it was claimed that fusion could occur in a test tube at room temperature, but this was not confirmed.

nuclearize /'nju:kliəraɪz/ *v.t.* to supply or equip (a nation) with nuclear weapons. —**nuclearization** /-'zeɪʃən/ *n.*

nuclear reaction a reaction involving the nuclei of atoms. Atomic nuclei can undergo changes either as a result of ◊radioactive decay, or as a result of particle bombardment in a machine or device, as in the production of cobalt-60 by the bombardment of cobalt-59 with neutrons. Nuclear ◊fission and nuclear ◊fusion are examples of nuclear reactions. The enormous amounts of energy released arise from the mass–energy relation put forward by Einstein, stating that $E = mc^2$ (where E is energy, m is mass, and c is the velocity of light). In nuclear reactions the sum of the masses of all the products (on the atomic mass unit scale) is less than the sum of the masses of the reacting particles. This lost mass is converted into energy according to Einstein's equation.

nuclear reactor a device for producing nuclear energy in a controlled manner. There are various types of reactor in use, all using nuclear fission. In a **gas-cooled reactor**, a circulating gas under pressure (such as carbon dioxide) removes heat from the core of the reactor, which usually contains natural uranium. The efficiency of the fission process is increased by slowing neutrons in the core by using a ◊moderator such as carbon. The reaction is controlled with neutron-absorbing rods made of boron. See also ◊AGR (advanced gas-cooled reactor). A **water-cooled reactor**, such as the steam-generating heavy water (deuterium oxide) reactor, has water circulating through the hot core. This is converted to steam, which drives turbo-alternators for generating electricity. See also ◊pressurized-water reactor and ◊fast reactor. Concerns about safety have led to study of reactors incorporating process-inherent ultimate safety (PIVS), a safety system for the emergency cooling of a reactor by automatically flooding an overheated core with water.

nuclear warfare war involving the use of nuclear weapons. Nuclear-weapons research began in Britain in 1940, but was transferred to the USA after it entered World War II. The research programme, known as the Manhattan Project, was directed by J Robert Oppenheimer. The first ◊atom bomb relied on the use of a chemical explosion to trigger a chain reaction. The first test explosion was at Alamogordo, New Mexico, 16 July 1945; the first use in war was by the USA against Japan 6 Aug 1945 at ◊Hiroshima. The worldwide total of nuclear weapons in 1989 was about 50,000, and the number of countries possessing nuclear weapons stood officially at five – USA, USSR, UK, France, and China – although many other nations were thought either to have a usable stockpile (Israel, South Africa) or the ability to produce them quickly (India, Pakistan, and others). See also ◊hydrogen bomb, neutron bomb (see ◊neutron).

nuclear waste the radioactive and toxic by-products of the nuclear-energy and nuclear-weapons industries. Reactor waste is of three types: **high-level** spent fuel, or the residue when nuclear fuel has been removed from a reactor and reprocessed; **intermediate**, which may be long-or short-lived; and **low-level**, but bulky, waste from reactors, which has only short-lived radioactivity. Disposal, by burial on land or at sea, has raised problems of safety, environmental pollution, and security. In absolute terms, nuclear waste cannot be safely relocated or disposed of.

nucleate /'nju:klieɪt/ *v.t./i.* 1. to form (into) a nucleus. 2. (in *past participle*) possessing a nucleus. [from Latin]

nucleic acid /nju:'kli:ɪk/ a complex organic acid made up of a long chain of nucleotides. The two types, known as DNA (deoxyribonucleic acid) and RNA (ribonucleic acid), form the basis of heredity. The nucleotides are made up of a sugar (deoxyribose or ribose), a phosphate group, and one of four purine or pyrimidine bases. The order of the bases along the nucleic acid strand contains the genetic code.

nucleolus *n.* in biology, a structure found in the nucleus of ◊eukaryotic cells. It produces the RNA that makes up the ◊ribosomes, from instructions in the DNA.

nucleon /'njup:kliɒn/ *n.* a particle found inside the nucleus of an ◊atom, either a ◊proton or a ◊neutron.

nucleonic /nju:kli'ɒnɪk/ *adj.* of nucleons or nucleonics. —**nucleonics** *n.pl.* (usually treated as *singular*) the branch of science and technology concerned with atomic nuclei and nucleons, especially the practical use of nuclear phenomena. [after *electronics*]

nucleon number the number of nucleons (protons or neutrons) in the nucleus of an ◊atom. The nucleon number (also called the mass number) is the sum of the proton number and the neutron number. In symbols, such as $^{14}_{6}C$, which represent nuclear ◊isotopes, the lower, or subscript, number is the proton number. The upper, or superscript, number is the nucleon number.

nucleoprotein /nju:kliəu'prəuti:n/ *n.* a compound of a protein with nucleic acid.

nucleosynthesis /nju:kliəu'sɪnθɪsɪs/ *n.* the formation of atoms more complicated than the hydrogen atom by cosmic processes.

nucleus /'nju:kliəs/ *n.* (*plural* **nuclei** /-iaɪ/) 1. the central part or thing around which others collect; in physics, the positively charged central part of an ◊atom, which constitutes almost all its mass. Except for hydrogen nuclei, which have only ◊protons, nuclei are composed of both protons and ◊neutrons. In biology, the central, membrane-enclosed part of a ◊eukaryotic cell, containing the chromosomes. 2. a kernel, an initial part meant to receive additions. [Latin = kernel (*nux* = nut)]

nude /nju:d/ *adj.* naked, bare, unclothed. —*n.* a picture or sculpture etc., of a nude human figure; a nude person. —**in the nude,** in an unclothed state, naked. —**nudity** *n.* [from Latin *nudus*]

nudge *v.t./i.* 1. to prod gently with the elbow to attract attention. 2. to push gradually. —*n.* such a prod or push.

nudist /'nju:dɪst/ *n.* a person who advocates or practises going unclothed. —**nudism** *n.*

Nuer /'nu:ə/ *n.* (*plural* the same) a member or the language of an African people living in south-eastern Sudan. —*adj.* of this people or their language. [local name]

Nuffield /'nʌfiːld/ William Richard Morris, Viscount Nuffield 1877–1963. English manufacturer and philanthropist. Starting with a small cycle-repairing business, in 1910 he designed a car that could be produced cheaply, and built up Morris Motors Ltd at Cowley, Oxford.

nugatory /'nju:gətərɪ/ *adj.* 1. futile, trifling. 2. inoperative, not valid. [from Latin *nugari* = to trifle]

nugget /'nʌgɪt/ *n.* 1. a lump of gold etc., found as a lump of the ◊native ore. Nuggets occur in ◊alluvial deposits where river-borne particles of the metal have adhered to one another. 2. something valuable. [from dialect *nug* = lump]

nuisance /'nju:səns/ *n.* 1. a source of trouble or annoyance; an annoying person, thing, or circumstance. 2. in law, interference with enjoyment of, or rights over, land. There are two kinds of nuisance. **Private nuisance** affects a particular occupier of land, such as noise from a neighbour; the aggrieved occupier can apply for an ◊injunction and claim ◊damages. **Public nuisance** affects an indefinite number of members of the public, such as obstructing the highway; it is a criminal offence. In this case, individuals can claim damages only if they are affected more than the general public. [from Old French = hurt (*nuire* = to hurt)]

Nujoma /nu:'dʒəumə/ Sam 1929– . Namibian left-wing politician, president from 1990, founder and leader of ◊SWAPO (the South-West Africa People's Organization) from 1959. He was exiled in 1960 and controlled guerrillas from Angolan bases until the first free elections were held in 1989, taking office early the following year.

nuke /nju:k/ *n.* (*slang, especially US*) a nuclear bomb, weapon etc. —*v.t.* to attack with nuclear weapons.

Nukua'lofa /nu:kuə'ləufə/ capital and port of Tonga on Tongatapu; population (1986) 29,000.

null *adj.* 1. void, not valid. 2. characterless, expressionless. 3. non-existent. —**nullity** *n.* [from French or Latin *nullus* = none]

nullify /'nʌlɪfaɪ/ *v.t.* to neutralize, to invalidate. —**nullification** /-'keɪʃən/ *n.*

nulli secundus second to none. [Latin]

numb /nʌm/ *adj.* deprived of feeling or the power of motion. —*v.t.* to make numb; to stupefy, to paralyse. —**numbly** *adv.*, **numbness** *n.* [from *nome* past participle of obsolete *nim* = take]

numbat /'nʌmbæt/ *n.* the banded anteater *Myrmecobius fasciatus*, a small rare marsupial native to SW Australia. It is brown with white stripes on the back, and has a long tubular tongue to gather termites and ants. The body is about 25 cm/10 in long, and the tongue can be extended 10 cm/4 in. [Aboriginal]

number *n.* 1. a count, sum, or aggregate of persons, things, or abstract units. 2. an arithmetical value showing position in a series; a symbol or figure representing this. The everyday number system is the decimal system, which uses the base ten. ◊Real numbers include all rational numbers (integers, or whole numbers, and fractions) and irrational numbers (those not expressible as fractions). ◊Complex numbers include the real and unreal numbers (real-number multiples of the square root of –1). 3. a person or thing having a place in a series; a single issue of a magazine; an item in a programme etc. 4. numerical reckoning. The ◊binary number system, used in computers, has two as its base. 5. a company, a collection, a group. 6. (in *plural*) numerical preponderance. 7. in grammar, the class of word-forms including all singular, all plural, or all dual etc., forms. —*v.t.* 1. to count. 2. to assign a number or numbers to. 3. to have or amount to a specified number. 4. to include as a member of a class. 5. (in *passive*) to be restricted in number. —**by numbers**, following simple instructions identified by numbers. **have a person's number**, (*slang*) to understand the person, or his or her motives. **one's number is up**, (*colloquial*) one is doomed to die. **number one**, (*colloquial*) oneself; the most important. **number-plate** *n.* a plate on a vehicle giving the registration number. **without number**, innumerable. [from Anglo-French from Latin *numerus*]

numberless *adj.* innumerable.

numerable /'nju:mərəbəl/ *adj.* countable. [from Latin]

numeral /'nju:mərəl/ *n.* a symbol denoting a number. —*adj.* of or denoting a number.

numerate /'nju:mərət/ *adj.* acquainted with the basic principles of mathematics and science. —**numeracy** *n.* [after *literate*]

numeration /nju:mə'reɪʃən/ *n.* a method or process of numbering; calculation.

numerator /'nju:məreɪtə/ *n.* the number above the line in a vulgar fraction showing how many of the parts indicated by the denominator are taken.

numerical /nju:'merɪkəl/ *adj.* of, in, or denoting a number or numbers. —**numerically** *adv.*

numerology /nju:mə'rɒlədʒɪ/ *n.* the study of the occult significance of numbers.

numerous /'nju:mərəs/ *adj.* many; consisting of many. [from Latin *numerosus*]

numinous /'nju:mɪnəs/ *adj.* indicating the presence of a divinity; spiritual, awe-inspiring. [from Latin (*numen* = deity)]

numismatic /nju:mɪz'mætɪk/ *adj.* of coins or coinage or medals. —**numismatist** /-'mɪzmətɪst/ *n.* [from French from Latin from Greek *nomisma* = current coin]

numismatics *n. pl.* (usually treated as *singular*) the study of ◊coins, or ◊medals and decorations.

numskull *n.* a stupid person.

nun *n.* a member of a community of women living apart under religious vows. Christian nuns take vows of poverty, chastity and obedience; their convents are ruled by a superior (often elected), who is subject to the authority of the bishop of the diocese or sometimes directly to the pope. See ◊monasticism. [Old English and from Old French from Latin *nonna* = elderly woman]

nuncio /'nʌnʃɪəʊ/ *n.* (*plural* **nuncios**) an ambassador of the pope, accredited to a civil government. The office dates from the 16th century. [Italian, from Latin *nuntius* = messenger]

Nunn /nʌn/ Trevor 1940– . British stage director, linked with the Royal Shakespeare Company from 1968. He received a Tony award (with John Caird 1948–) for his production of *Nicholas Nickleby* 1982 and for the musical *Les Misérables* 1987.

nunnery *n.* a convent of nuns.

nuptial /'nʌpʃəl/ *adj.* of marriage or a wedding. —*n.* (usually in *plural*) a wedding. [French or from Latin (*nuptiae* = wedding)]

Nuremberg /'njuərəmbɜ:g/ (German **Nürnberg**) industrial city in Bavaria, S Germany; population (1988) 467,000; products include electrical and other machinery, precision instruments, textiles, and toys. From 1933 the Nuremberg rallies were held here, and in 1945–1946 the Nuremberg trials of war criminals.

Nuremberg rallies annual meetings 1933–38 of the German ◊Nazi Party. They were characterized by extensive torchlight parades, marches in party formations, and mass rallies addressed by Nazi leaders such as Hitler and Goebbels.

Nuremberg trials after World War II, the trials of the 24 chief ◊Nazi war criminals between Nov 1945 and Oct 1946 by an international military tribunal consisting of four judges and four prosecutors: one of each from the USA, UK, USSR, and France. An appendix accused the German cabinet, general staff, high command, Nazi leadership corps, ◊SS, ◊Sturmabteilung, and ◊Gestapo of criminal behaviour.

Nureyev /nju'reɪef/ Rudolf 1938– . Soviet dancer and choreographer. A soloist with the Kirov Ballet, he defected to the West in 1961, where he was mainly associated with the Royal Ballet and was Margot ◊Fonteyn's principal partner.

nurse *n.* 1. a person trained to care for the sick, injured, or infirm. 2. a person employed to take charge of young children. —*v.t./i.* 1. to work as a nurse; to attend to (a sick person). 2. to feed or be fed at the breast. 3. to hold or treat carefully. 4. to foster, to promote the development of; to pay special attention to. —**nursing home**, a privately run hospital or home for invalids, old people etc. [from Old French *norice* from Latin *nutrire* = nourish]

nurseling *n.* or **nursling** an infant that is being suckled.

nursemaid *n.* a young woman employed to take charge of a child or children.

nursery /'nɜ:sərɪ/ *n.* 1. a room or place equipped for young children; a day nursery. 2. a place where plants are reared for sale. —**nursery rhyme**, a simple traditional song or story in rhyme for children. **nursery school**, a school for children below normal school age. **nursery slopes**, slopes suitable for beginners at skiing.

nurseryman *n.* (*plural* **nurserymen**) a male owner of or worker in a plant nursery.

nursing *n.* care of the sick, the very young, the very old, and the disabled. Organized training originated in 1836 in Germany, and was developed in Britain by the work of Florence ◊Nightingale, who, during the Crimean War, established standards of scientific, humanitarian care in military hospitals. Nurses give day-to-day care and carry out routine medical and surgical procedures under the supervision of a physician.

nurture /'nɜ:tʃə/ *n.* 1. bringing up, fostering care. 2. nourishment. —*v.t.* to bring up, to rear. [from Old French *nour(e)ture* from Latin *nutrire* = nourish]

nut *n.* 1. a fruit consisting of a hard or tough shell round an edible kernel; this kernel. A nut is formed from more than one carpel, but only one seed becomes fully formed; the remainder is aborted. The wall of the fruit, the pericarp, becomes hard and woody, forming the outer shell. Examples are the acorn, hazelnut, and sweet chestnut. 2. a pod containing hard seeds. 3. a small usually hexagonal piece of metal with a hole through it screwed on the end of a bolt to secure it: a common method of fastening pieces of metal together. They came into use at the turn of the 19th century. 4. (*slang*) the head. 5. (*slang*) a crazy person. 6. a small lump (of coal etc.). —*v.i.* (**-tt-**) to seek or gather nuts. —**do one's nut**, (*slang*) to be very angry. **nut-case** *n.* (*slang*) a crazy person. **nut and bolt** a common method of fastening pieces of metal or wood together. The nut consists of a small block (usually metal) with a threaded hole in the centre for screwing on to a threaded rod or pin (bolt or screw). **nuts and bolts**, the practical details. **nut-tree** *n.* a tree bearing nuts, especially the hazel. [Old English]

nutation /nju:'teɪʃən/ *n.* 1. nodding. 2. the oscillation of the Earth's axis, caused by the varying gravitational pulls of the Sun and Moon. Nutation changes the angle of the Earth's axial tilt (average 23.5°) by about 9 seconds of arc to either side of its mean position, a complete cycle taking just over 18.5 years. 3. (in botany) the spiral movement exhibited by the tips of certain stems during growth; it enables a climbing plant to find a suitable support. Nutation sometimes also occurs in tendrils and flower stalks. [from Latin *nutare* = nod]

nutcracker *n*. **1.** (usually in *plural*) an instrument for cracking nuts. **2.** a bird *Nucifraga caryocatactes* of the crow family found in areas of coniferous forest in Asia and parts of Europe, particularly mountains. About 33 cm/1.1 ft long, it has speckled plumage and a powerful beak. It feeds on conifer seeds. Irregularly, there is a mass migration of nutcrackers from Siberia to W Europe.

nuthatch /'nʌthætʃ/ *n*. a small European climbing bird *Sitta europaea*. It has a blue-grey back and a buff breast. It feeds on nuts, insects etc. The nest is built in a hole in a tree, and five to eight white eggs with reddish-brown spots are laid in early summer.

nutmeg *n*. the kernel of the seed of the evergreen tree *Myristica fragrans*, native to the Moluccas. Both the nutmeg and its secondary covering, known as **mace**, are used as spice in cookery. [partial translation of Old French *nois muguede* = musky nut]

nutria /'njuːtrɪə/ *n*. the skin or fur of the coypu. [Spanish = otter]

nutrient /'njuːtrɪənt/ *adj*. serving as or providing nourishment. —*n*. a nutrient substance. [from Latin *nutrire* = nourish]

nutriment /'njuːtrɪmənt/ *n*. nourishing food *literal* or *figurative*). [from Latin]

nutrition /njuː'trɪʃən/ *n*. food, nourishment; the science of food and its effect on human and animal health and disease. The study of the basic nutrients required to sustain life, their bioavailability in foods and overall diet, and the effect of cooking and storage. —**nutritional** *adj*., **nutritionally** *adv*. [French or from Latin]

nutritious /njuː'trɪʃəs/ *adj*. efficient as food. —**nutritiously** *adv*., **nutritiousness** *n*. [from Latin]

nutritive /'njuːtrɪtɪv/ *adj*. of nutrition; nutritious. [from French from Latin]

nuts *adj*. (*slang*) crazy, mad. —**nuts about** or **on**, (*slang*) very fond of or enthusiastic about.

nutshell *n*. the hard exterior covering of a nut. —**in a nutshell**, in a few words.

nutter *n*. (*slang*) a crazy person.

nutty *adj*. **1.** full of nuts. **2.** tasting like nuts. **3.** (*slang*) crazy. —**nuttily** *adv*., **nuttiness** *n*.

Nuuk /nuːk/ Inuit for ◊Godthaab, capital of Greenland.

nux vomica /nʌks 'vɒmɪkə/ the seed of an East Indian tree *Strychnos nux-vomica*, yielding strychnine. [Latin (*nux*= nut, and *vomitus* = vomit]

nuzzle *v.t./i*. **1.** to press or rub gently with the nose. **2.** to nestle, to lie snug. [from *nose*]

NW abbreviation of north-west, north-western.

NY abbreviation of New York.

nyala *n*. an antelope *Tragelaphus angasi* found in the thick bush of S Africa. About 1 m/3 ft at the shoulder, it is greyish-brown with thin vertical white stripes. Males have horns up to 80 cm/2.6 ft long.

Nyasa /'niːæsə/ former name for Lake ◊Malawi.

Nyasaland /'niːæsəlænd/ former name (until 1964) of ◊Malawi.

Nyerere /njə'reəri/ Julius (Kambarage) 1922– . Tanzanian socialist politician, president 1964–85. Originally a teacher, he devoted himself from 1954 to the formation of the Tanganyika African National Union and subsequent campaigning for independence. He became chief minister in 1960, was prime minister of Tanganyika 1961–62, president of the newly formed Tanganyika Republic 1962–64, and first president of Tanzania 1964–85.

Nyers /njeəʃ/ Rezso 1923– . Hungarian socialist leader. As secretary of the ruling Hungarian Socialist Worker's Party's central committee 1962–74 and a member of its

Nyerere Tanzanian politician and premier Dr Julius Nyerere, in London, 1960.

politburo 1966–74, he was the architect of Hungary's liberalizing economic reforms in 1968.

Nykvist /'niːkvɪst/ Sven 1922– . Swedish director of photography, associated with the film director Ingmar Bergman. He worked frequently in the USA from the mid-1970s. His films include *The Virgin Spring* 1960 (for Bergman), *Pretty Baby* 1978 (for Louis Malle), and *Fanny and Alexander* 1982 (for Bergman).

nylon /'nailɒn/ *n*. **1.** a strong light synthetic polymer that may be produced as filaments, bristles, or sheets and as moulded objects. It is similar in chemical structure to protein. Nylon was the first all-synthesized fibre, made from petroleum, natural gas, air, and water by the Du Pont firm in 1938. It is used in the manufacture of moulded articles, textiles, and medical sutures. Nylon fibres are stronger and more elastic than silk and are relatively insensitive to moisture and mildew. **2.** fabric made from nylon yarn. **3.** (in *plural*) nylon stockings. [invented word, with *-on* suggested by *cotton* and *rayon*; there is no evidence to support the derivations frequently given for this word in popular sources]

nymph /nɪmf/ *n*. **1.** in Greek mythology, a guardian spirit of nature. **Hamadryads** or **dryads** guarded trees; **naiads**, springs and pools; **oreads**, hills and rocks; and **nereids**, the sea. **2.** (*poetic*) a maiden. **3.** in entomology, the immature form of insects that do not have a pupal stage – for example, grasshoppers and dragonflies. Nymphs generally resemble the adult, but do not have fully formed reproductive organs or wings. [from Old French from Latin from Greek *numphē*]

nymphet /'nɪmfet, -'fet/ *n*. **1.** a young nymph. **2.** a nymphlike or sexually attractive girl.

nympho /'nɪmfəʊ/ *n*. (*plural* **nymphos**) (*colloquial*) a nymphomaniac. [abbreviation]

nymphomania /nɪmfəʊ'meɪnɪə/ *n*. excessive sexual desire in women. —**nymphomaniac** *n*.

nystagmus /nɪ'stægməs/ *n*. continual rapid oscillation of the eyeballs; an eye-disease characterized by this. [from Greek *nustagmos* = nodding (*nustazō* = nod)]

NZ abbreviation of New Zealand.

o, O /əu/ n. (plural os, o's) the 15th letter of the alphabet; (as a numeral, in telephone numbers etc.) nought, zero.

o' /ə/ prep. of, on (especially in phrases, e.g. o'clock, will-o'-the-wisp). [abbreviation]

O /əu/ interjection prefixed to a name in the vocative or expressing a wish, entreaty etc. [natural exclamation; variant of ◊oh]

O symbol for oxygen.

o/a abbreviation of on account.

oaf n. (plural oafs) an awkward lout. —**oafish** adj. [from Old Norse]

oak n. a forest tree Quercus robur or Q. petraea, one of over 300 known species widely distributed in temperate zones, with hard, straight-grained wood, acorns, and lobed leaves; its wood; an allied or similar tree; (attributive) of oak. —**oak-apple** or **oak-gall** (see ◊gall). **Oak-apple Day**, 29 May, the day of Charles II's restoration in 1660, when oak-apples or oak leaves were worn to commemorate the occasion after the Battle of Worcester 1651 when Charles II hid in an oak tree. —**oaken** adj. [Old English]

Oakley /'əukli/ Annie (Phoebe Anne Oakley Mozee) 1860–1926. US sharpshooter, a member of Buffalo Bill's Wild West Show (see William ◊Cody).

Oaks n. a horse race, one of the English classics, run at Epsom racecourse in June (normally two days after the ◊Derby), for three-year-old fillies only. The race is named after the Epsom home of the 12th Earl of Derby.

oakum /'əukəm/ n. loose fibre obtained by picking old rope to pieces. [Old English = off-combings]

OAP abbreviation of old-age pension(er).

oar /ɔ:/ n. **1.** a pole with a blade used to propel a boat by leverage against the water. **2.** a rower. —**put one's oar in**, to interfere. [Old English]

oarfish n. an oceanic fish (Regalecus glesne), in the family of ribbon-fishes. Occasionally up to 9 m/30 ft long, it has no scales, a small mouth, large eyes, and a compressed head.

oarsman n. (plural oarsmen) a rower. —**oarsmanship** n., **oarswoman** n.fem.

OAS abbreviation of ◊Organization of American States.

oasis /əu'eisis/ n. (plural oases /-i:z/) **1.** a fertile spot in the desert, with a spring or well of water. **2.** a thing or circumstance offering relief in difficulty. [Latin from Greek, apparently of Egyptian origin]

oast n. a kiln for drying hops. —**oast-house** n. a building containing this. [Old English]

Oastler /'əustlə/ Richard 1789–1861. English social reformer. He opposed child labour and the ◊Poor Law 1834, which restricted relief, and was largely responsible for securing the Factory Act 1833 and the Ten Hours Act 1847. He was born in Leeds, and was given the nickname of the 'Factory King' for his achievements on behalf of workers.

oat n. **1.** a type of grass of the genus Avena, a cereal food. The plant has long, narrow leaves and a stiff straw stem; the panicles of flowers, and later of grain, hang downwards. The cultivated oat Avena sativa is produced for human and animal food. **2.** an oat-plant or a variety of it. —**off one's oats**, (colloquial) lacking appetite for food. —**oaten** adj. [Old English]

oatcake n. a thin unleavened cake made of oatmeal.

Oates /əuts/ Titus 1649–1705. English conspirator. A priest, he entered the Jesuit colleges at Valladolid, Spain, and St Omer, France, as a spy in 1677–78, and on his return to England announced he had discovered a 'Popish Plot' to murder Charles II and re-establish Catholicism. Although this story was almost entirely false, many innocent Roman Catholics were executed during 1678–80 on Oates's evidence. In 1685 he was flogged, pilloried, and imprisoned for perjury. He was pardoned and granted a pension after the revolution of 1688.

oath n. (plural /əuðz/) **1.** a solemn declaration or undertaking naming God or a revered object as witness. In English courts witnesses normally swear to tell the truth holding a ◊New Testament in their right hand. People who object to the taking of oaths, such as ◊Quakers and atheists, give a solemn promise (◊affirmation) to tell the truth. In the USA witnesses raise their right hand in taking the oath. **2.** casual use of the name of God etc. in anger or emphasis; an obscenity. —**on** or **under oath**, having made a solemn oath. [Old English]

oatmeal n. meal made from oats.

OAU abbreviation of ◊Organisation of African Unity.

Oaxaca /wə'hɑːkə/ capital of a state of the same name in the Sierra Madre del Sur mountain range, central Mexico; population (1980) 157,300; former home town of presidents Benito Juárez and Porfirio Diaz; industries include food processing, textiles, and handicrafts.

Ob /ɒb/ river in Asian USSR, flowing 3,380 km/2,100 mi from the Altai mountains through the W Siberian Plain to

oat

grain

cross section of a grain

the Gulf of Ob in the Arctic Ocean. With its main tributary, the Irtysh, it is 5,600 km/3,480 mi.

ob. abbreviation of he or she died. [from Latin *obiit*]

ob- prefix used (usually **oc-** before *c*, **of-** before *f*, **op-** before *p*) especially in words from Latin, expressing exposure, meeting, facing, direction, compliance, opposition, resistance, hindrance, concealment, finality, completeness. [Latin *ob* = towards, against, in the way of]

obbligato /ɒbliˈgaːtəʊ/ *n.* (*plural* **obbligatos**) in music, a part or accompaniment forming an integral part of a composition. [Italian = obligatory]

obdurate /ˈɒbdjʊrət/ *adj.* hardened, stubborn. —**obduracy** *n.* [from Latin *durare* = harden]

OBE abbreviation of Officer of the Order of the British Empire, a British honour.

obedient /əʊˈbiːdiənt/ *adj.* obeying, ready to obey; submissive to another's will. —**obedience** *n.*, **obediently** *adv.*

obeisance /əʊˈbeɪsəns/ *n.* a bow, curtsey, or other respectful gesture; homage. —**obeisant** *adj.* [from Old French]

obelisk /ˈɒbəlɪsk/ *n.* a tapering usually four-sided stone pillar as a monument. [from Latin from Greek, diminutive of *obelus*]

obelus /ˈɒbələs/ *n.* (*plural* **obeli** /-laɪ/) a dagger-shaped mark of reference (†). [Latin from Greek = spit]

Oberammergau /əʊbərˈæməgaʊ/ village in Bavaria, Germany; population (1980) 5,000. A Christian ◊passion play has been performed here every ten years since 1634 (except during World Wars I and II) to commemorate the ending of the Black Death.

Oberon /ˈəʊbərɒn/ in folklore, king of the elves or fairies, and, according to the 13th-century French romance *Huon of Bordeaux*, an illegitimate son of Julius Caesar. Shakespeare used the character in *A Midsummer Night's Dream*.

Oberon Merle. Stage name of Estelle Merle O'Brien Thompson 1911–1979. Tasmanian-born British actress who starred in several films of Alexander Korda (to whom she was briefly married), including *The Scarlet Pimpernel* 1935. She played Cathy to Laurence Olivier's Heathcliff in *Wuthering Heights* 1939, and after 1940 worked successfully in the USA.

obese /əʊˈbiːs/ *adj.* very fat. —**obesity** *n.* [from Latin = having eaten oneself fat (*edere* = eat)]

obesity *n.* the condition of being overweight (generally, 20% or more above the desirable weight for one's sex, build, and height).

obey /əʊˈbeɪ/ *v.t./i.* 1. to do what is commanded by. 2. to be obedient. 3. to be actuated by (a force or impulse). [from Old French from Latin *obedire* (*audire* = hear)]

obfuscate /ˈɒbfʌskeɪt/ *v.t.* 1. to obscure or confuse (the mind, a topic etc.). 2. to stupefy, to bewilder. —**obfuscation** /-ˈkeɪʃən/ *n.* [from Latin *fuscus* = dark]

obi *n.* or **obeah** a form of witchcraft practised in the West Indies. It combines elements of Christianity and African religions, such as snake worship.

obiit a term found in, for example, inscriptions on tombstones, followed by a date. [Latin = he/she died]

obituary /əˈbɪtjʊərɪ/ *n.* a notice of a person's death especially in a newspaper, often with an account of the life of the deceased person. —*adj.* of or serving as an obituary. [from Latin *obitus* = death]

object /ˈɒbdʒɪkt/ *n.* 1. a material thing that can be seen or touched. 2. a person or thing to which an action or feeling is directed. 3. a thing sought or aimed at. 4. in grammar, a noun or its equivalent governed by an active transitive verb or by a preposition. 5. in philosophy, a thing external to the thinking mind or subject. —/əbˈdʒekt/ *v.t./i.* 1. to express opposition; to feel or express dislike or reluctance. 2. to adduce as contrary or damaging. —**no object**, not forming an important or restricting factor. **object-glass** *n.* the lens in a telescope etc. nearest to the object observed. **object-lesson** *n.* a striking practical example of some principle. —**objector** /əbˈdʒektə/ *n.* [from Latin *jacere* = throw]

objectify /ɒbˈdʒektɪfaɪ/ *v.t.* 1. to make objective. 2. to embody.

objection /əbˈdʒekʃən/ *n.* 1. a feeling of disapproval or opposition; a statement of this. 2. a reason for objecting; a drawback in a plan etc.

objectionable *adj.* open to objection; unpleasant, offensive. —**objectionably** *adv.*

objective /əbˈdʒektɪv/ *adj.* 1. external to the mind, actually existing. 2. dealing with outward things or exhibiting facts uncoloured by feelings or opinions. 3. in grammar, (of a case or word) constructed as or appropriate to the object. 4. aimed at. —*n.* 1. something sought or aimed at. 2. in grammar, the objective case. 3. an object-glass. —**objectively** *adv.*, **objectivity** /ɒbdʒekˈtɪvɪtɪ/ *n.*

object-oriented programming (OOP) a type of computer programming based on 'objects', in which data are closely linked to the procedures that operate on them. For example, a circle on the screen might be an object; it has data, such as a centre point and a radius, as well as procedures for moving it, erasing it, changing its size, and so on.

objet d'art /ɒbʒeɪ ˈdaː/ (*plural* **objets d'art** pronounced the same) a small decorative object. [French = object of art]

objurgate /ˈɒbdʒɜːgeɪt/ *v.t.* (*literary*) to rebuke, to scold. —**objurgation** /-ˈgeɪʃən/ *n.* [from Latin *objurgare* = quarrel]

oblate /ˈɒbleɪt, əˈbleɪt/ *adj.* (of a spheroid) flattened at the poles. [from Latin = brought forward, prolonged]

oblation /əˈbleɪʃən/ *n.* a thing offered to a divine being. [from Old French or Latin]

obligate /ˈɒbligeɪt/ *v.t.* (usually in *past participle*) to oblige (a person legally or morally) to do a thing.

obligation /ɒbliˈgeɪʃən/ *n.* 1. being obliged to do something; the compelling power of a law, contract, duty etc. 2. a duty, a task one must perform. 3. indebtedness for a service or benefit. —**under (an) obligation**, owing gratitude.

obligatory /əˈblɪgətərɪ/ *adj.* required by law, contract, or custom etc., not optional. —**obligatorily** *adv.* [from Latin]

oblige /əˈblaɪdʒ/ *v.t./i.* 1. to compel by law, contract, custom etc., or necessity. 2. to help or gratify by performing a small service. —**be obliged to a person**, to be indebted or grateful to him or her. **much obliged**, thank you. [from Old French from Latin *ligare* = bind)]

obliging *adj.* courteous and helpful, accommodating. —**obligingly** *adv.*

oblique /əˈbliːk/ *adj.* 1. declining from the vertical or horizontal, diverging from a straight line or course. 2. not going straight to the point, roundabout, indirect. 3. in grammar (of a case), other than the nominative or vocative. —*n.* an oblique stroke (/). —**obliquely** *adv.*, **obliquity** /əˈblɪkwɪtɪ/ *n.* [from French from Latin *obliquus*]

obliterate /əˈblɪtəreɪt/ *v.t.* to blot out, to destroy and leave no clear traces of —**obliteration** /-ˈreɪʃən/ *n.*, **obliterator** *n.* [from Latin *oblit(t)erare* = erase (*litera* = letter)]

oblivion /əˈblɪvɪən/ *n.* 1. the state of being forgotten. 2. the state of being oblivious. [from Old French from Latin *oblivisci* = forget]

oblivious /əˈblɪvɪəs/ *adj.* unaware or unconscious (with *of* or *to*).

oblong /ˈɒblɒŋ/ *adj.* of a rectangular shape with adjacent sides unequal. —*n.* an oblong figure or object. [from Latin, originally = somewhat long]

obloquy /ˈɒbləkwɪ/ *n.* 1. abuse intended to damage a person's reputation. 2. discredit brought by this. [from Latin *obloquium* = contradiction (*loqui* = speak)]

obnoxious /əbˈnɒkʃəs/ *adj.* offensive, objectionable, disliked. —**obnoxiously** *adv.* [from Latin *noxa* = hard]

oboe /ˈəʊbəʊ/ *n.* 1. a musical instrument of the ◊woodwind family. It is a wooden tube with a bell, is double-reeded, and has a yearning, poignant tone. It is played held in a vertical position. Its range is almost three octaves. 2. its player in an orchestra. 3. an organ reed-stop of similar quality. —**oboist** /-ˈbəʊɪst/ *n.* [from French *hautbois* (*haut* = high and *bois* = wood)]

Obote /əʊˈbəʊtɪ/ (Apollo) Milton 1924– . Ugandan politician who led the independence movement from 1961. He became prime minister in 1962 and announced a new constitution which made him president 1966–71 and 1980–85; he was overthrown twice, in 1971 by Idi ◊Amin and in 1985 by Lt-Gen Tito Okello.

Obrenovich /əˈbrenəvɪtʃ/ Serbian dynasty that ruled 1816–42 and 1859–1903. The dynasty engaged in a feud with the rival house of Karageorgevich, which obtained the throne by the murder of the last Obrenovich 1903.

O'Brien Willis H 1886–1962. US film animator and special-effects creator, responsible for one of the cinema's most memorable monsters, *King Kong* 1933.

obscene /əb'si:n/ *adj.* offensively indecent; in law, of a publication tending to deprave or corrupt; (*colloquial*) highly offensive. —**obscenely** *adv.*, **obscenity** /-'senɪtɪ/ *n.* [from French or Latin *obsc(a)enus*, originally = ill-omened]

obscenity law a law prohibiting the publishing of any material that tends to deprave or corrupt.

obscure /əb'skjuə/ *adj.* 1. not clearly expressed, not easily understood. 2. dark, indistinct. 3. hidden, unnoticed; (of a person) undistinguished, hardly known. —*v.t.* to make obscure or unintelligible; to conceal. —**obscurely** *adv.*, **obscurity** *n.* [from Old French from Latin *obscurus*]

obsequies /'ɒbsɪkwɪz/ *n. pl.* funeral rites. [from Anglo-French from Latin *obsequiae*]

obsequious /əb'si:kwiəs/ *adj.* excessively or sickeningly respectful. —**obsequiously** *adv.*, **obsequiousness** *n.* [from Latin *obsequium* = compliance]

observance /əb'zɜ:vəns/ *n.* 1. the keeping or performance of a law, duty etc. 2. a rite, a ceremonial act. [from Old French from Latin *observantia*]

observant *adj.* 1. quick at noticing things. 2. attentive in observance. —**observantly** *adv.*

observation /ɒbzə'veɪʃən/ *n.* 1. observing, being observed. 2. a comment or remark. 3. facts or data; the recording of these. —**observational** *adj.*

observatory /əb'zɜ:vətərɪ/ *n.* a building designed and equipped for scientific observation of the stars or weather etc. The earliest recorded observatory was at Alexandria, built by Ptolemy Soter, about 300 BC. The erection of observatories was revived in W Asia about AD 1000, and extended to Europe. The one built on the island of Hven (now Ven) in Denmark in 1576, for Tycho ◊Brahe, was followed by one in France, built in 1667 in Paris, and two in England, near London: the ◊Royal Greenwich Observatory, built in 1675, and one in Kew. The modern observatory dates from the invention of the telescope. The most powerful optical telescopes covering the sky are at ◊Mauna Kea; Mount ◊Palomar; Kitt Peak, Arizona; La Palma, the Canary Islands; and Mount Semirodniki, Caucasus, USSR. ◊Siding Springs Mountain in Australia is the site of the first computer-controlled one. ◊Radio astronomy observatories include ◊Jodrell Bank; the Mullard, Cambridge, England; ◊Arecibo; Effelsberg, Germany; and ◊Parkes in New South Wales, Australia. Observatories are also carried on aircraft or sent into orbit as satellites, in space stations, and on the Space Shuttle. The ◊Hubble Space Telescope was launched into orbit in April 1990. The Very Large Telescope is under construction by the European Southern Observatory (ESO), in the mountains of N Chile, and is expected to be in operation by 1997.

observe /əb'zɜ:v/ *v.t./i.* 1. to see and notice; to watch carefully. 2. to keep or pay attention to (rules etc.). 3. to celebrate or perform (an occasion, rite etc.). 4. to note and record (facts or data). 5. to remark. —**observable** *adj.* & *n.* [from Old French from Latin *servare* = watch]

observer *n.* one who observes; an interested spectator.

obsess /əb'ses/ *v.t.* to occupy the thoughts of (a person) continually. [from Latin *obsidere* = besiege]

obsession /əb'seʃən/ *n.* 1. obsessing, being obsessed. 2. a repetitive unwanted thought or compulsive action that is often recognized by the sufferer as being irrational, but which nevertheless causes distress. —**obsessional** *adj.*

obsessive /əb'sesɪv/ *adj.* of, causing, or showing obsession. —**obsessively** *adv.*

obsidian /əb'sɪdiən/ *n.* a dark vitreous lava or volcanic rock that looks like a coarse glass, chemically similar to ◊granite, but formed by cooling rapidly on the Earth's surface at low pressure. [from Latin from *Obsius*, name of finder of a similar stone, mentioned by Pliny]

obsolescent /ɒbsə'lesənt/ *adj.* becoming obsolete. —**obsolescence** *n.* [from Latin *obsolescere* (*solēre* = be accustomed)]

obsolete /'ɒbsəli:t/ *adj.* no longer used, antiquated.

obstacle /'ɒbstəkəl/ *n.* a thing obstructing progress. [from Old French from Latin *obstare* = stand in the way]

obstetrician /ɒbstɪ'trɪʃən/ *n.* a specialist in obstetrics.

obstetrics /ɒb'stetrɪks/ *n. pl.* (usually treated as *singular*) the branch of medicine and surgery dealing with the management of pregnancy, childbirth, and the immediate post-natal period. —**obstetric** *adj.*, **obstetrical** *adj.* [from Latin *obstetricius* (*obstetrix* = midwife)]

obstinate /'ɒbstɪnət/ *n.* stubborn, intractable; firmly continuing in one's action or opinion and not yielding to persuasion. —**obstinacy** *n.*, **obstinately** *adv.* [from Latin *obstinare* = persist]

obstreperous /əb'strepərəs/ *adj.* noisy, unruly. —**obstreperously** *adv.* [from Latin *obstrepere* = shout against]

obstruct /əb'strʌkt/ *v.t.* 1. to prevent or hinder passage along (a path etc.) by means of an object etc. placed in it. 2. to prevent or hinder the movement, progress, or activities of. —**obstructor** *n.* [from Latin *struere* = build]

obstruction /əb'strʌkʃən/ *n.* 1. obstructing, being obstructive. 2. a thing that obstructs, a blockage.

obstructive *adj.* causing or intended to cause obstruction.

obtain /əb'teɪn/ *v.t./i.* 1. to get, to come into possession of (a thing) by effort or as a gift. 2. to be established or in use as a rule or customary practice. —**obtainment** *n.* [from Old French from Latin *obtinēre* (*tenēre* = hold)]

obtainable *adj.* that may be obtained.

obtrude /əb'tru:d/ *v.t./i.* to force (oneself or one's ideas) upon others; to be or become obtrusive. —**obtrusion** *n.* [from Latin *trudere* = thrust]

obtrusive /əb'tru:sɪv/ *adj.* obtruding oneself; unpleasantly noticeable. —**obtrusively** *adv.*

obtuse /əb'tju:s/ *adj.* 1. stupid, slow at understanding. 2. of blunt shape, not sharp-edged or pointed. 3. (of an angle) more than 90° but less than 180°. —**obtusely** *adv.*, **obtuseness** *n.* [from Latin *tundere* = beat]

obverse /'ɒbvɜ:s/ *n.* 1. the side of a coin or medal etc. that bears the head or principal design; the front or proper or top side of a thing. 2. the counterpart. [from Latin *obvertere* = turn towards]

obviate /'ɒbvieɪt/ *v.t.* to make unnecessary; to get round (a danger or hindrance etc.). [from Latin *obviare* = withstand]

obvious /'ɒbviəs/ *adj.* easily seen or recognized or understood. —**obviously** *adv.* [from Latin *ob viam* = in the way]

oc- see ◊ob-.

OC abbreviation of Officer Commanding.

ocarina /ɒkə'ri:nə/ *n.* a small egg-shaped terracotta or metal wind instrument with holes for the fingers. [Italian *oca* = goose, from its shape]

O'Casey /əu'keɪsi/ Sean. Adopted name of John Casey 1884–1964. Irish dramatist. His early plays are tragicomedies, blending realism with symbolism and poetic with vernacular speech: *The Shadow of a Gunman* 1922, *Juno and the Paycock* 1925, and *The Plough and the Stars* 1926. Later plays include *Red Roses for Me* 1946 and *The Drums of Father Ned* 1960.

occasion /ə'keɪʒən/ *n.* 1. a special event or happening; a particular time marked by this. 2. a reason, a need. 3. a suitable juncture, an opportunity. 4. an immediate but subordinate cause. 5. (in *plural*) affairs, business. —*v.t.* to cause (especially incidentally). —**on occasion**, now and then, when the need arises. [from Old French or Latin *occidere* = go down]

occasional *adj.* 1. happening irregularly and infrequently. 2. made, intended for, or acting on a special occasion. —**occasionally** *adv.*

Occident /'ɒksɪdənt/ *n.* (*poetic* or *rhetorically*) the West (especially Europe and the USA) as opposed to the Orient. [from Old French from Latin = sunset, west]

occidental /ɒksi'dentəl/ *adj.* of the Occident, western. —*n.* a native or inhabitant of the Occident.

occiput /'ɒksɪpʌt/ *n.* the back of the head. —**occipital** /ɒk'sɪpɪtəl/ *adj.* [from Latin *caput* = head]

occlude /ɒ'klu:d/ *v.t.* 1. to obstruct, to stop up. 2. to absorb and retain (gases). —**occluded front,** the atmospheric condition that occurs when a cold front overtakes a mass of warm air, and warm air is driven upwards, producing a long period of steady rain. —**occlusion** *n.* [from Latin *occludere* (*claudere* = shut)]

occult[1] /ɒ'kʌlt/ *adj.* 1. involving the supernatural, mystical, magical. 2. esoteric, recondite. —**the occult,** occult phenomena generally. [from Latin *occulere* = to hide]

occult[2] *v.t.* to conceal, to cut off from view by passing in front (usually used in astronomy, to describe the effect of a concealing body much greater in apparent size than the concealed body). [from Latin *occultare* frequentative of *occulere*]

occultation /ɒ-'teɪʃ(ə)n/ n. in astronomy, the temporary obscuring of a star by a body in the solar system. Occultations are used to provide information about changes in an orbit, and the structure of objects in space, such as radio sources. The exact shapes and sizes of planets and asteroids can be found when they occult stars. The rings of Uranus were discovered when that planet occulted a star in 1977. See also ◊eclipse.

occupant /'ɒkjupənt/ n. a person occupying a dwelling, office, or position. —**occupancy** n.

occupation /ɒkju'peɪʃən/ n. 1. an activity that keeps a person busy; one's employment. 2. occupying, being occupied; taking or holding possession of a country or district by military force.

occupational adj. of or connected with one's occupation. —**occupational disease** or **hazard**, a disease or hazard to which a particular occupation renders one especially liable. **occupational therapy**, mental or physical activity to assist recovery from a disease or injury.

occupational psychology the study of human behaviour at work. It includes dealing with problems in organizations, advising on management difficulties, and investigating the relationship between humans and machines (as in the design of aircraft controls; see also ◊ergonomics). Another area is ◊psychometrics and the use of assessment to assist in selection of personnel.

occupier /'ɒkjupaɪə/ n. a person residing in a house etc. as its owner or tenant.

occupy /'ɒkjupaɪ/ v.t. 1. to reside in, to be a tenant of. 2. to take up or fill (a space or time or place). 3. to hold (a position or office). 4. to take military possession of; to place oneself in (a building etc.) forcibly or without authority. 5. to keep (a person or his time) filled with activity. [from Old French from Latin occupare = seize]

occur /ə'kɜ:/ v.i. (-rr-) 1. to come into being as an event or process. 2. to be met with or found to exist in some place or condition. —**occur to**, to come into the mind of. [from Latin occurrere = present itself]

occurrence /ə'kʌrəns/ n. 1. occurring. 2. a thing that occurs, an event.

ocean /'əuʃən/ n. 1. the sea surrounding the continents of the Earth, especially one of the named divisions of this: ◊Atlantic; ◊Pacific; ◊Indian; ◊Arctic; and ◊Antarctic Oceans (although only the first three are oceans, of which the Arctic and Antarctic form a part). They cover approximately 70%, or 363,000,000 sq km/140,000,000 sq mi of the total surface area of the Earth, recorded water levels having shown an increase of 2.4 mm/0.1 in for the pasts 100 years. 2. an immense expanse or quantity. —**ocean-going** adj. (of a ship) able to cross the ocean. —**oceanic** /əuʃi'ænɪk/ adj. [from Old French from Latin from Greek = stream encircling the Earth]

oceanarium n. a large display tank in which aquatic animals and plants live together much as they would in their natural environment. The first oceanarium was created by the explorer and naturalist W Douglas Burden in 1938 in Florida, USA.

Oceania /əuʃi'ɑːniə/ the islands of the S Pacific (◊Micronesia, ◊Melanesia, ◊Polynesia). The term is sometimes used to include ◊Australasia and the ◊Malay archipelago.

oceanography /əuʃə'nɒɡrəfi/ n. the study of oceans. It is a very wide science and its subdivisions deal with the individual ocean's extent and depth, the water's evolution and composition, its physics and chemistry, the bottom topography, currents and wind effects, tidal ranges, the biology, and the various aspects of human use. —**oceanographer** n.

ocean ridge a topographical feature of the seabed indicating the presence of a constructive plate margin produced by the rise of magma to the surface, see ◊plate tectonics. It can rise many thousands of feet or metres above the surrounding abyssal plain.

ocean trench a topographical feature of the seabed indicating the presence of a destructive plate margin (produced by the movements of ◊plate tectonics). The subduction or dragging downward of one plate of the ◊lithosphere beneath another means that the ocean floor is pulled down.

Oceanus /əu'siənəs/ in Greek mythology, one of the ◊Titans, the god of a river supposed to encircle the earth. He was the ancestor of other river gods, and of the nymphs of the seas and rivers.

ocellus /ə'seləs/ n. (plural ocelli /-laɪ/) 1. any of the simple (as opposed to compound) eyes of insects etc. 2. a facet of a compound eye. [Latin, diminutive of oculus = eye]

ocelot /'əusɪlɒt, 'ɒ-/ n. wild ◊cat (Felis pardalis) of Central and South America, up to 1 m/3 ft long with a 45 cm/1.5 ft tail. It weighs about 18 kg/40 lbs, and has a pale yellowish coat marked with longitudinal stripes and blotches. It is close to extinction, having been hunted for its fur. [French, abbreviation by Buffon from Nahuatl tlalocelotl = jaguar of the field, and applied to a different animal]

och /ɒx/ (Scottish and Irish) interjection meaning oh, ah. [Gaelic and Irish]

oche /'ɒki/ variant of ◊hockey[2].

Ochoa /əu'tʃəuə/ Severo 1905– . US biochemist. In 1955, while working at New York University, he discovered an enzyme able to assemble units of the ◊nucleic acid RNA. For his work towards the synthesis of RNA, Ochoa shared the 1959 Nobel Prize for Medicine with Arthur ◊Kornberg.

ochre /'əukə/ n. 1. an earth used as a yellow or brown or red pigment. 2. a pale brownish-yellow colour. —**ochrous** adj. [from Old French from Latin from Greek ōkhros = pale yellow]

o'clock /ə'klɒk/= of the clock, used to specify an hour.

O'Connell /əu'kɒnl/ Daniel 1775–1847. Irish politician, called 'the Liberator'. In 1823 he founded the Catholic Association to press Roman Catholic claims. Although ineligible, as a Roman Catholic, to take his seat, he was elected member of Parliament for County Clare 1828 and so forced the government to grant Catholic emancipation. In Parliament he cooperated with the Whigs in the hope of obtaining concessions until 1841, when he launched his campaign for repeal of the union.

O'Connor /əu'kɒnə/ Feargus 1794–1855. Irish parliamentary follower of Daniel ◊O'Connell. He sat in parliament 1832–35, and as editor of the Northern Star became an influential figure of the radical working-class Chartist movement (see ◊Chartism).

O'Connor Flannery 1925–1964. US novelist and short-story writer. Her works have a great sense of evil and sin, and often explore the religious sensibility of the Deep South. Her short stories include A Good Man Is Hard to Find 1955 and Everything That Rises Must Converge 1965.

OCR abbreviation of optical character recognition. In computing, a technique whereby a program can understand words or figures by 'reading' a printed image of the text. The image is first input from paper by ◊scanning. The program then uses its knowledge of the shapes of characters to convert the image to a set of internal codes.

Oct. abbreviation of October.

octagon /'ɒktəɡən/ n. a plane figure with eight sides and angles. —**octagonal** /-'tæɡənəl/ adj. [from Latin from Greek (gōnos = angled)]

octahedron /ɒktə'hi:drən/ n. (plural octahedrons) a solid figure contained by eight plane faces and usually by eight triangles. —**octahedral** adj. [from Greek (hedra = base)]

octal number system a number system to the ◊base eight, used in computing, in which all numbers are made up of the digits 0 to 7. For example, decimal 8 is represented as octal 10, and decimal 17 as octal 21. See also ◊hexadecimal number system.

octane /'ɒkteɪn/ n. a hydrocarbon compound of the paraffin series occurring in petrol. —**high-octane** adj. (of fuel used in internal-combustion engines) not detonating rapidly during the power stroke. **octane number**, a number indicating the anti-knock properties of fuel.

octane rating a numerical classification of petroleum fuels indicating their combustion characteristics.

Octans /'ɒktænz/ n. constellation in the southern hemisphere containing the southern celestial pole.

octave /'ɒktɪv/ n. 1. in music, a distance of eight notes as measured on the white notes of a piano keyboard. It corresponds to the consonance of first and second harmonics. 2. the seventh day after a religious festival; the period of eight days including the festival and its octave. 3. an eight-line stanza. [from Old French from Latin octavus = eighth]

Octavian /ɒk'teɪviən/ original name of ◊Augustus, the first Roman emperor.

octavo /ɒk'teɪvəu/ n. (plural octavos) the size of a book or page given by folding a sheet of standard size three times to form eight leaves; a book or sheet of this size.

octet /ɒk'tet/ *n.* (also **octette**) 1. a musical composition for eight performers; these performers. 2. any group of eight. 3. the set of eight lines beginning a sonnet. [from Italian or German]

octo- in combinations, eight. See ♢oct-, octa-.

October /ɒk'təʊbə/ *n.* the tenth month of the year. [Old English from Latin (*octō*= eight, because originally the eighth month in the Roman calendar)]

October Revolution the second stage of the ♢Russian Revolution when, on 24 Oct (6 Nov Western calendar), the Red Guards under Trotsky, and on orders from Lenin, seized the Winter Palace and arrested members of the Provisional Government. The following day the Second All-Russian Congress of Soviets handed over power to the Bolsheviks.

Octobrists /ɒk'təʊbrɪsts/ *n.* a group of Russian liberal constitutional politicians who accepted the reforming October Manifesto instituted by Tsar Nicholas II after the 1905 revolution and rejected more radical reforms.

oct-, octa- in combinations, eight. [from Latin or Greek (Latin *octo*, Greek *oktō* = eight)]

octogenarian /ɒktəʊdʒɪ'neərɪən/ *n.* a person from 80 to 89 years old. [from Latin (*octogeni* = 80 each)]

octopus /'ɒktəpəs/ *n.* (*plural* **octopuses**) a sea-mollusc of the family Octopodidae, a type of ♢cephalopod, with a round or oval body, and eight suckered tentacles. Octopuses occur in all temperate and tropical seas, where they feed on crabs and other small animals. They can vary their coloration according to their background, and can swim with their arms or by a type of jet propulsion by means of their funnel. They are as intelligent as some vertebrates, and are not dangerous. [from Greek (*pous* = foot)]

ocular /'ɒkjʊlə/ *adj.* of or connected with the eyes or sight, visual. [from French from Latin *oculus* = eye]

oculist /'ɒkjʊlɪst/ *n.* a specialist in the treatment of eye diseases and defects.

Ocussi Ambeno /ɒ'kusi m'beɪnəʊ/ port on the N coast of Indonesian West Timor, until 1975 an exclave of the Portuguese colony of East Timor. The port is an outlet for rice, copra, and sandalwood.

ODA abbreviation of ♢Overseas Development Administration.

odalisque /'əʊdəlɪsk/ *n.* (*historical*) an Oriental female slave or concubine, especially in the Turkish sultan's seraglio. [French from Turkish (*oda* = chamber and *lik* = function)]

odd *adj.* 1. unusual, strange, eccentric. 2. not regular, occasional; not normally noticed or considered; unconnected. 3. (of numbers such as 3 and 5) not integrally divisible by two; bearing such a number. 4. left over when the rest have been distributed or divided into pairs; detached from a set or series. 5. (appended to a number, sum, weight etc.) something more than; by which a round number, given sum etc., is exceeded. —**odd man out**, a person or thing differing from all others of a group in some respect. —**oddly** *adv.*, **oddness** *n.* [from Old Norse *odda-* in *odda-mathr* = third man (*oddi* = angle, triangle)]

oddball *n.* (*colloquial*) an eccentric person.

oddity /'ɒdɪtɪ/ *n.* 1. strangeness; a peculiar trait. 2. a strange person, thing, or event.

oddment *n.* an odd article, something left over; (in *plural*) odds and ends.

odds *n.pl.* (sometimes treated as *singular*). 1. the ratio between the amounts staked by the parties to a bet, based on the expected probability either way. 2. the balance of advantage or probability. 3. advantageous difference. —**at odds**, in conflict, at variance. **odds and ends**, remnants, stray articles. **odds-on** *n.* a state when success is expected to be more likely than failure. **over the odds**, above the generally agreed price etc.

ode *n.* in ancient literature, a poem intended or adapted to be sung; (in modern use) a rhymed (rarely unrhymed) lyric, often in the form of an address, generally dignified or exalted in subject, feeling, and style, but sometimes (in earlier use) simple and familiar (though less so than a song). From ancient Greece exponents include Sappho, Pindar, Horace, and Catullus; and among English poets, Spenser, Milton, Dryden, and Keats. [from French from Latin from Greek *ōidē* = song]

Odessa /ə'desə/ seaport in Ukraine, USSR, on the Black Sea, capital of Odessa region; population (1987) 1,141,000. Products include chemicals, pharmaceuticals, and machinery. Odessa was founded by Catherine II in 1795 near the site of an ancient Greek settlement.

Odin /'əʊdɪn/ chief god of Scandinavian mythology, the Woden or Wotan of the Germanic peoples. A sky god, he lives in Asgard, at the top of the world-tree, and from the Valkyries (the divine maidens) receives the souls of heroic slain warriors, feasting with them in his great hall, Valhalla. The wife of Odin is Freya, or Frigga, and Thor is their son. Wednesday is named after Odin.

odious /'əʊdɪəs/ *adj.* hateful, repulsive. —**odiously** *adv.*, **odiousness** *n.*

odium /'əʊdɪəm/ *n.* widespread dislike or disapproval felt towards a person or action. [Latin = hatred]

Odoacer /ɒdəʊ'eɪsə/ 433–493. King of Italy from 476, when he deposed Romulus Augustulus, the last Roman emperor. He was a leader of the barbarian mercenaries employed by Rome. He was overthrown and killed by Theodoric the Great, king of the Ostrogoths.

odometer /əʊ'dɒmɪtə/ *n.* an instrument for measuring the distance travelled by a wheeled vehicle. [from French (Greek *hodos* = way)]

odoriferous /əʊdə'rɪfərəs/ *adj.* diffusing a (usually agreeable) odour. [from Latin (*odor* = smell and *ferro* = carry)]

odour /'əʊdə/ *n.* 1. a smell. 2. a savour, a trace. 3. favour, repute. —**odorous** *adj.* [from Anglo-French from Latin *odor*]

Odysseus /ə'dɪsju:s/ the chief character of Homer's *Odyssey*, mentioned also in the *Iliad* as one of the foremost leaders of the Greek forces at the siege of Troy, a man of courage and ingenuity. He is said to have been the ruler of the island of Ithaca.

odyssey /'ɒdɪsɪ/ *n.* a long adventurous journey. [from *Odyssey*]

Odyssey /'ɒdɪsɪ/ Greek epic poem in 24 books, probably written before 700 BC, attributed to ♢Homer. It describes the voyage of Odysseus after the fall of Troy and the vengeance he takes on the suitors of his wife, Penelope, on his return. During his ten-year wanderings he has many adventures, including encounters with the Cyclops, Circe, Scylla and Charybdis, and the Sirens.

OE abbreviation of Old English; see ♢English language.

OECD abbreviation of ♢Organization for Economic Co-operation and Development.

OED abbreviation of Oxford English Dictionary.

oedema /i:'di:mə, i'd-/ *n.* any abnormal accumulation of fluid in tissues or cavities of the body; waterlogging of the tissues due to excessive loss of ♢plasma through the capillary walls. It may be generalized (the condition once known as dropsy) or confined to one area, such as the ankles. —**oedematous** *adj.* [Latin from Greek *oideō* = swell]

Oedipus /'i:dɪpəs/ in Greek legend, king of Thebes. Left to die at birth because his father Laius had been warned by an oracle that his son would kill him, he was saved and brought up by the king of Corinth. Oedipus killed Laius in a quarrel (without recognizing him). Because Oedipus saved Thebes from the Sphinx, he was granted the Theban kingdom and Jocasta (wife of Laius and his own mother) as his wife. After four children had been born, the truth was discovered. Jocasta hanged herself, Oedipus blinded himself, and as an exiled wanderer was guided by his daughter Antigone. —**Oedipal** *adj.*

Oedipus complex /'i:dɪpəs/ in psychology, the unconscious antagonism of a son to his father, whom he sees as a rival for his mother's affection. For a girl antagonistic to her mother, as a rival for her father's affection, the term is **Electra complex**. The terms were coined by ♢Freud.

Oedipus Tyrannus /'i:dɪpəs ti'rænəs/ or **Oedipus the King** 409 BC and **Oedipus at Colonus** 401 BC two Greek tragedies by ♢Sophocles based on the legend of Oedipus, king of Thebes.

o'er /'əʊə/ *prep.* & *adv.* (chiefly *poetic*) = as **over** [contraction]

oersted *n.* the c.g.s. unit (symbol Oe) of ♢magnetic field strength, now replaced by the SI unit ampere per metre. The Earth's magnetic field is about 0.5 oersted; the field near the poles of a small bar magnet is several hundred oersteds; and a powerful ◊electromagnet can have a field strength of 30,000 oersteds.

Oersted /'ɜːsted/ Hans Christian 1777–1851. Danish physicist who founded the science of electromagnetism. In 1820 he discovered the ◊magnetic field associated with an electric current.

oesophagus /iːˈsɒfəɡəs/ n. (plural **oesophagi** /-dʒaɪ/) the passage through which food travels from mouth to stomach. The human oesophagus is about 23 cm/9 in long. Its upper end is at the bottom of the ◊pharynx, immediately behind the windpipe. [from Greek]

oestrogen /'iːstrədʒ(ə)n/ n. a group of hormones produced by the ◊ovaries of vertebrates; the term is also used for various synthetic hormones which mimic their effects. The principal oestrogen in mammals is oestradiol. Oestrogens promote the development of female secondary sexual characteristics; stimulate egg production; and, in mammals, prepare the lining of the uterus for pregnancy. [from Greek *oistros* = frenzy]

oestrus n. in mammals, the period during a female's reproductive cycle (also known as the oestrus cycle or ◊menstrual cycle) when mating is most likely to occur. It usually coincides with ovulation.

oeuvre /œvr/ n. 1. a work of art, music, or literature. 2. the corpus of work produced by an artist, composer, or writer, considered as a whole. [French = work, from Latin *opera*]

of /əv, emphatic ɒv/ prep. 1. belonging to; originating from. 2. concerning. 3. composed or made from. 4. with reference or regard to. 5. for, involving, directed towards. 6. so as to bring separation or relief from. 7. during; regularly on a specified day or time. —**of itself**, by or in itself. [Old English]

of- see ◊ob-.

off adv. 1. away, at, or to a distance. 2. out of position; not on or touching or attached, loose, separate; gone; so as to be rid of; incorrect, insufficient. 3. so as to break continuity or continuance; discontinued, stopped; not available on the menu etc. 4. to the end, entirely, so as to be clear. 5. situated as regards money, supplies etc. 6. off-stage. 7. (of food etc.) beginning to decay. —prep. 1. from, away or down or up from, not on. 2. temporarily relieved of or abstaining from or not achieving. 3. using as a source or means of support. 4. leading from, not far from; at a short distance to sea from. —adj. far, further; (of a part of a vehicle, animal, or road) further from the side of a road when facing forward; (in cricket) designating the half of the field (as divided lengthways through the pitch) to which the striker's feet are pointed. —n. 1. the off side in cricket. 2. the start of a race. —**a bit off**, (slang) rather annoying or unfair or unwell. **off and on**, intermittently, now and then. **off-beat** adj. eccentric, unconventional. **off chance**, a remote possibility. **off colour**, not in good health; (US) somewhat indecent. **off-day** n. a day when one is not at one's best. **off-key** adj. out of tune; not quite suitable or fitting. **off-licence** n. a shop selling alcoholic drink for consumption elsewhere; a licence for this. **off-line** adj. (of computer equipment or a computer process) not directly controlled by or connected to a central processor. **off-load** v.t. to unload. **off-peak** adj. used or for use at times other than those of greatest demand. **off-putting** adj. (colloquial) disconcerting; repellent. **off-season** n. a time when business etc. is slack. **off-stage** adj. & adv. not on the stage and so not visible or audible to the audience. **off-white** adj. white with a grey or yellowish tinge.

Offa /'ɒfə/ died 796. King of Mercia, England, from 757. He conquered Essex, Kent, Sussex, and Surrey; defeated the Welsh and the West Saxons; and established Mercian supremacy over all England south of the river Humber.

offal /'ɒfəl/ n. 1. the edible parts of a carcass (especially the heart, liver etc.) cut off as less valuable. 2. refuse, scraps. [from Middle Dutch *afval*]

Offaly /'ɒfəli/ county of the Republic of Ireland, in the province of Leinster, between Galway on the west and Kildare on the east; area 2,000 sq km/772 sq mi; population (1986) 60,000.

Offa's Dyke /'ɒfəz/ a defensive earthwork along the Welsh border, of which there are remains from the mouth of the river Dee to that of the river Severn. It represents the boundary secured by ◊Offa's wars with Wales.

offcut n. a remnant of timber etc. after cutting.

Offenbach /'ɒfənbɑːk/ Jacques 1819–1880. French composer. He wrote light opera, including *Orphée aux enfers*/*Orpheus in the Underworld* 1858, *La belle Hélène* 1864, and *Les contes d'Hoffmann*/*The Tales of Hoffmann* 1881.

offence /əˈfens/ n. 1. an illegal act, a transgression. 2. wounding of the feelings; annoyance or resentment caused thus. 3. an aggressive action.

offend /əˈfend/ v.t./i. 1. to cause offence to; to displease or anger. 2. to do wrong. —**offender** n. [from Old French from Latin *offendere*, originally = strike against]

offensive /əˈfensɪv/ adj. 1. causing offence, insulting. 2. disgusting, repulsive. 3. aggressive, attacking; (of a weapon) meant for attacking. —n. an aggressive attitude, action, or campaign. —**offensively** adv., **offensiveness** n.

offer v.t./i. 1. to present for acceptance or refusal or for consideration. 2. to express readiness or show intention to do, pay, or give. 3. to provide, to give opportunity for. 4. to make available for sale. 5. to present to sight or notice; to present itself, to occur. —n. 1. an expression of readiness to do or give if desired, or to buy or sell (for a certain amount); the amount offered; a bid. 2. a proposal, especially of marriage. —**on offer**, for sale at a certain (especially reduced) price. [Old English or from Old French from Latin *offerre*]

offering n. a thing offered as a gift, contribution, sacrifice etc.

offertory /'ɒfətərɪ/ n. 1. in the Christian church, the offering of bread and wine at the Eucharist. 2. a collection of money at a religious service.

offhand adj. 1. curt or casual in manner. 2. without preparation etc. —adv. in an offhand way. —**offhanded** /-ˈhændɪd/ adj., **offhandedly** adv.

office /'ɒfɪs/ n. 1. a room or building used as a place of business, especially for clerical or administrative work; a room or department for a particular business. 2. a position with duties attached to it; tenure of an official position. 3. the quarters, staff, or collective authority of a government department. 4. a duty, a task, a function. 5. a piece of kindness, a service. 6. an authorized form of religious worship. 7. (in plural) rooms in a house that are devoted to household work, storage etc. [from Old French from Latin *officium* (*opus* = work, *facere* = do)]

officer /'ɒfɪsə/ n. 1. a person holding a position of authority or trust, especially one with a commission in the armed services or mercantile marine, or on a passenger ship. 2. a policeman or woman. 3. a holder of a post in a society (e.g. the president or secretary). —v.t. (usually in past participle) to provide with officers.

official /əˈfɪʃəl/ adj. 1. of an office or its tenure. 2. characteristic of officials and bureaucracy. 3. properly authorized. —n. a person holding office or engaged in official duties. —**officialdom** n., **officially** adv.

Official Secrets Act UK act of Parliament 1989, making disclosure of confidential material from government sources by employees subject to disciplinary procedures; it replaced Section 2 of an act of 1911. There is no public-interest defence, and disclosure of information already in the public domain is still a crime. Journalists who repeat disclosures may also be prosecuted.

officiate /əˈfɪʃɪeɪt/ v.i. 1. to act in an official capacity. 2. to perform divine service.

officious /əˈfɪʃəs/ adj. asserting one's authority, domineering; intrusively kind. —**officiously** adv.

offing n. the more distant part of the sea in view —**in the offing**, not far away; likely to appear or happen.

offish adj. (colloquial) inclined to be aloof.

offprint n. a printed copy of an article etc. originally forming part of a larger publication.

offset n. 1. a side-shoot from a plant serving for propagation. 2. compensation, a consideration or amount diminishing or neutralizing the effect of a contrary one. 3. a sloping ledge in a wall etc.; a bend in a pipe etc. to carry it past an obstacle. 4. (in full **offset process**) see ◊offset printing. —/also -'set/ v.t. (-tt-; past participle **offset**) 1. to counterbalance, to compensate. 2. to print by the offset process.

offset printing or **offset process** the most commonly used method of ◊printing, with the transfer of ink from a plate or stone to a smooth surface, often of rubber, and

ohmic heating *An ohmic heating system, in which liquid food is sterilized by passing an electric current through it.*

thence to paper. It works on the principle of ◊lithography: that grease and water repel one another. The printing plate is prepared using a photographic technique, resulting in a type image that attracts greasy printing ink. On the printing press the plate is wrapped around a cylinder, and wetted, then inked. The ink adheres only to the type area, and the image thus created is then transferred via an intermediate blanket cylinder to the paper.

offshoot *n.* 1. a side-shoot or branch. 2. a derivative.

offshore *adj.* 1. at sea some distance from the shore. 2. (of a wind) blowing from the land towards the sea.

offside /ɒf'saɪd/ *adj.* (of a player in a field game) in a position where he may not play the ball.

offspring *n.* (*plural* the same) a person's child or children or descendants; an animal's young or descendants. [Old English (as of = from, spring)]

O'Flaherty /əu'flɑ:həti/ Liam 1897–1984. Irish author whose novels, set in County Mayo, include *The Neighbour's Wife* 1923, *The Informer* 1925, and *Land* 1946.

oft /ɒft/ *adv.* (*archaic*) often. [Old English]

often /'ɒfən/ *adv.* 1. frequently, many times. 2. at short intervals. 3. in many instances. —**every so often,** from time to time. [Old English *oft*]

Ogallala Aquifer /əugə'læle/ the largest source of groundwater in the USA, stretching from southern South Dakota to NW Texas.

Ogbomosho /ɒgbə'məuʃəu/ city and commercial centre in W Nigeria, 80 km/50 mi NE of Ibadan; population (1981) 590,600.

ogee /'əudʒi:, -'dʒi:/ *n.* a sinuous line of a double continuous curve as in S; a moulding with such a section.

ogham /'ɒgəm/ *n.* 1. an ancient British and Irish alphabet of 20 characters, formed by parallel strokes on either side of or across a continuous line. 2. an inscription in this. 3. any of the characters. [Old Irish *ogam*, referred to *Ogma* supposed inventor]

ogive /'əudʒaɪv, -'dʒaɪv/ *n.* 1. the diagonal rib of a vault. 2. a pointed arch. [from French]

ogle /'əugəl/ *v.t./i.* to look amorously (at). —*n.* an amorous glance.

ogre /'əugə/ *n.* 1. a human-eating giant in folklore. 2. a terrifying person. —**ogress** *n. fem.*, **ogrish** *adj.* [from French]

Ogun /'əugun/ a state of SW Nigeria; population (1982) 2,473,300; area 16,762 sq km/6,474 sq mi; capital Abeokuta.

oh /əu/ interjection expressing surprise, pain, entreaty etc. [variant of ◊O]

O'Higgins /əu'hɪgɪnz/ Bernardo 1778–1842. Chilean revolutionary, known as 'the Liberator of Chile'. He was a leader of the struggle for independence from Spanish rule 1810–17 and head of the first permanent national government 1817–23.

Ohio /əu'haɪəu/ state of the midwest USA; nickname Buckeye State; **area** 107,100 sq km/41,341 sq mi; **capital** Columbus; **population** (1986) 10,752,000; **history** ceded to Britain by France in 1763; first settled by Europeans in 1788; created a state in 1803.

ohm /əum/ *n.* the SI unit (symbol Ω) of electrical ◊resistance (the property of a substance that restricts the flow of electrons through it), transmitting a current of one ampere when subjected to a potential difference of one volt.

Ohm /əum/ Georg Simon 1787–1854. German physicist who studied electricity and discovered the fundamental law that bears his name. The SI unit of electrical resistance is named after him.

ohmic heating a method of heating used in the food-processing industry, in which an electric current is passed through foodstuffs to sterilize them before packing. Electrical energy is transformed into heat throughout the whole volume of the food, not just at the surface. It is an alternative to in-can sterilization.

OHMS abbreviation of On Her (His) Majesty's Service.

Ohm's law a law proposed by Georg Ohm in 1827 that states that the steady electrical current in a metallic circuit is directly proportional to the constant total ◊electromotive force in the circuit.

oho /əu'həu/ interjection expressing surprise or exultation.

Ohrid, Lake /'ɒxrɪd/ lake on the frontier between Albania and Yugoslavia; area 350 sq km/135 sq mi.

oil *n.* 1. any of various liquid viscid unctuous, usually inflammable, chemically neutral substances lighter than and insoluble in water but soluble in alcohol and ether. The three main types are: essential oils, obtained from plants; fixed oils, obtained from animals and plants; and mineral oils, obtained chiefly from the refining of ◊petroleum. 2. (*US*) petroleum. 3. (often in *plural*) oil-colour. 4. an oil-painting.

5. (*colloquial*, usually in *plural*) oilskins. —*v.t.* **1.** to apply oil to; to lubricate, impregnate, or treat with oil. **2.** to supply oil to. —**oil-colour** *n.* (usually in *plural*) a paint made by mixing powdered pigment in oil. **oil-fired** *adj.* using oil as a fuel. **oil-paint** *n.* oil-colour. **oil-painting** *n.* the art of painting in oil-colours; a picture painted thus. **oil rig,** equipment for drilling an oil well. **oil-slick** *n.* a smooth patch of oil, especially on the sea. **oil well,** a well from which mineral oil is drawn. [from Anglo-French from Latin *oleum* = olive oil]

oilcake *n.* compressed linseed from which oil has been expressed, used as cattle food or manure.

oilcloth *n.* a fabric, especially canvas, water-proofed with oil.

oil crop any plant from which vegetable oils are pressed from the seeds. Cool temperate areas grow rapeseed and linseed; warm temperate regions produce sunflowers, olives, and soya beans; tropical regions produce groundnuts (such as peanuts), palm oil, and coconuts. Some vegetable oils, such as soya-bean oil, peanut oil, and cottonseed oil, are derived from crops grown primarily for other purposes. Most vegetable oils are used both as edible oils and as ingredients in industrial products such as soaps, varnishes, printing inks, and paints.

oiled *adj.* (*slang*) drunk.

oilfield *n.* a district yielding mineral oil.

oil palm African ◊palm tree *Elaeis guineensis*, the fruit of which yields valuable oils, used as food or processed into margarine, soap, and livestock feed.

oilskin *n.* a cloth waterproofed with oil; a garment of this; (in *plural*) a suit of this.

oil spill leakage or discharge of oil from a tanker, pipeline, or other source. Oil spills are frequent and may cause enormous ecological harm. In March 1989 the *Exxon Valdez* went aground, covering in oil 1,850 sq km/4,800 sq mi in Prince William Sound, Alaska, and killing 34,434 sea birds, 9,994 otters, and at least nine whales. The ecological cost of the spillage of crude oil into the Persian Gulf during the ◊Gulf War has still to be assessed.

oily *adj.* **1.** of or like oil. **2.** covered or soaked with oil. **3.** unpleasantly smooth in manner; ingratiating. —**oiliness** *n.*

ointment /'ɔɪntmənt/ *n.* a smooth greasy healing or beautifying preparation for the skin. [from Old French from Latin *unguere* = anoint]

OK /əu'keɪ/ *adj. & adv.* or **okay** all right, satisfactory; (as *interjection*) I agree. —*n.* approval, agreement to a plan etc. —*v.t.* to give one's approval or agreement to. [US, 19th century of disputed origin]

okapi /ə'kɑːpɪ/ *n.* an animal *Okapia johnstoni* of the giraffe family, though with much shorter legs and neck, found in the tropical rainforests of central Africa. Purplish brown with creamy face and black and white stripes on the legs and hindquarters, it is excellently camouflaged. Okapis have remained virtually unchanged for millions of years. Only a few hundred are thought to survive. [Central African]

okay variant of ◊OK.

Okhotsk, Sea of /əu'xɒtsk/ arm of the N Pacific between the Kamchatka Peninsula and Sakhalin and bordered southward by the Kuril Islands; area 937,000 sq km/ 361,700 sq mi. Free of ice only in summer, it is often fogbound.

Okinawa /ɒkiˈnɑːwə/ largest of the Japanese ◊Ryukyu Islands in the W Pacific; **area** 2,250 sq km/869 sq mi; **capital** Naha; **population** (1986) 1,190,000; **history** captured by the USA in the Battle of Okinawa 1 April–21 June 1945, with 47,000 US casualties (12,000 dead) and 60,000 Japanese (only a few hundred survived as prisoners); the island was returned to Japan in 1972.

Oklahoma /əukləˈhəumə/ state of the S central USA; nickname Sooner State; **area** 181,100 sq km/69,905 sq mi; **capital** Oklahoma City; **population** (1986) 3,305,000; **history** the region was acquired with the ◊Louisiana Purchase in 1803.

Oklahoma City industrial city (oil refining, machinery, aircraft, telephone equipment), capital of Oklahoma, USA, on the Canadian River; population (1984) 443,500.

okra /'əukrə, 'ɒk-/ *n.* a tall originally African ◊hisbiscus plant *Hibiscus esculentus* with seed-pods known as **bhindi** or ladies fingers used for food. [W African]

Okubo /əu'kuːbəu/ Toshimichi 1831–1878. Japanese ◊samurai leader whose opposition to the Tokugawa shogunate made him a leader in the ◊Meiji restoration 1866–88.

Okuma /əu'kuːmə/ Shigenobu 1838–1922. Japanese politician and prime minister 1898 and 1914–16. He presided over Japanese pressure for territorial concessions in China, before retiring 1916.

Olaf /'əulaf/ five kings of Norway, including:

Olaf I Tryggvesson 969–1000. King of Norway from 995. He began the conversion of Norway to Christianity and was killed in a sea battle against the Danes and Swedes.

Olaf II Haraldsson 995–1030. King of Norway from 1015. He offended his subjects by his centralizing policy and zeal for Christianity, and was killed in battle by Norwegian rebel chiefs backed by ◊Canute of Denmark. He was declared the patron saint of Norway in 1164.

Olaf V 1903– . King of Norway from 1957, when he succeeded his father Haakon VII.

Olbrich /'ɒlbrɪʃ/ Joseph Maria 1867–1908. Viennese architect who worked under Otto ◊Wagner and was opposed to the over-ornamentation of Art Nouveau. His major buildings, however, remain Art Nouveau in spirit: the Vienna Sezession 1897–98, the Hochzeitsturm 1907, and the Tietz department store in Düsseldorf, Germany.

old /əuld/ *adj.* **1.** having lived or existed for a long time. **2.** made long ago; used, established, or known for a long time; shabby from age or wear. **3.** having the characteristics, experience, feebleness etc. of age; skilled through long experience. **4.** not recent or modern; belonging chiefly to the past; former, original. **5.** of a specified age (*ten years old*). **6.** (*colloquial*) as a term of fondness or casual reference. —**the old,** old people. **of old,** of or in past times. **old age,** the later part of normal lifetime. **old age pension** see ◊pension; **old boy,** a former member of a school; (*colloquial*) an elderly man; (as a form of address) old man. **the old country,** one's mother country. **old-fashioned** *adj.* in or according to fashion or tastes no longer current, antiquated. **old girl,** a former member of a school; (*colloquial*) an elderly woman; (*colloquial*) as a fond form of address. **Old Glory,** (*US*) the Stars and Stripes. **old gold,** a dull brownish gold colour. **Old Guard,** the French Imperial Guard created by Napoleon I in 1804. **old guard,** the original or past or conservative members of a group. **old hat,** (*colloquial*) something tediously familiar. **old maid,** an elderly spinster; a prim and fussy person; a card game in which the object is to avoid the holding of an unpaired card. **old man,** (*colloquial*) one's father, husband, or employer etc.; (*colloquial*) as a fond form of address. **old man's beard,** a kind of clematis *Clematis vitalba* with grey fluffy hairs round the seeds. **old master,** a great painter of former times, especially of the 13th–17th centuries in Europe, a painting by such a painter. **Old Nick,** the Devil. **Old Pals Act,** the doctrine that friends should always help one another. **Old Style,** (of a date) reckoned by the Julian calendar. **old-time** *adj.* belonging to former times. **old-timer** *n.* a person with long experience or standing. **old wives' tale,** an old but foolish belief. **old woman,** (*colloquial*) a wife or mother; a fussy or timid man. **Old World,** Europe, Asia, and Africa, the part known by the

okapi

ancients to exist. **old year,** the year just ended or about to end. —**oldness** *n.* [Old English]

Old Bailey /ˈəʊld ˈbeɪlɪ/ popular name for the Central Criminal Court in London, situated in a street of that name in the City of London, off Ludgate Hill.

Old Catholic one of various breakaway groups from Roman Catholicism—including those in Holland (such as the **Church of Utrecht**, who separated from Rome in 1724 after accusations of ◊Jansenism) and groups in Austria, Czechoslovakia, Germany, and Switzerland—who rejected the proclamation of ◊papal infallibility of 1870. Old Catholic clergy are not celibate.

olden *adj.* (*archaic*) old; of old.

Oldenbarneveldt /ˈəʊldən'bɑːnəvelt/ Johan van 1547–1619. Dutch politician, a leading figure in the Netherlands' struggle for independence from Spain, who helped William the Silent negotiate the Union of Utrecht in 1579.

Oldenburg /ˈəʊldənbɜːg/ Claes 1929– . US pop artist, known for 'soft sculptures', gigantic replicas of everyday objects and foods, made of stuffed canvas or vinyl.

Oldenburg Henry 1615–1677. German official who came to London in 1652. In 1663 he was appointed to the new post of secretary to the Royal Society, a position he held until his death. He founded and edited the first scientific periodical, *Philosophical Transactions* (first issue 1665), and, through his extensive correspondence, acted as a clearing house for the science of the day.

Old English another term for ◊Anglo-Saxon; see also ◊English language.

Oldfield /ˈəʊldfiːld/ Bruce 1950– . English fashion designer who set up his own business in 1975. His evening wear has been worn by the British royal family.

oldie *n.* (*colloquial*) an old person or thing.

Old Man of the Sea in the ◊*Arabian Nights*, a man who compels strangers to carry him until they drop, encountered by Sinbad the Sailor on his fifth voyage. Sinbad escapes by getting him drunk. The Old Man of the Sea is also used in Greek mythology to describe ◊Proteus, an attendant of the sea god Poseidon.

Old Pretender nickname of ◊James Edward Stuart, the son of James II of England.

Old Testament Christian term for the Hebrew ◊Bible, which is the first part of the Christian Bible. The Christian Old Testament contains 39 books, and the Hebrew Bible 24. They include accounts of the origins of the world, the history of the ancient Hebrews and their covenant with God, prophetical writings, and religious poetry. The first five books are traditionally ascribed to Moses and called the Pentateuch by Christians and the Torah by Jews.

Old Trafford /ˈəʊld ˈtræfəd/ two sporting centres in Manchester, England. **Old Trafford football ground** is the home of Manchester United Football Club and was opened in 1910. The crowd capacity is 50,726. It was used for the 1966 World Cup competition and has also hosted the Football Association Cup Final and replays. **Old Trafford cricket ground** was opened in 1857 and has staged test matches regularly since 1884. The crowd capacity is 40,000.

Olduvai Gorge /ˈɒlduvaɪ ˈgɔːdʒ/ deep cleft in the Serengeti steppe, Tanzania, where the ◊Leakeys found prehistoric stone tools in the 1930s. They discovered Pleistocene remains of prehumans and gigantic animals in 1958–59. The gorge has given its name to the **Olduvai culture**, a simple stone-tool culture of prehistoric hominids, dating from 2–0.5 million years ago.

Old Vic /ˈəʊld ˈvɪk/ a theatre in S London, England, former home of the National Theatre (1963–76).

oleaginous /əʊliˈædʒɪnəs/ *adj.* 1. having the properties of or producing oil. 2. oily (*literal* or *figurative*). [from French from Latin *oleum* = olive oil]

oleander /əʊliˈændə(r)/ *n.* or **rose bay** an evergreen Mediterranean shrub *Nerium oleander* with pink or white flowers and aromatic leaves that secrete the poison oleandrin. [Latin]

oleaster /əʊliˈæstə/ *n.* a wild olive *Olea oleaster*. [from Latin]

olefin /ˈəʊləfɪn/ *n.* common name for ◊alkene, a hydrocarbon. [from French *oléfiant* = oil-forming]

O level, General Certificate of Education or **Ordinary level** an examination formerly taken in the UK by school children at age 16. It was superseded by the ◊GCSE in 1988.

olfactory /ɒlˈfæktərɪ/ *adj.* concerned with smelling. [from Latin *olfacere* = to smell]

olfactory cell in mammals, receptor cells found high up inside the nose, associated with the sense of smell. They are stimulated by chemicals in the air and enhance the related sense of taste.

oligarch /ˈɒlɪgɑːk/ *n.* a member of an oligarchy. [from French or Latin from Greek (*oligoi* = few and *arkhō* = rule)]

oligarchy /ˈɒlɪgɑːkɪ/ *n.* a form of government in which power is in the hands of a small group of people; this group; a state governed in this way. —**oligarchic** /-ˈgɑːkɪk/ *adj.*, **oligarchical** /-ˈgɑː-/ *adj.*

Oligocene /ˈɒlɪgəsiːn/ *adj.* of the third epoch of the Tertiary period of geological time. —*n.* this epoch 38–25 million years ago. [from Greek *oligos* = small and *kainos* = new]

oligopoly *n.* in economics, a situation in which a few companies control the major part of a particular market and concert their actions to perpetuate such control. This may include an agreement to fix prices (a ◊cartel).

oligosaccharide *n.* ◊carbohydrate comprising a few ◊monosaccharide units linked together. It is a general term used to indicate that a carbohydrate is larger than a simple di- or trisaccharide but not as large as a polysaccharide.

Olivares /ɒliˈvɑːres/ Count-Duke of (born Gaspar de Guzmán) 1587–1645. Spanish prime minister 1621–43. He committed Spain to recapturing the Netherlands and to involvement in the Thirty Years' War 1618–48, and his efforts to centralize power led to revolts in Catalonia and Portugal, which brought about his downfall.

olive /ˈɒlɪv/ *n.* 1. a small oval hard-stoned fruit, green when unripe and bluish-black when ripe. 2. the tree bearing it *Olea europaea*; its wood. Native to Asia but widely cultivated in Mediterranean and subtropical areas, it grows up to 15 m/50 ft high. 3. leaves or a branch or wreath of olive as an emblem of peace. 4. the colour of an unripe olive. —*adj.* 1. of green colour like an unripe olive. 2. (of the complexion) yellowish-brown. —**olive-branch** *n.* something done or offered as the sign of a wish to make peace. **olive oil,** oil extracted from olives. [from Old French from Latin *oliva* from Greek]

Oliver /ˈɒlɪvə/ Isaac c.1556–1617. English painter of miniatures, originally a Huguenot refugee, who studied under Nicholas ◊Hilliard. He became a court artist in the reign of James I.

Olives, Mount of /ˈɒlɪvz/ a range of hills E of Jerusalem, associated with the Christian religion: a former chapel (now a mosque) marks the traditional site of Jesus' ascension to heaven, with the Garden of Gethsemane at its foot.

Olivier /əˈlɪvieɪ/ Laurence (Kerr), Baron Olivier 1907–1989. English actor and director. For many years associated with the Old Vic theatre, he was director of the National Theatre company 1962–73. His stage roles include Henry V, Hamlet, Richard III, and Archie Rice in John Osborne's *The Entertainer*. His acting in and direction of filmed versions of Shakespeare's plays received critical acclaim, for example *Henry V* 1944 and *Hamlet* 1948.

olivine /ˈɒlɪviːn/ *n.* greenish mineral, magnesium iron silicate, $(Mg,Fe)_2SiO_4$. It is a rock-forming mineral, present in, for example, peridotite, gabbro, and basalt. Olivine is called **peridot** when pale green and transparent, and used in jewellery. [from Latin *oliva* = olive]

olm *n.* a cave-dwelling aquatic salamander (*Proteus anguinus*), found along the E Adriatic seaboard in Italy and Yugoslavia. The adult is permanently larval in form, about 25 cm/10 in long, with external gills; it is an instance of ◊neoteny.

Olympia /əˈlɪmpɪə/ a sanctuary in the W Peloponnese, ancient Greece, with a temple of Zeus and the stadium (for foot races, boxing, wrestling) and hippodrome (for chariot and horse races) where the original Olympic Games were held.

Olympiad /əˈlɪmpɪæd/ *n.* 1. a period of four years between Olympic Games, used by the ancient Greeks in dating events. 2. a celebration of the modern Olympic Games. 3. a regular international contest in chess etc.

Olympian /əˈlɪmpɪən/ *adj.* 1. of Olympus, celestial. 2. (of manner etc.) magnificent, condescending, superior. 3.

Olympic Games Bas relief on the base of a statue c.510 BC, Athens Museum, showing a pair of wrestlers practising, a runner in the start position, and a javelin thrower.

Olympic. —*n.* **1.** a dweller in Olympus, a Greek god. **2.** a person of great attainments or superhuman calm.

Olympic /ə'lɪmpɪk/ *adj.* of the Olympic Games. —*n.* (in *plural*) the Olympic Games. [from Latin from Greek *Olumpikos* = of **Olympus** or Olympia]

Olympic Games sporting contests originally held in Olympia, ancient Greece, every four years during a sacred truce; records were kept from 776 BC. Women were forbidden to be present, and the male contestants were naked. The ancient games were abolished in AD 394. The present-day games have been held every four years since 1896. Since 1924 there has been a separate winter games programme. From 1994 the winter and summer games will be held two years apart.

Olympus /ə'lɪmpəs/ (Greek **Olimbos**) several mountains in Greece and elsewhere, one of which is **Mount Olympus** in N Thessaly, Greece, 2,918 m/9,577 ft high. In ancient Greece it was considered the home of the gods.

om (especially in Buddhism and Hinduism) a mystic syllable, considered the most sacred mantra. It appears at the beginning and end of most Sanskrit recitations, prayers, and texts. [Sanskrit, a universal affirmation]

OM abbreviation of (member of the) ◊**Order of Merit**.

Oman /əʊ'mɑːn/ Sultanate of; country on the Arabian peninsula, bounded to the W by the United Arab Emirates, Saudi Arabia, and Yemen, and to the E by the Arabian Sea; **area** 272,000 sq km/105,000 sq mi; **capital** Muscat; **physical** Jebel Akhdar highlands, high arid plateau, fertile coastal strip, Kuria Muria islands; **head of state and government** Qaboos bin Said from 1970; **political system** absolute monarchy; **exports** oil, dates, silverware; **population** (1990 est) 1,305,000; **language** Arabic (official); English, Urdu; **recent history** the Sultanate of Muscat and Oman achieved full independence from Britain in 1951; Treaty of Friendship signed with Britain. In 1970 after 38 years' rule, Sultan Said bin Taimur was replaced in a coup by his son Qaboos bin Said, who instituted a more liberal and expansionist regime and changed the country's name to Sultanate of Oman. A rebellion in the south was defeated in 1975. In 1982 a Memorandum of Understanding was signed with the UK, providing for regular consultation on international issues. In 1985 diplomatic ties were established with the USSR, part of a policy of nonalignment.

Omar /'əʊmɑː/ 581–644. Adviser of the prophet Muhammad. In 634 he succeeded Abu Bakr as caliph (civic and religious leader of Islam) and conquered Syria, Palestine, Egypt, and Persia. He was assassinated by a slave.

Omar Khayyám /'əʊmɑː kəi'jæm/ *c.*1050–1123. Persian astronomer, mathematician, and poet. Born in Nishapur, he founded a school of astronomical research and assisted in reforming the calendar. His study of algebra was known in Europe, as well as in the East. In the West, Omar Khayyám is chiefly known as a poet through Edward ◊Fitzgerald's version of *The Rubáiyát of Omár Khayyám* 1859.

Omayyad dynasty /əʊ'maɪædz/ an Arabian ruling family of the Islamic empire who reigned as caliphs (civic and religious leaders of Islam) 661–750. They were overthrown by Abbasids, but a member of the family escaped to Spain and in 756 assumed the title of emir of Córdoba. His dynasty,

which took the title of caliph in 929, ruled in Córdoba until the early 11th century.

ombudsman /'ɒmbʊdzmæn/ *n.* (*plural* **ombudsmen**) an official appointed to investigate complaints by individuals against maladministration, especially by public authorities. The post is of Scandinavian origin; it was introduced in Sweden 1809, Denmark 1954, and Norway 1962, and spread to other countries from the 1960s. [Swedish = legal representative]

Omdurman /ɒmdə'mɑːn/ city in Sudan, on the White Nile, a suburb of Khartoum; population (1983) 526,000. It was the residence of the Sudanese sheik known as the Mahdi 1884–98.

Omdurman, Battle of battle on 2 Sept 1898 in which the Sudanese, led by the Khalifa, were defeated by British and Egyptian troops under General Kitchener.

omega /'əʊmɪɡə/ *n.* **1.** the last letter of the Greek alphabet, (ω, Ω) = o. **2.** the last of a series; the final development. [Greek *ōmega* = great O]

omelette /'ɒmlɪt/ *n.* beaten eggs cooked in a frying pan and often served folded round a savoury or sweet filling. [French]

omen /'əʊmen/ *n.* an occurrence or thing regarded as a prophetic sign; prophetic significance. [Latin]

omicron /ə'maɪkrɒn/ *n.* the 15th letter of the Greek alphabet, (o, O) = o. [Greek *o micron* = small O]

ominous /'ɒmɪnəs/ *adj.* looking or seeming as if trouble is at hand, inauspicious. —**ominously** *adv.* [from Latin]

omission /ə'mɪʃən/ *n.* **1.** omitting, being omitted. **2.** a thing omitted or not done. [from Old French or Latin]

omit /ə'mɪt/ *v.t.* (**-tt-**) **1.** to leave out, not to insert or include. **2.** to leave not done, to neglect or fail to do. [from Latin *omittere*]

omni- in combinations, all. [Latin *omnis* = all]

omnibus /'ɒmnɪbəs/ *n.* **1.** a bus. **2.** a volume containing several novels etc. previously published separately. —*adj.* serving several objects at once; comprising several items. [French from Latin = for everybody]

omnifarious /ɒmnɪ'feərɪəs/ *adj.* of all sorts. [from Latin]

omnipotent /ɒm'nɪpətənt/ *adj.* all-powerful. —**omnipotence** *n.*, **omnipotently** *adv.* [from Old French from Latin *potens* (from *posse* = be at hand]

omnipresent /ɒmnɪ'prezənt/ *adj.* present everywhere at the same time; ubiquitous. —**omnipresence** *n.* [from Latin *praeesse* = be at hand]

omniscient /ɒm'nɪsɪənt/ *adj.* knowing everything or much. —**omniscience** *n.* [from Latin *scire* = know]

omnivore *n.* an animal that feeds on both plant and animal material. Omnivores have digestive adaptations intermediate between those of ◊herbivores and ◊carnivores, with relatively unspecialized digestive systems and gut microorganisms that can digest a variety of foodstuffs. [from Latin *vorare* = devour]

omnivorous /ɒm'nɪvərəs/ *adj.* **1.** feeding on many kinds of food, especially on both plants and flesh. **2.** reading or observing etc. whatever comes one's way.

Omsk /ɒmsk/ industrial city (agricultural and other machinery, food processing, sawmills, oil refining) in the USSR, capital of Omsk region, W Siberia; population (1987)

1,134,000. Its oil refineries are linked with Tuimazy in Bashkiria by a 1,600 km/1,000 mi pipeline.

on *prep*. 1. supported by, attached to, covering, enclosing; carried with. 2. during; exactly at; contemporaneously with; immediately after or before; as a result of. 3. having or so as to have membership of (a committee etc.). 4. supported financially by. 5. close to, just by; in the direction of, against, so as to threaten. 6. touching, striking. 7. having as a basis or motive; having as a standard, confirmation, or guarantee. 8. concerning; using, engaged with; so as to affect; to be paid by. 9. added to. 10. in a specified manner or state. —*adv*. 1. so as to be supported by, attached to, or covering something. 2. in an appropriate direction, towards something. 3. further toward; in an advanced position or state. 4. with continued movement or action. 5. in operation or activity; being shown or performed. —*adj*. (in cricket) being in, from, or towards the part of the field on the striker's side and in front of his wicket. —*n*. the on side in cricket. —**be on**, (of an event) to be due to take place; (*colloquial*) to be willing to participate or approve; to accept a proposition or wager; to be practicable or acceptable. **be on at**, (*colloquial*) to nag or grumble at. **be on to**, to realize the significance or intentions of. **on and off**, intermittently, now and then. **on and on**, continually, at tedious length. **on-line** *adj*. (of computer equipment or a computer process) directly controlled by or connected to a central processor. **on time**, punctual, punctually. **on to**, to a position on. [Old English]

onager /ˈɒnəgə/ *n*. a wild ass (especially *Equus hemionus*). [from Latin from Greek *onos* = ass and *agrios* = wild]

onanism /ˈəʊnənɪzəm/ *n*. masturbation. [from French from *Onan* (Genesis 38: 9)]

Onassis /əʊˈnæsɪs/ Aristotle (Socrates) 1906–1975. Turkish-born Greek shipowner. In 1932 he started what became the largest independent shipping line and during the 1950s he was one of the first to construct supertankers. In 1968 he married Jacqueline Kennedy, widow of US president John F Kennedy.

> After a certain point money is meaningless. It ceases to be the goal. The game is what counts.
> **Aristotle Onassis**
> in *Esquire* 1969

once /wʌns/ *adv*. 1. on one occasion only. 2. at some point or period in the past. 3. ever, at all. 4. multiplied by one; by one degree. —*conj*. as soon as. —*n*. one time or occasion. —**all at once**, without warning, suddenly; all together. **at once**, immediately; simultaneously. **(every) once in a while**, from time to time. **for once**, on this (or that) occasion, even if at no other. **once again** *or* **more**, another time. **once and for all**, in a final manner, especially after much hesitation or uncertainty. **once or twice**, a few times. **once-over** *n*. (*colloquial*) a rapid preliminary inspection. **once upon a time**, at some vague time in the past. [Old English, originally genitive of one]

oncogene *n*. a gene carried by a virus that induces a cell to divide abnormally, forming a Ôtumour. Oncogenes arise from mutations in genes (proto-oncogenes) found in all normal cells. They are usually also found in viruses that are capable of transforming normal cells to tumour cells. Such viruses are able to insert their oncogenes into the host cell's DNA, causing it to divide uncontrollably. More than one oncogene may be necessary to transform a cell in this way. [from Greek *ogkos* = mass]

oncology /ɒŋˈkɒlədʒɪ/ *n*. branch of medicine concerned with the diagnosis and treatment of Ôneoplasms, especially cancer.

oncoming *adj*. approaching from the front.

ondes Martenot /ˈɒnd mɑːtəˈnəʊ/ electronic musical instrument invented by Maurice Martenot (1898–1980) and first demonstrated in 1928. A melody of considerable range and voice-like timbre is produced by sliding a contact along a conductive ribbon, the left hand controlling the tone colour. [French = Martenot waves]

one /wʌn/ *adj*. 1. single and integral in number. 2. (with a noun implied) a single person or thing of a kind expressed or

O'Neill *Previously a sailor, gold prospector, actor, and reporter, US playwright Eugene O'Neill was awarded the Nobel Prize for Literature in 1936.*

implied. 3. particular but undefined, especially as contrasted with another. 4. only such. 5. forming a unity. 6. identical, the same. —*n*. 1. the lowest cardinal numeral, a thing numbered with it (1, i, I); unity, a unit. 2. a single thing, person, or example (often referring to a noun previously expressed or implied). 3. a drink. 4. a story or joke. —*pron*. 1. a person of a specified kind. 2. any person, as representing people in general. 3. (*colloquial*) I. —**all one**, a matter of indifference (*to*). **at one**, in agreement. **one another**, each the other (as a formula of reciprocity). **one-armed bandit**, (*slang*) a fruit machine with a long handle. **one day**, on an unspecified day; at some unspecified future date. **one-horse** *adj*. using a single horse; (*slang*) small, poorly equipped. **one-man** *adj*. involving or operated by only one man. **one-off** *adj*. (*colloquial*) made as the only one, not repeated. **one or two**, (*colloquial*) a few. **one-sided** *adj*. unfair, partial. **one-time** *adj*. former. **one-track mind**, a mind preoccupied with one subject. **one-up** *adj*. (*colloquial*) having a particular advantage. **one-upmanship** *n*. (*colloquial*) the art of maintaining a psychological advantage. **one-way** *adj*. allowing movement, travel etc., in one direction only. [Old English]

Onega, Lake /əʊˈneɪgə/ second largest lake in Europe, NE of Leningrad, partly in Karelia, USSR; area 9,600 sq km/3,710 sq mi. The **Onega canal**, along its S shore, is part of the Mariinsk system linking Leningrad with the river Volga.

O'Neill /əʊˈniːl/ Eugene (Gladstone) 1888–1953. US playwright, the leading American dramatist between World Wars I and II. His plays include *Anna Christie* 1922, *Desire under the Elms* 1924, *The Iceman Cometh* 1946, and the posthumously produced autobiographical drama *Long Day's Journey into Night* 1956 (written in 1940). He was awarded the Nobel Prize for Literature in 1936.

> Our lives are merely strange dark interludes in the electric display of God the Father.
> **Eugene O'Neill**
> *Strange Interlude*

O'Neill Terence, Baron O'Neill of the Maine 1914–1990. Northern Irish Unionist politician. In the Ulster government he was minister of finance 1956–63, then prime minister 1963–69. He resigned when opposed by his party on measures to extend rights to Roman Catholics, including a universal franchise.

Ontario

oneness *n.* **1.** being one, singleness, uniqueness. **2.** agreement. **3.** sameness, changelessness.

one-party state a state in which there is a ban, constitutional or unofficial, on the number of political parties permitted to stand for election. In some cases there may be no legal alternative parties. For example, in the USSR members of only one political party stand for election; in others there may be limited tolerance of a few token members of an opposition party, as in Mexico; or one party may be permanently in power with no elections.

onerous /'ɒnərəs, 'əʊn-/ *adj.* burdensome. [from Old French from Latin *onus* = burden]

oneself /wʌn'self/ *pron.* the reflexive and emphatic form of *one.*

ongoing *adj.* continuing, in progress.

onion /'ʌnjən/ *n.* a vegetable *Allium cepa* with an edible bulb of pungent smell and flavour. —**oniony** *adj.* [from Anglo-French from Latin *unio*]

online system in computing, a system that allows the computer to work interactively with its users, responding to each instruction as it is given and prompting users for information when necessary, as opposed to a ◊batch system.

onlooker *n.* a spectator.

only /'əʊnlɪ/ *attrib. adj.* **1.** existing alone of its or their kind. **2.** best or alone worth knowing. —*adv.* **1.** without anything or anyone else, and that is all. **2.** no longer ago than; not until. **3.** with no better result than. —*conj.* except that, but then. —**if only**, I wish that. **only too**, extremely. [Old English]

Onnes /'ɒnəs/ Kamerlingh 1853–1926. Dutch physicist who worked mainly in the field of low-temperature physics. In 1911, he discovered the phenomenon of ◊superconductivity (enhanced electrical conductivity at very low temperatures), for which he was awarded the 1913 Nobel Prize for Physics.

o.n.o. abbreviation of or near(est) offer.

onomatopoeia /ɒnəmætə'piːə/ *n.* formation of a word or a ◊figure of speech that copies natural sounds. Thus the word or name 'cuckoo' imitates the sound that the cuckoo makes. —**onomatopoeic** *adj.* [Latin from Greek *onoma* = name and *poieō* = make]

onrush *n.* an onward rush.

onset *n.* **1.** an attack. **2.** a beginning.

onshore *adj.* **1.** on the shore. **2.** (of a wind) blowing from the sea towards the land.

onside *adj.* (of a player in a field game) not offside.

onslaught /'ɒnslɔt/ *n.* a fierce attack. [from *on* and Middle Dutch *slag* = blow]

Ontario /ɒn'teərɪəʊ/ province of central Canada; **area** 1,068,600 sq km/412,480 sq mi; **capital** Toronto; **population** (1986) 9,114,000; **history** first explored by the French in the 17th century, Ontario came under British control in 1763 (Treaty of Paris). An attempt in 1841 to form a merged province with French-speaking Québec failed, and Ontario became a separate province of Canada from 1867.

Ontario, Lake smallest and easternmost of the Great Lakes, on the US-Canadian border; area 19,200 sq km/ 7,400 sq mi. It is connected to Lake Erie by the Welland Canal and the Niagara River, and drains into the St Lawrence River. Its main port is Toronto.

ontogeny *n.* the process of development of a living organism, including the part of development that takes place after hatching or birth. The idea that 'ontogeny recapitulates phylogeny' (the development of an organism goes through the same stages as its evolutionary history), proposed by the German scientist Haeckel, is now discredited.

ontology /ɒn'tɒlədʒɪ/ *n.* the branch of metaphysics dealing with the nature of being. —**ontological** /-'lɒdʒɪkəl/ *adj.* [from Greek *ont-* = being]

onus /'əʊnəs/ *n.* a burden, a duty, a responsibility. [Latin]

onward /'ɒnwəd/ *adv.* (also **onwards**) further on; towards the front; with advancing motion. — *adj.* directed onwards.

onyx /'ɒnɪks/ *n.* a semiprecious variety of chalcedonic ◊silica (SiO_2) in which the crystals are too fine to be detected under a microscope, a state known as cryptocrystalline. It has straight parallel bands of different colours: milk white, black, and red. [from Old French from Latin from Greek, originally = finger-nail]

oodles /'uːdəlz/ *n. pl.* (*colloquial*) a very great amount. [originally US]

ooh /uː/ interjection expressing surprise, delight, pain etc. [natural exclamation]

oolite /'əʊəlaɪt/ *n.* a limestone made up of tiny spherical carbonate particles called **ooliths**. Ooliths have a concentric structure with a diameter up to 2 mm/0.08 in. They were formed by chemical precipitation and accumulation on ancient sea floors. —**oolitic** /-'lɪtɪk/ *adj.* [from French Greek *ōon* = egg and *lithos* = stone]

oops /ʊps, uːps/ interjection on making an obvious mistake. [natural exclamation]

Oort /ɔːt/ Jan Hendrik 1900– . Dutch astronomer. In 1927, he calculated the mass and size of our Galaxy, the Milky Way, and the Sun's distance from its centre, from the observed movements of stars around the Galaxy's centre. In 1950 Oort proposed that comets exist in a vast swarm, now called the **Oort Cloud**, at the edge of the solar system.

oosphere *n.* another name for the female gamete or ◊ovum of certain plants such as algae.

ooze *v.t./i.* **1.** (of a fluid) to trickle or leak slowly out. **2.** to exude moisture. **3.** to exude or exhibit (a feeling) freely. —*n.* **1.** wet mud, especially sediment of fine texture consisting mainly of organic matter found on the ocean floor at depths greater than 2,000 m/6,600 ft. **2.** a sluggish flow —**oozy** *adj.* [from Old English *wos* = juice, sap]

op *n.* (*colloquial*) an operation. [abbreviation]

op. opus.

op- prefix, see ◊ob-.

opacity /əʊ'pæsɪtɪ/ *n.* opaqueness. [from French from Latin *opacus*]

opal /'əʊp(ə)l/ *n.* a cryptocrystalline form of ◊silica, SiO_2, often occurring as stalactites and found in many types of rock. The common opal is translucent, milk white, yellow, red, blue, or green, and lustrous. Precious opal is iridescent, due to close-packed silica spheres diffracting light rays within the stone. [from French and Latin, probably ultimately from Sanskrit *upalas* = precious stone]

opalescent /əʊpə'lesənt/ *adj.* iridescent. —**opalescence** *n.* [from opal]

opaline /'əʊpəlaɪn/ *adj.* opal-like, opalescent.

opaque /əʊ'peɪk/ *adj.* **1.** not transmitting light, impenetrable to sight. **2.** unclear, obscure. [from Latin *opacus*]

Op Art a movement in modern art, popular in the 1960s. It uses scientifically based optical effects that confuse the spectator's eye. Precisely painted lines or dots are arranged in carefully regulated patterns to create an illusion of surface movement. Exponents include Victor Vasarely and Bridget Riley. [abbreviation of *optical art*]

op. cit. in the work already quoted. [abbreviation of Latin *opere citato*]

OPEC /'əʊpek/ acronym from ◊Organization of the Petroleum-Exporting Countries.

open /'əʊpən/ *adj.* **1.** not closed or locked or blocked up; not sealed; giving access. **2.** not covered or concealed or confined; not restricted. **3.** spread out, unfolded, expanded. **4.** with wide spaces between solid parts. **5.** undisguised, public, manifest. **6.** (of an exhibition, shop etc.) admitting visitors or customers, ready for business. **7.** (of a competition etc.) unrestricted as to who may compete. **8.** not yet settled or decided; (of an offer or vacancy) still available; (with *to*) willing or liable to receive. **9.** (of the bowels) not constipated. —*n.* **1.** *the* open air; *the* country. **2.** an open competition or championship. —*v.t./i.* 1. to make or become open or more open. 2. to begin or establish; to make a start. 3. to declare ceremonially to be open to the public. **open air**, outdoors. **open-and-shut** *adj.* (*colloquial*) perfectly straightforward. **open book**, one who is easily understood; not having secrets. **open day**, a day when the public may visit a place normally closed to them. **open-ended** *adj.* without limit or restriction. **open a person's eyes**, to make him realize something unexpected. **open-handed** *adj.* generous. **open-hearted** *adj.* frank and kindly. **open-heart surgery**, surgery with the heart exposed and blood made to bypass it. **open letter**, a letter of protest etc. addressed to a person by name but printed in a newspaper etc. **open-minded** *adj.* accessible to new ideas, unprejudiced; undecided. **open-plan** *adj.* with few interior walls. **open prison**, a prison with few physical restraints on prisoners. **open question**, a matter on which no final verdict has yet been made or on which none is possible. **open sandwich**, a slice of bread covered with a layer of meat or cheese etc. **open sea**, the expanse of sea away from the land. **open secret**, one known to so many people that it is no longer a secret. **open society**, one without a rigid structure and with freedom of belief. **open verdict**, one affirming the commission of a crime but not specifying a criminal or (in the case of violent death) a cause. —**openness** *n.* [Old English]

opencast mining or **open-pit mining** or **strip mining** with removal of surface layers and working from above, not from shafts underground. Coal, iron ore, and phosphates are often extracted by opencast mining.

Open College in the UK, an initiative launched by the Manpower Services Commission (subsequently the ◊Training Commission) to enable people to gain and update technical and vocational skills by means of distance teaching, such as correspondence, radio, and television.

open-door policy the economic philosophy of equal access by all nations to another nation's markets.

opener *n.* 1. a person or thing that opens something. 2. a device for opening tins or bottles etc.

open-hearth furnace a method of steelmaking, now largely superseded by the ◊basic-oxygen process. The open-hearth furnace was developed in England by German-born William and Friedrich Siemens, and improved by Pierre and Emile Martin in 1864. In the furnace, which has a wide, saucer-shaped hearth and a low roof, molten pig iron and scrap are packed into the shallow hearth and heated by overhead gas burners using preheated air.

opening *n.* 1. a space or gap; a place where something opens. 2. the beginning of something. 3. an opportunity. —**opening-time** *n.* the time at which public houses may legally open for custom.

openly *adv.* without concealment, publicly; frankly.

open shop a factory or other business employing men and women not belonging to trade unions, as opposed to the ◊closed shop, which employs trade unionists only.

Open University an institution established in the UK in 1969 to enable mature students without qualifications to study to degree level without regular attendance. Open University teaching is based on a mixture of correspondence courses, TV and radio lectures and demonstrations, personal tuition organized on a regional basis, and summer schools.

opera *n.* a dramatic musical work in which singing takes the place of speech. Dancing and spectacular staging may also play their parts. Opera originated in late 16th-century Florence. —**opera-glasses** *n.pl.* small binoculars for use at the opera or theatre. **opera-hat** *n.* a man's collapsible hat. **opera-house** *n.* a theatre for operas. [Italian from Latin = labour, work]

operable /ˈɒpərəbəl/ *adj.* 1. that can be operated. 2. suitable for treatment by a surgical operation.

operate /ˈɒpəreɪt/ *v.t./i.* 1. to be in action; to produce an effect. 2. to control the functioning of. 3. to perform a surgical operation. —**operating-theatre** *n.* a room for surgical operations. [from Latin *operari* = to work]

operatic /ɒpəˈrætɪk/ *adj.* of or like an opera. —**operatically** *adv.*

operating system (OS) in computing, a program that controls the basic operation of a computer. A typical OS controls the ◊peripheral devices, organizes the filing system, provides a means of communicating with the operator, and runs other programs.

operation /ɒpəˈreɪʃən/ *n.* 1. operating, being operated; the way a thing works; validity, scope. 2. a piece of work, something to be done. 3. an act performed by a surgeon on any part of the body to remove or deal with a diseased, injured, or deformed part. 4. a piece of military activity. 5. a financial or other transaction. 6. in mathematics, the subjection of a number, quantity, or function to a process affecting its value or form, e.g. multiplication, differentiation. [from Old French from Latin *operari* = to work]

operational *adj.* 1. of, engaged in, or used for operations. 2. able or ready to function. —**operational amplifier** an electronic circuit used to increase the size of an alternating voltage signal without distorting it. —**operational research**, the application of scientific principles to business etc. management. —**operationally** *adv.*

operations research a business discipline that uses logical analysis to find solutions to managerial and administrative problems, such as the allocation of resources, inventory control, competition, and the identification of information needed for decision-making.

operative /ˈɒpərətɪv/ *adj.* 1. in operation, having an effect; practical; having principal relevance. 2. of or by surgery. —*n.* a worker, especially in a factory. —**operatively** *adv.*

operator /ˈɒpəreɪtə/ *n.* 1. a person who operates a machine etc.; one who engages in business; (*colloquial*) a person acting in a specified way. 2. one who makes connections of lines at a telephone exchange. 3. in mathematics, a symbol or function denoting an operation.

operculum /əˈpɜːkjʊləm/ *n.* (*plural* **opercula**) a fish's gill-cover; a similar structure in a plant; the valve closing the mouth of a shell. [Latin *operire* = to cover]

operetta /ɒpəˈretə/ *n.* a one-act or short opera; a light opera. [Italian (diminutive of opera)]

operon *n.* a group of genes that are found next to each other on a chromosome, and are turned on and off as an integrated unit. They usually produce enzymes that control different steps in the same biochemical pathway. Operons were discovered in 1961 (by the French biochemists F Jacob and J Monod) in bacteria; they are less common in higher organisms, where the control of metabolism is a more complex process.

ophidian /əˈfɪdiən/ *n.* a member of the Ophidia or Serpentes, a suborder of reptiles including the ◊snakes; a snake. —*adj.* of this order; snakelike. [from Greek *ophis* = snake]

Ophiuchus /ɒˈfjuːkəs/ *n.* a large constellation along the celestial equator, known as the **serpent bearer** because the constellation Serpens is wrapped around it. The Sun passes through Ophiuchus each Dec, but the constellation is not part of the zodiac. Ophiuchus contains ◊Barnard's Star.

ophthalmia /ɒfˈθælmiə/ *n.* inflammation of the eye, especially conjunctivitis. [Latin from Greek *ophthalmos* = eye]

ophthalmic /ɒfˈθælmɪk/ *adj.* 1. of or for the eye. 2. of, for, or affected with ophthalmia. —**ophthalmic optician**, an optician qualified to prescribe as well as dispense spectacles etc.

ophthalmology /ɒfθælˈmɒlədʒɪ/ *n.* the study of the eye and its diseases. —**ophthalmologist** *n.*

ophthalmoscope /ɒfˈθælməskəʊp/ *n.* an instrument for examining the eye.

Ophüls /ˈɒphʊls/ Max. Adopted name of Max Oppenheimer 1902–1957. German film director. He moved to cinema from the theatre, and his work used intricate camera movements. He worked in Europe and the USA, attracting much critical praise for films such as *Letter from an Unknown Woman* 1948 and *Lola Montes* 1955.

opiate, endogenous a naturally produced chemical in the body that has effects similar to morphine and other opiate drugs. Examples include ◊endorphins and ◊encephalins.

opiate /ˈəʊpiət/ *adj.* 1. containing opium. 2. narcotic, soporific. —*n.* 1. a drug containing opium and easing pain or inducing sleep. 2. a soothing influence. [from Latin from Greek *opion*]

opine /əʊˈpaɪn/ *v.t.* to express or hold as one's opinion. [from Latin *opinari* = believe]

opinion /ə'pɪnjən/ n. 1. a belief based on grounds short of proof, a view held as probable. 2. what one thinks about something. 3. a piece of professional advice. —**opinion poll,** an estimate of public opinion made by questioning a representative sample of people. The first accurate sampled opinion poll was carried out by the statistician George ◊Gallup during the US presidential election of 1936. [from Old French from Latin *opinio*]

opinionated /ə'pɪnjəneɪtɪd/ adj. having strong opinions and holding them dogmatically.

opinion poll attempt to measure public opinion by taking a survey of the views of a representative sample of the electorate. The first accurately sampled opinion poll was carried out by the statistician George ◊Gallup during the US presidential election 1936. Opinion polls have encountered criticism on the grounds that their publication may influence the outcome of an election.

opium /'əupiəm/ n. a drug extracted from the unripe seeds of the opium poppy *Papaver somniferum* of SW Asia. It is an addictive narcotic, containing several alkaloids, including ◊morphine, one of the most powerful natural pain-killers and addictive narcotics known, and codeine, a milder painkiller. [from Latin from Greek *opion*]

Opium Wars wars waged in the mid-19th century by the UK against China to enforce the opening of Chinese ports to trade in opium. Opium from British India paid for Britain's imports from China, such as porcelain, silk, and, above all, tea.

Oporto /ə'pɔːtəu/ English form of ◊Porto, in Portugal.

opossum /ə'pɒsəm/ n. 1. an American marsupial of the family Didelphidae. Opossums are tree-living, nocturnal animals, with prehensile tails, and hands and feet well adapted for grasping. They can grow to the size of a cat, and are carnivorous and insectivorous. 2. a similar Australian marsupial of the family Phalangeridae, living in trees. [from Virginian Indian]

opp. abbreviation of opposite, meaning as opposed to.

Oppenheimer /'ɒpənhaɪmə/ J(ulius) Robert 1904–1967. US physicist. As director of the Los Alamos Science Laboratory 1943–45, he was in charge of the development of the atom bomb (the Manhattan Project). He objected to the development of the hydrogen bomb, and was alleged to be a security risk in 1953 by the US Atomic Energy Commission.

opponent /ə'pəunənt/ n. a person or group opposing another in a contest or war. [from Latin *opponere* = set against (*ponere* = place)]

opportune /'ɒpətjuːn/ adj. (of time) well-chosen, favourable; (of an action or event) well-timed. —**opportunely** adv. [from Old French from Latin *opportunus* (*portus* = harbour), originally of wind driving ship towards harbour]

opportunism /'ɒpətjuːnɪzəm/ n. the grasping of opportunities, often in an unprincipled way. —**opportunist** n.

opportunity /ɒpə'tjuːnɪtɪ/ n. a time or set of circumstances suitable for a particular purpose.

opportunity cost in economics, that which is forgone in order to achieve an objective. A family may choose to buy a new television set and forgo their annual holiday; the holiday represents the opportunity cost.

oppose /ə'pəuz/ v.t. 1. to place in opposition or contrast. 2. to set oneself against, to resist; to argue against. —**as opposed to,** in contrast with. [from Old French from Latin *opponere* = set against]

opposite /'ɒpəzɪt/ adj. 1. (often with *to*) having a position on the other or further side, facing or back to back. 2. of a contrary kind, as different as possible. —n. an opposite thing, person, or term. —adv. in the opposite position. —prep. opposite to. —**opposite number,** a person holding the equivalent position in another group or organization.

opposition /ɒpə'zɪʃən/ n. 1. resistance, being hostile or in conflict or disagreement. 2. placing or being placed opposite, contrast; a diametrically opposite position, especially of two heavenly bodies when their longitude differs by 180° (as opposed to *conjunction*). 3. the people who oppose a proposal etc.; a group of opponents or rivals. —**the Opposition,** the chief parliamentary party opposed to that in office. [from Old French from Latin *ponere* = place]

oppress /ə'pres/ v.t. 1. to govern harshly, to treat with continual cruelty or injustice; to keep in subservience. 2. to weigh down with cares or unhappiness. —**oppression**

optical illusion

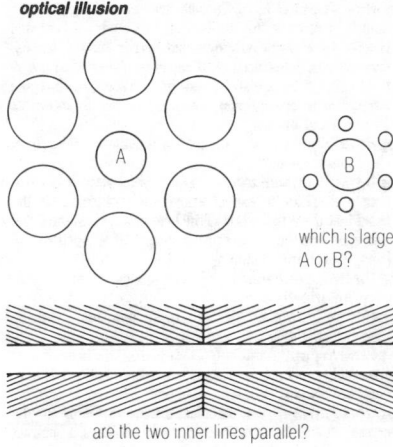

which is larger A or B?

are the two inner lines parallel?

n., **oppressor** n. [from Old French from Latin *pressare* (*premere* = press)]

oppressive adj. 1. oppressing. 2. difficult to endure. 3. (of weather) sultry and tiring. —**oppressively** adv., oppressiveness n.

opprobrious /ə'prəubriəs/ adj. (of language) severely scornful, abusive.

opprobrium /ə'prəubriəm/ n. great disgrace brought by shameful conduct. [Latin, from *opprobrium* = disgraceful act]

oppugn /ə'pjuːn/ v.t. to controvert, to call in question. [from Latin *oppugnare* = attack (*pugnare* -fight)]

opt v.i. to make a choice, to decide (*for* an alternative). —**opt out (of),** to choose not to participate (in). [from French from Latin *optare* = choose, wish]

optative /ɒp'teɪtɪv, 'ɒptə-/ adj. in grammar, (especially of a mood in Greek) expressing a wish.

optic /'ɒptɪk/ adj. of the eye or sight. [from French or Latin from Greek *optos* = seen]

optical /'ɒptɪkəl/ adj. 1. of sight, visual. 2. aiding sight. 3. of or according to optics. —**optical art** see ◊Op Art. **optical contouring,** computerized monitoring of a light pattern projected onto a patient to detect discrepancies in movements during breathing. **optical fibre,** thin optically pure glass fibre used in ◊fibre optics. **optical illusion,** an involuntary mental misinterpretation of a thing seen, due to its deceptive appearance (e.g. a mirage). —**optically** adv.

optical contouring computerized monitoring of a light pattern projected onto a patient to detect discrepancies in movements during breathing.

optical fibre very fine, optically pure glass fibre through which light can be reflected to transmit an image or information from one end to the other. Bundles of such fibres are used in ◊endoscopes to inspect otherwise inaccessible parts of machines or of the living body. Optical fibres are increasingly being used to replace copper wire in telephone cables, the messages being coded as pulses of light rather than a fluctuating electric current. In 1989 a 2,700 km/1,690 mi optical-fibre link was opened between Adelaide and Perth, Australia.

optical illusion a scene or picture that fools the eye. An example of a natural optical illusion is that the Moon appears bigger when it is on the horizon than when it is high in the sky, owing to the ◊refraction of light rays by the Earth's atmosphere.

optical instrument a device that uses one or more ◊lenses or ◊mirrors to produce an image. See ◊eye, ◊microscope, ◊periscope, ◊projector, and ◊telescope.

optician /ɒp'tɪʃən/ n. a maker or seller of spectacles and other optical instruments; one trained to provide means to correct the defects of people's eyesight. [from French from Latin]

optic nerve large nerve passing from the eye to the brain, carrying visual information. In mammals it may contain up to a million nerve fibres, connecting the sensory cells of the retina to the optical centres in the brain. Embryologically, the optic nerve develops as an outgrowth of the brain.

optics /'ɒptɪks/ *n. pl.* (usually treated as *singular*) the branch of physics that deals with the study of light and vision—for example shadows and mirror images, lenses, microscopes, telescopes, and cameras. On striking a surface, light rays are reflected or refracted with some absorption of energy, and the study of this is known as **geometrical optics.**

optimal /'ɒptɪməl/ *adj.* the best or most favourable. [from Latin *optimus* = best]

optimism /'ɒptɪmɪzəm/ *n.* 1. a hopeful view or disposition; a tendency to expect a favourable outcome. 2. the belief that the actual world is the best possible. 3. the belief that good must ultimately prevail over evil. —**optimist** *n.* [from French from Latin]

optimistic /ɒpti'mɪstɪk/ *adj.* showing optimism; hopeful. —**optimistically** *adv.*

optimize /'ɒptɪmaɪz/ *v.t.* to make optimum, to make the most of.

optimum /'ɒptɪməm/ *n.* (*plural* **optima**) the best or most favourable conditions or amount etc. —*adj.* optimal. [Latin, neuter of *optimus* = best]

option /'ɒpʃən/ *n.* 1. a choice; a thing that is or may be chosen. 2. the liberty of choosing. 3. in business, a contract giving the owner the right to buy or sell a specific quantity of a particular commodity or currency at a future date and at an agreed price, in return for a premium. The buyer or seller can decide not to exercise the option if it would prove disadvantageous. —**keep** *or* **leave one's options open**, to remain uncommitted. [French or from Latin *optare* = choose, wish]

optional *adj.* open to choice, not obligatory. —**optionally** *adv.*

optoelectronics *n.* branch of electronics concerned with the development of devices (based on the ◊semiconductor gallium arsenide) that respond not only to the ◊electrons of electronic data transmission, but also to ◊photons. An optoelectronic chip can detect and process data at a speed of 1 billion bits per second.

opulent /'ɒpjʊlənt/ *adj.* 1. wealthy. 2. abundant, luxuriant. 3. luxurious. —**opulence** *n.*, **opulently** *adv.* [from Latin *opes* = wealth]

opus /'əʊpəs, 'ɒ-/ *n.* (*plural* **opuses** or **opera** /'ɒpərə/) a musical composition numbered as one of a composer's works. [Latin = work]

or[1] *conj.* introducing an alternative or another name for the same thing or an afterthought. [Old English]

or[2] *n.* & *adj.* (usually placed after *n.*) in heraldry, gold, yellow [French from Latin *aurum*]

oracle /'ɒrəkəl/ *n.* 1. in classical antiquity, a place where deities were consulted through the medium of a priest etc. for advice or prophecy; the reply given. The earliest was probably at Dodona (in ◊Epirus), where priests interpreted the sounds made by the sacred oaks of ◊Zeus, but the most celebrated was that of Apollo at ◊Delphi. 2. a person or thing regarded as a source of wisdom etc. —**oracular** /ɒ'rækjʊlə/ *adj.* [from Old French from Latin *orare* = speak]

Oracle *n.* the ◊teletext system operated in Britain by Independent Television, introduced 1973. See also ◊Ceefax.

oral /'ɔːrəl/ *adj.* 1. spoken, verbal, by word of mouth. 2. done or taken by mouth. —*n.* (*colloquial*) a spoken examination. —**orally** *adv.* [from Latin *os* = mouth]

oral literature stories that are or have been transmitted in spoken form, such as public recitation, rather than through writing or printing. Most preliterate societies have had a tradition of oral literature, including short folk tales, legends, myths, proverbs, and riddles, as well as longer narrative works; and most of the ancient epics – such as the Greek *Odyssey* and the Mesopotamian *Gilgamesh* – seem to have been composed and added to over many centuries before they were committed to writing.

Oran /ɔː'rɑːn/ (Arabic *Wahran*) seaport in Algeria; population (1984) 663,500. Products include iron, textiles, footwear, and processed food; the port trades in grain, wool, and vegetables, and exports grass.

orange /'ɒrɪndʒ/ *n.* 1. a round juicy citrus fruit with reddish-yellow peel; the tree bearing it (*Citrus aurantium*). Thought to have originated in SE Asia, orange trees are commercially cultivated in Spain, Israel, the USA, Brazil, South Africa, and elsewhere. 2. reddish-yellow colour.

—*adj.* orange-coloured. —**orangeblossom** *n.* the fragrant white flowers of the orange, traditionally worn by brides. [from Old French ultimately from Arabic *nāranj* from Persian]

orangeade /ɒrɪndʒ'eɪd/ *n.* a drink made from orange-juice or a synthetic substitute.

Orange Free State /'ɒrɪndʒ friː 'steɪt/ province of the Republic of South Africa; **area** 127,993 sq km/49,405 sq mi; **capital** Bloemfontein; **population** (1987) 1,863,000; 82% ethnic Africans; **history** settlements from 1810 were complemented by the ◊Great Trek, and the state was recognized by Britain as independent in 1854. Following the South African, or Boer, War 1899–1902, it was annexed by Britain until it entered the union as a province in 1910.

Orange, House of /'ɒrɪndʒ/ the royal family of the Netherlands. The title is derived from the small principality of Orange, in S France, held by the family from the 8th century to 1713. They held considerable possessions in the Netherlands, to which, after 1530, was added the German county of Nassau.

Orangeman /'ɒrɪndʒmən/ *n.* (*plural* **Orangemen**) a member of the Ulster Protestant **Orange Society** established 1795 in opposition to the United Irishmen and the Roman Catholic secret societies. It was a revival of the Orange Institution of 1688, formed in support of William (III) of Orange, whose victory over the Catholic James II at the Battle of the Boyne in 1690 is commemorated annually in Northern Ireland by Protestants in parades on 12 July.

orangery /'ɒrɪndʒərɪ/ *n.* a building or hot-house for orange-trees.

orang-utan /ɔːræŋuː'tæn/ an anthropoid ape *Pongo pygmaeus*, found solely in Borneo and Sumatra. Up to 1.65 m/5.5 ft in height, it is covered with long red-brown hair, and mainly lives a solitary, arboreal life, feeding chiefly on fruit. Now an endangered species. [Malay = wild man]

oration /ɔː'reɪʃən/ *n.* a formal or ceremonial speech. [from Latin *oratio* (*orare* = speak, pray)]

orator /'ɒrətə/ *n.* a maker of a formal speech; a skilful speaker. [from Anglo-French from Latin]

Oratorian /ɒrə'tɔːrɪən/ *n.* a member of the Roman Catholic order of secular priests, called in full **Congregation of the Oratory of St Philip Neri**, formally constituted by Philip Neri in 1575 in Rome, and characterized by the degree of freedom allowed to individual communities.

oratorical /ɒrə'tɒrɪkəl/ *adj.* of or like oratory.

oratorio /ɒrə'tɔːrɪəʊ/ *n.* (*plural* **oratorios**) 1. a musical composition, usually on a sacred theme, for solo voices, chorus, and orchestra. 2. this as a musical form. [Italian, originally of musical services held at Oratory of St Philip Neri in Rome]

oratory[1] /'ɒrətərɪ/ *n.* the art of or skill in public speaking. [from Latin *oratoria* (*ars* = art) of speaking]

oratory[2] *n.* a small chapel, a place for private worship. [from Anglo-French from Latin *oratorium*]

orb *n.* 1. a sphere, a globe. 2. a globe surmounted by a cross as part of the royal regalia; a heavenly body. 3. (*poetic*) the eye. [from Latin *orbis* = ring]

orbicular /ɔː'bɪkjʊlə/ *adj.* spherical, circular. [from Latin *orbiculus* diminutive of *orbis* = ring]

Orbison /'ɔːbɪsən/ Roy 1936–1988. US pop singer and songwriter, composer of ballads such as 'Only The Lonely' 1960 and 'Running Scared' 1961. His biggest hit was the jaunty 'Oh, Pretty Woman' 1964.

orbit /'ɔːbɪt/ *n.* 1. the curved (usually closed) course of a planet, comet, satellite, spacecraft etc., the closed path followed by an object constrained by a tangential velocity to remain bound to a massive body (a planet or star) while not falling directly towards the centre of attraction. 2. the path of an electron round an atomic nucleus. 3. a range or sphere of action. —*v.t./i.* 1. to move in an orbit (round). 2. to put into orbit. —**orbiter** *n.* [from Latin = track of wheel or moon (*orbis* = ring)]

orbital /'ɔːbɪtəl/ *adj.* 1. of an orbit or orbits. 2. (of a road) passing round the outside of a city.

orbital, atomic the region around the nucleus of an atom (or, in a molecule, around several nuclei) in which an ◊electron is most likely to be found. According to ◊quantum theory, the position of an electron is uncertain; it may be found at any point. However, it is more likely to be found in some places than others, and these make up the orbital. An atom or molecule has numerous orbitals, each of which is characterised by three numbers, called **quantum numbers**, representing its energy (and hence size), its angular momentum (and hence shape), and its orientation. Each orbital can be occupied by one or two electrons (by two only if their spins are aligned in opposite electrons).

Orcadian /ɔːˈkeɪdɪən/ *n.* a native or inhabitant of the Islands of Orkney, Scotland. —*adj.* of Orkney. [from Latin *Orcades* = Orkney Islands]

orchard /ˈɔːtʃəd/ *n.* an enclosed piece of land planted with fruit-trees. [Old English (Latin *hortus* = garden)]

orchestra /ˈɔːkɪstrə/ *n.* **1.** a body of musicians playing together on stringed, wind, and percussion instruments according to an established scheme. **2.** the area in a theatre etc. assigned to them (called orchestra-pit when on a lower level). **3.** the semicircular space in front of the stage of an ancient Greek theatre, where the chorus danced and sang. —**orchestral** /ɔːˈkestrəl/ *adj.* [Latin from Greek *orkheomai* = to dance]

orchestrate /ˈɔːkɪstreɪt/ *v.t.* **1.** to compose, arrange, or score for an orchestral performance. **2.** to arrange or combine (various elements) harmoniously or for maximum effect. —**orchestration** /-ˈstreɪʃən/ *n.*

orchid /ˈɔːkɪd/ *n.* any plant of the family Orchidaceae, which contains some 18,000 species, distributed throughout the world except in the coldest areas, and most numerous in damp equatorial regions. The flowers have three sepals and three petals and are sometimes solitary, but more usually borne in spikes, racemes, or panicles, either erect or drooping. [from Latin *orchis* from Greek, originally = testicle (from shape of tuber in some species)]

Orczy /ˈɔːtsi/ Baroness Emmusca 1865–1947. Hungarian-born British novelist who wrote the historical adventure *The Scarlet Pimpernel* 1905. The foppish Sir Percy Blakeney, the bold rescuer of victims of the French Revolution, appeared in many sequels.

ordain /ɔːˈdeɪn/ *v.t.* **1.** to appoint ceremonially to perform religious duties in the Christian church. **2.** to destine. **3.** to appoint or decree authoritatively. [from Anglo-French from Latin *ordinare*]

ordeal /ɔːˈdiːl/ *n.* **1.** a severe or testing trial or experience. **2.** (*historical*) a method of determining guilt by making a suspect undergo physical harm, the safe endurance of which betokened innocence. [Old English]

ordeal, trial by in medieval times, a method of testing guilt of an accused person based on the belief in heaven's protection of the innocent. Examples of such ordeals are walking barefoot over heated iron, dipping the hand into boiling water, and swallowing consecrated bread (causing the guilty to choke).

order¹ *n.* **1.** a condition in which every part or unit is in its right place or in a normal or efficient state; the arrangement of things relative to one another; a proper or customary sequence. **2.** the prevalence of constitutional authority and obedience to the law. **3.** a system of rules or procedure. **4.** a command, an authoritative instruction; a direction to supply something, the thing (to be) supplied; a written instruction to pay money or giving authority to do something. **5.** a social class or rank. **6.** a monastic organization or institution; a Masonic or similar fraternity; a company to which distinguished persons are admitted as an honour or reward; the insignia of this. —*v.t.* **1.** to put in order, to arrange methodically. **2.** to command; to prescribe. **3.** to give an order for (goods etc.); to tell a waiter etc. to serve. —**holy orders,** the status of an ordained cleric. **in order,** in correct sequence or position; according to rules

orchid

etc.; in good condition. **in order to** *or* **that,** with the intention that; for the purpose of. **on order,** ordered but not yet received. **Order in Council,** a British sovereign's order on an administrative matter given by the advice of the Privy Council; in practice it is issued only on the advice of the cabinet. Acts of Parliament often provide for the issue of orders in council to regulate the detailed administration of their provisions. **order-paper** *n.* in the UK, a written or printed order of a day's proceedings, especially in Parliament. [from Old French *ordre* from Latin *ordo*]

order² *n.* in Classical architecture, the ◊column (including capital, shaft, and base) and the entablature, considered as an architectural whole. The earliest of the five orders was the Doric (with no base), which originated before the 5th century BC. It was followed by the Ionic, which was first found in Asia Minor. The Corinthian (with leafs in the capitals) dates from the end of the 5th century BC. The Composite appears first on the arch of Titus in Rome AD 82. No Tuscan columns survive from antiquity, but the order is thought to have originated in Etruscan times.

order³ *n.* in biological classification, a group of related families (allied genera, see ◊genus). For example, the horse, rhinoceros, and tapir families are grouped in the order Perissodactyla, the odd-toed ungulates, because they all have either one or three toes on each foot. The names of orders are not shown in italic (unlike genus and species names) and by convention they have the ending '-formes' in birds and fish; '-a' in mammals, amphibians, reptiles, and other animals; and '-ales' in fungi and plants. Related orders are grouped together in a ◊class.

orderly /ˈɔːdəli/ *adj.* **1.** well arranged, in good order; tidy. **2.** methodical. **3.** obedient to discipline, well-behaved. —*n.* **1.** a soldier in attendance on an officer to assist, take messages etc. **2.** an attendant in a hospital. —**orderly officer,** the officer on duty on a particular day. **orderly room,** a room where business is conducted in a military barracks. —**orderliness** *n.*

Order of Merit a British order of chivalry founded in 1902 by Edward VII and limited in number to 24 at any one time.

ordinal /ˈɔːdɪnəl/ *adj.* (of a number) defining a thing's position in a series (e.g. *first, tenth, hundredth*). —*n.* an ordinal number. [from Latin *ordo*]

ordinance /ˈɔːdɪnəns/ *n.* **1.** a decree. **2.** a religious rite. [from Old French from Latin *ordinare*]

ordinand /ˈɔːdɪnænd/ *n.* a candidate for ordination.

ordinary /ˈɔːdɪnəri/ *adj.* usual, customary, not exceptional. —*n.* a rule or book laying down the order of Christian service. —**in the ordinary way,** in normal circumstances, usually. **ordinary level,** former UK school examination, see ◊O level. **ordinary seaman,** a sailor of a lower rating than an able seaman. **out of the ordinary,** unusual. —**ordinarily** *adv.* [from Latin *ordinarius*]

ordinate /ˈɔːdɪnət/ *n.* in mathematics, a coordinate measured usually vertically. [from Latin *ordinare*]

ordination /ɔːdɪˈneɪʃ(ə)n/ *n.* religious ceremony by which a person is accepted into the priesthood or monastic life in various religions. Within the Christian church, ordination authorizes a priest to administer the sacraments. The Roman Catholic and Eastern Orthodox churches and the Church of England refuse to ordain women. [from Old French or Latin]

ordnance /ˈɔːdnəns/ *n.* artillery and military supplies; the government department dealing with these. [variant of ordinance]

Ordnance Survey the official state department for the mapping of Britain, established in 1791. In 1989, it began the process of conversion from a map archive to a data system, using digital techniques for both the storage and the creation of maps. Revision is continuous.

Ordovician /ɔːdəˈvɪsɪən/ *n.* the period of geological time 505–438 million years ago; the second period of the ◊Palaeozoic era. Animal life was confined to the sea: reef-building algae and the first jawless fish are characteristic.

ordure /ˈɔːdjuə/ *n.* dung. [from Old French *ord* = foul from Latin *horridus*]

ore /ɔː/ *n.* solid rock or mineral from which metal or other valuable substances can be extracted. [Old English]

oregano /ɒrɪˈɡɑːnəʊ/ *n.* dried wild marjoram as a seasoning. [Spanish = *origan*]

Oregon /ˈɒrɪɡən/ state of the NW USA, on the Pacific; nickname Beaver State; **area** 251,500 sq km/97,079 sq mi; **capital** Salem; **towns** Portland, Eugene; **population** (1987) 2,690,000; **history** settled 1811 by the Pacific Fur Company, Oregon Territory included Washington until 1853; Oregon became a state in 1859. The Oregon Trail (3,200 km/2,000 mi from Independence, Missouri, to the Columbia River) was the pioneer route across the USA 1841–60.

Oresteia /ɒrɪ'staɪə/ trilogy of Greek plays by ◊Aeschylus – *Agamemnon, Choephoroe,* and *Eumenides* – which won first prize at the festival of Dionysus in 458 BC. They describe the murder of Agamemnon by his wife Clytemnestra and the consequent vengeance of his son Orestes and daughter Electra.

Orestes /ɒ'restiːz/ in Greek legend, the son of ◊Agamemnon and ◊Clytemnestra, who killed his mother because she and her lover Aegisthus had murdered his father.

orfe *n.* fish *Leuciscus idus* of the carp family. It grows up to 50 cm/1.7 ft, and feeds on small aquatic animals. Generally greyish-black, an ornamental variety is orange. It lives in rivers and lakes of Europe and NW Asia.

Orff /ɔːf/ Carl 1895–1982. German composer, an individual stylist whose work is characterized by sharp dissonances and percussion. Among his compositions are the cantata *Carmina Burana* 1937 and the opera *Antigone* 1949.

organ /'ɔːgən/ *n.* **1.** a musical instrument consisting of pipes that sound when air is forced through them, operated by keyboards and pedals; a similar electronic instrument without pipes; a harmonium. Electrically controlled organs substitute electrical impulses and relays for some of the air-pressure controls. In electronic organs the notes are produced by electronic oscillators and are amplified at will. **2.** a part of an animal or plant body serving a particular function. **3.** a medium of communication (e.g. a newspaper) representing a party or interest. **—organ-grinder** *n.* the player of a barrel-organ. **organ-loft** *n.* a gallery for an organ. [Old English and from Old French from Latin from Greek *organon* = tool]

organdie /'ɔːgəndɪ, -'gændɪ/ *n.* fine translucent muslin, usually stiffened. [from French]

organelle *n.* a discrete and specialized structure in a living cell; organelles include mitochondria, chloroplasts, lysosomes, ribosomes, and the nucleus.

organic /ɔː'gænɪk/ *adj.* **1.** of or affecting a bodily organ or organs. **2.** (of plants or animals) having organs or an organized physical structure. **3.** (of food etc.) produced without the use of artificial fertilizers or pesticides. **4.** organized or arranged as a system of related parts. **5.** (of a compound etc.) containing carbon in its molecules. **6.** inherent, structural. **—organic chemistry,** the chemistry of carbon compounds, which are present in all living matter and in substances derived from it. In a typical organic compound, each carbon atom forms a bond with each of its neighbouring carbon atoms in the chain or ring, and two more with hydrogen atoms (carbon has a valency of four). Other atoms that may be involved in organic molecules include oxygen and nitrogen. Compounds containing only carbon and hydrogen are known as hydrocarbons. **—organically** *adv.* [from French from Latin from Greek *organikos*]

organic farming farming without the use of synthetic fertilizers (such as ◊nitrates and phosphates) or ◊pesticides (herbicides, insecticides, and fungicides) or other agrochemicals (such as hormones, growth stimulants, or fruit regulators).

organism /'ɔːgənɪzəm/ *n.* **1.** an individual animal or plant. **2.** an organized body. [from French]

organist /'ɔːgənɪst/ *n.* the player of an organ.

organization /ɔːgənaɪ'zeɪʃən/ *n.* **1.** organizing, being organized. **2.** an organized body of people; an organized system. **—organizational** *adj.*

Organization for Economic Cooperation and Development (OECD) Paris-based international organization of 24 industrialized countries, founded in 1961 to coordinate member states' economic policy strategies and to promote world trade. The OECD's subsidiary bodies include the International Energy Agency 1974, set up in the face of a world oil crisis.

Organization of African Unity (OAU) an association established in 1963 to eradicate colonialism and improve economic, cultural, and political co-operation in Africa; headquarters Addis Ababa, Ethiopia. The French-speaking Joint African and Mauritian Organization/Organisation Commune Africaine et Mauritienne: **OCAM** (1962) works within the framework of the OAU for African solidarity; headquarters Yaoundé, Cameroon.

Organization of American States (OAS) an association founded in 1948 by a charter signed by representatives of 30 North, Central, and South American states. Canada became a full member in 1990. It aims to maintain peace and solidarity within the hemisphere, and is concerned with the social and economic development of Latin America. Its headquarters are in Washington DC. It is based on the International Union of American Republics 1890–1910 and Pan-American Union 1910–48, set up to encourage friendly relations between countries of North and South America.

Organization of Central American States (*Organización de Estados Centro Americanos:* **ODECA**) an international association promoting common economic, political, educational, and military aims in Central America. The first organization, established in 1951, was superseded in 1962. Its members are Costa Rica, El Salvador, Guatemala, Honduras, and Nicaragua, provision being made for Panama to join at a later date. The permanent headquarters are in Guatemala City.

Organization of the Petroleum-Exporting Countries (OPEC) an international body established in 1960 to

organic chemistry

common organic molecule groupings

formula	name	atomic bonding
CH_3	Methyl	
CH_2CH_3	Ethyl	
CC	Double bond	
CHO	Aldehyde	
CH_2OH	Alcohol	
CO	Ketone	
COOH	Acid	
CH_2NH_2	Amine	
C_6H_6	Benzene ring	

co-ordinate price and supply policies of oil-producing states, and to improve the position of Third World states by forcing Western states to open their markets to their products. Its concerted action in raising prices in the 1970s triggered worldwide recession, but it also lessened demand, so the influence of OPEC was reduced by the mid-1980s. OPEC members are: Algeria, Ecuador, Gabon, Indonesia, Iran, Iraq, Kuwait, Libya, Nigeria, Qatar, Saudi Arabia, United Arab Emirates, and Venezuela.

organize /ˈɔːɡənaɪz/ v.t. **1.** to give an orderly structure to, to systematize. **2.** to initiate or make arrangements for; to enlist (a person or group) in this. **3.** to make organic, to make into living tissue. —**organizer** n. [from Old French from Latin from Greek *organon* = tool]

organizer n. in embryology, a part of the embryo that causes changes to occur in another part, through ◊induction, thus 'organizing' development and ◊differentiation.

organum n. in music, a form of early medieval harmony in which voices move in parallel.

organza /ɔːˈɡænzə/ n. a thin stiff transparent dress-fabric of silk or synthetic fibre.

orgasm /ˈɔːɡæzəm/ n. the climax of sexual excitement. **orgasmic** /-ˈɡæzmɪk/ adj. [from French from Greek *orgaō* = swell]

orgy /ˈɔːdʒɪ/ n. **1.** a wild drunken or licentious party or revelry. **2.** excessive indulgence in an activity. **3.** (in ancient Greece and Rome) secret rites in the worship of various gods, especially Bacchus, with wild drinking etc. —**orgiastic** /-ˈæstɪk/ adj. [from French from Latin from Greek *orgia* plural]

oriel /ˈɔːrɪəl/ n. a polygonal recess with windows projecting from the wall of a house at an upper level. [from Old French *oriol* = gallery]

orient /ˈɔːrɪənt/ v.t. **1.** to place or determine the position of with regard to the points of the compass. **2.** to site (a building etc.) so that it faces east. **3.** to face or turn (towards a specified direction); to bring into clearly understood relations, to direct. —**orient oneself**, to get one's bearings; to accustom oneself to a new situation etc.

Orient n. the East, the countries east of the Mediterranean, especially East Asia. [from Old French from Latin *oriens* = rising, sunrise (*oriri* = rise)]

oriental /ɔːrɪˈentəl, ɒr-/ adj. of the Orient, of the eastern or East Asian world or its civilization. —n. a native or inhabitant of the Orient.

orientate /ˈɔːrɪənteɪt/ v.t./i. to orient.

orientation /ɔːrɪənˈteɪʃən/ n. **1.** orienting, being oriented. **2.** position relative to surroundings.

orienteering /ɔːrɪənˈtɪərɪŋ/ n. the competitive sport of finding one's way on foot across rough country with map and compass. World championships have been held since 1966. Orienteering was invented in Sweden in 1918. [from Swedish *orientering*]

orifice /ˈɒrɪfɪs/ n. an aperture, the mouth of a cavity, a vent. [French from Latin *orificium* (*os* = mouth)]

origami /ɒrɪˈɡɑːmɪ/ n. the art of folding paper intricately into decorative shapes, originating in Japan in the 10th century. [Japanese]

origan /ˈɒrɪɡən/ n. (or **origanum** /-ˈɡɑːnəm/) wild marjoram *Origanum vulgare*. [from Latin from Greek]

Origen /ˈɒrɪdʒen/ c.185–c.254. Christian theologian, born in Alexandria, who produced a fancifully allegorical interpretation of the Bible. He castrated himself to ensure his celibacy.

origin /ˈɒrɪdʒɪn/ n. **1.** the point, source, or cause from which a thing begins its existence. **2.** parentage, ancestry. **3.** in mathematics, a point from which coordinates are measured. [from French or Latin *origo* (*oriri* = rise)]

original /əˈrɪdʒɪnəl/ adj. **1.** existing from the first, earliest; primitive; innate. **2.** that has served as a pattern, of which a copy or translation has been made. **3.** new in concept, not derived or imitative. **4.** thinking or acting for oneself, inventive, creative. —n. the first form of something, the thing from which another is copied or translated. —**original sin,** (in Christian theology) the innate depravity held to be common to all human beings in consequence of the Fall. —**originality** /-ˈnælɪtɪ/ n., **originally** adv. [from Old French or Latin]

originate /əˈrɪdʒɪneɪt/ v.t./i. **1.** to have its origin, to begin. **2.** to initiate or give origin to; to be the origin of. —**origination** /-ˈneɪʃən/ n., **originator** n. [from Latin]

Orkney Islands *The houses of the Neolithic village of Skara Brae are of drystone construction.*

Orinoco /ɒrɪˈnəʊkəʊ/ river in N South America, flowing for about 2,400 km/1,500 mi through Venezuela and forming for about 320 km/200 mi the boundary with Colombia; tributaries include the Guaviare, Meta, Apure, Ventuari, Caura, and Caroni. It is navigable by large steamers for 1,125 km/700 mi from its Atlantic delta; rapids obstruct the upper river.

oriole /ˈɔːrɪəʊl/ n. brightly coloured songbird. In Africa and Eurasia, orioles belong to the family Oriolidae, such as the golden oriole *Oriolus oriolus*; in the Americas to the Icteridae, such as the bobolink and the Baltimore oriole. [from Old French from Latin *aureus* = golden]

Orion in Greek mythology, a giant of ◊Boeotia, famed as a hunter.

Orion n. in astronomy, a very prominent constellation in the equatorial region of the sky (the celestial region), near Taurus, and represented as the hunter of Greek mythology. It contains the bright stars Betelgeuse and Rigel, as well as a distinctive row of three stars that make up Orion's belt. Beneath the belt, marking the sword of Orion, is the Orion nebula; nearby is one of the most distinctive dark nebulae, the Horsehead.

Orion nebula a luminous cloud of gas and dust 1,500 light years away, in the constellation Orion, from which stars are forming. It is about 15 light years in diameter and contains enough gas to make a cluster of thousands of stars. At the nebula's centre is a group of hot young stars, called the **Trapezium**, which make the surrounding gas glow. The nebula is visible to the naked eye as a misty patch below the belt of Orion.

Orissa /ɒˈrɪsə/ state of NE India; **area** 155,800 sq km/60,139 sq mi; **capital** Bhubaneswar; **population** (1981) 26,272,000; **language** Oriya (official); **religion** 90% Hindu; **history** administered by the British 1803–1912 as a subdivision of Bengal, it joined with Bihar to become a province. In 1936 Orissa became a separate province, and in 1948–49 its area was almost doubled before its designation as a state in 1950.

Orkney Causeway /ˈɔːknɪ/ or **Churchill Barriers** a construction in N Scotland put up in World War I, completed in 1943, joining four of the Orkney Islands, built to protect the British fleet from intrusion through the eastern entrances to Scapa Flow. The Orkney Causeway links the E mainland with the islands of Lambholm, Glimsholm, Burray, and South Ronaldsay.

Orkney Islands island group off the NE coast of Scotland; **area** 970 sq km/375 sq mi; **administrative headquarters** Kirkwall; **population** (1987) 19,000; **history** Harald I (Fairhair) of Norway conquered the islands in 876; they were pledged to James III of Scotland in 1468 for the dowry of Margaret of Denmark and annexed by Scotland (the dowry unpaid) in 1472.

Orlando /ɔːˈlændəʊ/ Vittorio Emanuele 1860–1952. Italian politician, prime minister 1917–19. He attended the Paris Peace Conference after World War I, but dissatisfaction with his handling of the Adriatic settlement led to his resignation. He initially supported Mussolini but was in retirement 1925–46, when he returned to the assembly and then the senate.

Orlando Furioso a poem by the Italian Renaissance writer Ariosto, published in 1532 as a sequel to Boiardo's *Orlando Innamorato* (1441–94). The poem describes the unrequited love of Orlando for Angelica, set against the war between Saracens (Arabs) and Christians during Charlemagne's reign. It influenced Shakespeare, Byron, and Milton, and is considered to be the greatest poem of the Italian Renaissance.

Orly /ˈɔːli/ international airport, the busiest in France, situated in a suburb of Paris in the *département* of Val-de-Marne; population about 17,000.

ormolu /ˈɔːməluː/ n. 1. gilded bronze. 2. a gold-coloured alloy. 3. articles made of or decorated with ormolu. [from French *or moulu* = powdered gold]

Ormuz /ˈɔːmuːz/ alternative name for the Iranian island ◊Hormuz.

Ormuzd /ˈɔːmʊzd/ another name for **Ahura Mazda**, the good god of ◊Zoroastrianism.

ornament /ˈɔːnəmənt/ n. 1. a decorative object or detail. 2. decoration, adornment. 3. a person or quality that brings honour or adds distinction. —/-ment/ v.t. to decorate; to be an ornament to. —**ornamental** /-ˈmentəl/ adj., **ornamentally** adv., **ornamentation** /-ˈteɪʃən/ n. [from Anglo-French from Latin *ornare* = adorn]

ornate /ɔːˈneɪt/ adj. elaborately ornamented; (of literary style) embellished with flowery language. [from Latin]

ornithology /ɔːnɪˈθɒlədʒɪ/ n. the study of birds. It covers scientific aspects relating to their structure and classification, and their habits, song, flight, and value to agriculture as destroyers of insect pests. It also covers the activities of people interested in birds. —**ornithological** /-ˈlɒdʒɪkəl/ adj., **ornithologist** n. [from Greek *ornis* = bird]

ornithophily n. the ◊pollination of flowers by birds. Ornithophilous flowers are typically brightly coloured, often red or orange. They produce large quantities of thin, watery nectar, and are scentless because most birds do not respond well to smell. They are found mostly in tropical areas, with hummingbirds being important pollinators in North and South America, and the sunbirds in Africa and Asia.

orogenesis /ɒrəˈdʒenɪsɪs/ n. the process of formation of mountains. —**orogenetic** /-dʒiˈnetɪk/ adj. [from Greek *oros* = mountain and *genesis* = origin]

orogeny /ɒˈrɒdʒənɪ/ n. 1. orogenesis. 2. a geological period of mountain-building. —**orogenic** /ɒrəˈdʒenɪk/ adj.

orotund /ˈɒrətʌnd/ adj. (of an utterance) dignified, imposing; pompous. [from Latin *ore rotundo*, literally 'with round mouth']

orphan /ˈɔːfən/ n. a child whose parents are dead. —adj. being an orphan; of or for orphans. —v.t. to make (a child) an orphan. [from Latin from Greek = bereaved]

orphanage n. an institution where orphans are housed and cared for.

Orpheus /ˈɔːfjuːs/ a mythical Greek poet and musician. The son of Apollo and a muse, he married Eurydice, who died from the bite of a snake. Orpheus went down to ◊Hades to bring her back, and her return to life was granted on condition that he walk ahead of her without looking back. He broke this condition, and Eurydice was irretrievably lost. In his grief, he offended the Maenad women of Thrace, and was torn to pieces by them.

Orphic /ˈɔːfɪk/ adj. of Orpheus or Orphism, the mystic religion associated with him.

Orphism n. an ancient Greek mystery cult. The Orphic hymns, poems attributed to Orpheus, now lost, were its scriptures. They recommended the purging of the evil in human nature through participation in secret purification rites and by a harsh lifestyle, in order to secure immortality.

orpiment /ˈɔːpɪmənt/ n. arsenic trisulphide as a mineral, formerly used as a yellow dye and artists' pigment. [from Old French from Latin *auripigmentum* (*aurum* = gold and *pigmentum* = pigment)]

Orr /ɔː/ Bobby (Robert) 1948– . Canadian hockey player, who played for the Boston Bruins 1967–76 and the Chicago Blackhawks 1976–79 of the National Hockey League. He was voted the best defence every year 1967–75, and was Most Valuable Player 1970–72. He was the first defence to score 100 points in a season, and was the leading scorer in 1970 and 1975.

orrery /ˈɒrərɪ/ n. a clockwork model of the planetary system. Invented about 1710 by George Graham, it was named after his patron, the 4th Earl of Orrery. It is the forerunner of the ◊planetarium.

orris /ˈɒrɪs/ n. a kind of iris, especially *Iris florentina*.—**orrisroot** n. a violet-scented iris root used in perfumery etc., grown in S Europe [apparently an alteration of *iris*]

Orsini /ɔːˈsiːnɪ/ Felice 1819–1858. Italian political activist, a member of the ◊Carbonari secret revolutionary group, who attempted unsuccessfully to assassinate Napoleon III in Paris in Jan 1858. He was subsequently executed, but the Orsini affair awakened Napoleon's interest in Italy and led to a secret alliance with Piedmont at Plombières in 1858, directed against Italy.

Ortega (Saavedra) /ɔːˈteɪɡə/ Daniel 1945– . Nicaraguan socialist politician, head of state 1981–90. He was a member of the Sandinista Liberation Front (FSLN), which overthrew the regime of Anastasio Somoza in 1979. US-sponsored ◊Contra guerrillas opposed his government from 1982.

ortho- in combinations, right, straight, correct. [from Greek *orthos* = straight]

orthochromatic n. a photographic film or paper of decreased sensitivity that can be processed with a red safelight. Using it, blue objects appear lighter and red ones darker because of increased blue sensitivity.

orthoclase /ˈɔːθəkleɪz/ n. common felspar in crystals with two cleavages at right angles. [from Greek *klasis* = breaking]

orthodontics /ɔːθəˈdɒntɪks/ n. a branch of ◊dentistry, mainly dealing with correction of irregularities in the teeth and jaws. —**orthodontic** adj., **orthodontist** n. [from Greek *odous* = tooth]

orthodox /ˈɔːθədɒks/ adj. holding the usual or currently accepted views, especially on religion; generally approved, conventional. —**Orthodox Church** or **Eastern Orthodox Church** or **Greek Orthodox Church**, a federation of self-governing Christian churches mainly found in E and SE Europe, the USSR, and parts of Asia. The centre of worship is the Eucharist. There is a married clergy, except for bishops; the Immaculate Conception is not accepted. The highest rank in the church is that of Ecumenical Patriarch, or Bishop of Istanbul. There are approximately 130 million adherents. —**orthodoxy** n. [from Latin from Greek *doxa* = opinion]

orthography /ɔːˈθɒɡrəfɪ/ n. spelling (especially with reference to its correctness). —**orthographic** /-ˈɡræfɪk/ adj., **orthographical** adj. [from Old French from Latin from Greek *graphia* = writing]

orthopaedics /ɔːθəˈpiːdɪks/ n. the branch of surgery dealing with the correction of deformities of the bones or muscles, originally in children. —**orthopaedic** adj., **orthopaedist** n. [from French from Greek *paideia* = rearing of children]

orthoptic /ɔːˈθɒptɪk/ adj. relating to the correct or normal use of the eyes. [from Greek *optos* = seen]

orthoptics /ɔːˈθɒptɪks/ n. remedial treatment of the eye muscles. —**orthoptist** n.

ortolan /ˈɔːtələn/ n. a bird *Emberiza hortulana* of the bunting family, common in Europe and W Asia, migrating to Africa in the winter. It is brownish, with a grey head, and nests on the ground. [French from Latin *hortulanus*]

Orton /ˈɔːtn/ Joe 1933–1967. English dramatist in whose black comedies surreal and violent action takes place in genteel and unlikely settings. Plays include *Entertaining Mr Sloane* 1964, *Loot* 1966, and *What the Butler Saw* 1968. His diaries deal frankly with his personal life. He was murdered by his lover Kenneth Halliwell.

The kind of people who always go on about whether a thing is in good taste invariably have very bad taste.
Joe Orton
(attrib.)

Orwell /'ɔ:wel/ George. Pen name of Eric Arthur Blair 1903–1950. English author. Among his books are the satire *Animal Farm* 1945, which includes such sayings as 'All animals are equal, but some are more equal than others', and the prophetic *Nineteen Eighty-Four* 1949, portraying the dangers of excessive state control over the individual. Other works include *Down and Out in Paris and London* 1933 and *Homage to Catalonia* 1938.

oryx /'ɒrɪks/ *n.* a large straight-horned African antelope of the genus *Oryx*. The Arabian oryx (*Oryx leucoryx*) was extinct in the wild but bred in captivity, and has been successfully reintroduced into the wild. The scimitar-horned oryx of the Sahara is also rare. Beisa oryx in E Africa and gemsbok in the Kalahari are more common. [from Latin from Greek *orux* = stonemason's pickaxe, from its pointed horns]

Os symbol for ◊osmium.

OS abbreviation of 1. old style. 2. ordinary seaman. 3. ◊Ordnance Survey. 4. outsize.

OS/2 a single-user computer ◊operating system, produced jointly by Microsoft Corporation and IBM, for use on large microcomputers. Its main features are ◊multitasking and the ability to access large amounts of internal memory.

Osaka /əu'sɑːkə/ industrial port on Honshu Island, Japan; **products** iron, steel, shipbuilding, chemicals, and textiles; **population** (1987) 2,546,000, metropolitan area 8,000,000. It is the oldest city of Japan and was at times the seat of government in the 4th–8th centuries.

Osborne /'ɒzbɔːn/ John (James) 1929– . English dramatist. He was one of the first ◊Angry Young Men (antiestablishment writers of the 1950s) of British theatre with his debut play, *Look Back in Anger*, in 1956. Other plays include *The Entertainer* 1957, *Luther* 1960, and *Watch It Come Down* 1976.

Damn you, England. You're rotting now, and quite soon you'll disappear.
John Osborne
in a letter to *Tribune* 1961

Oscar /'ɒskə/ *n.* each of several gold statuettes awarded annually by the Academy of Motion Picture Arts and Sciences (Hollywood, USA) for excellence in film acting, directing etc.; official name ◊Academy Award. [man's given name; the statuette is said to have reminded a librarian of the Academy of her uncle Oscar]

oscillate /'ɒsɪleɪt/ *v.t./i.* 1. to swing to and fro; to cause to do this. 2. to vacillate, to vary between extremes. 3. (of an electric current) to reverse its direction with high frequency. —**oscillation** /-'leɪʃən/ *n.* [from Latin *oscillare* = swing]

oscillating universe in astronomy, the theory that the gravitational attraction of the mass within the universe will eventually slow down and stop the expansion of the universe. The outward motions of the galaxies will then be reversed, eventually resulting in a 'Big Crunch', when all the matter in the universe will be contracted into a small volume of high density. This could undergo a further ◊Big Bang, thereby creating another expansion phase. The theory suggests that the universe could alternately expand and collapse through alternate Big Bangs and Big Crunches.

oscillator *n.* a generator or other instrument producing a desired oscillation (vibration). There are many types of oscillator for different purposes, involving various arrangements of valves or components such as ◊transistors, ◊inductors, ◊capacitors, and ◊resistors. An oscillator is an essential part of a radio transmitter, generating the high-frequency carrier signal necessary for radio communication.

Orwell English novelist and essayist George Orwell.

The ◊frequency is often controlled by the vibrations set up in a crystal, such as quartz.

oscillograph /ə'sɪlɒɡrɑːf/ *n.* an instrument for displaying or recording the values of rapidly changing oscillations, electrical or mechanical.

oscilloscope /ə'sɪləskəup/ *n.* a device for displaying oscillations, especially on the screen of a cathode-ray tube by deflecting a beam of ◊electrons.

Oshima /'əuʃɪmə/ Nagisa 1932– . Japanese film director whose violent and sexually explicit *Ai No Corrida*/*In the Realm of the Senses* 1977 caused controversy when first released. His other work includes *Death by Hanging* 1968 and *Merry Christmas Mr Lawrence* 1983, which starred the singer David Bowie.

Oshogbo /ɒ'ʃɒɡbəu/ city and trading centre on the river Niger, in W Nigeria, 200 km/125 mi NE of Lagos; population (1986) 405,000. Industries include cotton and brewing.

osier /'əuziə(r), 'əuʒə(r)/ *n.* any of several trees and shrubs of the willow genus *Salix*, cultivated for basket making; in particular, *S. viminalis*; a shoot of this. [from Old French]

Osiris /əu'saɪrɪs/ an ancient Egyptian god, the embodiment of goodness, who ruled the underworld after being killed by ◊Set. The sister-wife of Osiris was ◊Isis or Hathor, and their son ◊Horus captured his father's murderer.

-osis /-əusɪs/ suffix forming nouns denoting a process or condition (*metamorphosis*), especially a pathological state (*neurosis, thrombosis*). [from Latin or Greek]

Oslo /'ɒzləu/ capital and industrial port in Norway; **products** textiles, engineering, and timber; **population** (1988) 454,000; **history** the first recorded settlement was made in the 11th century by Harald III, but after a fire in 1624 the town was entirely replanned by Christian IV and renamed **Christiania** 1624–1924.

Osman I /'ɒzmən/ or **Othman I** 1259–1326. Turkish ruler from 1299. He began his career in the service of the ◊Seljuk Turks, but in 1299 he set up a kingdom of his own in Bithynia, NW Asia, and assumed the title of sultan. He conquered a great part of Anatolia, so founding a Turkish empire. His successors were known as 'sons of Osman', from which the term ◊Ottoman Empire is derived.

osmium /'ɒzmɪəm/ *n.* a hard, heavy, bluish-white, metallic element, symbol Os, atomic number 76, relative atomic mass 190.2. It is the densest of the elements, and is resistant to tarnish and corrosion. It occurs in platinum ores and as a free metal with iridium in a natural alloy called osmiridium, containing traces of platinum, ruthenium, and rhodium. It is a catalyst and it is used to make pen points and light-bulb filaments. [from Greek *osmē* = smell (from the pungent smell of its tetroxide)]

osmosis /ɒz'məusɪs/ *n.* the tendency of a solvent to pass from a less concentrated solution into a more concentrated one through a semipermeable membrane, permeable to the solvent but not to the solute. —**osmotic** /-'mɒtɪk/ *adj.* [ultimately from Greek *ōsmos* = thrust]

osprey /'ɒsprɪ/ n. a bird of prey *Pandion haliaetus*, known in North America from its diet as the **fish hawk**. It is dark brown above and a striking white below, and measures 60 cm/2 ft with a 2 m/6 ft wingspan. [from Old French ultimately from Latin *ossifraga* (*os* = bone and *frangere* = break]

Ossa, Mount /'ɒsə/ the highest peak on the island of Tasmania, Australia; height 1,617 m/5,250 ft.

osseous /'ɒsɪəs/ adj. of bone; having bones, bony. [from Latin *osseus* (*os* = bone)]

Ossian /'ɒsɪən/ (Celtic *Oisin*) a legendary Irish hero, invented by the Scottish writer James ◊Macpherson. He is sometimes represented as the son of ◊Finn Mac Cumhaill, about 250, and as having lived to tell the tales of Finn and the Ulster heroes to St Patrick, about 400. The publication in 1760 of Macpherson's poems, attributed to Ossian, made Ossian's name familiar throughout Europe.

ossicle /'ɒsɪkəl/ n. a small bone or piece of hard substance in an animal structure. [from Latin *ossiculum*]

ossify /'ɒsɪfaɪ/ v.t./i. **1.** to turn into bone, to harden. Bone is formed in vertebrate animals by **osteoblasts**, cells that secrete layers of ◊extracellular matrix on the surface of cartilage. Conversion to bone occurs through the deposition of calcium phosphate crystals within the matrix. **2.** to make or become rigid and unprogressive. —**ossification** /-fɪ'keɪʃən/ n. [from French from Latin *os* = bone]

ostensible /ɒ'stensɪb()l/ adj. pretended, professed, put forward to conceal what is real. —**ostensibly** adv. [French from Latin *ostendere* = show]

ostensive /ɒ'stensɪv/ adj. directly showing. —**ostensively** adv. [from Latin]

ostentation /ɒsten'teɪʃən/ n. a pretentious display of wealth etc., showing off. —**ostentatious** adj., **ostentatiously** adv. [from Old French from Latin]

osteo- /ɒstɪə(ʊ)-/ in combinations, bone. [from Greek *osteon* = bone]

osteomyelitis n. infection of bone, with spread of pus along the marrow cavity. The condition is now quite rare, but may follow a compound fracture, if broken bone protrudes through the skin, or from infectious disease elsewhere in the body.

osteopath /'ɒstɪəpæθ/ n. a practitioner of osteopathy.

osteopathy /ɒstɪ'ɒpəθɪ/ n. the treatment of disease by manipulation of bones, especially the spine, and muscles (their deformity being the supposed cause of problems). It claims to relieve not only postural problems and muscle pain, but asthma and other disorders. [from Greek *patheia* = suffering]

osteoporosis n. a disease in which the bone substance becomes porous and brittle. It is common in older people, affecting more women than men. It may occur in women whose ovaries have been removed, unless hormone-replacement therapy is instituted. Osteoporosis may occur as a side effect of long-term treatment with ◊corticosteroids. Early menopause in women, childlessness, small body build, lack of exercise, heavy drinking, smoking, and hereditary factors may also contribute.

Ostia /'ɒstɪə/ ancient Roman town near the mouth of the river Tiber. Founded about 330 BC, it was the port of Rome and had become a major commercial centre by the 2nd century AD. It was abandoned in the 9th century. The present-day seaside resort **Ostia Mare** is situated nearby.

ostinato n. a persistently repeated melodic or rhythmic figure. [Italian = obstinate]

ostler /'ɒslə/ n. a person in charge of stabling horses at an inn. [from Anglo-French *hosteler* ultimately from Latin *hospes* = host]

Ostmark /'ɒstmɑːk/ n. the currency unit in East Germany until 1990. [German, from *Ost* = east and ◊*marks²*]

Ostpolitik n. the policy of a West European country with regard to the communist countries of East Europe, especially West German chancellor ◊Brandt's policy of reconciliation with the communist bloc from 1971, pursued to a modified extent by his successors Schmidt and Kohl. The policy attained its goal with the reunification of Germany in 1990. [German *ost* = east and *politik* = politics]

ostracize /'ɒstrəsaɪz/ v.t. **1.** (in ancient Athens) to banish (a dangerously powerful or unpopular citizen) by a voting system in which the name of the person proposed for banishment was written on a potsherd. **2.** to exclude from society, favour, or common privileges. —**ostracism** n. [from Greek *ostrakon* = potsherd]

Ostrava /'ɒstrəvə/ an industrial city in Czechoslovakia, capital of Severomoravsky region, NE of Brno; **products** iron works, furnaces, coal, chemicals; **population** (1984) 324,000.

ostrich /'ɒstrɪtʃ/ n. **1.** a large flightless bird *Struthio camelus* found in Africa. The male, the largest living bird, may be about 2.5 m/8 ft tall and weigh 135 kg/300 lb. It has exceptionally strong legs and feet which, being two-toed, enable it to run at high speed, and are used in defence. It lives in family groups of one cock with several hens. It swallows hard substances to assist the working of its gizzard and is reputed to bury its head in the sand when pursued, believing that it cannot then be seen. **2.** a person who refuses to acknowledge an awkward truth. [from Old French from Latin *avis* = bird and *struthio* = ostrich from Greek]

Ostrogoth /'ɒstrəgɒθ/ n. a member of the eastern branch of the ◊Goths, an E Germanic people. —**Ostrogothic** /-'gɒθɪk/ adj. [from Latin = eastern Goth]

Ostrovsky /ɒ'strɒfski/ Alexander Nikolaevich 1823–1886. Russian playwright, founder of the modern Russian theatre. He dealt satirically with the manners of the middle class in numerous plays, for example *A Family Affair* 1850. His fairy-tale play *The Snow Maiden* 1873 inspired the composers Tchaikovsky and Rimsky-Korsakov.

Ostwald /'ɒstvælt/ Wilhelm 1853–1932. German chemist who devised the Ostwald process (the oxidation of ammonia over a platinum catalyst to give nitric acid). His work on catalysts laid the foundations of the petrochemical industry. He was awarded the Nobel Prize for Chemistry in 1909.

Oswald, St /'ɒzwəld/ c.605–642. King of Northumbria from 634, after killing the Welsh king Cadwallon.

OT abbreviation of Old Testament (see ◊Bible).

Otago /əʊ'tɑːgəʊ/ a peninsula and coastal plain on South Island, New Zealand, constituting a district; area 64,230 sq km/25,220 sq mi; chief cities include Dunedin and Invercargill.

Othello /ə'θeləʊ/ a tragedy by William Shakespeare, first performed 1604–05.

other /'ʌðə/ adj. **1.** not the same as one or some already mentioned or implied; separate in identity, distinct in kind. **2.** alternative; additional; being the remaining one of a set of two or more. —*n.* or *pron.* another person or thing. —*adv.* otherwise. —**the other day** etc., a few days, nights etc., ago. **other than**, different from. **other-worldly** adj. concerned or preoccupied with life after death or in some imagined world to the neglect of the present or real one. [Old English]

otherwise adv. **1.** in a different way. **2.** in other respects. **3.** in different circumstances. **4.** or else. —*adj.* in a different state. [Old English]

Othman /ɒθ'mɑːn/ c.574–656. Third caliph (leader of the Islamic empire) from 644, a son-in-law of the prophet Muhammad. Under his rule the Arabs became a naval power and extended their rule to N Africa and Cyprus,

ostrich

but Othman's personal weaknesses led to his assassination. He was responsible for the compilation of the authoritative version of the Koran, the sacred book of Islam.

Othman I another name for the Turkish sultan ◊Osman I.

Otho I /'əʊθəʊ/ 1815–1867. King of Greece 1832–62. As the 17-year-old son of King Ludwig I of Bavaria, he was selected by the European powers as the first king of independent Greece. He was overthrown by a popular revolt.

otiose /'əʊʃiəʊs, 'əʊt-/ adj. not required, serving no practical purpose. [from Latin otiosus (otium = leisure)]

Otis /'əʊtɪs/ Elisha Graves 1811–1861. US engineer who developed a lift that incorporated a safety device, making it acceptable for passenger use in the first skyscrapers. The device, invented in 1852, consisted of vertical ratchets on the sides of the lift shaft into which spring-loaded catches would engage and lock the lift in position in the event of cable failure.

otitis n. inflammation of the ear. Otitis externa, occurring in the outer ear canal, is easily treated with antibiotics. Inflamed conditions of the middle ear (otitis media) or inner ear (otitis interna) are more serious, carrying the risk of deafness and infection of the brain.

O'Toole /əʊ'tuːl/ Peter 1932– . Irish-born English actor who made his name as Lawrence of Arabia in 1962, and who then starred in films such as Beckett 1964 and The Lion in Winter 1968.

otosclerosis n. overgrowth of bone in the middle ear, causing progressive deafness. This inherited condition is gradual in onset, developing usually before middle age. It is twice as common in women as in men.

Ottawa /'ɒtəwə/ capital of Canada, in E Ontario, on the hills overlooking the Ottawa River and divided by the Rideau Canal into the Upper (western) and Lower (eastern) towns; population (1986) 301,000, metropolitan area (with adjoining Hull, Québec) 819,000. Industries include timber, pulp and paper, engineering, food processing, and publishing. It was founded in 1826–32 as **Bytown**, in honour of John By (1781–1836), whose army engineers were building the Rideau Canal. It was renamed in 1854 after the Outaouac Indians.

otter /'ɒtə/ n. an aquatic fish-eating mammal of the genus Lutra etc. with webbed feet, thick brown fur, and a pointed tail somewhat flattened horizontally, found on all continents except Australia; its fur. [Old English]

Otto /'ɒtəʊ/ four Holy Roman emperors, including:

Otto I 912–973. Holy Roman emperor from 936. He restored the power of the empire, asserted his authority over the pope and the nobles, ended the Magyar menace by his victory at the Lechfeld in 955, and refounded the East Mark, or Austria, as a barrier against them.

Otto IV c. 1182–1218. Holy Roman emperor, elected in 1198. He engaged in controversy with Pope Innocent III, and was defeated by the pope's ally, Philip of France, at Bouvines in 1214.

Otto cycle an alternative name for the ◊four-stroke cycle, introduced by the German engineer Nikolaus Otto (1832–1891) in 1876. It improved on existing piston engines by compressing the fuel mixture in the cylinder before it was ignited.

ottoman /'ɒtəmən/ n. 1. a long cushioned seat without back or arms. 2. a storage box with a padded top.

Ottoman adj. of the dynasty of ◊Osman I, his branch of the Turks, or the empire ruled by his descendants. —n. an Ottoman person. [French from Arabic]

Ottoman Empire the Muslim empire of the Turks 1300–1920, the successor of the ◊Seljuk Empire. It was founded by ◊Osman I and reached its height with ◊Suleiman in the 16th century. Its capital was Istanbul (formerly Constantinople). At its greatest extent its boundaries were Europe as far as Hungary, part of S Russia, Iran, the Palestinian coastline, Egypt, and N Africa. From the 17th century it was in decline. There was an attempted revival and reform under the Young Turk party in 1908, but the regime crumbled when Turkey sided with Germany in World War I. The sultanate was abolished by Atatürk in 1922; the last sultan was Muhammad VI.

Otway /'ɒtweɪ/ Thomas 1652–1685. English dramatist. His plays include the tragedies Alcibiades 1675, Don Carlos 1676, The Orphan 1680, and Venice Preserv'd 1682.

Otztal Alps /'ɜːtstɑːl/ range of the Alps in Italy and Austria, rising to 3,774 m/12,382 ft at Wildspitze, Austria's second highest peak.

Ouagadougou /wægə'duːguː/ capital and industrial centre of Burkina Faso; population (1985) 442,000. Products include textiles, vegetable oil, and soap.

oubliette /uːbli'et/ n. a secret dungeon with a trapdoor entrance. [French oublier = forget]

ouch interjection expressing sharp or sudden pain. [natural exclamation]

ought¹ /ɔːt/ v.aux. (as present and past, the only form now in use; negative **ought not**) expressing rightness or duty, advisability, or strong probability. [Old English, past tense of owe]

ought² n. (colloquial) the figure 0, nought. [from an ought for a nought]

Ouija /'wiːdʒə/ n. or **Ouija-board** the trade name of a board marked with the alphabet and other signs used with a movable pointer to obtain messages in spiritualistic seances. [from French oui = yes and German ja = yes]

Oujda /uː'ʒdɑː/ industrial and commercial city (lead and coalmining) in N Morocco, near the border with Algeria; population (1982) 471,000. It trades in wool, grain, and fruit.

ounce¹ /aʊns/ n. 1. a unit of weight equal to one-sixteenth of a pound ◊avoirdupois, equal to 437.5 grains (28.35 g); also one-twelfth of a pound troy, equal to 480 grains. 2. a very small quantity. [from Old French from Latin uncia = twelfth part of pound or foot]

ounce² n. an Asian feline Panthera uncia, the mountain panther or snow-leopard, smaller than the leopard but similarly marked. [from Old French once for earlier lonce (l mistaken for the definite article), ultimately from Latin lynx]

our poss. adj. of or belonging to us; that we are concerned with or thinking of. —**Our Father**, the Lord's Prayer, beginning with these words (Matthew 6: 9–13). **Our Lady**, the Virgin Mary. [Old English]

ours /'aʊəz/ poss. pron. of or belonging to us; the thing(s) belonging to us.

ourself /aʊə'self/ pron. corresponding to myself when used by a sovereign etc.

ourselves /aʊə'selvz/ pron. emphatic and reflexive form we, us.

ousel variant of ◊ouzel.

Ousmane /uː'smɑːn/ Sembene 1923– . Senegalese writer and film director. His novels, written in French, include Le docker noir/The Black Docker 1956, about his experiences as a union leader in Marseille; Les bouts de bois/God's Bits of Wood 1960; Le mandat/The Money Order, and Xala, the last two of which he made into films.

oust /aʊst/ v.t. to eject, to drive out of office or power; to seize the place of. [from Anglo-French from Latin obstare oppose]

out adv. 1. expressing movement or position away from a centre or beyond or regardless of stated or implied limits, or a state other than the right or usual one; away from or not in a place; not at home, not in one's office etc.; not in its normal or usual state. 2. (so as to be) excluded. 3. not in effective or favourable action; no longer in fashion or season or office; (in cricket etc.) having had one's innings ended; (of workers) on strike; (of a light or fire etc.) no longer burning; no longer visible. 4. in or into the open; so as to be clear or perceptible; (of flowers) open, (of plants) in bloom; (of a secret) revealed; (of a book) published; (after a superlative) among known examples etc. 5. to or at an end, completely. 6. in error. 7. unconscious. 8. (of a jury) considering its verdict in private. 9. with attentiveness (watch out). —prep. out of. —n. a way of escape. —int. get out!—v.t. 1. to put out. 2. (colloquial) to eject forcibly. 3. (in boxing) to knock out. —**out and about**, active outdoors. **out and away**, by far. **out and out**, thoroughly, **out-and-out** adj. complete, thorough. **out for**, intent on, determined to get. **out of**, from within; from among; beyond the range of; because of; by the use of, (of an animal) having as its dam; so as to be without a supply of. **out of doors**, in or into the open air. **out to**, determined to. [Old English]

out- prefix meaning: 1. out of, away from, outward. 2. external, separate. 3. so as to surpass or exceed.

outage /'aʊtɪdʒ/ n. a period of non-operation of a power-supply etc.

outback *n.* the immense inland region of Australia. Its main inhabitants are Aborigines, miners, and cattleranchers. Its harsh beauty has been recorded by artists such as Sidney Nolan.

outbid /aʊt'bɪd/ *v.t.* (-dd-) to bid higher than.

outboard *adj.* 1. towards the outside of a ship, aircraft, or vehicle. 2. (of a motor) attached externally to the stern of a boat; (of a boat) using such a motor.

outbreak *n.* a breaking out of anger, war, disease, fire etc.

outbuilding *n.* an outhouse.

outburst *n.* a bursting out, especially of emotion in vehement words.

outcast *n.* a person cast out of his home or rejected by society. —*adj.* homeless, rejected.

outclass /aʊt'klɑːs/ *v.t.* to surpass in quality.

outcome *n.* the result or effect of an event etc.

outcrop *n.* 1. part of an underlying stratum, vein, or rock that emerges on the surface of the ground etc.; such emergence. 2. a breaking out, a noticeable manifestation.

outcry *n.* 1. a loud cry. 2. a strong protest.

outdated /aʊt'deɪtɪd/ *adj.* out of date, obsolete.

outdistance /aʊt'dɪstəns/ *v.t.* to get far ahead of.

outdo /aʊt'duː/ *v.t.* (third person *singular present* outdoes /-'dʌz/; *past* outdid; *past participle* outdone) to do better than, to surpass.

outdoor *adj.* of, done, or for use out of doors; fond of the open air.

outdoors /aʊt'dɔːz/ *n.* the open air. —*adv.* in or into the open air.

outer *adj.* further from the centre or the inside; external, exterior. —**outer space,** the universe beyond the Earth's atmosphere. —**outermost** *adj.*

outface /aʊt'feɪs/ *v.t.* to disconcert by staring or by a display of confidence.

outfall *n.* an outlet of a river, drain etc.

outfield *n.* the outer part of a cricket or baseball pitch.

outfit *n.* 1. a set of equipment or clothes. 2. (*colloquial*) a group of persons, an organization.

outfitter *n.* a supplier of equipment, especially men's clothes.

outflank /aʊt'flæŋk/ *v.t.* to extend beyond or get round the flank of (an enemy); to outmanoeuvre, outwit.

outflow *n.* an outward flow; what flows out.

outfox /aʊt'fɒks/ *v.t.* to outwit.

outgoing *adj.* 1. going out; retiring from office. 2. sociable and friendly. —*n.* (in *plural*) expenditure.

outgrow /aʊt'grəʊ/ *v.t.* (*past* outgrew; *past participle* outgrown) 1. to grow faster or taller than. 2. to grow too big for; to be too old or developed for.

outgrowth *n.* 1. an offshoot. 2. a natural development or product.

outhouse *n.* a small building belonging to but separate from the main house.

outing *n.* a pleasure-trip or excursion.

outlandish /aʊt'lændɪʃ/ *adj.* looking or sounding very strange or foreign, bizarre. —**outlandishness** *n.* [Old English *ūtland* = foreign country]

outlast /aʊt'lɑːst/ *v.t.* to last longer than.

outlaw *n.* a fugitive from the law (originally one placed beyond the protection of the law). —*v.t.* 1. to declare (a person) an outlaw. 2. to make illegal, to proscribe.

outlawry *n.* in medieval England, a declaration that a criminal was outside the protection of the law, with his or her lands and goods forfeited to the crown, and all civil rights being set aside. It was a lucrative royal 'privilege'; the ◊Magna Carta restricted its use, and under Edward III it was further modified. Some outlaws, such as ◊Robin Hood, became popular heroes.

outlay *n.* expenditure.

outlet *n.* 1. a means of exit or escape. 2. a means of expressing feelings. 3. a market for goods.

outline *n.* 1. a line or lines showing the shape or boundary of something. 2. a summary; a statement of the chief facts. —*v.t.* to draw or describe in outline; to mark the outline of. —**in outline,** giving only an outline.

outlive /aʊt'lɪv/ *v.t.* to live longer than (a person) or beyond (a period); to live through (an experience).

outlook *n.* 1. a view on which one looks out. 2. a mental attitude. 3. future prospects.

outlying *adj.* situated far from a centre, remote.

outmanoeuvre /aʊtmə'nuːvə/ *v.t.* to outdo in manoeuvring.

outmatch /aʊt'mætʃ/ *v.t.* to be more than a match for.

outmoded /aʊt'məʊdɪd/ *adj.* out of fashion; obsolete.

outnumber /aʊt'nʌmbə/ *v.t.* to exceed in number.

outpace /aʊt'peɪs/ *v.t.* to go faster than; to outdo in a contest.

out-patient *n.* a patient not residing in hospital during treatment.

outpost *n.* 1. a detachment stationed at some distance from an army. 2. a distant branch or settlement.

output *n.* 1. the amount produced. 2. the electrical power etc. delivered by an apparatus. 3. the place where energy, information etc., leaves a system. 4. the results etc. supplied by a computer. —*v.t./i.* (*past & past participle* output or outputted) (of a computer) to supply (results etc.).

output device in computing, any device for displaying, in a form intelligible to the user, the results of processing done by a computer. The most common output devices are the VDU (visual display unit, or screen) and the printer.

outrage *n.* 1. an extreme or shocking violation of others' rights, sentiments etc.; a gross offence or indignity. 2. fierce resentment. —*v.t.* to subject to an outrage, to commit an outrage against; to shock and anger. [from Old French (*outrer* = exceed from Latin *ultra* = beyond)]

outrageous /aʊt'reɪdʒəs/ *adj.* greatly exceeding what is moderate or reasonable; grossly cruel, immoral, or offensive. —**outrageously** *adv.*

outrank /aʊt'ræŋk/ *v.t.* to be superior in rank to.

outré /'uːtreɪ/ *adj.* eccentric, violating decorum. [French, *past participle* of *outrer* from Latin *ultra* = beyond]

outrider *n.* a mounted attendant or motor-cyclist riding ahead of a procession etc.

outrigger *n.* 1. a spar or framework projecting from or over a ship's side. 2. a strip of wood fixed parallel to a canoe to stabilize it; a canoe with this.

outright /aʊt'raɪt/ *adv.* altogether, entirely, not gradually; without reservation, openly. —/'aʊtraɪt/ *adj.* complete, thorough.

outrun /aʊt'rʌn/ *v.t.* (-nn-; *past* outran; *past participle* outrun) 1. to run faster or further than. 2. to go beyond (a point or limit).

outsell /aʊt'sel/ *v.t.* (*past & past participle* outsold /-'səʊld/) to sell more than; to be sold in greater quantities than.

outset *n.* the beginning (usually in at or from the outset).

outshine /aʊt'ʃaɪn/ *v.t.* (*past & past participle* outshone /-'ʃɒn/) to shine brighter than; to surpass in excellence etc.

outside /aʊt'saɪd, 'aʊt-/ *n.* 1. the outer side of a surface or part. 2. the outer part(s). 3. outward appearance; all that is without. 4. a position on the outer side. —/'aʊtsaɪd/ *adj.* 1. of, on, or coming from the outside; outer. 2. not belonging to some circle or institution. 3. nearer to the outside of a games field. 4. the greatest existent or possible. —/aʊt'saɪd/ *adv.* on, at, or to the outside; in or into the open air. —/aʊt'saɪd/ *prep.* 1. on the outer side of; not in; at or to the outer side of. 2. other than. 3. not included in. —**at the outside,** (of amounts) at the most. **outside broadcast,** one not made from a studio. **outside chance,** a remote possibility.

outsider *n.* 1. a non-member of some circle, party, profession etc. 2. a competitor thought to have little chance.

outsize *adj.* unusually large. —*n.* an outsize garment etc. or person.

outskirts *n.pl.* the outer area of a town etc.

outsmart /aʊt'smɑːt/ *v.t.* to outwit, to be cleverer than.

outspoken /aʊt'spəʊkən/ *adj.* speaking or spoken without reserve, frank.

outspread /aʊt'spred/ *adj.* spread out. —*v.t.* to spread out.

outstanding /aʊt'stændɪŋ/ *adj.* 1. conspicuous, especially from excellence. 2. still to be dealt with. —**outstandingly** *adv.*

outstay /aʊt'steɪ/ *v.t.* to stay longer than.

outstretched /aʊt'stretʃt/ *adj.* stretched out.

outstrip /aʊt'strɪp/ *v.t.* (-pp-) 1. to go faster than. 2. to surpass.

out-tray *n.* a tray for outgoing documents.

outvote /aʊt'vəʊt/ *v.t.* to defeat by a majority of votes.

outward /'autwəd/ *adj.* 1. situated on or directed towards the outside. 2. going towards the outside. 3. external, material, apparent. — *adv.* (also **outwards**) in an outward direction, towards the outside. —**outward bound**, going away from home. [Old English]

outwardly *adv.* on the outside; in appearance.

outwardness *n.* external existence, objectivity.

outweigh /aut'wei/ *v.t.* to exceed in weight, value, importance, or influence.

outwit /aut'wɪt/ *v.t.* (-tt-) to be too clever for, to overcome by greater ingenuity.

outwork *n.* an advanced or detached part of a fortification.

outworn /aut'wɔn/ *adj.* worn out, obsolete, exhausted.

ouzel /'uːzəl/ *n.* 1. a small bird *Turdus torquatus* of the thrush family (**ring ouzel**), similar to a blackbird, but with a white band across the breast. It is found in Europe in mountainous and rocky country. 2. a diving bird of the genus *Cinclus* (**water ouzel**), a ◊dipper. [Old English = blackbird]

ouzo /'uːzəʊ/ *n.* a Greek drink of aniseed-flavoured spirits. [modern Greek]

ova plural of **ovum**.

oval /'əʊvəl/ *adj.* having a rounded symmetrical shape longer than it is broad, elliptical or ellipsoidal. —*n.* a thing of oval shape or outline. [from Latin *ovum* = egg]

Oval, the cricket ground in Kennington, London, England, the home of Surrey County Cricket Club. It was the venue for the first test match between England and Australia 1880.

Ovamboland /əʊ'væmbəʊlænd/ region of N Namibia stretching along the Namibia–Angola frontier; the scene of conflict between SWAPO guerrillas and South African forces in the 1970s and 1980s.

ovary /'əʊvərɪ/ *n.* 1. either of two reproductive organs in which ova are produced in female animals. In humans, the ovaries are two whitish rounded bodies about 25 mm/1 in by 35 mm/1.5 in, located in the abdomen near the ends of the ◊Fallopian tubes; see also ◊menstrual cycle. They are hollow with a thick wall to protect the ◊ovules. 2. the lower part of the pistil in a plant, from which the fruit is formed. Following fertilization of the ovum, it develops into the fruit wall or pericarp. —**ovarian** /-'veərɪən/ *adj.*

ovate /'əʊveɪt/ *adj.* egg-shaped (as a solid or in outline), oval.

ovation /ə'veɪʃən/ *n.* enthusiastic applause or reception. [from Latin *ovare* = exult]

oven /'ʌvən/ *n.* an enclosed compartment for heating or cooking food etc. [Old English]

ovenware *n.* dishes in which food can be cooked in an oven.

over /'əʊvə/ *adv.* expressing movement or position or state above or beyond something stated or implied: 1. outward and downward from the brink or from an erect position. 2. so as to cover or touch a whole surface. 3. with movement from one side to the other or so that a different side is showing; upside down; across a street or other space; with transference or change from one hand, part etc., to another. 4. with motion above something, so as to pass across. 5. from beginning to end, with repetition; thoroughly, with detailed consideration. 6. too, in excess, in addition, besides. 7. apart; until a later time. 8. at an end, settled. 9. (in a radio conversation) it is your turn to transmit. 10. (as an umpire's call in cricket) change ends for bowling etc. —*prep.* 1. in or to a position higher than. 2. out and down from; down from the edge of. 3. so as to clear; on or to the other side of. 4. so as to cover. 5. concerning. 6. while occupied with. 7. with or achieving superiority or preference to. 8. throughout the length or extent of; during. 9. beyond; more than. 10. transmitted by. 11. in comparison with. —*n.* a sequence of six (or eight) balls in cricket, bowled between two calls of 'over', play resulting from this. —*adj.* upper, outer, superior, extra (usually as prefix; see ◊over-). —**over and above**, besides. **over and over**, repeatedly. **over to you**, it is your turn to act. [Old English]

over- prefix added to verbs, nouns, adjectives, and adverbs, meaning: 1.excessively; to an unwanted degree (*overheat; overdue*). 2.upper, outer, extra (*overcoat; overtime*). 3.'over' in various senses (*overhang; overshadow*). 4. complete, utterly (*overawe; overjoyed*).

overact /əʊvər'ækt/ *v.t./i.* to act with exaggeration.

overall *adj.* 1. from end to end. 2. total, inclusive of all. —*adv.* in all parts, taken as a whole. —*n.* a protective outer garment; (in *plural*) protective outer trousers or suit.

overarm *adj. & adv.* with the arm brought forward and down from above shoulder level.

overawe /əʊvər'ɔ/ *v.t.* to overcome with awe.

overbalance /əʊvə'bæləns/ *v.t./i.* to lose one's balance and fall; to cause to do this.

overbear /əʊvə'beə/ *v.t.* (*past* -**bore**; *past participle* —**borne**) 1. to bear down by weight or force. 2. to repress by power or authority.

overbearing *adj.* domineering, bullying.

overblown /əʊvə'bləʊn/ *adj.* 1. pretentious. 2. (of a flower) too fully open, past its prime.

overboard *adv.* from within a ship into the water. —**go overboard**, (*colloquial*) to show extreme enthusiasm.

overbook /əʊvə'buk/ *v.t.* to make too many bookings for (an aircraft flight, hotel etc., or *absolutely*).

overcast /əʊvə'kɑːst/ *adv.* (of the sky) covered with cloud. —*v.t.* (*past & past participle* -**cast**) to stitch over (an edge) to prevent fraying.

overcharge /əʊvə'tʃɑːdʒ/ *v.t.* 1. to charge too high a price to (a person) or for (a thing). 2. to put an excessive charge into; to overfill.

overcheck *n.* a check pattern superimposed on a pattern of smaller checks.

overcoat *n.* a warm outdoor coat.

overcome /əʊvə'kʌm/ *v.t./i.* (*past* -**came**; *past participle* -**come**) 1. to win a victory over, to succeed in subduing; to be victorious. 2. to make helpless, to deprive of proper self-control. 3. to find a way of dealing with (a problem etc.).

overcrowd /əʊvə'kraʊd/ *v.t.* to crowd too many people into (a place or vehicle etc.).

overdevelop /əʊvədi'veləp/ *v.t.* to develop excessively.

overdo /əʊvə'duː/ *v.t.* (third person *singular present* –**does** /-'dʌz/; *past* -**did**; *past participle* -**done** /-'dʌn/) 1. to do (a thing) excessively, to go too far in. 2. to cook too much. 3. to exhaust. —**overdo it**, to work too hard; to exaggerate; to carry an action too far.

overdose *n.* an excessive dose, especially of a drug.

overdraft *n.* in banking, a loan facility on a current account; the amount by which an account is overdrawn. By agreement, the account holder may overdraw on his or her account up to a certain limit and for a specified time, and interest is payable on the amount borrowed.

overdraw /əʊvə'drɔ/ *v.t.* (*past* -**drew**; *past participle* –**drawn**) to draw more from (a bank account) than the amount in credit; (in *past participle*) having overdrawn one's account.

overdress /əʊvə'dres/ *v.t./i.* to dress ostentatiously or with too much formality.

overdrive *n.* a mechanism in a vehicle providing a gear ratio higher than that of the usual gears.

overdue /əʊvə'djuː/ *adj.* past the due time for payment, arrival etc.

overeat /əʊvər'iːt/ *v.i.* (*past* -**ate**; *past participle* -**eaten**) to eat too much.

over-emphasize /əʊvər'emfəsaɪz/ *v.t.* to emphasize excessively. —**over-emphasis** *n.*

overestimate /əʊvər'estɪmeɪt/ *v.t.* to form too high an estimate of. —/-ət/ *n.* too high an estimate.

over-expose /əʊvərɪk'spəʊz/ *v.t.* to expose for too long. —**over-exposure** *n.*

overfeed /əʊvə'fiːd/ *v.t./i.* (*past & past participle* -**fed**) to feed too much.

overfish /əʊvə'fɪʃ/ *v.t.* to fish (a river etc.) too much so that next season's supply is reduced.

overflow /əʊvə'fləʊ/ *v.t./i.* 1. to flow over (a brim etc.); to flood (a surface or area). 2. (of a crowd etc.) to spread beyond the limits of (a room etc.). 3. (of a receptacle etc.) to be so full that the contents overflow; (of kindness, a harvest etc.) to be very abundant. —/'əʊvə-/ *n.* 1. what overflows or is superfluous. 2. an outlet for excess liquid.

overfly /əʊvə'flaɪ/ *v.t.* (*past* -**flew**; *past participle* -**flown** /-'fləʊn/) to fly over or beyond (a place or territory).

overfull /əʊvə'fʊl/ *adj.* filled too much, too full.

overgrown /əʊvə'grəʊn/ *adj.* 1. covered with plants, weeds etc. 2. grown too big. —**overgrowth** *n.*

overhang /əʊvə'hæŋ/ *v.t./i.* (*past & past participle* -**hung**) to jut out (over). —/'əʊvə-/ *n.* overhanging; an overhanging part or amount.

overhaul /əʊvə'hɔl/ v.t. **1.** to check over thoroughly and make any necessary repairs to. **2.** to overtake. —/'əʊvə-/ n. a thorough check with repairs if necessary.

overhead /əʊvə'hed/ adv. above one's head, in the sky. —/'əʊvə-/ adj. placed overhead. —/'əʊvə-/ n. (in plural) the routine administrative and maintenance expenses of a business. These might include property rental, heating and lighting, insurance, and administration costs.

overhear /əʊvə'hɪə/ v.t. (past & past participle **-heard** /-'hɜːd/) to hear unintentionally or without the speaker's knowledge.

overheat /əʊvə'hiːt/ v.t./i. to make or become too hot.

Overijssel /əʊvər'aɪsəl/ province of the E central Netherlands; **capital** Zwolle; **area** 3,340 sq km/1,289 sq mi; **population** (1988) 1,010,000; **physical** it is generally flat and contains the rivers Ijssel and Vecht; **history** ruled by the bishops of Utrecht during the Middle Ages, Overijssel was sold to Charles V of Spain in 1527. It joined the revolt against Spanish authority, becomimg one of the United Provinces of the Netherlands in 1579.

overjoyed /əʊvə'dʒɔɪd/ adj. filled with extreme joy.

overkill n. a surplus of capacity for destruction above what is needed to defeat or destroy an enemy.

overland /əʊvə'lænd/ adv. by land. —/'əʊvə-/ adj. entirely or mainly by land.

overlander n. one of the Australian drovers in the 19th century who opened up new territory by driving their cattle to new stations, or to market, before the establishment of regular stock routes.

overland telegraph cable erected 1870–72 linking Port Augusta in South Australia and Darwin in Northern Territory, and the latter by undersea cable to Java; it ended the communications isolation of the Australian continent.

overlap /əʊvə'læp/ v.t./i. (-pp-) **1.** to extend beyond the edge of and partly cover. **2.** to coincide partly. —/'əʊvə-/ n. overlapping; an overlapping part or amount.

overlay /əʊvə'leɪ/ v.t. (past & past participle **-laid**) **1.** to lie on top of. **2.** to cover the surface of with a coating etc. —/'əʊvə-/ n. a thing laid over another.

overleaf /əʊvə'liːf/ adv. on the other side of a leaf of a book.

overlie /əʊvə'laɪ/ v.t. (past **-lay**; past participle **-lain**; partic. **-lying**) to lie on top of; to smother thus.

overload /əʊvə'ləʊd/ v.t. to put too great a load on or into. —/'əʊvə-/ n. a load that is too great.

overlook /əʊvə'lʊk/ v.t. **1.** to fail to observe or consider. **2.** to take no notice of, to allow (an offence) to go unpunished. **3.** to have a view of from above. **4.** to supervise.

Overlord, Operation the Allied invasion of Normandy, France, on 6 June 1944 (D-Day) during World War II.

overlord n. a supreme lord.

overly adv. (chiefly Scottish and US) excessively, too.

overman /əʊvə'mæn/ v.t. (-nn-) to provide with too many people as staff or crew.

overmantel n. ornamental shelves etc. over a mantelpiece.

overmuch /əʊvə'mʌtʃ/ adv. too much.

overnight /əʊvə'naɪt/ adv. **1.** during the course of a night. **2.** on the preceding evening regarded from the next day. **3.** (colloquial) instantly. —/'əʊvə-/ adj. done or for use etc. during a night.

overpass /'əʊvəpɑːs/ n. a road that passes over another by means of a bridge.

overpay /əʊvə'peɪ/ v.t. to pay too highly.

overplay /əʊvə'pleɪ/ v.t. to give too much importance to. —**overplay one's hand,** to act with overestimation of one's strength.

overpower /əʊvə'paʊə/ v.t. to overcome by greater strength or numbers.

overpowering adj. extreme, too intense.

overprint /əʊvə'prɪnt/ v.t. to print over (something already printed). —/'əʊvə-/ n. a thing overprinted.

overrate /əʊvə'reɪt/ v.t. to have too high an opinion of.

overreach /əʊvə'riːtʃ/ v.t. to outwit, to circumvent. —**overreach oneself,** to fail through being too ambitious.

over-react /əʊvəri'ækt/ v.i. to respond more strongly than is justified.

override /əʊvə'raɪd/ v.t. (past **-rode**; past participle **-ridden**) **1.** to have or claim superior authority or precedence over; to set aside (an order etc.) thus. **2.**

to intervene and cancel the operation of. **3.** to move so as to extend over or overlap.

overrider n. either of a pair of vertical attachments to the bumper of a car to prevent another bumper from becoming locked behind it.

overripe /əʊvə'raɪp/ adj. too ripe.

overrule /əʊvə'ruːl/ v.t. to set aside (a decision etc.) by superior authority; to set aside a decision of (a person) thus.

overrun /əʊvə'rʌn/ v.t. (-nn-; past **-ran**; past participle **-run**) **1.** to swarm or spread over. **2.** to conquer (a territory) by force of numbers. **3.** to exceed (a limit).

overseas adj. & adv. across or beyond the sea.

Overseas Development Administration (ODA) a UK official body that deals with development assistance to overseas countries, including financial aid on concessionary terms and technical assistance, usually in the form of sending specialists to other countries and giving training in the UK.

oversee /əʊvə'siː/ v.t. (past **-saw**; past participle **-seen**) to superintend.

overseer /'əʊvəsɪə/ n. a superintendent.

overset /əʊvə'set/ v.t. (-tt-; past & past participle **-set**) to overturn, to upset.

oversew /əʊvə'səʊ/ v.t. (past participle **-sewn** or **-sewed**) to sew together (two edges) with stitches lying over them.

overshadow /əʊvə'ʃædəʊ/ v.t. **1.** to appear much more prominent or important than. **2.** to cast into the shade.

overshoe /'əʊvəʃuː/ n. an outer protective shoe worn over an ordinary shoe.

overshoot /əʊvə'ʃuːt/ v.t. (past & past participle **-shot**) to pass or send beyond (a target or limit).

overshot adj. (of a water-wheel) turned by water falling on it from above.

oversight /'əʊvəsaɪt/ n. **1.** failure to do or note something; an inadvertent mistake. **2.** supervision.

over-simplify /əʊvə'sɪmplɪfaɪ/ v.t. to distort or misrepresent by putting in too simple terms.

overskirt n. an outer skirt.

oversleep /əʊvə'sliːp/ v.i. (past & past participle **-slept**) to sleep beyond an intended time of waking.

overspend /əʊvə'spend/ v.i. (past & past participle **-spent**) to spend beyond one's means.

overspill n. **1.** what spills over or overflows. **2.** surplus population moving to a new area.

overstaff /əʊvə'stɑːf/ v.t. (especially in past participle) to provide with too many staff.

overstate /əʊvə'steɪt/ v.t. to state too strongly, to exaggerate. —**overstatement** n.

overstay /əʊvə'steɪ/ v.t. to stay longer than.

oversteer v.i. (of a vehicle) to have a tendency to turn more sharply than was intended. —n. this tendency.

overstep /əʊvə'step/ v.t. (-pp-) to pass beyond (a limit).

overstock /əʊvə'stɒk/ v.t. to stock too many of; to stock with too many items.

overstrung /əʊvə'strʌŋ/ adj. **1.** (of a person or the nerves) too highly strung. **2.** (of a piano) with strings arranged in sets crossing each other obliquely.

overstuffed /əʊvə'stʌft/ adj. (of cushions etc.) filled with much or too much stuffing.

oversubscribed /əʊvəsəb'skraɪbd/ adj. (especially of shares for sale) not enough to meet the amount subscribed.

overt /əʊ'vɜːt, 'əʊ-/ adj. done openly, unconcealed. —**overtly** adv. [from Old French, past participle of ovrir = open from Latin]

overtake /əʊvə'teɪk/ v.t. (p.t. **-took** /-tʊk/, past participle **-taken**) **1.** to pass (a person or vehicle travelling in the same direction); to come abreast or level with. **2.** to exceed (a compared value or amount).

overtax /əʊvə'tæks/ v.t. **1.** to make excessive demands on. **2.** to tax too highly.

overthrow /əʊvə'θrəʊ/ v.t. (past **-threw** /-'θruː/; past participle **-thrown**) **1.** to remove forcibly from power. **2.** to conquer. **3.** to knock down, to upset. —/'əʊvə-/ n. **1.** defeat, downfall. **2.** a fielder's throwing of a ball beyond an intended point.

overthrust n. a thrust of (especially lower) strata on one side of a fault over those on the other side.

overtime n. time worked in addition to one's regular hours; payment for this. —adv. as or during overtime.

overtone *n.* 1. a subtle extra quality or implication. 2. in music, any of the tones above the lowest in a harmonic series.

overtrick *n.* a trick taken in excess of one's contract in the game of bridge.

overture /ˈəʊvətjʊə/ *n.* 1. an orchestral piece opening an opera etc.; a composition in this style. 2. (often in *plural*) a friendly approach showing willingness to begin negotiations; a formal proposal or offer. [from Old French from Latin *apertura = opening*]

overturn /əʊvəˈtɜːn/ *v.t./i.* 1. to turn over or fall down; to cause to do this. 2. to overthrow, to subvert.

over-use /əʊvəˈjuːz/ *v.t.* to use excessively. —/-ˈjuːs/ *n.* excessive use.

overview *n.* a general survey.

overweening /əʊvəˈwiːnɪŋ/ *adj.* arrogant, presumptuous. [from obsolete *ween = think*]

overweight /əʊvəˈweɪt/ *adj.* more than the allowed or normal or desired weight. —/ˈəʊvə-/ *n.* excess weight.

overwhelm /əʊvəˈwelm/ *v.t.* 1. to overpower, especially with an emotion or burden. 2. to overcome by force of numbers. 3. to bury or drown beneath a huge mass.

overwind /əʊvəˈwaɪnd/ *v.t.* (*past & past participle* —**wound**) to wind (a watch etc.) beyond the proper stopping-point.

overwork /əʊvəˈwɜːk/ *v.t./i.* to work or cause to work too hard; to weary or exhaust with too much work. —*n.* excessive work.

overwrought /əʊvəˈrɔːt/ *adj.* suffering a nervous reaction from over-excitement.

ovi- /əʊvɪ-/ in combinations, egg, ovum. [from Latin *ovum = egg*]

Ovid /ˈɒvɪd/ (Publius Ovidius Naso) 43–17 BC. Roman poet. His poetry deals mainly with the themes of love (*Amores* 20 BC, *Ars amatoria* 1 BC), mythology (*Metamorphoses* AD 2), and exile (*Tristia* AD 9–12).

oviduct /ˈəʊvɪdʌkt/ *n.* a canal through which ova pass from the ovary, especially in oviparous animals.

oviform /ˈəʊvɪfɔːm/ *adj.* egg-shaped.

ovine /ˈəʊvaɪn/ *adj.* of or like sheep. [from Latin *ovis = sheep*]

oviparous /əʊˈvɪpərəs/ *adj.* producing young from eggs expelled from the body before being hatched [from Latin *ovi-, and -parous = bearing*)]

ovipary *n.* a method of animal reproduction in which eggs are laid by the female and develop outside her body, in contrast to ◊ovovivipary and ◊vivipary. It is the most common form of reproduction.

ovipositor /əʊvɪˈpɒzɪtə/ *n.* a pointed tubular organ by which a female insect deposits eggs. [from Latin *ponere = to place*]

ovoid /ˈəʊvɔɪd/ *adj.* (of a solid) egg-shaped. [from French]

ovovivipary *n.* a method of animal reproduction in which fertilized eggs develop within the female (unlike ◊ovipary), and the embryo gains no nutritional substances from the female (unlike ◊vivipary). It occurs in some invertebrates, fishes, and reptiles.

ovulate /ˈɒvjʊleɪt/ *v.i.* to discharge an ovum or ova from an ovary; to produce ova. —**ovulation** /-ˈleɪʃən/ *n.* in mammals it occurs as part of the ◊menstrual cycle.

ovulation *n.* in female animals, the process of making and releasing egg cells. In mammals it occurs as part of the ◊menstrual cycle.

ovule /ˈəʊvjuːl/ *n.* 1. a germ-cell in a female plant, which develops into a seed after fertilization. It consists of an ◊embryo sac containing the female gamete (◊ovum or egg cell), surrounded by nutritive tissue, the nucellus. Outside this there are one or two coverings that provide protection, developing into the testa, or seed coat, following fertilization. 2. an unfertilized ovum. [French from Latin (diminutive of *ovum*)]

ovum *n.* (*plural* **ova**) 1. the female gamete (germ-cell) before fertilization, from which by fertilization with male sperm the young is developed. In animals it is called an egg, and is produced in the ovaries. In plants it is also known as an egg cell or oosphere, and is produced in an ovule. The ovum is nonmotile, and it must be fertilized by a male gamete before it can develop further, except in cases of ◊parthenogenesis.

ow interjection expressing sudden pain. [natural exclamation]

Owens *US track and field athlete Jesse Owens during an exhibition of the long jump in 1936.*

owe /əʊ/ *v.t.* 1. to be under an obligation to pay or repay (money etc. to a person); to be in debt. 2. to have a duty to render. 3. to feel (gratitude etc. towards another) in return for a service. 4. to be indebted for (a thing) to a cause or to another's work etc. [Old English]

Owen /ˈəʊɪn/ David 1938– . British politician, originally a doctor. He entered Parliament in 1966, and was Labour foreign secretary 1977–79. In 1981 he was one of the founders of the ◊Social Democratic Party (SDP), and in 1983 became its leader. Opposed to the decision of the majority of the party to merge with the Liberals in 1987, Owen stood down, but led a rump SDP from 1988, which was eventually disbanded in 1990.

Owen Robert 1771–1858. British socialist, born in Wales. In 1800 he became manager of a mill at New Lanark, Scotland, where by improving working and housing conditions and providing schools he created a model community. His ideas stimulated the ◊cooperative movement.

Owen Wilfred 1893–1918. English poet. His verse, owing much to the encouragement of Siegfried ◊Sassoon, expresses his hatred of war, for example *Anthem for Doomed Youth*, published in 1921.

Owens /ˈəʊɪnz/ Jesse (James Cleveland) 1913–1980. US track and field athlete, who excelled in the sprints, hurdles, and the long jump. At the 1936 Berlin Olympics he won four gold medals.

owing *predic. adj.* owed, not yet paid. —**owing to,** caused by, because of.

owl *n.* any bird of the order Strigiformes, found worldwide. Owls are mainly nocturnal birds of prey, with mobile heads, hooked beaks, acute hearing, forward-facing eyes, set round with rayed feathers, and soundless flight. They disgorge indigestible remains of their prey in pellets (castings). [Old English]

owlet /ˈaʊlɪt/ *n.* a small or young owl. [earlier *howlet*, diminutive of *owl/howl*]

owlish *adj.* like an owl; solemn and dull. —**owlishly** *adv.*

own /əʊn/ *adj.* belonging to oneself or itself. —*v.t./i.* 1. to have as property, to possess. 2. to acknowledge paternity, authorship, or possession of. 3. to admit as existent, valid, true etc. —**come into one's own,** to receive one's due, to achieve recognition. **of one's own,** belonging to oneself exclusively. **on one's own,** alone; independent, independently, without help. **own goal,** a goal scored by a member of a team against his own side. **own to,** to confess to. **own up (to),** to confess frankly. —**owned** *adj.* [Old English]

owner *n.* a possessor. **owner-occupier,** one who owns and occupies a house. —**ownership** *n.*

ox *n.* (*plural* **oxen**) 1. the castrated male of domestic species of cattle, used in Third World countries for ploughing and other agricultural purposes; also the extinct wild ox or aurochs of Europe, and surviving wild species. 2. a full-grown bullock of the domesticated species of cattle,

Bos taurus. —**ox-bow** *n.* a horseshoe bend in a river; a lake formed from this when the river cuts across the narrow end. In the USA, the term ◊bayou is often used.

ox-eye *n.* any of several plants (especially *Leucanthemum vulgare*) with flowers with dark centres. [Old English]

oxalic acid a solid, white alcohol (COOH)$_2$·2H$_2$, soluble in water, alcohol, and ether. Oxalic acid is sour and highly poisonous. It is found in rhubarb, and its salts (oxalates) occur in wood sorrel (genus *Oxalis*, family Oxalidaceae) and other plants. It is used in the leather and textile industries, ink manufacture, metal polishes, and for removing rust and ink stains. [from French from Latin from Greek *oxalis* = wood sorrel]

Oxbridge /'ɒksbrɪdʒ/ generic term for Oxford and Cambridge, the two oldest universities in the UK. —*adj.* characteristic of these.

oxen plural of ox.

OXFAM /'ɒksfæm/ (acronym from Oxford Committee for **Famine** Relief) a charity established in the UK in 1942 by Canon Theodore Richard Milford (1896–1987), initially to assist the starving people of Greece and subsequently to relieve poverty and famine worldwide.

Oxford industrial and university city in S England, the administrative capital of Oxfordshire, at the confluence of the rivers Cherwell and Thames. Industrial products include motor vehicles. **Oxford University** is the oldest British university, which started to develop during the 12th century.

Oxford Movement also known as **Tractarian Movement** or **Catholic Revival** a movement that attempted to revive Catholic religion in the Church of England. Cardinal Newman dated the movement from ◊Keble's sermon in Oxford in 1833. The Oxford Movement by the turn of the century had transformed the Anglican communion, and survives today as Anglo-Catholicism.

Oxfordshire /'ɒksfədʃə/ county in S central England; **area** 2,610 sq km/1,007 sq mi; **administrative headquarters** Oxford; **physical** river Thames and tributaries; Cotswolds and Chiltern Hills; **products** cereals, cars, paper, bricks, cement; **population** (1987) 578,000.

oxherd *n.* a cowherd.

oxhide *n.* the hide of an ox; leather from this.

oxidant /'ɒksɪdənt/ *n.* an oxidizing agent. [French, participle of *oxider* from Greek *oxys* = acid]

oxidation /ɒksi'deɪʃ(ə)n/ oxidizing, being oxidized; in chemistry, the loss of ◊electrons, gain of oxygen, or loss of hydrogen by an atom, ion, or molecule during a chemical reaction. [French from Greek]

oxide /'ɒksaɪd/ *n.* a compound of oxygen and another element, frequently produced by burning the element or a compound of it in air or oxygen.

oxidize /'ɒksɪdaɪz/ *v.t./i.* **1.** to combine or cause to combine with oxygen. **2.** to make or become rusty. **3.** to coat (metal) with an oxide. —**oxidization** /-'zeɪʃən/ *n.*

oxlip *n.* a plant closely related to the ◊cowslip.

Oxon. abbreviation of **1.** Oxfordshire. **2.** of Oxford University. [from Latin *Oxoniensis* = of Oxford]

Oxonian /ɒk'səʊnɪən/ *adj.* of Oxford or Oxford University. —*n.* **1.** a member of Oxford University. **2.** a citizen of Oxford. [from *Oxonia* Latinized form of *Ox(en)ford*]

oxpecker an African bird, genus *Buphagus*, of the starling family. It clambers about the bodies of large mammals, feeding on ticks and other parasites. Its vigilance may help to warn the host of approaching dangers.

oxtail *n.* the tail of an ox, much used for soup-making.

oxyacetylene torch /ɒksɪə'setɪli:n/ a gas torch that burns acetylene in pure oxygen, producing a high-temperature flame (3,000°C/5,400°F). It is widely used in welding to fuse metals. In the cutting torch, a jet of oxygen burns through metal already melted by the flame. [from oxygenate plus acetylene]

oxygen *n.* a colourless, odourless, tasteless, non-metallic, gaseous element, symbol O, atomic number 8, relative atomic mass 15.9994. It is the most abundant element in the Earth's crust (almost 50% by mass), forms about 21% by volume of the atmosphere, and is present in combined form in water, carbon dioxide, silicon dioxide (quartz), iron ore, calcium carbonate (limestone), and many other substances. Life on Earth evolved using oxygen, which is a by-product of ◊photosynthesis and the basis for ◊respiration in plants and animals. ◊Ozone is an ◊allotrope of oxygen. —**oxygen debt**, a physiological state produced by vigorous exercise, in which the lungs cannot supply all the oxygen the muscles need. —**oxygen mask**, a mask placed over the nose and mouth to supply oxygen for breathing. **oxygen tent**, a tentlike enclosure supplying a patient with air having increased oxygen content. [from French *oxygène* from Greek *oxys* = acid and *genes* = forming, because it was at first held to be the essential principle in the formation of acids]

oxygenate /'ɒksɪdʒəneɪt/ *v.t.* to supply, treat, or mix with oxygen, to oxidize. —**oxygenation** /-'neɪʃən/ *n.*

oxyhaemoglobin *n.* the oxygenated form of ◊haemoglobin, the pigment found in the red blood cells. All vertebrates, and some invertebrates, use haemoglobin for oxygen transport because the two substances can combine reversibly. In mammals oxyhaemoglobin forms in the lungs and is transported to the rest of the body, where the oxygen is released. The deoxygenated blood is then returned to the lungs. Haemoglobin will combine also with carbon monoxide to form carboxyhaemoglobin, but in this case the reaction is irreversible. Asphyxiation can result when oxyhaemoglobin cannot form in sufficient quantities.

oxymoron /ɒksi'mɔːrɒn/ *n.* a ◊figure of speech, combining two or more words with contradictory meanings, the effect being to startle. Examples include *cheerful pessimism*, *bittersweet*, *cruel to be kind* and *beloved enemy*. [from Greek, = pointedly foolish (*oxus* = sharp and *môros* = foolish)]

oxytocin /ɒksi'təʊsɪn/ *n.* a pituitary hormone controlling uterine contraction and the release of milk, used in synthetic form to induce labour etc. reducing bleeding at the site where the placenta was attached. etc. [from Greek *oxutokia* (*tokos* = childbirth)]

oyez /əʊ'jes/ or **oyes** an interjection uttered usually three times by a public crier or court officer to call for attention. [from Anglo-French, imperative of *oïr* = hear from Latin *audire*]

oyster *n.* **1.** a bivalve ◊mollusc of the genus *Ostrea* or family Ostreidae, used as a food and in some types producing a pearl. The upper valve is flat, the lower concave, hinged by an elastic ligament. The mantle, lying against the shell, protects the inner body, which includes respiratory, digestive, and reproductive organs. Oysters are distinguished by their change of sex, which may alternate annually or more frequently, and by the number of their eggs—a female may discharge up to a million eggs during a spawning period. **2.** a symbol of all one desires. **3.** white with a grey tinge. [from Old French from Latin *ostrea*, *ostreum* from Greek]

oyster catcher a shore-bird of the genus *Haematopus*, related to the plovers. The common oyster catcher of European coasts *H. ostralegus* is black and white, with a long red beak to open shellfish.

oz or **oz.** abbreviation of ◊ounce(s).

Ozal /əu'za:l/ Turgut 1927– . Turkish Islamic right-wing politician, prime minister 1983–89, president from 1989.

Ozalid process trademarked copying process used to produce positive prints from drawn or printed materials or film, such as printing proofs from film images. The film is placed on top of chemically treated paper and then exposed to ultraviolet light. The image is developed dry using ammonia vapour.

Ozark Mountains /'əʊzɑ:k/ area in the USA (shared by Arkansas, Illinois, Kansas, Mississippi, Oklahoma) of ridges, valleys, and streams; highest point only 700 m/2,300 ft; area 130,000 sq km/50,000 sq .ni.

ozone /'əʊzəʊn/ *n.* **1.** a form of oxygen with three atoms in the molecule (O$_3$), having a pungent smell. It is formed when the molecule of the stable form of oxygen, O$_2$, is split by ultraviolet radiation or electrical discharge. It forms a layer in the upper atmosphere, which protects life on Earth from ultraviolet rays, a cause of skin cancer. At lower levels it contributes to the ◊greenhouse effect. **2.** (*popularly*) invigorating air at the seaside etc. [from German from Greek *ozō* = smell]

Ozu /'əʊzu:/ Yasujiro 1903–1963. Japanese film director, who became known in the West only in his last years. *Tōkyō Monogatari/Tokyo Story* 1953 illustrates his typical low camera angles and his theme of middle-class family life.

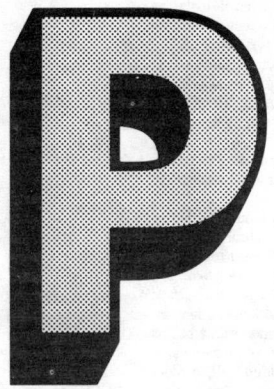

p, P /pi:/ *n.* (**ps, p's**) the 16th letter of the alphabet.
p abbreviation of 1. penny, pence. 2. in music, piano.
p. abbreviation of page.
P abbreviation of pawn (in chess).
P symbol for phosphorus.
pa /pɑː/ (*colloquial*) father. [abbreviation of *papa*]
p.a. abbreviation of per annum. [Latin = yearly]
Pa 1. abbreviation of ◊pascal. 2. symbol for ◊protactinium.
PA abbreviation of 1. personal assistant. 2. public address.
3. Press Association.
Paarl /pɑːl/ town on the Great Berg River, Cape Province, South Africa; population (1980) 71,300. It is the centre of a noted wine-producing area, 50 km/31 mi NE of Cape Town. Nelson Mandela served the last days of his imprisonment at the Victor Vester prison near here.
Pabst /pɑːpst/ G(eorg) W(ilhelm) 1885–1967. German film director, whose films include *Die Büchse der Pandora/Pandora's Box* 1928, *Das Tagebuch einer Verlorenen/The Diary of a Lost Girl* 1929, both starring Louise ◊Brooks, and *Die Dreigroschenoper/The Threepenny Opera* 1931.
paca *n.* a large nocturnal, burrowing ◊rodent of Central and South America, about 60 cm/2 ft long.
pace¹ *n.* 1. a single step in walking or running; the space traversed in this. 2. speed in walking or running. 3. any of the various gaits of (especially a trained) horse etc. —*v.t./i.* 1. to walk with a slow or regular pace; to traverse by pacing. 2. to set the pace for (a rider, runner etc.). 3. to measure (a distance) by pacing. 4. (of a horse) to amble. —**keep pace**, to advance at an equal rate. **put a person through his/her paces**, to test his/her qualities in action etc. **set the pace**, to set the speed, especially by leading. [from Old French *pas* from Latin *passus*]
pace² /'peɪsɪ, 'pɑːtʃeɪ/ *prep.* (in announcing a contrary opinion) with all due deference to (the person named). [Latin, ablative of *pax* = peace]
pacemaker *n.* 1. a runner etc. who sets the pace in a race. 2. a structure or device for stimulating the heart muscle. It delivers minute electric shocks at regular intervals and restores normal heartbeat. The latest ones are powered by radioactive isotopes for long life and weigh no more than 15 grams/0.5 oz. They are implanted under the skin.
Pachomius, St /pəˈkəʊmɪəs/ 292–346. Egyptian Christian, the founder of the first Christian monastery, near Dendera on the river Nile.
pachyderm /'pækɪdɜːm/ *n.* a thick-skinned mammal, especially an elephant or rhinoceros. —**pachydermatous** /-'dɜːmətəs/ *adj.* [from French from Greek *pakhus* = thick and *derma* = skin]
pacific /pəˈsɪfɪk/ *adj.* peaceful; making or loving peace. —**pacifically** *adv.* [from French or Latin *pax* = peace]
Pacific Islands United Nations trust territory in the W Pacific comprising over 2,000 islands and atolls, under Japanese mandate 1919–47, and administered by the USA 1947–80, when all its members, the ◊Carolines, ◊Mariana Islands (except ◊Guam), and ◊Marshall Islands, became independent.
Pacific Ocean the world's largest ocean, separating Asia and Australia from North and South America; area 166,242,500 sq km/64,170,000 sq mi; average depth

4,188 m/13,749 ft; greatest depth of any ocean 11,034 m/36,210 ft in the ◊Mariana Trench.
Pacific Security Treaty a military alliance agreement between Australia, New Zealand, and the USA, signed in 1951 (see ◊Anzus). Military cooperation between the USA and New Zealand has been restricted by the latter's policy of banning ships that might be carrying nuclear weapons.
Pacific War the war of 1879–83 fought by an alliance of Bolivia and Peru against Chile. Chile seized Antofagasta and the coast between the mouths of the rivers Loa and Paposo, rendering Bolivia landlocked, and also annexed the southern Peruvian coastline from Arica to the mouth of the Loa, including the nitrate fields of the Atacama Desert.
pacifist /'pæsɪfɪst/ *n.* one who rejects war and violence and believes that disputes should be settled by peaceful means. —**pacifism** *n.* [from French]
pacify /'pæsɪfaɪ/ *v.t.* 1. to calm and quieten, to appease. 2. to establish peace in. —**pacification** /-fɪˈkeɪʃən/ *n.*, **pacificatory** /pəˈsɪfɪkətərɪ/ *adj.* [from Old French or Latin *pax* = peace]
Pacino /pəˈtʃiːnəʊ/ Al(berto) 1940– . US film actor who played introverted but violent roles in films such as *The Godfather* 1972 and *Scarface* 1983. *Dick Tracy* 1990 added comedy to his range of acting styles.
pack¹ *n.* 1. a collection of things wrapped up or tied together for carrying. 2. (usually *derogatory*) a lot or set. 3. a set of playing cards. 4. a group of wild animals, hounds etc.; an organized group of Cub Scouts or Brownies. 5. a team's forwards in rugby football. 6. a medicinal or cosmetic substance applied to the skin. 7. an area of pack ice. 8. a method of packing. —*v.t./i.* 1. to put (things) together in a bundle, bag etc. for transport, storing, or marketing etc.; to fill with things thus; to fill a case etc. with one's belongings. 2. to be able to be packed. 3. to put closely together; to fill (a space) in this way; to fill (a theatre or meeting etc.) with people. 4. to cover or protect with something pressed tightly round or inside. 5. to carry (a gun etc.); to be capable of delivering (a punch) with skill or force. 6. (of animals) to form a pack. —**pack drill**, a military punishment of drill in full marching equipment (*no names no pack drill*, discretion will prevent punishment). **packhorse** *n.* a horse for carrying packs. **pack ice**, large crowded floating pieces of ice in the sea. **pack it in**, (*slang*) to cease doing something. **pack off**, to send away. **pack saddle** *n.* a saddle adapted for supporting packs. **pack up**, to put one's things together in readiness for departure or ceasing work; *slang*, of machinery etc.) to break down. **send packing**, (*colloquial*) to dismiss summarily. —**packer** *n.* [from Middle Dutch or Middle Low German]
pack² *v.t.* to select (a jury etc.) so as to secure a decision biased in one's favour.
package *n.* 1. a bundle of things packed. 2. a parcel, a box etc., in which things are packed. 3. a package deal. —*v.t.* to make up into or enclose in a package. —**package deal**, a transaction or proposals offered or agreed to as a whole. **package holiday** *or* **tour** etc., one with all arrangements made at an inclusive price.
packaging *n.* wrapping(s) or container(s) for goods.
Packer Kerry (Francis Bullmore) 1937– . Australian media proprietor, chair of Consolidated Press Holdings

Ltd in Australia. He is an energetic promoter of Australian sport, and in 1977 was instrumental in contracting Australian test cricketers to make up a world series cricket team.

packet /'pækɪt/ *n.* 1. a small package. 2. (*colloquial*) a large sum of money won or lost. —**packet boat**, a mail boat.

packing *n.* material used to pack and protect fragile articles etc. —**packing case**, a wooden case or framework for packing goods.

packthread *n.* stout thread for sewing or tying up packs.

pact *n.* an agreement, a treaty. [from Old French from Latin *pactum* (*pacisci* = agree)]

pad[1] *n.* 1. a piece of soft stuff used to reduce friction or jarring, rub things, fill out hollows, hold or absorb liquid etc. 2. a number of sheets of blank paper fastened together at one edge. 3. the fleshy underpart of an animal's foot. 4. a guard for the leg and ankle in cricket etc. 5. a flat surface for a helicopter takeoff and landing or a rocket launching. 6. (*slang*) a lodging. —*v.t.* (**-dd-**) 1. to provide with a pad or padding; to stuff. 2. to fill (a book etc.) with unnecessary material in order to lengthen it. —**padded cell,** a room with padded walls in a mental hospital.

pad[2] *v.t./i.* (**-dd-**) 1. to walk with a soft, dull, steady sound of steps. 2. to travel (along) on foot. [from Low German *pad* = path or *padden* = tread]

padding *n.* 1. material used to pad things. 2. superfluous words in a book, sentence etc.

Paddington Bear /'pædɪŋtən/ a bear who features in a series of children's stories by British writer Michael Bond (1926–), beginning with *A Bear called Paddington* 1958. He is found abandoned on Paddington Station in London by the Brown family, who adopt him; he likes marmalade sandwiches and customarily wears a hat, duffle coat, and wellington boots.

paddle[1] *n.* 1. a short, broad-bladed oar used without a rowlock. 2. a paddle-shaped instrument or part. 3. a fin, a flipper. 4. any of the boards fitted round the circumference of a paddle wheel or mill wheel. 5. an act or spell of paddling. —*v.t./i.* to move on water or propel (a canoe) by means of paddles; to row gently. —**paddle boat,** a boat propelled by a paddle wheel. **paddle wheel,** a wheel for propelling a ship, with boards round the circumference so as to press backward against the water as the wheel revolves. —**paddler** *n.*

paddle[2] *v.t./i.* to walk barefoot in shallow water; to dabble (the feet or hands) in shallow water. —*n.* an act or spell of paddling. [compare Low German *paddeln* = tramp about]

paddock /'pædək/ *n.* 1. a small field, especially for keeping horses in. 2. a turf enclosure adjoining a racecourse where horses are assembled before a race; a similar enclosure at a motor-racing circuit. 3. (*Australian and New Zealand*) a field, a plot of land.

paddy[1] *n.* 1. (in full **paddy field**) a field where rice is grown. 2. rice before threshing or in the husk. [from Malay]

paddy[2] *n.* (*colloquial*) a rage, a fit of temper.

Paddy *n.* (*colloquial*) a nickname for an Irishman. [pet form of Irish *Padraig* = Patrick]

padlock *n.* a detachable lock hanging by a pivoted hook from the object it fastens. —*v.t.* to secure with a padlock. [Old English]

padre /'pɑːdrɪ/ *n.* (*colloquial*) a chaplain in an army etc. [Italian, Spanish, and Portuguese = father]

Padua /'pædjuə/ (Italian *Padova*) city in N Italy, 45 km/28 mi W of Venice; population (1988) 224,000. The astronomer Galileo taught at the university, founded in 1222.

paean /'piːən/ *n.* a song of praise or triumph. [Latin from Doric Greek *paian* = hymn to Apollo]

paediatrics /piːdɪ'ætrɪks/ *n.pl.* (*US* pediatrics) the branch of medicine dealing with children and their diseases. —**paediatric** *adj.*, **paediatrician** /piːdɪə'trɪʃən/ *n.* [from *paedo-* = child and Greek *iatros* = physician]

paedo- /piːdə(ʊ)-/ in combinations, child. [from Greek *pais* = boy, child]

paedomorphosis *n.* in biology, an alternative term for ◊neoteny.

paedophilia /piːdə'fɪlɪə/ *n.* sexual love directed towards children. [Greek *philos* = loving]

paella /pɑː'elə/ *n.* a Spanish dish of rice, saffron, chicken, seafood etc., cooked and served in a large shallow pan. [Catalan, from Old French from Latin *patella* = pan]

Paganini *A drawing by Ingres of the Italian violinist and composer Paganini.*

pagan /'peɪgən/ *adj.* 1. heathen; irreligious. 2. holding the belief that deity exists in natural forces; nature-worshipping, especially in contrast to believing in Christianity, Judaism etc. —*n.* 1. a pagan person. 2. one with pagan beliefs. —**paganism** *n.* [from Latin *paganus* (*pagus* = village)]

Pagan /pə'gɑːn/ archaeological site in Myanmar with the ruins of the former capital (founded in 847, taken by Kublai Khan in 1287). These include Buddhist pagodas, shrines, and temples with wall paintings of the great period of Burmese art (11th–13th centuries).

Paganini /pægə'niːnɪ/ Niccolò 1782–1840. Italian violinist and composer, a virtuoso soloist from the age of nine. His works for the violin ingeniously exploit the potential of the instrument. His appearance, wild amours, and virtuosity (especially on a single string) fostered a rumour of his being in league with the devil.

page[1] /peɪdʒ/ *n.* a leaf of a book etc.; one side of this; what is written or printed on this; an episode that might fill a page in a written history etc. —*v.t.* to paginate. [French from Latin *pagina*]

page[2] *n.* a boy or man, usually in livery, employed to run errands, attend to a door etc.; a boy employed as a personal attendant of a person of rank, a bride etc. —*v.t.* to summon (as) by a page. [from Old French, perhaps ultimately from Greek *paidion* = small boy]

Page Earle (Christmas Grafton) 1880–1961. Australian politician, leader of the Country Party 1920–39 and briefly prime minister in April 1939. He represented Australia in the British war cabinet 1941–42 and was minister of health 1949–55. He introduced Australia's health scheme in 1953.

Page Frederick Handley 1885–1962. British aircraft engineer, founder of one of the earliest aircraft-manufacturing companies in 1909 and designer of long-range civil aeroplanes and multi-engined bombers in both world wars; for example, the Halifax, flown in World War II.

pageant /'pædʒənt/ *n.* a brilliant spectacle, especially an elaborate parade; a spectacular procession, or play performed in the open, illustrating historical events; a tableau etc. on a fixed stage or moving vehicle. A pageant was originally the wagon on which medieval ◊mystery plays were performed.

pageantry *n.* a spectacular show or display; what serves to make a pageant.

paginate /'pædʒɪneɪt/ *v.t.* to number the pages of (a book etc.). —**pagination** /-'neɪʃən/ *n.* [from French from Latin *pagina*]

paging *n.* in computing, a way of increasing the apparent memory capacity of a machine. See ◊virtual memory (under ◊virtual).

Pagnol /pæn'jɒl/ Marcel 1895–1974. French film director, author, and playwright, whose work includes *Fanny* 1932 and *Manon des Sources* 1953. He regarded the cinema as recorded theatre; thus his films, although strong on character and background, fail to exploit the medium fully as an independent art form.

pagoda /pəˈgəʊdə/ n. a Hindu or Buddhist temple or sacred building, especially a tower, in India and the Far East; an ornamental imitation of this. [from Portuguese, probably ultimately from Persian]

pah /pɑː/ interjection expressing disgust or contempt. [natural exclamation]

Pahlavi dynasty /ˈpɑːləvɪ/ an Iranian dynasty founded by Riza Khan (1877–1944), an army officer who seized control of the government in 1921 and was proclaimed shah in 1925. During World War II, Britain and the USSR were nervous of his German sympathies and occupied Iran 1941–46. They compelled him to abdicate in 1941 in favour of his son Muhammad Riza Shah Pahlavi, who took office in 1956, with US support, and who was deposed in the Islamic revolution of 1979.

paid past and past participle of **pay**.

pail n. a bucket. —**pailful** n. [Old English]

pain n. 1. the sense that gives an awareness of harmful effects on or in the body; mental suffering. It may be triggered by stimuli such as ◊trauma, inflammation, and heat. Pain is transmitted by specialized nerves and also has psychological components controlled by higher centres in the brain. 2. (in *plural*) careful effort. 3. punishment, the threat of this. —*v.t.* to inflict pain on; (in *past participle*) expressing pain. —**pain in the neck**, (*colloquial*) an annoying or tiresome person or thing. **painkiller** n. a medicine for alleviating pain, also known as an ◊analgesic. [from Old French *peine* from Latin *poena* = punishment]

Paine /peɪn/ Thomas 1737–1809. English left-wing political writer, active in the American and French revolutions. His pamphlet *Common Sense* 1776 ignited passions in the American Revolution; others include *The Rights of Man* 1791 and *The Age of Reason* 1793. He advocated republicanism, deism, the abolition of slavery, and the emancipation of women.

Character is much easier kept than recovered.
Thomas Paine
The American Crisis

---

painful adj. 1. causing pain; (of a part of the body) suffering pain. 2. causing trouble or difficulty, laborious. —**painfully** adv., **painfulness** n.

painless adj. not causing pain.

painstaking /ˈpeɪnzteɪkɪŋ/ adj. careful, industrious.

paint n. 1. any of various materials used to give a protective and decorative finish to surfaces or for making pictures. A paint consists of a pigment suspended in a vehicle, or binder, usually with added solvents. It is the vehicle that dries and hardens to form an adhesive film of paint. Among the most common kinds are cellulose paints (or lacquers), oil-based paints, emulsion paints, and special types such as enamels and primers. 2. (in *plural*) a collection of tubes or cakes of paint. —*v.t./i.* 1. to coat or decorate with paint; to colour thus. 2. to depict or portray with paint(s); to make pictures thus. 3. to describe. 4. to apply a liquid or cosmetic to (the skin or face); to apply (liquid etc.) thus. —**painted lady**, an orange-red butterfly *Vanessa cardui* with black and white spots. **paint the town red**, (*slang*) to enjoy oneself flamboyantly. [from Old French from Latin *pingere*]

paintbox n. a box holding dry paints for use by an artist.

paintbrush n. a brush for applying paint.

painter[1] n. one who paints, especially as an artist or decorator. —**painterly** adj.

painter[2] n. a rope attached to the bow of a boat for tying it to a quay etc. [probably from Old French *penteur* = rope from masthead]

painting n. 1. the application of colour, pigment, or paint to a surface. 2. a painted picture.

pair n. 1. a set of two persons or things used together or regarded as a unit. 2. an article consisting of two joined or corresponding parts. 3. an engaged or married couple; a mated couple of animals. 4. the other member of a pair. 5. two playing cards of the same denomination. 6. either or both of two MPs of opposing parties who are absent from a division by mutual arrangement. —*v.t./i.* 1. to arrange or be arranged in couples. 2. (of animals) to mate. 3. to partner (a person) with a member of the opposite sex. 4. to make a pair in Parliament. —**pair** off, to form into pairs. [from Old French from Latin *paria* (*par* = equal)]

Paisley /ˈpeɪzlɪ/ adj. having a distinctive pattern of curved abstract figures. [from *Paisley* in Scotland]

Pakhtoonistan /pɑːktuːniˈstɑːn/ independent state desired by the ◊Pathan people.

Pakistan /pɑːkiˈstɑːn/ Islamic Republic of; country in S Asia, stretching from the Himalayas to the Arabian Sea, bounded to the W by Iran, NW by Afghanistan, NE by China, and E by India; **area** 796,100 sq km/307,295 sq mi; one-third of Kashmir under Pakistani control; **capital** Islamabad; **physical** fertile Indus plain in E; Baluchistan plateau in W, mountains in N and NW; **head of state** Ghulam Ishaq Khan from 1988; **head of government** Nawaz Sharif from 1990; **political system** emergent democracy; **exports** cotton textiles, rice, leather, carpets; **population** (1990 est) 113,163,000 (66% Punjabi, 13% Sindhi); **language** Urdu and English (official); Punjabi, Sindhi, Pashto, Baluchi; **recent history** independence was achieved from Britain in 1947 and Pakistan was formed following the partition of India; proclaimed a republic in 1956. East Pakistan became the separate country of Bangladesh in 1971. After civil war, power was transferred to Zulfiqar Ali Bhutto; he was overthrown by Gen Zia ul-haq in 1977 and executed in 1979. Agitation for free elections was launched by Benazir Bhutto in 1986; she was elected president in 1988 (dismissed in 1990). Pakistan rejoined the Commonwealth in 1989.

Pakula /pəˈkuːlə/ Alan J 1928– . US film director, formerly a producer, whose best films are among the finest of the 1970s cinema and include *Klute* 1971 and *All the President's Men* 1976. His later work includes *Sophie's Choice* 1982 and *Presumed Innocent* 1990.

pal n. (*colloquial*) a friend, a mate. —*v.i.* (-ll-) (with *up*) (*colloquial*) to become friends. [from Romany, ultimately from Old English]

palace /ˈpælɪs/ n. 1. an official residence of a sovereign, president, archbishop, or bishop. 2. a splendid mansion, a spacious building. —**palace revolution**, the overthrow of a sovereign etc. without a civil war. [from Old French from Latin *Palatium*, house of Augustus at Rome]

paladin /ˈpælədɪn/ n. 1. any of the Twelve Peers of Charlemagne's court, of whom the Count Palatine was the chief. 2. a knight errant, a champion. [from French from Italian from Latin]

palaeo- /ˈpælɪə(ʊ)-/ in combinations, ancient, of ancient times. [from Greek *palaios*]

Palaeocene /ˈpælɪəsiːn/ adj. of the first epoch of the Tertiary period of geological time, 65–55 million years ago. —n. this era. During the Palaeocene era many types of mammals spread rapidly after the disappearance of the great reptiles of the Mesozoic. [from Greek *palaios* = ancient and *kainos* = new (the ancient part of the early recent)]

palaeography /pælɪˈɒgrəfɪ/ n. the study of ancient writing and documents. —**palaeographer** n., **palaeographic** /-ˈgræfɪk/ adj. [from French]

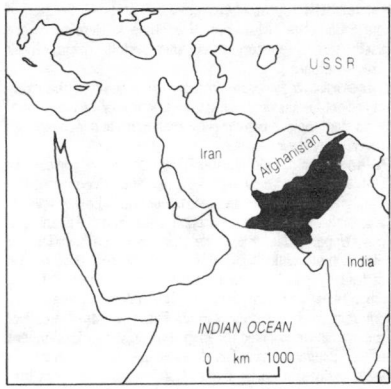

Pakistan

Palaeolithic /pæliə'lɪθɪk, peɪ-/ *adj.* of the earlier part of the Stone Age, when primitive stone implements were used; see ◊prehistory. —*n.* this period. [from Greek *lithos* = stone]

palaeontology /pælion'tolədʒɪ/ *n.* in geology, the study of ancient life encompassing the structure of ancient organisms and their environment, evolution, and ecology, as revealed by their ◊fossils.

Palaeozoic /pæliəu'zəuɪk/ *adj.* of the geological era 590–248 million years ago. —*n.* this era. It comprises the Cambrian, Ordovician and Silurian periods (Lower Palaeozoic) and the Devonian, Carboniferous, and Permian periods (Upper Palaeozoic). The Palaeozoic era includes the evolution of multicellular life forms in the sea; the invasion of land by plants and animals; and the evolution of fish, amphibians, and early reptiles. The continents were very different from the present ones but, towards the end of the era, all were joined together as a single world continent called ◊Pangaea. [from Greek *zōē* = life, *zōos* = living]

palais /'pæleɪ/ *n.* a public hall for dancing. —**palais glide**, a type of ballroom dance in which large groups dance simultaneously. [French *palais* (*de danse*) = public hall (for dancing)]

Palamedes /pælə'miːdiːz/ Greek mythological hero and inventor of writing. He exposed ◊Odysseus' pretence of madness before the Greek expedition sailed to ◊Troy. In revenge he was falsely denounced as a traitor by Odysseus, and stoned to death by the Greek army. [= 'Contriver']

Palance /'pæləns/ Jack. Stage name of Walter Jack Palahnuik 1920–. US film actor, often cast as a villain. His films include *Shane* 1953 and *Batman* 1989.

palanquin /pælən'kiːn/ *n.* or **palankeen** an eastern covered litter for one person. [from Portuguese]

palatable /'pælətəbəl/ *adj.* pleasant to the taste; agreeable to the mind.

palatal *adj.* of the palate; (of a sound) made by placing the tongue against the palate. —*n.* a palatal sound. —**palatally** *adv.* [French]

palate /'pælət/ *n.* 1. the structure forming the upper part of the mouth cavity in vertebrates. 2. the sense of taste. 3. mental taste, liking. [from Latin *palatum*]

palatial /pə'leɪʃəl/ *adj.* like a palace, spacious, splendid. —**palatially** *adv.* [from Latin]

palatinate /pə'lætɪneɪt/ *n.* a territory under a count palatine. —**Palatinate**, (German *Pfalz*) a historic division of Germany, dating from before the 8th century, ruled by a count palatine.

palatine /'pælətaɪn/ *adj.* possessing royal privileges, having jurisdiction (within a territory) such as elsewhere belongs only to the sovereign. [from French from Latin *Palatium*, house of Augustus at Rome]

Palau /pə'laʊ/ former name (until 1981) of the Republic of ◊Belau.

palaver /pə'lɑːvə(r)/ *n.* 1. fuss; profuse or idle talk. 2. (*slang*) an affair, a business. 3. (especially *historical*) a parley between African or other natives and traders etc. —*v.t./i.* to talk profusely; to wheedle. [from Portuguese *palavra* = word, from Latin]

pale[1] *adj.* 1. (of a person or complexion) having little colour, lighter than normal. 2. (of colour or light) faint, not bright or vivid; only faintly coloured. —*v.t./i.* 1. to make or become pale. 2. to become feeble in comparison. —**paleface** *n.* a supposed North American Indian name for a white man. —**palely** *adv.*, **paleness** *n.* [from Old French from Latin *pallidus*]

pale[2] *n.* 1. a stake used in a fence etc.; a boundary. 2. (*historical*) a district or territory within determined bounds or subject to a particular jurisdiction. 3. in heraldry, a vertical stripe in the middle of a field. —**beyond the pale**, outside the bounds of civilized behaviour etc. [from Old French from Latin *palus* = stake]

Palermo /pə'leəməʊ/ capital and seaport of Sicily; population (1988) 729,000. Industries include shipbuilding, steel, glass, and chemicals. It was founded by the Phoenicians in the 8th century BC.

Palestine /'pælɪstaɪn/ (also called the **Holy Land** because of its links with Judaism, Christianity, and Islam) area between the Mediterranean and the river Jordan, with Lebanon to the N and Sinai to the S. It was in ancient times dominated in turn by Egypt, Assyria, Babylonia, Persia, Macedonia, the Ptolemies, the Seleucids, and the Roman and Byzantine empires. Today it forms part of Israel. The Palestinian people (about 500,000 in the West Bank, E Jerusalem, and the Gaza Strip; 1.2 million in Jordan; 1.2 million in Israel; 300,000 in Lebanon; and 100,000 in the USA) are descendants of the people of ◊Canaan. [from Latin *Palaestina* (name of Roman province), from *Philistia*, land of the Philistines]

Palestine Liberation Organization (PLO) an Arab organization founded in 1964 to bring about an independent state of Palestine. It consists of several distinct groupings, the chief of which is al-◊Fatah, led by Yasser ◊Arafat, the president of the PLO since 1969. To achieve its ends it has pursued diplomatic initiatives, but also operates as a guerrilla army. In 1988, the Palestine National Council voted to create a state of Palestine, but at the same time endorsed United Nations resolution 242, recognizing Israel's right to exist.

Palestrina /pæli'striːnə/ Giovanni Pierluigi da 1525–1594. Italian composer of secular and sacred choral music. Apart from motets and madrigals, he also wrote 105 masses, including *Missa Papae Marcelli*.

palette /'pælət/ *n.* an artist's thin wooden slab etc. used for laying and mixing colours on. —**palette knife**, a thin steel blade with a handle for mixing colours or applying paint; a kitchen knife with a long, blunt, round-ended, flexible blade. [French, diminutive of *pale* = shovel from Latin]

palfrey /'pɒlfrɪ/ *n.* (*archaic*) a horse for ordinary riding, especially for ladies. [from Old French from Latin *paraveredus* (Greek *para* = beside, extra and Latin *veredus* = light horse)]

Pali /'pɑːli/ *n.* an ancient Indo-European language of N India, related to Sanskrit, and a classical language of Buddhism. [from Sanskrit *pālī-bhāsā* (*pālī* = canon and *bhāsā* = language)]

palimpsest /'pælɪmpsest/ *n.* a writing material or manuscript on which the original writing has been effaced to make room for other writing; a monumental brass turned and re-engraved on the reverse side. [from Latin from Greek *palin* = again and *psaō* = rub smooth]

palindrome /'pælɪndrəʊm/ *n.* a word or verse etc. that reads the same backwards as forwards (e.g. *rotator*, *nurses run*). —**palindromic** /-'drɒmɪk/ *adj.* [from Latin *palindromos* (*palin* = back again and *drom-* = run)]

paling /'peɪlɪŋ/ *n.* 1. a fence of pales. 2. a pale.

palisade /pæli'seɪd/ *n.* 1. a fence of pales or of iron railings. 2. a strong pointed wooden stake. —*v.t.* to enclose or furnish with a palisade. [from French from Provençal from Latin *palus* = stake]

palisade cell a cylindrical cell lying immediately beneath the upper epidermis of a leaf. Palisade cells normally exist as one closely packed row and contain many ◊chloroplasts. During the hours of daylight palisade cells are photosynthetic, using the energy of the Sun to create carbohydrates from water and carbon dioxide.

Palk Strait /pɔːlk/ a channel separating SE India from the island of Sri Lanka. It is 53 km/33 mi at its widest point.

pall[1] /pɔl/ *n.* 1. a cloth spread over a coffin, hearse, or tomb. 2. a woollen shoulder band with front and back pendants, worn by the pope and some metropolitans and archbishops. 3. something forming a dark heavy covering. [Old English from Latin *pallium* = cloak]

pall[2] *v.t./i.* to become uninteresting; to satiate, to cloy. —**pall on**, to cease to interest or attract. [from Old French *apalir* = grow pale]

Palladio /pə'lɑːdɪəʊ/ Andrea 1518–1580. Italian architect. His country houses (for example, Malcontenta, and the Villa Rotonda near Vicenza) were designed from 1540 for patrician families of the Venetian Republic. His style, which became known as **Palladian**, influenced Neo-Classical architecture, such as Washington's home at Mount Vernon, USA, the palace of Tsraskoe Selo in Russia, and Prior Park, England.

palladium /pə'leɪdɪəm/ *n.* a lightweight, ductile and malleable, silver-white, metallic element, symbol Pd, atomic number 46, relative atomic mass 106.4. It is one of the so-called platinum group of metals, and is resistant to tarnish and corrosion. It often occurs in nature as a free metal in a natural alloy with platinum. First isolated in 1803, palladium is used as a catalyst, in alloys of gold (to make white gold) and silver, in electroplating, and in dentistry. [from *Pallas*, an asteroid discovered just previously]

Pallas /'pæləs/ a title of the goddess ◊Athena in Greek mythology and religion.

pallbearer *n.* a person helping to carry the coffin at a funeral.

pallet[1] /'pælɪt/ *n.* a straw mattress; a mean or makeshift bed. [from Anglo-French from Latin *palea* = straw]

pallet[2] *n.* a portable platform for transporting and storing loads. [from French, diminutive of *pale* = shovel from Latin]

palliasse /'pæliæs/ *n.* a straw mattress. [from French *paillasse* from Italian from Latin]

palliate /'pælieɪt/ *v.t.* 1. to alleviate (a disease) without curing. 2. to excuse, to extenuate. —**palliative** *adj. & n.*, **palliation** /-'eɪʃən/ *n.* [from Latin *palliare* = to cloak]

pallid /'pælɪd/ *adj.* pale, especially from illness. [from Latin *pallidus*]

pallor /'pælə/ *n.* pallidness, paleness. [Latin *pallēre* = be pale]

pally *adj.* (*colloquial*) friendly. —**palliness** *n.*

palm[1] /pɑ:m/ *n.* 1. a chiefly tropical tree of the family Palmae, characterized by a single tall stem bearing a thick cluster of large palmate or pinnate leaves at the top. Some, such as the coconut, date, sago, and oil palms, are important economically. 2. a leaf of this as the symbol of victory. 3. supreme excellence; the prize for this. —**palm oil**, the oil from various palms. [Old English from Latin *palma*]

palm[2] *n.* the inner surface of the hand between the wrist and the fingers; the part of a glove that covers this. —*v.t.* to conceal in the hand. —**palm off**, to impose or thrust fraudulently *on* a person; to put (a person) off *with*. —**palmar** /'pɑ:mə/ *adj.* [from Old French from Latin *palma*]

Palma /'pælmə/ (Spanish *Palma de Mallorca*) industrial port (textiles, cement, paper, pottery), resort, and capital of the Balearic Islands, Spain, on Majorca; population (1986) 321,000. Palma was founded in 276 BC as a Roman colony.

Palmas, Las /'pælməs/ port in the Canary Islands; see ◊Las Palmas.

palmate /'pælmeɪt/ *adj.* shaped like the palm of the hand, having lobes etc. like spread fingers. —**palmately** *adv.* [from Latin]

Palme /'pɑ:lmə/ (Sven) Olof 1927–1986. Swedish social-democratic politician, prime minister 1969–76 and 1982–86. He entered government in 1963, holding several posts before becoming leader of the Social Democratic Labour Party (SAP) in 1969. He was assassinated in Feb 1986.

Palmer Arnold (Daniel) 1929– . US golfer, who helped to popularize the professional sport in the USA in the 1950s and 1960s. He won the Masters in 1958, 1960, 1962, and 1964; the US Open in 1960; and the British Open in 1961 and 1962.

Palmer Geoffrey Winston Russell 1942– . New Zealand Labour politician, prime minister 1989–90, deputy prime minister and attorney-general 1984–89.

Palmer Samuel 1805–1881. English landscape painter and etcher. He lived 1826–35 in Shoreham, Kent, with a group of artists who were all followers of William Blake and called themselves 'the Ancients'. Palmer's expressive landscape style during that period reflected a strongly spiritual inspiration.

Palmerston /'pɑ:məstən/ Henry John Temple, 3rd Viscount Palmerston 1784–1865. British politician. Initially a Tory, in Parliament from 1807, he was secretary-at-war 1809–28. He broke with the Tories in 1830 and sat in the Whig cabinets of 1830–34, 1835–41, and 1846–51 as foreign secretary. He was prime minister 1855–58 (when he rectified Aberdeen's mismanagement of the Crimean War, suppressed the Indian Mutiny, and carried through the Second Opium War) and 1859–65 (when he almost involved Britain in the American Civil War on the side of the South).

Die, my dear Doctor, that's the last thing I shall do!
Lord Palmerston
(last words)

---

palmetto /pæl'metəʊ/ *n.* (*plural* **palmettos**) a palm tree, especially of small size. [from Spanish *palmito*]

palmistry /'pɑ:mɪstrɪ/ *n.* the pseudo-science of divination by the lines and swellings of the hand. —**palmist** *n.*

Palm Sunday in the Christian calendar, the Sunday before Easter and first day of Holy Week, commemorating Jesus' entry into Jerusalem, when the crowd strewed palm leaves in his path.

palmy /'pɑ:mɪ/ *adj.* 1. of, like, or abounding in palms. 2. full of success, flourishing.

Palmyra /pæl'maɪrə/ ancient city and oasis in the desert of Syria, about 240 km/150 mi NE of Damascus. Palmyra, the biblical **Tadmor**, was flourishing by about 300 BC. It was destroyed in AD 272 after Queen Zenobia had led a revolt against the Romans. Extensive temple ruins exist, and on the site is a village called Tadmor.

Palo Alto /'pæləʊ 'æltəʊ/ city in California, USA, situated SE of San Francisco at the centre of the high-tech region known as 'Silicon Valley'; site of Stanford University.

Palomar, Mount /'pæləmɑ:/ the location, since 1948, of an observatory, 80 km/50 mi NE of San Diego, California, USA. It has a 5 m/200 in diameter reflecting telescope called the Hale.

palomino /pælə'mi:nəʊ/ *n.* (*plural* **palominos**) a golden or cream-coloured horse with a light-coloured mane and tail. [from Spanish = young pigeon]

palp *n.* a segmented organ at or near the mouth of certain insects and crustaceans, used for feeling and tasting things. [from Latin *palpare* = touch gently]

palpable /'pælpəbəl/ *adj.* that can be touched or felt; readily perceived by the senses or mind. —**palpability** /-'bɪlɪtɪ/ *n.*, **palpably** *adv.*

palpate /pæl'peɪt/ *v.t.* to examine (especially medically) by touch. —**palpation** /-'peɪʃən/ *n.*

palpitate /'pælpɪteɪt/ *v.i.* to pulsate, to throb; to tremble (with pleasure, fear etc.). [from Latin *palpitare*, frequentative of *palpare* = touch gently]

palpitation /pælpɪ'teɪʃən/ *n.* throbbing, trembling; increased activity of the heart due to exertion, agitation, or disease.

palsy /'pɔlzɪ/ *n.* paralysis, especially with involuntary tremors; a cause or state of powerlessness. —*v.t.* to affect with palsy. [from Old French from Latin]

paltry /'pɔltrɪ/ *adj.* worthless, contemptible, trivial. —**paltriness** *n.* [from dialect *palt* = rubbish]

palynology /pæli'nɒlədʒɪ/ *n.* the study of pollen in connection with plant geography, the dating of fossils, allergies etc. —**palynological** /-ə'lɒdʒɪkəl/ *adj.* [from Greek *palunō* = sprinkle]

Pamirs /pə'mɪəz/ central Asian plateau mainly in the USSR, but extending into China and Afghanistan, traversed by mountain ranges. Its highest peak is Mount Communism (Kommunizma Pik, 7,495 m/24,600 ft) in the Akademiya Nauk range, the highest mountain in the USSR.

pampas /'pæmpəs/ *n.pl.* the large treeless plains in South America lying between the Andes and the Atlantic and rising gradually from the coast to the lower slopes of the mountains. The eastern pampas contain large cattle ranches and the flax-and grain-growing area of Argentina; the western pampas are arid and unproductive. —**pampas grass**, a type of large grass, genus *Cortaderia*, originally from South America. It is grown as an ornamental grass in gardens. [Spanish from Quechua]

pamper *v.t.* to overindulge (a person, taste etc.); to spoil (a person) with luxury. [from obsolete *pamp* = cram]

pamphlet /'pæmflɪt/ *n.* a small, usually unbound booklet or leaflet containing information or a treatise. [from *Pamphilet* = pet name of *Pamphilus*, a 12th-century amatory poem]

pamphleteer /pæmfli'tɪə/ *n.* a writer of (especially political) pamphlets.

Pamyat /'pæmjæt/ *n.* a nationalist Russian popular movement. Founded in 1979 as a cultural and historical group attached to the Soviet Ministry of Aviation Industry, it grew from the mid-1980s, propounding a violently conservative and anti-Semitic Russian nationalist message. [Russian = memory]

pan[1] *n.* 1. a metal, earthenware, or plastic vessel used for cooking and other domestic purposes; a panlike vessel in which substances are heated etc. 2. the bowl of a pair of scales; the bowl of a lavatory. 3. the part of the lock that held the priming in obsolete types of gun. 4. a hollow in the ground. —*v.t.* (**-nn-**) to criticize severely. —**pan out,** (of gravel) to yield gold; (of an action etc.) to turn out (well etc.); to be successful. —**panful** *n.* [Old English]

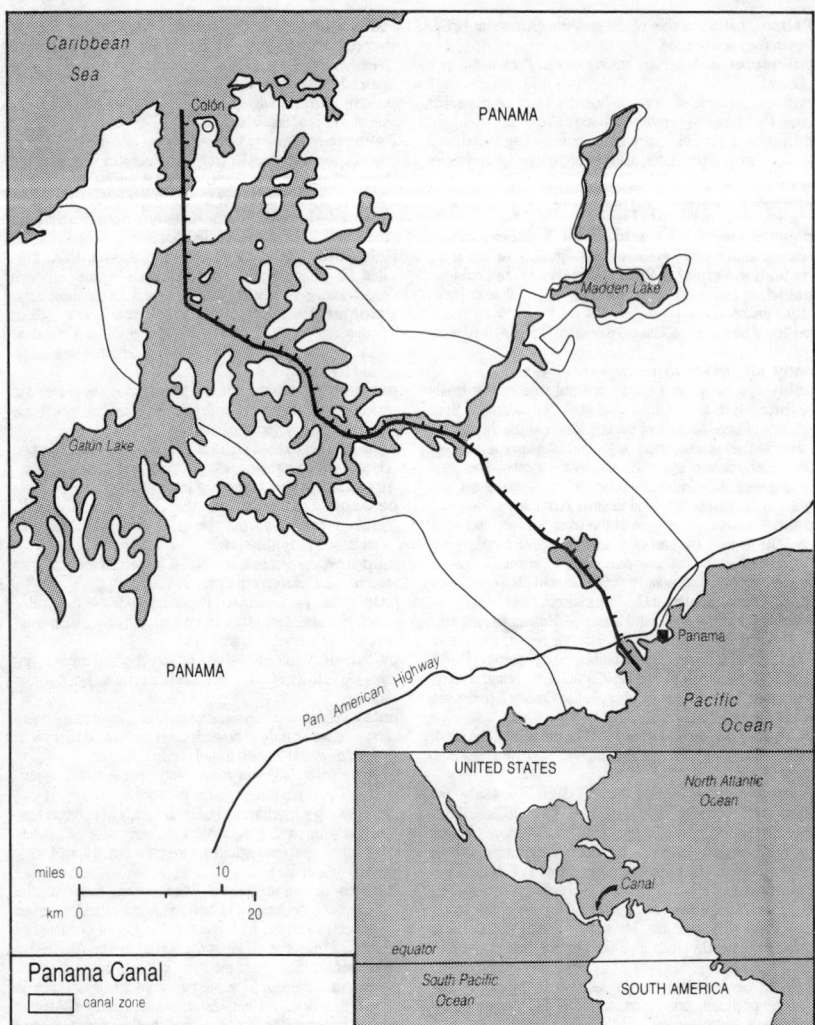

Caribbean
Sea

Colón

PANAMA

Madden Lake

Gatun Lake

PANAMA

Pan American Highway

Panama

Pacific
Ocean

miles 0   10

km 0   20

UNITED STATES

North Atlantic
Ocean

equator

Canal

South Pacific
Ocean

SOUTH AMERICA

Panama Canal

▢ canal zone

Panama Canal

pan² *v.t./i.* (**-nn-**) to swing (a cine camera) horizontally to
give a panoramic effect or follow a moving object; (of a
camera) to be moved thus. —*n.* a panning movement.

pan- in combinations, all, relating to the whole of a continent, racial group, religion etc. (e.g. *pan-American*).
[Greek *pan* = neuter of *pas* = all]

Pan in Greek mythology, a god (Roman Sylvanus) of flocks
and herds, shown as a man with the horns, ears, and hoofed
legs of a goat, and playing a shepherd's pipe.

panacea /pænə'siə/ *n.* any supposed remedy for all
known disease; a cure-all. [Latin from Greek *akos* =
remedy]

panache /pə'næʃ/ *n.* an assertively or flamboyantly confident style or manner. [French = plume]

Pan-Africanist Congress /pæn'æfrɪkənɪst/ (PAC) a
militant black South African nationalist group, which broke
away from the African National Congress (ANC) in 1959.
More radical than the ANC, the Pan-Africanist Congress
has a black-only policy for Africa. Since the 1970s, it has
been weakened by internal dissent.

panama /'pænəmɑː/ *n.* a hat of strawlike material made
from the leaves of a pine tree.

Panama /pænə'mɑː/ Republic of; country in Central
America, on a narrow isthmus between the Caribbean and
the Pacific Ocean, bounded to the W by Costa Rica and
to the E by Colombia; **area** 77,100 sq km/29,768 sq mi;

capital Panama City; **physical** mountain ranges; tropical
rainforest; Pearl Islands in Gulf of Panama; **head of state
and government** Guillermo Endara from 1989; **political
system** emergent democratic republic; **exports** bananas,
petroleum products, copper, shrimps, sugar; **population**
(1990 est) 2,423,000; **language** Spanish (official), English;
recent history independence from Spain was achieved in
1821; Panama joined with Colombia until 1903 when full
independence was gained. USA–Panama treaties transferred the Panama Canal to Panama in 1977. Gen Noriega,
effective ruler of the country from 1983, was charged with
drug smuggling by the USA in 1988. In 1989 he declared
the opposition's electoral victory invalid and was himself
declared 'maximum leader' by the assembly. A state of war
with the USA was announced; the US invasion in 1989
deposed Noriega and installed Guillermo Endara.

Panama Canal canal across the Panama isthmus in Central America, connecting the Pacific and Atlantic oceans;
length 80 km/50 mi, with 12 locks. Built by the USA
1904–14 after an unsuccessful attempt by the French, it
was formally opened in 1920. The **Panama Canal Zone**
was acquired 'in perpetuity' by the USA in 1903, comprising
land extending about 5 km/3 mi on either side of the canal.
The zone passed to Panama in 1979, and control of the canal
itself was ceded to Panama by the USA in Jan 1990 under
the terms of the Panama Canal Treaty of 1977.

Panama City capital of the Republic of Panama, near the Pacific end of the Panama Canal; population (1980) 386,000. Products include chemicals, plastics, and clothing. An earlier Panama, to the NE, founded in 1519, was destroyed in 1671, and the city was founded on the present site in 1673.

Pan-American Union /pænə'merɪkən/ the former name 1910–48 of the ◊Organization of American States.

panatella /pænə'telə/ n. a long thin cigar. [from Spanish = long thin biscuit]

pancake n. 1. a thin, flat batter cake usually fried in a pan. 2. a flat cake (e.g. of make-up). —**Pancake Day,** Shrove Tuesday (on which pancakes are traditionally eaten). **pancake landing,** a heavy landing of an aircraft descending too steeply in a level horizontal position.

Panchen Lama /'pɑːntʃən 'lɑːmə/ 10th incarnation 1935–1989. Tibetan spiritual leader, second in importance to the ◊Dalai Lama. A protégé of the Chinese since childhood, he is not indisputably·recognized. When the Dalai Lama left Tibet in 1959, the Panchen Lama was deputed by the Chinese to take over, but was stripped of power in 1964 for refusing to denounce the Dalai Lama. He did not appear again in public until 1978.

panchromatic /pænkrə'mætɪk/ adj. in photography, sensitive to all visible colours of the spectrum. Panchromatic film is a highly sensitive black-and-white film made to render all visible spectral colours in correct grey tones. It is always developed in total darkness.

pancreas /'pæŋkriəs/ n. in vertebrates, an accessory gland of the digestive system located close to the duodenum. When stimulated by ◊secretin, it secretes enzymes into the duodenum that digest starches, proteins, and fats. It also secretes the hormones insulin and glucagon that regulate the blood sugar level. —**pancreatic** /-'ætɪk/ adj. [from Greek kreas = flesh]

panda /'pændə/ n. a mammal of NW China and Tibet. The **giant panda** Ailuropoda melanoleuca, native to limited mountainous forested areas in China, has black and white fur with black eye patches, and feeds solely on bamboo shoots. It can grow up to 1.5 m/4.5 ft long, and weigh up to 140 kg/300 lbs. The **lesser panda** Ailurus fulgens, 50 cm/1.5 ft long, is black and chestnut, with a long tail. Destruction of pandas' natural habitats have made their extinction possible in the wild. —**panda car,** a police patrol car (originally white with black stripes on the doors). [Nepáli name]

pandemic /pæn'demɪk/ adj. (of a disease) prevalent over a whole region or the world. [from Greek dēmos = people]

pandemonium /pændi'məuniəm/ n. uproar, utter confusion; a scene of this. [name of capital of hell in Milton's Paradise Lost, from pan- and demon]

pander v.i. (with to) to gratify or indulge a person or weakness etc. —n. 1. a go-between in illicit love affairs; a procurer. 2. one who panders. [from Pandarus, name of Cressida's uncle in the medieval legend of Troilus and Cressida, who acted as go-between for the lovers]

P. & O. abbreviation of Peninsular and Oriental Steamship Company.

Pandora /pæn'dɔːrə/ in Greek mythology, the first mortal woman. Zeus sent her to Earth with a box of evils (to counteract the blessings brought to mortals by ◊Prometheus's gift of fire); she opened it, and they all flew out. Only hope was left inside as a consolation.

p. & p. abbreviation of postage and packing.

pane n. a single sheet of glass in a window or door. [from Old French pan from Latin pannus = piece of cloth]

panegyric /pæni'dʒɪrɪk/ n. a laudatory discourse, a eulogy. —**panegyrical** adj. [from French from Latin from Greek agora = assembly]

panel /'pænəl/ n. 1. a distinct, usually rectangular section of a surface (e.g. of a wall, door, vehicle). 2. a strip of material as part of a garment. 3. a team in a broadcast or public quiz programme etc.; a body of experts assembled for discussion or consultation. 4. a list of jurors, a jury. —v.t. (-ll-) to cover or decorate with panels. —**panel game,** a quiz etc. played by a panel. **panel saw,** a saw with small teeth for cutting thin wood for panels. [from Old French = piece of cloth]

panelling n. panelled work; wood for making panels.

panellist n. a member of a panel.

pang n. a sudden sharp pain or painful emotion. [variant of earlier pronge, compare Middle Low German prange = pinching]

Pangaea /pæn'dʒiːə/ or **Pangea** a world continent, named by Alfred ◊Wegener, that may have existed between 250 and 200 million years ago, made up of all the continental masses. It may be regarded as a combination of ◊Laurasia in the north and ◊Gondwanaland in the south, the rest of the Earth being covered by the ◊Panthalassa ocean.

pangolin /pæŋ'gəulɪn/ n. or **scaly anteater** an African and Asian toothless long-tailed mammal, order Pholidota, up to 1 m/3 ft long. The upper part of the body is covered with horny plates for defence. It is nocturnal and eats ants and termites. [from Malay = roller (because it rolls itself up)]

panic n. a sudden uncontrollable fear or alarm; infectious fright. —adj. of, connected with, or resulting from panic. —v.t./i. (-ck-) to affect or be affected with panic. —**panic-stricken** or **panic-struck** adj. affected with panic. —**panicky** adj. [from French from Greek]

panicle /'pænɪkəl/ n. a loose branching cluster of flowers. [from Latin paniculum, diminutive of panus = thread]

panjandrum /pæn'dʒændrəm/ n. a mock title of an exalted personage. [invented by S Foote in nonsense verse, 1755]

Panjshir Valley /'pʌndʒɪə(r)/ the valley of the river Panjshir, which rises in the Panjshir range to the N of Kabul, E Afghanistan. It was the chief centre of ◊Mujaheddin rebel resistance against the Soviet-backed Najibullah government in the 1980s.

Pankhurst /'pæŋkhɜːst/ Emmeline (born Goulden) 1858–1928. English suffragette. She founded the Women's Social and Political Union in 1903, and launched the militant suffragette campaign in 1905. In 1926 she joined the Conservative Party and was a prospective Parliamentary candidate. She was supported by her daughters **Christabel Pankhurst** (1880–1958) and **Sylvia Pankhurst** (1882–1960).

Women had always fought for men, and for their children. Now they were ready to fight for their own human rights. Our militant movement was established.

Emmeline Pankhurst
My Own Story

pannier /'pæniə/ n. 1. a basket, especially one of a pair carried by a beast of burden or on a bicycle, motor cycle etc. 2. (historical) a part of a skirt looped up round the hips; a frame supporting this. [from Old French from Latin panarium = breadbasket (panis = bread)]

panoply /'pænəplɪ/ n. 1. a complete suit of armour. 2. a complete or splendid array. [from French from Greek hopla = arms]

panorama /pænə'rɑːmə/ n. 1. a view of a wide area; a picture or photograph of this. 2. a view of a constantly changing scene or series of events etc. —**panoramic** /-'ræmɪk/ adj. [from Greek horama = view (horaō = see)]

pan pipe (in singular or plural) a musical instrument formed from three or more tubes of different lengths joined in a row (or, in some areas, a block of wood with tubes drilled down into it) with mouthpieces in line, and sounded by blowing across the top. [from Pan, Greek god]

pansy /'pænzɪ/ n. 1. a cultivated violet derived from the European wild pansy Viola tricolor, and including many different varieties and strains. The flowers are usually purple, yellow, cream, or a mixture, and there are many highly developed varieties bred for size, colour, or special markings. 2. (colloquial) an effeminate man; a male homosexual. [from French pensée = thought, pansy (penser = think from Latin pensare, frequentative of pendere = weigh)]

pant v.t./i. to breathe with short quick breaths; to utter breathlessly; to yearn; (of the heart etc.) to throb violently. —n. a panting breath; a throb. [from Old French pantaisier, ultimately from Greek]

pantaloons /pæntə'luːnz/ n.pl. (especially US) trousers. [from French from Italian]

Pantanal /pæntə'nɑːl/ large area of swamp land in the Mato Grosso of SW Brazil, occupying 220,000 sq km/ 84,975 sq mi in the upper reaches of the Paraguay river;

one of the world's great wildlife refuges; 1,370 sq km/ 530 sq mi were designated as a national park in 1981.

pantechnicon /pæn'teknɪkən/ n. a large van for transporting furniture etc. [short for pantechnicon van (*pantechnicon* = furniture warehouse, originally a bazaar)]

Panthalassa /pænθə'læsə/ an ocean that may have covered the surface of the Earth not occupied by the world continent ◊Pangaea between 250 and 200 million years ago.

pantheism /'pænθiɪzəm/ n. the doctrine that regards all of reality as divine, and God as present in all of nature and the universe. It is expressed in Egyptian religion and Brahmanism; Stoicism, Neo-Platonism, Judaism, Christianity, and Islam can be interpreted in pantheistic terms. Pantheistic philosophers include Bruno, Spinoza, Fichte, Schelling, and Hegel. —**pantheist** n., **pantheistic** /-'ɪstɪk/ adj. [from Greek *theos* = God]

pantheon /'pænθɪən/ n. 1. a temple dedicated to all the gods, such as that in ancient Rome, rebuilt by ◊Hadrian and still used as a church. 2. the deities of a people collectively. 3. **Pantheon**, a building in which the illustrious dead are buried or have memorials, e.g. the Panthéon in Paris. [from Latin from Greek *theios* = divine]

panther /'pænθə/ n. another name for a ◊leopard. [from Old French from Latin from Greek]

panties /'pæntɪz/ n.pl. (*colloquial*) short-legged or legless knickers worn by women and girls. [diminutive of *pants*]

pantihose /'pæntɪhəʊz/ n. women's tights.

pantile /'pæntaɪl/ n. a curved roof tile.

panto /'pæntəʊ/ n. (*colloquial*) a ◊pantomime. [abbreviation]

pantograph /'pæntəɡrɑːf/ n. 1. an instrument with jointed rods for enlarging or reducing a plan etc. 2. a jointed framework conveying current to an electric vehicle from overhead wires. [from *panto-* = all and *graphō* = write]

pantomime /'pæntəmaɪm/ n. 1. in the British theatre, a traditional Christmas entertainment with its origins in the harlequin spectacle of the 18th century and burlesque of the 19th century, which gave rise to the tradition of the principal boy being played by an actress and the dame by an actor. The harlequin's role diminished altogether as themes developed on folktales such as *The Sleeping Beauty* and *Cinderella*, and with the introduction of additional material such as popular songs, topical comedy, and audience participation. 2. gestures and facial expression used to convey meaning. —**pantomimic** /-'mɪmɪk/ adj. [French or from Latin from Greek *panto-* = all and *mimos*]

pantothenic acid $C_9H_{17}NO_5$, one of the water-soluble 'B' ◊vitamins, occurring widely throughout a normal diet. There is no specific deficiency disease associated with pantothenic acid but it is known to be involved in the breakdown of fats and carbohydrates.

pantry /'pæntrɪ/ n. 1. a room or cupboard in which crockery, cutlery, table linen etc. are kept. 2. a larder. [from Old French *panetier* = baker from Latin *panis* = bread]

pants n.pl. 1. (*colloquial*) underpants, panties. 2. (*US*) trousers. [abbreviation of *pantaloons*]

Panufnik /pə'nuːfnɪk/ Andrzej 1914–. Polish composer and conductor. He studied under Austrian composer Felix Weingartner (1863–1942), and came to Britain in 1954. His music is based on an intense working out of small motifs.

panzer n. a German mechanized division or regiment in World War II, used in connection with armoured vehicles, mainly tanks.

Paolozzi /paʊ'lɒtsi/ Eduardo 1924–. British sculptor, a major force in the ◊pop art movement in London in the mid-1950s. He typically uses bronze casts of pieces of machinery to create robotlike structures.

pap[1] n. 1. soft or semiliquid food for infants or invalids. 2. undemanding reading matter. [probably from Middle Low German or Middle Dutch from Latin *pappare* = eat]

pap[2] n. (*archaic* or *dialect*) a nipple of the breast. [from Scandinavian, imitative of sucking]

papa /pə'pɑː/ n. (*archaic*; especially as child's word) father. [French from Latin from Greek *pap(p)as*]

papacy /'peɪpəsɪ/ n. 1. the office or tenure of the pope or bishop of Rome, as head of the Roman Catholic Church. 2. the papal system. [from Latin *papatia* (*papa* = pope)]

papal /'peɪpəl/ adj. of the pope or his office. —**papally** adv. [from Old French from Latin]

papal infallibility the doctrine formulated by the Roman Catholic Vatican Council in 1870, which stated that the pope, when speaking officially on certain doctrinal or moral matters, was protected from error by God, and therefore such rulings could not be challenged.

Papal States an area of central Italy in which the pope was temporal ruler from 756 to the time of the country's unification in 1870.

Papandreou /pæpæn'dreɪuː/ Andreas 1919– . Greek socialist politician, founder of the Pan-Hellenic Socialist Movement (PASOK), and prime minister 1981–89, when he became implicated in the alleged embezzlement and diversion of funds to the Greek government of $200 million from the Bank of Crete, headed by George Koskotas, and lost the election.

papaw /pə'pɔː, 'pɔːpɔː/ n. or **pawpaw** 1. an oblong orange fruit with a thick fleshy rind, and numerous black seeds embedded in this pulp, used as food. 2. the palmlike tropical American tree *Carica papaya* bearing this. 3. (*US*) a North American tree *Asimina triloba* bearing purple flowers and an oblong edible fruit. [earlier *papay(a)* from Spanish and Portuguese]

papaya another name for papaw.

Papeete /pɑː'piːeɪtɪ/ capital and port of French Polynesia on the NW coast of Tahiti; population (1983) 79,000. Products include vanilla, copra, and mother-of-pearl.

Papen /'pɑːpən/ Franz von 1879–1969. German rightwing politician. As chancellor in 1932, he negotiated the Nazi-Conservative alliance that made Hitler chancellor in 1933. He was envoy to Austria 1934–38 and ambassador to Turkey 1939–44. Although acquitted at the ◊Nuremberg trials, he was imprisoned by a German denazification court for three years.

paper /'peɪpə/ n. 1. a substance in thin sheets made from pulp of wood or other fibrous material, used for writing or drawing or printing on, as a wrapping material etc. The invention of true paper, originally made of pulped fishing nets and rags, is credited to Tsai Lun, Chinese minister of agriculture, in AD 105. 2. a document; documents attesting identity or credentials; the documents belonging to a person or relating to a matter. 3. a newspaper. 4. wallpaper. 5. a piece of paper, especially as a wrapper etc. 6. a set of questions to be answered at one session in an examination; the written answers to these. 7. an essay or dissertation, especially one read to a learned society. —adj. made of or flimsy like paper; existing only in theory. —v.t. to decorate (a wall etc.) with paper. —**on paper**, in writing; in theory; to judge from written or printed evidence. **paperboy**, **papergirl** ns. one who delivers or sells newspapers. **paperclip** n. a clip of bent wire or of plastic for holding a few sheets of paper together. **paperknife** n. a blunt knife for opening letters etc. **paper money**, money in the form of banknotes. **paper tiger**, a threatening but ineffectual person or thing. [from Anglo-French from Latin = papyrus]

paperback adj. bound in stiff paper, not boards. —n. a paperback book.

paper sizes standard European sizes for paper, designated by a letter (A, B, or C) and a number (0–6). The letter indicates the size of the basic sheet at manufacture; the number is how many times it has been folded. A4 is obtained by folding an A3 sheet in half, which is half an A2 sheet, and so on.

paperweight n. a small, heavy object for keeping loose papers in place.

paperwork n. routine clerical or administrative work.

papery adj. like paper in thinness or texture.

papier mâché /pæpjeɪ'mæʃeɪ/ a craft technique that involves building up layer upon layer of pasted paper, which is then baked or left to harden. Used for trays, decorative objects, and even furniture, it is often painted, lacquered, or decorated with mother-of-pearl. [French = chewed paper]

papilla /pə'pɪlə/ n. (*plural* **papillae** /-liː/) a small nipplelike protuberance in or on the body. [Latin = nipple]

papillary /pə'pɪlərɪ/ adj. papilla-shaped.

papillon /'pæpɪjɔ̃/ n. a dog of a toy breed related to the spaniel, having a white coat with a few darker patches and erect ears resembling the shape of a butterfly's wings. [French = butterfly]

Papineau /pæpi'nəʊ/ Louis Joseph 1786–1871. Canadian politician. He led a mission to England to protest against the planned union of Lower Canada (Québec) and Upper Canada (Ontario), and demanded economic reform and an elected provincial legislature. In 1835 he gained the cooperation of William Lyon ◊Mackenzie in Upper Canada, and in 1837 organized an unsuccessful rebellion of the French against British rule in Lower Canada. He fled the country, but returned in 1847 to sit in the United Canadian legislature until 1854.

papist /'peɪpɪst/ n. an advocate of papal supremacy; (usually *derogatory*) a Roman Catholic. [from French from Latin *papa* = pope]

papoose /pə'puːs/ n. a North American Indian baby. [Algonquin]

Papp /pæp/ Joseph 1921– . US theatre director, and founder of the New York Shakespeare Festival in 1954, free to the public and held in an open-air theatre in Central Park. He also founded the New York Public Theatre in 1967, an off-Broadway forum for new talent.

paprika /'pæprɪkə/ n. a ripe red pepper; the red condiment made from it. [Magyar]

Papua New Guinea /'pɑːpuə nju:ˈgɪni/ country in the SW Pacific, comprising the eastern part of the island of New Guinea, the New Guinea islands, the Admiralty islands, and part of the Solomon islands; **area** 462,840 sq km/178,656 sq mi; **capital** Port Moresby (on E New Guinea); **physical** mountainous; includes islands of New Ireland, New Britain, and Bougainville; Admiralty Islands, D'Entrecasteaux Islands, and Louisiade Archipelago; **head of state** Elizabeth II represented by governor general; **head of government** Rabbie Namaliu from 1988; **political system** constitutional monarchy; **exports** copra, coconut oil, palm oil, tea, copper; **population** (1989 est) 3,613,000 (Papuans, Melanesians, Pygmies, (various minorities); **language** English (official); pidgin English, 715 local languages; **recent history** independence was achieved from Australia, within the Commonwealth, in 1975.

papyrology /pæpɪˈrɒlədʒɪ/ n. the study of ancient papyri. —**papyrologist** n.

papyrus /pə'paɪrəs/ n. (*plural* **papyri** /-riː/) 1. an aquatic plant *Cyperus papyrus* of the sedge family. 2. a type of paper made from the stem of this by the ancient Egyptians; a manuscript written on it. [from Latin from Greek]

par n. 1. an average or normal amount, degree, condition etc. 2. equality, an equal status or footing. 3. in golf, the number of strokes a scratch player should normally require for a hole or course. 4. the face value of stocks and shares etc. 5. (in full **par of exchange**) the recognized value of one country's currency in terms of another's. [Latin = equal]

para /'pærə/ n. (*colloquial*) a paratrooper. [abbreviation]

para. abbreviation of paragraph.

para-¹ /'pærə-/ prefix meaning 1. beside (e.g. *parabola*, *paramilitary*). 2. beyond (e.g. *paradox*, *paranormal*). [from Greek]

para-² in combinations, to protect, to ward off (e.g. *parachute*, *parasol*). [French from Italian *parare* = defend]

parable /'pærəbəl/ n. a narrative of imagined events used to illustrate a moral or spiritual lesson; an allegory. [from Old French from Latin *parabola* = comparison]

parabola /pə'ræbələ/ n. in mathematics, a curve formed by cutting a right circular cone with a plane parallel to the sloping side of the cone; one of the family of curves known as ◊conic sections (see under ◊conic). [from Greek *parabolē* = placing side by side]

parabolic /pærə'bɒlɪk/ adj. 1. of or expressed in a parable. 2. of or like a parabola. —**parabolically** adv. [from Latin from Greek]

Paracelsus /pærə'selsəs/ Adopted name of Theophrastus Bombastus von Hohenheim 1493–1541. Swiss physician, alchemist, and scientist. He developed the idea that minerals and chemicals might have medical uses (iatrochemistry). He introduced the use of ◊laudanum (which he named) for pain-killing purposes. Although Paracelsus was something of a charlatan, and his books contain much mystical nonsense, his rejection of the ancients and insistence on the value of experimentation make him a leading figure in early science.

paracentesis n. the evacuation of unwanted fluid from a body tissue or cavity by means of a drainage tube.

paracetamol /pærə'siːtəmɒl, -set-/ n. a compound forming a white powder, used to relieve pain and reduce fever; a tablet of this. It is as effective as aspirin in reducing

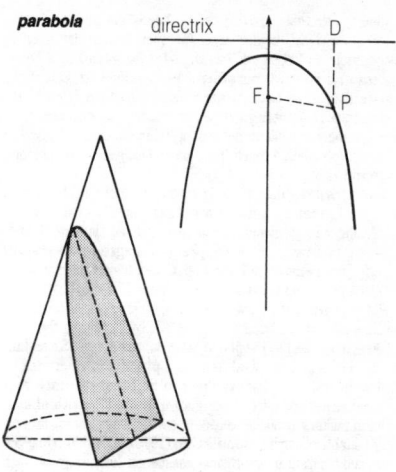

parabola

directrix   D

F   P

fever, and less irritating to the stomach, but has little anti-inflammatory action (as for joint pain). An overdose can cause severe, often irreversible, liver and kidney damage. [from its chemical name]

parachute /'pærəʃuːt/ n. an umbrella-shaped or rectangular apparatus of silk, nylon etc. strapped to a person or a package, used to slow down their descent from a high altitude, or for a missile to a safe speed for landing, or sometimes to aid (through braking) the landing of a plane or missile itself. Modern designs enable the parachutist to exercise considerable control of direction, as in ◊skydiving. (*attributive*) (to be) dropped by parachute. —*v.t./i.* to descend or convey by parachute. —**parachutist** n. [French, from Italian *parare* = defend and French *chute* = fall]

Paraclete /'pærəkliːt/ n. the Holy Spirit as an advocate or counsellor. [from Old French from Latin from Greek = called in aid (from *para¹* and *kaleō* = call)]

parade /pə'reɪd/ n. 1. a muster of troops for inspection. 2. a public procession. 3. an ostentatious display. 4. a public square or promenade. 5. a parade ground. —*v.t./i.* 1. to assemble for a parade. 2. to march through (streets etc.) in procession, to march ceremonially. 3. to display ostentatiously. —**parade ground**, a place for the muster of troops. [French = show, from Italian and Spanish from Latin *parare* = prepare]

paradigm /'pærədaɪm/ n. 1. an example or pattern, especially of the inflexions of a noun, verb etc. 2. all those factors, both scientific and sociological, that influence the research of the scientist. The term, first used by the US historian of science T S ◊Kuhn, has subsequently spread to social studies and politics. —**paradigmatic** /-dɪg'mætɪk/ adj. [from Latin from Greek *deiknumi* = show]

paradise /'pærədaɪs/ n. 1. the abode of God and of the righteous after death, heaven. 2. a region or state of supreme bliss. 3. in Genesis 2, 3, the garden of Eden. 4. in the Koran, a place of sensual pleasure. —**paradisiac** /-'daɪsɪæk/ adj., **paradisiacal** /-dɪ'saɪəkəl/ adj., **paradisal** adj. [from Old French, ultimately from Avestan *pairidaēza* = park]

Paradise Lost an epic poem by John Milton, first published in 1667. The poem describes the Fall of Man and the battle between God and Satan, as enacted through the story of Adam and Eve in the Garden of Eden. A sequel, *Paradise Regained*, was published in 1671.

paradox /'pærədɒks/ n. 1. a seemingly absurd though perhaps actually well-founded statement. 2. a self-contradictory or essentially absurd statement. 3. a person or thing conflicting with a preconceived notion of what is reasonable or possible. 4. paradoxical nature. —**paradoxical** /-'dɒksɪkəl/ adj., **paradoxically** adj. [from Latin from Greek *doxa* = opinion]

paraffin /'pærəfɪn/ n. the common name for ◊alkane, any member of the series of hydrocarbons with the general formula C_nH_{2n+2}. The lower members are gases, such as methane (marsh or natural gas). The middle ones (mainly liquid) form the basis of petrol, kerosene, and lubricating oils, while the higher ones (paraffin waxes) are used in ointment and cosmetic bases. —**liquid paraffin**, a tasteless mild laxative. **paraffin wax**, paraffin in a solid form. [German, from Latin *parum* = little and *affinis* = related]

paragon /'pærəgən/ n. a model of excellence, a supremely excellent person or thing; a model (*of* virtue etc.). [obsolete French from Italian *paragone* = touchstone from Greek]

paragraph /'pærəgrɑːf/ n. one or more sentences on a single theme, forming a distinct section of a piece of writing and beginning on a new (usually indented) line. —*v.t.* to arrange in paragraphs. —**paragraphic** /-'græfɪk/ *adj.* [from French or Latin from Greek *paragraphos* = short stroke marking break in sense (*graphō* = write)]

Paraguay /'pærəgwaɪ/ Republic of; landlocked country in South America, bounded to the NE by Brazil, to the S by Argentina, and to the NW by Bolivia; **area** 406,752 sq km/157,006 sq mi; **capital** Asunción; **physical** flat; divided by Paraguay River, Paraná River in S; **head of state and government** Andrés Rodriguez from 1989; **political system** military republic; **exports** cotton, soya beans, timber, vegetable oil, maté; **population** (1990 est) 4,660,000 (95% mixed Guaraní Indian-Spanish descent); **language** Spanish 6% (official); Guaraní 90%; **recent history** independence was achieved from Spain in 1811. Much territory was lost during the war with Argentina, Brazil, and Uruguay 1865–70; territory was won from Bolivia during the Chaco War 1932–35. Paraguay has experienced political instability under a series of different presidents since the late 1940s.

parakeet /'pærəkiːt/ n. any of various small, usually long-tailed species of ◊parrot. [from Old French, perhaps ultimately from diminutive of *Pierre* = Peter]

parallax /'pærəlæks/ n. the apparent difference in position or direction of an object caused by a change of the point of observation; the angular amount of this. In astronomy, nearby stars show a shift owing to parallax when viewed from different positions on the Earth's orbit around the Sun. A star's parallax is used to deduce its distance from the Earth. —**parallactic** /-'læktɪk/ *adj.* [from French from Greek *parallaxis* = change, alternation]

parallel /'pærəlel/ *adj.* 1. (of lines or planes) continuously equidistant; (of a line or plane) having this relation. 2. analogous, having features that correspond. —*n.* 1. a person or thing that is analogous to another. 2. a comparison. 3. (in full **parallel of latitude**) each of the imaginary parallel circles of constant latitude on the Earth's surface; a corresponding line on a map. 3. two parallel lines (‖) as a reference mark. —*v.t.* (*past tense* **paralleled**) 1. to be parallel to, to correspond to. 2. to represent as similar, to compare. 3. to adduce a parallel instance to. —**in parallel**, (of an electric circuit) arranged so as to join at common points at each end. **parallel bars**, a pair of parallel rails on posts for gymnastics. [from French from Latin from Greek = alongside each other (*para-* = beside and *allēlos* = one another)]

parallel circuit an electrical circuit in which the components are connected side by side. The current flowing in the circuit is shared by the components.

parallel computing or **parallel processing** an emerging computer technology that allows more than one computation at the same time. Currently, this means having a few computer processors working in parallel, but in future the number could run to thousands or millions.

parallelepiped /pærəle'lepɪped, -ə'paɪped/ n. a solid body of which each face is a parallelogram. [from Greek *epipedon* = plane surface (*pedon* = ground)]

parallelism n. being parallel; correspondence.

parallel lines and parallel planes in mathematics, straight lines or planes that always remain the same perpendicular distance from one another no matter how far they are extended. This is a principle of Euclidean geometry. Some non-Euclidean geometries, such as elliptical and hyperbolic geometry, however, reject Euclid's parallel axiom.

parallelogram /pærə'leləgræm/ n. in mathematics, a quadrilateral (four-sided plane figure) with opposite pairs of sides equal in length and parallel, and opposite angles equal. In the special case when all four sides are equal in length, the parallelogram is known as a **rhombus**, and when the internal angles are right angles, it is a **rectangle**

or **square**. [from French from Latin from Greek *para-* = beside and *grammē* = line]

paralyse /'pærəlaɪz/ *v.t.* 1. to affect with paralysis. 2. to render powerless; to bring to a standstill. [from French]

paralysis /pə'rælɪsɪs/ n. 1. impairment or loss of the power of movement, caused by disease or injury to nerves. Paralysis may also involve loss of sensation due to sensory-nerve disorder. 2. a state of powerlessness; inability to move or operate normally. [Latin from Greek *luō* = loosen]

paralytic /pærə'lɪtɪk/ *adj.* 1. affected by paralysis. 2. (*slang*) very drunk. —*n.* a person affected by paralysis. [from Old French from Latin from Greek]

Paramaribo /pærə'mærɪbəu/ port and capital of Surinam, South America, 24 km/15 mi from the sea on the river Surinam; population (1980) 193,000. Products include coffee, fruit, timber, and bauxite. It was founded by the French on an Indian village in 1540, made the capital of British Surinam in 1650, and placed under Dutch rule from 1816 to 1975.

paramedical /pærə'medɪkəl/ *adj.* (of services etc.) supplementing and supporting medical work.

parameter /pə'ræmɪtə/ n. 1. a quantity that is constant in the case considered but which varies in different cases. 2. a variable quantity or quality that restricts or gives a particular form to the thing it characterizes. [from Greek *para-* = beside and *metron* = measure]

paramilitary /pærə'mɪlɪtəri/ *adj.* organized like a military force but not part of the armed services. —*n.* a member of a paramilitary organization.

paramount /'pærəmaunt/ *adj.* supreme; in supreme authority. [from Anglo-French (Old French *par* = by and *amont* = above]

Paramount Studios a US film production and distribution company, founded in 1912 as the Famous Players Film Company by Adolph Zukor (1873–1976). In 1914 it merged with the distribution company Paramount Pictures. A major studio from the silent days of cinema, Paramount was adept at discovering new talent and Cecil B de Mille made many of his films for the studio. Despite its success, the company was often in financial trouble and in 1966 was taken over by Gulf and Western Industries. In recent years it has produced such successful films as *Grease* 1978 and *Raiders of the Lost Ark* 1981.

paramour /'pærəmuə/ n. (*archaic*) a married person's illicit lover. [from Old French *par amour* = by love]

Paraná /pærə'nɑː/ river in South America, formed by the confluence of the Río Grande and Paranaiba; the Paraguay joins it at Corrientes, and it flows into the Río de la Plata with the Uruguay; length 4,500 km/2,800 mi. It is used for hydroelectric power by Argentina, Brazil, and Paraguay.

parang /'pɑːræŋ/ n. a heavy Malayan sheath knife. [Malay]

paranoia /pærə'nɔɪə/ n. 1. a mental disorder with delusions of grandeur, persecution etc. 2. an abnormal tendency to suspect and mistrust others. [from Greek *noos* = mind]

paranoiac /pærə'nɔɪæk/ *adj.* or **paranoic** /pærə'nəuɪk/ paranoid. —*n.* a paranoid person.

paranoid /'pærənɔɪd/ *adj.* affected by paranoia. —*n.* a paranoid person.

paranormal /pærə'nɔːməl/ *adj.* (of phenomena or powers) presumed to operate according to natural laws beyond or outside those considered normal or known.

parapet /'pærəpɪt/ n. a low wall at the edge of a roof, balcony etc., or along the sides of a bridge etc.; a defence of earth or stone to conceal and protect troops. [French or from Italian = breast-high wall (*parare* = defend and *petto* = breast)]

paraphernalia /pærəfə'neɪliə/ *n.pl.* miscellaneous belongings, accessories etc. [Latin from Greek = personal articles which a woman could keep after marriage, as opposed to her dowry which went to her husband (*para-* = beside, beyond and *phernē* = dowry)]

paraphrase /'pærəfreɪz/ n. expression of the meaning of a passage in other words. —*v.t.* to express the meaning of (a passage) in other words. [French or from Latin from Greek *phrazō* = tell]

paraplegia /pærə'pliːdʒə/ n. paralysis of the legs and part or the whole of the trunk, usually due to spinal injury. [from Greek *plēssō* = strike]

paraplegic /pærə'pliːdʒɪk/ *adj.* of paraplegia. —*n.* one who suffers from paraplegia.

parapsychology /pærəsaɪ'kɒlədʒɪ/ *n.* the study of mental phenomena outside the sphere of ordinary psychology (hypnosis, telepathy etc.).

paraquat /'pærəkwɒt/ *n.* a nonselective herbicide. Although quickly degraded by soil microorganisms, it is deadly to human beings if ingested. [from *para-* and *quater*nary (with reference to its chemical composition)]

parasite /'pærəsaɪt/ *n.* **1.** an animal or plant living in or on another (called the 'host') and drawing nutriment directly from it. Parasites that live inside the host, such as liver flukes and tapeworms, are called **endoparasites**; those that live on the outside, such as fleas and lice, are called **ectoparasites. 2.** a person who lives off or exploits another or others. —**parasitic** /-'sɪtɪk/ *adj.*, **parasitically** /-'sɪtɪkəlɪ/ *adv.*, **parasitism** *n.* [from Latin from Greek = one who eats at another's table (*sitos* = food)]

parasol /'pærəsɒl/ *n.* a light umbrella used to give shade from the sun. [French from Italian *parare* = defend and *sole* = sun]

paratrooper /'pærətruː,pə/ *n.* a member of the paratroops.

paratroops /'pærətruːps/ *n.pl.* parachute troops.

paratyphoid /pærə'taɪfɔɪd/ *n.* a fever resembling typhoid but caused by a different bacterium.

parboil /'paːbɔɪl/ *v.t.* **1.** to boil (food) until it is partly cooked. **2.** to subject (a person) to great heat. [from Old French from Latin *perbullire* (*per-* = thoroughly, confused with *part* and *bullire* = boil)]

Parc des Princes /'paːk deɪ 'præns/ a French sports stadium and home of the national rugby union team. It has also staged international association football and is the home for Paris's two senior football teams, Paris St Germain and Racing Club.

parcel /'paːsəl/ *n.* **1.** a thing or things wrapped as a single package for carrying or for sending by post. **2.** a piece of land. **3.** the quantity dealt with in one commercial transaction. —*v.t.* (**-ll-**) **1.** to wrap up as a parcel. **2.** to divide (*out*) into portions. [from Old French, diminutive of Latin *particula*]

parch *v.t./i.* **1.** to make or become hot and dry. **2.** to roast (peas, corn etc.) slightly.

parchment /'paːtʃmənt/ *n.* **1.** a heavy paperlike material made from animal skins. **2.** a manuscript written on this. **3.** a high-grade paper made to resemble parchment. [from Old French from Latin *pergamina* from Pergamum which from the 2nd century BC was noted for the production of parchment]

pardon /'paːdən/ *n.* **1.** forgiveness. **2.** remission of the legal consequences of a crime or conviction. **3.** courteous forbearance. —*v.t.* **1.** to forgive. **2.** to make courteous allowances for, to excuse. —**I beg your pardon,** (*colloquial*) **pardon (me),** a formula of apology or disagreement, or a request to repeat something said. [from Old French from Latin *perdonare* = concede]

pardonable *adj.* that may be pardoned, easily excused. —**pardonably** *adv.*

pare *v.t.* **1.** to trim or shave by cutting away the surface or edge. **2.** to diminish little by little. [from Old French from Latin *parare* = prepare]

Paré /pæ'reɪ/ Ambroise 1509–1590. French surgeon who introduced modern principles to the treatment of wounds. As a military surgeon, Paré developed new ways of treating wounds and amputations, which greatly reduced the death rate among the wounded. He abandoned the practice of cauterization (sealing with heat), using balms and soothing lotions instead, and used ligatures to tie off blood vessels.

paregoric /pærɪ'gɒrɪk/ *n.* a camphorated tincture of opium used as an analgesic; an anodyne. —*adj.* soothing. [from Latin from Greek (*agoros* = speaking from *agora* = assembly)]

parenchyma *n.* a plant tissue composed of loosely packed, more or less spherical cells, with thin cellulose walls. Although parenchyma often has no specialized function, it is usually present in large amounts, forming a packing or ground tissue. It usually has many intercellular spaces.

parent /'peərənt/ *n.* **1.** one who has begotten or borne offspring, a father or mother. **2.** a forefather. **3.** a person who has adopted a child. **4.** an animal or plant from which others are derived. **5.** a source from which other things are derived. —*v.t./i.* to be a parent (of). —**parent governor,** an elected parent representative on the governing body of a state school. **parent–teacher association** (PTA) an organization consisting of, and promoting good relations between, teachers and the parents of their pupils. A PTA also supports the school by fund raising and other activities. —**parental** /pə'rentəl/ *adj.*, **parentally** *adv.*, **parenthood** *n.* [from Old French from Latin *parere* = bring forth]

parentage *n.* lineage, descent from parents.

parenthesis /pə'renθəsɪs/ *n.* (*plural* **parentheses** /-əsiːz/) **1.** a word, clause, or sentence inserted as an explanation or afterthought into a passage which is grammatically complete without it, and usually marked off by brackets, dashes, or commas. **2.** (in *plural*) a pair of round brackets ( ) used for this. —**in parenthesis,** as a parenthesis; as an aside or digression. [Latin from Greek *parentithēmi* = put in beside]

parenthesize /pə'renθəsaɪz/ *v.t.* to insert as a parenthesis; to put (words) between parentheses.

parenthetic /pærən'θetɪk/ *adj.* of or inserted as a parenthesis. —**parenthetical** *adj.*, **parenthetically** *adv.*

Pareto /pə'reɪtəʊ/ Vilfredo 1848–1923. Italian economist and political philosopher, born in Paris. He produced the first account of society as a self-regulating and interdependent system that operates independently of human attempts at voluntary control. A vigorous opponent of socialism and liberalism, Pareto justified inequality of income on the grounds of his empirical observation (**Pareto's law**) that income distribution remained constant whatever efforts were made to change it.

par excellence /paːr eksə'lɑ̃s/ above all others that may be so called. [French = by virtue of special excellence]

parfait /'paːfeɪ/ *n.* **1.** a rich iced pudding of whipped cream, eggs etc. **2.** layers of ice cream, fruit etc., served in a tall glass. [French = perfect]

parget /'paːdʒɪt/ *v.t.* to plaster (a wall etc.) especially with an ornamental pattern; to roughcast. —*n.* plaster; roughcast. [from Old French *pargeter* (*par* = all over and *jeter* = throw)]

pariah /pə'raɪə/ *n.* **1.** a member of a low or no caste. **2.** a social outcast. [from Tamil]

parietal /pə'raɪətəl/ *adj.* of the wall of the body or any of its cavities. —**parietal bone,** either of a pair of bones forming part of the skull. [from French or Latin *paries* = wall]

paring /'peərɪŋ/ *n.* a strip or piece cut off. [from Latin *parare*]

Paris /'pærɪs/ port and capital of France, on the River Seine; *département* in the Île de France region; area 105 sq km/40.5 sq mi; population (1982, metropolitan area) 8,707,000. Products include metal, leather, and luxury goods and chemicals, glass, and tobacco.

Paris in Greek legend, a prince of Troy whose abduction of Helen, wife of King Menelaus of Sparta, caused the Trojan war.

Paris Club an international forum dating from the 1950s for the rescheduling of debts granted or guaranteed by official bilateral creditors; it has no fixed membership nor an institutional structure. In the 1980s it was closely involved in seeking solutions to the serious debt crises affecting many developing countries.

Paris Commune two periods of government in France: **The Paris municipal government 1789–94** was established after the storming of the ◊Bastille and remained powerful in the French Revolution until the fall of Robespierre in 1794. **The provisional national government 18 March–May 1871** was formed while Paris was besieged by the Germans during the Franco-Prussian War. It consisted of socialists and left-wing republicans, and is often considered the first socialist government in history. Elected after the right-wing National Assembly at Versailles tried to disarm the National Guard, it fell when the Versailles troops captured Paris and massacred 20,000–30,000 people 21–28 May.

parish /'pærɪʃ/ *n.* **1.** an area having its own church and member of the clergy. **2.** a district constituted for the purposes of local government. **3.** the inhabitants of a parish. —**parish clerk,** an official performing various duties concerned with a church. **parish council,** a unit of local government in England and Wales, based on church parishes. **parish register,** a book recording christenings, marriages, and burials, at a parish church. [from Old French from Latin *parochia* from Greek = sojourning (*oikeō* = dwell)]

parishioner /pəˈrɪʃənə/ *n.* an inhabitant of a parish. [from obsolete *parishen*]

Parisian /pəˈrɪsɪən/ *adj.* of the city of Paris. —*n.* a native or inhabitant of Paris.

Paris, Treaty of any of various peace treaties signed in Paris. They include:

1763 ending the ◊Seven Years' War.

1783 recognizing American independence.

1814 and **1815** following the abdication and final defeat of ◊Napoleon I.

1856 ending the ◊Crimean War.

1898 ending the ◊Spanish-American War.

1919–20 conference preparing the Treaty of ◊Versailles at the end of World War I, held in Paris.

1946 after World War II, the peace treaties between the ◊Allies and Italy, Romania, Hungary, Bulgaria, and Finland.

1951 signed by France, West Germany, Italy, Belgium, Netherlands and Luxembourg, embodying the Schuman Plan to set up a single coal and steel authority.

1973 ending US participation in the ◊Vietnam War.

parity /ˈpærɪtɪ/ *n.* 1. equality of price, rate of exchange, wages, and buying power. Parity ratios may be used in the setting of wages to establish similar status to different work groups. 2. the equivalence of one currency in another; being at par. 3. the state of a number, being either even or odd. In computing, a parity bit (see ◊bit³) is sometimes added to numbers to help ensure accuracy. [from French or Latin *paritas* (*par* = equal)]

park /pɑːk/ *n.* 1. a large public garden in a town, for recreation. 2. a large enclosed piece of ground, usually with woodland and pasture, attached to a country house etc. 3. a large tract of land in its natural state for public enjoyment. 4. an area for motor cars etc. to be left in. 5. (*US*) a sports ground. —*v.t.* 1. to place and leave (a vehicle, or *absolute*) temporarily. 2. (*colloquial*) to deposit temporarily. —**park oneself**, (*colloquial*) to sit down. **parking lot**, (*US*) an outdoor area for parking vehicles. **parking meter**, a coin-operated meter which receives the fees for vehicles parked in a street and indicates the time available. **parking ticket**, a notice of a fine etc. imposed for parking a vehicle illegally. [from Old French *parc*]

Park Mungo 1771–1806. Scottish surgeon and explorer. He traced the course of the Niger river 1795–97 and probably drowned during a second expedition in 1805–06. He published *Travels in the Interior of Africa* 1799.

parka /ˈpɑːkə/ *n.* a skin jacket with a hood, worn by Eskimos; a similar windproof fabric garment worn by mountaineers etc. [Aleutian]

Park Chung Hee /ˈpɑːk tʃʊŋ ˈhiː/ 1917–1979. President of South Korea 1963–79. Under his rule South Korea had one of the world's fastest-growing economies, but recession and his increasing authoritarianism led to his assassination in 1979.

Parker /ˈpɑːkə/ Bonnie 1911–1943. US criminal; see ◊Bonnie and Clyde.

Parker Charlie (Charles Christopher), nicknamed 'Bird', 'Yardbird', 1920–1955. US alto saxophonist and jazz composer, associated with the trumpeter Dizzy Gillespie in developing the ◊bebop style. His mastery of improvisation inspired performers on all jazz instruments.

Parker Dorothy (born Rothschild) 1893–1967. US writer and wit, a leading member of the Algonquin Round Table. She reviewed for the magazines *Vanity Fair* and *The New Yorker*, and wrote wittily ironic verses, collected in several volumes including *Not So Deep As a Well* 1940, and short stories.

Parkes /pɑːks/ the site in New South Wales of the Australian National Radio Astronomy Observatory, featuring a radio telescope of 64 m/210 ft aperture, run by the Commonwealth Scientific and Industrial Research Organization.

Parkes Henry 1815–1896. Australian politician, born in the UK. He promoted education and the cause of federation, and suggested the official name 'Commonwealth of Australia'. He was five times premier of New South Wales 1872–91. Parkes, New South Wales, is named after him.

Parkinson /ˈpɑːkɪnsən/ Cecil (Edward) 1931– . British Conservative politician. He was chair of the party 1981–83,

Parker *A virtuoso on the alto saxophone, Charlie Parker.*

and became minister for trade and industry, but resigned in Oct 1984 following the disclosure of an affair with his secretary. In 1987 he rejoined the cabinet as secretary of state for energy, and was transport secretary 1989–90.

Parkinson's disease /ˈpɑːkɪnsənz/ or **Parkinsonism** a degenerative disease of the brain characterized by a progressive loss of mobility, muscular rigidity, tremor, and speech difficulties. The condition is mainly seen in people over the age of 50. [from J *Parkinson*, English surgeon, who described it in 1817 under the names 'shaking palsy' and 'paralysis agitans']

Parkinson's law /ˈpɑːkɪnsənz/ the notion that 'work expands so as to fill the time available for its completion'. [from C N *Parkinson*, English writer (1909–)]

parkland *n.* open grassland with clumps of trees etc.

Parkman /ˈpɑːkmən/ Francis 1823–1893. US historian and traveller, whose work chronicles the European exploration and conquest of North America, in such books as *The California and Oregon Trail* 1849 and *La Salle and the Discovery of the Great West* 1879.

parky *adj.* (*slang*) chilly.

parlance *n.* a way of speaking, phraseology. [Old French (*parler* = speak, ultimately from Latin *parabola*)]

parley /ˈpɑːlɪ/ *n.* a conference for debating points in dispute, especially a discussion of the terms for an armistice etc. —*v.i.* to hold a parley. [perhaps from Old French *parlée*, feminine past participle of *parler*]

parliament /ˈpɑːləmənt/ *n.* the legislative body of a country. The world's oldest parliament is the Icelandic Althing dating from about 930. The UK Parliament is usually dated from 1265. The Supreme Soviet of the USSR, with 1,500 members, may be the world's largest legislature. In the UK, Parliament is the supreme legislature, comprising the ◊House of Commons and the ◊House of Lords. Parliament originated in the 13th century, but its powers were not established until the late 17th century. The powers of the Lords were curtailed in 1911, and the duration of parliaments was fixed at five years, but any parliament may extend its own life, as happened during both World Wars. It meets in the Palace of Westminster, London. [from Old French *parlement* = speaking]

parliamentarian /pɑːləmenˈteərɪən/ *n.* a skilled debater in parliament.

parliamentary /pɑːləˈmentərɪ/ *adj.* 1. of parliament; enacted or established by a parliament. 2. (of language) admissible in Parliament, (*colloquial*) polite. —**parliamentary paper**, in UK politics, an official document, such as a White Paper or a report of a select committee, which is prepared for the information of members of Parliament.

Parliament, European the governing body of the European Community; see ◊European Parliament.

Parliament, Houses of the building where the UK legislative assembly meets. The present Houses of Parliament in London, designed in Gothic Revival style by the architects Charles Barry and A W Pugin, were built 1840–60, the previous building having burned down in 1834. It incorporates portions of the medieval Palace of Westminster.

parlour /'pɑːlə/ n. 1. a sitting room in a private house. 2. a room in a hotel, convent etc., for private conversation. 3. a shop providing specified goods or services. —**parlour game**, an indoor game, especially a word game. [from Anglo-French]

parlous /'pɑːləs/ adj. (archaic) perilous, hard to deal with. —adv. (archaic) extremely.

Parmesan /pɑːmɪ'zæn, (attributive) 'pɑː-/ n. a kind of hard cheese made originally at Parma and used especially in a grated form. [French from Italian parmegiano (from Parma in Italy)]

Parnassus /pɑː'næsəs/ mountain in central Greece, height 2,457 m/8,064 ft, revered as the abode of Apollo and the Muses. Delphi lies on its southern flank.

Parnell /pɑː'nel/ Charles Stewart 1846–1891. Irish nationalist politician. He supported a policy of obstruction and violence to attain ◊Home Rule, and became the president of the Nationalist Party in 1877. In 1879 he approved the ◊Land League, and his attitude led to his imprisonment in 1881. His career was ruined in 1890 when he was cited as co-respondent in a divorce case.

parochial /pə'rəʊkɪəl/ adj. 1. of a parish. 2. (of affairs, views etc.) merely local, confined to a narrow area. —**parochialism** n., **parochially** adv. [from Anglo-French from Latin parochia]

parody /'pærədɪ/ n. 1. a humorous exaggerated imitation of an author, literary work, style, etc. 2. a grotesque imitation, a travesty. —v.t. to compose a parody of, to mimic humorously. —**parodist** n. [from Latin or Greek parōidia = burlesque poem (ōidē = song)]

parole /pə'rəʊl/ n. 1. release of a prisoner (temporarily for a special purpose, or completely) before expiry of the sentence, on promise of good behaviour; such a promise. 2. a person's word of honour. —v.t. to release on parole. [French = word, from Latin parabola]

parotid /pə'rɒtɪd/ adj. situated near the ear. —n. the parotid gland. —**parotid gland**, the salivary gland in front of the ear. [from French or Latin from Greek parōtis (ous = ear)]

paroxysm /'pærəksɪzəm/ n. a sudden attack or outburst of rage, laughter etc.; a spasm. —**paroxysmal** /-'sɪzməl/ adj. [from French from Latin from Greek paroxunō = exasperate]

parquet /'pɑːkeɪ, -kɪ/ n. flooring of wooden blocks arranged in a pattern. —v.t. to floor (a room) thus. —**parquetry** /-kɪtrɪ/ n. [French = small compartment]

parr /pɑː/ n. a young salmon.

Parr Catherine 1512–1548. Sixth wife of Henry VIII of England. She had already lost two husbands when she married Henry VIII in 1543. She survived him, and in 1547 married Lord Seymour of Sudeley (1508–1549).

parricide /'pærɪsaɪd/ n. 1. the crime of killing one's own parent or other near relative. 2. one who is guilty of this. —**parricidal** adj. [French, or from Latin (associated with pater = father, parens = parent)]

parrot /'pærət/ n. 1. a bird of the order Psittaciformes, abundant in the tropics, especially in Australia and South America. The smaller species are commonly referred to as **parakeets**. They are mainly vegetarian, and range in size from the 8.5 cm/3.5 in **pygmy parrot** to the 100 cm/40 in **Amazon parrot**. The plumage is very colourful, and the call is commonly a harsh screech. The talent for imitating human speech is marked in the **grey parrot** Psittacus erithacus of Africa. 2. a person who mechanically repeats another's words or imitates his or her actions. —v.t. to repeat mechanically.

parry /'pærɪ/ v.t. 1. to ward off (a weapon or blow) by using one's own weapon etc. to block the thrust. 2. to evade (an awkward question) by an adroit reply. —n. parrying. [probably from French parer from Italian parare = ward off]

Parry William Edward 1790–1855. English admiral and Arctic explorer. He made detailed charts during explorations of the Northwest Passage 1819–20, 1821–23, and 1824–25. He made an attempt to reach the North Pole in 1827.

The Parry Islands, Northwest Territories, Canada, are named after him.

parse /pɑːz/ v.t. to describe (a word in context) grammatically, stating its inflexion, relation to the sentence etc.; to resolve (a sentence) into its component parts and describe them grammatically. [perhaps from obsolete pars = parts of speech from Old French]

parsec /'pɑːsek/ n. a unit of distance used in astronomy (symbol pc). One parsec is equal to 3.2617 ◊light years, 2.063×10^5 ◊astronomical units, and 3.086×10^{13} km, the distance at which a star would have a parallax of one second of an arc, i.e. at which the mean radius of the Earth's orbit subtends this angle. [from parallax and second]

Parsee /pɑː'siː/ n. an adherent of Zoroastrianism in India, a descendant of the Persians who fled to India from Muslim persecution in the 7th–8th centuries. About 100,000 Parsees now live mainly in Bombay State. [from Persian Parsi = Persian]

Parsifal /'pɑːsɪfəl/ in Germanic legend, the father of ◊Lohengrin and one of the knights who sought the Holy Grail.

parsimony /'pɑːsɪmənɪ/ n. carefulness in the use of money or resources; meanness, stinginess. —**parsimonious** /-'məʊnɪəs/ adj., **parsimoniously** adv. [from Latin parcere = spare]

parsley /'pɑːslɪ/ n. a biennial herb Petroselinum crispum of the carrot family Umbelliferae, cultivated for flavouring and garnishing dishes. It grows up to 45 cm/1.5 ft high and has pinnate, aromatic leaves and yellow umbelliferous flowers. [from Old French from Latin from Greek petroselinon (petra = rock and selinon = parsley)]

parsnip /'pɑːsnɪp/ n. a plant Pastinaca sativa of the carrot family Umbelliferae with a pale yellow tapering root used as a culinary vegetable; its root. [from Old French pasnaie from Latin pastinaca, assimilated to nep = turnip]

parson /'pɑːsən/ n. a rector; a vicar or any beneficed member of the clergy; (colloquial) any (especially Protestant) clergyperson. —**parson's nose**, the rump of a (cooked) fowl. [from Old French from Latin persona]

parsonage n. the house provided for a parson.

Parsons /'pɑːsənz/ Charles Algernon 1854–1931. English engineer who invented the Parsons steam ◊turbine in 1884, a landmark in marine engineering and later universally used in electricity generation (to drive an alternator).

part. in grammar, abbreviation of ◊participle.

part n. 1. some but not all of a thing or number of things. 2. an integral member or component. 3. a division of a book, broadcast serial etc., especially as much as is issued etc. at one time. 4. each of several equal portions of a whole. 5. a portion allotted, a share; a person's share in an action, his or her duty. 6. a character assigned to an actor on the stage; the words spoken by an actor on the stage; a copy of these. 7. in music, a melody or other constituent of harmony assigned to a particular voice or instrument. 8. a side in an agreement or dispute. 9. (in plural) a region, a district. 10. (in plural) abilities. —v.t./i. 1. to divide or separate into parts; to cause to do this. 2. to separate (the hair of the head on either side of a parting) with a comb. 3. to quit one another's company. 4. (colloquial) to part with one's money, to pay. —adv. in part, partly. —**for my part**, so far as I am concerned. **in part**, partly. **on the part of**, proceeding from, done etc. by. **part and parcel**, an essential part of. **part exchange**, a transaction in which an article is given as part of the payment for a more expensive one. **part of speech**, each of the grammatical classes of words (in English usually noun, adjective, article, pronoun, verb, adverb, preposition, conjunction, interjection). **part song**, a song for several voice parts, often unaccompanied. **part time**, less than full time. **part-time** adj. occupying or using only part of the available working time. **part-timer** n. one employed in part-time work. **part with**, to give up possession of, to hand over. **take in good part**, not to be offended by. **take part**, to assist or have a share (in). **take the part of**, to support, to back up. [from Old French from Latin pars]

partake /pɑː'teɪk/ v.i. (past **partook** /-'tʊk/, past participle **partaken**) 1. to participate. 2. to take a share, especially of food or drink. —**partaker** n. [back formation from partaker = part taker]

Parthenon The west front of the Parthenon, on the Acropolis in Athens, Greece.

parterre /pɑːˈteə/ n. 1. a level space in a garden occupied by flowerbeds. 2. the pit of a theatre. [French par terre = on the ground]

parthenocarpy n. in botany, the formation of fruits without seeds. This phenomenon, of no obvious benefit to the plant, occurs naturally in some plants, such as bananas. It can also be induced in some fruit crops, either by breeding or by applying certain plant hormones.

parthenogenesis /pɑːθɪnəʊˈdʒenəsɪs/ n. reproduction from gametes without fertilization. Parthenogenesis is the normal means of reproduction in a few plants (for example, dandelions) and animals (for example, certain fish). Some sexually reproducing species, such as aphids, show parthenogenesis at some stage in their life cycle. —**parthenogenetic** /-dʒiˈnetɪk/ adj. [from Greek parthenos = virgin and genesis = origin]

Parthenon /ˈpɑːθənən/ n. the temple of Athena Parthenos ('the Virgin') on the Acropolis at Athens; built 447–438 BC under the supervision of Phidias, and the most perfect example of Doric architecture (by Callicrates and Ictinus). In turn a Christian church and Turkish mosque, it was reduced to ruins when the Venetians bombarded the Acropolis in 1687. Greek sculptures from the Parthenon were removed by Lord Elgin in the early 19th century; these are popularly known as the ◊Elgin marbles.

Parthia /ˈpɑːθɪə/ ancient country in W Asia in what is now NE Iran, capital Ctesiphon. Originating in about 248 BC, it reached the peak of its power under Mithridates I in the 2nd century BC, and was annexed to Persia under the Sassanids in AD 226. Parthian horsemen feigned retreat and shot their arrows unexpectedly backwards, hence the expression **Parthian shot**, a remark delivered in parting. —**Parthian** adj.

partial /ˈpɑːʃəl/ adj. 1. not complete, forming only a part. 2. biased, unfair. —**partial eclipse**, an eclipse in which only part of the luminary is covered or darkened. **partial to**, having a liking for. —**partially** adv. [from Old French from Latin pars]

partiality /pɑːʃiˈælɪti/ n. 1. bias, favouritism. 2. a strong liking. [from Old French from Latin]

participant /pɑːˈtɪsɪpənt/ n. a participator.

participate /pɑːˈtɪsɪpeɪt/ v.i. to have a share, to take part. —**participation** /-ˈpeɪʃən/ n., **participator** n. [from Latin particeps = taking part from pars = part and -cip- from capere = take]

participle /ˈpɑːtɪsɪpəl/ n. in grammar, a form of the verb, in English either a **present participle** ending in -ing (for example, 'working' in 'They were working', 'working' men', and 'a hard-working team') or a **past participle** ending in -ed in regular verbs (for example, 'trained' in 'They have been trained well', 'trained soldiers', and 'a well-trained team'). —**participial** /-ˈsɪpɪəl/ adj. [from Old French from Latin participium]

particle /ˈpɑːtɪkəl/ n. 1. a minute portion of matter; see ◊particle, subatomic. 2. the least possible amount. 3. a minor part of speech, especially a short indeclinable one; a common prefix or suffix such as un-, -ship. [from Latin particula]

particle physics the study of elementary particles that make up all ◊atoms. Atoms are made up of positively charged ◊protons and, except for hydrogen, ◊neutrons (which have no charge) in the nucleus, surrounded by negatively charged ◊electrons. Nuclei do not split apart easily; they usually need to be bombarded by particles such as protons, raised to very high kinetic energies by particle accelerators.

particle, subatomic a particle which is smaller than an ◊atom. The ◊proton, ◊electron, and ◊neutrino are the only stable particles. The ◊neutron is stable only when in the atomic nucleus. Over 200 other unstable particles are known. All decay rapidly into other particles and are characterized by such properties as their mass, charge, spin, and lifetime. Particles that are influenced by the 'strong' nuclear force are known as hadrons. These are divided into heavy particles, baryons, which include the proton and neutron, and intermediate-mass particles, mesons. Light particles that are influenced by the 'weak' nuclear force are known as leptons.

particoloured /ˈpɑːtɪkʌləd/ adj. partly in one colour and partly in another. [from Old French parti = divided]

particular /pəˈtɪkjʊlə/ adj. 1. relating to one person or thing as distinct from others, individual. 2. more than usual, special. 3. scrupulously exact, fastidious; detailed. —n. 1. a detail, an item. 2. (in plural) information, a detailed account. —**in particular**, especially; specifically. [from Old French from Latin particula]

particularity /pətɪkjuˈlærɪti/ n. 1. the quality of being individual or particular. 2. fullness or minuteness of detail in description.

particularize /pəˈtɪkjʊləraɪz/ v.t. to name specially or one by one; to specify (items). —**particularization** /-ˈzeɪʃən/ n. [from French]

particularly adv. especially, very.

parting n. 1. leave-taking; departure. 2. the dividing line where hair is combed in different directions. 3. division, separating.

partisan /pɑːtiˈzæn, ˈpɑː-/ n. a member of an armed group that operates behind enemy lines or in occupied territories during wars. The name 'partisans' was first given to armed bands of Russians who operated against Napoleon's army in Russia during 1812, but has since been used to describe Russian, Yugoslav, Italian, Greek, and Polish ◊Resistance groups against the Germans during World War II. —**partisanship** n. [French from Italian dialect partigiano]

partition /pɑːˈtɪʃən/ n. 1. division into parts or (of a country) into nations. 2. a part or nation formed thus. 3. a structure separating two such parts, a thin wall. —v.t. 1. to divide into parts; to share out thus. 2. to divide, to separate (part of a room etc.) by means of a partition. [from Old French from Latin partiri = divide]

partitive /ˈpɑːtɪtɪv/ adj. in grammar, (of a word, form, etc.) denoting a part of a group or quantity. —n. a partitive word (e.g. some, any) or form. —**partitively** adv. [from French or Latin]

partly adv. with respect to a part, in some degree.

partner /ˈpɑːtnə/ n. 1. one who shares or takes part with another or others, especially in a business firm with shared risks and profits. 2. either of two people dancing together or playing tennis or cards etc. on the same side and scoring jointly. 3. a husband or wife; a person with whom one lives as if married. —v.t. to be a partner of; to associate as partners. —**partnership** n. [alteration of parcener = joint heir]

partridge /ˈpɑːtrɪdʒ/ n. a gamebird of the family Phasianidae which includes pheasants and quail. Two species common in the UK are the **grey partridge** Perdix perdix and the **French partridge** Alectoris rufa. [from Old French from Latin from Greek perdix]

parturient /pɑːˈtjʊərɪənt/ adj. about to give birth. [from Latin parturire to be in labour (parere = bring forth)]

parturition /pɑːtjʊəˈrɪʃən/ n. the act of bringing forth young, childbirth.

party n. 1. a social gathering, usually of invited guests. 2. a body of persons working or travelling together. 3. a group of people united in a cause, opinion, etc., especially a political group organized on a national basis. 4. a person or persons forming one side in an agreement or dispute. 5. an accessory (to an action etc.) 6. (colloquial) a person. —**party line**, the policy adopted by a political party; a telephone line shared by two or more subscribers. **party wall**, a wall common to the two buildings or rooms that it divides. [from Old French partie]

Parvati /'pɑːvəti/ in Hindu mythology, the consort of ◊Siva in one of her gentler manifestations, and the mother of Ganesa, the god of prophecy; she is said to be the daughter of the Himalayas.

parvenu *n.* or (*feminine*) **parvenue**, a social upstart. [French = arrived]

pas /pɑː/ *n.* (*plural* the same) a step in dancing. —*pas de deux* /də'dɜː/, a dance for two people. A *grand pas de deux* is danced by the prima ballerina and the premier danseur. [French = step]

pascal /'pæskəl/ *n.* an SI unit (symbol Pa) of pressure, equal to one newton per square metre. It replaces bars (see ◊bar²) and millibars (10^5 Pa equals one bar). [from B *Pascal*]

Pascal Blaise 1623–1662. French philosopher, mathematician, and physicist. He went into the Jansenist monastery of Port Royal in 1654 and defended a prominent Jansenist, Antoine Arnauld (1612–1694), against the Jesuits in his *Lettres provinciales* 1656. His *Pensées* 1670 was part of an unfinished defence of the Christian religion. Pascal contributed to the development of hydraulics, the ◊calculus, and the mathematical theory of ◊probability. **Pascal's principle** states that pressure everywhere in a fluid is the same, so that pressure applied at one point is transmitted equally to all parts of the container. This is the principle of the hydraulic press and jack. **Pascal's triangle** is a triangular array of numbers in which each number is the sum of the pair of numbers above it. Plotted at equal distances along a horizontal axis, the numbers in the rows give the binomial probability distribution with equal probability of success and failure, such as when tossing a fair coin.

PASCAL /pæ'skɑːl/ *n.* a high-level computer-programming language. Designed by Niklaus Wirth (1934–) in the 1960s as an aid to teaching programming, it is still widely used as such in universities, but is also recognized as a good general purpose programming language. [from B *Pascal*]

paschal /'pæskəl, 'pɑː-/ *adj.* 1. of the Jewish ◊Passover. 2. of Easter. —**paschal lamb**, a lamb sacrificed at Passover; (*figurative*) Christ. [from Old French from Latin *pascha* = Passover from Greek from Aramaic]

pasha /'pɑːʃə/ *n.* (*historical*) the title (placed after the name) of a Turkish officer of high rank. [from Turkish]

Pashto /'pʌʃtəʊ/ *n.* or **Pushtu** an Indo-European language, officially that of Afghanistan, also spoken in another dialect in N Pakistan. —*adj.* of or in this language. [Pashto]

Pasiphae /pə'sɪfiiː/ in Greek mythology, the wife of ◊Minos and mother of ◊Phaedra and of the ◊Minotaur, the offspring of her sexual union with a bull sent from the sea by the god ◊Poseidon.

Pasolini /pæsə'liːni/ Pier Paolo 1922–1975. Italian poet, novelist, and film director, an influential figure of the postwar years. His writings (making much use of first Friulan and later Roman dialect) include the novels *Ragazzi di vita/The Ragazzi* 1955 and *Una vita violenta/A Violent Life* 1959. Among his films are *Il vangelo secondo Mateo/The Gospel According to St Matthew* 1964 and *I racconti de Canterbury/The Canterbury Tales* 1972.

pass[1] /pɑːs/ *v.t./i.* (*past participle* passed /pɑːst/ or as *adj.* past) 1. to go or move onward or past something, to proceed; to leave (a thing) on one side or behind, to disregard. 2. to go from one person or place etc. to another, to be transferred. 3. to surpass, to be too great for. 4. to cause to move across, over, or past; (in football etc.) to send (the ball, or *absolute*) to a player of one's own side. 5. to discharge from the body as or with excreta. 6. to change from one state or condition etc. into another; to cease or come to an end; (of time) to go by. 7. to happen, to be done or said. 8. to occupy (time). 9. to circulate or cause to circulate; to be accepted or currently known in a certain way. 10. to be tolerated, to go uncensured. 11. to examine and declare satisfactory; to approve (a law etc.), especially by vote. 12. to achieve the required standard in performing (a test); to be accepted as satisfactory. 13. to go beyond. 14. to utter; to pronounce as a decision. 15. (in cards etc.) to refuse one's turn, e.g. in bidding. —*n.* 1. passing, especially of a test or at cards; a status of degree etc. without honours. 2. a permit to go into or out of a place or be absent from one's quarters. 3. (in football etc.) transference of the ball to a player of one's own side. 4. a movement made with the hand(s) or with something held. 5. a critical state of affairs. —**bring to pass**, to cause to happen. **come to pass**, to

happen, to occur. **in passing**, by the way, in the course of speech. **make a pass at**, (*colloquial*) to try to attract sexually. **pass away**, (euphemism) to die. **pass for**, to be accepted as. **pass off**, to cease gradually; (of an event) to take place and be completed (in a specified way); to offer or dispose of (a thing) under false pretences; to evade or dismiss (an awkward remark etc.) lightly. **pass out**, to become unconscious; to complete one's military training. **pass over**, to omit, ignore, or disregard; to ignore the claims of (a person) to promotion etc. **pass up**, (*colloquial*) to refuse or neglect (an opportunity etc.). [from Old French *passer* from Latin *passus*]

pass[2] *n.* a narrow route through mountains.

passable /'pɑːsəbəl/ *adj.* 1. (barely) satisfactory, adequate. 2. that can be passed. —**passably** *adv.*

passage /'pæsɪdʒ/ *n.* 1. passing; transition from one state to another; a journey by sea or air. 2. or **passageway** a narrow way for passing along, especially with walls on either side. 3. a tubelike structure through which air or secretions etc. pass in the body. 4. the liberty or right to pass through; the right of conveyance as a passenger by sea or air. 5. a short section of a book etc. or of a piece of music. 6. (in *plural*) an interchange of words etc. —**passage of arms**, a fight; a dispute. [from Old French]

passant /'pæsənt/ *adj.* in heraldry, (of an animal) walking and looking to the dexter side, with three paws on the ground and the right forepaw raised. [from Old French from *passer* = pass]

passbook *n.* a book issued by a bank or building society to an account holder, recording the sums deposited and withdrawn.

Passchendaele /'pæʃəndeɪl/ village in W Flanders, Belgium, near Ypres. The Passchendaele ridge before Ypres was the object of a costly and unsuccessful British offensive in World War I, between July and Nov 1917; British casualties numbered nearly 400,000.

passé /'pæseɪ/ *adj.* 1. behind the times. 2. past the prime. [French, past participle of *passer*]

passenger /'pæsɪndʒə/ *n.* 1. a traveller in or on a public or private conveyance (other than the driver, pilot, crew, etc.). 2. (*colloquial*) a member of a team, crew, etc. who does no effective work. [from Old French *passager*]

passer-by *n.* one who goes past, especially by chance.

passerine /'pæsəraɪn/ *adj.* of the order Passeriformes, the perching birds, whose feet are adapted for gripping branches and stems. —*n.* a passerine bird. [from Latin *passer* = sparrow]

passim /'pæsɪm/ *adv.* throughout or at many points in a book or article etc. [Latin *passus* = spread out]

passion /'pæʃən/ *n.* 1. strong emotion. 2. an outburst of anger. 3. sexual love. 4. great enthusiasm. 5. **Passion**, the sufferings of Christ on the cross; a narrative of this from the Gospels; a musical setting of this narrative. —**Passion Sunday**, the fifth Sunday in Lent. [from Old French from Latin *pati* = suffer]

passionate /'pæʃənət/ *adj.* 1. full of passion; showing or moved by strong emotion. 2. (of emotion) intense. —**passionately** *adv.* [from Latin]

passion flower a climbing plant of the tropical American genus *Passiflora*, family Passifloraceae. It bears distinctive flower heads comprising a saucer-shaped petal base, a fringelike corona, and a central stalk bearing the stamens and ovary. It is thought to resemble the crown of thorns and other symbols of the crucifixion. Some species produce edible fruit.

passion play a play representing the death and resurrection of a god, such as Osiris, Dionysus, or Jesus; it has its origins in medieval ◊mystery plays. Traditionally, a passion play takes place every ten years at ◊Oberammergau, Germany.

passive /'pæsɪv/ *adj.* 1. suffering an action, acted upon. 2. not resisting, submissive. 3. (of substances) not active, inert. 4. in grammar, indicating that the subject undergoes the action of the verb (e.g. in *he was seen*). —**passive resistance**, resistance by nonviolent refusal to cooperate. **passive voice**, in grammar, that comprising the passive forms of verbs. —**passively** *adv.*, **passiveness** *n.*, **passivity** /-'sɪvɪtɪ/ *n.* [from Old French or Latin *pati* = suffer]

passkey *n.* 1. a private key to a door or gate etc. 2. a master key.

pasteurization

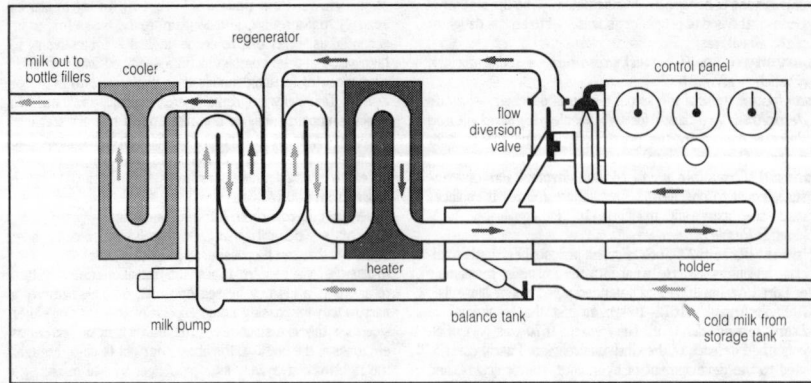

pass laws South African laws that required the black population to carry passbooks (identity documents) at all times and severely restricted freedom of movement. The laws, a major cause of discontent, formed a central part of the policies of ◊apartheid. They were repealed in 1986.

Passover *n.* **1.** (Hebrew *Pesach*) the Jewish festival celebrated each spring, held from 14 to 21 Nisan and commemorating the liberation of the Israelites from slavery in Egypt. **2.** the paschal lamb. [from *pass over*, with reference to the exemption of the Israelites from the death of the firstborn which afflicted the Egyptians (Old Testament, Exodus 12)]

passport /'pɑːspɔːt/ *n.* **1.** an official document issued by a government certifying the holder's identity and citizenship, and entitling him or her to travel under its protection to and from a foreign country. Some countries require an intending visitor to obtain a special endorsement or visa. From 1978 the member states of the European Community have begun to introduce a common passport. **2.** a thing that secures admission to or attainment of something. [from French]

password *n.* a selected word or phrase known only to one's own side, enabling sentries to distinguish friend from enemy.

Passy /'pæsi/ Frédéric 1822–1912. French economist, who shared the first Nobel Peace Prize in 1901 with Jean-Henri Dunant. He founded the International League for Permanent Peace in 1867, and was cofounder, with the English politician William Cremer (1828–1908), of the Inter-Parliamentary Conferences on Peace and on Arbitration in 1889.

past /pɑːst/ *adj.* **1.** belonging to the time before the present; (of time) gone by. **2.** in grammar, expressing a past action or state. —*n.* **1.** (especially **the past**) past time; past events. **2.** a person's past life or career, especially one that is discreditable. **3.** the past tense. —*prep.* **1.** beyond in time or place. **2.** beyond the range, limits, powers, or stage of. —*adv.* so as to pass by. —**not put it past**, (*colloquial*) to believe it possible of (a person). **past it**, (*slang*) incompetent or unusable through age. **past master**, an expert; a former master of a Freemason's lodge etc.

pasta /'pæstə/ *n.* dried paste made with flour and produced in various shapes (e.g. lasagne, macaroni); a cooked dish made with this. [Italian]

paste /peɪst/ *n.* **1.** any moist, fairly stiff mixture, especially of a powder and liquid. **2.** a dough of flour with fat, water etc. **3.** a liquid adhesive for paper etc. **4.** an easily spread preparation of ground meat, fish etc. **5.** a hard vitreous composition used in making imitation gems. —*v.t.* **1.** to fasten or coat with paste. **2.** (*slang*) to beat, thrash, bomb, etc. heavily. —**paste-up** *n.* a document prepared for copying etc. by pasting sections on a backing. [from Old French from Latin *pastē* = lozenge from Greek *pastē* (*pastos* = sprinkled)]

pasteboard *n.* a kind of thin board made of layers of paper or wood fibres pasted together.

pastel /'pæstəl/ *n.* **1.** a crayon made of dried paste compounded of pigments with gum solution. **2.** a drawing made with this. **3.** a light, delicate shade of colour. [French or from Italian]

pastern /'pæstɜːn/ *n.* the part of a horse's foot between fetlock and hoof. [from Old French *pasturon* (*pasture* = cord used to tether, from Latin)]

Pasternak /'pæstənæk/ Boris Leonidovich 1890–1960. Russian poet and novelist. His volumes of lyric poems include *A Twin Cloud* 1914 and *On Early Trains* 1943, and he translated Shakespeare's tragedies. His novel *Dr Zhivago* 1957 was banned in the USSR as a 'hostile act', and followed by a Nobel prize (which he declined). *Dr Zhivago* has since been unbanned and Pasternak posthumously rehabilitated.

Pasteur /'pæstɜː/ Louis 1822–1895. French chemist and microbiologist who discovered that fermentation is caused by microorganisms. **Pasteurization** is based on his discoveries. He also developed a vaccine for ◊rabies, which led to the foundation of the Institut Pasteur in Paris in 1888.

> There are no such things as applied sciences, only applications of science.
>
> **Louis Pasteur**
> address, 11 Sept 1872

pasteurization /ˌpɑːstʃərəˈzeɪʃən/ *n.* the treatment of food to reduce the number of microorganisms it contains and so protect consumers from disease. Harmful bacteria are killed and the development of others is delayed. For milk, the method involves heating it to 72°C/161°F for 15 seconds followed by rapid cooling to 10°C/50°F or lower. —**pasteurize** /'pɑːstʃəraɪz/ *v.t.* [from L *Pasteur*]

pastiche /pæˈstiːʃ/ *n.* **1.** a picture or musical or literary composition made up of selections from various sources. **2.** a literary or other work composed in the style of a well-known author. The intention is normally homage, rather than ridicule (as in parody). [French, from Italian *pasticcio* from Latin *pasta* = paste]

pastille /'pæstɪl, -stiːl/ *n.* **1.** a small medicinal or flavoured lozenge. **2.** a small roll of aromatic paste burnt as a fumigator etc. [French from Latin = little loaf, lozenge (*panis* = loaf)]

pastime /'pɑːstaɪm/ *n.* something done to pass time pleasantly, a recreation.

pastor /'pɑːstə/ *n.* a minister in charge of a church or congregation; a person exercising spiritual guidance. [from Old French from Latin = shepherd *pascere* = feed]

pastoral /'pɑːstərəl/ *adj.* **1.** of or portraying shepherds or country life. **2.** (of land) used for pasture. **3.** of a pastor; concerned with Christian spiritual guidance. —*n.* **1.** a pastoral poem, play, picture, etc. **2.** a letter from a pastor (especially a bishop) to the clergy or people. —**pastorally** *adv.* [from Latin]

pastoralist /'pɑːstərəlɪst/ *n.* (*Australian*) a sheep or cattle farmer.

pastorate /'pɑːstərət/ *n.* **1.** a pastor's office or tenure. **2.** a body of pastors.

past participle see ◊participle.

pastrami /pæˈstrɑːmɪ/ *n.* seasoned smoked beef. [Yiddish]

pastry /'peɪstrɪ/ n. 1. a dough made of flour, fat, and water, used for covering pies or holding filling. 2. food made with this. 3. a cake made wholly or partly of pastry. —**pastry cook,** a cook who makes pastry, especially for public sale.

pasturage /'pɑːstʃərɪdʒ/ n. 1. pasture land. 2. pasturing.

pasture /'pɑːstʃə/ n. 1. land covered with grass etc. suitable for grazing animals; a piece of such land. 2. grass etc. on this. —v.t./i. to put (animals) to graze in a pasture; (of animals) to graze. [from Old French from Latin pastura]

pasty[1] /'pæstɪ/ n. pastry with a sweet or savoury filling baked without a dish. [from Old French pasté(e) from Latin pasta = paste]

pasty[2] /'peɪstɪ/ adj. 1. of, like, or covered in paste. 2. unhealthily pale. —**pastily** adv., **pastiness** n.

pat v.t. (-tt-) to strike gently with the hand or a flat surface; to flatten or mould thus. —n. 1. a light stroke or tap; the sound made by this. 2. a small mass of butter or other soft substance. —adj. 1. apposite, opportune. 2. known thoroughly and ready for any occasion. —adv. in a pat manner, appositely. —**have off pat,** to know or have memorized perfectly. **pat on the back,** a congratulatory acknowledgement.

pat. abbreviation of ◊**patent.**

Patagonia /pætə'gəʊnɪə/ geographic area of South America, south of latitude 40° S, with sheep farming, and coal and oil resources. Sighted by Magellan in 1520, it was claimed by both Argentina and Chile until divided between them in 1881.

patch n. 1. a piece of material or metal etc. put on to mend a hole or as a reinforcement. 2. a piece of plaster or a pad put over a wound; a shield worn to protect an injured eye. 3. a distinguishable area on a surface; an isolated area or period of time. 4. a piece of ground; this covered by specified plants; (colloquial) an area assigned to a particular policeman etc. 5. a scrap, a remnant. —v.t. 1. to put a patch or patches on; (of a material) to serve as a patch to. 2. to piece together (literally or figuratively). —**not a patch on,** (colloquial) greatly inferior to. **patch pocket,** one made of a piece of cloth sewn on a garment. **patch up,** to repair with patches; to settle (a quarrel etc.) especially hastily or temporarily; to put together hastily.

patchouli /'pætʃʊlɪ/ n. a fragrant plant of the genus Pogostemon, family Labiateae, grown in the Far East, the leaves of which yield an essential oil; perfume made from this. [native name in Madras]

patchwork n. 1. needlework in which assorted small pieces of cloth are joined edge to edge, often in a pattern. 2. a thing made of assorted pieces.

patchy adj. 1. uneven in quality. 2. having or existing in patches. —**patchily** adv., **patchiness** n.

pate n. (archaic or colloquial) the head, often as the seat of the intellect.

pâté /'pæteɪ/ n. 1. a paste of meat etc. 2. a pie, a patty. —**pâté de foie gras,** /də fwɑː grɑː/ a paste of fatted goose liver. [French]

patella /pə'telə/ n. (plural patellae /-liː/) or **kneecap,** a flat bone embedded in the knee tendon of birds and mammals, which protects the joint from injury. —**patellar** adj. [Latin = small pan]

paten /'pætən/ n. a flat dish of gold or silver used in the Christian church for holding the consecrated bread at the ◊Eucharist. [from Old French or Latin patina]

patent /'peɪtənt, 'pæ-/ n. 1. an official document (originally **letters patent**) conferring a right or title etc., especially the sole right to make, use, or sell some invention for a limited period; the right granted by this. Ideas are not eligible; neither is anything not new. 2. an invention or process so protected. —adj. 1. conferred or protected by a patent; (of a food, medicine etc.) proprietary. 2. obvious, plain. 3. (colloquial) ingenious, well-contrived. —v.t. to obtain a patent for (an invention). —**patent leather,** leather with a glossy varnished surface. **Patent Office,** the government office from which patents are issued. —**patently** adv. [from Old French or Latin patēre = lie open]

patentee /peɪtən'tiː/ n. one who takes out or holds a patent; a person for the time being entitled to the benefit of a patent.

pater /'peɪtə/ n. (archaic, slang) father. [Latin]

Pater Walter Horatio 1839–1894. English critic. A stylist and supporter of 'art for art's sake', he published Studies in the History of the Renaissance 1873, Marius the Epicurean 1885, Imaginary Portraits 1887, and other works.

paternal /pə'tɜːnəl/ adj. 1. of or like a father. 2. related through the father. 3. (of a government etc.) limiting freedom and responsibility by well meant regulations. —**paternally** adv. [from Latin paternalis (pater = father)]

paternalism n. the policy of governing in a paternal way. —**paternalistic** /-'lɪstɪk/ adj.

paternity /pə'tɜːnɪtɪ/ n. 1. fatherhood. 2. one's paternal origin. 3. authorship, source. [from Old French or Latin paternalis]

Paternoster /pætə'nɒstə/ n. in the Roman Catholic Church, the Lord's Prayer. The opening words of the Latin version are Pater noster. [Latin = our father]

Paterson /'pætəsən/ Banjo (Andrew Barton) 1864–1941. Australian journalist, author of volumes of light verse and the popular song 'Waltzing Matilda', adapted from a folk song.

path /pɑːθ/ n. (plural /pɑːðz/) 1. a way or track laid down for walking or made by walking. 2. a line along which a person or thing moves. 3. a course of action. [Old English]

Pathan /pə'tɑːn/ n. a member of a Muslim people inhabiting NW Pakistan and SE Afghanistan. Formerly a constant threat to the British Raj, the Pakistani Pathans are now claiming independence, with the Afghani Pathans, in their own state of Pakhtoonistan, although this has not yet been recognized. —adj. of this people. [Hindi]

Pathé /'pæθeɪ/ Charles 1863–1957. French film pioneer, who began his career selling projectors in 1896 and with the profits formed Pathé Frères with his brothers. In 1901 he embarked on film production and by 1908 had become the world's biggest producer, with branches worldwide. He also developed an early colour process and established a weekly newsreel, Pathé Journal. World War I disrupted his enterprises and by 1918 he was gradually forced out of business by foreign competition.

pathetic /pə'θetɪk/ adj. arousing pity or sadness; arousing contempt; miserably inadequate. —**pathetic fallacy,** crediting inanimate things with human emotions. —**pathetically** adv. [from French from Latin from Greek pathos = suffering]

pathfinder n. an explorer. [Old English]

pathogen /'pæθədʒən/ n. an agent causing disease. —**pathogenic** /-'dʒenɪk/ adj. [from Greek pathos = suffering]

pathological /pæθə'lɒdʒɪkəl/ adj. 1. of pathology. 2. of or caused by a physical or mental disorder. —**pathologically** adv.

pathology /pə'θɒlədʒɪ/ n. 1. the science of bodily diseases. 2. abnormal changes in body tissue, caused by disease. —**pathologist** n. [from French]

pathos /'peɪθɒs/ n. a quality in speech, writing, events, etc., that arouses pity or sadness. [from Greek = suffering (paskhō = suffer)]

pathway n. a footway or track, especially one made by walking.

patience /'peɪʃəns/ n. 1. calm endurance of hardship, annoyance, inconvenience, delay, etc. 2. perseverance. 3. a card game (usually for one player) in which cards are brought into a specified arrangement. [from Old French from Latin]

patient /'peɪʃənt/ adj. having or showing patience. —n. a person receiving (or registered to receive) medical or dental treatment. —**patiently** adv. [from Old French from Latin pati = suffer]

patina /'pætɪnə/ n. 1. an incrustation, usually green, on the surface of old bronze; a similar alteration on other surfaces. 2. the gloss produced by age on woodwork. [Italian from Latin]

Patinir /pɑː'tiːnɪə/ (also **Patenier** or **Patinier**) Joachim c.1485–1524. Flemish painter, active in Antwerp, whose inspired landscape backgrounds dominated his religious subjects. He is known to have worked with Matsys and to have painted landscape backgrounds for other artists' works.

patio /'pætɪəʊ/ n. (plural patios) 1. a paved, usually roofless area adjoining a house. 2. an inner court open to the sky in a Spanish or Spanish American house. [Spanish]

patisserie /pə'tiːsərɪ/ n. a pastry cook's shop or wares. [from French from Latin pasticium = pastry]

patois /'pætwɑ:/ n. (plural the same /-ɑ:z/) 1. the dialect of the common people of a region, differing fundamentally from the literary language. 2. jargon. [French = rough speech]

Paton /'peɪtn/ Alan 1903–1988. South African writer. His novel Cry, the Beloved Country 1948 focused on racial inequality in South Africa. Later books include the study Land and People of South Africa 1956, The Long View 1968, and his autobiography Towards the Mountain 1980.

Patras /'pætrəs/ (Greek Patrai) industrial city (hydroelectric installations, textiles, paper) in the NW Peloponnese, Greece, on the Gulf of Patras; population (1981) 141,500. The ancient Patrae is the only one of the 12 cities of ◊Achaea to survive.

patriarch /'peɪtriɑ:k/ n. 1. the male head of a family or tribe. 2. (in the Eastern Orthodox and Roman Catholic Churches) a bishop of high rank. 3. a venerable old man. —the Patriarchs, the men named in the Bible (Genesis) as the ancestors of humankind, especially the ancestors of the ancient Hebrews, from Adam to Abraham, Isaac, Jacob, and his sons (who became Patriarchs of the Hebrew tribes). —patriarchal /-'ɑ:kəl/ adj. [from Old French from Latin from Greek patria = family and -arkhēs- = ruler]

patriarchate /'peɪtriɑ:kət/ n. the office, see, or residence of an ecclesiastical patriarch. [from Latin]

patriarchy /'peɪtriɑ:kɪ/ n. a patriarchal system of society, government etc. [from Latin from Greek]

patrician /pə'trɪʃən/ n. an ancient Roman noble, descended from the original citizens. After the 4th century BC the rights formerly exercised by the patricians alone were made available to the ◊plebeians, and patrician descent became only a matter of prestige. —adj. 1. noble, aristocratic. 2. of the ancient Roman nobility. [from Old French from Latin = having a noble father (pater = father)]

patricide /'pætrɪsaɪd/ n. 1. the crime of killing one's own father. 2. one who is guilty of this. —patricidal adj. [from Latin, alteration of parricida]

Patrick, St /'pætrɪk/ 389–c. 461. Patron saint of Ireland. Born in Britain, probably in S Wales, he was carried off by pirates to six years' slavery in Antrim, Ireland before escaping either to Britain or Gaul (his poor Latin suggests the former) to train as a missionary. He is variously said to have landed again in Ireland in 432 or 456, and his work was a vital factor in the spread of Christian influence there. His symbols are a snake and a shamrock; feast day 17 March.

patrilineal /pætri'lɪniəl/ adj. of or based on kinship with the father or the male line of ancestors. [from Latin pater = father]

patrimony /'pætrɪmənɪ/ n. property inherited from one's father or ancestors; a heritage (literal or figurative). —patrimonial /-'məʊniəl/ adj. [from Old French from Latin pater]

patriot /'pætrɪət, 'peɪ-/ n. one who is devoted to and ready to defend his or her country. —patriot missile, a ground-to-air medium-range missile system used in the air defence role. It has high-altitude coverage, electronic jamming capability, and excellent mobility. It was tested in battle against ◊SCUD missiles fired by the Iraqis in the 1991 ◊Gulf War. —patriotic /-'ɒtɪk/ adj., patriotically /-'ɒtɪkəlɪ/ adv., patriotism n. [from French from Latin from Greek patrios = of one's father]

patristic /pə'trɪstɪk/ adj. of the early Christian writers (the Church Fathers) or their work. [from German from Latin]

patrol /pə'trəʊl/ v.t./i. (-ll-) to walk or travel round (an area, or absolute) in order to protect or supervise it; to act as a patrol. —n. 1. patrolling. 2. a person or vehicle(s) assigned or sent out to patrol. 2. a unit of usually six in a Scout troop or Guide company. [from French patrouiller = paddle in mud]

patron /'peɪtrən/ n. 1. one who gives financial or other support to a person, activity, or cause. 2. a customer of a shop, restaurant etc. —patron saint, a saint regarded as protecting a person or place etc. —patroness n.fem. [from Old French from Latin patronus = protector of clients]

patronage /'pætrənɪdʒ/ n. 1. a patron's or customer's support. Patronage was for centuries bestowed mainly by individuals (often royal or noble) or by the church. In this century, patrons have tended to be political parties, the state, and, in the arts, private industry and foundations.

2. the right of bestowing or recommending for an appointment. 3. patronizing airs. [from Old French]

patronize /'pætrənaɪz/ v.t. 1. to act as a patron towards, to support. 2. to treat condescendingly. —patronizing adj., patronizingly adv. [from obsolete French or Latin]

patronymic /pætrə'nɪmɪk/ n. a name derived from that of a father or male ancestor. [from Latin from Greek pater = father and onoma = name]

patten /'pætən/ n. a shoe with the sole set on an iron ring etc. to raise the wearer's foot above the level of surface mud etc. [from Old French patin (patte = paw)]

Patten /'pætn/ Chris(topher Francis) 1944– . English Conservative politician. A former director of the Conservative Party research department, he held junior ministerial posts under Margaret Thatcher. He was environment secretary 1989–90 and chairman of the Conservative Party Organization from 1990.

patter[1] v.i. 1. to make a rapid succession of taps, as rain on a windowpane. 2. to run with short quick steps. —n. a series of taps or short light steps.

patter[2] n. rapid and often glib or deceptive speech, e.g. that used by a salesman or conjuror. —v.t./i. to repeat (prayers etc.) in a rapid mechanical way; to talk glibly. [from pater (Paternoster = Lord's Prayer)]

pattern /'pætən/ n. 1. a decorative design as executed on a carpet, wallpaper, cloth etc. 2. a model, design, or instructions from which a thing is to be made. 3. an excellent example or model. 4. a regular form or order. 5. a sample of cloth etc. —v.t. 1. to model (a thing after or on a design etc.). 2. to decorate with a pattern.

Patterson /'pætəsən/ Harry 1929– . English novelist, born in Newcastle. He has written many thrillers under his own name, including Dillinger 1983, as well as under the pseudonym Jack Higgins, including The Eagle Has Landed 1975.

Patti /'pætɪ/ Adelina 1843–1919. Anglo-Italian soprano renowned for her performances of Lucia in Lucia di Lammermoor and Amina in La sonnambula. At the age of 62 she was persuaded out of retirement to make a number of gramophone recordings, thus becoming one of the first opera singers to be recorded.

Patton /'pætn/ George (Smith) 1885–1945. US general in World War II, known as 'Blood and Guts'. He commanded the 2nd Armoured Division in 1940, and in 1942 led the Western Task Force that landed at Casablanca, Morocco. After commanding the 7th Army, he led the 3rd Army across France and into Germany, and in 1945 took over the 15th Army.

patty n. 1. a small pie or pasty. 2. (US) a small, flat cake of minced meat etc. [from French pâté]

paucity /'pɔ:sɪtɪ/ n. smallness of quantity or supply. [from Old French or Latin paucitas (paucus = few)]

Paul /pɔ:l/ Les. Adopted name of Lester Polfuss 1915– . US inventor of the solid-body electric guitar in the early 1940s, and a pioneer of recording techniques including overdubbing and electronic echo. The Gibson Les Paul guitar was first marketed in 1952 (the first commercial solid-body guitar was made by Leo ◊Fender). As a guitarist in the late 1940s and 1950s he recorded with the singer Mary Ford (1928–1977).

Paul 1901–1964. King of the Hellenes from 1947, when he succeeded his brother George II. He was the son of Constantine I. In 1938 he married Princess Frederika (1917–), daughter of the Duke of Brunswick. Her involvement in politics brought her under attack.

Paul six popes, including:

Paul VI Giovanni Battista Montini 1897–1978. Pope from 1963. His encyclical Humanae Vitae/Of Human Life 1968 reaffirmed the church's traditional teaching on birth control, thus following the minority report of the commission originally appointed by Pope John, rather than the majority view.

Paul I 1754–1801. Tsar of Russia from 1796, in succession to his mother Catherine II. Mentally unstable, he pursued an erratic foreign policy and was assassinated.

Pauli /'paʊlɪ/ Wolfgang 1900–1958. Austrian physicist, who originated Pauli's exclusion principle: in a given system no two electrons, protons, neutrons, or other elementary particles of half-integral spin can be characterized by the same set of ◊quantum numbers. He also predicted the existence of neutrinos. He won the Nobel Prize for Physics in 1945 for his work on atomic structure.

Pauline /'pɔːlaɪn/ adj. of St Paul.

Pauling /'pɔːlɪŋ/ Linus Carl 1901– . US chemist, author of fundamental work on the nature of the chemical bond and on the discovery of the helical structure of many proteins.

Paulinus /pɔːˈlaɪnəs/ died 644. Roman missionary to Britain who joined St ◊Augustine in Kent in 601, converted the Northumbrians in 625, and became the first archbishop of York. Excavations in 1978 revealed a church he built in Lincoln.

Paul Pry /'praɪ/ an inquisitive person. [character in US song 1820]

Paul, St /pɔːl/ c.3–c. AD 68. Christian missionary and martyr; in the New Testament, one of the apostles and author of 13 epistles. He is said to have been converted by a vision on the road to Damascus. After his conversion he made great missionary journeys, for example to ◊Philippi and ◊Ephesus, becoming known as the Apostle of the Gentiles (non-Jews). His emblems are a sword and a book; feast day 29 June.

Paulus /'paʊlʊs/ Friedrich von 1890–1957. German field marshal in World War II, commander of the forces that besieged Stalingrad (now Volgograd) in the USSR 1942–43; he was captured and gave evidence at the Nuremberg trials before settling in East Germany.

paunch /pɔntʃ/ n. 1. the stomach or belly. 2. a protruding abdomen. —v.t. to disembowel (an animal). —**paunchy** adj. [from Anglo-French from Latin pantex = bowels]

pauper /'pɔpə/ n. a very poor person; (historical) a recipient of poor law relief. —**pauperism** n. [Latin = poor]

pauperize /'pɔpəraɪz/ v.t. to make into a pauper; to impoverish greatly.

Pausanias /pɔːˈseɪnɪæs/ 2nd century AD. Greek geographer, author of a valuably accurate description of Greece compiled from his own travels, Description of Greece, also translated as Itinerary of Greece.

pause /pɔz/ n. 1. a temporary stop in action, sound, speech etc. 2. in music, a character placed over a note or rest indicating that it is to be lengthened at the performer's discretion. —v.i. to make a pause. —**give pause to**, to cause to hesitate. [from Old French or Latin pausa from Greek pauō = stop]

pavan /pəˈvæn/ n. or **pavane** a stately dance in slow duple time; the music for this. [from French from Spanish pavón = peacock]

Pavarotti /pævəˈrɒti/ Luciano 1935– . Italian tenor, whose operatic roles have included Rodolfo in La Bohème, Cavaradossi in Tosca, the Duke of Mantua in Rigoletto, and Nemorino in L'Elisir d'amore.

pave v.t. to cover (a street, floor etc.) with a durable surface. —**pave the way**, to make preparations. [from Old French paver]

pavement n. a paved surface or path, especially (for pedestrians) at the side of a road. [from Old French from Latin pavimentum (pavire = ram)]

pavilion /pəˈvɪljən/ n. 1. a light building in a park etc. used as a shelter. 2. a building on a sports ground for players and spectators. 3. an ornamental building for public entertainment. 4. a large tent. [from Old French from Latin papilio, originally = butterfly]

paving /'peɪvɪŋ/ n. a paved surface; the material for this.

Pavlov /'pævlɒv/ Ivan Petrovich 1849–1936. Russian physiologist who studied conditioned reflexes in animals. His work had a great impact on behavioural theory (see ◊behaviourism) and ◊learning theory. See also ◊conditioning.

pavlova /pævˈləʊvə/ n. a meringue cake served with cream and fruit. [from Anna Pavlova]

Pavlova /'pævləvə/ Anna 1881–1931. Russian dancer. Prima ballerina of the Imperial Ballet from 1906, she left Russia in 1913, and went on to become the world's most celebrated exponent of classical ballet. With London as her home, she toured extensively with her own company, influencing dancers worldwide with roles such as Mikhail ◊Fokine's The Dying Swan solo in 1905.

As is the case in all branches of art, success depends in a very large measure upon individual initiative and exertion, and cannot be achieved except by dint of hard work.

Anna Pavlova

paw n. 1. the foot of an animal having claws or nails. 2. (colloquial) a person's hand. —v.t./i. 1. to strike with a paw. 2. to scrape (the ground) with a hoof. 3. (colloquial) to touch awkwardly or rudely with the hand(s). [from Old French poue]

pawky adj. (Scottish and dialect) drily humorous. —**pawkily** adv., **pawkiness** n. [from Scottish and north of England dialect pawk = trick]

pawl n. 1. a lever with a catch for the teeth of a wheel or bar. 2. (nautical) a short bar to prevent a capstan etc. from recoiling. [perhaps from Low German and Dutch pal]

pawn[1] n. 1. a chessman of the smallest size and value. 2. an unimportant person subservient to others' plans. [from Anglo-French poun from Latin pedo = foot soldier]

pawn[2] v.t. 1. to deposit (a thing) with a pawnbroker as security for money borrowed. 2. to pledge in the hope of receiving something in return. —n. the state of being pawned. [from Old French pan, pand etc. = pledge]

pawnbroker n. one who lends money at interest on the security of personal property deposited. The traditional sign of the premises is three gold balls, the symbol used in front of the houses of the medieval Lombard merchants. —**pawnbroking** n. the business of a pawnbroker.

pawnshop n. a pawnbroker's place of business.

pawpaw variant of ◊papaw.

Pax /pæks/ Roman goddess of peace; her Greek counterpart is ◊Irene.

Paxton /'pækstən/ Joseph 1801–1865. English architect, garden superintendent to the Duke of Devonshire from 1826 and designer of the Great Exhibition building of 1851 (◊Crystal Palace), revolutionary in its structural use of glass and iron.

pay v.t./i. (past and past participle **paid**) 1. to hand over (money) in return for goods or services or in discharge of a debt; to give (a person) what is owed; to hand over the amount of (wages, a debt, ransom etc.). 2. to bear the cost of something. 3. to be profitable, beneficial, or worthwhile (to). 4. to bestow, render, or express. 5. to suffer (a penalty etc.). 6. to let out (a rope) by slackening it. —n. payment; wages. —**in the pay of**, employed by. **pay for**, to suffer or be punished because of. **pay in**, to pay into a bank account etc. **paying guest**, one who pays for his or her board and lodging. **pay its way**, to make enough profit to cover expenses. **pay off**, to pay in full and be free from (a debt) or discharge (an employee); (colloquial) to yield good results. **payoff** n. (slang) payment; reward or retribution; a climax, especially of a joke or story. **pay one's way**, not get into debt. **pay out**, to punish or be revenged on. **pay packet**, a packet containing an employee's wages. **pay phone**, a telephone with a coinbox for prepayment of calls. **pay up**, to pay in full; to pay what is demanded. —**payer** n. [from Old French payer from Latin pacare = appease (pax = peace)]

payable adj. that must or may be paid.

PAYE abbreviation of pay as you earn. In the UK, this is a system of tax collection in which a proportional amount of income tax is deducted on a regular basis by the employer before wages are paid and transferred to the Inland Revenue, reliefs due being notified to the employer by a code number for each employee.

payee /peɪˈiː/ n. a person to whom money is (to be) paid.

payload n. the part of an aircraft's load from which revenue is derived; the total weight of bombs or instruments carried by an aircraft or rocket etc.; goods etc. carried on a road vehicle.

paymaster n. an official who pays troops, workers etc. —**Paymaster-General**, the head of the Paymaster-General's Office, the British government department (established in 1835) that acts as paying agent for most other departments.

payment n. 1. paying. 2. an amount paid. 3. reward, recompense.

payola /peɪˈəʊlə/ n. a bribe or bribery offered in return for illicit or unfair help in promoting a commercial product. [from *pay* and *-ola* after *Pianola* etc.]

payroll n. a list of employees receiving regular pay.

Paysandú /paɪsænˈduː/ city in Uruguay, capital of Paysandú department, on the river Uruguay; population (1985) 74,000. Tinned meat is the main product. The city dates from 1772 and is linked by bridge since 1976 with Puerto Colón in Argentina.

Pays de la Loire /peiˈi: də lɑ: ˈlwɑ:/ agricultural region of W France, comprising the *départements* of Loire-Atlantique, Maine-et-Loire, Mayenne, Sarthe, and Vendée; **capital** Nantes; **area** 32,100 sq km/12,391 sq mi; **population** (1986) 3,018,000. Industries include shipbuilding and wine.

Paz /pɑːs/ (Estenssoro) Victor 1907– . President of Bolivia 1952–56, 1960–64, and 1985–89. He founded and led the Movimiento Nacionalista Revolucionario which seized power in 1952. His regime extended the vote to Indians, nationalized the country's largest tin mines, embarked on a major programme of agrarian reform, and brought inflation under control.

Paz Octavio 1914– . Mexican poet and essayist. His works reflect many influences, including Marxism, surrealism and Aztec mythology. His most celebrated poem *Piedra del sol/Sun Stone* 1957 uses contrasting images, centring upon the Aztec Calendar Stone (representing the Aztec universe), to symbolize the loneliness of individuals and their search for union with others. He was awarded the Nobel Prize for Literature 1990.

Pb symbol for lead. [from Latin *plumbum*]

p.c. abbreviation of 1. per cent. 2. postcard.

PC abbreviation of 1. police constable. 2. Privy Counsellor. 3. personal computer.

PCB abbreviation of 1. ◊polychlorinated biphenyl. 2. ◊printed circuit board.

PCP abbreviation of phencyclidine hydrochloride, a drug popularly known as angel dust.

pd abbreviation of ◊potential difference.

pd. abbreviation of paid.

Pd symbol for ◊palladium.

PE abbreviation of physical education.

pea n. 1. a hardy climbing plant *Pisum sativum*, family Leguminosae, whose seeds grow in pods and are used for food. 2. its seed. 3. any of various similar plants. —**pea green** adj. & n. bright green. **peashooter** n. a toy tube from which dried peas are shot by blowing. **peasouper** n. (*colloquial*) a thick yellow fog. [from *pease* taken as plural]

peace /piːs/ n. 1. quiet, tranquillity; mental calm. 2. freedom from or cessation of war. 3. a treaty ending a war. 4. freedom from civil disorder. —**at peace**, in a state of peace, not in strife. **hold one's peace**, to keep quiet. **keep the peace**, to prevent or refrain from strife. **make one's peace**, to bring oneself back into friendly relations (*with*). **peace offering**, something offered to show that one is willing to make peace. **peace pipe**, a tobacco pipe as a token of peace among North American Indians. **peacetime** n. a period when a country is not at war. [from Anglo-French from Latin *pax*]

peaceable /ˈpiːsəbəl/ adj. 1. desiring to be at peace with others, not quarrelsome. 2. peaceful. —**peaceably** adv. [from Old French from Latin *placabilis* = pleasing]

Peace Corps an organization of trained men and women, established in the USA by President Kennedy in 1961, providing skilled volunteer workers for the developing countries, especially in the fields of teaching, agriculture, and health. Living among the country's inhabitants, workers are paid only a small allowance to cover their basic needs and maintain health. The Peace Corps was inspired by the British programme Voluntary Service Overseas (VSO).

peaceful adj. characterized by or concerned with peace; not violating or infringing peace. —**peacefully** adv., **peacefulness** n.

peacemaker n. one who brings about peace.

peace movement the collective opposition to war. The Western peace movements of the late 20th century can trace their origins to the pacifists of the 19th century and conscientious objectors during World War I. The campaigns after World War II have tended to concentrate on nuclear weapons, but there are numerous organizations devoted to peace, some wholly pacifist, some merely opposed to escalation.

peach n. 1. a round, juicy fruit with a downy yellowish or reddish skin; the ◊nectarine is a smooth-skinned variety. 2. the tree *Prunus persica*, family Rosaceae, bearing it, with ovate leaves and small, usually pink flowers. 3. the yellowish-pink colour of the fruit. 4. (*slang*) a person or thing of superlative merit; an attractive young woman. —**peach Melba**, a dish of ice cream and peaches with a raspberry sauce. —**peachy** adj. [from Old French *peche* from Latin *persicum* (*malum*) = peach (literally 'Persian apple')]

peacock /ˈpiːkɒk/ n. the male peafowl, a bird of the pheasant family, native to S Asia. The common peacock *Pavo cristatus* is rather larger than a pheasant. The male has a large, brilliantly coloured tail with blue, green, and purple 'eyes' on a chestnut ground that can be spread upright like a fan. The female, or peahen, is brown with a small tail. —**peacock blue**, the lustrous blue of the peacock's neck. **peacock butterfly**, a butterfly *Inachis io* with conspicuous 'eyes' on its wings. [Old English from Latin *pavo* = peacock]

Peacock Thomas Love 1785–1866. English satirical novelist and poet. His works include *Headlong Hall* 1816, *Nightmare Abbey* 1818, *Crotchet Castle* 1831, and *Gryll Grange* 1860.

Marriage may often be a stormy lake, but celibacy is almost always a muddy horsepond.

                       Thomas Love Peacock
                              Melincourt

---

peafowl n. a kind of pheasant of the genus *Pavo*, a peacock or peahen.

peahen n. the female of the peafowl.

pea jacket /ˈpiːdʒækɪt/ a sailor's short double-breasted overcoat of coarse woollen cloth. [probably from Dutch *pijjakker*]

peak[1] n. 1. a pointed top, especially of a mountain. 2. any shape, edge, or part that tapers to form a point. 3. the projecting part (usually at the front) of the brim of a cap. 4. the highest point of achievement, intensity etc. 5. (*attributive*) maximum, most busy or intense etc. —*v.i.* to reach the highest value, quality etc. —**Peak District**, an area in Derbyshire, England, where there are many peaks. [from dialect *picked* = pointed]

peak[2] *v.i.* 1. to waste away. 2. (in *past participle*) pinched, drawn.

Peake /piːk/ Mervyn (Lawrence) 1911–1968. English writer and illustrator, born in China. His novels include the grotesque fantasy trilogy *Titus Groan* 1946, *Gormenghast* 1950, and *Titus Alone* 1959.

peaky adj. sickly, peaked. —**peakiness** n.

peal n. 1. the loud ringing of a bell or bells, especially a series of changes on a set of bells. 2. a set of bells with different notes. 3. a loud outburst of sound, especially of thunder or laughter. —*v.t./i.* to sound or cause to sound in a peal. [from *appellare* = address (*pellere* = drive)]

Peale /piːl/ Charles Willson 1741–1827. American artist, head of a large family of painters. His portraits of leading figures in the Revolutionary War include the earliest known portrait of George Washington (1772).

peanut n. or **groundnut** or **monkey nut** 1. a South American vinelike annual plant *Arachis hypogaea*, family Leguminosae. After flowering, the flower stalks bend and force the pods into the earth to ripen underground. The nuts are a staple food in many tropical countries and widely grown in the southern USA. They yield a valuable edible oil and are the basis for numerous processed foods. 2. the seed, or nut of this plant. 3. (in *plural, slang*) a paltry or trivial thing or amount, especially of money. —**peanut butter**, a paste of ground roasted peanuts.

pear /peə/ n. 1. a rounded fleshy fruit tapering towards the stalk. 2. the tree bearing it *Pyrus communis*, family Rosaceae, native to temperate regions of Eurasia. [Old English, ultimately from Latin *pirum*]

pearl /pɜːl/ n. 1. a smooth, lustrous, usually white or bluish-grey, calcareous substance (nacre) secreted by many molluscs, and deposited in thin layers on the inside of the shell around a parasite, a grain of sand, or some other irritant body. After several years of the mantle secreting this substance, a pearl is formed. See also ◊mother-of-pearl (under ◊mother). **2.** a thing like a pearl in form. **3.** a precious thing, the finest example. —*adj.* like a pearl in form or colour. —*v.t./i.* **1.** to fish for pearls. **2.** to reduce (barley etc.) to small rounded grains. **3.** to form pearl-like drops. **4.** to sprinkle with pearly drops. —**pearl barley,** barley rubbed into small rounded grains. **pearl button,** a button of real or imitation mother-of-pearl. **pearl diver,** one who dives for oysters containing pearls. [from Old French *perle*, probably ultimately from Latin *perna* = leg (applied to a kind of bivalve)]

Pearl Harbor /'pɜːl 'hɑːbə/ US Pacific naval base in Oahu, Hawaii, USA, the scene of a Japanese attack on 7 Dec 1941, which brought the USA into World War II. It took place while Japanese envoys were holding so-called peace talks in Washington. More than 2,000 US servicemen were killed, and a large part of the US Pacific fleet was destroyed or damaged during the attack.

pearly *adj.* like or adorned with pearls. —*n.* (in *plural*) costermongers' clothes decorated with pearl buttons. —**Pearly Gates,** the gates of heaven. **pearly king** (*or* **queen**), a leading London costermonger (or his wife) wearing pearlies.

Pearse /piəs/ Patrick Henry 1879–1916. Irish poet prominent in the Gaelic revival, a leader of the ◊Easter Rising of 1916. Proclaimed president of the provisional government, he was court-martialled and shot after its suppression.

Pearson /'piəsən/ Karl 1857–1936. British statistician, who followed Francis ◊Galton in introducing statistics and probability into genetics and who developed the concept of eugenics (improving the human race by selective breeding). He introduced the term ◊standard deviation into statistics.

Pearson Lester Bowles 1897–1972. Canadian politician, leader of the Liberal Party from 1958, prime minister 1963–68. As foreign minister 1948–57, he represented Canada at the United Nations, playing a key role in settling the ◊Suez Crisis in 1956. He was awarded the Nobel Peace Prize in 1957.

Peary /'piəri/ Robert Edwin 1856–1920. US polar explorer who, after several unsuccessful attempts, became the first person to reach the North Pole on 6 April 1909. In 1988 an astronomer claimed Peary's measurements were incorrect.

peasant /'pezənt/ *n.* a country dweller engaged in small-scale farming. A peasant normally owns or rents a small amount of land, aiming to be self-sufficent and to sell surplus supplies locally. —**peasantry** *n.* [from Anglo-French *paisant* (*païs* = country from Latin *pagus* = village)]

Peasants' Revolt the rising of the English peasantry in June 1381. Severe economic conditions following the Black Death together with the introduction of a poll tax in 1379 led to riots throughout England, especially in Kent and Essex. Led by Wat ◊Tyler and John ◊Ball, the rebels marched to London and demanded an end to serfdom and feudalism. King Richard II made concessions to the rebels which, after the death of Tyler at the hands of William Walworth, Lord Mayor of London, succeeded in dispersing them. These concessions were, however, revoked immediately.

pease /piːz/ *n.* (*archaic*) peas. —**pease pudding,** a pudding of boiled peas, eggs etc. [Old English *pise* = pea from Latin *pisum*]

peat *n.* a fibrous organic substance found in ◊bogs and formed by the incomplete decomposition of plants such as sphagnum moss. The USSR, Canada, Finland, Ireland, and other places have large deposits, which have been dried and used as fuel from ancient times. Peat can also be used as a soil additive.

peatbog *n.* a bog composed of peat.

pebble *n.* a small stone worn and rounded by the action of water. —**pebbledash** *n.* mortar with pebbles in it as a coating for a wall. —**pebbly** *adj.* [Old English]

pecan /'piːkən, pi'kæn/ *n.* a nut-producing ◊hickory tree *Carya illinoensis* or *C. pecan*, native to central USA and N Mexico and now widely cultivated. The tree grows to over 45 m/150 ft, and the edible nuts are smooth-shelled, the kernel resembling a smoothly ovate walnut. [from Algonquian]

peccadillo /pekə'dɪləʊ/ *n.* (*plural* **peccadilloes**) a trivial offence. [from Spanish (diminutive of *pecado* = sin from Latin *peccare* = to sin)]

peccary /'pekərɪ/ *n.* a tropical American genus of piglike animals *Tayassu*, having a gland in the middle of the back which secretes a strong-smelling substance. They are blackish in colour, covered with bristles, and have tusks which point downwards. Adults reach a height of 40 cm/16 in, and a weight of 25 kg/60 lbs. [from Carib]

peck[1] /pek/ *v.t./i.* **1.** to strike, nip, or pick up with the beak; to make (a hole) with the beak. **2.** to kiss hastily or perfunctorily. **3.** (*colloquial*) to eat in a nibbling or listless fashion. **4.** to carp *at.* **5.** to mark with short strokes. —*n.* **1.** a stroke, nip, or mark made by a beak. **2.** a hasty or perfunctory kiss. —**pecking order,** a social hierarchy, originally as observed among domestic fowls, where aggressive behaviour towards those of inferior status took the form of pecking.

peck[2] *n.* **1.** a measure of capacity for dry goods equal to 2 gallons or 8 quarts. **2.** a lot. [from Anglo-French]

Peck (Eldred) Gregory 1916–. US film actor. One of Hollywood's most enduring stars, he was often cast as a decent man of great moral and physical strength, as in *The Old Gringo* 1989. His other films include *Spellbound* 1945 and *To Kill a Mockingbird* 1962.

pecker *n.* in combinations, a bird that pecks. —**keep your pecker up,** (*slang*) stay cheerful.

Peckinpah /'pekɪnpɑː/ Sam 1925–1985. US film director, often of westerns, usually associated with slow-motion, blood-spurting violence. His best films, such as *The Wild Bunch* 1969, exhibit a thoughtful, if depressing, view of the world and human nature.

peckish *adj.* (*colloquial*) hungry.

Pécs /peɪtʃ/ city in SW Hungary, the centre of a coalmining area on the Yugoslav frontier; population (1988) 182,000. Industries include metal, leather, and wine. The town dates from Roman times and was under Turkish rule 1543–1686.

pectin /'pektɪn/ *n.* a soluble gelatinous carbohydrate found in ripe fruits etc. and used as a setting agent in jams and jellies. [from Greek *pēktos* = congealed]

pectoral /'pektərəl/ *adj.* of or for the breast, chest, or the upper area of the thorax associated with the muscles and bones used in moving the arms or forelimbs. —*n.* a pectoral fin or muscle. In birds, the *pectoralis major* is the very large muscle used to produce a powerful downbeat of the wing during flight. [from Old French from Latin *pectus* = breast]

peculate /'pekjʊleɪt/ *v.t./i.* to embezzle (money). —**peculation** /-'leɪʃən/ *n.*, **peculator** *n.* [from Latin]

peculiar /pi'kjuːlɪə/ *adj.* **1.** strange, eccentric. **2.** belonging exclusively *to*; belonging to the individual. **3.** particular, special. —**peculiarly** *adv.* [from Latin *peculium* = private property]

peculiarity /pɪkjuː'lɪærɪtɪ/ *n.* **1.** being peculiar. **2.** a characteristic. **3.** an oddity, an eccentricity.

pecuniary /pi'kjuːnɪərɪ/ *adj.* of or consisting of money. [from Latin *pecunia* = money from *pecu* = cattle, because in early Rome wealth consisted of cattle and sheep]

pedagogue /'pedəgɒg/ *n.* (*archaic*) a schoolmaster; (*derogatory*) one who teaches in a pedantic way. [from Latin from Greek *paidagōgos* (*pais* = boy and *agōgos* = guide)]

pedagogy /'pedəgɒdʒɪ/ *n.* the science of teaching. —**pedagogic** /-'gɒdʒɪk/ *adj.*, **pedagogical** /-'gɒdʒɪkəl/ *adj.* [from French from Greek]

pedal /'pedəl/ *n.* a lever or key operated by the foot, especially in a bicycle or motor vehicle or some musical instruments (e.g. the organ and the harp). —*v.t./i.* (-ll-) **1.** to move or operate by means of pedals. **2.** to ride a bicycle. —/also 'piː-/ *adj.* of the foot or feet. [from Latin or from French from Italian from Latin *pes* = foot]

pedalo /'pedələʊ/ *n.* (*plural* **pedalos**) a small pedal-operated pleasure boat.

pedant /'pedənt/ *n.* one who lays excessive emphasis on detailed points of learning or procedure. —**pedantic** /pi'dæntɪk/ *adj.*, **pedantically** /pi'dæntɪkəlɪ/ *adv.*, **pedantry** *n.* [from French from Italian]

peddle *v.t.* to sell (goods) as a pedlar; to carry about and offer for sale (*literally and figuratively*).

pederast /'pedəræst/ *n.* one who commits pederasty.

pederasty *n.* a homosexual act with a boy. [from Greek *pais* = boy and *erastēs* = lover]

pedestal /'pedɪstəl/ *n.* **1.** a base supporting a column, pillar, or statue etc. **2.** each of the two supporting columns of a knee-hole desk etc. —**put on a pedestal,**

to admire or respect greatly. [from French *piédestal* from Italian *piede* = foot]

pedestrian /pɪ'destrɪən/ *n.* a person who is walking, especially in a street. —*adj.* **1.** prosaic, dull. **2.** of walking; going or performed on foot. **3.** for walkers. —**pedestrian crossing,** a part of a road where crossing pedestrians have priority over the traffic. —**pedestrianism** *n.* [from French or Latin *pedester* (*pes* = foot)]

pedicel *n.* the stalk of an individual flower, which attaches it to the main floral axis, often developing in the axil of a bract.

pedicure /'pedɪkjuə/ *n.* **1.** care or treatment of the feet and toenails. **2.** a person who practises this professionally. [from French (Latin *pes* = foot and *curare* = care for)]

pedigree /'pedɪgri:/ *n.* **1.** a genealogical table. **2.** ancestral line (especially a distinguished one) of a person or animal. **3.** derivation. **4.** (*attributive*) having a recorded line of descent, especially one showing pure breeding. [from earlier *pedegru* from Anglo-French and Old French = crane's foot, mark denoting succession in pedigrees]

pediment /'pedɪmənt/ *n.* a triangular part crowning the front of a building, especially over a portico. The pediment was a distinctive feature of Greek temples. [earlier *periment*, perhaps corruption of *pyramid*]

pedlar /'pedlə/ *n.* **1.** a travelling vendor of small articles that are usually carried in a pack. **2.** a seller of illegal drugs. **3.** a retailer *of* gossip etc. [alteration of obsolete *pedder* (*ped* = pannier]

pedology /pɪ'dɒlədʒɪ/ *n.* the science of natural soils. —**pedological** /-də'lɒdʒɪkəl/ *adj.*, **pedologist** *n.* [from Russian from Greek *pedon* = ground]

pedometer /pɪ'dɒmɪtə/ *n.* an instrument for estimating the distance travelled on foot by recording the number of steps taken. Each step sets in motion a swinging weight within the instrument, causing the mechanism to rotate, and the number of rotations are registered on the instrument face. [from French from Latin *pedester* (*pes* = foot)]

Pedro /'pedrəʊ/ two emperors of Brazil:

Pedro I 1798–1834. Emperor of Brazil 1822–31. The son of John VI of Portugal, he escaped to Brazil on Napoleon's invasion, and was appointed regent in 1821. He proclaimed Brazil independent in 1822 and was crowned emperor, but abdicated in 1831 and returned to Portugal.

Pedro II 1825–1891. Emperor of Brazil 1831–89. He proved an enlightened ruler, but his antislavery measures alienated the landowners, who compelled him to abdicate.

peduncle /pɪ'dʌnkəl/ *n.* the stalk of a flower, fruit, or cluster, especially the main stalk bearing a solitary flower or subordinate stalks. —**peduncular** /pɪ'dʌnkjulə/ *adj.* [from Latin *pes* = foot]

pee *v.i.* (*colloquial*) to urinate. —*n.* (*colloquial*) **1.** urination. **2.** urine. [from *piss*]

Peeblesshire /'pi:bəlzʃə/ former county of S Scotland, included from 1975 in Borders region; Peebles was the county town.

peek *v.i.* to peep, to glance. —*n.* a peep, a glance.

peel *n.* the outer skin of certain fruits and vegetables; the outer coating of prawns etc. —*v.t./i.* **1.** to remove the peel from; to take *off* (peel etc.); to be able to be peeled. **2.** to come *off* in strips or layers; to lose skin or bark etc. thus. **3.** (*slang*) to strip off one's clothes before exercise. —**peel off,** to veer away from a formation of which one formed part. —**peeler** *n.* [from earlier *pill*, perhaps from Latin *pilare* = remove hair from (*pilus* = hair)]

Peel /pi:l/ Robert 1788–1850. British Conservative politician. As home secretary 1822–27 and 1828–30, he founded the modern police force and in 1829 introduced Roman Catholic emancipation. He was prime minister 1834–35 and 1841–46, when his repeal of the ◊Corn Laws caused him and his followers to break with the party.

peeling *n.* a piece peeled off, especially the skin of a fruit or vegetable.

Peenemünde /peɪnə'mʊndə/ fishing village in E Germany, used from 1937 by the Germans to develop the V2 rockets used in World War II.

peep[1] *v.i.* **1.** to look quickly or surreptitiously; to look through a narrow opening or from a concealed place. **2.** to come briefly or partially into view; to emerge slightly. —*n.* **1.** a brief or surreptitious look. **2.** the first appearance (of dawn, day etc.). —**peephole** *n.* a small hole to peep through. **Peeping Tom,** a furtive voyeur (from the name of

Peel *A portrait of Robert Peel, founder of the police force, by H W Pickersgill.*

a Coventry tailor said to have peeped at Lady Godiva when she rode naked through Coventry). **peep-of-day boys,** a Protestant organization in Ireland (1784–95) searching opponents' houses at daybreak for arms. **peepshow** *n.* a device, usually in the form of a box, with a small eyepiece, inside which are arranged the receding elements of a perspective view. **peep-toe(d)** *adj.* (of shoes) with a small opening at the tip of the toe.

peep[2] *n.* a weak high chirping sound like that made by young birds. —*v.i.* to make this sound. [imitative]

peepul another name for ◊bo tree.

peer[1] *v.i.* **1.** to peer searchingly or with difficulty. **2.** (*archaic*) to appear, to come into view. [variant of earlier *pire* from Low German]

peer[2] *n.* **1.** one who is equal to another in rank, standing, merit etc.; a member of the same age group or social set. **2.** a member of one of the degrees (duke, marquis, earl, viscount, baron) of nobility in the United Kingdom; a noble of any country. —**peer group,** a group of people who have a common identity based on such characteristics as similar social status, interests, age, or ethnic group. [from Anglo-French from Latin *par* = equal]

peerage *n.* **1.** peers, the nobility. **2.** the rank of peer or peeress. **3.** a book containing a list of peers.

peeress /'pɪərɪs/ *n.* a female holder of a peerage; a peer's wife.

peerless *adj.* unrivalled, superb.

peeve *v.t./i.* (*slang*) **1.** to irritate, to annoy. **2.** to grumble. —*n.* (*slang*) **1.** a cause of annoyance. **2.** a mood of vexation. [back formation from *peevish*]

peeved /pi:vd/ *adj.* (*slang*) annoyed, vexed.

peevish /'pi:vɪʃ/ *adj.* irritable, querulous. —**peevishly** *adv.*, **peevishness** *n.* [earlier = silly, mad, spiteful]

peewit /'pi:wɪt/ *n.* another name for the ◊lapwing, a kind of plover. [imitative of its cry]

peg *n.* **1.** a pin or bolt of wood, metal etc., for holding things together, hanging things on, holding a tent rope taut, marking a position, or as a stopper. **2.** a clothes peg. **3.** any of a series of pins or screws for adjusting the tension in a string of a violin etc. **4.** an occasion or opportunity, a pretext. **5.** a drink or measure of spirits. —*v.t./i.* (-gg-) **1.** to fix or mark with a peg or pegs. **2.** to maintain (prices or wages) at a certain level. —**off the peg,** (of clothes) ready-made. **peg away,** to work diligently, to be persistent. **pegboard** *n.* a board with holes and pegs for displaying or hanging things on. **peg leg,** an artificial leg; a person with this. **peg out,** to mark out the boundaries of; (*slang*) to die. **square peg in a round hole,** a person not suited to his or her surroundings, position etc. **take a person down a peg (or two),** to humble or humiliate him or her.

Pegasus /'pegəsəs/ **1.** in Greek mythology, the winged horse that sprang from the blood of Medusa, the steed of Bellerophon. Hippocrene, the spring of the Muses on Mount Helicon, Greece, is said to have sprung from a blow of his hoof. He was transformed into a constellation. 2. in astronomy, a constellation of the northern hemisphere, near Cygnus, and represented as a winged horse.

pegmatite *n.* an extremely coarse-grained igneous rock found in veins usually associated with large granite masses.

Pegu /pe'guː/ city in S Myanmar on the river Pegu, NE of Yangon; population (1983) 254,762. It was founded in 573 and is the home of the celebrated Shwemawdaw pagoda.

Péguy /peɪ'giː/ Charles 1873–1914. French Catholic socialist, who established a socialist publishing house in Paris. From 1900 he published on political topics *Les Cahiers de la Quinzaine/Fortnightly Notebooks* and on poetry, including *Le Mystère de la charité de Jeanne d'Arc/The Mystery of the Charity of Joan of Arc* 1897.

> The classical artist can be recognized by his sincerity, the romantic by his laborious insincerity.
>
> **Charles Péguy**
> preface to Jean Hugues' *La Grève*

Pei /peɪ/ Ieoh Ming 1917– . Chinese modernist/high-tech architect, who became a US citizen in 1948. His buildings include Dallas City Hall, Texas; East Building, National Gallery of Art, Washington DC, 1978; John F Kennedy Library Complex and the John Hancock Tower, Boston 1979; the Bank of China Tower, Hong Kong, 1987; and the glass pyramid in front of the Louvre, Paris, 1989.

PEI abbreviation of Prince Edward Island.

pejorative /pɪ'dʒɒrətɪv, 'piː dʒə-/ *adj.* derogatory, disparaging. —*n.* a pejorative word. —**pejoratively** *adv.* [from French from Latin *pejorare* (*pejor* = worse)]

pekan *n.* or **fisher marten** a North American marten (carnivorous mammal) about 1.2 m/4 ft long, with a doglike face, and brown fur with white patches on the chest.

peke /piːk/ *n.* (*colloquial*) a Pekingese dog. [abbreviation]

Peking /piː'kɪŋ/ former name of ◊Beijing, capital of China.

Pekingese /piː kiː'niː z/ *n.* (*plural* the same) 1. a native or inhabitant of Peking (now Beijing). 2. a dog of a short-legged snub-nosed breed with long silky hair, originally brought to Europe from the Summer Palace at Peking, China, in 1860.

Peking man the Chinese representative of an early species of human being, found as fossils, 500,000–750,000 years old, near Beijing (formerly Peking) in 1927. They had primitive stone tools, hunted game, and used fire. Similar varieties have been found in Java and E Africa. Their classification is disputed: some anthropologists classify them as *Homo erectus*, others as *Homo sapiens pithecanthropus*.

pekoe /'piː kəʊ/ *n.* a superior kind of black tea. [from Chinese dialect *pek-ho* = white down (the leaves being picked young with down on them)]

Pelagius /pe'leɪdʒəs/ 360–420. British theologian. He taught that each person possesses free will (and hence the possibility of salvation), denying Augustine's doctrines of predestination and original sin. Cleared of heresy by a synod in Jerusalem in 415, he was later condemned by the pope and the emperor.

pelargonium /pelɑː'gəʊniəm/ *n.* a plant of the genus *Pelargonium*, with showy flowers. [from Greek *pelargos* = stork]

Pelé /'peleɪ/ Adopted name of Edson Arantes do Nascimento 1940– . Brazilian soccer player. A prolific goal scorer, he appeared in four World Cup competitions 1958–70 and led Brazil to three championships. He spent most of his playing career with the Brazilian team, Santos, before ending it with the New York Cosmos in the USA.

pelf *n.* (usually *derogatory* or *jocular*) money, wealth. [related to Old French *pelfre* = spoils]

Pelham /'peləm/ Henry 1696–1754. British Whig politician. He held a succession of offices in Walpole's cabinet 1721–42, and was prime minister 1743–54.

pelican /'pelɪkən/ *n.* a type of large water bird of the family Pelecanidae, remarkable for the pouch beneath the bill used as a fishing net and temporary store for its catches of fish. Some species grow up to 1.8 m/6 ft, and have wingspans of 3 m/10 ft. —**pelican crossing**, a pedestrian crossing with traffic lights operated by pedestrians. [Old

English and from Old French from Latin from Greek *pelekus* = axe, with reference to its bill]

Pelion /'piːliən/ mountain in Thessaly, Greece, near Mount ◊Ossa; height 1,548 m/5,079 ft. In Greek mythology it was the home of the ◊Centaurs.

pelisse /pe'liː s/ *n.* 1. a woman's cloaklike garment with armholes or sleeves, reaching to the ankles. 2. a fur-lined mantle or cloak, especially as part of a hussar's uniform. [French from Latin *pellicia* = fur garment (*pellis* = skin)]

pellagra /pɪ'lægrə, -'leɪgrə/ *n.* a deficiency disease with cracking of the skin, often ending in insanity. [Italian *pelle* = skin]

pellet /'pelɪt/ *n.* 1. a small, rounded, closely packed mass of a soft substance. 2. a slug of small shot. [from Old French from Latin *pila* = ball]

pellicle /'pelɪkəl/ *n.* a thin skin; a membrane; a thin layer. [from French from Latin *pellicula*, diminutive of *pellis* = skin]

pell-mell /'pel'mel/ *adv.* & *adj.* in a hurrying, disorderly manner; headlong. [from French from Old French *peslemesle*, reduplication of *mesle* (*mesler* = mix)]

pellucid /pɪ'ljuː sɪd, -'luː-/ *adj.* 1. transparent, not distorting images or diffusing the light. 2. clear in style, expression, or thought. [from Latin]

pelmet /'pelmɪt/ *n.* a valance or pendent border, especially over a window or door to conceal curtain rods. [probably from French *palmette* = palm-leaf ornament]

Peloponnese /peləpə'niː s/ (Greek *Peloponnesos*) peninsula forming the S part of Greece; area 21,549 sq km/8,318 sq mi; population (1981) 1,012,500. It is joined to the mainland by the narrow isthmus of Corinth and is divided into the nomes (administrative areas) of Argolis, Arcadia, Achaea, Elis, Corinth, Lakonia, and Messenia, representing its seven ancient states.

Peloponnesian War /peləpə'niː ʃən/ the conflict between Athens and Sparta and their allies, 431–404 BC, originating in suspicions about the 'empire-building' ambitions of Pericles. It was ended by ◊Lysander's destruction of the political power of Athens.

pelota /pɪ'ləʊtə/ *n.* or **jai alai** (merry festival) a very fast ball game of Basque derivation, popular in Latin American countries and in the USA where it is a betting sport. It is played by two, four, or six players, in a walled court, or *cancha*, and somewhat resembles squash, but each player uses a long, curved, wickerwork basket, or *cesta*, strapped to the hand, to hurl the ball, or pelota (about the size of a baseball), against the walls. [Spanish = ball]

pelt[1] *v.t./i.* 1. to attack or strike repeatedly with missiles. 2. (of rain etc.) to beat down fast. 3. to run fast. —*n.* pelting. —**at full pelt**, as fast as possible.

pelt[2] *n.* an animal skin, especially with the hair or fur still on it. [from Old French, ultimately from Latin *pellis* = skin]

Peltier effect /'peltieɪ/ in physics, a change in temperature at the junction of two different metals produced when an electric current flows through them. The extent of the change depends on what the conducting metals are, and the nature of change (rise or fall in temperature) depends on the direction of current flow. It is the reverse of the ◊Seebeck effect. [from French physicist Jean Charles *Peltier* (1785–1845) who discovered it in 1834]

pelvis /'pelvɪs/ *n.* the basin-shaped cavity formed by the bones of the haunch with the sacrum and other vertebrae. —**pelvic** *adj.* —**pelvic girdle**, a set of bones that allows movement of the legs in relation to the rest of the body and provides sites for the attachment of relevant muscles. [Latin = basin]

Pembrokeshire /'pembrʊkʃə/ former extreme SW county of Wales, which became part of Dyfed in 1974; the county town was Haverfordwest.

pemmican /'pemɪkən/ *n.* a North American Indian cake of dried and pounded meat mixed with melted fat; beef so treated and flavoured with currants etc. for Arctic and other travellers. [from Cree *pimecan* (*pime* = fat)]

pen[1] *n.* 1. an instrument for writing in ink (originally a sharpened quill, now usually a device with a metal nib). 2. writing, especially as a profession. —*v.t.* (**-nn-**) to write (a letter etc.). —**pen friend**, a friend acquired and known mainly or only from correspondence. **pen name**, a literary pseudonym. **penpushing** *n.* (*colloquial*) clerical work. [from Old French from Latin *penna* = feather]

pen² *n.* a small enclosure for cows, sheep, poultry etc. —*v.t.* (**-nn-**) to enclose, to shut in or as if in a pen. [Old English *penn*]

pen³ *n.* a female swan.

penal /'pi:nəl/ *adj.* of or involving punishment, especially by law; (of an offence) punishable. —**penally** *adv.* [from Old French or Latin *poena* = punishment]

penalize /'pi:nəlaɪz/ *v.t.* **1.** to inflict a penalty on. **2.** to place at a comparative disadvantage. **3.** to make or declare (an action) penal.

penalty /'penəltɪ/ *n.* **1.** a punishment for breaking a law, rule, or contract; a fine or loss etc. incurred by this. **2.** a disadvantage imposed by an action or circumstances. **3.** a disadvantage to which a player or team in a sport must submit for breach of a rule. —**penalty area**, the area in front of the goal on a football field in which a foul by the defenders involves the award of a penalty kick. [from French from Latin *penalitas*]

penance /'penəns/ *n.* **1.** an act of self-mortification as an expression of repentance. **2.** in the Roman Catholic and Orthodox churches, a sacrament involving confession, absolution, and an act of repentance imposed by a priest. Penance is worked out now in terms of good deeds rather than routine repetition of prayers. —**do penance**, to perform such an act. [from Old French from Latin *poenitentia*]

Penang /pi'næŋ/ (Malay *Pulau Pinang*) state in W Peninsular Malaysia, formed of Penang Island, Province Wellesley, and the Dindings on the mainland; **area** 1,030 sq km/398 sq mi; **capital** Penang (George Town); **population** (1980) 955,000; **history** Penang Island was bought by Britain from the ruler of Kedah in 1785; Province Wellesley was acquired in 1800.

pence plural of **penny**.

penchant /'pɑ̃ʃɑ̃/ *n.* an inclination or liking. [French (*pencher* = incline)]

pencil /'pensəl/ *n.* **1.** an instrument for drawing or writing, especially of graphite, chalk etc., enclosed in a cylinder of wood or a metal etc. case with a tapering end. **2.** something used or shaped like this. —*v.t.* (**-ll-**) to write, draw, or mark with a pencil. [from Old French from Latin *penicillum* = paintbrush]

Penda /'pendə/ *c.*577–654. King of Mercia from about 632. He raised Mercia to a powerful kingdom, and defeated and killed two Northumbrian kings, Edwin in 632 and ◊Oswald in 642. He was killed in battle by Oswy, king of Northumbria.

pendant /'pendənt/ *n.* a hanging ornament, especially one attached to a necklace, bracelet etc. [from Old French from Latin *pendēre* = hang]

pendent *adj.* **1.** hanging, overhanging. **2.** undecided, pending. —**pendency** *n.* [variant of *pendant*]

pendentive /pen'dentɪv/ *n.* a spherical triangle formed by the intersection of a dome with two adjacent arches springing from supporting columns. [from French]

Penderecki /pendə'retski/ Krzysztof 1933– . Polish composer. His Expressionist works, such as the *Threnody for the Victims of Hiroshima* 1961 for strings, employ cluster and percusssion effects. He later turned to religious subjects and a more orthodox style, as in the *Magnificat* 1974 and the *Polish Requiem* 1980–83.

pending *adj.* **1.** waiting to be decided or settled. **2.** about to come into existence. —*prep.* **1.** until. **2.** during. [after French *pendant*]

pendulous /'pendjʊləs/ *adj.* hanging down, hanging so as to swing freely. [from Latin *pendēre* = hang]

pendulum /'pendjʊləm/ *n.* **1.** a body suspended so that it can swing freely or oscillate. **2.** an instrument consisting of a rod with a weight or 'bob' at the end, so suspended as to swing to and fro by the action of gravity.

Penelope /pə'neləpi/ in Greek legend, the wife of ◊Odysseus. During his absence after the siege of Troy she kept her many suitors at bay by asking them to wait until she had woven a shroud for her father-in-law, but unravelled her work each night. When Odysseus returned, he killed her suitors.

peneplain /'peniːpleɪn/ *n.* a region that has become almost a plain as a result of erosion. [Latin *paene* = almost]

penetrable /'penɪtrəbəl/ *adj.* that can be penetrated. —**penetrability** /-'bɪlɪtɪ/ *n.*

penetrate /'penɪtreɪt/ *v.t./i.* **1.** to make a way into or through. **2.** to enter and permeate. **3.** to see into or through (darkness etc.). **4.** to explore or comprehend mentally. **5.** to be absorbed by the mind. —**penetration** /-'treɪʃən/ *n.* [from Latin *penetrare* (*penitus* = inmost)]

penetrating *adj.* **1.** having or showing great insight. **2.** (of a voice or sound) easily heard through or above other sounds, carrying. —**penetratingly** *adv.*

penetration technology the development of missiles that have low radar, infrared, and optical signatures and thus can penetrate an enemy's defences undetected. In 1980 the USA announced that it had developed such a piloted aircraft, known as Stealth. It comes in both fighter and bomber versions. In 1989 two out of three tests failed, and by 1990 the cost of the Stealth had risen to $815 million per aircraft.

penguin /'peŋgwɪn/ *n.* a flightless sea bird of the family Spheniscidae of the southern hemisphere. Penguins are usually black and white, and they range in size from 40 cm/1.6 ft to 1.2 m/4 ft tall and have thick feathers to protect them from the intense cold. They are awkward on land, but their wings have evolved into flippers, making them excellent underwater swimmers. [originally = great auk]

penicillin /peni'sɪlɪn/ *n.* any of a group of ◊antibiotic compounds obtained from filtrates of moulds of the genus *Penicillium* (especially *P. notatum*) or produced synthetically. Penicillin was the first antibiotic to be discovered (by Alexander ◊Fleming), and kills a broad spectrum of bacteria, many of which cause disease in humans. [from Latin]

peninsula /pi'nɪnsjʊlə/ *n.* a tongue of land surrounded on three sides by water but still attached to a larger landmass. Florida, USA, is an example. —**peninsular** *adj.* [from Latin *paeninsula* (*paene* = almost and *insula* = island)]

Peninsular War the war 1808–14 caused by the French emperor Napoleon's invasion of Portugal and Spain. British expeditionary forces, combined with Spanish and Portuguese resistance, succeeded in defeating the French at Vimeiro in 1808, Talavera in 1809, ◊Salamanca in 1812, and Vittoria in 1813. The results were inconclusive, and the war was ended by Napoleon's abdication.

penis /'pi:nɪs/ *n.* the male reproductive organ, used for internal fertilization; it transfers sperm to the female reproductive tract. In mammals, the penis is made erect by vessels that fill with blood, and in most mammals (but not humans) is stiffened by a bone. It also contains the urethra, through which urine is passed. [Latin, originally = tail]

penitent /'penɪtənt/ *adj.* repentant. —*n.* a repentant sinner; a person doing penance under the direction of a confessor. —**penitence** *n.*, **penitently** *adv.* [from Old French from Latin *paenitēre* = repent]

penitential /peni'tenʃəl/ *adj.* of penitence or penance.

penitentiary /peni'tenʃərɪ/ *n.* (*US*) a prison for offenders convicted of serious crimes. —*adj.* **1.** of penance. **2.** of reformatory treatment. [from Latin]

penknife *n.* a small folding knife, especially for carrying in the pocket.

penmanship *n.* **1.** skill or style in writing or handwriting. **2.** the process of literary composition.

Penn /pen/ Irving 1917– . US fashion, advertising, portrait, editorial, and fine art photographer. In 1948 he took the first of many journeys to Africa and the Far East, resulting in a series of portrait photographs of local people, avoiding sophisticated technique. He was associated for many years with *Vogue* magazine in the USA.

Penn William 1644–1718. English Quaker, born in London. He joined the Quakers in 1667, and in 1681 obtained a grant of land in America (in settlement of a debt owed by the king to his father) on which he established the colony of Pennsylvania as a refuge for the persecuted Quakers.

pennant /'penənt/ *n.* a tapering flag, especially that flown at the masthead of a vessel in commission; a pennon. [blend of *pendant* and *pennon*]

Penney /'peni/ William 1909– . British scientist. He worked at Los Alamos 1944–45, designed the first British atomic bomb, and developed the advanced gas-cooled nuclear reactor used in some power stations.

penniless /'penɪlɪs/ *adj.* having no money; poor, destitute.

Pennines /'penaɪnz/ mountain system, 'the backbone of England', broken by a gap through which the river Aire flows to the E and the Ribble to the W; length (Scottish border to the Peaks in Derbyshire) 400 km/250 mi.

pennon /'penən/ n. 1. a long, narrow flag, triangular or swallow-tailed. 2. a long, pointed streamer of a ship. [from Old French from Latin *penna* = feather]

Pennsylvania /ˌpensɪl'veɪnɪə/ state of NE USA; nickname Keystone State; **area** 117,400 sq km/45,316 sq mi; **capital** Harrisburg; **towns** Philadelphia, Pittsburgh, Eerie, Allentown, Scranton; **features** Allegheny mountains; Ohio, Susquehanna, and Delaware rivers; **products** mushrooms, fruit, flowers, cereals, tobacco, meat, poultry, dairy products, anthracite, electrical equipment; **population** (1986) 11,889,000; **history** founded and named by William ◊Penn in 1682, following a land grant by Charles II. It was one of the original Thirteen States. There was a breakdown at the Three Mile Island nuclear reactor plant in Harrisburg in 1979.

penny n. (*plural* **pennies** for separate coins, **pence** for a sum of money) 1. a British bronze coin worth 1/100 of a pound, or formerly a coin worth 1/12 of a shilling; the monetary unit represented by this. 2. (*US colloquial*) a cent. —**in for a penny, in for a pound,** a thing once begun should be concluded at all costs. **in penny numbers,** in small quantities at a time. **pennies from heaven,** unexpected benefits. **penny black,** the first adhesive postage stamp (1840), printed in black. **the penny drops,** understanding dawns (from the use of a coin to operate slot machines etc.). **penny farthing,** a former type of bicycle with a large front wheel and a small rear one. **penny-pinching** adj. niggardly; (n.) niggardliness. **penny whistle,** one with six holes for the different notes. **penny wise (and pound foolish),** careful or thrifty in small matters (but wasteful in large ones). **a pretty penny,** a large sum of money. **two a penny,** commonly found and of little value. [Old English]

pennyroyal /peni'rɔɪəl/ n. a European perennial plant *Mentha pulegium* of the mint family, with oblong leaves and whorls of purplish flowers. It is found growing in wet places on sandy soil.

pennyweight n. a unit of weight equal to 24 grains, 1/20 ounce troy.

pennywort n. a plant with rounded leaves, **wall pennywort** *Umbilicus rupestris* or **marsh pennywort** *Hydrocotyle vulgaris*.

pennyworth n. as much as can be bought for a penny.

penology /piː'nɒlədʒɪ/ n. the study of punishment and prison management. —**penological** /-'lɒdʒɪkəl/ adj., **penologist** n. [from Latin *poena* = penalty]

pension¹ /'penʃən/ n. a periodic payment made by the State or by a private institution, to persons who have reached a specified age, to widowed or disabled persons, who are eligible for such assistance, or by employers to retired employees. **pension scheme** an organized method of saving for retirement, which may be government-run or privately administered. Contributors to such a scheme make regular payments for a qualifying period; on retirement, a payment is made at regular intervals from the invested pension fund. Pension funds have today become influential investors in major industries. In the UK, the age at which pensions become payable is under review, but is currently 65 for men and 60 for women. —v.t. to grant a pension to. —**pension off,** to dismiss with a pension; to cease to employ (a person) or use (a thing). [from Old French from Latin = payment (*pendere* = pay)]

pension² /'pɑ̃sjɔ̃/ n. a continental boarding house. [French]

pensionable adj. entitled or entitling one to a pension.

pensionary adj. of a pension. —n. a recipient of a pension. [from Latin]

pensioner n. a recipient of a retirement or other pension.

pensive /'pensɪv/ adj. deep in thought. —**pensively** adv., **pensiveness** n. [from Old French *penser* = think from Latin *pensare*)]

penstock /'penstɒk/ n. a sluice, a floodgate. [from *pen*² in sense 'mill-dam']

pent adj. shut in a confined space. [past participle of *pend*, variant of *pen*²]

penta- in combinations, five. [Greek *pente* = five]

pentacle /'pentəkl/ n. a figure used as a symbol, especially in magic, e.g. a pentagram. [from Latin *pentaculum*]

pentadactyl limb the typical limb of the mammals, birds, reptiles and amphibians. These ◊vertebrates are all descended from primitive amphibians whose immediate ancestors were fleshy-finned fish.

pentagon /'pentəgən/ n. a plane figure with five sides and angles. —**pentagonal** /-'tægənəl/ adj. [from French or Latin from Greek *pente* = five and *-gōnos-* = angled]

Pentagon n. the headquarters of the US Department of Defense, Arlington, Virginia. One of the world's largest office buildings (five-sided with a pentagonal central court), it houses the administrative and command headquarters for the US armed forces and has become synonymous with the defence-establishment bureaucracy.

pentagram /'pentəgræm/ n. a five-pointed star. [from Greek]

pentameter /pen'tæmɪtə/ n. a line of five metrical feet. [Latin from Greek]

pentanol n. $C_5H_{11}OH$ (common name **amyl alcohol**), a clear, colourless, oily liquid, usually having a characteristic choking odour. It is obtained by the fermentation of starches and from the distillation of petroleum.

Pentateuch /'pentətjuːk/ n. the Greek (and Christian) name for the first five books of the Bible, ascribed to Moses, and called the **Torah** by Jews. [from Latin from Greek *teuchos* = implement, book]

pentathlon /pen'tæθlən/ n. a five-sport competition. Modern pentathlon consists of former military training pursuits: swimming, fencing, running, horsemanship, and shooting. Formerly a five-event track and field competition for women, it was superseded by the ◊heptathlon in 1981. [from Greek *athlon* = contest]

pentatonic /pentə'tɒnɪk/ adj. of a five-note musical scale.

Pentecost /'pentɪkɒst/ n. 1. in Judaism, the festival of *Shavuot*, celebrated on the 50th day after ◊Passover in commemoration of the giving of the Ten Commandments to Moses on Mount Sinai, and the end of the grain harvest. 2. in the Christian church, the day on which the apostles experienced inspiration of the Holy Spirit, commemorated on Whit Sunday. —**pentecostal** /-'kɒstəl/ adj. [Old English and Old French from Latin from Greek = 50th day]

Pentecostal movement a Christian revivalist movement inspired by the baptism in the Holy Spirit with 'speaking in tongues' experienced by the apostles at the time of Pentecost. It represents a reaction against rigid theology and formal worship of the traditional churches. Pentecostalists believe in the literal word of the Bible and disapprove of alcohol, tobacco, dancing, theatre, and so on. It is an intensely missionary faith, and recruitment has been rapid since the 1960s: worldwide membership is more than 10 million.

penthouse /'penthaʊs/ n. 1. a separate apartment or flat etc. on the roof of a tall building. 2. a sloping roof, especially as a subsidiary structure attached to the wall of a main building. [from Old French *apentis* from Latin *appendicium* (*pendere* = hang)]

penult /pi'nʌlt, 'piː-/ adj. & n. (especially of a syllable) penultimate. [abbreviation]

penultimate /pi'nʌltɪmət/ adj. & n. last but one. [from Latin *paenultimus* (*paene* = almost and *ultimus* = last]

penumbra /pi'nʌmbrə/ n. (*plural* **penumbrae** /-iː/ or **penumbras**) a partly shaded region round the shadow of an opaque body, especially of the Moon or Earth in eclipse; partial shadow. —**penumbral** adj. [from Latin *paene* = almost and *umbra* = shadow]

penurious /pi'njʊərɪəs/ adj. 1. poverty-stricken. 2. scanty. 3. grudging, stingy. [from Latin]

penury /'penjʊrɪ/ n. 1. extreme poverty. 2. lack, scarcity. [from Latin *penuria*]

peony /'piːənɪ/ n. or **paeony** any perennial plant of the genus *Paeonia*, family Paeoniaceae, remarkable for their brilliant red, pink, or white flowers. Most popular are the **common peony** P. *officinalis*, the **white peony** P. *lactiflora*, and the taller **tree peony** P. *suffruticosa*. [Old English from Latin from Greek *Paean* = physician of the gods]

people /'piːpl/ n. 1. human beings in general. 2. persons belonging to a place or forming a group or social class; the subjects or citizens of a state. 3. ordinary persons, those not having high rank or office etc. 4. a person's parents or other relatives. —v.t. to fill with people, to populate. [from Anglo-French from Latin *populus*]

People's Budget in UK history, the Liberal government's budget of 1909 to finance social reforms and naval rearmament. The chancellor of the Exchequer, David Lloyd George, proposed graded and increased income tax and a 'supertax' on high incomes. The budget aroused great debate and precipitated a constitutional crisis.

People's Charter the key document of ◊Chartism, a movement for reform of the British political system in the 1830s. It was used to mobilize working-class support following the restricted extension of the franchise specified by the 1832 Reform Act. It was drawn up in Feb 1837.

pep n. (slang) vigour, spirit. —v.t. (-pp-) (slang) to fill with vigour, to enliven. —**pep pill,** a pill containing a stimulant drug. **pep talk,** a talk urging the listener to greater effort or courage. —**peppy** adj. [abbreviation of pepper]

Pepin /ˈpepɪn/ **the Short** c. 714–c. 768. King of the Franks from 751. The son of Charles Martel, he acted as Mayor of the Palace to the last Merovingian king, Childeric III, deposed him and assumed the royal title himself, founding the ◊Carolingian dynasty. He was ◊Charlemagne's father.

pepper n. a climbing plant Piper nigrum native to the E Indies, of the Old World pepper family Piperaceae. When gathered green, the berries are crushed to produce the seeds for the spice called **black pepper.** When the berries are ripe, the seeds are removed and the outer skin discarded, to produce **white pepper. Sweet pepper** comes from ◊capsicums native to the New World. —v.t. **1.** to sprinkle with or as with pepper. **2.** to pelt with missiles. —**pepper-and-salt** adj. (of cloth) woven so as to show small dots of dark and light colour intermingled. **pepper mill,** a mill for grinding peppercorns by hand. **pepper pot,** a small container with a perforated lid for sprinkling pepper. [Old English from Latin piper from Greek from Sanskrit]

peppercorn n. a dried pepper berry. —**peppercorn rent,** a nominal or very low rent.

peppermint n. **1.** a kind of mint Mentha piperita with ovate, aromatic leaves and purple flowers, grown for its strong fragrant oil. **2.** a lozenge or sweet flavoured with this. **3.** the oil itself.

peppery adj. **1.** of, like, or abounding in pepper; hot and spicy. **2** (of people) irascible; (of remarks etc.) pungent.

pepsin /ˈpepsɪn/ n. an enzyme that breaks down proteins during digestion. It requires a strongly acidic environment and is found in the stomach. [German, from Greek pepsis = digestion]

peptic /ˈpeptɪk/ adj. digestive. —**peptic ulcer,** an ulcer in the stomach or duodenum. —**peptically** adv. [from Greek peptos = cooked]

peptide /ˈpeptaɪd/ n. a molecule comprising two or more ◊amino acid molecules (not necessarily different) joined by **peptide bonds,** whereby the acid group of one acid is linked to the amino group of the other, CO.NH. The number of amino acid molecules in the peptide is indicated by reference to it as a di-, tri-, or polypeptide (two, three, or many amino acids). [from German]

Pepusch /ˈpeɪpʊʃ/ Johann Christoph 1667–1752. German composer who settled in England in about 1700. He contributed to John Gay's ballad operas The Beggar's Opera and Polly.

Pepys /piːps/ Samuel 1633–1703. English diarist. His diary, written 1659–69 (when his sight failed) in shorthand, was a unique record of both the daily life of the period and the intimate feelings of the man. It was not deciphered until 1825.

Strange to see how a good dinner and feasting reconciles everybody.

Samuel Pepys
Diary Nov 9 1665

---

per prep. **1.** for each. **2.** through, by, by means of. —**as per,** in accordance with. **as per usual,** (colloquial) as usual. [Latin = through]

per- prefix meaning **1.** through or all over (e.g. pervade). **2.** completely, very (e.g. perturb). **3.** to destruction (e.g. perdition); to the bad (e.g. pervert). [from Latin]

peradventure /pərədˈventʃə/ adv. (archaic or jocular) perhaps; by chance. —n. uncertainty, chance, conjecture; doubt. [from Old French = by chance]

perambulate /pəˈræmbjʊleɪt/ v.t./i. to walk through, over, or about (a place); to walk about or from place

to place. —**perambulation** /-ˈleɪʃən/ n. [from Latin ambulare = walk]

perambulator /pəˈræmbjʊleɪtə/ n. a pram.

per annum /pɜːr ˈænəm/ for each year. [Latin]

percale /pəˈkeɪl/ n. a closely-woven cotton fabric. [French]

per caput /pɜː ˈkæpʊt/ or **per capita** /pɜː ˈkæpɪtə/ for each person. [Latin = by head(s)]

perceive /pəˈsiːv/ v.t. to become aware of with the mind or through one of the senses; to see or notice. [from Old French from Latin percipere, originally = seize (capere = take)]

per cent /pəˈsent/ in every hundred. —n. a percentage; one part in every hundred. [from Latin centum = hundred]

percentage /pəˈsentɪdʒ/ n. a way of representing a number as a ◊fraction of 100. Thus 45 per cent (45%) equals 45/100, and 45% of 20 is 45/100 × 20 = 9.

perceptible /pəˈseptɪbəl/ adj. that can be perceived. —**perceptibility** /-ˈbɪlɪtɪ/ n., **perceptibly** adv. [Old French or from Latin percipere]

perception /pəˈsepʃən/ n. perceiving; the ability to perceive. [from Latin]

perceptive /pəˈseptɪv/ adj. **1.** of perception. **2.** having or showing insight and sensitive understanding. —**perceptively** adv., **perceptiveness** n., **perceptivity** /-ˈtɪvɪtɪ/ n. [from Latin]

perceptual /pəˈseptjuəl/ adj. of or involving perception.

Perceval /ˈpɜːsɪvəl/ Spencer 1762–1812. British Tory politician. He became chancellor of the Exchequer in 1807 and prime minister in 1809. He was shot in the lobby of the House of Commons in 1812 by a merchant who blamed government measures for his bankruptcy.

perch[1] n. **1.** a branch or bar etc. serving as a bird's resting place. **2.** an elevated position. **3.** a former measure of length (especially for land) equal to 5½ yards. —v.t./i. to rest or place on or as if on a perch. —**percher** n. [from Old French from Latin pertica = pole]

perch[2] n. (plural the same) a spiny-finned freshwater fish of the genus Perca found in Europe, Asia, and North America. Perch have varied shapes, and are usually a greenish colour. They are very prolific, spawning when three years old, and have voracious appetites. [from Old French from Latin perca from Greek]

perchance /pəˈtʃɑːns/ adv. (archaic) **1.** by chance. **2.** possibly, maybe. [from Anglo-French par chance]

percipient /pəˈsɪpɪənt/ adj. perceiving, perceptive. —**percipience** n. [from Latin percipere]

percolate /ˈpɜːkəleɪt/ v.t./i. **1.** to filter or cause to filter, especially through small holes. **2.** to permeate. **3.** to prepare (coffee) in a percolator. —**percolation** /-ˈleɪʃən/ n. [from Latin percolare (colum = strainer)]

percolator /ˈpɜːkəleɪtə/ n. a pot for making and serving coffee, in which boiling water is made to rise up a central tube and down through a perforated drum of ground coffee.

percussion /pəˈkʌʃən/ n. **1.** the forcible striking of one object against another. **2.** the group of percussion instruments in an orchestra. **3.** a gentle tapping of the body in medical diagnosis. —**percussion cap,** a small metal or paper device containing explosive powder and exploded by the fall of a hammer, used as a detonator or in a toy pistol. **percussion instrument,** a musical instrument played by striking a resonating surface. Percussion instruments can be divided into those that can be tuned to produce a sound of definite pitch, and those without pitch. —**percussive** adj. [French or from Latin percutere = strike]

Percy /ˈpɜːsɪ/ Henry 'Hotspur' 1364–1403. English soldier, son of the 1st Earl of Northumberland. In repelling a border raid, he defeated the Scots at Homildon Hill in Durham in 1402. He was killed at the battle of Shrewsbury while in revolt against Henry IV.

Percy Thomas 1729–1811. English scholar and bishop of Dromore from 1782. He discovered a manuscript collection of songs, ballads, and romances, from which he published a selection as Reliques of Ancient English Poetry 1765, influential in the Romantic revival.

perdition /pəˈdɪʃən/ n. damnation; eternal death. [from Old French or Latin perdere = destroy]

peregrination /perɪgrɪnˈeɪʃən/ n. travelling; a journey. [from Latin peregrinari]

peregrine /ˈperɪgrɪn/ n. a kind of falcon Falco peregrinus found in rocky coastal areas around the world. The male is bluish-grey with black and white underparts while the

Pérez de Cuéllar *Peruvian diplomat and secretary-general of the United Nations since 1982, General Javier Pérez de Cuéllar, Mexico City, 1984.*

female is browner; both have long pointed wings and tail. They soar and dive from great heights to catch their prey. Peregrines are used in falconry. [from Latin *peregrinus* = foreign (*peregre* = abroad)]

peremptory /pə'remptəri, 'perim-/ *adj.* imperious, insisting on obedience. —**peremptorily** *adv.*, **peremptoriness** *n.* [from Anglo-French from Latin *perimere* = destroy, put an end to]

perennial /pə'reniəl/ *adj.* lasting through the year; lasting long or for ever; (of a plant) living for several years. —*n.* a perennial plant. Herbaceous perennials have aerial stems and leaves that die each autumn. They survive the winter by means of an underground storage (perennating) organ, such as a bulb or rhizome. Trees and shrubs or woody perennials have stems that persist above ground throughout the year, and may be either ◊deciduous or ◊evergreen. See also ◊annual plant, ◊biennial plant. —**perennially** *adv.* [from Latin *perennis* (*annus* = year)]

Peres /'peres/ Shimon 1923– . Israeli socialist politician, prime minister 1984–86. Peres emigrated from Poland to Palestine in 1934, but was educated in the USA. In 1959 he was elected to the Knesset (Israeli parliament). He became leader of the Labour Party in 1977. Peres was prime minister, then foreign minister, under a power-sharing agreement with the leader of the Consolidation Party (Likud), Yitzhak ◊Shamir. From 1989 he was finance minister in a new Labour–Likud coalition.

perestroika /pere'strɔikə/ *n.* in Soviet politics, a term referring to the wide-ranging economic and political reforms initiated under Mikhail ◊Gorbachev's leadership. The term was first proposed at the 26th Party Congress in 1979 and actively promoted by Gorbachev from 1985. Originally, in the economic sphere, perestroika was conceived as involving the 'switching onto a track of intensive development' by automation and improved labour efficiency. It has evolved to attend increasingly to market indicators and incentives ('market socialism') and a gradual dismantlement of the Stalinist central-planning system, with decision-taking authority being devolved to self-financing enterprises. [Russian = restructuring]

Pérez de Cuéllar /'peres də 'kweijɑː/ Javier 1920– . Peruvian diplomat, secretary-general of the United Nations from 1982. A delegate to the first UN General Assembly 1946–47, he subsequently held several ambassadorial posts. He raised the standing of the UN by his successful diplomacy in ending the Iran–Iraq war in 1988 and securing the independence of Namibia in 1989. He was, however, unable to resolve the Gulf conflict resulting from Iraq's invasion of Kuwait in 1990.

perfect /'pɜːfɪkt/ *adj.* **1.** complete and with all necessary qualities; faultless; not deficient. **2.** exact, precise. **3.** (*colloquial*) excellent, most satisfactory. **4.** entire, unqualified. **5.** in grammar, (of a tense) denoting a completed event or action viewed in relation to the present (e.g. *he has gone*).

—*n.* in grammar, the perfect tense. —/pə'fekt/ *v.t.* to make perfect. —**perfect interval,** in music, an interval between the tonic and the fourth or fifth or octave in a major or minor scale. —**perfectly** *adv.* [from Old French from Latin *perficere* = complete]

perfect competition see ◊competition, perfect.

perfectible /pə'fektɪbəl/ *adj.* that can be perfected. —**perfectibility** /-'bɪlɪti/ *n.*

perfection /pə'fekʃən/ *n.* **1.** making or being perfect; faultlessness. **2.** a perfect person or thing. —**to perfection,** perfectly. [from Old French from Latin]

perfectionist *n.* one who is satisfied with nothing less than what he or she thinks is perfect. —**perfectionism** *n.*

perfidy /'pɜːfɪdi/ *n.* a breach of faith, treachery. —**perfidious** /pə'fɪdiəs/ *adj.*, **perfidiously** *adv.* [from Latin *perfidus* = treacherous]

perforate /'pɜːfəreɪt/ *v.t.* to make a hole or holes through, to pierce; to make a row of small holes in (paper etc.) so that part may be torn off easily. —**perforation** /-'reɪʃən/ *n.* [from Latin *perforare* = bore through]

perforce /pə'fɔːs/ *adv.* unavoidably, necessarily. [from Old French *par force*]

perform /pə'fɔːm/ *v.t./i.* **1.** to carry into effect, to be the agent of, to do. **2.** to go through (some process), to execute (a function, piece of music etc.). **3.** to act in a play etc., to play an instrument or sing etc. before an audience. **4.** to function. —**performing arts,** those (such as drama) that require public performance. —**performer** *n.* [from Anglo-French from Old French *parfournir*]

performance /pə'fɔːməns/ *n.* **1.** the process or manner of performing. **2.** a notable or (*colloquial*) a ridiculous action. **3.** the performing of or in a play etc. —**performance art,** one of a variety of staged artistic events, sometimes including music, painting, and sculpture. The events, which originated in the 1950s, are akin to happenings but less spontaneous.

perfume /'pɜːfjuːm/ *n.* **1.** a sweet smell. **2.** a fragrant essence used to scent the body, cosmetics, and candles. More than 100 natural aromatic chemicals may be blended from a range of 60,000 flowers, leaves, fruits, seeds, woods, barks, resins, and roots, combined by natural animal fixatives and various synthetics, the latter increasingly used even in expensive products. —*v.t.* to give a sweet smell to; to apply perfume to. [from French *parfumer* from obsolete Italian; originally of smoke from burning substance]

perfumery /pə'fjuːməri/ *n.* perfumes; the making or selling of these.

perfunctory /pə'fʌŋktəri/ *adj.* done superficially or without much care or interest, as a duty or routine; (of a person) acting thus. —**perfunctorily** *adv.*, **perfunctoriness** *n.* [from Latin *fungi* = perform]

Perga /'pɜːgə/ ruined city of Pamphylia, 16 km/10 mi NE of Adalia, Turkey, noted for its local cult of Artemis. It was visited by the apostle Paul.

Pergamum /'pɜːgəməm/ ancient Greek city in W Asia Minor, which became the capital of an independent kingdom 283 BC. As the ally of Rome it achieved great political importance in the 2nd century BC, and became a centre of art and culture.

pergola /'pɜːgələ/ *n.* an arbour or covered walk formed of growing plants trained over trelliswork. [Italian from Latin *pergula* = projecting roof]

perhaps /pə'hæps, præps/ *adv.* it may be, possibly.

peri /'piəri/ *n.* in Persian mythology, a fairy, a good (originally evil) genius; a beautiful or graceful being. [from Persian]

peri- /perɪ-/ prefix meaning round, about. [from Greek]

Peri /'peəri/ Jacopo 1561–1633. Italian composer, who served the ◊Medici family. His experimental melodic opera *Euridice* 1600 established the opera form and influenced Monteverdi. His first opera, *Dafne* 1597, is now lost.

perianth /'periænθ/ *n.* in botany, a collective term for the outer whorls of the flower, which protect the reproductive parts during development. In most ◊dicotyledons the perianth is composed of two distinct whorls, the calyx of ◊sepals and the corolla of petals, whereas in many ◊monocotyledons they are indistinguishable and the segments of the perianth are then known individually as tepals. [from French (Greek *anthos* = flower)]

periodic table of the elements

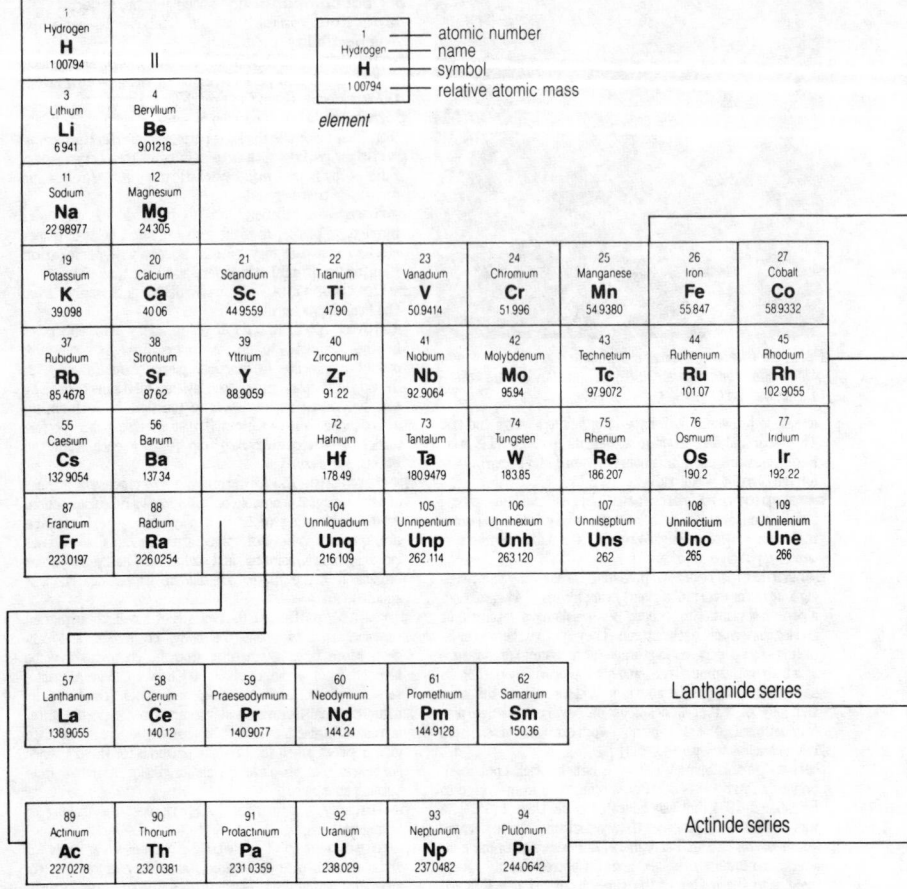

pericardium /peri'ka:diəm/ *n.* (*plural* **pericardia**) the membranous sac enclosing the heart. [from Greek *kardia* = heart]

pericarp /'perika:p/ *n.* the wall of a fruit. It encloses the seeds and is derived from the ◊ovary wall. In fruits such as the acorn, the pericarp becomes dry and hard, forming a shell around the seed. In fleshy fruits the pericarp is typically made up of three distinct layers. The **epicarp**, or **exocarp**, forms the tough outer skin of the fruit, while the **mesocarp** is often fleshy and forms the middle layers. The innermost layer or **endocarp**, which surrounds the seeds, may be membranous or thick and hard, as in the ◊drupe (stone) of cherries, plums, and apricots. [from French (Greek *karpos* = fruit, shell)]

Pericles /'perikli:z/ *c.*490–429 BC. Athenian politician, who dominated the city's affairs from 461 BC (as leader of the democratic party), and under whom Greek culture reached its height. He created a confederation of cities under the leadership of Athens, but the disasters of the ◊Peloponnesian War led to his overthrow in 430 BC. Although quickly reinstated, he died soon after.

peridotite *n.* a rock consisting largely of the mineral olivine; pyroxene and other minerals may also be present. Peridotite is an ultrabasic rock containing less than 45% silica by weight. It is believed to be one of the rock types making up the Earth's upper mantle, and is sometimes brought from the depths to the surface by major movements, or as inclusions in lavas.

perigee /'peridʒi:/ *n.* the point at which an object, travelling in an elliptical orbit around the Earth, is at its closest to the Earth. [from French from Greek *gē* = Earth]

perihelion /peri'hi:liən/ *n.* (*plural* **perihelia**) the point at which an object, travelling in an elliptical orbit around the Sun, is at its closest to the Sun. [from Greek *hēlios* = Sun]

peril /'peril/ *n.* serious danger. —**perilous** *adj.*, **perilously** *adv.* [from Old French from Latin *peric(u)lum*]

perimeter /pə'rimitə/ *n.* 1. the circumference or outline of a closed figure; the length of this. 2. the outer boundary of an enclosed area. [from French or Latin from Greek *metron* = measure]

perinatal *adj.* relating to the period shortly before, during, and after the birth of a child.

perineum /peri'ni:əm/ *n.* the region of the body between the anus and the scrotum or vulva. —**perineal** *adj.* [from Latin from Greek *perinaion*]

period /'piəriəd/ *n.* 1. a length or portion of time; a distinct portion of history, life etc.; a time forming part of a geological era. 2. the interval between recurrences of an astronomical or other phenomenon. 3. the time allocated for a lesson in school. 4. an occurrence of menstruation; the time of this. 5. a complete sentence, especially one consisting of several clauses. 6. a ◊full stop in punctuation. —*adj.* belonging to or characteristic of some past

periodic table of the elements

			III	IV	V	VI	VII	0
								2 Helium **He** 4.00260
			5 Boron **B** 10.81	6 Carbon **C** 12.011	7 Nitrogen **N** 14.0067	8 Oxygen **O** 15.9994	9 Fluorine **F** 18.99840	10 Neon **Ne** 20.179
			13 Aluminium **Al** 26.98154	14 Silicon **Si** 28.086	15 Phosphorus **P** 30.97376P	16 Sulphur **S** 32.06	17 Chlorine **Cl** 35.453	18 Argon **Ar** 39.948
28 Nickel **Ni** 58.70	29 Copper **Cu** 63.546	30 Zinc **Zn** 65.38	31 Gallium **Ga** 69.72	32 Germanium **Ge** 72.59	33 Arsenic **As** 74.9216	34 Selenium **Se** 78.96	35 Bromine **Br** 79.904	36 Krypton **Kr** 83.80
46 Palladium **Pd** 106.4	47 Silver **Ag** 107.868	48 Cadmium **Cd** 112.40	49 Indium **In** 114.82	50 Tin **Sn** 118.69	51 Antimony **Sb** 121.75	52 Tellurium **Te** 127.75	53 Iodine **I** 126.9045	54 Xenon **Xe** 131.30
78 Platinum **Pt** 195.09	79 Gold **Au** 196.9665	80 Mercury **Hg** 200.59	81 Thallium **Tl** 204.37	82 Lead **Pb** 207.37	83 Bismuth **Bi** 207.2	84 Polonium **Po** 210	85 Astatine **At** 211	86 Radon **Rn** 222.0176

63 Europium **Eu** 151.96	64 Gadolinium **Gd** 157.25	65 Terbium **Tb** 158.9254	66 Dysprosium **Dy** 162.50	67 Holmium **Ho** 164.9304	68 Erbium **Er** 167.26	69 Thulium **Tm** 168.9342	70 Ytterbium **Yb** 173.04	71 Lutetium **Lu** 174.97

95 Americium **Am** 243.0614	96 Curium **Cm** 247.0703	97 Berkelium **Bk** 247.0703	98 Californium **Cf** 251.0786	99 Einsteinium **Es** 252.0828	100 Fermium **Fm** 257.0951	101 Mendelevium **Md** 258.0986	012 Nobelium **No** 259.1009	103 Lawrencium **Lr** 260.1054

period. [from Old French from Latin from Greek *periodos* (*hodos* = way)]

periodic /piəri'ɒdık/ *adj.* appearing or occurring at intervals.

periodical /piəri'ɒdıkəl/ *adj.* periodic. —*n.* a magazine etc. published at regular intervals. —**periodically** *adv.*

periodicity /pırıə'dısıtı/ *n.* being periodic; the tendency to recur at intervals.

periodic table of the elements the classification of the elements following the statement by Mendeleyev in 1869 that 'the properties of elements are in periodic dependence upon their atomic weight'. (Today elements are classified by their atomic numbers rather than by their relative molecular masses.) There are striking similarities in the chemical properties of the elements in each of the vertical columns (called **groups**), which are numbered I–VII, and a gradation of properties along the horizontal rows (called **periods**). These features are a direct consequence of the electronic (and nuclear) structure of the atoms of the elements. The periodic table summarizes the major properties of the elements and how they change, and enables predictions to be made.

periodontal /periə'dɒntəl/ *adj.* of the tissues surrounding the teeth. —**periodontal disease,** (formerly known as **pyorrhoea**) a disease of the gums and bone supporting the teeth, caused by the accumulation of plaque and microorganisms; the gums recede, and the teeth eventually become loose and may drop out unless treatment is sought. [from Greek *odous odontos* = tooth]

peripatetic /peripə'tetık/ *adj.* 1. going from place to place, itinerant. 2. **Peripatetic** of the Greek philosopher Aristotle (died 322 BC) or his ideas. —*n.* 1. a traveller, an itinerant. 2. **Peripatetic** an adherent of Aristotle. [from Old French or Latin from Greek *pateō* = walk; sense 2 from Aristotle's custom of walking in the Lyceum in Athens while teaching]

peripheral /pə'rıfərəl/ *adj.* 1. of minor but not central importance. 2. of a periphery. —**peripheral device,** in computing, any item of equipment attached to and controlled by a computer. Peripherals are typically for input from and output to the user (for example, a keyboard or printer), storing data (for example, a disc drive), communications (such as a modem) or for performing physical tasks (such as a robot).

periphery /pə'rıfərı/ *n.* the boundary of a surface, area, or subject etc.; the region just outside or inside this. [from Latin from Greek = circumference (*pherō* = bear)]

periphrasis /pə'rıfrəsıs/ *n.* (*plural* **periphrases** /–əsi:z/) a roundabout phrase or way of speaking, a circumlocution. —**periphrastic** /peri'fræstık/ *adj.* [Latin from Greek *phrazō* = declare]

periscope /'perıskəup/ *n.* an apparatus with a tube and mirrors by which an observer in a submerged submarine, a trench, the rear of a crowd etc., can see things otherwise out of sight. —**periscopic** /-'skɒpɪk/ adj.

perish /'perɪʃ/ v.t./i. 1. to be destroyed, to suffer death or ruin. 2. to lose or cause (a fabric etc.) to lose its normal qualities, to rot. 3. to distress or wither by cold or exposure; to suffer thus. [from Old French from Latin perire]

perishable adj. liable to perish, subject to speedy decay. —n. (usually in plural) perishable goods (especially foods).

perisher n. (slang) an annoying person, especially a child.

perishing adj. 1. (colloquial) intensely cold. 2. (colloquial) confounded.

peristalsis n. the series of wavelike contractions, produced by the contraction of smooth ◊muscle, that pass along tubular organs, such as the intestines. The same term describes the wavelike motion of earthworms and other invertebrates, in which part of the body contracts as another part elongates.

peristyle /'perɪstaɪl/ n. a row of columns surrounding a temple, court, cloister etc.; the space surrounded by these. [from French from Latin from Greek stulon = pillar]

peritoneum /perɪtə'niəm/ n. (plural **peritoneums**) the tissue lining the abdominal cavity and digestive organs of vertebrates. —**peritoneal** adj. [Latin from Greek -tonos = stretched]

peritonitis /perɪtə'naɪtɪs/ n. inflammation within the peritoneum, due to infection or other irritation. It is sometimes seen following a burst appendix. Peritonitis quickly proves fatal without treatment.

periwig /'perɪwɪg/ n. (especially historical) a wig. [alteration of peruke]

periwinkle[1] /'perɪwɪŋkəl/ n. in botany, an evergreen trailing plant of the genus Vinca, of the dogbane family Apocynaceae, with blue or white flowers. [from Anglo-French pervenke from Latin pervinca]

periwinkle[2] /'perɪwɪŋkəl/ n. in zoology, a snail-like marine mollusc found on the shores of Europe and E North America. It has a conical spiral shell, and feeds on algae.

perjure /'pɜːdʒə/ v.refl. to cause oneself to be guilty of perjury; (in past participle) guilty of or involving perjury. [from Old French from Latin jurare = swear]

perjury /'pɜːdʒərɪ/ n. wilful utterance of a false statement while on oath (or affirmation) when appearing as a witness in legal proceedings, on a point material to the question at issue. In Britain and the USA it is punishable by a fine, imprisonment, or both. —**perjurious** /-'dʒuəriəs/ adj. [from Anglo-French from Latin perjurium]

perk[1] v.t./i. (colloquial, usually with up) 1. to regain or cause to regain courage, confidence, or liveliness. 2. to smarten. 3. to raise (the head etc.) briskly.

perk[2] (colloquial) abbreviation of perquisite.

Perkin /'pɜːkɪn/ William Henry 1838–1907. British chemist. In 1856 he discovered the mauve dye that originated from the aniline dye industry.

perky adj. lively and cheerful. —**perkily** adv., **perkiness** n.

Perm /pɜːm/ industrial city (shipbuilding, oil refining, aircraft, chemicals, sawmills), and capital of Perm region, USSR, on the Kama near the Ural mountains; population (1987) 1,075,000. It was called Molotov 1940–57.

perm[1] (colloquial) abbreviation of permanent wave. —v.t. (colloquial) to give a permanent wave to.

perm[2] n. (colloquial) abbreviation of permutation. —v.t. (colloquial) to make a permutation of.

permafrost /'pɜːməfrɒst/ n. ground in which a deep layer of soil does not thaw out during the summer but remains at below 0°C/32°F for at least two years, despite thawing of the soil above. It is claimed that 26% of the world's land surface is permafrost.

permanency /'pɜːmənənsɪ/ n. a permanent thing or arrangement.

permanent /'pɜːmənənt/ adj. lasting or intended to last or function indefinitely. **permanent wave**, a long-lasting artificial wave in the hair. **permanent way**, the finished roadbed of a railway. —**permanence** n., **permanently** adv. [from Old French from Latin manēre = remain]

permeable /'pɜːmiəbəl/ adj. admitting the passage of liquid etc. —**permeability** /-'bɪlɪtɪ/ n.

permeate /'pɜːmieɪt/ v.t./i. to pass, flow, or spread into every part of; to diffuse itself. —**permeation** /-'eɪʃən/ n. [from Latin meare = pass]

Permian /'pɜːmiən/ adj. of the period of geological time 286–248 million years ago, the last period of the Palaeozoic era. —n. this period. Its end was marked by a significant change in marine life, including the extinction of many corals and trilobites. Deserts were widespread, and terrestrial amphibians and mammal-like reptiles flourished. Cone-bearing plants (gymnosperms) came to prominence. [from Perm in the USSR]

permissible /pə'mɪsɪbəl/ adj. that can be permitted. —**permissibility** /-'bɪlɪtɪ/ n., **permissibly** adv. [from French or Latin]

permission /pə'mɪʃən/ n. consent or authorization to do something. [from Old French or Latin]

permissive /pə'mɪsɪv/ adj. 1. tolerant, allowing much freedom, especially in social conduct and sexual matters. The term **permissive society** often describes the years in the West from the 1950s to the 1970s. 2. giving permission. —**permissively** adv., **permissiveness** n. [from Old French or Latin]

permit /pə'mɪt/ v.t./i. (-tt-) 1. to give permission or consent to; to authorize, to allow. 2. to give an opportunity; to make possible; to admit of (alteration, delay etc.). —/'pɜːmɪt/ n. a written order giving permission to act, especially for entry into a place; permission. [from Latin mittere = let go, send]

permittivity /pəmɪ'tɪvɪtɪ/ n. a quantity measuring a substance's ability to store energy in an electric field.

permutation /pɜːmju:'teɪʃən/ n. 1. variation of the order of a set of things. 2. any one such arrangement. 3. in mathematics, the arrangement of a distinct objects taken b at a time in all possible orders. It is given by $a!/(a − b)!$, where '!' stands for ◊factorial. For example, the number of permutations of four letters taken from any group of six different letters is $6!/2! = (1 × 2 × 3 × 4 × 5 × 6)/(1 × 2) = 360$. 4. a combination or selection of a specified number of items from a larger group (especially of matches in a football pool). [from Old French or Latin mutare = change]

pernicious /pə'nɪʃəs/ adj. having a very harmful effect. —**pernicious anaemia**, a severe (formerly often fatal) form of anaemia. [from Latin pernicies = ruin]

pernickety /pə'nɪkɪtɪ/ adj. (colloquial) fastidious; over-precise. [origin Scottish]

Perón /pe'rɒn/ 'Evita' (Maria Eva) (born Duarte) 1919–1952. Argentine populist leader, born in Buenos Aires. She was a successful radio actress. In 1945 she married Juan Perón. After he became president she virtually ran the health and labour ministries, and did a lot of charitable work. In 1951 she stood for the post of vice president, but was opposed by the army and withdrew; she died of cancer soon afterwards.

Perón (María Estela) Isabel (born Martínez) 1931– . President of Argentina 1974–76, and third wife of Juan Perón. She succeeded him after he died in office, but labour unrest, inflation, and political violence pushed the country to the brink of chaos. Accused of corruption, she was held under house arrest for five years. She went into exile in Spain.

Perón Juan (Domingo) 1895–1974. Argentine politician, dictator 1946–55 and from 1973 until his death. He took part in the military coup of 1943, and his popularity with the descamisados ('shirtless ones') led to his election as president in 1946. He instituted social reforms, but encountered economic difficulties. After the death of his second wife Eva Perón he lost popularity, and was deposed in a military coup in 1955. He returned from exile to the presidency in 1973, but died in office in 1974, and was succeeded by his third wife Isabel Perón.

peroration /perə'reɪʃən/ n. a lengthy speech; the concluding part of a speech. [from Latin orare = speak]

Perotin /perəu'tæn/ the Great c.1160–c.1220. French composer. His church music has a timeless quality and introduced new concepts of harmony and part-writing to traditional organum.

peroxide /pə'rɒksaɪd/ n. a compound of oxygen with another element containing the maximum proportion of oxygen; (in full **hydrogen peroxide**) a colourless liquid used in a water solution, especially to bleach the hair. —v.t. to bleach (hair) with peroxide.

perpendicular /pɜːpən'dɪkjulə/ adj. 1. at right angles to a given line, plane, or surface. 2. upright, at right angles to the horizontal. 3. (of a cliff etc.) having a vertical face; very steep. 4. **Perpendicular** of the style of English Gothic architecture (14th–16th centuries) characterized by vertical tracery in large windows, two or four arc arches, lavishly decorated vaults and use of traceried panels. Examples include the choir and cloister of Gloucester Cathedral, and King's College Chapel, Cambridge. —*n.* a perpendicular line; a perpendicular position or direction. —**perpendicularity** /-'lærɪtɪ/ *n.*, **perpendicularly** *adv.* [from Latin *perpendiculum* = plumb line]

perpetrate /'pɜːpɪtreɪt/ *v.t.* to commit or perform (a blunder, crime, hoax, thing regarded as outrageous). —**perpetration** /-'treɪʃən/ *n.*, **perpetrator** *n.* [from Latin *patrare* = effect]

perpetual /pə'petjuəl/ *adj.* lasting for ever or indefinitely; unceasing; continuous; (*colloquial*) frequent, much repeated. —**perpetual motion**, the motion of a hypothetical machine running for ever unless subject to external forces or wear. —**perpetually** *adv.* [from Old French from Latin *perpetuus* from *perpes* = continuous]

perpetuate /pə'petjueɪt/ *v.t.* to make perpetual, to cause to be always remembered. —**perpetuation** /-'eɪʃən/ *n.*, **perpetuator** *n.* [from Latin]

perpetuity /pɜːpɪ'tjuːɪtɪ/ *n.* 1. the state or quality of being perpetual. 2. a perpetual possession, or position, or annuity. —**in perpetuity**, for ever. [from Old French from Latin]

perplex /pə'pleks/ *v.t.* 1. to bewilder, to puzzle greatly. 2. to complicate or confuse (a matter). [from Old French or Latin *perplexus* = involved (*plectere* = plait)]

perplexedly /pə'pleksɪdlɪ/ *adv.* in a perplexed manner.

perplexity /pə'pleksɪtɪ/ *n.* 1. perplexing, being perplexed. 2. a thing that perplexes.

per pro. abbreviation of by proxy, through an agent. [from Latin *per procurationem*]

perquisite /'pɜːkwɪzɪt/ *n.* a profit, allowance, or privilege etc. given or looked upon as one's right in addition to wages or salary etc. [from Latin *perquirere* = search diligently for (*quaerere* = seek)]

Perrault /pe'rəʊ/ Charles 1628–1703. French author of the fairy tales *Contes de ma mère l'oye*/*Mother Goose's Fairy Tales* 1697, which include 'Sleeping Beauty', 'Little Red Riding Hood', 'Blue Beard', 'Puss in Boots', and 'Cinderella'.

Perrin /pe'ræn/ Jean 1870–1942. French physicist who produced the crucial evidence that finally established the atomic nature of matter. Assuming the atomic hypothesis, Perrin demonstrated how the phenomenon of ◊Brownian movement could be used to derive precise values for ◊Avogadro's number. He was awarded the 1926 Nobel Prize for Physics.

perry /'perɪ/ *n.* a drink made from fermented pear juice. [from Old French *peré* from Latin *pirum* = pear]

Perry Matthew Calbraith 1794–1858. US naval officer, commander of the expedition of 1853 that reopened communication between Japan and the outside world after 250 years' isolation. Evident military superiority enabled him to negotiate the Treaty of Kanagawa in 1854 giving the USA trading rights with Japan.

per se /pɜː 'seɪ/ by or in itself, intrinsically. [Latin]

persecute /'pɜːsɪkjuːt/ *v.t.* to subject to constant hostility and ill treatment, especially because of religious or political beliefs; to harass. —**persecution** /-'kjuːʃən/ *n.*, **persecutor** *n.* [from Old French from Latin *persequi* = pursue]

Persephone /pɜː'sefənɪ/ Greek goddess (Roman Proserpina), the daughter of Zeus and Demeter. She was carried off to the underworld as the bride of Pluto, who later agreed that she should spend six months of the year with her mother. The myth symbolizes the growth and decay of vegetation.

Persepolis /pɜː'sepəlɪs/ ancient capital of the Persian Empire, 65 km/40 mi NE of Shiraz. It was burned down after its capture in 331 BC by Alexander the Great.

Perseus /'pɜːsjuːs/ 1. in Greek mythology, the son of Zeus and Danaë. He slew ◊Medusa, the Gorgon, rescued ◊Andromeda, and became king of Tiryns. 2. in astronomy, a constellation of the northern hemisphere, near Cassiopeia, represented as the mythological hero. The eye of the decapitated Gorgon is represented by the variable star Algol. Perseus lies in the Milky Way and contains the Double Cluster, a twin cluster of stars. Every August the Perseid meteor shower radiates from its northern part.

persevere /pɜːsɪ'vɪə/ *v.i.* to continue steadfastly, especially in something that is difficult or tedious. —**perseverance** *n.*, **persevering** *adj.* & *n.* [from Old French from Latin *perseverare* (*severus* = strict)]

Persia /'pɜːʃə/ 1. an ancient kingdom in SW Asia. In the 7th century BC the Persians established themselves in the present-day region of Fars (Iran), which then belonged to the Assyrians. Cyrus the Great overthrew the empire of the Medes in 550 BC and founded the Persian Empire. After a period of expansion and domination under Cyrus and Darius I, internal dynastic struggles weakened the empire and the Persian Wars with Greece 499–449 BC ended the Persian domination of the ancient world. In 331 BC Alexander the Great drove the Persians under Darius III (died 330 BC) into retreat, marking the end of the Persian Empire and the beginning of the Hellenistic period under the Seleucids. 2. modern-day Iran (known as Persia until 1935).

Persian /'pɜːʃən/ *n.* 1. a native or inhabitant of (especially ancient) Persia. 2. the language of Persia (modern-day Iran), a member of the Indo-Iranian branch of the Indo-European language family. —*adj.* of Persia or its people or language. —**Persian cat**, a cat of a breed with long silky hair. **Persian lamb**, the silky tightly-curled fur of karacul lambs. [from Old French from Latin]

Persian Gulf or **Arabian Gulf** a large shallow inlet of the Arabian Sea; area 233,000 sq km/90,000 sq mi. It divides the Arabian peninsula from Iran and is linked by the Strait of Hormuz and the Gulf of Oman to the Arabian Sea. Oilfields surround it in the Gulf States of Bahrain, Iran, Iraq, Kuwait, Oman, Qatar, Saudi Arabia, and the United Arab Emirates.

Persian Wars a series of conflicts between Greece and Persia 499–449 BC. The eventual victory of Greece marked the end of Persian domination of the ancient world and the beginning of Greek supremacy.

persiflage /'pɜːsɪflɑːʒ/ *n.* banter. [French (*siffler* = whistle)]

persimmon /pɜː'sɪmən/ *n.* any tree of the genus *Diospyros* of the ebony family Ebenaceae, especially the **common persimmon** *D. virginiana* of the eastern USA. The persimmon grows up to 19 m/60 ft high, and has alternate oval leaves and yellow-green unisexual flowers. The small, sweet, orange fruits are edible. [corruption of Algonquian word]

persist /pə'sɪst/ *v.i.* 1. to continue firmly or obstinately. 2. to continue in existence, to survive. —**persistence** *n.*, **persistency** *n.*, **persistent** *adj.*, **persistently** *adv.* [from Latin *sistere* = stand]

person /'pɜːsən/ *n.* 1. an individual human being. 2. the living body of a human being. 3. in grammar, each of the three classes of personal pronouns, verb forms etc., denoting respectively the person etc. speaking (**first person**), spoken to (**second person**), or spoken of (**third person**). 4. God as Father, Son, or Holy Ghost. —**in person**, physically present. [from Old French from Latin *persona*]

persona /pɜː'səʊnə/ *n.* (*plural* **personae** /-iː/) an aspect of one's personality as perceived by others. [Latin, originally = actor's mask]

personable *adj.* pleasing in appearance or behaviour.

personage /'pɜːsənɪdʒ/ *n.* a person, especially an important one.

persona grata /pɜː'səʊnə 'grɑːtə/ a person acceptable to certain others, especially a diplomat acceptable to a foreign government. —***persona non grata***, one who is not acceptable. [Latin]

personal /'pɜːsənəl/ *adj.* 1. of one's own or a particular person's own. 2. done or made etc. in person. 3. directed to or concerning an individual; of one's own or another's private life; referring (especially in a hostile way) to an individual's private life or concerns. 4. of the body. 5. of or existing as a person; in grammar, of or denoting one of the three persons. —**personal column**, a column of private advertisements or messages in a newspaper. **personal computer**, (PC) another name for ◊microcomputer. The term is also used, more specifically, to mean the IBM Personal Computer and machines based on it. **personal property**, all property except land and those interests in land that pass to one's heirs.

personal equity plan (PEP) an investment scheme introduced in the UK in 1987. Shares of public companies listed on the UK stock exchange are purchased by PEP managers on behalf of their clients. Up to certain limits, individuals may purchase such shares and, provided they hold them for at least a year, enjoy any capital gains and reinvested dividends tax-free.

personality /pɜːsəˈnælɪtɪ/ n. **1.** the distinctive character or qualities of a person. **2.** personal existence or identity, being a person. **3.** a famous person, a celebrity. **4.** (in *plural*) personal remarks.

personalize /ˈpɜːsənəlaɪz/ v.t. **1.** to make personal, especially by marking with the owner's name etc. **2.** to personify.

personally adv. **1.** in person. **2.** for one's own part.

personate /ˈpɜːsəneɪt/ v.t. **1.** to play the part of (a character in a drama etc.). **2.** to impersonate for fraudulent purposes. —**personation** /-ˈneɪʃən/ n., **personator** n. [from Latin *personare*]

personify /pɜːˈsɒnɪfaɪ/ v.t. **1.** to represent (a thing or abstraction) as having a personal nature. **2.** to symbolize (a quality) by a figure in human form. **3.** (especially in *past participle*) to embody in one's own person or exemplify (a quality). —**personification** /-fɪˈkeɪʃən/ n. [from French]

personnel /pɜːsəˈnel/ n. the body of employees, the staff (in a public undertaking, armed forces, an office etc.). —**personnel department,** the department of a firm etc. dealing with the appointment and welfare of employees. [French = personal]

perspective /pəˈspektɪv/ n. **1.** the art of drawing solid objects on a plane surface so as to give the right impression of their relative positions, size etc.; a picture so drawn. **2.** the apparent relation between visible objects as to position, distance etc. **3.** a mental view of the relative importance of things. **4.** a view or prospect (*literal* or *figurative*). —adj. of or in perspective. —**in perspective,** drawn or viewed according to the rules of perspective; correctly regarded as to relative importance. [from Latin (*ars*) *perspectiva* (*perspicere* = look through, examine)]

Perspex /ˈpɜːspeks/ n. trade name of a tough, light, transparent plastic, first produced in 1930. It is widely used for watch glasses, advertising signs, domestic baths, motorboat windshields, aircraft canopies, and protective shields. Its chemical name is polymethylmethacrylate (PMMA). It is manufactured under other names: Plexiglas (in the USA), Oroglas (in Europe), and Lucite.

perspicacious /pɜːspɪˈkeɪʃəs/ adj. having or showing great insight. —**perspicaciously** adv., **perspicacity** /-ˈkæsɪtɪ/ n. [from Latin *perspicax*]

perspicuous /pəˈspɪkjuəs/ adj. **1.** easily understood, clearly expressed. **2.** expressing things clearly. —**perspicuity** /pɜːspɪˈkjuːɪtɪ/ n., **perspicuously** adv., **perspicuousness** n. [from Latin originally = transparent]

perspiration /pɜːspɪˈreɪʃən/ n. the excretion of water and dissolved substances from the ◊sweat glands of the skin of mammals. Perspiration has two main functions: body cooling by the evaporation of water from the skin surface, and excretion of waste products such as salts. [French]

perspire /pəˈspaɪə/ v.t./i to sweat. [from French from Latin *spirare* = breathe]

persuade /pəˈsweɪd/ v.t. to cause (a person) to do or believe something, especially by reasoning, to induce. —**persuadable** adj., **persuasible** adj. [from Latin *suadēre* = induce]

persuasion /pəˈsweɪʒən/ n. **1.** persuading. **2.** persuasiveness. **3.** a belief or conviction; a sect holding a particular religious belief. [from Latin]

persuasive /pəˈsweɪsɪv/ adj. able or tending to persuade. —**persuasively** adv., **persuasiveness** n. [from French or Latin]

pert adj. **1.** cheeky. **2.** jaunty, lively. —**pertly** adv., **pertness** n. [from Old French *apert* from Latin *apertus* = open, and from Old French *aspert* from Latin *expertus*]

pertain /pəˈteɪn/ v.i. **1.** to be relevant or appropriate. **2.** to belong as a part, appendage, or accessory. [from Old French from Latin *pertinēre* = belong]

Perth /pɜːθ/ capital of Western Australia, with its port at nearby Fremantle on the Swan river; population (1986) 1,025,300. Products include textiles, cement, furniture, and vehicles. It was founded in 1829 and is the commercial and cultural centre of the state.

Perthshire /ˈpɜːθʃə/ former inland county of central Scotland, of which the major part was included in Tayside

in 1975, the SW being included in Central Region; Perth was the administrative headquarters.

pertinacious adj. holding firmly to an opinion or course of action; persistent, determined. —**pertinaciously** adv., **pertinacity** /-ˈnæsɪtɪ/ n. [from Latin *pertinax*]

pertinent /ˈpɜːtɪnənt/ adj. relevant to the matter in hand; to the point. —**pertinence** n., **pertinency** n., **pertinently** adv. [from Old French or Latin]

perturb /pəˈtɜːb/ v.t. to disturb greatly, to make anxious or uneasy. —**perturbation** /pɜːtɜːˈbeɪʃən/ n. [from Old French from Latin *turbare* = disturb]

Peru /pəˈruː/ Republic of; country in South America, on the Pacific, bounded to the N by Ecuador and Colombia, to the E by Brazil and Bolivia, and to the S by Chile; **area** 1,285,200 sq km/496,216 sq mi; **capital** Lima, including port of Callao; **physical** Andes mountains N–S cover 27%; Amazon river-basin jungle in NE; coastal plain in W; desert along coast N–S; **head of state and government** Alberto Fujimoro from 1990; **political system** democratic republic; **exports** coca, coffee, alpaca, llama and vicuna wool, fish meal, lead, copper, iron, oil; **population** (1990 est) 21,904,000 (46% Indian, mainly Quechua and Aymara; 43% mixed Spanish-Indian descent); **language** Spanish 68%, Quechua 27% (both official), Aymara 3%; **recent history** independence was achieved from Spain in 1824. Boundary disputes were settled with Bolivia in 1902, Colombia in 1927, and Ecuador in 1942; the dispute with Ecuador was renewed in 1981. Peru has been ruled by military and civilian governments alternately since 1948. Civilian rule was restored in 1980.

Peru Current formerly known as **Humboldt Current** a cold ocean ◊current flowing N from the Antarctic along the W coast of South America to S Ecuador, then W. It reduces the coastal temperature, making the W slopes of the Andes arid because winds are already chilled and dry when they meet the coast.

Perugino /peruˈdʒiːnəʊ/ Pietro. Original name of Pietro Vannucci 1446–1523. Italian painter, active chiefly in Perugia. He taught Raphael, who absorbed his soft and graceful figure style. Perugino produced paintings for the lower walls of the Sistine Chapel in 1481 (Vatican) and in 1500 decorated the Sala del Cambio in Perugia.

peruke /pəˈruːk/ n. (especially *historical*) a wig. [from French from Italian]

peruse /pəˈruːz/ v.t. to read or study (a document etc.) thoroughly or carefully. —**perusal** n.

Perutz /pəˈruːts/ Max 1914– . British biochemist, who shared the 1962 Nobel Prize for Chemistry with John Kendrew for work on the structure of the haemoglobin molecule.

pervade /pəˈveɪd/ v.t. to spread or be present throughout, to permeate. —**pervasion** n. [from Latin *vadere* = go]

pervasive /pəˈveɪsɪv/ adj. pervading. —**pervasiveness** n.

perverse /pəˈvɜːs/ adj. deliberately or stubbornly doing something different from what is reasonable or required; having this tendency, intractable. —**perversely** adv., **perverseness** n., **perversity** n. [from Old French from Latin]

perversion /pəˈvɜːʃən/ n. **1.** perverting, being perverted. **2.** preference for a form of sexual activity that is considered abnormal or unacceptable. [from Latin]

pervert /pəˈvɜːt/ v.t. **1.** to turn (a thing) from its proper use or nature; to misapply (words etc.). **2.** to lead astray from right behaviour or beliefs. **3.** (in *past participle*) showing perversion. —**perverting the course of justice,** in English law, the criminal offence of acting in such a way as to prevent justice being done. Examples are tampering with evidence, misleading the police or a court, and threatening witnesses or jurors. —/ˈpɜːvɜːt/ n. a perverted person; one showing perversion of sexual instincts. [from Old French or Latin *vertere* = turn]

pervious /ˈpɜːvɪəs/ adj. **1.** permeable, allowing passage. **2.** accessible (*to* reason etc.). [from Latin *pervius* (*via* = way)]

Pesach /ˈpeɪsɑːk/ the Jewish name for the ◊Passover festival.

peseta /pəˈseɪtə/ n. the currency unit of Spain. [Spanish, diminutive of *pesa* = weight]

Peshawar /pəˈʃaʊə/ capital of North-West Frontier Province, Pakistan, 18 km/11 mi E of the Khyber Pass; population (1981) 555,000. Products include textiles, leather, and copper.

pesky /ˈpeskɪ/ adj. (US colloquial) troublesome, annoying.

peso /ˈpeɪsəʊ/ n. (plural **pesos**) the currency unit of Chile, several Latin American countries, and the Philippines. [Spanish = weight, from Latin *pensum*]

pessary /ˈpesərɪ/ n. a device worn in the vagina to prevent uterine displacement or as a contraceptive; a vaginal suppository. [from Latin from Greek *pessos* = oval stone]

pessimism /ˈpesɪmɪzəm/ n. **1.** a gloomy view or disposition; a tendency to expect an unfavourable outcome. **2.** the belief that the actual world is the worst possible, or that all things tend to be evil. —**pessimist** n. [from Latin *pessimus* = worst]

pessimistic /pesɪˈmɪstɪk/ adj. showing pessimism; gloomy. —**pessimistically** adv.

pest n. **1.** a troublesome or annoying person or thing. **2.** in biology, any insect, fungus, rodent, or other living organism that has a harmful effect on human beings, other than those that directly cause human diseases. Most pests damage crops or livestock, but the term also covers those that damage buildings, destroy food stores, and spread disease. [from French or Latin *pestis* = plague]

pester v.t. to trouble or annoy, especially with frequent or persistent requests. [probably from French *empestrer* = encumber]

pesticide /ˈpestɪsaɪd/ n. any chemical used in farming, gardening, and indoors to combat pests and the diseases they carry. Pesticides are of three main types: **insecticides** (to kill insects), **fungicides** (to kill fungal diseases), and **herbicides** (to kill plants, mainly those considered weeds). The safest pesticides are those made from plants, such as the insecticides pyrethrum and derris. More potent are synthetic products, such as chlorinated hydrocarbons. These products, including DDT and dieldrin, are highly toxic to wildlife and human beings, so their use is now restricted by law in some areas and is declining.

pestiferous /peˈstɪfərəs/ adj. troublesome, harmful. [from Latin *pestis* = plague and *ferre* = bear]

pestilence /ˈpestɪləns/ n. a fatal epidemic disease, especially bubonic plague. [from Old French from Latin]

pestilent /ˈpestɪlənt/ adj. **1.** destructive to life, deadly; harmful. **2.** (colloquial) troublesome, annoying. [from Latin *pestis* = plague]

pestilential /pestɪˈlenʃəl/ adj. of a pestilence, pestilent. [from Latin]

pestle /ˈpesəl/ n. a club-shaped instrument for pounding substances in a mortar. [from Old French from Latin *pistillum* (*pinsere* = pound)]

pestology /peˈstɒlədʒɪ/ n. the scientific study of harmful insects and of the methods of dealing with them.

pet[1] n. **1.** a domesticated animal treated with affection and kept for pleasure or companionship. **2.** a darling, a favourite. —adj. **1.** of, for, or in the nature of a pet. **2.** favourite, particular. **3.** expressing fondness or familiarity. —v.t. (**-tt-**) **1.** to fondle (especially erotically). **2.** to treat with affection.

pet[2] n. offence at being slighted, ill humour.

peta- /ˈpetə-/ in combinations, denoting a factor of 10^{15}. [perhaps from *penta-*]

Pétain /peˈtæn/ Henri Philippe 1856–1951. French general and right-wing politician. His defence of Verdun in 1916 during World War I made him a national hero. During World War II he became prime minister in June 1940 and signed an armistice with Germany. Removing the seat of government to ◊Vichy, he established an authoritarian regime. He was imprisoned after the war.

To make a union with Great Britain would be a fusion with a corpse.
Henri Philippe Pétain
(to Churchill's proposal of an Anglo-French union, 1940)

---

petal /ˈpetəl/ n. part of a flower whose function is to attract pollinators such as insects or birds. Petals are frequently large and brightly coloured and may also be scented. Some

Peter I A portrait engraved from a painting by I Kupetsky in 1737.

have a nectary at the base and markings on the petal surface, known as ◊honey guides, to direct pollinators to the source of the nectar. In wind-pollinated plants, however, the petals are usually small and insignificant, and sometimes absent altogether. Petals are derived from modified leaves, and are known collectively as a ◊corolla. —**petalled** adj. [from Latin from Greek *petalon* = leaf]

petard /pɪˈtɑːd/ n. (historical) a small bomb used to blast down a door etc. —**hoist with his/her own petard**, injured by his/her own devices against others. [from French *péter* = break wind]

peter /ˈpiːtə/ v.i. **peter out**, to diminish gradually and come to an end.

Peter three tsars of Russia:

Peter I the Great 1672–1725. Tsar of Russia from 1682, on the death of his brother Tsar Feodor; he assumed control of the government in 1689. He attempted to reorganize the country on Western lines; the army was modernized, a fleet was built, the administrative and legal systems were remodelled, education was encouraged, and the church was brought under state control. On the Baltic coast, where he had conquered territory from Sweden, Peter built his new capital, St Petersburg (now Leningrad).

Peter II 1715–1730. Tsar of Russia from 1727. Son of Peter the Great, he had been passed over in favour of Catherine I in 1725 but succeeded her in 1727. He died of smallpox.

Peter III 1728–1762. Tsar of Russia in 1762. The weak-minded son of Peter I's eldest daughter, Anne, he was adopted in 1741 by his aunt ◊Elizabeth, Empress of Russia, and at her command married the future Catherine II in 1745. He was deposed in favour of his wife and probably murdered by her lover Alexius Orlov.

Peter I 1844–1921. King of Serbia from 1903. He was the son of Prince Alexander Karageorgevich and was elected king when the last Obrenovich king was murdered 1903. He took part in the retreat of the Serbian army 1915, and in 1918 was proclaimed first king of the Serbs, Croats, and Slovenes (renamed Yugoslavia in 1921).

Peter Lombard /ˈlɒmbɑːd/ 1100–1160. Italian Christian theologian whose *Sententiarum libri quatuor/Books of Sentences* 1148–51 considerably influenced Catholic doctrine.

Peterloo massacre /piːtəˈluː/ the events in St Peter's Fields, Manchester, England, on 16 Aug 1819, when an open-air meeting in support of parliamentary reform was charged by yeomanry and hussars. Eleven people were

petroleum

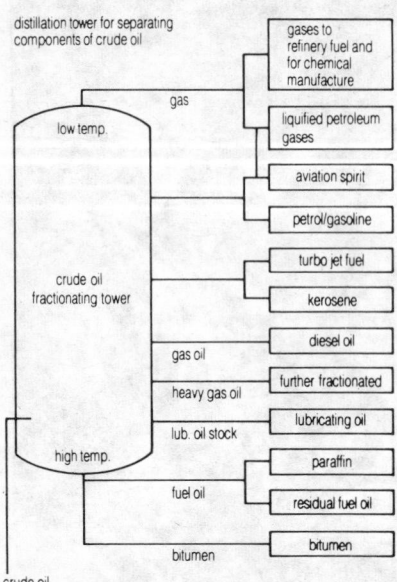

distillation tower for separating components of crude oil

gases to refinery fuel and for chemical manufacture

gas

liquified petroleum gases

low temp.

aviation spirit

petrol/gasoline

turbo jet fuel

crude oil fractionating tower

kerosene

diesel oil

gas oil

further fractionated

heavy gas oil

lubricating oil

lub. oil stock

high temp.

paraffin

fuel oil

residual fuel oil

bitumen

bitumen

crude oil

killed and 500 wounded. [name given in analogy with the Battle of Waterloo]

Peter Pan the hero of a play for children by James ◊Barrie, first performed in 1904. Peter Pan is an orphan with magical powers who arrives in the night nursery of the Darling children, Wendy, John, and Michael. He teaches them to fly and introduces them to the Never Never Land inhabited by fantastic characters, including the fairy Tinkerbell, the Lost Boys, and the pirate Captain Hook.

Peter, St Christian martyr, the author of two epistles in the New Testament and leader of the apostles. Originally a fisherman of Capernaum, on the Sea of Galilee, Peter was the first to acknowledge Jesus as the Messiah. His real name was Simon, but he was nicknamed Kephas ('Peter', from the Greek for 'rock') by Jesus, as being the rock upon which he would build his church. He is regarded as the first bishop of Rome, whose mantle the pope inherits. His emblem is two keys; feast day 29 June.

petersham /'pi:təʃəm/ n. a thick ribbed silk ribbon. [from Lord *Petersham*, English army officer (died 1851)]

Peter's pence in the Roman Catholic Church, a voluntary annual contribution to papal administrative costs; during the 10th–16th centuries it was a compulsory levy of one penny per household.

Peter the Hermit 1050–1115. French priest whose eloquent preaching of the First ◊Crusade sent thousands of peasants marching against the Turks, who massacred them in Asia Minor. Peter escaped and accompanied the main body of crusaders to Jerusalem.

petiole /'petiəul/ n. in botany, a slender stalk joining a leaf to a stem. Typically it is continuous with the midrib of the leaf and attached to the base of the leaf blade or ◊lamina, but occasionally it is attached to the lower surface of the lamina (a peltate leaf), as in the nasturtium. [from French from Latin *petiolus* = little foot, stalk]

Petit /pə'ti:/ Alexis 1791–1820. French physicist, co-discoverer of **Dulong and Petit's law**, which states that the ◊specific heat capacity of an element is inversely proportional to its ◊atomic mass.

petit bourgeois /pəti: 'buəʒwa:/ a member of the lower middle classes. [French]

petite /pə'ti:t/ adj. (of a woman) small and dainty in build. [French, feminine of *petit* = small]

petit four /pəti: 'fuə/ (*plural petits fours pronounced* the same) a very small fancy cake. [French = little oven]

petition /pə'tɪʃən/ n. **1.** asking, supplication. **2.** a formal written request, especially one signed by many people, appealing to an authority for a right or benefit etc. **3.**

an application to a court for a writ, order etc. —*v.t./i.* **1.** to make or address a petition to. **2.** to ask earnestly or humbly. —**petitioner** n. [from Old French from Latin *petere* = seek]

petition of right in British law, the procedure whereby, before the passing of the ◊Crown Proceedings Act 1947, a subject petitioned for legal relief against the crown, for example for money due under a contract, or for property of which the crown had taken possession. An example is the Petition of Right presented by Parliament and accepted by Charles I in 1628, declaring illegal taxation without parliamentary consent, imprisonment without trial, billeting of soldiers on private persons, and use of martial law.

petit mal /pəti: 'mæl/ a form of epilepsy without loss of consciousness. [French = small sickness]

petit point /pəti: 'pwæ/ or **tent stitch** a short, slanting embroidery stitch used on open-net canvas for upholstery and cushions to form a solid background. It was common in the 18th century. [French]

Petőfi /'petɜ:fi/ Sándor 1823–1849. Hungarian nationalist poet. He published his first volume of poems in 1844. He expressed his revolutionary ideas in the semi-autobiographical poem 'The Apostle', and died fighting the Austrians in the battle of Segesvár.

Petra /'petrə/ (Arabic **Wadi Musa**) ancient city carved out of the red rock at a site in Jordan, on the E slopes of the Wadi el Araba, 90 km/56 mi S of the Dead Sea. An Edomite stronghold and capital of the Nabataeans in the 2nd century, it was captured by the Roman emperor Trajan in 106 and destroyed by the Arabs in the 7th century. It was forgotten in Europe until 1812 when the Swiss traveller Jacob Burckhardt (1818–1897) came across it.

Petrarch /'petra:k/ (Italian **Petrarca**) Francesco 1304–1374. Italian poet, born in Arezzo, a devotee of the Classical tradition. His *Il Canzoniere* is composed of sonnets in praise of his idealized love 'Laura', whom he first saw in 1327 (she was a married woman and refused to become his mistress). The **Petrarchan sonnet** is associated with him; see ◊sonnet.

petrel /'petrəl/ n. either of two families of seabirds (Procellariidae and Hydrobatidae) that fly far from land. They include albatrosses, fulmars, and shearwaters.

Petrie /'pi:tri/ (William Matthew) Flinders 1853–1942. English archaeologist who excavated sites in Egypt (the pyramids at Gîza, the temple at Tanis, the Greek city of Naucratis in the Nile delta, Tell el Amarna, Naquada, Abydos, and Memphis) and Palestine from 1880.

petrify /'petrifai/ v.t./i. **1.** to paralyse with fear, astonishment etc. **2.** to turn or be turned into stone. —**petrification** /-fi'keɪʃən/ n. [from French from Latin *petrificare* (*petra* = rock from Greek)]

petrochemical /petrəu'kemikəl/ n. a chemical derived from the processing of ◊petroleum. —*adj.*, **petrochemical industry**, an industry based on industrial manufacturing processes that obtain their raw materials from the processing of petroleum.

petrodollar /'petrəudɒlə/ n. a dollar held by a petroleum-exporting country, a member of the ◊Organization of Petroleum Exporting Countries (OPEC).

Petrograd /'petrəgræd/ former name (1914–24) of ◊Leningrad, city in the USSR.

petrography /pi'trɒgrəfi/ n. the scientific description of the composition and formation of rocks. —**petrographic** /petrə'græfik/ adj. [from Greek *petra* = rock and *graphia* = writing]

petrol /'petrəl/ n. a mixture of hydrocarbons derived from petroleum, mainly used as a fuel for internal combustion engines. It is colourless and highly volatile. In the USA, petrol is called gasoline. —**petrol station**, a filling station. [from French from Latin]

petrol engine the most commonly used source of power for motor vehicles, introduced by the German engineers Gottlieb Daimler and Karl Benz in 1885. The petrol engine is a complex piece of machinery made up of about 150 moving parts. It is a reciprocating piston engine (see ◊internal-combustion engine), in which a number of pistons move up and down in cylinders. The motion of the pistons rotate a crankshaft, at the end of which is a heavy flywheel. From the flywheel the power is transferred to the car's driving wheels via the transmission system of clutch, gearbox, and final drive.

petroleum /pɪˈtrəʊlɪəm/ *n.* a natural mineral oil, a thick greenish-brown flammable liquid found underground in permeable rocks. Petroleum consists of hydrocarbons mixed with oxygen, sulphur, nitrogen, and other elements in varying proportions. It is thought to be derived from ancient organic material that has been converted by, first, bacterial action, then heat and pressure (but its origin may be chemical also). From crude petroleum, various products are made by distillation and other processes; for example, fuel oil, gasoline (petrol), kerosene, diesel, lubricating oil, paraffin wax, and petroleum jelly. [Latin *petra* = rock from Greek and *oleum* = oil]

petrology /pɪˈtrɒlədʒɪ/ *n.* the branch of ◊geology that deals with the study of rocks, their mineral compositions, and their origins. —**petrological** /-ˈlɒdʒɪkəl/ *adj.* [from Greek *petra* = rock]

Petronius /pəˈtrəʊnɪəs/ Gaius, known as **Petronius Arbiter** Roman author of the licentious romance *Satyricon*. He was a companion of the emperor Nero and supervisor of his pleasures.

Petropavlovsk-Kamchatskiy /petrəʊpævˈlɒvskkæm ˈtʃætski/ Pacific seaport and Soviet naval base on the E coast of the Kamchatka peninsula, USSR; population (1987) 252,000.

petticoat /ˈpetɪkəʊt/ *n.* 1. a woman's or girl's dress-length undergarment hanging from the waist or shoulders. 2. (*attributive*) feminine, of or by women. [from *petty coat*]

pettifogging /ˈpetɪfɒgɪŋ/ *adj.* 1. quibbling or wrangling about unimportant details. 2. practising legal chicanery. [from *pettifogger* = inferior legal practitioner (*fogger* = underhand dealer)]

pettish *adj.* peevish, petulant, irritable. —**pettishly** *adv.*, **pettishness** *n.*

petty *adj.* 1. unimportant, trivial. 2. small-minded. 3. minor; inferior; on a small scale. —**petty cash**, money kept for small cash items of expenditure. **petty officer**, a naval noncommissioned officer (NCO). **petty sessions**, a meeting of two or more magistrates for the summary trial of certain offences. —**pettily** *adv.*, **pettiness** *n.* [from Old French *petit* = small]

petulant /ˈpetjʊlənt/ *adj.* peevishly impatient or irritable. —**petulance** *n.*, **petulantly** *adv.* [from French from Latin *petere* = seek]

petunia /pɪˈtjuːnɪə/ *n.* a plant of the genus *Petunia* with funnel-shaped flowers of vivid purple, red, white etc. [from French from Guarani = tobacco]

pew *n.* 1. a long backed bench or enclosed compartment in a church. 2. (*colloquial*) a seat. [from Old French *puye* = balcony from Latin]

pewter /ˈpjuːtə/ *n.* any of various alloys of mostly tin with varying amounts of lead, copper, or antimony. Pewter has been known for centuries and was once widely used for domestic utensils but is now mainly used for ornamental ware. [from Old French *peutre*]

peyote /peɪˈəʊtɪ/ *n.* a spineless cactus *Lophophora williamsii* of N Mexico and SW USA. It has white or pink flowers. Its buttonlike tops contain the hallucinogen mescaline, which is used by American Indians in religious ceremonies. [American Spanish, from Nahuatl]

Pfalz /pfælts/ the German name of the historic division of Germany, the ◊Palatinate.

pfennig /ˈpfenɪg/ *n.* a small German coin worth 1/100 of a mark. [German]

PG abbreviation of paying guest.

pH /piːˈeɪtʃ/ *n.* a measure of the acidity or alkaline level of a solution. A pH of 7.0 (distilled water) indicates neutrality, below 7 is acid, while above 7 is alkaline. [German *potenz* = power and *H* (symbol for hydrogen) = dissolved hydrogen ions]

Phaedra /ˈfiːdrə/ in Greek mythology, a Cretan, the daughter of Minos and Pasiphae, married to ◊Theseus of Athens. Her adulterous passion for her stepson ◊Hippolytus leads to her death in plays by Euripides and Seneca, adapted by Racine.

Phaethon /ˈfeɪəθən/ in Greek mythology, the son of ◊Helios, who was allowed for one day to drive the chariot of the Sun. Losing control of the horses, he almost set the Earth on fire, and was killed by Zeus with a thunderbolt.

phage another name for a ◊bacteriophage, a virus that attacks bacteria.

phagocyte /ˈfægəsaɪt/ *n.* a type of white blood cell, or ◊leucocyte, that can engulf a bacterium or other invading microorganism. Phagocytes are found in blood, lymph, and other body tissues, where they also ingest foreign matter and dead tissue. [Greek *phag-* = eat]

phalanger /fəˈlændʒə/ *n.* in Australia and New Zealand, a tree-dwelling marsupial of the family Phalangeridae, with webbed hind feet. [from Greek *phalaggion* = spider's web, from its webbed toes]

Phalangist /fəˈlændʒɪst/ *n.* a member of a Lebanese military organization (**Phalanges Libanaises**), since 1958 the political and military force of the ◊Maronite Church in Lebanon. Its unbending right-wing policies and resistance to the introduction of democratic institutions helped contribute to the civil war in Lebanon.

phalanx /ˈfælæŋks/ *n.* (*plural* **phalanxes**) 1. in ancient Greece, a line of battle, especially a body of infantry drawn up in close order. 2. a set of persons etc. forming a compact mass or banded together for a common purpose. 3. (*plural* **phalanges**) a bone of the finger or toe. [Latin from Greek]

Phalaris /ˈfælərɪs/ 570–554 BC. Tyrant of the Greek colony of Acragas (Argrigento) in Sicily. He is said to have built a hollow bronze bull in which his victims were roasted alive. He was killed in a people's revolt.

phalarope *n.* a genus of seabirds related to plovers and resembling sandpipers. The **red-necked** *Phalaropus ilobatus* and grey *Phalaropus fulicarius* visit Britain from the Arctic; *Phalaropus tricolor* is exclusively North American. The male is courted by the female and hatches the eggs. The female is larger and more colourful.

phallus /ˈfæləs/ *n.* (*plural* **phalluses**) an image of the penis (usually in erection) as a symbol of generative power. —**phallic** *adj.* [Latin from Greek]

Phanerozoic *adj.* of an aeon in Earth history, consisting of the most recent 590 million years. —*n.* this aeon. It comprises the Palaeozoic, Mesozoic, and Cenozoic eras. The vast majority of fossils come from the Phanerozoic, owing to the evolution of hard shells and internal skeletons. [= interval of well-displayed life (from Greek *phanero* = visible)]

phantasm /ˈfæntæzəm/ *n.* an illusion, a phantom. —**phantasmal** /-ˈtæzməl/ *adj.* [from Old French from Latin from Greek *phantazō* = make visible]

phantasmagoria /fæntæzməˈgɒːrɪə/ *n.* a shifting scene of real or imagined figures. —**phantasmagoric** /-ˈgɒrɪk/ *adj.*

phantom /ˈfæntəm/ *n.* 1. a ghost, an apparition. 2. something without substance or reality, a mental illusion. —*adj.* merely apparent, illusory. [from Old French *fantosme* from Greek]

Pharaoh /ˈfeərəʊ/ *n.* the title of the ruler of ancient Egypt, originally applied to the royal household, and after about 950 BC to the king. [from Latin from Greek from Hebrew from Egyptian = great house]

Pharisee /ˈfærɪsiː/ *n.* 1. a member of a conservative Jewish sect that arose in the 2nd century BC in protest against all movements favouring compromise with Hellenistic culture. They were devout adherents of the law, both as found in the Torah and in the oral tradition known as the Mishnah. 2. a self-righteous person, a hypocrite. —**Pharisaic** /-ˈseɪk/ *adj.* [Old English, ultimately from Aramaic, from Hebrew *parush* = separated]

pharmaceutical /faːməˈsjuːtɪkəl/ *adj.* of or engaged in pharmacy; of the use or sale of medicinal drugs. [from Latin from Greek *pharmakeutēs* = druggist from *pharmakon* = drug]

pharmaceutics *n.pl.* (usually treated as *singular*) pharmacy (see ◊pharmacy sense 1).

pharmacist /ˈfaːməsɪst/ *n.* a person engaged in pharmacy.

pharmacology /faːməˈkɒlədʒɪ/ *n.* the science of the action of drugs on the body. —**pharmacological** /-ˈlɒdʒɪkəl/ *adj.*, **pharmacologist** *n.* [from Greek *pharmakon* = drug]

pharmacopoeia /faːməkəˈpiːə/ *n.* 1. a book (especially one published officially) containing a list of drugs with directions for their use. 2. a stock of drugs. [from Greek *pharmakopoios* = drug maker]

pharmacy /ˈfaːməsɪ/ *n.* 1. the preparation and dispensing of drugs. 2. a pharmacist's shop; a dispensary. [from Old French from Latin from Greek *pharmakeus* = druggist]

pharyngitis /ˌfærɪnˈdʒaɪtɪs/ *n.* inflammation of the pharynx.

pharynx /ˈfærɪŋks/ *n.* the interior of the throat, the cavity at the back of the mouth. Its walls are made of muscle strengthened with a fibrous layer and lined with mucous membrane. The internal nostrils lead backwards into the pharynx, which continues downwards into the oesophagus and (through the epiglottis) into the windpipe. On each side, a Eustachian tube enters the pharynx from the middle ear cavity. —**pharyngeal** /-ɪnˈdʒiːəl/ *adj.* [from Greek *pharugx*]

phase /feɪz/ *n.* **1.** a stage of change or development. **2.** in astronomy, the apparent shape of the Moon or a planet when all or part of its illuminated hemisphere is facing the Earth. The Moon undergoes a full cycle of phases from new (when between the Earth and the Sun) through first quarter (when at 90° eastern elongation from the Sun), full (when opposite the Sun), and last quarter (when at 90° western elongation from the Sun). The ◊inferior planets can also undergo a full cycle of phases, as can an asteroid passing inside the Earth's orbit. **3.** in chemistry, a physical state of matter: for example, ice and liquid water are different phases of water; a mixture of the two is termed a two-phase system. **4.** in physics, a stage in an oscillatory motion, such as a wave motion: two waves are in phase when their peaks and their troughs coincide. Otherwise, there is a **phase difference**, which has consequences in ◊interference phenomena and ◊alternating current electricity. —*v.t.* to carry out (a programme etc.) in phases or stages. —**phase in** or **out**, to bring gradually into (or out of) use. [from French from Greek *phasis* = appearance]

PhD abbreviation of Doctor of Philosophy. [from Latin *philosophiae doctor*]

pheasant /ˈfezənt/ *n.* a long-tailed game bird of the family Phasianidae, especially the common pheasant *Phasianus colchicus*, originally Asian but long naturalized in Europe. The plumage of the male is richly tinted with brownish-green, yellow, and red markings, but the female is a camouflaged brownish colour. The nest is made in the ground. [from Anglo-French from Greek *phasianus* (*Phasis* = river in Asia Minor)]

phenol /ˈfiːnɒl/ *n.* a member of a group of aromatic chemical compounds with weakly acidic properties, which are characterized by a hydroxyl (-OH) group attached directly to an aromatic ring. The simplest of the phenols, derived from benzene, is also known as phenol and has the formula C_6H_5OH. It is sometimes called **carbolic acid** and can be extracted from coal tar. Pure phenol consists of colourless, needle-shaped crystals which take up moisture from the atmosphere. It has a strong and characteristic smell and was once used as an antiseptic. It is, however, toxic by absorption through the skin. [from French *phène* = benzene]

phenomenal /fɪˈnɒmɪnəl/ *adj.* of the nature of a phenomenon; extraordinary, remarkable. —**phenomenally** *adv.*

phenomenalism *n.* a philosophical position that argues that statements about objects can be reduced to statements about what is perceived or perceivable. Thus J S Mill defined material objects as 'permanent possibilities of sensation'. Phenomenalism is closely connected with certain forms of ◊empiricism.

phenomenology *n.* the philosophical perspective, founded by the German philosopher ◊Husserl, that in the social sciences concentrates on phenomena as objects of perception (rather than as facts or occurrences that exist independently) in attempting to examine the ways people think about and interpret the world around them. It has been practised by the philosophers Heidegger, Sartre, and Merleau-Ponty.

phenomenon /fɪˈnɒmɪnən/ *n.* (*plural* **phenomena**) **1.** a fact or occurrence that appears or is perceived, especially a thing the cause of which is in question. **2.** a remarkable person or thing. [from Latin from Greek *phainomai* = appear]

phenotype *n.* in genetics, the traits actually displayed by an organism. The phenotype is not a direct reflection of the ◊genotype because some alleles are masked by the presence of other, dominant alleles (see ◊dominance). The phenotype is further modified by the effects of the environment (for example, poor food stunting growth).

pheromone /ˈferəməʊn/ *n.* a chemical substance secreted and released by an animal (such as an odour) for detection and response by another of the same (or a closely related) species. Pheromones are used by many animal species to attract mates. [from Greek *pherō* = convey and *hormone*]

phew /fjuː/ interjection expressing relief, weariness, surprise etc. [imitative of puffing]

phi /faɪ/ *n.* the 21st letter of the Greek alphabet, (φ, Φ) = ph. [Greek]

phial /ˈfaɪəl/ *n.* a small glass bottle, especially for liquid medicine. [from Old French from Latin from Greek]

Phidias /ˈfɪdiæs/ mid-5th century BC. Greek Classical sculptor. He supervised the sculptural programme for the Parthenon (most of it preserved in the British Museum, London, and known as the Elgin marbles). He also executed the colossal statue of Zeus at Olympia, one of the Seven Wonders of the World.

phil- see ◊philo-.

Philadelphia /fɪləˈdelfiə/ industrial city and port on the Delaware river in Pennsylvania, USA; population (1980) 1,688,000, metropolitan area 3,700,000. Products include refined oil, chemicals, textiles, processed food, printing and publishing. Founded in 1682, it was the first capital of the USA 1790–1800. [= city of brotherly love]

philander /fɪˈlændə/ *v.i.* (of a man) to flirt. —**philanderer** *n.* [from Greek *philandros* = fond of men, taken as name of lover]

philanthropy /fɪˈlænθrəpɪ/ *n.* concern for the welfare of mankind, especially as shown by acts of benevolence. —**philanthropic** /-ˈθrɒpɪk/ *adj.*, **philanthropically** /-ˈθrɒpɪkəlɪ/ *adv.*, **philanthropist** *n.* [from Latin from Greek *phileō* = to love and *anthrōpos* = human being]

philately /fɪˈlætəlɪ/ *n.* the collecting and study of postage stamps. It originated as a hobby in France about 1860. —**philatelic** /-ˈtelɪk/ *adj.*, **philatelist** *n.* [from French from Greek *phileō* = to love and *ateleia* = exemption from payment]

Philby /ˈfɪlbɪ/ Kim (Harold) 1912–1988. British intelligence officer from 1940 and Soviet agent from 1933. He was liaison officer in Washington 1949–51, when he was confirmed to be a double agent and asked to resign. Named in 1963 as having warned Guy Burgess and Donald Maclean (similarly double agents) that their activities were known, he fled to the USSR and became a Soviet citizen and general in the KGB. A fourth member of the ring was Anthony ◊Blunt.

To betray you must first belong.

Kim Philby
The New York Times 1967

-phile /-faɪl/ or **-phil** suffix forming nouns and adjectives in the sense 'one who is fond of' (e.g. *bibliophile*). [from Greek *philos* = loving]

philharmonic /fɪlɑːˈmɒnɪk/ *adj.* in the names of orchestras and music societies, fond of music. [from French from Italian]

Philip /ˈfɪlɪp/ Duke of Edinburgh 1921– . Prince of the UK, husband of Elizabeth II, and a grandson of George I of Greece and a great-great-grandson of Queen Victoria. He was born in Corfu, Greece but brought up in England.

Philip six kings of France, including:

Philip II (Philip Augustus) 1165–1223. King of France from 1180. As part of his efforts to establish a strong monarchy and evict the English from their French possessions, he waged war in turn against the English kings Henry II, Richard I (with whom he also went on the Third Crusade), and John (against whom he won the decisive battle of Bouvines in Flanders in 1214).

Philip IV the Fair 1268–1314. King of France from 1285. He engaged in a feud with Pope Boniface VIII and made him a prisoner in 1303. Clement V (1264–1314), elected pope through Philip's influence in 1305, moved the papal seat to Avignon in 1309 and collaborated with Philip to suppress the Templars, a powerful order of knights. Philip allied with the Scots against England and invaded Flanders.

Philip VI 1293–1350. King of France from 1328, first of the house of Valois, elected by the barons on the death of his cousin, Charles IV. His claim was challenged by Edward III of England, who defeated him at Crécy in 1346.

Philip II of Macedon /'fɪlɪp/ 382–336 BC. King of Macedonia from 359 BC. He seized the throne from his nephew, for whom he was regent, conquered the Greek city states, and formed them into a league whose forces could be united against Persia. He was assassinated while he was planning this expedition, and was succeeded by his son ◊Alexander the Great. His tomb was discovered at Vergina, N Greece, in 1978.

Philip five kings of Spain, including:

Philip I the Handsome 1478–1506. King of Castile from 1504, through his marriage in 1496 to Joanna the Mad (1479–1555). He was the son of the Holy Roman emperor Maximilian I.

Philip II 1527–1598. King of Spain from 1556. He was born at Valladolid, the son of the Habsburg emperor Charles V, and in 1554 married Queen Mary of England. On his father's abdication in 1556 he inherited Spain, the Netherlands, and the Spanish possessions in Italy and the Americas, and in 1580 annexed Portugal. His intolerance and lack of understanding of the Netherlanders drove them into revolt. Political and religious differences combined to involve him in war with England and, after 1589, with France. The defeat of the ◊Spanish Armada marked the beginning of the decline of Spanish power.

Philip V 1683–1746. King of Spain from 1700. A grandson of Louis XIV of France, he was the first Bourbon king of Spain. He was not recognized by the major European powers until 1713. See ◊Spanish Succession, War of the.

Philip the Good 1396–1467. Duke of Burgundy from 1419. He engaged in the Hundred Years' War as an ally of England until he made peace with the French at the Council of Arras in 1435. He made the Netherlands a centre of art and learning.

Philip Neri, St /'nɪəri/ 1515–1595. Italian Roman Catholic priest who organized the Congregation of the Oratory (see ◊Oratorian). He built the oratory over the church of St Jerome, Rome, where prayer meetings were held and scenes from the Bible performed with music, originating the musical form ◊oratorio. Feast day 26 May.

Philippi /fɪ'lɪpaɪ/ ancient city of Macedonia founded by Philip of Macedon in 358 BC. Near Philippi, Mark Antony and Augustus defeated Brutus and Cassius in 42 BC. It was the first European town where St Paul preached the Epistle to the Philippians (about AD 53).

philippic /fɪ'lɪpɪk/ *n.* a bitter invective. [from Latin from Greek (*Philippos* = Philip); originally applied to the orations of Demosthenes against Philip II of Macedon]

Philippines /'fɪlɪpi:nz/ Republic of the; country on an archipelago E of the Pacific Ocean and W of the South China Sea; **area** 300,000 sq km/115,800 sq mi; **capital** Manila (on Luzon); **physical** comprises over 7,000 islands; volcanic mountain ranges traverse main chain N–S; 50% still forested. The largest islands are Luzon 108,172 sq km/41,754 sq mi and Mindanao 94,227 sq km/36,372 sq mi; others include Samar, Negros, Palawan, Panay, Mindoro, Leyte, Cebu, and the Sulu group; **head of state and government** Corazón Aquino from 1986; **political system** emergent democracy; **exports** sugar, copra and coconut oil, timber, iron ore, copper concentrates; **population** (1990 est) 66,647,000 (93% Malaysian); **language** Filipino; English and Spanish; **recent history** independence was achieved from the USA in 1946. President Marcos was overthrown by Corazón Aquino's People's Power movement in 1986; seven coup attempts have been made between 1987 and 1990 but President Aquino remains in power.

Philip, St 1st century AD. In the New Testament, one of the 12 apostles. He was an inhabitant of Bethsaida (N Israel), and is said to have worked as a missionary in Anatolia. Feast day 3 May.

philistine /'fɪlɪstaɪn/ *n.* one who is hostile or indifferent to culture, or whose interests are material or commonplace. —*adj.* having such characteristics. —**philistinism** /-ɪnɪzəm/ *n.*

Philistine *n.* a member of a seafaring, warlike people of non-Semitic origin who founded city states on the Palestinian coastal plain in the 12th century BC, adopting a Semitic language and religion. They were at war with the Israelites in the 11th–10th centuries BC but were largely absorbed into the kingdom of Israel under King David, in about 1000 BC. —*adj.* of the Philistines. [ultimately from Hebrew]

Phillip /'fɪlɪp/ Arthur 1738–1814. British vice admiral, founder and governor of the convict settlement at Sydney, Australia, 1788–92, and hence founder of New South Wales.

Philips /'fɪlɪps/ Anton 1874–1951. Dutch industrialist and founder of an electronics firm. The Philips Bulb and Radio Works was founded in 1891 with his brother Gerard, at Eindhoven. Anton served as chair of the company 1921–51, during which time the firm became the largest producer of electrical goods outside the USA.

Phillips curve a graph showing the relationship between percentage changes in wages and unemployment, and indicating that wages rise faster during periods of low unemployment as employers compete for labour. The implication is that the dual objectives of low unemployment and low inflation are inconsistent. The concept has been widely questioned since the early 1960s because of the apparent instability of the wages/unemployment relationship. It was developed by the British economist A(lban) W(illiam) Phillips (1914–75), who plotted graphically wage and unemployment changes between 1861 and 1957.

philo- /-fɪlə(ʊ)-/ in combinations, (**phil-** before a vowel or *h*) liking, fond of. [from Greek *phileō* = to love]

philology /fɪ'lɒlədʒɪ/ *n.* 1. the study (especially historical and comparative) of language(s). 2. (*US*) the study of literature. 3. (*archaic*) love of learning and literature. —**philologian** /-'ləʊdʒiən/ *n.*, **philological** /-'lɒdʒɪkəl/ *adj.*, **philologist** *n.* [from French, ultimately from Greek = love of learning]

philosopher /fɪ'lɒsəfə/ *n.* 1. one engaged or learned in philosophy or a branch of it. 2. one who lives by philosophy or acts philosophically. —**philosopher's stone**, an object sought by alchemists as a means of turning other metals into gold or silver. [from Anglo-French from Latin from Greek = love of wisdom]

philosophize /fɪ'lɒsəfaɪz/ *v.i.* to reason like a philosopher; to speculate, to theorize; to moralize. [apparently from French *philosopher*]

philosophical /fɪlə'sɒfɪkəl/ *adj.* or **philosophic** 1. of or according to philosophy. 2. skilled in or devoted to philosophy. 3. calmly reasonable; bearing unavoidable misfortune unemotionally. —**philosophically** *adv.* [from Latin]

philosophy /fɪ'lɒsəfɪ/ *n.* 1. the use of reason and argument in the search for truth and the knowledge of reality, especially of the causes and nature of things, and of the principles governing existence, perception, human behaviour, and the material universe. As a branch of learning, philosophy includes metaphysics (the nature of being), epistemology (theory of knowledge), logic (study of valid inference), ethics, and aesthetics. Contemporary philosophers are inclined to think of philosophy as an investigation of the fundamental assumptions that govern our ways of understanding and acting in the world. 2. a particular system or set of beliefs preached by the above. 3. a system of conduct in life. 4. a philosophical attitude to misfortune etc. 5. advanced learning in general. [from Old French, ultimately from Greek = love of wisdom]

philtre /'fɪltə/ *n.* a drink supposed to be able to excite sexual love. [from French from Latin from Greek *philtron* (*phileō* = love)]

Phiz /fɪz/ pseudonym of Hablot Knight Browne 1815–1882. British artist who illustrated the greater part of *The Pickwick Papers* and other works by Charles Dickens.

phlebitis /fli'baɪtɪs/ *n.* inflammation of the walls of a vein. It is sometimes associated with blockage by a blood clot (◊thrombosis), in which case it is more accurately described as thrombophlebitis. —**phlebitic** /-'bɪtɪk/ *adj.* [from Greek *phleps* = vein]

phlebotomy *n.* the practice of blood-letting, withdrawing blood from a vein as a therapeutic measure.

phlegm /flem/ *n.* 1. a thick viscous substance secreted by the mucous membranes of the respiratory passages, discharged by coughing. 2. (*archaic*) this substance regarded as a humour (see ◊humour sense 4). 3. calmness; sluggishness. [from Old French from Latin from Greek = inflammation]

phlegmatic /fleg'mætɪk/ *adj.* calm, not easily agitated; sluggish. —**phlegmatically** *adv.*

phloem /'fləʊem/ n. the soft tissue of stems (as opposed to ◊xylem) that carries the sugars and other food materials made by photosynthesis from the leaves to all parts of the plant. [from Greek *phloos* = bark]

phlogiston /flɒ'dʒɪstən/ n. a substance formerly supposed to cause combustion. [from Greek *phlogizō* = set on fire, from *phlox* = flame]

phlox /flɒks/ n. any plant of the genus *Phlox*, native to North America and Siberia. They are small with alternate leaves and clusters of showy white, pink, red, or purple flowers. [Latin from Greek name of a plant (literally = 'flame')]

Phnom Penh /'nɒm 'pen/ capital of Cambodia, on the Mekong River, 210 km/130 mi NW of Saigon; population (1981) 600,000. Industries include textiles and food processing.

-phobe /-fəʊb/ suffix forming nouns and adjectives in the sense '(a person) disliking or fearing' (e.g. *Anglophobe*). [French from Latin from Greek *phobos* = fear]

phobia /'fəʊbiə/ n. an excessive irrational fear of an object or situation, for example, agoraphobia (fear of open spaces and crowded places), acrophobia (fear of heights), claustrophobia (fear of enclosed places). Behaviour therapy is one form of treatment.

-phobia /-fəʊbiə/ suffix forming abstract nouns corresponding to adjectives in -*phobe* (e.g. *xenophobia*). —**phobic** *adj.* [Latin from Greek *phobos* = fear]

Phobos /'fəʊbɒs/ one of the two moons of Mars, discovered in 1877 by the US astronomer Asaph Hall. It is an irregularly shaped lump of rock, cratered by ◊meteorite impacts. Phobos is $27 \times 21 \times 19$ km/$17 \times 13 \times 12$ mi across, and orbits Mars every 0.32 days at a height of 9,400 km/5,840 mi. It is thought to be an asteroid captured by Mars' gravity.

Phoenicia /fə'nɪʃiə/ ancient Greek name for N ◊Canaan on the E coast of the Mediterranean. —**Phoenician,** one of the people of this area who lived about 1200–332 BC. Seafaring traders and artisans, they are said to have circumnavigated Africa and established colonies in Cyprus, N Africa (for example Carthage), Malta, Sicily, and Spain. Their cities (Tyre, Sidon, and Byblos were the main ones) were independent states ruled by hereditary kings but dominated by merchant ruling classes. The fall of Tyre to Alexander the Great ended the separate history of Phoenicia. —*adj.* of Phoenicia. [from French from Latin from Greek]

phoenix /'fiːnɪks/ n. a mythical bird of the Arabian desert, the only one of its kind, said to live for five or six centuries and then burn itself on a funeral pyre, rising from its ashes with renewed youth to live through another cycle. [Old English, ultimately from Greek *phoinix* = Phoenician, purple, phoenix]

Phoenix capital of Arizona, USA; industrial city (steel, aluminium, electrical goods, food processing) and tourist centre on the Salt River; population (1986) 882,000.

Phoenix Park Murders the murder of several prominent members of the British government in Phoenix Park, Dublin on 6 May 1882. It threatened the conciliation between the Liberal government and the Irish nationalist members at Westminster which had been secured by the Kilmainham Treaty.

phon n. a unit of loudness, equal to the value in decibels of an equally loud tone with frequency 1,000 Hz. The higher the frequency, the louder a noise sounds for the same decibel value; thus an 80-decibel tone with a frequency of 20 Hz sounds as loud as 20 decibels at 1,000 Hz, and the phon value of both tones is 20. An aircraft engine has a loudness of around 140 phons.

phone /fəʊn/ n. (*colloquial*) a telephone. —*v.t./i.* (*colloquial*) to telephone. —**phone-in** n. a broadcast programme in which listeners participate by telephoning the studio. [abbreviation]

phoneme /'fəʊniːm/ n. a unit of significant sound in a specified language (e.g. the sound of *c* in *cat*, which differs from the *b* in *bat* and distinguishes the two words). —**phonemic** /-'niːmɪk/ *adj.*, **phonemics** n.pl. (also as *singular*) [from French from Greek = sound, speech]

phonetic /fə'netɪk/ *adj.* of or representing vocal sounds; (of a spelling) corresponding to the pronunciation. —**phonetically** *adv.* [from Greek *phōneō* = speak]

phonetician /fəʊni'tɪʃən/ n. an expert in phonetics.

phonetics /fə'netɪks/ n.pl. the identification, description, and classification of sounds used in articulate speech. These sounds are codified in the International Phonetic Alphabet (a highly modified version of the English/Roman alphabet).

phoney /'fəʊni/ *adj.* (*slang*) sham, counterfeit, fictitious. —*n.* (*slang*) a phoney person or thing.

phonic /'fəʊnɪk, 'fɒ-/ *adj.* of sound; of vocal sound. —**phonically** *adv.* [from Greek *phōnē* = voice, sound]

phono- /fəʊnə(ʊ)-/ in combinations, sound. [from Greek *phōnē*]

phonograph /'fəʊnəɡrɑːf/ n. an early form of gramophone; the name Thomas ◊Edison gave to his sound-recording apparatus, which developed into the ◊record player. The word 'phonograph' is still used in the USA.

phonology /fə'nɒlədʒɪ/ n. the study of the sounds in a language. —**phonological** /-'lɒdʒɪkəl/ *adj.*

phosphate /'fɒsfeɪt/ n. a salt or ester of phosphoric acid; an artificial fertilizer composed of or containing this. Incomplete neutralization of phosphoric acid gives rise to acid phosphates (see ◊acid salts and ◊buffer¹ sense 2). [French]

phosphor /'fɒsfə/ n. any substance that gives out visible light when it is illuminated by a beam of electrons or ultraviolet light. The television screen is coated on the inside with phosphors that glow when beams of electrons strike them. Fluorescent lamp tubes are also phosphor-coated. [German from Latin *phosphoros*]

phosphoresce /fɒsfə'res/ *v.i.* to show phosphorescence.

phosphorescence n. in physics, the emission of light by certain substances after they have absorbed energy, whether from visible light, other electromagnetic radiation such as ultraviolet rays or X-rays, or cathode rays (a beam of electrons). When the stimulating energy is removed phosphorescence ceases, although it may persist for a short time after (unlike ◊fluorescence, which stops immediately). —**phosphorescent** *adj.*

phosphoric acid an acid derived from phosphorus and oxygen. Its commonest form, H_3PO_4, is also known as orthophosphoric acid, and is produced by the action of phosphorus pentoxide, P_2O_5, on water. It is used in rust removers and for rust-proofing iron and steel.

phosphorus /'fɒsfərəs/ n. a nonmetallic element, symbol P, atomic number 15, relative atomic mass 30.9738. It occurs in nature as phosphates in the soil, in particular the mineral ◊apatite, and is essential to both plant and animal life. The element has three allotropic forms: a black powder; a white-yellow, waxy solid that ignites spontaneously in air to form the poisonous gas phosphorous pentoxide; and a red-brown powder that neither ignites spontaneously nor is poisonous. Compounds of phosphorus are used in fertilizers, various organic chemicals, for matches and fireworks, and in glass and steel. —**phosphoric** /-'fɒrɪk/ *adj.*, **phosphorous** *adj.* [Latin = morning star, from Greek *phôs* = light and *-phoros* = bringing]

photo n. (*plural* photos) a photograph. —**photo finish,** a close finish of a race with the winner determined by scrutiny of a photograph; any close-run thing. [abbreviation]

photo- /fəʊtə(ʊ)-/ in combinations, 1. light. 2. photography. [from Greek *phôs* = light]

photocell n. or **photoelectric cell** a device for measuring or detecting light or other electromagnetic radiation.

photochemical reaction any chemical reaction in which light is produced or light initiates the reaction. Light can initiate reactions by exciting atoms or molecules and making them more reactive: the light energy becomes converted to chemical energy.

photocopier /'fəʊtəʊkɒpiə(r)/ n. a machine that uses some form of photographic process to reproduce copies of documents or illustrations. Most modern photocopiers, as pioneered by the Xerox Corporation, use electrostatic photocopying, or xerography ('dry writing'). This employs a drum coated with a light-sensitive material, such as selenium, which holds a pattern of static electricity charges corresponding to the dark areas of an image projected on to the drum by a lens. Finely divided pigment (toner) of opposite electric charge sticks to the charged areas of the drum and is transferred to a sheet of paper, which is heated briefly to melt the toner and stick it to the paper.

photocopy /'fəʊtəʊkɒpi/ n. a copy of a document etc. made on a photocopier. —*v.t.* to make a photocopy of.

photoelectric /fəʊtəʊiˈlektrɪk/ *adj.* with or using the emission of electrons from a substance (usually a metallic surface) when it is struck by ◊photons (quanta of electromagnetic radiation), usually those of visible light or ultraviolet radiation. —**photoelectric cell**, a device using this effect to generate current. —**photoelectricity** /-ˈtrɪsɪtɪ/ *n.*

photofit /ˈfəʊtəʊfɪt/ *n.* a composite picture made from photographs of separate features assembled from descriptions put together to form a likeness, especially of a person sought by the police. It was developed from the ◊identikit system by Jacques Penry in 1970 for the police of Scotland Yard, London.

photogenic /fəʊtəʊˈdʒenɪk, -dʒiːnɪk/ *adj.* 1. apt to be a good subject for photography, coming out well in photographs. 2. producing, or emitting light. —**photogenically** *adv.* [from *photo-* = light and Greek *-genēs* = born]

photogram *n.* a picture produced on photographic material by exposing it to light, but without using a camera.

photograph /ˈfəʊtəɡrɑːf/ *n.* a picture formed by the chemical action of light or other radiation on a sensitive film. —*v.t.* 1. to take a photograph of. 2. to come out in a specified way when photographed.

photographer /fəˈtɒɡrəfə/ *n.* one who takes photographs.

photographic /fəʊtəˈɡræfɪk/ *adj.* 1. of or produced by photography. 2. (of the memory) recalling in detail from a single sight. —**photographically** *adv.*

photography /fəˈtɒɡrəfɪ/ *n.* the taking and processing of photographs; the process for producing images on sensitized materials by various forms of radiant energy, including visible light, ultraviolet, infrared, X-rays; radioactive radiation and electron beam.

photogravure /fəʊtəɡrəˈvjʊə/ *n.* a picture produced from a photographic negative transferred to a metal plate and etched in; this process. [French (*gravure* = etching)]

photolithography /fəʊtəʊliˈθɒɡrəfɪ/ *n.* lithography with the plates made by photography.

photometer /fəʊˈtɒmɪtə/ *n.* an instrument that measures luminous intensity, especially relative intensities from different sources. Bunsen's grease-spot photometer of 1844 compares the intensity of a light source with a known source by each illuminating one half of a translucent area. Modern photometers use ◊photocells, as in a photographer's exposure meter. A ◊photomultiplier can also be used as a photometer. —**photometric** /fəʊtəˈmetrɪk/ *adj.*, **photometry** *n.*

photosynthesis

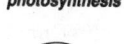

photomultiplier *n.* an instrument that detects low levels of electromagnetic radiation (usually visible light or ◊infrared radiation) and amplifies it to produce a detectable signal.

photon /ˈfəʊtɒn/ *n.* in physics, the smallest 'package', 'particle', or quantum of energy in which light, or any other form of electromagnetic radiation, is emitted. [from Greek *phōs* = light, after *electron*]

photoperiodism *n.* a biological mechanism that determines the timing of certain activities by responding to changes in day length. The flowering of many plants is initiated in this way. Photoperiodism in plants is regulated by a light-sensitive pigment, **phytochrome**. The breeding seasons of many temperate-zone animals are also triggered by increasing or declining day length, as part of their ◊biorhythms.

photosensitive /fəʊtəʊˈsensɪtɪv/ *adj.* reacting chemically etc. to light.

photosphere *n.* the visible surface of the Sun, which emits light and heat. About 300 km/200 mi deep, it consists of incandescent gas at a temperature of 5,800K (5,530°C/9,980°F).

Photostat /ˈfəʊtəʊstæt/ *n.* trade name of a photographic copy of a document etc. made by the Photostat process. —*v.t.* (**-tt-**) to make a Photostat of. [as in *thermostat* etc.]

photosynthesis /fəʊtəʊˈsɪnθɪsɪs/ *n.* the process by which green plants, photosynthetic bacteria, and cyanobacteria utilize light energy from the Sun to produce food molecules (◊carbohydrates) from carbon dioxide and water. There are two stages. During the **light reaction** sunlight is used to split water, H_2O, into oxygen, O_2; protons (hydrogen ions, H^+); and electrons, and oxygen is given off as a by-product. In the second-stage **dark reaction**, where sunlight is not required, the protons and electrons are used to convert carbon dioxide, CO_2, into carbohydrates, CH_2O. Photosynthesis depends on the ability of ◊chlorophyll to capture the energy of sunlight and to use it to split water molecules.

phototropism *n.* the movement of part of a plant towards or away from a source of light. Leaves are positively phototropic, detecting the source of light and orientating themselves to receive the maximum amount.

phrase /freɪz/ *n.* 1. a group of words forming a conceptual unit and usually without a predicate, grammatically equivalent to a noun, adjective, or adverb. 2. an idiomatic or short, pithy expression; a mode of expression. 3. in music, a group of notes forming a distinct unit within a

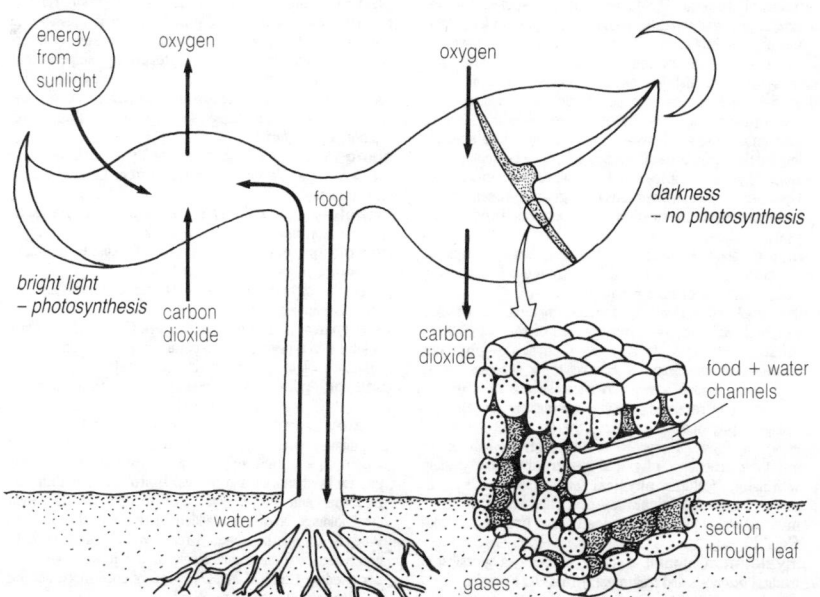

energy from sunlight

oxygen

oxygen

food

darkness – no photosynthesis

bright light – photosynthesis

carbon dioxide

carbon dioxide

food + water channels

water

section through leaf

gases

longer melody. —*v.t.* 1. to express in words. 2. to divide (music) into phrases, especially in performance. —**phrase book,** a book for travellers, listing phrases and their foreign equivalents. **phrase-structure grammar,** a theory of language structure that proposes that a given language has several different potential sentence patterns, consisting of various sorts of phrases, which can be expanded in various ways. —**phrasal** *adj.* [from Latin *phrasis* from Greek *phrazō* = declare]

phraseology /freɪzɪˈɒlədʒɪ/ *n.* choice or arrangement of words; mode of expression. —**phraseological** /-ˈlɒdʒɪkəl/ *adj.*

phrenology /frɪˈnɒlədʒɪ/ *n.* the study of the external form of the cranium as a supposed indication of a person's character and mental faculties. —**phrenological** /frenəˈlɒdʒɪkəl/ *adj.*, **phrenologist** *n.* [from Greek *phrēn* = mind]

Phrygia /ˈfrɪdʒɪə/ former kingdom of W Asia covering the Anatolian plateau. It was inhabited in ancient times by an Indo-European people and achieved great prosperity in the 8th century BC under a line of kings bearing in turn the names Gordius and Midas, but then fell under Lydian rule. From Phrygia the cult of ◊Cybele was introduced into Greece and Rome.

phthisis /ˈθaɪsɪs/ *n.* a progressive wasting disease, now especially pulmonary tuberculosis. [Latin from Greek *phthinō* = decay]

phut /fʌt/ *n.* a dull sound of impact, the collapse of an inflated object etc. —**go phut,** to explode or collapse with this sound; (*colloquial*) to collapse; to come to nothing. [from Hindi = to burst]

phylactery /fɪˈlæktərɪ/ *n.* 1. a small leather box containing Hebrew texts, worn by Jews at morning weekday prayer to remind them to keep their law. 2. an amulet or charm. [from Latin from Greek = amulet (*phulassō* = guard)]

phyllotaxis *n.* the arrangement of leaves on a plant stem. Leaves are nearly always arranged in a regular pattern and in the majority of plants they are inserted singly, either in a spiral arrangement up the stem, or on alternate sides. Other principal forms are opposite leaves, where two arise from the same node, and whorled, where three or more arise from the same node.

phylloxera *n.* a genus of aphidlike lice.

phylogeny *n.* the historical sequence of changes that occurs in a given species during the course of its evolution. It was once erroneously associated with ontogeny (the process of development of a living organism).

phylum /ˈfaɪləm/ *n.* (*plural* **phyla**) a major grouping in biological classification. Mammals, birds, reptiles, amphibians, fishes, and tunicates belong to the phylum Chordata; the phylum Mollusca consists of snails, slugs, mussels, clams, squid, and octopuses; the phylum Porifera contains sponges; and the phylum Echinodermata includes starfish, sea urchins, and sea cucumbers. In classifying plants (where the term 'division' often takes the place of 'phylum'), there are between four and nine phyla depending on the criteria used; all flowering plants belong to a single phylum, Angiospermata, and all conifers to another, Gymnospermata. Related phyla are grouped together in a ◊kingdom; phyla are subdivided into ◊classes. [from Greek *phulon* = race]

physic /ˈfɪzɪk/ *n.* (*archaic*) 1. the art of healing, medicine (excluding surgery). 2. a medicine. [from Old French from Latin from Greek *phusis* = nature]

physical /ˈfɪzɪkəl/ *adj.* 1. of matter, material (as opposed to moral, spiritual, or imaginary). 2. of the body. 3. of nature, according to its laws. 4. of physics. —**physical change,** in chemistry, a change to a substance that does not produce a new chemical substance and that can be easily reversed. Boiling and melting are physical changes. **physical chemistry,** the branch of chemistry in which physics is applied to the study of substances and their reactions. **physical geography,** that dealing with natural features. **physical jerks,** (*colloquial*) physical exercises. **physical science,** the study of inanimate natural objects. —**physically** *adv.* [from Latin from Greek]

physician /fɪˈzɪʃən/ *n.* a doctor, especially a specialist in medical diagnosis and treatment. [from Old French]

physicist /ˈfɪzɪsɪst/ *n.* an expert in physics.

physics /ˈfɪzɪks/ *n.pl.* (usually treated as *singular*) the branch of science concerned with the ultimate laws that govern the structure of the universe, and the forms of matter and energy and their interactions. For convenience, physics is often divided into branches such as nuclear physics, particle physics, solid-and liquid-state physics, electricity, electronics, magnetism, optics, acoustics, heat, and thermodynamics. Before this century, physics was known as **natural philosophy.**

physiognomy /fɪzɪˈɒnəmɪ/ *n.* 1. the features of the face; a type of face. 2. the art of judging character from facial or bodily features. 3. the external features of a country etc. —**physiognomist** *n.* [from Old French from Latin from Greek *phusis* = nature and *gnomon* = indicator]

physiography /fɪzɪˈɒɡrəfɪ/ *n.* 1. the description of nature or natural phenomena, or of a class of objects. 2. physical geography. —**physiographer** *n.* [from French from Greek *phusis* = nature and *graphia* = writing]

physiological psychology an aspect of ◊experimental psychology.

physiology /fɪzɪˈɒlədʒɪ/ *n.* the science of the functions and phenomena of living organisms and their parts as opposed to anatomy, which studies their structures; these functions. —**physiological** /-ˈlɒdʒɪkəl/ *adj.*, **physiologist** *n.* [from French or Latin from Greek *phusis* = nature]

physiotherapy /fɪzɪəʊˈθerəpɪ/ *n.* the treatment of disease or injury or deformity by massage, exercises, heat etc., not by drugs. —**physiotherapist** *n.* [from Greek *phusis* = nature and *therapeia* = healing]

physique /fɪˈziːk/ *n.* bodily structure and development. [French]

pi /paɪ/ *n.* 1. the 16th letter of the Greek alphabet, (π, Π) = p. 2. (π) the symbol of the ratio of the circumference of a circle to the diameter (approximately 3.14159). [Greek]

Piaf /ˈpiːæf/ Edith. Stage name of Edith Gassion 1915–1963. Parisian singer and songwriter who achieved success as a cabaret singer from the late 1930s and subsequently as a concert performer. She is celebrated for her defiant song '*Je ne regrette rien*/I Regret Nothing' and for '*La Vie en rose*' 1946. [French slang *piaf* = sparrow]

Piaget /piˈæʒeɪ/ Jean 1896–1980. Swiss psychologist distinguished by his studies of child development in relation to thought processes, and concepts of space, time, causality, and objectivity.

pianissimo /piæˈnɪsɪməʊ/ *adv.* in music, very softly. —*n.* in music, a passage to be played very softly. [Italian, superlative of *piano*]

pianist /ˈpiənɪst/ *n.* a player of the piano. [from French]

piano[1] /piˈænəʊ/ *n.* (*plural* **pianos**) a musical instrument with metal strings struck by hammers worked by levers from a keyboard (vibration being stopped by dampers when keys are released), and with pedals regulating the quality of the tone. —**piano accordion,** an accordion with the melody played on a small pianolike keyboard. [Italian, abbreviation of *pianoforte*]

piano[2] /piˈɑːnəʊ/ *adv.* in music, softly. —*n.* in music, a passage to be played softly. [Italian from Latin *planus* = flat, (of sound) soft]

pianoforte /piænəʊˈfɔːtɪ/ *n.* (*formal* or *archaic*) a piano. [from Italian *piano e forte* = soft and loud]

Pianola /piəˈnəʊlə/ *n.* trade name of a kind of automatic mechanical piano. [diminutive of *piano*]

pibroch /ˈpiːbrɒk/ *n.* a series of variations for the bagpipe. [from Gaelic = art of piping]

pica /ˈpaɪkə/ *n.* 1. a unit of type size (1/6 inch). 2. a size of letters in typewriting (ten per inch). [from Latin = 15th-century book of rules about church feasts]

picador /ˈpɪkədɔː/ *n.* a mounted man with a lance in a bullfight. [Spanish *picar* = prick]

Picardy /ˈpɪkədɪ/ (French *Picardie*) region of N France, including Aisne, Oise, and Somme *départements*; **area** 19,400 sq km/7,488 sq mi; **population** (1986) 1,774,000; **products** chemicals and metals; **history** in the 13th century the name Picardy was used to describe the feudal smallholdings N of Paris added to the French crown by Philip II. During the Hundred Years' War the area was hotly contested by France and England, but it was eventually occupied by Louis XI in 1477. Picardy once more became a major battlefield in World War I.

picaresque /pɪkə'resk/ *adj.* (of a style of fiction) dealing with the adventures of rogues and villains, telling their story in a series of loosely linked episodes. Examples include Daniel Defoe's *Moll Flanders*, Henry Fielding's *Tom Jones*, and Mark Twain's *Huckleberry Finn*. [French from Spanish *pícaro* = rogue]

Picasso /pɪ'kæsəʊ/ Pablo 1881–1973. Spanish artist, active chiefly in France, one of the most inventive and prolific talents in 20th-century art. His Blue Period 1901–04 and Rose Period 1905–06 preceded the revolutionary *Les Demoiselles d'Avignon* 1907 (Metropolitan Museum of Art, New York), which paved the way for ◊Cubism. In the early 1920s he was considered a leader of the Surrealist movement (see ◊Surrealism). In the 1930s his work included metal sculpture, book illustration, and the mural *Guernica* 1937 (Casón del Buen Retiro, Madrid), a comment on the bombing of civilians in the Spanish Civil War. He continued to paint into his eighties.

Art is a lie that makes us realize the truth.
Pablo Picasso

---

picayune /pɪkə'juːn/ *n.* (*US*) 1. a small coin. 2. (*colloquial*) an insignificant person or thing. —*adj.* (*US colloquial*) mean, contemptible; petty. [from French *picaillon* = Piedmontese coin]

piccalilli /pɪkə'lɪlɪ/ *n.* a pickle of chopped vegetables, mustard, and spices.

piccaninny /pɪkə'nɪnɪ/ *n.* a small black or Australian Aboriginal child. [West Indian Negro from Spanish *pequeño* = little]

Piccard /pɪ'kɑː/ Auguste 1884–1962. Swiss scientist. In 1931–32, he and his twin brother, **Jean Félix Piccard** (1884–1963), made ascents to 17,000 m/55,000 ft in a balloon of his own design, resulting in useful discoveries concerning stratospheric phenomena such as ◊cosmic rays (see under ◊cosmic). He also built and used, with his son **Jacques Ernest Piccard** (1922–), bathyscaphs for research under the sea.

piccolo /'pɪkələʊ/ *n.* (*plural* piccolos) the smallest member of the ◊flute family, sounding an octave higher than the ordinary. [Italian = small]

pick *v.t./i.* 1. to select (especially carefully or thoughtfully). 2. to detach (a flower, fruit etc.) from the plant bearing it. 3. to make a hole in or break the surface of with the fingers or a sharp instrument; to make (a hole) thus. 4. to open (a lock) with a pointed instrument, especially to force entry. 5. to probe or dig at to remove unwanted matter. 6. to eat (food) desultorily or in small bits. 7. to clear (a bone or carcass) of its flesh. —*n.* 1. picking, selection; the right to select. 2. the best or most wanted part. 3. a pickaxe. 4. an instrument for picking; a plectrum. —**pick and choose**, to select fastidiously. **pick at**, to find fault with; to eat desultorily. **pick a person's brains**, to extract ideas or information from him or her for one's own use. **pick holes in**, to find fault with. **pick-me-up**, *n.* a tonic (*literal* or *figurative*) to restore health or revive the spirits. **pick off**, to pluck off; to select and shoot (a target or succession of targets) with care. **pick on**, to find fault with, to nag at; to select. **pick out**, to take from a large number; to identify or recognize; to distinguish from the surrounding objects; to play (a tune) by ear on a piano etc. **pick over**, to look over item by item; to choose the best from. **pick a person's pocket**, to steal its contents from him or her. **pick a quarrel**, to provoke or seize an opportunity for one. **pick to pieces**, to criticize harshly. **pick up**, to take hold of and lift; to learn routinely; to stop for and take with one; to take (cargo etc.) on board; (of the police) to catch and take into custody; to acquire by chance or casually; to encounter and get to know (a person); to manage to receive (a broadcast signal etc.); to improve, to recover health, (of an engine) to recover speed. **pickup** *n.* picking up; a person met casually; the part of a record player carrying the stylus; a small open motor truck. —**picker** *n.*

pickaback /'pɪkəbæk/ variant of ◊piggyback.

pickaxe /'pɪkæks/ *n.* a heavy iron tool with a point at one end and a wooden handle at right angles to it, for breaking up hard ground etc. [from Old French *picois*, related to *pike*]

picket /'pɪkɪt/ *n.* 1. a gathering of workers and their trade union representatives, usually at the entrance to their place of work, to try to persuade others to support them in an industrial dispute. 2. a small body of troops acting as a patrol, a party of sentries. 3. a pointed stake driven into the ground. —*v.t./i.* 1. to place or act as a picket outside (a place of work). 2. to post as a military picket. 3. to tether (an animal). 4. to secure (a place) with stakes. [from French *piquet* = pointed stake (*piquer* = prick)]

Pickford /'pɪkfəd/ Mary. Adopted name of Gladys Smith 1893–1979. US silent film actress, born in Toronto, Canada. In 1919 she formed United Artists with Charlie Chaplin, D W Griffith, and her second husband (1920–36) Douglas Fairbanks. She often appeared as a young girl, even when she was well into her twenties. The public did not like her talking films, and she retired in 1933. She was known as 'America's Sweetheart'.

pickings *n.pl.* 1. casual profits or perquisites. 2. gains from pilfering. 3. the remaining scraps, gleanings.

pickle *n.* 1. a food, especially a vegetable, preserved in brine, vinegar, or a similar liquor; the liquor used. 2. (*colloquial*) a plight. —*v.t.* 1. to preserve in or treat with pickle. 2. (in *past participle, slang*) drunk. [from Middle Dutch or Middle Low German *pekel*]

pickpocket *n.* one who steals from people's pockets.

Pickwickian /pɪk'wɪkɪən/ *adj.* (of words or their sense) not in accordance with the usual meaning, conveniently interpreted so as to avoid offence etc. [from *Pickwick*, character in Charles Dickens's *Pickwick Papers* (1836–37)]

picky *adj.* (*colloquial*) excessively fastidious.

picnic /'pɪknɪk/ *n.* 1. a pleasure outing including an informal outdoor meal; the meal itself. 2. (*colloquial*) something readily or easily accomplished. —*v.i.* (-ck-) to take part in a picnic. —**picnicker** *n.* [from French *pique-nique*]

pico- /paɪkəʊ-, pi-/ in combinations, denoting a factor of 10^{-12}, one billionth (e.g. *picometre*). [from Spanish *pico* = beak, peak, little bit]

picot /'piːkəʊ/ *n.* a small loop of twisted thread in an edging to lace etc. [French, diminutive of *pic* = peak, point]

picric acid /'pɪkrɪk/ a yellow bitter substance used in dyeing and explosives. [from Greek *pikros* = bitter]

Pict *n.* a member of the ancient peoples of N Scotland. Of pre-Celtic origin, and speaking a non-Celtic language, the Picts are thought to have inhabited much of England before the arrival of the Celtic Britons. They were united with the Celtic Scots under the rule of Kenneth MacAlpin in 844. —**Pictish** *adj.* [from Latin *Picti*, perhaps = painted people, or perhaps assimilated to native name]

pictograph /'pɪktəgrɑːf/ *n.* or **pictogram** 1. a pictorial symbol used as a form of writing. 2. a pictorial representation of statistics. —**pictographic** /-'græfɪk/ *adj.* [from Latin *pingere* = paint]

pictorial /pɪk'tɔːrɪəl/ *adj.* of or expressed in a picture or pictures: illustrated. —*n.* a periodical with pictures as the main feature. —**pictorially** *adv.* [from Latin *pictorius* (*pictor* = painter)]

picture /'pɪktʃə/ *n.* 1. a likeness or representation of a subject produced by painting, drawing, or photography; a portrait. 2. a beautiful object or person. 3. a scene, a total visual or mental impression produced. 4. an image on a television screen. 5. a cinema film; (in *plural*) a performance at a cinema. —*v.t.* 1. to form a mental picture of, to imagine. 2. to represent in a picture. 3. to describe graphically. —**in the picture**, fully informed; noticed. **picture postcard**, a postcard with a picture on one side. **picture window**, a large window facing an attractive view. [from Latin *pingere* = paint]

picturesque /pɪktʃə'resk/ *adj.* 1. striking and pleasant to look at. 2. (of language) graphic, expressive. —**picturesquely** *adv.*, **picturesqueness** *n.* [from French *pittoresque* from Italian]

piddle *v.i.* 1. to work or act in a trifling way. 2. (*colloquial*) to urinate.

piddling *adj.* (*colloquial*) trifling, trivial.

pidgin /'pɪdʒɪn/ *n.* a simplified form of a language, used for communication between persons of different nationality etc. Pidgin languages are trade jargons, contact languages, or ◊lingua francas, arising in ports and markets where people of different linguistic backgrounds meet for commercial and other purposes. —**pidgin English**, a jargon, chiefly of English words, used originally between the

British and the Chinese in the 19th century. [corruption of *business*]

pi-dog variant of ◊pye-dog.

pie[1] *n.* 1. a dish of meat, fish, or fruit etc. enclosed in or covered with pastry or other crust and baked. 2. a confused mass of printers' type; chaos. **—easy as pie,** very easy. **pie chart,** a diagram representing various quantities as sectors of a circle. **pie in the sky,** a delusive prospect of future happiness, especially as a reward in heaven for virtue or suffering on Earth.

pie[2] *n.* a magpie. [from Old French from Latin *pica*]

piebald /'paɪbɔːld/ *adj.* (of a horse etc.) with irregular patches of white and black or other dark colour. **—n.** a piebald animal.

piece /piːs/ *n.* 1. any of the distinct portions of which a thing is composed or into which it is divided or broken; a detached portion. 2. a single example or specimen, an item. 3. a distinct section or area (of land etc.). 4. any of the things of which a set is composed. 5. a definite quantity in which a thing is made up for sale etc. 6. a fixed unit of work. 7. a (usually short) literary, dramatic, or musical composition. 8. a coin. 9. a man in board games, especially a chessman (usually other than a pawn). 10. a firearm; an artillery weapon. 11. (*derogatory*) a person, especially a woman. **—v.t.** to form into a whole, to join the pieces of. **—go to pieces,** to lose self-control; to collapse. **in one piece,** not broken, unharmed. **of a piece,** uniform, consistent. **piece goods,** textile fabrics woven in standard lengths. **pieces of eight,** (*historical*) Spanish dollars. **piecework** *n.* work paid at a rate per piece. **say one's piece,** to give one's opinion; to make a prepared statement. **take to pieces,** to separate the parts of; to be divisible thus. [from Anglo-French, probably from Celtic]

pièce de résistance /pjes də reˈzistɑ̃s/ the most outstanding item in a collection; the main dish of a meal. [French]

piecemeal /'piːsmiːl/ *adv.* piece by piece or part at a time. **—adj.** done etc. piecemeal.

Pieck /piːk/ Wilhelm 1876–1960. German communist politician. He was a leader of the 1919 ◊Spartacist revolt and a founder of the Socialist Unity Party in 1946. He opposed both the Weimar Republic and Nazism. From 1949 he was president of East Germany; the office was abolished on his death.

pied /paɪd/ *adj.* particoloured. [from *pie*[2]]

pied-à-terre /pjeɪdɑːˈteə/ *n.* (*plural* **pieds-à-terre** *pronounced* the same) a convenient second home, usually small and in a town or city. [French, literally 'foot to earth']

Piedmont /'piːdmɒnt/ (Italian *Piemonte*) region of N Italy, bordering Switzerland in the N and France in the W, and surrounded, except in the E, by the Alps and the Apennines; area 25,400 sq km/9,804 sq mi; population (1988) 4,377,000. Its capital is Turin. It also includes the fertile Po river valley. Products include fruit, grain, cattle, cars, and textiles. The movement for the unification of Italy started in the 19th century in Piedmont, under the house of Savoy.

pie-dog variant of ◊pye-dog.

pier /pɪə/ *n.* 1. a structure running out into the sea and serving as a promenade, or landing stage, or breakwater. The first British pier was built at Ryde, Isle of Wight, in 1814. Eugenius Birch (1818–1883) designed the West Pier, Brighton, 1866 (339 m/1,115 ft); Margate Pier, 1856; and the North Pier, Blackpool, 1863. 2. a support of an arch or of a span of a bridge; a pillar. 3. the solid masonry between windows etc. **—pier glass,** a large mirror of a kind originally placed between windows. [from Latin *pera*]

pierce /pɪəs/ *v.t./i.* 1. to penetrate (*literally* and *figuratively*). 2. to prick with or like a sharp instrument; to make (a hole) thus. 3. to force one's way through or into. [from Old French ultimately from Latin *pertundere* = bore through (*tundere* = thrust)]

piercing *adj.* 1. (of pain or cold etc.) intense, penetrating sharply. 2. (of a look or sound) sharp or shrill, fierce.

Piero della Francesca /piˈeərəʊ delə frænˈtʃeskə/ *c.*1420–1492. Italian painter, active in Arezzo and Urbino; one of the major artists of the 15th century. His work has a solemn stillness and unusually solid figures, luminous colour, and compositional harmony. It includes a fresco series *The Legend of the True Cross* (S Francesco, Arezzo), begun in about 1452. Piero wrote two treatises, one on mathematics, one on the laws of perspective in painting.

Piggott *Champion jockey Lester Piggott weighing in after the Handicap Stakes, Nottingham, 29 Oct 1985. He retired in 1985 but returned to racing in 1990.*

Pierrot /'pɪərəʊ/ *n.* a stock character in the French and English theatres (*feminine* **Pierrette**), with a whitened face and loose white costume. [French, diminutive of *Pierre* = Peter]

pietà /pjeɪˈtɑː/ *n.* a picture or sculpture of the Virgin Mary holding the dead body of Christ on her lap. [Italian from Latin *pius*]

pietism /'paɪətɪzəm/ *n.* 1. pious sentiment; exaggeration or affectation of this. 2. **Pietism** a religious movement within Lutheranism in the 17th century which emphasized spiritual and devotional faith rather than theology and dogma. [from German]

pietra dura an Italian technique of inlaying furniture with semiprecious stones, such as agate or quartz, in different colours, to create pictures or patterns. [Italian = hard stone]

piety /'paɪətɪ/ *n.* piousness; an act etc. showing this. [from Old French from Latin *pius*]

piezoelectricity /paiːˌzəʊɪlekˈtrɪsɪtɪ, piːˌzəʊ-/ *n.* the phenomenon, exhibited especially by certain crystals such as quartz, in which a substance becomes electrically polarized when subjected to pressure. **—piezoelectric** *adj.* [from Greek *piezō* = press]

piffle *n.* (*slang*) nonsense, worthless talk. **—v.i.** (*slang*) to talk or act feebly or frivolously. [imitative]

piffling *adj.* (*slang*) trivial, worthless.

pig *n.* 1. a wild or domesticated hoofed mammal of the family Suidae with a broad snout, stout bristly body, and short legs. The European **wild boar** *Sus scrofa* is the ancestor of domesticated breeds. Pigs are omnivorous and have simple stomachs. 2. pork. 3. (*colloquial*) a greedy, dirty, or unpleasant person. 4. (*slang, derogatory*) a policeman or policewoman. 5. an oblong mass of metal (especially iron or lead) from a smelting furnace. **—v.t./i.** to live or behave like a pig (especially *pig it*). **—pig in a poke,** a thing acquired or offered without previous sight or knowledge of it. **pig iron,** crude iron from a smelting furnace (see ◊iron). [from Old English]

Pigalle /piːˈgæl/ Jean Baptiste 1714–1785. French sculptor. In 1744 he made the marble *Mercury* (Louvre, Paris), a lively, naturalistic work. His subjects ranged from the intimate to the formal, and included portraits.

pigeon /ˈpɪdʒən/ n. any member of the family Columbidae, sometimes also called doves, distinguished by their large crops which, becoming glandular in the breeding season, secrete a milky fluid ('pigeon's milk') which aids digestion of food for the young. They are found worldwide. [from Old French from Latin *pipio*]

pigeon hawk another name for the ◊merlin.

pigeonhole n. 1. a small recess for a pigeon to rest in. 2. each of a set of small compartments in a cabinet or on a wall for papers, letters etc. —v.t. 1. to put in a pigeonhole. 2. to put aside for future consideration or indefinitely. 3. to classify mentally.

pigeon racing the sport of racing pigeons against a clock. The birds are taken from their loft(s) and transported to a starting point, often hundreds of miles away. They have to return to their loft and a special clock times their arrival.

piggery n. a place where pigs are bred; a pigsty.

piggish adj. like a pig, greedy or dirty.

Piggott /ˈpɪɡət/ Lester 1935–. English jockey. He was regarded as a brilliant tactician and adopted a unique high riding style. A champion jockey 11 times between 1960 and 1982, Piggott won all the major races and rode a record nine ◊Derby winners. He retired from riding in 1985 and took up training. In 1987 he was imprisoned for tax evasion. He returned to racing in 1990.

piggy n. a little pig. —**piggy bank,** a money box in the form of a hollow pig.

piggyback n. a ride on the shoulders and back of another. —adv. by means of a piggyback. [for earlier *pick-a-back*]

pigheaded adj. obstinate, stubborn.

piglet /ˈpɪɡlɪt/ n. a young pig.

pigment /ˈpɪɡmənt/ n. colouring matter. —v.t. to colour (skin or other tissue) with natural pigment. —**pigmentation** /-ˈteɪʃən/ n. [from Latin *pigmentum* (*pingere* = paint)]

pigskin n. a pig's skin; leather made from this.

pigsty n. 1. a partly covered pen for pigs. 2. a very dirty or untidy place.

pigswill n. the swill of a kitchen or brewery fed to pigs.

pigtail n. a plait of hair hanging from the back of the head.

pika n. or **mouse-hare** a small mammal of the family Ochotonidae, belonging to the order Lagomorpha (rabbits and hares). Pikas have short rounded ears, and most species are about 20 cm/8 in long, with greyish-brown fur and no visible tail. They live in mountainous regions of Asia and North America.

pike n. 1. (*plural* the same) a long, thin, freshwater fish *Esox lucius*, family Esocidae, of Europe, Asia and North America; it is a voracious feeder and may reach 2.2 m/7 ft, and 9 kg/20 lbs. 2. a peaked top of a hill. 3. (*historical*) an infantry weapon consisting of a long wooden shaft with a pointed metal head. [Old English = point]

piked /paɪkt/ adj. in diving and gymnastics, with the legs straight and forming an angle with the body at the hips.

pikelet /ˈpaɪklɪt/ n. a crumpet. [from Welsh (*bara*) *pyglyd* = pitchy (bread)]

pike-perch n. a freshwater fish *Stizostedion lucioperca*, related to the perch, common in Europe, W Asia, and North America. It reaches over 1 m/3 ft.

pikestaff n. the wooden shaft of a pike. —**plain as a pikestaff,** quite plain or obvious.

pilaff /ˈpɪlæf/ n. an oriental dish of rice with meat, spices etc. [from Turkish]

pilaster /pɪˈlæstə/ n. a rectangular column, especially one fastened into a wall. [from French from Italian from Latin *pila* = pillar]

Pilate /ˈpaɪlət/ Pontius early 1st century AD. Roman procurator of Judea AD 26–36. Unsympathetic to the Jews, his actions several times provoked riots, and in AD 36 he was recalled to Rome to account for the brutal suppression of a Samaritan revolt. The New Testament Gospels describe his reluctant ordering of Jesus' crucifixion, but there has been considerable debate about his actual role in it; many believe that pressure was put on him by Jewish conservative priests. The Greek historian Eusebius says he committed suicide, but another tradition says he became a Christian, and he is regarded as a saint and martyr in the Ethiopian Coptic and Greek Orthodox churches.

pilau /pɪˈlaʊ/ variant of ◊pilaff.

pilchard /ˈpɪltʃəd/ n. a small fish *Sardina pilchardus* of the herring family. Bluish-green above and silvery beneath, it grows to 25 cm/10 in long. It is most abundant in the W Mediterranean.

pile[1] n. 1. a number of things lying one upon another. 2. (*colloquial*) a large quantity, especially of money. 3. a grand or lofty building. 4. (in full **funeral pile**) a heap of wood etc. on which a corpse is burnt. 5. a series of plates of dissimilar metals laid alternately to produce an electric current. 6. (in full **atomic pile**) a nuclear reactor. —v.t./i. 1. to heap, stack, or load. 2. to crowd. —**pile it on,** (*colloquial*) to exaggerate. **pile up,** to accumulate, to cause (a vehicle or aircraft) to crash. **pile-up** n. a collision of several motor vehicles. [from Old French from Latin *pila* = pillar]

pile[2] n. 1. a pointed stake or post. 2. a heavy beam of metal, concrete, or timber driven vertically into the ground as a foundation or support for a building or bridge. —**pile driver,** a machine for driving piles into the ground. **pile dwelling,** n. a lake dwelling (see ◊lake[1]). [Old English from Latin *pilum* = javelin]

pile[3] n. the soft surface of a fabric with a tangible depth formed by cut or uncut loops. [probably from Anglo-French from Latin *pilus* = hair]

pile[4] n. (usually in *plural*) a haemorrhoid. [probably from Latin *pila* = ball]

pilfer v.t./i. to steal, especially in small quantities. —**pilferer** n. [from Anglo-French *pelfrer* = pillage]

pilgrim /ˈpɪlɡrɪm/ n. 1. one who journeys to a sacred or revered place as an act of religious devotion. 2. **Pilgrim** or **Pilgrim Father** one of the emigrants who sailed from Plymouth, Devon, England, in the *Mayflower* on 16 Sept 1620 to found the first colony in New England at New Plymouth, Massachusetts. Of the 102 passengers fewer than a quarter were Puritan refugees. [from Provençal from Latin *peregrinus* = foreign]

pilgrimage n. a pilgrim's journey to a sacred place inspired by religious devotion. For Hindus, the holy places include Varanasi and the purifying river Ganges; for Buddhists, the places connected with the crises of Buddha's career; for the ancient Greeks, the shrines at Delphi and Ephesus among others; for Jews, the sanctuary at Jerusalem; and for Muslims, Mecca. The great centres of Christian pilgrimages have been, or still are, Jerusalem, Rome, the tomb of St James of Compostela in Spain, the shrine of Becket in Canterbury, England, and the holy places at La Salette and Lourdes in France.

Pilgrimage of Grace the rebellion against Henry VIII of England in 1536–37, originating in Yorkshire and Lincolnshire. The uprising was directed against the policies of the monarch (such as the dissolution of the monasteries and the effects of ◊enclosure).

Pilgrim's Progress an allegory by John Bunyan, published 1678–84, that describes the journey through life to the Celestial City of a man called Christian. On his way through the Slough of Despond, the House Beautiful, Vanity Fair, Doubting Castle, and other landmarks, he meets a number of allegorical figures.

Pilgrims' Way the track running from Winchester to Canterbury, England, which was the route taken by medieval pilgrims visiting the shrine of Thomas à Becket. Some 195 km/120 mi long, the Pilgrims' Way can still be traced for most of its length.

pill n. 1. a small ball or flat piece of medicinal substance for swallowing whole. 2. something that has to be endured, a humiliation. —**the pill,** (*colloquial*) the contraceptive pill, based on female hormones. The combined pill, which contains oestrogen and progesterone, stops the production of eggs and makes the mucus produced by the cervix hostile to sperm. It is the most reliable form of contraception apart from sterilization, being more than 99% effective. [from Middle Dutch or Middle Low German]

pillage /ˈpɪlɪdʒ/ n. plundering, especially in war. —v.t. to plunder. —**pillager** n. [from Old French *piller* = plunder]

pillar /ˈpɪlə/ n. 1. a slender vertical structure of stone etc. used as a support or ornament. 2. an upright mass of air, water, rock etc. 3. a person regarded as a main supporter of a cause or principle. —**from pillar to post,** rapidly from one place or situation to another. **pillar box,** a hollow pillar in which letters may be posted. [from Anglo-French *piler*, ultimately from Latin *pila* = pillar]

pillbox n. 1. a shallow cylindrical box for holding pills. 2. a small concrete shelter for a gun emplacement.

pillion /ˈpɪljən/ n. a seat for a passenger behind a motor-cyclist etc. —**ride pillion**, to ride on this as a passenger. [from Gaelic = small cushion, from Latin *pellis* = skin]

pillory /ˈpɪlərɪ/ n. a wooden framework with holes for the head and hands, into which offenders were formerly locked for exposure to public ridicule. Bystanders threw whatever was available at the miscreant. —v.t. 1. to put in a pillory. 2. to expose to ridicule. [from Old French]

pillow /ˈpɪləʊ/ n. 1. a cushion used as a support for the head, especially in a bed. 2. a pillow-shaped block or support. —v.t. to rest or prop up on a pillow. [Old English, ultimately from Latin *pulvinus* = cushion]

pillowcase n. or **pillowslip** a washable cover of cotton etc. for a pillow.

pilot /ˈpaɪlət/ n. 1. a person who operates the controls of an aircraft. 2. a person qualified to take charge of ships entering or leaving a harbour or travelling through certain waters. 3. a guide. —v.t. 1. to act as the pilot of. 2. to guide. —adj. experimental, testing (on a small scale) how a scheme etc. will work. —**pilot light**, a small gas burner kept alight and lighting a larger burner when this is turned on; an electric indicator light or control light. **pilot officer**, (*British*) the lowest commissioned rank in the Royal Air Force. [from French from Latin ultimately from Greek *pēdon* = oar]

pilotfish n. a small marine fish *Naucrates ductor*, of the family Carangidae. It hides below sharks, turtles, or boats, using the shade as a base from which to prey on smaller fish. It is found in all warm oceans and grows to about 36 cm/14 in.

Pilsener /ˈpɪlznə, -s-/ n. a pale-coloured lager beer with a strong hop flavour, of the type brewed at Pilsen (Plzeň) in Czechoslovakia.

pilule /ˈpɪljuːl/ n. a small pill. [French from Latin *pilula*, diminutive of *pila* = ball]

pimento /pɪˈmentəʊ/ n. (*plural* pimentos) 1. a West Indian tree *Pimenta dioica*, the ground berry of which produces ◊allspice. 2. this spice. 3. a sweet variety of ◊capsicum pepper (more correctly spelled **pimiento**). [from Spanish from Latin]

pimp n. one who solicits clients for a prostitute or brothel. —v.i. to act as a pimp.

pimpernel /ˈpɪmpənel/ n. any plant of the genus *Anagallis* of the primrose family Primulaceae, with small red, blue, or white flowers. The European **scarlet pimpernel** *A. arvensis* grows in cornfields, the small flowers opening only in full sunshine. [from Old French, ultimately from Latin *piper* = pepper]

pimple n. a small, hard, inflamed spot on the skin; a similar slight swelling on a surface. —**pimply** adj. [Old English = break out in pustules]

pin n. 1. a thin, usually cylindrical, piece of metal with a sharp point and round broadened head for fastening together papers, fabrics etc. or (with an ornamental head) as a decoration. 2. a larger similar object of wood or metal for various purposes. 3. the projecting part of a dovetail joint. 4. in golf, a stick with a flag on it marking the position of a hole. 5. (in *plural, colloquial*) the legs. —v.t. (**-nn-**) 1. to fasten with a pin or pins. 2. to fix the responsibility for (a deed *on* a person). 3. to seize and hold fast (against a wall etc.). 4. to transfix with a pin, lance etc. —**pinball** n. a game in which small metal balls are shot across a sloping board and strike against pins. **pin down**, to make (a person) declare his or her intentions etc. clearly; to restrict the actions of (an enemy etc.); to specify (a thing) precisely. **pin one's faith** or **hopes on**, to rely absolutely on. **pin money**, a small sum of money, originally that allowed to a woman or earned by her for private expenses. **pins and needles**, a tingling sensation in a limb recovering from numbness. **pinstripe** n. a very narrow stripe in cloth. **pin table**, a table used in pinball. **pin tuck**, a very narrow ornamental tuck. **pin-up** n. a picture of an attractive or famous person, pinned up on a wall etc.; such a person. **pinwheel** n. a small Catherine wheel. [Old English from Latin *pinna* = point etc.]

pinafore /ˈpɪnəfɔː/ n. a full-length apron. —**pinafore dress**, a dress without a collar and sleeves, worn over a blouse or jumper.

pince-nez /ˈpæ̃sneɪ/ n. (*plural* the same) a pair of eye-glasses with a spring that clips on the nose. [French = pinch-nose]

pincers /ˈpɪnsəz/ n.pl. 1. or **pair of pincers** a gripping tool of two pivoted limbs forming jaws. 2. a similar organ of crustaceans etc. —**pincer movement**, a military movement in which forces converge from each side on an enemy position. [from Anglo-French (Old French *pincier* = pinch)]

pinch v.t./i. 1. to squeeze tightly between two surfaces, especially between finger and thumb. 2. (of cold, hunger etc.) to affect painfully; to cause to shrivel. 3. to stint, to be niggardly. 4. (*slang*) to steal. 5. (*slang*) to arrest. —n. 1. pinching, squeezing. 2. the stress of circumstances. 3. as much as can be taken up with the tips of the finger and thumb. —**at a pinch**, in an emergency, if necessary. **pinch off** or **out**, to shorten or remove (buds etc.) by pinching. [from Old French *pincier*, ultimately from Latin *pungere* = prick]

pinchbeck n. a goldlike alloy of copper and zinc used in cheap jewellery etc. —adj. counterfeit, sham. [from C *Pinchbeck*, English watchmaker (died 1732)]

Pincus /ˈpɪŋkəs/ Gregory Goodwin 1903–1967. US biologist who, together with Min Chueh Chang and John Rock, developed the contraceptive ◊pill in the 1950s.

pincushion n. a small cushion or pad into which pins are stuck to keep them ready for use.

Pindar /ˈpɪndə(r)/ c.552–442 BC. Greek poet, born near Thebes. He is renowned for his choral lyrics, 'Pindaric odes', written in honour of victors of athletic games.

Pindling /ˈpɪndlɪŋ/ Lynden (Oscar) 1930– . Bahamian prime minister from 1967. After studying law in London, he returned to the island to join the newly formed Progressive Liberal Party and then became the first black prime minister of the Bahamas.

pine[1] n. an evergreen coniferous tree of the genus *Pinus*; its wood. There are some 70–100 species, belonging to the Pinaceae, the largest family of conifers. Pine trees have needle-shaped leaves growing in clusters. The **Scots pine** *P. sylvestris* is grown commercially for soft timber and its yield of turpentine, tar, and pitch. —**pine cone**, the seed head of the pine. [Old English and from Old French from Latin *pinus*]

pine[2] v.i. 1. to waste away through grief or yearning. 2. to feel an intense longing. [Old English]

pineal /ˈpɪnɪəl/ adj. shaped like a pine cone. [from French from Latin *pinea* = pine cone]

pineal body or **pineal gland** a cone-shaped outgrowth of the vertebrate brain. In some lower vertebrates, this develops a rudimentary lens and retina, which show it to be derived from an eye, or pair of eyes, situated on the top of the head in ancestral vertebrates. The pineal still detects light (through the skull) in some fishes, lizards, and birds. Some lizards and the ◊tuatara have an opening in the skull for their pineal or 'third eye'. In fishes that can change colour to match the background, the pineal perceives the light level and controls the colour change. In birds, the pineal detects changes in daylight and stimulates breeding behaviour as spring approaches.

pineapple /ˈpaɪnæpəl/ n. 1. a large, juicy, tropical fruit with a yellow flesh and tough, segmented skin. 2. the plant *Ananas comosus* of the bromeliad family, native to South and Central America, but now cultivated in many other tropical areas, such as Hawaii and Queensland, Australia. The mauvish flowers are produced in the second year, and subsequently consolidate with their bracts into the fruit. [from *pine*[1] and *apple* (from the resemblance of the fruit to a pine cone)]

ping n. an abrupt single ringing sound. —v.t./i. to make or cause to make this sound. —**pinger** n. [imitative]

ping pong table tennis. [imitative, from sound of bat striking ball]

pinion[1] /ˈpɪnjən/ n. a small cog wheel engaging with a larger one; a cogged spindle engaging with a wheel. [from French *pignon* from Latin]

pinion[2] n. 1. the outer segment of a bird's wing. 2. (*poetic*) a wing. 3. a flight feather. —v.t. 1. to clip the wings of (a bird) to prevent it from flying. 2. to restrain (a person) by holding or binding his or her arms; to bind (arms) thus. [from Old French, ultimately from Latin *pinna* = feather]

pink[1] n. 1. pale red colour. 2. pink clothes or material. 3. any annual or perennial plant of the genus *Dianthus* of the family Carophyllaceae. The stems have characteristically swollen nodes, and the flowers range in colour from white through pink to purple. Deptford pink *D. armeria*, with deep pink flowers with pale dots, is native to Europe and naturalized in the USA. Other members of the pink family include carnations, sweet williams, and baby's breath *Gypsophila paniculata*. **4.** the best or most perfect condition. —*adj*. **1.** of pale red colour. **2.** (*slang*) mildly communist. —**in the pink**, (*slang*) in very good health. **pink gin**, gin flavoured with angostura bitters. —**pinkness** *n*.

pink² *v.t.* **1.** to pierce slightly. **2.** to cut a scalloped or zig-zag edge on. —**pinking shears**, a dressmaker's serrated scissors for cutting a zigzag edge.

pink³ *v.i.* (of a vehicle engine) to emit high-pitched explosive sounds when running faultily. [imitative]

Pinkerton /'pɪŋkətən/ Allan 1819–1884. US detective, born in Glasgow. In 1852 he founded **Pinkerton's National Detective Agency**, and built up the federal secret service from the espionage system he developed during the US Civil War.

Pink Floyd British psychedelic rock group, formed in 1965. The original members were Syd Barrett (1946–), Roger Waters (1944–), Richard Wright (1945–), and Nick Mason (1945–). Their albums include *The Dark Side of the Moon* 1973 and *The Wall* 1979, with its spin-off film starring Bob Geldof.

pinnace /'pɪnɪs/ *n*. a warship's or other ship's small boat. [from French]

pinnacle /'pɪnəkəl/ *n*. **1.** a small ornamental turret crowning a buttress, roof etc. **2.** a natural peak. **3.** the highest point (of fame, success etc.). [from Old French from Latin *pinnaculum* (*pinna* = wing, point)]

pinnate /'pɪnɪt/ *adj*. (of a compound ◊leaf) with leaflets on each side of the leaf stalk, as in ash trees (*Fraxinus*). Each leaflet is known as a **pinna**, and where the pinnae are themselves divided, the secondary divisions are known as pinnules. —**pinnately** *adv*. [from Latin *pinnatus* = feathered]

pinny *n*. (*colloquial*) a pinafore. [abbreviation]

Pinocchio /pɪ'nəukɪəu/ a wooden puppet that comes to life and assumes the characteristics of a human boy. His story is told in a fantasy for children by Carlo ◊Collodi, published in Italy in 1883 and in an English translation in 1892. Pinocchio's nose grows longer every time he tells a lie. A Walt Disney cartoon film, based on Collodi's story, was released in 1940 and brought the character to a much wider audience.

Pinochet (Ugarte) /'pi:nəuʃeɪ u:'gɑ:teɪ/ Augusto 1915– . Military ruler of Chile from 1973, when a coup backed by the US Central Intelligence Agency ousted and killed President Salvador Allende. Pinochet took over the presidency and governed ruthlessly, crushing all opposition. He was voted out of power when general elections were held in Dec 1989 but remains head of the armed forces until 1997. In 1990 his attempt to reassert political influence was firmly censured by President Patricio Aylwin.

pinpoint *n*. **1.** the point of a pin. **2.** something very small or sharp. —*v.t.* to locate or designate with high precision. —*adj*. **1.** seeming as small or sharp as the point of a pin. **2.** performed with or exhibiting high precision.

pinprick *n*. a trifling irritation.

pint /paɪnt/ *n*. **1.** an imperial dry or liquid measure of capacity equal to 20 fluid ounces, half a quart, one-eighth of a gallon, or 0.568 litre. In the USA, a liquid pint is equal to 0.473 litre, while a dry pint is equal to 0.550 litre. **2.** this quantity of liquid, especially milk or beer. —**pint-sized** *adj*. (*colloquial*) diminutive. [from Old French]

pinta /'paɪntə/ *n*. (*colloquial*) a pint of milk etc. [corruption (originally in advertising slogan) of *pint of*]

pintail *n*. a duck of the genus *Anas*, 70 cm/28 in long. The male has a dark brown head and neck with a white band running down the neck, and long, black, central tail feathers. The female is mottled brown. *A. acuta* is native to the northern hemisphere; two species are native to South America.

Pinter /'pɪntə/ Harold 1930– . English dramatist, originally an actor. He specializes in the tragicomedy of the breakdown of communication, broadly in the tradition of the Theatre of the ◊Absurd, for example *The Birthday Party* 1958 and *The Caretaker* 1960. Later plays include *The Homecoming* 1965, *Old Times* 1971, *Betrayal* 1978, and *Mountain Language* 1988.

pintle /'pɪt(ə)l/ *n*. a bolt or pin, especially one on which some other part turns. [Old English = penis]

Pinturicchio /pɪntu'rɪkɪəu/ (or **Pintoricchio**) pseudonym of Bernardino di Betto *c*.1454–1513. Italian painter, active in Rome, Perugia, and Siena. His chief works are the frescoes in the Borgia Apartments in the Vatican, 1490s, and in the Piccolomini Library of Siena Cathedral, 1503–08. He is thought to have assisted ◊Perugino in decorating the Sistine Chapel, Rome.

pinworm *n*. a ◊nematode worm *Enterobius vermicularis*, an intestinal parasite of humans.

Pinyin /pɪn'jɪn/ *n*. a Chinese phonetic alphabet approved in 1956 by the People's Republic of China, and used since 1979 in transcribing all names of people and places from Chinese ideograms into other languages using the English/Roman alphabet. For example, the former transcription Chou En-lai becomes Zhou Enlai, Hua Kuo-feng became Hua Guofeng, Teng Hsiao-ping became Deng Xiaoping, and Peking became Beijing.

pioneer /paɪə'nɪə/ *n*. an original explorer or settler or investigator of a subject etc.; an initiator of an enterprise. **pioneer species**, in ecology, those species that are the first to colonize and thrive in new areas. Coal tips, recently cleared woodland, and new roadsides are areas where pioneer species will quickly appear. —*v.t.* to be a pioneer; to originate (a course of action etc. followed later by others). [from French *pionnier* = foot soldier]

Pioneer probe one of a series of US solar-system space probes 1958–78. The probes *Pioneer 4–9* went into solar orbit to monitor the Sun's activity during the 1960s and early 1970s. *Pioneer 5*, launched in 1960, was the first of a series to study the solar wind between the planets. *Pioneer 10*, launched in March 1972, was the first probe to reach Jupiter (Dec 1973) and to leave the solar system (1983). *Pioneer 11*, launched in April 1973, passed Jupiter in Dec 1974, and was the first probe to reach Saturn (Sept 1979), before also leaving the solar system. *Pioneer 10* and *11* carry plaques containing messages from Earth in case they are found by other civilizations among the stars. Pioneer Venus probes were launched in May and Aug 1978. One orbited Venus, and the other dropped three probes onto the surface. In early 1990 *Pioneer 10* was 7.1 billion km from the Sun. Both it and *Pioneer 11* were still returning data measurements of starlight intensity to Earth.

pious /'paɪəs/ *adj*. **1.** devout in religion. **2.** ostentatiously virtuous. **3.** dutiful. —**piously** *adv*., **piousness** *n*. [from Latin *pius*]

pip¹ *n*. a seed of an apple, orange, grape etc. [abbreviation of *pippin*]

pip² *n*. **1.** each spot on playing cards, dice, or dominoes. **2.** a star (up to three according to rank) on the shoulder of an army officer's uniform. [earlier *peep*]

pip³ *v.t.* (**-pp-**) **1.** (*colloquial*) to hit with a shot. **2.** or **pip at the post** to forestall; to defeat narrowly or at the last moment.

pip⁴ *n*. a short high-pitched sound, especially one produced electronically e.g. as a time signal. [imitative]

pip⁵ *n*. **1.** a disease of poultry, hawks etc. **2.** (*slang*) a fit of disgust, depression, or bad temper. [from Middle Dutch or Middle Low German, perhaps ultimately from Latin *pituita* = slime]

pipe *n*. **1.** a tube of metal, plastic etc., especially for conveying water, gas etc. **2.** a narrow tube with a bowl at one end containing tobacco for smoking; the quantity of tobacco held by this. **3.** a wind instrument of a single tube; each tube by which the sound is produced in an organ; (in *plural*) bagpipes. **4.** a tubular organ, vessel etc., in an animal body. **5.** a boatswain's whistle; the sounding of this. **6.** a cask for wine, especially as a measure (usually = 105 gallons). —*v.t./i.* **1.** to convey (oil, water, gas etc.) by pipes. **2.** to transmit (recorded music etc.) by wire or cable for hearing elsewhere. **3.** to play on a pipe or pipes. **4.** to utter in a shrill voice. **5.** to lead or bring (a person etc.) by the sound of a pipe; to summon by sounding a whistle. **6.** to decorate or trim with piping. **7.** to furnish with pipes. —**pipe cleaner**, a piece of flexible tuft-covered wire to clean inside a tobacco pipe. **pipe down**, (*colloquial*) to be quiet or less insistent. **pipe dream**, an unattainable or fanciful hope or scheme, as indulged in when smoking a pipe (originally of opium). **pipe up**, to begin to sing, play a tune etc.; to interject a remark. [Old English, ultimately from Latin *pipare* = chirp]

pipeclay *n*. a fine white clay for tobacco pipes or for whitening leather etc.

piranha

red
piranha

pipefish *n.* a fish related to the seahorse but long and thin like a length of pipe. The **great pipefish** *Syngnathus acus* grows up to 50 cm/1.6 ft, and the male has a brood pouch for eggs and developing young.

pipeline *n.* 1. any extended line of conduits for carrying water, oil, gas, or other material over long distances. They are widely used in water-supply and oil-and gas-distribution schemes. The USA has over 300,000 km/200,000 mi of oil pipelines alone. One of the longest is the Trans-Alaskan Pipeline in Alaska. 2. a channel of supply or information. **—in the pipeline,** being considered, prepared etc.

pip emma /pip 'emə/(*colloquial*) p.m. [former signallers' names for letters *P* and *M*]

piper /'paipə/ *n.* one who plays on a pipe, especially the bagpipes.

Piper John 1903– . British painter, printmaker, and designer. His subjects include traditional Romantic views of landscape and architecture. As an official war artist he depicted damaged buildings. He also designed theatre sets and stained-glass windows for Coventry Cathedral and the Catholic Cathedral, Liverpool, England.

pipette /pi'pet/ *n.* a slender tube for the accurate measurement of a known volume of liquid, usually for transfer from one container to another, used in chemistry and biology laboratories. [French diminutive]

piping /'paipiŋ/ *n.* 1. a length of pipe; a system of pipes. 2. a pipelike fold enclosing a cord as a decoration for the edges or seams of upholstery etc. 3. ornamental cordlike lines of icing on a cake. *—adj.* **piping hot,** (of food or water) very hot.

pipistrelle /pipi'strel/ *n.* a small bat of the genus *Pipistrellus.* [from French from Italian from Latin *vespertilio* = bat (*vesper* = evening)]

pipit /'pipit/ *n.* any of several birds in the family Motacillidae, related to the wagtails. The European **meadow pipit** *Anthus pratensis* is about the size of a sparrow and streaky brown, but has a slender bill. It lives in open country and feeds on the ground. [probably imitative]

pippin /'pipin/ *n.* an apple grown from seed; any of various red and yellow desert apples. [from Old French *pepin*]

pipsqueak *n.* (*slang*) a small or unimportant but self-assertive person.

piquant /'pi:kənt/ *adj.* 1. pleasantly sharp in its taste or smell, appetizing. 2. pleasantly stimulating or exciting to the mind. **—piquancy** *n.*, **piquantly** *adv.* [French *piquer* = prick]

pique /pi:k/ *v.t.* 1. to wound the pride or self-respect of. 2. to irritate to arouse (curiosity or interest). *—n.* a feeling of resentment or hurt pride. [from French]

piquet /pi'ket/ *n.* a card game for two players with a pack of 32 cards (omitting the low cards two to six). [French]

Pirandello /pirən'deləu/ Luigi 1867–1936. Italian writer. His novel *Il fu Mattia Pascal/The Late Mattia Pascal* 1904 was highly acclaimed, along with many short stories. His plays include *La Morsa/The Vice* 1912, *Sei personaggi in cerca d'autore/Six Characters in Search of an Author* 1921, and *Enrico IV/Henry IV* 1922. The themes and treatment of his plays anticipated the work of Brecht, O'Neill, Anouilh, and Genet. He was awarded the Nobel Prize for Literature in 1934.

Piranesi /pirə'neizi/ Giambattista 1720–1778. Italian architect, most significant for his powerful etchings of Roman antiquities and as a theorist of architecture, advocating imaginative use of Roman models. Only one of his designs was built, Sta Maria del Priorato, Rome.

piranha /pi'rɑ:nə, -njə/ *n.* a South American freshwater fish, genus *Serrusalmus.* It can grow to 60 cm/2 ft long. Piranhas have razor-sharp teeth, and some species may

rapidly devour animals, especially if attracted by blood. [Portuguese from Tupi]

Piran, St /'pirən/ *c.* AD 500. Christian missionary sent to Cornwall by St Patrick. There are remains of his oratory at Perranzabuloe, and he is the patron saint of Cornwall and its nationalist movement; feast day 5 March.

pirate /'paiərət/ *n.* 1. originally a seafaring robber attacking other ships etc.; a ship used by a pirate. The term also applies to anyone taking a ship, aircraft, or any of its contents, from lawful ownership, punishable under international law by the court of any country where the pirate may be found or taken. The contemporary equivalent is hijacking. 2. one who infringes another's copyright or business rights or who broadcasts without authorization. **—pirate radio,** in the UK, illegal radio broadcasting set up to promote an alternative to the state-owned monopoly. The early pirate radio stations broadcast from ships offshore, outside territorial waters; the first was Radio Atlanta (later Radio Caroline), set up in 1964. *—v.t.* 1. to plunder. 2. to reproduce (a book etc.) or trade (goods) without due authorization. **—piracy** *n.*, **piratical** /pai'rætikəl/ *adj.* [from Latin from Greek *peiraō* = attempt, assault]

Pirithous /pai'riθəuəs/ in Greek mythology, the king of the Lapiths, and friend of ◊Theseus. His marriage with Hippodamia was the occasion of a battle between the Lapiths and their guests, the ◊Centaurs, which is a recurrent subject of Greek art.

pirouette /piru:'et/ *n.* in dance, a movement comprising a complete turn of the body on one leg with the other raised. *—v.i.* to perform a pirouette. [French = spinning top]

Pisa /'pi:zə/ city in Tuscany, Italy; population (1988) 104,000. It has a 11th–12th-century cathedral. Its famous campanile, the Leaning Tower of Pisa (repaired in 1990) is 55 m/180 ft high and about 5 m/16.5 ft out of the perpendicular.

Pisanello /pi:zə'neləu/ nickname of Antonio Pisano *c.* 1395–1455. Italian artist active in Verona, Venice, Naples, Rome, and elsewhere. His panel paintings reveal a rich International Gothic style; his frescoes are largely lost. He was also an outstanding portrait medallist.

Pisano /pi:'sɑ:nəu/ Nicola (died *c.* 1284) and his son Giovanni (died after 1314). Italian sculptors and architects. They made decorated marble pulpits in churches in Pisa, Siena, and Pistoia. Giovanni also created figures for Pisa's baptistery and designed the façade of Siena Cathedral.

Pisano Andrea *c.* 1290–1348. Italian sculptor who made the earliest bronze doors for the baptistery of Florence Cathedral, completed in 1336.

piscatorial /piskə'tɔ:riəl/ *adj.* of fishermen or fishing. [from Latin *piscator* = fisherman]

Pisces /'paisi:z/ *n.* a zodiac constellation, mainly in the northern hemisphere between Aries and Aquarius, near Pegasus. It is represented by two fishes tied together by their tails. The constellation contains the vernal ◊equinox, the point at which the Sun's path around the sky (the ◊ecliptic) crosses the celestial equator. The Sun reaches this point around 21 March each year as it passes through Pisces from mid-March to late April. In astrology, the dates for Pisces are between about 19 Feb and 20 March (see ◊precession). **—Piscean** *adj. & n.* [Latin = fishes]

piscina /pi'si:nə/ *n.* 1. a perforated stone basin near the altar in a church for carrying away water used in rinsing the chalice etc. 2. a fishpond. [Latin]

Piscis Austrinus /'paisis ɒ'strainəs/ or **Southern Fish** a constellation of the southern hemisphere near Capricornus. Its brightest star is ◊Fomalhaut.

Pisistratus /pai'sistrətəs/ *c.* 605–527 BC. Athenian politician. Although of noble family, he assumed the leadership of the peasant party, and seized power in 561 BC. He was twice expelled, but recovered power from 541 BC until his death. Ruling as a dictator under constitutional forms, he was the first to have the Homeric poems written down, and founded Greek drama by introducing the Dionysiac peasant festivals into Athens.

piss *v.t./i.* (*vulgar*) 1. to urinate. 2. (in *past participle*) drunk. *—n.* (*vulgar*) urine; urination. [from Old French *pisser* (imitative)]

Pissarro /pi'sɑ:rəu/ Camille 1831–1903. French Impressionist painter, born in the West Indies. He went to Paris in

1855, met Corot, then Monet, and became a leading member of the Impressionists. He experimented with various styles, including ◊pointillism, in the 1880s.

pistachio /pɪˈstæʃɪəʊ/ n. (plural **pistachios**) a nut with a greenish edible kernel; the deciduous Eurasian tree *Pistacia vera*, of the cashew family Anacardiaceae, bearing this. [from Italian and Spanish, ultimately from Persian *pistah*]

piste /piːst/ n. a ski track of compacted snow. [French = racetrack]

pistil n. a general term for the female part of a flower, either referring to one single ◊carpel or a group of several fused carpels. —**pistillate** adj. [from French or Latin *pistillum*]

pistol /ˈpɪstl/ n. any small ◊firearm designed to be fired with one hand. Pistols were in use from the early 15th century. —v.t. (-ll-) to shoot with a pistol. —**pistol grip,** a handle shaped like the butt of a pistol. **pistol-whip** v.t. to beat with a pistol. [from French from German from Czech]

piston /ˈpɪstn/ n. **1.** a barrel-shaped device used in reciprocating engines (◊steam, ◊petrol, ◊diesel) to harness power. Pistons are driven up and down in cylinders by expanding steam or hot gases. They pass on their motion via a connecting rod and crank to a ◊crankshaft, which turns the driving wheels. In a pump or ◊compressor, the role of the piston is reversed, being used to move gases and liquids. See also ◊internal-combustion engine. **2.** a sliding valve in a trumpet etc. —**piston rod,** the rod by which a piston imparts motion. [French from Italian]

Piston /ˈpɪstn/ Walter (Hamor) 1894–1976. US composer and teacher. He wrote a number of textbooks, including *Harmony* 1941 and *Orchestration* 1955. His Neo-Classical works include eight symphonies, a number of concertos, chamber music, the orchestral suite *Three New England Sketches* 1959, and the ballet *The Incredible Flautist* 1938.

pit n. **1.** a large hole in the ground, especially one made in digging for a mineral etc. or for industrial purposes. **2.** a coal mine. **3.** a covered hole as a trap for animals. **4.** a hollow on a surface. **5.** a part of the auditorium of a theatre on the floor of the house; the sunken part before the stage, accommodating the orchestra. **6.** a sunken area in a workshop floor for access to the underside of motor vehicles. **7.** an area of the side of the track at a racecourse, where racing cars are serviced etc. during a race. —v.t. **1.** to match or set in competition. **2.** (especially in *past participle*) to make pits or scars in. **3.** to put into a pit. —**pithead** n. the top of the shaft of a coal mine; the area surrounding this. **pit of the stomach,** the depression below the breastbone. [Old English from Latin *puteus* = well]

pita /ˈpiːtə/ n. or **pitta** a flat bread originating in Greece and the Middle East. [modern Greek = cake]

pit-a-pat /ˈpɪtəpæt/ n. a sound as of quick light steps or quick tapping. —adv. with this sound. [imitative]

Pitcairn Islands /ˈpɪtkeən/ British colony in Polynesia, 5,300 km/3,300 mi NE of New Zealand; **area** 27 sq km/10 sq mi; **capital** Adamstown; **features** includes the uninhabited Henderson Islands, an unspoiled coral atoll with a rare ecology, and tiny Ducie and Oeno, annexed by Britain in 1902; **government** the governor is the British high commissioner in New Zealand; **products** fruit and souvenirs to passing ships; **population** (1982) 54; **language** English; **history** first settled in 1790 by nine mutineers from the *Bounty* together with some Tahitians, their occupation remaining unknown until 1808.

pitch[1] v.t./i. **1.** to erect and fix (a tent or camp); to fix in a definite position. **2.** to throw or fling. **3.** to cause (a bowled ball in cricket) to strike the ground at a particular point; (of a ball) to strike the ground thus. **4.** to express in a particular style or at a particular level. **5.** to fall heavily; (of a ship or aircraft) to plunge alternately backwards and forwards in a lengthwise direction. **6.** in music, to set at a particular pitch. **7.** (*slang*) to tell (a tale, a yarn). —n. **1.** the act or process of pitching. **2.** an area marked out for play in outdoor games; in cricket, the area between or near the wickets. **3.** in music, the relative sound of a note, governed by the rate of vibration of a string etc.; the degree of highness or lowness of tone. **4.** the place at which a street vendor etc. is stationed. **5.** an approach taken in advertising or sales talk. **6.** the intensity of a quality etc. **7.** the distance between successive ridges of a screw, teeth of a cog etc.; the steepness of a slope. —**absolute pitch,** ability to recognize or reproduce the pitch of a note (also

perfect pitch); a fixed standard of pitch. **pitched battle,** a battle fought between armies in prepared positions and formations; a fierce argument. **pitched roof,** one that slopes. **pitch in,** (*colloquial*) to set to work vigorously. **pitch into,** (*colloquial*) to attack forcefully.

pitch[2] n. a black, sticky substance, hard when cold, but liquid when hot, used for waterproofing, roofing, and paving. It is made by the destructive distillation of wood or coal tar, and has been used since antiquity for caulking wooden ships. —v.t. to coat with pitch. —**pitch-black** or **pitch-dark** adj. dark with no light at all. **pitch pine,** a pine tree *Pinus rigida* yielding much resin. —**pitchy** adj. [Old English from Latin *pix*]

pitchblende /ˈpɪtʃblend/ n. or **uraninite** a brownish-black mineral, the major constituent of uranium ore, consisting mainly of uranium oxide, UO_2. It also contains some lead (the final, stable product of uranium decay) and variable amounts of most of the naturally occurring radioactive elements, which are products of either the decay or the fissioning of uranium isotopes. The uranium yield is 50–80%; it is also a source of radium, polonium, and actinium. [from German *blende*]

pitcher[1] n. a large jug with a handle or two ears and usually a lip, for holding liquids. —**pitcher plant,** any of various insectivorous plants of the family Sarraceniaceae, especially the genera *Nepenthes* and *Sarracenia*, the leaves of which are shaped like a pitcher and filled with a fluid that traps and digests insects. [from Old French]

pitcher[2] n. the player who delivers the ball in baseball.

pitchfork n. a long-handled fork with two prongs, used for pitching hay. —v.t. **1.** to throw (as) with a pitchfork. **2.** to thrust (a person) forcibly into a position, office etc.

piteous /ˈpɪtɪəs/ adj. deserving or arousing pity. —**piteously** adv. [from Anglo-French]

pitfall n. **1.** an unsuspected danger or difficulty. **2.** a covered hole as a trap for animals.

pith n. **1.** the spongy tissue in plant stems and branches or lining the rind of an orange etc. **2.** the essential part. **3.** physical strength, vigour. [Old English]

pithy adj. **1.** terse, condensed, and forcible. **2.** of or like pith. —**pithiness** n.

pitiable /ˈpɪtɪəbl/ adj. deserving or arousing pity or contempt. —**pitiably** adv. [from Old French]

pitiful /ˈpɪtɪfʊl/ adj. **1.** causing pity. **2.** contemptible. —**pitifully** adv.

pitiless /ˈpɪtɪlɪs/ adj. showing no pity. —**pitilessly** adv.

Pitman /ˈpɪtmən/ Isaac 1813–1897. English teacher and inventor of Pitman's shorthand. He studied Samuel Taylor's scheme for shorthand writing, and in 1837 published his own system, *Stenographic Soundhand*, fast, accurate, and adapted for use in many languages.

piton /ˈpiːtɒn/ n. a spike or peg with a hole through which a rope can be passed, driven into rock or crack as a support in rock climbing. [French = eyebolt]

Pitot tube /ˈpiːtəʊ/ an instrument that measures fluid (gas and liquid) flow. It is used to measure the speed of aircraft, and works by sensing pressure differences in different directions in the airstream. It was invented in the 1730s by the French scientist Henri Pitot (1695–1771).

Pitt /pɪt/ William, **the Elder,** 1st Earl of Chatham 1708–1778. British Whig politician, 'the Great Commoner'. As paymaster of the forces 1746–55, he broke with tradition by refusing to enrich himself; he was dismissed for attacking Newcastle, the prime minister. He served effectively as prime minister in coalition governments 1756–61 (successfully conducting the Seven Years' War) and 1766–68.

Pitt William, **the Younger** 1759–1806. British Tory prime minister 1783–1801 and 1804–06. He raised the importance of the House of Commons, clamped down on corruption, carried out fiscal reforms and effected the union with Ireland. He attempted to keep Britain at peace but underestimated the importance of the French Revolution and became embroiled in wars with France from 1793; he died on hearing of Napoleon's victory at Austerlitz.

pittance /ˈpɪtns/ n. **1.** a very small allowance or remuneration. **2.** in medieval monasteries, a small dish of food, distributed by a monk called the pittancer, either to sick monks or to celebrate a feast day. [from Old French from Latin]

pitter-patter /ˈpɪtəpætə/ n. & adv. pit-a-pat. [imitative]

Pittsburgh /ˈpɪtsbɜːg/ industrial city (machinery and chemicals) and inland port, where the Allegheny and Monongahela join to form the Ohio River in Pennsylvania, USA; population (1980) 423,940, metropolitan area 2,264,000. Established by the French as Fort Duquesne in 1750, the site was taken by the British in 1758 and renamed Fort Pitt.

pituitary /pɪˈtjuːɪtərɪ/ n. the pituitary gland. —**pituitary gland** or **body**, a pea-sized endocrine gland at the base of the brain. The anterior lobe secretes hormones, some of which control the activities of other glands (thyroid, gonads, and adrenal cortex); others are direct-acting hormones affecting milk secretion, and controlling growth. Secretions of the posterior lobe control body water balance, and contraction of the uterus. The posterior lobe is regulated by nerves from the ◊hypothalamus, and thus forms a link between the nervous and hormonal systems. [from Latin *pituita* = slime, phlegm, referring to the fact that the gland was once thought to secrete nasal mucus]

pity /ˈpɪtɪ/ n. 1. a feeling of sorrow for another's suffering. 2. a cause for regret. —v.t. to feel pity (often with contempt) for. —**take pity on**, to feel or act compassionately towards. [from Old French *pité* from Latin]

Pius /ˈpaɪəs/ 12 popes, including:

Pius IV 1499–1565. Pope from 1559, of the ◊Medici family. He reassembled the Council of ◊Trent and completed its work in 1563.

Pius V 1504–1572. Pope from 1566. He excommunicated Elizabeth I of England, and organized the expedition against the Turks that won the victory of ◊Lepanto.

Pius VI (Giovanni Angelo Braschi) 1717–1799. Pope from 1775. He strongly opposed the French Revolution, and died a prisoner in French hands.

Pius VII 1742–1823. Pope from 1800. He concluded a ◊concordat with France in 1801 and took part in Napoleon's coronation, but relations became strained. Napoleon annexed the papal states, and Pius was imprisoned 1809–14. After his return to Rome in 1814, he revived the Jesuit order.

Pius IX 1792–1878. Pope from 1846. He never accepted the incorporation of the Papal States and of Rome in the kingdom of Italy, and proclaimed the dogmas of the Immaculate Conception of the Virgin in 1854 and papal infallibility in 1870; his pontificate was the longest in history.

Pius X (Giuseppe Melchiore Sarto) 1835–1914. Pope from 1903, canonized in 1954. He condemned ◊Modernism in a manifesto of 1907.

Pius XI (Achille Ratti) 1857–1939. Pope from 1922. He signed the ◊concordat with Mussolini in 1929.

Pius XII (Eugenio Pacelli) 1876–1958. Pope from 1939. He was conservative in doctrine and politics, and condemned ◊Modernism. He proclaimed the dogma of the bodily assumption of the Virgin Mary in 1950 and in 1951 restated the doctrine (strongly criticized by many) that the life of an infant must not be sacrificed to save a mother in labour. He was widely criticized for failing to speak out against atrocities committed by the Germans during World War II and has been accused of collusion with the Nazis.

pivot /ˈpɪvət/ n. 1. a short pin or shaft on which something turns or oscillates. 2. a person or point that is crucial. —v.t./i. 1. to turn (as) on a pivot. 2. to provide with a pivot. 3. to depend crucially, to hinge. —**pivotal** adj. [French]

pixel n. a single dot on a computer screen. All screen images are made up of a collection of pixels, with each pixel being either off (dark) or on (illuminated, possibly in colour). The number of pixels available determines the screen's resolution. Typical resolutions of microcomputer screens vary from 320 × 200 pixels to 640 × 480 pixels, but screens with over 1,000 × 1,000 pixels are now quite common for graphic (pictorial) displays. [from *pix* = pictures and *element*]

pixie /ˈpɪksɪ/ n. or **pixy** a supernatural being akin to a fairy. —**pixie hood**, a hood with a pointed crown.

Pizarro /pɪˈzɑːrəʊ/ Francisco c.1475–1541. Spanish conquistador who took part in the expeditions of Balboa and others. He explored the NW coast of South America in 1526–27, and conquered Peru in 1531 with 180 followers. The Inca king Atahualpa was seized and murdered. In 1535 Pizarro founded Lima. Internal feuding led to Pizarro's assassination.

pizza /ˈpiːtsə/ n. an Italian dish of a layer of dough baked with a savoury topping. [Italian = pie]

pizzicato /pɪtsɪˈkɑːtəʊ/ adv. in music, with a string of the violin etc. plucked instead of played with the bow. —n. (plural **pizzicatos**) a note or passage to be played in this way. [Italian = pinched]

pl. abbreviation of plural.

Plaatje /ˈplɑːtʃɪ/ Solomon Tshekiso 1876–1932. Pioneer South African black community leader who was the first secretary-general and founder of the ◊African National Congress in 1912.

placable /ˈplækəbəl/ adj. easily appeased, forgiving. —**placability** /-ˈbɪlɪtɪ/ n. [from Old French or Latin *placare* = appease]

placard /ˈplækɑːd/ n. a large notice for public display. —v.t. 1. to put placards on (a wall etc.). 2. to advertise by placards. 3. to display as a placard. [from Old French *plaquier* = to plaster from Middle Dutch]

placate /pləˈkeɪt/ v.t. to conciliate, to pacify. —**placatory** adj. [from Latin *placare*]

place n. 1. a particular part of space or of an area on a surface. 2. a particular town, district, building etc. 3. in names, a short street; a square or the buildings round it; a country mansion. 4. a passage or part in a book etc.; the point one has reached in reading. 5. a proper space for a thing; position in a series. 6. rank, position in a community etc.; a duty appropriate to this. 7. a position of employment. 8. a space, seat, or accommodation for a person; one's home or dwelling. 9. in racing, a position among placed competitors, especially other than the winner. 10. a step in the progression of an argument or statement etc. 11. the position of a figure in a series as indicating its value in decimal or other notation. —v.t. 1. to put into a particular or proper place, state, rank, order etc.; to find a place for. 2. to locate; to identify in relation to circumstances etc. 3. to put or give (goods, an order for these) into the hands of a firm etc.; to invest (money). —**be placed**, to be among the first three in a race. **give place to**, to make room for; to yield precedence to; to be succeeded by. **go places**, (colloquial) to be successful. **in place**, in the right place; suitable. **in place of**, in exchange for, instead of. **in places**, at some places but not others. **out of place**, in the wrong place; unsuitable. **place kick**, a kick in football with the ball placed on the ground. **place mat**, a table mat for a person's place at table. **place setting**, a set of cutlery or dishes for one person at table. **put a person in his/her place**, to snub a presumptuous person. **take place**, to occur. **take the place of**, to be substituted for. —**placement** n. [from Old French from Latin *platea* = broad way from Greek]

Place /pleɪs/ Francis 1771–1854. English Radical. He showed great powers as a political organizer, and made Westminster a centre of Radicalism. He secured the repeal of the anti-union Combination Acts in 1824.

placebo /pləˈsiːbəʊ/ n. (plural **placebos**) a medicine intended to cure by reassuring the patient rather than by its physiological effect; a dummy pill etc. used in a controlled trial. [Latin = I shall be acceptable (*placere* = please)]

placenta /pləˈsentə/ n. (plural **placentae** /-iː/ or **placentas**) 1. a flattened, circular, spongy vascular structure that develops in the uterus of pregnant mammals through which the developing ◊fetus is supplied with nutriment and rid of waste products, and to which it is attached by the umbilical cord. The placenta also produces hormones that regulate the progress of pregnancy. It is shed as part of the afterbirth. 2. in plants, the part of the ◊carpel to which ◊ovules are attached. —**placental** adj. [Latin from Greek = flat cake]

placer /ˈpleɪsə, ˈplæ-/ n. a deposit of sand or gravel etc. containing valuable minerals in particles. [American Spanish]

placid /ˈplæsɪd/ adj. calm and peaceful; not easily made anxious or upset. —**placidity** /pləˈsɪdɪtɪ/ n., **placidly** adv. [from French or Latin *placidus* (*placere* = please)]

placket /ˈplækɪt/ n. an opening or slit in a woman's skirt, for fastenings or access to a pocket. [variant of *placard*]

plagiarize /ˈpleɪdʒəraɪz/ v.t. to pass off (another's ideas, writings, or inventions) as one's own. —**plagiarism** n., **plagiarist** n. [from Latin *plagiarius* = kidnapper]

plague /pleɪg/ n. 1. a deadly contagious disease transmitted by fleas (carried by the black ◊rat) which infect the sufferer with the bacillus *Pasteurella pestis*. An early symptom is swelling of lymph nodes, usually in the armpit and groin; such swellings are called 'buboes', hence **bubonic** plague. It causes virulent blood poisoning and the death rate is high. 2. an infestation of a pest. 3. a great trouble or affliction; (*colloquial*) a nuisance. —*v.t.* 1. to afflict with plague. 2. (*colloquial*) to pester, to annoy. [from Latin *plaga* = stroke]

plaice *n.* (*plural* the same) a kind of edible marine flatfish *Pleuronectes platessa*, abundant in the N Atlantic. It is white beneath and brownish with orange spots on the 'eyed' side. It can grow to 75 cm/2.5 ft long, and weigh about 2 kg/4.5 lbs. [from Old French from Latin *platessa*]

plaid /plæd/ *n.* a long piece of twilled woollen cloth with a chequered or tartan pattern, the outer article of Highland costume; the cloth used for this. —*adj.* made of or having a plaidlike pattern. [Gaelic]

Plaid Cymru /plaɪd ˈkʌmrɪ/ the Welsh nationalist party, founded in 1925 and dedicated to seeking autonomy for Wales. In 1966 the first Plaid Cymru member of Parliament was elected. [Welsh = party of Wales]

plain *adj.* 1. clear and unmistakable, easily perceived or understood. 2. not elaborate or intricate; not luxurious; (of food) not rich or highly seasoned. 3. straightforward, candid. 4. undistinguished in appearance, not beautiful or good-looking. 5. homely in manner, without affectation. —*n.* 1. or **grassland** a large level tract of country, upon which grass predominates. The plains cover large areas of the Earth's surface, especially between the deserts of the tropics and the rainforests of the equator, and have rain in one season only. Examples include the North European Plain, the High Plains of the USA and Canada, and the Russian Plain also known as the ◊steppe. 2. the ordinary stitch in knitting, producing a smooth surface towards the knitter. —*adv.* plainly, simply. —**plain chocolate**, chocolate made without milk. **plain clothes**, civilian clothes as distinct from uniform or official dress. **plain flour**, flour that does not contain a raising agent. **plain sailing**, a simple situation or course of action. **plain-spoken** *adj.* frank. —**plainly** *adv.*, **plainness** *n.* [from Old French from Latin *planus*]

Plains Indian a member of any of the North American Indian peoples of the Great Plains, which extend over 3,000 km/2,000 mi from Alberta to Texas. The Plains Indians were drawn from diverse linguistic stocks fringing the Plains, but shared many cultural traits, especially the nomadic hunting of bison herds once horses became available in the 18th century. The various groups include Blackfoot, Cheyenne, Comanche, Pawnee, and the Dakota or Sioux.

plainsong *n.* or **plainchant** traditional church music in medieval modes and in free rhythm depending on accentuation of the words, sung in unison, with a single line of vocal melody to words taken from the liturgy. See ◊Gregorian chant.

plaint *n.* 1. in law, an accusation, a charge. 2. (*poetic*) a lamentation, a complaint. [from Old French from Latin *plangere* = lament]

plaintiff /ˈpleɪntɪf/ *n.* the party who brings a suit into a lawcourt. [from Old French]

plaintive /ˈpleɪntɪv/ *adj.* mournful-sounding. —**plaintively** *adv.* [from Old French]

plait /plæt/ *n.* an interlacing of three or more strands of hair or ribbon or straw etc.; material thus interlaced. —*v.t.* to form into a plait. [from Old French from Latin *plicare* = fold]

plan *n.* 1. a method or procedure, thought out in advance, by which a thing is to be done. 2. a map of a town or district. 3. a drawing showing the relative position and size of the parts of a building or structure. 4. a scheme of arrangement. —*v.t./i.* (**-nn-**) 1. to arrange or work out the details of (a procedure, enterprise etc.) beforehand; to make plans. 2. to make a plan of or design for. 3. (in *past participle*) done in accordance with a plan. —**plan on**, (*colloquial*) to aim at or envisage. —**planner** *n.* [French from Italian *pianta* = plan of building]

planchette /plɑːnˈʃɛt/ *n.* a small board supported on castors and a pencil, said to trace letters etc. at spiritualist seances without conscious direction when one or more people rest their fingers lightly on the board. [French diminutive from Latin *planca*]

Planck /plæŋk/ Max 1858–1947. German physicist who framed the ◊quantum theory in 1900. He was awarded the Nobel Prize for Physics in 1918.

plane

Planck's constant in physics, a fundamental constant (symbol *h*) that is the energy of one quantum of electromagnetic radiation (the smallest possible 'packet' of energy; see ◊quantum theory) divided by the frequency of its radiation. Its value is 6.626196×10^{-34} joule seconds. [from M *Planck*]

plane[1] *n.* 1. a surface such that a straight line joining any two points in it lies wholly in it; a level surface. 2. a level of attainment or knowledge etc. 3. an aeroplane; a main aerofoil. —*adj.* level as or lying in a plane. [from Latin *planus*]

plane[2] *n.* a tool for smoothing the surface of wood by paring shavings from it. —*v.t.* to pare or make smooth with a plane. [Old French from Latin]

plane[3] *n.* a tall, spreading, broad-leaved tree of the genus *Platanus*. Species include the **oriental plane** *P. orientalis*, a favourite plantation tree of the Greeks and Romans; the hybrid **London plane** *P.* × *hispanica*, with palmate, usually five-lobed leaves; and the **American plane** or **buttonwood** *P. occidentalis*. [from Old French from Latin *platanus* from Greek]

planet /ˈplænɪt/ *n.* a large celestial body in orbit around a star, composed of rock, metal, or gas. There are nine planets in the ◊solar system. The inner four, called the **terrestrial planets**, are small and rocky, and include the planet Earth. The outer planets, with the exception of Pluto, are large balls of liquid and gas; the largest is Jupiter, which contains more than twice as much mass as all the other planets combined. Planets do not produce light, but reflect the light of their parent star. —**planetary** *adj.* [from Old French from Latin from Greek, literally = wanderer (*planaomai* = wander), originally distinguished from fixed stars by apparently having a motion of its own, and including the Sun and Moon]

planetarium /plænɪˈtɛərɪəm/ *n.* (*plural* **planetariums**) a device for projecting an image of the night sky as seen at various times and places; a building containing this.

planetary nebula a shell of gas thrown off by a star at the end of its life. Planetary nebulae have nothing to do with planets. They were named by William Herschel, who thought their rounded shape resembled the disc of a planet. After a star such as the Sun has expanded to become a ◊red giant, its outer layers are ejected into space to form a planetary nebula, leaving the core as a ◊white dwarf at the centre.

plangent /ˈplændʒənt/ *adj.* 1. loud and reverberating. 2. loud and plaintive. —**plangency** *n.* [from Latin *plangere* = lament]

planimeter *n.* a simple integrating instrument for measuring the area of a regular or irregular plane surface. It consists of two hinged arms: one is kept fixed and the other is traced around the boundary of the area. This actuates a small graduated wheel; the area is calculated from the wheel's change in position.

plank *n.* 1. a long flat piece of timber. 2. an item of a political or other programme. —*v.t.* 1. to furnish or cover with planks. 2. (*colloquial*) to put down roughly or violently; to pay (money) on the spot. —**walk the plank**, (*historical*) to be made to walk blindfold into the sea along a plank laid over the side of a ship. [from Old French from Latin *planca*]

planking *n.* planks collectively; a structure or surface of planks.

plankton /'plæŋktən/ *n.* small, often microscopic, forms of plant and animal life that drift in fresh or salt water, and are a source of food for larger animals. —**planktonic** /-'tɒnɪk/ *adj.* [German from Greek = wandering]

plano- /pleɪnəʊ-/ in combinations, level, flat; having one surface plane. [from Latin *planus* = flat]

planographic /pleɪnə'græfɪk/ *adj.* printing from a flat surface.

plant /plɑːnt/ *n.* **1.** an organism that obtains its food by photosynthesis or by absorption, and that has neither power of locomotion nor special organs of sensation or digestion; a small organism of this kind as distinguished from a tree or shrub. Plants are autotrophs, that is, they make carbohydrates from water and carbon dioxide, and are the primary producers in all food chains, so that all animal life is dependent on them. They play a vital part in the carbon cycle, removing carbon dioxide from the atmosphere and generating oxygen. **2.** the machinery and implements etc. used in industrial processes; a factory and its equipment. **3.** (*slang*) a thing deliberately placed for discovery by others; a hoax or trap. —*v.t.* **1.** to place in the ground or soil for growing; to put plants or seeds into (the ground or soil). **2.** to put or fix firmly in position. **3.** to station (a person), especially as a lookout or spy. **4.** to cause (an idea etc.) to be established in the mind. **5.** to deliver (a blow or thrust) with deliberate aim. **6.** (*slang*) to conceal, especially with a view to misleading a later discoverer. **7.** to settle or establish (a colony, community etc.). [from Old English and French from Latin *planta* = sprout, cutting]

Plantagenet /plæn'tædʒənɪt/ *n.* the English royal house, reigning 1154–1399. In the 1450s, Richard, duke of York, took it as a surname to emphasize his superior claim to the throne over Henry VI's. [from the nickname of Geoffrey, Count of Anjou (1113–1151), father of Henry II, who often wore in his hat a sprig of broom, *planta genista*]

plantain[1] /'plæntɪn/ *n.* a herb of the genus *Plantago* with broad, flat leaves spread close to the ground and seeds used for food for cage birds. [from Old French from Latin *plantago* (*planta* = sole of foot)]

plantain[2] *n.* a tropical bananalike fruit; the treelike plant *Musca paradisiaca* bearing this. [from Spanish *pla(n)tano* = plane tree]

plantation /plɑːn'teɪʃən/ *n.* **1.** an extensive collection or area of cultivated trees or plants. **2.** an estate for the cultivation of cotton, tobacco, rubber etc. **3.** (*historical*) colonization; a settlement in a new or conquered country, a colony. [from Old French or Latin *planta*]

plant classification the taxonomy or classification of plants. Originally the plant kingdom included bacteria, diatoms, dinoflagellates, fungi, and slime moulds, but these are not now thought of as plants. The groups that are always classified as plants are the bryophytes (mosses and liverworts), pteridophytes (ferns, horsetails, and club mosses), gymnosperms (conifers, yews, cycads, and ginkgos), and angiosperms (flowering plants).

planter *n.* **1.** the owner or manager of a plantation. **2.** a container for house plants.

plant hormone a substance produced by a plant that has a marked effect on its growth, flowering, leaf fall, fruit ripening, or some other process. Examples include ◊auxin, ◊gibberellin, ◊ethylene, and ◊cytokine.

plaque /plɑːk, plæk/ *n.* **1.** a flat tablet or plate of metal or porcelain etc. fixed on a wall as an ornament or memorial. **2.** a mixture of saliva, food particles, and bacteria. It builds up on teeth and converts sugars to acid, which eats through the hard exterior enamel into the dentine, causing decay. Plaque can be removed by regular brushing. [French from Dutch *plak*]

plasma /'plæzmə/ *n.* **1.** the colourless coagulable part of blood, lymph, or milk, in which corpuscles or fat globules float. **2.** in physics, an ionized gas produced at extremely high temperatures, as in the Sun and other stars, and which contains positive and negative charges in approximately equal numbers. It is a good electrical conductor. **3.** any analogous collection of charged particles in which one or both kinds are mobile, as the conduction electrons in a metal or the ions in a salt solution. [Latin = mould, from Greek *plassō* = to shape]

plasmapheresis *n.* the removal from the body of large quantities of blood, which is then divided into its components (plasma and blood cells) by centrifugal force in a continuous-flow cell separator. Once separated, the elements of the blood are isolated and available for specific treatment. Restored blood is then returned to the venous system of the patient.

plasmid /'plæzmɪd/ *n.* a small, mobile piece of ◊DNA found in bacteria and used in ◊genetic engineering.

plaster /'plɑːstə/ *n.* **1.** a soft mixture of lime, sand, and water, for spreading on walls etc. to form a smooth surface and harden by drying. **2.** a medicinal or protective substance spread on fabric and applied to the body. **3.** sticking plaster. **4.** plaster of Paris. —*v.t.* **1.** to cover (a wall etc.) with plaster or a similar substance. **2.** to coat or daub, to cover thickly. **3.** to stick or fix (a thing) like plaster on a surface; to make (hair) smooth with a fixative etc. **4.** (*slang*) to bomb or shell heavily. **5.** (in *past participle*, *slang*) drunk. —**plaster of Paris,** a fine white plaster obtained from gypsum used for making moulds or casts. —**plasterer** *n.* [Old English and Old French from Latin from Greek *emplastron*]

plasterboard *n.* board with a core of plaster used for partitions, walls etc.

plastic /'plæstɪk/ *n.* any of the stable synthetic materials that are fluid at some stage in their manufacture, when they can be shaped, and that later set to rigid or semirigid solids. Plastics today are chiefly derived from petroleum. Most are polymers, made up of long chains of identical molecules. —*adj.* **1.** made of plastic. **2.** capable of being moulded; pliant, supple. **3.** giving form to clay or wax etc. —**plastic arts,** the arts concerned with modelling or with the representation of solid objects. **plastic bomb,** one containing puttylike explosive. **plastic surgeon,** a specialist in plastic surgery. **plastic surgery,** the repair or replacement of injured or defective tissue; cosmetic surgery is carried out for reasons of vanity to conform to some aesthetic norm or counter the effects of ageing, for example, the removal of bags under the eyes or a double chin. —**plasticity** /plæ'stɪsɪtɪ/ *n.* [from French or Latin from Greek *plassō* = to shape]

Plasticine /'plæstɪsiːn/ *n.* trade name of a plastic substance used for modelling.

plasticize /'plæstɪsaɪz/ *v.t./i.* to make or become plastic. —**plasticizer** *n.*

plastid *n.* the general name for a cell ◊organelle of plants that is enclosed by a double membrane and contains a series of internal membranes and vesicles. Plastids contain DNA and are produced by division of existing plastids. They can be classified into two main groups: the **chromoplasts,** which contain pigments such as ◊carotenes and ◊chlorophyll, and the **leucoplasts,** which are colourless; however, the distinction between the two is not always clear-cut.

plastron /'plæstrən/ *n.* (*historical*) **1.** a steel breastplate. **2.** an ornamental front on a woman's bodice. [French, from Italian *piastra* from Latin *emplastrum* = plaster]

Plataea, Battle of a battle in 479 BC, in which the Greeks defeated the Persians during the ◊Persian Wars.

plate *n.* **1.** a shallow, usually circular, vessel from which food is eaten or served; the contents of this. **2.** a similar vessel used for the collection of money in churches etc. **3.** (*collective*) utensils of silver, gold, or other metal; objects of plated metal. **4.** a piece of metal with a name or inscription for affixing to something. **5.** an illustration on special paper in a book. **6.** a thin sheet of metal, glass etc., coated with a sensitive film for use in photography etc. **7.** a flat, thin, usually rigid sheet of metal etc. **8.** each of a number of nearly rigid pieces of the Earth's crust which each cover a large area, some of them including whole continents, and which together constitute the surface of the Earth. **9.** a smooth piece of metal etc. for engraving; an impression from this. **10.** a silver or gold cup as a prize for a horserace etc.; such a race. **11.** a thin piece of plastic material, moulded to the shape of the gums etc., to which artificial teeth are attached; (*colloquial*) a denture. —*v.t.* **1.** to cover (another metal) with a thin coat especially of silver, gold, or tin. **2.** to cover with plates of metal. —**on a plate,** (*colloquial*) available with little trouble to the recipient. **on one's plate,** for one to deal with or consider. [from Old French from Latin *plata* = plate armour]

plateau /'plætəʊ/ *n.* (*plural* **plateaux** /-əʊz/) **1.** an area of fairly level high ground or a mountainous region in which the peaks are at the same height. An **intermontane plateau** is one surrounded by mountains. A **piedmont plateau** is one that lies between the mountains and low-lying land. A **continental plateau** rises abruptly from low-lying lands or the sea. 2. a state of little variation after an increase. [French from Old French *platel* (*plat* = flat)]

plateful *n.* 1. as much as a plate will hold. 2. (*colloquial*) a great deal (of work etc.).

platelayer *n.* a person employed in fixing and repairing railway rails.

platelet /ˈpleɪtlɪt/ *n.* a tiny 'cell' found in the blood, which helps it to clot. Platelets are not true cells, but membrane-bound cell fragments that bud off from large cells in the bone marrow.

platen /ˈplætən/ *n.* a plate in a printing press by which the paper is pressed against the type; the roller in a typewriter against which the paper rests as it is struck by the letters. [from Old French *platine* = flat piece]

plateresque /plætəˈresk/ *adj.* richly ornamented in a style suggesting silverware. [from Spanish *platero* = silversmith from *plata* = silver]

Plate, river /pleɪt/ English name of Río de ◊la Plata, estuary in South America.

plate tectonics the concept that attributes ◊continental drift and ◊seafloor spreading to the continual formation and destruction of the outermost layer of the Earth. This layer is seen as consisting of major and minor plates, curved to the planet's spherical shape and with a jigsaw fit to one another. Convection currents within the Earth's mantle produce upwellings of new material along joint lines at the surface, forming ridges (for example the ◊Mid-Atlantic Ridge). The new material extends the plates, and these move away from the ridges. Where two plates collide, one overrides

plate tectonics

sea floor spreading

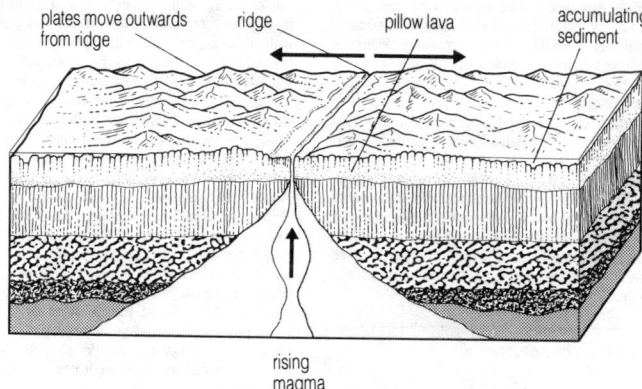

plates move outwards from ridge — ridge — pillow lava — accumulating sediment

rising magma

subduction zone

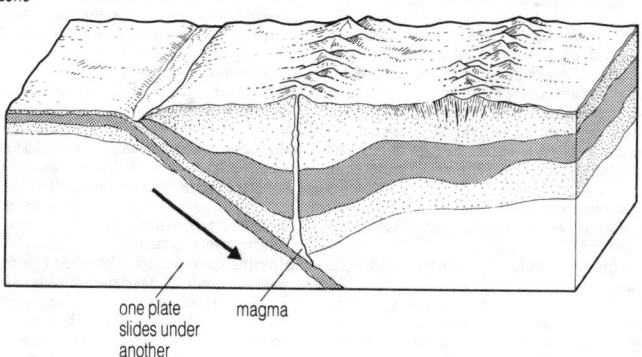

one plate slides under another — magma

collision zone

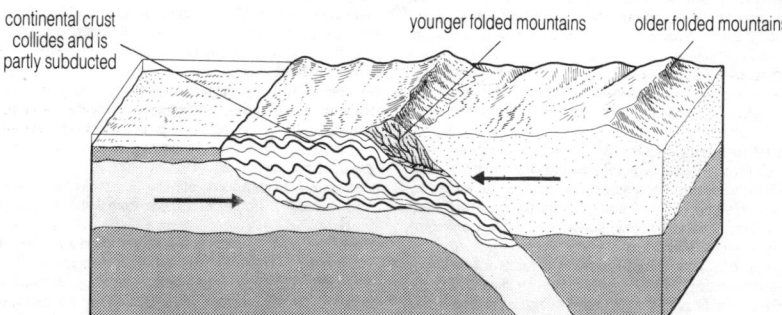

continental crust collides and is partly subducted — younger folded mountains — older folded mountains

the other and the lower is absorbed back into the mantle. These 'subduction zones' occur in the ocean trenches.

platform *n.* 1. a raised level surface, especially one from which a speaker addresses an audience. 2. a raised area along the side of a line at a railway station, where passengers board or alight from trains. 3. the floor area at the entrance to a bus. 4. a thick sole of a shoe. 5. the declared policy of a political party. [from French = ground plan]

Plath /plæθ/ Sylvia 1932–1963. US poet and novelist. Plath's powerful, highly personal poems, often expressing a sense of desolation, are distinguished by their intensity and sharp imagery. Collections include *The Colossus* 1960; *Ariel* 1965, published after her death; and *Collected Poems* 1981, which was awarded a Pulitzer Prize. Her autobiographical novel, *The Bell Jar* 1961, deals with the events surrounding a young woman's emotional breakdown.

platinum /'plætɪnəm/ *n.* a heavy, soft, silver-white, malleable and ductile rare metallic element, symbol Pt, atomic number 78, relative atomic mass 195.09. It is the first of a group of six metallic elements (platinum, osmium, iridium, rhodium, ruthenium, and palladium) that possess similar traits, such as resistance to tarnish, corrosion, and attack by acid, and that often occur as free metals (native metals). Both pure and as an alloy, platinum is used in dentistry, jewellery, and as a catalyst. —**platinum blonde**, a woman with silvery-blonde hair; this colour. [from earlier *platina* from Spanish, diminutive of *plata* = silver]

platitude /'plætɪtjuːd/ *n.* a commonplace remark, especially one solemnly delivered. —**platitudinous** /-'tjuːdɪnəs/ *adj.* [French *plat* = flat]

Plato /'pleɪtəʊ/ *c.*428–347 BC. Greek philosopher, a pupil of Socrates, teacher of Aristotle, and founder of the Academy. He was the author of philosophical dialogues on such topics as metaphysics, ethics, and politics. Central to his teachings is the notion of Forms, which are located outside the everyday world: timeless, motionless, and absolutely real.

Democracy passes into despotism.

Plato
Republic

Platonic /plə'tɒnɪk/ *adj.* 1. of Plato or his philosophy. 2. **platonic**, confined to words or theory, not leading to action, harmless; (of love or friendship) purely spiritual, not sexual. [from Latin from Greek *Platōn* = Plato]

Platonism /'pleɪtənɪzəm/ *n.* 1. the doctrines of Plato or his followers. 2. any of various revivals of these doctrines or related ideas, especially Neo-Platonism (3rd–5th centuries AD), and Cambridge Platonism (17th century) centred on Cambridge. —**Platonist** *n.*

platoon /plə'tuːn/ *n.* 1. a subdivision of a military company. 2. a group of people acting together. [from French *peloton* = small ball]

platter *n.* a flat dish or plate, especially for food. [Anglo-French *plater*]

platypus /'plætɪpəs/ *n.* an Australian egg-laying, aquatic, burrowing mammal *Ornithorhynchus anatinus* with a duck-like beak and flat tail. It feeds on water worms and insects, and when full-grown is 60 cm/2 ft long. [from Greek *platus* = broad, flat and *pous* = foot]

plaudit /'plɔːdɪt/ *n.* (usually in *plural*) a round of applause; an emphatic expression of approval. [from Latin *plaudite*, imperative of *plaudere* = clap (said by Roman actors at end of play)]

plausible /'plɔːzɪbəl/ *adj.* (of a statement etc.) seeming reasonable or probable; (of a person) persuasive but deceptive. —**plausibility** /-'bɪlɪtɪ/ *n.*, **plausibly** *adv.* [from Latin]

Plautus /'plɔːtəs/ *c.*254–184 BC. Roman dramatist, born in Umbria, who settled in Rome and worked in a bakery before achieving success as a dramatist. He wrote at least 56 comedies, freely adapted from Greek originals, of which 20 survive. Shakespeare based *The Comedy of Errors* on his *Menaechmi*.

play *v.t./i.* 1. to occupy oneself in a game or other recreational activity; to act light-heartedly or flippantly. 2. to take part in (a game). 3. to compete against in a game. 4. to occupy (a specified position) in a team for a game; to

assign (a player) to a position. 5. to move (a piece) or put (a card) on the table or strike (a ball etc.) in a game. 6. to perform on (a musical instrument); to perform (a piece of music etc.); to cause (a record or record player etc.) to produce sound. 7. to act in a drama etc.; to act the part of; to perform (a drama or role) on stage. 8. to move about lightly or irregularly; to allow (light or water etc.) to fall on something; (of a fountain or hosepipe) to discharge water. 9. to allow (a fish) to exhaust itself pulling against the line. —*n.* 1. playing; recreation, amusement, especially as the spontaneous activity of children. 2. the playing of a game; the action or manner of this. 3. a literary work written for performance on the stage; a similar work for broadcasting. 4. activity, operation. 5. free movement; space or scope for this. 6. a brisk, light, or fitful movement. 7. gambling. —**in** (*or* **out of**) **play**, (of the ball etc. in a game) in (or not in) position for continued play according to the rules. **make a play for**, (*slang*) to seek to acquire. **make play with**, to use effectively or ostentatiously. **play about** *or* **around**, to behave irresponsibly. **play along**, to pretend to cooperate. **play at**, to perform or engage in half-heartedly. **play back**, to play (sounds recently recorded). **playback** *n.* the playing back of sound. **play by ear**, to perform (music) without having seen a score; to proceed step by step going by one's instinct or by results. **play down**, to minimize the importance of. **played out**, exhausted of energy or usefulness. **play fast and loose**, to act unreliably. **play for time**, to seek to gain time by delaying. **play the game**, to observe the rules, to behave honourably. **play havoc** *or* **hell with**, (*colloquial*) to produce great disorder in. **play into a person's hands**, to act so as unwittingly to give him or her an advantage. **play the market**, to speculate in stocks etc. **play off**, to oppose (a person *against* another) especially for one's own advantage; to play an extra match to decide a draw or tie. **play-off** *n.* a match so played. **play on**, to take advantage of (a person's feelings etc.). **play on words**, to pun; a pun. **playpen** *n.* a portable enclosure for a young child to play in. **play safe** *or* **for safety**, to avoid risks. **play up**, to behave mischievously; to cause annoyance thus, to put all one's energy into a game. **play up to**, to flatter so as to win favour etc. **play with fire**, to take foolish risks. [Old English]

playbill *n.* a poster announcing a theatre programme.

playboy *n.* a pleasure-seeking, usually wealthy man.

player *n.* 1. a person taking part in a game. 2. a performer on a musical instrument. 3. an actor. 4. a record player.

playfellow *n.* a playmate.

playful *adj.* 1. full of fun. 2. in a mood for play, not serious; done in fun. —**playfully** *adv.*, **playfulness** *n.*

playgoer *n.* one who goes to the theatre.

playground *n.* an outdoor area for children to play on.

playgroup *n.* in the UK, a voluntary, usually part-time pre-school group, run by parents or sometimes by charitable organizations, to provide nursery education for children from three to five.

playhouse *n.* a theatre.

playing card a small oblong card with rounded corners used in games. A standard set consists of a 'deck' of 52 cards divided into four suits: hearts, clubs, diamonds, and spades. Within each suit there are 13 cards: nine are numbered two through to ten), three are called face, picture (or court) cards (jack, queen, and king) and one is called the ace.

playing field a field used for outdoor games.

playmate *n.* a child's companion in play.

plaything *n.* a toy or other thing to play with.

playtime *n.* time for play or recreation.

playwright *n.* a dramatist.

plc abbreviation of public limited company.

plea *n.* 1. an appeal, an entreaty. 2. in law, a formal statement by or on behalf of a defendant. 3. a pleading argument, an excuse. [from Anglo-French from Latin *placitum* = decree]

pleach *v.t.* to entwine or interlace (especially branches to form a hedge). [from Old French from Latin *plectere* = plait]

plead *v.t./i.* 1. to address a lawcourt as an advocate; to put forward (a case) in a lawcourt. 2. to declare oneself to be (guilty or not guilty) to a charge; to allege formally as a plea. 3. to offer as an excuse. 4. to make an appeal or entreaty. —**plead with**, to entreat earnestly. **pleadings**

n.pl. in law, documents exchanged between the parties to court actions, which set out the facts that form the basis of the case they intend to present in court, and (where relevant) stating what damages or other remedy they are claiming. [from Anglo-French]

Pleasance /'plezəns/ Donald 1919– . English actor. He has been acclaimed for roles in Luigi Pirandello's *The Rules of the Game*, in Harold Pinter's *The Caretaker*, and also in the title role of the film *Dr Crippen* 1962, conveying the sinister aspect of the outcast from society. Other films include *THX-1138* 1971 and *The Eagle has Landed* 1976.

pleasant /'plezənt/ *adj.* pleasing to the mind, feelings, or senses. —**pleasantly** *adv.*, **pleasantness** *n.* [from Old French]

pleasantry *n.* 1. jocularity. 2. humorous speech; a joking or polite remark. [from French]

please /pli:z/ *v.t./i.* 1. to give pleasure (to); to make satisfied or glad. 2. to think fit; to have the desire; to be the wish of. 3. (short for *may it please you*) used in polite requests. —**if you please**, if you are willing, especially (*ironically*) to indicate unreasonableness. **please oneself**, to do as one likes. [from Old French *plaisir* from Latin *placēre*]

pleasurable /'pleʒərəbəl/ *adj.* causing pleasure. —**pleasurably** *adv.*

pleasure /'pleʒə/ *n.* 1. a feeling of satisfaction or joy, enjoyment. 2. a source of pleasure or gratification. 3. one's will or desire. 4. (*attributive*) done or used for pleasure. [Old French]

pleat *n.* a fold or crease, especially a flattened fold in cloth doubled upon itself. —*v.t.* to make a pleat or pleats in. [variant of *plait*]

pleb *n.* (*slang*) a person of the lower classes. [abbreviation of *plebeian*]

plebeian /pli'bi:ən/ *n.* a member of the unprivileged class in ancient Rome, composed of aliens, freed slaves, and their descendants. During the 5th–4th centuries BC plebeians waged a long struggle to win political and social equality with the ◊patricians, eventually securing admission to the offices formerly reserved for patricians. —*adj.* of low birth, of the common people; uncultured; coarse, ignoble. [from Latin *plebs* = common people]

plebiscite /'plebisit/ *n.* a referendum or direct vote by all the electors of a country or district on a specific and important public question. Since the 18th century it has been employed on many occasions to decide to what country a particular area should belong; for example, in Upper Silesia and elsewhere after World War I, and in the Saar in 1935. [from French from Latin *scitum* = decree]

plectrum *n.* (*plural* **plectra**) a small, thin piece of horn or metal etc. for plucking the strings of a guitar etc. [Latin from Greek *plēssō* = strike]

pledge *n.* 1. a thing given as security for the fulfilment of a contract, payment of a debt etc., and liable to forfeiture in case of failure; a thing put in pawn. 2. a thing given as a token of favour etc. or of something to come. 3. a solemn promise. 4. the drinking of a health, a toast. —*v.t.* 1. to deposit as a security, to pawn. 2. to promise solemnly by pledge of (one's honour, word etc.); to bind by a solemn promise. 3. to drink to the health of. [Old French]

Pléiade, La /pleɪ'ɑ:d/ a group of seven poets in 16th-century France led by Pierre Ronsard, who were inspired by Classical models to improve French verse. [name derived from the seven stars of the Pleiades group]

Pleiades /'plaɪədi:z/ *n.pl.* 1. in Greek mythology, seven daughters of ◊Atlas, who asked to be changed into a cluster of stars to escape the pursuit of ◊Orion. 2. in astronomy, a star cluster about 400 light years away in the constellation Taurus, representing the seven sisters of Greek mythology. Its brightest stars (highly luminous, very young blue-white giants only a few million years old) are visible to the naked eye, but there are many fainter ones.

plein-air /plen 'eə/ *adj.* in painting, representing effects of atmosphere and light that are not observable in a studio. —**plein-airism** *n.* [French = open air, originally of French Impressionists around 1870]

pleiotropy *n.* a process whereby a given gene influences several different observed characteristics of an organism.

Pleistocene /'plaɪstəsi:n/ *adj.* of the first of the two epochs forming the Quaternary period of geological time. —*n.* this epoch, beginning 1.8 million years ago and ending 10,000 years ago. Glaciers were abundant during the

◊Ice Age, and humans evolved into modern *Homo sapiens*, appearing about 100,000 years ago. [from Greek *pleistos* = most and *kainos* = new]

Plekhanov /pli'xɑ:nɒf/ Georgi Valentinovich 1857–1918. Russian Marxist revolutionary and theorist, founder of the ◊Menshevik party. He led the first populist demonstration in St Petersburg, became a Marxist and, with Lenin, edited the newspaper *Iskra* (spark). In 1903 his opposition to Lenin led to the Bolshevik–Menshevik split.

plenary /'pli:nəri/ *adj.* 1. entire, unqualified. 2. (of an assembly) to be attended by all members. [from Latin *plenus* = full]

plenipotentiary /plenipə'tenʃəri/ *n.* a person (especially a diplomat) invested with full power of independent action. —*adj.* having this power. [from Latin *potentia* = power]

plenitude /'plenitju:d/ *n.* fullness, completeness; abundance. [from Old French from Latin *plenitas*)]

plenteous /'plentiəs/ *adj.* (*literary*) plentiful. [from Old French]

plentiful /'plentiful/ *adj.* existing in ample quantity. —**plentifully** *adv.*

plenty *n.* quite enough, as much as one could need or desire. —*adv.* (*colloquial*) quite, fully. [from Old French from Latin *plenitas*]

pleonasm /'pli:ənæzəm/ *n.* the use of extra words not needed to give the sense (e.g. *hear with one's ears*). —**pleonastic** /-'næstɪk/ *adj.* [from Latin from Greek *pleonazō* = be superfluous]

plesiosaurus /pli:siə'sɔ:rɪs/ *n.* an extinct carnivorous marine reptile of the Jurassic and Cretaceous periods, which reached a length of 12 m/36 ft, and had a long neck and paddlelike limbs. The ◊pliosaurs evolved from the plesiosaurs. [from Greek *plēsios* = near and *sauros* = lizard]

plethora /'pleθərə/ *n.* an overabundance. [Latin from Greek *plēthōrē* (*plēthō* = be full)]

pleura /'pluərə/ *n.* (*plural* **pleurae** /-i:/) one of a pair of membranes enveloping the lungs, protecting and lubricating them during breathing movements. —**pleural** *adj.* [Latin from Greek = rib]

pleurisy /'pluərisi/ *n.* inflammation of the pleura. Pleurisy is nearly always due to bacterial or viral infection, which can be treated with antibiotics. It renders breathing painful. —**pleuritic** /-'rɪtɪk/ *adj.* [from Old French from Latin from Greek *pleuritis*]

plexus /'pleksəs/ *n.* the network of nerves or vessels in an animal body. [Latin *plectere* = plait]

pliable /'plaɪəbəl/ *adj.* 1. bending easily, flexible. 2. easily influenced; compliant. —**pliability** /-'bɪlɪti/ *n.*, **pliably** *adv.* [French (*plier* = bend from Latin *plicare*)]

pliant /'plaɪənt/ *adj.* pliable. —**pliancy** *n.*, **pliantly** *adv.* [from Old French]

pliers /'plaɪəz/ *n.pl.* pincers with parallel flat surfaces for holding small objects, bending wire etc. [from dialect *ply* = bend]

plight[1] /plaɪt/ *n.* a condition or state, especially an unfortunate one. [Anglo-French *plit*]

plight[2] *v.t.* (*archaic*) to pledge. [from Old English = danger]

plimsoll /'plɪmsəl/ *n.* a rubber-soled canvas sports shoe.

Plimsoll Samuel 1824–1898. English social reformer, born in Bristol. He sat in Parliament as a Radical 1868–80, and through his efforts the Merchant Shipping Act was passed in 1876, providing for Board of Trade inspection of ships, and the compulsory painting of a **Plimsoll line** to indicate safe loading limits.

plinth *n.* the lower square member of the base of a column; a base supporting a vase or statue etc. [from French or Latin from Greek = tile]

Pliny the Elder /'plɪni/ (Gaius Plinius Secundus) *c.*23–79. Roman scientist and historian; only his works on astronomy, geography, and natural history survive. He was killed in an eruption of Vesuvius.

Pliny the Younger (Gaius Plinius Caecilius Secundus) *c.*61–113. Roman administrator, nephew of Pliny the Elder, whose correspondence is of great interest. Among his surviving letters are those describing the eruption of Vesuvius, his uncle's death, and his correspondence with the emperor ◊Trajan.

Pliocene /'plaɪəsi:n/ *adj.* of the fifth and final epoch of the Tertiary period of geological time, 5–1.8 million years ago. —*n.* this epoch. Humanlike apes ('australopithecines') evolved in Africa. [from Greek *pleiōn* = more and *kainos* = new]

pliosaur *n.* a prehistoric, carnivorous, marine reptile, descended from the ◊plesiosaurs, but with a shorter neck, and longer head and jaws. It was approximately 5 m/15 ft long. In 1989 the skeleton of one of a previously unknown species was discovered in northern Queensland. A hundred million years old, it lived in the sea which once covered the Great Artesian Basin.

Plisetskaya /pliˈsetskiə/ Maya 1925– . Soviet ballerina and actress. She attended the Moscow Bolshoi Ballet School and succeeded Ulanova as prima ballerina of the Bolshoi Ballet.

PLO abbreviation of ◊Palestine Liberation Organization.

plod *v.i.* (-dd-) 1. to walk doggedly or laboriously, to trudge. 2. to work slowly and steadily. —*n.* a spell of plodding. —**plodder** *n.*

plonk[1] *n.* a heavy thud. —*v.t.* to set down hurriedly or clumsily; to put firmly. [imitative]

plonk[2] *n.* (*slang*) cheap or inferior wine. [perhaps from *plonk*[1] or French *vin blanc* = white wine]

plop *n.* a sound as of an object dropping into water without a splash. —*v.t./i.* (-pp-) to fall or cause to fall with a plop. —*adv.* with a plop. [imitative]

plosive /ˈpləʊsɪv/ *adj.* (of a consonant, e.g. p, d, k) pronounced with a sudden release of the breath. —*n.* a consonant of this kind.

plot *n.* 1. a defined and usually small piece of ground. 2. the interrelationship of main events in a play, novel, film etc. 3. a conspiracy, a secret plan. —*v.t.* (-tt-) 1. to make a plan or map of. 2. to mark on a chart or diagram; to make (a curve etc.) by marking out a number of points. 3. to plan or contrive (a crime etc.); to plan secretly. —**plotter** *n.* [Old English and from Old French *complot* = secret plan]

plotter *n.* an ◊output device that draws pictures or diagrams under computer control. They are often used for producing business charts, architectural plans and engineering drawings. **Flatbed plotters** move a pen up and down across a flat drawing surface, while **roller plotters** roll the drawing paper past the pen as it moves from side to side.

plough /plaʊ/ *n.* 1. an implement for cutting furrows in soil and turning it up. The plough dates from about 3500 BC, when oxen were used to pull a simple wooden blade, or ard. In about 500 BC the iron share came into use. 2. an implement resembling this (e.g. a snowplough). 3. **the Plough,** a popular name for the most prominent part of the constellation ◊Ursa Major (the Great Bear). —*v.t.* 1. to turn up (earth, or *absolute*) or cast out (roots etc.) with a plough; to cut (a furrow). 2. to make one's way or advance laboriously (through snow, a book etc.). 3. to advance with irresistible penetration and damage. 4. (*slang*) to fail in (an examination); to declare that (a candidate) has failed. —**plough back,** to turn (growing grass etc.) into the soil to enrich it; to reinvest (profits) in the business producing them. [Old English from Old Norse]

ploughman *n.* (*plural* **ploughmen**) a person who guides a plough. —**ploughman's lunch,** a meal of bread and cheese etc.

ploughshare *n.* the cutting blade of a plough.

Plovdiv /ˈplɒvdɪv/ industrial city (textiles, chemicals, leather, tobacco) in Bulgaria, on the river Maritsa; population (1987) 357,000. Conquered by Philip of Macedon in the 4th century BC, it was known as Philippopolis ('Philip's city').

plover /ˈplʌvə/ *n.* a medium-sized wading bird of the family Charadriidae, found worldwide, e.g. the lapwing. Plovers are usually black or brown above, and white below. They have short bills. [Anglo-French, ultimately from Latin *pluvia* = rain]

ploy *n.* (*colloquial*) a cunning manœuvre used to gain an advantage. [origin Scottish]

PLR abbreviation of ◊public lending right.

pluck *v.t./i.* 1. to pick or pull out or away. 2. to strip (a bird) of feathers. 3. to pull at, to twitch. 4. to sound (the string of a musical instrument) with the finger or a plectrum. 5. to plunder, to swindle. —*n.* 1. courage, spirit. 2. plucking, a twitch. 3. an animal's heart and liver and lungs as food. —**pluck up courage,** to summon up one's courage. [Old English]

plucky *adj.* brave, spirited. —**pluckily** *adv.*, **pluckiness** *n.*

plug *n.* 1. a piece of solid material fitting tightly into a hole, used to fill a gap or cavity or act as a wedge or stopper. 2. a device of metal pins in an insulated casing fitting into holes in a socket for making an electrical connection; (*colloquial*) the socket. 3. a sparking plug. 4. (*colloquial*) favourable publicity for a commercial product etc. 5. (*colloquial*) the release mechanism of a water closet flushing apparatus. 6. a cake or stick of tobacco; a piece of this for chewing. —*v.t./i.* (-gg-) 1. to put a plug into; to stop with a plug. 2. (*slang*) to shoot or strike (a person etc.). 3. (*colloquial*) to mention favourably; to seek to popularize (a song, product, policy, etc.) by constant recommendation. 4. (*colloquial*) to work steadily. —**plug in,** to connect electrically by inserting a plug into a socket. **plug-in** *adj.* able to be connected thus. [from Middle Dutch and Middle Low German *plugge*]

plum *n.* 1. a roundish fleshy fruit with sweet pulp and a flattish pointed stone; the tree *Prunus domestica* bearing it. There are many varieties of plum, including the Victoria, czar, egg-plum, greengage, and damson; the sloe *P. spinosa* is closely related. Dried plums, known as prunes, are used in cooking. 2. a thing that is highly prized or the best of its kind. —**plum pudding,** a boiled pudding containing raisins etc. [Old English, ultimately from Latin *prunum*]

plumage /ˈpluːmɪdʒ/ *n.* a bird's feathers. [from Old French from Latin *pluma*]

plumb[1] /plʌm/ *n.* a ball of lead, especially attached to the end of a line for finding the depth of water or testing whether a wall etc. is vertical. —*adj.* vertical. —*adv.* 1. exactly; vertically. 2. (*US slang*) quite, utterly. —*v.t.* 1. to measure or test with a plumb line. 2. to reach or experience (depths of feeling etc.). 3. to get to the bottom of (a matter). —**out of plumb,** not vertical. **plumb line,** a line with a plumb attached. [from Latin *plumbum* = lead]

plumb[2] /plʌm/ *v.t./i.* 1. to work as a plumber. 2. to provide with a plumbing system; to fit (a thing) as part of this. [back formation from *plumber*]

plumbago /plʌmˈbeɪgəʊ/ *n.* 1. graphite. 2. a herbaceous plant of the genus *Plumbago* with spikes of tubular white, blue, or purplish flowers. [Latin *plumbum* = lead]

plumber /ˈplʌmə/ *n.* a person who fits and repairs the domestic apparatus of a water supply.

plumbing /ˈplʌmɪŋ/ *n.* 1. the system or apparatus of a water supply. 2. the work of a plumber. 3. (*colloquial*) lavatory installations.

plume /pluːm/ *n.* a feather, especially a large one used for ornament; an ornament of feathers etc. attached to a helmet or hat or worn in the hair; something resembling this. —*v.t.* 1. to furnish with a plume or plumes. 2. to pride (oneself). 3. (of a bird) to preen (itself or its feathers). [from Old French from Latin *pluma*]

plummet /ˈplʌmɪt/ *n.* 1. a plumb; a plumb line; a sounding lead. 2. a weight attached to a fishing line to keep a float upright. —*v.i.* to fall or plunge rapidly. [from Old French *plommet*]

plummy *adj.* 1. of plums; full of plums. 2. (*colloquial*) good, desirable. 3. (of a voice) sounding affectedly rich in tone.

plump[1] *adj.* having a full rounded shape, fleshy. —*v.t./i.* to make or become plump; to fatten. —**plumpness** *n.* [from Middle Dutch or Middle Low German = blunt, shapeless]

plump[2] *v.t./i.* to drop or plunge with an abrupt descent. —*n.* an abrupt or heavy fall. —*adv.* with a plump. —**plump for,** to choose; to decide on. [from Middle Low German or Middle Dutch (imitative)]

plumule *n.* the part of a seed embryo that develops into the shoot, bearing the first true leaves of the plant.

plumy /ˈpluːmɪ/ *adj.* 1. plumelike, feathery. 2. adorned with plumes.

plunder *v.t.* to rob (a place or person) forcibly of goods, especially (as) in war; to rob systematically; to steal or embezzle. —*n.* the violent or dishonest acquisition of property; the property so acquired; (*slang*) profit, gain. —**plunderer** *n.* [from Low German *plündern*]

plunge /plʌndʒ/ *v.t./i.* 1. to thrust or go suddenly or violently into something; to jump or dive into water; to immerse completely. 2. to enter or cause to enter a condition, course, or set of circumstances. 3. to descend suddenly; to move with a rush. 4. (*slang*) to gamble heavily; to run deeply into debt. —*n.* a plunging action or movement,

841

a dive. —**take the plunge**, to take a bold decisive step. [from Old French, ultimately from Latin *plumbum* = lead]

plunger *n.* 1. a part of a mechanism that works with a plunging or thrusting movement. 2. a rubber cup on a handle for the removal of blockages from pipes by a plunging action. 3. (*slang*) a reckless gambler.

pluperfect /pluːˈpɜːfɪkt/ *adj.* in grammar, (of a tense) denoting action completed prior to some past point of time (e.g. *he had said*). —*n.* in grammar, the pluperfect tense. [from Latin *plus quam perfectum* = more than perfect]

plur. abbreviation of plural.

plural /ˈplʊərəl/ *adj.* 1. more than one in number. 2. in grammar, (of a word or form) denoting more than one. —*n.* in grammar, a plural word or form; the plural number. [from Old French from Latin *plus* = more]

pluralism /ˈplʊərəlɪzəm/ *n.* 1. a form of society in which members of minority groups maintain independent traditions. 2. the holding of more than one office at a time. 3. in political science, the view that decision making in contemporary liberal democracies is the outcome of competition among several interest groups in a political system characterized by free elections, representative institutions, and open access to the organs of power. —**pluralist** *n.*, **pluralistic** /-ˈlɪstɪk/ *adj.*

plurality /plʊəˈrælɪtɪ/ *n.* 1. the state of being plural. 2. pluralism, a benefice or office held with another. 3. (*US*) a majority that is not absolute.

plus *prep.* 1. with addition of (symbol +). 2. (of a temperature) above zero. 3. (*colloquial*) with, having gained; possessing. —*adj.* 1. additional, extra. 2. (after a number) at least, rather better than. 3. in mathematics, positive. 4. having positive electrical charge. —*n.* 1. the symbol +. 2. an additional quantity; a positive quantity. 3. an advantage. [Latin = more]

plus ça change, plus c'est la même chose the more things change, the more they stay the same. [French]

plus fours /plʌsˈfɔːz/ long, wide knickerbockers. [so named because, to produce the overhang, four inches are added to ordinary knickerbockers]

plush *n.* a cloth of silk or cotton etc. with a long soft nap. —*adj.* 1. made of plush. 2. plushy. [from French *peluche* from Italian, ultimately from Latin *pilus* = hair]

plushy *adj.* luxurious. —**plushiness** *n.*

Plutarch /ˈpluːtɑːk/ *c.*AD 46–120. Greek biographer whose *Parallel Lives* has the life stories of pairs of Greek and Roman soldiers and politicians, followed by comparisons between the two. Thomas North's 1579 translation inspired Shakespeare's Roman plays.

Our nature holds so much envy and malice that our pleasure in our own advantages is not so great as our distress at others'.

Plutarch
Moralia

Pluto /ˈpluːtəʊ/ 1. in Greek mythology (Roman Dis), the lord of Hades, the underworld. He was the brother of Zeus and Poseidon. 2. in astronomy, the smallest and, usually, outermost planet of the solar system. It orbits the Sun every 248.5 years at an average distance of 5.8 billion km/ 3.6 billion mi. Its highly elliptical orbit occasionally takes it within the orbit of Neptune, such as 1979–99. Pluto has a diameter of about 3,000 km/2,000 mi, and a mass about 0.005 that of Earth. It is of low density, composed of rock and ice, with frozen methane on its surface and a thin atmosphere.

plutocracy /pluːˈtɒkrəsɪ/ *n.* 1. government by the wealthy; a state so governed. 2. a wealthy élite. [from Greek *ploutos* = wealth]

plutocrat /ˈpluːtəkræt/ *n.* 1. a member of a plutocracy. 2. a wealthy person. —**plutocratic** /-ˈkrætɪk/ *adj.*

plutonic /pluːˈtɒnɪk/ *adj.* 1. (of igneous rocks) formed by crystallization of molten material at a great depth underground; granites and gabbros are examples of plutonic rocks. 2. attributing most geological phenomena to the action of internal heat. [from Latin *Pluto*, lord of the underworld, from Greek]

plutonium /pluːˈtəʊnɪəm/ *n.* a silvery-white, radioactive, metallic element of the ◊actinide series, symbol Pu, atomic number 94, relative atomic mass 239.13. It occurs in nature in minute quantities in ◊pitchblende and other ores, but is produced in quantity only synthetically. It has six allotropic forms (see ◊allotropy) and is one of three fissile elements (elements capable of splitting into other elements; the others are thorium and uranium). The element has awkward physical properties and is the most toxic substance known. [from *Pluto*, planet next beyond Neptune]

pluvial /ˈpluːvɪəl/ *adj.* 1. of rain, rainy. 2. in geology, caused by rain. [from Latin *pluvia* = rain]

ply[1] /plaɪ/ *n.* 1. a thickness or layer of cloth or wood etc. 2. a strand of rope or yarn etc. [from French *pli*]

ply[2] *v.t./i.* 1. to use or wield (a tool or weapon). 2. to work steadily (at). 3. to supply continuously with food or drink etc.; to approach repeatedly with questions etc. 4. (of a vehicle etc.) to travel regularly to and fro between; to work (a route) thus. 5. (of a taxi driver etc.) to attend regularly for custom. [from Latin *applicare* = fasten to]

Plymouth /ˈplɪməθ/ city and seaport in Devon, England, at the mouth of the river Plym, with a dockyard, barracks, and naval base at Devonport; population (1981) 244,000.

Plymouth Brethren a fundamentalist Christian Protestant sect characterized by extreme simplicity of belief, founded in Dublin in about 1827 by the Reverend John Nelson Darby (1800–82). They have no ordained priesthood, affirming the ministry of all believers, and maintain no church buildings. They hold prayer meetings and Bible study in members' houses. An assembly of Brethren was held in Plymouth in 1831 to celebrate the sect's arrival in England, but by 1848 the movement had split into 'Open' and 'Close' Brethren. The latter refuse communion with all those not of their persuasion. [from *Plymouth* in Devon]

plywood /ˈplaɪwʊd/ *n.* a manufactured panel of wood widely used in building. It consists of several thin sheets, or plies, of wood, glued together with the grain (direction of the wood fibres) of one sheet at right angles to the grain of the adjacent plies. This construction gives plywood equal strength in every direction.

Plzeň /ˈpɪlzɛn/ (German *Pilsen*) industrial city (heavy machinery, cars, beer) in W Czechoslovakia, capital of Západočeský region; 84 km/52 mi SW of Prague; population (1984) 174,000.

p.m. abbreviation of after noon. [from Latin *post meridiem*]

Pm symbol for ◊promethium.

PM abbreviation of 1. Prime Minister. 2. postmortem.

pneumatic /njuːˈmætɪk/ *adj.* 1. filled with wind or air. 2. working by means of compressed air. —**pneumatic drill**, a drill operated by compressed air, used in mining and tunnelling, for drilling shot holes (for explosives), and in road repairs for breaking up pavements. It contains an air-operated piston that delivers hammer blows to the drill bit (see ◊bit[2] sense 2) many times a second. The French engineer Germain Sommeiller (1815–1871) developed the pneumatic drill in 1861 for tunnelling in the Alps. **pneumatic tyre**, a tyre inflated with air. —**pneumatically** *adv.* [from French or Latin from Greek *pneuma* = wind]

pneumatophore *n.* an erect root that rises up above the soil or water and promotes ◊gas exchange. Pneumatophores, or breathing roots, are formed by certain swamp-dwelling trees, such as mangroves, since there is little oxygen available to the roots in waterlogged conditions. They have numerous pores or ◊lenticels over their surface, allowing gas exchange.

pneumoconiosis *n.* a disease of the lungs caused by dust, especially from coal, asbestos, or silica. Inhaled particles make the lungs gradually fibrous and the victim has difficulty breathing.

pneumonectomy *n.* the surgical removal of all or part of a lung.

pneumonia /njuːˈməʊnɪə/ *n.* inflammation of one or both lungs, generally due to bacterial or viral infection but also to particulate matter or gases. It is characterized by a build-up of fluid in the alveoli, the clustered air sacs (at the end of the air passages) where oxygen exchange takes place. [Latin from Greek *pneumōn* = lung]

pneumothorax *n.* the presence of air in the pleural cavity, between a lung and the chest wall. It may be due to a penetrating injury of the lung or to lung disease, or it may arise without apparent cause. Prevented from expanding normally, the lung is liable to collapse.

Pnom Penh /ˈnɒm ˈpen/ alternative form of ◊Phnom Penh, capital of Cambodia.

pnp in electronics, abbreviation meaning in which an n-type layer occurs between two p-type layers.

po /pəʊ/ n. (plural **pos**) (colloquial) a chamberpot. —**po-faced** adj. (colloquial) solemn-faced, humourless. [French pronunciation of pot]

Po symbol for ◊polonium.

Po /pəʊ/ longest river in Italy, flowing from the Cottian Alps to the Adriatic; length 668 km/415 mi. Its valley is fertile and contains natural gas. The river is heavily polluted with nitrates, phosphates, and arsenic.

PO abbreviation of 1. Post Office. 2. postal order. 3. Petty Officer. 4. Pilot Officer.

Pocahontas /ˌpɒkəˈhɒntəs/ c.1595–1617. American Indian princess alleged to have saved the life of John Smith, the English colonist, when he was captured by her father Powhatan.

poach[1] v.t./i. 1. to catch (game or fish, or absolute) illegally. Since the creation of hunting grounds in the early middle ages, poaching has attracted heavy punishments. 2. to trespass or encroach (on the property or idea etc. of another). [perhaps from French pocher]

poach[2] v.t./i. 1. to cook (an egg) without the shell in boiling water or in a poacher. 2. to cook by simmering in a small amount of liquid. [from Old French pochier (poche = bag)]

poacher[1] n. one who poaches (see ◊poach[1]).

poacher[2] n. a pan with one or more cup-shaped containers in which eggs (without the shells) are placed for cooking over boiling water.

pochard n. a type of diving duck found in Europe and North America. The male **common pochard** Aythya ferina has a red head, black breast, whitish body and wings with black markings, and is about 45 cm/1.5 ft long. The female is greyish-brown, with greyish-white below.

Po Chu-i former transliteration of ◊Bo Zhu Yi, Chinese poet.

pock n. an eruptive spot on the skin, especially in smallpox. —**pock-marked** adj. bearing the scars left by such spots. [Old English]

pocket /ˈpɒkɪt/ n. 1. a small bag sewn into or on clothing, for carrying small articles. 2. a pouchlike compartment in a suitcase, car door etc. 3. money resources. 4. an isolated group or area. 5. a cavity in the Earth filled with gold or other ore. 6. a pouch at the corner or on the side of a billiard table into which balls are driven. 7. an air pocket. —adj. 1. of suitable size or shape for carrying in a pocket. 2. smaller than the usual size. —v.t. 1. to put into one's pocket. 2. to appropriate (especially dishonestly). 3. to confine as in a pocket. 4. to submit to (an injury or affront). 5. to conceal or suppress (feelings). 6. to drive (a billiard ball) into a pocket. —**in a person's pocket,** close to or intimate with him/her, under his/her control. **in pocket,** having gained in a transaction. **out of pocket,** having lost. **pocketbook** n. a notebook; a booklike case for papers or money carried in the pocket. **pocketknife** n. a knife with a folding blade or blades, for carrying in the pocket. **pocket money,** money for minor expenses, especially that allowed to children. [from Anglo-French diminutive]

pocketful n. (plural **pocketfuls**) as much as a pocket will hold.

pod n. in botany, a type of fruit that is characteristic of legumes (plants belonging to the Leguminosae family), such as peas and beans. It develops from a single ◊carpel and splits down both sides when ripe to release the seeds. —v.t./i. (-dd-) 1. to bear or form pods. 2. to remove (seeds etc.) from pods. [from dialect podware, podder = field crops]

podgy /ˈpɒdʒɪ/ adj. short and fat; plump, fleshy. —**podgily** adv., **podginess** n. [from podge = short fat person]

podium /ˈpəʊdɪəm/ n. (plural **podia**) 1. a continuous projecting base or pedestal round a room or house etc. 2. a rostrum. [Latin from Greek podion (diminutive of pous = foot)]

podzol n. or **podsol** a type of light-coloured soil found predominantly under coniferous forests and moorlands in cool regions where rainfall exceeds evaporation. The constant downward movement of water leaches nutrients from the upper layers, making podzols poor agricultural soils.

Poe /pəʊ/ Edgar Allan 1809–1849. US writer and poet. His short stories are renowned for their horrific atmosphere (as in The Fall of the House of Usher 1839) and acute reasoning

(for example, The Gold Bug 1843 and The Murders in the Rue Morgue 1841, in which the investigators Legrand and Dupin anticipate Conan Doyle's Sherlock Holmes). His poems include 'The Raven' 1844. His novel, The Narrative of Arthur Gordon Pym of Nantucket 1838, has attracted critical attention.

To villify a great man is the readiest way in which a little man can himself attain greatness.

Edgar Allan Poe
Marginalia

---

poem /ˈpəʊɪm/ n. 1. a metrical composition, especially one concerned with feeling or imaginative description; an elevated composition in verse or prose. 2. something with poetic qualities. [from French or Latin from Greek poēma (poieō = make)]

poesy /ˈpəʊɪsɪ/ n. (archaic) poetry. [from Old French from Latin from Greek poēsis]

poet /ˈpəʊɪt/ n. a writer of poems; one possessing high powers of imagination or expression etc. —**poetess** n.fem. [from Old French from Latin from Greek poētēs]

poetaster /pəʊɪˈtæstə/ n. a paltry or inferior poetical poet. [Latin -aster = derogatory suffix]

poetic /pəʊˈetɪk/ adj. of or like poetry or poets. —**poetic justice,** well-deserved punishment or reward. **poetic licence,** a writer's or artist's exaggeration or disregard of rules, for effect. —**poetically** adv. [from French from Latin from Greek]

poetical /pəʊˈetɪkəl/ adj. poetic; written in verse. —**poetically** adv.

poet laureate a poet of the British royal household, so called because of the laurel wreath awarded to eminent poets in the Graeco-Roman world. Early poets with unofficial status were Chaucer, Skelton, Spenser, Daniel, and Jonson. Among later poet laureates have been Wordsworth, Tennyson, Cecil Day Lewis, John Betjeman, and Ted Hughes.

poetry /ˈpəʊɪtrɪ/ n. 1. the art or work of a poet; the imaginative expression of emotion, thought, or narrative, frequently in metrical form and often using figurative language. Poetry has traditionally been distinguished from prose (ordinary written language) by rhyme or the rhythmical arrangement of words (metre), although the distinction is not always clear-cut. 2. poems collectively. 3. a quality that pleases the mind as poetry does. [from Latin poetria]

pogo /ˈpəʊgəʊ/ n. (plural **pogos**) or **pogo stick** a stiltlike toy with a spring, used for jumping about on.

pogrom /ˈpɒgrəm/ n. an unprovoked violent attack on an ethnic group, particularly Jews, carried out with official sanction. The Russian pogroms against Jews began in 1881, after the assassination of Tsar Alexander II, and again in 1903–06; persecution of the Jews remained constant until the Russian Revolution. Later there were pogroms in E Europe, especially in Poland after 1918, and in Germany under Hitler (see ◊Holocaust). [Russian = devastation]

poignant /ˈpɔɪnjənt/ adj. 1. painfully sharp to the senses or feelings, deeply moving. 2. sharp or pungent in taste or smell; pleasantly piquant. 3. arousing sympathy. —**poignancy** n., **poignantly** adv. [from Old French from Latin punctum, puncta (pungere = prick)]

poikilothermy n. the condition in which an animal's body temperature is largely dependent on the temperature of the air or water in which it lives. It is characteristic of all animals except birds and mammals, which maintain their body temperatures by ◊homeothermy. Poikilotherms have some means of warming themselves up, such as basking in the sun, or shivering, and can cool themselves down by sheltering from the sun under a rock or by bathing in water.

Poincaré /ˈpwæŋkæreɪ/ Jules Henri 1854–1912. French mathematician, who developed the theory of differential equations and was a pioneer in ◊relativity theory. He suggested that Isaac Newton's laws for the behaviour of the universe could be the exception rather than the rule. However, the calculation was so complex and time-consuming that he never managed to realise its full implication. He also published the first paper devoted entirely to ◊topology.

Poincaré Raymond Nicolas Landry 1860–1934. French politician, prime minister 1912–13, president 1913–20, and again prime minister 1922–24 (when he ordered the occupation of the Ruhr, Germany) and 1926–29.

Poindexter /'pɔɪndekstə/ John Marlan 1936–. US rear admiral and Republican government official. In 1981 he joined the Reagan administration's National Security Council (NSC) and became national security adviser in 1985. As a result of the ◊Irangate scandal, Poindexter was forced to resign in 1986, along with his assistant, Oliver North.

poinsettia /pɔɪn'setiə/ n. or **Christmas flower** a winter-flowering shrub *Euphorbia pulcherrima*, with large red leaves encircling small greenish-yellow flowers. It is native to Mexico and tropical America and is a popular houseplant in North America and Europe. [from J R *Poinsett*, American ambassador to Mexico (1799–1851)]

point n. 1. the sharp or tapered end of something; the tip or extremity. 2. in geometry, that which has position but no magnitude (e.g. the intersection of two lines). 3. a dot; this used as a punctuation mark; a dot or small stroke used in Semitic languages to indicate vowels or distinguish consonants; a decimal point. 4. a particular place or spot; an exact moment; a stage or degree of progress or increase; the level of temperature at which a change occurs. 5. each of the 32 directions marked on the compass; a corresponding direction towards the horizon. 6. a unit of measurement or value or scoring. 7. a separate item or detail. 8. a distinctive or significant feature; the essential thing; the thing intended or under discussion; the salient feature of a story, joke, remark etc. 9. effectiveness, purpose, value. 10. (usually in *plural*) a tapering movable rail by which a train may pass from one line to another. 11. an electrical socket, a power point. 12. (usually in *plural*) an electrical contact device in the distributor of an internal-combustion engine. 13. in cricket, a fieldsman on the off side near the batsman; his position. —*v.t./i.* 1. to direct or aim; to be directed or aimed; to direct attention, to indicate. 2. to provide with a point or points. 3. to give force to (words or actions). 4. to fill the joints of (brickwork etc.) with smoothed mortar or cement. —**at** or **on the point of,** on the verge of. **beside the point,** irrelevant, irrelevantly. **in point of,** as a matter of (fact etc.). **make a point of,** to indicate the necessity of; to call particular attention to (an action). **point duty,** (of a policeman etc.) being stationed at a particular point to control traffic. **point of no return,** the point in a journey or enterprise at which it becomes essential or more practical to continue to the end. **point of view,** a position from which a thing is viewed; a way of considering a matter. **point out,** to indicate, to draw attention to. **point-to-point** n. a horse race over a course defined only by certain landmarks. **point up,** to emphasize. **to the point,** relevant, relevantly. **up to a point,** to some extent but not completely. [from French from Latin *punctum, puncta* (*pungere* = prick)]

point-blank adj. 1. (of a shot) aimed or fired at a range very close to the target; (of range) very close. 2. (of a remark etc.) blunt, direct. —adv. 1. at point-blank range. 2. bluntly, directly.

pointe n. in dance, the tip of the toe. A dancer *sur les pointes* is dancing on his or her toes in blocked shoes, as popularized by Marie ◊Taglioni in 1832. [French = toe of shoe]

pointed adj. 1. sharpened or tapering to a point. 2. (of a remark or manner etc.) clearly aimed at a particular person or thing; emphasized. —**pointedly** adv.

Pointe-Noire /'pwænt 'nwa:/ chief port of the Congo, formerly (1950–58) the capital; population (1984) 297,000. Industries include oil refining and shipbuilding.

pointer n. 1. a thing that points, e.g. the index hand of a gauge etc.; a rod for pointing to the features on a chart etc. 2. (*colloquial*) a hint. 3. a dog of a breed that on scenting game stands rigid looking towards it. Pointers are often white mixed with black, tan, or dark brown. They stand about 60 cm/2 ft tall, and weigh about 28 kg/62 lbs.

pointillism /'pwæntɪlɪzəm/ n. 1. a technique in oil painting developed in the 1880s by the Neo-Impressionist Seurat. He used small dabs of pure colour laid side by side to create an impression of shimmering light when viewed from a distance. 2. in music, a form of 1950s serialism in which melody and harmony are replaced by complexes of isolated tones. —**pointillist** n. [from French *pointiller* = mark with dots]

pointing n. the cement filling the joints of brickwork; the facing produced by this.

pointless adj. without point or force; lacking purpose or meaning. —**pointlessly** adv.

point of sale (POS) in business premises, the point where a sale is transacted, for example, a supermarket checkout. In conjunction with electronic funds transfer, point of sale is part of the terminology of 'cashless shopping', enabling buyers to transfer funds directly from their bank accounts to the shop's (◊EFTPOS).

poise /pɔɪz/ v.t./i. 1. to balance or be balanced. 2. to hold suspended or supported. 3. to carry (one's head etc.) in a specified way. —n. 1. balance, the way something is poised. 2. a dignified and self-assured manner. [from Old French from Latin *pensare* (*pendere* = weigh)]

poison /'pɔɪzən/ n. 1. a substance that when introduced into or absorbed by a living organism causes death or injury, especially one that kills by rapid action even in a small quantity. 2. a harmful influence. —v.t. 1. to administer poison to; to kill, injure, or infect with poison; (especially in *past participle*) to smear (a weapon) with poison. 2. to corrupt or pervert (a person or the mind). 3. to spoil or destroy (a person's pleasure etc.). —**poison ivy,** a North American climbing plant *Rhus toxicodendron* secreting an irritant oil from the leaves. **poison pen,** an anonymous writer of libellous or scurrilous letters; the practice of writing these. **poison pill,** in business, a tactic to avoid hostile takeover by making the target unattractive. For example, a company may give a certain class of shareholders the right to have their shares redeemed at a very good price in the event of the company being taken over, thus involving the potential predator in considerable extra cost. —**poisoner** n., **poisonous** adj. [from Old French from Latin *potus* = having drunk]

Poisson /pwæsn/ Siméon Denis 1781–1840. French applied mathematician. In probability theory he formulated the **Poisson distribution**, which is widely used in probability calculations. He published four treatises and several papers on aspects of physics, including mechanics, heat, electricity and magnetism, elasticity, and astronomy.

Poitevin /'pɔɪtəvɪn/ adj. in English history, relating to the reigns of King John and King Henry III. [from the region of France S of the Loire (Poitou), which was controlled by the English for most of this period]

Poitier /pwɒtie/ Sidney 1924– . US actor and film director, the first black actor to become a star in Hollywood. His films as an actor included *In the Heat of the Night* 1967 and, as director, *Stir Crazy* 1980.

Poitou-Charentes /pwa:'tu: ʃæ'rɒnt/ region of western central France, comprising the *départements* of Charente, Charente-Maritime, Deux-Sèvres, and Vienne; **capital** Poitiers; **area** 25,800 sq km/9,959 sq mi; **population** (1986) 1,584,000; **products** dairy products, wheat, chemicals, metal goods; brandy is made at Cognac; **history** the area was contested by the English and French until the end of the Hundred Years' War, when it was incorporated into France by Charles II.

poke[1] v.t./i. 1. to thrust with the end of a finger or a stick etc. 2. to stir (a fire) with a poker. 3. to produce (a hole etc.) by poking. 4. to thrust or be thrust forward, to protrude. 5. to pry or search. 6. to potter. —n. the act of poking; a thrust or nudge. —**poke fun at,** to ridicule. **poke one's nose into,** to pry or intrude into. [from Middle Dutch and Middle Low German *poken*]

poke[2] n. a bag, a sack (*dialect* except in *a pig in a poke*). [from Old French]

poker[1] n. a stiff metal rod with a handle, for stirring a fire.

poker[2] n. a card game of US origin, in which two to eight people play (usually for stakes), and try to obtain a hand of five cards ranking higher than those of their opponents. The one with the best scoring hand wins the central pool. —**poker face,** an impassive countenance appropriate to a poker player; a person with this. [compare German *pochen* = to brag]

poky /'pəʊkɪ/ adj. (of a room etc.) small and cramped. —**pokiness** n.

Poland /'pəʊlənd/ Republic of; country in E Europe, bounded to the E by the USSR, to the S by Czechoslovakia, and to the W by Germany; **area** 312,700 sq km/120,733 sq mi; **capital** Warsaw; **physical** part of the great plain of Europe; Vistula, Oder, and Neisse rivers; Sudeten, Tatra,

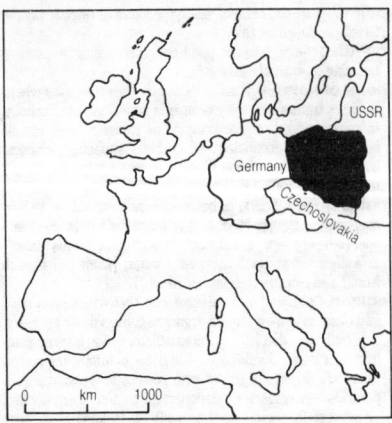

Poland

and Carpathian mountains; **head of state** Lech Walesa from 1990; **political system** socialist pluralist republic; **exports** coal, softwood timber, chemicals, machinery, ships; **population** (1990 est) 38,363,000; **language** Polish; **recent history** Poland was revived as an independent republic in 1918; occupied by the Germans 1939–44; the Polish boundaries were redrawn at the Potsdam Conference in 1945. The Communist People's Republic was proclaimed in 1947. Solidarity emerged as a free trade union in 1980 following the Gdańsk riots. Martial law was imposed by Gen Jaruzelski 1981–83. A referendum on economic reform was rejected in 1985. In 1988, following Solidarity strikes and demonstrations, pay increases were granted and the government held a church–state–union conference in 1989 when a new 'socialist pluralist' constitution was drawn up. Solidarity swept the board in national assembly elections in 1989; the Social Democrat Party and breakaway Union of Social Democrats came to power and Lech Walesa was elected head of state in 1990.

Polanski /pə'lænski/ Roman 1933– . Polish film director, born in Paris. He suffered a traumatic childhood in Nazi-occupied Poland, and later his wife, actress Sharon Tate, was the victim of murder by the Charles Manson 'family'. His tragic personal life is reflected in a fascination with horror and violence in his work. His films include *Repulsion* 1965, *Cul de Sac* 1966, *Rosemary's Baby* 1968, *Tess* 1979, and *Frantic* 1988.

polar /'pəulə/ *adj.* 1. of or near either pole of the Earth or the celestial sphere. 2. having electric or magnetic polarity. 3. directly opposite in character. —**polar bear,** a large white bear *Thalarctos maritimus* living in Arctic regions. Its skin is black to conserve 80–90% of the solar energy trapped and channelled down the hollow hairs of its fur. **polar circles,** the parallels at 23° 27' from the poles. [from French from Latin from Greek *polos* = axis]

polar coordinates in mathematics, a pair of coordinates used to define the position of a point in terms of its distance *r* from a fixed point (the origin) and its angle θ to a fixed line or axis. The coordinates of the point are $(r, θ)$.

Polaris /pə'lɑːrɪs/ *n.* or **Pole Star** or **North Star** the bright star closest to the north celestial pole, and the brightest star in the constellation Ursa Minor. Its position is indicated by the 'pointers' in Ursa Major. Polaris is a yellow ◊supergiant about 700 light years away.

polariscope /pə'lærɪskəup/ *n.* an instrument for showing the polarization of light or for viewing objects in polarized light.

polarity /pəu'lærɪtɪ/ *n.* 1. the tendency of a magnet etc. to point with its extremities to the Earth's magnetic poles, or of a body to lie with its axis in a particular direction. 2. the possession of two poles having contrary qualities. 3. the electrical condition of a body as positive or negative.

polarize /'pəulərɑɪz/ *v.t./i.* 1. to restrict the vibrations of (light waves etc.) so that they have different amplitudes in different planes. Light is said to be polarized when the vibrations take place in one particular plane. Polarized

light is used to test the strength of sugar solutions, to measure stresses in transparent materials, and to prevent glare. 2. to give electric or magnetic polarity to. 3. to set or become set at opposite extremes of opinion. —**polarization** /-'zeɪʃən/ *n.*

Polaroid /'pəulərɔɪd/ *n.* trade name of a material in thin sheets polarizing light passing through it; a camera able to develop a negative and produce a print within a short time of exposure. Invented by Edwin Land in the USA in 1947, the original camera produced black-and-white prints in about one minute. Modern cameras can produce black-and-white prints in a few seconds, and colour prints in less than a minute. An advanced model has automatic focusing and exposure. It ejects a piece of film on paper immediately after the picture has been taken. The film consists of layers of emulsion and colour dyes together with a pod of chemical developer. When the film is ejected the pod bursts and processing occurs in the light, producing a paper-backed print.

polar reversal the changeover in polarity of the Earth's magnetic poles. Studies of the magnetism retained in rocks at the time of their formation have shown that in the past the Earth's north magnetic pole repeatedly became the south magnetic pole, and vice versa.

polder /'pəuldə/ *n.* a piece of low-lying land reclaimed from the sea or a river, especially in the Netherlands. [from Middle Dutch]

pole[1] /pəul/ *n.* 1. a long, slender, rounded piece of wood or metal, especially one used as part of a supporting structure or in propelling a barge etc. 2. (as a measure) a perch (as ◊perch[1] sense 3). —**pole jump** *or* **pole vault,** a vault over a high bar with the help of a pole held in the hands. **up the pole,** (*slang*) in a difficulty; crazy. [Old English from Latin *palus* = stake]

pole[2] *n.* 1. either of the ends of the Earth's axis of rotation; either of two points in the celestial sphere about which the stars appear to revolve; the North Pole or South Pole. 2. each of the two opposite points on the surface of a magnet at which the magnetic forces are concentrated. 3. each of the two terminals (positive and negative) of an electric cell or battery etc. 4. each of two opposed principles. —**be poles apart,** to differ greatly. **Pole Star,** ◊Polaris, the northern pole star. [from Latin from Greek *polos* = axis]

Pole *n.* a native or inhabitant of Poland. [German from Polish]

Pole Reginald 1500–1558. English cardinal from 1536, who returned from Rome as papal legatee on the accession of Mary I in order to readmit England to the Catholic Church. He succeeded Cranmer as archbishop of Canterbury in 1556.

poleaxe *n.* 1. a battleaxe with a long handle. 2. a butcher's axe with a hammer at the back. —*v.t.* to slaughter or strike with a poleaxe. [from Middle Dutch or Middle Low German]

polecat /'pəulkæt/ *n.* 1. a small dark-brown mammal of the weasel family, especially *Mustela putorius*, with a brown back and dark belly. The body is about 50 cm/20 in long and it has a strong smell. It is native to Asia, Europe, and North America. 2. (*US*) a skunk.

polemic /pə'lemɪk/ *n.* a verbal attack; a controversial discussion. —*adj.* or **polemical** controversial, involving dispute. —**polemically** *adv.* [from Latin from Greek *polemos* = war]

polemics /pə'lemɪks/ *n.pl.* the art or practice of controversial discussion.

police /pə'liːs/ *n.* 1. a civil force responsible for maintaining public order; (as *plural*) its members. In the UK, the police force is responsible to the Home Office, with 56 autonomous police forces, generally organized on a county basis; mutual aid is given in circumstances such as mass picketing in the 1984–85 miners' strike, but there is no national police force or police riot unit (such as the French CRS riot squad). The predecessors of these forces were the ineffective medieval watch and London's Bow Street runners, introduced in 1749 by Henry ◊Fielding which formed a model for the London police force established by Robert ◊Peel's government in 1829 (hence 'peelers' or 'bobbies'); the system was introduced throughout the country from 1856. 2. a force with a similar function of enforcing the regulations of an organization etc. —*v.t.* 1. to maintain order in (a place) by means of police; to provide with police. 2. to keep order in, to control. —**police**

state, a totalitarian state regulated by means of a national police force controlling citizens' activities. **police station,** an office of a local police force. [French from Latin from Greek *politeia*]

Police Complaints Authority in the UK, an independent group of a dozen people set up under the Police and Criminal Evidence Act 1984 to supervise the investigation of serious complaints against the police by members of the public.

policeman *n.* (*plural* **policemen**) a man who is a member of a police force. —**policewoman** *n.fem.* (*plural* **policewomen**).

policy[1] /'pɒlɪsɪ/ *n.* **1.** a course of action adopted by a government or party or person. **2.** prudent conduct, sagacity. [from Old French from Latin from Greek *politeia*]

policy[2] *n.* a contract of insurance; a document containing this. [from French = bill of lading, ultimately from Greek *apodeixis* = evidence]

Policy Research, Institute for a British left-wing think-tank established in 1988 with Baroness Blackstone as chair of the board of trustees. It was designed to set the agenda for a future Labour government and challenge the Conservative government's belief in the advantages of the free market economy.

polio /'pəʊlɪəʊ/ (*colloquial*) abbreviation of poliomyelitis.

poliomyelitis /pəʊlɪəʊmaɪɪ'laɪtɪs/ *n.* an infectious viral disease which may cause temporary or permanent localized paralysis as a result of the infection and death of nerve cells in the spinal column or brain stem. The disease used to be known as infantile paralysis. The World Health Organization expects that polio will be eradicated by the year 2000. [from Greek *polios* = grey and *muelos* = marrow]

polish /'pɒlɪʃ/ *v.t./i.* **1.** to make or become smooth and glossy by rubbing. **2.** (especially in *past participle*) to refine or improve, to add finishing touches to. —*n.* **1.** a substance used for polishing things. **2.** smoothness or glossiness produced by friction. **3.** refinement, elegance. —**polish off,** to finish off quickly. —**polisher** *n.* [from Old French from Latin *polire*]

Polish /'pəʊlɪʃ/ *adj.* of Poland or the Poles or their language. —*n.* the language of Poland, a member of the Slavonic branch of the Indo-European language family. Polish is written in the Roman and not the Cyrillic alphabet and its standard form is based on the dialect of Poznań in W Poland.

Polish Corridor a strip of land designated under the Treaty of ◊Versailles in 1919 to give Poland access to the Baltic. It cut off East Prussia from the rest of Germany. When Poland took over the southern part of East Prussia in 1945, it was absorbed.

Politburo /'pɒlɪtbjʊərəʊ/ *n.* a subcommittee (known as the Praesidium 1952–66) of the Central Committee of the Communist Party in the USSR and some other communist states, which lays down party policy. It consists of about 12 voting and 6 candidate (nonvoting) members. [from Russian = political bureau]

polite /pə'laɪt/ *adj.* **1.** having good manners, socially correct. **2.** cultivated, cultured; refined, elegant. —**politely** *adv.*, **politeness** *n.* [from Latin *politus*]

Politian /pɒ'lɪʃən/ (Angelo Poliziano) Pen name of Angelo Ambrogini 1454–1494. Italian poet, playwright, and exponent of humanist ideals. He was tutor to Lorenzo de ◊Medici's children, and professor at the University of Florence; he wrote commentaries and essays on Classical authors.

politic /'pɒlɪtɪk/ *adj.* (of an action) judicious, expedient; (of a person) prudent, sagacious. —*v.i.* (**-ck-**) to engage in politics. [from Old French from Latin from Greek *politēs* = citizen]

political /pə'lɪtɪkəl/ *adj.* **1.** of or engaged in politics. **2.** of or affecting the state or its government; of public affairs. **3.** relating to a person's or organization's status or influence. —**political economy,** the study of the economic problems of government. **political geography,** that dealing with the boundaries and possessions of states. **political prisoner,** a person imprisoned for a political offence. **political science,** the study of the factors involved in politics; the scientific analysis of political activity and behaviour. —**politically** *adv.* [from Latin]

political action committee (PAC) in the USA, any organization that raises funds for political candidates and in return seeks to commit them to a particular policy. It also spends money on changing public opinion. There were about 3,500 PACs in 1990, and they controlled some 25% of all funds spent in elections for ◊Congress.

politician /pɒlɪ'tɪʃən/ *n.* one who is engaged in politics, especially as a profession; one who is skilled in political affairs.

politicize /pə'lɪtɪsaɪz/ *v.t./i.* **1.** to engage in or talk politics. **2.** to give a political character to. —**politicization** /-'zeɪʃən/ *n.*

politics /'pɒlɪtɪks/ *n.pl.* **1.** (also treated as *singular*) the science and art of government; political affairs or life. **2.** political principles or practice.

polity /'pɒlɪtɪ/ *n.* **1.** the form or process of civil government. **2.** an organized society, a state. [from Latin from Greek *politeia* (*politēs* = citizen from *polis* = city)]

Polk /pəʊk/ James Knox 1795–1849. 11th president of the USA 1845–49, a Democrat, born in North Carolina. He allowed Texas admission to the Union, and forced the war on Mexico that resulted in the annexation of California and New Mexico.

polka /'pɒlkə/ *n.* a folk dance in lively two-four time. The basic step is a hop followed by three short steps. It originated in Bohemia and spread with German immigrants to the USA, becoming a style of Texas country music. —*v.i.* to dance the polka. —**polka dot,** a round dot as one of many forming a regular pattern on a textile fabric etc. [French and German from Czech = half step]

poll /pəʊl/ *n.* **1.** voting at an election; the result of voting; the number of persons voting or of votes recorded. **2.** an opinion poll (see ◊opinion). **3.** the head; the crown or top of the head. —*v.t./i.* **1.** to vote at an election. **2.** (of a candidate) to receive as votes. **3.** to cut off the horns of (cattle) or the top of (a tree etc.).

pollack /'pɒlæk/ *n.* a marine fish *Pollachius pollachius* of the cod family, growing to 75 cm/2.5 ft, and found inshore. [from earlier *podlock*]

Pollaiuolo /pɒlaɪʊ:'əʊləʊ/ Antonio *c.*1432–1498 and Piero *c.*1441–1496. Italian artists, active in Florence. Both brothers were painters, sculptors, goldsmiths, engravers, and designers. Antonio is said to have been the first Renaissance artist to make a serious study of anatomy. The *Martyrdom of St Sebastian* 1475 (National Gallery, London) is considered a joint work.

pollard /'pɒləd/ *n.* **1.** an animal that has cast or lost its horns; an ox, sheep, or goat of a hornless breed. **2.** a tree polled so as to produce a close rounded head of young branches. Pollarding is often practised on willows, where the new branches or 'poles' are cut at intervals of a year or more, and used for fencing and firewood. It is also used to restrict the height of many street trees. See also ◊coppice. —*v.t.* to make (a tree) into a pollard.

pollen /'pɒlən/ *n.* the grains of ◊seed plants that contain the male gametes. In ◊angiosperms pollen is produced within ◊anthers; in most ◊gymnosperms it is produced in male cones. A pollen grain is typically yellow and, when mature, has a hard outer wall. Pollen of insect-pollinated plants (see ◊pollination) is often sticky and spiny and larger than the smooth, light grains produced by wind-pollinated species. —**pollen analysis,** ◊palynology. **pollen count,** an index of the amount of pollen in the air, published as a warning to those allergic to it. **pollen tube,** an outgrowth from a pollen grain that grows towards the ◊ovule, following germination of the grain on the ◊stigma. In angiosperms the pollen tube reaches the ovule by growing down through the ◊style (sense 7), carrying the male gametes inside. The gametes are discharged into the ovule and one fertilizes the egg cell. [Latin = fine flour]

pollination /'pɒlɪneʃən/ *n.* the process by which fertilization occurs in the sexual reproduction of higher plants. The male gametes are contained in ◊pollen grains, which must be transferred from the ◊anther to the ◊stigma in ◊angiosperms, and from the male cone to the female cone in ◊gymnosperms. Self-pollination occurs when pollen is transferred to a stigma of the same flower, or to another flower on the same plant; cross-pollination occurs when pollen is transferred to another plant. This involves external pollen-carrying agents, such as wind (see ◊anemophily), water, insects, birds (see ◊ornithophily), bats, and other small mammals. —**pollinate** /'pɒlɪneɪt/ *v.t.*, **pollinator** *n.*

pollinium *n.* (*plural* **pollinia**) a group of pollen grains that is transported as a single unit during pollination. Pollinia are common in orchids.

pollock variant of ◊pollack.

Pollock /ˈpɒlək/ Jackson 1912–1956. US painter, a pioneer of Abstract Expressionism and the foremost exponent of the technique ◊action painting, a style he developed around 1946.

pollster /ˈpəʊlstə/ *n.* a person who organizes an opinion poll.

poll tax a tax levied on every individual, without reference to their income or property. Being simple to administer, it was among the earliest sorts of tax (introduced in England in 1377), but because of its indiscriminate nature (it is a regressive tax, in that it falls proportionately more on poorer people) it has often proved unpopular. Poll tax or the **community charge** was introduced by the UK Conservative government in Scotland on 1 April 1989, and in England and Wales on 1 April 1990, replacing the property-based local taxation (previously ◊rates). Amendments to the tax were considered in the wake of widespread opposition and regional demonstrations, notably the Central London anti-poll tax rally in March 1990, which culminated in police–civilian violence and high-street looting. Its abolition was announced in March 1991.

pollute /pəˈluːt/ *v.t.* **1.** to make foul or impure. **2.** to corrupt. —**pollutant** *adj. & n.*, **pollution** *n.* the harmful effect on the environment of by-products of human activity, principally industrial and agricultural processes, for example noise, smoke, car emissions, chemical effluents in seas and rivers, pesticides, sewage, and household waste. Pollution contributes to the ◊greenhouse effect. [from Latin *polluere*]

Pollux 1. in Greek mythology, the twin brother of Castor (see ◊Castor and Pollux/Polydeuces). **2.** in astronomy, the brightest star in the constellation Gemini, and the 17th brightest star in the sky. Pollux is a yellowish star with a true luminosity 35 times that of the Sun. It is 35 light years away.

polo /ˈpəʊləʊ/ *n.* a four-a-side game resembling hockey, played on horseback with a long-handled mallet (polo stick). A typical game lasts about an hour, divided into 'chukkas' of 7½ minutes. The small ball is struck with the side of the mallet through goals at each end of the field. It originated in Iran, spread to India, and was first played in England in 1869. —**polo neck**, a high, round, turned-over collar on a jumper etc. [Kashmir dialect = ball]

Polo Marco 1254–1324. Venetian traveller and writer. He travelled overland to China 1271–75, and served the emperor Kublai Khan until he returned to Europe by sea 1292–95. He was captured while fighting for Venice against Genoa, and, while in prison 1296–98, dictated an account of his travels.

I have not told half of what I saw.
Marco Polo
(last words)

polonaise /pɒləˈneɪz/ *n.* a Polish dance in stately three-four time, that was common in 18th-century Europe; music for this. Chopin developed the polonaise as a pianistic form. [French = Polish]

polonium /pəˈləʊnɪəm/ *n.* a radioactive, metallic element, symbol Po, atomic number 84, relative atomic mass 210. Polonium occurs in nature in small amounts and was isolated from ◊pitchblende in 1898. It is the element having the largest number of isotopes (27) and is 5,000 times as radioactive as radium, liberating considerable amounts of heat. It was the first element to have its radioactive properties recognized and investigated. [from Latin *Polonia* = Poland (native country of its discoverer, Marie Curie)]

polony /pəˈləʊnɪ/ *n.* a sausage of partly cooked pork etc. [apparently for *Bologna* sausage]

Pol Pot /ˈpɒl ˈpɒt/ (also known as **Saloth Sar, Tol Saut,** and **Pol Porth**) 1925–. Cambodian politician and Communist party leader; a member of the anti-French resistance under Ho Chi Minh in the 1940s. As leader of the Khmer Rouge, he overthrew the government in 1975 and proclaimed Democratic Kampuchea with himself as premier. His policies were to evacuate cities and put

people to work in the countryside. The Khmer Rouge also carried out a systematic large-scale extermination of the Western-influenced educated and middle classes (3–4 million) before the regime was overthrown by a Vietnamese invasion in 1979. Pol Pot continued to help lead the Khmer Rouge until their withdrawal in 1989; in the same year he resigned from his last position within the Khmer Rouge.

poltergeist /ˈpɒltəgaɪst/ *n.* a mischievous ghost or spirit manifesting itself by making a noisy disturbance. [German *poltern* = create disturbance and *geist* = ghost]

poltroon /pɒlˈtruːn/ *n.* (*archaic*) a spiritless coward. —**poltroonery** *n.* [from French from Italian *poltro* = sluggard]

poly /ˈpɒlɪ/ (*plural* **polys**) (*colloquial*) abbreviation of polytechnic.

poly- prefix meaning **1.** many (e.g. *polygamy*). **2.** polymerized (e.g. *polyester*). [from Greek *polus* = much]

polyandry /ˈpɒliændrɪ/ *n.* a system whereby a woman has more than one husband at the same time. It is found in many parts of the world, for example, in Madagascar, Malaysia, and certain Pacific isles, and among certain Inuit and South American Indian groups. In Tibet and parts of India, polyandry takes the form of the marriage of one woman to several brothers, as a means of keeping intact a family's heritage and property. —**polyandrous** /-ˈændrəs/ *adj.* [from Greek *anēr* = man, husband]

polyanthus /pɒliˈænθəs/ *n.* a cultivated variety of ◊primrose, with multiple flowers on one stalk, bred from hybridized primulas in a variety of colours. [from Greek *anthos* = flower]

Polybius /pəˈlɪbɪəs/ *c.*201–120 BC. Greek politician and historian. He was involved with the ◊Achaean League against the Romans and, following the defeat of the Macedonians at Pydna in 168 BC, he was taken as a political hostage to Rome. He returned to Greece in 151 and was present at the capture of Carthage by his friend Scipio in 146. His history of Rome in 40 books, covering the years 220–146, has largely disappeared.

polychlorinated biphenyl (PCB) any of a group of chlorinated isomers of biphenal, $(C_6H_5)_2$. They are dangerous industrial chemicals, valuable for their fire-resisting qualities. They constitute an environmental hazard because of their persistent toxicity. Since 1973 their use has been limited by international agreement.

polychromatic /pɒlɪkrəˈmætɪk/ *adj.* **1.** many-coloured. **2.** (of radiation) consisting of more than one wavelength. —**polychromatically** *adv.*

polychrome /ˈpɒlɪkrəʊm/ *adj.* in many colours. —*n.* a polychrome work of art. [French from Greek *khrōma* = colour]

polyester /pɒliˈestə/ *n.* a synthetic resin formed by the ◊condensation of polyhydric alcohols (alcohols containing more than one hydroxyl group) with dibasic acids (acids containing two replaceable hydrogen atoms). Polyesters are thermosetting ◊plastics, used in making synthetic fibres, such as Dacron and Terylene, and constructional plastics. With glass fibre added as reinforcement, polyesters are used in car bodies and boat hulls.

polyethylene *n.* a polymer of the gas ethylene (technically called ethene, C_2H_4). It is a tough, white translucent waxy thermoplastic (which means it can be repeatedly softened by heating). It is used for packaging, bottles, toys, electric cable, pipes and tubing. In the UK it is better known under the trademark Polythene.

polygamy /pəˈlɪgəmɪ/ *n.* the practice of having more than one spouse at the same time. It is found among many peoples, and is common in Africa. Normally it is confined to chiefs and nobles, as among ancient Egyptians, Teutons, Irish, and Slavs. Islam limits the number of legal wives a man may have to four. Certain Christian sects, for example, the Anabaptists of Münster, Germany, and the Mormons, have practised polygamy. —**polygamist** *n.*, **polygamous** *adj.* [from French from Greek *gamos* = marriage]

polyglot /ˈpɒlɪglɒt/ *adj.* knowing or using or written in several languages. —*n.* a polyglot person. [from French from Greek *glōtta* = tongue]

polygon /ˈpɒlɪgən/ *n.* in geometry, a plane (two-dimensional) figure with three or more straight-line sides. Common polygons have their own names, which define the number of sides (for example, triangle, quadrilateral,

polygon

	number of sides	sum of interior angles (degrees)
triangle	3	180
quadrilateral	4	360
pentagon	5	540
hexagon	6	720
heptagon	7	900
octagon	8	1,080
decagon	10	1,440
duodecagon	12	1,800
icosagon	20	3,240

pentagon). —**polygonal** /pə'lɪgənəl/ *adj.* [from Latin from Greek *-gōnos* = angled]

polygraph /'pɒlɪgrɑːf/ *n.* or **lie detector** an instrument that records graphically certain body activities, such as thoracic and abdominal respiration, blood pressure, pulse rate, and galvanic skin response (changes in electrical resistance of the skin). Marked changes in these activities when a person answers a question may indicate that the person is lying. [from Greek]

polygyny /pə'lɪdʒɪnɪ/ *n.* polygamy in which one man has more than one wife. —**polygynous** *adj.* [from Greek *gunē* = woman, wife]

polyhedron /pɒli'hiːdrən/ *n.* (*plural* **polyhedra**) in geometry, a solid figure with four or more plane faces. The more faces there are on a polyhedron, the more closely it approximates to a sphere. —**polyhedral** *adj.* [from Greek *hedra* = base]

Polykleitos /pɒli'klaɪtɒs/ 5th century BC. Greek sculptor whose *Spear Carrier* 450–440 BC (Roman copies survive) exemplifies the naturalism and harmonious proportions of his work. He created the legendary colossal statue of *Hera* in Argos, in ivory and gold.

polymath /'pɒlɪmæθ/ *n.* a person with wide knowledge of many subjects. [from Greek *manthanō* = learn]

polymer /'pɒlɪmə/ *n.* a compound made up of large, long-chain molecules composed of many repeated simple units (**monomers**). There are many polymers, both natural (cellulose, chitin, lignin) and synthetic (polyethylene and nylon, types of plastic). Synthetic polymers belong to two groups: thermosoftening and thermosetting (see ◊plastic). —**polymeric** /-'merɪk/ *adj.* [German from Greek *polumeros* = having many parts]

polymerization /'pɒlɪməraɪzeɪʃən/ *n.* the chemical union of two or more (usually small) molecules of the same kind to form a new compound. —**polymerize** /'pɒlɪməraɪz/ *v.t./i.*

polymorphic /pɒli'mɔːfɪk/ *adj.* or **polymorphous** /-əs/ varying in individuals, passing through successive variations. [from Greek *morphē* = form]

polymorphism *n.* 1. in genetics, the coexistence of several distinctly different types in a ◊population. Examples include the different blood groups in humans and different colour forms in some butterflies. 2. in minerology, the ability of a substance to adopt different internal structures and external forms, in response to different conditions of temperature and/or pressure. For example, diamond and graphite are both forms of the element carbon, but they have very different properties and appearance.

Polynesia /pɒli'niːzɪə/ islands of Oceania E of 170° E latitude, including Hawaii, Kiribati, Tuvalu, Fiji, Tonga, Tokelau, Samoa, Cook Islands, and French Polynesia. —**Polynesian,** of Polynesia; an inhabitant of the Polynesian islands. Polynesians, who include the ◊Maori of New Zealand, are probably of Asian origin, and are distinct from the Melanesians, with whom there has been a degree of mixture.

Polynesian languages see ◊Malayo-Polynesian.

polynomial /pɒli'nəʊmɪəl/ *adj.* (of an algebraic expression) consisting of three or more terms. —*n.* in mathematics, an algebraic expression that has only one ◊variable (denoted by a letter). A polynomial of degree one, that is, whose highest ◊power (sense 13) of x is 1, as in $2x + 1$, is called a linear polynomial; $3x^2 + 2x + 1$ is quadratic; $4x^3 + 3x^2 + 2x + 1$ is cubic. [after *binomial*]

polyp /'pɒlɪp/ *n.* or **polypus** 1. a simple organism with a tube-shaped body, e.g. an individual coelenterate. 2. a small 'talked' benign tumour, most usually found on mucous membrane of the nose or bowels. Intestinal polyps are usually removed, since some have been found to be precursors of cancer. [from French from Latin from Greek *pous* = foot]

polypeptide /pɒli'peptaɪd/ *n.* a peptide formed by combination of many amino acids.

polyphonic /pɒli'fɒnɪk/ *adj.* 1. in music, combining two or more 'voices' or parts, each with an individual melody. 2. contrapuntal. 3. (of a letter or symbol) representing more than one sound. —**polyphony** /pə'lɪfənɪ/ *n.* [from Greek *phōnē* = voice, sound]

polyploid /'pɒlɪplɔɪd/ *adj.* in genetics, possessing three or more sets of chromosomes in cases where the normal complement is two sets (◊diploid). Polyploidy arises spontaneously and is common in plants (mainly among angiosperms), but rare in animals. Many crop plants are natural polyploids, including wheat, which has four sets of chromosomes per cell (durum wheat) or six sets (common wheat). Plant breeders can induce the formation of polyploids by treatment with a chemical, colchicine. —*n.* a polyploid cell or organism. [German, after *haploid*]

polysaccharide *n.* a long-chain ◊carbohydrate made up of hundreds or thousands of linked simple sugars (monosaccharides) such as glucose and closely related molecules.

polystyrene /pɒli'staɪriːn/ *n.* a kind of plastic, a polymer of styrene.

polysyliabic /pɒlɪsɪ'læbɪk/ *adj.* 1. having many syllables. 2. characterized by polysyllables.

polysyllable /'pɒlɪsɪləbəl/ *n.* a polysyllabic word.

polytechnic /pɒli'teknɪk/ *n.* a polytechnic institution, especially a college, for further education offering courses mainly at degree level and concentrating on full-time vocational courses, although many polytechnics provide a wide range of part-time courses at advanced levels. From April 1989 the 29 polytechnics in England became independent corporations. —*adj.* giving instruction in many (including vocational) subjects at an advanced level. [from French from Greek *tekhnē* = art]

polytheism /'pɒliθiːɪzəm/ *n.* the belief in or worship of many gods, as opposed to monotheism (belief in one god). Examples are the religions of ancient Egypt, Babylon, Greece, Rome, Mexico, and modern Hinduism. —**polytheist** *n.*, **polytheistic** /-'ɪstɪk/ *adj.* [from French from Greek *theos* = god]

polythene /'pɒliθiːn/ *n.* a tough, light plastic. [from *polyethylene*]

polyunsaturate *n.* a type of triglyceride (◊fat or oil) in which the long carbon chains of the ◊fatty acids contain several double bonds. —**polyunsaturated** *adj.* of this kind of fat or oil, not associated with the formation of cholesterol in the blood.

polyurethane /pɒli'juərəθeɪn/ *n.* a synthetic resin or plastic used especially as foam, as an electrical insulator, and in varnish. [from *poly-* and *urea* and *ethane*]

polyvinyl chloride /pɒli'vaɪnɪl/ a vinyl plastic used as an insulation or as a fabric.

pom *n.* 1. a Pomeranian. 2. (*Australian* and *New Zealand slang*) abbreviation of ◊pommy.

pomace /'pʌmɪs/ *n.* the mass of crushed apples in cider making. [from Latin = cider (*pomum* = apple)]

pomade /pə'mɑːd/ *n.* a scented ointment for the hair and the skin of the head. [from French from Italian]

pomander /pə'mændə/ *n.* a ball of mixed aromatic substances; a round container for this. [from Old French from Latin = apple of ambergris]

pome *n.* a type of ◊pseudocarp, or false fruit, typical of certain plants belonging to the Rosaceae family. The outer skin and fleshy tissues are developed after fertilization, and the five ◊carpels (the true fruit) form the pome's core, which surrounds the seeds. Examples of pomes are apples, pears, and quinces.

pomegranate /'pɒmɪgrænɪt/ *n.* 1. a tropical fruit, with a tough rind and reddish pulp enclosing many seeds, that can be eaten fresh or made into wine. 2. the tree *Punica granatum*, family Punicaceae. It is native to SW Asia but cultivated widely in tropical and subtropical areas. [from Old French from Latin, literally = many-seeded apple]

pomelo /'pʌmɪləʊ/ *n.* (*plural* **pomelos**) a shaddock or grapefruit.

Pomeranian /pɒməˈreɪnɪən/ n. a small breed of dog, about 15 cm/6 in, and 3 kg/6.5 lbs. It has long, straight hair with a neck frill, and the tail is carried over the back. [from *Pomerania*, region in Germany and Poland]

pomfret cake /ˈpʌmfrɪt, ˈpɒ-/ a small, round, flat liquorice sweet. [from Pontefract (earlier *Pomfret*) in West Yorkshire, England]

pommel /ˈpʌməl/ n. 1. a knob, especially at the end of a sword hilt. 2. the upward projecting front of a saddle. 3. either of pair of handgrips fitted to a vaulting horse. —v.t. (-ll-) to pummel. [from Old French *pomel*, diminutive from Latin *pomum* = apple]

pommy n. or **pommie** (*Australian* and *New Zealand slang*) a British person, especially a recent immigrant.

pomp n. 1. a stately and splendid display. 2. specious glory. [from Old French from Latin from Greek = procession]

Pompadour /ˈpɒmpəduə/ Jeanne Antoinette Poisson, Marquise de Pompadour 1721–1764. Mistress of ◊Louis XV of France from 1744, born in Paris. She largely dictated the government's ill-fated policy of reversing France's anti-Austrian policy for an anti-Prussian one. She acted as the patron of the Enlightenment philosophers Voltaire and Diderot.

Pompeii /pɒmˈpeɪi/ ancient city in Italy, near ◊Vesuvius, 21 km/13 mi SE of Naples. In AD 63 an earthquake destroyed much of the city, which had been a Roman port and pleasure resort; it was completely buried beneath volcanic ash when Vesuvius erupted in AD 79. Over 2,000 people were killed. Pompeii was rediscovered in 1748 and the systematic excavation, begun in 1763, still continues.

Pompey /ˈpɒmpi/ **the Great** (Gnaeus Pompeius Magnus) 106–48 BC. Roman soldier and politician. Originally a supporter of ◊Sulla and the aristocratic party, he joined the democrats when he became consul with ◊Crassus in 70 BC. He defeated ◊Mithridates VI of Pontus, and annexed Syria and Palestine. In 60 BC he formed the First Triumvirate with Julius ◊Caesar (whose daughter Julia he married) and Crassus, and when it broke down after 53 BC he returned to the aristocratic party. On the outbreak of civil war in 49 BC he withdrew to Greece, was defeated by Caesar at Pharsalus in 48 BC, and was murdered in Egypt.

Pompidou /pɒmpiˈduː/ Georges 1911–1974. French conservative politician, president 1969–74. An adviser on General de Gaulle's staff 1944–46, he held administrative posts until he became director-general of the French House of Rothschild in 1954, and even then continued in close association with de Gaulle, helping to draft the constitution of the Fifth Republic 1958–59. He negotiated a settlement with the Algerians in 1961 and, as prime minister 1962–68, with the students in the revolt of May 1968, and was elected to the presidency on de Gaulle's resignation.

pom-pom[1] /ˈpɒmpɒm/ n. an automatic quick-firing gun. [imitative]

pom-pom[2] variant of **pompon**.

pompon /ˈpɒmpɒn/ n. 1. a decorative tuft or ball on a hat or shoe etc. 2. a dahlia etc. with small tightly clustered petals. [French]

pompous /ˈpɒmpəs/ adj. ostentatiously or affectedly grand or solemn; (of language) pretentious, unduly grand. —**pomposity** /-ˈpɒsɪtɪ/ n., **pompously** adv. [from Old French from Latin from Greek = procession]

ponce n. 1. a man who lives off a prostitute's earnings. 2. (*slang*) an effeminate or homosexual man. —v.i. 1. to act as a ponce. 2. (*slang*) to move in an effeminate way; to potter.

Ponce de León /ˈpɒnseɪ deɪ leɪˈɒn/ Juan c.1460–1521. Spanish soldier and explorer. He is believed to have sailed with Columbus in 1493, and served 1502–04 in Hispaniola. He conquered Puerto Rico in 1508, and was made governor in 1509. In 1513 he was the first European to reach Florida.

Poncelet /pɒnsəˈleɪ/ Jean 1788–1867. French mathematician who worked on projective geometry. His book, started in 1814 and completed in 1822, deals with the properties of plane figures unchanged when projected.

poncho /ˈpɒntʃəʊ/ n. (*plural* ponchos) a blanketlike piece of cloth with a slit in the middle for the head, worn as a cloak; a garment shaped like this. [South American Spanish]

pond n. a small area of still water.

ponder v.t./i. 1. to think over, to consider. 2. to muse, to be deep in thought. [from Old French from Latin *ponderare* = weigh]

ponderable adj. having appreciable weight or significance. [from Latin]

ponderous /ˈpɒndərəs/ adj. 1. heavy, unwieldy. 2. (of a style) dull, tedious. —**ponderously** adv. [from Latin *pondus* = weight]

Pondicherry /pɒndɪˈtʃeri/ Union Territory of SE India; area 480 sq km/185 sq mi; population (1981) 604,000. Its capital is Pondicherry, and products include rice, peanuts, cotton, and sugar. Languages spoken include French, English, Tamil, Telugu, and Malayalam. Together with Karaikal, Yanam, and Mahé (on the Malabar Coast) it formed a French colony until 1954 when all were transferred to the government of India; since 1962 they have formed the Union Territory of Pondicherry.

pond-skater n. a water ◊bug that rows itself across the surface by using its middle legs. It feeds on smaller insects.

pondweed n. any aquatic plant of the genus *Potamogeton* that either floats on the water or is submerged. The leaves of floating pondweeds are broad and leathery, whereas leaves of the submerged forms are narrower and translucent; the flowers grow in green spikes.

pong n. (*slang*) a stink. —v.i. (*slang*) to stink.

poniard /ˈpɒnjəd/ n. (*historical*) a dagger. [from French from Latin *pugnale* (*pugnus* = fist)]

Pontefract cake a small, round, flat cake of liquorice, made at Pontefract in West Yorkshire, England.

Pontiac /ˈpɒntiæk/ a motor-manufacturing city in Michigan, USA, 38 km/24 mi NW of Detroit; population (1980) 76,700.

Pontiac c.1720–1769. North American Indian, chief of the Ottawa from 1755. In 1763–64 he led the 'Conspiracy of Pontiac' in an attempt to stop British encroachment on Indian lands. He achieved remarkable success against overwhelming odds, but eventually signed a peace treaty in 1766, and was murdered by an Illinois Indian at the instigation of a British trader.

pontiff n. a bishop, a chief priest; the pope. [from French from Latin *pontifex*]

pontifical /pɒnˈtɪfɪkəl/ adj. 1. of or befitting a pontiff. 2. pompously dogmatic. —**pontifically** adv. [from French or Latin]

pontificate /pɒnˈtɪfɪkeɪt/ v.i. 1. to speak in a pontifical way. 2. to play the pontiff. —/pɒnˈtɪfɪkət/ n. the office of bishop or pope; the period of this. [from Latin]

pontoon[1] /pɒnˈtuːn/ n. a card game in which players try to acquire cards with a face value totalling 21 and no more. [probable corruption of *vingt-un* = vingt-et-un (21)]

pontoon[2] n. 1. a flat-bottomed boat used as a ferryboat or to carry lifting gear etc. 2. each of several boats etc. used to support a temporary bridge (**pontoon bridge**). [from French from Latin *ponto* (*pons* = bridge)]

Pontormo /pɒnˈtɔːməʊ/ Jacopo Carucci 1494–1557. Italian painter, active in Florence. He developed a dramatic Mannerist style, with lurid colours. His mature style is demonstrated in *The Deposition* of about 1525 (Sta Felicità, Florence), an extraordinary composition of interlocked figures, with rosy pinks, lime yellows, and pale apple greens illuminating the scene.

Pontus /ˈpɒntəs/ kingdom of NE Asia Minor on the Black Sea from about 300–65 BC when its greatest ruler, ◊Mithridates VI, was defeated by ◊Pompey.

pony /ˈpəʊnɪ/ n. a small horse under 1.47 m/58 in (14.2 hands shoulder height). —**ponytail** n. hair drawn back, tied, and hanging down behind the head. **pony trekking** travelling across country on ponies for pleasure. [perhaps from French *poulenet*, diminutive of *poulain* = foal]

poodle n. a breed of dog, including **standard** (above 38 cm/15 in at shoulder), **miniature** (below 38 cm/15 in), and **toy** (below 28 cm/11 in) types. The long curly coat, often cut into an elaborate style, is usually either black or white, although greys and browns are also bred. [from German *pudel(hund)*]

poof /puːf/ n. (*slang*) an effeminate or homosexual man.

pooh /puː/ interjection expressing contempt or impatience. [imitative]

Pooh-Bah /puːˈbɑː/ n. a holder of many offices at once. [character in W S Gilbert's *The Mikado* 1885]

pooh-pooh /puːˈpuː/ v.t. to express contempt for, to ridicule. [reduplication of *pooh*]

pool[1] n. 1. a small body of still water, usually of natural formation. 2. a small shallow body of any liquid.

3. a deep place in a river. 4. a swimming pool. [Old English]

pool² *n.* 1. a common fund, e.g. of the profits of separate firms or of players' stakes in gambling. 2. a common supply of persons, vehicles, commodities etc., for sharing by a group of people; a group of persons sharing duties etc. 3. an arrangement between competing parties to fix prices and share business. 4. (*US*) or **pocket billiards** a game derived from ◊billiards and played in many different forms. Originally popular in the USA, it is now also played in Europe. —*v.t.* to put into a common fund; to share in common. —**the pools,** football pools, especially as conducted on a weekly basis. [from French *poule*, originally = hen]

Poona /'pu:nə/ former English spelling of ◊Pune, city in India; after independence in 1947 the form Poona was gradually superseded by Pune.

poop *n.* 1. the stern of a ship. 2. the aftermost and highest deck. [from Old French from Latin *puppis*]

poor /puə/ *adj.* 1. having little money or means. 2. deficient in a specified quality or possession. 3. scanty, inadequate; less good than is usual or expected. 4. deserving pity or sympathy, unfortunate. 5. spiritless, despicable. 6. humble, insignificant. —**poor man's,** an inferior or cheaper substitute for. **poor white,** (*US derogatory*) a member of a socially inferior group of white people. —**poorness** *n.* [from Old French *povre* from Latin *pauper*]

poorhouse *n.* (*historical*) the workhouse.

poor law the English system for poor relief, established by the Poor Relief Act of 1601. Each parish was responsible for its own poor, paid for by a parish tax. Relief today is provided by national social security benefits.

poorly *adv.* in a poor manner, badly. —*predic.adj.* unwell.

Pop Iggy. Stage name of James Jewel Osterberg 1947– . US rock singer and songwriter, initially known as **Iggy Stooge,** lead singer with a seminal garage band called the Stooges (1967–74), famed for his self-destructive protopunk performances. Later on in Pop's solo career his friend, David Bowie, contributed to *The Idiot* 1977, *Lust for Life* 1977, and *Blah, Blah, Blah* 1986.

pop¹ *n.* 1. a sudden sharp explosive sound, as of a cork when drawn. 2. an effervescing drink. —*v.t./i.* 1. to make or cause to make a pop. 2. to go, move, or put abruptly. 3. (*slang*) to pawn. —*adv.* with the sound of a pop. —**popeyed** *adj.* with eyes bulging or wide open. **pop off,** (*slang*) to die. **pop the question,** (*colloquial*) to propose marriage. **pop shop,** (*slang*) a pawnbroker's shop. **pop-up** *adj.* involving parts that pop up automatically. [imitative]

pop² *adj.* (*colloquial*) 1. in a popular modern style. 2. performing popular music. —*n.* (*colloquial*) pop music or records (see ◊pop music). [abbreviation of *popular*]

pop³ *n.* (*colloquial*) father; any older man. [from *papa*]

Pope *English poet and satirist Alexander Pope. The painting is by William Hore c.1739.*

Pop Art a movement of young artists in the mid-1950s and 1960s, reacting against the elitism of abstract art. Pop art used popular imagery drawn from advertising, comic strips, film, and television. It originated in Britain in 1956 with Richard Hamilton, Peter Blake (1932–), and others, and broke through in the USA with the paintings of flags and numbers by Jasper Johns in 1958 and Andy Warhol's first series of soup cans in 1962. [named by British critic Lawrence Alloway (1926–)]

popcorn *n.* maize which when heated bursts open to form fluffy balls.

pope¹ *n.* 1. the bishop of Rome, head of the Roman Catholic Church, which claims he is the spiritual descendant of St Peter. Elected by the Sacred College of Cardinals, a pope dates his pontificate from his coronation with the tiara, or triple crown, at St Peter's Basilica, Rome. The pope had great political power in Europe from the early Middle Ages until the Reformation. 2. the head of the Coptic Church. [Old English from Latin *papa* from Greek = father]

pope² *n.* a parish priest of the Orthodox Church in Russia etc. [from Russian *pop*]

Pope /pəup/ Alexander 1688–1744. English poet and satirist. He established his reputation with the precocious *Pastorals* 1709 and *Essay on Criticism* 1711, which were followed by a parody of the heroic epic *The Rape of the Lock* 1712–14 and 'Eloisa to Abelard' 1717. Other works include a highly Neo-Classical translation of Homer's *Iliad* and *Odyssey* 1715–26.

And gentle dullness ever loves a joke.

Alexander Pope
The Dunciad

popery /'pəupəri/ *n.* (*derogatory*) the papal system; the Roman Catholic religion.

popgun *n.* a child's toy gun firing a cork etc. by the action of compressed air.

popinjay /'pɒpɪndʒeɪ/ *n.* a fop; a conceited person. [from Old French *papingay* from Spanish from Arabic]

popish /'pəupɪʃ/ *adj.* (*derogatory*) of popery.

Popish Plot a supposed plot to murder Charles II; see under Titus ◊Oates.

poplar /'pɒplə/ *n.* a tall, slender tree of the genus *Populus*, with a straight trunk and often tremulous leaves. Poplars are often grown as windbreaks in commercial orchards. [from Anglo-French *popler* (*pople* from Latin *populus*)]

poplin /'pɒplɪn/ *n.* a strong fabric, originally with a warp of silk and a weft of worsted, but now usually made from cotton, in a plain weave with a finely ribbed surface. [from obsolete French *papeline*, perhaps from Italian]

pop music an umbrella term for contemporary music not classifiable as jazz or classical. Pop became distinct from folk music with the advent of sound-recording techniques, but it incorporates blues, country and western, and music hall sounds; electronic amplification and other technological innovations have played a large part in the creation of new styles. The traditional format is a song of roughly three minutes with verse, chorus, and middle eight bars. [abbreviation of *popular music*]

Popocatépetl /pɒpəkætə'petl/ volcano in central Mexico, 50 km/30 mi SE of Mexico City; 5,340 m/17,526 ft. It last erupted in 1920. [Aztec = smoking mountain]

Popov /'pɒpɒv/ Alexander 1859–1905. Russian physicist who devised the first ◊aerial, in advance of ◊Marconi (although he did not use it for radio communication). He also invented a detector for radio waves.

poppadam /'pɒpədəm/ *n.* a thin, crisp biscuit made with lentil flour. [from Tamil]

popper *n.* (*colloquial*) a press stud.

Popper /'pɒpə/ Karl (Raimund) 1902– . Austrian philosopher of science. His theory of falsificationism says that although scientific generalizations cannot be conclusively verified, they can be conclusively falsified by a counterinstance; therefore, science is not certain knowledge but a series of 'conjectures and refutations', approaching, though never reaching, a definitive truth. For Popper, psychoanalysis and Marxism are unfalsifiable and therefore unscientific.

poppet /'pɒpɪt/ n. (colloquial) (especially as a term of endearment) a small or dainty person. [ultimately from Latin pu(p)pa = doll]

popping crease in cricket, the line in front of and parallel to the wicket within which a batsman stands.

poppy n. any plant of the genus Papaver, family Papaveraceae, that bears brightly coloured, often dark-centred, flowers and yields a milky sap. Species include the crimson European **field poppy** P. rhoeas and the Asian **opium poppies**. Closely related are the **California poppy** Eschscholtzia californica and the yellow **horned** or **sea poppy** Glaucium flavum. —**Poppy Day,** ◊Remembrance Sunday, on which artificial poppies are worn. [Old English from Latin papaver]

poppycock n. (slang) nonsense. [Old English from Dutch dialect pappekak]

populace /'pɒpjʊləs/ n. the common people. [French from Italian popolaccio (popolo = people)]

popular /'pɒpjʊlə/ adj. 1. liked or admired by many people. 2. of, for, or prevalent among the general public. —**popularity** /-'lærɪtɪ/ n., **popularly** adv. [from Anglo-French or Latin populus = people]

popular front a political alliance of liberals, socialists, communists, and other centre and left-wing parties against fascism. This policy was proposed by the Communist International in 1935 and was adopted in France and Spain, where popular-front governments were elected in 1936; that in France was overthrown in 1938 and in Spain in 1939. In Britain a popular-front policy was advocated by Sir Stafford Cripps and others, but rejected by the Labour Party. The resistance movements in the occupied countries during World War II represented a revival of the popular-front idea, and in postwar politics the term tends to recur whenever a strong right-wing party can be counterbalanced only by an alliance of those on the left.

popularize v.t. 1. to make generally liked. 2. to present (a subject) in a readily understandable form. —**popularization** /-'zeɪʃən/ n., **popularizer** n.

populate /'pɒpjʊleɪt/ v.t. 1. to inhabit, to form the population of. 2. to supply with inhabitants. [from Latin populare]

population /pɒpju'leɪʃən/ n. 1. the inhabitants of a place or country etc.; the total number of these. **Population statistics** are derived from many sources, for example through the registration of births and deaths; and from censuses of the population. The first national censuses were taken in 1800 and 1801 and provided population statistics for Italy, Spain, the UK, Ireland and the USA; and the cities of London, Paris, Vienna, Berlin, and New York. 2. the extent to which a place is populated. 3. in biology and ecology, a group of animals of one species, living in a certain area and able to interbreed; the members of a given species in a community of living things. —**population explosion,** a sudden large increase of population. [from Latin populus]

population cycle in biology, regular fluctuations in the size of a population, as seen in lemmings, for example. Such cycles are often caused by density-dependent mortality: high mortality due to overcrowding causes a sudden decline in the population, which then gradually builds up again. Population cycles may also result from an interaction between a predator and its prey.

population genetics the branch of genetics that studies the way in which the frequencies of different ◊alleles in populations of organisms change, as a result of natural selection and other processes.

Populism n. in US history, a late 19th-century political movement that developed out of farmers' protests against economic hardship. The Populist, or People's party was founded in 1892 and ran several presidential candidates. It failed, however, to reverse increasing industrialization and the relative decline of agriculture in the USA. —**populist,** an adherent of a political party claiming to support the interests of ordinary people. [from Latin populus = people]

populous /'pɒpjʊləs/ adj. thickly inhabited. [from Latin populosus]

porcelain /'pɔːslɪn/ n. fine earthenware with a translucent body and a transparent glaze; articles made of this. [French from Italian porcellana = cowrie shell, china ware resembling this polished substance, from porcella, diminutive of porca = sow (perhaps from resemblance of shells to a sow's vulva)]

porcupine

North American porcupine

porch n. a covered approach to the entrance of a building. [from Old French from Latin porticus]

porcine /'pɔːsaɪn/ adj. of or like a pig. [from French or Latin porcus]

porcupine /'pɔːkjʊpaɪn/ n. a rodent of the family Hystricidae with a body and tail covered with erectile spines. The colouring is brown with black and white quills. North American porcupines, family Erethizontidae, differ from the Old World varieties by living in trees and having a prehensile tail and much shorter spines. [from Old French porcespin]

pore[1] n. a minute opening in the surface of a skin or leaf etc. through which fluids may pass. [from Old French from Latin from Greek poros]

pore[2] v.i. (with over) to be absorbed in studying (a book etc.); to meditate or think intently about.

Porgy and Bess /'pɔːgi, 'bes/ classic US folk opera 1935 by George and Ira Gershwin, based on the novel Porgy 1925 by DuBose Heyward, a story of the black residents of Catfish Row in Charleston, South Carolina.

pork n. the flesh (especially unsalted) of a pig used as food. —**pork pie,** a raised pie of minced pork etc., eaten cold. **porkpie hat,** a hat with a flat rimmed crown and the brim turned up all round. [Old French porc from Latin porcus = pig]

porker n. a pig raised for pork.

porky adj. 1. of or like pork. 2. (colloquial) fleshy. —**porkiness** n.

porn (colloquial) abbreviation of pornography.

pornography /pɔː'nɒgrəfɪ/ n. the explicit representation of sexual activity visually or descriptively to stimulate erotic rather than aesthetic feelings; pictures or literature etc. containing this. —**pornographer** n., **pornographic** /-'græfɪk/ adj. [from Greek pornē = prostitute]

porous /'pɔːrəs/ adj. 1. containing pores. 2. able to be permeated by fluid or air. —**porosity** /-'rɒsɪtɪ/ n. [from Old French from Latin from Greek poros]

porphyria n. a group of genetic disorders caused by an enzyme defect. It affects the digestive tract, causing abdominal distress; the nervous system, causing psychotic disorder, epilepsy, and weakness; the circulatory system, causing high blood pressure; and the skin, causing extreme sensitivity to light. No specific treatments exist.

porphyry /'pɔːfɪrɪ/ n. a hard igneous rock composed of crystals of red or white feldspar in a red matrix. —**porphyritic** /-'rɪtɪk/ adj. [from Latin porphyreum ultimately from Greek porphura = purple dye]

porpoise /'pɔːpəs/ n. a sea mammal of the genus Phocaena, the smallest member of the whale group, with a blunt, rounded snout. It can grow to 1.8 m/6 ft long, and feeds on fish and crustaceans. [from Old French from Latin porcus = pig and piscis = fish]

porridge /'pɒrɪdʒ/ n. a food made by boiling oatmeal or other meal or cereal in water or milk. [alteration from pottage]

porringer /'pɒrɪndʒə/ n. (archaic) a small soup basin, especially for a child. [alteration from earlier pottinger from Old French potager]

Porritt /'pɒrɪt/ Jonathon 1950– . British environmental campaigner, director of ◊Friends of the Earth 1984–1990. He has stood for election in both British and European elections as an Ecology (Green) Party candidate.

Porsche /pɔːʃ/ Ferdinand 1875–1951. German car designer. He was an engineer with Daimler–Benz before becoming a designer with the Auto-Union racing team in 1930. Among his designs were the Volkswagen (German 'people's car', popularly known as the Beetle), first produced in the 1930s, which became an international success in the 1950s–1970s, and Porsche sports cars. His son, Terry, formed the

Porsche Company in 1948 and produced Grand Prix cars, sports cars, and prototypes.

port[1] *n.* a harbour; a town or place possessing a harbour; a place where customs officers are stationed to supervise the entry of goods into a country. —**port of call,** a place where a ship or person stops during a journey. [Old English from Latin *portus*]

port[2] *n.* a sweet, fortified (with brandy) dessert wine (red, tawny, or white) made from grapes grown in the Douro basin of Portugal and exported from Porto. [from *Oporto* in Portugal, from where it is shipped]

port[3] *n.* the left-hand side (when facing forward) of a ship or aircraft. —*v.t.* to turn (the helm) to port. —**port tack,** a tack with the wind on the port side. [probably originally the side turned towards port]

port[4] *n.* **1.** an opening in a ship's side for entrance or loading etc. **2.** a porthole. [Old French from Latin *porta* = gate]

port[5] *v.t.* to carry (a rifle) diagonally across and close to the body. [from French from Latin *portare* = carry]

portable /'pɔːtəbəl/ *adj.* easily movable, convenient for carrying. —*n.* a portable form of typewriter, television set etc. —**portability** /-'bɪlɪtɪ/ *n.* [from Old French or Latin]

portage /'pɔːtɪdʒ/ *n.* the carrying of boats or goods between two navigable waters; a place at which this is necessary; the charge for it. —*v.t.* to convey (a boat or goods) over a portage. [from Old French]

portal /'pɔːtəl/ *n.* a gate or doorway etc., especially an elaborate one. —**portal vein,** a vein conveying blood to the liver or some other organ except the heart. [from Old French from Latin *portale*]

Port Arthur /pɔːt ˈɑːθə/ former name (until 1905) of the port and naval base of Lüshun in NE China, now part of Lüdz.

Port-au-Prince /pɔːtəʊˈprɪns/ capital and industrial port (sugar, rum, textiles, plastics) of Haiti; population (1982) 763,000.

portcullis /pɔːt'kʌlɪs/ *n.* a strong heavy grating sliding up and down in vertical grooves, lowered to block a gateway in a fortress etc. [from Old French = sliding door]

Port Elizabeth /iˈlɪzəbəθ/ industrial port (engineering, steel, food processing) in Cape province, South Africa, about 710 km/440 mi E of Cape Town on Algoa Bay; population (1980) 492,140.

portend /pɔːˈtend/ *v.t.* to foreshadow, as an omen, to give warning of. [from Latin *portendere*]

portent /'pɔːtent/ *n.* **1.** an omen; a significant sign of something to come. **2.** a prodigy, a marvellous thing. [from Latin *portentum*]

portentous /pɔːˈtentəs/ *adj.* **1.** being or like a portent. **2.** pompously solemn.

porter[1] /'pɔːtə(r)/ *n.* **1.** a person employed to carry luggage etc. **2.** a dark beer brewed from charred or browned malt. [from Old French from Latin *portator*]

porter[2] *n.* a doorman or gatekeeper, especially of a large building. [Anglo-French from Latin *portarius*]

Porter Cole (Albert) 1892–1964. US composer and lyricist of musical comedies. His shows, many of which were made into films, include *The Gay Divorcee* 1932 and *Kiss Me Kate* 1948.

Porter Edwin Stanton 1869–1941. US director of silent films, a pioneer of his time. His 1903 film *The Great Train Robbery* lasted 12 minutes which, for the period, was unusually long, and contained an early use of the close-up. More concerned with the technical than the artistic side of his films, which include *The Teddy Bears* 1907 and *The Final Pardon* 1912, Porter abandoned film-making in 1916.

Porter Eric 1928– . English actor. His numerous classical roles include title parts in *Uncle Vanya*, *Volpone*, and *King Lear*; on television he played Soames in *The Forsyte Saga*.

Porter Rodney Robert 1917–1985. British biochemist. In 1962 Porter proposed a structure for the antibody, gamma globulin (IgG) in which the molecule was seen as consisting of four chains. Porter was awarded, with Gerald ◊Edelman, the 1972 Nobel Prize for Medicine.

porterage *n.* the hire of porters.

porterhouse steak a thick choice steak of beef. [said to derive its name from a porterhouse, i.e. one selling porter (dark beer), in New York]

portfolio /pɔːt'fəʊliəʊ/ *n.* (*plural* **portfolios**) **1.** a case for loose drawings, sheets of paper etc. **2.** a list of investments held by a person or company etc. **3.** the office of a minister

of state. —**minister without portfolio,** a minister not in charge of any department of state. [from Italian *portafogli* (*portare* = carry and *foglio* = sheet of paper)]

porthole *n.* an aperture, usually glazed, in a ship's or aircraft's side for the admission of light and air to a ship or light to an aircraft.

portico /'pɔːtɪkəʊ/ *n.* (*plural* **porticoes**) a colonnade, a roof supported by columns at regular intervals, usually attached as a porch to a building. [Italian from Latin *porticus*]

portion /'pɔːʃən/ *n.* **1.** a part or share. **2.** the amount of food allotted to one person. **3.** a dowry. **4.** one's destiny or lot. —*v.t./i.* **1.** to divide into portions; to distribute. **2.** to give a dowry to. [from Old French from Latin *portio*]

Portland /'pɔːtlənd/ William Henry Cavendish Bentinck, 3rd Duke of Portland 1738–1809. British politician, originally a Whig, who in 1783 became nominal prime minister in the Fox–North coalition government. During the French Revolution he joined the Tories, and was prime minister 1807–09.

Portland cement /'pɔːtlənd/cement manufactured from chalk and clay. [from Isle of *Portland*, Dorset]

Portland stone a valuable building limestone.

Port Louis /pɔːt ˈluːi/ capital of Mauritius, on the island's NW coast; population (1987) 139,000. Exports include sugar, textiles, watches, and electronic goods.

portly *adj.* corpulent and dignified. —**portliness** *n.* [from Old French *port* = deportment]

portmanteau /pɔːt'mæntəʊ/ *n.* (*plural* **portmanteaus**) a trunk for clothes etc., opening into two equal parts. —**portmanteau word,** a factitious word blending the sounds and combining the meanings of two others. (e.g. *chortle*, from *chuckle* and *snort*). [from French]

Port Moresby /'mɔːzbi/ capital and port of Papua New Guinea on the S coast of New Guinea; population (1987) 152,000.

Porto /'pɔːtəʊ/ (English **Oporto**) industrial city (textiles, leather, pottery) in Portugal, on the river Douro, 5 km/3 mi from its mouth; population (1984) 327,000. It exports port.

Pôrto Alegre /pɔːtəʊ əˈleɪgri/ port and capital of Rio Grande do Sul state, S Brazil; population (1986) 2,705,000. It is a freshwater port for ocean-going vessels, and is Brazil's major commercial centre.

Port-of-Spain /'pɔːt əv ˈspeɪn/ port and capital of Trinidad and Tobago, on Trinidad; population (1988) 58,000.

Porton Down /'pɔːtn ˈdaʊn/ site of the Chemical Defence Establishment (CDE) of the Ministry of Defence in Wiltshire, SW England. Its prime role is to conduct research into means of protection from chemical attack.

Porto Novo /'pɔːtəʊ ˈnəʊvəʊ/ capital of Benin, W Africa; population (1982) 208,258. It was a former Portuguese centre for the slave and tobacco trade with Brazil and became a French protectorate in 1863.

portrait /'pɔːtrɪt/ *n.* **1.** a likeness of a person or animal made by drawing, painting, or photography. **2.** a description in words. —**portraitist** *n.* [French]

portraiture /'pɔːtrɪtʃə/ *n.* **1.** portraying. **2.** a portrait. **3.** a description in words.

Port Rashid /ræ'ʃiːd/ port serving Dubai in the United Arab Emirates.

portray /pɔːˈtreɪ/ *v.t.* **1.** to make a picture of. **2.** to describe in words. —**portrayal** *n.* [from Old French *portraire*]

Port Said /saɪd/ port in Egypt, on reclaimed land at the north end of the ◊Suez Canal; population (1983) 364,000. During the 1967 Arab–Israeli war the city was damaged and the canal blocked; Port Said was evacuated by 1969 but by 1975 had been largely reconstructed.

Portsmouth /'pɔːtsməθ/ city and naval port in Hampshire, England, opposite the Isle of Wight; population (1981) 179,500.

Portugal /'pɔːtjʊgəl/ Republic of; country in SW Europe, on the Atlantic, bounded to the N and E by Spain; **area** 92,000 sq km/35,521 sq mi (including Azores and Madeira); **capital** Lisbon; **physical** mountainous in the N, plains in S; **head of state** Mario Alberto Nobre Lopes Soares from 1986; **head of government** Cavaco Silva from 1985; **political system** democratic republic; **exports** port wine, sherry, olive oil, resin, cork, sardines, textiles, pottery, pulpwood; **population** (1990 est) 10,528,000; **language** Portuguese; **recent history** Portugal was a military dictatorship 1928–68 under Antonio de Oliveira Salazar. Its African colonies became independent in 1975 and in 1976 a new constitution, providing for return to civilian rule, was adopted. A new draft constitution was approved in 1982, reducing the powers of the presidency. In 1986 Mario Soares was elected the first civilian president for 60 years. Portugal joined the EC in the same year.

Portuguese /pɔːtjuˈgiːz/ *adj.* of Portugal or its people or language. —*n.* (*plural* the same) **1.** a native or inhabitant of Portugal. **2.** the language of Portugal, Brazil, Angola, Mozambique, and other former Portuguese colonies. A member of the Romance branch of the Indo-European language family, it is closely related to Spanish and strongly influenced by Arabic. [from Portuguese from Latin *portugalensis*]

Portuguese East Africa former name of ◊Mozambique.
Portuguese Guinea /ˈgɪni/ former name of ◊Guinea-Bissau.
Portuguese man-of-war a tropical or subtropical coelenterate with the appearance of a large jellyfish, of the genus *Physalia*. There is a gas-filled float on the surface, below which hang feeding, stinging, and reproductive tentacles. The float can be 30 cm/1 ft long.
Portuguese West Africa former name of ◊Angola.
pose /pəʊz/ *v.t./i.* **1.** to put into or assume a desired position for a portrait or photograph etc. **2.** to take a particular attitude for effect or to impress others. **3.** (with *as*) to pretend to be. **4.** to present (a question or problem). —*n.* **1.** an attitude in which a person etc. is posed. **2.** an affectation, a pretence. [from French from Latin *pausare* = pause; confused in part with Latin *ponere* = place]
Poseidon /pəˈsaɪdn/ Greek god (Roman Neptune), the brother of Zeus and Pluto. The brothers dethroned their father, Kronos, and divided his realm, Poseidon taking the sea; he was also worshipped as god of earthquakes. His son was ◊Triton.
poser *n.* a puzzling question or problem.
poseur /pəʊˈzɜː/ *n.* a person who poses for effect or behaves affectedly. [French]
posh *adj.* (*slang*) high-class, smart. —*v.t.* (*slang*) to smarten. [perhaps from slang *posh* = money, a dandy]
posit /ˈpɒzɪt/ *v.t.* to assume as a fact, to postulate. [from Latin]
position /pəˈzɪʃən/ *n.* **1.** the place occupied by a person or thing. **2.** the proper place. **3.** being advantageously placed. **4.** the way in which a thing or its parts are placed or arranged. **5.** a mental attitude; a way of looking at a question. **6.** a situation in relation to others. **7.** rank or status; high social standing. **8.** paid (official or domestic) employment. **9.** a place where troops are posted for strategic purposes. **10.** a configuration of chessmen etc. during a game. —*v.t.* to place in a position. —**positional** *adj.* [from Old French or Latin *ponere* = place]
positive /ˈpɒzɪtɪv/ *adj.* **1.** formally or explicitly stated. **2.** definite, unquestionable. **3.** (of a person) convinced, confident or over-confident in an opinion. **4.** absolute, not relative. **5.** (*colloquial*) downright, out-and-out. **6.** constructive. **7.** marked by the presence and not absence of qualities. **8.** dealing only with matters of fact, practical. **9.** tending in the direction naturally or arbitrarily taken as that of increase or progress. **10.** (of a quantity in algebra) greater than zero. **11.** of, containing, or producing the kind of electrical charge produced by rubbing glass with silk. **12.** (of a photograph) showing the lights and shades or colours as in the original image cast on a film etc. **13.** in grammar, (of an adjective or adverb) in the primary form expressing a simple quality without comparison. —*n.* a positive adjective, photograph, quantity etc. —**positive vetting,** an intensive inquiry into the background and character of a candidate for a senior post in the civil service etc. —**positively** *adv.*, **positiveness** *n.* [from Old French or Latin]
positivism /ˈpɒzɪtɪvɪzəm/ *n.* a theory associated with the French philosopher Comte (1798–1857), and ◊empiricism, which confines genuine knowledge within the bounds of science and observation. The theory is hostile to theology and to metaphysics that overstep this boundary. —**logical positivism,** a form of positivism which rejected any metaphysical world beyond everyday science and common sense, and confined statements to those of formal logic or mathematics. Developed in the 1920s, it influenced,

Temple of Poseidon NE corner, Cape Sounion, Greece.

and became more widely known through, the work of A J Ayer and the Vienna Circle. —**positivist** *n.*, **positivistic** /-ˈvɪstɪk/ *adj.* [from French]
positron /ˈpɒzɪtrɒn/ *n.* an ◊elementary particle, produced in some radioactive decay processes, which is similar in every respect to an ◊electron, except that it carries a positive electric charge. It is thus the ◊antiparticle to the electron.
positron emission tomography (PET) a technique which enables doctors to observe the operation of the human body by following the progress of a radioactive chemical that has been inhaled or injected. PET scanners pinpoint the location of the chemical by bombarding the body with low energy ◊gamma radiation. The technique has been used to study a wide range of diseases including schizophrenia, Alzheimer's disease and Parkinson's disease.
posse /ˈpɒsi/ *n.* a body (of constables); a strong force or company. [Latin = to be able]
possess /pəˈzes/ *v.t.* **1.** to hold as belonging to oneself, to have or own. **2.** to have (a faculty or quality etc.). **3.** to occupy or dominate the mind of. —**like one possessed,** with great energy. —**possessor** *n.* [from Old French from Latin *possidere*]
possession /pəˈzeʃən/ *n.* **1.** possessing, being possessed. **2.** a thing possessed. **3.** occupancy. **4.** (in *plural*) property, wealth. **5.** a subject territory. —**take possession of,** to become the owner or possessor of. [from Old French or Latin]
possessive /pəˈzesɪv/ *adj.* **1.** showing a desire to possess or to retain what one possesses. **2.** in grammar, (of a word or form) indicating possession (e.g. *Anne's, my, mine*). —*n.* in grammar, a possessive case or word. —**possessively** *adv.*, **possessiveness** *n.* [from Latin]
possibility /pɒsɪˈbɪlɪti/ *n.* **1.** the fact or condition of being possible. **2.** something that may exist or happen. **3.** capability of being used or of producing good results.
possible /ˈpɒsɪbəl/ *adj.* capable of existing, happening, being done etc. —*n.* **1.** a possible candidate, member of a team etc. **2.** the highest possible score, especially in shooting. [from Old French or Latin]
possibly /ˈpɒsɪbli/ *adv.* **1.** in accordance with possibility. **2.** perhaps, for all one knows to the contrary.
possum /ˈpɒsəm/ *n.* **1.** (*colloquial*) abbreviation of opossum. **2.** (*Australian* and *New Zealand*) a member of a large family of arboreal phalangers, some of which have a prehensile tail. —**play possum,** (*colloquial*) to pretend to be unconscious or unaware of something (from the opossum's habit of seeming to feign death if attacked).
post¹ /pəʊst/ *n.* **1.** a long, stout piece of timber or metal set upright in the ground etc. to support something, mark a position or boundary etc. **2.** the pole marking the start or finish of a race. —*v.t.* (also with *up*) **1.** to attach (a paper etc.) in a prominent place. **2.** to announce or advertise by a placard or in a published list. [Old English from Latin *postis*]
post² /pəʊst/ *n.* **1.** the official conveying of parcels, letters etc. **2.** the letters etc. conveyed; a single collection or delivery of these. **3.** a place where letters etc. are dealt with. —*v.t.* **1.** to put (a letter etc.) into the post. **2.** (especially in *past participle*) to supply (a person) with information. **3.** to enter (an item) in a ledger; to complete (a ledger) thus. —**postbag** *n.* a mailbag. **post-box** *n.* a box into which letters are inserted for dispatch or are delivered.

postcode n. a group of letters and numerals in a postal address to assist sorting. **post-free** adj. & adv. carried by post without charge to the recipient. **posthaste** adv. with great speed. **post office**, a building or room where postal business is carried on. **Post Office**, (PO) the public department or corporation responsible for postal services. **post-paid** adj. on which postage has been paid. [from French from Italian posta from Latin]

post[3] /pəʊst/ n. **1.** a situation of paid employment. **2.** the appointed place of a soldier etc. on watch; a place of duty. **3.** a place (especially a frontier fort) manned by soldiers; the soldiers there. **4.** a trading station. —v.t. **1.** to place (a soldier etc.) at his post. **2.** to appoint to a post or command. —**last post**, a military bugle call at the time of retiring for the night or at a funeral. [from French from Italian posto]

post- /pəʊst-/ prefix meaning after, behind. [from Latin post adv. & prep.]

postage /'pəʊstɪdʒ/ n. the amount charged for sending a letter etc. by post. —**postage stamp**, an official adhesive stamp for sticking on a letter etc. indicating the amount of postage paid.

postal /'pəʊstəl/ adj. of or by post. —**postal code**, a postcode. **postal order**, a kind of money order issued by the Post Office. —**postally** adv. [French]

postcard n. a card with space for a written message that can be sent through the mail without an envelope. The postcard's inventor was Emmanual Hermann, of Vienna, who in 1869 proposed a 'postal telegram', sent at a lower fee than a normal letter with an envelope. The first picture postcard was produced in 1894.

postdate /pəʊst'deɪt/ v.t. **1.** to follow in time. **2.** to give a date later than the true date to.

poster /'pəʊstə/ n. **1.** an advertising announcement for public display, often illustrated, first produced in France during the mid-19th century, when colour ◊lithography came into its own. **2.** a large printed picture.

poste restante /pəʊst re'stɑːt/ a department in a post office where letters are kept until called for. [French = letters remaining]

posterior /pɒ'stɪərɪə/ adj. **1.** later, coming after in a series or in order of time. **2.** situated behind or at the back. —n. the buttocks. [Latin, comparative of posterus = following]

posterity /pɒ'sterɪtɪ/ n. **1.** future generations. **2.** a person's descendants. [from Old French from Latin]

postern /'pɒstɜːn/ n. a small entrance at the back or side of a fortress etc. [from Old French from Latin posterula, diminutive from posterus]

postgraduate /pəʊst'grædjʊət/ adj. (of studies) carried on after taking a first degree; (of a student) engaged in such studies. —n. a postgraduate student.

post hoc after this, therefore on account of this. [Latin, abbreviation of post hoc, ergo propter hoc]

posthumous /'pɒstjʊməs/ adj. **1.** occurring after death. **2.** published after the author's death. **3.** born after the father's death. —**posthumously** adv. [from Latin postumus = last, associated with humus = ground]

postilion /pə'stɪljən/ n. a rider on the near horse drawing a coach etc. where there is no coachman. [from French from Italian = postboy]

Post-Impressionism n. the theory or practice of the Post-Impressionist school in art in the 1880s and 1890s, an extension of Impressionism. The term was first used by the British critic Roger Fry in 1911 to describe the works of Cézanne, van Gogh, and Gauguin. —**Post-Impressionist** n. a member of the Post-Impressionist movement, especially in French painting. The Post-Impressionists moved away from the spontaneity of Impressionism, seeking to reveal the subject's structural form without strict fidelity to its natural appearance, and attempting to give their work more serious meaning and permanence.

postman n. (plural **postmen**) one who delivers or collects letters etc. —**postwoman** n.fem.

postmark n. an official mark on a letter etc. cancelling the stamp and giving the place and date. —v.t. to stamp with a postmark.

postmaster n. the official in charge of certain post offices. —**postmistress** n.fem.

Post-Modernism n. a late 20th-century movement in the arts that rejects the preoccupation of ◊Modernism with pure form and technique rather than content. In the visual arts and architecture, Post-Modern designers use an amalgam of styles from the past, such as the Classical and the Baroque, and apply them to spare modern forms. Their slightly off-key familiarity creates a more immediate appeal than the austerities of Modernism.

postmortem /pəʊst'mɔːtəm/ n. **1.** the dissection of a dead body to determine the cause of death. It is also known as an **autopsy**. **2.** (colloquial) a discussion after the conclusion of a game, election etc. —adv. & adj. after death. [Latin]

postnatal /pəʊst'neɪtəl/ adj. of or concerning the period after childbirth.

postpone /pəʊst'pəʊn/ v.t. to cause or arrange to take place at a later time. —**postponement** n. [from Latin ponere = place]

postprandial /pəʊst'prændɪəl/ adj. (usually jocular) after lunch or dinner. [from Latin prandium = dinner]

postscript /'pəʊstskrɪpt/ n. an additional paragraph, especially at the end of a letter after the signature. [from Latin scribere = write]

postulant /'pɒstjʊlənt/ n. a candidate, especially for admission to a religious order. [French or from Latin]

postulate /'pɒstjʊleɪt/ v.t. to assume or require to be true, especially as a basis for reasoning; to claim; to take for granted. —/'pɒstjʊlət/ n. a thing postulated. —**postulation** /-'leɪʃən/ n. [from Latin postulare = demand]

posture /'pɒstʃə/ n. **1.** an attitude of the body or mind; the relative position of parts, especially of the body. **2.** a condition or state (of affairs etc.). —v.t./i. **1.** to assume a posture, especially for effect. **2.** to dispose the limbs of (a person) in a particular way. —**postural** adj., **posturer** n. [French from Italian from Latin]

postwar /pəʊst'wɔː, attributive 'pəʊst-/ adj. occurring after or existing after a war.

posy /'pəʊzɪ/ n. a small bunch of flowers. [contraction of poesy]

pot[1] n. **1.** a rounded vessel of earthenware, metal, or glass, for holding liquids or solids or for cooking in. **2.** a chamber pot, teapot etc. **3.** the contents of a pot. **4.** the total amount bet in a game etc.; (colloquial) a large sum. **5.** (slang) a prize in an athletic contest, especially a silver cup. **6.** (slang) a potbelly. —v.t./i. (**-tt-**) **1.** to plant in a pot. **2.** to sit (a child) on a chamber pot. **3.** to send (a ball) into the pocket in billiards etc. **4.** to shoot, to hit or kill (an animal) by a pot shot. **5.** to seize or secure. **6.** to abridge or epitomize. **7.** (especially in past participle) to preserve (food) in a sealed pot etc. —**go to pot**, (colloquial) to deteriorate, to be ruined. **potbelly** n. a protruding belly; a person with this. **pot boiler**, a piece of art, writing etc., done merely to earn money. **potherb** n. a herb used in cooking. **pothole** n. a deep hole in rock; a rough hole worn in a road surface. **potholing** n. exploring potholes in rock. **pothook** n. a hook over a fireplace for hanging or lifting a pot; a curved stroke in handwriting. **pothunter** n. a sportsman or sportswoman who shoots at random; a person who takes part in a contest merely for the sake of the prize. **pot luck**, whatever is available for a meal etc. **pot plant**, a plant grown in a flowerpot. **pot roast**, a piece of meat cooked slowly in a covered dish; (v.t.) to cook thus. **pot shot**, a random shot; a casual attempt. **potting shed**, a shed in which plants are grown in pots for planting out later. [Old English]

pot[2] n. (slang) marijuana. [probably from Mexican Spanish potiguaya]

potable /'pəʊtəbəl/ adj. drinkable. [French or from Latin potare = drink]

potage /pɒ'tɑːʒ/ n. thick soup. [French = pottage]

potash /'pɒtæʃ/ n. a general name for any potassium-containing mineral, most often applied to potassium carbonate, K_2CO_3, or potassium hydroxide, KOH. Potassium carbonate, originally made by roasting plants to ashes in earthenware pots, is commercially produced from the mineral sylvite (potassium chloride, KCl) and is used mainly in making artificial fertilizers, glass, and soap. [from Dutch]

potassium /pə'tæsɪəm/ n. a soft, waxlike, silver-white, metallic element, symbol K (Latin Kalium), atomic number 19, relative atomic mass 39.0983. It is one of the ◊alkali metals and has a very low density; it floats on water, and is the second lightest metal (after lithium). It oxidizes rapidly when exposed to air and reacts violently with water. Of great abundance in the Earth's crust, it is widely distributed with other elements and found in salt and mineral deposits in the form of potassium aluminium silicates. [Dutch *potassa* = potash]

potation /pəˈteɪʃən/ *n.* drinking; a drink. [from Old French or Latin]

potato /pəˈteɪtəʊ/ *n.* (*plural* potatoes) a perennial plant *Solanum tuberosum*, family Solanaceae, with edible tuberous roots that are rich in starch. Used by the Andean Indians for at least 2,000 years before the Spanish Conquest, the potato was introduced to Europe by the mid-16th century, and reputedly to England by Walter Raleigh. See also ◊sweet potato (under ◊sweet). [from Spanish *patata* from South American Indian name]

poteen /pɒˈtiːn/ *n.* in Ireland, whisky from an illicit still. [from Irish *poitín*, diminutive]

Potemkin /pəˈtemkɪn/ Grigory Aleksandrovich, Prince Potemkin 1739–1791. Russian politician. He entered the army and attracted the notice of Catherine II, whose friendship he kept throughout his life. He was an active administrator who reformed the army, built the Black Sea Fleet, conquered the Crimea, developed S Russia, and founded the Kherson arsenal in 1788 (the first Russian naval base on the Black Sea).

potent[1] /ˈpəʊtənt/ *adj.* 1. powerful, strong; (of a reason) forceful, cogent. 2. (of a man) not sexually impotent. —**potency** *n.* [from Latin *potens* (*posse* = be able)]

potent[2] *adj.* in heraldry, with a crutch-head shape; formed by a series of such shapes. —*n.* in heraldry, a fur formed thus. [from Old French *potence* crutch from Latin *potentia* power (as prec.)]

potentate /ˈpəʊtənteɪt/ *n.* a monarch or ruler with great power. [from Old French or Latin]

potential /pəˈtenʃəl/ *adj.* capable of coming into being or of being developed or used etc. —*n.* 1. ability or capacity available for use or development; usable resources. 2. a quantity determining the energy of a mass in a gravitational field, of a charge in an electric field etc. A charged ◊conductor (sense 3), for example, has a higher potential than the earth, whose potential is taken by convention to be zero. An electric cell (battery) has a potential in relation to e.m.f. (◊electromotive force), which can make current flow in an external circuit. The difference in potential between two points (the potential difference) is expressed in ◊volts; that is, a 12V battery has a potential difference of 12 volts between its negative and positive terminals. —**potentiality** /-ʃiˈælɪtɪ/ *n.*, **potentially** *adv.* [from Old French or Latin *potentia* = power]

potential difference see ◊potential, sense 2.

potential energy ◊energy possessed by an object by virtue of its relative position or state (for example, as in a compressed spring). It is contrasted with ◊kinetic energy (see under ◊kinetic).

potentiometer *n.* in physics, an electrical ◊resistor that can be divided so as to compare, measure, or control voltages. A simple type consists of a length of uniform resistance wire (about 1 m/3 ft long) carrying a constant current provided by a battery connected across the ends of the wire. The source of potential difference (voltage) to be measured is connected (to oppose the cell) between one end of the wire, through a ◊galvanometer (instrument for measuring small currents), to a contact free to slide along the wire. The sliding contact is moved until the galvanometer shows no deflection. The ratio of the length of potentiometer wire in the galvanometer circuit to the total length of wire is then equal to the ratio of the unknown potential difference to that of the battery. In radio circuits, any rotary variable resistance (such as volume control) is referred to as a potentiometer.

pother /ˈpɒðə/ *n.* (*literary*) a commotion, fuss.

potion /ˈpəʊʃən/ *n.* a liquid for drinking as a medicine or drug. [from Old French from Latin *potus* = having drunk]

Potomac /pəˈtəʊmək/ river in W Virgina, Virginia and Maryland states, USA, rising in the Allegheny mountains, and flowing SE through Washington DC, into Chesapeake Bay. It is formed by the junction of the N Potomac, about 153 km/95 mi long, and S Potomac, about 209 km/130 mi long, and is itself 459 km/285 mi long.

potpourri *n.* 1. a scented mixture of dried petals and spices. 2. a musical or literary medley. [French = rotten pot]

Potter Beatrix Potter's classic picture books began as a series of letters to children.

Potsdam Conference a conference held at Potsdam, East Germany, in July 1945 between representatives of the USA, the UK, and the USSR. They established the political and economic principles governing the treatment of Germany in the initial period of Allied control at the end of World War II, and sent an ultimatum to Japan demanding unconditional surrender on pain of utter destruction.

potsherd /ˈpɒtʃɜːd/ *n.* a broken piece of earthenware (especially in archaeology).

pottage *n.* (*archaic*) a soup, a stew. [from Old French *potage*]

potter[1] *v.i.* to work on trivial tasks in a leisurely relaxed way. —**potterer** *n.* [frequentative of dialect *pote* = push]

potter[2] *n.* a maker of earthenware vessels. [Old English]

Potter /ˈpɒtə/ Beatrix 1866–1943. English writer and illustrator of children's books, beginning with *The Tale of Peter Rabbit* 1900. The series, which included *The Tailor of Gloucester* 1902, *The Tale of Mrs Tiggy Winkle* 1904, *The Tale of Jeremy Fisher* 1906, and a sequel to Peter Rabbit, *The Tale of the Flopsy Bunnies* 1909, was based on her observation of family, pets, and the wildlife around her home in the Lake Distric. Her diaries, written in a secret code, were translated and published in 1966.

Potter Stephen 1900–1969. British author of humorous studies in how to outwit and outshine others, including *Gamesmanship* 1947, *Lifemanship* 1950, and *One Upmanship* 1952.

pottery *n.* 1. vessels etc. made of baked clay. 2. a potter's work or workshop. —**the Potteries**, a district in N Staffordshire, seat of the English china and earthenware industry. Wedgwood and Minton are factory names associated with the Potteries. [from Old French]

potto *n.* an arboreal, nocturnal, African mammal *Perodicticus potto* belonging to the loris family of primates. It has a thick body, strong limbs, grasping feet and hands, and grows to 40 cm/16 in long. It has horny spines along its backbone, which it uses in self-defence. It climbs slowly, and eats insects, snails, fruit, and leaves.

potty[1] *adj.* (*slang*) 1. crazy, foolish. 2. insignificant, trivial.

potty[2] *n.* (*colloquial*) a chamber pot, especially for a child.

pouch *n.* 1. a small bag or detachable outside pocket. 2. a baglike formation. —*v.t.* 1. to put into a pouch; to pocket. 2. to make (part of a dress etc.) hang like a pouch. [from Old French]

pouffe /puːf/ *n.* a padded stool without legs, large enough to be used as a seat. [French]

poujadist *n.* a member of an extreme right-wing political movement in France led by Pierre Poujade (1920–), which was prominent in French politics 1954–58. Known in France as the *Union de Défense des Commerçants et Artisans*, it won 52 seats in the national election in 1956. Its voting strength came mainly from the lower-middle-class and petit-bourgeois sections of society but the return of ◊de Gaulle to power in 1958, and the foundation of the Fifth Republic led to a rapid decline in the movement's fortunes. [from P *Poujade*]

Poulenc /ˈpuːlæŋk/ Francis (Jean Marcel) 1899–1963. French composer and pianist. A self-taught composer of witty and irreverent music, he was a member of the group of French composers known as *Les* ◊*Six*. Among his many works are the operas *Les Mamelles de Tirésias* 1947, and *Dialogues des Carmélites* 1957, and the ballet *Les Biches* 1923.

Poulsen /ˈpəʊlsən/ Valdemar 1869–1942. Danish engineer who in 1900 was the first to demonstrate that sound could be recorded magnetically, originally on a moving steel wire or tape; this was the forerunner of the tape recorder.

poult /pəʊlt/ *n.* a young domestic fowl, turkey, or game bird. [contraction of *pullet*]

poulterer /ˈpəʊltərə/ *n.* a dealer in poultry and, usually, game. [from earlier *poulter* from Old French *pouletier*]

poultice /ˈpəʊltɪs/ *n.* a soft heated mass of bread or kaolin etc. applied to a sore part of the body. —*v.t.* to apply a poultice to. [originally *pultes*, plural from Latin *puls* = pottage, pap]

poultry /ˈpəʊltrɪ/ *n.* domestic fowls, ducks, geese, turkeys etc., especially as a source of food. [from Old French *pouletier*]

pounce *v.i.* 1. to spring or swoop down in a sudden attack. 2. to seize *on* (an opportunity, mistake etc.) eagerly. —*n.* a pouncing movement.

pound[1] /paʊnd/ *n.* 1. an imperial unit (symbol lb) of weight. The commonly used avoirdupois pound, also called the **imperial standard pound** (7,000 grains/0.45 kg), differs from the **pound troy** (5,760 grains/0.37 kg), which is used for weighing precious metals. 2. (*plural* **pounds** or **pound**) the currency unit of the UK (in full **pound sterling**); the currency unit of some other countries. —**pound note,** a banknote for one pound. **pound of flesh,** any legal but morally offensive demand (with allusion to Shylock's demand for a pound of Antonio's flesh, pledged as security for a loan, in Shakespeare's *Merchant of Venice*). [Old English from Latin *pondo* = Roman pound weight]

pound[2] *v.t./i.* 1. to crush or beat with heavy repeated strokes. 2. to deliver heavy blows or gunfire etc. 3. to make one's way heavily. 4. (of the heart) to beat heavily. [Old English]

pound[3] *n.* an enclosure where stray animals or officially removed vehicles are kept until claimed. [from Old English]

Pound Ezra 1885–1972. US poet, who lived in London from 1908. His *Personae* and *Exultations* 1909 established the principles of the Imagist movement (see ◊Imagism). His largest work was the series of *Cantos* 1925–69 (intended to number 100), which attempted a massive reappraisal of history.

poundage *n.* a commission or fee of so much per pound in money or weight.

pounder *n.* a thing that weighs a pound or (**-pounder**) so many pounds; a gun carrying a shell of such weight.

pour /pɔː/ *v.t./i.* 1. to flow or cause to flow especially downwards in a stream or shower; to serve by pouring. 2. to rain heavily. 3. to come or go in profusion or rapid succession. 4. to discharge or send freely. 5. to utter at length or in a rush. —**pourer** *n.*

Poussin /puːˈsæŋ/ Nicolas 1594–1665. French painter, active chiefly in Rome; court painter to Louis XIII 1640–43. He was one of France's foremost landscape painters in the 17th century. He painted mythological and literary scenes in a strongly classical style: for example, *Rape of the Sabine Women* about 1636–37 (Metropolitan Museum of Art, New York).

pout *v.t./i.* to push forward one's lips as a sign of displeasure or sulking; to protrude (the lips); (of the lips) to be pushed forward thus. —*n.* a pouting expression.

pouter *n.* a kind of pigeon that can inflate its crop greatly.

poverty /ˈpɒvətɪ/ *n.* 1. the condition that exists when the basic needs of human beings (shelter, food and clothing) are not being met. 2. scarcity, lack. 3. inferiority, poorness. —**poverty line,** the minimum income level needed to secure the necessities of life. **poverty-stricken** *adj.* greatly affected by poverty. **poverty trap,** a situation in which an increase of income incurs loss of state benefits

so that the recipient is no better off than before. [from Old French from Latin *paupertas*]

POW abbreviation of prisoner of war.

powder *n.* 1. a mass of fine dry particles. 2. a medicine or cosmetic in this form. 3. gunpowder. —*v.t.* 1. to apply powder to. 2. to reduce to a fine powder. —**powder blue,** pale blue. **powder puff,** a soft pad for applying powder to the skin. **powder room,** a ladies' lavatory in a public building. —**powdery** *adj.,* **powderiness** *n.* [from Old French *poudre* from Latin *pulvis*]

powder metallurgy a method of shaping heat-resistant metals such as tungsten. Metal is pressed into a mould in powdered form and then sintered (heated to very high temperatures).

Powell /ˈpəʊəl/ Anthony (Dymoke) 1905– . English novelist who wrote the monumental series of 12 volumes *A Dance to the Music of Time* 1951–75 that begins shortly after World War I and chronicles a period of 50 years in the lives of Nicholas Jenkins and his circle of upper-class friends.

Powell /ˈpəʊəl/ Cecil Frank 1903–1969. English physicist, awarded the Nobel Prize for Physics in 1950 for his use of photographic emulsion as a method of tracking charged nuclear particles.

Powell (John) Enoch 1912– . British Conservative politician. He was minister of health 1960–63, and contested the party leadership in 1965. In 1968 he made a speech against immigration that led to his dismissal from the shadow cabinet. He resigned from the party in 1974, and was Official Unionist Party member for South Down, Northern Ireland 1974–87.

Powell Michael 1905–1990. English film director, who collaborated with screenwriter Emeric Pressburger. Their work, often criticized for extravagance, is richly imaginative, and includes the films *A Matter of Life and Death* 1946, and *Black Narcissus* 1947.

Powell William 1892–1984. US film actor who co-starred with Myrna Loy in the *Thin Man* series of films 1934–1947. He also played leading roles in *My Man Godfrey* 1936, *Life with Father* 1947, and *Mister Roberts* 1955. He retired in 1955.

power *n.* 1. the ability to do something; a particular faculty of the body or mind. 2. vigour, energy. 3. an active property or function. 4. (*colloquial*) a large amount. 5. control, influence; ascendancy. 6. authorization. 7. an influential person or organization etc.; a state having international influence. 8. a deity. 9. capacity for exerting mechanical force. 10. mechanical or electrical energy as opposed to hand labour; (*attributive*) operated by this. 11. in physics, the rate of doing work or consuming energy. It is measured in watts, or other units of work per unit time. 12. the electricity supply. 13. in mathematics, that which is represented by an ◊exponent (sense 4) or index, denoted by a superior small numeral. A number or symbol raised to the power of two, that is, multiplied by itself, is said to be squared (for example, 3^2, x^2), and something raised to the power of three is said to be cubed (for example, 2^3, y^3). 14. the magnifying capacity of a lens. —*v.t.* to supply with mechanical or electrical energy. —**power point,** a socket in a wall etc. for connecting an electrical device to the mains. **the powers that be,** those in authority. [Anglo-French *poer* from Latin]

powerboat *n.* any ◊motorboat used for racing.

powerful *adj.* having great power or influence. —**powerfully** *adv.,* **powerfulness** *n.*

powerhouse *n.* 1. a power station. 2. a person etc. of great energy.

powerless *adj.* without power; wholly unable. —**powerlessly** *adv.,* **powerlessness** *n.*

power of attorney in law, legal authority to act on behalf of another, for a specific transaction, or for a particular period.

power station a building where electrical power is generated for distribution (see ◊electricity). The largest in Europe is the Drax near Selby, Yorkshire, England, which supplies 10% of Britain's electricity.

powwow /ˈpaʊwaʊ/ *n.* a conference or meeting for discussion (originally among North American Indians). —*v.i.* to hold a powwow. [from Algonquian = magician]

Powys /ˈpəʊɪs/ county in central Wales; **area** 5,080 sq km/ 1,961 sq mi; **administrative headquarters** Llandrindod Wells; **physical** Brecon Beacons National Park; Black mountains; rivers: Wye, Severn, which both rise on Plynlimon (see ◊Dyfed); **products** agriculture, dairy cattle, sheep; **population** (1987) 113,000; **language** 20% Welsh, English.

Powys John Cowper 1872–1963. English novelist. His mystic and erotic books include *Wolf Solent* 1929 and *A Glastonbury Romance* 1933. He was one of three brothers (**Theodore Francis Powys** (1875–1953) and **Llewelyn Powys** (1884–1939)), all writers.

pox *n.* a virus disease with pocks; (*colloquial*) syphilis. [alternative spelling of *pocks*, plural of *pock*]

Poznań /'pɒznæn/ (German *Posen*) industrial city (machinery, aircraft, beer) in W Poland; population (1985) 553,000. Settled by German immigrants in 1253, it passed to Prussia in 1793 but was restored to Poland in 1919.

Pozsgay /'pɒʒgaɪ/ Imre 1933– . Hungarian socialist politician, presidential candidate for the Hungarian Socialist Party from 1989. Influential in the democratization of Hungary 1988–89, he was rejected by the electorate in the parliamentary elections of March 1990, coming a poor third in his constituency.

pp abbreviation of 1. per pro(curationem). [Latin = by proxy] 2. in music, pianissimo. [Italian = very softly]

pp. abbreviation of pages.

ppm abbreviation of parts per million.

PPS abbreviation of 1. Parliamentary Private Secretary. 2. additional postscript (*postpostscript*).

Pr symbol for ◊praseodymium.

PR abbreviation of 1. proportional representation. 2. public relations.

practicable /'præktɪkəbəl/ *adj.* that can be done or used; possible in practice. —**practicability** /-'bɪlɪtɪ/ *n.* [from French]

practical /'præktɪkəl/ *adj.* 1. involving activity as distinct from study or theory. 2. suited to use or action. 3. (of a person) inclined to action; able to do or make functional things well. 4. virtual. —*n.* a practical examination or lesson. —**practical joke**, a humorous trick played on a person. —**practicality** /-'kælɪtɪ/ *n.* [from obsolete French or Latin from Greek *prattō* = do]

practically *adv.* 1. virtually, almost. 2. in a practical way.

practice /'præktɪs/ *n.* 1. a habitual action, a custom. 2. repeated exercise to improve a skill; a spell of this. 3. action as opposed to theory. 4. the professional work of a doctor, lawyer etc.; this as a business; the patients or clients regularly consulting these. —**out of practice**, temporarily lacking a former skill etc.

practise /'præktɪs/ *v.t./i.* 1. to do habitually; to carry out in action. 2. to do repeatedly as an exercise to improve a skill. 3. to pursue (a profession, religion etc.; also *absolute*). 4. (in *past participle*) experienced, expert. [from Old French or Latin from Greek *prattō* = do]

practitioner /præk'tɪʃənə/ *n.* a person practising a profession, especially medicine.

Prado /'prɑːdəʊ/ Spanish art gallery (*Réal Museo de Pintura del Prado*/Royal Picture Gallery of the Prado), containing the national collection of pictures, founded by Charles III in 1785.

praemunire *n.* (one of) three English acts of Parliament passed in 1353, 1365, and 1393, aimed to prevent appeal to the pope against the power of the king, and therefore an early demonstration of independence from Rome. The statutes were opposed by English bishops.

praenomen /priː'nəʊmen/ *n.* an ancient Roman's first or personal name (e.g. *Marcus* Tullius Cicero). [Latin *prae* = before and *nomen* = name]

praesidium variant of ◊presidium.

praetor /'priːtə/ *n.* in ancient Rome, a magistrate, elected annually, who assisted the ◊consuls (sense 2) and presided over the civil courts. After a year in office, a praetor would act as a provincial governor for a further year. The number of praetors was finally increased to eight. [from French or Latin, perhaps from *prae* = before and *ire* = go]

praetorian /priː'tɔːrɪən/ *adj.* of a praetor. —**Praetorian Guard**, in ancient Rome, soldiers who formed the bodyguard of a general or of the emperor. [from Latin]

pragmatic /præg'mætɪk/ *adj.* 1. dealing with matters from a practical point of view. 2. treating the facts of history with reference to their practical lessons. —**pragmatically** *adv.* [from Latin from Greek *pragma* = deed]

pragmatism /'prægmətɪzəm/ *n.* 1. the matter-of-fact treatment of things. 2. a philosophy that evaluates assertions solely by their practical consequences and bearing on human interests. —**pragmatist** *n.* [from Greek *pragma*]

Prague /prɑːg/ (Czech *Praha*) city and capital of Czechoslovakia on the river Vltava; population (1985) 1,190,000. Industries include cars, aircraft, chemicals, paper and printing, clothing, brewing, and food processing. It became the capital in 1918.

Prague Spring the 1968 programme of liberalization, begun under a new Communist Party leader in Czechoslovakia. In Aug 1968 Soviet tanks invaded Czechoslavkia and entered the capital Prague to put down the liberalization movement initiated by the prime minister Alexander Dubček, who had earlier sought to assure the Soviets that his planned reforms would not threaten socialism. Dubček was arrested but released soon afterwards. Most of the Prague Spring reforms were reversed.

Praha Czech name for ◊Prague.

Praia /'praɪə/ port and capital of the Republic of Cape Verde, on the island of São Tiago (Santiago); population (1980) 37,500. Industries include fishing and shipping.

prairie /'preərɪ/ *n.* a large treeless area of grassland, especially in North America. —**prairie dog**, a North American rodent of the genus *Cynomys* with a bark like a dog's. See ◊marmot. **prairie oyster**, a raw egg seasoned and swallowed whole. [from Old French, ultimately from Latin *pratum* = meadow]

praise /preɪz/ *v.t.* 1. to express warm approval or admiration of. 2. to glorify (God) in words. —*n.* praising; approval expressed in words. [from Old French *preisier* from Latin *pretiare* (*pretium* = price)]

praiseworthy *adj.* worthy of praise.

Prakrit /'prɑːkrɪt/ *n.* a general name for the ancient Indo-European dialects of N India, contrasted with the sacred classical language Sanskrit. The Prakrits are considered to be the ancestors of such modern N Indian languages as Hindi, Punjabi, and Bengali. [Prakrit (Sanskrit word) = natural]

praline /'prɑːliːn/ *n.* a sweet made by browning nuts in boiling sugar. [French, from Marshal de Plessis-*Pralin* (1598–1675), whose cook invented it]

pram *n.* a four-wheeled carriage for a baby, pushed by a person walking. The invention dates from the mid-19th century. [abbreviation of *perambulator*]

prance /prɑːns/ *v.i.* 1. to walk or behave in an elated or arrogant manner. 2. (of a horse) to raise the forelegs and spring from the hind legs. —*n.* prancing; a prancing movement.

prang *v.t.* (*slang*) 1. to crash (an aircraft or vehicle); to damage by impact. 2. to bomb (a target) successfully. —*n.* (*slang*) a crash; damage by impact. [imitative]

prank *n.* a practical joke, a piece of mischief.

prankster *n.* a person fond of playing pranks.

praseodymium /preɪsɪə'dɪmɪəm/ *n.* a silver-white, malleable, metallic element of the ◊lanthanide series, symbol Pr, atomic number 59, relative atomic mass 140.907. It occurs in nature in the minerals monzanite and bastnasite, and its green salts are used to colour glass and ceramics. [from German from Greek *prasios* = leek-green (from its green salts) and *dymium*]

prat *n.* (*slang*) 1. a fool. 2. the buttocks.

prate *v.i.* to chatter, to talk too much; to talk foolishly or irrelevantly. —*n.* prating, idle talk. [from Middle Dutch or Middle Low German]

prattle *v.i.* to chatter or say in a childish way. —*n.* childish chatter; inconsequential talk.

prawn *n.* an edible shellfish of the genus *Palaemon*, *Penaeus* etc. The **common prawn** *Leander serratus*, of temperate seas has a long saw-edged spike or rostrum just in front of its eyes, and antennae much longer than its body length. It is distinguished from the shrimp not only by its larger size, but by having pincers on its second pair of legs.

Praxiteles /præk'sɪtəliːz/ mid-4th century BC. Greek sculptor, active in Athens. His *Aphrodite of Knidos* of about 350 BC (known through Roman copies) is thought to have initiated the tradition of life-size freestanding female nudes in Greek sculpture.

pray *v.t./i.* 1. to say prayers. 2. to make a devout supplication; to entreat; to ask earnestly (for). 3. (*archaic*, before an imperative) please. —**praying mantis,** see ◊mantis. [from Old French *preier* from Latin *precari*]

prayer[1] /ˈpreə/ *n.* **1.** a solemn request or thanksgiving to God or to an object of worship; a formula used in praying. Within Christianity, the Catholic and Orthodox churches sanction prayer to the Virgin Mary, angels, and saints as intercessors, whereas Protestantism limits prayer to God alone. **2.** the act of praying; a religious service consisting largely of prayers. **3.** an entreaty to a person. —**prayer book,** a book of set prayers. **prayer mat,** a small rug on which Muslims kneel to pray. **prayer wheel,** a revolving cylindrical box inscribed with or containing prayers, used especially by the Buddhists of Tibet. [from Old French from Latin *prex* = prayer]

prayer[2] /ˈpreɪə/ *n.* one who prays.

pre- prefix meaning before (in time, place, order, degree, or importance). [from Latin *prae* = before]

preach *v.t./i.* **1.** to deliver a sermon or religious address; to deliver (a sermon); to make (the Gospel) known by preaching. **2.** to give moral advice in an obtrusive way. **3.** to advocate or urge people to (a quality or practice etc.). —**preacher** *n.* [from Old French from Latin *praedicare* = proclaim]

preamble *n.* a preliminary statement; the introductory part of a statute or document etc. [from Old French from Latin *ambulare* = walk]

prearrange /priːəˈreɪndʒ/ *v.t.* to arrange beforehand. —**prearrangement** *n.*

prebend /ˈprebənd/ *n.* the stipend of a canon or member of a chapter; the portion of land or tithe from which this is drawn. —**prebendal** *adj.* [from Old French from Latin *praebenda* = pension (*praebēre* = grant)]

prebendary /ˈprebəndərɪ/ *n.* a holder of a prebend; an honorary canon. [from Latin]

Precambrian /priːˈkæmbrɪən/ *adj.* of the geological era preceding the Cambrian period and Palaeozoic era. —*n.* this era, the time from the formation of Earth (4.6 billion years ago) up to 590 million years ago. Its boundary with the Cambrian period marks the time when animals first developed hard outer parts (exoskeletons) and so left abundant fossil remains. It comprises about 85% of geological time and is divided into two periods: the Archaean and the Proterozoic.

precarious /prɪˈkeərɪəs/ *adj.* uncertain, dependent on chance; insecure. —**precariously** *adv.*, **precariousness** *n.* [from Latin = obtained by entreaty (*prex* = prayer)]

precast /priːˈkɑːst/ *adj.* (of concrete) cast in blocks before use.

precaution /prɪˈkɔːʃən/ *n.* an action taken beforehand to avoid a risk or ensure a good result. —**precautionary** *adj.* [from French from Latin *cavere* = take heed]

precede /prɪˈsiːd/ *v.t.* to come, go, or place before in time, order, importance etc. [from Old French from Latin *praecedere* (*prae* = before and *cedere* = go)]

precedence /ˈpresɪdəns/ *n.* priority in time or order etc.; the right of preceding others.

precedent /ˈpresɪdənt/ *n.* **1.** a previous case taken as an example for subsequent cases or as a justification. **2.** the ◊common law principle (see under ◊common) that, in deciding a particular case, judges are bound to follow any applicable principles of law laid down by superior courts in earlier reported cases. —*adj.* preceding in time or order etc. [from Old French]

precentor /prɪˈsentə/ *n.* one who leads the singing or (in a synagogue) the prayers of a congregation. [from French or Latin *praecentor* (*prae* = before and *canere* = sing)]

precept /ˈpriːsept/ *n.* **1.** a command, a rule of conduct. **2.** a writ, a warrant. [from Latin *praeceptum* from *praecipere* = warn, instruct]

preceptor /prɪˈseptə/ *n.* a teacher, an instructor. —**preceptorial** /-ˈtɔːrɪəl/ *adj.*, **preceptress** *n.fem.*

precession /prɪˈseʃən/ *n.* the slow movement of the axis of a spinning body round another axis (e.g. that of a spinning top, initially vertical but describing a cone round its original position as the top slows down). The gravitational pulls of the Sun and Moon on the Earth's equatorial bulge cause the Earth's axis to trace out a circle on the sky every 25,800 years. The position of the celestial poles (see ◊celestial sphere) is constantly changing owing to precession, as are the positions of the equinoxes (the points at which the celestial equator intersects the Sun's path around the

sky). —**precession of the equinoxes,** the apparent slow retrograde motion of the equinoctial points along the ecliptic (the path that the Sun appears to follow); the resulting earlier occurrence of the equinoxes in each successive sidereal year. [from Latin]

pre-Christian /priːˈkrɪstjən/ *adj.* before Christianity.

precinct /ˈpriːsɪŋkt/ *n.* **1.** an enclosed area, especially round a place of worship. **2.** (in full **pedestrian precinct**) an area in a town where traffic is prohibited. **3.** (in *plural*) environs. **4.** (*US*) a subdivision of a county, city, or ward for election and police purposes. [from Latin *praecingere* = encircle]

preciosity /preʃɪˈɒsɪtɪ/ *n.* overrefinement, especially in choice of words. [from Old French from Latin]

precious /ˈpreʃəs/ *adj.* **1.** of great value or worth. **2.** beloved; much prized. **3.** affectedly refined. **4.** (*colloquial*, often *ironic*) considerable. —*adv.* (*colloquial*) extremely, very. —**precious metals,** gold, silver, and platinum. **precious stone,** a piece of mineral having great value, especially as used in jewellery. —**preciously** *adv.*, **preciousness** *n.* [from Old French from Latin *pretiosus* (*pretium* = price)]

precipice /ˈpresɪpɪs/ *n.* a vertical or steep face of a rock, cliff, mountain etc. [from French from Latin *praecipitare*]

precipitance /prɪˈsɪpɪtəns/ *n.* or **precipitancy** rash haste. [from obsolete French]

precipitate /prɪˈsɪpɪteɪt/ *v.t.* **1.** to cause to happen suddenly or soon; to make occur prematurely. **2.** to send rapidly into a certain state or condition. **3.** to throw down headlong. **4.** to cause (a substance) to be deposited in solid form from a solution. **5.** to condense (a vapour) into drops which fall as rain etc. —/-tət/ *adj.* headlong, violently hurried; (of a person or act) hasty, rash, inconsiderate. —/-tət/ *n.* a substance precipitated from a solution; moisture condensed from vapour and falling as rain etc. In chemistry, a precipitate (ppt) is often represented by the symbol (s) in equations. —**precipitately** *adv.* [from Latin *praecipitare* (*praeceps* = headlong)]

precipitation /prɪsɪpɪˈteɪʃən/ *n.* **1.** precipitating, being precipitated. **2.** rash haste. **3.** the meteorological term for water that falls to the Earth from the atmosphere; the quantity of this. It includes rain, snow, sleet, hail, dew, and frost. [from French or Latin]

precipitous /prɪˈsɪpɪtəs/ *adj.* of or like a precipice, dangerously steep; precipitate. —**precipitously** *adv.* [from obsolete French from Latin]

précis /ˈpreɪsiː/ *n.* (*plural* the same /-iːz/) a summary, an abstract. —*v.t.* to make a précis of. [French]

precise /prɪˈsaɪs/ *adj.* **1.** accurately expressed. **2.** exact, definite. **3.** scrupulous in being exact. [from French from Latin *praecidere* = cut short]

precisely *adv.* **1.** in a precise manner, exactly. **2.** in exact terms. **3.** (as a reply) quite so, as you say.

precision /prɪˈsɪʒən/ *n.* **1.** accuracy. **2.** (*attributive*) characterized by or adapted for precision. [from French or Latin]

preclude /prɪˈkluːd/ *v.t.* to exclude the possibility of, to prevent. [from Latin *praecludere* (*prae* = before and *claudere* = shut)]

precocious /prɪˈkəʊʃəs/ *adj.* (of a person) having developed certain abilities or characteristics earlier than is usual; (of abilities etc.) showing such development. —**precocity** /prɪˈkɒsɪtɪ/ *n.*, **precociously** *adv.* [from Latin *praecox* = prematurely ripe]

precognition /priːkɒgˈnɪʃən/ *n.* (supposed) foreknowledge, especially of a supernatural kind.

Pre-Columbian /prɪkəˈlʌmbɪən/ *adj.* of the period before the discovery of America by Columbus.

preconceive /priːkənˈsiːv/ *v.t.* to form (an idea or opinion etc.) beforehand.

preconception /priːkənˈsepʃən/ *n.* a preconceived idea; a prejudice.

precondition /priːkənˈdɪʃən/ *n.* a condition that must be fulfilled before something else can happen.

precursor /priːˈkɜːsə/ *n.* **1.** a forerunner, a harbinger. **2.** a thing that precedes a later and more developed form. [from Latin *praecurrere* = run before]

predacious /prɪˈdeɪʃəs/ *adj.* (of an animal) predatory. [from Latin *praeda* = plunder]

predate /priːˈdeɪt/ *v.t.* to antedate.

predator /'predətə/ n. a predatory animal, one that hunts and kills other animals for food. [from Latin *praedari* = seize as plunder]

predatory /'predətərɪ/ adj. 1. (of an animal) preying naturally upon others. 2. plundering or exploiting others.

predecease /pri:dɪ'si:s/ v.t. to die earlier than (another person).

predecessor /'pri:dɪsesə/ n. 1. a former holder of an office or position with respect to a later holder. 2. an ancestor. 3. a thing to which something else has succeeded. [from Old French from Latin]

predella /prɪ'delə/ n. 1. an altar step; a painting on the vertical face of this. 2. a raised shelf at the back of an altar; a painting or sculpture on this. [Italian = stool]

predestination /prɪdestɪ'neɪʃən/ n. in Christian theology, the doctrine asserting that God has determined all events beforehand, including the ultimate salvation or damnation of the individual human soul. Today Christianity in general accepts that humanity has free will, though some forms, such as Calvinism, believe that salvation can only be attained by the gift of God. The concept of predestination is also found in Islam. [from Latin *praedestinare* (*prae* = before and *destinare* = destine)]

predestine /pri:'destɪn/ v.t. to determine beforehand; to ordain by divine will or as if by fate.

predetermine /pri:dɪ'tɜ:mɪn/ v.t. to decide beforehand, to predestine. —**predetermination** /-'neɪʃən/ n.

predicable /'predɪkəbəl/ adj. that may be predicated or affirmed.

predicament /prɪ'dɪkəmənt/ n. a difficult or unpleasant situation.

predicate /'predɪkeɪt/ v.t. to assert or affirm as true or existent. —/-kət/ n. 1. in logic, what is predicated (e.g. *mortal* in *all men are mortal*). 2. in grammar, what is said about the subject of a sentence etc. (e.g. *went home* in *John went home*). —**predication** /-'keɪʃən/ n. [from Latin *praedicare* = proclaim]

predicative /prɪ'dɪkətɪv/ adj. forming part or all of the predicate (e.g. *old* in *the dog is old* but not in *the old dog*). —**predicatively** adv.

predict /prɪ'dɪkt/ v.t. to foretell, to prophesy. —**predictor** n. [from Latin *praedicere* (*prae* = before and *dicere* = say)]

predictable adj. that can be predicted or is to be expected. —**predictability** /-'bɪlɪtɪ/ n., **predictably** adv.

prediction /prɪ'dɪkʃən/ n. 1. predicting, being predicted. 2. a thing predicted.

predilection /pri:dɪ'lekʃən/ n. a preference or special liking. [from French from Latin *praediligere* = prefer]

predispose /pri:dɪ'spəʊz/ v.t. 1. to influence favourably in advance. 2. to render liable or inclined. —**predisposition** /-pə'zɪʃən/ n.

predominant /prɪ'dɒmɪnənt/ adj. predominating; being the strongest or main element. —**predominance** n., **predominantly** adv.

predominate /prɪ'dɒmɪneɪt/ v.i. 1. to have or exert control, to be superior. 2. to be the stronger or main element. [from Latin *prae* = before and *dominari* = dominate]

predynastic /pri:daɪ'næstɪk/ adj. of the period before dynasties, especially in ancient Egypt.

pre-eminent /pri:'emɪnənt/ adj. excelling others, outstanding. —**pre-eminence** n., **pre-eminently** adv.

pre-empt /pri:'empt/ v.t. to obtain by pre-emption; to appropriate beforehand; to forestall. [back formation from *pre-emption*]

pre-emption /pri:'empʃən/ n. the purchase or taking of a thing by one person or party before an opportunity is offered to others. [from Latin *prae* = before and *emere* = buy]

pre-emptive /pri:'emptɪv/ adj. pre-empting; (of a military action) intended to prevent an attack by disabling the enemy.

preen v.t. (of a bird) to tidy (the feathers) with the beak; (of a person) to smarten (oneself or one's clothes etc.). —**preen oneself**, to congratulate oneself, to show self-satisfaction. [variant of obsolete verb *prune*, associated with dialect *preen* = pierce]

pre-exist /pri:ɪg'zɪst/ v.t./i. to exist beforehand or prior to. —**pre-existence** n.

pref. abbreviation of 1. prefix. 2. preface. 3. prefatory. 4. preference. 5. preferred.

prefab /'pri:fæb/ (*colloquial*) abbreviation of prefabricated building.

prefabricate /pri:'fæbrɪkeɪt/ v.t. to manufacture in sections that are ready for assembly on a site. —**prefabrication** /-'keɪʃən/ n.

preface /'prefəs/ n. 1. an introduction to a book, stating its subject, scope etc. 2. the preliminary part of a speech. —v.t. 1. to provide or introduce with a preface. 2. to lead up to (an event). [from Old French from Latin *prae* = before and *fari* = speak]

prefatory /'prefətərɪ/ adj. of or serving as a preface, introductory.

prefect /'pri:fekt/ n. 1. the chief administrative officer of a department (in France, Italy, Japan etc.). In France prefects were replaced by presidents of elected councils in 1984. 2. a senior pupil in a school etc. authorized to maintain discipline. [from Old French from Latin *praeficere* = set in authority]

prefecture /'pri:fektjʊə/ n. a district under the government of a prefect; a prefect's office or tenure. [from French or Latin]

prefer /prɪ'fɜ:/ v.t. (-rr-) 1. to choose as more desirable, to like better. 2. to submit (information, an accusation etc.) for consideration. 3. to promote (a person) to an office. [from Old French from Latin *praeferre* (*prae* = before and *ferre* = bear)]

preferable /'prefərəbəl/ adj. to be preferred; more desirable. —**preferably** adv.

preference /'prefərəns/ n. 1. preferring, being preferred. 2. a thing preferred. 3. the favouring of one person etc. before others. 4. a prior right. —**in preference to**, as a thing preferred over (another). **preference shares** *or* **stock**, shares or stock on which a dividend is paid before profits are distributed to holders of ordinary shares etc. [from French from Latin]

preferential /prefə'renʃəl/ adj. of or involving preference; giving or receiving favour. —**preferentially** adv.

preferment /prɪ'fɜ:mənt/ n. promotion to an office.

prefigure /pri:'fɪgə/ v.t. to represent or imagine beforehand.

prefix /'pri:fɪks/ n. 1. a verbal element placed at the beginning of a word to qualify the meaning (e.g. *ex-*, *non-*). 2. a title placed before a name (e.g. *Mr*). —v.t. 1. to put as an introduction. 2. to join as a prefix (to a word).

preform /pri:'fɔ:m/ v.t. to form beforehand.

pregnant /'pregnənt/ adj. 1. (of a woman or female animal) having a child or young developing in the womb. 2. full of meaning, significant or suggestive. 3. (with *with*) full of. 4. fruitful in results. —**pregnancy** n. the period during which an embryo grows within the womb, beginning at conception and ending at birth. In humans the normal length is 40 weeks. After the second month, the breasts become tense and tender, and the area round the nipples becomes darker. Enlargement of the uterus can be felt at about the end of the third month, and thereafter the abdomen enlarges progressively. Pregnancy in animals is called ◊gestation. [from French or Latin, probably from *prae* = before and (*g*)*nasci* = be born]

prehensile /prɪ'hensaɪl/ adj. (of a tail or limb) capable of grasping things. [from French from Latin *prehendere* = seize]

prehistoric /pri:hɪ'stɒrɪk/ adj. 1. of the period before written records. 2. (*derogatory*) antiquated, long out of date. —**prehistorically** adv. [from French]

prehistoric life the diverse organisms that inhabited the Earth from the origin of life about 3.5 billion years ago to the time when humans began to keep written records in about 3500 BC. During the course of evolution, new forms of life developed and many other forms, such as the dinosaurs, became extinct. Prehistoric life evolved over this vast timespan from simple bacteria-like cells in the oceans to algae and protozoans and complex multicellar forms such as worms, molluscs, crustaceans, fishes, insects, land plants, amphibians, reptiles, birds, and mammals. On a geological timescale human beings evolved relatively recently, about 4 million years ago, although the exact dating is a matter of some debate. See also ◊geological time.

prehistory /pri:'hɪstərɪ/ n. human cultures before the use of writing. A classification system was devised in 1816 by the Danish archaeologist Christian Thomsen (1788–1865), based on the predominant materials used by early humans for tools and weapons.

Stone Age Stone, mainly flint, was predominant. The Stone Age is divided into the Old, Middle, and New Stone Ages:

Old Stone Age (Palaeolithic) 3,500,000–5000 BC. Tools were chipped into shape by early humans, or hominids, from Africa, Asia, the Middle East, and Europe as well as later Neanderthal and Cro-Magnon people; the only domesticated animals were dogs. Some Asians crossed the Bering land bridge to inhabit the Americas. Cave paintings were produced 20,000–8,000 years ago in many parts of the world, for example, Altamira, Spain; Lascaux, France; central Sahara; India; and Australia. **Middle Stone Age** (Mesolithic) and **New Stone Age** (Neolithic). Stone and bone tools were ground and polished as well as chipped. In Neolithic times, agriculture and the domestication of goats, sheep, and cattle began. Stone Age cultures survived in the Americas, Asia, Africa, Oceania, and Australia until the 19th and 20th centuries.

Bronze Age Bronze tools and weapons began to be used in approximately 6000 BC in the Far East, and continued in the Middle East until about 1200 BC; in Britain the Bronze Age lasted from about 2000 to 500 BC. The heroes of the Greek poet Homer lived in the Bronze Age.

Iron Age Iron was hardened (alloyed) by the addition of carbon, so that it superseded bronze for tools and weapons; in the Old World this was generally from about 1000 BC.

pre-ignition /priːɪgˈnɪʃən/ n. the premature firing of an explosive mixture in an internal-combustion engine.

prejudge /priːˈdʒʌdʒ/ v.t. to pass judgement on (a person) before a trial or proper enquiry; to form a premature judgement on.

prejudice /ˈpredʒʊdɪs/ n. 1. a preconceived opinion, like, or dislike. 2. injury to someone's rights etc. —v.t. 1. (especially in past participle) to cause to have a prejudice. 2. to injure (a person's right etc.). —**without prejudice**, without detriment to an existing right or claim. [from Old French from Latin prae = before and judicium = judgement]

prejudicial /predʒuˈdɪʃəl/ adj. causing prejudice; detrimental (to rights, interests etc.). —**prejudicially** adv.

prelacy /ˈprelǝsɪ/ n. 1. church government by prelates. 2. prelates collectively. 3. the office or rank of prelate. [from Anglo-French from Latin]

prelate /ˈprelǝt/ n. a high ecclesiastical dignitary, e.g. a bishop. —**prelatical** /prɪˈlætɪkǝl/ adj. [from Old French from Latin praelatus]

prelim /ˈpriːlɪm/ n. 1. (colloquial) a preliminary examination. 2. (in plural; also /ˈpriːlɪmz/) the front matter of a book, the pages preceding the text. [abbreviation]

preliminary /prɪˈlɪmɪnərɪ/ adj. introductory, preparatory. —n. (usually in plural) a preliminary action or arrangement. —adv. preparatory. —**preliminarily** adv. [from French from Latin limen = threshold]

prelude /ˈpreljuːd/ n. 1. an action, event, or situation that precedes another and leads up to it. 2. the introductory part of a poem etc. 3. in music, a composition intended as the preface to further music, to set a mood for a stage work, as in Wagner's Lohengrin; as used by Chopin, a short piano work. —v.t./i. to serve as a prelude to; to introduce with a prelude. [from French or Latin praeludium (prae = before and ludere = play)]

Premadasa /premǝˈdɑːsǝ/ Ranasinghe 1924– . Sri Lankan politician, a United National Party member of Parliament from 1960, prime minister from 1978, and president from 1988, having gained popularity through overseeing a major house-building and poverty-alleviation programme. He has sought peace talks with the Tamil Tigers.

premarital /priːˈmærɪtǝl/ adj. of the time before marriage; occurring before marriage.

premature /ˈpremǝtjʊǝ/ adj. occurring or done before the usual or proper time, too early; hasty; (of a baby) born at least three weeks before the expected time. —**prematurely** adv., **prematureness** n., **prematurity** /-ˈtjʊǝrɪtɪ/ n. [from Latin = very early (prae = early and maturus = mature)]

premedication /priːmediˈkeɪʃǝn/ n. or (colloquial) **premed** medication in preparation for an operation etc.

premeditate /priːˈmedɪteɪt/ v.t. (especially in past participle) to plan beforehand. —**premeditation** /-ˈteɪʃǝn/ n.

premenstrual /priːˈmenstrʊǝl/ adj. of the time immediately before each menstruation. —**premenstrual tension**, (PMT) the popular name for **premenstrual syndrome**, a medical condition caused by hormone changes and comprising a number of physical and emotional features that occur cyclically before menstruation and disappear with its onset. Symptoms include mood changes, breast tenderness, a feeling of bloatedness, and headache.

premier adj. first in importance, order, or time. —n. 1. (originally short for premier minister) a prime minister. 2. the head of the government of a province of Canada or state of Australia. —**premiership** n. [from Old French = first, from Latin primarius]

première /ˈpremɪǝ/ n. the first performance or showing of a play or film. —v.t. to give a première of. [French, feminine of premier adj.]

Preminger /ˈpremɪŋgǝ/ Otto (Ludwig) 1906–1986. US film producer, director, and actor. Born in Vienna, he went to the USA in 1935. He directed Margin for Error 1942, Laura 1944, The Moon is Blue 1953, The Man With the Golden Arm 1955, Anatomy of a Murder 1959, Skidoo! 1968, and Rosebud 1974. His films are characterized by an intricate technique of storytelling, and a masterly use of the wide screen and the travelling camera.

premise /ˈpremɪs/ n. 1. a premiss. 2. (in plural) a house or building with its grounds and appurtenances. 3. in law, the houses, lands, or tenements previously specified in a document etc. —**on the premises**, in the house etc. concerned. [from Old French from Latin praemissa (praemittere = send in front)]

premiss /ˈpremɪs/ n. a statement from which another is inferred. [variant of premise]

premium /ˈpriːmɪǝm/ n. 1. an amount to be paid for a contract of insurance. 2. a sum added to interest, wages etc. 3. a reward or prize. —**at a premium**, above the usual or nominal price, highly valued. **Premium (Savings) Bond**, a British government security without interest but with chances of cash prizes. **put a premium on**, to provide or act as an incentive to; to attach special value to. [from Latin praemium = reward]

premolar /priːˈmǝʊlǝ/ n. in mammals, one of the large teeth towards the back of the mouth, between the molar and canine teeth. In herbivores they are adapted for grinding. In carnivores they may be carnassials. Premolars are present in milk ◊dentition as well as permanent dentition. —adj. of these teeth.

premonition /priːmǝˈnɪʃǝn, pre-/ n. a forewarning, a presentiment. —**premonitory** /prɪˈmɒnɪtǝrɪ/ adj. [from French or Latin praemonēre = warn]

Premonstratensian /priːmɒnstrǝˈtensiǝn/ n. a Roman Catholic monastic order founded in 1120 by St Norbert (c.1080–1134), a German bishop, at Prémontré, N France. Members were known as White Canons. The rule was a stricter version of that of the Augustinian Canons.

Prempeh I /ˈprempeɪ/ chief of the Ashanti people in W Africa. He became king in 1888, and later opposed British attempts to take over the region. He was deported and in 1900 the Ashanti were defeated. He returned to Kumasi (capital of the Ashanti region) in 1924 as chief of the people.

prenatal /priːˈneɪtǝl/ adj. of the period before being born or before childbirth.

preoccupation /priːɒkjuˈpeɪʃǝn/ n. 1. the state of being preoccupied. 2. a thing that engrosses one's mind.

preoccupy /priːˈɒkjʊpaɪ/ v.t. 1. (of a thought etc.) to dominate or engross the mind of so as to exclude other thoughts; (in past participle) inattentive because of this. 2. to appropriate beforehand.

preordain /priːɔːˈdeɪn/ v.t. to decree or determine beforehand.

prep n. school work that a pupil is required to do outside lessons; a school period when this is done. —**prep school**, abbreviation of ◊preparatory school.

preparation /prepǝˈreɪʃǝn/ n. 1. preparing, being prepared. 2. a specially prepared substance. 3. = ◊prep. 4. (usually in plural) a thing done to make ready. [from Old French from Latin praeparare]

preparatory /prɪˈpærǝtǝrɪ/ adj. serving to prepare, introductory. —adv. in a preparatory way. —**preparatory school**, a fee-paying independent school. In the UK, it is a junior school which prepares students for entry to a senior school at about age 13. In the USA, it is a school which prepares children for university entrance at about age 18. [from Latin]

prepare /pri'peə/ v.t. 1. to make or get ready. 2. to make (food or other substances) ready for use; to assemble (a meal etc.) for eating. —**be prepared to,** to be disposed or willing to. [from French or Latin *praeparare* (*prae* = before and *parare* = make ready)]

prepay /pri:'peɪ/ v.t. to pay (a charge) beforehand; to pay the postage on (a letter or parcel etc.) beforehand, e.g. by buying and affixing a stamp. —**prepayment** n.

preponderate /pri'pɒndəreɪt/ v.i. to be greater in influence, quantity, or number; to weigh more; to predominate. —**preponderance** n., **preponderant** adj., **preponderantly** adv. [from Latin *praeponderare* (*prae* = before and *pondus* = weight)]

preposition /prepə'zɪʃən/ n. in grammar, a part of speech coming before a noun or a pronoun to show a location (*in*, *on*), time (*during*), or some other relationship (for example, figurative relationships in phrases like '*by heart*' or '*on* time'). —**prepositional** adj. [from Latin *praeponere* = place in front]

prepossess /pri:pə'zes/ v.t. 1. (usually in *passive*, of an idea etc.) to take possession of (a person). 2. to prejudice (usually favourably and at first sight). —**prepossession** n.

prepossessing adj. attractive, making a good impression on others.

preposterous /pri'pɒstərəs/ adj. utterly absurd, outrageous; contrary to nature, reason, or common sense. —**preposterously** adv. [from Latin, literally = back to front (*prae* = before and *posterus* = coming after)]

prepuce /'pri:pju:s/ n. the foreskin; a similar structure at the tip of the clitoris. [from Latin *praeputium*]

Pre-Raphaelite /pri:'ræfɪəlaɪt/ n. an artist or writer in the mid-19th century who aimed at producing work in the spirit that prevailed before the time of the Italian artist ◊Raphael. —**Pre-Raphaelite Brotherhood,** a group of British painters 1848–53; Dante Gabriel Rossetti, John Everett Millais, and Holman Hunt were founding members. They aimed to paint serious subjects, to study nature closely, and to shun the influence of painterly styles post-Raphael. Their subjects were mainly biblical and literary, painted with obsessive naturalism. Artists associated with the group include Edward Burne-Jones and William Morris.

prerequisite /pri:'rekwɪzɪt/ adj. required as a precondition. —n. a prerequisite thing.

prerogative /pri'rɒgətɪv/ n. a right or privilege exclusive to an individual or class. [from Old French or Latin *praerogativa*, originally = tribe voting first (*praerogare* = ask first)]

presage /'presɪdʒ/ n. 1. an omen, a portent. 2. a presentiment. —(also pri'seɪdʒ) v.t. 1. to portend, to be an advance sign of. 2. to predict, to have a presentiment of. [from French from Latin *praesagium* (*prae* = before and *sagire* = perceive keenly)]

Presbyopia see ◊long sight.

presbyter /'prezbɪtə/ n. in the Episcopal Church, a minister of the second order, a priest; in the Presbyterian Church, an elder. [Latin from Greek = elder]

Presbyterianism /prezbi'tɪərɪənɪzəm/ n. a system of Christian Protestant church government, expounded during the ◊Reformation by John Calvin, which gives its name to the established Church of Scotland, and is also practised in England, Ireland, Switzerland, North America, and elsewhere. There is no compulsory form of worship and each congregation is governed by presbyters or elders (clerical or lay), who are of equal rank. Congregations are grouped in presbyteries, synods, and general assemblies. —**Presbyterian** n. a member of the Presbyterian Church; an adherent of the Presbyterian system. —adj. of or relating to Presbyterianism. [from Latin *presbyterium*]

presbytery /'prezbɪtərɪ/ n. 1. a body of presbyters, especially the court next above the kirk session. 2. the eastern part of a chancel. 3. the house of a Roman Catholic priest. [from Old French from Latin from Greek = elder]

preschool /'pri:sku:l/ adj. of the time before a child is old enough to attend school.

prescient /'presɪənt/ adj. having foreknowledge or foresight. —**prescience** n. [from Latin *praescire* (*prae* = before and *scire* = know)]

Prescott /'preskət/ John Leslie 1938– . British Labour Party politician, a member of the ◊Kinnock shadow cabinet. A strong parliamentary debater and television performer, he is sometimes critical of his colleagues. In 1988 he unsuccessfully challenged Roy Hattersley for the deputy leadership.

prescribe /pri'skraɪb/ v.t. 1. to lay down as a course or rule to be followed. 2. to advise the use of (a medicine etc.). [from Latin *praescribere* = direct in writing]

prescript /'pri:skrɪpt/ n. an ordinance, a law, a command. [from Latin *praescriptum*]

prescription /pri'skrɪpʃən/ n. 1. prescribing. 2. an order written in a recognized form by a practitioner of medicine, dentistry, or veterinary surgery to a pharmacist for a preparation of medications to be used in treatment; a medication thus prescribed. 3. in English law, the legal acquisition of title or right (such as an ◊easement) by uninterrupted use or possession. [from Old French from Latin]

prescriptive /pri'skrɪptɪv/ adj. 1. prescribing; laying down rules. 2. based on prescription; prescribed by custom.

presence /'prezəns/ n. 1. being present in a place; the place where a person is. 2. a person's appearance or bearing, especially when imposing. 3. a person or thing that is present. —**presence of mind,** calmness and self-command in a sudden difficulty etc. [from Old French from Latin]

present[1] /'prezənt/ adj. 1. being in the place in question. 2. now existing, occurring, or being such. 3. now being considered etc. 4. in grammar, expressing an action etc. now going on or habitually performed. —n. 1. the time now passing. 2. in grammar, the present tense. —**at present,** now. **by these presents,** in law, by this document. **for the present,** just now, as far as the present is concerned. **present-day** adj. of this time, modern. [from Old French from Latin *praeesse* = be at hand]

present[2] /'prezənt/ n. a thing given.

present[3] /pri'zent/ v.t. 1. to introduce (a person) to another or others. 2. to give as a gift or award; to offer for acceptance, attention, consideration etc. 3. to show, to reveal (a quality etc.). 4. to level or aim (a weapon). —**present arms,** to hold a rifle etc. vertically in front of the body as a salute. —**presenter** n. [from Old French from Latin *praesentare*]

presentable /pri'zentəbəl/ adj. of good appearance, fit to be presented. —**presentability** /-'bɪltɪ/ n., **presentably** adv.

presentation /prezən'teɪʃən/ n. 1. presenting, being presented. 2. a thing presented.

presentiment /pri'zentɪmənt/ n. a vague expectation, a foreboding (especially of evil). [from obsolete French]

presently /'prezəntlɪ/ adv. 1. soon, after a short time. 2. (especially *US* and *Scottish*) at the present time, now.

present participle see ◊participle.

preservative /pri'zɜːvətɪv/ n. a food ◊additive used to inhibit the growth of bacteria, yeasts, mould, and other microorganisms to extend the shelf life of foods. The term sometimes refers to ◊antioxidants as well. All preservatives are potentially damaging to health if eaten in sufficient quantity. Both the amount used, and the foods in which they can be used, are restricted by law. —adj. tending to preserve.

preserve /pri'zɜːv/ v.t. 1. to keep safe; to keep in an unchanged condition; to retain (a quality or condition). 2. to keep from decay; to treat (food etc.) so as to prevent decomposition or fermentation. 3. to protect (game, or a river etc.) for private use. —n. 1. (also in *plural*) preserved fruit, jam. 2. a place where game etc. is preserved. 3. a sphere regarded by a person as being for him or her alone. —**preservation** /prezə'veɪʃən/ n., **preserver** n. [from Old French from Latin *praeservare* (*prae* = before and *servare* = keep)]

preside /pri'zaɪd/ v.i. to be chairperson or president; to have the position of authority or control. [from French from Latin *praesidēre* (*prae* = before and *sedēre* = sit)]

presidency /'prezɪdənsɪ/ n. the office of president; the period of this. [from Spanish or Italian from Latin]

president /'prezɪdənt/ n. 1. the usual title of the head of state in a republic; the power of the office may range from the equivalent of a constitutional monarch to the actual head of the government. 2. a person who is head of a society or council etc.; the head of some colleges; (*US*)

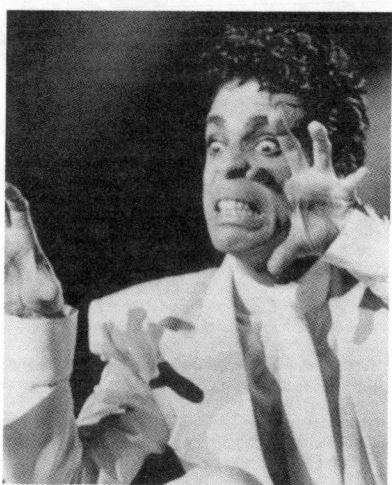

Prince US pop singer and versatile musician, Prince.

the head of a university or company etc.; the person in charge of a meeting. —**presidential** /-'denʃəl/ *adj.* [from Old French from Latin]

presidium /prɪ'sɪdɪəm/ *n.* or **praesidium** a standing committee in a communist organization, especially that of the Supreme Soviet in the Soviet Union which functions as the ultimate legislative authority when the Soviet itself is not sitting. The ◊Politburo was also known as the Praesidium 1952–66. [from Russian from Latin *praesidium* = garrison]

Presley /'prezli/ Elvis (Aaron) 1935–1977. US singer and guitarist, born in Tupelo, Mississippi. With his recordings for Sun Records in Memphis, Tennessee, 1954–55 and early hits such as 'Heartbreak Hotel' 1956, 'Hound Dog' 1956, and 'Love Me Tender' 1956, he created an individual vocal style, influenced by Southern blues, gospel music, country music, and rhythm and blues.

press[1] *v.t./i.* 1. to apply steady force to (a thing in contact). 2. to compress or squeeze (a thing) so as to flatten, shape, or smooth it or extract juice etc.; to make by pressing; to squeeze out (juice etc.); to iron (clothes etc.). 3. to be urgent, to require immediate action. 4. to throng closely; to push one's way; to hasten. 5. to exert pressure on (an enemy etc.); to oppress. 6. to urge or entreat; to make an insistent demand (upon). 7. to force the acceptance of; to insist upon. 8. in golf, to strike the ball imperfectly by trying too hard for a long hit. —*n.* 1. pressing. 2. a device or machinery for compressing, flattening, or shaping something, or for extracting juice. 3. a printing press; a printing or publishing firm. 4. the news media, in particular the newspapers, journals, and periodical literature generally; journalists and photographers etc. involved in these; publicity in newspapers etc. 5. crowding; a throng of people. 6. haste; the pressure of affairs. 7. a large, usually shelved cupboard for clothes, books etc. —**be pressed for,** to have barely enough (time etc.). **go** *or* **send to press,** to go or send to be printed. **press agent,** a person employed to attend to advertising and press publicity. **press conference,** an interview given to a body of journalists. **press gallery,** a gallery for reporters, especially in a legislative assembly. **press stud,** a small fastening device engaged by pressing the two parts together. **press-up** *n.* (usually in *plural*) an exercise in which a person lying prone presses down on the hands to straighten the arms so that head, shoulders, and trunk are raised. [from Old French from Latin *pressare*, frequentative of *premere* = press]

press[2] *v.t.* (*historical*) to force to serve in the army or navy. —**press gang,** (*historical*) a body of men employed to force men to serve in the army or navy; a group using coercive methods; (*v.t.*) to force into service. **press into service,** to bring into use as a makeshift. [alteration of obsolete *prest* from Old French = loan, advance pay, from Latin *praestare* = furnish]

Pressburger /'presbɜːgə/ Emeric 1902–1988. Hungarian director, producer, and screenwriter, known for his partnership with Michael ◊Powell.

Press Council in the UK, the organization (established in 1953) that aims to preserve the freedom of the press, to maintain standards, consider complaints, and report on monopoly developments.

pressing *adj.* urgent; urging strongly. —*n.* a thing made by pressing, especially a gramophone record; a series of such made at one time.

pressure /'preʃə/ *n.* 1. the exertion of continuous force on or against a body by another in contact with it; the force so exerted; the amount of this. 2. in physics, force per unit area. At the edge of the Earth's atmosphere, pressure is zero, whereas at ground level it is about 1013.25 millibars (or 1 atmosphere). Pressure at a depth h in a fluid of density d is equal to *hdg*, where g is the acceleration due to gravity. The SI unit of pressure is the ◊pascal (one newton per square metre), equal to 0.01 millibars. Pressure has also been measured using a mercury column (see ◊Torricelli) with 1 atmosphere equalling 760 mm of mercury. 3. urgency. 4. an affliction or difficulty. 5. a constraining influence. —*v.t.* to apply pressure to; to coerce, to persuade. [from Latin]

pressure cooker a sealed pan in which food is cooked in water under pressure, where water boils at a higher temperature than normal boiling point (100°C/212°F) and therefore cooks food quickly. The modern pressure cooker has a quick-sealing lid and a safety valve that can be adjusted to vary the steam pressure inside.

pressure group or **interest group** or **lobby** a group that puts pressure on governments or parties to ensure laws and treatment favourable to its own interest. Pressure groups have played an increasingly prominent role in contemporary Western democracies. In general they fall into two types: groups concerned with a single issue, such as nuclear disarmament, and groups attempting to promote their own interest, such as oil producers.

pressurize *v.t.* 1. to raise to a high pressure; (especially in *past participle*) to maintain normal atmospheric pressure in (an aircraft cabin etc.) at high altitude. 2. coerce. —**pressurized water reactor,** a nuclear reactor in which the coolant is water at high pressure. It contains a sealed system of pressurized water that is heated to form steam in heat exchangers in an external circuit. —**pressurization** *n.*

Prestel /'prestel/ *n.* the trade name of the ◊viewdata service provided by British Telecom (BT), which provides information on the television screen via the telephone network. BT pioneered the service in 1975.

Prester John /'prestə 'dʒɒn/ legendary Christian prince. During the 12th and 13th centuries, Prester John was believed to be the ruler of a powerful empire in Asia. From the 14th to the 16th century, he was generally believed to be the king of Abyssinia (now Ethiopia) in NE Africa.

prestidigitator /prestɪ'dɪdʒɪteɪtə/ *n.* a conjuror. —**prestidigitation** /-'teɪʃən/ *n.* [from French from Latin *praesto* = ready and *digitus* = finger, toe]

prestige /pre'stiːʒ/ *n.* influence or good reputation derived from past achievements, associations etc. —*adj.* having or conferring prestige. [French = illusion, glamour]

prestigious /pre'stɪdʒəs/ *adj.* having or showing prestige. [originally = deceptive, from Latin *praestigiae* = juggler's tricks]

presto /'prestəʊ/ *adv.* in music, in quick tempo. —*n.* (*plural* **prestos**) in music, a movement to be played this way. [Italian from Latin *praestus* (*praesto* = ready)]

prestressed /priː'strest/ *adj.* (of concrete) strengthened by means of stretched wires within it (see ◊concrete).

presumably /prɪ'zjuːməblɪ/ *adv.* it is or may be reasonably presumed.

presume /prɪ'zjuːm/ *v.t./i.* 1. to suppose to be true, to take for granted. 2. to take the liberty, to be impudent enough, to venture; to be presumptuous. —**presume on** *or* **upon,** to take advantage of or make unscrupulous use of (a person's good nature etc.). [from Old French from Latin *praesumere* = anticipate]

presumption /prɪ'zʌmpʃən/ *n.* 1. presumptuous behaviour. 2. presuming a thing to be true; a thing that is, or may be, presumed to be true; a ground for presuming something.

presumptive /prɪˈzʌmptɪv/ adj. giving grounds for presumption. —**presumptively** adv.

presumptuous /prɪˈzʌmptjuəs/ adj. behaving with impudent boldness; acting without due authority. —**presumptuously** adv., **presumptuousness** n.

presuppose /priːsəˈpəʊz/ v.t. 1. to assume beforehand. 2. to imply the existence of. —**presupposition** /-sʌpəˈzɪʃən/ n. [from Old French]

prêt-à-porter adj. (of clothes) ready-to-wear. [French]

pre-tax /priːˈtæks/ adj. (of income) before the deduction of taxes.

pretence /prɪˈtens/ n. 1. pretending, make-believe. 2. a claim, e.g. to merit or knowledge. 3. false profession of purpose, a pretext. 4. ostentation, show. —**in pretence**, in heraldry, borne on an inescutcheon to indicate pretension or claim. [from Anglo-French]

pretend /prɪˈtend/ v.t./i. 1. to claim or assert falsely so as to deceive. 2. to imagine to oneself in play. 3. (in past participle) falsely claimed to be such. —**pretend to**, to lay claim to (a right or title); to profess to have. —**pretendedly** adv. [from French or Latin praetendere (prae = before and tendere = stretch)]

pretender n. 1. one who pretends. 2. one who claims a throne or title. —**Old Pretender**, James Francis Edward Stuart; **Young Pretender**, Charles Edward Stuart, the son and grandson of James II, claimants to the British throne.

pretension /prɪˈtenʃən/ n. 1. the assertion of a claim; a justifiable claim. 2. pretentiousness. [from Latin]

pretentious /prɪˈtenʃəs/ adj. making an excessive claim to great merit or importance; ostentatious. —**pretentiously** adv., **pretentiousness** n. [from French]

preterite /ˈpretərɪt/ adj. in grammar, expressing a past action or state. —n. in grammar, the preterite tense of a verb. [from Old French or Latin praeterire = pass]

preternatural /priːtəˈnætʃrəl/ adj. outside the ordinary course of nature, unusual. —**preternaturally** adv. [from Latin praeter naturam = beyond nature]

pretext /ˈpriːtekst/ n. an ostensible reason, an excuse offered. [from Latin praetextus = outward display (prae = before and texere = weave)]

Pretoria /prɪˈtɔːrɪə/ administrative capital of the Republic of South Africa from 1910 and capital of Transvaal province from 1860; population (1985) 741,300. Industries include engineering, chemicals, iron, and steel. It was founded in 1855. [named after Boer leader Andries Pretorius (1799–1853)]

pretty /ˈprɪtɪ/ adj. 1. attractive in a delicate way. 2. fine or good of its kind. 3. (ironic) considerable. —adv. fairly, moderately. —**pretty much**, or **nearly** or **well**, almost, very nearly. **pretty-pretty** adj. with the prettiness overdone. —**prettily** adv., **prettiness** n. [Old English]

prevail /prɪˈveɪl/ v.i. 1. to be victorious, to gain the mastery. 2. to be more usual or prominent; to exist or occur in general use or experience. —**prevail on** or **upon**, to persuade. [from Latin praevalere (prae = before and valēre = have power)]

prevalent /ˈprevələnt/ adj. generally existing or occurring, predominant. —**prevalence** n., **prevalently** adv.

prevaricate /prɪˈværɪkeɪt/ v.i. to speak or act evasively or misleadingly; to quibble, to equivocate. —**prevarication** /-ˈkeɪʃən/ n., **prevaricator** n. [from Latin, originally = walk crookedly]

prevent /prɪˈvent/ v.t. to keep from happening or doing something; to hinder, to make impossible. —**prevention** n. [originally = anticipate, from Latin praevenire = come before]

preventable adj. that may be prevented.

preventative /prɪˈventətɪv/ adj. & n. preventive.

preventive /prɪˈventɪv/ adj. serving to prevent, especially preventing a disease. —n. a preventive agent, measure, drug etc. —**preventive detention**, the imprisonment of a person thought likely to commit a crime.

preview /ˈpriːvjuː/ n. a showing of a film or play etc. before it is seen by the general public. —v.t. to view or show in advance of public presentation.

Previn /ˈprevɪn/ André (George) 1929– . US conductor and composer, born in Berlin. After a period working as a composer and arranger in the US film industry, he concentrated on conducting. He was principal conductor of the London Symphony Orchestra 1968–79. He was appointed music director of Britain's Royal Philharmonic Orchestra in 1985 (a post he relinquished the following year, staying on as principal conductor), and of the Los Angeles Philharmonic in 1986.

previous /ˈpriːvɪəs/ adj. 1. coming before in time or order; prior. 2. done or acting hastily. —**previous to**, before. —**previously** adv. [from Latin praevius (prae = before and via = way)]

Prévost d'Exiles /preˈvəʊ degˈziːl/ Antoine François 1697–1763. French novelist, known as Abbé Prévost, who combined a military career with his life as a monk. His Manon Lescaut 1731 inspired operas by Massenet and Puccini.

prewar adj. occurring or existing before a war.

prey /preɪ/ n. 1. an animal that is hunted or killed by another for food. 2. a person or thing that falls victim to an enemy, disease, fear etc. —v.i. **prey on** or **upon**, to seek or take as prey; (of a disease or emotion etc.) to exert a harmful influence on. —**beast** or **bird of prey**, one that kills and devours other animals. [from Old French from Latin praeda = plunder]

Priam /ˈpraɪəm/ in Greek mythology, the last king of Troy. He was killed by Pyrrhus, the son of Achilles, when the Greeks entered the city of Troy concealed in a wooden horse.

Priapus /praɪˈeɪpəs/ Greek god of fertility, son of Dionysus and Aphrodite, represented as grotesquely ugly, with an exaggerated phallus. He was also a god of gardens, where his image was frequently used as a scarecrow.

price /praɪs/ n. 1. the amount of money for which a thing is bought or sold. 2. what must be given or done etc. to obtain or achieve something. 3. the odds in betting. —v.t. to fix or find the price of (a thing for sale); to estimate the value of. —**at a price**, at a high cost. **price-fixing** n. the maintaining of prices at a certain level by agreement between competing sellers. **price on a person's head**, a reward for his or her capture or death. **price tag**, a label on an item showing its price, the cost of an undertaking etc. **what price . . . ?** (colloquial) what is the chance of . . ?; the vaunted . . . has failed. [from Old French pris from Latin pretium]

Price Vincent 1911– . US actor, star of horror films including House of Wax 1953 and The Fall of the House of Usher 1960.

priceless adj. 1. invaluable. 2. (colloquial) very amusing or absurd.

pricey adj. (comparative **pricier**; superlative **priciest**) (colloquial) expensive.

prick v.t./i. 1. to pierce slightly, to make a small hole in. 2. to mark with pricks or dots. 3. to trouble mentally. 4. to feel a pricking sensation. —n. 1. a small hole or mark made by pricking. 2. a pain caused (as) by pricking. 3. (vulgar) the penis; (derogatory) a man. —**prick out**, to plant out (seedlings) in small holes pricked in soil. **prick up one's ears**, (of a dog) to make the ears erect when on the alert; (of a person) to become suddenly attentive. —**pricker** n. [Old English]

prickle n. 1. a small thorn. 2. the hard-pointed spine of a hedgehog etc. 3. a prickling sensation. —v.t./i. to affect or be affected with a sensation as of pricking. [Old English]

prickly adj. 1. having prickles. 2. (of a person) irritable. 3. tingling. —**prickly heat**, inflammation of the skin near the sweat glands with an eruption of vesicles and a prickly sensation, common in hot countries. —**prickly pear**, a cactus of the genus Opuntia, native to Central and South America, mainly Mexico and Chile, but naturalized in S Europe, N Africa, and Australia, where it is a pest. The common prickly pear O. vulgaris is low-growing, with flat, oval-stem joints, bright yellow flowers, and prickly, oval fruit; the flesh and seeds of the peeled fruit have a pleasant taste. —**prickliness** n.

pride n. 1. a feeling of elation or satisfaction at one's achievements, qualities, or possessions etc. 2. an object of this feeling. 3. unduly high opinion of one's own importance or merits etc. 4. a proper sense of what befits one's position, self-respect. 5. the best condition, the prime. 6. a group or company (of lions etc.). —v.refl. (with on or upon) to be proud of. —**pride of place**, the most important or prominent position. **take pride in**, to be proud of. [Old English from Old French prud = valiant]

Pride and Prejudice a novel by Jane Austen, published in the UK in 1813. Mr and Mrs Bennet, whose property is due to pass to a male cousin, William Collins, are anxious to secure good marriage settlements for their five daughters. Central to the story is the romance between the witty Elizabeth Bennet and the proud Mr Darcy.

Pride's purge the removal of about 100 Royalists and Presbyterians of the English House of Commons from Parliament by a detachment of soldiers led by Col Thomas Pride (died 1658) in 1648. They were accused of negotiating with Charles I and were seen as unreliable by the army. The remaining members were termed the ◊Rump and voted in favour of the king's trial.

prie-dieu /priː'djɜː/ *n.* a desk at which one kneels for prayer. [French = pray God]

priest /priːst/ *n.* an ordained minister of the Roman Catholic or Orthodox Church, or of the Anglican Church (above a deacon and below a bishop); an official minister of a non-Christian religion. —*v.t.* to make (a deacon) into a priest. —**priesthood** *n.* [Old English]

priestess /'priːstɪs/ *n.* a female priest of a non-Christian religion.

Priestley /'priːstli/ J(ohn) B(oynton) 1894–1984. English novelist and playwright. His first success was a novel about travelling theatre, *The Good Companions* 1929. He followed it with a realist novel about London life *Angel Pavement* 1930; later books include *Lost Empires* 1965 and *The Image Men* 1968. As a playwright he was often preoccupied with theories of time, as in *An Inspector Calls* 1945, but had also a gift for family comedy, for example, *When We Are Married* 1938.

priestly *adj.* of, like, or befitting a priest. —**priestliness** *n.*

prig *n.* a self-righteously correct or moralistic person. —**priggery** *n.*, **priggish** *adj.*

Prigogine /priˈɡəʊʒɪn/ Ilya 1917–. Russian-born Belgian chemist who, as a highly original theoretician, has made major contributions to the field of ◊thermodynamics for which work he was awarded the 1977 Nobel Prize for Physics. Earlier theories had considered systems at or about equilibrium. Prigogine began to study 'dissipative' or non-equilibrium structures frequently found in biological and chemical reactions.

prim *adj.* (of a person or manner) stiffly formal and precise, demure; disliking what is rough or improper, prudish. —**primly** *adv.*, **primness** *n.* [probably from Old French *prin* = fine, delicate]

prima ballerina /'priːmə/ a ballerina of the highest rank; the leading ballerina of a ballet company. [Italian = first female dancer]

primacy /'praɪməsi/ *n.* 1. pre-eminence. 2. the office of primate. [from Latin *primus* = first]

prima donna /priːmə 'dɒnə/ 1. the chief female singer in an opera. 2. a temperamentally self-important person. [Italian = first lady]

prima facie /praɪmə 'feɪʃiː/ at first sight; (of evidence) based on the first impression. [Latin]

primal /'praɪməl/ *adj.* 1. primitive, primeval. 2. chief, fundamental. —**primally** *adv.* [from Latin *primus* = first]

primary /'praɪməri/ *adj.* 1. earliest in time or order; first in a series, not derived. 2. of the first importance, chief. —*n.* a thing that is primary; a primary feather etc.; (*US*) a primary election. —**primary battery,** a battery producing electricity by an irreversible chemical action. **primary education,** the first stage of education in which the rudiments of knowledge are taught. **primary election,** (*US*) an election to appoint party conference delegates or to select candidates for a principal election. **primary feather,** any of the large flight feathers of a bird's wing. **primary school,** a school where primary education is given. —**primarily** *adv.* [from Latin *primarius*]

primary growth in plants, an increase in size due to cell division and cell expansion. It is restricted to the meristems, those areas of the plant that contain actively dividing cells. The main result of primary growth is the lengthening of the stem and the root.

primary sexual characteristic the endocrine gland producing maleness and femaleness. In males it is the testis and in females the ovary.

primate /'praɪmət, -eɪt/ *n.* 1. in the Christian church, the official title of an archbishop. 2. a member of the order Primates, the highest order of mammals, including man,

apes, monkeys, tarsiers, and lemurs. Generally, they have forward-directed eyes, gripping hands and feet, and opposable thumbs and big toes. They tend to have nails rather than claws, with gripping pads on the ends of the digits, all adaptations to the climbing mode of life. —**Primate of England,** the Archbishop of York. **Primate of all England,** the Archbishop of Canterbury. [from Old French from Latin = of first rank (*primus* = first)]

prime[1] *adj.* 1. chief, most important. 2. first-rate, excellent. 3. primary, fundamental. —*n.* 1. the state of highest perfection; the best part. 2. a beginning. 3. the second canonical hour of prayer. 4. a prime number. **prime time,** the time at which a television etc. audience is expected to be largest. [from Old French from Latin *primus* = first]

prime[2] *v.t.* 1. to prepare (a thing) for use or action; to prepare (a gun) for firing or (an explosive) for detonation. 2. to pour (liquid) into a pump to make it start working. 3. to prepare (wood etc.) for painting by applying a substance that prevents the paint from being absorbed. 4. to equip (a person) with information. 5. to ply (a person) with food or drink in preparation for something.

prime minister or **premier** the head of a parliamentary government, usually the leader of the largest party. The first in Britain is usually considered to have been Robert ◊Walpole, but the office was not officially recognized until 1905. In some countries, such as Australia, a distinction is drawn between the prime minister of the whole country, and the premier of an individual state. In countries with an executive president, such as France, the prime minister is of lesser standing.

prime number a number that can be divided only by 1 or itself, that is, having no other factors. There is an infinite number of primes, the first ten of which are 2, 3, 5, 7, 11, 13, 17, 19, 23, and 29 (by definition, the number 1 is excluded from the set of prime numbers). The number 2 is the only even prime because all other even numbers have 2 as a factor.

primer[1] *n.* a substance used to prime wood etc.

primer[2] *n.* 1. an elementary schoolbook for teaching children to read. 2. a small book introducing a subject. [from Anglo-French from Latin *primarius*]

prime rate the rate charged by commercial banks to their best customers. It is the base rate on which other rates are calculated according to the risk involved. Only borrowers who have the highest credit rating qualify for the prime rate.

primeval /praɪˈmiːvəl/ *adj.* of the first age of the world; ancient, primitive. —**primevally** *adv.* [from Latin *primus* = first and *aevum* = age]

primitive /'prɪmɪtɪv/ *adj.* 1. ancient, at an early stage of civilization. 2. undeveloped, crude, simple. —*n.* an untutored painter with a direct naïve style; a picture by such a painter. —**primitively** *adv.*, **primitiveness** *n.* [from Old French or Latin *primitivus* = first of its kind]

Primitive Methodism a Protestant Christian movement, an offshoot of Wesleyan ◊Methodism, that emerged in England in 1811 when evangelical enthusiasts organized camp meetings at places such as ◊Mow Cop in 1807. Inspired by American example, open-air sermons were accompanied by prayers and hymn singing. In 1932 the Primitive Methodists became a constituent of a unified Methodist church.

Primo de Rivera /'priːməʊ deɪ rɪ'veərə/ Miguel 1870–1930. Spanish soldier and politician, dictator from 1923 as well as premier from 1925. He was captain-general of Catalonia when he led a coup against the ineffective monarchy and became virtual dictator of Spain with the support of Alfonso XIII. He resigned in 1930.

primogeniture /praɪməʊˈdʒenɪtʃə/ *n.* 1. the fact of being the first-born child. 2. the right of succession or inheritance belonging to the eldest son. [from Latin *primo* = first and *genitura* = begetting]

primordial /praɪˈmɔːdiəl/ *adj.* existing at or from the beginning, primeval. —**primordially** *adv.* [from Latin *primus* = first and *ordiri* = begin]

Primorye territory of the USSR in SE Siberia on the Sea of Japan; area 165,900 sq km2/64,079 sq mi; population (1985) 2,136,000; the capital is Vladivostok. Timber and coal are produced.

primp *v.t.* to make (the hair etc.) tidy; to smarten. [dialect variant of *prime*]

printed circuit board   *A typical microcomputer PCB*

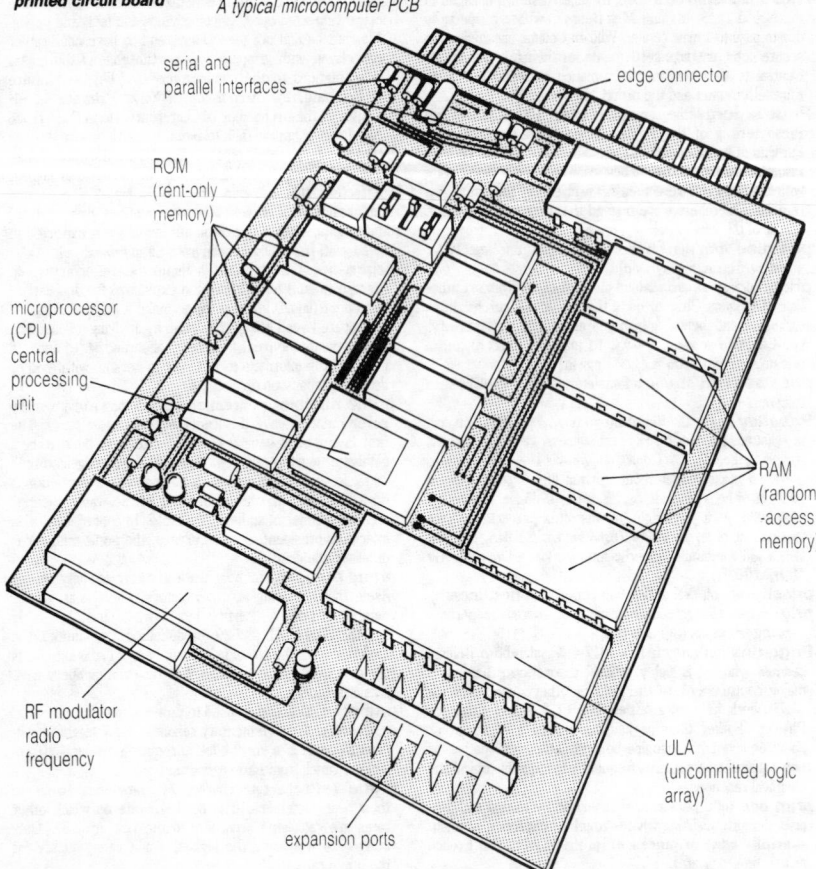

serial and
parallel interfaces

edge connector

ROM
(rent-only
memory)

microprocessor
(CPU)
central
processing
unit

RAM
(random
-access
memory)

RF modulator
radio
frequency

ULA
(uncommitted logic
array)

expansion ports

primrose /'prɪmrəʊz/ *n.* **1.** any plant of the genus *Primula*, family Primulaceae, with showy five-lobed, tube-shaped flowers; this flower. The common primrose *P. vulgaris* is a woodland plant, native to Europe, bearing pale yellow flowers in spring. **2.** the colour of this flower. —**primrose path,** the unjustified pursuit of ease or pleasure (with reference to Shakespeare *Hamlet* I. iii. 50). [from Old French from Latin = first rose]

primula /'prɪmjʊlə/ *n.* a herbaceous perennial of the genus *Primula* with flowers of various colours. [Latin, diminutive of *primus* = first]

Primus /'praɪməs/ *n.* trade name of a brand of portable stove burning vaporized paraffin for cooking etc. [Latin = first]

prince *n.* **1.** a male member of a royal family who is not a reigning king; in Britain, a son or grandson of the sovereign. In Rome and medieval Italy it was used as the title of certain officials, for example, *princeps senatus*. The title was granted to the king's sons in 15th-century France, and in England from Henry VII's time. **2.** a ruler, especially of a small state. **3.** a nobleman of some countries. **4.** a person who is outstanding of his kind. —**prince consort,** the husband of a reigning queen who is himself a prince. **Prince of Wales,** a title usually conferred on the heir apparent to the British throne. **Prince Regent,** a prince acting as regent, especially the future George IV who was regent 1811–20. [from Old French from Latin *princeps* = chieftain]

Prince /prɪns/ Stage name of Prince Rogers Nelson 1960– . US pop musician who composes, arranges, and produces his own records and often plays all the instruments. His albums, including *1999* 1982 and *Purple Rain* 1984, contain elements of rock, funk, and jazz. His hits include 'Little Red Corvette' from *1999*, 'Kiss' from *Parade*

1986, and 'Sign O' The Times' 1987 from the album of the same name.

Prince Edward Island /'edwəd/ province of E Canada; **area** 5,700 sq km/2,200 sq mi; **capital** Charlottetown; **physical** the smallest Canadian province; Prince Edward Island National Park; **products** potatoes, dairy products, lobsters, oysters, farm vehicles; **population** (1986) 127,000; **history** taken by the British in 1758; annexed to Nova Scotia in 1763; separate colony 1769; settled by the Scottish in 1803; joined the Confederation in 1873. [named after Prince Edward of Kent, father of Queen Victoria]

princeling /'prɪnslɪŋ/ *n.* a young or petty prince.

princely *adj.* **1.** of or worthy of a prince. **2.** sumptuous, splendid, generous.

princess /prɪn'ses, *attrib.* 'prɪn-/ *n.* **1.** the wife of a prince. **2.** a female member of a royal family who is not a reigning queen; in Britain, a daughter or granddaughter of the sovereign. —**Princess Royal,** a title borne only by the eldest daughter of the British sovereign, granted by royal declaration. It was first borne by Mary, eldest daughter of Charles I, probably in imitation of the French court where the eldest daughter of the king was styled 'Madame Royale'. The title is currently held by Princess Anne.

Prince William Sound /prɪns 'wɪljəm/ a channel in the Gulf of Alaska, extending 200 km/125 mi NW from Kayak Island. In March 1989 the oil tanker *Exxon Valdez* ran aground here, spilling 12 million gallons of crude oil in what was reckoned to be the world's greatest oil pollution disaster.

principal /'prɪnsɪpəl/ *adj.* (usually *attributive*) first in rank or importance, chief; main, leading. —*n.* **1.** the person with highest authority in an organization etc.; the head of some schools, colleges, and universities. **2.** a person who takes a leading part in an activity or in a play etc. **3.** a capital sum as distinct from interest or income. **4.** a person for whom another is agent. **5.** a civil servant of the grade below secretaries. —**principal boy,** the leading male part in a pantomime, usually played by a woman. **principal parts,** the parts of a verb from which all the other parts can be deduced. —**principally** *adv.*

principality /prɪnsɪ'pælɪtɪ/ *n.* a state ruled by a prince. —**the Principality,** Wales.

principle /'prɪnsɪpəl/ *n.* **1.** a fundamental truth or a general law or doctrine that is used as a basis of reasoning or action. **2.** a personal code of right conduct; (*in plural*) such rules of conduct. **3.** a general law in physics. **4.** a law of nature forming the basis for the construction or working of a machine. **5.** in chemistry, a constituent of a substance, especially one giving rise to some quality etc. **6.** a fundamental source, a primary element. —**in principle,** as regards fundamentals but not necessarily in detail. **on principle,** from a settled moral motive. [from Old French from Latin *principium* = source]

prink *v.t.* **1.** to make (oneself) smart. **2.** (of a bird) to preen. **3.** to walk daintily. [related to Dutch *pronk* = finery]

print *n.* **1.** an indentation or mark left on a surface by the pressure of a thing in contact. **2.** printed lettering or writing; words in printed form. **3.** a picture or design printed from a block or plate that holds ink or colour. The oldest form of print is the woodcut, common in medieval Europe, followed by line ◊engraving (from the 15th century), and ◊etching (from the 17th); coloured woodblock prints flourished in Japan from the 18th century. ◊Lithography was invented in 1796. **4.** a photograph produced from a negative. **5.** a printed cotton fabric. —*v.t.* **1.** to produce (a book, picture etc., or *absolute*) by applying inked types, blocks, or plates to paper etc.; to express or publish in print. **2.** to impress or stamp (a surface, or a mark or design in or on a surface). **3.** to write (words, letters, or *absolute*) without joining, in imitation of typography. **4.** to produce (a photograph) from a negative. **5.** to mark (a textile fabric) with a coloured design. **6.** to impress (an idea or scene etc. on the mind or memory). **7.** to make (a printed circuit or component). —**in** *or* **out of print,** (of a book etc.) available (or no longer available) from a publisher. [from Old French from Latin *premere*]

printed circuit board (PCB) an electrical circuit created by laying (printing) 'tracks' of a conductor such as copper onto one or both sides of an insulating board. The PCB was invented in 1936 by the Austrian scientist Paul Eisler, and was first used on a large scale in 1948.

printer *n.* **1.** one whose job or business is the printing of books, newspapers etc. **2.** any device that prints. **3.** in computing, an output device for producing printed copies of text or graphics. Types include the **daisywheel,** which produces good quality text but no graphics; the **dot matrix,** which creates character patterns from a matrix of small dots, producing text and graphics; and the ◊**laser printer,** which produces high quality text and graphics.

printing *n.* **1.** the reproduction of text or illustrative material on paper, as in books or newspapers, or on an increasing variety of materials; for example, on plastic containers. The first printing used woodblocks, followed by carved wood type or moulded metal type and hand-operated presses. Modern printing is effected by electronically controlled machinery. Current printing processes include electronic phototypesetting with ◊offset printing, and ◊gravure print. **2.** a single impression of a book. **3.** printed letters or writing imitating them. —**printing press,** a machine for printing from types or plates etc.

printout *n.* computer output in printed form.

prion *n.* an exceptionally small microorganism, a hundred times smaller than a virus. Composed of protein, and without any detectable amount of nucleic acid (genetic material), it is thought to cause diseases such as scrapie in sheep, and certain degenerative diseases of the nervous system in humans.

prior /'praɪə/ *adj.* earlier; coming before in time, order, or importance. —*n.* a superior of a religious house or order; in an abbey, the deputy of the abbot. —**prior to,** before. —**prioress** *n.fem.* [from Old French or Latin = former (*prae* = before)]

priority /praɪ'ɒrɪtɪ/ *n.* **1.** being earlier or more important; precedence in rank etc.; the right to be first. **2.** an interest having a prior claim to attention.

priory /'praɪərɪ/ *n.* a monastery governed by a prior; a nunnery governed by a prioress. [from Anglo-French]

prise /praɪz/ *v.t.* to force open or out by leverage. [Old French = levering instrument from Latin *prehendere* = seize]

prism /'prɪzəm/ *n.* **1.** in mathematics, a solid figure whose two ends are equal parallel rectilinear figures, and whose sides are parallelograms. **2.** in optics, a transparent body of this form, usually triangular, with refracting surfaces at an acute angle with each other. Prisms are used as mirrors to define the optical path in binoculars, camera viewfinders, and periscopes. The dispersive property of prisms is used in the ◊spectroscope. [from Latin from Greek *prisma* = thing sawn (*prizō* = saw)]

prismatic /prɪz'mætɪk/ *adj.* of or like a prism; (of colours) formed or distributed (as if) by a transparent prism. —**prismatically** *adv.* [from French from Greek]

prison /'prɪzən/ *n.* **1.** a place where people are confined after being convicted (or in certain cases accused) of crimes. Most countries claim to aim at rehabilitation. **2.** any place of custody or confinement. **3.** imprisonment, confinement. —**prison camp,** a camp serving as a prison for prisoners of war etc. [from Old French from Latin *prensio* (*prehendere* = seize)]

prisoner /'prɪzənə/ *n.* **1.** a person kept in prison. **2.** or **prisoner at the bar,** a person in custody on a criminal charge and on trial. **3.** a captive. **4.** a person or thing held in confinement or in another's grasp etc. —**prisoner of conscience,** a person in prison for an act of conscientious protest etc. **prisoner of war,** one who has been captured in a war. **take prisoner,** to seize and hold as a prisoner. [from Anglo-French]

prissy *adj.* prim. —**prissily** *adv.,* **prissiness** *n.*

pristine /'prɪstiːn, -aɪn/ *adj.* **1.** in the original condition, unspoilt. **2.** (*disputed usage*) spotless, fresh as if new. **3.** ancient, primitive. [from Latin *pristinus* = former]

privacy /'prɪvəsɪ, 'praɪ-/ *n.* being alone or undisturbed; the right to this; freedom from intrusion, public attention, secret surveillance (by scientific devices or other means), and from the disclosure to unauthorized persons of personal data, as accumulated in computer data banks.

private /'praɪvɪt/ *adj.* **1.** belonging to an individual, one's own, personal. **2.** confidential, not to be disclosed to others. **3.** kept from public knowledge or observation; (of a place) secluded. **4.** not open to the public. **5.** (of a person) not holding a public office or official position. **6.** (of medical treatment) conducted outside the state system, at the patient's expense. —*n.* **1.** a private soldier. **2.** (in *plural*) the genitals. —**in private,** privately, not in public. **private bill,** a parliamentary bill affecting an individual or corporation only. **private company,** one with restricted membership and no issue of shares. **private detective,** one engaged privately, outside the official police force. **private enterprise,** a business or businesses privately owned and free of direct state control. **private eye,** (*colloquial*) a private detective. **private hotel,** one not obliged to take all comers. **private means,** income from investments etc., apart from earned income. **private member,** an MP not holding a government appointment. **private parts,** the genitals. **private school,** a school supported wholly by pupils' fees and by endowments. **private sector,** the part of the economy free of direct state control. **private soldier,** an ordinary soldier, not an officer. —**privately** *adv.* [from Latin *privatus* (*privare* = deprive)]

privateer /praɪvə'tɪə/ *n.* **1.** an armed vessel owned and officered by private persons holding a commission from the government and authorized to use it against a hostile nation, especially in the capture of merchant shipping. Privateering existed from ancient times until the 19th century, when it was declared illegal by the Declaration of Paris in 1856. **2.** the commander of such a vessel. —**privateering** *n.*

private limited company (plc) a registered company which has limited liability (the shareholders cannot lose more than their original shareholdings), and a minimum of two shareholders and a maximum of fifty. It cannot offer its shares or debentures to the public and their transfer is restricted; a shareholder may relinquish shares with the permission of the other shareholders.

privation /praɪ'veɪʃən/ *n.* a lack of the comforts or necessaries of life. [from Latin *privatus* (*privare* = deprive)]

privative /ˈprɪvətɪv/ *adj.* consisting in or showing loss or absence; in grammar, indicating lack or absence. [from French or Latin]

privatization /ˌpraɪvətaɪˈzeɪʃən/ *n.* the policy or process of selling or transferring state-owned or public assets and services (nationalized industries) to private investors. Privatization of services takes place by the contracting out to private firms of the rendering of services previously supplied by public authorities. The proponents of privatization argue for the public benefit from its theoretically greater efficiency in a competitive market, and the release of resources for more appropriate use by government. Those against privatization believe that it removes a country's assets from all the people to a minority, whereas public utilities such as gas and water become private monopolies, and that a profit-making state-owned company raises revenue for the government. —**privatize** *v.t.*

privet /ˈprɪvɪt/ *n.* a bushy evergreen shrub of the genus *Ligustrum*, of the olive family Oleaceae, with smooth, dark-green leaves. The European **common privet** *L. vulgare* has white flowers and black berries and is naturalized in North America; the native North American **California privet** *L. ovalifolium* is also known as hedge privet.

privilege /ˈprɪvɪlɪdʒ/ *n.* a special right, advantage, or immunity belonging or granted to a person, group, or office; a special benefit or honour. —*v.t.* to invest with a privilege. [from Old French from Latin = law affecting an individual (*privus* = private and *lex legis* = law)]

privileged *adj.* having a privilege or privileges.

privy /ˈprɪvi/ *adj.* hidden, secluded, secret. —*n.* (*archaic* or *US*) a lavatory. —**Privy Council**, a sovereign's or governor-general's private counsellors. In the UK, it originally comprised the chief royal officials of the Norman kings and, under the Tudors and early Stuarts, became the chief governing body. It was replaced from 1688 by the ◊cabinet, originally a committee of the council, and the council itself now retains only formal powers in issuing royal proclamations and orders-in-council. Cabinet ministers are automatically members, and it is presided over by the Lord President of the Council. In the USA, an advisory council consisting of the heads of executive departments. **Privy Counsellor,** a member of the Privy Council of the UK. **privy purse,** an allowance from public revenue for the sovereign's private expenses. The office that deals with this expenditure is also known as the Privy Purse. **privy seal,** a state seal formerly attached to documents that were afterwards to pass the Great Seal, or to ones of lesser importance not requiring the Great Seal. **Lord Privy Seal,** until 1884, the UK officer of state in charge of the royal seal to prevent its misuse. The honorary title is now held by a senior cabinet minister who has special nondepartmental duties. **privy to,** sharing in the secret of (a person's plans etc.). —**privily** *adv.* [from Old French *privé* from Latin *privatus*]

Prix Goncourt /ˌpriː gɒŋˈkuə/ a French literary prize for fiction, given by the Académie ◊Goncourt from 1903.

prize[1] *n.* 1. something that can be won in a competition or lottery etc. 2. an award given as a symbol of victory or superiority. 3. something striven for or worth striving for. —*adj.* 1. to which a prize is awarded. 2. excellent of its kind. —*v.t.* to value highly. —**prizefighter** *n.* a professional boxer; (*historical*) one who fought to the finish (in bare fists) for a prize or stake, before the introduction of Queensberry Rules. [variant of *price*]

prize[2] *n.* a ship or property captured in naval warfare. [from Old French *prise* from Latin *prehendere* = seize]

prize[3] variant of ◊prise.

pro[1] /prəʊ/ *n.* (*plural* **pros**) (*colloquial*) a professional. [abbreviation]

pro[2] /prəʊ/ *adj. & prep.* (of an argument or reason) for, in favour (of). —*n.* (*plural* **pros**) a reason for or in favour (especially in **pros and cons**). [Latin = for, on behalf of]

PRO abbreviation of public relations officer.

pro-[1] prefix meaning 1. as a substitute or deputy for, substituted for. 2. favouring, siding with. 3. forwards (e.g. *produce*). 4. forwards and downwards (e.g. *prostrate*). 5. onwards (e.g. *proceed*). 6. in front of (e.g. *protect*). [from Latin]

pro-[2] prefix meaning before (in time, place, or order). [from Greek *pro* = before]

probability /ˌprɒbəˈbɪlɪti/ *n.* 1. being probable; likelihood. 2. something that is probable, the most probable event. 3. the extent to which an event is likely to occur, measured by the ratio of favourable cases to all possible cases. In general, the probability that *n* particular events will happen out of a total of *m* possible events is *n/m*. A certainty has a probability of 1; an impossibility has a probability of 0. Empirical probability is defined as the number of successful events divided by the total possible number of events. —**in all probability,** most probably. [from French or Latin]

probable /ˈprɒbəbəl/ *adj.* that may be expected to happen or prove true; likely. —*n.* a probable candidate, member of a team etc. —**probably** *adv.* [from Old French or Latin *probare* = test, demonstrate]

probate *n.* 1. the official proving of a will. 2. a verified copy of a will with a certificate as handed to the executors. [from Latin *probare* = test, demonstrate]

probation /prəˈbeɪʃən/ *n.* 1. the testing of the character or abilities of a person, especially of a candidate for employment or membership. 2. a system whereby certain offenders are supervised by an official as an alternative to imprisonment. There are strict limits placed on travel, associations, and behaviour. Often an offender is required to visit a probation officer on a regular schedule. Failure to abide by the regulations can result in imprisonment. —**on probation,** undergoing probation before full admission to employment or membership, or as a criminal offender. **probation officer,** an official supervising offenders on probation. —**probationary** *adj.* [from Latin *probare*]

probationer *n.* a person undergoing a probationary period of testing, e.g. a hospital nurse at an early stage of training.

probative /ˈprəʊbətɪv/ *adj.* affording proof.

probe *n.* 1. a device for exploring an otherwise inaccessible place or object etc.; a blunt-ended surgical instrument for exploring a wound. 2. an unmanned exploratory spacecraft transmitting information about its environment. 3. a penetrating investigation. —*v.t.* 1. to explore with a probe. 2. to penetrate (a thing) with a sharp instrument. 3. to examine or enquire into closely. [from Latin *proba*]

probity /ˈprəʊbɪti/ *n.* uprightness, honesty. [from French or Latin *probus* = good]

problem /ˈprɒbləm/ *n.* 1. a doubtful or difficult matter requiring solution. 2. something hard to understand, accomplish, or deal with. 3. an exercise in mathematics or chess etc. [from Old French or Latin from Greek *problēma* (*ballō* = throw)]

problematic /ˌprɒbləˈmætɪk/ *adj.* or **problematical** 1. hard to understand, accomplish, or deal with. 2. doubtful, questionable. —**problematically** *adv.* [from French or Latin from Greek]

proboscis /prəˈbɒsɪs/ *n.* (*plural* **proboscises**) 1. an elephant's trunk; the long flexible snout of the tapir etc. 2. an elongated part of the mouth of some insects, used for sucking things. [Latin from Greek *boskō* = feed]

procedure /prəˈsiːdjə, -dʒə/ *n.* 1. a mode of conducting business or a legal action. 2. a series of actions conducted in a certain order or manner. 3. in computing, a small part of a computer program, which performs a specific task, such as clearing the screen or sorting a file. —**procedural** *adj.* [from French]

proceed /prəˈsiːd/ *v.i.* 1. to go forward or onward; to make one's way. 2. to continue in an activity; (of an action) to be carried on or continued. 3. to adopt a course of action. 4. to go on to say. 5. to start a lawsuit (against a person). 6. to come forth, to originate. [from Old French from Latin *cedere* = go]

proceeding *n.* 1. an action, a piece of conduct. 2. (in *plural*) a legal action. 3. (in *plural*) a published report of discussions or a conference.

proceeds /ˈprəʊsiːdz/ *n.pl.* money produced by a sale or performance etc. [plural of obsolete *proceed*, noun from *proceed*]

process[1] /ˈprəʊses/ *n.* 1. a series of actions or proceedings used in making, manufacturing, or achieving something. 2. progress, course. 3. a natural or involuntary operation or series of changes. 4. a lawsuit; a summons or writ. 5. a natural appendage or outgrowth on an organism. —*v.t.* to put through a manufacturing or other process; to treat, especially so as to prevent decay.

process[2] /prəˈses/ *v.i.* (*colloquial*) to walk in procession. [back formation from *procession*]

processing cycle in computing, the sequence of steps performed repeatedly by a computer in the execution of a program. The computer's CPU (central processing unit) continuously works through a loop of fetching a program instruction from the memory, fetching any data it needs, operating on the data, and storing the result in the memory, before it fetches another program instruction.

procession /prəˈseʃən/ *n.* a number of persons or vehicles etc. going along in orderly succession, especially as a ceremony or demonstration or festivity; the action of this. [from Latin *cedere* = go]

processional *adj.* of processions; used, carried, or sung in processions. —*n.* a processional hymn. [from Latin]

processor /ˈprəʊsesə/ *n.* **1.** a machine that processes things. **2.** in computing, another name for the central processing unit (◊CPU) or ◊microprocessor of a computer.

proclaim /prəˈkleɪm/ *v.t.* **1.** to announce publicly or officially, to declare; to declare (a person) to be (a king, traitor etc.). **2.** to reveal as being. [from Latin *proclamare* = cry out (*clamare* = cry)]

proclamation /prɒkləˈmeɪʃən/ *n.* **1.** proclaiming. **2.** a thing proclaimed.

proclivity /prəˈklɪvɪtɪ/ *n.* a tendency or natural inclination. [from Latin *proclivis* = inclined from *clivus* = slope]

proconsul *n.* a Roman ◊consul (sense 2) who went on to govern a province when his term ended.

Proconsul *n.* a prehistoric ape skull found on Rusinga Island in Lake Victoria (Nyanza), E Africa, by Mary ◊Leakey. It is believed to be 20 million years old.

procrastinate /prəˈkræstɪneɪt/ *v.i.* to defer action; to be dilatory. —**procrastination** /-ˈneɪʃən/ *n.*, **procrastinator** *n.* [from Latin *crastinus* = of tomorrow]

procreate /ˈprəʊkrɪeɪt/ *v.t.* to bring (offspring) into existence by the natural process of reproduction. —**procreation** /-ˈeɪʃən/ *n.*, **procreative** *adj.* [from Latin *creare*]

Procrustean /prəˈkrʌstɪən/ *adj.* seeking to enforce uniformity by violent methods. [from *Procrustes*, robber in Greek legend, who made travellers fit a bed by lopping or stretching them]

proctor /ˈprɒktə/ *n.* each of two university officers at Oxford and Cambridge, appointed annually and having mainly disciplinary functions. —**Queen's** *or* **King's Proctor,** an official who has the right to intervene in probate, divorce, and nullity cases when collusion or suppression of facts is alleged. —**proctorial** /-ˈtɔːrɪəl/ *adj.*, **proctorship** *n.* [syncopation of *procurator*]

procuration /prɒkjuəˈreɪʃən/ *n.* **1.** procuring. **2.** the function or an authorized action of an attorney. [from Latin *curare* = look after]

procurator /ˈprɒkjuəreɪtə/ *n.* an agent or proxy, especially with power of attorney. —**procurator fiscal,** an officer of a sheriff's court in Scotland, acting as public prosecutor of a district and with other duties similar to those of a coroner. **procurator general,** the head of the Treasury law department.

procure /prəˈkjuə/ *v.t./i.* **1.** to obtain by care or effort, to acquire. **2.** to bring about. **3.** to act as a procurer or procuress (of). —**procurement** *n.* [from Old French from Latin *curare* = look after]

procurer *n.* one who obtains women for prostitution. —**procuress** *n.fem.* [from Old French from Latin]

Procyon /ˈprəʊsɪən/ *n.* or **Alpha Canis Minoris** the brightest star in the constellation Canis Minor and the eighth brightest star in the sky. Procyon is a white star 11.5 light years from Earth, with a mass of 1.7 Suns. It has a ◊white dwarf companion that orbits it every 40 years.

prod *v.t./i.* (**-dd-**) **1.** to poke. **2.** to urge or stimulate to action. —*n.* **1.** a poke. **2.** a stimulus to action. **3.** a pointed instrument for prodding things. [perhaps imitative]

prodigal /ˈprɒdɪgəl/ *adj.* **1.** recklessly wasteful or extravagant. **2.** lavish. —*n.* a prodigal person. —**prodigal son,** a repentant wastrel, a returned wanderer (New Testament, Luke 15: 11–32). —**prodigality** /-ˈgælɪtɪ/ *n.*, **prodigally** *adv.* [from Latin *prodigus* = lavish]

prodigious /prəˈdɪdʒəs/ *adj.* **1.** marvellous. **2.** enormous. **3.** abnormal. —**prodigiously** *adv.* [from Latin]

prodigy /ˈprɒdɪdʒɪ/ *n.* **1.** a person with exceptional qualities or abilities, especially a precocious child. **2.** a marvellous thing; a wonderful example of something. [from Latin *prodigium* = portent]

produce /prəˈdjuːs/ *v.t.* **1.** to bring forward for consideration, inspection, or use. **2.** to bring (a play or performance etc.) before the public; to be the producer of. **3.** to manufacture (goods) from raw materials etc. **4.** to bear or yield (offspring, fruit, a harvest etc.); to bring into existence; to cause or bring about (a reaction etc.). **5.** to extend or continue (a line). —/ˈprɒdjuːs/ *n.* what is produced, especially agricultural and natural products generally; the amount of this. [from Latin *ducere* = lead]

producer /prəˈdjuːsə/ *n.* **1.** one who produces articles or agricultural products etc. (as opposed to *consumer*). **2.** a person who directs the acting of a play. **3.** a person in charge of the expenditure, schedule, and quality of a film or a broadcast programme.

product /ˈprɒdʌkt/ *n.* **1.** a thing or substance produced by a natural process or by manufacture. **2.** a result. **3.** a quantity obtained by multiplying.

production /prəˈdʌkʃən/ *n.* **1.** producing; being produced or manufactured, especially in large quantities. **2.** the total yield. **3.** a thing produced, especially a literary or artistic work, a play or film etc. [from Old French from Latin]

productive /prəˈdʌktɪv/ *adj.* **1.** of or engaged in the production of goods; producing commodities of exchangeable value. **2.** producing much. **3.** (with *of*) producing, giving rise to. —**productively** *adv.*, **productiveness** *n.* [from French or Latin]

productivity /prɒdʌkˈtɪvɪtɪ/ *n.* **1.** capacity to produce; effectiveness of productive effort, especially in industry. **2.** in an ecosystem, the amount of material in the food chain produced by the primary producers (plants) that is available for consumption by animals.

proem /ˈprəʊem/ *n.* an introductory discourse. [from Old French or Latin from Greek *prooimion* (*oimē* = song)]

Prof. abbreviation of Professor.

profane /prəˈfeɪn/ *adj.* **1.** not sacred, secular. **2.** irreverent, blasphemous. —*v.t.* to treat (a sacred thing) with irreverence or disregard; to violate or pollute (what is entitled to respect). —**profanation** /-ˈneɪʃən/ *n.*, **profanely** *adv.* [from Old French from Latin = before (i.e. outside) the temple]

profanity /prəˈfænɪtɪ/ *n.* a profane act or profane language, blasphemy.

profess /prəˈfes/ *v.t.* **1.** to claim openly to have (a quality or feeling); to pretend, to allege. **2.** to declare. **3.** to affirm one's faith in or allegiance to. [from Latin *profitēri* = declare publicly (*fatēri* = confess)]

professed /prəˈfest/ *adj.* **1.** avowed, openly acknowledged by oneself. **2.** pretended, alleged. **3.** having taken the vows of a religious order. —**professedly** *adv.*

profession /prəˈfeʃən/ *n.* **1.** an occupation, especially in some branch of advanced learning or science. **2.** the body of persons engaged in this. **3.** a declaration, an avowal. [from Old French from Latin]

professional *adj.* **1.** of, belonging to, or connected with a profession. **2.** having or showing the skill of a professional. **3.** engaged in a specified activity as one's main paid occupation (often as distinct from *amateur*). —*n.* a professional person. —**professionalism** *n.*, **professionally** *adv.*

professor /prəˈfesə/ *n.* **1.** a university teacher of the highest (in the USA, of high) rank. **2.** one who makes a profession (of a religion etc.). —**professorial** /-ˈsɔːrɪəl/ *adj.*, **professorship** *n.* [from Old French or Latin]

proffer *v.t.* to offer. [from Anglo-French]

proficient /prəˈfɪʃənt/ *adj.* able to do something correctly or competently through training or practice, skilled. —**proficiency** *n.*, **proficiently** *adv.* [from Latin *proficere* = make progress]

profile /ˈprəʊfaɪl/ *n.* **1.** an outline (especially of a human face) as seen from one side; a representation of this. **2.** a short biographical or character sketch. **3.** a vertical cross-section of a structure or of layers of soil etc. —*v.t.* to represent in profile. —**keep a low profile,** to remain inconspicuous. [from obsolete Italian *profilare* = draw in outline]

profit /ˈprɒfɪt/ *n.* **1.** an advantage or benefit obtained from doing something. **2.** money gained in a business transaction; the excess of returns over outlay. —*v.t./i.* **1.** to be beneficial (to). **2.** to obtain an advantage or benefit. —**profit-sharing** *n.* the practice of allowing the employees of a company to share directly in its profits. [from Old French from Latin *profectus*]

profitable *adj.* bringing profit or benefits. —**profitability** /-'bɪlɪtɪ/ *n.*, **profitably** *adv.*

profiteer /prɒfɪ'tɪə/ *v.t./i.* to make or seek excessive profits out of others' needs, especially in times of scarcity. —*n.* a person who profiteers. [from Latin *profectus*]

profiterole /prə'fɪtərəʊl/ *n.* a small hollow cake of choux pastry with sweet or savoury filling. [French, diminutive of *profit* from Latin *profectus*]

profligate /'prɒflɪgət/ *adj.* 1. licentious, dissolute. 2. recklessly wasteful or extravagant. —*n.* a profligate person. —**profligacy** *n.* [from Latin *profligare* = overthrow, ruin]

pro forma /prəʊ'fɔːmə/1. for form's sake. 2. (in full **pro forma invoice**) an invoice sent to a purchaser in advance of the goods for the completion of business formalities. [Latin]

profound /prə'faʊnd/ *adj.* 1. having or showing great knowledge or insight into a subject. 2. requiring much study or thought. 3. deep, intense; far-reaching. —**profoundly** *adv.*, **profundity** /-'fʌndɪtɪ/ *n.* [from Old French from Latin *profundus* = deep]

Profumo /prə'fjuːməʊ/ John (Dennis) 1915– . British Conservative politician, secretary of state for war from 1960 to June 1963, when he resigned on the disclosure of his involvement with Christine Keeler, mistress also of a Soviet naval attaché. In 1982 Profumo became administrator of the social and educational settlement Toynbee Hall in London.

profuse /prə'fjuːs/ *adj.* 1. lavish, extravagant. 2. plentiful. —**profusely** *adv.*, **profuseness** *n.*, **profusion** /-'fjuːʒən/ *n.* [from Latin *profusus* (*fundere* = pour)]

progenitor /prəʊ'dʒenɪtə/ *n.* an ancestor; a predecessor, an original. [from Old French from Latin *gignere* = beget]

progeny /'prɒdʒənɪ/ *n.* 1. offspring. 2. an outcome. [from Old French from Latin *progenies*]

progesterone /prəʊ'dʒestərəʊn/ *n.* a ◊steroid hormone that occurs in vertebrates. In mammals, it regulates the menstrual cycle and pregnancy. Progesterone is secreted by the corpus luteum (the ruptured Graafian follicle of a discharged ovum). [from German (from *pro-*, *gestation*, and *steroid*]

prognosis /prɒg'nəʊsɪs/ *n.* (*plural* **prognoses** /-iːz/) a forecast or advance indication, especially of the course of a disease and the chance of recovery. [Latin from Greek *gignōskō* = know]

prognostic /prɒg'nɒstɪk/ *n.* an advance indication or omen; a prediction. —*adj.* foretelling, predictive. [from Old French from Latin from Greek]

prognosticate /prɒg'nɒstɪkeɪt/ *v.t.* to foretell or foresee; (of a thing) to betoken. —**prognostication** /-'keɪʃən/ *n.*, **prognosticator** *n.* [from Latin]

programmable *adj.* that may be programmed.

programme /'prəʊgræm/ *n.* (*US* and in computing **program**) *n.* 1. a plan of intended procedure. 2. a descriptive list or notice of a series of events; these events. 3. a broadcast performance or entertainment. 4. program, a series of instructions to control the operation of a computer. —*v.t.* (**-mm-**) 1. to make a programme of. 2. **program**, to express (a problem) or instruct (a computer etc.) by means of a program. —**programming**, in computing, the activity of writing instructions in a programming language for the control of a computer. **Applications programming** is for end-user programs, such as accounts programs or word-processing packages. **Systems programming** is for operating systems and the like, which are concerned more with the internal workings of the computer. —**programmatic** /-'mætɪk/ *adj.*, **programmer** *n.* [from Latin from Greek *prographō* = write publicly]

programme music music that tells a story, depicts a scene or painting, or illustrates a literary or philosophical idea, such as Richard Strauss' *Don Juan.*

programming language in computing, a special notation in which instructions for controlling a computer are written. Programming languages are designed to be easy for people to write and read, but must be capable of being mechanically translated (by a ◊compiler or ◊interpreter) (sense 2) into the ◊machine code that the computer can execute.

program trading the buying and selling of a group of shares using a computer program to generate orders automatically whenever there is an appreciable movement in prices.

progress /'prəʊgres/ *n.* 1. forward or onward movement. 2. an advance or development, especially to a better state. 3. (*archaic*) a state journey, especially by a royal person. —/prə'gres/ *v.t./i.* 1. to move forward or onward. 2. to advance or develop, especially to a better state. 3. to deal with at successive stages. —**in progress**, taking place, in the course of occurrence. [from Latin *progressus* (*progredi* = go forward)]

progression /prə'greʃən/ *n.* 1. progressing. 2. a succession or series. 3. in mathematics, a sequence of numbers each formed by a specific relationship to its predecessor. An **arithmetical progression** has numbers that increase or decrease by a common sum or difference (for example, 2, 4, 6, 8); a **geometric progression** has numbers each bearing a fixed ratio to its predecessor (for example, 3, 6, 12, 24); and a **harmonic progression** is a sequence with numbers whose ◊reciprocals are in arithmetical progression, for example 1, $1/2$, $1/3$, $1/4$. [from Old French or Latin]

progressive /prə'gresɪv/ *adj.* 1. making continuous forward movement. 2. proceeding steadily or in regular degrees. 3. favouring political or social reform; advancing in social conditions, efficiency etc. 4. (of a disease etc.) continuously increasing in severity or extent. 5. (of a card game, dance etc.) with a periodic change of partners. 6. (of taxation) at rates increasing with the sum taxed. 7. in grammar, of a tense, expressing an action in progress. —**progressive education**, teaching methods that take as their starting point children's own aptitudes and interests, and encourage them to follow their own investigations and lines of inquiry. —*n.* an advocate of a progressive policy. —**progressively** *adv.*, **progressiveness** *n.* [from French or Latin]

Progressivism *n.* in US history, the name of both a reform movement and a political party, active in the two decades before World War I. Mainly middle-class and urban-based, Progressives secured legislation at national, state, and local levels to improve the democratic system, working conditions, and welfare provision.

prohibit /prə'hɪbɪt/ *v.t.* to forbid or prevent. —**prohibitor** *n.*, **prohibitory** *adj.* [from Latin *prohibēre*]

prohibition /prəʊhɪ'bɪʃən, prəʊɪ-/ *n.* 1. forbidding, being forbidden. 2. an edict or order that forbids something. 3. the forbidding by law of the manufacture and sale of intoxicants, especially that established in the USA in 1920. It led to bootlegging (the illegal distribution of liquor, often illicitly distilled), to the financial advantage of organized crime, and public opinion insisted on repeal in 1933. [from Old French or Latin]

prohibitionist *n.* an advocate of legal prohibition.

prohibitive /prə'hɪbɪtɪv/ *adj.* prohibiting; (of prices, costs, taxes etc.) extremely high. —**prohibitively** *adv.* [from French or Latin]

project /'prɒdʒekt/ *n.* 1. a plan or scheme; a planned undertaking. 2. a task set as an educational exercise, requiring students to do their own research and present the results. —/prə'dʒekt/ *v.t./i.* 1. to plan or contrive (a scheme etc.). 2. to cause (a light, shadow, or image) to fall on a surface. 3. to send or throw outwards or forwards. 4. to extend outwards from a surface. 5. to imagine (a thing or person or oneself) as having another's feelings, being in another situation or in the future etc.; to attribute (one's own feelings) to another person or thing, especially unconsciously. 6. to extrapolate (results to a future time etc.). 7. to make a projection of (the Earth or sky etc.). [from Latin *projicere* = throw forward (*jacere* = throw)]

projectile /prə'dʒektaɪl/ *n.* an object to be hurled or projected forcibly, especially from a gun. —*adj.* of or serving as a projectile.

projection /prə'dʒekʃən/ *n.* 1. projecting, being projected. 2. a thing that projects from a surface. 3. a representation on a plane surface of (any part of) the surface of the Earth or of a celestial sphere. See also ◊map projection. 4. a mental image viewed as objective reality.

projectionist *n.* a person who operates a projector.

projector /prə'dʒektə/ *n.* an apparatus for projecting the image of a photographic slide (transparency) or film on a screen.

prokaryote *n.* in biology, an organism whose cells lack organelles (specialized segregated structures such as nuclei, mitochondria, and chloroplasts). Prokaryote DNA is not arranged in chromosomes but forms a coiled structure called a **nucleoid**. The prokaryotes comprise only the **bacteria** and **cyanobacteria**; all other organisms are eukaryotes.

Prokhorov /'prɒxərɒf/ Aleksandr 1916–. Russian physicist whose fundamental work on microwaves in 1955 led to the construction of the first practical ◊maser (the microwave equivalent of the laser) by Charles ◊Townes, for which they shared the 1964 Nobel Prize for Physics.

Prokofiev /prə'kɒfief/ Sergey (Sergeyevich) 1891–1953. Soviet composer. His music includes operas such as *The Love of Three Oranges* 1921; ballets for ◊Diaghilev, including *Romeo and Juliet* 1935; seven symphonies including *Classical Symphony* 1916–17; music for films; piano and violin concertos; songs and cantatas (for example, that composed for the 30th anniversary of the October Revolution); and *Peter and the Wolf* 1936.

prolapse /'prəʊlæps/ *n.* or **prolapsus** the slipping forward or downward of a part or organ due to the effects of strain in weakening the supporting tissues. The term is most often used with regard to the rectum (due to chronic bowel problems) or the uterus (following several pregnancies). —/prə'læps/ *v.i.* to undergo a prolapse. [from Latin *labi* = slip]

prolate /'prəʊleɪt/ *adj.* (of a spheroid) lengthened along the polar diameter. [from Latin = brought forward, prolonged]

prolegomena /prəʊli'gɒmmə/ *n.pl.* a preliminary discourse or matter prefixed to a book etc. [Latin from Greek, neuter passive participle of *prolegō* = say beforehand]

proletarian /prəʊli'teəriən/ *adj.* of the proletariat. —*n.* a member of the proletariat. [from Latin = one who served the state not with property but with offspring (*proles*)]

proletariat /prəʊli'teəriət/ *n.* **1.** the working class (contrasted with the bourgeoisie). **2.** in Marxist theory, those classes in society that possess no property, and therefore depend on the sale of their labour or expertise. They are usually divided into the industrial, agricultural, and intellectual proletariat. [from French]

proliferate /prə'lɪfəreɪt/ *v.t./i.* **1.** to reproduce itself or grow by the multiplication of elementary parts; to produce (cells) thus. **2.** to increase rapidly in numbers etc. —**proliferation** /-'reɪʃən/ *n.* [from French from Latin *proles* = offspring and *ferre* = bear]

prolific /prə'lɪfɪk/ *adj.* producing much offspring or output; abundantly productive. —**prolifically** *adv.* [from Latin]

prolix /'prəʊlɪks/ *adj.* lengthy, tediously wordy. —**prolixity** /prə'lɪksɪtɪ/ *n.* [from Old French or Latin *prolixus* = long, extended]

Prolog *n.* in computing, a programming language based on logic. Invented at the University of Marseille, France in 1971, it did not achieve widespread use until more than ten years later. It is used mainly for ◊artificial intelligence programming.

prologue *n.* **1.** an introduction to a poem or play etc. **2.** an act or event serving as an introduction. [from Old French from Latin from Greek *logos* = speech]

prolong /prə'lɒŋ/ *v.t.* to extend in duration or spatial length. —**prolongation** /prəʊlɒŋ'geɪʃən/ *n.* [from Old French and Latin *prolongare* (*longus* = long)]

PROM acronym from **programmable read-only memory**. In computing, a memory device in the form of a silicon chip that can be programmed to hold information permanently. PROM chips are empty of information when manufactured, unlike ROM chips, which have their memories built into them. Other memory devices are ◊EPROM and ◊RAM.

prom *n.* (*colloquial*) **1.** a promenade. **2.** abbreviation for promenade concert.

promenade /prɒmə'nɑːd/ *n.* **1.** a public place for walking, especially a paved area along the sea front in a seaside town. **2.** a leisurely walk, especially for pleasure. —*v.t./i.* **1.** to take a leisurely walk (through). **2.** to lead (a person) about a place, especially for display. —**promenade concert**, originally, a concert with an area for a part of the audience to stand and move about. Now, in the UK, the name of any one of an annual BBC series (**the Proms**) at the Royal Albert Hall, London, at which part of the audience stands. They were originated by Henry Wood in 1895. **promenade deck**, the

upper deck on a passenger ship. [French (*se promener* = walk)]

Prometheus /prə'miːθjuːs/ in Greek mythology, a ◊Titan who stole fire from heaven for the human race. In revenge, Zeus had him chained to a rock where an eagle came each day to feast on his liver, which grew back each night, until he was rescued by ◊Hercules.

promethium /prə'miːθɪəm/ *n.* a radioactive, metallic element of the ◊lanthanide series, symbol Pm, atomic number 61, relative atomic mass 145. It occurs in nature only in extremely minute amounts, produced as a fission product of uranium in ◊pitchblende and other uranium ores; for a long time it was considered not to occur in nature. The longest-lived isotope has a half-life of slightly more than 20 years. [from *Prometheus*]

prominence /'prɒmɪnəns/ *n.* **1.** being prominent. **2.** a prominent thing. **3.** a bright cloud of gas projecting from the Sun into space 100,000 km/60,000 mi or more. **Quiescent prominences** last for months, and are held in place by magnetic fields in the Sun's corona. **Surge prominences** shoot gas into space at speeds of 1,000 kps/600 mps. **Loop prominences** are gases falling back to the Sun's surface after a solar ◊flare. [obsolete French from Latin]

prominent *adj.* **1.** jutting out, projecting. **2.** conspicuous. **3.** distinguished, well-known. —**prominently** *adv.* [from Latin *prominēre* = project]

promiscuous /prə'mɪskjuəs/ *adj.* **1.** having casual sexual relations with many people. **2.** casual, indiscriminate. **3.** of mixed and indiscriminate composition or kinds. —**promiscuity** /prɒmɪ'skjuːɪtɪ/ *n.*, **promiscuously** *adv.* [from Latin *promiscuus* (*miscēre* = mix)]

promise /'prɒmɪs/ *n.* **1.** an assurance as to what one will or will not do, or of help or giving something. **2.** an indication of something that may be expected to come or occur. **3.** an indication of future achievement or good result. —*v.t./i.* **1.** to make a promise, to give an assurance; to give (a person) a promise of (a thing); (*colloquial*) to assure. **2.** to seem likely. —**promised land**, Canaan, promised by God to Abraham and his descendants (Old Testament, Genesis 17: 8); any place of expected happiness. [from Latin *promissum* (*promittere* = send forth, promise)]

promising *adj.* likely to turn out well or produce good results. —**promisingly** *adv.*

promissory /'prɒmɪsərɪ/ *adj.* conveying or implying a promise. —**promissory note**, a signed document containing a written promise to pay a stated sum.

promontory /'prɒməntərɪ/ *n.* a point of high land jutting out into the sea etc., a headland. [from Latin *promunturium* (perhaps from *mons* = mountain)]

promote /prə'məʊt/ *v.t.* **1.** to raise (a person) to a higher rank or office. **2.** to help forward or encourage (an enterprise or result). **3.** to publicize (a product) in order to sell it. **4.** to initiate (a project). **5.** to take the necessary steps for the passing of (a private bill in Parliament). —**promotion** *n.*, **promotional** *adj.* [from Latin *movēre* = move]

promoter *n.* one who promotes an enterprise financially, especially the formation of a joint-stock company or the holding of a sporting event etc.

prompt *adj.* **1.** acting or done without delay or at once. **2.** punctual. —*adv.* punctually. —*v.t.* **1.** to incite or stimulate (a person) to action. **2.** to inspire or give rise to (a feeling or action). **3.** to help (an actor etc., or *absolute*) by supplying the words that come next; to assist (a hesitant person) with a suggestion etc. —*n.* a thing said to help the memory, especially of an actor. —**prompt side**, the side of a stage (usually to the actors' left) where the prompter is placed. —**promptitude** *n.*, **promptly** *adv.*, **promptness** *n.* [from Old French or Latin *promere* = produce]

prompter *n.* a person (placed out of sight of the audience) who prompts the actors on a stage.

promulgate /'prɒməlgeɪt/ *v.t.* to make known to the public, to disseminate; to proclaim (a decree or news). —**promulgation** /-'geɪʃən/ *n.*, **promulgator** *n.* [from Latin *mulgēre* = milk, cause to come forth]

prone *adj.* **1.** lying face downwards (as opposed to *supine*); lying flat, prostrate. **2.** disposed (*to*), liable or likely (*to*). —**proneness** *n.* [from Latin *pronus* (*pro* = forwards)]

prong *n.* each of the two or more projecting pointed parts at the end of a fork etc. [perhaps related to Middle Low German *prange* = pinching instrument]

pronged *adj.* having a specified number or kind of prongs.

pronghorn *n.* a hoofed herbivorous mammal *Antilocapra americana* of the W USA. It is light brown, and about 1 m/ 3 ft high. It sheds its horns annually, and can reach speeds of 100 kph/60 mph. The loss of prairies to agriculture, combined with excessive hunting, has brought the pronghorn close to extinction.

pronominal /prə'nɒmɪnəl/ *adj.* of or of the nature of a pronoun. [from Latin]

pronoun /'prəʊnaʊn/ *n.* 1. in grammar, a part of speech that is used in place of a noun, usually to save repetition of the noun (for example 'The people arrived around nine o'clock. *They* behaved as though we were expecting *them*'). 2. a pronominal adjective. [from *pro-* = on behalf of, after Latin *pronomen*]

pronounce /prə'naʊns/ *v.t./i.* 1. to utter (a word or speech sound) distinctly or correctly or in a specified way. 2. to utter or declare formally. 3. to declare as one's opinion; to pass judgement. [from Old French from Latin *nuntiare* = announce]

pronounceable *adj.* (of a word etc.) that may be pronounced.

pronounced *adj.* noticeable, strongly marked.

pronouncement *n.* a formal statement, a declaration.

pronto /'prɒntəʊ/ *adv.* (*slang*) promptly, quickly. [Spanish from Latin = prompt]

pronunciation /prənʌnsi'eɪʃən/ *n.* the way in which words are rendered into human speech sounds. This can be a language as a whole ('French pronunciation'), a particular word or name ('what is the pronunciation of *allophony*?'), or a person's individual way of pronouncing words. The pronunciation of languages forms the academic subject of ◊phonetics. [from Old French or Latin]

proof *n.* 1. a fact or thing that shows or helps to show that something is true or exists. 2. a demonstration of the truth of something. 3. the process of testing whether something is true, good, or valid. 4. a standard of strength for distilled alcoholic liquors. See ◊proof spirit. 5. a trial impression of printed matter, produced for correction. 6. a trial print of a photograph. —*adj.* impervious to penetration, damage, or undesired action. —*v.t.* 1. to make a proof of (printed matter). 2. to make (a thing) proof, against something; to make (a fabric etc.) waterproof. —**proof** in combinations, in the sense 'impervious', 'resistant', forming adjectives (e.g. *bulletproof*, *waterproof*) and verbs (e.g. *soundproof*). —**proofread** *v.t.* to read and correct (printed proofs). **proofreader** *n.* a person who does this. [from Old French from Latin *proba*]

proof spirit a numerical scale used to indicate the alcohol content of an alcoholic drink. Proof spirit (or 100% proof spirit) acquired its name from a solution of alcohol in water which, when used to moisten gunpowder, contained just enough alcohol to permit it to burn. In practice, the degrees proof of an alcoholic drink is based on the specific gravity of an aqueous solution containing the same amount of alcohol as the drink. Typical values are: whisky, gin, rum 70 degrees proof (40% alcohol); vodka 65 degrees proof; sherry 28 degrees proof; table wine 20 degrees proof; beer 4 degrees proof. The USA uses a different proof scale to the UK; a US whisky of 80 degrees proof on the US scale would be 70 degrees proof on the UK scale.

prop[1] *n.* 1. a rigid support, especially not a structural part of the thing supported. 2. a person etc. depended on for help or support. —*v.t.* (**-pp-**) to support (as) with a prop (often with *up*).

prop[2] (*colloquial*) abbreviation of aircraft propeller.

prop[3] (*colloquial*) abbreviation of a stage property in a theatre.

propaganda /prɒpə'gændə/ *n.* the systematic spreading (propagation) of information or disinformation, usually to promote a religious or political doctrine with the intention of instilling particular attitudes or responses; (usually *derogatory*) the ideas etc. thus propagated. —**propagandist** *n.* [Italian from Latin *congregatio de propaganda fide*, title of Roman Catholic committee in charge of foreign missions]

propagate /'prɒpəgeɪt/ *v.t./i.* 1. to breed or reproduce from parent stock. 2. to disseminate (news or ideas etc.). 3. to transmit (a vibration, earthquake etc.). 4. to be propagated. —**propagation** /-'geɪʃən/ *n.*, **propagator** *n.* [from Latin *propagare* = multiply plants from layers (*pangere* = fix, layer)]

propane /'prəʊpeɪn/ *n.* C_3H_8, a gaseous hydrocarbon of the ◊alkane series, found in petroleum and used as fuel. [from *propionic acid* (Greek *piōn* = fat)]

propanol an alternative name for ◊propyl alcohol.

propanone *n.* CH_3COCH_3 (common name **acetone**), a colourless inflammable liquid used extensively as a solvent, as in nail varnish remover. It boils at 133.7°F/ 56.5°C, mixes with water in all proportions, and has a characteristic odour.

propel /prə'pel/ *v.t.* (**-ll-**) to drive or push forward, to give onward motion to. —**propellent** *adj.* [from Latin *propellere* (*pellere* = drive)]

propellant *n.* a propelling agent, for example the substance burned in a rocket for propulsion. The explosive charge that propels a projectile from a gun is also called a propellant.

propeller *n.* (in full **screw propeller**) a device with blades on a revolving shaft for propelling a ship or aircraft to which it is fitted. The curved blades describe a helical path as they rotate with the hub, and accelerate fluid (liquid or gas) backwards during rotation. Reaction to this backward movement of fluid sets up a propulsive thrust forwards.

propene *n.* $CH_3CH:CH_2$ (common name **propylene**), the second member of the alkene series of hydrocarbons. A colourless, inflammable gas, it is widely used by industry to make organic chemicals, including polypropylene plastics.

propenoic acid $H_2C:CHCOOH$ (common name **acrylic acid**), an acid obtained from the aldehyde propenal (acrolein) derived from glycerol or fats. Glasslike thermoplastic resins are made by polymerizing ◊esters of propenoic acid or methyl propenoic acid and used for transparent components, lenses, and dentures. Other acrylic compounds are used for adhesives, artificial fibres, and artists' acrylic paint.

propensity /prə'pensɪtɪ/ *n.* an inclination or tendency. [from Latin *propensus* = inclined]

proper /'prɒpə/ *adj.* 1. suitable, appropriate. 2. correct, according to rules. 3. respectable, in conformity with social standards or conventions. 4. real or genuine; rightly so called; (usually placed after the noun) strictly so called. 5. belonging or relating exclusively or distinctively (*to*). 6. (*colloquial*) thorough, complete. —**proper fraction**, a fraction less than unity, with the numerator less than the denominator. **proper name** *or* **noun**, the name of an individual person, place, or thing. —**properly** *adv.* [from Old French from Latin *proprius* = one's own]

proper motion the gradual change in the position of a star that results from its motion in orbit around our Galaxy, the Milky Way. Proper motions are slight and undetectable to the naked eye, but can be accurately measured on telescopic photographs taken many years apart. Barnard's Star is the star with the largest proper motion, 10.3 arc seconds per year.

propertied /'prɒpətɪd/ *adj.* having property, especially of real estate.

property /'prɒpətɪ/ *n.* 1. a thing or things owned. 2. real estate, a person's land or house etc. 3. a movable object used on a theatre stage or in a film etc. 4. in chemistry, a characteristic possessed by a substance by virtue of its composition. [from Old French from Latin *proprietas*]

prophecy /'prɒfɪsɪ/ *n.* 1. the power of prophesying. 2. a prophetic utterance. 3. the foretelling of future events.

prophesy /'prɒfɪsaɪ/ *v.t./i.* to speak as a prophet; to foretell future events; to foretell. [from Old French *profecier*]

prophet /'prɒfɪt/ *n.* 1. an inspired teacher, a person regarded as revealing or interpreting divine will. 2. any of the prophetical writers in the Old Testament; **the Prophets**, their writings. 3. one who foretells events. 4. a spokesman or advocate of a principle etc. **the Prophet**, Muhammad. —**prophetess** *n.fem.* [from Old French from Latin from Greek, originally = spokesman (*phēmi* = speak)]

prophetic /prə'fetɪk/ *adj.* or **prophetical** 1. of a prophet. 2. predicting or containing a prediction (of an event etc.). —**prophetically** *adv.* [from French or Latin from Greek]

prophylactic /prɒfɪ'læktɪk/ *adj.* tending to prevent a disease or other misfortune. —*n.* a prophylactic medicine or course of action. —**prophylactically** *adv.* [from French from Greek *phulassō* = guard]

prophylaxis /prɒfɪ'læksɪs/ *n.* preventive treatment against a disease etc., including exercise and vaccination (see ◊vaccine). Prophylactic medicine is an aspect of public health provision that is receiving increasing attention. [from Greek *phulaxis* = guarding]

propinquity /prə'pɪŋkwɪtɪ/ *n.* 1. nearness in place. 2. close kinship. [from Old French or Latin *propinquus* = near]

propitiate /prə'pɪʃieɪt/ *v.t.* to win the favour or forgiveness of, to placate. —**propitiation** /-'eɪʃən/ *n.* [from Latin *propitiare*]

propitiatory /prə'pɪʃətərɪ/ *adj.* serving or intended to propitiate.

propitious /prə'pɪʃəs/ *adj.* favourable, giving a good omen or a suitable opportunity. —**propitiously** *adv.* [from Old French or Latin *propitius*]

proponent /prə'pəʊnənt/ *n.* a person who puts forward a proposal; a person who supports a cause etc. [from Latin *proponere*]

proportion /prə'pɔ:ʃən/ *n.* 1. a fraction or comparative share of a whole. 2. a ratio. 3. the correct relation in size, amount, or degree between one thing and another or between a thing's parts. 4. (in *plural*) dimensions, size. —*v.t.* to give correct proportions to; to make (one thing) proportionate to another. —**proportionment** *n.* [from Old French or Latin *portio*]

proportional *adj.* in correct proportion; corresponding in size, amount, or degree. —**proportionally** *adv.* [from Latin]

proportional representation (PR) an electoral system in which the distribution of party seats corresponds to their proportion of the total votes cast, and minority votes are not wasted (as opposed to a simple majority, or 'first past the post', system). Forms include **party list** or **additional member system** and **single transferable vote**. Under party list, as recommended by the Hansard Society in 1976 for introduction in Britain, three-quarters of the members would be elected in single-member constituencies on the traditional majority-vote system, and the remaining seats would be allocated according to the overall number of votes cast for each party (a variant of this is used in Germany). Under the single transferable vote system candidates are numbered in order of preference by the voter, and any votes surplus to the minimum required for a candidate to win are transferred to second preferences, as are second-preference votes from the successive candidates at the bottom of the poll until the required number of elected candidates is achieved (this is in use in the Republic of Ireland).

proportionate /prə'pɔ:ʃənət/ *adj.* in due proportion. —**proportionately** *adv.*

proposal /prə'pəʊzəl/ *n.* 1. the proposing of something. 2. a course of action etc. proposed. 3. an offer of marriage.

propose /prə'pəʊz/ *v.t./i.* 1. to put forward for consideration. 2. to have and declare as one's plan or intention; to make a proposal. 3. to make an offer of marriage. 4. to offer (a person or a person's health) as the subject for the drinking of a toast. 5. to nominate (a person) as a member of a society etc. [from Old French from Latin *proponere*]

proposition /prɒpə'zɪʃən/ *n.* 1. a proposal, a scheme proposed. 2. a statement, an assertion. 3. (*colloquial*) a thing to be considered, dealt with, or undertaken. 4. a formal statement of a theorem or problem, often including a demonstration. —*v.t.* (*colloquial*) to put a proposal to; to suggest extramarital sexual intercourse to. [from Old French or Latin]

propound /prə'paʊnd/ *v.t.* to put forward for consideration. —**propounder** *n.* [from Latin *proponere*, literally = place in front]

proprietary /prə'praɪətərɪ/ *adj.* 1. of a proprietor. 2. holding property. 3. held in private ownership. 4. manufactured and sold by one particular firm, usually under a patent. [from Latin *proprietarius*]

proprietor /prə'praɪətə/ *n.* the holder of a property; the owner of a business. —**proprietorial** /-'tɔ:rɪəl/ *adj.*, **proprietress** *n.fem.*

propriety /prə'praɪɪtɪ/ *n.* 1. being proper or suitable. 2. correctness of behaviour or morals. 3. (in *plural*) the details of correct conduct. [from Old French from Latin *proprietas*]

propulsion /prə'pʌlʃən/ *n.* driving or pushing forward. —**propulsive** *adj.* [from obsolete verb *propulse* from Latin *propulsare*, frequentative of *propellere* = propel]

propulsor /prə'pʌlsə/ *n.* a ducted propeller which can be swivelled to give forward, upward, or downward flight to an airship.

propyl alcohol usually a mixture of two isomeric compounds (see ◊*isomer*): normal propyl alcohol and isopropyl alcohol, $CH_3CHOHCH_3$. The former is also known as 1-propanol, and the latter as 2-propanol. Both are colourless liquids that can be mixed with water and are used in perfumery.

propylene the common name for ◊*propene*.

pro rata /prəʊ 'rɑːtə/proportional; in proportion. [Latin = according to the rate]

prorogue /prə'rəʊg/ *v.t./i.* to discontinue the meetings of (a parliament etc.) without dissolving it; (of a parliament etc.) to be prorogued. —**prorogation** /prəʊrə'geɪʃən/ *n.* [from Old French from Latin *prorogare* = prolong (*rogare* = ask)]

prosaic /prə'zeɪɪk/ *adj.* 1. like prose, lacking in poetic beauty. 2. unromantic, commonplace, dull. —**prosaically** *adv.* [from French or Latin]

proscenium /prəʊ'siːnɪəm/ *n.* (*plural* **prosceniums**) the part of a theatre stage in front of a drop or curtain, especially with the enclosing arch. [Latin from Greek *skēnē* = tent, stage]

proscribe /prə'skraɪb/ *v.t.* 1. to forbid by law. 2. to denounce as dangerous etc. 3. to put (a person) outside the protection of the law; to banish, to exile. —**proscription** /-'skrɪpʃən/ *n.*, **proscriptive** /-'skrɪptɪv/ *adj.* [from Latin *scribere* = write]

prose /prəʊz/ *n.* 1. written or spoken language without metrical regularity; in literature, prose corresponds more closely to the patterns of everyday speech than ◊poetry. In modern literature, however, the distinction between verse and prose is not always clear-cut. 2. dull or matter-of-fact quality. —*v.i.* to talk tediously. —**prose poem**, an elevated prose composition. [from Old French from Latin *prosa* (*oratio*) = straightforward discourse (*prorsus* = direct)]

prosecute /'prɒsɪkjuːt/ *v.t.* 1. to institute legal proceedings against (a person, or *absolute*) or with reference to (a crime or claim etc.). 2. to carry on or be occupied with. [from Latin *prosequi* (*sequi* = follow)]

prosecution /prɒsɪ'kjuːʃən/ *n.* 1. the institution and carrying on of legal proceedings. 2. the prosecuting party. 3. prosecuting, being prosecuted. [from Old French or Latin]

Prosecution Service, Crown the body established by the Prosecution of Offences Act 1985, responsible for prosecuting all criminal offences in England and Wales. It is headed by the Director of Public Prosecutions (DPP), and brings England and Wales in line with Scotland (see ◊procurator fiscal) in having a prosecution service independent of the police.

prosecutor /'prɒsɪkjuːtə/ *n.* one who prosecutes, especially in a criminal court.

proselyte /'prɒsɪlaɪt/ *n.* 1. a person converted from one opinion or belief etc. to another. 2. a Gentile convert to the Jewish faith. [from Latin from Greek *proserkhomai* = come to a place]

proselytism /'prɒsɪlɪtɪzəm/ *n.* 1. being a proselyte. 2. the practice of proselytizing.

proselytize /'prɒsɪlɪtaɪz/ *v.t.* to seek to make a proselyte of (a person, or *absolute*).

Proserpina /prə'sɜːpɪnə/ the Roman equivalent of ◊Persephone, goddess of the underworld.

prosody /'prɒsədɪ/ *n.* the science of versification; the study of speech rhythms. —**prosodic** /prə'sɒdɪk/ *adj.*, **prosodically** /prə'sɒdɪkəlɪ/ *adv.*, **prosodist** *n.* [from Latin from Greek *pros* = to and *ōidē* = song]

prospect /'prɒspekt/ *n.* 1. what one is to expect; a chance (of success etc.). 2. an extensive view of a landscape etc.; a mental scene or view of matters. 3. (*colloquial*) a possible or likely customer etc. —/prə'spekt/ *v.t./i.* to explore or search (for gold etc.); to look out *for*. —**prospector** /prə'spektə/ *n.* [from Latin]

prospective /prə'spektɪv/ *adj.* expected to be or occur; future, possible. [from obsolete French or Latin]

prospectus /prə'spektəs/ *n.* a printed document describing the chief features of a school or business etc. [Latin = prospect (*prospicere* = look forward)]

prosper /'prɒspə/ *v.i.* to be successful, to thrive. [from obsolete French or Latin *prosperare*]

prosperity /prɒ'sperɪtɪ/ *n.* prosperous state or condition, wealth.

prosperous /'prɒspərəs/ *adj.* **1.** financially successful, thriving. **2.** auspicious. —**prosperously** *adv.* [from obsolete French from Latin *prosperus*]

Prost /prɒst/ Alain 1955–. French racing-car driver who won 44 races from 168 starts, and was world champion in 1985, 1986, and 1989. He raced in Formula One events from 1980 and had his first Grand Prix win in 1981 (French GP) driving a Renault. In 1984 he began driving for the McLaren team. He is known as 'the Professor'.

prostaglandin *n.* any of a group of complex fatty acids that act as messenger substances between cells. Effects include stimulating the contraction of smooth muscle (for example, of the womb during birth), regulating the production of stomach acid, and modifying hormonal activity. In excess, prostaglandins may produce inflammatory disorders such as arthritis. Synthetic prostaglandins are used to induce labour in humans and domestic animals.

prostate /'prɒsteɪt/ *n.* (in full **prostate gland**) the large gland surrounding, and opening into, the urethra at the base of the bladder in male mammals. The prostate gland produces an alkaline fluid that is released during ejaculation; this fluid activates sperm, and prevents their clumping together. —**prostatic** /-'tætɪk/ *adj.* [French from Greek *prostatēs* = one who stands before]

prosthesis /'prɒsθɪsɪs/ *n.* (*plural* **prostheses** /-iːz/) the replacement of a body part with an artificial substitute; the part supplied for this. Prostheses in the form of artificial limbs, such as wooden legs and metal hooks for hands, have been used for centuries, although artificial limbs are now more natural-looking and comfortable to wear. The comparatively new field of ◊bionics (see under ◊bionic) has developed myoelectric, or bionic, arms, which are electronically operated and worked by minute electrical impulses from body muscles. Other prostheses include hearing aids, false teeth and eyes, and, for the heart, a ◊pacemaker (sense 2) and plastic heart valves and blood vessels. —**prosthetic** /-'θetɪk/ *adj.* [Latin from Greek = placing in addition]

prostitute /'prɒstɪtjuːt/ *n.* a woman who engages in sexual intercourse for payment; a man who engages in homosexual acts for payment. —*v.t.* to make a prostitute of (especially *oneself*); to sell or make use of (one's honour or abilities etc.) unworthily. —**prostitution** /-'tjuːʃən/ *n.* [from Latin *prostituere* = offer for sale (*statuere* = set up)]

prostrate /'prɒstreɪt/ *adj.* **1.** lying with one's face to the ground, especially in submission or humility. **2.** lying in a horizontal position. **3.** overcome, overthrown. **4.** physically exhausted. —/prɒ'streɪt/ *v.t.* **1.** to throw (oneself) down prostrate. **2.** to overcome, to make submissive. **3.** (of fatigue etc.) to reduce to extreme physical weakness. —**prostration** /prɒ'streɪʃən/ *n.* [from Latin *sternere* = lay flat]

prosy /'prəʊzɪ/ *adj.* prosaic, dull. —**prosily** *adv.*, **prosiness** *n.*

protactinium /prəʊtæk'tɪnɪəm/ *n.* a silver-grey, radioactive, metallic element of the ◊actinide series, symbol Pa, atomic number 91, relative atomic mass 231.036. It occurs in nature in very small quantities, in ◊pitchblende and other uranium ores. It has 14 known isotopes; the longest-lived, Pa-231, has a half-life of 32,480 years. [German]

protagonist /prəʊ'tægənɪst/ *n.* **1.** the chief person in a drama or the plot of a story; the principal performer. **2.** (*disputed usage*) a champion or advocate of a course or method etc. [from Greek *prōtos* = first and *agonistēs* = actor]

protandry *n.* in a flower, the state in which the male reproductive organs reach maturity before those of the female. This is a common method of avoiding self-fertilization. See also ◊protogyny.

protean /'prəʊtɪən, -'tiːən/ *adj.* variable, versatile; taking many forms. [from *Proteus*]

protease *n.* a general term for an enzyme capable of splitting proteins. Examples include pepsin, found in the stomach, and trypsin, found in the small intestine.

protect /prə'tekt/ *v.t.* **1.** to keep from harm or injury. **2.** to guard (a home industry) against competition by import duties on foreign goods. [from Latin *tegere* = cover]

protection /prə'tekʃən/ *n.* **1.** protecting, being protected. **2.** a person or thing that protects. **3.** the system of protecting home industries. **4.** immunity from molestation obtained by payment under threat of violence; money so paid. [from Old French or Latin]

protectionism *n.* in economics, the imposition of heavy duties or import quotas by a government as a means of discouraging the import of foreign goods likely to compete with domestic products. Price controls, quota systems, and the reduction of surpluses are among the measures taken for agricultural products in the EC (see ◊agriculture). The opposite practice is ◊free trade. —**protectionist** *n.*

protective *adj.* protecting; giving or intended for protection. —**protective custody,** the detention of a person actually or allegedly for his/her own protection. —**protectively** *adv.*

protector *n.* **1.** a person or thing that protects. **2.** a regent in charge of a kingdom during the minority or absence of a sovereign. —**protectorship** *n.*, **protectress** *n.fem.* [from Old French from Latin]

protectorate /prə'tektərət/ *n.* formerly in international law, a small state under the direct or indirect control of a larger one. The 20th-century equivalent is a ◊trust territory. —**the Protectorate,** in English history, the rule of Oliver and Richard ◊Cromwell 1653–59.

protégé /'prɒteʒeɪ/ *n.* a person to whom another is protector or patron. —**protégée** *n.fem.* [French]

protein /'prəʊtiːn/ *n.* a long-chain molecule composed of amino acids joined by ◊peptide bonds. Proteins are essential to all living organisms. As **enzymes** they regulate all aspects of metabolism. Structural proteins such as **keratin** and **collagen** make up the skin, claws, bones, tendons, and ligaments; **muscle** proteins produce movement; **haemoglobin** transports oxygen; and **membrane** proteins regulate the movement of substances into and out of cells. [from French and German from Greek *prōteios* = primary]

pro tem /prəʊ 'tem/ (*colloquial*) abbreviation of *pro tempore.*

pro tempore /prəʊ 'tempərɪ/ for the time being. [Latin]

Proterozoic *adj.* of the period of geological time 2.5 billion to 590 million years ago. —*n.* this period; the second division of the Precambrian era. It is defined as the time of simple life, since many rocks dating from this aeon show traces of biological activity, and some contain the fossils of bacteria and algae.

protest /prə'test/ *v.t./i.* **1.** to express disapproval or dissent; (*US*) to object to (a decision etc.). **2.** to declare solemnly or firmly, especially in reply to an accusation etc. **3.** to write or obtain a protest in regard to (a bill). —/'prəʊtest/ *n.* **1.** a formal statement or action of disapproval or dissent. **2.** a written declaration that a bill has been presented and payment or acceptance refused. —**under protest,** unwillingly and after making protests. —**protestor** /prə'testə/ *n.* [from Old French from Latin *testari* = assert on oath]

Protestantism /'prɒtɪstəntɪzm/ *n.* one of the main divisions of Christianity, which emerged from Roman Catholicism at the ◊Reformation. The chief denominations are the Anglican Communion (Episcopalian in the USA), Baptists, Lutherans, Methodists, Pentecostals, and Presbyterians, with a total membership of about 300 million. —**Protestant,** a member or adherent of any of these denominations. —*adj.* of or relating to a Protestant denomination. [from Latin]

protestation /prɒte'steɪʃən/ *n.* a solemn affirmation; a protest.

Proteus /'prəʊtjəs/ in Greek mythology, an old man, the warden of the sea beasts of Poseidon, who possessed the gift of prophecy, and could transform himself into any form he chose to evade questioning.

protist /prə'tɪst/ *n.* in biology, a single-celled organism of the kingdom Protista, having a ◊eukaryotic cell, but distinguished from the plant, fungal, or animal kingdoms. The main protists are protozoa (see ◊protozoan). [from Greek *prōtos* = first]

proto- /prəʊtə(ʊ)-/ in combinations, first. [from Greek *prōtos* = first]

protocol /'prəʊtəkɒl/ *n.* **1.** official formality and etiquette; observance of this. **2.** the original draft of a diplomatic document, especially of the agreed terms of a treaty. **3.** in computing, an agreed set of standards for the transfer of data between different devices. They cover transmission speed, format of data, and the signals required to synchronize the transfer. See also ◊interface, sense 2. —*v.t./i.* (**-ll-**) to draw up a protocol or protocols; to record

Proust A photograph taken in the 1880s when Marcel Proust, novelist and critic, moved in the most fashionable Parisian circles.

in a protocol. [from Old French from Latin from Greek = flyleaf (*kolla* = glue)]

Protocols of Zion a forged document containing supposed plans for Jewish world conquest, alleged to have been submitted by ◊Herzl to the first Zionist Congress at Basel in 1897, and published in Russia in 1905. Although proved to be a forgery in 1921, the document was used by Hitler in his anti-Semitic campaign 1933–45.

protogyny *n.* in a flower, the state where the female reproductive organs reach maturity before those of the male. Like ◊protandry, this is a method of avoiding self-fertilization, but it is much less common.

proton /'prəutɒn/ *n.* a positively charged elementary particle found in the nuclei of all atoms. [from Greek *prōtos* = first, reflecting their character as primitive constituents of all atomic nuclei; also perhaps suggested by the name of William *Prout*, who suggested that hydrogen was a constituent of all the elements]

proton number the number, sometimes called the **atomic number**, of protons in the nucleus of an ◊atom. Adding the proton number to the number of neutrons in the nucleus (the neutron number) produces the ◊nucleon number.

Proton rocket a Soviet space rocket introduced in 1965, used to launch heavy satellites, space probes, and the Salyut and *Mir* space stations.

protoplasm /'prəutəplæzəm/ *n.* the contents of a living cell. Strictly speaking it includes all the discrete structures (organelles) in a cell, but it is often used simply to mean the jellylike material in which these float. The contents of a cell outside the nucleus are called ◊cytoplasm. —**protoplasmic** /-'plæzmɪk/ *adj.* [from Greek *prōtos* = first and *plassō* = mould]

protoplast /'prəutəplæst/ *n.* in biology, the contents of a cell after the cell wall has been removed. [from French or Latin from Greek *plastos*= moulded]

prototype /'prəutətaɪp/ *n.* an original thing or person in relation to a copy or imitation or developed form; a trial model, a preliminary version (e.g. of an aeroplane). Prototypes are tested for performance, reliability, economy, and safety; then the main design can be modified before full-scale production begins. [French or from Latin from Greek]

protozoan *n.* or **protozoon** (*plural* **protozoa**) a group of single-celled organisms without rigid cell walls. Some, such as amoeba, ingest other cells, but most are ◊saprotrophs or parasites. The group is polyphyletic (containing organisms which have different evolutionary origins).

protract /prə'trækt/ *v.t.* to prolong in duration. —**protraction** *n.* [from Latin *trahere* = draw]

protractor *n.* an instrument for measuring flat angles, usually a semicircle marked off in degrees.

protrude /prə'tru:d/ *v.t.i.* to project or cause to project from a surface; to thrust forward. —**protrusion** *n.*, **protrusive** /-'tru:sɪv/ *adj.* [from Latin *trudere* = thrust]

protuberant /prə'tju:bərənt/ *adj.* bulging out, prominent. —**protuberance** *n.* [from Latin *tuber* = bump]

proud *adj.* 1. feeling or showing justifiable pride; marked by or causing such feeling. 2. feeling oneself greatly honoured. 3. full of self-respect and independence. 4. having an unduly high opinion of one's own qualities or merits. 5. (of a thing) imposing, splendid. 6. slightly projecting; (of flesh) overgrown round a healing wound. —**do a person proud**, to treat him or her with great generosity or honour. —**proudly** *adv.* [Old English from Old French *prud* = valiant]

Proudhon /pru:'dɒn/ Pierre Joseph 1809–1865. French anarchist, born in Besançon. He sat in the Constituent Assembly of 1848, was imprisoned for three years, and had to go into exile in Brussels. He published *Qu'est-ce que la propriété*/*What is Property?* 1840 and *Philosophie de la misère*/*Philosophy of Poverty* 1846; the former contains the dictum 'property is theft'.

Proust /pru:st/ Marcel 1871–1922. French novelist and critic. His immense autobiographical work *À la recherche du temps perdu*/*Remembrance of Things Past* 1913–27, consisting of a series of novels, is the expression of his childhood memories coaxed from his subconscious; it is also a precise reflection of life in provincial France at the end of the 19th century.

The true paradises are paradises we have lost.
Marcel Proust
Le Temps Retrouvé

Prout /praut/ William 1785–1850. English physician and chemist. In 1815 Prout published his hypothesis that the atomic weight of every atom is an exact and integral multiple of the hydrogen atom. The discovery of isotopes (atoms of the same element that have different masses) in the 20th century bore out his idea.

provable /'pru:vəbəl/ *adj.* that may be proved. —**provability** /-'bɪltɪ/ *n.*

prove /pru:v/ *v.t.i.* 1. to give or be proof of. 2. to be found to be, to emerge as. 3. to establish the validity of (a will). 4. to rise or cause (dough) to rise. 5. (*archaic*) to test the qualities of. —**not proven**, in Scottish law, the evidence is insufficient to establish guilt or innocence. **prove oneself**, to demonstrate one's abilities etc. [from Old French from Latin *probare* = test, demonstrate (*probus* = good)]

provenance /'prɒvənəns/ *n.* origin, place of origin. [French, from Latin *provenire* = come forth (*venire* = come)]

Provençal /prɒvɑ̃'sɑ:l/ *adj.* of Provence in SE France or its people or language. —*n.* 1. a native or inhabitant of Provence. 2. the language spoken in and around Provence, a member of the Romance branch of the Indo-European language family. It is now regarded as a dialect or patois. [from *Provence* from Latin *provincia* = province]

Provence-Alpes-Côte d'Azur /prɒ'vɒns ælp kəut dæ'zjuə/ region of SE France, comprising the *départements* of Alpes-de-Haute-Provence, Hautes-Alpes, Alpes-Maritimes, Bouches-du Rhône, Var, and Vaucluse; area 31,400 sq km/12,120 sq mi; capital Marseille; population (1986) 4,059,000. The *Côte d'Azur*, on the Mediterranean, is a tourist centre. Provence was an independent kingdom in the 10th century, and the area still has its own language, Provençal.

provender /'prɒvɪndə/ *n.* fodder; (*colloquial*) food for humans. [from Old French from Latin *praebenda*]

proverb /'prɒvɜ:b/ *n.* 1. a short, pithy saying in general use, stating a truth or giving advice. 2. a person or thing that is widely known as exemplifying something. [from Old French or Latin *proverbium* (*verbum* = word)]

proverbial /prə'vɜ:bɪəl/ *adj.* 1. of or expressed in proverbs. 2. well-known, notorious. —**proverbially** *adv.* [from Latin]

provide /prə'vaɪd/ v.t./i. 1. to cause (a person) to have possession or use of something; to supply, to make available. 2. to supply the necessities of life. 3. to make due preparation (for or against a contingency). 4. to stipulate, to give as a condition. —**provided** or **providing** (**that**), on the condition or understanding that. [from Latin providēre = foresee (vidēre = see]

providence /'prɒvɪdəns/ n. 1. being provident; foresight, timely care. 2. the beneficent care of God or nature. 3. Providence, God in this aspect. [from Old French or Latin]

provident /'prɒvɪdənt/ adj. having or showing wise foresight for future needs or events; thrifty. —**Provident Society**, a Friendly Society.

providential /prɒvɪ'denʃəl/ adj. 1. of or by divine foresight or intervention. 2. opportune, lucky. —**providentially** adv.

provider /prə'vaɪdə/ n. one who provides; the breadwinner of a family etc.

province /'prɒvɪns/ n. 1. each of the principal administrative divisions of certain countries. 2. a district consisting of a group of adjacent dioceses, under the charge of an archbishop. 3. a sphere of responsibility or concern or of knowledge; a branch of learning. 4. in Roman history, a territory under Roman rule, outside Italy. —**the Province**, in recent use, Northern Ireland. **the provinces**, the whole of a country outside its capital city. [from Old French from Latin provincia]

provincial /prə'vɪnʃəl/ adj. 1. of a province or provinces. 2. having restricted views or the interests or manners etc. attributed to inhabitants of the provinces. —n. an inhabitant of a province or the provinces. —**provincialism** n.

provision /prə'vɪʒən/ n. 1. providing; preparation for a future contingency. 2. a provided amount of something; (in plural) a supply of food and drink. 3. a formally stated condition or stipulation. —v.t. to supply with provisions. [from Old French from Latin]

provisional /prə'vɪʒənəl/ adj. arranged or agreed upon temporarily but possibly to be altered later. —**Provisional**, a member of the Provisional wing of the IRA. The name is taken from the 'Provisional Government of the Republic of Ireland' which was declared in 1916. —**provisionally** adv.

proviso /prə'vaɪzəʊ/ n. (plural provisos) a stipulation, a clause giving a stipulation in a document. [from French or Latin]

provisory /prə'vaɪzərɪ/ adj. 1. conditional. 2. making provision. [from French or Latin]

provocation /prɒvə'keɪʃən/ n. 1. provoking, being provoked. 2. something that provokes anger or retaliation. [from Old French or Latin]

provocative /prə'vɒkətɪv/ adj. 1. tending or intended to arouse anger, interest, or sexual desire. 2. deliberately annoying. —**provocatively** adv. [from obsolete French from Latin]

provoke /prə'vəʊk/ v.t. 1. to rouse or incite (a person) to a feeling or action. 2. to annoy or irritate. 3. to cause or give rise to (a feeling or reaction etc.). 4. to tempt or allure. [from Old French from Latin vocare = summon]

provost /'prɒvəst/ n. 1. the head of some colleges. 2. the head of a Scottish municipal corporation or burgh, the approximate equivalent of an English mayor. 3. (in full **provost marshal** /prəʊ'vəʊ/) the head of the military police in a camp or on active service. [Old English and from Old French from Latin propositus for praepositus = placed in charge)]

prow /praʊ/ n. the projecting front part of a ship or boat. [from French, ultimately from Greek prōira]

prowess /'praʊɪs/ n. great ability or daring. [from Old French prud = valiant]

prowl v.t./i. to go about stealthily in search of prey or to catch others unawares; to traverse (a place) thus; to pace or wander restlessly. —n. prowling. —**prowler** n.

prox. abbreviation of ◊proximo.

Proxima Centauri /'prɒksɪmə sen'tɔːraɪ/ the closest star to the Sun, 4.3 light years away. It is a faint ◊red dwarf, visible only with a telescope, and is a member of the Alpha Centauri triple-star system. [from Latin proximus = nearest; so named because it is about 0.1 light years closer to Earth than its two partners]

proximate /'prɒksɪmət/ adj. 1. nearest, next before or after (in time or order, in causation etc.). 2. approximate. [from Latin proximus = nearest]

proximity /prɒk'sɪmɪtɪ/ n. 1. nearness in space or time. 2. neighbourhood. [from French or Latin]

proximo /'prɒksɪməʊ/ adj. in commerce, of the next month. [Latin = in the next (mense = month)]

proxy /'prɒksɪ/ n. 1. a person authorized to act for another; the agency of such a person. 2. a document authorizing a person to vote on behalf of another; a vote so given. [from obsolete procuracy from Latin curare = look after]

prude /pruːd/ n. a person of extreme or exaggerated propriety in conduct or speech, one who is easily shocked by sexual matters. —**prudery** n., **prudish** adj., **prudishly** adv., **prudishness** n. [French, from prudefemme, feminine of prud'homme = good man and true]

prudent /'pruːdənt/ adj. showing care and foresight, avoiding rashness. —**prudence** n., **prudently** adv. [from Old French or Latin providēre = foresee]

prudential /pruː'denʃəl/ adj. of, involving, or characterized by prudence. —**prudentially** adv.

prune[1] v.t. 1. to trim by cutting away dead or overgrown branches or shoots, especially to promote growth. 2. to remove or reduce (what is regarded as superfluous or excessive); to remove items thus from. [from Old French pr(o)ignier]

prune[2] n. a dried plum. [from Old French from Latin prunum = plum]

Prunus n. a genus of trees of the northern hemisphere, family Rosaceae, producing fruit with a fleshy, edible pericarp. The genus includes plums, cherries, peaches, apricots, and almonds.

prurient /'prʊərɪənt/ adj. given to or arising from the indulgence of lewd thoughts. —**prurience** n., **pruriently** adv. [from Latin prurire = itch]

Prussia /'prʌʃə/ N German state 1618–1945 on the Baltic coast. It was an independent kingdom until 1867, when it became, under ◊Bismarck, the military power of the North German Confederation and part of the German Empire in 1871 under the Prussian king Wilhelm I. West Prussia became part of Poland under the ◊Versailles Treaty, and East Prussia was largely incorporated into the USSR after 1945.

Prussian /'prʌʃən/ adj. of Prussia. —n. a native of Prussia. —**Prussian blue**, a deep blue pigment.

prussic /'prʌsɪk/ adj. of or obtained from Prussian blue. —**prussic acid**, the former name for ◊hydrocyanic acid, a highly poisonous aqueous solution of hydrogen cyanide. [from French]

Prut /pruːt/ a river that rises in the Carpathian Mountains of SW Ukraine, USSR and flows 900 km/565 mi to meet the Danube at Reni, USSR. For part of its course it follows the eastern frontier of Romania.

pry /praɪ/ v.i. to inquire impertinently (into a person's affairs etc.); to look or peer inquisitively and often furtively.

Przhevalsky /pʃe'vælski/ Nikolai Mikhailovitch 1839–1888. Russian explorer and soldier. In 1870 he crossed the Gobi Desert to Beijing and then went on to the upper reaches of the Chang Jiang River. His attempts to penetrate Tibet as far as Lhasa failed on three occasions, but he continued to explore the mountain regions between Tibet and Mongolia, where he made collections of plants and animals, including a wild camel and a wild horse (the species is now known as Przhevalsky's horse).

PS abbreviation of postscript. [Latin post scriptum = after writing]

psalm /sɑːm/ n. a sacred poem or song of praise, especially one of those in the Book of Psalms in the Old Testament. [Old English from Latin from Greek psalmos = song sung to the harp (psallō = pluck the strings)]

psalmist n. an author of psalms. [from Latin]

psalmody /'sɑːmədɪ, 'sælmədɪ/ n. the practice or art of singing psalms etc., especially in public worship. [from Latin from Greek ōidē = singing]

Psalter /'sɔːltə, 'sɒ-/ n. 1. the Book of Psalms. 2. **psalter**, a copy or version of this. [from Latin from Greek psaltērion = stringed instrument]

psaltery /'sɔːltərɪ, 'sɒ-/ n. an ancient and medieval instrument like a dulcimer but played by plucking the strings. [from Old French from Latin]

pseudocopulation

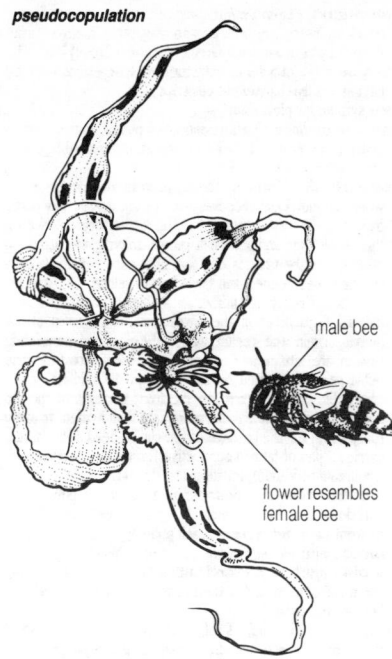

male bee

flower resembles
female bee

PSBR abbreviation of ◊public sector borrowing requirement.

psephology /se'fɒlədʒɪ, se-/ *n.* the study of trends in elections and voting. —**psephologist** *n.* [from Greek *psēphos* = pebble used in voting]

pseudo- /sju:dəʊ-/ in combinations, false, apparent, supposed but not real. [Greek *pseudēs* = false]

pseudocarp *n.* a fruitlike structure that incorporates tissue that is not derived from the ovary wall. The additional tissues may be derived from floral parts such as the ◊receptacle (sense 2) and ◊calyx. Different types of pseudocarp include pineapples, figs, apples, and pears.

pseudocopulation *n.* the attempted copulation by a male insect with a flower. It results in ◊pollination of the flower and is common in the orchid family, where the flowers of many species resemble a particular species of female bee. When a male bee attempts to mate with a flower, the pollinia (groups of pollen grains) stick to its body. They are transferred to the stigma of another flower when the insect attempts copulation again.

pseudomorph *n.* a mineral that has replaced another *in situ* and has retained the external crystal shape of the original mineral.

pseudonym /'sju:dənɪm/ *n.* a fictitious name, especially one assumed by an author. —**pseudonymity** /-'nɪmɪtɪ/ *n.*, **pseudonymous** /-'dɒnɪməs/ *adj.* [from French from Greek *onoma* = name]

pseudopodium /sju:də'pəʊdɪəm/ *n.* (*plural* **pseudopodia**) a temporary footlike protrusion of cell tissue, used for movement, feeding etc., by some protozoa and other animals. [from Greek *podion*, diminutive of *pous podos* = foot]

PSFD abbreviation of public sector financial deficit; see under ◊public sector borrowing requirement.

psi[1] /psaɪ/ *n.* the 23rd letter of the Greek alphabet (ψ, Ψ) = ps. [Greek]

psi[2] *n.* in parapsychology, a hypothetical faculty common to humans and other animals said to be responsible for extrasensory perception (ESP) and telekinesis.

Psilocybe *n.* a genus of mushroom with hallucinogenic properties, including the Mexican sacred mushroom *P. mexicana*, which contains compounds with effects similar to LSD. A related species *P. semilanceata* is found in N Europe.

psoriasis /sɔː'raɪəsɪs/ *n.* a chronic, recurring skin disease characterized by raised, red, scaly patches, usually on the scalp, back, arms, and/or legs. Tar preparations, steroid creams, and ultraviolet light are used to treat it, and sometimes it disappears spontaneously. Psoriasis may be accompanied by a form of arthritis. [from Greek *psōriaō* = have itch]

psst interjection to attract the attention surreptitiously. [imitative]

PSV abbreviation of public service vehicle.

psyche /'saɪkɪ/ *n.* the human soul or spirit; the human mind. [Latin from Greek]

Psyche a late Greek personification of the soul as a winged girl or young woman. The goddess Aphrodite was so jealous of Psyche's beauty that she ordered her son Eros, the god of love, to make Psyche fall in love with the worst of men. Instead, he fell in love with her himself.

psychedelic /saɪkɪ'delɪk/ *adj.* 1. hallucinatory, expanding the mind's awareness. 2. having intensely vivid colours or sounds etc. [Greek *dēlos* = clear]

psychedelic rock or **acid rock** a type of pop music involving advanced electronic equipment for both light and sound that appeared in about 1966. The free-form improvisations and light shows of the hippie years had by the 1980s evolved into stadium performances with lasers and other special effects.

psychiatric /saɪkɪ'ætrɪk/ *adj.* or **psychiatrical** of or concerning psychiatry. —**psychiatrically** *adv.*

psychiatry /saɪ'kaɪətrɪ/ *n.* the branch of medicine dealing with the diagnosis and treatment of mental disorder. —**psychiatrist** *n.* [Greek *iatreia* = healing]

psychic /'saɪkɪk/ *adj.* psychical, able to exercise psychical or occult powers. —*n.* 1. a person susceptible to psychical influence, a medium. 2. (in *plural*) the study of psychical phenomena. —**psychically** *adv.* [from Greek]

psychical /'saɪkɪkəl/ *adj.* of the soul or mind, of phenomena and conditions apparently outside the domain of physical law. —**psychically** *adv.*

psycho- /saɪkəʊ-/ in combinations, mind, soul. [from Greek]

psychoanalyse /saɪkəʊ'ænəlaɪz/ *v.t.* to treat by psychoanalysis. —**psychoanalyst** *n.*

psychoanalysis /saɪkəʊə'næləsɪs/ *n.* 1. a therapeutic method originated by ◊Freud for treating disorders of the personality or behaviour by bringing into a patient's consciousness his or her unconscious conflicts and fantasies. It is typically prolonged and expensive and its effectiveness has been disputed. 2. a theory of personality and psychical life derived from this, based on concepts of the ego, id, and superego, the conscious, preconscious, and unconscious levels of the mind, and the repression of the sexual instinct. —**psychoanalytic** /-ænə'lɪtɪk/ *adj.*, **psychoanalytical** /-ænə'lɪtɪkəl/ *adj.*

psychological /saɪkə'lɒdʒɪkəl/ *adj.* of the mind; of psychology. —**psychological moment,** the psychologically appropriate moment; (*colloquial*) the most appropriate time. **psychological warfare,** warfare achieving its aims by weakening the enemy's morale.

psychology /saɪ'kɒlədʒɪ/ *n.* 1. the systematic study of human and animal behaviour. The first psychology laboratory was founded in 1879 by Wilhelm ◊Wundt at Leipzig, Germany. The subject includes diverse areas of study and application, among them the roles of instinct, heredity, environment, and culture; the processes of sensation, perception, learning and memory; the bases of motivation and emotion; and the functioning of thought, intelligence, and language. 2. (*colloquial*) mental characteristics. —**psychologist** *n.*

psychometrics *n.* (as *singular*) the measurement of mental processes. This includes intelligence and aptitude testing to help in job selection and in the clinical assessment of cognitive deficiencies resulting from brain damage.

psychometry /saɪ'kɒmɪtrɪ/ *n.* 1. divination of facts concerning an object (e.g. its source, ownership) from contact with it. 2. measurement of mental abilities. —**psychometric** /-kə'metrɪk/ *adj.*

psychoneurosis /saɪkəʊnjuə'rəʊsɪs/ *n.* a neurosis, especially with indirect expression of emotional feelings. —**psychoneurotic** /-'rɒtɪk/ *adj.*

psychopath /'saɪkəpæθ/ *n.* a person suffering from chronic mental disorder especially with aggressive antisocial behaviour and an absence of feelings of guilt about the behaviour; a mentally or emotionally unstable person.

—**psychopathic** /-'pæθɪk/ adj., **psychopathy** /-'kɒpəθɪ/ n. [Greek -pathēs = sufferer]

psychopathology /saɪkəʊpə'θɒlədʒɪ/ n. the science of mental disorders.

psychosis /saɪ'kəʊsɪs/ n. (plural **psychoses** /-iːz/) or **psychotic disorder** a general term for a serious mental disorder where the individual commonly loses contact with reality and may experience hallucinations (seeing or hearing things that do not exist) or delusions (fixed false beliefs). For example, in a paranoid psychosis, an individual may believe that others are plotting against him or her. A major type of psychosis is ◊schizophrenia. [from Greek = principle of life]

psychosomatic /saɪkəʊsə'mætɪk/ adj. of the mind and the body; (of a disease etc.) caused or aggravated by mental stress. —**psychosomatically** adv.

psychosurgery /saɪkəʊ'sɜːdʒərɪ/ n. brain surgery as a means of treating mental disorder. For example, **lobotomy** is the separation of the white fibres in the prefrontal lobe of the brain, as a means of relieving a deep state of anxiety.

psychotherapy /saɪkəʊ'θerəpɪ/ n. treatment of mental disorders by psychological means rather than surgery or drugs. Examples include ◊cognitive therapy and ◊psychoanalysis. —**psychotherapeutic** /-'pjuː'tɪk/ adj., **psychotherapist** n.

psychotic /saɪ'kɒtɪk/ adj. of or suffering from psychosis. —n. a psychotic person.

psychotic disorder another name for ◊psychosis.

pt. abbreviation of 1. part. 2. pint. 3. point. 4. port.

Pt symbol for platinum.

PT abbreviation of physical training.

PTA abbreviation of parent–teacher association.

ptarmigan /'tɑːmɪɡən/ n. a type of grouse *Lagopus mutus* found in N Europe. It is about 36 cm/1.2 ft long, and has white plumage in winter. [from Gaelic]

Pte abbreviation of Private (soldier).

pteridophyte /'terɪdəfaɪt/ n. a simple type of ◊vascular plant. The pteridophytes comprise four classes: the Psilosida, including the most primitive vascular plants, found mainly in the tropics; the Lycopsida, including the club mosses; the Sphenopsida, including the horsetails; and the Pteropsida, including the ferns. They are mainly terrestrial, nonflowering plants characterized by the presence of a vascular system; the possession of true stems, roots, and leaves; and by a marked ◊alternation of generations, with the sporophyte forming the dominant generation in the life cycle. They do not produce seeds. [from Greek *pteris* = fern and *phuton* = plant]

pterodactyl /terə'dæktɪl/ n. see ◊pterosaur. [from Greek *pteron* = wing and *daktulos* = finger]

pterosaur n. any extinct flying reptile of the order Pterosauria, existing in the Mesozoic age. Pterosaurs were formerly assumed to be smooth-skinned gliders, but recent discoveries show that at least some were furry, probably warm-blooded, and may have had muscle fibres and blood vessels on their wings, stiffened by moving the hind legs, thus allowing controlled and strong flapping flight. They ranged from starling size to the largest with 12 m/40 ft wingspan. The term 'pterodactyl' is sometimes used for any pterosaur, but it actually refers only to the starling-sized genus *Pterodactylus*.

PTFE abbreviation of polytetrafluoroethylene, a nonstick coating known by the trade name ◊Teflon.

PTO abbreviation of please turn over.

Ptolemy /'tɒləmɪ/ (Claudius Ptolemaeus) c.100–AD 170. Egyptian astronomer and geographer, who worked in Alexandria. His major work, the *Almagest*, developed the theory that Earth is the centre of the universe, with the Sun, Moon, and stars revolving around it. In 1543 the Polish astronomer ◊Copernicus disproved the **Ptolemaic system**. Ptolemy's *Geography* was a standard source of information until the 16th century.

Ptolemy a dynasty of kings of Macedonian origin who ruled Egypt over a period of 300 years, including:

Ptolemy I c.367–283 BC. Ruler of Egypt from 323 BC, king from 304. He was one of ◊Alexander the Great's generals, and possibly his half-brother (and married his lover, ◊Thaïs). He established the library in Alexandria.

Ptolemy XIII 63–47 BC. Joint ruler of Egypt with his sister–wife Cleopatra; she put him to death.

ptomaine /'təʊmeɪn/ n. any of various amines (some toxic) in putrefying animal and vegetable matter. [from French from Italian from Greek *ptōma* = corpse]

p-type adj. (of a semiconductor device or a region in this) having positive carriers of electricity.

Pu symbol for plutonium.

pub n. (colloquial) abbreviation of public house. —**pub crawl**, a series of visits to several pubs with drinking at each.

puberty /'pjuːbətɪ/ n. the stage in human development when the individual becomes sexually mature. It may occur from the age of ten upwards. The sexual organs take on their adult form and pubic hair grows. In girls, menstruation begins, and the breasts develop; in boys, the voice breaks and becomes deeper, and facial hair develops. —**pubertal** adj. [from French or Latin *puber* = adult]

pubes /'pjuː.biːz/ n. the lowest part of the front of the human trunk, the region where the external generative organs are situated. The underlying bony structure, the pubic arch, is formed by the union in the midline of the two pubic bones, which are the front portions of the hip bones. In women it is more prominent than in men, to allow more room for the passage of the child's head at birth, and carries a pad of fat and connective tissue, the *mons veneris* (mountain of Venus), for its protection. [Latin]

pubescence /pjuː'besəns/ n. 1. arrival at puberty. 2. soft down on a plant or animal. —**pubescent** adj. [French or from Latin *pubescere* = reach puberty]

pubic /'pjuː.bɪk/ adj. of the pubes or pubis.

pubis /'pjuː.bɪs/ n. (plural **pubes** /-iːz/) the bone forming the front of each half of the pelvis. [from Latin *os pubis* = bone of the pubes]

public /'pʌblɪk/ adj. 1. of, concerning, or for the use of the people as a whole. 2. representing the people; done by or for the people. 3. open to general observation or knowledge, openly done or existing. 4. of or engaged in the people's affairs or service. —n. the community in general; members of it; a section of the community. —**in public**, openly, for all to see or know. **public-address system**, a system of loudspeakers etc. for a speaker at a large gathering. **public company**, one with shares available to all buyers. **public house**, a place licensed for and mainly concerned with selling alcoholic drink for consumption on the premises. **public relations**, the promotion of good relations between a business etc. and the public. **public servant**, a state official. **public-spirited** adj. ready to do things for the benefit of people in general. **public transport**, buses, trains etc., available to the public and having fixed routes. **public utility**, an organization supplying gas or electricity or water etc., and regarded as a public service. **public works**, building operations undertaken by the state.

—**publicly** adv. [from Old French or Latin *publicus* (*populus* = people, influenced by *pubes* = adult population)]

Public Against Violence (Slovak *Verejnost Proti Násil'u*) the Slovak half of the Czechoslovak democratic movement, counterpart of the Czech organization ◊Civic Forum.

publican /'pʌblɪkən/ n. 1. the keeper of a public house. 2. in Roman history and in the New Testament, a tax collector. [from Old French from Latin = tax collector]

publication /pʌblɪ'keɪʃən/ n. 1. the issuing of a book or periodical etc. to the public. 2. a book etc. so issued. 3. making publicly known. [from Old French from Latin *publicare*]

public corporation a company structure that is similar in organization to a public limited company but with no shareholder rights. Such corporations are established to carry out state-owned activities, but are financially independent of the state and are run by a board. The first public corporation to be formed in the UK was the Central Electricity Board in the 1920s.

Public Health Acts 1848, 1872, 1875. In the UK, legislation enacted by Parliament to deal with squalor and disease and to establish a code of sanitary law. The first act established a central board of health with three members who were responsible to Parliament to impose local boards of health in districts where the death rate was above the national average and made provision for other local boards of health to be established by petition. The 1872 act made it obligatory for every local authority to appoint a medical officer of health. The 1875 act consolidated previous acts and provided a comprehensive code for public health.

public inquiry in English law, a legal investigation where witnesses are called and evidence is produced in a similar fashion to a court of law. Inquiries may be held as part of legal procedure, or into a matter of public concern.

publicist /'pʌblɪsɪst/ n. 1. a writer on or a person skilled in current public affairs. 2. an expert in publicity. [from French from Latin (*jus*) *publicum* = public (law)]

publicity /pʌb'lɪsɪtɪ/ n. 1. public attention; the means of attracting it, the business of advertising. 2. being open to general observation; notoriety. [from French]

publicize /'pʌblɪsaɪz/ v.t. to make publicly known, especially by advertisement.

public lending right (PLR) the right of authors to payment when their books are lent by public libraries, similar to a royalty on performance of a play or piece of music. Payment to the copyright holder for such borrowings was introduced in Australia in 1974 and in the UK in 1984.

public limited company (plc) a registered company in which shares and debentures may be offered to the public. It must have a minimum of seven shareholders and there is no upper limit. The company's financial records must be available for any member of the public to scrutinize, and the company's name must carry the words 'public limited company' or initials *plc*. A public company can raise enormous financial resources to fuel its development and expansion by inviting the public to buy shares.

Public Order Act a UK act of Parliament in 1986 to control ◊riots. It abolished the common law offences of riot, rout, unlawful assembly and affray and created a new expanded range of statutory offences: riot, violent disorder, affray, threatening behaviour, and disorderly conduct. These are all arrestable offences that may be committed in both private and public places. Prosecution for riot requires the consent of the Director of Public Prosecutions.

public school in England, a fee-paying independent school. In Scotland, the USA, and many other English-speaking countries, a 'public' school is a state-maintained school, and independent schools are generally known as 'private' schools.

public-sector borrowing requirement (PSBR) the amount of money needed by a government to cover any deficit in financing its own activities, including loans to local authorities and public corporations, and also the funds raised by local authorities and public corporations from other sources.

public spending expenditure by the government, covering the military, health, education, infrastructure, development projects, and the cost of servicing overseas borrowing.

publish /'pʌblɪʃ/ v.t. 1. to issue copies of (a book, or periodical, newspaper etc., or *absolute*) for sale to the public. 2. to make generally known, to announce formally. [from Old French from Latin *publicare*]

publisher n. a person or firm that issues and distributes copies of a book, periodical, newspaper etc.

Puccini /puˈtʃiːnɪ/ Giacomo (Antonio Domenico Michele Secondo Maria) 1858–1924. Italian opera composer whose music shows a strong gift for melody and dramatic effect. His realist works include *Manon Lescaut* 1893, *La Bohème* 1896, *Tosca* 1900, *Madame Butterfly* 1904, and the unfinished *Turandot* (published 1926).

puce adj. & n. brownish-purple. [French = flea, flea colour, from Latin *pulex*]

puck n. a rubber disc used in ice hockey.

pucker v.t./i. to gather or cause to gather into wrinkles, folds, or bulges, intentionally or as a fault. —n. such a wrinkle or bulge.

pud /pud/ (*colloquial*) abbreviation of pudding.

pudding /'pudɪŋ/ n. 1. any sweet food made with sugar, eggs etc.; a dessert. 2. food of various kinds containing or enclosed in a mixture of flour (or a similar substance) and other ingredients and cooked by baking, boiling, or steaming. 3. a kind of sausage. 4. a dumpy slow-witted person. —**puddingy** adj. [from Old French *boudin* = black pudding, ultimately from Latin *botellus* = sausage]

puddle n. 1. a small pool especially of rain on a road etc. 2. clay made into a watertight coating. —v.t. 1. to make muddy. 2. to knead (clay and sand) with water into a muddy mixture. 3. to stir (molten iron) to produce wrought iron

by expelling the carbon. —**puddly** adj. [diminutive of Old English *pudd* = ditch]

puddle clay clay, with sand or gravel, that has had water added and mixed thoroughly so that it becomes watertight. The term was coined in 1762 by the canal builder James Brindley, although its use in dams goes back to Roman times.

pudenda /pjuˈdendə/ n.pl. the genitals, especially of a woman. [Latin = things to be ashamed of]

Pudovkin /puːˈdɒfkɪn/ Vsevolod Illationovich 1893–1953. Russian film director, whose films include the silent *Mother* 1926, *The End of St Petersburg* 1927, and *Storm over Asia* 1928; and the sound films *Deserter* 1933 and *Suvorov* 1941.

pueblo /'pwebləʊ/ n. (*plural* **pueblos**) a type of settlement in the SW USA and Latin America, especially of Indians, with multistorey adobe dwellings occupied by a number of families. [Spanish = people, village, from Latin *populus*]

Pueblo /'pweɪbləʊ/ n. a generic name for the North American Indians known for their communal terraced villages of mud brick or stone. Surviving groups include the ◊Hopi.

puerile /'pjʊəraɪl/ adj. suitable only for children, silly and immature. —**puerility** /-'rɪlɪtɪ/ n. [from French or Latin *puer* = boy]

puerperal /pjuːˈɜːpərəl/ adj. of or due to childbirth. —**puerperal fever,** a fever following childbirth and caused by uterine infection. [from Latin *puerperus* (*puer* = child and *-parus* = bearing)]

Puerto Rico /'pweətəʊ 'riːkəʊ/ the Commonwealth of; easternmost island of the Greater Antilles situated between the US Virgin Islands and the Dominican Republic; **area** 9,000 sq km/3,475 sq mi; **capital** San Juan; **physical** smallest island of the Greater Antilles; **exports** sugar, tobacco, rum, pineapples, textiles, plastics, chemicals, processed foods; **population** (1980) 3,197,000, 67% urban; **language** Spanish and English (official); **government** under the constitution of 1952, similar to that of the USA, with a governor elected for four years, and a legislative assembly with a senate and house of representatives; **recent history** ceded to the USA after the ◊Spanish-American War in 1898; achieved Commonwealth status with local self-government in 1952.

Puerto Sandino /'pweətəʊ sænˈdiːnaʊ/ a major port on the Pacific west coast of Nicaragua, known as **Puerto Somoza**, until 1979.

puff n. 1. a short quick blowing of breath or wind etc.; its sound; a small quantity of smoke or vapour etc. emitted at a puff. 2. the act of smoking a pipe etc. 3. a powder puff. 4. a cake of light pastry. 5. a piece of extravagant praise as a review or advertisement etc. —v.t./i. 1. to emit a puff or puffs; to emit (smoke etc.) in puffs; to smoke (a pipe etc.) in puffs. 2. to come (out or up) in puffs. 3. to blow (dust etc.) away with a puff. 4. to breathe hard, to pant; to put out of breath. 5. to make or become inflated; to swell. 6. to advertise (goods etc.) with extravagant praise. —**puff adder,** a large, venomous African viper (especially *Bitis arietans*) that inflates the upper part of its body when excited. **puffball** n. a fungus of the genus *Lycoperdon* with a ball-shaped sporecase that cracks with maturity, releasing the enclosed spores in the form of a brown powder; for example, the common puffball *Lycoperdon perlatum*. **puff pastry,** light flaky pastry. **puff** or **puffed sleeve,** a short sleeve that is very full at the shoulder. **puff up,** (especially in *past participle*) to elate, to make proud. [probably imitative]

puffer fish a fish of the family Tetraodontidae. As a means of defence it inflates its body with air or water until it becomes spherical and the skin spines become erect. Puffer fish are mainly found in warm waters, where they feed on molluscs, crustaceans, and coral. They vary in size, up to 50 cm/20 in long. The skin of some puffer fish is poisonous (25 times more toxic than cyanide), but they are prized as a delicacy (fugu) in Japan after the poison has been removed.

puffin /'pʌfɪn/ n. a seabird *Fratercula arctica* of the ◊auk family, found in the N Atlantic. It is about 30 cm/1 ft long, with a white face and front, red legs, and a large deep bill, very brightly coloured in summer. It has short wings and webbed feet. It is a poor flyer, but an excellent swimmer. It nests in rock crevices, or makes burrows, and lays a single egg.

puffy *adj.* 1. puffed out, swollen. 2. short-winded. —**puffily** *adv.*, **puffiness** *n.*

pug *n.* a breed of small dog with a broad, flat nose and wrinkled face, chunky body, and tail curled over the hip. —**pug-nosed** *adj.* having a short, flattish nose.

Puget Sound /'pju:dʒɪt/ an inlet of the Pacific Ocean on the W coast of Washington state, USA.

pugilist /'pju:dʒɪlɪst/ *n.* a professional boxer. —**pugilism** *n.*, **pugilistic** /-'lɪstɪk/ *adj.* [from Latin *pugil*]

Pugin /'pju:dʒɪn/ Augustus Welby Northmore 1812–1852. English architect, collaborator with ◊Barry in the detailed design of the Houses of Parliament. He did much to revive Gothic architecture in England.

Puglia /'pju:liə/ (English **Apulia**) region of Italy, the southeastern 'heel'; area 19,300 sq km/7,450 sq mi; capital Bari; population (1988) 4,043,000. Products include wheat, grapes, almonds, olives, and vegetables. The main industrial centre is Taranto.

pugnacious /pʌg'neɪʃəs/ *adj.* disposed to fight, aggressive. —**pugnaciously** *adv.*, **pugnacity** /-'næsɪtɪ/ *n.* [from Latin *pugnax* (*pugnare* = fight)]

P'u-i /'pu:/ (formerly **Pu-Yi**) Henry 1906–1967. Last emperor of China (as Hsuan Tung) from 1908 until his deposition in 1912; he was restored for a week in 1917. After his deposition he chose to be called Henry. He was president 1932–34 and emperor 1934–45 of the Japanese puppet state of Manchukuo (see ◊Manchuria). Captured by Soviet troops, he was returned to China in 1949 and put on trial in the new People's Republic of China in 1950. Pardoned by Mao Zedong in 1959, he became a worker in a botanical garden in Beijing.

puisne /'pju:nɪ/ *n.* a judge of a superior court who is inferior in rank to a chief justice. [French (*puis* = after (from Latin *postea*) and *né* = born from Latin *natus*)]

puissance /'pwi:sɑ:ns/ *n.* in showjumping, a test of a horse's ability to jump high obstacles. [French]

puissant /'pju:ɪsənt, 'pwi:-/ *adj.* (*literary*) having great power or influence, mighty. [from Old French from Latin *posse* = be able]

pūjā *n.* worship, in Hinduism, Buddhism, and Jainism.

puke *v.t./i.* to vomit. —*n.* vomit. [probably imitative]

pukka /'pʌkə/ *adj.* (*colloquial*) genuine; of good quality. [from Hindi = cooked]

pulchritude /'pʌlkrɪtju:d/ *n.* (*literary*) beauty. —**pulchritudinous** /-'tju:dɪnəs/ *adj.* [from Latin *pulcher* = beautiful]

pule *v.i.* to whimper, to cry querulously or weakly. [probably imitative]

Pulitzer /'pulɪtsə/ Joseph 1847–1911. US newspaper proprietor, born in Hungary. He acquired the *New York World* in 1883 and in 1903 founded the school of journalism at Columbia University, which awards the annual Pulitzer prizes in journalism and letters.

pull /pul/ *v.t./i.* 1. to exert force on (a thing) so as to move it towards oneself or towards the origin of the force; to cause to move thus; to exert such a force. 2. to remove (a cork or tooth) by pulling. 3. to damage (a muscle etc.) by abnormal strain. 4. to move (a boat) by pulling on its oars; (of a boat etc.) to be caused to move, especially in a specified direction. 5. to proceed with effort. 6. to bring out (a weapon) for use. 7. to restrain the speed of (a horse). 8. to attract (customers). 9. to draw (liquor) from a barrel etc. 10. in cricket, to strike (a ball) to the leg side; in golf, to strike (a ball) widely to the left. 11. to print (a proof etc.). —*n.* 1. the act of pulling; the force thus exerted. 2. a means of exerting influence, an advantage. 3. a deep draught of liquor. 4. a prolonged effort, e.g. in going up a hill. 5. a handle etc. for applying pull. 6. a printer's rough proof. 7. a pulling stroke in cricket or golf. —**pull apart** *or* **to pieces**, to separate the parts forcibly; to criticize severely. **pull back**, to retreat or cause to retreat. **pull down**, to demolish; to humiliate. **pull a fast one**, (*slang*) to gain an advantage by unfair or deceitful means. **pull in**, to earn or acquire; (of a train etc.) to enter a station; (of a vehicle) to move to the side of or off a road; (*colloquial*) to arrest. **pull-in** *n.* a place for a vehicle to pull in off the road. **pull a person's leg**, to deceive him or her playfully. **pull off**, to remove by pulling; to succeed in achieving or winning. **pull oneself together**, to recover control of oneself. **pull out**, to depart; to withdraw from an undertaking; (of a train etc.) to leave a station; (of a vehicle) to move from the side of a road, or into position to overtake another.

pulley

20N

20N

simple pulley (above)
pulley system used for
heavy weights (below)

5N

20N   N = newton,
       a unit of force

pull one's punches, to avoid using one's full force. **pull rank**, to take unfair advantage of seniority. **pull round** *or* **through**, to recover from an illness. **pull strings**, to exert (especially clandestine) influence. **pull up**, to stop or cause to stop moving; to reprimand; to pull out of the ground; to check oneself. **pull one's weight**, to do one's fair share of work. [Old English]

pullet /'pulɪt/ *n.* a young domestic fowl, especially a hen that has begun to lay but not yet moulted. [from Old French diminutive of *poule* from Latin *pullus*]

pulley /'pulɪ/ *n.* 1. a grooved wheel for a cord etc. to pass over, set in a block and used for changing the direction of a force (as in a simple hoist for raising loads). The use of more than one pulley results in a mechanical advantage, so that a given effort can raise a heavier load. 2. a wheel or drum fixed on a shaft and turned by a belt, used especially to increase speed or power. [from Old French *polie*, probably ultimately from Greek *polos* = axis]

Pullman /'pulmən/ *n.* 1. a type of railway carriage with luxurious furnishings and without compartments; a luxurious motor coach. 2. a sleeping car. [from G M *Pullman*]

Pullman George 1831–1897. US engineer who developed the Pullman railway car. In an attempt to improve the standard of comfort of rail travel, he built his first Pioneer Sleeping Car in 1863. He formed the Pullman Palace Car Company in 1867 and in 1881 the town of Pullman, Illinois, was built for his workers.

pullover *n.* a knitted garment (with no fastenings) for the upper part of the body, put on over the head.

pullulate /'pʌljuleɪt/ v.i. **1.** to sprout; to develop. **2.** to abound *with*. —**pullulation** /-'leɪʃən/ n. [from Latin *pullulare* = sprout]

pulmonary /'pʌlmənərɪ/ adj. **1.** of, in, or affecting the lungs. **2.** affected with or subject to lung disease. [from Latin *pulmo* = lung]

pulp n. **1.** the fleshy part of a fruit, animal body etc. **2.** a soft shapeless mass, especially that of rags or wood etc., from which paper is made. **3.** (*attributive*, of a magazine etc.) of a kind originally printed on rough paper made from wood pulp, often with sensational or poor-quality writing. —v.t./i. to reduce to or become pulp. —**pulpy** adj., **pulpiness** n. [from Latin *pulpa*]

pulpit /'pulpɪt/ n. a raised enclosed platform in a church etc. from which a preacher delivers a sermon. [from Latin *pulpitum*]

pulsar /'pʌlsɑ:/ n. a celestial source that emits pulses of energy at regular intervals, ranging from a few seconds to small fractions of a second. Pulsars were discovered in 1967, and are thought to be rapidly rotating ◊neutron stars, which flash at radio and other wavelengths as they spin. Over 300 radio pulsars are now known in our Galaxy, although a million or so may exist. [from *pulsating star*]

pulsate /pʌl'seɪt, 'pʌl-/ v.i. to expand and contract rhythmically, to throb; to vibrate, to quiver. —**pulsation** /-'seɪʃən/ n., **pulsator** /-'seɪtə/ n., **pulsatory** /'pʌlsətərɪ/ adj. [from Latin *pulsare*]

pulse¹ n. **1.** the rhythmical throbbing of the arteries as blood is propelled along them; each successive beat of the arteries or heart; the rate of this beat, generally about 70 per minute. The pulse can be felt where an artery is near the surface, such as in the wrist or the neck. **2.** a single vibration of sound or light or electric current etc., especially as a signal. **3.** a throb or thrill of life or emotion; a latent feeling. —v.i. to pulsate. [from Latin *pulsus* (*pellere* = drive, beat)]

pulse² n. **1.** (as *singular* or *plural*) the edible seeds of leguminous plants, e.g. peas, beans, lentils. Pulses provide a concentrated source of vegetable protein, and make a vital contribution to human diets in poor countries where meat is scarce. **2.** any kind of these. [from Old French from Latin *puls* = meal porridge]

pulse-code modulation a method of converting a continuous electrical signal (such as that produced by a microphone) into a series of pulses (a digital signal) for transmission along a telephone line.

pulverize /'pʌlvəraɪz/ v.t./i. **1.** to reduce or crumble to powder or dust; to demolish. **2.** to defeat utterly. —**pulverization** /-'zeɪʃən/ n. [from Latin *pulvis* = dust]

puma /'pju:mə/ n. a large wild cat *Felis concolor* found in the Americas, also called the cougar or mountain lion. It has a tawny coat and is 1.5 m/4.5 ft long with a 90 cm/3 ft tail. Pumas have been hunted nearly to extinction. [Spanish, from Quechua]

pumice /'pʌmɪs/ n. or **pumice stone** a light volcanic rock produced by the frothing action of expanding gases during the solidification of lava; a piece of this. It has the texture of a hard sponge and is used as an abrasive and for polishing. [from Old French from Latin *pumex*]

pummel /'pʌməl/ v.t. (-ll-) to strike repeatedly, especially with the fist. [alteration from *pommel*]

pump¹ n. a machine or device of various kinds for raising or moving liquids or gases; a machine for raising water for domestic use. Some pumps, such as the traditional **lift pump** used to raise water from wells, work by a reciprocating (up-and-down) action. Movement of a piston in a cylinder with a one-way valve creates a partial vacuum in the cylinder, thereby sucking water into it. **Gear pumps**, used to pump oil in a car's lubrication system, have two meshing gears that rotate inside a housing, and the teeth move the oil. **Rotary pumps** contain a rotor with vanes projecting from it inside a casing, sweeping the oil round as they move. —v.t./i. **1.** to raise, move, or inflate by using a pump; to use a pump; to empty by using a pump. **2.** to pour or cause to pour forth as if by pumping. **3.** to move vigorously up and down like a pump handle. **4.** to question (a person) persistently to obtain information.

pump² n. **1.** a plimsoll. **2.** a light shoe for dancing etc. **3.** (*US*) a court shoe.

pumped storage hydroelectric plant that uses surplus electricity to pump water back into a high-level reservoir. In normal working the water flows from this reservoir through the ◊turbines to generate power for feeding into the grid. At times of low power demand, electricity is taken from the grid to turn the turbines into pumps that then pump the water back again. This ensures that there is always a maximum 'head' of water in the reservoir to give the maximum output when required.

pumpernickel /'pʌmpənɪkəl, 'pu-/ n. German wholemeal rye bread. [German, originally = lout, stinker (*pumpen* = break wind and *Nickel* = Nicholas)]

pumpkin n. **1.** the large, round, orange-coloured fruit of a trailing vine, *Cucurbita pepo* of the family Cucurbitaceae, used as a vegetable and (in the USA) a filling for pies. **2.** this vine. [from earlier *pompon*, ultimately from Greek *pepōn* = large melon]

pun n. a figure of speech, a play on words, or double meaning that is technically known as **paronomasia** (Greek = adapted meaning). Double meaning can be accidental, often resulting from homonymy, or the multiple meaning of words; puns, however, are deliberate, intended as jokes or as clever and compact remarks. —v.i. (-nn-) to make a pun or puns. [perhaps from obsolete *pundigrion*]

punch¹ v.t. **1.** to strike with the fist. **2.** to pierce a hole in (metal, paper, a ticket etc.) as or with a punch; to pierce (a hole) thus. —n. **1.** a blow with the fist; the ability to deliver this. **2.** (*slang*) vigour, effective force. **3.** an instrument or machine for cutting holes or impressing a design in leather, metal, paper etc. —**punchball** n. an inflated ball held on a stand etc. and punched as a form of exercise. **punch-drunk** adj. stupefied through having been severely punched (*literally* or *figuratively*). **punch line,** the words giving the point of a joke or story. **punch-up** n. a fist fight, a brawl. [variant of *pounce* = emboss]

punch² n. a drink usually of wine or spirits mixed with hot or cold water, spice etc. —**punchbowl** n. a bowl in which punch is mixed; a round deep hollow in a hill.

punch³ n. (in full **Suffolk punch**) a short-legged, thickset, chestnut-coloured draught horse.

Punch n. the male character in the traditional ◊puppet play *Punch and Judy*, a humpbacked, hooknosed figure who fights with his wife, Judy. —**as pleased** or **proud as Punch,** showing great pleasure or pride. [abbreviation of *Punchinello*, perhaps diminutive of Italian *pollecena* = young turkey cock (with hooked beak which the nose of Punch's mask resembles)]

punched card in computing, an early form of data storage and input, now almost obsolete. The 80-column card was widely used in the 1960s and 1970s. This was a thin card, measuring 190 × 84 mm, holding up to 80 characters of data encoded as small rectangular holes.

punchy adj. having vigour, forceful.

punctilio /pʌŋk'tɪlɪəʊ/ n. (*plural* **punctilios**) **1.** a delicate point of ceremony or honour; the etiquette of such points. **2.** petty formality. [from Italian and Spanish diminutive from Latin *punctum, puncta*]

punctilious /pʌŋk'tɪlɪəs/ adj. attentive to formality or etiquette; precise in behaviour. —**punctiliously** adv., **punctiliousness** n. [from French]

punctual /'pʌŋktjuəl/ adj. observant of the appointed time; neither early nor late. —**punctuality** /-'ælɪtɪ/ n., **punctually** adv. [from Latin]

punctuate /'pʌŋktjueɪt/ v.t. **1.** to insert punctuation marks so as to organize written and printed language to be as readable, clear, and logical as possible. **2.** to interrupt at intervals. **3.** to emphasize, to accentuate. [from Latin *punctuare*]

punctuated equilibrium model an evolutionary theory developed by Niles Eldridge and Stephen Jay Gould in 1972 to explain discontinuities in the fossil record. It claims that periods of rapid change alternate with periods of relative stability (stasis), and that the appearance of new lineages is a separate process from the gradual evolution of adaptive changes within a species.

punctuation /pʌŋktju'eɪʃən/ n. punctuating; the system used for this. —**punctuation mark,** any of the marks (e.g. full stop and comma) used in writing to separate sentences and phrases etc. and clarify meaning.

puncture /'pʌŋktʃə/ n. a prick or pricking, especially an accidental piercing of a pneumatic tyre; a hole thus made. —v.t./i. to make a puncture in; to undergo a puncture; to prick or pierce. [from Latin *punctura* (*pungere* = prick)]

pundit

pundit /'pʌndɪt/ n. 1. a learned Hindu. 2. a learned expert or teacher. —**punditry** n. [from Hindi from Sanskrit = learned]

Pune /'puːnə/ formerly **Poona** city in Maharashtra, India; population (1985) 1,685,000. Products include chemicals, rice, sugar, cotton, paper, and jewellery.

pungent /'pʌndʒənt/ adj. 1. having a sharp or strong taste or smell. 2. (of remarks) penetrating, biting, caustic. 3. mentally stimulating. —**pungency** n., **pungently** adv. [from Latin pungere = prick]

Punic /'pjuːnɪk/ adj. relating to ◊Carthage, ancient city in N Africa founded by the Phoenicians. [Latin Punicus = a Phoenician]

Punic Wars three wars between ◊Rome and ◊Carthage. The **First**, 264–241 BC, resulted in the defeat of the Carthaginians under ◊Hamilcar Barca and the cession of Sicily to Rome. During the **Second**, 218–201 BC, Hannibal invaded Italy, defeated the Romans under ◊Fabius Maximus at Cannae, but was finally defeated by ◊Scipio Africanus Major at Zama (now in Algeria). The **Third**, 149–146 BC, ended in the destruction of Carthage, and her possessions becoming the Roman province of Africa.

punish /'pʌnɪʃ/ v.t. 1. to cause (an offender) to suffer for an offence; to inflict a penalty for (an offence). 2. (colloquial) to inflict severe blows on (an opponent). 3. to tax severely, to subject to severe treatment. [from Old French from Latin punire (poena = penalty)]

punishable adj. liable to be punished, especially by law.

punishment n. 1. punishing, being punished. 2. that which an offender is made to suffer for his or her offence. 3. severe treatment or suffering.

punitive /'pjuːnɪtɪv/ adj. inflicting or intended to inflict punishment. [from French or Latin punire]

Punjab /pʌn'dʒɑːb/ former state of British India, now divided between India and Pakistan (see separate entries below). Punjab was annexed by Britain in 1849, after the Sikh Wars 1845–46 and 1848–49, and formed into a province with its capital at Lahore. Under the British, W Punjab was extensively irrigated, and land was granted to Indians who had served in the British army. [Sanskrit = five rivers: the Indus tributaries Jhelum, Chnab, Ravi, Beas, and Sutlej]

Punjab /pʌn'dʒɑːb/ state of NW India; **area** 50,400 sq km/19,454 sq mi; **capital** Chandigarh; **physical** mainly agricultural, crops chiefly under irrigation; **population** (1981) 16,670,000; **language** Punjabi.

Punjab /pʌn'dʒɑːb/ state of NE Pakistan; **area** 205,344 sq km/79,263 sq mi; **capital** Lahore; **physical** wheat cultivation (by irrigation); **population** (1981) 47,292,000; **language** Punjabi, Urdu.

Punjabi language /pʌn'dʒɑːbi/ a member of the Indo-Iranian branch of the Indo-European language family, spoken in the Punjab provinces of India and Pakistan. It is considered by some to be a variety of Hindi, by others to be a distinct language.

punk n. (colloquial) 1. a worthless person or thing. 2. a movement of disaffected youth of the late 1970s, manifesting itself in fashions and music designed to shock or intimidate. —**punk rock**, a type of pop music using aggressive and outrageous effects, as exemplified by such groups as the Sex Pistols 1975–78, the Slits 1977–82, and Johnny Thunders (with the Heartbreakers from 1975).

punnet /'pʌnɪt/ n. a small basket or container for fruit etc. [perhaps diminutive of dialect pun = pound]

punster n. a habitual maker of puns.

punt[1] n. a flat-bottomed shallow boat propelled by a long pole thrust against the bottom of a river etc. —v.t./i. to propel (a punt) with a pole in this way; to travel or convey in a punt. —**punter**[1] n. [from Middle Low German or Middle Dutch from Latin ponto = Gaulish transport vessel]

punt[2] v.t. to kick (a football) after it has dropped from the hands and before it reaches the ground. —n. such a kick. —**punter**[2] n. [probably from dialect punt = push forcibly]

punt[3] v.i. 1. in some card games, to lay a stake against the bank. 2. (colloquial) to bet on a horse etc.; to speculate in shares etc. [from French ponter (ponte = player against bank from Spanish)]

punter[3] n. 1. one who punts (see ◊punt[3]). 2. (colloquial) the victim of a swindler or confidence trickster; a customer or client etc., a spectator.

puny /'pjuːnɪ/ adj. undersized, weak, feeble. —**puniness** n. [phonetic spelling of puisne]

pup n. a young dog; a young wolf, rat, seal etc. —v.t. (-pp-) (of a bitch etc.) to bring forth (young, or absolute). —in **pup**, (of a bitch) pregnant. **sell a person a pup**, to swindle him or her, especially by selling a thing on its prospective value. [from puppy]

pupa /'pjuːpə/ n. (plural **pupae**) an insect in its passive phase of development between larva and imago when larval tissues are broken down, and adult tissues and structures are formed. —**pupal** adj. [Latin = doll]

pupate /pjuː'peɪt/ v.t. to become a pupa. —**pupation** /-'peɪʃən/ n.

pupil /'pjuːpɪl/ n. 1. one who is taught by another; a schoolchild; a disciple. 2. the circular opening in the centre of the iris of the eye. [from Old French from Latin pupillus, pupilla, diminutive of pupus = boy, pupa = girl]

puppet /'pʌpɪt/ n. 1. an inanimate figure representing a human being or an animal etc., ranging in size from a few inches to larger than life, moved by various means as an entertainment. The earliest known puppets are from 10th-century BC China. The types include **finger** or **glove puppets** (such as ◊Punch); **string marionettes** (which reached a high artistic level in ancient Burma and Sri Lanka and in Italian princely courts from the 16th to 18th centuries; **shadow silhouettes** (operated by rods and seen on a lit screen, as in Java); and **bunraku** (devised in Osaka, Japan), in which three or four black-clad operators on stage may combine to work each puppet about 1 m/3 ft high. 2. a person whose acts are controlled by another. —**puppet state,** a country that is apparently independent but actually under the control of another power. —**puppetry** n. [variant of poppet]

puppy n. 1. a young dog. 2. a vain, empty-headed young man. —**puppy fat,** temporary fatness of a child or adolescent. [perhaps from Old French po(u)pee = doll]

Purana /pu'rɑːnə/ n. one of a number of sacred Hindu writings dealing with ancient times and events, and dating from the 4th century AD onwards. The 18 main texts include the Vishnu Purāna and Bhāgavata, which encourage devotion to ◊Vishnu, above all in his incarnation as ◊Krishna.

purblind /'pɜːblaɪnd/ adj. 1. partly blind, dim-sighted. 2. stupid, dim-witted. [originally pur(e) (= utterly) blind]

Purcell /'pɜːsəl/ Henry 1659–1695. English Baroque composer. His work can be highly expressive, for example, the opera Dido and Aeneas 1689 and music for Dryden's King Arthur 1691 and for The Fairy Queen 1692. He wrote more than 500 works, ranging from secular operas and incidental music for plays to cantatas and church music.

purchase /'pɜːtʃəs/ v.t. 1. to buy. 2. to obtain or achieve with a specified cost or sacrifice. —n. 1. buying. 2. a thing bought. 3. an annual rent or return from land. 4. a firm hold on a thing to move it or prevent it slipping, leverage. —**purchaser** n. [from Anglo-French]

purchasing-power parity a system for comparing standards of living between different countries. Comparing the gross domestic product of different countries involves first converting them to a common currency (usually US dollars or pound sterling), a conversion which is subject to large fluctuations with variations in exchange rates. Purchasing power parity aims to overcome this by measuring how much money in the currency of those countries is required to buy a comparable range of goods and services.

purdah /'pɜːdə/ n. a system of screening Muslim or Hindu women from strangers by means of a veil or curtain. It had begun to disappear with the adoption of Western culture, but the fundamentalism of the 1980s revived it, for example, the wearing of the ◊chuddar (an all-enveloping black mantle), in Iran. The Koran requests only 'modesty' in dress. [from Urdu and Persian = veil, curtain]

pure adj. 1. not mixed with any other substance; free from impurities; of unmixed origin. 2. morally or sexually undefiled; chaste. 3. mere, nothing but. 4. (of sound) not discordant, perfectly in tune. 5. dealing with theory only, not with practical applications. —**pure breeding line**, in genetics, a strain of individuals that when interbred produce genetically identical progeny. A pure breeding tall pea plant is ◊homozygous for the allele controlling height. —**pureness** n. [from Old French from Latin purus]

purée /'pjuəreɪ/ *n.* a pulp of vegetables or fruit etc. reduced to a smooth cream. [French]

Pure Land Buddhism the dominant form of Buddhism in China and Japan. It emphasizes faith in and love of Buddha, in particular Amitābha (Amida in Japan, Amituofo in China), the ideal 'Buddha of boundless light', who has vowed that all believers who call on his name will be reborn in his Pure Land, or Western Paradise. This also applies to women, who had been debarred from attaining salvation through monastic life. There are over 16 million Pure Land Buddhists in Japan.

purely *adv.* in a pure manner; merely; solely, exclusively; entirely.

purgative /'pɜ:gətɪv/ *adj.* 1. serving to purify. 2. strongly laxative. —*n.* a purgative thing; a laxative. [from Old French or Latin *purgare*]

purgatory /'pɜ:gətərɪ/ *n.* 1. in Roman Catholic belief, a purificatory state or place where the souls of those who have died in a state of grace can expiate their venial sins, with a limited amount of suffering. 2. a place or state of temporary suffering or expiation. —**purgatorial** /-'tɔ:rɪəl/ *adj.* [from Anglo-French from Latin *purgare*]

purge *v.t.* 1. to make physically or spiritually clean; to remove by a cleansing process. 2. to rid of people regarded as undesirable. 3. to empty (the bowels); to empty the bowels of (a person). 4. in law, to atone for or wipe out (an offence, especially contempt of court). —*n.* 1. the act or process of purging. In 1934 the Nazis carried out a purge of their party and a number of party leaders were executed for an alleged plot against Hitler. During the 1930s purges were conducted in the USSR under Stalin, carried out by the secret police against political opponents, Communist Party members, minorities, civil servants, and large sections of the armed forces' officer corps. Some 10 million people were executed or deported to labour camps from 1934 to 1938. Later purges include Communist purges in Hungary (1949), Czechoslovakia (1951), and China (1955). 2. a purgative. [from Old French from Latin *purgare*]

purify /'pjuərɪfaɪ/ *v.t.* to cleanse or make pure; to make ceremonially clean; to clear of extraneous elements. —**purification** /-fɪ'keɪʃən/ *n.*, **purificatory** *adj.*, **purifier** *n.* [from Old French from Latin *purus*]

Purim *n.* a Jewish festival celebrated in February or March (the 14th of Adar in the Jewish calendar), commemorating ◊Esther, who saved the Jews from destruction in 473 BC during the Persian occupation.

purist /'pjuərɪst/ *n.* a stickler for or affecter of scrupulous purity, especially in language. —**purism** *n.*, **puristic** /-'rɪstɪk/ *adj.* [from French]

Puritan /'pjuərɪtən/ *n.* 1. from 1564, a member of the Church of England who wished to eliminate Roman Catholic survivals in church ritual, or substitute a presbyterian for an episcopal form of church government. The term also covers the separatists who withdrew from the church altogether. The Puritans were identified with the parliamentary opposition under James I and Charles I, and after the Restoration were driven from the church, and more usually known as ◊Dissenters or ◊Nonconformists. 2. **puritan** a person practising or affecting extreme strictness in religion or morals. —*adj.* 1. of the Puritans. 2. **puritan** scrupulous in religion or morals. —**puritanical** /-'tænɪkəl/ *adj.*, **puritanism** *n.* [from Latin *puritas* = purity (*purus* = pure)]

purity /'pjuərɪtɪ/ *n.* pureness, cleanness; freedom from physical or moral pollution. [from Old French]

purl[1] *n.* 1. a knitting stitch with the needle put into the stitch in an opposite to the normal direction, producing a ridge towards the knitter. 2. a chain of minute loops, a picot. —*v.t.* to make (a stitch, or *absolute*) purl. [from Scottish *pirl* = twist]

purl[2] *v.i.* (of a brook etc.) to flow with a swirling motion and babbling sound. [probably imitative]

purler *n.* (*colloquial*) a headlong fall. [from *purl* = overturn]

purlieu /'pɜ:lju:/ *n.* 1. one's bounds or limits or usual haunts. 2. (*historical*) a tract on the border of a forest. 3. (in *plural*) outskirts, an outlying region. [probable alteration of Anglo-French *purale(e)* = perambulation to settle boundaries]

purlin /'pɜ:lɪn/ *n.* a horizontal beam along a roof. [from Latin *perlio*]

purloin /pɜ:'lɔɪn/ *v.t.* to steal, to pilfer. [from Anglo-French (*loign* = far from Latin *longe*)]

purple *n.* 1. a colour between red and blue. 2. (in full **Tyrian purple**) a crimson colour obtained from some molluscs. 3. a purple robe, especially as the dress of an emperor etc. 4. the scarlet official dress of a cardinal. —*adj.* of a purple or Tyrian purple colour. —*v.t./i.* to make or become purple. —**born in the purple,** born to a reigning family; belonging to the most privileged class. [Latin *porphyrogenitus*, originally used of one born of the imperial family at Constantinople and (it is said) in a chamber called the *Porphyra*] **purple passage** *or* **patch,** an overornate passage in a literary composition. —**purplish** *adj.* [Old English from Latin *purpura* from Greek *porphura* (shellfish yielding) purple]

purport /pə'pɔ:t/ *v.t.* 1. to profess, to be intended to seem. 2. (of a document or speech) to have as its meaning, to state. —/'pɜ:pɔ:t/ *n.* an ostensible meaning; the sense or tenor of a document or statement. —**purportedly** *adv.* [from Anglo-French from Latin *portare* = carry]

purpose /'pɜ:pəs/ *n.* 1. an intended result, something for which effort is being made. 2. intention to act, determination. —*v.t.* to have as one's purpose, to intend. —**on purpose,** intentionally. **purpose-built** *or* **purpose-made** etc. *adj.* built etc. for a specific purpose. **to little** *or* **no purpose,** with little or no result or effect. **to the purpose,** relevant, useful. [from Anglo-French from Latin *proponere*, literally = put in front]

purposeful *adj.* having or indicating a (conscious) purpose; intentional; acting or done with determination. —**purposefully** *adv.*, **purposefulness** *n.*

purposely *adv.* on purpose.

purposive /'pɜ:pəsɪv/ *adj.* having, serving, or done with a purpose; purposeful.

purpura *n.* a condition marked by purplish patches on the skin or mucous membranes due to localized spontaneous bleeding. It may be harmless, as sometimes with the elderly, or linked with disease, allergy, or drug reactions.

purr /pɜ:/ *v.i.* (of a cat etc.) to make a low vibratory sound expressing pleasure; (of machinery etc.) to make a similar sound. —*n.* such a sound. [imitative]

purse *n.* 1. a small pouch of leather etc. for carrying money on the person. 2. (*US*) a handbag. 3. money, funds. 4. a sum given as a present or prize for a contest. —*v.t./i.* to pucker or contract (the lips or brow) in wrinkles; to become wrinkled. —**hold the purse strings,** to have control of expenditure. [Old English from Latin *bursa* from Greek = leather]

purser *n.* an officer on a ship who keeps the accounts, especially the head steward in a passenger vessel.

pursuance /pə'sju:əns/ *n.* carrying out or observance (of a plan, rules etc.).

pursuant /pə'sju:ənt/ *adj.* (with *to*) in accordance with. [from Old French]

pursue /pə'sju:/ *v.t./i.* 1. to follow with intent to overtake, capture, or do harm to. 2. to continue, to proceed along or with (a route, course of action, topic etc.). 3. to engage in (a study or other activity). 4. to seek to attain. 5. (of misfortune etc.) to assail persistently. —**pursuer** *n.* [from Anglo-French from Latin]

pursuit /pə'sju:t/ *n.* 1. pursuing. 2. an occupation or activity pursued. [from Old French]

pursuivant /'pɜ:sɪvənt/ *n.* an officer of the College of Arms below a herald. [from Old French]

purulent /'pjuərulənt/ *adj.* of, containing, or discharging pus. —**purulence** *n.* [French or from Latin *pus puris*]

purvey /pə'veɪ/ *v.t.* to provide or supply (articles of food) as one's business. —**purveyor** *n.* [from Anglo-French from Latin *providēre* = provide]

purview /'pɜ:vju:/ *n.* 1. the scope or range of a document or scheme etc. 2. the range of physical or mental vision.

pus /pʌs/ *n.* yellowish viscous matter that forms in the body as a result of bacterial attack; it includes white blood cells (leucocytes) 'killed in battle' with the bacteria, plasma, and broken-down tissue cells. An enclosed collection of pus is an abscess. [Latin *pus puris*]

Pusan /pu:'sæn/ *or* **Busan** chief industrial port (textiles, rubber, salt, fishing) of South Korea; population (1985) 3,517,000. It was invaded by the Japanese in 1592 and opened to foreign trade in 1883.

Pusey /'pju:zi/ Edward Bouverie 1800–1882. English Church of England priest from 1828. In 1835 he joined J H ◊Newman in issuing the *Tracts for the Times*. After

Newman's conversion to Catholicism, Pusey became leader of the High Church Party or Puseyites, striving until his death to keep them from conversion.

push /puʃ/ *v.t./i.* **1.** to exert force on (a thing) so as to move it away from oneself or from the origin of the force; to cause to move thus; to exert such a force. **2.** to thrust outwards; to cause to project. **3.** to move forward or extend by effort. **4.** to make a vigorous effort in order to succeed to surpass others. **5.** to urge or impel; to put a strain on the abilities or tolerance of. **6.** to promote the use or sale or adoption of (e.g. by advertising); to sell (a drug) illegally. —*n.* **1.** the act of pushing; the force thus exerted. **2.** a vigorous effort; a military attack in force. **3.** enterprise, determination to succeed; use of influence to advance a person. **4.** the pressure of affairs, a crisis. —**be pushed for,** (*colloquial*) to have very little of. **push around,** to bully. **push-bike** *n.* (*colloquial*) a pedal cycle. **push button,** a button to be pushed especially to operate an electrical device; (*adj.*) operated thus. **pushchair** *n.* a folding chair on wheels, in which a child can be pushed along. **push for,** to demand. **push one's luck,** see ◊luck. **push off,** to push with an oar etc. against the bank etc. in order to get a boat out into a stream; (*slang*) to go away. **pushover** *n.* (*colloquial*) something easily done; a person who is easily convinced or charmed. **push-start** *n.* the starting of a motor vehicle by pushing it to turn the engine; (*v.t.*) to start (a vehicle) thus. **push through,** to get completed or accepted quickly. —**pusher** *n.* [from Old French *pousser* from Latin *pulsare*]

pushful *adj.* self-assertive, determined to succeed. —**pushfully** *adv.*, **pushfulness** *n.*

pushing *adj.* **1.** (of a person) pushful. **2.** (*colloquial*) having nearly reached (a specified age).

Pushkin /ˈpuʃkɪn/ Aleksandr 1799–1837. Russian poet and writer. He was exiled in 1820 for his political verse and in 1824 was in trouble for his atheistic opinions. He wrote ballads such as *The Gypsies* 1827, and the novel in verse *Eugene Onegin* 1823–31. Other works include the tragic drama *Boris Godunov* 1825, and the prose pieces *The Captain's Daughter* 1836 and *The Queen of Spades* 1834. Pushkin's range was vast, and his willingness to experiment freed later Russian writers from many of the archaic conventions of the literature of his time.

Pushtu /ˈpʌʃtuː/ another name for the ◊Pashto language. —*n. & adj.* [from Persian]

pushy *adj.* (*colloquial*) pushful.

pusillanimous /pjuːsɪˈlænɪməs/ *adj.* lacking courage, timid. —**pusillanimity** /-ˈnɪmɪtɪ/ *n.*, **pusillanimously** *adv.* [from Latin *pusillus* = small and *animus* = mind]

puss /pus/ *n.* **1.** a cat (especially as a form of address). **2.** (*colloquial*) a playful or coquettish girl.

pussy /ˈpusɪ/ *n.* **1.** or **pussycat,** a cat. **2.** (*vulgar*) the vulva. —**pussy willow,** a willow with furry catkins.

pussyfoot *v.i.* (*colloquial*) **1.** to move stealthily. **2.** to shirk dealing with or referring directly to a problem etc.

pustulate /ˈpʌstjuleɪt/ *v.t./i.* to form into pustules. [from Latin *pustulare*]

pustule /ˈpʌstjuːl/ *n.* a pimple or blister, especially one containing pus. —**pustular** *adj.* [from Old French or Latin *pustula*]

put /put/ *v.t./i.* (**-tt-;** *past* and *past participle* **put**) **1.** to move to or cause to be in a specified place or position. **2.** to bring into a specified condition or state. **3.** to impose as a tax etc. **4.** to submit for consideration or attention. **5.** to express or state. **6.** to estimate. **7.** to place as an investment; to stake (money) in a bet. **8.** to lay (blame). **9.** (of a ship) to proceed. **10.** to hurl (the shot or weight) as an athletic exercise. —*n.* a throw of a shot or weight. —**put across,** to succeed in communicating (an idea etc.); to cause to seem acceptable. **put away,** (*colloquial*) to put into prison or into a mental home; (*colloquial*) to consume as food or drink. **put back,** to restore to a former place; to move back the hands of (a clock or watch). **put by,** to save for future use. **put down,** to suppress by force or authority; to snub; to have (an animal) destroyed; to record or enter in writing; to enter (a person's name) as one who will subscribe; to reckon or consider; to attribute. **put-down** *n.* a snub. **put in,** to make (an appearance); to enter (a claim etc.); to spend (time) in working etc. **put in for,** to apply for. **put it across,** (*slang*) to trick or get the better of. **put it to a person,** to challenge him or her to deny. **put off,** to postpone; to postpone

an engagement with (a person); to make excuses and try to avoid; to dissuade, to repel; to put (an electrical device or light etc.) out. **put on,** to stage (a play etc.); to cause (an electrical device or light etc.) to function; to advance the hands of (a clock or watch); to feign (an emotion); to increase one's weight by (so much). **put oneself in a person's place,** to imagine oneself in his or her situation etc. **put out,** to disconcert, to annoy, to inconvenience; to cause (a fire or light etc.) to cease to burn or function. **put over,** to put across. **put through,** to carry out or complete; to connect by telephone. **put under,** to make unconscious. **put up,** to build, to erect; to raise (a price etc.), to provide with or receive accommodation; to engage in (a fight, struggle etc.) as a form of resistance; to present (a proposal); to present oneself as a candidate; to provide (money as a backer); to offer for sale or competition; to concoct. **put-up** *adj.* fraudulently concocted. **put upon,** (*colloquial*) unfairly burdened or deceived. **put a person up to,** to instigate him or her in. **put up with,** to tolerate, to submit to. [from Old English]

putative /ˈpjuːtətɪv/ *adj.* reputed, supposed. [from Old French or Latin *putare* = think]

putlog /ˈpʌtlɒg/ *n.* each of the short horizontal timbers projecting from a wall, on which scaffold floorboards rest.

putrefy /ˈpjuːtrɪfaɪ/ *v.i.* to rot, to decay; to fester or suppurate. —**putrefaction** /-ˈfækʃən/ *n.* [from Latin *putrefacere* (*puter* = rotten and *facere* = make)]

putrescent /pjuːˈtresənt/ *adj.* decaying, rotting; of or accompanying this process. —**putrescence** *n.* [from Latin *putrescere*]

putrid /ˈpjuːtrɪd/ *adj.* **1.** decomposed, rotten. **2.** foul, noxious. **3.** (*slang*) of poor quality; very unpleasant. —**putridity** /-ˈtrɪdɪtɪ/ *n.* [from Latin *putrēre* = rot]

putsch /putʃ/ *n.* an attempt at a political revolution; a violent seizure of power, such as Hitler and Ludendorff's abortive beer-hall putsch in Nov 1923, which attempted to overthrow the Bavarian government. [Swiss German = thrust]

putt /pʌt/ *v.t./i.* to strike (a golfball) gently to get it into or nearer to a hole on a putting green. —*n.* such a stroke. —**putting green,** in golf, the smooth area of grass round a hole. [variant of *put*]

puttee /ˈpʌtɪ/ *n.* a long strip of cloth wound spirally round the leg from the ankle to the knee for protection and support. [from Hindi = bandage]

putter /ˈpʌtə/ *n.* a golf club used in putting.

Puttnam /ˈpʌtnəm/ David Terence 1941– . English film producer, who has played a major role in reviving the British film industry internationally. His films include *Chariots of Fire* 1981 and *The Killing Fields* 1984.

putty /ˈpʌtɪ/ *n.* a soft, hard-setting paste of chalk powder and linseed oil for fixing glass in a frame, filling up holes in woodwork etc. —*v.t.* to fix or fill with putty. [from French *potée*]

Pu-Yi former transliteration of the name of the last Chinese emperor, Henry ◊P'u-i.

puzzle *n.* **1.** a difficult or confusing problem. **2.** a problem or toy designed to test knowledge or ingenuity. —*v.t./i.* to confound or disconcert mentally; to require much thought to comprehend. —**puzzle about** *or* **over,** to be confused about; to ponder about. **puzzle out,** to solve or understand by hard thought. —**puzzlement** *n.*

puzzler *n.* a difficult question or problem.

PVC abbreviation of polyvinyl chloride.

PW abbreviation of Policewoman.

PWR abbreviation of pressurized water reactor, a nuclear reactor design used in nuclear power stations in many countries, and in nuclear-powered submarines. In the PWR, water under pressure is the coolant and ◊moderator. It circulates through a steam generator, where its heat boils water to provide steam to drive power ◊turbines.

pyaemia /paɪˈiːmɪə/ *n.* blood poisoning with formation of abscesses in the viscera. [from Greek *puon* = pus and *haima* = blood]

pye-dog /ˈpaɪdɒg/ *n.* a vagrant mongrel of the East. [from Hindi *pahi* = outsider]

pyelitis *n.* inflammation of the renal pelvis, the central part of the kidney where urine accumulates before discharge.

It is caused by bacterial infection and is more common in women than in men.

Pygmalion /pɪg'meɪlɪən/ in Greek legend, a king of Cyprus who fell in love with an ivory statue he had carved. When Aphrodite brought it to life as Galatea, he married her.

pygmy /'pɪgmɪ/ *n.* 1. a member of a population whose average male height is not greater than 150 cm (4 ft 11 in), e.g. the Bambuti of tropical central Africa (the term 'Negrito' is used of similar populations of SE Asia). 2. a very small person or thing. 3. an insignificant person or thing. —*adj.* 1. of pygmies. 2. very small. [from Latin from Greek *pugmē* = length from elbow to knuckles]

pyjamas /pi'dʒɑ:məz/ *n.pl.* a suit of loose trousers and jacket for sleeping in; a similar garment for beach or evening wear by women. [from Urdu = leg clothing]

pylon /'paɪlən/ *n.* 1. a tall latticework structure used as a support for overhead electricity cables or as a boundary. 2. a structure marking a path for aircraft. 3. a structure supporting the engine of an aircraft. 4. a gateway or gate tower, especially the monumental gateway to an Egyptian temple, usually formed by two truncated pyramidal towers connected by a lower architectural member containing the gate. [from Greek *pulōn* (*pulē* = gate)]

Pym /pɪm/ John 1584–1643. English Parliamentarian, largely responsible for the ◊Petition of Right of 1628. As leader of the Puritan opposition in the ◊Long Parliament from 1640, he played a leading role in the impeachment of Charles I's advisers Strafford and Laud, drew up the ◊Grand Remonstrance, and was the chief of five members of Parliament Charles I wanted arrested in 1642. The five took refuge in the City, from which they emerged triumphant when the king left London.

Pynchon /'pɪntʃən/ Thomas 1937– . US novelist who creates a bizarre, labyrinthine world in his books, which include *V* 1963, *The Crying of Lot 49* 1966, *Gravity's Rainbow* 1973, and *Vineland* 1990.

Pyongyang /pjɒŋ'jæŋ/ capital and industrial city (coal, iron, steel, textiles, chemicals) of North Korea; population (1984) 2,640,000.

pyorrhoea /paɪə'rɪə/ *n.* discharge of pus, especially in disease of the tooth sockets. [from Greek *puon* = pus and *rhoia* = flux]

pyracantha /paɪərə'kænθə/ *n.* an evergreen thorny shrub of the genus *Pyracantha* with white flowers and scarlet or orange berries. [Latin from Greek]

pyramid /'pɪrəmɪd/ *n.* 1. a monumental structure, especially as used in ancient Egypt to enclose a royal tomb, usually with a square base and with four equal triangular sides meeting at an apex. The Great Pyramid of Khufu/Cheops at Giza, near Cairo is an example; it is 230 m/755 ft square and 147 m/481 ft high. In Babylon and Assyria broadly stepped pyramids (ziggurats) were used as the base for a shrine to a god: the Tower of Babel (see also ◊Babylon) was probably one of these. 2. in geometry, a solid figure with triangular side faces meeting at a common vertex (point) and with a ◊polygon as its base. The volume *V* of a pyramid is given by *V* = $^1/_3Bh$, where *B* is the area of the base and *h* is the perpendicular height. 3. a thing or pile of things shaped like this. —**pyramid of numbers**, in ecology, a diagram that shows how many plants and animals there are at different levels in a ◊food chain. **pyramid selling**, a system of selling goods in which agency rights are sold to an increasing number of distributors at successively lower levels. —**pyramidal** /-'ræmɪdəl/ *adj.* [from Latin from Greek *puramis*]

pyre /'paɪə/ *n.* a heap of combustible material, especially a funeral pile for burning a corpse. [from Latin from Greek *pura* (*pur* = fire)]

Pyrenees /pɪrə'ni:z/ (French *Pyrénées*; Spanish *Pirineos*) mountain range in SW Europe between France and Spain; length about 435 km/270 mi; highest peak Aneto (French *Néthon*) 3,404 m/11,172 ft. ◊Andorra is entirely within the range. Hydroelectric power has encouraged industrial development in the foothills.

pyrethrum /paɪ'ri:θrəm/ *n.* 1. a chrysanthemum with finely divided leaves (especially *Chrysanthemum coccineum* and *C. cinerariifolium*). 2. a powerful contact pesticide for aphids and mosquitoes made from its dried flowers. [Latin from Greek = feverfew]

Pythagoras' theorem
for right-angled triangles

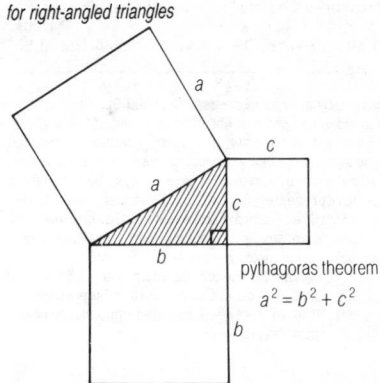

pythagoras theorem
$$a^2 = b^2 + c^2$$

pyretic /paɪ'retɪk, pɪ-/ *adj.* of or producing fever. [from Greek *puretos* = fever]

Pyrex /'paɪreks/ *n.* trade name of a hard heat-resistant glass. [invented word]

pyrexia /paɪ'reksɪə/ *n.* fever. [from Greek *purexis* (*puressō* = be feverish)]

pyridine *n.* C_5H_5N, a heterocyclic compound (see ◊cyclic compounds). It is a liquid with a sickly smell that occurs in coal tar. It is soluble in water, acts as a strong ◊base, and is used as a solvent, mainly in the manufacture of plastics.

pyridoxine *n.* or **vitamin B6**, $C_8H_{11}NO_3$, a member of the ◊vitamin B complex. There is no clearly identifiable disease associated with deficiency but its absence from the diet can give rise to malfunction of the central nervous system and general skin disorders. Good sources are liver, meat, milk, and cereal grains. Related compounds may also show vitamin B6 activity.

pyrite /'paɪraɪt/ *n.* or **iron pyrites** a common iron ore, iron sulphide FeS_2; also called **fool's gold** because of its yellow metallic lustre. Pyrite has a hardness of 6–6.5 on the Mohs' scale. It is used in the production of sulphuric acid. The term is also used for other sulphides, for example, **copper pyrites**, a sulphide of copper and iron. [Latin from Greek *pur* = fire]

pyro- /paɪrəʊ-/ in combinations, fire. [from Greek *pur* = fire]

pyroclastic *adj.* in geology, pertaining to fragments of solidified volcanic magma, ranging in size from fine ash to large boulders, that are extruded during an explosive volcanic eruption; also the rocks that are formed by consolidation of such material. Pyroclastic rocks include tuff (ash deposit) and agglomerate (volcanic breccia).

pyromania /paɪrəʊ'meɪnɪə/ *n.* an uncontrollable impulse to start fires. —**pyromaniac** *n. & adj.*

pyrometer *n.* a ◊thermometer used for measuring high temperatures.

pyrotechnics /paɪrəʊ'tekhnɪks/ *n.pl.* 1. the art of making fireworks. 2. a display of fireworks. 3. any loud or brilliant display. —**pyrotechnic** *adj.* [from Greek *tekhnē* = art]

pyroxene *n.* any one of a group of minerals, silicates of calcium, iron, and magnesium with a general formula $XYSi_2O_6$, found in igneous and metamorphic rocks. The internal structure is based on single chains of silicon and oxygen. Diopside, X=Ca,Y=Mg, and augite, X=Ca,Y=Mg,Fe,Al, are common pyroxenes.

pyrrhic /'pɪrɪk/ *adj.* (of a victory) won at too great a cost. [from *Pyrrhus*, king of Epirus]

Pyrrho /'pɪrəʊ/ *c.*360–*c.*270 BC. Greek philosopher, founder of ◊Scepticism, who maintained that since certainty was impossible, peace of mind lay in renouncing all claims to knowledge.

Pyrrhus /'pɪrəs/ *c.*318–272 BC. King of ◊Epirus from 307, who invaded Italy in 280, as an ally of the Tarentines against Rome. He twice defeated the Romans but with such heavy losses that the term **Pyrrhic victory** has come to mean a victory not worth winning. He returned to Greece in 275 after his defeat at Beneventum, and was killed in a riot in Argos.

One more such victory and we are lost.

Pyrrhus
after defeating the Romans at Asculum, 279 BC

Pythagoras /paɪˈθæɡərəs/ c.580–500 BC. Greek mathematician and philosopher, who formulated Pythagoras' theorem. Much of his work concerned numbers, to which he assigned mystical properties. For example, he classified numbers into triangular ones (1, 3, 6, 10, ...), which can be represented as a triangular array, and square ones (1, 4, 9, 16, ...), which form squares. He also observed that any two adjacent triangular numbers add to a square number (for example, $1 + 3 = 4$; $3 + 6 = 9$; $6 + 10 = 16$; ...). Pythagoras was the founder of a politically influential religious brotherhood in Croton, S Italy (suppressed in the 5th century). Its tenets included immortality of the soul and ◊transmigration.

Pythagoras' theorem in geometry, the theorem stating that in a right-angled triangle, the area of the square on the hypotenuse (the longest side) is equal to the sum of the areas of the squares drawn on the other two sides. If the hypotenuse is h units long and the lengths of the other sides are a and b, then $h^2 = a^2 + b^2$. [from *Pythagoras*]

python /ˈpaɪθən/ n. a type of snake (especially of the genus *Python*) that kills its prey by compressing and asphyxiating it. It is found in the tropics of Africa, Asia, and Australia. Some species are small, but the reticulated python of SE Asia can grow to 10 m/33 ft. [Latin from Greek *Puthōn* = huge serpent or monster slain near Delphi by Apollo in myth]

pyx n. 1. in Christian religion, a vessel in which bread consecrated for the Eucharist is kept. 2. a box in which specimen coins are deposited at the Royal Mint. —**trial of the pyx**, an annual test of specimen coins at the Royal Mint by a group of members (called a *jury*) of the Goldsmith's Company. [from Latin from Greek *puxis* (*puxos* = box)]

q, Q /kjuː/ *n.* (*plural* **qs, q's**) 17th letter of the alphabet.
Q. abbreviation of **1.** Queen('s). **2.** question.
Qaboos /kəˈbuːs/ bin Saidq 1940– . Sultan of Oman,
the 14th descendant of the Albusaid family. Opposed to
the conservative views of his father, he overthrew him
in 1970 in a bloodless coup and assumed the sultanship.
Since then he has followed more liberal and expansionist
policies, while maintaining his country's position of international nonalignment.
Qaddafi alternative form of ◊Khaddhafi, Libyan leader.

I am not afraid of anything. If you fear God you do not
fear anything else.
Colonel Muhammar Qaddafi

Qadisiya, Battle of /kɑːˈdiːsiːə/ the battle fought in
S Iraq in 637. A Muslim Arab force defeated a larger
Zoroastrian Persian army and ended the ◊Sassanian Empire.
The defeat is still resented in Iran, where Muslim Arab
nationalism threatens to break up the Iranian state.
qat *n.* a shrub *Catha edulis* of the staff-tree family
Celastraceae. The leaves are chewed as a mild narcotic in some Arab countries. Its use was banned in
◊Somalia in 1983.
Qatar /ˈkætɑː/ State of; country in the Middle East, occupying Qatar peninsula in the Arabian Gulf, bounded SW
by Saudi Arabia and S by United Arab Emirates; **area**
11,400 sq km/4,402 sq mi; **capital** and chief port Doha;
physical mostly flat desert with salt flats in S; **head
of state and government** Sheik Khalifa bin Hamad al-
Thani from 1972; **political system** absolute monarchy;
products oil, natural gas, petrochemicals, fertilizers, iron,
steel; **population** (1990 est) 498,000; **language** Arabic;
recent history independence was achieved from Britain in
1971. A British protectorate from 1916. A new constitution
confirmed the emirate as an absolute monarchy in 1970.
In 1971 independence was achieved from Britain and a
treaty of friendship was signed with the UK. The Emir
Sheik Ahmad was replaced in 1972 in a bloodless coup by
his cousin, Crown Prince Sheik Khalifa, who introduced a
programme of social and economic reform.
QC abbreviation of ◊Queen's Counsel.
QED abbreviation of *quod erat demonstrandum* [Latin =
which was to be proved]
Qin dynasty /tʃɪn/ Chinese imperial dynasty 221–206 BC.
◊Shi Huangdi was its most renowned emperor.
Qinghai /tʃɪŋˈhaɪ/ formerly **Tsinghai** province of NW
China; **area** 721,000 sq km/278,306 sq mi; **capital** Xin-
ing; **physical** mainly desert; **products** oil, livestock, medi-
cal products; **population** (1986) 4,120,000.
Qisarya /kiːˈsɑːriə/ Mediterranean port N of Tel Aviv,
Israel; there are underwater remains of Herod the Great's
port of Caesarea.
Qld. or **Qld** abbreviation of Queensland.
Qom /kʊm/ or **Qum** holy city of Shi'ite Muslims, in central
Iran, 145 km/90 mi S of Tehran; population (1986) 551,000.
qr. abbreviation of quarter(s).
qt. abbreviation of quart(s).

q.t. (*slang*) abbreviation of quiet (*on the q.t.*).
qua /kweɪ/ *conj.* in the capacity of. [Latin = in the manner in which]
quack[1] *n.* the harsh cry of a duck. —*v.i.* **1.** to utter a quack.
2. to talk loudly. [imitative]
quack[2] *n.* a person who falsely claims to have medical skill
or to provide remedies which will cure disease, a charlatan.
—*adj.* **1.** being a quack. **2.** characteristic of or used by a
quack. —**quackery** *n.* [abbreviation of Dutch *quacksalver*,
from *quacken* = boast and *salf* = salve, ointment]
quad[1] /kwɒd/ *n.* (*colloquial*) **1.** a quadruplet. **2.** a quadrangle. **3.** quadraphony. —*adj.* quadraphonic. [abbreviation]
quad[2] *n.* a small metal block used by printers in spacing. [abbreviation of *quadrat*, from Latin *quadratus* =
made square]
Quadragesima /kwɒdrəˈdʒesɪmə/ *n.* in the Christian
calendar, the first Sunday in Lent. [from Latin = fortieth
(day), Lent having 40 days]
quadrangle /ˈkwɒdræŋgəl/ *n.* **1.** a four-cornered figure, especially a square or rectangle. **2.** a four-sided
court bordered by large buildings, especially in colleges.
—**quadrangular** /-ˈræŋgjʊlə/ *adj.* [from Old French from
Latin *quattuor* = four and *angulus* = angle]
quadrant /ˈkwɒdrənt/ *n.* **1.** a quarter of a circle's circumference; a quarter of a circle as cut by two diameters at
right angles; a quarter of a sphere as cut by two planes
intersecting at right angles at the centre. **2.** a thing shaped
like a quarter-circle, especially a graduated strip of metal
etc.; an instrument including this for taking angular measurements. [from Latin *quadrans* = quarter]
quadraphonic /kwɒdrəˈfɒnɪk/ *adj.* (of sound reproduction) using four transmission channels. —**quadraphonic-
ally** *adv.*, **quadraphony** /-ˈrɒfənɪ/ *n.*
quadrat /ˈkwɒdræt/ *n.* a small area marked out for study
of the plants and animals it contains. [from Latin *quadratus*
= made square]
quadrate /ˈkwɒdreɪt/ *adj.* square, rectangular.
quadrathon *n.* a sports event in which the competitors
must swim two miles, walk 30 miles, cycle 100 miles, and
run 26.2 miles (a marathon) within 22 hours.
quadratic equation /kwɒdˈrætɪk/ an equation in
mathematics, a polynomial equation of second degree
(that is, an equation containing as its highest power
the square of a single unknown variable, such as x^2).
The general formula of such equations is $ax^2 + bx +
c = 0$, in which a, b, and c are real numbers, and only
the coefficient a cannot equal 0. In ◊coordinate geometry, a quadratic function represents a ◊parabola. [from
French or Latin]
quadrature *n.* the position of the Moon or an outer planet
where a line between it and Earth makes a right angle with
a line joining Earth to the Sun.
quadrennial /kwɒdˈrenɪəl/ *adj.* **1.** lasting for four years.
2. recurring every four years. —**quadrennially** *adv.*
quadrennium /kwɒdˈrenɪəm/ *n.* (*plural* **quadren-
niums**) a period of four years. [from Latin *quadrennium*]
quadri- /kwɒdrɪ/ in combinations, four. [Latin *quattuor* =
four]
quadrilateral /kwɒdrɪˈlætərəl/ *adj.* having four sides.
—*n.* a quadrilateral figure. [from Latin *latus* = side]

quadrille[1] /kwə'drɪl/ *n.* a square dance usually containing five figures; music for this. [French from Spanish *cuadrilla* = squadron (*cuadra* = square)]

quadrille[2] *n.* a card game fashionable in the 18th century, played by four persons with 40 cards (i.e. an ordinary pack without the 8s, 9s, and 10s). [French]

quadrillion /kwə'drɪljən/ *n.* (for *plural* usage see ◊hundred) **1.** a million raised to the fourth power (1 followed by 24 ciphers). **2.** (*US*) a thousand raised to the fifth power (1 followed by 15 ciphers).

quadriplegia /kwɒdrɪ'pliːdʒiə/ *n.* paralysis of all four limbs. —**quadriplegic** *adj.* & *n.* [from Greek *plēgē* = blow]

quadroon /kwə'druːn/ *n.* the offspring of a white and a mulatto, a person who is one-quarter black. [from Spanish *cuarterón* (*cuarto* = fourth)]

quadruped /'kwɒdrʊped/ *n.* a four-footed animal, especially a mammal. [from French or Latin (*quadri-*and *pes* = foot)]

quadruple /'kwɒdrʊpəl/ *adj.* **1.** fourfold; having four parts; being four times as many or as much. **2.** (of time in music) having four beats in a bar. —*n.* a fourfold number or amount. —*v.t./i.* to multiply by four. —**quadruply** *adv.* [from French from Latin *quadruplus*]

Quadruple Alliance in European history, three military alliances of four nations: **the Quadruple Alliance 1718** Austria, Britain, France, and the United Provinces (Netherlands) joined forces to prevent Spain from annexing Sardinia and Sicily; **the Quadruple Alliance 1813** Austria, Britain, Prussia, and Russia allied to defeat the French emperor Napoleon; renewed 1815 and 1818. See ◊Vienna, Congress of; **the Quadruple Alliance 1834** of Britain, France, Portugal, and Spain guaranteed the constitutional monarchies of Spain and Portugal against rebels in the Carlist War.

quadruplet /'kwɒdrʊplɪt, -'ruː-/ *n.* each of four children born at one birth.

quadruplicate /kwɒ'druːplɪkət/ *adj.* **1.** fourfold. **2.** of which four copies are made. —/-eɪt/ *v.t.* **1.** to multiply by four. **2.** to make four copies of. —**in quadruplicate,** in four copies. [from Latin *quadruplex* = fourfold]

quaestor /'kwiːstə/ *n.* a magistrate in ancient Rome whose duties were mainly concerned with public finances. The quaestors originated as assistants to the consuls. Both urban and military quaestors existed, the latter being attached to the commanding generals in the provinces. [from Latin *quaerere* = seek]

quaff /kwɒf, kwɑːf/ *v.t./i.* (*literary*) to drain (a cup etc.) in copious draughts; to drink deeply.

quagga *n.* a South African wild horse which became extinct in the 1880s. It was brown, with a white tail and legs and a striped head and neck.

quagmire /'kwægmaɪə, 'kwɒg-/ *n.* a quaking bog, a marsh, a slough. [from *quag* = marsh or dialect *quag* = to shake and *mire*]

quail[1] *n.* (*plural* the same or **quails**) a bird of the smallest species of the partridge family. The common quail *Coturnix coturnix* is about 18 cm/7 in long, reddish-brown, with a white throat and a yellowish belly. It is found in Europe, Asia, and Africa, and has been introduced to North America. [from Old French from Latin *coacula*]

quail[2] *v.i.* to flinch, to show fear.

quaint *adj.* piquantly or attractively unfamiliar or old-fashioned, daintily odd. —**quaintly** *adv.*, **quaintness** *n.* [originally = cunning, from Old French from Latin *cognitus* (*cognoscere* = ascertain)]

quake *v.i.* to shake or tremble from unsteadiness; (of a person) to shake with fear etc. —*n.* (*colloquial*) an earthquake. [Old English]

Quaker /'kweɪkə(r)/ *n.* a member of the Society of ◊Friends. The name was once derogatory. —**Quakerism** *n.*

qualification /kwɒlɪfɪ'keɪʃən/ *n.* **1.** qualifying. **2.** an accomplishment fitting a person for a position or purpose. **3.** a thing that modifies or limits a meaning etc. —**qualificatory** *adj.* [French or from Latin]

qualify /'kwɒlɪfaɪ/ *v.t./i.* **1.** to make competent or fit for a position or purpose; to make legally entitled. **2.** (of a person) to satisfy the conditions or requirements. **3.** to modify or make (a statement etc.) less absolute. **4.** to moderate, to mitigate, to make less extreme. **5.** to attribute a quality to, to describe as. —**qualifier** *n.* [from French from Latin *qualis* = such as, of what kind]

qualitative /'kwɒlɪtətɪv/ *adj.* concerned with or depending on quality. [from Latin]

qualitative analysis the procedure for determining the identity of the component(s) of a substance or mixture.

quality /'kwɒlɪti/ *n.* **1.** degree or level of excellence. **2.** general excellence. **3.** an attribute or faculty. **4.** (of a voice or sound) timbre. **5.** (*archaic*) high social standing. [from Old French from Latin]

qualm /kwɑːm/ *n.* **1.** a misgiving, an uneasy doubt, a scruple of conscience. **2.** a momentary faint or sick feeling.

quandary /'kwɒndərɪ/ *n.* a perplexed state, a practical dilemma.

quango /'kwæŋgəʊ/ *n.* (*plural* **quangos**) a semipublic body with financial support from and senior appointments made by the government. [acronym from *quasi-*autonomous *non-governmental organization*]

quanta *n.* plural of ◊quantum.

quantifiable /'kwɒntɪfaɪəbəl/ *adj.* that may be quantified.

quantify /'kwɒntɪfaɪ/ *v.t.* to express as a quantity; to determine the quantity of. —**quantification** /-fɪ'keɪʃən/ *n.* [from Latin *quantus* = how much]

quantitative /'kwɒntɪtətɪv/ *adj.* concerned with quantity; measured or measurable by quantity. [from Latin]

quantitative analysis the procedure for determining the precise amount of a known component present in a single substance or mixture. A known amount of the substance is subjected to particular procedures. **Gravimetric analysis** determines the mass of each constituent present; ◊**volumetric analysis** determines the concentration of a solution by titration (see ◊titrate) against a solution of known concentration.

quantity /'kwɒntɪti/ *n.* **1.** ability to be measured through having size, weight, amount, or number. **2.** an amount or number of things; a specified or considerable amount or number. **3.** length or shortness of vowel sounds or syllables. **4.** a thing having quantity. —**quantity surveyor,** a person who measures and prices the work of builders. **quantity theory of money,** economic theory claiming that an increase in the amount of money in circulation causes a proportionate increase in prices. [from Old French from Latin]

quant. suff. abbreviation of *quantum sufficit* [Latin = as much as suffices]

quantum /'kwɒntəm/ *n.* (*plural* **quanta**) **1.** a minimum amount of a physical quantity (such as energy or momentum) which can exist in a given situation and by multiples of which changes in the quantity occur. **2.** a required, desired, or allowed amount. —**quantum mechanics,** a mathematical form of quantum theory dealing with the motion and interaction of (especially subatomic) particles and incorporating the concept that these particles can also be regarded as waves. [Latin, neuter of *quantus* = how much]

quantum number in physics, one of a set of four numbers that uniquely characterize an ◊electron and its state in an ◊atom. The **principal quantum number** n (= 1, 2, 3, and so on) defines the electron's main energy level. The **orbital quantum number** l (= n - 1, n - 2, and so on to l = 0) relates to angular momentum. The **magnetic quantum number** m (= l, l - 1, l - 2, and so on to 0 and then on to ... - (l - 2), - (l - 1) and -l) describes the energies of electrons in a magnetic field. The **spin quantum number** m_s (= + 1/2 or -1/2) gives the spin direction of the electron.

quantum theory in physics, the theory that many quantities, such as ◊energy, cannot have a continuous range of values, but only a number of discrete (particular) ones, because they are packaged in 'quanta of energy'. Just as earlier theory showed how light, generally seen as a wave motion, could also in some ways be seen as composed of discrete particles (◊photons), quantum mechanics shows how atomic particles such as electrons may also be seen as having wavelike properties. Quantum mechanics is the basis of particle physics, modern theoretical chemistry, and the solid-state physics that describes the behaviour of the silicon chips used in computers.

quarantine /'kwɒrəntiːn/ *n.* isolation imposed on a ship, persons, or animals to prevent infection or contagion; the period of this. —*v.t.* to put into quarantine. [from Italian *quaranta* = forty]

quark /kwɑːk, kwɔk/ *n.* any of at least five hypothetical ◊elementary particles which, together with their antiparticles, are believed to be fundamental constituents of the elementary particles, mesons and baryons. [from phrase 'Three quarks for Muster Mark!' in James Joyce's *Finnegans Wake* 1939]

quarrel /'kwɒrəl/ *n.* 1. a violent disagreement; a break in friendly relations. 2. a cause for complaint. —*v.i.* (-ll-) 1. to engage in a quarrel; to break off friendly relations. 2. to find fault. [from Old French from Latin *querel(l)a* = complaint]

quarrelsome *adj.* given to quarrelling. —**quarrelsomeness** *n.*

quarry[1] /'kwɒrɪ/ *n.* a place from which stone is extracted for building etc. —*v.t./i.* to extract (stone) from a quarry. —**quarry tile,** an unglazed floor tile. [from Latin from Old French *quarriere* from Latin *quadrum* = square]

quarry[2] *n.* an intended prey or victim being hunted; something sought or pursued. [from Old French *cuiree,* ultimately from Latin *cor* = heart; originally = parts of deer given to hounds]

quart /kwɔt/ *n.* an imperial liquid or dry measure, equal to two pints or 1.136 litres (one quarter of a gallon). [from Old French from Latin *quartus* = fourth]

quarter /'kwɔtə/ *n.* 1. each of four equal parts into which a thing is divided. 2. a period of three months, especially one ending on a quarter-day. 3. a point of time 15 minutes before or after any hour. 4. 25 US or Canadian cents; a coin for this. 5. a division of a town, especially as occupied by a particular class. 6. a point of the compass; the region at this; a direction; a district; a person or group regarded as a possible source of supply. 7. (in *plural*) lodgings; an abode, a station of troops. 8. one fourth of a lunar month; the Moon's position between the first two (**first quarter**) and the last two (**last quarter**) of these. 9. each of the four parts into which a carcass is divided. 10. (in *plural*) the hind legs and adjoining parts of a quadruped; the hindquarters. 11. exemption from being put to death, on condition of surrender. 12. a grain-measure of eight bushels, one quarter of a hundredweight. —*v.t.* 1. to divide into quarters; (*historical*) to divide (the body of an executed person) thus. 2. to put (troops etc.) into quarters; to provide with lodgings. 3. to place (coats of arms) on four parts of a shield's surface. —**cry quarter,** to ask for mercy. **quarter-day** *n.* any of the four days beginning an official quarter of the year for fiscal purposes (in England 25 Mar, 24 June, 29 Sept, 25 Dec; in Scotland 2 Feb, 15 May, 1 August, 11 Nov). **quarterfinal** *n.* a match or round preceding a semifinal. **quarterlight** *n.* a small vertically opening window in a motor vehicle. **quarter sessions,** (*historical*) in England, a court with limited criminal and civil jurisdiction, usually held quarterly, replaced 1972 by crown courts (see also ◊law courts). [from Anglo-French from Latin *quartarius*]

quarterdeck *n.* the part of a ship's upper deck near the stern, usually reserved for officers.

quartering *n.* (often in *plural*) coats of arms arranged on one shield to denote alliances of families.

quarterly *adv.* 1. once in each quarter of a year. 2. (in heraldry) in the four, or in two diagonally opposite, quarters of a shield. —*adj.* 1. done, published, or due quarterly. 2. (in heraldry, of a shield) quartered. —*n.* a quarterly publication.

quartermaster *n.* 1. a regimental officer in charge of quartering, rations, etc. 2. a naval petty officer in charge of steering, signals, etc.

quarterstaff *n.* a stout pole, about two metres long, formerly used by peasantry as a weapon.

quartet /kwɔ'tet/ *n.* or **quartette** 1. a musical composition for four performers; these performers. 2. any group of four. [from French from Italian *quarto* = fourth, from Latin *quartus* = four]

quarto /'kwɔtəʊ/ *n.* (*plural* **quartos**) the size of a book or page given by twice folding a sheet to form four leaves; a book or sheet of this size. [from Latin (*in*) *quarto* = (in) fourth (of sheet)]

quartz /kwɔts/ *n.* a crystalline form of ◊silica SiO_2, one of the most abundant minerals of the Earth's crust (12% by volume). Quartz occurs in many different kinds of rock, including sandstone and granite. It ranks 7 on the Mohs' scale of hardness and is resistant to chemical or mechanical breakdown. Quartzes vary according to the size and purity

Quayle *Vice president of the USA from 1989, Dan Quayle.*

of their crystals. Crystals of pure quartz are coarse, colourless, and transparent, and this form is usually called rock crystal. Impure coloured varieties, often used as gemstones, include agate, citrine quartz, and amethyst. Quartz is used in ornamental work and industry, where its reaction to electricity makes it valuable in electronic instruments (see ◊piezoelectricity). Quartz can also be made synthetically. —**quartz clock** *or* **watch,** one operated by electric vibrations of a quartz crystal. **quartz lamp,** a quartz tube with mercury vapour as the light source. [from German from Slavonic]

quartzite *n.* a ◊metamorphic rock consisting of pure quartz sandstone that has recrystallized under increasing heat and pressure.

quasar /'kweɪsɑː(r)/ *n.* in astronomy, a class of star-like celestial objects far beyond our Galaxy. Although quasars are small, with diameters less than a light year, each emits more energy than 100 giant galaxies. Quasars are thought to be at the centre of distant galaxies, their brilliance emanating from the stars and gas falling towards an immense ◊black hole at their nucleus. Quasar light shows a large ◊red shift, placing quasars far off in the universe, the most distant lying over 10 billion light years away.

quash /kwɒʃ/ *v.t.* 1. annul, regard as not valid, especially by legal procedure. 2. suppress, crush. [from Old French *quasser* from Latin *quassare* = shake violently]

quasi- /'kweɪzaɪ/ prefix for seeming(ly), not real(ly); almost. [from Latin *quasi* = as if]

Quasimodo /kwɑːzi'məʊdəʊ/ Salvatore 1901–1968. Italian poet. His first book *Acque e terre/Waters and Land* appeared 1930. Later books, including *Nuove poesie/New Poetry* 1942, and *Il falso e vero verde/The False and True Green* 1956, reflect a growing preoccupation with the political and social problems of his time. He won the Nobel Prize for Literature in 1959.

Poetry is the revelation of a feeling that the poet believes to be interior and personal [but] which the reader recognizes as his own.

Salvatore Quasimodo
The New York Times, May 14 1960.

---

quassia /'kwɒʃə/ *n.* 1. a tropical American tree of the genus *Quassia,* especially *Q. amara;* its wood, bark, or root. 2. a bitter tonic from these now used in insecticides. [from G *Quassi,* an 18th-century Surinamer, who discovered its medicinal properties]

quaternary /kwə'tɜːnərɪ/ *adj.* 1. having four parts. 2. Quaternary, of the period of geological time that began 1.8 million years ago and is still in process. It is divided into the ◊Pleistocene and ◊Holocene epochs. —**Quaternary** *n.* this period. [from Latin *quaterni* = four each]

quatrain /'kwɒtreɪn/ *n.* a four-line stanza. [French *quatre* = four]

quatrefoil /'kætrəfɔɪl/ *n.* 1. a four-cusped figure. 2. a four-lobed leaf or flower. [from Anglo-French *quatre* = four and *foil* = leaf]

quattrocento /kwɔːtruˈtʃɛntʊ/ *n.* Italian art of the 15th century. [Italian = 1400]

quaver /ˈkweɪvə/ *v.t./i.* 1. to tremble, to vibrate. 2. to say or speak in a trembling voice; to sing with trembling. —*n.* 1. a quavering sound; quavering speech. 2. a trill. 3. in music, a note half as long as a crotchet. —**quavery** *adj.*

quay /kiː/ *n.* an artificial landing-place for loading and unloading ships. [from Old French *kay*]

Quayle /kweɪl/ (J) Dan(forth) 1947– . US Republican politician, an Indiana congressman from 1977, senator from 1981, vice president from 1989.

queasy /ˈkwiːzɪ/ *adj.* 1. feeling slight nausea; having an easily upset digestion. 2. (of food) causing nausea. 3. (of a conscience or person) over-scrupulous. —**queasily** *adv.*, **queasiness** *n.*

Québec /kwiˈbek/ capital and industrial port (textiles, leather, timber, paper, printing and publishing) of Québec province, on the St Lawrence River, Canada; population (1986) 165,000, metropolitan area 603,000.

Québec province of E Canada; **area** 1,540,700 sq km/594,710 sq mi; **capital** Québec; **products** iron, copper, gold, zinc, cereals, potatoes, paper, textiles, fish, maple syrup (70% of world's output); **population** (1986) 6,540,000; **language** French (the only official language since 1974, although 17% speak English). Language laws 1989 prohibit the use of English on street signs; **history** known as New France 1534–1763; captured by the British and became province of Québec 1763–90, Lower Canada 1791–1846, Canada East 1846–67; one of the original provinces 1867. Nationalist feelings in the 1960s were strong enough to lead to an uprising by Québec Liberation Front (FLQ) separatists in 1970; the separatist Parti Québecois was defeated by Liberal Party 1989.

Québec Conference two conferences of Allied leaders in the city of Québec during World War II. The **first conference** in 1943 approved the British admiral Mountbatten as supreme Allied commander in SE Asia and made plans for the invasion of France, for which the US general Eisenhower was to be supreme commander. The **second conference** in Sept 1944 adopted plans for intensified air attacks on Germany, created a unified strategy against Japan, and established a postwar policy for a defeated Germany.

Quechua /ˈketʃwə/ *n.* also **Quichua** or **Kechua** a member of a group of South American Indians of the Andean region, whose ancestors include the ◊Inca. The Quechua language is the second official language of Peru, and is still spoken in Ecuador, Bolivia, Columbia, Argentina, and Chile.

queen *n.* 1. a female sovereign (especially hereditary) ruler of an independent state. 2. a king's wife. 3. a woman, country, or thing regarded as pre-eminent in a specified field, area, or class. 4. a perfect fertile female of the bee, ant, etc. 5. the most powerful piece in chess. 6. a court card with a picture of a queen. 7. (*slang*) a male homosexual. —*v.t.* to convert (a pawn in chess) to a queen when it reaches the opponent's end of the board; (of a pawn) to be thus converted. —**Queen-Anne** *adj.* in the style of English design characteristic of the early 18th century with plain, simple lines. **queen consort**, a king's wife. **queen it**, to act the queen. **queen mother**, a king's widow who is the mother of a sovereign. **queen post** either of the two upright posts between the tie beam and the main rafters. —**queenly** *adj.*, **queenliness** *n.* [Old English]

Queen Maud Land /kwiːn ˈmɔːd/ a region of Antarctica west of Enderby Land, claimed by Norway since 1939.

Queens /kwinz/ a borough and county at the western end of Long Island, New York City, USA; population (1980) 1,891,300.

Queensberry /ˈkwiːnzbəri/ John Sholto Douglas, 8th Marquess of 1844–1900. British patron of boxing. In 1867 he formulated the Queensberry Rules, the standard rules of boxing. A keen all-round sportsman, Douglas was an expert horseman and excelled at steeplechasing. He was the father of Lord Alfred ◊Douglas.

Queen's Counsel (QC) in England, a barrister appointed to senior rank by the Lord Chancellor. When the monarch is a king the term is **King's Counsel** (KC).

Queensland /ˈkwiːnzlænd/ state in NE Australia; **area** 1,727,200 sq km/666,699 sq mi; **capital** Brisbane; **physical** Great Dividing Range, including Mount Bartle Frere

'*Québec Province*

1,657 m/5,438 ft; Great Barrier Reef (collection of coral reefs and islands about 2,000 km/1,250 mi long off the E coast); **products** sugar, pineapples, beef, cotton, wool, tobacco, copper, gold, silver, lead, zinc, coal, nickel, bauxite, uranium, natural gas; **population** (1987) 2,650,000; **history** part of New South Wales until 1859, when it became self-governing. In 1989 the ruling National Party was defeated after 32 years in power and replaced by the Labour Party.

queer *adj.* 1. strange, odd, eccentric. 2. suspect, of questionable character. 3. slightly ill, faint. 4. (*slang*, especially of a man) homosexual. —*n.* (*derogatory slang*) a homosexual (especially male) person. —*v.t.* (*slang*) to spoil, to put out of order. —**in Queer Street**, (*slang*) in debt or trouble or disrepute. **queer the pitch for**, to spoil the chances of (a person) beforehand. —**queerly** *adv.*, **queerness** *n.*

quell *v.t.* to suppress; to reduce to submission. [Old English = kill]

quench *v.t.* 1. to satisfy (one's thirst) by drinking. 2. to extinguish (a fire or light). 3. to cool, especially with water. 4. to stifle or suppress (a desire etc.). [Old English]

quenching *n.* ◊heat treatment used to harden metals. They are heated to a certain temperature and then quickly plunged into cold water or oil.

quern /kwɜːn/ *n.* 1. a simple apparatus for grinding corn, consisting of two hard stones, the upper of which is rubbed to and fro, or rotated, on the lower one. 2. a small hand-mill for pepper etc. [Old English]

querulous /ˈkwerʊləs/ *adj.* complaining peevishly. —**querulously** *adv.*, **querulousness** *n.* [from Latin *queri* = complain]

query /ˈkwɪərɪ/ *n.* 1. a question. 2. a question mark or the word *query* spoken or written as a mark of interrogation. —*v.t.* to ask or enquire. 2. to call in question, to dispute the accuracy of. [anglicized form of Latin *quaere* = ask]

quest *n.* 1. seeking, a search. 2. a thing sought. —*v.i.* to seek or search for something. —**in quest of**, seeking. [from Old French from Latin *quaerere* = seek]

question /ˈkwestʃən/ *n.* 1. a sentence so worded or expressed as to seek information. 2. a doubt or dispute about a matter; the raising of such doubt etc. 3. the matters to be discussed or decided. 4. a problem for solution. 5. a thing depending on the conditions of. —*v.t.* 1. to ask questions of; to subject to examination. 2. to call in question; to throw doubt on. —**beyond (all) question**, certainly. **call in question**, to express doubts about, to dispute. **in question**, being mentioned or discussed. **out of the question**, impracticable, not worth considering. **question mark**, the punctuation mark (?) indicating a question. **question master** the person who puts the questions to people taking part in a quiz game or similar entertainment. **question time**, a period in the British Parliament when MPs may question ministers. —**questioner** *n.*

questionable *adj.* of doubtful truth, validity, or advisability; suspect. —**questionably** *adv.*

questionnaire /kwestʃəˈneə/ *n.* a formulated series of questions put to a number of people, especially as part of a survey. [French]

quetzal *n.* a long-tailed, Central American bird. The male is brightly coloured, with green, red, blue, and white feathers, and is about 1.3 m/4.3 ft long including tail. The female is smaller and lacks the tail and plumage. It eats fruit, insects, and small frogs and lizards. It is the national emblem of Guatemala, and was considered sacred by the Mayans and the Aztecs. The quetzal's forest habitat is rapidly being destroyed, and hunting of birds for trophies or souvenirs also threatens its survival.

Quetzalcoatl /ketsǝlkǝu'ætl/ feathered serpent god of air and water in the pre-Columbian ◊Aztec and ◊Toltec cultures of Central America. In legendary human form, he was said to have been fair-skinned and bearded, and to have reigned on Earth during a golden age. He disappeared across the sea, with a promise to return; ◊Cortés exploited the coincidence of description when he invaded. Ruins of one of Quetzalcoatl's temples survive at Teotihuacán in Mexico.

queue /kju:/ n. 1. a line or sequence of persons or vehicles etc. awaiting their turn. 2. a pigtail. —v. i. (often with *up*) to stand in or join a queue. [French from Latin *cauda* = tail]

Quevedo y Villegas Francisco Gómez de 1580-1645. Spanish novelist and satirist. His picaresque novel *La Vida del Buscón/The Life of a Scoundrel* 1626 follows the tradition of the roguish hero who has a series of adventures. *Sueños/Visions* 1627 is a brilliant series of satirical portraits of contemporary society.

Quezon City /'keɪsɒn 'sɪti/ former capital of the Philippines 1948-76, NE part of metropolitan ◊Manila, on Luzon Island; population (1980) 1,166,000. It was named after the Philippines' first president, Manuel Luis Quezon (1878-1944).

quibble n. 1. a petty objection, a trivial point of criticism. 2. a play on words, a pun. 3. an equivocation, an evasion; an argument depending on the ambiguity of a word or phrase. —v. i. to use quibbles. —**quibbler** n.

quiche /ki:ʃ/ n. an open tart, usually with a savoury filling. [French]

quick adj. 1. taking only a short time to do something or to traverse a distance or to be done or obtained etc. 2. able to notice or learn or think quickly; alert. 3. (of temper) easily roused. 4. (*archaic*) living, alive. —adv. quickly, at a rapid rate; in a fairly short time. —n. 1. the sensitive flesh below the nails or skin or a sore. 2. the seat of feeling or emotion. —**quick-freeze** v.t. to freeze (food) rapidly for storing, so that it keeps its natural qualities. **quick-witted** adj. alert; quick to understand a situation; quick at making jokes. —**quickly** adv. **quickness** n. [Old English, originally = alive]

quicken v.t./i. 1. to make or become quicker, to accelerate. 2. to make or become livelier, to stimulate. 3. (of a woman or fetus) to reach the stage of pregnancy when the fetus makes movements that can be felt by the mother.

quickie n. (*colloquial*) a thing made or done quickly.

quicklime n. unslaked lime.

quicksand n. an area of loose wet sand into which heavy objects readily sink.

quickset adj. formed of live plants set to grow in a hedge. —n. a hedge formed thus.

quicksilver n. 1. former name for the element ◊mercury. 2. a mercurial temperament.

quickstep n. a ballroom dance with quick steps; the music for this.

quid[1] n. (*plural* the same) (*slang*) one pound sterling. —**quids in**, able to profit.

quid[2] n. a lump of tobacco for chewing. [dialect variant of cud]

quiddity /'kwɪdɪtɪ/ n. 1. the essence of a thing. 2. a quibble, a captious subtlety. [from Latin *quidditas* (*quid* = what)]

quid pro quo /kwɪd prǝu 'kwǝu/a thing given as compensation. [Latin = something for something]

quiescent /kwi'esǝnt/ adj. inactive, dormant. —**quiescence** n.

quiet /'kwaɪǝt/ adj. 1. with little or no sound or motion. 2. of gentle or peaceful disposition. 3. unobtrusive, not showy. 4. not overt, private, disguised. 5. undisturbed, uninterrupted; free or far from vigorous action; informal. 6. enjoyed in quiet; not anxious or remorseful. —n. an undisturbed state, tranquillity; repose; stillness, silence. —v.t./i. to make or become quiet or calm. —**be quiet**, (*colloquial*) to cease talking etc. **keep quiet**, to say

nothing. **on the quiet**, unobtrusively, secretly. —**quietly** adv., **quietness** n. [from Old French from Latin *quiescere* = become calm]

quieten v.t./i. to make or become quiet.

quietism /'kwaɪǝtɪzǝm/ n. a passive, contemplative attitude to life, as a form of Christian religious mysticism. The founder of modern quietism was the Spanish priest Molinos who published a *Guida Spirituale/Spiritual Guide* 1675. —**quietist** n. & adj. [from Italian]

quietude /'kwaɪɪtjuːd/ n. quietness.

quietus /kwaɪ'iːtǝs/ n. release from life, final riddance. [from Latin *quietus* quit, used in receipts]

quiff n. a lock of hair plastered down or brushed up on the forehead.

quill n. 1. a large feather of a bird's wing or tail; a pen made from this. 2. the hollow stem of a feather; a plectrum or other device made from this. 3. one of a porcupine's spines.

quilt n. a coverlet, especially of quilted material. —v.t. to line (a coverlet or garment) with padding held between two layers of cloth etc. by crosslines of stitching. [from Old French *coilte* from Latin *culcita* = cushion]

quin n. (*colloquial*) a quintuplet. [abbreviation]

quince n. an acid, pear-shaped fruit used in jams etc.; the tree *Cydonia oblonga* bearing it. It is native to W Asia.

quincentenary /kwɪnsen'tiːnǝrɪ/ n. a 500th anniversary; a celebration of this. —adj. of a quincentenary. [from Latin *quinque* = five and **centenary**]

quincunx /'kwɪnkʌŋks/ n. 1. the centre and four corner points of a square or rectangle. 2. five trees etc. so placed. [Latin = five-twelfths (*quinque* = five and *uncia* = twelfth part)]

quinine /'kwɪniːn/ n. antimalarial drug extracted from the bark of the cinchona tree. Peruvian Indians taught French missionaries how to use the bark 1630, but quinine was not isolated for another two centuries. It is a bitter alkaloid, $C_{20}H_{24}N_2O_2$. [from *quina* = cinchona bark (Spanish from Quechua *kina* = bark)]

Quinn /kwɪn/ Anthony 1915- . Mexican actor, in films from 1935, including the title role in *Zorba the Greek* 1964. He later often played variations on this larger-than-life character.

> In Europe an actor is an artist. In Hollywood, if he isn't working, he's a bum.
>
> **Anthony Quinn**

Quinquagesima /kwɪŋkwǝ'dʒesɪmǝ/ n. in the Christian calendar, the Sunday before Lent (50 days before Easter). [Latin *quinquagesimus* = fiftieth]

quinquennial /kwɪŋ'kwenɪǝl/ adj. lasting or recurring every five years. —**quinquenially** adv.

quinquennium /kwɪŋ'kwenɪǝm/ n. (*plural* **quinquenniums**) a period of five years. [Latin *quinque* = five and *annus* = year]

quinquereme /'kwɪŋkwɪriːm/ n. an ancient ◊galley, probably with five men at each oar. [from Latin *quinque* = five and *remus* = oar]

quince

quinsy /'kwɪnzɪ/ n. inflammation of the throat, especially with an abscess on the tonsil(s). [from Old French from Latin *quinancia* from Greek]

Quintero /kɪn'teːəʊ/ Serafin Alvárez and Joaquin Alvárez. Spanish dramatists; see ◊Alvárez Quintero.

quintessence /kwɪn'tesəns/ n. 1. the purest and most perfect form or manifestation or embodiment of a quality etc. 2. a highly refined extract. —**quintessential** /-'ti'senʃəl/ adj., **quintessentially** adv. [from French from Latin *quinta essentia* = fifth essence (underlying the four elements)]

quintet /kwɪn'tet/ n. 1. a musical composition for five performers; these performers. 2. any group of five. [from French from Italian *quinto* = fifth, from Latin]

Quintilian /kwɪn'tɪlɪən/ (Marcus Fabius Quintilianus) c.AD 35–95. Roman rhetorician. He was born in Calgurris, Spain, taught rhetoric in Rome from AD 68, and composed the *Institutio oratorio/The Education of an Orator*, in which he advocated a simple and sincere style of public speaking.

Evil habits, once settled, are more easily broken than mended.

Marcus Fabius Quintilian
De Institutione Oratoria

---

quintuple /'kwɪntjʊpəl/ adj. fivefold; having five parts; being five times as many or as much. —n. a fivefold number or amount. —v.t./i. to multiply by five. [from French from Latin *quintus* = fifth]

quintuplet /'kwɪntjʊplɪt, -'tjuː-/ n. each of five children born at one birth.

quintuplicate /kwɪn'tjuːplɪkət/ adj. 1. fivefold. 2. of which five copies are made.

quip n. a clever saying, an epigram. -v.i. (-**pp**-) to make quips.

quire n. 1. 25 (formerly 24) sheets of writing paper. 2. each of the folded sheets that are sewn together in bookbinding. —**in quires**, unbound. [from Old French from Latin *quaterni* = four each]

Quirinal /'kwɪrɪnəl/ one of the seven hills on which ancient Rome was built. Its summit is occupied by a palace built 1574 as a summer residence for the pope and occupied 1870–1946 by the kings of Italy. [from *Quirinus* local god of the ◊Sabines]

quirk n. 1. a peculiarity of behaviour. 2. a trick of fate. 3. a flourish in writing. —**quirky** adj.

quisling /'kwɪzlɪŋ/ n. a traitor, especially one who collaborates with an enemy occupying his country. [from V. *Quisling*]

Quisling Vidkun 1887–1945. Norwegian politician. Leader from 1933 of the Norwegian Fascist Party, he aided the Nazi invasion of Norway 1940 by delaying mobilization and urging non-resistance. He was made premier by Hitler in 1942, and was arrested and shot as a traitor by the Norwegians in 1945.

quit v.t. (-**tt**-) 1. to give up, to abandon. 2. to cease. 3. to leave or depart (from). —*predic. adj.* rid. [earlier = release, from Old French from Latin *quittus, quietus* (*quiescere* = become calm)]

quitch n. a weed with long creeping roots, couch-grass *Agropyron repens.* [Old English]

quite adv. 1. completely, entirely, wholly. 2. really, actually. 3. somewhat, to some extent. —**quite a few**, a fair number. **quite (so)**, I grant the truth of that. **quite something**, remarkable. [variant of *quit* adj.]

Quito /'kiːtəʊ/ capital and industrial city (textiles, chemicals, leather, gold, silver) of Ecuador, about 3,000 m/9,850 ft above sea level; population (1982) 1,110,250. It was an ancient settlement, taken by the Incas about 1470 and by the Spanish in 1534. It has a temperate climate the year round.

quits *predicative adj.* on even terms by retaliation or repayment. —**call it** *or* **cry quits**, to acknowledge that things are now even, to agree to stop quarrelling etc.

quittance /'kwɪtəns/ n. (*archaic*) 1. release from an obligation. 2. an acknowledgement of payment. [from Old French]

quitter n. a deserter, a shirker.

quiver[1] /'kwɪvə/ v.i. to tremble or vibrate with a slight,

rapid motion. —n. a quivering motion or sound. [from obsolete *quiver* = nimble]

quiver[2] n. a case for holding arrows. [from Old French *quivre*]

qui vive /kiː 'viː v/on the qui vive, on the alert. [French = (long) live who? (as sentry's challenge)]

Quixote, Don /'kwɪksəʊt/ a novel by the Spanish writer ◊Cervantes, with a hero of the same name.

quixotic /kwɪk'sɒtɪk/ adj. chivalrous and unselfish to an extravagant or impractical extent. —**quixotically** adv., **quixotry** /'kwɪksətrɪ/ n.

quiz n. (*plural* **quizzes**) a series of questions testing people's knowledge, especially as a form of entertainment. —v.t. (-**zz**-) 1. to interrogate. 2. (*archaic*) to stare at curiously or critically. 3. (*archaic*) to make fun of.

quizzical /'kwɪzɪkəl/ adj. 1. expressing or done with mild or amused perplexity. 2. strange, comical. —**quizzically** adv.

Qum /kuːm/ alternative spelling of ◊Qom, city of Iran.

Qumran /'kumraːn/ or **Khirbet Qumran** archaeological site in Jordan, excavated from 1951, in the foothills NW of the Dead Sea. Originally an Iron Age fort (6th century BC), it was occupied in the late 2nd century BC by a monastic community, the ◊Essenes, until the buildings were burned by Romans in AD 68. The monastery library had contained the ◊Dead Sea Scrolls, which had been hidden in caves for safekeeping and were discovered in 1947.

quod n. (*slang*) prison.

quod erat demonstrandum (QED) a phrase added at the end of a geometry proof. [Latin = which was to be proved]

quod vide (qv) indicates a cross-reference. [Latin = which see]

quoin /kɔɪn/ n. 1. an outside corner of a building. 2. a corner-stone. 3. an inside corner of a room. 4. a wedge used for various purposes. [variant of *coin* from Latin *cuneus* = wedge]

quoit n. 1. a ring thrown at a mark or to encircle a peg. 2. (in *plural*) a game in which a rubber, rope, or metal ring is thrown at a peg (hob) from a point 16.5 m/54 ft away.

quondam adj. that once was, sometime, former. [Latin = formerly]

quorum /'kwɔːrəm/ n. the minimum number of members that must be present to constitute a valid meeting. —**quorate** adj. [Latin = of which people]

quota /'kwəʊtə/ n. 1. the share to be contributed to or received from a total by one of the parties concerned. 2. the total number or amount required or permitted; in international trade, a limitation on the quantities exported or imported. The justification of quotas include protection of a home industry from an influx of cheap goods, prevention of a heavy outflow of goods (usually raw materials) because there are insufficient quantities to meet domestic demand, allowance for a new industry to develop before it is exposed to competition, or prevention of a decline in the world price of a particular commodity. [from Latin *quota (pars)* = how great (a part) (*quot* = how many)]

quotable /'kwəʊtəbəl/ adj. worth quoting.

quotation /kwəʊ'teɪʃən/ n. 1. quoting. 2. a passage or price quoted. —**quotation-marks** n.pl. inverted commas (' ' or " ") used at the beginning and end of quoted passages or words.

quote v.t./i. 1. to cite or appeal to (an author or book) in confirmation of some view 2. to repeat or copy out a passage from; to repeat or copy out (a passage). 3. to enclose (words) in quotation marks. 4. to state the price of (usually *at* a figure). —n. (*colloquial*) 1. a passage or price quoted. 2. (usually in *plural*) a quotation mark. [from Latin *quotare* = mark with numbers]

quoth /kwəʊθ/ v.t. (*archaic*) (only with *I* or *he* or *she* placed after) said. [Old English]

quotidian /kwə'tɪdɪən/ adj. 1. daily; (of a fever) recurring every day. 2. everyday, commonplace. [from Old French from Latin *quotidie* = daily]

quotient /'kwəʊʃənt/ n. the result of a division sum. [from Latin *quotiens* = how many times]

quo vadis? where are you going? [Latin]

qv or **q.v.** abbreviation of ◊quod vide.

QwaQwa /kwaːkwaː/ a black homeland of South Africa that achieved self-governing status in 1974; population (1985) 181,600.

qy. or **qy** abbreviation of query.

r, R /ɑː/ *n.* (*plural* **rs, r's**) the 18th letter of the alphabet.
—**the three Rs**, reading, (w)riting, (a)rithmetic.
R abbreviation (in chess) of rook.
Ⓡ symbol for registered as a trademark.
r. abbreviation of right.
R. abbreviation of 1. *Regina.* 2. *Rex.* 3. River.
Ra symbol for radium.
RA abbreviation of 1. Royal Academician; Royal Academy of Art, London, founded 1768. 2. Royal Artillery.
Rabat /rə'bɑːt/ capital of Morocco, industrial port on the Atlantic coast, 177 km/110 mi W of Fez; **products** cotton textiles, carpets, leather goods; **population** (1982) 519,000, Rabat-Salé 842,000. It is named after the *ribat* or fortified monastery, around which it developed.
rabbet /'ræbɪt/ *n. & v.t.* = ◊rebate². [from Old French *rab(b)at* = recess]
rabbi /'ræbaɪ/ *n.* in Judaism, the chief religious leader of a synagogue or the spiritual leader of a Jewish congregation; also, a scholar of Judaic law and ritual from the 1st century AD. —**rabbinical** /-'bɪnɪkəl/ *adj.* [ultimately from Hebrew = my master]
rabbit /'ræbɪt/ *n.* 1. a herbivorous, long-eared, burrowing mammal *Oryctolagus cuniculus* of the Leporidae family, allied to the hare but with shorter legs and smaller ears, brownish-grey in the natural state, also black, white, or pied in domestication. It has legs and feet adapted for running and hopping, large front teeth, and can grow up to 40 cm/16 in long. It is native to Europe and N Africa, but is now found worldwide. 2. (*US*) a hare. 3. (*colloquial*) a poor performer at a game. —*v.i.* 1. to hunt rabbits. 2. (*slang*) to talk lengthily or in a rambling way. —**rabbit punch**, a short chop with the edge of the hand to an opponent's nape, a blow used to break a rabbit's neck. —**rabbity** *adj.*
rabble *n.* a disorderly crowd, a mob; a contemptible or inferior set of people; the lower or disorderly classes of the populace.
Rabelais /'ræbəleɪ/ François 1495–1553. French satirist, monk, and physician, whose name has become synonymous with bawdy humour. He was educated in the Renaissance humanist tradition and was the author of satirical allegories, including *La Vie inestimable de Gargantua/The Inestimable Life of Gargantua* 1535 and *Faits et dits héroïques du grand Pantagruel/Deeds and Sayings of the Great Pantagruel* 1533, about two giants (father and son) Gargantua and Pantagruel.
Rabi /'rɑːbi/ Isidor Isaac 1898–1988. Russian-born US physicist who developed techniques to measure accurately the strength of the weak magnetic fields generated when charged elementary particles, such as the electron, spin about their axes. The work won him the 1944 Nobel Prize for Physics.
rabid /'ræbɪd/ *adj.* 1. furious, raging. 2. fanatical. 3. of or affected with rabies. —**rabidity** /rə'bɪdɪtɪ/ *n.*, **rabidly** *adv.* [from Latin *rabere* = rave]
rabies /'reɪbiːz, -ɪz/ *n.* or **hydrophobia** a contagious virus disease of the central nervous system that can afflict all warm-blooded creatures. It is almost invariably fatal once symptoms have developed. Its transmission to humans is generally by a bite from a rabid dog. [Greek = fear of water]

Rabin /ræ'biːn/ Itzhak 1922– . Israeli prime minister 1974–77, who succeeded Golda ◊Meir.
RAC abbreviation of Royal Automobile Club.
raccoon /rə'kuːn/ *n.* or **racoon** an omnivorous nocturnal mammal of the Americas. The common raccoon *Procyon lotor* is about 60 cm/2 ft long, with a grey-brown body, a black and white ringed tail, and a black 'mask' around its eyes. The crab-eating raccoon *P. cancrivorus* of South America is slightly smaller and has shorter fur. [American Indian]
race¹ *n.* 1. a contest of speed in reaching a certain point or in doing or achieving something; (in *plural*) a series of these for horses or dogs at a fixed time on a regular course. 2. a strong, fast current of water. 3. a channel for the balls in a ball-bearing. —*v.t./i.* 1. to compete in a race; to have a race with; to cause to race. 2. to move or cause to move or operate at full or excessive speed. 3. to take part in horse-racing. —**race-meeting** *n.* a series of horse-races at one venue at fixed times. **race-track** *n.* a course for racing horses, vehicles etc. —**racer** *n.* [originally = running, from Old Norse]
race² *n.* 1. in anthropology, a term sometimes applied to a physically distinctive group of people, on the basis of difference from other groups in skin colour, head shape, hair type, and physique. Anthropologists formerly divided the human race into three hypothetical racial groups: Caucasoid, Mongoloid, and Negroid. However, scientific studies have failed to indicate any absolute confirmation of genetic racial divisions. Many anthropologists today thus completely reject the concept of race, and social scientists tend to prefer the term ethnic group (see ◊ethnicity). 2. a group of persons, animals, or plants connected by common descent; a genus, species, breed, or variety of animals or plants. —**the human race**, human kind. **race relations**, relations between members of different ethnic groups in the same country or community. **race riot**, an outbreak of violence due to ethnic antagonism. [French from Italian *razza*]
racecourse *n.* a ground for horse racing.
racegoer *n.* one who frequents horse races.
racehorse *n.* a horse bred or kept for racing.
raceme /rə'siːm/ *n.* a flower-cluster with flowers attached by short stalks at intervals along a stem. [from Latin *racemus* = grape-bunch]
race relations acts UK acts of Parliament 1965, 1968, and 1976 to improve race relations. The Race Relations Act 1965 set up the Race Relations Board to promote racial harmony, prevent racial discrimination, and deal with complaints. It made stirring up racial hatred or practising discrimination in a public place illegal. The Race Relations Act 1968 increased the powers of the Race Relations Board, who were enabled to make their own investigations. Discrimination in housing and employment was made illegal. The act also set up the Community Relations Commission. The Race Relations Act 1976 set up the Commission for Racial Equality with powers to investigate discrimination. It made racially offensive comments illegal and provided for complaints to be taken to a race relations tribunal.
rachel /rə'ʃel/ *n.* a light, tannish colour of face powder. [from *Rachel*, stage-name of Elisa Félix (1820–1858), French actress]

Rachmaninov /ræk'mænɪnɒf/ Sergei (Vasilevich) 1873–1943. Russian composer, conductor, and pianist. After the 1917 Revolution he went to the USA. His dramatically emotional Romantic music has a strong melodic basis and includes operas, such as *Francesca da Rimini* 1906, three symphonies, four piano concertos, piano pieces, and songs. Among his other works are the *Prelude in C-sharp Minor* 1892 and *Rhapsody on a Theme of Paganini* 1934 for piano and orchestra.

racial /'reɪʃəl/ *adj.* of or characteristic of a race; concerning or caused by race. —**racially** *adv.*

racialism *n.* 1. belief in the superiority of a particular race. 2. antagonism towards a particular race. —**racialist** *n.* & *adj.*

Racine /ræ'si:n/ Jean 1639–1699. French dramatist and exponent of the classical tragedy in French drama. His subjects came from Greek mythology and he observed the rules of classical Greek drama. Most of his tragedies have women in the title role, for example *Andromaque* 1667, *Iphigénie* 1674, and *Phèdre* 1677. After the contemporary failure of *Phèdre* he no longer wrote for the secular stage, but influenced by Madame de ◊Maintenon wrote two religious dramas, *Esther* 1689 and *Athalie* 1691, which achieved posthumous success.

> Love is not dumb. The heart speaks many ways.
> **Jean Racine**
> *Britannicus*

racism /'reɪsɪzəm/ *n.* 1. racialism; belief in, or a set of implicit assumptions about, the superiority of one's own race or ethnic group, often accompanied by prejudice against members of an ethnic group different from one's own. Racism may be used to justify discrimination (see under ◊discriminate), verbal or physical abuse, or even genocide, as in Nazi Germany or as practised by European settlers against American Indians in both North and South America. 2. the theory that human abilities etc. are determined by race. —**racist** *n.* & *adj.*

rack[1] *n.* 1. a framework, usually with bars or pegs etc., for holding things or hanging things on. 2. a cogged or toothed bar or rail engaging with a wheel or pinion etc. 3. (*historical*) an instrument of torture, a frame with a roller at each end to which a person's wrists and ankles were tied so that the joints were stretched when the rollers were turned. —*v.t.* 1. (of a disease or pain) to inflict suffering on. 2. (*historical*) to torture (a person) on a rack. 3. to place on or in a rack. 4. to shake violently; to injure by straining. —**on the rack**, in pain or distress. **rack one's brains**, to try hard to remember or think of something. **rack railway**, a mountain railway with a cogged rail in which a pinion on the locomotive engages, and a rack running usually between the rails, enabling the locomotive to climb slopes as steep as 1 in 2.1. **rack-rent** *n.* an exorbitant rent. [from Dutch or Middle Low German]

rack[2] *n.* destruction (especially in *rack and ruin*). [variant of *wrack*]

racket[1] /'rækɪt/ *n.* a bat having a round or oval frame strung with catgut or nylon etc., used in ball-games such as tennis and rackets. [from French, ultimately from Arabic = palm of the hand]

racket[2] *n.* 1. a din, a noisy fuss. 2. a business or other scheme in which dishonest means are used. 3. (*slang*) a line of business; a dodge. —*v.i.* to move about noisily; to engage in wild social activities. —**stand the racket**, (*colloquial*) to bear the costs or consequences.

racketeer /rækɪ'tɪə/ *n.* one who operates a dishonest scheme. —**racketeering** *n.*

rackets *n.* or **racquets** an indoor game played on an enclosed court. It is regarded as the forerunner of many racket and ball games. It is played on a court usually 18.3 m/60 ft long by 9.1 m/30 ft wide, by two or four persons each with a racket about 75 cm/2.5 ft long, weighing 255 g/9 oz. The ball is 25 mm/1 in in diameter and weighs 28 g/1 oz. Play begins from a service box, one is marked at each side of mid-court, and the ball must hit above a 2.75 m/9 ft line on the end wall. After service it may be played anywhere above a line 68.5 cm/27 in high on the end wall, the general rules of tennis applying thereafter.

rackety *adj.* noisy, rowdy.

raconteur /rækɒn'tɜː/ *n.* a teller of anecdotes. —**raconteuse** /-'tɜːz/ *n.fem.* [French *raconter* = relate]

racoon /rə'ku:n/ *n.* alternative spelling of ◊raccoon.

racy /'reɪsɪ/ *adj.* 1. lively and vigorous in style. 2. (*US*) risqué. 3. of a distinctive quality; retaining traces of its origin. —**racily** *adv.*, **raciness** *n.* [from *race*[2]]

rad abbreviation of 1. ◊radian(s). 2. radical. 3. radiation unit, the SI unit of absorbed dose of radiation. It is the dose when one kilogram of matter absorbs 0.01 joule of energy (formerly, the dose when one gram absorbs 100 ergs). Different types of radiation cause different amounts of damage for the same absorbed dose; the **dose equivalent** is measured in ◊rems.

radar /'reɪdɑː/ *n.* 1. a system for detecting the presence of objects at a distance, or ascertaining their position and motion, by transmitting short radio waves and detecting or measuring their return after they are reflected; a similar system in which the return signal consists of radio waves a suitably equipped target automatically transmits when it receives the outgoing waves. 2. an apparatus or installation used for this system. —**radar trap**, an arrangement using radar to detect vehicles etc. travelling faster than the speed limitative [acronym from *ra*dio *d*etection *a*nd *r*anging]

Radcliffe /'rædklɪf/ Ann (born Ward) 1764–1823. English novelist, a chief exponent of the ◊Gothic novel or 'romance of terror', for example, *The Mysteries of Udolpho* 1794.

raddle *n.* red ochre. —*v.t.* to colour with raddle, or with much rouge crudely used.

raddled *adj.* worn out.

Radha /'rɑːdə/ in the Hindu epic ◊*Mahābhārata*, the wife of a cowherd who leaves her husband for love of Krishna (an incarnation of the god Vishnu). Her devotion to Krishna is seen by the mystical *bhakti* movement as the ideal of the love between humans and God.

radial /'reɪdɪəl/ *adj.* 1. of or arranged like rays or radii; having spokes or lines radiating from a centre. 2. acting or moving along lines that diverge from a centre. 3. (of a tyre; also **radial-ply**) having fabric layers with cords lying radial to the hub of the wheel (not crossing each other). —*n.* a radial-ply tyre. —**radial circuit** a circuit used in household electric wiring in which all electrical appliances are connected to cables that radiate out from the main supply point or fuse box. —**radially** *adv.* [from Latin *radius* = spoke, ray]

radian /'reɪdɪən/ *n.* in mathematics, an alternative unit to the ◊degree for measuring angles. It is the angle at the centre of a circle when the centre is joined to the two ends of an arc (part of the circumference) equal in length to the radius of the circle. There are 2π (approximately 6.284) radians in a full circle (360°).

radiant /'reɪdɪənt/ *adj.* 1. emitting rays of light. 2. looking very bright and happy; (of beauty) splendid, dazzling. 3. (of light) issuing in rays. —*n.* a point or object from which light or heat radiates. —**radiant heat**, heat transmitted by radiation. —**radiance** *n.*, **radiancy** *n.*, **radiantly** *adv.* [from Latin *radiare*]

radiate /'reɪdɪeɪt/ *v.t.i.* 1. to emit rays of light, heat or other radiation; to emit from a centre; (of light or heat) to issue in rays. 2. to diverge or spread from a central point; to cause to do this. 3. to exude or show (a feeling etc.) clearly. —/'reɪdɪət/ *adj.* having the parts radially arranged.

radiation /reɪdɪ'eɪʃən/ *n.* 1. radiating, being radiated. 2. the emission of energy as electromagnetic waves or as moving particles for example, heat light, alpha particles, and beta particles (see ◊radioactivity). 3. energy thus transmitted. —**radiation biology**, the study of how living things are affected by radioactive (ionizing) emissions (see ◊radioactivity) and by electromagnetic (nonionizing) radiation (◊electromagnetic waves). Both can be used therapeutically, for example to treat cancer, when the radiation dose is very carefully controlled (**radio therapy** or **X-ray therapy**). —**radiation unit**, a unit of measurement for radioactivity and radiation doses. Continued use of the units introduced earlier this century (the curie, rad, rem, and roentgen) has been approved while the derived SI units (becquerel, gray, sievert, coulomb) become familiar. One curie equals 3.7×10^{-10} becquerels (activity); one rad equals 10^{-2} gray (absorbed dose); one rem equals 10^{-2} sievert (dose equivalent); one roentgen equals 2.58×10^{-4} coulomb/kg (exposure to ionizing radiation).

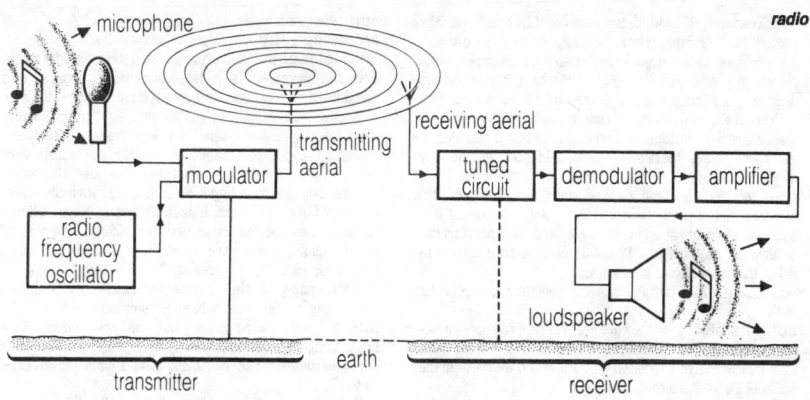

radio

radiation sickness sickness resulting from exposure to radiation, including X-rays, gamma rays, neutrons, and other nuclear radiation, as from weapons and fallout. Such radiation ionizes atoms in the body and causes nausea, vomiting, diarrhoea, and other symptoms. The body cells may be damaged even by very small doses, causing ◊leukaemia; and genetic changes may be induced in the germ plasm, causing infants to be born damaged or mutated.

radiation units units of measurement for radioactivity and radiation doses. Continued use of the units introduced earlier this century (the curie, rad, rem, and roentgen) has been approved while the derived SI units (becquerel, gray, sievert, coulomb) become familiar. One curie equals 3.7×10^{-10} becquerels (activity); one rad equals 10^{-2} gray (absorbed dose); one rem equals 10^{-2} sievert (dose equivalent); one roentgen equals 2.58×10^{-4} coulomb/kg (exposure to ionizing radiation).

radiator /ˈreɪdɪeɪtə/ n. 1. an apparatus for heating a room etc. by the radiation of heat, especially a metal structure through which steam or hot water circulates, or one heated electrically. 2. an engine-cooling apparatus in a motor vehicle or aeroplane, with a large surface for cooling circulating water.

Radić /ˈrɑːdɪtʃ/ Stjepan 1871–1928. Yugoslav nationalist politician, founder of the Croatian Peasant Party 1904. He led the Croat national movement within the Austro-Hungarian Empire and advocated a federal state with Croatian autonomy. His opposition to Serbian supremacy within Yugoslavia led to his assassination in parliament.

radical /ˈrædɪkəl/ adj. 1. fundamental, far-reaching, thorough. 2. advocating radical reforms; holding extreme views, revolutionary. 3. forming the basis, primary. 4. of the root of a number or quantity. 5. of the roots of words. —n. 1. in politics, anyone with opinions more extreme than the main current of a country's major political party or parties, especially those with left-wing opinions. 2. a group of atoms forming part of a compound and remaining unaltered during its ordinary chemical changes, yet often unable to exist alone. 3. the root of a word. 4. a mathematical quantity forming or expressed as the root of another. —**radicalism** n., **radically** adv. [from Latin radix= root]

Radical n. in Britain, a supporter of parliamentary reform before the Reform Bill 1832. As a group the Radicals later became the progressive wing of the Liberal Party. During the 1860s (led by Cobden, Bright, and J S Mill) they campaigned for extension of the franchise, free trade, and ◊laissez-faire, but after 1870, under the leadership of Joseph Chamberlain and Dilke, they adopted a republican and semi-socialist programme. With the growth of ◊socialism in the later 19th century, Radicalism ceased to exist as an organized movement.

radicle /ˈrædɪk(ə)l/ n. the part of a plant embryo that develops into the primary root. It usually emerges from the seed before the embryonic shoot, or ◊plumule, its tip protected by a root cap, or calyptra, as it pushes through the soil. The radicle may form the basis of the entire root system, or it may be replaced by adventitious roots (positioned on the stem). [from Latin radicula diminutive of radix = root]

radii plural of **radius**.

radio /ˈreɪdɪəʊ/ n. (plural **radios**) 1. the transmission and reception of messages etc. by electromagnetic waves of radio frequency, without a connecting wire. In radio transmission a microphone converts ◊sound¹ waves (pressure variations in the air) into ◊electromagnetic waves; these are picked up by a receiving aerial and fed to a loudspeaker, which converts them back into sound waves. 2. an apparatus for transmitting or receiving signals by radio. 3. sound broadcasting; a station engaged in this. —adj. 1. of, using, or sent by radio; equipped with radio. 2. of or concerned with stars or other celestial bodies from which radio waves are received or reflected. —v.t./i. to send (a message) by radio; to communicate (with) or broadcast by radio. —**radio star**, a small celestial object emitting strong radio waves. [short for radio-telegraphy etc.]

radio- in combinations, of or connected with rays, radiation, radioactivity, or radio. [from Latin radius = spoke, ray]

radioactive /reɪdɪəʊˈæktɪv/ adj. of or exhibiting radioactivity.

radioactive decay spontaneous alteration of the nucleus of a radioactive atom; this changes its atomic number, thus transmuting one element into another, and is accompanied by the emission of radiation. Alpha and beta decay are the most common forms. In **alpha decay** (the loss of a helium nucleus—two protons and two neutrons) the atomic number decreases by two; in **beta decay** (the loss of an electron) the atomic number increases by one.

Radioactive Incident Monitoring Network (RIMNET) a monitoring network at 46 Meteorological Office sites throughout the UK (to be raised to about 90). It feeds into a central computer, and was installed in 1989 to record contamination levels from nuclear incidents such as the ◊Chernobyl disaster.

radioactive tracer a radioactive isotope used in a labelled compound; see ◊tracer.

radioactive waste any waste that emits radiation in excess of the background level. See ◊nuclear waste.

radioactivity n. spontaneous alteration of the nuclei of radioactive atoms, accompanied by the emmission of radiation. It is the property exhibited by the radioactive ◊isotopes of stable elements and all isotopes of radioactive elements, and can be either natural or induced. See ◊radioactive decay.

radio astronomy the study of radio waves emitted naturally by objects in space, by means of a ◊radio telescope. Radio emission comes from hot gas (**thermal radiation**); electrons spiralling in magnetic fields (**synchroton radiation**); and specific wavelengths (**lines**) emitted by atoms and molecules in space, such as the 21 cm/8 in line emitted by hydrogen gas. Radio astronomy began in 1932 when Karl ◊Jansky detected radio waves from the centre of our Galaxy, but the subject did not develop until after World War II. Radio astronomy has greatly improved our understanding of the evolution of stars, the structure of galaxies, and the origin of the universe.

radio beacon a radio transmitter in a fixed location, used in marine and aerial navigation. Ships and aircraft pinpoint their positions by reference to continuous signals given out by two or more beacons.

radiocarbon *n*. a radioactive isotope of carbon, especially carbon 14. —**radiocarbon dating**, or **carbon dating**, a method of dating organic materials (for example, bone or wood), used in archaeology. Plants take up carbon dioxide gas from the atmosphere and incorporate it into their tissues, and some of that carbon dioxide contains the radioactive isotope of carbon, carbon-14. On death, the plant ceases to take up carbon-14 and that already taken up decays at a known rate, the half-life of 5,730 years, so that the time elapsed since the plant died can be measured in a laboratory. Animals take carbon-14 into their bodies from eating plant tissues and their remains can be similarly dated. After 120,000 years so little carbon-14 is left that no measure is possible.

radio, cellular a portable telephone system; see ◊cellular radio.

radiochemistry *n*. the chemical study of radioactive isotopes and their compounds (whether produced from naturally radioactive or irradiated materials) and their use in the study of other chemical processes.

radio-controlled *adj*. controlled from a distance by radio.

radio frequency frequency of radio waves, between about 10 kilohertz and 0.1 terahertz; for classification of radio frequencies and wavelengths, see ◊electromagnetic waves.

radio galaxy a galaxy that is a strong source of electromagnetic waves of radio wavelengths. All galaxies, including our own, emit some radio waves, but radio galaxies are up to a million times more powerful.

radiogram /'reɪdiəʊgræm/ *n*. **1.** a combined radio and gramophone. **2.** a telegram sent by radio. **3.** a picture obtained by X-rays etc.

radiograph /'reɪdiəgrɑːf/ *n*. **1.** a picture obtained by X-rays etc. X-rays penetrate matter according to its nature, density, and thickness. In doing so they can cast shadows on photographic film, producing a radiograph. **2.** an instrument for recording the intensity of radiation. —*v.t.* to obtain a picture by X-rays etc. —**radiographer** /-'ɒgrəfə/ *n*., **radiography** /-'ɒgrəfɪ/ *n*. the branch of science concerned with the use of radiation (particularly X-rays) to produce images on photographic film or fluorescent screens. Radiography is widely used in medicine for examining bones and tissues and in industry for examining solid materials; for example, to check welded seams in pipelines.

radioisotope *n*. a radioactive isotope, a naturally occurring or synthetic radioactive form of an element. Most radioisotopes are made by bombarding a stable element with neutrons in the core of a nuclear reactor. The radiations given off by radioisotopes are easy to detect (hence their use as ◊tracers). They can in some instances penetrate substantial thicknesses of materials, and they have profound effects on living matter. Although they are dangerous, they are used in the fields of medicine, industry, agriculture, and research.

radioisotope scanning the use of radioactive materials (radioisotopes or radionuclides) to pinpoint disease. It reveals the size and shape of the target organ and whether any part of it is failing to take up radioactive material, usually an indication of disease.

radiolarian /reɪdiə'leəriən/ *n*. a protozoan of the order Radiolaria, with a silicious skeleton and radiating pseudopodia. [from Latin *radiolus*]

radiology /reɪdi'ɒlədʒɪ/ *n*. the study of X-rays and other high-energy radiation, especially for use in medicine. —**radiologist** *n*.

radiometric dating a method of dating rock by assessing the amount of ◊radioactive decay of naturally occurring ◊isotopes. The dating of rocks may be based on the gradual decay of uranium into lead. The ratio of the amounts of 'parent' to 'daughter' isotopes in a sample gives a measure of the time it has been decaying, that is, of its age. Different elements and isotopes are used depending on the isotopes present and the age of the rocks to be dated. Once-living matter can often be dated by ◊radiocarbon dating, employing the half-life of the isotope carbon-14, which is naturally present in organic tissue.

radiometry /reɪdi'ɒmətrɪ/ *n*. the measurement of radioactivity or ionizing radiation. —**radiometric** /-ə'metrɪk/ *adj*.

radioscopy /reɪdi'ɒskəpɪ/ *n*. the examination by X-rays etc. of objects opaque to light.

radiotelegraphy *n*. telegraphy using radio.

radiotelephony *n*. telephony using radio.

radio telescope an instrument for detecting radio waves from the universe. Radio telescopes usually consist of a metal bowl that collects and focuses radio waves the way a concave mirror collects and focuses light waves. Other radio telescopes are shaped like long troughs, and some consist of simple, rod-shaped aerials. Radio telescopes are much larger than optical telescopes, because the wavelengths they are detecting are much longer than the wavelength of light. A large dish such as that at ◊Jodrell Bank, England, can see the radio sky less clearly than a small optical telescope sees the visible sky. The largest single dish is 305 m/1,000 ft across, at Arecibo, Puerto Rico.

radiotherapy *n*. the treatment of disease by ◊radiation from X-ray machines or radioactive sources.

radish /'rædɪʃ/ *n*. an annual plant *Raphanus sativus* with a crisp, pungent root eaten raw; this root is usually reddish but sometimes white or black. [Old English from Latin *radix*= root]

radium /'reɪdiəm/ *n*. a white, metallic, radioactive element, symbol Ra, atomic number 88, relative atomic mass 226.02, the heaviest member of the alkaline-earth metal group. It is found in nature in ◊pitchblende and other uranium ores. Of the 16 isotopes, the commonest, Ra-226, has a half-life of 1.622 years. The element was discovered and named in 1898 by Pierre and Marie ◊Curie, who were investigating the residues of pitchblende. [from Latin *radius* = ray]

radius /'reɪdiəs/ *n*. (*plural* **radii** /-iaɪ/) **1.** a straight line from the centre to the circumference of a circle or sphere; the length of this; distance from a centre. **2.** any of a set of lines diverging from a point like the radii of a circle. **3.** the thicker and shorter of the two bones in the forearm, on the same side as the thumb; the corresponding bone in an animal's foreleg or bird's wing. [Latin = spoke, ray]

radix /'reɪdɪks/ *n*. (*plural* **radices** /-siːz/) a number or symbol used as the basis of a numeration scale. [Latin = root]

Radnorshire /'rædnəʃə/ former border county of Wales, merged with Powys 1974. Presteign was the county town.

radon /'reɪdɒn/ *n*. a colourless, odourless, gaseous, radioactive, non-metallic element, symbol Rn, atomic number 86, relative atomic mass 222. It is grouped with the ◊inert gases and was formerly considered non-reactive, but is now known to form some compounds with fluorine. Of the 20 known isotopes, only three occur in nature; the longest half-life is 3.82 days. [from *radium*, after *argon* etc.]

Raeburn /'reɪbɜːn/ Henry 1756–1823. Scottish portrait painter, active mainly in Edinburgh. He developed a technique of painting with broad brushstrokes directly on the canvas without preparatory drawing. He was appointed painter to George IV in 1823. *The Reverend Robert Walker Skating c*.1784 (National Gallery, Edinburgh) 1784 is typical.

RAF abbreviation of ◊Royal Air Force.

Rafelson /'reɪfəlsən/ Bob (Robert) 1934– . US film director who gained critical acclaim for his second film, *Five Easy Pieces* 1971. His other films include *Head* 1968, *The Postman Always Rings Twice* 1981, and *Black Widow* 1987.

raffia /'ræfiə/ *n*. a fibre from the leaves of a kind of palm-tree, used for tying up plants and making mats and baskets etc.; this tree *Raphia ruffia*. [Malagasy]

raffish *adj*. disreputable, rakish; tawdry. —**raffishness** *n*. [from *raff* = rubbish]

raffle *n*. a sale of articles by lottery, especially for charity. —*v.t.* to sell by a raffle. [originally = dice-game, from Old French *raf(f)le*]

Raffles /'ræfəlz/ Thomas Stamford 1781–1826. British colonial administrator, born in Jamaica. He served in the British East India Company, took part in the capture of Java from the Dutch in 1811, and while governor of Sumatra 1818–23 was responsible for the acquisition and founding of Singapore 1819.

rafflesia *n*. or **stinking corpse lily** any parasitic plant without stems of the genus *Rafflesia*, family Rafflesiaceae, native to Malaysia, Indonesia, and Thailand. There are 14 species, several of which are endangered by logging of the forests where they grow; the fruit is used locally for medicine. The largest flowers in the world are produced by *R. arnoldiana*. About 1 m/3 ft across, they exude a smell of rotting flesh, which attracts flies to pollinate them.

Rafsanjani President of Iran Ali Akbar Rafsanjani. He is viewed as the most pragmatic and influential member of Iran's post-Khomeini collective leadership.

Rafsanjani /ræfsænʒɑ:'ni:/ Hojatoleslam Ali Akbar Hashemi 1934– . Iranian politician and cleric, president from 1989. After training as a mullah (Islamic teacher) under Ayatollah ◊Khomeini in Qom, he acquired considerable wealth through his construction business but kept in touch with his exiled mentor. When the Ayatollah returned after the revolution of 1979–80, Rafsanjani became the speaker of the Iranian parliament and, after Khomeini's death, state president and effective political leader.

raft /rɑ:ft/ n. a flat, floating structure of wood or fastened logs etc., used in water for transport or as an emergency boat. [from Old Norse]

Raft George. Stage name of George Ranft 1895–1980. US film actor, usually cast as a gangster (as in *Scarface* 1932). His later work included the comedy *Some Like it Hot* 1959.

rafter /'rɑ:ftə/ n. any of the sloping beams forming the framework of a roof. [Old English]

rag[1] n. 1. a torn, frayed or worn piece of woven material. 2. (in *plural*) old or torn or worn clothes. 3. (*collective*) rags used as a material for making paper, stuffing etc. 4. (*derogatory*) a newspaper. —**in rags**, much torn. **rag-and-bone man,** n. an itinerant dealer in old clothes, furniture etc. **ragbag** n. a bag for old rags; a miscellaneous collection. **rags to riches**, poverty to affluence. **rag trade**, (*colloquial*) the clothing business. [probably back-formation from *ragged*]

rag[2] n. 1. a programme of stunts, parades, and entertainment, staged by students to collect money for charity. 2. (*colloquial*) a prank. 3. (*slang*) a rowdy celebration; a noisy disorderly scene. —*v.t./i.* (-gg-) (*slang*) 1. to tease, to play rough jokes on. 2. to engage in rough play, to be riotous.

rag[3] n. a piece of ◊ragtime.

raga n. in Indian music, a scale of notes and style of ornament for music associated with a particular mood or time of day; the equivalent term in rhythm is **tala**. A choice of raga and tala forms the basis of improvised music; however, a written composition may also be based on (and called) a raga. [Sanskrit *rāga* = tone or colour]

ragamuffin /'rægəmʌfɪn/ n. a person in ragged dirty clothes. [from *rag*[1] with fanciful ending]

rage n. 1. fierce or violent anger; a fit of this. 2. the violent operation of a natural force. —*v.i.* 1. to be fiercely angry; to speak furiously or madly. 2. (of a wind or battle etc.) to be violent, to be at its height. —**be all the rage,** to be

temporarily very popular or fashionable. [from Old French from Latin *rabere* = rave]

ragged /'rægɪd/ adj. 1. torn, frayed. 2. wearing ragged clothes. 3. having a broken jagged outline or surface. 4. faulty, lacking finish or smoothness or uniformity. —**run a person ragged,** to exhaust or debilitate him or her. —**raggedly** adv., **raggedness** n. [from Old Norse = tufted]

raglan /'ræglən/ n. (usually *attributive*) a garment, especially an overcoat, with sleeves that continue to the neck and are joined to the body of the garment by sloping seams. —**raglan sleeve,** a sleeve of this kind. [from Lord *Raglan*]

Don't carry away that arm till I have taken off my ring.
Lord Raglan
(after his arm had been amputated following the Battle of Waterloo)

Raglan FitzRoy James Henry Somerset, 1st Baron Raglan 1788–1855. English general. He took part in the Peninsular War under Wellington, and lost his right arm at Waterloo. He commanded the British forces in the Crimean War from 1854.

Ragnarök /'ræfnərək/ or (German) **Götterdämmerung** in Norse mythology, the ultimate cataclysmic battle between gods and forces of evil from which a new order will come. [Icelandic = judgement of the gods]

ragout /'rægu:/ n. a highly seasoned stew of meat and vegetables. [from French *ragoûter* = revive taste of]

ragtag (and bobtail) riff-raff, disreputable people. [from *rag*[1]]

ragtime n. music with a syncopated melodic line and regularly accented accompaniment. It developed in the USA among black musicians in the late 19th century; it was influenced by folk tradition, minstrel shows, and marching bands, and was later incorporated into jazz. Scott ◊Joplin was a leading writer of ragtime pieces, called rags.

ragwort /'rægwɜ:t/ n. any wild plant of the genus *Senecio*, especially S. *jacobaea*, the common ragwort of Europe, with yellow flowers and ragged leaves.

Rahman /'rɑ:mən, mu:'dʒi:buə/ Sheik Mujibur 1921–1975. Bangladeshi Nationalist politician, president 1975. He was arrested several times for campaigning for the autonomy of East Pakistan. He won the elections in 1970 as leader of the Awami League but was again arrested when negotiations with the Pakistan government broke down. After the civil war of 1971, he became prime minister of the newly independent Bangladesh. He was presidential dictator Jan– Aug 1975, when he was assassinated.

Rahman Tunku Abdul 1903– . Malaysian politician, first prime minister of independent Malaya 1957–63 and of Malaysia 1963–70.

raï n. Algerian pop music developed in the 1970s from the Bedouin song form *melhoun*, using synthesizers and electronic drums.

raid n. 1. a sudden attack and withdrawal made by a military party or by ships or aircraft. 2. an attack made in order to steal or do harm. 3. a surprise visit by police etc. to arrest suspected persons or to seize illicit goods. —*v.t./i.* to make a raid (on). —**raider** n. [Scottish form of *road*]

Raikes /reɪks/ Robert 1735–1811. English printer who started the first Sunday school (for religious purposes) in Gloucester 1780 and who stimulated the growth of weekday voluntary 'ragged schools' for poor children.

rail[1] n. 1. a level or sloping bar or series of bars on which to hang things, as the top of banisters, as part of a fence, as a protection against contact or falling over etc. 2. a horizontal piece in the frame of a panelled door etc. 3. a steel bar or continuous line of bars laid on the ground usually as one of two forming a railway track. 3. railways as a means of transport. —*v.t.* 1. to furnish with a rail. 2. to enclose with rails. —**off the rails**, disorganized, out of order or control; crazy. [from Old French *reille* from Latin *regula* = rule]

rail[2] *v.i.* to complain or protest fiercely or abusively. [from French *railler*]

rail[3] n. a small wading bird of the family Rallidae including corncrakes, coots, moorhens, and gallinules. Many oceanic islands have their own species of rail, often flightless, such as the Guam rail and Auckland Island rail. Several of these species have declined sharply, usually because of introduced predators such as rats and cats. [from Old French *raille*]

railcar *n.* a self-propelled railway coach.

railhead *n.* **1.** the furthest point reached by a railway under construction. **2.** the point on a railway at which the road transport of goods begins or ends.

railing *n.* a fence or barrier made of rails.

raillery /'reɪlərɪ/ *n.* good-humoured ridicule. [from French *raillerie*]

railroad *n.* (*US*) a railway. —*v.t.* to rush or force into hasty action.

railway *n.* **1.** a track or set of tracks of steel rails for the passage of trains conveying passengers and goods. **2.** a system of transport using these; the organization and personnel required for its working. Following the work of English steam pioneers such as James ◊Watt, George ◊Stephenson built the first public steam railway, from Stockton to Darlington, in 1825. This heralded extensive railway building in Britain, continental Europe, and North America, providing a fast and economical means of transport and communication. After World War II, steam was replaced by electric and diesel engines. At the same time, the growth of road building, air services, and car ownership destroyed the supremacy of the railways. **3.** a track on which wheeled equipment is run.

railwayman *n.* (*plural* **railwaymen**) a male railway employee.

raiment /'reɪmənt/ *n.* (*archaic*) clothing. [from obsolete *arrayment*]

rain *n.* **1.** condensed moisture of the atmosphere falling in drops; a fall of these; (in *plural*) falls of rain, the season of these. **2.** falling liquid or solid particles or objects (*literal* or *figurative*); a rainlike descent of these. —*v.t./i.* **1.** to fall or send down as or like rain; to send down rain. **2.** to supply in large quantities. —**it rains** *or* **is raining**, rain falls or is falling. **rain off**, (especially in *passive*) to cause to be cancelled because of rain. **rain shadow**, a region in the lee of mountains where rainfall is low because it is sheltered from the prevailing winds. **rainwater** *n.* water that has fallen as rain, not obtained from wells etc. [Old English]

rainbow /'reɪnbəʊ/ *n.* an arch displaying the colours of the ◊spectrum formed in the sky by the refraction and dispersion of the Sun's rays in falling rain or in spray or mist. Its cause was discovered by Theodoric of Freiburg in the 14th century. —*adj.* many-coloured. —**rainbow trout**, a large trout *Salmo gairdnerii* originally of the Pacific coast of North America. [Old English]

rainbow coalition or **rainbow alliance** in politics, from the mid-1980s, a loose, left-of-centre grouping of disparate elements, encompassing sections of society that are traditionally politically underrepresented, such as nonwhite ethnic groups. Its aims include promoting minority rights and equal opportunities. 'Rainbow' is a translation of French *Arc-en-Ciel*, a name applied in 1984 to an alliance of 20 Euro-MPs from various countries who supported Green environmental policies. The term was taken up by Jesse Jackson's US presidential campaign, which sought to represent an alliance of nonwhite political groupings.

raincoat *n.* a waterproof or water-resistant coat.

raindrop *n.* a single drop of rain.

Raine /reɪn/ Kathleen 1908– . English poet. Her volumes of poetry include *Stone and Flower* 1943 and *The Lost Country* 1971, and reflect both the Northumberland landscape of her upbringing and the religious feeling which led her to the Roman Catholic Church in 1944.

rainfall *n.* a fall of rain; the quantity of rain falling within a given area in a given time.

rainforest *n.* dense forest found on or near the ◊equator where the climate is hot and wet. Over half the tropical rainforests are in Central and South America, the rest in SE Asia and Africa. Although covering approximately 8% of the Earth's land surface, they comprise about 50% of all growing wood on the planet, and harbour at least 40% of the Earth's species (plants and animals). Rainforests are being destroyed at an increasing rate as their valuable timber is harvested and land cleared for agriculture, causing problems of ◊deforestation, soil ◊erosion, and flooding. By 1990 50% of the world's rainforest had been removed.

Rainier III /'reɪnɪeɪ/ 1923– . Prince of Monaco from 1949. He was married to the US film actress Grace ◊Kelly.

rainy *adj.* (of the weather, a day, region etc.) in or on which rain is falling or much rain usually falls. —**rainy day**, a time of special need in the future. [Old English]

Rais /reɪ/ Gilles de 1404–1440. French marshal who fought alongside Joan of Arc. In 1440 he was hanged for the torture and murder of 140 children, but the court proceedings were irregular. He is the historical basis of the ◊Bluebeard character.

raise /reɪz/ *v.t.* **1.** to put or take into a higher position; to cause to rise or stand up or be vertical. **2.** to construct or build up. **3.** to levy, to collect, to manage to obtain. **3.** to cause to be heard or considered. **4.** to set going or bring into being; to breed (animals) or grow (crops). **5.** to bring up, to educate. **6.** to increase the amount, value, or strength of. **7.** to promote to a higher rank. **8.** to multiply (a quantity to a power). **9.** to cause (bread) to rise. **10.** (in a card-game) to bet more than (another player). **11.** to abandon or force an enemy to abandon (a siege etc.). **12.** to remove (a barrier). **13.** to cause (a ghost etc.) to appear. **14.** (*colloquial*) to find (a person etc. who is wanted). —*n.* an increase in a stake or bid; (*US*) an increase in salary. —**raise from the dead**, to restore to life. **raise a laugh**, to cause others to laugh. **raise one's eyebrows**, to look supercilious or shocked. **raise the wind**, to procure money for a purpose. [from Old Norse]

raisin /'reɪzən/ *n.* a partially dried grape. used for eating, baking, and the confectionery trade. The chief kinds are the common raisin, the sultana or seedless raisin, and the currant. They are produced in the Mediterranean area, California, and Australia. [from Old French from Latin *racemus* grape-bunch]

raison d'être /reɪz 'detr/ the purpose or reason that accounts for or justifies or originally caused a thing's existence. [French]

raj /rɑːdʒ/ *n.* British sovereignty in India. [Hindi = reign]

raja /'rɑːdʒə/ *n.* or **rajah** (*historical*) an Indian king or prince; a noble or petty dignitary. [from Hindi from Sanskrit *rājan* = king]

Rajasthan /rɑːdʒə'stɑːn/ state of NW India; **area** 342,200 sq km/132,089 sq mi; **capital** Jaipur; **physical** includes the larger part of the Thar Desert; **products** oilseed, cotton, sugar, asbestos, copper, textiles, cement, glass; **population** (1981) 34,103,000; **language** Rajasthani, Hindi; **history** formed 1948; enlarged 1956.

Rajneesh meditation /rɑːdʒ'niːʃ/ a system of meditation based on the teachings of the Indian Shree Rajneesh (born Chaadra Mohan Jain), established in the early 1970s. Until 1989 he called himself **Bhagwan** (Hindi = God). His followers, who number about half a million worldwide, regard themselves as Sannyas, or Hindu ascetics; they wear orange robes and carry a string of prayer beads. They are not expected to observe any specific prohibitions, but are to be guided by their instincts.

rake[1] *n.* an implement of a pole with a toothed cross-bar at the end for drawing together hay etc. or smoothing loose soil or gravel; an implement like this, e.g. to draw in money at a gaming-table. —*v.t./i.* **1.** to collect or gather (as) with a rake; to make tidy or smooth with a rake; to use a rake. **2.** to search thoroughly, to ransack. **3.** to direct gunfire along (a line) from end to end; to direct one's eyes or a camera thus. **4.** to scratch or scrape. —**rake in**, (*colloquial*) to amass (profits etc.). **rake-off** *n.* (*colloquial*) a commission or share, especially in a disreputable deal. **rake up**, to revive (unwelcome memories etc.). [Old English]

rake[2] *n.* a dissipated or immoral man of fashion. [from *rakehell*]

rake[3] *v.t./i.* to set or be set at a sloping angle; (of a mast or funnel) to incline from the perpendicular towards the stern. —*n.* a raking position or build; the amount by which a thing rakes.

rakish /'reɪkɪʃ/ *adj.* like a rake (**rake**[2]); dashing, jaunty. —**rakishly** *adv.*, **rakishness** *n.*

Raleigh /'rɔːlɪ/ or **Ralegh** Walter *c.*1552–1618. English adventurer. He made colonizing and exploring voyages to North America 1584–87 and South America in 1595, and naval attacks on Spanish ports. His aggressive actions against Spanish interests brought him into conflict with the pacific James I. He was imprisoned for treason 1603–16 and executed on his return from an unsuccessful final expedition to South America.

'Tis a sharp remedy, but a sure one for all ills.
Walter Raleigh
(feeling the edge of the axe before his execution)

---

rallentando /ˌrælənˈtændəʊ/ *adv.* in music, with a gradual decrease of speed. —*n.* (*plural* **rallentandos**) a musical passage to be played this way. [Italian]
rally[1] /ˈrælɪ/ *v.t./i.* **1.** to bring or come together as support
or for united effort. **2.** to bring or come together again after
a rout or dispersion. **3.** to rouse or revive (courage etc.); to
recover after an illness; (of share-prices etc.) to increase
after a fall. —*n.* **1.** rallying, being rallied. **2.** a mass meeting
of supporters or persons having a common interest. **3.** a
competition for motor vehicles, usually over public roads.
4. a series of strokes in tennis etc. before a point is decided.
[from French *rallier*]
rally[2] *v.t.* to subject to good-humoured ridicule. [from
French *railler*]
ram *n.* **1.** an uncastrated male sheep. **2.** the Ram, the
constellation or sign of the zodiac Aries. **3.** a battering-ram.
4. the falling weight of a pile-driving machine. **5.** a hydraulic
water-raising or lifting machine. —*v.t.* (**-mm-**) **1.** to force or
squeeze into place by pressure; to beat or drive (*down* or *in*
etc.) by heavy blows. **2.** to strike and push heavily, to crash
against. —**ram-jet** *n.* a simple form of jet engine in which
the air used for combustion is compressed solely by the
forward motion of the engine. —**rammer** *n.* [Old English]
RAM abbreviation of random-access memory. In computing,
a form of storage frequently used for the internal ◊memory
of microcomputers. It is made up of a collection of ◊inte-
grated circuits (chips). Unlike ◊ROM, RAM can be both
read from and written to by the computer, but its contents are lost when the power is switched off. Today's
microcomputers have up to eight megabytes of RAM.
Rama /ˈrɑːmə/ an incarnation of ◊Vishnu, the supreme
spirit of Hinduism. He is the hero of the epic poem the
Rāmāyana, and he is regarded as an example of morality and virtue.
Ramadan /ˌræməˈdɑːn / *n.* the ninth month of the
lunar calendar of Islam. Throughout Ramadan a strict
fast is observed during the hours of daylight; Muslims are
encouraged to read the whole Koran in commemoration of
the Night of Power (which falls during the month) when, it is
believed, Muhammad first received his revelations from the
angel Gabriel. [from Arabic *ramada* = be hot]
Ramakrishna /ˌrɑːməˈkrɪʃnə/ 1834–1886. Hindu sage,
teacher, and mystic (one dedicated to achieving oneness
with or a direct experience of God or some force beyond the
normal world). Ramakrishna claimed that mystical experience was the ultimate aim of religions, and that all religions
which led to this goal were equally valid.
Rāmāyana /rɑːˈmaɪənə/ a Sanskrit epic of about 300 BC,
in which Rama (an incarnation of the god Vishnu) and
his friend Hanuman (the monkey chieftain) strive to
recover Rama's wife, Sita, abducted by demon king
Ravana.
Rambert /ˈrɒmbeə/ Marie. Adopted name of Cyvia
Rambam 1888–1982. British ballet dancer and teacher
born in Warsaw, Poland, who became a British citizen in
1918. One of the major innovative and influential figures in
modern ballet, she was with the Diaghilev ballet 1912–13,
opened the Rambert School in 1920, and in 1926 founded the
Ballet Rambert, which she directed (renamed Rambert
Dance Company 1987).
ramble *v.i.* **1.** to walk for pleasure, with or without a
definite route. **2.** to talk or write disconnectedly. —*n.* a
walk taken for pleasure.
rambler *n.* **1.** one who rambles. **2.** a vigorously growing
and straggling climbing rose.
rambling *adj.* that rambles; (of a house, street etc.)
irregularly arranged; (of a plant) straggling, climbing.
Ram Das /rɑːm dɑːs/ 1534–1581. Indian religious
leader, fourth guru (teacher) of Sikhism 1574–81, who
founded the Sikh holy city of Amritsar.
Rameau /ræˈməʊ/ Jean-Philippe 1683–1764. French
organist and composer. He wrote *Treatise on Harmony*
1722 and his varied works include keyboard and vocal music
and many operas, such as *Castor and Pollux* 1737.

Rambert *As teacher and promoter to many dancers,
choreographers, and stage designers, Marie Rambert was one
of modern ballet's most influential figures.*

ramekin /ˈræmɪkɪn/ *n.* a small dish for baking and serving
an individual portion of food; food served in this. [from
French *ramequin*]
ramify /ˈræmɪfaɪ/ *v.t./i.* **1.** to form branches or subdivisions or offshoots, to branch out. **2.** (usually in *passive*)
to cause to branch out; to arrange in a branching manner.
—**ramification** /-fɪˈkeɪʃən/ *n.* [from French from Latin
ramus = branch]
Ramillies, Battle of /ˈræmɪliz/ battle in which the British
commander Marlborough defeated the French army on 23
May 1706, during the War of the ◊Spanish Succession, at a
village in Brabant, Belgium, 21 km/13 mi N of Namur.
ramjet *n.* a simple ◊jet engine used in some guided missiles. It only comes into operation at high speeds. Air is
then 'rammed' into the combustion chamber, into which fuel
is sprayed and ignited.
Ram Mohun Roy /rɑːm ˈməʊhʊn ˈrɔɪ/ 1770–1833.
Indian religious reformer, founder 1830 of Brahma Samaj,
a mystic cult.
ramp[1] *n.* **1.** a slope joining two levels of ground or floor etc.
2. movable stairs for entering or leaving an aircraft. —*v.t./i.*
1. to furnish or build with a ramp. **2.** to take a threatening
posture. **3.** to rampage. [from French *rampe* (Old French
ramper = creep)]
ramp[2] *n.* (slang) a swindle, a racket, especially one
involving exorbitant prices. —*v.t./i.* (slang) to engage in
a ramp; to subject (a person etc.) to a ramp.
rampage /ræmˈpeɪdʒ/ *v.i.* to rush wildly or violently
about; to rage, to storm. —/ˈræmpeɪdʒ/ *n.* wild or violent behaviour. —**on the rampage**, rampaging. —**ram-
pageous** /ræmˈpeɪdʒəs/ *adj.*
rampant /ˈræmpənt/ *adj.* **1.** (in heraldry, especially
of a lion) standing on the left hind foot with forefeet
raised, right higher than left, facing dexter (right). **2.**
unrestrained, flourishing excessively. **3.** violent or extravagant in action or opinion. —**rampancy** *n.* [from Old
French]
rampart /ˈræmpɑːt/ *n.* **1.** a defensive wall with a broad
top and usually a stone parapet; a walkway on this.
2. a defence, a protection. [from French *remparer* =
fortify]
Ramphal /ˈræmfɑːl/ Shridath Surendranath ('Sonny')
1928– . Guyanese politician. He was minister of foreign
affairs and justice 1972–75 and secretary-general of the
British Commonwealth 1975–90.
Rampling /ˈræmplɪŋ/ Charlotte 1945– . British actress,
whose sometimes controversial films include *Georgy Girl*
1966, *The Night Porter/Il Portiere di Notti* 1974, and *Farewell My Lovely* 1975.

ramrod /'ræmrɒd/ *n.* **1.** a rod for ramming down the charge of a muzzle-loaded firearm. **2.** a thing that is very straight or rigid.

Ramsay /'ræmzi/ Allan 1686–1758. Scottish poet. He published *The Tea-Table Miscellany* 1724–37 and *The Evergreen* 1724, collections of ancient and modern Scottish song, including revivals of the work of such poets as Dunbar and Henryson.

Ramsay Allan 1713–1784. Scottish portrait painter. After studying in Edinburgh and Italy, he established himself as a portraitist in London and became painter to George III in 1760. His portraits include *The Artist's Wife* about 1755 (National Gallery, Edinburgh).

Ramsay William 1852–1916. Scottish chemist who, with Lord Rayleigh, discovered argon in 1894. In 1895 Ramsay produced helium and in 1898, in cooperation with Morris Travers, identified neon, krypton, and xenon. In 1903, with Frederick Soddy, he noted the transmutation of radium into helium, which led to the discovery of the density and relative atomic mass of radium. He was awarded the Nobel Prize for Chemistry in 1904.

Ramses /'ræmɪsiːz/ or **Rameses** 11 kings of ancient Egypt, including:

Ramses II or **Rameses II** king of Egypt about 1304–1236 BC, the son of Seti I. He campaigned successfully against the Hittites, and built two rock temples at ◊Abu Simbel in Upper Egypt.

Ramses III or **Rameses III** king of Egypt about 1200–1168 BC. He won a naval victory over the Philistines and other Middle Eastern peoples, and asserted his control over Palestine.

ramshackle /'ræmʃækəl/ *adj.* tumbledown, rickety. [from past participle of obsolete *ransackle*]

ran past of **run**.

ranch /rɑːntʃ/ *n.* **1.** a cattle-breeding establishment especially in the USA and Canada. **2.** a farm where certain other animals are bred. —*v.i.* to farm on a ranch. —**rancher** *n.* [from Spanish *rancho* = persons eating together]

rancid /'rænsɪd/ *adj.* smelling or tasting like rank stale fat. —**rancidity** /-'sɪdɪti/ *n.* [from Latin *rancidus*]

rancour /'ræŋkə/ *n.* inveterate bitterness, malignant hate. —**rancorous** *adj.*, **rancorously** *adv.* [from Old French from Latin]

rand /rænd, rɑːnt/ *n.* the currency unit of South Africa. [from the *Rand*, gold-field near Johannesburg]

R & D abbreviation of research and development.

random /'rændəm/ *adj.* made or done etc. without method or conscious choice. —**at random**, without aim or purpose or principle. **random access**, (in computers, usually *attributive*) a memory or file all parts of which are directly accessible so that it need not be processed sequentially. —**randomly** *adv.* [from Old French *randon* = great speed]

random number one of a series of numbers with no detectable pattern used in ◊computer simulation and ◊computer games. It is impossible for an ordinary computer to generate true random numbers, but various techniques are available for obtaining pseudo-random numbers, these being close enough to true randomness for most purposes.

randy *adj.* lustful, eager for sexual gratification; —**randily** *adv.*, **randiness** *n.*

ranee /'rɑːni/ *n.* a raja's wife or widow. [from Hindi from Sanskrit *rājni*feminine of *rājan* = king]

rang past of ◊**ring**[2].

range /reɪndʒ/ *n.* **1.** the area over which a thing is found or has effect or relevance, scope. **2.** the region between limits of variation; such limits. **3.** the distance attainable or to be covered by a gun or missile etc.; the distance that can be covered by a vehicle or aircraft without refuelling; the distance between a camera and the subject to be photographed. **4.** a row or series, especially of mountains. **5.** an open or enclosed area with targets for shooting. **6.** a fireplace with ovens and hotplates for cooking. **7.** a large open area for grazing or hunting. —*v.t.i.* **1.** to place in a row or rows or in a specified arrangement. **2.** to rove or wander. **3.** to reach; to lie; to spread out; to be found over a specified area; to vary between limits. **4.** to traverse in all directions. —**rangefinder** *n.* an instrument to determine the distance of an object for shooting or photography. [from Old French = row]

ranger /'reɪndʒə/ *n.* **1.** a keeper of a royal or national park or forest. **2.** a member of a body of mounted troops. **3. Ranger** a senior Guide.

Rangoon /ræŋ'guːn/ former name (until 1989) of ◊Yangon, capital of Myanmar.

rangy /'reɪndʒɪ/ *adj.* tall and lanky.

Ranjit Singh /'rændʒɪt 'sɪŋ/ 1780–1839. Indian maharajah. He succeeded his father as a minor Sikh leader 1792, and created a Sikh army that conquered Kashmir and the Punjab. In alliance with the British, he established himself as 'Lion of the Punjab', ruler of the strongest of the independent Indian states.

rank[1] /ræŋk/ *n.* **1.** a place in a scale of quality or value etc.; a position or grade. **2.** high social position. **3.** a line of people or things. **4.** a place where taxis stand to await hire. —*v.t.i.* **1.** to have a specified rank or place. **2.** to assign a rank to, to classify. **3.** to arrange in a rank. —**close ranks**, to maintain solidarity. **rank and file**, ordinary undistinguished people. **the ranks**, common soldiers. [from Old French]

rank[2] *adj.* **1.** too luxuriant, coarse; choked with or apt to produce weeds or excessive foliage. **2.** foul-smelling; loathsome, corrupt. **3.** flagrant, unmistakably bad, complete. —**rankly** *adv.*, **rankness** *n.* [Old English]

Rank Joseph Arthur 1888–1972. British film magnate. Having entered films in 1933 to promote the Methodist cause, he proceeded to gain control of much of the industry through takeovers and forming new businesses. The Rank Organization still owns the Odeon chain of cinemas and Pinewood Studios, although film is now a minor part of its activities.

Ranke /'ræŋkə/ Leopold von 1795–1886. German historian whose quest for objectivity in history had great impact on the discipline. His attempts to explain 'how it really was' dominated both German and outside historical thought until 1914 and beyond.

rankle *v.i.* (of envy or disappointment etc. or their cause) to cause persistent annoyance or resentment. [from Old French = festering sore, from Latin *dra(cu)nculus* diminutive of *draco* = serpent]

ransack /'rænsæk/ *v.t.* **1.** to pillage or plunder. **2.** to search thoroughly. [from Old Norse *rann* = house and *-saka* = seek]

ransom /'rænsəm/ *n.* a sum of money or other payment demanded or paid for the release of a prisoner; liberation of a prisoner in return for this. —*v.t.* **1.** to buy the freedom or restoration of, to redeem. **2.** to hold to ransom. **3.** to release for a ransom. —**hold to ransom**, to hold (a captive) and demand a ransom for his release; to demand concessions from (a person etc.) by threatening some damaging action. [from Old French from Latin = redemption]

Ransome /'rænsəm/ Arthur 1884–1967. English journalist (correspondent in Russia for the *Daily News* during World War I and the Revolution) and writer of adventure stories for children, such as *Swallows and Amazons* 1930 and *Peter Duck* 1932.

rant *v.t.i.* to use bombastic language; to declaim, to recite theatrically; to preach noisily. —*n.* a piece of ranting. [from Dutch]

ranunculus /rə'nʌŋkjʊləs/ *n.* (*plural* **ranunculuses**) a plant of the genus *Ranunculus*, including the buttercup. [Latin originally diminutive of *rana* = frog]

Rao /rau/ Raja 1909– . Indian writer, educated in France. He wrote about Indian independence from the perspective of a village in S India in *Kanthapura* 1938 and later, in *The Serpent and the Rope* 1960, about a young cosmopolitan intellectual seeking enlightenment. Collections of stories include *The Cow of the Barricades* 1947 and *The Policeman and the Rose* 1978.

Raoult /rɑː'uː/ Francois 1830–1901. French chemist. In 1882, while working at the University of Grenoble, Raoult formulated one of the basic laws of chemistry. **Raoult's law** enables the relative molecular mass of a substance to be determined by noting how much of it is required to depress the freezing point of a solvent by a certain amount.

rap[1] *n.* **1.** a quick sharp blow. **2.** a knock, a sharp tapping sound. **3.** (*slang*) blame, punishment. **4.** a rhythmic recitation to music; see ◊rap music. —*v.t.i.* (**-pp-**) **1.** to strike quickly and sharply. **2.** to knock, to make the sound of a rap. **3.** to criticize adversely. —**rap out**, to utter abruptly; to express by raps.

rap² *n.* a small amount, the least bit. [originally = counterfeit halfpenny, abbreviation of Irish *ropaire*]

rapacious /rəˈpeɪʃəs/ *adj.* grasping, extortionate; predatory. —**rapaciously** *adv.*, **rapacity** /rəˈpæsɪtɪ/ *n.* [from Latin *rapere* = snatch]

Rapa Nui /ˈrɑːpə ˈnuːi/ another name for ◊Easter Island, an island in the Pacific.

rape¹ *n.* **1.** the act or crime of having sexual intercourse with a person (usually a woman) without freely given consent. **2.** violent assault or interference. —*v.t.* to commit rape on. [from Anglo-French from Latin *rapere* = snatch]

rape² *n.* a plant *Brassica napus* grown as fodder and for its seed from which oil is made. [from Latin *rapum*, *rapa* = turnip]

rape³ *n.* the refuse of grapes that is left after wine-making. [from French from Latin *raspa*]

Raphael /ˈræfeɪəl ˈsænziəʊ/ (Raffaello Sanzio) 1483–1520. Italian painter, one of the greatest of the High Renaissance, active in Perugia, Florence, and Rome (from 1508), where he painted frescoes in the Vatican and for secular patrons. His religious and mythological scenes are harmoniously composed; his portraits enhance the character of his sitters and express dignity. Many of his designs were engraved. Much of his later work was the product of his studio.

rapid /ˈræpɪd/ *adj.* **1.** quick, swift; acting or completed in a short time. **2.** (of a slope) descending steeply. —*n.* (usually in *plural*) a steep descent in a river-bed with a swift current. —**rapidity** /rəˈpɪdɪtɪ/ *n.*, **rapidly** *adv.* [from Latin *rapidus*]

Rapid Deployment Force former name (until 1983) of US ◊Central Command, a military strike force.

rapier /ˈreɪpɪə/ *n.* a light, slender, double-edged sword used for thrusting.

rapine /ˈræpaɪn/ *n.* plundering. [from Old French or Latin *rapina* (*rapere* = seize)]

rapist /ˈreɪpɪst/ *n.* one who commits rape.

rap music a rapid, rhythmic chant over a prerecorded repetitive backing track. Rap emerged in New York from 1979 as part of the ◊hip-hop culture, although the usually macho, swaggering lyrics have roots in ritual boasts and insults.

rapport /ræˈpɔː/ *n.* an understanding relationship or communication between people. [French *rapporter*, from Latin *portare* = carry]

rapprochement /ræˈprɒʃmɑ̃/ *n.* resumption of harmonious relations, especially between states. [French]

rapscallion /ræpˈskæliən/ *n.* a rascal. [earlier *rascallion*]

rapt *adj.* fully intent or absorbed, enraptured; carried away with emotion or lofty thought. [from Latin *raptus* past participle of *rapere* = seize]

raptorial /ræpˈtɔːrɪəl/ *adj.* predatory. —*n.* a predatory animal or bird. [from Latin *raptor* = ravisher, plunderer]

rapture /ˈræptʃə/ *n.* ecstatic delight; (in *plural*) great pleasure or enthusiasm, the expression of this. —**rapturous** *adj.*, **rapturously** *adv.* [obsolete French or from Latin *raptura*]

rare¹ *adj.* **1.** seldom done or found or occurring, very uncommon, unusual. **2.** exceptionally good. **3.** of less than usual density. —**rare earth**, any of a class of 17 chemically similar metallic elements or their oxides, including scandium, yttrium, and the lanthanides (the term is sometimes applied to the lanthanides alone). —**rareness** *n.* [from Latin *rarus*]

rare² *adj.* (of meat) underdone. [Old English]

rarebit /ˈreəbɪt/ *n.* melted cheese on toast. [alteration of (Welsh) *rabbit*]

rarefy /ˈreərɪfaɪ/ *v.t./i.* **1.** to make or become less solid or dense. **2.** to refine. **3.** to make (an idea etc.) subtle. —**rarefaction** /-ˈfækʃən/ *n.* [from Old French or Latin *rarus* = rare and *facere* = make]

rare gas alternative name for ◊inert gas.

rarely *adv.* seldom, not often; exceptionally.

raring /ˈreərɪŋ/ *adj.* (*colloquial*) enthusiastic, eager (*to go* etc.). [participle of *rare*, dialect variant of *rear²*]

rarity /ˈreərɪtɪ/ *n.* **1.** rareness. **2.** an uncommon thing. [from French or Latin]

rascal /ˈrɑːskəl/ *n.* a dishonest or mischievous person. —**rascally** *adj.* [from Old French *rascaille* = rabble]

rash¹ *adj.* acting or done without due consideration of the

possible consequences or risks. —**rashly** *adv.*, **rashness** *n.* [from Old English = Middle Dutch *rasch*]

rash² *n.* **1.** an eruption of spots or patches on the skin. **2.** a sudden widespread onset. [compare Old French *ra(s)che* = eruptive sores]

Rashdun /ræʃˈduːn/ the first four caliphs (heads) of Islam: Abu Bakr, Umar, Uthman, and Ali. [rightly guided ones]

rasher *n.* a thin slice of bacon or ham.

rasp /rɑːsp/ *n.* **1.** a coarse file having separate teeth. **2.** a grating sound. —*v.t./i.* **1.** to scrape with a rasp; to scrape roughly. **2.** to make a grating sound; to say gratingly. **3.** to grate upon (a person or his feelings). [from Old French *raspe*, *rasper*]

raspberry /ˈrɑːzbərɪ/ *n.* **1.** an edible sweet, usually red, conical berry; the prickly cane plant *Rubus idaeus* of the Rosaceae family, bearing this. **2.** (*slang*) a sound expressing derision or dislike. —**raspberry-cane** *n.* a raspberry plant.

Rasputin /ræsˈpjuːtɪn/ Grigory Efimovich 1871–1916. Siberian Eastern Orthodox mystic and wandering 'holy man', the illiterate son of a peasant. He acquired influence over the tsarina Alexandra, wife of ◊Nicholas II, because of her faith in his power to ease her son's suffering from haemophilia, and he was able to make political and ecclesiastical appointments. His abuse of power and his notorious debauchery (reputedly including the tsarina) led to his being murdered by a group of nobles who, when poison had no effect, dumped him in the river Neva after shooting him. [Russian = dissolute]

Rasta /ˈræstə/ *n.* a Rastafarian. [abbreviation]

Rastafarian /ræstəˈfeərɪən/ *adj.* of the Rastafari sect. —*n.* a member of this sect. [from the title and name *Ras Tafari* Amharic *ras* = chief by which Haile Selassie was known from 1916 until his accession in 1930]

Rastafarianism *n.* a religion originating in the West Indies, based on the ideas of Marcus ◊Garvey, who called on black people to return to Africa and set up a black-governed country there. When Haile Selassie (Ras Tafari, was crowned emperor of Ethiopia in 1930, this was seen as a fulfilment of prophecy and Rastafarians acknowledged him as the Messiah, the incarnation of God (**Jah**). The use of ganja (marijuana) is a sacrament. There are no churches. There were about one million Rastafarians by 1990.

rat *n.* **1.** a rodent of the genus *Rattus* like a large mouse; a similar rodent, particularly the large members of the family Muridae. They usually have pointed snouts and scaly tails. **2.** (*colloquial*) an unpleasant or treacherous person. —*v.i.* (-tt-) **1.** to hunt or kill rats. **2.** to act as an informer. —**rat on**, to desert or betray (a person). **rat race**, a fiercely competitive struggle, especially to maintain one's position in work or life. **smell a rat**, to begin to suspect treachery etc. [Old English and Old French]

ratafia /rætəˈfiːə/ *n.* **1.** a liqueur flavoured with almonds or fruit-kernels. **2.** a small almond biscuit. [French]

ratatouille /rɑːtɑːˈtuːi/ *n.* a Provençal dish of vegetables (chiefly aubergines, tomatoes, onions, and peppers) stewed in oil. [French dialect]

ratchet /ˈrætʃɪt/ *n.* **1.** a set of teeth on the edge of a bar or wheel with a catch allowing motion in one direction only. **2.** (in full **ratchet-wheel**) a wheel with a rim so toothed. [from French *rochet* = lance-head]

rate¹ *n.* **1.** a stated numerical proportion between two sets of things (the second usually expressed as unity), especially as a measure of amount or degree or as the basis of calculating an amount or value. **2.** a fixed or appropriate charge, cost, or value; a measure of this. **3.** rapidity of movement or change. **4.** class, rank. **5.** (until 1989–90) an assessment by a local authority levied on the value of buildings and land owned or leased; (in *plural*) the amount payable. —*v.t./i.* **1.** to estimate or assign the worth or value of. **2.** to consider, to regard as; to rank or be regarded in a specified way. **3.** to subject to the payment of a local rate; to value for the assessment of rates. **4.** (*US*) to be worthy of, to deserve. —**at any rate**, in any case, whatever happens. **at this rate**, if this example is typical. [from Old French from Latin *rata* (*rēri* = reckon)]

rate² *v.t./i.* to scold angrily.

rateable /ˈreɪtəbəl/ *adj.* liable to rates. —**rateable value**, the value at which a house etc. was assessed for rates.

rate of reaction the speed at which a chemical reaction proceeds. It is usually expressed in terms of the concentration (usually in ◊moles per litre) of a reactant consumed or product formed in unit time; so the units would be moles per litre per second (mol l^{-1} s^{-1}). The rate of a reaction is affected by the concentration of the reactants, the temperature of the reactants, and the presence of a ◊catalyst. If the reaction is entirely in the gas state, pressure affects the rate, and, for solids, the particle size.

ratepayer *n.* a person liable to pay rates.

rates *n.* in the UK, tax that was levied on residential, industrial, and commercial property by local authorities to cover their expenditure (see ◊county council, ◊local government). The rate for a household with several wage-earners may be identical with that for a single person of retirement age, and rebates are given to ratepayers whose income falls below a certain level. The Conservative government (1979–) curbed high-spending councils by cutting the government supplementary grant aid to them and limiting the level of rate that could be levied (**ratecapping**), and in 1989–90 replaced the rate with a **community charge** or ◊poll tax on each individual. In Jan 1990 the UK government revised all valuations of business property in England and Wales as part of its new Uniform Business Rate. All commercial property users pay 34.8% of the valuation. Rates were revalued proportionally higher in the south than the north.

rate support grant in the UK 1967–90, an amount of money made available annually by central government to supplement rates as a source of income for local government; replaced by a revenue support grant (see ◊poll tax).

rath /rɑ:θ/ *n.* (in Ireland and SW Wales) a small circular hillfort. [Irish]

Rathbone /ˈræθbəʊn/ (Philip St John) Basil 1892–1967. South African-born British character actor, one of the cinema's great villains; he also played Sherlock Holmes (the fictional detective created by Arthur Conan Doyle) in several films. He worked mainly in Hollywood, in films such as *The Adventures of Robin Hood* 1938 and *The Hound of the Baskervilles* 1939.

Rathenau /ˈrɑːtənaʊ/ Walther 1867–1922. German politician. He was a leading industrialist and was appointed economic director during World War I, developing a system of economic planning in combination with capitalism. After the war he founded the Democratic Party, and became foreign minister in 1922. The same year he signed the Rapallo Treaty of Friendship with the USSR, cancelling German and Soviet counterclaims for indemnities for World War I, and soon after was assassinated by right-wing fanatics.

rather /ˈrɑːðə/ *adv.* 1. by preference, more willingly. 2. more truly; as the more likely alternative. 3. more precisely. 4. slightly, to some extent. 5. (*colloquial*, in an answer) most certainly. —**had rather,** would rather. [from Old English = earlier]

ratify /ˈrætɪfaɪ/ *v.t.* to confirm or accept (an agreement made in one's name) by formal consent, signature etc. —**ratification** /-fɪˈkeɪʃən/ *n.* [from Old French from Latin *ratificare*]

rating[1] /ˈreɪtɪŋ/ *n.* 1. a place in a rank or class. 2. the estimated standing of a person as regards credit etc. 3. a noncommissioned sailor. 4. the amount fixed as a local rate. 5. the relative popularity of a broadcast programme as determined by the estimated size of the audience.

rating[2] *n.* an angry reprimand.

ratio /ˈreɪʃɪəʊ/ *n.* (*plural* **ratios**) the quantitative relation between two similar magnitudes determined by the number of times one contains the other. [Latin]

ratiocinate /rætɪˈɒsɪneɪt/ *v.i.* to reason, especially using syllogisms. —**ratiocination** /-ˈneɪʃən/ *n.* [from Latin]

ration /ˈræʃən/ *n.* an allowance or portion of food or clothing etc., especially an official allowance in time of shortage; (usually in *plural*) a fixed daily allowance of food in the armed forces etc. —*v.t.* to limit (persons or provisions) to a fixed ration; to share (food etc.) in fixed quantities. [French, from Italian or Spanish from Latin *ratio* = reckoning, ratio]

rational /ˈræʃənl/ *adj.* 1. of or based on reason; sane, sensible. 2. endowed with reason. 3. rejecting what is unreasonable or cannot be tested by reason in religion or custom. 4. (of a quantity or ratio) expressible as a ratio of integers; see ◊rational number. —**rationality** /-ˈnælɪtɪ/ *n.*, **rationally** *adv.* [from Latin]

rationale /ræʃəˈnɑːl/ *n.* a fundamental reason; a logical basis. [neuter of Latin *rationalis*]

rationalism /ˈræʃənəlɪzəm/ *n.* 1. the practice of explaining the supernatural in religion in a way that is consonant with reason, or of treating reason as the ultimate authority in religion as elsewhere. 2. the theory that self-evident propositions deduced by reason are the sole basis of all knowledge (disregarding experience of the senses). It is usually contrasted with empiricism and sensationalism. —**rationalist** *n.*, **rationalistic** /-ˈlɪstɪk/ *adj.*

rationalize *v.t.* 1. to offer a reasoned but specious explanation of (behaviour or an attitude). 2. to make logical and consistent. 3. to make (an industry) more efficient by reorganizing it to reduce or eliminate waste. 4. to explain by rationalism. —**rationalization** /-ˈzeɪʃən/ *n.*

rationalized unit a unit for which the defining equation conforms to the geometry of the system. Equations involving circular symmetry contain the factor 2π; those involving spherical symmetry 4π. ◊SI units are rationalized, ◊c.g.s. units are not.

rational number in mathematics, any number that can be expressed as an exact fraction (with a denominator not equal to 0), that is, as $a \div b$ where a and b are integers. For example, 2, 1/4, 15/4, $-3/5$ are all rational numbers, whereas π (which represents the constant 3.141592...) is not. Numbers such as π are called ◊irrational numbers.

rationing *n.* a restricted allowance of provisions or other supplies in time of war or shortage. Food rationing was introduced in Germany and in Britain during World War I. During World War II food rationing, organized by the government, began in Britain in 1940. Each person was issued with a ration book of coupons. Bacon, butter, and sugar were restricted, followed by other goods including sweets, petrol, clothing, soap, and furniture. Some people tried to buy extra on the black market. In 1946 the world wheat shortage led to bread rationing. Clothes rationing ended in Britain in 1949. During the Suez crisis of 1956 petrol rationing was introduced in Britain.

ratite *n.* a flightless bird with a breastbone without the keel to which flight muscles are attached. Examples are ostrich, rhea, emu, cassowary, and kiwi.

ratline /ˈrætlɪn/ *n.* or **ratlin** any of the small lines fastened across a sailing ship's shrouds like ladder rungs.

rat-tail *n.* or **grenadier** fish of the family Macrouridae. They have stout heads and bodies, and long tapering tails. They are common in deep oceanic waters on the continental slopes. Some species have a light-emitting organ in front of the anus.

rattan /rəˈtæn/ *n.* 1. a palm of the genus *Calamus* etc. with long, thin, many-jointed pliable stems. 2. a piece of rattan stem used as a cane etc. [from Malay]

rat-tat /ˈrætˈtæt/ *n.* a rapping sound, especially of a knocker. [imitative]

Rattigan /ˈrætɪɡən/ Terence 1911–1977. English playwright. His play *Ross* 1960 was based on T E Lawrence (Lawrence of Arabia). Rattigan's work ranges from the comedy *French Without Tears* 1936 to the psychological intensity of *The Winslow Boy* 1945. Other plays include *The Browning Version* 1948 and *Separate Tables* 1954.

A novelist may lose his readers for a few pages; a playwright never dares lose his audience for a minute.

Terence Rattigan
New York Journal American 1956

---

rattle *v.t./i.* 1. to make or cause to make a rapid succession of short, sharp, hard sounds; to cause such sounds by shaking something. 2. to move or travel with a rattling noise. 3. (usually with *off*) to say or recite rapidly; (usually with *on*) to talk in a lively thoughtless way. 4. (*slang*) to disconcert, to alarm. —*n.* 1. a rattling sound. 2. a device or toy etc. for making a rattling sound.

Rattle /ˈrætl/ Simon 1955– . English conductor. Principal conductor of the Birmingham Symphony Orchestra from 1980, he is renowned for his eclectic range and for interpretations of Mahler and Sibelius.

rattlesnake *n.* a snake of the North American genus *Crotalus* and related genera, distinguished by the horny, flat rings of the tail, which rattle when vibrated as a warning to attackers. They can grow to 2.5 m/8 ft long. The venom injected by some rattlesnakes can be fatal.

rattlesnake

*diamond backed
rattle snake*

rattletrap *n.* a rickety old vehicle etc.
rattling *adj.* brisk, vigorous. —*adv.* remarkably.
ratty *adj.* **1.** relating to or infested with rats. **2.** (*slang*) irritable, angry.
raucous /ˈrɔːkəs/ *adj.* harsh-sounding, loud and hoarse. —**raucously** *adv.*, **raucousness** *n.* [from Latin *raucus*]
raunchy /ˈrɔːntʃɪ/ *adj.* coarse, earthy; boisterous.
Raunkiaer system /ˈraʊŋkiə/ a method of classification devised by the Danish ecologist Christen Raunkiaer (1860–1938) whereby plants are divided into groups according to the position of their ◊perennating (overwintering) buds in relation to the soil surface. For example, plants in cold areas, such as the tundra, generally have their buds protected below ground, whereas in hot, tropical areas they are above ground and freely exposed. This scheme is useful for comparing vegetation types in different parts of the world.
Rauschenberg /ˈraʊʃənbəːg/ Robert 1925– . US pop artist, a creator of happenings (art in live performance) and incongruous multimedia works such as *Monogram* 1959 (Moderna Museet, Stockholm), a car tyre around the body of a stuffed goat daubed with paint. In the 1960s he returned to painting and used the silk-screen printing process to transfer images to canvas. He also made collages.
ravage /ˈrævɪdʒ/ *v.t./i.* to devastate, to plunder, to make havoc (in). —*n.* **1.** devastation. **2.** (usually in *plural*) destructive effect. [from French, alteration of *ravine* = rush of water]
Ravana /ˈrɑːvənə/ in the Hindu epic *Rāmāyana*, demon king of Lankā (Sri Lanka) who abducted Sita, the wife of Rama.
rave *v.i.* **1.** to talk wildly or furiously (as) in delirium. **2.** to speak with rapturous admiration. —*n.* **1.** (*colloquial*) a highly enthusiastic review (of a film or play etc.). **2.** (*slang*) an infatuation. —**rave-up** *n.* (*slang*) a lively party. **raving beauty**, an excitingly beautiful person. **raving mad**, completely mad.
ravel /ˈrævəl/ *v.t./i.* (**-ll-**) **1.** to entangle or become entangled. **2.** to confuse or complicate (a question or problem). **3.** to fray out. **4.** to disentangle, to unravel; to distinguish the separate threads or subdivisions of. —*n.* a tangle, a knot; a complication.
Ravel /ræˈvel/ (Joseph) Maurice 1875–1937. French composer. His work is characterized by its sensuousness, unresolved dissonances, and 'tone colour'. Examples are the piano pieces *Pavane pour une infante défunte* 1899 and *Jeux d'eau* 1901, and the ballets *Daphnis et Chloë* 1912 and *Boléro* 1928.
raven[1] /ˈreɪvən/ *n.* a large crow *Corvus corax* with glossy, blue-black feathers and a hoarse cry. It is about 60 cm/2 ft long, and a scavenger, found only in the northern hemisphere. —*adj.* (usually of hair) glossy black. [Old English]
raven[2] /ˈrævən/ *v.t./i.* **1.** to plunder, to seek prey or booty. **2.** to devour voraciously. [from Old French *raviner* = ravage]
ravenous /ˈrævənəs/ *adj.* very hungry; voracious; rapacious. —**ravenously** *adv.* [from Old French]
ravine /rəˈviːn/ *n.* a deep, narrow gorge. [French from Latin]
ravioli /ræviˈəʊlɪ/ *n.* small pasta cases containing meat etc. [Italian]
ravish /ˈrævɪʃ/ *v.t.* **1.** to commit rape on. **2.** to enrapture, to fill with delight. —**ravishment** *n.* [from Old French from Latin *rapere* = seize]
raw *adj.* **1.** uncooked. **2.** in its natural state, not yet or not fully processed or manufactured. **3.** inexperienced; untrained. **4.** stripped of skin and having the underlying flesh exposed; sensitive to the touch from being so exposed. **5.**

(of atmosphere or a day etc.) damp and chilly. **6.** crude in artistic quality, lacking finish. **7.** (of an edge of cloth) not a selvage and not hemmed. —**in the raw**, in its natural state without mitigation; naked. **raw-boned** *adj.* gaunt. **raw deal**, see ◊deal[1]. **raw material**, that from which a process of manufacture makes articles. **touch a person on the raw**, to wound his feelings on a point where he is sensitive. —**rawness** *n.* [Old English]
Rawalpindi /rɔːlˈpɪndɪ/ city in Punjab province, Pakistan, in the foothills of the Himalayas; population (1981) 928,400. Industries include oil refining, iron, chemicals, and furniture.
rawhide *n.* untanned leather; a rope or whip of this.
Rawlinson /ˈrɔːlɪnsən/ Henry Creswicke 1810–1895. English orientalist and political agent in Baghdad in the Ottoman Empire from 1844. He deciphered the Babylonian cuneiform and Old Persian scripts of ◊Darius I's trilingual inscription at Behistun, Persia, continued the excavation work of A H ◊Layard, and published a *History of Assyria* 1852.
Rawlplug /ˈrɔːlplʌg/ *n.* the trade name of a thin, cylindrical plug for holding a screw or nail in masonry. [from J J & W R *Rawl*ings, English electrical engineers]
Rawls /rɔːlz/ John 1921– . US philosopher. In *A Theory of Justice* 1971, he revived the concept of the ◊'social contract' and its enforcement by civil disobedience.
ray[1] /reɪ/ *n.* **1.** a single line or narrow beam of light or other radiation. **2.** a straight line in which radiation is propagated to a given point; (in *plural*) radiation of a specified type. **3.** a remnant or beginning of an enlightening or cheering influence. **4.** any of a set of radiating lines, parts, or things. **5.** the marginal part of a composite flower (e.g. a daisy). [from Old French *rai* from Latin *radius* = ray]
ray[2] *n.* a large, cartilaginous sea-fish of the order *Rajiformes*. It has a flattened body, winglike pectoral fins and a tail like a whip. [from Old French from Latin *raia*]
ray[3] *n.* in music, the second note of the major scale in ◊tonic sol-fa. [from *resonare*]
Ray John 1627–1705. English naturalist who devised a classification system accounting for nearly 18,000 plant species. It was the first system to divide flowering plants into ◊monocotyledons and ◊dicotyledons, with additional divisions made on the basis of leaf and flower characters and fruit types.
Ray Nicholas. Adopted name of Raymond Nicholas Kienzle 1911–1979. US film director, critically acclaimed for his socially aware dramas such as *Rebel Without a Cause* 1955. His later epics, such as *King of Kings* 1961, were less successful.
Ray Satyajit 1921– . Indian film director, renowned for his trilogy of life in his native Bengal: *Pather Panchali*, *Unvanquished*, and *The World of Apu* 1955–59. Later films include *The Chess Players* 1977 and *The Home and the World* 1984.
Raynaud's disease /ˈreɪnəʊz/ a chronic condition in which the blood supply to the extremities is reduced by periodic spasm of the blood vessels on exposure to cold. It is most often seen in young women.
rayon /ˈreɪɒn/ *n.* an artificial textile fibre or fabric made from cellulose. A common type is ◊viscose, which consists of regenerated filaments of pure cellulose. Acetate and triacetate are kinds of rayon consisting of filaments of cellulose acetate and triacetate.
raze *v.t.* to destroy completely, to tear down (usually *to the ground*). [from Old French = shave close, ultimately from Latin *radere* = scrape]
razor /ˈreɪzə/ *n.* an instrument with a sharp blade used in cutting hair especially from the skin. Razors were known in the Bronze Age. The safety razor was patented by William Henson in 1847; a disposable version was produced by King Gillette (1855–1932) at the start of the 20th century. The earliest electric razors date from the 1920s. **razor-blade** *n.* a blade used in a razor, especially a flat piece of metal with two sharp edges used in a safety razor. **razor-edge** *n.* a keen edge; a sharp mountain ridge; a critical situation; a sharp line of division. [from Old French]
razorbill *n.* N Atlantic seabird *Alca torda*, of the auk family, which breeds on cliffs, and migrates to the Mediterranean in winter. It has a curved, sharp-edged beak, and is black above and white below. It uses its wings as paddles when diving.

razor-shell *n.* or **razor-fish** or (*US*) **razor-clam**, two genera of bivalve molluscs, *Ensis* and *Solen*, with narrow elongated shells, resembling an old-fashioned razor handle and delicately coloured. They are found in sand among rocks.

razzle *n.* (*slang*) a spree, a lively outing.

razzle-dazzle /ˈræzəldæzəl/ *n.* (*slang*) 1. excitement, bustle, a spree. 2. (*slang*) noisy advertising.

razzmatazz /ˌræzməˈtæz/ *n.* (*colloquial*) 1. excitement, bustle. 2. noisy advertising. 3. insincere actions, humbug.

Rb symbol for rubidium.

RC abbreviation of Roman Catholic.

Rd abbreviation of road.

re[1] /riː/ *prep.* in the matter of (as the first word in a heading, especially of a legal document; (*colloquial*) about, concerning. [Latin, ablative of *res* = thing]

re[2] /reɪ/ variant of ◊ray[3].

're abbreviation of are.

re-[1] (sometimes **red-** before vowels: *redolent*) prefix in verbs and verbal derivatives denoting: in return, mutually (*react, resemble*), opposition (*repel, resist*), behind or after (*relic, remain*), retirement or secrecy (*recluse, reticence*), off, away, down (*recede, relegate, repress*), frequentative or intensive force (*redouble, refine, resplendent*), negative force (*recant, reveal*). [from Latin]

re-[2] prefix attachable to almost any verb or its derivative in senses (1) once more, afresh, anew; (2) back, with return to a previous state. A hyphen is normally used when the word begins in *e-* (*re-enact*) or to distinguish the compound from a more familiar one-word form (*re-form* = form again).

Re symbol for rhenium.

reach *v.t./i.* 1. to stretch out or extend. 2. to stretch out the hand etc. in order to touch or grasp or take something; to make a reaching motion or effort (*literal* or *figurative*). 3. to get as far as, to arrive at, to attain. 4. to make contact by hand etc. or by telephone etc. 5. to sail with the wind abeam or abaft the beam. —*n.* 1. an act of reaching. 2. the extent to which a hand etc. can be reached out, an influence exerted, or a mental power used. 3. a continuous extent, especially the part of a river that can be looked along at once between two bends, or part of a canal between locks. 4. in sailing, the distance traversed in reaching (**broad reach**, with the wind aft the beam but not so far aft that the vessel is running. **close reach**, with the wind forward of the beam but not so far forward that the vessel is close-hauled). —**reach-me-down** *adj.* (*colloquial*) ready-made. [Old English]

reachable *adj.* that may be reached.

react /riːˈækt/ *v.i.* 1. to respond *to* a stimulus, to undergo a change or show behaviour that is due to some influence. 2. to be actuated by repulsion *against*, to tend in a reverse or backward direction.

reaction /riːˈækʃən/ *n.* 1. reacting; a responsive feeling. 2. an occurrence of a condition after its opposite. 3. tendency to oppose change or to return to a former system, especially in politics. 4. the interaction of substances undergoing chemical change; in chemistry, the coming together of two or more atoms, ions or molecules resulting in a ◊chemical change. The nature of the reaction is portrayed by a chemical equation.

reactionary /riːˈækʃənərɪ/ *adj.* showing reaction; opposed to progress or reform. —*n.* a reactionary person.

reaction principle a principle stated by Isaac ◊Newton as his third law of motion: to every action, there is an equal and opposite reaction.

reactivate /riːˈæktɪveɪt/ *v.t.* to restore to a state of activity. —**reactivation** /-ˈveɪʃən/ *n.*

reactive /riːˈæktɪv/ *adj.* showing reaction. —**reactivity** /-ˈtɪvɪtɪ/ *n.*

reactivity series chemical series produced by arranging the metals in order of their ease of reaction with reagents such as oxygen, water, and acids. This arrangement aids in understanding the properties of metals, helps to explain differences, and enables predictions to be made about a certain metal based on a knowledge of its position or properties.

reactor /riːˈæktə/ *n.* a ◊nuclear reactor.

read /riːd/ *v.t./i.* (*past* and *past participle* **read** /red/) 1. to reproduce mentally or vocally the words of (an author, book, letter etc.) while following their symbols with the eyes or fingers. 2. to be able to understand the meaning

Reagan The Hollywood actor who became president of the USA.

of (written or printed words or symbols). 3. to interpret mentally, to find implications; to declare the interpretation of. 4. (of a measuring instrument) to show (a figure etc.). 5. to have a specified wording. 6. to study or discover by reading; to study (a subject at university); to carry out a course of study. 7. (of a computer) to copy or transfer (data). —*n.* a spell of reading. —**read between the lines**, to look for and find a hidden or implicit meaning. **read-only memory**, (in computers) a memory whose contents can usually be read at high speed but cannot be changed by program instructions; see ◊ROM. **read up**, to make a special study of (a subject). **take as read**, to dispense with actual reading or discussion of. **well read**, (of a person) having knowledge of a subject or good general acquaintance with literature through reading. [Old English]

readable *adj.* able to be read; interesting to read.

readdress /riːəˈdres/ *v.t.* to alter the address on (a letter).

reader *n.* 1. one who reads. 2. a book containing passages for practice in reading by students learning a language. 3. a device to produce an image that can be read from a microfilm etc. 4. a university lecturer of a higher grade. 5. a publisher's employee who reports on submitted manuscripts; a printer's proof-corrector.

Reader's Digest a magazine founded 1922 in the USA to publish condensed articles and books, usually of an uplifting and conservative kind, along with in-house features. It has editions in many different languages and had the world's largest circulation until the mid-1980s.

readership *n.* the readers of a newspaper etc.

readily /ˈredɪlɪ/ *adv.* 1. without showing reluctance, willingly. 2. without difficulty.

readiness *n.* 1. a ready or prepared state. 2. willingness. 3. facility, quickness in argument or action.

reading *n.* 1. the act of one who reads. 2. an entertainment at which a thing is read. 3. matter to be read; its specified quality. 4. literary knowledge. 5. a figure etc. given by a measuring instrument. 6. an interpretation. 7. each of the three occasions on which a bill must be presented to a legislature for acceptance. —**reading-room** *n.* a room in a club, library etc., for those wishing to read.

readjust /riːəˈdʒʌst/ *v.t./i.* to adjust (a thing) again; to adapt oneself again. —**readjustment** *n.*

ready /ˈredɪ/ *adj.* 1. with preparations complete; in a fit state for immediate use or action. 2. willing; about or inclined to do something. 3. easily available; within reach. 4. prompt, quick, facile. —*adv.* beforehand, so as to be ready when the time comes. —*n.* (*slang*) ready money. —*v.t.* to make ready, to prepare. —**at the ready**, ready for action. **ready-made** *adj.* (especially of clothes) made for immediate wear, not to measure. **ready money**, actual coin or notes; payment on the spot. **ready reckoner**, a book or table of the results of arithmetical computations of the kind commonly wanted in business etc. [Old English]

Reagan /'reɪgən/ Ronald (Wilson) 1911–　. US Republican politician, governor of California 1966–74, president 1981–89. A former Hollywood actor, Reagan was a hawkish and popular president. He adopted an aggressive policy in Central America, attempting to overthrow the government of Nicaragua, and invading ◊Grenada in 1983. In 1987, ◊Irangate was investigated by the Tower Commission; Reagan admitted that USA–Iran negotiations had become an 'arms for hostages deal', but denied knowledge of resultant funds being illegally sent to the Contras in Nicaragua. He increased military spending (sending the national budget deficit to record levels), cut social programmes, introduced deregulation of domestic markets, and cut taxes. His ◊Strategic Defense Initiative, announced in 1983, proved controversial owing to the cost and unfeasibility. He was succeeded by George ◊Bush.

You know, by the time you reach my age, you've made plenty of mistakes if you've lived your life properly.

Ronald Reagan
The Observer 1987

---

reagent /riː'eɪdʒənt/ *n.* a substance used to cause a chemical reaction, especially to detect another substance.

real[1] /'rɪəl/ *adj.* **1.** existing as a thing or occurring in fact, not imaginary. **2.** genuine, rightly so called; not artificial or imitation. **3.** in law, consisting of immovable property such as land or houses. **4.** (of income or value etc.) appraised by purchasing power. —*adv.* (*Scottish* and *US colloquial*) really, very. —**real money,** coin, cash. **real time,** the actual time of a process analysed by a computer. [Anglo-French and from Latin *res* = thing]

real[2] /reɪ'ɑːl/ *n.* (*historical*) a silver coin in Spanish-speaking countries. [Spanish]

realgar /riː'ælgə/ *n.* a mineral consisting of arsenic sulphide, used as a pigment and in fireworks. [from Latin from Arabic = dust of the cave]

realign /riː'ə'laɪn/ *v.t./i.* **1.** to align again. **2.** to regroup in politics etc. —**realignment** *n.*

realism /'rɪəlɪzəm/ *n.* **1.** the practice of regarding things in their true nature, and dealing with them as they are; practical views and policy. **2.** fidelity of representation, truth to nature, insistence upon details; the showing of life as it is without glossing over what is ugly or painful. **3.** the medieval theory that universal or general ideas have objective existence. It is opposed to nominalism. **4.** in contemporary philosophy, the doctrine that there is an intuitively appreciated reality apart from what is presented to the consciousness. It is opposed to idealism. —**realist** *n.*

realistic /rɪə'lɪstɪk/ *adj.* **1.** regarding things as they are, following a policy of realism. **2.** based on facts rather than ideals. **3.** (of wages or prices) high enough to pay the worker or seller adequately. —**realistically** *adv.*

reality /ri'ælɪtɪ/ *n.* **1.** what is real or existent or underlies appearances. **2.** real existence, being real. **3.** resemblance to an original. [from Latin or French]

realize /'rɪəlaɪz/ *v.t.* **1.** to be fully aware of; to present or conceive as real; to understand clearly. **2.** (usually in *passive*) to convert (a hope or plan) into a fact. **3.** to convert (securities or profit) into money by selling. **4.** to acquire (a profit); to be sold for (a specified price). —**realization** /-'zeɪʃən/ *n.*

really /'rɪəlɪ/ *adv.* **1.** in reality, in fact. **2.** indeed, I assure you. **3.** as an expression of interest, surprise, or mild protest.

realm /relm/ *n.* **1.** a kingdom. **2.** a field of activity or interest. [from Old French from Latin]

real number in mathematics, any ◊rational (which include the integers) or ◊irrational number. Real numbers exclude ◊imaginary numbers, found in ◊complex numbers of the general form $a + bi$ where $i = \sqrt{-1}$, although these do include a real component a.

Realpolitik *n.* the pragmatic pursuit of self-interest and power, backed up by force when convenient. The term was coined in 1853 to describe ◊Bismarck's policies in Prussia during the 1848 revolutions. [German = politics of realism]

real tennis a racket and ball game played in France, from about the 12th century, over a central net in an indoor court,

but with a sloping roof let into each end and one side of the court, against which the ball may be hit. Basic scoring is as for lawn ◊tennis, but with various modifications.

real-time system in computing, a program that responds to events in the world as they happen, as, for example, an automatic-pilot program in an aircraft must respond instantly to correct course deviations. Process control, robotics, games, and many military applications are examples of real-time systems.

realty /'rɪəltɪ/ *n.* real estate.

ream[1] *n.* **1.** 20 quires of paper (about 500 sheets). **2.** (usually in *plural*) a large quantity of writing. [from Old French ultimately from Arabic = bundle]

ream[2] *v.t.* to enlarge or give a smooth finish to (a hole drilled in metal etc.) by a borer. —**reamer** *n.*

reap *v.t.* **1.** to cut or gather (a crop, especially grain) as harvest; to harvest the crop of (a field etc.). **2.** to receive as the consequence of one's own or another's actions. [Old English]

reaper *n.* **1.** a person who reaps. **2.** a machine for reaping crops. **3.** death personified.

reappear /riː'ə'pɪə/ *v.i.* to appear again. —**reappearance** *n.*

reappraise /riː'ə'preɪz/ *v.t.* to appraise again, to reconsider. —**reappraisal** *n.*

rear[1] *n.* **1.** the back part, the space behind, position at the back of something. **2.** (*colloquial*) the buttocks. —*adj.* at the back, in the rear. —**bring up the rear,** to come last. **rear admiral,** the lowest grade of admiral. **rear lamp** *or* **rear light,** a light, usually red, on the back of a vehicle.

rear[2] *v.t./i.* **1.** to bring up and educate (children); to breed and care for (animals); to cultivate (crops). **2.** (of a horse etc.) to raise itself on its hind legs. **3.** to set upright, to build; to hold upwards. **4.** to extend to a great height. [Old English]

rearguard *n.* a body of troops detached to protect the rear of the main force; especially in retreats. —**rearguard action,** an engagement between the rearguard and the enemy (*literal* or *figurative*). [from Old French *rereguarde* (Latin *retro* = backwards)]

rearm /riː'ɑːm/ *v.t./i.* to arm again, especially with improved weapons. —**rearmament** *n.*

rearmost *adj.* furthest back.

rearrange /riː'ə'reɪndʒ/ *v.t.* to arrange in a different way. —**rearrangement** *n.*

rearward /'rɪəwəd/ *n.* the rear (especially in prepositional phrases: *to the rearward of, in the rearward*). —*adj.* to the rear. —*adv.* (also **rearwards**) towards the rear. [from Anglo-French *rerewarde*]

reason /'riːzən/ *n.* **1.** a motive, cause, or justification; a fact adduced or serving as this. **2.** the intellectual faculty by which conclusions are drawn from premises. **3.** sanity. **4.** good sense, sensible conduct; what is right or practical or practicable; moderation. —*v.t./i.* **1.** to form or try to reach conclusions by connected thought, to state as a step in this. **2.** to try to persuade a person by giving reasons. —**by reason of,** owing to. **in** or **within reason,** within the bounds of moderation. **with reason,** not unjustifiably. [from Old French from Latin]

reasonable *adj.* **1.** having or based on sound judgement or moderation; sensible, not expecting too much. **2.** not excessive, not expensive or extortionate. **3.** ready to listen to reason. —**reasonableness** *n.*, **reasonably** *adv.*

reassemble /riː'ə'sembəl/ *v.t./i.* to assemble again.

reassure /riː'ə'ʃuə/ *v.t.* to restore confidence to, to dispel the apprehensions of. —**reassurance** *n.*

Réaumur /reɪ'əʊmjuər/ Réné Antoine Ferchault de 1683–1757. French metallurgist and entomologist. His definitive work on the early steel industry, published in 1722, described how to convert iron into steel and laid the foundations of the modern steel industry. He produced a six-volume work between 1734 and 1742 on the natural history of insects, the first books on entomology.

reave *v.t.* (*past* and *past participle* **reft**) (*archaic*) to deprive forcibly; to take by force or carry off. [Old English]

rebarbative /riː'bɑːbətɪv/ *adj.* (*literary*) repellent, unattractive. [from French *barbe* = beard]

rebate[1] /'riːbeɪt/ *n.* a deduction from a sum to be paid, a discount; a partial refund. [from Old French *rebattre*]

rebate[2] *n.* a step-shaped channel etc. cut along the edge or face of wood etc., usually to receive the edge or tongue of another piece. —*v.t.* to join or fix with a rebate; to make a rebate in.

rebel /'rebəl/ *n.* 1. a person who fights against, resists, or refuses allegiance to the established government; a person or thing that resists authority or control. 2. (*attributive*) rebellious; of rebels; in rebellion. —/ri'bel/ *v.i.* (-ll-) 1. to act as a rebel. 2. to feel or display repugnance (against a custom etc.). [from Old French from Latin *rebellare* (*bellum* = war)]

rebellion /ri'beljən/ *n.* open resistance to authority, especially organized armed resistance to the established government.

rebellious /ri'beljəs/ *adj.* 1. in rebellion. 2. disposed to rebel, defying lawful authority. 3. (of a thing) unmanageable, refractory. —**rebelliously** *adv.*, **rebelliousness** *n.*

rebirth /ri:'bɜ:θ/ *n.* 1. a new incarnation; a return to life or activity, a revival. 2. spiritual enlightenment.

rebound /ri'baund/ *v.i.* 1. to spring back after impact. 2. (of an action) to have an adverse effect upon the originator. —/'ri:baund/ *n.* 1. an act of rebounding, a recoil. 2. reaction after disappointment or other emotion. [from Old French]

rebuff /ri'bʌf/ *n.* an unkind or contemptuous rejection; snub. —*v.t.* to give a rebuff to. [from French from Italian *buffo* = puff]

rebuild /ri:'bɪld/ *v.t.* (*past* and *past participle* **rebuilt**) to build again after destruction or demolition.

rebuke /ri'bju:k/ *v.t.* to reprove sharply or severely. —*n.* a sharp or severe reproof. [from Anglo-French *rebuker* (Old French *buchier* = beat)]

rebus /'ri:bəs/ *n.* a representation of a word (especially a name) by pictures etc. suggesting its syllables. [from French from Latin *rebus*, ablative plural of *res* = thing]

rebut /ri'bʌt/ *v.t.* (-tt-) 1. to refute or disprove (evidence or an accusation). 2. to force or turn back. —**rebutment** *n.* **rebuttal** *n.* [from Anglo-French]

recalcitrant /ri'kælsɪtrənt/ *adj.* obstinately disobedient, resisting authority or discipline. —**recalcitrance** *n.* [from Latin *recalcitrare* = kick out]

recall /ri'kɔ:l/ *v.t.* 1. to summon to return. 2. to bring back to the attention or memory etc. 3. to recollect, to remember. 4. to revoke or annul (an action or decision). —*n.* 1. a summons to come back. 2. the act of remembering; ability to remember. 3. the possiblity of revoking or annulling; a process by which voters can demand the dismissal from office of elected officials, as in some states of the USA.

recant /ri'kænt/ *v.t./i.* to withdraw and renounce (a former belief or statement etc.) as erroneous or heretical; to disavow a former opinion, especially with a public confession of error. —**recantation** /ri:kæn'teɪʃən/ *n.* [from Latin *cantare* = sing]

recap /'ri:kæp/ *v.t.* (*colloquial*) (-pp-) to recapitulate. —*n.* (*colloquial*) recapitulation. [abbreviation]

recapitulate /ri:kə'pɪtjʌleɪt/ *v.t./i.* to state again briefly; to repeat the main points of. [from Latin *capitulum* = chapter]

recapitulation /ri:kəpɪtjʌ'leɪʃən/ *n.* 1. recapitulating. 2. in music, the part of a movement in which the themes from the exposition are restated. [from Old French or Latin]

recapture /ri:'kæptʃə/ *v.t.* 1. to capture again (a person or thing that has escaped or been lost to an enemy). 2. to re-experience (a past emotion etc.). —*n.* recapturing.

recast /ri:'kɑ:st/ *v.t.* (*past* and *past participle* **recast**) to put into a new form, to improve the arrangement of. —*n.* 1. recasting. 2. a recast form.

recce /'rekɪ/ *n.* (*slang*) a reconnaissance. —*v.t./i.* (*slang*) to reconnoitre. [abbreviation]

recede /ri'si:d/ *v.i.* 1. to go or shrink back or further off; to be left at an increasing distance by the observer's motion. 2. to slope backwards. 3. to decline in force or value etc. [from Latin *cedere* = go]

receipt /ri'si:t/ *n.* 1. receiving, being received. 2. a written acknowledgement that something has been received or that money has been paid. 3. (*archaic*) a recipe. —*v.t.* to put a written receipt on (a bill). [from Anglo-French *receite*]

receive /ri'si:v/ *v.t.* 1. to acquire, accept, or take in (something offered, sent, or given). 2. to have conferred or inflicted upon one, to experience; to be treated with. 3. to take the force, weight, or impact of. 4. to consent to hear (a confession or an oath) or consider (a petition). 5. to accept (stolen goods knowingly; also *absolute*). 6. to serve as a receptacle for; to be able to hold or accommodate. 7. to

allow to enter as a member or guest; to greet or welcome in a specified manner. 8. to be marked (*literal* or *figurative*) more or less permanently with (an impression etc.). 9. to convert (broadcast signals) into sound or a picture. 10. (especially in *past participle*) to give credit to, to accept as authoritative or true. —**be at** *or* **on the receiving end**, (*colloquial*) to bear the brunt of something unpleasant. **received pronunciation**, the standard educated form of southern English speech formerly used for example by BBC announcers. [from Old French from Latin *capere* = take]

receiver *n.* 1. a person or thing that receives something. 2. an official who administers property under a receiving-order. 3. a person who accepts stolen goods while knowing them to be stolen. 4. the part of a telephone that receives incoming sound and is held to the ear. 5. a radio or television receiving apparatus.

receiving-order *n.* the order of a court of law to an official (the **receiver**) to take charge of the property of an individual, company, or partnership in serious financial difficulties or an insane person or of property that is the subject of litigation. In the case of bankruptcy, the assets may be sold and distributed by the receiver to creditors.

recent /'ri:sənt/ *adj.* not long past, that happened or began to exist or existed shortly before the present. —**recency** *n.*, **recently** *adv.* [from French or Latin *recens recentis*]

receptacle /ri'septəkəl/ *n.* 1. a container, something for holding or containing what is put into it. 2. the enlarged end of a flower stalk to which the floral parts are attached. Normally the receptacle is rounded, but in some plants it is flattened or cup-shaped. 3. the region on that part of some seaweeds which becomes swollen at certain times of the year and bears the reproductive organs.

reception /ri'sepʃən/ *n.* 1. receiving, being received. 2. the way in which a person or thing is received. 3. a social occasion for receiving guests, especially after a wedding. 4. the place where guests or clients are registered or welcomed on arrival at a hotel or office etc. 5. the receiving of broadcast signals; the quality of this. —**reception room**, a room available or suitable for receiving company or visitors. [from Old French or Latin]

receptionist *n.* a person employed to receive guests or clients etc.

receptive /ri'septɪv/ *adj.* able or quick to receive knowledge, impressions, ideas etc. —**receptiveness** *n.*, **receptivity** /ri:sep'tɪvɪtɪ/ *n.* [from French or Latin]

receptor *n.* any cell capable of detecting stimuli. Receptors form part of the nervous system and are used by the body to gather information about the internal or external environment. There are several types, classified according to function. Some respond to light, some to mechanical force, and some to heat. They are essential for ◊homeostasis.

recess /ri'ses/ *n.* 1. a part or space set back from the line of a wall etc.; a small, hollow place inside something; a remote or secret place. 2. temporary cessation from business (especially of Parliament); a time of this. —*v.t./i.* 1. to make a recess in or of (a wall etc.). 2. (US) to take a recess, to adjourn. [from Latin *recessus*]

recession /ri'seʃ(ə)n/ *n.* in economics, a fall in business activity lasting more than a few months, causing stagnation in a country's output. A serious recession is called a **slump**.

recessional /ri'seʃənəl/ *adj.* in the Christian church, sung while the clergy and choir withdraw after a service. —*n.* a recessional hymn.

recessive /ri'sesɪv/ *adj.* 1. tending to recede. 2. in genetics, a recessive allele can only produce a detectable effect on the organism bearing it when both chromosomes carry it, that is, when the same allele has been inherited from both parents. The individual is then said to be homozygous. In a heterozygous individual, the effect of a recessive allele will be masked by a dominant allele (see ◊dominance). —**recessively** *adv.*

recharge /ri:'tʃɑ:dʒ/ *v.t.* to charge (a battery or gun) again. —**recharge one's batteries**, to have a period of rest and recovery.

rechargeable /ri:'tʃɑ:dʒəbəl/ *adj.* that may be recharged.

recherché /rə'ʃeəʃeɪ/ *adj.* devised or selected with care or difficulty; far-fetched. [French *chercher* = seek]

rechristen /riːˈkrɪsən/ v.t. to christen again; to give a new name to.

recidivist /rɪˈsɪdɪvɪst/ n. one who relapses into crime. —**recidivism** n. [from French from Latin *recidivus* = falling back]

Recife /reˈsiːfə/ industrial seaport (cotton textiles, sugar refining, fruit canning, flour milling) and naval base in Brazil; capital of Pernambuco state, at the mouth of the river Capibaribe; population (1980) 1,184,215. It was founded in 1504.

recipe /ˈresɪpɪ/ n. 1. a statement of the ingredients and procedure for preparing a dish etc. in cookery. 2. a procedure to be followed in order to achieve something. [Latin, imperative of *recipere* = receive]

recipient /rɪˈsɪpɪənt/ n. a person who receives something. [from French from Italian or Latin]

reciprocal /rɪsɪprəkəl/ adj. 1. given or received in return. 2. mutual; in grammar, (of a pronoun) expressing mutual relation (e.g. *each other*). 3. corresponding but the other way round. —n. a mathematical expression or function so related to another that their product is unity. Thus the reciprocal of 2 is $1/2$; of $2/3$ is $3/2$; of x^2 is $1/x^2$ or x^{-2}. —**reciprocally** adv. [from Latin *reciprocus* originally = moving backwards and forwards]

reciprocate /rɪˈsɪprəkeɪt/ v.t./i. 1. to give and receive mutually; to make a return for something done, given or felt. 2. (of a machine part) to go with alternate backward and forward motion. —**reciprocation** /-ˈkeɪʃən/ n. [from Latin *reciprocare*]

reciprocity /resɪˈprɒsɪtɪ/ n. 1. the condition of being reciprocal. 2. a mutual action. 3. give-and-take, especially the interchange of privileges. [from French]

recital /rɪˈsaɪtəl/ n. 1. reciting. 2. a long account of a series of facts or events. 3. a musical entertainment given by one performer or group; a similar entertainment of any kind (e.g. by a dancer).

recitation /resɪˈteɪʃən/ n. 1. reciting. 2. a thing recited.

recitative /resɪtəˈtiːv/ n. musical declamation of the kind usual in the narrative and dialogue parts of opera and oratorio. [from Italian *recitativo*]

recite /rɪˈsaɪt/ v.t./i. 1. to repeat aloud or declaim (a poem or passage) from memory; to give a recitation. 2. to state (facts) in order. [from Old French or Latin *recitare*]

reckless /ˈreklɪs/ adj. regardless of consequences or danger etc. —**recklessly** adv., **recklessness** n. [Old English *reck* = concern oneself]

reckon /ˈrekən/ v.t./i. 1. to count up; to compute by calculation. 2. to include in a total or as a member of a particular class. 3. to have as one's opinion; to consider or regard; to feel confident. —**day of reckoning**, the time when something must be atoned for or avenged. **reckon on**, to rely or count or base plans on. **reckon with**, to take into account; to settle accounts with (a person). [Old English]

reckoner n. an aid to reckoning, a ready reckoner. See ◊ready.

reclaim /rɪˈkleɪm/ v.t. 1. to seek the return of (one's property); to take action so as to recover possession of. 2. to bring (flooded or waste land) under cultivation. 3. to win back or away from vice, error, or waste condition. —**reclamation** /reklәˈmeɪʃən/ n. [from Old French from Latin *clamare* = shout]

recline /rɪˈklaɪn/ v.t./i. to assume or be in a horizontal or leaning position, to put in this position. [from Old French or Latin *clinare* = bend]

recluse /rɪˈkluːs/ n. a person given to or living in seclusion or isolation. [from Old French from Latin *claudere* = shut]

recognition /rekəgˈnɪʃən/ n. recognizing, being recognized.

recognizable /ˈrekəgnaɪzəbəl/ adj. that can be identified or detected. —**recognizably** adv.

recognizance /rɪˈkɒgnɪzəns/ n. a bond by which a person undertakes before a court or magistrate to observe some condition, e.g. to appear when summoned; a sum pledged as surety for such an observance.

recognize /ˈrekəgnaɪz/ v.t. 1. to identify as known before. 2. to realize or discover the nature of. 3. to realize or admit (a fact). 4. to acknowledge the existence, validity, character, or claims of. 5. to show appreciation of, to reward. [from Old French from Latin *cognoscere* = learn]

recoil /rɪˈkɔɪl/ v.i. 1. to move suddenly or spring back, or shrink mentally, in horror, disgust, or fear. 2. to rebound

after impact. 3. to have an adverse reactive effect upon the originator. 4. (of a gun) to be driven backwards by a discharge. —/ˈriːkɔɪl/ n. the act or sensation of recoiling. [from Old French *reculer* from Latin *culus* = buttocks]

recollect /rekəˈlekt/ v.t. to remember; to succeed in remembering, to call to mind. [from Latin *colligere* = collect]

recollection /rekəˈlekʃən/ n. 1. recollecting. 2. a thing recollected. 3. a person's memory; the time over which it extends. [French or from Latin]

recombination n. in genetics, any process that recombines, or 'shuffles', the genetic material, thus increasing genetic variation in the offspring. The two main processes of recombination both occur during meiosis (reduction division). One is ◊crossing over, in which chromosome pairs exchange segments; the other is the random reassortment of chromosomes that occurs when each gamete (sperm or egg) receives only one of each chromosome pair. —**recombinant** adj.

recommence /riːkəˈmens/ v.t./i. to begin again. —**recommencement** n.

recommend /rekəˈmend/ v.t. 1. to suggest as fit for employment or favour or trial. 2. to advise (a course of action etc.). 3. (of qualities or conduct etc.) to make acceptable or desirable. 4. to commend or entrust (to a person or his care). —**recommendation** /-ˈdeɪʃən/ n. [from Latin *commendare* = commend]

recompense /ˈrekəmpens/ v.t. 1. to make amends to (a person) or for (a loss etc.). 2. to requite, reward, or punish (a person or action). —n. a reward, a requital; retribution. [from Old French from Latin *compensare* = compensate]

reconcilable /ˈrekənsaɪləbəl/ adj. that may be reconciled.

reconcile /ˈrekənsaɪl/ v.t. 1. to make friendly again after an estrangement or quarrel. 2. to induce to accept or be submissive (to an unwelcome fact or situation). 3. to harmonize (facts), to show the compatibility of. —**reconciliation** /-sɪlɪˈeɪʃən/ n. [from Old French or Latin *conciliare* = conciliate]

recondite /ˈrekəndaɪt/ adj. (of a subject or knowledge) abstruse, out of the way, little known; (of an author or style) dealing in recondite knowledge or allusion, obscure. [from Latin *condere* = hide]

recondition /riːkənˈdɪʃən/ v.t. to overhaul, to renovate to make usable again.

reconnaissance /rɪˈkɒnɪsəns/ n. a survey of a region, especially a military examination to locate an enemy or ascertain strategic features; a preliminary survey.

reconnoitre /rekəˈnɔɪtə/ v.t./i. to make a reconnaissance (of). [from obsolete French from Latin]

reconquer /riːˈkɒŋkə/ v.t. to conquer again. —**reconquest** /riːˈkɒŋkwest/ n.

Reconquista /reɪkɒŋˈkiːstə/ n. the Christian defeat of the ◊Moors in the 9th–15th centuries, and their expulsion from Spain. [Spanish = reconquest]

reconsider /riːkənˈsɪdə/ v.t. to consider again, especially for a possible change of decision. —**reconsideration** /-ˈreɪʃən/ n.

reconstitute /riːˈkɒnstɪtjuːt/ v.t. 1. to reconstruct, to reorganize. 2. to restore the previous constitution of (dried food etc.) by adding water. —**reconstitution** /-ˈtjuːʃən/ n.

reconstruct /riːkənˈstrʌkt/ v.t. 1. to construct or build again. 2. to piece together (past events) into an intelligible whole, by imagination or by re-enacting them. 3. to reorganize. —**reconstruction** n.

Reconstruction n. (*historical*) the period 1865–77 after the US Civil War during which the nation was reunited under the federal government after the defeat of the Southern Confederacy.

recopy /riːˈkɒpɪ/ v.t. to make a fresh copy of.

record /rɪˈkɔːd/ v.t. 1. to set down for remembrance or reference, to put in writing or other permanent form. 2. to convert (sound or visual scenes, especially television pictures) to a permanent form for later reproduction. 3. (of a measuring instrument) to register. —/ˈrekɔːd/ n. 1. the state of being recorded or preserved in writing etc. 2. a piece of recorded evidence or information; an account of a fact preserved in a permanent form; a document or monument preserving it. 3. an official report of public or legal proceedings. 4. the known facts about a person's past;

a list and the details of previous offences. **5.** a disc (formerly a cylinder) from which recorded sound can be reproduced. **6.** an object serving as a memorial, portrait etc. **7.** (often *attributive*) the best performance or most remarkable event of its kind on record. —**for the record,** so that facts may be recorded officially. **go on record,** to state an opinion openly so that it is published. **have a record,** to have been convicted on a previous occasion. **off the record,** unofficially, confidentially. **on record,** officially recorded, publicly known. **recorded delivery,** a Post Office service whereby safe delivery is recorded by the signature of the recipient. [from Old French from Latin *recordari* = remember]

recorder /rɪˈkɔːdə/ *n.* **1.** a keeper of records. **2.** in the English legal system, a barrister or solicitor appointed to act for a period as a part-time judge of a Crown Court; (*historical*) a judge in certain courts. **3.** an apparatus for recording things, especially a tape-recorder. **4.** in music, an instrument of the ◊woodwind family, blown through one end, in which different notes are obtained by covering the holes in the instrument. Recorders are played in a consort (ensemble) of matching tone and comprise sopranino, descant, treble, and bass.

recording /rɪˈkɔːdɪŋ/ *n.* **1.** the process of storing information especially audio or video signals. Sounds and pictures can be stored on discs or tape. The gramophone record or ◊compact disc stores music or speech as a spiral groove on a plastic disc and the sounds are reproduced by a record player. In ◊tape recording, sounds are stored as a magnetic pattern on plastic tape. The best-quality reproduction is achieved using ◊digital audio tape. **2.** the material or programme thus recorded.

recordist /rɪˈkɔːdɪst/ *n.* a person who records sound.

Record Office, Public a government office containing the English national records since the Norman Conquest, brought together from courts of law and government departments, including the Domesday Book, the Gunpowder Plot papers, and the log of HMS *Victory* at Trafalgar. It was established in 1838 in Chancery Lane, London; records from the 18th century onwards have been housed at Kew, London, since 1976.

record player a device for reproducing sound recorded, usually in a spiral groove on a vinyl disc. A motor-driven turntable rotates the record at a constant speed, and a stylus or needle on the head of a pick-up is made to vibrate by the undulations in the record groove. These vibrations are then converted to electrical signals by a ◊transducer in the head (often a ◊piezoelectric crystal). After amplification, the signals pass to one or more loudspeakers, which convert them into sound.

recount /rɪˈkaʊnt/ *v.t.* to narrate, to tell in detail. [from Anglo-French *reconter*]

re-count /riːˈkaʊnt/ *v.t.* to count again. —/ˈriːkaʊnt/ *n.* re-counting, especially of election votes.

recoup /rɪˈkuːp/ *v.t.* **1.** to recover or regain (a loss). **2.** to compensate or reimburse for loss. —**recoup oneself,** to recover a loss. —**recoupment** *n.* [from French *couper* = cut]

recourse /rɪˈkɔːs/ *n.* **1.** resorting to a possible source of help. **2.** person or thing forming such a source. —**have recourse to,** to adopt as an adviser or helper or as an expedient. [from Old French from Latin *cursus* = course]

recover /rɪˈkʌvə/ *v.t./i.* **1.** to regain possession, use, or control of. **2.** to come back to health or consciousness or to a normal state or position. **3.** to obtain or secure by legal process. **4.** to retrieve or make up for (a loss or setback etc.). —**recover oneself,** to regain calmness or consciousness or control of one's limbs. [from Anglo-French *recoverer*]

recoverable *adj.* that may be recovered.

recovery *n.* the act or process of recovering or being recovered. [from Anglo-French *recoverie*]

recreant /ˈrekrɪənt/ *adj.* (*literary*) craven, cowardly. —*n.* a coward. [from Old French (*recroire* = yield in trial by combat]

re-create /riːkriˈeɪt/ *v.t.* to create again.

recreation /rekriˈeɪʃən/ *n.* the process or a means of refreshing or entertaining oneself after work by some pleasurable activity. —**recreational** *adj.* [from Old French from Latin]

recriminate /rɪˈkrɪmɪneɪt/ *v.i.* to make mutual or counter accusations. —**recrimination** /-ˈneɪʃən/ *n.,* **recriminatory** *adj.* [from Latin *recriminare* = accuse]

recross /riːˈkrɒs/ *v.t./i.* to cross again, to go back across.

recrudesce /riːkruːˈdes, rek-/ *v.i.* (of a disease or sore or discontent etc.) to break out again. —**recrudescence** *n.,* **recrudescent** *adj.* [from Latin *crudus* = raw]

recruit /rɪˈkruːt/ *n.* a soldier newly enlisted and not yet fully trained; a new member of a society etc.; a beginner. —*v.t./i.* **1.** to enlist (a person) as a recruit; to enlist recruits for (an army etc.); to get or seek recruits. **2.** to replenish or reinvigorate (numbers or strength etc.). —**recruitment** *n.* [from obsolete French dialect *recrute* from Latin *recrescere* = grow again]

Recruit scandal in Japanese politics, the revelation in 1988 that a number of politicians and business leaders had profited from insider trading. It led to the resignation of several cabinet ministers, including Prime Minister Takeshita, whose closest aide committed suicide, and to the arrest of 20 people.

rectal /ˈrektəl/ *adj.* of or by means of the rectum.

rectangle /ˈrektæŋgəl/ *n.* a four-sided plane rectilinear figure with four right angles, especially one with adjacent sides unequal. Its area A is the product of the length l and width w; that is, $A = l \times w$. A rectangle with all four sides equal is a ◊square. —**rectangular** /-ˈtæŋgʊlə/ *adj.* [French or from Latin *rectus* = straight and *angulus* = angle]

rectifiable /ˈrektɪfaɪəbəl/ *adj.* that may be rectified.

rectify /ˈrektɪfaɪ/ *v.t.* **1.** to put right, to correct. **2.** to purify or refine, especially by repeated distillation. **3.** to convert (alternating current) to direct current. —**rectification** /-fɪˈkeɪʃən/ *n.,* **rectifier** *n.* a device used for obtaining one-directional current (DC) from an alternating source of supply (AC). Types include plate rectifiers, thermionic ◊diodes, and ◊semiconductor diodes. [from Old French from Latin *rectus* = straight, right and *facere* = make]

rectilinear /rektɪˈlɪnɪə/ *adj.* **1.** bounded or characterized by straight lines. **2.** in or forming a straight line. [from Latin *linea* = line]

rectitude /ˈrektɪtjuːd/ *n.* moral goodness; correctness of behaviour or procedure. [from Old French or Latin *rectitudo*]

recto /ˈrektəʊ/ *n.* (*plural* rectos) the right-hand page of an open book; the front of a leaf of a manuscript etc. (as opposed to **verso**). [from Latin *recto (folio)* = on the right leaf]

rector /ˈrektə/ *n.* **1.** an incumbent of a Church of England parish where all the tithes formerly passed to the incumbent as opposed to a vicar, who was only entitled to part; the head priest of a Roman Catholic church. **2.** the head of a university, college, or religious institution. —**rectorship** *n.* [from Old French or Latin = ruler (*regere* = rule)]

rectory *n.* the house provided for a rector. [from Anglo-French or Latin]

rectrix /ˈrektrɪks/ *n.* (*plural* rectrices /-iːsiːz/) any of a bird's strong tail-feathers, directing its flight. [Latin, feminine of **rector**]

rectum /ˈrektəm/ *n.* (*plural* rectums) the final section of the large intestine, terminating at the anus. [from Latin = straight (intestine)]

recumbent /rɪˈkʌmbənt/ *adj.* lying down, reclining. [from Latin *cumbere* = lie]

recuperate /rɪˈkjuːpəreɪt, -ˈkuː-/ *v.t./i.* to recover from illness, exhaustion, or loss etc.; to regain (health or losses etc.). —**recuperation** /-ˈreɪʃən/ *n.* **recuperative** *adj.* [from Latin *recuperare*]

recur /rɪˈkɜː/ *v.i.* (-**rr**-) **1.** to occur again, to be repeated. **2.** to go back in thought or speech. —**recurring decimal,** a decimal fraction in which the same figures are repeated indefinitely. [from Latin *recurrere* = run back]

recurrent /rɪˈkʌrənt/ *adj.* recurring, happening repeatedly. —**recurrence** *n.*

recursion *n.* in computing, a technique whereby a ◊function or ◊procedure calls itself, enabling a complex problem to be broken down into simpler steps. For example, a function which returns the factorial of a number, n, would obtain its result by multiplying n by the factorial of $n - 1$.

recusant /ˈrekjʊzənt/ *n.* one who refuses submission to authority or compliance with a regulation. —**recusancy** *n.* [from Latin *recusare* = refuse]

recycle /riːˈsaɪkəl/ v.t. to return (a material) to a previous stage of a cyclic process; to convert (waste) into a form in which it can be reused.

recycling n. the processing of industrial and household waste (such as paper, glass, and some metals) so that it can be reused, thus saving expenditure on scarce raw materials, slowing down the depletion of nonrenewable resources, and helping to reduce pollution.

red adj. 1. of the colour of blood or a colour approaching this (ranging to pink or orange); flushed in the face with shame, anger etc.; (of the eyes) sore, bloodshot; (of the hair) reddish-brown, tawny. 2. having to do with bloodshed, burning, violence, or revolution. 3. **Red**, Russian, Soviet; socialist, communist. —n. 1. red colour or pigment. 2. red clothes or material. 3. a socialist, revolutionary, or communist. The term originated in the 19th century in the form 'red republican', meaning a republican who favoured a social as well as a political revolution, generally by armed violence. Red is the colour adopted by socialist parties. —**in the red**, in debt. **red admiral**, a butterfly; see ◊admiral. **red-blooded** adj. virile, vigorous. **red card**, such a card shown by the referee at a football match to a player whom he is sending off the field. **red carpet**, privileged treatment of an important visitor. **red cent**, (US) the smallest (originally copper) coin. **Red Crescent**, the equivalent of the ◊Red Cross in Muslim countries. **red-handed** adj. in the act of committing a crime or doing wrong etc. **red hat**, a cardinal's hat, the symbol of his office. **red herring**, an irrelevant distraction. **red-hot** adj. heated to redness; highly exciting or excited; angry; (of news) fresh, completely new. **red-hot poker**, a garden plant of the genus Kniphofia with spikes of red or yellow flowers. **Red Indian**, (derogatory) a North American Indian. **red lead**, a pigment made from red oxide of lead. **red-letter day**, one that is pleasantly noteworthy or memorable (originally a festival marked in red on a calendar). **red light**, a signal to stop on a road or railway; a warning. **red-light district**, one containing many brothels. **red pepper**, cayenne pepper; the ripe fruit of a capsicum plant. **red rag**, a thing that excites a person's rage. **red rose**, the emblem of Lancashire or Lancastrians. **red squirrel**, a squirrel of the native English species (Sciurus leucouros) with reddish fur. **red tape**, excessive use of or adherence to formalities especially in public business; the term derives from the fastening for department bundles of documents in Britain. —**reddish** adj., **redly** adv., **redness** n. [Old English]

red- prefix; see ◊re-[2]

Red and the Black, The French Le Rouge et le noir novel by Stendhal, published 1830. Julien Sorel, a carpenter's son, pursues social advancement by dishonourable means. Marriage to a marquis's daughter, a title, and an army commission are within his grasp when revelation of his murky past by a former lover destroys him.

Red Army former name of the army of the USSR. It developed from the Red Guards, volunteers who carried out the Bolshevik revolution, and received its name because it fought under the red flag. It was officially renamed the Soviet Army in 1946. The Chinese revolutionary army was also called the Red Army.

red blood cell or **erythrocyte** an oxygen-transporting cell of the ◊blood. Red cells are the most numerous type of blood cell and contain the red pigment haemoglobin. Mammalian erythrocytes are disclike with a depression in the centre and no nucleus; those of other vertebrates are oval and nucleated.

redbreast n. a ◊robin.

redbrick adj. (of English universities) founded in the 19th century or early 20th century, as distinct from Oxford and Cambridge (Oxbridge).

Red Brigades Italian Brigate rosse extreme left-wing guerrilla groups active in Italy during the 1970s and early 1980s. They were implicated in many kidnappings and killings, including that of Christian Democrat leader Aldo Moro 1978.

redcap n. a member of the military police.

redcoat n. (historical) a British soldier.

Red Cross, the an international relief agency founded by the Geneva Convention in 1864 at the instigation of the Swiss doctor Henri ◊Dunant to assist the wounded and prisoners in war. Its symbol is a symmetrical red cross on a white ground. In addition to dealing with associated problems of war, such as refugees and the care of the disabled, the Red Cross is increasingly concerned with victims of natural disasters—floods, earthquakes, epidemics, and accidents.

redcurrant n. a small, round, red edible berry; the shrub Ribes sylvestre bearing it.

redden /ˈredən/ v.t./i. to make or become red.

Redding /ˈredɪŋ/ Otis 1941–1967. US soul singer and songwriter. He had a number of hits in the mid-1960s such as 'My Girl' 1965, 'Respect' 1967, and '(Sittin' on the) Dock of the Bay' 1968, released after his death in a plane crash.

red dwarf any star that is cool, faint, and small (about one-tenth the mass and diameter of the Sun). A red dwarf burns slowly and has an estimated lifetime of 100 billion years. Red dwarfs may be the most abundant type of star, but are difficult to see because they are so faint. Two of the closest stars to the Sun, ◊Proxima Centauri and ◊Barnard's Star, are red dwarfs.

redecorate /riːˈdekəreɪt/ v.t. to decorate freshly. —**redecoration** /-ˈreɪʃən/ n.

redeem /rɪˈdiːm/ v.t. 1. to buy back, recover by expenditure of effort or by a stipulated payment. 2. to make a single payment to cancel (a regular charge or obligation). 3. to convert (tokens or bonds) into goods or cash. 4. to save, rescue, or reclaim; to deliver from damnation or from the consequences of sin. 5. to make amends for, to serve as a compensating factor; to save from a defect or from blame. 6. to purchase the freedom of (a person); to save (a person's life) by a ransom. 7. to fulfil (a promise). [from Old French or Latin emere = buy]

redeemable adj. that may be redeemed.

redeemer n. one who redeems. —**the Redeemer**, Jesus who, in Christian belief, redeemed humankind.

redemption /rɪˈdempʃən/ n. 1. redeeming, being redeemed. 2. a thing that redeems.

redeploy /riːdɪˈplɔɪ/ v.t. to send (troops or workers etc.) to a new place or task. —**redeployment** n.

redevelop /riːdɪˈveləp/ v.t. to develop (especially land) afresh. —**redevelopment** n.

red flag a symbol of danger or revolution; the international symbol of socialism. In France it was used as a revolutionary emblem from 1792 onward, and was adopted officially as its flag by the Paris Commune of 1871. Since the revolution of Nov 1917, it has been the national flag of the USSR; as such it bears a golden hammer and sickle crossed, symbolizing the unity of the industrial workers and peasants, under a gold-rimmed five-pointed star, signifying peace between the five continents. The British Labour Party anthem, called 'The Red Flag', was written by Jim ◊Connell in 1889.

Redford /ˈredfəd/ (Charles) Robert 1937– . US actor and film director. His first starring role was in Butch Cassidy and the Sundance Kid 1969, and his other films as an actor include All the President's Men 1976 and Out of Africa 1985. He directed Ordinary People 1980 and The Milagro Beanfield War 1988.

red giant any large bright star with a cool surface. A red giant is thought to represent a late stage in the evolution of a star like the Sun, as it runs out of hydrogen fuel at its centre. It has a diameter between 10 and 100 times that of the Sun, and because it is so large it is very bright, but the surface temperature is lower than that of the Sun, about 2,000–3,000K ($1,700°C/3,000°F–2,700°C/5,000°F$).

Redgrave /ˈredɡreɪv/ Michael 1908–1985. British actor. His stage roles included Hamlet and Lear (Shakespeare), Uncle Vanya (Chekhov), and the schoolmaster in Rattigan's The Browning Version. He also appeared in films. He was the father of Vanessa and Lynn Redgrave, both actresses.

Redgrave Vanessa 1937– . British actress. She has played Shakespeare's Lady Macbeth and Cleopatra on the stage, and the title role in the film Julia 1976 (Academy Award). She is active in left-wing politics. Daughter of Michael Redgrave.

Red Guards the armed workers who took part in the ◊Russian Revolution of 1917. The name was also given to the school and college students, wearing red armbands, active in the Cultural Revolution in China 1966–68.

rediffusion /riːdɪˈfjuːʒən/ n. the relaying of broadcast programmes, especially by wire from a central receiver.

redirect /riːdɪˈrekt/ v.t. to direct or send to another place, to readdress. —**redirection** n.

red shift

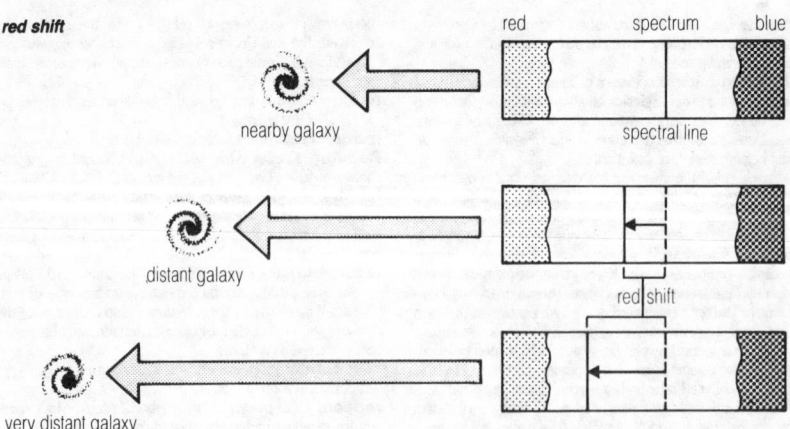

red spectrum blue

nearby galaxy

spectral line

distant galaxy

red shift

very distant galaxy

rediscover /riː diˈskʌvə/ *v.t.* to discover again (what has been lost).

Redmond /ˈredmənd/ John Edward 1856–1918. Irish politician, Parnell's successor as leader of the Nationalist Party 1890–1916. The 1910 elections saw him holding the balance of power in the House of Commons, and he secured the introduction of a ◊Home Rule bill, which was opposed by Protestant Ulster.

redo /riː duː/ *v.t.* (*past* **redid;** *past participle* **redone** /–ˈdʌn/) 1. to do again. 2. to redecorate.

redolent /ˈredələnt/ *adj.* strongly smelling or suggestive or reminiscent *of*; fragrant. —**redolence** *n.* [from Latin *olēre* = smell]

Redon /rəˈdɒn/ Odilon 1840–1916. French Symbolist painter and graphic artist. He used fantastic symbols and images, sometimes mythological. From the 1890s he painted still lifes and landscapes. His work was much admired by the Surrealists.

redouble /riː dʌbəl/ *v.t./i.* 1. to make or grow greater or more intense or numerous. 2. to double again a bid in bridge already doubled by an opponent. —*n.* redoubling of a bid in bridge.

redoubt /riˈdaʊt/ *n.* an outwork or fieldwork without flanking defences. [from French from Italian from Latin *reductus* = refuge]

redoubtable /riˈdaʊtəbəl/ *adj.* formidable, especially an opponent. [from Old French *redouter* = fear]

Redoubt, Mount /riˈdaʊt/ active volcanic peak rising to 3,140 m/10,197 ft W of Cook inlet in S Alaska, USA. There were recent eruptions in 1966 and 1989.

redound /riˈdaʊnd/ *v.i.* to come back as an advantage or disadvantage, to accrue. [from Old French from Latin *redundare* = overflow]

redox reaction a chemical change in which one reactant is reduced and the other oxidized. The reaction can occur only if both are present and each changes simultaneously. For example, hydrogen reduces copper(II) oxide to copper while it is itself oxidized to water.

$$CuO + H_2 \rightarrow Cu + H_2O$$

Many chemical changes can be classified as redox. Corrosion of iron, the reactions in chemical cells, and electrolysis are just a few instances in which redox reactions occur.

redpoll *n.* 1. a bird with a red forehead (especially *Carduelis flammea*) similar to a linnet. 2. an animal of a red breed of polled cattle.

redress /riˈdres/ *v.t.* to set right; to rectify (a wrong or grievance etc.). —*n.* reparation, amends for a wrong done; redressing of a grievance etc. —**redress the balance,** to restore equality. [from Old French]

Red Riding Hood a traditional European fairy story. Little Red Riding Hood is on her way to visit her sick grandmother when she meets a wolf. After discovering where she is going he gets there before her, and eats and impersonates the grandmother. In Charles Perrault's version (1697) Red Riding Hood is eaten too, but later writers introduced a woodcutter to rescue her.

Red Scare (*historical*) campaign against radicals and dissenters in the USA which took place in the aftermath of

World War I and the Russian Revolution, during a period of labour disorders and violence.

Red Sea a submerged section of the ◊Great Rift Valley (2,000 km/1,200 mi long and up to 320 km/200 mi wide). Egypt, Sudan, and Ethiopia (in Africa) and Saudi Arabia (Asia) are on its shores.

redshank *n.* a large wading bird, *Tringa totanus*, of N Europe and Asia, a type of sandpiper. It nests in swampy areas, although most winter in the south. It is greyish and speckled black, and has long red legs.

red shift in astronomy, the lengthening of the wavelengths of light from an object as a result of the object's motion away from us. It is an example of the ◊Doppler effect. The red shift in light from galaxies is evidence that the universe is expanding.

redskin *n.* (*derogatory*) an American Indian.

redstart *n.* a small, red-tailed songbird of the genus *Phoenicurus*. A member of the thrush family, it winters in Africa and spends the summer in Eurasia. The male has a dark-grey head (with white mark on the forehead and black face) and back, brown wings with lighter underparts, and a red tail. [Old English *steort* = tail]

Red Terror the term used by opponents to describe the Bolshevik seizure and retention of power in Russia after Oct 1917.

reduce /riˈdjuːs/ *v.t./i.* 1. to make or become smaller or less. 2. to bring by force or necessity to some state or action. 3. to convert to another (especially simpler) form; to convert (a fraction) to the form with the lowest terms; to bring, simplify, or adapt by classification or analysis to its components etc. 4. to subdue, to bring back to obedience. 5. to make lower in status or rank. 6. to slim. 7. to weaken; to impoverish. 8. to convert (an oxide etc.) to a metal; to remove oxygen from or add hydrogen or electrons to. 9. to restore (a broken or dislocated part) to its original or proper position; to remedy (a dislocation) thus. —**reducer** *n.* [from Latin *ducere* = bring]

reducible *adj.* that may be reduced.

reductio ad absurdum /rɪdʌktɪəʊ æd əbˈsɜːdəm/ proof of falsity by showing the absurd logical consequence; the carrying of a principle to unpractical lengths. [Latin = reduction to the absurd]

reduction /riˈdʌkʃən/ *n.* 1. reducing, being reduced; an instance of this. 2. the amount by which something is reduced, especially in price. 3. a reduced copy of a picture or version of a musical score etc. 4. in chemistry, the gain of electrons, loss of oxygen, or gain of hydrogen by an atom, ion, or molecule during a chemical reaction. [from Old French or Latin]

reductive /riˈdʌktɪv/ *adj.* causing reduction.

redundancy rights in British law, the rights of employees to a payment (linked to the length of their employment) if they lose their jobs because they are no longer needed. The statutory right was introduced in 1965, but payments are often made in excess of the statutory scheme.

redundant /riˈdʌndənt/ *adj.* 1. superfluous; that can be omitted without loss of significance. 2. (of a worker) no longer needed for any available job and therefore liable to dismissal. —**redundancy** *n.* [from Latin]

reduplicate /ri'dju:plɪkeɪt/ *v.t.* to make double, to repeat; to repeat (a word or syllable) exactly or with a slight change (e.g. *hurly-burly*, *see-saw*). —**reduplication** /-'keɪʃən/ *n.*, **reduplicative** /-kətɪv/ *adj.* [from Latin *duplicare* = duplicate]

redwing *n.* a thrush, *Turdus iliacus*, smaller than the song thrush, with reddish wing and body markings. It breeds in the north of Europe and Asia, flying south in winter.

redwood *n.* a giant North American coniferous tree *Sequoia sempervirens* yielding reddish wood. See ◊sequoia.

re-echo /ri:'ekəʊ/ *v.t./i.* to echo repeatedly, to resound.

reed /ri:d/ *n.* 1. a water or marsh plant of the genus *Phragmites* with a firm stem; a tall straight stalk of this. The common reed *P. australis* attains a height of 3 m/ 10 ft, having stiff, erect leaves and straight stems bearing a plume of purplish flowers. 2. the vibrating part of some wind instruments. 3. (usually in *plural*) such an instrument. —**reed stop**, a reeded organ-stop. [Old English]

Reed Lou 1942– . US rock singer, songwriter, guitarist, and former member (1965–70) of the seminal New York avant-garde band **Velvet Underground**. His solo work deals largely with urban alienation and angst, and includes the albums *Berlin* 1973, *Street Hassle* 1978, and *New York* 1989.

Reed Oliver 1938– . British actor, nephew of the director Carol Reed. He became a star through such films as *Women in Love* 1969, *The Devils* 1971, and *Castaway* 1987.

reeded *adj.* with a vibrating reed.

reedy *adj.* 1. full of reeds. 2. like a reed in slenderness or (of grass) thickness. 3. like a reed instrument in tone. —**reediness** *n.*

reef[1] *n.* 1. a ridge of rock or sand etc. at or near the surface of the sea etc. 2. a lode of ore; the bedrock surrounding this. [from Middle Dutch or Middle Low German from Old Norse]

reef[2] *n.* each of several strips along the top or bottom of a sail that can be taken in or rolled up to reduce the sail's surface in high wind. —*v.t.* to take in the reef(s) of (a sail). —**reef knot**, a double knot made symmetrically. [from Dutch from Old Norse]

reefer *n.* 1. a marijuana cigarette. 2. a thick double-breasted jacket.

reek *v.i.* to smell strongly or unpleasantly; to have unpleasant or suspicious associations. —*n.* 1. a foul or stale smell. 2. (especially *Scottish*) smoke, vapour, a visible exhalation. [Old English]

reel *n.* 1. a cylindrical device on which thread, silk, yarn, paper, film, wire etc., are wound; a quantity of thread etc. wound on a reel; a device for winding and unwinding a line as required, especially in fishing. 2. a revolving part in various machines. 3. a lively folk-dance or Scottish dance; the music for this. —*v.t./i.* 1. to wind (thread, a fishing-line etc.) on or off reel. 2. to draw (a fish etc.) in by using a reel. 3. to stand, walk, or run unsteadily; to be shaken physically or mentally; to rock from side to side, to swing violently. 4. to dance a reel. —**reel off**, to say or recite very rapidly and without apparent effort. [Old English]

reel *n.* in cinema, plastic or metal spool used for winding and storing film. As the size of cinema reels became standardized it came to refer to the running time of the film: a standard 35-mm reel holds 313 m/900 ft of film, which runs for ten minutes when projected at 24 frames per second; hence a 'two-reeler' was a film lasting 20 minutes. Today's projectors, however, hold bigger reels.

re-elect /ri:ɪ'lekt/ *v.t.* to elect again. —**re-election** *n.*

re-enter /ri:'entə/ *v.t./i.* to enter again. —**re-entry** *n.*

re-entrant /ri:'entrənt/ *adj.* (of an angle) pointing inwards, reflex.

Rees-Mogg /ri:s 'mɒg/ Lord William 1928– . British journalist, editor of *The Times* 1967–81, chair of the Arts Council 1982–89, and from 1988 chair of the Broadcasting Standards Council.

re-establish /ri:ɪ'stæblɪʃ/ *v.t.* to establish again. —**re-establishment** *n.*

reeve[1] *n.* (*historical*) the chief magistrate of a town or district. In Anglo-Saxon England, a reeve was an official charged with the administration of a shire or burgh, fulfilling functions similar to those of the later sheriff. After the Norman Conquest, the term tended to be restricted to the person elected by the villeins to oversee the work of the manor and to communicate with the manorial lord. [Old English]

reeve[2] *v.t.* (*past* rove) (*nautical*) to thread (a rope or rod etc.) through a ring or other aperture; to fasten (a rope or block etc.) thus.

reeve[3] *n.* a female ruff (bird of the sandpiper family).

Reeves /ri:vz/ William Pember 1857–1932. New Zealand politician and writer. He was New Zealand minister of education 1891–96, and director of the London School of Economics 1908–19. He wrote poetry and the classic description of New Zealand, *Long White Cloud* 1898.

re-examine /ri:ɪg'zæmɪn/ *v.t.* to examine again. —**re-examination** /-'neɪʃən/ *n.*

ref *n.* (*colloquial*) a referee in sports. [abbreviation]

reface /ri:'feɪs/ *v.t.* to put a new facing on (a building).

refectory /rɪ'fektərɪ, 'refɪk-/ *n.* a room for communal meals, especially in a monastery or college. —**refectory table**, a long narrow table. [from Latin *refectorium* (*reficere* = refresh)]

refer /rɪ'fɜː/ *v.t./i.* (-rr-) 1. to ascribe; to consider as belonging to a specified date, place or class. 2. to send on or direct (a person, a question for discussion) to an authority or source of information; to make an appeal or have recourse thus. 3. to make an allusion; to direct attention by words; to interpret (a statement) as being directed, (of a statement) to have relation or be directed (to what is specified). —**referred pain**, pain felt in a part of the body other than its true source. —**referral** *n.* [from Old French from Latin *referre* = carry back]

referable /rɪ'fɜːrəbl, 'refər-/ *adj.* that may be referred.

referee /refə'riː/ *n.* 1. a person to whom a dispute is or may be referred for decision. 2. an umpire, especially in football or boxing. 3. a person willing to testify to the character of an applicant for employment etc. 4. in law, a member of the court of referees appointed by the House of Commons to give judgement on petitions against private bills; also one of the three officials to whom cases before the high court may be submitted. —*v.t./i.* to act as a referee (for).

reference /'refərəns/ *n.* 1. the referring of a matter for decision, settlement, or consideration to some authority. 2. the scope given to such an authority. 3. relation, respect, or correspondence *to*. 4. allusion. 5. a direction to a book etc. (or a passage in it) where information may be found; a book or passage so cited. 6. the act of looking up a passage etc. or of referring to a person etc. for information. 7. a written testimonial supporting an applicant for employment etc.; a person giving this. —**in** *or* **with reference to**, regarding, as regards, about. **reference book**, a book for occasional consultation, providing information for reference but not designed to be read straight through. **reference library** *or* **room**, one providing books that may be consulted but not taken away. —**referential** /-'renʃəl/ *adj.*

referendum /refə'rendəm/ *n.* (*plural* **referendums**) the referring of a political question to the electorate for a direct decision by a general vote. It is most frequently employed in Switzerland, the first country to use it, but has also been used in Australia, New Zealand, Québec, and certain states of the USA. It was used in the UK for the first time in 1975 on the issue of membership of the European Community. A similar device is the ◊recall. See also ◊initiative. [Latin, gerund of *referre* = refer]

refill /ri:'fɪl/ *v.t.* to fill again. —/'ri:fɪl/ *n.* a new filling; the material for this.

refine /rɪ'faɪn/ *v.t./i.* 1. to free from impurities or defects. 2. to make or become more polished or elegant or cultured. [from French *raffiner*]

refined *adj.* characterized by polish, elegance, or subtlety.

refinement *n.* 1. refining, being refined. 2. fineness of feeling or taste; polish or elegance in behaviour or manners. 3. an added development or improvement. 4. a piece of subtle reasoning, a fine distinction.

refiner *n.* one who refines, especially one whose business is to refine crude oil or sugar or metal etc.

refinery *n.* a place where oil etc. is refined.

refining *n.* any process that purifies or converts something into a more useful form. Metals usually need refining after they have been extracted from their ores by such processes as smelting (see ◊smelt[1]). Petroleum, or crude oil, needs refining before it can be used; the process involves

◊fractionation, the separation of the substance into separate components or 'fractions'.

refit /ri:'fit/ *v.t./i.* (**-tt-**) to make or become fit again (especially of a ship undergoing renewal and repairs). —/'ri:fit/ *n.* refitting. —**refitment** *n.*

reflate /ri:'fleit/ *v.t.* to cause the reflation of (a currency or economy etc.).

reflation /ri:'fleiʃən/ *n.* the inflation of a financial system to restore the previous condition after deflation. —**reflationary** *adj.*

reflect /ri'flekt/ *v.t./i.* **1.** (of a surface or body) to throw back (heat, light, or sound). **2.** (of a mirror etc.) to show an image of; to reproduce to the eye or mind; to correspond in appearance or effect to. **3.** (of an action or result etc.) to show or bring (credit etc.) on the person or method responsible; (*absolute*) to bring discredit on the person etc. responsible. **4.** to think deeply, to consider; to remind oneself of past events. [from Old French or Latin *flectere*= bend]

reflection /ri'flekʃən/ *n.* or **reflexion 1.** reflecting, being reflected. **2.** reflected light or heat etc; a reflected image; the throwing back or deflection of waves, such as ◊light[1] or ◊sound[1] waves, when they hit a surface. The **law of reflection** states that the angle of incidence (the angle between the ray and a perpendicular line drawn to the surface) is equal to the angle of reflection (the angle between the reflected ray and a perpendicular to the surface). **3.** discredit; a thing bringing this. **4.** reconsideration. **5.** deep thought; an idea or statement produced by this.

reflective *adj.* **1.** (of a surface etc.) giving back a reflection or image. **2.** (of mental faculties) concerned in reflection or thought; (of a person or mood etc.) thoughtful, given to meditation.

reflector *n.* **1.** a piece of glass or metal etc. for reflecting light in a required direction, e.g. a red one on the back of a motor vehicle. **2.** a mirror producing images; a telescope equipped with this.

reflex /'ri:fleks/ *adj.* **1.** (of an action) independent of the will, as an automatic response to nerve-stimulation (e.g. a sneeze). **2.** (of an angle) exceeding 180°. —*n.* **1.** a reflex action, controlled by the ◊nervous system. The receptor (e.g. a sense organ) and the effector (such as a muscle) are linked directly (via the spinal ganglia or the lower brain, in vertebrates), making responses to stimuli very rapid. Reflex actions are most common in simple animals. **2.** a secondary manifestation, a corresponding result. **3.** reflected light; a reflected image. [Latin *reflexus*]

reflex camera a camera that uses a mirror and prisms to reflect light passing through the lens into the viewfinder, showing the photographer the exact scene that is being shot. When the shutter button is released, the mirror springs out of the way, allowing light to reach the film. The most common type is the single-lens reflex (◊SLR) camera. The twin-lens reflex (◊TLR) camera has one lens with a mirror for viewing, the other is used for exposing the film.

reflexive /ri'fleksiv/ *adj.* in grammar, of a word or form, implying the subject's action on himself or itself. —*n.* a reflexive word or form, especially a pronoun (e.g. *myself*).

refloat /ri:'fləʊt/ *v.t.* to set (a stranded ship) afloat again.

reflux /'ri:flʌks/ *n.* backward flow; in chemistry, a method of boiling in which vapour is liquefied and returned to the boiler.

reform /ri'fɔ:m/ *v.t./i.* to make or become better by the removal of faults or errors; to abolish or cure (an abuse or malpractice). —*n.* the removal of faults or abuses, especially of a moral or political or social kind; an improvement made or suggested. **Reformed Church,** any of the Protestant churches which have accepted the principles of the Reformation, especially of those following Calvinist rather than Lutheran doctrines. —**reformer** *n.* [from Old French or Latin *formare* = form]

re-form /ri:'fɔ:m/ *v.t./i.* to form again.

Reform Acts UK acts of Parliament 1832, 1867, and 1884 that extended voting rights and redistributed parliamentary seats.

Reformation *n.* a religious and political movement in 16th-century Europe to reform the Roman Catholic Church, and leading to the establishment of Protestant churches. Anticipated from the 12th century by the Waldenses, Lollards, and Hussites, it became effective in the 16th century when the absolute monarchies gave it support by

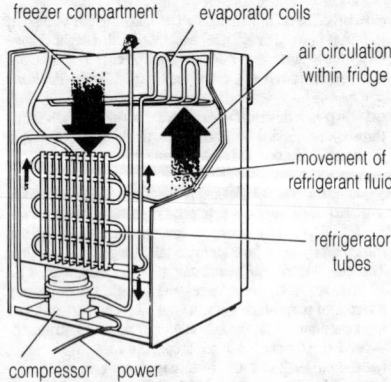

challenging the political power of the papacy and confiscating church wealth.

reformation /refə'meiʃən/ *n.* reforming, being reformed, especially a radical change for the better in public affairs.

reformative /ri'fɔ:mətiv/ *adj.* tending or intended to produce reform. [from Old French or Latin]

reformatory /ri'fɔ:mətəri/ *adj.* reformative. —*n.* (*US* and *historical*) an institution to which young offenders are sent.

refract /ri'frækt/ *v.t.* (of water, air, glass etc.) to deflect (a ray of light etc.) at a certain angle when it enters obliquely from another medium of different density.

refraction *n.* the bending of a wave of light, heat, or sound when it passes from one medium to another. Refraction occurs because waves travel at different velocities in different media. **refractive** *adj.* [from Latin *refringere* (*frangere*= break)]

refractor *n.* a refracting medium or lens; a telescope using a lens to produce an image.

refractory /ri'fræktəri/ *adj.* **1.** resisting control or discipline, stubborn. **2.** (of a disease or wound etc.) not yielding to treatment. **3.** (of a substance) resistant to heat; hard to fuse or work; e.g. ◊ceramics made from clay, minerals, or other earthy materials. Furnaces are lined with silica and dolomite. Alumina (aluminium oxide) is an excellent refractory, often used for the bodies of spark plugs. Titanium and tungsten are often called refractory metals because they are temperature resistant. ◊Cermets are refractory materials made up of ceramics and metals. [from Latin *refractarius*]

refrain[1] /ri'frein/ *v.i.* to abstain or keep oneself (*from* a thing or action). [from Old French from Latin *refrenare* (*frenum* = bridle)]

refrain[2] *n.* a recurring phrase or lines especially at the end of stanzas; the music accompanying this. [from Old French ultimately from Latin]

refrangible /ri'frændʒibəl/ *adj.* that can be refracted.

refresh /ri'freʃ/ *v.t.* to give fresh spirit or vigour to; to stimulate (one's memory). [from Old French]

refresher *n.* **1.** an extra fee to counsel in a prolonged lawsuit. **2.** (*colloquial*) a drink. —**refresher course,** a course reviewing previous studies, or giving instruction in modern methods etc.

refreshment *n.* **1.** refreshing, being refreshed. **2.** a thing that refreshes, especially food and drink, (usually in *plural*) this when not regarded as constituting a meal.

refrigerant /ri'fridʒərənt/ *n.* a substance used for refrigeration. The most commonly used refrigerants in modern systems were ◊chlorofluorocarbons, but these are now being replaced by coolants that do not damage the ozone layer. —*adj.* refrigerating. [from French or Latin]

refrigerate /ri'fridʒəreit/ *v.t./i.* to make or become cool or cold; to subject (food etc.) to cold in order to freeze or preserve it.

refrigeration *n.* the use of technology to transfer heat from cold to warm, against the normal temperature gradient, so that a body can remain substantially colder than its surroundings. Refrigeration equipment is used for the chilling and deep freezing of food (see ◊food technology) and in air conditioners and industrial processes. Refrigeration is commonly achieved by a vapour-compression cycle, in which a suitable chemical (the refrigerant) travels through a long circuit of tubing, during which it changes from a vapour to a liquid and back again. A compression chamber makes it condense, and thus give out heat. In another part of the circuit, called the evaporator coils, the pressure is much lower, so the refrigerant evaporates, absorbing heat as it does so. The evaporation process takes place near the central part of the refrigerator, which therefore becomes colder, while the compression process takes place near a ventilation grille, transfering the heat to the air outside. [from Latin *frigus* = cold]

refrigerator *n*. a cabinet or room in which food etc. is refrigerated.

reft *past* and *past participle* ◊reave.

refuel /ri:'fju:əl/ *v.t./i.* (-ll-) to replenish the fuel supply (of).

refuge /'refju:dʒ/ *n*. shelter from pursuit or danger or trouble; a person or place etc. offering this. [from Old French from Latin *fugere* = flee]

refugee /refju'dʒi:/ *n*. a person taking refuge, especially in a foreign country, from political, religious, or military persecution or natural disaster. In 1990 there were an estimated 15 million refugees worldwide, whose resettlement and welfare were the responsibility of the United Nations High Commission for Refugees (UNCHR). [from French *réfugié*]

refulgent /ri'fʌldʒənt/ *adj*. shining, gloriously bright. —**refulgence** *n*. [from Latin *fulgēre* = shine]

refund /ri:'fʌnd/ *v.t./i.* to pay back (money or expenses); to reimburse (a person); to make repayment. —/'ri:fʌnd/ *n*. refunding, repayment. [originally = pour back, from Old French or Latin *fundere* = pour]

refurbish /ri:'fɜ:bɪʃ/ *v.t.* to brighten up, to redecorate.

refusal /ri'fju:zəl/ *n*. 1. refusing, being refused. 2. the right or privilege of deciding to accept or refuse a thing before it is offered to others.

refuse[1] /ri'fju:z/ *v.t./i.* 1. to say or show that one is unwilling to accept, give, or do (what is requested); to indicate unwillingness; not to grant a request made by (a person). 2. (of a horse) to be unwilling to jump (a fence etc.). [from Old French]

refuse[2] /'refju:s/ *n*. what is rejected as worthless, waste.

refutable /ri'fju:təbəl/ *adj*. that may be refuted.

refute /ri'fju:t/ *v.t.* to prove the falsity or error of (a statement etc. or a person advancing it); to rebut by argument. —**refutation** /refju'teɪʃən/ *n*. [from Latin *refutare*]

regain /ri'geɪn/ *v.t.* 1. to obtain possession, use, or control of after loss. 2. to reach (a place) again.

regal /'ri:gəl/ *adj*. of or by a monarch or monarchs; fit for a king or queen, magnificent. —**regality** /ri'gælɪti/ *n.*, **regally** *adv*. [from Old French or Latin *regalis* (*rex* = king)]

regale /ri'geɪl/ *v.t.* to entertain lavishly with feasting or talk etc.; (of beauty, flowers etc.) to give delight to. [from Old French *gale* = pleasure]

regalia /ri'geɪljə/ *n.pl.* the insignia of royalty used at coronations; the insignia of an order or civic dignity. The British **crown jewels** (except for the Ampulla and the Anointing Spoon) were broken up at the time of Oliver Cromwell, and now date from the Restoration. In 1671 Colonel ◊Blood attempted to steal them, but was captured, then pardoned and pensioned by Charles II. They are kept in the Tower of London in the Crown Jewel House (1967). [Latin]

Regan /'ri:gən/ Donald 1918– . US Republican political adviser to Ronald ◊Reagan. He was secretary of the Treasury 1981–85, and chief of White House staff 1985–87, when he was forced to resign because of widespread belief of his complicity in the ◊Irangate scandal.

regard /ri'gɑ:d/ *v.t.* 1. to gaze steadily at (usually in a specified way). 2. to give heed to, to take into account. 3. to look upon or contemplate mentally in a specified way, to consider to be. —*n*. 1. a steady gaze. 2. heed, consideration. 3. respectful or kindly feeling. 4. reference, a point attended to. 5. (in *plural*) an expression of friendliness in a letter etc., compliments. —**as regards,** about, concerning, in respect of. **in** *or* **with regard to,** regarding, in respect of. [from French *regarder*]

regardant /ri'gɑ:dənt/ *adj*. in heraldry, looking backwards. [from Anglo-French and Old French]

regardful *adj*. mindful *of*.

regarding *prep*. about, concerning, with reference to.

regardless *adj*. without regard or consideration (*of*). —*adv*. without paying attention.

regatta /ri'gætə/ *n*. a meeting for boat or yacht races. [Venetian dialect]

regelation *n*. a phenomenon in which water refreezes to ice after it has been melted by pressure at a temperature below the freezing point of water. Pressure makes an ice skate, for example, form a film of water that freezes once again after the skater has passed.

regency /'ri:dʒənsi/ *n*. the office of a regent; a commission acting as regent; a regent's or regency commission's period of office. —**the Regency,** the period of 1811–20 in Britain when George, Prince of Wales, (later ◊George IV) acted as regent, or 1715–23 in France with Philip, Duke of Orleans, as regent. [from Latin]

Regency style a style of architecture and interior furnishings popular in England during the late 18th and early 19th centuries. The style is characterized by its restrained simplicity and its imitation of ancient classical elements, often Greek.

regenerate /ri'dʒenəreɪt/ *v.t./i.* 1. to generate again; to form afresh. 2. to give new life or vigour to. 3. to reform spiritually or morally. —/ri'dʒenərət/ *adj*. spiritually born again, reformed. —**regeneration** /-'reɪʃən/ *n*. **regenerative** *adj*. [from Latin *generare* = beget]

regeneration *n*. in biology, regrowth of a new organ or tissue after the loss or removal of the original. It is common in plants, where a new individual can often be produced from a cutting of the original. In animals, regeneration of major structures is limited to lower organisms; certain lizards can regrow their tails if these are lost, and new flatworms can grow from a tiny fragment of an old one. In mammals, regeneration is limited to the repair of tissue in wound healing and the regrowth of peripheral nerves following damage.

regent /'ri:dʒənt/ *n*. a person discharging the royal functions during a sovereign's minority or incapacity, or during a lengthy absence from the country. —*adj*. (placed after a noun) acting as regent. [from Old French or Latin *regere* = rule]

Reger /'reɪgə/ (Johann Baptist Joseph) Max(imilian) 1873–1916. German composer and pianist. He taught at Munich 1905–07, was professor at the Leipzig Conservatoire from 1907, and was conductor of the Meiningen ducal orchestra 1911–14. His works include organ and piano music, chamber music, and songs.

reggae /'regeɪ/ *n*. the predominant form of Jamaican popular music of the 1970s and 1980s, characterized by a strongly accentuated subsidiary beat and a prominent bass. The lyrics often refer to Rastafarianism. Musicians include Bob Marley (1945–1981), Lee 'Scratch' Perry (1940– , performer and producer), and the group Black Uhuru. Reggae is widely popular outside the West Indies, with many exponents especially in South Africa and the UK.

regicide /'redʒɪsaɪd/ *n*. 1. the killing of a king. 2. a person guilty of or involved in this. —**regicidal** /-'saɪdəl/ *adj*. [from Latin *rex regis* = king]

regime /reɪ'ʒi:m/ *n*. a method or system of government; the prevailing order or system of things. [from French]

regimen /'redʒɪmen/ *n*. a prescribed course of exercise, way of life, and especially diet. [Latin *regere* = rule]

regiment /'redʒɪmənt/ *n*. 1. a permanent unit of the army usually commanded by a colonel and divided into several companies, troops, or batteries and often into two or more battalions. 2. an operational unit of artillery etc. 3. a large array or number of things. —/also -ment/ *v.t.* to organize rigidly into groups or according to a system; to form into regiment(s). — **regimentation** /-'teɪʃən/ *n*. [from Old French from Latin]

regimental /redʒi'mentəl/ *adj*. of a regiment. —*n*. (in *plural*) military uniform, especially of a particular regiment. —**regimentally** *adv*.

Regina /ri'dʒaɪnə/ *n*. the reigning queen (in the titles of lawsuits, e.g. *Regina* v. *Jones*, the Crown versus Jones). [Latin = queen]

indubitable. **7.** bound by a religious rule; belonging to a religious or monastic order. —*n.* **1.** a regular soldier. **2.** (*colloquial*) a regular customer, visitor etc. **3.** a member of the regular clergy. —**regularity** /-'lærɪtɪ/ *n.* **regularly** *adv.* [from Old French and Latin *regula* = rule]

regularize /'regjʊləraɪz/ *v.t.* to make regular.

regulate /'regjʊleɪt/ *v.t.* **1.** to control or direct by rule(s); to subject to restrictions. **2.** to adapt to requirements; to alter the speed of (a machine or clock) so that it will work accurately. —**regulator** *n.* [from Latin *regulare*]

regulation /regjʊ'leɪʃən/ *n.* **1.** regulating, being regulated. **2.** a prescribed rule. —*adj.* in accordance with regulations, of the correct type etc.; usual. —**the Queen's Regulations,** those applying to the armed forces.

Regulus /'regjʊləs/ *n.* the brightest star in the constellation Leo, and the 21st brightest star in the sky. Regulus has a true luminosity 160 times that of the Sun, and is 85 light years from Earth.

regurgitate /rɪ'gɜːdʒɪteɪt/ *v.t./i.* **1.** to bring (swallowed food) up again to the mouth. **2.** to cast or pour out again; to gush back. —**regurgitation** /-'teɪʃən/ *n.* [from Latin *regurgitare* (*gurges* = whirlpool)]

rehabilitate /riːhə'bɪlɪteɪt/ *v.t.* **1.** to restore to effectiveness or normal life by training, especially after imprisonment or illness. **2.** to restore to privileges, reputation, or proper condition. —**rehabilitation** /-'teɪʃən/ *n.*

rehash /riː'hæʃ/ *v.t.* to put (old material) into a new form without significant change or improvement. —/'riːhæʃ/ *n.* rehashing; material rehashed.

rehearsal /rɪ'hɜːsəl/ *n.* rehearsing; a trial performance or practice.

rehearse /rɪ'hɜːs/ *v.t./i.* **1.** to practise before performing in public. **2.** to train by rehearsal. **3.** to recite, to say over; to give a list of, to enumerate. [from Anglo-French and Old French]

reheat /riː'hiːt/ *v.t.* to heat again. —**reheater** *n.*

Rehnquist /'renkwɪst/ William 1924– . Chief justice of the US ◊Supreme Court. Active within the Republican Party, he was appointed head of the office of legal counsel by President Nixon in 1969 and controversially defended such measures as pre-trial detention and wiretapping.

Rehoboam /riːhə'bəʊəm/ king of Judah about 932–915 BC, son of Solomon. Under his rule the Jewish nation split into the two kingdoms of **Israel** and **Judah**. Ten of the tribes revolted against him and took Jeroboam as their ruler, leaving Rehoboam only the tribes of Judah and Benjamin.

rehoboam /riːhə'bəʊəm/ *n.* a large winebottle, twice the size of a jeroboam. [from *Rehoboam*]

Rehoboth Gebiet /rɪ'həʊbəθ/ district of Namibia to the south of Windhoek; area 32,168 sq km/12,420 sq mi; chief town Rehoboth. The area is occupied by the Basters, an ethnic group of European-Nama descent.

rehouse /riː'haʊz/ *v.t.* to provide with new accommodation.

Reich /raɪx, -k/ *n.* the three periods in European history. The **First Reich** was the Holy Roman Empire 962–1806, the **Second Reich** the German Empire 1871–1918, and the ◊**Third Reich** Nazi Germany 1933–45. [German = kingdom, realm, state]

Reich /raɪk/ Steve 1936– . US composer. His Minimalist music consists of simple patterns carefully superimposed and modified to highlight constantly changing melodies and rhythms; examples are *Phase Patterns* for four electronic organs 1970, *Music for Mallet Instruments, Voices, and Organ* 1973, and *Music for Percussion and Keyboards* 1984.

Reich Wilhelm 1897–1957. Austrian doctor, who emigrated to the USA 1939. He combined ◊Marxism and ◊psychoanalysis to advocate the positive effects of directed sexual energies and sexual freedom.

Reichstadt, Duke of /'raɪkʃtæt/ title of ◊Napoleon II, son of Napoleon I.

Reichstag /'raɪkstɑːg/ *n.* the German parliament building and lower legislative house during the German Empire 1871–1918 and Weimar Republic 1919–33.

Reichstag Fire the burning of the German parliament building in Berlin on 27 Feb 1933, less than a month after the Nazi leader Hitler became chancellor. The fire was used as a justification for the suspension of many constitutional guarantees and also as an excuse to attack the communists. There is still debate over Nazi involvement in the crime, not least because they were the main beneficiaries.

Regina /rə'dʒaɪnə/ industrial city (oil refining, cement, steel, farm machinery, fertilizers), and capital of Saskatchewan, Canada; population (1986) 175,000. It was founded in 1882 as **Pile O'Bones**, and renamed in honour of Queen Victoria of England.

region /'riːdʒən/ *n.* **1.** a continuous part of a surface, space, or body, with or without definite boundaries or with certain characteristics. **2.** an administrative division of a country, especially in Scotland. **3.** the sphere or realm of a subject etc. —**in the region of,** approximately. —**regional** *adj.*, **regionally** *adv.* [from Old French from Latin *regio* = direction, district]

Regional Crime Squad in the UK, a local police force that deals with serious crime; see under ◊Scotland Yard, New.

register /'redʒɪstər/ *n.* **1.** an official list of names, items, attendances etc.; the book or other document(s) in which this is kept. **2.** a mechanical device for indicating or recording speed, force, numbers etc., automatically. **3.** an adjustable plate for widening or narrowing an opening and regulating draught, especially in a fire-grate. **4.** the compass of a voice or instrument; a part of the voice-compass. **5.** a set of organ-pipes; a sliding device controlling this. **6.** exact correspondence of position in printing etc. —*v.t./i.* **1.** to enter or cause to be entered in a register. **2.** to set down formally in writing; to present for consideration. **3.** to entrust (a letter etc.) to a post office for transmission by registered post. **4.** (of an instrument) to indicate or record automatically. **5.** to notice and remember. **6.** to express (an emotion) facially or by a gesture. **7.** to make an impression on a person's mind. —**registered post,** a procedure with special precautions for safety and for compensation in case of loss. **register office,** a place where records of births, marriages, and deaths are made and where civil marriages are performed. [from Old French or Latin *regesta* = things recorded]

register *n.* in computing, a fast type of memory, often built into the computer's central processing unit. Some registers are reserved for special tasks, such as keeping track of the next command to be executed; others are used for holding frequently used data and for storing intermediate results.

registrar /redʒɪ'strɑː/ *n.* **1.** a person charged with keeping a register; the senior administrative officer in a university etc. **2.** a doctor undergoing hospital training as a specialist. [from Latin]

registration /redʒɪ'streɪʃən/ *n.* registering, being registered. —**registration mark** *or* **number,** a combination of letters and figures uniquely identifying a motor vehicle. [from obsolete French or Latin]

registry /'redʒɪstrɪ/ *n.* a place or office where registers are kept. —**registry office,** a register office. [from Latin *registerium*]

Regius professor /'riːdʒɪəs/ the holder of a chair founded by a sovereign (especially one at Oxford or Cambridge instituted by Henry VIII) or filled by crown appointment. [Latin = royal (*rex regis* = king)]

regnant /'regnənt/ *adj.* reigning. [from Latin *regnare* = reign]

regress /rɪ'gres/ *v.i.* **1.** to move backwards. **2.** to go back to an earlier or more primitive state. —/'riːgres/ *n.* regressing; relapse, backward tendency. —**regression** *n.*, **regressive** *adj.* [from Latin *gradi* = to step]

regret /rɪ'gret/ *v.t.* (-tt-) to feel or express sorrow, repentance, or distress over (an action or loss etc.); to say with sorrow or remorse. —*n.* a feeling of sorrow or repentance etc. over an action or loss etc. —**give** *or* **send** etc. **one's regrets,** to decline an invitation. [from Old French *regreter* = bewail]

regretful *adj.* feeling or showing regret. —**regretfully** *adv.*

regrettable *adj.* (of events or conduct) undesirable, unwelcome, deserving censure. —**regrettably** *adv.*

regroup /riː'gruːp/ *v.t./i.* to form into new groups.

regular /'regjʊlə/ *adj.* **1.** conforming to a rule or principle or to a standard of procedure; consistent; symmetrical. **2.** acting, done, or recurring uniformly or calculably in time or manner; habitual, constant, orderly. **3.** conforming to a standard of etiquette or procedure. **4.** properly constituted or qualified; devoted exclusively or primarily to its nominal function. **5.** in grammar, (of a noun, verb etc.) following the normal type of inflexion. **6.** (*colloquial*) thorough,

Reichstein /'raɪkstaɪn/ Tadeus 1897– . Swiss biochemist who investigated the chemical activity of the adrenal glands. By 1946 Reichstein had identified a large number of steroids secreted by the adrenal cortex, some of which would later be used in the treatment of Addison's disease. Reichstein shared the 1950 Nobel Prize for Physiology or Medicine with Edward Kendall (1886–1972) and Philip Hench (1896–1965).

reign /reɪn/ n. sovereignty, rule; the period during which a sovereign reigns. —v.i. 1. to be king or queen. 2. to prevail. [from Old French from Latin regnum = kingdom]

reimburse /riːɪmˈbɜːs/ v.t. to repay (a person who has expended money, a person's expenses). —**reimbursement** n. [from obsolete imburse from Latin bursa = purse]

Reims /riːmz/, French ræns/ (English **Rheims**) capital of Champagne-Ardenne region, France; population (1982) 199,000. It is the centre of the champagne industry and has textile industries as well. It was known in Roman times as Durocorturum. From 987 all but six French kings were crowned here. Ceded to England in 1420 under the Treaty of Troyes, it was retaken by Joan of Arc, who had Charles VII consecrated in the 13th-century cathedral. In World War II, the German High Command formally surrendered here to US general Eisenhower on 7 May 1945.

rein /reɪn/ n. (in singular or plural) 1. a long narrow strap with each end attached to a bit, used to guide or check a horse etc. in riding or driving; a similar device to restrain a child etc. 2. a means of control. —v.t. 1. to check or control with reins; to pull or hold (as) with reins. 2. to restrain, to control. —**give free rein to**, to allow free scope to. **keep a tight rein on**, to allow little freedom to. [from Old French from Latin tenēre = hold]

reincarnation /riːɪnkɑːˈneɪʃ(ə)n/ n. the rebirth of a human soul or the spirit of a plant or animal in another human or animal. The belief is part of the teachings of many religions and philosophies, for example ancient Egyptian and Greek (the philosophies of Pythagoras and Plato), Buddhism, Hinduism, Jainism, certain Christian heresies (such as the Cathars), and theosophy. It is also referred to as **transmigration** or metempsychosis. —**reincarnate** /-ɪnˈkɑːnɪt/ adj.

reindeer /'reɪndɪə/ n. (North American **caribou**) (plural the same) a deer, Rangifer tarandus, of Arctic and subarctic regions, common to both eastern and western hemispheres. About 120 cm/4 ft at the shoulder, it has a thick, brownish coat and broad hooves well adapted to travel over snow. It is the only deer in which both sexes have antlers; up to 150 cm/5 ft long, they are shed in winter. [from Old Norse]

reinforce /riːɪnˈfɔːs/ v.t. to strengthen or support, especially by additional men or material or by an increase of numbers, quantity, size etc. [from French renforcer from Latin fortis = strong]

reinforcement n. 1. reinforcing, being reinforced. 2. a thing that reinforces; (in plural) additional personnel, ships etc. sent to reinforce armed forces etc.

Reinhardt /'raɪnhɑːt/ Django (Jean Baptiste) 1910–1953. Belgian jazz guitarist and composer, who was co-leader, with Stephane Grappelli, of Quintet de Hot Club de France 1934–39.

Reinhardt Max 1873–1943. Austrian producer and director whose Expressionist style was predominant in German theatre and film during the 1920s and 1930s. Directors such as Murnau and Lubitsch and actors such as Dietrich worked with him. He co-directed the US film A Midsummer Night's Dream 1935.

reinstate /riːɪnˈsteɪt/ v.t. to restore to or replace in a lost position or privileges etc. —**reinstatement** n. [from instate = establish in office]

reinsure /riːɪnˈʃʊə/ v.t./i. to insure again (especially of an insurer securing himself by transferring risk to another insurer). —**reinsurance** n.

reissue /riːˈɪsjuː/ v.t. to issue (a thing) again. —n. a thing reissued.

Reisz /raɪs/ Karel 1926– . Czech film director, originally a writer and film critic, who lived in Britain from 1938. His first feature film, Saturday Night and Sunday Morning 1960, was a critical and commercial success. His other movies include Morgan 1966, The French Lieutenant's Woman 1981, and Sweet Dreams 1986.

reiterate /riːˈɪtəreɪt/ v.t. to say or do again or repeatedly. —**reiteration** /-ˈreɪʃən/ n., **reiterative** /-ˈɪtərətɪv/ adj.

reject /rɪˈdʒekt/ v.t. 1. to refuse to accept or believe in. 2. to put aside or send back as not to be used or done or complied with etc. —/'riːdʒekt/ n. a person or thing rejected. —**rejection** /rɪˈdʒekʃən/ n., **rejector** n. [from Latin rejicere (jacere = throw)]

rejig /riːˈdʒɪg/ v.t. (-gg-) to re-equip (a factory etc.) for a new kind of work; (colloquial) to rearrange.

rejoice /rɪˈdʒɔɪs/ v.t./i. 1. to feel or show great joy; to take delight. 2. to cause joy to. —**rejoicing** n. [from Old French rejoir]

rejoin[1] /rɪˈdʒɔɪn/ v.t./i. to join together again, to reunite.

rejoin[2] v.t./i. to say in answer, to retort; to reply to a charge or pleading in a lawsuit. [from Old French rejoindre]

rejoinder /rɪˈdʒɔɪndə/ n. what is said in reply or rejoined, a retort.

rejuvenate /rɪˈdʒuːvəneɪt/ v.t. to make (as if) young again. —**rejuvenation** /-ˈneɪʃən/ n., **rejuvenator** n. [from Latin juvenis = young]

relapse /rɪˈlæps/ v.i. to fall back into a previous condition, or into a worse state after improvement. —n. relapsing, especially after partial recovery from illness. [from Latin labi = slip]

relate /rɪˈleɪt/ v.t./i. 1. to narrate, to tell in detail. 2. to bring into relation. 3. to have reference. 4. to bring oneself into a sympathetic or successful relationship (to a person or thing). [from Latin]

related adj. connected, especially by blood or marriage; having a common descent or origin.

relation /rɪˈleɪʃən/ n. 1. the way in which one person or thing is related to another; a similarity, correspondence, or contrast between people or things or events. 2. (in plural) dealings with others; sexual intercourse. 3. a person who is a relative. 4. being related. 5. narration, a narrative. —**in relation to**, as regards. —**relationship** n. [from Old French or Latin]

relational database in computing, a type of ◊database in which data are viewed as a collection of linked tables. It is the most popular of the three basic database models, the others being **network** and **hierarchical**.

relative /'relətɪv/ adj. 1. considered in relation to something else. 2. proportionate; comparative. 3. corresponding in some way, related to each other; having reference or relating to. 4. in grammar, (of a word) referring to an expressed or implied antecedent and attaching a subordinate clause to it; (of a clause) attached to an antecedent by a relative word. —n. 1. a person who is related to another by parentage, descent, or marriage. 2. a species related to another by a common origin. 3. in grammar, a relative word, especially a pronoun. —**relatively** adv., **relativeness** n. [from Old French or Latin]

relative atomic mass the mass of an atom. It depends on the number of protons and neutrons in the atom, the electrons having negligible mass. It is calculated relative to one-twelfth the mass of an atom of carbon-12. If more than one ◊isotope of the element is present, the relative atomic mass is calculated by taking an average that takes account of the relative proportions of each isotope, resulting in values that are not whole numbers. The term **atomic weight**, although commonly used, is strictly speaking incorrect.

relative biological effectiveness the relative damage caused to living tissue by different types of radiation. Some radiations do much more damage than others; alpha particles, for example, cause 20 times as much destruction as electrons (beta particles).

relative density or **specific gravity** the density (at 20°C/68°F) of a solid or liquid relative to (divided by) the maximum density of water (at 4°C/39.2°F). The relative density of a gas is its density divided by the density of hydrogen (or sometimes dry air) at the same temperature and pressure.

relative humidity the concentration of water vapour in the air. It is expressed as a percentage of the maximum amount that the air could contain at the same temperature and pressure. The higher the temperature the more water vapour the air can hold.

relative molecular mass the mass of a molecule, calculated relative to one-twelfth the mass of an atom of carbon-12. It is found by adding the relative atomic masses of the atoms that make up the molecule. The

religion – festivals

Month	Festival	Religion	Commemorating
Jan 6th	Epiphany	Western Christian	coming of the Magi
6th–7th	Christmas	Orthodox Christian	birth of Christ
18th–19th	Epiphany	Orthodox Christian	coming of the Magi
Jan–Feb	New Year	Chinese	Return of Kitchen God to heaven
Feb–Mar	Shrove Tuesday	Christian	day before Lent
	Ash Wednesday	Christian	first day of Lent
	Purim	Jewish	story of Esther
	Mahashivaratri	Hindu	Siva
Mar–Apr	Palm Sunday	Western Christian	first day of Holy Week
	Good Friday	Western Christian	Crucifixion of Christ
	Easter	Western Christian	Resurrection of Christ
	Passover	Jewish	escape from slavery in Egypt
	Holi	Hindu	Krishna
	Holi Mohalla	Sikh	(coincides with Holi)
	Rama Naumi	Hindu	birth of Rama
	Ching Ming	Chinese	remembrance of dead
Apr 13th	Baisakhi	Sikh	founding of the Khalsa
Apr–May	Easter	Orthodox Christian	Resurrection of Christ
May–Jun	Shavuot	Jewish	giving of Ten Commandments to Moses
	Whitsun	Western Christian	filling of Jesus's followers with Holy Spirit
	Wesak	Buddhist	day of Buddha's birth, enlightenment and death
	Martyrdom of Guru Arjan	Sikh	death of fifth guru of Sikhism
Jun	Dragon Boat Festival	Chinese	Chinese martyr
	Whitsun	Orthodox Christian	filling of Jesus's followers with Holy Spirit
Jul	Dhammacakka	Buddhist	preaching of Buddha's first sermon
Aug	Raksha Bandhan	Hindu	family
Aug–Sept	Janmashtami	Hindu	birthday of Krishna
Sept	Moon Festival	Chinese	Chinese hero
Sept–Oct	Rosh Hashana	Jewish	start of Jewish New Year
	Yom Kippur	Jewish	day of fasting
	Succot	Jewish	Israelites' time in the wilderness
Oct	Dusshera	Hindu	goddess Devi
Oct–Nov	Divali	Hindu	goddess Lakshmi
	Divali	Sikh	release of Guru Hargobind from prison
Nov	Guru Nanak's Birthday	Sikh	founder of Sikhism
	Advent	Western Christian	preparation for Christmas
Nov–Dec	Bodhi Day	Buddhist (Mahayana)	Buddha's enlightenment
Dec	Hanukkah	Jewish	recapture of Temple of Jerusalem
	Winter Festival	Chinese	time of feasting
25th	Christmas	Western Christian	birth of Christ
Dec–Jan	Birthday of Guru Gobind Singh	Sikh	last (tenth) human guru of Sikhism
	Martyrdom of Guru Tegh Bahadur	Sikh	ninth guru of Sikhism

term **molecular weight** is often used, but strictly this is incorrect.

relativity /relə'tɪvɪtɪ/ *n.* 1. being relative. 2. a theory based on the principle that all motion is relative and that light travels with a constant maximum speed in a vacuum (also **special relativity**); a theory extending this to gravitation and accelerated motion (**general relativity**).

relax /rɪ'læks/ *v.t./i.* 1. to make or become less stiff, rigid, or tense. 2. to make or become less formal or strict. 3. to reduce or abate (one's attention or efforts etc.). 4. to cease work or effort; to indulge in recreation. —**relaxation** /-'seɪʃən/ *n.* [from Latin *laxus* = lax]

relay /'riːleɪ/ *n.* 1. a fresh set of people or animals taking the place of others who have completed a spell of work. 2. a fresh supply of material to be used or worked on. 3. a relay race. 4. a device activating an electric circuit; a device that receives and transmits a telegraph message or broadcast etc. A small current passing through a coil of wire wound around an iron core attracts an ()armature whose movement closes a pair of sprung contacts to complete a secondary circuit, which may carry a large current or activate other devices. The solid-state equivalent is a thyristor switching device. 5. a relayed message or transmission. —/also riː'leɪ/ *v.t.* to receive (a message, broadcast etc.) and transmit to others. —**relay race**, a race between teams of which each member in turn covers part of the distance. [from Old French *relai* from Latin *laxare*]

re-lay /riː'leɪ/ *v.t.* (*past* and *past participle* **re-laid**) to lay again.

relay neurone a nerve cell in the spinal cord, connecting motor neurones to sensory neurones. Relay neurones allow information to pass straight through the spinal cord, bypassing the brain. In humans such reflex actions, which are extremely rapid, cause the sudden removal of a limb from a painful stimulus.

release /rɪ'liːs/ *v.t.* 1. to set free (*literal* or *figurative*); to unfasten. 2. to remove or allow to move from a fixed position; to allow to fall or fly etc. 3. to make (information or a recording etc.) public; to issue (a film etc.) for general exhibition. —*n.* 1. releasing, being released. 2. a handle or catch etc. that unfastens a device or machine-part. 3. a document etc. made available for publication; a film or record etc. that is released; the releasing of a document or film etc. thus. [from Old French *relesser* from Latin *relaxare* = relax]

relegate /'relɪgeɪt/ *v.t.* to consign or dismiss to an inferior position; to transfer (a sports team) to a lower division of a league etc.; to banish. —**relegation** /-'geɪʃən/ *n.* [from Latin *legare* = send]

relent /rɪ'lent/ *v.i.* to relax one's severity, to abandon a harsh intention, to yield to compassion. [from Latin *lentare* = bend]

relentless *adj.* unrelenting. —**relentlessly** *adv.*, re-lentlessness *n.*

relevant /'relɪvənt/ *adj.* related to the matter in hand. —**relevance** *n.* [from Latin *relevare* = lift]

reliable /rɪ'laɪəbəl/ *adj.* that may be relied on. —**reliability** /-'bɪlɪtɪ/ *n.*, **reliably** *adv.*

reliance /rɪ'laɪəns/ *n.* relying; trust, confidence.

relic /'relɪk/ *n.* 1. something that survives from an earlier age; a surviving custom or belief from a past age; an object that is interesting because of its age or associations. 2. a part of a holy person's body or belongings kept after his or her death as an object of reverence. Christian examples include the arm of St Teresa of Avila, the blood of St Januarius, and the ◊True Cross. Buddhist relics include the funeral ashes of the historic Buddha, placed in a number of stupas or burial mounds. 3. (in *plural*) residue, surviving scraps; the dead body or remains of a person. [from Old French from Latin *reliquiae* from *relinquere* = leave behind]

relict /'relɪkt/ *n.* 1. a person's widow 2. a geological or other object surviving in a primitive form.

relief /rɪ'liːf/ *n.* 1. alleviation of or deliverance from pain, distress, anxiety etc. 2. a feature etc. that breaks up monotony or relaxes tension. 3. assistance given to persons in special danger, need, or difficulty. 4. the replacing of a person or persons on duty by another or others; the person(s) thus taking over. 5. a thing supplementing another in some service. 6. a method of moulding, carving, or stamping in which the design stands out from the surface; a piece of sculpture etc. in relief; representation of relief given by the arrangement of line, colour, or shading. The Italian terms *basso-rilievo* (low relief), *mezzo-rilievo* (middle relief), and *alto-rilievo* (high relief) are used according to the extent to which the sculpture projects. The French term *bas-relief* is commonly used to mean low relief. 7. deliverance of a besieged place, especially by raising the siege. 8. redress of a hardship or grievance. —**relief map,** a map showing hills and valleys by shading or colouring etc. rather than by contour lines alone. **relief road,** a road by which traffic can avoid a congested area. [from Anglo-French and French from Italian]

relieve /rɪ'liːv/ *v.t.* 1. to give relief, bring or be a relief to. 2. to mitigate the tedium or monotony of. 3. to release (a person) from duty by taking his place or providing a substitute. —**relieve one's feelings,** to use strong language or vigorous behaviour when annoyed. **relieve oneself,** to urinate or defecate. **relieve a person of,** to take (a burden or responsibility etc.) from him. [from Old French *relever* from Latin *relevare* = lift]

religion /rɪ'lɪdʒən/ *n.* 1. belief in a superhuman controlling power, especially in a personal God or gods entitled to obedience and worship; the expression of this in worship. 2. a particular system of faith. 3. a thing that one is devoted to. 4. life under monastic vows. [from Anglo-French from Latin *religio* = obligation, bond, reverence]

religious /rɪ'lɪdʒəs/ *adj.* 1. believing firmly in a religion and paying attention to its practices. 2. of or concerned with religion. 3. of or belonging to a monastic order. 4. scrupulous, conscientious. —*n.* (*plural* the same) a person bound by monastic vows. —**religiously** *adv.*

relinquish /rɪ'lɪŋkwɪʃ/ *v.t.* 1. to give up or cease from (a habit, plan, or belief etc.). 2. to resign or surrender (a right or possession). 3. to relax one's hold of. —**relinquishment** *n.* [from Old French from Latin *relinquere* = leave behind]

reliquary /'relɪkwərɪ/ *n.* a receptacle for relics. [from French *reliquaire*]

relish /'relɪʃ/ *n.* 1. great liking or enjoyment. 2. appetizing flavour, attractive quality. 3. a thing eaten with plainer food to add flavour. 4. a distinctive taste or tinge *of.* —*v.t.* to get pleasure from, to enjoy greatly. [from Old French = remainder]

relive /riː'lɪv/ *v.t.* to live (an experience etc.) over again, especially in the imagination.

reload /riː'ləʊd/ *v.t./i.* to load again.

relocate /riː'ləʊkeɪt/ *v.t./i.* to locate in or move to a new place. —**relocation** /-'keɪʃən/ *n.*

reluctant /rɪ'lʌktənt/ *adj.* unwilling, with consent grudgingly given. —**reluctance** *n.*, **reluctantly** *adv.* [from Latin *luctari* = struggle]

rely /rɪ'laɪ/ *v.i.* (with *on* or *upon*) to trust confidently, to depend on for help. [originally = rally, be vassal of, from Old French *relier* = bind together]

rem acronym from roentgen equivalent man SI unit of radiation dose equivalent. Some types of radiation do more damage than others for the same absorbed dose; the equivalent dose in rems is equal to the dose in ◊rads multiplied by the relative biological effectiveness. Humans can absorb up to 25 rems without immediate ill effects; 100 rems may produce radiation sickness; and more than 800 rems causes death.

remain /rɪ'meɪn/ *v.i.* 1. to be left after other parts have been removed, used, or dealt with. 2. to be in the same place or condition during further time; to continue to be. [from Old French from Latin *manēre* = stay]

remainder /rɪ'meɪndə/ *n.* 1. the remaining persons, things, or part. 2. the number left after subtraction or division. 3. the copies of a book left unsold when demand has almost ceased. —*v.t.* to dispose of (the remainder of the copies of a book) at a reduced price. [from Anglo-French]

remains *n.pl.* 1. what remains after other parts have been removed or used etc. 2. relics of antiquity, especially of buildings. 3. a dead body. [from Old French]

remand /rɪ'mɑːnd/ *v.t.* to send back (a prisoner) into custody while further evidence is sought. —*n.* remanding, being remanded. —**on remand,** held in custody after being remanded. **remand centre** *or* **home,** an institution to which young offenders may be sent. [from Latin *mandare* = commit]

remanent /'remənənt/ *adj.* remaining, residual. —**remanent magnetism,** magnetization remaining after the source of excitation has been removed. [from Latin]

remark /rɪ'mɑːk/ *v.t./i.* 1. to say by way of comment. 2. to take notice of, to regard with attention. —*n.* 1. a written or spoken comment, anything said. 2. noticing. [from French *remarquer*]

remarkable *adj.* worth notice, exceptional, unusual. —**remarkably** *adv.*

Remarque /rə'mɑːk/ Erich Maria 1898–1970. German novelist, a soldier in World War I, whose *All Quiet on the Western Front* 1929, one of the first antiwar novels, led to his being deprived of German nationality. He lived in Switzerland 1929–39 and then in the USA.

remarry /riː'mærɪ/ *v.t./i.* to marry again. —**remarriage** *n.*

Rembrandt /'rembrænt/ Harmensz van Rijn 1606–1669. Dutch painter and etcher, one of the most prolific and significant artists in Europe of the 17th century. Between 1629 and 1669 he painted some 60 penetrating self-portraits. He also painted religious subjects, and produced about 300 etchings and over 1,000 drawings. His group portraits include *The Anatomy Lesson of Dr Tulp* 1632 (Mauritshuis, The Hague) and *The Night Watch* 1642 (Rijksmuseum, Amsterdam).

remediable /rɪ'miːdiəbəl/ *adj.* that may be remedied.

remedial /rɪ'miːdiəl/ *adj.* providing a remedy for a disease or deficiency. —**remedially** *adv.* [from Latin]

remedial education special classes, or teaching strategies, that aim to help children with learning difficulties to catch up with children within the normal range of achievement.

remedy /'remɪdɪ/ *n.* 1. something that cures or relieves a disease or that puts right a matter. 2. redress, legal or other reparation. —*v.t.* to be a remedy for; to put right. [from Anglo-French from Latin *remedium* (*medēri* = heal)]

remember /rɪ'membə/ *v.t.* 1. to keep in one's mind, not to forget. 2. to recall (knowledge or an experience etc.) to one's mind; to be able to do this. 3. to think of (a person), especially in making a gift etc. 4. to convey greetings from. [from Old French from Latin *memor* = mindful]

remembrance /rɪˈmembrəns/ *n. & adj.* 1. remembering, being remembered; memory. 2. a memento; a memorial. 3. (in *plural*) greetings conveyed through a third person. [from Old French]

Remembrance Sunday (known until 1945 as **Armistice Day**) in the UK, national day of remembrance for those killed in both world wars and later conflicts, on the second Sunday of Nov. In Canada 11 Nov is **Remembrance Day**. The US equivalent is ◊Veterans Day.

remind /rɪˈmaɪnd/ *v.t.* to cause (a person) to remember or think *of*.

reminder *n.* a thing that reminds or is a memento.

Remington /ˈremɪŋtən/ Frederic 1861–1909. US sculptor, painter, and illustrator. His exploratory trips to the American West inspired lively images of cowboys and horses, such as his sculpture *Off the Range* (Corcoran Gallery of Art, Washington, DC) and his bronze *Bronco Buster* 1895, of which there are over 300 copies.

Remington Philo 1816–1889. US inventor of the typewriter and breech-loading rifle that bear his name. He began manufacturing typewriters 1873, using the patent of Christopher Sholes (1819–1890), and made improvements that resulted five years later in the first machine with a shift key, thus providing lower-case letters as well as capital letters. The Remington rifle and carbine, which had a falling block breech and a tubular magazine, were developed in collaboration with his father.

reminisce /remɪˈnɪs/ *v.i.* to indulge in reminiscences.

reminiscence /remɪˈnɪsəns/ *n.* 1. remembering of things past. 2. (in *plural*) an account of facts and incidents remembered, especially in literary form. 3. a thing that is reminiscent of something else. [from Latin *reminisci* = remember]

reminiscent *adj.* 1. inclined to reminisce. 2. suggestive *of.* —**reminiscently** *adv.*

remiss /rɪˈmɪs/ *adj.* careless of one's duty, lax, negligent. [from Latin *remissus*]

remission /rɪˈmɪʃən/ *n.* 1. shortening of a prison sentence on account of good behaviour; the remitting of a debt or penalty etc. 2. diminution of force or intensity especially of a disease or pain; temporary disappearance of symptoms during the course of a disease. 3. God's pardon or forgiveness of sins. [from Old French or Latin]

remit /rɪˈmɪt/ *v.t./i.* (-**tt**-) 1. to cancel (a debt etc.); to refrain from inflicting (a punishment). 2. to make or become less intense; to cease. 3. to send (money etc.) in payment. 4. to refer (a matter for decision etc.) to some authority. 5. to postpone. 6. (of God) to pardon or forgive (sins). —/also ˈriːmɪt/ *n.* 1. an item remitted for consideration. 2. the terms of reference of a committee etc. [from Latin *mittere* = send]

remittance /rɪˈmɪtəns/ *n.* the sending of money to a person; the money sent.

remittent *adj.* that abates at intervals.

remnant /ˈremnənt/ *n.* 1. a small remaining quantity, part, or number of people or things; a surviving trace. 2. a piece of cloth etc. left when the greater part has been used or sold. [from Old French *remenant*]

remodel /riːˈmɒdəl/ *v.t.* to model again or differently; to reconstruct or reorganize.

remonstrance /rɪˈmɒnstrəns/ *n.* 1. (*historical*) a formal statement of public grievances. 2. remonstrating, a protest.

remonstrate /ˈremənstreɪt/ *v.t./i.* to make a protest (*with* a person). [from Latin *monstrare* = show]

remora *n.* a warm-water fish that has an adhesive disc on the head, by which it attaches itself to whales, sharks, and turtles. These provide the remora with shelter, transport, and food in the form of parasites on the host's skin.

remorse /rɪˈmɔːs/ *n.* deep regret for a wrong committed; compunction. [from Old French from Latin *remordēre* = vex (*mordēre* = bite)]

remorseful *adj.* filled with remorse. —**remorsefully** *adv.*

remorseless *adj.* relentless, without compassion. —**remorselessly** *adv.*

remote /rɪˈməʊt/ *adj.* 1. far apart; far away in place or time. 2. far from civilization etc.; secluded. 3. not closely related. 4. slight. 5. aloof, not friendly. —**remote control**, control of apparatus etc. from a distance, usually by means

of an electrically operated device, radio etc. —**remotely** *adv.,* **remoteness** *n.* [from Latin *remotus*]

remote sensing gathering and recording information from a distance, developed as a result of space technology. Space probes have sent back photographs and data about planets as distant as Neptune. Satellites such as *Landsat* have surveyed all the Earth's surface from orbit. Computer processing of data obtained by their scanning instruments, and the application of so-called false colours (generated by the computer), have made it possible to reveal surface features invisible in ordinary light. This has proved valuable in agriculture, forestry, and urban planning, and has led to the discovery of new deposits of minerals.

remould /riːˈməʊld/ *v.t.* to mould again, to refashion; to reconstruct the tread of (a tyre). —/ˈriːməʊld/ *n.* a remoulded tyre.

removable /rɪˈmuːvəbəl/ *adj.* that may be removed.

removal /rɪˈmuːvəl/ *n.* removing, being removed; transfer of furniture etc. to a different house.

remove /rɪˈmuːv/ *v.t./i.* 1. to take off or away from the place occupied; to convey to another place. 2. to get rid of. 3. to dismiss from office. 4. to take off (clothing). 5. (in *past participle*) distant, remote. —*n.* 1. distance, degree of remoteness. 2. a stage in gradation. 3. a form or division in some British schools. —**cousin once, twice** etc., **removed,** see ◊cousin. —**remover** *n.* [from Old French from Latin]

REM sleep or **rapid-eye-movement sleep** a phase of sleep that recurs several times nightly in humans and is associated with dreaming. The eyes flicker quickly beneath closed lids.

remunerate /rɪˈmjuːnəreɪt/ *v.t.* to pay or reward (a person) for a service rendered; to pay for or reward (work etc.). —**remuneration** /-ˈreɪʃən/ *n.,* **remunerative** *adj.* [from Latin *remunerari* (*munus* = gift)]

Renaissance /rɪˈneɪsəns, -sãs/ *n.* 1. the revival of art and learning under the influence of Classical models which began in Italy in the late Middle Ages and reached its peak at the end of the 15th century before spreading northwards into the rest of Europe; the period of this. 2. **renaissance,** any similar revival. [French = rebirth]

Renaissance art in painting and sculpture the ◊Renaissance movement led to greater naturalism and interest in anatomy and perspective. Renaissance art peaked around 1500 with the careers of Leonardo da Vinci, Raphael, Michelangelo, and Titian in Italy and Dürer in Germany. The revival of interest in classical Greek and Roman culture also inspired poets such as Petrarch and prose writers such as Boccaccio, and scientists and explorers proliferated.

renal /ˈriːnəl/ *adj.* of the kidneys. [from French from Latin *renes* = kidneys]

rename /riːˈneɪm/ *v.t.* to give a fresh name to.

renascent /rɪˈnæsənt/ *adj.* springing up anew, being reborn. —**renascence** *n.* [from Latin *nasci* = be born]

Renault /ˈrenəʊ/ Mary. Pen name of Mary Challans 1905–1983. English novelist who recreated the world of ancient Greece, with a trilogy on ◊Theseus and two novels on ◊Alexander: *Fire from Heaven* 1970 and *The Persian Boy* 1972.

rend *v.t./i.* (*past* and *past participle* **rent**) (*archaic*) to tear or wrench forcibly. [Old English]

Rendell /ˈrendl/ Ruth 1930– . English novelist and short-story writer, author of a detective series featuring Chief Inspector Wexford. Her psychological crime novels explore the minds of people who commit murder, often through obsession or social inadequacy, as in *A Demon in my View* 1976 and *Heartstones* 1987.

render *v.t.* 1. to cause to be or become. 2. to give or pay (money, a service etc.) especially in return or as a thing due; to give (assistance). 3. to present, to send in. 4. to represent or portray; to act (a role); to perform (music). 5. to translate. 6. to melt down (fat). 7. to cover (stone or brick) with a first coat of plaster. [from Anglo-French *rendre* from Latin *reddere* (*dare* = give)]

rendezvous /ˈrɒndeɪvuː/ *n.* (*plural* the same /-uːz/) an agreed or regular meeting-place; a meeting by agreement. —*v.i.* (*third person singular present* **rendezvouses** /-vuːz/, *past* **rendezvoused** /-vuːd/, *participle* **rendezvousing** /-vuːɪŋ/) to meet at a rendezvous. [from French *rendezvous* = present yourselves]

rendition /ren'dɪʃən/ *n.* the rendering or interpretation of a dramatic role, musical piece etc. [obsolete French]

René /rə'neɪ/ France-Albert 1935– . Seychelles left-wing politician, president from 1977 following a coup.

renegade /'renɪgeɪd/ *n.* one who deserts his or her party or principles. [from Spanish *renegado* from Latin]

renege /rɪ'niːg, -'neɪg/ *v.t/i.* 1. to deny, to renounce. 2. (*US*, in cards) to revoke. —**renege on,** to fail to keep (a promise etc.); to disappoint (a person). [from Latin *negare* = deny]

renew /rɪ'njuː/ *v.t.* 1. to restore to its original state; to revive, to regenerate. 2. to replace with a fresh supply etc. 3. to repeat, to re-establish; to make, get, or give again; to arrange for a continuation or continued validity of (a licence, subscription, lease etc.). —**renewal** *n.*

renewable resource a natural resource that is replaced by natural processes in a reasonable amount of time. Soil, water, forests, plants, and animals are all renewable resources as long as they are properly conserved. Solar, wind, wave, and geothermal energies are based on renewable resources.

Reni /'reɪni/ Guido 1575–1642. Italian painter, active in Bologna and Rome (about 1600–14), who is considered one of the greatest Italian artists of the 17th century. His work includes the fresco *Phoebus and the Hours Preceded by Aurora* 1613 (Casino Rospigliosi, Rome). His workshop in Bologna produced numerous religious images, including Madonnas.

Rennes /ren/ industrial city (oil refining, chemicals, electronics, cars) and capital of Ille-et-Vilaine *département*, W France, at the confluence of the Ille and Vilaine, 56 km/35 mi SE of St Malo; population (1982) 234,000. It was the old capital of Brittany.

rennet /'renɪt/ *n.* curdled milk found in the stomach of an unweaned calf, or a preparation of a bovine stomach-membrane or of a plant, used in curdling milk for cheese or junket. It contains the enzyme rennin, which can now be chemically produced.

Rennie /'reni/ John 1761–1821. Scottish engineer who built the old Waterloo Bridge and old London Bridge (reconstructed in Arizona, USA).

rennin *n.* or **chymase** enzyme found in the gastric juice of young mammals, used in the digestion of milk.

Renoir /'renwɑː/ Jean 1894–1979. French film director, son of the painter Auguste Renoir, whose films include *La grande Illusion* 1937, and *La Règle du jeu/The Rules of the Game* 1939. In 1975 he received an honorary Academy Award for his life's work.

Renoir Pierre-Auguste 1841–1919. French Impressionist painter. He met Monet and Sisley in the early 1860s, and together they formed the nucleus of the Impressionist movement. He developed a lively, colourful painting style with feathery brushwork and painted many voluptuous female nudes, such as *The Bathers* about 1884–87 (Philadelphia Museum of Art, USA). In his later years he turned to sculpture.

renounce /rɪ'naʊns/ *v.t.* 1. to give up (a claim or right etc.) formally. 2. to repudiate, to refuse to recognize any longer; to decline further association or disclaim a relationship with. [from Old French *renoncer* from Latin (*nuntiare* = announce)]

renovate /'renəveɪt/ *v.t.* to restore to a good condition, to repair. —**renovation** /-'veɪʃən/ *n.,* **renovator** *n.* [from Latin *novus* = new]

renown /rɪ'naʊn/ *n.* fame, high distinction. [from Anglo-French and Old French from Latin *nomen* = make famous]

renowned *adj.* famous, celebrated.

rent[1] *n.* a tenant's periodical payment to an owner or landlord for the use of land or premises; payment for the use of equipment etc. —*v.t./i.* 1. to pay rent for occupation or use of. 2. to let or hire for rent; to be let at a specified rent. [from Old French *rente*]

rent[2] *n.* a large tear in a garment etc.; an opening in clouds etc.

rent[3] *past* and *past participle* of ◊**rend.**

rentable /'rentəbəl/ *adj.* that may be rented.

rental /'rentəl/ *n.* 1. the amount paid or received as rent. 2. renting. [from Anglo-French or Latin]

Rentenmark /'rentənmɑːk/ *n.* the currency introduced in Germany at the end of 1923 by the president of the Reichsbank, Hjalmar Schacht (1877–1970), to replace old Reichsmarks which had been rendered worthless by inflation.

rentier /'rãtieɪ/ *n.* a person living on income from property or investments. [French *rente* = dividend]

renumber /riː'nʌmbə/ *v.t.* to change the numbering of.

renunciation /rɪnʌnsi'eɪʃən/ *n.* renouncing; the giving up of things.

reopen /riː'əʊpən/ *v.t./i.* to open again.

reorder /riː'ɔːdə/ *v.t.* 1. to order again. 2. to put into a new order.

reorganize /riː'ɔːgənaɪz/ *v.t.* to organize again in a different way. —**reorganization** /-'zeɪʃən/ *n.*

rep[1] *n.* a textile fabric with a corded surface, used in curtains and upholstery. [from French *reps*]

rep[2] *n.* (*colloquial*) a representative, especially a commercial traveller. [abbreviation]

rep[3] *n.* (*colloquial*) a repertory theatre or company. [abbreviation]

repaint /riː'peɪnt/ *v.t.* to paint again or differently. —/'riːpeɪnt/ *n.* 1. repainting. 2. a repainted thing.

repair[1] /rɪ'peə/ *v.t.* 1. to restore to a good condition after damage or wear. 2. to set right or make amends for (a loss or wrong etc.). —*n.* 1. restoring to a sound condition; the act or result of doing this. 2. condition as regards being repaired. —**repairer** *n.* [from Old French *reparer* from Latin *parare* = make ready]

repair[2] *v.i.* to go, resort, or have recourse to. [from Old French from Latin *repatriare*]

reparable /'repərəbəl/ *adj.* (of a loss etc.) that can be made good. [French from Latin]

reparation /repə'reɪʃən/ *n.* making amends; compensation. [from Old French from Latin]

repartee /repɑː'tiː/ *n.* a witty retort; the making of witty retorts. [from French *repartir* = reply promptly]

repast /rɪ'pɑːst/ *n.* a meal; the food and drink for a meal. [from Old French from Latin *repascere* = feed]

repatriate /riː'pætrieɪt/ *v.t./i.* to restore (a person) to his native land; to return thus. —/-ət/ *n.* a repatriated person. —**repatriation** /-'eɪʃən/ *n.* [from Latin *patria* = native land]

repay /riː'peɪ/ *v.t./i.* 1. to pay back (money); to pay back money to (a person). 2. to give in return or recompense; to make recompense for (a service etc.); to requite (an action). —**repayment** *n.*

repayable *adj.* that can or must be repaid.

repeal /rɪ'piːl/ *v.t.* to annul or revoke (a law etc.). —*n.* repealing. [from Anglo-French and Old French]

repeat /rɪ'piːt/ *v.t./i.* 1. to say, do, or provide again. 2. to say, recite, or report (something heard or learnt). 3. to recur, to appear again or repeatedly. 4. (of food) to be tasted intermittently for some time after being swallowed. —*n.* 1. repeating. 2. a thing repeated; a repeated broadcast programme; (*Music*) a passage intended to be repeated, a mark indicating this; each occurrence of a pattern repeated in wallpaper etc. —**repeat itself,** to recur in the same form. **repeat oneself,** to say or do the same thing over again. [from Old French from Latin *petere* = seek]

repeatable *adj.* that may be repeated; suitable for being repeated.

repeatedly *adv.* many times over.

repeater *n.* a person or thing that repeats, especially a firearm that fires several shots without reloading, or a watch etc. that strikes the last quarter etc. again when required; a device that repeats a signal.

repel /rɪ'pel/ *v.t.* (**-ll-**) 1. to drive back, to ward off; to refuse admission, approach, or acceptance to. 2. to be impenetrable by. 3. to be repulsive or distasteful to. [from Latin *pellere* = drive]

repellent *adj.* that repels. —*n.* a substance that repels something (especially insects).

repent /rɪ'pent/ *v.t./i.* to feel deep sorrow or regret about (one's wrongdoing or omission etc.). —**repentance** *n.,* **repentant** *adj.* [from Old French *repentir*]

repercussion /riːpə'kʌʃən/ *n.* 1. an indirect effect or reaction of an event or act. 2. a recoil after impact. 3. an echo. [from Old French or Latin *percutere* = strike]

repertoire /'repətwɑː/ *n.* a stock of pieces that a performer or company knows or is prepared to give; a stock of regularly performed pieces, regularly used techniques etc. [from French from Latin]

repertory /'repətərɪ/ n. **1.** a repertoire. **2.** theatrical performance of various plays for short periods by one company. **3.** a store or collection, especially of information or instances etc. [from Latin *repertorium* (*reperire* = find)]

repetition /repɪ'tɪʃən/ n. **1.** repeating, being repeated. **2.** a thing repeated; a copy. —**repetitious** adj., **repetitive** /rɪ'petɪtɪv/ adj., **repetitively** adv. [from French or Latin]

repine /rɪ'paɪn/ v.i. to fret, to be discontented.

replace /rɪ'pleɪs/ v.t. **1.** to put back in place. **2.** to take the place of. **3.** to find or provide a substitute for.

replaceable adj. that may be replaced.

replacement n. **1.** replacing, being replaced. **2.** a person or thing that takes the place of another.

replant /ri:'plɑ:nt/ v.t. to plant again or differently.

replantation /ri:plɑ:n'teɪʃ(e)n/ n. **1.** replanting. **2.** permanent reattachment to the body of a part which has been removed or severed.

replay /ri:'pleɪ/ v.t. to play (a match, recording etc.) over again. —/'ri:pleɪ/ n. the replaying (of a match, a recording of an incident in a game etc.).

replenish /rɪ'plenɪʃ/ v.t. to fill up again (*with*); to renew (a supply etc.). —**replenishment** n. [from Old French *replenir* (*plein* = full)]

replete /rɪ'pli:t/ adj. filled or well supplied; full, gorged, sated. —**repletion** n. [from Old French or Latin *plēre* = fill]

replica /'replɪkə/ n. an exact copy, especially a duplicate made by an original artist of his picture etc.; a model, especially on a smaller scale. [Italian]

replication n. in biology, production of copies of the genetic material, DNA; it occurs during cell division (◊mitosis and ◊meiosis). Most mutations are caused by mistakes during replication.

reply /rɪ'plaɪ/ v.t./i. to make an answer; to say in answer. —n. **1.** replying. **2.** what is replied, an answer. [from Old French from Latin *replicare*, literally = fold again]

reply, right of the right of a member of the public to respond to a media statement. A statutory right of reply, enforceable by a Press Commission, as exists in many Western European countries, failed to reach the statute book in the UK in 1989. There is no legal provision in the UK that any correction should receive the same prominence as the original statement and legal aid is not available in defamation cases, so that only the wealthy are able to sue. However, the major newspapers signed a Code of Practice in 1989 that promised some public protection.

report /rɪ'pɔ:t/ v.t./i. **1.** to bring back or give an account of; to state as a fact or news; to narrate, describe, or repeat, especially as a eyewitness or hearer etc.; to describe (an event etc.) for publication or broadcasting; to make an official or formal statement about. **2.** to make a formal accusation about (an offence or offender). **3.** to present oneself as having returned or arrived. **4.** to be responsible to a specified person as one's superior or supervisor. —n. **1.** a spoken or written account of something seen, done, or studied. **2.** a description for publication or broadcasting. **3.** a periodical statement on a pupil's work, conduct etc. **4.** rumour, a piece of gossip. **5.** the sound of an explosion or firing of a gun. —**reported speech**, a speaker's words as given in a report of them, with person and tense etc. adapted. [from Old French from Latin *portare* = carry]

reporter n. a person employed to gather and report news for a newspaper or broadcast.

repose[1] /rɪ'pəʊz/ n. **1.** cessation of activity, excitement, or toil; sleep. **2.** a peaceful or quiescent state, tranquillity. —v.t./i. to rest, to lie; to be supported. [from Old French from Latin *pausare* = pause]

repose[2] v.t. to place (trust etc.) *in*.

reposeful adj. inducing or exhibiting repose. —**reposefully** adv.

repository /rɪ'pɒzɪtərɪ/ n. a place where things are stored, especially a warehouse or museum; a receptacle; a recipient of secrets etc. [from obsolete French or Latin]

repossess /ri:pə'zes/ v.t. to regain possession of (especially goods on which hire-purchase payments are in arrears). —**repossession** n.

repp variant of ◊rep[1].

reprehend /reprɪ'hend/ v.t. to rebuke, to blame. [from Latin *prehendere* = seize]

reprehensible /reprɪ'hensɪbəl/ adj. deserving rebuke. —**reprehensibly** adv.

represent /reprɪ'zent/ v.t. **1.** to be an example or embodiment of. **2.** to symbolize. **3.** to present a likeness or description of to the mind or senses. **4.** to describe or depict, *as*, to declare *to be*; to declare. **5.** to show or play the part of in a picture or stage play etc. **6.** to be a deputy, agent, or spokesperson for; to be the elected representative of (the people of an area) in a legislative assembly. [from Old French or Latin *praesentare* = present]

representation /reprɪzen'teɪʃən/ n. **1.** representing, being represented. **2.** a thing that represents something. **3.** (especially in *plural*) a statement made by way of an allegation or to convey an opinion. —**representational** adj.

Representation of the People Acts a series of UK acts of Parliament from 1867 that extended voting rights, creating universal suffrage in 1928. See also ◊Reform Acts.

representative /reprɪ'zentətɪv/ adj. **1.** typical of a group or class. **2.** containing examples of all or many types. **3.** consisting of elected deputies or representatives; based on the representation of a nation etc. by such deputies. **4.** serving as a portrayal or symbol of. —n. **1.** a sample, or specimen, or typical embodiment. **2.** an agent of a person, or firm, or society; a firm's travelling salesman or -woman **3.** a delegate, a person chosen to represent another or others, or to take part in a legislative assembly on their behalf. —**House of Representatives**, the lower and larger branch of the legislative assembly in the USA. [from Old French or Latin]

repress /rɪ'pres/ v.t. to keep down, to suppress; to keep (emotions etc.) from finding an outlet; (in *past participle*) suffering from repression of the emotions. —**repression** n., in psychology, an unconscious process said to protect a person from ideas, impulses, or memories that would threaten emotional stability were they to become conscious. **repressive** adj., **repressively** adv. [from Latin *reprimere* (*premere* = press)]

reprieve /rɪ'pri:v/ v.t. **1.** to postpone or remit the execution of (a condemned person). **2.** to give a respite to. —n. **1.** reprieving, being reprieved; a legal temporary suspension of the execution of a sentence of a criminal court; a warrant for this. It is usually associated with the death penalty. It is distinct from a pardon (extinguishing the sentence) and commutation (alteration) of a sentence (e.g. from death to life imprisonment). **2.** a respite. [from Anglo-French *repris* (*reprendre* = take back)]

reprimand /'reprɪmɑ:nd/ n. a formal or official rebuke. —v.t. to administer a reprimand to. [from French from Spanish from Latin *reprimenda*]

reprint /ri:'prɪnt/ v.t. to print again. —/'ri:prɪnt/ n. the reprinting of a book etc.; a book etc. reprinted.

reprisal /rɪ'praɪzəl/ n. an act of retaliation. [from Anglo-French from Latin]

reprise /rɪ'pri:z/ n. a repeated passage in music; a repeated song etc. in a musical programme. [French]

reproach /rɪ'prəʊtʃ/ v.t. to express disapproval to (a person) for a fault or offence. —n. **1.** reproaching; an instance of this. **2.** a thing that brings disgrace or discredit. **3.** disgraced or discredited state. —**beyond reproach**, deserving no blame, perfect. [from Old French *reprocher* from Latin *prope* = near]

reproachful adj. inclined to or expressing reproach. —**reproachfully** adv.

reprobate /'reprəbeɪt/ n. an unprincipled or immoral person. [from Latin *reprobare* = disapprove]

reprobation /reprə'beɪʃən/ n. strong condemnation.

reproduce /ri:prə'dju:s/ v.t./i. **1.** to produce a copy or representation of. **2.** to cause to be seen or heard etc. again or to occur again. **3.** to produce further members of the same species by natural means; to produce offspring of.

reproducible adj. that may be reproduced.

reproduction /ri:prə'dʌkʃən/ n. **1.** reproducing, being reproduced. In biology, the process by which a living organism produces other organisms similar to itself. There are two kinds: asexual reproduction and sexual reproduction. The former is a biological term for reproductive processes that are not ◊sexual and thus do not involve fusion of ◊gametes. The production of offspring from an unfertilized gamete is called ◊parthenogenesis. Asexual processes include ◊binary fission, in which the parent organism splits into two or more 'daughter' organisms, and ◊budding, in which a new organism is formed initially as an outgrowth of the parent organism. The asexual production of spores, as in ferns and mosses, is also common, and many plants reproduce asexually by means of runners, rhizomes, bulbs, and corms; see ◊vegetative reproduction. Unlike sexual reproduction, these processes do not involve the fusion of two gametes. See also ◊parthenogenesis. Sexual reproduction is a reproductive process in organisms that requires the union, or fertilization, of gametes. These are usually produced by two different individuals, although self-fertilization occurs in a few ◊hermaphrodites such as tapeworms. Except in some lower organisms, the gametes are of two distinct types called eggs and sperm. The organisms producing the eggs are called females, and those producing the sperm, males. The fusion of a male and female gamete produces a **zygote**, from which a new individual develops. 2. a copy of a painting etc. 3. (*attributive*, of furniture etc.) made in imitation of an earlier style. —**reproduction rate** or **fecundity**, in ecology, the rate at which a population or species reproduces itself.

reproductive /riːprəˈdʌktɪv/ *adj.* of or concerning reproduction.

reprography /rɪˈprɒɡrəfɪ/ *n.* the science and practice of copying documents by photography, xerography etc. —**reprographic** /riːprəˈɡræfɪk/ *adj.*

reproof /rɪˈpruːf/ *n.* an expression of condemnation for a fault or offence. [from Old French *reprove*]

reprove /rɪˈpruːv/ *v.t.* to give a reproof to (a person) or for (conduct etc.). [from Old French *reprover* from Latin *reprobare* = disapprove]

reptile /ˈreptaɪl/ *n.* a vertebrate animal of the class Reptilia, which includes snakes, lizards, crocodiles, turtles, and tortoises. They breathe by means of lungs; this distinguishes them from ◊amphibians, the larvae of which breathe through gills. They are cold-blooded, produced from eggs, and the skin is usually covered with scales. The metabolism is slow, and in some cases (some large snakes) intervals between meals may be months. Reptiles date back over 300 million years. [from Latin *reptilis* (*repere* = crawl)]

reptilian /repˈtɪlɪən/ *adj.* 1. of reptiles. 2. (of animals) creeping. —*n.* a reptile.

republic /rɪˈpʌblɪk/ *n.* where the head of state is not a monarch, either hereditary or elected, but usually a president whose role may or may not include political functions [from French from Latin *respublica* (*res* = concern and *publicus* = public)]

Republic, The a treatise by the Greek philosopher Plato in which the voice of ◊Socrates is used to describe the ideal state, where the cultivation of truth, beauty, and goodness achieves perfection.

republican *adj.* 1. of or constituted as a republic; characteristic of republics. 2. advocating or supporting republican government. —*n.* 1. a person advocating or supporting republican government. 2. **Republican**, a member of the Republican Party. —**republicanism** *n.*

Republican Party one of the USA's two main political parties, formed 1854 by a coalition of ◊slavery opponents, who elected their first president, Abraham ◊Lincoln, in 1860. The early Republican Party supported protective tariffs and favoured genuine settlers (homesteaders) over land speculators. Towards the end of the century the Republican Party was identified with US imperialism and industrial expansion. With few intermissions, the Republican Party controlled Congress from the 1860s until defeated by the New Deal Democrats in 1932. After an isolationist period before World War II, the Republican Party adopted an active foreign policy under ◊Nixon and ◊Ford, but the latter was defeated by Carter in the presidential election of 1976. However, the party enjoyed landslide presidential victories for ◊Reagan and also carried the Senate 1980–86. ◊Bush won the 1988 presidential election but faced a Democratic Senate and House of Representatives.

repudiate /rɪˈpjuːdɪeɪt/ *v.t.* to reject or disown utterly; to deny; to refuse to recognize or obey (an authority or treaty) or discharge (an obligation or debt). —**repudiation** /-ˈeɪʃən/ *n.*, **repudiator** *n.* [from Latin *repudiare* (*repudium* = divorce)]

repugnant /rɪˈpʌɡnənt/ *adj.* 1. strongly distasteful or objectionable. 2. (of ideas etc.) inconsistent, incompatible. —**repugnance** *n.* [from French or Latin *repugnare* = fight against]

repulse /rɪˈpʌls/ *v.t.* 1. to drive back (an attack or attacking enemy) by force of arms. 2. to rebuff. 3. to refuse (a request or offer, or its maker). —*n.* 1. repulsing, being repulsed. 2. a rebuff. [from Latin *pellere* = drive]

repulsion /rɪˈpʌlʃən/ *n.* 1. repelling, being repelled. 2. a feeling of strong distaste, revulsion.

repulsive /rɪˈpʌlsɪv/ *adj.* 1. arousing strong distaste, loathsome. 2. causing repulsion. —**repulsively** *adv.*, **repulsiveness** *n.* [from French *répulsif* from Latin]

reputable /ˈrepjʊtəbəl/ *adj.* of good repute, respected. —**reputably** *adv.* [obsolete French or from Latin]

reputation /repjuˈteɪʃən/ *n.* 1. what is generally said or believed about a person or thing. 2. the state of being well thought of. [from Latin]

repute /rɪˈpjuːt/ *n.* reputation. —*v.t.* (in *passive*) to be generally considered. [from Old French or Latin *putare* = think]

reputed /rɪˈpjuːtɪd/ *adj.* said or thought to be but possibly not. —**reputed pint** etc., a bottle of wine or spirits etc. sold as a pint etc. but not guaranteed as an imperial measure. —**reputedly** *adv.*

request /rɪˈkwest/ *n.* 1. asking for something. 2. a thing asked for. 3. the state of being sought after, demand. —*v.t.* to make a request for (a thing) or of (a person); to seek permission. —**by** or **on request**, in response to an expressed wish. **request stop**, a place where a bus etc. stops only on a passenger's (or intended passenger's) request. [from Old French from Latin *requaerere*]

requiem /ˈrekwɪəm/ *n.* in the Roman Catholic church, a mass for the dead; the music for this. Musical settings include those by Palestrina, Mozart, Berlioz, and Verdi. [from Latin accusative of *requies* = repose]

require /rɪˈkwaɪə/ *v.t.* 1. to be unable to do without, to depend on for success, fulfilment, growth etc. 2. to lay down as imperative; to order or oblige. 3. to wish to have. [from Old French from Latin *requirere* (*quaerere* = seek)]

requirement *n.* a thing required; a need.

requisite /ˈrekwɪzɪt/ *adj.* required by circumstances, necessary to success. —*n.* a thing needed for some purpose. [from Latin *requisitus*]

requisition /rekwɪˈzɪʃən/ *n.* 1. an official order laying claim to the use of property or materials; a formal written demand that some duty should be performed. 2. being called or put into service. —*v.t.* to demand use or supply of, especially by a formal requisition. [from French or Latin]

requite /rɪˈkwaɪt/ *v.t.* to make a return for (a service) to avenge (a wrong or injury etc.); to make a return to (a person); to repay with good or evil. —**requital** *n.* [from *quite* variant of *quit*]

reredos /ˈrɪədɒs/ *n.* ornamental screen or wall-facing behind a church altar. [from Old French *areredos* (*arere* = behind and *dos* = back]

re-route /riːˈruːt/ *v.t.* to send or carry by a different route.

rerun /riːˈrʌn/ *v.t.* (-nn-) to run again. —/ˈriːrʌn/ *n.* an act of rerunning; a repeat of a film etc.

resale /riːˈseɪl/ *n.* sale to another person of something one has bought.

rescind /rɪˈsɪnd/ *v.t.* to abrogate, to revoke, to cancel. —**rescission** /-ʒən/ *n.* [from Latin *scindere* = cut]

rescript /ˈriːskrɪpt/ *n.* 1. a Roman emperor's or pope's written reply to an appeal for a decision; any papal decision. 2. an official edict or announcement. [from Latin *rescriptum* (*rescribere* = write back)]

rescue /ˈreskjuː/ *v.t.* to save or bring away from capture, danger, harm etc. —*n.* rescuing, being rescued. —**rescuer** *n.* [from Old French *rescoure* (Latin *executere* = shake out)]

research /rɪˈsɜːtʃ, ˈriː-/ *n.* systematic investigation and study in order to establish facts and reach new conclusions. Scientific research is commonly classified into two types: **pure research**, involving theories with little apparent relevance to human concerns; and **research**, concerned with finding solutions to problems of social importance, for instance, in medicine and engineering. The two types are linked in that theories developed from pure research may eventually be found to be of great value to society. —*v.t./i.* to do research (into). —**researcher** *n.* [from obsolete French]

resell /riːˈsel/ *v.t.* (*past* and *past participle* **resold** /-ˈsəʊld/) to sell (what one has bought) to another person.

resemble /rɪ'zembəl/ *v.t.* to be like (another person or thing). —**resemblance** *n.* [from Old French *resembler* from Latin *similis* = like]

resent /rɪ'zent/ *v.t.* to feel indignation at or retain bitter feelings about (an action or injury etc.); to feel offended by (a person). [from obsolete French *resentir* (Latin *sentire* = feel)]

resentful *adj.* feeling resentment. —**resentfully** *adv.*

resentment *n.* indignant or bitter feelings. [from French or Italian]

reservation /rezə'veɪʃən/ *n.* 1. reserving, being reserved. 2. a reserved seat or hotel accommodation etc.; a record of this. 3. a limitation on one's agreement or acceptance of an idea etc. 4. a strip of land between the carriageways of a road. 5. a tract of land set apart by a government for some special purpose or for ethnic groups whose land has been seized, e.g. North American Indians, African blacks, Australian Aborigines.

reserve /rɪ'zɜːv/ *v.t.* 1. to put aside or keep back for a later occasion or special use. 2. to order to be specially retained or allocated for a particular person at a particular time. 3. to retain (a right etc.). 4. to postpone delivery of (a judgement). —*n.* 1. a thing reserved for future use; an extra amount or stock kept available for use when needed. 2. a limitation or exception attached to something. 3. self-restraint, reticence; coolness of manner. 4. a company's profit added to the capital. 5. (in *singular* or *plural*) troops withheld from action to reinforce or protect others; forces outside the regular ones but available in an emergency. 6. a member of a military reserve. 7. an extra player chosen in case a substitute should be needed in a team. 8. a place reserved for special use, especially as a habitat. —**in reserve**, unused and available if needed. **reserve price**, the lowest acceptable price stipulated for an item sold at an auction. [from Old French from Latin *servare* = keep]

reserve currency in economics, a country's holding of internationally acceptable means of payment (major foreign currencies or gold); central banks also hold the ultimate reserve of money for their domestic banking sector. On the asset side of company balance sheets, undistributed profits are listed as reserves.

reserved *adj.* reticent, uncommunicative; tending not to reveal emotions or opinions.

reservist *n.* a member of a military reserve.

reservoir /'rezəvwɑː/ *n.* 1. a large natural or artificial lake as the source of an area's water supply. 2. a container for a supply of fuel or other liquid. 3. a supply of information etc. [from French]

reshuffle /riː'ʃʌfəl/ *v.t.* to shuffle (cards) again; to interchange the posts or responsibilities of (a group of people). —*n.* reshuffling.

reside /rɪ'zaɪd/ *v.i.* 1. to have one's home or dwell permanently (in a specified place). 2. (of power, right, or quality etc.) to be vested or present (in a specified person etc.).

residence /'rezɪdəns/ *n.* 1. residing. 2. a place where one resides. 3. a house, especially of considerable pretension. —**in residence**, dwelling at a specified place especially for the performance of duties or work.

resident /'rezɪdənt/ *n.* a permanent inhabitant, not a visitor; (in a hotel) a person staying overnight. —*adj.* having quarters on the spot; residing; in residence; located. [from Old French or Latin *sedēre* = sit]

residential /rezɪ'denʃəl/ *adj.* 1. suitable for or occupied by private houses. 2. used as a residence. 3. based on or connected with residence. —**residentially** *adv.*

residual /rɪ'zɪdjuəl/ *adj.* left as a residue or residuum. —*n.* a residual quantity. —**residually** *adv.*

residual current device or **earth leakage circuit breaker** device that protects users of electrical equipment from electric shock by interrupting the electricity supply if a short circuit or current leakage occurs.

residuary /rɪ'zɪdjuərɪ/ *adj.* 1. of the residue of an estate. 2. residual.

residue /'rezɪdjuː/ *n.* 1. the remainder, what is left or remains over. 2. what remains of an estate after the payment of charges, debts, and bequests. 3. in chemistry, a substance or mixture of substances remaining in the original container after the removal of one or more components by a separation process. [from Old French from Latin]

residuum /rɪ'zɪdjuːəm/ *n.* (*plural* **residua**) what remains, especially a substance left after combustion or evaporation. [Latin *residuus* = remaining]

resign /rɪ'zaɪn/ *v.t./i.* to give up or surrender (one's job, property, claim etc.); to give up one's job. —**resign oneself to,** to come to accept or tolerate; to regard as inevitable. [from Old French from Latin *resignare* = unseal, cancel]

resignation /rezɪg'neɪʃən/ *n.* 1. resigning, especially of a job. 2. a letter etc. conveying that one wishes to resign. 3. a resigned attitude or expression.

resigned /rɪ'zaɪnd/ *adj.* having resigned oneself; content to endure, showing patient acceptance of an unwelcome task or situation. —**resignedly** /-nɪdlɪ/ *adv.*

resilient /rɪ'zɪlɪənt/ *adj.* 1. springing back to its original form after compression etc. 2. (of a person) readily recovering from shock or depression etc. —**resilience** *n.*, **resiliently** *adv.* [from Latin *resilire* = spring back]

resin /'rezɪn/ *n.* 1. a sticky substance secreted by many plants and trees, especially pines and firs, in gummy drops that harden in air. Varnishes are common products of the hard resins, and ointments come from the soft resins. 2. a similar synthetic substance, especially an organic compound made by polymerization and used as a plastic or in plastics. —*v.t.* to rub or treat with resin. —**resinous** *adj.* [from Latin *resina*]

resist /rɪ'zɪst/ *v.t./i.* 1. to be undamaged or unaffected by; to stop the course of. 2. to refrain from accepting or yielding to (a pleasure or temptation etc.). 3. to oppose, to strive against, to try to impede; to refuse to comply (with). [from Old French or Latin *resistere* = stop]

resistance /rɪ'zɪstəns/ *n.* 1. resisting, refusal to comply; the power to resist; ability to resist harsh or bad conditions. 2. an influence that hinders or stops something. 3. in physics, that property of a substance that restricts the flow of electricity through it, associated with the conversion of electrical energy to heat; also the magnitude of this property. Resistance depends on many factors, such as the nature of the material, its temperature, dimensions, and thermal properties; degree of impurity; the nature and state of illumination of the surface; and the frequency and magnitude of the current. The practical unit of resistance is the ◊ohm. —**line of least resistance,** the easiest method or course. —**resistant** *adj.* [from French from Latin]

resistance movement opposition movement in a country occupied by an enemy or colonial power, especially in the 20th century. During World War II, resistance in E Europe took the form of ◊guerrilla warfare, for example in Yugoslavia, Greece, Poland, and by ◊partisan bands behind the German lines in the USSR. In more industrialized countries, such as France (where the underground movement was called the **maquis**), Belgium, and Czechoslovakia, sabotage in factories and on the railways, propaganda, and the assassination of Germans and collaborators were a priority.

resistivity /rezɪs'tɪvɪtɪ/ *n.* the power of a specified material to resist the passage of an electric current.

resistor /rɪ'zɪstə(r)/ *n.* in physics, any component in an electrical circuit used to introduce ◊resistance to a current. Resistors are often made from wire-wound coils or pieces of carbon. ◊Rheostats and ◊potentiometers are variable resistors.

resit /riː'sɪt/ *v.t.* (**-tt-**) to take (an examination) again, usually after failing.

Resnais /re'neɪ/ Alain 1922– . French film director whose work is characterized by the themes of memory and unconventional concepts of time. His films include *Hiroshima mon amour* 1959, *L'Année dernière à Marienbad*/*Last Year at Marienbad* 1961, and *Providence* 1977.

resoluble /rɪ'zɒljubəl/ *adj.* that can be resolved; analysable. [from French or Latin]

resolute /'rezəluːt, -ljuːt/ *adj.* showing great determination, not vacillating or shrinking. —**resolutely** *adv.*, **resoluteness** *n.*

resolution /rezə'luːʃən, -'ljuː-/ *n.* 1. the quality of being resolute, great determination. 2. a thing resolved on, an intention. 3. a formal expression of opinion agreed on by a committee or assembly. 4. the solving of a doubt, problem, or question. 5. separation into constituent parts; conversion into another form; causing musical discord to pass into concord; the smallest interval measurable by a scientific instrument.

resolve /ri'zɒlv/ *v.t./i.* 1. to decide firmly; to cause to do this. 2. (of an assembly or meeting) to pass a resolution. 3. to separate into constituent parts; to analyse mentally. 4. to solve or settle (a doubt, argument etc.). 5. in music, to convert (discord) or be converted into concord. —*n.* 1. a firm decision or intention. 2. determination. —**resolving power,** the ability of a lens etc. to distinguish very small or very close objects. [from Latin *solvere*= solve]

resolved *adj.* resolute, determined.

resonance *n.* rapid and uncontrolled increase in the size of a vibration when the vibrating object is subject to a force varying at its ◊natural frequency. In a trombone, for example, the length of the air column in the instrument is adjusted until it resonates with the note being sounded. Resonance effects are also produced by many electrical circuits. Tuning a radio, for example, is done by adjusting the natural frequency of the receiver circuit until it coincides with the frequency of the radio waves falling on the aerial.

resonant /'rezənənt/ *adj.* resounding, echoing. —**resonance** *n.* [from French or Latin *sonare* = sound]

resonate /'rezəneɪt/ *v.i.* to produce or show resonance, to resound.

resonator /'rezəneɪtə/ *n.* 1. an instrument responding to a single note and used for detecting it in combinations. 2. an appliance for giving resonance to sounds or other vibrations.

resort /ri'zɔ:t/ *n.* 1. a place frequented especially for holidays or for a specified purpose. 2. a thing to which recourse is had, an expedient; recourse. 3. frequenting, or being frequented. —*v.i.* 1. to turn for aid or as an expedient. 2. to go in large numbers or as a frequent or customary practice. —**in the last resort,** when all else has failed, as a final attempt. [from Old French *sortir* = go out]

resound /ri'zaʊnd/ *v.t./i.* 1. (of a place) to be filled with sound, to echo; to re-echo (a sound). 2. (of a voice, instrument, sound etc.) to produce echoes; to go on sounding; to fill a place with sound. 3. (of a reputation etc.) to be much talked of, to produce a sensation.

resounding *adj.* 1. that resounds. 2. notable, decisive. —**resoundingly** *adv.*

resource /ri'sɔ:s, -'zɔ:s/ *n.* 1. something to which one can turn for help or support or to achieve one's purpose. 2. (usually in *plural*) available assets, a stock that can be drawn on; (in *plural*) materials that can be used to satisfy human needs. Because human needs are diverse and extend from basic physical requirements, such as food and shelter, to ill-defined aesthetic needs, resources encompass a vast range of items. The intellectual resources of a society—its ideas and technologies – determine which aspects of the environment meet that society's needs, and therefore become resources. For example, in the 19th century, uranium was used only in the manufacture of coloured glass. Today, with the advent of nuclear technology, it is a military and energy resource. Resources are often categorized into **human resources,** such as labour, supplies, and skills, and **natural resources,** such as climate, fossil fuels, and water. Natural resources are divided into ◊nonrenewable resources and ◊renewable resources. 3. ingenuity; quick wit. [from French Latin *surgere* = rise]

resourceful *adj.* good at devising expedients. —**resourcefully** *adv.,* **resourcefulness** *n.*

respect /ri'spekt/ *n.* 1. admiration felt or shown towards a person or thing that has good qualities or achievements; politeness arising from this. 2. heed, consideration for something. 3. an aspect or detail. 4. reference, relation. 5. (in *plural*) polite greetings. —*v.t.* 1. to feel or show respect for. 2. to avoid interfering with or harming; to refrain from offending. —**in respect of,** as concerns, with reference to. **pay one's respects,** to make a polite visit. **pay one's last respects,** to show respect for a dead person, especially by attending the funeral. [from Old French or Latin *respectus* (*respicere* = look back at)]

respectable /ri'spektəbəl/ *adj.* 1. deserving respect. 2. of moderately good social standing; honest and decent; proper in appearance or behaviour. 3. of a moderately good standard or size etc.; not bringing disgrace or embarrassment. —**respectability** /-'bɪlɪtɪ/ *n.,* **respectably** *adv.*

respecter *n.* one who respects. —**be no respecter of persons,** to treat everyone in the same way without being influenced by their importance etc.

respectful *adj.* showing respect. —**respectfully** *adv.,* **respectfulness** *n.*

respecting *prep.* in respect of, concerning.

respective *adj.* concerning or appropriate to each of several individually; comparative. [from French or Latin]

respectively *adv.* for each separately or in turn, and in the order mentioned.

Respighi /res'pi:gi/ Ottorino 1879–1936. Italian composer, a student of ◊Rimsky-Korsakov, whose works include the symphonic poems *The Fountains of Rome* 1917 and *The Pines of Rome* 1924 (incorporating the recorded song of a nightingale), operas, and chamber music.

respiration /respə'reɪʃən/ *n.* 1. breathing (more accurately described as a form of ◊gas exchange). 2. a plant's absorption of oxygen and emission of carbon dioxide. 3. the biochemical process within living cells by which food molecules are progressively broken down (oxidised) to release energy in the form of ◊ATP. In most organisms this requires oxygen, but in some bacteria the oxidant is the nitrate or sulphate ion instead. In all higher organisms, respiration occurs in the ◊mitochondria. 4. a single inspiration and expiration, a breath. [French or from Latin]

respirator /'respəreɪtə/ *n.* 1. an apparatus worn over the mouth and nose to warm, filter, or purify inhaled air or to prevent inhalation of a poison, gas etc. 2. an apparatus for maintaining artificial respiration.

respiratory /'respəreɪtərɪ, rɪ'spaɪərət-/ *adj.* of respiration.

respiratory distress syndrome (RDS) formerly **hyaline membrane disease** a condition in which a newborn baby's lungs are insufficiently expanded to permit adequate oxygenation. Premature babies are most at risk. Such babies survive with the aid of intravenous fluids and oxygen, sometimes with assisted ventilation.

respire /ri'spaɪə/ *v.t./i.* to breathe; (of plants) to perform the process of respiration. [from Old French or Latin *spirare* = breathe]

respite /'respaɪt, -ɪt/ *n.* 1. an interval of rest or relief. 2. a delay permitted before an obligation must be discharged or a penalty suffered. —*v.t.* to grant or bring respite to. [from Old French *respit* from Latin *respicere* = look back at]

resplendent /ri'splendənt/ *adj.* brilliant with colour or decorations. —**resplendence** *n.,* **resplendency** *n.,* **resplendently** *adv.* [from Latin *splendēre* = glitter]

respond /ri'spɒnd/ *v.i.* 1. to make an answer; to act or behave in an answering or corresponding manner. 2. to show sensitiveness to a stimulus or action etc., by behaviour or change. [from Latin *spondēre* = pledge]

respondent *n.* a defendant, especially in an appeal or divorce case. —*adj.* in the position of a defendant.

response /ri'spɒns/ *n.* 1. an answer given in word or act. 2. a feeling, movement, or change etc. caused by a stimulus or influence. 3. in the Christian church, any part of the liturgy said or sung in answer to a priest etc. —**response time,** in computing, the delay between entering a command and seeing its effect. [from Old French or Latin *responsum*]

responsibility /rɪspɒnsɪ'bɪlɪtɪ/ *n.* 1. being responsible. 2. something for which one is responsible. 3. responsible quality.

responsible /ri'spɒnsɪbəl/ *adj.* 1. legally or morally obliged to take care of something or to carry out a duty, liable to be blamed for loss of favour etc.; having to account for one's actions *to* a specified person. 2. capable of rational conduct. 3. evidently trustworthy, of good credit or repute. 4. being the primary cause. 5. involving important duties. —**responsibly** *adv.* [obsolete French from Latin]

responsive /ri'spɒnsɪv/ *adj.* 1. responding readily to a stimulus; responding warmly and favourably. 2. answering; by way of answer. —**responsively** *adv.,* **responsiveness** *n.* [from French or Latin]

respray /ri:'spreɪ/ *v.t.* to spray again, especially to change the colour of paint on a vehicle. —/'ri:spreɪ/ *n.* the act or process of respraying.

rest[1] *v.t./i.* 1. to cease from work, exertion, or action etc.; to be still or asleep, especially in order to regain one's vigour; to cause or allow to do this. 2. to place or be placed for support. 3. to rely. 4. (of a look etc.) to alight, to be directed. 5. (of a subject) to be left without further

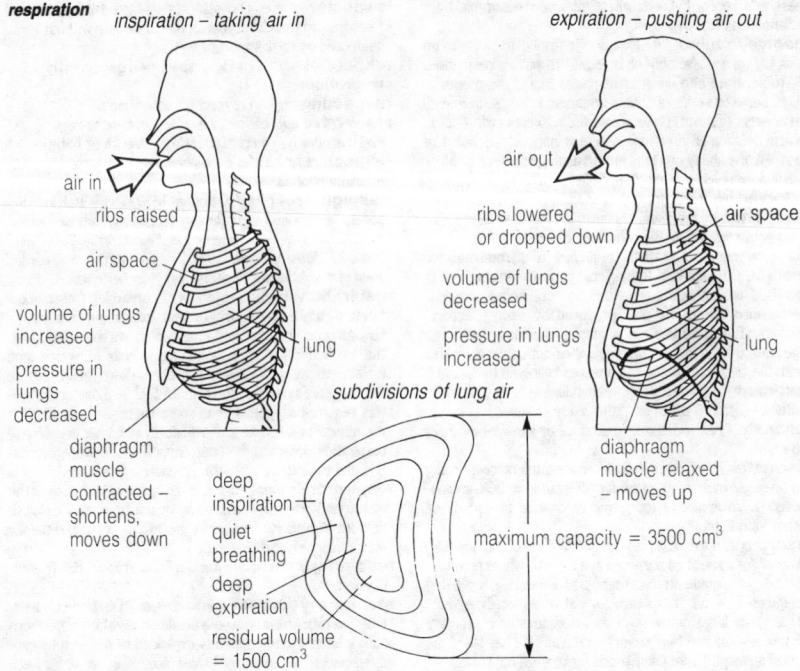

respiration

inspiration – taking air in

expiration – pushing air out

air in
ribs raised
air space
volume of lungs increased
pressure in lungs decreased
diaphragm muscle contracted – shortens, moves down
lung

air out
ribs lowered or dropped down
air space
volume of lungs decreased
pressure in lungs increased
diaphragm muscle relaxed – moves up
lung

subdivisions of lung air

deep inspiration
quiet breathing
deep expiration
residual volume = 1500 cm³

maximum capacity = 3500 cm³

investigation or discussion. **6.** to lie buried. **7.** (in *past participle*) refreshed or invigorated by resting. —*n.* **1.** inactivity or sleep as a way of regaining vigour; a period of this. **2.** a support for holding or steadying something. **3.** in music, an interval of silence between notes; a sign indicating this. —**at rest**, not moving; no longer anxious; (of the dead) free from trouble or anxiety. **be resting**, (of an actor) to be out of work. **rest mass**, in physics, the mass of a particle at rest or moving at only a low velocity compared with that of light. According to the theory of ◊relativity, at very high velocities, there is a relativistic effect that increases the mass of the particle. **rest one's case**, to conclude presentation of it. **rest-cure** *n.* a prolonged period of rest (usually in bed) as medical treatment. **rest on one's oars,** to relax one's efforts. **rest room,** a lavatory and other facilities for employees or customers. [Old English]

rest² *n.* **the rest,** the remaining part(s) or individuals, the others; the remaining quantity etc. —*v.i.* to remain in a specified state. —**rest with,** to be left in the hands or charge of. [from Old French *reste* (*rester* = remain behind, from Latin *stare* = stand]

restaurant /'restərɒnt/ *n.* a place where meals can be bought and eaten. —**restaurant car,** a dining car. [French *restaure* = restore]

restaurateur /restərə'tɜ:/ *n.* a restaurant-keeper.

restful *adj.* inducing or giving a feeling of rest. —**restfully** *adv.*, **restfulness** *n.*

restitution /resti'tju:ʃən/ *n.* **1.** restoration of a thing to its proper owner or to its original state. **2.** reparation for injury or damage. [from Old French or Latin *restituere* = restore]

restive /'restɪv/ *adj.* restless, resisting control because made impatient by delay or restraint. —**restively** *adv.*, **restiveness** *n.* [from Old French]

restless *adj.* **1.** unable to rest or to be still; constantly in motion or fidgeting. **2.** without rest or sleep. —**restlessly** *adv.*, **restlessness** *n.*

restock /ri:'stɒk/ *v.t./i.* to stock again, to replenish one's stock.

restoration /restə'reɪʃən/ *n.* **1.** restoring, being restored. **2.** a model, drawing, or reconstruction representing the supposed original form of an extinct animal, ruined building etc.

Restoration *n.* in English history, period when the monarchy, in the person of Charles II, was re-established after the English Civil War and the fall of the ◊Protectorate 1660.

Restoration comedy a style of English theatre, dating from the Restoration. It witnessed the first appearance of women on the English stage, most notably in the 'breeches part', specially created in order to costume the actress in male attire, thus revealing her figure to its best advantage. The genre placed much emphasis on sexual antics. Examples include Wycherley's *The Country Wife* 1675, Congreve's *The Way of the World* 1700, and Farquhar's *The Beaux' Stratagem* 1707.

restorative /rɪ'stɔrətɪv/ *adj.* that tends to restore health or strength. —*n.* a restorative food or medicine etc.

restore /rɪ'stɔ:/ *v.t.* **1.** to bring back to its original state, e.g. by rebuilding or repairing. **2.** to bring back to good health or vigour. **3.** to put back in its former position; to reinstate; to give back to its original owner. **4.** to make a representation of the supposed original form of (an extinct animal, a ruin etc.). —**restorer** *n.* [from Old French from Latin *restaurare*]

restrain /rɪ'streɪn/ *v.t.* to hold back from movement or action; to keep under control or within bounds. [from Old French from Latin *stringere* = tie]

restraint /rɪ'streɪnt/ *n.* **1.** restraining, being restrained. **2.** an agency or influence that restrains. **3.** self-control; avoidance of excess or exaggeration; reserve of manner. **4.** confinement, especially because of insanity.

restrict /rɪ'strɪkt/ *v.t.* to put a limit on, to subject to limitations. —**restriction** *n.* [from Latin *restringere*]

restrictive /rɪ'strɪktɪv/ *adj.* restricting. —**restrictive practice,** an agreement or practice in a particular trade or business that keeps the cost of goods or services artificially high (for example, an agreement to restrict output) or provides barriers to outsiders entering the trade or business. [from Old French or Latin]

restructure /ri:'strʌktʃə/ *v.t.* to give a new structure to; to rebuild, to rearrange.

result /rɪ'zʌlt/ *n.* **1.** that which is produced by an activity or operation, an effect, a consequence; a satisfactory outcome. **2.** a quantity or formula etc. obtained by calculation. **3.** a statement of the score, marks, or name of the winner in a sporting event, competition, or examination; (in *plural*) a list of these. —*v.i.* **1.** to occur as a result. **2.** to have a specified result. [from Latin *resultare* = spring back]

resultant /rɪ'zʌltənt/ adj. occurring as a result, especially as the total outcome of more or less opposed forces. —n. a force etc. equivalent to two or more acting in different directions at the same point.

resume /rɪ'zju:m/ v.t./i. 1. to begin again or go on after interruption, to begin to speak, work, or use again. 2. to get or take again or back. [from Old French or Latin *sumere* = take up]

résumé /'rezju:meɪ/ n. a summary. [French]

resumption /rɪ'zʌmpʃən/ n. resuming. —**resumptive** adj.

resurface /ri:'sɜ:fɪs/ v.t./i. 1. to put a new surface on. 2. to return to the surface.

resurgent /rɪ'sɜ:dʒənt/ adj. rising or arising again after defeat, destruction, or disappearance. —**resurgence** n. [from Latin *surgere* = rise]

resurrect /rezə'rekt/ v.t. 1. to revive the practice or memory of. 2. to take from the grave, to exhume. 3. to dig up.

resurrection /rezə'rekʃən/ n. 1. rising from the dead, especially, in Christian, Jewish, and Muslim belief, the rising from the dead that all souls will experience at the Last Judgement. The **Resurrection** also refers to Jesus Christ rising from the dead on the third day after his crucifixion, a belief central to Christianity and celebrated at Easter. 2. revival after disuse, inactivity, or decay. [from Old French from Latin]

resuscitate /rɪ'sʌsɪteɪt/ v.t./i. 1. to revive from unconsciousness or apparent death. 2. to revive (an old custom or institution etc.); to return or restore to vogue, vigour, or vividness. —**resuscitation** /-'teɪʃən/ n. [from Latin *suscitare* = rouse]

resuscitation n. steps taken to revive anyone on the brink of death. The most successful technique for life-threatening emergencies, such as electrocution, near-drowning, or heart attack, is mouth-to-mouth resuscitation. Medical and paramedical staff are trained in cardiopulmonary resuscitation: the use of specialized equipment and techniques to attempt to restart the breathing and/or heartbeat and stabilize the patient long enough for more definitive treatment.

retable /rɪ'teɪbəl/ n. a shelf, or frame enclosing decorative panels, above the back of an altar. [from French from Latin *retrotabulum* = rear table]

retail /'ri:teɪl/ n. the selling of things in small quantities to the general public and usually not for resale. The retailer is the last link in the distribution chain. A retailer's purchases are usually made from a wholesaler. —adj. of retail. —adv. by retail. —v.t./i. 1. to sell or be sold by retail. 2. /also ri:'teɪl/ to recount, to relate details of. —**retailer** n. [from Old French *retaille* = piece cut off]

retail price index (RPI) indicator of variations in the ◊cost of living.

retail price maintenance (RPM) in the UK, exceptions to the general rule that shops can charge whatever price they choose for goods. The main areas where RPM applies are books (where the Net Book Agreement prevents booksellers charging less than the publisher's price) and some pharmaceutical products.

retain /rɪ'teɪn/ v.t. 1. to keep possession of, not to lose; to continue to have, practise, or recognize. 2. to keep in one's memory. 3. to keep in place, to hold fixed. 4. to secure the services of (a person, especially a barrister) with a preliminary payment. [from Anglo-French from Latin *tenēre* = hold]

retainer n. 1. a person or thing that retains. 2. a fee for retaining a barrister etc. 3. (*historical*) a dependant or follower of a person of rank. —**old retainer**, (*jocular*) a faithful old servant.

retake /ri:'teɪk/ v.t. (*past* retook; *past participle* retaken) to take again; to recapture.

retaliate /rɪ'tælieɪt/ v.t./i. to repay (an injury or insult etc.) in kind; to make a counterattack. —**retaliation** /-'eɪʃən/ n., **retaliatory** /-ljətərɪ/ adj. [from Latin *retaliare* (*talis* = such)]

retard /rɪ'tɑ:d/ v.t. to make slow or late, to delay the progress or accomplishment of. —**retardation** /ri:tɑ:'deɪʃən/ n. [from French from Latin *retardare* (*tardus* = slow)]

retarded adj. backward in mental or physical development.

retch v.i. to make a motion as in vomiting, especially involuntarily and without effect. [Old English = spit (imitative)]

retell /ri:'tel/ v.t. (*past* and *past participle* retold /-'təʊld/) to tell (a story etc.) again.

retention /rɪ'tenʃən/ n. retaining, being retained. [from Old French or Latin]

retentive /rɪ'tentɪv/ adj. tending to retain; (of the memory) not forgetful. —**retentiveness** n.

rethink /ri:'θɪŋk/ v.t. (*past* and *past participle* rethought /-'θɔ:t/) to consider afresh, especially with a view to making changes. —/'ri:θɪŋk/ n. rethinking, a reassessment.

reticence /'retɪsəns/ n. avoidance of expressing all one knows or feels or more than is necessary; disposition to silence, taciturnity. —**reticent** adj., **reticently** adv. [from Latin *reticentia* (*tacēre* = be silent)]

reticle /'retɪkəl/ n. a network of fine threads or lines in the focal plane of an optical instrument to help accurate observation. [from Latin *reticulum* diminutive of *rete* = net]

reticulate /rɪ'tɪkjuleɪt/ v.t./i. to divide or be divided in fact or appearance into a network. —/rɪ'tɪkjʊlət/ adj. reticulated. [from Latin]

reticulation /rɪtɪkju'leɪʃən/ n. (usually in *plural*) a netlike marking or arrangement.

reticule /'retɪkju:l/ n. 1. a reticle. 2. a woman's bag of woven or other material, carried or worn to serve the purpose of a pocket. [from French from Latin]

reticulum /rɪ'tɪkjʊləm/ n. (*plural* reticula) 1. a ruminant's second stomach. 2. a netlike structure, a fine network in cytoplasm etc., a reticulated membrane etc. [Latin, diminutive of *rete* = net]

retina n. (*plural* retinas) light-sensitive area at the back of the ◊eye connected to the brain by the optic nerve. It has several layers and in humans contains over a million rods and cones, sensory cells capable of converting light into nervous messages that pass down the optic nerve to the brain. —**retinal** adj. [from Latin *rete* = net]

retinue /'retɪnju:/ n. a body of attendants accompanying an important person. [from Old French]

retire /rɪ'taɪə/ v.t./i. 1. to give up one's regular work because of advancing age; to cause (an employee) to do this. 2. to withdraw; to go away; to retreat. 3. to seek seclusion or shelter; to go to bed. 4. (of a batsman at cricket) to terminate voluntarily or be compelled to suspend one's innings. —**retire into oneself**, to become uncommunicative or unsociable. —**retirement** n. [from French *tirer* = draw]

retired adj. 1. who has retired. 2. withdrawn from society or observation, secluded.

retiring adj. shy, avoiding society, fond of seclusion.

retort[1] /rɪ'tɔ:t/ n. an incisive, witty, or angry reply. —v.t./i. 1. to say by way of retort; to make a retort. 2. to repay (an insult or attack) in kind. [from Latin *torquēre* = twist]

retort[2] n. 1. a vessel (usually of glass) with a long, downward-bent neck, used in distilling liquids. 2. a vessel for heating mercury for purification, coal to generate gas, or iron and carbon to make steel. [from French from Latin]

retouch /ri:'tʌtʃ/ v.t. to improve (a picture or photograph etc.) by fresh touches or alterations. [from French]

retrace /rɪ'treɪs/ v.t. to go back over; to trace back to the source or beginning; to recall the course of in memory. [from French]

retraceable adj. that may be retraced.

retract /rɪ'trækt/ v.t./i. 1. to draw or be drawn back or in. 2. to withdraw (a statement or opinion etc.); to refuse to keep (an agreement). —**retraction** n., **retractor** n. [from Old French or Latin *retractare*]

retractable adj. that may be retracted.

retractile /rɪ'træktaɪl/ adj. (especially of a bodily part) retractable.

retread /ri:'tred/ v.t. to put a fresh tread on (a tyre). —/'ri:tred/ n. a retreaded tyre.

retreat /rɪ'tri:t/ v.i. 1. to withdraw after defeat or when faced with danger or difficulty; to go away to a place of shelter. 2. to recede. —n. 1. retreating; the military signal for this; a military bugle-call at sunset. 2. withdrawal into privacy or security; a place of shelter or seclusion. 3. a period of withdrawal from worldly activities for prayer and meditation. —**beat a retreat**, to retreat, to abandon an undertaking. [from Old French from Latin *trahere* = draw]

retrench /rɪ'trentʃ/ v.t./i. to reduce the amount of (expense or its cause); to reduce one's expenditure or operations. —**retrenchment** n. [from obsolete French *retrencher* = cut back]

retrial /riːˈtraɪəl/ *n.* the retrying of a lawsuit.

retribution /retrɪˈbjuːʃən/ *n.* a deserved punishment, requital, usually for evil done. —**retributive** /rɪˈtrɪbjutɪv/ *adj.* [from Latin *tribuere* = assign]

retrievable /rɪˈtriːvəbəl/ *adj.* that may be retrieved.

retrieve /rɪˈtriː/ *v.t.* 1. to regain possession of; to recover by investigation or effort of memory. 2. to find again (stored information etc.). 3. (of a dog) to find and bring in (killed or wounded game etc.). 4. to rescue, to restore to a flourishing state. 5. to repair or set right (a loss or error etc.). —*n.* possibility of recovery. —**retrieval** *n.* [from Old French *trover* = find]

retriever *n.* a type of dog. The commonest breeds are the Labrador retriever, large, smooth-coated, and usually black or yellow; and the golden retriever, with either flat or wavy coat. They can grow to 60 cm/2 ft high and weigh 40 kg/90 lbs. They were traditionally used for retrieving game.

retro- /retrəʊ-/ *prefix.* 1. backwards; back again; in return. 2. behind. [from Latin *retro* = backwards]

retroactive /retrəʊˈæktɪv/ *adj.* having a retrospective effect. —**retroactively** *adv.*

retrograde /ˈretrəɡreɪd/ *adj.* 1. directed backwards. 2. reverting, especially to an inferior state; declining. 3. reversed. —*v.i.* to move backwards, to recede; to decline, to revert. [from Latin *retrogradi* = move backwards]

retrogress /retrəˈɡres/ *v.i.* to move backwards, to deteriorate. —**retrogression** /-eʃən/ *n.*, **retrogressive** *adj.*

retrorocket /ˈretrəʊrɒkɪt/ *n.* an auxiliary rocket for slowing down a spacecraft etc.

retrospect /ˈretrəspekt/ *n.* a survey of or reference to past time or events etc. —**in retrospect**, when one looks back on a past event or situation.

retrospection /retrəˈspekʃən/ *n.* looking back, especially on the past.

retrospective /retrəˈspektɪv/ *adj.* 1. looking back on or dealing with the past. 2. (of a statute etc.) applying to the past as well as the future. —**retrospectively** *adv.*

retroussé /rəˈtruːseɪ/ *adj.* (of the nose) turned up at the tip. [French, past participle of *retrousser* = tuck up]

retroverted /ˈretrəvɜːtɪd/ *adj.* (especially of the womb) turned backwards. [from Latin *vertere* = turn]

retrovirus *n.* any of a family (*Retroviridae*) of ◊viruses containing the genetic material ◊RNA rather than the more usual ◊DNA.

retry /riːˈtraɪ/ *v.t.* to try (a defendant or lawsuit) again.

retsina /retˈsiːnə/ *n.* a resin-flavoured Greek wine. [modern Greek]

return /rɪˈtɜːn/ *v.t.i.* 1. to come or go back. 2. to bring, give, put, or send back; to pay back or reciprocate, to give in response; to yield (a profit). 3. to say in reply, to retort. 4. to send (a ball) back in cricket or tennis etc. 5. to state or describe officially, especially in answer to a writ or formal demand. 6. (of a constituency) to elect as an MP etc. —*n.* 1. coming or going back. 2. bringing, giving, putting, or sending back; paying back. 3. a thing given etc. back. 4. a return ticket. 5. (in *singular* or *plural*) the proceeds or profit of an undertaking; the coming in of these. 6. a formal report compiled or submitted by order. —**by return (of post)**, by the next available post in the return direction. **in return**, as an exchange or reciprocal action. **many happy returns (of the day)**, a birthday or festival greeting. **return crease**, in cricket, each of two lines joining the popping-crease and bowling-crease and extending beyond the latter. In his delivery stride the bowler's back foot must land within the return crease. **returning officer**, an official conducting an election in a constituency and announcing the name of the person elected. **return ticket**, a ticket for the journey to a place and back to the starting point. [from Old French *retorner*]

retype /riːˈtaɪp/ *v.t.* to type again.

Retz /res/ Jean François Paul de Gondi, Cardinal de Retz 1614–1679. French politician. A priest with political ambitions, he stirred up and largely led the insurrection known as the ◊Fronde. After a period of imprisonment and exile he was restored to favour in 1662 and created abbot of St Denis.

reunion /riːˈjuːnjən/ *n.* 1. reuniting, being reunited. 2. a social gathering of people who were formerly associated. [from French]

Réunion /reɪuːˈnjɒn/ French island of the Mascarenes group, in the Indian Ocean, 650 km/400 mi E of Madagascar and 180 km/110 mi SW of Mauritius; **area** 2,512 sq km/970 sq mi; **capital** St Denis; **physical** forested, rising in Piton de Neiges to 3,069 m/10,072 ft; **products** sugar, maize, vanilla, tobacco, rum; **population** (1987) 565,000; **history** explored by Portuguese (the first European visitors) in 1513; annexed by Louis XIII of France in 1642; overseas *département* of France from 1946; overseas region from 1972.

reunite /riːjuːˈnaɪt/ *v.t.i.* to unite again after separation.

Reus /ˈreɪus/ industrial city with an international airport in Catalonia, E Spain, 10 km/6 mi NW of Tarragona.

reuse /riːˈjuːz/ *v.t.* to use again. —/-ˈjuːs/ *n.* using or being used again.

Reuter /ˈrɔɪtə/ Paul Julius, Baron de Reuter 1816–1899. German founder of the international news agency Reuters. He began a continental pigeon post in 1849, and in 1851 he set up a news agency in London. In 1858 he persuaded the press to use his news telegrams, and the service became worldwide.

rev *n.* (*colloquial*) a revolution (of an engine). —*v.t.i.* (**-vv-**) (*colloquial*) 1. (of an engine) to cause the crankshaft to rotate. 2. to rev up. —**rev up**, to cause (an engine) to run quickly, to increase the speed of its revolution. [abbreviation]

Rev. abbreviation of Reverend.

revalue /riːˈvæljuː/ *v.t.* to reassess the value of; to give a new (higher) value to a currency etc. —**revaluation** /-ˈeɪʃən/ *n.*

revamp /riːˈvæmp/ *v.t.* to renovate, to give a new appearance to.

Revd abbreviation of Reverend.

reveal /rɪˈviːl/ *v.t.* to make known (a secret etc.); to uncover and allow to be seen. —*n.* the internal side surface of an opening or recess, especially the aperture of a door or window. [from Old French or Latin *velum* = veil]

reveille /rɪˈvælɪ/ *n.* a military waking-signal. [from French *réveillez* imperative of *réveiller* = wake up]

revel /ˈrevəl/ *v.i.* (**-ll-**) 1. to make merry, to be riotously festive. 2. to take keen delight. —*n.* (in *singular* or *plural*) revelling, merry-making; an instance of this. —**reveller** *n.* [from Old French *reveler* = riot]

revelation /revəˈleɪʃən/ *n.* 1. the revealing of a fact. 2. the disclosing of knowledge, or knowledge disclosed, to man by a divine or supernatural agency; **the Revelation (of St John the Divine)**, the last book of the New Testament traditionally attributed to the author of the Gospel of St John but now generally held to be the work of another writer. It describes a vision of the end of the world (the ◊apocalypse), of the Last Judgement, and of a new heaven and earth ruled by God from Jerusalem. 3. something revealed, a startling disclosure.

revelry /ˈrevəlrɪ/ *n.* revelling, revels.

revenge /rɪˈvendʒ/ *n.* 1. punishment or injury inflicted in return for what one has suffered; desire to inflict this; the act of retaliation. 2. opportunity to defeat in a return game an opponent who won an earlier game etc. —*v.t.* to avenge. —**be revenged** or **revenge oneself**, to obtain revenge. [from Old French from Latin *revindicare*]

revengeful *adj.* eager for revenge. —**revengefully** *adv.*

revenue /ˈrevənjuː/, **-vɪn-** *n.* 1. income, especially of a large amount, from any source; (in *plural*) items constituting this. 2. a state's annual income from which public expenses are met; the department of the civil service collecting this. [from Old French *revenir* = come back]

reverberate /rɪˈvɜːbəreɪt/ *v.t.i.* (of sound, light, or heat) to be returned or reflected; to return (a sound etc.) thus. —**reverberant** *adj.*, **reverberation** /-ˈreɪʃən/ *n.*, **reverberative** *adj.* [from Latin *verberare* = lash]

revere /rɪˈvɪə/ *v.t.* to feel deep respect or religious veneration for. [from French or Latin *vererī* = fear]

Revere Paul 1735–1818. American nationalist, a Boston silversmith, who carried the news of the approach of British troops to Lexington and Concord (see ◊American Revolution) on the night of 18 Apr 1775. Longfellow's poem 'Paul Revere's Ride' commemorates the event.

reverence /ˈrevərəns/ *n.* 1. revering, being revered. 2. a feeling of awe and respect or veneration. —*v.t.* to regard or treat with reverence. —**His, Your, etc. Reverence,**

(*archaic* or *jocular*) a title used in addressing or referring to a cleric. [from Old French from Latin]

reverend /ˈrevərənd/ *adj.* deserving reverence. **—the Reverend,** the title of a Christian cleric (**Very Reverend,** of a dean; **Right Reverend,** of a bishop; **Most Reverend,** of an archbishop). **Reverend Mother,** the Mother Superior of a convent. [from Old French or Latin *reverendus*]

reverent /ˈrevərənt/ *adj.* feeling or showing reverence. **—reverently** *adv.* [from Latin *reverens*]

reverential /revəˈrenʃ(ə)l/ *adj.* of the nature of, due to, or characterized by reverence. **—reverentially** *adv.*

reverie /ˈrevəri/ *n.* a fit of abstracted musing, a daydream; being engaged in this. [from Old French = rejoicing, revelry (*rever* = be delirious)]

revers /rɪˈvɪə/ *n.* (*plural* the same /-ɪəz/) a turned-back edge of a garment revealing the undersurface; the material on this surface. [French]

reversal /rɪˈvɜːsəl/ *n.* reversing, being reversed.

reverse /rɪˈvɜːs/ *v.t./i.* 1. to turn the other way round or up or inside out. 2. to change to the opposite character or effect. 3. to travel or cause to travel backwards; to make (an engine etc.) work in the contrary direction. 4. to revoke or annul (a decree, act etc.). **—adj.** 1. facing or moving in the opposite direction. 2. opposite in character or order. 3. upside down. **—n.** 1. the opposite; the opposite of the usual manner. 2. a piece of misfortune; a defeat in battle. 3. reverse gear or motion. 4. the reverse side; the back of a coin etc. bearing a secondary design; the verso of a leaf. **—reverse arms,** to hold rifles butt upwards. **reverse the charges,** to make the recipient of a telephone call responsible for payment. **reverse gear,** the gear used to make a vehicle etc. travel backwards. **reverse takeover,** in business, a ◊takeover where a company sells itself to another, to avoid being itself the target of a purchase by an unwelcome predator. **the reverse of,** far from, not at all. **reversing light,** a white light at the rear of a vehicle, operated when a vehicle travels backwards. **—reversely** *adv.* [from Old French from Latin *versare* frequentative of *vertere* = turn]

reversible *adj.* that may be reversed.

reversion /rɪˈvɜːʃən/ *n.* 1. the legal right (especially of an original owner or his or her heirs) to possess or succeed to property on the death of the present possessor. 2. return to a previous state, especially in biology to an earlier type.

revert /rɪˈvɜːt/ *v.i.* 1. to return to a former state, practice, subject etc. 2. (of property, an office etc.) to return by reversion.

revetment /rɪˈvetmənt/ *n.* a facing of masonry on a rampart or wall; a retaining wall. [from French *revêtir* from Latin]

review /rɪˈvjuː/ *n.* 1. a general survey or assessment of a subject or thing; a survey of past events. 2. re-examination, reconsideration. 3. a display and formal inspection of troops etc. 4. a published report assessing the merits of a book or play etc.; a periodical publication with critical articles on current events, the arts etc. **—v.t.** 1. to survey or look back on. 2. to re-examine, to reconsider. 3. to hold a review of (troops etc.). 4. to write a review of (a book or play etc.). **—reviewer** *n.* [from obsolete French *revoir* = see again]

revile /rɪˈvaɪl/ *v.t.* to criticize abusively. **—revilement** *n.* [from Old French *reviler*]

revise /rɪˈvaɪz/ *v.t.* 1. to re-examine and alter or correct. 2. to go over (work learnt or done) in preparation for an examination. **—n.** a printer's proof-sheet embodying corrections made in an earlier proof. **—Revised Version,** the revision made in 1870–84 of the Authorized Version of the Bible. **Revised Standard Version,** the revision made in 1946–57 of the American Standard Version of the Bible (the latter was based on the English RV and published in 1901). [from French or Latin *visere* intensive of *vidēre* = see]

revision /rɪˈvɪʒən/ *n.* 1. revising, being revised. 2. a revised edition or form. [from Latin]

revisionism *n.* a political theory derived from Marxism that moderates one or more of the basic tenets of Marx, and is hence condemned by orthodox Marxists. The first noted Marxist revisionist was Eduard Bernstein, who in Germany in the 1890s questioned the inevitability of a breakdown in capitalism. After World War II the term became widely used by established Communist parties, both in E Europe and Asia, to condemn movements

(whether more or less radical) that threatened the official party policy.

revisit /riːˈvɪzɪt/ *v.t.* to pay another visit to (a place).

revisory /rɪˈvaɪzərɪ/ *adj.* of revision.

revival /rɪˈvaɪvəl/ *n.* 1. reviving, being revived. 2. something brought back into use or fashion; a new production of an old play etc. 3. a reawakening of religious fervour; a campaign to promote this.

revivalist *n.* one who promotes a religious revival. **—revivalism** *n.*

revive /rɪˈvaɪv/ *v.t./i.* 1. to come or bring back to consciousness, life, or strength. 2. to come or bring back to existence, use, notice etc. **—reviver** *n.* [from Old French or Latin *vivere* = live]

revivify /riːˈvɪvɪfaɪ/ *v.t.* to restore to life or strength or activity. **—revivification** /-fɪˈkeɪʃən/ *n.* [from French or Latin *revivificare* (*vivus* = alive and *facere* = make)]

revocable /ˈrevəkəbəl/ *adj.* that may be revoked. [Old French or from Latin]

revoke /rɪˈvəʊk/ *v.t./i.* 1. to withdraw or cancel (a decree or promise etc.). 2. to fail to follow suit in a card-game when able to do so. **—n.** revoking in a card game. [from Old French or Latin *vocare* = call]

revolt /rɪˈvəʊlt/ *v.t./i.* 1. to rise in rebellion; to be in a mood of protest or defiance. 2. to affect with strong disgust. 3. to feel or turn away in strong disgust. **—n.** 1. an act or state of rebelling or defying authority. 2. a sense of strong disgust. [from French, ultimately from Latin *volvere* = roll]

revolting *adj.* disgusting.

revolution /revəˈluːʃən/ *n.* 1. the forcible overthrow of a government or social order, in favour of a new system; for example, the American Revolution, where colonists broke free from their colonial ties and established a sovereign, independent nation; the French Revolution, where an absolute monarchy was overthrown by opposition from inside the country and a popular uprising; and the Russian Revolution, where a repressive monarchy was overthrown by those seeking to institute widespread social and economic changes based on a socialist model. 2. any fundamental change or reversal of conditions or ideas. 3. revolving; a single completion of an orbit or rotation; the time taken for this; cyclic recurrence. [from Old French or Latin]

revolutionary *adj.* 1. involving great change. 2. of or causing political revolution. **—n.** an instigator or supporter of political revolution.

Revolutionary Wars a series of wars 1791–1802 between France and the combined armies of England, Austria, Prussia, and others, during the period of the French Revolution.

revolutionize *v.t.* to introduce fundamental change to.

revolutions of 1848 a series of revolts in various parts of Europe against monarchical rule. While some of the revolutionaries had republican ideas, many more were motivated by economic grievances. The revolution began in France with the overthrow of Louis Philippe and then spread to Italy, the Austrian Empire, and Germany, where the short-lived ◊Frankfurt Parliament put forward ideas about political unity in Germany. None of the revolutions enjoyed any lasting success, and most were violently suppressed within a few months.

revolve /rɪˈvɒlv/ *v.t./i.* 1. to turn or cause to turn round, especially on an axis. 2. to move in orbit. 3. to ponder (a problem etc.) in one's mind. **—revolving door,** a door with several radial partitions turning round a central axis. [from Latin *volvere* = roll]

revolver /rɪˈvɒlvə/ *n.* a small handgun with revolving chambers that hold the bullets, enabling several shots to be fired without reloading. The Colt revolver was patented in 1835.

revue /rɪˈvjuː/ *n.* a stage presentation involving short satirical and topical items in the form of songs, sketches, and monologues; it originated in Europe in the late 19th century. In Britain the first revue seems to have been *Under the Clock* 1893 by Seymour Hicks (1871–1949) and Charles Brookfield. The 1920s revues were spectacular entertainments, but the 'intimate revue' became increasingly popular, employing writers such as Noël Coward. During the 1960s the satirical revue took off with the Cambridge Footlights' production *Beyond the Fringe*, establishing the revue tradition among the young and at fringe theatrical events. [French = review]

revulsion /rɪˈvʌlʃən/ *n.* 1. a feeling of strong disgust. 2. a sudden violent change of feeling. [French or from Latin *vellere* = pluck]

reward /rɪˈwɔːd/ *n.* 1. something given or received in return for what was done, or for a service or merit. 2. a sum of money offered for the detection of a criminal, recovery of lost property etc. —*v.t.* to give a reward to (a person) or for (a service etc.). [from Anglo-French = *regard*]

rewarding *adj.* (of an activity etc.) well worth doing.

rewind /riːˈwaɪnd/ *v.t.* (*past* and *past participle* **rewound**) to wind (a film or tape etc.) back to the beginning.

rewire /riːˈwaɪə/ *v.t.* to renew the wiring of (a house etc.).

reword /riːˈwɜːd/ *v.t.* to change the wording of.

rewrite /riːˈraɪt/ *v.t.* (*past* **rewrote**; *past participle* **rewritten**) to write again or differently. —/ˈriːraɪt/ *n.* a thing rewritten.

Rex /reks/ *n.* the reigning king (in use as ◊regina). [Latin = king]

Reykjavik /ˈreɪkjəviːk/ capital (from 1918) and chief port of Iceland, on the SW coast; population (1988) 93,000. Fish processing is the main industry. Reykjavik is heated by underground mains fed by volcanic springs. It was a seat of Danish administration from 1801 to 1918.

Reynolds /ˈrenldz/ Burt 1936– . US film actor in adventure films and comedies. His films include *Deliverance* 1972, *Hustle* 1975, and *City Heat* 1984.

Reynolds Joshua 1723–1792. English portrait painter, active in London from 1752. He became the first president of the Royal Academy in 1768. His portraits display a facility for striking and characterful compositions in a consciously grand manner. He often borrowed classical poses, for example *Mrs Siddons as the Tragic Muse* 1784 (San Marino, California, USA).

A mere copier of nature can never produce anything great.

Joshua Reynolds
discourse to students of the Royal Academy
14 Dec 1770

Reynolds Osborne 1842–1912. British physicist and engineer who studied ◊fluid flow and devised the **Reynolds number**, which relates to turbulence in flowing fluids.

Rf symbol for rutherfordium.

RGB abbreviation of **red-green-blue** a method of connecting a colour screen to a computer, involving three separate signals: red, green, and blue. All the colours displayed by the screen can be made up from these three component colours.

Rh symbol for rhodium.

r.h. abbreviation of right hand.

rhapsodize /ˈræpsədaɪz/ *v.i.* to utter or write rhapsodies.

rhapsody /ˈræpsədɪ/ *n.* 1. an ecstatic spoken or written statement. 2. a romantic musical composition in an irregular form, often based on folk melodies, such as Liszt's *Hungarian Rhapsodies* 1853–1854. —**rhapsodic** /-ˈsɒdɪk/ *adj.*, **rhapsodical** /-ˈsɒdɪkəl/ *adj.* [from Greek *rhapsōidos* (*rhaptō* = stitch and *ōdē* = song)]

rhea *n.* a flightless bird, family Rheidae, found only in South America. There are two species: *Rhea americana* and the smaller *Pterocnemia pennata*. They differ from the ostrich in having a feathered neck and head and three-toed feet, no plumelike tail feathers, and in their smaller size (up to 1.5 m/5 ft high and 25 kg/55 lbs).

Rhea /ˈriːə/ in Greek mythology, a fertility goddess, one of the Titans, wife of Kronos and mother of several gods, including Zeus.

Rhee /riː/ Syngman 1875–1965. Korean right-wing politician. A rebel under Chinese and Japanese rule, he became president of South Korea from 1948 until riots forced him to resign and leave the country in 1960.

Rheims /riːmz/ English version of ◊Reims, city in France.

Rheinland-Pfalz /ˈraɪnlænt ˈpfælts/ German name for the ◊Rhineland-Palatinate region of Germany.

Rhenish /ˈriːnɪʃ, ˈren-/ *adj.* (*archaic*) of the Rhine or neighbouring regions. [from Anglo-French from Latin *Rhenus* = Rhine]

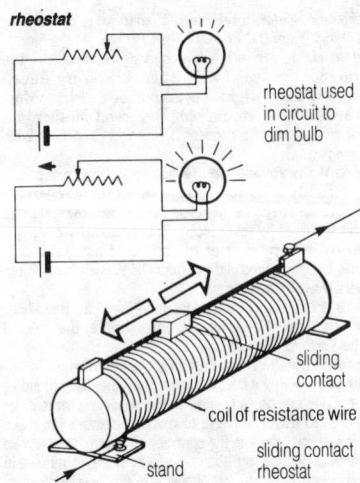

rheostat

rheostat used in circuit to dim bulb

sliding contact

coil of resistance wire

sliding contact rheostat

stand

rhenium /ˈriːnɪəm/ *n.* a rare, hard, heavy metallic element, symbol Re, atomic number 75, relative atomic mass 186.22. It was identified in 1925 in the minerals columbite, tantalite, and wolframite. It is a grey metal, used in thermocouples (electric temperature-measuring devices) and as a catalyst. [from Latin *Rhenus* = Rhine]

rheostat *n.* in physics, a variable ◊resistor, usually consisting of a high-resistance wire-wound coil with a sliding contact. It is used to vary the electrical resistance without interrupting the current (e.g., when dimming lights). The circular type in electronics (which can be used, for example, as the volume control of an amplifier) is also known as a ◊potentiometer.

rhesus /ˈriːsəs/ *n.* or **bandar** a small macaque monkey *Macaca mulatta*, found in N India and SE Asia. It has long, straight, brown-grey hair, pinkish face, and red buttocks. It can grow up to 60 cm/2 ft long, with a 20 cm/8 in tail. —**rhesus factor,** a ◊protein on the surface of red blood cells of humans and some animals, which is involved in the rhesus blood group system. Most individuals possess the main rhesus factor (Rh+), but those without this factor (Rh–) produce ◊antibodies if they come into contact with it. **rhesus negative,** not having this factor. **rhesus positive,** having this factor. [from *Rhesus* mythical king of Thrace]

rhetoric /ˈretərɪk/ *n.* 1. the art of speaking or writing impressively; the art of public speaking and debate. 2. language used for its impressive sound (often with an implication of insincerity, exaggeration etc.). [from Old French from Latin from Greek *rhētōr* = orator]

rhetorical /rɪˈtɒrɪkəl/ *adj.* expressed with a view to impressive effect; the nature of rhetoric. —**rhetorical question,** a question asked not for information but to produce an effect (e.g. *who cares?*). —**rhetorically** *adv.* [from Latin from Greek]

rheumatic /ruːˈmætɪk/ *adj.* of, caused by, or suffering from rheumatism. —*n.* (in *plural*, *colloquial*) rheumatism. —**rheumatic fever,** *or* **acute rheumatism,** an acute illness characterized by fever and painful swelling of joints. Some victims also experience involuntary movements of the limbs and head, a form of chorea. —**rheumatically** *adv.*, **rheumaticky** *adj.* [from Old French or Latin from Greek *rheuma* = watery secretion]

rheumatism /ˈruːmətɪzəm/ *n.* any of several diseases causing pain in the joints, muscles, or fibrous tissue, especially rheumatoid arthritis.

rheumatoid /ˈruːmətɔɪd/ *adj.* having the character of rheumatism. —**rheumatoid arthritis,** a chronic progressive disease causing inflammation and stiffening of the joints.

rheumatology /ruːməˈtɒlədʒɪ/ *n.* the study of rheumatic diseases. —**rheumatologist** *n.*

Rhine /raɪn/ (German *Rhein*, French *Rhin*) European river rising in Switzerland and reaching the North Sea via Germany and the Netherlands; length 1,320 km/820 mi.

Tributaries include the Moselle and the Ruhr. The Rhine is linked with the Mediterranean by the Rhine-Rhône Waterway, and with the Black Sea by the Rhine-Main-Danube Waterway.

Rhine Joseph Banks 1895–1980. US parapsychologist. His work at Duke University, North Carolina, involving controlled laboratory experiments in telepathy, clairvoyance, precognition, and psychokinesis, described in *Extra-Sensory Perception* 1934, made ESP a common term. See also ◊parapsychology.

Rhineland-Palatinate /'raɪnlænd pə'lætɪnət/ (German *Rheinland-Pfalz*) administrative region (German *Land*) of Germany; **area** 19,800 sq km/7,643 sq mi; **capital** Mainz; **physical** wooded mountain country, river valleys of Rhine and Moselle; **products** wine (75% of German output). tobacco, chemicals, machinery, leather goods, pottery; **population** (1988) 3,611,000. **history** formed 1946 of the Rhenish Palatinate and parts of Hessen, Rhine province, and Hessen-Nassau.

rhinestone /'raɪnstəʊn/ n. an imitation diamond.

rhino /'raɪnəʊ/ n. (*plural* the same or **rhinos**) (*colloquial*) a rhinoceros. [abbreviation]

rhinoceros /raɪ'nɒsərəs/ n. (*plural* **rhinoceroses** or the same) a hoofed mammal of the family Rhinocerotidae. The one-horned Indian rhinoceros *Rhinoceros unicornis* is up to 2 m/6 ft at the shoulder, with a tubercled skin, folded into shield-like pieces; the African black rhinoceros *Diceros bicornis* is 1.5 m/5 ft high, with a prehensile upper lip for feeding on shrubs; the broad-lipped or 'white' rhinoceros *Ceratotherium simum* is actually slaty-grey, with a squarish mouth for browsing grass. The latter two are smooth-skinned and two-horned. They are solitary and vegetarian, with poor eyesight but excellent hearing and smell. Needless slaughter has led to the near extinction of all species of rhinoceros, particularly the Sumatran rhinoceros and Javan rhinoceros. [from Latin from Greek *rhino-* = nostril, nose and *keras* = horn]

rhizoid n. a hairlike outgrowth found on the ◊gametophyte generation of ferns, mosses and liverworts. Rhizoids anchor the plant to the substrate and can absorb water and nutrients. They may be composed of many cells, as in mosses, where they are usually brownish, or unicellular, as in liverworts, where they are usually colourless. Rhizoids fulfil the same functions as the ◊roots of higher plants but are simpler in construction.

rhizome /'raɪzəʊm/ n. a rootlike stem growing along or under the ground and emitting both roots and shoots. It is a ◊perennating organ in some species, where it is generally thick and fleshy, while in other species it is mainly a means of ◊vegetative reproduction, and is therefore long and slender, with buds all along it that send up new plants. The potato is a rhizome that has two distinct parts, the tuber being the swollen end of a long, cordlike rhizome. [from Greek *rhizoō* = take root]

rhm abbreviation of **roentgen-hour-metre** the unit of effective strength of a radioactive source that produces gamma rays. It is used for substances for which it is difficult to establish radioactive disintegration rates.

rho /rəʊ/ n. the 17th letter of the Greek alphabet (ρ, P) = rh. [Greek]

Rhode Island /rəʊd 'aɪlənd/ smallest state of the USA, in New England; nickname Little Rhody or the Ocean State; **area** 3,100 sq km/1,197 sq mi; **capital** Providence; **features** Narragansett Bay runs inland 45 km/28 mi; **products** apples, potatoes, poultry (notably Rhode Island Reds), dairy products, jewellery (30% of the workforce), textiles, silverware, machinery, rubber, plastics, electronics; **population** (1987) 986,000; **history** founded in 1636 by Roger Williams, exiled from Massachusetts Bay colony for religious dissent; one of the original Thirteen States.

Rhodes /rəʊdz/ Cecil (John) 1853–1902. South African politician, born in the UK, prime minister of Cape Colony 1890–96. Aiming at the formation of a South African federation and of a block of British territory from the Cape to Cairo, he was responsible for the annexation of Bechuanaland (now Botswana) in 1885. He formed the British South Africa Company in 1889, which occupied Mashonaland and Matabeleland, thus forming Rhodesia (now Zambia and Zimbabwe).

Rhodes Greek *Rodhos* Greek island, largest of the Dodecanese, in the E Aegean Sea; **area** 1,412 sq km/

545 sq mi; **capital** Rhodes; **products** grapes, olives; **population** (1981) 88,000; **history** settled by Greeks about 1000 BC; the ◊Colossus of Rhodes (fell 224 BC) was one of the Seven Wonders of the World; held by the Knights Hospitallers of St John 1306–1522; taken from Turkish rule by the Italian occupation of 1912; ceded to Greece in 1947.

Rhodes Wilfred 1877–1973. English cricketer. He took more wickets than anyone else in the game – 4,187 wickets 1898–1930 – and also scored 39,802 first-class runs.

Rhodes Zandra 1940– . English fashion designer known for the extravagant fantasy and luxury of her dress creations.

Rhodesia /rəʊ'diːʃə/ former name of ◊Zambia (North Rhodesia) and ◊Zimbabwe (South Rhodesia).

rhodium /'rəʊdɪəm/ n. a hard, white metallic element, symbol Rh, atomic number 45, atomic mass 102.905. It is one of the so-called platinum group of metals and is resistant to tarnish, corrosion, and acid. It occurs as a free metal in the natural alloy osmiridium and is used in jewellery, electroplating, and the manufacture of thermocouples. [from Greek *rhodon* = rose (from colour of solution of its salts)]

rhododendron n. any of numerous shrubs of the genus *Rhododendron* of the heath family Ericaceae. Most species are evergreen. The leaves are usually dark and leathery, and the large racemes of flowers occur in all colours except blue. They thrive on acid soils. ◊Azaleas belong to the same genus. [Latin = oleander, from Greek (*rhodon* = rose and *dendron* = tree)]

Rhodope Mountains /'rɒdəpi/ range of mountains on the frontier between Greece and Bulgaria, rising to 2,925 m/9,497 ft at Musala.

rhomboid /'rɒmbɔɪd/ adj. like a rhombus. —n. a quadrilateral of which only the opposite sides and angles are equal. —**rhomboidal** adj. [from French or Latin from Greek]

rhombus n. (*plural* **rhombuses**) in geometry, an oblique equilateral (all sides equal) ◊parallelogram, such as the diamond on a playing card. Its diagonals bisect each other at right angles, and its area is half the product of the lengths of the two diagonals. A rhombus whose internal angles are 90° is called a square. [Latin from Greek *rhombos*]

Rhône /rəʊn/ river of S Europe; length 810 km/500 mi. It rises in Switzerland and flows through Lake Geneva to Lyon in France, where at its confluence with the Saône the upper limit of navigation is reached. The river turns due south, passes Vienne and Avignon, and takes in the Isère and other tributaries. Near Arles it divides into the **Grand** and **Petit Rhône**, flowing respectively SE and SW into the Mediterranean west of Marseille.

Rhône-Alpes /rəʊn 'ælps/ region of E France in the upper reaches of the Rhône; **area** 43,700 sq km/16,868 sq mi; **population** (1986) 5,154,000. It consists of the *départements* of Ain, Ardèche, Drôme, Isère, Loire, Rhône, Savoie, and Haute-Savoie. The chief town is Lyon. There are several notable wine-producing areas, including Chenas, Fleurie, and Beaujolais. Industrial products include chemicals, textiles, and motor vehicles.

rhubarb /'ruːbɑːb/ n. **1.** a garden plant of the genus *Rheum rhaponticum* of the buckwheat family Polygonaceae, grown for its pink, fleshy, edible leaf stalks. The leaves are poisonous. There are also wild rhubarbs (genus *Rheum* native to Europe and Asia; these stalks. **2.** the root of a Chinese plant of the genus *Rheum*; a purgative made from this. [from Old French from Latin *rhabarbarum*]

rhumb /rʌm/ n. **1.** any of the 32 points of the compass. **2.** the angle between the directions of any two successive compass-points. **3.** a rhumb line. —**rhumb line**, a line cutting all meridians at the same angle; the line followed by a ship sailing according to a fixed compass-bearing. [from French probably from Dutch *ruim* = room, associated with Latin *rhombus*]

rhyme /raɪm/ n. **1.** identity of sound between the endings of words or of verse-lines, such as *wing* and *sing*. Avoided in Japanese, it is a common literary device in other Asian and European languages. Rhyme first appeared in Europe in late Latin poetry but was not used in Classical Greek and Latin. **2.** (in *singular* or *plural*) a verse having rhymes. **3.** the use of rhyme. **4.** a word providing a rhyme to another. —v. t/i. **1.** to form a rhyme; to have rhymes. **2.** to write rhymes; to put or make (a story etc.) into rhyme. **3.** to treat (a word) as rhyming with another. —**rhyming slang,** slang that replaces words by words or phrases that rhyme with them (e.g. *stairs* by *apples and pears*). **without rhyme or reason,** lacking discernible sense or logic. [from Old French *rime* from Latin from Greek]

rhymester /ˈraɪmstə/ *n.* a writer of (especially simple) rhymes.

rhyolite *n.* an ◊igneous rock, the fine-grained volcanic (extrusive) equivalent of granite.

Rhys /riːs/ Jean 1894–1979. British novelist, born in Dominica. Her works include *Wide Sargasso Sea* 1966, a recreation, set in a Caribbean island, of the life of Rochester's mad wife in *Jane Eyre* by Charlotte Brontë.

rhythm /ˈrɪðəm/ *n.* **1.** the pattern produced by various relations of emphasis and duration of notes in music or by long and short or accented and unaccented syllables; the aspect of composition concerned with this. **2.** a movement with a regular succession of strong and weak elements. **3.** a regularly recurring sequence of events. —**rhythmic** *adj.*, **rhythmical** *adj.*, **rhythmically** *adv.* [from French or Latin from Greek *rhuthmos*]

rhythm and blues (R & B) US popular music of the 1940s–60s, which drew on swing and jump-jazz rhythms and blues vocals and was a progenitor of rock and roll. It diversified into soul, funk, and other styles. R & B artists include Bo Diddley (1928–), Jackie Wilson (1934–84), and Etta James (*c.* 1938–).

rhythm method method of natural contraception that relies on avoiding intercourse when the woman is producing egg cells (ovulating). The time of ovulation can be worked out by the calendar (counting days from the last period), by temperature changes, or by inspection of the cervical mucus. All these methods are unreliable because it is possible for ovulation to occur at any stage of the menstrual cycle.

ria *n.* a long, narrow sea inlet, usually branching and surrounded by hills. A ria is deeper and wider towards its mouth, unlike a ◊fjord. It is formed by the flooding of a river valley due to either a rise in sea level or a lowering of a landmass.

rib *n.* **1.** each of the bones articulated in pairs to the ◊spine in invertebrates and curving round to protect the thoracic cavity and its organs. Most fishes and many reptiles have ribs along most of the spine, but in mammals they are found only in the chest area. In humans, there are 12 pairs of ribs. The ribs protect the lungs and heart, and allow the chest to expand and contract easily **2.** a joint of meat from this part of an animal. **3.** a ridge or long, raised piece, often of stronger or thicker material, across a surface or through a structure, serving to support or strengthen; any of the hinged rods forming the framework of an umbrella. **4.** a combination of plain and purl stitches in knitting, producing a ribbed somewhat elastic fabric. —*v.t.* (**-bb-**) **1.** to provide with ribs. **2.** to knit as rib. **3.** (*colloquial*) to tease. —**ribcage** *n.* the framework of ribs round the thoracic cavity. [Old English]

RIBA abbreviation of Royal Institute of British Architects.

ribald /ˈrɪbəld/ *adj.* (of language or its user) coarsely or disrespectfully humorous. [originally = low-born retainer, from Old French *ribault* (*riber* = pursue licentious pleasures)]

ribaldry /ˈrɪbəldrɪ/ *n.* ribald talk.

riband /ˈrɪbənd/ *n.* a ribbon. [from Old French *riban*]

ribbed /rɪbd/ *adj.* **1.** having ribs or riblike markings. **2.** knitted in rib.

Ribbentrop /ˈrɪbəntrɒp/ Joachim von 1893–1946. German Nazi politician and diplomat, born in the Rhineland. He joined the Nazi party in 1932 and acted as Hitler's adviser on foreign affairs; he was German ambassador to Britain 1936–38 and foreign minister 1938–45, during which time he negotiated the Non-Aggression Pact between Germany and the Soviet Union. He was tried at Nuremberg as a war criminal 1946 and hanged.

ribbon /ˈrɪbən/ *n.* **1.** a narrow strip or band of silk or other ornamental material, used for decoration or for tying something; material in this form. **2.** a ribbon of a special colour or pattern worn to indicate some honour or membership of a sports team etc. **3.** a long narrow strip of anything, e.g. inked material used in a typewriter. **4.** (in *plural*) ragged strips. —**ribbon development,** the building of houses in a narrow strip along a road outwards from a town or village. [variant of *riband*]

rice

grain   cross section of a grain

Ribera /riˈbiərə/ José (Jusepe) de 1591–1652. Spanish painter, active in Italy from 1616 under the patronage of the viceroys of Naples. His early work shows the impact of Caravaggio, but his colours gradually lightened. He painted many full-length saints and mythological figures and genre scenes, which he produced without preliminary drawing.

riboflavin *n.* or **vitamin B₂** a ◊vitamin of the B complex whose absence in the diet causes stunted growth.

ribonucleic acid /raɪbəʊnjuːˈkliːɪk/ full name of ◊RNA. [from *ribose* a sugar and Latin *nucleus* = kernal]

ribosome *n.* in biology, the protein-making machinery of the cell. Ribosomes are located on the endoplasmic reticulum of eukaryotic cells, and are made of proteins and a special type of ◊RNA, ribosomal RNA. They receive messenger RNA (copied from the ◊DNA) and ◊amino acids, and 'translate' the messenger RNA by using its chemically coded instructions to link amino acids in a specific order, to make a strand of a particular protein.

Ricardo /rɪˈkɑːdəʊ/ David 1772–1823. English economist, author of *Principles of Political Economy* 1817. Among his discoveries were the principle of ◊comparative advantage (that countries can benefit by specializing in goods they produce efficiently and trading internationally to buy others) and the law of diminishing returns (that continued increments of capital and labour applied to a given quantity of land will eventually show a declining rate of increase in output).

rice /raɪs/ *n.* the principal cereal of the wet regions of the tropics; derived from grass of the species *Oryza sativa*, probably native to India and SE Asia. The yield is very large, and rice is said to be the staple food of one-third of the world population. —**rice paper,** paper made from the pith of an oriental tree, *Tetrapanax papyriferum*, and used for painting and in cookery. [from Old French *ris* from Italian from Latin from Greek *oruza*]

Rice Elmer 1892–1967. US playwright. His works include *The Adding Machine* 1923 and *Street Scene* 1929, which won a Pulitzer Prize and was made into an opera by Kurt Weill. Many of his plays deal with such economic and political issues as the Depression (*We, the People* 1933) and racism (*American Landscape* 1939).

rich /rɪtʃ/ *adj.* **1.** having much wealth. **2.** having a large supply of something; having great natural resources; (of soil) full of nutrients, fertile. **3.** splendid, made of costly materials, elaborate. **4.** producing or produced abundantly. **5.** (of food or diet) containing a large proportion of fat, oil, eggs, spice etc. **6.** (of a mixture in an internal-combustion engine) containing a high proportion of fuel. **7.** (of colour, sound, or smell) pleasantly deep or strong. **8.** (of an incident or assertion etc.) highly amusing or ludicrous. —**richness** *n.* [Old English and from Old French *riche*]

Rich Adrienne 1929– . US radical feminist poet, writer, and critic. Her poetry is both subjective and political,

Richter scale

value	relative amount of energy released	examples
1		
2		
3		
4	1	Carlisle, 1979
5	30	San Francisco, 1979
		New England, 1979
		Wrexham, Wales 1990
6	100	San Fernando, 1971
7	30,000	Chimbote, 1970
		San Francisco, 1989
8	1,000,000	Tangshan, 1976
		San Francisco, 1906
		Lisbon, 1755
		Alaska, 1964

concerned with female consciousness, peace, and gay rights. Her works include *On Lies, Secrets and Silence* 1979 and *The Fact of a Doorframe: Poems Selected and New* 1984.

Richard /'rɪtʃəd/ Cliff. Stage name of Harry Roger Webb 1940– . English pop singer. In the late 1950s he was influenced by Elvis Presley, but became a Christian family entertainer, continuing to have hits in the UK throughout the 1980s. His original backing group was the **Shadows** (1958–68 and later re-formed).

Richard /'rɪtʃəd/ three kings of England:

Richard I the Lion-Hearted (French *Coeur-de-Lion*) 1157–1199. King of England from 1189, who spent all but six months of his reign abroad. He was the third son of Henry II, against whom he twice rebelled. In the third ◊Crusade 1191–92 he won victories at Cyprus, Acre, and Arsuf (against ◊Saladin), but failed to recover Jerusalem. While returning overland he was captured by the Duke of Austria, who handed him over to the emperor Henry VI, and he was held prisoner until a large ransom was raised. He then returned briefly to England, where his brother John I had been ruling in his stead. His later years were spent in warfare in France, where he was killed.

Richard II 1367–1400. King of England from 1377, effectively from 1389, son of Edward the Black Prince. He reigned in conflict with Parliament; they executed some of his associates in 1388 and he some of the opposing barons in 1397, whereupon he made himself absolute. Two years later, forced to abdicate in favour of ◊Henry IV, he was jailed and probably assassinated.

Richard III 1452–1485. King of England from 1483. The son of Richard, Duke of York, he was created Duke of Gloucester by his brother Edward IV, and distinguished himself in the Wars of the ◊Roses. On Edward's death in 1483 he became protector to his nephew Edward V, and soon secured the crown for himself on the plea that Edward IV's sons were illegitimate. He proved a capable ruler, but the suspicion that he had murdered Edward V and his brother undermined his popularity. In 1485 Henry, Earl of Richmond (later ◊Henry VII), raised a rebellion, and Richard III was defeated and killed at ◊Bosworth. Scholars now tend to minimize the evidence for his crimes as Tudor propaganda.

Richards /'rɪtʃədz/ Frank. Pen name of Charles Harold St John Hamilton 1875–1961. English writer for the children's papers *Magnet* and *Gem*, who invented Greyfriars public school and the fat boy Billy Bunter.

Richards Gordon 1905–1986. English jockey and trainer who was champion on the flat a record 26 times between 1925 and 1953.

Mother always told me my day was coming, but I never realized that I'd end up being the shortest knight of the year.
Gordon Richards
Champion jockey, on learning of his knighthood
(attrib.)

Richards Theodore 1868–1928. US chemist. Working at Harvard University, Boston for much of his career, Richards concentrated on determining as accurately as possible the atomic weights of a large number of elements. He was awarded the Nobel Prize for Chemistry in 1914.

Richardson /'rɪtʃədsən/ Dorothy 1873–1957. English novelist whose works were collected under the title *Pilgrimage* 1938. She pioneered the 'stream of consciousness' technique and has been linked with Virginia ◊Woolf, who credited her with having invented 'the psychological sentence of the feminine gender'.

Richardson Ralph (David) 1902–1983. English actor. He played many stage parts, including Falstaff (Shakespeare), Peer Gynt (Ibsen), and Cyrano de Bergerac (Rostand). He shared the management of the Old Vic theatre with Laurence Olivier 1944–50.

Richardson Samuel 1689–1761. English novelist, one of the founders of the modern novel. *Pamela* 1740–41, written in the form of a series of letters and containing much dramatic conversation, was sensationally popular all across Europe, and was followed by *Clarissa* 1747–48 and *Sir Charles Grandison* 1753–54.

Richardson Tony 1928– . English director and producer. With George Devine he established the English Stage Company 1955 at the Royal Court Theatre, with productions such as *Look Back in Anger* 1956. His films include *Saturday Night and Sunday Morning* 1960.

Richelieu /'ri:ʃljə:/ Armand Jean du Plessis de 1585–1642. French cardinal and politician, chief minister from 1624. He aimed to make the monarchy absolute; he ruthlessly crushed opposition by the nobility and destroyed the political power of the ◊Huguenots, while leaving them religious freedom. Abroad, he sought to establish French supremacy by breaking the power of the Habsburgs; he therefore supported the Swedish king Gustavus Adolphus and the German Protestant princes against Austria and in 1635 brought France into the Thirty Years' War.

Nothing is as dangerous for the state as those who would govern kingdoms with maxims found in books.
Cardinal Richelieu
Political Testament

riches /'rɪtʃɪz/ *n.pl.* a great quantity of money, property, valuable possessions, natural resources etc.

richly *adv.* 1. in a rich way. 2. fully, thoroughly.

Richter /'rɪktə/ Burton 1931– . US high-energy physicist who, in the 1960s, designed the Stanford Positron Accelerating Ring (SPEAR). In 1974 Richter used SPEAR to produce a new particle, later named the ψ (psi) particle, thought to be formed from the charmed quark postulated by Sheldon ◊Glashow. Richter shared the 1976 Nobel Physics Prize with Samuel ◊Ting.

Richter Charles Francis 1900–1985. US seismologist, deviser of the ◊Richter scale used to measure the strength of the waves from earthquakes.

Richter Johann Paul Friedrich 1763–1825. German author, commonly known as Jean Paul. He created a series of comic eccentrics in works such as the romance *Titan* 1800–03 and *Die Flegeljahre/The Awkward Age* 1804–05.

Richter scale a scale based on measurement of seismic waves, used to determine the magnitude of an earthquake at the epicentre. The magnitude of an earthquake differs from the intensity, measured by the Mercalli scale, which is subjective and varies from place to place for the same earthquake.

Richthofen /'rɪkthəʊfən/ Manfred, Freiherr von (the 'Red Baron') 1892–1918. German aviator. In World War I he commanded the 11th Chasing Squadron, known as **Richthofen's Flying Circus**, and shot down 80 aircraft before being killed in action.

ricin *n.* an extremely toxic extract from the seeds of the ◊castor-oil plant. When combined with ◊monoclonal antibodies, ricin can attack cancer cells, particularly in the treatment of lymphoma and leukaemia.

rick[1] *n.* a stack of hay etc. [Old English]

rick[2] *v.t.* to sprain or strain slightly. —*n.* a slight sprain or strain. [from Middle Low German *wricken*]

rickets /'rɪkɪts/ *n.* (as *singular* or *plural*) defective growth of bone in children due to an insufficiency of calcium deposits. The bones, which do not harden adequately, are bent out of shape. It is usually caused by a lack of vitamin D

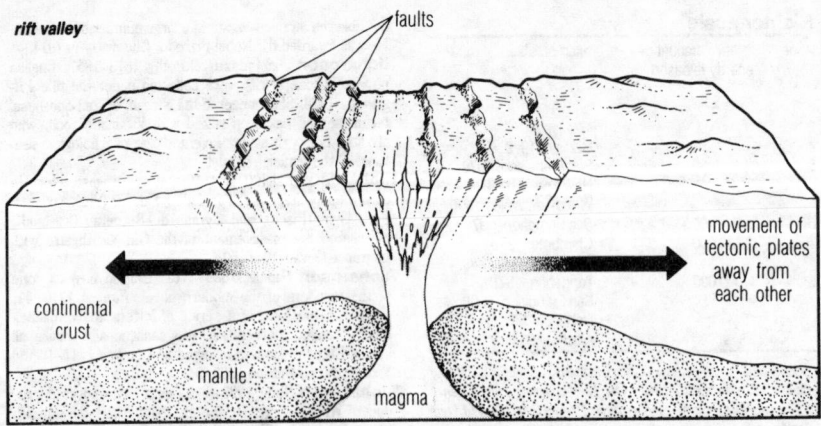

rift valley — faults — movement of tectonic plates away from each other — continental crust — mantle — magma

and insufficient exposure to sunlight. Renal rickets, also a condition of malformed bone, is associated with kidney disease. —**rickettsial** /rɪˈketsɪəl/ *adj.*

rickety /ˈrɪkɪtɪ/ *adj.* 1. shaky, weak-jointed, insecure. 2. suffering from rickets. —**ricketiness** *n.*

rickrack variant of ◊ricrac.

rickshaw /ˈrɪkʃɔː/ *n.* or **ricksha** a light two-wheeled hooded vehicle drawn by one or more persons. [abbreviation of *jinricksha(w)* from Japanese *jin* = person, *riki* = power and *sha* = vehicle]

ricochet /ˈrɪkəʃeɪ, -ʃet/ *v.i.* (*past* **ricocheted** /-eɪd/; *participle* **ricocheting** /-eɪɪŋ/) to rebound from a surface as a missile does when it strikes with a glancing blow —*n.* a rebound of this kind; a hit made after it. [French]

ricrac /ˈrɪkræk/ *n.* a zigzag braided trimming for garments. [reduplication of *rack*[1]]

rid *v.t.* (-**dd**-; *past* and *past participle* **rid**) to free from something unpleasant or unwanted. —**get rid of**, to cause to go away; (*colloquial*) to succeed in selling. [originally = clear (land etc.), from Old Norse]

riddance /ˈrɪdəns/ *n.* ridding. —**good riddance**, welcome deliverance from an unwanted person or thing.

ridden past participle of *ride.*

riddle[1] *n.* 1. a question or statement testing ingenuity in finding its answer or meaning. 2. a puzzling fact, thing, or person. —*v.i.* to speak in or propound riddles. [Old English, relative to *read*]

riddle[2] *v.t.* 1. to pierce with many holes. 2. (in *past participle*) thoroughly permeated (with faults etc.). 3. to pass through a riddle. —*n.* a coarse sieve for gravel or cinders etc. [Old English]

ride *v.t./i.* (*past* **rode**; *past participle* **ridden** /ˈrɪdən/) 1. to sit on and control or be carried by (a horse etc.). 2. to travel on horseback, a bicycle, train, or other conveyance; to travel thus over or through. 3. to be carried on or conveyed by, to be supported on; to float or seem to float. 4. to yield to (a blow) so as to reduce its impact. 5. to give a ride to. —*n.* 1. a spell of riding; a journey on a horse etc. or in a vehicle. 2. a track for riding on, especially through woods. 3. a roundabout or other device on which people ride at a fairground etc. 4. the quality of sensations felt when riding. —**let a thing ride**, to leave it undisturbed. **ride down**, to overtake or trample on horseback. **ride out**, to come safely through (a storm etc., or a danger or difficulty). **ride up**, (of a garment) to work upwards when worn. **riding light**, a light shown by a ship at anchor. **take for a ride**, (*slang*) to hoax or deceive. [Old English]

rider *n.* 1. one who rides a horse or bicycle etc. 2. an additional clause amending or supplementing a document, a corollary; a recommendation etc. added to a verdict; in mathematics, a problem arising as a corollary of a theorem etc.

riderless *adj.* without a rider.

ridge /rɪdʒ/ *n.* 1. the line of junction of two surfaces sloping upwards towards each other; a long narrow hill-top, a mountain range, a watershed; any narrow elevation across a surface. 2. an elongated region of high barometric pressure. 3. a raised strip of arable land, usually one of a set separated by furrows. —**ridge-piece** *n.* a beam along the ridge of a

roof. **ridgepole** *n.* a horizontal pole of a long tent. —**ridgy** *adj.* [Old English]

ridgeway /ˈrɪdʒweɪ/ *n.* a road along a ridge, sometimes dating back to medieval or perhaps even prehistoric times.

ridicule /ˈrɪdɪkjuːl/ *n.* making or being made an object of derision. —*v.t.* to make fun of, to subject to ridicule. [French or from Latin *ridiculum* (*ridēre* = laugh)]

ridiculous /rɪˈdɪkjuləs/ *adj.* 1. deserving to be laughed at, especially in a malicious or scornful way. 2. not worth serious consideration, preposterous. —**ridiculously** *adv.* or [from French or from Latin *ridiculosus*]

riding /ˈraɪdɪŋ/ *n.* a former administrative division of Yorkshire (*East*, *North*, and *West Riding*). [Old English from Old Norse = third part]

Ridley /ˈrɪdlɪ/ Nicholas *c.*1500–1555. English Protestant bishop. He became chaplain to Henry VIII in 1541 and bishop of London in 1550. He took an active part in the Reformation and supported Lady Jane Grey's claim to the throne. After Mary's accession he was arrested and burned as a heretic.

Ridley Nicholas 1929– . British Conservative politician, cabinet minister 1983–90. After a period in industry he became active as a 'dry' right-winger in the Conservative Party: a 'Thatcherite' before Margaret Thatcher had brought the term to public attention. He served under Harold Macmillan, Edward Heath, and Alec Douglas-Home, but did not become a member of the cabinet until 1983. His apparent disdain for public opinion caused his transfer, in 1989, from the politically sensitive Department of the Environment to that of Trade and Industry, and his resignation in July 1990 after criticisms of European colleagues and Germany.

Rie /riː/ Lucie 1902–. Austrian-born potter who worked in England from the 1930s. Her pottery, exhibited all over the world, is simple and pure in form, showing a debt to Bernard ◊Leach.

Riefenstahl /ˈriːfənʃtaːl/ Leni 1902– . German filmmaker. Her film of the Nazi rallies at Nuremberg, *Triumph des Willens/Triumph of the Will* 1934, vividly illustrated Hitler's charismatic appeal but tainted her career. After World War II her work was blacklisted by the Allies until 1952.

Riel /riˈel/ Louis 1844–1885. French-Canadian rebel, a champion of the Métis (an Indian-French people); he established a provisional government in Winnipeg in an unsuccessful revolt 1869–70 and was hanged for treason after leading a second revolt in Saskatchewan in 1885.

Riesling /ˈriːslɪŋ/ *n.* a kind of dry white wine made from a European variety of grape; this grape. [German]

Riesman /ˈriːsmən/ David 1909– . US sociologist, author of *The Lonely Crowd: A Study of the Changing American Character* 1950. He made a distinction among 'inner-directed', 'tradition-directed', and 'other-directed' societies; the first using individual internal values, the second using established tradition, and the third, other people's expectations, to develop cohesiveness and conformity within a society

Rietvelt /ˈriːtfelt/ Gerrit Thomas 1888–1964. Dutch architect, an exponent of De ◊Stijl. He designed the Schroeder

House at Utrecht 1924; he is also well known for colourful, minimalist chair design.

rife *predic. adj.* 1. of common occurrence, widespread. 2. well provided, full. [Old English]

Riff *n.* member of a ◊Berber people of N Morocco, who under ◊Abd el-Krim long resisted the Spanish and French.

riffle *v.t./i.* to turn (pages) in quick succession; to leaf quickly (through a book); to thumb (a block of paper or pack of cards etc.), releasing the edges in (rapid) sucession.

riffraff /'rɪfræf/ *n.* a rabble, disreputable or undesirable persons. [from Old French *rif et raf*]

rifle /'raɪfəl/ *n.* 1. a ◊firearm that has spiral grooves (rifling) in its barrel, especially one fired from shoulder level. Rifled guns came into use in the 16th century. 2. (in *plural*) soldiers with rifles. —*v.t.* 1. to search and rob. 2. to make spiral grooves in (a gun or its barrel or bore) to make the bullet spin and so travel more accurately when fired. [from Old French *rifler* = scratch, plunder, from Old Dutch]

rifleman *n.* (*plural* **riflemen**) a male soldier armed with a rifle.

rifling /'raɪflɪŋ/ *n.* the arrangement of grooves in a rifle.

rift /rɪft/ *n.* 1. a crack or split in an object. 2. a cleft in the Earth or a rock. 3. a disagreement, a breach in friendly relations. [Scandinavian relative to *riven*]

rift valley a valley formed by the subsidence of a block of the Earth's ◊crust between two or more parallel ◊faults. Rift valleys are steep-sided and form where the crust is being pulled apart, as at ◊ocean ridges, or in the Great Rift Valley (see ◊Rift Valley, Great) of E Africa.

Rift Valley, Great volcanic valley formed 10–20 million years ago by a crack in the Earth's crust and running about 6,400 km/4,000 mi from the Jordan valley in Syria through the Red Sea to Mozambique in SE Africa. At some points its traces have been lost by erosion, but elsewhere, as in S Kenya, cliffs rise thousands of metres. It is marked by a series of lakes, including Lake Turkana (formerly Lake Rudolph), and volcanoes, such as Mount Kilimanjaro.

rig[1] /rɪg/ *v.t.* (-**gg**-) 1. to provide (a ship) with spars and ropes etc. 2. (often *with out* or *up*) to provide with clothes or other equipment. 3. to set up hastily or as a makeshift. 4. to assemble and adjust the parts of (an aircraft). —*n.* 1. the arrangement of a ship's masts and sails etc. 2. equipment for a special purpose, e.g. a radio transmitter. 3. an oil-rig. —**rigout** *n.* (*colloquial*) an outfit of clothes.

rig[2] *v.t.* (-**gg**-) to manage or conduct fraudulently. —**rig the market**, to cause an artificial rise or fall in prices.

Riga /'ri:gə/ capital and port of Latvian Republic, USSR; population (1987) 900,000. A member of the ◊Hanseatic League from 1282, Riga has belonged in turn to Poland from 1582, Sweden from 1621, and Russia from 1710. It was the capital of independent Latvia 1918–40 and was occupied by Germany 1941–44, before being annexed by the USSR.

Rigel /'raɪgəl/ *n.* the brightest star in the constellation Orion. It is a blue-white supergiant, with an estimated diameter 50 times that of the Sun. It is 900 light years from Earth and is 50,000 times more luminous than our Sun. It is the seventh brightest star in the sky.

Rigg Diana 1938– . English actress. Her stage roles include Héloïse in *Abelard and Héloïse* 1970, and television roles include Emma Peel in *The Avengers* 1965–67 and Lady Deadlock in *Bleak House* 1985. She became the hostess for *Mystery Theater* on US public TV from 1989.

rigging *n.* a ship's spars and ropes etc. used to support masts and set or work the sails.

right /raɪt/ *adj.* 1. (of conduct etc.) morally good, in accordance with justice, equity, or duty. 2. proper, correct, true; preferable, most suitable; (of a side of a fabric) meant for show or use. 3. in a good or normal condition; sane; well-advised, not mistaken. 4. on or towards the right-hand side. 5. politically to the right (see sense 4 below). 6. (*archaic* or *colloquial*) real, properly so called. —*n.* 1. what is just; a fair claim or treatment. 2. being entitled to a privilege or immunity; a thing one is entitled to. 3. the right-hand part, region, or direction; the right hand; a blow with this; (in marching) the right foot. 4. (often **Right**) the right wing of a political party or other group; conservatives collectively. —*v.t.* 1. to restore to a proper, correct, or vertical position. 2. to set right, to make amends or take vengeance for; to vindicate, to justify; to rehabilitate. 3. to correct. —*adv.* 1. straight. 2. (*colloquial*) immediately. 3. all the way, completely. 4. exactly, quite. 5. on or to the right-hand side.

6. rightly. 7. all right; what you say is correct; I agree. 8. (*archaic*) very, to the full. —**by right(s)**, if right were done. **in one's own right**, through one's own position or effort etc. **in the right**, having justice or truth on one's side. **on the right side of**, in the favour of (a person); somewhat less than (a stated age). **put** *or* **set to rights**, to arrange in proper order. **right and left**, on all sides. **right angle**, an angle of 90°, made by lines meeting with equal angles on either side (**at right angles**, placed to form a right angle). **right ascension**, the celestial co-ordinate corresponding to longitude, measured eastwards on the celestial sphere from the point known as the First Point of Aries, where the ecliptic intersects the celestial equator. **right bank**, the bank of a river on the right as one faces downstream. **right hand**, the hand that, in most people, is used more than the left, on the side opposite the left hand; a right-hand person. **right-hand** *adj.* of, on, or towards this side of a person or the corresponding side of a thing. **right-handed** *adj.* using the right hand by preference as more serviceable; made by or for the right hand; turning to the right. **right-hander** *n.* a right-handed person or blow. **right-hand person**, an indispensable or chief assistant. **Right Honourable**, the title of earls, viscounts, barons, Privy Counsellors, and certain others. **right-minded** *adj.* having proper or honest principles. **right of way**, the right to pass over another's ground; a path that is subject to such a right; the right to proceed while another vehicle etc. must wait. **right-oh!**, (*colloquial*) an expression of agreement to what is suggested. **Right Reverend**, title of a bishop. **rights issue**, an issue of shares offered by a company at a special price to its existing shareholders. **rights of man**, = ◊human rights. **right wing**, the right-hand side of a football team etc. on the field; a player in this position; the more conservative or reactionary section of a political party or spectrum. **right-winger** *n.* a person on the right wing. —**rightly** *adv.*, **rightness** *n.* [Old English]

right-angled triangle triangle in which one of the angles is a right angle (90°). It is the basic form of triangle for defining trigonometrical ratios (for example, sine, cosine, and tangent) and for which ◊Pythagoras' theorem holds true. The longest side of a right-angled triangle is called the hypotenuse.

righteous /'raɪtʃəs/ *adj.* doing what is morally right; making a show of this; morally justifiable. —**righteously** *adv.*, **righteousness** *n.* [Old English] after *bounteous* etc.]

rightful *adj.* in accordance with what is just, proper, or legal; (of property etc.) to which one is entitled. —**rightfully** *adv.* [Old English]

rightism *n.* political conservatism. —**rightist** *n.*

Rights of Man and the Citizen, Declaration of a historic French document. According to the statement of the French National Assembly in 1789, these rights include representation in the legislature; equality before the law; equality of opportunity; freedom from arbitrary imprisonment; freedom of speech and religion; taxation in proportion to ability to pay; and security of property. In 1946 were added equal rights for women; right to work, join a union, and strike; leisure, social security, and support in old age; and free education.

rightward /'raɪtwəd/ *adv.* or **rightwards** towards the right. —*adj.* going towards or facing the right.

right wing the more conservative or reactionary section of a political party or spectrum. It originated in the French national assembly in 1789, where the nobles sat in the place of honour on the president's right, whereas the commons were on his left (hence ◊left wing).

rigid /'rɪdʒɪd/ *adj.* 1. not flexible, that cannot be bent. 2. inflexible, strict. —**rigidity** /-'dʒɪdɪti/ *n.*, **rigidly** *adv.* [from French or Latin *rigidus*]

rigmarole /'rɪgmərəʊl/ *n.* 1. a rambling statement; meaningless talk. 2. a lengthy procedure. [alteration from obsolete *ragman roll* = catalogue]

rigor /'raɪgɔ:, 'rɪgə/ *n.* medical term for shivering. —**rigor mortis**, stiffening of the body after death. [from Latin *rigēre* = be stiff]

rigour /'rɪgə/ *n.* 1. severity, strictness. 2. (in *plural*) harshness of weather or conditions. 3. logical exactitude. —**rigorous** *adj.*, **rigorously** *adv.* [from Old French from Latin]

Rigveda /rɪg'veɪdə/ *n.* the oldest of the ◊Vedas, the chief sacred writings of Hinduism. It consists of hymns to the Aryan gods, such as Indra, and to nature gods.

rile *v.t.* (*colloquial*) to anger, to irritate. [variant of *roil* = make turbid]

Riley /'raili/ Bridget (Louise) 1931– . English Op Art painter. In the early 1960s she invented her characteristic style, arranging hard-edged black and white dots or lines in regular patterns that created disturbing effects of scintillating light and movement. *Fission* 1963 (Museum of Modern Art, New York) is an example. She introduced colour in the late 1960s and experimented with silk-screen prints on Perspex.

Rilke /'rɪlkə/ Rainer Maria 1875–1926. Austrian writer, born in Prague. His prose works include the semi-autobiographical *Die Aufzeichnungen des Malte Laurids Brigge*/*Notebook of Malte Laurids Brigge* 1910, and his poetical works include *Die Sonnette an Orpheus*/*Sonnets to Orpheus* 1923 and *Duisener Elegien*/*Duino Elegies* 1923. His verse is characterized by a form of mystic pantheism that seeks to achieve a state of ecstasy in which existence can be apprehended as a whole.

rill *n.* a small stream.

rim *n.* a raised edge or border; the outer edge of a wheel, on which a tyre is fitted. [Old English]

Rimbaud /ræm'bəu/ (Jean Nicolas) Arthur 1854–1891. French Symbolist poet. His verse was chiefly written before the age of 20, notably *Les Illuminations* published 1886. From 1871 he lived with ◊Verlaine.

rime *n.* frost; (*poetic*) hoar-frost. —*v.t.* to cover with rime. [Old English]

rimmed *adj.* edged, bordered.

Rimsky-Korsakov /'rɪmski 'kɔːsəkɒf/ Nikolay Andreyevich 1844–1908. Russian composer. He used Russian folk idiom and rhythms in his Romantic compositions and published a text on orchestration. His operas include *The Maid of Pskov* 1873, *The Snow Maiden* 1882, *Mozart and Salieri* 1898, and *The Golden Cockerel* 1907, a satirical attack on despotism that was banned until 1909.

rind /raɪnd/ *n.* a tough outer layer or skin on fruit, vegetables, cheese, bacon etc. [Old English]

rinderpest /'rɪndəpest/ *n.* a disease of ruminants (especially cattle). [German *rinder* = cattle]

ring[1] *n.* 1. a circlet, usually of precious metal, worn on a finger. 2. a circular band of any material; (in *plural*) a pair of metal or wooden rings 236 mm/9.5 in in diameter suspended 500 mm/20 in apart and 2 m/8 ft above the ground, used in gymnastics competitions in which swinging and balancing movements are performed. 3. a line or band round, or the rim of, a cylindrical or circular object. 4. a mark or part etc. having the form of a circular band. 5. a circular or other enclosure for a circus, boxing, betting at races, the showing of cattle etc. 6. persons or things arranged in a circle; such an arrangement; a combination of traders, politicians, spies etc., acting together for the control of operations. 7. a circular or spiral course. —*v.t.* 1. to enclose with a ring, to encircle, to put a ring on (a bird etc.) to identify it. 3. to cut a ring in the bark of (a tree), especially to retard its growth and improve fruit-production. —**the ring**, bookmakers. **make** *or* **run rings round,** to do things much better than (another person). **ringdove** *n.* a large species of pigeon, *Columba palumbus*. **ring finger,** the third finger especially of the left hand, on which a wedding ring is usually worn. **ring main** *or* **circuit,** an electrical circuit serving many sockets in a continuous ring. **ring road,** a bypass encircling a town. [Old English]

ring[2] *v.t./i.* (*past* rang; *past participle* rung) 1. to give out a clear resonant sound of or like that of a bell when struck. 2. to make (a bell) ring; to sound (a peal etc.) on bells; to sound a bell as a summons; to signal by ringing. 3. to make a telephone call (to). 4. to resound. 5. (of the ears) to be filled with a sensation of ringing. 6. (*colloquial*) to alter and sell (a stolen vehicle). —*n.* 1. a ringing sound or tone. 2. the act of ringing a bell; the sound caused by this. 3. a specified feeling conveyed by an utterance. 4. (*colloquial*) a telephone call. 5. a set of (church) bells. —**ring a bell,** (*colloquial*) to begin to revive a memory. **ring down** (or **up**) **the curtain,** to cause it to be lowered (or raised). **ring off,** to end a telephone call. **ring up,** to call by telephone; to record (an amount) on a cash register. [Old English]

ringer *n.* 1. a person who rings bells. 2. (*US*) a race-horse etc. fraudulently substituted for another. 3. a person's double.

ringleader *n.* a leading instigator in crime, mischief etc.

ringlet /'rɪŋlɪt/ *n.* a long tubular curl of hair. —**ringleted** *adj.*

ringmaster *n.* a person directing a circus performance.

ringside *n.* the area immediately beside a boxing or circus ring. —*adj.* (of a seat etc.) close to the scene of action.

ringworm *n.* a contagious fungus skin-disease forming circular patches, usually on the scalp and feet (athlete's foot). It is treated with ◊antifungal preparations.

rink *n.* 1. an area of natural or artificial ice for skating or a game of curling etc.; a floor for roller-skating; a building containing either of these. 2. a strip of bowling green. 3. a team in bowls or curling.

rinse *v.t.* to wash out with clean water; to wash lightly; to put (clothes etc.) through clean water to remove soap etc.; to remove (impurities) by rinsing. —*n.* 1. rinsing. 2. a solution washed through hair to tint or condition it. [from Old French *rincer*]

Rinzai /'rɪnzaɪ/ *n.* (Chinese **Lin-ch'i**) school of Zen Buddhism introduced to Japan from China in the 12th century by the monk Eisai and others. It emphasizes rigorous monastic discipline and sudden enlightenment by meditation on a *kōan* (paradoxical question).

Río de Janeiro /'riːəu də ʒə'nɪərəu/ port and resort in Brazil; population (1980) 5,091,000, metropolitan area 10,217,000. The name commemorates the arrival of Portuguese explorers on 1 Jan 1502, but there is in fact no river. Sugar Loaf Mountain stands at the entrance to the harbour. It was the capital of Brazil 1822–1960. [Portuguese = river of January]

Río Grande /'riːəu 'grænd, 'grændi/ river rising in the Rocky Mountains in S Colorado, USA, and flowing south to the Gulf of Mexico, where it is reduced to a trickle by irrigation demands on its upper reaches; length 3,050 km/1,900 mi. Its last 2,400 km/1,500 mi form the US-Mexican border.

Riom /ri'ɒm/ town on the river Ambène, in the Puy-de-Dôme *département* of central France. In World War II, it was the scene in Feb–Apr 1942 of the 'war guilt' trials of several prominent French people by the ◊Vichy government. The accused included the former prime ministers ◊Blum and ◊Daladier, and General ◊Gamelin. The occasion turned into a wrangle over the reasons for French unpreparedness for war, and at the German dictator Hitler's instigation, the court was dissolved. The defendants remained in prison until released by the Allies in 1945.

Río Muni /'riːəu 'muːni/ the mainland portion of ◊Equatorial Guinea.

riot *n.* 1. a disturbance caused by a potentially violent mob. In the UK, riots formerly suppressed under the Riot Act are now governed by the ◊Public Order Act 1986. Methods of riot control include plastic bullets, stun bags (soft canvas pouches filled with buckshot which spread out in flight), water cannon, and CS gas (tear gas). Riots in Britain include the Spitalfields weavers' riot of 1736, the ◊Gordon riots of 1780, the Newport riots of 1839, and riots over the Reform Bill in Hyde Park, London, in 1866; in the 1980s inner-city riots occurred in Toxteth, Liverpool; St Paul's, Bristol; Broadwater Farm, Tottenham, and Brixton, London; and in 1990 rioting took place in central London and several other cities after demonstrations against the ◊poll tax. 2. loud revelry; a lavish display or enjoyment. 3. (*colloquial*) a very amusing thing or person. —*v.i.* to make or take part in a riot. —**riot helmet, riot shield,** a helmet or shield for use by police or soldiers dealing with riots. **run riot,** to behave in an unruly way; (of plants) to grow or spread uncontrolled. —**rioter** *n.* [from Old French *riote, rioter*]

Riot Act in the UK, an act of Parliament passed in 1714 to suppress the ◊Jacobite disorders. If three or more persons assembled unlawfully to the disturbance of the public peace, a magistrate could read a proclamation ordering them to disperse ('reading the Riot Act'); after which they might be dispersed by force. It was superseded by the 1986 ◊Public Order Act.

riotous /'raɪətəs/ *adj.* 1. disorderly, unruly. 2. boisterous, unrestrained. —**riotously** *adv.*

RIP abbreviation for *requiescat in pace* [Latin 'may he/she rest in peace'].

rip[1] *v.t./i.* (-pp-) 1. to tear or cut (a thing) quickly or forcibly away or apart; to make (a hole etc.) thus; to make a long tear or cut in. 2. to come violently apart, to split. 3. to rush along. —*n.* 1. a long tear or cut. 2. an act of ripping. 3.

a stretch of rough water. —**let rip,** (*colloquial*) to refrain from holding back the speed of or from interfering with (a person or thing); to speak violently. **rip-cord** *n.* a cord for releasing a parachute from its pack. **rip off,** (*slang*) to defraud; to steal. **rip-off** *n.* (*slang*) a fraud; a theft. **rip-roaring** *adj.* wildly noisy. **ripsaw** *n.* a saw for sawing wood along the grain. —**ripper** *n.*

rip² *n.* 1. a dissolute person. 2. a worthless horse.

riparian /raɪˈpeəriən/ *adj.* of or on a river-bank. [from Latin *ripa* = bank]

ripe *adj.* 1. (of grain or fruit etc.) ready to be gathered and used; (of cheese or wine etc.) matured and ready to be eaten or drunk. 2. mature, fully developed; (of a person's age) advanced. 3. ready, in a fit state. —**ripely** *adv.*, **ripeness** *n.* [Old English]

ripen *v.t./i.* to make or become ripe.

riposte /rɪˈpɒst/ *n.* 1. a quick counterstroke; a retort. 2. a quick return thrust in fencing. —*v.i.* to deliver a riposte. [from French from Italian]

ripple *n.* 1. a ruffling of the surface of water, a small wave or series of waves. 2. a gentle, lively sound that rises and falls. 3. a wavy appearance in hair etc. —*v.t./i.* 1. to form or flow in ripples; to cause to do this. 2. to show or sound like ripples. —**ripply** *adj.*

ripple tank in physics, a shallow water-filled tray used to demonstrate various properties of waves, such as reflection, refraction, diffraction, and interference, by programming and manipulating their movement.

Rip Van Winkle /ˈrɪp væn ˈwɪŋkl/ a legendary character created by Washington Irving in his 1819 tale of a man who falls into a magical 20-year sleep, and wakes to find he has slumbered through the American Revolution.

RISC acronym from reduced instruction-set computer, a processor on a single silicon chip that is faster and more powerful than others in common use today. By reducing the range of operations the processor can carry out, the chips are able to optimize those operations to execute more quickly. Computers based on RISC chips became commercially available in the late 1980s but are less widespread than traditional processors.

rise /raɪz/ *v.i.* (*past* **rose** /rəʊz/; *past participle* **risen** /ˈrɪzən/) 1. to come or go up; to grow, project, swell, or incline upwards; to become higher; to reach a higher position, level, intensity, or amount; to come to the surface; to become or be visible above the surroundings or horizon; (of bread or cake etc.) to swell by the action of yeast etc.; (of fish) to come to the surface to feed; (of a person's spirits) to become more cheerful. 2. to get up from lying, sitting, or kneeling, or from a bed; (of a meeting etc.) to cease to sit for business, to recover a standing or vertical position, to become erect; to leave the ground; to come to life again. 3. to cease to be quiet or submissive, to rebel; (of the wind) to begin to blow, to strengthen. 4. (of a river etc.) to have its origin, to begin or begin to flow. —*n.* 1. the act, manner, or amount of rising. 2. an upward slope, a small hill. 3. social advancement, upward progress; an increase in power, rank, price, amount, height, wages etc. 4. a movement of fish to the surface. 5. origin. —**get a rise out of,** to cause to display temper or characteristic behaviour. **give rise to,** to cause. **rise to,** to develop powers equal to dealing with (an occasion). [Old English]

riser *n.* the vertical piece between the treads of a staircase.

risible /ˈrɪzɪbəl/ *adj.* 1. laughable, ludicrous. 2. inclined to laugh. [from Latin *risibilis* (*ridēre* = laugh)]

rising /ˈraɪzɪŋ/ *adj.* 1. advancing to maturity or high standing. 2. approaching (a specified age). 3. (of ground) sloping upwards. —*n.* a revolt.

risk *n.* 1. the possibility of meeting danger or suffering harm or loss; exposure to this. 2. a person or thing causing risk or regarded in relation to risk. —*v.t.* to expose to risk; to accept the risk of; to venture on. —**at risk,** exposed to danger. **run a** *or* **the risk,** to expose oneself to danger or loss etc. [from French *risque, risquer* from Italian]

risk capital or **venture capital** finance provided by venture capital companies, individuals, and merchant banks for medium or long-term business ventures that are not their own and in which there is a strong element of risk.

risky *adj.* 1. full of risk. 2. risqué. —**riskily** *adv.*, **riskiness** *n.*

Risorgimento /rɪˌsɔːdʒiˈmentəʊ/ *n.* the movement for Italian national unity and independence from 1815. Leading figures in the movement included ◊Cavour, ◊Mazzini, and ◊Garibaldi. Uprisings in 1848–49 failed, but with help from France in a war against Austria—to oust it from Italian provinces in the north—an Italian kingdom was founded in 1861. Unification was finally completed with the addition of Venetia in 1866 and the Papal States in 1870.

risotto /rɪˈzɒtəʊ/ *n.* (*plural* **risottos**) an Italian dish of rice containing chopped meat or cheese and vegetables. [Italian]

risqué /ˈrɪskeɪ/ *adj.* (of a story etc.) slightly indecent. [French]

rissole /ˈrɪsəʊl/ *n.* a ball or cake of minced meat or nuts mixed with potato or breadcrumbs etc. and usually fried. [French, ultimately from Latin *russeolus* = reddish]

ritardando /riːtɑːˈdændəʊ/ *adv.* & *n.* (*plural* **ritardandos**) in music, with a gradual decrease of speed; also called rallentando. [Italian]

rite *n.* a religious or other solemn ceremony; an action required or usual in this; the body of usage characteristic of a church. [from Old French or Latin *ritus*]

Ritter /ˈrɪtə/ Tex (Woodward Maurice) 1905–1974. US singer and actor who was popular as a singing cowboy in B-films in the 1930s and 1940s. He sang the title song to *High Noon* 1952, and his other films include *Sing Cowboy Sing* 1937 and *Arizona Trail* 1943.

ritual /ˈrɪtjʊəl/ *n.* 1. the series of actions used in a religious or other rite; a particular form of this. 2. a procedure regularly followed. —*adj.* of or done as a ritual. —**ritually** *adv.* [from Latin]

ritualism *n.* regular or excessive practice of ritual. —**ritualist** *n.*, **ritualistic** /-ˈlɪstɪk/ *adj.*, **ritualistically** /-ˈlɪstɪkəli/ *adv.*

ritualization *n.* in ethology, a stereotype that occurs in certain behaviour patterns when these are incorporated into displays. For example, the exaggerated and stylized head toss of the goldeneye drake during courtship is a ritualization of the bathing movement used to wet the feathers; its duration and form have become fixed. Ritualization may make displays clearly recognizable, so ensuring that individuals mate only with members of their own species.

ritzy /ˈrɪtsi/ *adj.* (*colloquial*) high-class, luxurious, ostentatiously smart. [from *Ritz*, name of luxurious hotels, from C. *Ritz* (died 1918) Swiss hotel-owner]

rival /ˈraɪvəl/ *n.* 1. a person or thing competing with another. 2. a person or thing that equals another in quality. —*attrib. adj.* being a rival or rivals. —*v.t.* (**-ll-**) to be a rival of or comparable to; to seem or claim to be as good as. —**rivalry** *n.* [from Latin *rivus* = stream; originally = one using the same stream]

riven /ˈrɪvən/ *adj.* split, torn violently. [*past participle* of archaic *rive* from Old Norse]

river /ˈrɪvə/ *n.* 1. a copious natural stream of water flowing in a channel to the sea etc. 2. a copious flow. —**sell down the river,** (*colloquial*) to defraud or betray. [from Anglo-French *river(e)* = river (bank)]

Rivera /rɪˈveərə/ Diego 1886–1957. Mexican painter, active in Europe until 1921. He received many public commissions for murals exalting the Mexican revolution. A vast cycle on historical themes (National Palace, Mexico City) was begun in 1929. In the 1930s he visited the USA and produced murals for the Rockefeller Center, New York (later overpainted because he included a portrait of Lenin).

Rivera Primo de Spanish politician; see ◊Primo de Rivera.

riverside *n.* the ground along a river-bank.

rivet /ˈrɪvɪt/ *n.* a nail or bolt for holding metal plates etc. together, its headless end being beaten out or pressed down when in place. —*v.t.* 1. to join or fasten with a rivet or rivets. Riveting is used in building construction, boilermaking, and shipbuilding. 2. to beat out or press down the end of (a nail or bolt). 3. to fix, to make immovable; to direct (the eyes or attention etc.) intently; to engross (a person or his attention). —**riveter** *n.* [from Old French *river* = clench]

Riviera /rɪviˈeərə/ the Mediterranean coast of France and Italy from Marseille to La Spezia. The most exclusive section, with the finest climate, is the ◊Côte d'Azur, Menton–St Tropez, which includes Monaco. It has the highest property prices in the world. [Italian = seashore]

rivulet /ˈrɪvjʊlɪt/ *n.* a small stream. [alteration from obsolete *riveret* (French, diminutive of *river*)]

Rix /rɪks/ Brian 1924– . British actor and manager. He became known for his series of farces at London's Whitehall Theatre, notably *Dry Rot* 1954–58. He made several films for cinema and television, including *A Roof Over My Head* 1977, and is extremely active in organizations and charities aiding the mentally handicapped.

Riyadh /'riːæd/ (Arabic *Ar Riyad*) capital of Saudi Arabia and of the Central Province, formerly the sultanate of Nejd, in an oasis, connected by rail with Damman on the Arabian Gulf; population (1986) 1,500,000.

Rizzio /'rɪtsɪəʊ/ David 1533–1566. Italian adventurer at the court of Mary Queen of Scots. After her marriage to ◊Darnley, Rizzio's influence over her incited her husband's jealousy, and he was murdered by Darnley and his friends.

RKO (Radio Keith Orpheum) US film production and distribution company, formed in 1928 through mergers and acquisitions. It was the most financially unstable of the major Hollywood studios, despite the success of many of its films, including *King Kong* 1933 and the series of musicals starring Fred Astaire and Ginger Rogers. In 1948, Howard ◊Hughes bought the studio and accelerated its decline by poor management. The company ceased production in 1953.

RM abbreviation of Royal Marines.

Rn symbol for radon.

RN abbreviation for Royal Navy; see under ◊navy.

RNA abbreviation of **ribonucleic acid**; nucleic acid involved in the process of translating ◊DNA, the genetic material into proteins. It is usually single-stranded, unlike the double-stranded DNA, and consists of a large number of nucleotides strung together, each of which comprises the sugar ribose, a phosphate group, and one of four bases (uracil, cytosine, adenine, or guanine). RNA is copied from DNA by the formation of ◊base pairs, with uracil taking the place of thymine. Although RNA is normally associated only with the process of protein synthesis, it makes up the hereditary material itself in some viruses, such as ◊retroviruses.

RNLI abbreviation of Royal National Lifeboat Institution.

roach /rəʊtʃ/ *n.* a small freshwater fish (especially *Rutilus rutilus*) of the carp family of N Europe, dark green above, whitish below, with reddish lower fins. It grows to 35 cm/1.2 ft. [from Old French *roc(h)e*]

Roach Hal 1892– . US film producer, usually of comedies who was active from the 1910s to the 1940s. He worked with ◊Laurel and Hardy, and also produced films for Harold Lloyd and Charley Chase. His work includes *The Music Box* 1932, *Way Out West* 1936, and *Of Mice and Men* 1939.

road *n.* 1. a way by which people, animals, or vehicles may pass between places, especially one with a prepared surface. Reinforced tracks became necessary with the invention of wheeled vehicles in about 3000 BC and most ancient civilizations had some form of road network. The Romans developed engineering techniques that were not equalled for another 1,400 years. 2. a way of getting to or achieving something. 3. one's way or route. 4. (usually in *plural*; also **roadstead**) a piece of water near a shore in which ships can ride at anchor. —**one for the road**, (*colloquial*) a final drink before departure. **on the road**, travelling, especially as a commercial traveller, itinerant performer, or vagrant. **roadblock** *n.* a barricade set up by police etc. on a road to enable them to stop and search traffic. **road hog**, a reckless or inconsiderate motorist or cyclist. **roadholding** *n.* the stability of a moving vehicle. **road show**, a theatrical performance by a company on tour. **road test**, a test of a vehicle by use on the road. **road train**, (*Austral.*) a very large lorry hauling two or three trailers. **roadworks** *n.pl.* construction or repair of roads. [Old English]

roadie /'rəʊdɪ/ *n.* (*colloquial*) an assistant of a touring band, responsible for equipment. [from *road*]

roadrunner *n.* a crested bird, *Geococcyx californianus*, of the ◊cuckoo family. It can run 25 kph/15 mph, and is native to the SW USA.

roadside *n.* the border of a road.

roadstead *n.* see ◊road sense 4.

roadster *n.* an open car without rear seats.

roadway *n.* a road; the part of a road intended for vehicles.

roadworthy *adj.* (of a vehicle) fit for use on a road. —**roadworthiness** *n.*

roam *v.t./i.* to wander (through). —*n.* a wander.

roan *adj.* (of an animal) with a coat of which the prevailing colour is thickly interspersed with another, especially bay,

roadrunner

greater roadrunner

sorrel, or chestnut mixed with white or grey. —*n.* a roan animal, especially a horse. [Old English]

roar *n.* 1. a long, loud, deep sound like that made by a lion. 2. loud laughter. —*v.t./i.* 1. to utter a roar; to express in this way. 2. to function with the sound of a roar; to travel in a vehicle at high speed while the engine roaring. —**roarer** *n.* [Old English (imitative)]

roaring *adj.* 1. noisy. 2. briskly active. —*adv.* **roaring drunk**, very or noisily drunk. —**roaring forties**, stormy ocean tracts between latitudes 40° and 50° S.

roast *v.t./i.* 1. to cook (food, especially meat) by exposure to heat or in an oven. 2. to heat (coffee-beans) before grinding. 3. to expose to fire or great heat. 4. (*US*) to censure. 5. to undergo roasting. —*attrib. adj.* (of meat, a potato, chestnut etc.) roasted. —*n.* 1. roast meat; a joint of meat for roasting. 2. the operation of roasting. [from Old French *rostir*]

roaster *n.* 1. a fowl etc. suitable for roasting. 2. an apparatus that will roast meat etc.

roasting *adj.* very hot.

rob *v.t.* (-bb-) 1. to steal from; to deprive unlawfully. 2. to deprive of what is due or normal. —**robber** *n.*, **robbery** *n.* in law, a variety of ◊theft; stealing from the person, using force, or the threat of force, to intimidate the victim. [from Old French *rob(b)er*]

Robbe-Grillet /rɒb griːˈjeɪ/ Alain 1922– . French writer, the leading theorist of *le nouveau roman* (the new novel), for example his own *Les Gommes/The Erasers* 1953, *La Jalousie/Jealousy* 1957, and *Dans le labyrinthe/In the Labyrinth* 1959, which concentrates on the detailed description of physical objects. He also wrote the script for the film *L'Année dernière à Marienbad/Last Year in Marienbad* 1961.

Robben Island /'rɒbɪn/ prison island in Table Bay, Cape Town, South Africa.

Robbia, della /'rɒbɪə/ Italian family of sculptors and architects, active in Florence. **Luca della Robbia** (1400–1482) created a number of major works in Florence, notably the marble *cantoria* (singing gallery) in the cathedral 1431–38 (Museo del Duomo), with lively groups of choristers. Luca also developed a characteristic style of glazed terracotta work.

Robbins /'rɒbɪnz/ Jerome 1918– . US dancer and choreographer. He choreographed the musicals *The King and I* 1951, *West Side Story* 1957, and *Fiddler on the Roof* 1964. Robbins was ballet master of the New York City Ballet 1969–83, when he became joint ballet master in chief.

robe *n.* 1. a long loose garment. 2. (often in *plural*) a long outer garment worn as an indication of the wearer's rank or office etc. 3. a dressing-gown. —*v.t./i.* to put on robes; to clothe in a robe; to dress. [from Old French]

Robert /'rɒbət/ two dukes of Normandy:

Robert I the **Devil** Duke of Normandy from 1028. He was the father of William the Conqueror, and is the hero of several romances; he was legendary for his cruelty.

Robert II *c.* 1054–1134. Eldest son of ◊William I (the Conqueror), succeeding him as duke of Normandy (but not on the English throne) in 1087. His brother ◊William II ascended the English throne, and they warred until 1096, after which Robert took part in the First Crusade. When his other brother ◊Henry I claimed the English throne in 1100, Robert contested the claim and invaded England unsuccessfully in 1101. Henry invaded Normandy in 1106, and captured Robert, who remained a prisoner in England until his death.

Robert three kings of Scotland:

Robert I Robert the Bruce 1274–1329. King of Scotland from 1306, and grandson of Robert de ◊Bruce. He shared in the national uprising led by William ◊Wallace, and, after Wallace's execution in 1305, rose once more against Edward I of England, and was crowned at Scone in 1306. He defeated Edward II at ◊Bannockburn in 1314. In 1328 the treaty of Northampton recognized Scotland's independence and Robert as king.

Robert II 1316–1390. King of Scotland from 1371. He was the son of Walter (1293–1326), steward of Scotland, who married Marjory, daughter of Robert I. He was the first king of the house of Stuart.

Robert III *c.* 1340–1406. King of Scotland from 1390, son of Robert II. He was unable to control the nobles, and the government fell largely into the hands of his brother, Robert, duke of Albany (*c.* 1340–1420).

Roberts /'rɒbəts/ Frederick Sleigh ('Bobs'), 1st Earl Roberts 1832–1914. British field marshal. During the Afghan War of 1878–80 he occupied Kabul, and during the Second South African War 1899–1902 he made possible the annexation of the Transvaal and Orange Free State.

Roberts Tom (Thomas William) 1856–1931. Australian painter, founder of the **Heidelberg School** that introduced Impressionism to Australia. Roberts, born in England, arrived in Australia in 1869, returning to Europe to study 1881–85. He received official commissions, including one to paint the opening of the first Australian federal parliament but is better known for his scenes of pioneering life.

Robertson /'rɒbətsən/ Thomas William 1829–1871. English dramatist. Initially an actor, he had his first success as a dramatist with *David Garrick* 1864, which set a new, realistic trend in English drama of the time; later plays included *Society* 1865 and *Caste* 1867.

Robeson /'rəʊbsən/ Paul 1898–1976. US bass singer and actor. He graduated from Columbia University as a lawyer, but limited opportunities for blacks led him instead to the stage. He appeared in *The Emperor Jones* 1924 and *Showboat* 1928, in which he sang 'Ol' Man River'. He played *Othello* in 1930, and his films include *Sanders of the River* 1935 and *King Solomon's Mines* 1937. An ardent advocate of black rights, he had his passport withdrawn 1950–58 because of his association with left-wing movements. He then left the USA to live in England.

Robespierre /'rəʊbzpjeə/ Maximilien François Marie Isidore de 1758–1794. French politician in the ◊French Revolution. As leader of the ◊Jacobins in the National Convention, he supported the execution of Louis XVI and the overthrow of the right-wing republican Girondins, and in July 1793 was elected to the Committee of Public Safety. A year later he was guillotined; many believe that he was a scapegoat for the Reign of ◊Terror since he ordered only 72 executions personally.

Any institution which does not suppose the people good, and the magistrate corruptible, is evil.
Maximilien Robespierre
Déclaration des Droits de l'Homme

---

robin *n.* a migratory songbird, *Erithacus rubecula*, of the thrush family, found in Europe, W Asia, Africa, and the Azores. About 13 cm/5 in long, both sexes are olive brown with a red breast. The nest is constructed in a sheltered place, and from five to seven white freckled eggs are laid. The larger North American robin, *Turdus migratorius*, belongs to the same family. In Australia members of several unrelated genera have been given the familiar name, and may have white, yellowish, or red breasts. [from Old French, pet form of man's name *Robert*]

Robin Hood /'rɒbɪn hʊd/ a legendary English outlaw and champion of the poor against the rich. He is said to have lived in Sherwood Forest, Nottinghamshire, during the reign of Richard I (1189–99). He feuded with the sheriff of Nottingham, accompanied by Maid Marian and a band of followers known as his 'merry men'. He appears in ballads from the 13th century, but his first datable appearance is in Langland's *Piers Plowman* about 1377.

Robinson /'rɒbɪnsən/ Edward G. Stage name of Emanuel Goldenberg 1893–1973. Romanian-born US film actor who emigrated with his family to the US in 1903. He was

robot

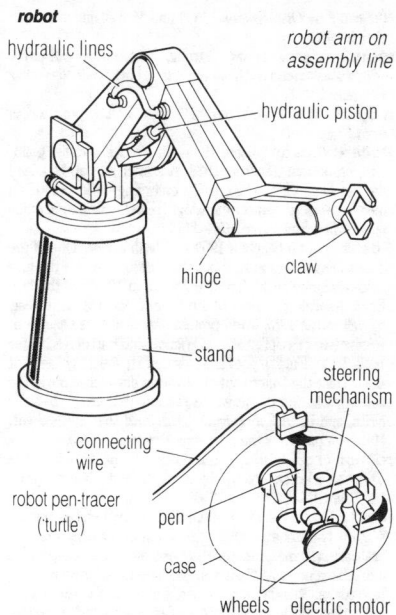

robot arm on assembly line

hydraulic lines
hydraulic piston
hinge
claw
stand
steering mechanism
connecting wire
robot pen-tracer ('turtle')
pen
case
wheels   electric motor

associated with gangster roles, such as *Little Caesar* 1930. He also performed in dramatic and comedy roles in film and on the stage and was a great art collector. He wrote two autobiographical volumes, *My Father, My Son* 1958 and *All My Yesterdays* 1973. His other films include *Dr Ehrlich's Magic Bullet* 1944, *The Ten Commandments* 1940, *Double Indemnity* 1956 and *Soylent Green* 1973.

Robinson Henry Crabb 1775–1867. English writer, whose diaries, journals, and letters are a valuable source of information on his literary friends ◊Lamb, ◊Coleridge, ◊Wordsworth, and ◊Southey.

Robinson Sugar Ray. Adopted name of Walker Smith 1920–1989. US boxer, world welterweight champion 1945–51, defending his title five times. He defeated Jake LaMotta in 1951 to take the middleweight title. He lost the title six times and won it seven times. He retired at the age of 45.

Robinson W(illiam) Heath 1872–1944. English cartoonist and illustrator, who made humorous drawings of bizarre machinery for performing simple tasks, such as raising one's hat. A clumsy design is often described as a 'Heath Robinson' contraption.

Robinson Crusoe /'kruːsəʊ/ *The Life and strange and surprising Adventures of Robinson Crusoe* novel by Daniel Defoe, published 1719, in which the hero is shipwrecked on an island and survives for years by his own ingenuity until rescued; based on the adventures of Alexander Selkirk. The book had many imitators and is the first major English novel.

robot /'rəʊbɒt/ *n.* **1.** any machine controlled by electronic chip or computer that can be programmed to do work (robotics, as opposed to mechanical work, called automation). The most common types are robotic 'arms'; when fixed to the floor or a workbench, they perform functions such as paint spraying or assembling parts in factories. Others include radio-directed or computer-controlled vehicles for carrying materials, and a miscellany of devices from cruise missiles and deep-sea and space-exploration craft to robotic toys. **2.** an apparently human automaton; a machinelike person. **3.** (*South African*) an automatic traffic-signal. [Czech, from *robota* = forced labour; used by K. ◊Capek in his play *R.U.R.* (Rossum's Universal Robots) 1920]

robotic /rə'bɒtɪk/ *adj.* of robots; resembling a robot. —**robotics** *n.pl.* the design, construction, operation, and application of robots; the study of robots.

Robson /'rɒbsən/ Flora 1902–1984. English actress. Her successes include her roles as Queen Elizabeth in the film *Fire Over England* 1931 and Mrs Alving in Ibsen's *Ghosts* 1959.

robust /rəʊ'bʌst/ *adj.* strong, vigorous. —**robustly** *adv.*, **robustness** *n.* [from French or Latin *robustus* (*robur* = strength)]

roc /rɒk/ *n.* a gigantic bird of Arab legend. [from Spanish from Arabic]

Rocard /'rɒkɑː/ Michel 1930– . French socialist politician, prime minister from 1988. A former radical, he joined the Socialist Party (PS) 1973, emerging as leader of its moderate social-democratic wing. He held ministerial office under Mitterrand from 1981–85.

Roche /rəʊʃ/ Stephen 1959– . Irish cyclist. One of the outstanding riders in Europe in the 1980s, he was the first British winner of the Tour de France in 1987 and the first English-speaking winner of the Tour of Italy the same year, as well as the 1987 world professional road-race champion.

Rochester /'rɒtʃɪstə/ John Wilmot, 2nd Earl of Rochester 1647–1680. English poet and courtier. He fought gallantly at sea against the Dutch, but chiefly led a debauched life at the court of Charles II. He wrote graceful (but often obscene) lyrics, and his *A Satire against Mankind* 1675 rivals Swift. He was a patron of the poet John Dryden.

rochet /'rɒtʃɪt/ *n.* a surplice-like vestment used in the Christian church chiefly by bishops and abbots. [from Old French]

rock[1] *n.* 1. the hard part of the Earth's crust underlying the soil; the hard, compact material of which rock consists: mineral particles and/or materials of organic origin consolidated into a hard mass as ◊igneous, ◊sedimentary, or ◊metamorphic rocks. 2. a large detached stone. 3. a mass of rock projecting and forming a hill, cliff etc., or standing up into or out of water from the bottom. 4. a hard sweet made in a cylindrical stick, usually flavoured with peppermint. —**on the rocks,** (*colloquial*) short of money, (of a drink) served neat with ice. **rock-bottom** *adj.* & *n.* (*colloquial* of prices etc.) the very lowest. **rock-bound** *adj.* (of a coast) rocky, very rugged. **rock cake,** a small fruit cake with a rugged surface. **rock climbing,** a sport originally an integral part of mountaineering. It began as a form of training for Alpine expeditions and is now divided into three categories: the **outcrop climb** for climbs of up to 30 m/100 ft; the **crag climb** on cliffs of 30 m–300 m/100–1,000 ft, and the **big wall climb,** which is the nearest thing to Alpine climbing, but without the hazards of snow and ice. **rock crystal,** transparent colourless quartz usually in hexagonal prisms. **rock garden,** a rockery; a garden in which rockeries are the chief feature. **rock-plant** *n.* a plant growing on or among rocks. **rock salmon,** dogfish as sold for food. **rock salt,** common salt as a solid mineral. [from Old French *ro(c)que, roche*]

rock[2] *v.t./i.* 1. to move or be moved gently to and fro while supported on something. 2. to sway or shake violently. 3. to disturb greatly by shock. —*n.* 1. a rocking motion. 2. modern popular music with a strong beat; rock and roll. —**rocking chair,** a chair mounted on rockers or springs so that it can be rocked by the sitter. **rocking horse,** a wooden horse mounted on rockers or springs so that it can be rocked by a child sitting on it. [Old English]

rock and roll or **rock 'n' roll** pop music born of a fusion of rhythm and blues and country and western and based on electric guitar and drums. In the mid-1950s, with the advent of Elvis Presley, it became the heartbeat of teenage rebellion in the West but was soon adopted worldwide. It found perhaps its purest form in late-1950s **rockabilly**; the blanket term 'rock' later came to comprise a multitude of styles. The term was popularized by US disc jockey Alan Freed (1922–1965) from 1951. Leading rock-and-roll singers and songwriters of the 1950s included Chuck ◊Berry, Buddy ◊Holly, and Gene Vincent (1935–1971).

Rockefeller /'rɒkəfelə/ John D(avison) 1839–1937. US millionaire, founder of Standard Oil in 1870 (which achieved control of 90% of US refineries by 1882). The activities of the Standard Oil Trust led to an outcry against monopolies and the passing of the Sherman Anti-Trust Act of 1890. A lawsuit of 1892 prompted the dissolution of the trust, only for it to be refounded in 1899 as a holding company. In 1911, this was also declared illegal by the Supreme Court. He founded the philanthropic **Rockefeller Foundation** in 1913, to which his son **John D(avison) Rockefeller Jr** (1874–1960) devoted his life.

rocket
the Saturn V moon rocket

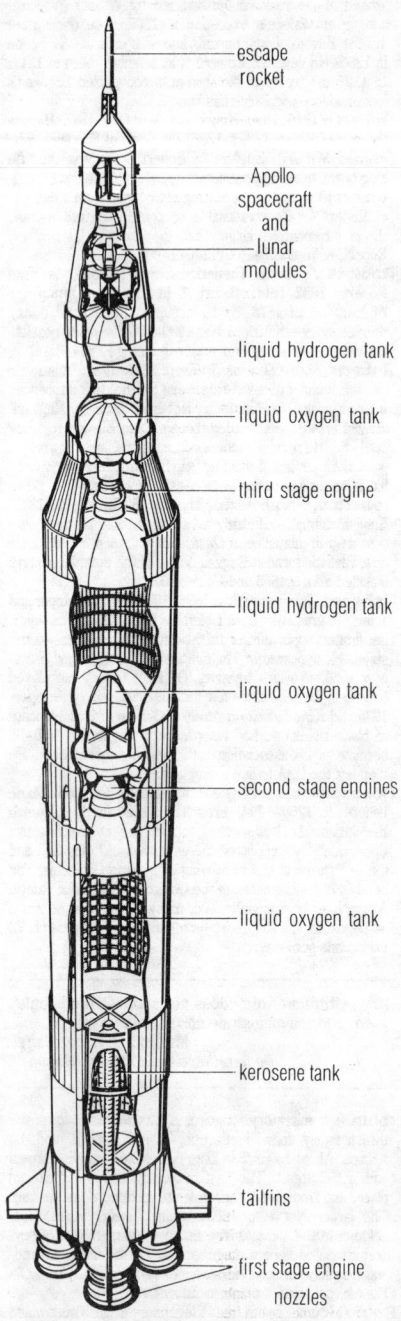

escape rocket

Apollo spacecraft and lunar modules

liquid hydrogen tank

liquid oxygen tank

third stage engine

liquid hydrogen tank

liquid oxygen tank

second stage engines

liquid oxygen tank

kerosene tank

tailfins

first stage engine nozzles

rocker *n.* 1. a device for rocking or being rocked. 2. each of the curved bars on which a rocking chair etc. is mounted. —**off one's rocker,** (*slang*) crazy.

rockery /'rɒkərɪ/ *n.* an artificial mound or bank containing large stones and planted with rock-plants.

rocket /'rɒkɪt/ *n.* 1. a firework or similar device (e.g. as a signal) that rises into the air when ignited and then explodes. 2. a projectile operating by the reaction of a continuous jet of gases released in the combustion of a propellant within it; a device propelled by this, especially a bomb or spacecraft. Unlike jet engines, which are also reaction engines, modern rockets carry their own oxygen supply to burn their fuel and are totally independent of any surrounding atmosphere. As rockets are the only form of propulsion available that can function in a vacuum, they are essential to exploration in outer space. ◊Multistage rockets have to be used, consisting of a number of rockets joined together. 3. (slang) a reprimand. —v.t./i. 1. to move rapidly upwards or away. 2. to bombard with rockets. [from French roquette from Italian rocca = distaff]

rocketry n. the science or practice of rocket propulsion.

rocky[1] /'rɒki/ adj. of or like a rock; abounding in rocks.

rocky[2] adj. (colloquial) unsteady, tottering. —**rockily** adv., **rockiness** n.

Rocky Mountains or **Rockies** largest North American mountain system. They extend from the junction with the Mexican plateau northward through the west central states of the USA and through Canada to the Alaskan border. The highest mountain is Mount McKinley (6,194 m/20,320 ft).

Rococo /rə'kəʊkəʊ/ n. movement in the arts in 18th-century Europe, a trend towards lightness, elegance, delicacy, and decorative charm. The term 'Rococo' refers to rocaille, a style of interior decoration based on S-curves and scroll-like forms. Watteau's paintings and Sèvres porcelain belong to the French Rococo vogue. In the 1730s the movement became widespread in Europe, notably in the churches and palaces of S Germany and Austria. [French, jocular alteration of rocaille fancy shell-and rock-work for fountains and grottoes, from roc = rock]

rod n. 1. a slender, straight stick or metal bar. 2. a cane or birch for use in flogging people. 3. a fishing rod; an angler with the right to use this on a specified stretch of water. 4. (as an obsolete measure) 5½ yd, also called a perch (see ◊Gunter). —**make a rod for one's own back**, to cause future trouble or effort for oneself. [Old English]

Roddick /'rɒdɪk/ Anita 1943–   . British entrepreneur, founder of the Body Shop, which now has branches worldwide. Roddick started with one shop in Brighton, England, 1976, selling only natural toiletries in refillable plastic containers.

rode past of ride.

rodent /'rəʊd(ə)nt/ n. a mammal of the worldwide order Rodentia. Besides ordinary 'cheek teeth', they have a single front pair of incisor teeth in both upper and lower jaw, which continue to grow as they are worn down. They are subdivided into three suborders, Myomorpha, Scuiromorpha, and Hystricomorpha, of which the rat, squirrel, and porcupine respectively are the typical members. —adj. gnawing; (of an ulcer) spreading slowly. —**rodent officer**, an official rat-catcher. [from Latin rodere = gnaw]

rodeo /rəʊ'deɪəʊ/ n. (plural rodeos) 1. an exhibition of cowboys' skill in handling animals. Originally a practical means of rounding up cattle in North America, it is now a professional sport in the USA and Canada. Ranching skills such as bronco busting, bull riding, steer wrestling, and calf roping are rodeo events. 2. a round-up of cattle on a ranch for branding etc. [Spanish rodear = go round]

Rodgers /'rɒdʒəz/ Richard (Charles) 1902–1979. US composer. He collaborated with librettist Lorenz Hart (1895–1943) on songs such as 'Blue Moon' 1934 and musicals such as On Your Toes 1936, and with Oscar Hammerstein II (1895–1960) wrote musicals such as Oklahoma! 1943, South Pacific 1949, The King and I 1951, and The Sound of Music 1959.

Rodhos /'rɒðɒs/ Greek name for the island of ◊Rhodes.

Rodin /'rəʊdæn/ Auguste 1840–1917. French sculptor, often considered the greatest of his day. Through his work he freed sculpture from the idealizing conventions of the time by his realistic treatment of the human figure, introducing a new boldness of style and expression. Examples are Le Penseur/The Thinker 1880, Le Baiser/The Kiss 1886 (marble version in the Louvre, Paris), and Les Bourgeois de Calais/The Burghers of Calais 1885–95 (copy in Embankment Gardens, Westminster, London).

Rodnina /rɒd'niːnə/ Irina 1949–   . Soviet ice skater. Between 1969 and 1980 she won 23 world, Olympic, and European gold medals in pairs competitions. Her partners were Alexei Ulanov and then Alexsandr Zaitsev.

roe[1] /rəʊ/ n. a mass of eggs in a female fish's ovary (**hard roe**); a male fish's milt (**soft roe**). [from Middle Low German or Middle Dutch]

roe[2] n. (plural **roes** or **roe**) or **roe-deer** a small kind of deer Capreolus capreolus. [Old English]

roebuck n. a male roe-deer.

Roeg /rəʊg/ Nicolas 1928–   . English film director. His work has stylish visual appeal and imaginative, often offbeat treatment of subjects. His films include Performance 1970, Walkabout 1971, Don't Look Now 1973, The Man Who Fell to Earth 1976, Insignificance 1984, and Track 29 1988.

roentgen /'rʌntjən/ n. or **röntgen** the SI unit (symbol r) of radiation exposure, used for X-and gamma rays. It is defined in terms of the number of ions produced in one cubic centimetre of air by the radiation. Exposure to 1,000 roentgens gives rise to an absorbed dose of about 870 rads (8.7 grays), which is a dose equivalent of 870 rems (8.7 sieverts). The annual dose equivalent from natural sources in the UK is 1,100 microsieverts. [from W C Roentgen]

Roethke /'retki/ Theodore 1908–1963. US poet. His father owned a large nursery business, and the greenhouses and plants of his childhood provide the detail and imagery for much of his lyrical, personal, and visionary poetry. Collections include Open House 1941, The Lost Son 1948, The Waking 1953 (Pulitzer Prize), and the posthumous Collected Poems 1968.

rogation /rə'geɪʃən/ n. (usually in plural) in the Christian church the litany of the saints chanted on the three Rogation Days before Ascension Day. —**Rogation Days**, certain days prescribed in the Western Church for prayer and fasting; the three days before Ascension Day which used to be marked by processions round the parish boundaries ('beating the bounds') and blessing of crops; now only rarely observed. **Rogation Sunday**, the Sunday before Ascension Day. [from Latin rogare = ask]

roger /'rɒdʒə/ interjection, in telegraphy etc., your message has been received and understood; (slang) I agree. [man's name Roger, used in signalling code for letter R]

Rogers /'rɒdʒəz/ Carl 1902–1987. US psychologist who developed the client-centred approach to counselling and psychotherapy. This stressed the importance of clients making their own decisions and developing their own potential (self-actualization).

Rogers Ginger. Stage name of Virginia Katherine McMath 1911–   . US actress, dancer, and singer. She worked from the 1930s to the 1950s, often starring with Fred Astaire in such films as Top Hat 1935 and Swing Time 1936. Her later work includes Bachelor Mother 1939 and Kitty Foyle 1940.

Rogers Richard 1933–   . British architect. His works include the Centre Pompidou in Paris 1977 (jointly with Renzo Piano) and the Lloyd's building in London 1986.

Rogers Roy. Stage name of Leonard Slye 1912–   . US actor who moved to the cinema from radio. He was one of the original singing cowboys of the 1930s and 1940s. Confined to B-films for most of his career, he appeared opposite Bob Hope and Jane Russell in Son of Paleface 1952. His other films include The Big Show 1936 and My Pal Trigger 1946 (Trigger was his horse).

Roget /'rəʊmə/ Peter Mark 1779–1869. English physician, one of the founders of the University of London, and author of a Thesaurus of English Words and Phrases 1852, a text constantly revised and still in print, offering synonyms.

rogue /rəʊg/ n. 1. a dishonest or unprincipled person. 2. a mischievous person, especially a child. 3. a wild animal driven away or living apart from the herd and of savage temper. 4. an inferior or defective specimen among many acceptable ones. —**rogue's gallery**, a collection of photographs of known criminals etc. —**roguery** n., **roguish** adj., **roguishly** adv., **roguishness** n.

Röhm /rɜːm/ Ernst 1887–1934. German leader of the Nazi Brownshirts, the SA (◊Sturmabteilung). On the pretext of an intended SA putsch (uprising) by the Brownshirts, the Nazis had some hundred of them, including Röhm, killed on 29–30 June 1934 (an event known as the ◊Night of the Long Knives).

Rohmer /'rəʊmə/ Eric. Adopted name of Jean-Marie Maurice Schérer 1920–. French film director and writer who was formerly a critic and television director. Part of the French new wave, his films are often concerned with the psychology of self-deception. They include My Night at Maud's/Ma Nuit chez Maud 1969, Claire's Knee/Le Genou *de Claire* 1970, and *The Marquise of O/La Marquise d'O/Die Marquise von O* 1976.

Rohmer Sax. Pen name of Arthur Sarsfield Ward 1886–1959. English crime writer who created the sinister Chinese character Fu Manchu.

Roh Tae-woo /'rəʊ teɪ'wu:/ 1932– . South Korean right-wing politician and general. He held ministerial office from 1981 under President Chun, and became chair of the ruling Democratic Justice Party 1985. He was elected president in 1987, amid allegations of fraud and despite being connected with the massacre of about 2,000 anti-government demonstrators in 1980.

roister *v.i.* to revel noisily, to be uproarious. [from French *rustre* = ruffian, from Latin *rus* = the country]

Roland /'rəʊlənd/ French hero, whose real and legendary deeds of valour and chivalry inspired many medieval and later romances, including the 11th-century *Chanson de Roland* and Ariosto's *Orlando Furioso*. A knight of ◊Charlemagne, Roland was killed in 778 with his friend Oliver and the 12 peers of France at Roncesvalles (in the Pyrenees) by Basques. He headed the rearguard during Charlemagne's retreat from his invasion of Spain.

Roland de la Platière /'rəʊ'lɒŋ də lɑː plætiˈeə/ Jeanne Manon (born Philipon) 1754–1793. French intellectual politician, whose salon from 1789 was a focus of democratic discussion. Her ideas were influential after her husband Jean Marie Roland de la Platière (1734–1793) became minister of the interior in 1792. As a supporter of the ◊Girondin party, opposed to Robespierre and Danton, she was condemned to the guillotine in 1793 without being allowed to speak in her own defence. Her last words were 'O liberty! What crimes are committed in thy name!' While in prison she wrote *Mémoires*.

Oh liberty! what crimes are committed in your name!

Madam Roland de la Platière
last words (attrib.)

---

role /rəʊl/ *n.* 1. an actor's part. 2. a person's or thing's function. 3. in the social sciences, the part(s) a person plays in society, either in helping the social system to work or in fulfilling social responsibilities towards others. **role play,** the way children learn adult roles by acting them out in play (mothers and fathers, cops and robbers). [from French]

Rolfe /rəʊf/ Frederick 1860–1913. English writer, who called himself Baron Corvo. A Roman Catholic convert, frustrated in his desire to enter the priesthood, he wrote the novel *Hadrian VII* 1904, in which the character of the title rose from being a poor writer to become pope. In *Desire and Pursuit of the Whole* 1934 he wrote about his homosexual fantasies and friends, earning the poet Auden's description of him as 'a master of vituperation'.

roll /rəʊl/ *n.* 1. a cylinder formed by turning a flexible material over and over on itself without folding; a thing of similar form. 2. a small individual portion of bread separately baked. 3. an official list or register. 4. a rolling motion or gait; a spell of rolling. 5. a continuous, rhythmic sound of thunder or a drum. 6. a complete revolution of an aircraft about its longitudinal axis. —*v.t./i.* 1. to move, send, or go in some direction by turning on an axis. 2. (of a vehicle) to advance or convey on wheels; (of a person) to be so conveyed. 3. to turn over and over into a cylindrical or spherical shape; to make thus. 4. to flatten by passing under or between rollers. 5. to walk with a swaying gait; (of a ship or vehicle) to sway to and fro sideways; (of an aircraft) to turn (partially or completely) on its horizontal axis. 6. to undulate; to show an undulating surface or motion; to go, propel, or carry with such a motion. 7. to sound with a vibration or trill. —**be rolling in,** to have a large supply of. **Master of the Rolls,** one of the judges of the Court of Appeal, and Keeper of the Records at the Public Record Office. **roll by** or **on,** (of time) to pass steadily. **roll call,** the calling of a list of names to establish presence. **rolled gold,** a thin coating of gold applied to a base metal. **rolled into one,** combined in one person etc. **roll film,** a length of photographic film backed with opaque paper and rolled on a spool. **roll one's eyes,** to show the whites in various directions. **roll in,** to arrive in great numbers. **rolling mill,** a machine or factory for rolling metal into shape.

rolling pin, a roller for pastry. **rolling stock,** stock of railway (or (*US*) road) vehicles. **rolling stone,** a person unwilling to settle for long in one place. **roll of honour,** a list of those honoured, especially the dead in a war. **roll-on** *n.* a light, elastic corset; (*adj.*) (of a ship) on to which motor vehicles can be driven; (of a cosmetic) applied from a container with a rotating ball in its neck. **roll-top desk,** a desk with a flexible cover sliding in curved grooves. **roll up,** to make into or form a roll; (*colloquial*) to arrive in a vehicle or on the scene. **strike off the rolls,** to debar from practising as a solicitor. [from Old French from Latin *rotulus* (*rota* wheel)]

roller /'rəʊlə/ *n.* 1. a hard cylinder for smoothing, spreading, or crushing things etc. 2. a small cylinder on which the hair is rolled for setting. 3. a long, swelling wave. 4. a brightly coloured bird of the family Coraciidae, somewhat resembling crows but related to kingfishers, found in the Old World (eastern hemisphere). They grow up to 32 cm/13 in long. The name is derived from their habit of rolling over in flight. —**roller coaster,** a switchback at a fair etc. **roller skate,** see ◊skate. **roller towel,** a towel with the ends joined, hung on a roller.

rollicking /'rɒlɪkɪŋ/ *adj.* jovial and boisterous.

rolling *n.* common method of shaping metal. Rolling is carried out by giant mangles, consisting of several sets, or stands, of heavy rollers positioned one above the other. Red-hot metal slabs are rolled into sheet and also (using shaped rollers) girders and rails. Metal sheets are often cold-rolled finally to impart a harder surface.

Rolling Stones, the British band formed in 1962, once notorious as the 'bad boys' of rock. Original members were Mick Jagger (1943–), Keith Richards (1943–), Brian Jones (1942–1969), Bill Wyman (1936–), Charlie Watts (1941–), and later, the pianist Ian Stewart (1938–1985). A rock-and-roll institution, the Rolling Stones were still performing and recording in the 1990s.

rollmops /'rəʊlmɒps/ *n.* (sometimes erroneously treated as *plural*) a rolled fillet of herring, flavoured with sliced onions, spices etc., and pickled in brine. [German]

Rollo /'rɒləʊ/ 1st Duke of Normandy *c.*860–932. Viking leader. He left Norway about 875 and marauded, sailing up the Seine to Rouen. He besieged Paris 886, and in 912 was baptized and granted the province of Normandy by Charles III of France. He was its duke until his retirement to a monastery 927. He was an ancestor of William the Conqueror.

Rolls /rəʊlz/ Charles Stewart 1877–1910. British engineer who joined with Henry ◊Royce in 1905 to design and produce cars.

Rolls-Royce /'rəʊlz 'rɔɪs/ *n.* industrial company manufacturing cars and aeroplane engines, founded in 1906 by Henry ◊Royce and Charles Rolls. The Silver Ghost car model was designed in 1906 and produced until 1925, when the Phantom was introduced. In 1914, Royce designed the Eagle aircraft engine, used extensively in World War I. Royce also designed the Merlin engine, used in Spitfires and Hurricanes in World War II. Jet engines followed and became an important part of the company.

roly-poly /'rəʊli'pəʊli/ *n.* a pudding made of a sheet of suet pastry covered with jam etc., formed into a roll, and boiled or baked. —*adj.* (usually of a child) podgy, plump.

ROM acronym from read-only memory in computing, an electronic memory device; a computer's permanent store of vital information or programs. ROM holds data or programs that will rarely or never need to be changed but must always be readily available, for example, a computer's operating system. It is an ◊integrated circuit (chip) and its capacity is measured in ◊kilobytes (thousands of characters).

rom. abbreviation of roman (type).

Romains /rəʊ'mæn/ Jules. Pen name of Louis Farigoule 1885–1972. French novelist, playwright and poet. His plays include the farce *Knock, ou le triomphe de la médecine/Dr Knock* 1923 and *Donogoo* 1930, and his novels include *Mort de quelqu'un/Death of a Nobody* 1911, *Les Copains/The Boys in the Back Room* 1913, and *Les Hommes de bonne volonté/Men of Good Will* (27 volumes) 1932–47.

Roman /'rəʊmən/ *adj.* 1. of ancient or modern Rome or the Roman republic or Empire. 2. of the Roman Catholic Church. 3. (of the nose) having a prominent upper part or bridge like those seen in portraits of ancient Romans. 4. of the plain upright lettering or type used in ordinary print (as opposed to *Gothic* or *black letter*, and *italic*). **5.** (of the alphabet) based on the ancient Roman system with letters A–Z. —*n.* **1.** a native or inhabitant of ancient or modern Rome, a citizen of the Roman republic or Empire. **2.** a Roman Catholic. **3.** roman type. —**Roman candle**, a tubular firework discharging a shower of sparks with coloured balls of flame. [from Old French from Latin *Roma* = Rome]

Roman art the sculpture and painting of ancient Rome, from the 4th century BC onwards to the fall of the empire. Much Roman art was intended for public education, notably the sculpted triumphal arches and giant columns, such as *Trajan's Column* AD 106–113 and portrait sculptures of soldiers, politicians, and emperors. Surviving mural paintings (in Pompeii, Rome, and Ostia) and mosaic decorations show Greek influence. Roman art was to prove a lasting inspiration in the West.

Roman Britain the period in British history from the mid-1st century BC to the mid-4th century AD. Roman relations with Britain began with Caesar's invasions of 55 and 54 BC, but the actual conquest was not begun until AD 43. England was rapidly Romanized, but north of York fewer remains of Roman civilization have been found. After several unsuccessful attempts to conquer Scotland the northern frontier was fixed at ◊Hadrian's Wall. During the 4th century Britain was raided by the Saxons, Picts, and Scots. The Roman armies were withdrawn in 407 but there were partial re-occupations 417–*c.*427 and about 450. Roman towns include London, York, Chester, St Albans, Colchester, Lincoln, Gloucester, and Bath. The most permanent remains of the occupation were the system of military roads radiating from London.

Roman Catholicism one of the main divisions of the Christian religion, separate from the Eastern Orthodox Church from 1054, and headed by the pope. For history and beliefs, see ◊Christianity. Membership is about 585 million worldwide, concentrated in S Europe, Latin America, and the Philippines. The Protestant churches separated from the Catholic with the Reformation in the 16th century, to which the Counter-Reformation was a response. An attempt to update Catholic doctrines in the late 19th century was condemned by Pope Pius X in 1907, and more recent moves have been rejected by John Paul II.

romance /rəˈmæns/ *n.* **1.** an episode or story centred on highly imaginative and emotive scenes of love or heroism etc., originally a long verse narrative written in a Romance language; such stories as a genre; the atmosphere characterizing them; a mental tendency to be influenced by it, sympathetic imaginativeness. Tales of love and adventure, in verse or prose, became popular in France about 1200 and spread throughout Europe. There were Arthurian romances about the legendary King Arthur and his knights, and romances based on the adventures of Charlemagne and on classical themes. **2.** a love affair viewed as resembling a tale of romance; a love-story (often used disparagingly, to imply a contrast with a realist novel). **3.** a picturesque exaggeration or falsehood; an instance of this. —*v.i.* to exaggerate or distort the truth in an imaginative way.

Romance *adj.* of the branch of Indo-European languages descended from the Latin of the Roman Empire ('popular' or 'vulgar' as opposed to 'classical' Latin. —*n.* this group, of which the present-day languages with national status are French, Spanish, Portuguese, Italian, and Romanian. [from Old French from Latin *Romanicus*]

Romanesque /rəʊməˈnesk/ *n.* a style of art and architecture prevalent in Europe in the 8th to 12 centuries, with massive vaulting and round arches, solid volumes, and emphasis on perpendicular elements. In England the style is called ◊Norman. —*adj.* of this style. See also ◊medieval art. [French]

roman-fleuve /rəʊmɑ̃ˈflɜːv/ *n.* (plural **romans-fleuves**, pronounced the same) a sequence of self-contained novels [French = river novel]

Romania /rəʊˈmeɪnɪə/ country in SE Europe, on the Black Sea, bounded to the N and E by the USSR, to the S by Bulgaria, to the SW by Yugoslavia, and to the NW by Hungary. **area** 237,500 sq km/91,699 sq mi; **capital** Bucharest; **physical** mountains, surrounding a plateau, with river plains S and E, Carpathian mountains and Transylvanian Alps, Danube river, Black Sea coast; **head of state** Ion Iliescu from 1989; **head of government** Petra Roman

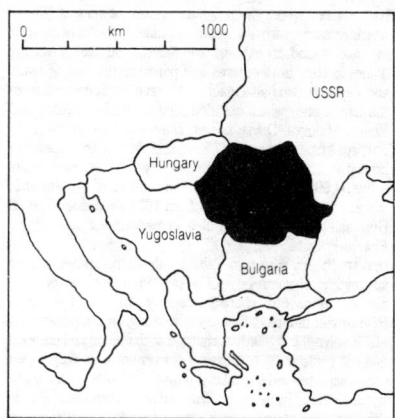

Romania

from 1989; **political system** emergency provisional government from Dec 1989; **exports** petroleum products and oilfield equipment, electrical goods, cars; **population** (1990 est) 23,269,000; **language** Romanian (official); Hungarian, German; **recent history** pro-Nazi Antonescu government overthrown 1944; Communist-dominated government appointed 1945; King Michael abdicated and People's Republic proclaimed 1947, boundaries redrawn. Joined Comecon in 1949 and the Warsaw Pact in 1955. Soviet occupation forces were removed in 1965. Ceausescu created president 1974. In 1987 workers demonstrated against austerity programme introduced after two winters of austerity and power cuts. In 1989 'Christmas revolution' the Ceausescu regime was overthrown and power assumed by the military-dissident-reform communist National Salvation Front. Ceausescu was tried and executed and the Securitate intelligence removed. Strikes and protests against the effects of the market economy followed in 1990.

Romanian language a member of the Romance branch of the Indo-European language family, spoken in Romania, Macedonia, Albania, and parts of N Greece. It has been strongly influenced by the Slavonic languages and by Greek. The Cyrillic alphabet was used until the 19th century, when a variant of the Roman alphabet was adopted.

romanize /ˈrəʊmənaɪz/ *v.t.* **1.** to make Roman or Roman Catholic in character. **2.** to put into the Roman alphabet or roman type. —**romanization** /-ˈzeɪʃən/ *n.*

Roman law the legal system of ancient Rome that is now the basis of ◊civil law, one of the main European legal systems.

Roman numerals an ancient European number system using symbols different from Arabic numerals (the ordinary numbers 1, 2, 3, 4, 5, and so on). The seven key symbols in Roman numerals, as represented today, are I (1), V (5), X (10), L (50), C (100), D (500) and M (1,000). There is no zero, and therefore no place-value as is fundamental to the Arabic system. The first ten Roman numerals are I, II, III, IV (or IIII), V, VI, VII, VIII, IX, and X. When a Roman symbol is preceded by a symbol of equal or greater value, the values of the symbols are added (XVI = 16). When a symbol is preceded by a symbol of less value, the values are subtracted (XL = 40). A horizontal bar over a symbol indicates a factor of 1,000 ($\bar{\text{X}}$ = 10,000). Although addition and subtraction are fairly straightforward using Roman numerals, the absence of a zero makes other arithmetic calculations (such as multiplication) clumsy and difficult.

Romano- /rəməɪnəʊ-/ in combinations of Roman.

Romano Giulio. see ◊Giulio Romano, Italian painter and architect.

Romanov dynasty /ˈrəʊmənɒf/ rulers of Russia from 1613 to the ◊Russian Revolution in 1917. Under the Romanovs, Russia developed into an absolutist empire. The last tsar, Nicholas II, abdicated in Mar 1917 and was murdered in July 1918, together with his family.

Roman religion the religious system of ancient Rome, which retained early elements of animism (with reverence for stones and trees) and totemism, and had a strong domestic base in the ◊lares and penates, the cult of Janus and Vesta. It also had a main pantheon of gods derived from the Greek one, which included Jupiter and Juno, Mars and Venus, Minerva, Diana, Ceres, and many lesser deities.

Romansch /rəʊˈmænʃ/ n. a member of the Romance branch of the Indo-European language family, spoken by some 50,000 people in the eastern cantons of Switzerland. It was accorded official status from 1937 alongside French, German, and Italian. It is also known among scholars as Rhaeto-Romanic.

romantic /rəˈmæntɪk/ adj. 1. of, characterized by, or suggestive of romance; (of a person) enjoying romance and situations etc. characterized by this. 2. (frequently **Romantic**; of music, literature, painting, or the composers etc. involved) imaginative, charged with feeling and emotion and not conforming to classical conventions. 3. (of an idea etc.) characterized by fantasy, unpractical. —n. 1. a romantic person. 2. (frequently **Romantic**) a composer etc. in the Romantic style. —**romantically** adv. [from romaunt = tale of chivalry, from Old French]

romanticism /rəˈmæntɪsɪzəm/ n. 1. a tendency towards romance or romantic views. 2. (frequently **Romanticism**) the distinctive qualities or spirit of the Romantic movement in music, literature, and painting. The term is often used to characterize the culture of 19th-century Europe, as contrasted with 18th-century ◊Classicism. In music, it generally refers to a preoccupation with the expression of emotion and with nature and folk history as a source of inspiration. Often linked with nationalistic feelings, the Romantic movement reached its height in the late 19th century, as in the works of Schumann and Wagner. —**romanticist** n.

romanticize v.t./i. 1. to make romantic. 2. to indulge in romantic ideas etc.

Romany /ˈrɒmənɪ/ n. a nomadic people, also called **Gypsy** (a corruption of 'Egyptian', since they were erroneously thought to come from Egypt). They are now believed to have originated in NW India, and live throughout the world. 2. their language. —adj. of the Romanies or their language. [from Romany Rom = man]

Rome /rəʊm/ (Italian **Roma**) capital of Italy and of Lazio region, on the river Tiber, 27 km/17 mi from the Tyrrhenian Sea; population (1988) 2,817,000. Rome has few industries but is an important cultural, road, and rail centre. A large section of the population finds employment in government offices. Remains of the ancient city include the Forum, Colosseum, and Pantheon.

Romeo /ˈrəʊmɪəʊ/ n. a romantic lover.

Romeo and Juliet /ˈrəʊmɪəʊ, ˈdʒuːliːˈɛt/ a romantic tragedy by William Shakespeare, first performed 1594–95. The play is concerned with the doomed love of Romeo and Juliet, victims of the bitter enmity between their respective families in Verona.

romer /ˈrəʊmə/ n. a small piece of plastic or card marked with scales along two edges meeting at a right angle, or (if transparent) bearing a grid, used for measuring grid references on a map. [from C. Romer (died 1951), British barrister, its inventor]

Rome, Sack of AD 410. The invasion and capture of the city of Rome by the Goths, generally accepted as marking the effective end of the Roman Empire.

Rome, Treaties of international agreements signed in March 1957 by Belgium, France, Germany, Italy, Luxemburg, and the Netherlands, which formally set up the European Economic Community (◊EEC). Its terms proposed the abolition of internal tariffs between the six member countries, uniform external tariffs, the free movement of goods, capital, and people. A second Treaty set up the European Atomic Energy Commission (EURATOM) to develop nuclear energy for peaceful uses.

Rommel /ˈrɒməl/ Erwin 1891–1944. German field marshal. He served in World War I, and in World War II he played an important part in the invasions of central Europe and France. He was commander of the N African offensive from 1941 (when he was nicknamed 'Desert Fox') until defeated in the Battles of El ◊Alamein. He was commander in chief for a short time against the Allies in Europe during 1944 but (as a sympathizer with the ◊Stauffenberg plot against Hitler) was forced to commit suicide.

Romney /ˈrʌmnɪ/ George 1734–1802. English portrait painter, active in London from 1762. He painted several portraits of Lady Hamilton, Admiral Nelson's mistress.

romp v.i. 1. to play about roughly and energetically. 2. to succeed easily. —n. a spell of romping.

rompers n.pl. a young child's play-garment, usually covering the trunk only.

Romulus /ˈrɒmjʊləs/ in Roman mythology, legendary founder and first king of Rome, the son of Mars and Rhea Silvia, daughter of Numitor, king of Alba Longa. Romulus and his twin brother Remus were thrown into the Tiber by their great-uncle Amulius, who had deposed Numitor, but were suckled by a she-wolf and rescued by a shepherd. On reaching adulthood they killed Amulius and founded Rome.

Romulus Augustulus /ɔːˈɡʌstəs/ born c. AD 461. Last Roman emperor in the West. He was made emperor by his father Orestes, a soldier, about 475 but was compelled to abdicate in 476 by Odoacer, leader of the barbarian mercenaries, who nicknamed him Augustulus. Orestes was executed and Romulus Augustulus confined to a Neapolitan villa.

rondeau /ˈrɒndəʊ/ n. a short poem with only two rhymes throughout and the opening words used twice as a refrain. [French]

rondel /ˈrɒndəl/ n. a rondeau, especially of a special form. [from Old French from Latin rotundus = round]

rondo /ˈrɒndəʊ/ n. or **rondeau** (plural rondos) a piece of music with a leading theme which recurs several times. Rondo form is often used for the last movement of a sonata or concerto. [Italian from French]

Rondônia /rɒnˈdəʊnɪə/ state in NW Brazil; the centre of Amazonian tin and gold mining and of experiments in agricultural colonization; area 243,044 sq km/93,876 sq mi; population (1986) 776,000. Known as the Federal Territory of Guaporé until 1956, it became a state in 1981.

Ronsard /rɒnˈsɑː/ Pierre de 1524–1585. French poet, leader of the ◊Pléiade group of poets. Under the patronage of Charles IX, he published original verse in a lightly sensitive style, including odes and love sonnets, such as Odes 1550, Les Amours/Lovers 1552–53, and the 'Marie' cycle, Continuation des amours/Lovers Continued 1555–56.

röntgen n. alternative spelling for ◊roentgen, unit of X-and gamma-ray exposure.

Röntgen /ˈrʌntgən/ (or Roentgen) Wilhelm Konrad 1845–1923. German physicist who discovered X-rays in 1895. While investigating the passage of electricity through gases, he noticed the ◊fluorescence of a barium platinocyanide screen. This radiation passed through some substances opaque to light, and affected photographic plates. Developments from this discovery have revolutionized medical diagnosis.

rood n. 1. a crucifix, especially one raised on the middle of a rood screen. 2. a quarter-acre. —**rood loft**, a gallery above a rood screen. **rood screen**, a carved wooden or stone screen separating the nave from the chancel in a church, found in England and mainland Europe especially in the 14th–mid-16th centuries. [Old English]

roof n. the upper covering of a building; the top of a covered vehicle; the overhead rock in a cave or mine etc. —v.t. to cover with a roof; to be the roof of. —**hit** or **raise the roof**, (colloquial) to become very angry. **roof garden**, a garden on the flat roof of a building. **roof of the mouth**, the palate. **roof rack**, a framework to carry luggage etc. on the roof of a car. **rooftop** n. the outer surface of a roof. **rooftree** n. the ridge-piece of a roof. [Old English]

roofing n. material used for a roof.

rook[1] /rʊk/ n. a gregarious bird Corvus frugilegus of the crow family. The plumage is black and lustrous and the face bare; it can grow to 45 cm/1.5 ft in length. Rooks nest in colonies at the tops of trees. —v.t. 1. to win money from at cards etc., especially by swindling. 2. to charge (a customer) extortionately. [Old English]

rook[2] n. a chess piece with a battlement-shaped top. [from Old French from Arabic]

rookery /ˈrʊkərɪ/ n. 1. a colony of rooks, penguins, or seals. 2. (archaic) a crowded cluster of mean houses or tenements.

rookie /ˈrʊkɪ/ n. (slang) a recruit. [corruption of recruit]

room /ruːm, rʊm/ n. 1. space that is or could be occupied by something. 2. a part of a house enclosed by walls or partitions; the people in this; (in plural) apartments, lodgings.

3. opportunity, scope. —*v.i.* (*US*) to have a room or rooms, to lodge. —**rooming house,** a lodging-house. **roommate** *n.* a person sharing a room. **room service,** provision of food etc. in a hotel bedroom. [Old English]

roomy /'ru:mɪ/ *adj.* having much room, spacious. —**roominess** *n.*

Roon /rəʊn/ Albrecht Theodor Emil, Graf von 1803–1879. Prussian field marshal. As war minister from 1859, he reorganized the army and made possible the victories over Austria 1866 (see ◊Prussia) and those in the ◊Franco-Prussian War 1870–71.

Rooney /'ru:nɪ/ Mickey. Stage name of Joe Yule 1920– . US actor who began his career in his parents' stage act when he was two years old. He played Andy Hardy in the Hardy family series of B-films 1936–46 and starred opposite Judy Garland in several musicals, including *Babes in Arms* 1939. He also played Puck in *A Midsummer Night's Dream* 1935 and starred in *Boys' Town* 1938.

Roosevelt /'rəʊzəvelt/ (Anna) Eleanor 1884–1962. US social worker, lecturer and First Lady; her newspaper column 'My Day' was widely syndicated. She was a delegate to the UN general assembly and later chair of the UN commission on human rights 1946–51. She helped to draw up the Declaration of Human Rights at the UN in 1945. Within the Democratic Party she formed the left-wing Americans for Democratic Action group in 1947. She was married to President Franklin Roosevelt.

Roosevelt Franklin Delano 1882–1945. 32nd president of the USA 1933–45, a Democrat. He served as governor of New York 1929–33. Becoming president amid the ◊Depression, he launched the ◊**New Deal** economic and social reform programme, which made him popular with the people. After the outbreak of World War II he introduced ◊Lend-Lease for the supply of war materials and services to the Allies and drew up the ◊Atlantic Charter of solidarity. Once the USA had entered the war in 1941, he spent much time in meetings with Allied leaders (see ◊Québec, ◊Tehran, and ◊Yalta conferences).

A radical is a man with both feet firmly planted in the air.

Franklin D Roosevelt
broadcast address to Forum on Current Problems,
1939

Roosevelt Theodore 1858–1919. 26th president of the USA 1901–09, a Republican. After serving as governor of New York 1898–1900 he became vice president to ◊McKinley, whom he succeeded as president on McKinley's assassination in 1901. He campaigned against the great trusts (combines that reduce competition), while carrying on a jingoist foreign policy designed to enforce US supremacy over Latin America.

roost *n.* a bird's perching or resting place, especially a place where fowls sleep. —*v.i.* (of a bird or person) to settle for sleep; to be perched or lodged for the night. —**come home to roost,** to recoil upon the originator. [Old English]

rooster *n.* (*US*) a domestic cock.

root[1] *n.* **1.** the part of a plant that attaches it to the earth and conveys water and nourishment from the soil; (in *plural*) fibres or branches of this. Roots usually grow downwards and towards water. Plants, such as epiphytic orchids that grow above ground, produce aerial roots that absorb moisture from the atmosphere. Others, such as ivy, have climbing roots arising from the stems that serve to attach the plant to trees and walls. **2.** a small plant with a root for transplanting. **3.** a plant with an edible root, such a root. **4.** the embedded part of a hair, tooth etc. **5.** (in *plural*) what causes close emotional attachment to a place etc. **6.** a source or origin; a basis; a means of continuance. **7.** a number that when multiplied by itself a given number of times yields a given number, especially a ◊square root; the value of a quantity such that a given equation is satisfied. **8.** an ultimate element of a language from which words have been made by addition or modification. —*v.t./i.* **1.** to take root; to cause to do this. **2.** (especially in *past participle*) to fix or establish firmly. **3.** to drag or dig up by the roots. —**root and branch,** thoroughly, radically. **root out,** to find and get rid of. **rootstock** *n.* a ◊rhizome; a plant into

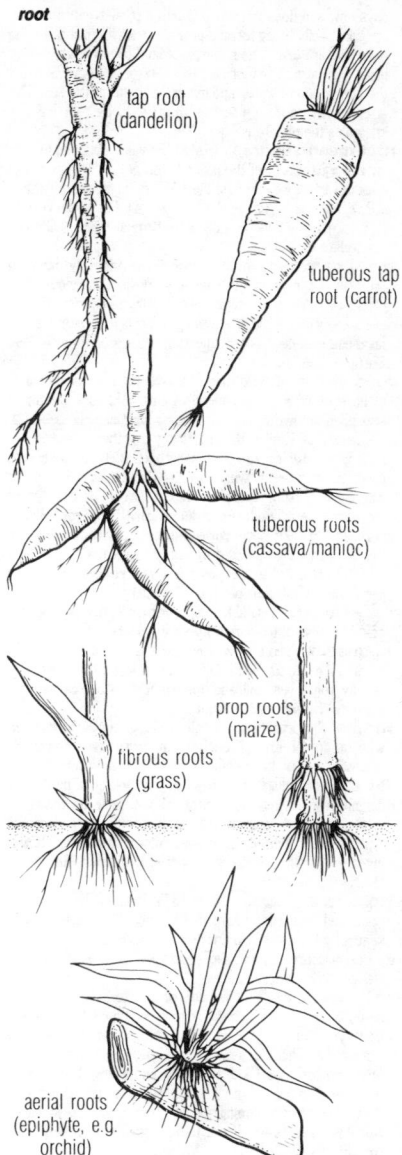

root

tap root (dandelion)

tuberous tap root (carrot)

tuberous roots (cassava/manioc)

prop roots (maize)

fibrous roots (grass)

aerial roots (epiphyte, e.g. orchid)

which a graft is inserted; a source from which offshoots have arisen. **take root,** to begin to draw nourishment from the soil; to become established. [Old English]

root[2] *v.t./i.* **1.** to dig or turn up (the ground etc.) with the snout or beak in search of food. **2.** to rummage; to find or extract by rummaging —**root for,** (*US slang*) to encourage by applause or support. [Old English]

root crop ambiguous term for several different types of crop; in agriculture, it refers to turnips, swedes, and beets, which are actually enlarged hypocotyls and contain little root, whereas in trade statistics it refers to the tubers of potatoes, cassava, and yams. Roots have a high carbohydrate content, but their protein content rarely exceeds 2%. Consequently, communities relying almost exclusively upon roots may suffer from protein deficiency. Potatoes, cassava, and yams are second in importance only to cereals as human food. Food production for a given area from roots is greater than from cereals.

root hair tubular outgrowth from a cell on the surface of a plant root. It is a delicate structure, which survives for a few days only and does not develop into a root. New root hairs are continually being formed near the root tip to replace the ones that are lost. The majority of land plants possess root hairs, which greatly increase the surface area available for the absorption of water and mineral salts from the soil. The layer of the root's epidermis that produces root hairs is known as the piliferous layer.

root-mean-square *n.* (RMS) the value obtained by taking the square root of the mean (average) of the squares of a set of values; for example the RMS value of four quantities *a, b, c,* and *d* is $\sqrt{[(a^2 + b^2 + c^2 + d^2)/4]}$. For an alternating current, the RMS value is equal to the peak value divided by the square root of 2.

roots music or **world music** term originally denoting ◊reggae, later encompassing any music indigenous to a particular culture. Examples are W African *mbalax,* E African *soukous,* S African *mbaqanga,* French Antillean *zouk,* Javanese gamelan, Latin American salsa, Cajun music, and European folk music.

rope *n.* 1. stout cord made by twisting together strands of fibre or wire etc.; a piece of this. Although ◊hemp is still used to make rope, nylon is increasingly used. 2. a quantity of similar things strung together. —*v.t.* 1. to fasten, secure, or catch with a rope. 2. to enclose with rope. 3. to connect with rope. —**the rope,** a halter for hanging a person. **know** *or* **learn the ropes,** to know (or learn) the procedure for doing something. **rope in,** to persuade to take part. **rope-ladder** *n.* a ladder made of two long ropes connected by rungs. **ropewalk** *n.* a long piece of ground where ropes are made. **rope-walker** *n.* a performer on a tightrope. [Old English]

ropy /'rəʊpɪ/ *adj.* 1. like a rope; forming viscous or gelatinous threads. 2. (*colloquial*) poor in quality.

Roquefort /'rɒkfɔː/ *n.* the trade name of blue cheese originally made at Roquefort, a town in southern France, usually from ewes' milk and ripened in limestone caves, with a strong characteristic flavour.

rorqual /'rɔːkwəl/ *n.* a whale of the genus *Balaenoptera,* with a dorsal fin. [French from Norwegian from Old Icelandic. *reythr* the specific name and *hvalr* = whale]

Rorschach test /'rɔːʃɑːk/ in psychology, a method of diagnosis involving the use of inkblot patterns that subjects are asked to interpret, to help indicate personality type, degree of intelligence, and emotional stability. It was invented by the Swiss psychiatrist Hermann Rorschach (1884–1922).

Rosa /'rəʊzə/ Salvator 1615–1673. Italian painter, etcher, poet, and musician, active in Florence 1640–49 and subsequently in Rome. He created wild, romantic, and sometimes macabre landscapes, seascapes, and battle scenes. He also wrote verse satires.

rosaceous /rəʊ'zeɪʃəs/ *adj.* of the Rosaceae, the large family of plants of which the rose is the type. [from Latin]

rosary /'rəʊzərɪ/ *n.* 1. a form of prayer used by Roman Catholics, consisting of 150 ◊Ave Marias and 15 ◊Paternosters and Glorias; a book containing this; a string of 55 or 165 beads for keeping count of these prayers. 2. a similar bead-string used in other religions, including Buddhism and Islam. [from Latin *rosarium* = rose-garden (*rosa* = rose)]

Roscius Gallus /'rɒskɪəs 'gæləs/ Quintus *c.*126–62 BC. Roman actor, originally a slave, so gifted that his name became a byword for a great actor.

Roscoff /'rɒskɒf/ port on the Brittany coast of France with a ferry link to Plymouth in England; population (1982) 4,000.

Roscommon /rɒs'kɒmən/ (originally Ros-Comain, 'wood around a monastery') county of the Republic of Ireland in the province of Connacht; **area** 2,460 sq km/ 950 sq mi; **physical** bounded on the E by the river Shannon; lakes: Gara, Key, Allen; rich pastures; **population** (1986) 55,000.

rose[1] /rəʊz/ *n.* 1. a prickly bush or shrub of the genus *Rosa,* bearing ornamental, usually fragrant, flowers; its flower; a flowering plant resembling this. Numerous cultivated forms have been derived from the Eurasian sweet briar or eglantine, *R. rubiginosa,* and dogrose, *R. canina.* There are many climbing varieties, but the forms more commonly cultivated are bush roses and standards, (cultivated roses grafted on to a briar stem). 2. deep pink colour. 3. a representation of the flower; a design based on it. 4.

the sprinkling-nozzle of a hose or watering-can. —*adj.* deep pink. —**rosebay** *n.* a willow-herb *Epilobium angustifolium.* **rosebud** *n.* the bud of a rose. **rose-water** *n.* a fragrant liquid perfumed with roses. **rose window,** a circular window with a roselike pattern of tracery. **see things through rose-coloured spectacles,** to take an unduly cheerful view of things. [from Old English from Latin *rosa*]

rose[2] past participle of **rise.**

rosé /'rəʊzeɪ/ *n.* a light, pink wine, coloured by only brief contact with the grape-skins. [French = pink]

roseate /'rəʊzɪət/ *adj.* 1. deep pink. 2. unduly cheerful. [from Latin *roseus*]

Roseau /rəʊ'zəʊ/ formerly **Charlotte Town** capital of ◊Dominica, West Indies; population (1981) 20,000.

rosebay willowherb common perennial weed. See ◊willowherb.

Roseirs /rɒ'seərəs/ port at the head of navigation of the Blue Nile in Sudan. A hydroelectric scheme here provides the country with 70% of its electrical power.

rosemary /'rəʊzmərɪ/ *n.* an evergreen shrub, *Rosemarinus officinalis,* of the mint family Labiatae, native to the Mediterranean and W Asia, with small, scented leaves. It is widely cultivated as a culinary herb and for the aromatic oil extracted from the clusters of pale, purple flowers, and regarded as an emblem of remembrance. [from Old French or Middle Dutch or Latin *ros marinus* = dew of the sea]

Rosenberg /'rəʊzənbɜːg/ Alfred 1893–1946. German politician, born in Tallinn, Estonia. He became the chief Nazi ideologist and was minister for eastern occupied territories 1941–44. He was tried at ◊Nuremberg in 1946 as a war criminal and hanged.

Rosenberg Isaac 1890–1918. English poet of the World War I period. Trained as an artist at the Slade school in London, Rosenberg enlisted in the British army in 1915. He wrote about the horror of life on the front line, as in 'Break of Day in the Trenches'.

Rosenberg Julius 1918–1953 and Ethel 1915–1953. US married couple, accused of being leaders of a nuclear-espionage ring passing information to the USSR; both were executed.

rosery /'rəʊzərɪ/ *n.* a rose-garden.

Roses, Wars of the civil wars in England 1455–85 between the houses of ◊Lancaster (badge, red rose) and ◊York (badge, white rose):

1455 Opened with battle of St Albans on 22 May, a Yorkist victory (◊Henry VI made prisoner).

1459–61 War renewed until ◊Edward IV, having become king, confirmed his position by a victory at Towton on 29 Mar 1461.

1470 ◊Warwick (who had helped Edward to the throne) allied instead with Henry VI's widow, ◊Margaret of Anjou, but was defeated by Edward at Barnet on 14 Apr and by Margaret at Tewkesbury on 4 May.

1485 Yorkist regime ended with the defeat of ◊Richard III by the future ◊Henry VII at ◊Bosworth on 22 Aug.
The name was given in the 19th century by novelist Walter Scott.

Rose Theatre the former London theatre near Southwark Bridge where many of Shakespeare's plays were performed. The excavation and preservation of the remains of the theatre, discovered in 1989, caused controversy between government bodies and archaeologists.

Rosetta Stone /rəʊ'zetə/ a slab of basalt with inscriptions from 197 BC, found near the town of Rosetta, Egypt, in 1799. Giving the same text in three versions—Greek, hieroglyphic, and demotic script—it became the key to deciphering other Egyptian inscriptions.

rosette /rə'zet/ *n.* a roselike object, symbol, or arrangement of parts; a rose-shaped ornament of ribbons etc., especially as a supporter's badge, or as an award or a symbol of an award in a competition; a rose-shaped carving. [French diminutive of *rose*]

rosewood *n.* any of several fragrant close-grained woods used in making furniture.

Rosh Hashanah /'rɒʃ hə'ʃɑːnə/ a two-day holiday that marks the start of the Jewish New Year (first new moon after the autumn equinox), traditionally announced by blowing a ram's horn (a ◊shofar).

Rosicrucians /rəʊzɪ'kruːʃ(ə)n/ *n.* group of early 17th-century philosophers who claimed occult powers and employed the terminology of ◊alchemy to expound their mystical doctrines (said to derive from ◊Paracelsus). The name comes from books published in 1614 and 1615, attributed to Christian Rosenkreutz ('rosy cross'), most probably a pen name but allegedly a writer living around 1460. Several societies have been founded in Britain and the USA that claim to be their successors, such as the Rosicrucian Fraternity (1614 in Germany, 1861 in USA). —*adj.* of the Rosicrucians. [from Latin *rosa crucis* (or *crux*, literally = rose cross) as Latinization of Rosenkreutz]

rosin /'rɒzɪn/ *n.* resin, especially in a solid form. —*v.t.* to rub (especially the bow of a violin etc.) with rosin. [alteration from *resin*]

Ross /rɒs/ James Clark 1800–1862. English explorer who discovered the magnetic North Pole in 1831. He also went to the Antarctic in 1839; Ross Island, Ross Sea, and Ross Dependency are named after him.

Ross Martin. Pen name of Violet Florence ◊Martin, Irish novelist.

Ross Ronald 1857–1932. British physician and bacteriologist, born in India. From 1881 to 1899 he served in the Indian medical service, and during 1895–98 identified mosquitoes of the genus *Anopheles* as being responsible for the spread of malaria. He was awarded the Nobel Prize for Medicine in 1902.

Ross Dependency all the Antarctic islands and territories between 160° E and 150° W longitude and south of 60° S latitude; it includes Edward VII Land, Ross Sea and its islands, and parts of Victoria Land; **area** 450,000 sq km/173,700 sq mi; **features** the Ross Ice Shelf (or Ross Barrier), a permanent layer of ice across the Ross Sea about 425 m/1,400 ft thick; **population** a few scientific bases with about 250 staff members, 12 of whom are present during winter; **history** given to New Zealand 1923. It is probable that marine organisms beneath the ice shelf had been undisturbed from the Pleistocene period until drillings were made 1976.

Rossellini /rɒsə'liːni/ Roberto 1906–1977. Italian film director. His World War II trilogy of films, *Roma città aperta*/Rome, *Open City* 1945, *Paisá*/*Paisan* 1946, and *Germania anno zero*/*Germany Year Zero* 1947 are considered landmarks in postwar European cinema.

Rossetti /rə'zeti/ Christina (Georgina) 1830–1894. English poet, sister of Dante Rossetti and a devout High Anglican (see ◊Oxford movement). Her verse includes *Goblin Market and Other Poems* 1862 and expresses unfulfilled spiritual yearning and frustrated love. She was a skilful technician and made use of irregular rhyme and line length.

Better by far you should forget and smile
Than you should remember and be sad.
Christina Rossetti
'Remember'

Rossetti Dante Gabriel 1828–1882. British painter and poet, a founding member of the ◊Pre-Raphaelite Brotherhood (PRB) in 1848. As well as romantic medieval scenes, he produced many idealized portraits of women. His verse includes 'The Blessed Damozel' 1850. His sister was the poet Christina Rossetti.

Rossini /rɒ'siːni/ Gioachino (Antonio) 1792–1868. Italian composer. His first success was the opera *Tancredi* 1813. In 1816 his 'opera buffa' *Il barbiere di Siviglia*/*The Barber of Seville* was produced in Rome. During his fertile composition period 1815–23 he produced 20 operas, and created (with ◊Donizetti and ◊Bellini) the 19th-century Italian operatic style. After *Guillaume Tell*/*William Tell* 1829 he gave up writing opera and his later years were spent in Bologna and Paris.

Rostand /rɒs'tɒn/ Edmond 1869–1918. French dramatist, who wrote *Cyrano de Bergerac* 1897 and *L'Aiglon* 1900 (based on the life of Napoleon III), in which Sarah Bernhardt played a leading role.

roster /'rɒstə/ *n.* a list or plan showing turns of duty etc. —*v.t.* to put on a roster. [from Dutch, originally = grid-iron, with reference to parallel lines]

rostrum /'rɒstrəm/ *n.* (*plural* **rostra**) a platform for public speaking or for an orchestral conductor. [Latin = beak (originally *rostra* in Roman forum adorned with beaks of captured galleys)]

rosy /'rəʊzɪ/ *adj.* 1. rose-coloured, deep pink. 2. promising, cheerful, helpful. —**rosily** *adv.*, **rosiness** *n.*

rot *v.t./i.* (-tt-) 1. (of animal or vegetable matter) to lose its original form by chemical action caused by bacteria or fungi etc. 2. to perish or become weak through lack of use or activity. 3. to cause to rot. —*n.* 1. rotting; rottenness. 2. (*slang*) nonsense, an absurd statement or argument. 3. a series of failures, a rapid decline. —*int.* expressing incredulity or ridicule. —**rot-gut** *n.* (*slang*) inferior or harmful liquor. [Old English]

rota /'rəʊtə/ *n.* a list of persons acting, or duties to be done, in rotation; a roster. [Latin = wheel]

Rotarian /rəʊ'teəriən/ *n.* a member of Rotary. —*adj.* of Rotary.

rotary /'rəʊtərɪ/ *adj.* acting by rotation. [from Latin *rotarius*]

Rotary *n.* (in full **Rotary International**) a worldwide society for business and professional people having as its aim the promotion of unselfish service and international goodwill. Its name derives from the fact that the first local group, formed in Chicago in 1905, met at each member's premises in rotation. —**Rotary Club**, a local branch of Rotary.

rotate /rəʊ'teɪt/ *v.t./i.* 1. to move round an axis or centre, to revolve or cause to revolve. 2. to arrange or deal with in rotation. —**rotator** *n.* [from Latin *rotare*]

rotation /rəʊ'teɪʃən/ *n.* 1. rotating, being rotated. 2. recurrence; a recurrent series or period; a regular succession of various members of a group. 3. the practice of growing a different crop each year on a plot of land in a regular order, to avoid exhausting the soil. —**rotational** *adj.*

rotatory /'rəʊtətərɪ/ *adj.* rotating; of rotation.

rote *n.* **by rote**, by memory without thought of the meaning; by a fixed procedure.

Roth /rɒθ/ Philip 1933– . US novelist, known for his portrayals of 20th-century Jewish-American life. His books include *Goodbye Columbus* 1959; *Portnoy's Complaint* 1969; and a series of semi-autobiographical novels about a writer, Nathan Zuckerman, including *The Ghost Writer* 1979, *Zuckerman Unbound* 1981, *The Anatomy Lesson* 1984, and *The Counterlife* 1987. Psychosexual themes are prominent in his work.

Rothamsted /'rɒθəmsted/ agricultural research centre in Hertfordshire, England, NW of St Albans.

Rotherhithe Tunnel /'rɒðəhaɪð/ road tunnel extending 7,776 km/4,860 ft under the river Thames E of Wapping, London, connecting Roherhithe with Shadwell. It was built 1904–08 to a design by Maurice Fitzmarice.

Rothko /'rɒθkəʊ/ Mark 1903–1970. Russian-born US painter, an Abstract Expressionist and a pioneer of **Colour Field** painting (abstract, dominated by areas of unmodulated, strong colour). Rothko produced several series of paintings in the 1950s and 1960s, including one at Harvard University; one in the Tate Gallery, London; and one for a chapel in Houston, Texas, 1967–69.

Rothschild /'rɒθstʃaɪld/ European family active in the financial world for two centuries. **Mayer Anselm** (1744–1812) set up as a moneylender in Frankfurt-am-Main, Germany, and business houses were established throughout Europe by his ten children.

rotifer *n.* any of the tiny invertebrates, also called 'wheel animalcules', of the phylum Aschelminthes. Mainly freshwater, some marine, rotifers have a ring of cilia that carries food to the mouth and also provides propulsion. Smallest of multicellular animals, few reach 0.05 cm/0.02 in.

rotisserie /rə'tɪsərɪ/ *n.* a cooking-device for roasting food on a revolving spit. [from French from Old French *rostir* = roast]

rotor /'rəʊtə/ *n.* 1. a rotary part of a machine. 2. a horizontally rotating vane of a helicopter. [irregular for *rotator*]

rotten /'rɒtən/ *adj.* 1. rotting, rotted; falling to pieces or liable to break or tear from age or use. 2. morally or politically corrupt; effete. 3. contemptible, worthless. 4. (*colloquial*) unpleasant. —**rottenly** *adv.*, **rottenness** *n.* [from Old Norse]

rotten borough English Parliamentary constituency, before the Great Reform Act 1832, that returned members to Parliament in spite of having small numbers of electors. Such a borough could easily be manipulated by those with sufficient money or influence.

rotter *n.* (*slang*) an objectionable or contemptible person.

Rotterdam /'rɒtədæm/ industrial port (brewing, distilling, shipbuilding, sugar and petroleum refining, margarine, tobacco) in the Netherlands and one of the foremost ocean cargo ports in the world, in the Rhine-Maas delta, linked by canal 1866–90 with the North Sea; population (1988) 1,036,000.

Rottweiler /'rɒtwaɪlə/ n. breed of guard dog originating from Rottweil in S Germany. Large and powerful, it needs regular exercise, and has not proved successful as a pet.

rotund /rəʊ'tʌnd/ adj. 1. (of a person) rounded, plump. 2. (of speech or literary style etc.) sonorous, grandiloquent. —**rotundity** n. [from Latin *rotundus* from *rota* = wheel]

rotunda /rəʊ'tʌndə/ n. a circular building or hall, especially one with a dome. [from Italian *rotonda*]

Rouault /ru:'əʊ/ Georges 1871–1958. French painter, etcher, illustrator, and designer. Early in his career he was associated with the ◊Fauves but created his own style using heavy, dark colours and bold brushwork. His subjects included sad clowns, prostitutes, and evil lawyers; from about 1940 he painted mainly religious works.

Roubiliac /ru:bi'jæk/ or **Roubillac**, Louis François c.1705–1762. French sculptor, a Huguenot who fled religious persecution to settle in England in 1732. He became a leading sculptor of the day, creating a statue of Handel for Vauxhall Gardens 1737 (Victoria and Albert Museum, London).

rouble /'ru:bəl/ n. the currency unit of the USSR. [French from Russian]

roué /'ru:eɪ/ n. a dissolute person, especially an elderly one. [French *rouer* = break on wheel—one deserving this]

rouge /ru:ʒ/ n. a red cosmetic used to colour the cheeks. —v.t. to colour with rouge. [French = red, from Latin *rubeus*]

rough /rʌf/ adj. 1. having an uneven or irregular surface, not smooth or level. 2. not gentle or restrained or careful; violent, boisterous, harsh; severe, unpleasant, demanding. 3. lacking finish or delicacy; not perfected or detailed; approximate. —adv. in a rough manner. —n. 1. hardship. 2. a hooligan, a ruffian. 3. something rough, rough ground etc. 4. an unfinished or natural state; a rough drawing or design etc. —v.t. 1. to make rough. 2. to shape, plan, or sketch *out* roughly. —**rough-and-ready** adj. rough or crude but effective; not elaborate or overparticular. **rough-and-tumble** adj. disorderly, irregular; (n.) a disorderly fight. **rough deal**, see ◊deal[1]. **rough diamond**, an uncut diamond; a person of good nature but rough manners. **rough-dry** v.t. to dry (clothes) without ironing. **roughhouse** n. (slang) a disturbance, violent behaviour. **rough it**, do without basic comforts. **rough justice**, treatment that is approximately fair. **rough-rider** n. one who rides unbroken horses. **rough shooting**, shooting (as a sport) without the help of beaters. **rough up**, (slang) to attack (a person) violently. —**roughly** adv., **roughness** n. [Old English]

roughage /'rʌfɪdʒ/ n. indigestible fibrous material in plants which are used as food (e.g. bran, green vegetables, and certain fruits) that stimulates the action of the intestines.

roughcast n. a plaster of lime and gravel, used on outside walls. —v.t. to coat with this.

roughen /'rʌfən/ v.t./i. to make or become rough.

roughneck n. 1. (colloquial) a driller on an oil rig. 2. (US slang) a rough person.

roughshod adj. (of a horse) having shoes with nail-heads projecting to prevent slipping. —**ride roughshod over**, to treat inconsiderately or arrogantly.

roulette /ru:'let/ n. a gambling game played with a revolving compartmented wheel (numbered 0–36 and alternately coloured red and black) in which a ball rolls randomly. [French from Latin (diminutive of *rota* = wheel)]

round adj. 1. having a curved shape or outline; shaped like a circle, sphere, or cylinder. 2. done with a circular motion. 3. full, complete; candid. —n. 1. a round object; a rung of a ladder; a slice of bread cut across the loaf; a sandwich made from whole slices of bread. 2. a revolving motion; a circular or recurring course or series; a route on which things are to be delivered or inspected. 3. a single provision of drinks etc. to each member of a group. 4. one spell of play in a game etc.; one stage in a competition or struggle; one section of a boxing-match. 5. the playing of all the holes in a golf-course once. 6. a single shot or volley of shots from one or more firearms; ammunition for this. 7. a solid form of sculpture

etc. 8. a musical composition for two or more voices in which each sings the same melody but starts at a different time. —adv. 1. with a circular motion; in a circle or curve; with return to the starting-point or an earlier state; into consciousness after unconsciousness; so as to change to an opposite position (literal or figurative). 2. to, at, or affecting all or many points of a circumference or area or members of a company etc.; in every direction from a centre or within a radius. 3. by a circuitous route; to a person's house etc. 4. measuring (a specified distance) in girth. —prep. 1. so as to encircle or enclose. 2. with successive visits to; to all points of interest in. 3. having as an axis or central point; coming close from various sides but not into contact (literal or figurative). 4. so as to pass in a curved course; having thus passed; in a position thus reached. —v.t./i. 1. to give or take a round shape. 2. (with *up* or *down*) to make (a number etc.) round by omitting units or fractions. 3. to travel round (a cape, corner etc.). —**go the rounds,** to go from person to person. **in the round,** with all features shown or considered; (of a sculpture) with all sides shown, not in relief; (of a theatre) with the audience all round the stage. **round about,** all round, on all sides (of); approximately. **round and round,** several times round. **round dance,** a dance with a circular movement or in which the dancers form a ring. **round figure,** or number, a figure or number without odd units or fractions. **round off,** to bring to a complete state. **round on,** to make an unexpected retort to or retaliation against. **round robin,** a petition with signatures in a circle to conceal the order of signing. **round shoulders,** shoulders bent forward so that the back is rounded. **round-table conference,** one with discussion by members round a table. **round trip,** a trip to one or more places and back again. **round up,** to gather or bring together. **round-up** n. a rounding up; a summary. [from Old French from Latin *rotundus*]

roundabout n. 1. a road junction with traffic passing in one direction round a central island. 2. a merry-go-round or other revolving structure at a funfair. —adj. circuitous.

roundel /'raʊndəl/ n. 1. a small disc, a medallion. 2. a circular identifying mark. 3. a rondeau. [from Old French *rondel(le)*]

roundelay /'raʊndɪleɪ/ n. a short, simple song with a refrain. [from French *rondelet*]

rounders /'raʊndəz/ n. an outdoor game played with a bat and ball between teams of nine players, having features in common with baseball (its original name) but played on a much smaller pitch.

Roundhead n. a member of the party (also known as **Parliamentarians**) opposing the royalist Cavaliers during the English Civil War 1640–60, so called because of the style in which the Puritans, who were an important element in the forces, wore their hair.

roundly adv. 1. thoroughly, severely. 2. in a rounded shape.

roundsman n. (plural **roundsmen**) a retailer's employee delivering goods on a regular round.

roundworm n. a worm with a rounded body, especially one of the genus *Ascaris*.

rouse /raʊz/ v.t./i. 1. to wake; to cause to wake. 2. to make active or excited.

rousing adj. vigorous, stirring.

Rousseau /ru:'səʊ/ Henri 'Le Douanier' 1844–1910. French painter, a self-taught naive artist. His subjects included scenes of the Parisian suburbs and exotic junglescapes, painted with painstaking detail, for example *Surprised! Tropical Storm with a Tiger* 1891 (National Gallery, London).

Rousseau Jean-Jacques 1712–1778. French social philosopher and writer, born in Geneva, Switzerland. *Discourses on the Origins of Inequality* 1754 made his name: he denounced civilized society and postulated the paradox of the superiority of the 'noble savage'. *Social Contract* 1762 emphasized the rights of the people over those of the government, and stated that a government could be legitimately overthrown if it failed to express the general will of the people. It was a significant influence on the French Revolution. In the novel *Emile* 1762 he outlined a new theory of education, based on natural development and the power of example, to elicit the unspoiled nature and abilities of children. *Confessions*, published posthumously 1782, was a frank account of

Rowlandson *This boisterous watercolour by the English artist Thomas Rowlandson is typical of his Dr Syntax series. It is from the first series* Tour of Dr Syntax in Search of the Picturesque *1809, for which William Combe wrote accompanying verses. It was a parody of popular picturesque travels of the day.*

his occasionally immoral life and was a founding work of autobiography.

Man was born free, and everywhere he is in chains.
Jean-Jacques Rousseau
Du Contrat Social

---

roustabout /'raʊstəbaʊt/ n. 1. a labourer on an oil rig. 2. an unskilled or casual labourer. [from dialect *roust* = rout out]

rout[1] n. a disorderly retreat of defeated troops; utter defeat. —v.t. to put to flight, to defeat utterly. [from Anglo-French *rute*]

rout[2] variant of ◊root[2].

route /ruːt/ n. the way taken in getting from a starting-point to a destination. —v.t. (participle **routeing**) to send by a particular route. —**route march**, a training-march for troops. [from Old French = road, ultimately from Latin *rumpere* = break]

router /'raʊtə/ n. a type of two-handled plane for cutting grooves etc.

routine /ruː'tiːn/ n. 1. a regular course of procedure; the unvarying performance of certain acts. 2. a set sequence of movements in a dance or other performance. 3. a sequence of instructions to a computer. —adj. performed as a routine. —**routinely** adv. [French]

roux /ruː/ n. (plural the same) a mixture of fat and flour used as a basis for making a sauce etc. [French = browned]

rove[1] v.i. to wander. —**rove beetle**, a long-bodied beetle of the family Staphylinidae. **roving commission**, authority to travel as may be necessary in conducting an inquiry or other work. **roving eye**, a tendency to flirt. [originally archery term = shoot at casual mark with range not determined, perhaps from dialect *rave* = stray]

rove[2] past of ◊reeve[2].

rover[1] /'rəʊvə/ n. a roving person, a wanderer.

rover[2] n. a pirate. [from Middle Low German or Middle Dutch *roven* = rob]

row[1] /rəʊ/ n. 1. a number of persons or things in a more or less straight line. 2. a line of seats across a theatre etc. 3. a street with houses along one or each side. —**in a row**, (colloquial) in succession. [Old English]

row[2] v.t./i. to propel (a boat) with oars; to convey (a passenger) in a boat thus. —n. a spell of rowing. Rowing is practised as a competitive sport either by one rower with two oars (sculling) or by crews (two, four, or eight persons)

with one ear each, often with a coxswain. —**rowing-boat** or **rowboat** n. a boat propelled by oars. [Old English]

row[3] /raʊ/ n. (colloquial) 1. a loud noise or commotion. 2. a fierce quarrel or dispute. —v.i. (colloquial) to make or engage in a row.

rowan /'rəʊən, 'raʊ-/ n. the ◊mountain ash tree *Sorbus aucuparia*; its scarlet berry. [from Scandinavian]

Rowbotham /'rəʊbɒtəm/ Sheila 1943– . British socialist, feminist, historian, lecturer, and writer. Her pamphlet *Women's Liberation and the New Politics* 1970 laid down fundamental approaches and demands of the emerging women's movement.

rowdy /'raʊdɪ/ adj. noisy and disorderly. —n. a rowdy person. —**rowdily** adv., **rowdiness** n., **rowdyism** n.

Rowe /rəʊ/ Nicholas 1674–1718. English playwright and poet, whose dramas include *The Fair Penitent* 1702 and *Jane Shore* 1714, in which Mrs Siddons played. He edited Shakespeare, and was poet laureate from 1715.

rowel /'raʊəl/ n. a spiked, revolving disc at the end of a spur. [from Old French *roel(e)* from Latin *rota* = wheel]

Rowlandson /'rəʊləndsən/ Thomas 1756–1827. English painter and illustrator, a caricaturist of Georgian social life. He published the series of drawings *Tour of Dr Syntax in Search of the Picturesque* 1809 and its two sequels 1812–21.

Rowley /'rəʊlɪ/ William c.1585–c.1642. English actor and dramatist, collaborator with ◊Middleton in *The Changeling* 1621 and with ◊Dekker and ◊Ford in *The Witch of Edmonton* published 1658.

Rowling /'rəʊlɪŋ/ Wallace 'Bill' 1927– . New Zealand Labour politician, party leader 1969–75, prime minister 1974–75.

rowlock /'rɒlək/ n. a device for holding an oar in place and serving as a fulcrum.

Rowntree /'raʊntriː/ Benjamin Seebohm 1871–1954. British entrepreneur and philanthropist. Much of the money he acquired as chair (1925–41) of the family firm of confectioners, H I Rowntree, he used to fund investigations into social conditions. His writings include *Poverty* 1900. The three **Rowntree Trusts**, which were founded by his father **Joseph Rowntree** (1836–1925) in 1904, fund research into housing, social care, and social policy, support projects relating to social justice, and give grants to pressure groups working in these areas.

Rowse /raʊs/ A(lfred) L(eslie) 1903– . English popular historian. He published a biography of Shakespeare 1963, and in 1973 controversially identified the 'Dark Lady' of Shakespeare's sonnets as Emilia Lanier, half-Italian daughter of a court musician, with whom the Bard is alleged to have had an affair 1593–95.

Roy /rɔɪ/ Manabendra Nakh 1887–1954. Founder of the Indian Communist Party in exile in Tashkent in 1920. Expelled from the Comintern in 1929, he returned to India and was imprisoned for five years. A steadfast communist, he finally became disillusioned after World War II and developed his ideas on practical humanism.

Roy Rajah Ram Rohan. Bengali religious and social reformer known as ◊Ram Mohun Roy.

royal /'rɔɪəl/ *adj.* 1. of, suited to, or worthy of a king or queen. 2. in the service or under the patronage of royalty; belonging to a king or queen or their family. 3. splendid; on a great scale, of exceptional size etc. —*n.* 1. (*colloquial*) a member of a royal family. 2. a royal mast or sail (that above the topgallant). —**royal blue**, deep vivid blue. **royal flush**, see ◊flush³. **royal icing**, hard icing for cakes, made with icing sugar and egg-white. **royal jelly**, a substance secreted by worker-bees and fed by them to future queen bees. **royal oak**, a sprig of oak worn on 29 May to commemorate the restoration of Charles II (1660) who hid in an oak-tree after the battle of Worcester in 1651. **royal warrant**, a warrant authorizing a manufacturer or retailer to supply goods to a specified royal person. —**royally** *adv.* [from Old French *roial* from Latin = regal]

Royal Academy of Dramatic Art (RADA) British college founded by Herbert Beerbohm Tree in 1904 to train young actors. Since 1905 its headquarters have been in Gower Street, London. A royal charter was granted 1920.

Royal Aeronautical Society oldest British aviation body, formed in 1866. Its members discussed and explored the possibilities of flight long before its successful achievement.

Royal Air Force (RAF) the air force of Britain. The RAF was formed in 1918 by the merger of the Royal Naval Air Service and the Royal Flying Corps.

royal assent in the UK, formal consent given by a British sovereign to the passage of a bill through Parliament, after which it becomes an ◊act of Parliament. The last instance of a royal refusal was the rejection of the Scottish Militia Bill of 1702 by Queen Anne.

Royal Ballet the title under which the British Sadler's Wells Ballet (at Covent Garden), Sadler's Wells Theatre Ballet, and the Sadler's Wells Ballet School were incorporated in 1956.

Royal Botanic Gardens, Kew botanic gardens in Richmond, Surrey, England, popularly known as ◊Kew Gardens.

Royal British Legion full name of the ◊British Legion, a nonpolitical body promoting the welfare of war veterans and their dependants.

Royal Canadian Mounted Police (RCMP) Canadian national police force, known as the Mounties and famed for their uniform of red jackets and broad-brimmed hats. Their Security Service, established 1950, was disbanded in 1981 and replaced by the independent Canadian Security Intelligence Service.

royal commission in the UK and Canada, a group of people appointed by the government (nominally appointed by the sovereign) to investigate a matter of public concern and make recommendations on any actions to be taken in connection with it, including changes in the law. In cases where agreement on recommendations cannot be reached, a minority report can be submitted by dissenters. No royal commissions have been set up under the Conservative governments since 1979.

Royal Greenwich Observatory the national astronomical observatory of the UK, founded in 1675 at Greenwich, E London, England, to provide navigational information for sailors. After World War II it was moved to Herstmonceux Castle, Sussex; in 1990 it was transferred to Cambridge. It also operates telescopes on La Palma in the Canary Islands, including the 4.2 m/165 in William Herschel Telescope, commissioned in 1987.

royal household the personal staff of a sovereign. In Britain the chief officers are the Lord Chamberlain, the Lord Steward, and the Master of the Horse. The other principal members of the royal family also maintain their own households.

Royal Institution of Great Britain an organization for the promotion, diffusion, and extension of science and knowledge, founded in London in 1799 by the Anglo-American physicist Count Rumford (1753–1814). Michael ◊Faraday and Humphry ◊Davy were among its directors.

royalist /'rɔɪəlɪst/ *n.* a monarchist, a supporter of a monarchy or the royal side in a civil war etc.; **Royalist,** a supporter of the Stuarts in the English Civil War.

Royal Marines a British military force trained for amphibious warfare.

Royal Military Academy a British officer-training college popularly known as ◊Sandhurst.

Royal Opera House the leading British opera house, Covent Garden, London; the original theatre opened in 1732 and the present building dates from 1858.

Royal Shakespeare Company (RSC) a British professional theatre company that performs Shakespearean and other plays. It was founded 1961 from the company at the Shakespeare Memorial Theatre 1932 (now the Royal Shakespeare Theatre) in Stratford-upon-Avon, Warwickshire, England.

Royal Society the oldest and premier scientific society in Britain, originating from 1645 and chartered in 1660; Christopher ◊Wren and Isaac ◊Newton were prominent early members. Its Scottish equivalent is the Royal Society of Edinburgh 1783.

Royal Society for the Prevention of Cruelty to Animals (RSPCA) the British organization formed in 1824 to safeguard the welfare of animals; it promotes legislation, has an inspectorate to secure enforcement of existing laws, and runs clinics.

royalty *n.* 1. being royal. 2. a royal person or persons. 3. the sum paid to a patentee for the use of a patent or to an author etc. for each copy of his book etc. sold or for each public performance of his work. 4. a royal right (now especially over minerals) granted by a sovereign to an individual or a corporation. [from Old French]

Royal Worcester Porcelain Factory see ◊Worcester Porcelain Factory.

Royce /rɔɪs/ (Frederick) Henry 1863–1933. British engineer who so impressed Charles ◊Rolls by the car he built for his own personal use in 1904 that ◊Rolls-Royce Ltd was formed in 1906 to produce automobiles and engines.

RPI abbreviation of retail price index; see ◊cost of living.

rpm abbreviation of *r*evolutions *p*er *m*inute.

RSFSR abbreviation for ◊Russian Soviet Federal Socialist Republic, the largest constituent republic of the USSR.

RSM abbreviation of regimental sergeant major.

RSPB abbreviation of Royal Society for the Protection of Birds; see ◊birdwatching.

RSPCA abbreviation for ◊Royal Society for the Prevention of Cruelty to Animals.

RSV abbreviation of Revised Standard Version (of the Bible).

RSVP abbreviation for *répondez s'il vous plaît* (French 'please reply').

rt. or **rt** abbreviation of right.

Rt Hon. abbreviation of Right Honourable, the title of British members of Parliament.

Rt Revd abbreviation of Right Reverend.

Ru symbol for ruthenium.

Ruanda alternative spelling of ◊Rwanda, country in central Africa.

ruat coelum whatever happens. [Latin = though the heavens may fall]

rub *v.t./i.* (-bb-) 1. to press one's hand or an object etc. against (a surface) and slide it to and fro; to apply thus. 2. to clean or polish by rubbing; to make or become dry, smooth, or sore etc. in this way; to remove by rubbing. 3. to move or slide (objects) against each other. —*n.* 1. the act or process of rubbing. 2. an impediment or difficulty. —**rub along,** (*colloquial*) to manage to get on without undue difficulty. **rub down,** to dry, smooth, or clean by rubbing. **rub it in,** to emphasize or repeat an embarrassing fact etc. **rub off on,** to be transferred to by contact (*literal* or *figurative*). **rub shoulders with,** to associate with. **rub up,** to polish; to brush up (a subject etc.). **rub up the wrong way,** to irritate or repel.

rubato /ruːˈbɑːtəʊ/ *n.* (*plural* **rubatos**) in music, a pushing or dragging against the beat for extra expressive effect. [from *tempo rubato,* Italian = robbed time]

rubber¹ *n.* 1. a tough elastic substance made from the latex of tropical plants or synthetically. Most important is Para rubber, which derives from the tree *Hevea brasiliensis*. It was introduced from Brazil to SE Asia, where most of the world supply is now produced, the chief exporters being Malaysia, Indonesia, Sri Lanka, Cambodia, Thailand, Sarawak, and Brunei. At about seven years the tree, which may grow to 20 m/60 ft, is ready for 'tapping'. Small incisions are made in the trunk and the latex drips into collecting cups. In pure form, rubber is white and has the formula $(C_5H_8)_n$. 2. a piece of this or some other substance for erasing pencil or ink marks. 3. a device for rubbing things. 4. (*slang*) a ◊condom. 5. (in *plural*, *US*) galoshes. —**rubber band**, a loop of rubber to hold papers etc. together. **rubber plant**, a plant yielding rubber, especially *Ficus elastica* grown as a houseplant with shiny, oval leaves. **rubber stamp**, a device for inking and imprinting on a surface; one who mechanically agrees to others' actions; an indication of such agreement. **rubber-stamp**, *v.t.* to approve (an action) automatically without proper consideration. —**rubbery** *adj*.

rubber[2] *n.* a match of usually three successive games between the same sides or persons at bridge etc. or cricket.

rubberneck *n.* (*US colloquial*) an inquisitive person; a gaping sightseer. —*v.i.* (*US colloquial*) to behave as a rubberneck.

rubbing *n.* a reproduction or impression made of a memorial brass or other relief design by placing paper over it and rubbing with pigment.

rubbish *n.* 1. waste or worthless matter. 2. absurd ideas or suggestions, nonsense (often as an exclamation of contempt). —**rubbishy** *adj*. [from Anglo-French *rubbous*]

rubble *n.* waste or rough fragments of stone or brick etc. –**rubbly** *adj*.

Rubbra /ˈrʌbrə/ Edmund 1901–1986. British composer. He studied under ◊Holst and was a master of contrapuntal writing, as exemplified in his study *Counterpoint* 1960. His compositions include 11 symphonies, chamber music, and songs.

rubella /ruˈbelə/ *n.* technical term for ◊German measles. [from Latin *rubellus* = reddish]

Rubens /ˈruːbɪnz/ Peter Paul 1577–1640. Flemish painter, who brought the exuberance of Italian Baroque to N Europe, creating, with an army of assistants, innumerable religious and allegorical paintings for churches and palaces. These show mastery of drama in large compositions, and love of rich colour. He also painted portraits and, in his last years, landscapes.

Rubicon /ˈruːbɪkən/ ancient name of the small river flowing into the Adriatic which, under the Roman Republic, marked the boundary between Italy proper and Cisalpine Gaul. When ◊Caesar led his army across it in 49 BC he therefore declared war on the republic; hence to 'cross the Rubicon' means to take an irrevocable step. It is believed to be the present-day **Fiumicino**, which rises in the Etruscan Apennines 16 km/10 mi WNW of San Marino and enters the Adriatic 16 km/10 mi NW of Rimini.

rubicund /ˈruːbɪkʌnd/ *adj.* (of a person or complexion) ruddy, high-coloured. [from French or Latin *rubicundus* (*rubēre* = be red)]

rubidium *n.* a soft, silver-white, metallic element, symbol Rb, atomic number 37, relative atomic mass 85.47. It is one of the ◊alkali metals, ignites spontaneously in air, and reacts violently with water. It is used in photoelectric cells and vacuum-tube filaments. [from Latin *rubidus* = reddish (with reference to its spectrum lines)] [Latin *rubidus* 'red']

Rubik /ˈruːbɪk/ Erno 1944– . Hungarian architect who invented the **Rubik cube**, a multicoloured puzzle that can be manipulated and rearranged in only one correct way, but about 43 trillion wrong ones. Intended to help his students understand three-dimensional design, it became a fad that swept around the world.

Rubinstein /ˈruːbɪnstaɪn/ Helena 1882–1965. Polish-born cosmetics tycoon, who emigrated to Australia 1902, where she started a cosmetics business. She moved to Europe 1904 and later to the USA, opening salons in London, Paris, and New York.

rubric /ˈruːbrɪk/ *n.* 1. in the Christian churches, a direction for the conduct of service inserted in a liturgical book. 2. explanatory words. 3. a heading or passage in red or special lettering. [from Old French or Latin *rubrica* = red ochre]

ruby /ˈruːbɪ/ *n.* 1. a rare precious stone with a colour varying from deep crimson to pale rose. It is the red transparent gem variety of the mineral ◊corundum Al_2O_3, aluminium oxide. Small amounts of chromium oxide, Cr_2O_3, substituting for aluminium oxide, give ruby its colour. Natural rubies are found mainly in Myanmar (Burma), but rubies can also be produced artificially and such synthetic stones are used in ◊lasers. 2. a deep red colour. —*adj.* deep red. —**ruby wedding**, the 40th anniversary of a wedding. [from Old French *rubi* from Latin *rubeus* = red]

ruche /ruː/ *n.* a frill or gathering of lace etc. [French, from Latin *rusca* = tree-bark]

ruck[1] *n.* 1. the main body of competitors not likely to overtake the leaders. 2. the undistinguished crowd of persons or things. 3. in rugby football, a loose scrum with the ball on the ground. [originally = stack of fuel; apparently Scandinavian]

ruck[2] *v.t./i.* to crease or wrinkle. [from Old Norse]

rucksack /ˈrʌksæk, ˈrʊk-/ *n.* a bag slung by straps from both shoulders and resting on the back. [German *Rücken* = back]

ruction /ˈrʌkʃən/ *n.* (especially in *plural*, *colloquial*) protests and noisy argument, a row; a disturbance.

rudd *n.* a freshwater fish, *Scardinius erythrophthalmus*, common in lakes and slow rivers of Europe. Brownish green above and silvery below, with red fins and golden eyes, it can grow to a length of 45 cm/1.5 ft, and a weight of 1 kg/2.2 lbs.

rudder *n.* a flat piece hinged vertically to the stern of a vessel or the rear of an aircraft for steering. [Old English]

ruddy *adj.* 1. (of a person or complexion) freshly or healthily red. 2. reddish. 3. (*colloquial*) bloody, damnable. —**ruddily** *adv.*, **ruddiness** *n.* [Old English]

rude /ruːd/ *adj.* 1. impolite, showing no respect or consideration; coarse. 2. roughly made or done; primitive, uneducated. 3. abrupt, sudden. 4. vigorous, hearty. —**rudely** *adv.*, **rudeness** *n.* [from Old French from Latin *rudis* = unwrought]

Rude François 1784–1855. French Romantic sculptor. He produced the low-relief scene on the Arc de Triomphe, Paris, showing the capped figure of Liberty leading the revolutionaries (1833, known as *The Volunteers of 1792* or *The Marseillaise*).

rudiment /ˈruːdɪmənt/ *n.* 1. (in *plural*) the elements or first principles of knowledge or some subject. 2. (in *plural*) the imperfect beginnings of something undeveloped. 3. a part or organ imperfectly developed because it is vestigial or has no function (e.g. the breast in males). —**rudimentary** /-ˈmentərɪ/ *adj.* [French or from Latin]

Rudolf /ˈruːdɒlf/ former name of Lake ◊Turkana in E Africa.

Rudolph /ˈruːdɒlf/ 1858–1889. Crown prince of Austria, the only son of Emperor Franz Joseph. In 1889 he and his mistress, Baroness Marie Vetsera, were found shot in his hunting lodge at Mayerling, near Vienna. The official verdict was suicide, although there were rumours that it was perpetrated by Jesuits, Hungarian nobles, or the baroness's husband.

Rudolph two Holy Roman emperors:

Rudolph I 1218–1291. Holy Roman emperor from 1273. Originally count of Habsburg, he was the first Habsburg emperor and expanded his dynasty by investing his sons with the duchies of Austria and Styria.

Rudolph II 1552–1612. Holy Roman emperor from 1576, when he succeeded his father Maximilian II. His policies led to unrest in Hungary and Bohemia, which led to the surrender of Hungary to his brother Matthias in 1608 and religious freedom for Bohemia.

Rudra /ˈrʊdrə/ early Hindu storm god, most of whose attributes were later taken over by ◊Siva.

rue[1] *v.t.* (*participle* **ruing**) to repent of, to regret; to wish undone or non-existent. [Old English]

rue[2] *n.* an evergreen, shrubby, perennial herb *Ruta graveolens*, family Rutaceae, native to S Europe and temperate Asia. It bears clusters of yellow flowers. An oil extracted from the bitter, strongly scented, blue-green leaves is used in perfumery. [from Old French from Latin *ruta* from Greek]

rueful /ˈruːfəl/ *adj.* expressing good-humoured regret. —**ruefully** *adv.*

ruff[1] *n.* 1. a projecting starched frill worn round the neck especially in the 16th century 2. a projecting or conspicuously coloured ring of feathers or hair round a bird's or animal's neck. **3.** a bird *Philomachus pugnax* of the snipe family. The name is taken from the frill of erectile feathers developed in breeding time round the neck of the male. The ruff is found across N Europe and Asia, and migrates south in winter. **4.** a kind of pigeon.

ruff² *v.t./i.* to trump at cards. —*n.* trumping. [originally name of card game from Old French *ro(u)ffle*]

ruffian /'rʌfiən/ *n.* a violent, lawless person. —**ruffianism** *n.*, **ruffianly** *adj.* [from French from Italian *ruffiano*]

ruffle *v.t./i.* **1.** to disturb the smoothness or evenness of. **2.** to upset the calmness or even temper of (a person). **3.** to undergo ruffling. —*n.* a frill of lace etc. worn especially round the wrist or neck.

rufous /'ru:fəs/ *adj.* (especially of animals) reddish-brown. [from Latin *rufus*]

rug *n.* **1.** a thick floor-mat. **2.** a piece of thick material used as a blanket or coverlet. —**pull the rug from under,** to deprive of support, to weaken, to unsettle.

rugby /'rʌgbi/ *n.* (in full **rugby football**) a contact sport played with an oval ball which may be carried as well as kicked. —**Rugby League,** a partly professional form of rugby football founded in England in 1895 as the Northern Union when a dispute about pay caused northern clubs to break away from the Rugby Football Union. The game is similar to Rugby Union, but the number of players was reduced from 15 to 13 in 1906, and other rule changes have made the game more open and fast-moving. **Rugby Union,** the amateur form of rugby football in which there are 15 players on each side. 'Tries' are scored by 'touching down' the ball beyond the goal line or by kicking goals from penalties. The Rugby Football Union was formed in 1871 and has its headquarters in England (Twickenham, Middlesex). [from *Rugby School*, Warwickshire, England, where it developed]

rugged /'rʌgɪd/ *adj.* **1.** having a rough, uneven surface or outline; (of the features) irregular and strongly marked. **2.** (of manner etc.) rough but kindly and sincere. **3.** harsh-sounding. **4.** sturdy. —**ruggedly** *adv.*, **ruggedness** *n.*

rugger /'rʌgə/ *n.* (*colloquial*) rugby football.

Ruhr /ruə/ river in West Germany; it rises in the Rothaargebirge and flows W to join the Rhine at Duisburg. The **Ruhr valley** (228 km/142 mi), a metropolitan industrial area (petrochemicals, cars; iron and steel at Duisburg and Dortmund) was formerly a coalmining centre.

ruin /'ru:ɪn/ *n.* **1.** severe damage or destruction; a destroyed or wrecked state. **2.** complete loss of fortune, resources, or prospects. **3.** (in *singular* or *plural*) the remains of something that has suffered ruin. **4.** a cause of ruin. —*v.t.* to bring into a state of ruin; to damage so severely that it is in ruins; (in *past participle*) reduced to ruins. —**ruination** /-'neɪʃən/ *n.* [from Old French from Latin *ruina* (*ruere* = fall)]

ruinous /'ru:ɪnəs/ *adj.* **1.** bringing or likely to bring ruin, disastrous. **2.** in ruins, dilapidated. —**ruinously** *adv.* [from Latin *ruinosus*]

Ruisdael /'raɪzdɑːl/ or **Ruysdael** Jacob van *c.*1628–1682. Dutch landscape painter, active in Amsterdam from about 1655. He painted rural scenes near his native town of Haarlem and in Germany, and excelled in depicting gnarled and weatherbeaten trees. The few figures in his pictures were painted by other artists.

rule *n.* **1.** a statement of what can, must, or should be done in a certain set of circumstances or in playing a game; the customary or normal state of things or course of action. **2.** government, exercise of authority, control. **3.** a graduated, straight, often jointed, measuring device used by carpenters etc. **4.** a thin line or dash in printing. **5.** the code of discipline of a religious order. **6.** in law, an order made by a judge or court with reference to a particular case only. —*v.t./i.* **1.** to have authoritative control over, to govern. **2.** to keep under control; to exercise a decisive influence over. **3.** to give a decision as judge or other authority. **4.** to mark parallel lines across (paper); to make (a straight line) with a ruler etc. —**as a rule,** usually, more often than not. **rule of law,** the doctrine that no individual, however powerful, is above the law. The principle had a significant influence on attempts to restrain the arbitrary use of power by rulers and on the growth of legally enforceable human rights in many Western countries. It is often used as a justification for separating legislative from judicial power. **rule of thumb,** a rule based on experience or practice, not on theory. **rule**

out, to exclude, to pronounce irrelevant or ineligible. **rule the roost,** to be in control, to dominate. [from Old French from Latin *regula*]

ruler *n.* **1.** a person who rules by authority, especially over a country etc. **2.** a straight strip of wood or metal etc. used for measuring or for drawing straight lines.

ruling *n.* an authoritative pronouncement.

rum¹ *n.* a spirit fermented and distilled from sugar cane. Scummings from the sugar-pans produce the best rum, molasses the lowest grade.

rum² *adj.* (*colloquial*) strange, odd. [16th-century slang, originally = excellent]

rumba /'rʌmbə/ *n.* a ballroom dance of Cuban origin, danced on the spot with a pronounced movement of the hips; the music for this. [American Spanish]

rumble¹ *v.i.* to make a continuous deep sound as of distant thunder; (of a person or vehicle) to go along making such a sound. —*n.* a rumbling sound.

rumble² *v.t.* (*slang*) to see through (a deception), to detect the true character of.

rumbustious /rʌm'bʌstʃəs/ *adj.* (*colloquial*) boisterous, uproarious.

ruminant /'ru:mɪnənt/ *n.* an even-toed, hoofed mammal with a rumen, the 'first stomach' of the complex digestive system. Plant food is stored and fermented before being brought back to the mouth for chewing (chewing the cud), and then is swallowed to the next stomach. Ruminants include cattle, antelopes, goats, deer, and giraffes. —*adj.* **1.** belonging to the ruminants. **2.** meditative.

ruminate /'ru:mɪneɪt/ *v.i.* **1.** to chew the cud. **2.** to ponder, to meditate. —**rumination** /-'neɪʃən/ *n.*, **ruminative** *adj.* [from Latin *ruminari* (*rumen* = throat)]

rummage /'rʌmɪdʒ/ *v.t./i.* **1.** to search by turning things over or disarranging them. **2.** to discover thus. —*n.* a search of this kind. —**rummage sale,** a jumble sale. [originally = arranging of casks in hold, from Old French *arrumer* = stow]

rummy *n.* a card game played usually with two packs, each player seeking to dispose of his cards by forming sequences or sets. It probably derives from mah-jongg.

rumour /'ru:mə/ *n.* information spread by word of mouth, of doubtful accuracy. —*v.t.* (usually in *passive*) to spread as a rumour. [from Old French from Latin *rumor* = noise]

rump *n.* **1.** the tail-end or buttocks of an animal, person, or bird. **2.** a cut of meat from an animal's hindquarters. **3.** an unimportant remnant. —**rump steak,** a steak cut from a rump of beef.

rumple *v.t./i.* to make or become crumpled; to make (something smooth) untidy. [from Middle Dutch *rompe* = wrinkle]

Rump, the the English Parliament formed between Dec 1648 and Nov 1653 after ◊Pride's Purge of the ◊Long Parliament to ensure a majority in favour of trying Charles I. It was dismissed in 1653 by Cromwell, who replaced it with the ◊Barebones Parliament. Reinstated after the Protectorate ended in 1659 and the full membership of the Long Parliament restored by ◊Monk in 1660, it dissolved itself shortly afterwards and was replaced by the Convention Parliament which brought about the restoration of the monarchy.

rumpus /'rʌmpəs/ *n.* (*colloquial*) an uproar; an angry dispute.

run *v.t./i.* (**-nn-**; *past* **ran**; *past participle* **run**) **1.** to move with quick steps, never having both or all feet on the ground at once; in cricket, to traverse the pitch to score a run. **2.** to flee. **3.** to go or travel hurriedly or swiftly; (of a ship) to go straight and fast; (of salmon) to go up river in large numbers from the sea. **4.** to compete in a race or contest; to seek election. **5.** to advance (as) by rolling or on wheels, or smoothly or easily. **6.** to be in action or operation; to be current or valid. **7.** (of a bus, train etc.) to travel from point to point; to convey (a person) in a vehicle; to smuggle (guns etc.). **8.** to extend; to have a course, order, or tendency. **9.** to flow or cause to flow; to fill (a bath etc.) thus; to exude liquid; to be wet. **10.** to spread rapidly or beyond the intended limit. **11.** to make one's way through or over (a course, race, distance etc.); to perform (an errand). **12.** to own and use (a vehicle etc.); to operate (a business). **13.** to cause to run, go, extend, or function. **14.** (of a newspaper) to print as an item. **15.** to sew (fabric) with running stitches. —*n.* **1.** an act or spell of running. **2.** a short excursion; a distance travelled. **3.** a general tendency of development; a regular route. **4.** a continuous or long stretch, spell, or course; a high general demand; a quantity produced in one period of operation. **5.** the general or average type or class. **6.** a point scored in cricket or baseball. **7.** permission to make unrestricted use of something. **8.** an animal's regular track; an enclosure where domestic animals can range; a track for some purpose. **9.** a large number of salmon going up river from the sea. **10.** a ladder in a stocking etc. **—on the run,** fleeing from pursuit or capture. **run across,** to happen to meet or find. **run away,** to leave secretly or hastily. **run away with,** to elope with; to win (a prize etc.) easily; to accept (an idea) too hastily; to require (much money) in expense. **run down,** to knock down with a moving vehicle or ship; to reduce the numbers of; (of a clock) to stop because not rewound; to discover after searching; to disparage; (in *passive*) to be weak or exhausted from overwork or undernourishment. **run-down** *n.* a reduction in numbers; a detailed analysis; (*adj.*) decayed after being prosperous. **run dry,** to cease to flow. **run for it,** to seek safety by fleeing. **run for one's money,** some return for outlay or effort. **run in,** to run (a new engine or vehicle) carefully in the early stages; (*colloquial*) to arrest. **run into,** to collide with; to encounter; to reach as many as. **run off,** to run away; to produce (copies etc.) on a machine; to decide (a race) after a tie or heats; to flow or cause to flow away; to write or recite fluently. **run-of-the-mill** *adj.* ordinary, undistinguished. **run out,** to come to an end, to become used up; to exhaust one's stock; to jut out; to put down the wicket of (a batsman who is running). **run out on,** (*colloquial*) to desert (a person). **run over,** to overflow; to study or repeat quickly; (of a vehicle or driver) to pass over, to knock down or crush. **run through,** to examine or rehearse briefly; to deal successively with. **run to,** to have the money or ability for; to reach (an amount or number; to show a tendency to (fat etc.). **run up,** to accumulate (a debt etc.) quickly; to build hurriedly; to make quickly by sewing; to add up (a column of figures); to raise (a flag). **run-up** *n.* the period preceding an important event. **run up against,** to meet with (a difficulty). [Old English]

runaway *n.* a fugitive. —*adj.* **1.** fugitive. **2.** (of a victory) won easily.

Runcie /ˈrʌnsi/ Robert (Alexander Kennedy) 1921– . English cleric, archbishop of Canterbury 1980–91, the first to be appointed on the suggestion of the Church Crown Appointments Commission (formed in 1977) rather than by political consultation. He favoured ecclesiastical remarriage for the divorced and the eventual introduction of the ordination of women.

Rundstedt /ˈrʊndstet/ Karl Rudolf Gerd von 1875–1953. German field marshal in World War II. Largely responsible for the German breakthrough in France in 1940, he was defeated on the Ukrainian front in 1941. As commander in chief in France from 1942, he resisted the Allied invasion of 1944 and in Dec launched the temporarily successful Ardennes offensive.

rune /ruːn/ *n.* **1.** any letter of the earliest Germanic alphabet, used especially by the Scandinavians and Anglo-Saxons from about the 3rd century and formed by modifying Roman or Greek characters to suit carving. Runes were scratched on wood, metal, stone or bone. **2.** a letter of a similar alphabet of 8th-century Mongolian Turks. **3.** a similar mark of mysterious or magical significance. **4.** a Finnish poem; a division of this. **—runic** *adj.* [from Old Norse = magic signs]

rung[1] *n.* **1.** a cross-piece of a ladder (*literal* or *figurative*). **2.** a short stick fixed as a cross bar in a chair etc. [Old English]

rung[2] past participle of ◊ring[2].

runnel /ˈrʌnəl/ *n.* **1.** a brook. **2.** a gutter. [Old English]

runner *n.* **1.** one who or that which runs; a person or animal that runs in a race. **2.** a messenger. **3.** a creeping plant-stem that can take root, a type of ◊stolon. **4.** a rod, groove, or roller for a thing to move on; each of the long strips on which a sledge etc. slides. **5.** a long, narrow strip of carpet, or of ornamental cloth for a table etc. **—runner bean,** a kind of climbing bean *Phaseolus multiflorus.* **runner-up** *n.* a person or team finishing second in a competition.

running *n.* the action of runners in a race etc.; the way a race proceeds. —*adj.* **1.** performed while running. **2.** continuous. **3.** consecutive. **—in** *or* **out of the running,**

with a good (or no) chance of succeeding. **make the running,** to set the pace (*literal* or *figurative*). **running commentary,** a spoken description of events as they occur. **running knot,** a knot that slips along a rope etc. so that the size of the loop is changed. **running repairs,** minor repairs and replacements. **running stitch,** a line of evenly spaced stitches made by a straight thread passing in and out of the material.

runny *adj.* **1.** tending to flow or exude fluid. **2.** semi-liquid; excessively fluid.

runt *n.* an undersized person or animal; the smallest of a litter.

runway *n.* a specially prepared surface for the taking off and landing of aircraft.

Runyon /ˈrʌnjən/ Damon 1884–1946. US journalist, primarily a sports reporter, whose short stories in *Guys and Dolls* 1932 deal wryly with the seamier side of New York City life in his own invented jargon.

rupee /ruːˈpiː/ *n.* the currency unit of India, Pakistan, Nepál, Bhutan, Sri Lanka, Mauritius, the Maldives, and the Seychelles. [from Hindi from Sanskrit = wrought silver]

Rupert /ˈruːpət/ Prince 1619–1682. English Royalist general and admiral, born in Prague, son of the Elector Palatine Frederick V (1596–1632) and James I's daughter Elizabeth. Defeated by Cromwell at ◊Marston Moor and ◊Naseby in the Civil War, he commanded a privateering fleet 1649–52, until routed by Admiral Robert Blake, and, returning after the Restoration, was a distinguished admiral in the Dutch Wars. He founded the ◊Hudson's Bay Company.

rupture /ˈrʌptʃə/ *n.* **1.** breaking, breach. **2.** a breach of harmonious relations, disagreement and parting. **3.** an abdominal ◊hernia. —*v.t./i.* **1.** to burst or break (tissue etc.); to become burst or broken. **2.** to sever (a connection). **3.** to affect with or suffer a hernia. [from Old French or from Latin *rumpere* = break]

rural /ˈrʊərəl/ *adj.* in, of, or suggesting the countryside. **—rural dean, Christian clerics,** see ◊dean[1]. **rural district,** (*historical*) a group of country parishes governed by an elected council. [from Old French or Latin *rus* = the country]

ruse /ruːz/ *n.* a stratagem, a trick. [from Old French *ruser* = drive back]

rush[1] *v.t./i.* **1.** to go, move, or pass precipitately or with great speed. **2.** to impel or carry along rapidly. **3.** to act hastily; to force into hasty action. **4.** to attack or capture with a sudden assault. —*n.* **1.** rushing; an instance of this. **2.** a period of great activity. **3.** a sudden migration of large numbers. **4.** a sudden great demand for goods etc. **5.** (in *plural, colloquial*) the first print or showing of a film after shooting, before it is cut and edited. **—rush one's fences,** to act with undue haste. **rush-hour** *n.* the time each morning and evening when traffic or business is heaviest. [Anglo-French *russher* = Old French *ruser*]

rush[2] *n.* a marsh plant of the genus *Juncus* with slender pith-filled stems, found in cold and temperate regions, used for making chair-seats or baskets etc.; a stem of this. **—rush candle,** a candle made by dipping the pith of a rush in tallow. **—rushy** *adj.* [Old English]

Rushdie /ˈrʊʃdi/ (Ahmed) Salman 1947– . British writer, born in India of a Muslim family. His novel *The Satanic Verses* 1988 (the title refers to verses deleted from the Koran) offended many Muslims with alleged blasphemy. In 1989 the Ayatollah Khomeini of Iran called for Rushdie and his publishers to be killed.

rusk *n.* a slice of bread rebaked as a light biscuit, especially for feeding infants. [from Spanish or Portuguese *rosca* = twist, roll of bread]

Rusk /rʌsk/ Dean 1909– . US Democrat politician. He was secretary of state to presidents Kennedy and L B Johnson 1961–69, and became unpopular through his involvement with the ◊Vietnam War.

Ruskin /ˈrʌskɪn/ John 1819–1900. English art critic and social critic. He published five volumes of *Modern Painters* 1843–60; *The Seven Lamps of Architecture* 1849, in which he stated his philosophy of art; and *The Stones of Venice* 1851–53, in which he drew moral lessons from architectural history. His writings hastened the appreciation of painters considered unorthodox at the time, such as ◊Turner and the ◊Pre-Raphaelite Brotherhood. His later writings were concerned with social and economic problems.

Russian history

	The southern steppes of Russia were originally inhabited by nomadic peoples, and the northern forests by Slavonic peoples who slowly spread southwards.
9th–10th centuries	Viking chieftains established their own rule in Novgorod, Kiev, and other cities.
10th–12th centuries	Kiev temporarily united the Russian peoples into an empire. Christianity was introduced from Constantinople in 988.
13th century	The Mongols (the Golden Horde) overran the southern steppes 1223, compelling the Russian princes to pay tribute.
14th century	Byelorussia and Ukraine came under Polish rule.
1462–1505	Ivan III (the Great), prince of Moscow, threw off the Mongol yoke and united the northwest.
1547–84	Ivan IV (the Terrible) assumed the title of tsar and conquered Kazan and Astrakhan. During his reign the colonization of Siberia began.
1613	The first Romanov tsar, Michael, was elected after a period of chaos.
1667	Following a Cossack revolt, E Ukraine was reunited with Russia.
1682–1725	Peter I (the Great) modernized the bureaucracy and army. He founded a navy and a new capital, St Petersburg (now Leningrad); introduced Western education; and wrested the Baltic seaboard from Sweden. By 1700 the colonization of Siberia had reached the Pacific.
1762–96	Catherine II (the Great) annexed the Crimea and part of Poland and recovered W Ukraine and White Russia.
1798–1814	Russia intervened in the Revolutionary and Napoleonic Wars (1798–1801, 1805–07) and after repelling Napoleon's invasion, took part in his overthrow (1812–14).
1827–29	War with Turkey resulted from Russian attempts to dominate the Balkans.
1853–56	The ◊Crimean War.
1858–60	The treaties of Aigun 1858 and Peking 1860 were imposed on China, annexing territories north of the Amur and east of the Ussuri rivers.
1861	Serfdom was abolished (on terms unfavourable to the peasants). A rapid growth of industry followed, a working-class movement developed, and revolutionary ideas spread, culminating in the assassination of Alexander II in 1881.
1877–78	Balkan war with Turkey.
1898	The Social Democratic Party was founded.
1904–05	The occupation of Manchuria resulted in war with Japan (see ◊Russo-Japanese War).
1905	A revolution, although suppressed, compelled the tsar to accept a parliament (the Duma) with limited powers.
1914	Russo-German rivalries in the Balkans, which had brought Russia into an alliance with France 1895 and Britain 1907, were one of the causes of the outbreak of World War I.
1917	During World I, the ◊Russian Revolution began.
	For subsequent history, see ◊Union of Soviet Socialist Republics.

Remember that the most beautiful things in the world are the most useless; peacocks and lilies for instance.
John Ruskin
The Stones of Venice

Russell /ˈrʌsəl/ Bertrand (Arthur William), 3rd Earl Russell 1872–1970. English philosopher and mathematician, who contributed to the development of modern mathematical logic and wrote about social issues. His works include *Principia Mathematica* 1910–13 (with A N ◊Whitehead), in which he attempted to show that mathematics could be reduced to a branch of logic; *The Problems of Philosophy* 1912; and *A History of Western Philosophy* 1946. He was an outspoken liberal pacifist.

Russell George William 1867–1935. Irish poet and essayist. An ardent nationalist, he helped found the Irish national theatre, and his poetry, published under the pseudonym 'AE', includes *Gods of War* 1915 and reflects his interest in mysticism and theosophy.

Russell Jane 1921– . US actress who was discovered by producer Howard Hughes. Her first film, *The Outlaw* 1943, was not properly released for several years owing to censorship problems. Her other films include *The Paleface* 1948, *Gentlemen Prefer Blondes* 1953, and *The Revolt of Mamie Stover* 1957. She retired in 1970.

Russell John, 1st Earl Russell 1792–1878. British Liberal politician, son of the 6th Duke of Bedford. He entered the House of Commons in 1813 and supported Catholic emancipation and the Reform Bill. He held cabinet posts 1830–41, became prime minister 1846–52, and was again a cabinet minister until becoming prime minister again 1865–66. He retired after the defeat of his Reform Bill in 1866.

Russell Ken 1927– . English film director whose work includes *Women in Love* 1969, *Altered States* 1979, and *Salome's Last Dance* 1988.

Russell Lord William 1639–1683. British Whig politician. Son of the 1st Duke of Bedford, he was among the founders of the Whig Party, and actively supported attempts in

Parliament to exclude the Roman Catholic James II from succeeding to the throne. In 1683 he was accused, on dubious evidence, of complicity in the ◊Rye House Plot to murder Charles II, and was executed.

russet /ˈrʌsit/ adj. reddish-brown —n. 1. russet colour. 2. an apple with a rough skin of this colour. [from Anglo-French, ultimately from Latin *russus* = red]

Russia /ˈrʌʃə/ originally the name of the pre-revolutionary Russian Empire (until 1917), and now accurately restricted to the ◊Russian Soviet Federative Socialist Republic only. It is incorrectly used to refer to the whole of the present ◊Union of Soviet Socialist Republics.

Russian /ˈrʌʃən/ adj. of Russia (the largest republic in the USSR) or its people or language; (loosely) of the USSR. —n. 1. a native or inhabitant of Russia or (loosely) of the USSR. 2. the official language of the USSR; see ◊Russian language. —**Russian roulette**, the firing of a revolver held to one's head after spinning the cylinder with one chamber loaded. **Russian salad**, a salad of mixed diced vegetables coated with mayonnaise.

Russian art painting and other products of the visual arts made in Russia and later in the USSR. From the 10th to the 17th century Russian art was dominated by the Eastern Orthodox Church and was influenced by various styles of Byzantine art. Painters such as Andrei Rublev produced icons, images of holy figures that were often considered precious. By the 17th century European influence had grown strong and in the 18th century the tsars imported European sculptors and painters. Early Russian Modernism 1910–30 anticipated Western trends but was then suppressed in favour of art geared to the sentimental glorification of workers.

Russian civil war a bitter conflict of nearly three years which followed Russian setbacks in World War I and the upheavals of the 1917 Revolution. In Dec 1917 counterrevolutionary armies, the 'Whites' began to organize resistance to the October Revolution of 1917. The Red Army (Bolsheviks), improvised by Leon Trotsky, opposed them and civil war resulted. Hostilities continued for nearly three years with the Bolsheviks being successful.

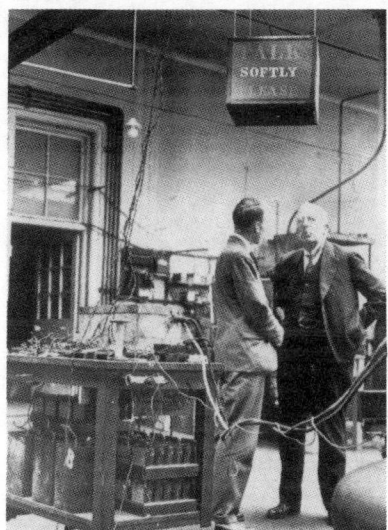

Rutherford British physicist Ernest Rutherford (right) with J Ratcliffe in Cambridge, 1935. He discovered the core of the atom which he called the nucleus,and three kinds of radiation, alpha, beta, and gamma rays.

Russian language a member of the Slavonic branch of the Indo-European language family. The people of Russia proper refer to it as Great Russian, in contrast with Ukrainian (which they call Little Russian) and the language of Byelorussia (White Russian). It is written in the Cyrillic alphabet and is the standard means of communication throughout the USSR.

Russian Revolution two revolutions of Feb and Oct 1917 (Julian calendar) that began with the overthrow of the Romanov dynasty and ended with the establishment of a communist soviet (council) state, the Union of Socialist Soviet Republics (USSR). The **February Revolution** (Mar Western calendar) arose because of food and fuel shortages, the ongoing repressiveness of the tsarist government, and military incompetence in World War I. Riots in Petrograd led to the abdication of Tsar Nicholas II and the formation of a provisional government under Prince Lvov. They had little support as troops, communications, and transport were controlled by the Petrograd workers' and soldiers' council. ◊Lenin returned to Russia in Apr as head of the ◊Bolsheviks. Kerensky replaced Lvov as head of government in July. During this period, the Bolsheviks gained control of the soviets and advocated land reform (under the slogan 'All power to the soviets') and an end to their involvement in World War I.

The **October Revolution** was a coup on the night of 25–26 Oct (6–7 Nov Western calendar). Bolshevik workers and sailors seized the government buildings and the Winter Palace, Petrograd. The second All-Russian Congress of Soviets, which met the following day, proclaimed itself the new government of Russia, and Lenin became leader. Bolsheviks soon took control of the cities, established worker control in factories, and nationalized the banks. The ◊Cheka (secret police) was set up to silence the opposition. The government concluded peace with Germany early in 1918 through the Treaty of ◊Brest-Litovsk, but civil war broke out in that year when anti-Bolshevik elements within the army attempted to seize power. The war lasted until 1922, when the Red Army, organized by ◊Trotsky, finally overcame 'White' (Tsarist) opposition, but with huge losses, after which communist control was complete.

Russian Soviet Federal Socialist Republic (abbreviated RSFSR; Russian *Rossiyskaya*) constituent republic of the USSR; **area** 17,075,000 sq km/6,592,658 sq mi; **capital** Moscow; **physical** largest of the Soviet republics (occupies about three-quarters of the USSR); includes the fertile Black Earth district; extensive forests; the Ural

Mountains with large mineral resources; **features** the heavily industrialized area around Moscow; Siberia; includes 16 autonomous republics; **products** three-quarters of the agricultural and industrial output of the USSR; **population** (1987) 145,311,000; 83% Russian; **language** Great Russian; **recent history** see ◊Union of Soviet Socialist Republics; **Autonomous Soviet Socialist Republics** (capitals in brackets): Bashkir (Ufa); Buryat (Ulan-Udé); Checheno-Ingush (Grozny); Chuvash (Cheboksary); Dagestan (Makhachkala); Kabardino-Balkar (Nalchik); Kalmyk (Elista); Karelia (Petrozavodsk); Komi (Syktyvkar); Mari (Yoshkar-Ola); Mordovia (Saransk); North Ossetia (Ordzhonikidze); Tatar (Kazan); Tuva (Kizyl); Udmurt (Izhevsk); Yakut (Yakutsk).

Russo-Japanese War war between Russia and Japan 1904–05, which arose from conflicting ambitions in Korea and ◊Manchuria, specifically, the Russian occupation of Port Arthur (modern Lüda) in 1896 and of the Amur province in 1900. Japan successfully besieged Port Arthur from May 1904 to Jan 1905, took Mukden between 29 Feb and 10 Mar, and on 27 May defeated the Russian Baltic fleet, which had sailed halfway around the world to Tsushima Strait. A peace was signed in Portsmouth, New Hampshire, USA, on 23 Aug 1905. Russia surrendered its lease on Port Arthur, ceded S Sakhalin to Japan, evacuated Manchuria, and recognized Japan's interests in Korea.

russula *n.* any fungus of the genus *Russula*, comprising many species. They are medium to large mushrooms with flattened caps, and many are brightly coloured. *R. emetica* is a common species found in damp places under conifers. Up to 9 cm/3.5 in across, the cap is scarlet, fading to cherry, and the gills are white. This toadstool tastes acrid and causes vomiting eaten raw, but some russulas are edible.

rust /rʌst/ *n.* **1.** a reddish or yellowish-brown corrosive coating (hydrated iron (III) or ferric oxide $Fe_2O_3.H_2O$) formed on iron or steel by oxidation. **2.** reddish-brown. **3.** minute parasitic fungi of the order Uredinales, which appear on the leaves of their hosts as orange-red spots, later becoming darker. The commonest is the wheat rust, *Puccinia graminis*. **4.** an impaired state due to disuse or inactivity. —*v.t./i.* **1.** to make or become rusty. **2.** to lose quality or efficiency by disuse or inactivity. [Old English, relative to *red*]

Rust Mathias 1968– . German aviator who in May 1987 piloted a light plane from Finland to Moscow, landing in Red Square. Found guilty of 'malicious hooliganism', he was imprisoned until 1988.

rustic /'rʌstɪk/ *adj.* **1.** having the appearance or qualities ascribed to country people or peasants, simple and unsophisticated, rough and unrefined. **2.** made of untrimmed branches or rough timber. —*n.* a country dweller, a peasant. —**rustically** *adv.*, **rusticity** /-'tɪsɪtɪ/ *n.* [from Latin *rusticus* (*rus* = the country)]

rusticate /'rʌstɪkeɪt/ *v.t./i.* **1.** to send down temporarily from a university as a punishment. **2.** to retire to or live in the country. **3.** to mark (masonry) with sunk joints or a roughened surface. —**rustication** /-'keɪʃən/ *n.* [from Latin *rusticare* = live in the country]

rustle /'rʌsəl/ *v.t./i.* **1.** to make or cause to make a gentle sound as of dry leaves blown in a breeze. **2.** to steal (cattle or horses). —*n.* a rustling sound. —**rustle up**, (*colloquial*) to produce when needed. —**rustler** *n.*

rustless *adj.* not liable to rust.

rusty *adj.* **1.** rusted, affected by rust. **2.** stiff with age or disuse; (of knowledge etc.) faded or impaired by neglect. **3.** rust-coloured; (of black clothes) discoloured by age. —**rustily** *adv.* **rustiness** *n.*

rut¹ *n.* **1.** a deep track made by the passage of wheels. **2.** a fixed pattern of behaviour difficult to change; a habitual usually dull course of life. [probably from Old French = road]

rut² *n.* the periodic sexual excitement of male deer etc. —*v.i.* (-tt-) to be affected with rut. [from Old French from Latin *rugitus* (*rugire* = roar)]

Ruth /ruːθ/ in the Old Testament, Moabite (see ◊Moab) ancestress of David (king of Israel) by her second marriage to Boaz. When her first husband died, she preferred to stay with her mother-in-law, Naomi, rather than return to her own people.

Ruthenia /ruːˈθiːnɪə/ or **Carpathian Ukraine** region of central Europe, on the southern slopes of the Carpathian mountains, home of the Ruthenes or Russniaks. Dominated by Hungary from the 10th century, it was part of Austria-Hungary until World War I. Divided among Czechoslovakia, Poland, and Romania in 1918, it was independent for a single day in 1938, immediately occupied by Hungary, captured by the USSR in 1944, and 1945–47 became incorporated into Ukraine Republic, USSR.

ruthenium /ruːˈθiːnɪəm/ n. a rare hard, brittle, silver-white, metallic element, symbol Ru, atomic number 44, relative atomic mass 101.07. It is one of the so-called platinum group of metals; it occurs in platinum ores as a free metal and in the natural alloy osmiridium. It is used as a hardener in alloys and as a catalyst; its compounds are used as colouring agents in glass and ceramics. [from Latin *Ruthenia = Russia (from its discovery in ores from the Urals*]

Rutherford /ˈrʌðəfəd/ Ernest 1871–1937. New Zealand physicist, a pioneer of modern atomic science. His main research was in the field of radioactivity, and he discovered alpha, beta, and gamma rays. He named the nucleus, and was the first to recognize the ionizing nature of the atom. He won the Nobel Prize for Physics in 1908.

Rutherford Margaret 1892–1972. English film and theatre actress who specialized in playing formidable yet jovially eccentric roles. She played Agatha Christie's Miss Marple in four films in the early 1960s and won an Academy Award for her role in *The VIPs* 1963.

rutherfordium /rʌðəˈfɔːdɪəm/ n. a name proposed by US scientists for the element currently known as ◊unnilquadium (atomic number 104), to honour New Zealand physicist Ernest Rutherford.

ruthless /ˈruːθlɪs/ adj. having no pity or compassion. —**ruthlessly** adv., **ruthlessness** n. [from *ruth* = pity, from *rue*[1]]

rutile n. TiO$_2$, titanium oxide, a naturally occurring mineral of titanium. It is usually reddish brown to black, with a very bright (adamantine) surface lustre. It crystallizes in the tetragonal system. Rutile is common in a wide range of igneous and metamorphic rocks and also occurs concentrated in sands; the coastal sands of E and W Australia are a major source. Rutile is also used as a pigment that gives a brilliant white to paint, paper, and plastics.

Rutland /ˈrʌtlənd/ formerly the smallest English county, now part of ◊Leicestershire.

rutted /ˈrʌtɪd/ adj. marked with ruts.

Ruwenzori /ruːənˈzɔːri/ mountain range on the frontier between Zaïre and Uganda, rising to 5,119 m/16,794 ft at Mount Stanley.

Ruysdael Jacob van see ◊Ruisdael, Dutch painter.

Ruyter /ˈraɪtə/ Michael Adrianszoon de 1607–1676. Dutch admiral who led his country's fleet in the wars against England. On 1–4 June 1666 he forced the British fleet under Rupert and Albemarle to retire into the Thames, but on 25 July was heavily defeated off the North Foreland, Kent. In 1667 he sailed up the Medway to burn three men-of-war at Chatham, and captured others.

RV abbreviation of Revised Version (of the Bible).

Rwanda /ruːˈændə/ landlocked country in central Africa, bounded to the N by Uganda, to the E by Tanzania, to the S by Burundi, and to the W by Zaïre; **area** 26,338 sq km/10,173 sq mi; **capital** Kigali; **physical** high savanna and hills with volcanic mountains in NW; part of lake Kivu; highest peak Mount Karisimbi 4,507 m/14,792 ft; Kagera river (whose headwaters are the source of the Nile) and National Park; **head of state and government** Juvenal Habyarimana from 1973; **political system** one-party military republic; **exports** coffee, tea, pyrethrum, tin, tungsten; **population** (1990 est) 7,603,000; **language** Kinyarwanda, French (official), Kiswahili; **recent history** 1916 League of Nations mandated Rwanda and Burundi to Belgium as Territory of Ruanda-Urundi; 1962 independence from Belgium achieved; 1973 military coup led by Major-Gen Juvenal Habyarimana; 1980 civilian rule adopted; 1990 Rwandan Patriotic Army attacked government, constitutional reforms promised.

Ryan /ˈraɪən/ Robert 1909–1973. US theatre and film actor who was equally impressive in leading and character roles. His films include *Woman on the Beach* 1947, *The Set-Up* 1949, and *The Wild Bunch* 1969.

Rybinsk /ˈrɪbɪnsk/ port and industrial city (engineering) on the Volga, NE of Moscow in the Russian Soviet Federal

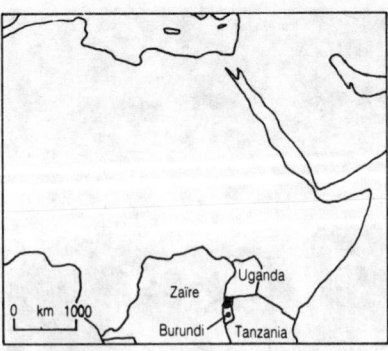

Rwanda

Socialist Republic; population (1987) 254,000. Between 1984 and 1988 it was named **Andropov** after a president of the USSR.

Rydberg constant /ˈrɪdbɜːg/ in physics, a constant that relates atomic spectra to the ◊spectrum of hydrogen. Its value is 1.0977×10^7 per metre.

Ryder /ˈraɪdə/ Albert Pinkham 1847–1917. US painter who developed one of the most original styles of his time. He painted with broad strokes that tended to simplify form and used yellowish colours that gave his works an eerie, haunted quality. His works are poetic, romantic, and filled with unreality; *Death on a Pale Horse* 1910 (Cleveland Museum of Art) is typical.

Ryder Cup a golf tournament for professional men's teams from the USA and Europe. It is played every two years, and the match is made up of a series of singles, foursomes, and fourballs played over three days.

rye /raɪ/ n. **1.** a cereal plant *Secale cereale*; the grain of this, used for bread and fodder. Rye is grown extensively in N Europe. In Britain, it is principally a forage crop, but the grain is used in the production of crispbread and some health cereals. **2.** (in full **rye whisky**) whisky distilled from rye. [Old English]

rye-grass /ˈraɪgrɑːs/ n. a fodder grass of the genus *Lolium* especially *L. perenne*, common in pastures and waste places. It grows up to 60 cm/24 in high, flowers in midsummer, and sends up abundant nutritious leaves, good for cattle. It is a Eurasian species but has been introduced to Australia and North America.

Ryle /raɪl/ Martin 1918–1984. English radioastronomer. At the Mullard Radio Astronomy Observatory, Cambridge, he developed the technique of sky-mapping using 'aperture synthesis', combining smaller dish aerials to give the characteristics of one large one. His work on the distribution of radio sources in the universe brought confirmation of the ◊Big Bang theory. He won, with Antony ◊Hewish, the Nobel Prize for Physics 1974.

Ryukyu Islands /riˈuːkjuː/ southernmost island group of Japan, stretching towards Taiwan and including Okinawa, Miyako, and Ishigaki; **area** 2,254 sq km/870 sq mi; **capital** Naha, on Okinawa; **features** 73 islands, some uninhabited; subject to typhoons; **products** sugar, pineapples, fish; **population** (1985) 1,179,000; **history** originally an independent kingdom; ruled by China from the late 14th century until seized by Japan in 1609 and controlled by the Satsuma feudal lords until 1868, when the Japanese government took over. Chinese claims to the islands were relinquished in 1895. In World War II the islands were taken by USA in 1945 (see under ◊Okinawa); northernmost group, Oshima, restored to Japan in 1953, the rest in 1972.

Ryzhkov /ˈrɪʒkof/ Nikolai Ivanovich 1929– . Soviet communist politician. He held governmental and party posts from 1975 before being brought into the Politburo and made prime minister in 1985 by Gorbachev. A low-profile technocrat, Ryzhkov is viewed as a more cautious and centralist reformer than Gorbachev. As the author of unpopular economic reforms, he was nearly forced to resign, surviving with the support of Mikhail Gorbachev, only to suffer a heart attack early in 1991.

s, S /es/ *n.* (*plural* **ss, s's** /'esɪz/) **1.** the 19th letter of the alphabet. **2.** an S-shaped thing.

s. abbreviation of **1.** second(s). **2.** shilling(s) [from Latin *solidus*, originally = gold coin of the Roman Empire]. **3.** singular. **4.** son.

's abbreviation of has, is, us.

S abbreviation of **1.** Saint. **2.** south, southern. **3.** siemens.

S symbol for sulphur.

SA abbreviation of **1.** Salvation Army. **2.** South Africa. **3.** South Australia.

SAARC abbreviation of South Asian Association for Regional Cooperation.

Saarinen /'saːrɪnən/ Eero 1910–1961. Finnish-born US architect distinguished for a wide range of innovative modern designs using a variety of creative shapes for buildings. His works include the US embassy, London, the TWA terminal, New York, and Dulles Airport, Washington DC. He collaborated on a number of projects with his father, Eliel Saarinen.

Saarinen Eliel 1873–1950. Finnish architect and town planner, founder of the Finnish Romantic school. In 1923 he emigrated to the USA, where he contributed to US skyscraper design by his work in Chicago, and later turned to functionalism.

Saarland /'saːlænd, German 'zaːlænt/ (French *Sarre*) *Land* (state) of Germany, crossed NW–S by the river Saar; **area** 2,570 sq km/992 sq mi; **capital** Saarbrücken; **physical** one-third of the state is forest; **products** cereals and other crops; cattle, pigs, poultry. Former flourishing coal and steel industries survive only by government subsidy; **population** (1988) 1,034,000; **recent history** in 1919, the Saar district was administered by France under the auspices of the League of Nations; a plebiscite returned it to Germany in 1935; Hitler gave it the name Saarbrücken. Part of the French zone of occupation in 1945, it was part of the economic union with France in 1947. It was returned to Germany in 1957.

Sabatini /sæbə'tiːni/ Gabriela 1970– . Argentine tennis player who in 1986 became the youngest Wimbledon semi-finalist for 99 years. She was ranked number three in the world behind Steffi Graf and Martina Navratilova in 1989 after capturing the Italian Open title.

Sabbatarian /sæbə'teərɪən/ *n.* a person who observes the Sabbath strictly. —**Sabbatarianism** *n.* the belief, held by some Protestant Christians, in the strict observance of the Sabbath, Sunday, following the fourth commandment of the Bible. It began in the 17th century. [from Latin]

Sabbath /'sæbəθ/ *n.* the seventh day of the week, commanded by God in the Old Testament as a sacred day of rest; in Judaism, from sunset Friday to sunset Saturday; in Christianity, Sunday (or, in some sects, Saturday). [Old English, ultimately from Hebrew *shābath* = to rest]

sabbatical /sə'bætɪkəl/ *adj.* **1.** of the Sabbath. **2.** (of leave) granted at intervals to a university professor etc. for study or travel etc. —*n.* a period of sabbatical leave. [from Latin from Greek]

sabin *n.* a unit of sound absorption, used in acoustical engineering. One sabin is the absorption of one square foot (0.093 square metre) of a perfectly absorbing surface (such as an open window).

Sabin /'seɪbɪn/ Albert 1906– . Polish-born US microbiologist whose involvement in the antipolio campaigns led to the development of a new, highly effective, live vaccine. The earlier vaccine, developed by the physicist Jonas ◊Salk, was based on heat-killed viruses. Sabin was convinced that a live form would be longer-lasting and more effective, and he succeeded in weakening the virus so that it lost its virulence. The vaccine can be orally administered.

Sabine /'sæbaɪn/ *n.* a member of an ancient people of central Italy, conquered by the Romans and amalgamated with them in the 3rd century BC. The so-called rape of the Sabine women, a mythical attempt by ◊Romulus in the early days of Rome to carry off the Sabine women to colonize the new city, is frequently depicted in art.

sable /'seɪbəl/ *n.* **1.** a small dark-furred arctic mammal *Martes zibellina* or *M. americana*; its fur or skin. **2.** in heraldry, the colour black. —*adj.* black, gloomy. [from Old French, ultimately from Slavonic]

sabot /'sæbəʊ/ *n.* a heavy wooden or wooden-soled shoe. [French]

sabotage /'sæbətaːʒ/ *n.* malicious or wanton damage or destruction, especially for an industrial or political purpose. —*v.t.* to commit sabotage on; to destroy or render useless, to spoil. [French, from *saboter* = make a noise with sabots, perform or execute badly, destroy (tools, machinery etc.) wilfully]

saboteur /sæbə'tɜː/ *n.* one who commits sabotage. [French]

sabre /'seɪbə/ *n.* **1.** a cavalry sword with a curved blade. **2.** a light fencing sword with a tapering blade. —**sabre-rattling** *n.* a display or threats of military force. [French, earlier *sable*, ultimately from Polish or Magyar]

sac /sæk/ *n.* a membranous bag in an animal or vegetable organism. [French or from Latin *saccus* = sack]

saccharide *n.* the scientific term for a ◊sugar molecule. Saccharides can be joined together in long chains to form ◊polysaccharides.

saccharin /'sækərɪn/ *n.* $C_7H_5NO_3S$ (technical name **ortho-sulpho benzimide**) a sweet, white, crystalline solid derived from coal tar and substituted for sugar. Since 1977 it has been regarded as potentially carcinogenic. [German from Latin *saccharum* = sugar]

saccharine /'sækəriːn/ *adj.* intensely sweet, cloying.

Sacco-Vanzetti case /'sækəʊvæn'zeti/ a murder trial in Massachusetts, USA, 1920–21. Italian immigrants Nicola Sacco (1891–1927) and Bartolomeo Vanzetti (1888–1927) were convicted of murder during an alleged robbery. The conviction was upheld on appeal, with application for retrial denied. Prolonged controversy delayed execution until 1927. In 1977 the verdict was declared unjust because of the judge's prejudice against the accuseds' anarchist views.

sacerdotal /sækə'dəʊtəl/ *adj.* of priests or priestly office. [from Old French or Latin *sacerdos* = priest]

Sacher-Masoch /'zæxə 'maːzɒx/ Leopold von 1836–1895. Austrian novelist. His books dealt with the sexual pleasure of having pain inflicted on oneself, hence ◊masochism.

sachet /'sæʃeɪ/ *n.* a small bag or packet containing a portion of a substance or filled with a perfumed substance for

Sacco-Vanzetti case *The Italian-American anarchists, Sacco and Vanzetti, entering a Massachusetts courthouse during their trial for murder, 1920–21.*

laying among clothes etc. [French, diminutive of *sac* from Latin *saccus* from Greek]

Sachs /zæks/ Hans 1494–1576. German poet and composer who worked as a master shoemaker in Nuremberg. He composed 4,275 *Meisterlieder/Mastersongs*, and figures prominently in ◊Wagner's opera *Die Meistersinger von Nürnberg.*

sack[1] *n.* **1.** a large, strong bag for storing or conveying goods. **2.** the quantity contained in a sack. **3.** a woman's loose-fitting dress. **4.** (*slang*) a bed. —*v.t.* **1.** to put into a sack or sacks. **2.** (*colloquial*) to dismiss from a job etc. —**the sack,** (*colloquial*) dismissal from a job etc. **hit the sack,** (*slang*) to go to bed. —**sackful** *n.* [Old English from Latin *saccus* from Greek]

sack[2] *v.t.* to plunder and destroy (a captured town etc.). —*n.* the sacking of a town etc. [from French *sac* (in phrase *mettre à sac*), from Italian *sacco*]

sack[3] *n.* (*historical*) a white wine formerly imported from Spain and the Canary Islands. [originally *wyne seck*, from French *vin sec* = dry wine]

sackbut /'sækbʌt/ *n.* a musical instrument of the ◊brass family, a form of trombone, common from the 14th century. [from French *saqueboute* = hook for pulling man off horse]

sackcloth *n.* **1.** a coarse fabric of flax or hemp. **2.** mourning or penitential garb (especially in *sackcloth and ashes*).

sacking *n.* material for making sacks, sackcloth.

Sackville /'sækvɪl/ Thomas, 1st Earl of Dorset 1536–1608. English poet, collaborator with Thomas Norton on *Gorboduc* 1561, written in blank verse and one of the earliest English tragedies.

sacral /'seɪkrəl/ *adj.* **1.** of the ◊sacrum. **2.** of or for sacred rites.

sacrament /'sækrəmənt/ *n.* **1.** a religious ceremony or act regarded as an outward and visible sign of inward and spiritual grace. In the Roman Catholic Church there are seven sacraments: baptism, Holy Communion (Eucharist or mass), confirmation, rite of reconciliation (confession and penance), holy orders, matrimony, and the anointing of the sick. Only the first two are held to be essential by the Church of England. **2.** (in full **Blessed** or **Holy Sacrament**) the Eucharist. **3.** a sacred thing, influence, etc. —**sacramental** /-'mentəl/ *adj.* [from Old French from Latin *sacrare* = hallow, from *sacer* = holy]

sacred /'seɪkrɪd/ *adj.* **1.** associated with or dedicated to God or a god; regarded with reverence because of this. **2.** connected with religion, not secular. **3.** dedicated to some purpose or purpose. **4.** safeguarded or required by religion or tradition, inviolable. —**sacred cow,** any person, institution, or custom that is considered above criticism [from the Hindu belief that cows are sacred and must not be killed]. **Sacred Heart,** in the Roman Catholic Church, the heart of Jesus (or *of Mary*) as an object of devotion. **Sacred Thread ceremony,** a Hindu initiation ceremony that marks the passage to maturity for boys of the upper

three castes; it usually takes place between the ages of five and 12. [past participle of obsolete *sacre* = consecrate from Old French *sacrer* from Latin *sacrare*]

sacrifice /'sækrɪfaɪs/ *n.* **1.** the giving up of a valued thing for the sake of something else that is more important, worthy, or urgent. **2.** the slaughter of a victim or presenting of a gift to win the favour of a deity. **3.** the thing thus given up or offered. **4.** in games, a loss deliberately incurred to avoid greater loss or obtain a compensating advantage. —*v.t./i.* **1.** to give up or offer as a sacrifice. **2.** to devote *to.* —**sacrificial** /-'fɪʃəl/ *adj.* [from Old French from Latin]

sacrilege /'sækrɪlɪdʒ/ *n.* disrespect or damage to something regarded as sacred. —**sacrilegious** /-'lɪdʒəs/ *adj.* [from Old French from Latin *sacrilegus* = stealer of sacred things, from *sacer* = sacred and *legere* = take possession of]

sacristan /'sækrɪstən/ *n.* the person in charge of the sacristy and church contents. [from Latin]

sacristy /'sækrɪstɪ/ *n.* the repository for a church's vestments, vessels, etc. [from French or Italian or Latin *sacristia*]

sacro- /seɪkrəʊ-/ in combinations, of the ◊sacrum.

sacrosanct /'sækrəʊsæŋkt/ *adj.* reverenced or respected and therefore not to be violated or damaged. —**sacrosanctity** /-'sæŋkt-/ *n.* [from Latin *sacer* = sacred and *sanctus* = holy]

sacrum /'seɪkrəm/ *n.* the composite triangular bone forming the back of the pelvis. [from Latin *os sacrum* = sacred bone (from sacrificial use)]

sad *adj.* **1.** showing or causing sorrow, unhappy. **2.** regrettable; deplorably bad. **3.** (of cake or pastry) dense from not having risen. —**sadly** *adv.*, **sadness** *n.* [Old English]

SAD acronym from ◊seasonal affective disorder.

Sadat /sə'dæt/ Anwar 1918–1981. Egyptian politician. Succeeding ◊Nasser as president in 1970, he restored morale by his handling of the Egyptian campaign in the 1973 war against Israel. In 1974 his plan for economic, social, and political reform to transform Egypt was unanimously adopted in a referendum. In 1977 he visited Israel to reconcile the two countries, and in 1978 shared the Nobel Peace Prize with Israeli prime minister Menachem Begin. He was assassinated by Islamic fundamentalists.

sadden *v.t./i.* to make or become sad.

saddle *n.* **1.** a seat of leather etc., usually raised at the front and rear, fastened on a horse etc. for riding. **2.** the seat for the rider of a bicycle etc. **3.** a joint of meat consisting of the two loins. **4.** a ridge rising to a summit at each end. —*v.t.* **1.** to put a saddle on (a horse etc.). **2.** to burden (a person) with a task etc.; to put (a burden etc.) on a person. —**saddlebag** *n.* one of a pair of bags laid across the back of a horse etc.; a bag attached behind the saddle of a bicycle etc. —**in the saddle,** on horseback; in office or control. [Old English]

saddleback *n.* **1.** a saddlebacked hill or roof. **2.** a black pig with a white stripe across its back.

saddlebacked *adj.* with a concave upper outline.

saddler *n.* a maker of or dealer in saddles etc.

saddlery *n.* a saddler's trade or goods.

Sadducee /'sædjusiː/ *n.* a member of an ancient Hebrew sect opposed to the ◊Pharisees. They were an aristocratic group centred on the priesthood in Jerusalem until the final destruction of the Temple. Sadducees denied the immortality of the soul and the existence of angels, and maintained the religious law in all its strictness. Many of their ideas and practices resurfaced in medieval Jewish sects. [Old English ultimately from Hebrew]

Sade /saɪd/ Donatien Alphonse François, Comte de, known as the **Marquis de Sade** 1740–1814. French writer. He was imprisoned for sexual offences and finally committed to an asylum. He wrote plays and novels dealing explicitly with a variety of sexual practices, including ◊sadism.

sadhu /'sɑːduː/ *n.* a Hindu or Jain ascetic and holy mendicant who devotes himself to the goal of *moksha*, or liberation from the cycle of reincarnation. [Sanskrit = holy man]

S'adi or **Saadi** /sɑː'diː/ pen name of Sheikh Moslih Addin *c.*1184–*c.*1291. Persian poet, author of *Bustan/Tree Garden* and *Gulistan/Flower Garden.*

sadism /'seɪdɪzəm/ *n.* enjoyment of cruelty to others; a sexual perversion characterized by this. —**sadist** *n.*,

Sadat *former President Anwar Sadat of Egypt. He shared the 1978 Nobel Peace Prize with the Israeli prime minister Menachem Begin for their efforts to reconcile the two countries.*

sadistic /sə'dɪstɪk/ *adj.*, **sadistically** *adv.* [from French from Marquis de *Sade*]

Sadler's Wells /'sædləz 'welz/ a theatre in Islington, N London, England. Originally a music hall, it was developed by Lilian Baylis as a northern annexe to the ◊Old Vic in 1931. For many years it housed the Sadler's Wells Opera Company and the Sadler's Wells Ballet, which later became the ◊Royal Ballet (transferred to Birmingham (Hippodrome) in 1990).

Sadowa, Battle of /'sædəvɑː/ (also known as the **Battle of Königgrätz**) the Prussian victory over the Austrian army on 3 July 1866, ending the ◊Seven Weeks' War. It confirmed Prussian hegemony over the German states and led to the formation of the North German Confederation in 1867. It took place near the village of Sadowa (Czech *Sadová*) 13 km/8 mi NW of Hradec Kralove (German *Königgrätz*) in Czechoslovakia.

s.a.e. abbreviation of stamped addressed envelope.

safari /sə'fɑːrɪ/ *n.* an overland expedition, especially in Africa. —**safari park**, an area where wild animals are kept in the open for viewing from vehicles. [Swahili, from Arabic *safara* = travel]

safe *adj.* **1.** free from risk or danger; not dangerous. **2.** providing security or protection. —*n.* **1.** a strong lockable cupboard or cabinet for valuables. **2.** a ventilated cabinet for storing food. —**on the safe side**, having a margin of security against risks. **safe conduct**, the right to pass through a district on a particular occasion without risk of arrest or harm; a document granting this. **safe deposit**, a building containing safes and strongrooms that are let separately. **safe period**, the time during and near a menstrual period when sexual intercourse is least likely to result in conception. —**safely** *adv.*, **safeness** *n.* [from Anglo-French *saf* from Latin *salvus* = uninjured]

safeguard *n.* a stipulation, circumstance, etc., that tends to prevent something undesirable. —*v.t.* to protect by a stipulation or precaution.

safety *n.* being safe, freedom from risk or danger. —**safety belt**, a strap securing a person safely, especially a seat belt. **safety catch**, a device for locking a gun trigger or preventing the accidental or dangerous operation of machinery. **safety curtain**, a fireproof curtain in a theatre to divide the auditorium from the stage in case of fire etc. **safety match**, a match that ignites only on a specially prepared surface. **safety net**, a net placed to catch an acrobat etc. in case of a fall from a height. **safety razor**, one with a guard to prevent the blade cutting the skin. Its

invention dates from the mid-19th century. **safety valve,** a valve that opens automatically to relieve excessive pressure in a boiler etc.; a means of harmlessly releasing excitement, anger, etc. [from Old French from Latin]

safety glass glass that does not splinter into sharp pieces when smashed. **Toughened glass** is made by heating a glass sheet and then rapidly cooling it with a blast of cold air; it shatters into rounded pieces when smashed. **Laminated glass** is a 'sandwich' of a clear plastic film between two glass sheets; when this is struck, it simply cracks, the plastic holding the glass in place.

safety lamp a portable lamp designed for use in places where flammable gases such as methane may be encountered, for example in coal mines. The electric head lamp used as a miner's working light has the bulb and contacts in protected enclosures. The flame safety lamp, now used primarily for gas detection, has the wick enclosed within a strong glass cylinder surmounted by wire gauzes. Humphrey ◊Davy (in 1815) and George ◊Stephenson each invented flame safety lamps.

safety pin a pin with a point that is bent back to the head and can be held in a guard so that the user may not be pricked nor the pin come out unintentionally.

Saffir–Simpson damage-potential scale /'sæfə'sɪmpsən/ a scale of potential damage from wind and sea when a hurricane is in progress: 1 is minimal damage, 5 is catastrophic.

safflower *n.* an Asian plant *Carthamus tinctorius*, family Compositae. It is thistlelike, and widely grown for the oil from its seeds, which is used in cooking, margarine, and paints and varnishes; the seed residue is used as cattle feed.

saffron /'sæfrən/ *n.* the orange-coloured stigmas of the crocus *Crocus sativus* used for colouring and flavouring; the colour of this. The plant is of the iris family, probably native to SW Asia, and formerly widely cultivated in Europe. —*adj.* saffron-coloured. [from Old French from Arabic]

sag *v.i.* (-**gg**-) **1.** to hang or subside loosely and unevenly; to sink or curve downwards in the middle under weight or pressure. **2.** (of prices) to fall. —*n.* the state or amount of sagging. [from Middle Low German or Dutch = subside]

saga /'sɑːgə/ *n.* **1.** a long story of heroic achievement. **2.** a series of connected books telling the story of a family etc. **3.** a prose narrative written down in the 11th–13th centuries in Norway and Iceland. The sagas range from family chronicles, such as the *Landnamabok* of Ari (1067–1148), to legendary and anonymous works such as the *Njala* saga. Other sagas include the *Heimskringla* of Snorri Sturluson celebrating Norwegian kings (1178–1241), the *Sturlunga* of Sturla Thordsson (1214–1284), and the legendary and anonymous *Laxdaela* and *Grettla* sagas. [Old Norse = narrative]

sagacious /sə'geɪʃəs/ *adj.* having or showing insight or good judgement. —**sagaciously** *adv.*, **sagacity** /-'gæsɪtɪ/ *n.* [from Latin *sagax*]

Sagan /sæ'gɒn/ Françoise 1935– . French novelist. Her studies of love relationships include *Bonjour Tristesse*/*Hello Sadness* 1954, *Un Certain Sourire*/*A Certain Smile* 1956, and *Aimez-vous Brahms?*/*Do You Like Brahms?* 1959.

sage¹ *n.* a kitchen herb *Salvia officinalis* with greyish-green leaves. It grows up to 50 cm/1.6 ft high and has bluish-lilac or pink flowers. —**sagebrush** *n.* the growth of plants (especially of the genus *Artemisia*) in some sterile alkaline regions of the USA. [from Old French from Latin *salvia* = healing plant]

sage² *adj.* profoundly wise, having wisdom gained from experience. —*n.* a profoundly wise man. —**sagely** *adv.* [from Old French from Latin *sapere* = be wise]

saggar /'sægə/ *n.* a case of baked, fireproof clay enclosing pottery while it is baked.

Sagittarius /sædʒɪ'teərɪəs/ *n.* the ninth sign of the zodiac, the Archer: a constellation in the southern hemisphere, represented as a centaur aiming a bow and arrow at neighbouring Scorpius. The Sun passes through Sagittarius from mid-Dec to mid-Jan, including the winter solstice, when it is farthest south of the equator. The constellation contains many nebulae and ◊globular clusters, and open ◊star clusters. Kaus Australis and Nunki are its brightest stars. The centre of our Galaxy, the Milky Way, is marked by the radio source Sagittarius A. In astrology, the dates for Sagittarius are between about 22

Nov and 21 Dec (see ◊precession). —**Sagittarian** *adj.* & *n.* [Latin = archer]

sago /ˈseɪgəʊ/ *n.* (*plural* **sagos**) **1.** a starch used in puddings, for manufacturing glucose, and sizing textiles. **2.** a palm (especially of the genus *Metroxylon*) with a pith yielding this. [from Malay]

Sahara /səˈhɑːrə/ the largest desert in the world, occupying 5,500,000 sq km/2,123,000 sq mi of N Africa from the Atlantic to the Nile, covering: W Egypt; part of W Sudan; large parts of Mauritania, Mali, Niger, and Chad; and southern parts of Morocco, Algeria, Tunisia, and Libya. Small areas in Algeria and Tunisia are below sea level, but it is mainly a plateau with a central mountain system. The area of the Sahara has expanded by 650,000 sq km/251,000 sq mi in the last half century, but reafforestation is being attempted in certain areas.

sahib /sɑːb, ˈsɑːɪb/ *n.* (*historical*) a form of address to European men in India. [Urdu from Arabic = lord]

said past and past participle of **say**.

saiga *n.* an antelope *Saiga tartarica* of E European and W Asian steppes and deserts. Buff-coloured, whitish in winter, it stands 75 cm/2.5 ft at the shoulder, with a body about 1.5 m/5 ft long. Its nose is unusually large and swollen, an adaptation which may help warm and moisten the air inhaled, and keep out the desert dust. The saiga can run at 80 kph/50 mph.

Saigon /saɪˈgɒn/ former name (until 1976) of ◊Ho Chi Minh City, Vietnam.

Saigon, Battle of during the Vietnam War, the battle from 29 Jan to 23 Feb 1968, when 5,000 Vietcong were expelled by South Vietnamese and US forces. The city was finally taken by North Vietnamese forces on 30 April 1975, after South Vietnamese withdrawal from the central highlands.

sail *n.* **1.** a piece of canvas or other material extended on rigging to catch the wind and propel a vessel; a ship's sails collectively. **2.** a voyage or excursion in a sailing vessel. **3.** a ship, especially as discerned from its sails. **4.** the wind-catching apparatus on a windmill. —*v.t./i.* **1.** to travel on water by the use of sails or engine power. **2.** to navigate (the sea, a ship, etc.); to set (a toy boat) afloat. **3.** to start on a voyage. **4.** to glide or move smoothly or in a stately manner. —**sail close to the wind**, to sail as nearly against the wind as possible; to come close to indecency or dishonesty. **sailing boat** *or* **ship**, one moved by sails. **sail into**, to attack with blows or words. **under sail**, with the sails set. [Old English]

sailboard *n.* a kind of surfboard with a sail, a windsurfer.

sailboarding *n.* the sport of riding on a sailboard, ◊windsurfing. —**sailboarder** *n.*

sailcloth *n.* **1.** canvas for sails. **2.** a canvaslike dress material.

sailor *n.* **1.** a seaman or mariner, especially one below the rank of officer. **2.** a person considered as liable or not liable to seasickness (*bad* or *good sailor*). [variant of *sailer*]

sailplane *n.* a glider designed for soaring.

sainfoin /ˈsænfɔɪn/ *n.* a pink-flowered fodder plant *Onobrychis sativa*. [from obsolete French *saintfoin*, originally = lucerne, from Latin *sanctum foenum* = holy hay]

saint (*abbreviation* St or S., in *plural* Sts or SS) *n.* **1.** a holy person, one declared (in the Roman Catholic or Eastern Orthodox Church) worthy of veneration, whose intercession may be publicly sought (see ◊canonization). The term is also used in Buddhism for individuals who have led a virtuous and holy life. For individual saints, see under forename, for example ◊Paul, St. **2.** the title of such a person or of one receiving veneration, or used in the name of a church not named after a saint (e.g. St Saviour's, St Cross). **3.** each of the souls of the dead in paradise. **4.** a member of the Christian church or (in certain religious bodies) of one's own branch of it. **5.** a very good, patient, or unselfish person. —*v.t.* to canonize; to call or regard as a saint; (in *past participle*) sacred, worthy of sainthood. —**sainthood** *n.* [from Old French from Latin *sanctus* = holy (*sancire* = consecrate)]

St Andrews /sənt ˈændruːz/ town at the E tip of Fife, Scotland, 19 km/12 mi SE of Dundee; **population** (1981) 11,400. Its university (1411) is the oldest in Scotland, and the Royal and Ancient Club (1754) is the ruling body in the sporting world of golf.

St Bartholomew, Massacre of /bɑːˈθɒləmjuː/ the slaughter of ◊Huguenots in Paris from 24 Aug to 17 Sept 1572 and until 3 Oct in the provinces. About 25,000 people are believed to have been killed. When ◊Catherine de' Medici's plot to have ◊Coligny assassinated failed, she resolved to have all the Huguenot leaders killed, persuading her son Charles IX it was in the interests of public safety. Catherine received congratulations from all the Catholic powers, and the pope ordered a medal to be struck.

St Bernard /ˈbɜːnəd/ a large, heavily built dog, 70 cm/2.5 ft high at the shoulder, weighing about 70 kg/150 lbs. St Bernards have pendulous ears and lips, large feet, and drooping lower eyelids. They are usually orange and white. [from the Augustinian monks of Grand *St Bernard* Hospice, Switzerland, who kept them for finding lost travellers in the Alps and to act as guides]

St Christopher (St Kitts)-Nevis /sənt ˈkrɪstəfə ˈniːvɪs/ Federation of; country in the West Indies, in the Leeward Islands; **area** 269 sq km/104 sq mi; **capital** Basseterre (on St Kitts); **physical** two volcanic islands in the Lesser Antilles; **head of state** Elizabeth II from 1983 represented by governor-general; **head of government** Kennedy Alphonse Simmonds from 1980; **political system** federal constitutional monarchy; **exports** sugar, molasses, cotton; **population** (1990 est) 40,000; **language** English **recent history** granted internal self-government within the British Commonwealth in 1967; full independence within the Commonwealth was achieved in 1983.

St Elmo's fire a bluish, flamelike electrical discharge that sometimes occurs above ships' masts and other pointed objects or about aircraft in stormy weather. Although high voltage, it is low current and therefore harmless. St Elmo (or St Erasmus) is the patron saint of sailors.

Saint-Exupéry /sænt eksjuːpəˈriː/ Antoine de 1900–1944. French author, who wrote the autobiographical *Vol de nuit/Night Flight* 1931 and *Terre des hommes/Wind, Sand, and Stars* 1939. His celebrated children's book *Le petit Prince/The Little Prince* 1943 is also an adult allegory.

Saint-Gaudens /seɪntˈgɔːdnz/ Augustus 1848–1907. Irish-born US sculptor; one of the leading Neo-Classical sculptors of his time. His monuments include the *Admiral Farragut* 1877 in Madison Square Park and the giant nude *Diana* that topped Stanford ◊White's Madison Square Garden, both in New York City, and the *Adams Memorial* 1891 in Rock Creek Cemetery, Washington DC.

St George's /sənt ˈdʒɔːdʒɪz/ port and capital of Grenada; population (1986) 7,500, urban area 29,000.

St Helena /sənt hiˈliːnə/ British island in the S Atlantic, 1,900 km/1,200 mi W of Africa, area 122 sq km/47 sq mi; population (1985) 5,900. Its capital is Jamestown, and it exports fish and timber. Ascension and Tristan da Cunha are dependencies.

St Helens, Mount /seɪnt ˈhelənz/ volcanic mountain in Washington State, USA. When it erupted in 1980 after being quiescent since 1857, it devastated an area of 600 sq km /230 sq mi and its height was reduced from 2,950 m/9,682 ft to 2,560 m/8,402 ft.

St James's Palace /sənt ˈdʒeɪmzɪz/ a palace in Pall Mall, London, a royal residence 1698–1837.

St John, Order of (full title **Knights Hospitallers of St John of Jerusalem**) the oldest order of Christian chivalry, named from the hospital at Jerusalem founded about 1048 by merchants of Amalfi for pilgrims, whose travel routes the knights defended from the Muslims. Today there are about 8,000 knights (male and female), and the Grand Master is the world's highest-ranking Roman Catholic lay person.

St John's /seɪnt ˈdʒɒnz/ capital and chief port of Newfoundland, Canada; population (1986) 96,000, urban area 162,000. The main industry is cod-fish processing.

St John's port and capital of Antigua and Barbuda, on Antigua; population (1982) 30,000.

Saint-Just /sænˈʒuːst/ Louis Antoine Léon Florelle de 1767–1794. French revolutionary. A close associate of ◊Robespierre, he became a member of the Committee of Public Safety 1793, and was guillotined with Robespierre.

St Kitts-Nevis /sənt ˈkɪts ˈniːvɪs/ contracted form of ◊St Christopher-Nevis.

Saint-Laurent /sæn ləuˈrɒŋ/ Yves (Henri Donat Mathieu) 1936– . French couturier, partner to Christian ◊Dior from 1954 and his successor in 1957. He opened his own fashion house in 1962.

St Lawrence /seɪnt 'lɒrəns/ river in E North America. From ports on the ◊Great Lakes, it forms, with linking canals (which also give great hydroelectric capacity to the river), the St Lawrence Seaway for ocean-going ships, ending in the Gulf of St Lawrence. It is 1,050 km/650 mi long, and is ice-bound for four months a year.

St Leger /'ledʒə(r)/ a horse race held at Doncaster, England every Sept. It is a flat race over 2.8 km/1.7 mi, and is the last of the season. First held in 1776, it is the oldest of the English classic races.

St Louis /seɪnt 'luːɪs/ city in Missouri, USA, on the Mississippi River; population (1986) 426,300, metropolitan area 2,356,000. Its products include aerospace equipment, aircraft, vehicles, chemicals, electrical goods, steel, and beer.

Saint Lucia /sənt 'luːʃə/ country in the West Indies, one of the Windward Islands; **area** 617 sq km/238 sq mi; **capital** Castries; **physical** mountainous; mainly tropical forest; volcanic peaks; Gros and Petit Pitons; **head of state** Elizabeth II from 1979 represented by governor-general; **head of government** John G M Compton from 1982; **political system** constitutional monarchy; **exports** coconut oil, bananas, cocoa, copra; **population** (1990 est) 153,000; **language** English; French patois; **recent history** independence from Britain was achieved in 1979; St Lucia remains within the Commonwealth.

St Moritz /sæn mə'rɪts/ winter sports centre in SE Switzerland; it contains the Cresta Run (built in 1885) for tobogggans, bobsleighs, and luges. It was the site of the Winter Olympics in 1928 and 1948.

St Petersburg /'piːtəbɜːg/ former name (until 1914) of the city of ◊Leningrad, USSR. A recent vote favoured the restoration of the old name.

St Pierre and Miquelon /sæmpi'eə 'miːkəlɒn/ territorial collectivity of France, eight small islands off the S coast of Newfoundland, Canada; **area** St Pierre group 26 sq km/10 sq mi; Miquelon-Langlade group 216 sq km/ 83 sq mi; **capital** St Pierre; **physical** the last surviving remnant of France's North American empire; **government** French-appointed commissioner and elected local council; one representative in the National Assembly in France; **products** fish; **population** (1987) 6,300; **language** French; **recent history** French territory until 1976; overseas *département* until 1985. There were violent protests in 1989 when France tried to impose its claim to a 320 km/200 mi fishing zone around the islands; Canada maintains that there is only a 19 km/12 mi zone.

Saint-Saëns /sæn'sɒns/ (Charles) Camille 1835–1921. French composer, pianist, and organist. Among his many lyrical Romantic pieces are concertos, the symphonic poem *Danse macabre* 1875, the opera *Samson et Dalila* 1877, and the orchestral *Carnaval des animaux/Carnival of the Animals* 1886.

Saint-Simon /sænsi:'mɒn/ Claude Henri, Comte de 1760–1825. French socialist, who fought in the American Revolution and was imprisoned during the French Revolution. He advocated an atheist society ruled by technicians and industrialists in *Du Système industrielle/The Industrial System* 1821.

Saint-Simon Louis de Rouvroy, Duc de 1675–1755. French soldier, courtier, and politician, whose *Mémoires* 1691–1723 are unrivalled as a description of the French court.

St Valentine's Day Massacre the murder in Chicago, USA, of seven unarmed members of the 'Bugs' Moran gang on 14 Feb 1929 by members of Al ◊Capone's gang disguised as policemen. The killings testified to the intensity of gangland warfare for the control of the trade in illicit liquor during ◊prohibition.

St Vincent and the Grenadines /sənt 'vinsənt, 'grenədi:nz/ country in the Windward Islands, West Indies; **area** 388 sq km/150 sq mi, including Northern Grenadines (43 sq km/17 sq mi); **capital** Kingstown; **physical** volcanic mountains, thickly forested; **head of state** Elizabeth II from 1979 represented by governor-general; **head of government** James Mitchell from 1984; **political system** constitutional monarchy; **exports** bananas, tarros, sweet potatoes, arrowroot, copra; **population** (1990 est) 106,000; **language** English; French patois; **recent history** achieved full independence from Britain within the Commonwealth in 1979.

St Vitus's dance /'vaɪtəs/ the former name for ◊chorea, a nervous disorder. [from St Vitus, martyred under the Roman emperor Diocletian, the patron saint of dancers]

sake[1] *n.* for the sake of, for (a person's) sake, out of consideration for, in the interest of; in order to please, honour, get, or keep. for heaven's *or* God's etc. sake, an exclamation of dismay, annoyance, or supplication. [Old English = contention, charge]

sake[2] /'sɑːkɪ/ *n.* a Japanese fermented liquor made from rice. [Japanese]

Sakhalin /sæxə'liːn/ (Japanese *Karafuto*) island in the Pacific, N of Japan, that since 1947 forms with the ◊Kurils a region of the USSR; **area** 74,000 sq km/28,564 sq mi; **capital** Yuzhno-Sakhalinsk (Japanese *Toyohara*); **population** (1981) 650,000, including aboriginal ◊Ainu and Gilyaks.

Sakharov /'sækərɒv/ Andrei Dmitrievich 1921–1989. Soviet physicist, known both as the 'father of the Soviet H-bomb' and as an outspoken human-rights campaigner. He received the Nobel Peace Prize in 1975. In 1989 he was elected to the Congress of the USSR People's Deputies (CUPD), where he emerged as leader of its radical reform grouping.

Saki /'sɑːki/ pen name of H(ugh) H(ector) Munro 1870–1916. Burmese-born British writer of ingeniously witty and bizarre short stories, often with surprise endings. He also wrote two novels *The Unbearable Bassington* 1912 and *When William Came* 1913.

Sakti /'ʃʌkti/ *n.* the female principle in ◊Hinduism.

Śākyamuni /ʃɑːkjə'muni/ *n.* the historical ◊Buddha, called *Shaka* in Japan (because Gautama was of the Śakya clan).

salaam /sə'lɑːm/ *n.* **1.** an oriental salutation 'Peace'; an Indian obeisance with or without this, a bow with the right palm on the forehead. **2.** (in *plural*) respectful compliments. —*v.t./i.* to make a salaam (to). [from Arabic]

salacious /sə'leɪʃəs/ *adj.* indecently erotic, lewd. —**salaciously** *adv.*, **salaciousness** *n.*, **salacity** /-'læsɪtɪ/ *n.* [from Latin *salax* (*salire* = leap)]

salad /'sæləd/ *n.* a mixture of raw or cold vegetables, herbs, etc., usually seasoned with oil, vinegar etc., and often eaten with or including cold meat, cheese etc.; a vegetable or herb suitable for eating raw. —**salad days**, one's period of youthful inexperience. **salad dressing**, a mixture of oil, vinegar etc., used with a salad. [from Old French from Provençal, ultimately from Latin *sal* = salt]

Saint-Simon *Ahead of his time, the Comte de Saint-Simon advocated a 'meritocracy', the equality of women, and a plan to link the Atlantic and Pacific by canal.*

salamander

fire salamander

Saladin /'sælədɪn/ or *Sala-ud-din* 1138–1193. Born a Kurd, he was sultan of Egypt from 1175, in succession to the Atabeg of Mosul, on whose behalf he conquered Egypt 1164–74. He subsequently conquered Syria 1174–87 and precipitated the third ◊Crusade by his recovery of Jerusalem from the Christians in 1187. Renowned for knightly courtesy, Saladin made peace with Richard I of England in 1192.

Salamanca, Battle of /sælə'mæŋkə/ the victory on 22 July 1812 of British troops under their commander Wellington over the French army in the ◊Peninsular War.

salamander /sælə'mændə/ *n.* **1.** in mythology, a lizardlike animal living in fire. **2.** any tailed amphibian, family Salamandridae, of the order Caudata, which live in the northern hemisphere. The European **spotted** or **fire salamander** *Salamandra salamandra* is black with bright yellow, orange, or red markings, and up to 20 cm/8 in long. Other types include the **giant salamander** of Japan *Andrias japonicus*, 1.5 m/5 ft long, and the **Mexican salamander** *Ambystoma mexicanum*, or ◊axolotl. [from Old French from Latin from Greek]

salami /sə'lɑːmɪ/ *n.* a highly seasoned sausage, originally from Italy. [Italian, ultimately from Latin *sal* = salt]

Salamis ancient city on the E coast of Cyprus, the capital under the early Ptolemies until its harbour silted up about 200 BC, when it was succeeded by Paphos in the SW.

Salamis, Battle of /'sæləmɪs/ the naval battle off the coast of the island of Salamis, SE Greece, in which the Greeks defeated the Persians in 480 BC.

sal ammoniac /sæl ə'məʊniæk/ ◊ammonium chloride, originally said to have been made from camels' dung near the temple of Jupiter Ammon. [from Latin *sal* = salt and *ammoniacus* = of Jupiter Ammon]

Salang Highway /'sɑːlæŋ/ the main N–S route between Kabul, capital of Afghanistan, and the Soviet frontier; length 422 km/264 mi. The high-altitude **Salang Pass** and **Salang Tunnel** cross a natural break in the Hindu Kush mountains about 100 km/60 mi N of Kabul. This supply route was a major target of the Mujaheddin resistance fighters during the Soviet occupation of Afghanistan.

salary /'sælərɪ/ *n.* a fixed regular payment, usually calculated on an annual basis and paid monthly, made by an employer to an employee. —*v.t.* (especially in *past participle*) to pay a salary to. [from Anglo-French from Latin *salarium* = originally soldier's salt money]

salat *n.* the daily prayers that are one of the Five Pillars of ◊Islam.

Salazar /sælə'zɑː/ Antonio de Oliveira 1889–1970. Portuguese prime minister 1932–68, who exercised a virtual dictatorship. Salazar was also foreign minister 1936–47 and during World War II he maintained Portuguese neutrality. He fought long colonial wars in Africa (Angola and Mozambique) that impeded his country's economic development.

sale *n.* **1.** selling, being sold. **2.** an instance of this; the amount sold. **3.** an event at which goods are sold, especially by public auction or for charity. **4.** disposal of a shop's stock at reduced prices, e.g. at the end of a season. **5.** (in *plural*) the department of a firm concerned with selling its products. —**for** or **on sale**, offered for purchase. **sale of work**, a sale for charity etc. of goods provided by supporters. **sale or return**, an arrangement by which a retailer can return to a wholesaler without payment any goods left unsold. **saleroom** *n.* a room in which auctions are held. **sales talk**, persuasive talk to promote the sale

of goods or the acceptance of an idea etc. [Old English from Old Norse]

saleable *adj.* fit for sale; likely to find a purchaser. —**saleability** /-'bɪlɪtɪ/ *n.*

Salesian /sə'liːʒən/ *adj.* of a Roman Catholic educational religious order named after St ◊Francis of Sales. —*n.* a member of this order.

salesman *n.* (*plural* **salesmen**) a man employed to sell goods in a shop etc. or as a middleman between producer and retailer.

salesmanship *n.* skill in selling.

salesperson *n.* a salesman or saleswoman.

saleswoman *n.* (*plural* **saleswomen**) a woman employed to sell goods.

salicylic acid /sæli'sɪlɪk/ HOC_6H_4COOH, the active chemical constituent of aspirin, an analgesic drug. The acid and its salts (salicylates) occur naturally in many plants; concentrated sources include willow bark and oil of wintergreen. [from French *salicyle* from Latin *salix* = willow]

salient /'seɪliənt/ *adj.* prominent, conspicuous; standing or pointing outwards. —*n.* a salient angle; a bulge in the line of a military attack or defence. [from Latin *salire* = leap]

Salieri /sæli'eəri/ Antonio 1750–1825. Italian composer. He taught Beethoven, Schubert, and Liszt, and was the musical rival of Mozart, whom it has been suggested, without proof, that he poisoned, at the Emperor's court in Vienna.

Salinas de Gortiari /sə'liːnəs də gɔːti'ɑːri/ Carlos 1948– . Mexican politician, president from 1988, a member of the dominant Institutional Revolutionary Party (PRI).

saline /'seɪlaɪn/ *adj.* of salt or salts; containing or tasting of salt(s). —*n.* **1.** a saline substance, especially a medicine. **2.** a salt lake, spring etc. —**salinity** /sə'lɪnɪtɪ/ *n.* [from Latin *salinus* (*sal* = salt)]

Salinger /'sælɪndʒə/ J(erome) D(avid) 1919– . US writer of the novel of adolescence *The Catcher in the Rye* 1951 and stories of a Jewish family, including *Franny and Zooey* 1961.

Salisbury /'sɔːlzbəri/ former name (until 1980) of ◊Harare, capital of Zimbabwe.

Salisbury Robert Cecil, 1st Earl of Salisbury. Title conferred on Robert ◊Cecil, secretary of state to Elizabeth I of England.

Salisbury Robert Arthur Talbot Gascoyne-Cecil, 3rd Marquess of Salisbury 1830–1903. British Conservative politician. As foreign secretary 1878–80, he took part in the Congress of Berlin, and as prime minister 1885–86, 1886–92, and 1895–1902 gave his main attention to foreign policy, remaining also as foreign secretary for most of this time.

saliva /sə'laɪvə/ *n.* the colourless liquid produced by glands in the mouth, assisting in chewing and digestion in vertebrates. In some animals, it contains the ◊enzyme ptyalin, which digests starch, and in blood-feeding species, it contains ◊anticoagulants. —**salivary** *adj.* [Latin]

salivate /'sælɪveɪt/ *v.i.* to secrete or discharge saliva, especially in excess. —**salivation** /-'veɪʃən/ *n.* [from Latin *salivare*]

Salk /sɔːlk/ Jonas Edward 1914– . US physician and microbiologist. In 1954 he developed the vaccine that led to virtual eradication of paralytic ◊polio in industrialized countries. He was director of the Salk Institute for Biological Studies, University of California, San Diego, 1963–75.

Sallinen /'sælɪnen/ Tyko 1879–1955. Finnish Expressionist painter. Inspired by ◊Fauvism on visits to France in 1909 and 1914, he created visionary works relating partly to his childhood experiences of religion. He also painted Finnish landscapes and peasant life, such as *Washerwoman* 1911 (Ateneum, Helsinki).

sallow[1] /'sæləʊ/ *adj.* (especially of the complexion) of sickly yellow or pale brown. —*v.t./i.* to make or become sallow. —**sallowness** *n.* [Old English = dusky]

sallow[2] /'sæləʊ/ *n.* a low-growing willow; a shoot or the wood of this. [Old English]

Sallust /'sæləst/ Gaius Sallustius Crispus 86–*c.*34 BC. Roman historian, and a supporter of Julius Caesar. He wrote accounts of Catiline's conspiracy and the Jugurthine War in an epigrammatic style.

To like and dislike the same things, that is indeed true friendship.

Sallust (Gaius Sallustius Crispus)
Bellum Catilinae

sally /'sælɪ/ *n.* **1.** a rush from a besieged place upon the besiegers, a sortie. **2.** an excursion. **3.** a lively or witty remark. —*v.i.* to make a sally. —**sally forth** *or* **out,** to go on a journey or walk etc. [from French *saillie* from Latin *salire* = leap]

Sally Lunn /sæli 'lʌn/ a kind of sweet light teacake served hot. [perhaps from name of girl hawking them in Bath about 1800]

salmagundi /sælmə'gʌndɪ/ *n.* **1.** a dish of chopped meat, anchovies, eggs, onions etc., and seasoning. **2.** a miscellaneous collection. [from French *salmigondis*]

salmi /'sælmɪ/ *n.* a ragout or casserole, especially of game birds. [French]

salmon /'sæmən/ *n.* (*plural* usually the same) **1.** a large fish of the family Salmonidae with orange-pink flesh, highly valued for food and sport. The normal colour of the scales is silvery with a few dark spots, but the colour changes at the spawning season. Salmon live in the sea, but return to spawn in the place they were spawned, often overcoming great obstacles to get there. **2.** the colour of the salmon's flesh. —*adj.* orange-pink. —**salmon trout,** a sea ◊trout. [from Anglo-French from Latin *salmo*]

salmonella /sælmə'nelə/ *n.* any of a very varied group of bacteria of the genus *Salmonella*. They can be divided into three broad groups. One of these, *S. typhosa,* causes typhoid and paratyphoid fevers, while a second group causes salmonella ◊food poisoning, which is characterized by stomach pains, vomiting, diarrhoea, and headache. It can be fatal in elderly people, but others usually recover in a few days without antibiotics. Most cases are caused by contaminated animal products, especially poultry meat. [from D E *Salmon,* American veterinary surgeon]

Salome /sə'ləumɪ/ 1st century AD. In the New Testament, granddaughter of the king of Judea, Herod the Great. Rewarded for her skill in dancing, she requested the head of John the Baptist from her stepfather ◊Herod Antipas.

salon /'sælɒn/ *n.* **1.** the reception room of a large continental house. **2.** a meeting there of eminent people. **3.** a room or establishment where a hairdresser or couturier etc. receives clients. [French from Italian *salone* (*sala* = hall)]

saloon /sə'lu:n/ *n.* **1.** a large public room for a specified purpose. **2.** a public room on a ship. **3.** (*US*) a place where alcoholic drinks may be bought and drunk. **4.** a saloon car. —**saloon bar,** a first-class bar in a public house. **saloon car,** a motor car with a closed body for driver and passengers. [from French *salon*]

salsa *n.* a Latin big-band dance music popularized by Puerto Ricans in New York City in the 1980s and by, among others, the Panamanian singer Rubén Blades (1948–   ).

salsify /'sælsɪfɪ/ *n.* or **vegetable oyster** a hardy plant biennial *Tragopogon porrifolius,* family Compositae. Its white, fleshy roots and spring shoots are cooked and eaten. [from French from Italian *salsefica*]

salt /sɔlt, sɒlt/ *n.* **1.** or **common salt** sodium chloride, NaCl, a substance found dissolved in sea water and as rock salt (halite) in large deposits and salt domes. Common salt is used extensively in the food industry as a preservative and for flavouring, and in the chemical industry to make chlorine and sodium. **2.** in chemistry, any compound formed from an acid and a base through the replacement of all or part of the hydrogen in the acid by a metal or electropositive radical. **3.** (often in *plural*) a substance resembling common salt in taste, form etc.; (in *plural*) such a substance used as a laxative. **4.** piquancy, pungency, wit. **5.** a saltcellar. **6.** or **old salt,** an experienced sailor. —*adj.* containing or tasting of salt; cured, preserved, or seasoned with salt. —*v.t.* **1.** to cure, preserve, or season with salt or brine. **2.** to sprinkle with salt. **3.** (*slang*) to make (a mine) appear rich by fraudulently inserting precious metal into it before it is viewed (also *figurative*); to make fraudulent entries in (accounts etc.). —**salt away** *or* **down,** (*colloquial*) to save

or put aside for the future. **saltcellar** *n.* a container for salt at table. **salt lick,** a place where animals lick earth impregnated with salt. **salt mine,** a mine yielding rock salt; a place of unremitting toil. **the salt of the Earth,** the finest people, those who keep society wholesome. **saltpan** *n.* a hollow near the sea where salt is got by evaporation. **take with a grain** *or* **pinch of salt,** to regard sceptically. **worth one's salt,** deserving one's position, competent. [Old English]

SALT acronym from ◊Strategic Arms Limitation Talks, a series of US-Soviet negotiations 1969–79.

saltation *n.* the idea that an abrupt genetic change can occur in an individual, which then gives rise to a new species. The idea has now been largely discredited, although the appearance of ◊polyploid individuals can be considered an example. [Latin *saltare* = to leap]

salting /'sɔltɪŋ, 'sɒ-/ *n.* a marsh overflowed by the sea.

saltire /'sæltaɪə/ *n.* an X-shaped cross; this dividing a shield etc. into four sections. [from Old French *sau(l)toir* = stirrup cord, stile, from Latin *saltare* = leap]

Salt Lake City /sɔ:lt leɪk 'sɪtɪ/ capital of Utah, USA, on the river Jordan, 18 km/11 mi SE of the Great Salt Lake; population (1982) 164,000. Founded in 1847, it is the headquarters of the ◊Mormon Church. Mining, construction, and other industries are being replaced by high technology.

Salt March in Indian history, an episode during the period of nationalist agitation against British rule, forming part of Mahatma Gandhi's campaign of ◊civil disobedience.

saltpetre /sɒlt'pi:tə/ *n.* potassium nitrate, KNO$_3$, a white, crystalline, salty substance used as a constituent of gunpowder, in preserving meat, and medicinally. It occurs naturally, being deposited during dry periods in places with warm climates such as India. [from Old French from Latin *salpetra,* probably = salt of the rock]

salty /'sɔltɪ, 'sɒ-/ *adj.* **1.** containing or tasting of salt. **2.** piquant, pungent. —**saltiness** *n.*

salubrious *adj.* health-giving, healthy. —**salubrity** *n.* [from Latin *salubris* (*salus* = health)]

saluki /sə'lu:kɪ/ *n.* or **gazelle hound** a tall, slender, silky-coated dog resembling the greyhound. It is about 65 cm/26 in high, and usually fawn, cream, or white in colour. [from Arabic]

salutary /'sæljutərɪ/ *adj.* producing good effects. —**salutarily** *adv.* [from French or Latin *salutaris* (*salus* = health)]

salutation /sæljuː'teɪʃən/ *n.* a sign or expression of greeting or respect; the use of these. —**salutatory** /sə'ljuːtətərɪ/ *adj.*

salute /sə'luːt, -'ljuːt/ *n.* **1.** a gesture of respect or courteous recognition. **2.** a prescribed military movement of the hand or the firing of a gun or guns etc. as a formal or ceremonial sign of respect. —*v.t.* **1.** to greet with a polite gesture. **2.** to perform a military salute; to greet with this. **3.** to express respect for, to commend. [from Old French or Latin *salutare* (*salus* = health)]

Salvador /sælvə'dɔ:/ port and naval base in Bahia state, NE Brazil, on the inner side of a peninsula separating Todos Santos Bay from the Atlantic; population (1985) 2,126,000. Products include cocoa, tobacco, and sugar. Founded in 1510, it was the capital of Brazil 1549–1763.

Salvador, El /el'sælvədɔ:/ republic in Central America; see ◊El Salvador.

salvage /'sælvɪdʒ/ *n.* **1.** the rescue of property from loss at sea or from fire etc.; payment made or due for this; property so saved. **2.** the saving and utilization of waste materials; materials salvaged. —*v.t.* **1.** to save from a wreck etc. **2.** to make salvage of. [French from Latin *salvagium*]

salvation /sæl'veɪʃən/ *n.* **1.** the saving of the soul from sin and its consequences; the state of being saved. **2.** preservation from loss or calamity; a thing that preserves from these. —**salvationist** *n.* [from Old French from Latin *salvare* = save]

Salvation Army a Christian evangelical, social-service, and social-reform organization, originating in 1865 in London, England, with the work of William ◊Booth; now a worldwide organization. It has military titles for its officials, is renowned for its brass bands, and its weekly journal is the *War Cry.*

salve[1] *n.* **1.** a healing ointment. **2.** a thing that soothes or consoles. —*v.t.* to soothe. [Old English]

salve[2] *v.t.* to save from a wreck or fire etc. —**salvor** *n.* [back formation from *salvage*]

salver

salver *n.* a tray, usually metal, on which letters or refreshments etc. are handed. [from French from Spanish *salva* = assaying of food]

salvia /'sælvɪə/ *n.* a garden plant of the genus *Salvia*, especially a species with red flowers *S. splendens*. [Latin = *sage*[1]]

salvo /'sælvəʊ/ *n.* (*plural* **salvoes**) 1. a simultaneous discharge of guns or bombs. 2. a round of applause. [from French from Italian *salva* = salutation]

sal volatile /sæl və'lætɪlɪ/ another name for ◊smelling salts. [Latin = volatile salt]

Salyut *n.* a series of seven space stations launched by the USSR 1971–82. Salyut was cylindrical in shape, 15 m/50 ft long, and weighed 19 tonnes. It housed two or three cosmonauts at a time, for missions lasting up to eight months. [Russian = salute]

Salzburg /'sæltsbɜː g/ 1. capital of the province of Salzburg, W Austria, on the river Salzach; population (1981) 139,400. It is the seat of an archbishopric founded by St Boniface about 700 and has a 17th-century cathedral. Salzburg is the birthplace of the composer Wolfgang Amadeus Mozart and an annual music festival has been held here since 1920. 2. federal province of Austria; area 7,200 sq km/2,779 sq mi; population (1987) 462,000. Industries include stock rearing, dairy farming, forestry, and tourism.

samara *n.* in botany, a winged fruit, a type of ◊achene.

Samaria /sə'meərɪə/ region of ancient Israel. The town of Samaria (now **Sebastiyeh**) on the W bank of the river Jordan was the capital of Israel in the 10th–8th centuries BC. It was renamed **Sebarte** in the 1st century BC by the Roman administrator Herod the Great. Extensive remains have been excavated.

Samaritan *n.* 1. *or* good **Samaritan** a person who readily gives help to one in distress who has no claim upon him or her (with reference to the Bible, Luke 10: 30 ff.). 2. a member of an organization that gives comfort and help (especially through the telephone service) to people in distress. 3. a member or descendant of the colonists forced to settle in Samaria (now N Israel) by the Assyrians after their occupation of the ancient kingdom of Israel in 722 BC. Samaritans adopted a form of Judaism, but adopted only the *Pentateuch*, the five books of Moses of the Old Testament, and regarded their temple on Mount Gerizim as the true sanctuary. [from Latin from Greek *Samareia* = Samaria]

samarium /sə'meərɪəm/ *n.* a hard, brittle, grey-white, metallic element of the ◊lanthanide series, symbol Sm, atomic number 62, relative atomic mass 150.4. It is widely distributed in nature and is obtained commercially from the minerals monzanite and bastnasite. It is used only occasionally in industry, mainly as a catalyst in organic reactions. Samarium was discovered by spectroscopic analysis of the mineral samarskite. [named in 1879 by French chemist Paul Lecoq de Boisbaudran (1838–1912) after its source]

Samarkand /sæmɑː'kænd/ city in Uzbek Republic, USSR; capital of Samarkand region, near the river Zerafshan, 217 km/135 mi E of Bukhara; population (1987) 388,000. Industries include cotton-ginning, silk manufacture, and engineering.

samba /'sæmbə/ *n.* a ballroom dance of Brazilian origin; the music for this. —*v.i.* to dance the samba. [Portuguese, of African origin]

same *adj.* 1. being of one kind, not different; unchanged, unvarying. 2. just mentioned. —*pron.* (**the same**) the same person or thing; the person or thing just mentioned. —*adv.* (**the same**) in the same way, similarly. —**all** *or* **just the same**, nevertheless. **be all** *or* **just the same**, to make no difference (to a person). **same here**, (*colloquial*) the same applies to me, I agree. —**sameness** *n.* [from Old Norse]

samizdat /'sæmɪzdæt/ *n.* in the USSR and E Europe before the 1989 uprisings, written material circulated underground to evade state censorship, for example reviews of Solzhenitsyn's banned novel *August 1914* 1972. [Russian = self-published]

Samoa /sə'məʊə/ volcanic island chain in the SW Pacific. It is divided into Western Samoa and American Samoa.

Samoa, American group of islands 4,200 km/2,610 miles S of Hawaii, an unincorporated territory of the USA, administered by the US Department of the Interior; **area** 200 sq km/77 sq mi; **capital** Fagatogo on Tutuila;

population (1981) 34,000; **exports** canned tuna, handicrafts; **currency** US dollar; **population** (1981) 34,000; **language** Samoan and English; **history** the islands were acquired by the USA Dec 1899 by agreement with Britain and Germany under the Treaty of Berlin. A constitution was adopted 1960 and revised 1967.

Samoa, Western Independent State of; country in the SW Pacific, in ◊Polynesia, NE of Fiji; **area** 2,830 sq km/1,093 sq mi; **capital** Apia (on Upolu island); **physical** comprises South Pacific islands of Savai'i and Upolu, with two smaller tropical islands and islets; mountain ranges on main islands; lava flows on Savai'i; **head of state** King Malietoa Tanumafili II from 1962; **head of government** Tofilau Eti Alesana from 1988; **political system** constitutional monarchy; **exports** coconut oil, copra, cocoa, fruit juice, cigarettes; **population** (1989) 169,000; **language** English, Samoan (official); **recent history** independence was achieved within the Commonwealth in 1962. Tupuola Taisi Efi was the country's first nonroyal prime minister in 1975.

samovar /'sæməvɑː(r)/ *n.* an urn, heated by charcoal, used for making tea. [Russian = self-boiling]

samoyed *n.* a breed of dog, originating in Siberia. It is about 50 cm/1.9 ft in height and weighs about 25 g/60 lbs. It resembles a ◊chow, but has a more pointed face and a white coat.

sampan *n.* a small boat used on the rivers and coasts of China, Japan, and neighbouring islands, rowed with a scull (or two sculls) from the stern and usually having a sail of matting and an awning. [from Chinese *san ban* (*san* = three and *ban* = board)]

samphire *n.* or **glasswort** or **sea asparagus** a perennial plant *Crithmum maritimum* found on sea cliffs in Europe. The aromatic leaves are fleshy and sharply pointed; the flowers grow in yellow-green umbels. It is used in salads, or pickled. [from French (*herbe de*) *Saint Pierre* = St Peter's herb]

sample /'sɑːmpəl/ *n.* a small, separated part or quantity intended to show what the whole is like; a specimen; an illustrative or typical example. —*v.t.* to take or give a sample of; to try the qualities of; to get representative experience of. [from Anglo-French *assample* = example]

sampler *n.* a piece of embroidery worked in various stitches as a specimen of proficiency. [from Old French *essamplaire* from Latin *exemplum*]

Samson /'sæmsən/ 11th century BC. In the Old Testament, a hero of Israel. He was renowned for exploits of strength against the Philistines, which ended when his mistress Delilah cut off his hair, the source of his strength, as told in the Book of Judges.

Samsun Black Sea port and capital of a province of the same name in N Turkey; situated at the mouth of the Murat river in a tobacco-growing area; site of the ancient city of Amisus; population (1985) 280,000.

Samuel /'sæmjuəl/ 11th–10th century BC. In the Old Testament, the last of the judges who ruled the ancient Hebrews before their adoption of a monarchy, and the first of the prophets; the two books bearing his name cover the story of Samuel and the reigns of kings Saul and David.

samurai /'sæmuraɪ/ *n.* (*plural* the same) a member of the feudal military caste in Japan from the mid-12th century until 1869, when the feudal system was abolished and all samurai pensioned off by the government. Many became leaders in various spheres of modern life. A samurai was an armed retainer of a *daimyō* (large landowner) with specific duties and privileges and a strict code of honour. A *rōnin* was a samurai without feudal allegiance. [Japanese]

San /sɑːn/ *n.* a member of a hunter-gatherer people of the Kalahari Desert. Living in Botswana, Namibia, and South Africa, they number approximately 50,000. Their languages belong to the Khoisan family. [Khoisan]

San'a /sæ'nɑː/ capital of Yemen, SW Arabia, 320 km/200 mi N of Aden; population (1986) 427,000. A walled city, with fine mosques and traditional architecture, it is rapidly being modernized.

San Andreas fault /sæn æn'dreɪəs/ a geological fault line stretching for 1,125 km/700 mi in a NW–SE direction through the state of California, USA.

San Antonio /sæn æn'təʊniəʊ/ city in S Texas, USA; population (1986) 914,350. A commercial and financial centre; industries include aircraft maintenance, oil refining, and meat packing. Founded in 1718, it grew up round the site of the ◊Alamo fort.

sanatorium /sænə'tɔ:riəm/ *n.* (*plural* **sanatoriums**) **1.** an establishment for treating chronic diseases (e.g. tuberculosis) or convalescents. **2.** accommodation for sick persons in a school etc. [from Latin *sanare* = heal]

sanctify /'sæŋktɪfaɪ/ *v.t.* **1.** to make holy or sacred. **2.** to justify. —**sanctification** /-fɪ'keɪʃən/ *n.* [from Old French from Latin *sanctus* = holy]

sanctimonious /sæŋktɪ'məʊnɪəs/ *adj.* making a show of righteousness or piety. —**sanctimoniously** *adv.*, **sanctimoniousness** *n.* [from Latin *sanctimonia* = sanctity]

sanction /'sæŋkʃən/ *n.* **1.** permission or approval for an action or behaviour etc. **2.** confirmation or ratification of a law etc. **3.** a penalty for disobeying a law or a reward for obeying it; (especially in *plural*) action taken by a country etc. to penalize and coerce a country or organization that is considered to have violated a law, code of practice, or basic human rights. Examples of the use of sanctions are the attempted economic boycott of Italy (1935–36) during the Abyssinian War by the League of Nations and the call for measures against South Africa on human-rights grounds by the United Nations and other organizations from 1985. —*v.t.* **1.** to give sanction or approval to, to authorize. **2.** to ratify. **3.** to attach a penalty or reward to (a law). [French from Latin *sancire* = make holy]

sanctity /'sæŋktɪtɪ/ *n.* holiness, sacredness. [from Old French or Latin *sanctitas*]

Sanctorius /sæŋk'tɔ:rɪəs/ Sanctorius 1561–1636. Italian physiologist who pioneered the study of ◊metabolism and invented the clinical thermometer and a device for measuring pulse rate.

sanctuary /'sæŋktjʊərɪ/ *n.* **1.** a sacred place. **2.** the holiest part of a temple; the part of the chancel containing the altar. **3.** a place where birds or wild animals etc. are protected and encouraged to breed. **4.** (especially *historical*) a sacred place where a fugitive from the law, or a debtor, was secured by medieval Christian church law against arrest or violence; a place in which similar immunity was established by custom or law. In England the right of a criminal to seek sanctuary was removed by legislation in 1623 and again in 1697, though for civil offenders it remained until 1723. Immunity was valid for 40 days only, after which the claimant must either surrender, become an outlaw, or go into permanent exile. **5.** a place of refuge. [from Anglo-French from Latin *sanctuarium*]

sanctum /'sæŋktəm/ *n.* **1.** a holy place. **2.** a person's private room or study. [Latin]

Sanctus /'sæŋktəs/ *n.* in the Christian church, the hymn (from Isaiah 6: 3) beginning 'Sanctus, sanctus, sanctus' or 'Holy, holy, holy', forming the conclusion of the Eucharistic preface; the music for this. —**Sanctus bell**, a bell in the turret at the junction of nave and chancel, or a handbell, rung at the Sanctus or at the elevation of the host. [Latin = holy]

sand *n.* the loose, granular substance resulting from the wearing down of siliceous and other rocks and found on the seashore, riverbeds, deserts etc.; (in *plural*) grains of sand, an expanse of sand, a sandbank. Grains of sand are sized 0.02–2.00 mm/0.0008–0.0800 in in diameter, consisting chiefly of ◊quartz, but owing their varying colour to mixtures of other minerals. Sand is used in cement-making, as an abrasive, in glass-making, and for other purposes. —*v.t.* **1.** to smooth or polish with sandpaper. **2.** to sprinkle, cover, or treat with sand. —**sandblast** *n.* a jet of sand driven by compressed air or steam for cleaning a glass or stone etc. surface; (*v.t.*) to treat with this. **sand castle**, a structure of sand made by or for a child on the seashore. **sand dune** *or* **hill**, a dune. **sandglass** *n.* a wasp-waisted reversible glass with two bulbs containing enough sand to take a definite time in passing from the upper to the lower bulb. **sand martin**, a bird *Riparia riparia* nesting in sandy banks. **sandpit** *n.* a pit etc. containing sand for children to play in. **sand wasp**, a wasp of the family Sphecidae that makes its nest in sand. **sand yacht**, a yachtlike vehicle on wheels for use on sand. [Old English]

Sand /sɒnd/ George. Pen name of Amandine Aurore Lucie Dupin 1804–1876. French author, whose prolific literary

Sand French novelist George Sand. Her affairs with a succession of artists and poets provided the inspiration for much of her work.

output was often autobiographical. In 1831 she left her husband after nine years of marriage and, while living in Paris as a writer, had love affairs with Alfred de ◊Musset, ◊Chopin, and others. Her first novel, *Indiana* 1832, was a plea for women's right to independence.

sandal¹ /sændəl/ *n.* a shoe with an open-work upper or no upper, usually fastened with straps. [from Latin from Greek *sandalion*]

sandal² *n. or* **sandalwood** a scented wood; a tree with this, especially one of the genus *Santalum*. [from Latin ultimately from Sanskrit]

sandbag *n.* a bag filled with sand, used to protect a wall or building (e.g. during flooding, in war) or to make temporary defences, or as a ruffian's weapon. —*v.t.* (**-gg-**) **1.** to protect with sandbags. **2.** to hit with a sandbag.

sandbank *n.* a deposit of sand forming a shallow place in a sea or river.

sandbar *n.* a ridge of sand built up by the currents across the mouth of a river or bay. A sandbar may be entirely underwater or it may form an elongated island that breaks the surface. A sandbar stretching out from a headland is a **sand spit**.

Sandburg /'sændbɜ:g/ Carl August 1878–1967. US poet. His poetry celebrates ordinary US life, as in *Chicago Poems* 1916, and *The People, Yes* 1936. *Always the Young Strangers* 1953 is an autobiography. Both his poetry and his biography of Abraham Lincoln won Pulitzer prizes.

sander *n.* a device for sanding things.

Sanders /'sɑ:ndəz/ George 1906–1972. Russian-born British actor, usually cast as a smooth-talking cad. Most of his film career was spent in the USA where he starred in such films as *Rebecca* 1940, *The Moon and Sixpence* 1942, and *The Picture of Dorian Gray* 1944.

sandgrouse *n.* a bird of the family Pteroclidae, related to the pigeons. It lives in warm, dry areas of Europe and Africa and has long wings, short legs, and hard skin.

sandhopper *n.* a crustacean *Talitrus saltator* about 1.6 cm/0.6 in long, without a shell. It is found above the high-tide mark on seashores. The term also refers to some other amphipod crustaceans.

San Diego /sæn di'eɪgəʊ/ city and military and naval base in California, USA; population (1986) 1,015,200. Industries include biomedical technology, aircraft missiles, and fish canning. ◊Tijuana adjoins San Diego across the Mexican border.

Sandinista /sændi'ni:stə/ *n.* a Nicaraguan left-wing revolutionary; see ◊Nicaraguan revolution.

sandman *n.* an imaginary person causing sleepiness in children, the personification of tiredness causing children's eyes to smart towards bedtime.

sandpaper *n.* paper with a coating of sand or other abrasive for smoothing or polishing things. —*v.t.* to smooth or polish with sandpaper.

sandpiper *n.* a bird belonging to the snipe family Scolopacidae, inhabiting wet, sandy places. The common sandpiper *Tringa hypoleucos* is a small, graceful bird with a long, slender bill and short tail, drab above and white below. It is common in the northern hemisphere.

Sandringham House /'sændrɪŋəm/ a private residence of the British sovereign, built in 1863 by the Prince of Wales (afterwards Edward VII) 1869–1971 on the estate he had bought in Norfolk, NE of Kings Lynn, in 1863.

sandstone *n.* any ◊sedimentary rock formed from the consolidation of sand, with sand-sized grains (0.0625–2 mm/0.0025–0.08 in) in a matrix or cement. The principal component is quartz. Sandstones are classified according to the matrix or cement material (whether derived from clay or silt, for example as calcareous sandstone; ferruginous sandstone; siliceous sandstone).

sandstorm *n.* a storm with clouds of sand raised by the wind.

sandwich /'sænwɪdʒ/ *n.* 1. two or more slices of bread with a filling between. 2. a cake of two or more layers with jam or cream etc. between. —*v.t.* to put (a thing, statement, etc.) between two others of a different kind. —**sandwich board**, each of the two advertisement boards carried by a sandwich man. **sandwich course**, a course of training with alternate periods of practical and theoretical work. **sandwich man**, a person walking in the street with advertisement boards displayed on the body, one before and one behind. [from 4th Earl of *Sandwich*, said to have eaten only slices of bread and meat while gaming for 24 hours]

Sandwich /'sænwɪtʃ/ John Montagu, 4th Earl of Sandwich 1718–1792. English politician, an inept First Lord of the Admiralty 1771–82 during the American Revolution, whose corrupt practices were blamed for the British navy's inadequacies.

Sandwich Islands former name of ◊Hawaii, a group of islands in the Pacific.

sandy *adj.* 1. having much sand. 2. sand-coloured. 3. (of hair) yellowish-red; (of a person) having hair of this colour. —**sandiness** *n.*

Sandys /sændz/ Duncan Edwin. Original name of British politician Baron ◊Duncan-Sandys.

sane *adj.* 1. having a sound mind, not mad. 2. showing good judgement, sensible and practical. —**sanely** *adv.* [from Latin *sanus* = healthy]

San Francisco /sæn frænˈsɪskəʊ/ chief Pacific port of the USA, in California; population (1986) 749,000, metropolitan area of San Francisco and Oakland 3,192,000. The city stands on a peninsula, S of the Golden Gate (1937), the world's second longest single-span bridge, 1,280 m/4,200 ft. The strait gives access to San Francisco Bay. Industries include meat packing, fruit canning, printing and publishing, and the manufacture of metal goods.

sang past of **sing**.

Sanger /'sæŋə/ Frederick 1918– . English biochemist, the first person to win a Nobel Prize for Chemistry twice: in 1958 for determining the structure of insulin, and in 1980 for work on the chemical structure of genes.

sang-froid /sɑ̃'frwɑ/ *n.* calmness in danger or difficulty. [French = cold blood]

sangha /'sɑːŋə/ *n.* the Buddhist monastic order, including monks, nuns, and novices. [from Sanskrit = community (*sam* = together and *lan* = come in contact)]

sangria /sæŋˈɡriːə/ *n.* a Spanish drink of red wine with lemonade etc. [Spanish = bleeding]

sanguinary /'sæŋɡwɪnəri/ *adj.* accompanied by or delighting in bloodshed; bloody, bloodthirsty. [from Latin *sanguis* = blood]

sanguine /'sæŋɡwɪn/ *adj.* 1. optimistic. 2. (of the complexion) bright and florid. [from Old French from Latin *sanguineus*]

Sanhedrin /'sænɪdrɪn/ *n.* the supreme Jewish council and highest court of justice in Jerusalem in New Testament times. It pronounced the sentence of death on Jesus Christ. [from Hebrew from Greek *sunedrion* (*sun* = with and *hedra* = seat)]

sanitarium /sæni'teəriəm/ *n.* (*US*) a sanatorium.

sanitary /'sænɪtəri/ *adj.* 1. of or assisting hygiene, hygienic. 2. of sanitation. —**sanitary towel**, an absorbent pad used during menstruation. [from French from Latin *sanitas* (*sanus* = healthy)]

sanitation /sæni'teɪʃən/ *n.* sanitary conditions, the maintenance or improvement of these; the disposal of sewage and refuse etc.

sanitize /'sænɪtaɪz/ *v.t.* to make sanitary.

sanity /'sænɪti/ *n.* being sane. [from Latin *sanitas*]

San José /sæn həʊ'zeɪ/ 1. capital of Costa Rica; population (1984) 245,370. Products include coffee, cocoa, and sugar cane. It was founded in 1737 and has been the capital since 1823. 2. city in Santa Clara Valley, California, USA; population (1986) 712,000. Industries include aerospace research and development, electronics, flowers, fruit canning, and wine making. It was the first capital of California 1849–51.

San Juan /sæn 'wɑːn/ capital of Puerto Rico; population (1980) 434,850. It is a port and industrial city. Products include sugar, rum, and cigars.

sank past of **sink**.

San Luis Potosí /sæn luːˈiːs pɒtəʊ'siː/ silver-mining city and capital of San Luis Potosí state, central Mexico; population (1986) 602,000. Founded in 1586 as a Franciscan mission, it became the colonial administrative headquarters and has fine buildings of the period.

San Marino /sæn mə'riːnəʊ/ Republic of; landlocked country within north central Italy; **area** 61 sq km/24 sq mi; **capital** San Marino; **physical** on the slope of Mount Titano; **head of state and government** two captains-regent, elected for a six-month period; **political system** direct democracy; **exports** wine, ceramics, paint, chemicals; **population** (1990 est) 23,000; **language** Italian; **recent history** independence was recognized under Italy's protection in 1862. Governed by a series of left-wing and centre-left coalitions 1947–86; Communist and Christian Democrat 'grand coalition' formed in 1986.

San Martín /sæn mɑːˈtiːn/ José de San Martín 1778–1850. South American nationalist. Born in Argentina, he served in the Spanish army during the Peninsular War, but after 1812 he devoted himself to the South American struggle for independence, playing a large part in the liberation of Argentina, Chile, and Peru from Spanish rule.

sannyasin /sʌnˈjɑːsɪn/ *n.* in Hinduism, a person who has renounced worldly goods to live a life of asceticism and seek *moksha*, or liberation from reincarnation, through meditation and prayer.

San Pedro Sula /sæn 'pedrəʊ 'suːlə/ main industrial and commercial city in NW Honduras, the second largest city in the country; population (1986) 400,000. It trades in bananas, coffee, sugar, and timber and manufactures textiles, plastics, furniture, and cement.

San Salvador /sæn 'sælvədɔː/ capital of El Salvador 48 km/30 mi from the Pacific, at the foot of San Salvador volcano (2,548 m/8,360 ft); population (1984) 453,000. Industries include food processing and textiles. Since its foundation in 1525, it has suffered from several earthquakes.

sans-culotte *n.* in the French Revolution, a member of the working classes, who wore trousers, as opposed to the aristocracy and bourgeoisie, who wore knee breeches. [French = without knee breeches]

sanserif /sæn'serɪf/ *adj.* without serifs. —*n.* a form of typeface without serifs.

Sanskrit *n.* the dominant classical language of the Indian subcontinent, a member of the Indo-Iranian group of the Indo-European language family, and the sacred language of Hinduism. The oldest form of Sanskrit is *Vedic*, the variety used in the *Vedas* and *Upanishads* (about 1500–700 BC). —*adj.* of or in Sanskrit. —**Sanskritic** /-'krɪtɪk/ *adj.* [from Sanskrit = composed (*sam* = together and *kr* = make)]

sans souci without cares or worries. [French]

Santa Ana /'sæntə 'ænə/ a periodic warm Californian ◊wind.

Santa Anna /'sæntə 'ænə/ Antonio López de 1795–1876. Mexican revolutionary. A leader in achieving independence from Spain in 1821, he pursued a chequered career of victory and defeat and was in and out of office as president or dictator for the rest of his life; he led the attack on the ◊Alamo fort in Texas in 1836.

Santa Claus /klɔ:z/ another name for Father Christmas; see under St ◊Nicholas.

Santa Fé Trail a US trade route 1821–80 from Independence, Missouri, to Santa Fé, New Mexico.

Santayana /sænti'ænə/ George 1863–1952. Spanish-born US philosopher and critic. He developed his philosophy based on naturalism and taught that everything has a natural basis.

Sant'Elia /sæn'teliə/ Antonio 1888–1916. Italian architect. His drawings convey a Futurist vision of a metropolis with skyscrapers, traffic lanes, and streamlined factories.

Santiago /sænti'ɑ:gəu/ capital of Chile; population (1987) 4,858,000. Industries include textiles, chemicals, and food processing. It was founded in 1541 and is laid out with broad avenues.

Santo Domingo /'sæntəu də'mɪŋgəu/ capital and chief sea port of the Dominican Republic; population (1982) 1,600,000. Founded in 1496 by Bartolomeo, brother of Christopher Columbus, it is the oldest colonial city in the Americas. Its cathedral was built 1515–40.

Sānusī /sə'nu:si/ Sidi Muhammad ibn 'Ali as- c.1787–1859. Algerian-born Muslim religious reformer. He preached a return to the puritanism of early Islam and met with much success in Libya, where he founded the sect named after him.

San Yu /sæn'ju:/ 1919– . Myanmar (Burmese) politician. A member of the Revolutionary Council that came to power in 1962, he became president in 1981 and was re-elected in 1985. He was forced to resign in July 1988, along with Ne Win, after riots in Yangon (formerly Rangoon).

Sâo Paulo /sau 'pauləu/ city in Brazil, 72 km/45 mi NW of its port Santos; population (1986) 8,490,700, metropolitan area 15,280,000. It is South America's leading industrial city, producing electronics, steel, and chemicals; it has meat-packing plants and is the centre of Brazil's coffee trade. It originated as a Jesuit mission in 1554.

Sâo Tomé e Principe /'saun tu'mei, 'prɪnsɪpə/ Democratic Republic of; country in the Gulf of Guinea, off the coast of W Africa; **area** 1,000 sq km/386 sq mi; **capital** Sâo Tomé; **physical** comprises two main islands and several smaller ones, all volcanic; thickly forested and fertile; **head of state and government** Manual Pinto da Costa from 1975; **political system** one-party Socialist republic; **exports** cocoa, copra, coffee, palm oil and kernels; **population** (1990 est) 125,000; **language** Portuguese (official); **recent history** independence from Portugal was achieved in 1975. The first multiparty elections were held in 1991.

sap[1] n. 1. the vital juice circulating in ◊vascular plants, especially woody ones, carrying nutriment to all parts. Sap can be milky (as in rubber trees), resinous (as in pines), or syrupy (as in maples). Sap contains alkaloids, protein, and starch. 2. vigour, vitality. 3. sapwood. 4. (*slang*) a foolish person. —*v.t.* (**-pp-**) 1. to drain or dry (wood) of sap. 2. to exhaust the vigour of, to weaken. [Old English]

sap[2] n. 1. a tunnel or trench to conceal assailants' approach to a fortified place. 2. the insidious undermining of belief etc. —*v.t./i.* (**-pp-**) 1. to dig saps; to undermine (a wall etc.). 2. to destroy insidiously, to weaken. [from French or Latin *zappa* = spade, spadework]

sapid /'sæpɪd/ adj. 1. savoury, palatable. 2. (of writings etc.) not insipid or vapid. —**sapidity** /sə'pɪdɪtɪ/ n. [from Latin *sapidus* (*sapere* = have flavour)]

sapient /'seɪpɪənt/ adj. (*literary*) wise, pretending to be wise. —**sapience** n. [from Old French or Latin *sapiens* (*sapere* = be wise)]

sapling n. a young tree.

saponification n. in chemistry, the ◊hydrolysis (splitting) of an ◊ester by treatment with a strong alkali, resulting in the liberation of the alcohol from which the ester had been derived and a salt of the constituent fatty acid. The process is used in the manufacture of soap.

sapper n. 1. one who digs saps. 2. a soldier of the Royal Engineers (especially as the official term for a private).

Sapphic /'sæfɪk/ adj. 1. of the Greek poetess Sappho (7th century BC) or her poetry, especially (of a stanza or verse) in four-line form with a short fourth line. 2. another word for ◊lesbian. [from French from Latin from Greek = of Sappho]

sapphire /'sæfaɪə/ n. 1. the deep blue, transparent gem variety of the mineral ◊corundum Al_2O_3, aluminium oxide. Small amounts of iron and titanium give it its colour. 2. its bright blue colour. 3. a corundum gem of any colour except red (which is a ruby). —*adj.* of sapphire blue. [from Old French from Latin from Greek = lapis lazuli]

Sappho /'sæfəu/ c.612–580 BC. Greek lyric poetess, friend of the poet ◊Alcaeus and leader of a female literary coterie at Mytilene (now **Lesvos**). Legend says she committed suicide when her love for the boatman Phaon was unrequited. Only fragments of her poems have survived.

Sapporo /sə'pɔ:rəu/ capital of ◊Hokkaido, Japan; population (1987) 1,555,000. Industries include rubber and food processing. It is a winter sports centre and was the site of the 1972 Winter Olympics. Giant figures are sculpted in ice at the annual snow festival.

sappy adj. 1. full of sap. 2. young and vigorous. 3. (*slang*) foolish.

saprophyte /'sæprəfaɪt/ n. in botany, an obsolete term for a saprotroph, an organism that lives in dead or decaying matter. —**saprophytic** /-'fɪtɪk/ adj. [from Greek *sapros* = putrid and *phuð* = grow]

saprotroph n. (formerly **saprophyte**) an organism that feeds on the excrement or the dead bodies or tissues of others. Saprotrophs include most fungi (the rest being parasites); many bacteria and protozoa; animals such as dung beetles and vultures; and a few unusual plants, including several orchids. Saprotrophs cannot make food for themselves, so they are a type of ◊heterotroph. They are useful scavengers, and in sewage farms and refuse dumps break down organic matter into nutrients easily assimilable by green plants.

sapwood n. the soft outer layers of recently formed wood between the heartwood and the bark.

saraband /'særəbænd/ n. a slow Spanish dance; the music for this. [from French from Spanish and Italian *zarabanda*]

Saracen /'særəsən/ n. an ancient Greek and Roman term for an Arab, used in the Middle Ages by Europeans for all Muslims. The equivalent term used in Spain was ◊Moor. [from Old French]

Saragossa /særə'gɒsə/ English spelling of ◊Zaragoza, city in Aragon, Spain.

Sarajevo /særə'jeɪvəu/ capital of Bosnia and Herzegovina, Yugoslavia; population (1982) 449,000. Industries include engineering, brewing, chemicals, carpets, and ceramics. It was the site of the 1984 Winter Olympics.

Saratov /sə'rɑ:tɒf/ industrial port (chemicals, oil refining) on the river Volga in the USSR; population (1987) 918,000. It was established in the 1590s as a fortress to protect the Volga trade route.

Sarawak /sə'rɑ:wæk/ state of Malaysia, on the NW corner of the island of Borneo; **area** 124,400 sq km/48,018 sq mi; **capital** Kuching; **products** timber, oil, rice, pepper, rubber, and coconuts; **population** (1986) 1,550,000.

sarcasm /'sɑ:kæzəm/ n. an ironical remark or comment; the use of such remarks. [from French or Latin from Greek *sarkazō* = speak bitterly]

sarcastic /sɑ:'kæstɪk/ adj. using or showing sarcasm. —**sarcastically** adv.

sarcoma /sɑ:'kəumə/ n. (*plural* **sarcomata**) a type of malignant ◊tumour arising from the fat, muscles, bones, cartilage, or blood and lymph vessels and connective tissues. Sarcomas are much less common than ◊carcinomas. [from Greek *sarkoô* = become fleshy from *sarx* = flesh]

sarcophagus /sɑ:'kɒfəgəs/ n. (*plural* **sarcophagi** /-gaɪ/) a stone coffin. [Latin from Greek = flesh-consuming (*phagos* = eating)]

sardine /sɑ:'di:n/ n. a young pilchard or similar small fish in the ◊herring family, often tinned tightly packed in oil. —**like sardines,** crowded close together. [from Old French from Latin *sardina*]

Sardinia /sɑ:'dɪnɪə/ (Italian *Sardegna*) mountainous island, special autonomous region of Italy; area 24,100 sq km/9,303 sq mi; population (1988) 1,651,000. Its capital is Cagliari, and it exports cork and petrochemicals. After centuries of foreign rule, it became linked in 1720 with Piedmont, and this dual kingdom became the basis of a united Italy from 1861.

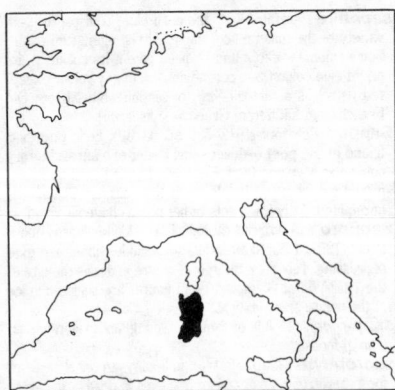

Sardinia

sardonic /saːˈdɒnɪk/ *adj.* humorous in a grim or sarcastic way; full of bitter mockery; cynical. —**sardonically** *adv.* [from French from Latin from Greek *Sardonios* (= Sardinian), substituted for Homeric *sardanios* (epithet of bitter or scornful laughter) because of belief that eating a Sardinian plant could result in convulsive laughter ending in death]

sardonyx /saːˈdɒnɪks/ *n.* an onyx in which white layers alternate with yellow or orange ones. [from Latin from Greek *sardios* = a precious stone and *onyx*]

sargasso /saːˈɡæsəʊ/ *n.* (*plural* **sargassos**) a seaweed of the genus *Sargassum*, with berrylike air vessels, found floating in islandlike masses. [from Portuguese]

Sargasso Sea /saːˈɡæsəʊ/ part of the N Atlantic (between 40° and 80°W and 25° and 30°N) left static by circling ocean currents, and covered with floating weed *Sargassum natans*.

sarge *n.* (slang) a sergeant. [abbreviation]

Sargent /saːˈdʒənt/ John Singer 1856–1925. US portrait painter. Born in Florence of American parents, he studied there and in Paris, then settled in London around 1885. He was a fashionable and prolific painter.

Sargeson /saːˈdʒsən/ Frank 1903–1982. New Zealand writer of short stories and novels including *The Hangover* 1967 and *Man of England Now* 1972.

Sargon /ˈsaːɡɒn/ two Mesopotamian kings:

Sargon I king of Akkad *c.*2370–2230 BC, and founder of the first Babylonian empire. Like Moses, he was said to have been found floating in a cradle on the local river, in his case the Euphrates.

Sargon II died 705 BC. King of Assyria from 722 BC, who assumed the name of his predecessor. To keep conquered peoples from rising against him, he had whole populations moved from their homelands, including the Israelites from Samaria.

sari /ˈsaːrɪ/ *n.* a length of material draped around the body, worn as the main garment by Hindu women. [from Hindi]

Sark /saːk/ one of the ◊Channel Islands, 10 km/6 mi E of Guernsey; area 5 sq km/2 sq mi; there is no town or village. It is divided into Great and Little Sark, linked by an isthmus, and is of great natural beauty. The Seigneurie of Sark was established by Elizabeth I, the ruler being known as Seigneur/Dame, and has its own parliament, the Chief Pleas.

Sarney (Costa) /saːˈneɪ/ José 1930– . Brazilian politician, member of the Democratic Movement (PMDB), president 1985–90.

sarong /səˈrɒŋ/ *n.* a Malay and Javanese garment worn by both sexes, consisting of a long strip of cloth tucked round the waist or under the armpits. [Malay, literally = sheath]

Sarraute /sæˈrəʊt/ Nathalie 1920– . Russian-born French novelist whose books include *Portrait d'un inconnu/Portrait of a Man Unknown* 1948, *Les Fruits d'or/The Golden Fruits* 1964, and *Vous les entendez?/Do You Hear Them?* 1972. An exponent of the *nouveau roman*, Sarraute bypasses plot, character, and style for the half-conscious interaction of minds.

sarsaparilla /saːsəpəˈrɪlə/ *n.* a tropical American smilax plant, especially *Smilax ornata*; its dried roots; a tonic made from these. [from Spanish *zarzaparilla* (*zarza* = bramble)]

sarsen /ˈsaːsən/ *n.* a sandstone etc. boulder, a relict carried by ice in the glacial period.

sarsenet /ˈsaːsnɪt/ *n.* a soft silk fabric used especially as a lining. [from Anglo-French *sarzinett*]

sartorial /saːˈtɔːrɪəl/ *adj.* of clothes or tailoring. —**sartorially** *adv.* [from Latin *sartor* = tailor]

Sartre /ˈsaːtrə/ Jean-Paul 1905–1980. French author and philosopher, a leading proponent of ◊existentialism in postwar philosophy. He published his first novel, *La Nausée/Nausea*, in 1937, followed by the trilogy *Les Chemins de la Liberté/Roads to Freedom* 1944–45 and many plays, including *Huis Clos/In Camera* 1944. *L'Être et le néant/Being and Nothingness* 1943, his first major philosophical work, sets out a radical doctrine of human freedom. In the later work *Critique de la raison dialectique/Critique of Dialectical Reason* 1960 he tried to produce a fusion of existentialism and Marxism.

Three o'clock is always too late or too early for anything you want to do.

Jean-Paul Sartre
Nausea

SAS abbreviation of **1.** ◊Special Air Service. **2.** Scandinavian Airlines System.

sash[1] *n.* a long strip or loop of cloth etc. worn over one shoulder or round the waist as part of a uniform or insignia, or (by a woman or child) round the waist for ornament. [from Arabic = muslin, turban]

sash[2] *n.* a frame holding the glass in a sash window. —**sash cord**, a strong cord attaching sash weights to a sash. **sash weight**, a weight attached to each end of a sash to balance it at any height. **sash window**, a window usually made to slide up and down in grooves. [from *sashes*, corruption of *chassis*]

Saskatchewan /sæˈskætʃəwən/ province of W Canada; **area** 652,300 sq km/251,788 sq mi; **capital** Regina; **physical** prairies in the S; to the N, forests, lakes, and subarctic tundra; **products** more than 60% of Canada's wheat; oil, natural gas, uranium, zinc, potash (world's largest reserves), copper, helium; **population** (1986) 1,010,000; **recent history** ceded to Canadian government in 1870 as part of Northwest Territories; became a province in 1905. [Cree *Kis-is-ska-tche-wan* = swift flowing]

sassafras /ˈsæsəfræs/ *n.* **1.** a small tree of the genus *Sassafras*, especially a North American species yielding bark that is used medicinally and in perfumes. **2.** this bark. [from Spanish or Portuguese]

Sassanian Empire /səˈseɪnɪən/ Persian empire founded in AD 224 by Ardashir, a chieftain in the area of what is now Fars, in Iran, who had taken over ◊Parthia; it was named for his grandfather, Sasan. The capital was Ctesiphon, near modern ◊Baghdad, Iraq. After a rapid period of expansion, when it contested supremacy with Rome, it was destroyed in 637 by Muslim Arabs at the Battle of ◊Qadisiya.

Sassau-Nguesso /sæsaʊŋˈɡesəʊ/ Denis 1943– . Congolese socialist politician, president from 1979. He progressively consolidated his position within the ruling left-wing Congolese Labour Party (PCT), at the same time as improving relations with France and the USA.

Sassenach /ˈsæsənæx, -æk/ *n.* (*Scottish* and *Irish*, usually *derogatory*) an English person. [from Gaelic or Irish from Latin *Saxo* = Saxon]

Sassoon /səˈsuːn/ Siegfried 1886–1967. English writer, author of the autobiography *Memoirs of a Foxhunting Man* 1928. His *War Poems* 1919 express the disillusionment of his generation.

sat *n.* in Hinduism, true existence or reality: the converse of illusion (*maya*).

sat past and past participle of **sit**.

Sat. abbreviation of Saturday.

Satan /ˈseɪtən/ another name for the ◊devil. [Old English, ultimately from Hebrew = adversary]

satanic /səˈtænɪk/ *adj.* of or like Satan; devilish, evil. —**satanically** *adv.*

Satanism /'seɪtənɪzəm/ n. 1. the worship of Satan, with a travesty of Christian forms. 2. the pursuit of evil. —**Satanist** n.

satchel /'sætʃəl/ n. a small bag, usually with a shoulder strap, especially for carrying school books. [from Old French from Latin *saccellus* (*saccus* = sack)]

sate v.t. to satiate.

sateen /sæ'tiːn/ n. a glossy cotton fabric woven like satin. [from *satin* after *velveteen*]

satellite /'sætəlaɪt/ n. 1. a heavenly body revolving round a planet; a moon. 2. an artificial body placed in orbit round the Earth or other planet for purposes of military observation, research, navigation, or communications. The first artificial satellite was ◊*Sputnik*, launched in 1957. 3. a follower, a hanger-on; a member of a retinue. 4. a small country etc. controlled by or dependent on another and following its lead. [French or from Latin *satelles* = guard]

satellite television the transmission of broadcast signals through artificial communications satellites. Mainly positioned in ◊geostationary orbit, satellites have been used since the 1960s to relay television pictures around the world. Higher-power satellites have more recently been developed to broadcast signals to cable systems or directly to people's homes. Direct broadcasting began in the UK in 1989.

satellite town a ◊new town planned and built to serve a particular local industry, or as a dormitory or overspill town for people who work in a nearby metropolis. Satellite towns in Britain include Port Sunlight near Birkenhead (Cheshire), built to house workers at Lever Brothers soap factories, and Milton Keynes (N Buckinghamshire) built in 1967.

satiable /'seɪʃəbəl/ adj. that may be satiated.

satiate /'seɪʃieɪt/ v.t. to gratify fully, to surfeit. —**satiation** /-'eɪʃən/ n. [from Latin *satiare* (*satis* = enough)]

Satie /sæ'tiː/ Erik (Alfred Leslie) 1866–1925. French composer. His piano pieces, such as *Gymnopédies* 1888, often combine wit and melancholy. His orchestral works include *Parade* 1917, among whose sound effects is a typewriter. He was the mentor of the group of composers known as ◊*Les Six*.

satiety /sə'taɪətɪ/ n. the state or feeling of being satiated.

satin /'sætɪn/ n. a silky fabric so woven that it has a glossy surface on one side. —*adj.* smooth as satin. —*v.t.* to give a glossy surface to (paper). —**satiny** adj. [from Old French from Arabic = of Tseutung in China]

satinwood n. a kind of choice glossy timber of any of various trees.

satire /'sætaɪə/ n. 1. the use of ridicule, irony, or sarcasm to expose folly or vice etc. 2. a work or composition using satire. —**satirical** /sə'tɪrɪkəl/ adj., **satirically** adv. [French or from Latin, originally = medley]

satirist /'sætɪrɪst/ n. a writer or performer of satires.

satirize /'sætɪraɪz/ v.t. to attack with satire; to describe satirically. [from French]

satisfaction /sætɪs'fækʃən/ n. 1. satisfying, being satisfied. 2. a thing that satisfies a desire or gratifies a feeling. 3. a thing that settles an obligation or debt, or compensates for an injury or loss.

satisfactory /sætɪs'fæktərɪ/ adj. satisfying expectations or needs; adequate. —**satisfactorily** adv., **satisfactoriness** n. [from French or Latin]

satisfy /'sætɪsfaɪ/ v.t./i. 1. to give (a person) what he or she wants, demands, or needs; to make pleased or contented; to be adequate. 2. to deal adequately with (an obligation, debt etc.); to pay (a creditor). 3. to put an end to (a demand or craving etc.) by giving what is required. 4. to provide with sufficient information or proof; to convince. [from Old French from Latin *satisfacere* (*satis* = enough and *facere* = make)]

Satō /'saːtəu/ Eisaku 1901–1975. Japanese conservative politician, prime minister 1964–72. He contested Hayato Ikeda (1899–1965) for the Liberal Democratic Party leadership and succeeded him as prime minister, pledged to a more independent foreign policy. He shared the Nobel Peace Prize in 1974 for his rejection of nuclear weapons.

satori n. in Zen Buddhism, awakening, the experience of sudden ◊enlightenment.

satrap /'sætræp/ n. 1. (*historical*) a provincial governor in the ancient Persian empire. 2. (derogatory) any local ruler. [from Old French or Latin from Greek from Old Persian = country protector]

satsuma /sæt'suːmə/ n. a kind of mandarin orange originally grown in Japan. The fruit withstands cold conditions well. [from *Satsuma*, province of Japan]

saturate /'sætʃəreɪt, -tjur-/ v.t. 1. to make thoroughly wet, to soak. 2. to cause to absorb or accept as much as possible. [from Latin *saturare* (*satur* = full)]

saturated compound in chemistry, any organic compound that contains only single covalent bonds, such as propane. Saturated organic compounds can only undergo further reaction by ◊substitution reactions such as the production of chloropropane from propane. They have fewer reactions than unsaturated compounds such as alkenes.

saturated solution in physics, a solution obtained when a solvent (liquid) can dissolve no more of a solute (usually a solid) at a particular temperature. Normally, a slight fall in temperature causes some of the solute to crystallize out of solution. If this does not happen the phenomenon is called supercooling, and the solution is said to be **supersaturated**.

saturation /sætʃə'reɪʃən, -tjur-/ n. the act or result of being saturated. —**saturation point,** the point beyond which no more can be absorbed or accepted.

Saturday /'sætədeɪ, -dɪ/ n. the day of the week following Friday. —*adv.* (*colloquial*) on Saturday. [Old English = day of Saturn]

Saturn /'sætɜːn/ 1. in Roman mythology, the god of agriculture (Greek *Kronos*), whose period of rule was the ancient Golden Age. He was dethroned by his sons Jupiter, Neptune, and Pluto. 2. in astronomy, the second largest planet in the solar system, sixth from the Sun, and encircled by bright and easily visible equatorial rings. Saturn orbits the Sun every 29.46 years at an average distance of 1,427,000,000 km/886,700,000 mi. Its equatorial diameter is 120,000 km/75,000 mi, but its polar diameter is 12,000 km/7,450 mi smaller, a result of its fast rotation and low density, the lowest of any planet. Saturn spins on its axis every 10 hours 14 minutes at its equator, slowing to 10 hours 40 minutes at high latitudes. Its mass is 95 times that of Earth, and its magnetic field 1,000 times stronger. Saturn is believed to have a small core of rock and iron, encased in ice and topped by a deep layer of liquid hydrogen. There are over 20 known moons, its largest being ◊Titan. The visible rings begin about 11,000 km/7,000 mi from the planet's surface and extend out to about 56,000 km/35,000 mi. Made of small chunks of ice and rock (averaging 1 m/3 ft across), they are 275,000 km/170,000 mi rim to rim, but only 100 m/300 ft thick. The ◊Voyager probes showed that the rings actually consist of thousands of closely spaced ringlets.

Saturnalia /sætə'neɪliə/ n. 1. the ancient Roman festival of Saturn in December, observed as a time of unrestrained merrymaking. Gifts were exchanged, and slaves were briefly treated as their masters' equals. 2. **saturnalia,** a scene or time of wild revelry or tumult.

saturnine /'sætənaɪn/ adj. of gloomy forbidding temperament or appearance. [from Old French from Latin]

Saturn rocket a family of large US rockets, developed by Wernher von Braun for the ◊Apollo project. The two-stage Saturn IB was used for launching Apollo spacecraft into orbit around the Earth. The three-stage Saturn V sent Apollo spacecraft to the Moon, and launched the ◊Skylab space station. The lift-off thrust of a Saturn V was 3,500 tonnes. After Apollo and *Skylab*, the Saturn rockets were retired in favour of the ◊space shuttle.

satyr /'sætə/ n. 1. in Greek mythology, a lustful, drunken woodland creature characterized by pointed ears, two horns on the forehead, and a tail. Satyrs attended the god of wine, ◊Dionysus. Roman writers confused satyrs with goat-footed fauns. 2. a grossly lustful man. [from Old French or Latin from Greek]

sauce /sɔːs/ n. 1. a liquid or soft preparation served with food to add moisture, flavour, and richness. 2. impudence. —*v.t.* (*colloquial*) to be impudent to (a person). [from Old French ultimately from Latin *salsus* = salted]

saucepan n. a metal cooking vessel, usually round and with a long handle at the side, for use on top of a cooker etc.

saucer /'sɔːsə/ n. 1. a small shallow dish, especially for standing a cup on. 2. a thing of this shape. [from Old French]

saucy /'sɔːsɪ/ adj. 1. impudent. 2. (*colloquial*) stylish, smart-looking. —**saucily** adv., **sauciness** n.

Saudi /'saʊdɪ/ n. 1. a native or inhabitant of Saudi Arabia. 2. a member of the dynasty founded by ◊Ibn Saud. —adj. of the Saudis or Saudi Arabia.

Saudi Arabia /'saʊdi ə'reɪbiə/ Kingdom of; country on the Arabian peninsula, stretching from the Red Sea to the Arabian Gulf, bounded to the N by Jordan, Iraq, and Kuwait; to the E by Qatar and the United Arab Emirates; to the SE by Oman; and to the S by Yemen; **area** 2,200,518 sq km/ 849,400 sq mi; **capital** Riyadh; **physical** desert, sloping to the Persian Gulf from a height of 2,750 m/9,000 ft in the W; Naful desert in N and the Rub'ai Khali (Empty Quarter) in S, area 650,000 sq km/250,000 sq mi; **head of state and government** King Fahd Ibn Abdul Aziz from 1982; **political system** absolute monarchy; **exports** oil, petroleum products; **population** (1990 est) 16,758,000 (16% nomadic); **language** Arabic; **recent history** the territories were united and the kingdom established 1926–32. Rioting by Iranian pilgrims in 1987 led to severing of diplomatic relations with Iran. In 1990 when Iraqi troops invaded Kuwait and massed on the Saudi Arabian border King Fahd called for help from US and UK forces; the subsequent ◊Gulf War in 1991 ensured Saudi Arabia's security.

sauerkraut /'saʊəkraʊt/ n. a German dish of chopped pickled cabbage. [German (sauer = sour and kraut = vegetable)]

Saul /sɔːl/ in the Old Testament, the first king of Israel. He was anointed by Samuel and warred successfully against the neighbouring Ammonites and Philistines, but fell from God's favour in his battle against the Amalekites. He became jealous and suspicious of David and turned against him and Samuel. After being wounded in battle with the Philistines, in which his three sons died, he committed suicide.

sauna /'sɔːnə/ n. a type of bath causing perspiration by means of dry heat; a building or room for this. The bather typically spends a few minutes in a small room in which the temperature is raised to about 90°C/200°F. This is then followed by a cold shower or swim. [Finnish]

Saunders /'sɔːndəz/ Cicely 1918– . English philanthropist, founder of the hospice movement, which aims to provide a caring and comfortable environment in which people with terminal illnesses can die.

saunter /'sɔːntə/ v.i. to walk in a leisurely way. —n. a leisurely walk or walking pace.

saurian /'sɔːriən/ n. an animal of the lizard family. —adj. of or like a lizard. [from Greek saura = lizard]

sausage /'sɒsɪdʒ/ n. 1. minced meat seasoned and enclosed in a cylindrical case of thin membrane; a length of this. 2. a sausage-shaped object. —**not a sausage,** (slang) nothing at all. **sausage roll,** sausage meat baked in a cylindrical pastry case. [from Old French saussiche from Latin salsicia (salsus = salted)]

sauté /'səʊteɪ/ adj. quickly and lightly fried in a little fat. —n. food cooked thus. —v.t. (past and past participle **sautéd**) to cook thus. [French (sauter = jump)]

Sauternes /səʊ'tɜːn/ n. a sweet white French wine. [from Sauternes, a district of SW France]

savage /'sævɪdʒ/ adj. 1. in a primitive or uncivilized state. 2. wild and fierce. 3. cruel and hostile. 4. (colloquial) very angry. —n. 1. a member of a savage tribe. 2. a brutal or barbarous person. —v.t. 1. (of an animal) to attack savagely, to maul. 2. (of a critic etc.) to attack fiercely. —**savagely** adv., **savageness** n. [from Old French sauvage from Latin silvaticus (silva = forest)]

savagery /'sævɪdʒrɪ/ n. savage behaviour or state.

savanna /sə'vænə/ n. or **savannah** extensive open tropical or subtropical grasslands, with scattered trees and shrubs. Savannas cover large areas of Africa, North and South America, and N Australia. [from Spanish zavana]

savant /'sævənt/ n. a learned person. [French (savoir = know)]

save v.t./i. 1. to rescue, to keep from danger, harm, or capture. 2. to keep for future use or enjoyment; to put aside (money) for future use. 3. to make unnecessary (for); to avoid wasting. 4. to effect the spiritual salvation of. 5. to avoid losing (a match or game etc.); in football etc., to prevent an opponent from scoring. —n. in football etc., the act of preventing an opponent from scoring. —prep. except, but. —conj. (archaic) unless, except. —**save-as-you-earn** n. a method of saving by regular deduction from earnings. —**saver** n. [from Anglo-French sa(u)ver from Latin salvare (salvus = safe)]

Savonarola Italian Dominican monk Savonarola established a democratic republic in Florence. His portrait is by Fra Bartolommeo.

saveloy /'sævəlɔɪ/ n. a highly seasoned dried sausage. [corruption of French cervelas from Italian cervello = brain]

Savery /'seɪvəri/ Thomas c.1650–1715. English engineer who invented the steam-driven water pump, precursor of the steam engine, in 1696.

Savimbi /sə'vɪmbi/ Jonas 1934– . Angolan soldier and right-wing revolutionary, founder of the National Union for the Total Independence of Angola (UNITA).

saving /'seɪvɪŋ/ n. 1. the act of rescuing or keeping from danger etc. 2. (usually in plural) money put aside for future use; unspent income, after deduction of tax. In economics a distinction is made between ◊investment, involving the purchase of capital goods, such as buying a house, and saving (where capital goods are not directly purchased, for example, buying shares). —adj. 1. that saves or redeems. 2. that makes economical use of (labour etc.). 3. (of a clause etc.) stipulating an exception or reservation. —prep. 1. except; with the exception of. 2. without offence to. —**savings and loan association,** in the USA, an institution which makes loans for home improvements, construction, and purchase. It also offers financial services such as insurance and annuities. **savings bank,** a bank paying interest on small deposits. **savings certificate,** an interest-bearing document issued by the government for savers.

saviour /'seɪvjə/ n. a person who saves others from harm or danger. —**our** or **the Saviour,** Jesus Christ. [from Old French from Latin salvator]

savoir-faire /sævwɑː 'feə(r)/ n. knowledge of how to behave in any situation that may arise, tact. [French = know how to do]

Savonarola /sævənə'rəʊlə/ Girolamo 1452–1498. Italian reformer, a Dominican friar and an eloquent preacher. His crusade against political and religious corruption won him popular support, and in 1494 he led a revolt in Florence that expelled the ruling Medici family and established a democratic republic. His denunciations of Pope ◊Alexander VI led to his excommunication in 1497, and in 1498 he was arrested, tortured, hanged, and burned for heresy.

savory /'seɪvəri/ n. an aromatic herb of the genus Satureia, used in cookery.

savour /'seɪvə/ n. 1. a characteristic taste or smell (literal or figurative). 2. the power to arouse enjoyment. —v.t./i. 1. to taste or smell (a thing) with enjoyment or deliberation (literally or figuratively). 2. to have a certain taste or smell. 3. to give a specified impression. [from Old French from Latin sapor (sapere = taste)]

savoury /'seɪvəri/ adj. 1. having an appetizing taste or smell. 2. having a salt or piquant and not a sweet taste.

—*n.* a savoury dish, especially at the end of a meal or as an appetizer. —**savouriness** *n.*

savoy /sə'vɔɪ/ *n.* a ◊cabbage with wrinkled leaves.

Savoy area of France between the Alps, Lake Geneva, and the river Rhône. A medieval duchy, it was made into the *départements* of Savoie and Haute-Savoie, in the Rhône-Alpes region.

savvy /'sævɪ/ *v.t./i.* (*slang*) to know. —*n.* (*slang*) knowingness, understanding. —*adj.* (*US*) knowing, wise. [from Spanish *sabe usted* = you know]

saw[1] *n.* a tool with a toothed metal blade or edge for cutting wood, metal, stone etc., by a to-and-fro or rotary motion. —*v.t./i.* (*past participle* **sawn** or **sawed**) **1.** to cut (wood etc.) with a saw; to make (boards etc.) with a saw. **2.** to move to and fro, to divide (the air etc.) with the motion as of a saw or a person sawing. —**saw off**, to remove or reduce by sawing. **sawtooth** or **sawtoothed** *adj.* shaped like the teeth of a saw, serrated. [Old English]

saw[2] *n.* an old saying, a maxim. [Old English, related to *say*]

saw[3] past of **see**[1].

Sawchuk /'sɔ:tʃʌk/ Terry (Terrance Gordon) 1929–1970. Canadian ice-hockey player, a goaltender. He played for Detroit, Boston, Toronto, Los Angeles, and New York Rangers 1950–67, and holds the National Hockey League (NHL) record of 103 shut-outs (games in which he did not concede a goal).

sawdust *n.* powdery fragments of wood produced in sawing.

sawfish *n.* a fish of the ◊ray order. The **common sawfish** *Pristis pectinatus*, family Pristidae, is more than 6 m/19 ft long. It resembles a shark and has some 24 teeth along an elongated snout (2 m/6 ft), which can be used as a weapon.

sawfly *n.* an insect of the order Hymenoptera, related to bees, wasps, and ants, but lacking a 'waist' on the body. The egg-laying tube (ovipositor) of the female has a saw edge, which she uses to make a slit in a plant stem to lay her eggs.

Saw Maung /sɔ:/ 1929– . Myanmar (Burmese) soldier and politician. Appointed head of the armed forces in 1985 by ◊Ne Win, he led a coup to remove Ne Win's successor, Maung Maung, in 1988 and became leader of an emergency government, which, despite being defeated in the May 1990 election, remained in office.

sawmill *n.* a mill for the mechanical sawing of wood.

sawn past participle of **saw**[1].

sawyer *n.* a workman who saws timber.

sax *n.* (*colloquial*) a ◊saxophone. [abbreviation]

saxe /sæks/ *n.* or **saxe blue** light blue with a greyish tinge. [French = Saxony]

Saxe /sæks/ Maurice, Comte de 1696–1750. Soldier, illegitimate son of the Elector of Saxony, who served under Prince Eugène of Savoy and was created marshal of France in 1743 for his exploits in the War of the Austrian Succession.

Saxe-Coburg-Gotha /'sæks 'kəubɜːg 'gəutə/ Saxon duchy. Albert, the Prince Consort of Britain's Queen Victoria, was a son of the 1st Duke, Ernest I (1784–1844), who was succeeded by Albert's elder brother, Ernest II (1818–1893). It remained the name of the British royal house until 1917, when it was changed to Windsor.

saxhorn /'sækshɔːn/ *n.* a family of brass musical instruments played with valves, invented by the Belgian Adolphe Sax (1814–1894) in 1845.

saxifrage /'sæksɪfrɪdʒ/ *n.* any plant of the genus *Saxifraga*, family Saxifragaceae, occurring in rocky, mountainous, and alpine situations in the northern hemisphere. Saxifrages are low plants with groups of small white, pink, or yellow flowers. [from Old French or Latin *saxifraga* (*saxum* = rock and *frangere* = break]

Saxon *n.* **1.** a member of a Teutonic people, one branch of which invaded Britain in the early Middle Ages; see under ◊Anglo-Saxon. **2.** or **Old Saxon** the language of this tribe. **3.** Anglo-Saxon. **4.** a native of modern Saxony. **5.** the Germanic (as opposed to Latin or Romance) elements of English. —*adj.* of the Saxons or their language. [from French from Latin *Saxo*]

Saxony (German *Sachsen*) administrative *Land* (state) · of Germany; **area** 17,036 sq km/6,580 sq mi; **capital** Dresden; **products** electronics, textiles, vehicles, machinery, chemicals, coal; **population** (1990) 5,000,000; **recent**

history in 1946 Saxony became a region of East Germany and in 1952 it was split into the districts of Leipzig, Dresden, and Chemnitz (later named Karl-Marx-Stadt). The state of Saxony was restored in 1990 following German reunification and the abolition of the former East German districts.

Saxony-Anhalt /'sæksənɪ 'ænhælt/ administrative *Land* (state) of Germany; **area** 25,000 sq km/10,000 sq mi; **capital** Magdeburg; **products** chemicals, electronics, rolling stock, footwear, cereals, vegetables; **population** (1990) 3,000,000; **recent history** in 1946 Saxony-Anhalt was joined to the former Prussian province of Saxony as a region of East Germany and in 1952 it was divided into the districts of Halle and Magdeburg. Following the reunification of Germany in 1990, Saxony-Anhalt was reconstituted as one of the five new *Länder* of the Federal Republic.

saxophone /'sæksəfəun/ *n.* a large family of wind instruments combining woodwind and brass features, the single reed of the clarinet and the wide bore of the bugle. Patented in 1846 by Adolphe Sax (1814–1894), a Belgian instrument maker, the saxophone is a lively and versatile instrument that has played a prominent part in the history of jazz. Four of the original eight sizes remain in common use: soprano, alto, tenor, and baritone. The soprano is usually straight, the others curved back at the mouthpiece end, and with an upturned bell. —**saxophonist** /-'səfnɪst/ *n.*

say *v.t./i.* (*past and past participle* **said** /sed/; third person singular present of **says** /sez/) **1.** to utter or recite in a speaking voice. **2.** to state; to have a specified wording. **3.** to put into words; to convey information; to indicate or show. **4.** to give as an argument or excuse. **5.** to give as an opinion or decision. **6.** to suppose as a possibility; to select as an example etc.; to take (a specified amount etc.) as being near enough. —*n.* **1.** what one wishes to say; an opportunity of saying this. **2.** a share in a discussion or decision; the power of final decision. —**go without saying**, to be obvious. **I'll say**, (*colloquial*) yes indeed. **I say**, an exclamation drawing attention, opening a conversation, or expressing surprise. **say-so** *n.* the power of decision; mere assertion. **says you**, (*slang*) I disagree. **that is to say**, in other words. [Old English]

SAYE abbreviation of save-as-you-earn (see ◊save).

Sayers /'seɪəz/ Dorothy L(eigh) 1893–1957. English writer of crime novels featuring detective Lord Peter Wimsey and heroine Harriet Vane, including *Strong Poison* 1930, *The Nine Tailors* 1934, and *Gaudy Night* 1935. She also wrote religious plays for radio, and translations of Dante.

saying *n.* a frequent or proverbial remark.

Say's law /seɪz/ in economics, the 'law of markets' formulated by Jean-Baptiste Say (1767–1832) to the effect that supply creates its own demand and that resources can never be underused.

Sb symbol for ◊antimony. [from Latin *stibium*]

sc. abbreviation of ◊scilicet.

Sc symbol for ◊scandium.

scab *n.* **1.** a crust formed over a sore in healing. **2.** a kind of skin disease or plant disease with scabs or scablike roughness. **3.** (*derogatory*) a blackleg in a strike. —*v.i.* (-bb-) **1.** to form a scab; to heal over thus. **2.** (*derogatory*) act as a blackleg. —**scabby** *adj.*

scabbard /'skæbəd/ *n.* the sheath of a sword etc. [from Anglo-French]

scabies /'skeɪbiː/ *n.* a contagious infection of the skin caused by the parasitic itch mite *Sarcoptes scaboi*, which burrows under the skin to deposit eggs. Treatment is by antiparasitic creams and lotions. [Latin *scabere* = scratch]

scabious /'skeɪbiəs/ *n.* any plant of the Eurasian genus *Scabiosa* of the teasel family Dipsacaceae, with many small, usually blue, flowers borne in a single head on a tall stalk. The field scabious *Knautia arvensis*, although of a different genus, is closely related. [from Latin *scabiosa* (*herba*) = plant curing itch]

scabrous /'skeɪbrəs/ *adj.* **1.** (of the skin etc.) rough and scaly. **2.** indecent. [from French or Latin *scaber* = rough]

scaffold /'skæfəld/ *n.* **1.** a platform on which criminals are executed. **2.** scaffolding. [from Old French]

scaffolding *n.* **1.** a temporary structure of poles or tubes and planks providing platforms for building work; the materials for this. **2.** any temporary framework.

scalar

scalar /'skeɪlə/ *adj.* in mathematics, having magnitude but not direction. —**scalar quantity**, a quantity that has magnitude but no direction, as distinct from a ◊vector quantity, which has a direction as well as a magnitude. Temperature, mass, and volume are scalar quantities. [from Latin *scala* = ladder]

scalawag *n.* or **scallywag 1.** a rascal. **2.** (*US historical, derogatory*) a white Southerner who, during and after the Civil War of 1861–65, supported the Republican Party and black emancipation and enfranchisement.

scald[1] /skɔld, skɒld/ *v.t.* **1.** to injure or pain with hot liquid or vapour. **2.** to heat (especially milk or cream) to near boiling point. **3.** to cleanse (a vessel) with boiling water. —*n.* an injury to the skin by scalding. [from Anglo-French from Latin *excaldare* (*calidus* = hot)]

scald[2] variant of ◊skald.

scale[1] *n.* **1.** a set of marks at fixed distances on a line for use in measuring etc.; a rule determining the intervals between these; a piece of metal etc. on which they are marked. **2.** relative dimensions or extent; the ratio of reduction or enlargement in a map, drawing etc. **3.** a series of degrees; a ladderlike arrangement, a graded system. **4.** in music, a sequence of pitches that establishes a key, and in some respects the character of a composition. A scale is defined by its starting note and may be major or minor depending on the order of intervals. A **chromatic scale** is the full range of 12 notes: it has no key because there is no fixed starting point. A **whole-tone scale** is a six-note scale and is also indeterminate in key: only two are possible. A **diatonic scale** has seven notes, a **pentatonic scale** has five. —*v.t.* **1.** to climb (a wall, precipice etc.) with a ladder or by clambering. **2.** to represent in dimensions different from but proportional to the actual ones. —**in scale**, in proportion. **on a large** (*or* **small**) **scale**, to a large (or small) extent. **scale down** (*or* **up**), to make smaller (or larger) in proportion; to reduce (or increase) in size. **to scale**, with uniform reduction or enlargement. [from Latin *scala* = ladder]

scale[2] *n.* **1.** any of the small, thin, horny overlapping plates protecting the skin of many fishes and reptiles. **2.** a thin plate or flake resembling this. **3.** an incrustation of calcium carbonate deposits inside a boiler or kettle etc. in which hard water is regularly used; tartar on teeth. —*v.t./i.* **1.** to remove scale(s) from. **2.** to form or drop off in scales. —**scaly** *adj.* [from Old French *escale*]

scale[3] *n.* **1.** the pan of a weighing balance. **2.** (in *plural*) a weighing instrument; **the Scales**, the constellation or sign of the zodiac ◊Libra. —*v.t.* to be found to weigh (a specified amount). —**pair of scales**, a simple balance. **tip** *or* **turn the scale(s)**, to outweigh the opposite scale; to be the decisive factor. [from Old Norse = bowl]

scalene /'skeɪliːn/ *adj.* in geometry, (of a triangle etc.) having unequal sides. [from Latin from Greek *skalēnos* = unequal]

scallion /'skæljən/ *n.* a ◊shallot; a long-necked bulbless onion. [from Anglo-French from Latin = onion of *Ascalon* in Palestine]

scallop *n.* **1.** a marine ◊mollusc of the family Pectinidae, with a bivalve fan-shaped shell. Scallops use 'jet propulsion' to move through the water to escape predators such as starfish. **2.** one shell of this used as a container in which food is cooked and served. **3.** each of a series of ornamental semicircular curves edging a fabric etc. —*v.t.* **1.** to cook in a scallop. **2.** to ornament (material etc.) with scallops. **3.** (usually in *past participle*) to bake (slices of potato) overlapping in a scalloplike arrangement. [from Old French = escalope]

scalloping *n.* a scallop edging.

scallywag /'skæliwæg/ alternative spelling of ◊scalawag.

scalp *n.* the skin and hair of the top of the head; this formerly cut off as a trophy by an American Indian. —*v.t.* **1.** to remove the scalp of. **2.** to criticize savagely. **3.** (*US colloquial*) to resell at a high or quick profit.

scalpel /'skælpəl/ *n.* a small surgical knife. [French or from Latin diminutive of *scalprum* = chisel (*scalpere* = scratch, carve)]

scaly anteater another name for the ◊pangolin.

scamp *n.* a rascal. —*v.t.* to do (work etc.) perfunctorily or inadequately. [from *scamp* = rob on highway, probably from Middle Dutch = decamp]

scamper *v.i.* to move or run hastily or impulsively, to run about playfully. —*n.* an act of scampering.

scampi /'skæmpi/ *n.pl.* large prawns; these as food. [Italian]

scan *v.t./i.* (**-nn-**) **1.** to look at all parts of (a thing) successively. **2.** to look over quickly or cursorily. **3.** to traverse with a controlled electronic or radar beam. **4.** to resolve (a picture) into its elements of light and shade for television transmission. **5.** to test the metre of (a line etc. of verse) by examining the nature and number of its feet and syllables; (of a line etc.) to be metrically correct. —*n.* an act or process of scanning. —**scanner** *n.* any device, usually electronic, used to sense and reproduce an image; see ◊scanning. [from Latin *scandere*, originally = climb]

scandal *n.* **1.** a general feeling of (especially moral) outrage or indignation; a thing causing this. **2.** malicious gossip about people's faults and wrongdoing. [from Old French from Latin from Greek = stumbling block]

scandalize /'skændəlaɪz/ *v.t.* to offend the moral feelings or sense of propriety of.

scandalmonger *n.* a person who disseminates scandal.

scandalous /'skændələs/ *adj.* containing or arousing scandal, outrageous, shocking. —**scandalously** *adv.*

Scandinavia /skændɪ'neɪvɪə/ peninsula in NW Europe, comprising Norway and Sweden; politically and culturally it also includes Denmark, Finland, and Iceland.

Scandinavian /skændɪ'neɪvɪən/ *adj.* of Scandinavia or its people or languages. —*n.* **1.** a native of Scandinavia. **2.** the languages of Scandinavia.

scandium /'skændɪəm/ *n.* a silver-white, metallic element of the ◊lanthanide series, symbol Sc, atomic number 21, relative atomic mass 44.956. Its compounds are found widely distributed in nature, but only in minute amounts. The metal has little industrial importance. [from Latin *Scandia* = Scandinavia (source of minerals containing it)]

scanning *n.* in medicine, the noninvasive examination of body organs to detect abnormalities of structure or function. Detectable waves, for example ◊ultrasound, magnetic, or ◊X-rays, are passed through the part to be scanned. Their absorption pattern is recorded, analysed by computer, and displayed pictorially on a screen.

scansion /'skænʃən/ *n.* metrical scanning. [from Latin]

scant *adj.* scanty, insufficient. —*v.t.* (*archaic*) to skimp, to stint. [from Old Norse *skammr* = short]

scantling *n.* **1.** a timber beam of small cross section. **2.** the size to which stone or timber is to be cut. **3.** a set of standard dimensions for parts of a structure, especially in shipbuilding. [from obsolete *scantlon* from Old French = sample]

scanty *adj.* **1.** of small amount or extent. **2.** barely sufficient. —**scantily** *adv.*, **scantiness** *n.*

scapegoat /'skeɪpgəʊt/ *n.* **1.** in the Old Testament, a goat allowed to escape when the Jewish chief priest had symbolically laid the sins of the people upon it (Leviticus 16). **2.** a person who is made to bear blame or punishment that should rightly fall on others. [from archaic *scape* = escape]

scapegrace /'skeɪpgreɪs/ *n.* a wild and foolish or rash person, especially a child or young person who constantly gets into trouble. [= one who *escapes* the *grace* of God]

scapula *n.* or **shoulder blade** (*plural* **scapulae** /-liː/) a large bone forming part of the pectoral girdle, assisting in the articulation of the arm with the chest region. Its flattened shape allows a large region for the attachment of muscles. [Latin]

scapular /'skæpjʊlə/ *adj.* of the scapula. —*n.* **1.** a monastic short cloak. **2.** a scapular feather.

scar[1] *n.* **1.** a mark left by damage, especially on the skin by a healed wound or on a plant by the loss of a leaf etc. **2.** the lasting effect of grief etc. —*v.t./i.* (**-rr-**) to mark with a scar; to form a scar or scars. [from Old French from Latin from Greek *eskhara* = scab]

scar[2] *n.* a precipitous craggy part of a mountainside or cliff. [from Old Norse = reef]

scarab /'skærəb/ *n.* **1.** a beetle of the family Scarabaeidae. **2.** the sacred dung beetle *Scarabeus sacer*, revered by the ancient Egyptians as the symbol of resurrection. **3.** a carving of a beetle, engraved with symbols on the flat side and used in ancient Egypt as a charm. [from Latin *scarabaeus* from Greek]

scarce /skeəs/ *adj.* **1.** (usually *predicative*) not plentiful, insufficient for demand or need. **2.** seldom found, rare.

—adv. (literary) scarcely. **—make oneself scarce,** to go away; to keep out of the way. [from Anglo-French ultimately from Latin *excerpere* from *carpere* = pluck]

scarcely *adv.* **1.** almost not; not quite; only just. **2.** not; surely not; probably not.

scarcity /'skeəsɪtɪ/ *n.* being scarce; a shortage.

scare *v.t./i.* to strike or be struck with sudden fear, to startle and frighten; to drive (away, off etc.) by fright; *(in past participle)* frightened. *—n.* a sudden outbreak of fear; alarm caused by a rumour. [from Old Norse *skirra* = frighten]

scarecrow *n.* **1.** a figure of a person dressed in old clothes and set up in a field to scare birds away from crops. **2.** a badly dressed or grotesque person.

scaremonger *n.* a person who raises unnecessary or excessive alarm. **—scaremongering** *n.*

scarf[1] *n. (plural* **scarves** /skɑːvz/) **1.** a long, narrow strip of material worn for warmth or ornament round the neck. **2.** a square piece of material worn round the neck or over a woman's hair. [probably from Old French *escarpe* = sash]

scarf[2] *n.* a joint made by thinning the ends of two pieces of timber etc. so that they overlap without an increase of thickness and fastening them with bolts etc. *—v.t.* to join with a scarf. [related to French *écarver*]

Scargill Arthur 1938– . British trade-union leader. Elected president of the National Union of Miners (NUM) in 1981, he embarked on a collision course with the Conservative government of Margaret Thatcher. The damaging strike of 1984–85 split the miners' movement. In 1990 an independent inquiry, commissioned by the NUM, found him guilty of breach of duty and maintaining double accounts during the strike.

scarify[1] /'skeərɪfaɪ, 'skæ-/ *v.t.* **1.** to loosen the surface of (soil etc.). **2.** to make slight incisions in (skin etc.); to cut off skin from. **3.** to criticize etc. mercilessly. **—scarification** /-fɪ'keɪʃən/ *n.* [from French from Latin from Greek *skariphos* = stylus]

scarify[2] /'skeərɪfaɪ/ *v.t. (colloquial)* to scare, to terrify.

scarlatina /skɑːlə'tiːnə/ *n.* ◊scarlet fever. [Italian]

Scarlatti /skɑː'læti/ (Giuseppe) Domenico 1685–1757. Italian composer, eldest son of Alessandro Scarlatti, who lived most of his life in Portugal and Spain in the service of the Queen of Spain. He wrote highly original harpsichord sonatas.

Scarlatti (Pietro) Alessandro (Gaspare) 1660–1725. Italian Baroque composer, Master of the Chapel at the court of Naples, who developed the opera form. He composed more than 100 operas, including *Tigrane* 1715, as well as church music and oratorios.

scarlet /'skɑːlɪt/ *adj.* of brilliant red colour. *—n.* **1.** scarlet colour or pigment. **2.** scarlet clothes or material. **—scarlet runner,** a kind of bean; the scarlet-flowered climbing plant *Phaseolus multiflorus* bearing this. [from Old French *escarlate*]

scarlet fever or **scarlatina** an acute infectious disease, especially of children, caused by the bacterium *Streptococcus pyogenes*. It is marked by a sore throat and a bright red rash spreading from the upper to the lower part of the body. The rash is followed by the skin peeling in flakes. It is treated with antibiotics.

scarp *n.* a steep slope, especially the inner side of a ditch in a fortification. *—v.t.* to make steep or perpendicular. **—scarp and dip,** in geology, the two slopes formed when a sedimentary bed outcrops as a landscape feature. The scarp is the slope that cuts across the bedding plane; the dip is the opposite slope which follows the bedding plane. The scarp is usually steep, while the dip is a gentle slope. [from Italian *scarpa*]

scarper *v.i. (slang)* to escape, to run away. [probably from Italian *scappare* = escape, influenced by rhyming slang *Scapa Flow* = go]

scary /'skeərɪ/ *adj. (colloquial)* frightening.

scat[1] *v.i.* (-tt-) *(colloquial)* to depart quickly. *—int. (colloquial)* depart quickly.

scat[2] *n.* wordless jazz singing using the voice as an instrument. *—v.i.* to sing in this style.

scathe /skeɪð/ *v.t. (archaic)* to harm or injure. *—n. (archaic)* harm, injury. [from Old Norse; compare Old English *sceatha* = malefactor, injury]

scathing /'skeɪðɪŋ/ *adj.* (of a look, criticism etc.) harsh, severe.

scatology /skæ'tɒlədʒɪ/ *n.* preoccupation with obscene literature or with excrement. **—scatological** /skætə'lɒdʒɪkəl/ *adj.* [from Greek *skōr* = dung]

scatter *v.t./i.* **1.** to throw or put here and there; to cover thus. **2.** to go or send in different directions. **3.** to deflect or diffuse (light or particles etc.). **4.** (in *past participle*) not situated together, wide apart. *—n.* **1.** scattering. **2.** a small amount scattered. **3.** the extent of distribution, especially of shot. **—scatterbrain** *n.* a scatterbrained person. **scatterbrained** *adj.* lacking concentration; disorganized; flighty.

scatty *adj. (slang)* scatterbrained, crazy. **—scattily** *adv.,* **scattiness** *n.*

scaup *n.* a diving duck of the genus *Aythya*, frequenting northern coasts. [from *scaup*, Scottish variant of *scalp* = musselbed, which it frequents]

scaur variant of ◊scar[2].

scavenge /'skævɪndʒ/ *v.t./i.* **1.** to be or act as a scavenger (of). **2.** to remove dirt, waste, or impurities etc. from. [back formation from *scavenger*]

scavenger /'skævɪndʒə/ *n.* **1.** a person who searches among or collects things unwanted by others. **2.** an animal or bird that feeds on carrion. [originally = inspector of imports, from Anglo-French]

Sc.D. abbreviation of Doctor of Science. [from Latin *scientiae doctor*]

scenario /sɪ'nɑːrɪəʊ/ *n. (plural* **scenarios**) **1.** the script or synopsis of a film, play etc. **2.** an imagined sequence of future events. [Italian]

scene /siːn/ *n.* **1.** the place in which an event or series of events takes or took place. **2.** a portion of a play during which the action is continuous; a subdivision of an act; a similar portion of a film, book etc. **3.** an incident thought of as resembling this. **4.** a dramatic outburst of temper or emotion; a stormy interview. **5.** a landscape or view as seen by a spectator. **6.** stage scenery. **7.** *(slang)* an area or subject of activity or interest; a way of life. **—behind the scenes,** behind stage, out of sight of the audience; not known to the public, working secretly. **come on the scene,** to arrive. **set the scene,** to describe the location of events etc. **scene shifter,** a person engaged in changing the scenery in a theatre. [from Latin from Greek *skēnē* = tent, stage]

scenery /'siːnərɪ/ *n.* **1.** structures used on a theatre stage to represent features in the scene of the action. **2.** the general appearance of a landscape; its picturesque features. [earlier *scenary* from Italian *scenario*]

scenic /'siːnɪk/ *adj.* **1.** having fine natural scenery. **2.** of scenery. **3.** of or on the stage. **—scenic railway,** a miniature railway running through artificial picturesque scenery as an amusement at a fair. **—scenically** *adv.*

scent /sent/ *n.* **1.** a characteristic odour, especially a pleasant one. **2.** liquid perfume. **3.** the smell or trail left by an animal; a line of investigation or pursuit. **4.** the power of detecting or distinguishing smells or discovering the presence of something. *—v.t.* **1.** to discern by sense of smell. **2.** to sniff out. **3.** to begin to suspect the presence or existence of. **4.** to make fragrant, to apply perfume to. **—off the scent,** misled by false information etc. **—scented** *adj.* [from Old French *sentir* = perceive, smell, from Latin *sentire* = feel, sense]

scent gland a gland that opens onto the outer surface of animals, producing odorous compounds that are used for communicating between members of the same species (◊pheromones), or for discouraging predators.

sceptic /'skeptɪk/ *n.* **1.** a sceptical person; one who doubts the truth of religious doctrines. **2.** a philosopher who questions the possibility of knowledge. **—scepticism** /-sɪzəm/ *n.* **—Scepticism,** an ancient philosophical view that absolute knowledge of things is ultimately unobtainable, hence the only proper attitude is to suspend judgement. Its origins lay in the teachings of the Greek philosopher Pyrrho, who maintained that peace of mind lay in renouncing all claims to knowledge. [from French or Latin from Greek *skeptomai* = consider]

sceptical /'skeptɪkəl/ *adj.* inclined to disbelieve things; doubting or questioning the truth of claims or statements etc. **—sceptically** *adv.*

sceptre /'septə/ *n.* a staff borne as a symbol of sovereignty. [from Old French from Latin from Greek *skē ptron* (*skē ptō* = lean on)]

Schadenfreude /'ʃadənfrɔɪdə/ n. malicious enjoyment of others' misfortunes. [German (*Schaden* = harm and *Freude* = joy)]

schedule /'ʃedju:l/ n. 1. a timetable or programme of planned events or work etc. 2. a table of details or items, especially as an appendix to a document. —v.t. 1. to make a schedule of; to include in a schedule; to appoint a time for. 2. to include (an ancient monument) in a list of those considered to be of national importance and so to be preserved. —**on schedule**, to time, not late. **scheduled flight**, one operated on a regular timetable. [from Old French from Latin *schedula* = slip of paper, diminutive of *scheda* from Greek *skhēdē* = papyrus leaf]

Scheele /'ʃeɪlə/ Karl 1742–1786. Swedish chemist and pharmacist. In the book *Experiments on Air and Fire* 1777, he argued that the atmosphere was composed of two gases. One, which supported combustion (oxygen), he called 'fire air', and the other, which inhibited combustion (nitrogen), he called 'vitiated air'. He thus anticipated Joseph ◊Priestley's discovery of oxygen by two years.

Scheer /ʃeə/ Reinhard 1863–1928. German admiral in World War I, commander of the High Sea Fleet in 1916 at the Battle of ◊Jutland.

Scheherazade /ʃəherə'zɑ:d/ n. the storyteller in the ◊*Arabian Nights*.

schematic /skiˈmætɪk/ adj. in the form of a diagram or chart. —n. a schematic diagram. —**schematically** adv.

schematize /'ski:mətaɪz/ v.t. to put into schematic form; to formulate in regular order. —**schematization** /-'zeɪʃən/ n. [from Greek = assume a form]

scheme /ski:m/ n. 1. a plan of work or action. 2. an orderly planned arrangement. 3. a secret or underhand plan. —v.t./i. to make plans; to plan, especially in secret or in an underhand way. —**schemer** n. [from Latin from Greek *skhēma* = form, figure]

Scherchen /'ʃeəʃən/ Hermann 1891–1966. German conductor. He collaborated with ◊Schoenberg, and in 1919 founded the journal *Melos* to promote contemporary music. He moved to Switzerland in 1933, and was active as a conductor and teacher. He wrote two texts, *Handbook of Conducting* and *The Nature of Music*. During the 1950s he founded a music publishing house, Ars Viva Verlag, and an electronic studio at Gravesano.

scherzo /'skeətsəʊ/ n. (*plural* **scherzos**) in music, a lively piece, usually in rapid triple (3/4) time; often used for the third movement of a symphony, sonata, or quartet. [Italian = jest]

Schiaparelli /skjæpə'reli/ Elsa 1896–1973. Italian couturier and knitwear designer. Her innovative fashion ideas included padded shoulders, sophisticated colours ('shocking pink'), and the pioneering use of zips and synthetic fabrics.

Schiaparelli Giovanni (Virginio) 1835–1910. Italian astronomer who discovered the so-called 'Martian canals'. He studied ancient and medieval astronomy, discovered the asteroid 69 (Hesperia) in 1861, observed double stars, and revealed the connection between comets and meteors. In 1877 he was the first to draw attention to the linear markings on Mars, which gave rise to the 'Martian canal' controversy. These markings are now known to be optical effects and not real lines.

Schiele /'ʃi:lə/ Egon 1890–1918. Austrian Expressionist artist. Originally a landscape painter, he was strongly influenced by Art Nouveau and developed a contorted linear style. His subject matter included portraits and nudes. In 1911 he was arrested for alleged obscenity.

Schiller /'ʃɪlə/ Johann Christoph Friedrich von 1759–1805. German dramatist, poet, and historian. He wrote *Sturm und Drang* ('storm and stress') verse and plays, including the dramatic trilogy *Wallenstein* 1798–99. Much of his work concerns the aspirations for political freedom and the avoidance of mediocrity.

Against stupidity the gods themselves struggle in vain.

Friedrich von Schiller
Die Jungfrau von Orleans

Schinkel /'ʃɪŋkəl/ Karl Friedrich 1781–1841. Prussian Neo-Classical architect. Major works include the Old

Museum, Berlin, 1823–30, the Nikolaikirche in Potsdam 1830–37, and the Roman Bath 1833 in the park of Potsdam.

schism /'sɪzəm, 'skɪ-/ n. division into opposing groups because of a difference in belief or opinion, especially in a religious body, as in the ◊Great Schism in the Roman Catholic Church; over the doctrine of papal infallibility, as with the Old Catholics in 1879; and over the use of the Latin Tridentine mass in 1988. —**schismatic** /-'mætɪk/ adj., **schismatically** adv. [from Old French from Latin from Greek *skhisma* = cleft (*skhizō* = split)]

schist /ʃɪst/ n. a foliated (laminated) ◊metamorphic rock arranged in parallel layers of ◊minerals, for example, mica, which easily splits off into thin plates. [from French from Latin from Greek *skhistos* = split]

schizo /'skɪtsəʊ/ n. (*plural* **schizos**) (*colloquial*) a schizophrenic. [abbreviation]

schizocarp n. a type of dry ◊fruit that develops from two or more carpels and splits, when mature, to form separate one-seeded units known as mericarps.

schizoid /'skɪtsɔɪd/ adj. of or resembling schizophrenia or a schizophrenic. —n. a schizoid person.

schizophrenia /skɪtsə'fri:nɪə/ n. a mental disorder, a psychosis of unknown origin, which can lead to profound changes in personality and behaviour including paranoia and hallucinations. Modern treatment approaches include drugs, family therapy, stress reduction, and rehabilitation. —**schizophrenic** /-'frenɪk/ adj. & n. [from Greek *skhizō* = split and *phrēn* = mind]

Schlegel /'ʃleɪgəl/ August Wilhelm von 1767–1845. German Romantic author, translator of Shakespeare, whose *Über dramatische Kunst und Literatur/Lectures on Dramatic Art and Literature* 1809–11 broke down the formalism of the old classical criteria of literary composition.

Schlegel Friedrich von 1772–1829. German critic, who (with his brother August) was a founder of the Romantic movement, and a pioneer in the comparative study of languages.

Schlesinger /'ʃlesɪndʒə/ John 1926– . English film and television director who was responsible for such British films as *Billy Liar* 1963 and *Darling* 1965. His first US film, *Midnight Cowboy* 1969, was a big commercial success and was followed by *Sunday, Bloody Sunday* 1971, *Marathon Man* 1976, and *Yanks* 1979.

Schleswig-Holstein /'ʃlezwɪg 'hɒlstaɪn/ *Land* (state) of Germany; **area** 15,700 sq km/6,060 sq mi; **capital** Kiel; **physical** river Elbe, Kiel Canal, Heligoland; **products** shipbuilding, mechanical and electrical engineering, food processing; **population** (1988) 2,613,000; **recent history** formerly held by Denmark, the two duchies of Schleswig and Holstein were annexed by Prussia in 1866. A plebiscite held in 1920 returned the northern part of Schleswig to Denmark, which made it the province of Haderslev and Aabenraa; the rest, with Holstein, remained part of Germany.

Schlieffen Plan /'ʃli:fən/ a military plan produced by the German chief of general staff, General Count Alfred von Schlieffen (1833–1913), in Dec 1905, which formed the basis of German military planning before World War I, and which inspired Hitler's plans for the conquest of Europe in World War II. It involved a simultaneous attack on Russia and France, the object being to defeat France quickly and then deploy all available resources against the Russians.

Schliemann /'ʃli:mən/ Heinrich 1822–1890. German archaeologist. He earned a fortune in business, retiring in 1863 to pursue his lifelong ambition to discover a historical basis for Homer's *Iliad*. In 1871 he began excavating at Hissarlik, Turkey, a site which yielded the ruins of nine consecutive cities and was indeed the site of Troy. His later excavations were at Mycenae 1874–76, where he discovered the ruins of the ◊Mycenaean civilization.

schmaltz /ʃmɒlts/ n. sugary sentimentalism, especially in music or literature. [Yiddish from German = dripping]

Schmidt /ʃmɪt/ Helmut 1918– . German socialist politician, member of the Social Democratic Party (SPD), chancellor of West Germany 1974–83. As chancellor, Schmidt introduced social reforms and continued Brandt's policy of ◊Ostpolitik. With the French president Giscard d'Estaing, he instigated annual world and European economic summits. He was a firm supporter of ◊NATO and of the deployment of US nuclear missiles in West Germany during the early 1980s.

Schoenberg *Arnold Schoenberg teaching at the University of California.*

Schmidt-Rottluff /ʃmɪt ˈrɒtluf/ Karl 1884–1974. German Expressionist painter and printmaker, a founding member of the movement **Die ◊Brücke** in Dresden in 1905, active in Berlin from 1911. Inspired by Vincent van Gogh and ◊Fauvism, he developed a vigorous style of brushwork and a bold palette. He painted portraits and landscapes and produced numerous woodcuts and lithographs.

schnapps /ʃnæps/ *n.* a kind of strong gin. [German, = dram of liquor, from Low German and Dutch *snaps* = mouthful]

Schneider /ˈʃnaɪdə/ Romy. Stage name of Rosemarie Albach-Retty 1938–1982. Austrian film actress who starred in *Boccaccio '70* 1962, *Le Procès/Der Prozess* 1962, and *Ludwig* 1972.

schnitzel /ˈʃnɪtsəl/ *n.* a veal cutlet. [German]

Schoenberg /ˈʃɜ:nbɜ:g/ Arnold (Franz Walter) 1874–1951. Austro-Hungarian composer, a US citizen from 1941. After Romantic early work such as *Verklärte Nacht* 1899 and the *Gurrelieder/Songs of Gurra* 1900–11, he experimented with ◊atonality (absence of key), producing works such as *Pierrot Lunaire* 1912 for chamber ensemble and voice, before developing the 12-tone system of musical composition. This was further developed by his pupils ◊Berg and ◊Webern.

scholar /ˈskɒlə/ *n.* **1.** a person with great learning in a particular subject; one who is skilled in academic work. **2.** a person who learns. **3.** a person who holds a scholarship. —**scholarly** *adj.* [from Old French from Latin *scholaris*]

scholarship *n.* **1.** an award of money towards education, usually gained by means of a competitive examination. **2.** learning or knowledge in a particular subject. **3.** the methods and achievements characteristic of scholars and academic work.

scholastic /skɒˈlæstɪk/ *adj.* of schools or education, academic. —**scholastically** *adv.* [from Latin from Greek]

scholasticism /skəˈlæstɪsɪzəm/ *n.* the theological and philosophical systems that were studied in both Christian and Judaic schools in Europe in the medieval period. Scholasticism sought to integrate biblical teaching with Platonic and Aristotelian philosophy.

school[1] /skuːl/ *n.* **1.** an institution for educating children or giving instruction. **2.** (*US*) a university; a department of this. **3.** the buildings or pupils of such an institution; the time during which teaching is done. **4.** the process of being educated in a school; circumstances or an occupation serving to educate or discipline. **5.** a branch of study at a university. **6.** a group of thinkers, artists etc., sharing the same principles, methods, characteristics, or inspirations. **7.** a group of card players or gamblers. **8.** a medieval lecture room. —*v.t.* **1.** to educate; to send to school. **2.** to discipline; to train or accustom. —**school-leaver** *n.* a person who has just left school. **school year**, the period when schools are in session, reckoned from the autumn term. [from Old English, ultimately from Latin *schola* = school from Greek *skholē* = leisure, disputation, philosophy, lecture place]

school[2] *n.* a shoal of fish, whales etc. [from Middle Low German or Middle Dutch = Old English *scolu* = troop]

schoolchild *n.* (*plural* **schoolchildren**) (also **schoolboy, schoolgirl**) a child who attends school.

schoolhouse *n.* the building of a school, especially that of a village.

schooling *n.* education, especially in a school.

schoolman *n.* (*plural* **schoolmen**) **1.** a teacher in a medieval European university. **2.** a theologian seeking to deal with religious doctrines by the rules of Aristotelian logic.

schoolmaster *n.* a male teacher in a school. —**schoolmistress** *n.fem.*

schoolroom *n.* a room used for lessons in a school or private house.

schoolteacher *n.* a teacher in a school.

schooner /ˈskuːnə/ *n.* **1.** a fore-and-aft-rigged ship with more than one mast. **2.** a large glass of sherry etc.

Schopenhauer /ˈʃəʊpənhaʊə/ Arthur 1788–1860. German philosopher whose *The World as Will and Idea* 1818 expounded an atheistic and pessimistic world view: an irrational will is considered as the inner principle of the world, producing an ever-frustrated cycle of desire, of which the only escape is aesthetic contemplation or absorption into nothingness.

schottische /ʃɒˈtiː.ʃ/ *n.* a kind of slow polka; the music for this. [from German *der schottische Tanz* = the Scottish dance]

Schreiner /ˈʃraɪnə/ Olive 1862–1920. South African novelist and supporter of women's rights. Her autobiographical *The Story of an African Farm* 1883 describes life on the South African veld.

Schubert /ˈʃuːbət/ Franz (Peter) 1797–1828. Austrian composer. His ten symphonies include the incomplete eighth in B minor (the 'Unfinished') and the 'Great' in C major. He wrote chamber and piano music, including the 'Trout Quintet', and over 600 Lieder (songs) combining the Romantic expression of emotion with pure melody. They include the cycles *Die schöne Müllerin/The Beautiful Maid of the Mill* 1823 and *Die Winterreise/The Winter Journey* 1827.

Schumacher /ˈʃuːmækə/ Fritz. Ernst Friedrich 1911–1977. German writer and economist, whose *Small is Beautiful: Economics as if People Mattered* 1973 makes a case for small-scale economic growth without great capital expenditure.

Schuman /ˈʃuːmɒn/ Robert 1886–1963. French politician. He was prime minister 1947–48, and as foreign minister 1948–53 he proposed in May 1950 a common market for coal and steel (the **Schuman Plan**), which was established as the European Coal and Steel Community in 1952, the basis of the European Community.

Schumann /ˈʃuːmən/ Robert Alexander 1810–1856. German Romantic composer. His songs and short piano pieces show simplicity combined with an ability to portray mood and emotion. Among his compositions are four symphonies, a violin concerto, a piano concerto, sonatas, and song cycles, such as *Dichterliebe/Poet's Love* 1840. Mendelssohn championed many of his works.

Schuschnigg /ˈʃuʃnɪg/ Kurt von 1897–1977. Austrian chancellor 1934–38, in succession to ◊Dollfuss. He tried in vain to prevent Nazi annexation (*Anschluss*); in Feb 1938 he was forced to accept a Nazi minister of the interior, and a month later Austria was occupied and annexed by Germany. He was imprisoned in Germany until 1945, when he went to the USA; he returned to Austria in 1967.

Schütz /ʃʊtz/ Heinrich 1585–1672. German composer, musical director to the Elector of Saxony from 1614. His works include *The Seven Last Words* about 1645, *Musicalische Exequien* 1636, and the *Deutsche Magnificat/German Magnificat* 1671.

schwa /ʃwaː, ʃvaː/ *n.* an indeterminate vowel sound (as in *another*); the symbol ə representing this. [German from Hebrew, apparently = emptiness]

Schwinger /ˈʃwɪŋə/ Julian 1918– . US quantum physicist. His research concerned the behaviour of charged particles in electrical fields. This work, expressed entirely through mathematics, combines elements from quantum theory and relativity theory.

Schwitters /ˈʃvɪtəz/ Kurt 1887–1948. German artist, a member of the ◊Dada movement. He moved to Norway in 1937 and to England in 1940. From 1918 he developed a variation on collage, using discarded rubbish such as buttons and bus tickets to create pictures and structures.

sciatic /saɪˈætɪk/ *adj.* 1. of the hip; affecting the hip or sciatic nerve. 2. suffering from or liable to sciatica. —**sciatic nerve**, the large nerve from the pelvis to the thigh. [from French from Latin from Greek *iskhiadikos* (*iskhion* = hip joint)]

sciatica /saɪˈætɪkə/ *n.* persistent pain in the leg, along the sciatic nerve and its branches. Causes of sciatica include inflammation of the nerve or pressure on, or inflammation of, a nerve root leading out of the lower spine. [Latin]

science /ˈsaɪəns/ *n.* 1. any systematic field of study or body of knowledge that aims, through experiment, observation, and deduction, to produce reliable explanation of phenomena, with reference to the material and physical world. Science is divided into separate areas of study, some combined under such headings as ◊life sciences and ◊earth sciences. These areas are usually jointly referred to as the **natural sciences**. Physics and chemistry are sometimes separated out and called the **physical sciences**, with **mathematics** left in a category of its own. The application of science for practical purposes is called **technology**. **Social science** is the systematic study of human behaviour, and includes such areas as anthropology, economics, psychology, and sociology. 2. an organized body of knowledge on a subject. 3. skilful technique. [from Old French from Latin *scientia* = knowledge (*scire* = know)]

science fiction or **speculative fiction** also known as **SF** or **sci-fi** a genre of fiction and film with an imaginary scientific, technological, or futuristic basis. It is sometimes held to have its roots in the works of Mary Shelley, notably *Frankenstein* 1818. Often taking its ideas and concerns from current ideas in science and the social sciences, science fiction aims to shake up standard perceptions of reality.

science park a site on which high-technology industrial businesses are housed near a university, so that they can benefit from the research expertise of the university's scientists. Science parks originated in the USA in the 1950s.

scientific /saɪənˈtɪfɪk/ *adj.* 1. of science; used or engaged in science. 2. following the systematic methods of science. 3. having, using, or requiring trained skill. —**scientifically** *adv.* [from French or Latin]

scientific law in science, one or several principles that are taken to be universally applicable.

scientist /ˈsaɪəntɪst/ *n.* a student of or expert in one or more of the natural or physical sciences.

Scientology /saɪənˈtɒlədʒi/ *n.* an 'applied religious philosophy' based on ◊dianetics, founded in California in 1954 by L Ron ◊Hubbard as the **Church of Scientology**. It claims to 'increase man's spiritual awareness', but its methods of recruiting and retaining converts have been criticized. Its headquarters have been in Sussex, England, from 1959. —**Scientologist** *n.* [from Latin *scientia* = knowledge and Greek *logos* = branch of learning]

sci-fi /ˈsaɪfaɪ/ *n.* (*colloquial*) ◊science fiction. [abbreviation]

scilicet /ˈsaɪlɪset/ *adv.* that is to say (introducing a word to be supplied or an explanation of an ambiguous word). [Latin]

scilla *n.* any bulbous plant of the genus *Scilla*, family Liliaceae, bearing blue, pink, or white flowers, and including the spring squill *S. verna*.

Scilly Islands /ˈsɪli/ or **Isles of Scilly** group of 140 islands and islets lying 40 km/25 mi SW of Land's End, England; administered by the Duchy of Cornwall; area 16 sq km/6.3 sq mi; population (1981) 1,850. The five inhabited islands are **St Mary's**, the largest, on which is Hugh Town, capital of the Scillies; **Tresco**, the second largest, with subtropical gardens; **St Martin's**, noted for beautiful shells; **St Agnes**; and **Bryher**. The numerous wreck sites off the islands include many of Sir Cloudesley ◊Shovell's fleet in 1707. The Isles of Scilly are an important birdwatching centre with breeding sea birds in summer and rare migrants in the spring and autumn.

scimitar /ˈsɪmɪtə/ *n.* a curved oriental sword. [from French or Italian]

scintilla /sɪnˈtɪlə/ *n.* a sign or trace. [Latin = spark]

scintillate /ˈsɪntɪleɪt/ *v.i.* 1. to sparkle; to give off sparks. 2. to talk or act with brilliance. —**scintillation** /-ˈleɪʃən/ *n.* [from Latin *scintillare*]

scintillation counter an instrument for measuring very low levels of radiation. The radiation strikes a scintillator (a device that emits a unit of light when a charged elementary particle collides with it), whose light output is 'amplified' by a ◊photomultiplier; the current pulses of its output are in turn counted or added by a scaler to give a numerical reading.

sciolism /ˈsaɪəlɪzəm/ *n.* superficial knowledge; a display of this. —**sciolist** *n.*, **sciolistic** /-ˈlɪstɪk/ *adj.* [from Latin *sciolus* = smatterer, diminutive of *scius* = knowing]

scion /ˈsaɪən/ *n.* 1. a shoot of a plant, especially one cut for grafting. 2. a descendant; a young member of a family. [from Old French = shoot, twig]

Scipio Africanus Major /ˈskɪpiəʊ æfriˈkɑːnəs ˈmeɪdzə/ 237–c.183 BC. Roman general. He defeated the Carthaginians in Spain 210–206, invaded Africa in 204, and defeated Hannibal at Zama in 202.

Scipio Africanus Minor /ˈskɪpiəʊ æfriˈkɑːnəs ˈmaɪnə/ c.185–129 BC. Roman general, the adopted grandson of Scipio Africanus Major, also known as **Scipio Aemilianus**. He destroyed Carthage in 146, and subdued Spain in 134. He was opposed to his brothers-in-law, under the Gracchi (see under ◊Gracchus), and his wife is thought to have shared in his murder.

scissors /ˈsɪzəz/ *n.pl.* or **pair of scissors** a cutting instrument made of two blades so pivoted that their cutting edges close on what is to be cut. [from Old French from Latin *cisorium* = cutting instrument, related to *scindere* = cut]

SCLC abbreviation of US civil-rights organization ◊Southern Christian Leadership Conference.

sclerenchyma *n.* a plant tissue whose function is to strengthen and support, composed of thick-walled cells that are heavily lignified (toughened). On maturity the cell inside dies, and only the cell walls remain.

sclerosis /sklɪəˈrəʊsɪs/ *n.* abnormal hardening of body tissue. —**disseminated** or ◊**multiple sclerosis**, sclerosis spreading to all or many parts of the body. —**sclerotic** /-ˈrɒtɪk/ *adj.* [from Latin from Greek *sklēroō* = harden]

scoff[1] *v.i.* to speak derisively; to jeer. —*n.* a scoffing remark, a jeer. —**scoffer** *n.*

scoff[2] *v.t./i.* (*slang*) to eat greedily. —*n.* (*slang*) food, a meal. [from Afrikaans *schoff* = quarter of a day]

Scofield /ˈskəʊfiːld/ Paul 1922– . English actor. His wide-ranging roles include the drunken priest in Greene's *The Power and the Glory*, Harry in Pinter's *The Homecoming*, and Salieri in Shaffer's *Amadeus*. He appeared as Sir Thomas More in both stage and film versions of Bott's *A Man for All Seasons*.

scold /skəʊld/ *v.t./i.* to rebuke (especially a child). —*n.* a nagging woman.

scolding *n.* a lengthy rebuke (especially a child).

scoliosis *n.* lateral curvature of the spine. Correction by operations to insert bone grafts (thus creating a straight but rigid spine) has been replaced by insertion of an electronic stimulative device in the lower back to contract the muscles adequately.

scollop variant of ◊scallop.

sconce[1] *n.* a wall bracket holding a candlestick or light fitting. [from Old French from Latin *absconsa* = covered light]

sconce[2] *n.* a small fort or earthwork. [from Dutch *schans* = brushwood]

scone /skɒn, skəʊn/ *n.* a small, soft cake of flour, oatmeal, or barley meal baked quickly and eaten buttered.

scoop *n.* 1. a deep shovel-like tool for taking up and moving grain, sugar, coal etc. 2. a ladle; a device with a small round bowl and a handle, for serving portions of ice cream etc. 3. the quantity taken with a scoop. 4. a scooping movement. 5. a large profit made quickly or by anticipating one's competitors. 6. an exclusive item in a newspaper etc. —*v.t.* 1. to lift or hollow with or as with a scoop. 2. to secure (a large profit etc.) by sudden action or luck. 3. to forestall (a rival newspaper etc.) with a news scoop. [from Middle Dutch or Middle Low German = bucket]

scoot *v.i.* (*colloquial*) to run or dart; to go away hastily.

scooter *n.* 1. a child's toy vehicle consisting of a footboard with a wheel at front and back and a long steering handle, propelled by thrusting one foot against the ground while the other rests on the footboard. 2. or **motor scooter** a kind of lightweight motorcycle with a protective shield extending from below the handles to where the rider's feet rest. —**scooterist** *n.*

scope *n.* **1.** the reach or sphere of observation or action; the extent to which it is possible or permissible to range or develop etc. **2.** opportunity, outlet. [from Italian from Greek = target]

-scope suffix forming nouns denoting a thing looked at or through (e.g. *telescope*) or an instrument for observing or showing (e.g. *oscilloscope*). [from Greek *skopeō* = look at]

scorbutic /skɔːˈbjuːtɪk/ *adj.* of, like, or affected with scurvy. [from Latin *scorbutus* = scurvy]

scorch *v.t./i.* **1.** to burn or discolour the surface of with dry heat; to become burnt or discoloured thus. **2.** (*slang*) to go at a very high speed. —*n.* a mark made by scorching. —**scorched earth policy,** in warfare, the policy of burning and destroying everything that might be of use to an invading army, especially the crops in the fields. It was used to great effect in Russia in 1812 against the invasion of the French emperor Napoleon and again during World War II to hinder the advance of German forces in 1941.

scorcher *n.* (*colloquial*) a very hot day.

score *n.* **1.** the number of points or goals etc. made by a player or side in a game, or gained in a competition etc.; a list or total of these, a reckoning. **2.** (*plural* the same) a set of 20; (*plural* scores) very many. **3.** a copy of a musical composition with the parts on a series of staves. **4.** the music for a musical comedy, film etc. **5.** a reason or motive; a topic. **6.** (*colloquial*) a remark or act by which a person scores off another. **7.** a line or mark cut into a surface. **8.** a record of money owing. —*v.t./i.* **1.** to gain (a point or points) in a game etc.; to make a score; to achieve (a success, victory etc.). **2.** to keep a record of the score; to record in a score. **3.** to have an advantage; to be successful, to have good luck; to make a clever retort that puts an opponent at a disadvantage. **4.** to cut a line or mark(s) into. **5.** to write out as a musical score; to arrange (a piece of music) for specified instruments. —**know the score,** to be aware of essential facts. **on that score,** so far as that matter is concerned. **pay off old scores,** to get one's revenge. **scoreboard** *or* **scorebook, scorecard, scoresheet** *n.* a board etc. on which a score is entered or displayed. **score off,** (*colloquial*) to humiliate; to defeat in argument or repartee. **score out,** to delete. —**scorer** *n.* [from Old Norse = notch, tally, 20]

scoria /ˈskɔːrɪə/ *n.* (*plural* **scoriae** /-iː/) slag, a clinkerlike mass of lava. —**scoriaceous** /-ˈeɪʃəs/ *adj.* [Latin from Greek = refuse (*skōr* = dung)]

scorn *n.* **1.** strong contempt. **2.** an object of this. —*v.t.* **1.** to feel or show strong contempt for. **2.** to reject as unworthy, to refuse scornfully. [from Old French]

scornful *adj.* feeling or showing scorn. —**scornfully** *adv.,* **scornfulness** *n.*

Scorpio /ˈskɔːpɪəʊ / *n.*   an alternative term for ◊Scorpius, the eighth sign of the zodiac.

scorpion /ˈskɔːpɪən/ *n.* **1.** a lobsterlike arachnid of the order Scorpionida. Common in the tropics and subtropics, the scorpion has a segmented body with a long tail ending in a poisonous sting. Some species reach 25 cm/10 in. They produce live young rather than eggs, and hunt chiefly by night. **2. the Scorpion,** the constellation or sign of the zodiac Scorpius. [from Old French from Latin]

scorpion fly an insect of the order Mecoptera. They have a characteristic downturned beak with jaws at the tip, and many males have a turned-up tail, giving them their common name. Most feed on insects or carrion. They are an ancient group with relatively few living representatives.

Scorpius /ˈskɔːpɪəs/ *n.* or **Scorpio** a zodiac constellation in the southern hemisphere between Libra and Sagittarius, represented as a scorpion. The Sun passes briefly through Scorpius in the last week of Nov. The heart of the scorpion

scorpion

is marked by the red supergiant star Antares. Scorpius contains rich Milky Way star fields, plus the strongest ◊X-ray source in the sky, Scorpius X-1. In astrology, the dates for Scorpius are between about 24 Oct and 21 Nov (see ◊precession). —**Scorpian** *adj.* & *n.* [Latin from Greek = scorpion]

Scorsese /skɔːˈseɪzi/ Martin 1942– . US director whose films concentrate on complex characterization and the themes of alienation and guilt. His work includes *Mean Streets* 1973, *Taxi Driver* 1976, *Raging Bull* 1979, *After Hours* 1987, and *The Last Temptation of Christ* 1988.

Scot *n.* **1.** a native of Scotland. **2.** (*historical*) a member of a Gaelic tribe that migrated from Ireland to Scotland about the 6th century. [Old English from Latin *Scottus*]

scotch /ˈskɒtʃ/ *v.t.* **1.** to put an end to decisively; to frustrate (a plan etc.). **2.** (*archaic*) to wound without killing. —*n.* a line on the ground for hopscotch.

Scotch *adj.* of Scotland or Scottish people or their form of English. —*n.* **1.** the form of English used (especially in the Lowlands) in Scotland. **2.** Scotch whisky. —**Scotch broth,** soup made from beef or mutton with vegetables, pearl barley etc. **Scotch cap,** a man's wide beret, like that worn as part of Highland dress. **Scotch egg,** a hard-boiled egg enclosed in sausage meat. **Scotch fir** *or* **pine,** a type of ◊pine tree *Pinus sylvestris.* **Scotch mist,** thick mist and drizzle. **Scotch terrier,** a small rough-haired short-legged kind of terrier. **Scotch whisky,** ◊whisky distilled in Scotland. **Scotch woodcock,** scrambled eggs on toast, garnished with anchovies. [contraction of *Scottish*]

scot-free *adj.* unharmed, unpunished. [from obsolete *scot* = tax, from Old Norse *skot*]

Scotland /ˈskɒtlənd/ the northernmost part of Britain, formerly an independent country, now part of the UK; **area** 78,470 sq km/30,297 sq mi; **capital** Edinburgh; **physical** the Highlands in the north (see ◊Grampian Mountains); central Lowlands, including valleys of the Clyde and Forth, with most of the country's population and industries; Southern Uplands (including the ◊Lammermuir Hills); and islands of the Orkneys, Shetlands, and Western Isles; **government** Scotland sends members to the UK Parliament at Westminster. Local government is on similar lines to that of England (see under ◊provost), but there is a differing legal system (see ◊Scots law); **products** electronics, aero and marine engines, oil, natural gas, chemicals, textiles, clothing, printing, paper, food processing, tourism; **population** (1987) 5,113,000; **language** English; Gaelic spoken by 1.3%, mainly in the Highlands; **recent history** the first Scottish member of Parliament was elected in 1945. A referendum on a Scottish directly elected assembly failed in 1979; the movement for an independent or devolved Scottish assembly continues. The poll tax was introduced first in Scotland in 1989, despite widespread opposition.

Scotland Yard, New the headquarters of the ◊Criminal Investigation Department (CID) of Britain's London Metropolitan Police, established in 1878. It is named from its original location in Scotland Yard, off Whitehall.

Scots /skɒts/ *adj.* & *n.* Scottish. [originally *Scottis,* northern variant of *Scottish*]

Scots language the form of the English language as traditionally spoken and written in Scotland, regarded by some scholars as a distinct language.

Scots law the legal system of Scotland. Owing to its separate development, Scotland has a system differing from the rest of the UK, being based on ◊civil law. Its continued separate existence was guaranteed by the Act of Union with England in 1707.

Scotsman /ˈskɒtsmən/ *n.* (*plural* **Scotsmen**) a native of Scotland. —**Scotswoman** *n.fem.* (*plural* **Scotswomen**)

Scott /skɒt/ (George) Gilbert 1811–1878. English architect. As the leading practical architect in the mid-19th-century Gothic revival in England, Scott was responsible for the building or restoration of many public buildings, including the Albert Memorial, the Foreign Office, and St Pancras Station, all in London.

Scott George C(ampbell) 1927– . US actor who played mostly tough, authoritarian film roles. His work includes *Dr Strangelove* 1964, *Patton* 1970, *The Hospital* 1971, and *Firestarter* 1984.

Scott Giles Gilbert 1880–1960. English architect, grandson of George Gilbert Scott. He designed Liverpool Anglican Cathedral, Cambridge University Library, and Waterloo

Scotland: kings and queens

(from the unification of Scotland to the union of the crowns of Scotland and England)

Celtic kings	Year of accession
Malcolm II	1005
Duncan I	1034
Macbeth	1040
Malcolm III Canmore	1057
Donald Ban (restored)	1095
Edgar	1097
Alexander I	1107
David I	1124
Malcolm IV	1153
William the Lion	1165
Alexander II	1214
Alexander III	1249
Margaret of Norway	1286–90
English Domination	
John Balliol	1292–96
Annexed to England	*1296–1306*
House of Bruce	
Robert I Bruce	1306
David II	1329
House of Stuart	
Robert II	1371
Robert III	1390
James I	1406
James II	1437
James III	1460
James IV	1488
James V	1513
Mary	1542
James VI	1567
Union of Crowns	*1603*

Bridge, London 1945. He supervised the rebuilding of the House of Commons after World War II.

Scott Peter (Markham) 1909–1989. English naturalist, artist, and explorer, founder of the Wildfowl Trust at Slimbridge, Gloucestershire, England, and a founder of the World Wildlife Fund (now World Wide Fund for Nature). He was the son of the Antarctic explorer R F Scott.

Scott Randolph. Stage name of Randolph Crane 1903–1987. US actor. He began his career in romantic films before becoming one of Hollywood's Western stars in the 1930s. His films include *Roberta* 1934, *Jesse James* 1939, and *Ride the High Country* 1962.

Scott Robert Falcon, known as **Scott of the Antarctic**, 1868–1912. English explorer who commanded two Antarctic expeditions, 1901–04 and 1910–12. On 18 Jan 1912 he reached the South Pole, shortly after ◊Amundsen, but on the return journey he and his companions died in a blizzard only a few miles from their base camp.

Scott Walter 1771–1832. Scottish novelist and poet. His first works were translations of German ballads, followed by poems such as 'The Lady of the Lake' 1810 and 'Lord of the Isles' 1815. He gained a European reputation for his historical novels such as *Heart of Midlothian* 1818, *Ivanhoe* 1819, and *The Fair Maid of Perth* 1828. His last years were marked by frantic writing to pay off his debts, after the bankruptcy of his publishing company in 1826.

There is a Southern proverb – fine words butter no parsnips.

Walter Scott
The Legend of Montrose

Scottie /'skɒtɪ/ *n.* (*colloquial*) 1. a ◊Scot. 2. a Scotch terrier.

Scottish /'skɒtɪʃ/ *adj.* of Scotland or its inhabitants. —**Scottish National Party,** a political party formed in 1934 by an amalgamation of the National Party of Scotland and the Scottish Party, which seeks autonomous government for Scotland. **Scottish Nationalist,** a member of this party.

Scottish Gaelic language see ◊Gaelic language.

scoundrel /'skaʊndrəl/ *n.* an unscrupulous person, a villain. —**scoundrelly** *adj.*

scour[1] *v.t.* 1. to clean or brighten by rubbing; to rub away (rust or a stain etc.). 2. to clear (a channel or pipe etc.) by the force of water flowing over or through it. 3. to purge drastically. —*n.* 1. scouring. 2. the action of water on a channel etc. [from Middle Dutch and Middle Low German from Latin *excurare* = clean off]

scour[2] *v.t./i.* to search rapidly or thoroughly.

scourer *n.* an abrasive pad or powder for scouring things.

scourge /skɜːdʒ/ *n.* 1. a person or thing regarded as a bringer of vengeance or punishment. 2. a whip for flogging people. —*v.t.* 1. to chastise, to afflict greatly. 2. to whip. [from Old French from Latin *corrigia* = whip]

scouse /skaʊs/ *adj.* (*slang*) of Liverpool. —*n.* (*slang*) 1. a native of Liverpool. 2. Liverpool dialect. [from *lobscouse* (a type of stew)]

scout[1] *n.* 1. a person, especially a soldier, sent out to get information about an enemy etc. 2. an act of seeking information. 3. a talent scout. 4. Scout, a member of the Scout Association. 5. a college servant at Oxford. 6. (*colloquial*) a fellow, a person. —*v.i.* to act as a scout. —**scout about** *or* **around,** to search. **Scout Association,** an international youth organization (originally called the Boy Scouts) founded in England in 1908 by Robert Baden-Powell for helping boys to develop character by training them in open-air activities. There are four branches: Beaver Scouts (aged 6–8), Cub Scouts (aged 8–10$1/2$), Scouts (10$1/2$–15$1/2$), and Venture Scouts (15$1/2$–20). Around a third of all Venture Scouts are girls and in 1990 younger girls were admitted to the Scouts (see also ◊Girl Guides). [from Old French *escoute* from Latin *auscultare* = listen]

scout[2] *v.t.* to reject (an idea etc.) with scorn. [from Scandinavian]

Scouter *n.* an adult leader in the Scout Association.

scow *n.* a flat-bottomed boat. [from Dutch = ferryboat]

scowl *n.* a sullen or bad-tempered look on a person's face. —*v.i.* to make a scowl.

scrabble *v.i.* 1. to make a scratching movement or sound with the hands or feet. 2. to grope busily; to struggle to find or obtain something. —*n.* scrabbling. [from Middle Dutch, frequentative of *schrabben* = scrape]

Scrabble *n.* the trade name of a board game for two to four players, based on the crossword puzzle, in which lettered tiles of varying point values are used to form words. International competitions are held.

scrag *n.* 1. or **scrag end** the bony part of an animal's carcass as food; neck of mutton; the less meaty end of this. 2. a skinny person or animal. —*v.t.* (-**gg**-) to seize roughly by the neck; to handle roughly, to beat up.

scraggy *adj.* thin and bony. —**scraggily** *adv.*, **scragginess** *n.*

scram *v.i.* (-**mm**-) (*slang*, especially in *imperative*) to go away.

scramble *v.t./i.* 1. to move as best one can over rough ground or by clambering; to move hastily and awkwardly. 2. to struggle eagerly to do or obtain something. 3. (of aircraft or their crew) to hurry and take off quickly in an emergency. 4. to mix together indiscriminately; to cook (egg) by mixing its contents and heating the mixture in a pan until it thickens. 5. to make (a telephone conversation etc.) unintelligible except to a person with a special receiver by altering the frequencies on which it is transmitted. —*n.* 1. a climb or walk over rough ground. 2. an eager struggle to do or obtain something. 3. a motorcycle race over rough ground (see ◊motocross). —**scrambled egg,** (*colloquial*) gold braid on an officer's cap. [imitative]

scrambler *n.* a device for scrambling telephone conversations.

scrap[1] *n.* 1. a small detached piece, a fragment. 2. rubbish, waste material; discarded metal suitable for reprocessing. 3. (with negative) the smallest piece or amount. 4. (in *plural*) odds and ends, bits of uneaten food. —*v.t.* (-**pp**-) to discard as useless. —**scrapbook** *n.* a book in which newspaper cuttings or similar souvenirs are mounted. **scrap merchant,** a dealer in scrap. **scrap yard,** a place where scrap is collected. [from Old Norse]

scrap[2] *n.* (*colloquial*) a fight or rough quarrel. —*v.i.* (-**pp**-) to have a scrap.

scrape *v.t./i.* **1.** to make (a thing) level, clean, or smooth by causing a hard edge to move across the surface; to apply (a hard edge) thus; to remove by scraping. **2.** to scratch or damage by scraping. **3.** to dig (a hollow etc.) by scraping. **4.** to draw or move with a sound (as) of scraping; to produce such a sound. **5.** to pass along or through something with difficulty, with or without touching it. **6.** to obtain or amass with effort or by parsimony. **7.** to be very economical. **8.** to draw back the foot in making a clumsy bow. —*n.* **1.** a scraping movement or sound. **2.** a scraped place or mark. **3.** a thinly applied layer of butter etc. on bread. **4.** an awkward situation resulting from an escapade. —**scrape acquaintance,** to contrive to become acquainted. **scrape the barrel,** to be driven to using one's last and inferior resources because the better ones are finished. **scrape through** etc., to get through a difficult situation or pass an examination by only a very narrow margin. [from Old Norse or Middle Dutch]

scraper *n.* a device used for scraping things; an earth-moving machine used in road construction. Self-propelled or hauled by a ◊bulldozer, a scraper consists of an open bowl, with a cutting blade at the lower front edge.

scrapie /'skreɪpɪ/ *n.* a fatal disease of sheep and goats that attacks the central nervous system, causing deterioration of the brain cells. It is believed to be caused by a submicroscopic organism known as a prion and may be related to ◊bovine spongiform encephalopathy, the disease of cattle known as 'mad cow disease'.

scraping *n.* (especially in *plural*) a fragment produced by scraping.

scrappy *adj.* consisting of scraps or disconnected elements. —**scrappily** *adv.,* **scrappiness** *n.*

scratch /skrætʃ/ *v.t.* **1.** to make a shallow mark or wound on (a surface) with something sharp. **2.** to make or form by scratching. **3.** to scrape with the fingernail(s) in order to relieve itching. **4.** to make a thin scraping sound. **5.** to obtain with difficulty. **6.** (with *off, out,* or *through*) to delete by drawing a line through; to withdraw from a race, competition, or (*US*) election. —*n.* **1.** a mark, wound, or sound made by scratching; (*colloquial*) a trifling wound. **2.** a spell of scratching oneself. **3.** a line from which competitors start in a race, especially those receiving no handicap. —*adj.* **1.** collected by chance or from whatever is available. **2.** with no handicap given. —**from scratch,** from the beginning; without help or advantage. **scratch one's head,** to be perplexed. **scratch the surface,** to deal with a matter only superficially. **up to scratch,** up to the required standard.

scratchy *adj.* **1.** tending to make scratches or a scratching noise. **2.** tending to cause itchiness. **3.** (of a drawing etc.) done in scratches or carelessly. —**scratchily** *adv.,* **scratchiness** *n.*

scrawl *v.t./i.* **1.** to write in a hurried, untidy way. **2.** to cross *out* thus. —*n.* hurried writing; a scrawled note.

scrawny *adj.* lean, scraggy. [variant of dialect *scranny*]

scream *v.t./i.* **1.** to emit a piercing cry of pain, terror, annoyance, or excitement. **2.** to speak or sing (words etc.) in such a tone. **3.** to make or move with a shrill sound like a scream. **4.** to laugh uncontrollably. **5.** to be blatantly obvious. —*n.* **1.** a screaming cry or sound. **2.** (*colloquial*) an irresistibly funny occurrence or person. [Old English]

screamer *n.* a South American marsh-dwelling bird of the family Anhimidae; there are only three species. They are about 80 cm/2.6 ft long, with short, curved beaks, dark plumage, spurs on the front of the wings, and a crest or a horn on the head.

scree *n.* (in *singular* or *plural*) a mass of small, loose stones, sliding when trodden on; a mountain slope covered with these. [from Old Norse = landslip]

screech *n.* a harsh, high-pitched scream. —*v.t./i.* to utter with or make a screech. —**screech owl,** an ◊owl that screeches instead of hooting, especially a barn owl. [variant of earlier *scritch* (imitative)]

screed *n.* **1.** a tiresomely long letter or other document. **2.** a level strip of material formed or placed on a floor, road etc., as a guide for the accurate finishing of it. **3.** a levelled layer of material forming part of a floor etc. —*v.t.* to level by means of a screed; to apply (material) as a screed.

screen *n.* **1.** an upright structure used to conceal, protect, or divide something. **2.** anything serving a similar purpose; an expression or measure etc. adopted for concealment; the protection given by this. **3.** a blank surface on which a film,

televised picture, radar image etc., is projected; the cinema industry. **4.** a sight screen; a windscreen. **5.** a large sieve or riddle. **6.** a frame with fine wire netting to keep out flies, mosquitoes etc. **7.** a system for showing the presence or absence of a disease, quality etc. **8.** in printing, a transparent, finely ruled plate or film used in half-tone reproduction. —*v.t.* **1.** to shelter, conceal, or protect. **2.** to protect from discovery or deserved blame by diverting suspicion. **3.** to show (images or a film etc.) on a screen. **4.** to prevent from causing electrical interference. **5.** to sieve. **6.** to test for the presence or absence of a disease, quality (especially reliability or loyalty) etc. —**screen printing,** a process like stencilling with ink forced through a prepared sheet of fine material; see ◊silk-screen printing. [from Old French *escren* from Old High German *skrank* = barrier]

screenplay *n.* the script of a film.

screw /skruː/ *n.* **1.** a cylinder or cone with a spiral ridge round the outside (**male screw**) or the inside (**female screw**); a metal male screw with a slotted head and a sharp point for fastening things (especially of wood) together. Each turn of a screw moves it forward or backwards by a distance equal to the pitch (the spacing between neighbouring threads). **2.** a wooden or metal screw used to exert pressure; (in *singular* or *plural*) an instrument of torture operating thus. **3.** a propeller or other device acting like a screw. **4.** one turn of a screw. **5.** a small, twisted-up paper of tobacco etc. **6.** (in billiards etc.) an oblique curling motion of the ball. **7.** (*slang*) a prison warder. **8.** (*British slang*) the amount of one's salary or wages. **9.** (*vulgar*) sexual intercourse; a partner in this. —*v.t./i.* **1.** to fasten or tighten with a screw or screws. **2.** to turn (a screw); to twist or turn round like a screw. **3.** (of a ball etc.) to swerve. **4.** to put the screws on, to oppress; to extort (consent, money etc.). **5.** to contort or contract (one's face etc.). **6.** (*vulgar*) to have sexual intercourse (with). —**have a screw loose,** (*colloquial*) to be slightly crazy. **put the screws on,** to exert pressure (on), to intimidate or extort money. **screw cap** *or* **screw top,** a cap or top that screws on to a bottle etc. **screw up,** to contort or contract (one's eyes, face etc.); to summon up (one's courage); (*slang*) to bungle or mismanage. [from Old French *escroue* = female screw, nut, from Latin *scrofa* = female pig used for breeding]

screwball *n.* (*US slang*) a crazy or eccentric person.

screwdriver *n.* a tool with a shaped tip fitting into the slot of a screw to turn it.

screwed *adj.* (*slang*) drunk.

screwy *adj.* (*slang*) crazy, eccentric; absurd.

Scriabin /skri'æbɪn/ alternative transcription of ◊Skryabin, Russian composer.

scribble *v.t./i.* **1.** to write carelessly or hurriedly. **2.** to make meaningless marks. —*n.* something scribbled; hurried or careless writing; scribbled, meaningless marks. —**scribbler** *n.* [from Latin *scribillare*, diminutive of Latin *scribere* = write]

scribe *n.* **1.** an ancient or medieval copyist of manuscripts. **2.** a professional Jewish religious scholar in New Testament times. **3.** a pointed instrument for making marks on wood etc. —*v.t.* to mark with a scribe. —**scribal** *adj.* [from Latin *scriba*]

scrim *n.* an open-weave fabric for lining or upholstery etc.

scrimmage /'skrɪmɪdʒ/ *n.* a confused struggle; a skirmish. —*v.i.* to engage in a scrimmage. [variant of *skirmish*]

scrimp *v.t./i.* to skimp.

scrimshank /'skrɪmʃæŋk/ *v.i.* (*slang*) to shirk work, to malinger.

scrip *n.* **1.** in finance, a provisional certificate of money subscribed entitling the holder to dividends; (*collective*) such certificates. **2.** an extra share or shares issued to existing shareholders based on their holdings. It does not involve the raising of new capital as in a ◊rights issue. [abbreviation of *subscription receipt*]

script *n.* **1.** handwriting, written characters. **2.** type imitating handwriting. **3.** an alphabet or system of writing. **4.** the text of a play, film, broadcast talk etc. **5.** an examinee's written answer. —*v.t.* to write the script for (a film etc.). —**scriptwriter** *n.* a writer for broadcasting or films etc. [from Old French from Latin *scriptum*]

scripture /'skrɪptʃə/ *n.* **1.** sacred writings. **2. Scripture** *or* **the Scriptures,** the sacred writings of the Christians (the Old and New Testaments) or the Jews (the Old Testament). —**scriptural** *adj.* [from Latin]

scrivener /'skrɪvənə/ n. (historical) a drafter of documents, a copyist, a notary. [from Old French escrivein from Latin scriba]

scrofula /'skrɒfjʊlə/ n. a disease with glandular swellings, probably a form of tuberculosis. —**scrofulous** adj. [Latin diminutive of scrofulae (plural) = scrofulous swelling from scrofa = female pig]

scroll /skrəʊl/ n. 1. a roll of parchment or paper, especially with writing; a book of the ancient roll form. 2. an ornamental design imitating a roll of parchment. —v.t. to move (the display on a VDU screen) up or down as new material appears. [originally scrowle, alteration from rowle = roll]

scrolled /skrəʊld/ adj. having a scroll ornament.

Scrooge /skru:dʒ/ n. a miser. [character in Charles Dickens's novel A Christmas Carol]

scrotum /'skrəʊtəm/ n. (plural scrota) the pouch of skin containing the testicles. —**scrotal** adj. [Latin]

scrounge v.t./i. (slang) to cadge; to collect by foraging. —**scrounger** n. [variant of dialect scrunge = steal]

scrub[1] v.t./i. (-bb-) 1. to rub hard so as to clean or brighten, especially with a hard brush; to use a brush thus. 2. to remove impurities from (gas) in a scrubber. 3. (slang) to scrap or cancel (a plan, order etc.) —n. scrubbing, being scrubbed. —**scrub up**, (of a surgeon etc.) to clean the hands and arms by scrubbing before an operation.

scrub[2] n. 1. brushwood or stunted forest growth; land covered with this. 2. a stunted or insignificant person etc. —**scrubby** adj. [variant of shrub]

scrubber[1] n. 1. an apparatus for cleaning gases. 2. (derogatory slang) an immoral or sluttish woman.

scrubber[2] n. (Australian) an inferior animal, especially a bullock, living in scrub country.

scruff n. the back of the neck.

scruffy adj. (colloquial) shabby and untidy. —**scruffily** adv., **scruffiness** n. [from scruff, variant of scurf]

scrum n. a scrummage. —**scrum half**, in rugby, the half-back who puts the ball into the scrum. [abbreviation]

scrummage /'skrʌmɪdʒ/ n. in rugby, the grouping of all forwards on each side to push against those of the other and seek possession of the ball thrown on the ground between them. [variant of skirmish]

scrump v.t./i. (dialect or slang) to steal (apples), especially from orchards. [from dialect scrump = small apple]

scrumptious /'skrʌmpʃəs/ adj. (colloquial) delicious, delightful.

scrumpy n. (colloquial, originally dialect) rough cider.

scrunch n. a crunch. —v.t. to crunch.

scruple /'skru:pəl/ n. 1. due regard to the morality or propriety of an action etc.; doubt or hesitation caused by this. 2. (historical) a unit of weight of 20 grains. —v.i. to feel or be influenced by scruples; (especially with negative) to be reluctant because of scruples. [from French or Latin scrupulus (scrupus = rough pebble)]

scrupulous /'skru:pjʊləs/ adj. 1. careful to avoid doing wrong. 2. conscientious or thorough even in small matters; painstakingly careful and thorough. —**scrupulosity** /-'lɒsɪtɪ/ n., **scrupulously** adv., **scrupulousness** n.

scrutineer /skru:tɪ'nɪə/ n. a person who scrutinizes ballot papers.

scrutinize /'skru:tɪnaɪz/ v.t. to subject to scrutiny.

scrutiny /'skru:tɪnɪ/ n. a careful look or examination; an official examination of ballot papers to check their validity or the accuracy of counting. [from Latin scrutinium (scrutari = search)]

scuba /'sku:bə/ n. acronym from self-contained underwater breathing apparatus, an apparatus designed to enable a swimmer to breathe while under the water; also called ◊aqualung.

scud v.i. (-dd-) 1. to run or fly straight and fast, to skim along. 2. (nautical) to run before the wind. —n. 1. a spell of scudding; a scudding motion. 2. vapoury driving clouds; a driving shower.

Scud a surface-to-surface missile designed and produced in the USSR, which can be armed with a nuclear, chemical, or conventional warhead. The **Scud-B**, deployed on a mobile launcher, was the version most commonly used by the Iraqi army in the ◊Gulf War 1991. It is a relatively inaccurate weapon.

Scudamore /'skju:dəmɔ:/ Peter 1958– . British National Hunt jockey. He was champion jockey in 1982 (shared with John Francome) and from 1986 to 1990. In the 1988–89 season he became the third jockey to ride 1,000 National Hunt winners; in Feb 1989 he became the first person to ride 150 winners in a season and went on to increase his total to 221.

scuff v.t./i. 1. to walk with dragging feet, to shuffle. 2. to graze or brush against; to mark or wear out (shoes etc.) thus. —n. a mark of scuffing. [imitative]

scuffle n. a confused struggle or fight at close quarters. —v.i. to engage in a scuffle.

scull n. 1. each of a pair of small oars used by a single rower. 2. an oar that rests on the stern of a boat, used with a screwlike motion. 3. (in plural) a sculling race. —v.t. to propel (a boat, or absolute) with sculls.

sculler n. 1. a user of a scull or sculls. 2. a boat for sculling.

scullery /'skʌlərɪ/ n. a back kitchen; a room in which dishes etc. are washed. [from Old French escuelerie (escuele = dish from Latin scutella = salver, diminutive of scutra = wooden platter)]

Scullin /'skʌlɪn/ James Henry 1876–1953. Australian Labor politician. He was leader of the Federal Parliamentary Labor Party 1928–35, and prime minister and minister of industry 1929–31.

scullion /'skʌljən/ n. (archaic) a cook's boy, one who washes dishes.

sculpt v.t./i. (colloquial) to sculpture. [abbreviation]

sculptor /'skʌlptə/ n. one who sculptures. —**sculptress** n.fem. [Latin]

sculpture /'skʌlptʃə/ n. 1. the artistic shaping in relief or in the round of materials such as wood, stone, metal, and, more recently, plastic and other synthetics. All ancient civilizations, including the Assyrian, Egyptian, Indian, Chinese, and Mayan, have left examples of sculpture. Traditional European sculpture descends from that of Greece, Rome, and Renaissance Italy. 2. a work of sculpture. —v.t./i. to represent in or adorn with sculpture; to practise sculpture. —**sculptural** adj., **sculpturally** adv. [from Latin sculptura (sculpere = carve)]

scum n. 1. a layer of dirt, froth, or impurities etc. that rises to the top of a liquid. 2. a worthless part; a worthless person or persons. —v.t./i. (-mm-) to remove the scum from; to form a scum (on). —**scummy** adj. [from Middle Low German or Middle Dutch]

scuncheon /'skʌntʃən/ n. the inside face of a doorjamb, window frame etc. [from Old French escoinson from Latin cuneus = wedge]

scupper n. a hole in a ship's side to carry off water from the deck. —v.t. (slang) 1. to sink (a ship) deliberately. 2. to defeat or ruin (a plan etc.). 3. to kill.

scurf n. flakes of dead skin, especially on the scalp. —**scurfy** adj. [Old English]

scurrilous /'skʌrɪləs/ adj. 1. abusive and insulting. 2. coarsely humorous. —**scurrility** /-'rɪlɪtɪ/ n., **scurrilously** adv. [from Latin scurrilis (scurra = buffoon)]

scurry /'skʌrɪ/ v.i. to run or move hurriedly, especially with short quick steps; to scamper. —n. 1. an act or sound of scurrying; a rush. 2. a flurry of rain or snow. [abbreviation of hurry-scurry, reduplication of hurry]

scurvy /'skɜ:vɪ/ n. a disease caused by deficiency of vitamin C (ascorbic acid), which is contained in fresh vegetables and fruit. The signs are weakness and aching joints and muscles, progressing to bleeding of the gums and then other organs, and drying up of the skin and hair. —adj. paltry, dishonourable, contemptible. —**scurvily** adv., **scurviness** n. [from scurf]

scut n. a short tail, especially of a rabbit, hare, or deer.

scutter v.i. (colloquial) to scurry. —n. (colloquial) a scurry.

scuttle[1] n. 1. a receptacle for carrying and holding a small supply of coal. 2. the part of a motor-car body between the windscreen and bonnet. [from Old Norse or Old High German from Latin scutella = dish]

scuttle[2] n. a hole with a lid in a ship's deck or side. —v.t. to let water into (a ship), especially to sink it.

scuttle[3] v.i. to scurry, to flee from danger or difficulty. —n. 1. a scuttling run. 2. a precipitate flight or departure.

scythe /saɪð/ n. a mowing and reaping instrument with a long, curved blade swung over the ground. It is similar to a ◊sickle. The scythe was in common use in the Middle East and Europe from the dawn of agriculture until the early 20th century, by which time it had generally been replaced by machinery. —*v.t.* to cut with a scythe. [Old English]

Scythia /'sɪðɪə/ region north of the Black Sea between the Carpathian mountains and the river Don, inhabited by the Scythians in the 7th–1st centuries BC. From the middle of the 4th century, they were slowly superseded by the Sarmatians. The Scythians produced ornaments and vases in gold and electrum with animal decoration.

SDI abbreviation of ◊Strategic Defense Initiative.

SDLP abbreviation of ◊Social Democratic and Labour Party (Northern Ireland).

SDP abbreviation of ◊Social Democratic Party.

SDR abbreviation of ◊special drawing right.

Se symbol for ◊selenium.

SE abbreviation of southeast, southeastern.

sea *n.* 1. the expanse of salt water that covers most of the Earth's surface and surrounds the continents (see ◊ocean); any part of this as opposed to land or fresh water. 2. a named tract of salt water partly or wholly enclosed by land; a large freshwater inland lake. 3. the waves of the sea; their motion or state. 4. a vast quantity or expanse. —*attrib.* living or used in, on, or near the sea (often prefixed to the name of a marine animal, plant etc., having a superficial resemblance to what it is named after). —**at sea**, in a ship on the sea; perplexed, confused. **by sea**, in a ship or ships. **go to sea**, to become a sailor. **on the sea**, in a ship at sea; situated on the coast. **sea anchor**, a bag to retard the drifting of a ship. **sea bird**, a bird frequenting the sea or land near the sea. **seaborne** *adj.* conveyed by the sea. **sea change**, a notable or unexpected transformation. **sea cow**, a ◊sirenian; a walrus; a hippopotamus. **sea dog**, an old sailor, especially an Elizabethan captain. **sea-girt** *adj.* surrounded by sea. **sea-green** *adj. & n.* bluish-green. **sea legs**, the ability to walk on the deck of a rolling ship. **sea level**, the mean level of the sea's surface, used in reckoning the height of hills etc. and as a barometric standard. **Sea Lord**, in the UK, a naval member of the Admiralty Board. **sea mile**, a ◊nautical mile. **seaport** *n.* a port on the coast. **sea room**, space for a ship to turn etc. at sea. **sea salt**, salt produced by evaporating sea water. **seascape** *n.* a picture or view of the sea. **Sea Scout**, a member of the maritime branch of the ◊Scout Association. **seashell** *n.* the shell of a salt-water mollusc. **seashore** *n.* land close to the sea. **seaside** *n.* the sea coast, especially as a holiday resort. **seaway** *n.* a ship's progress; a place where a ship lies in open water; an inland waterway open to seagoing ships. [Old English]

sea anemone an invertebrate marine animal of the class Cnidaria with a tubelike body attached by the base to a rock or shell. The other end has an open 'mouth' surrounded by stinging tentacles, which capture crustaceans and other small organisms. Many sea anemones are beautifully coloured, especially those in tropical waters.

seaboard *n.* the seashore or line of a coast; a coastal region.

sea cucumber an echinoderm of the class Holothuroidea with a cylindrical body that is tough-skinned, knobbed, or spiny. The body may be several feet in length. Sea cucumbers are sometimes called **cotton-spinners** from the sticky filaments they eject from the anus in self-defence.

seafarer *n.* a sailor, a traveller by sea.

seafaring *adj. & n.* travelling by sea, especially as one's regular occupation.

seafloor spreading the growth of the ocean ◊crust outwards (sideways) from mid-ocean ridges. The concept of seafloor spreading has been combined with that of continental drift and incorporated into ◊plate tectonics.

seafood *n.* edible marine fish or shellfish.

seagoing *adj.* 1. (of ships) fit for crossing the sea. 2. (of a person) seafaring.

seagull *n.* a ◊gull.

sea horse 1. a fish of one of several genera, of which *Hippocampus* is typical. The body is small and compressed and covered with bony plates raised into tubercles or spines. The tail is prehensile, the head at right angles to its body, and the tubular mouth sucks in small animals and a fish's food. 2. a mythical creature with a horse's head and a fish's tail.

sea kale a perennial plant *Crambe maritima* of the family Cruciferae. In Europe the young shoots are cultivated as a vegetable.

seal[1] *n.* 1. a piece of wax, lead, paper etc., with a stamped design, attached to a document as a guarantee of authenticity or to a receptacle, room, envelope etc., as a sign that (while the seal is unbroken) the contents have not been tampered with since it was affixed. 2. an engraved piece of metal etc. for stamping such a design. Seals were used in ancient China and medieval Europe and are still used in China, Korea, and Japan. 3. a substance or device to close an aperture etc. 4. an act, gesture, or event regarded as a confirmation or guarantee. 5. a decorative adhesive stamp. —*v.t.* 1. to stamp or fasten with a seal; to fix a seal to; to certify as correct with a seal or stamp. 2. to close securely or hermetically. 3. to confine securely. 4. to settle or decide. —**sealing wax**, a mixture of shellac and rosin softened by heating and used for seals. **seal off**, to prevent entry to and exit from (an area). **seals of office**, those held during tenure of office, especially by a lord chancellor or secretary of state. In medieval England, the **great seal** of the nation was kept by the chancellor. The **privy seal** of the monarch was initially kept for less serious matters, but by the 14th century it had become the most important seal. **set one's seal to**, to authorize or confirm. [from Anglo-French from Latin *sigillum*, diminutive of *signum* = sign]

seal[2] *n.* 1. an amphibious marine mammal of the family Phocidae. Seals have a streamlined body with thick blubber for insulation, no external earflaps, and small front flippers. The hind flippers provide the thrust for swimming, but they cannot be brought under the body for walking on land. Seals feed on fish, squid, or crustaceans, and are commonly found in Arctic and Antarctic waters, but also in Mediterranean, Caribbean, and Hawaiian waters. 2. sealskin. —*v.i.* to hunt seals. They are killed for blubber and for their skins, which are made into coats or capes, in Canada and Scandinavia. Conservationists have campaigned to stop the practice. [Old English]

sealant *n.* material for sealing things, especially to make them airtight or watertight.

sea law a set of laws dealing with fishing areas, ships, and navigation; see ◊maritime law.

sealer *n.* a ship or person engaged in hunting seals.

sea lily a deep-water ◊echinoderm of the class Crinoidea. The rayed, cuplike body is borne on a stalk, and has feathery arms in multiples of five encircling the mouth.

sea lion a marine mammal of the family Otariidae which also includes the fur seals. This streamlined animal has large fore flippers which it uses to row itself through the water. The hind flippers can be turned beneath the body to walk on land. A small earflap is present.

sealskin *n.* the skin or prepared fur of a seal; a garment made from this.

Sealyham /'siːlɪəm/ *n.* a wire-haired short-legged terrier. [from *Sealyham* in Dyfed, Wales]

seam *n.* 1. the line where two edges join, especially of cloth or leather etc. or boards. 2. a fissure between parallel edges. 3. a wrinkle. 4. a stratum of coal etc. —*v.t.* 1. to join by a seam. 2. (especially in *past participle*) to mark or score with a seam, fissure, or scar. —**seam bowler**, a bowler in cricket who makes the ball spin by bouncing it off its seam. [Old English]

seaman *n.* (*plural* **seamen**) one whose occupation is on the sea; a sailor, especially below the rank of officer.

seamanship *n.* skill in managing a ship or boat.

seamstress /'semstrɪs/ *n.* a woman who sews, especially as a job. [Old English]

seamy *adj.* marked with or showing seams. —**seamy side**, the disreputable or unattractive side.

Seanad /'ʃænəð/ *n.* the upper house of parliament in the Republic of Ireland. [Irish = senate]

seance /'seɪɑːs/ *n.* a meeting for the exhibition or investigation of spiritualistic phenomena. [from French = a sitting]

Sea Peoples unidentified seafaring warriors who may have been ◊Achaeans, Etruscans, or ◊Philistines, who ravaged and settled the Mediterranean coasts in the 12th–13th centuries BC. They were defeated by Ramses III of Egypt in 1191.

seaplane *n.* any aeroplane capable of taking off from, and landing on, water. There are two major types: the **floatplane** is similar to an ordinary aeroplane but has floats in place of wheels; the **flying boat** has a broad hull shaped like a boat and may also have floats attached to the wing tips.

sear *v.t.* 1. to scorch, to cauterize. 2. to make (the conscience or feelings etc.) callous. [Old English]

search /sɜːtʃ/ *v.t./i.* 1. to look through or go over thoroughly in order to find something. 2. to examine the clothes and body of (a person) to see if anything is concealed there. 3. to examine thoroughly (*literally* or *figuratively*). 4. in computing, to extract a specific item from a large body of data, such as a file or table. —*n.* an act of searching; an investigation. —**in search of**, trying to find. **search me**, (*colloquial*) I do not know. **search out**, to look for, to seek out. **search party**, a group of people organized to look for a lost person or thing. **search warrant**, an official authority to enter and search a building. —**searcher** *n.* [from Anglo-French from Latin *circare* = go round]

searchlight *n.* an electric lamp with a powerful concentrated beam that can be turned in any direction; the light or beam from this.

Searle /sɜːl/ Ronald 1920– . English cartoonist and illustrator, who created the schoolgirls of St Trinian's in 1941 and has made numerous cartoons of cats.

seasick *adj.* suffering from sickness or nausea from the motion of a ship etc. —**seasickness** *n.*

sea slug a marine gastropod mollusc in which the shell is reduced or absent. Nudibranch sea slugs include some very colourful forms, especially in the tropics. Tentacles on the back help take in oxygen. They are largely carnivorous, feeding on hydroids and sponges. Most are under 2.5 cm/ 1 in long, and live on the sea bottom or on vegetation, although some live in open waters.

season /'siːzən/ *n.* 1. each of the divisions of the year associated with a type of weather and a stage of vegetation. In temperate latitudes four seasons are recognized: spring, summer, autumn, and winter. Tropical regions have two seasons: the wet and the dry. Monsoon areas around the Indian Ocean have three seasons: the cold, the hot, and the rainy. The change in seasons is mainly due to the change in attitude of the Earth's axis in relation to the Sun, and hence the position of the Sun in the sky in relation to a particular place. 2. a proper or suitable time; the time when something is plentiful, active, or in vogue; the high season. 3. the time of year regularly devoted to an activity, or to social life generally. 4. an indefinite period. 5. (*colloquial*) a season ticket. —*v.t./i.* 1. to flavour or make palatable with salt, herbs etc.; to enhance with wit etc.; to temper or moderate. 2. to make or become suitable or in a desired condition, especially by exposure to air or weather. —**in season**, (of food) available in good condition and plentifully; (of an animal) on heat. **season ticket**, a ticket entitling the holder to any number of journeys, admittances etc., in a given period. [from Old French *saison* from Latin *satio* = sowing]

seasonable *adj.* 1. suitable or usual to the season. 2. opportune; meeting the needs of the occasion. —**seasonably** *adv.*

seasonal *adj.* of, depending on, or varying with the season. —**seasonally** *adv.*

seasonal adjustment in statistics, an adjustment of figures designed to take into account influences that are purely seasonal, and relevant only for a short time. The resulting figures are then thought to reflect long-term trends more accurately.

seasonal affective disorder (SAD) recurrent depression characterized by an increased incidence at a particular time of year. One type of seasonal affective disorder increases in incidence in autumn and winter, and is associated with increased sleeping and appetite.

seasonal unemployment unemployment arising from the seasonal nature of some economic activities. An example is agriculture, which uses a smaller labour force in winter.

seasoning *n.* flavouring added to food.

sea squirt a ◊chordate of the class Ascidiacea. A pouch-shaped animal attached to a rock or other base, it draws in food-carrying water through one siphon, and expels it through another after straining it through the gills. The young are free-swimming tadpole-shaped organisms.

seat *n.* 1. a thing made or used for sitting on; a place for one person in a theatre, vehicle etc. 2. occupation of a seat; the right to this, e.g. as a member of a board or of a parliament. 3. the buttocks; the part of the trousers etc. covering them. 4. the part of a chair etc. on which the sitter's weight directly rests; the part of a machine that supports or guides another part. 5. a site or location. 6. a country mansion, especially with large grounds. 7. a person's manner of sitting on a horse etc. —*v.t.* 1. to cause to sit. 2. to provide sitting accommodation for. 3. (in *past participle*) sitting. 4. to put or fit in position. —**be seated**, to sit down. **by the seat of one's pants**, by instinct rather than knowledge or logic. **seat belt**, a belt securing a person in the seat of a car or aircraft. **take a seat**, to sit down. **take one's seat**, to sit down, especially in one's appointed place; to assume one's official position, to be formally admitted to a parliament or congress. [from Old Norse]

-seater in combinations, having a specified number of seats.

seating *n.* seats collectively, sitting accommodation.

SEATO abbreviation of ◊South East Asia Treaty Organization.

Seattle /si'ætl/ port (grain, timber, fruit, fish) of the state of Washington, USA, situated between Puget Sound and Lake Washington; population (1980) 493,846, metropolitan area (with Everett) 1,601,000. It is a centre for the manufacture of jet aircraft (Boeing), and also has shipbuilding, food processing, and paper industries. [from the Indian *Sealth*]

sea urchin a type of ◊echinoderm with a globular body enclosed with plates of lime and covered with spines. Sometimes the spines are holding organs, and they also assist in locomotion. Sea urchins feed on seaweed and the animals frequenting them, and some are edible.

seaward /'siːwəd/ *adv.* or **seawards** towards the sea. —*adj.* going or facing towards the sea. —*n.* such a direction or position.

season

how the Earth's tilt and its orbit
around the Sun cause the seasons

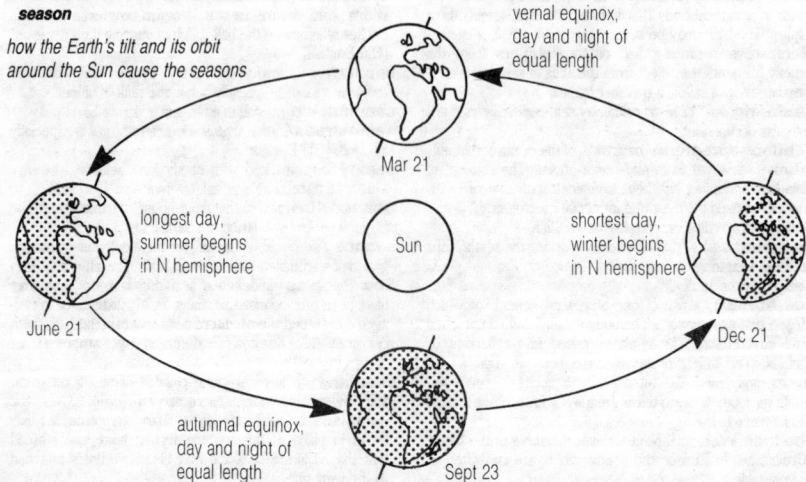

vernal equinox,
day and night of
equal length

Mar 21

longest day,
summer begins
in N hemisphere

Sun

shortest day,
winter begins
in N hemisphere

June 21

Dec 21

autumnal equinox,
day and night of
equal length

Sept 23

seaweed *n.* any of a vast collection of marine and fresh-water, simple, multicellular plant forms belonging to the ◊algae and found growing from about high-water mark to depths of 100–200 m/300–600 ft. Some have holdfasts, stalks, and fronds, sometimes with air bladders to keep them afloat, and are green, blue-green, red, or brown.

seaworthy *adj.* fit to put to sea.

sebaceous /si'beɪʃəs/ *adj.* fatty, secreting or conveying oily matter. [from Latin *sebum* = tallow]

Sebastiano del Piombo /sɪbæsti'ɑːnəu del pi'ɒmbəu/ *c.*1485–1547. Italian painter, born in Venice, one of the great painters of the High Renaissance. Sebastiano was a pupil of ◊Giorgione and developed a similar style of painting. In 1511 he moved to Rome, where his friendship with Michelangelo (and rivalry with Raphael) inspired him to his greatest works, such as *The Raising of Lazarus* 1517–19 (National Gallery, London). He also painted powerful portraits.

Sebastian, St /si'bæstiən/ Roman soldier, traditionally a member of Emperor Diocletian's bodyguard until his Christian faith was discovered. He was martyred by being shot with arrows. Feast day 20 Jan.

sec or **s** abbreviation of second, a unit of time.

sec *adj.* (of wine) dry. [French from Latin *siccus* = dry]

sec. abbreviation of secretary.

secant /'siːkənt/ *n.* a straight line that cuts a curve, especially a circle, at two points; the radius of a circle produced through one end of an arc to meet the tangent to the other end; the ratio of this to the radius. —**secant of an angle**, the ratio of the length of the hypotenuse to the length of the side adjacent to that angle in a right-angled triangle. It is the ◊reciprocal of the cosine (sec = 1/cos). [from French from Latin *secare* = cut]

secateurs /sekə'tɜːz/ *n.pl.* pruning clippers used with one hand. [from French from Latin *secare* = cut]

secede /si'siːd/ *v.i.* to withdraw formally from an organization, e.g. a political federation. [from Latin *secedere* (*se-* = aside and *cedere* = go)]

secession /si'seʃən/ *n.* seceding. —**secessionist** *n.* [from French or Latin]

seclude /si'kluːd/ *v.t.* to keep (a person) apart from others; to keep (a place) screened or sheltered from view. [from Latin *secludere* (*se-* = aside and *claudere* = shut)]

seclusion /si'kluːʒən/ *n.* 1. secluding, being secluded; privacy. 2. a secluded place.

second[1] /'sekənd/ *adj.* 1. next after first. 2. another besides one or the first, additional. 3. of subordinate importance or position etc., inferior. 4. in music, performing a lower or subordinate part. 5. metaphorical, such as to be comparable to. —*n.* 1. the person or thing that is second; the second day of a month. 2. another person or thing besides the previously mentioned or principal one. 3. second-class honours in a university degree. 4. an assistant to a combatant in a duel, boxing match etc. 5. (in *plural*) a second helping of food; a second course of a meal. —*v.t.* 1. to back up, to assist. 2. to support, (a resolution etc. or its proposer) formally so as to show that the proposer is not isolated or as a means of bringing it to a vote. —**second-best** *adj.* & *n.* next after the best; inferior in quality (*come off second-best*, to fail to win). **second chamber**, the upper house of a parliament. **second class**, the second-best group or category or accommodation etc.; the class of mail that does not have priority in delivery. **second-class** *adj.* & *adv.* of or by the second or inferior class. **second fiddle**, a subordinate position or role. **second-guess** *v.t./i.* (*US*) to anticipate the action of; to predict; to criticize by hindsight. **second-hand** *adj.* having had a previous owner, not new; (of a shop etc.) supplying such goods; (*adv.*) from a secondary source (*at second hand*, indirectly). **second lieutenant**, an army officer next below lieutenant. **second nature**, an acquired tendency that has become instinctive. **second officer**, an assistant mate on a merchant ship. **second person**, in grammar, see ◊person. **second-rate** *adj.* in the second class, inferior. **second sight**, the supposed power of perceiving future events. **second teeth**, the permanent teeth of an adult. **second thoughts**, a new opinion or resolution reached after further consideration. **second wind**, recovery of regular breathing during continued exertion after breathlessness; renewed capacity for effort after tiredness. —**seconder** *n.* [from Old French from Latin *secundus* (*sequi* = follow)]

second[2] /si'kɒnd/ *v.t.* to transfer (an officer or official) temporarily to another appointment or department. —**secondment** *n.*

second[3] /'sekənd/ *n.* 1. the basic SI unit (symbol sec or s) of time, one-sixtieth of a minute. It is defined as the duration of 9,192,631,770 periods of the radiation corresponding to the transition between two hyperfine levels of the ground state of the caesium-133 isotope. 2. in mathematics, the second is a unit (symbol ϑ) of angular measurement, equalling one-sixtieth of a minute, which in turn is one-sixtieth of a degree. 3. (*colloquial*) a very short time. [from Old French from Latin *secunda* (*minuta*) = secondary minute, i.e. minute of a minute]

secondary /'sekəndəri/ *adj.* 1. coming after or next below what is primary; derived from, depending on, or supplementing what is primary; of lesser importance or rank etc. than the first. 2. (of education, a school etc.) for those who have received primary education but have not yet proceeded to a university or occupation. —*n.* a thing that is secondary. —**secondary colours**, see ◊colour. **secondary picketing**, furtherance of an industrial dispute by picketing the premises of a firm not directly involved in it. —**secondarily** *adv.* [from Latin]

secondary emission in physics, an emission of electrons from the surface of certain substances when they are struck by high-speed electrons or other particles from an external source. See also ◊photomultiplier.

secondary growth or **secondary thickening** the increase in diameter of the roots and stems of certain plants (notably shrubs and trees) that results from the production of new cells by the ◊cambium. It provides the plant with additional mechanical support and new conducting cells, the secondary ◊xylem and ◊phloem. Secondary growth is generally confined to ◊gymnosperms and, among the ◊angiosperms, to the dicotyledons. With just a few exceptions, the monocotyledons (grasses, lilies) exhibit only primary growth, resulting from cell division at the apical ◊meristems.

secondary market a market for resale or purchase of shares, bonds, and commodities outside of organized stock exchanges and primary markets.

secondary modern school in the UK, a secondary school that normally takes children who have failed to gain a ◊grammar school place, in those few areas which retain academic selection at 11 or 12.

secondary sexual characteristic in biology, an external feature of an organism that is characteristic of its gender (male or female), but not the reproductive organs themselves. They include facial hair in men and breasts in women, combs in cockerels, brightly coloured plumage in many male birds, and manes in male lions. In many cases, they are involved in displays and contests for mates and have evolved by ◊sexual selection. Their development is stimulated by sex hormones.

Second Front in World War II, the battle line opened against Germany on 6 June 1944 by the Allies (Britain and the USA). Following Germany's invasion of Russia in June 1941 (the 'first front'), Russian leader Joseph Stalin asked Britain to invade the European mainland, to relieve pressure on the ◊Red Army. An Anglo-American invasion fleet landed on the Normandy beaches and, after overcoming fierce German resistance, Paris was liberated by the Allied forces on 25 Aug 1944.

secondly *adv.* in the second place, furthermore.

Second World War an alternative name for ◊World War II.

secrecy /'siːkrəsi/ *n.* keeping things secret; being kept secret. —**sworn to secrecy**, having promised to keep a secret.

secret /'siːkrɪt/ *adj.* 1. kept or meant to be kept from the knowledge or view of others or of all but a few; to be known only by specified people. 2. acting or operating secretly. 3. fond of secrecy. —*n.* 1. a thing kept or meant to be kept secret. 2. a mystery, a thing for which an explanation is unknown or not widely known. 3. a valid but not generally known method for achieving something. —**in secret**, in a secret manner. **secret agent**, a spy acting for a country. **secret ballot**, one in which individual voters' choices are not made public. **secret police**, a police force operating in secret for political ends. **secret service**, any government ◊intelligence organization. In the USA the Secret Service is a law-enforcement unit of the Treasury Department and provides the president's bodyguard. **secret society,** a society with membership by invitation only, often involving initiation rites, secret rituals, and dire punishments for those who break the code. Often founded for religious reasons or benefit, some have become the province of corrupt politicians or gangsters, like the ◊Mafia, ◊Ku Klux Klan, ◊Freemasonry, and the ◊Triad. —**secretly** *adv.* [from Old French from Latin *secretus* from *secernere*= separate, set apart (*se*-= aside and *cernere* = sift)]

secretaire /sekri'teə/ *n.* an escritoire. [French]

secretariat /sekrə'teəriət/ *n.* an administrative office or department; its members or premises. [from French from Latin]

secretary /'sekrətəri/ *n.* **1.** a person employed to assist with correspondence, keep records, make appointments, etc. **2.** an official appointed by a society etc. to conduct its correspondence, keep its records etc. **3.** the principal assistant of a government minister, ambassador etc. —**secretary-general** *n.* the principal administrator of an organization. **secretary of state,** the head of a major government department; (*US*) the foreign secretary. —**secretarial** /-'teəriəl/ *adj.,* **secretaryship** *n.* [from Latin *secretarius*]

secretary bird a long-legged, mainly grey-plumaged bird of prey *Sagittarius serpentarius*, about 1.2 m/4 ft tall, with an erectile head crest. It is protected in S Africa because it eats poisonous snakes. [from its crest which is likened to quill pens placed behind a writer's ear]

secrete /si'kri:t/ *v.t.* **1.** to put into a place of concealment. **2.** to separate (a substance) in a gland etc. from blood or sap for a function in the organism or for excretion. —**secretor** *n.* [from *secret* or as back formation from *secretion*]

secretin *n.* a ◊hormone produced by the small intestine of vertebrates that stimulates the production of digestive secretions by the pancreas and liver.

secretion /si'kri:ʃən/ *n.* **1.** secreting, being secreted. **2.** in biology, any substance (normally a fluid) produced by a cell or specialized gland, for example, sweat, saliva, enzymes, and hormones. [from French or Latin *secretio*]

secretive /'si:krətɪv/ *adj.* making a secret of things unnecessarily, uncommunicative. —**secretively** *adv.,* **secretiveness** *n.* [back formation from *secretiveness* after French *secrétiveté*]

secretory /si'kri:təri/ *adj.* of physiological secretion.

sect *n.* a group of people with religious or other beliefs that differ from those more generally accepted; the followers of a particular philosophy or school of thought. [from Old French or Latin *secta* (*sequi* = follow)]

sectarian /sek'teəriən/ *adj.* of or concerning a sect; bigoted or narrow-minded in following one's sect. —*n.* a member of a sect. —**sectarianism** *n.* [from Latin *sectarius* = adherent]

section /'sekʃən/ *n.* **1.** a part cut off; one of the parts into which a thing is divided or divisible or out of which a structure can be fitted together; a subdivision of a book, statute, group of people etc.; (*US*) an area of land, a district of a town; a subdivision of an army platoon. **2.** separation by cutting. **3.** the cutting of a solid by a plane; the resulting figure or area of this. —*v.t.* to arrange in or divide into sections. —**section mark,** a sign (§) used to indicate the start of a section of a book etc. [French or from Latin *secare* = cut]

sectional *adj.* **1.** of a section. **2.** made in sections. **3.** local rather than general; partisan. —**sectionally** *adv.*

sector /'sektə/ *n.* **1.** a distinct part or branch of an enterprise, of society or the economy etc. **2.** the plane figure enclosed between two radii of a circle, ellipse etc., and the arc cut off by them. **3.** any of the parts into which a battle area is divided for control of operations. [Latin, originally = cutter]

secular /'sekjulə/ *adj.* **1.** concerned with the affairs of this world, not spiritual or sacred. **2.** not ecclesiastical or monastic. **3.** occurring once in an age or century. —**secularity** /-'lærɪtɪ/ *n.* [from French or Latin *saecularis* (*saeculum* = an age)]

secularism *n.* the belief that morality or education should not be based on religion. —**secularist** *n.*

secularization *n.* the process through which religious thinking, practice, and institutions lose their religious and/or social significance. The concept is based on the theory, held by some sociologists, that as societies become industrialized their religious morals, values, and institutions give way to secular ones and some religious traits become common secular practices.

secure /si'kjuə/ *adj.* **1.** safe, especially against attack. **2.** certain not to slip or fail; reliable. —*v.t.* **1.** to make secure; to fasten or close securely. **2.** to succeed in obtaining. **3.** to guarantee, to make safe against loss. —**securely** *adv.* [from Latin *securus,* originally = free from worry (*se*-= aside and *cura* = care)]

Securities and Exchange Commission (SEC) an official US agency created in 1934 to ensure full disclosure to the investing public and protection against malpractice in the securities (stocks and shares) and financial markets (such as insider trading).

Securities and Investment Board the UK body with the overall responsibility for policing financial dealings in the City of London. Introduced in 1987 following the deregulation process of the so-called ◊Big Bang, it acts as an umbrella organization to such self-regulating bodies as the Stock Exchange.

security /si'kjuərɪtɪ/ *n.* **1.** the state or feeling of being secure; a thing that gives this. **2.** the safety of a state, organization etc., against espionage, theft, or other danger; an organization for ensuring this. **3.** a thing deposited or pledged as a guarantee of the fulfilment of an undertaking or payment of a loan, to be forfeited in case of failure. **4.** (often in *plural*) a document as evidence of a loan; a certificate of stock, a bond etc. —**security risk,** a person whose presence may threaten security. [from Old French or Latin]

sedan /si'dæn/ *n.* **1.** or **sedan chair** an enclosed chair for one passenger carried on horizontal poles by two bearers. Introduced into England by Sir Sanders Duncombe in 1634, by the 18th century it was the equivalent of a one-person taxi. **2.** (*US*) an enclosed motorcar for four or more persons. [ultimately from Latin *sella* = saddle (*sedēre* = sit)]

sedate[1] /si'deɪt/ *adj.* tranquil and dignified, not lively. —**sedately** *adv.,* **sedateness** *n.* [from Latin *sedare* = make calm (*sedēre* = sit)]

sedate[2] /si'deɪt/ *v.t.* to treat with sedatives. —**sedation** /-'deɪʃən/ *n.* [back formation from *sedation* from French or Latin]

sedative /'sedətɪv/ *adj.* tending to calm or soothe. —*n.* a sedative medicine or influence. Sedative medication will induce sleep in larger doses. Examples are ◊barbiturates, ◊narcotics, and ◊benzodiazepines. [from Old French or Latin]

Seddon /'sedn/ Richard John 1845–1906. New Zealand Liberal politician, prime minister 1893–1906.

sedentary /'sedəntərɪ/ *adj.* sitting; (of work etc.) characterized by much sitting and little physical exercise; (of a person) having or inclined to work etc. of this kind. [from French or Latin *sedēre* = sit]

seder *n.* a meal that forms part of the Jewish festival of Passover, which celebrates the ◊Exodus.

sedge *n.* any perennial grasslike plant of the family Cyperaceae, especially the genus *Carex,* usually with three-cornered solid stems, common in low water or on wet and marshy ground. —**sedgy** *adj.* [Old English]

Sedgemoor, Battle of /'sedʒmuə/ in English history, a battle on 6 July 1685 in which ◊Monmouth's rebellion was crushed by the forces of James II, on a tract of marshy land 5 km/3 mi SE of Bridgwater, Somerset.

sediment /'sedimənt/ *n.* **1.** very fine particles of solid matter suspended in a liquid or settling to the bottom of it. **2.** solid matter carried by water or wind and deposited on the surface of the land. Typical sediments are, in order of increasing coarseness, clay, mud, silt, sand, gravel, pebbles, cobbles, and boulders. —**sedimentation** /-'teɪʃən/ *n.* [from French or Latin *sedēre* = sit]

sedimentary /sedi'mentərɪ/ *adj.* **1.** of or like sediment. **2.** (of rock) formed by the accumulation and cementation of deposits that have been laid down by water, wind, ice, or gravity. Sedimentary rocks cover more than two-thirds of the Earth's surface and comprise three major categories: **clastic, chemically precipitated,** and **organic.** Clastic sediments are the largest group and are composed of fragments of pre-existing rocks; they include clays, sands, and gravels. Chemical precipitates include limestones such as chalk, and evaporated deposits such as gypsum and halite (rock salt). Coal, oil shale, and limestone made of fossil material are examples of organic sedimentary rocks.

sedition /sɪˈdɪʃən/ *n.* conduct or speech inciting people to rebellion: in the UK, the offence of inciting unlawful opposition to the crown and government. —**seditious** *adj.* [from Old French or Latin *seditio* (*se*- = aside and *ire* = go)]

seduce /sɪˈdjuːs/ *v.t.* to tempt into (especially extramarital) sexual intercourse; to persuade (especially into wrongdoing) by offering temptations. —**seducer** *n.*, **seductress** /-ˈdʌktrɪs/ *n.fem.* [from Latin *se*- = aside and *ducere* = lead]

seduction /sɪˈdʌkʃən/ *n.* 1. seducing, being seduced. 2. a tempting or attractive thing or quality. [from French or Latin]

seductive /sɪˈdʌktɪv/ *adj.* tending to seduce, alluring, enticing. —**seductively** *adv.*, **seductiveness** *n.*

sedulous /ˈsedjʊləs/ *adj.* diligent and persevering. —**sedulity** /sɪˈdjuːlɪtɪ/ *n.*, **sedulously** *adv.*, **sedulousness** *n.* [from Latin *sedulus* = zealous]

sedum /ˈsiːdəm/ *n.* a fleshy-leaved plant of the genus *Sedum*, with pink, white, or yellow flowers. [Latin = houseleek]

see[1] *v.t./i.* (*past* **saw**; *past participle* **seen**) 1. to perceive with the eyes; to have or use the power of doing this. 2. to perceive with the mind, to understand; to ascertain; to consider, to take time to do this; to foresee; to find attractive qualities (in a person etc.). 3. to watch, to be a spectator of. 4. to look at for information; to learn (a fact) from a newspaper or other visual source. 5. to meet; to be near and recognize. 6. to grant or obtain an interview (with); to visit in order to consult. 7. to interpret, to have an opinion of. 8. to supervise, to ensure. 9. to experience; to have presented to one's attention. 10. to call up a mental picture of, to imagine. 11. to escort or conduct. 12. in gambling, especially poker, to equal (a bet); to equal the bet of (a player). —**see about**, to attend to. **see after**, to take care of. **see the back of**, to be rid of (an unwanted person or thing). **see into**, to investigate. **see the light**, to realize one's mistakes etc.; to undergo a religious conversion. **see off**, to accompany to a place of departure; to ensure the departure of (a person). **see out**, to accompany out of a building etc.; to finish (a project etc.) completely; to wait until the end of (a period). **see over**, to inspect, to tour and examine. **see red**, to become suddenly enraged. **see stars**, to see lights before one's eyes as a result of a blow on the head. **see through**, not to be deceived by, to detect the nature of. **see a person through**, to support him or her during a difficult time. **see a thing through**, to finish it completely. **see-through** *adj.* (especially of clothing) transparent, diaphanous. **see to**, to attend to; to organize; to put right. [Old English]

see[2] *n.* the area under the authority of a bishop or archbishop; the bishop's or archbishop's office or jurisdiction. [from Anglo-French from Latin *sedes* = seat]

Seebeck effect /ˈsiːbek/ or **thermoelectric effect** in physics, the generation of a voltage in a circuit containing two different metals, or semiconductors, by keeping the junctions between them at different temperatures; the basis of the ◊thermocouple. It is the opposite of the ◊Peltier effect (in which current flow causes a temperature difference between the junctions of different metals). [from German physicist Thomas *Seebeck* (1770–1831) who discovered it]

seed *n.* 1. the unit of reproduction of a plant (◊angiosperm or ◊gymnosperm), a fertilized ovule capable of developing into another such plant; (*collective*) seeds in any quantity, especially as collected for sowing. A seed consists of an embryo and a food store, surrounded and protected by an outer seed coat, called the testa. The food store is contained either in a specialized nutritive tissue, the ◊endosperm, or in the ◊cotyledons of the embryo itself. In angiosperms the seed is enclosed within a fruit, whereas in gymnosperms it is usually naked and unprotected, once shed from the female cone. Following germination the seed develops into a new plant. 2. semen, milt. 3. something from which a tendency or feeling etc. can develop. 4. offspring, descendants. 5. in tennis etc., a seeded player. —*v.t./i.* 1. to plant seeds (in); to sprinkle (as) with seed. 2. to produce or drop seed. 3. to remove seeds from (fruit etc.). 4. to place crystal etc. in (a cloud) to produce rain. 5. to name (a strong player) as not to be matched against another named in this way in the early rounds of a

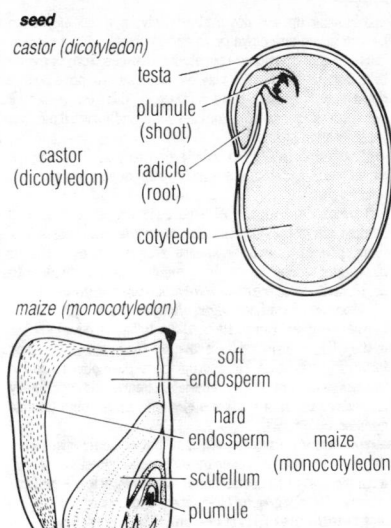

seed

castor (dicotyledon)

testa
plumule (shoot)
castor (dicotyledon)
radicle (root)
cotyledon

maize (monocotyledon)

soft endosperm
hard endosperm
scutellum
plumule
radicle
maize (monocotyledon)

knockout tournament, so as to increase the interest of later rounds; to arrange (the order of play) thus. —**go** or **run to seed**, to cease flowering as the seed develops; to become degenerate or unkempt etc. **seedbed** *n.* a bed of fine soil in which to sow seeds; a place of development. **seed pearl,** a very small pearl. **seed potato,** a potato kept for seed. [Old English]

seed drill a machine for sowing cereals and other seeds, developed by Jethro ◊Tull in England in 1701, although simple seeding devices were known in Babylon by 2000 BC. The seed is stored in a hopper and delivered by tubes into furrows in the ground. The furrows are made by a set of blades, or coulters, attached to the front of the drill. A ◊harrow is drawn behind the drill to cover up the seeds.

seedling *n.* a young plant, especially one raised from seed and not from a cutting etc.

seed plant or **spermatophyte** any seed-bearing plant. The seed plants are subdivided into two classes: the ◊angiosperms, or flowering plants, and the ◊gymnosperms, principally the cycads and conifers. Together, they comprise the major types of vegetation found on land.

seedsman *n.* (*plural* **seedsmen**) a dealer in seeds.

seedy *adj.* 1. full of seed; going to seed. 2. shabby-looking. 3. (*colloquial*) unwell. —**seedily** *adv.*, **seediness** *n.*

seeing *n.* use of the eyes. —*conj.* or **seeing that** considering that, inasmuch as, because.

seek *v.t./i.* (*past* and *past participle* **sought** /sɔt/) 1. to make a search or inquiry (for); to try or want to find, obtain, or reach or do. 2. (*archaic*) to aim at, to attempt. —**seek out**, to seek specially, to single out for companionship etc. [Old English]

seem *v.i.* to have the air, appearance, or feeling of being; to give a certain impression as to an action or state. —**it seems**, it appears to be true or the fact. [from Old Norse = honour]

seeming *adj.* apparent but perhaps not real.

seemly *adj.* conforming to accepted standards of good taste; proper; suitable. —**seemliness** *n.*

seen past participle of **see**[1].

seep *v.i.* to ooze slowly out of or through; to percolate slowly.

seepage *n.* seeping; the quantity that seeps out.

seer *n.* 1. one who sees. 2. a person who sees visions, a prophet.

seersucker /ˈsɪəsʌkə/ *n.* a striped material of linen or cotton etc. woven with a puckered surface. [from Persian, literally = milk and sugar]

seesaw *n.* 1. a device for children, with a long plank balanced on a central support and a child sitting at each end moving up and down alternately; a game played on this. **2.** an up-and-down or to-and-fro motion. **3.** a contest in which the advantage repeatedly changes from one side to the other. —*v.i.* **1.** to play on a seesaw; to move up and down as on a seesaw. **2.** to vacillate in policy etc. —*adj.* & *adv.* with an up-and-down or backward-and-forward motion. [reduplication of *saw*[1]]

seethe /siːð/ *v.i.* **1.** to bubble or surge as in boiling. **2.** to be very agitated (especially with anger) or excited. [Old English]

segment /ˈsegmənt/ *n.* a part cut off or separable or marked off as though separable from the other parts of a thing; part of a circle or sphere etc. cut off by a line or plane intersecting it. —*also* -ˈment/ *v.t./i.* to divide into segments. —**segmental** /-ˈmentəl/ *adj.*, **segmentation** /-ˈteɪʃən/ *n.* [from Latin *segmentum* (*secare* = cut)]

Segrè /seˈgreɪ/ Emilio 1905–1989. Italian physicist settled in the USA, who in 1955 discovered the antiproton, a new form of ◊antimatter. He shared the 1959 Nobel Prize for Physics with Owen Chamberlain. Segrè had previously discovered the first synthetic element, technetium (atomic number 43), in 1937.

segregate /ˈsegrɪgeɪt/ *v.t./i.* to put or come apart from the rest, to isolate; to separate (especially a racial group) from the rest of the community. —**segregation** /-ˈgeɪʃən/ *n.* [from Latin *segregare* (*se-* = apart and *grex* = flock)]

segregationist /segrɪˈgeɪʃənɪst/ *n.* a person who is in favour of racial segregation.

Seifert /ˈsiːfət/ Jaroslav 1901–1986. Czech poet who won state prizes but became an original member of the Charter 77 human-rights movement. His works include *Mozart in Prague* 1970 and *Umbrella from Piccadilly* 1978. He received the Nobel Prize for Literature in 1984.

seigneur /seɪnˈjɜː/ *n.* a feudal lord. —**seigneurial** *adj.* [from Old French from Latin = senior]

seine /seɪn/ *n.* a fishing net for encircling fish, with floats at the top and weights at the bottom edge. Purse seine nets, usually towed by two boats, may be up to 30 nautical miles in length. —*v.t./i.* to fish or catch with a seine. [from Old French and Old English, ultimately from Greek *sagēnē*]

Seine French river rising on the Langres plateau NW of Dijon, and flowing 774 km/472 mi in a NW direction to join the English Channel near Le Havre, passing through Paris and Rouen.

seise see ◊seize[5].

seismic /ˈsaɪzmɪk/ *adj.* of earthquakes; of earth vibrations produced artificially by explosions. —**seismic survey**, a survey of an area that is being explored for oil and gas, employing seismic methods. —**seismically** *adv.* [from Greek *seismos* = earthquake (*seiō* = shake)]

seismogram /ˈsaɪzməgræm/ *n.* the record given by a seismograph.

seismograph /ˈsaɪzməgrɑːf/ *n.* an instrument for detecting, recording, and measuring the force and direction etc. of earthquakes.

seismography /saɪzˈmɒgrəfɪ/ *n.* the recording of natural or artificially produced seismic phenomena. —**seismographer** *n.*, **seismographic** /-ˈgræfɪk/ *adj.*

seismology /saɪzˈmɒlədʒɪ/ *n.* the study of earthquakes and how their shock waves travel through the Earth. By examining the global pattern of waves produced by an earthquake, experts can deduce the nature of the materials through which they have passed. This leads to an understanding of the Earth's internal structure. —**seismological** /-ˈlɒdʒɪkəl/ *adj.*, **seismologist** *n.*

seize /siːz/ *v.t./i.* **1.** to take hold of (a thing) forcibly, suddenly, or eagerly. **2.** to take possession of forcibly or by legal power. **3.** to understand suddenly. **4.** to grasp with the mind quickly or clearly. **5.** in law also **seise** /siːz/ to put in possession of. **6.** (*nautical*) to fasten by binding with turns of yarn etc. **seize on** *or* **upon**, to seize eagerly. **seize up**, (of a mechanism) to become stuck or jammed from undue heat or friction. [from Old French]

seizure /ˈsiːʒə/ *n.* **1.** seizing, being seized. **2.** a sudden attack of apoplexy etc., a stroke.

sejant /ˈsiːʒənt/ *adj.* in heraldry, (of an animal) sitting upright on its haunches. [from Old French = sitting from Latin *sedēre* = sit]

Sekhmet /ˈsekmet/ ancient Egyptian goddess of heat and fire. She was represented with the head of a lioness, and worshipped at Memphis as the wife of ◊Ptah.

seldom /ˈseldəm/ *adv.* rarely, not often. [Old English]

select /sɪˈlekt/ *v.t.* to pick out as the best or most suitable. —*adj.* **1.** chosen for excellence or fitness. **2.** (of a society etc.) exclusive, cautious in admitting members. [from Latin *seligere* (*se-* = apart and *legere* = pick)]

select committee any of several long-standing committees of the UK House of Commons, such as the Environment Committee and the Treasury and Civil Service Committee. These were intended to restore parliamentary control of the executive, improve the quality of legislation, and scrutinize public spending and the work of government departments. Select committees represent the major parliamentary reform of the 20th century, and a possible means (through their all-party membership) of avoiding the automatic repeal of one government's measures by its successor.

selection /sɪˈlekʃən/ *n.* **1.** selecting, being selected. **2.** the selected person(s) or thing(s). **3.** a collection of things from which a choice may be made. **4.** the process by which some animals or plants thrive more than others, as a factor in evolution. [from Latin *selectio*]

selective *adj.* **1.** chosen or choosing carefully. **2.** able to select. —**selectively** *adv.*, **selectivity** /-ˈtɪvɪtɪ/ *n.*

selector *n.* **1.** a person who selects; a member of a committee selecting a national sports team. **2.** a device in machinery making the required selection of gear etc.

Selene /sɪˈliːnɪ/ in Greek mythology, the goddess of the Moon. She was the daughter of Titan and the sister of Helios and Eos. In later times she was identified with ◊Artemis.

selenium /sɪˈliːnɪəm/ *n.* a grey, non-metallic element, symbol Se, atomic number 34, relative atomic mass 78.96. It belongs to the sulphur group and occurs in several allotropic forms that differ in their physical and chemical properties. It is an essential trace element in human nutrition. Obtained from many sulphide ores and selenides, it is used as a red colouring for glass and enamel. [from Greek *selēnē* = moon]

Seleucus I /səˈluːkəs/ Nicator *c.*358–280 BC. Macedonian general under Alexander the Great and founder of the **Seleucid Empire**. After Alexander's death in 323 BC, Seleucus became governor and then (in 312 BC) ruler of Babylonia, founding the city of Seleucia on the river Tigris. He conquered Syria and had himself crowned king in 306 BC, but his expansionist policies brought him into conflict with the Ptolemies of Egypt, and he was assassinated by Ptolemy Ceraunus. He was succeeded by his son Antiochus I.

self *n.* (*plural* **selves**) /selvz/) **1.** a person's or thing's own individuality or essence. **2.** a person or thing as the object of introspection or reflexive action. **3.** one's own interests or pleasure; concentration on these. **4.** (in commerce, or *colloquial*) myself, yourself, herself etc. —*adj.* of the same colour as the rest or throughout. [Old English]

self- prefix expressing a reflexive action in the senses 'of or by oneself or itself', 'on, in, for, or relating to oneself or itself'.

self-abnegation *n.* self-sacrifice.

self-abuse *n.* masturbation.

self-addressed *adj.* addressed to oneself.

self-appointed *adj.* appointed by himself or herself, especially in an officious or self-righteous way, and not necessarily recognized by others.

self-assertive /selfəˈsɜːtɪv/ *adj.* asserting onself, one's rights etc., confidently. —**self-assertion** *n.*

self-assured /selfəˈʃʊəd/ *adj.* self-confident. —**self-assurance** *n.*

self-catering *adj.* catering for oneself, providing one's own meals, especially while on holiday.

self-centred /selfˈsentəd/ *adj.* preoccupied with oneself or one's own affairs.

self-confessed *adj.* openly confessing oneself to be.

self-confident *adj.* having confidence in one's own abilities. —**self-confidence** *n.*

self-conscious *adj.* embarrassed or unnatural in manner from knowing that one is observed by others. —**self-consciousness** *n.*

self-contained *adj.* **1.** complete in itself; (of accommodation) having all the necessary facilities and not sharing these. **2.** (of a person) independent, able to do without the company of others; not communicating freely.

self-control *n*. ability to control one's behaviour and not act emotionally. —**self-controlled** *adj*.

self-deception *n*. deceiving oneself, especially about one's feelings etc.

self-defeating *adj*. (of a course of action etc.) frustrating the purpose it was intended to serve.

self-defence *n*. defence of oneself or of one's rights or good reputation etc.

self-denial *n*. deliberately going without the pleasures etc. that one would like to have.

self-determination *n*. 1. determination of one's own fate or course of action, free will. 2. a nation's determination of its own form of government or its allegiance.

self-discipline *n*. discipline and training of oneself.

self-drive *adj*. (of a hired vehicle) driven by the hirer.

self-educated *adj*. educated by oneself, with little or no help from schools etc.

self-effacing *adj*. keeping oneself in the background. —**self-effacement** *n*.

self-employed *adj*. working independently and not for an employer.

self-esteem *n*. good opinion of oneself.

self-evident *adj*. evident without proof, explanation, or further evidence.

self-explanatory *adj*. that needs no (further) explanation.

self-fertilizing *adj*. (of a plant) fertilizing itself by its own pollen, not from others. —**self-fertilization** *n*.

self-fulfilment *n*. fulfilment of one's own hopes and ambitions etc.

self-governing *adj*. governing itself. —**self-government** *n*.

self-help *n*. use of one's own abilities or resources to achieve success, without dependence on others.

self-important *adj*. having a high opinion of one's own importance, pompous. —**self-importance** *n*.

self-imposed *adj*. (of a task etc.) imposed by oneself on oneself.

self-induced *adj*. induced by oneself or itself.

self-induction *n*. or **self-inductance** in physics, the creation of a counter emf (◊electromotive force) in a coil because of variations in the current flowing through it.

self-indulgent *adj*. greatly indulging one's own desires for comfort and pleasure. —**self-indulgence** *n*.

self-inflicted *adj*. inflicted by oneself on oneself.

self-interest *n*. one's personal interest or advantage. —**self-interested** *adj*.

selfish *adj*. acting or done according to one's own interests and needs without regard for those of others; keeping good things for oneself and not sharing. —**selfishly** *adv*., **selfishness** *n*.

selfless *adj*. disregarding oneself or one's own interests, unselfish. —**selflessly** *adv*., **selflessness** *n*.

self-loading *adj*. (of a firearm) reloading itself after firing, automatic.

self-locking *adj*. locking automatically when closed.

self-made *adj*. having risen from poverty or obscurity and achieved success by one's own efforts.

self-opinionated *adj*. stubbornly adhering to one's own opinions.

self-pity *n*. pity for oneself.

self-portrait *n*. a portrait of him-or herself by an artist; an account of him-or herself by a writer.

self-possessed *adj*. feeling or remaining calm and dignified, especially in difficulty. —**self-possession** *n*.

self-preservation *n*. protection of oneself from death, harm, or injury etc.; the instinct to ensure one's own survival.

self-propelled *adj*. propelled by itself or its own motor etc., not drawn or pushed. —**self-propulsion** *n*.

self-raising *adj*. (of flour) containing a raising agent and for use without additional baking powder.

self-recording *adj*. (of a scientific instrument) recording measurements or changes etc. automatically.

self-regard *n*. regard for oneself.

self-reliant *adj*. reliant on or confident in one's own abilities and resources. —**self-reliance** *n*.

self-reproach *n*. reproach or blame directed by oneself at oneself.

self-respect *n*. respect for oneself, the feeling that one is behaving with honour, dignity etc. —**self-respecting** *adj*.

self-restrained *adj*. able to restrain one's own emotions. —**self-restraint** *n*.

Selfridge /'selfrɪdʒ/ Harry Gordon 1857–1947. US entrepreneur who in 1909 founded Selfridges in London, the first large department store in Britain.

The customer is always right.
Harry Gordon Selfridge
(slogan adopted at his shops)

---

self-righteous *adj*. conceitedly aware of or asserting one's own righteousness. —**self-righteously** *adv*.

self-sacrifice *n*. sacrifice of one's own interests and wishes so that others may benefit. —**self-sacrificing** *adj*.

selfsame *adj*. the very same, identical.

self-satisfied *adj*. pleased or unduly satisfied with oneself or one's own achievements, conceited. —**self-satisfaction** *n*.

self-sealing *adj*. sealing automatically; (of a tyre etc.) having the means of automatically sealing small punctures.

self-seeking *adj*. & *n*. seeking to promote one's own interests rather than those of others.

self-service *n*. (often *attributive*) the system in a shop or restaurant etc. by which customers serve themselves and pay for what they have taken.

self-sown *adj*. grown from seed that has dropped naturally from the plant.

self-starter *n*. an electric device for starting an internal-combustion engine.

self-styled *adj*. using a title or name etc. that one has given oneself, especially without authorization or right.

self-sufficient *adj*. able to supply one's own needs without outside help. —**self-sufficiency** *n*.

self-supporting *adj*. that supports oneself or itself without help; self-sufficient.

self-taught *adj*. having taught oneself without formal help from a teacher etc.

self-willed *adj*. obstinately determined to follow one's own wishes, intentions etc.; stubborn. —**self-will** *n*.

self-winding *adj*. (of a watch or clock) having a mechanism that winds it automatically.

Seljuk Empire an empire of the Turkish people (converted to Islam during the 7th century) under the leadership of the invading Tatars or Seljuk Turks. The Seljuk Empire 1055–1243 included all Anatolia and most of Syria. It was succeeded by the ◊Ottoman Empire.

sell *v.t./i.* (*past* and *past participle* **sold** /səʊld/) 1. to make over or dispose of in exchange for money. 2. to keep a stock of (goods) for sale. 3. (of goods) to find purchasers; to have a specified price. 4. to betray or offer dishonourably for money or other reward. 5. to promote sales of; to inspire with a desire to buy, acquire, or agree to. —*n*. (*colloquial*) 1. the manner of selling. 2. a deception, a disappointment. —**be sold on**, to be enthusiastic about. **selling point**, an advantage recommending a thing. **sell off**, to sell the remainder of (goods) at reduced prices. **sell out**, to sell (all one's stock, shares etc., or *absolute*); to betray; to be treacherous or disloyal to. **sellout** *n*. the selling of all tickets for a show etc., a commercial success; a betrayal. **sell short**, to disparage; to underestimate. **sell up**, to sell one's business, house etc. [Old English]

sellable *adj*. that may be sold, able to find purchasers.

Sellafield /'seləfi:ld/ the site of a nuclear power station on the coast of Cumbria, NW England. It was known as **Windscale** until 1971, when the management of the site was transferred from the UK Atomic Energy Authority to British Nuclear Fuels Ltd. The plant is the world's greatest discharger of radioactive waste: between 1968 and 1979 180 kg of plutonium was discharged into the Irish Sea.

seller *n*. one who sells. —**seller's market,** a situation in which a commodity is scarce and therefore expensive.

Sellers /'seləz/ Peter 1925–1980. English comedian and film actor. He made his name in the British radio comedy series *The Goon Show* 1949–60, and his films include *Dr Strangelove* 1964, five *Pink Panther* films 1964–78 (as the bumbling Inspector Clouseau), and *Being There* 1979.

Sellotape /'seləʊteɪp/ *n*. the trade name of an adhesive, usually transparent, cellulose or plastic tape. —**sellotape** *v.t.* to fix or seal with tape of this kind.

selva n. equatorial rainforest, such as that in the Amazon basin in South America.

selvage /'selvɪdʒ/ n. 1. an edge of cloth so woven that it does not unravel. 2. a tapelike border along the edge of cloth, intended to be removed or hidden. [from *self* and *edge*]

selves plural of **self**.

Selwyn Lloyd /'selwɪn 'lɔɪd/ John, Baron 1904–1978. English Conservative politician. He was foreign secretary 1955–60 and chancellor of the Exchequer 1960–62, responsible for the creation of the National Economic Development Council. The unpopularity of his policy of wage restraint in an attempt to defeat inflation forced his resignation. He was Speaker of the House of Commons 1971–76.

Selznick /'selznɪk/ David O(liver) 1902–1965. US film producer whose early work includes *King Kong*, *Dinner at Eight*, and *Little Women* all 1933. His independent company, Selznick International (1935–40), made such lavish films as *Gone With the Wind* 1939, *Rebecca* 1940, and *Duel in the Sun* 1946.

semantic /sɪ'mæntɪk/ adj. of meaning in language; of connotation. —**semantically** adv. [from French from Greek *sēmainō* = signify]

semantics n.pl. (usually treated as *singular*) 1. the branch of ◊linguistics dealing with the meaning of words. 2. meaning, connotation. 3. interpretation of symbols (e.g. road signs) other than words.

semaphore /'seməfɔ:/ n. 1. a system of signalling by holding the arms or two flags in certain positions to indicate letters of the alphabet. 2. a signalling apparatus consisting of a post with movable arm(s) etc. used on railways etc. —v.t./i. to signal or send by semaphore. [from French from Greek *sēma* = sign and *pherō* = bear]

Semarang /sə'mɑːræŋ/ port in N Java, Indonesia; population (1980) 1,027,000. There is a shipbuilding industry, and exports include coffee, teak, sugar, tobacco, kapok, and petroleum from nearby oilfields.

semblance /'sembləns/ n. 1. an outward appearance (either real or pretended), a show. 2. a resemblance or likeness. [from Old French from Latin *similis* = like]

Semele /'semɪli/ in Greek mythology, the mother of Dionysus by Zeus. At Hera's suggestion, she demanded that Zeus should appear to her in all his glory, but when he did so she was consumed by lightning.

semelparity n. in biology, the occurrence of a single act of reproduction during an organism's lifetime. Most semelparous species produce very large numbers of offspring when they do reproduce, and normally die soon afterwards. Examples include the Pacific salmon and the pine-looper moth. Many plants are semelparous, or ◊monocarpic. Repeated reproduction is called ◊iteroparity.

semen /'si:men/ n. the whitish reproductive fluid produced by male animals, containing spermatozoa. [Latin = seed]

Semenov /sə'mjɒnɒf/ Nikoly 1896– . Russian physical chemist who made significant contributions to the study of chemical chain reactions. In 1956 he became the first Russian to receive the Nobel Prize for Chemistry, which he shared with Cyril ◊Hinshelwood.

semester /sɪ'mestə/ n. a half-year course or term in (especially German and US) universities. [German from Latin *semestris* = six-monthly (*sex* = six and *mensis* = month)]

semi /'semɪ/ n. (*colloquial*) a semidetached house. [abbreviation]

semi- prefix with the meaning of 1. half, partly. 2. occurring or appearing twice in a specified period (e.g. *semiannual*). [French or Latin = half]

semibreve /'semɪbri:v/ n. in music, the longest note in common use.

semicircle /'semɪsɜːkəl/ n. half of a circle or of its circumference.

semicircular /semɪ'sɜːkjuːlə/ adj. arranged in or shaped like a semicircle. —**semicircular canal**, each of three fluid-filled channels in the inner ◊ear giving information to the brain to help to maintain balance.

semicolon /semɪ'kəʊlən/ n. a punctuation mark (;) used where there is a more distinct break than that indicated by a comma but less than that indicated by a full stop. It also helps separate items in a complex list.

semiconductor /semɪkən'dʌktə/ n. a crystalline material with an electrical conductivity between that of metals (good) and insulators (poor). —**semiconducting** adj.

semidetached adj. (of a house) joined to another on one side only.

semifinal /semi'faɪnəl/ n. the match or round preceding the final. —**semifinalist** n.

seminal /'semɪnəl/ adj. 1. of seed or semen; of reproduction. 2. (of ideas etc.) providing a basis for future development. —**seminal fluid**, semen. [from Old French or Latin]

seminar /'semɪnɑː/ n. 1. a small class at a university etc. for discussion and research. 2. a short, intensive course of study. [German]

seminary /'semɪnərɪ/ n. a training college for priests or rabbis etc. —**seminarist** n. [from Latin = seed plot]

semiology /siːmɪ'ɒlədʒɪ/ n. or **semiotics** the study of the function of signs and symbols in human communication, both in language and by various nonlinguistic means. Beginning with the notion of the Swiss linguist Ferdinand de Saussure (1857–1913) that no word or other sign (**signifier**) is intrinsically linked with its meaning (**signified**), it was developed as a scientific discipline, especially by ◊Lévi-Strauss and ◊Barthes. —**semiotic** adj. [from Greek *sēmeion* = sign (*sēma* = mark)]

semi-permeable adj. (of a membrane etc.) allowing small molecules to pass through but not large ones; permeable to molecules of water but not to those of any dissolved substance.

semiprecious /semi'preʃəs/ adj. (of a gem) less valuable than the stones called precious.

semiquaver /'semɪkweɪvə/ n. in music, a note equal to half a quaver.

Semiramis /se'mɪrəmɪs/ lived c.800 BC. Assyrian queen, later identified with the chief Assyrian goddess ◊Ishtar.

semirigid adj. (of an airship) having a flexible gas container to which is attached a stiffened keel or framework.

semiskilled adj. (of work or a worker) having or needing some training but at or of a less qualified level than a skilled worker.

Semite /'si:maɪt/ n. a member of any of the peoples of the Middle East originally speaking a Semitic language, and traditionally said to be descended from Shem, a son of Noah in the Bible. Ancient Semitic peoples include the Hebrews, Ammonites, Moabites, Edomites, Babylonians, Assyrians, Chaldaeans, Phoenicians, and Canaanites. The Semitic peoples founded the monotheistic religions of Judaism, Christianity, and Islam. —adj. of the Semites. [from Latin from Greek *Sēm* = Shem]

Semitic /si'mɪtɪk/ adj. 1. of the ◊Hamito-Semitic family of languages that includes Hebrew, Arabic, and Aramaic, and certain ancient languages such as Phoenician, Assyrian, and Babylonian. 2. of Semites; of the Jews.

semitone /'semɪtəʊn/ n. half a tone in the musical scale.

semitrailer /semi'treɪlə/ n. a trailer having wheels at the back and supported at the front by a towing vehicle.

semitropical /semi'trɒpɪkəl/ adj. subtropical.

semivowel /'semɪvaʊəl/ n. a sound intermediate between a vowel and a consonant (e.g. *w*, *y*); a letter representing this.

Semmelweis /'seməlvaɪs/ Ignaz Philipp 1818–1865. Hungarian obstetrician who pioneered ◊asepsis (better medical hygiene), later popularized by the British surgeon Joseph ◊Lister. He was dismissed from the General Hospital in Vienna for his efforts, which were not widely adopted at the time.

semolina /semə'li:nə/ n. the hard grains left after the milling of flour, used in milk puddings etc.; a pudding made of this. [from Italian *semolino* (*semola* = bran)]

sempstress variant of **seamstress**.

Semtex n. the trade name of a plastic explosive, manufactured in Czechoslovakia. It is safe to handle (it can only be ignited by a detonator), and difficult to trace, since it has no smell. It has been used by extremist groups in the Middle East and by the IRA in Northern Ireland.

sen. abbreviation of 1. senator. 2. senior.

SEN abbreviation of State Enrolled Nurse.

Senanayake /senə'naɪəkə/ Don Stephen 1884–1952. First prime minister of independent Sri Lanka (formerly Ceylon) 1947–52.

Senanayake Dudley 1911–1973. Prime minister of Sri Lanka 1952–53, 1960, and 1965–70; son of Don Senanayake.

senate /'senət/ *n.* **1.** the state council of the ancient Roman republic and empire, composed (after the early period) of ex-magistrates and having a variety of administrative, legislative, and judicial functions. Although nominally advisory, it controlled finance and foreign policy. **2.** the upper and smaller branch of the legislative assembly in the USA, France, states of the USA etc. The US Senate consists of 100 members, two from each state, elected for a six-year term. **3.** the governing (academic) body of certain universities or (*US*) colleges. [from Old French from Latin *senatus* (*senex* = old man)]

senator *n.* a member of a senate. —**senatorial** /-'tɔːrɪəl/ *adj.*

send *v.t./i.* (*past* and *past participle* **sent**) **1.** to order, cause, or enable to go to a certain destination; to have (a thing) conveyed. **2.** to send a message or letter. **3.** (of God, providence etc.) to grant, bestow, or inflict. **4.** to cause to move or go. **5.** to cause to become. **6.** (*slang*) to affect emotionally, to put into ecstasy. —**send away for,** to order (goods etc.) by post from a dealer. **send down,** to rusticate or expel from a university; to put in prison. **send for,** to order (a person) to come to one's presence; to order (a thing) to be brought or delivered from elsewhere. **send off,** to dispatch (a letter etc.); to attend the departure of (a person) as a sign of respect etc.; (of a referee) to order (a player) to leave the field and take no further part in the game. **sendoff** *n.* a demonstration of goodwill etc. at the departure of a person, the start of a project, etc. **send on,** to transmit to a further destination or in advance of one's own arrival. **send up,** to cause to go up; to transmit to higher authority; (*colloquial*) to satirize, to ridicule by comic imitation. **send-up** *n.* (*colloquial*) a satire or parody. **send word,** to send information. —**sender** *n.* [Old English]

Sendak /'sendæk/ Maurice 1928– . US illustrator and writer of children's books. His deliberately archaic books include *Where the Wild Things Are* 1963, *In the Night Kitchen* 1970, and *Outside Over There* 1981.

Sendero Luminoso a Maoist guerrilla group active in Peru, formed in 1980 to overthrow the government. Until 1988 its activity was confined to rural areas. By June 1988 an estimated 9,000 people had been killed in the insurgency, about half of them guerrillas. [Spanish = Shining Path]

Seneca /'senɪkə/ Lucius Annaeus *c.* 4 BC–AD 65. Roman Stoic playwright, author of essays and nine tragedies. He was tutor to the future emperor Nero but lost favour after the latter's accession to the throne and was ordered to commit suicide. His tragedies were accepted as classical models by 16th-century dramatists.

> Live among men as if God beheld you; speak to God as if man were listening.
> **Lucius Annaeus Seneca**
> *Epistles*

Senefelder /'zeɪnəfeldə/ Alois 1771–1834. German engraver, born in Prague. He is thought to have invented ◊lithography.

Senegal /senɪgɔːl/ Republic of; country in W Africa, on the Atlantic, bounded to the N by Mauritania, E by Mali, S by Guinea and Guinea-Bissau, and enclosing Gambia on three sides; **area** 196,200 sq km/75,753 sq mi; **capital** and chief port Dakar; **physical** plains rising to hills in SE; swamp and tropical forest in SW; river Senegal; **head of state and government** Abdou Diouf from 1981; **political system** emergent Socialist democratic republic; **exports** peanuts, cotton, fish, phosphates; **population** (1990 est) 7,740,000; **language** French (official); African dialects; **recent history** independence was achieved from France in 1960. Military assistance was provided to Gambia in 1980–81; the confederation of Senegambia came into effect in 1982 but was abandoned in 1989.

senescence *n.* in biology, the deterioration in physical and reproductive capacities associated with old age. See ◊ageing.

senescent /sɪ'nesənt/ *adj.* growing old. [from Latin *senescere* (*senex* = old)]

seneschal /'senɪʃəl/ *n.* the steward of a medieval great house. [from Old French from Latin *seniscalus*]

Senghor /sɒŋ'gɔː/ Léopold (Sédar) 1906– . First president of independent Senegal 1960–80, a believer in pan-African unity, and a poet and essayist.

senile /'siːnaɪl/ *adj.* of or characteristic of old age; having the symptoms and weaknesses of old age. —**senility** /sɪ'nɪlɪtɪ/ *n.* [from French or Latin *senilis* (*senex* = old)]

senile dementia see ◊dementia and ◊Alzheimer's Disease.

senior /'siːnɪə/ *adj.* **1.** older or oldest in age; (placed after a name) older than another of the same name. **2.** higher in rank or authority. **3.** for older children. —*n.* **1.** a senior person; one's senior in age or rank etc. **2.** a member of a senior school. —**senior citizen,** an elderly person, especially an old-age pensioner. **senior nursing officer,** a person in charge of nurses in a hospital. **senior school,** a school for

Sendak *Condemned as disturbing by some parents and teachers, the creatures portrayed in* Where the Wild Things Are *by Maurice Sendak nonetheless convey extremely well the dreams and imaginings of childhood.*

older children (especially those over 11). **senior service,** (*UK*) the Royal Navy. [Latin, comparative of *senex* = old]

seniority /siːni'ɒrɪtɪ/ *n.* the state of being senior.

senna /'senə/ *n.* cassia; a laxative prepared from this. [from Latin from Arabic]

Senna /'senə/ Ayrton 1960– . Brazilian motor-racing driver. He had his first Grand Prix win in the 1985 Portuguese Grand Prix, has since surpassed Jim Clark's record for most pole positions and, in 1988, was world champion, winning a championship record eight races. He won his second world title in 1990.

Sennacherib /si'nækərɪb/ died 681 BC. King of Assyria from 705 BC. Son of ◊Sargon II, he rebuilt the city of Nineveh on a grand scale, sacked Babylon in 689, and defeated ◊Hezekiah, king of Judah, but failed to take Jerusalem. He was assassinated by his sons, and one of them, Esarhaddon, succeeded him.

Sennett /'senɪt/ Mack. Stage name of Michael Sinnott 1880–1960. US film producer, originally an actor, responsible for 1920s slapstick silent films featuring the Keystone Kops, 'Fatty' Arbuckle, and Charlie Chaplin. He did not make the transition to sound with much enthusiasm and retired in 1935. His films include *Tillie's Punctured Romance* 1914, *The Shriek of Araby* 1923, and *The Barber Shop* (sound) 1933.

señor /sen'jɔː/ *n.* (*plural señores* /-rez/) a title used of or to a Spanish-speaking man. [Spanish from Latin = senior]

señora /sen'jɔːrə/ *n.* a title used of or to a Spanish-speaking married woman.

señorita /senjə'riːtə/ *n.* a title used of or to a Spanish-speaking unmarried woman.

sensation /sen'seɪʃən/ *n.* 1. an awareness or feeling produced by stimulation of a sense organ or of the mind, emotions etc. 2. ability to feel such stimulation. 3. a condition of eager interest, excitement, or admiration aroused in a community or group of people; a person or thing arousing this. [from Latin *sensatio* from *sensus* = sense]

sensational *adj.* 1. arousing eager interest, excitement, or admiration in a community or group of people. 2. (*colloquial*) extraordinary. —**sensationally** *adv.*

sensationalism *n.* 1. pursuit of the sensational; use of subject matter, words, or style etc. in order to produce excessive emotional excitement in people. 2. the theory that ideas are derived solely from sensation (as opposed to ◊rationalism). —**sensationalist** *n.*

sense *n.* 1. any of the special powers (usually reckoned as sight, hearing, smell, taste, touch) by which a living thing becomes aware of external objects and of changes in the condition of its own body. 2. ability to perceive, feel, or be conscious of a thing; awareness or recognition of something. 3. practical wisdom or judgement; conformity to this; common sense. 4. the meaning of a word etc.; possession of a meaning or of reasonableness. 5. the prevailing opinion. 6. (in *plural*) a person's sanity or normal state of mind. —*v.t.* 1. to perceive by one or more of the senses. 2. to become aware of by receiving a mental impression; to realize. 3. (of a machine etc.) to detect. —**come to one's senses,** to regain consciousness; to be sensible after acting foolishly. **in a** *or* **one sense,** if the statement is understood in a particular way. **make sense,** to be intelligible or practicable. **make sense of,** to show or find the meaning of. **sense datum,** whatever is the immediate object of any of the senses, usually (but not always) with the implication that it is not a material object. [from Latin *sensus* (*sentire* = feel)]

senseless *adj.* 1. unconscious. 2. not showing good sense, wildly foolish; without meaning or purpose. —**senselessness** *n.*

sensibility /sensi'bɪlɪtɪ/ *n.* 1. the capacity to feel physically or emotionally. 2. exceptional or excessive sensitiveness; delicacy of feeling, susceptibility. 3. (in *plural*) a tendency to feel offended etc. [from Latin]

sensible /'sensɪbəl/ *adj.* 1. having or showing good sense. 2. aware. 3. perceptible by the senses; great enough to be perceived. 4. (of clothing etc.) practical and functional rather than fashionable. —**sensibly** *adv.* [from Old French or Latin *sensibilis*]

sensitive /'sensɪtɪv/ *adj.* 1. affected by stimuli or mental impressions; receiving impressions quickly and easily. 2. alert and considerate about the feelings of others. 3. easily hurt or offended. 4. (of an instrument etc.) readily responsive to or recording slight changes; (of photographic

materials etc.) prepared so as to respond to the action of light. 5. (of a topic) requiring tactful treatment so as to avoid embarrassment, ensure security etc. —**sensitive plant,** a mimosa *Mimosa pudica* or other plant that droops or closes when touched; a sensitive person. —**sensitively** *adv.* [from Old French or Latin]

sensitivity /sensi'tɪvɪtɪ/ *n.* the quality or degree of being sensitive.

sensitize /'sensɪtaɪz/ *v.t.* to make sensitive. —**sensitization** /-'zeɪʃən/ *n.*

sensor /'sensə/ *n.* a device to detect, record, or measure a physical property.

sensory /'sensərɪ/ *adj.* of sensation or the senses; receiving or transmitting sensation. [from Latin *sensorium* = seat of feeling]

sensual /'sensjuəl/ *adj.* 1. physical, gratifying to the body. 2. indulging oneself with physical pleasures; showing that one does this. —**sensualism** *n.*, **sensuality** /-'ælɪtɪ/ *n.*, **sensually** *adv.* [from Latin]

sensuous /'sensjuəs/ *adj.* of, affecting, or appealing to the senses, especially aesthetically. —**sensuously** *adv.*

sent past and past participle of **send.**

sentence /'sentəns/ *n.* 1. a set of words (or occasionally one word) that is complete in itself as an expression of thought, containing or implying a subject and a predicate and expressing a statement, question, exclamation, or command. 2. the decision of a lawcourt, especially the punishment allotted to a person convicted in a criminal trial; the declaration of this. —*v.t.* to pass sentence upon (a convicted person); to condemn to a specified punishment. —**sentential** /-'tenʃəl/ *adj.* (in grammatical sense). [from Old French from Latin *sententia* = opinion]

sententious /sen'tenʃəs/ *adj.* affectedly or pompously formal or moralizing; aphoristic. —**sententiously** *adv.*, **sententiousness** *n.* [from Latin]

sentient /'senʃənt/ *adj.* perceiving or capable of perceiving things by means of the senses. —**sentience** *n.*, **sentiency** *n.* [from Latin *sentire* = feel]

sentiment /'sentɪmənt/ *n.* 1. a mental attitude produced by one's feeling about something; a verbal expression of this; an opinion. 2. emotion as opposed to reason; sentimentality. [from Old French from Latin]

sentimental /senti'mentəl/ *adj.* 1. of or characterized by romantic or nostalgic feeling. 2. showing or affected by emotion rather than reason. —**sentimental value,** the value of a thing to a particular person because of its associations. —**sentimentalism** *n.*, **sentimentalist** *n.*, **sentimentality** /-'tælɪtɪ/ *n.*, **sentimentally** *adv.*

sentimentalize /senti'mentəlaɪz/ *v.t.* to show sentimentality.

sentinel /'sentɪnəl/ *n.* a lookout, a sentry. [from French from Italian]

sentry /'sentrɪ/ *n.* a soldier etc. stationed to keep guard. —**sentry box,** a wooden cabin large enough to shelter a standing sentry. **sentry go,** the duty of pacing up and down as a sentry.

Seoul /səʊl/ or **Sôul** capital of South Korea, near the Han River, and with its chief port at Inchon; population (1985) 9,646,000. Industries include engineering, textiles, and food processing.

sepal /'sepəl/ *n.* the part of a flower, usually green, that surrounds and protects the flower in bud. The sepals are derived from modified leaves, and are collectively known as the ◊calyx. [from French (coined in 1790)]

separable /'sepərəbəl/ *adj.* that may be separated. —**separability** /-'bɪlɪtɪ/ *n.* **separably** *adv.* [from French or Latin]

separate /'sepərət/ *adj.* not joined or united with others; forming a unit that is or may be regarded as apart or by itself, distinct, individual. —*n.* (in *plural*) separate articles of dress suitable for wearing together in various combinations. —/-eɪt/ *v.t./i.* 1. to make separate, to divide, to keep apart; to prevent the union or contact of; to be between. 2. to become separate; to go different ways; to withdraw oneself from a union; to cease to live together as a (married) couple. 3. to divide into sorts or sizes etc.; to extract (an item or set of items etc.) thus. —**separately** *adv.* [from Latin *separare* (*se-* = apart and *parare* = make ready)]

separation /sepə'reɪʃən/ *n.* 1. separating, being separate. 2. (in full **judicial** or **legal separation**) an arrangement by which a husband and wife remain married but live apart. —**separation of powers,** an approach to limiting the powers of government by separating governmental functions into the executive, legislative, and judiciary. The concept has its fullest practical expression in the US constitution. [from Old French from Latin]

separatism /'sepərətizəm/ n. a policy of separation, especially for political or ecclesiastical independence. —**separatist** n.

separative /'sepərətiv/ adj. tending to cause separation.

separator /'sepəreitə/ n. a machine for separating things, e.g. cream from milk.

Sephardi /si'fɑ:di/ n. (plural **Sephardim**) a Jew descended from those expelled from Spain and Portugal in the 15th century, or from those forcibly converted to Christianity (Marranos) at that time (compare ◊Ashkenazi). Many settled in N Africa, and some in other Mediterranean countries, in the Netherlands, and in England. —**Sephardic** adj. [Hebrew, from name of country (*Sepharad*) mentioned in the Old Testament, Obadiah 20, and held in late Jewish tradition to be Spain]

sepia /'si:piə/ n. a dark, reddish-brown colour or paint. [Latin from Greek = cuttlefish]

sepoy /'si:pɔi/ n. (*historical*) an Indian soldier in the service of the British or Indian army in the days of British rule in India. [from Urdu and Persian *sipāhī* = soldier]

Sepoy Rebellion the revolt 1857–58 of the Indian soldiers (sepoys) against the British in India; also known as the **Sepoy,** or **Indian, Mutiny.** The uprising was confined to the north, from Bengal to the Punjab, and central India. The majority of support came from the army and recently dethroned princes, but in some areas it developed into a peasant uprising and general revolt. It included the seizure of Delhi by the rebels, its siege and recapture by the British, and the defence of Lucknow by a British garrison. The mutiny led to the end of rule by the ◊British East India Company and its replacement by direct British crown administration.

sepsis /'sepsis/ n. infection; any poisoned state due to the introduction of disease-causing organisms from outside into the bloodstream. [Greek]

sept n. a clan, especially in Ireland.

Sept. abbreviation of September.

September /sep'tembə/ n. the ninth month of the year. [from Latin *septem* = seven, because it was originally the seventh month in the Roman calendar]

septennial /sep'teniəl/ adj. lasting or recurring every seven years. —**septennially** adv. [from Latin *septennium* (*septem* = seven and *annus* = year)]

septet /sep'tet/ n. 1. a musical composition for seven performers; these performers. 2. any group of seven. [from German from Latin *septem* = seven]

septic /'septik/ adj. infected with harmful microorganisms that cause pus to form. —**septic tank,** a tank into which sewage is conveyed and in which it remains until the activity of bacteria makes it liquid enough to drain away. —**septically** adv. [from Latin from Greek *sebl ptikos* (*sēpō* = make rotten)]

septicaemia /septi'si:miə/ n. the technical term for ◊blood poisoning. —**septicaemic** adj. [Greek *haima* = blood]

septuagenarian /septjuədʒi'neəriən/ adj. from 70 to 79 years old. —n. a septuagenarian person. [from Latin *septuageni* = 70 each]

Septuagesima /septjuə'dʒesimə/ n. in the Christian calendar, the Sunday before Sexagesima. [Latin = 70th (day), with reference to period of 70 days from Septuagesima to the Saturday after Easter]

Septuagint /'septjuədʒint/ n. the oldest Greek version of the Old Testament or Hebrew Bible, traditionally made by 70 scholars. [Latin = 70]

septum /'septəm/ n. (*plural* **septa**) a partition such as that between the nostrils or the chambers of a poppy fruit or a shell. [from Latin *saepire* = fence off]

septuple /'septjupəl/ adj. sevenfold; having seven parts; being seven times as many or as much. —n. a sevenfold number or amount. [from Latin *septuplus* (*septem* = seven)]

sepulchral /si'pʌlkrəl/ adj. 1. of a sepulchre or interment. 2. gloomy, funereal. [from French or Latin]

sepulchre /'sepəlkə/ n. a tomb, especially one cut in rock or built of stone or brick. —v.t. to place in a sepulchre;

to serve as a sepulchre for. [from Old French from Latin *sepulc(h)rum* (*sepelire* = bury)]

sepulture /'sepəltʃə/ n. burying, placing in a grave. [from Old French from Latin *sepultura*]

sequel /'si:kwəl/ n. 1. what follows or arises out of an earlier event. 2. a novel or film etc. that continues the story of an earlier one. [from Old French or Latin *sequela* (*sequi* = follow)]

sequence /'si:kwəns/ n. 1. a succession; the order of succession. 2. a set of things belonging next to one another, an unbroken series. 3. a section of a cinema film, dealing with one scene or topic. [from Latin *sequentia*]

sequential /si'kwenʃəl/ adj. forming a sequence or consequence. —**sequentially** adv.

sequester /si'kwestə/ v.t. 1. to seclude, to isolate. 2. to sequestrate. [from Old French or Latin *sequestrare* (*sequester* = person with whom a contested thing is deposited)]

sequestrate /si'kwestreit, 'si:-/ v.t. to confiscate; to take temporary possession of (a debtor's estate etc.). —**sequestration** /si:kwe'streiʃən/ n., **sequestrator** n. [from Latin]

sequin /'si:kwin/ n. a circular spangle on a dress etc. —**sequinned** adj. [French from Italian *zecchino* = gold coin]

sequoia /si'kwɔiə/ n. either of two species of conifer in the redwood family Taxodiaceae, native to the western USA. The **redwood** *Sequoia sempervirens* is a long-lived timber tree, and one specimen, the Howard Libbey Redwood, is the world's tallest tree at 110 m/361 ft, with a circumference of 13.4 m/44 ft. The **giant sequoia** *Sequoiadendron giganteum* reaches up to 30 m/100 ft in circumference at the base, and grows almost as tall as the redwood. It is also (except for the bristlecone pine) the oldest living tree, some specimens being estimated at over 3,500 years of age. [from G G *Sequoya*]

Sequoya /sə'kwɔiə/ George Guess 1770–1843. American Indian scholar and leader. After serving with the US army in the Creek War 1813–14, he made a study of his own Cherokee language and created a syllabary which was approved by the Cherokee council in 1821. This helped thousands of Indians towards literacy and resulted in the publication of books and newspapers in their own language.

serac /se'ræk/ n. each of the castellated masses into which a glacier is divided at steep points by the crossing of crevasses. [from Swiss French *sérac*, originally the name of a compact white cheese]

seraglio /se'rɑ:liəu/ n. (*plural* **seraglios**) 1. a harem. 2. (*historical*) a Turkish palace. [from Italian from Turkish from Persian *sarāy* = palace]

seraph /'seræf/ n. (*plural* **seraphim** or **seraphs**) in Christian and Judaic belief, an ◊angel of the highest order. They are mentioned in the book of Isaiah in the Old Testament. —**seraphic** /sə'ræfik/ adj., **seraphically** adv. [back formation from *seraphim* (ultimately from Hebrew)]

Serapis /'serəpis/ ancient Greco-Egyptian god, a combination of Hades and Osiris, invented by the Ptolemies; his finest temple was the Serapeum in Alexandria.

Serbia /'sɜ:biə/ (Serbo-Croat **Srbija**) constituent republic of Yugoslavia, which includes the autonomous provinces of Kosovo and Vojvodina; **area** 88,400 sq km/ 34,122 sq mi; **capital** Belgrade; **physical** fertile Danube plains in the N, mountainous in the S; **population** (1986) 9,660,000; **language** the Serbian variant of Serbo-Croat, sometimes written in Cyrillic script; **recent history** uprisings in the 19th century secured autonomy after more than three centuries of Ottoman rule. In the Balkan wars 1912–13 Serbia encroached on Turkish and Bulgarian territory. The Kingdom of the Serbs, Croats and Slovenes, formed in 1918 and led by Serbian Peter ◊Karageorgevic, became Yugoslavia in 1921. After unrest in Kosovo in the 1980s a campaign by the hard-line Serbian party chief, Milosevic, culminated in the adoption of a new multiparty constitution in 1990, stripping the republics of Kosovo and Vojvodina of their autonomy. The election of Milosevic as president in Dec 1990 sparked more uprisings. In 1991 Serbia called for secession and Serb-Croatian clashes broke out in Croatia. The federal army intervened, but fighting continued.

SERC abbreviation of Science and Engineering Research Council.

serenade /serə'neɪd/ *n.* **1.** a piece of music sung or played by a lover to his lady, or suitable for this. **2.** an orchestral suite for a small ensemble. —*v.t.* to sing or play a serenade to. [from French or Italian *serenata* from Latin *serenus* = calm]

serendipity /serən'dɪpɪtɪ/ *n.* the faculty of making happy discoveries by accident. —**serendipitous** *adj.* [coined by Horace Walpole in 1754 from *The Three Princes of Serendip* (Sri Lanka), a fairy tale]

serene /sɪ'riːn/ *adj.* **1.** (of the sky, air etc.) clear and calm; (of the sea) unruffled. **2.** tranquil, calm and unperturbed. —**His, Her, Your Serene Highness**, titles used of or to members of some European royal families. —**serenely** *adv.*, **serenity** /-'renɪtɪ/ *n.* [from Latin *serenus*]

serf *n.* **1.** a labourer or peasant under ◊feudalism. Serfs could not be sold like slaves, but they were not free to leave their master's estate without his permission. They had to work the lord's land without pay for a number of days every week and pay a percentage of their produce to the lord every year. They also served as soldiers in the event of conflict. Serfs had to perform extra labour at harvest time and other busy seasons; in return they were allowed to cultivate a portion of the estate for their own benefit. **2.** an oppressed labourer, a drudge. —**serfdom** *n.* [Old French from Latin *servus* = slave]

serge *n.* a durable, twilled worsted etc. fabric used for making clothes. [from Old French from Latin *serica* (*lana*) (*sericum* = silk)]

sergeant /'saːdʒənt/ *n.* **1.** a noncommissioned army or airforce officer, in the UK next below warrant officer. **2.** (*British*) a police officer below inspector. —(**regimental**) **sergeant major**, a warrant officer assisting the adjutant of a regiment or battalion. [from Old French from Latin *serviens* = servant]

Sergius, St /'saːdʒɪəs/ of Radonezh 1314–1392. Patron saint of Russia, who founded the Eastern Orthodox monastery of the Blessed Trinity near Moscow in 1334. He acted as a mediator among Russian feudal princes, and inspired the victory of Dmitri, Grand Duke of Moscow, over the Tatar khan Mamai at Kulikovo, on the upper Don, in 1380.

serial /'sɪərɪəl/ *n.* a story published or broadcast etc. in regular instalments. —*adj.* **1.** of, in, or forming a series. **2.** (of a story etc.) in the form of a serial. **3.** (of music) using serial composition. —**serial composition**, in music, an alternative name for the ◊twelve-note system of composition. **serial number**, a number identifying an item in a series. —**serialism** *n.*, **serially** *adv.*

serialize /'sɪərɪəlaɪz/ *v.t.* to publish or produce in instalments. —**serialization** /-'zeɪʃən/ *n.*

series /'sɪəriːz, -ɪz/ *n.* (*plural* the same) **1.** a number of things of the same kind, or related to each other in a similar way, occurring, arranged, or produced in order. **2.** a set of geological strata with a common characteristic. **3.** a set of stamps or coins etc. issued at one time or in one reign. **4.** an arrangement of the 12 notes of the chromatic scale as the basis for serial composition (see ◊twelve-note system). —**in series**, in an ordered succession. **series circuit**, an electric circuit in which the components are connected end to end, so that the current flows through them all one after the other. [Latin = row, chain (*serere* = join)]

serif /'serɪf/ *n.* a slight projection finishing off the stroke of a printed letter (as in T, contrasted with sanserif T).

seriocomic /sɪərɪəʊ'kɒmɪk/ *adj.* combining the serious and the comic. —**seriocomically** *adv.*

serious *adj.* **1.** solemn and thoughtful, not smiling. **2.** sincere, in earnest, not casual or light-hearted. **3.** important, demanding thought. **4.** causing great concern, not slight. —**seriously** *adv.*, **seriousness** *n.* [from Old French or Latin *seriosus*]

serjeant /'saːdʒənt/ *n.* or **serjeant at law** (*British historical*) a barrister of the highest rank. —**serjeant at arms**, an official of a court, city, or parliament, with ceremonial duties; (*British*) an officer of each House of Parliament with the duty of enforcing the commands of the house, arresting offenders etc. [variant of *serjeant*]

sermon /'saːmən/ *n.* **1.** a spoken or written discourse on religion or morals etc., especially one delivered by a clergyperson during a religious service. **2.** a long, moralizing talk. [from Anglo-French from Latin *sermo* = discourse]

sermonize *v.t./i.* to deliver a moral lecture (to).

serous /'sɪərəs/ *adj.* **1.** of or like ◊serum, watery. **2.** (of a gland etc.) having a serous secretion. —**serosity** /-'rɒsɪtɪ/ *n.* [from French or Latin]

Serpens *n.* a constellation of the equatorial region of the sky, represented as a serpent coiled around the body of ◊Ophiuchus. It is the only constellation divided into two halves: **Serpens Caput**, the head (on one side of Ophiuchus), and **Serpens Cauda**, the tail (on the other side). Its main feature is the Eagle Nebula.

serpent /'saːpənt/ *n.* **1.** a snake, especially of a large kind. **2.** a sly or treacherous person. [from Old French from Latin *serpens* (*serpere* = creep)]

serpentine /'saːpəntaɪn/ *adj.* of or like a serpent, twisting and turning; cunning, treacherous. —*n.* one of a group of minerals, hydrous magnesium silicate, $Mg_3Si_2O_5(OH)_4$, occurring in soft ◊metamorphic rocks and usually dark green. The fibrous form **chrysotile** is a source of ◊asbestos; other forms are **antigorite**, **talc**, and **meerschaum**. Serpentine minerals are formed by hydration of ultrabasic rocks during metamorphism. Rare snake-patterned forms are used in ornamental carving.

SERPS abbreviation of State Earnings-Related Pension Scheme, the UK state ◊pension scheme.

serrated /se'reɪtɪd/ *adj.* with a toothed edge like a saw. —**serration** *n.* [from Latin *serra* = saw]

serried /'serɪd/ *adj.* (of ranks of soldiers) close together. [from *serry* = press close from French *serrer* = to close]

serum /'sɪərəm/ *n.* (*plural* **sera** or **serums**) **1.** the thin, amber-coloured fluid that remains from blood when the rest has clotted; this taken from an immunized animal and used for inoculation. It is blood plasma with the anticoagulant proteins removed, and contains ◊antibodies and other proteins, as well as the fats and sugars of the blood. It can be produced synthetically. **2.** any watery fluid from animal tissue (e.g. in a blister). [Latin = whey]

servant /'saːvənt/ *n.* **1.** a person employed to do domestic work in a household or as a personal attendant. **2.** an employee considered as performing services for his or her employer. **3.** a devoted follower, a person willing to serve another. [from Old French]

serve *v.t./i.* **1.** to perform services for; to be a servant to; to work for. **2.** to be employed or performing a spell of duty; to be a member of the armed forces. **3.** to be useful to or serviceable for; to do what is required; to provide a facility for. **4.** to go through a due period of (office, apprenticeship, a prison sentence etc.). **5.** to set out or present (food) for those about to eat it; to act as a waiter; to attend to (a customer in a shop). **6.** (of a quantity of food) to be enough for. **7.** to treat or act towards (a person) in a specified way. **8.** to assist (the officiating priest) in a religious service. **9.** to make legal delivery of (a writ etc.). **10.** in tennis etc., to set the ball in play. **11.** (of an animal) to copulate with (a female). —*n.* a service in tennis etc.; a person's turn for this. —**serve a person right**, to be his or her deserved punishment or misfortune. **serve up**, to offer for acceptance. —**server** *n.* [from Old French *servir* from Latin *servus* = slave]

servery /'saːvərɪ/ *n.* **1.** a room from which meals are served and in which utensils are kept. **2.** a serving hatch.

Servetus /saː'viːtəs/ Michael (Miguel Serveto) 1511–1553. Spanish Christian Anabaptist theologian and physician. He was a pioneer in the study of the circulation of the blood and found that it circulates to the lungs from the right chamber of the heart. He was burned alive by the church reformer John Calvin in Geneva, Switzerland, for publishing attacks on the doctrine of the Trinity.

service /'saːvɪs/ *n.* **1.** the doing of work for another or for a community etc.; the work done; assistance or benefit given to someone; readiness to perform this. **2.** a provision or system of supplying some public need, e.g. transport or (in *plural*) a supply of water, gas, electricity etc. **3.** being a servant; employment or position as a servant. **4.** employment in a public organization or crown department; such an organization or department; a branch of the armed forces; (*attributive*) of the kind issued to the armed forces. **5.** a ceremony of worship; a form of liturgy for this. **6.** maintenance and repair of a vehicle, machine, appliance etc., at intervals. **7.** assistance or advice given to customers after the sale of goods. **8.** the serving of food etc.; an extra charge nominally made for this. **9.** a set of dishes, plates etc., required for serving a meal. **10.** the act or manner

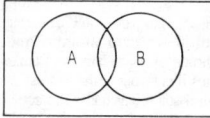

A and B are overlapping sets

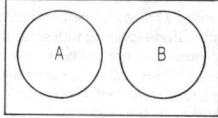

A and B are disjoint sets

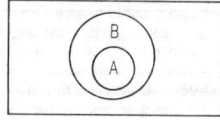

A is the subset of B

of serving in tennis etc.; a game in which one serves. —*v.t.* 1. to maintain or repair (machinery etc.). 2. to provide with service(s), to repair (a car or machine etc.). —**at a person's service,** ready to serve him or her. **in service,** employed as a servant; in use. **of service,** useful, helpful. **on active service,** serving in the armed forces in wartime. **see service,** to have experience of serving, especially in the armed forces; (of a thing) to be much used. **service area,** an area beside a major road for the supply of petrol, refreshments etc.; an area served by a broadcasting station. **service box,** the marked area of a squash court within which a validly served ball must fall. **service charge,** an additional charge for service. **service court,** in tennis etc., the marked area within which a validly served ball must fall. **service flat,** a flat in which domestic service and sometimes meals are provided by the management. **service industry,** any commercial activity that provides and charges for various services to customers (as opposed to manufacturing or supplying goods), such as restaurants, the tourist industry, cleaning, hotels, and the retail trade (shops and supermarkets). **service line,** in tennis, the line bounding a service court. **service road,** a road serving houses lying back from a main road. **service station,** a place beside a road selling petrol and oil etc. to motorists. [from Old French or Latin *servitium*]

Service /'sɜːvɪs/ Robert William 1874–1938. Canadian author, born in England. He was popular for his ballads of the Yukon in the days of the Gold Rush, for example 'The Shooting of Dan McGrew' 1907.

serviceable *adj.* useful or usable, able to render service; durable, suited for use rather than ornament. —**serviceability** /-'bɪlɪtɪ/ *n.,* **serviceably** *adv.*

serviceman *n.* (*plural* **servicemen**) 1. a man in the armed forces. 2. a man providing service or maintenance.

services, armed the air, sea, and land forces of a country; see ◊army, ◊navy, ◊air force; also called the armed forces. In the UK the army and navy can be traced back to the locally raised forces that prevented King Alfred's Wessex from being overrun by the Danes. All three armed services are professionals, with no conscript element. The **Royal Navy** is known as the Senior Service, because of its formal origin under Henry VIII, whereas no permanent standing **army** was raised until the time of Charles II (see also ◊marines). The ◊Territorial Army is a backup force of volunteers. The ◊**Royal Air Force** was formed in 1918. ◊**Women's services** originated in World War I.

service tree a deciduous Eurasian tree *Sorbus domestica* of the rose family Rosaceae, with alternate pinnate leaves, white flowers, and small, edible, oval fruit. The **wild service tree** *S. torminalis* has oblong rather than pointed leaflets. It is related to the ◊mountain ash.

servicewoman *n.* (*plural* **servicewomen**) a woman in the armed forces.

serviette /sɜːvɪ'et/ *n.* a table napkin. [from Old French]

servile /'sɜːvaɪl/ *adj.* 1. of or like a slave; suitable for a servant, menial. 2. excessively submissive, lacking independence. —**servilely** *adv.,* **servility** /-'vɪlɪtɪ/ *n.* [from Latin *servilis* (*servus* = slave)]

serving *n.* a quantity of food for one person. —**serving hatch** *n.* an aperture through which food is served.

servitor /'sɜːvɪtə/ *n.* (*archaic*) a servant, an attendant. [from Old French or Latin]

servitude /'sɜːvɪtjuːd/ *n.* slavery, subjection. [from Old French from Latin]

servo /'sɜːvəʊ/ *n.* (*plural* **servos**) a servomotor or ◊servomechanism. [abbreviation]

servo- /sɜːvəʊ-/ in combinations, a means of powered automatic control of a larger system (e.g. *servo-assisted, servomotor*). [from French from Latin *servus* = slave]

servomechanism *n.* an automatic control system used in aircraft, motor cars, and other complex machines. A specific input, such as moving a lever or joystick, causes a specific output, such as feeding current to an electric motor that moves, for example, the rudder of the aircraft. At the same time, the position of the rudder is detected and fed back to the central control, so that small adjustments can continually be made to maintain the desired course.

sesame /'sesəmɪ/ *n.* an annual plant *Sesamum indicum* of the family Pedaliaceae, probably native to SE Asia; its oily seeds, used for food and soap making. —**open sesame,** a magic formula used in an Arabian Nights tale to cause a door to open; a magical or mysterious means of access to what is usually inaccessible. [from Latin from Greek, of Asian origin]

sesqui- /seskwɪ/ prefix denoting one and a half (e.g. *sesquicentenary*). [Latin]

sessile /'sesaɪl/ *adj.* 1. in botany, of a leaf, flower, or fruit that lacks a stalk and sits directly on the stem, as do the acorns of the **sessile oak** *Quercus petraea*; in zoology, of the eyes of crustaceans when these lack stalks and sit directly on the head. 2. fixed in one position, immobile; in zoology, of an animal that normally stays in the same place, such as a barnacle or mussel. [from Latin *sessilis* (*sedēre* = sit)]

session /'seʃən/ *n.* 1. an assembly for deliberative or judicial business; a single meeting for such a purpose; a period during which such meetings are regularly held. 2. an academic year; (*US*) a university term. 3. a period devoted to an activity. —**in session,** assembled for business, not on vacation. —**sessional** *adj.* [from Old French or Latin *sessio*]

Session, Court of one of the civil courts in Scotland (see ◊Scots law).

sestet /ses'tet/ *n.* 1. the set of six lines ending a sonnet. 2. a sextet. [from Italian *sesto* from Latin *sextus* = sixth]

set[1] *v.t./i.* (**-tt-**; *past* and *past participle* **set**) 1. to put or place; to cause to stand in position. 2. to put in contact with, to apply (one thing) to another. 3. to fix ready or in position; to adjust the hands of (a clock or watch); to adjust (an alarm clock) to sound at the required time; to adjust the mechanism of (a trap etc.); to lay (a table) for a meal. 4. to fix, decide, or appoint. 5. to arrange and protect (a broken bone, limb, etc.) into the right relative position so that it will heal after fracture or dislocation; to arrange (the hair) while damp so that it will dry in the required style; to insert (a jewel) in a ring, framework etc.; to decorate or provide (a surface etc.) with jewels, ornaments etc. 6. to put into a specified state, to cause to be or to do or begin doing. 7. to represent (a story etc.) as happening at a certain time or place. 8. to present or assign as work to be done. 9. to exhibit as a type or model; to initiate (a fashion etc.); to establish (a record). 10. to make or become hard, firm, or established. 11. to provide a tune for (words). 12. to arrange (type) or type for (a book etc.). 13. to cause (a hen) to sit on eggs; to place (eggs) for a hen to sit on. 14. (of the Sun, Moon, etc.) to be brought towards or below the horizon by the Earth's movement. 15. (of a tide or current etc.) to have a specified motion or direction. 16. in certain dances, to face another dancer and make certain steps. 17. (*vulgar* or *dialect*) to sit. —**set about,** to begin (a task); to attack with blows or words. **set back,** to place further back in space or time; to impede the progress of; to cause a change for the worse; to cost (a person) a specified sum. **setback** *n.* impeding of progress; a change for the worse. **set foot in** *or* **on,** to enter or arrive at (a place etc.). **set forth**, to set out. **set in**, to begin and become established. **set off**, to begin a journey; to cause to begin; to ignite (a firework etc.) or cause to explode; to serve as an adornment or foil to, to enhance; to use as a compensating item. **set on** *or* **upon**, to attack violently; to cause or urge to attack. **set out,** to begin a journey; to have a specified aim or intention; to arrange or exhibit; to declare, to make known. **set sail**, to hoist sail; to begin a voyage. **set to,** to begin doing something vigorously; to begin fighting, arguing, or eating; to begin making a loud sound); to cause; to supply adequately; to restore or enhance the health of; to establish (a record). **setup** *n.* an arrangement or organization; the structure of this. **set up house**, to establish a household. [Old English]

set² *n.* **1.** a number of things or persons that are grouped together as similar or forming a unit; a section of society whose members consort together or have similar interests etc. **2.** a collection of implements, vessels etc., needed for a specified purpose. **3.** a radio or television receiver. **4.** in tennis etc., a group of games forming a unit or part of a match. **5.** the way something sets or is set, placed, or arranged; the process or style of setting hair. **6.** the scenery in use for a play or film; the stage etc. where this is performed. **7.** in mathematics, any collection of defined things (elements), provided the elements are distinct and that there is a rule to decide whether an element is a member of a set. It is usually denoted by a capital letter and indicated by curly brackets. **8.** or **sett** a badger's burrow; a granite paving block; a slip, shoot, bulb, or tuber for planting. —**dead set**, a determined attack or initiative. **set theory**, the branch of mathematics which deals with sets. [sense 1 from Old French *sette* from Latin *secta* (*sequi* = follow); senses 2–3 from *set¹*]

set³ *adj.* **1.** prescribed or determined in advance; unchanging, unmoving; (of a phrase or speech etc.) having an invariable or predetermined wording, not extempore. **2.** prepared for action. —**set on** *or* **upon,** determined to get or achieve etc. **set piece**, a formal or elaborate arrangement especially in art or literature; fireworks arranged on scaffolding etc. **set square**, a draughtsperson's right-angled triangular plate for drawing lines in a certain relation to each other, especially at 90°, 45°, or 30°. [past participle of *set¹*]

Set in Egyptian mythology, the god of night, the desert, and of all evils. He was the murderer of ◊Osiris, and is portrayed as a grotesque animal.

sett variant of ◊set² sense 8.

settee /se'ti:/ *n.* a long seat, with a back and, usually, arms, for more than one person.

setter *n.* a breed of dog, about 60 cm/2 ft high, and weighing about 25 kg/55 lbs. It has a long, smooth coat, a feathered tail, and a spaniel-like face. Originally gun dogs, setters were trained to stand rigid, or 'set', when they scented game.

setting *n.* **1.** the position, place, or manner etc. in which something is set. **2.** music for the words of a song etc. **3.** a set of cutlery or crockery for one person at table.

settle¹ *v.t./i.* **1.** to place (a thing etc.) so that it stays in position. **2.** to establish or be established more or less permanently; to make one's home; to occupy as settlers. **3.** to sink or come to rest; to cause to do this; to become compact in this way. **4.** to make or become calm or orderly; to stop being restless. **5.** to arrange as desired; to end or arrange conclusively; to deal with; to pay (a debt etc., or *absolute*). **6.** to bestow by legal process. **7.** (in *past participle*) not soon changing. —**settle down**, to become settled after disturbance or movement etc.; to adopt a regular or secure style of life; to apply oneself (to work etc.). **settle up**, to pay what is owing. **settle with**, to pay all or part of the amount due to (a creditor); to get revenge on. [Old English]

settle² *n.* a wooden seat for two or more people, with a high back and arms and often with a box below the seat. [Old English = place to sit]

settlement *n.* **1.** settling, being settled. **2.** a place occupied by settlers. **3.** a political or financial etc. agreement; an arrangement ending a dispute; the terms on which property is settled on a person by legal process; a deed stating these; the amount of property given. —**settlement out of court**, a compromise reached between the parties to a legal dispute. Most civil legal actions are settled out of

court, reducing legal costs and avoiding the uncertainty of the outcome of a trial.

Settlement, Act of in Britain, a law passed in 1701 during the reign of King William III, designed to ensure a Protestant succession to the throne by excluding the Roman Catholic descendants of James II in favour of the Protestant House of Hanover. Elizabeth II still reigns under this act.

settler *n.* one who goes to live permanently in a previously unoccupied land, a colonist.

Seurat /'sɜːrɑː/ Georges 1859–1891. French artist. He originated, with Paul Signac, the Neo-Impressionist technique of ◊**Pointillism** (painting with small dabs rather than long brushstrokes). Examples of his work are *The Bathers, Asnières* 1884 (National Gallery, London) and *Sunday on the Island of La Grande Jatte* 1886 (Art Institute of Chicago).

seven /'sevən/ *adj. & n.* **1.** one more than six; the symbol for this (7, vii, VII). **2.** the size etc. denoted by seven. [Old English]

seven deadly sins in Christian theology, anger, avarice, envy, gluttony, lust, pride, and sloth.

sevenfold *adj. & adv.* seven times as much or as many; consisting of seven parts.

seventeen /sevən'tiːn/ *adj. & n.* **1.** one more than 16; the symbol for this (17, xvii, XVII). **2.** the size etc. denoted by 17. —**seventeenth** *adj. & n.* [Old English]

seventh *adj.* next after the sixth. —*n.* each of seven equal parts of a thing. —**seventh heaven**, a state of intense joy; the highest of seven heavens in Muslim and some Jewish systems. —**seventhly** *adv.*

Seventh Day Adventist a member of the Protestant religious sect of the same name. The group has its main following in the USA, and distinctive tenets are that Saturday is the Sabbath and that Jesus's second coming is imminent. They originally expected the second coming in 1844.

seventy /'sevəntɪ/ *adj. & n.* **1.** seven times ten; the symbol for this (70, lxx, LXX). **2.** (in *plural*) the numbers, years, or degrees of temperature from 70 to 79. —**seventieth** or **70th** *adj. & n.* [Old English]

Seven Weeks' War a war in 1866 between Austria and Prussia, engineered by the German chancellor ◊Bismarck. It was nominally over the possession of ◊Schleswig-Holstein, but it was actually to confirm Prussia's superseding Austria as the leading German state. The Battle of ◊Sadowa was the culmination of von ◊Moltke's victories.

Seven Wonders of the World in antiquity, the pyramids of Egypt, the hanging gardens of Babylon, the temple of Artemis at Ephesus, the statue of Zeus at Olympia, the mausoleum at Halicarnassus, the Colossus of Rhodes, and the Pharos (lighthouse) at Alexandria.

Seven Years' War (in North America known as the **French and Indian War**) a war 1756–63 arising from the conflict between Austria and Prussia, and between France and Britain over colonial supremacy. Britain and Prussia defeated France, Austria, Spain, and Russia; Britain gained control of India and many of France's colonies, including Canada. Spain ceded Florida to Britain in exchange for Cuba. Fighting against great odds, Prussia was eventually successful in becoming established as one of the great European powers. The war ended with the Treaty of Paris of 1763, signed by Britain, France, and Spain.

sever /'sevə/ *v.t./i.* **1.** to divide, break, or make separate, especially by cutting. **2.** to terminate the employment contract of (a person). [from Anglo-French from Latin *separare*]

several /'sevrəl/ *adj. & pron.* **1.** a few, more than two but not many. **2.** separate, respective. —**severally** *adv.*

severance /'sevərəns/ *n.* severing, being severed; a severed state. —**severance pay,** the amount paid to an employee on the termination of his or her contract.

severe /si'vɪə/ *adj.* **1.** strict; without sympathy; imposing harsh treatment. **2.** intense, forceful. **3.** making great demands on endurance, energy, ability etc. **4.** plain and without decoration. —**severely** *adv.*, **severity** /si'verɪtɪ/ *n.* [from French or Latin *severus*]

Severin /'sevərɪn/ Tim 1940– . Writer, historian, and traveller who has retraced the routes of a number of historical and mythological figures.

Severn /'sevən/ river of Wales and England, rising on the NE side of Plynlimmon, N Wales, and flowing 338 km/210 mi through Shrewsbury, Worcester, and Gloucester to the Bristol Channel. The **Severn bore** is a tidal wave up to 2 m/6 ft high.

Severus /si'viərəs/ Lucius Septimius AD 146–211. Roman emperor, born in N Africa. He held a command on the Danube when in AD 193 the emperor Pertinax was murdered. Proclaimed emperor by his troops, Severus proved an able administrator; he was the only African to become emperor. He died at York while campaigning in Britain against the Caledonians.

Seville /si'vil/ (Spanish *Sevilla*) city in Andalucia, Spain, on the Guadalquivir River, 96 km/60 mi N of Cadiz; population (1986) 668,000. Products include machinery, spirits, porcelain, pharmaceuticals, silk, and tobacco.

Sèvres /'seivrə/ *n.* fine porcelain produced at a factory in Sèvres, France, since the early 18th century. It is characterized by the use of intensely coloured backgrounds (such as pink and royal blue), against which flowers are painted in elaborately embellished frames, often in gold.

Sèvres, Treaty of the last of the treaties that ended World War I. It was negotiated between the Allied powers and the Ottoman Empire and finalized in Aug 1920, but never ratified by the Turkish government.

sew /səʊ/ *v.t./i.* (*past participle* **sewn** or **sewed**) to fasten by passing thread again and again through material, using a threaded needle, an awl etc., or a sewing machine; to make or attach by sewing; to use a needle and thread or a sewing machine thus. —**sew up**, to join or enclose by sewing; (*colloquial*, especially in *past participle*) to arrange or finish dealing with (a project etc.). [Old English]

sewage /'sjuːidʒ, 'suː-/ *n.* liquid waste matter drained away from houses, towns, factories etc., for disposal. —**sewage disposal**, the disposal of human excreta and other waterborne waste products. These waste products are conveyed through sewers to **sewage works**, where they have to undergo a series of purification treatments to be acceptable for discharge into rivers or the sea, according to various local laws and ordinances. In 1987, Britain dumped more than 4,700 tonnes of sewage sludge into the North Sea, and 4,200 tonnes into the Irish Sea and other coastal areas. **sewage farm**, a farm on which a town's sewage is treated and used for manure.

Sewell /'sjuːəl/ Anna 1820–1878. English author whose only published work, *Black Beauty* 1877, tells the life story of a horse. Although now read as a children's book, it was written to encourage sympathetic treatment of horses by adults.

sewer /'sjuːə, 'suː-/ *n.* a public drain for carrying away sewage and drainage water. —*v.t.* to provide or drain with sewers. [from Anglo-French, originally = channel to carry off overflow from a fish pond, ultimately from Latin *aqua* = water (related to *ewer*)]

sewerage /'sjuːərɪdʒ, 'suː-/ *n.* a system of sewers; drainage by sewers.

sewing machine an apparatus for the mechanical sewing of cloth, leather, and other materials by a needle, powered by hand, treadle, or belted electric motor. The popular lock-stitch machine, using a double thread, was invented independently in the USA by both Walter Hunt in 1834 and Elias ◊Howe in 1846. Howe's machine was the basis of the machine patented in 1851 by Isaac ◊Singer. In the latest microprocessor-controlled sewing machines, as many as 25 different stitching patterns can be selected by push button.

sewn past participle of **sew**.

sex *n.* **1.** either of the two main divisions (male and female) into which living things are placed on the basis of their reproductive functions; the fact of belonging to one of these. **2.** sexual instincts, desires etc., or their manifestation. **3.** (*colloquial*) sexual intercourse. —*adj.* of sex; arising from the difference or consciousness of sex. —*v.t.* **1.** to determine the sex of (a young animal etc.). **2.** (in *past participle*) having sexual characteristics or instincts etc. —**sex appeal**, sexual attractiveness. **sex life,** a person's sexual activities. **sex-starved** *adj.* lacking sexual gratification. **sex symbol,** a person who is for many the epitome of sexual attraction and glamour. —**sexer** *n.* [from Old French or Latin *sexus*]

sexagenarian /seksədʒi'neəriən/ *adj.* from 60 to 69 years old. —*n.* a sexagenarian person. [from Latin *sexageni* = 60 each]

Sexagesima /seksə'dʒesimə/ *n.* in the Christian calendar, the Sunday before Quinquagesima. [Latin = 60th (day)]

sexagesimal *adj.* of 60ths or 60; reckoning or reckoned by 60ths. [from Latin *sexagesimus* = 60th]

sex determination the process by which the sex of an organism is determined. In many species, the sex of an individual is dictated by the two sex chromosomes (X and Y) it receives from its parents. In mammals, some plants, and a few insects, males are XY, and females XX; in birds, reptiles, some amphibians, and butterflies the reverse is the case. In bees and wasps, males are produced from unfertilized eggs, females from fertilized eggs. Environmental factors can affect some fish and reptiles, such as turtles, where sex is influenced by the temperature at which the eggs develop.

sexism *n.* **1.** prejudice or ◊discrimination against people (especially women) because of their sex. **2.** the assumption that a person's abilities and social functions are predetermined because of his or her sex (a form of ◊stereotype). —**sexist** *adj.* & *n.*

sexless *adj.* **1.** lacking sex, neuter. **2.** not involving sexual feelings or attraction. —**sexlessly** *adv.*

sex linkage in genetics, the tendency for certain characteristics to occur exclusively, or predominantly, in one sex only. Human examples include red-green colour blindness and haemophilia, both found predominantly in males. In both cases, these characteristics are ◊recessive and are determined by genes on the ◊X chromosome.

sexology /sek'sɒlədʒɪ/ *n.* the study of human sexual life or relationships. —**sexological** /-'lɒdʒɪkəl/ *adj.*, **sexologist** *n.*

Sex Pistols, the a UK punk-rock group (1975–78) that became notorious under the guidance of their manager, Malcolm McLaren (1946–). They released one album, *Never Mind the Bollocks, Here's the Sex Pistols* 1977. Members included Johnny Rotten (real name John Lydon, 1956–) and Sid Vicious (real name John Ritchie, 1957–1979).

sextant /'sekstənt/ *n.* a navigational instrument for determining latitude by measuring the angle between some heavenly body and the horizon. It was invented by John Hadley (1682–1744) in 1730 and can be used only in clear weather. [from Latin *sextans* = sixth part (*sexus* = sixth), because early sextants all contained 60°, i.e. one sixth of a circle]

sextet /sek'stet/ *n.* **1.** a musical composition for six performers; these performers. **2.** any group of six. [alteration of *sestet*]

sexton /'sekstən/ *n.* a person who looks after a church and churchyard, often acting as bell-ringer and grave-digger. [from Anglo-French from Latin *sacer* = holy]

Sexton Anne 1928–1974. US poet. She studied with Robert Lowell and wrote similarly confessional poetry, as in *To Bedlam and Part Way Back* 1960 and *All My Pretty Ones* 1962. She committed suicide, and her *Complete Poems* appeared posthumously in 1981.

sextuple /'sekstjʊpəl/ *adj.* sixfold, having six parts; being six times as many or as much. —*n.* a sixfold number or amount. [from Latin *sextuplus* (*sex* = six)]

sextant

simplified diagram of a sextant

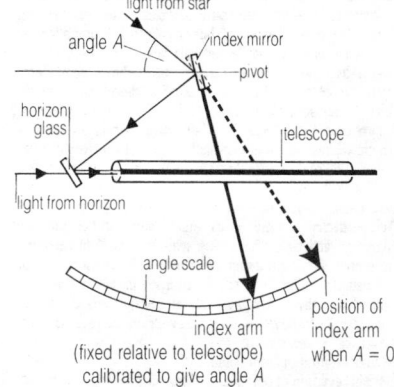

light from star

angle A

index mirror

pivot

horizon glass

telescope

light from horizon

angle scale

index arm
(fixed relative to telescope)
calibrated to give angle A

position of index arm when A = 0

sextuplet /'sekstju:plɪt/ *n.* each of six children born at one birth. [after *triplet* etc.]

sexual /'seksjuəl, 'sekʃ-/ *adj.* 1. of sex or the sexes or the relationship or feelings etc. between them. 2. (of reproduction) occurring by fusion of male and female gametes. —**sexual intercourse,** copulation (especially of a man and a woman); insertion of the penis into the vagina, usually followed by the ejaculation of semen. —**sexuality** /-'ælɪtɪ/ *n.* **sexually** *adv.* [from Latin *sexualis* (*sexus* = sex)]

sexual reproduction a reproductive process in organisms that requires the union, or ◊fertilization, of gametes (such as eggs and sperm). These are usually produced by two different individuals, although self-fertilization occurs in a few ◊hermaphrodites such as tapeworms. Most organisms other than bacteria and cyanobacteria show some sort of sexual process. Except in some lower organisms, the gametes are of two distinct types called eggs and sperm. The organisms producing the eggs are called females, and those producing the sperm, males. The fusion of a male and female gamete produces a **zygote,** from which a new individual develops. The alternatives to sexual reproduction are binary fission, budding, vegetative reproduction, parthenogenesis, and spore formation.

sexual selection a process similar to ◊natural selection but relating exclusively to success in finding a mate for the purpose of sexual reproduction and producing offspring. Sexual selection occurs when one sex (usually but not always the female) invests more effort in producing young than the other. Members of the other sex compete for access to this limited resource (usually males competing for the chance to mate with females). Sexual selection often favours features that increase a male's attractiveness to females (such as the pheasant's tail) or enable males to fight with one another (such as a deer's antlers). More subtly, it can produce hormonal effects by which the male makes the female unreceptive to other males, causes the abortion of fetuses already conceived, or removes the sperm of males who have already mated with a female.

sexy *adj.* sexually attractive or stimulating. —**sexily** *adv.* **sexiness** *n.*

Seychelles /seɪ'ʃelz/ Republic of; country in the Indian Ocean, off E Africa, N of Madagascar; **area** 453 sq km/175 sq mi; **capital** Victoria (on Mahé island); **physical** comprises two distinct island groups, one concentrated, the other widely scattered, totalling over 100 islands and islets; Aldabra atoll, containing world's largest tropical lagoon; **head of state and government** France-Albert René from 1977; **political system** one-party Socialist republic; **exports** copra, cinnamon; **population** (1990) 71,000; **language** Creole 95%, English, French (all official); **recent history** independence was achieved from Britain as a republic within the Commonwealth in 1976. René ousted former president Mancham in an armed coup and took over the presidency in 1977; a new constitution was adopted in 1979 with the Seychelles People's Progressive Front (SPPF) as the sole legal party. Further coups in 1981 and 1987 failed.

Seyfert galaxy /'saɪfət/ a type of galaxy whose small, bright centre is caused by hot gas moving at high speed around a massive central object, possibly a ◊black hole. Almost all Seyferts are spiral galaxies. They seem to be closely related to ◊quasars, but are about 100 times fainter. [named after their discoverer Carl *Seyfert* (1911–1960)]

Seymour /'si:mɔ:/ Jane *c.*1509–1537. Third wife of Henry VIII, whom she married in 1536. She died soon after the birth of her son, Edward VI.

Seymour Lynn 1939– . Canadian ballerina of rare dramatic talent. She was principal dancer of the Royal Ballet from 1959 and artistic director of the Munich State Opera Ballet 1978–80.

sez (*slang*) says.

Sezession *n.* any of various groups of German and Austrian artists in the 1890s who 'seceded' from official academic art institutions in order to found new schools of painting. The first was in Munich in 1892; the next, linked with the paintings of Gustav ◊Klimt, was the Vienna Sezession of 1897; the Berlin Sezession followed in 1899. [German = secession]

sf abbreviation of ◊sforzando.

SF abbreviation of ◊science fiction.

Sforza /'sfɔ:tsə/ Italian family that ruled the duchy of Milan 1450–99, 1512–15, and 1522–35. Its court was a centre of Renaissance culture and its rulers prominent patrons of the arts. **Ludovico Sforza** (1451–1508) made Milan one of the most powerful Italian states.

sforzando /sfɔt'sændəʊ/ *adj. & adv.* in music, with sudden emphasis. [Italian (*sforzare* = use force)]

sh interjection meaning hush.

Shaanxi /ʃɑ:n'ʃi:/ or **Shensi** province of NW China; **area** 195,800 sq km/75,579 sq mi; **capital** Xian; **physical** mountains; Huang He valley, one of the earliest settled areas of China; **products** iron, steel, mining, textiles, fruit, tea, rice, wheat; **population** (1986) 30,430,000.

shabby *adj.* 1. worn and faded; not kept in good condition; (of a person) poorly dressed. 2. contemptible, dishonourable. —**shabbily** *adj.*, **shabbiness** *n.* [from *shab* = scab from Old English]

shack *n.* a roughly built hut or shed. —**shack up,** (*slang*) to cohabit.

shackle *n.* 1. a metal loop or link, closed by a bolt, to connect chains etc. 2. a fetter enclosing an ankle or wrist. 3. a restraint, an impediment. 4. a unit of length, used at sea for measuring cable or chain. One shackle is 15 fathoms (27 m/90 ft). —*v.t.* 1. to put shackles on. 2. to impede, to restrict. [Old English]

Shackleton /'ʃækəltən/ Ernest 1874–1922. Irish Antarctic explorer. In 1907–09, he commanded an expedition that reached 88° 23⌐ ⌐S latitude, located the magnetic South Pole, and climbed Mount ◊Erebus.

shad *n.* (*plural* **shads** or **shad**) an edible fish of the genus *Alosa*, the largest (2.7 kg/6 lbs) of the herring family. They migrate in shoals to breed in rivers. They are Atlantic fish but have been introduced to the Pacific. [from Old English]

shade *n.* 1. comparative darkness (and usually coolness) caused by shelter from direct light and heat; a place or area sheltered from the Sun. 2. the darker part of a picture etc. 3. a colour, especially with regard to its depth or as distinguished from one nearly like it. 4. a slight amount or difference. 5. a translucent cover for a lamp etc.; a screen excluding or moderating light; (*US*) a window blind; (*US*, in *plural*) sunglasses. 6. a ghost; (in *plural*) reminders of some person or thing. —*v.t./i.* 1. to screen from light. 2. to cover, moderate, or exclude the light of. 3. to darken (parts of a drawing etc.), especially with parallel lines to represent shadow etc. 4. to change or pass gradually into another colour or variety. —**in the shade,** in comparative obscurity. [Old English]

shadoof /ʃæ'du:f/ *n.* or **shaduf** a machine for lifting water, consisting typically of a long, pivoted wooden pole acting as a lever, with a weight at one end. The other end is positioned over a well, for example. The shadoof was in use in ancient Egypt and is still used in Arab countries today. [from Egyptian Arabic]

shadow /'ʃædəʊ/ *n.* 1. shade; a patch of shade; a dark figure projected by a body intercepting rays of light. 2. one's inseparable attendant or companion; a person secretly following another. 3. a very slight trace. 4. a weak or insubstantial thing, a remnant. 5. the shaded part of a picture. 6. gloom, sadness. —*v.t.* 1. to cast a shadow over. 2. to follow and watch secretly. —**shadow-boxing** *n.* boxing against an imaginary opponent as a form of training. —**shadower** *n.* [Old English]

shadow cabinet the chief members of the British parliamentary opposition, each of whom is responsible for commenting on the policies and performance of a government ministry.

shadowy *adj.* like a shadow; full of shadows; vague, indistinct.

shady /'ʃeɪdɪ/ *adj.* 1. giving shade. 2. situated in the shade. 3. disreputable, of doubtful honesty. —**shadily** *adv.*, **shadiness** *n.*

SHAEF acronym from Supreme Headquarters Allied Expeditionary Force, the World War II military centre established on 15 Feb 1944 in London, where final plans for the Allied invasion of Europe (under US general Eisenhower) were worked out.

Shaffer /'ʃæfə/ Peter 1926– . English playwright. His plays include *Five Finger Exercise* 1958, the historical epic *The Royal Hunt of the Sun* 1964, *Equus* 1973, and *Amadeus* 1979 about the composer Mozart.

shaft /ʃɑːft/ *n.* **1.** an arrow, spear, or similar device; its long slender stem. **2.** a remark intended to hurt or stimulate. **3.** a ray (of light); a bolt (of lightning). **4.** a stem or stalk; the central stem of a feather; the stem or long handle of a tool, implement etc.; a long narrow part supporting, connecting, or driving a part or parts of greater thickness etc.; a column, especially between the base and the capital. **5.** a long narrow vertical or sloping passage or opening giving access to a mine, or as an outlet for air or smoke; a vertical passage for movement of a lift etc. **6.** each of a pair of poles between which a horse is harnessed to a vehicle. **7.** (*US slang*) harsh or unjust treatment. —*v.t.* to treat harshly or unjustly. [Old English]

Shaftesbury /'ʃɑːftsbəri/ market town and agricultural centre in Dorset, England, 30 km/19 mi SW of Salisbury; population (1985) 6,000. King Alfred is said to have founded an abbey on the site in 880; Canute died at Shaftesbury in 1035.

Shaftesbury Anthony Ashley Cooper, 1st Earl of Shaftesbury 1621–1683. English politician, a supporter of the Restoration of the monarchy. He became Lord Chancellor in 1672, but went into opposition in 1673 and began to organize the ◊Whig Party. He headed the Whigs' demand for the exclusion of the future James II from the succession, secured the passing of the ◊Habeas Corpus Act in 1679, then, when accused of treason in 1681, fled to Holland.

Shaftesbury Anthony Ashley Cooper, 7th Earl of Shaftesbury 1801–1885. English Tory politician. He strongly supported the Ten Hours Act of 1847 and other factory legislation, including the 1842 act forbidding the employment of women and children underground in mines. He was also associated with the movement to provide free education for the poor.

shag *n.* **1.** a rough growth or mass of hair or fibre. **2.** a strong coarse kind of tobacco. **3.** a ◊cormorant, especially the **crested cormorant** *Phalacrocorax aristotelis.* —*v.t./i.* (*vulgar*) to have sexual intercourse (with). [Old English]

shaggy *adj.* **1.** having long rough hair or fibre. **2.** (of hair etc.) rough, thick, and untidy. —**shaggy-dog story,** a long, inconsequential narrative or joke. —**shaggily** *adv.,* **shagginess** *n.*

shagreen /ʃæ'griːn/ *n.* a kind of untanned leather with a granulated surface; sharkskin (rough with natural papillae) used for rasping and polishing things. [variant of *chagrin* in sense 'rough skin']

shah /ʃɑː/ *n.* (more formally, *Shahanshah* = king of kings) the traditional title of ancient Persian rulers, and also of those of the recent ◊Pahlavi dynasty in Iran; the person bearing this title. [from Persian = king]

Shah Jahan /'ʃɑː dʒə'hɑːn/ 1592–1666. Mogul emperor of India 1628–58. During his reign the ◊Taj Mahal and the Pearl Mosque at Agra were built. From 1658 he was a prisoner of his son Aurangzeb.

Shahn /ʃɑːn/ Ben 1898–1969. US artist, born in Lithuania, a Social Realist painter. His work included drawings and paintings on the ◊Dreyfus case and the ◊Sacco and Vanzetti case in which two Italian anarchists were accused of murders. He painted murals for the Rockefeller Center, New York (with the Mexican artist Diego Rivera), and the Federal Security Building, Washington, 1940–42.

Shaka /'ʃɑːgə/ or **Chaka** *c.*1787–1828. Zulu chief who formed a Zulu empire in SE Africa. He seized power from his half-brother in 1816 and then embarked on a bloody military campaign to unite the Zulu clans, initiating the period of warfare known as the ◊Mfecane. He was assassinated in 1828 by two half-brothers.

shake *v.t./i.* (*past* **shook** /ʃʊk/; *past participle* **shaken**) **1.** to move violently or quickly up and down or to and fro; to tremble or vibrate, to cause to do this. **2.** to agitate or shock; (*colloquial*) to upset the composure of. **3.** to weaken or impair; to make less convincing or firm or courageous. **4.** (of a voice etc.) to make tremulous or rapidly alternating sounds, to trill. **5.** to make a threatening gesture with (one's fist, stick etc.). **6.** (*colloquial*) to shake hands. —*n.* **1.** shaking, being shaken; a jerk or shock. **2.** a milk shake. **3.** in music, a trill. **4.** (*colloquial*) a moment. —**the shakes,** a fit of trembling. **no great shakes,** (*colloquial*) not very good or significant. **shake down,** to settle or cause to fall by shaking; to settle down, to become established. **shake hands,** to clasp hands (with another person), especially when meeting or parting, in reconciliation or congratulation, or as a sign of a bargain. **shake one's head,** to move one's head from side to side in refusal, denial, disapproval, or concern. **shake off,** to get rid of (an unwanted thing, bad habit, illness, undesirable companion, worry etc.). **shake out,** to empty by shaking; to spread or open (a sail, flag, etc.) by shaking. **shake up,** to mix (ingredients) by shaking; to restore to shape by shaking; to disturb or make uncomfortable; to rouse from lethargy, apathy, conventionality etc. **shake-up** *n.* an upheaval, a reorganization. [Old English]

shaker *n.* **1.** a person or thing that shakes. **2.** a container for shaking together the ingredients of cocktails etc. **3.** **Shaker,** a member of the Christian sect of the **United Society of Believers in Christ's Second Appearing,** so called because of their ecstatic shakings in worship. The movement was founded by James and Jane Wardley in England about 1747, and taken to North America in 1774 by Ann Lee (1736–1784). They anticipated modern spiritualist beliefs, but their doctrine of celibacy led to their virtual extinction. **Shaker furniture** has been admired in the 20th century for its simple and robust design.

Shakespeare /'ʃeɪkspɪə/ William 1564–1616. English dramatist and poet. He established himself in London by 1589 as an actor and a playwright and remained England's unrivalled dramatist until his death. Shakespeare is today still considered the greatest English playwright. His plays, written in blank verse, can be broadly divided into lyric plays, including ◊*Romeo and Juliet* and ◊*A Midsummer Night's Dream*; comedies, including *The Comedy of Errors, As You Like It, Much Ado About Nothing,* and *Measure For Measure*; historical plays, such as *Henry VI* (in three parts), *Richard III,* and *Henry IV* (in two parts), which often showed cynical political wisdom; and tragedies, such as ◊*Hamlet,* ◊*Macbeth,* and ◊*King Lear.* He also wrote numerous sonnets. For the first 200 years after his death, Shakespeare's plays were frequently performed in cut or revised form (Nahum Tate's *King Lear* was given a happy ending), and it was not until the 19th century, with the critical assessment of Samuel Taylor ◊Coleridge and William ◊Hazlitt, that the original texts were restored.

O! it is excellent
To have a lion's strength,
but it is tyrannous
To use it like a giant.

William Shakespeare
Measure for Measure

Shakespearian /'ʃeɪks'pɪərɪən/ *adj.* of Shakespeare.

Shakespeare *The title page engraving by M Droeshout for the First Folio of Shakespeare's plays.*

shako /ˈʃækəʊ/ n. (plural **shakos**) a cylindrical, peaked military hat with an upright plume or tuft. [from French from Magyar = peaked (cap)]

shaky adj. 1. unsteady, apt to shake, trembling. 2. unsound, infirm; unreliable, wavering. —**shakily** adv., **shakiness** n.

shale n. a fine-grained and finely laminated ◊sedimentary rock composed of silt and clay that parts easily along bedding planes. It differs from mudstone in that the latter splits into flakes. Oil shale contains kerogen, a solid bituminous material that yields ◊petroleum when heated. —**shaly** adj.

shall /ʃəl, emphat. ʃæl/ v.aux. (third person singular **shall**, archaic second person singular (with thou) **shalt**; past **should**) expressing **a.** (in the first person) a future action or state, **b.** (in other persons) a strong assertion, promise, or command. —**shall I?** do you want me to? [Old English]

shallot /ʃəˈlɒt/ n. a small onion Allium ascalonicum in which bulbs are clustered like garlic; it is used for cooking and in pickles. [from French from Latin = onion of Ascalon in Palestine]

shallow /ˈʃæləʊ/ adj. 1. of little depth. 2. not thinking deeply; not thought out deeply. 3. not capable of deep feelings. —n. (often in plural) a shallow place. —v.t./i. to make or become shallow. —**shallowly** adv., **shallowness** n.

shalom /ʃəˈlɒm/ n. & int. a Jewish salutation at a meeting or parting. [from Hebrew = peace]

shalt archaic form of ◊**shall**.

shalwar /ˈʃʌlvɑː/ n. loose trousers worn by both sexes in some S Asian countries. [from Persian]

sham v.t./i. (-mm-) to pretend; to pretend to be. —n. a pretence; a thing or feeling that is not genuine; a person pretending to be something that he or she is not. —adj. pretended, not genuine. —**shammer** n.

shaman /ˈʃæmən/ n. a ritual leader, one who acts as intermediary between society and the supernatural world in many indigenous cultures of Asia, Africa, and the Americas. Also known as a **medicine man**, **seer**, or **sorcerer**, the shaman is expected to use white magic powers to cure illness and control good and evil spirits. —**shamanism** n. [from German and Russian from Tungusian]

shamateur /ˈʃæmətə/ n. a sports player classed as an amateur though often profiting like a professional. —**shamateurism** n.

shamble v.i. to walk or run with a shuffling, awkward, or lazy gait. —n. a shambling gait.

shambles /ˈʃæmbəlz/ n.pl. (usually treated as singular) (colloquial) 1. a butcher's slaughterhouse. 2. a scene or condition of great bloodshed or disorder. [plural of shamble = stall, Old English from Latin scamellum, diminutive of scamnum = bench]

shambolic /ʃæmˈbɒlɪk/ adj. (colloquial) chaotic, disorganized. [after symbolic]

shame n. 1. a feeling of distress or humiliation caused by consciousness of one's guilt or folly etc.; capacity for experiencing this feeling. 2. a state of disgrace or discredit. 3. a person or thing that brings disgrace etc.; a thing that is wrong or regrettable, a pity. —v.t. to bring shame on, to make ashamed; to put to shame; to force by shame. —**for shame!** a reproof to a person for not showing shame. **put to shame**, to disgrace or humiliate by revealing superior qualities etc. [Old English]

shamefaced adj. 1. showing shame. 2. bashful, shy.

shameful adj. causing shame, disgraceful. —**shamefully** adv.

shameless adj. having or showing no feeling of shame; impudent. —**shamelessly** adv.

Shamir /ʃæˈmɪə/ Yitzhak 1915– . Israeli politician, born in Poland; foreign minister under Menachem Begin 1980–83, prime minister 1983–84, and again foreign minister in the ◊Peres unity government from 1984. In Oct 1986, he and Peres exchanged positions, Shamir becoming prime minister and Peres taking over as foreign minister. He was re-elected in 1989 and formed a new coalition government with Peres in 1990. Shamir was a leader of the ◊Stern Gang of guerrillas (1940–48) during the British mandate rule of Palestine.

shammy n. a chamois leather. [corrupt pronunciation of chamois]

shampoo /ʃæmˈpuː/ n. 1. a liquid or cream used to lather and wash the hair. 2. a liquid or chemical for washing a car

or carpet etc. 3. the act or process of shampooing. —v.t. to wash with shampoo. [from Hindi imperative of chāmpnā = to press]

shamrock n. any of several trifoliate ◊clovers and cloverlike plants (especially Trifolium minus) of the family Leguminosae. One is said to have been used by St Patrick to illustrate the doctrine of the Holy Trinity, and it was made the national badge of Ireland. [from Irish, diminutive of seamar = clover]

Shan /ʃɑːn/ n. a member of a people of the mountainous borderlands separating Thailand, Myanmar (Burma), and China. They are related to the Laos and Thais, and their language belongs to the Sino-Tibetan family.

Shandong /ʃænˈdʌŋ/ or **Shantung** province of NE China; **area** 153,300 sq km/59,174 sq mi; **capital** Jinan; **physical** crossed by the Huang He River and the ◊Grand Canal; Shandong Peninsula; **products** cereals, cotton, wild silk, varied minerals; **population** (1986) 77,760,000.

shandy /ˈʃændɪ/ n. beer mixed with lemonade or ginger beer. [from earlier shandygaff]

shanghai /ʃænˈhaɪ/ v.t. 1. (historical) to force (a person or people) aboard a ship to serve as a sailor, usually after stupefying them by drugs etc. 2. to transfer forcibly, to abduct; to compel. [from Shanghai]

Shanghai port on the Huang-pu and Wusong rivers, Jiangsu province, China, 24 km/15 mi from the Chang Jiang estuary; **population** (1986) 6,980,000, the largest city in China. The municipality of Shanghai has an area of 5,800 sq km/2,239 sq mi and a population of 12,320,000. Industries include textiles, paper, chemicals, steel, agricultural machinery, precision instruments, shipbuilding, flour and vegetable-oil milling, and oil refining. It handles about 50% of China's imports and exports.

shank n. 1. the leg; the lower part of the leg; a shinbone. 2. a shaft or stem; the long narrow part of an implement etc. —**Shank's mare** or **pony**, one's own legs as a means of conveyance. [Old English, related to Middle High German schenkel = thigh]

Shankar /ˈʃæŋkɑː/ Ravi 1920– . Indian composer and musician. A virtuoso of the ◊sitar, he has composed film music and founded music schools in Bombay and Los Angeles.

Shankara /ʃəˈriːə/ 799–833. Hindu philosopher who wrote commentaries on some of the major Hindu scriptures, as well as hymns and essays on religious ideas. Shankara was responsible for the final form of the Advaita Vedanta school of Hindu philosophy, which teaches that Brahman, the supreme being, is all that exists in the universe, everything else is illusion. Shankara was fiercely opposed to Buddhism and may have influenced its decline in India.

Shannon /ˈʃænən/ longest river in Ireland, rising in County Cavan and flowing 386 km/240 mi through Loughs Allen and Ree and past Athlone, to reach the Atlantic through a wide estuary below Limerick. It is also the major source of electric power in the republic, with hydroelectric installations at and above Ardnacrusha, 5 km/3 mi N of Limerick.

Shannon Claude Elwood 1916– . US mathematician, whose paper The Mathematical Theory of Communication 1948 marks the beginning of the science of information theory. He argued that information data and ◊entropy are analogous, and obtained a quantitive measure of the amount of information in a given message.

shan't /ʃɑːnt/ = shall not.

shantung /ʃænˈtʌŋ/ n. a soft, undressed Chinese silk, usually undyed; fabric resembling this. [from Shantung, alternative spelling of Shandong province, China]

shanty[1] /ˈʃæntɪ/ n. a shack. —**shanty town**, a town consisting of shanties. [originally N American]

shanty[2] n. a song traditionally sung by sailors while hauling ropes etc. [probably from French chantez, imperative of chanter = sing]

Shanxi /ʃænˈʃiː/ or **Shansi** province of NE China; **area** 157,100 sq km/60,641 sq mi; **capital** Taiyuan; **physical** a drought-ridden plateau, partly surrounded by the ◊Great Wall; **products** coal, iron, fruit; **population** (1986) 26,550,000; **recent history** the province saw the outbreak of the Boxer Rebellion in 1900.

shape n. 1. an external form or appearance, the total effect produced by a thing's outlines. 2. a specific form or guise in which something appears. **3.** a kind, sort, or way. **4.** a definite or proper arrangement; condition, good condition. **5.** a person or thing as seen, especially as indistinctly seen or imagined. **6.** a mould or pattern; a jelly etc. shaped in a mould; a piece of material, paper etc., made or cut in a particular form. —*v.t./i.* **1.** to give a certain shape or form to. **2.** to adapt or modify (one's ideas etc.); to frame mentally, to imagine. **3.** to assume or develop into a certain shape or condition; to give signs of future development. —**shape up,** to take (a specified form); to show promise; to make good progress. —**shaper** *n.* [Old English = creation]

SHAPE acronym from Supreme Headquarters Allied Powers Europe; SHAPE is situated near Mons, Belgium, and is the headquarters of NATO's Supreme Allied Commander Europe (SACEUR).

shapeless *adj.* lacking proper shape or shapeliness. —**shapelessly** *adv.,* **shapelessness** *n.*

shapely *adj.* well formed or proportioned; of an elegant or pleasing shape or appearance. —**shapeliness** *n.*

Shapley /'ʃæpli/ Harlow 1885–1972. US astronomer, whose study of ◊globular clusters showed that they were arranged in a halo around the Galaxy, and that the Galaxy was much larger than previously thought. He realized that the Sun was not at the centre of the Galaxy as then assumed, but two-thirds of the way out to the rim.

shard *n.* a broken piece of glass, eggshell etc. [Old English = crack]

share[1] *n.* **1.** a part given to an individual out of a larger amount which is being divided or of a commitment or achievement; the part one is entitled to have or obliged to give or do. **2.** each of the equal parts forming a business company's capital and entitling the holder to a proportion of the profits. Shares may be numbered and are issued as units of definite face value; shareholders are not always called on to pay the full face value of their shares, though they bind themselves to do so. —*v.t./i.* **1.** to give portions of (a thing) to two or more people; to give away part of. **2.** to have a share of; to use, possess, endure, or benefit from (a thing) jointly with others. —**go shares,** to share. **sharecropper** *n.* a tenant farmer who pays part of his or her crop as rent to the owner. **sharecropping** *n.* this process. **share-out** *n.* a division and distribution, especially of profits or proceeds. —**sharer** *n.* [Old English]

share[2] *n.* a ploughshare. [Old English]

shareholder *n.* an owner of shares in a company.

Shari'a /ʃæ'ri:ə/ or **shariah** the law of ◊Islam believed by Muslims to be based on divine revelation, and drawn from a number of sources, including the Koran, the Hadith, and the consensus of the Muslim community. From the latter part of the 19th century, the role of the Shari'a courts in the majority of Muslim countries began to be taken over by secular courts, and the Shari'a to be largely restricted to family law. [from Arabic]

Sharif /ʃæ'ri:f/ Omar. Stage name of Michael Shalhoub 1932– . Egyptian actor, in international films after his successful appearance in *Lawrence of Arabia* 1962. His other films include *Dr Zhivago* 1965 and *Funny Girl* 1968.

Sharjah /'ʃɑ:dʒə/ or **Shariqah** third largest of the seven member states of the ◊United Arab Emirates, situated on the Arabian Gulf NE of Dubai; area 2,600 sq km/1,004 sq mi; population (1985) 269,000. Since 1952 it has included the small state of Kalba. In 1974 oil was discovered offshore. Industries include ship repair, cement, paint, and metal products.

shark *n.* **1.** a large, voracious, sea fish of the order Selachii, with a cartilaginous skeleton. Sharks are found worldwide. They have streamlined bodies and high-speed manoeuvrability, and their eyes, though lacking acuity of vision or sense of colour, are highly sensitive to light. Their sense of smell is so acute that one-third of the brain is given up to interpreting its signals; they can detect blood in the water up to 1 km/0.6 mi away. They also respond to electrical charges emanating from other animals. **2.** a rapacious person; a swindler.

sharkskin *n.* **1.** the skin of a shark. **2.** a wool, silk, or rayon fabric with a smooth, slightly lustrous finish.

sharp /ʃɑ:p/ *adj.* **1.** having an edge or point able to cut or pierce; tapering to a point or edge; abrupt, not gradual; steep, angular. **2.** well-defined, clean-cut, distinct. **3.** intense, forceful; loud and shrill; irritable, speaking harshly and angrily; (of tastes or smells) producing a smarting sensation. **4.** quick to see, hear, or notice things, intelligent. **5.** quick to take advantage; artful, unscrupulous, dishonest. **6.** vigorous, brisk. **7.** in music, (of a note) above the correct or normal pitch; a semitone higher than the corresponding note or key of natural pitch. —*adv.* **1.** punctually. **2.** suddenly. **3.** at a sharp angle. **4.** in music, above the correct pitch. —*n.* **1.** in music, a note that is a semitone higher than the corresponding one of natural pitch; the sign indicating this. **2.** (*colloquial*) a swindler, a cheat. —**sharp end,** (*colloquial*) the bow of a ship; the place where decisions are made and correct action is taken. **sharp-eyed** *adj.* quick at noticing things. —**sharp practice,** dishonest or barely honest dealings. —**sharply** *adv.,* **sharpness** *n.* [Old English]

Sharp Granville 1735–1813. English philanthropist. He was prominent in the antislavery movement and in 1772 secured a legal decision 'that as soon as any slave sets foot on English territory he becomes free'.

sharpen *v.t./i.* to make or become sharp. —**sharpener** *n.*

sharper *n.* a swindler, especially at cards.

Sharpeville /'ʃɑ:pvɪl/ black township in South Africa, 65 km/40 mi S of Johannesburg and N of Vereeniging; 69 people were killed here when police fired on a crowd of anti-apartheid demonstrators on 21 March 1960.

Sharpey-Schäfer /'ʃɑ:pi 'ʃeɪfə/ Edward Albert 1850–1935. English physiologist, one of the founders of endocrinology. He made important discoveries relating to the hormone ◊adrenaline, and to the ◊pituitary and other ◊endocrine, or ductless, glands.

sharpish *adj.* (*colloquial*) fairly sharp. —*adv.* (*colloquial*) fairly sharply, quite quickly.

sharpshooter *n.* a person who shoots accurately.

Shastri /'ʃæstri/ Lal Bahadur 1904–1966. Indian politician, prime minister 1964–66. He campaigned for national integration, and secured a declaration of peace with Pakistan at the Tashkent peace conference of 1966.

Shatt-al-Arab /ʃæt æl 'æræb/ (Persian *Arvand*) waterway formed by the confluence of the rivers ◊Euphrates and ◊Tigris; length 190 km/120 mi to the Persian Gulf. Basra, Khorramshahr, and Abadan stand on it. [= river of Arabia]

shatter *v.t./i.* **1.** to break or become broken violently into small pieces. **2.** to destroy utterly. **3.** to disturb or upset the calmness of.

shave *v.t./i.* (*past participle* **shaved** or (especially as *adj.*) **shaven** /'ʃeɪvən/) **1.** to cut (growing hair) from the chin etc. with a razor; to remove hair from the chin etc. (of). **2.** to cut thin slices from the surface of (wood etc.) to shape it. **3.** to graze gently in passing. **4.** to reduce or remove. —*n.* **1.** shaving, being shaved. **2.** (especially **close shave**) a narrow miss or escape. **3.** a tool for shaving wood etc. [Old English]

shaver *n.* **1.** a thing that shaves, especially an electric razor. **2.** (*colloquial*) a young lad.

shaving *n.* (especially in *plural*) a thin strip shaved from the surface of wood etc.

Shaw /ʃɔ:/ George Bernard 1856–1950. Irish dramatist. He was also a critic and novelist, and an early member of the socialist ◊Fabian Society. His plays combine comedy with political, philosophical, and polemic aspects, aiming to make an impact on his audience's social conscience as well as their emotions. They include *Arms and the Man* 1894, *Devil's Disciple* 1897, *Man and Superman* 1905, *Pygmalion* 1913, and *St Joan* 1924. He was awarded the Nobel Prize for Literature in 1925.

shawl *n.* a large piece of fabric, usually rectangular and often folded into a triangle, worn over the shoulders or head or wrapped round a baby. —*v.t.* (especially in *past participle*) to put a shawl on (a person). [from Urdu from Persian]

shawm *n.* in music, an early form of oboe. [from Old French, ultimately from Greek *kalamos* = reed]

Shchedrin /ʃtʃi'dri:n/ N. Pen name of Mikhail Evgrafovich Saltykov 1826–1889. Russian writer, whose works include *Fables* 1884–85, in which he depicts misplaced 'good intentions', and the novel *The Golovlevs* 1880. He was a satirist of pessimistic outlook.

she /ʃi:/ *pron.* (*objective* **her**; *possessive* **her, hers**; *plural* **they**) the woman, girl, or female animal (or thing regarded as female, e.g. a ship) previously named or in question.

—*n.* a female animal. —*adj.* (usually with hyphen) female (e.g. *she-ass*). [Old English]

sheaf *n.* (*plural* **sheaves**) 1. a bundle of stalks of corn etc. tied together after reaping. 2. a bundle of arrows, papers, etc., laid lengthways together. —*v.t.* to make into sheaves. [Old English]

shear *v.t./i.* (*past* **sheared**; *past participle* **shorn** or **sheared**). 1. to cut or trim with scissors, shears etc.; to remove or take off by cutting; to clip wool off (a sheep etc.). 2. to strip bare, to deprive. 3. to break or distort by shear; to be broken or distorted by shear. —*n.* 1. a type of distortion or fracture produced by pressure, in which each successive layer (e.g. of a mass of rock) slides over the next; transformation of a geometrical figure or solid in which one line or plane remains fixed and those parallel to it move sideways. 2. (in *plural*; also **pair of shears**) a clipping or cutting instrument working like scissors but much larger and usually operated with both hands. [Old English]

Shearer /'ʃiərə/ (Edith) Norma 1900–1983. Canadian actress who starred in such films as *Private Lives* 1931, *Romeo and Juliet* 1936, and *Marie Antoinette* 1938. She was married to MGM executive Irving Thalberg.

shearwater *n.* a sea bird related to petrels and albatrosses. The **Manx shearwater** *Puffinus puffinus* is the only species that breeds in Britain.

sheath /ʃiːθ/ *n.* (*plural* /ʃiːðz/) 1. a covering into which a blade is thrust when not in use; a protective covering. 2. a sheathlike covering in various animal and vegetable structures; the tubular fold of skin into which the penis of a horse, bull, dog etc., is retracted. 3. a ◊condom. 4. a woman's close-fitting dress. —**sheath knife**, a daggerlike knife carried in a sheath. [Old English]

sheathe /ʃiːð/ *v.t.* to put into a sheath; to encase or protect with a sheath.

sheave *v.t.* to make into sheaves.

sheaves plural of **sheaf**.

Sheba /'ʃiːbə/ ancient name for SE ◊Yemen (Sha'abijah). It was once renowned for gold and spices. According to the Old Testament, its queen visited Solomon; the former Ethiopian royal house traced its descent from their union.

shebeen /ʃi'biːn/ *n.* (*Irish*) an unlicensed house selling alcoholic liquor. [from Anglo-Irish (Gaelic *séibe* = mugful)]

Shechem /'ʃiːkem/ ancient town in Palestine, capital of Samaria. In the Old Testament, it is the traditional burial place of Joseph; nearby is Jacob's well. Shechem was destroyed about AD 67 by the Roman emperor Vespasian; on its site stands Nablus (a corruption of Neapolis) built by the Roman emperor ◊Hadrian.

shed[1] *n.* a one-storeyed building for storing things or as a shelter for livestock etc., or for use as a workshop.

shed[2] *v.t.* (**-dd-**; *past* and *past participle* **shed**) 1. to lose (a thing) by a natural falling off. 2. to take off (clothes etc.). 3. to reduce (an electrical power load) by disconnection etc. 4. to allow to pour forth. 5. to send forth, to diffuse, to radiate. —**shed light on**, to help to explain. [Old English]

sheen *n.* gloss, lustre. —**sheeny** *adj.* [from obsolete *sheen* = beautiful from Old English]

sheep *n.* (*plural* **sheep**) 1. a grass-eating animal of the genus *Ovis* of the family Bovidae with a thick woolly coat. Wild species survive in the uplands of central Asia, and their domesticated descendants are reared worldwide for meat, wool, milk, and cheese, and for rotation on arable land to maintain its fertility. Over 50 breeds of sheep have evolved in the UK, and many more worldwide, to suit different requirements and a range of geographical and climatic conditions. 2. a bashful, timid, or silly person. 3. (usually in *plural*) a member of a minister's congregation. —**separate the sheep from the goats**, to separate the good from the wicked. **sheep-dip** *n.* a preparation for cleansing sheep of vermin etc.; a place where sheep are dipped in this. **sheepfold** *n.* an enclosure for sheep. [Old English]

sheepdog *n.* a dog trained to guard and herd sheep; a rough-coated breed of dog. The **Old English sheepdog** is grey or blue-grey, with white markings, and is about 56 cm/22 in tall at the shoulder. The **Shetland sheepdog** is much smaller, 36 cm/14 in tall, and shaped more like a long-coated collie. Sheepdogs were fomerly used by shepherds and farmers to tend sheep. **Border collies** are now used for this job.

sheepish *adj.* bashful; embarrassed through shame. —**sheepishly** *adv.*, **sheepishness** *n.*

sheep

Scottish blackface

Dorset down

Suffolk

Welsh mountain

sheepshank *n.* a knot used to shorten a rope temporarily.

sheepskin *n.* 1. a garment or rug of sheep's skin with the wool on. 2. leather of sheep's skin used in bookbinding etc.

sheer[1] *adj.* 1. mere, pure, not mixed or qualified. 2. (of a cliff or ascent etc.) with little or no slope, perpendicular. 3. (of a textile) very thin, diaphanous. —*adv.* perpendicularly, directly.

sheer[2] *v.i.* to swerve or change course. —**sheer off**, to go away, to leave a person or topic that one dislikes or fears.

sheerlegs *n.* or **sheers** a hoisting apparatus of two (or more) poles attached at or near the top and separated at the bottom, used for fitting masts to ships or putting in engines etc. [variant of *shear*]

sheet[1] *n.* 1. a large, rectangular piece of cotton or other fabric, used especially in pairs as inner bedclothes. 2. a thin, broad, usually flat piece of material (e.g. paper or glass). 3. a wide expanse of water, ice, flame, falling rain etc. 4. a newspaper. —*v.t./i.* 1. to provide or cover with sheets. 2. to form into sheets. 3. (of rain etc.) to fall in sheets. —**sheet lightning**, lightning that looks like a sheet of light across the sky. **sheet metal**, metal formed into thin sheets by rolling, hammering etc. **sheet music**, music published in separate sheets. [Old English]

sheet[2] *n.* a rope or chain attached to the lower corner of a sail for securing or controlling it. —**sheet anchor**, a second anchor for use in emergencies; a person or thing depended on for security or stability. [Old English]

sheeting *n.* material for making sheets.

Sheffield /'ʃefiːld/ industrial city on the river Don, South Yorkshire, England; population (1986) 538,700. From the 12th century, iron smelting was the chief industry, and by the 14th century, Sheffield cutlery, silverware, and plate were made. During the Industrial Revolution the iron and steel industries developed rapidly. It now produces alloys and special steels, cutlery of all kinds, permanent magnets, drills, and precision tools.

sheikh /ʃeɪk, ʃiːk/ *n.* or **sheik** the head of an Arab family or village; a Muslim leader. —**sheikhdom** *n.* [ultimately from Arabic = old man]

sheila /ˈʃiːlə/ *n.* (*Australian* and *NZ slang*) a young woman, a girl. [originally *shaler*]

shekel /ˈʃekəl/ *n.* **1.** the currency unit of Israel. **2.** an ancient Jewish etc. weight and silver coin. **3.** (in *plural, colloquial*) money, riches. [from Hebrew *shākal* = weigh]

Shelburne /ˈʃelbən/ William Petty FitzMaurice, 2nd Earl of Shelburne 1737–1805. English Whig politician. He was an opponent of George III's American policy, and as prime minister in 1783 he concluded peace with the USA.

sheldrake /ˈʃeldreɪk/ *n.* a male shelduck.

shelduck *n.* a bright-plumaged wild duck of the genus *Tadorna*, especially *T. tadorna*, with a dark-green head and red bill and the rest of the plumage strikingly marked in black, white, and chestnut. Shelducks are widely distributed in Europe and Asia. They lay 10–12 white eggs in rabbit burrows on sandy coasts, and are usually seen on estuary mudflats.

shelf *n.* (*plural* **shelves**) **1.** a horizontal board or slab etc. projecting from a wall or forming one tier of a bookcase or cupboard. **2.** something resembling this; a ledge, a horizontal stepline projection in a cliff face etc.; a reef or sandbank. —**on the shelf,** (especially of a person) no longer active or of use; past the age when he or she might expect to get married. **shelf life,** the time for which a stored thing remains usable. **shelf-mark** *n.* a mark on a book to show its place in a library. **shelf sea,** a relatively shallow sea, usually no deeper than 200 m/650 ft, overlying the continental shelf around the coastlines. [from Middle Low German, related to Old English *scylfe* = partition, *scylf* = crag]

shell *n.* **1.** the hard outer covering of a nut kernel, egg, seed, or fruit, or of an animal such as a crab, snail, or tortoise. **2.** a structure that forms a firm framework or covering. **3.** the walls or framework of an unfinished or gutted building or ship etc. **4.** an explosive projectile for firing from a large gun etc.; the hollow case containing explosives for a cartridge, firework etc. **5.** a light rowing boat for racing. **6.** a group of electrons in an atom, with almost equal energy. —*v.t.* **1.** to take out of a shell, to remove the shell or pod from. **2.** to fire shells at. —**come out of one's shell,** to become more communicative and less shy. **shell out,** (*slang*) to pay out (money). —**shell-less** *adj.*, **shelly** *adj.* [Old English]

shellac /ʃəˈlæk/ *n.* a resin derived from secretions of the ◊lac insect. —*v.t.* (**-ck-**) to varnish with shellac.

shelled *adj.* **1.** having a shell. **2.** deprived of its shell.

Shelley /ˈʃeli/ Mary Wollstonecraft 1797–1851. English writer, the daughter of Mary Wollstonecraft and William Godwin. In 1814 she eloped with the poet Percy Bysshe Shelley, whom she married in 1816. Her novels include ◊*Frankenstein* 1818, *The Last Man* 1826, and *Valperga* 1823.

Shelley Percy Bysshe 1792–1822. English lyric poet, a leading figure in the Romantic movement. Expelled from Oxford for atheism, he fought all his life against religion and for political freedom. This is reflected in his early poems such as *Queen Mab* 1813. He later wrote tragedies including *The Cenci* 1818, lyric dramas such as *Prometheus Unbound* 1820, and lyrical poems such as 'Ode to the West Wind'. He drowned while sailing in Italy.

Hell is a city much like London – A populous and smoky city.
Percy Bysshe Shelley
Peter Bell the Third

shellfish *n.* (*plural* the same) a water animal with a shell, especially an edible mollusc or a crustacean.

shell shock or **combat neurosis** or **battle fatigue** any of the various forms of mental disorder that affect soldiers exposed to heavy explosions or extreme ◊stress. Shell shock was first diagnosed during World War I.

shelter *n.* **1.** something that serves as a shield or barrier against attack, danger, heat, wind etc.; a structure providing this. **2.** refuge, a shielded condition. —*v.t./i.* **1.** to

provide with shelter. **2.** to protect from blame, trouble, or competition. **3.** to find or take shelter. —**sheltered housing** etc., that provided for people who are old or handicapped, with special facilities or services.

shelve *v.t./i.* **1.** to arrange on a shelf or shelves. **2.** to fit with shelves. **3.** to defer consideration of (a plan etc.); to remove (a person) from active work etc. **4.** (of ground) to slope away.

shelves plural of **shelf.**

shelving *n.* shelves collectively; material for shelves.

Shema /ʃeˈmɑ/ *n.* in Judaism, a prayer from the Torah, recited by orthodox men every morning and evening, which affirms the special relationship of the Jews with God.

shemozzle /ʃiˈmɒzəl/ *n.* (*slang*) a rumpus, a brawl; a muddle. [from Yiddish after Hebrew = of no luck]

shenanigan /ʃiˈnænigən/ *n.* (*colloquial*) nonsense; trickery; high-spirited behaviour.

Shenyang /ʃenˈjæŋ/ industrial city and capital of Liaoning province, China; population (1986) 4,200,000. It was the capital of the Manchu emperors 1644–1912.

Shenzen /ʃʌnˈdzʌn/ a special economic zone established in 1980 opposite Hong Kong on the coast of Guangdong province, S China. Its status provided much of the driving force of its spectacular development in the 1980s when its population rose from 20,000 in 1980 to 600,000 in 1989. Part of the population consists of 'rotated' newcomers from other provinces who return to their homes after a few years spent learning foreign business techniques.

Shepard /ˈʃepəd/ E(rnest) H(oward) 1879–1976. English illustrator of books by A A Milne (*Winnie-the-Pooh* 1926) and Kenneth Grahame (*The Wind in the Willows* 1908).

Shepard Sam 1943– . US dramatist and actor. His work combines colloquial American dialogue with striking visual imagery, and includes *The Tooth of Crime* 1972 and *Buried Child* 1978, for which he won the Pulitzer Prize. He has acted in a number of films, including *The Right Stuff* 1983, *Fool for Love* 1986, based on his play of the same name, and *Steel Magnolias* 1989.

shepherd /ˈʃepəd/ *n.* **1.** a person who tends a flock of sheep at pasture. **2.** a spiritual leader, a priest. —*v.t.* **1.** to tend (sheep). **2.** to lead spiritually. **3.** to marshal, conduct, or drive (a crowd etc.) like sheep. —**shepherd's pie,** ◊cottage pie. —**shepherdess** *n.fem.* [Old English]

Sheraton /ˈʃerətən/ *n.* a style of furniture introduced in England about 1790, with delicate and graceful forms. [from Thomas *Sheraton,* English furniture-maker (*c.*1751–1806)]

sherbet /ˈʃɜːbət/ *n.* **1.** an oriental drink of sweetened diluted fruit juice. **2.** a fizzy, flavoured drink; the powder for this. [from Turkish or Persian from Arabic = drink]

sherd *n.* a ◊potsherd. [variant of *shard*]

Sheridan /ˈʃerɪdən/ Richard Brinsley 1751–1816. Irish dramatist and politician, born in Dublin. His social comedies include *The Rivals* 1775, celebrated for the character of Mrs Malaprop, *The School for Scandal* 1777, and *The Critic* 1779. In 1776 he became lessee of the Drury Lane Theatre. He became a member of Parliament in 1780.

If it is abuse—why one is sure to hear of it from one damned good-natured friend or other!
Richard Brinsley Sheridan
The Critic

sheriff /ˈʃerɪf/ *n.* **1.** or **high sheriff** in England and Wales, the crown's chief executive officer in a county for ceremonial purposes. **2.** an honorary officer elected annually in some towns. **3.** (*Scottish*; also **sheriff-depute**) the chief judge of a county or district; the equivalent of the English county-court judge, but also dealing with criminal cases. **4.** (*US*) the popularly elected head law-enforcement officer of a county, combining judicial authority with administrative duties. [Old English *scir* = shire and *gerēfa* = reeve]

Sherlock /ˈʃɜːlɒk/ *n.* a person who investigates mysteries or shows great perceptiveness; a private detective. [from *Sherlock* Holmes]

Sherlock Holmes /ˈʃɜːlɒk ˈhəʊmz/ a fictitious private detective, created by the English writer Arthur Conan ◊Doyle in *A Study in Scarlet* 1887 and recurring in novels and stories until 1914. Holmes's ability to make inferences from slight clues always astonishes the narrator, Dr Watson.

Sherman /ˈʃɜːmən/ William Tecumseh 1820–1891. US Union general in the American Civil War. In 1864 he captured and burned Atlanta, from where he marched to the sea, laying Georgia waste, and then drove the Confederates northwards. He was US Army Chief of Staff 1869–83.

Sherpa /ˈʃɜːpə/ n. a member of a people in NE Nepál related to the Tibetans, and renowned for their mountaineering skill. They frequently work as support staff and guides for climbing expeditions. A Sherpa, Tensing Norgay, was one of the first two people to climb Mount Everest.

Sherrington /ˈʃerɪŋtən/ Charles Scott 1857–1952. English neurophysiologist who studied the structure and function of the nervous system. *The Integrative Action of the Nervous System* 1906 formulated the principles of reflex action. He was awarded the Nobel Prize for Medicine (with E D ◊Adrian) in 1932.

sherry n. a white, usually fortified wine originally from S Spain; a glass of this. [from *Xeres* (now *Jerez de la Frontera*) in Spain]

Sherwood Forest /ˈʃɜːwʊd/ a hilly stretch of parkland in W Nottinghamshire, England, area about 520 sq km/ 200 sq mi. It was formerly a royal forest. It is associated with the legendary outlaw ◊Robin Hood.

Shetland /ˈʃetlənd/ adj. of the Shetland Islands, Scotland. —**Shetland pony,** a small, hardy, rough-coated pony. **Shetland wool,** fine, loosely twisted wool from Shetland sheep. —**Shetlander** n.

Shetland Islands group of islands to the N–NW of Scotland; **area** 1,400 sq km/541 sq mi; **administrative headquarters** Lerwick on Mainland, largest of the 19 inhabited islands; **physical** over 100 islands including Muckle Flugga (latitude 60° 51′ N) the northernmost of the British Isles; **products** processed fish, handknits from Fair Isle and Unst, miniature ponies; Europe's largest oil port is Sullom Voe, Mainland; **population** (1987) 22,000; **language** dialect derived from Norse, the islands having been a Norse dependency from the 8th century until 1472.

Shevardnadze /ʃevədˈnɑːdzə/ Edvard 1928– . Soviet politician, foreign minister 1985–1990. A supporter of ◊Gorbachev, he was first secretary of the Georgian Communist Party from 1972 and an advocate of economic reform. In 1985 he became foreign minister and a member of the Politburo, and worked for détente and disarmament. At the end of 1990 he announced his intention to resign in an unexpected and unusually outspoken attack on the Soviet leadership.

shew archaic variant of **show.**

Shiah /ˈʃiːə/ n. the ◊Shi'ite branch of Islam. [from Arabic = party (of Ali Muhammad's cousin and son-in-law)]

shibboleth n. an old-fashioned doctrine or formula of a party or sect; a catchword; a word, custom, or principle etc. regarded as revealing a person's orthodoxy etc. [from Hebrew = ear of corn, from a story in the Bible, Judges 12: 6, where it was a kind of password distinguishing those who could pronounce it from those who could not]

Shidehara /ʃɪdeɪˈhɑːrə/ Kijurō 1872–1951. Japanese politician and diplomat, prime minister 1945–46. As foreign minister 1924–27 and 1929–31, he promoted conciliation with China, and economic rather than military expansion. After a brief period as prime minister 1945–46, he became speaker of the Japanese Diet (parliament) 1946–51.

shield n. 1. a piece of defensive armour carried in the hand or on the arm to protect the body against missiles or thrusts. 2. an object, structure, or layer of material that protects something; a person giving protection; a shieldlike part in an animal or plant. See also ◊biological shield and ◊heat shield. 3. in geology, an alternative name for ◊craton, the ancient core of a continent. 4. a representation of a shield as a heraldic device displaying a coat of arms. 5. a trophy in the form of a shield. —v.t. to protect or screen; to protect from discovery. [Old English]

shift v.t./i. 1. to change or move from one position to another. 2. to change form or character. 3. to pass (responsibility etc.) on to someone else. 4. (*slang*) to move quickly; to consume (food or drink). 5. (*US*) to change gear in a motor vehicle. —n. 1. a change of place, position, form, or character. 2. a set of workers who start work as another set finishes; the period for which they work. 3. a scheme

for achieving something, an expedient. 4. a trick, a piece of evasion. 5. a woman's straight-cut dress. 6. a change of position of typewriter typebars to type capitals etc. 7. a displacement of the lines of the spectrum. 8. (*US*) a gear change in a motor vehicle. —**make shift,** to manage in less than ideal circumstances. **shift for oneself,** to depend on one's own efforts. **shift one's ground,** to take a new position in an argument etc. —**shifter** n. [Old English = arrange, divide]

shiftless adj. lazy and inefficient; lacking resourcefulness. —**shiftlessly** adv., **shiftlessness** n.

shifty adj. evasive, deceitful, untrustworthy. —**shiftily** adv., **shiftiness** n.

Shi Huangdi /ˈʃiː hwændɪ/ or **Shih Huang Ti** 259–210 BC. Emperor of China. He succeeded to the throne of the state of Qin in 246 and reunited the country as an empire by 228. He burned almost all existing books in 213 to destroy ties with the past; rebuilt the ◊Great Wall; and was buried at Xian in a tomb complex guarded by 10,000 life-size terracotta warriors (excavated by archaeologists in the 1980s).

Shi'ite /ˈʃiːaɪt/ or **Shiite** or **Shiah** a member of one of the two major groups of ◊Islam who believe that ◊Ali was Muhammad's first true successor. Shi'ites are doctrinally opposed to the Sunni Muslims. Holy men have greater authority in the Shi'ite sect than in the Sunni sect. They are prominent in Iran and Lebanon and are also found in Iraq and Bahrain. Breakaway subsects include the **Alawite** sect, to which the ruling party in Syria belongs; and the **Ismaili** sect, with the Aga Khan IV (1936–) as its spiritual head.

Shikoku /ʃiːˈkəʊkuː/ smallest of the four main islands of Japan, S of Honshu, E of Kyushu; **area** 18,800 sq km/ 7,257 sq mi; **chief town** Matsuyama; **products** rice, wheat, soya beans, sugar cane, orchard fruits, salt, and copper; **population** (1986) 4,226,000. [Japanese = four provinces]

shillelagh /ʃɪˈleɪlə, -lɪ/ n. an Irish cudgel. [from *Shillelagh* in County Wicklow, Ireland]

shilling n. a former British currency unit and coin worth one-twentieth of a pound; a monetary unit in East African countries. [Old English]

shilly-shally /ˈʃɪlɪʃælɪ/ v.i. to vacillate, to hesitate or be undecided. [reduplication of *shall I?*]

Shilton /ˈʃɪltən/ Peter 1949– . English international footballer, an outstanding goalkeeper. He has made more than 900 Football League appearances, an all-time record, and won a record number of England caps (125).

shim n. a thin wedge used in machinery etc. to make parts fit. —v.t. (**-mm-**) to fit or fill up thus.

shimmer v.i. to shine with a tremulous or faint, diffused light. —n. such a light. [Old English]

shin n. 1. the front of the leg below the knee. 2. **shin of beef** an ox's (especially fore-)shank as a cut of meat. —v.t./i. (**-nn-**) to climb by clinging with arms and legs. —**shinbone** n. the inner and usually larger of the two bones from knee to ankle. [Old English]

shindig /ˈʃɪndɪg/ n. or **shindy** (*colloquial*) 1. a festive gathering, especially a boisterous one. 2. a din, a brawl.

shine v.t./i. (*past* and *past participle* **shone** /ʃɒn/) 1. to emit or reflect light, to be bright, to glow. 2. (of the Sun, a star etc.) to be clearly visible. 3. to be brilliant, to excel. 4. to cause to shine (in a certain direction etc.). 5. (*past participle* **shined**) to polish so as to produce a shine. —n. brightness, a lustre, a polish; light, sunshine. —**take a shine to,** (*colloquial*) to take a liking to. [Old English]

shiner /ˈʃaɪnə/ n. (*colloquial*) a black eye.

shingle[1] /ˈʃɪŋgəl/ n. (in *singular* or *plural*) pebbles in a mass, as on a seashore. —**shingly** adj.

shingle[2] n. 1. a rectangular piece of wood used as a roof tile. 2. shingled hair; shingling the hair. —v.t. 1. to roof with shingles. 2. to cut (a woman's hair) short so that it tapers from the back of the head to the nape of the neck so that all ends are exposed like roof shingles.

shingles /ˈʃɪŋgəlz/ n.pl. (usually treated as *singular*) the common name for herpes zoster, an acute painful viral inflammation of the nerve ganglia, with a skin eruption of blisters along the course of the affected nerves, often forming a girdle around the middle of the body. [from Latin *cingulus* = girdle (*cingere* = gird)]

Shinkansen /ˈʃɪnkænsen/ n. the fast railway network operated by Japanese Railways, on which the bullet trains run. The network, opened in 1964, uses specially built straight and level track, on which average speeds of 160 kph/100 mph are attained. [Japanese = new trunk line]

Shinto /'ʃɪntəʊ 'ʃɪntəʊ/ n. the indigenous religion of Japan. It combines an empathetic oneness with natural forces and loyalty to the reigning dynasty as descendants of the Sun goddess, Amaterasu-Omikami. An aggressive nationalistic aspect was developed from 1868 by the Meiji rulers and discarded after World War II. —**Shintoist,** n. [Japanese *shintō* from Chinese *shen tao*= way of the gods]

shinty /'ʃɪntɪ/ n. **1.** a game like hockey between teams of 12 players, brought to Scotland by the invading Irish Gaels and sharing its history with ◊hurling until the mid-14th century. **2.** the stick or ball used in this. [earlier *shinny*, apparently from cry (*shin ye*) used in the game]

shiny /'ʃaɪnɪ/ adj. having a shine; (of clothes) with the nap worn off. —**shinily** adv., **shininess** n.

ship n. **1.** a large seagoing vessel. The Greeks, Phoenicians, Romans, and Vikings used ships extensively for trade, exploration, and warfare. The 14th century was the era of European exploration by sailing ship, largely aided by the invention of the compass. In the 15th century Britain's Royal Navy was first formed, but in the 16th–19th centuries Spanish and Dutch ships reigned supreme. The ultimate sailing ships, the fast US and British tea clippers, were built in the 19th century. Also in the 19th century, iron was first used for some shipbuilding instead of wood. Steam-propelled ships of the late 19th century were followed by compound engine and turbine-propelled vessels from the early 20th century. **2.** (*colloquial*) a spacecraft; (*US*) an aircraft. —v.t./i. (**-pp-**) **1.** to put, send, or take on board a ship for conveyance to a destination. **2.** to transport. **3.** to fix (a mast, rudder etc.) in its place on a ship. **4.** to embark; (of a sailor) to take service on a ship. **5.** to take (oars) from the rowlocks and lay them inside the boat. **6.** to have (water, a sea) come into a boat etc. over the gunwale. **take ship,** to go on board a ship for a journey. **when one's ship comes home** *or* **in,** when one's fortune is made. [Old English]

-ship suffix forming nouns denoting quality or condition (e.g. *friendship, hardship*), status, office, or honour (e.g. *authorship, lordship*), tenure of an office (e.g. *secretaryship*), skill in a certain capacity (e.g. *leadership*), the collective individuals of a group (e.g. *membership*). [Old English]

shipboard n. especially in **on shipboard,** on board a ship.

shipbuilder n. a person engaged in the business of building ships. —**shipbuilding** n.

shipload n. the quantity of cargo or passengers that a ship can carry.

shipmate n. a person belonging to or sailing on the same ship as another.

shipment n. the placing of goods on a ship; the amount shipped.

shipowner n. a person owning or having shares in a ship or ships.

shipper n. one who ships goods, especially in import or export.

shipping n. ships collectively; transport of goods by ship.

shipshape adv. & predic. adj. in good order, neat and tidy.

shipwreck n. **1.** destruction of a ship at sea by storm or by striking rocks etc. **2.** the remains of a ship destroyed thus. **3.** the ruin of plans etc. —v.t. to cause to suffer a shipwreck.

shipwright n. **1.** a shipbuilder. **2.** a ship's carpenter.

shipyard n. a place where ships are built.

shire n. **1.** a county; (*historical*) an administrative area formed in Britain for the purpose of raising taxes in Anglo-Saxon times. By AD 1000 most of S England had been divided into shires with fortified strongholds at their centres. **2.** (*Australian*) a rural area with its own elected council. —**shire horse,** a draught horse of a heavy, powerful breed, with long, white hair covering the lower part of the legs. **the shires,** the band of English counties with names (formerly) ending in *-shire*, extending NE from Hampshire and Devon; the Midland counties of England; the fox-hunting district of England, comprising mainly Leicestershire and Northamptonshire. [Old English]

shirk v.t. to avoid (a duty or work etc., or *absolute*) from laziness, cowardice etc. —**shirker** n.

shirr v.t. to gather (fabric), especially with elastic or parallel threads run through it.

shirt n. a loose-sleeved garment of cotton or silk etc. for the upper part of the body. —**keep one's shirt on,** (*slang*) to keep one's temper. **put one's shirt on,** (*slang*) to bet all one's money on (a horse etc.). **shirt dress,** a woman's dress with a bodice like a shirt. [Old English]

shirting n. material for shirts.

shirtwaister n. a shirt dress.

shirty adj. (*slang*) angry, annoyed. —**shirtily** adv., **shirtiness** n.

shish kebab /ʃɪʃ kɪˈbæb/ pieces of meat and vegetable grilled on skewers. [from Turkish *shish* = skewer and *kebab* = roast meat]

shit v.t./i. (**-tt-**; past and past participle **shit**) (*vulgar*) to defecate; to get rid of as excrement. —n. (*vulgar*) **1.** faeces. **2.** an act of defecating. **3.** nonsense. **4.** a despicable person. —int. (*vulgar*) an expression of anger or annoyance. [Old English]

shiver[1] /'ʃɪvə/ v.i. to tremble slightly, especially with cold or fear. —n. a shivering movement. —**the shivers,** an attack of shivering; a feeling of fear or horror. —**shivery** adj.

shiver[2] /'ʃɪvə/ n. (usually in *plural*) a small fragment, a splinter. —v.t./i. to break into shivers. [related to Old High German *scivaro* = splinter]

shoal[1] n. a multitude, a great number, especially of fish swimming together. —v.i. (of fish) to form a shoal or shoals.

shoal[2] n. **1.** a shallow place in the sea; a submerged sandbank, especially one that shows at low water. **2.** (usually in *plural*) hidden danger. —v.i. to become shallow. [Old English, related to *shallow*]

shock[1] n. **1.** the effect of a violent impact or shake; a violent shake or tremor of the Earth's crust in an earthquake. **2.** a sudden violent effect upon the mind or emotions; in medicine, circulatory failure marked by a sudden fall of blood pressure and resulting in pallor, sweating, a fast (but weak) pulse, and sometimes complete collapse, caused by physical injury or pain or by mental trauma; an electric shock. **3.** great disturbance of or injury to an organization, stability, etc. —v.t./i. **1.** to affect with an electrical or mental shock. **2.** to appear horrifying or outrageous to. —**shock absorber,** a device on a vehicle etc. for absorbing vibration and shock. Shock absorbers are used in conjunction with coil springs in most motor-vehicle suspension systems and are usually of the telescopic type, consisting of a piston in an oil-filled cylinder. **shock therapy** *or* **treatment,** psychiatric treatment by means of a shock induced artificially by electricity or drugs. **shock troops,** troops specially trained for violent assaults. **shock wave,** an air wave caused by an explosion or by a body moving faster than sound. [from French *choc, choquer*]

shock[2] n. a group of corn sheaves propped up together in a field. —v.t. to arrange (corn) in shocks. [= Middle Dutch and Middle Low German *schok*]

shock[3] n. an unkempt or shaggy mass of hair.

shocker n. (*colloquial*) a person or thing that shocks; a very bad specimen of something; a sordid or sensational novel, film etc.

shocking adj. causing shock; scandalous; (*colloquial*) very bad. —**shocking pink,** a vibrant shade of pink. —**shockingly** adv.

Shockley /'ʃɒklɪ/ William 1910–1989. US physicist and amateur geneticist, who worked with John ◊Bardeen and Walter ◊Brattain on the invention of the ◊transistor. They were jointly awarded the Nobel Prize for Physics in 1956. During the 1970s Shockley was severely criticized for his claim that blacks were genetically inferior to whites in terms of intelligence.

shod past and past participle of **shoe.**

shoddy n. fibre made from shredded old cloth; cloth made partly from this. —adj. of poor quality or badly made. —**shoddily** adv., **shoddiness** n.

shoe /ʃuː/ n. **1.** an outer foot covering of leather etc., especially one not reaching above the ankle. **2.** a thing like a shoe in shape or use. **3.** a metal rim nailed to a horse's hoof. **4.** a brake shoe (see ◊brake[1]). —v.t. (past and past participle **shod;** participle **shoeing**) **1.** to fit (a horse etc.) with a shoe or shoes. **2.** (in *past participle*) having shoes etc. of a specified kind. —**in a person's shoes,** in his or her position or predicament. **shoehorn** *n*. a curved piece of horn or metal etc. for easing the heel into a shoe. **shoelace** *n*. a cord for lacing a shoe. **shoestring** *n*. a shoelace; (*colloquial*) a small or inadequate amount of money (especially as capital). **shoetree** *n*. a shaped block for keeping a shoe in shape. [Old English]

shoebill *n*. or **whale-headed stork** a large, grey, long-legged, swamp-dwelling African bird *Balaeniceps rex*. It stands up to 1.5 m/5 ft tall and has a large, wide beak, 20 cm/8 in long, with which it scoops fish, molluscs, reptiles, and carrion out of the mud.

shoemaker /'ʃuːmeɪkə/ *n*. a person whose business is making and repairing boots and shoes. —**shoemaking** *n*.

Shoemaker Willie (William Lee) 1931– . US jockey, whose career 1949–90 was outstandingly successful. He rode 8,833 winners from 40,351 mounts and his earnings exceeded $123 million. He was the leading US jockey ten times.

shoeshine *n*. (*US*) the polishing of shoes.

shofar *n*. in Judaism, a ram's horn blown in the synagogue as a call to repentance at the new year festivals of Rosh Hashanah and Yom Kippur.

shogun /'ʃəʊɡʊn/ *n*. in Japanese history, the commander in chief of the army. Although nominally appointed by and subject to the emperor and acting in his name, the shoguns, by successive usurpations of power, became the real rulers of Japan from 1192 to 1867. With the abolition of the feudal system in 1867 the emperor reassumed actual sovereignty and the power of the shoguns came to an end, the office being abolished in 1868. —**shogunate** *n*. [Japanese *shōgun* = general, from Chinese *jiang jung*]

Sholokhov /'ʃɒləkɒf/, Russian /ʃɒləxəf/ Mikhail Aleksandrovich 1905–1984. Soviet novelist. His *And Quiet Flows the Don* 1926–40 depicts the Don Cossacks through World War I and the Russian Revolution. He received the 1965 Nobel Prize for Literature.

Shona /'ʃɒnə/ *n*. a member of a S African people; their language. The Shona form approximately 80% of the population of Zimbabwe. They also occupy the land between the Save and Pungure rivers in Mozambique, and smaller groups are found in South Africa, Botswana, and Zambia. The Shona language belongs to the Bantu group of the Niger-Congo family.

shone past and past participle of **shine**.

shoo interjection used to frighten animals away. —*v.t./i.* to utter such a sound; to drive away thus. [imitative]

shook past of **shake**.

shoot *v.t./i.* (*past* and *past participle* **shot**) 1. to cause (a weapon, or *absolute*) to discharge a missile; to kill or wound with a missile from a weapon. 2. to hunt with a gun for sport. 3. to come, go, or send swiftly or violently. 4. to pass swiftly over (rapids etc.) or under (a bridge). 5. in football etc., to take a shot at goal; to score (a goal). 6. to photograph; to film. 7. (of a plant) to put forth buds; (of a bud) to appear. 8. (as *interjection, US*) say what you have to say. —*n.* 1. a young branch or sucker; the new growth of a plant; in botany, the part of a ◊vascular plant growing above ground, comprising a stem bearing leaves, buds, and flowers. 2. an expedition or party for shooting game; land in which game is shot. 3. a chute. —**be** *or* **get shot of**, to be rid of. **shoot down**, to kill (a person) cold-bloodedly by shooting; to cause (an aircraft or its pilot) to fall to the ground by shooting; to argue effectively against (a proposal etc.). **shooting brake**, (*British*) an estate car. **shooting gallery**, a place for shooting at targets with rifles etc. **shooting star**, a small meteor moving rapidly. **shooting stick**, a walking stick with a handle folding out to form a small seat. **shoot one's mouth off**, (*slang*) to talk freely or indiscreetly. **shoot up**, to rise or grow rapidly; to destroy or terrorize by shooting. **the whole shoot**, (*slang*) everything. —**shooter** *n*. [Old English]

shop *n*. 1. a building or room where goods or services are on sale to the public. 2. a place where manufacturing or repairing is done. 3. one's work or profession as a subject of conversation (*to talk shop*). 4. (*slang*) an institution, an establishment, a place of business etc. —*v.t./i.* (**-pp-**) 1. to go to shops to make purchases etc. 2. (*slang*) to inform against, especially to the police. —**all over the shop**, (*slang*) in great disorder, scattered everywhere. **shop around**, to look for the best bargain. **shop assistant**, an employee in a retail shop. **shop floor**, the production area

in a factory etc.; workers as distinct from management. **shop-soiled** *adj*. soiled or faded by having been on display in a shop. **shop steward**, an official of a trade union elected by fellow workers as their representative who recruits for the union, inspects contribution cards, and reports grievances to the district committee. [from Anglo-French and Old French *eschoppe* = booth, from Middle Low German]

shopkeeper *n*. the owner or manager of a shop.

shoplifter *n*. a person who steals goods from a shop after entering as a customer. —**shoplifting** *n*.

shopper *n*. 1. a person who shops. 2. a shopping bag.

shopping *n*. 1. buying goods from shops. 2. the goods bought. —**shopping bag**, a bag for holding shopping. **shopping centre**, an area or complex of buildings where shops are concentrated. **shopping trolley**, a trolley with a large shopping bag mounted on it.

shopwalker *n*. a supervisor in a large shop.

shore[1] *n*. the land that adjoins the sea or a large body of water. —**on shore**, ashore. [from Middle Dutch or Middle Low German]

shore[2] *n*. a prop, a beam set obliquely against a wall or ship etc. as a support. —*v.t.* to prop or support with shores. [from Middle Dutch or Middle Low German = prop]

shoreline *n*. the line of a shore.

shorn past participle of **shear**.

short *adj*. 1. measuring little from end to end in space or time; soon traversed or finished. 2. of small stature, not tall. 3. not lasting, not reaching far into the past or future. 4. not far-reaching, acting near at hand; insufficient, having an insufficient supply; (seemingly) less than the stated or usual amount etc. 5. concise, brief; curt; (of temper) easily lost. 6. (of an alcoholic drink) small and concentrated, made with spirits. 7. (of a vowel sound or a syllable) relatively brief or light (compare ◊long[1] 7). 8. (of pastry) rich and crumbly through containing much fat. 9. (of a sale in stocks etc.) effected with borrowed stock in expectation of acquiring stock later at a lower price. 10. in cricket, (of a fielding position) close to the batsman. —*adv.* 1. abruptly, suddenly. 2. before the natural or expected time or place. 3. in a short manner. —*n.* 1. a short thing, especially a short syllable or vowel; a short film. 2. (*colloquial*) a short circuit. 3. (*colloquial*) a short drink. —*v.t./i.* (*colloquial*) to short-circuit. —**be caught** *or* **taken short**, to be put at a disadvantage; (*colloquial*) to have a sudden need to go to the toilet. **come** *or* **fall short of**, to fail to reach or amount to. **for short**, as a short name. **in short**, briefly. **short-change** *v.t.* to rob or cheat, especially by giving insufficient change. **short circuit**, a connection (usually a fault) in an electrical circuit in which current flows through small resistance, bypassing the rest of the circuit. A large current flowing through a short circuit may cause the circuit to overheat dangerously. **short-circuit** *v.t./i.* to cause a short circuit in; to have a short circuit; to shorten or avoid by taking a short cut. **short cut**, a shorter way or method than that usually followed. **short division**, division of numbers without writing down details of the calculation. **short for**, serving as an abbreviation of. **short-handed** *adj*. understaffed, with insufficient help. **short list**, a list of selected candidates from which the final choice will be made. **short-list** *v.t.* to put on a short list. **short-lived** *adj*. having a short life, ephemeral. **short of**, not having enough of; less than; distant from; without going so far as. **short on**, (*colloquial*) deficient in. **short-range** *adj*. having a short range; relating to a short period of future time. **short shrift**, curt attention or treatment. **short-term** *adj*. occurring in or relating to a short period of time. **short wave**, a radio wave of frequency greater than 3 MHz. **short-winded** *adj*. easily becoming breathless. —**shortness** *n*. [Old English]

shortage *n*. a deficiency; the amount of this.

shortbread *n*. a rich, crumbly biscuit made with flour, butter, and sugar.

shortcake *n*. 1. shortbread. 2. a cake of short pastry, usually served with fruit.

shortcoming *n*. failure to reach a required standard, a deficiency.

shorten *v.t./i.* to make or become short or shorter.

shortening *n*. fat used for making short pastry.

shortfall *n*. a deficit.

· **shorthand** *n*. 1. any system of rapid writing, such as the abbreviations practised by the Greeks and Romans. The

Shostakovich *Soviet composer Dmitry Shostakovich pictured in his study in 1954.*

first perfecter of an entirely phonetic system was Isaac ◊Pitman, by which system speeds of about 300 words a minute are said to be attainable. **2.** an abbreviated or symbolic mode of expression.

shorthorn *n.* one of a breed of cattle with short horns.

shortly *adv.* **1.** soon, not long, in a short time. **2.** in a few words. **3.** curtly.

Short Parliament the English Parliament that was summoned by Charles I on 13 April 1640 to raise funds for his war against the Scots. It was succeeded later in the year by the ◊Long Parliament.

shorts *n.pl.* **1.** trousers that do not reach to the knee. **2.** (*US*) underpants.

short sight or **myopia** the inability of the ◊eye to focus on distant objects. Short sight occurs when the lens loses its ability to become flatter, or when the eyeball is too long. As a result, the image is focused on a point in front of the ◊retina. The problem can be corrected by use of a diverging or concave lens. **—short-sighted** *adj.* having short sight; lacking imagination or foresight.

short story a short work of prose ﬁction, which typically either sets up and resolves a single narrative point or depicts a mood or an atmosphere. Celebrated short-story writers include Chekhov, Kipling, Maupassant, Saki, Borges, and Hemingway.

short tennis a variation of lawn tennis. It is played on a smaller court, largely by children. It can be played indoors or outdoors.

shorty *n.* or **shortie** (*colloquial*) a person or garment shorter than average.

Shostakovich /ʃɒstəˈkəʊvɪtʃ/ Dmitry (Dmitriyevich) 1906–1975. Soviet composer. His music is tonal, expressive, and sometimes highly dramatic; it has not always been to official Soviet taste. He wrote 15 symphonies, chamber music, ballets, and operas, the latter including *Lady Macbeth of Mtsensk* 1934, which was suppressed as 'too divorced from the proletariat', but revived as *Katerina Izmaylova* in 1963.

shot[1] *n.* **1.** the discharge of a gun etc.; the sound of this; an attempt to hit something by shooting or throwing etc. **2.** a stroke or kick in a ball game. **3.** an attempt to do something. **4.** a possessor of a specified skill in shooting. **5.** a single missile for a gun etc., especially a nonexplosive projectile; a small lead pellet of which several are used for a single charge; (as *plural*) these collectively. **6.** the heavy metal ball used in shot put. **7.** a photograph; the scene photographed; a film sequence taken by one camera. **8.** the launch of a space rocket. **9.** the injection of a drug etc. **10.** (*colloquial*) a dram of spirits. **—like a shot,** very quickly; without hesitation, willingly. **shot in the arm,** a stimulus or encouragement. **shot in the dark,** a mere guess. [Old English]

shot[2] past and past participle of **shoot.** **—adj. 1.** that has been shot. **2.** (of fabric) woven or dyed so as to show different colours at different angles. **—shot through,** permeated, suffused.

shotgun *n.* a gun for firing small shot at short range. **—shotgun wedding,** one that is enforced, especially because of the bride's pregnancy.

shot put or **putting the shot** in athletics, the sport of throwing (or putting) overhand from the shoulder a metal ball (or shot). Standard shot weights are 7.26 kg/16 lb for men and 4 kg/8.8 lb for women.

should /ʃəd, *emphatic* ʃʊd/ *v.aux.* (*third person singular* **should**) past tense of **shall,** used especially in reported speech or to express obligation, condition, likelihood, or a tentative suggestion.

shoulder /ˈʃəʊldə/ *n.* **1.** the part of the body to which the arm, wing, or foreleg is attached; either lateral projection below or behind the neck. **2.** the part of a garment covering the shoulder. **3.** an animal's upper foreleg as a joint of meat. **4.** (in *plural*) the body regarded as bearing a burden, blame, etc. **5.** a part or projection resembling a human shoulder; a strip of land adjoining a metalled road surface. **—v.t./i. 1.** to push with one's shoulder; to make one's way thus. **2.** to take a burden on one's shoulders; to assume the responsibility or blame for. **—put one's shoulder to the wheel,** to make a strong effort. **shoulder arms,** to move a rifle to a position with the barrel against the shoulder and the butt in the hand. **shoulder blade,** either large flat bone of the upper back. **shoulder strap,** a strap passing over the shoulder to support something; a strap from the shoulder to the collar of a garment, especially with indication of military rank. **shoulder to shoulder,** side by side; with a united effort. **straight from the shoulder,** (of a blow) well delivered; (of criticism etc.) frank, direct. [Old English]

shouldn't /'ʃʊdənt/= should not.

shout n. 1. a loud utterance or vocal sound calling attention or expressing joy, excitement, disapproval etc. 2. (*Australian* and *New Zealand colloquial*) one's turn to buy a round of drinks. —v.t./i. 1. to emit a shout; to speak, say, or call loudly. 2. (*Australian* and *New Zealand colloquial*) to buy drinks etc. for. —**shout down,** to reduce to silence by shouting.

shove /ʃʌv/ v.t./i. to push vigorously; (*colloquial*) to put casually. —n. an act of shoving. —**shove-halfpenny** n. a game in which coins etc. are pushed along a marked board. **shove off,** to start from the shore in a boat; (*colloquial*) to depart. [Old English]

shovel /'ʃʌvəl/ n. an implement shaped like a spade with the side edges turned up, used for scooping up earth, snow, coal etc.; a machine or part of a machine with a similar function. —v.t. (-**ll**-) 1. to move with or as with a shovel. 2. to scoop or thrust roughly. —**shovel hat,** a broad-brimmed hat. —**shovelful** n. [Old English]

shovelboard n. or **shuffleboard** a game played especially on a ship's deck by pushing discs over a marked surface.

shoveler n. a freshwater duck *Anas clypeata*. The male has a green head and white and brown body plumage, and can grow up to 50 cm/1.7 ft long. The female is speckled brown. Spending the summer in N Europe or North America, it winters further south. [so named because of its long and broad, flattened beak]

Shovell /'ʃʌvəl/ Cloudesley c.1650–1707. English admiral who took part, with George Rooke (1650–1709), in the capture of Gibraltar in 1704. In 1707 his flagship *Association* was wrecked off the Isles of Scilly and he was strangled for his rings by an islander when he came ashore.

show /ʃəʊ/ v.t./i. 1. to allow or cause to be seen; to offer for inspection or viewing; to exhibit in a show. 2. to demonstrate, to point out, to prove; to cause to understand. 3. to conduct. 4. to give (specified treatment to a person or thing). 5. to be visible or noticeable. —n. 1. showing, being shown. 2. a display; a public exhibition for competition, entertainment, or advertisement etc.; a pageant; (*colloquial*) any public entertainment or performance. 3. (*slang*) a concern or undertaking; a business. 4. an outward appearance; the impression produced; ostentation, mere display. 5. a discharge of blood from the vagina in menstruation or at the start of childbirth. —**show business,** the entertainment industry. **showcase** n. a glazed case for displaying exhibits. **showdown** n. a final test or battle etc.; a disclosure of achievements or possibilities. **show one's hand,** to reveal one's intentions. **show house,** one house in an estate etc. furnished and prepared for inspection. **showjumping** n. competitive jumping on horseback. **show off,** to display to advantage; to act in a flamboyant way in order to impress. **show-off** n. a person who shows off. **show of hands,** the raising of hands to vote for or against a proposal etc. **showpiece** n. an excellent specimen suitable for display. **showplace** n. an attractive or much visited place. **show trial,** a judicial trial regarded as intended mainly to impress public opinion. **show up,** to make or be visible or conspicuous; to expose or humiliate; (*colloquial*) to appear or arrive. [Old English]

shower /'ʃaʊə/ n. 1. a brief fall of rain or snow etc., or of bullets, stones, dust etc.; a sudden copious arrival of gifts or honours etc. 2. (in full **shower bath**) a bath in which water is sprayed from above; a room or device for this. 3. (*slang*) a contemptible or unpleasant person or group. 4. (*US*) a party for giving gifts, especially to a prospective bride. —v.t./i. 1. to descend in a shower. 2. to discharge (water or missiles etc.) in a shower; to bestow (gifts etc.) lavishly. 3. to use a shower bath. [Old English]

showery /'ʃaʊərɪ/ adj. (of weather) with many showers.

showing n. a display or performance; the quality or appearance of a performance or achievement etc.; the evidence or putting of a case.

showman n. (*plural* **showmen**) 1. a proprietor or organizer of public entertainment. 2. a person skilled in showmanship.

showmanship n. capacity for exhibiting one's goods or capabilities to the best advantage.

shown past participle of **show**.

showroom n. a room where goods are displayed or kept for inspection.

showy /'ʃəʊɪ/ adj. making a good or conspicuous display; gaudy. —**showily** adv., **showiness** n.

shrank past of **shrink**.

shrapnel /'ʃræpnəl/ n. 1. fragments of exploded bombs or shells. 2. an artillery shell containing metal pieces which it scatters on explosion. [from Gen H *Shrapnel* (1761–1842), British army officer who invented this shell about 1804]

shred n. 1. a piece torn, scraped, or broken off; a scrap or fragment. 2. the least amount. —v.t. (-**dd**-) to tear or cut into shreds. —**shredder** n. [Old English]

shrew /ʃruː/ n. 1. a small, insectivorous, mouselike animal of the family Soricidae, with a long snout, found in Eurasia and the Americas. Its high metabolic rate means that it must eat almost constantly. 2. a bad-tempered or scolding woman. [Old English]

shrewd /ʃruːd/ adj. showing astute powers of judgement, clever and judicious. —**shrewdly** adv., **shrewdness** n.

shrewish adj. scolding, bad-tempered.

shriek /ʃriːk/ n. a shrill scream or sound. —v.t./i. to make a shriek; to say in shrill tones. [imitative]

shrift n. (*archaic*) confession and absolution. —**short shrift,** see ◊short. [Old English from Latin *scribere* = write]

shrike n. or **butcherbird** a bird of the family Laniidae, with a strong hooked and toothed bill. There are over 70 species, living mostly in Africa but also in Eurasia and North America. They often impale insects and small vertebrates on thorns. They can grow to 35 cm/14 in long, and have grey, black, or brown plumage.

shrill adj. piercing and high-pitched in sound. —v.t./i. to sound or utter shrilly. —**shrilly** adv., **shrillness** n. [related to Low German *schrell* = sharp in tone]

shrimp n. 1. a small, edible crustacean related to the ◊prawn, especially of the genus *Crangon*, pink when boiled. It has a cylindrical, semitransparent body, with ten jointed legs. Some shrimps grow up to 25 cm/10 in long. 2. (*colloquial*) a very small person. —v.i. to go in search of shrimps.

shrine n. 1. a place for special worship or devotion. 2. a tomb or casket containing sacred relics. 3. a place hallowed by some memory or association etc. [Old English from Latin *scrinium* = bookcase]

shrink v.t./i. (*past* **shrank**; *past participle* **shrunk** or (*especially as adj.*) **shrunken**) 1. to make or become smaller, especially by the action of moisture, heat, or cold. 2. to draw back so as to avoid something; to withdraw; to be averse (from an action). —n. 1. the act of shrinking. 2. (*slang*, short for *headshrinker*) a psychiatrist. —**shrink-wrap** v.t. to enclose (an article) in material that shrinks tightly round it. [Old English]

shrinkage n. 1. the process or amount of shrinking. 2. (in commerce) loss by theft or wastage etc.

shrive v.t. (*past* **shrove**; *past participle* **shriven** /'ʃrɪvən/) (*archaic*) in the Christian church, to hear the confession of and give absolution to; to submit (oneself) for this. [Old English = impose as penance from Latin *scribere* = write]

shrivel /'ʃrɪvəl/ v.t./i. (-**ll**-) to contract into a wrinkled or curled-up state.

Shropshire /'ʃrɒpʃə/ county in W England. Sometimes abbreviated to **Salop,** it was officially so known from 1974 until local protest reversed the decision in 1980; **area** 3,490 sq km/1,347 sq mi; **administrative headquarters** Shrewsbury; **physical** bisected, on the Welsh border, NW to SE by the river Severn; Ellesmere, the largest of several lakes; the Clee Hills rise to about 610 m/1,800 ft in the SW; **products** chiefly agricultural: sheep and cattle; **population** (1987) 397,000.

shroud n. 1. a winding sheet. 2. something that conceals. 3. (in *plural*) the ropes supporting a ship's mast. —v.t. 1. to clothe (a corpse) for burial. 2. to cover and conceal or disguise. —**shroud of Turin,** a Christian relic; see ◊Turin shroud. [Old English]

shrove past of ◊shrive.

Shrovetide n. Shrove Tuesday and the two preceding days.

Shrove Tuesday in the Christian calendar, the day before the beginning of Lent, on which it was customary to be shriven. It is also known as **Mardi Gras**.

shrub n. a perennial woody plant that typically produces several separate stems, at or near ground level, rather than the single trunk of most trees. A shrub is usually smaller than a tree, but there is no clear distinction between large shrubs and small trees. —**shrubby** adj. [from Old English = shrubbery]

shrubbery n. an area planted with shrubs.

shrug v.t./i. (-gg-) to raise (one's shoulders) slightly and momentarily to express indifference, helplessness, doubt, etc. —n. a shrugging movement. —**shrug off**, to dismiss as unimportant.

shrunk past participle of **shrink**.

shrunken n. see ◊shrink.

shudder n. a sudden or convulsive shivering or quivering; a vibrating motion. —v.i. 1. to experience a shudder; to feel strong repugnance or fear etc. 2. to vibrate strongly. [from Middle Dutch or Middle Low German]

shuffle v.t./i. 1. to walk without lifting the feet clear of the ground; to move (one's feet) thus. 2. to slide (cards) over one another so as to change their order; to rearrange, to jumble. 3. to keep shifting one's position; to prevaricate, to be evasive. —n. 1. a shuffling movement or walk; a shuffling dance. 2. shuffling of cards etc. 3. a general rearrangement. —**shuffleboard**, another spelling of ◊shovelboard. **shuffle off**, to remove or get rid of. —**shuffler** n. [from Low German = walk clumsily]

Shultz /ʃults/ George P 1920–　. US Republican politician, economics adviser to President ◊Reagan 1980–82 and secretary of state 1982–89.

shun v.t. (-nn-) to avoid, to keep away from; to abstain from. [Old English]

shunt v.t./i. 1. to move (a train etc.) to another track; (of a train) to be shunted. 2. to move or put aside; to redirect. —n. 1. shunting, being shunted. 2. a conductor joining two points of an electrical circuit for the diversion of current. 3. in surgery, an alternative path for the circulation of blood. 4. (slang) a collision of vehicles, especially nose to tail. —**shunter** n.

shush interjection meaning hush! —v.t./i. to call for silence (from); to be silent. [imitative]

shut v.t./i. (-tt-; past and past participle **shut**) 1. to move (a door, window, lid etc.) into position to block an opening; (of a door etc.) to move or admit of being moved thus; to shut the door or lid etc. of (a room, box, eye etc.). 2. to bring (a book, telescope etc.) into a folded-up or contracted state. 3. to catch or pinch (a finger, dress, etc.) by shutting something on it. 4. to bar access to (a place). —**be shut of**, (slang) to be rid of. **shut down**, to cease working or business, either at the end of a day or permanently; to cause to do this. **shutdown** n. this process. **shuteye** n. (slang) sleep. **shut off**, to stop the flow of (water, gas etc.); to separate from society etc. **shut up**, to shut securely or permanently; to imprison; to put away in a box etc.; (colloquial, especially in imperative) to stop talking. **shut up shop**, to cease business or work at the end of the day or permanently. [Old English]

Shute /ʃuːt/ Nevil. Pen name of English novelist Nevil Shute Norway 1899–1960. Among his books are A Town Like Alice 1949 and On the Beach 1957.

shutter n. 1. a movable hinged cover for a window. 2. a device that opens and closes the lens aperture of a camera to allow light to fall on the film. —v.t. to provide with shutters. —**put up the shutters**, to cease business at the end of the day or permanently.

shuttle n. 1. a holder carrying the weft thread to and fro between the threads of the warp in weaving. 2. a moving holder carrying the lower thread in a sewing machine. 3. a vehicle used in a shuttle service; a ◊space shuttle. 4. a shuttlecock. —v.t./i. to move, travel, or send to and fro. —**shuttle diplomacy**, negotiations conducted by a mediator who travels to several countries at brief intervals. **shuttle service**, a transport system operating to and fro over a relatively short distance. [Old English = a dart]

shuttlecock n. a small, rounded piece of cork etc. with a ring of feathers attached, or of other material made in this shape, struck to and fro with a battledore in the old game of battledore and shuttlecock, and with a racket in badminton.

shy[1] /ʃaɪ/ adj. 1. timid and lacking self-confidence in the presence of others; avoiding company; reserved; (of behaviour) showing shyness. 2. (of an animal) timid and avoiding observation. 3. (as suffix) showing fear or distaste of (e.g. workshy). —v.i. to jump or move suddenly in alarm. —n. an act of shying. —**shy of**, wary of. [Old English]

shy[2] v.t. (colloquial) to fling or throw. —n. (colloquial) a throw.

shyster /ˈʃaɪstə/ n. (colloquial) a person who acts unscrupulously or unprofessionally.

si /siː/ n. in music, te. [perhaps from initials of Sancte Iohannes (see ◊gamut)]

Si symbol for ◊silicon.

SI abbreviation of Système International (d'Unités); see ◊SI units. [French = International System (of Units)]

sial n. in geochemistry and geophysics, the substance of the Earth's continental ◊crust, as distinct from the sima of the ocean crust. [from silica and alumina, its two main chemical constituents]

siamang n. the largest ◊gibbon Symphalangus syndactylus, native to Malaysia and Sumatra. Siamangs have a large throat pouch to amplify the voice, making the territorial 'song' extremely loud. They are black-haired, up to 90 cm/3 ft tall, with very long arms (a span of 150 cm/5 ft).

Siamese /saɪəˈmiːz/ adj. of Siam or its people or language. —n. 1. a native or the language (also called ◊Thai) of Siam. 2. a Siamese cat. —**Siamese cat**, a cat of a breed with short, pale fur and dark markings. **Siamese twins**, identical twins that are physically conjoined at birth. [from Siam, former name of Thailand]

sib n. a sibling. [Old English]

Sibelius /siˈbeɪliəs/ Jean (Christian) 1865–1957. Finnish composer. His works include nationalistic symphonic poems such as En Saga 1893 and Finlandia 1900, a violin concerto 1904, and seven symphonies.

Siberia /saɪˈbɪəriə/ Asian region of the USSR, extending from the Urals to the Pacific; it was used from the 18th century to exile political and criminal prisoners; **area** 12,050,000 sq km/4,650,000 sq mi; **towns** Novosibirsk, Omsk, Krasnoyarsk, Irkutsk; **products** hydroelectric power from rivers Lena, Ob, and Yenisei; forestry; mineral resources, including gold, diamonds, oil, natural gas, iron, copper, nickel, cobalt.

sibilant /ˈsɪbɪlənt/ adj. sounded with a hiss; hissing. —n. a sibilant letter or sound. —**sibilance** n., **sibilancy** n. [from Latin sibilare = hiss]

Sibley /ˈsɪbli/ Antoinette 1939–　. British dancer. Joining the Royal Ballet in 1956, she became senior soloist in 1960. Her roles included Odette/Odile, Giselle, and the betrayed girl in The Rake's Progress.

sibling n. each of two or more children having one or both parents in common. [from sib]

sibyl /ˈsɪbɪl/ n. any of the women who in ancient times acted as the reputed mouthpiece of a god, uttering prophecies and oracles. —**Sibyl**, in Roman mythology, a priestess of Apollo. She offered to sell to ◊Tarquinius nine collections of prophecies, the **Sibylline Books**, but the price was too high. When she had destroyed all but three, he bought those for the identical price, and these were kept for consultation in emergency at Rome. [from Old French or Latin from Greek Sibulla]

sibylline /ˈsɪbɪlaɪn/ adj. issuing from a sibyl; oracular, mysteriously prophetic. [from Latin]

sic /sɪk/ adv. thus used, spelled etc. (used in brackets to confirm or call attention to the form of quoted words). [Latin = thus]

Sichuan /sɪtʃˈwɑːn/ or **Szechwan** province of central China; **area** 569,000 sq km/219,634 sq mi; **capital** Chengdu; **physical** surrounded by mountains; **products** rice, coal, oil, natural gas; **population** (1986) 103,200,000.

Sicily /ˈsɪsəli/ (Italian Sicilia) largest Mediterranean island, an autonomous region of Italy; **area** 25,700 sq km/9,920 sq mi; **capital** Palermo; **physical** includes the islands of ◊Lipari, Egadi, Ustica, and ◊Pantelleria; Etna, 3,323 m/10,906 ft high, is the highest volcano in Europe; **exports** Marsala wine, olives, citrus fruits, refined oil and petrochemicals, pharmaceuticals, potash, asphalt, and marble; **population** (1988) 5,141,000.

sick adj. 1. physically or mentally unwell, feeling the effects of a disease. 2. vomiting, tending to vomit. 3. of or for those who are sick (sickbed, sickroom etc.). 4. greatly distressed or disgusted. 5. (of humour) finding amusement in misfortune or in morbid subjects. —v.t. (colloquial) to vomit (especially with up). —**be sick**, to vomit. **sickbay** n. a room or rooms for sick people in an institution or on a ship etc. **sick of,** tired of, bored with through having already had too much of. [Old English]

sick building syndrome a malaise diagnosed in the early 1980s among office workers and thought to be caused by such pollutants as formaldehyde (from furniture and insulating materials), benzene (from paint), and the solvent trichloroethylene, concentrated in air-conditioned buildings. Symptoms include headache, sore throat, tiredness, colds, and flu. Studies have found that it can cause a 40% drop in productivity and a 30% rise in absenteeism.

sicken *v.t./i.* to make or become sick or disgusted etc. —**sicken for,** to be in the first stages of (an illness).

Sickert /'sɪkət/ Walter (Richard) 1860–1942. English artist. His Impressionist cityscapes of London and Venice, portraits, and domestic and music-hall interiors capture subtleties of tone and light, often with a melancholy atmosphere.

sickle *n.* **1.** a harvesting tool with a curved blade and a short handle. It was widely used in the Middle East and Europe for cutting wheat, barley, and oats from about 10,000 BC to the 19th century. **2.** something shaped like this. —**sickle cell,** a sickle-shaped red blood corpuscle. [Old English, from Latin *sicula* (*secare* = cut)]

sickle-cell disease a hereditary chronic blood disorder common among people of black African descent. It is characterized by distortion and fragility of the red blood cells, which are lost too rapidly from the circulation. This often results in ◊anaemia.

sickly *adj.* **1.** liable to be ill, of weak health. **2.** unhealthy-looking, faint, pale. **3.** causing ill health. **4.** inducing or connected with nausea; mawkish, weakly sentimental. —**sickliness** *n.*

sickness *n.* **1.** being ill, disease. **2.** a specified disease. **3.** vomiting.

Siddons /'sɪdnz/ Sarah 1755–1831. Welsh actress. Her majestic presence made her suited to tragic and heroic roles such as Lady Macbeth, Zara in Congreve's *The Mourning Bride*, and Constance in *King John*.

side *n.* **1.** any of the surfaces bounding an object, especially the vertical inner or outer surface or one of those distinguished from the top and bottom or front and back or ends. **2.** in mathematics, each of the lines bounding a triangle, rectangle etc.; each of the two quantities stated to be equal in an equation. **3.** either surface of a thing regarded as having only two; the amount of writing filling one side of a sheet of paper. **4.** the right or left part of a person's or animal's body; the corresponding half of a carcass. **5.** a direction; the part of an object or place etc. that faces a specified direction or is on an observer's right or left. **6.** the region to the right or left of (or nearer or further than) a real or imaginary dividing line; the part or area near the edge or away from the centre. **7.** a partial aspect of a thing; an aspect differing from or opposed to other aspects. **8.** each of two sets of opponents at war or competing in some way; the cause represented by these. **9.** the line of descent through one parent. **10.** (in billiards etc.) the spinning motion given to a ball by striking it on one side. **11.** (*slang*) assumption of superiority, swagger. —in combinations, **1.** situated at or directed to or from a side (e.g. *side door, side glance*). **2.** secondary, minor, incidental (e.g. *side effect, side issue, side street*). —*v.i.* to take part or be on the same side. —**sided** *adj.* having a specified number or type of sides. —**by the side of,** close to; compared with. **on one side,** not in the main or central position; aside. **on the side,** as a sideline. **on the —side,** somewhat. **side by side,** standing close together, especially for mutual encouragement. **sidecar** *n.* a passenger car attachable to the side of a motorcycle. **side drum** *n.* a small double-headed drum. **side-saddle** *n.* a saddle enabling a rider to have both feet on the same side of a horse; (*adv.*) sitting thus on a horse. **sideshow** *n.* a small show at a fair or exhibition; a minor or subsidiary activity or affair. **sideslip** *n.* a skid, a movement sideways; (*v.i.*) to move sideways. **side-splitting** *adj.* causing hearty laughter. **sidestep** *n.* a step sideways; (*v.t.*) to avoid by stepping sideways; to evade (an issue etc.). **sideswipe** *n.* a glancing blow along the side; an indirect or incidental criticism etc.; (*v.t.*) to hit with a sideswipe. **sidetrack** *v.t.* to divert (a person) from the main course or issue. **side whiskers** *n.pl.* those growing on the cheek. **side wind,** a wind coming from one side. [Old English]

Sidney *Renaissance man Philip Sidney was a poet, politician, courtier, and soldier.*

sideboard *n.* a table or flat-topped chest with drawers and cupboards for china etc.

sideburns *n.pl.* short side whiskers. [from US general *Burnside* (1824–1881), who sported a moustache, whiskers, and clean-shaven chin]

sidekick *n.* (*US colloquial*) a close associate; a subordinate member of a pair or group.

sidelight *n.* **1.** light from the side. **2.** a piece of incidental information about a subject etc. **3.** each of a pair of small lights at the front of a vehicle. **4.** a light at the side of a moving ship.

sideline *n.* **1.** work etc. carried on in addition to one's main activity. **2.** (in *plural*) the lines bounding the sides of a football pitch etc.; the space just outside these. **3.** a place for spectators as distinct from participants.

sidelong *adj.* directed to the side, oblique. —*adv.* to the side.

sidereal /saɪ'dɪərɪəl/ *adj.* of or determined by means of the stars. —**sidereal day,** the time between successive passages of any given star over a meridian. [from Latin *sidereus* (*sidus* = star)]

sidesman *n.* (*plural* **sidesmen**) an assistant churchwarden who takes the collection etc.

sidewalk *n.* (*US*) a pavement at the side of a road.

sideways *adj.* & *adv.* **1.** with the side foremost. **2.** to or from one side.

sidewinder *n.* a rattlesnake *Crotalus cerastes* that lives in the deserts of the SW USA and Mexico, and moves by throwing its coils sideways across the sand. It can grow up to 75 cm/2.5 ft long.

siding /'saɪdɪŋ/ *n.* a short railway track to the side of a railway line, used for shunting.

Siding Spring Mountain a peak 400 km/250 mi NW of Sydney, site of the 3.9 m/154 in **Anglo-Australian Telescope,** opened in 1974, which was the first big telescope to be fully computer-controlled. It is one of the most powerful telescopes in the southern hemisphere.

sidle /'saɪdəl/ *v.i.* to walk obliquely; to move timidly or furtively. [back formation from *sideling* = sidelong]

Sidney /'sɪdni/ Philip 1554–1586. English poet and soldier, author of the sonnet sequence *Astrophel and Stella* 1591, *Arcadia* 1590, a prose romance, and *Apologie for Poetrie* 1595, the earliest work of English literary criticism. He entered Parliament in 1581. In 1585 he was made governor of Flushing in the Netherlands, and died at Zutphen, fighting the Spaniards.

siege /siːdʒ/ *n.* the surrounding and blockading of a fortified place; the surrounding by the police etc. of a house occupied by a gunman etc. —**lay siege to,** to conduct a siege of. **raise a siege,** to end it. [from Old French *sege* = seat]

Siegel /'siːgəl/ Don(ald) 1912– . US film director who made thrillers, Westerns, and police dramas. He also directed *Invasion of the Body Snatchers* 1956. His other films include *Madigan* 1968, *Dirty Harry* 1971, and *The Shootist* 1976.

Siegfried /'siːgfriːd, German 'ziːkfriːt/ legendary Germanic hero, also known as ◊Sigurd. It is uncertain whether his story has a historical basis, but it was current about

AD 700. In the poems of the Norse Elder ◊Edda and in the prose Völsunga Saga, Siegfried appears under the name of ◊Sigurd. A version of the story is in the German *Nibelungenlied/Song of the Nibelung.*

Siegfried Line in World War I, the defensive line established in 1918 by the Germans in France; in World War II, the Allies' name for the West Wall, the German defensive line established along its western frontier, from the Netherlands to Switzerland.

siemens /ˈsiːmənz/ n. the SI unit (symbol S) of electrical conductance, the reciprocal of the ◊impedance of an electrical circuit. One siemens equals one ampere per volt. It was formerly called the mho or reciprocal ohm. [from E W von *Siemens*]

Siemens German family of four brothers, creators of a vast industrial empire. The eldest, **Ernst Werner von Siemens** (1812–1892), founded the original electrical firm of Siemens und Halske in 1847 and made many advances in telegraphy. **William (Karl Wilhelm)** (1823–1883) moved to England and perfected the open-hearth production of steel, pioneered the development of the electric locomotive and the laying of transoceanic cables, and improved the electric generator.

Sienkiewicz /ʃɛŋkiˈeɪvɪtʃ/ Henryk 1846–1916. Polish author. His books include *Quo Vadis?* 1895, set in Rome at the time of Nero, and the 17th-century historical trilogy *With Fire and Sword, The Deluge,* and *Pan Michael* 1890–93.

sienna /siˈenə/ n. a kind of clay used as a pigment; its colour of reddish-brown (**burnt sienna**) or yellowish-brown (**raw sienna**). [from *Siena* in Italy]

sierra /siˈerə/ n. a long, jagged mountain chain in Spain or Spanish America. [Spanish, from Latin *serra* = saw]

Sierra Leone /siˈerə liˈəʊn/ Republic of; country in W Africa, on the Atlantic, bounded to the N and E by Guinea and to the SE by Liberia; **area** 71,740 sq km/27,710 sq mi; **capital** Freetown; **physical** mountains in E; hills and forest; coastal mangrove swamps; **head of state and government** Joseph Saidu Momoh from 1985; **political system** one-party republic; **exports** palm kernels, cocoa, coffee, ginger, diamonds, bauxite, rutile; **population** (1990 est) 4,168,000; **language** English (official); local languages; **recent history** independence was achieved from Britain within the Commonwealth in 1961. An army revolt in 1968 was followed by a new constitution in 1971, making Sierra Leone a republic with Siaka Stevens as president. Stevens retired in 1985. An attempted coup against his successor Momoh in 1989 was foiled.

Sierra Madre /siˈerə ˈmɑːdreɪ/ chief mountain system of Mexico, consisting of three ranges, enclosing the central plateau of the country; highest point Pico de Orizaba 5,700 m/18,700 ft. The Sierra Madre del Sur [= of the south] runs along the SW Pacific coast.

siesta n. an afternoon nap or rest, especially in hot countries. [Spanish, from Latin *sexta (hora)* = sixth hour]

sieve /sɪv/ n. a utensil with a network or perforated bottom through which liquids or fine particles can pass while solid or coarser matter is retained, or used for reducing a soft mixture pressed through it to a uniform pulp. —*v.t.* to put through a sieve. [Old English]

sievert n. the SI unit (symbol Sv) of radiation dose equivalent. It is defined as the absorbed dose of ionizing radiation (modified to account for different types of radiation causing different effects in biological tissue) of one joule per kilogram. One sievert equals 100 ◊rem. [from Swedish physicist Rolf *Sievert* (1896–1966)]

Sieyes /siːˈeɪjes/ Emmanuel-Joseph 1748–1836. French cleric and constitutional theorist who led the bourgeois attack on royal and aristocratic privilege in the ◊States General (parliament) 1788–89. Active in the early years of the French Revolution, he later retired from politics, but re-emerged as an organizer of the coup that brought Napoleon I to power in 1799.

sift v.t./i. **1.** to separate with or cause to pass through a sieve. **2.** to sprinkle (flour etc.) from a sieve or perforated container. **3.** to subject (information etc.) to close scrutiny or analysis. **4.** (of snow etc.) to fall as if from a sieve. —**sifter** n. [Old English]

sigh /saɪ/ n. a long deep audible breath expressing sadness, weariness, longing, relief etc.; an act of making this; a sound resembling it. —*v.t./i.* **1.** to make a sigh; to express

with sighs. **2.** to yearn *for* a person or thing desired or lost. [Old English]

sight /saɪt/ n. **1.** the faculty of perception through the response of the brain to the action of light on the ◊eye. **2.** seeing, being seen. **3.** the range of vision; the region open to vision. **4.** the way of regarding something, opinion. **5.** a thing seen or visible or worth seeing; (in *plural*) the noteworthy or attractive features of a town etc. **6.** a person or thing regarded as unsightly or ridiculous-looking. **7.** a precise aim with a gun or observation with an optical instrument; a device for assisting this. **8.** (*colloquial*) a great quantity. —*v.t.* **1.** to get a sight of, to observe the presence of. **2.** to aim (a gun etc.) by using the sights. —**at first sight,** on the first glimpse or impression. **at** *or* **on sight,** as soon as a person or thing is seen. **catch sight of,** to begin to see or be aware of. **in sight,** visible, imminent. **set one's sights on,** to be determined to acquire or achieve etc. a **sight for sore eyes,** a person or thing one is delighted to see. **sight-read** *v.t.* to read (music) at sight, without preliminary practice or study of the score. **sightscreen** n. in cricket, a large, white screen placed near the boundary in line with the wicket to help the batsman see the ball. **sight unseen,** without previous inspection. [Old English]

sighted adj. having sight, not blind.

sightless adj. blind.

sightly adj. attractive to look at. —**sightliness** n.

sightseer n. a person visiting the sights of a place. —**sightseeing** n.

Sigismund /ˈsɪɡɪsmənd/ 1368–1437. Holy Roman emperor from 1411. He convened and presided over the council of Constance 1414–18, where he promised protection to the religious reformer ◊Huss, but imprisoned him after his condemnation for heresy and acquiesced in his burning. King of Bohemia from 1419, he led the military campaign against the ◊Hussites.

sigma /ˈsɪɡmə/ n. the 18th letter of the Greek alphabet (σ, Σ) = s. [Latin from Greek]

Sigma Octantis /ˈsɪɡmə ɒkˈtæntɪs/ the star closest to the south celestial pole (see ◊celestial sphere), in effect the southern equivalent of ◊Polaris, although far less conspicuous. Situated just less than 1° from the south celestial pole in the constellation Octans, Sigma Octantis is 120 light years away.

sign /saɪn/ n. **1.** a thing perceived that suggests the existence of a fact, quality, or condition, either past, present, or future. **2.** a mark or device with a special meaning, a symbol. **3.** a motion or gesture used instead of words to convey information, a demand etc. **4.** each of the 12 divisions of the ◊zodiac. **5.** a publicly displayed symbol or device giving information; a signboard. —*v.t./i.* **1.** to write one's name on (a document) to show its authenticity or one's agreement or acceptance; to write (one's name) thus. **2.** to engage or be engaged by signing a contract. **3.** to indicate or communicate by a gesture. —**sign away,** to relinquish a right to by signing. **sign language,** a series of signs used by deaf or dumb people for communication. **sign off,** to end work or a contract etc.; to indicate the end of a broadcast etc. **sign on,** to sign a contract of employment etc.; to register oneself (e.g. as available for employment); to indicate the start of a broadcast etc. [from Old French from Latin *signum* = mark, token]

Signac /siːnˈjæk/ Paul 1863–1935. French artist. In 1884 he joined with Georges Seurat in founding the *Société des Artistes Indépendants* and developing the technique of ◊Pointillism.

signal /ˈsɪɡnəl/ n. **1.** a sign (especially a prearranged one) conveying information or giving an instruction; a message made up of such signs. **2.** a device on a railway giving instructions or warnings to train drivers etc. (◊semaphore). **3.** an event which causes immediate activity. **4.** transmitted electrical impulses or radio waves; a sequence of these. —*v.t./i.* (-ll-) to make a signal or signals (to); to transmit or announce by a signal; to direct by a signal. —*adj.* remarkably good or bad, noteworthy. —**signal box,** a building from which railway signals are controlled. —**signaller** n. [from Old French from Latin *signalis*]

signalize v.t. to make noteworthy or remarkable.

signally adv. remarkably, notably.

signalman n. (*plural* **signalmen**) a person responsible for displaying or operating signals.

signatory /'sɪgnətərɪ/ *adj.* that has signed an agreement, especially a treaty. —*n.* a signatory party, especially a state.

signature /'sɪgnətʃə/ *n.* **1.** a person's name or initials used in signing. **2.** the act of signing. **3.** in music, a sign put after the clef to indicate the key or time. **4.** a section of a book made from one sheet folded and cut; a letter or figure indicating a sequence of these. —**signature tune,** a tune used, especially in broadcasting, to announce a particular programme or performer etc. [from Latin *signatura* (*signare* = to mark)]

signboard *n.* a board with a name or symbol etc. displayed outside a shop or hotel etc.

signet /'sɪgnɪt/ *n.* a small seal used with or instead of a person's signature. —**signet ring,** a finger ring with a signet set in it. [from Old French or Latin *signum* = mark, token]

significance /sɪg'nɪfɪkəns/ *n.* **1.** signifying. **2.** what is meant. **3.** importance. —**significancy** *n.* [Old French or from Latin]

significant *adj.* **1.** having or conveying a meaning, especially an important or noteworthy one. **2.** important. —**significant figure,** in mathematics, a digit conveying information about a number containing it, and not a zero used simply to fill a vacant place at the beginning or end. —**significantly** *adv.* [from Latin]

signify *v.t./i.* **1.** to be a sign, symbol, or indication of. **2.** to mean, to have as a meaning. **3.** to make known. **4.** to be of importance. —**signification** /-fɪ'keɪʃən/ *n.* [from Old French from Latin *significare* (*signum* = mark and *facere* = make)]

signor /'siːnjɔː/ *n.* (plural *signori* /-'njɔːrɪ/) the title used of or to an Italian man. [Italian from Latin = senior]

signora /siːn'jɔːrə/ *n.* the title used of or to an Italian married woman.

signorina /siːnjə'riːnə/ *n.* the title used of or to an Italian unmarried woman.

signpost *n.* a post bearing a sign, especially one indicating direction. —*v.t.* to provide with a post or posts of this kind.

Sigurd /'sɪguəd/ in Norse mythology, a hero who appears in both the ◊*Nibelungenlied/Song of the Nibelung* (under his German name of ◊Siegfried) and the ◊*Edda.*

Sihanouk /siːə'nuːk/ Norodom 1922– . Cambodian politician, king 1941–55, prime minister 1955–70, when his government was overthrown by a military coup led by Lon Nol. With Pol Pot's resistance front, he overthrew Lon Nol in 1975 and again became prime minister 1975–76, when he was forced to resign by the ◊Khmer Rouge.

Sikh /siːk, sɪk/ *n.* an adherent of Sikhism. [Hindi = disciple, from Sanskrit]

Sikhism /'siːkɪzəm, 'sɪ-‒'siːkɪzəm, 'sɪ-/ *n.* a religion professed by 16 million Indians, living mainly in the Punjab. Sikhism was founded by Nanak (1469–*c.*1539). Sikhs believe in a single God who is the immortal creator of the universe and who has never been incarnate in any form, and in the equality of all human beings; Sikhism is strongly opposed to caste divisions. Their holy book is the ◊*Guru Granth Sahib.* Guru Gobind Singh (1666–1708) instituted the Khanda-di-Pahul, the Baptism of the Sword, and established the *Khalsa* ('pure'), the company of the faithful. The Khalsa wear the five Ks: *kes,* long hair; *kangha,* a comb; *kirpan,* a sword; *kachh,* short trousers; and *kara,* a steel bracelet. Sikh men take the last name 'Singh' ('lion') and women 'Kaur' ('princess').

Sikh Wars two wars in India between the Sikhs and the British: The **First Sikh War** 1845–46 followed an invasion of British India by Punjabi Sikhs. The Sikhs were defeated and part of their territory annexed. The **Second Sikh War** 1848–49 arose from a Sikh revolt in Multan. They were defeated, and the British annexed the Punjab.

Sikkim /'sɪkɪm/ or **Denjong** state of NE India; formerly a protected state, it was absorbed by India in 1975, the monarchy being abolished. China does not recognize India's sovereignty; **area** 7,300 sq km/2,818 mi; **capital** Gangtok; **physical** in the Himalayas; highest peak Mount Kangchenjunga (8,600 m/28,216 ft); **products** rice, grain, tea, fruit, soya beans, carpets, cigarettes, lead, zinc, copper; **population** (1981) 316,000; **language** Bhutia, Lepecha, Khaskura (Nepali), all official.

Sikorski /si'kɔːski/ Wladyslaw 1881–1943. Polish general and statesman; prime minister 1922–23, and 1939–45 of the Polish government-in-exile in London during World War II. He was killed in an aeroplane crash near Gibraltar in controversial circumstances.

Sikorsky Igor 1889–1972. Ukrainian-born US engineer who built the first successful helicopter. He emigrated to the USA in 1918, where he first constructed multi-engined flying boats. His first helicopter (the VS300) flew in 1939 and a commercial version (the R3) went into production in 1943.

silage *n.* **1.** storage in a ◊silo. **2.** green fodder so stored. [alteration from *ensilage* after *silo*]

Silbury Hill a steep, rounded, artificial mound (40 m/130 ft high) of the Bronze Age about 2660 BC, in Wiltshire, near ◊Avebury, England. Excavation has shown it not to be a barrow (grave), as was previously thought.

Silchester /'sɪltʃɪstə/ archaeological site, a major town in Roman Britain. It is 10 km/6 mi N of Basingstoke, Hampshire.

silence /'saɪləns/ *n.* **1.** absence of sound. **2.** avoidance of or abstinence from speech or making a noise. **3.** avoidance of mentioning a thing or of betraying a secret etc. —*v.t.* to make silent by coercion or superior argument; to stop the sound of. —**in silence,** without speech or other sound. [from Old French or Latin *silentium*]

silencer *n.* **1.** (*North American* **muffler**) a device in the exhaust system of cars and motorbikes. Gases leave the engine at supersonic speeds, and the exhaust system and silencer are designed to slow them down, thereby silencing them. **2.** a device for reducing the noise made by a gun.

silent /'saɪlənt/ *adj.* not speaking; not making or accompanied by a sound; saying little. —**silent majority,** people of moderate opinions who rarely make themselves heard. —**silently** *adv.* [from Latin *silēre* = be silent]

Silesia /saɪ'liːzɪə/ a long-disputed region of Europe because of its geographical position, mineral resources, and industrial potential; now in Poland and Czechoslovakia. Dispute began in the 17th century with claims on the area by both Austria and Prussia. It was seized by Prussia's Frederick the Great, which started the War of the ◊Austrian Succession; this was finally recognized by Austria in 1763, after the Seven Years' War. After World War I, it was divided in 1919 among newly formed Czechoslovakia, revived Poland, and Germany, which retained the major part. In 1945, after World War II, all German Silesia east of the Oder-Neisse line was transferred to Polish administration; about ten million inhabitants of German origin, both there and in Czechoslovak Silesia, were expelled.

silhouette /sɪlu:'et/ *n.* **1.** a picture of a person in profile or of a thing in outline only, either dark against a light background or vice versa, or cut out in pages (a common pictorial technique in the late 18th and early 19th centuries). **2.** an appearance of a person or thing against the light so that only the outline is distinguishable. —*v.t.* to represent or (usually in *passive*) show in silhouette. [from Étienne de *Silhouette* (1709–1767), French author and politician, amateur maker of paper cutouts]

silica /'sɪlɪkə/ *n.* silicon dioxide, SiO_2, the composition of the most common mineral group, of which the most familiar form is quartz. Other silica forms are ◊chalcedony, chert, opal, tridymite, and cristobalite. Chalcedony includes some semiprecious forms: gem varieties include agate, onyx, sardonyx, carnelian, and tiger's eye. —**siliceous** /sɪ'lɪʃəs/ *adj.* [from Latin *silex* = flint]

silicate /'sɪlɪkeɪt/ *n.* a compound containing silicon and oxygen combined together as a negative ion (◊anion), together with one or more metal ◊cations.

silicon /'sɪlɪkən/ *n.* a brittle, nonmetallic element, symbol Si, atomic number 14, relative atomic mass 28.086. It is the second most abundant element (after oxygen) in the Earth's crust and occurs in amorphous and crystalline forms. In nature it is found only in combination with other elements, chiefly with oxygen in silica (silicon dioxide, SiO_2) and silicates. These form the mineral ◊quartz, which makes up most sands, gravels, and beaches. —**silicon chip,** an ◊integrated circuit with microscopically small electrical components on a piece of silicon crystal only a few millimetres square. **Silicon Valley,** nickname of Santa Clara County, California, since the 1950s the site of many high-technology electronic firms, whose prosperity is based on the silicon chip. [Latin *silicium* = silica]

silicone /'sɪlɪkəʊn/ *n.* one of many polymeric organic compounds of silicon with high resistance to cold, heat, water, and the passage of electricity, used in polishes, paints, lubricants etc.

silicosis /sɪlɪ'kəʊsɪs/ *n.* a chronic disease of miners and stone cutters who inhale ◊silica dust, which makes the lung tissues fibrous and less capable of aerating the blood. It is a form of ◊pneumoconiosis.

silk *n.* **1.** the fine, soft, strong fibre produced by a silkworm in making its cocoon; thread or cloth made from or resembling this; (in *plural*) clothing made from silk. The introduction of synthetics originally harmed the silk industry, but rising standards of living have produced an increased demand for real silk. It is manufactured in China, India, Japan, and Thailand. **2.** a similar fibre produced by spiders or some insects. **3.** (*British colloquial*) a King's or ◊Queen's Counsel, as having the right to wear a silk gown. **4.** fine, soft strands like threads of silk. **5.** (*attributive*) made of silk. **—silk hat,** a tall cylindrical hat covered with silk plush. **take silk,** to become a King's or ◊Queen's Counsel. [Old English from Latin *sericum* (*seres* from Greek *Seres* = the Chinese or neighbouring peoples)]

silken *adj.* of or resembling silk; soft, smooth, or lustrous.

Silk Road an ancient and medieval overland route of about 6,400 km/4,000 mi by which silk was brought from China to Europe in return for trade goods; it ran west via the Gobi Desert, Samarkand, and Antioch to Mediterranean ports in Greece, Italy, the Middle East, and Egypt.

silk-screen printing or **serigraphy** a method of ◊printing based on stencils. It can be used to print on most surfaces, including paper, plastic, cloth, and wood. An impermeable stencil (either paper or photographic) is attached to a finely meshed silk screen that has been stretched on a wooden frame, so that the ink passes through to the area beneath only where the image is required. The design can also be painted directly on the screen with varnish. A series of screens can be used to add successive layers of colour to the design. The process was developed in the early 20th century for commercial use and adopted by many artists from the 1930s onwards.

silkworm *n.* usually the larva of the **common silkworm moth** *Bombyx mori.* After hatching from the egg and maturing on the leaves of white mulberry trees (or a synthetic substitute), it spins a protective cocoon of fine silk thread 275 m/900 ft long. It is killed before emerging as a moth to keep the thread intact, and several threads are combined to form the commercial silk thread woven into textiles.

silky *adj.* **1.** soft and smooth like silk. **2.** suave. **—silkily** *adv.,* **silkiness** *n.*

sill *n.* **1.** a slab of wood or stone etc. at the base of a window or doorway etc. **2.** a sheet of igneous rock intruded between other rocks. [Old English]

sillabub variant of ◊syllabub.

sillimanite *n.* aluminium silicate, Al$_2$SiO$_5$, a mineral that occurs either as white to brownish prismatic crystals or as minute white fibres. It is an indicator of high temperature conditions in metamorphic rocks formed from clay sediments. Andalusite, kyanite, and sillimanite are all polymorphs of Al$_2$SiO$_5$.

silly *adj.* **1.** lacking good sense, foolish, unwise. **2.** weakminded. **3.** in cricket, (of a fielding position) very close to the batsman. **—n.** (*colloquial*) a foolish person. **—silly-billy** *n.* (*colloquial*) a foolish person. **—silliness** *n.* [Old English = happy]

silo /'saɪləʊ/ *n.* (*plural* **silos**) **1.** in farming, a pit or airtight tower in which ◊silage is made by the fermentation of freshly cut grass and other forage crops. **2.** a tower or pit for the storage of cement or grain etc. **3.** in military technology, an underground chamber for housing and launching a ballistic missile. [Spanish from Latin from Greek *siros* = pit for corn]

silt *n.* sediment deposited by water in a channel or harbour etc. **—v.t./i.** to block or be blocked with silt. **—siltation** /-'teɪʃən/ *n.*

Silurian /saɪ'ljʊərɪən/ *adj.* of a period of geological time 408–438 million years ago, the third period of the Palaeozoic era. **—n.** this period. Silurian sediments are mostly marine and consist of shales and limestone. Luxuriant reefs were built by coral-like organisms. The first land plants began to evolve during this period, and there were many ostracoderms (armoured jawless fishes). The first jawed fishes (called acanthodians) also appeared.

silvan /'sɪlvən/ *adj.* of the woods; having woods, rural. [from French or Latin *silva* = wood]

silver *n.* **1.** a white, lustrous, extremely malleable and ductile metallic element, symbol Ag [from Latin *argentum*], atomic number 47, relative atomic mass 107.868. It occurs in nature in ores and as a free metal; the chief ores are sulphides, from which the metal is extracted by smelting with lead. It is the best metallic conductor of both heat and electricity; its most useful compounds are the chloride and bromide, which darken on exposure to light and are the basis of photographic emulsions. Silver is used ornamentally, for jewellery and tableware, for coinage, in electroplating, electrical contacts, and dentistry, and as a solder. It has been mined since prehistory. **2.** coins or articles made of or looking like silver. **3.** the colour of silver. **4.** a silver medal. **—adj.** of or coloured like silver. **—v.t./i.** **1.** to coat or plate with silver. **2.** to give a silvery appearance to. **3.** to provide (a mirror glass) with a backing of tin amalgam etc. **4.** (of hair) to turn grey or white. **—silver birch,** the common ◊birch. **silverfish** *n.* a silver-coloured fish; a silvery ◊bristletail found in books and damp places. **silver jubilee,** a 25th anniversary. **silver lining,** a consolation or hopeful feature in misfortune. **silver medal,** a medal of silver awarded as second prize. **silver paper,** tin foil. **silver plate,** articles plated with silver. **silver-plated** *adj.* plated with silver. **silver sand,** fine, pure sand used in gardening. **silver wedding,** the 25th anniversary of a wedding. [Old English]

silverside *n.* the upper (and usually best) side of a round of beef.

silversmith *n.* one who makes articles in silver.

Silverstone Britain's oldest motor-racing circuit. It is situated near Towcester, Northamptonshire, and was built on a disused airfield after World War II. It staged the first world championship Grand Prix on 13 May 1950 and has staged 23 since, becoming the permanent home of the British Grand Prix in 1987.

silverware *n.* articles made of or plated with silver.

silvery *adj.* **1.** like silver in colour or appearance. **2.** having a clear gentle ringing sound.

silviculture *n.* cultivation of forest trees. [French from Latin *silva* = wood]

Sim /sɪm/ Alistair 1900–1976. Scottish comedy actor. Possessed of a marvellously expressive face, he was ideally cast in eccentric roles, as in the title role in *Scrooge* 1951. His other films include *Inspector Hornleigh* 1939, *Green for Danger* 1945, and *The Belles of St Trinians* 1954.

sima *n.* in geochemistry and geophysics, the substance of the Earth's oceanic ◊crust, as distinct from the sial of the continental crust. [from *silica* and *magnesia*, its two main chemical constituents]

Simenon /'si:mənɒn/ Georges 1903–1989. Belgian crime writer. Initially a pulp-fiction writer, in 1931 he created Inspector Maigret of the *Paris Sûreté* who appeared in a series of detective novels.

Simeon Stylites, St /'sɪmɪən staɪ'laɪtiːz/ *c.*390–459. Syrian Christian ascetic who practised his ideal of self-denial by living for 37 years on a platform on top of a high pillar. Feast day 5 Jan.

simian /'sɪmɪən/ *adj.* resembling an ape or monkey. **—n.** an ape or monkey. [from Latin *simia* = monkey]

similar /'sɪmɪlə/ *adv.* **1.** like, alike; having a resemblance but not quite the same. **2.** of the same kind, nature, shape, or amount. **—similarity** /-'lærɪtɪ/ *n.,* **similarly** *adv.* [from French or Latin *similis* = like]

simile /'sɪmɪlɪ/ *n.* a ◊figure of speech that in English uses the conjunctions *like* and *as* to express comparisons (for example, 'run like the devil'; 'as deaf as a post'). It is sometimes confused with ◊metaphor. [Latin]

similitude /sɪ'mɪlɪtjuːd/ *n.* **1.** similarity, outward appearance. **2.** comparison; expression of comparison. [from Old French or Latin]

simmer *v.t./i.* **1.** to keep or be kept bubbling or boiling gently. **2.** to be in a state of anger or laughter which is only just suppressed. **—n.** a simmering condition. **—simmer down,** to become less agitated. [alteration from earlier *simper*]

Simmons /'sɪmənz/ Jean 1929– . English actress who starred in the films *Black Narcissus* 1947, *Guys and Dolls* 1955, and *Spartacus* 1960. She worked in Hollywood from the 1950s onwards, and retired in the early 1970s.

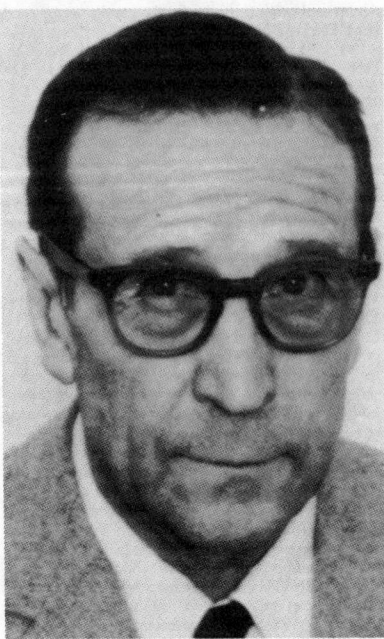

Simenon *Georges Simenon, novelist of the world of crime.*

simnel /'sɪmnəl/ *n.* a rich cake, especially for Mothering Sunday or Easter, covered with marzipan and decorated. [from Old French, ultimately from Latin *simila* = fine flour]

Simon /si:'mɒn/ Claude 1913– . French novelist. Originally an artist, he abandoned time structure in such novels as *La Route de Flandres/The Flanders Road* 1960, *Le Palace* 1962, and *Histoire* 1967. His later novels include *Les Géorgiques* 1981 and *L'Acacia* 1989. He was awarded the Nobel Prize for Literature in 1985.

Simon /'saɪmən/ Herbert 1916– . US social scientist. He researched decision-making in business corporations, and argued that maximum profit was seldom the chief motive. He received the 1978 Nobel Prize for Economics.

Simon (Marvin) Neil 1927– . US playwright. His stage plays (which were made into films) include the wryly comic *Barefoot in the Park* 1963, *The Odd Couple* 1965, and *The Sunshine Boys* 1972, and the more serious, autobiographical *Brighton Beach Memoirs* 1983 and *Biloxi Blues* 1985. He has also written screenplays and co-written musicals.

Simon Paul 1942– . US pop singer and songwriter. In a folk-rock duo with Art Garfunkel (1942–), he had such hits as 'Mrs Robinson' 1968 and 'Bridge Over Troubled Water' 1970. Simon's solo work includes the critically acclaimed album *Graceland* 1986, for which he drew on Cajun and African music, and *The Rhythm of the Saints* 1990.

Like a bridge over troubled water, I will ease your mind.

Paul Simon
'Bridge Over Troubled Water'

Simone Martini Sienese painter; see ◊Martini, Simone.

si monumentum requiris, circumspice the epitaph of English architect Christopher Wren in St Paul's Cathedral, London. [Latin = if you seek his monument, look about you]

simony /'saɪmənɪ/ *n.* in the Christian church, the buying and selling of church preferments, now usually regarded as a sin. [from Old French from Latin (*Simon* Magus (Acts 8: 18), with allusion to his offer of money to the apostles to purchase the power of giving the Holy Ghost by the laying on of hands)]

simoom /si'mu:m/ *n.* a hot, dry, dust-laden desert wind. [from Arabic *samma* = to poison]

simper *v.t./i.* to smile in a silly or affected way; to express by or with simpering. —*n.* such a smile.

simple *adj.* 1. easily understood or done, presenting no difficulty. 2. not complicated or elaborate; without luxury or sophistication. 3. not compound, consisting of or involving only one element or operation etc. 4. absolute, unqualified; straightforward. 5. foolish, ignorant; gullible; feeble-minded. —**simple fracture**, a fracture of the bone only. **simple interest**, see ◊interest. **simple-minded** *adj.* unsophisticated, without cunning; feeble-minded. **simple time**, in music, that with a binary subdivision of the unit (e.g. into two, four, eight). [from Old French from Latin *simplus*]

simple harmonic motion (SHM) the oscillatory or vibrational motion in which an object (or point) moves so that its acceleration towards a central point is proportional to its distance from it. A simple example is a pendulum, which also demonstrates another feature of SHM, that the maximum deflection is the same on each side of the central point.

simpleton /'sɪmpəltən/ *n.* a stupid or gullible person.

simplicity /sɪm'plɪsɪtɪ/ *n.* the fact or quality of being simple. [from Latin *simplex*]

simplify *v.t.* to make simple or less difficult. —**simplification** /-fɪ'keɪʃən/ *n.* [from French from Latin *simplificare* = make simple]

simplistic /sɪm'plɪstɪk/ *adj.* excessively or affectedly simple or simplified. —**simplistically** *adv.*

simply *adv.* 1. in a simple manner. 2. absolutely, without doubt. 3. merely.

Simpson /'sɪmpsən/ Wallis Warfield, Duchess of Windsor 1896–1986. US socialite, twice divorced, who married the Duke of Windsor (formerly ◊Edward VIII) in 1937, following his abdication.

simulate /'sɪmjʊleɪt/ *v.t.* 1. to pretend to be, have, or feel. 2. to imitate or counterfeit; to imitate the conditions of (a situation etc.), e.g. for training. —**simulation** /-'leɪʃən/ *n.*, **simulator** *n.* [from Latin *simulare*]

simultaneous /sɪməl'teɪnɪəs/ *adj.* occurring or operating at the same time. —**simultaneity** /-tə'neɪtɪ/ *n.*, **simultaneously** *adv.* [from Latin *simul* = at the same time]

simultaneous equation in mathematics, one of two or more algebraic equations that contain two or more unknown quantities that may have a unique solution. For example, in the case of two linear equations with two unknown variables, such as (i) $x + 3y = 6$ and (ii) $3y - 2x = 4$, the solution will be those unique values of x and y that are valid for both equations. Linear simultaneous equations can be solved by using algebraic manipulation to eliminate one of the variables, ◊coordinate geometry, or matrices (see ◊matrix).

sin[1] *n.* 1. the breaking of a religious or moral law, especially by a conscious act; an act that does this. In Roman Catholic theology, a distinction is made between **mortal sin**, which, if unforgiven, results in damnation, and **venial sin**, which is less serious. In Islam, the one unforgivable sin is **shirk**, denial that Allah is the only god. 2. a serious fault or offence. 3. an act that is contrary to common sense. —*v.i.* (**-nn-**) to commit a sin. [Old English]

sin[2] /saɪn/ abbreviation of ◊sine.

Sinai /'saɪnaɪ/ Egyptian peninsula, at the head of the Red Sea; area 65,000 sq km/25,000 sq mi. Resources include oil, natural gas, manganese, and coal; irrigation water from the river Nile is carried under the Suez Canal.

Sinai, Battle of a battle on 6–24 Oct 1973 which took place during the Yom Kippur War between Israel and Egypt. After one of the longest tank battles ever, the Israelis crossed the Suez canal on 16 Oct, cutting off the Egyptian 3rd Army.

Sinan /si'nɑ:n/ 1489–1588. Ottoman architect, chief architect from 1538 to ◊Suleiman the Magnificent. Among the hundreds of buildings he designed are the Suleimaniye in Istanbul, a mosque complex, and the Topkapi Saray, palace of the Sultan (now a museum).

Sinatra /si'nɑ:trə/ Frank (Francis Albert) 1915– . US singer and film actor. In the 1940s he sang songs such as 'Night and Day' and 'You'd Be So Nice To Come Home To' with Harvey James's and Tommy Dorsey's bands. He was celebrated for his love ballads, which were unmatched in phrasing and emotion.

sine wave

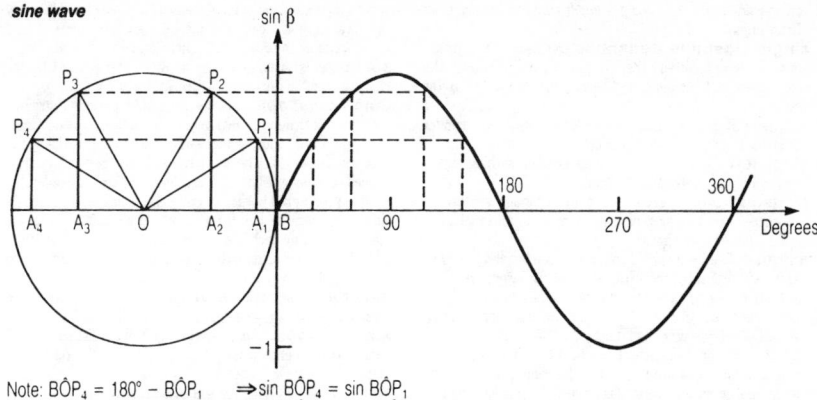

Note: $B\hat{O}P_4 = 180° - B\hat{O}P_1$ $\Rightarrow \sin B\hat{O}P_4 = \sin B\hat{O}P_1$
      $B\hat{O}P_3 = 180° - B\hat{O}P_2$ $\&\ \sin B\hat{O}P_3 = \sin B\hat{O}P_2$

since *prep.* after (a specified past event or time); between (a past event or time) and now. —*conj.* 1. during or in the time after. 2. for the reason that, because. —*adv.* 1. from that time or event until now. 2. ago. [Old English = after that]

sincere /sɪn'sɪə/ *adj.* free from pretence or deceit. —**sincerity** /sɪn'serɪtɪ/ *n.* [from Latin *sincerus* = clean, pure]

sincerely *adv.* in a sincere manner. —**yours sincerely,** a formula for ending a letter.

Sinclair /'sɪŋkleə/ Clive 1940– . British electronics engineer who produced the first widely available pocket calculator, pocket and wristwatch televisions, a series of home computers, and the innovative but commercially disastrous 'C5' personal transport (a low cyclelike three-wheeled device powered by a washing-machine motor).

Sinclair Upton 1878–1968. US novelist. His concern for social reforms is reflected in *The Jungle* 1906, which exposed the horrors of the Chicago stockyards and led to a change in food-processing laws; *Boston* 1928; and his Lanny Budd series 1940–53, including *Dragon's Teeth* 1942, which won the Pulitzer Prize.

sine /saɪn/ *n.* in trigonometry, a function of an angle in a right-angled triangle defined as the ratio of the length of the side opposite the angle to the length of the hypotenuse (the longest side). [from Latin *sinus* = curve, fold of toga]

sinecure /'saɪnɪkjuə/ *n.* a position that requires little or no work but yields profit or honour. [from Latin *sine cura* = without care]

sine die /saɪnɪ 'daɪɪ:, sɪneɪ 'diːeɪ/ in law or of business, adjourned indefinitely, with no appointed date. [Latin = without a day]

sine qua non /saɪneɪ kwɑː 'nəʊn, saɪnɪ kweɪ 'nɒn/ an indispensable condition or qualification. [Latin = without which not]

sinew /'sɪnjuː/ *n.* 1. tough, fibrous tissue joining a muscle to a bone; a piece of this. 2. (in *plural*) muscles, bodily strength. 3. a thing that strengthens or sustains. [Old English]

sinewy *adj.* having strong sinews.

sinfonietta *n.* 1. an orchestral work that is of a shorter, lighter nature than a ◊symphony. 2. a small symphony orchestra.

sinful *adj.* committing or involving sin; wicked. —**sinfully** *adv.*, **sinfulness** *n.*

sing *v.t./i.* (*past* **sang**; *past participle* **sung**) 1. to utter musical sounds with the voice, especially with a set tune; to utter or produce by singing. 2. (of the wind, a kettle etc.) to make a humming, buzzing, or ringing sound; (of the ears) to be affected with a ringing or buzzing sound. 3. (*slang*) to act as an informer. —**sing-along** *n.* a song or recording to which one can sing in accompaniment; a singsong to the accompaniment of a leader or tune. **sing out,** to shout. **sing the praises of,** to praise enthusiastically or continually. —**singer** *n.* [Old English]

sing. abbreviation of singular.

Singapore /sɪŋə'pɔː/ Republic of; country in SE Asia, off the tip of the Malay Peninsula; **area** 620 sq km/239 sq mi;

capital Singapore city; **physical** comprises Singapore Island, low and flat, and 57 small islands; **head of state** Wee Kim Wee from 1985; **head of government** Goh Chok Tong from 1990; **political system** liberal democratic republic; **exports** electronics, petroleum products, rubber, machinery, vehicles; **population** (1990 est) 2,703,000 (Chinese 75%, Malay 14%, Tamil 7%); **language** Malay, Chinese, Tamil, English (all official); **recent history** independence from Britain was achieved in 1959. Singapore joined the new Federation of Malaysia in 1963 but left to become an independent republic in 1965. The ruling conservative party exercises an increasingly authoritarian rule.

singe /sɪndʒ/ *v.t./i.* (*participle* **singeing**) to burn superficially or lightly; to burn off the tips or ends of. —*n.* 1. a superficial burn. 2. an act of singeing. [Old English]

Singer /'sɪŋə/ Isaac Bashevis 1904– . Polish novelist and short-story writer. His works, written in Yiddish, often portray traditional Jewish life in Poland and the USA, and the loneliness of old age. They include *Gimpel the Fool* 1957, *The Slave* 1960, *Shosha* 1978, and *Old Love* 1979. He was awarded the Nobel Prize for Literature in 1978.

Singer Isaac Merit 1811–1875. US inventor of domestic and industrial sewing machines. Within a few years of opening his first factory in 1851, he became the world's largest manufacturer (despite charges of patent infringement by Elias ◊Howe), and by the late 1860s more than 100,000 Singer sewing machines were in use in the USA alone. To make his machines available to the widest market, Singer became the first manufacturer to offer attractive hire-purchase terms.

Singh /sɪŋ/ Vishwanath Pratap 1931– . Indian politician, prime minister 1989–90. As a member of the Congress (I) Party, he held ministerial posts under Indira Gandhi and Rajiv Gandhi, and from 1984 led an anticorruption drive. When he unearthed an arms sales scandal in 1988, he was ousted from the government and party and formed a broad-based opposition alliance, the ◊**Janata Dal,** which won the Nov 1989 election. Mounting caste and communal conflict split the Janata Dal and forced him out of office in Nov 1990.

Singhalese /sɪn'liːz/ variant of ◊Sinhalese.

Singh, Gobind see ◊Gobind Singh, Sikh guru.

single /'sɪŋgəl/ *adj.* 1. one only, not double or multiple; united, undivided; designed for or used or done by one person etc. 2. one by itself; regarded separately; not married. 3. (of a ticket) valid for the outward journey only, not a return. 4. (with negative or interrogative) even one. 5. (of a flower) having only one set of petals. —*n.* 1. a thing that is single, a single item in a series. 2. a single ticket. 3. a pop record with one piece of music on the A side. 4. in cricket, a hit for one run. 5. (usually in *plural*) a game with one player on each side. —*v.t.* (with *out*) to choose for special attention etc.; to distinguish from others. —**single-breasted** *adj.* (of a coat etc.) having only one set of buttons and overlapping little across the breast. **single combat,** a duel. **single file,** a file of persons in one line. **single-handed** *adv.* without help from another; (*adj.*) done single-handed. **single-minded** *adj.* having or intent on only one purpose. —**singly** *adv.* [from Old French from Latin *singulus*]

single-sideband transmission radio-wave transmission using either the frequency band above the carrier-wave frequency, or below, instead of both (as now).

singlet /'sɪŋglɪt/ *n.* a man's sleeveless garment worn under or instead of a shirt. [after *doublet*]

singleton /'sɪŋgəltən/ *n.* a single person or thing, especially a player's only card of a suit.

singsong *adj.* uttered with a monotonous rhythm or cadence. —*n.* 1. a singsong manner. 2. an informal gathering for singing in chorus.

singular /'sɪŋgjʊlə/ *adj.* 1. unique; much beyond the average; extraordinary; eccentric, strange. 2. in grammar, (of a word or form) denoting one person or thing. —*n.* in grammar, a singular word or form, the singular number. —**singularity** /-'lærɪtɪ/ *n.* 1. the condition of being singular. 2. in astrophysics, the point at the centre of a ◊black hole at which it is predicted that the infinite gravitational forces will compress the infalling mass of the collapsing star to infinite density. It is a point in space-time at which the known laws of physics break down. **singularly** *adv.* [from Old French from Latin *singularis*]

Sinhala /'sɪnhələ/ *adj.* & *n.* Sinhalese. [Sinhalese]

Sinhalese /sɪnhə'liːz/ *adj.* of the Sinhalese or their language. —*n.* (*plural* the same) 1. a member of an Aryan people deriving from northern India and forming the majority of the population in Sri Lanka. 2. their language, belonging to the Indo-Iranian branch of the Indo-European family. [from Sanskrit *Sinhalam* = Sri Lanka]

sinister /'sɪnɪstə/ *adj.* 1. suggestive of evil, looking malignant or villainous; wicked, criminal; of evil omen. 2. in heraldry, of or on the left-hand side (the observer's right) of a shield etc. [from Old French or Latin = left]

sink *v.t./i.* (*past* sank; *past participle* sunk or (as *adj.*) sunken) 1. to fall slowly downwards; to come gradually to a lower level or pitch; to disappear below the horizon; to go or penetrate below the surface, especially of a liquid; (of a ship) to go to the bottom of the sea etc. 2. to pass into a less active condition; to lose value or strength etc. gradually. 3. to cause or allow to sink; to overlook or forget (one's differences etc.) to cause the failure or discomfiture of. 4. to dig (a well); to bore (a shaft). 5. to engrave (a die). 6. to invest (money). 7. to cause (a ball) to enter a pocket in billiards, a hole in golf etc. —*n.* 1. a fixed basin with a drainage pipe and usually with a water supply. 2. a place where foul liquid collects; a place of rampant vice etc. —**sink in**, to penetrate; to become understood. **sinking feeling**, a feeling of hunger or fear. **sinking fund**, a fund for the gradual repayment of a debt. For a company, a sinking fund is used to allow annually for ◊depreciation; in the case of a nation, a sinking fund pays off a part of the national debt. **sunk fence**, a fence formed by or built along the bottom of a ditch. [Old English]

sinker *n.* a weight used to sink a fishing line or sounding line.

sinner *n.* one who sins.

Sinn Féin /ˌʃɪn 'feɪn/ Irish nationalist party founded by Arthur Griffith (1872–1922) in 1905; in 1917 ◊de Valera became its president. It is the political wing of the Irish Republican Army, and is similarly split between comparative moderates and extremists. In 1985 it gained representation in 17 out of 26 district councils in Northern Ireland. [Gaelic = we ourselves]

Sino- /saɪnəʊ-/ in combinations, Chinese (and) (e.g. *Sino-American*; *Sinophobia*). [from Greek *Sinai* = the Chinese]

Sino-Japanese Wars /saɪnəʊdʒæpə'niːz/ two wars waged by Japan against China to expand to the mainland. During the **First Sino-Japanese War** 1894–95, Japan secured the 'independence' of Korea, cession of Taiwan and the nearby Pescadores Islands, and the Liaodong peninsula (for a naval base). France, Germany, and Russia pressured Japan into returning the last-named, which Russia occupied in 1896; this led to the Russo-Japanese War 1904–06. During the **Second Sino-Japanese War** 1931–45, the Japanese occupied Manchuria, which they formed into the puppet state of Manchukuo. They also attacked Shanghai and moved into NE China. In 1937 the Chinese leaders Chiang Kai-shek and Mao Zedong allied to fight the Japanese. In 1941 the Japanese attack on the USA (see ◊Pearl Harbor)

led to the extension of lend-lease aid to China and US entry into war against Japan. The Japanese surrendered to China in 1945, after the Allies had concluded World War II.

sinology /sɪ'nɒlədʒɪ, saɪ-/ *n.* the study of the Chinese language and history etc. —**sinologist** *n.*

Sino-Soviet split /saɪnəʊ'səʊvɪət/ a period of strained relations between the two major communist powers, China and the USSR, during the early 1960s, thus dividing the communist world. The tension was based partly on differences in ideology but also involved rivalry for leadership and old territorial border claims. The Chinese communists also criticized the USSR for supplying aircraft to India and for withdrawing technical and military aid to China in 1960. The USSR supported India in its border warfare with China between 1961 and 1962.

sinter *n.* a solid coalesced by heating. —*v.t./i.* to form into a sinter. [German = cinder]

sinuate /'sɪnjuːət/ *adj.* wavy-edged, with distinct inward and outward bends along the edge. [from Latin, past participle of *sinuare* = to bend]

Sinuiju /sɪnwiː'dʒuː/ capital of North Pyongan province, near the mouth of the Yalu River, North Korea; population (1984) 754,000. It was founded in 1910.

sinuous /'sɪnjuəs/ *adj.* with many curves, undulating, meandering. —**sinuosity** /-'ɒsɪtɪ/ *n.*, **sinuously** *adv.* [from French or Latin]

sinus /'saɪnəs/ *n.* a cavity of bone or tissue, especially in the skull communicating with the nostrils. [Latin = bosom, recess]

sinusitis /saɪnə'saɪtɪs/ *n.* painful inflammation of one of the sinuses that surround the nasal passages. Most cases clear with antibiotics and nasal decongestants, but some require surgical drainage.

Sioux /suː/ *n.* (*plural* the same) a member or the language of a group of North American ◊Plains Indians (also called the Dakota), now living on reservations in South Dakota and Nebraska, and among the general public. Under chiefs Crazy Horse and Sitting Bull they defeated General George Custer at Little Bighorn, Montana; as a result, Congress abrogated the Fort Laramie Treaty of 1868 (which had given the Sioux a large area in the Black Hills of Dakota). Gold, uranium, coal, oil, and natural gas have been found there since, and the Sioux pressed for and were awarded $160 million compensation in 1980. —*adj.* of the Sioux or their language. —**Siouan** /'suːən/ *adj.* [French, from Sioux name]

sip *v.t./i.* (-pp-) to drink in repeated small mouthfuls or spoonfuls. —*n.* a small mouthful of liquid; an act of taking this.

siphon /'saɪfən/ *n.* 1. a pipe or tube shaped like an inverted V or U with unequal arms, to convey liquid from a container. When it is filled with liquid and the shorter arm is placed in a tank or reservoir, liquid flows out of the longer arm provided that its exit is below the level of the surface of the liquid in the tank. 2. a bottle from which aerated water is forced out by the pressure of a gas. 3. the sucking tube of some insects or small animals. —*v.t./i.* to conduct or flow (as) through a siphon. [French or from Latin from Greek *siphōn* = pipe]

sir /sɜː/ *n.* 1. a polite or respectful form of address or reference to a man. 2. Sir, the title prefixed to the Christian name of a knight or baronet. [reduced form of *sire*]

sire *n.* 1. the male parent of an animal, especially a stallion kept for breeding. 2. (*archaic*) a form of address to a king. 3. (*archaic*) a father or male ancestor. —*v.t.* (especially of a stallion) to beget. [from Old French from Latin *senior*]

siren /'saɪərən/ *n.* 1. in Greek mythology, a sea nymph who lured sailors to their death by her singing. ◊Odysseus, in order to hear the sirens safely, tied himself to the mast of his ship and stuffed his crew's ears with wax. The Argonauts escaped them because the singing of Orpheus surpassed that of the sirens. 2. a dangerously fascinating woman, a temptress; (*attributive*) irresistibly tempting. 3. a device for making a loud prolonged signal or warning sound; the sound made. [from Old French from Latin from Greek]

sirenian /saɪ'riːnɪən/ *adj.* of the order Sirenia of large aquatic plant-eating mammals that includes the dugong and the ◊manatee. —*n.* a member of this order.

Sirius /'sɪrɪəs/ *n.* or **Dog Star** or **Alpha Canis Majoris** the brightest star in the sky, 8.7 light years from Earth in the constellation Canis Major. Sirius is a white star with a mass 2.35 that of the Sun, a diameter 1.8 times that of the Sun, and a luminosity of 23 Suns. It is orbited every 50 years by a white dwarf, Sirius B.

sirloin /'sɜːlɔɪn/ n. **1.** the upper and choicer part of a loin of beef. **2.** (US) a rump steak. [from Old French]

sirocco /si'rɒkəʊ/ n. (plural **siroccos**) **1.** a hot, normally dry and dust-laden wind that blows from the deserts of N Africa, across the Mediterranean into S Europe. It occurs mainly in the spring. **2.** any hot, oppressive wind. [French from Italian ultimately from Arabic = east wind]

sis n. (colloquial) sister. [abbreviation]

sisal /'saɪsəl/ n. strong fibre made from various species of ◊agave, such as Agave sisalina. [from Sisal, port in Yucatán, Mexico]

siskin /'sɪskɪn/ n. **1.** a greenish-yellow bird Carduelis spinus in the finch family Fringillidae, about 12 cm/5 in long, found in Eurasia. **2.** a small North American songbird Spinus spinus. [from Middle Dutch]

Sisley /'sɪzli/ Alfred 1839–1899. French Impressionist painter, whose landscapes include views of Port-Marly and the river Seine, painted during floods in 1876.

sissy n. an effeminate or cowardly person. —adj. characteristic of a sissy. [from sis]

sister n. **1.** a woman or girl in relation to the other sons and daughters of her parents. **2.** a close woman friend or associate; a female fellow member of the same church, trade union, or other association, or of the human race. **3.** a member of a sisterhood, especially a nun. **4.** a female hospital nurse in authority over others; (colloquial) any female nurse. **5.** (attributive) of the same type, design, origin etc. —**sister-in-law** n. (plural **sisters-in-law**) the sister of one's husband or wife; one's brother's wife. —**sisterly** adj. [from Old Norse]

sisterhood n. **1.** the relationship (as) of sisters. **2.** a society of women bound by monastic views or devoting themselves to religious or charitable work.

Sistine Chapel a chapel in the Vatican, Rome, begun under Pope Sixtus IV in 1473 by Giovanni del Dolci, and decorated by (among others) Michelangelo. It houses the conclave that meets to select a new pope.

Sisulu /si'suːluː/ Walter 1912– . South African civil-rights activist, one of the first full-time secretary generals of the African National Congress (ANC), in 1964, with Nelson Mandela. He was imprisoned following the 1964 ◊Rivonia Trial for opposition to the apartheid system and released, at the age of 77, as a gesture of reform by President F W ◊de Klerk in 1989.

Sisyphean /sɪsɪ'fiːən/ adj. endlessly laborious. [from Sisyphus]

Sisyphus /'sɪsɪfəs/ in Greek mythology, a king of Corinth who, after his evil life, was condemned in the underworld to push a huge stone up a hill, which always rolled back down again before he could reach the top.

sit v.t./i. (**-tt-**; past and past participle **sat**) **1.** to take or be in a position in which the body is supported more or less upright by the buttocks resting on the ground or a raised seat etc. **2.** to cause to sit, to place in a sitting position. **3.** (of a bird) to perch; (of an animal) to rest with the hind legs bent and the body close to the ground. **4.** (of a bird) to remain on the nest to hatch eggs. **5.** to be engaged in an occupation in which the sitting position is usual; to pose for a portrait; to be a member of Parliament for a constituency; to be a candidate for an examination etc.; to undergo (an examination). **6.** (of a parliament or court etc.) to be in session. **7.** to be in a more or less permanent position or condition. **8.** (of clothes etc.) to fit or hang in a certain way. **9.** to keep or have one's seat on (a horse etc.). —**be sitting pretty**, to be comfortably or advantageously placed. **sit at a person's feet**, to be his or her pupil. **sit back**, to relax one's efforts. **sit down**, to sit after standing; to cause to sit; to suffer tamely (under humiliation etc.). **sit-down** adj. (of a meal) eaten sitting. **sit-down strike**, a strike in which workers refuse to leave their place of work. **sit in**, to occupy a place as a protest. **sit-in** n. such a protest. **sit in judgement**, to assume the right of judging others; to be censorious. **sit in on**, to be present as a guest or observer at (a meeting). **sit on**, to be a member of (a committee etc.); to hold a session or inquiry concerning; (colloquial) to delay action about; (slang) to repress, rebuke, or snub. **sit on the fence**, to remain neutral or undecided. **sit out**, to take no part in (a dance etc.); to stay until the end of

(an ordeal etc.). **sit tight**, (colloquial) to remain firmly in one's place; not to yield. **sit up**, to rise from a lying to a sitting position; to sit firmly upright; not to go to bed (until later than the usual time); (colloquial) to have one's interest or attention suddenly aroused. **sit-upon** n. (colloquial) the buttocks. [from Old English]

Sita /'siːtɑ/ in Hinduism, the wife of Rama, an avatar (manifestation) of the god Vishnu; a character in the ◊Rāmāyana epic, characterized by chastity and kindness.

sitar /si'tɑː(r)/ n. an Indian stringed instrument. It has a pear-shaped body, long neck, and an additional gourd resonator at the opposite end. A principal solo instrument, it has seven metal strings extending over movable frets and two concealed strings that provide a continuous singing drone. [from Hindi from Persian]

sitatunga n. or **marshbuck** a herbivorous antelope Tragelaphus spekei found in several swamp regions in Central Africa. The hooves are long and splayed to help progress on soft surfaces. They are up to about 1.2 m/4 ft high at the shoulder; the males have thick horns up to 90 cm/3 ft long.

sitcom /'sɪtkɒm/ n. (colloquial) a situation comedy. [abbreviation]

site n. **1.** the ground on which a town or building stood, stands, or is to stand. **2.** the place where some activity or event takes place or took place. —v.t. to locate; to provide with a site. [from Anglo-French or Latin situs = local position]

sitter n. **1.** one who sits, especially for a portrait. **2.** a baby-sitter. **3.** (slang) an easy catch or shot; something easy to do.

sitting n. **1.** the time during which a person or assembly etc. sits continuously. **2.** a clutch of eggs. —adj. **1.** having sat down. **2.** (of an animal or bird) not running or flying. —**sitting duck** or **target**, a person or thing that is a helpless victim of attack. **sitting room**, a room for sitting in; space enough to accommodate seated persons. **sitting tenant**, one already occupying a house etc.

Sitting Bull /'sɪtɪŋ 'bʊl/ c.1834–1893. North American Indian chief who fought a rearguard action against white incursions into Indian lands. He led the ◊Sioux onslaught against General ◊Custer and defeated him at the Battle of Little Big Horn on 25 June 1876.

situate /'sɪtjuːeɪt/ v.t. **1.** to place or put in a specified position, situation etc.; (in past participle) in specified circumstances. **2.** to establish or indicate the place of; to put in a context. —/-ət/ adj. (archaic or in law) situated. [from Latin situare from situs = site]

situation /sɪtju:'eɪʃən/ n. **1.** a place (with its surroundings) that is occupied by something. **2.** a set of circumstances; a state of affairs; a condition. **3.** an employee's position or job. —**situation comedy**, a comedy (especially a serial) in which the humour derives largely from the particular conjunction of characters and circumstances. —**situational** adj. [from French or Latin]

Sitwell /'sɪtwəl/ Edith 1887–1964. English poet whose series of poems Façade was performed as recitations to the specially written music of William ◊Walton from 1923.

My poems are hymns of praise to the glory of life.
Edith Sitwell
Collected Poems: 'Some Notes on My Poetry'

SI units (French Système International (d'Unités)) a standard system of units of measurement used by scientists worldwide. Originally proposed in 1960, it replaces the ◊m.k.s., ◊c.g.s., and ◊f.p.s. systems. It is based on seven basic units: the metre (m) for length, kilogram (kg) for weight, second (s) for time, ampere (A) for electrical current, kelvin (K) for temperature, mole (mol) for amount of substance, and candela (cd) for luminosity.

Siva /'ʃiːvə/ or **Shiva** in Hinduism, the third chief god (with Brahma and Vishnu). As Mahadeva (great lord), he is the creator, symbolized by the phallic lingam, who restores what as Mahakala he destroys. He is often sculpted as Nataraja, performing his fruitful cosmic dance. His consort or female principle (sakti) is Parvati, otherwise known as Durga or Kali. [Sanskrit = propitious]

six *adj. & n.* **1.** one more than five; the symbol for this (6, vi, VI). **2.** the size etc. denoted by six. —**at sixes and sevens,** in confusion or disagreement. **hit** *or* **knock for six,** (*colloquial*) to surprise utterly or overwhelm. **six-gun** *or* **six-shooter** *n.* (*US*) a revolver with six chambers. [Old English]

Six Acts in British history, the acts of Parliament passed in 1819 by Lord Liverpool's Tory administration to curtail political radicalism in the aftermath of the ◊Peterloo massacre and during a period of agitation for reform when ◊habeas corpus was suspended and the powers of magistrates extended.

Six Counties the six counties that form Northern Ireland: Antrim, Armagh, Down, Fermanagh, Londonderry, and Tyrone.

sixfold *adj. & adv.* six times as much or as many; consisting of six parts.

Six, Les a group of French 20th-century composers; see ◊Les Six.

sixpence *n.* (*British*) the sum of 6p; (*formerly*) the sum of 6d., a silver coin worth this.

sixpenny *adj.* costing or worth sixpence.

sixteen /siks'ti:n/ *adj.* **1.** one more than 15; the symbol for this (16, xvi, XVI). **2.** the size etc. denoted by 16. —**sixteenth** *adj. & n.* [Old English]

sixth *adj.* next after the fifth. —*n.* each of six equal parts of a thing. —**sixth form,** in UK education, a form in a secondary school for pupils who study for one or two years beyond school-leaving age in order to gain ◊A-level or other post-15 qualifications. **sixth-form college,** a college with special courses for such pupils. **sixth sense,** a supposed faculty giving intuitive or extrasensory knowledge. —**sixthly** *adv.*

sixty /'siksti/ *adj. & n.* **1.** six times ten; the symbol for this (60, lx, LX). **2.** (in *plural*) the numbers, years, or degrees of temperature from 60 to 69. —**sixtieth** *adj. & n.* [Old English]

size[1] *n.* **1.** the extent of a thing; dimensions, magnitude. **2.** each of the series of standard measurements in which things of the same kind are made, grouped, sold etc. —*v.t.* to group or sort according to size. —**size up,** to estimate the size of; (*colloquial*) to form a judgement of. **that is the size of it,** (*colloquial*) that is the truth of the matter. —**sized** *adj.* of a specific size (e.g. *large-sized*). [from Old French]

size[2] *n.* a gelatinous solution used in glazing paper, stiffening textiles etc. —*v.t.* to treat with size.

sizeable *adj.* fairly large.

sizzle *v.i.* **1.** to make a spluttering or hissing noise as of frying. **2.** (*colloquial*) to be in a state of great heat or excitement etc. —*n.* a sizzling sound. [imitative]

SJ abbreviation of Society of Jesus; see ◊Jesuit.

sjambok /'ʃæmbɒk/ *n.* in South Africa, a rhinoceros-hide whip. [Afrikaans from Malay from Urdu]

skald /skɔld, skɒld/ *n.* an ancient-Scandinavian poet. [from Old Norse]

Skara Brae /'skærə 'breɪ/ preserved Neolithic village in the Orkney Islands, Scotland, on Mainland.

skate[1] *n.* each of a pair of blades, or (**roller skate**) metal frames with four small wheels, fitted to the soles of boots or shoes so that the wearer can glide over ice or a hard surface. —*v.t./i.* to move on skates, to perform (a specified figure) on skates. The chief competitive ice-skating events are figure skating, for singles or pairs, ice-dancing, and simple speed skating. —**get one's skates on,** (*slang*) to make haste. **skate on thin ice,** to behave rashly, to risk danger etc. **skate over,** to make only a passing reference (or no reference) to. —**skater** *n.* [from Dutch *schaats* from Old French *eschasse* = stilt]

skate[2] *n.* (*plural* **skate**) any of several species of flatfish of the ray group. The **common skate** *Raja batis* is up to 1.8 m/6 ft long and greyish, with black specks. [from Old Norse]

skate[3] *n.* (*slang*) or **cheapskate** a contemptible or dishonest person.

skateboard *n.* a short, narrow board on roller-skate wheels for riding on while standing, and steerable by weight positioning. As a land alternative to surfing, skateboards developed in California in the 1960s and became a worldwide craze in the 1970s. Skateboarding is practised in urban environments and enjoyed a revival in the late 1980s. —**skateboarder** *n.*, **skateboarding** *n.*

skedaddle /ski'dædəl/ *colloquial v.i.* to depart hurriedly. —*n.* a hurried departure.

skein /skeɪn/ *n.* **1.** a loosely coiled bundle of yarn or thread. **2.** a flock of wild geese etc. in flight. [from Old French *escaigne*]

skeleton /'skelɪtən/ *n.* **1.** the rigid or semirigid framework that supports an animal's body, protects its internal organs, and provides anchorage points for its muscles. The skeleton may be composed of bone and cartilage (vertebrates), chitin (arthropods), calcium carbonate (molluscs and other invertebrates), or silica (many protists). **2.** any supporting framework or structure. **3.** a very thin person or animal. **4.** the remaining part of something after its life or usefulness is gone. **5.** an outline sketch, an epitome. **6.** (*attributive*) having only the essential or minimum number of persons or parts etc. —**skeleton in the cupboard,** a discreditable or embarrassing fact kept secret. **skeleton key,** a key fitting many locks. —**skeletal** *adj.* [Greek, neuter of *skeletos* = dried up]

skep *n.* **1.** a wooden or wicker basket, the quantity contained in this. **2.** a straw or wicker beehive. [from Old Norse]

skerry *n.* a reef, a rocky island. [Orkney dialect from Old Norse]

sketch *n.* **1.** a rough drawing or painting. **2.** a brief account of something. **3.** a short, usually humorous play. **4.** a short descriptive piece of writing. **5.** a musical composition of a single movement. —*v.t./i.* to make a sketch or sketches (of). —**sketchbook** *n.* sheets of drawing paper made up in the form of a book. **sketch in,** to indicate briefly or in outline. **sketch map,** a roughly drawn map with few details. —**sketcher** *n.* [from Dutch from Italian ultimately from Greek *skhedios* = extempore]

sketchy *adj.* like a sketch, rough and not detailed; unsubstantial or imperfect, especially through haste. —**sketchily** *adv.*, **sketchiness** *n.*

skew *adj.* set askew, slanting, oblique; distorted. —*n.* a skewed position, a slant. —*v.t./i.* **1.** to make skew; to distort. **2.** to move obliquely. —**on the skew,** askew. **skewwhiff** *adj.* (*colloquial*) askew. [from Old French from Germanic]

skewbald /'skju:bɔld/ *adj.* (of an animal) with irregular patches of white and another colour. —*n.* a skewbald animal, especially a horse. [from obsolete *skued*, after *piebald*]

skewer *n.* a long pin designed for holding meat compactly together while it is cooking. —*v.t.* to fasten together or pierce (as) with a skewer. [variant of dialect *skiver*]

ski /ski:/ *n.* (*plural* **skis**) each of a pair of long, narrow pieces of wood etc. fastened under the feet for travelling over snow; a similar device under a vehicle. —*v.i.* (*past* and *past participle* **skied** or **ski'd** /ski:d/; *participle* **skiing**) to travel on skis. —**ski jump** a steep slope levelling off before a sharp drop to allow a skier to leap through the air. **ski lift,** a device for carrying skiers up a slope, usually on seats hung from an overhead cable. **ski run,** a slope suitable for skiing. —**skier** *n.* [Norwegian, from Old Norse *skíth* = billet, snowshoe]

skid /skɪd/ *v.t./i.* (**-dd-**) (of a vehicle etc.) to slide (especially sideways or obliquely) on a slippery road etc.; to cause (a vehicle) to skid. —*n.* **1.** an act of skidding. **2.** a piece of wood etc. serving as a support or fender etc. **3.** a braking device, especially a wooden or metal shoe on a wheel. **4.** a runner on an aircraft for use when landing. —**on the skids,** (*colloquial*) about to be discarded or defeated. **put the skids under,** to hasten the downfall or failure of. **skidpan** *n.* a slippery surface prepared for vehicle drivers to practise control of skidding. **skid row,** (*US*) a district frequented by vagrants.

skiff *n.* a light rowing or sailing boat. [from French *esquif*]

skiffle *n.* a style of British popular music, introduced by singer and banjo player Lonnie Donegan (1931–) in 1956, using improvised percussion instruments such as tea chests and washboards.

skilful *adj.* having or showing skill. —**skilfully** *adv.*

skill *n.* the ability to do something well. [from Old Norse = distinction (*skilja* = distinguish)]

skilled *adj.* **1.** skilful. **2.** (of a worker) highly trained or experienced; (of work) requiring skill or special training.

skillet /'skɪlɪt/ *n.* **1.** a small metal cooking pot with a long handle and, usually, legs. **2.** (*US*) a frying pan.

skim *v.t./i.* (-mm-) 1. to take floating matter or cream etc. from the surface of a liquid; to clear (a liquid) thus. 2. to pass over (a surface) almost touching it or touching it lightly; to glide along. 3. to read or look at cursorily. —**skim milk** *or* **skimmed milk,** milk from which the cream has been skimmed. —**skimmer** *n.* [back formation from *skimmer*]

skimmer *n.* 1. a ladle etc. for skimming liquids. 2. a long-winged marine bird of the genus *Rynchops* that feeds by skimming over water with its knifelike lower mandible immersed. [from Old French *escume* = scum]

skimp *v.t./i.* to supply or use a meagre amount or rather less than what is needed (of); to be parsimonious.

skimpy *adj.* meagre, not ample; scanty. —**skimpily** *adv.,* **skimpiness** *n.*

skin *n.* 1. the flexible, continuous covering of the body of a vertebrate. In mammals, the outer layer (epidermis) is dead and protective, and its cells are constantly being rubbed away and replaced from below. The lower layer (dermis) contains blood vessels, nerves, hair roots, and sweat and sebaceous glands, and is supported by a network of fibrous and elastic cells. 2. a skin (with or without hair) removed from an animal; material made from this; a container for water or wine, made from an animal's whole skin. 3. the colour or complexion of a person's skin. 4. outer layer or covering; a film like a skin on the surface of a liquid. 5. a ship's planking or plating. —*v.t./i.* (-nn-) 1. to strip or scrape the skin from. 2. to cover or become covered (as) with skin. 3. (*slang*) to fleece, to swindle. —**be (all) skin and bone,** to be very thin. **by the skin of one's teeth,** by a very narrow margin. **get under a person's skin,** (*colloquial*) to interest or annoy him or her intensely. **have a thick (or thin) skin,** to be insensitive (or sensitive) to criticism etc. **no skin off one's nose,** (*colloquial*) of no consequence to one. **save one's skin,** to avoid death or harm etc. **skin-deep** *adj.* superficial, not deep or lasting. **skin-diver** *n.* one who swims underwater without a diving suit, usually with an aqualung and flippers. **skin diving,** such swimming. **skin flick,** (*slang*) a pornographic film. **skin graft,** a surgical transplanting of skin; the skin thus transferred. **skin-tight** *adj.* very close-fitting. [Old English from Old Norse; compare Old High German *scinden* = flay]

skinflint *n.* a miserly person.

skinful *n.* (*colloquial*) enough alcoholic liquor to make one drunk.

skinhead *n.* a youth with hair shaved off or cut very short, especially one of a group adopting this style.

skink *n.* a lizard of the family Scincidae, a large family of about 700 species found throughout the tropics and subtropics. The body is usually long, and the legs reduced. Some are actually legless and rather snakelike. Many are good burrowers, or can 'swim' through sand, like the **sandfish,** genus *Scincus,* of N Africa. Some skinks lay eggs, others bear live young.

Skinner /'skɪnə/ B(urrhus) F(rederic) 1903–1990. US psychologist, a radical behaviourist who studied operant conditioning and maintained that behaviour is shaped and maintained by its consequences. He applied his conditioning technique to education (he pioneered programmed learning) and to clinical work with psychotic patients. He rejected almost all previous psychology.

skinny *adj.* thin or emaciated. —**skinniness** *n.*

skint *adj.* (*slang*) having no money. [= *skinned*]

skip[1] *v.t./i.* (-pp-) 1. to move along lightly, especially by taking two steps with each foot in turn. 2. to jump lightly from the ground; to jump using a skipping rope. 3. to pass quickly from one subject or point to another. 4. to omit in reading or dealing with; (*colloquial*) not to participate in. 5. (*colloquial*) to leave hurriedly. —*n.* a skipping movement or action. —**skip bail,** to jump bail. **skip it!** (*slang*) abandon the topic etc. **skipping rope,** a length of rope (usually with two handles) revolved over the head and under the feet while jumping as a game or exercise.

skip[2] *n.* 1. a large container for refuse etc. 2. a cage or bucket etc. in which people or materials are raised or lowered in mines etc.

skipper *n.* the captain of a ship, especially of a small trading or fishing vessel; the captain of an aircraft; the captain of a side in games. —*v.t.* to act as captain of. [from Middle Dutch or Middle Low German *schipper*]

skirl *n.* the shrill sound characteristic of bagpipes. —*v.i.* to make a skirl.

skirmish *n.* a minor fight especially between small or outlying parts of armies or fleets; a short argument or contest of wit etc. —*v.i.* to engage in a skirmish. [from Old French *eskirmir*]

skirt *n.* 1. a woman's outer garment hanging from the waist; the part of a coat etc. that hangs below the waist. 2. the hanging part round the base of a hovercraft. 3. an edge, a border, an extreme part; skirt of beef (see below). —*v.t./i.* 1. to go or lie along or round the edge of. 2. to avoid dealing with (an issue etc.). —**skirting board,** a narrow board etc. along the bottom of a room wall. **skirt of beef,** the diaphragm etc. as food; meat from the lower flank. [from Old Norse = *shirt*]

skit *n.* a light, usually short piece of satire or burlesque. [related to *skit* = move lightly]

skittish /'skɪtɪʃ/ *adj.* lively, playful; (of a horse etc.) nervous, inclined to shy. —**skittishly** *adv.,* **skittishness** *n.*

skittle *n.* 1. (in *plural*) a game played with usually nine wooden pins set up at the end of an alley to be bowled down usually with a wooden ball or disc; a game played with similar pins set up on a board to be knocked down by a swinging suspended ball. Two or more players can compete. Skittles resembles ◊tenpin bowling. 2. a pin used in these games. —*v.t.* in cricket, (with *out*) to get (batsmen) out in rapid succession.

skive *v.t./i.* (*slang*) to evade (a duty). —**skive off,** to depart evasively. —**skiver** *n.* [originally = split (leather), from Old Norse]

skivvy /'skɪvi/ *n.* (*colloquial, derogatory*) a domestic servant, especially female.

Skopje /'skɒpjeɪ/ capital and industrial city of Macedonia, Yugoslavia; population (1981) 506,547. Industries include iron, steel, chromium mining, and food processing.

Skryabin /skri'æbin/ or **Scriabin** Alexander (Nikolayevich) 1872–1915. Russian composer and pianist. His powerfully emotional tone poems such as *Prometheus* 1911, and symphonies such as *Divine Poem* 1903, employed unusual harmonies.

skua /'skuːə/ *n.* a dark-coloured gull-like seabird of the genus *Stercorarius* etc. living in arctic and antarctic waters. Skuas can grow up to 60 cm/2 ft long, and are good fliers. They are aggressive scavengers, and will seldom fish for themselves but force gulls to disgorge their catch, and will also eat chicks of other birds. [from Faeroese and Old Norse]

skulduggery /skʌl'dʌgərɪ/ *n.* trickery; unscrupulous behaviour. [originally Scottish = unchastity]

skulk *v.i.* to loiter, move, or conceal oneself stealthily, especially in cowardice, evasion of duty, or because intending mischief. [from Scandinavian; compare Norwegian *skulka* = lurk]

skull *n.* 1. in vertebrates, the collection of flat and regularly shaped bones (or cartilage) that enclose the brain and the organs of sight, hearing, and smell, and provide support for the jaws. In mammals, the skull consists of 22 bones joined by sutures. The floor of the skull is pierced by a large hole for the spinal cord and a number of smaller apertures through which other nerves and blood vessels pass. The bones of the face include the upper jaw, enclose the sinuses, and form the framework for the nose, eyes, and roof of the mouth cavity. Inside, the skull has various shallow cavities into which fit different parts of the brain. 2. the bony framework of the head; a representation of this. 3. the head as the site of the intelligence. —**skull and crossbones,** a representation of a skull with two thighbones crossed below it as an emblem of piracy or death. **skullcap** *n.* a small, close-fitting, peakless cap.

skunk *n.* 1. a black, white-striped, bushy-tailed American animal of the genus *Mephitis* etc. of the weasel family, about the size of a cat and able to emit a powerful stench from liquid secreted by its anal glands when attacked; its fur. 2. a contemptible person. [from American Indian]

sky /skaɪ/ *n.* (in *singular* or *plural*) the region of the clouds, atmosphere, and outer space seen from the Earth. —*v.t.* to hit (a cricket ball) high into the air. —**sky-blue** *adj.* & *n.* bright clear blue. **sky-high** *adv.* & *adj.* reaching the sky; very high. **skyrocket** *n.* a rocket exploding high in the air. —*v.t.* to rise very steeply or rapidly. **skywriting** *n.* legible smoke trails emitted by an aeroplane. **to the skies,** without reserve. [originally = cloud(s), from Old Norse]

skull

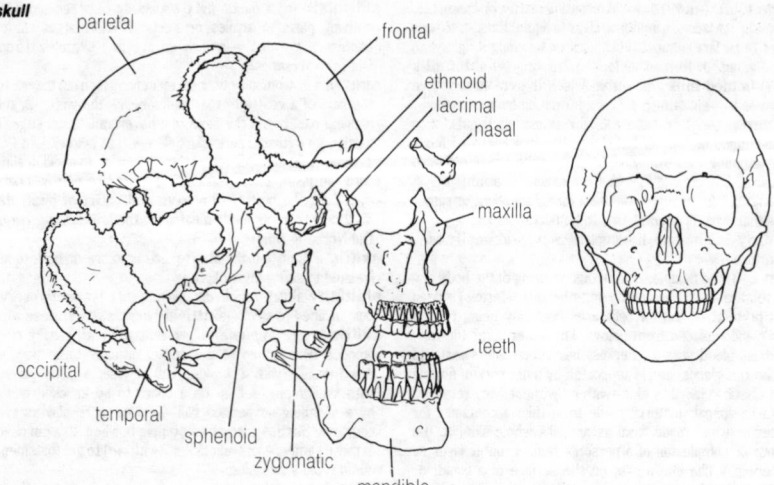

parietal
frontal
ethmoid
lacrimal
nasal
maxilla
occipital
teeth
temporal
sphenoid
zygomatic
mandible

skydiving *n.* the sport of freefalling from an aircraft at a height of up to 3,650 m/12,000 ft, performing aerobatics, and opening a parachute when 600 m/2,000 ft from the ground.

Skye /skaɪ/ largest island of the Inner Hebrides, Scotland; area 1,740 sq km/672 sq mi; population (1987) 8,100. It is separated from the mainland by the Sound of Sleat. The chief port is Portree. The economy is based on crofting, tourism, and livestock.

skyjack *v.t.* (*slang*) to hijack (an aircraft).

Skylab /'skaɪlæb/ *n.* US space station, in orbit 1973–79, made from the adapted upper stage of a Saturn V rocket. At 75 tonnes, it was the heaviest object ever put into space, and was 25.6 m/84 ft long. *Skylab* contained a workshop for carrying out experiments in weightlessness, an observatory for monitoring the Sun, and cameras for photographing the Earth's surface.

skylark *n.* a ◊lark *Alauda arvensis* that soars while singing. —*v.i.* to play tricks and practical jokes.

skylight *n.* a window in a roof.

skyline *n.* the outline of hills, buildings etc., defined against the sky.

skyscraper *n.* a building so tall that it appears to 'scrape the sky', developed from 1868 in New York, USA, where land prices were high and the geology adapted to such methods of construction. Skyscrapers are now found in cities throughout the world. The world's tallest free-standing structure is the CN (Canadian National) Tower, Toronto, 555 m/1,821 ft.

skyward /'skaɪwəd/ *adv.* or **skywards** & *adj.* towards the sky.

slab *n.* a flat, thick, usually square or rectangular piece of solid matter.

slack[1] *adj.* 1. lacking firmness or tautness. 2. lacking energy or activity; sluggish; negligent. 3. (of the tide etc.) neither ebbing nor flowing. —*n.* 1. a slack period, slack part of a rope etc.; (*colloquial*) a spell of inactivity. 2. (in *plural*) informal trousers. —*v.t./i.* 1. to slacken. 2. (*colloquial*) to take a rest; to be lazy. —**slack off**, to loosen, to lose or cause to lose vigour. **slack up**, to reduce speed. —**slackly** *adv.*, **slackness** *n.* [Old English]

slack[2] *n.* coal dust.

slacken *v.t./i.* to make or become slack.

slacker *n.* a shirker, an indolent person.

slag *n.* in chemistry, the molten mass of impurities that is produced in the smelting or refining of metals. —*v.i.* (-gg-) to form slag. —**slag heap**, a hill of refuse from a mine etc. —**slaggy** *adj.* [from Middle Low German]

slain past participle of *slay.*

slake *v.t.* 1. to assuage or satisfy (one's thirst, revenge, etc.). 2. to disintegrate (lime) by combination with water. [Old English]

slaked lime Ca(OH)$_2$ (technical name **calcium hydroxide**) the substance produced by adding water to quicklime (calcium oxide, CaO). Much heat is given out and the solid crumbles as it absorbs water. A solution of slaked lime is called ◊limewater.

slalom /'slɑːləm/ *n.* a ski race down a zigzag course with artificial obstacles; an obstacle race in canoes. [Norwegian = sloping track]

slam[1] *v.t./i.* (-mm-) 1. to shut forcefully with a loud bang; to put, knock, or move with a similar sound or violently. 2. (*slang*) to criticize severely; to hit, to beat; to gain an easy victory over. —*n.* the sound or action of slamming.

slam[2] *n.* the gaining of every trick at cards. —**grand slam**, the winning of 13 tricks in bridge; the winning of all of a group of championships in a sport.

slander /'slɑːndə/ *n.* a false statement maliciously uttered that is damaging to a person's reputation; the uttering of this. If broadcast on radio or television it constitutes ◊libel. —*v.t.* to utter a slander about. —**slanderous** *adj.*, **slanderously** *adv.* [from Anglo-French and Old French from Latin]

slang *n.* words and phrases, or particular meanings of these, that are found only in very informal language or in that of restricted groups of people. —*v.t./i.* to use abusive language (to). —**slanging match**, a prolonged exchange of insults. —**slangy** *adj.*

slant /slɑːnt/ *v.t./i.* 1. to slope, to lie or go at an angle from the vertical or horizontal; to cause to do this. 2. to present (information etc.) from a particular point of view or unfairly. —*n.* 1. a slope, an oblique position. 2. the way information etc. is presented; an attitude or bias. —*adj.* sloping, oblique. —**on a** *or* **the slant**, aslant. [variant of dialect *slent*, from Old Norse *sletta* = dash]

slantwise *adv.* aslant.

slap *v.t./i.* (-pp-) 1. to strike with the palm of the hand or a flat object, or so as to make a similar noise. 2. to lay forcefully. 3. to put hastily or carelessly. —*n.* a blow with the palm of the hand or a flat object; a slapping sound. —*adv.* with a slap; directly, suddenly; exactly. —**slap and tickle**, (*colloquial*) lively (especially amorous) amusement. **slap-bang** *adv.* violently, noisily, headlong. **slap down**, (*colloquial*) to snub; to reprimand. **slap-happy** *adj.* (*colloquial*) cheerfully casual or flippant. **slap in the face**, a rebuff or insult. **slap on the back**, congratulations. **slap-up** *adj.* lavish, first-class. [from Low German (imitative)]

slapdash *adj.* hasty and careless. —*adv.* in a slapdash manner.

slapstick *n.* boisterous knockabout comedy.

slash *v.t./i.* 1. to make a sweeping stroke or strokes with a sword, knife, whip etc.; to strike or cut thus. 2. to make an ornamental slit in (a garment), especially so as to show underlying fabric. 3. to reduce (prices etc.) drastically. 4. (in *participle*) vigorously incisive or effective. 5. to censure vigorously. —*n.* a slashing cut or stroke.

slat *n.* a thin, narrow piece of wood or plastic etc., especially used in an overlapping series as in a fence or Venetian blind. [from Old French *esclat* = splinter]

slate *n.* **1.** a fine-grained, usually grey metamorphic rock that splits readily into thin slabs along its ◊cleavage plane. It is the metamorphic equivalent of ◊shale. **2.** a piece of such a plate used as a roofing material or for writing on. **3.** the dull blue or grey colour of slate. —*v.t.* **1.** to cover with slates. **2.** (*colloquial*) to criticize severely. **3.** (*US*) to make arrangements for (an event etc.). **4.** (*US*) to nominate for office etc. —**clean slate**, no discreditable history. **clean the slate**, to remove obligations, grievances etc. —**slaty** *adj.* [from Old French *esclate* feminine of *esclat*]

slattern /'slætɜ:n/ *n.* a slovenly woman. —**slatternliness** *n.*, **slatternly** *adj.*

slaughter *n.* **1.** the killing of animals for food etc. **2.** the ruthless killing of many persons or animals. —*v.t.* **1.** to kill (animals) for food etc. **2.** to kill ruthlessly in great numbers. **3.** (*colloquial*) to defeat utterly. —**slaughterer** *n.* [from Old Norse]

slaughterhouse *n.* a place for the slaughter of animals as food.

Slav /slɑ:v/ *n.* a member of a group of peoples in central and E Europe, including the Russians, Poles, Czechs, Bulgarians, Serbo-Croats etc., speaking languages of the Slavonic group. —*adj.* of the Slavs. [from Latin *Sclavus*]

slave *n.* **1.** a person who is owned by another and has to serve him or her. **2.** a drudge, a person working very hard. **3.** a helpless victim of some dominating influence. **4.** a part of a machine directly controlled by another. —*v.i.* to work very hard. —**slave-driver** *n.* an overseer of slaves at work; a hard taskmaster. **slave labour**, forced labour. **slave trade**, the procuring, transporting, and selling of slaves, see ◊slavery. [from Old French *esclave* from Latin *Sclavus* = Slav, the Slavonic peoples in parts of Central Europe having been reduced to bondage by conquest]

slaver[1] /'sleɪvə/ *n.* a ship or person engaged in the slave trade.

slaver[2] /'slævə/ *n.* **1.** saliva running from the mouth. **2.** flattery; drivel. —*v.i.* to let saliva run from the mouth, to dribble.

slavery /'sleɪvərɪ/ *n.* **1.** the condition or work of a slave. **2.** very hard work, drudgery. **3.** the custom of having slaves. Slavery goes back to prehistoric times, but declined in Europe after the fall of the Roman Empire. During the imperialism of Spain, Portugal, and Britain in the 16th–18th centuries and in the American South in the 17th–19th centuries, slavery became a mainstay of an agricultural factory economy, with millions of Africans abducted to work on plantations in North and South America. Millions more died in the process, but the profits from this trade were enormous. Slavery was abolished in the British Empire in 1833 and in the USA at the end of the Civil War 1863–65, but continues illegally in some countries with cases reported in the 1980s in, for example, China and Sudan.

slavish /'sleɪvɪʃ/ *adj.* **1.** of or like slaves; excessively submissive. **2.** showing no independence or originality. —**slavishly** *adv.*, **slavishness** *n.*

Slavonic /slə'vɒnɪk/ *adj.* or (*US*) **Slavic 1.** of the branch of the Indo-European language family spoken in central and E Europe, the Balkans, and parts of N Asia. The family comprises the **southern group** (Serbo-Croatian, Slovene, and Macedonian in Yugoslavia, and Bulgarian in Bulgaria); the **western group** (Czech and Slovak in Czechoslovakia, Sorbian in E Germany, and Polish and its related dialects); and the **eastern group** (Russian, Ukrainian, and Byelorussian in the USSR). **2.** of the Slavs. —*n.* the Slavonic group of languages. [from Latin *S(c)lavonia* = country of the Slavs]

Slavophile *n.* a member of an intellectual and political group in 19th-century Russia that promoted the idea of an Eastern orientation for the empire in opposition to those who wanted the country to adopt Western methods and ideas of development.

slay *v.t.* (*past* **slew** /slu:/; *past participle* **slain**) to kill. [Old English]

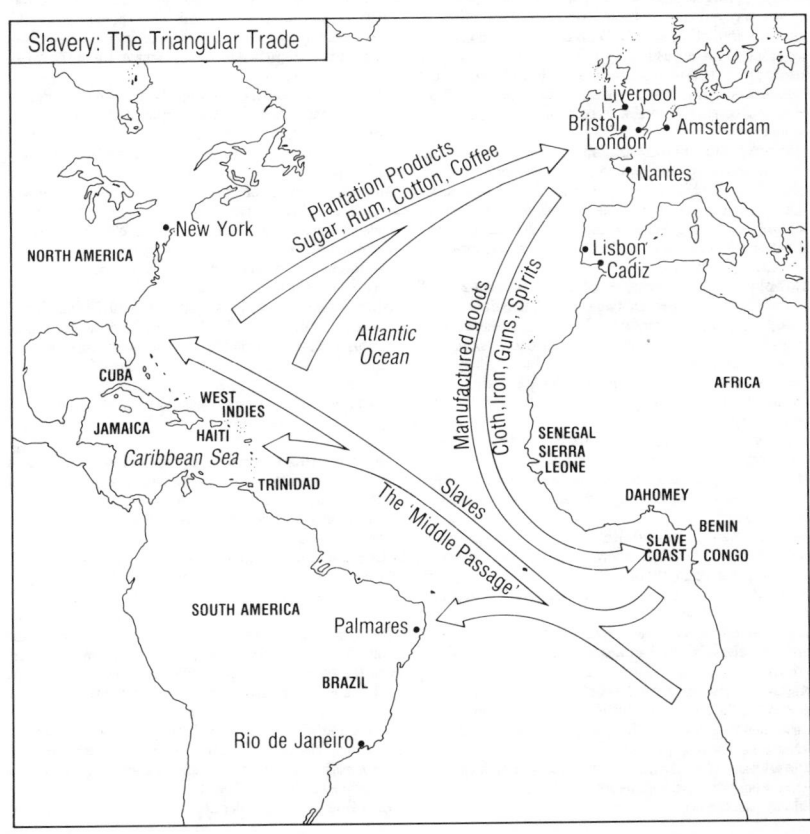

Slavery: The Triangular Trade

SLD abbreviation of ◊Social and Liberal Democrats.

sleazy *adj.* squalid, tawdry; slatternly. —**sleazily** *adv.*, **sleaziness** *n.*

sled *n.* (*US*) a sledge. —*v.t./i.* (**-dd-**) (*US*) to sledge. [from Middle Low German]

sledge *n.* a vehicle on runners instead of wheels for conveying loads or passengers, especially over snow. —*v.t./i.* to travel or convey by sledge. [from Middle Dutch *sleedse*]

sledgehammer *n.* 1. a large, heavy hammer. 2. (*attributive*) heavy and powerful. [Old English *slecg* = slay]

sleek *adj.* 1. (of hair or skin etc.) smooth and glossy. 2. looking well fed and comfortable. 3. ingratiating. —*v.t.* to make sleek. —**sleekly** *adv.*, **sleekness** *n.* [variant of *slick*]

sleep /sli:p/ *n.* 1. the naturally recurring condition of rest in animals, in which the eyes are closed, postural muscles relaxed, and consciousness suspended; a sleeplike state. The function of sleep is unclear. People deprived of sleep become irritable, uncoordinated, forgetful, hallucinatory, and even psychotic. 2. a spell of sleeping. 3. the inert condition of hibernating animals. —*v.t./i.* 1. to be in a state of sleep; to fall asleep. 2. to stay for a night's sleep. 3. to have sexual intercourse in bed *together* or *with*. 4. to spend (time) in sleeping. 5. to provide sleeping accommodation for. 6. to be inactive or dead. —**go to sleep**, to enter the state of sleep; (of a limb etc.) to become numbed. **last sleep**, death. **put to sleep**, to anaesthetize; to kill (an animal) painlessly. **sleep around**, (*colloquial*) to be sexually promiscuous. **sleep in**, to remain asleep later than usual. **sleeping bag**, a lined or padded bag to sleep in, especially when camping etc. **sleeping car** *or* **carriage**, a railway coach with beds or berths. **sleeping partner**, one not sharing in the actual work of a firm. **sleeping pill**, a pill (especially one of the ◊barbiturates) to induce sleep. **sleep off**, to get rid of (a headache etc.) by sleeping. **sleep on it**, to refrain from deciding (a question etc.) until the next day. **sleepwalker** *n.* a person who walks about while asleep. **sleepwalking** *n.* this condition. [Old English]

Sleep Wayne 1948–. British dancer who was principal dancer with the Royal Ballet 1973–83 and formed his own company, Dash, in 1980.

sleeper *n.* 1. one who sleeps. 2. each of the beams on which railway rails run. 3. a sleeping car; a berth in this. 4. a ring or stud worn in a pierced ear to keep the hole from closing.

sleeping sickness or **trypanosomiasis** an infectious disease of tropical Africa. Early symptoms include fever, headache, and chills, followed by ◊anaemia and joint pains. Later, the disease attacks the central nervous system, causing drowsiness, lethargy, and, if left untreated, death. Control is by eradication of the tsetse fly, which transmits the disease to humans.

sleepless *adj.* 1. lacking sleep; unable to sleep. 2. continually active. —**sleeplessly** *adv.*, **sleeplessness** *n.*

sleepy *adj.* 1. ready for sleep, about to fall asleep. 2. lacking activity or bustle. —**sleepily** *adv.*, **sleepiness** *n.*

sleet *n.* snow and rain together; hail or snow melting as it falls. —*v.i.* to fall as sleet. —**it sleets** *or* **is sleeting**, sleet is falling. —**sleety** *adj.* [related to Middle Low German *sloten* = hail]

sleeve *n.* 1. the part of a garment that encloses the arm or a part of it. 2. the cover of a gramophone record. 3. a tube enclosing a rod or smaller tube. 4. a windsock. —**up one's sleeve**, concealed but ready for use. —**sleeved** *adj.* [Old English]

sleeveless *adj.* without sleeves.

sleigh /slei/ *n.* a sledge, especially one for riding on. —*v.i.* to travel on a sleigh. [from Dutch *slee*]

sleight /slait/ *n.* (*archaic*) dexterity, cunning. —**sleight of hand**, a display of dexterity; conjuring. [from Old Norse]

slender *adj.* 1. of small girth or breadth; slim and graceful. 2. relatively small in amount etc.; scanty. —**slenderness** *n.*

slept past and past participle of **sleep**.

sleuth /slu:θ/ *n.* a detective. —**sleuthhound** *n.* a bloodhound; a detective. [originally *sleuthhound*, from Old Norse *slóth* = track]

slew¹ /slu:/ *v.t./i.* to turn or swing forcibly or with effort to a new position. —*n.* such a turn.

slew² past of **slay**.

slice *n.* 1. a thin, broad, 'or wedge-shaped piece cut from something. 2. a share or portion. 3. an implement with a broad, flat blade for lifting or serving fish etc. or for scraping or chipping things. 4. in golf, a slicing stroke. —*v.t./i.* 1. to cut into slices; to cut from a larger piece. 2. to cut cleanly or easily with or like a knife. 3. in golf, to strike (a ball) badly so that it deviates from the direction intended, going to the right of a right-handed player. —**sliced bread**, bread that is sliced and wrapped before being sold. —**slicer** *n.* [from Old French *esclice* = splinter]

slick *adj.* 1. skilful or efficient, especially in a superficial or pretentious way or with some trickery. 2. smooth in manner or speech. 3. shrewd, wily. 4. smooth and slippery. —*n.* a slippery place or patch; a thick patch of oil floating on the sea. —*v.t.* to make sleek. —**slickness** *n.*

slide *v.t./i.* (*past* and *past participle* **slid**) 1. to move or cause to move along a smooth surface with constant friction on the same part of the thing moving. 2. to move or go smoothly or quietly. 3. to pass gradually or imperceptibly into a condition or habit. 4. to glide more or less erect over ice or other smooth surface without using skates. —*n.* 1. an act of sliding. 2. a smooth surface for sliding on; an inclined plane down which goods etc. are slid or for children to play on. 3. a sliding part of a machine or instrument. 4. a thing slid into place; a mounted picture or transparency for showing by means of a projector; a small glass plate holding an object for examination under a microscope. 5. a hair slide. —**let things slide**, to fail to give them proper attention or control; to allow deterioration. **slide over**, to skate over (a delicate subject etc.). **slide rule**, a mathematical instrument with pairs of logarithmic sliding scales, used for rapid calculations, including multiplication, division, and the extraction of square roots. It has been largely superseded by the electronic calculator. **sliding scale**, a scale of fees, taxes, wages etc., that varies as a whole according to changes in some standard. —**slider** *n.* [Old English]

slight /slait/ *adj.* 1. not much, not great, not thorough; inconsiderable. 2. slender and frail-looking, not heavily built. —*v.t.* to treat or speak of (a person etc.) with disrespect or as not worth attention. —*n.* an act of slighting. —**slightly** *adv.*, **slightness** *n.* [from Old Norse = level, smooth]

Sligo /'slaigəʊ/ county in the province of Connacht, Republic of Ireland, situated on the Atlantic coast of NW Ireland; area 1,800 sq km/695 sq mi; population (1986) 56,000. The county town is Sligo; there is livestock and dairy farming.

slim /slim/ *adj.* 1. of small girth or thickness, not heavily built. 2. relatively small. —*v.t./i.* (**-mm-**) 1. to make oneself slimmer by dieting, exercise etc. 2. to reduce (a workforce etc.) in size. —**slimly** *adv.*, **slimmer** *n.*, **slimness** *n.* [Dutch or Low German = Middle Low German *slim(m)* = slanting]

Slim William Joseph, 1st Viscount 1891–1970. English field marshal in World War II. He commanded the 1st Burma Corps 1942–45, stemming the Japanese invasion of India, and then forcing them out of Burma (now Myanmar). He was governor general of Australia 1953–60.

slime *n.* an unpleasant, slippery, thick liquid substance. [Old English, related to Latin *limus* = mud, Greek *limnē* = marsh]

slime mould or **myxomycete** an extraordinary organism which shows some features of ◊fungi and some of ◊protozoa. Slime moulds are not closely related to any other group, although they are often classed, for convenience, with the fungi.

Cellular slime moulds go through a phase of living as single cells, looking like amoebae, and feed by engulfing the bacteria found in rotting wood, dung, or damp soil. When a food supply is exhausted, up to 100,000 of these amoebae form into a colony resembling a single sluglike animal and migrate to a fresh source of bacteria. The colony then takes on the aspect of a fungus, and forms long-stalked fruiting bodies which release spores. These germinate to release amoebae, which repeat the life cycle.

Plasmodial slime moulds have a more complex life cycle involving sexual reproduction. They form a slimy mass of protoplasm with no internal cell walls, which slowly spreads over the bark or branches of trees.

slimline *adj.* of slender design.

slimy /'slɪmɪ/ adj. 1. like slime; covered with or full of slime. 2. disgustingly obsequious, meek, or dishonest. —**slimily** adv., **sliminess** n.

sling[1] n. 1. a belt, strap, or chain(s) etc. looped round an object to lift it or support it as it hangs. 2. a bandage etc. looped round the neck to support an injured arm. 3. a looped strap used to throw a stone or other missile. —v.t. (past and past participle **slung**) 1. to suspend or lift with a sling; to arrange so as to be held or moved from above. 2. to hurl with a sling; (colloquial) to throw. —**slingback** n. a shoe held in place by a strap above and behind the heel. **sling one's hook,** (slang) to make off.

sling[2] n. (US) a sweetened drink of gin or other spirits and water.

slink v.i. (past and past participle **slunk**) to move in a stealthy, guilty, or shamefaced manner. [Old English = crawl]

slinky adj. 1. moving in a slinking manner; stealthy. 2. smooth and sinuous; (of clothes) close-fitting and sinuous. —**slinkily** adv., **slinkiness** n.

slip[1] v.t./i. (-pp-) 1. to slide unintentionally or momentarily; to lose one's footing or one's balance thus. 2. to go or put with a smooth movement or stealthily. 3. to escape restraint or capture by being slippery or not grasped firmly. 4. to make one's way quietly or unobserved. 5. to make a careless or casual error; to fall below one's normal standard. 6. to release from restraint or connection. 7. in knitting, to move (a stitch) to the other needle without looping the yarn through it. 8. to escape from; to evade. —n. 1. an act of slipping. 2. an accidental or slight error. 3. a loose covering or garment; a petticoat. 4. a reduction in the movement or speed of a pulley or propeller etc. 5. (in singular or plural) a slipway. 6. in cricket, a fieldsman close behind the wicket; (in singular or plural) this part of the ground. —**give a person the slip,** to escape from or evade him or her. **let slip,** to release accidentally or deliberately; to miss (an opportunity); to utter inadvertently. **slipcase** or **slipcover** n. a fitted cover for a book or furniture etc. **slipknot** n. a knot that can be undone at a pull, a running knot. **slip of the pen** (or **tongue**), a small mistake in which something is written (or said) unintentionally. **slip-on** adj. (of shoes or clothes) that can be easily slipped on or off. **slipped disc,** a disc between the vertebrae that has become displaced and causes lumbar pain. **slip road,** a road for entering or leaving a motorway etc. **slipstream** n. a current of air or water driven back by a propeller or moving vehicle. **slip up,** (colloquial) to make a mistake. **slip-up** n. (colloquial) a mistake, a blunder.

slip[2] n. 1. a small piece of paper, especially for writing on. 2. a cutting taken from a plant for grafting or planting. —**slip of a girl** etc., a small, slim girl etc.

slip[3] n. finely ground clay mixed with water for coating or decorating earthenware. [Old English = slime]

slipper n. a light, loose shoe for indoor wear.

slippery adj. 1. difficult to grasp because of smoothness or wetness etc. 2. (of a surface) on which slipping is likely. 3. (of a person) unreliable, unscrupulous. —**slipperiness** n.

slippy adj. (colloquial) slippery. —**look slippy,** to make haste.

slipshod adj. 1. slovenly, careless. 2. having shoes that are down at heel.

slipway n. a sloping structure used for building ships or as a landing stage.

slit n. a straight, narrow incision or opening. —v.t (-tt-; past and past participle **slit**) to make a slit in; to cut into strips. [from Old English]

slither /'slɪðə/ v.i. to slip or slide unsteadily. —n. an act of slithering. —**slithery** adj. [Old English frequentative of slide)]

sliver /'slɪvə/ n. a thin strip or piece of wood etc. —v.t./i. to break off as a sliver; to break or form into slivers. [related to dialect slive = cleave]

Sloane /sləʊn/ Hans 1660–1753. British physician, born in County Down, Ireland. He settled in London, and in 1721 founded the Chelsea Physic Garden. He was president of the Royal College of Physicians 1719–35, and in 1727 succeeded the physicist Isaac Newton as president of the Royal Society. His library, which he bequeathed to the nation, formed the nucleus of the British Museum.

slob n. (colloquial) a large and coarse or stupid person. [from Irish slab = mud]

slobber v.t./i. 1. to slaver or dribble. 2. to show excessive sentiment over a person etc. —n. slaver. —**slobbery** adj. [= Dutch slobbern (imitative)]

sloe /sləʊ/ n. the ♦blackthorn; its fruit. [Old English]

slog v.t./i. (-gg-) 1. to hit hard. 2. to work or walk doggedly. —n. 1. a hard hit. 2. hard, steady work; a spell of this. —**slogger** n.

slogan /'sləʊgən/ n. a short, catchy phrase used in advertising etc.; a party cry, a watchword. [from Gaelic = war cry]

sloop n. a small, one-masted, fore-and-aft-rigged vessel. [from Dutch sloep]

slop v.t./i. (-pp-) 1. to spill (liquid); to be spilt; to splash liquid on. 2. to behave effusively. 3. to plod clumsily through mud or puddles etc.; to move in a slovenly way. —n. 1. slopped liquid. 2. weak sentimentality. 3. (in plural) household liquid refuse; the contents of chamber pots; dregs from teacups etc. 4. (in singular or plural) unappetizing liquid food. —**slop basin,** a basin for the dregs of cups at table. **slop out,** in prison, to carry slops out from cells. **slop pail,** a pail for removing bedroom or kitchen slops. [earlier = slush, related to Old English slyppe = slimy substance]

slope n. 1. a position, direction, or state at an angle from the horizontal or vertical; a state in which one end or side is at a higher level than the other; the difference in level between two ends or sides of a thing. 2. a piece of rising or falling ground; a place for skiing on the side of a mountain. —v.t./i. 1. to have or take a slope. 2. to cause to do this. —**slope arms,** to place a rifle in a sloping position against the shoulder. **slope off,** (slang) to go away. [from aslope = crosswise]

sloppy adj. 1. having a liquid consistency and splashing easily; excessively liquid. 2. unsystematic, careless. 3. untidy and ill-fitting; loose-fitting. 4. weakly sentimental. —**sloppily** adv., **sloppiness** n.

slosh v.t./i. 1. to splash; to move with a splashing sound. 2. to hit heavily. 3. to pour (liquid) clumsily (on). —n. 1. slush. 2. an act or sound of splashing. 3. (slang) a heavy blow. [variant of slush]

sloshed adj. (slang) drunk.

slot n. 1. a slit or other narrow aperture in a machine etc. for something (especially a coin) to be inserted. 2. a groove, channel, or slit into which something fits or in which something works. 3. an allotted place in an arrangement or scheme. —v.t./i. (-tt-) 1. to put into or be placed in a slot. 2. to make a slot or slots in. —**slot machine,** a machine worked by the insertion of a coin, especially delivering small purchased articles or providing amusement. [originally = hollow of the breast, from Old French esclot]

sloth /sləʊθ/ n. 1. laziness, indolence. 2. a South and Central American slow-moving arboreal mammal of the genera Choloepus and Bradypus, of the order Edentata. Sloths are greyish brown, about 70 cm/2.3 ft long, and have small rounded heads, rudimentary tails, and prolonged forelimbs. Each foot has long, curved claws adapted to clinging upside down from trees. They are vegetarian. [from slow]

slothful adj. lazy. —**slothfully** adv.

slouch v.i. to stand, move, or sit in a drooping, ungainly fashion. —n. 1. a slouching posture or movement. 2. the downward bend of a hat brim. 3. (slang) a lazy, incompetent, or slovenly worker etc. —**slouch hat,** a hat with a wide, flexible brim. —**sloucher** n.

slough[1] /slaʊ/ n. a swamp, a miry place. [Old English]

slough[2] /slʌf/ n. a snake's cast skin; dead tissue that drops away. —v.t./i. to cast or drop as slough.

Slovak /'sləʊvæk/ n. a native or the language of Slovakia. —adj. of the Slovaks. [from Slovak etc. Slovák]

Slovakia /sləʊ'vɑːkiə/ region of E ♦Czechoslovakia settled in the 5th–6th centuries by Slavs; occupied by the Magyars in the 10th century; part of the kingdom of Hungary until 1918, when it became a province of Czechoslovakia. Slovakia was a puppet state under German domination 1939–45, and was abolished as an administrative division in 1949. Its capital and chief town was Bratislava. Following the overthrow of the communist regime in Czechoslovakia in 1989, the Slovaks have demanded independence.

sloven /'slʌvən/ n. a slovenly person.

Slovenia /sləʊ'viːniə/ or **Slovenija** constituent republic of NW Yugoslavia; **area** 20,300 sq km/7,836 sq mi; **capital** Ljubljana; **physical** mountainous; rivers Sava and Drava; **products** grain, sugar beet, livestock, timber, cotton and woollen textiles, steel, vehicles; **population** (1986) 1,930,000; 89% Slovenes; **language** Slovene, resembling Serbo-Croat, written in Roman characters; **recent history** until 1918 the Austrian province of Carniola; an autonomous republic of Yugoslavia from 1946. In Sept 1989 it voted to give itself the right to secede from Yugoslavia and to prevent the Yugoslavian government from interfering in Slovene affairs and in June 1991 Slovenia declared itself independent.

slovenly adj. careless and untidy, unmethodical. —adv. in a slovenly manner. —**slovenliness** n.

slow /sləʊ/ adj. **1.** not quick or fast; acting, moving, or done without haste or rapidity. **2.** tending to cause slowness. **3.** (of a clock etc.) showing a time earlier than the correct one. **4.** dull-witted, stupid; not understanding readily. **5.** lacking liveliness, slack or sluggish. **6.** (of a fire or oven) giving low heat. **7.** (of photographic film) not very sensitive to light, needing a long exposure; (of a lens) having only a small aperture. **8.** lacking the inclination. —adv. slowly (used when slow gives the essential point, as in go slow). —v.t./i. (with down or up) to reduce the speed of; to go more slowly. —**slowdown** n. the action of slowing down. **slow motion**, a speed of cinema film in which movements appear much slower than in real life; a simulation of this. —**slowly** adv., **slowness** n. [Old English]

slowcoach n. a person who is slow in his or her actions, understanding, or work etc.

slowworm n. a harmless species of lizard *Anguis fragilis*, common in Europe. Superficially resembling a snake, it is distinguished by its small mouth and movable eyelids. It is about 30 cm/1 ft long, and eats worms and slugs. [Old English, first element of uncertain origin but not from slow]

SLR abbreviation of single-lens reflex, a type of ◊camera in which the image is seen in the lens used for taking the photograph.

sludge n. **1.** thick greasy mud; muddy or slushy sediment. **2.** sewage. —**sludgy** adj.

slug[1] n. **1.** a small air-breathing gastropod related to the snails, but with absent or much reduced shell. The **grey field slug** *Agriolimax reticulatus* is a common British species, and a pest to crops and garden plants. **2.** a piece of metal; a bullet of irregular shape; a missile for an airgun. **3.** (US) a tot of liquor. [from earlier *slugg(e)* = sluggard]

slug[2] v.t./i. (US) (-gg-) to hit hard. —n. (US) a hard hit.

sluggard /'slʌɡəd/ n. a lazy person. [from slug = be slothful]

sluggish adj. inert, slow-moving. —**sluggishly** adv., **sluggishness** n.

sluice /sluːs/ n. **1.** (or **sluicegate** a sliding gate or other contrivance for regulating the flow or level of water. **2.** the water regulated by this. **3.** or **sluiceway** an artificial channel for carrying off water. **4.** a place for rinsing things. —v.t./i. **1.** to let out (water) by means of a sluice; (of water) to rush out freely (as) from a sluice. **2.** to flood, scour, or rinse with a flow of water. [from Old French *escluse* from Latin *excludere* (*claudere* = shut)]

slum n. a dirty overcrowded district inhabited by poor people. —v.i. (-mm-) **1.** to live in slumlike conditions. **2.** to visit a slum for curiosity or for charitable purposes. —**slummy** adj. [19th-century slang]

slumber v.t./i. to sleep (literally or figuratively). —n. sleep (literal or figurative). —**slumberer** n., **slumberous** adj., **slumbrous** adj. [from Old English]

slump n. a sudden severe or prolonged fall in prices and values and in demand for goods etc. —v.i. **1.** to undergo a slump. **2.** to sit or fall down limply. [originally = sink in bog (imitative)]

slung past and past participle of sling[1].

slunk past and past participle of slink.

slur v.t./i. (-rr-) **1.** to sound or write (words, musical notes, etc.) so that they run into one another. **2.** to put a slur upon (a person or character). **3.** to pass lightly or deceptively (over a fact etc.). —n. **1.** an imputation; discredit. **2.** an act of slurring. **3.** in music, a curved line joining notes to be slurred.

slurp v.t. (colloquial) to eat or drink with a noisy sucking sound. —n. (colloquial) this sound. [from Dutch]

slurry /'slʌrɪ/ n. thin mud; a suspension of fine solid material in water or other liquid; thin liquid cement. [related to dialect slur = thin mud]

slush n. **1.** thawing snow; watery mud. **2.** silly sentimental talk or writing. —**slush fund,** money used to bribe officials etc., e.g. by illicit commission. —**slushy** adj.

slut n. a slovenly woman. —**sluttish** adj.

Sluter /'sluːtə/ Claus c.1380–1406. N European Gothic sculptor, probably of Dutch origin, active in Dijon, France. His work includes the *Well of Moses* c.1395–1403 (now in the grounds of a hospital in Dijon); and the kneeling mourners, or *gisants*, for the tomb of his patron Philip the Bold, Duke of Burgundy (Dijon Museum and Cleveland Museum, Ohio).

sly /slaɪ/ adj. **1.** done or doing things in an unpleasantly cunning and secret way. **2.** mischievous and knowing. —**on the sly**, secretly. —**slyly** adv., **slyness** n. [from Old Norse, originally = able to strike]

Sm symbol for ◊samarium.

smack[1] n. **1.** a sharp slap or blow; a hard hit. **2.** a sharp sound as of a surface struck by a flat object; a loud kiss. —v.t. to slap; to move with a smack. —adv. (colloquial) with a smack; suddenly, directly, violently. —**smack in the eye,** a rebuff. [from Middle Dutch (imitative)]

smack[2] v.t./i. to have a slight flavour or trace of something. —n. **1.** a slight flavour or trace. **2.** (slang) ◊heroin, an addictive depressant drug. [Old English]

smack[3] n. a boat with a single mast, used for sailing or fishing. [from Dutch]

smacker n. (slang) **1.** a loud kiss, a sounding blow. **2.** (US) $1.

small adj. **1.** not large or big. **2.** not great in importance, amount, power etc.; not much, insignificant. **3.** consisting of small particles. **4.** doing things on a small scale. **5.** socially undistinguished, poor or humble. **6.** mean, ungenerous; paltry. —n. **1.** the slenderest part of something (especially **small of the back**). **2.** (in plural, colloquial) small articles of laundry, especially underwear. —adv. into small pieces. —**feel** or **look small,** to be humiliated or ashamed. **small beer,** an insignificant thing. **small change,** coins, especially low denominations as opposed to notes. **small fry,** see ◊fry[2]. **small hours,** the period soon after midnight. **small-minded** adj. narrow or selfish in outlook. **small-scale** adj. made or occurring on a small scale. **small talk,** social conversation on unimportant matters. **small-time** adj. unimportant, petty. —**smallness** n. [Old English]

small arms one of the two main divisions of firearms, guns that can be carried by hand. The first small arms were portable handguns in use in the late 14th century, supported on the ground and ignited by hand. Today's small arms range from breech-loading single-shot rifles and shotguns to sophisticated automatic and semiautomatic weapons. In 1980, there were 11,522 deaths in the USA caused by hand-held guns; in the UK, there were 8.

small claims court 1. in the USA, a court that deals with small civil claims, using a simple procedure, often without attorney intervention. **2.** a similar body introduced experimentally in London and Manchester for a time in the 1980s. **3.** a county court in the UK, where a simplified procedure applies for small claims.

smallholder n. an owner or user of a smallholding.

smallholding n. a piece of agricultural land smaller than a farm.

small intestine the length of gut between the stomach and the large intestine, consisting of the duodenum and the ileum. It is responsible for digesting and absorbing food.

smallpox /'smɔːlpɒks/ n. an acute, highly contagious viral disease, marked by aches, fever, vomiting, and skin eruptions leaving pitted scars. Widespread vaccination programmes have almost eradicated this often fatal disease.

smarm v.t. (colloquial) **1.** to smooth, to slick. **2.** to flatter fulsomely.

smarmy adj. (colloquial) ingratiating. —**smarminess** n.

smart adj. **1.** clever, ingenious; quick-witted. **2.** neat and elegant; fashionable. **3.** forceful; brisk. —v.i. to feel acute pain or distress. —n. a stinging sensation or mental feeling. —**look smart,** to make haste. **smart alec,** a know-all. —**smartly** adv., **smartness** n. [Old English]

smart card a plastic card with an embedded microprocessor and memory. It can store, for example, personal data, identification, and bank account details, to enable it to be used as a credit or debit card. The card can be 'loaded' with credits that are then spent electronically, and reloaded as needed. Possible other uses range from hotel door 'keys' to passports.

smarten *v.t./i.* (usually with *up*) to make or become smart.

smart pill in medicine, a peanut-sized pill containing a computer and sensors to take measurements as it passes through the body. The information is transmitted, by ultrasound, to an external computer. The pill can discharge drugs, for example, it can detect stones in the gallbladder and release chemicals to dissolve them.

smash *v.t./i.* 1. to break or become broken suddenly and noisily into pieces. 2. to destroy, defeat, or overthrow suddenly and completely; to suffer such destruction etc. 3. to strike or move with great force; to strike (a ball) forcefully downwards in tennis etc. —*n.* 1. an act or sound of smashing; a collision; a disaster, financial ruin. 2. or **smash hit** a very successful play or song etc. —*adv.* with a smash. —**smash-and-grab** *adj.* (of a robbery) in which a thief smashes a window and seizes goods. [imitative]

smasher *n.* (*colloquial*) a very pleasing or beautiful person or thing.

smashing *adj.* (*colloquial*) excellent, wonderful; beautiful.

smattering /'smætərıŋ/ *n.* a slight knowledge of something. [from *smatter* = talk ignorantly]

smear *v.t.* 1. to daub or stain with a greasy or sticky substance. 2. to smudge. 3. to discredit or defame; to seek to do this. —*n.* 1. the action or result of smearing. 2. material smeared on a microscope slide etc. for examination; a specimen of this. 3. discrediting, defaming; an attempt at this. —**smeary** *adj.* [Old English]

smell *n.* 1. the faculty of perception through the response of the brain to chemical molecules in the air. It works by having receptors in the nose for particular chemical groups, into which the airborne chemicals must fit to trigger a message to the brain. 2. the quality in substances that affects this sense. 3. an unpleasant odour. 4. an act of inhaling to ascertain a smell. —*v.t./i.* (*past* and *past participle* **smelt** or **smelled**) 1. to perceive, detect, or examine by smell; to have or use the sense of smell. 2. to give off a smell; to seem by smell to be; to be redolent *of* something specified. —**smell out**, to seek or discover by smelling or investigation.

smelling salts or **sal volatile** a mixture of ammonium carbonate, bicarbonate, and carbamate together with other strong-smelling substances, formerly used as a restorative for dizziness or fainting.

smelly *adj.* having a strong or unpleasant smell. —**smelliness** *n.*

smelt[1] *v.t.* to extract metal from (ore) by melting; to extract (metal) thus. Oxide ores such as iron ore are smelted in a furnace with coke (carbon), which reduces the ore into metal and also provides fuel for the process. [from Middle Dutch or Middle Low German]

smelt[2] *n.* a small edible fish, usually marine, although some species are freshwater and some live in lakes. They occur in Europe and North America. The most common European smelt is the **sparling** *Osmerus eperlanus*. [Old English]

smelt[3] past and past participle of **smell**.

Smersh /smɑː∫/ *n.* formerly the main administration of counterintelligence in the USSR, established in 1942. It was a subsection of the ◊KGB.

Smetana /'smetənə/ Bedřich 1824–1884. Czech composer, whose music has a distinct national character, as in for example the operas *The Bartered Bride* 1866 and *Dalibor* 1868, and the symphonic suite *My Country* 1875–80. He conducted the National Theatre of Prague 1866–74.

smidgen /'smıdʒən/ *n.* (*colloquial*) a small bit or amount.

smilax /'smaılæks/ *n.* 1. a climbing plant, often with a prickly stem, of the genus *Smilax*, some tropical species of which yield sarsaparilla from tuberous root stocks. 2. a South African climbing asparagus *Asparagus asparagoides* much used in decoration. [Latin from Greek = bindweed]

smile *v.t./i.* to make or have a facial expression indicating pleasure or amusement, with the lips stretched and turning upwards at their ends; to express by smiling; to give (a smile) of a specified kind. —*n.* an act of smiling; a smiling expression or aspect. —**smile on** *or* **at**, to look encouragingly on; (of a circumstance etc.) to favour. —**smiler** *n.*

smirch *v.t.* to besmirch. —*n.* 1. a smear or stain. 2. discredit.

smirk *n.* a silly or self-satisfied smile. —*v.i.* to give a smirk. [Old English (*smerian* = laugh at)]

smite *v.t./i.* (*past* **smote**; *past participle* **smitten** /'smıtən/) 1. (*archaic*) to hit hard; to chastise, to defeat. 2. to have a sudden effect on. 3. (especially in *past participle*) to strike with a disease, desire, emotion, or fascination. [Old English *smitan* = smear]

smith /smıθ/ *n.* 1. a worker in metal. 2. a blacksmith. 3. one who creates something (e.g. *songsmith*). [Old English]

Smith Adam 1723–1790. Scottish economist, often regarded as the founder of political economy. His *The Wealth of Nations* 1776 defined national wealth in terms of labour. The cause of wealth is explained by the division of labour: dividing a production process into several repetitive operations, each carried out by different workers. Smith advocated the free working of individual enterprise, and the necessity of 'free trade'.

Smith Bessie 1894–1937. US jazz and blues singer, born in Chattanooga, Tennessee. Known as the 'Empress of the Blues', she established herself in the 1920s after she was discovered by Columbia Records. She made over 150 recordings accompanied by such greats as Louis Armstrong and Benny Goodman. Her popularity waned in the Depression, and she died after a car crash when she was refused admission to a whites-only hospital.

Smith David 1906–1965. US sculptor and painter, whose work made a lasting impact on sculpture after World War II. He trained as a steel welder in a car factory. His pieces are large openwork metal abstracts.

Smith Ian (Douglas) 1919– . Rhodesian politician. He was a founder of the Rhodesian Front in 1962 and prime minister 1964–79. In 1965 he made a unilateral declaration of Rhodesia's independence and, despite United Nations sanctions, maintained his regime with tenacity. In 1979 he was succeeded as prime minister by Bishop Abel Muzorewa, when the country was renamed Zimbabwe. He was suspended from the Zimbabwe parliament in April 1987 and resigned in May as head of the white opposition party.

Smith John 1580–1631. English colonist. He took part in the colonization of Virginia, acting as president of the North American colony 1608–09. He explored New England in 1614, which he named, and published pamphlets on America and an autobiography. He also traded with the Indians, which may have kept the colonists alive in the early years.

Smith John Maynard. British biologist, see ◊Maynard Smith.

Smith Joseph 1805–1844. US founder of the ◊Mormon religious sect. In 1827 he claimed to have been granted the revelation of the *Book of Mormon* (an ancient prophet), inscribed on gold plates and concealed a thousand years before in a hill near Palmyra, New York State. He founded the Church of Jesus Christ of Latter-day Saints in Fayette, New York, in 1830.

Smith Maggie (Margaret Natalie) 1934– . English actress, a highly talented comedienne. Her films include *The Prime of Miss Jean Brodie* 1969 (Academy Award), *California Suite* 1978, *A Private Function* 1984, and *A Room with a View* 1986.

Smith Stevie (Florence Margaret) 1902–1971. English poet and novelist. She published her first book *Novel on Yellow Paper* in 1936, and her first collection of poems *A Good Time Was Had by All* in 1937. She wrote a further eight volumes of eccentrically direct verse, including *Not Waving but Drowning* 1957, and two more novels. *Collected Poems* was published in 1975.

Smith William 1769–1839. English geologist, the founder of stratigraphy. Working as a canal engineer, he observed while supervising excavations that different beds of rock could be identified by their fossils, and so established the basis of ◊stratigraphy. He also produced the first geological maps of England and Wales.

smithereens /smıðə'riːnz/ *n.pl.* small fragments.

Smiths, the /smıθs/ English four-piece rock group (1982–87) from Manchester. Their songs, with lyrics by singer Morrissey (1959–) and tunes by guitarist Johnny Marr (1964–), drew on diverse sources such as rockabilly, Mersey beat, and the Byrds, with confessional humour and images of urban desolation.

smithy /'smıðı/ *n.* a blacksmith's workshop, a forge.

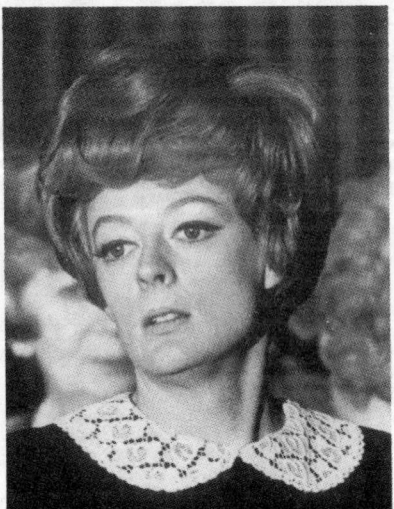

Smith *English actress Maggie Smith playing the title role in the film* The Prime of Miss Jean Brodie *1968.*

smitten past participle of **smite.**

smock *n.* 1. a loose overall. 2. or **smock frock** a loose shirtlike garment often ornamented with smocking. —*v.t.* to decorate with smocking. [Old English]

smocking *n.* ornamentation on cloth made by gathering it tightly with stitches into a honeycomb pattern.

smog *n.* fog intensified by smoke. —**smoggy** *adj.* [portmanteau word]

smoke *n.* 1. the visible vapour given off by a burning substance. 2. an act or period of smoking ◊tobacco. 3. (*colloquial*) a ◊cigarette or cigar. —*v.t./i.* 1. to emit smoke or other visible vapour. 2. to inhale and exhale the smoke of a cigarette, cigar, or pipe; to do this habitually; to use (a cigarette etc.) thus. The practice can be habit-forming and is dangerous to health, since carbon monoxide and other toxic materials result from the combustion process. A direct link between lung cancer and tobacco smoking was established in 1950; the habit is also linked to respiratory and coronary heart diseases. In the West, smoking is now forbidden in many public places because even **passive smoking** (breathing in fumes from other people's cigarettes) can be harmful. In the UK in 1988 33% of men and 30% of women were smokers. (1972 figures 52% and 41%.) 3. to darken or preserve by the action of smoke. —**go up in smoke,** to come to nothing. **smoke bomb,** a bomb that emits dense smoke on exploding. **smoke out,** to drive out by means of smoke; to drive out of hiding or secrecy etc. —**smokestack** *n.* a chimney or funnel for discharging the smoke of a locomotive or steamer. [Old English]

smokeless *adj.* having or producing little or no smoke. —**smokeless fuel,** fuel in which, when burned, all the carbon is fully oxidized to carbon dioxide, CO_2. Natural gas, oil, and coke are smokeless fuels.

smoker *n.* 1. a person who smokes tobacco habitually. 2. a part of a railway coach in which smoking is allowed. 3. a vent on the ocean floor through which hot, mineral-rich groundwater erupts into the sea, forming thick clouds of suspension.

smokescreen *n.* 1. a cloud of smoke concealing military or other operations. 2. a device or ruse for disguising activities.

smoky *adj.* 1. producing or emitting much smoke. 2. covered or filled with smoke; obscured (as) with smoke. 3. suggestive of or having the greyish colour of smoke. —**smokily** *adv.,* **smokiness** *n.*

Smollett /'smɒlɪt/ Tobias George 1721–1771. Scottish novelist who wrote the picaresque novels *Roderick Random* 1748, *Peregrine Pickle* 1751, *Ferdinand Count Fathom* 1753, *Sir Lancelot Greaves* 1760–62, and *Humphrey Clinker* 1771.

I think for my part half of the nation is mad – and the other not very sound.

> **Tobias Smollett**
> *The Adventures of Sir Launcelot Greaves*

smolt /smɔult/ *n.* a young salmon at the stage between parr and grilse, when it is covered with silvery scales and migrates to the sea for the first time. [originally Scottish and north of England]

smooch *v.i.* (*colloquial*) to kiss and caress; to dance slowly and closely to a lazy, romantic melody. —*n.* a spell of smooching; music for this. [imitative]

smooth /smuːð/ *adj.* 1. having an even surface; without roughness, projections, or indentations; not hairy; (of water) without waves. 2. having an even texture, without lumps. 3. not harsh in sound or taste; moving evenly without jolts or bumping; progressing without hindrance. 4. pleasantly polite but perhaps insincere. —*v.t./i.* 1. to make or become smooth. 2. to remove problems or dangers from. —*adv.* smoothly. —*n.* a smoothing touch or stroke. —**smoothly** *adv.,* **smoothness** *n.* [Old English]

smooth muscle a muscle capable of slow contraction over a period of time. Its presence in the wall of the alimentary canal allows slow rhythmic movements known as ◊peristalsis, which cause food to be mixed and forced along the gut. Smooth muscle has a microscopic structure distinct from other forms, and is not under conscious control.

smorgasbord /'smɔːɡəsbɔːd/ *n.* Swedish hors d'œuvres typically consisting of open sandwiches with an assortment of delicacies; a buffet meal with a variety of dishes. [Swedish (*smörgås* = (slice of) bread and butter and *bord* = table)]

smote past of **smite.**

smother /'smʌðə/ *v.t./i.* 1. to suffocate or stifle; to be suffocated. 2. to cover thickly; to overwhelm (with gifts, kindness etc.). 3. to put out or keep down (a fire) by heaping ashes etc. on it. 4. to repress or conceal. —*n.* a cloud of smoke or dust etc.; obscurity caused by this. [from Old English *smorian* = suffocate]

smoulder /'smǝuldǝ/ *v.i.* 1. to burn slowly without flame or in a suppressed way. 2. to burn inwardly with concealed anger or jealousy etc. 3. (of feelings) to exist in a suppressed state.

smudge *n.* a blurred or smeared mark. —*v.t./i.* 1. to make a smudge on or of. 2. to become smeared or blurred. —**smudgy** *adj.*

smug *adj.* self-satisfied, complacent; consciously respectable. —**smugly** *adv.,* **smugness** *n.* [from Low German *smuk* = pretty]

smuggle *v.t.* to import or export (goods) illegally, especially without paying customs duties; to convey secretly. Smuggling has a long tradition in most border and coastal regions; goods smuggled include tobacco, spirits, diamonds, gold, and illegal drugs. —**smuggler** *n.* [from Low German]

smut *n.* 1. a small flake of soot; a small black mark made (as) by this. 2. obscene talk, pictures, or stories. 3. a cereal disease turning parts of the plant to black powder. —*v.t./i.* (**-tt-**) 1. to mark with smuts. 2. to infect with or contract smut disease. —**smutty** *adj.,* **smuttiness** *n.*

Smuts /smʌts/ Jan Christian 1870–1950. South African politician and soldier; prime minister 1919–24 and 1939–48. He supported the Allies in both world wars and was a member of the British imperial war cabinet 1917–18. Although more of an internationalist than his contemporaries, Smuts was a segregationalist, voting in favour of legislation that took away black rights and land ownership.

Smythson /'smaɪðsən/ Robert 1535–1614. English architect, who built Elizabethan country houses including Longleat 1568–75, Wollaton Hall 1580–88, and Hardwick Hall 1590–97. Their castlelike silhouettes, symmetry, and large gridded windows are a uniquely romantic, English version of Classicism.

Sn symbol for ◊tin. [from Latin *stannum* = tin]

snack *n.* a small, casual, or hurried meal. —**snack bar,** a place where snacks are served. [originally = a snap or bite, from Middle Dutch verb *snacken,* variant of *snappen* = snap]

snaffle *n.* a simple bridle bit without a curb. —*v.t.* 1. to put a snaffle on. 2. (*slang*) to take, to steal.

snag *n.* 1. an unexpected or hidden difficulty. 2. a jagged projection. 3. a tear in fabric caused by a snag. —*v.t./i.* (-**gg**-) to catch, tear, or be caught on a snag. —**snaggy** *adj.*

snail *n.* a slow-moving, air-breathing gastropod mollusc, especially of the family Helicidae, with a spiral shell. There are thousands of species, on land and in water. —**snail's pace,** very slow movement. [Old English]

snake *n.* 1. a reptile of the suborder Serpentes (or Ophidia) of the order Squamata, which also includes lizards. Snakes are characterized by an elongated limbless body, possibly evolved because of subterranean ancestors. One of the internal modifications is the absence or greatly reduced size of the left lung. The skin is covered in scales, which are markedly wider underneath, where they form. There are 3,000 species found in the tropic and temperate zones, but none in New Zealand, Ireland, Iceland, and near the poles. Only three species are found in Britain: the adder, smooth snake, and grass snake. 2. or **snake in the grass** a treacherous person; a secret enemy. —*v.i.* to move or twist etc. like a snake. —**snake charmer,** a person appearing to make snakes move to music etc. **snakes and ladders,** a game with counters moved, according to the throw of the dice, along a board with sudden advances up 'ladders' or returns down 'snakes' depicted on the board. [Old English]

snaky /'sneɪkɪ/ *adj.* 1. snakelike in appearance or movements or in cunning, treachery etc. 2. infested with snakes. —**snakily** *adv.*

snap *v.t./i.* (-**pp**-) 1. to make or cause to make a sharp cracking sound; to open or close thus. 2. to break suddenly or with a cracking sound. 3. to speak or say with sudden irritation. 4. to make a sudden audible bite. 5. to move quickly. 6. to take a snapshot of. —*n.* 1. an act or sound of snapping. 2. a catch that fastens with a snap. 3. a crisp, brittle cake or biscuit. 4. a snapshot. 5. or **cold snap** a sudden brief spell of cold weather. 6. a card game in which players call 'Snap' when two similar cards are exposed (also as interjection at the unexpected similarity of two things). 7. vigour, liveliness. —*adv.* with a snapping sound. —*adj.* sudden; done or arranged etc. quickly or at short notice. —**snap fastener,** a press stud. **snap one's fingers at,** to defy; to regard with contempt. **snap out of,** (*slang*) to throw off (a mood etc.) by a sudden effort. **snap up,** to pick up or buy hastily or eagerly.

snapdragon *n.* a perennial herbaceous plant of the genus *Antirrhinum,* family Scrophulariaceae, with spikes of brightly coloured two-lipped flowers.

snapper *n.* any of several food fish, especially of the family Lutianidae.

snappish *adj.* inclined to snap; irritable, petulant. —**snappishly** *adv.*

snappy *adj.* (*colloquial*) 1. brisk, full of zest. 2. neat and elegant. —**make it snappy,** (*colloquial*) to be quick. —**snappily** *adv.*

snapshot *n.* a photograph taken informally or casually.

snare *n.* 1. a trap, especially with a noose, for catching birds or animals. 2. a thing that tempts or exposes one to danger or failure etc. 3. (often in *plural*) an arrangement of twisted gut or wire etc. stretched across the lower head of a side drum to produce a rattling sound; or **snare drum** a drum fitted with snares. —*v.t.* to catch in a snare; to ensnare. [Old English from Old Norse]

snarl[1] *v.t./i.* 1. to growl angrily with bared teeth. 2. to speak irritably or cynically. —*n.* an act or sound of snarling. [from Low German]

snarl[2] *v.t./i.* (often with *up*) to tangle; to become entangled; to confuse and hamper the movement of (traffic etc.). —*n.* a tangle. —**snarl-up** *n.* a confusion or jam of traffic etc.

snatch *v.t./i.* to seize quickly, eagerly, or unexpectedly; to take quickly or when a chance occurs. —*n.* 1. an act of snatching. 2. a fragment of song or talk etc. 3. a short spell of activity etc.

snazzy /'snæzɪ/ *adj.* (*slang*) smart, stylish; excellent. —**snazzily** *adv.,* **snazziness** *n.*

sneak *v.t./i.* 1. to go or convey furtively. 2. (*slang*) to steal unobserved. 3. (*slang*) to tell tales, especially at school. —*n.* a cowardly underhand person; (*slang*)

a telltale, especially at school. —*adj.* acting or done without warning; secret. —**sneak thief,** a petty thief; a person who steals from open rooms etc. —**sneaky** *adj.*

sneakers *n.pl.* soft-soled shoes.

sneaking *adj.* (of a feeling or suspicion etc.) persistent but not openly acknowledged.

sneer *n.* a scornful smile or remark. —*v.t./i.* to show scorn by a sneer; to utter thus.

sneeze *n.* a sudden involuntary expulsion of air from the nose and mouth caused by irritation in the nostrils. —*v.i.* to make a sneeze. —**not to be sneezed at,** (*colloquial*) not contemptible, worth having. [earlier *snese, nese, fnese,* from Old Norse]

Snell /snel/ Willebrord 1581–1626. Dutch mathematician and physicist who devised the basic law of refraction, known as **Snell's law,** in 1621. This states that the ratio between the sine of the angle of incidence and the sine of the angle of refraction is constant. The laws describing the reflection of light were well known in antiquity, but the principles governing the refraction of light were little understood. Snell's law was published by ◊Descartes in 1637.

snellen *n.* a unit expressing the visual power of the eye.

snick *v.t.* 1. to make a small notch or incision in. 2. in cricket, to hit (the ball) with a light glancing stroke. —*n.* such a notch or stroke. [suggested by *snickersnee* = large knife]

snicker *v.i.* to snigger. —*n.* a snigger. [imitative]

snide *adj.* (*colloquial*) 1. sneering, slyly derogatory. 2. counterfeit. 3. (*US*) mean, underhand. [19th-century slang]

sniff *v.t./i.* to draw up air audibly through the nose; to smell thus. —*n.* an act or sound of sniffing. —**sniff at,** to try the smell of; to show contempt for or disapproval of. [imitative]

sniffle *v.i.* to sniff repeatedly or slightly. —*n.* an act of sniffling; (in *plural*) a cold in the head causing sniffling. [imitative]

sniffy *adj.* (*colloquial*) disdainful. —**sniffily** *adv.,* **sniffiness** *n.*

snifter *n.* (*slang*) a small drink of alcoholic liquor. [from dialect *snift* = sniff]

snigger *n.* a sly giggle. —*v.i.* to utter a snigger.

snip *v.t./i.* (-**pp**-) to cut with scissors or shears, especially in small quick strokes. —*n.* 1. an act of snipping. 2. a piece snipped off. 3. (*slang*) something cheaply acquired or easily done. [from Low German or Dutch (imitative)]

snipe *n.* (*plural* **snipes** or *collective* **snipe**) a European marsh bird of the family Scolopacidae, order Charadriiformes, with a long, straight bill. Species include the **common snipe** *Gallinago gallinago* and the rare **great snipe** *Gallinago media,* of which the males hold spring gatherings to show their prowess. The snipe is closely related to the ◊woodcock. —*v.i.* 1. to fire shots from a hiding place, usually at long range. 2. to make a sly critical remark attacking a person or thing. —**sniper** *n.*

snippet /'snɪpɪt/ *n.* 1. a small piece cut off. 2. (usually in *plural*) a scrap or fragment of information or knowledge etc.; a short extract from a book etc.

snitch *v.t.* (*slang*) to steal. [originally = fillip on the nose]

snivel /'snɪvəl/ *v.i.* (-**ll**-) 1. to cry or complain in a miserable whining way; to weep with sniffling. 2. to run at the nose. —*n.* 1. an act of snivelling. 2. running mucus. —**sniveller** *n.* [from Old English (*snofl* = mucus)]

snob *n.* a person who has an exaggerated respect for social position or wealth, or attainments or tastes, and despises those he considers inferior. —**snobbery** *n.,* **snobbish** *adj.,* **snobbishly** *adv.,* **snobbishness** *n.* [originally = cobbler]

snoek /snuːk/ *n.* (*South African*) a ◊barracuda. [Afrikaans, from Dutch = pike]

snog *v.i.* (-**gg**-) (*slang*) to engage in kissing and caressing. —*n.* (*slang*) a spell of snogging.

snood *n.* a loose, baglike, ornamental net in which a woman's hair is held at the back. [Old English *snōd*]

snook /snuːk/ *n.* (*colloquial*) a contemptuous gesture with the thumb to the nose and the fingers spread. —**cock a snook at,** to make this gesture at; to show cheeky contempt for.

snooker /'snuːkə/ *n.* 1. an indoor game derived from ◊billiards (via ◊pool). It is played with 22 balls: 15 red, one each of yellow, green, brown, blue, pink, and black, and one white cueball. Red balls are worth one point when sunk, while the coloured balls have ascending values from two points for the yellow to seven points for the black. The world professional championship was first held in 1927. The world amateur championship was first held in 1963. The game was invented by British army officers in India, in 1875. 2. a position in this game where a direct shot would lose points. —*v.t.* to subject to a snooker; (*slang*, especially in *passive*) to thwart, to defeat.

snoop *v.i.* to pry inquisitively. —*n.* an act of snooping. —**snooper** *n.*, **snoopy** *adj.* [from Dutch = eat on the sly]

snoot *n.* (*slang*) the nose. [variant of *snout*]

snooty *adj.* (*colloquial*) supercilious, haughty, snobbish. —**snootily** *adv.*

snooze *n.* a short sleep, especially in the daytime. —*v.i.* to take a snooze.

snore *n.* a loud noise during sleep made by vibration of the soft palate (the rear part of the roof of the mouth) caused by streams of air entering the nose and mouth at the same time. It is most common when the nose is partially blocked. —*v.i.* to make such sounds. —**snorer** *n.*

snorkel *n.* 1. a breathing tube for supplying air to an underwater swimmer. 2. a device by which a submerged submarine can take in and expel air. —*v.i.* (-ll-) to swim with a snorkel. [from German *schnorchel*]

Snorkel /'snɔːkəl/ *n.* trade name of a piece of apparatus consisting of a platform which may be elevated and extended, used in fighting fires in tall buildings.

snort *n.* 1. an explosive sound made by the sudden forcing of breath through the nose, especially expressing indignation or incredulity; a similar sound made by an engine etc. 2. (*colloquial*) a small drink of liquor. —*v.t./i.* to make a snort; to express or utter with a snort.

snorter *n.* (*slang*) something notably vigorous or difficult etc.

snot *n.* (*slang*) 1. nasal mucus. 2. a contemptible person.

snotty *adj.* (*slang*) 1. running or foul with nasal mucus. 2. contemptible, bad-tempered. 3. supercilious. —**snottily** *adv.*, **snottiness** *n.*

snout *n.* the projecting nose (and mouth) of an animal; (*derogatory*) the human nose; the pointed front of a thing. [from Middle Dutch or Middle Low German]

snow /snəʊ/ *n.* 1. frozen atmospheric vapour falling to earth in light white flakes; a fall of this; a layer of it on the ground. Light reflecting in the crystals, which have a basic hexagonal (six-sided) geometry, gives snow its white appearance. 2. a thing resembling snow in whiteness or texture etc.; (*slang*) cocaine. —*v.i.* to fall as or like snow; to come in large numbers or quantities. —**it snows** *or* **is snowing**, snow falls or is falling. **snowberry** *n.* a garden shrub *Symphoricarpos rivularis* with white berries. **snow-blind** *adj.* temporarily blinded by the glare from snow. **snowbound** *adj.* prevented by snow from going out or travelling. **snowcapped** *adj.* (of a mountain) covered at the top with snow. **snowdrift** *n.* a bank of snow heaped by the wind. **snowed in** *or* **up**, snowbound. **snowed under**, covered (as) with snow; overwhelmed with a quantity of letters, work etc. **snow goose**, the arctic white goose *Anser caerulescens*. **snow line**, the level above which snow never melts entirely. **snowplough** *n.* a device for clearing a road or railway of snow; a skiing movement turning the points of the skis inwards so as to stop. **snowshoe** *n.* a flat device like a racket attached to the foot for walking on snow without sinking in. **snow-white** *adj.* pure white. [Old English]

Snow /snəʊ/ C(harles) P(ercy), Baron Snow 1905–1980. English novelist and physicist. He held government scientific posts in World War II and 1964–66. His sequence of novels *Strangers and Brothers* 1940–64 portrayed English life from 1920 onwards. His *Two Cultures* (Cambridge Rede lecture 1959) discussed the absence of communication between literary and scientific intellectuals in the West, and added the phrase 'the two cultures' to the language.

snowball *n.* snow pressed together into a ball for throwing in play. —*v.t./i.* 1. to throw or pelt with snowballs. 2. to increase rapidly. —**snowball tree**, a variety of guelder rose *Viburnum opulus* variant *roseum*.

Snowdon /'snəʊdn/ Anthony Armstrong-Jones, Earl of Snowdon 1930– . English portrait photographer. In 1960 he married Princess Margaret; they were divorced in 1978.

snowdrop

snowdrop *n.* a spring-flowering plant *Galanthus nivalis* with white drooping flowers, native to Europe.

snowfall *n.* the amount of fallen snow.

snowflake *n.* each of the small collections of crystals in which snow falls.

snow leopard a type of ◊leopard.

snowman *n.* (*plural* **snowmen**) a figure made of compressed snow roughly in the shape of a person.

snowmobile /'snəʊməbiːl/ *n.* a motor vehicle, especially with runners or caterpillar tracks, for travel over snow.

snowstorm *n.* a heavy fall of snow, especially with a high wind.

Snow White a traditional European fairy tale. Snow White is a princess persecuted by her jealous stepmother. Taking refuge in a remote cottage inhabited by seven dwarfs, she is tricked by the disguised queen into eating a poisoned apple. She is woken from apparent death by a prince.

snowy *adj.* 1. with snow falling; with much snow. 2. covered with snow. 3. as white as snow. —**snowy owl**, a large white ◊owl *Nyctea nyctea*.

SNP abbreviation of ◊Scottish National Party.

Snr abbreviation of Senior.

snub[1] *v.t.* (-bb-) to rebuff or humiliate with sharp words or a marked lack of cordiality. —*n.* an act of snubbing. [from Old Norse = chide]

snub[2] *adj.* (of the nose) short and stumpy. **snub-nosed** *adj.*

snuff[1] *n.* the charred part of a candlewick. —*v.t./i.* to remove the snuff from (a candle). —**snuff it**, (*slang*) to die. **snuff out**, to extinguish (a candle) by snuffing; to kill or put an end to (hopes etc.); (*slang*) to die.

snuff[2] *n.* 1. powdered tobacco or medicine taken by sniffing it up the nostrils. Snuff taking was common in 17th-century England and the Netherlands, and spread in the 18th century to other parts of Europe, but was largely superseded by cigarette smoking. 2. a sniff. —*v.t./i.* 1. to take snuff. 2. to sniff. —**snuffbox** *n.* a small box for holding snuff. **snuff-coloured** *adj.* dark yellowish-brown. [from Middle Dutch = snuffle]

snuffer *n.* a device for snuffing or extinguishing a candle.

snuffle *v.t./i.* 1. to sniff in a noisy way; to breathe noisily (as) through a partly blocked nose. 2. to speak or say with snuffles. —*n.* a snuffling sound.

snug *adj.* cosy, sheltered and comfortable; (of a garment) close-fitting. —*n.* a small bar in a public house, with comfortable seating for a few people. —**snugly** *adv.*

snuggery *n.* a snug place, especially a person's private room.

snuggle *v.t./i.* to settle or draw into a warm comfortable position.

Snyders /'snaɪdəs/ Frans 1579–1657. Flemish painter of hunting scenes and still lifes. Based in Antwerp, he was a pupil of ◊Brueghel the Younger and later assisted ◊Rubens and worked with ◊Jordaens. In 1608–09 he travelled in Italy. He excelled at painting fur, feathers, and animals fighting.

so /səʊ/ *adv. & conj.* 1. in this or that way; in the manner, position, or state described or implied; to that or to such an extent. 2. to a great or notable degree. 3. (with verbs of saying or thinking etc.) thus, this, that. 4. consequently, therefore; indeed, in actual fact. 5. also. —**and so on** *or* **forth**, and others of the same kind; and in other similar ways. **or so**, approximately. **so as to**, in order to, in such a way as to. **so be it**, an expression of acceptance of or resignation to an event etc. **so-called** *adj.* called or named thus (but perhaps wrongly or inaccurately). **so long**, (*colloquial*) goodbye. **so many** (*or* **much**), a definite number (or amount); nothing but. **so much for**, that is all that need be said or done about. **so-so** *adj. & adv.* only moderately good or well. **so that**, in order that. **so to say** *or* **speak**, an expression of reserve or apology for an exaggeration or neologism etc. **so what?** that is irrelevant or of no importance. [Old English]

soak *v. t./i.* 1. to place or lie in a liquid so as to become thoroughly wet. 2. (of liquid) to penetrate gradually; (of rain) to drench. 3. to absorb (literally or figuratively). 4. (*slang*) to extort money from. —*n.* 1. the act or process of soaking. 2. (*colloquial*) a hard drinker. —**soakaway** *n.* an arrangement for the disposal of water by percolation through the soil. **soak oneself in**, to absorb (a liquid or knowledge etc.). **soak through**, (of moisture) to penetrate, to make thoroughly wet. [Old English]

Soames /sǝumz/ Christopher, Baron Soames 1920–1987. British Conservative politician. He held ministerial posts 1958–64, was vice president of the Commission of the European Communities 1973–77 and governor of (Southern) Rhodesia in the period of its transition to independence as Zimbabwe, Dec 1979– April 1980.

so-and-so /'sǝuǝnsǝu/ *n.* (*plural* **so-and-so's**) 1. a particular person or thing not needing to be specified. 2. (*colloquial*, to avoid use of a vulgar word) an unpleasant or objectionable person.

Soane /sǝun/ John 1753–1837. English architect whose individual Neo-Classical designs anticipated contemporary taste. He designed his own house in Lincoln's Inn Fields, London, now the **Soane Museum**. Little remains of his extensive work at the Bank of England, London.

soap *n.* a cleansing substance yielding lather when rubbed in water. A mixture of the sodium salts of various ◊fatty acids (palmitic, stearic, and oleic acid), it is made by the action of caustic soda or caustic potash on fats of animal or vegetable origin. Soap makes grease and dirt disperse in water in a similar manner to a ◊detergent. —*v.t.* to apply soap to; to rub with soap. —**soapbox** *n.* a makeshift stand for a street orator. **soap flakes**, flakes of soap prepared for washing clothes etc. **soap opera**, a sentimental domestic broadcast serial. **soap powder**, a powder, especially with additives, for washing clothes etc. [Old English]

soapstone *n.* a compact, massive form of impure ◊talc; see ◊steatite.

soapsuds *n.pl.* suds.

soapy *adj.* 1. of or like soap. 2. containing or smeared with soap. 3. unctuous, flattering. —**soapily** *adv.*, **soapiness** *n.*

soar *v.i.* 1. to rise high in flight. 2. to reach a high level or standard. [from Old French *essorer*, ultimately from Latin *aura* = breeze]

Soares /'swɑːres/ Mario 1924– . Portuguese socialist politician, president from 1986. Exiled in 1970, he returned to Portugal in 1974, and, as leader of the Portuguese Socialist Party, was prime minister 1976–78. He resigned as party leader in 1980, but in 1986 he was elected Portugal's first socialist president.

sob *v.t./i.* (**-bb-**) to draw the breath in convulsive gasps, usually with weeping; to utter with sobs. —*n.* the act or sound of sobbing. —**sob story**, (*colloquial*) a narrative meant to evoke sympathy. **sob stuff**, (*colloquial*) pathos, sentimental writing or behaviour.

sober *adj.* 1. not intoxicated; not given to heavy drinking. 2. serious, sedate, not frivolous. 3. moderate, well-balanced. 4. (of colour etc.) quiet and inconspicuous. —*v.t./i.* to make or become sober. —**soberly** *adv.*, **sobriety** /sǝ'braiǝti/ *n.* [from Old French from Latin]

Sobers /'sǝubǝz/ Gary (Garfield St Aubrun) 1936– . West Indian test cricketer. One of the game's great all-rounders, he scored more than 8,000 test runs, took over 200 wickets, held more than 100 catches, and holds the record for the highest test innings: 365 not out.

Sobieski /sɒb'jeski/ John, alternative name for ◊John III, king of Poland.

sobriquet /'sǝubrikei/ *n.* a nickname. [French, originally = tap under chin]

Soc. abbreviation of 1. Socialist. 2. Society.

soccer /'sɒkǝ/ *n.* (*colloquial*) Association ◊football. [from abbreviation of *Association*]

sociable /'sǝuʃǝbǝl/ *adj.* fond of company; characterized by friendly companionship. —**sociability** /-'bilɪti/ *n.*, **sociably** *adv.* [French, or from Latin *sociare* = unite]

social /'sǝuʃǝl/ *adj.* 1. of society or its organization; concerned with the mutual relationships of people or classes living in association. 2. living in organized communities, not solitary. 3. sociable. 4. of or designed for companionship and sociability. —*n.* a social gathering, especially one organized by a club etc. —**social climber**, a person seeking to gain a higher rank in society. **social services**, the welfare services provided by the state, including education, health, housing, and ◊social security. **social work**, organized work to alleviate social problems. **social worker**, a person engaged in this. —**socially** *adv.* [French or from Latin *socius* = companion]

Social and Liberal Democrats the official name for the British political party formed in 1988 from the former Liberal Party and most of the Social Democratic Party. The common name for the party is the **Liberal Democrats**. Its leader (from July 1988) is Paddy ◊Ashdown.

social behaviour in zoology, behaviour concerned with altering the behaviour of other individuals of the same species. Social behaviour allows animals to live harmoniously in groups by establishing hierarchies of dominance to discourage disabling fighting. It may be aggressive or submissive (for example, cowering and other signals of appeasement), or designed to establish bonds (such as social grooming or preening).

social contract 1. the idea that government authority derives originally from an agreement between ruler and ruled in which the former agrees to provide order in return for obedience from the latter. It has been used to support both absolutism (◊Hobbes) and democracy (◊Locke, ◊Rousseau). 2. an unofficial agreement or **social compact** between a government and organized labour that, in return for control of prices, rents, and so on, the unions would refrain from economically disruptive wage demands.

social democracy the political ideology or belief in the gradual evolution of a democratic ◊socialism within existing political structures. The earliest was the German *Sozialdemokratische Partei* (SPD), today one of the two major German parties, created in 1875 from August Bebel's earlier German Social Democratic Workers' Party, itself founded in 1869. Parties along the lines of the German model were founded in the last two decades of the 19th century in a number of countries including Austria, Belgium, the Netherlands, Hungary, Poland, and Russia. The British Labour Party is in the social-democratic tradition.

Social Democratic Federation (SDF) in British history, a socialist society, founded as the Democratic Federation in 1881 and renamed in 1884. It was led by H M Hyndman (1842–1921), a former conservative journalist and stockbroker who claimed Karl ◊Marx as his inspiration without obtaining recognition from his mentor. In 1911 it became the British Socialist Party.

Social Democratic Labour Party (SDLP) a Northern Irish left-wing political party, formed in 1970. It aims ultimately at Irish unification, but distances itself from the violent tactics of the Irish Republican Army, adopting a constitutional, conciliatory role. The SDLP, led by John Hume (1937–), was responsible for setting up the ◊New Ireland Forum in 1983.

Social Democratic Party (SDP) a British centrist political party 1981–90 formed by members of Parliament who resigned from the Labour Party. The 1983 and 1987 general elections were fought in alliance with the Liberal Party as the **Liberal/SDP Alliance**. A merger of the two parties was voted for by the SDP in 1987, and the new party became the ◊Social and Liberal Democrats, leaving a rump SDP that folded in 1990.

social history the branch of history that documents the living and working conditions of people rather than affairs of state.

socialism /'sǝuʃǝlɪzǝm/ *n.* a political and economic theory of social organization which advocates that the community as a whole should own and control the means of production, distribution, and exchange; a policy or practice based on this theory. The term has been used to describe positions as widely apart as anarchism and social democracy. Socialist ideas appeared in classical times; in early Christianity; among later Christian sects such as the ◊Anabaptists and ◊Diggers; and, in the 18th and early 19th centuries, were put forward as systematic political aims by Jean-Jacques ◊Rousseau, Claude ◊Saint-Simon, François ◊Fourier, and Robert ◊Owen, among others. See also Karl ◊Marx and Friedrich ◊Engels. In the later 19th century socialist parties arose in most European countries; for example, in Britain the ◊Independent Labour Party. —**socialist** *n.*, **socialistic** /-'lɪstɪk/ *adj.* [from French]

'socialism in one country' a concept proposed by the Soviet dictator Stalin in 1924. In contrast to ◊Trotsky's theory of the permanent revolution, Stalin suggested that the emphasis be changed away from promoting revolutions abroad to the idea of building socialism, economically and politically, in the USSR without help from other countries.

socialist realism an artistic doctrine imposed in the USSR during the 1930s setting out the optimistic, socialist terms in which society should be portrayed in works of art (in music and the visual arts as well as writing).

socialite /'səʊʃəlaɪt/ *n.* a person prominent in fashionable society.

socialize /'səʊʃəlaɪz/ *v.t./i.* **1.** to behave sociably; to make social. **2.** to organize in a socialistic manner. —**socialization** *n.* the process, beginning in childhood, by which a person learns how to become a member of a society, learning its norms, customs, laws, and ways of living. The main agents of socialization are the family, school, peer groups, work, religion, and the mass media. The main methods of socialization are direct instruction, rewards and punishment, imitation, experimentation, role play, and interaction.

Social Realism in painting, art that realistically depicts subjects of social concern, such as poverty and deprivation. The French artist Courbet provides a 19th-century example of the genre. Subsequently, in the USA, the Ashcan school and Ben Shahn are among those described as Social Realists.

social science one of the group of academic disciplines that investigate how and why people behave the way they do, as individuals and in groups. The term originated with the 19th-century French thinker Auguste ◊Comte. The academic social sciences are generally listed as sociology, economics, anthropology, political science, and psychology.

social security the state provision of financial aid to alleviate poverty. The term 'social security' was first applied officially in the USA, in the Social Security Act 1935. It was first used officially in Britain in 1944, and following the ◊Beveridge Report of 1942 a series of acts was passed from 1945 to widen the scope of social security. Basic entitlements of those paying National Insurance contributions in Britain include an old-age pension, unemployment benefit, widow's pension, and payment during a period of sickness in one's working life. Other benefits include family credit, child benefit, and attendance allowance for those looking after sick or disabled people. Entitlements under National Insurance, such as unemployment benefit, are paid at flat rates regardless of need; other benefits, such as income support, are 'means-tested', that is, claimants' income must be below a certain level. Most payments, with the exception of unemployment benefit, are made by the Department of Social Security (DSS).

society /sə'saɪəti/ *n.* **1.** an organized and interdependent community; the system of living in this. **2.** people of the higher social classes. **3.** company, companionship. **4.** an association of persons sharing a common aim or interest etc. —**Society of Friends**, official name of the Quakers; see ◊Friends, Society of. **Society of Jesus**, the ◊Jesuits. [from French from Latin]

Society Islands (French *Archipel de la Société*) an archipelago in ◊French Polynesia, divided into Windward Islands and Leeward Islands; area 1,685 sq km/650 sq mi; population (1983) 142,000. The administrative headquarters is Papeete on ◊Tahiti. The **Windward Islands** (French *Îles du Vent*) have an area of 1,200 sq km/460 sq mi and a population (1983) of 123,000. They comprise Tahiti, Moorea (area 132 sq km/51 sq mi; population 7,000), Maio (or Tubuai Manu; 9 sq km/3.5 sq mi; population 200), and the smaller Tetiaroa and Mehetia. The **Leeward Islands** (French *Îles sous le Vent*) have an area of 404 sq km/156 sq mi and a population of 19,000. They comprise the volcanic islands of Raiatea (including the main town of Uturoa), Huahine, Bora-Bora, Maupiti, Tahaa, and four small atolls. Claimed by France in 1768, the group became a French protectorate in 1843 and a colony in 1880.

Socinianism /səʊ'sɪnɪənɪzəm/ *n.* a form of 17th-century Christian belief which rejects such traditional doctrines as the Trinity and original sin. It is an early form of ◊Unitarianism. [from **Socinus**, Latinized name of Lelio

Francesco Maria Sozzini (1525–1562), Italian Protestant theologian]

socio- /səʊsɪəʊ-, -ʃɪəʊ-/ in combinations, of society or sociology (and). [from Latin *socius* = companion]

sociobiology /səʊʃɪəʊbaɪ'ɒlədʒɪ/ *n.* the study of the biological basis of all human and animal social behaviour, including the application of ◊population genetics to the evolution of behaviour. It builds on the concept of ◊inclusive fitness. Contrary to some popular interpretations, it does not assume that all behaviour is genetically determined.

sociology /səʊsɪ'ɒlədʒɪ/ *n.* the systematic study of society, in particular of social order and social change, social conflict and social problems. It studies institutions such as the family, law, and the church, as well as concepts such as norm, role, and culture. —**sociological** /-sɪə'lɒdʒɪkəl/ *adj.* **sociologist** *n.*

sock[1] *n.* **1.** a short stocking, usually not reaching the knee. **2.** a loose insole. —**pull one's socks up**, (*colloquial*) to make an effort to improve. **put a sock in it**, (*slang*) to be quiet. [Old English from Latin *soccus* = actor's shoe]

sock[2] *v.t.* (*slang*) to hit (a person) hard. —*n.* (*slang*) a hard blow. —**sock it to**, to attack or address (a person) vigorously.

socket /'sɒkɪt/ *n.* a natural or artificial hollow for something to fit into or stand firm or revolve in, especially a device receiving a plug or light bulb etc. to make an electrical connection. [from Anglo-French, diminutive of Old French *soc* = ploughshare]

Socrates /'sɒkrəti:z/ *c.*469–399 BC. Athenian philosopher. He wrote nothing himself but was immortalized in the dialogues of his pupil Plato. In his desire to combat the scepticism of the ◊Sophists, Socrates asserted the possibility of genuine knowledge. In ethics, he put forward the view that the good person never knowingly does wrong. True knowledge emerges through dialogue and systematic questioning and an abandoning of uncritical claims to knowledge.

The unexamined life is not worth living.
Socrates

Socratic /sə'krætɪk/ *adj.* of Socrates or his philosophy. —**Socratic irony**, see ◊irony. **Socratic method**, the method of teaching used by Socrates, in which he aimed to guide pupils to clear thinking on ethics and politics by asking questions and then exposing their inconsistencies in cross-examination. This method was effective against the ◊Sophists.

sod[1] *n.* turf, a piece of turf; the surface of the ground. —**under the sod**, in the grave. [from Middle Dutch or Middle Low German]

sod[2] *n.* (*vulgar*) an unpleasant or despicable person; a fellow. —*v.t.* (**-dd-**) (*vulgar*) to damn. [abbreviation of *sodomite*]

soda /'səʊdə/ *n.* **1.** a compound of sodium in common use, especially sodium carbonate (**washing soda**), bicarbonate (**baking soda**, see ◊bicarbonate of soda), or hydroxide (**caustic soda**). **2.** or **soda water** water made effervescent with carbon dioxide and used as a drink alone or with spirits etc. —**soda ash**, the former name for ◊sodium carbonate, Na_2CO_3. **soda bread**, bread leavened with baking soda. **soda fountain**, a device supplying soda water; a shop equipped with this. **soda lime**, a powdery mixture of calcium hydroxide and sodium hydroxide or potassium hydroxide, used in medicine and as a drying agent. [Latin]

sodden /'sɒdən/ *adj.* **1.** saturated with liquid, soaked through. **2.** rendered stupid or dull etc. with drunkenness. [past participle of *seethe*]

Soddy /'sɒdi/ Frederick 1877–1956. English physical chemist, who pioneered research into atomic disintegration and coined the term '◊isotope'. He was awarded the Nobel Prize for Physics in 1921 for investigating the origin and nature of isotopes.

Söderberg /'səʊdəberj/ Hjalmar (Eric Fredrik) 1869–1941. Swedish writer. His work includes the short, melancholy novels *Förvillelser/Aberrations* 1895, *Martin Bircks ungdom/The Youth of Martin Birck* 1901, *Doktor Glas/Dr Glass* 1906, and the play *Gertrud* 1906.

sodium *n.* a soft, waxlike, silver-white, metallic element, symbol Na (from Latin *natrium*), atomic number 11, relative atomic mass 22.898. It is one of the ◊alkali metals and has a very low density, being light enough to float on water. It is the sixth most abundant element (the fourth most abundant metal) in the Earth's crust. Sodium is highly reactive, oxidizing rapidly when exposed to air and reacting violently with water. Sodium compounds used industrially include sodium nitrate (saltpetre, $NaNO_3$, used as a fertilizer) and sodium thiosulphate (hypo, $Na_2S_2O_3$, used as a photographic fixer). Thousands of tons of these are manufactured annually. Sodium metal is used to a limited extent in spectroscopy, in discharge lamps, and alloyed with potassium as a heat-transfer medium in nuclear reactors. It was isolated from caustic soda in 1807 by Humphry Davy. —**sodium bicarbonate,** see ◊bicarbonate of soda. **sodium carbonate,** ◊washing soda, Na_2CO_3. **sodium chloride** or **common salt,** NaCl, a white, crystalline compound which occurs naturally in the oceans and in salt deposits left by dried-up ancient seas. It is a typical ionic solid with a high melting point (801°C); it is soluble in water, insoluble in organic solvents, and is a strong electrolyte when molten or in aqueous solution. It is widely used in the food industry as a flavouring and preservative, and in the chemical industry in the manufacture of sodium, chlorine, and sodium carbonate. **sodium hydroxide,** caustic soda, NaOH. **sodium lamp,** a lamp giving a yellow light from an electrical discharge in sodium vapour. [from *soda*]

Sodom and Gomorrah /'sɒdəm, gə'mɒrə/ two ancient cities in the Dead Sea area of the Middle East, recorded in the Old Testament (Genesis) as being destroyed by fire and brimstone for their wickedness.

sodomite /'sɒdəmaɪt/ *n.* a person practising sodomy. [from Old French from Latin from Greek]

sodomy /'sɒdəmɪ/ *n.* an anal or other copulationlike act, especially between males or between a person and an animal. [from Latin from *Sodom*]

soever /səʊ'evə/ *adv.* (*literary*) of any possible kind or extent.

sofa /'səʊfə/ *n.* a long upholstered seat with a back and raised ends or arms. [French, ultimately from Arabic]

soffit *n.* an undersurface of an arch or lintel etc. [from French or Italian from Latin *sub* = under and *figere* = fix]

Sofia /'səʊfiə/ or **Sofiya** capital of Bulgaria since 1878; population (1987) 1,129,000. Industries include textiles, rubber, machinery, and electrical equipment. It lies at the foot of the Vitosha Mountains.

soft *adj.* **1.** not hard or firm, yielding to pressure; malleable, plastic, easily cut. **2.** (of cloth etc.) smooth or fine in texture, not rough or stiff. **3.** (of air etc.) mild, balmy. **4.** (of water) free from mineral salts that prevent soap from lathering. **5.** (of light or colour etc.) not brilliant or glaring; (of sound) not loud or strident. **6.** (of a consonant) sibilant (as *c* in *ice*, *g* in *age*). **7.** (of an outline etc.) not sharply defined. **8.** (of an action or manner etc.) gentle, conciliatory; complimentary, amorous; (of the heart or feelings etc.) compassionate, sympathetic. **9.** (of character etc.) feeble, effeminate, silly, sentimental. **10.** (*slang*) (of a job etc.) easy. **11.** (of drugs) not likely to cause addiction. **12.** (of currency, prices etc.) likely to depreciate. **13.** (of pornography) not highly obscene. —*adv.* softly. —**be soft on,** (*colloquial*) to be lenient towards; to be infatuated with. **soft-boiled** *adj.* (of an egg) boiled so as to leave the yolk still soft. **soft drink,** a nonalcoholic drink. **soft fruit,** small stoneless fruits such as strawberries and currants. **soft furnishings,** curtains and rugs etc. **soft-hearted** *adj.* compassionate. **soft landing,** one made with little or no damage. **soft option,** the easier alternative. **soft palate,** the back part of the palate, which is not bony. **soft pedal,** the pedal on a piano making the tone softer. **soft-pedal** *v.t./i.* to refrain from emphasizing. **soft roe,** see ◊roe[1]. **soft sell,** restrained salesmanship. **soft-soap** *v.t.* (*colloquial*) to persuade (a person) with flattery. **soft-spoken** *adj.* speaking with a soft voice. **soft spot,** a feeling of affection for a person or thing. **soft touch,** (*slang*) a person readily parting with money when asked. —**softly** *adv.*, **softness** *n.* [Old English *sōfte* = agreeable]

softball *n.* a modified form of baseball using a softer and larger ball, originally devised (about 1887) as an indoor game. The two main differences are the distances between the bases (18.29 m/60 ft) and that the ball is pitched underhand in softball. There are two forms of softball, fast pitch and slow pitch; in the latter the ball must be delivered to home plate in an arc that must be not less than 2.4 m/8 ft at its height.

soft currency a vulnerable currency that tends to fall in value on foreign-exchange markets because of political or economic uncertainty. Governments are unwilling to hold soft currencies in their foreign-exchange reserves, preferring strong or hard currencies, which are easily convertible.

soften /'sɒfən/ *v.t./i.* to make or become soft or softer. —**soften up,** to make weaker by a preliminary attack; to make more persuasible by preliminary approaches etc. —**softener** *n.*

softie /'sɒftɪ/ *n.* (*colloquial*) a person who is physically weak or not hardy, or who is soft-hearted.

software *n.* in computing, a collection of programs and procedures for making a computer perform a specific task, as opposed to ◊hardware, which is the machine itself. Software is created by programmers and either distributed on a suitable medium, such as the floppy disc, or built into the computer in the form of ◊firmware.

soft water water that contains very few dissolved metal ions such as calcium (Ca^{2+}) or magnesium (Mg^{2+}). It lathers easily with soap, and no ◊scale is formed inside kettles or boilers.

softwood *n.* any coniferous tree, or the wood from it. In general this type of wood is softer and easier to work, but in some cases less durable, than wood from flowering (or angiosperm) trees.

soggy *adj.* **1.** sodden. **2.** moist and heavy in texture. —**soggily** *adv.*, **sogginess** *n.* [from dialect *sog* = a swamp]

soh /səʊ/ *n.* in music, the fifth note of the major scale in tonic sol-fa. [from *solve* (see ◊gamut)]

soigné /swɑː'njeɪ/ *adj.* (*feminine* **soignée**) carefully finished or arranged; well-groomed and sophisticated. [past participle of French *soigner* = take care of]

soil[1] *n.* **1.** the loose covering of broken rocky material and decaying organic matter overlying the bedrock of the Earth's surface. Deep soils form in warm wet climates and in valleys; shallow soils form in cool dry areas and on slopes. The study of soil (**pedology**) is significant because of the relative importance of different soil types to agriculture. **2.** the ground belonging to a nation, territory. [from Anglo-French]

soil[2] *v.t./i.* **1.** to make or become dirty. **2.** to defile, to bring discredit to. —*n.* **1.** a dirty mark; defilement. **2.** filth; refuse matter. —**soil pipe,** the discharge pipe of a water closet. [from Old French *suill(i)er* ultimately from Latin *sus* = pig]

Soil Association a pioneer British ecological organization founded in 1945, which campaigns against pesticides and promotes organic farming.

soil creep the gradual movement of soil down a slope. As each soil particle is dislodged by a raindrop, it moves slightly further downhill. This eventually results in a mass downward movement of soil on the slope.

soil erosion the wearing away and redistribution of the Earth's soil layer. It is caused by the action of water, wind, and ice, and also by improper methods of ◊agriculture. If unchecked, soil erosion results in the formation of ◊deserts.

soil mechanics a branch of engineering that studies the nature and properties of the soil. Soil is investigated during construction work to ensure that it has the mechanical properties necessary to support the foundations of dams, bridges, and roads.

soirée /'swɑːreɪ/ *n.* an evening party, especially for conversation or music. [French *soir* = evening]

sojourn /'sɒdʒɜːn/ *n.* a temporary stay. —*v.i.* to make a sojourn. [from Old French *sojorn(er)* from Latin *diurnum* = day]

sol[1] *n.* a colloidal suspension of very small solid particles in a liquid that retains the physical properties of a liquid (see ◊colloid). [abbreviation of *solution*]

sol[2] variant of ◊soh.

sola /'səʊlə/ *n.* a pithy-stemmed East Indian swamp plant *Aeschynomene aspera*. —**sola topi,** a sun helmet made from its pith. [from Urdu or Bengali]

solar system

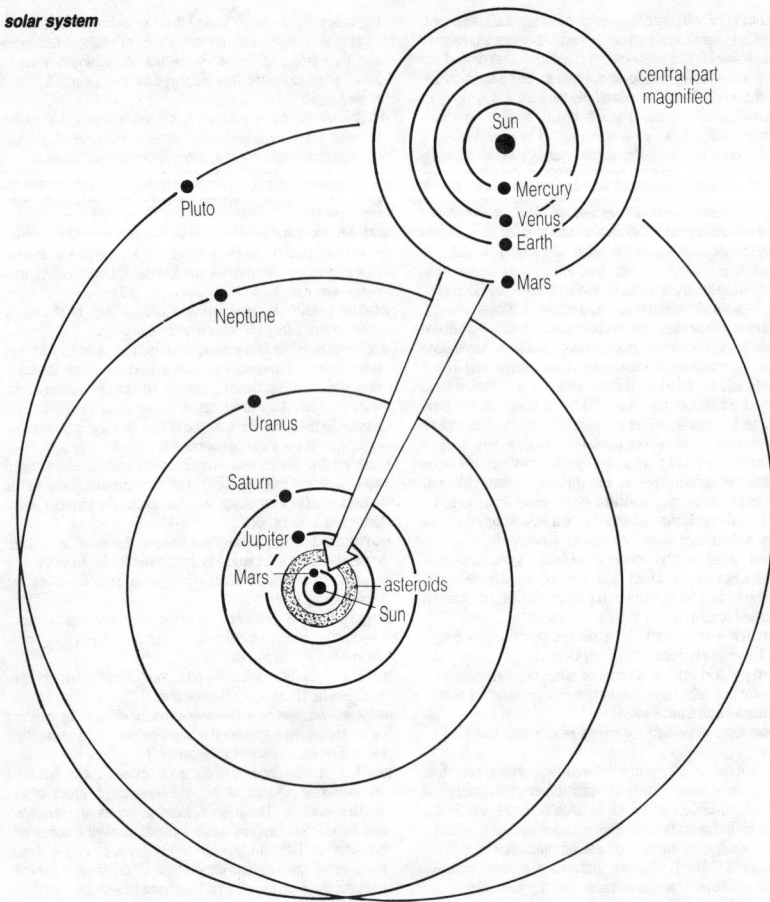

solace /ˈsɒləs/ *n.* comfort in distress or disappointment or in tedium. —*v.t.* to give solace to. [from Old French from Latin *solatium* (*solari* = console)]

solan /ˈsəʊlən/ *n.* a large gooselike ◊gannet *Sula bassana*.

solar /ˈsəʊlə/ *adj.* of or reckoned by the Sun. —*n.* **1.** a solarium. **2.** the upper chamber in a medieval house. —**solar battery** *or* **cell,** a device converting solar radiation into electricity. **solar day,** the interval between meridian transits of the Sun. **solar plexus,** the complex of radiating nerves at the pit of the stomach. **solar year,** see ◊year. [from Latin *solaris* (*sol* = sun)]

solar energy energy derived from the Sun's radiation. The amount of energy falling on just 1 sq km/0.3861 sq mi is about 4,000 megawatts, enough to heat and light a small town. In one second the Sun gives off 13 million times more energy than all the electricity used in the USA in one year. It is a nonpolluting and renewable energy source used as far north as Scandinavia as well as in the SW USA, in Mediterranean countries, and elsewhere. **Solar heaters** have industrial or domestic uses. They usually consist of a black (heat-absorbing) panel containing pipes through which air or water, heated by the Sun, is circulated, either by thermal ◊convection or by a pump. Solar energy may also be harnessed indirectly using solar cells (photovoltaic cells) made of panels of ◊semiconductor material (usually silicon), which generate electricity when illuminated by sunlight.

solarium /səˈleərɪəm/ *n.* (*plural* **solaria**) a place for the enjoyment or medical use of sunshine. [Latin]

solar pond a natural or artificial body of salt water, for example the Dead Sea, in which salt becomes more soluble in the Sun's heat. Water at the bottom becomes saltier and hotter, and is insulated by the less salty water layer at the

top. Temperatures at the bottom reach about 100°C/212°F and can be used to generate electricity.

solar radiation the radiation given off by the Sun, consisting mainly of visible light, ◊ultraviolet radiation, and ◊infrared radiation, although the whole spectrum of ◊electromagnetic waves is present, from radio waves to X-rays. High-energy charged particles such as electrons are also emitted, especially from solar ◊flares. When these reach the Earth, they cause magnetic storms (disruptions of the Earth's magnetic field), which interfere with radio communications.

solar system the Sun and all the bodies orbiting it: the nine planets (Mercury, Venus, Earth, Mars, Jupiter, Saturn, Uranus, Neptune, and Pluto), their moons, the asteroids, and the comets. It is thought to have formed from a cloud of gas and dust in space about 4.6 billion years ago. The Sun contains 99% of the mass of the solar system. The edge of the solar system is not clearly defined, marked only by the limit of the Sun's gravitational influence, which extends about 1.5 light years, almost halfway to the nearest star, Alpha Centauri, 4.3 light years away.

solar wind a stream of atomic particles, mostly protons and electrons, from the Sun's corona, flowing outwards at speeds of between 300 kps/186 mps and 1,000 kps/621 mps.

sold past and past participle of **sell.**

solder /ˈsəʊldə, ˈsɒd-/ *n.* any of various alloys used when melted for joining metals such as copper, its common alloys (brass and bronze), and tin-plated steel, as used for making food cans. Soft solders (usually alloys of tin and lead, sometimes with added antimony) melt at low temperatures (about 200°C/392°F), and are widely used in the electrical industry for joining copper wires. Hard (or brazing) solders, such as silver solder (an alloy of copper, silver, and zinc), melt at much higher temperatures and form a much stronger joint. —*v.t.* to join with solder. —**soldering iron**, a tool to melt and apply solder. [from Old French *soudure* (*souder* from Latin *solidare* = fasten]

soldier /'səʊldʒə/ *n.* **1.** a member of an army or a **common soldier**; a private or noncommissioned officer in an army. **2.** a military commander of specified ability. —*v.i.* to serve as a soldier. —**soldier of fortune**, an adventurous person ready to serve any state or person, a mercenary. **soldier on**, (*colloquial*) to persevere doggedly. —**soldierly** *adj.* [from Old French *sou(l)de* = soldier's pay, from Latin]

soldiery *n.* soldiers, especially of a specified character.

sole[1] *n.* **1.** the undersurface of the foot; the part of a shoe or sock etc. below the foot, especially the part other than the heel. **2.** the lower surface or base of a plough, golf-club head etc. —*v.t.* to provide (a shoe etc.) with a sole. [Old English from Latin *solea* = sandal]

sole[2] *n.* a flatfish of the genus *Solea* found in temperate and tropical waters. [from Old French from Latin from its shape]

sole[3] *adj.* one and only, single, exclusive. —**solely** *adv.* [from Old French from Latin *solus* = alone]

solecism /'sɒlɪsɪzəm/ *n.* an offence against grammar, idiom, or etiquette. —**solecistic** /-'sɪstɪk/ *adj.* [from French or Latin from Greek *soloikos* = speaking incorrectly]

solemn /'sɒləm/ *adj.* **1.** not smiling or cheerful. **2.** dignified and impressive. **3.** formal, accompanied by ceremony. —**solemnly** *adv.*, **solemnness** *n.* [from Old French from Latin *sollemnis* = customary]

solemnity /sə'lemnɪtɪ/ *n.* **1.** being solemn. **2.** a solemn rite.

solemnize /'sɒləmnaɪz/ *v.t.* **1.** to perform (a ceremony, especially of marriage) with formal rites. **2.** to make solemn. —**solemnization** /-'zeɪʃən/ *n.*

solenoid /'səʊlənɔɪd/ *n.* a coil of wire, usually cylindrical, in which a magnetic field is created by passing an electric current through it (see ◊electromagnet). This field can be used to move an iron rod placed on its axis. Mechanical valves attached to the rod can be operated by switching the current on or off, so converting electrical energy into mechanical energy. Solenoids are used to relay energy from the battery of a car to the starter motor by means of the ignition switch. [from French from Greek *sōlēn* = tube]

sol-fa /sɒl'fɑː/ *n.* a method of teaching music, usually singing; see ◊tonic sol-fa.

Solferino, Battle of /sɒlfə'riːnəʊ/ Napoleon III's victory over the Austrian army in 1859 at a village near Verona, N Italy, 8 km/5 mi S of Lake Garda.

soli see ◊solo.

solicit /sə'lɪsɪt/ *v.t./i.* **1.** to ask repeatedly or earnestly for; to seek to obtain. **2.** to make an immoral sexual offer; to accost and offer one's services as a prostitute. —**solicitation** /-'teɪʃən/ *n.* [from Old French from Latin *sollicitare* = agitate (*sollicitus* = anxious from *sollus* = entire and *citus* = set in motion)]

solicitor *n.* (*British*) a member of the legal profession, formerly one competent to advise clients and instruct barristers but not appearing as an advocate except in certain lower courts. A solicitor is a lawyer who provides all-round legal services (making wills, winding up estates, conveyancing, divorce, and litigation). In the USA the general term is lawyer or attorney.

Solicitor General in the UK, a law officer of the crown, deputy to the ◊Attorney General, a political appointee with ministerial rank.

solicitous /sə'lɪsɪtəs/ *adj.* anxious and concerned, especially about a person's welfare or comfort. —**solicitously** *adv.* [from Latin *sollicitus*]

solicitude /sə'lɪsɪtjuːd/ *n.* solicitous concern.

solid /'sɒlɪd/ *adj.* **1.** firm and stable in shape, not liquid or fluid. **2.** of solid material throughout, not hollow; of the same substance throughout. **3.** of strong material, construction, or build, not flimsy or slender etc. **4.** having three dimensions; concerned with solids. **5.** sound and reliable; sound but without special flair etc.; financially sound. **6.** (*colloquial*) (of time) uninterrupted. **7.** (*colloquial*) unanimous, undivided. —*n.* **1.** a solid substance or body. **2.** (in *plural*) solid food. —**solid state**, a state of matter in which the constituent atoms or molecules, according to ◊kinetic theory, are not free to move but merely vibrate about fixed positions, such as those in crystal lattices. **solid-state** *adj.* of or relating to the solid state; using the electronic properties of solids, especially semiconductors, to replace those of valves. **solid-state circuit**, a circuit where all the components (resistors, capacitors, transistors, and diodes) and interconnections are made at the same time, and by the same processes, in or on one piece of single-crystal silicon. The small size of this construction accounts for its use in electronics for space vehicles and aircraft. —**solidly** *adv.* [from Old French or Latin *solidus* (related to *salvus* = safe and *sollus* = entire)]

solidarity /sɒlɪ'dærɪtɪ/ *n.* unity or agreement of feeling or action, especially among individuals with a common interest; mutual dependence. [from French]

Solidarity *n.* (Polish *Solidarność*) the national confederation of independent trade unions in Poland, formed under the leadership of Lech ◊Walesa in Sept 1980. An illegal organization from 1981 to 1989, it now heads the Polish government and divisions have emerged in the leadership.

solidify /sə'lɪdɪfaɪ/ *v.t./i.* to make or become solid. —**solidification** /-fɪ'keɪʃən/ *n.* the change of state of a substance from liquid or vapour to solid on cooling. It is the opposite of melting or sublimation. [from French]

solidity /sə'lɪdɪtɪ/ *n.* the state of being solid, firmness.

soliloquize /sə'lɪləkwaɪz/ *v.i.* to utter a soliloquy.

soliloquy /sə'lɪləkwɪ/ *n.* a speech in which a person expresses his or her thoughts aloud without addressing any specific person, especially in a play; a period of this. [from Latin *solus* = alone and *loqui* = speak]

solipsism /'sɒlɪpsɪzəm/ *n.* in philosophy, a view that maintains that the self is the only thing that can be known to exist. It is an extreme form of ◊scepticism. The solipsist sees himself or herself as the only individual in existence, assuming other people to be a reflection of his or her own consciousness. —**solipsist** *n.* [from Latin *solus* = alone and *ipse* = self]

solitaire /sɒlɪ'teə/ *n.* **1.** a jewel set by itself; a piece of jewellery containing this. **2.** a game played on a special board by one person with marbles etc. removed one at a time after another has been jumped over each. **3.** (*US*) the card game of patience, which is played by one person. [French from Latin]

solitary /'sɒlɪtərɪ/ *adj.* **1.** alone, without companions; living alone, not gregarious. **2.** single, sole. **3.** (of a place) unfrequented, lonely. —*n.* **1.** a recluse. **2.** (*slang*) solitary confinement. —**solitary confinement**, isolation in a separate cell as a punishment. —**solitarily** *adv.*, **solitariness** *n.* [from Latin *solus* = alone]

soliton *n.* a nonlinear solitary wave that maintains its shape and velocity, and does not widen and disperse in the normal way. Such behaviour is characteristic of the waves of ◊energy that constitute the particles of atomic physics, and the mathematical equations that sum up the behaviour of solitons are being used to further research in nuclear fusion and superconductivity. [from a *solitary* wave seen on a canal by Scottish engineer John Scott Russell (1808–1882)]

solitude /'sɒlɪtjuːd/ *n.* **1.** being solitary. **2.** a solitary place. [from Old French or Latin]

solmization /sɒlmɪ'zeɪʃən/ *n.* the system of associating each note of the musical scale with a particular syllable (e.g. *do*, *re*, *mi*, etc., or doh, ray, me etc.; see ◊tonic sol-fa). [from French]

solo /'səʊləʊ/ *n.* (*plural* solos) **1.** (*plural* also solli /-liː/) a musical composition or passage for a single voice or instrument, with or without accompaniment. **2.** a performance by one person; a pilot's flight in an aircraft without an instructor or companion. **3.** (in full **solo whist**) a card game like whist in which one player may oppose the others. —*adj. & adv.* performed as a solo; unaccompanied, alone. [Italian from Latin *solus* = alone]

soloist /'səʊləʊɪst/ *n.* a performer of a solo, especially in music.

Solomon /'sɒləmən/ *c.*974–*c.*937 BC. in the Old Testament, third king of Israel, son of David by Bathsheba. During a peaceful reign, he was famed for his wisdom and his alliances with Egypt and Phoenicia. The much later biblical Proverbs, Ecclesiastes, and Song of Songs are attributed to him. He built the temple in Jerusalem with the aid of heavy taxation and forced labour, resulting in the revolt of N Israel.

Solomon Islands country in the W Pacific, E of New Guinea, comprising many hundreds of islands, the largest of which is Guadalcanal; **area** 27,600 sq km/10,656 sq mi; **capital** Honiara (on Guadalcanal); **physical** comprises all but the northernmost islands (which belong to Papua New Guinea) of a Melanesian archipelago stretching nearly 1,500 km/900 mi. The largest is Guadalcanal (area 6,500 sq km/2,510 sq mi); others are Malaita, San Cristobal, New Georgia, Santa Isabel, Choiseul; mainly mountainous and forested; **head of state** Elizabeth II represented by governor-general; **head of government** Solomon Mamaloni from 1989; **political system** constitutional monarchy; **exports** fish products, palm oil, copra, cocoa, timber; **population** (1990 est) 314,000 (Melanesian 95%, Polynesian 4%); **language** English (official); 120 Melanesian dialects; **recent history** independence was achieved from Britain within the Commonwealth in 1978 with Peter Kenilorea as prime minister. Solomon Mamaloni replaced him in 1981; Kenilorea returned to power in 1984 but resigned in 1986. Mamaloni formed a People's Action Party (PAP)-dominated coalition government in 1989.

Solomon's seal any perennial plant of the genus *Polygonatum* of the lily family Liliaceae, found growing in moist, shady woodland areas. They have bell-like white or greenish-white flowers drooping from the leaf axils of arching stems, followed by blue or black berries.

Solon /'səʊlɒn/ *c.* 638–558 BC. Athenian statesman. As one of the chief magistrates about 594 BC, he carried out the revision of the constitution that laid the foundations of Athenian democracy.

solstice /'sɒlstɪs/ *n.* each of two occasions during the year when the Sun is at its highest or lowest point above the celestial equator (and appears to pause before returning) and the number of hours of daylight greatest (at the **summer solstice**, about 21 June) or smallest (**winter solstice**, about 22 Dec). [from Old French from Latin *sol* = sun and *sistere* = stand still]

Solti /'ʃɒlti/ Georg 1912– . Hungarian-born British conductor. He was music director at Covent Garden 1961–71 and became director of the Chicago Symphony Orchestra in 1969. He was also principal conductor of the London Philharmonic Orchestra 1979–83.

solubility *n.* in physics, a measure of the amount of solute (usually a solid or gas) that will dissolve in a given amount of solvent (usually a liquid) at a particular temperature. Solubility may be expressed as grams of solute per 100 grams of solvent or, for a gas, in parts per million (ppm) of solvent.

soluble /'sɒljuːbəl/ *adj.* that can be dissolved (especially in water) or solved. —**solubility** /-'bɪlɪtɪ/ *n.*, **solubly** *adv.* [from Old French from Latin]

solute /'sɒljuːt/ *n.* a substance that is dissolved in another substance.

solution /sə'luːʃən, -'ljuː-/ *n.* **1.** solving or the means of solving a problem or difficulty. **2.** the conversion of a solid or gas into a liquid by mixture with a liquid; the state resulting from this. One of the substances is the **solvent** and the others (**solutes**) are said to be dissolved in it. **3.** dissolving, being dissolved. [from Old French from Latin]

solvable *adj.* that may be solved.

Solvay process /'sɒlveɪ/a manufacturing process for obtaining sodium carbonate (= washing soda) from limestone, ammonia, and brine. [from E *Solvay* (1838–1922), Belgian chemist, who developed the process]

solve *v.t.* to find the answer to (a problem or puzzle); to find an action or course that removes or effectively deals with (a problem or difficulty). —**solver** *n.* [from Latin *solvere* = unfasten, release]

solvent /'sɒlvənt/ *adj.* **1.** able to dissolve or form a solution with something. **2.** having enough money to meet one's liabilities. —*n.* a substance, usually a liquid, that will dissolve another substance (see ◊solution). Although the commonest solvent is water, in popular use the term refers to low-boiling-point organic liquids that are harmful if used in a confined space. They can give rise to respiratory problems, liver damage, and neurological complaints. —**solvency** *n.*

Solyman I alternative spelling of ◊Suleiman, Ottoman sultan.

Solzhenitsyn /sɒlʒə'nɪtsɪn/ Alexander (Isayevich) 1918– . Soviet novelist, a US citizen from 1974. After military service, he was in prison and exile 1945–57 for anti-Stalinist comments. Much of his writing is semi-autobiographical and highly critical of the system, including *One Day in the Life of Ivan Denisovich* 1962 which deals with the labour camps under Stalin, and *The Gulag Archipelago* 1973, an exposé of the whole Soviet labour-camp network. This led to his expulsion from the USSR in 1974.

> The salvation of mankind lies only in making everything the concern of all.
> **Alexander Solzhenitsyn**
> Nobel Lecture, 1970

Som. abbreviation of Somerset, county in England.

soma /'səʊmə/ *n.* an intoxicating drink made from the fermented sap of the *Asclepias acida* plant, used in Indian religious ritual as a sacrifice to the gods. As *haoma*, its consumption also constituted the central rite in Zoroastrian ritual. Some have argued that the plant was in fact a hallucogenic mushroom. [from Sanskrit *sōma*]

Somalia /sə'mɑːlɪə/ Somali Democratic Republic; country in the Horn of Africa, on the Indian Ocean; **area** 637,700 sq km/246,220 sq mi; **capital** Mogadishu; **physical** mainly flat, with hills in the N; **head of state** Mohammed Siyad Barre from 1969; **head of government** Mohammed Ali Samantar from 1987; **political system** one-party socialist republic; **exports** livestock, skins, hides, bananas; **population** (1990 est) 8,415,000 (including 350,000 refugees from Ethiopia and 50,000 in Djibouti); **language** Somali, Arabic (both official), Italian, English; **recent history** independence was achieved from Britain and Italy in 1960. Following an army coup in 1969, the constitution was suspended, a Supreme Revolutionary Council was set up, and the name of the country was changed to Somali Democratic Republic. After defeat in an eight-month war with Ethiopia in 1978, armed insurrection began in the N, leading to civil war. Constitutional reforms were promised in 1990.

Somaliland /sə'mɑːlɪlænd/ region of Somali-speaking peoples in E Africa, including the former British Somaliland Protectorate (established in 1887) and Italian Somaliland (made a colony in 1927, conquered by Britain in 1941 and administered by Britain until 1950), which both became independent in 1960 as the Somali Democratic Republic, the official name for ◊Somalia. It also includes former French Somaliland, which was established in 1892, became known as the Territory of the Afars and Issas in 1967, and became independent as ◊Djibouti in 1977.

somatic /sə'mætɪk/ *adj.* of the body, not of the mind. —**somatically** *adv.* [from Greek *sōma* = body]

sombre /'sɒmbə/ *adj.* dark, gloomy, dismal. —**sombrely** *adv.* [French from Latin *umbra* = shade]

sombrero /sɒm'breərəʊ/ *n.* (*plural* **sombreros**) a broad-brimmed hat worn especially in Latin American countries. [Spanish (*sombra* = shade)]

some /səm, *emphatic* sʌm/ *adj.* **1.** an unspecified amount or number of. **2.** that is unknown or unnamed. **3.** approximately. **4.** a considerable amount or number of; at least a small amount of. **5.** such to a certain extent; (*slang*) notably such. —*pron.* some people or things; some number or amount. —*adv.* (*colloquial*) to some extent. [Old English]

-some /-səm/ suffix forming **1.** adjectives in the senses 'adapted to, productive of' (e.g. *cuddlesome, fearsome*), 'characterized by being' (e.g. *fulsome*), 'apt to' (e.g. *tiresome, meddlesome*); **2.** nouns from numerals in the sense 'a group of' (e.g. *foursome*). [Old English]

somebody *n.* & *pron.* **1.** some person. **2.** a person of importance.

somehow *adv.* **1.** in some unspecified or unexplained manner. **2.** for some reason or other.

someone *n.* & *pron.* somebody.

someplace *adv.* (*US*) somewhere.

somersault /'sʌməsɒlt/ *n.* an acrobatic movement in which the body rolls head over heels either on the ground or in the air; a similar overturning movement. —*v.i.* to perform a somersault. [from Old French from Latin *supra* = above and *saltus* = leap]

Somerville *Scottish scientific writer Mary Somerville, portrayed by James Swinton.*

Somerset /'sʌməset/ county in SW England; **area** 3,460 sq km/1,336 sq mi; **administrative headquarters** Taunton; **physical** rivers Avon, Parret, and Exe; marshy coastline on the Bristol Channel; Mendip Hills (including Cheddar Gorge and Wookey Hole, a series of limestone caves where Old Stone Age flint implements and bones of extinct animals have been found); the Quantock Hills; Exmoor; **products** engineering, dairy products, cider, Exmoor ponies; **population** (1987) 452,000.

Somerset /'sʌməset/ Edward Seymour, 1st Duke of Somerset *c.*1506–1552. English politician. Created Earl of Hertford after Henry VIII's marriage to his sister Jane, he became Duke of Somerset and Protector (regent) for Edward VI in 1547. His attempt to check ◊enclosure (the transfer of land from common to private ownership) offended landowners and his moderation in religion upset the Protestants, and he was beheaded on a fake treason charge in 1552.

Somerville /'sʌməvɪl/ Mary (born Fairfax) 1780–1872. Scottish scientific writer who produced several widely used textbooks, despite having just one year of formal education. Somerville College, Oxford, is named after her.

something *n. & pron.* 1. some unspecified or unknown thing. 2. a known or understood but unexpressed quantity or quality or extent. 3. an important or notable person or thing. —**see something of,** to meet (a person) occasionally or for a short time. [Old English]

sometime *adv.* 1. at some time. 2. formerly. —*adj.* former.

sometimes *adv.* at some times.

somewhat *adv.* to some extent.

somewhere *adv.* in or to some place.

Somme, Battle of the /sɒm/ an Allied offensive in World War I in July–Nov 1916 at Beaumont-Hamel-Chaulnes, on the river Somme in N France, during which severe losses were suffered by both sides. It was the first battle in which tanks were used. The German offensive around St Quentin in March–April 1918 is sometimes called the Second Battle of the Somme.

Sommerfeld /'zɒməfelt/ Arnold 1868–1951. German physicist who demonstrated that difficulties with Niels ◊Bohr's model of the atom, in which electrons move around a central nucleus in circular orbits, could be overcome by supposing that electrons adopt elliptical orbits.

somnambulism /sɒm'næmbjuːlizəm/ *n.* sleepwalking. —**somnambulant** *adj.*, **somnambulist** *n.* [from Latin *somnus* = sleep and *ambulare* = walk]

somnolent /'sɒmnələnt/ *adj.* sleepy, asleep; inducing drowsiness. —**somnolence** *n.* [from Old French or Latin]

Somoza Debayle /sə'məusə/ Anastasio 1925–1980. Nicaraguan soldier and politician, president 1967–72 and 1974–79. The second son of Anastasio Somoza García, he succeeded his brother Luis Somoza Debayle (1922–1967;

president 1956–63) as president of Nicaragua in 1967, to head an even more oppressive regime. He was removed by Sandinista guerrillas in 1979, and assassinated in Paraguay in 1980.

Somoza García /sə'məusə gɑː'siːə/ Anastasio 1896–1956. Nicaraguan soldier and politician, president 1937–47 and 1950–56. A protégé of the USA, who wanted a reliable ally to protect their interests in Central America, he was virtual dictator of Nicaragua from 1937 until his assassination in 1956. He exiled most of his political opponents and amassed a considerable fortune in land and businesses. Members of his family retained control of the country until 1979, when they were overthrown by popular forces.

son /sʌn/ *n.* 1. a male child in relation to his parent(s). 2. a male descendant, a male member of a family etc. 3. a person regarded as inheriting an occupation or quality etc. 4. a form of address to a boy. —**son-in-law** *n.* (*plural* **sons-in-law**) a daughter's husband. **the Son of God** *or* **of Man,** in the Christian religion, Jesus. [Old English]

sonar /'səunɑː(r)/ acronym from sound navigation and ranging, a method of locating underwater objects by the reflection of ultrasonic waves; the apparatus for this. The time taken for an acoustic beam to travel to the object and back to the source enables the distance to be found since the velocity of sound in water is known. The process is similar to that used in ◊radar. Sonar devices, or **echo sounders**, were developed during World War I and after for detecting the presence of enemy U-boats, hence the original name, **asdic**, acronym from Allied Submarine Detection Investigation Committee. The name was changed to sonar in 1963.

sonata /sə'nɑːtə/ *n.* a composition for one instrument or two, normally with three or four movements contrasted in rhythm and speed but related in key. —**sonata form,** a type of composition in which two themes ('subjects') are successively set forth, developed, and restated. It is the framework for much classical music, including sonatas, ◊symphonies, and ◊concertos. [Italian, from *sonare* = sound (i.e. a piece to be played rather than sung)]

Sondheim /'sɒndhaɪm/ Stephen (Joshua) 1930– . US composer and lyricist. He wrote the witty and sophisticated lyrics of Leonard Bernstein's *West Side Story* 1957 and composed musicals, including *A Little Night Music* 1973, *Pacific Overtures* 1976, *Sweeney Todd* 1979, *Into the Woods* 1987, and *Sunday in the Park with George* 1989.

son et lumière /sɒn eɪ luː'mjeə(r)/ the outdoor night-time dramatization of the history of a notable building, monument, town, and so on, using theatrical lighting effects, sound effects, music, and narration; invented by Paul Robert Houdin, curator of the Château de Chambord, France. [French = sound and light]

song *n.* 1. singing, vocal music. 2. a piece of music for singing, a short poem etc. set to music or meant to be sung; a musical composition suggestive of a song. The term 'song' is used for secular music, whereas ◊motet and ◊cantata tend to be forms of sacred music. —**for a song,** very cheaply. **song and dance,** an outcry, a commotion. **song thrush,** a common thrush *Turdus philomelos* noted for its singing. [from Old English *sang*]

songbird *n.* a bird with a melodious cry.

song cycle a sequence of songs related in mood and sung as a group, used by Romantic composers such as Schubert, Schumann, and Hugo Wolf.

Songhai Empire /sɒŋ'gaɪ/ a former kingdom of NW Africa, founded in the 8th century, which developed into a powerful Muslim empire under the rule of Sonni Ali (reigned 1464–92). It superseded ◊Mali and extended its territory, occupying an area that included parts of present-day Guinea, Burkina Faso, Senegal, Gambia, Mali, Mauritania, Niger, and Nigeria. In 1591 it was invaded and overthrown by Morocco.

Song of Solomon a book of the Old Testament; see ◊Solomon.

songster *n.* a singer, a songbird. —**songstress** *n.fem.* [Old English]

sonic /'sɒnɪk/ *adj.* of or involving sound or sound waves. —**sonic barrier,** the ◊sound barrier. **sonic boom,** the noise like a thunderclap that occurs when an aircraft passes through the sound barrier, or begins to travel faster than the speed of sound. It happens when the cone-shaped shock wave caused by the plane touches the ground. [from Latin *sonus* = sound]

sonnet /'sɒnɪt/ *n.* a poem of 14 lines with lengths and rhymes in accordance with one of several schemes, in English usually having ten syllables per line. The sonnet is of Italian origin and was introduced to England by Sir Thomas ◊Wyatt in the form used by Petrarch (rhyming *abba abba cdcdcd* or *cdecde*) and followed by Milton and Wordsworth; Shakespeare used the form *abab cdcd efef gg*. [French or from Italian *sonetto*, diminutive of *suono* = sound]

sonny /'sʌnɪ/ *n.* (*colloquial*) a familiar form of address to a young boy.

sonoluminescence *n.* the emission of light by a liquid that is subjected to high-frequency sound waves. The rapid changes of pressure induced by the sound cause minute bubbles to form in the liquid, which then collapse. Light is emitted at the final stage of the collapse, probably because it squeezes and heats gas inside the bubbles.

sonorous /'sɒnərəs sə'nɔːrəs/ *adj.* resonant, having a loud, full, or deep sound; (of speech etc.) sounding imposing. —**sonority** /sə'nɒrɪtɪ/ *n.*, **sonorously** *adv.* [from Latin *sonor* = sound]

soon *adv.* 1. after no long interval of time. 2. relatively early, quickly. 3. (after *as* or in comparative) readily, willingly. —**as** *or* **so soon as,** at the moment that; not later than, as early as. **sooner or later,** at some future time, eventually. [Old English]

Soong Ching-ling /'suːn tʃɪŋ'lɪŋ/ 1890–1981. Chinese politician, wife of the ◊Guomindang Nationalist leader founder ◊Sun Yat-sen; she remained a prominent figure in Chinese politics after his death, being a vice chair of the People's Republic of China from 1959.

soot /sʊt/ *n.* a black, powdery substance rising in smoke and deposited by it on surfaces. —*v.t.* to cover with soot. [Old English]

sooth *n.* (*archaic*) truth. [Old English *sōth* (originally adjective = true)]

soothe /suːð/ *v.t.* to calm (a person or feelings etc.); to soften or mitigate (a pain etc.). —**soothing** *adj.* [Old English = verify]

soothsayer /'suːθseɪə/ *n.* one who foretells the future, a diviner.

sooty /'sʊtɪ/ *adj.* 1. covered with soot. 2. like soot; black or brownish-black.

sop *n.* 1. a piece of bread etc. dipped in liquid before being eaten or cooked. 2. a concession made in order to pacify or bribe a troublesome person. 3. a milksop. —*v.t./i.* (-**pp**-) 1. to dip in liquid. 2. to soak up (liquid) with something absorbent. [Old English]

Sophia /sə'faɪə/ Electress of Hanover 1630–1714. Twelfth child of Frederick V, elector palatine of the Rhine and king of Bohemia, and Elizabeth, daughter of James I of England. She married the elector of Hanover in 1658. Widowed in 1698, she was recognized in the succession to the English throne in 1701, and when Queen Anne died without issue in 1714, her son George I founded the Hanoverian dynasty.

sophism /'sɒfɪzəm/ *n.* a false argument, especially one intended to deceive. [from Old French from Latin from Greek *sophisma* = clever device (*sophizomai* = become wise from *sophos* = wise)]

sophist /'sɒfɪst/ *n.* 1. a captious or fallacious reasoner, a quibbler. 2. **Sophist,** one of a group of Greek 5th-century BC lecturers on culture, rhetoric, and politics. Sceptical about the possibility of achieving genuine knowledge, they applied bogus reasoning and were concerned with winning arguments rather than establishing the truth. —**sophistic** /-'fɪstɪk/ *adj.*

sophisticate /sə'fɪstɪkeɪt/ *v.t.* (especially in *past participle*) 1. to make (a person etc.) worldly-wise, cultured, or refined. 2. to make (equipment or techniques etc.) highly developed or complex. —/-kət/ *adj.* sophisticated. —/-kət/ *n.* a sophisticated person. —**sophistication** /-'keɪʃən/ *n.* [from Latin = tamper with]

sophistry /'sɒfɪstrɪ/ *n.* fallacious reasoning, the use of sophisms; a sophism.

Sophocles /'sɒfəkliːz/ 495–406 BC. Greek dramatist who, with Aeschylus and Euripides, is one of the three great ancient tragedians. He modified the form of tragedy by introducing a third actor and developing stage scenery. He wrote some 120 plays, of which seven tragedies survive. These are *Antigone* 441 BC, *Oedipus Tyrannus*,

Electra, *Ajax*, *Trachiniae*, *Philoctetes* 409 BC, and *Oedipus at Colonus* 401 BC. Human will plays a greater part than that of the gods in his tragedies, and his characters are generally heroic.

sophomore /'sɒfəmɔː/ *n.* (*US*) a second-year student at a university or high school.

soporific /sɒpə'rɪfɪk/ *adj.* tending to produce sleep. —*n.* a soporific drug or influence. —**soporifically** *adv.* [from Latin *sopor* = sleep and *facere* = make]

sopping *adj.* drenched.

soppy *adj.* 1. very wet. 2. (*colloquial*) mawkishly sentimental; silly. —**soppily** *adv.*, **soppiness** *n.*

soprano /sə'prɑːnəʊ/ *n.* (*plural* **sopranos**) 1. the highest female or boy's singing voice. 2. a singer with such a voice; the part written for it. 3. an instrument of the higher or highest pitch in its family. [Italian (*sopra* = above from Latin *supra*)]

Sopwith /'sɒpwɪθ/ Thomas Octave Murdoch 1888–1989. English designer of the Sopwith Camel biplane, used in World War I, and joint developer of the Hawker Hurricane fighter plane used in World War II. In 1912 he founded the Sopwith Aviation Company, which in 1920 he wound up and reopened as the Hawker Company.

sorbet /'sɔːbət/ *n.* a water ice; a sherbet. [French from Italian, ultimately from Arabic = drink]

sorbic acid CH₂CH:CHCH:CHCOOH, a tasteless acid found in the fruit of the mountain ash (genus *Sorbus*) and prepared synthetically. It is widely used in the preservation of food, for example, cider, wine, soft drinks, animal feeds, bread, and cheese.

Sorbonne /sɔː'bɒn/ the common name for the University of Paris, originally a theological institute founded in 1253 by Robert de Sorbon, chaplain to Louis IX.

sorcerer /'sɔːsərə/ *n.* a magician, a wizard. —**sorceress** *n.fem.*, **sorcery** *n.* [from Old French *sorcier* from Latin *sors* = lot]

sordid *adj.* 1. dirty, squalid. 2. ignoble, not honourable; mercenary. —**sordidly** *adv.*, **sordidness** *n.* [from French or Latin *sordidus* (*sordēre* = be dirty)]

sore *adj.* 1. causing or feeling pain from injury or disease. 2. causing or feeling mental distress or annoyance. 3. (*archaic*) serious, severe. —*n.* 1. a sore place on the body. 2. a source of distress or annoyance. —*adv.* (*archaic*) sorely. —**soreness** *n.* [Old English]

sorely *adv.* very much; severely.

Sørensen /'sɜːrənsən/ Søren 1868–1939. Danish chemist, who in 1909 introduced the concept of using the ◊pH scale as a measure of the acidity of a solution. On Sørensen's scale, still used today, a pH of 7 is neutral; higher numbers represent alkalinity, and lower numbers acidity.

sorghum /'sɔːgəm/ *n.* or **great millet** or **Guinea corn** any cereal grass of the genus *Sorghum*, native to Africa but cultivated widely in India, China, the USA, and S Europe. The seeds are used for making bread. ◊Durra is a member of the genus. [from Italian *sorgo*]

Soroptimist /sə'rɒptɪmɪst/ *n.* a member of the Soroptimist Club, an international club for professional and business women, with the aim of providing service to the community. [apparently from Latin *soror* = sister and *optimist*]

sorority /sə'rɒrɪtɪ/ *n.* 1. a devotional sisterhood. 2. (*US*) a women's society in a university or college; the men's equivalent is a fraternity. [from Latin *soror* = sister]

sorrel¹ /'sɒrəl/ *n.* any of several plants of the genus *Rumex* of the buckwheat family Polygonaceae. *R. acetosa* is grown for its bitter salad leaves. ◊Dock plants are of the same genus. [from Old French *sur* = sour]

sorrel² /'sɒrəl/ *adj.* of a light reddish-brown colour. —*n.* 1. this colour. 2. a sorrel animal, especially a horse. [from Old French *sorel* (*sor* = yellowish)]

sorrow /'sɒrəʊ/ *n.* 1. mental distress caused by loss or disappointment etc. 2. a thing causing sorrow. —*v.i.* to feel sorrow, to grieve. [Old English]

sorrowful *adj.* feeling or showing sorrow; distressing. —**sorrowfully** *adv.*

sorry /'sɒrɪ/ *adj.* 1. (*predicative*) feeling pity, regret, or sympathy. 2. an expression of apology. 3. (*attributive*) wretched; paltry. —**sorry for oneself,** (*colloquial*) dejected. [Old English]

sort *n.* 1. a particular kind or variety. 2. (*colloquial*) a person with regard to his or her (specified) character. —*v.t.* 1.

to arrange according to sort, size, destination etc. **2.** in computing, to arrange data in sequence. The choice of sorting method involves a compromise between running time, memory usage, and complexity. **—of a sort or of sorts,** not fully deserving the name given. **out of sorts,** slightly unwell; in low spirits. **sort of,** (*colloquial*) as it were, to some extent. **sort out,** to separate into sorts; to select (things of one or more sorts) from a miscellaneous group; to disentangle; to put into order; to solve; (*slang*) to deal with or punish. **—sorter** *n.* [from Old French from Latin *sors* = lot, condition]

sortie /ˈsɔːtiː/ *n.* **1.** a sally, especially from a besieged garrison. **2.** an operational flight by a military aircraft. [French (*sortir* = go out)]

sorus *n.* in ferns, a group of sporangia, the reproductive structures that produce ◊spores. They occur on the lower surface of fern fronds.

SOS /esəʊˈes/ *n.* (*plural* **SOSs**) the international code signal of extreme distress; an urgent appeal for help etc. [letters chosen as easily recognized in Morse code]

Sosnowiec /sɒˈsnɒvjets/ chief city of the Darowa coal region in the Upper Silesian province of Katowice, S Poland; population (1985) 255,000.

sostenuto /sɒstəˈnuːtəʊ/ *adv.* in music, in a sustained manner. **—n.** (*plural* **sostenutos**) a passage to be played in this way. [Italian from Latin *sustinere* = sustain]

sot *n.* a habitual drunkard. **—sottish** *adj.* [Old English and from Old French = foolish]

sotto voce /ˈsɒtəʊ ˈvəʊtʃi/ in an undertone. [Italian = under the voice]

sou /suː/ *n.* **1.** a former French coin of low value. **2.** (*colloquial*) a very small amount of money. **—not a sou,** no money at all. [French from Old French from Latin *solidus* = Roman gold coin]

soubrette *n.* a pert maidservant etc. in comedy; an actress taking this part. [French from Provençal *soubret* = coy]

soubriquet variant of ◊sobriquet.

soufflé /ˈsuːfleɪ/ *n.* a light, spongy dish usually made with stiffly beaten egg whites. [French = blown]

sough /sʌf, saʊ/ *n.* a moaning or whispering sound as of the wind in trees. **—v.i.** to make this sound. [from Old English = resound]

sought past and past participle of **seek.**

souk /suːk/ *n.* a marketplace in Muslim countries. [from Arabic]

soul /səʊl/ *n.* **1.** the spiritual or immaterial element in a person, in many religions regarded as immortal. **2.** the moral, emotional, or intellectual nature of a person or animal. **3.** a personification or pattern. **4.** an individual; a person regarded with familiarity or pity etc. **5.** a person regarded as the animating or essential part. **6.** emotional or intellectual energy or intensity, especially as revealed in a work of art. **7.** the emotional or spiritual quality of black American life and culture; soul music. **—soul-destroying** *adj.* deadeningly monotonous or depressing. **soul mate,** a person ideally suited to another. **soul music,** a style of ◊rhythm and blues sung by, among others, Sam Cooke (1931–1964), Aretha Franklin (1942–), and Al Green (1946–). Soul is a synthesis of blues, gospel music, and jazz which emerged in the 1950s. Its lyrics are emotionally intense and earthy. **soul-searching** *adj.* examining one's own emotions or motives. **upon my soul,** an exclamation of surprise. [Old English]

soulful *adj.* having, expressing, or evoking deep feeling. **—soulfully** *adv.*

soulless *adj.* **1.** lacking sensitivity or noble qualities. **2.** undistinguished, uninteresting.

sound¹ *n.* **1.** waves of pressure that travel through the air or other elastic medium (such as water) and are detectable at certain frequencies by the ear. **2.** the sensation produced by these; a particular kind of it. **3.** a sound made in speech. **4.** sound reproduced in a film etc. **5.** the mental impression produced by a statement or description etc. **—v.t./i. 1.** to emit or cause to emit sound. **2.** to utter, to pronounce. **3.** to convey an impression when heard. **4.** to give an audible signal for (an alarm etc.). **5.** to test (the lungs etc.) by noting the sound produced. **—sound effects,** sounds other than speech or music produced artificially for use in a play or film etc. **sounding board,** a canopy projecting sound towards an audience; a means of disseminating opinions

etc. **sound off,** (*colloquial*) to talk loudly, to express one's opinions forcefully. **sound wave,** a wave of condensation and rarefaction, by which sound is transmitted in the air etc. All sound waves in air travel with a speed dependent on the temperature; under ordinary conditions, this is about 330 m/1,070 ft per second. The pitch of the sound depends on the number of vibrations imposed on the air per second, but the speed is unaffected. The loudness of a sound is dependent primarily on the amplitude of the vibration of the air. **—sounder** *n.* [from Anglo-French from Latin *sonus*]

sound² *adj.* **1.** healthy, not diseased or injured or rotten. **2.** (of an opinion or policy etc.) correct, orthodox, well-founded. **3.** financially secure. **4.** undisturbed. **5.** thorough. **—adv.** soundly. **—soundly** *adv.*, **soundness** *n.* [from Old English]

sound³ *v.t.* **1.** to test the depth or quality of the bottom of (the sea or a river etc.). **2.** (also with *out*) to inquire into the opinions or feelings of. **—sounder** *n.* [from Old French *sonder* from Latin *sub* = under and *unda* = wave]

sound⁴ *n.* a strait (of water). [Old English = swimming]

sound barrier the concept that the speed of sound, or sonic speed (about 1,220 kph/760 mph at sea level), constitutes a speed limit to flight through the atmosphere, since a badly designed aircraft suffers severe buffeting at near sonic speed owing to the formation of shock waves. US test pilot Chuck Yeager first flew through the 'barrier' in 1947 in a Bell X-1 rocket plane. Now, by careful design, aircraft such as Concorde can fly at supersonic speed with ease, though they create in their wake a ◊sonic boom.

sounding *n.* **1.** measurement of the depth of water. **2.** (in *plural*) the region near enough to the shore to allow sounding.

soundproof *adj.* impervious to sound. **—v.t.** to make soundproof.

sound synthesis the generation of sound (usually music) by electronic ◊synthesizer.

soundtrack *n.* a band at one side of a cine film or videotape on which the accompanying sound is recorded; the sound itself. Usually the sound is recorded in the form of an optical track (a pattern of light and shade). The pattern is produced on the film when signals from the recording microphone are made to vary the intensity of a light beam. During playback, a light is shone through the track on to a photocell, which converts the pattern of light falling on it into appropriate electrical signals. These signals are then fed to loudspeakers to recreate the original sounds.

soup /suːp/ *n.* a liquid food made by stewing bones, vegetables etc. **—v.t.** (usually with *up*) (*colloquial*) **1.** to increase the power of (an engine etc.). **2.** to enliven. **—in the soup,** (*slang*) in difficulties or trouble. **soup kitchen,** an establishment supplying free soup etc. to the poor or in times of distress. **soup plate,** a large deep plate for soup. **—soupy** *adj.* [from French *soupe* from Latin]

soupçon /ˈsuːpsɒ̃/ *n.* a very small quantity, a trace or tinge. [French from Latin = suspicion]

Souphanouvong /suːfænuːˈvɒŋ/ Prince 1912– . Laotian politician, president 1975–86. After an abortive revolt against French rule in 1945, he led the guerrilla organization Pathet Lao, and in 1975 became the first president of the Republic of Laos. He resigned after suffering a stroke.

sour *adj.* **1.** tasting or smelling sharp like unripe fruit; not fresh, tasting or smelling sharp or unpleasant from fermentation or staleness. **2.** (of soil) excessively acid; deficient in lime. **3.** bad-tempered, disagreeable in manner. **—n.** an acid drink, especially of whisky with lemon juice or lime juice. **—v.t./i.** to make or become sour. **—go or turn sour,** to turn out badly; to lose one's keenness. **sour grapes,** said when a person disparages what he or she desires but cannot attain. [from the fable of the fox who wanted some grapes but found that they were out of reach and so pretended that they were sour and undesirable anyway] **—sourly** *adv.*, **sourness** *n.* [Old English]

source /sɔːs/ *n.* **1.** the place from which a thing comes or is obtained. **2.** a person or book etc. providing information. **3.** the starting point of a river or stream. **—at source,** at the point of origin or issue. [from Old French *sors*, *sourse* from *sourdre* = rise from Latin *surgere*]

source language in computing, the language in which programs are originally written, as opposed to ◊machine code, which is the form in which they are carried out by the computer. The translation from source language to machine code is done by a ◊compiler or ◊interpreter program within the computer.

souring *n.* the change that occurs to wine on prolonged exposure to air. The ethanol in the wine is oxidized by the air (oxygen) to ethanoic acid. It is the presence of the ethanoic (acetic) acid that produces the sour taste.

sourpuss *n.* (*slang*) a bad-tempered person.

Sousa /ˈsuːzə/ John Philip 1854–1932. US bandmaster and composer of marches such as 'The Stars and Stripes Forever!' 1897.

sousaphone *n.* a form of large bass ◊tuba, suggested by John Sousa, designed to wrap round the player in a circle and having a forward-facing bell.

souse /saʊs/ *v.t./i.* 1. to steep in pickle. 2. to plunge or soak in liquid; to drench; to throw (liquid) over a thing. 3. (in *past participle, slang*) drunk. —*n.* 1. pickle made with salt. 2. (*US*) food in pickle. 3. a plunge or soaking. [from Old French *sous* = pickle from Old High German *sulza* = brine]

soutane /suːˈtɑːn/ *n.* the cassock of a Roman Catholic priest. [French from Italian *sottana* (*sotto* = under)]

south *n.* 1. the point of the horizon opposite north; the compass point corresponding to this; the direction in which this lies. 2. or **South** the part of a country or town lying to the south. —*adj.* 1. towards, at, near, or facing the south. 2. (of wind) blowing from the south. —*adv.* towards, at, or near the south. —**South Pole,** the southern end of the Earth's axis of rotation; see ◊pole. **south-southeast** *n., adj.,* & *adv.* midway between south and southeast. **south-southwest** *n., adj.,* & *adv.* midway between south and southwest. [Old English]

South Africa /saʊθ ˈæfrɪkə/ Republic of; country on the S tip of Africa, bounded to the N by Namibia, Botswana, and Zimbabwe and NE by Swaziland and Mozambique; **area** 1,223,181 sq km/472,148 sq mi; **capital** Cape Town (legislative), Pretoria (administrative), Bloemfontein (judicial); **physical** S end of large plateau, fringed by mountains and lowland coastal margin; Drakensberg Mountains, Table Mountain; Limpopo and Orange rivers; the Veld and the Karroo; part of Kalahari Desert; **territories** Prince Edward Island in the Antarctic; **head of state and government** F W de Klerk from 1989; **political system** racist, nationalist republic, restricted democracy; **exports** corn, sugar, fruit, wool, gold, platinum, diamonds; **population** (1990 est) 39,550,000 (73% black: Zulu, Xhosa, Sotho, Tswana; 18% white: 3% mixed, 3% Asiatic); **language** Afrikaans and English (both official); Bantu; **recent history** the Union of South Africa was formed in 1910 from two British colonies and two Boer republics. The apartheid system of racial discrimination was initiated in 1948 by Daniel Malan, leader of the National Party (NP). In 1960 the African National Congress (ANC) was banned. South Africa withdrew from the Commonwealth and became a republic in 1961. Harsh repression of black South Africans continued; important landmarks were the sentencing to life imprisonment of ANC leaders in 1964, violent suppression of the Soweto uprising in 1976, the death in custody of Pan African Congress activist Steve Biko in 1977. In 1984 a new constitution was adopted, giving segregated representation to coloureds. Violence continued to grow in black townships. The Commonwealth agreed on limited sanctions in 1986. The Democratic Party (DP) was launched in 1989 and President F W de Klerk announced the lifting of the ban on the ANC in 1990 and the repeal of apartheid laws in 1991.

South African Wars two wars between the Boers (settlers of Dutch origin) and the British; essentially fought for the gold and diamonds of the Transvaal. The **War of 1881** was triggered by the attempt of the Boers of the ◊Transvaal to reassert the independence surrendered in 1877 in return for British aid against African peoples. The British were defeated at Majuba, and the Transvaal again became independent. The **War of 1899–1902,** also known as the **Boer War,** was preceded by the armed ◊Jameson Raid into the Boer Transvaal; a failed attempt, inspired by the Cape Colony prime minister Rhodes, to precipitate a revolt against Kruger, the Transvaal president. The *uitlanders* (non-Boer immigrants) were still not given the vote by the Boers, negotiations failed, and the Boers invaded British territory, besieging Ladysmith, Mafeking (now Mafikeng), and Kimberley. British commander ◊Kitchener countered Boer guerrilla warfare by putting the noncombatants who

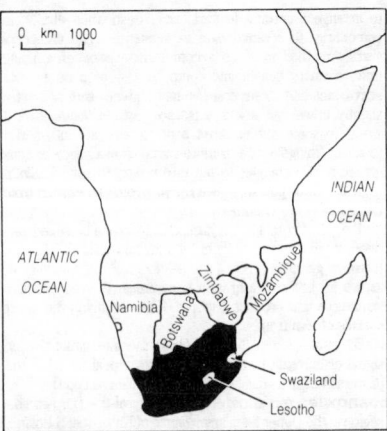

South Africa

supported them into concentration camps (about 26,000 women and children died of sickness). The war ended with the Peace of Vereeniging following the Boer defeat.

South America /saʊθ əˈmerɪkə/ fourth largest of the continents, nearly twice as large as Europe, extending S from ◊Central America; **area** 17,854,000 sq km/6,893,429 sq mi; **largest cities** (over 3.5 million inhabitants) Buenos Aires, São Paulo, Rio de Janeiro, Bogotá, Santiago, Lima, Caracas; **physical** Andes in the W; Brazilian and Guiana highlands; central plains from the Orinoco basin to Patagonia; Parana-Paraguay-Uruguay system flowing to form the La Plata estuary; Amazon river basin, with its remaining great forests and their rich fauna and flora; **products** coffee, cocoa, sugar, bananas, oranges, wine, meat and fish products, cotton, wool, handicrafts, minerals incuding oil, silver, iron ore, copper; **population** (1985) 263,300,000; originally ◊American Indians, who survive chiefly in Bolivia, Peru, and Ecuador and are increasing in number. In addition there are many mestizo (people of mixed Spanish or Portuguese and Indian ancestry) elsewhere; many people originally from Europe, largely Spanish, Italian, and Portuguese; and many of African descent, originally imported as slaves; **language** Spanish, Portuguese (chief language in Brazil), many Indian languages.

Southampton /saʊθˈhæmptən/ port in Hampshire, S England; population (1981) 204,604. Industries include engineering, chemicals, plastics, flour-milling, and tobacco; it is also a passenger and container port.

Southampton Henry Wriothesley, 3rd Earl of Southampton 1573–1624. English courtier, patron of Shakespeare. Shakespeare dedicated *Venus and Adonis* and *The Rape of Lucrece* to him and may have addressed him in the sonnets.

South Asia Regional Cooperation Committee (SARCC) an organization established in 1983 by India, Pakistan, Bangladesh, Nepál, Sri Lanka, Bhutan, and the Maldives to cover agriculture, telecommunications, health, population, sports, art, and culture.

South Australia state of the Commonwealth of Australia; **area** 984,000 sq km/379,824 sq mi; **capital** Adelaide (chief port); **physical** Murray Valley irrigated area, including wine-growing Barossa Valley; lakes: ◊Eyre, ◊Torrens; mountains: Mount Lofty, Musgrave, Flinders; parts of the ◊Nullarbor Plain, and Great Victoria and Simpson deserts; **products** meat and wool (80% of area cattle and sheep grazing), wines and spirits, dried and canned fruit, iron (Middleback Range), coal (Leigh Creek), copper, uranium (Roxby Downs), oil and natural gas in the NE, lead, zinc, iron, opals, household and electrical goods, vehicles; **population** (1987) 1,388,000; 1% Aborigines; **recent history** the first European settlement was in 1834; South Australia was a province from 1836 and a state from 1901.

South Carolina /saʊθ kærəˈlaɪnə/ state of the SE USA; nickname Palmetto State; **area** 80,600 sq km/ 31,112 sq mi; **capital** Columbia; **physical** large areas of woodland; subtropical climate in coastal areas; **products** tobacco, cotton, fruit, soya beans, meat, textiles, clothing, paper, woodwulp, furniture, bricks, chemicals, machinery; **population** (1988) 3,493,000; **history** one of the original Thirteen States in 1776; joined the Confederacy in 1860; readmitted to Union in 1868.

South Dakota /sauθ də'kəutə/ state of the USA; nickname Coyote or Sunshine State; **area** 199,800 sq km/ 77,123 sq mi; **capital** Pierre; **physical** Great Plains; Black Hills; Badlands; **products** cereals, livestock, gold (greatest US producer); **population** (1986) 708,000; **recent history** state from 1889.

southeast n. **1.** the point midway between south and east; the direction in which this lies. **2.** or **South-East** the part of a country or town lying to the southeast. —*adj.* of, towards, or coming from the southeast. —*adv.* towards, at, or near the southeast. —**southeasterly** *adj.* & *adv.*, **southeastern** *adj.*

southeaster n. a southeast wind.

southerly /'sʌðəlɪ/ *adj.* & *adv.* **1.** in a southern position or direction. **2.** (of wind) blowing from the south (approximately).

southern /'sʌðən/ *adj.* of or in the south. —**Southern states**, those in the south (especially southeast) of the USA. [Old English]

Southern Uplands one of the three geographical divisions of Scotland, occupying most of the hilly Scottish Borderland to the south of a geological fault line that stretches from Dunbar on the North Sea to Girvan on the Firth of Clyde. The Southern Uplands, largely formed by rocks of the Silurian and Ordovician age, are intersected by the broad valleys of the Nith and Tweed rivers.

Southern Cross the popular name for the constellation ◊Crux.

Southerne /'sʌðən/ Thomas 1660–1746. English playwright and poet, author of the tragicomedies *Oroonoko* 1695–96 and *The Fatal Marriage* 1694.

southerner n. a native or inhabitant of the south.

southern lights the common name for the ◊aurora australis, coloured light in southern skies.

Southey /'sauðɪ/ Robert 1774–1843. English poet and author, friend of Coleridge and Wordsworth. In 1813 he became poet laureate but is better known for his *Life of Nelson* 1813 and for his letters.

Curses are like young chickens, they always come home to roost.

Robert Southey
The Curse of Kehama

South Georgia /sauθ 'dʒɔːdʒə/ island in the S Atlantic, a British crown colony administered with the South Sandwich Islands; area 3,757 sq km/1,450 sq mi. South Georgia lies 1,300 km/800 mi SE of the Falkland Islands, of which it was a dependency until 1985. The British Antarctic Survey has a station on nearby Bird Island.

South Glamorgan /sauθ glə'mɔːgən/ county in S Wales; **area** 420 sq km/162 sq mi; **administrative headquarters** Cardiff; **physical** fertile Vale of Glamorgan; **products** dairy farming, industry (steel, plastics, engineering) in the Cardiff area; **population** (1987) 400,000; **language** 6% Welsh; English.

South Holland (Dutch *Zuid-Holland*) low-lying coastal province of the Netherlands; **area** 2,910 sq km/1,123 sq mi; **population** (1988) 3,208,000; **capital** The Hague; **products** bulbs, horticulture, livestock, dairy products, chemicals, textiles; **history** once part of the former county of Holland that was divided into two provinces (North and South) in 1840.

South Korea see ◊Korea, South.

southpaw *adj.* (*colloquial*) left-handed. —*n.* (*colloquial*) a left-handed person, especially a boxer.

South Sea Bubble a financial crisis in Britain in 1720. The South Sea Company, founded in 1711, which had a monopoly of trade with South America, offered in 1719 to take over more than half the national debt in return for further concessions. Its £100 shares rapidly rose to £1,000, and an orgy of speculation followed. When the 'bubble' burst, thousands were ruined. The discovery that cabinet ministers had been guilty of corruption led to a political crisis.

southward /'sauθwəd/ *adj.* & (also **southwards**) *adv.* towards the south. —*n.* a southward direction or region.

southwest n. **1.** the point midway between south and west; the direction in which this lies. **2.** or **South-West** the part of a country or town lying to the southwest. —*adj.* of, towards, or coming from the southwest. —*adv.* towards, at, or near the southwest. —**southwesterly** *adj.* & *adv.*, **southwestern** *adj.*

South West Africa /sauθ west 'æfrɪkə/ former name (until 1968) of ◊Namibia.

South West Africa People's Organization (SWAPO) an organization formed in 1959 in South West Africa (now ◊Namibia) to oppose South African rule. SWAPO guerrillas, led by Sam Nujoma, began attacking with support from Angola. In 1966 SWAPO was recognized by the United Nations as the legitimate government of Namibia, and won the first independent election in 1989.

southwester n. a southwest wind.

South Yorkshire /sauθ 'jɔːkʃə/ metropolitan county of England, created in 1976, originally administered by an elected council; its powers reverted to district councils from 1986; **area** 1,560 sq km/602 sq mi; **administrative headquarters** Barnsley; **physical** river Don; part of Peak District National Park; **products** metalwork, coal, dairy, sheep, arable farming; **population** (1987) 1,296,000.

Soutine /su:'ti:n/ Chaim 1894–1943. Lithuanian-born French Expressionist artist. He painted landscapes and portraits, including many of painters active in Paris in the 1920s and 1930s. He had a distorted style, using thick application of paint (impasto) and brilliant colours.

souvenir /su:və'nɪə/ n. a thing kept as a reminder of a place, person, or event. [French from Latin *subvenire* = occur to the mind]

sou'wester /sau'westə/**1.** a waterproof hat with a broad flap at the back. **2.** a southwest wind.

sovereign /'sɒvrɪn/ n. **1.** a supreme ruler, especially a monarch. **2.** a British gold coin nominally worth £1. It was introduced by Henry VII and became the standard monetary unit in 1817. Minting ceased for currency purposes in the UK in 1914, but the sovereign continued to be used as 'unofficial' currency in the Middle East. It was minted for the last time in 1987 and has now been replaced by the **Britannia**. —*adj.* **1.** supreme; unmitigated. **2.** possessing sovereign power; independent; royal. **3.** very good or effective. [from Old French *so(u)verain* ultimately from Latin *super* = over]

sovereignty n. absolute authority within a given territory. The possession of sovereignty is taken to be the distinguishing feature of the state, as against other forms of community. The term has an internal aspect, in that it refers to the ultimate source of authority within a state, such as a parliament or monarch, and an external aspect, where it denotes the independence of the state from any outside authority.

Soviet /'səuviət, 'sɒv-/ *adj.* of the USSR. —*n.* a citizen of the USSR. —**soviet** n. an elected council in a district of the USSR. A soviet was originally a strike committee elected by Russian workers in the 1905 revolution; in 1917 these were set up by peasants, soldiers, and factory workers. The soviets sent delegates to the All-Russian Congress of Soviets to represent their opinions to a future government. They were later taken over by the ◊Bolsheviks. —**Supreme Soviet**, until 1989, the governing council of the USSR or of any of its constituent republics. [from Russian *sovet* = council]

Soviet Central Asia formerly **Turkestan** an area of the USSR comprising the constituent republics of ◊Kazakhstan, ◊Uzbekistan, ◊Tadzhikistan, ◊Turkmenistan, and ◊Kirghizia.

Soviet Union /'səuviət 'ju:niən/ alternative name for the ◊Union of Soviet Socialist Republics (USSR).

sovkhoz n. a state-owned farm in the USSR where the workers are state employees. The sovkhoz differs from the *kolkhoz* where the farm is run by a ◊collective.

sow[1] /səu/ *v.t.* (*past* **sowed**; *past participle* **sown** or **sowed**) **1.** to put (seed) on or in the earth for the purpose of growth; to plant (land) with seed. **2.** to implant or spread (feelings or ideas). —**sower** n. [Old English]

sow[2] /sau/ n. an adult female pig. [Old English]

Soweto /sə'weɪtəu/ (South West Township) racially segregated urban settlement in South Africa, SW of Johannesburg; population (1983) 915,872. It has experienced civil unrest because of the ◊apartheid regime; there were serious riots in 1976 and 1985, continuing into the 1990s.

soy *n.* **1.** a sauce made from pickled soya beans. **2.** (*US*) **soybean** a soya bean. [Japanese *shōyu* from Chinese *shi-you* (*shi* = salted beans and *you* = oil)]

soya /'sɔɪə/ *n.* a leguminous plant *Glycine max*, native to E Asia, in particular Japan and China, originally grown as a forage crop. —**soya bean**, the seed of this plant. It is used in cooking oils and margarine, as a flour, soya milk, or processed into tofu, miso, or textured vegetable protein. [from Dutch from Malay]

Soyinka /ʃɔɪ'ɪŋkə/ Wole 1934– . Nigerian author, who was a political prisoner in Nigeria 1967–69. His works include the play *The Lion and the Jewel* 1963; his prison memoirs *The Man Died* 1972; *Aké, The Years of Childhood* 1982, an autobiography, and *Isara*, a fictionalized memoir 1989. He was the first African to receive the Nobel Prize for Literature, in 1986.

Soyuz /sɔɪ'u:z/ *n.* a series of Soviet spacecraft, capable of carrying up to three cosmonauts. Soyuz spacecraft consist of three parts: a rear section containing engines; the central crew compartment; and a forward compartment that gives additional room for working and living space. They are used for ferrying crews up to space stations. [Russian = union]

sozzled /'sɒzəld/ *adj.* (*slang*) very drunk. [from dialect *sozzle* = mix sloppily (imitative)]

spa /spɑ:/ *n.* a curative mineral spring; a place with this. [from *Spa* in Belgium, celebrated since medieval times for the curative properties of its mineral springs]

Spaak /spɑ:k/ Paul-Henri 1899–1972. Belgian socialist politician. From 1936 to 1966 he held office almost continuously as foreign minister or prime minister. He was an ardent advocate of international peace.

space *n.* **1.** the continuous expanse in which things exist and move; a portion of this; the amount of this taken by a particular thing or available for a particular purpose. **2.** the interval between points or objects; an empty area. **3.** an interval of time. **4.** the area of paper used in writing or printing something. **5.** outer space, the void that exists beyond Earth's atmosphere. Above 120 km/75 mi, very little atmosphere remains, so objects can continue to move quickly without extra energy. The space between the planets is not entirely empty, but filled with the tenuous gas of the ◊solar wind as well as dust specks. **6.** a large area. —*attributive* of or used for travel etc. in outer space. —*v.t.* to set or arrange at intervals; to put spaces between. —**space age**, the era of space travel. [from Old French *espace* from Latin *spatium*]

spacecraft *n.* a vehicle for travelling in outer space.

Spacek /'speɪsek/ Sissy (Mary Elizabeth) 1949– . US film actress who starred in *Badlands* 1973 and *Carrie* 1976, in which she played a repressed telekinetic teenager. Her other films include *Coal Miner's Daughter* 1979 and *Missing* 1982.

Spacelab *n.* a small space station built by the European Space Agency, carried in the cargo bay of the space shuttle, in which it remains throughout each flight, returning to Earth with the shuttle. Spacelab consists of a pressurized module in which astronauts can work, and a series of pallets, open to the vacuum of space, on which equipment is mounted.

spaceman *n.* (*plural* **spacemen**) a space traveller.

space probe any instrumented object sent beyond Earth to collect data from other parts of the solar system and from deep space. The first probe was the Soviet *Lunik 1*, which flew past the Moon in 1959. Other probes include *Giotto*, the Moon probes, and the Mariner, Pioneer, Viking, and Voyager series.

spaceship *n.* a spacecraft.

space shuttle a spacecraft travelling repeatedly e.g. between Earth and a space station. The US crewed space shuttle was first launched on 12 April 1981. It was developed by ◊NASA to reduce the cost of using space for commercial, scientific, and military purposes. After leaving its payload in space, the rocket component can be flown back to Earth like any conventional aeroplane. The space-shuttle orbiter, the part that goes into space, is 37.2 m/122 ft long and weighs 68 tonnes. Two to eight crew members occupy the orbiter's nose section, and missions last up to 30 days. In its cargo bay the orbiter

space shuttle The space shuttle Columbia.

can carry up to 29 tonnes of satellites, scientific equipment, ◊Spacelab, or military payloads.

space station any large structure designed for human occupation in space for extended periods of time. Space stations are used for carrying out astronomical observations and surveys of Earth, as well as for biological studies and the processing of materials in weightlessness. The first space station was ◊*Salyut 1*, and the USA has launched ◊*Skylab*.

spacesuit *n.* a sealed, pressurized suit allowing the wearer to survive in outer space.

space-time *n.* in physics, a combination of space and time used in the theory of ◊relativity. When developing relativity, Einstein showed that time was in many respects like an extra dimension (or direction) to space. Space and time can thus be considered as entwined into a single entity, rather than two separate things.

spacious /'speɪʃəs/ *adj.* providing much space, roomy. —**spaciousness** *n.* [from Old French or Latin]

spade[1] *n.* a digging tool with a sharp-edged, broad, usually metal blade; a similar tool for various purposes. —**call a spade a spade**, to speak plainly or bluntly. —**spadeful!** *n.* [Old English]

spade[2] *n.* a playing card of the suit (**spades**) marked with black figures shaped like an inverted heart with a short stem. [from Italian *spada* = sword from Latin from Greek]

spadework *n.* hard preparatory work.

spadix /'speɪdɪks/ *n.* a spike of flowers closely arranged round a fleshy axis and usually enclosed in a spathe. [Latin from Greek = palm branch]

spaghetti /spə'getɪ/ *n.* pasta made in solid strings, between macaroni and vermicelli in thickness. [Italian, plural of diminutive of *spago* = string]

Spain /speɪn/ country in SW Europe, on the Iberian Peninsula between the Atlantic and the Mediterranean, bounded to the N by France and to the W by Portugal; **area** 504,750 sq km/194,960 sq mi; **capital** Madrid; **physical** central plateau with mountain ranges; lowlands in S; includes Balearic and Canary Islands, and Ceuta and Melilla; rivers Ebro, Douro, Tagus, Guadiana, Guadalquivir; Iberian Plateau (Meseta); Pyrenees, Cantabrian Mountains, Andalusian Mountains, Sierra Nevada; **head of state** Juan Carlos I from 1975; **head of government** Felipe González Marquez from 1982; **political system** constitutional monarchy; **exports** citrus fruits, grapes, pomegranates, vegetables, wine, sherry, olive oil, canned fruit and fish, iron ore, cork, vehicles, leather goods, ceramics; **population** (1990 est) 39,623,000;

Spain 1270-1492

language Spanish (Castilian, official), Basque, Catalan, Galician, Valencian, and Majorcan; **recent history** civil war 1936–39; Gen Francisco Franco became head of state and government, with the fascist Falange party as the only legal political organization until his death in 1975. He was succeeded by King Juan Carlos I; restoration of the monarchy and adoption of a new constitution. The Socialist Workers' Party (PSOE) won a sweeping electoral victory in 1982. Spain joined the European Community in 1986.

Spallanzani /spæl∂nt'sɑ:ni/ Lazzaro 1729–1799. Italian biologist and priest. He disproved the theory that microbes spontaneously generate out of rotten food by showing that they would not grow in flasks of broth that had been boiled for 30 minutes and then sealed.

Spam *n.* trade name of a tinned meat made mainly from ham. [arbitrary formation or from *sp*iced h*am*]

span[1] *n.* **1.** the full extent from end to end or across; the maximum lateral extent of an aeroplane or its wing. **2.** each part of a bridge between the supports. **3.** the maximum distance between the tips of the thumb and little finger, especially as a measure = 9 in. **4.** length in time from beginning to end. —*v.t.* (**-nn-**) to extend from side to side or end to end of; to bridge (a river etc.). [Old English]

span[2] see ◊spick and span.

Spandau /'ʃpændaʊ/ suburb of W Berlin, Germany. The chief war criminals condemned at the Nuremberg Trials in 1946 were imprisoned in the fortress there. The last of them was the Nazi leader Rudolf Hess, and the prison was demolished following his death in 1987.

spandrel /'spændr∂l/ *n.* the space between the curve of an arch and the surrounding rectangular moulding or framework or between the curves of adjoining arches and the moulding above.

spangle *n.* a small piece of glittering material, especially one of many as an ornament of a dress etc. —*v.t.* (especially in *past participle*) to cover (as) with spangles. [from *spang* from Middle Dutch and Old High German, Old Norse *spöng* = brooch]

Spaniard /'spænj∂d/ *n.* a native of Spain. [from Old French *Espaigne* = Spain]

spaniel /'spænj∂l/ *n.* a dog of a breed with a long, silky coat and drooping ears. The **Clumber spaniel**, weighing up to 32 kg/70 lb, takes its name from the estate of the duke of Newcastle, who imported them from France; it is white with lemon markings. The **cocker** (English and American) is smaller (12 kg/25 lb, 40 cm/15 in tall), and of various colours. The **springer** (English and Welsh), about 20 kg/45 lb and 50 cm/20 in tall, is so called because of its use for 'springing' game. The **Sussex spaniel** is believed to be the oldest variety, weighs 20 kg/45 lb, is 40 cm/15 in tall, and is a golden liver colour. Toy spaniels include the **King Charles, Japanese, Tibetan,** and **Pekingese.** [from Old French = Spanish dog]

Spanish /'spænɪʃ/ *adj.* of Spain or its people or language. —*n.* the Spanish language, a member of the Romance branch of the Indo-European language family, traditionally known as Castilian and originally spoken only in NE Spain. As the language of the court, it has been the standard and literary language of the Spanish state since the 13th century. It is now a world language, spoken in Mexico and all South and Central American countries (except Brazil, Guyana, Suriname, and French Guiana) as well as in the Philippines, Cuba, Puerto Rico, and much of the USA that borders on Spanish-speaking countries or has large Latin American immigrant communities. —**the Spanish,** the people of Spain. **Spanish fly,** a dried insect *Lytta vesicatoria* used in medicine and as a supposed aphrodisiac.

Spanish-American War a war in 1898 by Cuban revolutionaries (with US backing) against Spanish rule. The Treaty of Paris ceded Cuba, the Philippines, Guam, and Puerto Rico to the USA.

Spanish Armada the fleet sent by Philip II of Spain against England in 1588. Consisting of 130 ships, it sailed from Lisbon and carried on a running fight up the Channel with the English fleet of 197 small ships under Howard of Effingham and Francis ◊Drake. The Armada anchored off Calais but was forced to put to sea by fireships, and a general action followed off Gravelines. What remained of the Armada escaped around the N of Scotland and W of Ireland, suffering many losses by storm and shipwreck on the way. Only about half the original fleet returned to Spain.

Spanish Civil War 1936–39. See ◊Civil War, Spanish.

Spanish Guinea /'spænɪʃ 'gɪnɪ/ former name of the Republic of ◊Equatorial Guinea.

Spanish Main a term often used to describe the Caribbean in the 16th–17th centuries, but more properly the South American mainland between the river Orinoco and Panama.

Spanish Sahara /'spænɪʃ s∂'hɑːr∂/ former name for ◊Western Sahara.

Spanish Succession, War of the a war 1701–14 waged by Britain, Austria, the Netherlands, Portugal, and Denmark (the Allies) against France, Spain, and Bavaria.

It was caused by Louis XIV's acceptance of the Spanish throne on behalf of his grandson, Philip V of Spain, in defiance of the Partition Treaty of 1700, under which it would have passed to Archduke Charles of Austria (later Holy Roman Emperor Charles VI). By the Treaties of Utrecht 1713 and Rastat 1714 the Allies recognized Philip as King of Spain, but Gibraltar, Minorca, and Nova Scotia were ceded to Britain, and Belgium, Milan, and Naples to Austria.

spank *v.t./i.* 1. to slap on the buttocks. 2. (of a horse etc.) to move briskly. —*n.* a slap given in spanking.

spanker *n.* a fore-and-aft sail on the after side of the mizenmast.

spanking *n.* the process of spanking or being spanked. —*adj.* (*colloquial*) brisk, lively; excellent. —*adv.* (*colloquial*) briskly; excellently.

spanner *n.* a tool for turning a nut on a bolt etc. —**spanner in the works,** an upsetting element or influence. [German *spannen* = draw tight]

spar[1] *n.* 1. a stout pole as used for a ship's mast etc. 2. the main longitudinal beam of an aeroplane wing. [from Old French *esparre* or Old Norse *sperra*]

spar[2] *v.i.* (**-rr-**) 1. to make the motions of attack and defence with closed fists; to use the hands (as) in boxing. 2. to engage in argument etc. —*n.* a sparring motion; a boxing match. —**sparring partner,** a boxer employed to practise with another in training; a person with whom one enjoys arguing. [Old English]

spar[3] *n.* an easily split crystalline mineral. [Middle Low German, related to Old English *spæren* = of plaster, *spærstān* = gypsum]

spare *v.t.* 1. to refrain from hurting, harming, or destroying; to be merciful towards. 2. to use with great restraint; to refrain from using. 3. to part with, to be able to afford to give; to do without; to allow to have (a thing etc., especially that one does not need). —*adj.* 1. additional to what is usually needed or used; reserved for occasional or emergency use. 2. (of a person etc.) thin; lean. 3. small in quantity; frugal. —*n.* a spare part. —**go spare,** (*slang*) to become very angry. **not spare oneself,** to exert one's utmost efforts. **spare part,** a duplicate to replace a lost or damaged part. **sparerib** *n.* a cut of pork from the lower ribs. **spare time,** leisure. **spare tyre,** (*colloquial*) a circle of fatness round or above the waist. —**sparely** *adv.,* **spareness** *n.* [Old English]

sparing /'speərɪŋ/ *adj.* economical, not generous or wasteful; restrained. —**sparingly** *adv.*

spark *n.* 1. a fiery particle, e.g. one thrown off by a burning substance or caused by friction. 2. a flash of light produced by an electrical discharge; such a discharge serving to fire an explosive mixture in an internal-combustion engine. 3. a flash of wit etc. 4. a minute amount of a quality etc. 5. a lively person. —*v.t./i.* 1. to emit a spark or sparks. 2. (also with *off*) to stir into activity, to initiate. [Old English]

Spark /spɑːk/ Muriel 1918– . Scottish novelist. She is a Catholic convert, and her works are enigmatic satires: *The Ballad of Peckham Rye* 1960, *The Prime of Miss Jean Brodie* 1961, *The Only Problem* 1984, and *Symposium* 1990.

spark chamber an electronic device for recording tracks of subatomic ◊particles. In combination with a stack of photographic plates, a spark chamber enables the point where an interaction has taken place to be located to, within a cubic centimetre. At its simplest, it consists of two smooth, threadlike ◊electrodes that are positioned 1–2 cm apart, the space between being filled by gas.

sparkle *v.i.* 1. to shine brightly with flashes of light. 2. to show brilliant wit or liveliness. 3. (of wine) to effervesce. —*n.* sparkling light or brightness.

sparkler *n.* 1. a sparking firework. 2. (in *plural, slang*) diamonds.

spark plug a plug that produces an electric spark in the cylinder of a petrol engine to ignite the fuel mixture. It consists essentially of two electrodes insulated from one another. High-voltage (18,000 V) electricity is fed to a central electrode via the distributor. At the base of the electrode, inside the cylinder, the electricity jumps to another electrode earthed to the engine body, creating a spark. See also ◊ignition coil.

sparrow /'spærəʊ/ *n.* a small, thick-beaked, brownish-grey bird, especially of the genus *Passer*. They are up to 18 cm/7 in long and are found worldwide. [Old English]

sparrowhawk *n.* a woodland bird of prey *Accipiter nisus* found in Eurasia and N Africa. It has a long tail and short wings. The male grows to 28 cm/1.1 ft long, and the female 38 cm/1.5 ft. It hunts small birds.

sparse *adj.* thinly scattered, not dense; infrequent. —**sparsely** *adv.,* **sparseness** *n.,* **sparsity** *n.* [from Latin *sparsus* (*spargere* = scatter)]

Sparta /'spɑːtə/ ancient Greek city-state in the S Peloponnese (near Sparte), developed from Dorian settlements in the 10th century BC. The Spartans, known for their military discipline and austerity, took part in the Persian and Peloponnesian wars.

Spartacist /'spɑːtəsɪst/ *n.* a member of a group of left-wing radicals in Germany at the end of World War I, founders of the **Spartacus League,** which became the German Communist party in 1919. The league participated in the Berlin workers' revolt of Jan 1919, which was suppressed by the Freikorps on the orders of the socialist government. The agitation ended with the murder of Spartacist leaders Karl ◊Liebknecht and Rosa ◊Luxemburg.

Spartacus /'spɑːtəkəs/ died 71 BC. Thracian gladiator who in 73 BC led a revolt of gladiators and slaves at Capua. He was eventually caught by ◊Crassus and crucified.

Spartan /'spɑːtən/ *adj.* 1. of Sparta or its inhabitants. 2. (of conditions) simple and sometimes harsh, without comfort or luxuries (with allusion to the hardy and austere life of Spartans). —*n.* 1. a native of Sparta. 2. an austere person.

spasm /'spæzəm/ *n.* 1. a sudden involuntary muscular contraction. 2. a sudden convulsive movement or emotion etc.; a brief spell of activity. [from Old French or Latin from Greek *spaō* = pull]

spasmodic /spæz'mɒdɪk/ *adj.* of or occurring in spasms, intermittent. —**spasmodically** *adv.* [from Greek *spasmōdēs*]

spastic /'spæstɪk/ *adj.* suffering from ◊cerebral palsy. The term is also applied generally to limbs with impaired movement, stiffness, and resistance to passive movement, and to any body part (such as the colon) affected with spasm. —*n.* a spastic person. —**spastically** *adv.* [from Latin from Greek]

spat[1] *n.* (usually in *plural*) a short gaiter covering the instep and reaching a little above the ankle. Spats were worn by men in the 1920s and 1930s. [abbreviation of *spatterdash*]

spat[2] *n.* the spawn of a shellfish, especially of the oyster. [Anglo-French]

spat[3] *n.* (*US colloquial*) a petty or brief quarrel.

spat[4] past and past participle of ◊spit[1].

spate *n.* 1. a sudden flood. 2. a large or excessive amount. —**in spate,** (of a river) flowing strongly at an abnormally high level. [originally Scottish and north of England]

spathe /speɪð/ *n.* a large bract or bracts enveloping a ◊spadix or a flower cluster. [from Latin from Greek = broad blade]

spatial /'speɪʃəl/ *adj.* of space. —**spatially** *adv.* [from Latin *spatium* = space]

spatter *v.t./i.* to splash or scatter in small drops. —*n.* a splash or splashes; the sound of spattering.

spatula /'spætjʊlə/ *n.* 1. a tool like a knife with a broad blunt flexible blade, used especially by artists and in cookery. 2. a strip of stiff material used by a doctor for pressing down the tongue etc. [Latin]

spavin /'spævɪn/ *n.* a disease of a horse's hock with a hard bony swelling. —**spavined** *adj.* [from Old French *espavin*]

spawn *v.t./i.* 1. (of fish, frogs, molluscs etc.) to deposit spawn; to produce (spawn); to be produced as spawn or young. 2. (*derogatory*) to produce as offspring. 3. to produce or generate in large numbers. —*n.* 1. the eggs of fish, frogs, etc. 2. (*derogatory*) human or other offspring. 3. the white fibrous matter from which fungi grow. [from Anglo-French *espaundre* from Latin *expandere* = spread]

spay *v.t.* to remove the ovaries of (a female animal). [from Anglo-French = cut with sword]

speak *v.t./i.* (*past* **spoke**; *past participle* **spoken**) 1. to utter words in an ordinary voice (not singing). 2. to hold a conversation; to make a speech. 3. to utter or pronounce (words); to use (a specified language) in speaking; to make known in words. 4. to convey an idea, to be evidence of something. —**generally** (*or* **strictly** etc.) **speaking,** in the general (or strict etc.) sense of the words. **not** (*or* **nothing**) **to speak of,** not (or nothing) worth mentioning.

on speaking terms, sufficiently friendly or acquainted to hold a conversation. **speak for,** to act as a spokesperson for; to speak in defence of; to bespeak. **speak for itself,** to be sufficient evidence. **speak out** *or* **up,** to speak loudly or freely; to give one's opinion etc. without hesitation or fear. **speak volumes (for),** to be very significant (in terms of). [Old English]

speakeasy *n.* a bar that illegally sold alcoholic beverages during the ◊Prohibition period (1920–33) in the USA. [probably from the need to speak quickly or quietly to the doorkeeper in order to gain admission]

speaker *n.* **1.** one who speaks, especially in public; a person of a specified skill in speech-making; one who speaks a specified language. **2.** a loudspeaker. **3. Speaker,** the presiding officer of a legislative assembly. In the UK, in the House of Commons the Speaker is elected for each parliament, usually on an agreed basis among the parties, but often holds the office for many years. The original appointment dates from 1377. The equivalent of Speaker in the House of Lords is the Lord Chancellor.

spear *n.* a thrusting or hurling weapon consisting of a stout staff with a pointed tip of metal etc. —*v.t.* to pierce or strike (as) with a spear. [Old English]

spearhead *n.* **1.** the pointed tip of a spear. **2.** a person or group leading an attack or challenge etc. —*v.t.* to act as the spearhead of (an attack etc.).

spearmint *n.* a common garden mint *Mentha spicata* used in cookery and to flavour chewing gum.

spec *n.* (*colloquial*) a speculation. —**on spec,** as a speculation.

special /'speʃəl/ *adj.* **1.** of a particular or peculiar kind, not general; for a particular purpose. **2.** exceptional in amount or degree etc. —*n.* a special constable, edition of a newspaper, dish on a menu etc. —**special correspondent,** one appointed by a newspaper to report on a special event or facts. **special delivery,** a delivery of mail separately from the regular delivery. **special edition,** an edition of a newspaper including later news than the ordinary edition. **special licence,** a licence allowing a marriage to take place within a short time without banns. **special pleading,** in law, pleading with particular reference to the circumstances of a case, as opposed to general pleading; (*popularly*) persuasive but unfair reasoning. —**specially** *adv.* [from Old French (= especial) or Latin *specialis*]

Special Air Service (SAS) a specialist British regiment recruited mainly from Parachute Regiment volunteers. It has served in Malaysia, Oman, Northern Ireland, and against international terrorism, as in the siege of the Iranian embassy in London in 1980.

Special Areas Acts UK acts of Parliament 1936 and 1937, aimed at dealing with high unemployment in some regions of Britain. These areas, designated 'special areas', attracted government assistance in the form of loans and subsidies to generate new employment. Other measures included setting up industrial and trading estates that could be leased at subsidized rates. The acts were an early example of regional aid.

Special Branch a section of the British police originally established in 1883 to deal with Irish Fenian activists. All 42 police forces in Britain now have their own Special Branches. They act as the executive arm of MI5 (British ◊intelligence) in its duty of preventing or investigating espionage, subversion, and sabotage; carry out duties at air and sea ports in respect of naturalization and immigration; and provide armed bodyguards for public figures.

special constable in the UK, a part-time volunteer who supplements local police forces as required. Special constables were established by the Special Constabulary Act 1831. They number some 16,000. They have no extra powers other than normal rights as citizens, although they wear a police-style uniform. They work alongside the police at football matches, demonstrations, and similar events.

special drawing right (SDR) the right of a member state of the ◊International Monetary Fund to apply for money to finance its balance-of-payments deficit. Originally, the SDR was linked to gold and the US dollar. After 1974 SDRs were defined in terms of a 'basket' of the 16 currencies of countries doing 1% or more of the world's trade. In 1981 the SDR was simplified to a weighted average of US dollars, French francs, German marks, Japanese yen, and UK sterling.

special education education, often in separate 'special schools', for children with specific physical or mental problems or disabilities.

specialist *n.* one who specializes in a particular branch of a profession, especially medicine.

speciality /speʃiˈælɪtɪ/ *n.* **1.** a special feature. **2.** a special thing or activity; a special product; a subject in which one specializes.

specialize /'speʃəlaɪz/ *v.t./i.* **1.** to be or become a specialist. **2.** to make or become individual; to adapt for a particular purpose. —**specialization** /-'zeɪʃən/ *n.* [from French]

special relationship the belief that ties of common language, culture, and shared aims should sustain a political relationship between the USA and the UK, and that the same would not apply to relationships between the USA and other European states.

specialty /'speʃəltɪ/ *n.* a speciality. [from Old French]

specie /'spiːʃiː, -ʃɪ/ *n.* coin as opposed to paper money. [Latin, ablative of *species*]

species /'spiːʃiːz, -ʃɪz/ *n.* (*plural* the same) **1.** a class of things having some common characteristics. **2.** in biology, a distinguishable group of organisms that resemble each other or consist of a few distinctive types (as in ◊polymorphism), and that can all interbreed to produce fertile offspring. Species are the lowest level in the system of biological classification. A **native** species is a species that has existed in the same country at least from prehistoric times; a **naturalized** species is one known to have been introduced by humans from its mother country, but which now maintains itself; while an **exotic** species is one that requires human intervention to survive. **3.** a kind or sort. [Latin, originally = appearance (*specere* = look)]

specific /spɪˈsɪfɪk/ *adj.* **1.** particular, clearly distinguished from others. **2.** exact, giving full details. **3.** peculiar, relating to a particular thing; (of a medicine etc.) having a distinct effect in curing a certain disease. —*n.* a specific detail or aspect; a specific medicine. —**specifically** *adv.*, **specificity** /-'fɪsɪtɪ/ *n.* [from Latin *specere* = look and *facere* = make]

specification /spesɪfɪ'keɪʃən/ *n.* (usually in *plural*) a detail of the design and materials etc. (to be) used in a machine or project etc. [from Latin]

specific gravity an alternative term for ◊relative density.

specific heat capacity in physics, the quantity of heat required to raise unit mass (1 kg) of a substance by one ◊kelvin (1°C). The unit of specific heat capacity in the SI system is the ◊joule per kilogram kelvin (J kg⁻¹ K⁻¹).

specify /'spesɪfaɪ/ *v.t.* to name expressly, to mention definitely; to include in specifications. [from Old French or Latin]

specimen /'spesɪmɪn/ *n.* an individual or part taken as an example of a class or whole, especially when used for investigation; (*colloquial*, usually *derogatory*) a person of a specified sort. [Latin]

specious /'spiːʃəs/ *adj.* apparently good or sound but not really so; superficially plausible. —**speciously** *adv.* [from Latin *speciosus* = attractive]

speck *n.* a small spot or stain; a particle. —*v.t.* (especially in *past participle*) to mark with specks. [Old English]

speckle *n.* a speck, especially one of many markings on the skin etc. —*v.t.* (especially in *past participle*) to mark with speckles. [from Middle Dutch]

specs *n.pl.* (*colloquial*) spectacles.

spectacle /'spektəkəl/ *n.* **1.** an object of sight, especially of public attention; a striking, impressive, or ridiculous sight. **2.** a public show. **3.** (in *plural*) a pair of lenses to correct or assist defective sight, set in a frame to rest on the nose and ears. —**spectacled** *adj.* [from Old French from Latin *spectaculum* (*spectare* = look)]

spectacular /spek'tækjʊlə/ *adj.* striking, impressive, amazing. —*n.* a spectacular performance; a lavishly produced film etc. —**spectacularly** *adv.*

spectator /spek'teɪtə/ *n.* one who watches a show, game, or incident etc. —**spectator sport,** a sport which attracts many spectators. [from French or Latin]

Spector /'spektə/ Phil 1940– . US record producer, known for the 'wall of sound', created using a large orchestra, which distinguished his work in the early 1960s with vocal groups such as the Crystals and the Ronettes. He withdrew into semi-retirement in 1966.

spectra plural of **spectrum**.

spectral /'spektrəl/ adj. 1. of a spectre or spectres; ghostlike. 2. of the spectrum or spectra. —**spectrally** adv.

spectre /'spektə/ n. 1. a ghost. 2. a haunting presentiment. [French or from Latin spectrum = image]

spectrograph /'spektrəgrɑːf/ n. an apparatus for photographing or otherwise reproducing spectra. —**spectrographic** /-'græfɪk/ adj. (see ◊spectrum)

spectrometer /spek'trɒmɪtə/ n. a spectroscope that can be used for measuring observed spectra (see ◊spectrum). [from German or French]

spectroscope /'spektrəskəʊp/ n. an instrument for producing and examining spectra (see ◊spectrum). —**spectroscopic** /-'skɒpɪk/ adj., **spectroscopically** /-'skɒpɪkəlɪ/ adv. [from German or French]

spectroscopy /spek'trɒskəpɪ/ n. the study of spectra (see ◊spectrum) associated with atoms or molecules in solid, liquid, or gaseous phase. Spectroscopy can be used to identify unknown compounds and is an invaluable tool to scientists, industry (for example, pharmaceuticals for purity checks), and medical workers.

spectrum /'spektrəm/ n. (plural **spectra**) 1. the range of colours as seen in a rainbow or when white light is passed through a prism or a diffraction grating. 2. in physics, a range of frequencies or wavelengths when electromagnetic radiations are separated into their constituent parts. 3. such a range characteristic of a body or substance when emitting or absorbing radiation. An incandescent body gives rise to a **continuous spectrum** where the dispersed radiation is distributed uninterruptedly over a range of wavelengths. An element gives a **line spectrum** – one or more bright discrete lines at characteristic wavelengths. Molecular gases give **band spectra** in which there are groups of close-packed lines shaded in one direction of wavelength. In an **absorption spectrum** dark lines or spaces replace the characteristic bright lines of the absorbing medium. The **mass spectrum** of an element is obtained from a mass spectrometer and shows the relative proportions of its constituent ◊isotopes. 4. a similar range of component parts of anything, arranged by degree, quality etc. [Latin, = image, apparition (specere = look)]

speculate /'spekjʊleɪt/ v.i. 1. to form or put forward opinions by conjecture, without definite knowledge. 2. to engage in risky financial transactions. —**speculation** /-'leɪʃən/ n., **speculator** n. [from Latin speculari = spy out]

speculative /'spekjʊlətɪv/ adj. involving speculation. —**speculative action**, a law case taken on a 'no win, no fee' basis, legal in the USA and Scotland, but not in England. —**speculatively** adv., **speculativeness** n.

sped past and past participle of **speed**.

speech n. 1. the act, faculty, or manner of speaking. 2. words spoken; a spoken communication to an audience. 3. the language of a nation or group etc. —**speech day**, an annual celebration at school when speeches are made. **speech therapy**, treatment to improve defective speech. [Old English]

speechify /'spiːtʃɪfaɪ/ v.i. (colloquial) to make a speech or speeches.

speechless adj. silent, temporarily unable to speak through emotion or surprise etc. —**speechlessly** adv., **speechlessness** n.

speech recognition in computing, techniques whereby a computer can understand ordinary speech. Spoken words are divided into 'frames', each lasting about one-30th of a second, which are converted to a wave form. These are then compared with a series of stored frames to determine the most likely word. Research into speech recognition started in 1938, but the technology became sufficiently developed for commercial applications only in the late 1980s.

speech synthesis a computer-based technology for the generation of speech. A speech synthesizer is controlled by a computer, which supplies strings of codes representing basic speech sounds (phonemes) and these together make up words. Speech-synthesis applications include children's toys, car and aircraft warning systems, and talking books for the blind.

speed n. 1. rapidity of movement or operation; quick motion. 2. the rate at which something moves. Speed in

kilometres per hour is calculated by dividing the distance travelled in kilometres by the time taken in hours. Speed is a ◊scalar quantity, as the direction of motion is not involved. This makes it different from velocity, which is a ◊vector quantity. 3. the gear appropriate to a range of speeds on a bicycle etc. 4. the relative sensitivity of a photographic film to light; the lightgathering power of a lens. 5. (slang) ◊amphetamine, a stimulant drug. 6. (archaic) success, prosperity. —v.t./i. (past and past participle **sped**) 1. to go or send quickly. 2. (of a motorist etc.; past and past participle **speeded**) to travel at an illegal or dangerous speed. 3. (archaic) to be or make prosperous or successful. —**at full speed**, as fast as one can go or work. **at speed**, moving quickly. **speed limit**, the maximum permitted speed of a vehicle on a road etc. **speed up**, to move or work faster; to cause to do this. **speed-up** n. [Old English]

speedboat n. a motor boat designed for high speed.

speedo /'spiːdəʊ/ n. (plural **speedos**) (colloquial) a speedometer.

speed of light the speed at which light and other ◊electromagnetic waves travel through empty space. Its value is 299,792,458 metres per second/186,281 miles per second. The speed of light is the highest speed possible, according to the theory of ◊relativity, and its value is independent of the motion of its source and of the observer. It is impossible to accelerate any material body to this speed because it would require an infinite amount of energy.

speed of sound the speed at which sound travels through a medium, such as air or water. In air at a temperature of 0°C (32°F), the speed of sound is 331 m/1,087 ft per second. At higher temperatures, the speed of sound is greater; at 18°C (64°F) it is 342 m/1,123 ft per second. It is greater in liquids and solids; for example, in water it is around 1,440 m/4,724 ft per second, depending on the temperature.

speedometer /spiː'dɒmɪtə/ n. a device indicating the speed of a vehicle, attached to the transmission of the vehicle by a flexible drive shaft.

speedway n. 1. motorcycle racing on a dirt track; an arena for this. Four riders compete in each heat over four laps. A series of heats make up a match or competition. In Britain there are two leagues, the British League and the National League. World championships exist for individuals, pairs (first held in 1970), four-rider teams (first held in 1960), long-track racing, and ice speedway. 2. (US) a road or track for fast traffic.

speedwell n. any flowering plant of the genus Veronica of the snapdragon family Scrophulariaceae. Of the many wild species, most are low-growing with small, bluish flowers.

speedy adj. 1. moving quickly, rapid. 2. done or coming etc. without delay. —**speedily** adv., **speediness** n.

speleology /speli'ɒlədʒɪ, spiː-/ n. the scientific study of caves, their origin, development, physical structure, flora, fauna, folklore, exploration, mapping, photography, cave diving, and rescue work. —**speleological** /-'lɒdʒɪkəl/ adj., **speleologist** n. [from French from Latin from Greek spēlaion = cave]

spell¹ n. 1. words supposed to have magic power; the effect of these. 2. the fascination exercised by a person or activity etc. [Old English]

spell² v.t./i. (past and past participle **spelt** or **spelled**) 1. to write or name in their correct sequence the letters of (a word). 2. (of letters) to make up (a word). 3. (of circumstances etc.) to have as a consequence, to involve. —**spell out**, to make out (words etc.) laboriously or slowly; to spell aloud; to explain in detail. —**speller** n. [from Old French espel(l)er]

spell³ n. a period of time or work; a period of some activity; a period of a certain type of weather. —v.t. to relieve (a person) in work etc. by taking one's turn.

spellbound adj. held as if by a spell, fascinated.

spelling n. 1. the way a word is spelled. 2. ability to spell.

spelt¹ n. a kind of wheat Triticum spelta giving very fine flour. [Old English]

spelt² past and past participle of ◊spell².

Spence /spens/ Basil 1907–1976. Scottish architect. He was professor of architecture at the Royal Academy, London, 1961–68, and his works include Coventry Cathedral, Sussex University, and the British embassy in Rome.

Spencer /'spensə/ Stanley 1891–1959. English painter, who was born and lived in Cookham-on-Thames, Berkshire, and recreated the Christian story in a Cookham setting. His detailed, dreamlike compositions had little regard for perspective and used generalized human figures.

spend *v.t./i.* (*past* and *past participle* **spent**) **1.** to pay out (money) in buying something. **2.** to use up, to consume (material or energy etc.). **3.** to pass or occupy (time etc.). **4.** (in *past participle*) having lost its original force or strength. —**spend a penny,** (*colloquial*) to urinate or defecate. —**spender** *n.* [Old English from Latin]

Spender /'spendə/ Stephen (Harold) 1909– . English poet and critic. His earlier poetry has a left-wing political content, as in *Twenty Poems* 1930 and *Poems of Dedication* 1946. Other works include the autobiography *World within World* 1951 and translations. He cofounded the magazine *Horizon* and was coeditor of *Encounter* 1953–67.

> My parents kept me from children who were rough
> Who threw words like stones and who wore torn
> clothes.
>
> **Stephen Spender**
> *Collected Poems*

spendthrift *n.* an extravagant person.

Spenser /'spensə/ Edmund *c.*1552–1599. English poet who has been called the 'poet's poet' because of his rich imagery and command of versification. He is known for his moral allegory *The Faerie Queene*, of which six books survive (three published 1590 and three 1596). Other books include *The Shepheard's Calendar* 1579, *Astrophel* 1586, the love sonnets *Amoretti*, and the *Epithalamion* 1595.

> What more felicity can fall to creature,
> Than to enjoy delight with liberty.
>
> **Edmund Spenser**
> *Complaints*

sperm *n.* (*plural* **sperms** or **sperm**) semen; a spermatozoon, the male ◊gamete of animals. Each sperm cell has a head capsule containing a nucleus, a middle portion containing ◊mitochondria (which provide energy), and a long tail (flagellum). —**sperm whale,** a large ◊whale *Physeter catodon* yielding spermaceti. —**spermatic** /-'mætɪk/ *adj.* [from Latin from Greek *sperma* = seed]

spermaceti /spɜːmə'setɪ/ *n.* a white, waxy substance formerly used for ointments etc. [from Latin *sperma* = sperm and *ceti* = of whale, it being regarded as whale spawn]

spermatophore *n.* a small, nutrient-rich packet of ◊sperm produced in invertebrates, newts, and cephalopods.

spermatophyte *n.* in botany, another name for a ◊seed plant.

spermatozoon /spɜːmətə'zəuən/ *n.* (*plural* **spermatozoa**) a ◊sperm cell. [from Greek *zōion* = living creature]

spermicide /'spɜːmɪsaɪd/ *n.* any cream, jelly, pessary, or other preparation that kills the sperm cells in semen. Spermicides are used for contraceptive purposes, usually in combination with a ◊condom or ◊diaphragm. Sponges impregnated with spermicide have been developed but are not yet in widespread use. Spermicide used alone is only 75% effective in preventing pregnancy. —**spermicidal** *adj.*

Sperry /'sperɪ/ Elmer Ambrose 1860–1930. US engineer who developed various devices using ◊gyroscopes, such as gyrostabilizers (for ships and torpedoes) and gyro-controlled autopilots.

spew *v.t./i.* **1.** to vomit. **2.** to gush out; to cause to do this. [Old English (imitative)]

SPF abbreviation of South Pacific Forum.

sphagnum /'sfægnəm/ *n.* (*plural* **sphagna**) a ◊moss of the genus *Sphagnum* growing in bogs and peat. [from Greek *sphagnos* = a moss]

sphalerite *n.* the chief ore of zinc, composed of zinc sulphide with a small proportion of iron, formula (Zn,Fe)S. It is brown with a nonmetallic lustre unless an appreciable amount of iron is present (up to 26% by weight). Sphalerite

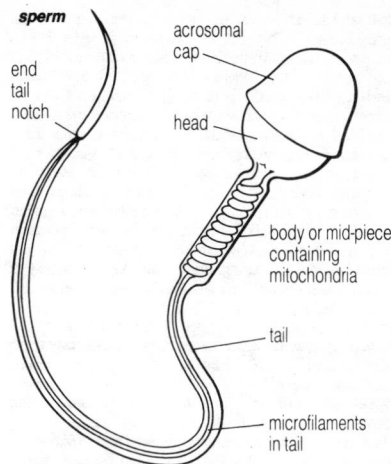

sperm

end
tail
notch

acrosomal
cap

head

body or mid-piece
containing
mitochondria

tail

microfilaments
in tail

usually occurs in ore veins in limestones, where it is often associated with galena. It crystallizes in the cubic system but does not normally form perfect cubes.

sphenoid /'sfiːnɔɪd/ *adj.* wedge-shaped. —**sphenoid bone,** in the skeleton of vertebrates, a compound bone between the temporal bone and the eye. [from Greek *sphēn* = wedge]

sphere /sfɪə/ *n.* **1.** in mathematics, a circular solid figure with all points on its surface the same distance from the centre; the surface of this. For a sphere of radius r, the volume $V = \frac{4}{3}\pi r^3$ and the surface area $A = 4\pi r^2$. **2.** a globe, a ball. **3.** a field of action, influence, or existence; one's place in society. **4.** each of the revolving shells in which the heavenly bodies were formerly thought to be set. [from Old French from Latin from Greek *sphaira* = ball]

spherical /'sferɪkəl/ *adj.* **1.** shaped like a sphere. **2.** of spheres. **3.** (of a triangle etc.) bounded by the arcs of the great circles of a sphere. —**spherically** *adv.*, **sphericity** /-'rɪsɪtɪ/ *n.* [from Latin from Greek]

spheroid /'sfɪərɔɪd/ *n.* a spherelike but not perfectly spherical body. —**spheroidal** /-'rɔɪdəl/ *adj.* [from Latin from Greek]

sphincter /'sfɪŋktə/ *n.* a ring of muscle closing and opening an orifice. Found at various points in the alimentary canal, sphincters contract and relax to control the movement of food. [Latin from Greek *sphiggō* = bind tight]

sphinx /sfɪŋks/ *n.* or **Sphinx 1.** a mythological creature, represented in Egyptian, Assyrian, and Greek art as a lion with a human head. The Sphinx in Greek mythology was female, and killed travellers who failed to answer a riddle; she killed herself when ◊Oedipus gave the right answer. **2.** an enigmatic or inscrutable person. [Latin from Greek]

sphygmomanometer *n.* an instrument for measuring blood pressure. Consisting of an inflatable arm cuff joined by a rubber tube to a pressure-recording device (often a column-of-mercury scale), it is used, together with a stethoscope, to measure arterial blood pressure.

spice *n.* **1.** an aromatic or pungent vegetable substance used to flavour food; spices collectively. Spices are mostly obtained from tropical plants, and include pepper, nutmeg, ginger, and cinnamon. **2.** an interesting or piquant quality. **3.** a trace. —*v.t.* **1.** to flavour with spice. **2.** to enhance (with wit etc.). [from Old French *espice* from Latin]

spick and span /spɪk ənd 'spæn/ clean and tidy; new-looking. [from earlier *spick and span new,* extension of obsolete *span new* (Old Norse)]

spicule, solar in astronomy, a short-lived jet of hot gas in the upper ◊chromosphere of the Sun. Spicules are spiky in appearance and move at high velocities along lines of magnetic force to which they owe their shapes. They are usually seen to form at about 45° to the vertical, and appear to disperse material into the ◊corona.

spicy /'spaɪsɪ/ *adj.* **1.** of or flavoured with spice. **2.** piquant; slightly scandalous or improper. —**spicily** *adv.*, **spiciness** *n.*

spider /'spaɪdə/ n. **1.** an eight-legged arthropod of the order Araneida, many species of which spin webs. Unlike insects, spiders have the head and breast merged to form the cephalothorax, connected to the abdomen by a characteristic narrow waist. There are up to eight eyes. On the undersurface of the abdomen of many species are spinnerets which exude a viscid fluid. This hardens on exposure to the air to form silky threads, used to spin webs in which the spider nests and catches its prey. Its fangs inject substances to subdue and digest prey, the juices of which are then sucked in by the spider. **2.** a thing resembling a spider. —**spider crab**, a crab of the superfamily Oxyrhyncha, with long thin legs. **spiderman** n. a person working at a great height on a building. **spider monkey**, a monkey of the genus *Ateles* with long limbs and a long prehensile tail. [Old English]

spidery adj. of or like a spider; very thin or long.

spiel /spi:l/ n. (*slang*) a speech or story, especially a glib or long one. —v.t./i. (*slang*) to speak lengthily or glibly. [German = game]

Spielberg /'spi:lbɜ:g/ Steven 1947– . US film director, writer, and producer. His highly successful films, including *Jaws* 1975, *Close Encounters of the Third Kind* 1977, *Raiders of the Lost Ark* 1981, and *ET* 1982 have gained him popular rather than critical acclaim. He also directed *Indiana Jones and the Temple of Doom* 1984, *The Color Purple* 1985, *Empire of the Sun* 1987, and *Indiana Jones and the Last Crusade* 1989.

spigot /'spɪgət/ n. a small peg or plug; a device for controlling the flow of liquor from a cask etc.

spike[1] n. **1.** a sharp, projecting point; a pointed piece of metal, e.g. one of a set forming the top of an iron fence or worn on the bottom of a running shoe to prevent slipping. **2.** (in *plural*) running shoes fitted with spikes. **3.** a large nail. **4.** a pointed metal rod standing upright on a base and used e.g. to hold unused matter in a newspaper office. —v.t. **1.** to put spikes on or into; to fix on a spike. **2.** (*colloquial*) to add alcohol to (a drink). **3.** (*historical*) to plug the vent of (a gun) with a spike. —**spike a person's guns**, to spoil his or her plans.

spike[2] n. a cluster of sessile flowers arranged closely on a long common axis; a separate sprig of any plant in which flowers form a spikelike cluster; an ear of corn. [from Latin *spica* = ear of corn]

spikelet n. in botany, one of the units of a grass ◊inflorescence; a small spike.

spikenard /'spaɪknɑ:d/ n. **1.** a tall, sweet-smelling plant *Nardostachys jatamansi*. **2.** an aromatic ointment formerly made from this. [from Latin]

spiky adj. **1.** like a spike; having a spike or spikes. **2.** (*colloquial*) dogmatic; bad-tempered. —**spikily** adv., **spikiness** n.

spill[1] v.t./i. (*past* and *past participle* **spilt** or **spilled**) **1.** to cause or allow (a liquid or powder etc.) to run over the edge of its container. **2.** to become spilt. **3.** to shed (others' blood). **4.** to throw accidentally from a saddle or vehicle. **5.** (*slang*) to disclose (information etc.). —n. **1.** spilling, being spilt. **2.** being thrown from a saddle etc.; a tumble, a fall. —**spill the beans**, see ◊bean. [Old English = kill]

spill[2] n. a thin strip of wood or paper used for transferring flame, e.g. for lighting a fire or pipe. [related to *spile* = wooden peg, from Middle Dutch or Middle Low German]

spillage n. **1.** the action of spilling. **2.** the amount spilt.

spillikin /'spɪlɪkɪn/ n. a splinter of wood etc.; (in *plural*) a game in which a heap of these is removed by taking one at a time without disturbing the others.

spillway n. a passage for surplus water from a dam.

spin v.t./i. (-**nn-**; *past* and *past participle* **spun**) **1.** to turn or cause to turn rapidly on its own axis. **2.** to draw out and twist (raw cotton or wool etc.) into threads; to make (yarn) thus. Synthetic fibres are extruded as a liquid through the holes of a spinneret. **3.** (of a spider or silkworm) to make (a web or cocoon) by emitting a viscous thread. **4.** (of a person's head etc.) to be in a whirl through dizziness or astonishment; to toss (a coin). **5.** to spin-dry. **6.** to tell or compose (a story etc.). —n. **1.** a spinning movement. **2.** a short drive in a motor vehicle. **3.** a rotating dive of an aircraft. **4.** in physics, the intrinsic angular momentum of an elementary particle. —**spin bowler**, in cricket, a bowler who imparts spin to a ball. **spin-drier** or **spin-dryer** n. a machine for drying clothes by spinning them in a rotating

Spielberg *US film director Steven Spielberg.*

drum so that moisture is squeezed out by centrifugal force. **spin-dry** v.t. to dry thus. **spin-off** n. an incidental or secondary result or benefit, especially in technology. **spin out**, to prolong (a speech or discussion etc.). **spun silk**, a cheap material of short-fibred and waste silk, often mixed with cotton. [Old English]

spina bifida /'spaɪnə 'bɪfɪdə/ a congenital defect of the spine in which part of the spinal cord and its membranes are exposed, due to incomplete development of the spine. [Latin = cleft spine]

spinach /'spɪnɪdʒ/ n. an annual plant *Spinacia oleracea* of the goosefoot family Chenopodiaceae. It is native to Asia and widely cultivated for its leaves, which are eaten as a vegetable.

spinal /'spaɪnəl/ adj. of the spine. —**spinal column,** the spine. **spinal cord,** the cylindrical nervous structure within the spine. [from Latin]

spindle n. **1.** a slender rod or bar, often with tapered ends, to twist and wind thread. **2.** a pin or axis that revolves or on which a thing revolves. —**spindle-shanks** n. a person with long, thin legs. **spindle tree,** a tree of the genus *Euonymus*, especially *E. europaeus*, with a hard wood formerly used for spindles. [Old English]

spindly adj. long or tall or thin.

spindrift /'spɪndrɪft/ n. spray blown along the surface of the sea. [Scottish variant of *spoondrift* (*spoon* = run before the wind)]

spine n. **1.** the backbone of vertebrates. In most mammals, it contains 26 small bones called vertebrae, which enclose and protect the spinal cord (which links the peripheral nervous system to the brain). The spine connects with the skull, ribs, back muscles, and pelvis. **2.** a sharp, needlelike outgrowth of an animal or plant. **3.** the part of a book's cover or jacket that encloses its page fastening. **4.** a sharp ridge or projection. —**spine-chiller** n. a spine-chilling book or film etc. **spine-chilling** adj. frighteningly thrilling or exciting. [from Old French *espine* or Latin *spina* = thorn]

spineless adj. **1.** lacking a backbone. **2.** lacking resoluteness or strength of character, feeble. —**spinelessness** n.

spinet /spɪ'net/ n. a keyboard instrument, similar to a ◊harpsichord but smaller, which has only one string for each note. [from French from Italian *spinetta*]

spinnaker /'spɪnəkə/ n. a large triangular sail carried opposite the mainsail of a racing yacht running before the wind. [from *Sphinx*, name of first yacht to use it]

spinner n. **1.** a person or thing that spins, especially a manufacturer engaged in cotton spinning. **2.** a spin bowler. **3.** in fishing, a revolving bait as a lure.

spinneret /'spɪnəret/ n. **1.** the spinning organ of a spider etc. **2.** a device for forming synthetic fibre.

spinney /'spɪnɪ/ n. a small wood, a thicket. [from Old French from Latin *spinetum*]

spinning machine a machine for drawing out fibres and twisting them into a long thread, or yarn. Spinning was originally done by hand, then with the **spinning wheel**, and in about 1767 in England James ◊Hargreaves built the **spinning jenny**, a machine that could spin 8, then 16, bobbins at once. Later, Samuel ◊Crompton's **spinning mule** of 1779 had a moving carriage carrying the spindles and is still in use today.

spinning top = ◊top[2].

spinning wheel a household device for spinning yarn or thread, with a spindle driven by a wheel operated originally by hand, later by a crank or treadle.

Spinoza /spɪˈnəʊzə/ Benedict or Baruch 1632–1677. Dutch philosopher who believed in a rationalistic pantheism that owed much to Descartes' mathematical appreciation of the universe. Mind and matter are two modes of an infinite substance that he called God or Nature, good and evil being relative. He was a determinist, believing that human action was motivated by self-preservation.

spinster *n.* an unmarried woman; an (elderly) woman thought unlikely to marry. [originally = woman who spins]

spiny /ˈspaɪnɪ/ *adj.* having (many) spines. —**spininess** *n.*

spiny anteater an alternative name for the ◊echidna.

spiracle /ˈspaɪərəkəl/ *n.* 1. in insects, the opening of a ◊trachea, through which oxygen enters the body and carbon dioxide is expelled. 2. in cartilaginous fishes (sharks and rays), a circular opening that marks the remains of the first gill slit. [from Latin *spirare* = breathe]

spiraea /spaɪˈriːə/ *n.* any herbaceous plant or shrub of the genus *Spiraea*, family Rosaceae, which includes many cultivated species with ornamental panicles of flowers. [Latin from Greek *speira* = coil]

spiral /ˈspaɪərəl/ *adj.* coiled in a plane or as round a cylinder or cone; having this shape. —*n.* 1. a spiral curve; a thing of spiral form. Various kinds of spirals can be generated mathematically, for example, an equiangular or logarithmic spiral (in which a tangent at any point on the curve always makes the same angle with it) and an ◊involute. It also occurs in nature as a normal consequence of accelerating growth, such as the spiral shape of the shells of snails and some other molluscs. 2. a continuous increase or decrease in two or more quantities alternately or in succession, because of their dependence on each other. —*v.i.* (**-ll-**) to move in a spiral course. —**spiral staircase**, a staircase rising round a central axis. —**spirally** *adv.* [French or from Latin *spira* = coil from Greek]

spirant /ˈspaɪərənt/ *adj.* uttered with a continuous expulsion of the breath. —*n.* a spirant consonant. [from Latin *spirare* = breathe]

spire *n.* a tapering structure like a tall cone or pyramid rising above a tower; any tapering body. [Old English]

spirit /ˈspɪrɪt/ *n.* 1. a person's animating principle or intelligence. 2. a person's soul. 3. a person from an intellectual or moral viewpoint. 4. a disembodied person or incorporeal being. 5. a person's mental or moral nature. 6. an attitude or mood. 7. courage, self-assertion, vivacity. 8. (in *plural*) a state of mind. 9. a tendency prevailing at a particular time etc. 10. a principle or purpose underlying the form of a law etc. 11. a volatile liquid produced by distillation; purified alcohol; (usually in *plural*) a strong distilled ◊alcoholic liquor. —*v.t.* to convey rapidly or mysteriously. —**in spirit**, inwardly. **spirit gum**, a quick-drying gum for attaching false hair. **spirit lamp**, a lamp burning methylated or other volatile spirit instead of oil. **spirit level**, a device consisting of a sealed glass tube nearly filled with liquid and containing an air bubble, used to test levelness by the position of this bubble. [from Anglo-French from Latin *spiritus* = breath]

spirited *adj.* 1. full of spirit, lively, courageous. 2. having a specified spirit or disposition (e.g. *poor-spirited*). —**spiritedly** *adv.*

spiritless *adj.* lacking vigour or courage.

spiritual /ˈspɪrɪtjuəl/ *adj.* of or concerned with the spirit, not physical or worldly; of the church or religion. —*n.* a religious song, especially of American blacks, predecessor of ◊gospel music. —**spirituality** /-ˈælɪtɪ/ *n.*, **spiritually** *adv.* [from Old French from Latin]

spiritualism /ˈspɪrɪtjuəlɪzəm/ *n.* the belief that the spirits of the dead communicate with the living, especially through mediums. —**spiritualist** *n.*, **spiritualistic** /-ˈlɪstɪk/ *adj.*

spirituous /ˈspɪrɪtjuəs/ *adj.* alcoholic, distilled and not only fermented.

spit[1] *v.t./i.* (**-tt-**; *past* and *past participle* **spat** or **spit**) 1. to eject from the mouth; to eject saliva from the mouth; to do this as a gesture of contempt. 2. to utter (oaths or threats etc.) vehemently. 3. to make a noise as of spitting. 4. (of a fire or gun etc.) to throw out with an explosion. 5. (of rain) to fall lightly. —*n.* 1. spittle. 2. spitting. —**the (dead or very) spit**, a spitting image. **spit and polish**, a soldier's cleaning and polishing work. **spit it out**, (*colloquial*) to speak candidly or louder. **spitting image**, an exact counterpart or likeness. [Old English, originally imitative]

spit[2] *n.* 1. a rod on which meat is fixed for roasting over a fire etc. 2. a long narrow strip of land projecting into the sea; a ◊sandbar deposited by a current carrying material from one direction to another across the mouth of an inlet. —*v.t.* (**-tt-**) to pierce (as) with a spit. [Old English]

spit[3] *n.* a spade's depth of earth. [from Old English *spittan* = dig with spade]

spite *n.* malicious desire to hurt, annoy, or frustrate another person. —*v.t.* to hurt or annoy etc. through spite. —**in spite of**, not being prevented by, regardless of. [from Old French from Latin *despectus* = looked down on]

spiteful *adj.* full of spite; showing or caused by spite. —**spitefully** *adv.*, **spitefulness** *n.*

spitfire *n.* a person of fiery temper.

Spitsbergen /ˈspɪtsbɜːgən/ the main island in the Norwegian archipelago of ◊Svalbard.

spittle /ˈspɪtəl/ *n.* 1. saliva, especially as ejected from the mouth. 2. an alternative name for ◊cuckoo spit.

spittlebug an alternative name for ◊froghopper.

spittoon /spɪˈtuːn/ *n.* a vessel for spitting into.

Spitz /spɪts/ Mark Andrew 1950– . US swimmer. He won a record seven gold medals at the 1972 Olympic Games, all in world record times, and retired the same year.

spiv *n.* a man, especially a flashily dressed one, living from shady dealings rather than regular work. —**spivish** *adj.*

splash *v.t./i.* 1. to cause (liquid) to fly about in drops; to wet with such drops; (of liquid) to be splashed. 2. to move or fall with splashing. 3. to decorate with scattered patches of colour etc. 4. to display (news) prominently. 5. to spend (money) freely and ostentatiously. —*n.* 1. the act or sound of splashing. 2. a quantity of liquid splashed; a mark etc. made by splashing. 3. a patch of colour or light. 4. a striking or ostentatious display. 5. (*colloquial*) a small quantity of soda water etc. (in a drink). —**make a splash**, to attract much attention. **splashdown** *n.* the alighting of a spacecraft on the sea. **splash out**, (*colloquial*) to spend money freely. —**splashy** *adj.* [alteration from *plash*]

splashback *n.* a panel behind a sink etc. to protect a wall from splashes.

splatter *v.t./i.* to splash noisily; to spatter. —*n.* a noisy splashing sound. [imitative]

splay *v.t./i.* to spread apart; (of an opening) to have the sides diverging; to make (an opening) have divergent sides. —*n.* a surface at an oblique angle to another. —*adj.* splayed. [from *display*]

spleen *n.* 1. an organ in vertebrates, part of the lymphatic system, which helps to process ◊lymphocytes. It also regulates the number of red blood cells in circulation by destroying old cells, and stores iron. It is situated behind the stomach. 2. moroseness, irritability. [from Old French *esplen* from Latin from Greek *splēn*]

spleenwort /ˈspliːnwɔːt/ *n.* a fern of the genus *Asplenium*, formerly used as a remedy for disorders of the spleen.

splendid /ˈsplendɪd/ *adj.* 1. magnificent, displaying splendour. 2. (*colloquial*) excellent. —**splendidly** *adv.* [from French or Latin *splendēre* = shine]

splendiferous /splenˈdɪfərəs/ *adj.* (*colloquial*) splendid. [from Latin *ferre* = bear]

splendour /ˈsplendə/ *n.* brilliance, magnificent display or appearance; grandeur. [from Anglo-French or Latin]

splenetic /splɪˈnetɪk/ *adj.* bad-tempered, peevish. —**splenetically** *adv.* [from Latin]

splenic /ˈspliːnɪk, ˈsple-/ *adj.* of or in the spleen. [from French or Latin from Greek]

splice *v.t.* 1. to join pieces of (ropes) by interweaving strands. 2. to join (pieces of wood or tape etc.) in an overlapping position. 3. (*colloquial*, especially in *passive*) to join in marriage. —*n.* a junction made by splicing. —**splice the mainbrace**, (*nautical*) to serve a free drink of spirits.

splint *n.* 1. a strip of wood etc. bound to a limb, especially to keep a broken bone in the right position while it heals. 2. a tumour or bony excrescence on the inside of a horse's leg. 3. or **splint bone** either of two small bones in a horse's foreleg lying behind and close to the cannon bone; the human fibula. —*v.t.* to secure with a splint. [from Middle Dutch or Middle Low German = metal plate or pin]

splinter *n.* a small, sharp piece broken off wood or glass etc. —*v.t./i.* to break or become broken into splinters. —**splinter group**, a small (especially political) group that has broken away from a larger one. —**splintery** *adj.* [from Middle Dutch]

split /splɪt/ *v.t./i.* (**-tt-**; *past* and *past participle* **split**) 1. to break or become broken into parts, especially lengthwise or with the grain or the plane of cleavage. 2. to divide into parts; to divide and share. 3. to remove or be removed by breaking or dividing. 4. to divide or become divided into disagreeing or hostile parties. 5. to cause fission of (an atom). 6. (*slang*) to betray secrets, to inform (on a person). —*n.* 1. an act or the result of splitting. 2. a disagreement or schism. 3. a dish made of bananas etc. split open, with ice cream etc. 4. (in *plural*) the feat of sitting down or leaping with the legs widely spread out at right angles to the body. 5. a half bottle of mineral water; a half glass of liquor. —**be splitting**, (of the head) to feel acute pain from a headache. **split hairs**, see ◊hair. **split infinitive**, one with an adverb etc. inserted between *to* and the verb. **split-level** *adj.* built or having components at more than one level. **split pea**, a pea dried and split for cooking. **split personality**, a change of personality as in schizophrenia. **split pin**, a pin or bolt etc. held in place by the splaying of its split end. **split second**, a very brief moment. **split one's sides**, to laugh heartily. **splitting headache**, a very severe headache. **split up**, to separate; (of a couple etc.) to cease living together. [originally nautical, from Middle Dutch]

Split (Italian *Spalato*) port in Yugoslavia, on the Adriatic; population (1981) 236,000. Industries include engineering, cement, and textiles, and it is also a tourist resort.

splodge variant of **splotch**.

splosh *v.t./i.* (*colloquial*) to splash. —*n.* (*colloquial*) a splash. [imitative]

splotch *n.* a daub, blot, or smear. —*v.t.* to daub, to blot, to smear.

splurge *n.* an ostentatious display or effort. —*v.i.* to make a splurge.

splutter *v.t./i.* 1. to make a rapid series of spitting sounds. 2. to speak or utter rapidly or incoherently. —*n.* a spluttering sound. [from *sputter* by association with *splash*]

Spock /spɒk/ Benjamin McLane 1903– . US paediatrician and writer on child care. His *Common Sense Book of Baby and Child Care* 1946 urged less rigidity in bringing up children than had been advised by previous generations of writers on the subject, but this was misunderstood as advocating permissiveness. He was also active in the peace movement, especially during the Vietnam War.

Spode /spəʊd/ Josiah 1754–1827. English potter. He developed bone porcelain (made from bone ash, china stone, and china clay) around 1800, which was produced at all English factories in the 19th century. Spode became potter to King George III in 1806.

spoil *v.t./i.* (*past* and *past participle* **spoilt** or **spoiled**) 1. to make or become useless or unsatisfactory. 2. to diminish a person's enjoyment of. 3. to harm the character of (a person) by indulgence. 4. (of food etc.) to go bad. —*n.* (in *singular* or *plural*) 1. plunder, stolen goods, especially those taken by a victor. 2. profits; advantages accruing from success or an official position. —**be spoiling for**, to seek eagerly or aggressively. **spoilsport** *n.* one who spoils other's enjoyment. [from Old French from Latin *spoliare* (*spolium* = plunder)]

spoiler *n.* a device on an aircraft to retard it by interrupting the airflow; a similar device on a vehicle to prevent it from being lifted off the ground at speed.

spoils system in the USA, the granting of offices and favours among the supporters of a party in office. The spoils system, a type of ◊patronage, was used by President Jefferson and was enlarged in scope by the 1820 Tenure of Office Act, which gave the president and Senate the power to reappoint posts that were the gift of the government after each four-yearly election. The practice remained common in the 20th century in US local government.

spoke[1] *n.* 1. each of the bars or rods running from the hub to the rim of a wheel. 2. a rung of a ladder. —*v.t.* 1. to provide with spokes. 2. to obstruct (a wheel etc.) by thrusting a spoke in. —**put a spoke in a person's wheel**, to hinder or thwart his or her purpose. [Old English]

spoke[2] past of **speak**.

spoken past participle of **speak**. —*adj.* speaking in a specified way (e.g. *soft-spoken, well-spoken*).

spokeshave /'spəʊkʃeɪv/ *n.* a tool for planing curved surfaces.

spokesman /'spəʊksmən/ *n.* (*plural* **spokesmen**) one who speaks on behalf of a group. —**spokeswoman** *n.fem.*

spoliation /spəʊlɪ'eɪʃən/ *n.* plundering, pillage. [from Latin]

spondee /'spɒndiː/ *n.* a metrical foot with two long or stressed syllables. —**spondaic** /-'deɪk/ *adj.* [from Old French or Latin from Greek *spondē* = libation, as being characteristic of music accompanying libations]

sponge /spʌndʒ/ *n.* 1. a water animal of the phylum Porifera, with a porous body wall and a tough elastic skeleton. Its hollow body is lined by cells bearing flagellae, whose whiplike movements keep water circulating, bringing a stream of food particles. 2. this skeleton, or a piece of a substance of similar texture, used for washing, cleaning, or padding things. 3. a thing of spongelike absorbency or consistency. 4. a sponge cake. 5. the act of sponging; a wash with a sponge. —*v.t./i.* 1. to wipe or wash with a sponge. 2. to live parasitically on others, to scrounge. —**sponge bag**, a waterproof bag for toilet articles. **sponge cake** (or **sponge pudding**), a light cake (or pudding) of spongelike consistency. **sponge rubber**, rubber made porous like a sponge. **throw in** *or* **up the sponge**, to abandon a contest, to admit defeat. [Old English from Latin from Greek *spoggia*]

spongeable /'spʌndʒəbəl/ *adj.* that may be sponged.

sponger /'spʌndʒə/ *n.* a person who habitually sponges on others.

spongy /'spʌndʒɪ/ *adj.* like sponge in texture or absorbency, soft and springy. —**spongily** *adv.*, **sponginess** *n.*

sponson /'spɒnsən/ *n.* 1. a projection from the side of a warship or tank to enable a gun to be trained forward and aft. 2. an air-filled structure fitted along the gunwale of a canoe to make it more stable and buoyant. 3. a short winglike projection from the hull of a seaplane, to stabilize it on water.

sponsor /'spɒnsə/ *n.* 1. a person who makes him-or herself responsible for another, presents a candidate for baptism, introduces legislation, or contributes to a charity in return for a specified activity by another. 2. an advertiser who pays for a sporting event, broadcast etc. which includes an advertisement of his, her, or their goods. —*v.t.* to be a sponsor for. —**sponsorial** /spɒn'sɔːrɪəl/ *adj.*, **sponsorship** *n.* [Latin (*spondēre* = promise solemnly)]

spontaneous /spɒn'teɪnɪəs/ *adj.* acting, done, or occurring without external cause or incitement; resulting from natural impulse; (of a style or manner) gracefully natural and unconstrained. —**spontaneous combustion**, ignition of a substance by chemical changes within it, not by flame etc. from an external source. **spontaneous generation** or **abiogenesis** the erroneous belief that living organisms can arise spontaneously from nonliving matter. This survived until the mid-19th century, when the French chemist Louis Pasteur demonstrated that a nutrient broth would not generate microorganisms if it was adequately sterilized. The theory of ◊biogenesis holds that spontaneous generation cannot now occur; it is thought, however, to have played an essential role in the origin of ◊life on this planet four billion years ago. **spontaneity** /spɒntə'niːɪtɪ/ *n.*, **spontaneously** *adv.* [from Latin *sponte* = of one's own accord]

spoof *n.* (*colloquial*) a parody; a hoax, a swindle. —*v.t.* (*colloquial*) to parody; to hoax, to swindle. [invented by A Roberts, English comedian (1852–1933)]

spook *n.* (*colloquial*) a ghost. [Dutch]

spooky *adj.* (*colloquial*) ghostly, eerie. —**spookiness** *n.*

spool *n.* a reel on which something is wound, e.g. yarn or magnetic tape; the revolving cylinder of an angler's reel. —*v.t.* to wind on a spool. [from Old French *espole* or Middle Low German or Middle Dutch]

spooling *n.* in computing, a process in which information to be printed is temporarily stored in a file, the actual printing being carried out later. It is used to prevent a relatively slow printer from holding up the system at critical times, and to enable several computers or programs to share one printer.

spoon *n.* 1. a utensil with an oval or round bowl and a handle, for conveying food (especially liquid) to the mouth or for stirring or measuring things. 2. a spoon-shaped thing. 3. or **spoonbait** a revolving, spoon-shaped, metal fish lure. —*v.t./i.* 1. to take or lift with a spoon. 2. to hit (a ball) feebly upwards. 3. (*colloquial*) to behave in an amorous way. —**spoon-feed** *v.t.* to feed (a baby etc.) with a spoon; to give such extensive help etc. to (a person) that they need make no effort for themselves. —**spoonful** *n.* [Old English = chip of wood]

spoonbill *n.* a wading bird of the family Threskiornithidae, characterized by a long, flat bill, dilated at the tip in the shape of a spoon, which it uses to sift for food in shallow, open water. Spoonbills are usually white, and up to 90 cm/3 ft tall.

spoonerism /'spu:nərɪzəm/ *n.* the exchange of elements in a flow of words. Usually a slip of the tongue, a spoonerism can also be contrived for comic effect (for example 'a troop of Boy Scouts' becoming 'a scoop of Boy Trouts'). [from William *Spooner* (1844–1930), English scholar reputed to have made such errors in speaking]

spoor *n.* an animal's track or scent. [Afrikaans from Middle Dutch]

sporadic /spə'rædɪk/ *adj.* occurring only here and there or occasionally. —**sporadically** *adv.* [from Latin from Greek *sporas* = scattered]

spore *n.* a small reproductive or resting body, usually consisting of just one cell. Unlike a ◊gamete, it does not need to fuse with another cell in order to develop into a new organism. Spores are produced by the lower plants, most fungi, some bacteria, and certain protozoa. They are generally light and easily dispersed by wind movements. [from Greek *spora* = sowing, seed]

sporophyte *n.* the diploid spore-producing generation in the life cycle of a plant that undergoes ◊alternation of generations.

sporran /'spɒrən/ *n.* a pouch worn in front of a kilt. [from Gaelic from Latin *bursa* = purse]

sport *n.* **1.** an athletic (especially outdoor) activity; any game or pastime; an outdoor pastime such as hunting or fishing. **2.** such activities or pastimes collectively; the world of sport; (in *plural*) a meeting for competing in sports, especially athletics. **3.** amusement, diversion, fun. **4.** (*colloquial*) a good fellow, a sportsmanlike person. **5.** an animal or plant differing from the normal type. —*v.t./i.* **1.** to play, to amuse oneself. **2.** to wear or display ostentatiously. —**in sport**, jestingly. **make sport of**, to ridicule. **sports car**, a low-built fast car. **sports coat** *or* **jacket**, a man's jacket for informal wear. [from *disport*]

sporting *adj.* **1.** interested or concerned in sport. **2.** sportsmanlike. —**a sporting chance**, some possibility of success.

sportive *adj.* playful. —**sportively** *adv.*

sportsman *n.* (*plural* **sportsmen**) **1.** a person fond of sport. **2.** a person who behaves fairly and generously. —**sportsmanlike** *adj.*, **sportsmanship** *n.*, **sportswoman** *n.fem.*

sporty *adj.* (*colloquial*) **1.** fond of sport. **2.** rakish, showy. —**sportily** *adv.*, **sportiness** *n.*

spot *n.* **1.** a small, roundish area or mark differing in colour or texture etc. from the surface it is on; a blemish or stain; a pimple. **2.** a particular place, a definite locality. **3.** (*colloquial*) one's (regular) position in an organization or programme etc. **4.** a small quantity of something; a drop (of liquid). **5.** a spotlight. —*v.t./i.* (**-tt-**) **1.** to mark with a spot or spots; to become marked thus. **2.** to make spots, to rain slightly. **3.** (*colloquial*) to pick out, to recognize, to catch sight of; to watch for and take note of (trains, talent etc.). **4.** (in *past participle*) marked or decorated with spots. —**in a** (**tight** etc.) **spot**, (*colloquial*) in difficulty. **on the spot**, at the scene of an action or event; (*colloquial*) in a position such that a response or action is required. **spot cash**, money paid immediately on a sale. **spot check**, a sudden or random check. **spot-on** *adj.* (*colloquial*) precise, on target. **spotted dick**, a suet pudding containing currants. **spot welding**, welding between points of metal surfaces in contact. —**spotter** *n.*

spotless *adj.* free from stain or blemish, perfectly clean.

spotlight *n.* **1.** a beam of light directed on a small area; a lamp projecting this. **2.** full attention or publicity. —*v.t.* **1.** to direct a spotlight on. **2.** to make conspicuous, to draw attention to.

spotty *adj.* **1.** marked with spots. **2.** patchy, irregular. —**spottily** *adv.*, **spottiness** *n.*

spouse /spaʊs/ *n.* a husband or wife. [from Old French from Latin *sponsus, sponsa*, past participle of *spondēre* = betroth]

spout *n.* **1.** a projecting tube or lip through which liquid etc. is poured or issues from a teapot, jug, roof gutter, fountain, etc. **2.** a jet or column of liquid etc. —*v.t./i.* **1.** to discharge or issue forcefully or in a jet. **2.** to utter in

a declamatory manner. —**up the spout**, (*slang*) useless, ruined; in trouble; pawned. [from Middle Dutch (imitative)]

sprain *v.t.* to injure (a joint or its muscles or ligaments) by wrenching it violently. —*n.* such an injury.

sprang past of **spring**.

sprat *n.* a small sea fish *Sprattus sprattus*. [Old English]

Spratly Islands /'sprætli/ (Chinese **Nanshan Islands**) a group of small islands, coral reefs, and sandbars dispersed over a distance of 965 km/600 mi in the South China Sea. They are of strategic importance, commanding the sea passage from Japan to Singapore, and were used as a submarine base by the Japanese during World War II. The islands are claimed in whole or part by the People's Republic of China, Taiwan, Malaysia, Vietnam (which calls the islands **Truong Sa**), and the Philippines (which calls them **Kalayaan**). Oil was discovered here in 1976.

sprawl *v.t./i.* **1.** to sit, lie, or fall with the limbs flung out or in an ungainly way; to spread (one's limbs) thus. **2.** to be of an irregular or straggling form. —*n.* a sprawling position, movement, or mass. [Old English]

spray[1] *n.* **1.** water or other liquid flying in very small drops. **2.** a liquid preparation to be applied in this way with an atomizer etc.; a device for such an application. —*v.t.* to send out (a liquid) in very small drops; to sprinkle thus; to sprinkle (plants etc.) thus with insecticides. —**spray gun**, a gunlike device for spraying paint etc. —**sprayer** *n.*

spray[2] *n.* **1.** a single shoot or branch with its leaves, twigs, and flowers. **2.** a bunch of cut flowers etc. arranged decoratively. **3.** an ornament in similar form.

spread /spred/ *v.t./i.* (*past* and *past participle* **spread**) **1.** to open out, to extend the surface of, to unroll or unfold; to cause to cover a larger surface, to display thus. **2.** to have a wide or specified extent; to become longer or wider. **3.** to cover the surface of, to apply as a layer; to be able to be spread. **4.** to make or become widely known or felt. **5.** to distribute or become distributed over an area or period. —*n.* **1.** spreading, being spread. **2.** a thing's extent, expanse, or breadth. **3.** expansion; increased bodily girth. **4.** the range of prices, rates etc. **5.** (*colloquial*) a lavish meal. **6.** a sweet or savoury paste for spreading on bread etc. **7.** a bedspread. **8.** printed matter spread across more than one column. —**spread eagle**, a figure of an eagle with the legs and wings extended, as an emblem. **spread-eagle** *v.t.* to place (a person) in a position with the arms and legs spread out; to defeat utterly. **spread oneself**, to be lavish or discursive. [Old English]

spreadsheet *n.* in computing, a program that mimics a sheet of ruled paper, divided into columns and rows. The user enters values in the sheet, then instructs the program to perform some operation on them, such as totalling a column or finding the average of a series of numbers. Highly complex numerical analyses may be built up from these simple steps. Spreadsheets are widely used in business for forecasting and financial control.

spree *n.* a lively outing, especially where one spends money freely; a bout of fun or drinking etc.

sprig *n.* **1.** a small branch, a shoot. **2.** an ornament resembling this, especially on fabric. **3.** (usually *derogatory*) a young man. —*v.t.* (**-gg-**) to ornament (fabric etc.) with sprigs.

sprightly /'spraɪtli/ *adj.* lively, full of energy; brisk. —**sprightliness** *n.* [from *sprite*]

spring *v.t./i.* (*past* **sprang**; *past participle* **sprung**) **1.** to jump, to move rapidly or suddenly, especially in a single movement. **2.** to originate or arise (from ancestors or a source etc.). **3.** to produce, develop, or operate suddenly or unexpectedly. **4.** to rouse (game) from an earth or covert; to contrive the escape of (a prisoner etc.). **5.** (of wood etc.) to become warped or split. **6.** (usually in *past participle*) to provide with springs. —*n.* **1.** the act of springing, a jump. **2.** elasticity. **3.** a device, usually a metal coil, that returns to its original shape after being stretched or compressed. Springs are used in some machines (such as clocks) to store energy; in other machines (such as engines) to close valves; or (in groups) to make a seat etc. more comfortable. **4.** the season in which vegetation begins to appear, from March to May in the northern hemisphere. **5.** a place where water or oil comes up naturally from the ground; a basin or flow so formed. A water spring is formed at the point of intersection of the water table and the ground's surface. **6.** a motive or origin of an action or custom etc. —**spring**

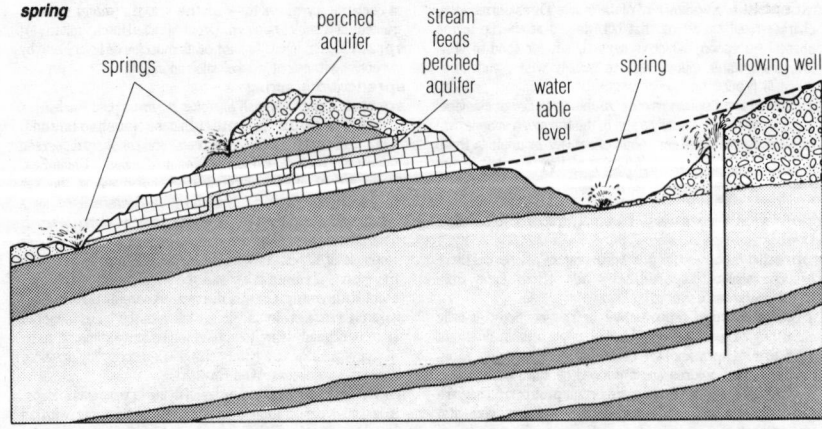

spring

springs · perched aquifer · stream feeds perched aquifer · water table level · spring · flowing well

balance, a ◊balance that measures weight by the tension of a spring. **spring chicken,** a young fowl for eating; a youthful person. **spring-clean** *n.* a thorough cleaning of a house, especially in spring; (*v.t.*) to clean thus. **spring onion,** a young onion eaten raw. **spring roll,** a Chinese snack consisting of a pancake filled with vegetables and fried in the shape of a roll. **spring tide,** a tide of maximum height. **spring up,** to come into being, to appear. **sprung rhythm,** a poetic rhythm approximating to speech, each foot having one stressed syllable followed by a varying number of unstressed. [Old English]

springboard *n.* a springy board giving an impetus in leaping or diving etc.; a source of impetus.

springbok /'sprɪŋbɒk/ *n.* **1.** a South African antelope *Antidorcas marsupialis* about 80 cm/2.6 ft at the shoulder, with head and body 1.3 m/4 ft long. They may leap 3 m/10 ft or more in the air when startled or playing, and have a fold of skin along the middle of the back which is raised to a crest in alarm. They once migrated in herds of over a million, but are now found only in small numbers where protected. **2. Springboks,** a South African national sporting team or touring party. [Afrikaans, from Dutch *springen* = spring and *bok* = antelope]

springer *n.* **1.** a small ◊spaniel of a breed used to spring game. **2.** the part of an arch where the curve begins; the lowest stone of this.

Springsteen /'sprɪŋstiːn/ Bruce 1949– . US rock singer, songwriter, and guitarist, born in New Jersey. His music combines melodies in traditional rock idiom and reflective lyrics about working-class life on albums such as *Born to Run* 1975 and *Born in the USA* 1984. His vast stadium concerts with the E Street Band were marked by his ability to overcome the distance between audience and artist, making him one of rock's finest live performers.

springtail *n.* a wingless insect of the order Collembola, leaping by means of a springlike caudal part.

springtime *n.* the season of spring.

springy *adj.* elastic, springing back quickly when squeezed or stretched. —**springily** *adv.,* **springiness** *n.*

sprinkle *v.t.* **1.** to scatter in small drops or particles. **2.** to scatter small drops etc. on (a surface). **3.** to distribute in small amounts. —*n.* sprinkling; a light shower.

sprinkler *n.* a device for sprinkling water.

sprinkling *n.* a small, thinly distributed number or amount.

sprint *v.t./i.* to run at full speed, especially over a short distance. —*n.* such a run; a similar spell of maximum effort in swimming, cycling etc. —**sprinter** *n.* [from Old Norse and Icelandic *spretta*]

sprit *n.* a small diagonal spar from a mast to the upper outer corner of a sail. [Old English *sprēot* = pole]

sprite *n.* an elf, fairy, or goblin. [from *sprit,* variant of *spirit*]

spritely /'spraɪtlɪ/ *adj.* (*US*) sprightly.

spritsail /'sprɪtsəl/ *n.* a sail extended by a sprit; a sail extended by a yard set under the bowsprit.

sprocket /'sprɒkɪt/ *n.* each of the several teeth on a wheel engaging with the links of a chain.

sprout *v.t./i.* to begin to grow or appear, to put forth shoots; to produce thus. —*n.* **1.** shoot of a plant. **2.** a Brussels sprout, a variety of ◊cabbage. [Old English]

spruce[1] /spruːs/ *adj.* neat in dress and appearance, smart. —*v.t./i.* to make or become spruce. —**sprucely** *adv.,* **spruceness** *n.*

spruce[2] *n.* a coniferous tree of the genus *Picea* of the pine family, found over much of the northern hemisphere; its wood. Spruces are pyramidal in shape and have rigid, prickly needles and drooping, leathery cones. Some are important forestry trees, such as the **sitka spruce** *P. sitchensis,* native to W North America, and the **Norway spruce** *P. abies,* now planted widely in North America. [alteration from obsolete *Pruce* = Prussia]

sprung past participle of **spring.**

spry /spraɪ/ *adj.* (*comparative* **spryer**; *superlative* **spryest**) lively, nimble. —**spryly** *adv.,* **spryness** *n.*

spud *n.* **1.** a small, narrow spade for weeding. **2.** (*slang*) a potato. —*v.t.* (**-dd-**) to dig with a spud.

spume *n.* froth, foam. —*v.i.* to foam. —**spumy** *adj.* [from Old French or Latin *spuma*]

spun past participle of **spin.**

spunk *n.* **1.** touchwood. **2.** (*colloquial*) mettle, spirit. **3.** (*slang*) semen. —**spunky** *adj.*

spur *n.* **1.** a device with a small spike or spiked wheel attached to a rider's heel for urging a horse forward. **2.** a stimulus, an incentive. **3.** a spur-shaped thing, especially the hard projection on a cock's leg; a projection from a mountain or mountain range; a branch road or railway. —*v.t./i.* (**-rr-**) **1.** to prick (a horse) with a spur. **2.** to incite or stimulate; to urge on. **3.** (especially in *past participle*) to provide with spurs. —**on the spur of the moment,** on a momentary impulse. [Old English]

spurge *n.* a plant of the genus *Euphorbia,* with an acrid milky juice. [from Old French *espurge* (*espurgier* from Latin *purgare* = cleanse)]

spurious /'spjʊərɪəs/ *adj.* not genuine, not what it purports to be. —**spuriously** *adv.* [from Latin *spurius,* originally = illegitimate]

spurn *v.t.* to reject with disdain, to treat with contempt; to repel with one's foot. [Old English]

spurt *v.t./i.* **1.** to gush, to send out (liquid) suddenly. **2.** to increase speed suddenly. —*n.* **1.** a sudden gush. **2.** a sudden increase in speed; a short burst of activity.

Sputnik /'spʊtnɪk, 'spʌ-/ *n.* a series of ten Soviet Earth-orbiting satellites. *Sputnik 1* was the first artificial satellite, launched on 4 Oct 1957. It weighed 84 kg/185 lb, with a 58 cm/23 in diameter, and carried only a simple radio transmitter which allowed scientists to track it as it orbited Earth. It burned up in the atmosphere 92 days later. *Sputnik 2,* launched on 3 Nov 1957, carried the dog Laika, the first living creature in space. Later Sputniks were test flights of the Vostok spacecraft. They were superseded by the Cosmos series. [Russian = fellow traveller]

sputter *v.t./i.* to splutter, to make a series of quick explosive sounds. —*n.* a sputtering sound. [from Dutch *sputteren* (imitative)]

sputum /'spju:təm/ n. (plural **sputa**) saliva; expectorated matter, especially as used to diagnose disease. [Latin, past participle of *spuere* = spit]

spy /spaɪ/ n. a person secretly collecting and reporting information on the activities or movements of an enemy or competitor etc. as an ◊intelligence agent or otherwise; a person keeping a secret watch on others. —v.t./i. 1. to discern, especially by careful observation. 2. to act as a spy; to keep watch secretly. 3. to pry. [from Old French *espier* = espy]

Spycatcher the controversial memoirs (published in 1987) of former UK intelligence officer Peter ◊Wright. The Law Lords unanimously rejected the UK government's attempt to prevent allegations of MI5 misconduct being reported in the British media.

spyglass n. a small telescope.

spyhole n. a peephole.

sq abbreviation of square (measure).

SQL abbreviation of Structured Query Language, in computing, a language designed for use with ◊relational databases. Although it can be used by programmers in the same way as other languages, it is often used as a means for programs to communicate among themselves. Typically, one program (called the 'client') uses SQL to request data from a database 'server'.

squab /skwɒb/ n. 1. a short, fat person. 2. a young (unfledged) pigeon or other bird. 3. a stuffed seat or cushion, especially as part (usually the back) of a seat in a motor car. —adj. short and fat, squat.

squabble /'skwɒbəl/ n. a petty or noisy quarrel. —v.i. to engage in a squabble.

squad /skwɒd/ n. a small group of people sharing a task etc., especially a small number of soldiers. [from French *escouade* from Italian *squadra* from Latin *quadra* = square]

squadron n. an organized body of persons etc., especially a cavalry division of two troops; a detachment of warships employed on a particular service; in the UK, a unit of the Royal Air Force with 10 to 18 aircraft. —**squadron leader**, in the UK, an officer commanding an RAF squadron, next below wing commander. [from Italian *squadrone*]

squalid /'skwɒlɪd/ adj. 1. dirty and unpleasant, especially because of neglect or poverty. 2. morally degrading. —**squalidly** adv. [from Latin *squalēre* = be rough or dirty]

squall n. 1. a sudden or violent wind storm, especially with rain or snow or sleet. 2. a discordant cry, a scream (especially of a baby). —v.t./i. to utter (with) a squall; to scream. —**squally** adj.

squalor /'skwɒlə/ n. a squalid state. [Latin]

squander /'skwɒndə/ v.t. to spend wastefully.

square n. 1. in geometry, a quadrilateral (four-sided) plane figure with all sides equal and each angle a right angle. Its diagonals bisect each other at right angles. The area A of a square is the length l of one side multiplied by itself (A = l × l). 2. an object or arrangement of (approximately) this shape. 3. an open, usually four-sided area surrounded by buildings. 4. in astrology, the aspect of two planets 90° apart, regarded as having an unfavourable influence. 5. the product obtained when a number is multiplied by itself, represented by an exponent (power) of 2; for example, 4 × 4 = 4^2 = 16 and 6.8 × 6.8 = 6.8^2 = 46.24. 6. an L- or T-shaped instrument for obtaining or testing right angles. 7. (slang) a conventional or old-fashioned person. —adj. 1. having the shape of a square. 2. having or in the form of a right angle; at right angles, 90° apart; angular, not round. 3. of or using units that express the measure of an area; (of a unit of measure) equal to the area of a square having each side one specified unit in length. 4. level, parallel. 5. properly arranged, settled; or **all square** not in debt, with no money owed; (of scores etc.) balanced, equal. 6. fair and honest. 7. direct, uncompromising. 8. (slang) conventional, or old-fashioned. —adv. squarely; directly; fairly, honestly. —v.t./i. 1. to make right-angled. 2. to mark with squares. 3. to multiply (a number) by itself. 4. to place evenly or squarely. 5. to make or be consistent. 6. to settle or pay (a bill etc.); (colloquial) to pay or bribe (a person); to make the scores of (a match etc.) equal. —**back to square one**, (colloquial) back to the starting point with no progress made. **on the square**, (colloquial) honest, honestly; fair, fairly. **out of square**, not at right angles. **square-bashing** n. (slang) military drill on a barrack square. **square the circle**, to construct a square equal in area to a given circle;

to do what is impossible. **square dance**, a dance with usually four couples facing inwards from four sides. **square deal**, a fair bargain or treatment. **square leg**, in cricket, the position of the fieldsman at some distance on the batsman's leg side and nearly opposite the stumps. **square meal**, a substantial and satisfying meal. **square-rigged** adj. with the principal sails at right angles to the length of the ship. **square root**, in mathematics, a number that when squared (multiplied by itself) equals a given number. For example, the square root of 25 (written $\sqrt{25}$) is ±5, because 5 × 5 = 25, and (–5) × (–5) = 25. As an ◊exponent, a square root is represented by $1/2$, for example, $16^{1/2}$ = 4. **square up**, to settle an account etc. **square up to**, to move towards (a person) in a fighting attitude; to face and tackle (a difficulty) resolutely. —**squarely** adv., **squareness** n. [from Old French *esquare*, ultimately from Latin *quadra* = square]

squash[1] /skwɒʃ/ v.t./i. 1. to crush, to squeeze or become squeezed flat or into pulp. 2. to pack tightly, to crowd, to squeeze into a small space. 3. to suppress. 4. to silence (a person) with a crushing reply etc. —n. 1. a crowd of people squashed together; a crowded state. 2. a sound (as) of something being squashed. 3. a drink made of crushed fruit. 4. squash rackets. —**squash rackets**, a game played with rackets and a small, soft ball in a closed court, derived from ◊rackets. There are two forms of squash: the American form, which is played in North and some South American countries, and the English, which is played mainly in Europe, Pakistan, and Commonwealth countries such as Australia and New Zealand. The Squash Rackets Association was formed in 1928. The world open championship was first held in 1975. —**squashy** adj. [alteration from *quash*]

squash[2] n. a trailing annual plant of the genus *Cucurbita*; a gourd of this, eaten as a vegetable. [from Narraganset]

squat /skwɒt/ v.t./i. (**-tt-**) 1. to sit on one's heels, or on the ground with the knees drawn up, or in a hunched position. 2. to put into a squatting position. 3. (colloquial) to sit down. 4. to act as a squatter. —adj. 1. short and thick, dumpy. 2. squatting. —n. 1. a squatting posture. 2. a place occupied by squatters. 3. being a squatter. [from Old French *esquatir* = flatten]

squatter n. 1. a person who takes unauthorized possession of unoccupied premises etc. 2. (historical) a sheep farmer in 19th-century Australia and New Zealand. Squatters were legal tenants of crown grazing land. Those who survived droughts and held on to their wealth established a politically powerful 'squattocracy', and built elegant mansions. As closer agricultural settlement spread at the end of the century, their influence waned.

squaw n. a North American Indian woman or wife. [from Narraganset]

squawk n. 1. a loud, harsh cry, especially of a bird. 2. a complaint. —v.i. to utter a squawk. [imitative]

squeak n. 1. a short high-pitched cry or sound. 2. or **narrow squeak** a narrow escape; a success barely attained. —v.t./i. 1. to make a squeak. 2. to utter shrilly. 3. (with *through* or *by* etc.; colloquial) to pass or succeed narrowly. 4. (slang) to turn informer. —**squeaker** n. [imitative]

squeaky adj. making a squeaking sound. —**squeakily** adv., **squeakiness** n.

squeal n. a prolonged shrill sound or cry. —v.t./i. 1. to make a squeal. 2. to utter with a squeal. 3. (slang) to turn informer. 4. (slang) to protest vociferously. [imitative]

squeamish /'skwi:mɪʃ/ adj. 1. easily nauseated, disgusted, or shocked. 2. over-scrupulous about principles. —**squeamishly** adv., **squeamishness** n. [from Anglo-French *escoymos*]

squeegee /skwi:'dʒi:/ n. an instrument with a rubber edge or roller on a long handle, used to remove liquid from surfaces. —v.t. to treat with a squeegee. [from *squeege*, strengthened form of *squeeze*]

squeeze v.t./i. 1. to exert pressure on from opposite or all sides. 2. to treat this so as to extract moisture or juice; to extract (juice) by squeezing; to reduce the size of or alter the shape of by squeezing. 3. to force into or through; to force one's way; to crowd. 4. to produce by pressure or effort. 5. to obtain by compulsion or strong urging; to extort money from; to harass thus. —n. 1. squeezing, being squeezed. 2. an affectionate clasp or hug. 3. a small amount of liquid produced by squeezing. 4. a crowd or crush; the pressure of this. 5. hardship or

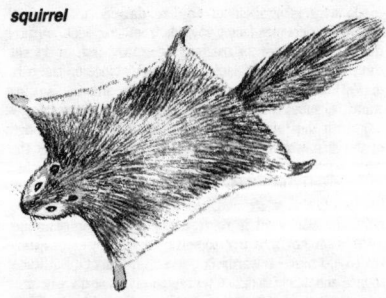

squirrel

difficulty caused by a shortage of money or time etc. **6.** restrictions on borrowing and investment during a financial crisis. [earlier *squise*]

squelch *v.t./i.* **1.** to make a sucking sound as of treading in thick mud; to move with a squelching sound. **2.** to disconcert, to silence. —*n.* an act or sound of squelching. [imitative]

squib *n.* a small firework burning with a hissing sound and usually with a final explosion. —**damp squib**, an unsuccessful attempt to impress etc.

squid *n.* a ten-armed marine ◊cephalopod, especially of the genus *Loligo*.

squiffy /'skwɪfɪ/ *adj.* (*slang*) slightly drunk.

squiggle *n.* a short, curling line, especially in handwriting. —**squiggly** *adj.* [imitative]

squill *n.* **1.** a plant of the genus *Scilla*, family Liliaceae, growing from a bulb, resembling a bluebell. It is found growing in dry places near the sea in W Europe. **2.** a crustacean of the genus *Squilla*. [from Latin from Greek *skilla*]

squinch *n.* a straight or arched structure across the interior angle of a square tower to carry a dome etc. [variant of obsolete *scunch*, abbreviation of *scuncheon*]

squint *v.i.* **1.** to have the eyes turned in different directions; to have a squint. **2.** to look obliquely or with half-shut eyes or through a narrow opening. —*n.* **1.** or **strabismus** a common condition in which one eye deviates in any direction. A squint may be convergent (with the bad eye turned inward), divergent (outward), or, in rare cases, vertical. A convergent squint is also called **cross-eye**. **2.** a stealthy or sidelong glance; (*colloquial*) a glance, a look. **3.** a narrow opening in a church wall giving a view of the altar. —*adj.* (*colloquial*) askew. [from *asquint* adverb (compare Dutch *schuinte* = slant)]

squire *n.* **1.** a country gentleman, especially the chief landowner in a country district. **2.** a woman's escort or gallant. **3.** (*historical*) a knight's attendant. **4.** (*jocular*, as a form of address to a man) sir. —*v.t.* (of a man) to attend or escort (a woman). [from Old French = esquire]

squirearchy /'skwaɪərɑːkɪ/ *n.* landowners collectively, especially as having political or social influence. [after *hierarchy* etc.]

squirm *v.i.* **1.** to wriggle, to writhe. **2.** to show or feel embarrassment or discomfiture. —*n.* a squirming movement. [imitative]

squirrel *n.* a bushy-tailed, usually arboreal rodent of the family Sciuridae; its fur. Squirrels are found worldwide except for Australia, Madagascar, and polar regions. —*v.t.* (-ll-) (with *away*) to hoard. [from Anglo-French ultimately from Greek *skiouros* (*skia* = shade and *oura* = tail)]

squirt *v.t./i.* to eject (liquid etc.) in a jet; to be ejected thus. —*n.* **1.** a jet of water etc. **2.** a device for ejecting this. **3.** (*colloquial*) an insignificant, self-assertive person. [imitative]

squish *n.* a slight squelching sound. —*v.i.* to move with a squish. —**squishy** *adj.* [imitative]

sr abbreviation of ◊steradian.

Sr symbol for ◊strontium.

Sr. abbreviation of **1.** Senior. **2.** *Señor.*

Sra. abbreviation of *señora.*

Sri Lanka /sri: 'læŋkə/ Democratic Socialist Republic of; (until 1972 Ceylon) island in the Indian Ocean, off the SE coast of India; **area** 65,600 sq km/25,328 sq mi; **capital** and chief port Colombo; **physical** flat in N and around the coast; hills and mountains in S and central interior; Adam's Peak 2,243 m/7,538 ft; **head of state** Ranasinghe Premadsa from 1989; **head of government** Dingiri Banda Wijetunge from 1989; **political system** liberal democratic republic; **exports** tea, rubber, coconut products, graphite, sapphires, rubies, gemstones; **population** (1990 est) 17,135,000 (Sinhalese 74%, Tamils 17%, Moors 7%); **language** Sinhala, Tamil (both official); English; **recent history** independence from Britain within the Commonwealth was achieved in 1948. The Socialist Republic of Sri Lanka was proclaimed in 1972. Tamil guerrilla violence escalated in 1983; a ceasefire was policed by Indian troops but left-wing guerrillas campaigned against an Indo-Sri Lankan peace pact in 1988. India agreed to withdraw its peace-keeping forces in 1990.

SRN abbreviation of State Registered Nurse.

SS abbreviation of **1.** Saints. **2.** steamship. **3.** (*historical*) the Nazi special police force established in 1925. [German *Schutz-Staffel* = protective squadron] Under ◊Himmler its 500,000 membership included the full-time **Waffen-SS** (armed SS), which fought in World War II, and spare-time members. The SS was brutal in its treatment of the Jews and others in the concentration camps and occupied territories. It was condemned at the Nuremberg Trials of war criminals.

SSE abbreviation of south-southeast.

SSR abbreviation of Soviet Socialist Republic.

SSW abbreviation of south-southwest.

st. abbreviation of stone.

St abbreviation of Saint, Street.

stab *v.t./i.* (-bb-) **1.** to pierce or wound with a pointed tool or weapon; to aim a blow with such a weapon. **2.** to cause a sensation like being stabbed. **3.** to hurt or distress (a person or feelings etc.). —*n.* **1.** an act or the result of stabbing; a wound or harm. **2.** (*colloquial*) an attempt. —**stab in the back**, a treacherous or slanderous attack.

stability /stə'bɪlɪtɪ/ *n.* **1.** being stable. **2.** in physics, how difficult it is to move an object from a position of ◊equilibrium. A stable object returns to its rest position after being shifted slightly. An unstable object topples or falls when shifted slightly.

stabilize /'steɪbɪlaɪz/ *v.t./i.* to make or become stable. —**stabilization** /-'zeɪʃən/ *n.*

stabilizer *n.* a device to keep a ship, aircraft, or child's bicycle steady. A ship may be stabilized by a pair of fins fitted to the sides, governed automatically by a ◊gyroscope mechanism.

stable[1] /'steɪbəl/ *adj.* firmly fixed or established, not easily moved or changed or destroyed or decomposed; resolute, constant. [from Anglo-French from Latin *stabilis* (*stare* = stand)]

stable[2] *n.* **1.** a building in which horses are kept. **2.** a place where racehorses are kept and trained; the racehorses of a particular stable. **3.** persons or products etc. having a common origin or affiliation; such an origin or affiliation. —*v.t.* to put or keep (a horse) in a stable. —**stable companion** *or* **stable mate**, a horse of the same stable; a member of the same organization. —**stably** *adv.* [from Old French from Latin *stabulum*]

stabling /'steɪbəlɪŋ/ *n.* accommodation for horses.

staccato /stə'kɑːtəʊ/ *adj. & adv.* especially in music, in a sharp disconnected manner, not running on smoothly. [Italian, past participle of *staccare* from Old French = detach]

stack *n.* **1.** a pile or heap, especially in an orderly arrangement. **2.** a haystack. **3.** (*colloquial*) a large quantity. **4.** a chimney stack; a tall factory chimney; a chimney or funnel for smoke on a steamer etc.; a tall steel structure from which unwanted gas produced in association with oil is burnt off. **5.** a stacked group of aircraft. **6.** a library's store of books to which readers do not usually have direct access. **7.** a high detached rock, especially off the coast of Scotland. —*v.t.* **1.** to pile in a stack or stacks. **2.** to arrange (cards) secretly for cheating; to manipulate (circumstances etc.) to one's advantage. **3.** to cause (aircraft) to fly round the same point at different levels while waiting to land. **4.** in computing, to store data so that the most recent item stored will be the next to be retrieved. The technique is commonly called 'last in, first out'. [from Old Norse *stakkr* = haystack]

stadholder *n.* or **stadtholder** the leader of the United Provinces of the Netherlands from the 15th to the 18th century.

stadium /'steɪdɪəm/ *n.* an enclosed athletic or sports ground with tiers of seats for spectators. [Latin from Greek *stadion*]

Staël /staːl/ Anne Louise Germaine Necker, Madame de Staël 1766–1817. French author, daughter of the financier ◊Necker. She wrote semi-autobiographical novels such as *Delphine* 1802 and *Corinne* 1807, and the critical work *De l'Allemagne* 1810, on German literature. She was banished from Paris by Napoleon in 1803 because of her advocacy of political freedom.

staff *n.* **1.** a stick or pole used as a weapon, support, or measuring stick, or as a symbol of office. **2.** a body of officers assisting a commanding officer and concerned with an army, regiment, or fleet etc. as a whole. **3.** a group of persons by whom a business is carried on; those responsible to a manager or other person in authority. **4.** persons in authority within an organization (as distinct from pupils etc.); those engaged in administrative as distinct from manual work. **5.** (*plural* also **staves**) in music, the set of usually five parallel lines to indicate the pitch of notes by position —*v.t.* to provide (an institution etc.) with a staff. —**staff college,** a college where officers are trained for staff duties. **staff nurse,** a nurse ranking just below a sister. **staff officer,** a member of a military staff. [Old English]

Staffordshire /'stæfədʃə/ county in west central England; **area** 2,720 sq km/1,050 sq mi; **administrative headquarters** Stafford; **physical** largely flat, comprising the Vale of Trent and its tributaries; **products** coal in the north; china and earthenware in the Potteries and the upper Trent basin; **population** (1987) 1,028,000.

Staffordshire porcelain pottery from Staffordshire, England, one of the largest pottery-producing regions in the world, built up around an area rich in clay. Different companies, the first of which was Longton, have produced stoneware and earthenware from the 17th century onwards. See also the ◊Potteries, and ◊pottery and porcelain.

Staffs. abbreviation of Staffordshire.

stag *n.* **1.** a male deer. **2.** a person who seeks to buy new shares and sell at once for profit. —**stag beetle,** a beetle of the family Lucanidae with branched mandibles like antlers. **stag party,** a party for men only.

stage *n.* **1.** a point or period in the course of a development or process. **2.** a platform, especially a raised one on which plays etc. are performed before an audience. **3.** the acting or theatrical profession; dramatic art or literature. **4.** a scene of action. **5.** a regular stopping place on a route; the distance between two of these. **6.** a section of a space rocket with a separate means of propulsion. —*v.t.* **1.** to present (a play etc.) on the stage. **2.** to organize and carry out. —**stage direction,** an instruction in a play about an actor's movement, the sounds to be heard etc. **stage fright,** nervousness on facing an audience, especially for the first time. **stagehand** *n.* a person handling scenery etc. in a theatre. **stage-manage** *v.t.* to be the stage manager of; to arrange and control for effect. **stage manager,** the person responsible for lighting and mechanical arrangements etc. on a stage. **stage-struck** *adj.* strongly wishing to be an actor or actress. **stage whisper,** an aside, a loud whisper meant to be heard by others than the person addressed. [from Old French *estage* ultimately from Latin *stare* = stand]

stagecoach *n.* a large, horse-drawn, closed coach that formerly ran regularly by stages between two places.

stagecraft *n.* skill or experience in writing or staging plays.

stager *n.* (especially **old stager**) an experienced person.

stagflation /stæg'fleɪʃən/ *n.* an economic condition in which rapid inflation is accompanied by stagnating, even declining, output and by increasing unemployment. Its cause is often sharp increases in costs of raw materials and/or labour. Stagflation was experienced in Europe in the 1970s.

stagger *v.t./i.* **1.** to walk or move unsteadily; to cause to do this. **2.** (of news etc.) to shock or confuse (a person). **3.** to arrange (events or hours of work etc.) so that they do not coincide. **4.** to arrange (objects) so that they are not in line. —*n.* a staggering movement; (in *plural*) a disease, especially of horses and cattle, causing staggering. [from Old Norse *staka* = push, stagger]

staggering *adj.* astonishing, bewildering.

staghound *n.* a large hound used in hunting deer.

staging *n.* **1.** the presentation of a play etc. **2.** a platform or support, especially a temporary one; shelves for plants in a greenhouse. —**staging post,** a regular stopping place, especially on an air route.

stagnant /'stægnənt/ *adj.* **1.** (of water etc.) motionless, not flowing, still and stale. **2.** showing no activity. —**stagnancy** *n.*

stagnate *v.i.* to be or become stagnant. —**stagnation** *n.* [from Latin *stagnare* (*stagnum* = pool)]

stagy /'steɪdʒɪ/ *adj.* theatrical in style or manner.

Stahl /ʃtaːl/ Georg Ernst 1660–1734. German chemist who produced a fallacious theory of combustion. He argued that objects burn because they contain a combustible substance, phlogiston. Chemists spent much of the 18th century evaluating Stahl's theories before they were finally proved false by ◊Lavoisier.

staid *adj.* of quiet and sober character or demeanour, sedate. [= *stayed*, past participle of *stay*[1]]

stain *v.t.* **1.** to discolour or be discoloured by the action of a liquid sinking in. **2.** to spoil or damage (a reputation or character etc.). **3.** to colour (wood or glass etc.) with a substance that penetrates the material; to treat (a microscopic specimen) with a colouring agent. —*n.* **1.** an act or the result of staining. **2.** a blot or blemish. **3.** damage to a reputation etc. **4.** in chemistry, a coloured compound that will bind to other substances. Stains are used extensively in microbiology to colour microorganisms and in histochemistry to detect the presence and whereabouts in plant and animal tissue of substances such as fats, cellulose, and proteins. —**stained glass,** pieces of glass, either dyed or superficially coloured, set in a framework (usually of lead) to form decorative or pictorial designs. [from earlier *distain* from Old French *desteindre* from Latin *tingere*]

stainless *adj.* **1.** without stains. **2.** not liable to stain. —**stainless steel,** a widely used ◊alloy of iron, chromium, and nickel that resists rusting under oxidizing conditions because it is protected by the film of oxide which forms on its surface. Its chromium content also gives it a high tensile strength. It is used for cutlery and kitchen fittings. Stainless steel was first produced in the UK in 1913 and in Germany in 1914.

stair *n.* each of a set of fixed indoor steps; (in *plural*) a set of these. —**stair rod,** a rod for securing a carpet in the angle between two steps. [Old English]

staircase *n.* a flight of stairs and the supporting structure; the part of a building containing this.

stairway *n.* a flight of stairs; the way up this.

stake *n.* **1.** a stout stick pointed at one end for driving into the ground as a support or marker etc.; (*historical*) a post to which a person was tied to be burnt alive; this death as a punishment. **2.** the money etc. wagered on an event. **3.** an interest or concern, especially financial. **4.** (in *plural*) the money offered as the prize in a horse race; the race itself. —*v.t.* **1.** to secure or support with stakes. **2.** to mark (an area) with stakes. **3.** to establish (a claim). **4.** to wager (money etc. *on* an event). **5.** (*US colloquial*) to give financial or other support to. —**at stake,** wagered, risked, to be won or lost. **stake out,** to place under surveillance. [Old English]

stakeholder *n.* a third party with whom money etc. wagered is deposited.

Stakhanovite /stə'kɑːnəvaɪt/ *n.* one who is exceptionally hard-working and productive. —**Stakhanovism** *n.* [from Aleksei *Stakhanov*, Russian coal miner (1906–1977), who in 1935 produced a phenomenal amount of coal by a combination of new methods and great energy]

stalactite /'stæləktaɪt/ *n.* an iciclelike deposit of calcium carbonate hanging from the roof of a cave etc. [from Greek *stalaktos* = dripping (*stalassō* = drip)]

stalagmite /'stæləgmaɪt/ *n.* a deposit like a stalactite rising like a spike from the floor of a cave etc. [from Greek *stalagma* = a dripping]

stale *adj.* **1.** not fresh; musty, insipid, or otherwise the worse for age or use; trite or unoriginal. **2.** (of an athlete or musician etc.) having his or her ability impaired by excessive exertion or practice. —*v.t./i.* to make or become stale. —**stalely** *adv.,* **staleness** *n.*

stalemate *n.* **1.** the state of a chess game counting as a draw, in which one player cannot move without going into check. **2.** a deadlock in proceedings. —*v.t.* **1.** to bring (a player) to a stalemate. **2.** to bring a deadlock. [from obsolete *stale* in same sense and *mate*[2]]

Stalin /'stɑːlɪn/ Joseph. Adopted name of Joseph Vissarionovich Djugashvili 1879–1953. Soviet politician. A member of the October Revolution Committee in 1917, Stalin became general secretary of the Communist Party in 1922. After ◊Lenin's death in 1924, Stalin sought to create '◊socialism in one country' and clashed with ◊Trotsky, who denied the possibility of socialism inside Russia until revolution had occurred in W Europe. Stalin won this ideological struggle by 1927, and a series of five-year plans was launched to collectivize industry and agriculture from 1928. All opposition was eliminated in the Great Purge 1936–38. During World War II, Stalin intervened in the military direction of the campaigns against Nazi Germany. His role was denounced after his death by Khrushchev and other members of the Soviet regime. [Russian = steel]

> A single death is a tragedy; a million is a statistic.
> **Joseph Stalin**
> (attrib.)

Stalingrad /'stɑːlɪŋɡræd/ former name (1925–61) of the Soviet city of ◊Volgograd.

stalk[1] /stɔːk/ *n.* a stem, especially the main stem of a herbaceous plant or the slender stem supporting a leaf or flower or fruit etc.; a similar support of an organ etc. in animals.

stalk[2] *v.t./i.* **1.** to pursue or approach (a wild animal or an enemy etc.) stealthily. **2.** to stride, to walk in a stately or imposing manner. —*n.* **1.** a stalking of game. **2.** an imposing gait. —**stalking horse,** a horse behind which a hunter hides; a pretext concealing one's real intentions or actions. —**stalker** *n.* [from Old English]

Stalker affair /'stɔːkə/ an inquiry begun in 1984 by John Stalker, deputy chief constable in Manchester, England, into the killing of six unarmed men in 1982 by Royal Ulster Constabulary special units in Northern Ireland. The inquiry was halted and Stalker suspended from duty in 1986. Although he was later reinstated, the inquiry did not reopen, and no reason for his suspension was given.

stall[1] /stɔːl/ *n.* **1.** a stable or cowhouse; a compartment for one animal in this. **2.** a trader's booth in a market etc. **3.** a fixed seat in a choir or chancel, more or less enclosed at the back and sides. **4.** (usually in *plural*) each of the seats on the ground floor of a theatre. **5.** a compartment for one person in a shower bath, one horse at the start of a race etc. **6.** the stalling of an engine or aircraft; the condition resulting from this. —*v.t./i.* **1.** (of a motor vehicle or its engine) to stop because of inadequate fuel supply or overloading of the engine etc.; (of an aircraft) to get out of control because its speed is insufficient. **2.** to cause (an engine etc.) to stall. **3.** to put or keep (cattle etc.) in a stall or stalls. [Old English]

stall[2] *v.t./i.* to play for time when being questioned etc.; to delay or obstruct (a person). [from *stall* = pickpocket's confederate, originally = decoy, from Anglo-French *estale* = position]

stallion /'stæljən/ *n.* an uncastrated male horse. [from Old French *estalon*]

Stallone /stə'ləʊn/ Sylvester 1946–. US film actor. He played bit parts and occasional leads in exploitation films before starring in *Rocky* 1976 and its sequels, which he also wrote. His later films have mostly been based around violence, and include *F.I.S.T.* 1978, *First Blood* 1982, and *Rambo* 1985.

stalwart /'stɔːlwət/ *adj.* **1.** strongly built, sturdy. **2.** courageous; strong and faithful; resolute. —*n.* a stalwart person, especially a loyal, uncompromising partisan. [Old English = place worthy]

Stamboul /stæm'buːl/ the old part of the Turkish city of ◊Istanbul, the area formerly occupied by ◊Byzantium.

stamen /'steɪmen/ *n.* the male reproductive organ of a flower. The stamens are collectively referred to as the ◊androecium. A typical stamen consists of a stalk, or filament, with an anther, the pollen-bearing organ, at its apex. [Latin, literally = warp thread]

stamina /'stæmɪnə/ *n.* ability to endure prolonged physical or mental strain. [Latin, plural of *stamen*]

stammer *v.t./i.* to speak with halting articulation, especially with pauses or rapid repetitions of the same syllable; to utter (words) thus. —*n.* an act or the habit of stammering. —**stammerer** *n.* [Old English]

stamp *v.t./i.* **1.** to bring down (one's foot) heavily on the ground etc.; to crush or flatten thus; to walk with heavy steps. **2.** to impress (a pattern or mark etc.) on a surface; to impress (a surface) with a pattern or mark etc. **3.** to affix a postage or other stamp to. **4.** to assign a specific character to; to mark out. —*n.* **1.** an instrument for stamping things. **2.** a mark or design made by this. **3.** or **postage stamp** a small adhesive piece of paper showing the amount paid, affixed to letters etc. to be posted; a piece of paper impressed with an official mark as evidence of payment of a tax or fee, for affixing to a licence or deed etc.; a similar decorative device sold in aid of a charity. **4.** a mark impressed on or a label etc. fixed to a commodity as evidence of its quality etc. **5.** an act or sound of stamping of the foot. **6.** a characteristic mark or quality. —**stamp collector,** one who collects postage stamps as a hobby. **stamp duty,** a duty imposed on certain kinds of legal document. **stamping ground,** a favourite place of resort or action. **stamp on,** to impress on (the memory etc.); to suppress. **stamp out,** to produce by cutting out with a die etc.; to put an end to, to destroy. [= Old High German *stampfōn* = to pound]

Stamp Act a UK act of Parliament in 1765 that sought to raise enough money from the American colonies to cover the cost of their defence. Refusal to use the required tax stamps and a blockade of British merchant shipping in the colonies forced repeal of the act the following year. It was a precursor of the ◊American Revolution. The act taxed (by requiring an official stamp) all publications and legal documents published in British colonies.

stampede /stæm'piːd/ *n.* a sudden hurried rush of cattle or people etc., especially in fright; an uncontrolled or unreasoning action by a large number of people. —*v.t./i.* to take part in a stampede; to cause to do this. [from Spanish *estampida*]

stance /stɑːns, stæns/ *n.* **1.** an attitude or position of the body. **2.** a standpoint, an attitude. [French from Italian *stanza* = standing place]

stamen

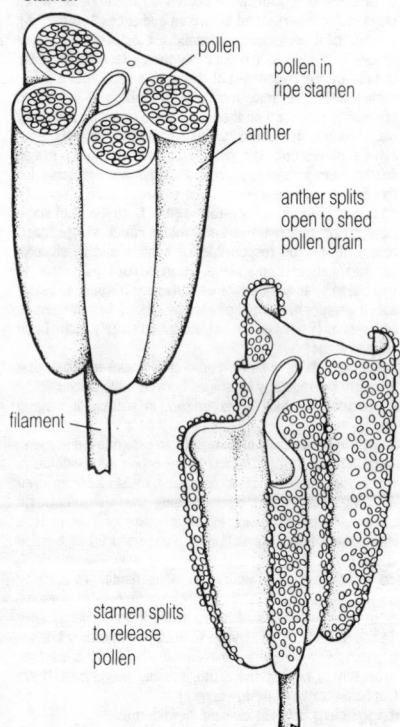

pollen

pollen in
ripe stamen

anther

anther splits
open to shed
pollen grain

filament

stamen splits
to release
pollen

stanch /stɑːntʃ/ v.t. to stop the flow of (blood) etc.); to stop the flow from (a wound). [from Old French *estanchier*]

stanchion /'stɑːnʃən/ n. an upright post or support; a device for confining cattle in a stall etc. [from Anglo-French ultimately from Latin *stare* = stand]

stand v.t./i. (*past* and *past participle* **stood** /stʊd/) **1.** to have, take, or maintain an upright position, especially on the feet or a base. **2.** to be situated. **3.** to place, to set upright. **4.** to be of a specified height. **5.** to remain firm or valid, or in a specified condition. **6.** to move to and remain in a specified position; to take a specified attitude (*literally* or *figuratively*); (of ships) to hold a specified course. **7.** to maintain a position; to avoid falling, moving, or being moved; to remain stationary or unused. **8.** to undergo; to endure or tolerate. **9.** to provide at one's own expense. **10.** to act as. —n. **1.** a standing or stationary condition. **2.** a position taken up, an attitude adopted (*literal* or *figurative*). **3.** resistance to attack or compulsion. **4.** a rack or pedestal etc. on which something may be placed. **5.** a table, booth, or other (often temporary) structure on which things are exhibited or sold. **6.** a standing place for vehicles. **7.** a raised structure for persons to sit or stand on, e.g. at a sports ground. **8.** (*US*) a witness box. **9.** a halt made by a touring company etc. to give a performance or performances. **10.** in cricket, a prolonged stay at the wicket by two batsmen. **11.** a group of growing trees etc. —**as it stands**, in its present condition; in the present circumstances. **stand by**, to stand ready for action; to stand near; to look without interfering; to uphold or support (a person); to adhere to (a promise etc.). **stand-by** n. (*plural* **stand-bys**) a person or thing ready if needed in an emergency etc.; (*especially attributive*) a system of allocating spare seats on an aircraft to passengers who have not booked in advance. **stand corrected**, to accept that one was wrong. **stand down**, to withdraw from a position or candidacy. **stand for**, to represent; to be a candidate for (especially public office); (*colloquial*) to tolerate. **stand one's ground**, not to yield. **stand in**, to deputize. **stand-in** n. a deputy or substitute, especially for a principal film actor or actress while the cameras and lighting for a scene are set. **stand off**, to move or keep away; to dispense temporarily with the services of (an employee). **stand-off half**, a half-back in rugby football who forms a link between the scrum half and the three-quarters. **stand-offish** adj. cold or distant in manner. **stand on**, to insist on; to observe scrupulously. **stand on one's own (two) feet**, to be self-reliant or independent. **stand out**, to be prominent or outstanding; to persist in resistance or support. **stand to**, to stand ready for action; to abide by; to be likely or certain to. **stand to reason**, to be obvious or logical. **stand up**, to come to or remain in or place in a standing position; to be valid; (*colloquial*) to fail to keep an appointment with. **stand-up** adj. (of a meal) eaten standing; (of a fight) violent and thorough; (of a collar) upright, not turned down. **stand up for**, to defend or support, to side with. **stand up to**, to face (an opponent) courageously; to be resistant to the harmful effects of (use or wear etc.). **take one's stand**, to base an argument or reliance (*on*). [Old English]

standard /'stændəd/ n. **1.** an object, quality, or specification serving as an example or principle to which others should conform or by which others are judged. **2.** a required or specified level of excellence etc. **3.** the average quality; the ordinary design or procedure etc. without added or novel features. **4.** a distinctive flag. **5.** an upright support or pipe. **6.** a treelike shrub with (or grafted on) an upright stem. —adj. **1.** serving or used as a standard. **2.** having a recognized and permanent value, authoritative. **3.** of normal or prescribed quality or size etc.; (of language) conforming to established educated usage. —**standard-bearer** n. a person who carries a distinctive flag; a prominent leader in a cause. **standard lamp**, a domestic lamp on a tall upright with a base. **standard time**, that established in a country or region by law or custom and based on the longitude. [from Anglo-French from Latin *tendere* = stretch]

standard atmosphere an alternative term for ◊atmosphere, a unit of pressure.

standard deviation in statistics, a measure of the spread of data. The deviation (difference) of each of the data items from the mean is found, and their values squared. The mean value of these squares is then calculated. The standard deviation is the square root of this mean.

standard form a method of writing numbers often used by scientists, particularly for very large or very small numbers. The numbers are written with one digit before the decimal point and multiplied by a power of 10. The number of digits given after the decimal point depends on the accuracy required. For example, the ◊speed of light is 2.9979×10^8 metres per second.

standard gravity the acceleration due to gravity, generally taken as 9.81274 metres per second. See ◊g scale.

standard illuminants three standard light intensities, A, B, and C, used for illumination when phenomena involving colour are measured. A is the light from a filament at 2,848 K (2,575°C), B is noon sunlight, and C is normal daylight. B and C are defined with respect to A. Standardization is necessary because colours appear different when viewed in different lights.

standardize v.t. to cause to conform to a standard. —**standardization** /-'zeɪʃən/ n.

standard of living in economics, the measure of consumption and welfare of a country, community, class, or person. Individual standard-of-living expectations are heavily influenced by the income and consumption of other people in similar jobs.

standard temperature and pressure (STP) in chemistry, a standard set of conditions for experimental measurements, to enable comparisons to be made between sets of results. Standard temperature is 0°C and standard pressure 1 atmosphere (101,325 Pa).

standard volume in physics, the volume occupied by one kilogram molecule (the molecular mass in kilograms) of any gas at standard temperature and pressure. Its value is approximately 22.414 cubic metres.

standee /stæn'diː/ n. (*colloquial*) one who stands, especially when all seats are occupied.

standing n. **1.** status; esteem, high repute. **2.** past duration. —adj. **1.** that stands, upright; (of corn) not yet harvested. **2.** (of a jump or start) performed from rest without a run-up. **3.** permanent, remaining effective or valid. **4.** (of water) not flowing. —**standing joke**, an object of permanent ridicule. **standing order**, an instruction (banker's order) by a depositor with the bank to pay a certain sum of money at regular intervals, or to a newsagent etc. for the regular supply of a periodical etc. It is similar to ◊direct debit. **standing orders**, the rules governing procedure in Parliament or a council etc. **standing room**, space to stand in.

standing committee a committee of the UK House of Commons that examines parliamentary bills (proposed acts of Parliament) for detailed correction and amendment. The committee comprises members of Parliament from the main political parties, with a majority usually held by the government. Several standing committees may be in existence at any time, each usually created for a particular bill.

standing crop in ecology, the total number of individuals of a given species alive in a particular area at any moment. It is sometimes measured as the weight (or ◊biomass) of a given species in a sample section.

standing order in banking, an instruction (banker's order) by a depositor with the bank to pay a certain sum of money at regular intervals. In some cases, the bank may be billed by a third party such as a supplier of gas or electricity, who is authorized by the depositor to invoice the bank directly, which in turn will pay out the sum demanded (known as **direct debit**).

standing wave a wave in which the positions of ◊nodes (positions of zero vibration) and antinodes (positions of maximum vibration) do not move. Standing waves result when two similar waves travel in opposite directions through the same space. For example, when a sound wave is reflected back along its own path, as when a stretched string is plucked, a standing wave is formed. In this case the antinode remains fixed at the centre and the nodes are at the two ends. Water and ◊electromagnetic waves can form standing waves in the same way.

standpipe n. a vertical pipe for fluid to rise in, e.g. to provide a water supply outside or at a distance from buildings.

standpoint n. a point of view.

standstill n. a stoppage, inability to proceed.

Stanford /'stænfəd/ Charles Villiers 1852–1924. British composer and teacher, born in Ireland. A leading figure in the 19th-century renaissance of British music, his many

Stanhope

works include operas such as *Shamus O'Brien* 1896, seven symphonies, chamber music, and church music. Among his pupils were Vaughan Williams, Holst, and Bridge.

Stanhope /ˈstænəp/ Hester Lucy 1776–1839. English traveller who left England in 1810 to tour the Middle East with Bedouins and eventually settled there. She adopted local dress and became involved in Eastern politics.

Stanislavsky /ˌstæniˈslævski/ Konstantin Sergeivich 1863–1938. Russian actor, director, and teacher. He founded the Moscow Art Theatre in 1898 and directed productions of Chekhov and Gorky. He was the originator of ◊Method acting, described in *My Life in Art* 1924 and other works.

stank past of **stink**.

Stanley /ˈstænli/ family name of the earls of ◊Derby.

Stanley town on E Falkland, capital of the ◊Falkland Islands; population (1986) 1,200. After changing its name only once between 1843 and 1982, it was renamed five times in the space of six weeks during the Falklands War in April–June 1982.

Stanley Henry Morton 1841–1904. Welsh-born US explorer and journalist who made four expeditions to Africa. He and David ◊Livingstone met at Ujiji in 1871 and explored Lake Tanganyika. He traced the course of the river Zaïre (Congo) to the sea 1874–77, established the Congo Free State (Zaïre) 1879–84, and charted much of the interior 1887–89.

Stanley Wendell 1904–1971. US biochemist. Working at the Rockefeller Institute, Princeton, Stanley succeeded, in 1935, in crystallizing a virus: the tobacco mosaic virus (TMV). He went on to demonstrate that, despite its crystalline state, TMV remained infectious. With John Northrop and James Sumner, Stanley received the 1946 Nobel Chemistry Prize.

Stannaries, the /ˈstænərɪz/ the tin-mining district of Cornwall and Devon. —**Stannary court,** a lawcourt for the regulation of tin mines in the Stannaries. [from Latin *stannum* = tin]

Stanton /ˈstæntən/ Elizabeth Cady 1815–1902. US feminist who, with Susan B ◊Anthony, founded the National Woman Suffrage Association in 1869, the first women's movement in the USA, and was its first president. She and Anthony wrote and compiled the *History of Women's Suffrage* 1881–86. Stanton also worked for the abolition of slavery.

Stanwyck /ˈstænwɪk/ Barbara. Stage name of Ruby Stevens 1907–1990. US film actress of the 1930s to 1950s. Often cast as an independently minded woman of the world, she also excelled in villainous roles, as in *Double Indemnity* 1944. Her other films include *Stella Dallas* 1937, *Ball of Fire* 1942, and *Executive Suite* 1954.

stanza /ˈstænzə/ *n.* a group of lines in a poem. Each stanza has a set, repeatable pattern of metre and rhyme and is normally divided from the following stanza by a blank line. [Italian, originally = standing place, from *stare* = stand]

staphylococcus /ˌstæfɪləˈkɒkəs/ *n.* (*plural* **staphylococci** /-iː/) a form of pus-producing bacterium. —**staphylococcal** *adj.* [from Greek *staphulē* = bunch of grapes and *kokkos* = berry]

staple[1] /ˈsteɪpəl/ *n.* **1.** a U-shaped metal bar or piece of wire with pointed ends, driven into wood etc. to hold something in place. **2.** a piece of metal or wire driven into sheets of paper etc. and clenched to fasten them together. —*v.t.* to fasten or furnish with a staple. —**stapler** *n.* [Old English = Old High German *staffal* = foundation, Old Norse *stöpull* = pillar]

staple[2] /ˈsteɪpəl/ *adj.* principal, standard; important as a product or export. —*n.* **1.** an important (usually principal) article of commerce in a district or country. **2.** a chief element or material. **3.** the fibre of cotton or wool etc. as determining its quality. [from Old French *estaple* = market from Middle Low German or Middle Dutch]

star *n.* **1.** a celestial body appearing as a luminous point in the night sky; a large self-luminous gaseous ball such as the Sun; a celestial body regarded as influencing a person's fortunes etc. Stars are born from ◊nebulae, and consist mostly of hydrogen and helium gases. They produce their own heat and light by nuclear reactions. Surface temperatures range from 2,000°C/3,600°F to above 30,000°C/54,000°F, and the corresponding colours range from blue-white to red. The brightest stars have masses 100 times that of the Sun, and emit as much light as millions of suns; they live for less

than a million years before exploding as ◊supernovae. The faintest stars are the ◊red dwarfs, less than one-thousandth the brightness of the Sun. **2.** a thing resembling a star in shape or appearance; a figure or object with radiating points, e.g. as a decoration or mark of rank, or showing a category of excellence. **3.** a famous or brilliant person, especially an actor, actress, or other performer; a principal performer in a play or film etc. —*v.t./i.* (**-rr-**) **1.** to mark or adorn (as) with a star or stars. **2.** to present or perform as a star actor etc. —**stardust** *n.* a multitude of stars looking like dust. **stargazer** *n.* (*colloquial*) an astronomer or astrologer. **star-studded** *adj.* covered with stars; including many famous actors etc. **star turn,** the main item in an entertainment etc. [Old English]

starboard /ˈstɑːbəd/ *n.* the right-hand side of a ship or aircraft looking forward. —*v.t.* to turn (the helm) to starboard. —**starboard tack,** a tack with the wind on the starboard side. [Old English from *steer*[1]]

starch *n.* **1.** a high-molecular-mass ◊carbohydrate, produced by plants as a food store; main dietary sources are cereals, legumes, and tubers, including potatoes. It consists of varying proportions of two ◊glucose polymers (◊polysaccharides): straight-chain (amylose) and branched (amylopectin) molecules. **2.** a preparation of this for stiffening linen etc. **3.** stiffness of manner, formality. —*v.t.* to stiffen (as) with starch. [compare Old High German *sterken* = stiffen]

Star Chamber 1. (*historical*) an English civil and criminal court, created in 1487 by Henry VII. It comprised some 20 or 30 judges. The Star Chamber became notorious under Charles I for judgements favourable to the king and to Archbishop ◊Laud and was abolished in 1641 by the ◊Long Parliament. **2.** In the UK, private ministerial meetings at which disputes between the Treasury and high-spending departments are resolved. [from the star-shaped ceiling decoration of the room in the Palace of Westminster, London, where its first meetings were held]

starchy *adj.* **1.** of or like starch; containing much starch. **2.** stiff and formal in manner. —**starchily** *adv.*, **starchiness** *n.*

star cluster a group of related stars, usually held together by gravity. Members of a star cluster are thought to form together from one large cloud of gas in space. **Open clusters** such as the Pleiades contain from a dozen to many hundreds of young stars, loosely scattered over several light years. ◊**Globular clusters** are larger and much more densely packed, containing perhaps 100,000 old stars.

stardom *n.* the position or fame of a star actor etc.

stare *v.t./i.* to look fixedly with the eyes wide open, especially with curiosity, surprise, or horror; to reduce (a person) to a specified condition by staring. —*n.* a staring gaze. —**stare a person in the face,** to be clearly evident or imminent. [Old English]

starfish *n.* an ◊echinoderm of the class Asteroidea with arms radiating from a central body. Usually there are five arms, but some species have more. They are covered with spines and small pincerlike organs. There are also a number of small tubular processes on the skin surface which assist in respiration. Starfish are predators, and vary in size from 1.2 cm/0.5 in to 90 cm/3 ft.

stark /stɑːk/ *adj.* **1.** desolate, bare; cheerless. **2.** sharply evident. **3.** downright, complete. **4.** completely naked. **5.** (*archaic*) stiff, rigid. —*adv.* completely, wholly. —**starkly** *adv.*, **starkness** *n.* [Old English]

Stark Freya 1893– . English traveller, mountaineer, and writer who for a long time has worked in South America. She described her explorations in the Middle East in many books, including *The Valley of the Assassins* 1934, *The Southern Gates of Arabia* 1936, and *A Winter in Arabia* 1940.

starlet /ˈstɑːlɪt/ *n.* a young film actress aspiring to become a star.

starlight *n.* light from the stars.

starling /ˈstɑːlɪŋ/ *n.* a bird *Sturnus vulgaris* that forms large flocks, common in N Eurasia and naturalized in North America from the late 19th century. The black, speckled plumage is glossed with green and purple. Its own call is a bright whistle, but it is a mimic of the songs of other birds. It is about 20 cm/8 in long. [Old English]

Starling Ernest Henry 1866–1927. English physiologist who discovered ◊secretin and coined the word 'hormone'.

He formulated **Starling's law**, which states that the force of the heart's contraction is a function of the length of the muscle fibres. He is considered one of the founders of endocrinology.

starlit *adj.* lighted by stars; with stars visible.

Star of David *or* **Magen David** a six-pointed star (made with two equilateral triangles), a symbol of Judaism since the 17th century. It is the central motif on the flag of Israel, and, since 1897, the emblem of Zionism. [Hebrew = shield of David]

starry *adj.* full of or bright with stars. —**starry-eyed** *adj.* (*colloquial*) bright-eyed, romantic but unpractical.

start *v.t./i.* **1.** to set in motion or action; to begin or cause to begin operating. **2.** to cause or enable to begin; to establish or found; to conceive (a baby). **3.** to begin a journey etc. **4.** to make a sudden movement from pain or surprise etc. **5.** to spring suddenly. **6.** to rouse (game etc.) from a lair. **7.** (of timber etc.) to become loose or displaced; to cause (timber) to do this. —*n.* **1.** the beginning; the place where a race is begun. **2.** an advantage granted in beginning a race; an advantageous initial position in life or business etc. **3.** a sudden movement of pain or surprise etc. —**for a start,** as a thing to start with. **starting block,** a shaped block against which a runner braces his feet at the start of a race. **starting price,** the final odds before the start of a horse race etc. **start off,** to begin; to start to move. **start out,** to begin; to begin a journey. **start up,** to rise suddenly; to come or bring into existence or action. [compare Old High German *sturzen* = overthrow, rush]

START acronym from ◊Strategic Arms Reduction Talks.

starter *n.* **1.** a device for starting the engine of a motor vehicle etc. **2.** a person giving the signal for the start of a race. **3.** a horse or competitor starting in a race. **4.** the first course of a meal.

startle *v.t.* to give a shock or surprise to. [Old English]

starve *v.t./i.* **1.** to die of hunger or suffer acutely from lack of food, to cause to do this; (*colloquial*) to feel very hungry or very cold. **2.** to be deprived or short of something needed or wanted; to cause to be in this position. **3.** to compel by starving. —**starvation** /-'veɪʃən/ *n.* [Old English = die]

starveling /'stɑːvlɪŋ/ *n.* a starving person or animal.

Star Wars the popular term for the ◊Strategic Defense Initiative announced by US president Reagan in 1983.

stash *v.t.* (*slang*) to conceal, to stow. —*n.* (*slang*) **1.** a hiding place. **2.** a thing hidden.

stasis /'steɪsɪs, 'stæ-/ *n.* (*plural* **stases** /-iːz/) a stoppage of flow or circulation. [Greek = standing]

state *n.* **1.** the quality of a person's or thing's characteristics or circumstances. **2.** (*colloquial*) an excited or agitated condition of mind. **3.** a territory that forms its own domestic and foreign policy, acting through laws that are typically decided by a government and carried out, by force if necessary, by agents of that government; part of a federal republic; civil government. **4.** pomp. —*adj.* of or concerned with the state or its ceremonial occasions. —*v.t.* **1.** to express in speech or writing. **2.** to fix or specify. **3.** in music, to play (a theme etc.), especially for the first time. —**in** *or* **into a fixed state,** in or into an excited or anxious or untidy condition. **lie in state,** to be laid in a public place of honour before burial. **State Enrolled Nurse,** in the UK, a nurse enrolled on a state register and having a qualification lower than that of a State Registered Nurse. **state of play,** the position in which a matter or business stands at a particular time. **State Registered Nurse,** in the UK, a nurse enrolled on a state register and more highly qualified than a State Enrolled Nurse. **the States,** the ◊United States of America. [from Latin *status* = standing]

state change in science, a change in the physical state of a material. For instance, melting, boiling, evaporation, and their opposites (solidification and condensing) are state changes.

State Department (Department of State) the US government department responsible for ◊foreign relations, headed by the ◊secretary of state, the senior cabinet officer.

statehood *n.* the condition of being a state.

stateless *adj.* having no nationality or citizenship.

stately *adj.* dignified, imposing. —**stately home,** a large grand house, especially one of historical interest. —**stateliness** *n.*

statement /'steɪtmənt/ *n.* **1.** stating, being stated. **2.** expression in words; a thing stated. **3.** a formal account

of facts, especially of transactions in a bank account or of the amount due to a shop or supplier.

stateroom *n.* **1.** a state apartment. **2.** a private compartment in a passenger ship.

States General 1. (*historical*) the former French parliament that consisted of three estates: nobility, clergy, and commons. First summoned in 1302, it declined in importance as the power of the crown grew. It was not called at all between 1614 and 1789; it was called in 1789 because the crown needed to institute fiscal reforms to avoid financial collapse. Once called, the demands made by the States General formed the first phase in the ◊French Revolution. **2.** the Dutch parliament.

statesman *n.* (*plural* **statesmen**) a person skilled in affairs of state; a sagacious, far-sighted politician. —**statesmanlike** *adj.*, **statesmanship** *n.*, **stateswoman** *n.fem.*

states of matter the forms (solid, liquid, or gas) in which material can exist. Whether a material is solid, liquid, or gas depends on its temperature and the pressure on it. The transition between states takes place at definite temperatures, called melting point and boiling point.

static /'stætɪk/ *adj.* **1.** stationary; not movable; not acting, not changing. **2.** concerned with bodies at rest or forces in equilibrium; of force acting by weight without motion (as opposed to *dynamic*). —*n.* **1.** static electricity. **2.** atmospherics. —**statically** *adv.* [from Greek *statikos* (*sta-* = stand)]

static electricity an ◊electric charge acquired by a body by means of electrostatic induction or friction and not flowing as current. Rubbing different materials can produce static electricity, seen in the sparks produced on combing one's hair or removing a nylon shirt. In some processes static electricity is useful, as in paint spraying, where the parts to be sprayed are charged with electricity of opposite polarity to that on the paint droplets, and in ◊xerography.

statics *n.pl.* (usually treated as *singular*) **1.** the branch of mechanics concerned with the behaviour of bodies at rest and forces in equilibrium, and distinguished from ◊dynamics. **2.** static.

station /'steɪʃən/ *n.* **1.** a place or building etc. where a person or thing stands or is placed or where a particular activity, especially a public service, is based or organized. **2.** a regular stopping place on a railway line; the buildings at this. **3.** an establishment engaged in broadcasting. **4.** a military or naval base; the inhabitants of this. **5.** position in life, rank or status. **6.** (*Australian*) a large sheep farm or cattle farm. —*v.t.* to assign a station to; to put in position. —**station manager** *or* **stationmaster,** the official in charge of a railway station. **station wagon,** (*US*) an estate car. [from Old French from Latin *statio* (*stare* = stand)]

stationary /'steɪʃənərɪ/ *adj.* not moving; not intended to be moved; not changing in amount or quantity. [from Latin]

stationer /'steɪʃənə/ *n.* a dealer in stationery. [from Latin in the sense 'shopkeeper' (who is stationary) as opposed to pedlar]

stationery /'steɪʃənərɪ/ *n.* writing materials, office supplies etc.

Stationery Office, His/Her Majesty's (HMSO) an office established in 1786 to supply books and stationery to British government departments, and to superintend the printing of government reports and other papers, and books and pamphlets on subjects ranging from national works of art to industrial and agricultural processes. The corresponding establishment in the USA is the Government Printing Office.

stations of the Cross in the Christian church, a series of 14 crosses, usually each with a picture or image, depicting the 14 stages in Jesus' journey to the Crucifixion.

statistic /stə'tɪstɪk/ *n.* a statistical fact or item. [from German from Latin *status* = standing]

statistical /stə'tɪstɪkəl/ *adj.* of or concerned with statistics. —**statistical inference,** the science of drawing reliable conclusions from apparently random collections of numerical data, and of estimating the probability of the truth of those conclusions. —**statistically** *adv.*

statistics /stə'tɪstɪks/ *n.pl.* **1.** numerical data systematically collected. **2.** (usually treated as *singular*) the art of organizing numerical data so as to exhibit what is significant, especially the norm or ◊mean and deviations from it. ◊Probability is the branch of statistics dealing with predictions of events. —**statistician** /stæti'stɪʃən/ n.

statuary /'stætjuərɪ/ adj. of or for statues. —n. 1. statues; the making of these. 2. a maker of statues. [from Latin]

statue /'stætjuː, -tʃuː/ n. a sculptured, moulded, or cast figure of a person or animal etc., usually of life size or larger. [from Old French from Latin statua (stare = stand)]

statuesque /stætju'esk, stætʃ-/ adj. like a statue in size, dignity, or stillness. —**statuesquely** adv., **statuesqueness** n.

statuette /stætju'et, stætʃ-/ n. a small statue.

stature /'stætjə, -tʃə/ n. 1. the natural height of the body. 2. greatness gained by ability or achievement. [from Old French from Latin statura (stare = stand)]

status /'steɪtəs/ n. 1. a person's position or rank in relation to others; a person's or thing's legal position. 2. high rank or prestige. —**status quo**, the state of affairs as it is or as it was before a recent change. **status symbol**, a possession or activity etc. regarded as evidence of a person's high status. [Latin = standing]

statute /'stætjuːt/ n. 1. a law passed by a legislative body. 2. a rule of an institution. —**statute book**, the statute law; a book or books containing this. **statute law**, a statute; statutes collectively. **statute mile**, see ◊mile. [from Old French from Latin statuere = set up]

statutory /'stætjutərɪ/ adj. enacted or required by statute. —**statutorily** adv.

Staudinger /'ʃtaudɪŋə/ Hermann 1881–1965. German organic chemist, founder of macromolecular chemistry, who carried out pioneering research into the structure of albumen and cellulose. He was awarded the Nobel Prize for Chemistry in 1953.

Stauffenberg /'ʃtaufənbeəg/ Claus von 1907–1944. German colonel in World War II who, in a conspiracy to assassinate Hitler, planted a bomb in the dictator's headquarters conference room in the Wolf's Lair at Rastenburg, East Prussia, on 20 July 1944. Hitler was merely injured, and Stauffenberg and 200 others were later executed by the Nazi regime.

staunch /stɔːntʃ/ adj. 1. firm in attitude, opinion, or loyalty. 2. (of a ship or joint etc.) watertight, airtight. —**staunchly** adv. [from Old French estanche]

staurolite n. a silicate mineral, $(Fe,Mg)_2(Al,Fe)_9Si_4O_{20}(OH)_2$. It forms brown crystals that may be twinned in the form of a cross. It is a useful indicator of medium grade (moderate temperature and pressure) in metamorphic rocks formed from clay sediments.

stave n. 1. each of the curved pieces of wood forming the sides of a cask or pail etc. 2. in music, a staff. 3. a stanza, a verse. —v.t. (past and past participle stove or staved) to break a hole in; to knock out of shape. —**stave in**, to crush by forcing inwards. **stave off**, to avert or defer (danger or misfortune etc.). [variant of staff]

staves see ◊staff.

Stavropol a territory of the Russian Soviet Federal Socialist Republic, lying N of the Caucasus mountains; area 80,600 sq km/31,128 sq mi; population (1985) 2,715,000. The capital is Stavropol. Irrigated land produces grain and sheep are also reared. There are natural gas deposits.

stay[1] v.t./i. 1. to continue to be in the same place or condition, not to depart or change. 2. to dwell temporarily, especially as a guest or visitor. 3. to stop or pause in movement, action, or speech; to cause to do this. 4. to postpone (judgement etc.). 5. to assuage (hunger etc.) especially for a short time. 6. to show endurance. —n. 1. an action or period of staying. 2. suspension or postponement of the execution of a sentence etc. —**stay-at-home** adj. remaining habitually at home; —n. a person who does this. **stay the course**, to endure a struggle etc. to the end. **stay in**, to remain indoors. **staying power**, endurance. **stay the night**, to remain until the next day. **stay put**, (colloquial) to remain where it is placed or where one is. [from Anglo-French estai from Latin stare = stand]

stay[2] n. 1. a prop or support. 2. a rope etc. supporting a mast or flagstaff etc. 3. a tie piece in an aircraft. 4. (in plural) a corset. [Old English]

stayer n. a person or animal with great endurance.

staysail /'steɪseɪl, -səl/ n. a sail extended on a stay.

STD abbreviation of 1. subscriber trunk dialling. 2. sexually transmitted disease, a term encompassing not only traditional ◊venereal disease, but also a growing list of conditions, such as ◊AIDS and scabies, which are known to be spread primarily by sexual contact.

stead /sted/ n. **in a person's** or **thing's stead**, instead of him or her or it; as a substitute. **stand in good stead**, to be advantageous or serviceable to (a person). [Old English]

steadfast adj. firm and not changing or yielding. —**steadfastly** adv., **steadfastness** n.

steady /'stedɪ/ adj. 1. firmly in position, not tottering or rocking or wavering. 2. done, operating, or happening in a uniform and regular manner. 3. constant in mind or conduct. 4. serious and dependable in character. —v.t./i. to make or become steady. —adv. steadily. —n. (colloquial) a regular boyfriend or girlfriend. —**go steady with**, (colloquial) to have as a regular boyfriend or girlfriend. **steady on!** be careful! —**steadily** adv., **steadiness** n. [from stead]

steady-state theory the theory that the universe appears the same wherever (and whenever) viewed. This seems, however, to be refuted by the existence of cosmic background radiation.

steak /steɪk/ n. 1. a thick slice of meat (especially beef) or fish, cut for grilling or frying. 2. beef from the front of the animal, cut for stewing or braising. —**steakhouse** n. a restaurant specializing in beefsteaks. [from Old Norse, related to stikna = be roasted]

steal v.t./i. (past stole; past participle stolen) 1. to take (another's property) illegally or without permission, especially secretly. 2. to obtain surreptitiously or by surprise; to gain insidiously or artfully etc. 3. to move or come silently or gradually. —n. (US colloquial) 1. stealing, theft. 2. an (unexpectedly) easy task or good bargain. —**steal a march on**, to gain an advantage over by acting surreptitiously or anticipating. **steal a person's thunder**, see ◊thunder. **steal the show**, to outshine the other performers unexpectedly. [Old English]

stealth /stelθ/ n. secrecy, secret or surreptitious behaviour.

stealthy /'stelθɪ/ adj. acting or done by stealth. —**stealthily** adv., **stealthiness** n.

steam n. 1. the invisible gas into which water is changed by boiling, used as motive power. 2. the visible vapour of minute suspended water particles that forms when steam condenses in the air. 3. (colloquial) energy, power. —v.t./i. 1. to give out steam. 2. to cook or treat by steam. 3. to move by the power of steam; (colloquial) to work or move vigorously or rapidly. —**steam-hammer** n. a forging hammer worked by steam. **steam iron**, an electric iron emitting steam from its flat surface. **steam radio**, (colloquial) radio broadcasting regarded as antiquated by comparison with television. **steam train**, a train pulled by a steam engine; see ◊railway. **steam up**, to cover or become covered with condensed steam. **be** or **get steamed up**, to be or become excited or agitated. [Old English]

steamboat n. a steam-driven boat, especially a paddle-wheel craft used widely on rivers in the 19th century.

steam engine an engine that uses the power of steam to produce useful work. It was the principal power source during the British Industrial Revolution in the 18th century. The first successful steam engine was built in 1712 by Thomas Newcomen: steam was admitted to a cylinder as a piston moved up, and was then condensed by a spray of water, allowing air pressure to force the piston downwards. James Watt improved Newcomen's engine in 1769 by condensing the steam outside the cylinder (thus saving energy formerly used to reheat the cylinder) and by using steam to force the piston upwards. Watt also introduced the **double-acting engine**, in which steam is alternately sent to each end of the cylinder. The **compound engine** of 1781 uses the exhaust from one cylinder to drive the piston of another. The **high-pressure steam engine** was developed in 1802 by Richard Trevithick, and led to the development of the steam locomotive. A later development was the steam ◊turbine, still used today to power ships and generators in power stations. A steam engine is an external combustion-engine.

steamer n. 1. a steamship. 2. a container for steaming food etc.

steamroller n. 1. a heavy, slow-moving locomotive with a roller, used in road-making. 2. a crushing power or force. —*v.t.* to crush or move along (as) with a steam-roller.

steamship *n.* a steam-driven ◊ship.

steamy *adj.* 1. of, like, or full of steam. 2. (*colloquial*) erotic. —**steamily** *adv.*, **steaminess** *n.*

stearic acid $CH_3(CH_2)_{16}COOH$, a saturated long-chain ◊fatty acid, soluble in alcohol and ether but not in water. It is found in many fats and oils, and is used to make soap and candles and as a lubricant. The salts of stearic acid are called stearates.

steatite /'sti:ətaɪt/ *n.* a kind of usually grey talc with a greasy feel. [from Latin from Greek *stear* = tallow]

steed *n.* (*literary*) a horse. [Old English *stēda* = stallion]

steel /sti:l/ *n.* 1. a malleable alloy of iron and up to 1.7% carbon, sometimes with other elements, such as manganese, phosphorus, sulphur, and silicon, capable of being tempered to many different degrees of hardness. The USA, the USSR, and Japan are the main steel producers. Steel has innumerable uses, including ship and automobile manufacture, skyscraper frames, and machinery of all kinds. 2. a steel rod for sharpening knives. 3. (*literary*; not in *plural*) a sword. 4. great strength or firmness. —*adj.* of or like steel. —*v.t.* to harden or make resolute. —**steel wool**, fine shavings of steel massed together for use as an abrasive. [Old English]

Steel David 1938– . British politician, leader of the Liberal Party 1976–88. He entered into a compact with the Labour government 1977–78, and into an alliance with the Social Democratic Party (SDP) in 1983. Having supported the Liberal-SDP merger (forming the ◊Social and Liberal Democrats), he resigned the leadership in 1988.

steel band a type of musical ensemble common in the West Indies, consisting mostly of percussion instruments made from oil drums that give a sweet, metallic, ringing tone.

Steele /sti:l/ Richard 1672–1729. Irish essayist who founded the journal *The Tatler* 1709–11, in which Joseph ◊Addison collaborated. They continued their joint work in *The Spectator*, also founded by Steele, 1711–12, and *The Guardian* 1713. He also wrote plays, such as *The Conscious Lovers* 1722.

steely *adj.* of or like steel; inflexibly severe. —**steeliness** *n.*

steelyard *n.* a weighing apparatus with a graduated arm along which a weight slides.

Steen /stem/ Jan 1626–1679. Dutch painter. Born in Leiden, he was also active in The Hague, Delft, and Haarlem. He painted humorous everyday scenes, mainly set in taverns or bourgeois households, as well as portraits and landscapes.

steep[1] *adj.* 1. sloping sharply, hard to climb. 2. (of a rise or fall) rapid. 3. (*colloquial*) exorbitant, unreasonable; exaggerated, incredible. —*n.* a steep slope, a precipice. —**steeply** *adv.*, **steepness** *n.* [Old English]

steep[2] *v.t.* to soak or bathe in a liquid. —*n.* 1. the action of steeping. 2. a liquid for steeping things in. —**steep in**, to pervade or imbue with; to make deeply acquainted with (a subject etc.).

steepen *v.t./i.* to make or become steep.

steeple *n.* a tall tower, especially one surmounted by a spire, above the roof of a church. [Old English]

steeplechase *n.* 1. a horse race across a tract of country or on a racecourse with hedges, ditches etc., to jump. 2. a cross-country foot race. —**steeplechasing** *n.* the sport of riding in steeplechases. —**steeplechaser** *n.*

steeplejack *n.* a person who climbs steeples, tall chimneys, etc., to repair them.

steer[1] *v.t./i.* 1. to direct the course of; to guide (a vehicle or boat etc.) by means of its mechanism. 2. to be able to be steered. —**steer clear of**, to take care to avoid. **steering column**, the column on which a steering wheel is mounted. **steering committee,** a committee deciding the order of business, the general course of operations etc. **steering wheel,** the wheel by which a vehicle, vessel etc., is steered. —**steerer** *n.* [Old English]

steer[2] *n.* a young male ox, especially a bullock. [Old English]

steerage *n.* 1. steering. 2. (*obsolete*) the part of a ship assigned to passengers travelling at the cheapest rate.

steersman *n.* (*plural* **steersmen**) one who steers a ship.

Steele *As founder of* The Tatler *in 1709, Richard Steele aimed to raise moral and Christian standards as well as to amuse.*

Stefan /'ʃtefæn/ Joseph 1835–1893. Austrian physicist who established one of the basic laws of heat radiation in 1874, since known as the ◊**Stefan–Boltzmann law.** This states that the heat radiated by a hot body is proportional to the fourth power of its absolute temperature.

Stefan–Boltzmann constant /'stefən 'bəʊltsmən/ in physics, a constant relating the energy emitted by a black body (a hypothetical body that absorbs or emits all the energy falling on it) to its temperature. Its value is $5.6697 \times 10^{-8} \text{ W m}^{-2} \text{ K}^{-4}$.

Stefan–Boltzmann law in physics, a law that relates the energy, E, radiated away from a perfect emitter (a ◊black body), to the temperature, T, of that body. It has the form $M = \sigma T^4$, where M is the energy radiated per unit area per second, T is the temperature, and σ is the Stefan–Boltzmann constant.

Steiermark /'ʃtaɪəmɑːk/ the German name for ◊Styria, province of Austria.

Steiger /'staɪgə/ Rod(ney Stephen) 1925– . US character actor who often played leading film roles. His work includes *On the Waterfront* 1954, *In the Heat of the Night* 1967, and the title role in *W C Fields and Me* 1976.

stein /staɪn/ *n.* a large earthenware mug, especially for beer. [German = stone]

Stein Gertrude 1874–1946. US writer. She influenced writers such as ◊Hemingway and Scott ◊Fitzgerald by her cinematic technique, use of repetition and absence of punctuation: devices to convey immediacy and realism. Her works include the self-portrait *The Autobiography of Alice B Toklas* 1933.

Steinbeck /'staɪnbek/ John (Ernst) 1902–1968. US novelist. His work includes *Of Mice and Men* 1937, *The Grapes of Wrath* 1939, *Cannery Row* 1945, *East of Eden* 1952 (a film was made with James Dean), and *Winter of our Discontent* 1961. Many of his books deal with the lives of working people. He received the Nobel Prize for Literature in 1962.

stela /'sti:lə/ *n.* or **stele** /-i:/ (*plural* **stelae** /-i:/) an ancient upright slab or pillar, usually inscribed and sculptured, especially as a gravestone. [Latin from Greek *stēlē* = standing block]

Stella /'stelə/ Frank 1936– . US painter, a pioneer of the hard-edged geometric trend in abstract art that followed Abstract Expressionism. From around 1960 he also experimented with the shape of his canvases.

stellar /'stelə/ *adj.* of a star or stars. [from Latin *stella* = star]

stem[1] *n.* 1. the main supporting axis of a plant that bears the leaves, buds, and reproductive structures; it may be simple or branched. The plant stem usually grows above ground, although some grow underground, including ◊rhizomes, ◊corms, ◊rootstocks, and ◊tubers. Stems contain a continuous vascular system that conducts water and food to and from all parts of the plant. 2. any stem-shaped part, e.g. the slender part of a wineglass between bowl and foot. 3. the root or main part of a noun or verb etc., to which case endings etc. are added. 4. the curved upright timber or metal piece at the fore end of a ship; a ship's bows. —*v.i.* (-mm-) 1. (with *from*) to originate. 2. to make headway against (the tide etc.). [Old English]

stem[2] *v.t./i.* (-mm-) 1. to restrain the flow of (*literally* or *figuratively*), to dam. 2. in skiing, to retard oneself by forcing the heel outwards. —*n.* in skiing, the act of stemming. —**stem turn**, a turn made by stemming with one ski. [from Old Norse]

stench *n.* a foul smell. [Old English *stenc* = (any) smell]

stencil /'stensəl/ *n.* a thin sheet in which a pattern is cut, used to produce a corresponding pattern on the surface beneath it by applying ink or paint etc.; a pattern so produced. —*v.t.* (-ll-) to produce (a pattern) with a stencil; to mark (a surface) thus. [originally = ornament, from Old French *estanceler* = cover with stars from Latin *scintilla* = spark]

Stendhal /stænˈdæl/ pen name of Marie Henri Beyle 1783–1842. French novelist. His two major novels *Le Rouge et le noir*/*The Red and the Black* 1830 and *La Chartreuse de Parme*/*The Charterhouse of Parme* 1839 were pioneering works in their treatment of disguise and hypocrisy; a review of the latter by ◊Balzac in 1840 furthered Stendhal's reputation.

stenography /steˈnɒɡrəfi/ *n.* the writing of shorthand. —**stenographer** *n.* [from Greek *stenos* = narrow and *graphia* = writing]

stenosis *n.* the narrowing of a body vessel, duct, or opening, usually due to disease.

stentorian /stenˈtɔːrɪən/ *adj.* (of a voice etc.) loud and powerful. [from Greek *Stentōr*, a herald in the Trojan War]

step *n.* 1. a complete action of moving and placing one leg in walking or running; the distance covered by this; a unit of movement in dancing. 2. a measure taken, especially one of several in a course of action. 3. a surface on which the foot is placed when ascending or descending, a stair or tread; (in *plural*) a stepladder. 4. a short distance. 5. a mark or sound made by a foot in walking etc.; a manner of stepping. 6. a stage in a scale of promotion or precedence etc. —*v.t./i.* (-pp-) 1. to lift and set down the foot or alternate feet as in walking. 2. to go a short distance or progress (as) by stepping. 3. to measure (a distance) by stepping. —**break step**, to get out of step. **in step**, putting the foot to the ground at the same time as others, especially in marching; conforming to the actions etc. of others. **keep step**, to remain in step. **mind** *or* **watch one's step**, to take care. **out of step**, not in step, **step by step**, gradually, cautiously. **step down**, to resign. **step in**, to enter; to intervene. **stepladder** *n.* a short self-supporting ladder with flat steps. **step on it**, (*slang*) to go or act faster. **step out**, to take long brisk steps; to go out to enjoy oneself socially. **stepping stone**, a raised stone (usually one of a series) as a means of crossing a stream etc.; a means of progress towards achieving something. **step up**, to come up or forward; to increase the rate or volume of. [Old English]

step- prefix denoting a relationship like the one specified but resulting from a parent's remarriage. [Old English]

stepbrother *n.* a male child of one's step-parent's previous marriage.

stepchild *n.* a spouse's child by a previous marriage.

stepdaughter *n.* a female stepchild.

stepfather *n.* a male step-parent.

stephanotis /stefəˈnəʊtɪs/ *n.* a fragrant tropical climbing plant of the genus *Stephanotis*. [from Greek = fit for a wreath (*stephanos*)]

Stephen /'stiːvən/ *c.*1097–1154. King of England from 1135. A grandson of William I, he was elected king in 1135, although he had previously recognized Henry I's daughter ◊Matilda as heiress to the throne. Matilda landed in England in 1139, and civil war disrupted the country until 1153, when Stephen acknowledged Matilda's son, Henry II, as his own heir.

Stephen Leslie 1832–1904. English critic, first editor of the *Dictionary of National Biography* and father of the novelist Virginia ◊Woolf.

Stephen, St died *c.*AD 35. The first Christian martyr; he was stoned to death. Feast day 26 Dec.

Stephenson /'stiːvənsən/ George 1781–1848. English engineer who built the first successful steam locomotive, and who also invented a safety lamp in 1815. He was appointed engineer of the Stockton and Darlington Railway, the world's first public railway, in 1821, and of the Liverpool and Manchester Railway in 1826. In 1829 he won a £500 prize with his locomotive *Rocket*.

Stephenson Robert 1803–1859. English civil engineer who constructed railway bridges such as the high-level bridge at Newcastle upon Tyne, England, and the Menai and Conway tubular bridges in Wales. He was the son of George Stephenson.

stepmother *n.* a female step-parent.

step-parent *n.* a mother's or father's later spouse.

steppe /step/ *n.* a level treeless plain; especially the temperate grasslands of Europe and Asia. [from Russian]

step rocket another term for ◊multi-stage rocket.

stepsister *n.* a female child of one's step-parent's previous marriage.

stepson *n.* a male stepchild.

Steptoe /'steptəʊ/ Patrick Christopher 1913–1988. English obstetrician who pioneered ◊in vitro fertilization. Steptoe, together with biologist Robert Edwards, was the first to succeed in implanting in the womb an egg fertilized outside the body. The first 'test-tube baby' was born in 1978.

steradian *n.* the unit (symbol sr) of solid (three-dimensional) angle, the three-dimensional equivalent of the ◊radian. One steradian is the angle at the centre of a sphere when an area on the surface of the sphere equal to the square of the sphere's radius is joined to the centre. [from *stereo* and *radian*]

Sterea Ellas-Evvoia /'sterɪə 'ɛlæs 'evɪə/ the region of central Greece and Euboea occupying the southern part of the Greek mainland between the Ionian and Aegean seas and including the island of Euboea; population (1981) 1,099,800; area 24,391 sq km/9,421 sq mi. The chief city is Athens.

stereo /'sterɪəʊ, 'stɪər-/ *n.* (*plural* **stereos**) 1. a stereophonic record player etc. 2. stereophony. 3. a stereoscope. 4. a stereotype. —*adj.* 1. stereophonic. 2. stereoscopic. [abbreviation]

stereo- /sterɪəʊ-, stɪərɪəʊ-/ in combinations, having three dimensions. [from Greek *stereos* = solid]

stereochemistry /sterɪəʊˈkemɪstrɪ, 'stɪər-/ *n.* the branch of chemistry dealing with the composition of matter as affected by the relations of atoms in space.

stereophonic /sterɪəˈfɒnɪk, stɪər-/ *adj.* (of sound reproduction) using two complementary channels leading to two loudspeakers, which gives a more natural depth to the sound. Stereo recording began with the introduction of two-track magnetic tape in the 1950s. See ◊hi-fi. —**stereophonically** *adv.*, **stereophony** /-'ɒfənɪ/ *n.*

stereoscope /'sterɪəskəʊp, 'stɪər-/ *n.* a device by which two slightly different photographs etc. are viewed together, giving the impression of depth and solidity. —**stereoscopic** /-'skɒpɪk/ *adj.*, **stereoscopically** /-'skɒpɪkəlɪ/ *adv.*

stereotype /'sterɪətaɪp, 'stɪər-/ *n.* 1. a fixed, exaggerated, and preconceived description about a certain group or society. It is based on prejudice rather than fact, but by repetition and with time, stereotypes become fixed in people's minds, resistant to change or factual evidence to the contrary. 2. a conventional idea or opinion or character etc. 3. a printing plate cast from a mould of composed type. —*v.t.* 1. (usually in *past participle*) to formalize, to make typical or conventional. 2. to print from a stereotype; to make a stereotype of. [from French]

sterile /'steraɪl/ *adj.* 1. not able to produce seed or offspring, barren. 2. free from living microorganisms. 3. without result, unproductive. —**sterility** /-'rɪlɪtɪ/ *n.* [from French or Latin *sterilis*]

sterilize /'sterɪlaɪz/ *v.t.* 1. to make sterile or free from living microorganisms. Methods include heat treatment (such as boiling), the use of chemicals (such as disinfectants), irradiation with gamma rays, and filtration. See also ◊asepsis. 2. to deprive of the power of reproduction, especially by removal or obstruction of reproductive organs. In women, this is normally achieved by sealing or tying off the ◊Fallopian tubes (tubal ligation) so that fertilization can no longer take place. In men, the transmission of sperm is blocked by ◊vasectomy. —**sterilization** /-'zeɪʃən/ n.

sterling /'stɜːlɪŋ/ adj. **1.** of or in British money. **2.** (of coin or precious metal) genuine, of standard value or purity. **3.** (of a person or qualities etc.) of solid worth, genuine, reliable. —n. British money. —**sterling silver,** silver of 92.5% purity. The rest is copper, which hardens the silver, making it more useful.

stern[1] adj. strict and severe, not lenient or cheerful or kindly. —**sternly** adv., **sternness** n. [Old English]

stern[2] n. the rear part of a ship or boat; any rear part. —**sternpost** n. the central upright timber etc. of the stern, usually bearing the rudder.

Sternberg /'ʃtɛənbeək/ Josef von 1894–1969. Austrian film director who lived in the USA from childhood. He worked with Marlene Dietrich on *The Blue Angel/Der blaue Engel* 1930 and other films. He favoured striking imagery over narrative in his work, which includes *Underworld* 1927 and *Blonde Venus* 1932.

Sterne /stɜːn/ Laurence 1713–1768. Irish writer, creator of the comic antihero Tristram Shandy. *The Life and Opinions of Tristram Shandy, Gent* 1760–67, an eccentrically whimsical and bawdy novel, foreshadowed many of the techniques and devices of 20th-century novelists, including James Joyce. His other works include *A Sentimental Journey through France and Italy* 1768.

sternum n. (*plural* **sternums** or **sterna**) the breastbone, a large, flat bone at the front of the chest, joined to the ribs. It gives protection to the heart and lungs. —**sternal** adj. [from Greek *sternon* = chest]

steroid /'stɪərɔɪd, 'steɪ-/ n. any of a large group of fat-soluble organic compounds whose molecules all have a basic structure that consists of four fused rings of carbon atoms. Steroids include the sex hormones, such as ◊testosterone, the corticosteroid hormones produced by the ◊adrenal gland, bile acids, and ◊cholesterol. The term is commonly used to refer to ◊anabolic steroid, a synthetic hormone.

sterol /'stɪərɒl, 'steɪ-/ n. any of a group of solid, cyclic, unsaturated alcohols, with a complex structure, consisting of four carbon rings; cholesterol is an example. They are important in vitamin synthesis. Steroids are derived from sterols. [from *cholesterol* etc.]

stertorous /'stɜːtərəs/ adj. (of breathing etc.) laboured and noisy. —**stertorously** adv. [from Latin *stertere* = snore]

stet v.imper. (placed beside a deleted word on a proof sheet etc.) let it stand as printed or written. [Latin, third person singular present subjunctive of *stare* = stand]

stethoscope /'steθəskəʊp/ n. an instrument used for listening to sounds within the body, e.g. those of the heart and lungs. It consists of two earpieces connected by flexible tubes to a small plate that is placed against the body. It was invented in 1819 in France by René Théophile Hyacinthe ◊Laënnec. —**stethoscopic** /-'skɒpɪk/ adj. [from French from Greek *stēthos* = breast and *skopeō* = look at]

stetson /'stetsən/ n. a slouch hat with a very wide brim and a high crown. [from J B *Stetson*, American hatmaker (1830–1906)]

stevedore /'stiːvədɔː/ n. a person employed in loading and unloading ships. [from Spanish *estivar* = stow a cargo from Latin *stipare* = pack tight]

Stevens /'stiːvənz/ George 1904–1975. US film director who began as a director of photography. He made films such as *Swing Time* 1936 and *Gunga Din* 1939, and his reputation grew steadily, as did the length of his films. His later work included *A Place in the Sun* 1951, *Shane* 1953, and *Giant* 1956.

Stevens Siaka Probin 1905–1988. Sierra Leone politician, president 1971–85. He was the leader of the moderate left-wing All People's Congress (APC), from 1978 the country's only legal political party.

Stevens Wallace 1879–1955. US poet. An insurance-company executive, he was not recognized as a major poet until late in life. His volumes of elegant and philosophical poems include *Harmonium* 1923, *The Man with the Blue Guitar* 1937, and *Transport to Summer* 1947. *The Necessary Angel* 1951 is a collection of essays. He won the Pulitzer Prize in 1954 for his *Collected Poems*.

Stevenson /'stiːvənsən/ Adlai 1900–1965. US Democrat politician. As governor of Illinois 1949–53 he campaigned vigorously against corruption in public life, and as Democratic candidate for the presidency in 1952 and 1956 was twice defeated by Eisenhower. In 1945 he was chief US delegate at the founding conference of the United Nations.

An editor is one who separates the wheat from the chaff and prints the chaff.

Adlai Stevenson
The Stevenson Wit

Stevenson Robert Louis 1850–1894. Scottish novelist and poet, author of the adventure novel *Treasure Island* 1883. Later works included the novels *Kidnapped* 1886, *The Master of Ballantrae* 1889, *Dr Jekyll and Mr Hyde* 1886, and the anthology *A Child's Garden of Verses* 1885.

stew v.t./i. **1.** to cook or be cooked by long simmering in a closed vessel with a liquid. **2.** (*colloquial*) to swelter. —n. **1.** a dish of stewed meat etc. **2.** (*colloquial*) an agitated or angry state. —**stew in one's own juice,** to be obliged to suffer the consequences of one's own actions without help or intervention from others. [from Old French *estuver*]

steward /'stjuːəd/ n. **1.** a person employed to manage another's property, especially a great house or estate. **2.** a person responsible for supplies of food etc. for a college or club etc. **3.** a passengers' attendant on a ship, aircraft, or train. **4.** an official in charge of a race meeting or show etc. —v.t./i. to act as a steward (of). —**Lord High Steward of England,** a high officer of state presiding at coronations. [Old English from *stig* = house and *weard* = ward]

stewardess n. a female steward, especially on a ship or aircraft.

stewardship n. **1.** the position or work of a steward. **2.** the organized pledging of specific amounts of money etc. to be given regularly to the church.

Stewart /'stjuːət/ Jackie (John Young) 1939– . Scottish motor-racing driver. He started in 99 races and, with manufacturer Ken Tyrrell, built up one of the sport's great partnerships. Until surpassed by Alain Prost of France in 1987, Stewart held the record for the most Formula One Grand Prix wins (27).

Stewart James 1908– . US actor who specialized in the role of the stubbornly honest, ordinary American in such films as *Mr Smith Goes to Washington* 1939, *The Philadelphia Story* 1940 (Academy Award), *It's a Wonderful Life* 1946, *Harvey* 1950, *The Man from Laramie* 1955, and *The FBI Story* 1959. His films with director Alfred ◊Hitchcock include *Rope* 1948, *Rear Window* 1954, *The Man Who Knew Too Much* 1956, and *Vertigo* 1958.

stewed adj. **1.** cooked by stewing. **2.** (of tea) bitter or strong from infusing for too long. **3.** (*slang*) drunk.

stick[1] n. **1.** a short slender branch or piece of wood, especially one trimmed for use as a support or weapon, or as firewood. **2.** a thin rod of wood etc. for a particular purpose; a thing resembling this in shape; the implement used to propel the ball in hockey or polo etc.; a gear lever; a conductor's baton; a more or less cylindrical piece of a substance, e.g. celery or dynamite; (*colloquial*) an item of furniture etc. **3.** punishment, especially by beating; adverse criticism. **4.** (*colloquial*) a person, especially one who is dull or unsociable. [Old English]

stick[2] v.t./i. (*past* and *past participle* **stuck**) **1.** to insert or thrust (a thing or its point) into something; to stab. **2.** to fix on or upon a pointed object; (*colloquial*) to put. **3.** to fix or be fixed (as) by glue or solution etc.; (*colloquial*) to remain in the same place; (*colloquial* of an accusation etc.) to be convincing or regarded as valid. **4.** to lose or deprive of the power of motion or action through friction, jamming, or some other impediment or difficulty. **5.** (*slang*) to endure, to tolerate. **6.** (*colloquial*) to impose a difficult or unpleasant task upon. **7.** to provide (a plant) with a stick as a support. —**be stuck for,** (*colloquial*) to be at a loss for or in need of. **be stuck on,** (*slang*) to be captivated by. **be stuck with,** (*colloquial*) to be unable to get rid of. **get stuck in** or **into,** (*slang*) to begin in earnest. **stick around,** (*slang*) to linger, to remain at the same place. **stick at,** (*colloquial*) to persevere with. **stick at nothing,** to allow nothing, especially no scruples, to deter one. **stick by** or **with,** to stay close or faithful to. **sticking plaster,** an adhesive plaster for wounds etc. **stick-in-the-mud** n. (*colloquial*) an unprogressive or old-fashioned person. **stick**

Stewart *Famous for his roles as the stubbornly honest, upright American, actor James Stewart is seen here portraying a dedicated investigator in the film* The FBI Story.

in one's throat, to be against one's principles. **stick it out**, (*colloquial*) to endure something unpleasant. **stick one's neck out**, to expose oneself to danger etc. by acting boldly. **stick out**, to protrude or cause to protrude. **stick out for**, to persist in demanding. **stick to**, to remain fixed on or to, to remain faithful to, to keep to (a subject etc.). **stick together**, (*colloquial*) to remain united or mutually loyal. **stick up**, to protrude or cause to protrude; to be or make erect; to fasten to an upright surface; (*slang*) to rob or threaten with a gun. **stick-up** *n*. (*slang*) a robbery with a gun. **stick up for**, to support or defend (a person or cause). [Old English]

sticker *n*. 1. an adhesive label. 2. a persistent person.

stick insect an insect of the order Phasmida, closely resembling a stick or twig. Many species are wingless. The longest reach a length of 30 cm/1 ft.

stickleback /'stɪkəlbæk/ *n*. a fish of the family Gasterosteidae, found in the northern hemisphere. It has a long body which can grow to 18 cm/7 in. It has spines along the back which take the place of the first dorsal fin, and which can be raised to make the fish difficult to eat for predators. [Old English = thorn-back]

stickler *n*. a person who insists on something. [from obsolete *stickle* = be umpire]

stickpin *n*. (*US*) a tiepin.

sticky *adj*. 1. sticking or tending to stick to what is touched. 2. (of weather) humid. 3. (*colloquial*) making or likely to make objections. 4. (*slang*) very unpleasant or difficult. —**sticky wicket**, in cricket, (*colloquial*) a pitch that is drying after rain and is difficult for batsmen; difficult circumstances. —**stickily** *adv*., **stickiness** *n*.

stiction /'stɪkʃən/ *n*. static friction, the friction which tends to prevent surfaces at rest from being set in motion. [from *static* and friction]

Stieglitz /'staɪglɪts/ Alfred 1864–1946. US photographer. After forming the Photo Secession group in 1903, he began the magazine *Camera Work*. Through exhibitions at his gallery '291' in New York he helped to establish photography as an art form. His works include 'Winter, Fifth Avenue' 1893 and 'Steerage' 1907. In 1924 he married the painter Georgia O'Keeffe, who was the model in many of his photographs.

stiff *adj*. 1. not flexible; not moving or changing its shape easily. 2. not fluid, thick and hard to stir. 3. difficult to move or deal with; (of a breeze) blowing strongly; (of a price or penalty) high, severe; (of a drink or dose) strong. 4. formal

in manner, not pleasantly sociable or friendly. 5. (*colloquial*) to an extreme degree. —*n*. (*slang*) 1. a corpse. 2. a foolish or useless person. —**stiff-necked** *adj*. obstinate; haughty. **stiff upper lip**, fortitude in enduring grief etc. **stiff with**, (*slang*) abundantly provided with. —**stiffly** *adv*., **stiffness** *n*. [Old English]

stiffen *v.t./i.* to make or become stiff. —**stiffener** *n*.

stifle[1] /'staɪfəl/ *v.t./i.* 1. to suffocate; to be or feel unable to breathe for lack of air. 2. to restrain, to suppress. —**stifling** *adj*.

stifle[2] /'staɪfəl/ *n*. the joint of a dog's or horse's etc. leg between hip and hock.

stigma /'stɪgmə/ *n*. (*plural* **stigmas**) 1. a mark or sign of disgrace or discredit. 2. in a flower, the surface at the tip of a ◊carpel that receives the ◊pollen. It often has short outgrowths, flaps, or hairs to trap pollen and may produce a sticky secretion to which the grains adhere. 3. (in *plural* **stigmata** /'stɪgmətə/) marks corresponding to those left on Jesus' body by the nails and spear at his crucifixion which are said to have appeared spontaneously on St Francis and other saints. [Latin from Greek = mark made by pointed instrument]

stigmatize /'stɪgmətaɪz/ *v.t.* to brand as unworthy or disgraceful. —**stigmatization** /-'zeɪʃən/ *n*. [from French or Latin from Greek]

Stijl, de /staɪl/ a group of 20th-century Dutch artists and architects led by ◊Mondrian from 1917. They believed in the concept of the 'designer'; that all life, work, and leisure should be surrounded by art; and that everything functional should also be aesthetic. The group had a strong influence on the ◊Bauhaus school. [Dutch = the style]

stile[1] *n*. an arrangement of steps allowing people but not animals to climb over a fence or wall. [Old English]

stile[2] *n*. a vertical piece in the frame of a panelled door, wainscot etc. A horizontal piece is a rail. [probably from Dutch *stijl* = pillar, doorpost]

stiletto /stɪ'letəʊ/ *n*. (*plural* **stilettos**) 1. a short dagger. 2. a pointed instrument for making eyelets etc. —**stiletto heel**, a high tapering heel of a shoe. [Italian, diminutive of *stilo* = dagger]

still[1] *adj*. 1. without or almost without motion or sound. 2. (of drinks) not effervescing. —*n*. 1. silence and calm. 2. an ordinary static photograph (as opposed to a motion picture), especially a single shot from a cinema film. —*adv*. 1. without moving. 2. even until or at a particular time. 3. nevertheless, all the same. 4. even, yet, increasingly. —*v.t./i.* to make or become still, to quieten. —**still birth**, a birth in which the child is born dead. **still life** (*plural* **still lifes**), a painting of inanimate objects, e.g. fruits. —**stillness** *n*. [Old English]

still[2] *n*. an apparatus for distilling spirituous liquors etc. —**still room**, a room for distilling, a housekeeper's storeroom in a large house. [from *distil*]

stillborn *adj*. 1. born dead. 2. (of an idea or plan etc.) not developing.

stilt *n*. 1. each of a pair of poles with supports for the feet enabling the user to walk at a distance above the ground. 2. each of a set of piles or posts supporting a building etc. [from Low German]

stilted *adj*. 1. (of literary style etc.) stiff and unnaturally formal. 2. standing on stilts. —**stiltedly** *adv*.

Stilton /'stɪltən/ *n*. a rich blue-veined cheese originally made at various places in Leicestershire, England, and formerly sold to travellers at a coaching inn at Stilton (now in Cambridgeshire) on the Great North Road from London.

Stilwell /'stɪlwel/ Joseph Warren 1883–1946. US general, nicknamed 'Vinegar Joe'. In 1942 he became US military representative in China, when he commanded the Chinese forces cooperating with the British (with whom he quarrelled) in Burma (now Myanmar); he later commanded all US forces in China, Burma, and India until recalled to the USA in 1944 after differences over nationalist policy with the ◊Guomindang (nationalist) leader Chiang Kai-shek. Subsequently he commanded the US 10th Army on the Japanese island of Okinawa.

stimulant /'stɪmjʊlənt/ *adj*. that stimulates, especially that increases bodily or mental activity. —*n*. a stimulant substance or influence; for example, ◊amphetamine. When given to children, stimulants may have a paradoxical, calming effect. Stimulants cause liver damage, are habit-forming, have limited therapeutic value, and are now prescribed only to treat ◊narcolepsy and to reduce the appetite in dieting. [from Latin]

stimulate /ˈstɪmjʊleɪt/ v.t. 1. to make more vigorous or active. 2. to apply a stimulus to. —**stimulation** /-ˈleɪʃən/ n., **stimulative** adj., **stimulator** n. [from Latin stimulare]

stimulus /ˈstɪmjʊləs/ n. (plural -li /-laɪ/) a stimulating thing or effect; something that produces a reaction in an organ or tissue. [Latin = goad]

sting n. 1. a sharp-pointed part or organ of an insect etc., used for wounding and often injecting poison. 2. a stiff sharp-pointed hair on certain plants, causing inflammation if touched. 3. infliction of a wound by a sting; the wound so inflicted. 4. any sharp bodily or mental pain; a wounding quality or effect. 5. (slang) a swindle. —v.t./i. (past and past participle **stung**) 1. to wound or affect with a sting; to be able to do this. 2. to cause to feel sharp bodily or mental pain. 3. to stimulate sharply as if by a sting. 4. (slang) to swindle, especially by overcharging; to extort money from. —**stinging nettle**, a ◊nettle that stings (as opposed to dead-nettle). **sting in the tail**, an unexpected pain or difficulty at the end. **stingray** n. a broad flatfish, especially of the family Dasyatidae, with a stinging tail; see ◊ray. [Old English]

stinger n. a thing that stings, especially a sharp, painful blow.

stingy /ˈstɪndʒɪ/ adj. spending, giving, or given grudgingly or in small amounts. —**stingily** adv., **stinginess** n.

stink v.t./i. (past **stank** or **stunk**; past participle **stunk**) 1. to give off an offensive smell. 2. (colloquial) to be or seem very unpleasant, unsavoury, or dishonest. —n. 1. an offensive smell. 2. (colloquial) an offensive complaint or fuss. —**stink bomb**, a device emitting a stink when exploded. **stink out**, to drive out by a stink; to fill (a place) with a stink. [Old English]

stinker n. 1. a person or thing that stinks. 2. (slang) a very objectionable person or thing; a difficult task; a letter etc. conveying strong disapproval.

stinkhorn n. any foul-smelling fungus of the genus Phallus, especially P. impudicus; they first appear on the surface as white balls.

stinking adj. that stinks; (slang) very objectionable. —adv. (slang) extremely and usually objectionably.

stinkwood n. any of various trees with unpleasant-smelling wood. The S African tree Ocotea bullata, family Lauraceae, has offensive-smelling wood when newly felled, but fine, durable timber used for furniture. Another stinkwood is Gustavia augusta from tropical America.

stint v.t. to restrict to a small allowance (of); to be niggardly with. —n. 1. a limitation of supply or effort. 2. a fixed or allotted amount of work. 3. a small ◊sandpiper of the genus Calidris. [Old English = to blunt]

stipend /ˈstaɪpend/ n. a salary, especially of a cleric. [from Old French or Latin stipendium (stips = wages and pendere = to pay)]

stipendiary /staɪˈpendjərɪ, stɪ-/ adj. receiving a stipend. —n. a person receiving a stipend. —**stipendiary magistrate**, a paid professional magistrate. [from Latin]

stipple v.t./i. 1. to paint, draw, or engrave with small dots (not with lines or strokes). 2. to roughen the surface of (paint or cement etc.). —n. stippling; this effect. [from Dutch stippelen, frequentative of stippen = to prick (stip = point)]

stipulate /ˈstɪpjʊleɪt/ v.t./i. to demand or specify as part of a bargain or agreement. —**stipulate for**, to mention or insist upon as essential. —**stipulation** /-ˈleɪʃən/ n. [from Latin stipulari]

stipule n. an outgrowth arising from the base of a leaf or leaf stalk in certain plants. Stipules usually occur in pairs or fused into a single semicircular structure. They may have a leaflike appearance, as in goosegrass Galium aparine, be spiny, as in false acacia Robina, or look like small scales.

stir[1] v.t./i. (-rr-) 1. to move a spoon etc. round and round in (a liquid etc.) so as to mix the ingredients. 2. to move or cause to move slightly; to be or begin to be in motion; to rise after sleeping. 3. to arouse, inspire, or excite (emotions etc., or a person as regards these). —n. 1. the act or process of stirring. 2. a commotion or disturbance;

excitement, a sensation. —**stir one's stumps**, (colloquial) to begin to move; to hurry. **stir up**, to mix thoroughly by stirring; to stimulate. [Old English]

stir[2] n. (slang) prison.

Stirling /ˈstɜːlɪŋ/ James 1926– . British architect, associated with collegiate and museum architecture. His works include the engineering building at Leicester University, and the Clore Gallery (the extension to house the ◊Turner collection) at the Tate Gallery, London, opened in 1987.

Stirling engine a hot-air engine invented by Scottish priest Robert Stirling (1790–1878) in 1876. It is a piston engine that uses hot air as a working fluid.

stirrup /ˈstɪrəp/ n. a metal or leather support for a horse rider's foot, hanging from the saddle. —**stirrup cup**, a drink offered to a person about to depart, originally on horseback. **stirrup leather**, a strap attaching a stirrup to a saddle. **stirrup pump**, a hand-operated water pump with a stirrup-shaped footrest, used to extinguish small fires. [Old English (stigan = climb and rope)]

stitch n. 1. a single pass of a threaded needle in and out of fabric in sewing or tissue in surgery; a thread etc. between two needle holes. 2. a single complete movement of a needle or hook in knitting or crochet; the loop of thread made thus. 3. a particular method of arranging the thread(s). 4. the least bit of clothing. 5. an acute pain in the side induced by running etc. —v.t./i. to sew, to make stitches (in). —**in stitches**, (colloquial) laughing uncontrollably. **stitch in time**, a timely remedy. **stitch up**, to join or mend by sewing. [Old English]

stoa /ˈstəʊə/ n. in ancient Greek architecture, a portico or roofed colonnade. [Greek]

stoat n. a carnivorous mammal Mustela erminea of the weasel family, about 37 cm/15 in long including the black-tipped tail. It has a long body and a flattened head. The upper parts and tail are red-brown, and the underparts are white. Stoats live in Europe, Asia, and North America. In the colder regions, the coat turns white (ermine) in winter.

stock n. 1. a store of goods etc. ready for sale or distribution etc.; a supply of things available for use. 2. livestock. 3. (British) the fully paid-up capital of a business company; a portion of this held by an investor (differing from shares in that it is not issued in fixed amounts); fixed-interest securities or, for example, those issued by central and local government; (US) an ordinary share. 4. one's reputation or popularity. 5. money lent to a government at fixed interest. 6. a line of ancestry. 7. liquid made by stewing bones, vegetables etc., as a basis for soup, sauce etc. 8. a base, support, or handle for an implement or machine etc.; the butt of a rifle etc. 9. a plant into which a graft is inserted; the main trunk of a tree etc. 10. a fragrant-flowered cruciferous plant of the genus Matthiola. 11. (in plural) supports for a ship during building. 12. (in plural, historical) a timber frame with holes used until the 19th century to confine the legs and sometimes the arms of minor offenders, and expose them to public humiliation. The ◊pillory had a similar purpose. 13. a cravat worn e.g. as part of riding kit; a piece of black or purple fabric worn over the shirt front by a cleric, hanging from a clerical collar. —adj. 1. kept in stock and readily available. 2. commonly used, conventional, hackneyed. —v.t./i. 1. to have (goods) in stock. 2. to provide with goods, equipment, or livestock. 3. to fit (a gun etc.) with a stock. —**in** (or out of) **stock**, available (or not available) immediately for sale etc. **on the stocks**, in construction or preparation. **stock car**, a specially strengthened car for use in ◊stock-car racing. **stock in trade**, all the requisites of a trade or profession. **stock market**, a ◊stock exchange; the transactions on this. **stockpot** n. a pot for making soup stock. **stockroom** n. a room for storing goods. **stock-still** adj. motionless. **stocktaking** n. making the inventory of the stock in a shop etc.; a review of one's position and resources. **stock up**, to provide with or get stocks or supplies. **stock up with**, to gather a stock of. **take stock**, to make an inventory of one's stock; to make a review or estimate of a situation etc. [Old English (Old Norse stokkr = trunk)]

stockade /stɒˈkeɪd/ n. a line or enclosure of upright stakes. —v.t. to fortify with a stockade. [from obsolete French from Spanish estacada]

stockbreeder n. a farmer who raises livestock.

stockbroker n. a broker on the stock exchange. —**stockbroking** n.

stock-car racing a sport popular in the UK and the USA, but in two different forms. In the UK, the cars are 'old bangers', which attempt to force the other cars off the track or immobilize them. This format is popular in the USA as 'demolition derbies'. In the USA, the cars are high-powered sports cars that race on purpose-built tracks at distances up to 640 km/500 mi.

stock exchange an institution for the buying and selling of stocks and shares (securities). The world's largest stock exchanges are London, New York (Wall Street), and Tokyo. London's is the oldest stock exchange in the world, opened in 1801. The former division on the London Stock Exchange between brokers (who bought shares from jobbers to sell to the public) and jobbers (who sold them only to brokers on commission, the 'jobbers' turn') was abolished in 1986.

Stock Exchange Automation System (SEAQ) a computerized system of share price monitoring. From October 1987, SEAQ began displaying market makers' quotations for UK stocks, having only been operational previously for overseas equities.

Stockhausen /ˈʃtɒkhauzən/ Karlheinz 1928– . German composer of avant-garde music, who has continued to explore new musical sounds and compositional techniques since the 1950s. His major works include *Gesang der Jünglinge* 1956 and *Kontakte* 1960 (electronic music); *Klavierstücke* 1952–85; *Momente* 1961–64, revised 1972, *Mikrophonie I* 1964, and *Sirius* 1977. Since 1977 all his works have been part of *Licht*, a cycle of seven musical ceremonies, intended for performance on the evenings of a week. He has completed *Donnerstag* 1980, *Samstag* 1984, and *Montag* 1988.

stockholder *n.* an owner of stocks or shares.

Stockholm /ˈstɒkhəʊm/ capital and industrial port of Sweden; population (1988) 667,000. It is built on a number of islands. Industries include engineering, brewing, electrical goods, paper, textiles, and pottery.

stockinet /stɒkiˈnet/ *n.* or **stockinette** fine stretchable machine-knitted fabric used for underwear etc. [probably from *stocking net*]

stocking *n.* 1. a close-fitting covering for the foot and all or part of the leg, usually knitted or woven of wool or nylon etc. 2. a differently coloured lower part of the leg of a horse etc. —**in one's stocking** *or* **stockinged feet,** wearing stockings but no shoes. **stocking mask,** a nylon stocking worn over the head as a criminal's disguise. **stocking stitch,** alternate rows of plain and purl in knitting, giving a plain, smooth surface on one side.

stockist *n.* one who stocks (certain) goods for sale.

stockjobber *n.* (*British*) a jobber on the Stock Exchange, until 1986 dealing with stockbrokers but not with the general public.

stockman *n.* (*plural* **stockmen**) (*Australian*) a person in charge of livestock.

stockpile *n.* an accumulated stock of goods etc. held in reserve. —*v.t.* to accumulate a stockpile of.

stockrider *n.* (*Australian*) a herder on an unfenced station.

stocky *adj.* short and strongly built. —**stockily** *adv.,* **stockiness** *n.*

stockyard *n.* an enclosure for sorting or temporary keeping of cattle.

stodge /stɒdʒ/ *n.* (*colloquial*) 1. food of a thick, heavy kind. 2. an unimaginative person or work. —*v.t./i.* (*colloquial*) 1. to stuff (oneself) with food etc. 2. to trudge through mud etc.; to work laboriously. [imitative, after *stuff* and *podge*]

stodgy /ˈstɒdʒɪ/ *adj.* 1. (of food) heavy and thick, indigestible. 2. dull and uninteresting. —**stodgily** *adv.,* **stodginess** *n.*

stoic /ˈstəʊɪk/ *n.* 1. a stoical person. 2. **Stoic** a member of an ancient Greek school of philosophy, see ◊stoicism.

stoical /ˈstəʊɪkəl/ *adj.* having or showing great self-control in adversity. —**stoically** *adv.*

stoicism *n.* 1. the exercise of self-control in adversity. 2. **Stoicism** a Greek school of philosophy, founded about 300 BC by Zeno of Citium. The Stoics were pantheistic materialists who believed that happiness lay in accepting the law of the universe. They emphasized human brotherhood, denounced slavery, and were internationalist. [Greek *stoa* = porch, from the porch on which Zeno taught]

stoke *v.t./i.* (often with *up*) 1. to tend and put fuel on (a fire or furnace etc.). 2. (*colloquial*) to consume food steadily and in large quantities. [back formation from *stoker*]

stokehold *n.* a compartment in which a steamer's fires are tended.

stokehole *n.* a space for stokers in front of a furnace.

stoker /ˈstəʊkə/ *n.* 1. a person who stokes a furnace etc., especially on a ship. 2. a mechanical device for doing this. [Dutch, from *stoken* = stoke from Middle Dutch *stoken* = push]

Stoker Bram (Abraham) 1847–1912. Irish novelist, actor, theatre manager, and author. His novel ◊*Dracula* 1897 crystallized most aspects of the traditional vampire legend and became the source for all subsequent popular fiction and films on the subject.

stokes *n.* a c.g.s. unit (symbol St) of kinematic viscosity (rate of flow of a liquid).

STOL /stɒl/ acronym from short takeoff and landing, used to describe aircraft fitted with special devices on the wings (such as sucking flaps) that increase aerodynamic lift at low speeds. Small passenger and freight STOL craft may become common with the demand for small airports, especially in difficult terrain.

stole[1] *n.* 1. a woman's long garment like a scarf, worn over the shoulders. 2. a strip of silk etc. worn similarly as a vestment by a priest. [Old English from Latin from Greek *stolē* = equipment]

stole[2] past of **steal**.

stolen past participle of **steal**.

stolid /ˈstɒlɪd/ *adj.* not feeling or showing emotion or animation; not easily excited or moved. —**stolidity** /-ˈlɪdɪtɪ/ *n.,* **stolidly** *adv.* [from obsolete French or Latin *stolidus*]

stolon *n.* a type of ◊runner.

stoma *n.* (*plural* **stomata**) in botany, a pore in the epidermis of a plant. Each stoma is surrounded by a pair of guard cells that are crescent-shaped when the stoma is open but can collapse to an oval shape, thus closing off the opening between them. Stomata allow the exchange of carbon dioxide and oxygen (needed for ◊photosynthesis and ◊respiration) between the internal tissues of the plant and the outside atmosphere. They are also the main route by which water is lost from the plant, and they can be closed to conserve water, the movements being controlled by changes in turgidity of the guard cells.

stomach /ˈstʌmək/ *n.* 1. the first cavity in the digestive system of animals. In mammals it is a bag of muscle situated just below the diaphragm. Food enters it from the oesophagus, is digested by the acid and ◊enzymes secreted by the stomach lining, and then passes into the duodenum. Some plant-eating mammals have multichambered stomachs that harbour bacteria in one of the chambers to assist in the digestion of ◊cellulose. 2. the lower front of the body. 3. an appetite or inclination. —*v.t.* to endure, to put up with. —**stomachache** *n.* a pain in the belly, especially in the bowels. **stomach pump,** a syringe for emptying the stomach or forcing liquid into it. **stomach upset,** a temporary slight digestive disorder. [from Old French from Latin from Greek, originally = gullet (*stoma* = mouth)]

stomacher /ˈstʌməkə/ *n.* (*historical*) a pointed front piece of a woman's dress, often jewelled or embroidered.

stomp *n.* a lively jazz dance with heavy stamping. —*v.t./i.* to tread heavily (on); to dance a stomp. [US dialect variant of *stamp*]

stone /stəʊn/ *n.* 1. the solid nonmetallic mineral matter of which rock is made. 2. a small piece of this; a piece of stone of a definite shape or for a particular purpose. 3. a thing resembling a stone in hardness or form, e.g. a hard morbid concretion in the body or a hard case of the kernel in some fruits. 4. a precious stone. 5. (*plural* the same) an imperial unit (symbol st) of mass. One stone is 14 pounds (6.35 kg). —*adj.* made of stone. —*v.t.* 1. to pelt with stones. 2. to remove the stones from (fruit). 3. (in *past participle, slang*) very drunk; incapacitated or stimulated by drugs. —**cast** *or* **throw stones,** to make aspersions on the character etc. **leave no stone unturned,** to try every possible means. **stone-cold** *adj.* completely cold. **stone-dead** *adj.* completely dead. **stone-deaf** *adj.* completely deaf. **stonefly** *n.* an insect of the order Plecoptera, with aquatic larvae found under stones, used as bait. **stone fruit,** a ◊drupe. **a stone's throw,** a short distance. [Old English]

Stone Lucy 1818–1893. US feminist orator and editor. Married to the radical Henry Blackwell in 1855, she gained wide publicity when, after a mutual declaration rejecting the legal superiority of the man in marriage, she chose to retain her own surname despite her marriage. The epithet 'Lucy Stoner' was coined to mean a woman who advocated doing the same.

Stone Age the developmental stage of humans in ◊prehistory before the use of metals, when tools and weapons were made chiefly of stone, especially flint. The Stone Age is subdivided into the Old or Palaeolithic, the Middle or Mesolithic, and the New or Neolithic. The people of the Old Stone Age were hunters, whereas the Neolithic people took the first steps in agriculture, the domestication of animals, weaving, and pottery.

stonechat *n.* a small bird *Saxicola torquata* of the thrush family Turdidae frequently found in Eurasia and Africa on open land with bushes. The male has a black head and throat, tawny breast, and dark back; the female is browner. Stonechats have an alarm note like the knocking of pebbles.

stonecrop *n.* any of several plants of the genus *Sedum* of the orpine family Crassulaceae, a succulent herb with fleshy leaves and clusters of starlike flowers. Stonecrops are characteristic of dry, rocky places and some grow on walls.

stonefish *n.* a fish *Synanceia verrucosa* that lives in shallow waters of the Indian and Pacific Oceans. It is about 35 cm/14 in long, and camouflaged to resemble encrusted rock. It has poisonous spines that can inflict painful venom.

Stonehenge /stəʊn'hendʒ/ *n.* a megalithic monument dating from about 2000 BC on Salisbury Plain, Wiltshire, England. It consisted originally of a circle of 30 upright stones, their tops linked by lintel stones to form a continuous circle about 30 m/100 ft across. Within the circle was a horseshoe arrangement of five trilithons (two uprights plus a lintel, set as five separate entities), and a so-called 'altar stone' (an upright pillar) on the axis of the horseshoe at the open, NE end, which faces in the direction of the rising sun. It has been suggested that it served as an observatory. Although Stonehenge is far older than ◊Druidism, an annual Druid ceremony is held here at the summer solstice. At that time it is also a spiritual focus for many people with a nomadic way of life, who on several consecutive midsummers in the 1980s were forcibly kept from access to Stonehenge by police.

stonemason *n.* a dresser of or builder in stone.

stonewall *v.i.* 1. to obstruct discussion etc. with noncommittal answers. 2. in cricket, to bat without attempting to score runs.

stoneware *n.* a very hard opaque pottery made of nonporous clay with feldspar and a high silica content, fired at high temperature.

stonework *n.* work built of stone, masonry.

stony /'stəʊnɪ/ *adj.* 1. full of stones. 2. like stone in texture, hard. 3. unfeeling, uncompromising, unresponsive. 4. (*slang*) = stony-broke. —**stony-broke** *adj.* (*slang*) = broke. —**stonily** *adv.*, **stoniness** *n.*

stood past and past participle of **stand**.

stooge *n.* (*colloquial*) 1. a comedian's assistant, used as a target for jokes. 2. a subordinate who does routine work. 3. a person whose actions are entirely controlled by another. —*v.i.* (*colloquial*) 1. to act as a stooge. 2. to move or wander aimlessly.

stool *n.* 1. a movable seat without a back or arms, usually for one person; a footstool. 2. (usually in *plural*) faeces. 3. a root or stump of a tree or plant from which shoots spring. —**stoolpigeon** *n.* a pigeon as a decoy; a police informer. [Old English]

stoolball *n.* an ancient game, considered the ancestor of cricket, the main differences being that in stoolball bowling is underarm and the ball is soft; the bat is wooden and shaped like a tennis racket.

stoop[1] *n.* 1. to bend (one's shoulders or body) forwards and downwards; to carry one's head and shoulders thus. 2. to condescend; to lower oneself morally. —*n.* a stooping posture. [Old English]

stoop[2] *n.* (*US*) a porch or small veranda or the steps in front of a house. [from Dutch *stoep* (related to *step*)]

stop *v.t./i.* (-pp-) 1. to put an end to the movement, progress, or operation etc. of; to cause to halt or pause. 2. to refrain from continuing, to cease motion or working.

3. (*slang*) to receive (a blow etc.) on one's body. 4. to remain, to stay for a short time. 5. to close by plugging or obstructing; to put a filling in (a tooth). 6. to keep back, to refuse to give or allow; to instruct a bank to withhold payment on (a cheque). 7. to obtain the desired pitch in a musical instrument by pressing (a string) or blocking (a hole). —*n.* 1. stopping, being stopped; a pause or check. 2. a place where a bus or train etc. regularly stops. 3. a sign to show a pause in written matter, especially a full stop. 4. a device for stopping motion at a particular point. 5. in music, a change of pitch effected by stopping a string; in an organ, a row of pipes of one character; a knob etc. operating these. 6. in optics and photography, a diaphragm; the effective diameter of a lens; a device reducing this. 7. a plosive sound. —**pull out all the stops**, to make an extreme effort. **stop at nothing**, to be ruthless or unscrupulous. **stop-go** *n.* the alternate suppression and stimulation of progress. **stop off** *or* **over**, to break one's journey. **stopping train**, a train stopping at many intermediate stations. **stop press**, late news inserted in a newspaper after printing has begun. **stopwatch** *n.* a watch with a mechanism for instantly starting and stopping it, used in timing races etc. [Old English]

stopcock *n.* an externally operated valve to regulate the flow in a pipe etc.

Stopes /stəʊps/ Marie (Carmichael) 1880–1958. Scottish birth-control campaigner. With her husband H V Roe (1878–1949), an aircraft manufacturer, she founded a London birth-control clinic in 1921. The Well Woman Centre in Marie Stopes House, London, commemorates her work. She wrote plays and verse as well as the best-selling manual *Married Love* 1918.

stopgap *n.* a temporary substitute.

stopoff *n.* or **stopover** a break in one's journey.

stoppage *n.* the condition of being blocked or stopped.

Stoppard /'stɒpɑːd/ Tom 1937–   . Czechoslovak-born British playwright, whose works use wit and wordplay to explore logical and philosophical ideas. He wrote *Rosencrantz and Guildenstern are Dead* 1967. This was followed by comedies including *The Real Inspector Hound* 1968, *Jumpers* 1972, *Travesties* 1974, *Dirty Linen* 1976, *The Real Thing* 1982, and *Hapgood* 1988. He has also written for radio, television, and the cinema.

Life is a gamble, at terrible odds—if it was a bet, you wouldn't take it.

Tom Stoppard
Rosencrantz and Guildenstern Are Dead

Stopes *Scottish birth-control campaigner Marie Stopes.*

stopper *n.* a plug for closing a bottle etc. —*v.t.* to close with a stopper. —**put a stopper on,** to cause to cease.
stopping *n.* a filling for a tooth.
storage /ˈstɔːrɪdʒ/ *n.* 1. the storing of goods etc. 2. a method of storing; the space available for this. 3. the cost of storing. 4. the storing of data. —**storage battery** *or* **cell,** a battery or cell for storing electricity. **storage heater,** an electric heater accumulating heat outside peak hours for later release.
store *n.* 1. a quantity of something or (also in *plural*) articles accumulated so as to be available for use. 2. a large shop selling goods of many kinds; (*US*) a shop. 3. a storehouse, a warehouse where things are stored. 4. a device in a computer for storing data. —*v.t.* 1. to accumulate for future use. 2. to put (furniture etc.) into a warehouse for temporary keeping. 3. to stock with something useful. 4. in computing, to enter or retain (data) for future retrieval. —**in store,** being stored; kept available for use; destined to happen, imminent. **set store by,** to consider important, to value greatly. **store cattle,** cattle kept for breeding or for future fattening. **storeroom** *n.* a room used for storing things. [from Old French *estore, estorer* from Latin *instaurare* = renew]
storehouse *n.* a place where things are stored.
storekeeper *n.* 1. a person in charge of a store or stores. 2. (*US*) a shopkeeper.
storey /ˈstɔːrɪ/ *n.* 1. each of the parts into which a building is divided horizontally; the whole of the rooms etc. having a continuous floor. 2. a thing forming a horizontal division. —**storeyed** *adj.* [from Latin *historia* = history]
storied /ˈstɔːrɪd/ *adj.* celebrated in or associated with stories or legends.
stork *n.* a tall, usually white, carnivorous wading bird of the mainly tropical order Ciconiiformes, with a long beak, slender body, long, powerful wings, and long thin neck and legs. Some species grow up to 150 cm/5 ft tall. [Old English]
storm *n.* 1. a violent disturbance of the atmosphere with thunder, strong wind, heavy rain or snow, or hail. 2. a violent disturbance or commotion in human affairs; a violent dispute etc. 3. a violent shower of missiles or blows; a violent outbreak of applause, abuse etc. 4. a direct military assault upon (and the capture of) a defended place. —*v.t./i.* 1. (of wind or rain) to rage, to be violent. 2. to move or behave violently or very angrily. 3. to attract or capture by storm. —**storm centre,** the centre of a storm or cyclone; a subject etc. upon which agitation is concentrated. **storm cloud,** a heavy rain cloud; something threatening. **storm door,** an additional outer door. **storm in a teacup,** great excitement over a trivial matter. **storm petrel,** a small black and white ◊petrel *Hydrobates pelagicus* of the North Atlantic, said to be active before storms. **storm trooper,** a member of storm troops. **storm troops,** shock troops; the Nazi political militia or ◊*Sturm Abteilung.* **take by storm,** to capture by storm; to captivate quickly. [Old English]
stormy *adj.* 1. full of storms; affected by storms. 2. (of wind etc.) violent as in a storm. 3. full of violent anger or outbursts. —**stormy petrel,** the ◊storm petrel; a person whose arrival seems to foreshadow or attract trouble. —**stormily** *adv.,* **storminess** *n.*
story *n.* 1. an account of an incident or of a series of incidents, either true or invented. 2. the past course of a person's or institution's life. 3. a report of an item of news; material suitable for this. 4. or **storyline** the plot of a novel or play etc. 5. (*colloquial*) a fib. [from Anglo-French *estorie* from Latin from Greek *historia*]
stoup /stuːp/ *n.* 1. a basin for holy water, especially in the wall of a church. 2. (*archaic*) a flagon, a beaker. [from Old Norse]
stout *adj.* 1. (of a person) solidly built and rather fat. 2. of considerable thickness or strength. 3. brave and resolute. —*n.* a strong, dark beer brewed with roasted malt or barley. —**stoutly** *adv.,* **stoutness** *n.* [from Anglo-French (e)*stout*]
stove[1] *n.* 1. an apparatus containing an oven or ovens. 2. a closed apparatus used for heating rooms etc. 3. a hothouse with artificial heat. —**stove enamel,** a heat-proof enamel produced by treating enamelled objects in a stove. **stove-enamelled** *adj.* [originally = sweating room, from Middle Dutch]
stove[2] past and past participle of **stave.**

stow /stəʊ/ *v.t.* 1. to place in a receptacle for storage. 2. (*slang,* especially in *imperative*) to cease from. —**stow away,** to put away in storage or in reserve; to conceal oneself as a stowaway. [from *bestow*]
stowage *n.* stowing, being stowed; the space available for this; the charge for it.
stowaway *n.* a person who hides on board a ship or aircraft etc. so as to travel without charge or unseen.
Stowe /stəʊ/ Harriet Beecher 1811–1896. US suffragist, abolitionist, and author of of the antislavery novel ◊*Uncle Tom's Cabin,* first published as a serial 1851–52. Her book was radical in its time and did much to spread antislavery sentiment, but it has later been criticized for sentimentality and racism.
STP abbreviation of ◊standard temperature and pressure.
strabismus /strəˈbɪzməs/ *n.* squinting; a squint. [from Greek *strabizō* = squint]
Strachey /ˈstreɪtʃɪ/ (Giles) Lytton 1880–1932. English critic and biographer, a member of the ◊Bloomsbury Group of writers and artists. He wrote *Landmarks in French Literature* 1912. The mocking and witty treatment of Cardinal Manning, Florence Nightingale, Thomas Arnold, and General Gordon in *Eminent Victorians* 1918 won him recognition. His biography *Queen Victoria* 1921 was more affectionate.
straddle *v.t./i.* 1. to sit or stand (across) with the legs wide apart; to part (one's legs) widely. 2. to drop shots or bombs short of and beyond (a specified point). —*n.* the act of straddling. [from *striddlings* = astride]
Stradivari /strædɪˈvɑːrɪ/ Antonio. In Latin form **Stradivarius** 1644–1737. Italian stringed instrument maker, generally considered the greatest of all violin makers. He was born in Cremona and studied there with Nicolo ◊Amati. He produced more than 1,100 instruments from his family workshops.
strafe /strɑːf, streɪf/ *v.t.* to harass with gunfire or bombs. —*n.* an act of strafing. [adaptation of German 1914 catchword *Gott strafe* (God punish) *England*]
Strafford /ˈstræfəd/ Thomas Wentworth, 1st Earl of Strafford 1593–1641. English politician, originally an opponent of Charles I, but from 1628 on the Royalist side. He ruled despotically as Lord Deputy of Ireland 1632–39, when he returned to England as Charles's chief adviser and received an earldom. He was impeached in 1640 by Parliament, abandoned by Charles as a scapegoat, and beheaded.
straggle *v.i.* 1. to lack or lose compactness, to grow or spread in an irregular or untidy way. 2. to go or wander separately, not in a group; to drop behind others. —*n.* a straggling group. —**straggler** *n.,* **straggly** *adj.*
straight /streɪt/ *adj.* 1. extending or moving uniformly in the same direction, without a curve or bend etc. 2. direct. 3. in unbroken succession. 4. level, tidy; in the proper order, place, or condition. 5. honest; candid; not evasive. 6. not modified or elaborate, without additions; (of a drink) undiluted. 7. conventional, respectable; heterosexual. —*n.* 1. the straight part of something, especially the concluding stretch of a racecourse. 2. a straight condition. 3. a sequence of five cards in poker. 4. (*slang*) a heterosexual person. —*adv.* in a straight line, direct; in the right direction, correctly. —**go straight,** to live an honest life after being a criminal. **on the straight,** not on the bias. **straight away,** immediately. **straight eye,** the ability to draw or cut etc. in a straight line or to detect deviation from the straight. **straight face,** an expression concealing or not showing one's amusement etc. **straight fight,** a contest between two candidates only. **straight man,** the member of a comic act who makes remarks for the comedian to joke about. **straight off,** (*colloquial*) immediately; without hesitation. —**straightly** *adv.,* **straightness** *n.* [past participle of *stretch*]
straighten /ˈstreɪtən/ *v.t./i.* to make or become straight. —**straighten up,** to stand erect after bending.
straightforward /streɪtˈfɔːwəd/ *adj.* 1. honest, frank. 2. (of a task etc.) uncomplicated. —**straightforwardly** *adv.,* **straightforwardness** *n.*
strain[1] *v.t./i.* 1. to stretch tightly, to make or become taut or tense. 2. to injure or weaken by excessive stretching or by overexertion. 3. to make an intensive effort; to use in this. 4. to apply (a rule or meaning etc.) beyond its true application. 5. to hold in a tight embrace. 6. to pass (liquid)

through a sieve or similar device in order to separate solids from the liquid in which they are dispersed; to filter out (solids) thus. —*n.* **1.** straining, being strained; the force exerted in straining. **2.** an injury caused by straining a muscle etc. **3.** a severe demand on mental or physical strength or on resources; distress caused by this. **4.** a passage from a piece of music or poetry. **5.** a tone or tendency in speech or writing. [from Old French *estreindre* from Latin *stringere* = draw tight]

strain[2] *n.* **1.** a line of descent of animals, plants, or microorganisms; a variety or breed of these. **2.** a slight or inherited tendency as part of character. [Old English = progeny]

strained *adj.* **1.** (of behaviour or manner) produced by effort, not arising from genuine feeling. **2.** (of a relationship) characterized by unpleasant tension.

strainer *n.* a device for straining liquids.

strait *n.* **1.** (in *singular* or *plural*) a narrow passage of water connecting two large bodies of water. **2.** (usually in *plural*) a difficult state of affairs. —*adj.* (*archaic*) narrow, limited, strict. —**strait-laced** *adj.* very prim and proper, puritanical. [from Old French *estreit* = tight from Latin *stringere* = draw tight]

straiten /'streɪtən/ *v.t.* to restrict; (in *past participle*) of or characterized by poverty.

straitjacket *n.* **1.** a strong garment put on a violent person to confine his or her arms. **2.** restrictive measures. —*v.t.* **1.** to restrain with a straitjacket. **2.** to restrict severely.

Straits Settlements /'streɪts 'setlmənts/ former province of the ◊East India Company 1826–58, and British crown colony 1867–1946; it comprised Singapore, Malacca, Penang, Cocos Islands, Christmas Island, and Labuan.

strake *n.* a continuous line of planking or plates from stem to stern of a ship. [related to Old English *streccan* = stretch]

stramonium /strə'məʊnɪəm/ *n.* a drug used to treat asthma; the plant yielding it (*Datura stramonium*).

strand[1] *v.t./i.* **1.** to run or cause to run aground. **2.** (in *past participle*) in difficulties, especially without money or means of transport. —*n.* a shore. [Old English]

strand[2] *n.* **1.** each of the threads or wires twisted round each other to make a rope or cable etc. **2.** a single thread or strip of fibre; a lock of hair. **3.** an element or strain in any composite whole.

strange /streɪndʒ/ *adj.* **1.** unusual, surprising; eccentric. **2.** unfamiliar, not one's own, alien. **3.** unaccustomed; not at one's ease. —**strangely** *adv.*, **strangeness** *n.* [from Old French *estrange* from Latin *extraneus* (*extra* = outside)]

strange attractor in physics, a point that moves irregularly within a given region at all times. Such movement describes, for example, the motion of turbulent fluids.

stranger /'streɪndʒə/ *n.* a person in a place or company that he or she does not know or belong to or where he or she is unknown; a person one does not know. —**a** (*or* **no**) **stranger to**, unaccustomed (or accustomed) to. [from Old French *estrangier* from Latin]

strangle *v.t.* **1.** to squeeze the windpipe or neck of, especially so as to kill. **2.** to restrict or prevent the proper growth, operation, or utterance of. —**strangler** *n.* [from Old French from Latin *strangulare* from Greek *straggalē* = halter]

stranglehold *n.* **1.** a strangling or deadly grip. **2.** firm or exclusive control.

strangulate /'stræŋgjʊleɪt/ *v.t.* to compress (a vein or intestine etc.) so that nothing can pass through. [from Latin]

strangulation /stræŋgjʊ'leɪʃən/ *n.* **1.** strangling. **2.** strangulating.

strap *n.* **1.** a strip of leather or other flexible material often with a buckle, for holding things together or in place. **2.** a shoulder strap. **3.** a loop for grasping to steady oneself in a moving vehicle. —*v.t.* (**-pp-**) **1.** to secure with a strap or straps. **2.** to beat with a strap. —**strapped for,** (*slang*) short of (cash etc.). [dialect form of *strop*]

strapping *adj.* tall and healthy-looking. —*n.* **1.** straps; material for these. **2.** sticking plaster etc. used for binding wounds or injuries.

Strasberg /'stræzbɜːg/ Lee 1902–1982. US actor and artistic director of the ◊Actors Studio from 1948, who developed Method acting from ◊Stanislavsky's system; pupils have included Jane Fonda, John Garfield, Sidney Poitier, and Paul Newman.

Strasbourg /'stræzbʊəg/ city on the river Ill, in Bas-Rhin *département*, capital of Alsace, France; population (1982) 373,000. Industries include car manufacture, tobacco, printing and publishing, and preserves. The ◊Council of Europe meets here, and sessions of the European Parliament alternate between Strasbourg and Luxembourg.

strata plural of **stratum**.

stratagem /'strætədʒəm/ *n.* a cunning plan or scheme; trickery. [from French from Latin from Greek *stratēgēma* (*stratēgos* = a general)]

strategic /strə'tiːdʒɪk/ *adj.* **1.** of strategy. **2.** giving an advantage. **3.** (of materials) essential in war. **4.** (of bombing) designed to destroy an area's economy and demoralize the enemy. Heavy bombardment of cities is regarded as strategic bombing. —**strategic weapons,** missiles etc. that can reach the enemy's home territory (as opposed to **tactical weapons** which are for use at close quarters or in battle). —**strategically** *adv.* [from French from Greek]

Strategic Arms Limitation Talks (SALT) a series of US-Soviet discussions aimed at reducing the rate of nuclear arms build-up. The talks, delayed by the Soviet invasion of Czechoslovakia in 1968, began in 1969 between the US president Lyndon Johnson and the Soviet leader Brezhnev. Neither the SALT I accord (effective 1972–77) nor SALT II called for reductions in nuclear weaponry, merely a limit on the expansion of these forces. SALT II was never fully ratified because of the Soviet occupation of Afghanistan, although the terms of the accord were respected by both sides from 1979 until President ◊Reagan exceeded its limitations during his second term 1985–89. SALT talks were superseded by START (Strategic Arms Reduction Talks).

Strategic Arms Reduction Talks (START) a phase in US-Soviet peace discussions. START began with talks in Geneva in 1983, leading to the signing of the ◊Intermediate Nuclear Forces (INF) treaty in 1987. In 1989 proposals for reductions in conventional weapons were added to the agenda.

Strategic Defense Initiative (SDI) also called **Star Wars** an attempt by the USA to develop a defence system against incoming nuclear missiles, based in part outside the Earth's atmosphere. It was announced by President Reagan in March 1983, and the research had by 1990 cost over $16.5 billion. In 1988, the joint Chiefs of Staff announced that they expected to be able to intercept no more than 30% of incoming missiles.

strategic islands islands (Azores, Canary Islands, Cyprus, Iceland, Madeira, and Malta) of great political and military significance likely to affect their stability; they held their first international conference in 1979.

strategy /'strætɪdʒɪ/ *n.* **1.** the art of war, especially the planning of the movements of troops into favourable positions. **2.** a plan of action or policy in business or politics etc. —**strategist** *n.* [from French from Greek = generalship]

Stratford-upon-Avon /'strætfəd əpɒn 'eɪvən/ market town on the river Avon, in Warwickshire, England; population (1981) 21,000. It is the birthplace of William Shakespeare. His grave is in the parish church. The Royal Shakespeare Theatre 1932 replaced an earlier building 1877–79 that burned down in 1926.

strath *n.* (*Scottish*) a broad valley. [from Gaelic *srath*]

Strathclyde /stræθ'klaɪd/ region of Scotland; **area** 13,900 sq km/5,367 sq mi; **administrative headquarters** Glasgow; **physical** includes some of Inner ◊Hebrides; river Clyde; part of Loch Lomond; Glencoe in the S Highlands; islands: Arran, Bute, Mull; **products** dairy, pig, and poultry products; shipbuilding; engineering; coal from Ayr and Lanark; oil-related services; **population** (1987) 2,333,000, half the population of Scotland.

strathspey /stræθ'speɪ/ *n.* a slow Scottish dance; music for this. [from *Strathspey,* valley of the river Spey]

stratify /'strætɪfaɪ/ *v.t.* (especially in *past participle*) to arrange in strata or grades etc. —**stratification** /-fɪ'keɪʃən/ *n.* [from French]

stratigraphy /strə'tɪɡrəfɪ/ *n.* the order and relative positions of strata; the branch of geology that deals with the sequence of formation of ◊sedimentary rock layers and the conditions under which they were formed. Its basis was developed by William ◊Smith, a British canal engineer. —**stratigraphic**/-'ɡræfɪk/ *adj.*, **stratigraphically** /-'ɡræfɪkəlɪ/ *adv.*

stratocumulus /ˌstrætəʊˈkjuːmjʊləs/ n. dark masses of low cloud, frequently merging to cover the whole sky.

stratopause /ˈstrætəʊpɔːz/ n. the interface between the stratosphere and the ionosphere.

stratosphere /ˈstrætəsfɪə/ n. that part of the atmosphere 10–40 km/6–25 mi from Earth, where the temperature slowly rises from a low of −55°C/−67°F to around 0°C/32°F. The air is rarefied and at around 25 km/15 mi much ◊ozone is concentrated. —**stratospheric** /-ˈsferɪk/ adj.

stratum /ˈstrɑːtəm, ˈstreɪ-/ n. (plural strata) 1. each of a series of layers, especially of ◊beds of ◊sedimentary rock in the Earth's crust. 2. a social level or class. [Latin = something spread or laid down]

stratus /ˈstrɑːtəs, ˈstreɪ-/ n. (plural strati /-tiː/) a continuous horizontal sheet of cloud.

Strauss /straʊs/ Franz-Josef 1915–1988. German conservative politician, leader of the West German Bavarian Christian Social Union (CSU) party 1961–88, premier of Bavaria 1978–88. In 1962 he lost his post as minister of defence when he illegally shut down the offices of Der Spiegel for a month, after the magazine revealed details of a failed NATO exercise. In the 1970s, Strauss opposed Ostpolitik (the policy of reconciliation with the East).

Strauss Johann (Baptist) 1825–1899. Austrian conductor and composer, the son of Johann Strauss (1804–1849). In 1872 he gave up conducting and wrote operettas, such as Die Fledermaus 1874, and numerous waltzes, such as The Blue Danube and Tales from the Vienna Woods, which gained him the title 'The Waltz King'.

Strauss Richard (Georg) 1864–1949. German composer and conductor. He followed the German Romantic tradition but had a strongly personal style, characterized by his bold, colourful orchestration. He first wrote tone poems such as Don Juan 1889, Till Eulenspiegel's Merry Pranks 1895, and Also sprach Zarathustra 1896. He then moved on to opera with Salome 1905 and Elektra 1909, both of which have elements of polytonality. He reverted to a more traditional style with Der Rosenkavalier 1911.

Stravinsky /strəˈvɪnski/ Igor 1882–1971. Russian composer, later of French (1934) and US (1945) nationality. He studied under ◊Rimsky-Korsakov and wrote the music for the Diaghilev ballets The Firebird 1910, Petrushka 1911, and The Rite of Spring 1913 (controversial at the time for their unorthodox rhythms and harmonies). His versatile work ranges from his Neo-Classical ballet Pulcinella 1920, to the choral-orchestral Symphony of Psalms 1930. He later made use of serial techniques in works such as the Canticum Sacrum 1955 and the ballet Agon 1953–57.

straw n. 1. dry cut stalks of grain used as material for bedding, packing, fodder etc. 2. a single stalk or piece of straw. 3. a thin hollow tube for sucking drink through. 4. an insignificant thing. 5. the pale yellow colour of straw. —**clutch at straws**, to try a hopeless expedient in desperation. **straw in the wind**, a slight hint of future developments. **straw poll** or **vote**, an unofficial ballot as a test of opinion. [Old English]

strawberry /ˈstrɔːbərɪ/ n. a pulpy red fruit having the surface studded with yellow seeds; the low-growing perennial plant of the genus Fragaria bearing this. Commercial cultivated forms bear one crop of fruit in summer and multiply by runners. —**strawberry mark**, a reddish birthmark.

stray v.i. 1. to leave one's group or proper place with no settled destination or purpose; to roam. 2. to deviate from a direct course or from a subject. —n. a person or domestic animal that has strayed; a stray thing. —adj. 1. that has strayed, lost. 2. isolated, found or occurring occasionally or unexpectedly. 3. unwanted, unintentional. [from Anglo-French estrayer from Latin extra = away and vagari = wander]

streak n. 1. a long, thin, usually irregular line or band, especially distinguished by its colour. 2. a flash of lightning. 3. a strain or element in a character. 4. a spell or series. —v.t./i. 1. to mark with streaks. 2. to move very rapidly; (colloquial) to run naked through a public place. —**streaker** n. [Old English = pen stroke]

streaky adj. full of streaks; (of bacon) with alternate streaks of fat and lean. —**streakily** adv., **streakiness** n.

stream n. 1. a body of water flowing in its bed, a brook or river. 2. a flow of fluid or of a mass of things or people. 3. the current or direction of something flowing or moving. 4. in some schools, a section into which children with the same level of ability are placed. —v.t./i. 1. to flow or move as a stream. 2. to emit a stream of; to run with liquid. 3. to float or wave at full length. 4. to arrange (schoolchildren) in streams. —**on stream**, in active operation or production. **stream of consciousness**, the continuous flow of a person's thoughts and reactions to events; a literary style depicting this, as in James Joyce's novel Ulysses. [Old English]

streamer n. 1. a long narrow flag. 2. a long narrow ribbon or strip of paper attached at one or both ends. 3. a banner headline.

streamline v.t. 1. to give a smooth even shape to (a vehicle, boat etc.) so as to offer the least possible resistance to motion through air or water. Aircraft, for example, must be carefully streamlined to reduce air resistance, or ◊drag. 2. to make more efficient by simplifying, removing superfluities etc.

Streep /striːp/ Meryl 1949– . US actress known for her strong character roles. Her films include The Deer Hunter 1978, Kramer vs Kramer 1979, Out of Africa 1985, Ironweed 1988, A Cry in the Dark 1989, and Postcards from the Edge 1990.

street n. a public road in a city, town, or village; this with the houses or buildings on each side; the persons who live or work in a particular street. —**on the streets**, working as a prostitute. **streets ahead (of)**, (colloquial) much superior (to). **streetwalker** n. a prostitute seeking customers in the street. **up one's street**, (colloquial) within one's range of interest or knowledge, to one's liking. [Old English from Latin strata (via) = paved (way)]

streetcar n. (US) a tram; see ◊tramway.

street hockey a form of hockey played on roller skates. At one time played mostly on streets in the USA, it is now played in indoor arenas, also in the UK.

Streisand /ˈstraɪsænd/ Barbra (Barbara Joan) 1942– . US singer and actress, who became a film star in Funny Girl 1968. Her subsequent films include What's Up Doc? 1972, A Star is Born 1979, and Yentl 1983, which she also directed.

strength n. 1. the quality, extent, or manner of being strong. 2. what makes one strong. 3. the number of persons present or available; the full complement. —**from strength to strength**, with ever-increasing success. **in strength**, in large numbers. **on the strength of**, relying on, on the basis of. [Old English]

strengthen /ˈstreŋθən/ v.t./i. to make or become stronger. —**strengthener** n.

strength of acids and bases in chemistry, the ability of ◊acids and ◊bases to dissociate in solution with water, and hence to produce a high or low ◊pH.

strenuous /ˈstrenjʊəs/ adj. making or requiring great exertions, energetic. —**strenuously** adv., **strenuousness** n. [from Latin strenuus]

streptococcus /ˌstreptəˈkɒkəs/ n. (plural streptococci /-aɪ/) a bacterium causing serious infections. —**streptococcal** adj. [from Greek streptos = twisted and kokkos = berry]

streptomycin /ˌstreptəˈmaɪsɪn/ n. an antibiotic drug discovered in 1944, used to treat tuberculosis, influenzal meningitis, and other infections, some of which are unaffected by ◊penicillin. [from Greek mukēs = fungus]

Stresemann /ˈʃtreɪzəmæn/ Gustav 1878–1929. German politician, chancellor in 1923 and foreign minister from 1923 to 1929 of the Weimar Republic. His achievements included negotiating the Pact of ◊Locarno 1925. He shared the 1926 Nobel Peace Prize with Aristide Briand.

stress n. 1. pressure, tension; the measure of this. 2. a demand on physical or mental strength; distress caused by this. 3. emphasis; the extra force used on a syllable or on word(s) in speaking, or on a note or notes in music. —v.t. 1. to lay stress on. 2. to subject to stress. —**lay stress on**, to indicate as important. [from distress or partly from Old French estresse = narrowness, from Latin stringere = draw tight]

stress and strain in the science of materials, measures of the deforming force applied to a body (stress) and of the resulting change in its shape (strain). For a perfectly elastic material, stress is proportional to strain (◊Hooke's law).

stressful adj. causing stress. —**stressfully** adv.

stretch v.t./i. 1. to pull out tightly or into a greater length, extent, or size; to be able to be stretched without breaking;

to tend to become stretched. 2. to place or lie at full length or spread out; to extend one's limbs and tighten the muscles after being relaxed. 3. to be continuous from a point or between points; to have a specified length or extension. 4. to make great demands on the abilities of; to strain to the utmost or beyond a reasonable limit; to exaggerate (the truth). —*n.* 1. stretching, being stretched; the ability to be stretched. 2. a continuous expanse or tract; a continuous period of time. 3. (*slang*) a period of imprisonment. 4. (*US*) the straight part of a racetrack. —*adj.* able to be stretched, elastic. —**stretch one's legs,** to exercise oneself by walking. **stretch out,** to extend (a hand or foot etc.); to last for a longer period; to prolong. **stretch a point,** to agree to something not normally allowed. [Old English]

stretcher *n.* 1. a framework of two poles with canvas etc. between for carrying a sick or injured person in a lying position. 2. any of various devices for stretching things. 3. a brick etc. placed lengthwise in the face of a wall.

stretchy *adj.* (*colloquial*) able or tending to stretch. —**stretchiness** *n.*

strew /struː/ *v.t.* (*past participle* **strewn** or **strewed**) to scatter or spread about over a surface; to cover or partly cover with scattered things. [Old English]

stria /ˈstraɪə/ *n.* (*plural* **striae** /-iː/) a slight furrow or ridge on a surface. [Latin]

striated /straɪˈeɪtɪd/ *adj.* marked with striae. —**striation** *n.*

stricken (*archaic*) past participle of **strike.**

strict *adj.* 1. precisely limited or defined, without exception or deviation. 2. requiring or giving complete obedience or exact performance. —**strictly speaking,** if one uses words in their strict sense. —**strictly** *adv.,* **strictness** *n.* [from Latin *strictus* (*stringere* = draw tight)]

stricture /ˈstrɪktʃ(ə/ *n.* 1. (usually in *plural*) a critical or censorious remark. 2. abnormal constriction of a tubelike part of the body.

stride *v.t./i.* (*past* **strode;** *past participle* **stridden** /ˈstrɪdən/) 1. to walk with long steps. 2. to cross with one step. 3. to bestride. —*n.* 1. a single long step; the length of this; gait as determined by the length of the stride. 2. (usually in *plural*) progress. —**get into one's stride,** to settle into an efficient rate of work. **take in one's stride,** to manage without difficulty. [Old English]

strident /ˈstraɪdənt/ *adj.* loud and harsh. —**stridency** *n.,* **stridently** *adv.* [from Latin *stridere* = creak]

stridulatory organs in insects, organs that produce sound when rubbed together. Crickets rub their wings together, but grasshoppers rub a hind leg against a wing. Stridulation is thought to be used for attracting mates, but may also serve to mark territory.

strife *n.* quarrelling, a state of conflict; a struggle between opposed persons or things. [from Old French *estrif*]

strike *v.t./i.* (*past* and *past participle* **struck**) 1. to subject to an impact; to bring or come into sudden hard contact (with); to inflict (a blow), to knock or propel with a blow or stroke. 2. to attack suddenly; (of a disease) to afflict. 3. (of lightning) to descend upon and blast. 4. to produce (sparks or a sound etc.) by striking something; to produce (a musical note) by pressing a key; to make (a coin or medal) by stamping metal etc.; to ignite (a match) by friction. 5. (of a clock) to indicate (time) by a sound; (of time) to be indicated thus. 6. to bring suddenly into a specified state as if at one stroke. 7. to reach (gold or mineral oil etc.) by digging or drilling. 8. to agree on (a bargain). 9. to put oneself theatrically into (an attitude). 10. to occur to the mind of; to produce a mental impression on. 11. to penetrate; to cause to penetrate; to fill with sudden fear etc. 12. to insert (a plant cutting) in the soil to take root; (of a cutting) to take root. 13. to cease work in protest about a grievance. 14. to lower or take down (a flag or tent etc.). 15. to take a specified direction. 16. to arrive at (an average or balance) by balancing or equalizing the items. —*n.* 1. an act or instance of striking. 2. employees' concerted refusal to work unless a grievance is remedied; a similar concerted abstention from activity by persons attempting to obtain a concession or register a grievance. 3. a sudden find or success. 4. an attack, especially from the air. —**be struck on,** (*slang*) to be infatuated with. **on strike,** taking part in an industrial strike. **strikebreaker** *n.* a person working or brought in in place of a striker. **strike home,** to deal an effective blow, to have an intended effect. **strike off,** to

Strindberg *Drawing of Swedish dramatist August Strindberg by his friend Carl Larsson.*

remove with a stroke; to delete (a name etc.) from a list. **strike out,** to hit out; to act vigorously; to delete (an item or name etc.). **strike pay,** an allowance paid by a trade union to members on strike. **strike up,** to start (an acquaintance, conversation etc.) rapidly or casually; to begin playing (a tune etc.). [Old English = go, stroke]

striker *n.* 1. a person or thing that strikes. 2. an employee who is on strike. 3. in football, a player whose main function is to try to score goals.

striking *adj.* sure to be noticed; attractive and impressive. —**strikingly** *adv.*

Strindberg /ˈstrɪndbɜːg/ August 1849–1912. Swedish playwright and novelist. His plays, influential in the development of dramatic technique, are in a variety of styles including historical plays, symbolic dramas (the two-part *Dödsdansen/The Dance of Death* 1901) and 'chamber plays' such as *Spöksonaten/The Ghost* [*Spook*] *Sonata* 1907. *Fadren/The Father* 1887 and *Fröken Julie/Miss Julie* 1888 are among his works.

Strine /straɪn/ *n.* a comic transliteration of Australian speech; Australian English, especially of the uneducated type. [alleged pronunciation of 'Australian' in such speech]

string *n.* 1. narrow cord, twine; a piece of this or a similar material used for tying or holding things together, for pulling, or interwoven in a frame to form the head of a racket. 2. a piece of catgut, cord, or wire stretched and caused to vibrate so as to produce notes in a musical instrument; (in *plural*) the stringed instruments played with a bow in an orchestra etc.; (*attributive*) relating to or consisting of these. 3. (in *plural*) an awkward stipulation or complication. 4. a set of things strung together; a series of people or events; a group of racehorses trained at one stable. 5. a strip of tough fibre connecting two halves of a bean pod etc. —*v.t./i.* (*past* and *past participle* **strung**) 1. to fit or fasten with string(s). 2. to thread (beads etc.) on a string. 3. to arrange in or as a string. 4. to trim the tough fibre from (beans). 5. (especially in *past participle*) to make (the nerves or resolution etc.) tense and ready for action. —**on a string,** under one's control or influence. **string along,** (*colloquial*) to deceive. **string along with,** (*colloquial*) to accompany. **string course,** a raised horizontal band of bricks etc. on a building. **string up,** to hang up on strings etc.; to kill by hanging. **string vest,** a vest of a material with large mesh. [Old English]

stringed *adj.* (of musical instruments) having strings.

stringed instrument a musical instrument that produces a sound by making a stretched string vibrate. Types include: **bowed** violin family; viol family; **plucked**

guitar, ukelele, lute, sitar, harp, banjo, lyre; **plucked mechanically** harpsichord; **struck mechanically** piano, clavichord; **hammered** dulcimer.

stringent /'strɪndʒənt/ *adj.* (of rules etc.) strict, severe, leaving no loophole for discretion. —**stringency** *n.*, **stringently** *adv.* [from Latin *stringere* = draw tight]

stringer /'strɪŋə/ *n.* 1. a longitudinal structural member in a framework especially of a ship or aircraft. 2. a newspaper correspondent not on the regular staff.

string theory a mathematical theory developed in the 1980s; see ◊superstring theory.

stringy /'strɪŋɪ/ *adj.* like a string, fibrous. —**stringiness** *n.*

strip[1] *v.t./i.* (**-pp-**) 1. to remove the clothes or covering from; to undress oneself. 2. to deprive of property or titles. 3. to leave bare of accessories or fittings. 4. to remove the old paint from. 5. to damage the thread of (a screw) or the teeth of (a gear). —*n.* 1. an act of stripping, especially of undressing in a striptease. 2. (*colloquial*) the clothes worn by the members of a sports team. —**strip club,** a club where striptease is performed. **strip down,** to remove the accessory fittings of or take apart (a machine etc.). **striptease** *n.* an entertainment in which a person gradually undresses before an audience. [from Old English = despoil]

strip[2] *n.* a long narrow piece or area. —**strip cartoon,** a comic strip. **strip light,** a tubular fluorescent lamp. **tear a person off a strip,** (*slang*) to rebuke him or her. [from or related to Middle Low German *strippe* = strap]

stripe *n.* 1. a long narrow band or strip differing in colour or texture from the surface on either side of it. 2. a chevron etc. denoting military rank. 3. (*archaic*, usually in *plural*) a blow with a scourge or lash.

striped /straɪpt/ *adj.* marked with stripes.

stripling *n.* a youth not fully grown.

stripper *n.* 1. a person or thing that strips something. 2. a device or solvent for removing paint etc. 3. a striptease performer.

stripy /'straɪpɪ/ *adj.* striped.

strive *v.i.* (*past* strove; *past participle* striven /'strɪvən/) 1. to make great efforts. 2. to carry on a conflict. [from Old French *estriver*]

strobe *n.* (*colloquial*) a stroboscope. [abbreviation]

strobilus in botany, a reproductive structure found in most ◊gymnosperms and some pteridophytes, notably the club mosses. In conifers the strobilus is commonly known as a ◊cone.

stroboscope /'strəʊbəskəʊp/ *n.* a lamp made to flash intermittently; an instrument for studying continuous periodic motion by using light flashing at the same frequency as that of the motion; for example, rotating machinery can be optically 'stopped' by illuminating it with a stroboscope flashing at the exact rate of rotation. —**stroboscopic** /-'skɒpɪk/ *adj.* [from Greek *strobos* = whirling and *skopeō* = look at]

strode *past* of **stride**.

Stroessner /'stresnə/ Alfredo 1912– . Military leader and president of Paraguay 1954–89. As head of the armed forces from 1951, he seized power in a coup in 1954 sponsored by the right-wing ruling Colorado Party. Accused by his opponents of harsh repression, his regime spent heavily on the military to preserve his authority. He was overthrown by a military coup and gained asylum in Brazil.

stroganoff /'strɒgənɒf/ *n.* or **beef stroganoff** a dish of strips of beef cooked in a sauce containing sour cream. [from Count Paul *Stroganov*, 19th-century Russian diplomat]

Stroheim /'ʃtrəʊhaɪm/ Erich von. Assumed name of Erich Oswald Stroheim 1885–1957. Austrian actor and director who worked in Hollywood from 1914. Successful as an actor in villainous roles, his career as a director was wrecked by his extravagance and he returned to acting in international films such as *La Grande Illusion* 1937 and *Sunset Boulevard* 1950. His films as director include *Greed* 1923 and *Queen Kelly* 1928 (unfinished).

stroke *n.* 1. an act of striking. 2. in medicine, a sudden interruption of the blood supply to the brain. It is also termed a cerebrovascular accident or apoplexy. Strokes are caused by a sudden bleed in the brain (cerebral haemorrhage) or interruption of the blood supply to part of the brain due to ◊embolism or ◊thrombosis. They vary in severity from producing almost no symptoms to proving rapidly fatal. In between are those (often recurring) that leave a wide range of impaired function, depending on the size and location of the event. 3. an action or movement, especially as one of a series or in a game etc.; the slightest such action; a highly effective effort, action, or occurrence of a specified kind. 4. the sound made by a striking clock. 5. a movement in one direction of a pen or paintbrush etc.; a detail contributing to a general effect. 6. a mode or action of moving an oar in rowing; a mode of moving the limbs in swimming. 7. or **stroke oar** the rower nearest the stern, who sets the time of the stroke. 8. an act or spell of stroking. —*v.t.* 1. to pass the hand gently along the surface of (hair or fur etc.). 2. to act as stroke of (a boat or crew). —**at a stroke,** by a single action. **on the stroke (of),** punctually (at).

stroll /strəʊl/ *v.i.* to walk in a leisurely way. —*n.* a short leisurely walk. —**strolling players,** actors etc. going from place to place performing.

strong *adj.* 1. having the power of resistance to being broken, damaged, disturbed, overcome etc. 2. capable of exerting great force or of doing much; physically powerful; powerful through numbers, resources, or quality; powerful in effect; (of an argument etc.) convincing. 3. concentrated, having a large proportion of a flavouring or colouring element, or of a substance in water or other solvent; (of a drink) containing much alcohol. 4. (placed after a noun) having a specified number of members. —*adv.* strongly, vigorously. —**strong-arm** *adj.* using force. **strongbox** *n.* a strongly made small chest for valuables. **strong language,** forceful language, swearing. **strong-minded** *adj.* having a determined mind. **strong point,** a fortified position; a thing at which one excels. **strongroom** *n.* a strongly built room for the storage and protection of valuables. **strong suit,** a suit at cards in which one can take tricks; a thing at which one excels. **strong verb,** a verb forming inflexions by vowel change within the stem rather than by the addition of a suffix. —**strongly** *adv.* [Old English]

stronghold *n.* 1. a fortified place; a secure refuge. 2. a centre of support for a cause etc.

strontium /'strɒntɪəm/ *n.* a soft, ductile, pale-yellow, metallic element, symbol Sr, atomic number 38, relative atomic mass 87.62. It is one of the ◊alkaline-earth elements, widely distributed in small quantities only as a sulphate or carbonate. Strontium salts burn with a red flame and are used in fireworks and signal flames. [from *Strontian,* town in Scotland where the carbonate was discovered]

strop *n.* a device, especially a strip of leather, for sharpening razors. —*v.t.* (**-pp-**) to sharpen on or with a strop. [from Middle Dutch or Middle Low German]

strophanthus *n.* any tropical plant of the genus *Strophanthus* of the dogbane family Apocynaceae, native to Africa and Asia. Seeds of the handsome climber *S. gratus* yield a poison, strophantin, used on arrows in hunting, and in medicine as a heart stimulant.

stroppy /'strɒpɪ/ *adj.* (*slang*) bad-tempered, awkward to deal with.

strove *past* of **strive**.

struck *past* and past participle of **strike**.

structural /'strʌktʃərəl/ *adj.* 1. of a structure or framework. 2. used in the construction of buildings etc. —**structural linguistics,** the study of a language viewed as a system made up of interrelated elements without regard to their historical development. —**structurally** *adv.*

structuralism /'strʌktʃərəlɪzəm/ *n.* 1. any theory or method in which a discipline or field of study is envisaged as comprising elements interrelated in systems and structures at various levels, being regarded as more significant than the elements considered in isolation. 2. in psychology, a method of investigating the structure of consciousness through the introspective analysis of simple forms of sensation, thought, images etc. 3. any of the theories of linguistics in which language is considered as a system or structure comprising elements at various phonological, grammatical, and semantic levels, especially after the work of the Swiss linguist Ferdinand de Saussure (1857–1913). —**structuralist** *n.*

structure /'strʌktʃə/ *n.* 1. the way in which a thing is constructed or organized. 2. a supporting framework or the essential parts of a thing. 3. a constructed thing, a complex whole; a building. —*v.t.* to give a structure to, to organize. [from Old French or Latin *structura* (*struere* = build)]

structured programming the process of writing a computer program in small, independent parts. This allows a more easily controlled program development and the individual design and testing of the component parts. Structured programs are built up from units called modules, which normally correspond to single procedures or functions.

strudel /'stru:dəl/ *n.* a confection of thin pastry filled especially with apple. [German]

struggle *v.i.* **1.** to throw one's limbs or body about in a vigorous effort to get free. **2.** to make a vigorous or determined effort under difficulties; to make one's way or a living etc. with difficulty. **3.** (with *with* or *against*) to try to overcome (an opponent) or deal with (a problem). —*n.* an act or period of struggling, a vigorous effort; a hard contest.

strum *v.t./i.* (**-mm-**) to play unskilfully or monotonously on (a stringed or keyboard instrument). —*n.* the act or sound of strumming. [imitative]

strumpet /'strʌmpɪt/ *n.* (*archaic*) a prostitute.

strung past and past participle of **string**.

strut *n.* **1.** a bar forming part of a framework and designed to strengthen and brace it. **2.** a strutting gait. —*v.t./i.* (**-tt-**) to walk in a stiff, pompous way. **3.** to brace with struts. [Old English]

'struth /stru:θ/ (*colloquial interjection*) an exclamation of surprise. [*God's truth*]

strychnine /'strɪkni:n/ *n.* $C_{21}H_{22}O_2N_2$, a bitter-tasting, poisonous alkaloid. It is a poison that causes violent muscular spasms; used in small doses as a stimulant, it is usually obtained by powdering the seeds of plants of the genus *Strychnos* (for example *Strychnos nux vomica*). Curare is a related drug. [from Latin from Greek *strukhnos* = nightshade]

Stuart /'stju:ət/ or **Stewart** the royal family which inherited the Scottish throne in 1371 and the English throne in 1603.

stub *n.* **1.** a short stump; a remnant of a pencil or cigarette etc. after use. **2.** the counterfoil of a cheque or receipt etc. —*v.t.* (**-bb-**) to strike (one's toe) against a hard object; (usually with *out*) to extinguish (a cigarette etc.) by pressing the lighted end against something. [Old English]

stubble *n.* **1.** the lower ends of the stalks of cereal plants left sticking up from the ground after the harvest is cut. **2.** a short stiff growth of hair or beard, especially that growing after shaving. —**stubbly** *adj.* [from Anglo-French from Latin, variant of *stipula* = straw]

stubborn /'stʌbən/ *adj.* obstinate, not docile; not easy to control or deal with. —**stubbornly** *adv.*, **stubbornness** *n.*

Stubbs /stʌbz/ George 1724–1806. English artist, known for paintings of horses. After the publication of his book of engravings *The Anatomy of the Horse* 1766, he was widely commissioned as an animal painter.

stubby *adj.* short and thick. —**stubbiness** *n.*

stucco *n.* (*plural* **stuccoes**) plaster or cement for coating walls or for moulding to form architectural decorations. —*v.t.* to coat with stucco. [Italian]

stuck past and past participle of **stick**[2].

stuck-up *adj.* conceited, snobbish.

stud[1] *n.* **1.** a short, large-headed nail, a rivet; a small knob projecting from a surface, especially for ornament. **2.** a device like a button on a shank, used e.g. to fasten a detachable shirt collar. —*v.t.* (**-dd-**) to set (as) with stud. [Old English]

stud[2] *n.* **1.** a number of horses kept for breeding etc.; the place where these are kept. **2.** a stallion. —**at stud**, (of a stallion) available for breeding on payment of a fee. **studbook** *n.* a book containing pedigrees of horses. **stud farm**, a farm where horses are bred. **National Stud**, a British establishment founded in 1915, and from 1964 located at Newmarket, where stallions are kept for visiting mares in order to breed racehorses. It is now maintained by the Horserace Betting Levy Board. **stud poker**, poker with betting after the dealing of successive cards face up. [Old English]

studding *n.* the woodwork of a lath-and-plaster wall.

studdingsail /'stʌnsəl/ *n.* an extra sail set at the side of a square sail in light winds.

student /'stju:dənt/ *n.* a person who is studying, especially at a university or other place of higher education;

(*attributive*) studying in order to become. [from Latin *studēre*]

studio /'stju:diəʊ/ *n.* (*plural* **studios**) **1.** the workroom of a painter, sculptor, photographer etc. **2.** a room or premises where cinema films are made. **3.** a room from which radio or television programmes are regularly broadcast or in which recordings are made. —**studio couch**, a divanlike couch that can be converted into a bed. [Italian from Latin]

studious /'stju:diəs/ *adj.* **1.** assiduous in study or reading. **2.** painstaking; careful and deliberate. —**studiously** *adv.*, **studiousness** *n.* [from Latin *studiosus*]

study /'stʌdɪ/ *n.* **1.** giving one's attention to acquiring information or knowledge, especially from books. **2.** the object of this; a thing worth studying. **3.** a work presenting the result of investigations into a particular subject; a preliminary drawing; a written or other portrayal of an aspect of behaviour or character etc. **4.** a musical composition designed to develop a player's skill. **5.** a room used by a person for reading, writing etc. —*v.t./i.* **1.** to make a study of; to examine attentively; to apply oneself to study. **2.** to give care and consideration to. **3.** (in *past participle*) deliberate, carefully and intentionally contrived. [from Old French from Latin *studium* = zeal, study]

stuff *n.* **1.** the material that a thing is made of or that may be used for some purpose. **2.** a substance, things, or belongings of an indeterminate kind or quality or not needing to be specified; a particular knowledge or activity. **3.** (*slang*) valueless matter, trash. **4.** woollen fabric (as distinct from silk, cotton, or linen). —*v.t./i.* **1.** to pack or cram; to fill tightly; to stop up. **2.** to fill the empty skin of (an animal or bird etc.) with material to restore its original shape, e.g. for exhibition in a museum; to fill with padding; to fill (a fowl or rolled meat etc.) with minced seasoning etc. before cooking. **3.** to fill (a person or oneself) with food; to eat greedily. **4.** to push hastily or clumsily. **5.** (*slang*) to dispose of as unwanted. —**get stuffed!** (*slang*) go away; stop annoying me. **stuff and nonsense**, an exclamation of incredulity or ridicule. **stuffed shirt**, (*colloquial*) a pompous person. [from Old French *estoffe* (*estoffer* = equip from Greek *stuphō* = draw together)]

stuffing *n.* **1.** padding used to stuff cushions etc. **2.** a savoury mixture used to stuff fowl etc.

stuffy *adj.* **1.** (of a room etc.) lacking ventilation or fresh air. **2.** (of the nose) blocked with secretions so that breathing is difficult. **3.** (*colloquial*) prim and pompous, old-fashioned or narrow-minded. **4.** (*colloquial*) showing annoyance. —**stuffily** *adv.*, **stuffiness** *n.*

Stukeley /'stju:klɪ/ William 1687–1765. English antiquarian and pioneer archaeologist, who made some of the earliest accurate observations about Stonehenge, in 1740, and Avebury, in 1743. He originated the popular idea that both were built by Druids.

stultify /'stʌltɪfaɪ/ *v.t.* to make ineffective or useless, to impair. —**stultification** /-fɪ'keɪʃən/ *n.* [from Latin *stultificare* (*stultus* = foolish and *facere* = make)]

stum *n.* unfermented grape juice, must. —*v.t.* (**-mm-**) **1.** to prevent from fermenting, or from continuing to ferment, by using sulphur etc. **2.** to renew the fermentation of (wine) by adding stum. [from Dutch *stom* from *stom* (adj.) = dumb]

stumble *v.i.* **1.** to lurch forward or have a partial fall from catching or striking or misplacing the foot; to walk with repeated stumbling. **2.** to make a mistake or repeated mistakes in speaking or in playing music. —*n.* an act of stumbling. —**stumble across** *or* **on**, to discover accidentally. **stumbling block**, an obstacle or circumstance etc. causing difficulty or hesitation.

stump *n.* **1.** the projecting remnant of a tree remaining in the ground after the rest has fallen or been cut down; a corresponding remnant of a broken tooth, amputated limb, or of something worn down. **2.** in cricket, each of the three uprights of a wicket. —*v.t./i.* **1.** to walk stiffly or noisily. **2.** in cricket, to put (a batsman) out by touching the stumps with the ball while he is outside his crease. **3.** (*colloquial*) to be too difficult for, to baffle. —**stump up**, (*slang*) to pay or produce (money required); to pay what is owed. [from Middle Dutch or Old High German]

stumpy *adj.* short and thick. —**stumpiness** *n.*

stun *v.t.* (**-nn-**) **1.** to knock senseless. **2.** to daze or shock by the impact of strong emotion. [from Old French from Latin *tonare* = thunder]

stung past and past participle of **sting**.

stunk a past and past participle of **stink**.

stunner *n.* (*colloquial*) a stunning person or thing.

stunning *adj.* (*colloquial*) extremely good or attractive. —**stunningly** *adv.*

stunt[1] *v.t.* to retard the growth or development of. [*stunt* = foolish, Old Norse *stuttr* = short]

stunt[2] *n.* (*colloquial*) something unusual or difficult done as a performance or to attract attention. —*v.i.* (*colloquial*) to perform stunts. —**stunt man** *or* **woman,** a person employed to take an actor's place in performing dangerous stunts.

stupa /ˈstjuːpə/ *n.* a round, usually domed, Buddhist monument, usually containing a sacred relic. [from Sanskrit = heap, pile]

stupefy /ˈstjuːpɪfaɪ/ *v.t.* 1. to dull the wits or senses of. 2. to stun with astonishment. —**stupefaction** /-ˈfækʃən/ *n.* [from French from Latin *stupefacere* (*stupēre* = be amazed and *facere* = make)]

stupendous *adj.* amazing or prodigious, especially by its size or degree. —**stupendously** *adv.* [from Latin]

stupid /ˈstjuːpɪd/ *adj.* 1. not intelligent or clever, slow at learning or understanding things; typical of stupid persons. 2. uninteresting, boring. 3. in a state of stupor. —**stupidity** /-ˈpɪdɪtɪ/ *n.,* **stupidly** *adv.* [from French or Latin]

stupor /ˈstjuːpər/ *n.* a dazed or torpid or helplessly amazed state. [Latin]

sturdy /ˈstɜːdɪ/ *adj.* strongly built, hardy, vigorous. —**sturdily** *adv.,* **sturdiness** *n.* [originally = recklessly violent, from Old French *est(o)urdi* = dazed]

sturgeon *n.* a large edible fish of the subclass Chondrostei. Sturgeons have five rows of bony plates, small mouths, and four barbels. They are voracious feeders and yield caviare. [from Anglo-French]

Sturges /ˈstɜːdʒɪz/ Preston. Adopted name of Edmond Biden 1898–1959. US film director and writer who enjoyed great success with a series of comedies in the early 1940s, including *Sullivan's Travels* 1941, *The Palm Beach Story,* and *The Miracle of Morgan's Creek* 1943.

Sturluson /ˈstuəlusɒn/ Snorri 1179–1241. Icelandic author of the Old Norse poems called ◊Eddas and the *Heimskringla,* a saga chronicle of Norwegian kings until 1177.

Sturm Abteilung /ˈʃtuəm æptaɪluŋ/ (SA) the German terrorist militia, also known as **Brownshirts,** of the ◊Nazi Party, established in 1921 under the leadership of ◊Röhm, in charge of physical training and political indoctrination. [German = storm section]

Sturm und Drang /ˈʃtuəm unt ˈdræŋ/ a German early Romantic movement in literature and music, from about 1775, concerned with the depiction of extravagant passions. Writers associated with the movement include Herder, Goethe, and Schiller. [German = storm and stress, from a play by Friedrich von Klinger 1776]

stutter *v.t./i.* to stammer, especially by involuntarily repeating the first consonants of words; to utter (words) thus. —*n.* an act or habit of stuttering. —**stutterer** *n.* [frequentative of dialect *stut*]

Stuttgart /ˈʃtutɡɑːt/ capital of Baden-Württemberg, SW Germany; population (1988) 565,000. Industries include publishing and the manufacture of vehicles and electrical goods.

sty[1] /staɪ/ *n.* a pigsty. [Old English]

sty[2] *n.* an inflamed swelling on the edge of an eyelid. [from dialect *styany* = *styan eye* from Old English = swelling eye, shortened as though = *sty on eye*]

Stygian /ˈstɪdʒɪən/ *adj.* of or like the Styx or Hades; gloomy, murky. [from Latin from Greek *Stugios* = Styx, river of Hades]

style /staɪl/ *n.* 1. a kind or sort, especially in regard to appearance and form. 2. the manner of writing, speaking, or doing something; the distinctive manner of a person, school, or period. 3. the correct way of designating a person or thing. 4. elegance, distinction. 5. shape; pattern; fashion (in dress etc.). 6. a pointed implement for scratching or engraving things. 7. in flowers, the part of the ◊carpel bearing the ◊stigma at its tip. In some flowers it is very short or completely lacking, while in others it may be long and slender, positioning the stigma in the most effective place to receive the pollen. —*v.t./i.* 1. to design or make etc. in a particular (especially a fashionable) style. 2. to designate in a specified way. [from Old French from Latin *stilus* = stylus]

stylish *adj.* in fashionable style; elegant. —**stylishly** *adv.,* **stylishness** *n.*

stylist *n.* 1. a person concerned with style, especially a writer having or aiming at a good literary style, or a designer of fashionable styles. 2. a hairdresser who styles hair.

stylistic /staɪˈlɪstɪk/ *adj.* of literary or artistic style. —*n.* (in *plural*) the study of literary style. —**stylistically** *adv.*

stylite /ˈstaɪlaɪt/ *n.* any of the Christian ascetics who lived on a platform on top of a pillar, especially in Syria in the 5th century. [from Greek *stulos* = pillar]

stylized /ˈstaɪlaɪzd/ *adj.* (of a work of art etc.) made to conform to a conventional style.

stylus *n.* (*plural* **styluses**) 1. a needlelike point for producing or following a groove in a gramophone record. 2. a pointed writing implement. [erroneous spelling of Latin *stilus*]

stymie /ˈstaɪmɪ/ *n.* 1. in golf, the situation when an opponent's ball is between one's own ball and the hole. 2. a difficult situation that blocks or thwarts one's activities. —*v.t.* 1. to subject to a stymie. 2. to block or thwart the activities of.

styptic /ˈstɪptɪk/ *adj.* checking the flow of blood by causing blood vessels to contract. [from Latin from Greek *stuphō* = contract]

styrene /ˈstaɪriːn/ *n.* a liquid hydrocarbon easily polymerized and used in making plastics. [from Greek *sturax* = a resin]

Styx /stɪks/ in Greek mythology, the river surrounding the underworld.

Suárez González /ˈswɑːreθ ɡɒnˈθɑːleθ/ Adolfo 1933– . Spanish politician, prime minister 1976–81. A friend of King Juan Carlos, he was appointed by the king to guide Spain into democracy after the death of the fascist dictator Franco.

suasion /ˈsweɪʒən/ *n.* persuasion. —**moral suasion,** a strong recommendation appealing to the moral sense. [from Old French or Latin *suadēre* = urge]

suave /swɑːv/ *adj.* smooth-mannered. —**suavely** *adv.,* **suavity** *n.* [French or from Latin *suavis* = agreeable]

sub *n.* (*colloquial*) 1. a submarine. 2. a subscription. 3. a substitute. 4. a subeditor. —*v.t./i.* (**-bb-**) (*colloquial*) 1. to substitute. 2. to subedit. [abbreviation]

sub- prefix (in some Latin-derived words **suc-** before *c,* **suf-** before *f,* **sug-** before *g,* **sup-** before *p,* **sur-** before *r,* **sus-** before *s*) denoting 1. under, at, to, or from a lower position (e.g. *subordinate, submerge, subtract*). 2. secondary or inferior position (e.g. *subclass, sublieutenant, subtotal*). 3. nearly, more or less (e.g. *subarctic*). [from Latin *sub* = under]

subaltern /ˈsʌbəltən/ *n.* an officer of the rank next below a captain. [from Latin *alter* = other]

subaqua /sʌbˈækwə/ *adj.* (of a sport etc.) taking place underwater. [from Latin *sub aqua* = under the water]

subaquatic *adj.* underwater.

subaqueous /sʌbˈeɪkwɪəs/ *adj.* subaquatic.

subarctic /sʌbˈɑːktɪk/ *adj.* of or like the regions somewhat south of the Arctic Circle.

subatomic /sʌbəˈtɒmɪk/ *adj.* occurring in an atom; smaller than an atom.

subatomic particle see ◊particle, subatomic, and ◊elementary particle.

Subbuteo /səˈbuːtɪəu/ *n.* a game that simulates an association football match. Players manipulate plastic figures to pass the ball and score goals. A world cup championship is held every four years.

subcommittee /ˈsʌbkəmɪtɪ/ *n.* a committee formed for a special purpose from some members of the main committee.

subconscious /sʌbˈkɒnʃəs/ *n.* the part of the mind that is considered to be not fully conscious but able to influence actions etc. —*adj.* of the subconscious. —**subconsciously** *adv.*

subcontinent /sʌbˈkɒntɪnənt/ *n.* a landmass of great extent not classed as a continent.

subcontract /sʌbˈkɒntrækt/ *n.* an arrangement by which one who has contracted to do work arranges for it to be done by others. —/sʌbkənˈtrækt/ *v.t./i.* to make a subcontract (for). —**subcontractor** /-ˈtræktə/ *n.*

subculture /ˈsʌbkʌltʃə/ *n.* a social group or its culture within a larger culture.

subcutaneous /sʌbkju:'teɪnɪəs/ *adj.* under the skin.

subdivide /sʌbdɪ'vaɪd/ *v.t./i.* to divide again after the first division.

subdivision /'sʌbdɪvɪʒən/ *n.* 1. subdividing. 2. a subordinate division.

subdue /səb'dju:/ *v.t.* 1. to overcome, to bring under control. 2. (especially in *past participle*) to make softer, gentler, or less intense. [from Old French *souduire* = seduce from Latin *subducere* = withdraw, used with sense of Latin *subdere* = conquer]

subedit *v.t.* to act as subeditor of.

subeditor *n.* 1. an assistant editor. 2. one who prepares material for printing in a newspaper or book etc. —**subeditorial** /-'tɔːrɪəl/ *adj.*

subfusc /sʌb'fʌsk/ *n.* the dull-coloured clothing worn in some universities on formal occasions. [from Latin *fuscus* = dark brown]

subheading /'sʌbhedɪŋ/ *n.* a subordinate heading.

subhuman /sʌb'hju:mən/ *adj.* less than human; not fully human.

subject¹ /'sʌbdʒɪkt/ *n.* 1. the person or thing being discussed, described, represented, or studied. 2. a person under a particular political rule; any member of a state except the supreme ruler; a person owing obedience to another. 3. a circumstance, person, or thing that gives occasion for a specified feeling or action. 4. a branch of study. 5. in logic and grammar, the term about which something is predicated in a proposition; the word(s) in a sentence that name who or what does the action or undergoes what is stated in the verb. 6. in philosophy, the conscious self as opposed to all that is external to the mind; the substance as opposed to the attributes of something. 7. a principal theme in a piece of music. 8. especially in medicine, a person with a specified (usually undesirable) bodily or mental tendency. —*adj.* not politically independent, owing obedience to another state etc. —*adv.* (with *to*) provided that (a specified condition is fulfilled). —**subject to**, owing obedience to; liable to. [from Old French from Latin *subjicere* = place beneath (*jacere* = throw)]

subject² *v.t.* 1. (with *to*) to cause to undergo or experience. 2. to bring (a country etc.) under one's control. —**subjection** *n.*

subjective /səb'dʒektɪv/ *adj.* 1. of or due to the consciousness or thinking or the percipient subject as opposed to real or external things, not objective; imaginary. 2. giving prominence to or depending on personal opinions or idiosyncrasy. 3. in grammar, of the subject. —**subjectively** *adv.*, **subjectivity** /-'tɪvɪtɪ/ *n.* [from Latin]

subjoin /səb'dʒɔɪn/ *v.t.* to add (an anecdote or illustration etc.) at the end.

sub judice /sʌb 'dʒu:dɪsɪ/ under judicial consideration, not yet decided (and in the UK therefore not to be commented on). [Latin = under a judge]

subjugate /'sʌbdʒʊgeɪt/ *v.t.* to conquer, to bring into subjection or bondage. —**subjugation** /-'geɪʃən/ *n.*, **subjugator** *n.* [from Latin *subjugare* (*jugum* = yoke)]

subjunctive /səb'dʒʌŋktɪv/ *adj.* in grammar, (of a word) expressing a wish, supposition, or possibility (e.g. *if I were you; suffice it to say*). —*n.* a subjunctive mood or form. [from French or Latin]

subkingdom /'sʌbkɪŋdəm/ *n.* a taxonomic category below a kingdom.

sublease /'sʌblɪ:s/ *n.* a lease granted to a subtenant. —/sʌb'lɪ:s/ *v.t.* to lease by a sublease.

sublet /sʌb'let/ *v.t.* (-tt-; *past* and *past participle* sublet) to let to a subtenant.

sublimate /'sʌblɪmeɪt/ *v.t.* 1. to divert the energy of (a primitive impulse etc.) into a culturally higher activity. 2. to sublime (a substance); to refine, to purify. —/'sʌblɪmət/ *n.* a sublimed substance. —**sublimation** /-'meɪʃən/ *n.* 1. the diversion of energy into a culturally higher activity. 2. in chemistry, the conversion of a solid to vapour without passing through the liquid phase. [from Latin *sublimare*]

sublime /sə'blaɪm/ *adj.* 1. of the highest or most exalted sort, awe-inspiring. 2. characteristic of one who has no fear of the consequences. —*v.t./i.* to convert (a substance) from a solid into a vapour by heat (and usually allow to solidify again); (of a substance) to undergo this process; to purify or make sublime. —**sublimely** *adv.*, **sublimity** /-'lɪmɪtɪ/ *n.* [from Latin *sublimis*]

subliminal /sʌb'lɪmɪnəl/ *adj.* below the threshold of consciousness; too faint or rapid to be consciously perceived. It may be visual (words or images flashed between the frames of a cinema or TV film), or aural (a radio message broadcast constantly at very low volume). Subliminal advertising is illegal in many countries, including Britain. —**subliminally** *adv.* [from Latin *limen* = threshold]

sublunar /sʌb'lu:nə/ *adj.* or **sublunary** existing or situated beneath the Moon or between its orbit and that of Earth; subject to the Moon's influence.

sub-machine-gun *n.* a lightweight machine gun held in the hand.

submarine /sʌbmə'ri:n, 'sʌb-/ *n.* an underwater ship, especially an armed warship. The first underwater ship was constructed for James I of England by the Dutch scientist Cornelius van Drebbel (1572–1633) in 1620. In nuclear submarines, steam turbines use the heat given off by the nuclear reactor to drive a propeller. —*adj.* existing or occurring or done below the surface of the sea.

submerge /səb'mɜ:dʒ/ *v.t./i.* 1. to place below the surface of water or other liquid; to flood. 2. (of a submarine) to dive, to go below the surface. —**submergence** *n.*, **submersion** *n.* [from Latin *mergere* = dip]

submersible /səb'mɜ:sɪbəl/ *adj.* capable of submerging. —*n.* a vessel designed to operate under water, especially a small submarine used by engineers and research scientists as a ferry craft to support diving operations. The most advanced submersibles are the lock-out type, which have two compartments: one for the pilot, the other to carry divers. The diving compartment is pressurized and provides access to the sea.

submicroscopic /sʌbmaɪkrə'skɒpɪk/ *adj.* too small to be seen by an ordinary microscope.

submission /səb'mɪʃən/ *n.* 1. submitting, being submitted. 2. a thing submitted; a theory etc. submitted by counsel to a judge or jury. [from Old French or Latin]

submissive /səb'mɪsɪv/ *adj.* submitting to power or authority; meek, willing to obey. —**submissively** *adv.*, **submissiveness** *n.*

submit *v.t./i.* (-tt-) 1. to surrender (oneself) to the control or authority of another; to cease to resist or oppose. 2. to present for consideration or decision. 3. to subject (a person or thing) to a process or treatment. [from Latin *mittere* = send]

subnormal /'sʌbnɔːməl/ *adj.* 1. less than normal. 2. below the normal standard of intelligence. —**subnormality** /-'mælɪtɪ/ *n.*

suborder /'sʌbɔːdə/ *n.* a taxonomic category between order and family.

subordinate /sə'bɔ:dɪnət/ *adj.* 1. of lesser importance or rank. 2. working under the control or authority of another. —*n.* a person in a subordinate position. —/-eɪt/ *v.t.* to make or treat as subordinate. —**subordinate clause**, a clause serving as a noun, adjective, or adverb within a sentence. —**subordination** /-'neɪʃən/ *n.* [from Latin *ordinare* = ordain]

suborn /sə'bɔ:n/ *v.t.* to induce (especially by bribery) to commit perjury or some other crime. —**subornation** /-'neɪʃən/ *n.* [from Latin *subornare* = incite secretly (*ornare* = equip)]

subplot *n.* a subordinate plot in a play.

subpoena /səb'pi:nə/ *n.* in law, a writ requiring someone to give evidence before a court or judicial official at a specific time and place. —*v.t.* (*past* and *past participle* subpoenaed /-nəd/) to serve a subpoena on. [from Latin *sub poena* = under penalty]

sub rosa /sʌb 'rəʊzə/ in confidence or secretly. [Latin = under the rose, as emblem of secrecy]

subroutine *n.* in computing, a small section of a program that is executed ('called') from another part of the program. Subroutines provide a method of performing the same task at more than one point in the program, and also of separating the details of a program from its main logic. In some computer languages, subroutines are similar to ◊functions or ◊procedures.

subscribe /səb'skraɪb/ *v.t./i.* 1. to contribute (a sum of money); to pay regularly for membership of an organization, receipt of a publication etc. 2. to sign (one's name) at the foot of a document; to sign (a document) thus. 3. (with *to*) to express one's agreement with (an opinion or resolution). [from Latin *scribere* = write]

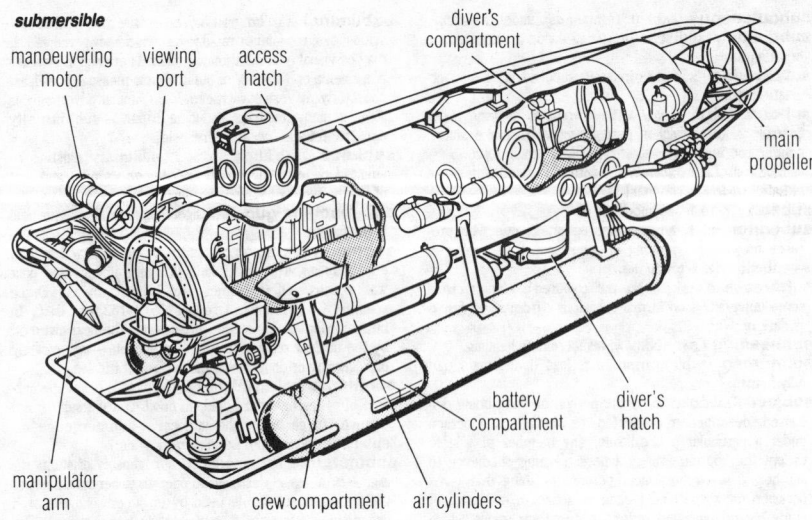

submersible

manoeuvering motor · viewing port · access hatch · diver's compartment · main propeller · battery compartment · diver's hatch · manipulator arm · crew compartment · air cylinders

subscriber *n.* 1. one who subscribes. 2. a person paying a regular sum for the hire of a telephone. —**subscriber trunk dialling**, the making of trunk calls by a subscriber without the assistance of an operator.

subscript /'sʌbskrɪpt/ *adj.* written or printed below. —*n.* a subscript number or symbol. [from Latin]

subscription /səb'skrɪpʃən/ *n.* 1. subscribing. 2. money subscribed; a fee for membership of an organization etc. —**subscription concert**, a concert (usually one of a series) paid for mainly by those who subscribe in advance.

subsection /'sʌbsekʃən/ *n.* a division of a section.

subsequent /'sʌbsɪkwənt/ *adj.* following a specified or implied event. —**subsequent to**, later than, after. —**subsequently** *adv.* [from Old French or Latin *sequi* = follow]

subservient *adj.* 1. subordinate. 2. servile, obsequious. 3. of use in a minor role. —**subservience** *n.*, **subserviently** *adv.* [from Latin *servire* = serve]

subside *v.i.* 1. to sink or settle to a lower level or to the bottom. 2. (of ground) to cave in, to sink. 3. to become less active or intense or prominent. 4. (of a person) to sink into a chair etc. —**subsidence** /səb'saɪdəns, 'sʌbsɪdəns/ *n.* [from Latin *sidere* = settle, related to *sedēre* = sit]

subsidiary /səb'sɪdɪərɪ/ *adj.* 1. of secondary (not primary) importance. 2. (of a company) legally controlled by another company having 50% or more of its shares. —*n.* a subsidiary company, thing, or person. [from Latin]

subsidize *v.t.* to provide with a subsidy; to reduce the cost of with a subsidy.

subsidy /'sʌbsɪdɪ/ *n.* payment or concession contributed by the state or a public body etc. to a state or private company, or an individual, to keep prices at a desired level or to assist in meeting expenses etc. [from Anglo-French from Latin *subsidium* = assistance]

subsist /səb'sɪst/ *v.i.* to exist, to continue to exist, to get sustenance or a livelihood. [from Latin *subsistere* = stand firm (*sistere* = set, stand)]

subsistence /səb'sɪstəns/ *n.* subsisting; a means of this. —**subsistence farming**, farming in which almost all the crops are consumed by the farmer's household. **subsistence level** *or* **wage**, merely enough to provide the bare necessities of life.

subsoil /'sʌbsɔɪl/ *n.* the soil immediately below the surface soil.

subsonic /sʌb'sɒnɪk/ *adj.* relating to speeds less than that of sound. —**subsonically** *adv.*

subspecies /'sʌbspiːʃiːz/ *n.* a taxonomic category below a species, usually a more or less permanent variety geographically isolated.

substance /'sʌbstəns/ *n.* 1. a particular kind of matter having more or less uniform properties. 2. the essence of what is spoken or written. 3. reality, solidity. 4. wealth and possessions. 5. content as distinct from form. —**in substance**, in the main points. [from Old French from Latin = essence]

substandard /sʌb'stændəd/ *adj.* below the usual or required standard.

substantial /səb'stænʃəl/ *adj.* 1. of real importance or value; considerable in amount. 2. of solid structure. 3. having substance, actually existing. 4. well-to-do. 5. essential, virtual. —**substantially** *adv.*

substantiate /səb'stænʃɪeɪt/ *v.t.* to support with evidence, to prove the truth of. —**substantiation** /-'eɪʃən/ *n.* [from Latin *substantiare* = give substance to]

substantive /'sʌbstəntɪv, səb'stæntɪv/ *adj.* 1. having independent existence, not subordinate. 2. actual, real, permanent. —/'sʌb-/ *n.* a noun. —**substantival** /-'taɪvəl/ *adj.*

substation /'sʌbsteɪʃən/ *n.* a subordinate station; a station at which electrical current is switched, transformed, or converted, intermediate between a generating station and a low-tension distribution network.

substitute /'sʌbstɪtjuːt/ *n.* a person or thing acting or serving in place of another. —*v.t.* to put, use, or serve as a substitute. —*adj.* acting as a substitute. —**substitution** /-'tjuːʃən/ *n.* —**substitution reaction**, in chemistry, the replacement of one atom or ◊functional group in an organic molecule by another. [from Latin *substituere* (*statuere* = set up)]

substrate *n.* in biochemistry, a compound or mixture of compounds acted on by an enzyme. The term also refers to a substance such as ◊agar that provides the nutrients for the metabolism of microorganisms. Since the enzyme systems of microorganisms regulate their metabolism, the essential meaning is the same.

substratum *n.* (*plural* **substrata**) an underlying layer or substance. [past participle of Latin *substernere* (*sternere* = strew)]

subsume *v.t.* to include (an instance etc.) under a particular rule or class. —**subsumption** /-'sʌmpʃən/ *n.* [from Latin *sumere* = take]

subtenant /'sʌbtenənt/ *n.* a person renting a room or house etc. from one who is a tenant of it. —**subtenancy** *n.*

subtend *v.t.* (of a line or arc) to form (an angle) at a point where lines drawn from each end of it meet; (of an angle or chord) to have bounding lines or points that meet or coincide with those of (a line or arc). [from Latin *tendere* = stretch]

subterfuge /'sʌbtəfjuːdʒ/ *n.* a piece of trickery or deceit etc. used to escape blame or defeat etc.; the use of this. [French, or from Latin *subterfugere* = escape secretly (*subter* = beneath and *fugere* = flee)]

subterranean /sʌbtə'reɪnɪən/ *adj.* underground. [from Latin *terra* = earth]

subtitle /'sʌbtaɪtəl/ *n.* 1. a subordinate or additional title of a book etc. 2. a caption of a cinema film, especially translating foreign dialogue. —*v.t.* to provide with a subtitle or subtitles.

subtle /'sʌtəl/ *adj.* **1.** slight and difficult to detect or describe. **2.** making or able to make fine distinctions. **3.** ingenious, crafty. —**subtlety** *n.*, **subtly** *adv.* [from Old French from Latin *subtilis*]

subtopia /sʌb'təʊpiə/ *n.* unsightly suburbs, especially those disfiguring a rural area. [from *sub(urb)* and *(u)topia*]

subtotal /'sʌbtəʊtəl/ *n.* the total of part of a group of figures to be added.

subtract /səb'trækt/ *v.t.* to deduct, to remove (a part, quantity, or number) from a greater one. —**subtraction** *n.* [from Latin *trahere* = draw]

subtropical /sʌb'trɒpikəl/ *adj.* **1.** bordering on the tropics. **2.** characteristic of subtropical regions.

suburb /'sʌbɜːb/ *n.* an outlying district of a city. [from Old French or Latin *suburbium* (*urbs* = city)]

suburban /sə'bɜːbən/ *adj.* of or characteristic of suburbs; having only limited interests and narrow-minded views. —**suburbanite** *n.* [from Latin]

Suburbia /sə'bɜːbiə/ *n.* (usually *derogatory*) the suburbs and their inhabitants.

subvention /səb'venʃən/ *n.* a subsidy. [from Old French from Latin *subvenire* = come to a person's aid from *venire* = come]

subversive /səb'vɜːsɪv/ *adj.* attempting subversion. —*n.* a subversive person. [from Latin]

subvert /səb'vɜːt/ *v.t.* to weaken or overthrow the authority of (a government etc.); to attempt to do this. —**subversion** *n.* [from Old French or Latin *subvertere* = overturn (*vertere* = turn)]

subway /'sʌbweɪ/ *n.* **1.** an underground passage, especially for pedestrians. **2.** (*US*) an ◊underground railway.

suc- prefix; see ◊sub-.

succeed /sək'siːd/ *v.t./i.* **1.** to be successful. **2.** to come next in time or order, to follow. **3.** to come by inheritance or due order (to an office or title). [from Old French or Latin *succedere* (*cedere* = go)]

success /sək'ses/ *n.* **1.** a favourable outcome, the accomplishment of what was aimed at; the attainment of wealth, fame, or position. **2.** a thing or person that turns out well. [from Latin *successus*]

successful *adj.* having success, prosperous. —**successfully** *adv.*

succession /sək'seʃən/ *n.* **1.** following in order; a series of people or things one after another. **2.** succeeding to the throne or to an office or inheritance; the right of doing this; a series of persons having such a right. **3.** in ecology, the series of changes that occur in the structure and composition of the vegetation in a given area from the time it is first colonized by plants (**primary succession**), or after it has been disturbed by fire, flood, or clearing (**secondary succession**). —**in succession**, one after another. **in succession to**, as the successor of.

successive /sək'sesɪv/ *adj.* following in succession; in an unbroken series. —**successively** *adv.* [from Latin]

successor /sək'sesə/ *n.* a person or thing that succeeds another.

succinct *adj.* concise, expressed briefly and clearly. —**succinctly** *adv.*, **succinctness** *n.* [from Latin *succingere* = tuck up (*cingere* = gird)]

Succot /'sʊkəs/ *n.* or **Sukkoth** in Judaism, a harvest festival celebrated in Oct, also known as the **Feast of Booths**, which commemorates the time when the Israelites lived in the wilderness during the ◊Exodus from Egypt. As a reminder of the shelters used in the wilderness, huts are built and used for eating and sleeping during the seven days of the festival.

succour /'sʌkə/ *n.* (*literary*) help given in time of need. —*v.t.* (*literary*) to give succour to. [from Old French from Latin *currere* = run]

succubus *n.* a female spirit; see ◊incubus.

succulent /'sʌkjʊlənt/ *adj.* **1.** juicy (*literally* or *figuratively*). **2.** (of a plant) having thick, fleshy leaves or stems. —*n.* a succulent plant: a thick, fleshy plant that stores water in its tissues; for example, cacti and stonecrops. Succulents live either in areas where water is very scarce, such as deserts, or in places where it is not easily obtainable because of the high concentrations of salts in the soil, as in salt marshes. See also ◊xerophyte. —**succulence** *n.* [from Latin *succus* = juice]

succumb /sə'kʌm/ *v.i.* to give way to something overpowering; to die. [from Old French or Latin *cumbere* = lie]

such *adj.* **1.** of the kind or degree indicated or suggested. **2.** of the same kind. **3.** so great or extreme. —*pron.* such a person or persons or thing(s). —**as such**, as being what has been specified; in itself. **such-and-such** *adj.* (a person or thing) of a particular kind but not needing to be specified. **such as**, for example. [Old English]

suchlike *adj.* of the same kind. —*pron.* (usually *plural*) things of this kind.

suck *v.t./i.* **1.** to draw (liquid) into the mouth by using the lip muscles; to draw liquid from (a thing) thus. **2.** to squeeze and extract the flavour from (a sweet etc.) in the mouth by using the tongue. **3.** to use a sucking action or make a sucking sound. **4.** to draw in; to obtain. —*n.* an act or period of sucking. —**suck dry**, to exhaust the contents of by sucking. **suck in** or **up**, to absorb; to engulf, to draw into itself. **suck up to**, (*slang*) to toady to. [Old English]

sucker *n.* **1.** a shoot springing from a plant's root or its stem below ground. Plants that produce suckers include the elm, the dandelion, and members of the rose family. **2.** an organ in animals or a part of an apparatus for adhering by suction to surfaces. **3.** (*slang*) a gullible or easily deceived person.

sucking pig a pig that is not yet weaned, especially one suitable for roasting whole.

suckle *v.t.* **1.** to feed (young) from the breast or udder. **2.** (of young) to take milk thus.

suckling *n.* an unweaned child or animal.

sucrase *n.* an enzyme capable of digesting sucrose into its constituent molecules of glucose and fructose.

Sucre /'suːkreɪ/ legal capital and judicial seat of Bolivia; population (1985) 87,000. It stands on the central plateau at an altitude of 2,840 m/9,320 ft. The first revolt against Spanish rule in South America began here on 25 May 1809.

Sucre Antonio José de 1795–1830. South American revolutionary leader. As chief lieutenant of Simón ◊Bolívar, he won several battles in freeing the colonies of Ecuador and Bolivia from Spanish rule, and in 1826 became president of Bolivia. After a mutiny by the army and invasion by Peru, he resigned in 1828 and was assassinated in 1830 on his way to join Bolívar.

sucrose *n.* $C_{12}H_{22}O_{11}$, a ◊disaccharide known commonly as ◊sugar, cane sugar, or beet sugar. [from French *sucre* = sugar]

suction /'sʌkʃən/ *n.* **1.** sucking. **2.** production of a partial vacuum causing adhesion of surfaces or enabling external atmospheric pressure to force a liquid etc. into the vacant space. [from Latin *suctio* (*sugere* = suck)]

Sudan /suː'dɑːn/ Democratic Republic of; country in NE Africa, S of Egypt, with a Red Sea coast; it is the largest country in Africa; **area** 2,505,800 sq km/967,489 sq mi; **capital** Khartoum; **physical** fertile valley of river Nile separates Libyan Desert in W from high rocky Nubian Desert in E; Sudd swamp; **head of state and government** Gen Omar Hasan Ahmed el-Bashir from 1989; **political system** military republic; **exports** cotton, gum arabic, sesame seed, peanuts, sorghum; **population** (1990 est) 25,164,000; **language** Arabic 51% (official); tribal languages; **recent history** Sudan achieved independence from Britain and Egypt as a republic in 1956; the name was changed to the Democratic Republic of Sudan in 1969. A new constitution was adopted in 1971 and a national assembly established in 1974. *Sharia* (Islamic law) was introduced in 1983. Following a series of unsatisfactory governments and coups since 1956, the country reached a state of virtual civil war with the Sudan People's Liberation Movement (SPLM) in 1987; a peace pact was signed in 1988 but civil war continued with a new SPLM offensive in 1990.

Sudbury /'sʌdbəri/ city. in Ontario, Canada; population (1986) 149,000. A buried meteorite there yields 90% of the world's nickel.

sudden /'sʌdən/ *adj.* done or occurring etc. abruptly or unexpectedly. —**all of a sudden,** suddenly. **sudden death,** (*colloquial*) a decision (especially in a drawn contest) by the result of a single event. —**suddenly** *adv.*, **suddenness** *n.* [from Anglo-French from Latin *subitus* = sudden]

sudden infant death syndrome (SIDS) the technical term for ◊cot death.

Sudetenland /suː'deɪtnlænd/ mountainous region of N Czechoslovakia, annexed by Germany under the ◊Munich Agreement of 1938; it was returned to Czechoslovakia in 1945.

sudorific /sjuːˈdɔrɪfɪk, suːˈ-/ *adj.* causing sweating. —*n.* a sudorific drug. [from Latin *sudor* = sweat and *facere* = make]

Sudra /ˈsuːdrə/ *n.* a member of the lowest of the four great Hindu classes (the labourer class), whose function is to serve the other three varnas; this class. [from Sanskrit]

suds /sʌdz/ *n.pl.* froth of soap and water. —**sudsy** *adj.*

sue /sjuː, suː/ *v.t./i.* **1.** to begin a lawsuit against (a person). **2.** to make an application. [from Anglo-French, ultimately from Latin *sequi* = follow]

suede /sweɪd/ *n.* **1.** kid or other skin with the flesh side rubbed to a nap. **2.** a cloth imitating this. [from French (*gants de*) *Suède* = (gloves of) Sweden]

suedette /sweɪˈdet/ *n.* a material designed to imitate the texture of suede, especially a type of cotton or rayon fabric with a suedelike nap.

suet /ˈsjuːɪt, ˈsuːˈ-/ *n.* the hard fat of the kidneys and loins of oxen or sheep etc. —**suety** *adj.* [from Old French from Latin *sebum* = tallow]

Suetonius /suːɪˈtəʊniəs/ (Gaius Suetonius Tranquillius) *c.* AD 69–140. Roman historian, author of *Lives of the Caesars* (Julius Caesar to Domitian).

Suez Canal /ˈsuːɪz/ artificial waterway, 160 km/100 mi long, from Port Said to Suez, linking the Mediterranean and Red seas, separating Africa from Asia, and providing the shortest eastwards sea route from Europe. It was opened in 1869, nationalized in 1956, blocked by Egypt during the Arab-Israeli war of 1967, and not reopened until 1975.

Suez Crisis the military confrontation of Oct–Dec 1956 following the nationalization of the Suez Canal by President Nasser of Egypt. In an attempt to reassert international control of the canal, Israel launched an attack, after which British and French troops landed. Widespread international censure (Soviet protest, US nonsupport, and considerable domestic opposition) forced the withdrawal of British and French troops. The crisis resulted in the resignation of British prime minister Eden.

suf- prefix; see ◊sub-.

suffer *v.t./i.* **1.** to experience the effects of (something unpleasant); to feel pain or grief; to be subjected to damage. **2.** to undergo (a change). **3.** to tolerate; (*archaic*) to permit. —**sufferer** *n.*, **suffering** *n.* [from Anglo-French from Latin *ferre* = bear]

sufferable *adj.* bearable.

sufferance *n.* tacit consent, abstention from an objection. —**on sufferance**, tolerated but not supported.

suffice /səˈfaɪs/ *v.t./i.* to be enough or adequate; to meet the needs of (a person etc.). —**suffice it to say,** I will content myself with saying. [from Old French from Latin *sufficere* (*facere* = make)]

sufficiency /səˈfɪʃənsɪ/ *n.* a sufficient amount. [from Latin]

sufficient /səˈfɪʃənt/ *adj.* enough. —**sufficiently** *adv.* [from Old French or Latin]

suffix /ˈsʌfɪks/ *n.* a letter or letters added at the end of a word to form a derivative. —*v.t.* to append, especially as a suffix. [from Latin *figere fix-* = fix]

suffocate /ˈsʌfəkeɪt/ *v.t./i.* **1.** to impede or stop the breathing of (a person etc.); to choke or kill thus. **2.** to be or feel suffocated. —**suffocation** /-ˈkeɪʃən/ *n.* [from Latin *suffocare* (*fauces* = throat)]

Suffolk /ˈsʌfək/ county of E England; **area** 3,800 sq km/1,467 sq mi; **administrative headquarters** Ipswich; **physical** low undulating surface and flat coastline; rivers: Waveney, Alde, Deben, Orwell, Stour; part of the Norfolk Broads; **products** cereals, sugar beet, working horses (Suffolk punches), fertilizers, agricultural machinery; **population** (1987) 635,000.

suffragan /ˈsʌfrəgən/ *n.* **1.** in the Christian church, a bishop appointed to assist a diocesan bishop. **2.** a bishop in relation to his archbishop. [from Anglo-French from Latin; originally of bishop summoned to vote in synod]

suffrage /ˈsʌfrɪdʒ/ *n.* **1.** the right of voting in political elections. **2.** a short prayer or petition. [from Latin *suffragium*]

suffragette /sʌfrəˈdʒet/ *n.* or **suffragist** (*historical*) a woman fighting for the right to vote. In the UK, women's suffrage bills were repeatedly introduced and defeated in Parliament between 1886 and 1911, and a militant campaign was launched in 1906 by Emmeline ◊Pankhurst and her daughters. In 1918 women were granted limited franchise; in 1928 it was extended to all women over 21. In the

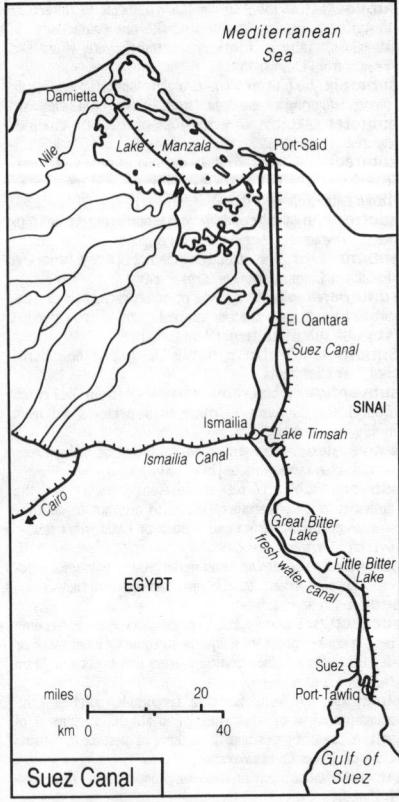

Suez Canal

USA the 19th amendment to the constitution in 1920 gave women the vote in federal and state elections. [term coined by a *Daily Mail* reporter]

suffuse /səˈfjuːz/ *v.t.* (of a colour or moisture etc.) to spread throughout or over. —**suffusion** *n.* [from Latin *fundere* = pour]

Sufi /ˈsuːfɪ/ *n.* a Muslim ascetic mystic. —**Sufic** *adj.*, **Sufism** *n.* a mystical movement of ◊Islam which originated in the 8th century. Sufis believe that deep intuition is the only real guide to knowledge. The movement has a strong strain of asceticism. There are a number of groups within Sufism, each with its own method of meditative practice, one of which is the whirling dance of the ◊dervishes. [from Arabic *suf* = wool (which was used for clothing by religious persons from pre-Islamic times)]

sug- prefix; see ◊sub-.

sugar /ˈʃʊgə/ *n.* **1.** a sweet, crystalline substance used in cookery, confectionery etc. The major sources are tropical cane sugar, which accounts for about two-thirds of production, and temperate sugar beet. Sugar was introduced to Europe in the 8th century, and became known in England around 1100 when the Crusaders brought it from the Middle East. It was first imported to England in 1319, but was taxed from 1685 to 1874, and only became widespread after then. In 1800 annual consumption in Britain was about 10 kg per person; in 1985 the average Briton consumed 0.8 kg of sugar per week. World production is about 100 million tonnes a year. Subsidies given to European sugar producers by the EC have reduced the export earnings of Third World sugar-producing countries. **2.** a sweet, soluble carbohydrate, either a monosaccharide or a disaccharide. **3.** (*US colloquial,* as a term of address) darling. —*v.t.* to sweeten or coat with sugar. —**sugar beet,** a ◊beet from whose roots sugar is made. **sugar cane,** a perennial tropical grass *Saccharum officinarum* with very tall stems from which sugar is made. **sugar daddy,** (*slang*) an elderly man who lavishes gifts on a young person to whom he is sexually attracted. **sugar loaf,** a conical moulded mass of sugar.

sugar soap, an alkaline compound for cleaning or removing paint. [from Old French, ultimately from Arabic *sukkar*]

Sugar Alan 1947– . British entrepreneur, founder in 1968 of the Amstrad electronics company which holds a major position in the European personal computer market. In 1985 he introduced a complete word-processing system at the price of £399. Subsequent models consolidated his success internationally.

sugar maple an E North American ◊maple tree *Acer saccharum.*

sugary *n.* 1. containing or resembling sugar. 2. attractively or excessively sweet or pleasant. —**sugariness** *n.*

suggest /sə'dʒest/ *v.t.* 1. to put forward for consideration or as a possibility; to propose tentatively. 2. to cause (an idea) to present itself; to bring (an idea) into the mind. —**suggest itself,** to come into the mind. [from Latin *gerere* = bring]

suggestible /sə'dʒestɪbəl/ *adj.* 1. easily influenced by suggestions. 2. that may be suggested. —**suggestibility** /-'bɪlɪti/ *n.*

suggestion /sə'dʒestʃən/ *n.* 1. suggesting. 2. a thing suggested. 3. the insinuation of a belief or impulse into the mind. 4. a hint or slight trace. [from Old French from Latin]

suggestive /sə'dʒestɪv/ *adj.* 1. conveying a suggestion. 2. tending to convey an indecent or improper meaning etc. —**suggestively** *adv.,* **suggestiveness** *n.*

Suharto /su:'hɑːtəʊ/ Raden 1921– . Indonesian politician and general who ousted Sukarno to become president in 1967. He ended confrontation with Malaysia, invaded East Timor in 1975, and reached a cooperation agreement with Papua New Guinea in 1979. His authoritarian rule has met domestic opposition from the left.

suicidal /'su:ɪsaɪdəl, 'sju:-, -'saɪ-/ *adj.* 1. of or tending to suicide; (of a person) liable to commit suicide. 2. extremely foolhardy, destructive to one's own interests etc. —**suicidally** *adv.*

suicide /'su:ɪsaɪd, sju:-/ *n.* 1. the intentional killing of oneself; an instance of this; a person who does this. Until 1961 suicide was a criminal offence in English law. To aid and abet another's suicide is an offence, and euthanasia or mercy killing may amount to aiding in this context. In Japan ◊hara-kiri is considered honourable. In 1986, the highest suicide rates per million of the population were 430 for men in Finland and 199 for women in Denmark. In 1988, there were 4,193 suicides in England and Wales, about 83 per million of the population. 2. an action destructive to one's own interests or reputation etc. [from Latin *sui* = of oneself and *caedere* = kill]

sui generis /sjuaɪ 'dʒenərɪs, su:i:/of its own kind, unique. [Latin]

suit /su:t, sju:t/ *n.* 1. a set of clothes for wearing together, especially of the same cloth and consisting of a jacket and trousers or skirt. 2. clothing for a particular purpose. 3. a set of pyjamas, armour etc. 4. any of the four sets (spades, hearts, diamonds, clubs) into which a pack of cards is divided. 5. a lawsuit. 6. (*archaic*) suing; the seeking of a woman's hand in marriage. —*v.t./i.* 1. to satisfy, to meet the demands or needs of. 2. to be convenient or right for. 3. to give a pleasing appearance or effect upon. 4. (of a climate, food etc.) to improve or not impair the health of, to agree with. 5. to adapt, to make suitable. —**suit oneself,** to do as one chooses; to find something that satisfies one. [from Anglo-French *suite*]

suitable *adj.* right or appropriate for the purpose or occasion etc. —**suitability** /-'bɪlɪti/ *n.,* **suitably** *adv.*

suitcase *n.* a rectangular case for carrying clothes etc., usually with a handle and a hinged lid.

suite /swi:t/ *n.* 1. a set of rooms or furniture. 2. a set of attendants, a retinue. 3. in music, a set of instrumental pieces. [French]

suitor /'su:tə, 'sju:-/ *n.* 1. a man wooing a woman. 2. a plaintiff or petitioner. [from Anglo-French from Latin *secutor* (*sequi* = follow)]

Sukarno /su:'kɑːnəʊ/ Achmed 1901–1970. Indonesian nationalist, president 1945–67. During World War II he cooperated in the local administration set up by the Japanese, replacing Dutch rule. After the war he became the first president of the new Indonesian republic, becoming president-for-life in 1966; he was ousted by ◊Suharto.

Sulawesi /su:lə'weɪsi/ formerly **Celebes** island in E Indonesia, one of the Sunda Islands; area (with dependent islands) 190,000 sq km/73,000 sq mi; population (1980) 10,410,000. It is mountainous and forested and produces copra and nickel.

Suleiman /su:li'mɑːn/ or **Solyman** 1494–1566. Ottoman sultan from 1520, known as **the Magnificent** and **the Lawgiver.** Under his rule, the Ottoman Empire flourished and reached its largest extent. He made conquests in the Balkans, the Mediterranean, Persia, and N Africa, but was defeated at Vienna in 1529 and Valletta (on Malta) in 1565. He was a patron of the arts, a poet, and an administrator.

sulfa variant of sulpha, short for ◊sulphonamide.

sulk *v.i.* to be sulky. —*n.* (usually in *plural*) a sulky fit.

sulky *adj.* sullen and unsociable from resentment or bad temper. —*n.* a light two-wheeled one-horse vehicle for a single person, especially as used in trotting races, so called because it admits only one person. —**sulkily** *adv.,* **sulkiness** *n.*

Sulla /'sʌlə/ Lucius Cornelius 138–78 BC. Roman general and politician, a leader of the senatorial party. Forcibly suppressing the democrats in 88 BC, he departed for a successful campaign against ◊Mithridates VI of Pontus. The democrats seized power in his absence, but on his return Sulla captured Rome and massacred all opponents. The reforms he made as dictator, which strengthened the Senate, were backward-looking and short-lived. He retired in 79 BC.

sullen /'sʌlən/ *adj.* passively resentful, stubbornly ill-humoured, unresponsive. —**sullenly** *adv.,* **sullenness** *n.* [alteration from earlier *solein* from Latin *solus* = alone]

Sullivan /'sʌlɪvən/ Arthur (Seymour) 1842–1900. English composer who wrote operettas in collaboration with William Gilbert, including *HMS Pinafore* 1878, *The Pirates of Penzance* 1879, and *The Mikado* 1885. Their partnership broke down in 1896. Sullivan also composed serious instrumental, choral, and operatic works, for example, the opera *Ivanhoe* 1890.

sully /'sʌli/ *v.t.* to stain or blemish; to diminish the purity or splendour of (a reputation etc.).

sulpha /'sʌlfə/ *adj.* sulphonamide. [abbreviation]

sulphate *n.* SO₄²⁻, any salt or ester derived from sulphuric acid. Most sulphates are water soluble (the exceptions are lead, calcium, strontium, and barium sulphates), and require a very high temperature to decompose them. [from French from Latin *sulphur*]

sulphide /'sʌlfaɪd/ *n.* a compound of sulphur and another element in which sulphur is the more ◊electronegative element. Sulphides occur in a number of minerals. Some of the more volatile sulphides have extremely unpleasant odours (hydrogen sulphide smells of bad eggs).

sulphite /'sʌlfaɪt/ *n.* SO₃²⁻, any salt or ester derived from sulphurous acid.

sulphonamide /sʌl'fɒnəmaɪd/ *n.* any of a group of compounds containing the chemical group sulphonamide, SO₂NH₂, or its derivatives, which were, and still are in some cases, used to treat bacterial diseases. Sulphadiazine, C₁₀H₁₀N₄O₂S, is an example.

sulphur /'sʌlfə/ *n.* 1. a brittle, pale-yellow, nonmetallic element, symbol S, atomic number 16, relative atomic mass 32.064. It occurs in three allotropic forms: two crystalline (rhombic and monoclinic) and one amorphous. It burns in air with a blue flame and a stifling odour. Insoluble in water but soluble in carbon disulphide, it is a good electrical insulator. Sulphur is widely used in the manufacture of sulphuric acid (used to treat phosphate rock to make fertilizers) and in making paper, matches, gunpowder and fireworks, in vulcanizing rubber, and in medicines and insecticides. 2. a pale, slightly greenish-yellow colour. 3. a yellow butterfly of the family Pieridae. [from Anglo-French from Latin]

sulphur dioxide SO₂, a pungent gas produced by burning sulphur in air or oxygen.

sulphureous /sʌl'fjʊəriəs/ *adj.* of or like sulphur.

sulphuric /sʌl'fjʊərɪk/ *adj.* containing sulphur in a higher valency. [from French]

sulphuric acid or **oil of vitriol** H₂SO₄, a dense, oily, colourless liquid which gives out heat when added to water. It is used extensively in the chemical industry, petrol refining, and in manufacturing fertilizers, detergents, explosives, and dyes.

sulphurous /'sʌlfərəs/ *adj.* 1. of or like sulphur. 2. containing sulphur in a lower valency. —**sulphurous acid,** an unstable, weak acid used as a reducing and bleaching agent.

sulphurous acid H_2SO_3, a solution of sulphur dioxide, SO_2, in water. It is a weak acid.

sultan /'sʌltən/ *n.* 1. a Muslim sovereign. 2. or **sweet sultan** a sweet-scented plant *Centaurea moschata* or *C. suaveolens*. [French or from Latin from Arabic = power, ruler]

sultana /sʌl'tɑːnə/ *n.* 1. a kind of seedless raisin. 2. a sultan's wife, mother, concubine, or daughter. [Italian]

sultanate /'sʌltənət/ *n.* the position of or territory ruled by a sultan.

sultry /'sʌltrɪ/ *adj.* 1. (of weather etc.) hot and humid. 2. of dark, mysterious beauty; passionate, sensual. —**sultrily** *adv.*, **sultriness** *n.* [from obsolete verb *sulter*; related to *swelter*]

sum *n.* 1. a total resulting from the addition of items. 2. a particular amount of money. 3. a problem in arithmetic; the working out of this. 4. the whole amount. 5. the substance, a summary (of facts etc.). —*v.t.* (**-mm-**) to find the sum of. —**in sum**, briefly, in summary. **sum up**, to find or give the total of; to express briefly, to summarize; to form or express a judgement or opinion of; (especially of a judge) to recapitulate the evidence or argument. [from Old French from Latin *summa* (*summus* = highest)]

sumac /'ʃuːmæk/ *n.* a shrub of the genus *Rhus* yielding leaves which are dried and ground for use in tanning and dyeing; these leaves. [from Old French or Latin from Arabic]

Sumatra /suːˈmɑːtrə/ or **Sumatera** second largest island of Indonesia, one of the Sunda Islands; area 473,600 sq km/182,800 sq mi; population (1980) 28,016,000. East of a longitudinal volcanic mountain range is a wide plain; both are heavily forested. Products include rubber, rice, tobacco, tea, timber, tin, and petroleum.

Sumer /'suːmə/ area of S Iraq where the Sumerian civilization was established; part of Babylonia (see ◊Babylon).

Sumerian civilization the world's earliest civilization, dated about 3500 BC, located at the confluence of the Tigris and Euphrates rivers in lower Mesopotamia (present-day Iraq). It was a city-state with priests as secular rulers. Sumerian culture was based on the taxation of the surplus produced by agricultural villagers to support the urban ruling class and its public works programme, which included state-controlled irrigation. Cities included ◊Lagash, ◊Eridu, and ◊Ur.

summarize /'sʌməraɪz/ *v.t.* to make or be a summary of.

summary /'sʌmərɪ/ *n.* a statement giving the main points of something. —*adj.* 1. brief, giving the main points only. 2. done or given without delay, details, or formalities. —**summarily** *adv.* [from Latin]

summation /sʌˈmeɪʃən/ *n.* 1. the finding of a total. 2. summarizing.

summer *n.* 1. the warmest season of the year, from June to Aug in the northern hemisphere. 2. the mature stage of life etc. —*adj.* characteristic of or suitable for summer. —**summerhouse** *n.* a light building in a garden or park, providing shade in summer. **Summer Palace**, a palace (now in ruins) of the Chinese emperors near Beijing. **summer pudding**, a dish made by pressing soft fruits into a bowl lined and covered with bread or sponge cake. **summer school**, a series of lectures etc. in summer, especially at a university. **summertime** *n.* the season or weather of summer. **summer time**, in the UK, an hour in advance of Greenwich mean time. The practice of advancing clocks in the spring and putting them back in autumn was introduced in the UK in 1916. In North America and Australia the practice is known as **daylight saving time**. —**summery** *adj.* [Old English]

summit /'sʌmɪt/ *n.* 1. the highest point, the top. 2. the highest level of achievement or status. 3. or **summit meeting** a discussion between heads of governments. [from Old French *somet* (*som* = top from Latin *summus* = highest)]

summon /'sʌmən/ *v.t.* 1. to demand the presence of, to call together. 2. to command (a person) to appear in a lawcourt. 3. to call upon (a person etc.) to do something. 4. to gather (one's strength, courage, or energy etc.) in order to do something). [from Old French *monēre* = warn]

summons /'sʌmənz/ *n.* an authoritative call to attend or do something; in law, a court order officially delivered,

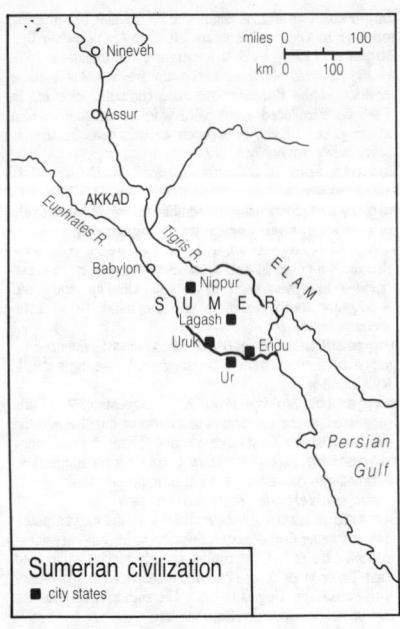

Sumerian civilization
■ city states

requiring someone to appear in court on a certain date. —*v.t.* to serve with a summons.

Sumner /'sʌmnə/ James 1887–1955. US biochemist. In 1926 he succeeded in crystallizing the enzyme urease and demonstrating its protein nature. For this work Sumner shared the 1946 Nobel Prize for Chemistry with John Northrop and Wendell Stanley.

sumo /'suːməʊ/ *n.* (*plural* **sumos**) 1. a kind of Japanese wrestling in which a person is considered defeated if he touches the ground except with his feet, or fails to keep within a marked area. 2. a person who takes part in this. Sumo wrestlers are men of large size, rarely weighing less than 130 kg/21 st or 285 lb. [Japanese *sumō*]

sump *n.* 1. a casing holding lubricating oil in an internal-combustion engine. 2. a pit, well, or low area into which waste or superfluous liquid drains. [originally = marsh, related to *swamp*]

sumptuary /'sʌmptʊərɪ/ *adj.* regulating expenditure. [from Latin *sumptus* = cost from *sumere* = take]

sumptuous /'sʌmptʊəs/ *adj.* splendid and costly-looking. —**sumptuously** *adv.*, **sumptuousness** *n.* [from Old French from Latin]

sun *n.* 1. or **Sun** the ◊star at the centre of the solar system. Its diameter is 1,392,000 km/865,000 mi; its temperature at the surface is about 6,000K (5,800°C/10,000°F) and at the centre 15,000,000K (15,000,000°C/27,000,000°F). It is composed of about 70% hydrogen and 30% helium, with other elements making up less than 1%. The Sun's energy is generated by nuclear fusion reactions that turn hydrogen into helium at its centre. It is about 4.7 billion years old, with a predicted lifetime of 10 billion years. Activity on the Sun, including sunspots, flares, and prominences, waxes and wanes during the solar cycle, which peaks every 11 years or so. 2. warmth or light from the Sun. 3. any fixed star with or without planets. 4. (*poetical*) a day or year. —*v.t./i.* (**-nn-**) to expose (oneself etc.) to the Sun. —**a place in the sun,** a favourable situation or condition. **sunglasses** *n.pl.* spectacles with tinted lenses to protect the eyes from sunlight or glare. **sun-god** *n.* the Sun worshipped as a deity. **Sun King,** ◊Louis XIV of France, so called from the magnificence of his reign. **sun lamp,** a lamp giving ultraviolet rays for therapy or an artificial suntan. **sun lounge,** a room designed to receive much sunlight. **sun roof,** a roof with a sliding section in a car. **suntan** *n.* tanning of the skin by exposure to the Sun. **suntanned** *adj.* tanned by the Sun. **suntrap** *n.* a sunny place, especially one sheltered from the wind. **sunup** *n.* (*US*) sunrise. **under the sun,** anywhere in the world. [Old English]

Sun. abbreviation of Sunday.

sunbathe *v.i.* to expose one's body to the Sun.

sunbeam *n.* a ray of sun.

sunburn *n.* tanning or inflammation of the skin caused by exposure to the Sun. **—sunburnt** *adj.*

Sun City /'sʌn 'sɪti/ alternative name for ◊Mmabatho, resort in Bophuthatswana, South Africa.

sundae /'sʌndeɪ/ *n.* a confection of ice cream with fruit, syrup etc.

Sunday /'sʌndeɪ/ *n.* **1.** the day of the week following Saturday, the Christian day of rest and worship. **2.** a newspaper published on Sundays. **—adv.** (*colloquial*) on Sunday. **—Sunday best,** one's best clothes (kept for use on Sundays). **Sunday painter,** an amateur painter, one who paints solely for pleasure. **Sunday school,** a school held on Sundays for children, now only for religious instruction. [Old English = day of the Sun]

sunder *v.t.* to break or tear apart, to sever. [Old English]

sundew *n.* any insectivorous plant of the genus *Drosera,* family Droseraceae, with viscid hairs on the leaves for catching prey.

sundial *n.* an instrument showing the time by the shadow of a rod or plate cast by the Sun on a scaled dial.

sundown *n.* sunset.

sundry /'sʌndrɪ/ *adj.* various, several. **—n.** (in *plural*) oddments, accessories, items not needed to be specified. **—all and sundry,** everyone. [Old English]

sunfish *n.* a large, globular fish, especially *Mola mola* with disc-shaped body 3 m/10 ft long found in all temperate and tropical oceans.

sunflower *n.* a tall plant of the genus *Helianthus,* family Compositae. The common sunflower *H. annuus,* probably native to Mexico, grows to 4.5 m/15 ft in favourable conditions. It is commercially cultivated in central Europe, the USA, and the USSR for the oil-bearing seeds that follow the large yellow-petalled flowers.

sung past participle of **sing.**

sunk past and past participle of **sink.**

sunken *adj.* lying below the level of a surrounding area; (of cheeks etc.) shrunken, hollow. [past participle of *sink*]

sunless *adj.* without sunshine.

sunlight *n.* light from the Sun.

sunlit *adj.* illuminated by sunlight.

Sunna /'sʌnə/ *n.* the traditional portion of Islamic law, based on Muhammad's words or acts but not written by him. [Arabic = form, way, rule]

Sunni /'sʊni/ *n.* a member of the larger of the two main sects of ◊Islam, with about 680 million adherents. Sunni Muslims believe that the first four caliphs were all legitimate successors of the prophet Muhammad, and that guidance on belief and life should come from the Koran, the Hadith, and the Shari'a, not from a human authority or spiritual leader. Imams in Sunni Islam are educated lay teachers of the faith and prayer leaders. [from the *Sunna*]

Sunningdale Agreement /'sʌnɪŋdeɪl/ an agreement reached by the UK and Irish governments, together with the Northern Ireland executive, in Dec 1973 in Sunningdale, England. The agreement included provisions for a power-sharing executive in Northern Ireland. However, the executive lasted only five weeks before the UK government was defeated in a general election, and a subsequent general strike in May 1974 brought down the Northern Ireland government.

Sunnite /'sʌnaɪt/ *n.* another word for ◊Sunni.

sunny *adj.* **1.** bright with or as sunlight; exposed to or warm with the Sun. **2.** happy, cheerful. **—sunnily** *adv.,* **sunniness** *n.*

sunrise *n.* the Sun's rising; the moment of this; the eastern sky with the colours of the sunrise.

sunset *n.* the Sun's setting; the moment of this; the western sky with the colours of the sunset.

sunshade *n.* a parasol or awning, giving shade from the Sun.

sunshine *n.* **1.** the light of the Sun; the area illuminated by it. **2.** fair weather. **3.** cheerfulness, bright influence.

sunspot *n.* a dark patch on the surface of the Sun, actually an area of cooler gas, thought to be caused by strong magnetic fields that block the outward flow of heat to the Sun's surface. Sunspots last from several days to over a month, ranging in size from 2,000 km/1,250 mi to groups stretching for over 100,000 km/62,000 mi. The number of

sunspots visible at a given time varies from none to over 100 in a cycle averaging 11 years.

sunstroke *n.* illness caused by excessive exposure to the Sun; ◊heatstroke.

sunwise *adv.* in the direction of the Sun's course (and hence lucky; as opposed to *widdershins*).

Sun Yat-sen /'sʌn jæt'sen/ or **Sun Zhong Shan** 1867–1925. Chinese revolutionary leader and statesman, founder of the ◊Guomindang (Nationalist party) in 1894, and provisional president of the Republic of China in 1912 after playing a vital part in deposing the emperor. He was president of a breakaway government from 1921.

Sun Zhong Shan /'sʌn dzʌŋ'ʃɑːn/ the Pinyin transliteration of ◊Sun Yat-sen.

sup *v.t./i.* (**-pp-**) **1.** to drink by sips or spoonfuls. **2.** to take supper. **3.** (*colloquial*) to drink (beer etc.). **—n.** a mouthful of liquid; (*colloquial*) a drink of beer etc. [Old English; in second sense of verb from Old French]

sup- prefix; see ◊sub-.

super /'suːpə, 'sjuː-/ *adj.* (*slang*) excellent, superb. **—n.** (*colloquial*) **1.** a supernumerary. **2.** a superintendent. [abbreviation]

super- /'suːpə-, sjuː-/ prefix with the meaning of above or beyond or over (e.g. *superstructure, supernormal*); to a great or extreme degree (e.g. *superabundant, supertanker*); higher in status (e.g. *superintendent*). [from Latin *super* = over]

superabundant /suːpərə'bʌndənt, sjuː-/ *adj.* very abundant, more than enough. **—superabundance** *n.*

superactinide *n.* any of a theoretical series of superheavy, radioactive elements, starting with atomic number 113, that extend beyond the ◊transactinide series in the periodic table. They do not occur in nature and none has yet been synthesized.

superannuate /suːpə'rænjueɪt, sjuː-/ *v.t.* **1.** to discharge (an employee) into retirement with a pension. **2.** to discard as too old for use. [from Latin *annus* = year]

superannuation /suːpərænju'eɪʃən, sjuː-/ *n.* **1.** superannuating. **2.** a pension granted to an employee on retirement; payment(s) contributed towards this during his or her employment.

superb /suː'pɜːb, sjuː-/ *adj.* of the most impressive or splendid kind, excellent. **—superbly** *adv.* [from French or Latin *superbus* = proud]

supercargo *n.* (*plural* **supercargoes**) a person in a merchant ship managing the sales etc. of cargo. [from Spanish *sobrecargo* (*sobre* = over)]

supercharge *v.t.* **1.** to charge to extreme or excess (with energy etc.). **2.** to use a supercharger on.

supercharger *n.* a device forcing extra air or fuel into an internal-combustion engine to increase its power.

superciliary /suːpə'sɪlɪərɪ, sjuː-/ *adj.* of the eyebrow; over the eye. [from Latin *supercilium* = eyebrow (*cilium* = eyelid)]

supercilious /suːpə'sɪlɪəs, sjuː-/ *adj.* with an air of superiority, haughty and scornful. **—superciliously** *adv.,* **superciliousness** *n.* [from Latin]

supercomputer *n.* the fastest, most powerful type of computer, capable of performing its basic operations in picoseconds (thousand-billionths of a second), rather than nanoseconds (billionths of a second) as most other computers.

superconductivity /suːpəkɒndʌk'tɪvɪtɪ, sjuː-/ *n.* in physics, an increase in electrical conductivity at low temperatures. The resistance of some metals and metallic compounds decreases uniformly with decreasing temperature until at a critical temperature (the superconducting point), within a few degrees of absolute zero (0K/–273.16°C/–459.67°F), the resistance suddenly falls to zero. The phenomenon was discovered by the Dutch scientist, Kamerlingh Onnes (1853–1926) in 1911. **—superconductive** /-kn'dʌktɪv/ *adj.*

supercool *v.t.* to cool (a ◊saturated solution) below its freezing point without its becoming solid or crystalline. Instead it forms a supersaturated solution. Usually crystallization rapidly follows the introduction of a small (seed) crystal or agitation of the supercooled solution.

superego /suːpər'iːgəu, -'egəu, sjuː-/ *n.* in Freudian psychology, the element of the human mind concerned with the ideal, responsible for ethics and self-imposed standards of behaviour. It is characterized as a form of conscience, restraining the ◊ego, and responsible for feelings of guilt when the moral code is broken.

supererogation /suːpərərəˈgeɪʃən, sjuː-/ n. the doing of more than duty requires. [from Latin *supererogare* = pay out in addition, originally public money after formal request for permission (*rogare* = ask)]

superfamily n. a taxonomic category between family and order.

superficial /suːpəˈfɪʃəl, sjuː-/ adj. 1. of or on the surface only. 2. without depth of knowledge or feeling etc. 3. (of measure) square. —**superficiality** /-ʃiˈælɪtɪ/ n., **superficially** adv. [from Latin *superficies* = surface from *facies* = face]

superfine adj. extremely fine or refined.

superfluity /suːpəˈfluːɪtɪ, sjuː-/ n. 1. a superfluous amount or thing. 2. being superfluous. [from Old French from Latin]

superfluous /suːˈpɜːfluəs, sjuː-/ adj. more than is needed or required; not needed. —**superfluously** adv., **superfluousness** n. [from Latin *fluere* = flow]

supergiant n. the largest and most luminous type of star known, with a diameter of up to 1,000 times that of the Sun and absolute magnitudes of between –5 and –9.

supergrass n. (*slang*) one who informs against a large number of persons.

superheat v.t. to heat (liquid) above its boiling point without allowing it to vaporize; to heat (vapour) above its boiling point. —**superheater** n.

superhighway n. (*US*) a broad main road for fast traffic.

superhuman /suːpəˈhjuːmən, sjuː-/ adj. 1. exceeding the normal human capacity or power. 2. higher than humanity, divine.

superimpose /suːpərɪmˈpəʊz, sjuː-/ v.t. to lay or place (a thing) on top of something else. —**superimposition** /-pəˈzɪʃən/ n.

superintend /suːpərɪnˈtend, sjuː-/ v.t./i. to supervise. —**superintendence** n. [from Latin *superintendere*]

superintendent n. 1. one who superintends. 2. the director of an institution etc. 3. (*British*) a police officer above the rank of inspector.

superior /suːˈpɪərɪə, sjuː-/ adj. 1. higher in position or rank; (of figures etc.) written or printed above the line. 2. better or greater in some way; of high or higher quality. 3. showing that one feels oneself to be better or wiser etc. than others; conceited, supercilious. 4. (with *to*) not influenced by; not yielding or resorting to. —n. 1. a person or thing of higher rank, ability, or quality. 2. the head of a monastery or other religious community. —**superiority** /-ˈɒrɪtɪ/ n. [from Old French from Latin, comparative of *superus* = situated above]

Superior, Lake /suːˈpɪərɪə/ largest and deepest of the ◊Great Lakes, and the second largest lake in the world; area 83,300 sq km/32,200 sq mi.

superior planet a planet that is farther away from the Sun than the Earth. All the planets from Mars outwards are described as superior planets.

superlative /suːˈpɜːlətɪv, sjuː-/ adj. of the highest degree or quality, excellent. —n. in grammar, the superlative degree; a superlative form. —**superlative adjective** (*or* **adverb**), an adjective (or adverb) in the superlative degree. **superlative degree**, the form expressing the highest or a very high degree of a quality (e.g. *bravest, most quickly*). —**superlatively** adv., **superlativeness** n. [from Old French from Latin *superlatus* = carried above]

superman n. (*plural* **supermen**) a man of superhuman powers or achievement. —**superwoman** n. *fem.*

Superman /ˈsuːpəmæn/ 1. a comic-strip hero created in 1938 in the USA by writer Jerome Siegel and artist, Joseph Shuster, later featured in television, films, and other media. Superman was born on the planet Krypton. He has extraordinary powers, including the ability to fly; he is vulnerable only to kryptonite, rock remnants of his exploded home planet. Between feats of crime-fighting or rescuing accident victims, he leads an ordinary life as a bespectacled journalist, Clark Kent. 2. in the German philosopher ◊Nietzsche's work, the ideal future human being, the ◊*Übermensch*, or Superman.

supermarket n. a large self-service shop selling food and household goods. The first, Piggly-Wiggly, was introduced by US retailer Clarence Saunders in Memphis, Tennessee, in 1919.

supernatural /suːpəˈnætʃərəl, sjuː-/ adj. of or manifesting phenomena not explicable by natural or physical laws. —**supernaturally** adv.

supernova /suːpəˈnəʊvə, sjuː-/ n. (*plural* **supernovae** or **supernovas**) a star that at the time of its explosive death temporarily attains a brightness 100 million times that of the Sun or more. It can shine as brilliantly as a small galaxy for a few days or weeks. In 1987 a supernova visible to the unaided eye occurred in the Large Magellanic Cloud, a small neighbouring galaxy. Eta Carinae, visible in the constellation Carina in the southern hemisphere, may become a supernova in a few hundred years.

supernumerary /suːpəˈnjuːmərərɪ, sjuː-/ adj. in excess of the normal number, extra. —n. a supernumerary person or thing. [from Latin *super numerum* = beyond the number]

superphosphate /suːpəˈfɒsfeɪt, sjuː-/ n. a fertilizer made from phosphate rock.

superpose /suːpəˈpəʊz, sjuː-/ v.t. to place (a geometrical figure) upon another so that their outlines coincide. —**superposition** /-pəˈzɪʃən/ n.

superpower n. a nation or state having a dominant position in world politics; the USA and the USSR from the end of World War II in 1945, when they emerged as significantly stronger than all other countries.

supersaturation n. in chemistry, the state of a solution that has a higher concentration of ◊solute than would normally be obtained in a ◊saturated solution.

superscribe /ˈsuːpəskraɪb, ˈsjuː-/ v.t. to write (an inscription) at the top of or outside a document etc. [from Latin *scribere* = write]

superscript /ˈsuːpəskrɪpt, ˈsjuː-/ adj. written or printed just above and to the right of a word, figure, or symbol. —n. a superscript figure or symbol.

superscription /suːpəˈskrɪpʃən, sjuː-/ n. superscribed words.

supersede /suːpəˈsiːd, sjuː-/ v.t. to take the place of; to put or use another in place of. —**supercession** /-ˈseʃən/ n. [from Old French from Latin *supersedēre* = be superior to (*sedēre* = sit)]

supersonic /suːpəˈsɒnɪk, sjuː-/ adj. of or having a speed greater than that of sound, measured in ◊Mach numbers. In dry air at 0°C/32°F, sound travels at about 1,170 kph/727 mph, but decreases with altitude until, at 12,000 m/39,000 ft, it is only 1,060 kph/658 mph, remaining constant below that height. When an aircraft passes the ◊sound barrier, shock waves are built up that give rise to ◊sonic boom, often heard at ground level. The first supersonic flight was achieved in 1948. —**supersonically** adv.

superstar n. a great star in entertainment etc.

superstition /suːpəˈstɪʃən, sjuː-/ n. 1. belief in the existence or power of the supernatural; irrational fear of the unknown or mysterious; misdirected reverence. 2. a religion, or practice, or opinion based on such tendencies. 3. a widely held but wrong idea. —**superstitious** adj., **superstitiously** adv., **superstitiousness** n. [from Old French or Latin *superstitio* from *superstare* (*stare* = stand)]

superstore n. a large supermarket, especially one with a sales area of at least 2,500 sq m/27,000 sq ft.

superstring theory a mathematical theory developed in the 1980s to explain the properties of the ◊fundamental particles and the forces between them (in particular, gravity and the nuclear forces) in a way that combines ◊relativity and ◊quantum theory. In string theory, the fundamental objects in the universe are not pointlike particles but extremely small stringlike objects. These objects exist in a universe of ten dimensions, although, for reasons not yet understood, only three space dimensions and one dimension of time are discernable. There are many unresolved difficulties with superstring theory, but some physicists think it may be the ultimate 'theory of everything' that explains all aspects of the universe within one framework.

superstructure n. a structure built on top of something else; a building as distinct from its foundations.

supertanker n. a very large tanker.

supervene /suːpəˈviːn, sjuː-/ v.i. to occur as an interruption in or change from some state or process. —**supervention** n. [from Latin *venire* = come]

supervise /ˈsuːpəvaɪz, ˈsjuː-/ v.t. to direct and inspect (work, workers, or the operation of an organization).

—supervision /-'vɪʒən/ *n.*, **supervisor** *n.*, **supervisory** *adj.* [from Latin *vidēre* = see]

supine /'su:paɪn, 'sju:-/ *adj.* 1. lying face upwards. 2. inactive, indolent. —*n.* a Latin verbal noun used only in the accusative and ablative cases. —**supinely** *adv.* [from Latin *supinus* (*super* = above)]

supper *n.* a light evening meal, the last meal of the day. [from Old French *soper, super*]

supplant /sə'plɑ:nt/ *v.t.* to oust and take the place of. —**supplanter** *n.* [from Old French or Latin *supplantare* = trip up (*planta* = sole)]

supple *adj.* bending easily, flexible, not stiff. —**supplely** *adv.*, **suppleness** *n.* [from Old French from Latin *supplex* = submissive]

supplement /'sʌplɪmənt/ *n.* 1. a thing added as an extra or to make up for a deficiency. 2. a part added to a book etc. to give further information or to treat a particular subject; a set of special pages issued with a newspaper. —*also* -'ment/ *v.t.* to provide or be a supplement to. —**supplemental** /-'mentəl/ *adj.*, **supplementary** /-'mentərɪ/ *adj.* —**supplementary benefit**, in Britain, former name (1966–88) for **income support**, weekly ◊social security payments by the state to those with low incomes. **supplementation** /-'teɪʃən/ *n.* [from Latin]

suppliant /'sʌplɪənt/ *n.* a humble petitioner. —*adj.* supplicating. [from French *supplier* from Latin]

supplicate /'sʌplɪkeɪt/ *v.t./i.* to petition humbly. —**supplication** /-'keɪʃən/ *n.*, **supplicatory** *adj.* [from Latin *plicare* = bend]

supply /sə'plaɪ/ *v.t.* 1. to give or provide with (something needed or useful); to make available for use. 2. to make up for (a deficiency or need). —*n.* 1. provision of what is needed. 2. a stock or store, an amount of something provided or obtainable. 3. (in *plural*) the collected necessaries for an army, expedition etc. 4. a person, especially a schoolteacher or cleric, acting as a temporary substitute for another. 5. in economics, the production of goods or services for a market in anticipation of an expected ◊demand. There is no guarantee that supply will match actual demand. —**on supply**, (of a schoolteacher etc.) acting as a supply. **supply and demand**, the quantities available and required, as factors regulating the price of commodities. For a typical commodity, the supply curve is upward-sloping (the higher the price, the more the manufacturer is willing to sell), while the demand curve is downward-sloping (the cheaper the commodity, the more demand there is for it). The point where the curves intersect is the equilibrium price at which supply equals demand. —**supplier** *n.* [from Old French from Latin *plēre* = fill]

support /sə'pɔ:t/ *v.t.* 1. to keep from falling or sinking; to hold in position; to bear all or part of the weight of. 2. to give strength to; to enable to last or continue; to supply with necessaries. 3. to assist by one's approval or presence or by subscription to funds; to speak in favour of (a resolution etc.); to be actively interested in (a particular sport or team). 4. to take a secondary part to (another performer). 5. to bring facts to confirm (a statement etc.); to corroborate. 6. to endure, to tolerate. —*n.* 1. supporting, being supported. 2. a person or thing that supports. —**in support of**, so as to support. **supporting film**, a less important film in a cinema programme. [from Old French from Latin *portare* = carry]

support environment in computing, a collection of programs (◊software) used to help people to design and write other programs. At its simplest, this includes a ◊text editor (word-processing software) and a ◊compiler for translating programs into executable form; but can also include interactive debuggers for helping to locate faults, data dictionaries for keeping track of the data used, and rapid prototyping tools for producing quick, experimental mock-ups of programs.

supporter *n.* 1. a person or thing that supports; a person supporting a team or sport. 2. in heraldry, a representation of a living creature holding up or standing beside an escutcheon, usually as one of a pair on either side.

supportive /sə'pɔ:tɪv/ *adj.* providing support or encouragement.

suppose /sə'pəʊz/ *v.t.* 1. to accept as true or probable, to be inclined to think. 2. to take as a possibility or hypothesis for the purpose of arguments; (in *imperative*) as a formula of proposal. 3. (of a theory or result etc.) to require as

a condition; to presuppose. 4. (in *past participle*) generally accepted as being so. —**be supposed to,** to be expected or required to; (*colloquial*, with *negative*) ought not to, not to be allowed to. [from Old French]

supposedly /sə'pəʊzɪdlɪ/ *adv.* as is generally supposed.

supposition /sʌpə'zɪʃən/ *n.* 1. a thing supposed. 2. supposing.

suppositious /sʌpə'zɪʃəs/ *adj.* hypothetical. —**suppositiously** *adv.*, **suppositiousness** *n.*

supposititious /sʌpɒzɪ'tɪʃəs/ *adj.* substituted for the real person or thing, spurious. —**supposititiously** *adv.*, **supposititiousness** *n.* [from Latin *supponere* = substitute (*ponere* = place)]

suppository /sə'pɒzɪtərɪ/ *n.* a medical preparation for insertion into the rectum or vagina, where it is left to melt. [from Latin]

suppress /sə'pres/ *v.t.* 1. to put an end to the activity or existence of, especially by force or authority. 2. to prevent from being seen, heard, or known. 3. to eliminate (electrical interference etc.) partially; to equip (a device) to reduce such interference as it produces. —**suppression** *n.*, **suppressor** *n.* [from Latin *supprimere* (*premere* = press)]

suppressible *adj.* that may be suppressed.

suppurate /'sʌpjʊreɪt/ *v.i.* to form pus, to fester. —**suppuration** /-'reɪʃən/ *n.* [from Latin *suppurare* (*pus puris* = pus)]

supra /'su:prə/ *adv.* above or further back in the book etc. [Latin = above]

supra- /su:prə-/ prefix meaning above.

supranational /su:prə'næʃənəl/ *adj.* transcending national limits.

supremacy /su:'preməsɪ, sju:-/ *n.* being supreme; the highest authority.

Supremacy, Acts of two UK acts of Parliament of 1534 and 1559, which established Henry VIII and Elizabeth I respectively as head of the English church in place of the pope.

Suprematism *n.* a Russian abstract-art movement developed about 1913 by ◊Malevich. The Suprematist paintings gradually became more severe, until in 1918 they reached a climax with the *White on White* series showing white geometrical shapes on a white ground.

supreme /su:'pri:m/ *adj.* 1. highest in rank or authority. 2. highest in importance, intensity, or quality; most outstanding; (of a penalty or sacrifice) involving death. —**Supreme Being**, God. [from Latin *supremus*, superlative of *superus* = situated above]

Supreme Court the highest judicial tribunal, in the USA composed of a chief justice (William Rehnquist from 1986) and eight associate justices. Appointments are made by the president, and members can be removed only by impeachment. In Britain, the Supreme Court of Judicature is made up of the Court of Appeal and the High Court.

Supremes, the US vocal group, pioneers of the Motown sound, formed in 1959 in Detroit. Beginning in 1962, the group was a trio comprising, initially, Diana Ross (1944–), Mary Wilson (1944–), and Florence Ballard (1943–1976). They were one of the most successful female groups of the 1960s, and had a string of pop hits beginning with 'Where Did Our Love Go?' 1964 and 'Baby Love' 1964. Diana Ross left to pursue a solo career in 1969.

supremo /su:'pri:məʊ, sju:-/ *n.* (*plural* **supremos**) a supreme leader or ruler. [Spanish]

sur-[1] prefix; see ◊sub-.

sur-[2] prefix meaning super- (e.g. *surcharge, surface, surrealism*). [Old French]

Surabaya /sʊərə'baɪə/ port on the island of Java, Indonesia; population (1980) 2,028,000. It has oil refineries and shipyards and is a naval base.

Suraj-ud-Dowlah /suˈrɑ:dʒ ʊd ˈdaʊlə/ 1728–1757. Nawab of Bengal, India. He captured Calcutta from the British in 1756 and imprisoned some of the British in the Black Hole of Calcutta (a small room in which a number of them died), but was defeated in 1757 by Robert ◊Clive, and lost Bengal to the British at the Battle of ◊Plassey. He was killed in his capital, Murshidabad.

surcease /sɜ:'si:s/ *n.* (*archaic*) cessation. —*v.i.* (*archaic*) to cease. [from Old French *sursis* (*surseoir* = refrain from Latin]

surcharge /'sɜ:tʃɑ:dʒ/ *n.* 1. an additional charge or payment. 2. a mark printed on a postage stamp, especially one changing its value. **3.** an additional or excessive load. —*also* -'tʃɑːdʒ/ *v.t.* **1.** to exact a surcharge from; to exact (a sum) as a surcharge. **2.** to mark (a postage stamp) with a surcharge. **3.** to overload. [from Old French]

surd *adj.* **1.** (of a number) ◊irrational. **2.** (of a sound) uttered with breath and not voice (e.g. *f, k, p, s, t*). —*n.* **1.** a surd number, the mathematical root of a quantity that can never be exactly expressed, especially the root of an integer; for example, $\sqrt{3} = 1.732050808...$. **2.** a surd sound. [from Latin *surdus* = deaf]

sure /ʃʊə, ʃɔː/ *adj.* **1.** having or seeming to have adequate reasons for one's belief; free from doubts; having satisfactory knowledge or trust. **2.** certain to do something or to happen. **3.** reliable, secure, unfailing. **4.** undoubtedly true or truthful. —*adv.* (*colloquial*) certainly. —**be sure to,** to take care to, not to fail to. **for sure,** (*colloquial*) without doubt. **make sure,** to make or become certain, to ensure. **sure enough,** (*colloquial*) in fact, certainly. **sure-fire** *adj.* (*colloquial*) certain to succeed. **sure-footed** *adj.* never stumbling or making a mistake. **to be sure,** it is undeniable or admitted. —**sureness** *n.* [from Old French *sur* from Latin = secure]

surely /'ʃʊəlɪ, 'ʃɔː-/ *adv.* **1.** in a sure manner; with certainty; securely. **2.** used for emphasis, or (in questions) as an appeal to likelihood or reason. **3.** (as an answer) certainly, yes.

surety /'ʃʊərətɪ/ *n.* **1.** a person who makes him- or herself responsible for another's performance of an undertaking or payment of a debt. **2.** (*archaic*) certainty. [from Old French from Latin *securitas* = security]

surf *n.* the foam of the sea breaking on the shore or on reefs. —*v.i.* to go ◊surfing. —**surfriding** *n.* another term for surfing. —**surfer** *n.* [from earlier *suff*]

surface /'sɜːfɪs/ *n.* **1.** the outside of a thing; any of the limits terminating a solid. **2.** the top of a liquid or of soil etc. **3.** the outward aspect, what is perceived on a casual view or consideration. **4.** in geometry, that which has length and breadth but no thickness. —(*attributive*) *adj.* of the surface; superficial. —*v.t./i.* **1.** to give a (special) surface to (a road, paper etc.). **2.** to rise to the surface; to become visible or known; (*colloquial*) to become conscious. **3.** to bring (a submarine) to the surface. —**surface mail,** mail carried overland and by sea. **surface tension,** tension of the surface of a liquid, tending to minimize its surface area because of unequal cohesive forces between ◊molecules at the surface. [French]

surface-area-to-volume ratio the ratio of an animal's surface area (the area covered by its skin) to its total volume. This is high for small animals, but low for large animals such as elephants.

surfboard *n.* a long, narrow board used in surfing.

surfeit /'sɜːfɪt/ *n.* an excess, especially in eating or drinking; the resulting satiety. —*v.t./i.* to overfeed; to be or cause to be wearied through excess. [from Old French; compare Latin *superficiens* = excessive]

surfing *n.* the sport of riding on the crest of large waves while standing on a narrow, keeled surfboard, usually of light synthetic material such as fibreglass, about 1.8 m/ 6 ft long (or 2.4–7 m/8–9 ft known as the Malibu), as first developed in Hawaii and Australia. ◊Windsurfing is a recent development.

surge *v.i.* **1.** to move to and fro (as) in waves. **2.** to move suddenly and powerfully; to increase in volume or intensity. —*n.* **1.** a powerful wave. **2.** a surging motion; an impetuous onset. [from Old French from Latin *surgere* = rise]

surgeon /'sɜːdʒən/ *n.* a person skilled in surgery; a naval or military medical officer. [from Anglo-French (Old French *sirurgie* from Latin *chirurgia* from Greek, literally = handiwork)]

surgeon fish a fish of the tropical marine family Acanthuridae. It has a flat body up to 50 cm/1.7 ft long, is brightly coloured, and has a moveable spine on each side of the tail which can be used as a weapon.

surgery /'sɜːdʒərɪ/ *n.* **1.** the treatment of bodily injuries, disorders, and disease by cutting or manipulation of the affected parts. It involves technologies such as beamed high-energy ultrasonic waves, binocular magnifiers for microsurgery, and lasers. **2.** the place where or time when a doctor or dentist etc. gives advice and treatment, or an MP or lawyer etc. is available for consultation. [from Old French]

surgical /'sɜːdʒɪkəl/ *adj.* of or by surgeons or surgery; (of an appliance) used for surgery or in conditions suitable for surgery. —**surgical spirit,** ◊ethanol to which a small amount of methanol has been added to render it unfit to drink. It is used to sterilize surfaces and to cleanse skin abrasions and sores. —**surgically** *adv.* [from earlier *chirurgical*]

Suriname /suəri'næm/ Republic of; country on the N coast of South America, on the Atlantic coast, between Guyana and French Guiana; **area** 163,820 sq km/63,243 sq mi; **capital** Paramaribo; **physical** hilly and forested, with flat coast; Surinam River; **head of state and government** (interim) Johan Kraag from 1991; **political system** emergent democratic republic; **exports** alumina, aluminium, bauxite, rice, timber; **population** (1990 est) 408,000 (Hindustani 37%, Creole 31%, Javanese 15%); **recent history** independence from the Netherlands was achieved in 1975; 40% of the population emigrated to the Netherlands. An army coup in 1980 overthrew the government; led by Lt-Col Desi Bouterse, the army set up a Revolutionary People's Front in 1982. A new constitution was approved in 1987, but Bouterse rejected the peace accord reached by President Shankar with guerrilla insurgents and vowed to continue fighting.

surly /'sɜːlɪ/ *adj.* bad-tempered and unfriendly. —**surlily** *adv.*, **surliness** *n.* [alteration of obsolete *sirly* = haughty from *sir*]

surmise /sə'maɪz/ *n.* a conjecture. —*v.t./i.* to conjecture. [from Anglo-French and Old French, past participle of *surmettre* = accuse from Latin *supermittere* (*mittere* = send)]

surmount /sə'maʊnt/ *v.t.* **1.** to overcome (a difficulty); to get over (an obstacle). **2.** (in *past participle*) capped or crowned by a specified thing. [from Old French *monter* = mount]

surmountable *adj.* that may be surmounted.

surname /'sɜːneɪm/ *n.* the name common to all members of a family, a person's hereditary name. —*v.t.* to give a surname to. [alteration of *surnoun* from Anglo-French (Latin *nomen* = name]

surpass /sə'pɑːs/ *v.t.* to do or be greater or better than, to excel; (in *participle*) excelling or exceeding others. —**surpassingly** *adv.* [from French]

surplice /'sɜːplɪs/ *n.* in the Christian church, a loose, white linen vestment worn by members of the clergy and choristers. [from Anglo-French from Latin *superpellicium* (*pellicia* = pelisse)]

surplus /'sɜːpləs/ *n.* an amount left over when requirements have been met; the excess of revenue over expenditure. —*adj.* exceeding what is needed or used. [from Anglo-French from Latin]

surprise /sə'praɪz/ *n.* **1.** the emotion aroused by something sudden or unexpected. **2.** an event or thing arousing such emotion. **3.** the catching of a person etc. unprepared. **4.** (*attributive*) made or done etc. unexpectedly, without warning. —*v.t.* **1.** to affect with surprise, to turn out contrary to the expectations of; to shock, to scandalize. **2.** to capture or attack by surprise; to come upon (a person) off his or her guard. **3.** to startle into action by surprise. **4.** to discover (a secret etc.) by unexpected action. —**by surprise,** unexpectedly. —**surprising** *adj.*, **surprisingly** *adv.* [Old French, past participle of *surprendre* (Latin *praehendere* = seize)]

Surrealism /sə'rɪːəlɪzəm/ *n.* a movement in art, literature, and film that developed out of ◊Dada around 1922. Led by André ◊Breton, who produced the *Surrealist Manifesto* 1924, the Surrealists were inspired by the thoughts and visions of the subconscious mind. They explored varied styles and techniques, and the movement was the dominant force in Western art between World Wars I and II. - –**Surrealist** or **surrealist** *n. & adj.*, **surrealistic** /-'lɪstɪk/ *adj.* of or similar to the work of the Surrealists, **surrealistically** /-'lɪstɪkəlɪ/ *adv.* [from French]

surrender /sə'rendə/ *v.t./i.* **1.** to hand over, to give into another's power or control, especially on demand or under compulsion. **2.** to give oneself up; to accept an enemy's demand for submission. **3.** to give up one's rights under (an insurance policy) in return for a small sum received immediately. —*n.* surrendering. —**surrender oneself to,** to give way to (an emotion). **surrender to one's bail,** to appear duly in a lawcourt after release on bail. [from Anglo-French]

surreptitious /sʌrəp'tɪʃəs/ *adj.* acting or done by stealth. —**surreptitiously** *adv.* [from Latin *surripere* = seize secretly (*rapere* = seize)]

Surrey /'sʌri/ county in S England; **area** 1,660 sq km/ 641 sq mi; **administrative headquarters** Kingston upon Thames; **physical** rivers: Thames, Mole, Wey; hills: Box and Leith; North Downs; **products** market garden vegetables, agricultural products, service industries; **population** (1987) 1,000,000.

Surrey Henry Howard, Earl of Surrey *c.*1517–1547. English courtier and poet, executed on a poorly based charge of high treason. With Thomas ◊Wyatt, he introduced the sonnet to England, and was a pioneer of ◊blank verse.

surrogate /'sʌrəgət/ *n.* a deputy, especially of a bishop; a substitute. —**surrogacy** *n.* the practice whereby a woman is sought, and usually paid, to bear a child for an infertile couple. Such commercial surrogacy is practised in some European countries and in the USA. [from Latin, past participle of *surrogare* = elect as substitute (*rogare* = ask)]

surround /sə'raʊnd/ *v.t.* to come to be all round; to enclose on all sides; to encircle with enemy forces. —*n.* a border or edging, especially between walls and carpet; a floor covering for this. —**surrounded by** *or* **with,** having on all sides. [originally = overflow, from Anglo-French from Latin *superundare* (*unda* = wave)]

surroundings *n.pl.* the things or conditions around and liable to affect a person or thing.

surtax /'sɜ:tæks/ *n.* an additional tax, especially on incomes over a certain amount. —*v.t.* to impose a surtax on. [from French]

surveillance /sɜ:'veɪləns/ *n.* close observation, especially of a suspected person. [French, from *surveiller* = keep watch on (Latin *vigilare* = keep watch)]

survey /sə'veɪ/ *v.t.* 1. to look at and take a general view of. 2. to make or present a survey of. 3. to examine the condition of (a building etc.). 4. to measure and map out the size, position, elevation etc. of (an area). Surveying is used to establish boundaries and to evaluate the topography for engineering work. The measurements used are both linear and angular, and geometry and trigonometry are applied in the calculations. —/'sɜ:veɪ/ *n.* 1. the act of surveying. 2. a general examination of a situation or subject; an account of this. 3. the surveying of land etc.; a map or plan produced by this. [from Anglo-French from Latin *vidēre* = see]

surveyor /sə'veɪə/ *n.* one who surveys land or buildings professionally.

survival /sə'vaɪvəl/ *n.* 1. surviving. 2. something that has survived from earlier times.

survive /sə'vaɪv/ *v.t.i./i.* 1. to continue to live or exist. 2. to live or exist longer than. 3. to come alive through or continue to exist in spite of (a danger or accident etc.). —**survivor** *n.* [from Anglo-French *survivre* from Latin *supervivere* (*vivere* = live)]

Sūrya /'suəriə/ in Hindu mythology, the sun-god, son of the sky-god Indra. His daughter, also named Sūrya, is a female personification of the Sun.

sus *n.* (*slang*) 1. suspicion. 2. a suspect. —*v.t.* (-ss-) (*slang,* often with *out*) to investigate, to reconnoitre. [abbreviation]

sus- prefix; see ◊sub-.

susceptibility /səsepti'bɪlɪti/ *n.* 1. being susceptible. 2. (in *plural*) a person's sensitive feelings.

susceptible /sə'septɪbəl/ *adj.* 1. impressionable; falling in love easily. 2. (*predicative,* with *to*) liable to be affected by, sensitive to; (with *of*) able to undergo, admitting. —**susceptibly** *adv.* [from Latin *suscipere* = take up (*capere* = take)]

susceptive /sə'septɪv/ *adj.* susceptible.

suspect /sə'spekt/ *v.t.* 1. to have an impression of the existence or presence of; to have a partial or unconfirmed belief. 2. to have suspicions or doubts about, to mistrust. —/'sʌspekt/ *n.* a suspected person. —/'sʌspekt/ *adj.* subject to suspicion or distrust. [from Latin *suspicere* (*specere* = look)]

suspend /sə'spend/ *v.t.* 1. to hang up; (in *past participle,* of solid particles etc. in a fluid) sustained somewhere between top and bottom, kept from falling or sinking. 2. to keep inoperative or undecided for a time, to postpone. 3. to put a temporary stop to; to deprive temporarily of a position or right. —**suspended sentence,** a sentence

of imprisonment that is not enforced, on condition of good behaviour. [from Old French or Latin *pendere* = hang]

suspender *n.* 1. an attachment to hold up a stocking or sock by its top. 2. (in *plural, US*) a pair of braces. —**suspender belt,** a woman's undergarment with suspenders.

suspense /sə'spens/ *n.* a state of anxious uncertainty or expectation. [from Anglo-French from Latin]

suspension /sə'spenʃən/ *n.* 1. suspending, being suspended. 2. the means by which a vehicle is supported on its axles. 3. in physics, a colloidal state consisting of small solid particles dispersed in a liquid or gas (see ◊colloid). —**suspension bridge,** a bridge with a roadway suspended from cables supported by towers. [French or from Latin]

suspensory ligament in the ◊eye, a ring of fibre supporting the lens.

suspicion /sə'spɪʃən/ *n.* 1. the feeling of one who suspects; a partial or unconfirmed belief. 2. suspecting, being suspected. 3. a slight trace. —**above suspicion,** too obviously good etc. to be suspected. **under suspicion,** suspected. [from Anglo-French from Latin]

suspicious /sə'spɪʃəs/ *adj.* 1. prone to or feeling suspicion. 2. indicating or justifying suspicion. —**suspiciously** *adv.*

suss variant of ◊sus.

Sussex /'sʌsɪks/ former county of England, on the S coast, now divided into ◊East Sussex and ◊West Sussex.

sustain /sə'steɪn/ *v.t.* 1. to bear the weight of, to support, especially for a long period. 2. to endure without giving way. 3. to undergo, to suffer (a defeat or injury etc.). 4. to confirm or uphold the validity of. 5. to keep (a sound or effort etc.) going continuously. [from Anglo-French from Latin *sustinēre* (*tenēre* = hold)]

sustenance /'sʌstɪnəns/ *n.* 1. the process of sustaining life by food. 2. the food itself, nourishment.

Sutherland /'sʌðələnd/ Donald 1934– . Canadian film actor who usually appears in offbeat roles. He starred in *M.A.S.H.* 1970, and his subsequent films include *Klute* 1971, *Don't Look Now* 1973, and *Revolution* 1986.

Sutherland /'sʌðələnd/ Graham (Vivian) 1903–1980. English painter, graphic artist, and designer, active mainly in France from the late 1940s. He painted portraits, landscapes, and religious subjects. His *Christ in Glory* tapestry of 1962 is in Coventry Cathedral.

sutler *n.* (*historical*) a camp follower selling food etc.[from obsolete Dutch *soeteler* (*soetelen* = perform mean duties)]

suttee /sʌ'ti:/ *n.* the former act or custom of a Hindu widow sacrificing herself on her husband's funeral pyre; a Hindu widow doing this. Although it was banned in the 17th century by the Mogul Emperors, the custom continued even after it was made illegal under British rule in 1829. There continue to be sporadic revivals. [Hindi and Urdu, from Sanskrit = faithful wife]

Sutton Hoo /'sʌtn 'hu:/ an archaeological site in Suffolk, England, where in 1939 a Saxon ship burial was excavated. It is the funeral monument of Raedwald, king of the East Angles, who died about 624 or 625. The jewellery, armour, and weapons discovered were placed in the British Museum, London.

suture /'su:tʃə/ *n.* 1. surgical stitching of a wound; a stitch or thread etc. used in this. 2. a seamlike line of junction of two bones at their edges, especially in the skull; a similar junction or parts in a plant or animal body. —*v.t.* to stitch (a wound). [French, or from Latin *sutura* (*suere* = sew)]

suzerain /'su:zəreɪn/ *n.* 1. a feudal overlord. 2. a sovereign or state having some control over another state that is internally autonomous. —**suzerainty** *n.* [French]

Suzhou /su:'dʒəʊ/ formerly **Soochow** and **Wuhsien** 1912–49 city S of the Yangtze River delta and E of the ◊Grand Canal, in Jiangsu province, China; population (1983) 670,000. It has embroidery and jade-carving traditions and Shizilin and Zhuozheng gardens. The city dates from about 1000 BC, and the name Suzhou from the 7th century AD; it was reputedly visited by the Venetian Marco ◊Polo.

Suzuki /su'zu:ki/ Zenkō 1911– . Japanese politician. Originally a socialist member of the Dietin 1947, he became a conservative (Liberal Democrat) in 1949, and was prime minister 1980–82.

Svalbard /'sva:lbɑ:/ Norwegian archipelago in the Arctic Ocean. The main island is Spitsbergen; other islands include North East Land, Edge Island, Barents Island, and Prince Charles Foreland.

Svedberg /ˈsvedberɪ/ Theodor 1884–1971. Swedish chemist. In 1924 he constructed the first ultracentrifuge, a machine that allowed the rapid separation of particles by mass. He was awarded the Nobel Prize for Chemistry in 1926.

svelte /svelt/ *adj.* slender and graceful. [French, from Italian *svelto*]

Svengali /svenˈgɑːli/ *n.* a person who moulds another into a performer and masterminds his or her career. The original Svengali was a character in the novel *Trilby* 1894 by George ◊Du Maurier.

Sverdlovsk /sviədˈlɒvsk/ formerly (until 1924) **Ekaterinburg** industrial town in W USSR, in the E foothills of the Urals; population (1987) 1,331,000. Industries include copper, iron, platinum, engineering, and chemicals. Tsar ◊Nicholas II and his family were murdered here in 1918.

SW abbreviation of southwest, southwestern.

swab /swɒb/ *n.* **1.** a mop or other absorbent device for cleansing, drying, or absorbing things. **2.** an absorbent pad used in surgery. **3.** a specimen of a secretion taken for examination. —*v.t.* (**-bb-**) to clean with a swab; to take up (moisture) with a swab. [from Dutch *zwabber* from Germanic = splash, sway]

Swabia /ˈsweɪbiə/ (German ***Schwaben***) historic region of SW Germany, an independent duchy in the Middle Ages. It includes Augsburg and Ulm and forms part of the *Länder* (states) of Baden-Württemberg, Bavaria, and Hessen.

swaddle /ˈswɒdəl/ *v.t.* to swathe in wraps, clothes, or warm garments. —**swaddling clothes,** the narrow bandages formerly wrapped round a new-born child to restrain its movements.

swag *n.* **1.** loot. **2.** a carved ornamental festoon of fruit, flowers etc., hung by its ends. **3.** (*Australian*) a bundle of personal belongings carried by a tramp etc. [from *swag* = sway]

swage *n.* **1.** a die or stamp for shaping wrought iron. **2.** a tool for bending metal etc. —*v.t.* to shape with a swage. [from French *s(o)uage* = decorative groove]

swagger *v.i.* to walk or behave with arrogance or self-importance. —*n.* a swaggering gait or behaviour; smartness. —*adj.* **1.** (*colloquial*) smart, fashionable. **2.** (of a coat) cut with a loose flare from the shoulders. —**swagger stick,** a short cane carried by a military officer.

Swahili /swɑːˈhiːlɪ/ *n.* **1.** a member of an African people inhabiting Zanzibar and adjoining coastal areas of Kenya and Tanzania. The Swahili are not an isolated group, but are part of a mixed coastal society engaged in fishing and trading. **2.** their language. It is of Bantu origin and strongly influenced by Arabic, a widespread ◊lingua franca of E Africa and the national language of Tanzania (1967) and Kenya (1973). [from Arabic, plural of *sāhil* = coast]

swain *n.* **1.** (*archaic*) a country youth. **2.** (*poetic*) a young lover or suitor. [from Old Norse *sveinn* = lad = Old English *swān* = swineherd]

swallow[1] /ˈswɒləʊ/ *v.t./i.* **1.** to cause or allow (food etc.) to pass down one's throat; to perform the muscular movement (as) of swallowing something. **2.** to accept (a statement) with ready credulity; to accept (an insult) meekly. **3.** to repress (a sound or emotion etc.). **4.** to take in so as to engulf or absorb. —*n.* **1.** the act of swallowing. **2.** the amount swallowed in one movement. [Old English]

swallow[2] /ˈswɒləʊ/ *n.* a migratory, swift-flying, insect-eating bird of the family Hirundinidae, found worldwide. It has a dark-blue back, brown head and throat, and pinkish breast. Its tail feathers are forked, and its wings are long and narrow. —**swallow dive,** a dive with the arms outspread until close to the water. —**swallowtail,** a deeply forked tail; a butterfly or hummingbird with a forked tail. [Old English]

swam past of **swim.**

swami /ˈswɑːmɪ/ *n.* a Hindu religious teacher. [from Hindi = master]

swamp /swɒmp/ *n.* a permanently or periodically waterlogged tract of wet, spongy land, often overgrown with plant growth. —*v.t.* to overwhelm, flood, or soak with water; to overwhelm or make invisible etc. with an excess or large amount of something. —**swampy** *adj.*

swan /swɒn/ *n.* a large, web-footed, swimming bird of the duck family, usually of the genus *Cygnus,* with a long, gracefully curved neck. The **mute swan** *C. olor* is up to 150 cm/5 ft long, has white plumage, an orange bill with a black knob surmounting it, and black legs; the voice is a harsh hiss. —*v.i.* (**-nn-**) (*slang*) to go in a leisurely, majestic way, like a swan. —**Swan of Avon,** the playwright Shakespeare. **swan song,** a person's final composition or performance etc. (from the old belief that a swan sang sweetly when about to die). **swan-upping** *n.* in the UK, the annual taking up and marking (by the appropriate authorities) of swans on the Thames. [Old English]

Swan /swɒn/ Joseph Wilson 1828–1914. English inventor of the incandescent-filament electric lamp and of bromide paper for use in developing photographs.

swank *n.* (*colloquial*) **1.** boastful behaviour, ostentation. **2.** a person who swanks. —*v.i.* (*colloquial*) to behave with swank. —**swanky** *adj.*, **swankily** *adv.*, **swankiness** *n.* [originally Midland dialect]

swannery /ˈswɒnərɪ/ *n.* a place where swans are kept.

swansdown /ˈswɒnzdaʊn/ *n.* **1.** the down of the swan used in trimmings etc. **2.** thick cotton cloth with soft nap on one side.

Swanson /ˈswɒnsən/ Gloria. Stage name of Gloria Josephine Mae Svenson 1897–1983. US actress, a star of silent films who retired in 1932 but made several comebacks. Her work includes *Sadie Thompson* 1928, *Queen Kelly* 1928 (unfinished), and *Sunset Boulevard*1950.

swap /swɒp/ *v.t./i.* (**-pp-**) to exchange or barter.—*n.* **1.** an act of swapping. **2.** a thing suitable for swapping. [originally = hit]

SWAPO /ˈswɔpəʊ/ acronym from ◊**South West Africa People's Organization.**

sward /swɔːd/ *n.* an expanse of short grass. [Old English = skin]

swarm[1] /swɔːm/ *n.* **1.** a large number of insects, birds, small animals, or people moving in a cluster. **2.** a cluster of bees leaving the hive with a queen bee, to form a new home. —*v.i.* **1.** to move in or form a swarm. **2.** (of a place) to be crowded or overrun. [Old English]

swarm[2] *v.i.* (with *up*) to climb by gripping with the hands or arms and legs.

swarthy /ˈswɔːðɪ/ *adj.* dark, dark-complexioned. —**swarthily** *adv.*, **swarthiness** *n.* [variant of earlier *swarty* (*swart,* from Old English)]

swashbuckler /ˈswɒʃbʌklə/ *n.* a person who swaggers aggressively. —**swashbuckling** *adj.* & *n.* [from *swash* = strike noisily and *buckler* = small shield]

swastika /ˈswɒstɪkə/ *n.* a symbol formed by a cross with equal arms each continued as far again at right angles and all in the same clockwise or anticlockwise direction. An ancient good-luck symbol in both the New and the Old World and an Aryan and Buddhist mystic sign, it was adopted by Hitler as the emblem of the Nazi Party and incorporated into the German national flag 1935–45. [from Sanskrit *svastika* (*svasti* = well-being from *sú* = good and *astí* = being)]

swat /swɒt/ *v.t.* (**-tt-**) to hit hard; to crush (a fly etc.) with a blow. —*n.* an act of swatting. [earlier = sit down, dialect variant of *squat*]

swatch /swɒtʃ/ *n.* a sample, especially of cloth; a collection of samples.

swath /swɔːθ/ *n.* (*plural* /swɔːθs, swɔːðz/) a ridge of grass or corn etc. lying after being cut; the space left clear after one passage of a mower etc.; a broad strip. [Old English]

swathe[1] /sweɪð/ *v.t.* to wrap in layers of bandage, wrappings, or warm garments etc. [Old English]

swathe[2] another word for ◊swath.

swatter /ˈswɒtə/ *n.* an implement for swatting flies.

sway *v.t./i.* **1.** to swing or cause to swing gently; to lean from side to side or to one side. **2.** to influence the opinions, sympathy, or action of. **3.** to waver in one's opinion or attitude. —*n.* **1.** a swaying movement. **2.** influence, power; rule. [compare Low German *swajen* = be blown to and fro, Dutch *zwaaien* = swing, wave]

Swazi kingdom /ˈswɑːzi/ a southern African kingdom, established by Sobhuza I (died 1839), and named after his successor Mswati (ruled 1840–75). The kingdom was established by Sobhuza as a result of the ◊Mfecane disturbances.

Swaziland /ˈswɑːzɪlænd/ Kingdom of; country in SE Africa, bounded by Mozambique and the Transvaal province of South Africa; **area** 17,400 sq km/6,716 sq mi; **capital** Mbabane; **physical** central valley; mountains in W; **head of state and government** King Mswati III from 1986; **political system** near-absolute monarchy; **exports** sugar, canned fruit, woodpulp, asbestos; **population** (1990 est)

779,000; **language** Swazi 90%, English (both official); **recent history** independence was achieved from Britain within the Commonwealth in 1968. A new constitution was adopted in 1978. King Sobhuza II died in 1982; a power struggle ensued between two of his wives. In 1984 the 18-year-old crown prince became king. A new government was elected in 1987 with Sotsha Dlamini as prime minister.

swear /sweə/ *v.t./i. (past* **swore**; *past participle* **sworn**) **1.** to state or promise solemnly or on oath; *(colloquial)* to state emphatically. **2.** to cause to take an oath. **3.** to use profane or obscene language in anger or surprise etc. —**swear by,** to appeal to as a witness in taking an oath; *(colloquial)* to have great confidence in. **swear in,** to induct into an office etc. by administering an oath. **swear off,** *(colloquial)* to promise to abstain from (drink etc.). **swear to,** *(colloquial)* to say that one is certain of. **swearword** *n.* a profane or obscene word. —**swearer** *n.* [Old English]

sweat /swet/ *n.* **1.** moisture exuded through the pores of the skin, especially from heat or nervousness. **2.** a state or period of sweating; *(colloquial)* a state of anxiety. **3.** *(colloquial)* drudgery, an effort, a laborious task or undertaking. **4.** condensed moisture on a surface. —*v.t./i. (past* and *past participle* **sweated,** *US* **sweat**) **1.** to exude sweat. **2.** to be terrified, suffering etc. **3.** (of a wall etc.) to exhibit surface moisture. **4.** to emit like sweat. **5.** to make (a horse or athlete etc.) sweat by exercise. **6.** to drudge or toil, to cause to do this. —**sweatband** *n.* a band of absorbent material inside a hat or round the wrist etc. to soak up sweat. **sweat blood,** to work strenuously; to be extremely anxious. **sweated labour,** labour employed for long hours at low wages. **sweat out,** *(colloquial)* to endure to the end. **sweatshirt,** a sleeved cotton sweater. —**sweaty** *adj.* [Old English]

sweater /'swetə/ *n.* a jumper or pullover.

sweat gland a ◊gland within the skin of mammals that produces surface perspiration. In primates, sweat glands are distributed over the whole body, but in most other mammals they are more localized; for example, in cats and dogs, they are restricted to the feet and around the face.

sweatshop *n.* a workshop or factory where employees work long hours for low wages. Conditions are generally poor, and employees may be under the legal working age. Exploitation of labour in this way is associated with unscrupulous employers, who often employ illegal immigrants or children in their labour force.

swede *n.* an annual or biennial plant *Brassica napus,* widely cultivated for its edible root, which is purple, white, or yellow. It is similar in taste to the turnip *Brassica rapa* but is of greater food value, firmer fleshed, and keeps longer. The yellow variety is commonly known as **rutabaga**. [from *Sweden* from where it was brought to Scotland in the 18th century]

Swede /swi:d/ *n.* a native of Sweden. [Middle Low German and Middle Dutch]

Sweden /'swi:dn/ Kingdom of; country in N Europe on the Baltic Sea, bounded to the W by Norway and to the NE by Finland; **area** 450,000 sq km/173,745 sq mi; **capital** Stockholm; **physical** mountains in NW; plains in S; thickly forested; more than 20,000 islands off the Stockholm coast; lakes, including Vänern, Vättern, Mälarn, Hjälmarn; islands of Öland and Gotland; **head of state** Carl XVI Gustaf from 1973; **head of government** Ingvar Carlsson from 1986; **political system** constitutional monarchy; **exports** aircraft, vehicles, ballbearings, drills, missiles, electronics, petrochemicals, textiles, furnishings, ornamental glass; **population** (1990 est) 8,407,000 (including 17,000 Lapps and 1.2 million postwar immigrants from Finland, Turkey, Yugoslavia, Greece, Iran, other Nordic countries); **language** Swedish; Finnish; **recent history** Sweden remained neutral in both World Wars. Under Social Democratic Labour Party (SAP) leader and prime minister Olof Palme, the constitution was amended in 1971, and the monarch's constitutional powers were reduced in 1975. Olof Palme was murdered in 1986; the SAP government was re-elected in 1988 but resigned in 1990. Sweden is applying for EC membership.

Swedenborg /'swi:dnbɔ:g/ Emanuel 1688–1772. Swedish theologian and philosopher. He trained as a scientist, but from 1747 concentrated on scriptural study, and in *Divine Love and Wisdom* 1763 concluded that the Last Judgment had taken place in 1757, and that the **New**

Church, of which he was the prophet, had now been inaugurated. His writings are the scriptures of the sect popularly known as Swedenborgians, and his works are kept in circulation by the Swedenborg Society, London.

Swedish /'swi:dɪʃ/ *adj.* of Sweden or its people or language. —*n.* the official language of Sweden, a member of the Germanic branch of the Indo-European language family, spoken in Sweden and Finland and closely related to Danish and Norwegian.

sweep *v.t./i. (past* and *past participle* **swept**) **1.** to clear away (dust or litter etc.) with or as with a broom or brush; to clean or clear (a surface or area) thus. **2.** to move or remove by pushing; to carry in an impetuous course; to clear forcefully. **3.** to go smoothly and swiftly or majestically. **4.** to pass or cause to pass quickly over or along; to touch lightly; to affect swiftly. **5.** to extend in a continuous line or slope. **6.** to make (a bow or curtsy) with a smooth movement. —*n.* **1.** a sweeping movement. **2.** a sweeping line or slope. **3.** the act of sweeping with a broom etc. **4.** a chimney sweep. **5.** a sortie by aircraft. **6.** *(colloquial)* a sweepstake. **7.** a long oar. **8.** the movement of a beam across the screen of a cathode-ray tube. —**make a clean sweep of,** to abolish or expel completely; to win all the prizes etc. in. **sweep the board,** to win all the money in a gambling game; to win all the possible prizes etc. **sweep (-second) hand,** an extra hand on a clock or watch, indicating seconds. **swept-wing** *adj.* (of an aircraft) having the wing placed at an acute angle to the axis. [Old English]

sweeper *n.* **1.** one who cleans by sweeping. **2.** a device for sweeping a carpet etc. **3.** in football, a defensive player positioned close to the goalkeeper.

sweeping *adj.* **1.** wide in range or effect. **2.** taking no account of particular cases or exceptions. —*n.* (in *plural*) dirt etc. collected by sweeping. —**sweepingly** *adv.*

sweepstake *n.* a form of gambling on horse races etc. in which all the competitors' stakes are paid to the winners; a race with betting of this kind; a prize or the prizes won in a sweepstake.

sweet *adj.* **1.** tasting as if containing sugar, not bitter. **2.** fragrant. **3.** melodious. **4.** fresh, (of food) not stale, (of water) not salt. **5.** pleasant, gratifying; *(colloquial)* pretty, charming. —*n.* **1.** a small shaped piece of sweet substance, usually made with sugar or chocolate. **2.** a sweet dish forming one course of a meal. **3.** (in *plural*) delights, gratifications. **4.** (especially as a form of address) darling, sweetheart. —**be sweet on,** *(colloquial)* to be fond of or in love with. **sweet-and-sour** *adj.* cooked in a sauce with both sweet and sour ingredients. **sweet brier,** a small wild ◊rose. **sweet corn,** a sweet-flavoured ◊maize. **sweet pea,** a climbing garden plant of the ◊pea family. **sweet potato,** a tropical American plant *Ipomoea batatas* of the morning-glory family Convolvulaceae; the white-orange tuberous root is used as a source of starch and alcohol and eaten as a vegetable. **sweet talk,** (*US*) flattery. **sweet-talk** *v.t.* (*US*) to persuade by flattery. **sweet tooth,** a liking for sweet-tasting things. **sweet william,** a biennial to perennial plant *Dianthus barbatus* of the pink family Caryophyllaceae, native to S Europe. It is grown for its fragrant red, white, and pink flowers. —**sweetly** *adv.,* **sweetness** *n.* [Old English]

sweetbread *n.* the pancreas or thymus gland of an animal, especially as food.

sweeten *v.t./i.* to make or become sweet or sweeter.

sweetener *n.* **1.** or **sweetening** a substance used to sweeten food or drink. **2.** *(colloquial)* a bribe.

sweetheart *n.* each of a pair of persons who are in love with each other (also as a term of endearment).

sweetie *n. (colloquial)* **1.** a sweet. **2.** a sweetheart.

sweetmeal *adj.* (of biscuits) sweetened with wholemeal.

sweetmeat *n.* a sweet; a small fancy cake.

swell *v.t./i. (past participle* **swollen** /'swəʊlən/ or **swelled**) **1.** to make or become larger because of pressure from within; to curve or cause to curve outwards. **2.** to make or become larger in amount, volume, numbers, or intensity. **1.** an act or the state of swelling. **2.** a heaving of the sea with waves that do not break. **3.** a crescendo; a mechanism in an organ etc. for obtaining a crescendo or diminuendo. **4.** *(colloquial)* a person of distinction or of dashing or fashionable appearance. **5.** a protuberant part. —*adj.* (*US colloquial*) smart, excellent. —**swelled** *or* **swollen head,** *(colloquial)* conceit. [Old English]

Swift *Nearly all Jonathan Swift's works were published anonymously, and with the exception of* Gulliver's Travels, *he received no payment for his work.*

swelling *n.* a part raised up from the surrounding surface; an abnormal protuberance.

swelter *v.i.* to be uncomfortably hot. —*n.* a sweltering condition. [from Old English = perish]

swept past and past participle of **sweep**.

swerve *v.t./i.* to turn or cause to turn aside from a straight course, especially in a sudden movement. —*n.* a swerving movement or course. [Old English = scour]

swift *adj.* quick, rapid. —*n.* a fast-flying, short-legged bird of the family Apodidae, of which there are about 75 species, found largely in the tropics. They are 9–23 cm/4–11 in long, with brown or grey plumage, long wings, and a forked tail. They are capable of flying 110 kph/70 mph. —**swiftly** *adv.*, **swiftness** *n.* [Old English]

Swift /swɪft/ Jonathan 1667–1745. Irish satirist and Anglican cleric, author of *Gulliver's Travels* 1726, an allegory describing travel to countries inhabited by giants, miniature people, and intelligent horses. Other works include *The Tale of a Tub* 1704, attacking corruption in religion and learning; contributions to the Tory paper *The Examiner*, of which he was editor 1710–11; the satirical *A Modest Proposal* 1729, which suggested that children of the poor should be eaten; and many essays and pamphlets.

Satire is a sort of glass wherein beholders do generally discover everybody's face but their own.
Jonathan Swift
The Battle of the Books

swig *v.t./i.* (-gg-) (*colloquial*) to take a drink or drinks (of). —*n.* (*colloquial*) a drink or swallow.

swill *v.t./i.* 1. to pour water over or through; to wash or rinse. 2. (of water etc.) to pour. 3. to drink greedily. —*n.* 1. a rinse. 2. a sloppy mixture of waste food fed to pigs. 3. inferior liquor. [Old English]

swim *v.t./i.* (-mm-; *past* swam; *past participle* swum) 1. to propel the body through water by movements of the limbs or fins, tail etc.; to traverse thus; to cause to swim. 2. to float. 3. to be covered or flooded with a liquid. 4. to seem to be whirling or undulating; to have a dizzy sensation. —*n.* 1. an act or spell of swimming. 2. a deep pool frequented by fish in a river. 3. the main current of affairs. —**swimming** *n.* self-propulsion of the body through the water. As a competitive sport there are four strokes: freestyle, breaststroke, backstroke, and butterfly. Distances of races vary between 50 and 1,500 m. Olympic-size pools are 50 m/55 yd long and have eight lanes. —**in the swim**, active in or knowing what is going on. **swim bladder**, a thin-walled,

air-filled sac found in bony fishes, between the gut and the spine. Air enters the bladder from the gut or from surrounding ◊capillaries, and changes of air pressure within the bladder maintain buoyancy whatever the water depth. **swimming bath** *or* **swimming pool**, a pool constructed for swimming. **swimsuit** a bathing suit. —**swimmer** *n.* [Old English]

swimmingly *adv.* with easy and unobstructed progress.

swimming, synchronized a swimming discipline that demands artistry as opposed to speed. Competitors, either individual (solo) or in pairs, perform rhythmic routines to music. Points are awarded for interpretation and style. It was introduced into the Olympic swimming programme in 1984.

Swinburne /'swɪnbɜːn/ Algernon Charles 1837–1909. English poet. He attracted attention with the choruses of his Greek-style tragedy *Atalanta in Calydon* 1865, but he and ◊Rossetti were attacked in 1871 as leaders of 'the fleshly school of poetry', and the revolutionary politics of *Songs before Sunrise* 1871 alienated others.

swindle *v.t./i.* to cheat (a person) in a business transaction; to obtain (money etc.) by fraud. —*n.* 1. a piece of swindling. 2. a fraudulent person or thing. —**swindler** *n.* [back formation from *swindler* from German = extravagant maker of schemes]

swine *n.* (*plural* the same) 1. a pig. 2. (*colloquial*) a disgusting or contemptible person or thing. [Old English]

swing *v.t./i.* (*past* and *past participle* swung) 1. to move to and fro while hanging or supported; to cause to do this; (*slang*) to be executed by hanging. 2. to suspend by its end(s). 3. to lift with a swinging movement; to move by gripping something and leaping; to walk or run with an easy rhythmical gait. 4. to turn (a wheel etc.) smoothly; to turn to one side or in a curve. 5. to change from one opinion or mood etc. to another; to influence (voters or voting etc.) decisively; (*slang*) to deal with, to arrange satisfactorily. 6. to play (music) with a swing rhythm. 7. (in *participle, slang*) lively. —*n.* 1. a swinging motion or action. 2. a seat slung by ropes or chains for swinging in; a swingboat; a spell of swinging in this. 3. the extent to which a thing swings; the amount by which votes, opinions, points scored etc., change from one side to another. 4. short for ◊swing music. —**in full swing**, with activity at its greatest. **swingboat** *n.* a boat-shaped swing at fairs. **swing bridge**, a bridge that can be swung aside to let ships pass. **swing door**, a door able to open in either direction and close itself when released. **swing the lead**, (*slang*) to malinger. —**swinger** *n.* [Old English *swingan* = to beat]

swingeing /'swɪndʒɪŋ/ *adj.* 1. (of a blow) forcible. 2. huge in amount, number, or scope. [from Old English *swengan* = shake, shatter]

swing music a jazz style popular in the 1930s–40s. A big-band sound with a simple harmonic base of varying tempo from the rhythm section (percussion, guitar, piano), harmonic brass and woodwind sections (sometimes strings), and superimposed solo melodic line from, for example, trumpet, clarinet, or saxophone. Exponents included Benny Goodman, Duke Ellington, and Glenn Miller, who introduced jazz to a mass white audience.

swing-wing *n.* or **variable-geometry wing** an aircraft wing that can be moved during flight to provide a suitable configuration for either low-speed or high-speed flight. The British engineer Barnes ◊Wallis developed the idea of the swing-wing, now used in several aircraft, including the US F-111 and the European Tornado. These craft have their wings projecting nearly at right angles for takeoff and landing and low-speed flight, and swung back for high-speed flight.

swinish /'swaɪnɪʃ/ *adj.* bestial; filthy.

swipe *v.t./i.* 1. (*colloquial*) to hit hard and recklessly. 2. (*slang*) to steal. —*n.* (*colloquial*) a reckless hard hit or attempt to hit.

swirl *v.t./i.* to move, flow, or carry along with a whirling motion. —*n.* a swirling motion; a twist, a curl. [originally Scottish]

swish *v.t./i.* to strike, move, or cause to move with a hissing sound. —*n.* a swishing action or sound. —*adj.* (*colloquial*) smart, fashionable. [imitative]

Swiss *adj.* of Switzerland or its people. —*n.* (*plural* the same) a native of Switzerland. —**Swiss cheese plant**, the common name for ◊monstera, a plant of the arum family. **Swiss guards,** Swiss mercenary troops employed formerly by sovereigns of France etc. and still at the Vatican. **Swissroll,** a thin, flat, sponge cake spread with jam etc. and rolled up. [from French *Suisse* from Middle High German]

switch *n.* **1.** a device for making and breaking a connection in an electric circuit. **2.** a transfer, a changeover; a deviation. **3.** a flexible shoot cut from a tree; a light tapering rod. **4.** a device at a junction of railway tracks for transferring a train from one track to another. —*v.t./i.* **1.** to turn (an electrical or other appliance) on or off by means of a switch; to control (an electric current) by means of a switch. **2.** to divert (thoughts or talk etc.) to another subject; to change or exchange (positions, methods, policy etc.). **3.** to transfer (a train) to another track. **4.** to swing round quickly; to snatch suddenly. **5.** to whip or flick with a switch.

switchback *n.* **1.** a railway used for amusement at fairs etc. in which a train's ascents are effected by the momentum of previous descents. **2.** a road or railway with alternate ascents and descents, or zigzagging on a slope.

switchboard *n.* a panel with a set of switches for making telephone connections or operating electric circuits.

Swithun, St /ˈswɪθən/ died 862. English priest, chancellor of King Ethelwolf and bishop of Winchester from 852. According to legend, the weather on his feast day (15 July) is said to continue as either wet or fine for 40 days.

Switzerland /ˈswɪtzələnd/ Swiss Confederation (German *Schweiz,* French *Suisse,* Romansch *Svizzera*); landlocked country in W Europe, bounded to the N by Germany, to the E by Austria, to the S by Italy, and to the W by France. **area** 41,300 sq km/15,946 sq mi; **capital** Bern; **physical** most mountainous country in Europe (Alps and Jura Mountains); highest peak Dufourspitze 4,634 m/15,203 ft in Appenines; lakes Maggiore, Lucerne, Geneva, Constance; **head of state and government** Arnold Koller from 1990; **political system** federal democratic republic; **exports** electrical goods, chemicals, pharmaceuticals, watches, precision instruments, confectionery; **population** (1990 est) 6,628,000; **language** German 65%, French 18%, Italian 12%, Romansch 1% (all official); **recent history** civil war in 1847 resulted in greater centralization of the former Helvetic Republic. Women were given the vote in federal elections in 1971. A referendum in 1986 rejected the proposal for membership of the United Nations.

swivel /ˈswɪvəl/ *n.* a coupling between two parts enabling one to revolve without the other. —*v.t./i.* (-ll-) to turn (as) on a swivel. —**swivel chair,** a chair with a seat turning horizontally. [from Old English = sweep]

swizz *n.* (*slang*) a swindle, a disappointment.

swizzle *n.* (*colloquial*) **1.** a compounded intoxicating drink especially of rum or gin and bitters made frothy. **2.** (*slang*)

swing-wing

forms delta wing
with tailplane

fully
extended
position
(low speed)

swept-back
position
(high-speed)

a swizz. —**swizzle stick,** a stick used for frothing or flattening drinks.

swollen past participle of **swell.**

swoon *v.i.* to faint. —*n.* a faint.

swoop *v.i.* to descend with a rushing movement like a bird upon its prey; to make a sudden attack. —*n.* a swooping or snatching movement or action.

swop variant of **swap.**

sword /sɔːd/ *n.* a weapon with a long blade and a hilt with a hand guard. —**the sword,** war, military power. **cross swords,** to have a fight or dispute. **put to the sword,** to kill, especially in war. **sword dance,** a dance in which the performer brandishes swords or steps about swords laid on the ground. **swordplay** *n.* fencing, repartee or lively arguing. **swordstick** *n.* a hollow walking stick containing a blade that can be used as a sword. [Old English]

swordfish *n.* a large sea fish *Xiphias gladius* with the upper jaw prolonged into a sharp swordlike beak. Swordfish may reach 4.5 m/15 ft in length and weigh 450 kg/1,000 lbs.

swordsman *n.* (*plural* **swordsmen**) a person of good or specified skill with a sword. —**swordsmanship** *n.*

swore past of **swear.**

sworn past participle of **swear.** —*adj.* bound (as) by an oath.

swot *v.t./i.* (*slang*) (-tt-) to study hard. —*n.* (*slang*) **1.** a person who swots. **2.** hard study. —**swot up,** to study (a subject) hard or hurriedly. [dialect variant of *sweat*]

swum past participle of **swim.**

swung past and past participle of **swing.**

sybarite /ˈsɪbəraɪt/ *n.* a person who is extremely fond of comfort and luxury. —**sybaritic** /-ˈrɪtɪk/ *adj.* [from *Sybaris,* ancient city in southern Italy, noted for its luxury]

sycamore /ˈsɪkəmɔː/ *n.* **1.** a large maple tree *Acer pseudoplatanus* native to Europe. The leaves are five-lobed, and the hanging racemes of flowers are followed by winged fruits. The timber is used for furniture-making. **2.** (*US*) a plane tree. **3.** the wood of either of these. [variant of *sycomore* = kind of fig tree, from Old French from Latin from Greek]

sycophant /ˈsɪkəfænt/ *n.* a person who tries to win favour by flattery. —**sycophancy** *n.*, **sycophantic** /-ˈfæntɪk/ *adj.*, **sycophantically** *adv.* [from French or Latin from Greek = informer]

Sydenham /ˈsɪdənəm/ Thomas 1624–1689. English physician, the first person to describe measles and to recommend the use of quinine for relieving symptoms of malaria. His original reputation as 'the English Hippocrates' rested upon his belief that careful observation is more useful than speculation. His *Observationes medicae* was published in 1676.

Sydney /ˈsɪdni/ capital and port of New South Wales, Australia; population (1986) 3,431,000. Industries include engineering, oil refining, electronics, scientific equipment, chemicals, clothing, and furniture. It is a financial centre.

Sydow /ˈsiːdəʊ/ Max von (Carl Adolf) 1929– . Swedish actor associated with the director Ingmar Bergman. He made his US debut as Jesus in *The Greatest Story Ever Told* 1965. His other films include *The Seventh Seal* 1957, *The Exorcist* 1973, and *Hannah and her Sisters* 1985.

syl- see ◊**syn-.**

syllabary /ˈsɪləbərɪ/ *n.* a list of characters representing syllables and serving the purpose, in some languages or stages of writing, of an alphabet.

syllabic /sɪˈlæbɪk/ *adj.* of or in syllables. —**syllabically** *adv.* [from French or Latin from Greek]

syllabification /sɪlæbɪfɪˈkeɪʃən/ *n.* a division into or utterance in syllables. [from Latin]

syllable /ˈsɪləbəl/ *n.* **1.** a unit of pronunciation forming the whole or a part of a word and usually having one vowel sound, often with a consonant or consonants before or after. **2.** a character or characters representing a syllable. **3.** the least amount of speech or writing. —**in words of one syllable,** simply, plainly. [from Anglo-French from Latin from Greek *sullabē* (*lambanō* = take)]

syllabub /ˈsɪləbʌb/ *n.* a dish of sweetened whipped cream flavoured with wine etc.

syllabus /ˈsɪləbəs/ *n.* (*plural* **syllabuses**) a programme or conspectus of a course of study, teaching etc. [misreading of Latin *sittybas* from Greek = title slips]

syllepsis /sɪ'lepsɪs/ *n.* (*plural* **syllepses** /-iːz/) a figure of speech applying a word to two others in different senses (e.g. *took the oath and his seat*), or to two others of which it grammatically suits one only (e.g. *neither you nor he knows*). [Latin from Greek = taking together]

syllogism /'sɪlədʒɪzəm/ *n.* a form of reasoning in which from two given or assumed propositions (the *premises*) a third is deduced (the *conclusion*). Syllogisms were devised by Aristotle in his work on logic. They establish the conditions under which a valid conclusion follows or does not follow by deduction from given premises. The following is an example of a valid syllogism: 'All men are mortal, Socrates is a man, therefore Socrates is mortal.' —**syllogistic** /-'dʒɪstɪk/ *adj.* [from Old French from Latin from Greek from *logizomai* = to reason]

sylph /sɪlf/ *n.* **1.** an elemental spirit of the air. **2.** a slender, graceful woman or girl.

sylvan variant of **silvan**.

Sylvanus in Roman mythology, another name for ◊Silvanus.

sym- see ◊syn-.

symbiosis /sɪmbi'əʊsɪs, -baɪ-/ *n.* (*plural* **symbioses** /-iːz/) **1.** any close relationship between two organisms of different species, especially where both partners benefit from the association. A well-known example is the pollination relationship between insects and flowers, where the insects feed on nectar and carry pollen from one flower to another. This is sometimes known as ◊mutualism. Symbiosis in a broader sense includes ◊commensalism and ◊parasitism. **2.** an association of cooperating persons. —**symbiotic** /-'ɒtɪk/ *adj.* [from Greek = living together (*bios* =life)]

symbol /'sɪmbəl/ *n.* **1.** a thing regarded as suggesting something or embodying certain characteristics; something that stands for something else. **2.** a mark or sign used to convey information visually, indicating an idea, object, process etc. [from Latin from Greek *sumbolon* = mark, token]

symbolic /sɪm'bɒlɪk/ *adj.* or **symbolical** of, using, or used as a symbol.

symbolic processor a computer purpose-built to run so-called symbol-manipulation programs rather than programs involving a great deal of numerical computation. Mostly, they exist for the ◊artificial intelligence language ◊Lisp, although some have also been built to run ◊Prolog.

symbolism /'sɪmbəlɪzəm/ *n.* **1.** use of symbols to represent things; symbols collectively. **2. Symbolism,** a late 19th-century movement in French poetry, associated with Verlaine, Mallarmé, and Rimbaud, who used words for their symbolic rather than concrete meaning. **3. Symbolism,** a movement in late 19th-century painting that emerged in France inspired by the trend in poetry. The subjects were often mythological, mystical, or fantastic. Gustave Moreau was a leading exponent. —**symbolist, Symbolist** *n.*

symbolize *v.t.* to be a symbol of; to represent by means of symbols. —**symbolization** /-'zeɪʃən/ *n.* [from French]

Symington /'sɪmɪŋtən/ William 1763–1831. Scottish engineer who built the first successful steamboat. He invented the steam road locomotive in 1787 and a steamboat engine in 1788. His steamboat the *Charlotte Dundas* was completed in 1802.

symmetry /'sɪmɪtrɪ/ *n.* **1.** correct proportion of parts; beauty resulting from this. **2.** a structure that allows an object to be divided into parts of equal shape and size; possession of such a structure; the repetition of exactly similar parts facing each other or a centre. —**symmetric** /-'metrɪk/ *adj.,* **symmetrical** /-'metrɪkəl/ *adj.,* **symmetrically** /-'metrɪkəlɪ/ *adv.* [from obsolete French or Latin from Greek *metron* = measure]

sympathetic /sɪmpə'θetɪk/ *adj.* **1.** of, showing, or expressing sympathy; due to sympathy. **2.** likeable. **3.** not antagonistic. —**sympathetic magic,** magic seeking to affect an event etc. by imitating the effect desired. **sympathetic string,** in music, a string which vibrates with sympathetic resonance, enriching the tone. —**sympathetically** *adv.*

sympathize /'sɪmpəθaɪz/ *v.i.* to feel or express sympathy. —**sympathizer** *n.* [from French]

sympathy /'sɪmpəθɪ/ *n.* **1.** sharing or the ability to share another's emotions or sensations. **2.** a feeling of pity or tenderness towards one suffering pain, grief, or trouble. **3.** liking for each other produced in people who have similar opinions or tastes. **4.** (in *singular* or *plural*) agreement with another person etc. in an opinion or desire. [from Latin from Greek *pathos* = feeling]

symphonic /sɪm'fɒnɪk/ *adj.* of or like a symphony or symphonies. —**symphonic poem,** an orchestral piece usually in one movement and usually descriptive or rhapsodic. The term was first used by Liszt for his 13 one-movement orchestral works that interpret a story from literature or history. Richard Strauss preferred the title **tone poem.** —**symphonically** *adv.*

symphony /'sɪmfənɪ/ *n.* **1.** an elaborate composition for a full orchestra, traditionally in four separate but closely related movements. It developed from the smaller ◊sonata form, the Italian overture, and the dance suite of the 18th century. **2.** (*US*) a symphony orchestra. —**symphony orchestra,** a large orchestra playing symphonies etc. [originally = harmony of sound, from Old French from Latin from Greek *phōnē* = sound]

symposium /sɪm'pəʊzɪəm/ *n.* (*plural* **symposia**) a conference or collection of essays etc. on a particular subject; a philosophical or other friendly discussion. [from Latin from Greek = drinking party (*potēs* = drinker)]

symptom /'sɪmptəm/ *n.* a sign of the existence of a condition, especially any change or manifestation in the body suggestive of disease as perceived by the sufferer. Symptoms are subjective phenomena. In strict usage, symptoms are events or changes reported by the patient; signs are noted by the doctor during the patient's examination. [from Latin from Greek *sumpiptō* = happen (*piptō* = fall)]

symptomatic /sɪmptə'mætɪk/ *adj.* serving as a symptom. —**symptomatically** *adv.*

syn- (**syl-** before *l,* **sym-** before *b, m, p*) prefix in senses 'together', 'at the same time', 'alike' etc. [from Greek *sun* = with]

synagogue /'sɪnəgɒg/ *n.* a place of worship of a Jewish assembly, also (in the USA) called a temple; the assembly itself. As an institution the synagogue dates from the destruction of the Temple in Jerusalem in AD 70, though it had been developing from the time of the Babylonian exile as a substitute for the Temple. In antiquity it was a public meeting hall where the Torah was also read, but today it is used primarily for prayer and services. —**synagogal** *adj.,* **synagogical** /-'gɒgɪkəl, -'gɒdʒɪkəl/ *adj.* [from Old French from Latin from Greek = assembly]

synapse *n.* the junction between two ◊nerve cells of an animal, or between a nerve cell and a muscle. The two cells involved are not in direct contact but separated by a narrow gap called the synaptic cleft. Across this gap flow chemical ◊neurotransmitters, which have a specific effect on the receiving cell when they bind to special receptors on its surface. The response may be a nervous impulse in a nerve cell or a contraction in a muscle cell.

sync /sɪŋk/ *n.* or **synch** (*colloquial*) synchronization. —*v.t.* (*colloquial*) to synchronize. [abbreviation]

synchromesh /'sɪŋkrəʊmeʃ/ *n.* a system of gear changing, especially in motor vehicles, in which the gear wheels revolve at the same speed while they are being brought into engagement. —*adj.* of this system. [abbreviation of *synchronized mesh*]

synchronic /sɪŋ'krɒnɪk/ *adj.* concerned with a subject as it exists at a particular time. —**synchronic linguistics,** = descriptive linguistics. —**synchronically** *adv.*

synchronism /'sɪŋkrənɪzəm/ *n.* **1.** being or treated as synchronous or synchronic. **2.** synchronizing. [from Greek]

synchronize /'sɪŋkrənaɪz/ *v.t./i.* to make or be synchronous with. —**synchronization** /-'zeɪʃən/ *n.,* **synchronizer** *n.*

synchronous /'sɪŋkrənəs/ *adj.* **1.** existing or occurring at the same time. **2.** having the same or a proportional speed and operating simultaneously. [from Latin from Greek *khronos* = time]

synchrotron /'sɪŋkrətrɒn/ *n.* a particle ◊accelerator, a cyclotron in which the strength of the magnetic field increases with the energy of the particles, keeping their orbital radius constant.

syncline /'sɪŋklaɪn/ *n.* a fold in the rocks of the Earth's crust in which the layers or ◊beds dip inwards, thus forming a troughlike structure with a sag in the middle. The opposite structure, with the beds arching upwards, is an ◊anticline. —**synclinal** /-'klaɪnəl/ *adj.* [from Greek *klinō* = lean]

syncopate /'sɪŋkəpeɪt/ v.t. 1. in music, to displace the beats or accents. 2. to shorten (a word) by dropping an interior letter or letters. —**syncopation** /-'peɪʃən/ n. [from Latin]

syncope /'sɪŋkəpɪ/ n. 1. syncopation. 2. temporary unconsciousness; a faint, ◊fainting. [from Latin from Greek koptō = cut off]

syncretize /'sɪŋkrɪtaɪz/ v.t./i. to combine (different beliefs or principles). [from Greek sugkrētizō = combine as two parties against a third]

syndic /'sɪndɪk/ n. any of various university or government officials. [French from Latin from Greek = advocate (dikē = justice)]

syndicalism /'sɪndɪkəlɪzəm/ n. a political movement that rejected parliamentary activity in favour of direct action, culminating in a revolutionary general strike to secure worker ownership and control of industry. The idea originated under Robert ◊Owen's influence in the 1830s, acquired its name and its more violent aspects in France from the philosopher ◊Sorel, and also reached the USA (see ◊Industrial Workers of the World). After 1918 syndicalism was absorbed in communism, although it continued to have an independent existence in Spain until the late 1930s. —**syndicalist** n. [from French syndicat = trade union]

syndicate /'sɪndɪkət/ n. 1. a combination of persons or commercial firms to promote some common interest. 2. an association supplying material simultaneously to a number of periodicals. 3. a committee of syndics. —/-keɪt/ v.t. 1. to form into a syndicate. 2. to publish (material) through a syndicate. —**syndication** /-'keɪʃən/ n.

syndrome /'sɪndrəʊm/ n. 1. a set of signs and symptoms that together indicate the presence of a disease or abnormal condition. 2. a combination of opinions, behaviour etc., characteristic of a particular condition. [from Greek dram- = run]

synecdoche /sɪ'nekdəkɪ/ n. a ◊figure of speech in which a part is named but the whole is understood, or conversely (e.g. several new faces in the team for new people, or England beat Australia at cricket for the English team beat the Australian team). [from Latin from Greek ekdekhomai = take up]

synergy n. in architecture, the augmented strength of systems, where the strength of a wall is greater than the added total of its individual units. [Greek = combined action]

Synge /sɪŋ/ J(ohn) M(illington) 1871–1909. Irish playwright, a leading figure in the Irish dramatic revival of the early 20th century. His six plays reflect the speech patterns of the Aran Islands and W Ireland. They include In the Shadow of the Glen 1903, Riders to the Sea 1904, and The Playboy of the Western World 1907, which caused riots at the Abbey Theatre, Dublin, when first performed.

Synge Richard 1914– . British biochemist who investigated paper ◊chromatography (a means of separating mixtures). By 1940 techniques of chromatography for separating proteins had been devised. Still lacking were comparable techniques for distinguishing the amino acids that constituted the proteins. By 1944, Synge and his colleague Archer Martin had worked out a procedure, known as ascending chromatography, which filled this gap and won them the 1952 Nobel Prize for Chemistry.

synod /'sɪnəd/ n. a council of clergy and church officials (and sometimes laity) convened for discussing ecclesiastical affairs. [from Latin from Greek = meeting (hodos = way)]

synonym /'sɪnənɪm/ n. a word or phrase that means exactly or nearly the same as another in the same language. There are very few strict synonyms in any language, although there may be near-synonyms, depending upon the contexts in which the words are used. Thus brotherly and fraternal are synonyms in English, but a brotherhood is not at all the same as a fraternity. **synonymy** n. [from Latin from Greek onoma = name]

synonymous /sɪ'nɒnɪməs/ adj. having the same meaning.

synopsis /sɪ'nɒpsɪs/ n. (plural synopses /-i:z/) a summary, a brief general survey. [Latin from Greek opsis = seeing]

synoptic /sɪ'nɒptɪk/ adj. of or giving a synopsis. —**Synoptic Gospels**, in the New Testament, those of Matthew, Mark, and Luke, which have many similarities (whereas that of John differs greatly). —**synoptically** adv. [from Greek]

synovia /saɪ'nəʊvɪə/ n. or **synovial fluid** a viscous yellow fluid that bathes movable joints between the bones of vertebrates. It nourishes and lubricates the ◊cartilage at the end of each bone. —**synovial** adj. [Latin]

syntax /'sɪntæks/ n. the arrangement of words and phrases to form sentences; the rules or analysis of this. —**syntactic**/-'tæktɪk/ adj., **syntactically** /-'tæktɪkəlɪ/adv. [from French or Latin from Greek = marshalling (tassō = arrange)]

synthesis /'sɪnθɪsɪs/ n. (plural syntheses /-si:z/) 1. the combination of separate parts or elements into a complex whole. 2. in chemistry, the formation of a substance or compound from more elementary compounds. The synthesis of a drug can involve several stages from the initial material to the final product; the complexity of these stages is a major factor in the cost of production. [Latin from Greek]

synthesize /'sɪnθɪsaɪz/ v.t. to make by synthesis.

synthesizer /'sɪnθɪsaɪzə/ n. an electronic device for combining sounds so as to reproduce the musical tones of conventional instruments or produce a variety of artificial ones. In **preset synthesizers** the sound of various instruments is produced by a built-in computer-type memory. In **programmable synthesizers** any number of new instrumental or other sounds may be produced at the will of the performer. **Speech synthesizers** can break down speech into 128 basic elements (allophones), which are then combined into words and sentences, as in the voices of electronic teaching aids.

synthetic /sɪn'θetɪk/ adj. 1. produced by synthesis; manufactured (as opposed to produced naturally). 2. (colloquial) affected, insincere. 3. in philosophy, a term employed by ◊Kant to describe a judgement in which the predicate is not contained within the subject; for example, 'The flower is blue' is synthetic, since every flower is not blue. It is the converse of ◊analytic. —n. a synthetic substance or fabric. Since the 1900s, more and more of the materials used in everyday life are synthetics, including plastics (polythene, polystyrene), synthetic fibres (nylon, acrylics, polyesters), synthetic resins, and synthetic rubber. Most naturally occurring organic substances are now made synthetically, especially pharmaceuticals. —**synthetic fibre**, a fibre made by chemical processes, unknown in nature. There are two kinds. One is made from natural materials that have been chemically processed in some way; ◊rayon, for example, is made by processing the cellulose in wood pulp. The other type is the true synthetic fibre, made entirely from chemicals. ◊Nylon was the original synthetic fibre, made from chemicals obtained from petroleum (crude oil). —**synthetically** adv. [from French from Greek]

syphilis /'sɪfɪlɪs/ n. a contagious venereal disease caused by the spiral-shaped bacterium (spirochete) Treponema pallidum. Untreated, it runs its course in three stages over many years, often starting with a painless hard sore, or chancre, developing within a month on the area of infection (usually the genitals). The second stage, months later, is a rash with arthritis, hepatitis, and/or meningitis. The third stage, years later, leads eventually to paralysis, blindness, insanity, and death. The Wassermann test is a diagnostic blood test for syphilis. —**syphilitic** /-'lɪtɪk/ adj. [from title of a Latin poem 1530 by a physician of Verona in Italy, about a shepherd Syphilus, the supposed first sufferer from the disease]

Syria /'sɪrɪə/ Syrian Arab Republic; country in W Asia, on the Mediterranean, bounded to the N by Turkey, to the E by Iraq, to the S by Jordan, and to the SW by Israel and Lebanon; **area** 185,200 sq km/71,506 sq mi; **capital** Damascus; **physical** mountains alternate with fertile plains and desert areas; Euphrates River; Mount Hermon, Golan Heights; **head of state and government** Hafez-al-Assad from 1971; **political system** Socialist republic; **exports** cotton, cereals, oil, phosphates, tobacco; **population** (1990 est) 12,471000; **language** Arabic 89% (official), Kurdish 6%, Armenian 3%; **recent history** Full independence was achieved from France in 1946. Syria merged with Egypt to from the United Arab Republic (UAR) in 1958; this disintegrated in 1961. Territory was lost to Israel in the Six-Day War of 1967; in 1984 a plan for government of national unity in Lebanon was approved. President Assad secured the release of US hostages. Further attempts to release Western hostages were made in 1987. Diplomatic relations were restored with Britain in 1990.

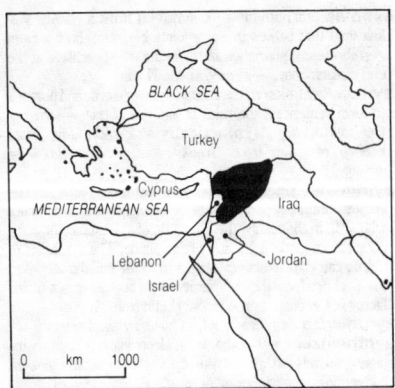

Syria

Syriac /'sɪriæk/ *n.* the language of ancient Syria, a Semitic language, originally the Aramaic dialect spoken in and around Edessa (now in Turkey) and widely used in W Asia from about 700 BC to AD 700. From the 3rd to 7th centuries it was a Christian liturgical and literary language. —*adj.* of this language. [from Latin from Greek *Suria* = Syria]

syringa /si'rɪŋgə/ *n.* 1. the ◊mock orange *Philadelphus.* 2. the botanical name for ◊lilac (*Syringa vulgaris*). [as following entry, from stems of mock orange being used for pipestems]

syringe /'sɪrɪndʒ, -'rɪndʒ/ *n.* a device for drawing in liquid by suction and then ejecting it in a fine stream. —*v.t.* to sluice or spray with a syringe. [from Latin *syringa* from Greek *surigx* = pipe]

syrup /'sɪrəp/ *n.* 1. a thick liquid of water (nearly) saturated with sugar; this flavoured or medicated. 2. condensed sugar-cane juice, molasses, treacle. 3. excessive sweetness of manner. —**syrupy** *adj.* [from Old French or Latin from Arabic]

system /'sɪstəm/ *n.* 1. a set of connected things or parts that form a whole or work together; a set of organs in the body with a common function. 2. an animal body as a whole. 3. a set of rules, principles, or practices forming a particular philosophy or form of government. 4. a major group of layers of rock that were deposited during a particular geological period and contain similar fossils. 5. a method of classification, notation, measurement etc. 6. being systematic, orderliness. —**get a thing out of one's system,** to be rid of its effects. [from French or Latin from Greek *sustēma* (*histēmi* = set up)]

systematic /sɪstə'mætɪk/ *adj.* methodical, according to a system, not casually or at random. —**systematically** *adv.*

systematize /'sɪstəmətaɪz/ *v.t.* to make systematic. —**systematization** /-'zeɪʃən/ *n.*

Système International d'Unités see ◊SI units. [French]

systemic /si'stemɪk/ *adj.* 1. in medicine, relating to or affecting the body as a whole. A systemic disease affects the whole body. 2. (of an insecticide etc.) entering plant tissues via the roots and shoots. —**systemically** *adv.*

systems analysis in computing, the investigation of a business activity or clerical procedure, with a view to deciding if and how it can be computerized. The analyst discusses the existing procedures with the people involved, observes the flow of data through the business, and draws up an outline specification of the required computer system.

systems design in computing, the detailed design of an ◊application. The designer breaks the system down into component programs and designs the required input forms, screen layouts, and printouts. Systems design forms a link between systems analysis and ◊programming.

System X in communications, a modular, computer-controlled, digital switching system used in telephone exchanges.

systole /'sɪstəlɪ/ *n.* the rhythmical contraction of the chambers of the heart, alternating with diastole to form the pulse. —**systolic** /si'stɒlɪk/ *adj.* [Latin from Greek *sustellō* = contract]

Szczecin /'ʃtʃetʃiːn/ (German *Stettin*) industrial port (shipbuilding, fish processing, synthetic fibres, tools, iron) on the river Oder, in NW Poland; population (1989) 391,000.

Székesfehérvár /'seɪkeʃfeheəvɑː/ industrial city (metal products) in west central Hungary; population (1988) 113,000. It is a market centre for wine, tobacco, and fruit.

Szent-Gyorgi /sent'dʒɜːdʒi/ Albert 1893–1986. Hungarian-born US biochemist who isolated vitamin C and studied the chemistry of muscular activity. He received the Nobel Prize for Medicine in 1937.

Szilard /'sɪlɑːd/ Leo 1898–1964. Hungarian-born US physicist who, in 1934, was one of the first scientists to realize that nuclear fission, or atom splitting, could lead to a chain reaction releasing enormous amounts of instantaneous energy. He emigrated to the USA in 1938 and there influenced ◊Einstein to advise President Roosevelt to begin the nuclear arms programme. After World War II he turned his attention to the newly emerging field of molecular biology.

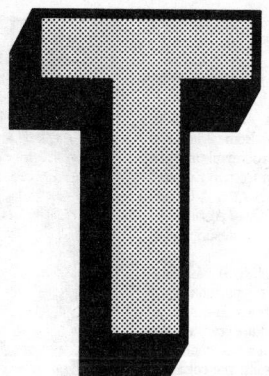

t, T /tiː/ *n.* (*plural* **ts, t's**) **1.** the 20th letter of the English alphabet; in the Greek alphabet (still called *tau*) its form was T, τ. **2.** a T-shaped thing. —**cross the t's,** to be minutely accurate. **to a T,** exactly, to a nicety.

t symbol for ton(s), tonne(s).

T 1. abbreviation of tesla. **2.** symbol for tritium.

ta /tɑː/ (*colloquial*) interjection meaning thank you. [infantile form]

Ta symbol for tantalum.

TA abbreviation of Territorial Army.

tab *n.* **1.** a small projecting flap or attached strip, especially one by which a thing can be hung, fastened, or identified. **2.** (*colloquial*) an account, a tally; (*US colloquial*) a bill; a price. —*v.t.* (**-bb-**) to provide with tabs. —**keep a tab** *or* **tabs on,** to keep account of; to have under observation or in check. [probably from dialect; compare *tag*]

TAB abbreviation of typhoid-paratyphoid A and B vaccine.

tabard /'tæbəd/ *n.* **1.** a short-sleeved or sleeveless jerkin emblazoned with the arms of the sovereign and forming the official dress of a herald or pursuivant. **2.** (*historical*) a short surcoat open at the sides and with short sleeves, worn by a knight over armour and emblazoned with armorial bearings. **3.** a woman's or girl's garment of similar shape. [from Old French *tabart*]

tabby /'tæbɪ/ *n.* **1.** a grey or brownish cat with dark stripes. **2.** a kind of watered silk. [from French from Arabic = quarter of Baghdad where tabby silk was produced; connection of sense 1 uncertain]

tabernacle /'tæbənækəl/ *n.* **1.** (in the Bible) a fixed or movable habitation, usually of light construction; a tent containing the Ark of the Covenant, used as a portable shrine by the Israelites during their wanderings in the wilderness. **2.** a meeting-place for worship used by non-Conformists (e. g. Baptists) or by Mormons; (*historical*) any of the temporary structures used during the rebuilding of churches after the Fire of London (1666). **3.** a canopied niche or recess in the wall of a church etc.; an ornamental receptacle for the pyx or consecrated elements of the Eucharist. [from Old French or Latin *tabernaculum* = tent, diminutive of *taberna* = hut]

tabla /'tæblə, 'tɑːblə/ *n.* a pair of small Indian drums played with the hands, often to accompany the sitar. [Urdu from Arabic *tabla* = drum]

table /'teɪbəl/ *n.* **1.** a piece of furniture with a flat top supported on one or more legs, providing a level surface for putting things on. **2.** the food provided at table. **3.** a set of facts or figures systematically arranged, especially in columns; the matter contained in such a set. **4.** a flat surface for working on or for machinery etc. **5.** a slab of wood or stone etc.; the matter inscribed on it. —*v.t.* **1.** to bring forward for discussion or consideration. **2.** to postpone consideration of (a matter). —**at table,** taking a meal at a table. **on the table,** submitted for discussion or consideration. **tablecloth** *n.* a cloth spread on a table, especially for meals. **table licence,** a licence to serve alcoholic drinks with meals only. **table linen,** tablecloths, napkins etc. **Table of the House,** the central table in either of the Houses of Parliament. **turn the tables on,** to reverse one's relations (with), especially to pass from a weaker to a stronger position. **under**

the table, drunk. [from Old French from Latin *tabula* = plank, tablet]

tableau /'tæbləʊ/ *n.* (*plural* **tableaux** /-əʊz/) **1.** a picturesque presentation; a group of silent motionless persons arranged to represent a scene. **2.** a dramatic or effective situation suddenly brought about. [French, diminutive of *table*]

table d'hôte /tɑːbl 'dəʊt/ a meal at a fixed time and price in a hotel etc., with less choice of dishes than à la carte. [French = host's table]

tableland *n.* a plateau of land.

tablespoon *n.* a large spoon for serving food; the amount held by this. —**tablespoonful** *n.* (*plural* **tablespoonfuls**)

tablet /'tæblɪt/ *n.* **1.** a small measured and compressed amount of a substance, especially of a medicine or drug. **2.** a small flat piece of soap etc. **3.** a small slab or panel, especially for the display of an inscription. [from Old French from Latin *tabula* = plank, tablet]

table tennis or **ping pong** indoor game played by two or four players with small bats and a ball bouncing on a table divided by a net. It was developed in Britain about 1880 and derived from lawn tennis.

tabloid /'tæblɔɪd/ *n.* a newspaper, usually popular in style, printed on sheets that are half the size of larger newspapers. [originally name of compressed drug-preparation]

taboo /tə'buː/ *n.* the system or an act of setting a person or thing apart as sacred or accursed; a prohibition or restriction imposed by social custom. —*adj.* avoided or prohibited, especially by social custom. —*v.t.* to put under a taboo; to exclude or prohibit by authority or social influence. [Polynesian *tabu* = forbidden]

tabor /'teɪbə/ *n.* (*historical*) a small drum, especially used to accompany a pipe. [from Old French from Persian *tabīra* = drum]

tabular /'tæbjʊlə/ *adj.* of or arranged in tables or lists. [from Latin]

tabula rasa a mind without any preconceived ideas. [Latin = scraped tablet, from the Romans' use of wax-covered tablets which could be written on with a pointed stick and cleared by smoothing over the surface]

tabulate /'tæbjʊleɪt/ *v.t.* to arrange (figures or facts) in tabular form. —**tabulation** /-'leɪʃən/ *n.* [from Latin *tabulare* (*tabula* = table)]

tabulator *n.* **1.** a person or thing that tabulates. **2.** a device on a typewriter for advancing to a sequence of set positions in tabular work.

tacet *n.* in music, score indication used when an instrument is to be silent for a complete movement or section of a movement. [Latin = it is silent]

tachisme /'tæʃɪzəm/ *n.* action painting. [French *tache* = stain]

tacho /'tækəʊ/ *n.* (*plural* **tachos**) (*colloquial*) a tachometer. [abbreviation]

tachograph /'tækəɡrɑːf/ *n.* a combined speedometer and clock that records a vehicle's speed (on a small card disc, magnetic disc, or tape) and the length of time the vehicle is moving or stationary. It is used to monitor a lorry driver's working hours. [from Greek *takhos* = speed]

tachometer /tæ'kɒmɪtə/ *n.* an instrument for measuring velocity or speed of rotation (especially of a vehicle engine).

tacit /'tæsɪt/ adj. understood or implied without being stated. —**tacitly** adv. [from Latin tacitus (tacēre = be silent)]

taciturn /'tæsɪtɜːn/ adj. habitually saying very little, uncommunicative. —**taciturnity** /-'tɜːnɪtɪ/ n.

Tacitus /'tæsɪtəs/ Publius Cornelius AD c.55–c.120. Roman historian. A public orator in Rome, he was consul under Nerva ADɪ 97–98 and proconsul of Asia AD 112–113. He wrote histories of the Roman Empire, *Arɴnales* and *Historiae*, covering the years AD 14–68 and 69–97 respectively. He also wrote a *Life of Agricola* 97 (he married Agricola's daughter in 77) and a description of the German tribes, *Germania* 98.

tack[1] n. 1. a small sharp broad-headed nail; (US) a drawing-pin. 2. a long stitch used in fastening fabric in position lightly or temporarily. 3. the direction in which a ship moves as determined by the position of its sails; a temporary change of direction in sailing to take advantage of a side wind etc.; a rope for securing the corner of some sails; the corner to which this is fastened. 4. a course of action or policy. 5. sticky condition of varnish etc. —v.t./i. 1. to fasten with a tack or tacks. 2. to stitch with tacks. 3. to add as an extra thing. 4. to change a ship's course by turning its head to the wind; to make a series of such tacks. 5. to change one's conduct or policy etc. [compare Old French tache = clasp]

tack[2] n. riding-harness, saddles etc. [from tackle]

tackle n. 1. the equipment for a task or sport. 2. a mechanism, especially of ropes, pulley-blocks, hooks etc., for lifting weights, managing sails etc.; a windlass with its ropes and hooks. 3. the act of tackling in football etc. —v.t. 1. to try to deal with (a problem or difficulty); to grapple with or try to overcome (an opponent); to enter into a discussion with (a person, especially about an awkward matter). 2. (in football etc.) to intercept or stop (a player running with the ball). —**tackler** n. [probably from Middle Low German (taken = lay hold of)]

tacky adj. (of glue or varnish etc.) in the sticky stage before complete dryness. —**tackiness** n. [from tack[1]]

tact n. skill in avoiding giving offence or in winning goodwill by saying or doing the right thing. [French from Latin tactus (= sense of) touch (tangere = to touch)]

tactful adj. having or showing tact. —**tactfully** adv., **tactfulness** n.

tactic /'tæktɪk/ n. a piece of tactics.

tactical /'tæktɪkəl/ adj. 1. of tactics. 2. (of bombing) done in immediate support of military or naval operations. 3. adroitly planning or planned. —**tactical weapons**, see ◊strategic weapons. —**tactically** adv.

tactician /tæk'tɪʃən/ n. an expert in tactics.

tactics n.pl. (also treated as singular) 1. the art of placing and manœuvring armed forces skilfully in a battle (distinguished from strategy). 2. the procedure adopted in carrying out a scheme or achieving some end. [from Greek taktika (tassō = arrange)]

tactile /'tæktaɪl/ adj. of or connected with the sense of touch; perceived by touch. —**tactility** /-'tɪlɪtɪ/ n. [from Latin tactilis (tangere = touch)]

tactless adj. having or showing no tact. —**tactlessly** adv., **tactlessness** n.

Tadmur /'tædmuə/ Arabic name for the ancient city of ◊Palmyra in Syria.

tadpole n. the larva of a frog or toad etc. at the stage when it lives in water and has gills and a tail. [from toad and poll, from size of head]

Tadzhik /tɑː'dʒiːk/ n. or **Tajik** a speaker of any of the Tadzhik dialects, which belong to the Iranian branch of the Indo-European family. The Tadzhiks have long been associated with neighbouring Turkic peoples and their language contains Altaic loan words. The Tadzhiks inhabit Tadzhikistan (part of the USSR) and Afghanistan.

Tadzhikistan /tædʒiːkɪ'stɑːn/ constituent republic of S central USSR from 1929, part of Soviet Central Asia; **area** 143,100 sq km/55,251 sq mi; **capital** Dushanbe; **features** few areas below 3,500 m/11,000 ft; **population** (1987) 4,807,000; 59% Tadzhik, 23% Uzbek, 11% Russian or Ukrainian; **language** Tadzhik, similar to Farsi (Persian); **recent history** formed in 1924 from the Tadzhik areas of Bokhara and Turkestan. It experienced a devastating earthquake in Jan 1989 (274 people died) and ethnic conflict 1989–90.

Tagore Nobel prize-winning Indian writer, Rabindranath Tagore, photographed in 1920.

Taegu /teɪ'guː/ largest inland city of South Korea after Seoul; population (1985) 2,031,000.

Taejon /teɪ'dʒɒn/ capital of South Chungchong province, central South Korea; population (1985) 866,000. Korea's tallest standing Buddha and oldest wooden building are found NE of the city at Popchusa in the Mount Songnisan National Park. [Korean = large rice paddy]

tae kwon do Korean ◊martial art similar to ◊karate, which includes punching and kicking. It was included in the 1988 Olympic Games as a demonstration sport.

Tafawa Balewa /tə'fɑːwə bə'leɪwə/ Alhaji Abubakar 1912–1966. Nigerian politician, prime minister from 1957 to 1966, when he was assassinated in a coup d'état.

taffeta /'tæfɪtə/ n. a fine lustrous silk or silklike fabric. [from Old French or Latin ultimately from Persian, past participle of tā ftan = twist]

taffrail /'tæfreɪl/ n. a rail round a ship's stern. [from Dutch taffereel = panel; assimilated to rail[1]]

Taffy /'tæfɪ/ n. (colloquial) a nickname for a Welshman. [supposed Welsh pronunciation of Davy = David]

Taft /tæft/ William Howard 1857–1930. 27th president of the USA 1909–13, a Republican. He was secretary of war 1904–08 in Theodore Roosevelt's administration, but as president his conservatism provoked Roosevelt to stand against him in the 1912 election. Taft served as chief justice of the Supreme Court 1921–30.

tag[1] n. 1. a loop, flap, or label for handling, hanging, or marking a thing. 2. a metal or plastic point of a shoelace etc. used to assist insertion. 3. a loose or ragged end. 4. a trite quotation, a stock phrase. —v.t./i. (-gg-) 1. to attach a tag to. 2. to attach, to add as an extra thing. 3. (colloquial) to follow; to trail behind. —**tag along**, (colloquial) to go along with another or others.

tag[2] n. a children's game of chasing and touching. —v.t. (-gg-) to touch in a game of tag.

Tagalog /'tægəlɒg/ n. 1. a member of the principal people of the Philippine Islands. 2. their language. [Tagalog (taga = native and ilog = river)]

Tagliacozzi /tæljə'kɒtsi/ Gaspare 1546–1599. Italian surgeon who pioneered plastic surgery. He was the first to repair noses lost in duels or through ◊syphilis. He also carried out repair of ears. His method involved taking flaps of skin from the arm and grafting them into place.

tagliatelle /tɑːljə'telɪ/ n. a ribbon-shaped form of pasta. [Italian]

Taglioni /tæl'jəʊni/ Marie 1804–1884. Italian dancer. A ballerina of ethereal style and exceptional lightness, she was the first to use ◊pointe work, or dancing on the toes, as an expressive part of ballet rather than as sheer technique. She created many roles, including the title role in *La Sylphide* 1832, first performed at the Paris Opéra, and choreographed by her father **Filippo** (1771–1871). Marie's brother **Paolo** (1808–1884) was a choreographer and ballet master at Berlin Court Opera 1856–83, and his daughter **Marie** (1833–1891) danced in Berlin and London, creating many roles in her father's ballets.

Tagore /tə'gɔː/ Rabindranath 1861–1941. Bengali Indian writer, born in Calcutta. One of the most influential Indian authors of the 20th century, he translated into English his own verse *Gitanjali* ('song offerings') 1912 and his verse play *Chitra* 1896. He was awarded the Nobel Prize for Literature 1913.

Tahiti /tɑ'hiːti/ largest of the Society Islands, in ◊French Polynesia; **area** 1,042 sq km/402 sq mi; **capital** Papeete; **population** (1983) 116,000. Tahiti was visited by Capt James ◊Cook in 1769 and by ◊Bligh of the *Bounty* in 1788. It came under French control in 1843 and became a colony in 1880.

Tai /tai/ *n.* a member of any of the groups of SE Asian peoples who speak Tai languages, all of which belong to the Sino-Tibetan language family. There are over 60 million speakers, the majority of whom live in Thailand. Tai peoples are also found in SW China, NW Myanmar (Burma), Laos, and N Vietnam.

T'ai Chi a series of 108 complex, slow-motion movements, each named and designed (for example, The White Crane Spreads its Wings) to ensure effective circulation of the *chi*, or intrinsic energy of the universe, through the mind and body. It derives partly from the Shaolin ◊martial arts of China and partly from ◊Taoism.

taiga /'taigə/ *n.* or **boreal forest** Russian name for the forest zone S of the ◊tundra, found across the N hemisphere. Here, dense forests of conifers (spruces and hemlocks), birches, and poplars occupy glaciated regions punctuated with cold lakes, streams, bogs, and marshes. Winters are prolonged and very cold, but the summer is warm enough to promote dense growth. The varied fauna and flora are in delicate balance because the conditions of life are so precarious. This ecology is threatened by mining, forestry, and pipeline construction.

tail[1] *n.* **1.** the hindmost part of an animal, especially when prolonged beyond the rest of the body. **2.** a thing like a tail in form or position, e. g. the part of a shirt below the waist, the hanging part of the back of a coat, the end of a procession; the part of a dovetail joint that is shaped like a dove's spread tail. **3.** the rear part of an aeroplane or rocket. **4.** the luminous train of a comet. **5.** the inferior or weaker part of anything. **6.** (in *plural, colloquial*) a tailcoat; evening dress including this. **7.** (usually in *plural*) the reverse of a coin turning up in a toss. **8.** (*slang*) a person following or shadowing another. —*v.t./i.* **1.** to remove the stalks of (fruit etc.). **2.** (*slang*) to shadow, to follow closely. —**on a person's tail**, closely following him. **tail away** *or* **off**, to become fewer or smaller or slighter; to fall behind or away in a scattered line; to end inconclusively. **tailback** *n.* a long line of traffic extending back from an obstruction. **tailboard** *n.* a hinged or removable back of a lorry etc. **tail end**, the hindmost, lowest, or last part. **tail gate**, a tailboard; a door at the back of a motor vehicle. **tail light** *or* **tail lamp**, a light at the rear of a motor vehicle or bicycle. **tailspin** *n.* the spin of an aircraft. **tail wind**, a wind blowing in the direction of travel of a vehicle or aircraft etc. **turn tail**, to turn one's back; to run away. **with one's tail between one's legs**, humiliated or dejected by defeat etc. [Old English]

tail[2] *n.* limitation of ownership, especially of an estate limited to a person and his heirs. —*adj.* so limited. —**in tail**, under such limitation. [from Old French *taille* (*taillier* = cut, from Latin *talea* = twig)]

tailcoat *n.* a man's coat with a long skirt divided at the back into tails and cut away in front, worn as part of formal dress.

tailless *adj.* having no tail.

tailor /'teilə/ *n.* a maker of men's clothes, especially to order. —*v.t.* **1.** to make (clothes) as a tailor; to make in a simple smoothly-fitting design. **2.** to make or adapt for a special purpose. —**tailorbird** *n.* a small Asian bird, especially of the genus *Orthotomus*, sewing leaves together to form a nest. **tailor-made** *adj.* made by a tailor;

entirely suited to a purpose. [from Anglo-French *taillour* (*taillier* = cut)]

tailpiece *n.* **1.** the final part of a thing. **2.** a decoration in the blank space at the end of a chapter etc.

tailpipe *n.* the rear section of the exhaust pipe of a motor vehicle.

tailplane *n.* the horizontal aerofoil at the tail of an aircraft.

tailstock *n.* the adjustable part of a lathe, with a fixed spindle to support one end of the workpiece.

Taine /tein/ Hippolyte Adolphe 1828–1893. French critic and historian. He analysed literary works as products of period and environment, as in *Histoire de la littérature anglaise/History of English Literature* 1863 and *Philosophie de l'art/Philosophy of Art* 1865–69.

taint *n.* a trace of some bad quality or of decay or infection. —*v.t./i.* to affect or become affected with a taint. [from Old French from Latin (*tingere* = dye)]

taipan *n.* a small-headed cobra *Oxyuranus scutellatus* found in NE Australia and New Guinea. It is about 3 m/10 ft long, and has a brown back and yellow belly. Its venom is fatal within minutes.

Taipei /tai'pei/ or **Taibei** capital and commercial centre of Taiwan; population (1987) 2,640,000. Industries include electronics, plastics, textiles, and machinery.

Taiwan country in SE Asia, officially the Republic of China, occupying the island of Taiwan between the E China Sea and the S China Sea; **area** 36,179 sq km/13,965 sq mi; **capital** Taipei; **head of state** Lee Teng-hui from 1988; **head of government** Lee Huan from 1989; **political system** emergent democracy; **population** (1990) 20,454,000 (84% Taiwanese, 14% mainlanders); **language** Mandarin Chinese (official); Taiwan, Hakka dialects; **recent history** annexed by China in 1683, Taiwan was ceded to Japan in 1895 but recovered by China in 1945. In 1989 the Kuomintang (Nationalist Party of China) won the first free assembly elections.

Taiyuan /taɪju'ɑːn/ capital of Shanxi province, NE China; population (1986) 1,880,000. Industries include iron, steel, agricultural machinery, and textiles. It is a walled city, founded in the 5th century AD, on the river Fen He, and is the seat of Shanxi University.

Ta'iz /tɑː'ɪz/ one of the main towns of Yemen; situated in the south of the country at the centre of a coffee-growing region; population (1980) 119,500. Cotton, leather, and jewellery are also produced.

Taizé /tei'zei/ *n.* ecumenical Christian community based in the village of that name in SE France. Founded in 1940 by Swiss theologian Roger Schutz (1915–), it has been since the 1960s a communal centre for young Christians.

Taj Mahal /'tɑːdʒ mə'hɑːl/ white marble mausoleum built 1634–56 on the river Jumna near Agra, India. Erected by Shah Jehan to the memory of his favourite wife, it is a celebrated example of Indo-Islamic architecture, the fusion of Muslim and Hindu styles.

takahe *n.* a bird *Notornis mantelli* of the rail family: native to New Zealand. A heavy flightless species, about 60 cm/2 ft tall, with blue and green plumage and a red beak, the takahe was thought to have become extinct at the end of the 19th century, but in 1948 small numbers were rediscovered in the tussock grass of a mountain valley on South Island.

Taj Mahal Over 20,000 labourers were employed in the construction of the Taj Mahal (1634–56), in Agra, N India.

take *v.t./i.* (*past* **took** /tʊk/; *past participle* **taken**) 1. to get into one's hands; to get possession of, to win. 2. to obtain after fulfilling the necessary conditions; to obtain the use of by payment; to buy (a specified newspaper etc.) regularly. 3. to assume possession of; to occupy (a position), especially as one's right; to avail oneself of; to indulge in; to use as a means of transport. 4. to consume (food or medicine). 5. to be successful or effective. 6. to require; to use up. 7. to cause to come or go with one; to carry; to remove from its place; to dispossess a person of. 8. to catch or be infected with (fire, fever etc.); to experience or be affected by; to exert (a feeling or effort). 9. to find out and note (a name, measurements, temperature etc.). 10. to grasp mentally, to understand; to deal with or interpret in a specified way. 11. to accept, to endure. 12. to perform; to move round or over; to teach or be taught (a subject); to sit for (an examination). 13. to make by photography; to photograph. 14. to use as an instance. 15. in grammar, to have or require as part of a construction. 16. to copulate with (a woman). —*n.* 1. the amount taken or caught. 2. a scene or sequence of a film photographed at one time without stopping the camera. —**take after,** to resemble (a parent etc.). **take against,** to begin to dislike. **take away,** to remove or carry elsewhere; to subtract. **takeaway** *adj.* (of food) bought at a restaurant for eating elsewhere; (*n.*) a restaurant selling this. **take back,** to retract (a statement); to carry (a person) in thought to a past time. **take down,** to write down (spoken words); to remove (a structure) by separating it into pieces. **take for,** to regard as being. **take in,** to receive as a lodger etc.; to undertake (work) at home; to include; to visit (a place) en route; to make (a garment etc.) smaller; to understand; to cheat. **take in hand,** to undertake; to start doing or dealing with; to undertake the control or reform of. **take in vain,** to use (a person's name) lightly or profanely. **take it,** to assume; (*colloquial*) to endure punishment etc. bravely. **take it or leave it,** to accept it or not. **take it out of,** to exhaust the strength of; to have revenge on. **take it out on,** to relieve frustration by attacking or treating harshly. **take it on** *or* **upon oneself,** to venture or presume to do a thing. **taken by** *or* **with,** attracted or charmed by. **taken ill,** suddenly affected by illness. **take off,** to remove (clothing) from the body; to deduct; to mimic humorously; to jump from the ground; to become airborne; to have (a day) as a holiday. **take-off** *n.* an act of becoming airborne; an act of mimicking; a place from which one jumps. **take oneself off,** to depart. **take on,** to undertake (work); to engage (an employee); to agree to oppose at a game; to acquire (a new meaning etc.); (*colloquial*) to show strong emotion. **take out,** to remove, to escort on an outing; to get (a licence or summons etc.) issued. **take a person out of himself,** to make him forget his worries etc. **take over,** to succeed to the management or ownership of; to assume control. **take-over** *n.* see ◊**takeover**. **take one's time,** not to hurry. **take to,** to begin or fall into the habit of; to have recourse to; to adapt oneself to; to form a liking for. **take up,** to become interested or engaged in (a pursuit); to adopt as a protégé; to occupy (time or space); to begin (residence etc.); to resume after an interruption; to interrupt or question (a speaker); to accept (an offer etc.); to shorten (a garment). **take a person up on,** to accept (his offer etc.). **take up with,** to begin to associate with. [Old English]

take-home pay a worker's actual wage or salary, after deductions have been made for such things as taxation, national insurance schemes, and employers' pension funds. **Disposable income** is take-home pay minus mortgage payments, rent, rates, bills, and so on.

takeover *n.* in business, the acquisition by one company of a sufficient number of shares in another company to have effective control of that company—usually 51%, although a controlling stake may be as little as 30%. Takeovers may be agreed or contested; methods employed include the ◊dawn raid, and methods of avoiding an unwelcome takeover include ◊reverse takeover, ◊poison pills or inviting a ◊white knight to make a takeover bid.

taker *n.* one who takes bets or accepts an offer etc.

taking *adj.* attractive, captivating. —*n.* (in *plural*) the amount of money taken in a business.

Talbot /ˈtɔːlbət/ William Henry Fox 1800–1877. English pioneer of photography. He invented the paper-based ◊calotype process, the first ◊negative/positive method. Talbot made ◊photograms several years before Daguerre's invention was announced.

talc *n.* a mineral, hydrous magnesium silicate, $Mg_3Si_4O_{10}(OH)_2$. A translucent material, it occurs in tabular crystals, but the massive impure form, known as **steatite** or **soapstone**, is more common. It is formed by the alteration of magnesium compounds, and usually found in metamorphic rocks. Talc is very soft, ranked 1 on the ◊Mohs' scale of hardness. It is used in powdered form in cosmetics, lubricants, and as an additive in paper manufacture. [French or from Latin *talcum* from Arabic from Persian]

talcum *n.* talc. —**talcum powder,** powdered talc for toilet use, usually perfumed. [Latin]

tale *n.* 1. a narrative or story, especially a fictitious one. 2. a report of an alleged fact, often malicious or in breach of a confidence. [Old English]

talebearer *n.* a person who maliciously gossips or reveals secrets.

talent /ˈtælənt/ *n.* 1. a special or very great ability; high mental ability. 2. persons who have this. 3. an ancient weight and unit of currency, especially among the Greeks. —**talent scout,** a seeker-out of talent, especially for the entertainment industries. [Old English, ultimately from Greek *talanton* = balance, weight, sum of money]

talented /ˈtæləntɪd/ *adj.* having great ability.

Taliesin /tælˈjesɪn/ lived *c.*550. Legendary Welsh poet, a bard at the court of the king of Rheged in Scotland. Taliesin allegedly died at Taliesin (named after him) in Dyfed.

talisman /ˈtælɪzmən/ *n.* an object supposed to be endowed with magic powers, especially of averting evil from or bringing good luck to its holder. —**talismanic** /-ˈmænɪk/ *adj.* [French and Spanish from Greek *telesma* = completion, religious rite (*telos* = end)]

talk /tɔːk/ *v.t./i.* 1. to convey or exchange ideas by spoken words. 2. to have the power of speech. 3. to express, utter, or discuss in words. 4. to use (a specified language) in speech. 5. to affect or influence by talking. 6. to betray secrets; to gossip. 7. to have influence. —*n.* 1. talking, conversation, discussion. 2. style of speech. 3. an informal lecture. 4. rumour, gossip; its theme. 5. talking or promises etc. without action or results. —**now you're talking,** (*colloquial*) I welcome that offer or suggestion. **talk back,** to reply defiantly. **talk down,** to silence by greater loudness or persistence; to speak patronizingly; to bring (a pilot or aircraft) to a landing by radio instructions from the ground. **talking book,** a recorded reading of a book, especially for the blind. **talk out,** to block the course of (a bill in Parliament) by prolonging the discussion to the time of adjournment. **talk over,** to discuss at length. **talk a person over** *or* **round,** to win him over by talking. **you can** *or* **can't talk,** (*colloquial*) you are just as bad yourself. —**talker** *n.*

talkative /ˈtɔːkətɪv/ *adj.* talking very much.

talkie /ˈtɔːkɪ/ *n.* (*colloquial*) a sound-film. [from *talking film*]

Talking Heads US new-wave rock group formed in 1975 in New York. Their nervy minimalist music is inspired by African rhythms; albums include *More Songs About Buildings and Food* 1978, *Little Creatures* 1985, and *Naked* 1988.

talking-to *n.* (*colloquial*) a reproof.

tall /tɔːl/ *adj.* 1. of more than average height. 2. having a specified height. —**talk tall,** to talk extravagantly or boastfully. **tall order,** a difficult task. **tall story,** (*colloquial*) one that is difficult to believe. **walk tall,** to feel justifiable pride. —**tallness** *n.* [from Old English = swift]

tallage *n.* English tax paid by cities, boroughs, and royal ◊demesnes, first levied under Henry II as a replacement for ◊danegeld. It was abolished in 1340 after it had been superseded by grants of taxation voted by Parliament.

Tallahassee /tæləˈhæsi/ capital of Florida, USA; population (1980) 82,000. It is an agricultural and lumbering centre. The explorer ◊De Soto found an Indian settlement here 1539. It has many pre–Civil War mansions. [Cree Indian 'old town']

tallboy *n.* a tall chest of drawers.

Talleyrand /ˈtælɪrænd/ Charles Maurice de Talleyrand-Périgord 1754–1838. French politician and diplomat. As bishop of Autun 1789–91 he supported moderate reform during the ◊French Revolution, was excommunicated by the pope, and fled to the USA during the Reign of Terror (persecution of anti-revolutionaries). He returned and became foreign minister under the Directory 1797–99 and under Napoleon 1799–1807. He represented France at the Congress of ◊Vienna 1814–15.

Tallinn /'tælɪn/ (German **Reval**) naval port and capital of Estonia, NW USSR; population (1987) 478,000. Industries include electrical and oil-drilling machinery, textiles, and paper. Founded in 1219, it was a member of the ◊Hanseatic League; passed to Sweden in 1561 and to Russia in 1750. Vyshgorod castle (13th century) and other medieval buildings remain. It is a yachting centre.

Tallis /'tælɪs/ Thomas c.1505–1585. English composer in the polyphonic style. He wrote masses, anthems, and other church music.

tallith *n.* a four-cornered, fringed shawl worn by Jewish men during morning prayers.

tallow /'tæləʊ/ *n.* the harder kinds of (especially animal) fat melted down for use in making candles, soap etc. —**tallowy** *adj.* [from Middle Low German]

tally /'tælɪ/ *v.i.* to correspond. —*n.* 1. the reckoning of a debt or score. 2. a mark registering a fixed number of objects delivered or received; such a number as a unit. 3. (*historical*) a piece of wood scored across with notches for the items of an account. 4. a ticket or label for identification. 5. a corresponding thing, a counterpart, a duplicate. [from Anglo-French from Latin *talea* = twig]

tally-ho /'tælɪ'həʊ/ *int.* a huntsman's cry to the hounds on seeing a fox. —*n.* (*plural* **tally-hos**) an utterance of this. —*v.t./i.* to utter the cry of 'tally-ho'; to indicate (a fox) or urge (hounds) with this. [compare French *taïant*]

Talmud /'tælmʊd/ *n.* the two most important works of post-Biblical Jewish literature, the Babylonian and the Palestinian (or Jerusalem) Talmud provide a compilation of ancient Jewish law and tradition. The Babylonian Talmud was edited at the end of the 5th century AD and is the more authoritative version for later Judaism; both Talmuds are written in a mix of Hebrew and Aramaic. They contain the Mishnah (early rabbinical commentaries compiled c. AD 200) and commentary (Gemara) on the Mishnah, and the material can be generally divided into *halakhah*, consisting of legal and ritual matters, and *aggadah*, concerned with ethical, theological, and folklorist matters. —**Talmudic** /-'mʊdɪk/ *adj.* [from Hebrew = instruction (*lamad* = learn)]

talon /'tælən/ *n.* a claw, especially of a bird of prey. [from Old French = heel, from Latin *talus* = ankle]

TAM abbreviation of (usually *attributive*) television audience measurement, denoting a measure of the number of people watching a particular television programme as estimated by the company Television Audience Measurement Ltd.

tamandua *n.* the tree-living toothless anteater *Tamandua tetradactyla* found in tropical forests and tree savannah from S Mexico to Brazil. About 56 cm/1.8 ft long with a prehensile tail of equal length, it has strong foreclaws with which it can break into nests of tree ants and termites, which it licks up with its narrow tongue.

Tamar /'teɪmɑː/ *n.* in the Old Testament, the sister of ◊Absalom. She was raped by her half-brother Amnon, who was then killed by Absalom.

Tamar /'teɪmɑː/ river flowing into Bass Strait, Tasmania, formed by the union of the North and South Esk; length 65 km/40 mi.

tamarind /'tæmərɪnd/ *n.* an evergreen tropical tree *Tamarindus indica*, family Leguminosae, native to the Old World, with pinnate leaves and reddish-yellow flowers, followed by pods. The acid pulp surrounding the seeds is used medicinally and as a flavouring; this fruit. [from Latin from Arabic = date of India]

tamarisk *n.* any small tree or shrub of the genus *Tamarix*, flourishing in warm, salty, desert regions of Europe and Asia where no other vegetation is found. The common tamarisk *T. gallica* has scalelike leaves and spikes of very small, pink flowers. [from Latin *tamarix*]

Tambo /'tæmbəʊ/ Oliver 1917– . South African nationalist politician, in exile 1960–90, president of the African National Congress (ANC) from 1977.

tambour /'tæmbʊə/ *n.* 1. a drum. 2. a circular frame for holding a fabric taut while it is being embroidered. 3. a sloping buttress or projection in a fives-court or real-tennis court etc. [French, from *tabour* = tabor]

tambourine /tæmbə'riːn/ *n.* a percussion instrument of a hoop with a parchment stretched over one side and jingling discs in slots round the hoop. [from French *tambourin*]

tame *adj.* 1. (of an animal) gentle and not afraid of human beings, not wild or fierce. 2. insipid, not exciting or interesting. 3. (of a person) docile and available. —*v.t.* to make tame or manageable; to subdue. —**tamely** *adv.*, **tameness** *n.* [from Old English]

tameable *adj.* that may be tamed.

Tamerlane /'tæmələɪn/ or **Tamburlaine** or **Timur i Leng** 1336–1405. Mongol ruler of ◊Samarkand from 1369 who conquered Persia, Azerbaijan, Armenia, and Georgia. He defeated the ◊Golden Horde in 1395, sacked Delhi in 1398, invaded Syria and Anatolia, and captured the Ottoman sultan in Ankara in 1402; he died invading China.

Tamil /'tæmɪl/ *n.* 1. a member of a Dravidian people inhabiting southern India and Sri Lanka. The majority of Tamils live in the Indian state of Tamil Nadu (formerly Madras), though there are approximately 3 million Tamils in Sri Lanka. 2. their language, a member of the Dravidian family of languages, written in its own distinctive script. —*adj.* of the Tamils or their language. [from native name *Tamil*]

Tamil Nadu /'tæmɪl nɑː'duː/ formerly (until 1968) **Madras State**; state of SE India; **area** 130,100 sq km/50,219 sq mi; **capital** Madras; **population** (1981) 48,297,000; **language** Tamil; **recent history** the present state was formed in 1956. Tamil Nadu comprises part of the former British Madras presidency (later province) formed from areas taken from France and Tipu Sahib, the sultan of Mysore, in the 18th century, which became a state of the Republic of India in 1950. The northeast was detached to form Andhra Pradesh in 1953; other areas went to Kerala and Mysore (now Karnataka) in 1956, and the Laccadive Islands (now Lakshadweep) became a separate Union Territory.

Taming of the Shrew, The comedy by William Shakespeare, first performed 1593–94. Bianca, who has many suitors, must not marry until her sister Katherina (the shrew) has done so. Petruchio agrees to woo Katherina so that his friend Hortensio may marry Bianca. Petruchio succeeds in 'taming' Katherina but Bianca marries another.

Tammany Hall /'tæmənɪ/ Democratic Party organization in New York. It originated in 1789 as the Society of St Tammany, named after an American Indian chief. It was dominant from 1800 until the 1930s and gained a reputation for gangsterism; its domination was broken by Mayor ◊La Guardia.

Tammuz /'tæmuːz/ in Sumerian legend, a vegetation god, who died at midsummer and was brought back from the underworld in spring by his lover Ishtar. His cult spread over Babylonia, Syria, Phoenicia, and Palestine. In Greek mythology Tammuz appears as ◊Adonis.

tam-o'-shanter /tæmə'ʃæntə/ a round Scottish cap, usually woollen. [from hero of Burns's *Tam o' Shanter*]

tamp *v.t.* to pack or ram down tightly. [perhaps from *tampion* = stopper for gun-muzzle]

Tampa /'tæmpə/ port and resort in W Florida, USA; population (1986) 279,000. Industries include fruit and vegetable canning, shipbuilding, and the manufacture of fertilizers, clothing, and cigars.

tamper *v.i.* **tamper with,** to meddle with, to make unauthorized changes in; to exert a secret or corrupt influence upon, to bribe. [variant of *temper*]

Tampere /'tæmpəreɪ/ (Swedish **Tammerfors**) city in SW Finland; population (1988) 171,000, metropolitan area 258,000. It is the second largest city in Finland. Industries include textiles, paper, footwear, and turbines.

tampon /'tæmpɒn/ *n.* a plug of cotton-wool etc. used to absorb natural secretions or stop a haemorrhage. —*v.t.* to plug with a tampon. [French]

tan[1] *n.* 1. yellowish-brown colour. 2. the brown colour in skin exposed to sun. 3. tree-bark used in tanning hides. —*adj.* yellowish-brown. —*v.t./i.* (**-nn-**) 1. to make or become brown by exposure to sun. 2. to convert (raw hide) into leather by soaking in a liquid containing tannic acid or by the use of mineral salts etc. 3. (*slang*) to thrash. [Old English, perhaps from Celtic]

tan[2] abbreviation of tangent.

Tanabata /tænə'bɑːtə/ *n.* Japanese 'star festival' celebrated annually on 7 July, introduced from China in the 8th century. It is dedicated to Altair and Vega, two stars

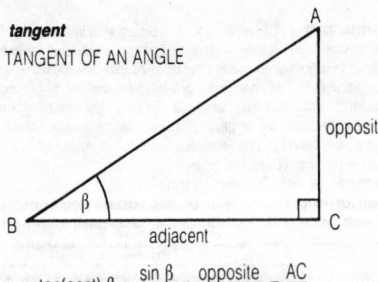

tangent

TANGENT OF AN ANGLE

$$\tan(\text{gent})\ \beta = \frac{\sin\beta}{\cos\beta} = \frac{\text{opposite}}{\text{adjacent}} = \frac{AC}{BC}$$

in the constellation Aquila, which are united once yearly in the Milky Way. According to legend they represent two star-crossed lovers allowed by the gods to meet on that night.

tanager *n.* any of various birds of the family Emberizidae, related to buntings. There are about 230 species in forests of Central and South America, all brilliantly coloured. They are 10–20 cm/4–8 in long, with plump bodies and conical beaks.

Tanagra /'tænəgrə/ ancient city in ◊Boeotia, central Greece. Sparta defeated Athens there in 457 BC. Terracotta statuettes called **tanagra** were excavated in 1874.

Tanaka /tɒ'nɑːkə/ Kakuei 1918– . Japanese right-wing politician, leader of the dominant Liberal Democratic Party (LDP) and prime minister 1972–74. In 1976 he was charged with corruption and resigned from the LDP but remained a powerful faction leader.

Tananarive /tənænə'riːv/ former name for ◊Antananarivo, the capital of Madagascar.

tandem /'tændəm/ *n.* **1.** a bicycle with seats and pedals for two or more persons one behind another. **2.** a group of two persons or machines etc. with one behind or following the other. **3.** a carriage driven tandem. —*adv.* with two or more horses harnessed one behind another. —**in tandem**, one behind another. [Latin = at length]

tandoor /'tænduə/ *n.* a clay oven. [Hindi]

tandoori /tæn'duərɪ/ *n.* food cooked over charcoal in a tandoor.

tang *n.* **1.** a strong taste, flavour, or smell; a characteristic quality. **2.** a projection on the blade of a tool by which the blade is held firm in the handle. [from Old Norse *tange* = point]

Tanganyika /tæŋgən'jiːkə/ former British colony in E Africa, which now forms the mainland of ◊Tanzania.

Tanganyika African National Union (TANU) a moderate socialist national party organized by Tanzanian politician Julius ◊Nyerere in the 1950s. TANU won electoral successes in 1958 and 1960, ensuring that Nyerere was recognized as prime minister on 1 May 1961, when Tanganyika prepared for independence from Britain.

Tanganyika, Lake lake 772 m/2,534 ft above sea level in the Great Rift Valley, E Africa, with Zaïre to the W, Zambia to the S, and Tanzania and Burundi to the E. It is about 645 km/400 mi long, with an area of about 31,000 sq km/12,000 sq mi, and is the deepest lake (1,435 m/4,710 ft) in Africa. The mountains around its shores rise to about 2,700 m/8,860 ft. The chief ports are Bujumbura (Burundi), Kigoma (Tanzania), and Kalémié (Zaïre).

Tange /'tæŋgeɪ/ Kenzo 1913– . Japanese architect. His works include the National Gymnasium, Tokyo, for the 1964 Olympics, and the city of Abuja, planned to replace Lagos as the capital of Nigeria.

tangent /'tændʒənt/ *n.* **1.** a straight line that meets a curve or curved surface at a point, but if extended does not intersect it at that point. **2.** the ratio of the sides opposite and adjacent to the angle in a right-angled triangle. —**at a tangent**, diverging from a previous course of action or thought etc. [from Latin *tangere* = touch]

tangential /tæn'dʒenʃəl/ *adj.* **1.** of or along a tangent. **2.** divergent. **3.** peripheral. —**tangentially** *adv.*

tangerine /tændʒə'riːn/ *n.* **1.** a small flattened orange *Citrus reticulata* from Tangier. **2.** its deep orange-yellow colour. [from *Tangier* in Morocco]

tangible /'tændʒɪbəl/ *adj.* **1.** perceptible by touch. **2.** definite, clearly intelligible; not elusive or visionary. —**tangibility** /-'bɪlɪtɪ/ *n.*, **tangibly** *adv.* [from Latin *tangere* = touch]

Tangier /tæn'dʒɪə/ or **Tangiers** or **Tanger** port in N Morocco, on the Strait of Gibraltar; population (1982) 436,227. It was a Phoenician trading centre in the 15th century BC. Captured by the Portuguese in 1471, it passed to England in 1662 as part of the dowry of Catherine of Braganza, but was abandoned in 1684, and later became a lair of the North African, or Barbary, pirates. From 1923 Tangier and a small surrounding enclave became an international zone, administered by Spain 1940–45. In 1956 it was transferred to independent Morocco and became a free port in 1962.

tangle *v.t./i.* **1.** to twist or become twisted into a confused mass. **2.** to entangle. **3.** to become involved in conflict. **4.** to complicate. —*n.* a tangled mass or condition.

tangly *adj.* tangled.

tango /'tæŋgəʊ/ *n.* (*plural* **tangos**) a slow South American ballroom dance in two-four time. It originated in Africa, and reached Europe via South America, where it had blended with Spanish elements (such as the ◊habanera); the music for this. —*v.i.* to dance the tango. [American Spanish]

tangram /'tæŋgræm/ *n.* a Chinese puzzle square cut into seven pieces to be combined into various figures.

Tanguy /tɒŋ'giː/ Yves 1900–1955. French Surrealist painter, who lived in the USA from 1939. His inventive canvases feature semi-abstract creatures in a barren landscape.

tangy /'tæŋgɪ/ *adj.* having a strong taste or flavour or smell.

Tanizaki /tæni'zɑːki/ Jun-ichirō 1886–1965. Japanese novelist. His works include a modern version of ◊Murasaki's *The Tale of Genji* 1939–41, *The Makioka Sisters* in three volumes 1943–48, and *The Key* 1956.

tank[1] *n.* **1.** a large receptacle for liquid or gas. —**tank up**, to fill the tank of a vehicle etc.; (*slang*) to drink heavily. [from Gujarati, perhaps from Sanskrit *tadaga* = pond]

tank[2] *n.* an armoured motor vehicle carrying guns and moving on caterpillar tracks. The term was originally a code name for the first effective tracked and armoured fighting vehicle, invented by the British soldier and scholar Ernest Swinton, and used in the battle of the Somme 1916.

tankard /'tæŋkəd/ *n.* a tall mug, especially a silver or pewter mug for beer. [compare Middle Dutch *tanckaert*]

tanker *n.* a ship, aircraft, or road vehicle for carrying liquids (especially mineral oils) in bulk. Currently the biggest oil tanker is the Greek-owned *Hellas Fos*, 555,051 tonnes deadweight.

Tannenberg, Battle of /'tænənbɜːg/ two battles, named after a village now in N Poland: **1410** the Poles and Lithuanians defeated the Teutonic Knights, establishing Poland as a major power; **1914** during World War I, when Tannenberg was part of East Prussia, ◊Hindenburg defeated the Russians.

tanner[1] *n.* one who tans hides.

tanner[2] *n.* (*historical*) a sixpence.

tannery /'tænərɪ/ *n.* a place where hides are tanned.

tannic /'tænɪk/ *adj.* of tan. [from French]

tannic acid or **tannin** $C_{14}H_{10}O_9$ yellow astringent substance, composed of several ◊phenol rings, occurring in the bark, wood, roots, fruits, and galls (growths) of certain trees, such as the oak. It precipitates gelatin to give an insoluble compound, used in the manufacture of leather from hides (tanning).

tanning *n.* treating animal skins to preserve them and make them into leather. In vegetable tanning, the prepared skins are soaked in tannic acid. Chrome tanning, which is much quicker, uses solutions of chromium salts.

Tannoy /'tænɔɪ/ *n.* trade name of a type of public-address system.

tansy *n.* a perennial herb *Tanacetum vulgare*, family Compositae, native to Europe. The yellow flower heads grow in clusters, and the aromatic leaves are used in cookery. [from Old French from Latin from Greek *athanasia* = immortality (*a*– = not and *thanatos* = death)]

tantalize /'tæntəlaɪz/ *v.t.* to tease or torment by the sight of something that is desired but kept out of reach or withheld. —**tantalization** /-'zeɪʃən/ *n.* [from *tantalus*]

tantalum /'tæntələm/ n. a rare hard white metallic element, symbol Ta, atomic number 73, relative atomic mass 180.948. It occurs with niobium in tantalite and other minerals. It can be drawn into wire with a very high melting point and great tenacity, useful for lamp filaments subject to vibration. It is also used in alloys, for corrosion-resistant laboratory apparatus and chemical equipment, as a catalyst in manufacturing synthetic rubber, in tools and instruments, and in rectifiers and capacitors.

tantalus /'tæntələs/ n. a stand in which decanters of spirits are locked up but visible. [from *Tantalus*, mythical king punished in Hades by sight of unattainable water and fruit]

tantamount /'tæntəmaʊnt/ *predic. adj.* equivalent. [from Italian *tanto montare* = to amount to so much]

tant mieux so much the better. [French]

tant pis so much the worse. [French]

tantra /'tæntrə/ n. each of a class of Hindu, Buddhist, or Jain sacred texts that deal with mystical and magical practices. —**tantric** *adj.* [Sanskrit = loom (*tan* = stretch, weave)]

Tantrism /'tæntrɪzəm/ n. forms of Hinduism and Buddhism that emphasize the division of the universe into male and female forces that maintain its unity by their interaction; this gives women equal status with men. Tantric Hinduism is associated with magical and sexual yoga practices that imitate the union of Siva and Sakti, as described in religious books known as the *Tantras*. In Buddhism, the *Tantras* are texts attributed to the Buddha, describing methods of attaining enlightenment.

tantrum /'tæntrəm/ n. an outburst of bad temper or petulance, especially in a child.

Tanzania /tænzə'niːə/ United Republic of; country in E Africa, on the Indian Ocean, bounded to the N by Uganda and Kenya; to the S by Mozambique, Malawi, and Zambia; and to the W by Zaïre, Burundi, and Rwanda; **area** 945,000 sq km/364,865 sq mi; **capital** Dodoma; **physical** central plateau; lakes in N and W; coastal plains; lakes Victoria, Tanganyika, and Niasa; **head of state and government** Ndugu Ali Hassan Mwinyi from 1985; **political system** one-party socialist republic; **population** (1990 est) 26,070,000; **language** Kiswahili, English (both official); **recent history** Zanzibar became a British protectorate in 1890; in 1961 independence was achieved, while Tanganyika became a republic in 1962. In 1964 Tanganyika and Zanzibar became the United Republic of Tanzania. In 1977 the Revolutionary Party of Tanzania (CCM) was proclaimed the only legal party.

Taoiseach /'tiːʃəx/ n. the Gaelic name for the prime minister of the Irish Republic. [Irish = chief, leader]

Taoism /'taːəʊɪzəm, 'taʊ-/ n. a Chinese philosophical system, traditionally founded by the Chinese philosopher Lao Zi in the 6th century BC, though the scriptures, *Tao Te Ching*, were apparently compiled in the 3rd century BC. The 'tao' or 'way' denotes the hidden principle of the universe, and less stress is laid on good deeds than on harmonious interaction with the environment, which automatically ensures right behaviour. The second major work is that of Zhuangzi (*c.*389–286 BC), *The Way of Zhuangzi*. The magical side of Taoism is illustrated by the *I Ching* or *Book of Changes*, a book of divination. —**Taoist** n. [from Chinese *dao* = right way]

tap[1] n. **1.** a device for drawing liquid from a cask or for allowing liquid or gas to come from a pipe or vessel in a controlled flow. **2.** a device for cutting a screw thread inside a cavity. **3.** a connection for tapping a telephone. —*v.t.* (-pp-) **1.** to fit a tap into (a cask); to let out (liquid) thus. **2.** to draw sap from (a tree) or fluid from (the body) by incision; to draw (fluid etc.) thus. **3.** to extract or obtain supplies or information from; to establish communication or trade with. **4.** to cut a screw-thread inside (a cavity). **5.** to make a connection in (a circuit etc.) so as to divert electricity or fit a listening-device for overhearing telephone conversations. —**on tap,** ready to be drawn off by tap; (*colloquial*) ready for immediate use. [Old English]

tap[2] *v.t./i.* (-pp-) **1.** to strike with a quick, light, but audible blow; to knock gently on (a door etc.). **2.** to strike (a thing) lightly against something. —n. a quick light blow; the sound of this. [imitative]

tap dancing to perform a dance with a sharp rhythmical tapping of the feet. Tap dancing is a rapid step dance, derived from clog dancing. Its main characteristic is the

tapping of toes and heels, accentuated by steel taps affixed to the shoes. It was popularized in ◊vaudeville and in 1930s films by dancers such as Fred Astaire and Bill 'Bojangles' Robinson (1878–1949).

tape n. **1.** a narrow strip of woven cotton etc. used for tying, fastening, or labelling things; such a strip stretched across a race-track at the finishing-line. **2.** a strip of paper or of transparent film etc. coated with adhesive for fastening packages etc. **3.** a magnetic tape; a tape-recording. **4.** a long strip of paper printed or punched to convey messages. **5.** a tape-measure. —*v.t.* **1.** to tie or fasten with tape. **2.** to record on magnetic tape. **3.** to measure with a tape. —**have a person** *or* **thing taped,** (*slang*) to understand him or it fully. **tape-machine** n. a machine for receiving and recording telegraph messages. **tape measure,** a strip of tape or thin flexible metal marked for measuring length.

tape-record *v.t.* to record (sounds) on magnetic tape. **tape recorder,** an apparatus for recording sounds on magnetic tape and afterwards reproducing them. **tape recording,** such a record or reproduction. [Old English]

taper /'teɪpə/ n. a wick coated thinly with wax, burnt to give a light or to light candles etc. —*v.t./i.* to make or become gradually narrower. —**taper off,** to make or become gradually less in amount etc.; to cease gradually. [Old English from Latin *papyrus*, whose pith was used for candle-wicks]

tape recording, magnetic method of recording electric signals on a layer of iron oxide, or other magnetic material, coating a thin plastic tape. The electrical impulses are fed to the electromagnetic recording head, which magnetizes the tape in accordance with the frequency and amplitude of the original signal. Impulses may be audio (for sound recording), video (for television), or data (for computer). For playback, the tape is passed over the same, or another, head to convert magnetic into electrical impulses, which are then amplified for reproduction. Tapes are easily demagnetized (erased) for reuse, and come in cassette, cartridge, or reel form.

tapestry /'tæpɪstrɪ/ n. a thick textile fabric in which coloured weft threads are woven (originally by hand) to form pictures or designs; embroidery imitating this, usually in wools on canvas; a piece of such embroidery. Tapestry-weaving is an ancient art, common to many countries. The great European centres of tapestry weaving were in Belgium, France, and England. The ◊Gobelins tapestry factory of Paris was made a royal establishment in the 17th century. In England, William ◊Morris established the Merton Abbey looms in the late 19th century. Other designers have included ◊Raphael, ◊Rubens, and ◊Burne-Jones. The ◊Bayeux Tapestry is an embroidery, not a woven tapestry. —**tapestried** *adj.* [from Old French *tapisserie* (*tapis* = carpet)]

tapeworm n. a flat parasitic worm in the class Cestoda, of the phylum Platyhelminthes (flatworms), with no digestive or sense organs. It can reach a length of 15 m/50 ft, and attaches itself to its host's intestines by means of hooks and suckers. Tapeworms usually reach humans in imperfectly cooked meat or fish, causing anaemia and intestinal disorders.

tapioca /tæp'iəʊkə/ n. a starchy substance in hard white grains obtained from cassava and used for puddings etc. [from Tupi and Guarani *tipioca* (*tipi* = dregs and *og, ok* = squeeze out)]

tapir /'teɪpə, -pɪə/ n. a vegetarian piglike mammal of the genus *Tapirus* of the forests of Central and South America, with a short flexible snout. Tapirs grow to a maximum of 1 m/3 ft at the shoulder, and weigh 350 kg/770 lb. They have thick, hairy, black skin, short tails and short trunks. They are shy and harmless. Their survival is in danger because of destruction of the forests. [from Tupi]

tappet /'tæpɪt/ n. a cam or other projecting part used in machinery to give intermittent motion. [apparently from *tap*[2]]

taproom n. a room in which alcoholic drinks are available on tap.

taproot n. in botany, a single, robust, main ◊root that is derived from the embryonic root, or ◊radicle, and grows vertically downwards, often to considerable depth. Taproots are often modified for food storage and are common in biennial plants such as the carrot *Daucus carota*.

tar¹ *n.* a dark thick inflammable liquid distilled from wood, coal, or peat etc. and used as a preservative of wood and iron, an antiseptic etc.; a similar substance formed in the combustion of tobacco etc. —*v.t.* (**-rr-**) to cover with tar. —**tar and feather,** to smear with tar and then cover with feathers as a punishment. **tarred with the same brush,** having the same faults. **tar-seal** *v.t.* (*Australian*) to surface (a road) with a mixture of tar and broken stone; (*n.*) a road surfaced thus. [Old English]

tar² *n.* (*colloquial*) a sailor. [abbreviation of *tarpaulin*]

taradiddle /ˈtærədɪdəl/ *n.* (*colloquial*) a petty lie; nonsense. [compare *diddle*]

Tara Hill /ˈtɑːrə/ ancient religious and political centre in County Meath, S Ireland. The site of a palace and coronation place of many Irish kings, abandoned in the 6th century. St ◊Patrick preached here.

tarantella /tærənˈtelə/ *n.* a rapid whirling South Italian dance; the music for this.

Taranto /təˈræntəʊ/ naval base and port in Puglia region, SE Italy; population (1988) 245,000. It is an important commercial centre, and its steelworks are part of the new industrial complex of S Italy. It was the site of the ancient Greek **Tarentum**, founded in the 8th century BC by ◊Sparta, and was captured by the Romans in 272 BC.

tarantula /təˈræntjʊlə/ *n.* 1. a large black spider of the genus *Lycosa* of southern Europe. In the Middle Ages, its bite was thought to cause hysterical ailments, for which dancing was the cure, hence the dance named tarantella. 2. a large hairy tropical spider. [Latin from Italian (*Taranto* in S Italy)]

tarboosh /tɑːˈbuːʃ/ *n.* a cap like a fez, worn alone or as part of a turban. [from Arabic, ultimately from Persian = head cover]

tardy /ˈtɑːdɪ/ *adj.* slow to act, move, or happen; delaying or delayed beyond the right or expected time. —**tardily** *adv.*, **tardiness** *n.* [from French *tardif* from Latin *tardus* = slow]

tare¹ *n.* 1. a kind of vetch, especially as a cornfield weed (*Vicia hirsuta*) or fodder (*V. sativa*). 2. (in *plural*, in the Bible) an injurious cornfield weed, thought to be darnel.

tare² *n.* an allowance made to the purchaser for the weight of the container in which goods are packed, or for the vehicle transporting them, in instances where the goods are weighed together with their container or vehicle. [from French = deficiency, ultimately from Arabic = what is rejected]

target /ˈtɑːgɪt/ *n.* 1. an object or mark that a person tries to hit in shooting etc.; a round or rectangular object painted with concentric circles for this purpose, especially in archery. 2. a person or thing against which criticism or scorn is directed. 3. an objective, a minimum result aimed at. —*v.t.* 1. to aim (a weapon etc.) at a target. 2. to plan or schedule (a thing) to attain an objective. [from old French, diminutive of *targe* = shield]

Targum /ˈtɑːgəm/ *n.* any of various ancient Aramaic paraphrases or interpretations of the Hebrew scriptures. [from Chaldee = interpretation]

tariff /ˈtærɪf/ *n.* 1. a list of fixed charges. 2. the duty on a particular class of imports or exports; a list of duties or customs to be paid. [from French ultimately from Arabic = notification]

Tariff Reform League organization set up in 1903 as a vehicle for the ideas of the Liberal politician Joseph ◊Chamberlain on protective tariffs. It aimed to unify the British Empire by promoting imperial preference in trade.

Tarkovsky /tɑːˈkɒfski/ Andrei 1932–1986. Soviet film director whose work is characterized by unorthodox cinematic techniques and visual beauty. His films include the science fiction *Solaris* 1972, *Mirror* 1975, and *The Sacrifice* 1986.

tarlatan /ˈtɑːlətən/ *n.* a thin stiff open kind of muslin. [from French; probably of Indian origin]

Tarmac /ˈtɑːmæk/ *n.* trade name of a tarmacadam; a runway etc. made of this. —**tarmac** *v.t.* (**-ck-**) to surface with tarmacadam. [abbreviation]

tarmacadam /ˌtɑːməˈkædəm/ *n.* road materials of stone or slag bound with tar. [from *tar¹* and *macadam*]

tarn /tɑːn/ *n.* a small mountain lake. [from Old Norse]

Tarn river in SW France, rising in the Cévennes and flowing 350 km/217 mi to the Garonne. It cuts the limestone plateaux in picturesque gorges.

tarnish /ˈtɑːnɪʃ/ *v.t./i.* 1. to lessen or destroy the lustre of (metal etc.). 2. to stain or blemish (a reputation etc.). 3. (of metal etc.) to lose its lustre. —*n.* 1. loss of lustre. 2. a blemish, a stain. [from French *ternir* (*terne* = dark)]

taro *n.* (*plural taros*) or **eddo** a plant *Colocasia esculenta* of the arum family Araceae, native to tropical Asia; the tubers are edible and are the source of Polynesian poi (a fermented food). [Polynesian]

tarot /ˈtærət/ *n.* 1. a card (especially one of 22 trumps) in a pack of 78 cards used in a game or for fortune-telling. The pack comprises the **minor arcana** in four suits (resembling playing cards) and the **major arcana**, 22 cards with densely symbolic illustrations, which have links with astrology and the ◊Kabbala. The origin of the tarot is unknown; the earliest known reference to tarot cards is from 1392. The pack may have been designed in Europe in the early 14th century as a repository of Gnostic ideas then being suppressed by the Christian church. Since the 18th century the tarot has interested occult scholars. 2. (also in *plural*) this game. [from Italian and French]

tarpaulin /tɑːˈpɔːlɪn/ *n.* a waterproof cloth especially of tarred canvas; a sheet or covering of this. [probably from *tar¹* and *pall¹*]

tarpon *n.* a marine herringlike fish *Tarpon atlanticus.* It reaches 2 m/6 ft and may weigh 135 kg/300 lb. It lives in warm Atlantic waters.

Tarquinius Superbus /tɑːˈkwɪniəs suːˈpɜːbəs/ lived in the 5th century BC. Last king of Rome 534–510 BC. He abolished certain rights of Romans, and made the city powerful. He was deposed when his son Sextus raped ◊Lucretia.

tarradiddle variant of ◊taradiddle.

tarragon /ˈtærəgən/ *n.* a perennial bushy herb *Artemisia dracunculus* of the daisy family Compositae, native to the Old World, growing to 1.5 m/5 ft, with narrow leaves and small green-white flower heads arranged in groups. Tarragon contains an aromatic oil; its leaves are used to flavour salads, pickles, and tartar sauce. It is closely related to wormwood. [Latin from Greek *tarkhōn*, perhaps through Arabic from Greek *drakōn* = dragon]

tarry¹ /ˈtɑːrɪ/ *adj.* of or smeared with tar. —**tarriness** *n.*

tarry² /ˈtærɪ/ *v.i.* (*archaic*) to delay in coming or going, to linger.

tarsal /ˈtɑːsəl/ *adj.* of the tarsus.

tarsier /ˈtɑːsɪə/ *n.* a Malaysian primate *Tarsius spectrum*, about the size of a rat. It has thick, light-brown fur, very large eyes, and long feet and hands. It is nocturnal, arboreal, and eats insects and lizards. [French (from *tarsus*, from the structure of its foot)]

tarsus /ˈtɑːsəs/ *n.* (*plural tarsi* /-siː/) 1. the small bones (seven in man) that make up the ankle. 2. the shank of a bird's leg. [from Greek *tarsos* = flat of the foot]

Tarsus city in İçel province, SE Turkey, on the river Pamuk; population (1980) 121,000. Formerly the capital of the Roman province of Cilicia, it was the birthplace of St ◊Paul.

tart¹ *n.* 1. a small round of pastry with jam etc. on top. 2. a pie with a fruit or sweet filling. [from Old French *tarte*]

tart² *n.* (*slang*) a prostitute, an immoral woman. —*v.t./i.* (*colloquial*) to dress or decorate gaudily or with cheap finery; to smarten. [probably abbreviation of *sweetheart*]

tart³ *adj.* 1. sharp-tasting, acid. 2. sharp in manner, biting. —**tartly** *adv.*, **tartness** *n.* [Old English]

tartan /ˈtɑːtən/ *n.* a pattern of coloured stripes crossing at right angles, especially a distinctive pattern worn by Scottish Highlanders to denote their clan; cloth woven in such a pattern. Tartan developed in the 17th century, but was banned after the 1745 ◊Jacobite rebellion, and not legalized again until 1782. [perhaps from Old French *tertaine, tiretaine*]

tartar /ˈtɑːtə/ *n.* 1. a hard chalky deposit that forms on the teeth. 2. a reddish deposit that forms on the side of a cask in which wine is fermented. [from Latin from Greek *tartaron*]

Tartar variant of ◊Tatar.

tartaric /tɑːˈtærɪk/ *adj.* of tartar or tartaric acid. —**tartaric acid,** HCOO(CHOH)₂COOH, an organic acid present in vegetable tissues, especially unripe grapes, in the form of salts of potassium, calcium, and magnesium. It is used in carbonated drinks and baking powders.

tartar sauce /ˈtɑːtə/ a sauce of mayonnaise containing chopped gherkins etc.

1093 tatting

Tasmanian devil

Tartarus /'tɑːtərəs/ in Greek mythology, a part of ◊Hades, the underworld, where the wicked were punished.

Tartini /tɑːˈtiːni/ Giuseppe 1692–1770. Italian composer and violinist. In 1728 he founded a school of violin playing in Padua. A leading exponent of violin technique, he composed the *Devil's Trill* sonata.

tartlet /'tɑːtlɪt/ *n.* a small tart.

Tarzan /'tɑːzən/ fictitious hero inhabiting the African rainforest, created by the US writer Edgar Rice ◊Burroughs in *Tarzan of the Apes* 1914, with numerous sequels. He and his partner Jane have featured in films, comic strips, and television serials. Tarzan, raised by apes from infancy, is in fact a British peer, Lord Greystoke. He has enormous physical strength and the ability to communicate with animals. Jane Porter, an American, falls in love with him while on safari and elects to stay. —*n.* a man of powerful physique and great agility.

Tasaday /'tɑːsədaɪ/ *n.* a member of an indigenous people of the rainforests of Mindanao in the ◊Philippines, discovered by anthropologists in the 1960s.

Tashkent /tæʃˈkent/ capital of Uzbekistan, S central USSR; population (1987) 2,124,000. Industries include the manufacture of mining machinery, chemicals, textiles, and leather goods. Founded in the 7th century, it was taken by the Turks in the 12th century and captured by Tamerlane in 1361. In 1865 it was taken by the Russians. It was severely damaged by an earthquake in 1966.

task /tɑːsk/ *n.* a piece of work to be done. —*v.t.* to make great demands on (a person's powers etc.). —**take to task,** to rebuke. **task force,** a unit specially organized for a task. [from Old French *tasque* from Latin *tasca*]

taskmaster *n.* one who imposes a task or burden.

Tasman /'tæzmən/ Abel Janszoon 1603–1659. Dutch navigator. In 1642, he was the first European to see Tasmania. He also made the first European sightings of New Zealand, Tonga, and Fiji.

Tasmania /tæzˈmeɪniə/ formerly (until 1856) **Van Diemen's Land**; island off the S coast of Australia; a state of the Commonwealth of Australia; **area** 67,800 sq km/26,171 sq mi; **capital** Hobart; **population** (1987) 448,000; **recent history** the first European to visit here was Abel Tasman in 1642; the last of the Tasmanian Aboriginals died in 1876. Tasmania joined the Australian Commonwealth as a state in 1901.

Tasmanian devil /tæzˈmeɪniən/ a bearlike marsupial *Sarcophilus harrisii*, about 65 cm/2.1 ft long with a 25 cm/10 in bushy tail. It has a large head, strong teeth, and is blackish with white patches on the chest and hind parts. It is nocturnal, carnivorous, and can be ferocious when cornered. It has recently become extinct in Australia, and survives only in remote parts of Tasmania.

Tasmanian tiger/wolf or **thylacine** carnivorous marsupial *Thylacinus cynocephalus*; which is doglike in appearance and can be nearly 2 m/6 ft from nose to tail tip. It was hunted to probable extinction in the 1930s, there are still occasional unconfirmed reports of sightings.

Tasman Sea /'tæzmən/ the ◊Pacific Ocean between SE Australia and NW New Zealand. It is named after the explorer Abel ◊Tasman.

Tass /tæs/ acronym from Telegrafnoye Agentstvo Sovyetskovo Soyuza; Soviet news agency.

tassel /'tæsəl/ *n.* 1. a bunch of threads or cords tied at one end and hanging loosely, attached as an ornament to a cushion, scarf etc. 2. a tassel-like catkin or head of certain plants (e. g. maize). [from Old French = clasp]

tasset /'tæsɪt/ *n.* (in *plural*) a series of overlapping plates in medieval armour, hanging from the corslet and protecting

the thighs. [from Old French *tasse* = purse, holster; connection of sense not clear]

Tasso /'tæssəʊ/ Torquato 1544–1595. Italian poet, author of the romantic epic poem of the First Crusade *La Gerusalemme Liberata/Jerusalem Delivered* 1574, followed by the *Gerusalemme Conquistata/Jerusalem Conquered*, written during the period from 1576 when he was mentally unstable.

taste /'teɪst/ *n.* 1. the sensation caused in the tongue by a soluble substance placed on it. The human ◊tongue can distinguish only four basic tastes (sweet, sour, bitter, and salty) but it is supplemented by the nose's sense of smell. 2. the faculty of perceiving this sensation. 3. a small portion of food or drink taken as a sample; a slight experience of something. 4. a liking. 5. aesthetic discernment in art, literature, or conduct; conformity to its dictates. —*v.t./i.* 1. to discern or test the flavour of (food etc., or *absolute*) by taking it into the mouth. 2. to eat or drink a small portion of. 3. to perceive the flavour of. 4. to have experience of. 5. to have a specified flavour. —**taste bud,** any of the cells on the surface of the tongue by which things are tasted. **to one's taste,** pleasing, suitable. [from Old French *tast* from *taster* = touch, try, perhaps from Latin *tangere* = touch and *gustare* = taste]

tasteful *adj.* having or showing good taste. —**tastefully** *adv.*, **tastefulness** *n.*

tasteless *adj.* 1. lacking flavour. 2. having or showing bad taste. —**tastelessly** *adv.*, **tastelessness** *n.*

taster /'teɪstə/ *n.* a person employed to judge teas or wines etc. by tasting them.

tasty /'teɪstɪ/ *adj.* having a strong flavour; appetizing. —**tastily** *adv.*, **tastiness** *n.*

tat[1] *n.* tatty things; a tatty person; tattiness.

tat[2] *v.t./i.* (**-tt-**) to do tatting; to make by tatting.

ta-ta /tæ'tɑː/ *int.* (*colloquial*) goodbye.

Tatar /'tɑːtə/ *n.* or **Tartar** 1. a member of a group of Central Asian peoples, including Mongols and Turks. They now live mainly in Tatar and Uzbekistan (where they were deported from the Crimea in 1944) and SW Siberia, USSR. 2. their Turkic language. 3. a violent-tempered or intractable person. —*adj.* of the Tartars or their language.

Tatar Autonomous Republic administrative region of W central USSR; **area** 68,000 sq km/26,250 sq mi; **capital** Kazan; **population** (1986) 3,537,000; **history** territory of Volga-Kama Bulgar state from 10th to 13th centuries; conquered by Mongols until 15th century; conquered by Russia in 1552; became an autonomous republic in 1920.

Tate /teɪt/ Nahum 1652–1715. Irish poet, born in Dublin. He wrote an adaptation of Shakespeare's *King Lear* with a happy ending. He also produced a version of the psalms, and hymns; among his poems is 'While shepherds watched'. He became British poet laureate in 1692.

Tate Phyllis (Margaret) 1911–1987. British composer. Her works include *Concerto for Saxophone and Strings* 1944, the opera *The Lodger* 1960, based on the story of Jack the Ripper, and *Serenade to Christmas* for soprano, chorus and orchestra 1972.

Tate Gallery a London art gallery exhibiting British art from late 16th century, and international from 1810. Endowed by the sugar merchant Henry Tate (1819–99), it was opened in 1897. A Liverpool branch of the Tate Gallery opened in 1988.

Tati /tæ'tiː/ Jacques. Stage name of Jacques Tatischeff 1908–1982. French comic actor, director, and writer. He portrayed Monsieur Hulot, a character who embodies polite opposition to modern mechanization, in a series of films including *Les Vacances de M Hulot/Monsieur Hulot's Holiday* 1953.

Tatlin /'tætlɪn/ Vladimir 1885–1953. Russian artist, co-founder of ◊Constructivism. After encountering Cubism in Paris in 1913 he evolved his first Constructivist works, using raw materials such as tin, glass, plaster, and wood to create abstract sculptures that he suspended in the air.

tattered /'tætəd/ *adj.* in tatters.

tatters *n.pl.* rags, irregularly torn pieces of cloth or paper etc. —**in tatters,** (of an argument etc.) ruined, demolished. [from Old Norse *tötrar* = rags]

tatting /'tætɪŋ/ *n.* 1. a kind of knotted lace made by hand with a small shuttle and used for trimming etc. 2. the process of making this.

tattle *v.i.* to chatter or gossip idly; to reveal information thus. —*n.* idle chatter or gossip. [from Flemish *tatelen* (imitative)]

tattoo[1] /tə'tuː/ *n.* 1. an evening drum or bugle signal recalling soldiers to quarters. 2. an elaboration of this with music and marching as an entertainment. 3. a rapping or drumming sound. [from earlier *tap-too* from Dutch = close the tap (of the cask)]

tattoo[2] *v.t.* to mark (the skin) with an indelible pattern by puncturing and inserting pigment; to make (a design) thus. —*n.* such a design. —**tattooist** *n.* [from Polynesian]

tatty /'tætɪ/ *adj.* (*colloquial*) 1. tattered, shabby and untidy. 2. tawdry, fussily ornate. —**tattily** *adv.*, **tattiness** *n.* [originally Scottish = shaggy]

Tatum /'teɪtəm/ Edward Lawrie 1909–1975. US microbiologist. For his work on biochemical genetics, he shared the 1958 Nobel Prize for Medicine with George Beadle and Joshua Lederberg.

tau /tau, tɔː/ *n.* the nineteenth letter of the Greek alphabet, (τ, Τ) = t. —**tau cross**, a T-shaped cross. [from Greek]

Taube /'tɔːbi/ Henry 1915– . US chemist who established the basis of inorganic chemistry through his study of the loss or gain of electrons by atoms during chemical reactions.

Tau Ceti /tɔː 'siːtaɪ/ one of the nearest stars visible to the naked eye, 11.9 light years from Earth in the constellation Cetus. It has a diameter slightly less than that of the Sun, and an actual luminosity of about 45% of the Sun's. Its similarity to the Sun is sufficient to suggest that Tau Ceti may possess a planetary system, although observations have yet to reveal definite evidence of this.

taught past and past participle of **teach**.

taunt *n.* a thing said to anger or wound a person. —*v.t.* to assail with taunts; to reproach (a person with conduct etc.) contemptuously. [from French *tant pour tant* = tit for tat, smart rejoinder]

taupe /təup/ *n.* grey with a tinge of another colour, usually brown. [French = mole[1]]

Taupo /'taupəu/ largest lake in New Zealand, in a volcanic area of hot springs; area 620 sq km/239 sq mi. It is the source of the Waikato River.

Taurus /'tɔːrəs/ *n.* a zodiac constellation in the northern hemisphere near Orion, represented as a bull. The Sun passes through Taurus from mid-May to late June. Its brightest star is Aldebaran, seen as the bull's red eye. Taurus contains the Hyades and Pleiades open ◊star clusters, and the Crab nebula. In astrology, the dates for Taurus are between about 20 April and 20 May (see ◊precession). —**Taurean** *adj.* & *n.* [Latin = bull]

Taussig /'tausɪg/ Helen Brooke 1898–1986. US cardiologist who developed surgery for 'blue' babies. Such babies never fully develop the shunting mechanism in the circulatory system that allows blood to be oxygenated in the lungs before passing to the rest of the body. The babies are born chronically short of oxygen and usually do not survive without surgery.

taut *adj.* 1. (of a rope etc.) tight, not slack; (of the nerves) tense. 2. (of a ship etc.) in good condition. —**tautly** *adv.*

tauten /'tɔːtən/ *v.t./i.* to make or become taut.

tautology /tɔː'tɒlədʒɪ/ *n.* the saying of the same thing twice over in different words, especially as a fault of style (e. g. *arrived one after the other in succession*). —**tautological** /tɔːtə'lɒdʒɪkəl/ *adj.*, **tautologous** /-ləgəs/ *adj.* [from Latin from Greek *tautologia* (*tauto* = the same)]

Tavener /'tævənə/ John (Kenneth) 1944– . English composer whose individual and sometimes abrasive works include the dramatic cantata *The Whale* 1968 and the opera *Thérèse* 1979. He has also composed music for the Eastern Orthodox Church.

tavern *n.* (*literary*) an inn, a public house. [from Old French from Latin *taberna* = hut, tavern]

Taverner /'tævənə/ John 1495–1545. English organist and composer. He wrote masses and motets in polyphonic style, showing great contrapuntal skill, but as a Protestant renounced his art. He was imprisoned in 1528 for heresy, and, as an agent of Thomas Cromwell, assisted in the dissolution of the monasteries.

tawdry /'tɔːdrɪ/ *adj.* showy but worthless, gaudy. —**tawdrily** *adv.*, **tawdriness** *n.* [short for *tawdry lace* from *St Audrey's lace* (*Audrey* = Etheldrida, patron saint of Ely, died 679) from the cheap finery sold at St Audrey's fair]

tawny /'tɔːnɪ/ *adj.* brownish-yellow, brownish-orange. —**tawniness** *n.* [from Anglo-French *tauné*]

tawse /tɔːz/ *n.* (*Scottish*) a leather strap with a slit end, used for punishing children. [plural of obsolete *taw* = leather made without tannin]

tax *n.* 1. a contribution to state revenue legally levied on persons, property, or business. 2. a heavy demand made upon a person, resources, etc. —*v.t.* 1. to impose a tax on; to require to pay tax. 2. to pay the tax on. 3. to make heavy demands on. 4. to accuse in a challenging way. —**tax-deductible** *adj.* (of expenses) that may be paid out of income before the deduction of income tax. **tax-free** *adj.* exempt from taxes. **tax return**, a declaration of income for taxation purposes. [from Old French from Latin *taxare* = censure, compute, perhaps from Greek *tassō* = fix]

taxable *adj.* that may be taxed.

taxation /tæk'seɪʃən/ *n.* the imposition or payment of tax. Taxation can be **direct** (a deduction from income) or **indirect** (added to the purchase price of goods or services, that is, a tax on consumption). The standard form of indirect taxation in Europe is **value-added tax** (VAT). **Income tax** is the most common form of direct taxation.

tax avoidance the conducting of financial affairs in such a way as to keep tax liability to a minimum within the law.

tax evasion failure to meet tax liabilities by illegal action, such as not declaring income. Tax evasion is a criminal offence.

tax haven a country or state where taxes are much lower than elsewhere. It is common practice for companies of one country to register in the tax haven of another, to avoid liability for taxation under their own country's laws. In a tax haven, any business transacted is treated as confidential. Tax havens include the Channel Islands, Switzerland, Bermuda, the Bahamas, and Liberia.

taxi /'tæksɪ/ *n.* (in full **taxi-cab**) a motor car plying for hire and usually fitted with a taximeter. —*v.t./i.* (*participle* **taxiing**) 1. (of an aircraft or pilot) to go along the ground or surface of the water under the machine's own power before or after flying. 2. to go or convey in a taxi. [abbreviation of *taximeter cab*]

taxidermy /'tæksɪdɜːmɪ/ *n.* the art of preparing, stuffing, and mounting the skins of animals with lifelike effect. —**taxidermist** *n.* [from Greek *taxis* = arrangement and *derma* = skin]

taximeter /'tæksɪmiːtə/ *n.* an automatic fare-indicator fitted to a taxi. [from French]

taxis *n.* (plural **taxes**) or **tactic movement** in botany, the movement of a single cell, such as a bacterium, protozoan, single-celled alga, or gamete, in response to an external stimulus. A movement directed towards the stimulus is described as positive taxis, and away from it as negative taxis. The alga *Chlamydomonas*, for example, demonstrates positive **phototaxis** by swimming towards a light source to increase the rate of photosynthesis. **Chemotaxis** is a response to a chemical stimulus, as seen in many bacteria that move towards higher concentrations of nutrients.

tax loophole gap in the law that can be exploited to gain a tax advantage not intended by the government when the law was made.

taxman *n.* (*plural* **taxmen**) an inspector or collector of taxes.

Taxodium *n.* a genus of tree of the redwood family Taxodiaceae. The deciduous swamp cypress *Taxodium distichum* grows in or near water in SE USA and Mexico, and is a valuable timber tree.

taxonomic /tæksə'nɒmɪk/ *adj.* (also **taxonomical**) of or using taxonomy. —**taxonomically** *adv.*

taxonomy /tæk'sɒnəmɪ/ *n.* classification, especially in biology; the principles of this. —**taxonomist** *n.* [from French from Greek *taxis* = arrangement and *-nomia* = distribution]

taxpayer *n.* one who pays taxes.

tax shelter an investment opportunity designed to reduce the tax burden on an individual or group of individuals but at the same time to stimulate finance in the direction of a particular location or activity. Such shelters might be tax exempt or lightly taxed securities in government or a local authority, or forestry or energy projects.

Tay /teɪ/ longest river in Scotland; length 189 km/118 mi. Rising in NW Central region, it flows NE through Loch Tay,

Taylor *English-born actress Elizabeth Taylor with co-star Montgomery Clift in a scene from* Raintree County *1957.*

then E and SE past Perth to the Firth of Tay, crossed at Dundee by the Tay Bridge, before joining the North Sea. The Tay has salmon fisheries; its main tributaries are the Tummel, Isla, and Earn.

Taylor /'teɪlə/ Elizabeth 1932– . English-born US actress whose films include *National Velvet* 1944, *Cat on a Hot Tin Roof* 1958, *Butterfield 8* 1960 (Academy Award), *Cleopatra* 1963, and *Who's Afraid of Virginia Woolf?* 1966 (Academy Award). Her seven husbands have included the actors Michael Wilding (1912–1979) and Richard ◊Burton (twice).

Taylor Frederick Winslow 1856–1915. US engineer and management consultant, the founder of scientific management. His ideas, published in *Principles of Scientific Management* 1911, were based on the breakdown of work to the simplest tasks, the separation of planning from execution of tasks, and the introduction of time-and-motion studies. His methods were clearly expressed in assembly-line factories, but have been criticized for degrading and alienating workers and producing managerial dictatorship.

Tay-Sachs disease /teɪ'sæks/ inherited disorder, due to a defective gene, causing an enzyme deficiency that leads to blindness, retardation, and death in childhood. Because of their enforced isolation and inbreeding during hundreds of years, it is most common in people of E European Jewish descent.

Tayside /'teɪsaɪd/ region of Scotland; **area** 7,700 sq km/ 2,973 sq mi; **administrative headquarters** Dundee; **population** (1987) 394,000.

Tb symbol for terbium.

TB abbreviation of **1.** tubercle bacillus; **2.** (*colloquial*) tuberculosis.

Tbilisi /dbi'liːsi/ formerly **Tiflis** capital of Georgia, SW USSR; population (1987) 1,194,000. Industries include textiles, machinery, ceramics, and tobacco. Dating from the 5th century, it is a centre of Georgian culture, with fine medieval churches. Anti-Russian demonstrations were quashed here by troops in 1981 and 1989, the latter following rejected demands for autonomy from the Abkhazia enclave, resulting in 19 or more deaths from poison gas (containing chloroacetophenone) and 100 injured.

T-bone /'tiː bəʊn/ *n.* a T-shaped bone, especially in a steak from the thin end of the loin.

T cell or **T lymphocyte** immune cell (see ◊immunity and ◊lymphocyte) that plays several roles in the body's defences. T cells are so called because they mature in the ◊thymus.

Tchaikovsky /tʃaɪ'kɒfski/ Pyotr Il'yich 1840–1893. Russian composer. His strong sense of melody, personal expression, and brilliant orchestration are clear throughout his many Romantic works, which include six symphonies, three piano concertos and a violin concerto, operas (for example, *Eugene Onegin* 1879), ballets (for example, *The Nutcracker* 1892), orchestral fantasies (for example, *Romeo and Juliet* 1870), and chamber and vocal music.

TD abbreviation of *Teachta Dála,* a member of the Irish parliament. [Irish]

te /tiː/ *n.* in music, the seventh note of the major scale in tonic sol-fa. [alteration from *si,* perhaps from *Sancte Iohannes*]

tea *n.* **1.** an evergreen shrub or small tree *Camellia sinensis.* Known in China as early as 2737 BC, tea was first brought to Europe in AD 1610 and rapidly became a fashionable drink. In 1823 it was found growing wild in N India, and plantations were later established in Assam and Sri Lanka; producers today include Africa, South America, the USSR, Indonesia, and Iran. **2.** the dried leaves of this plant. **3.** a drink made by infusing tea-leaves in boiling water; a similar drink made from the leaves of other plants or from some other substance. **4.** a meal at which tea is a main feature. —**tea bag,** a small porous bag of tea for infusion. **tea chest,** a light metal-lined wooden box in which tea is exported. **teacloth** *n.* a cloth for a teatable. **tea leaf,**

a leaf of tea especially (in *plural*) after infusion or as dregs; (*rhyming slang*) a thief. **tearoom** *or* **teashop** *n.* a place where tea and light refreshments are served to the public. **tea rose,** a rose *Rosa odorata* with a scent like tea. **tea towel,** a towel for drying washed crockery etc. [originally *tay* ultimately from Chinese *t'e*]

teacake *n.* a light usually sweet bun eaten at tea, usually served toasted and buttered.

teach *v.t./i.* (*past* and *past participle* **taught** /tɔt/) **1.** to impart information or skill to (a person) or about (a subject) systematically; to do this as a profession. **2.** to put forward as a fact or principle. **3.** to induce to adopt a practice etc. by example or experience; (*colloquial*) to deter by punishment etc. **—teach-in** *n.* a lecture and discussion, or a series of these, on a subject of public interest. [Old English]

teachable *adj.* **1.** apt at learning. **2.** (of a subject) that can be taught.

teacher *n.* one who teaches, especially in a school.

teaching *n.* **1.** what is taught, a doctrine. **2.** the teachers' profession.

teacup *n.* a cup from which tea and other hot drinks are drunk.

teak *n.* a heavy, durable, yellowish timber; the Asian tree *Tectona grandis* yielding this. [from Portuguese from Malayalam]

teal *n.* (*plural* the same) a small freshwater duck *Anas crecca* of the N hemisphere, about 35 cm/14 in long. The drake has a reddish-brown head with green and buff markings on either side, and a black and white line on the wing. The female is buff and brown. [related to Middle Dutch *teling*]

team *n.* **1.** a set of players forming one side in certain games and sports. **2.** a set of persons working together. **3.** two or more animals harnessed together to draw a vehicle or farm implement. **—v.t./i.** to combine into a team or set for a common purpose. **—team-mate** *n.* a fellow member of a team. **team spirit,** willingness to act for the benefit of one's group rather than oneself. **teamwork** *n.* combined effort, co-operation. [Old English = offspring]

teamster *n.* **1.** a driver of a team of animals. **2.** (*US*) a lorry-driver.

teapot *n.* a pot with a handle, spout, and lid, in which tea is brewed and from which it is poured.

Teapot Dome Scandal US political scandal which revealed the corruption of the Harding administration. It centred on the leasing of naval oil reserves in 1921 at Teapot Dome, Wyoming, without competitive bidding as a result of bribing the secretary of the interior, Albert B Fall (1861–1944). Fall was tried and imprisoned 1929.

tear[1] /teə/ *v.t./i.* (*past* **tore**; *past participle* **torn**) **1.** to pull forcibly apart, away, or to pieces; to make (a hole or rent) thus. **2.** to become torn; to be capable of being torn. **3.** to subject to conflicting desires or demands; to disrupt violently. **4.** to run, walk, or travel hurriedly or impetuously. **—n.** a hole or rent caused by tearing. **—tear fault,** a geological fault in which the fracture is approximately vertical and movement is horizontal. **tear oneself away,** leave in spite of a strong desire to stay. **tear one's hair,** to pull it in anger or frustration or despair. [Old English]

tear[2] /tiə/ *n.* a drop of clear salty liquid serving to moisten and wash the eye and falling from it in sorrow or distress etc. **—in tears,** weeping. **teardrop** *n.* a single tear. **tear gas,** *n.* a gas that disables by causing severe irritation to the eyes. **tear-jerker** *n.* (*colloquial*) a story etc. calculated to evoke sadness or sympathy. **without tears,** presented so as to be learned or done easily. [Old English]

tearaway /'teərəweɪ/ *n.* a reckless hooligan.

tearful /'tiəfəl/ *adj.* shedding or ready to shed tears; sad. **—tearfully** *adv.*

tear gas any of various volatile gases that produce irritation and tearing of the eyes. Tear gas is utilized by some police forces as a tool of crowd-control. It has also been used in chemical warfare. The gas is delivered in pressurized, liquid-filled canisters or grenades, thrown by hand or launched from a specially adapted rifle. Gases such as Mace cause violent coughing and blinding tears, which pass when the inhaler breathes fresh air, and there are no lasting effects.

tearing /'teərɪŋ/ *adj.* extreme, overwhelming.

tease /tiːz/ *v.t.* **1.** to try playfully or maliciously to provoke (a person) by jokes, questions, or petty annoyances. **2.** to

pick (wool etc.) into separate strands. **3.** to brush up the nap on (cloth). **—n.** (*colloquial*) a person who is fond of teasing others. **—tease out,** to separate by disentangling.

teasel /'tiːzəl/ *n.* **1.** a plant of the genus *Dipsacus* with prickly flower-heads. **2.** such a head dried and used for raising the nap on cloth; a device used thus. [Old English]

teaser /'tiːzə/ *n.* (*colloquial*) a hard question or task.

teaspoon *n.* a small spoon for stirring tea; the amount held by this. **—teaspoonful** *n.* (*plural* **teaspoonfuls**)

teat *n.* **1.** a mammary nipple, especially of an animal. **2.** a device, especially of rubber, for sucking milk from a bottle. [from Old French *tete*]

Tebaldi /te'bældi/ Renata 1922– . Italian dramatic soprano, renowned for the controlled purity of her voice and for her roles in ◊Puccini operas.

Tebbit /'tebɪt/ Norman 1931– . British Conservative politician. He was minister for employment 1981–83, minister for trade and industry 1983–85, chancellor of the Duchy of Lancaster 1985–87, and chair of the party 1985–87. As his relations with Margaret Thatcher cooled, he returned to the back benches in 1987.

tec *n.* (*slang*) a detective. [abbreviation]

Tech /tek/ *n.* (*colloquial*) a technical college or school. [abbreviation]

technetium /tek'niːʃəm/ *n.* an artificially produced radioactive metallic element, symbol Tc, atomic number 43. It is a superconductor and is used as a hardener in steel alloys and as a medical tracer. [from Greek *tekhnētos* = artificial (*tekhnē* = art)]

technical /'teknɪkəl/ *adj.* **1.** of or involving the mechanical arts and applied sciences. **2.** of or relating to a particular subject or craft etc. or its techniques. **3.** (of a book or discourse etc.) using technical language, requiring special knowledge to be understood. **4.** such in strict interpretation. **—technically** *adv.* [from Latin from Greek *tekhnikos* (*tekhnē* = art)]

technicality /tekni'kælɪtɪ/ *n.* **1.** being technical. **2.** a technical expression. **3.** a technical point or detail.

technician /tek'nɪʃən/ *n.* **1.** an expert in the techniques of a particular skill or craft. **2.** a mechanic; a person employed to look after technical equipment in a laboratory etc.

Technicolor *n.* **1.** trade name of a process of colour cinematography using three separate negatives of blue, green and red images. It was invented by Daniel F Comstock and Herbert T Kalmus in the USA in 1922. **2.** vivid colour, artificial brilliance. [from *technical* and *colour*]

technique /tek'niːk/ *n.* the method of doing or performing something, especially in an art or science; skill in this. [French]

technocracy /tek'nɒkrəsɪ/ *n.* government or control of a society or industry by technical experts. The term was invented by US engineer W H Smyth 1919 to describe his proposed 'rule by technicians', and was popularized by James Burham (1903–) in *Managerial Revolution* 1941. [from Greek *tekhnē* = art]

technocrat /'teknəkræt/ *n.* an exponent or advocate of technocracy.

technological /teknə'lɒdʒɪkəl/ *adj.* of or using technology. **—technologically** *adv.*

tectonics /tek'tɒnɪks/ *n.pl.* (usually treated as *singular*) in geology, the study of the movements of rocks on the Earth's surface. On a small scale tectonics involves the formation of ◊folds and ◊faults, but on a large scale ◊plate tectonics deals with the movement of the Earth's surface as a whole. [from Latin from Greek (*tektōn* = carpenter)]

Tecumseh /tɪ'kʌmsə/ 1768–1813. North American Indian chief of the Shawnee. He attempted to unite the Indian peoples from Canada to Florida against the encroachment of white settlers, but the defeat of his brother **Tenskwatawa**, 'The Prophet', at the battle of Tippecanoe Nov 1811 by Governor W H Harrison, largely destroyed the confederacy built up by Tecumseh. He was commissioned a brigadier general in the British army during the War of 1812, and died in battle.

Ted *n.* (*colloquial*) a Teddy boy. [abbreviation]

tedder *n.* a machine for drying hay. [from Old Norse *tethja* = spread manure]

teddy bear a soft furry toy bear. [from *Teddy*, pet name of *Theodore* Roosevelt, American president]

Teddy boy /'tedɪ/(*colloquial*) a youth with a supposedly Edwardian style of dress, especially in the 1950s. [from *Teddy*, pet-form of *Edward*]

tedious *adj.* tiresomely long, wearisome. —**tediously** *adv.*, **tediousness** *n.* [from Old French or Latin]

tedium /'tiːdɪəm/ *n.* tediousness. [from Latin *taedium* (*taedēre* = to weary)]

tee *n.* 1. a cleared space from which a golf ball is struck at the beginning of play for each hole. 2. a small support of wood or plastic from which a ball is thus struck. 3. the mark aimed at in bowls, quoits, etc. —*v.t.* to place (a ball) on a golf tee. —**tee off**, to play a ball from a tee, to start, to begin. [from earlier *teaz* (origin unknown); in last sense of *n.* perhaps = *tee*[1]]

teem[1] *v.i.* 1. to be abundant. 2. to be full, to swarm (*with*). [from Old English *team* = offspring]

teem[2] *v.i.* (of water etc.) to flow copiously. [from Old Norse]

-teen suffix forming the numerals 13–19. [Old English]

teenage /'tiːneɪdʒ/ *adj.* of or characteristic of teenagers.

teenager /'tiːneɪdʒə/ *n.* a person in his or her teens.

teens /tiːnz/ *n.pl.* the years of one's age from 13 to 19.

teeny /'tiːnɪ/ *adj.* (*colloquial*) tiny. [variant of *tiny*]

teeny-bopper *n.* a girl in her teens or younger who is a fan of pop music and follows the latest fashions.

Teesside /'tiːzsaɪd/ industrial area at the mouth of the river Tees, Cleveland, NE England; population (1981) 382,700. Industries include high-technology, capital-intensive steelmaking; chemicals; an oil-fuel terminal; and the main North Sea natural-gas terminal. Middlesbrough is a major port.

teeter *v.i.* to totter, to move unsteadily. [variant of dialect *titter*]

teeth plural of **tooth**.

teethe /tiːð/ *v.i.* to grow or cut teeth, especially the milk-teeth. —**teething ring**, a small ring for an infant to bite on while teething. **teething troubles**, initial troubles in an enterprise etc.

teetotal /tiː'təʊtəl/ *adj.* abstaining completely from alcoholic drinks. —**teetotalism** *n.*, **teetotaller** *n.* [reduplication of *total*]

tefillin *n.* or **phylacteries** in Judaism, two small leather boxes containing scrolls from the Torah, that are strapped to the left arm and the forehead by Jewish men for daily prayer.

Teflon /'teflɒn/ trade name of a tough, waxlike, heat-resistant plastic (polytetrafluoroethylene, or PTFE), used for coating nonsticking cookware and in gaskets and bearings.

Tegucigalpa /teɪgʊsɪ'gælpə/ capital of Honduras, population (1986) 605,000. It has textile and food-processing industries. It was founded in 1524 as a gold and silver mining centre.

Tehran /teə'rɑːn/ capital of Iran; population (1986) 6,043,000. Industries include textiles, chemicals, engineering, and tobacco. It was founded in the 12th century and made the capital in 1788 by Muhammad Shah. Much of the city was rebuilt in the 1920s and 1930s. Tehran is the site of the Gulistan Palace (the former royal residence).

Tehran Conference conference held in 1943 in Tehran, Iran, the first meeting of World War II Allied leaders Churchill, Roosevelt, and Stalin. The chief subject discussed was coordination of Allied strategy in W and E Europe.

Teilhard de Chardin /teɪ'ɑː də ʃɑ:'dæŋ/ Pierre 1881–1955. French Jesuit theologian, palaeontologist, and philosopher. He is best known for his creative synthesis of nature and religion, based on his fieldwork and fossil studies. Publication of his *Le Phénomène humain/The Phenomenon of Man*, written 1938–40, was delayed (due to his unorthodox views) until after his death by the embargo of his superiors. He saw humanity as being in a constant process of evolution, moving towards a perfect spiritual state.

Tej Bahadur /'teɪg bə'hɑːduə/ 1621–1675. Indian religious leader, ninth guru (teacher) of Sikhism 1664–75, executed for refusing to renounce his faith.

Te Kanawa /teɪ 'kɑːnəwə/ Kiri 1944– . New Zealand opera singer. Her first major role was the Countess in Mozart's *The Marriage of Figaro* at Covent Garden, London, 1971. She sang at the wedding of Prince Charles in 1980.

tektite /'tektaɪt/ *n.* a small roundish glassy solid body of unknown origin occurring in various parts of the Earth. [from German from Greek *tēktos* = molten (*tēkō* = melt)]

telamon /'teləmən/ *n.* (*plural* **telamones** /-'məʊniːz/) a sculptured male figure used as a pillar to support an entablature. [from Latin from Greek *Telamōn*, name of a mythical hero]

Tel Aviv /'tel ə'viːv/ officially **Tel Aviv-Jaffa** /'dʒæfə/ city in Israel, on the Mediterranean Sea; population (1987) 320,000. Industries include textiles, chemicals, sugar, printing, and publishing. Tel Aviv was founded in 1909 as a Jewish residential area in the Arab town of Jaffa, with which it was combined in 1949; their ports were superseded in 1965 by Ashdod to the S.

tele- /telɪ-/ in combinations 1. far, at a distance. 2. television. [in first sense from Greek (*tēle* = far off); in second sense from *television*]

telecommunication /telɪkəmjuːnɪ'keɪʃən/ *n.* communication over long distances by cable, telegraph, telephone, or broadcasting; (usually in *plural*) this branch of technology.

Telecom Tower formerly **Post Office Tower** building in London, 189 m/620 ft high. Completed in 1966, it is a microwave relay tower capable of handling up to 150,000 simultaneous telephone conversations and over 40 television channels.

telegram /'telɪgræm/ *n.* a message sent by telegraph and then usually delivered in printed form.

telegraph /'telɪgrɑːf/ *n.* transmitting messages or signals to a distance, especially by making and breaking an electrical connection; an apparatus for this. —*v.t./i.* to send a message by telegraph (to); to send (a message) thus; to send an instruction to by telegraph.

telegraphic /telɪ'græfɪk/ *adj.* 1. of telegraphs or telegrams. 2. worded economically like telegrams. —**telegraphically** *adv.*

telegraphist /tɪ'legrəfɪst/ *n.* a person skilled or employed in telegraphy.

telegraphy /tɪ'legrəfɪ/ *n.* the process of communication by telegraph.

telekinesis /telɪkaɪ'niːsɪs, -kɪ-/ *n.* movement of or in a body alleged to occur at a distance from, and without material connection with, the motive cause or agent. [from Greek *kinēsis* = motion]

Telemann /'teɪləmæn/ Georg Philipp 1681–1767. German Baroque composer, organist, and conductor at the Johanneum, Hamburg, from 1721. He was one of the most prolific composers ever, producing 25 operas, 1,800 church cantatas, hundreds of other vocal works, and 600 instrumental works.

telemeter /'telmiːtə/ *n.* an apparatus for recording the readings of an instrument and transmitting it by radio.

telemetry /tɪ'lemɪtrɪ/ *n.* the process of obtaining measurements at a point removed from the place where they are made; transmission of these, usually by radio. See ◊remote sensing.

teleology /telɪ'ɒlədʒɪ/ *n.* the doctrine of final causes, especially as related to the evidence of design or purpose in nature. —**teleological** /-ə'lɒdʒɪkəl/ *adj.* [from Greek *telos* = end]

telepath /'telɪpæθ/ *n.* a person able to communicate by telepathy.

telepathy /tɪ'lepəθɪ/ *n.* communication between minds otherwise than by the known senses. —**telepathic** /telɪ'pæθɪk/ *adj.*, **telepathist** *n.* [from Greek *pathos* = feeling]

telephone /'telɪfəʊn/ *n.* 1. an apparatus for transmitting sound (especially speech) to a distance by wire, cord, or radio, usually by converting acoustic vibrations into electrical signals for transmission, invented by Alexander Graham ◊Bell in 1876. 2. the transmitting and receiving instrument used in this. 3. the system of communication by a network of telephones. —*v.t./i.* to speak to (a person) by telephone; to send (a message) by telephone; to make a telephone call. —**telephone box, booth,** *or* **kiosk,** a boxlike kiosk containing a telephone for public use. **telephone directory** *or* **book,** a book listing the names and telephone numbers of people who are connected to a particular telephone system. **telephone number,** a number assigned to a particular telephone and used in making connections to it. —**telephonic** /-'fɒnɪk/ *adj.*, **telephonically** /-'fɒnɪkəlɪ/ *adv.* [from Greek *phōnē* = voice]

telecommunications chronology

1794	Claude Chappe in France built a long-distance signalling system using semaphore.
1839	Charles Wheatstone and William Cooke devised an electric telegraph in England.
1843	Samuel Morse transmitted the first message along a telegraph line in the USA, using his Morse code of signals—short (dots) and long (dashes).
1858	The first transatlantic telegraph cable was laid.
1876	Alexander Graham Bell invented the telephone.
1877	Thomas Edison invented the carbon transmitter for the telephone.
1894	Marconi pioneered wireless telegraphy in Italy, later moving to England.
1900	Fessenden in the USA first broadcast voice by radio.
1901	Marconi transmitted the first radio signals across the Atlantic.
1904	Fleming invented the thermionic valve.
1907	Charles Krumm introduced the forerunner of the teleprinter.
1920	Stations in Detroit and Pittsburgh began regular radio broadcasts.
1922	The BBC began its first radio transmissions, for the London station 2LO.
1932	The Post Office introduced the Telex in Britain.
1956	The first transatlantic telephone cable was laid.
1962	Telstar pioneers transatlantic satellite communications, transmitting live TV pictures.
1966	Charles Kao in England advanced the idea of using optical fibres for telecommunications transmissions.
1969	Live TV pictures were sent from astronauts on the Moon back to Earth.
1975	The Post Office announced Prestel, the world's first viewdata system, using the telephone lines to link a computer data bank with the TV screen.
1977	The first optical fibre cable was installed in California.
1986	*Voyager 2* transmitted images of the planet Uranus over a distance of 3 billion km/2 billion mi, the signals taking 2 hours 45 minutes to make the journey back to Earth.
1988	Videophones introduced in Japan.
1989	*Voyager 2* transmitted images of the planet Neptune; the first transoceanic optical fibre cable, capable of carrying 40,000 simultaneous telephone conversations, was laid between Europe and the USA.

telephone tapping a method of listening in on a telephone conversation; in the UK and the USA it is a criminal offence if done without a warrant or the consent of the person concerned.

telephonist /ti'lefənɪst/ n. an operator of a telephone exchange or at a switchboard.

telephony /ti'lefənɪ/ n. the use or system of telephones.

telephoto /teli'fəʊtəʊ/ adj. telephotographic. [abbreviation]

telephotography /telɪfə'tɒɡrəfɪ/ n. the photographing of distant objects with combined lenses giving a large image. —**telephotographic** /-fəʊtə'ɡræfɪk/ adj.

telephoto lens a photographic lens of longer focal length than normal that takes a very narrow view and gives a large image through a combination of telescopic and ordinary photographic lenses.

teleprinter /'telɪprɪntə/ n. or **teletypewriter** a device for typing and transmitting telegraph messages and for receiving and typing them.

telescope /'telɪskəʊp/ n. 1. an optical instrument using lenses or mirrors, or both, to focus light to produce a magnified image. A telescope makes distant objects appear nearer and larger, and shows objects fainter than can be seen by the eye alone. A telescope with a large aperture, or opening, can distinguish finer detail and fainter objects than one with a small aperture. The **refracting telescope** uses lenses, and the **reflecting telescope** uses mirrors. A third type, the **catadioptric telescope**, with a combination of lenses and mirrors, is used increasingly. 2. a ◊radio telescope. —v.t./i. 1. to press or drive (sections of tube, colliding vehicles, etc.) together so that one slides into another like the sections of a telescope; to close or be driven or be capable of closing thus. 2. to compress so as to occupy less space or time. [from Italian]

telescopic /teli'skɒpɪk/ adj. 1. of or made with a telescope. 2. consisting of sections which telescope. —**telescopic sight**, a telescope used for sighting on a rifle etc. —**telescopically** adv.

teletext /'telɪtekst/ n. a news and information service from a computer source transmitted to the television screens of subcribers.

Teletype /'telɪtaɪp/ n. trade name of a kind of teleprinter.

televangelist n. in North America, a fundamentalist Christian minister, often of a Pentecostal church, who hosts a television show and solicits donations from viewers.

televise /'telɪvaɪz/ v.t. to transmit by television.

television /'telɪvɪʒən, -'vɪʒən/ n. (TV) 1. a system for reproducing on a screen visual images transmitted (with sound) by radio signals. 2. (in full **television set**) a device for receiving these signals. 3. television broadcasting generally. —**televisual** /-'vɪʒuəl/ adj.

telex /'teleks/ n. a system of telegraphy using teleprinters and the public telecommunication network. —v.t. to send by telex; to communicate with by telex. [from *tele*printer and *ex*change]

Telford /'telfəd/ Thomas 1757–1834. Scottish civil engineer who opened up N Scotland by building roads and waterways. He constructed many aqueducts and canals, including the Caledonian Canal 1802–23, and erected the Menai road suspension bridge 1819–26, a type of structure scarcely tried previously in England. In Scotland he constructed over 1,600 km/1,000 mi of road and 1,200 bridges, churches, and harbours.

tell¹ /tel/ v.t./i. (*past* and *past participle* told /təʊld/) 1. to make known, especially in spoken or written words; to utter. 2. to give information to; to assure; to reveal a secret. 3. to direct or order. 4. to decide, to determine; to distinguish. 5. to produce a noticeable effect. 6. to count. —**tell off**, (*colloquial*) to reprimand, to scold; to count off or detach for duty. **tell on,** to reveal the activities of (a person) by telling others. **tell tales,** to report a discreditable fact about another. **tell the time,** to read it from the face of a clock or watch. **you're telling me,** (*slang*) I am well aware of what you say. [Old English]

tell² n. an artificial mound in the Middle East etc. formed by accumulated remains of ancient settlements superimposed on earlier ones. [from Arabic = hillock]

Tell Wilhelm (William). Legendary 14th-century Swiss archer, said to have refused to salute the Habsburg badge at Altdorf on Lake Lucerne. Sentenced to shoot an apple from his son's head, he did so, then shot the tyrannical Austrian ruler Gessler, symbolizing his people's refusal to submit to external authority.

Tell el Amarna /'tel el ə'mɑːnə/ site of the ancient Egyptian capital ◊Akhetaton. The ◊Amarna tablets were found there.

teller n. 1. a person employed to receive and pay out money in a bank etc. 2. a person appointed to count votes.

Teller /telə/ Edward 1908– . Hungarian-born US physicist known as the father of the ◊hydrogen bomb, which he worked upon, after taking part in the atom bomb project, at the Los Alamos research centre, New Mexico 1946–52. He was a key witness against his colleague, Robert ◊Oppenheimer at the security hearings in 1954. He was widely believed to be the model for the leading character in Stanley Kubrick's 1964 film *Dr Strangelove*. More recently he has been one of the leading supporters of the Star Wars programme (◊Strategic Defense Initiative).

telling adj. having a noticeable effect, striking.

telescope

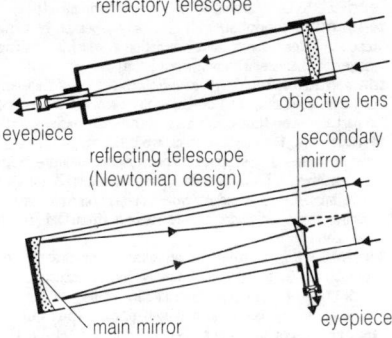

refractory telescope

objective lens

eyepiece

secondary mirror

reflecting telescope (Newtonian design)

main mirror   eyepiece

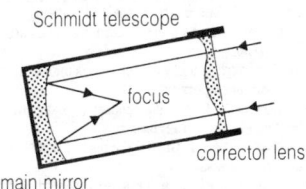

Schmidt telescope

focus

corrector lens

main mirror

telltale *n.* **1.** a person who discloses another's private affairs or misdeeds. **2.** an automatic registering device. **3.** a metal sheet extending across the front wall of a squash court, above which the ball must strike the wall. —*adj.* that reveals or betrays.

tellurium /te'ljuəriəm/ *n.* a rare semi-metallic element, symbol Te, atomic number 52, chemically related to sulphur and selenium. [from Latin *tellus -uris* = earth, probably named in contrast to uranium]

telly /'teli/ *n.* (*colloquial*) television; a television set. [abbreviation]

Telstar /'telsta:(r)/ *n.* US communications satellite, launched on 10 July 1962, which relayed the first live television transmissions between the USA and Europe. *Telstar* orbited the Earth in 158 minutes, and so had to be tracked by ground stations, unlike the geostationary satellites of today.

temerity /ti'meriti/ *n.* audacity, rashness. [from Latin *temeritas* (*temere* = rashly)]

temp *n.* (*colloquial*) a temporary employee, especially a secretary. [abbreviation]

temper *n.* **1.** the state of the mind as regards calmness or anger. **2.** a fit of anger; a tendency to have such fits. **3.** calmness under provocation. **4.** the condition of tempered metal as regards hardness and elasticity. —*v.t.* **1.** to bring (metal or clay) to the proper hardness or consistency. **2.** to moderate or mitigate. [Old English from Latin *temperare* = mingle]

tempera /'tempərə/ *n.* a method of painting with powdered colours mixed with egg or size. It was used in Europe from the 12th or early 13th century until the 15th century, when it began to give way to oil painting. [Italian, from Latin *temperare* = mix]

temperament /'temprəmənt/ *n.* **1.** a person's distinct nature and character, especially as determined by physical constitution and permanently affecting his or her behaviour. **2.** in music, the adjustment of intervals in the tuning of a piano etc. so as to fit the scale for use in all keys, especially (**equal temperament**) in which the twelve semitones are at equal intervals. [from Latin]

temperamental /temprə'mentəl/ *adj.* **1.** of the temperament. **2.** liable to erratic or moody behaviour. —**temperamentally** *adv.*

temperance /'tempərəns/ *n.* **1.** moderation or self-restraint, especially in eating and drinking. **2.** abstinence or partial abstinence from alcoholic drink. [from Anglo-French from Latin]

temperance movement societies dedicated to curtailing the consumption of alcohol by total prohibition, local restriction, or encouragement of declarations of personal abstinence ('the pledge'). They were first set up in the USA, Ireland, and Scotland, then in the N of England in the 1830s.

temperate /'tempərət/ *adj.* **1.** avoiding excess; moderate. **2.** of mild temperature. —**temperately** *adv.* [from Latin]

temperature /'tempritʃə/ *n.* **1.** the degree or intensity of the heat of a body in relation to others, especially as shown by a thermometer or perceived by touch; (*colloquial*) a body temperature above normal. Temperature is measured in degrees Celsius (before 1948 called centigrade), Kelvin, or Fahrenheit. **2.** a degree of excitement in a discussion etc.

temperature regulation the ability of an organism to control its body temperature.

tempering *n.* heat treatment for improving the properties of metals, often used for steel alloys. The metal is heated to a certain temperature and then cooled suddenly in a water or oil bath.

tempest /'tempist/ *n.* a violent storm. [from Old French from Latin *tempestas* = season, storm (*tempus* = time)]

Tempest, The romantic drama by William Shakespeare, first performed 1611–12. Prospero, usurped as duke of Milan by his brother Antonio, lives on a remote island with his daughter Miranda and Caliban, a deformed creature. Prospero uses magic to shipwreck Antonio and his party on the island and, with the help of the spirit Ariel, regains his dukedom.

tempestuous /tem'pestjuəs/ *adj.* stormy, turbulent. [from Latin]

Templar /'templə/ *n.* a member of the Knights Templars, a military and religious order (*c.*1120–1312) for protecting pilgrims to the Holy Land. [from Anglo-French]

template /'templeɪt/ *n.* a thin board or metal plate used as a guide in cutting, shaping, or drilling. [originally *templet*, probably diminutive of *temple* = device in loom for keeping cloth stretched, from Old French]

temple[1] /'tempəl/ *n.* a building devoted to the worship, or treated as a dwelling-place, of a god or gods; (*US*) another name for ◊synagogue. —**Inner** and **Middle Temple**, two Inns of Court in London. [Old English and from Old French from Latin *templum* = open or consecrated space]

temple[2] *n.* the flat part of either side of the head between the forehead and the ear. [from Old French from Latin *tempus*]

Temple *n.* the centre of Jewish national worship in Jerusalem in both ancient and modern days. The Western or **Wailing Wall** is the surviving part of the western wall of the enclosure of Herod's Temple. Since the destruction of the Temple AD 70, Jews have gone there to pray and to mourn their dispersion and the loss of their homeland.

Temple Shirley 1928– . US actress who became the most successful child star of the 1930s. Her films include *Bright Eyes* 1934 (Academy Award), in which she sang 'On the Good Ship Lollipop'. Her other films include *Curly Top* 1935 and *Rebecca of Sunnybrook Farm* 1938. Her career as a film star was virtually at an end by the time she was 12. As Shirley Temple Black, she became active in the Republican Party and was US chief of protocol 1976–77. She was appointed US ambassador to Czechoslovakia in 1989.

tempo *n.* (*plural* **tempos** or **tempi** /-i:/) **1.** the speed at which music is or should be played, especially as characteristic. **2.** a rate of motion or activity. [Italian, from Latin *tempus* = time]

temporal /'tempərəl/ *adj.* **1.** of worldly as opposed to spiritual affairs, secular. **2.** of or denoting time. **3.** of the temple(s) of the head (*temporal bone*). [from Old French or Latin]

temporary /'tempərəri/ *adj.* lasting or meant to last only for a limited time. —*n.* a person employed temporarily. —**temporarily** *adv.*, **temporariness** *n.* [from Latin (*tempus* = time)]

temporize /'tempəraɪz/ *v.i.* to avoid committing oneself, to act so as to gain time; to comply temporarily with the requirements of an occasion. —**temporization** /-'zeɪʃən/ *n.*, **temporizer** *n.* [from French from Latin]

tempt *v.t.* **1.** to entice or incite to do a wrong or forbidden thing. **2.** to arouse a desire in, to attract. **3.** to risk provoking (fate or Providence) by deliberate rashness. —**be tempted to,** to be strongly disposed to. —**tempter** *n.*, **temptress** *n. feminine* [from Old French from Latin *temptare* = test]

temptation /temp'teɪʃən/ n. 1. tempting, being tempted; an incitement, especially to wrongdoing. 2. an attractive thing or course of action. 3. (archaic) putting to the test.

tempting adj. attractive, inviting.

Temuco /te'muːkəʊ/ market town and capital of Araucanía region, Chile; population (1987) 218,000.

ten adj. & n. 1. one more than nine. 2. the symbol for this (10, x, X). 3. a size etc. denoted by ten. [Old English]

tenable /'tenəbəl/ adj. 1. that can be maintained against attack or objection. 2. (of an office etc.) that can be held for a specified period or by a specified class of person. —**tenability** /-'bɪlɪtɪ/ n. [French (tenir = hold from Latin tenēre)]

tenacious /tɪ'neɪʃəs/ adj. 1. keeping a firm hold (of property, principles, life, etc.). 2. (of memory) retentive. 3. holding tightly, not easily separable; tough. —**tenaciously** adv., **tenacity** /tɪ'næsɪtɪ/ n. [from Latin tenax (tenēre = hold)]

tenancy n. occupancy as a tenant.

tenant /'tenənt/ n. a person who rents land or property from a landlord; the occupant of a place. —**tenant farmer,** one farming hired land. [from Old French tenir = hold]

tenant farming system whereby farmers rent their holdings from a landowner in return for the use of agricultural land.

tenantry n. the tenants of an estate etc.

tench n. (plural the same) a European freshwater fish Tinca tinca. A member of the carp family, it is about 45 cm/ 18 in long, weighing 2 kg/4.5 lbs, coloured olive-green above and grey beneath. The scales are small and there is a barbel at each side of the mouth. [from Old French from Latin tinca]

Ten Commandments in the Old Testament, the laws given by God to the Hebrew leader Moses on Mt Sinai, engraved on two tablets of stone. They are: to have no other gods besides Jehovah; to make no idols; not to misuse the name of God; to keep the sabbath holy; to honour one's parents; not to commit murder, adultery, or theft; not to give false evidence; not to be covetous. They form the basis of Jewish and Christian moral codes; the 'tablets of the Law' given to Moses are also mentioned in the Koran. The giving of the Ten Commandments is celebrated in the Jewish festival of Shavuot.

tend[1] v.i. 1. to be likely to behave in a specified way or to have a specified characteristic or influence. 2. to take a specified direction (literal or figurative). [from Old French from Latin tendere = stretch]

tend[2] v.t. to take care of, to look after. [from attend]

tendency /'tendənsɪ/ n. 1. the way a person or thing tends to be or behave. 2. the direction in which something moves or changes, a trend. [from Latin]

tendentious /ten'denʃəs/ adj. (derogatory, of a speech or piece of writing etc.) designed to advance a cause, not impartial. —**tendentiously** adv., **tendentiousness** n.

tender[1] adj. 1. easily cut or chewed, not tough. 2. easily hurt or wounded, susceptible to pain or grief; delicate, fragile, sensitive. 3. loving, gentle. 4. requiring tact. 5. (of age) early, immature. —**tender spot,** a subject on which one is touchy. —**tenderly** adv., **tenderness** n. [from Old French from Latin tener]

tender[2] v.t.i. 1. to make an offer of or present for acceptance. 2. to send in a tender for the execution of work etc. —n. an offer, especially in writing, to execute work or supply goods at a stated price. —**put out to tender,** to seek offers in respect of (work etc.). [from Old French tendre]

tender[3] n. 1. one who looks after people or things. 2. a vessel attending a larger one and carrying stores etc. 3. a truck attached to a steam locomotive and carrying coal etc. [from tend[2]]

tenderfoot n. a newcomer who is unused to hardships, an inexperienced person.

tenderize v.t. to make tender; to make (meat) tender by beating etc. —**tenderizer** n.

tenderloin n. 1. the middle part of pork loin. 2. (US) the undercut of a sirloin.

tendon /'tendən/ n. or **sinew** a cord of tough, fibrous connective tissue that joins muscle to bone in vertebrates. [French or from Latin from Greek tenōn = sinew (teinō = stretch)]

tendril n. in botany, a slender, threadlike structure that supports a climbing plant by coiling around suitable supports, such as the stems and branches of other plants. It may be a modified stem, leaf, leaflet, flower, leaf stalk, or stipule (a small appendage on either side of the leaf stalk), and may be simple or branched. The tendrils of Virginia creeper Parthenocissus quinquefolia are modified flower heads with suckerlike pads at the end that stick to walls, while those of the grapevine Vitis grow away from the light and thus enter dark crevices where they expand to anchor

Tenniel The Mad Hatter's tea party, from Lewis Carroll's Alice in Wonderland.

the plant firmly. [probably from obsolete French *tendrillon* (*tendron* = young shoot, from Latin]

tenement /'tenɪmənt/ *n.* 1. a piece of land held by an owner; in law, any kind of permanent property held by a tenant. 2. a flat or room rented as a dwelling-place. 3. (*Scottish*) a house divided into and let in tenements. [from Old French from Latin (*tenēre* = hold)]

Tenerife /tenə'riːf/ largest of the ◊Canary Islands, Spain; **area** 2,060 sq km/795 sq mi; **main town** Santa Cruz; **population** (1981) 557,000. The island has an active volcano, Pico de Teide.

tenet /'tenɪt/ *n.* a doctrine held by a group or person. [Latin = he holds]

tenfold /'tenfəʊld/ *adj. & adv.* ten times as much or as many; consisting of ten parts.

Teng Hsiao-ping /'teŋ ʃaʊ'pɪŋ/ alternative spelling of ◊Deng Xiaoping, Chinese politician.

Ten Hours Act 1847 British act of Parliament that restricted the working day of all workers except adult males. It was prompted by the public campaign (the 'Ten Hours Movement') set up in 1831. Women and young people were restricted to a 10½ hour day, with 1½ hours for meals, between 6 am and 6 pm.

Teniers /'teniəz/ family of Flemish painters, active in Antwerp. **David Teniers the Younger** (David II, 1610–1690) became court painter to Archduke Leopold William, governor of the Netherlands, in Brussels. He painted scenes of peasant life.

tenner *n.* (*colloquial*) a £10 note.

Tennessee /tenə'siː/ state of the E central USA; nickname Volunteer State; **area** 109,200 sq km/42,151 sq mi; **capital** Nashville; **population** (1987) 4,855,000; **history** first settled in 1757, it became a state in 1796.

Tenniel /'tenjəl/ John 1820–1914. English illustrator and cartoonist, known for his illustrations for Lewis Carroll's *Alice's Adventures in Wonderland* 1865 and *Through the Looking-Glass* 1872.

tennis, lawn a racket and ball game, played by two or four players whose aim is to strike the ball into the prescribed area of the court in such a way that it cannot be returned. The game is won by those first winning four points (called 15, 30, 40, game), unless both sides reach 40 (deuce), when two consecutive points are needed to win. A set is won by winning six games with a margin of two over opponents, though a tie-break system operates, that is at six games to each side (or in some cases eight) except in the final set. Lawn tennis was invented towards the end of the 19th century, and derived from ◊real tennis. Although played on different surfaces (grass, wood, shale, clay, concrete) it is still called 'lawn tennis'. Major events include the ◊Davis Cup, first contested in 1900 for international men's competition, and the annual All England Tennis Club championships (originating in 1877), an open event for players of both sexes at ◊Wimbledon. The latter is one of the four **Grand Slam** events; the others are the US Open, first held in 1881 as US Championships becoming US Open in 1968, French Championships, and Australian Championships. [from French *tenez* = take, receive, called by server to his opponent]

Tennyson /'tenɪsən/ Alfred, 1st Baron Tennyson 1809–1892. English poet, poet laureate 1850–96, whose verse has a majestic, musical quality. His works include 'The Lady of Shalott', 'The Lotus Eaters', 'Ulysses', 'Break, Break, Break', 'The Charge of the Light Brigade'; the longer narratives *Locksley Hall* 1832 and *Maud* 1855; the elegy *In Memoriam* 1850; and a long series of poems on the Arthurian legends *The Idylls of the King* 1857–85.

No life that breathes with human breath
Has ever truly long'd for death.

Alfred, 1st Baron Tennyson
The Two Voices

tenon /'tenən/ *n.* a projection shaped to fit into a mortise. —**tenon-saw** *n.* a small saw with a strong brass or steel back, used for fine work. [from French (*tenir* = hold from Latin *tenēre*)]

tenor /'tenə/ *n.* 1. the highest ordinary adult male singing-voice; a singer with this; a part written for it. 2. a musical instrument with approximately the range of a tenor voice. 3. the general routine or course of something. 4. the general meaning or drift. [from Anglo-French from Latin *tenor* (*tenēre* = hold)]

tenpin bowling a form of skittles similar to ninepins.

tense[1] *adj.* 1. stretched tightly. 2. with muscles tight in attentiveness for what may happen; unable to relax, edgy. 3. causing tenseness. —*v.t./i.* to make or become tense. —**tensely** *adv.*, **tenseness** *n.* [from Latin *tensus* (*tendere* = stretch)]

tense[2] *n.* the form taken by a word to indicate the time (also continuance or completeness) of an action; a set of such forms. [from Old French from Latin *tempus* = time]

tensile /'tensaɪl/ *adj.* 1. of tension. 2. capable of being stretched. —**tensile strength,** resistance to breaking under tension. —**tensility** /-'sɪlɪtɪ/ *n.* [from Latin *tensilis*]

tension /'tenʃən/ *n.* 1. stretching, being stretched. 2. tenseness, the condition when feelings are tense. 3. the effect produced by forces pulling against each other. 4. electromotive force. 5. (in knitting) the number of stitches and rows to a unit of measurement. [French or from Latin]

tent *n.* 1. a portable shelter or dwelling of canvas or cloth etc. supported by poles and by ropes attached to pegs driven into the ground. 2. a cover etc. resembling a tent. [from Latin *tendere* = stretch]

tentacle /'tentəkəl/ *n.* 1. a long slender flexible appendage of an animal, used for feeling or grasping things or for moving. 2. a thing compared to a tentacle in use. —**tentacled** *adj.* [from Latin *tentare*]

tentative /'tentətɪv/ *adj.* done as a trial, hesitant, not definite. —**tentatively** *adv.*

tenter *n.* a machine for stretching cloth to dry in shape. [from Latin *tentorium* (*tentere* = stretch).

tenterhooks *n.pl.* hooks to which cloth is fastened on a tenter. —**on tenterhooks,** in a state of suspense or strain because of uncertainty.

tenth *adj.* next after the ninth. —*n.* each of ten equal parts of a thing. —**tenthly** *adv.*

tenuous /'tenjuəs/ *adj.* 1. having little substance or validity, very slight. 2. very thin in form or consistency. —**tenuity** /-'juːɪtɪ/ *n.*, **tenuously** *adv.*, **tenuousness** *n.* [from Latin *tenuis*]

tenure /'tenjə/ *n.* the holding of office or of land or other permanent property or of accommodation etc.; the period or condition of this. [from Old French (French *tenir* = hold)]

Teotihuacán /teɪəutiːwə'kaːn/ ancient city in central Mexico, the religious centre of the ◊Toltec civilization.

tepee /'tiːpiː/ *n.* a North American Indian conical tent. [from Dakota *tipī*]

tepid /'tepɪd/ *adj.* 1. slightly warm, lukewarm. 2. unenthusiastic. —**tepidity** /tɪ'pɪdɪtɪ/ *n.*, **tepidly** *adv.* [from Latin *tepidus* (*tepēre* = be lukewarm)]

tequila /te'kiːlə/ *n.* a Mexican liquor made from agave. [from *Tequila* in Mexico]

tera- /terə-/ in combinations, one million million. [from Greek *teras* = monster]

teratogen *n.* any nongenetic agent that can induce deformities in the fetus if absorbed by the mother during pregnancy. Teratogens include some drugs (notably alcohol and ◊thalidomide), other chemicals, certain disease organisms, and radioactivity.

terbium /'tɜːbiəm/ *n.* a soft, silver-grey, metallic element of the ◊lanthanide series, symbol Tb, atomic number 65, relative atomic mass 158.925. It occurs in gadolinite and other ores, with yttrium and ytterbium, and is used in lasers, semiconductors, and television tubes. [from *Ytterby*, Sweden, where it was first found]

Terborch /tə'bɔːx/ Gerard 1617–1681. Dutch painter of small-scale portraits and genre (everyday) scenes, mainly of soldiers at rest or wealthy families in their homes. He travelled widely in Europe. *The Peace of Münster* 1648 (National Gallery, London) is an official group portrait.

Terbrugghen /tə'bruxən/ Hendrik 1588–1629. Dutch painter, a leader of the **Utrecht school** with Honthorst. He visited Rome around 1604 and was inspired by Caravaggio's work. He painted religious subjects and genre (everyday) scenes.

tercel /'tɜːsəl/ *n.* a male hawk. [from Old French, ultimately from Latin *tertius* = third, because believed to come from third egg of clutch]

tercentenary /tɜːsenˈtiːnərɪ/ n. a three-hundredth anniversary; a celebration of this. [from Latin ter = thrice and centenary]

terebinth n. a South European tree Pistacia terebinthus yielding turpentine. [from Old French or Latin from Greek terebinthos]

teredo /təˈriːdəʊ/ n. (plural teredos) a mollusc of the genus Teredo that bores into submerged timber. [Latin from Greek terēdōn (teirō = rub hard, bore)]

Terence /ˈterəns/ (Publius Terentius Afer) 190–159 BC. Roman dramatist, born in Carthage and brought as a slave to Rome, where he was freed and came under the patronage of ◊Scipio Africanus Major. His surviving six comedies (including The Eunuch 161 BC) are subtly characterized and based on Greek models.

Teresa, St /təˈriːzə/ 1515–1582. Spanish mystic, born in Avila. She became a Carmelite nun, and in 1562 founded a new and stricter order. She was subject to fainting fits, during which she saw visions. She wrote The Way to Perfection 1583 and an autobiography, Life of the Mother Theresa of Jesus 1611. In 1622 she was canonized, and in 1970 was made the first female Doctor of the Church.

Tereshkova /terɪʃˈkəʊvə/ Valentina Vladimirovna 1937– . Soviet cosmonaut, the first woman to fly in space. In June 1963 she made a three-day flight in Vostok 6, orbiting the Earth 48 times.

tergiversation /tɜːdʒɪvɜːˈseɪʃən/ n. a change of party or principles, apostasy; the making of conflicting statements. [from Latin (tergum = the back and vertere = turn)]

term n. 1. a word used to express a definite concept, especially in a branch of study etc. 2. (in plural) language used, a mode of expression. 3. (in plural) a relation between people. 4. (in plural) conditions offered or accepted; stipulations. 5. (in plural) the charge or price. 6. a limited period of some state or activity; a period of action or of contemplated results; a period during which instruction is given in a school or university, or during which a lawcourt holds sessions. 7. a word or words that may be the subject or predicate of a logical proposition. 8. in mathematics, each quantity in a ratio or series; an item of a compound algebraic expression. 9. in architecture, a pillar in the form of a pedestal supporting the bust of a human or animal figure. 10. (archaic) an appointed limitative —v.t. to call by a specified term or expression. —come to terms, to reach agreement; to reconcile oneself (with a difficulty etc.). in terms of, in the language peculiar to; using as a basis of expression or thought. terms of reference, the points referred to an individual or body of persons for decision or report; the scope of an inquiry etc.; the definition of this. [from Old French from Latin (terminus = end, boundary]

termagant /ˈtɜːməgənt/ n. an overbearing woman, a virago. [from Old French Tervagan from Italian Trivigante = imaginary deity of violent character in morality plays]

terminable /ˈtɜːmɪnəbəl/ adj. that may be terminated.

terminal /ˈtɜːmɪnəl/ adj. 1. of or forming the last part or terminus. 2. forming or undergoing the last stage of a fatal disease. 3. of or done etc. each term. —n. 1. a terminating thing, an extremity. 2. a terminus for trains or long-distance buses; an air terminal (see ◊air). 3. a point of connection for closing an electric circuit. 4. an apparatus consisting of a keyboard and screen to enable an operator to communicate with a computer or communications system etc. —terminally adv. [from Latin (terminus = end, boundary]

terminate /ˈtɜːmɪneɪt/ v.t./i. to bring or come to an end. —terminator n. [from Latin terminare]

termination /tɜːmɪˈneɪʃən/ n. an ending; the way something ends; a word's final letter(s). [from Old French or Latin]

terminology /tɜːmɪˈnɒlədʒɪ/ n. 1. the system of terms used in a particular subject. 2. the science of the proper use of terms. —terminological /-nəˈlɒdʒɪkəl/ adj. [from German]

terminus /ˈtɜːmɪnəs/ n. (plural termini /-naɪ/) 1. a station at the end of a railway or bus route. 2. a point at the end of a pipeline etc. [Latin = end, boundary]

termite /ˈtɜːmaɪt/ n. a small antlike insect of the order Isoptera, destructive to timber. [from Latin termes, tarmes (terere = rub)]

tern n. a sea-bird of the genus Sterna, like a gull but usually smaller and with a forked tail. [of Scandinavian origin]

ternary /ˈtɜːnərɪ/ adj. composed of three parts. [from Latin ternarius (terni = three each)]

terotechnology /tɪərəʊtekˈnɒlədʒɪ, terəʊ-/ n. the branch of technology and engineering concerned with the installation, maintenance, and replacement of industrial plant and equipment and with related subjects and practices. [from Greek tērō = watch over, take care of]

terrace /ˈterəs/ n. 1. a raised level space, natural or artificial, especially for walking, standing, or cultivation. 2. a row of houses on a raised level or built in one block of uniform style. 3. a flight of wide shallow steps as for spectators at a sports ground. [Old French from Latin terra = earth]

terraced adj. formed into or having a terrace or terraces. —terraced roof, a flat roof especially of an Eastern house.

terracotta /terəˈkɒtə/ n. 1. an unglazed usually brownish-red pottery used as an ornamental building-material and in statuary. 2. a statuette of this. 3. its colour. [Italian = baked earth]

terra firma /terə ˈfɜːmə/ dry land, firm ground. [Latin]

terrain /teˈreɪn/ n. a tract of land as regards its natural features. [French from Latin terrenus (terra = earth)]

terra incognita an unknown region. [Latin]

terrapin /ˈterəpɪn/ n. a member of some species of the order Chelonia (◊turtles and ◊tortoises). Terrapins are small to medium-sized, aquatic or semi-aquatic, and found widely in temperate zones. They are omnivorous, but generally eat aquatic animals. Species include the diamond-back terrapin Malaclemys terrapin of the eastern USA, the yellow-bellied terrapin, and the red-eared terrapin Pseudemys scripta elegans. Some species are in danger of extinction owing to collection for the pet trade; most of the animals collected die in transit. [Algonquian]

terrarium /teˈreərɪəm/ n. (plural terrariums) 1. a place for keeping small land animals. 2. a sealed transparent globe etc. containing growing plants. [from Latin terra = earth]

terrazzo /tɪˈrætsəʊ/ n. (plural terrazzos) a flooring-material of stone chips set in concrete and given a smooth surface. [Italian = terrace]

terrene /teˈriːn/ adj. of the Earth, earthly; terrestrial. [from Anglo-French from Latin terrenus (terra = earth)]

terrestrial /təˈrestrɪəl/ adj. of or on the Earth; of or on dry land. [from Latin terrestris]

terrible /ˈterɪbəl/ adj. 1. appalling, distressing; causing or fit to cause terror. 2. (colloquial) extreme, hard to bear. 3. (colloquial) very bad or incompetent. —terribly adv. [from French from Latin (terrēre = frighten)]

terrier /ˈterɪə/ n. a usually small, hardy, active dog bred originally for turning out foxes etc. from their earths. Types include the bull, cairn, fox, Irish, Scottish, Sealyham, Skye, and Yorkshire terriers. The small Parson Jack Russell terrier was recognized by the Kennel Club in 1990 as a variant of the fox terrier. [from Old French from Latin terrarius (terra = earth)]

terrific /təˈrɪfɪk/ adj. 1. (colloquial) of great size or intensity. 2. (colloquial) excellent. 3. causing terror. —terrifically adv. [from Latin (terrēre = frighten and facere = make)]

terrify /ˈterɪfaɪ/ v.t. to frighten severely.

terrine /təˈriːn/ n. 1. a pâté or similar food. 2. an earthenware vessel holding this. [originally form of tureen]

territorial /terɪˈtɔːrɪəl/ adj. of a territory or districts. —territorial waters, the waters under a state's jurisdiction, especially the part of the sea within a stated distance of the shore. —territorially adv. [from Latin (terra = land)]

Territorial n. a member of the Territorial Army. —adj. of a Territory or Territories. —Territorial Army, a trained reserve force organized by localities, for use in an emergency.

territorial behaviour in biology, any behaviour that serves to exclude other members of the same species from a fixed area or territory. It may involve aggressively driving out intruders, marking the boundary (with dung piles or secretions from special scent glands), conspicuous visual displays, characteristic songs, or loud calls.

territory /ˈterɪtərɪ/ n. 1. the land under the jurisdiction of a ruler, state, or city etc. 2. Territory, a country or area forming part of the USA, Australia, or Canada, but not ranking as a State or province. 3. an area for which a person has responsibility or over which a salesman etc. operates. 4. a sphere of action or thought, a province. 5. an area claimed or dominated by one person or group and defended against others; an area defended by an animal against others of the same species. [from Latin (*terra* = land)]

terror /'terə/ *n.* 1. extreme fear. 2. a person or thing causing terror; (*colloquial*) a formidable person, a troublesome person or thing. —**the Terror** *or* **Reign of Terror,** the period of the French Revolution between mid-1793 and July 1794 when the ruling Jacobin faction, dominated by Robespierre, ruthlessly executed opponents and anyone else considered a threat to their regime. **terror-stricken** *or* **-struck** *adj.* affected with terror. [from Old French from Latin *terrēre* = frighten]

terrorism *n.* the practice of using violent and intimidating methods, especially to achieve political ends. —**terrorist** *n.* [from French]

terrorize *v.t.* to fill with terror; to coerce by terrorism. —**terrorization** /-'zeɪʃən/ *n.*

terry /'teri/ *n.* a pile fabric with the loops uncut, used especially for towels.

Terry (John) Quinlan 1937– . British Neo-Classical architect. His work includes country houses, for example Merks Hall, Great Dunmow, Essex, 1982, and the larger-scale Richmond, London, riverside project, commissioned in 1984.

Terry-Thomas /'tɒməs/ stage name of Thomas Terry Hoar Stevens 1911–1990. British film comedy actor, who portrayed upper-class English fools in such films as *I'm All Right Jack* 1959, *It's a Mad, Mad, Mad, Mad World* 1963, and *How to Murder Your Wife* 1965.

terse *adj.* concise, brief and forcible in style; curt. —**tersely** *adv.,* **terseness** *n.* [from Latin *tersus* (*tergēre* = wipe)]

tertiary /'tɜːʃəri/ *adj.* coming after secondary, of the third order or rank etc. —*n.* 1. a bird's flight feather of the third row. 2. in the Roman Catholic church, a member of a 'third order' (see under ◊holy orders); a lay person who, while marrying and following a normal employment, attempts to live in accordance with a modified version of the rule of one of the religious orders. The first such order was founded by St ◊Francis in 1221. [from Latin *tertiarius* (*tertius* third)]

Tertiary *adj.* 1. of the period of geological time 65–1.8 million years ago. —*n.* this period. It is divided into into five epochs: Palaeocene, Eocene, Oligocene, Miocene, and Pliocene. During the Tertiary, mammals took over all the ecological niches left vacant by the extinction of the dinosaurs, and became the prevalent land animals. The continents took on their present positions, and climatic and vegetation zones as we know them became established. Within the geological time column the Tertiary follows the Cretaceous period and is succeeded by the Quaternary period.

tertiary college in the UK, a college for students aged over 16 that combines the work of a ◊sixth form and a ◊further education college.

Tertullian /tɜː'tʌliən/ Quintus Septimius Florens AD 155–222. Carthaginian Father of the Church, the first major Christian writer in Latin; he became a leading exponent of ◊Montanism.

Terylene /'terɪliːn/ *n.* trade name of a synthetic polyester used as a textile fibre. [from *terephthalic* acid and *ethylene*]

terza rima a poetical metre used in Dante's *Divine Comedy*, consisting of three-line stanzas in which the second line rhymes with the first and third of the following stanza. Shelley's 'Ode to the West Wind' is another example.

tesla /'teslə/ *n.* the unit (symbol T) of magnetic flux density, = 10,000 gauss. [from N *Tesla*]

Tesla Nikola 1856–1943. Croatian electrical engineer, who emigrated to the USA in 1884. He invented fluorescent lighting, the Tesla induction motor, and the Tesla coil, and developed the ◊alternating current (AC) electrical supply system.

tessellated /'tesəleɪtɪd/ *adj.* of or resembling a mosaic; having a finely chequered surface. [from Latin (*tessella* = diminutive of *tessera*)]

tessellation /tesə'leɪʃən/ *n.* an arrangement of polygons without gaps or overlapping, especially in a repeating pattern. [from Latin *tessellare*]

tessera /'tesərə/ *n.* (*plural* **tesserae** /-iː/) each of the small cubes or blocks of which a mosaic consists. [Latin from Greek *tessares* = four]

test[1] *n.* 1. a critical examination or trial of a person's or thing's qualities. 2. the means, standard, or circumstances

suitable for or serving such an examination. 3. a minor examination, especially in a school. 4. (*colloquial*) a test match. —*v.t.* 1. to subject to a test. 2. to try severely, to tax. 3. in chemistry, to examine by means of a reagent. —**put to the test,** to cause to undergo a test. **stand the test,** not to fail or incur rejection. **test case,** a case whose decision is taken as settling other cases involving the same question of law. **test match,** a cricket or Rugby match between the teams of certain countries, usually one of a series in a tour. **test paper,** an examination paper used in a test; in chemistry, a paper impregnated with a substance changing colour under known conditions. **test pilot,** a pilot who tests the performance of newly designed aircraft. **test tube,** a thin glass tube closed at one end used for chemical tests etc. **test-tube baby,** (*colloquial*) a baby developed from an ovum fertilized outside the mother's body. —**tester** *n.* [from Old French from Latin *testu(m)* = earthen pot]

test[2] *n.* the hard continuous shell of some invertebrates. [from Latin *testa* = tile, shell, etc.]

testa /'testə/ *n.* (*plural* **testae** /-iː/) a seed-coat. [Latin]

testaceous /te'steɪʃəs/ *adj.* having a hard continuous shell.

testacy /'testəsi/ *n.* being testate.

testament /'testəmənt/ *n.* 1. (usually **last will and testament**) a will. 2. (*colloquial*) a written statement of one's beliefs etc. 3. a covenant, a dispensation; **Testament,** a portion of the Bible. [from Latin *testamentum* = will; in early Christian Latin rendering Greek *diathēkē*= covenant]

testamentary /testə'mentəri/ *adj.* of, by, or in a will.

testate /'testeɪt/ *adj.* having left a valid will at death. —*n.* a testate person. [from Latin (*testari* = testify from *testis* = witness)]

testator /te'steɪtə/ *n.* a person who has made a will, especially one who dies testate. —**testatrix** *n.fem.* [from Anglo-French from Latin]

Test Ban Treaty agreement signed by the USA, the USSR, and the UK on 5 Aug 1963 contracting to test nuclear weapons only underground. In the following two years 90 other nations signed the treaty, the only major nonsignatories being France and China, which continued underwater and ground-level tests.

tester *n.* a canopy, especially over a four-poster bed. [from Latin (*testa* = file)]

testicle /'testɪkəl/ *n.* the male organ that secretes spermatozoa etc., especially one of the pair in the scrotum behind the penis of man and most mammals. [from Latin *testiculus*, diminutive of *testis* = witness (of virility)]

testify /'testɪfaɪ/ *v.t./i.* to bear witness; to give evidence; to declare; to be evidence of. [from Latin (*testis* = witness and *facere* = make)]

testimonial /testi'məuniəl/ *n.* 1. a certificate of character, conduct, or qualifications. 2. a gift presented to a person (especially in public) as a mark of esteem. [from Old French or Latin]

testimony /'testɪmənɪ/ *n.* 1. a declaration of statement (written or spoken), especially one made under oath. 2. evidence in support of something. [from Latin (*testis* = witness)]

testis *n.* (*plural* **testes** /-iːz/) a testicle. [Latin *testis* = witness (of virility)]

testosterone /te'stɒstərəun/ *n.* a male sex hormone produced in the testicles and (in very much smaller quantities) in the ovaries and adrenal cortex. [from *testes* and *sterol*]

testy *adj.* irascible, short-tempered —**testily** *adv.,* **testiness** *n.* [from Anglo-French *testif* (*teste* = head)]

tetanus /'tetənəs/ *n.* or **lockjaw** an acute disease caused by the toxin of the bacillus *Clostridium tetani*, which usually enters the body through a wound. The bacterium is chiefly found in richly manured soil. Untreated, in seven to ten days tetanus produces muscular spasm and rigidity of the jaw spreading to the other muscles, convulsions, and death. There is a preventive vaccine series, and the disease may be treatable with tetanus antitoxin and antibiotics. [Latin from Greek *tetanos* (*teinō* = stretch)]

tetchy /'tetʃi/ *adj.* peevish, irritable, touchy. —**tetchily** *adv.,* **tetchiness** *n.* [probably from obsolete *tecche, tache* = blemish, fault, from Old French]

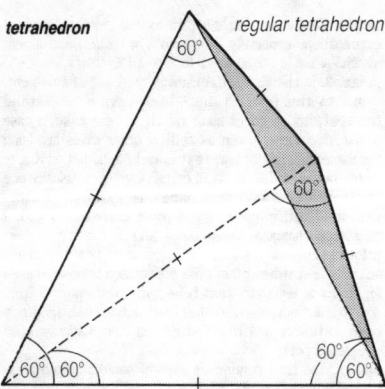

tetrahedron   *regular tetrahedron*

tête-à-tête /teita:'teit/ *n.* a private conversation or interview, usually between two people. —*adv.* & *adj.* together in private. [French, literally head-to-head]

tether /'teðə/ *n.* a rope or chain by which an animal is tied while grazing. —*v.t.* to tie with a tether. —**at the end of one's tether,** having reached the limit of one's patience or endurance etc. [from Old Norse]

Tet Offensive /tet/ in the Vietnam War, a prolonged attack mounted by the Vietcong against Saigon (now Ho Chi Minh City) and other South Vietnamese cities and hamlets beginning on 30 Jan 1968. Although the Vietcong were finally forced to withdraw, the Tet Offensive brought into question the ability of the South Vietnamese and their US allies to win the war.

tetra /tetrə/ *n.* a brightly coloured tropical fish of the family Characidae.

tetra- in combinations, four. [Greek *tessares* = four)]

tetrad /'tetræd/ *n.* a group of four. [from Greek]

tetragon /'tetrəgən/ *n.* a plane figure with four sides and angles. —**tetragonal** /-'rægənəl/ *adj.* [Greek *-gōnos* = -angled]

tetrahedron /tetrə'hi:drən/ *n.* (*plural* **tetrahedra**) in geometry, a solid figure (◊polyhedron) with four triangular faces; that is, a ◊pyramid on a triangular base. A regular tetrahedron has equilateral triangles as its faces. —**tetrahedral** *adj.* [Greek *hedra* = base)]

tetralogy /te'trælədʒɪ/ *n.* a group of four related literary or dramatic works. [from Greek]

tetrameter /te'træmɪtə/ *n.* a line of verse of four measures. [from Latin from Greek *metron* = measure]

tetrapod *n.* a type of ◊vertebrate. The group includes mammals, birds, reptiles, and amphibians. Birds are included because they evolved from four-legged ancestors, the forelimbs having become modified to form wings. Even snakes are tetrapods, since their lack of limbs is secondary. [Latin = four-legged]

Tetuán /te'twa:n/ or **Tétouan** town in NE Morocco, near the Mediterranean coast, 64 km/40 mi SE of Tangier; population (1982) 372,000. Products include textiles, leather, and soap. It was settled by Moorish exiles from Spain in the 16th century.

Teuton /'tju:tən/ *n.* **1.** a member of a Teutonic nation, especially a German. **2.** a member of a north-European tribe combining with others to carry out raids on NE and southern France during the Roman period. [from Latin from Indo-European = people, country]

Teutonic /tju:'tonɪk/ *adj.* **1.** of the Teutons. **2.** of the Germanic peoples or their languages. **3.** German.

Teutonic Knight a member of a German Christian military order, the **Knights of the Teutonic Order,** founded in 1190 by Hermann of Salza in Palestine. They crusaded against the pagan Prussians and Lithuanians from 1228 and controlled Prussia until the 16th century. Their capital was Marienburg (now Malbork, Poland).

Texas /'teksəs/ state of the SW USA; nickname Lone Star State; **area** 691,200 sq km/266,803 sq mi; **capital** Austin; **population** (1985) 16,370,000; **history** settled by the Spanish in 1682; part of Mexico 1821–36; Santa Anna massacred the Alamo garrison in 1836, but was defeated by Sam Houston at San Jacinto the same year; Texas became an independent republic 1836–45, with Houston

as president; in 1845 it became a state of the USA. Texas is the only state in the USA to have previously been an independent republic.

text *n.* **1.** the main body of a book or page etc. as distinct from the notes, illustrations, appendices, etc. **2.** the original words of an author or document, especially as distinct from a paraphrase or commentary. **3.** a passage of Scripture quoted or used as the subject of a sermon etc.; a subject, a theme. **4.** (in *plural*) books prescribed for study. [from Old French from Latin *textus* (*texere* = weave)]

textbook *n.* a book of information for use in studying a subject. —*adj.* exemplary, accurate; instructively typical.

text editor in computing, a program that allows the user to edit text on the screen and to store it in a file. Text editors are similar to ◊word processors, except that they lack the ability to format text into paragraphs and pages and to apply different typefaces and styles.

textile /'tekstaɪl/ *n.* a woven fabric; formerly a material woven from natural spun thread, now loosely extended to machine knits and spun-bonded fabrics (in which a web of fibre is created and then fuse-bonded by passing it through controlled heat). —*adj.* of weaving; woven. [from Latin *textilis* (*texere* = weave)]

textual /'tekstjuəl/ *adj.* of, in, or concerning a text. —**textually** *adv.* [from Latin *textus*]

texture /'tekstʃə/ *n.* the quality of a surface or substance when felt or looked at; the arrangement of threads in a textile fabric. —**textural** *adj.*, **texturally** *adv.* [from Latin *textura*]

textured *adj.* **1.** having a specified texture. **2.** provided with a texture, not smooth or plain.

textured vegetable protein a manufactured meat substitute; see ◊TVP.

TGV *n.* the French electrically powered train that provides the world's fastest rail service. Introduced in 1981, it holds the world speed record for a train of 482.4 kmh/301.5 mph (about half the speed of a passenger jet aircraft), reached at a stretch near Tours in 1989. In its regular service, the TGV covers the 425 km/264 mi distance between Paris and Lyons in two hours. [abbreviation of French *train à grande vitesse* = high speed train]

Thackeray /'θækərɪ/ William Makepeace 1811–1863. English novelist and essayist, born in Calcutta, India. He was a regular contributor to *Fraser's Magazine* and *Punch. Vanity Fair* 1847–48 was his first novel, followed by *Pendennis* 1848, *Henry Esmond* 1852 (and its sequel *The Virginians* 1857–59), and *The Newcomes* 1853–55, in which Thackeray's tendency to sentimentality is most marked.

He who meanly admires mean things is a snob.
William Makepeace Thackeray
The Book of Snobs

Thai /taɪ/ *adj.* of Thailand or its people or language. —*n.* **1.** a native or inhabitant of Thailand. **2.** the language of Thailand. [Thai = free]

Thailand /'taɪlænd/ Kingdom of; country in SE Asia on the Gulf of Siam, bounded to the east by Laos and Cambodia, to the south by Malaysia, and to the west by Myanmar (formerly Burma); **area** 513,100 sq km/198,108 sq mi; **capital** and chief port Bangkok; **physical** mountainous, semi-arid plateau in NE, fertile central region, tropical isthmus in S; **head of state** King Bhumibol Adulyadej from 1946; **head of government** Chatichai Choonhavan from 1988; **political system** emergent democracy; **population** (1990 est) 54,890,000 (Thai 75%, Chinese 14%); **language** Thai and Chinese (both official); regional dialects; **recent history** Anglo-French agreement in 1896 recognized Siam as an independent buffer state. In 1932 a constitutional monarchy was established, and the name of Thailand adopted in 1939. The Japanese occupied the country 1941–44. The military seized power in a coup in 1947, were overthrown in 1973, and reassumed control in 1976. A civilian government was formed in 1983 but martial law was maintained.

Thaïs /'θeɪɪs/ Greek courtesan, mistress of ◊*Alexander the Great* and later wife of ◊*Ptolemy* I, king of Egypt. She allegedly instigated the burning of ◊*Persepolis*.

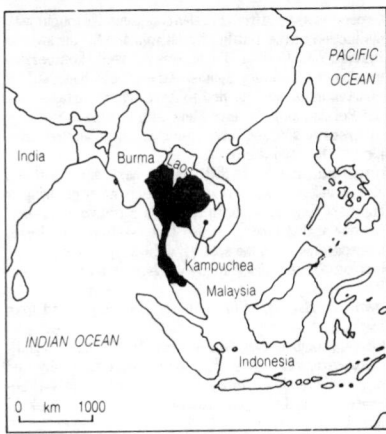

Thailand

thalamus /ˈθæləməs/ *n.* (*plural* **thalami** /-maɪ/) the interior region of the brain where the sensory nerves originate. [Latin from Greek = inner room]

thalassaemia *n.* or **Cooley's anaemia** a chronic hereditary blood disorder that is widespread in the Mediterranean countries and found also in Africa and Asia. It is characterized by an abnormality of the red blood cells and bone marrow, with enlargement of the spleen.

Thalberg /ˈθɔːlbɜːg/ Irving 1899–1936. US film production executive. At the age of 20 he was head of production at Universal Pictures, and in 1924 he became production supervisor of the newly formed Metro-Goldwyn-Mayer, (MGM). He was responsible for such prestige films as *Ben-Hur* 1926 and *Mutiny on the Bounty* 1935. With Louis B Mayer he built up MGM into one of the biggest Hollywood studios of the 1930s.

Thales /ˈθeɪliːz/ 640–546 BC. Greek philosopher and scientist. He made advances in geometry, predicted an eclipse of the Sun in 585 BC, and, as a philosophical materialist, theorized that water was the first principle of all things, that the Earth floated on water, and so proposed an explanation for earthquakes. He lived in Miletus in Asia Minor.

thalidomide /θəˈlɪdəmaɪd/ *n.* a ◊hypnotic drug developed in the 1950s for use as a sedative. When taken in early pregnancy, it caused malformation of the fetus (such as abnormalities in the limbs) in over 5,000 recognized cases, and the drug was withdrawn. [from ph*thalimidoglutarimide*]

thallium /ˈθæliəm/ *n.* a soft, bluish-white, malleable, metallic element, symbol Tl, atomic number 81, relative atomic mass 204.37. It is a poor conductor of electricity. Its compounds are poisonous and are used as insecticides and rodent poisons; some are used in the optical-glass and infrared-glass industries and in photoelectric cells. It was discovered and isolated by Crookes 1861, and by Lamy 1862. [from Greek *thallos* = green shoot (from the green line in its spectrum)]

thallius *n.* any plant body that is not divided into true leaves, stems, and roots. It is often thin and flattened, as in the body of a seaweed, lichen, or liverwort, and the gametophyte generation (◊prothallus) of a fern.

Thames /temz/ river in S England; length 338 km/210 mi. It rises in the Cotswolds above Cirencester and is tidal as far as Teddington. Below London there is protection from flooding by means of the Thames barrier. The headstreams unite at Lechlade. Tributaries from the north are the Windrush, Evenlode, Cherwell, Thame, Colne, Lea, and Roding; and from the south, Kennet, Loddon, Wey, Mole, Darent, and Medway. Above Oxford it is sometimes poetically called **Isis**.

Thames barrier a moveable barrier built across the river Thames at Woolwich, London, as part of the city's flood defences. Completed in 1982, the barrier comprises curved flood gates which are rotated 90° into position from beneath the water to form a barrier when exceptionally high tides are expected.

Thames Tunnel a tunnel extending 1,200 ft under the river Thames, London, linking Rotherhithe with Wapping. The first underwater tunnel in the world, it was designed by Marc Isambard Brunel, and completed in 1843. Originally intended as a road tunnel, lack of funds meant that it remained a foot tunnel until the 1860s, when it was converted into a railway tunnel for the East London Railway. Today it carries underground trains.

than /ðən, *emphatic* ðæn/ *conj.* introducing the second element in a comparison (*you are taller than he* (*is*); *we like you better than* (*her*), or a statement of difference (*anyone other than me*). [Old English, originally = *then*]

thane *n.* or **thegn** 1. (in Anglo-Saxon England) one who held land from the king or other superior in return for performing military service. 2. (in Scotland until the 15th century) one who held land from a Scottish king and ranked below an earl, a clan chief. [Old English = servant, soldier]

thank *v.t.* 1. to express gratitude to. 2. to hold responsible. —*n.* (in *plural*) gratitude, an expression of gratitude; (as a formula) thank you. —**thank goodness** *or* **heavens** etc., (*colloquial*) expressions of relief etc. **thank you,** a polite formula acknowledging a gift or service etc. [Old English]

thankful *adj.* feeling or expressing gratitude. —**thankfully** *adv.*, **thankfulness** *n.*

thankless *adj.* not likely to win thanks, giving no pleasure or profit. —**thanklessly** *adv.*, **thanklessness** *n.*

thanksgiving *n.* the expression of gratitude, especially to God. —**Thanksgiving (Day),** an annual holiday for giving thanks to God, the fourth Thur in Nov in the USA, usually the second Mon in Oct in Canada. It was first celebrated by the Pilgrim settlers in Massachusetts on their first harvest in 1621.

that /ðət, *emphatic* ðæt/ *pron.* (*plural* **those** /ðəʊz/) 1. the person or thing indicated, named, or understood. 2. the further or less obvious one of two (as opposed to *this*). 3. (as *relative pron.*) used instead of *which* or *who* to introduce a defining clause. —*adj.* (*plural* **those**) designating the person or thing indicated etc. —*adv.* to that degree or extent, so. —*conj.* introducing a dependent clause, especially a statement or hypothesis, purpose, or result. —**all that,** very. **that's that,** that is settled or finished. [Old English]

thatch *n.* 1. roofing of straw, or reeds, or similar material. 2. (*colloquial*) the hair of the head. —*v.t.* to roof with thatch. —**thatcher** *n.* [Old English from Old High German *dach* = roof]

Thatcher /ˈθætʃə/ Margaret Hilda (born Roberts) 1925–   . English Conservative politician, prime minister 1979–1990. She was education minister 1970–74, and Conservative party leader from 1975. In 1982 she sent British troops to recapture the Falkland Islands from Argentina. She confronted trade union power during the miners' strike 1984–85, sold off majority stakes in many public utilities to the private sector, and reduced the influence of local government through such measures as the abolition of metropolitan councils, the control of expenditure through 'rate-capping', and the introduction of the community charge or ◊poll tax from 1989. She was one of the most active opponents of the Iraqi invasion of Kuwait in 1990. In 1990 splits in the cabinet over the issues of Europe and consensus government forced her resignation. An astute Parliamentary tactician, she tolerated little disagreement, either from the opposition or from within her own party.

To those waiting with bated breath for that favourite media catch-phrase, the U-turn, I have only one thing to say. You turn if you want to. The lady's not for turning.

Margaret Hilda Thatcher
speech to the Conservative Party Conference, 1980

---

thaumatrope *n.* in photography, a disc with two different pictures at opposite ends of its surface. The images combine into one when rapidly rotated because of the persistence of visual impressions.

thaw *v.t./i.* 1. to pass into a liquid or unfrozen state after being frozen. 2. to become warm enough to melt ice etc. or to lose numbness. 3. to become less cool or less formal in manner. 4. to cause to thaw. —*n.* thawing; warmth of weather that thaws ice etc. [Old English]

the /before a vowel ðɪ; before a consonant ðə; emphatic ðiː/ —adj. serving to particularize as needing no further identification (have you seen the newspaper?), to describe as unique (the Queen; the Thames), to assist in defining with an adjective (Alfred the Great) or (stressed) distinguish as the best-known (do you mean the Kipling?), to indicate a following defining clause or phrase (the horse you mention); to confer generic or representative or distributive value on (diseases of the eye; the stage; 5p in the pound); or to precede an adjective used absolute (nothing but the best). —adv. (preceding comparatives in expressions of proportional variation) in or by that (or such) degree, on that account (the more the merrier; am not the more inclined to help him because he is poor). [Old English]

theatre /'θɪətə/ n. 1. a building or outdoor area for the performance of plays and similar entertainments. The first known European theatres were in Greece from about 600 BC. Historic London theatres include the Haymarket (1720, rebuilt 1821), Drury Lane (1663), and Her Majesty's (1705), both rebuilt several times. The English Stage Company was established at the Royal Court Theatre 1956 to provide a platform for new works. 2. performance by actors for an audience; it may include ◊drama, dancing, music, ◊mime, and ◊puppets. Theatre history can be traced to Egyptian religious ritualistic drama as long ago as 3200 BC. 3. the writing and production of plays. 4. a room or hall for lectures etc. with seats in tiers. 5. an operating theatre. —theatre-in-the-round n. a form of play presentation in which the audience is seated all round the acting area. theatre weapons, weapons intermediate between tactical and strategic (see ◊strategic). [from Old French or Latin from Greek theatron (theaomai = behold)]

theatrical /θɪˈætrɪkəl/ adj. 1. of or for the theatre or acting. 2. (of a person or manner etc.) calculated for effect, showy. — n. (in plural) dramatic performances (especially amateur) or behaviour —theatricality /-ˈkælɪtɪ/ n., theatrically adv. [from Latin from Greek]

Thebes /θiːbz/ capital of Boeotia in ancient Greece. In the Peloponnesian War it was allied with Sparta against Athens. For a short time after 371 BC when Thebes defeated Sparta at Leuctra, it was the most powerful state in Greece. Alexander the Great destroyed it in 336 BC and although it was restored, it never regained its former power.

Thebes Greek name of an ancient city (**Niut-Ammon**) in Upper Egypt, on the Nile. Probably founded under the first dynasty, it was the centre of the worship of Ammon, and the Egyptian capital under the New Kingdom in about 1600 BC. Temple ruins survive near the villages of Karnak and Luxor, and in the nearby **Valley of the Kings** are buried the 18th–20th dynasty kings, including Tutankhamen and Amenhotep III.

thee /ðiː/ pron. the objective case of **thou**.

theft n. stealing; an act or instance of this. In Britain, under the Theft Act 1968, the maximum penalty is ten years' imprisonment. The act placed under a single heading forms of theft that had formerly been dealt with individually, for example burglary and larceny. [Old English]

thegn alternative spelling of ◊thane.

their /ðeə/ poss. adj. of or belonging to them. [from Old Norse]

theirs /ðeəz/ poss. pron. of or belonging to them; the thing(s) belonging to them.

theism /'θiːɪzəm/ n. belief in the existence of gods or a god, especially a God supernaturally revealed to man (deism denies such revelation) and maintaining a personal relation to his creatures. —theist n., theistic /-ˈɪstɪk/ adj. [from Greek theos = god]

them /ðəm, emphatic ðem/ pron. the objective case of they; (colloquial) they. —adj. (vulgar) those. [from Old Norse]

theme /θiːm/ n. 1. the subject or topic of talk, writing, or thought. 2. in music, a basic melody or musical figure, which often occurs with variations. 3. (US) a school exercise on a given subject. —theme song or tune, a recurrent melody in a musical play or film; a signature tune. —thematic /θɪˈmætɪk/ adj., thematically /θɪˈmætɪkəlɪ/ adv. [from Latin from Greek thema (tithēmi = place)]

Themistocles /θəˈmɪstəkliːz/ c.525–c.460 BC. Athenian soldier and politician. Largely through his policies in Athens (creating its navy and strengthening its walls)

Greece was saved from Persian conquest. He fought with distinction in the Battle of ◊Salamis 480 BC during the Persian War. In about 470 he was accused of embezzlement and conspiracy against Athens, and banished by Spartan influence. He fled to Asia, where Artaxerxes, the Persian king, received him with favour.

themselves /ðəmˈselvz/ pron. emphatic and reflexive form of **they** and **them**.

then /ðen/ adv. 1. at that time. 2. next, after that, and also. 3. in that case, therefore. 4. used to imply grudging or impatient concession, or to resume a narrative etc. —adj. existing at that time. —n. that time. —then and there, immediately and on the spot. [Old English]

thence /ðens/ adv. 1. from that place. 2. for that reason. [Old English]

thenceforth /ðensˈfɔθ/ adv. or thenceforward from that time on.

theo- in combinations, God or a god. [Greek theos = god]

theocracy /θɪˈɒkrəsɪ/ n. a form of government by God or a god directly or through a priestly order etc. —theocratic /θɪəˈkrætɪk/ adj., theocratically /θɪəˈkrætɪkəlɪ/ adv. [from Greek]

Theocritus /θɪˈɒkrɪtəs/ c.310–c.250 BC. Greek poet whose Idylls became models for later pastoral poetry. Probably born in Syracuse, he spent much of his life in Alexandria.

theodolite /θɪˈɒdəlaɪt/ n. an instrument for the measurement of horizontal and vertical angles, used in surveying. It consists of a small telescope mounted so as to move on two graduated circles, one horizontal and the other vertical, while its axes pass through the centre of the circles. See also ◊triangulation.

Theodora /θiːəˈdɔːrə/ 508–548. Byzantine empress from 527. She was originally the mistress of Emperor Justinian before marrying him in 525. She earned a reputation for charity, courage, and championing the rights of women.

Theodorakis /θɪədəˈrɑːkɪs/ Mikis 1925– . Greek composer. He was imprisoned 1967–70 for attempting to overthrow the military regime of Greece.

Theodoric the Great /θɪˈɒdərɪk/ c.455–526. King of the Ostrogoths from 474 in succession to his father. He invaded Italy in 488, overthrew King Odoacer (whom he murdered) and established his own Ostrogothic kingdom there, with its capital in Ravenna. He had no strong successor, and his kingdom eventually became part of the Byzantine Empire of Justinian.

theogony /θɪˈɒgənɪ/ n. the genealogy of the gods; an account of this. [Greek theos = god and -gonia = begetting]

theologian /θɪəˈlɒdʒɪən/ n. an expert in theology.

theology /θɪˈɒlədʒɪ/ n. the study or system of (especially the Christian) religion, either by reasoned deduction from the natural world or through revelation, as in the scriptures. —theological /θɪəˈlɒdʒɪkəl/ adj., theologically adv. [from Old French from Latin from Greek]

Theophanes the Greek 14th century. Byzantine painter active in Russia. He influenced painting in Novgorod, where his frescoes in Our Saviour of the Transfiguration are dated to 1378.

theorbo n. a long-necked ◊lute that has additional strings.

theorem /'θɪərəm/ n. 1. a general proposition not self-evident but demonstrable by argument, especially in mathematics. 2. a rule in algebra etc., especially one expressed by symbols or formulae. [from French or Latin from Greek theōreō = behold]

theoretical /θɪəˈretɪkəl/ adj. 1. concerned with knowledge but not with its practical application. 2. based on theory rather than experience. —theoretically adv.

theoretician /θɪərɪˈtɪʃən/ n. a person concerned with the theoretical part of a subject.

theorist /'θɪərɪst/ n. a holder or inventor of a theory.

theorize /'θɪəraɪz/ v.i. to evolve or indulge in theories.

theory /'θɪərɪ/ n. 1. a system of ideas formulated (by reasoning from known facts) to explain something. 2. an opinion, a supposition; ideas or suppositions in general (as opposed to practice). 3. an exposition of the principles on which a subject is based. [from Latin from Greek theōreō = behold]

theosophy /θɪˈɒsəfɪ/ n. any of various philosophies professing to achieve a knowledge of God by spiritual ecstasy, direct intuition, or special individual relations, especially that of the Theosophical Society, founded in New York in 1875 by Madame Blavatsky and H S Olcott. It was based on Hindu ideas of ◊karma and ◊reincarnation, with ◊nirvana as the eventual aim. —**theosophist** *n.*, **theosophical** /-ə'spfɪkəl/ *adj.* [from Latin from Greek = wise concerning God]

therapeutic /θerə'pjuːtɪk/ *adj.* of, for, or contributing to the cure of a disease. —**therapeutically** *adv.* [from French or Latin from Greek *therapeuō* = wait on, cure]

therapeutics *n.pl.* (usually treated as *singular*) the branch of medicine concerned with the treatment and remedying of ill health.

therapy /'θerəpɪ/ *n.* 1. curative medical treatment. 2. physiotherapy, psychotherapy. —**therapist** *n.* [from Greek *therapeia* = healing]

Theravāda /θerə'vɑːdə/ *n.* one of the two major forms of ◊Buddhism, common in S Asia (Sri Lanka, Thailand, Cambodia, and Myanmar); the other is the later Mahāyāna.

there /ðeə/ *adv.* 1. in, at, or to that place or position; at that point (in a speech, performance, writing, etc.); in that respect; used for emphasis in calling attention. 2. used as an introductory word, usually with the verb *to be*, in a sentence where the verb precedes its subject, indicating a fact or the existence of something. —*n.* that place. —interjection expressing confirmation, satisfaction, reassurance, etc. [Old English]

thereabouts /'ðeərəbaʊts/ *adv.* or **thereabout** near that place; near that number, quantity, time, etc.

thereafter /ðeər'ɑːftə/ *adv.* (*formal*) after that.

thereby /ðeə'baɪ, 'ðeə-/ *adv.* by that means, as a result of that. —**thereby hangs a tale**, much could be said about that.

therefore /'ðeəfɔ/ *adv.* for that reason.

therein /ðeər'ɪn/ *adv.* (*formal*) in that place etc.; in that respect.

thereof /ðeər'ɒv/ *adv.* (*formal*) of that or it.

Theresa /tə'reɪzə/ Mother. Born Agnes Bojaxhiu 1910– . Roman Catholic nun. She was born in Skopje, Albania, and at 18 entered a Calcutta convent and became a teacher. In 1948 she became an Indian citizen and founded the Missionaries of Charity, an order for men and women based in Calcutta that helps abandoned children and the dying. Nobel Peace Prize 1979.

Thérèse of Lisieux, St /tə'reɪz, liː'sjɜː/ 1873–1897. French saint. She was born in Alençon, and entered a Carmelite convent in Lisieux at 15, where her holy life induced her superior to ask her to write her spiritual autobiography. She advocated the 'Little Way of Goodness' in small things in everyday life, and became known as the 'Little Flower of Jesus'. She died of tuberculosis and was canonized in 1925.

thereto /ðeə'tuː/ *adv.* (*formal*) to that or it; in addition.

thereupon /ðeərə'pɒn/ *adv.* in consequence of that; soon or immediately after that.

therm *n.* a unit of heat, in Britain especially the statutory unit of calorific value in a gas-supply (100,000 British thermal units); equivalent to 1.055×10^8 joules. It is no longer in scientific use. [from Greek *thermē* = heat]

thermal *adj.* of, for, or producing heat. —*n.* a rising current of heated air, used by gliders to gain height. **thermal unit**, a unit for measuring heat (**British thermal unit**, the amount of heat needed to raise 1 lb of water 1°F). —**thermally** *adv.* [French]

thermal capacity the heat energy, C, required to increase the temperature of an object by one degree. It is measured in joules per degree, $J/°C$ or J/K. If an object has mass m and is made of a substance with ◊specific heat capacity c, then $C = mc$.

thermal conductivity in physics, the ability of a substance to conduct heat. Good thermal conductors, like good electrical conductors, are generally materials with many free electrons (such as metals).

thermal expansion in physics, expansion that is due to a rise in temperature. It can be expressed in terms of linear, area, or volume expansion.

thermic lance a cutting tool consisting of a tube of mild steel, enclosing tightly packed small steel rods and fed with oxygen. On ignition temperatures above 3,000°C are produced and the thermic lance becomes its own sustaining fuel. It rapidly penetrates walls and a 23 cm/9 in steel door can be cut through in less than 30 seconds.

Thermidor *n.* the 11th month of the French Revolutionary calendar, which gave its name to the period after the fall of the Jacobins and the proscription of ◊Robespierre by the National Convention on 9 Thermidor 1794.

thermionics /θɜːmi'ɒnɪk/ *n.pl.* the branch of electronics dealing with the emission of electrons from matter under the influence of heat. [from *thermo-* and *ion*, named by O W Richardson]

thermionic valve a device consisting of a sealed tube containing two or more electrodes, one of which is heated to produce a flow of electrons in one direction. In most applications valves have been replaced by ◊transistors.

thermistor *n.* a device whose electrical ◊resistance falls as temperature rises. The current passing through a thermistor increases rapidly as its temperature rises, and so they are used in electrical thermometers.

thermite process a method used in incendiary devices and welding operations. It uses a powdered mixture of aluminium and (usually) iron oxide, which, when ignited, gives out enormous heat. The oxide is reduced to iron, which is molten at the high temperatures produced. This can be used to make a weld. The process was discovered in 1895 by German chemist Hans Goldschmidt (1861–1923).

thermo- /θɜːməʊ-/ in combinations, heat. [Greek *thermos* = hot and *thermē* = heat]

thermocouple /'θɜːməʊkʌpəl/ *n.* a device for measuring temperatures by means of the thermoelectric voltage developing between two pieces of wire of different metals joined to each other at each end. A current flows in the circuit when the two junctions are maintained at different temperatures (◊Seebeck effect). The electromotive force generated—measured by a millivoltmeter—is proportional to the temperature difference.

thermodynamics /θɜːməʊdaɪ'næmɪks/ *n.pl.* (usually treated as *singular*) the branch of physics dealing with the transformation of heat into and from other forms of energy. It is the basis of the study of the efficient working of engines, such as the steam and internal combustion engines. The three laws of thermodynamics are (1) energy can be neither created nor destroyed, heat and mechanical work being mutually convertible; (2) it is impossible for an unaided self-acting machine to convey heat from one body to another at a higher temperature; and (3) it is impossible by any procedure, no matter how idealized, to reduce any system to the ◊absolute zero of temperature (0K/–273°C) in a finite number of operations. —**thermodynamic** *adj.*, **thermodynamical** *adj.*, **thermodynamically** *adv.*

thermoelectric /θɜːməʊi'lektrɪk/ *adj.* producing electricity by difference of temperatures.

thermography *n.* the photographic recording of heat patterns. It is used medically as an imaging technique to identify 'hot spots' in the body—for example, tumours, where cells are more active than usual.

thermoluminescence *n.* the light released by a material that is heated after being exposed to ◊irradiation. It occurs with most crystalline substances to some extent. It is used in archaeology to date pottery, and by geologists in studying terrestrial rocks and meteorites.

thermometer /θə'mɒmɪtə/ *n.* an instrument for measuring temperature by means of a substance whose expansion and contraction under different degrees of heat and cold are capable of accurate measurement. There are many types, designed to measure different temperature ranges to varying degrees of accuracy. Each makes use of a different physical effect of temperature. Expansion of a liquid is employed in common **liquid-in-glass thermometers**, such as those containing mercury or alcohol. The more accurate **gas thermometer** uses the effect of temperature on the pressure of a gas held at constant volume. A **resistance thermometer** takes advantage of the change in resistance of a conductor (such as a platinum wire) with variation in temperature. Another electrical thermometer is the ◊thermocouple. Mechanically, temperature change can be indicated by the change in curvature of a **bimetallic strip** (as commonly used in a ◊thermostat). [from French]

thermonuclear /θɜːməʊ'njuːkliə/ *adj.* relating to nuclear reactions that occur only at very high temperatures; (of a bomb etc.) using such reactions.

thermoplastic /θɜːməʊ'plæstɪk/ *adj.* becoming plastic on heating and hardening on cooling. —*n.* a thermoplastic substance.

thermometer

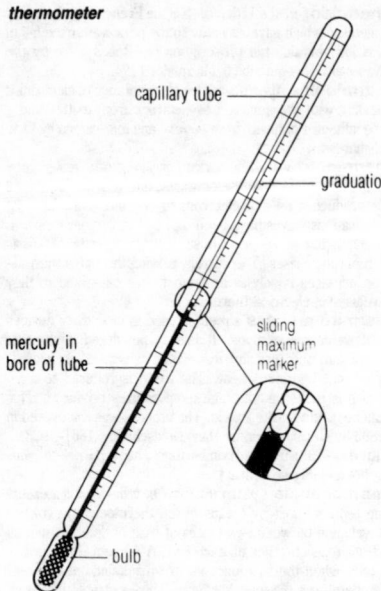

capillary tube

graduation

mercury in bore of tube

sliding maximum marker

bulb

Thermopylae, Battle of /θɜːˈmɒpɪliː/ a battle during the ◊Persian wars in 480 BC when Leonidas, king of Sparta, and 1,000 men defended the pass of Thermopylae to the death against a much greater force of Persians. The pass led from Thessaly to Locris in central Greece.

Thermos /ˈθɜːmɒs/ *n.* trade name of a kind of ◊vacuum flask. [from Greek *thermos* = hot]

thermosetting /θɜːməʊˈsetɪŋ/ *adj.* (of plastics) setting permanently when heated.

thermosphere /ˈθɜːməsfɪə/ *n.* the layer in the Earth's ◊atmosphere above the mesosphere and below the exosphere. Its lower level is about 80 km/50 mi above the ground, but its upper level is undefined. The ionosphere is located in the thermosphere. In the thermosphere the temperature rises with increasing height to several thousand degrees Celsius. However, because of the thinness of the air, very little heat is actually present.

thermostat /ˈθɜːməstæt/ *n.* a device for the automatic regulation of temperature. It employs a temperature sensor (often a bimetallic strip) to operate a switch or valve to control electricity or fuel supply. Thermostats are used in central heating, ovens, and car engines. —**thermostatic** /-ˈstætɪk/ *adj.*, **thermostatically** /-ˈstætɪkəlɪ/ *adv.* [Greek *statos* = standing]

thesaurus /θɪˈsɔːrəs/ *n.* (*plural* **thesauri** /-raɪ/) a collection of synonyms or words with related meaning. Thesaurus compilers include ◊Pliny, Francis ◊Bacon, Comenius (1592–1670), and Peter Mark ◊Roget, whose work was published in 1852. [Latin from Greek = treasury]

these plural of **this**.

Theseus legendary hero of ◊Attica, supposed to have united the states of the area under a constitutional government in Athens. Ariadne, whom he later abandoned on Naxos, helped him find his way through the labyrinth to kill the ◊Minotaur. He also fought the Amazons and was one of the ◊Argonauts.

thesis /ˈθiːsɪs/ *n.* (*plural* **theses** /-siːz/) 1. a proposition to be maintained or proved. 2. a dissertation, especially by a candidate for a degree. [Latin from Greek = putting]

Thespian /ˈθespɪən/ *adj.* of tragedy or the drama. —*n.* an actor or actress. [from *Thespis*]

Thespis /ˈθespɪs/ 6th century BC. Greek dramatic poet, born in Attica, said to have introduced the first actor into plays (previously presented by choruses only). He was also said to have invented tragedy and to have introduced the wearing of linen masks.

Thessaloniki /θesəlɒˈniːkiː/ (English **Salonika**) port in Macedonia, NE Greece, at the head of the Gulf of Thessaloniki, the second largest city of Greece; population

(1981) 706,200. Industries include textiles, shipbuilding, chemicals, brewing, and tanning. It was founded from Corinth by the Romans in 315 BC as **Thessalonica** (to whose inhabitants St Paul addressed two epistles), captured by the Saracens in AD 904 and by the Turks in 1430, and restored to Greece in 1912.

Thessaly /ˈθesəliː/ (Greek *Thessalia*) region of E central Greece, on the Aegean; **area** 13,904 sq km/5,367 sq mi; **population** (1981) 695,650. It is a major area of cereal production. It was an independent state in ancient Greece and later formed part of the Roman province of ◊Macedonia. It was Turkish from the 14th century until incorporated in Greece in 1881.

theta /ˈθiːtə/ *n.* the eighth letter of the Greek alphabet, (θ, Θ) = th. [Greek]

Thetford /ˈθetfəd/ market town in Norfolk, England; **population** (1982) 19,000. It is the birthplace of Thomas Paine.

Thetford Mines site of the world's largest asbestos deposits, 80 km/50 mi south of Québec, Canada. It was discovered in 1876.

thews /θjuːz/ *n.pl.* (*literary*) a person's muscular strength. [Old English = usage, conduct]

they /ðeɪ/ *pron.* (*objective* **them**; *possessive* **their, theirs**) plural of **he, she, it**[1]; people in general; those in authority. [from Old Norse]

thiamine *n.* or **vitamin B₁** vitamin of the B complex. Its absence from the diet causes the disease beriberi.

Thibault /tiːˈbəʊ/ Anatole-François. Real name of French writer Anatole ◊France.

thick *adj.* 1. of great or specified distance in diameter or between opposite surfaces; (of a line etc.) broad, not fine. 2. arranged closely, crowded together, dense; densely covered or filled; firm in consistency, containing much solid matter; made of thick material; muddy, cloudy, impenetrable by the sight. 3. (*colloquial*) stupid, dull. 4. (of the voice) indistinct. 5. (*colloquial*) intimate, very friendly. —*n.* the thick part of anything. —*adv.* thickly. —**a bit thick**, (*slang*) unreasonable, intolerable. **in the thick of it**, in the busiest part of an activity or fight etc. **thick-headed** *adj.* stupid. **thick-skinned** *adj.* not sensitive to reproach or criticism. **through thick and thin**, under all conditions, in spite of all difficulties. —**thickly** *adv.* [Old English]

thicken *v.t./i.* 1. to make or become thick or thicker. 2. to become more complicated. —**thickener** *n.*

thicket /ˈθɪkɪt/ *n.* a tangle of shrubs or trees. [Old English]

thickness *n.* 1. being thick; the extent to which a thing is thick. 2. a layer of material of known thickness. 3. the part between opposite surfaces.

thickset *adj.* 1. set or growing closely together. 2. having a stocky or burly body.

thief *n.* (*plural* **thieves** /θiːvz/) one who steals, especially stealthily and without violence. [Old English]

Thiers /tiˈeə/ Louis Adolphe 1797–1877. French politician and historian, first president of the Third Republic 1871–73. He held cabinet posts under Louis Philippe, led the parliamentary opposition to Napoleon III from 1863, and as head of the provisional government in 1871 negotiated peace with Prussia and suppressed the briefly autonomous ◊Paris Commune. His books include *Histoire de la Révolution française/History of the French Revolution* 1823–27.

thieve *v.t./i.* to be a thief; to steal. [Old English]

thievery *n.* stealing.

thievish *adj.* given to stealing.

thigh /θaɪ/ *n.* the part of the leg between the hip and the knee. [Old English]

thimble *n.* a metal or plastic cap, usually with a closed end, worn on the end of the finger to protect the finger-tip and push the needle in sewing. [Old English]

thimbleful *n.* (*plural* **thimblefuls**) a small quantity, especially of a liquid to drink.

Thimbu /ˈθɪmbuː/ or **Thimphu** capital since 1962 of the Himalayan state of Bhutan; population (1982) 15,000.

thin *adj.* 1. having the opposite surfaces close together, of small thickness. 2. (of a line) narrow, not broad. 3. made of thin material. 4. lean, not plump. 5. not dense or copious; not of thick consistency, (of liquid) flowing easily. 6. lacking strength or substance or an important ingredient; (of an excuse etc.) feeble, transparent. —*adv.* thinly. —*v.t./i.* to make or become thin or thinner. —**have a thin time**, (*slang*) to have a wretched or uncomfortable time. **thin on the ground**, few in number, rare. **thin on top**, balding.

thin out, to make or become fewer or less crowded. **thin-skinned** *adj.* sensitive to reproach or criticism. —**thinly** *adv.*, **thinness** *n.* [Old English]

thine /ðaɪn/ *poss. pron.* (*archaic*) of or belonging to thee; the thing(s) belonging to thee. —*poss. adj.* (*archaic*) the form of **thy** before a vowel. [Old English]

thing[1] *n.* **1.** whatever is or may be thought about or perceived. **2.** an inanimate object as distinct from a living creature. **3.** an unspecified object or item. **4.** (expressing pity, contempt, or affection) a creature. **5.** an act, fact, idea, quality, task, etc. **6.** a specimen or type of something. **7.** (*colloquial*) something remarkable. **8.** (in *plural*) personal belongings, clothing; implement, utensils. **9.** (in *plural*) affairs in general; circumstances, conditions. —**the thing,** what is conventionally proper or fashionable, what is needed or required, what is most important. **do one's own thing,** (*colloquial*) to pursue one's own interests or inclinations. **have a thing about,** (*colloquial*) to be obsessed or prejudiced about. **make a thing of,** to regard as essential; to cause a fuss about. [Old English]

thing[2] *n.* an assembly of freemen in the Norse lands (Scandinavia) during the medieval period. It could encompass a meeting of the whole nation (*Althing*) or of a small town or community (*Husthing*).

thingummy /'θɪŋəmɪ/ *n.* (also **thingumajig** etc.) (*colloquial*) a person or thing whose name one has forgotten or does not know. [from *thing*[1], with meaningless suffix]

think *v.t./i.* (*past* and *past participle* **thought** /θɔt/) **1.** to exercise the mind in an active way, to form connected ideas. **2.** to have as an idea or opinion. **3.** to form as an intention or plan. **4.** to take into consideration. **5.** to call to mind, to remember. —*n.* (*colloquial*) an act of thinking. —**think again,** to revise one's plans or opinions. **think aloud,** to utter one's thoughts as soon as they occur. **think better of,** to change one's mind about (an intention) after reconsideration. **think little** *or* **nothing of,** to consider insignificant. **think much** *or* **well** *or* **highly** etc. **of,** to have a high opinion of. **think out,** to consider carefully; to produce (an idea etc.) by thinking. **think over,** to reflect upon in order to reach a decision. **think through,** to reflect fully upon (a problem etc.). **think twice,** to use careful consideration, to avoid a hasty action etc. **think up,** (*colloquial*) to devise, to produce by thought. [Old English]

thinker *n.* one who thinks, especially in a specified way; a person with a skilled or powerful mind.

thinking *adj.* using thought or rational judgement. —*n.* opinion or judgement.

think-tank *n.* the popular name for research foundations, generally private, that gather experts to study policy questions and make recommendations. There are think-tanks representing positions across the political spectrum, and they are sometimes funded according to the viewpoints they represent.

thinner *n.* a volatile liquid used to make paint etc. thinner.

thiosulphate /θaɪə'sʌlfeɪt/ *n.* a sulphate in which some oxygen is replaced by sulphur. [from Greek *theion* = sulphur]

third *adj. & n.* **1.** next after second. **2.** each of three equal parts of a thing. —**third degree,** a long and severe questioning, especially by the police to obtain information or a confession. **third man,** a fielder in cricket near the boundary behind the slips. **third party,** another party besides the two principals; a bystander etc. **third party** *adj.* (of insurance) covering damage or injury suffered by a person other than the insured. **third person,** a third party; in grammar, see ◊person. **third-rate** *adj.* inferior, very poor. —**thirdly** *adv.* [Old English]

Third Reich a term used by the Nazis to describe Germany during the years of Hitler's dictatorship after 1933. [German *Reich* = Empire

Third World a term originally applied collectively to those countries of Africa, Asia, and Latin America that were not aligned with either the Western bloc (First World) or Communist bloc (Second World). The term later took on economic connotations and was applied to those 120 countries that were underdeveloped, as compared to the industrialized free-market countries of the West and the industrialized Communist countries. Third World countries are the poorest, as measured by their income per capita, and are concentrated in Asia, Africa, and Latin America. They are divided into low-income countries, including China and

India; middle-income countries, such as Nigeria, Indonesia, and Bolivia; and upper-middle-income countries, such as Brazil, Algeria, and Malaysia.

thirst *n.* **1.** the feeling caused by a desire or need to drink. **2.** a strong desire. —*v.i.* to feel a thirst. [Old English]

thirsty *adj.* **1.** feeling thirst. **2.** (of a country or season) in need of water, dry. **3.** eager. **4.** (*colloquial*) causing thirst. —**thirstily** *adv.*, **thirstiness** *n.* [Old English]

thirteen /θɜː'tiːn/ *adj. & n.* **1.** one more than 12; the symbol for this (13, xiii, XIII). **2.** the size etc. denoted by 13. —**thirteenth** *adj. & n.* [Old English]

Thirteen Colonies the 13 American colonies that signed the ◊Declaration of Independence from Britain in 1776. Led by George Washington, the Continental Army defeated the British army in the ◊American Revolution 1776–81 to become the original 13 United States of America: Connecticut, Delaware, Georgia, Maryland, Massachusetts, New Hampshire, New Jersey, New York, North Carolina, Pennsylvania, Rhode Island, South Carolina, and Virginia. They were united first under the ◊Articles of Confederation and from 1789, the US ◊constitution.

thirty /'θɜːtɪ/ *adj. & n.* **1.** three times ten; the symbol for this (30, xxx, XXX). **2.** (in *plural*) the numbers, years, or degrees of temperature from 30 to 39. —**thirtieth** *adj. & n.* [Old English]

35 mm a width of photographic film, the most popular format for the camera today. The 35-mm camera falls into two categories, the ◊SLR and the ◊rangefinder.

38th parallel the demarcation line between North (People's Democratic Republic of) and South (Republic of) Korea, agreed at the Yalta Conference in 1945 and largely unaltered by the Korean War of 1950–53.

Thirty-Nine Articles a set of articles of faith defining the doctrine of the Anglican Church; see under ◊Anglican Communion.

Thirty Years' War a major war 1618–48 in central Europe. Beginning as a German conflict between Protestants and Catholics, it gradually became transformed into a struggle to determine whether the ruling Austrian Habsburg family would gain control of all Germany. The war caused serious economic and demographic problems in central Europe.

this /ðɪs/ *pron.* (*plural* **these** /ðiːz/) **1.** the person or thing close at hand or indicated or already named or understood. **2.** the nearer or more obvious one of two (as opposed to *that*). **3.** the present day or time. —*adj.* (*plural* **these**) designating the person or thing close at hand etc. —*adv.* to this degree or extent. —**this and that,** various things. [Old English]

thistle /'θɪsəl/ *n.* a species of prickly plant of several genera, such as *Carduus* and *Cirsium*, in the family Compositae, found in the northern hemisphere. The stems are spiny, the flower heads purple, white, or yellow and cottony, and the leaves deeply indented with prickly margins. The thistle is the Scottish national emblem. [Old English]

Thistle, Order of the a Scottish order of ◊knighthood.

thistledown *n.* light fluffy stuff containing thistle seeds and blown about in the wind.

thistly *adj.* overgrown with thistles.

thither /'ðɪðə/ *adv.* (*archaic*) to or towards that place. [Old English]

thixotropy /θɪk'sɒtrəpɪ/ *n.* the property of becoming temporarily liquid when shaken, stirred, etc., and returning to a gel state on standing. —**thixotropic** /-ə'trɒpɪk/ *adj.* [from Greek *thixis* = touching and *tropē* = turning]

thole *n.* (in full **tholepin**) a pin in the gunwale of a boat as a fulcrum for an oar; each of two such pins forming a rowlock. [Old English from Old Norse *thollr* = fir tree, peg]

Thomas /'tɒməs/ Dylan (Marlais) 1914–1953. Welsh poet. His poems include the celebration of his 30th birthday 'Poem in October' and the evocation of his youth 'Fern Hill' 1946. His radio play *Under Milk Wood* 1954 and the short stories of *Portrait of the Artist as a Young Dog* 1940 are autobiographical.

Thomas Edward (Philip) 1878–1917. English poet, born in London of Welsh parents. He met the US poet Robert Frost and began writing poetry under his influence. Some of his poems were published early in 1917 under the pseudonym Edward Eastaway in *An Anthology of New Verse*. *Poems* was

Thompson *Daley Thompson, decathlon world record-breaker.*

published Oct 1917 after his death in World War I, followed by *Last Poems* 1918.

Thomas à Kempis /ə ˈkempɪs/ 1380–1471. German Augustinian monk who lived at the monastery of Zwolle. He took his name from his birthplace Kempen; his real surname was Hammerken. His *De Imitatio Christi/Imitation of Christ* is probably the most widely known devotional work ever written.

Thomas, St in the New Testament, one of the 12 apostles, said to have preached in S India, hence the ancient churches there were referred to as the 'Christians of St Thomas'. He is not the author of the Gospel of St Thomas, the Gnostic collection of Jesus' sayings.

Thompson /ˈtɒmpsən/ Daley (Francis Morgan) 1958– . English decathlete, who has broken the world record four times since winning the Commonwealth Games decathlon title in 1978. He has won two more Commonwealth titles (1982, 1986), two Olympic gold medals (1980, 1984), three European medals (silver 1978; gold 1982, 1986), and a world title (1983).

Thompson David 1770–1857. Canadian explorer and surveyor who mapped extensive areas of W Canada, including the Columbia River, for the Hudson's Bay Company 1789–1811.

Thompson Flora 1877–1948. English novelist, whose trilogy *Lark Rise to Candleford* 1945 describes Victorian rural life.

Thompson John Taliaferro 1860–1940. US colonel, inventor of the Thompson sub-machine-gun (see ◊machine gun).

Thomson /ˈtɒmsən/ Elihu 1853–1937. US inventor. He founded, with E J Houston, the Thomson–Houston Electric Company in 1882, later merging with the Edison Company to form the General Electric Company. He made advances into the nature of the ◊electric arc and invented the first high-frequency ◊dynamo and ◊transformer.

Thomson George Paget 1892–1975. English physicist. His work on ◊interference phenomena in the scattering of electrons by crystals helped to confirm the wave-like nature of particles. He shared a Nobel prize with C J ◊Davisson in 1937.

Thomson James 1700–1748. Scottish poet, whose descriptive blank verse poem *The Seasons* 1726–30 was a forerunner of the Romantic movement. He also wrote the words of 'Rule, Britannia'.

Thomson J(oseph) J(ohn) 1856–1940. English physicist who discovered the ◊electron. He was responsible for organizing the Cavendish atomic research laboratory at Cambridge University. His work inaugurated the electrical theory of the atom, and his elucidation of positive rays and their application to an analysis of neon led to ◊Aston's discovery of ◊isotopes. He was awarded the Nobel Prize for Physics in 1906.

Thomson Virgil 1896–1989. US composer and critic. His large body of work, characterized by a clarity and simplicity of style, includes operas such as *Four Saints in Three Acts* (libretto by Gertrude Stein) 1934; orchestral, choral, and chamber music; and film scores.

thong *n.* a narrow strip of hide or leather. [Old English]

Thor /θɔː/ in Norse mythology, the god of thunder (his hammer), and represented as a man of enormous strength defending humanity against demons. He was the son of Odin and Freya, and Thursday is named after him.

thorax /ˈθɔːræks/ *n.* (*plural* **thoraces** /-rəsiːz/) in tetrapod vertebrates, the part of the body containing the heart and lungs, and protected by the rib cage; in arthropods, the middle part of the body, between the head and abdomen. —**thoracic** /-ˈræsɪk/ *adj.* [Latin from Greek, originally = cuirass]

Thoreau /ˈθɔːrəʊ/ Henry David 1817–1862. US author and naturalist. His work *Walden, or Life in the Woods* 1854 stimulated the back-to-nature movement, and he completed some 30 volumes based on his daily nature walks. His essay 'Civil Disobedience' 1849, advocating peaceful resistance to unjust laws, had a wide impact.

The mass of men lead lives of quiet desperation.

Henry David Thoreau
Walden

---

thorium /ˈθɔːrɪəm/ *n.* a dark-grey, radioactive, metallic element of the ◊actinide series, symbol Th, atomic number 90, relative atomic mass 232.038. It occurs throughout the world in small quantities in minerals such as thorite and is widely distributed in monzanite beach sands. It is one of three fissile elements (the others are uranium and plutonium), and its longest-lived isotope has a half-life of 1.39×10^{10} years. Thorium is used to strengthen alloys. It was discovered by Jöns Berzelius in 1828 and was named by him. [from *Thor*, Norse god]

thorn *n.* **1.** a stiff sharp-pointed projection on a plant. **2.** a thorn-bearing shrub or tree. —**a thorn in one's flesh** *or* **side,** a constant source of annoyance. [Old English]

thorn apple *or* **jimson weed** an annual plant *Datura stramonium* of the nightshade family, growing to 2 m/ 6 ft in northern temperate and subtropical areas; native to America and naturalized worldwide. It bears white or violet trumpet-shaped flowers and capsulelike fruit that split to release black seeds. All parts of the plant are poisonous. The fruit of the ◊hawthorn is also called thorn apple.

thorny *adj.* **1.** full of thorns. **2.** like a thorn. **3.** (of a subject) hard to handle without offence. —**thornily** *adv.,* **thorniness** *n.* [Old English]

thorough /ˈθʌrə/ *adj.* complete and unqualified, not merely superficial; acting or done with great attention to detail; absolute. —**thoroughly** *adv.,* **thoroughness** *n.* [Old English]

thoroughbred *adj.* bred of pure or pedigree stock. —*n.* a thoroughbred animal, especially a horse. All racehorses are thoroughbreds, and all male thoroughbreds are direct descendants of one of three stallions imported into Britain during the 17th and 18th centuries: the Darley Arabian, Byerley Turk, and Godolphin Barb.

thoroughfare *n.* a road or path open at both ends, especially for traffic.

thoroughgoing *adj.* thorough; extreme.

Thorpe /θɔːp/ Jeremy 1929– . English Liberal politician, leader of the Liberal Party 1967–76.

those plural of **that.**

Thoth /təʊt/ in Egyptian mythology, god of wisdom and learning. He was represented as a scribe with the head of an ◊ibis, the bird sacred to him.

Thothmes /ˈtəʊtmɛs/ four Egyptian kings of the 18th dynasty, including:

Thothmes I king of Egypt 1540–1501 BC. He founded the Egyptian empire in Syria.

Thothmes III king of Egypt about 1500–1446 BC. He extended the empire to the river Euphrates, and conquered Nubia. He was a grandson of Thothmes I.

thou /ðaʊ/ *pron.* of the second person singular (now replaced by **you** except in some formal, liturgical, and poetic uses). [Old English]

though /ðəʊ/ *conj.* despite the fact that; even supposing that; and yet, nevertheless. —*adv.* however, all the same. [from Old Norse]

thought[1] /θɔːt/ *n.* **1.** the process, power, or manner of thinking; the faculty of reason. **2.** the way of thinking associated with a particular time or people etc. **3.** sober reflection, consideration. **4.** an idea or chain of reasoning produced by thinking. **5.** an intention. **6.** (usually in *plural*) what one is thinking, one's opinion. —**a thought,** somewhat. **in thought,** meditating. **thought reader** *n.* a person supposedly able to perceive another's thoughts without their being spoken. [Old English]

thought[2] past and past participle of **think.**

thoughtful *adj.* **1.** thinking deeply; often absorbed in thought. **2.** (of a book or writer etc.) showing signs of careful thought. **3.** showing thought for the needs of others, considerate. —**thoughtfully** *adv.,* **thoughtfulness** *n.*

thoughtless *adj.* careless of consequences or of others' feelings; caused by lack of thought. —**thoughtlessly** *adv.,* **thoughtlessness** *n.*

thousand /ˈθaʊzənd/ *adj.* & *n.* (for plural usage see ◊hundred) **1.** ten hundred; the symbol for this (1,000, m, M) **2.** (in *plural*) very many. —**thousandth** *adj.* & *n.* [Old English]

Thousand and One Nights a collection of Oriental tales, also known as the ◊*Arabian Nights.*

thousandfold *adj.* & *adv.* a thousand times as much or as many; consisting of a thousand parts.

Thrace /θreɪs/ (Greek *Thráki*) ancient empire (6000 BC–AD 300) in the Balkans, SE Europe, formed by parts of modern Greece and Bulgaria. It was held successively by the Greeks, Persians, Macedonians, and Romans.

thrall /θrɔːl/ *n.* (*literary*) **1.** a slave (of or to a person or thing). **2.** slavery. —**thraldom** *n.* [Old English from Old Norse]

thrash *v.t./i.* **1.** to beat severely with a stick or whip. **2.** to defeat thoroughly in a contest. **3.** to thresh (corn etc.). **4.** to act like a flail, to deliver repeated blows; to move violently. —**thrash out,** to discuss to a conclusion. [Old English]

thread /θrɛd/ *n.* **1.** a thin length of any substance. **2.** a length of spun cotton or wool etc. used in weaving or in sewing or knitting. **3.** anything regarded as threadlike with reference to its continuity or connectedness. **4.** the spiral ridge of a screw. —*v.t.* **1.** to pass a thread through the eye of (a needle). **2.** to put (beads) on a thread. **3.** to arrange (material in strip form, e.g. film) in the proper position on equipment. **4.** to pick one's way through (a maze, a crowded place, etc.); to make (one's way) thus. —**threader** *n.* [Old English]

threadbare *adj.* **1.** (of cloth) so worn that the nap is lost and the threads are visible; (of a person) wearing such clothes. **2.** hackneyed.

threadworm *n.* a small threadlike worm *Strongyloides stercoralis* infesting the intestines, a type of ◊nematode.

threat /θrɛt/ *n.* **1.** a declaration of intention to punish, hurt, or harm a person or thing. **2.** an indication of something undesirable coming. **3.** a person or thing as a likely cause of harm etc. [Old English]

threaten /ˈθrɛtən/ *v.t.* **1.** to make a threat or threats against. **2.** to be a sign or indication of (something undesirable). **3.** to announce one's intention to do an undesirable or unexpected thing. **4.** to give warning of the infliction of (harm etc.; or *absolute*). [Old English]

three *adj.* & *n.* **1.** one more than two; the symbol for this (3, iii, III). **2.** the size etc. denoted by three. —**threecornered** *adj.* triangular; (of a contest etc.) between three parties each for himself. **three-decker** *n.* a warship with three gun decks; a sandwich with three slices of bread; a three-volume novel. **three-dimensional** *adj.* having or appearing to have length, breadth, and depth. **three-legged race,** a race between pairs with the right leg of one tied to the other's left leg. **three-ply** *adj.* having three strands or layers; (*n.*) wool etc. having three strands; plywood having three layers. **three-point turn,** a method of turning a vehicle round in a narrow space by driving forwards, backwards, and forwards. **three-quarter** *n.* any of the three or four players just behind the half-backs in Rugby football. **three-quarters** *n.* three parts out of four. **the three Rs,** see ◊R. **three-way** *adj.* involving three ways or participants. [Old English]

threefold *adj. & adv.* three times as much or as many; consisting of three parts.

Three Mile Island island in the Shenandoah River near Harrisburg, Pennsylvania, site of a nuclear power station which was put out of action following a major accident in March 1979. Opposition to nuclear power in the USA was reinforced after this accident and safety standards reassessed.

threepence /ˈθrepəns/ *n.* the sum of three pence.

threepenny /ˈθrepənɪ/ *adj.* costing or worth three pence. —**threepenny bit,** a former coin worth 3d.

threescore *n.* (*archaic*) sixty.

Three Sisters, The a play by Anton Chekhov, first produced in 1901. A family, bored and frustrated by life in the provinces, dream that if they move to Moscow their problems will disappear. However, apathy prevents the dream becoming reality.

threesome /ˈθriːsəm/ *n.* a group of three persons.

threnody /ˈθrenədɪ/ *n.* a song of lamentation, especially on a person's death. [from Greek *thrēnos* = wailing and *ōidē* = ode]

thresh *v.t./i.* **1.** to beat out or separate grain from (husks of corn etc.). Traditionally, threshing was carried out by hand in winter months using the flail, a jointed beating stick. Today, it is done automatically inside the combine harvester at the time of cutting. **2.** to make violent movements. —**threshing floor** *n.* a hard level floor for threshing, especially with flails. [variant of *thrash*]

threshold /ˈθreʃəuld/ *n.* **1.** a strip of wood or stone forming the bottom of a doorway and crossed in entering a house etc. **2.** the point of entry or beginning of something. **3.** the limit below which a stimulus causes no reaction; the magnitude or intensity that must be exceeded for a certain reaction or phenomenon to occur. [Old English, related to **thrash** in sense 'tread']

threw past of **throw**.

thrice *adv.* (*archaic*) **1.** three times, on three occasions. **2.** (especially in combinations) highly. [Old English]

thrift *n.* **1.** economical management of money or resources. **2.** the sea pink *Armeria maritima*. [from Old Norse]

thriftless *adj.* wasteful.

thrifty *adj.* practising thrift, economical. —**thriftily** *adv.,* **thriftiness** *n.*

thrill *n.* a nervous tremor of emotion or sensation; a slight throb or pulsation. —*v.t./i.* to feel or cause to feel a thrill; to throb or pulsate slightly. [Old English = pierce]

thriller *n.* an exciting or sensational story or play etc., especially one involving crime or espionage.

thrips *n.* (*plural* the same) a tiny insect with feathery wings of the order Thysanoptera, many of which injure plants by feeding on their juices. [Latin from Greek = woodworm]

thrive *v.i.* (*past* **throve** or **thrived**; *past participle* **thriven** /ˈθrɪvən/ or **thrived**) **1.** to prosper, to be successful. **2.** to grow or develop well and vigorously. [from Old Norse]

throat *n.* **1.** the windpipe, the gullet; the front part of the neck containing this. **2.** a narrow passage, entrance or exit, such as the throat of a carburettor. **3.** the forward upper corner of a fore-and-aft sail. —**cut one's own throat,** to bring about one's own downfall. **ram** *or* **thrust down a person's throat,** to force (a thing) on his attention. **throat latch** *or* **lash,** the strap of a bridle passing under a horse's throat. [Old English]

throaty *adj.* **1.** uttered deep in the throat. **2.** hoarsely resonant. —**throatily** *adv.,* **throatiness** *n.*

throb *v.i.* (**-bb-**) **1.** (of the heart or pulse etc.) to beat with more than usual force or rapidity. **2.** to vibrate or sound with a persistent rhythm; to vibrate with emotion. —*n.* throbbing. [apparently imitative]

throe *n.* (usually in *plural*) a violent pang, especially of childbirth or death. —**in the throes of,** (*colloquial*) struggling with the task of. [alteration from earlier *throwe,* perhaps from Old English *thrēa* = calamity]

thrombosis /θrɒmˈbəusɪs/ *n.* (*plural* **thromboses** /-iːz/) a condition in which a blood clot forms in a vein or artery, causing loss of circulation to the area served by the vessel. If it breaks away, it often travels to the lungs, causing pulmonary embolism. —**thrombotic** /-ˈbɒtɪk/ *adj.* [from Greek = curdling (*thrombos* = lump, blood clot)]

throne *n.* **1.** a chair of state for a sovereign or bishop etc. **2.** sovereign power. —*v.t.* to enthrone. [from Old French from Latin from Greek *thronos* = high seat]

throng *n.* a crowded mass of people. —*v.t./i.* to come, go, or press in a throng; to fill with a throng. [Old English]

throstle /ˈθrɒsəl/ *n.* a song thrush. [Old English]

throttle *n.* **1.** a valve controlling the flow of fuel or steam etc. in an engine; a lever or pedal operating this valve. **2.** the throat, the gullet, the windpipe. —*v.t.* **1.** to choke, to strangle. **2.** to prevent the utterance etc. of. **3.** to control (an engine or steam etc.) with a throttle. —**throttle back** *or* **down,** to reduce the speed of (an engine or vehicle) by throttling.

through /θruː/ *prep.* **1.** from end to end or side to side of; entering at one side or end and coming out at the other. **2.** between, among. **3.** from beginning to end of. **4.** by reason of; by the agency, means, or fault of. **5.** (*US*) up to and including. —*adv.* **1.** through a thing; from side to side or end to end; from beginning to end. **2.** so as to be connected by telephone. —*adj.* going through, especially of travel where the whole journey is made without change of line or vehicle etc. or with one ticket; (of traffic) going through a place to its destination. —**be through,** to have finished; to cease to have dealings; to have no further prospects. **through and through,** through again and again; thoroughly, completely. [Old English]

throughout /θruːˈaut/ *prep.* right through, from end to end of. —*adv.* in every part or respect.

throughput *n.* the amount of material put through a process, especially in manufacturing or computing.

throve see ↓**thrive**.

throw /θrəu/ *v.t./i.* (*past* **threw** /θruː/; *past participle* **thrown**) **1.** to propel with some force through the air or in a particular direction. **2.** to force violently into a specified position or state; to compel to be in a specified condition. **3.** to turn or move (a part of the body) quickly or suddenly. **4.** to project or cast (a light, shadow, spell, etc.). **5.** to bring to the ground in wrestling; (of a horse) to unseat (a rider); (*colloquial*) to disconcert. **6.** to put (clothes etc.) on or off carelessly or hastily. **7.** to cause (dice) to fall on a table; to obtain (a specified number) thus. **8.** to cause to pass or extend suddenly. **9.** to move (a switch or lever) so as to operate it. **10.** to shape (round pottery) on a wheel. **11.** to have (a fit or tantrum etc.). **12.** (*slang*) to give (a party). **13.** (*US*) to lose (a contest or race etc.) intentionally. —*n.* **1.** an act of throwing. **2.** the distance a thing is or may be thrown. **3.** being thrown in wrestling. —**throw away,** to part with as useless or unwanted; to fail to make use of (an opportunity etc.). **throw-away** *adj.* meant to be thrown away after use. **throw back,** to revert to ancestral character; (usually in *passive*) to compel to rely on. **throwback** *n.* reversion to ancestral character; an instance of this. **throw in,** to interpose (a word or remark); to include with no extra charge; to throw (a football) from the edge of a pitch where it has gone out of play. **throw off,** to discard; to contrive to get rid of or free oneself from; to write or utter easily, as if without effort, or in an offhand way. **throw oneself at,** to seek energetically to win the friendship or love of. **throw oneself into,** to engage vigorously in. **throw oneself on** *or* **upon,** to rely completely on. **throw open,** to cause to be suddenly or widely open; to make accessible. **throw out,** to put out forcibly or suddenly; to throw away; to reject (a proposal etc.); to confuse or distract (a person). **throw over,** to desert, to abandon. **throw together,** to assemble hastily; to bring into casual contact. **throw up,** to abandon; to resign from; to vomit; to erect hastily; to bring to notice. —**thrower** *n.* [Old English = twist]

throwing event a field athletic contest. There are four at most major international track and field meetings: discus, hammer, javelin, and shot put. Caber tossing is also a throwing event but is found only at Highland Games.

thrum[1] *v.t./i.* (**-mm-**) to play (a stringed instrument) monotonously or unskilfully; to drum or tap idly (on). —*n.* such playing; the resulting sound. [imitative]

thrum[2] *n.* an unwoven end of a warp thread, or the whole of such ends, left when the finished web is cut away; any short loose thread. [Old English from Old High German *drum* = remnant, end piece]

thrush[1] *n.* a small bird of the family Turdidae, found worldwide, e. g. the blackbird, nightingale, or especially the song thrush *Turdus philomelos* or missel thrush. Thrushes are usually brown with speckles of other colours. They are between 12–30 cm/5–12 in long. [Old English]

thrush[2] *n.* infection usually of the mouth (particularly in infants), but also sometimes of the vagina, caused by a yeastlike fungus (genus *Candida*). It is seen as white patches on the mucous membranes.

thrust *v.t./i.* (*past & past participle* **thrust**) 1. to push forcibly. 2. to put forcibly into a specified position or condition; to force the acceptance of. 3. to make a forward stroke with a sword etc. —*n.* 1. a thrusting movement or force; the forward force exerted by a propeller or jet etc.; the stress between parts of an arch etc.; in geology, a compressive strain in the Earth's crust. 2. a strong attempt to penetrate an enemy's line or territory. 3. a hostile remark aimed at a person. 4. the chief theme or gist of remarks etc. —**thruster** *n.* [from Old Norse]

Thucydides /θjuːˈsɪdɪdiːz/ 460–400 BC. Athenian historian, who exercised command in the ◊Peloponnesian War with Sparta in 424 BC with so little success that he was banished until 404 BC. In his *History of the Peloponnesian War*, he attempted a scientific impartiality.

thud *n.* a low dull sound as of a blow on a non-resonant thing. —*v.i.* (**-dd-**) to make a thud; to fall with a thud. [probably Old English = thrust]

thug *n.* 1. a vicious or brutal ruffian. 2. **Thug** a member of a Hindu sect who strangled travellers as sacrifices to ◊Kali, the goddess of destruction. The sect was in suppressed in about 1830. —**thuggery** *n.* [from Hindi and Marathi = swindler]

Thule /ˈθjuːli/ Greek and Roman name for the northernmost land known. It was applied to the Shetlands, the Orkneys, and Iceland, and by later writers to Scandinavia.

thulium /ˈθuːliəm/ *n.* a soft, silver-white, malleable and ductile, metallic element, of the ◊lanthanide series, symbol Tm, atomic number 69, relative atomic mass 168.94. It is the least abundant of the rare-earth metals, and was first found in gadolinite and various other minerals. It is used in arc lighting. [from *Thule*]

thumb /θʌm/ *n.* 1. the short thick finger set apart from the other four. 2. the part of a glove covering the thumb. —*v.t./i.* 1. to wear or soil (pages etc.) with the thumb. 2. to turn over pages (as) with the thumb. 3. to request or get (a lift in a passing vehicle) by indicating the desired direction with the thumb. 4. to use the thumb (on) in a gesture. —**thumb index**, a set of lettered grooves cut down the side of a book's leaves to enable the user to open the book directly at a particular section. **thumbnail sketch**, a brief verbal description. **thumb one's nose**, to cock a snook. **thumbs down**, a gesture of rejection. **thumbs up**, a gesture or exclamation of satisfaction. **under a person's thumb**, completely dominated by him or her. [Old English]

thumbscrew *n.* an instrument of torture for compressing the thumb(s).

thump *v.t./i.* to beat, or strike, or knock heavily, especially with the fist. 2. to thud. —*n.* a heavy blow; the sound of this. [imitative]

thumping *adj.* (*colloquial*) big.

thunder *n.* 1. a loud noise heard after lightning and due to disturbance of the air by a discharge of electricity. 2. a resounding loud deep noise. 3. (in *singular* or *plural*) authoritative censure or threats. —*v.t./i.* 1. to give forth thunder (especially *it thunders, is thundering*). 2. to make a noise like thunder; to move with a loud noise. 3. to utter loudly; to make a forceful verbal attack. —**steal a person's thunder**, to forestall him by using his ideas or words etc. before he can do so himself (from the remark of John Dennis, English dramatist (*c.*1710), when the stage thunder he had intended for his own play was used for another). **thundercloud** *n.* a storm cloud charged with electricity and producing thunder and lightning. —**thunderer** *n.*, **thundery** *adj.* [Old English]

thunderbolt *n.* 1. a flash of lightning with a crash of thunder. 2. an imaginary destructive missile thought of as sent to earth with a lighting flash. 3. a very startling and formidable event or statement.

thunderclap *n.* 1. a crash of thunder. 2. a sudden terrible event or news.

thundering *adj.* (*colloquial*) very big or great.

thunderous *adj.* like thunder; very loud.

thunderstorm *n.* a storm with thunder and lightning and usually heavy rain or hail.

thunderstruck *adj.* amazed.

Thünen /ˈtjuːnən/ Johann von 1785–1850. German economist and geographer who believed that the success of a state depends on the wellbeing of its farmers. His book *The Isolated State* 1820, a pioneering study of land use, includes the earliest example of marginal productivity theory, a theory which he developed to calculate the natural wage for a farmworker. He has been described as the first modern economist.

Thur. abbreviation of Thursday.

Thurber /ˈθɜːbə/ James (Grover) 1894–1961. US humorist. His short stories, written mainly for the *New Yorker* magazine, include 'The Secret Life of Walter Mitty' 1932, and his doodle drawings include fanciful impressions of dogs.

thurible /ˈθjuərɪbəl/ *n.* a censer. [from Old French or Latin *t(h)uribulum* (*t(h)us* = incense)]

Thursday /ˈθɜːzdeɪ/ *n.* the day of the week following Wednesday. —*adv.* (*colloquial*) on Thursday. [Old English = day of Thor (Norse god), representing Latin *Jovis dies* = day of Jupiter]

thus /ðʌs/ *adv.* (*formal*) 1. in this way, like this. 2. as a result or inference. 3. to this extent, so. [Old English]

thwack *v.t.* to hit with a heavy blow. —*n.* a heavy blow. [imitative]

thwart /θwɔːt/ *v.t.* to frustrate (a person or purpose etc.). —*n.* a rower's seat, placed across the boat. [from Old Norse = transverse]

thy /ðaɪ/ *poss. adj.* of or belonging to thee; now replaced by **your** except in some formal, liturgical, and poetic uses. [Old English]

thylacine *n.* another name for the ◊Tasmanian tiger/wolf.

thyme /taɪm/ *n.* any of several herbs of the genus *Thymus* of the mint family, Labiatae. Garden thyme *T. vulgaris*, native to the Mediterranean, grows to 30 cm/1 ft high, and has pinkish flowers. Its aromatic leaves are used for seasoning. [from Old French from Latin from Greek *thumon* (*thuō* = burn sacrifice)]

thymol /ˈθaɪmɒl/ *n.* an antiseptic made from oil of thyme. [from *thyme*]

thymus /ˈθaɪməs/ *n.* a lymphoid organ in vertebrates, situated in the upper chest cavity in humans. The thymus processes ◊lymphocyte cells to produce T-lymphocytes (T denotes 'thymus-derived'), which are responsible for binding to specific invading organisms and killing them or rendering them harmless. [from Greek *thumos*]

thyristor /θaɪˈrɪstə/ *n.* a type of ◊rectifier, an electronic device that conducts electricity in one direction only. The thyristor is composed of layers of ◊semiconductor material sandwiched between two electrodes called the anode and cathode. The current can be switched on by using a third electrode called the gate. [Greek *thura* = door]

thyroid /ˈθaɪrɔɪd/ *n.* 1. the thyroid gland. 2. an extract from the thyroid gland of animals used in treating goitre etc. —**thyroid cartilage**, a large cartilage of the larynx, the projection of which in man forms the Adam's apple. **thyroid gland**, an ◊endocrine gland of vertebrates, situated in the neck in front of the trachea. It secretes several hormones, among them thyroxin, a hormone containing iodine. This stimulates growth, metabolism, and other functions of the body. Excessive action produces Graves's disease, characterized by bulging eyeballs and an elevated metabolism, while deficient action produces ◊myxoedema in adults and dwarfism in juveniles. [from obsolete French from Greek *thureos* = oblong shield]

thyself *pron.* the emphatic and reflexive form of **thou** and **thee**: now replaced in general use by **yourself**.

Thyssen /ˈtɪsən/ Fritz 1873–1951. German industrialist who based his business on the Ruhr iron and steel industry. Fearful of the communist threat, Thyssen became an early supporter of Hitler and contributed large amounts of money to his early political campaigns. By 1939 he had broken with the Nazis and fled first to Switzerland and later to Italy, where in 1941 he was sent to a concentration camp. Released in 1945, he was ordered to surrender 15% of his property.

Ti symbol for titanium.

Tiananmen Square /tjenənˈmen/ a paved open space in central Beijing (Peking), China, the largest public square in the world (area 0.4 sq km/0.14 sq mi). On 3–4 June 1989 over 1,000 unarmed protesters were killed by government troops in a massacre that crushed China's emerging pro-democracy movement. [Chinese = Square of Heavenly Peace]

Tianjin /tjen'dʒɪn/ or **Tientsin** port and industrial and commercial city in Hubei province, central China; population (1986) 5,380,000. The special municipality of Tianjin has an area of 4,000 sq km/1,544 sq mi and a population of 8,190,000. Its handmade silk and wool carpets are renowned. Dagan oilfield is nearby. Tianjin was opened to foreign trade in 1860 and occupied by the Japanese in 1937.

Tian Shan /ti'en 'ʃɑːn/ (Chinese *Tien Shan*) mountain system on the Soviet-Chinese border. **Pik Pobedy** on the Xinjiang–Kirghizia border is the highest peak at 7,440 m/24,415 ft.

tiara /ti'ɑːrə/ *n.* 1. a woman's ornamental crescent-shaped headdress, worn on ceremonial occasions. 2. a headdress worn by the pope, pointed at the top and surrounded by three crowns. [Latin from Greek]

Tiberias, Lake or **Sea of Galilee** lake in N Israel, 210 m/689 ft below sea level, into which the ◊Jordan flows; area 170 sq km/66 sq mi. The first Israeli ◊kibbutz (cooperative settlement) was founded nearby in 1909.

Tiberius /taɪ'bɪəriəs/ Claudius Nero 42 BC–AD 37. Roman emperor, the stepson, adopted son, and successor of Augustus from AD 14. A distinguished soldier, he was a conscientious ruler under whom the empire prospered.

It is the part of a good shepherd to shear his flock, not flay it.

Claudius Nero Tiberius

Tibet /tɪ'bet/ autonomous region of SW China (Pinyin form *Xizang*); **area** 1,221,600 sq km/471,538 sq mi; **capital** Lhasa; **features** barren plateau bounded to the S and SW by the Himalayas and to the N by the Kunlun Mountains, traversed W to E by the Bukamagna, Karakoram, and other mountain ranges, and having an average elevation of 4,000–4,500 m/13,000–15,000 ft; **population** (1986) 2,030,000; many Chinese have settled in Tibet; **recent history** under Chinese rule from about 1700. Independence was regained after a revolt in 1912. China regained control in 1951 when the historic ruler and religious leader, the ◊Dalai Lama, was driven from the country and the monks (who formed 25% of the population) were forced out of the monasteries. Between 1951 and 1959 the Chinese People's Liberation Army (PLA) controlled Tibet, although the Dalai Lama returned as nominal spiritual and temporal head of state. Suppression by the PLA of an uprising in 1959 prompted the Dalai Lama and 9,000 Tibetans to flee to India. In 1965 Tibet became an autonomous region of China.

tibia /'tɪbiə/ *n.* (*plural* **tibiae** /-iː/) the inner and usually larger of the two bones from knee to ankle; the corresponding bone in a bird. —**tibial** *adj.* [Latin = shinbone, flute]

tic *n.* a habitual spasmodic contraction of the muscles especially of the face; a kind of neuralgia. [French from Italian *ticchio*]

tick[1] *n.* 1. a slight recurring click, especially that of a watch or clock. 2. (*colloquial*) a moment, an instant. 3. a small mark set against items in a list etc. in checking. —*v.t./i.* 1. (of a clock etc.) to make ticks. 2. to mark (an item) with a tick. —**tick off,** (*slang*) to reprimand. **tick over,** (of an engine or *figurative*) to idle. **ticktack** *n.* a kind of manual semaphore signalling used by bookmakers on a racecourse. **ticktock** *n.* the ticking of a large clock etc. **what makes a person tick,** his or her motivation, what makes someone behave as he or she does. [compare Dutch *tik* = touch, tick]

tick[2] *n.* an arachnid of the order Acarina or a similar insect (e. g. *Melophagus*). Ticks are blood-sucking, disease-carrying parasites on humans, animals, and birds. [compare Middle Dutch or Middle Low German *teke*]

tick[3] *n.* (*colloquial*) credit. [apparent abbreviation of *ticket* in phrase *on the ticket*]

tick[4] *n.* the cover of a mattress or pillow; ticking. [from Middle Dutch or Middle Low German, ultimately from Greek *thēkē* = case]

ticker *n.* (*colloquial*) the heart; a watch; a tape machine. —**ticker tape** *n.* (*US*) a paper strip from a tape-machine;

this or similar material thrown in long strips from windows to greet a celebrity.

ticket /'tɪkɪt/ *n.* 1. a written or printed piece of paper or card entitling the holder to enter a place, participate in an event, travel by public transport, etc. 2. a certificate of discharge from the army or of qualification as a ship's master, pilot, etc. 3. a label attached to a thing and giving its price etc. 4. an official notification of a traffic offence etc. 5. a list of candidates put forward by one group, especially a political party. —*v.t.* to attach a ticket to. —**the ticket,** (*slang*) the correct or desirable thing. [from obsolete French *étiquet* (Old French *estiquier* = fix, from Middle Dutch)]

ticking *n.* a stout usually striped linen or cotton material used for covering mattresses etc.

tickle /'tɪkəl/ *v.t./i.* 1. to apply light touches or stroking to (a person or part of his or her body) so as to excite the nerves and usually produce laughter and spasmodic movement. 2. to feel this sensation. 3. to excite agreeably, to amuse, to divert. —*n.* an act or sensation of tickling. —**tickled pink** *or* **to death,** (*colloquial*) extremely amused or pleased. [probably from *tick* = touch lightly]

ticklish *adj.* 1. sensitive to tickling. 2. (of a matter or person to be dealt with) difficult, requiring careful handling. —**ticklishness** *n.*

tidal /'taɪdəl/ *adj.* of or affected by a tide or tides. —**tidal power station,** a ◊hydroelectric power plant that uses the 'head' of water created by the rise and fall of the ocean tides to spin the water turbines. **tidal wave,** a misleading name for a ◊tsunami; a widespread manifestation of feeling etc. —**tidally** *adv.*

tidbit variant of ◊titbit.

tiddler *n.* (*colloquial*) 1. a small fish, especially a stickleback or minnow. 2. an unusually small thing. [perhaps related to *tiddly* = little]

tiddly[1] *adj.* (*colloquial*) very small. [variant of *tiddy* (nursery word)]

tiddly[2] *adj.* (*slang*) slightly drunk.

tiddlywinks *n.* a game in which small counters are caused to spring from the table into a cup-shaped or cylindrical receptacle by pressing upon their edges with a larger counter. —**tiddlywink** *n.* a counter used in this game.

tide *n.* 1. the regular rise and fall of the sea due to the attraction of the Moon and Sun; water as moved by this. High water occurs at an average interval of 12 hr 24 min 30 sec. The highest or **spring tides** are at or near new and full Moon; the lowest or **neap tides** when the Moon is in its first or third quarter. Some seas, such as the Mediterranean, have very small tides. **Gravitational tides** (the pull of nearby groups of stars) have been observed to affect the galaxies. 2. a trend of opinion, fortune, or events. 3. a time or season (*archaic* except in *noontide, Christmastide*, etc.). —*v.i.* to be carried by the tide. —**tidemark** *n.* the mark made by the tide at high water; (*colloquial*) a line of dirt round a bath showing the level of the water that has been used, or on the body of a person showing the extent of his washing. **tide a person over,** to help him through a temporary need or difficulty. **tide table,** a list of the times of high tide at a place. **turn the tide,** to reverse the trend of events. [Old English = time]

tideway *n.* the tidal part of a river.

tidings /'taɪdɪŋz/ *n.* (as *singular* or *plural*) news. [Old English, probably from Old Norse = events]

tidy /'taɪdi/ *adj.* 1. neat and orderly, methodically arranged or inclined. 2. (*colloquial*) considerable. —*n.* 1. a receptacle for odds and ends. 2. a cover for a chair back etc. —*v.t.* to make tidy. —**tidily** *adv.*, **tidiness** *n.* [originally = timely, from *tide*]

tie /taɪ/ *v.t./i.* (*participle* **tying**) 1. to attach or fasten with a string or cord etc. 2. to form (a string, ribbon, shoelace, necktie, etc.) into a knot or bow; to form (a knot or bow) thus. 3. to restrict or limit (a person) in some way. 4. to make the same score as another competitor. 5. to bind (rafters etc.) by a crosspiece etc. 6. in music, to unite notes by a tie. —*n.* 1. a cord or chain etc. used for fastening. 2. a necktie. 3. a thing that unites or restricts persons. 4. equality of score or a draw or dead heat among persons. 5. a match between any pair of players or teams. 6. a rod or beam holding parts of a structure together. 7. in music, a curved line above or below two notes of the same pitch that are to be joined as one. —**tie beam** a horizontal beam connecting rafters. **tiebreak** *n.* a means of deciding the winner when

tide

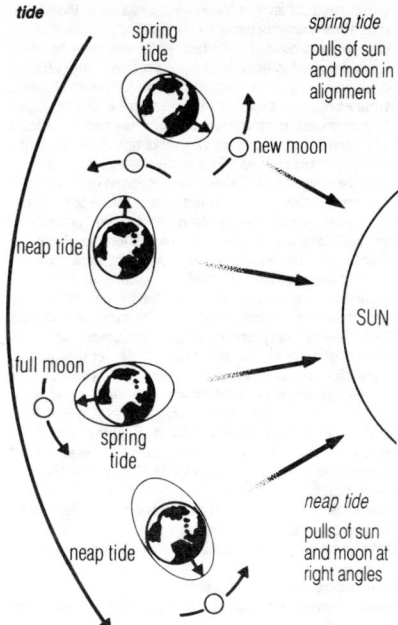

spring tide pulls of sun and moon in alignment

new moon

SUN

neap tide pulls of sun and moon at right angles

competitors have tied. **tied cottage,** a dwelling occupied subject to the tenant's working for the owner. **tied house,** a public house bound to supply only a particular brewer's beer. **tie-dyeing** *n.* a method of producing dyed patterns by tying parts of the fabric so that they are protected from the dye. **tie in** *or* **up,** to agree or be closely associated; to cause to do this. **tiepin** *n.* an ornamental pin holding a tie in place. **tie up,** to bind or fasten with cord etc.; to invest or reserve (capital etc.) so that it is not immediately available for use; to obstruct; (usually in *passive*) to occupy (a person) fully. [Old English]

Tieck /tiːk/ Johann Ludwig 1773–1853. German Romantic poet and collector of folk tales, some of which he dramatized, such as 'Puss in Boots'.

Tientsin /tjen'tsɪn/ alternative form of ◊Tianjin, industrial city in NE China.

Tiepolo /ti'epələʊ/ Giovanni Battista 1696–1770. Italian painter, born in Venice. He created monumental Rococo decorative schemes in palaces and churches in NE Italy, SW Germany, and Madrid (1762–70). The style is light-hearted, the palette light and warm, and he made great play with illusion.

tier /tɪə/ *n.* a row, rank, or unit of a structure as one of several placed one above another. —**tiered** *adj.* [from French *tire* (*tirer* = draw, elongate)]

Tierra del Fuego /ti'eərə del 'fweɪgəʊ/ island group divided between Chile and Argentina. It is separated from the mainland of South America by the Strait of Magellan, and Cape Horn is at the southernmost point. Chief town, Ushuaia, Argentina, is the world's southernmost town. Industries include oil and sheep farming.

tiff *n.* a petty quarrel.

Tiffany /'tɪfənɪ/ Louis Comfort 1848–1933. US artist and glassmaker, son of Charles Louis Tiffany, who founded Tiffany and Company, the New York City jewellers. He produced stained-glass windows, iridescent Favrile glass, and lampshades in the Art Nouveau style. He used glass that contained oxides of iron and other elements to produce rich colours.

tiffin /'tɪfɪn/ *n.* (in India) lunch. [apparently from *tiffing* = taking slight drink]

tiger /'taɪgə/ *n.* 1. the largest of the great cats *Panthera tigris,* formerly found in much of central and S Asia but nearing extinction because of hunting and the destruction of its natural habitat. The tiger can grow to 3.6 m/12 ft long and weigh 300 kg/660 lbs; it has a yellow-orange coat with black stripes. It is solitary, and feeds on deer and cattle.

It is a good swimmer. 2. a fierce, energetic, or formidable person. —**tiger cat** any moderate-sized feline resembling a tiger, e. g. an ocelot. **tiger lily** a tall garden lily *Lilium tigrinum* with dark-spotted orange flowers. **tiger moth** a moth of the family Arctiidae, especially *Arctia caja,* with richly spotted and streaked wings. [from Old French from Latin from Greek *tigris*]

tight /taɪt/ *adj.* 1. fixed, fastened, or drawn together firmly and hard to move or undo. 2. fitting closely, made impermeable to a specified thing. 3. with things or people arranged closely together. 4. tense, stretched so as to leave no slack. 5. (*colloquial*) drunk. 6. (of money or materials) not easily obtainable. 7. produced by or requiring great exertion or pressure; (of precautions, a programme, etc.) stringent, demanding; (*colloquial*) presenting difficulties. 8. (*colloquial*) stingy. —*adv.* tightly. —**tight-fisted** *adj.* stingy. **tight-lipped** *adj.* with the lips compressed to restrain emotion or speech. —**tightly** *adv.,* **tightness** *n.* [probably from Old Norse]

tighten *v.t./i.* to make or become tighter.

tightrope *n.* a rope stretched tightly high above the ground, on which acrobats perform.

tights *n.pl.* a thin close-fitting elastic garment covering the legs and the lower part of the body, worn by women in place of stockings; a similar garment worn by a dancer, acrobat, etc.

Tigré /'tiːgreɪ/ or **Tigray** region in the northern highlands of Ethiopia; **area** 65,900 sq km/25,444 sq mi; **chief town** is Mekele; **population** (est 1984, when drought and famine were driving large numbers of people to fertile land in the south or into neighbouring Sudan) 2.4 million. Since 1978 a guerrilla group known as the Tigré People's Liberation Front has been fighting for regional autonomy.

tigress /'taɪgrɪs/ *n.* a female tiger.

Tigris /'taɪgrɪs/ (Arabic *Shatt Dijla*) river flowing through Turkey and Iraq (see also ◊Mesopotamia), joining the ◊Euphrates above Basra, where it forms the ◊Shatt-al-Arab; length 1,600 km/1,000 mi.

Tihuanaco /tiːwə'nɑːkəʊ/ site of a Peruvian city, south of Lake Titicaca in the Andes, which gave its name to the 8th–14th-century civilization that preceded the Inca.

Tijuana /tiː'wɑːnə/ city and resort in NW Mexico; population (1980) 461,257; known for horse races and casinos. ◊San Diego adjoins it across the US border.

Tikhonov /'tiːxənɒf/ Nikolai 1905– . Soviet politician. He was a close associate of President Brezhnev, joining the Politburo in 1979, and was prime minister (chair of the Council of Ministers) 1980–85. In April 1989 he was removed from the central committee.

tilbury /'tɪlbərɪ/ *n.* a light, open, two-wheeled carriage fashionable in the first half of the 19th century. [from inventor's name]

tilde /'tɪldə/ *n.* the mark (˜) put over a letter, e. g. Spanish *n* when pronounced /nj/ (as in señor). [Spanish from Latin *titulus*]

tile *n.* 1. a thin slab of glazed or unglazed baked clay or other material used in series for covering a roof, wall, or floor. 2. a thin flat piece used in a game (especially mah-jong). —*v.t.* to cover with tiles. —**on the tiles,** (*slang*) on a nocturnal spree. [Old English from Latin *tegula*]

tiling /'taɪlɪŋ/ *n.* 1. the process of fixing tiles. 2. an area of tiles.

till[1] *prep.* & *conj.* until. [from Old English and Old Norse = to]

till[2] *n.* a drawer for money in a shop or bank etc., especially with a device recording the amount of each purchase.

till[3] *v.t.* to cultivate (land). [Old English = strive for]

till[4] *n.* a deposit of clay, mud, gravel, and boulders left by a glacier. Till is unsorted, all sizes of fragments mixed up together, and it shows no stratification; that is, it does not form clear layers or ◊beds.

tillage *n.* 1. preparation of land for crop bearing. 2. tilled land.

tiller *n.* a bar by which the rudder is turned. [from Anglo-French *telier* = weaver's beam]

Tilly /'tɪlɪ/ Jan Tserklaes, Count von Tilly 1559–1632. Flemish commander of the army of the Catholic League and imperial forces in the ◊Thirty Years' War. Notorious for his storming of Magdeburg, Germany, in 1631, he was defeated by the Swedish king Gustavus Adolphus at

Breitenfeld and at the river Lech in SW Germany, where he was mortally wounded.

tilt *v.t./i.* 1. to move or cause to move into a sloping position. 2. to run or thrust with a lance in jousting. —*n.* 1. tilting. 2. a sloping position. 3. an attack, especially with argument or satire. —**(at) full tilt**, at full speed; with full force. [perhaps from Old English *tealt* = unsteady]

tilt-rotor aircraft a type of vertical takeoff aircraft, also called a ◊convertiplane.

timber *n.* 1. wood used in construction, furniture, and paper pulp. **Hardwoods** include tropical mahogany, teak, ebony, rosewood, temperate oak, elm, beech, and eucalyptus. Most are slow-growing, and world supplies are near exhaustion. **Softwoods** comprise the ◊conifers (pine, fir, spruce, and larch), which are quick to grow and easy to work but inferior in quality of grain. **White woods** include ash, birch, and sycamore; all have light-coloured timber, are fast-growing, and can be used as veneers on cheaper timber. 2. a piece of wood, a beam, especially as a rib of a vessel. 3. large standing trees. 4. (especially as *interjection*) a tree about to fall. —**timber line** (on a mountain) the line or level above which no trees grow. [Old English = building]

timbered *adj.* 1. made wholly or partly of timber. 2. (of country) wooded.

timbre /tæbr, 'tæmbə/ *n.* the distinctive character of a musical sound or a voice apart from its pitch and intensity. [French, ultimately from Greek *tumpanon* = drum]

timbrel /'tɪmbrəl/ *n.* (*archaic*) a tambourine. [from Old French]

Timbuktu /tɪmbʌk'tuː/ or **Tombouctou** town in Mali; population (1976) 20,500. A camel caravan centre from the 11th century on the fringe of the Sahara, since 1960 it has been surrounded by the southward movement of the desert, and the former canal link with the river Niger is dry. Products include salt.

time *n.* 1. the indefinite continued existence of the universe in the past, present, and future regarded as a whole; the progress of this as affecting persons or things, recorded by division into hours, minutes, and seconds. Formerly the measurement of time was based on the Earth's rotation on its axis, but this was found to be irregular. Therefore the second, the standard ◊SI unit of time, was redefined in 1956 in terms of the Earth's annual orbit of the Sun, and in 1967 in terms of a radiation pattern of the element caesium. Universal time (UT), based on the Earth's actual rotation, was replaced by coordinated universal time (UTC) in 1972, the difference between the two involving the addition (or subtraction) of leap seconds on the last day of June or Dec. **Father Time,** time personified as an aged man, bald but having a forelock, carrying a scythe and an hourglass. 2. the portion of time belonging to particular events or circumstances. 3. a portion of time between two points; the point or period allotted, available, or suitable for something; a prison sentence; an apprenticeship; a period of gestation; the date of childbirth or of death. 4. a point of time stated in hours and minutes of the day. 5. any of the standard systems by which time is reckoned. 6. an occasion or instance; (in *plural*, expressing multiplication) a specified number of times. 7. (in *singular* or *plural*) the conditions of life or of a period. 8. measured time spent in work etc. 9. in music, the duration of a note; a style depending on the number and accentuation of beats in the bar; a rate of performance. —*v.t.* 1. to choose the time or moment for; to arrange the time of. 2. to measure the time taken by. —**against time**, with the utmost speed so as to finish by a specified time. **at the same time**, in spite of this, however. **at times**, sometimes, intermittently. **behind the times**, old-fashioned. **for the time being**, until some other arrangement is made. **from time to time**, occasionally, at intervals. **half the time**, (*colloquial*) as often as not. **have a time of it**, to undergo trouble or difficulty. **have no time for**, to be unable or unwilling to spend time on; to dislike. **in no time**, very soon or quickly. **in time**, not late, punctual; sooner or later; in accordance with the time of music etc. **keep time**, to move or sing etc. in time. **lose time**, to waste time. **on time**, in accordance with the timetable; punctual, punctually. **pass the time of day**, (*colloquial*) to exchange a greeting or casual remarks. **time after time**, on many occasions; in many instances. **time and (time) again**, on many occasions. **time and a half,** a

rate of payment for work at one-and-a-half times the normal rate. **time-and-motion** *adj.* concerned with measuring the efficiency of industrial and other operations. **time bomb,** a bomb designed to explode at a pre-set time. **time clock** a clock with a device for recording workers' hours of work. **time exposure,** exposure of a photographic film for longer than an instant. **time-honoured** *adj.* esteemed by tradition or custom. **time-lag** *n.* an interval of time between cause and effect. **time limit** a limit of time within which a thing must be done. **time of one's life,** a period of exceptional enjoyment. **time out of mind,** from before anyone can remember. **time and motion study,** the process of analysis applied to a job or number of jobs to check the efficiency of the work method, equipment used, and the worker. Its findings are used to improve performance. **time sharing** the use of a computer by several persons for different operations at one time; the ownership or right to the use of a property for a fixed limited time each year. **time signal** an audible indication of the exact time of day. **time signature**, (in music, see ◊signature 3. **time switch** a switch acting automatically at a pre-set time. **time was,** there was a time. **time zone,** a range of longitudes where a common standard time is used. [Old English]

timekeeper *n.* 1. one who records the time, especially of workers or in a game. 2. a watch or clock etc. as regards its accuracy.

timeless *adj.* not affected by the passage of time; not to be thought of as having duration.

timely *adj.* opportune, coming at the right time. —**timeliness** *n.*

timepiece *n.* a clock or watch.

timer /'taɪmə/ *n.* a person or device that measures the time taken.

timetable *n.* a list of the times at which events will take place, especially the arrival of buses or trains etc., or the series of lessons in a school etc.

timid /'tɪmɪd/ *adj.* easily frightened, not bold; shy. —**timidity** /tɪ'mɪdɪtɪ/ *n.*, **timidly** *adv.* [from French or Latin *timidus* (*timēre* = fear)]

timing /'taɪmɪŋ/ *n.* the way a thing is timed.

Timișoara /tɪmɪ'ʃwɑːrə/ capital of Timiș county, W Romania; population (1985) 319,000. The revolt against the Ceaușescu regime began here in Dec 1989 when demonstrators prevented the arrest and deportation of a popular protestant minister who was promoting the rights of ethnic Hungarians. This soon led to large pro-democracy rallies.

Timor /'tiːmɔː/ largest and most easterly of the Lesser Sunda Islands, part of Indonesia; area 33,610 sq km/12,973 sq mi. **West Timor** (capital Kupang) was formerly Dutch and was included in Indonesian independence. **East Timor** (capital Dili) was an overseas province of Portugal until it was annexed by Indonesia in 1975. Guerrilla warfare by local people seeking independence continues. Since 1975 over 500,000 have been killed or have resettled in West Timor, according to Amnesty International. Products include coffee, maize, rice, and coconuts.

timorous /'tɪmərəs/ *adj.* timid; frightened. —**timorously** *adv.,* **timorousness** *n.* [from Old French from Latin *timēre* = fear]

Timothy /'tɪməθɪ/ in the New Testament, companion to St ◊Paul, both on his missionary journeys and in prison. Two of the Pauline epistles are addressed to him.

timpano /'tɪmpənəʊ/ *n.* (obsolete except in *plural*, **timpani**) a kettledrum. —**timpanist** *n.* [Italian]

tin *n.* 1. a soft, silver-white, malleable and somewhat ductile, metallic element, symbol Sn (from Latin *stannum*), atomic number 50, relative atomic mass 118.69. Tin exhibits ◊allotropy, having three forms: the familiar lustrous metallic form above 55.8°F/13.2°C; a brittle form above 321.8°F/161°C; and a grey powder form below 55.8°F/13.2°C (commonly called tin pest or tin disease). The metal is quite soft (slightly harder than lead) and can be rolled, pressed, or hammered into extremely thin sheets; it has a low melting point. In nature it occurs rarely as a free metal. It resists corrosion and is therefore used for coating and plating other metals. 2. a container made of tin or tin plate, or of aluminium, especially one hermetically sealed for preserving food. 3. tin plate. —*v.t.* (-nn-) 1. to pack (food) in a tin for preservation. 2. to cover or coat with tin. —**tin foil**, foil made of tin, aluminium, or tin alloy, and used to wrap food for cooking, keeping fresh, etc. **tin**

god, an object of unjustified veneration. **tin-opener** *n.* a tool for opening tins of food. **tin plate,** sheet iron or sheet steel coated with tin. **tin-tack** *n.* a tin-coated iron tack. **tin whistle,** a penny whistle. [Old English]

Tinbergen /'tɪnbɜːgən/ Jan 1903–1988. Dutch economist. He shared a Nobel prize in 1969 with Ragnar Frisch for his work on ◊econometrics (the mathematical-statistical expression of economic theory).

tincture /'tɪŋktʃə/ *n.* **1.** a tinge or trace of some element or quality. **2.** a medicinal solution of a drug in alcohol. —*v.t.* to tinge. [from Latin *tingere* = stain]

tinder *n.* a dry substance that readily catches fire from a spark. —**tinderbox** *n.* a box containing tinder, flint, and steel, for kindling fires. —**tindery** *adj.* [Old English]

tine *n.* each of the points or prongs of a fork, harrow, antler, etc. [Old English]

Ting /tɪŋ/ Samuel 1936– . US high-energy physicist. In 1974 he detected a new subatomic particle, known as the J particle, similar to the ψ (psi) particle found by Burton ◊Richter, with whom he shared the 1976 Nobel Prize for Physics.

tinge *v.t.* to colour slightly; to give a slight trace of some element or quality to. —*n.* a slight colouring or trace. [from Latin *tingere* = stain]

tingle *v.i.* to feel a slight pricking, stinging, or throbbing sensation, especially in the ears or hands; to cause this. —*n.* a tingling sensation. [perhaps variant of *tinkle*]

tinker *n.* **1.** an itinerant mender of kettles and pans etc. **2.** (*Scottish* and *Irish*) a gypsy. **3.** (*colloquial*) a mischievous person or animal. **4.** a spell of tinkering. —*v.i.* **1.** to work at something casually trying to improve or repair it. **2.** to work as a tinker.

tinkle *n.* **1.** a series of short light ringing sounds. **2.** (*colloquial*) a telephone call. —*v.t./i.* to make or cause to make a tinkle. [from obsolete *tink* = to chink (imitative)]

tinnitus *n.* in medicine, constant internal sounds, inaudible to others. The phenomenon may originate from noisy conditions (drilling, machinery, or loud music) or from infection of the middle or inner ear. The victim may become overwhelmed by the relentless noise in the head.

tinny *adj.* **1.** of or like tin. **2.** (of a metal object) flimsy, insubstantial. **3.** having a metallic taste or a thin metallic sound. —**tinnily** *adv.,* **tinniness** *n.*

tin ore the mineral from which tin is extracted, principally cassiterite, SnO_2. The world's chief producers are Malaysia, Thailand, and Bolivia. The UK was a major producer in the 19th century but today only a few working mines remain, and production is small.

tinpot *adj.* (*colloquial, derogatory*) cheap, inferior.

tinsel /'tɪnsəl/ *n.* a glittering metallic substance used in strips or threads to give an inexpensive sparkling effect. —*adj.* superficially showy, gaudy. [probably from Anglo-French, ultimately from Latin *scintillare* = spark]

tinsmith *n.* a worker in tin and tin plate.

tint *n.* **1.** a variety of a colour, especially made by adding white. **2.** a slight trace of a different colour. **3.** a faint colour spread over a surface. —*v.t.* to apply a tint to; to colour. —**tinted** *adj.* [from Latin *tinctus*]

tintinnabulation /tɪntɪnæbjuˈleɪʃən/ *n.* a ringing or tinkling of bells. [from Latin *tintinnabulum* = bell]

Tintoretto /tɪntəˈretəʊ/ real name Jacopo Robusti 1518–1594. Italian painter, active in Venice. His dramatic religious paintings are spectacularly lit and full of movement, such as his canvases of the lives of Christ and the Virgin in the Scuola di San Rocco, Venice, 1564–88.

Grant me paradise in this world; I'm not so sure I'll reach it in the next.

Jacopo Tintoretto
(attrib. arguing that he be allowed to paint the Paradiso at the Doge's palace in Venice)

---

tiny /'taɪnɪ/ *adj.* very small or slight. —**tinily** *adv.,* **tininess** *n.*

tip¹ *n.* **1.** the very end, especially of a small or tapering thing. **2.** a small piece or part attached to an end of a thing. **3.** a leaf-bud of tea. —*v.t.* (**-pp-**) to provide with a tip. —**on the tip of one's tongue,** just about to be said,

Tipperary *Celtic crosses, with their characteristic intertwined ornamentation, are found in the Irish countryside. This is the east face of South Cross at Ahenny in Tipperary.*

or remembered and spoken. **tip of the iceberg,** the small evident part of something much larger. [from Old Norse]

tip² *v.t./i.* (**-pp-**) **1.** to tilt or topple; to cause to do this. **2.** to overturn, to cause to overbalance; to discharge (the contents of a truck or jug etc.) thus. **3.** to make a small present of money to, especially for service given. **4.** to name as the likely winner of a race or contest etc. **5.** to strike or touch lightly. —*n.* **1.** a small money present, especially for service given. **2.** private or special information (e. g. about a horse race or stock market); a small or casual piece of advice. **3.** a slight push or tilt. **4.** a place where material (especially rubbish) is tipped. **5.** a light stroke. —**tip a person off,** to give him or her a hint or special information, or a warning. **tip-off** *n.* such information etc. **tip-up** *adj.* able to be tipped, e. g. of a seat in a theatre to allow passage past. **tip a person the wink,** to give him private information.

Tipperary /tɪpəˈreərɪ/ county in the Republic of Ireland, province of Munster, divided into north and south regions. **North Tipperary: area** 2,000 sq km/772 sq mi; **administrative headquarters** Nenagh; **population** (1986) 59,000. **South Tipperary: area** 2,260 sq km/872 sq mi; **administrative headquarters** Clonmel; **population** (1986) 77,000. It includes part of the Golden Vale, a dairy-farming region.

tippet /'tɪpɪt/ *n.* a small cape or collar of fur etc. with the ends hanging down in front.

Tippett Michael (Kemp) 1905– . English composer whose works include the operas *The Midsummer Marriage* 1952 and *The Knot Garden* 1970; four symphonies; *Songs for Ariel* 1962; and choral music including *The Mask of Time* 1982.

tipple *v.t./i.* to drink (wine or spirits etc.); to be a habitual drinker. —*n.* (*colloquial*) alcoholic or other drink. —**tippler** *n.* [back formation from *tippler*]

tipstaff *n.* **1.** a sheriff's officer. **2.** the metal-tipped staff carried by him as a badge of office.

tipster *n.* one who gives tips about horse races etc.

tipsy /'tɪpsɪ/ *adj.* slightly intoxicated; caused by or showing slight intoxication. —**tipsy cake** a sponge cake soaked in wine or spirits and served with custard. —**tipsily** *adv.*, **tipsiness** *n.*

tiptoe *n.* the tips of the toes. —*v.i.* to walk on tiptoe or very stealthily. —*adv.* on tiptoe, with the heels off the ground.

tiptop /'tɪptɒp, -'tɒp/ *adj.* (*colloquial*) excellent. —*n.* (*colloquial*) the highest point of excellence. —*adv.* (*colloquial*) excellently.

TIR abbreviation of *Transport International Routier*. [French = international road transport]

tirade /taɪ'reɪd, tɪ–/ *n.* a long vehement denunciation or declamation. [French from Italian = volley]

Tirana /tɪ'rɑːnə/ or **Tiranë** capital (since 1920) of Albania; population (1983) 206,000. Industries include metallurgy, cotton textiles, soap, and cigarettes. It was founded in the early 17th century by Turks when part of the Ottoman Empire. Although the city is now largely composed of recent buildings, some older districts and mosques have been preserved.

tire[1] *v.t./i.* to make or become tired. [Old English]

tire[2] *n.* 1. a band of metal placed round the rim of a wheel to strengthen it. 2. (*US*) a tyre.

tired /'taɪəd/ *adj.* 1. feeling that one would like to sleep or rest. 2. (of an idea etc.) hackneyed. —**tired of**, having had enough of (a thing or activity) and feeling impatient or bored.

tireless *adj.* not tiring easily, having inexhaustible energy. —**tirelessly** *adv.*

Tiresias /taɪ'riːsiəs/ or **Teiresias** in Greek mythology, a man blinded by the gods and given the ability to predict the future.

tiresome *adj.* wearisome, tedious; (*colloquial*) annoying.

Tîrgu Mureş /'tɜːgu 'muəreʃ/ city in Transylvania, Romania, on the river Mureş; population (1978) 137,000. With a population comprising approximately equal numbers of ethnic Hungarians and Romanians, the city was the scene of rioting between the two groups following Hungarian demands for greater autonomy in 1990; six people were killed.

tiro /'taɪərəu/ *n.* (*plural* tiros) a beginner, a novice. [Latin = recruit]

Tirol /tɪ'rəul/ federal province of Austria; **area** 12,600 sq km/4,864 sq mi; **capital** Innsbruck; **population** (1987) 610,000. It produces diesel engines, optical instruments, and hydroelectric power. Tirol was formerly a province (from 1363) of the Austrian Empire, divided in 1919 between Austria and Italy (see ◊Trentino–Alto Adige).

Tirpitz /'tɜːpɪts/ Alfred von 1849–1930. German admiral. As secretary for the navy 1897–1916, he created the modern German navy and planned the World War I U-boat campaign.

Tirso de Molina /'tɪəsəu deɪ mə'liːnə/ pen name of Gabriel Telléz 1571–1648. Spanish dramatist and monk who wrote more than 400 plays, of which eight are extant, including comedies, historical and biblical dramas, and a series based on the legend of Don Juan.

Tiryns /'tɪrɪns/ ancient Greek city in the Peloponnese on the plain of Argos, with remains of the ◊Mycenaean culture.

'tis /tɪz/ (*archaic*) it is.

Tissot /tiː'səu/ James (Joseph Jacques) 1836–1902. French painter who produced detailed portraits of Victorian high society during a ten-year stay in England.

tissue /'tɪʃuː, 'tɪsjuː/ *n.* 1. in biology, any kind of cellular fabric that occurs in an organism's body. Several kinds of tissue can usually be distinguished, each consisting of cells of a particular kind bound together by cell walls (in plants) or extracellular matrix (in animals). Thus, nerve and muscle are different kinds of tissue in animals, as are ◊parenchyma and ◊sclerenchyma in plants. 2. tissue paper. 3. a disposable piece of thin soft absorbent paper for wiping or drying things. 4. a fine gauzy fabric. 5. a connected series (of lies etc.). —**tissue paper** thin soft unsized paper for wrapping or packing things. [from Old French *tissu* from Latin *texere* = weave]

tissue culture the process by which cells from a plant or animal are removed from the organism and grown under controlled conditions in a sterile medium containing all the necessary nutrients. Tissue culture can provide information on cell growth and differentiation, and is also used in plant propagation and drug production. See also ◊meristem.

tissue plasminogen activator (TPA) a naturally occurring substance in the body tissues that activates the enzyme plasmin, which is able to dissolve blood clots. Human TPA, produced in bacteria by genetic engineering, has been used to try to dissolve blood clots in the coronary arteries of heart-attack victims.

tit[1] *n.* or **titmouse** an insectivorous, acrobatic bird of the family Paridae, of which there are 65 species (e.g. *blue tit*, *coal tit*). They are 8–20 cm/3–8 in long and have grey or black plumage, often with blue or yellow markings. They are found in Eurasia and Africa, and also in North America, where they are called **chickadees**. [probably from Scandinavian]

tit[2] *n.* **tit for tat**, blow for blow, retaliation. [= earlier *tip* (*tip*[2]) *for tat*]

tit[3] *n.* (*vulgar*) a nipple; (in *plural*) a woman's breasts. [Old English]

Titan /'taɪtn/ *n.* 1. in astronomy, the largest moon of the planet Saturn, with a diameter of 5,150 km/3,200 mi and a mean distance from Saturn of 1,222,000 km/759,000 mi. It was discovered in 1655 by Christiaan Huygens, and is one of the two largest moons in the solar system (only Ganymede, of Jupiter, is larger). 2. in Greek mythology, any of the giant children of Uranus and Gaia, who included Kronos, Rhea, Themis (mother of Prometheus and personification of law and order), and Oceanus. Kronos and Rhea were in turn the parents of Zeus, who ousted Kronos as the ruler of the world.

titanic /taɪ'tænɪk/ *adj.* gigantic, colossal. —**titanically** *adv.* [from Greek *Titan*]

Titanic *n.* British passenger liner, supposedly unsinkable, that struck an iceberg and sank off the Grand Banks of Newfoundland on its first voyage 14–15 April 1912; 1,513 lives were lost. In 1985 it was located by robot submarine 4 km/2.5 mi down in an ocean canyon, preserved by the cold environment. In 1987 salvage operations began.

titanium /taɪ'teɪnɪəm, tɪ–/ *n.* a strong, light-weight, silver-grey, metallic element, symbol Ti, atomic number 22, relative atomic mass 47.90. The ninth most abundant element in the Earth's crust, its compounds occur in practically all igneous rocks and their sedimentary deposits. It is very strong and resistant to corrosion, so it is used in building high-speed aircraft and spacecraft; it is also widely used in making alloys, as it unites with almost every metal except copper and aluminium. Titanium oxide is used in high-grade white pigments. [from after *uranium*]

titanium ore one of the minerals from which titanium is extracted, principally ilmenite, $FeTiO_3$, and rutile, TiO_2. Both these ore minerals are found either in rick formations or concentrated in heavy mineral sands. Brazil, India, and Canada are major producers.

Titan rocket a family of US space rockets, developed from the Titan intercontinental missile. Two-stage Titan rockets launched the ◊Gemini crewed missions. More powerful Titans, with additional stages and strap-on boosters, were used to launch spy satellites and space probes, including ◊Viking and ◊Voyager.

titbit *n.* a dainty morsel; a piquant item of news etc. [probably from dialect *tid* = tender and *bit*[1]]

titfer *n.* (*slang*) a hat. [abbreviation of *tit* (*tit*[2]) *for tat*, rhyming slang = hat]

tithe /taɪð/ *n.* (*historical*) a tax of one tenth, especially a tenth part of the annual produce of land or labour formerly levied to support clergy and the Church. —*v.t./i.* to subject to tithes; to pay tithes. —**tithe barn**, a barn built to hold tithes paid in kind. [Old English = tenth]

Titian /'tɪʃən/ anglicized form of the name of Tiziano Vecellio *c.*1487–1576. Italian painter, active in Venice, one of the greatest artists of the High Renaissance. In 1533 he became court painter to Charles V, Holy Roman Emperor, whose son Philip II of Spain later became his patron. Titian's work is richly coloured, with inventive composition. He produced a vast number of portraits, religious paintings, and mythological scenes, including *Bacchus and Ariadne* 1520–23, *Venus and Adonis* 1554, and the *Entombment of Christ* 1559.

Titicaca /tɪti'kɑːkə/ lake in the Andes, 3,810 m/12,500 ft above sea level; area 8,300 sq km/3,200 sq mi, the largest lake in South America. It is divided between Bolivia (port at Guaqui) and Peru (ports at Puno and Huancane). It has enormous edible frogs.

titillate /'tɪtɪleɪt/ v.t. to excite pleasantly; to tickle. —**titillation** /-'leɪʃən/ n. [from Latin *titillare*]

titivate /'tɪtɪveɪt/ v.t. (*colloquial*) to smarten, to put the finishing touches to. —**titivation** /-veɪʃən/ n.

title /'taɪtəl/ n. 1. the name of a book, poem, or work of art etc. 2. the heading of a chapter or legal document etc.; a caption or credit title of a film. 3. a form of nomenclature indicating a person's status (e.g. *professor, queen*) or used as a form of address or reference (e.g. *Lord, Mr, Your Grace*). 4. a championship in sport. 5. the right to the ownership of property with or without possession; the facts constituting this; a just or recognized claim. —**title deed** a legal instrument as evidence of a right. **title page,** a page at the beginning of a book giving the title and particulars of authorship etc. **title-role** n. the part in a play etc. that gives it its name (e. g. *Othello*). [from Old French from Latin *titulus* = placard, title]

titled /'taɪtəld/ adj. having a title of nobility or rank.

titmouse n. (*plural* **titmice**) a tit (◊tit[1]). [from obsolete *mose* = titmouse]

Tito /'tiːtəʊ/ adopted name of Josip Broz 1892–1980. Yugoslav soldier and communist politician, in power from 1945. In World War II he organized the National Liberation Army to carry on guerrilla warfare against the German invasion in 1941, and was created marshal in 1943. As prime minister 1946–53 and president from 1953, he followed a foreign policy of 'positive neutralism'.

Titograd /'tiːtəʊɡræd/ formerly (until 1948) **Podgorica** capital of Montenegro, Yugoslavia; population (1981) 132,300. Industries include metal working, furniture making, and tobacco. It was damaged in World War II and after rebuilding was renamed in honour of Marshal Tito. It was the birthplace of the Roman emperor Diocletian.

titrate /taɪ'treɪt/ v.t. in analytical chemistry, to find the concentration of one compound in a solution by determining how much of it will react with a known amount of another compound in solution. —**titration** /-'treɪʃən/ n. [from French *titrer* (*titre* = title)]

titter v.i. to laugh covertly, to giggle. —n. such a laugh. [imitative]

tittle /'tɪtəl/ n. a small written or printed stroke or dot; a particle, a whit (especially *not one jot or tittle*). [from Latin *titulus*]

tittle-tattle v.i. to tattle. —n. tattle. [reduplication of *tattle*]

tittup /'tɪtəp/ v.i. to move in a lively or frisky way, to bob up and down. —n. such a movement. [perhaps imitative of hoof beats]

titular /'tɪtjʊlə/ adj. 1. of or relating to a title. 2. existing or being such in title only. [from French from Latin *titulus*]

Titus /'taɪtəs/ Flavius Sabinus Vespasianus AD 39–81. Roman emperor from AD 79. Eldest son of ◊Vespasian, he stormed Jerusalem in 70 to end the Jewish revolt in Roman Palestine. He completed the Colosseum, and enjoyed a peaceful reign, except for ◊Agricola's campaigns in Britain.

tizzy /'tɪzɪ/ n. (*slang*) a state of nervous agitation or confusion.

Tl symbol for thallium.

Tlingit /'tlɪŋɡɪt/ n. a member of a North American Indian people of the NW coast, living in S Alaska and N British Columbia. They are especially known for carving wooden totem poles that include such animals as the raven, whale, octopus, beaver, bear, wolf, and the mythical 'thunderbird'. Their language is related to the Athabaskan languages.

TLR camera a twin-lens reflex camera that has a viewing lens of the same angle of view and focal length mounted above and parallel to the taking lens.

Tm symbol for thulium.

TM abbreviation of ◊transcendental meditation.

TNT abbreviation of trinitrotoluene.

to /tə, *before a vowel* tʊ, *emphatic* tuː/ prep. 1. in the direction of; so as to approach, reach, or be in (a place, position, or state etc.). 2. as far as, not falling far short of. 3. as compared with; in respect of. 4. for (a person or thing) to hold, possess, or be affected etc. by. 5. (with a verb) introducing an infinitive; expressing purpose, consequence, or cause; used alone when an infinitive is understood (*I meant to call but forgot to*). —adv. to or in a normal or required position or condition; to a standstill; (of a door) into

toad

western spadefoot toad

a nearly closed position. —**to and fro,** backwards and forwards; repeatedly between the same places. [Old English]

toad n. 1. the general name for over 2,500 species of froglike tailless amphibians of the genus *Bufo,* which are slow-moving, stout, and have dry, warty skins. They live in cool, moist places, lay their eggs in water, and grow up to 25 cm/10 in long. 2. a repulsive person. —**toad-in-the-hole** n. sausages or other meat baked in batter. [Old English]

toadflax n. a plant of the genus *Linaria* or allied genera with spurred yellow or purple flowers.

toadstool n. an inedible or poisonous type of ◊fungus with a fleshy, gilled fruiting body on a stalk.

toady n. a sycophant, an obsequious hanger-on. —v.t./i. to behave as a toady (to). [from *toadeater,* originally the attendant of a charlatan, employed to eat or pretend to eat toads (held to be poisonous) to enable his master to exhibit his skill in expelling poison]

toast n. 1. a toasted slice of bread. 2. a person or thing in whose honour a company is requested to drink; the call to drink or an instance of drinking in this way. —v.t. 1. to brown the surface of (bread, a teacake, cheese, etc.) by placing it before a fire or other source of heat. 2. to warm (one's feet or oneself) thus. 3. to honour or pledge good wishes by drinking. —**have a person on toast,** (*slang*) to have him at one's mercy. **toasting fork,** a long-handled fork for holding a slice of bread before a fire to toast it. **toastmaster** n. a person announcing the toasts at a public dinner. **toast rack,** a rack for holding slices of toast at table. [from Old French *toster* from Latin *torrēre* = parch]

toaster n. an electrical device for making toast.

tobacco /tə'bækəʊ/ n. (*plural* **tobaccos**) a plant of the genus *Nicotiana,* of the nightshade family Solanaceae, native to tropical parts of the Americas. *N. tabacum* is widely cultivated in warm, dry climates, its narcotic leaves being used in cigars and cigarettes, and in powdered form as snuff. [from Spanish *tobaco,* of American Indian origin]

tobacconist /tə'bækənɪst/ n. a shopkeeper who sells tobacco and cigarettes etc.

Tobago /tə'beɪɡəʊ/ island in the West Indies; part of the republic of ◊Trinidad and Tobago.

toboggan /tə'bɒɡən/ n. a long light narrow sledge curved upwards at the front, used for sliding downhill especially over snow or ice. —v.i. to ride on a toboggan. [from Canadian French from Algonquian]

Tobruk /tə'brʊk/ Libyan port; population (1984) 94,000. Occupied by Italy in 1911, it was taken by Britain in 1941 during World War II, and unsuccessfully besieged by Axis forces April–Dec 1941. It was captured by Germany in June 1942 after the retreat of the main British force to Egypt, and this precipitated the replacement of Auchinleck by Montgomery as British commander.

toby jug a jug or mug in the form of a stout old man wearing a long full-skirted coat and a three-cornered hat (18th-century costume). [from *Toby,* man's name]

toccata /tə'kɑːtə/ n. a musical composition for a piano, organ, etc., designed to exhibit a performer's touch and technique. [Italian, past participle of *toccare* = touch]

Tocqueville /tɒk'viːl/ Alexis de 1805–1859. French politician and political scientist, author of the first analytical study of the US constitution, *De la Démocratie en Amérique/Democracy in America* 1835, and of a penetrating description of France before the Revolution, *L'Ancien Régime et la Révolution/The Old Regime and the Revolution* 1856.

tocsin /'tɒksɪn/ n. an alarm signal; a bell used to sound an alarm. [French from *touquesain, toquassen* from Provençal]

tod *n.* (*slang*) **on one's tod**, alone, on one's own. [perhaps from *on one's Tod Sloan* (jockey, died 1933), rhyming slang]

today /təˈdeɪ/ *adv.* on this present day; nowadays, in modern times. —*n.* this present day; modern times. [Old English]

Todd /tɒd/ Alexander, Baron Todd 1907– . Scottish organic chemist, who won a Nobel prize in 1957 for his work on the role of nucleic acids in genetics. He also synthesized vitamins B1, B12, and E.

Todd Ron(ald) 1927– . British trade-union leader. He rose from shop steward to general secretary of Britain's largest trade union, the Transport and General Workers' (TGWU). Although backing the Labour Party leadership, he has criticized its attitude towards nuclear disarmament.

toddle *v.i.* to walk with a young child's short unsteady steps; (*colloquial*, usually with *off*) to depart. —*n.* a toddling walk.

toddler *n.* a child who has only recently learnt to walk.

toddy /ˈtɒdɪ/ *n.* a drink of spirits with hot water and sugar. [from Hindi (*tar* = palm)]

to-do /təˈduː/ *n.* a commotion, a fuss. [from *to do* as in *What's to do?*]

toe *n.* 1. any of the terminal members (five in humans) of the front part of the foot; the corresponding part of an animal or bird. 2. the part of footwear that covers the toes. 3. the lower end or tip of an implement etc. —*v.t.* to touch with the toes. —**on one's toes**, alert, eager. **toecap** *n.* the reinforced toe of a boot or shoe. **toehold** *n.* a slight foothold (*literal* and *figurative*). **toe the line**, to conform (especially under compulsion) to the requirement of one's group or party. [Old English]

toff *n.* (*slang*) a distinguished or well-dressed person. [perhaps from *tuft* in archaic sense 'titled undergraduate', who formerly at Oxford and Cambridge Universities wore a gold tassel on the academic cap]

toffee /ˈtɒfɪ/ *n.* a kind of firm or hard sweet made by boiling sugar, butter, etc.; a small piece of this. —**can't do a thing for toffee**, (*slang*) is incompetent at it. **toffee-apple** *n.* a toffee-coated apple on a stick. **toffee-nosed** *adj.* (*slang*) snobbish, pretentious. [from earlier *taffy*]

tofu /ˈtəʊfuː/ *n.* (especially in China and Japan) a curd made from mashed soya beans. It is a good source of protein and naturally low in fat. [from Japanese from Chinese = rotten beans]

tog *n.* 1. (usually in *plural*, *slang*) a garment. 2. a unit of measure of thermal insulation used in the textile trade; a light summer suit provides 1.0 tog. —*v.t.* (**-gg-**) (with *out* or *up*) (*slang*) to dress. [abbreviation of 16th-century slang *togman* from French *toge* or Latin *toga*; sense 2 modelled on earlier US term *clo* (*clothes*)]

toga /ˈtəʊgə/ *n.* an ancient Roman citizen's loose flowing outer garment. —**toga'd** *adj.* [Latin (related to *tegere* = cover)]

together /təˈgeðə/ *adv.* 1. in or into company or conjunction; towards each other; so as to unite. 2. one with another. 3. simultaneously. 4. in an unbroken succession. 5. (*colloquial*) well organized or controlled. —**together with**, as well as, and also. [Old English]

togetherness *n.* being together; feeling or belonging together.

toggle *n.* a fastening device consisting of a short piece of wood or metal etc. secured by its centre and passed through a loop or hole etc. —**toggle switch**, a switch operated by a projecting lever.

Togliatti /tɒlˈjæti/ Palmiro 1893–1964. Founding member of the Italian Communist Party in 1921 and effectively its leader for almost 40 years from 1926 until his death. In exile from 1926 until 1944, he returned after the fall of the Fascist dictator Mussolini to become a member of Badoglio's government and held office until 1946.

Togo /ˈtəʊgəʊ/ Republic of; country in W Africa, bounded to the W by Ghana, to the E by Benin, and to the N by Burkina Faso; **area** 56,800 sq km/21,930 sq mi; **capital** Lomé; **physical** two savanna plains, divided by range of hills NE-SW; coastal lagoons and marsh; **head of state and government** Etienne Gnassingbé Eyadéma from 1967; **political system** one-party socialist republic; **population** (1990 est) 3,566,000; **language** French (official), local languages; **recent history** as Togoland, was a German protectorate from 1885 until captured by Anglo-French forces in 1914; divided between Britain and France

under League of Nations mandate in 1922. Independence was achieved from France in 1960, as the Republic of Togo. A military coup in 1963 installed Nicolas Grunitzky as president, replaced in 1967 by Lt-Gen Eyadema in another (bloodless) coup. A further attempted coup in 1986 failed.

Tōgō /ˈtəʊgəʊ/ Heihachirō 1846–1934. Japanese admiral who commanded the fleet at the battle of Tsushima in 1905, when Japan defeated the Russians and effectively ended the Russo-Japanese War of 1904–05.

Tohoku /təʊˈhəʊku:/ mountainous region of N Honshu island, Japan; **area** 66,971 sq km/25,867 sq mi; **chief city** Sendai; **population** (1986) 9,737,000. Timber, fruit, fish, and livestock are produced. The city of Aomori in the NE is linked to Hakodate on the island of Hokkaido by the **Seikan tunnel**, the world's longest underwater tunnel.

toil *v.i.* to work long or laboriously; to move laboriously. —*n.* hard or laborious work. —**toiler** *n.* [from Anglo-French = dispute, from Latin *tudiculare* = stir about (*tudicula* = machine for bruising olives, relative to *tundere* = beat)]

toilet /ˈtɔɪlɪt/ *n.* 1. a lavatory, a place where waste products from the body are excreted. Simple ◊latrines, pits dug in the ground, with ◊sewers to carry away waste, have been found in the Indus Valley and ancient Babylon; the medieval ◊garderobe is essentially the same. The valve ◊cistern, with a base that could be opened or closed, was invented by John Harington, godson of Queen Elizabeth I; following the introduction of the ◊ball valve in 1748, it was independently reinvented and patented by Alexander Cummings in 1775. Cumming's design included a U-bend to keep smells out. This design was then improved by Joseph ◊Bramah in 1778. 2. the process of washing oneself, dressing, etc. —**toilet paper**, paper for cleaning oneself after excreting. **toilet roll**, a roll of toilet paper. **toilet soap**, soap for washing oneself. **toilet training**, the training of a young child to use the lavatory. **toilet water**, a scented liquid used in or after cleansing the skin. [from French *toilette*]

toiletries /ˈtɔɪlɪtrɪz/ *n.pl.* articles used in making one's toilet.

toils /tɔɪlz/ *n.pl.* a snare. [from Old French *toile* = cloth from Latin *tela* = web]

toilsome /ˈtɔɪlsəm/ *adj.* involving toil.

Tōjō /ˈtəʊdʒəʊ/ Hideki 1884–1948. Japanese general and premier 1941–44 during World War II. Promoted to chief of staff of Japan's Guangdong army in Manchuria in 1937, he served as minister for war 1940–41. He was held responsible for defeats in the Pacific in 1944 and forced to resign. After Japan's defeat, he was hanged as a war criminal.

tokamak *n.* an experimental machine designed by Soviet scientists to investigate controlled nuclear fusion. It consists of a doughnut-shaped chamber surrounded by electromagnets capable of exerting very powerful magnetic fields. The fields are generated to confine a very hot (millions of degrees) ◊plasma of ions and electrons, keeping it away from the chamber walls. See also ◊JET.

Tokay /təˈkeɪ/ *n.* a sweet Hungarian wine; a similar wine from elsewhere. [from *Tokaj* in Hungary]

token /ˈtəʊkən/ *n.* 1. an indication; a thing serving as a symbol, reminder, keepsake, distinctive mark, or guarantee. 2. a voucher exchangeable for goods. 3. a thing used to represent something else; a device resembling a coin, bought for use in slot machines etc. or for making certain payments. —*adj.* serving as a token or pledge but often on a small scale. —**by this** *or* **the same token**, similarly; moreover; in corroboration of what I say. [Old English]

tokenism /ˈtəʊkənɪzəm/ *n.* making only a token effort or granting only minimum concessions, especially to minority or suppressed groups.

Tokugawa /tɒkuˈgɑːwə/ *n.* military family that controlled Japan as ◊shoguns 1603–1867. **Iyeyasu** or **Ieyasu Tokugawa** (1542–1616) was the Japanese general and politician who established the Tokugawa shogunate. The Tokugawa were feudal lords who ruled about one-quarter of Japan.

Tokyo /ˈtəʊkiəʊ/ capital of Japan, on Honshu Island; population (1987) 8,209,000, metropolitan area over 12,000,000. The Sumida river delta separates the city from its suburb of Honjo. It is Japan's main cultural and industrial centre (engineering, chemicals, textiles, electrical goods). Founded in the 16th century as *Yedo* (or *Edo*), it was renamed when the emperor moved his court there from Kyoto in 1868.

An earthquake in 1923 killed 58,000 people. The city was severely damaged by Allied bombing in World War II. The subsequent rebuilding has made it into one of the world's most modern cities.

tolbooth /'tɒlbuːθ/ variant of **tollbooth** (see ◊toll[1]).

told /təʊld/ past and past participle of **tell**.

Toledo /tɒ'leɪdəʊ/ city on the river Tagus, Castilla–La Mancha, central Spain; population (1982) 62,000. It was the capital of the Visigoth kingdom 534–711 (see ◊Goth), then became a Moorish city, and was the Castilian capital 1085–1560.

tolerable /'tɒlərəbəl/ adj. 1. able to be tolerated, endurable. 2. fairly good, passable. —**tolerableness** n., **tolerably** adv. [from Old French from Latin]

tolerance /'tɒlərəns/ n. 1. willingness or ability to tolerate a person or thing. 2. permissible variation in dimension or weight.

tolerant /'tɒlərənt/ adj. having or showing tolerance. —**tolerantly** adv.

tolerate /'tɒləreɪt/ v.t. 1. to permit without protest or interference. 2. to find or treat as endurable. 3. to be able to take (a medicine) or undergo (a process etc.) without harm. —**toleration** /-'reɪʃən/ n. [from Latin tolerare]

Tolkien /'tɒlkiːn/ J(ohn) R(onald) R(euel) 1892–1973. English writer who created the fictional world of Middle Earth in *The Hobbit* 1937 and the trilogy *The Lord of the Rings* 1954–55, fantasy novels peopled with hobbits, dwarves, and strange magical creatures. His work developed a cult following in the 1960s and had many imitators. At Oxford University he was professor of Anglo-Saxon 1925–45 and Merton professor of English 1945–59.

One Ring to rule them all, One Ring to find them, One Ring to bring them all and in the darkness bind them.

John Ronald Reuel Tolkien
The Lord of the Rings

---

toll[1] /təʊl/ n. 1. a charge payable for permission to pass a barrier or for the use of a bridge or road etc. 2. the cost or damage caused by a disaster or incurred in an achievement. —**take its toll**, to be accompanied by loss or injury etc. **tollbooth** n. (*archaic, Scottish*) a town hall or town gaol. **toll bridge,** a bridge at which a toll is charged. **tollgate** n. a gate preventing passage until a toll is paid. **tollhouse** n. (*historical*) a small house built near a tollgate for the use of the keeper, usually hexagonal in shape so that the windows commanded a view in all directions. **toll road,** a road maintained by the tolls collected on it. [Old English from Latin *toloneum* from Greek *telos* = tax]

toll[2] v.t./i. 1. (of a bell) to sound with a slow uniform succession of strokes. 2. to ring (a bell or knell) or strike (an hour) or announce or mark (a death etc.) thus. —n. the tolling or stroke of a bell. [from obsolete or dialect *toll* = pull]

Tolpuddle Martyrs /'tɒlpʌdl/ six farm labourers of Tolpuddle, near Dorchester, SW England, who were transported to Australia in 1834 for forming a trade union. After nationwide agitation they were pardoned two years later.

Tolstoy /'tɒlstɔɪ/ Leo Nikolaievich 1828–1910. Russian novelist who wrote *Tales from Sebastopol* 1856, ◊*War and Peace* 1863–69, and ◊*Anna Karenina* 1873–77. From 1880 Tolstoy underwent a profound spiritual crisis and took up various moral positions, including passive resistance to evil, rejection of authority (religious or civil) and private ownership, and a return to basic mystical Christianity. He was excommunicated by the Orthodox Church, and his later works were banned.

Toltec /'tɒltek/ n. a member of an ancient American Indian people who ruled much of Mexico in the 10th–12th centuries, with their capital at Tula, and built new ceremonial centres in the Mayan territories of Yucatán. After the Toltecs' fall in the 13th century, the Aztecs took over much of their former territory, except for the regions regained by the Maya.

tolu /tə'ljuː, 'təʊljuː/ n. a fragrant brown balsam from a South American tree *Myroxylon balsamum.* [from (Santiago de) *Tolu* in Colombia]

toluene /'tɒljuiːn/ n. or **methyl benzene** $C_6H_5CH_3$, a colourless, inflammable liquid, insoluble in water, derived from petroleum. It is used as a solvent, in aircraft fuels,

in preparing phenol (carbolic acid, used in making resins for adhesives, pharmaceuticals, and as a disinfectant), and the powerful high explosive TNT (see ◊trinitrotoluene). [from *tolu*]

toluol /'tɒljuɒl/ n. a commercial grade of toluene. [from *tolu*]

tom n. (in full **tom cat**) a male cat. —**Tom, Dick, and Harry,** (usually *derogatory*) persons taken at random, ordinary people (usually preceded by *any* or *every*). [abbreviation of man's name *Thomas*]

tomahawk /'tɒməhɔːk/ n. a North American Indian war axe. [from Algonquian *tämäham* = he cuts]

Tomasi /təʊ'mɑːsi/ Giuseppe, Prince of Lampedusa. Italian writer; see ◊Lampedusa.

tomato /tə'mɑːtəʊ/ n. (*plural* **tomatoes**) 1. an annual plant *Lycopersicon esculentum* of the nightshade family Solanaceae, native to South America. 2. the many-seeded red fruit of this plant (technically a berry), used in salads and cooking. [from French or Spanish and Portuguese from Mexican *tomatl*]

tomb /tuːm/ n. a grave or other place of burial; a burial vault; a sepulchral monument. [from Anglo-French, ultimately from Greek *tumbos*]

Tombaugh /'tɒmbɔː/ Clyde (William) 1906– . US astronomer who discovered the planet ◊Pluto in 1930.

tombola /tɒm'bəʊlə/ n. a kind of lottery with tickets and prizes. [French or from Italian *tombolare* = tumble]

tomboy n. a rough, boyish girl.

tombstone n. a stone standing or laid over a grave, usually with an epitaph.

Tombstone former silver-mining town in the desert of SE Arizona, USA. The **gunfight at the OK Corral,** with deputy marshal Wyatt Earp, his brothers, and 'Doc' Holliday against the Clanton gang, took place here on 26 Oct 1881.

tome n. a large book or volume. [French from Latin from Greek *tomos*, originally = section (*temnō* = cut)]

tomfool /tɒm'fuːl/ adj. extremely foolish. —n. a fool.

tomfoolery n. foolish behaviour.

Tom Jones, The History of a novel by Henry Fielding, published in 1749. It describes the complicated, and not always reputable, early life of Tom Jones, an orphan, who is good-natured but hot-headed.

Tommy /'tɒmi/ n. a British private soldier. [from *Tommy* (*Thomas*) *Atkins,* name used in specimens of completed official forms]

Tommy gun /'tɒmɪɡʌn/ the popular name for the Thompson sub-machine-gun; see ◊machine gun. [from co-inventor J T *Thompson*]

tommyrot /'tɒmɪrɒt/ n. (*slang*) nonsense.

tomography /tə'mɒɡrəfi/ n. radiography in which an image of a selected plane in the body or other object is obtained by rotating the detector and the source of radiation in such a way that points outside the plane give a blurred image. —**tomographic** /-'ɡræfɪk/ adj. [from Greek *tomē* = cutting]

tomorrow /tə'mɒrəʊ/ adv. on the day after today; at some future time. —n. the day after today; the near future.

Tom Sawyer, The Adventures of a novel by US author Mark Twain, published in 1876. It describes the childhood escapades of Tom Sawyer and his friends Huckleberry Finn and Joe Harper in a small Mississippi community before the Civil War. It and its sequel *The Adventures of Huckleberry Finn* 1885 are remarkable for their rejection of the high moral tone prevalent in 19th-century children's literature.

tomtit n. a ◊tit, especially a blue tit.

tom-tom /'tɒmtɒm/ n. a primitive drum beaten with the hands; a tall drum used in jazz bands etc. [from Hindi *tamtam* (imitative)]

-tomy /-təmi/ suffix forming nouns with sense 'cutting', especially in names of surgical operations or incision (e. g. *laparotomy*). [from Greek *-tomia* = cutting (*temnō* = cut)]

ton /tʌn/ n. 1. a measure of weight, 2,240 lb. The **long ton,** used in the UK, is 2,240 lb/1,016 kg; the **short ton,** used in the USA, is 2,000 lb/907 kg. The **metric ton** or **tonne** is 1,000 kg/2,205 lb. 2. a in shipping, unit of volume equal to 2.83 cubic metres/100 cubic feet. **Gross tonnage** is the total internal volume of a ship in tons; **net register tonnage** is the volume used for carrying cargo or passengers. **Displacement tonnage** is the weight of the vessel, in terms of the number of imperial tons of seawater displaced when the ship is loaded to its load line; it is used to describe warships. 3. (usually in *plural*) (*colloquial*) a large number or amount. 4. (*slang*) a speed of 100 mph 5. (*slang*) £100. —**ton-up boys,** motorcyclists who travel at high speed. **weighs a ton,** is very heavy. [different spelling of *tun*]

tonal /'təʊnəl/ *adj.* of or relating to tone or tonality. —**tonal language,** a tone language (see ◊tone). —**tonally** *adv.* [from Latin]

tonality /tə'næliti/ *n.* 1. the relationship between the notes of a musical scale; the observance of a single tonic key as the basis of a composition. 2. the colour scheme of a picture.

tone *n.* 1. a musical or vocal sound, especially with reference to its pitch, quality, and strength. 2. the modulation of the voice to express a particular feeling or mood. 3. a manner of expression in writing. 4. a musical sound, especially of a definite pitch and character; an interval of a major second, e. g. C–D. 5. the general effect of colour or of light and shade in a picture; a tint or shade of colour. 6. the prevailing character of morals and sentiments etc. in a group. 7. proper firmness of bodily organs and tissues; a state of good or specified health. —*v.t./i.* 1. to give a desired tone to; to modify the tone of; to attune. 2. to harmonize in colour. —**tone-deaf** *adj.* unable to perceive differences of musical pitch accurately. **tone down,** to make or become softer in the tone of sound or colour; to make (a statement etc.) less harsh or emphatic. **tone language,** a language which uses variations in pitch to distinguish words which would otherwise sound identical. **tone poem** *or* **symphonic poem,** an orchestral composition illustrating a poetic idea as used, for example, by Richard Strauss. **tone up,** to make or become brighter or more vigorous or intense. —**toner** *n.* [from Old French from Latin from Greek, originally = tension (*teinō* = stretch)]

Tone /təʊn/ (Theobald) Wolfe 1763–1798. Irish nationalist, prominent in the revolutionary society of the United Irishmen. In 1798 he accompanied the French invasion of Ireland, was captured and condemned to death, but slit his own throat in prison.

Tonga /'tɒŋə/ Kingdom of country in the SW Pacific, in ◊Polynesia; **area** 750 sq km/290 sq mi; **capital** Nuku'alofa (on Tongatapu island); **physical** three groups of islands in SW Pacific, mostly coral formations, but active volcano in W; **head of state and government** King Taufa'ahau Tupou IV from 1965; **political system** absolute monarchy; **population** (1988) 95,000; **language** Tongan (official), English; **recent history** became a British protectorate in 1900, independence achieved from Britain with the Commonwealth in 1970.

tongs /tɒŋz/ *n.pl.* an instrument with two arms joined at one end, used for grasping and holding things. [Old English]

tongue /tʌŋ/ *n.* 1. the fleshy muscular organ in the mouth used in tasting, licking, swallowing, and (in human beings) speech. It has a thick root attached to a U-shaped bone (hyoid), and is covered with a ◊mucous membrane containing nerves and 'taste buds'. 2. the tongue of an ox etc. as food. 3. the faculty of or a tendency in speech. 4. the language of a nation etc. 5. a thing like a tongue in shape, e. g. a long promontory, a strip of leather under the laces in a shoe, the clapper of a bell, the pin of a buckle; the projecting strip on a wooden etc. board fitting into the groove of another. —**find** (*or* **lose**) **one's tongue,** to be able (or unable) to express oneself after a shock etc. **hold one's tongue,** to remain silent. **tongue-tie** *n.* a speech impediment due to a malformation of the tongue. **tongue-tied** *adj.* too shy or embarrassed to speak; having a tongue-tie. **tongue twister,** a sequence of words difficult to pronounce quickly and correctly. **with one's tongue in one's cheek,** insincerely or ironically; with sly humour. [Old English]

tonguing *n.* in music, the use of the tongue to articulate certain notes in playing a wind instrument.

tonic /'tɒnik/ *n.* 1. an invigorating medicine; anything serving to invigorate. 2. tonic water. 3. in music, the first degree or key note of a scale (for example, the note C in the scale of C major). —*adj.* 1. serving as a tonic, invigorating. 2. of the tonic or keynote in music. —**tonic water,** a carbonated drink flavoured with quinine or another bitter. [from French from Greek]

tonic sol-fa /sɒl'fɑː/ a method of teaching music, usually singing, systematized in England by John ◊Curwen (1816-1880). The notes of a scale are named by syllables (doh, ray, me, fah, soh, lah, te, with the ◊key (sense 4) indicated) to simplify singing by sight.

tonight /tə'naɪt/ *adv.* on the present or approaching evening or night. —*n.* the present evening or night, the evening or night of today.

Tonkin resolution the act passed by the US Congress on 7 Aug 1964 after the **Tonkin Gulf Incident,** in which it was alleged that North Vietnamese patrol boats fired on two US destroyers. It allowed President Lyndon Johnson 'to take all necessary steps, including the use of armed forces' to help SEATO (South-East Asia Treaty Organization) members 'defend their freedom'. This resolution formed the basis for the considerable increase in US military involvement in the Vietnam War. The resolution was repealed in 1971 in light of evidence that the Johnson administration contrived to deceive Congress about the incident.

tonnage /'tʌnɪdʒ/ *n.* 1. a ship's internal cubic capacity or freight-carrying capacity. 2. the charge per ton on cargo or freight.

tonne /tʌn, tɒn/ *n.* the metric ton of 1,000 kg/2,204.6 lb; equivalent to 0.9842 of an imperial ◊ton. [French]

Tönnies Ferdinand 1855-1936. German social theorist and philosopher, one of the founders of the sociological tradition of community studies and urban sociology through his key work, ◊*Gemeinschaft-Gesellschaft* 1887. Tönnies contrasted the nature of social relationships in traditional societies and small organizations (*Gemeinschaft*, 'community') with those in industrial societies and large organizations (*Gesellschaft*, 'association'). He was pessimistic about the effect of industrialization and urbanization on the social and moral order, seeing them as a threat to traditional society's sense of community.

tonsil /'tɒnsəl/ *n.* in higher vertebrates, either of two small masses of lymphoid tissue situated at the back of the mouth and throat (palatine tonsils), and on the rear surface of the tongue (lingual tonsils). The tonsils contain many ◊lymphocytes and are part of the body's defence system against infection. —**tonsillar** /'tɒnsɪlə/ *adj.* [from French or Latin *tonsillae*]

tonsillectomy /tɒnsɪ'lektəmɪ/ *n.* surgical removal of the tonsils.

tonsillitis /tɒnsɪ'laɪtɪs/ *n.* inflammation of the tonsils.

tonsorial /tɒn'sɔːrɪəl/ *adj.* of a barber or a barber's work. [from Latin *tonsor* (*tondēre* = shave)]

tonsure /'tɒnʃə/ *n.* the full or partial shaving of the head as a symbol of entering the clerical or monastic orders. Until the early 1970s in the Roman Catholic Church, the crown was shaved (leaving a surrounding fringe to resemble Jesus' crown of thorns); in the Eastern Orthodox Church the hair is merely shorn close. For Buddhist monks, the entire head is shaved except for a topknot. —*v.t.* to give a tonsure to. [from Old French or Latin]

Tonton Macoute /'tɒntɒn mə'kuːt/ a member of a private army of death squads on Haiti. The Tontons Macoutes were initially organized by François Duvalier, president of Haiti 1957–71, and continued to terrorize the population under his successor J C Duvalier. It is alleged that the organization continued to operate after Duvalier's exile to France.

Tony award /'təʊni/ the annual award by the League of New York Theaters to playwrights, performers, and technicians in ◊Broadway plays. [named after US actress and producer Antoinette Perry (1888–1946)]

too *adv.* 1. to a greater extent than is desirable or permissible. 2. (*colloquial*) extremely. 3. in addition, moreover. —**none too,** rather less than. **too much,** intolerable. **too much for,** more than a match for; more than can be endured by. [stressed form of *to*]

took past of **take.**

tool *n.* 1. any implement (usually held in the hand) that gives the user a ◊mechanical advantage, such as a hammer or a saw; a **machine tool** is a tool operated by power. Tools are the basis of industrial production; the chief machine tool is the ◊lathe. The industrial potential of a country is often calculated by the number of machine tools available. Automatic control of machine tools, a milestone in industrial development, is known as ◊automation, and electronic control is called robotics (see ◊robot). 2. a thing used in an occupation or pursuit. **3.** a person used as a mere instrument by another. —*v.t./i.* **1.** to dress (stone) with a chisel. **2.** to impress a design on (a leather book cover etc.). **3.** (*slang*) to drive or ride in a casual or leisurely manner. —**tool pusher,** a worker directing drilling on an oil rig. [Old English]

toot *n.* a short sharp sound (as) of a horn or trumpet. —*v.t./i.* to sound (a horn etc.) thus; to give out such a sound. [probably from Middle Low German, or imitative]

tooth (*plural* **teeth**) **1.** in vertebrates, one of a set of hard, bonelike structures in the mouth, used for biting and chewing food, and in defence and aggression. In humans, the first set (20 milk teeth) appear from age six months to two and a half years. The permanent ◊dentition replaces these from the sixth year onwards, the wisdom teeth (third molars) sometimes not appearing until the age of 25 or 30. Adults have 32 teeth: two incisors, one canine (eye tooth), two premolars, and three molars on each side of each jaw. Each tooth consists of an enamel coat (hardened calcium deposits), dentine (a thick, bonelike layer), and an inner pulp cavity, housing nerves and blood vessels. The neck of the tooth is covered by the ◊gum, while the enamel-covered crown protrudes above the gum line. **2.** a toothlike part or projection, e. g. a cog of a gearwheel, a point of a saw or comb etc. **3.** sense of taste, an appetite. **4.** (in *plural*) force or effectiveness. —**armed to the teeth,** completely and elaborately armed or equipped. **fight tooth and nail,** to fight very fiercely. **get one's teeth into,** to devote oneself seriously to. **in the teeth of,** in spite of (opposition or difficulty etc.), in opposition to (instructions etc.); directly against (the wind etc.). **tooth comb,** a comb with fine close-set teeth (properly a fine-tooth comb; see ◊fine¹). **tooth powder,** a powder for cleaning the teeth. [Old English]

toothache *n.* pain in a tooth or the teeth.

toothbrush *n.* a brush for cleaning the teeth.

toothless *adj.* having no teeth.

toothpaste *n.* paste for cleaning the teeth.

toothpick *n.* a small sharp instrument for removing food etc. lodged between the teeth.

toothsome *adj.* (of food) delicious.

toothy *adj.* having large, numerous, or prominent teeth.

tootle *v.i.* **1.** to toot gently or repeatedly. **2.** (*colloquial*) to go in a casual or leisurely way.

top¹ *n.* **1.** the highest point or part. **2.** the upper surface; a thing forming the upper part; the cover or cap of a container etc. **3.** the highest rank; the foremost place or position; a person holding such a rank etc. **4.** a garment for the upper part of the body. **5.** (usually in *plural*) the leaves etc. of a plant grown chiefly for its root. **6.** the utmost degree or intensity. **7.** top gear. **8.** a platform round the head of the lower mast of a ship. **9.** (*predicative,* in *plural*) a person or thing of the very best quality. —*adj.* highest in position, degree, or importance. —*v.t.* (**-pp-**) **1.** to furnish with a top or cap. **2.** to be higher than; to be superior to, to surpass. **3.** to be at the top of; to reach the top of (a hill etc.) **4.** to hit (a ball in golf) above its centre. —**at the top,** in the highest rank of a profession etc. **on top,** above, in a superior position. **on top of,** fully in control of; in close proximity to; in addition to. **on top of the world,** exuberant. **over the top,** over the parapet of a trench; into a final or decisive state or a state of excess. **top brass,** (*colloquial*) high-ranking officers. **top dog,** (*colloquial*) the victor, the master. **top drawer,** a high social position or origin. **top-dress** *v.t.* to apply manure or fertilizer on the top of (the earth), not dig it in. **top-flight** *adj.* in the highest rank of achievement. **top gear,** the highest gear. **top hat,** a tall silk hat. **top-heavy** *adj.* overweighted at the top and so in danger of falling. **top-hole** *adj.* (*slang*) first-rate. **top-level** *adj.* of or at the highest rank or level. **topnotch** *adj.* (*colloquial*) first-rate. **top off,** to put an end or finishing touch to. **top out,** to put the highest stone on (a building). **top secret,** of the highest secrecy. **top up,** to fill up (a partly empty container); to add extra money or items to. [Old English]

top² *n.* a toy, usually conical or pear-shaped, with a sharp point at the bottom on which it rotates when set in motion. [Old English]

topaz /ˈtəʊpæz/ *n.* a mineral, aluminium fluosilicate, $Al_2SiO_4(F,OH)_2$. It is usually yellow, but pink if it has been heated, and is used as a gemstone when transparent.

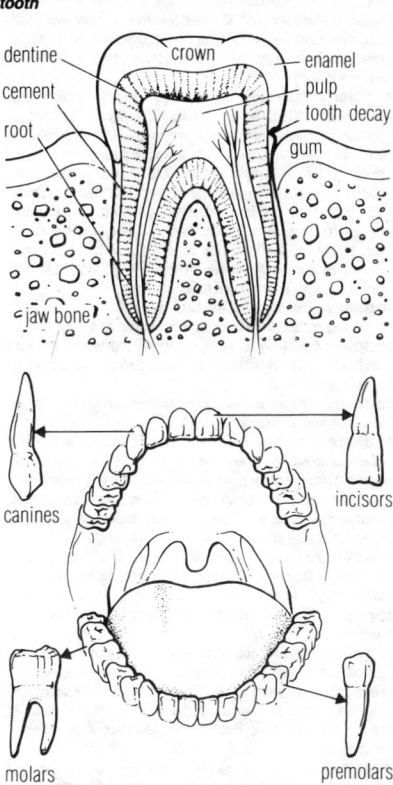

tooth

dentine · crown · enamel · pulp · cement · tooth decay · root · gum · jaw bone · incisors · canines · molars · premolars

It ranks 8 on the Mohs' scale of hardness. [from Old French from Latin from Greek *topazos*]

topcoat *n.* **1.** an overcoat. **2.** an outer coat of paint etc.

tope¹ *n.* a small shark of the genus *Galeorhinus*. [perhaps from Cornish]

tope² *v.i.* (*archaic*) to drink intoxicating liquor to excess, especially habitually. —**toper** *n.* [perhaps from obsolete *top* = quaff]

tope³ *n.* a tumulus found in India and SE Asia; a Buddhist monument usually built over a relic of Buddha or his disciples. Topes date from 400–300 BC including ones at Sanchi, near Bhilsa, central India.

topgallant /tɒpˈgælənt/ *n.* the mast, sail, yard, or rigging immediately above the topmast and topsail.

topi¹ /ˈtəʊpɪ/ *n.* (also **topee**) a sun helmet, especially a sola topi. [from Hindi]

topi² *n.* or **korrigum** an antelope *Damaliscus korrigum* of equatorial Africa, head and body about 1.7 m/5.5 ft long, 1.1 m/3.5 ft high at the shoulder, with a chocolate-brown coat. [from Hindi]

topiary /ˈtəʊpɪərɪ/ *n.* the art of clipping shrubs etc. into ornamental shapes, originated by the Romans in the 1st century and revived in the 16th–17th centuries in formal gardens. —*adj.* of this art. [from French from Latin *topiarius* = landscape-gardener ultimately from Greek *topos* = place]

topic /ˈtɒpɪk/ *n.* a theme for discussion, a subject of conversation or discourse. [from Latin from Greek *topos* = place, a commonplace]

topical *adj.* dealing with current topics. —**topicality** /-ˈkælɪtɪ/ *n.,* **topically** *adv.*

topknot *n.* a tuft or crest or bow of ribbon etc. worn or growing on the head.

topless *adj.* without a top; (of a woman's clothing) leaving the breasts bare, (of a woman) so clothed.

topmast *n.* the part of a mast next above the lower mast.

topmost *adj.* uppermost, highest.

topography /təˈpɒgrəfɪ/ *n.* the surface shape and aspect of the land; its study. Topography deals with relief and contours, the distribution of mountains and valleys, the patterns of rivers, and all other features, natural and artificial, that produce the landscape. —**topographer** *n.*, **topographical** /tɒpəˈɡræfɪkəl/ *adj.* [from Latin from Greek *topos* = place]

topology /təˈpɒlədʒɪ/ *n.* **1.** the branch of geometry that deals with those properties of a figure that remain unchanged even when the figure is transformed (bent or stretched) – for example, when a square painted on a rubber sheet is deformed by distorting the sheet. Topology has scientific applications, as in the study of turbulence in fluids. The map of the London Underground system is an example of the topological representation of the rail network. **2.** the branch of mathematics concerned with the abstract theory of continuity. —**topological** /tɒpəˈlɒdʒɪkəl/ *adj.* [from German from Greek *topos* = place]

topper *n.* (*colloquial*) a top hat.

topping *n.* decorative cream etc. on top of a cake etc.

topple *v.t./i.* **1.** to fall headlong or as if top-heavy; to cause to do this. **2.** to overthrow, to cause to fall from a position of authority.

topsail /ˈtɒpsəl/ *n.* **1.** a square sail next above the lowest. **2.** a fore-and-aft sail on a gaff.

topside *n.* **1.** the outer side of a round of beef. **2.** the side of a ship above the water line.

topsoil *n.* the upper, cultivated layer of soil, which may vary in depth from 8 to 45 cm/3 to 18 in. It contains organic matter, the decayed remains of vegetation, which plants need for active growth.

topsy-turvy /tɒpsɪˈtɜːvɪ/ *adv. & adj.* **1.** upside down. **2.** in or into utter confusion. [apparently from *top*[1] and obsolete *turve* = overturn]

toque /təʊk/ *n.* a woman's close-fitting brimless hat with a high crown. [French]

tor *n.* **1.** a rocky hill top. **2.** an isolated mass of rock, usually granite, left upstanding on a moor after the surrounding rock has been worn away. Erosion takes place along the joints in the rock, wearing the outcrop into a mass of rounded lumps. [Old English *torr*; compare Gaelic *tòrr* = bulging hill]

Torah /ˈtɔːrə/ *n.* **1.** in ◊Judaism, the Pentateuch, the first five books of the Hebrew Bible (Christian Old Testament), which are ascribed to Moses. It contains a traditional history of the world from the Creation to the death of Moses; it also includes the Hebrew people's ◊covenant with the one God, rules for religious observance, and guidelines for social conduct, including the Ten Commandments. **2.** a scroll containing this. [from Hebrew = instruction]

torch *n.* **1.** a small hand-held electric lamp powered by a battery or an electric power cell contained in a case. **2.** a burning piece of resinous wood, or combustible material fixed on a stick and ignited, used as a light for carrying in the hand. —**carry a torch for,** to feel (unreturned) love for. [from Old French from Latin *torqua* (*torquēre* = twist)]

tore past of **tear**[1].

toreador /ˈtɒrɪədɔː/ *n.* a bullfighter, especially on horseback. [Spanish (*toro* = bull from Latin *taurus*)]

Torgau /ˈtɔːɡaʊ/ town in Leipzig county, E Germany; population 20,000. In 1760, during the Seven Years' War, Frederick II of Prussia defeated the Austrians nearby, and in World War II the US and Soviet forces first met here.

torment /ˈtɔːment/ *n.* severe bodily or mental suffering; a cause of this. —/tɔːˈment/ *v.t.* to subject to torment; to tease or worry excessively. —**tormentor** /-ˈmentə/ *n.* [from Old French from Latin *tormentum*]

tormentil /ˈtɔːməntɪl/ *n.* a low-growing herb *Potentilla erecta* with yellow flowers. [from Old French from Latin]

torn past participle of **tear**[1].

tornado /tɔːˈneɪdəʊ/ *n.* (*plural* **tornadoes**) **1.** an extremely violent revolving storm with swirling, funnel-shaped clouds, caused by a rising column of warm air propelled by strong wind. A tornado can rise to a great height, but with a diameter of only a few hundred yards or metres or less. Tornadoes move with wind speeds of 160–480 kph/100–300 mph, destroying everything in their path. They are common in the central USA and Australia. **2.** a loud outburst. [apparently assimilation of Spanish *tronada* = thunderstorm]

Torness /tɔːˈnes/ site of an advanced gas-cooled nuclear reactor 7 km/4.5 mi SW of Dunbar, East Lothian, Scotland. It started to generate power in 1987.

Toronto /təˈrɒntəʊ/ formerly (until 1834) **York** port on Lake Ontario, capital of Ontario, Canada; metropolitan population (1985) 3,427,000. It is Canada's main industrial and commercial centre (banking, shipbuilding, cars, farm machinery, food processing, publishing) and also a cultural centre, with theatres and a film industry. The Skydome 1989, a sports arena with a retractable roof dome, seats up to 53,000 and is bigger than the Roman Coliseum. A French fort was established in 1749, and the site became the provincial capital in 1793. [North American Indian = place of meeting]

torpedo[1] /tɔːˈpiːdəʊ/ *n.* (*plural* **torpedoes**) a cigar-shaped self-propelled underwater missile fired at a ship from a submarine or surface ship or from an aircraft and exploding on impact. Modern torpedoes are homing missiles; some resemble mines in that they lie on the seabed until activated by the acoustic signal of a passing ship. A television camera enables them to be remotely controlled, and in the final stage of attack they lock on to the radar or sonar signals of the target ship. —*v.t.* **1.** to destroy or attack with a torpedo. **2.** to ruin (a policy or institution etc.) suddenly. —**torpedo boat,** a small fast warship armed with torpedoes. [Latin = electric ray (*torpēre* = be numb)]

torpedo[2] *n.* a type of ray (fish) whose electric organs between the pectoral fin and the head can give a powerful shock. Torpedoes can grow to 180 cm/6 ft in length. [Latin = electric ray]

torpid /ˈtɔːpɪd/ *adj.* sluggish, inactive, apathetic; (of a hibernating animal) dormant. —**torpidity** /-ˈpɪdɪtɪ/ *n.*, **torpidly** *adv.* [from Latin *torpidus*]

torpor /ˈtɔːpə/ *n.* a torpid condition. [Latin *torpēre* = be numb]

torque /tɔːk/ *n.* **1.** the turning effect of force on an object. A turbine produces a torque that turns an electricity generator in a power station. Torque is measured by multiplying the force by its perpendicular distance from the turning point. **2.** a necklace or collar usually of twisted metal, worn by the ancient Britons, Gauls, etc. [from Latin *torquēre* = twist]

torque converter a device similar to a turbine, filled with oil, used in automatic transmission systems in motor vehicles and locomotives to transmit power (torque) from the engine to the gears.

Torquemada /tɔːkiˈmɑːdə/ Tomás de 1420–1498. Spanish Dominican monk, confessor to Queen Isabella I. In 1483 he revived the ◊Inquisition on her behalf, and at least 2,000 'heretics' were burned; Torquemada also expelled the Jews from Spain in 1492, with a resultant decline of the economy.

torr *n.* a unit of pressure equal to 1/760 of an ◊atmosphere, used mainly in high-vacuum technology.

torrent /ˈtɒrənt/ *n.* **1.** a rushing stream of water or lava etc. **2.** (usually in *plural*) a great downpour of rain. **3.** a violent flow (of abuse, questions, etc.). —**torrential** /təˈrenʃəl/ *adj.* [French from Italian from Latin]

Torreón /tɒriˈɒn/ industrial and agricultural city in Coahuila state, N Mexico, on the river Nazas at an altitude of 1,127 m/3,700 ft; population (1986) 730,000. Before the arrival of the railway in 1907 Torreón was the largest of the three Laguna cotton-district cities (with Gómez Palacio and Ciudad Lerdo). Since then it has developed as a major thoroughfare and commercial centre.

Torricelli /tɒriˈtʃeli/ Evangelista 1608–1647. Italian physicist and pupil of ◊Galileo, who devised the mercury ◊barometer.

torrid /ˈtɒrɪd/ *adj.* **1.** (of land etc.) parched by the sun, very hot. **2.** intense, passionate. —**torrid zone,** the tropics. [from French or Latin *torridus* (*torrēre* = scorch)]

torsion /ˈtɔːʃən/ *n.* twisting, especially of one end of a thing while the other is held fixed. —**torsional** *adj.* [from Old French from Latin *torquēre* = twist]

torso /ˈtɔːsəʊ/ *n.* (*plural* **torsos**) **1.** the trunk of the human body or of a statue. **2.** a statue lacking the head and limbs. [Italian = stalk, stump, from Latin *thyrsus*]

tort *n.* in law, a wrongful act for which someone can be sued for damages in a civil court. It includes such acts as libel, trespass, injury done to someone (whether intentionally or by negligence), and inducement to break a contract (although breach of contract itself is not a tort). —**tortious** /ˈtɔːʃəs/ *adj.* [from Old French from Latin *tortum* = wrong (*torquēre* = twist)]

tortilla /tɔːˈtiːlə/ n. a Latin American flat maize cake eaten hot. [Spanish diminutive of *torta* = cake from Latin]

tortoise /ˈtɔːtəs/ n. a slow-moving reptile of the order Chelonia, family Testudinidae, with the body enclosed in a hard shell. Tortoises are related to the ◊terrapins and ◊turtles, and range in length from 10 cm/4 in to 150 cm/5 ft. The shell consists of a curved upper carapace and flattened lower plastron joined at the sides. The head and limbs may be withdrawn into it when the tortoise is in danger. Most land tortoises are herbivorous and have no teeth. The mouth forms a sharp-edged 'beak'. Eggs are laid in warm earth in great numbers, and are not incubated by the mother. Some tortoises are known to live for 150 years. [Old French from Latin *tortuca*]

tortoiseshell /ˈtɔːtəʃel/ n. 1. the yellowish-brown mottled and clouded shell of certain turtles. 2. a cat or butterfly with markings suggesting tortoiseshell. —adj. having such markings.

tortuous /ˈtɔːtjuəs/ adj. 1. full of twists and turns. 2. devious, not straightforward. —**tortuosity** /-ˈɒsɪtɪ/ n., **tortuously** adv. [from Old French from Latin *tortus* = a twist]

torture /ˈtɔːtʃə/ n. 1. the infliction of severe bodily pain especially as a punishment or to extort evidence or confession. Legally abolished in England about 1640, torture was allowed in Scotland until 1708 and until 1789 in France. In the 20th century torture is widely, though in most countries unofficially, used. 2. severe physical or mental pain. —v.t. 1. to subject to torture. 2. to force out of its natural shape or meaning, to distort. —**torturer** n. [French from Latin *tortum* = wrong (*torquēre* = twist)]

Torvill and Dean /ˈtɔːvɪl, ˈdiːn/ English ice-dance champions Jayne Torvill (1957–) and Christopher Dean (1959–), both from Nottingham. They won the world title four times 1981–84 and were the 1984 Olympic champions.

Tory /ˈtɔːrɪ/ n. (*colloquial* or *derogatory*) a member of the Conservative Party. —**Tory Party**, the forerunner of the British ◊Conservative Party about 1680–1830. It was the party of the squire and parson, as opposed to the Whigs (supported by the trading classes and Nonconformists). In the USA a Tory was an opponent of the break with Britain in the War of American Independence 1775–83. —adj. of Tories or the Tory Party. **Toryism** n. [originally = Irish outlaw (Irish *tóir* = pursue)]

Tory democracy a concept attributed to the 19th-century British Conservative Party, and to the campaign of Lord Randolph ◊Churchill against Stafford Northcote in the early 1880s. The slogan was not backed up by any specific policy proposals. 'Tory democracy' was revived in the 1980s as a rallying cry for Conservatives with a social conscience.

Toscana /tɒˈskɑːnə/ Italian name for the region of ◊Tuscany.

tosh n. (*slang*) nonsense, rubbish.

toss v.t./i. 1. to move with an uneven or restless to-and-fro motion. 2. to throw lightly, carelessly, or easily; to throw back (the head), especially in contempt or impatience. 3. to send (a coin) spinning in the air to decide a choice etc. by the way it falls; to settle a dispute with (a person) thus. 4. to coat (food) by gently shaking it in a dressing etc. —n. 1. a tossing action or movement. 2. the result obtained by tossing a coin. —**argue the toss**, to dispute a choice already made. **take a toss**, to be thrown by a horse etc. **toss off**, to compose or finish rapidly and effortlessly; to drink (liquor) in one draught. **toss up**, to toss a coin. **toss-up** n. the tossing of a coin; (*colloquial*) an even chance.

tot[1] n. 1. a small child. 2. a dram of liquor. [of dialect origin]

tot[2] v.t./i. (**-tt-**) (usually with *up*) to add up; (of items) to mount up. **-totting-up** n. the adding of separate items, especially of convictions towards disqualification from driving. **tot up to**, to amount to. [abbreviation of *total* or of Latin *totum* = the whole]

total /ˈtəʊtl/ adj. 1. including everything or everyone; comprising the whole. 2. absolute, unqualified. —n. the total number or quantity. —v.t./i. (**-ll-**) to reckon the total of; to amount in number (to). —**total internal reflection**, the complete reflection of a beam of light that occurs from the surface of an optically 'less dense' material. For example, a beam from an underwater light source can be reflected from the surface of the water, rather than escaping through the surface. Total internal reflection can only happen if a light beam hits a surface at an angle greater than the ◊critical angle for that particular pair of materials. **total war**, war in which all available weapons and resources are employed. [from Old French from Latin *totus* = entire]

totalitarian /təʊtælɪˈteərɪən/ adj. relating to a form of government permitting no rival loyalties or parties, usually demanding total submission of the individual to the requirement of the state. Examples of totalitarian regimes are Italy under Benito ◊Mussolini 1922–45; Germany under Adolph ◊Hitler 1933–45; the USSR under Joseph ◊Stalin from the 1930s until his death in 1953; more recently Romania under Nicolae ◊Ceauşescu 1974–89. —**totalitarianism** n.

totality /təʊˈtælɪtɪ/ n. 1. the total number or amount. 2. being total. [from Latin *totus* = entire]

totalizator /ˈtəʊtəlaɪzeɪtə/ n. a device showing the number and amount of the bets staked on a race to enable the total to be divided among those betting on the winner; this betting system.

totalize v.t. to combine into a total.

totally adv. completely.

tote[1] n. (*slang*) a totalizator. [abbreviation]

tote[2] v.t. (*colloquial*) to carry. —**tote bag**, a large bag for parcels etc. [17th-century US, probably of dialect origin]

totem /ˈtəʊtəm/ n. a natural object, especially an animal, adopted as the emblem of a clan or individual, especially among North American Indians; an image of this. —**totem pole**, a pole on which totems are carved, painted, or hung. —**totemic** /-ˈtemɪk/ adj. [Algonquian]

totemism /ˈtəʊtəmɪzəm/ n. the belief in individual or clan kinship with an animal, plant, or object. This totem is sacred to those concerned, and they are forbidden to eat or desecrate it; marriage within the clan is usually forbidden. Totemism occurs among Pacific Islanders and Australian Aborigines, and was formerly prevalent throughout Europe, Africa, and Asia. Most North and South American Indian societies also had totems. —**totemistic** /-ˈmɪstɪk/ adj. [Algonquin = mark of my family]

Totenkopfverbände /ˈtəʊtnkɒpffəbendə/ n. the 'death's head' units of the Nazi ◊SS organization. Originally used to guard concentration camps after 1935, they became an elite fighting division attached to the Waffen-SS during World War II.

t'other /ˈtʌðə/ adj. & pron. the other. [from *the tother*, for earlier *that other* 'the other']

Totò /ˈtəʊtəʊ/ Stage name of Antonio de Curtis Gagliardi Ducas Comneno di Bisanzio 1898–1967. Italian comedian who moved to films from the music hall. His films, such as *Totò le Moko* 1949 and *L'Oro di Napoli/Gold of Naples* 1954, made him something of a national institution.

totter v.i. 1. to walk unsteadily or feebly. 2. to rock or shake as if about to collapse; (of a state or system) to be shaken, to be on the point of collapse. —n. an unsteady or shaky movement or gait. —**tottery** adj. [from Middle Dutch = swing]

toucan /ˈtuːkən/ n. a South and Central American forest-dwelling bird of the family Ramphastidae. Toucans have very large, brilliantly coloured beaks and often handsome plumage. They live in small flocks, eat fruits, seeds, and insects, and lay their eggs in holes in trees. They grow to 64 cm/2 ft in length. There are 37 species. [from Tupi or Guarani]

touch /tʌtʃ/ v.t./i. 1. to be or come together so that there is no space between; to meet or cause to meet thus. 2. to put one's hand etc. lightly upon; to press or strike lightly. 3. to reach as far as; to reach momentarily; to approach in excellence. 4. (with *negative*) to move, harm, affect, or attempt in any degree; to have any dealings with; to eat or drink even a little of. 5. to arouse sympathy or other emotion in. 6. to modify; to draw or paint with light strokes. 7. (*slang*) to persuade to give money as a loan or gift. 8. (in *past participle*) slightly crazy. —n. 1. an act or the fact of touching. 2. the faculty of perception through the response of the brain to touching things, especially with the fingers. Many animals, such as nocturnal ones, rely on touch more than humans do. Some have specialized organs of touch that project from the body, such as whiskers or antennae. 3. small things done in producing a piece of work. 4. a small amount, a tinge or trace. 5. the manner of touching the keys or strings, of an instrument; the response of the keys etc. to this; a distinctive manner of workmanship or procedure.

toucan

6. a relationship of communication or knowledge. 7. the part of a football field beyond the side limits. 8. (*slang*) an act of obtaining money from a person; a person from whom money may be obtained. —**finishing touch(es)**, the final details completing and enhancing a piece of work etc. **touch-and-go** *adj.* uncertain as regards the result, risky. **touch at**, (of a ship) to call at (a port etc.) **touch bottom**, to reach the bottom of the water with the feet; to reach the lowest or worst point. **touch down,** (of an aircraft) to reach the ground in landing. **touch judge**, a linesman in rugby football. **touchline** *n.* the side limit of a football field. **touch off**, to explode by touching with a match etc.; to initiate (a process) suddenly. **touch on** *or* **upon**, to refer to or mention briefly or casually; to verge on. **touchpaper** *n.* a paper impregnated with nitre to burn slowly and ignite a firework etc. **touch-type** *v.t./i.* to use a typewriter without looking at the keys. **touch up**, to correct or improve with minor additions. **touch wood**, to put the hand on something wooden in the superstitious belief of averting bad luck (also used as a phrase implying such action). [from Old French *tochier* (probably imitative)]

touchdown *n.* the act of touching down by an aircraft.

touché /'tuː ʃeɪ/ *interjection* acknowledging a hit by a fencing opponent or a justified retort by another in a discussion. [French = touched]

touching /'tʌtʃɪŋ/ *adj.* raising sympathy or tender feelings. —*prep.* concerning. —**touchingly** *adv.*

touch screen in computing, an input device allowing the user to communicate with the computer by touching a display screen with a finger. In this way, the user can point to a required ◊menu option or item of data. Touch screens are used less widely than other pointing devices such as the ◊joystick or ◊mouse.

touch sensor in a computer-controlled ◊robot, a device used to give the robot a sense of touch, allowing it to manipulate delicate objects or move automatically about a room. Touch sensors provide the feedback necessary for the robot to adjust the force of its movements and the pressure of its grip. The main types include the strain gauge and the microswitch.

touchstone *n.* 1. dark schist or jasper for testing alloys by the marks they make on it. 2. a criterion.

touchwood *n.* readily inflammable rotten wood or similar substance.

touchy /'tʌtʃɪ/ *adj.* apt to take offence, over-sensitive. —**touchily** *adv.*, **touchiness** *n.*

tough /tʌf/ *adj.* 1. difficult to break, cut, tear, or chew. 2. able to endure hardship; not easily hurt, damaged, or injured. 3. unyielding, stubborn; resolute; (*colloquial*) acting sternly or viciously. 4. (*colloquial*, of luck etc.) hard. 5. (*US slang*) vicious, rough and violent. 6. (of clay etc.) stiff, tenacious. —*n.* a tough person, especially a ruffian. —**toughly** *adv.*, **toughness** *n.* [Old English]

toughen /'tʌfən/ *v.t./i.* to make or become tough or tougher.

Toulon /tuːˈlɒn/ port and capital of Var *département*, SE France, on the Mediterranean Sea, 48 km/30 mi SE of

Marseille; population (1983) 410,000. It is the chief Mediterranean naval station of France. Industries include oil refining, chemicals, furniture, and clothing. Toulon was the Roman *Telo Martius* and was made a port by Henry IV. It was occupied by the British in 1793, and Napoleon first distinguished himself in driving them out. In World War II the French fleet was scuttled here to avoid its passing to German control.

Toulouse /tuːˈluːz/ capital of Haute-Garonne *département*, S France, on the river Garonne SE of Bordeaux; population (1982) 541,000. The chief industries are textiles and aircraft construction (Concorde was built here). Toulouse was the capital of the Visigoths (see ◊Goth) and later of Aquitaine 781–843.

Toulouse-Lautrec /tuːˈluːz ləuˈtrek/ Henri Marie Raymond de 1864–1901. French artist, associated with the Impressionists. He was active in Paris, where he painted entertainers and prostitutes. From 1891 his lithograph posters were a great success.

toupee /'tuː peɪ/ *n.* a wig; an artifical patch of hair worn to cover a bald part of the head. [from *toupet* = hair-tuft]

tour /tuə/ *n.* 1. a journey through a country, town, or building etc. visiting various places or things of interest or giving performances. 2. a spell of duty on military or diplomatic service. —*v.t./i.* to make a tour (of). —**on tour**, touring. [from Old French from Latin from Greek *tornos* = lathe]

touraco *n.* a fruit-eating African bird of the family Musophagidae. Touracos have short, rounded wings, long tails, and erectile crests. The largest are 70 cm/28 in long.

tour de force /tuə də ˈfɔːs/ a great feat of strength or skill. [French]

Tour de France a French road race for professional cyclists held annually over approximately 4,800 km/3,000 mi of primarily French roads. The race takes about three weeks to complete and the route varies each year, often taking in adjoining countries, but always ending in Paris. A separate stage is held every day, and the overall leader at the end of each stage wears the coveted 'yellow jersey' (French *maillot jaune*). The **Milk Race** is the English equivalent of the Tour de France but on a smaller scale, and involves amateur and professional teams.

tourism /'tuərɪzəm/ *n.* 1. visiting places as a tourist. 2. the business of providing accommodation and services for tourists.

tourist /'tuərɪst/ *n.* a person who is travelling or visiting a place for recreation. —**tourist class**, a class of passenger accommodation in a ship or aircraft etc. lower than first class. **tourist trap**, a place that exploits tourists. **Tourist Trophy**, motorcycle races held annually on the Isle of Man.

touristy *adj.* (*derogatory*) suitable for tourists; frequented by tourists.

tourmaline /'tuəməlɪn, -iːn/ *n.* a hard, brittle mineral, a complex of various metal silicates, but mainly sodium aluminium borosilicate. It has unusual electric properties and is used as a gem. [French from Sinhalese (it was originally found in Sri Lanka)]

tournament /'tuənəmənt/ *n.* 1. a contest of skill between a number of competitors, involving a series of matches. 2. a medieval spectacle in which two sides contended with usually blunted weapons. 3. a modern display of military exercises, contests etc. [from Old French *tornei, torneier*]

tournedos /'tuənədəu/ *n.* (*plural* the same) a small round thick slice of fillet for one person, cooked with a strip of fat round it. [French]

Tourneur /'tɜːnə/ Cyril 1575–1626. English dramatist. Little is known about his life but *The Atheist's Tragedy* 1611 and *The Revenger's Tragedy* 1607 (thought by some scholars to be by ◊Middleton) are among the most powerful of Jacobean dramas.

tourney /'tuənɪ/ *n.* a tournament. —*v.i.* to take part in a tournament. [from Old French *tornei, torneier*]

tourniquet /'tuənɪkeɪ/ *n.* a device or strip of material drawn tightly round a limb to stop the flow of blood through an artery by compression. [French, probably from Old French *tournicle* = coat of mail, influenced by *tourner* = turn]

tousle /'tauzəl/ *v.t.* to pull about roughly, to make (the hair or clothes) untidy. [from dialect *touse*]

Toussaint L'Ouverture /tuːˈsæŋ luːvəˈtjuə/ Pierre Dominique *c.*1743–1803. Haitian revolutionary leader, born a slave. He joined the insurrection of 1791 against the French colonizers and was made governor by the revolutionary French government. He expelled the Spanish and British, but when the French emperor Napoleon reimposed slavery he revolted, was captured, and died in prison in France. In 1983 his remains were returned to Haiti.

tout *v.t./i.* 1. to pester possible customers with requests for orders; to solicit the custom of (a person) or for (a thing). 2. to spy out the movements and condition of racehorses in training. —*n.* a person who touts; a tipster touting information about racehorses etc. [originally = look out, from obsolete or dialect *toot*]

tout de suite immediately. [French]

tow¹ /təʊ/ *v.t.* to pull along behind, especially with a rope etc. —*n.* towing, being towed. —**in tow**, being towed; (*colloquial*) accompanying or under the charge of a person. **on tow**, being towed. **towbar** *n.* the bar by which a caravan is attached to the vehicle towing it. **towpath** *n.* or **towing path**, a path beside a river or canal for use when a horse is towing a barge etc. [Old English]

tow² *n.* fibres of flax or hemp prepared for spinning. —**towheaded** *adj.* having a head of very light-coloured or tousled hair. [from Middle Low German *touw*]

towards /tə'wɔːdz/*prep.* or **toward** 1. in the direction of. 2. as regards, in relation to. 3. for the purpose of achieving or promoting; as a contribution to. 4. near, approaching. [Old English = future]

towel /'taʊəl/ *n.* an absorbent cloth or paper etc. for drying with after washing. —*v.t./i.* (-**ll**-) to wipe or dry with a towel. —**throw in the towel**, to admit defeat. [from Old French *toail(l)e*]

towelling *n.* material for towels.

tower *n.* 1. a tall usually square or circular structure, either standing alone (e. g. as a fort) or forming part of a castle, church, or other large building; a similar structure housing machinery etc. 2. a tower block. —*v.i.* to be of great height; to be taller or more eminent than others. —**the Tower**, the ◊Tower of London. **tower block**, a very tall building containing flats or offices. **tower of strength**, a person who gives strong and reliable support. [Old English from Latin *turris*]

Tower /'taʊə/ John 1925–1991. US Republican politician, a senator from Texas 1961–83. Despite having been a paid arms-industry consultant, he was selected in 1989 by President Bush to serve as defence secretary, but the Senate refused to approve the appointment because of Tower's previous heavy drinking.

towering *adj.* 1. high, lofty. 2. (of rage etc.) violent.

Tower of London a fortress on the Thames bank to the east of the City. The keep, or White Tower, was built in about 1078 by Bishop Gundulf on the site of British and Roman fortifications. It is surrounded by two strong walls and a moat (now dry), and was for centuries a royal residence and the principal state prison.

town *n.* 1. a collection of dwellings and other buildings, larger than a village, especially one not creating a city; its inhabitants. 2. a town or city as distinct from country. 3. the central business and shopping area of a neighbourhood. 4. London. —**go to town**, to act or work with energy and enthusiasm. **on the town**, (*colloquial*) on a spree in town. **town clerk**, an officer of a town corporation, in charge of records etc. **town crier**, a person making official announcements in public places. **town gas**, manufactured inflammable gas for domestic use. **town hall**, a building for a town's official business, often with a hall that may be used for public events. **town house**, a residence in town as distinct from the country; a terrace house or a house in a compact group in a town. [Old English *tūn* = enclosure]

townee /taʊ'niː/ *n.* (also **townie** /'taʊnɪ/) (*derogatory*) an inhabitant of a town.

Townes /taʊnz/ Charles 1915– . US physicist who in 1953 designed and constructed the first ◊maser. For this work, he shared the 1964 Nobel prize with Soviet physicists Nikolai Basov (1922–) and Aleksandr ◊Prokhorov.

town planning the design of buildings or groups of buildings in a physical and social context, concentrating on the relationship between various buildings and their environment, as well as on their uses. See also ◊garden city; (under ◊new town).

townscape *n.* 1. a picture of a town. 2. the visual appearance of a town or towns.

Townsend /'taʊnzend/ Sue 1946– . English humorous novelist, author of *The Secret Diary of Adrian Mole, aged 13³/4* 1982 and later sequels.

townsfolk *n.* the inhabitants of a town or towns.

Townshend /'taʊnzend/ Pete 1945– . English rock musician, founder member of the ◊Who; his solo albums include *Empty Glass* 1980.

township *n.* (formerly in the UK) a small town or village that formed part of a large parish. 2. (*US* and *Canada*) an administrative division of a county, or a district six miles square. 3. (in some other countries) a small town or settlement; (in South Africa) an area set aside for non-white occupation.

townsman *n.* (*plural* **townsmen**) an inhabitant of a town. —**townswoman** *n.fem.* (*plural* **townswomen**)

townspeople *n.pl.* the inhabitants of a town.

Townswomen's Guilds, National Union of in the UK, an urban version of the ◊Women's Institute. It was founded in 1929.

toxaemia /tɒk'siːmɪə/ *n.* 1. a condition in which poisons are spread throughout the body by the bloodstream, such as those produced by ◊pathogens or by localized cells in the body. 2. the condition of abnormally high blood pressure in pregnancy. —**toxaemic** *adj.* [from Greek *toxikon pharmakon* = poison for arrows and *haima* = blood]

toxic *adj.* of, caused by, or acting as a poison. Lead from car exhausts, asbestos, and chlorinated solvents are some examples of toxic substances that occur in the environment; generally the effects take some time to become apparent (anything from a few hours to many years). The cumulative effects of toxic waste pose a serious threat to the ecological stability of the planet. —**toxicity** /tɒk'sɪsɪtɪ/ *n.* [from Latin from Greek *toxikon pharmakon* = poison for arrows (*toxa* = arrows)]

toxicity test a test carried out on new drugs, cosmetics, food additives, pesticides, and other synthetic chemicals to see whether they are safe for humans to use. Such tests aim to identify potential toxins, carcinogens, teratogens, and mutagens.

toxicology /tɒksi'kɒlədʒɪ/ *n.* the study of poisons. —**toxicological** /-'lɒdʒɪkəl/ *adj.*, **toxicologist** *n.*

toxic syndrome a fatal disease caused by adulterated industrial oil, illegally imported from France into Spain, re-refined, and sold for human consumption from 1981. More than 20,000 people became ill, and 600–700 died.

toxin /'tɒksɪn/ *n.* a poison, especially of animal or vegetable origin; a poison secreted by a microorganism and causing a particular disease. In vertebrates, toxins are broken down by ◊enzyme action, mainly in the liver.

toxocariasis *n.* the infection of humans by a canine intestinal worm, which results in a swollen liver and sometimes eye damage.

toxophilite /tɒk'sɒfɪlaɪt/ *n.* a student or lover of archery. —*adj.* of archery. —**toxophily** *n.* [from Ascham's *Toxophilus* (1545) from Greek *toxon* = bow and *phileō* = to love]

toy *n.* 1. a thing to play with, especially for a child. 2. a trinket or curiosity; a thing intended for amusement rather than for serious use. —*adj.* 1. that is a toy. 2. (of a dog) of a diminutive breed or variety, kept as a pet. —*v.i.* (with *with*) to handle or finger idly; to deal with or consider without great seriousness.

Toynbee /'tɔɪnbɪ/ Arnold 1852–1883. English economic historian, who coined the term 'industrial revolution' in his *Lectures on the Industrial Revolution*, published in 1884. Toynbee Hall, an education settlement in the east end of London, was named after him.

Toynbee Arnold Joseph 1889–1975. English historian whose *A Study of History* 1934–61 was an attempt to discover the laws governing the rise and fall of civilizations. He was the nephew of the economic historian Arnold Toynbee.

trace¹ *n.* 1. a mark left behind, as the track of an animal, a footprint, or the line made by a moving pen. 2. a perceptible sign of what has existed or happened. 3. a very small quantity. —*v.t.* 1. to follow or discover by observing marks, tracks, pieces of evidence etc. 2. to go along (a path etc.). 3. to mark out, to sketch the outline of; to form (letters etc.) laboriously. 4. to copy (a drawing etc.) by marking its lines on a piece of transparent paper placed over it. —**trace element**, a substance occurring or required (especially in soil) only in

trachea

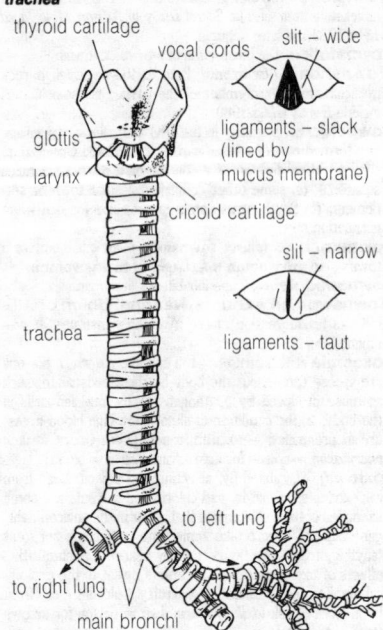

thyroid cartilage
vocal cords
slit – wide
glottis
ligaments – slack
(lined by
larynx
mucus membrane)
cricoid cartilage
slit – narrow
trachea
ligaments – taut
to left lung
to right lung
main bronchi

minute amounts. [from Old French *tracier* from Latin *tractus* = drawing]

trace² *n.* each of the two side straps, chains, or ropes by which a horse draws a vehicle. —**kick over the traces,** to become insubordinate or reckless. [from Old French *trais,* plural of *trait*]

traceable *adj.* that may be traced.

tracer /ˈtreɪsə/ *n.* **1.** a bullet that when ignited by the propellant emits light or a trail of smoke etc. by which its course may be observed, enabling the gunner to correct his aim. **2.** in science, a small quantity of a radioactive ◊isotope (form of an element) used to follow the path of a chemical reaction or a physical or biological process in the human body etc. The location (and possibly concentration) of the tracer is usually detected by using a Geiger–Muller counter.

tracery /ˈtreɪsərɪ/ *n.* stone ornamental openwork especially in the head of a Gothic window; a decorative lacelike pattern suggesting this.

trachea /trəˈkiːə, ˈtreɪkɪə/ *n.* a tube that forms an airway in air-breathing animals. In land-living ◊vertebrates, including humans, it is also known as the **windpipe** and runs from the larynx to the upper part of the chest. Its diameter is about 1.5 cm/0.6 in and its length 10 cm/4 in. It is strong and flexible, and reinforced by rings of ◊cartilage. In the upper chest, the trachea branches into two tubes: the left and right bronchi, which enter the lungs. Insects have a branching network of tubes called tracheae, which conduct air from holes (◊spiracles) in the body surface to all the body tissues. The finest branches of the tracheae are called tracheoles. [from Latin from Greek = rough artery (*trakhus* = rough)]

tracheid *n.* a cell found in the water-conducting tissue (◊xylem) of many plants, including gymnosperms (conifers) and pteridophytes (ferns). It is long and thin with pointed ends. The cell walls are thickened by ◊lignin, except for numerous small rounded areas, or pits, through which water and dissolved minerals pass from one cell to another. Once mature, the cell itself dies and only its walls remain.

tracheostomy *n.* a surgical opening in the windpipe (trachea), usually created for the insertion of a tube to enable the patient to breathe. It is done either to bypass the airway impaired by disease or injury, or to safeguard it during surgery or a prolonged period of mechanical ventilation.

tracheotomy /treɪkɪˈɒtəmɪ, træk-/ *n.* surgical incision of the trachea. [Greek *-tomia* = cutting]

trachoma /trəˈkəʊmə/ *n.* a chronic eye infection, resembling severe ◊conjunctivitis. The conjunctiva becomes inflamed, with scarring and formation of pus, and there may be damage to the cornea. It is caused by a viruslike organism (◊chlamydia), and is a disease of dry tropical regions. Although it responds well to antibiotics, numerically it remains the biggest single cause of blindness worldwide. [from Greek *trakhus* = rough]

tracing /ˈtreɪsɪŋ/ *n.* a traced copy of a map or drawing etc.; the process of making this. —**tracing paper,** transparent paper for making tracings.

track *n.* **1.** a mark or series of marks left by a person, or animal, or vehicle etc. in passing along. **2.** a path or rough road, especially one established by use. **3.** the course taken. **4.** a course, action, or procedure. **5.** a prepared course for racing etc. **6.** a continuous line of railway. **7.** a continuous band round the wheels of a tank or tractor etc. **8.** a soundtrack; a groove on a gramophone record; a particular recorded section of a gramophone record or magnetic tape. —*v.t./i.* **1.** to follow the track or course of; to find or observe by doing this. **2.** (of wheels) to run so that the back wheel is exactly in the first wheel's track. **3.** (of a stylus) to follow a groove. **4.** (of a cine camera) to move along a set path while taking a picture. —**in one's tracks,** (*colloquial*) where one stands, then and there. **keep** (*or* **lose**) **track of,** to follow (or fail to follow) the course or development of. **make tracks,** (*slang*) to go away. **make tracks for,** (*slang*) to go in pursuit of or towards. **off the track,** away from the subject in hand. **track down,** to reach or capture by tracking. **track event,** (in athletics) an event taking place on a track, e. g. running. **track record,** a person's past achievements. **track suit,** a suit worn by athletes etc. while training or before or after competing. [from Old French *trac,* perhaps from Lower Dutch *tre(c)k* = draught etc.]

tracked vehicle a vehicle, such as a tank or bulldozer, that runs on its own tracks (known as ◊caterpillar tracks).

tracker *n.* a person or thing that tracks. —**tracker dog,** a police dog tracing by scent.

tracklement /ˈtrækəlmənt/ *n.* an article of food, especially a jelly, for eating with meat.

tract¹ *n.* **1.** a region or area of indefinite (usually large) extent. **2.** a system of connected parts in an animal body, along which something passes. [from Latin *tractus* (*trahere* = draw, pull)]

tract² *n.* an essay or pamphlet, especially on a religious subject. [apparently abbreviation of Latin *tractatus* = treatise]

tractable /ˈtræktəbəl/ *adj.* easy to manage or deal with; docile. —**tractability** /-ˈbɪlɪtɪ/ *n.* [from Latin *tractare* = handle]

Tractarian /trækˈteərɪən/ *n.* an adherent or promoter of Tractarianism. —**Tractarianism** *n.* a name for the earlier stages of the ◊Oxford Movement, derived from the *Tracts for the Times,* the series of 90 pamphlets issued under its aegis.

traction /ˈtrækʃən/ *n.* **1.** pulling or drawing a load along a surface. **2.** a therapeutic sustained pull on a limb etc. —**traction engine,** a steam or diesel engine for drawing a heavy load on a road or across fields etc. [French or from Latin]

tractor /ˈtræktə/ *n.* **1.** in agriculture, a powerful motor vehicle, commonly having large rear wheels or caterpillar tracks, used for pulling farm machinery and loads. It is usually powered by a diesel engine and has a power-takeoff mechanism for driving machinery, and a hydraulic lift for raising and lowering implements. **2.** a traction engine.

Tracy /ˈtreɪsɪ/ Spencer 1900–1967. US actor distinguished for his understated, seemingly effortless natural performances. His films include *Captains Courageous* 1937 and *Boys' Town* 1938 (for both of which he won Academy Awards), and he starred with Katharine Hepburn in nine films, including *Adam's Rib* 1949 and *Guess Who's Coming to Dinner* 1967, his final performance.

trad *adj.* (*colloquial*) traditional. —*n.* (*colloquial*) traditional jazz. [abbreviation]

trade *n.* **1.** the exchange of goods for money or other goods. **2.** business done with a specified class or at a specified time. **3.** business carried on for earnings or profit (especially as distinct from a profession); a skilled handicraft. **4.** the persons engaged in a particular trade. **5.** (usually in *plural*) a trade wind. —*v.t./i.* **1.** to engage in trade, to buy and sell. **2.** to exchange (goods) in trade; to have a transaction (*with* a person). —**trade description,** a description of the characteristics of goods, including their quality, quantity, and fitness for the purpose for which they are required. **trade in,** to give (a used article) in part payment for another. **trade-in** *n.* an article given in this way. **trademark,** *n.* a device or word(s) legally registered or established by use to distinguish the goods of a particular manufacturer etc. **trade name,** a name by which a thing is known in the trade, or given by a manufacturer to a proprietary article, or under which a business is carried on. **trade off,** to exchange as a compromise. **trade-off** *n.* a thing given in this way. **trade on** *or* **upon,** to make great use of for one's own advantage. **trade secret,** a technique used in a trade and giving an advantage because it is not generally known. [from Middle Low German = track]

trade cycle or **business cycle** a period of time that includes a peak and trough of economic activity, as measured by a country's national income. In Keynesian economics, one of the main roles of the government is to smooth out the peaks and troughs of the trade cycle by intervening in the economy, thus minimizing 'overheating' and 'stagnation'. This is accomplished by regulating interest rates and government spending to maintain a proper balance of economic activity.

Trade Disputes Act 1906 the UK act of Parliament of 1906 which protected trade unions against claims by by their employers for damages resulting from trade disputes. The Act reversed the Taff Vale judgement in 1902 which made trade unions liable for their members' actions.

trader /ˈtreɪdə/ *n.* a person or ship engaged in trade.

Tradescant /trəˈdeskənt/ John 1570–1638. English gardener and botanist, who travelled widely in Europe and is thought to have introduced the cos lettuce to England from the Greek island bearing the same name. He was appointed gardener to Charles I and was succeeded by his son, **John Tradescant the Younger** (1608–62), after his death. The younger Tradescant undertook three plant-collecting trips to Virginia, USA, and the Swedish botanist Carl Linnaeus named the genus *Tradescantia* in his honour.

tradescantia /trædiˈskæntɪə/ *n.* any plant of the genus *Tradescantia* of the family Commelinaceae, native to North and Central America. The spiderwort *T. virginiana* is a cultivated garden plant; the wandering jew *T. albiflora* is a common house plant, with green oval leaves tinged with pink or purple or silver-striped. [from J *Tradescant*]

tradesman *n.* (*plural* **tradesmen**) a person engaged in trade, especially a shopkeeper.

Trades Union Congress (TUC) the voluntary organization of trade unions, founded in the UK in 1868, in which delegates of affiliated unions meet annually to consider matters affecting their members. In 1988 there were some 100 affiliated unions, with an aggregate membership of about 11 million.

trade union an organization of employed workers formed to undertake collective bargaining with employers and to try to achieve improved working conditions for its members. Attitudes of government to unions and of unions to management vary greatly from country to country. Probably the most effective trade-union system is that of Sweden, and the most internationally known is the Polish ◊Solidarity. —**trade unionism,** this style of organisation. **trade unionist,** an advocate of trade unionism; a member of a trade union.

trade unionism, international worldwide cooperation between unions. In 1973 a European Trade Union Confederation was established, membership 29 million, and there is an International Labour Organization, established in 1919 and affiliated to the United Nations from 1945, which formulates standards for labour and social conditions. Other organizations are the International Confederation of Free Trade Unions (1949), including the American Federation of Labor and Congress of Industrial Organizations and the UK Trades Union Congress, and the World Federation of Trade Unions (1945).

trade wind a prevailing wind that blows towards the equator from the northeast and southeast. Trade winds are caused by hot air rising at the equator and the consequent movement of air from north and south to take its place. The winds are deflected towards the west because of

the Earth's west-to-east rotation. The unpredictable calms known as the ◊doldrums lie at their convergence.

trading /ˈtreɪdɪŋ/ *n.* engaging in trade, buying and selling. —**trading estate,** an area designed to be occupied by industrial and commercial firms. **trading stamp,** stamp given by retailers to customers according to the value of goods purchased; when a sufficient number have been collected, the stamps can be redeemed for goods or money.

tradition /trəˈdɪʃən/ *n.* an opinion, belief, or custom handed down from one generation to another, especially orally; this process of handing down; an artistic or literary principle based on usage or experience. [from Old French or Latin *tradere* = hand on]

traditional *adj.* of, based on, or obtained by tradition; (of jazz) based on an early style. —**traditionally** *adv.*

traditionalism *n.* great or excessive respect for tradition. —**traditionalist** *n.* [from French]

traduce /trəˈdjuːs/ *v.t.* to misrepresent in an unfavourable way, to slander. —**traducement** *n.* [from Latin = disgrace (*ducere* = lead)]

Trafalgar, Battle of /trəˈfælgə, ˌtræfælˈgɑː/ the battle of 21 Oct 1805 in the ◊Napoleonic Wars. The British fleet under Admiral Nelson defeated a Franco-Spanish fleet; Nelson was mortally wounded. It is named after Cape Trafalgar, a low headland in SW Spain, near the western entrance to the Straits of Gibraltar.

traffic /ˈtræfɪk/ *n.* **1.** vehicles, ships, or aircraft moving along a route. **2.** trade, especially in illicit goods. **3.** the number of persons or amount of goods conveyed. **4.** the use of a service, the amount of this. **5.** dealings between persons etc. —*v.t./i.* (**-ck-**) to trade; to deal in. —**traffic island,** a paved etc. area in a road to direct the traffic and provide a refuge for pedestrians. **traffic light,** a signal controlling road traffic by coloured lights. **traffic warden,** a person employed to assist the police in controlling the movement and parking of road vehicles. —**trafficker** *n.* [from French or Spanish from Italian]

tragacanth /ˈtrægəkænθ/ *n.* a white or reddish gum from plants of the genus *Astragalus,* used in pharmacy etc. [from French from Latin from Greek *tragacantha,* name of shrub (*tragos* = goat and *acantha* = thorn)]

tragedian /trəˈdʒiːdɪən/ *n.* **1.** a writer of tragedies. **2.** an actor in tragedy.

tragedienne /trədʒiːdiˈen/ *n.* an actress in tragedy. [French]

tragedy /ˈtrædʒɪdɪ/ *n.* **1.** in the theatre, a play dealing with a serious theme, traditionally one in which a character meets disaster either as a result of personal failings or circumstances beyond his or her control. Historically the Greek view of tragedy, as defined by Aristotle and expressed by the great tragedians Aeschylus, Euripides, and Sophocles, has been predominant in the western tradition. In the 20th century tragedies in the narrow Greek sense of dealing with exalted personages in an elevated manner have virtually died out. Tragedy has been replaced by dramas with 'tragic' implications or overtones, as in the work of Ibsen, O'Neill, Tennessee Williams, Pinter, and Osborne, for example, or by the hybrid tragicomedy. **2.** a sad event; a serious accident; a calamity. [from Old French from Latin from Greek *tragōidia,* apparently = goat song (*tragos* = goat and *ōidē* = song)]

tragic /ˈtrædʒɪk/ *adj.* **1.** of or in the style of tragedy. **2.** sorrowful. **3.** causing great sadness; calamitous. [from French from Latin from Greek *tragos* = goat]

tragical /ˈtrædʒɪkəl/ *adj.* **1.** sorrowful. **2.** causing great sadness. —**tragically** *adv.*

tragicomedy /trædʒiˈkɒmɪdɪ/ *n.* a drama that contains elements of tragedy and comedy; for example, Shakespeare's 'reconciliation' plays, such as *The Winter's Tale,* which reach a tragic climax but then lighten to a happy conclusion. A tragicomedy is the usual form for plays in the tradition of the Theatre of the ◊Absurd, such as Samuel ◊Beckett's *En attendant Godot/Waiting for Godot* 1953 and Tom ◊Stoppard's *Rosencrantz and Guildenstern are Dead* 1967. —**tragicomic** *adj.,* **tragicomically** *adv.* [from French or Italian from Latin]

trahison des clercs involvement of intellectuals in active politics. [French = the treason of the intellectuals]

trail *v.t./i.* **1.** to drag or be dragged along behind, especially on the ground. **2.** to move wearily; to lag or straggle. **3.** to hang or float loosely; (of a plant) to hang or spread downwards. 4. to be losing in a contest; to be losing to (a specified team etc.). 5. to diminish, to become fainter. 6. to follow the trail of, to track. —*n.* 1. a mark left where something has passed; a track or scent followed in hunting. 2. a beaten path, especially through a wild region. 3. a thing that trails or hangs trailing. 4. a line of people or things following behind something. —**trailing edge**, the rear edge of a moving body. [from Old French or Middle Low German from Latin *tragula* = dragnet]

trailer *n.* 1. a truck etc. drawn by a vehicle and used to carry a load. 2. a set of short extracts from a film, shown in advance to advertise it. 3. a person or thing that trails. 4. (*US*) a caravan.

train *n.* 1. a series of railway carriages or trucks drawn by a locomotive. 2. a succession or series of persons or things; a set of parts in machinery, actuating one another in a series. 3. a body of followers, a retinue. 4. a thing drawn along behind or forming the back part, especially the elongated part of a long dress or robe that trails on the ground behind the wearer. 5. a line of combustible material placed to lead fire to an explosive. —*v.t./i.* 1. to bring to a desired standard of performance or behaviour by instruction and practice; to undergo such a process; to teach and accustom (a person or animal) to do something. 2. to bring or come to physical efficiency by exercise and diet. 3. to cause (a plant) to grow in the required direction. 4. to aim (a gun or camera etc.). —**in train**, in preparation; arranged. **trainbearer** *n.* an attendant holding up the train of a person's robe. **train spotter**, a collector of the identification numbers of railway engines seen. [from Old French ultimately from Latin *trahere* = draw]

trainable *adj.* that may be trained.

trainee /treɪˈniː/ *n.* a person being trained, especially for an occupation.

trainer *n.* 1. a person who trains horses or athletes etc. 2. an aircraft or device simulating it to train pilots. 3. a training shoe.

training *n.* the process by which one is trained for a sport or contest or for an occupation. —**training shoe**, a soft running shoe without spikes.

Training Agency the UK government-sponsored organization responsible for retraining of unemployed workers. Founded as the **Manpower Services Commission** in 1974, the organization operated such schemes as the Training Opportunities Scheme (TOPS), the Youth Opportunities Programme (YOP) 1978, the Youth Training Scheme (YTS) 1983, and the Technical and Vocational Initiative (TVEI).

traipse *v.i.* (*colloquial*) to trudge; to go about on errands etc.

trait /treɪ/ *n.* a distinguishing feature in a character, appearance, habit, or portrayal. [French, from Latin *tractus*]

traitor /ˈtreɪtə/ *n.* a person who behaves disloyally; one who betrays his country. —**traitorous** *adj.*, **traitress** *n.fem.* [from Old French from Latin *traditor*]

Trajan /ˈtreɪdʒən/ Marcus Ulpius (Trajanus) AD 52–117. Roman emperor and soldier, born in Seville. He was adopted as heir by ◊Nerva, whom he succeeded in AD 98.

trajectory /ˈtrædʒɪktərɪ, trəˈdʒek-/ *n.* the path of a body (e. g. a comet or bullet) moving under given forces. [from Latin *traicere* = throw across (*jacere* = throw]

tram *n.* or **tramcar**, a passenger vehicle running on rails laid in a public road. Trams are powered either by electric conductor rails below ground or conductor arms connected to overhead wires. Greater manoeuvrability is achieved with the ◊trolley bus, similarly powered by conductor arms overhead but without tracks. 2. a four-wheeled truck used in coal mines. [from Middle Low German and Middle Dutch *trame* = beam]

tramlines *n.pl.* 1. the rails for a tram. 2. (*colloquial*) the pair of parallel lines at the edge of a tennis or badminton court.

trammel /ˈtræməl/ *n.* 1. a kind of dragnet in which a fine net is hung loosely between vertical walls of coarser net, so that fish passing through carry some of the fine net through the coarser and are trapped in the pocket thus formed. 2. (usually in *plural*) things that hamper one's activities. —*v.t.* (**-ll-**) to hamper. [from Old French from Latin *tramaculum*, perhaps from *tri-* and *macula* = mail]

tramp *v.t./i.* 1. to walk with a firm heavy tread; to walk laboriously; to travel on foot across (an area or distance) thus. 2. to trample. 3. to live as a tramp. —*n.* 1. a person

who goes from place to place as a vagrant. 2. the sound of heavy footsteps. 3. a long walk. 4. (*slang*) a dissolute woman. 5. a freight vessel, especially a steamer, that does not travel on a regular route.

trample *v.t./i.* to tread repeatedly with heavy or crushing steps; to crush or harm thus.

trampoline /ˈtræmpəliːn/ *n.* a stretched canvas sheet connected by springs to a horizontal frame, used for jumping on in acrobatic leaps. —*v.i.* to use a trampoline. [from Italian *trampolino* (*trampoli* = stilts)]

trampolining *n.* gymnastics performed on a trampoline. Marks are gained for carrying out difficult manoeuvres. Synchronized trampolining and tumbling are also popular forms of the sport.

tramway *n.* 1. a transport system for use in cities, where wheeled vehicles (trams) run along parallel rails in the road. 2. the rails for a tram.

trance /trɑːns/ *n.* a sleeplike state in which the subject loses the ordinary perceptions of time and space, and even of his or her own body; a hypnotic or cataleptic state; mental abstraction from external things, rapture, ecstasy. [from Old French *transe* (*transir* = depart from, Latin *transitus*)]

tranche /trɑːnʃ/ *n.* a portion, especially of income or of a block of shares. [French = slice]

tranny /ˈtrænɪ/ *n.* (*slang*) a transistor radio. [abbreviation]

tranquil /ˈtræŋkwɪl/ *adj.* calm and undisturbed, not agitated. —**tranquillity** /-ˈkwɪlɪtɪ/ *n.*, **tranquilly** *adv.* [from French or Latin *tranquillus*]

tranquillize /ˈtræŋkwɪlaɪz/ *v.t.* to make tranquil, to calm, especially by a drug.

tranquillizer *n.* a drug used to diminish anxiety and induce calmness.

trans- /trænz-, trɑːnz-/prefix meaning across, through, beyond; to or on the farther side of. [from Latin *trans* = across]

transact /trænˈzækt, trɑː-/ *v.t.* to perform or carry out (business). —**transactor** *n.* [from Latin]

transactinide element any of a series of nine radioactive, metallic elements with atomic numbers that extend beyond the ◊actinide series, those from 104 (rutherfordium) to 112 (unnamed). They are grouped because of their expected chemical similarities (all are bivalent), the properties differing only slightly with atomic number. All have half-lives of less than two minutes.

transaction /trænˈzækʃən, trɑː-/ *n.* 1. transacting. 2. business transacted. 3. (in *plural*) the reports of discussions and lectures at the meetings of a learned society.

Trans-Alaskan Pipeline one of the world's greatest civil engineering projects, the construction of a pipeline to carry petroleum (crude oil) 1,285 km/800 mi from N Alaska to the ice-free port of Valdez. It was completed in 1977 after three years' work and much criticism by ecologists.

transalpine /trænzˈælpaɪn, trɑː-/ *adj.* on the north side of the Alps. [from Latin]

Trans-Amazonian Highway /trænzæməˈzəʊnɪən/ or **Transamazonica** the road linking Recife in the east with the provinces of Rondonia, Amazonas, and Acre in the west. Begun as part of the Brazilian National Integration Programme (PIN) in 1970, the Trans-Amazonian Highway was designed to enhance national security, aid the industrial development of the north of Brazil, and act as a safety valve for the overpopulated coastal regions.

transatlantic /trænzətˈlæntɪk, trɑː-/ *adj.* 1. crossing the Atlantic. 2. on or from the other side of the Atlantic; American; (*US*) European.

transceiver /trænˈsiːvə, trɑː-/ *n.* a combined radio transmitter and receiver. [from *transmitter* and *receiver*]

transcend /trænˈsend, trɑː-/ *v.t.* 1. to go or be beyond the range or grasp of (human experience, belief, description, etc.). 2. to surpass. [from Old French or Latin *transcendere* (*scandere* = climb)]

transcendent *adj.* 1. transcending human experience. 2. of supreme merit or quality, surpassing. 3. (of God) existing apart from, or not subject to the limitations of, the material universe. —**transcendence** *n.*, **transcendency** *n.*, **transcendently** *adv.*

transcendental /trænsenˈdentəl, trɑː-/ *adj.* 1. not based on experience, intuitively accepted, innate in the mind. 2. consisting of, dealing in, or inspired by abstraction, visionary. —**transcendental meditation,** (TM) a technique of focusing the mind, based in part on Hindu

transfer orbit

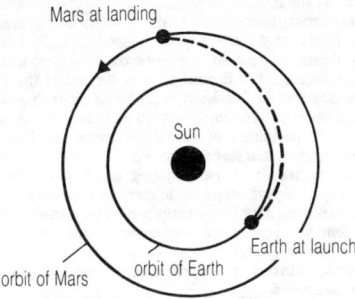

Mars at landing

Sun

Earth at launch

orbit of Mars   orbit of Earth

meditation. Meditators are given a *mantra* (a special word or phrase) to repeat over and over to themselves; such meditation is believed to benefit the practitioner by relieving stress and inducing a feeling of well-being and relaxation. It was introduced to the West by Maharishi Mahesh Yogi and popularized by the Beatles in the late 1960s. —**transcendentally** *adv.* [from Latin]

transcendentalism *n.* a philosophy or belief taking account of transcendental things. —**transcendentalist** *n.*

transcontinental /ˌtrænzkɒntiˈnentəl, trɑː-/ *adj.* extending or travelling across a continent.

transcribe /trænˈskraɪb, trɑː-/ *v.t.* 1. to copy in writing. 2. to write out (shorthand etc.) in ordinary characters. 3. in music, to adapt (a composition) for a voice or instrument other than that for which it was originally written. —**transcriber** *n.* [from Latin *scribere* = write]

transcript /ˈtrænskrɪpt, ˈtrɑː-/ *n.* a written copy. [from Old French from Latin]

transcription /trænˈskrɪpʃən, trɑː-/ *n.* 1. transcribing, the written representation of sounds. 2. a transcript; something transcribed. 3. in living cells, the process by which the information for the synthesis of a protein is transferred from the ◊DNA strand on which it is carried to the messenger ◊RNA strand involved in the actual synthesis. [French or from Latin]

transducer /trænzˈdjuːsə, trɑː-/ *n.* a power-transforming device that enables ◊energy in any form (electrical, acoustical, mechanical) to flow from one transmission system to another. [from Latin *transducere* = lead across]

transept /ˈtrænsept, ˈtrɑː-/ *n.* the part of a cruciform church at right angles to the nave; either arm of this.

transfer /trænsˈfɜː, trɑː-/ *v.t./i.* (**-rr-**) 1. to convey, move, or hand over from one person, group, or place to another; to make over possession of (property or rights etc.). 2. to convey (a design etc.) from one surface to another. 3. to change or be moved to another group or occupation. 4. to go from one station or route or conveyance to another in order to continue a journey. 5. to change (a meaning) by extension or metaphor. —/ˈtrænsfɜː, ˈtrɑː-/ *n.* 1. transferring, being transferred. 2. a document effecting the conveyance of property or a right. 3. a design or picture that is or can be conveyed from one surface to another. —**transference** /ˈtræ-, ˈtrɑː-/ *n.* [from French or Latin *ferre* = bear]

transferable /trænsˈfɜːrəbəl, trɑː-/ *adj.* that may be transferred.

transfer orbit the elliptical path followed by a spacecraft moving from one orbit to another, designed to save fuel by moving for most of the journey in free fall.

transfiguration *n.* 1. transfiguring, being transfigured. 2. Transfiguration, that of Christ (Matthew 17: 2), celebrated on 6 Aug.

transfigure /ˈtrænsˈfɪgə, trɑː-/ *v.t.* to change the appearance of, especially to something nobler or more beautiful. [from Old French or Latin]

transfinite /trænsˈfaɪnaɪt/ *adj.* beyond or surpassing what is finite; in mathematics, of a number, exceeding all finite numbers.

transfix /trænsˈfɪks, trɑː-/ *v.t.* 1. to pierce with or impale on something sharp-pointed. 2. to make motionless with fear or astonishment etc. [from Latin]

transform /trænsˈfɔːm, trɑː-/ *v.t.* 1. to make a considerable change in the form, appearance, or character of. 2. to

change the voltage of (an electric current). —**transformation** /-fəˈmeɪʃən/ *n.*, **transformational** /-fəˈmeɪʃənəl/ *adj.* [from Old French or Latin]

transformational grammar the theory of language structure initiated by Noam ◊Chomsky, which proposes that below the actual phrases and sentences of a language (its **surface structure**) there lies a more basic layer (its **deep structure**), which is processed by various transformational rules when we speak and write.

transformer *n.* a device in which, by electromagnetic induction, an alternating current (AC) of one voltage is transformed to another voltage, without change of ◊frequency. Transformers are widely used in electrical apparatus of all kinds, and in particular in power transmission where high voltages and low currents are utilized.

transfuse /trænsˈfjuːz, trɑː-/ *v.t.* 1. to cause (a fluid, colour, influence etc.) to permeate; to imbue thus. 2. to inject blood or blood products (plasma, red cells) into a patient's circulation to make up for deficiencies due to disease, injury, or surgical intervention. —**transfusion** /-ˈfjuːʒən/ *n.* [from Latin *fundere* = pour)]

transgenic organism a plant, animal, bacterium, or other living organism which has had a foreign gene added to it by means of ◊genetic engineering.

transgress /trænsˈgres, trɑː-/ *v.t./i.* 1. to break (a rule or law etc.); to go beyond (a limitation). 2. to sin. —**transgression** *n.*, **transgressor** *n.* [from French or Latin *gradi* = step, go]

transient /ˈtrænsiənt, ˈtrɑː-/ *adj.* quickly passing away, fleeting. —**transience** *n.* [from Latin *transire* = go across]

transistor /trænˈsɪstə, trɑː-/ *n.* 1. a semiconductor device, usually having three terminals and two junctions, in which the load current can be made to be proportional to a small input current, so that it is functionally equivalent to a valve but is much smaller and more robust, operates at lower voltages, and consumes less power and produces less heat. 2. (in full **transistor radio**) a portable radio set equipped with transistors. [from *transfer* and *resistor*]

transistorize *v.t.* to equip with transistors (rather than valves).

transit /ˈtrænsɪt, ˈtrɑː-/ *n.* 1. the process of going, conveying, or being conveyed across, over, or through. 2. a passage or route. 3. the apparent passage of a heavenly body across the disc of another or across the meridian of a place. Transits of the inferior planets occur when they pass directly between the Earth and Sun, and are seen as tiny dark spots against the Sun's disc. —**transit camp**, a camp for the temporary accommodation of soldiers, refugees, etc. [from Latin *transitus* (*transire* = go across)]

transition /trænˈsɪʃən, trɑː-/ *n.* 1. the process of changing from one state or subject etc. to another. 2. a period during which one style of art develops into another, especially of architecture between Norman and Early English. —**transitional** *adj.*, **transitionally** *adv.* [French or from Latin]

transition metal any of a group of metallic elements that have incomplete inner electron shells and exhibit variable valency—for example, cobalt, copper, iron, and molybdenum. They are excellent conductors of electricity, and generally form highly coloured compounds.

transitive /ˈtrænsɪtɪv, ˈtrɑː-/ *adj.* (of a verb) taking a direct object expressed or understood. —**transitively** *adv.* [from Latin *transitus*]

transitory /ˈtrænsɪtərɪ, ˈtrɑː-/ *adj.* existing for a time but not long-lasting, merely temporary. —**transitorily** *adv.*, **transitoriness** *n.* [from Anglo-French from Latin]

Transkei /trænsˈkaɪ/ largest of South Africa's Bantustans, or homelands, extending northeast from the Great Kei River, on the coast of Cape Province, to the border of Natal; area 43,808 sq km/16,910 sq mi; population (1985) 3,000,000, including small white and Asian minorities. It became self-governing in 1963, and achieved full 'independence' in 1976. Its capital is Umtata, and it has a port at Mnganzana. It is one of the two homelands of the Xhosa people (the other is Ciskei), and products include livestock, coffee, tea, sugar, maize, and sorghum. Its government consists of a president (paramount chief Tutor Nyangelizwe Vulinolela Ndamase from 1986) and single-chamber national assembly.

translate /trænsˈleɪt, trɑː-/ *v.t.* 1. to express the sense of (a word or text etc.) in another language, in plainer words, or in another form of representation. 2. to infer or declare the significance of, to interpret. 3. to move from one person, place, or condition to another; to remove (a bishop) to another see; to move (a saint's relics etc.) to another place; (in the Bible) to convey to heaven without death. 4. in living cells, to synthesize proteins. The information coded as a sequence of nucleotides in messenger ◊RNA is transformed into a sequence of amino acids in a peptide chain. The process involves the 'translation' of the ◊genetic code. See also ◊transcription. —**translation** n., **translator** n. [from Latin translatus, past participle of transferre (ferre = bear)]

transliterate /træns'lɪtəreɪt, trɑ:-/ v.t. to represent (a letter or word) in the corresponding character(s) of another alphabet or language. —**transliteration** n., **transliterator** n. [from Latin littera = letter]

translocation n. the movement of soluble materials through ◊vascular plants.

translucent /træns'lu:sənt, trɑ:-/ adj. allowing light to pass through, especially without being transparent. —**translucence** n., **translucency** n. [from Latin lucēre = shine]

transmigrate /trænsmaɪ'greɪt, trɑ:-/ v.i. 1. (of a soul) to pass into a different body. See ◊reincarnation. 2. to migrate. —**transmigration** n. [from Latin]

transmissible /træns'mɪsɪbəl, trɑ:-/ adj. transmittable. [from Latin transmittere]

transmission /træns'mɪʃən, trɑ:-/ n. 1. transmitting, being transmitted. 2. a broadcast programme. 3. the gear transmitting power from the engine to the axle in a motor vehicle. [from Latin]

transmit /træns'mɪt, trɑ:-/ v.t. (-tt-) 1. to send or pass on from one person, place, or thing to another. 2. to allow to pass through or along, to be a medium for. 3. to send out (a message, signal, or programme etc.) by telegraph wire or radio waves. [from Latin mittere = send]

transmittable /træns'mɪtəbəl/ adj. that may be transmitted.

transmitter n. 1. the equipment used to transmit a message, signal etc. 2. a person or thing that transmits.

transmogrify /træns'mɒgrɪfaɪ, trɑ:-/ v.t. to transform, especially in a magical or surprising manner. —**transmogrification** /-fɪ'keɪʃən/ n.

transmutation /trænsmju:'teɪʃən, trɑ:-/ n. transmuting, being transmuted. —**transmutation of metals,** the turning of other metals into gold as the alchemists' aim. [from Old French or Latin]

transmute /træns'mju:t, trɑ:-/ v.t. to change the form, nature, or substance of, to convert into a different thing. [from Latin mutare = change]

transoceanic /trænsəʊʃi'ænɪk, trɑ:-/ adj. 1. crossing the ocean. 2. on or from the other side of the ocean.

transom /'trænsəm/ n. a crossbeam, especially a horizontal bar of wood or stone above a door or above or in a window; a window above this. [from Old French traversin]

transparency /træns'pærənsɪ, trɑ:-/ n. 1. being transparent. 2. a picture (especially a photographic slide) to be viewed by light passing through it. [from Latin]

transparent /træns'pærənt, trɑ:-/ adj. 1. transmitting rays of light without diffusion so that bodies behind can be distinctly seen (compare translucent). 2. (of a disguise or pretext etc.) easily seen through. 3. clear and unmistakable; easily understood; free from affectation or disguise. —**transparently** adv. [from Old French from Latin transpārēre = shine through (parēre = appear)]

transpire /træns'paɪə, trɑ:-/ v.t./i. 1. (of a secret or fact etc.) to become known. 2. (disputed usage) to happen. 3. to emit (vapour or moisture) through the stomata (see stoma) in the leaves or the pores of the skin etc.; to be emitted thus. In plants, this causes a continuous upward flow of water from the roots via the ◊xylem, which is known as the transpiration stream. —**transpiration** /-pɪ'reɪʃən/ n. [from French or Latin spirare = breathe]

transplant /træns'plɑ:nt, trɑ:-/ v.t. 1. to uproot and replant or establish elsewhere (often figurative). 2. to transfer (living tissue or an organ) and implant in another part of the body or in another (human or animal) body. In most organ transplants, the operation is for life-saving purposes, though the immune system tends to reject foreign tissue. Careful matching and immunosuppressive drugs must be used, but these are not always successful. —/'træ-, 'trɑ:/ n. transplanting of tissue or an organ; a

thing transplanted. —**transplantation** /-plɑ:n'teɪʃən/ n. [from Latin transplantare]

transport /træns'pɔ:t, trɑ:-/ v.t. 1. to take (a person or goods etc.) from one place to another. 2. (historical) to deport (a criminal) to a penal colony. Transportation was introduced in England towards the end of the 17th century and was abolished in 1857 after many thousands had been transported, mostly to Australia. It was also used for punishment of criminals by France until 1938. 3. (especially in past participle) to affect with strong emotion. —/'træ-, trɑ:-/ n. 1. transporting. 2. means of conveyance; a ship or aircraft employed to carry soldiers, stores etc. 3. vehement emotion. —**transport café,** a café catering chiefly for long-distance lorry drivers. —**transportation** /-'teɪʃən/ n. [from Old French or Latin portare = carry]

transportable /træns'pɔ:təbəl, trɑ:-/ adj. that may be transported.

Transport and General Workers Union (TGWU) a UK trade union founded in 1921 by the amalgamation of a number of dockers' and road-transport workers' unions, previously associated in the Transport Workers' Federation. It is the largest trade union in Britain.

transporter /træns'pɔ:tə, trɑ:-/ n. a vehicle used to transport other vehicles, heavy machinery etc. —**transporter bridge,** a bridge carrying vehicles across water on a suspended platform.

transpose /træns'pəʊz, trɑ:-/ v.t. 1. to cause (two or more things) to change places; to change the position of (a thing) in a series; to change the natural or existing order or position of (a word or words) in a sentence. 2. to put (music) into a different key. —**transposition** /-pə'zɪʃən/ n. [from Old French]

transputer n. an electronic device introduced in computers to increase computing power. In the circuits of a standard computer the processing of data takes place in sequence. In a transputer's circuits processing takes place in parallel, greatly reducing computing time for programs written specifically for the transputer.

transsexual /trænz'seksjʊəl, trɑ:-/ adj. having the physical characteristics of one sex and the psychological characteristics of the other. —n. a transsexual person, one who identifies himself or herself completely with the opposite sex, believing that the wrong sex was assigned at birth. Transsexuals may undergo surgery to modify external sexual characteristics. —**transsexualism** n.

transship /træns'ʃɪp, trɑ:-/ v.t. (-pp-) to transfer from one ship or conveyance to another. —**transshipment** n.

Trans-Siberian Railway /trænssaɪ'bɪərɪən/ a railway line connecting the cities of European Russia with Omsk, Novosibirsk, Irkutsk, and Khabarovsk, and terminating at Vladivostok on the Pacific. It was built 1891–1905; from Leningrad to Vladivostok is about 8,700 km/5,400 mi. A 3,102 km/1,928 mi northern line was completed in 1984 after ten years' work.

transubstantiation /trænsəbstænʃi'eɪʃən/ n. the Roman Catholic doctrine that in the ◊Eucharist the whole substance of the bread and wine, after consecration, is converted into the body and blood of Christ, only the 'accidents' (i.e. appearances) of bread and wine remaining. (Compare ◊consubstantiation.) [from Latin transubstantiare]

transuranic element or **transuranium element** a chemical element with an atomic number of 93 or more, that is, with a greater number of protons in the nucleus than uranium. All transuranic elements are radioactive. Apart from neptunium and plutonium, none of these have been found in nature, but they have been created in nuclear reactions.

Transvaal /'trænzvɑ:l/ province of NE South Africa, bordering Zimbabwe to the N; area 262,499 sq km/101,325 sq mi; capital Pretoria; population (1985) 7,532,000. Products include diamonds, coal, iron ore, copper, lead, tin, manganese, meat, maize, tobacco, and fruit. The main rivers are the Vaal and Limpopo with their tributaries. Swaziland forms an enclave on the Natal border. It was settled by Voortrekkers, Boers who left Cape Colony in the Great Trek from 1831. Independence was recognized by Britain in 1852, until the settlers' difficulties with the conquered Zulus led to British annexation in 1877. It was made a British colony after the South African War 1899–1902, and in 1910 became a province of the Union of South Africa.

Transylvania

transverse /'trænzvɜ:s, 'trɑ:-, -'vɜ:s/ adj. situated, arranged, or acting in a crosswise direction. —**transversely** adv. [from Latin vertere = turn]

transvestism /trænz'vestɪzəm, trɑ:-/ n. clothing oneself in the garments of the opposite sex as a form of psychological abnormality. [from Latin vestire = clothe]

transvestite /trænz'vestaɪt, trɑ:-/ n. a person who indulges in transvestism.

Transylvania /trænsɪl'veɪnɪə/ mountainous area of central and NW Romania, bounded to the S by the Transylvanian Alps (an extension of the ◊Carpathians), formerly a province, with its capital at Cluj. It was part of Hungary from about 1000 until its people voted to unite with Romania in 1918. It is the home of the vampire legends.

trap[1] n. 1. a device, often baited, for catching and holding animals. 2. a trick betraying a person into speech or an act. 3. an arrangement to catch an unsuspecting person, e. g. a speeding motorist. 4. a device for effecting the sudden release e. g. of a greyhound in a race, of a ball to be struck at, of a clay pigeon to be shot at. 5. a curve in a drainpipe etc. serving when filled with liquid to seal it against the return of a gas. 6. a two-wheeled carriage. 7. a trapdoor. 8. (slang) the mouth. —v.t. (-pp-) 1. to catch in a trap to stop and retain (as) in a trap. 2. to furnish (a place) with traps. [Old English]

trap[2] n. a kind of dark volcanic rock. [from Swedish trapp (trappa = stair, from its stairlike appearance)]

trapdoor n. a door in a floor, ceiling, or roof.

trapeze /trə'pi:z/ n. a crossbar suspended by cords as a swing for acrobatics etc. [from French from Latin]

trapezium /trə'pi:zɪəm/ n. (plural trapezia or trapeziums) 1. in geometry, a four-sided plane figure (quadrilateral) with two of its sides parallel. If the parallel sides have lengths a and b and the perpendicular distance between them is h (the height of the trapezium), its area $A = \frac{1}{2}h(a + b)$. 2. (US) a trapezoid. [Latin from Greek trapezion (trapeza = table)]

trapezoid /'træpɪzɔɪd/ n. a quadrilateral with no sides parallel (the term quadrilateral is preferred). 2. (US) a trapezium. —**trapezoidal** /-'zɔɪdəl/ adj. [from Greek]

trapper n. a person who traps wild animals, especially for furs.

trappings /'træpɪŋz/ n.pl. ornamental accessories; the harness of a horse, especially when ornamental. [from obsolete trap from Old French drap = cloth]

Trappist /'træpɪst/ n. a member of the branch of the Cistercian order founded in 1664 at La Trappe in Normandy, following an austere rule and noted (at least until recently) for abstinence from meat and for practice of perpetual silence. —**Trappistine** /-tɪn/ n. a member of an affiliated order of nuns. [from French from La Trappe]

traps n.pl. (colloquial) baggage, belongings.

trasformismo n. government by coalition, using tactics of reforming new cabinets and political alliances, often between conflicting interest groups, in order to retain power. The term has been applied cynically to describe changing the appearance while the essence remains the same. It was first used to describe the way the Italian nationalist leader Cavour held on to power. [Italian = transformation]

trash n. 1. worthless or waste stuff, rubbish. 2. a worthless person; worthless people. —**trash can**, a dustbin. —**trashy** adj.

trattoria /træto'ri:ə/ n. an Italian eating house. [Italian]

trauma /'trɔ:mə/ n. (plural traumas) 1. in psychiatry, a painful emotional experience or shock with lasting psychic consequences. 2. in medicine, a wound or injury; the condition caused by this. [Greek = wound]

traumatic /trɔ:'mætɪk/ adj. 1. of or causing trauma. 2. (colloquial) very unpleasant. [from Latin from Greek]

travail /'træveɪl/ n. 1. (literary) painful or laborious effort. 2. (archaic) the pains of childbirth. —v.i. 1. (literary) to make a painful or laborious effort. 2. (archaic) to suffer the pains of childbirth. [from Old French from Latin trepalium = instrument of torture]

travel /'trævəl/ v.t./i. (-ll-) 1. to go from one place or point to another; to make a journey, especially of some length or abroad. 2. to journey along or through (a country); to cover (a distance) in travelling. 3. (colloquial) to withstand a long journey. 4. to go from place to place as a salesman. 5. to move or proceed in a specified manner or at a specified rate. 6. (colloquial) to move quickly. 7. (of a machine part) to move. —n. 1. travelling, especially in foreign countries. 2. the range, rate, or mode of movement of a machine part. —**travel agency** (or agent), an agency (or agent) making arrangements for travellers. **travelling crane**, a crane able to move along an overhead support.

travelled adj. experienced in travelling.

traveller n. 1. a person who travels or is travelling. 2. a commercial traveller. 3. an itinerant wanderer, the term is applied to the ◊Romany people and to vagabonds and peripatetic dissidents. —**traveller's cheque**, a cheque for a fixed amount, encashable on a signature usually in many countries. **traveller's joy**, wild clematis Clematis vitalba. **traveller's tale**, an incredible and probably untrue story.

travelogue /'trævəlɒg/ n. a film or illustrated lecture with a narrative of travel.

Traven /'trævən/ B(en). Pen name of Herman Feige 1882–1969. US novelist, born in Germany, whose true identity was not revealed until 1979. His books include the bestseller The Death Ship 1926 and The Treasure of the Sierra Madre 1934, which was made into a film starring Humphrey Bogart in 1948.

Travers /'trævəz/ Morris William 1872–1961. English chemist who, with William Ramsay, between 1894 and 1908 first identified what were called the ◊inert or noble gases: krypton, xenon, and radon.

traverse /trə'vɜːs/ *v.t./i.* 1. to travel or lie across. 2. to consider or discuss the whole extent of (a subject). 3. to turn (a large gun) horizontally. —/'trævəs/ *n.* 1. a sideways movement or course; traversing. 2. a thing that crosses another. —**traversal** /trə'vɜːsəl/ *n.* [from Old French from Latin *vertere* = turn]

travesty /'trævɪstɪ/ *n.* a grotesque misrepresentation or imitation. —*v.t.* to make or be a travesty of. [from French *travestir* = change clothes of, from Italian]

trawl *n.* a large wide-mouthed fishing net dragged by a boat along the bottom of the sea etc. —*v.t./i.* to catch with a trawl or seine; to catch by trawling. [probably from Middle Dutch *tragelen* = drag]

trawler *n.* a boat for use with a trawl.

tray *n.* 1. a flat utensil, usually with a raised edge, on which small articles are placed for display or carrying. 2. a meal on a tray. 3. an open receptacle for holding a person's correspondence etc. in an office. 4. a tray-like (often removable) receptacle forming a compartment in a trunk, cabinet, or other container. [Old English]

treacherous /'tretʃərəs/ *adj.* 1. guilty of or involving treachery. 2. (of the weather, ice, memory etc.) not to be relied on, likely to fail or give way. —**treacherously** *adv.*, **treacherousness** *n.* [from Old French *trechier*, *trichier* = deceive]

treachery /'tretʃərɪ/ *n.* violation of faith or trust, especially by secret desertion of the cause to which one professes allegiance.

treacle /'triːkəl/ *n.* the syrup produced in refining sugar; molasses. —**treacly** *adj.* [originally = antidote for snake-bite, from Old French from Latin *theriaca* from Greek]

tread /tred/ *v.t./i.* (*past* **trod**; *past participle* **trodden** or **trod**) 1. to set one's foot down; to walk or step; (of a foot) to be set down. 2. to walk on; to press or crush with the feet; to perform (steps etc.) by walking; to make (a path or hole etc.) by treading. 3. (of a male bird) to copulate with (a hen, or *absolute*). —*n.* 1. the manner or sound of walking. 2. the top surface of a step or stair. 3. the part of a wheel that touches the ground or rails; the part of a rail that the wheels touch; a thick moulded part of a vehicle tyre for gripping the road; a part of the sole of a boot etc. similarly moulded. —**tread the boards**, to be an actor. **tread on air**, to feel elated. **tread on a person's corns** *or* **toes**, to offend his feelings or encroach upon his privileges. **tread water**, to maintain an upright position in water by making treading movements with the feet and hands. [Old English]

treadle /'tredəl/ *n.* a lever worked by the foot and imparting motion to a machine. [Old English]

treadmill *n.* 1. a wide millwheel turned by people treading on steps fixed along the length of its circumference, formerly worked by prisoners as a punishment. 2. a similar device used for exercise. 3. tiring, monotonous, routine work.

treason /'triːzən/ *n.* an act of betrayal, in particular against the sovereign or the state to which the offender owes allegiance; a breach of faith, disloyalty. Treason is punishable in Britain by death. It includes: plotting the wounding or death of the sovereign or his or her spouse or heir; levying war against the sovereign in his or her realm; and giving aid or comfort to the sovereign's enemies in wartime. —**treasonous** *adj.* [from Anglo-French *treisoun* from Latin]

treasonable *adj.* involving or guilty of treason. —**treasonableness** *n.*, **treasonably** *adv.*

treasure /'treʒə/ *n.* 1. precious metals or gems; a hoard of these, accumulated wealth. 2. a thing valued for its rarity, workmanship, associations etc. 3. (*colloquial*) a beloved or highly valued person. —*v.t.* to store as valuable (*literally*, or *figuratively* in the memory); to value highly. —**treasure hunt** *n.* a search for treasure; a game in which the players seek a hidden object. **treasure trove**, gold or silver coins, plate, or bullion found hidden and of unknown ownership. Normally, treasure originally hidden, and not abandoned, belongs to the crown, but if the treasure was casually lost or intentionally abandoned, the first finder is entitled to it against all but the true owner. Objects buried with no intention of recovering them, for example in a burial mound, do not rank as treasure trove, and belong to the owner of the ground. The term is also used to describe something very useful or desirable that a person finds. [from Old French from Latin *thesaurus* from Greek]

Treasure Island an adventure story for children by R L ◊Stevenson, published in 1883. Jim Hawkins, the story's narrator, sets sail with Squire Trelawney in the *Hispaniola*, armed with a map showing the location of buried treasure. Attempts by the ship's crew of pirates, including Long John Silver, to seize the map are foiled after much fighting and the squire finds the treasure.

treasurer *n.* a person in charge of the funds of a society or municipality etc. [from Anglo-French and Old French]

treasury *n.* 1. a place where treasure is kept. 2. the funds or revenue of a state, or institution, or society. 3. the department managing the public revenue of a country; the offices and officers of this. —**Treasury bench**, the front bench in Parliament occupied by the prime minister, the chancellor of the Exchequer etc. **treasury bill**, a bill of exchange issued by a government to raise money for temporary needs.

treat *v.t./i.* 1. to act or behave towards (a person or thing) in a specified way. 2. to deal with or act upon (a person or thing) with a view to obtaining a particular result; to subject to a chemical or other process; to give medical or surgical treatment to. 3. to present or deal with (a subject). 4. to provide with food or entertainment at one's own expense. 5. to negotiate terms. —*n.* 1. a thing that gives pleasure, especially something unexpected or unusual; an entertainment designed to do this. 2. the treating of others to something at one's own expense. —**stand treat**, to bear the expense of an entertainment etc. [from Anglo-French *treter* from Latin *tractare* = handle]

treatise /'triːtɪs, -ɪz/ *n.* a written work dealing formally and systematically with a subject.

treatment *n.* 1. the process or manner of behaving towards or dealing with a person or thing. 2. something done to relieve or cure an illness or abnormality etc.

treaty /'triːtɪ/ *n.* 1. a formally concluded and ratified agreement between states. Treaties are binding in international law, the rules being laid down in the Vienna Convention on the Law of Treaties 1969. 2. an agreement between persons, especially for the purchase of property. [from Anglo-French from Latin *tractatus*]

treble /'trebəl/ *adj.* 1. threefold; triple; three times as much or many. 2. (of the voice) high-pitched; in music, soprano (especially of a boy or boy's voice; or of an instrument). —*n.* 1. a treble quantity or thing. 2. a hit at darts on the narrow ring between the two middle circles on the board, scoring treble. 3. a soprano, especially a boy or boy's voice; a high-pitched voice. —*v.t./i.* to multiply or be multiplied by three. —**trebly** *adv.* [from Old French from Latin *triplus*]

tree *n.* 1. a perennial plant with a single woody self-supporting stem (*trunk*) usually unbranched for some distance above the ground, and protected by an outer layer of ◊bark. It absorbs water through a ◊root system. There is no clear dividing line between ◊shrubs and trees, but sometimes a minimum height of 6 m/20 ft is used to define a tree. 2. a Christmas tree. 3. a piece or frame of wood for various purposes. 4. a family tree. —*v.t.* to force (an animal, or (also *figurative*) a person) to take refuge up a tree. —**grow on trees**, to be plentifully available without effort. **tree creeper**, a small, short-legged bird of the family Certhiidae, which spirals with a mouselike movement up tree trunks searching for food with its thin downcurved beak. **tree fern**, a large fern with an upright woody stem. **tree house**, a structure in a tree for children to play in. **tree ring** *or* **annual ring**, a ring in the cross section of a tree, from one year's growth. **tree surgeon**, one who specializes in the care of trees. [Old English]

trefoil /'trefɔɪl, 'triː-/ *n.* 1. one of several ◊clover plants of the genus *Trifolium* of the pea family Leguminosae, the leaves of which are divided into three leaflets. The name is also used for other plants with leaves divided into three lobes. 2. a three-lobed thing, especially an ornamentation in tracery. [from Anglo-French from Latin (*tri-* = three and *folium* = leaf)]

trek *v.i.* (-kk-) (originally *South African*) 1. to travel arduously. 2. to migrate or journey with one's belongings in ox wagons. —*n.* (originally *South African*) 1. such a journey; each stage of it. 2. an organized migration of a body of persons. [from South African Dutch *trekken* = draw, pull]

trellis /'trelɪs/ *n.* a lattice or grating of light wooden or metal bars used especially as a support for fruit trees or creepers and often fastened against a wall. [from Old French from Latin *trilix* = three-ply]

trematode /'trematəʊd/ *n.* a parasitic flatworm with an oval non-segmented body, of the class Trematoda, including the ◊fluke. [from Greek = perforated (*trēma* = hole)]

tremble *v.i.* to shake involuntarily with fear, excitement, weakness etc.; to be in a state of apprehension; to move in a quivering manner. —*n.* trembling, a quiver. [from Old French from Latin *tremulare*]

trembler *n.* an automatic vibrator for making and breaking an electric circuit.

trembly *adj.* (*colloquial*) trembling.

tremendous /trɪ'mendəs/ *adj.* 1. immense. 2. (*colloquial*) remarkable, excellent. —**tremendously** *adv.*, **tremendousness** *n.* [from Latin = to be trembled at]

tremolo /'tremələʊ/ *n.* (*plural* **tremolos**) a tremulous effect in playing music or in singing. [Italian]

tremor /'tremə/ *n.* 1. a slight shaking or trembling movement, a vibration; a slight earthquake. 2. a thrill of fear or other emotion. [from Old French and Latin *tremere* = tremble]

tremulous /'tremjʊləs/ *adj.* 1. trembling from nervousness or weakness. 2. easily made to quiver. —**tremulously** *adv.* [from Latin *tremulus*]

trench *n.* a long narrow usually deep ditch, especially one dug by troops to stand in and be sheltered from an enemy's fire. —*v.t.* to dig a trench or trenches in (the ground); to dig (soil or a garden) thus so as to bring the subsoil to the top. —**trench coat**, a belted coat or raincoat with pockets and flaps like those of a military uniform coat. **trench warfare**, hostilities conducted from defensive long, narrow, deeply dug trenches, which were first used widely during the American Civil War in 1864. Trenches were commonly used from the advent of mechanized war until increased mobility provided by the aeroplane and the motor car enabled attacking armies to avoid such large-scale, immobile forms of defence. [from Old French = cut, from Latin *truncare*]

trenchant /'trentʃənt/ *adj.* (of style or language etc.) incisive, strong and effective. —**trenchancy** *n.*, **trenchantly** *adv.*

Trenchard /'trentʃəd/ Hugh Montague, 1st Viscount Trenchard 1873–1956. British aviator and police commissioner. He commanded the Royal Flying Corps in World War I 1915–17, and organized the Royal Air Force 1918–29, becoming its first marshal in 1927. As commissioner of the Metropolitan Police, he established the Police College at Hendon and carried out the Trenchard Reforms, which introduced more scientific methods of detection.

trencher *n.* (*historical*) a wooden platter for serving food. [from Anglo-French *trenchour*]

trencherman *n.* (*plural* **trenchermen**) a person with regard to the amount he usually eats.

trend *n.* the general direction that something takes; a continuing tendency. —*v.i.* to have a specified trend. —**trendsetter** *n.* a person who leads the way in a fashion etc. [Old English = revolve]

trendy *adj.* (*colloquial*) up-to-date, following the latest trends of fashion. —*n.* (*colloquial*) a trendy person. —**trendily** *adv.*, **trendiness** *n.*

Trent, Council of /trent/ the conference held 1545–63 by the Roman Catholic Church at Trento, N Italy initiating the ◊Counter-Reformation; see also ◊Reformation.

Trent Bridge the test cricket ground in Nottingham, home of the Nottinghamshire county side. One of the oldest cricket grounds in Britain, it was opened in 1838.

Trentino–Alto Adige /tren'tiːnəʊ 'æltəʊ 'ædɪdʒeɪ/ autonomous region of N Italy, comprising the provinces of Bolzano and Trento; **area** 13,600 sq km/5,250 sq mi; **capital** Trento; chief towns Trento in the Italian-speaking southern area, and Bolzano-Bozen in the northern German-speaking area of South ◊Tirol (the region was Austrian until ceded to Italy in 1919); **population** (1988) 882,000.

trepan /trɪ'pæn/ *n.* a surgeon's cylindrical saw for removing part of the skull. —*v.t.* (-nn-) to perforate (a skull) with a trepan. [from Latin from Greek *trupanon* = auger (*trupē* = hole)]

trephine /trɪ'fiːn/ *n.* an improved form of trepan with a guiding centre-pin. —*v.t.* to operate on with this. [originally *trafine*, from Latin *tres fines* = three ends]

trepidation /trepi'deɪʃən/ *n.* a state of fear and anxiety, nervous agitation. [from Latin *trepidare* = be agitated]

trespass /'trespəs/ *v.i.* 1. to enter a person's land or property without authority. In law, a landowner has the right to eject a trespasser by the use of reasonable force and can sue for any damage caused. 2. to intrude or make use of unreasonably. 3. (*archaic*) to sin, to do wrong. —*n.* 1. an act of trespassing. 2. a sin, wrongdoing. —**trespasser** *n.* [from Old French from Latin]

tress *n.* a lock of human (especially female) hair; (in *plural*) a head of such hair. [from Old French, perhaps ultimately from Greek *trikha* = threefold]

Tressell /'tresəl/ Robert. Pseudonym of Robert Noonan 1868–1911. English author, whose *The Ragged Trousered Philanthropists*, published in an abridged form in 1914, gave a detailed account of the poverty of working people's lives.

trestle /'tresəl/ *n.* 1. each of a pair or set of supports on which a board is rested to form a table. 2. a trestlework. —**trestle table**, a table consisting of a board or boards laid on trestles or other supports. **trestlework** *n.* an open braced framework to support a bridge etc. [from Old French ultimately from Latin *transtrum* = crossbeam]

Treurnicht /'trɜːnɪxt/ Andries Petrus 1921– . South African Conservative Party politician. A former minister of the Dutch Reformed Church, he was elected to the South African parliament as a National Party member but left it to form a new right-wing Conservative Party, opposed to any dilution of the ◊apartheid system.

Trevithick /'trevɪθɪk/ Richard 1771–1833. British engineer, constructor of a steam road locomotive in 1801 and the first steam engine to run on rails in 1804.

trews /truːz/ *n.pl.* close-fitting usually tartan trousers. [from Irish or Gaelic]

TRH abbreviation of Their Royal Highnesses.

tri- in combinations, three, three times. [Latin and Greek (Latin *tres* and Greek *treis* = three)]

triad /'traɪæd, -əd/ *n.* 1. a group of three (especially notes in a chord). 2. the number three. —**triadic** /-'ædɪk/ *adj.*, **triadically** *adv.* [from French or Latin from Greek]

Triad any of various secret societies, originally founded in China as a Buddhist cult in AD 36. They became known as the Triads because the triangle played a significant part in the initiation ceremony. Today Triads are reputed to be involved in organized crime (drugs, gambling, prostitution) among overseas Chinese. The headquarters are alleged to be in Hong Kong.

trial /'traɪəl/ *n.* 1. a judicial examination and determination of issues between parties by a judge with or without a jury. 2. the process of testing qualities or performance by use and experience. 3. a sports match to test the ability of players who may be selected for an important team. 4. a test of individual ability on a motor cycle over rough ground or on a road. 5. a trying thing, experience, or person. —**on trial**, undergoing a trial; to be chosen or retained only if suitable. **trial and error**, the process of trying repeatedly and learning from one's errors until one succeeds. **trial by ordeal**, in the Middle Ages, a test of guilt or innocence by which God's judgement of the case was supposedly revealed through the accused's exposure to fire, water or blessed bread. **trial run**, a preliminary testing of a vehicle or vessel etc. [Anglo-French from Old French *trier*]

Trial, The (German *Der Prozess*) a novel by Franz Kafka, published in 1925. It deals with the sinister circumstances in which a man is arrested for no apparent reason, and with his consequent feelings of guilt and alienation, culminating in his 'execution'.

triangle /'traɪæŋgəl/ *n.* 1. in geometry, a three-sided plane figure, the sum of whose interior angles is 180°. Triangles can be classified by the relative lengths of their sides. A **scalene triangle** has no sides of equal length; an **isosceles triangle** has at least two equal sides; an **equilateral triangle** has three equal sides (and three equal angles of 60°). If the length of one side of a triangle is l and the perpendicular distance from that side to the opposite corner is h (the height or altitude of the triangle), its area $A = \frac{1}{2} l \times h$.

triangular /traɪ'æŋgjʊlə/ *adj.* 1. triangle-shaped, three-cornered. 2. (of a contest or treaty etc.) between three persons or parties. 3. (of a pyramid) having a three-sided base. [from Latin]

triangulate /traɪ'æŋgjʊleɪt/ *v.t.* to divide (an area) into triangles for surveying and navigation purposes. Surveyors measure a certain length exactly to provide a base line.

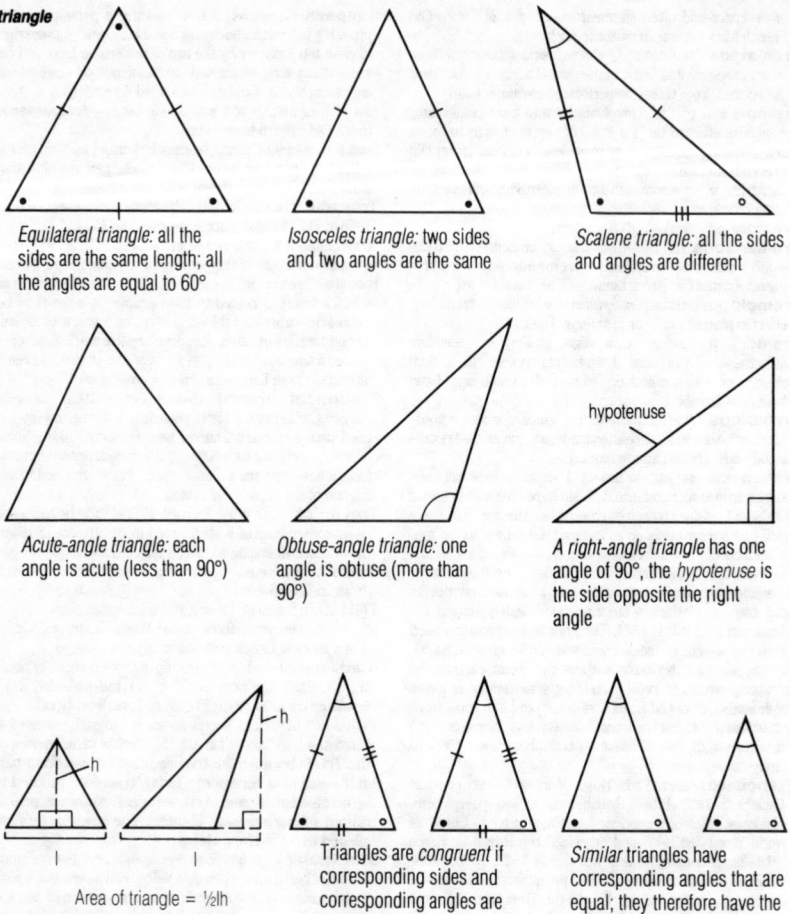

triangle

Equilateral triangle: all the sides are the same length; all the angles are equal to 60°

Isosceles triangle: two sides and two angles are the same

Scalene triangle: all the sides and angles are different

Acute-angle triangle: each angle is acute (less than 90°)

Obtuse-angle triangle: one angle is obtuse (more than 90°)

A right-angle triangle has one angle of 90°, the *hypotenuse* is the side opposite the right angle

Area of triangle = ½lh

Triangles are *congruent* if corresponding sides and corresponding angles are equal

Similar triangles have corresponding angles that are equal; they therefore have the same shape

From each end of this line they then measure the angle to a distant point, using a ◊theodolite. They now have a triangle in which they know the length of one side and the two adjacent angles. By simple trigonometry they can work out the lengths of the other two sides. —**triangulation** /-'leɪʃən/ *n.*

Trianon /'triːənɒŋ/ *n.* two palaces in the park at ◊Versailles, France: Le Grand Trianon built for Louis XIV, and Le Petit Trianon for Louis XV.

Triassic *adj.* of the period of geological time 248–213 million years ago, the first period of the Mesozoic era. The continents were fused together to form the world continent ◊Pangaea. Triassic sediments contain remains of early dinosaurs and other reptiles now extinct. By late Triassic times, the first mammals had evolved. The climate was generally dry; desert sandstones are typical Triassic rocks. —*n.* the Triassic period.

triathlon *n.* a test of stamina involving three sports: swimming 3.8 km/2.4 mi, cycling 180 km/112 mi, and running a marathon 42.195 km/26 mi 385 yd, each one immediately following the last.

tribe *n.* **1.** a group of families (especially in a primitive or nomadic culture) living as a community under one or more chiefs and usually claiming descent from a common ancestor; any similar natural or political division; any of the 12 divisions of the people of ancient Israel, each traditionally descended from one of the patriarchs. **2.** (usually *derogatory*) a set or number of persons, especially of one profession etc. or family. —**tribal** *adj.*, **tribally** *adv.* [from Old French or Latin *tribus*]

tribesman *n.* (*plural* **tribesmen**) a member of a tribe or one's own tribe.

tribology /traɪ'bɒlədʒɪ, traɪ-/ *n.* the study of the friction, wear, lubrication, and design of bearings. [from Greek *tribos* = rubbing]

tribulation /trɪbju'leɪʃən/ *n.* great affliction. [from Old French from Latin *tribulare* = oppress from *tribulum* = threshingsledge]

tribunal /traɪ'bjuːnəl, trɪ-/ *n.* **1.** strictly, a court of justice, but used in English law for a body appointed by the government to arbitrate in disputes, or investigate certain matters. Tribunals usually consist of a lawyer as chair, sitting with two lay assessors. **2.** a seat or bench for a judge or judges. [French or from Latin]

tribune[1] /'trɪbjuːn/ *n.* **1.** a popular leader or demagogue. **2.** in ancient Rome, a magistrate of ◊plebeian family, elected annually to defend the interests of the common people; only two were originally chosen in 494 BC, but there were later ten. They could veto the decisions of any other magistrate. **3.** in ancient Rome, an officer commanding a legion for two-month periods. —**tribunate** *n.* [from Latin *tribunus*]

tribune[2] *n.* **1.** a bishop's throne in a basilica; an apse containing this. **2.** a dais, a rostrum. [French from Italian from Latin]

tributary /'trɪbjutərɪ/ *n.* **1.** a river or stream flowing into a larger river or lake. **2.** a person or state paying or subject to tribute. —*adj.* **1.** that is a tributary. **2.** contributory.

tribute /'trɪbjuːt/ *n.* **1.** a thing said, done, or given as a mark of respect or affection etc. **2.** a payment formerly made periodically by one State or ruler to another as a sign of dependence. [from Latin *tributum* (*tribuere* = assign, originally divide between tribes)]

trice *n.* **in a trice**, in an instant. [from *trice* = haul up, from Middle Dutch and Middle Low German]

triceps /'traɪseps/ *n.* a muscle (especially in the upper arm) with three points of attachment. [Latin *caput* = head]

triceratops *n.* a rhinoceroslike dinosaur with three horns and a neck frill. Up to 8 m/25 ft long, it lived in the Cretaceous period.

trichinosis /trɪkɪ'nəʊsɪs/ *n.* a disease caused by hairlike worms in the muscles. [from *trichina* = hairlike worm from Greek *trikhinos* = hairlike]

trichloromethane *n.* the technical name for ◊chloroform.

trichology /trɪ'kɒlədʒɪ/ *n.* the study of hair. **—trichologist** *n.* [from Greek *thrix* = hair]

trichromatic /traɪkrə'mætɪk/ *adj.* **1.** three-coloured. **2.** (of vision) having the normal three colour-sensations (red, green, purple).

trick *n.* **1.** a thing done to fool, outwit, or deceive someone. **2.** an optical or other illusion. **3.** a special technique; the exact or best way to do something. **4.** a feat of skill done for entertainment. **5.** a mischievous, foolish, or discreditable act; a practical joke. **6.** a peculiar or characteristic habit. **7.** the cards played in one round of a card game; the winning of a round. **8.** (*attributive*) done to deceive or mystify. —*v.t.* to deceive or persuade by a trick, **(***colloquial***) to achieve what is required. how's tricks?** (*slang*) how are things? **trick or treat?** (*US*) a phrase said by children who call at houses at Hallowe'en seeking to be given sweets etc. and threatening to do mischief if these are not provided. **trick out** *or* **up**, to deck, to decorate. [from Old French *trique, triche* (*trichier* = deceive]

trickery *n.* deception, the use of tricks.

trickle *v.t./i.* **1.** to flow in drops or in a small stream; to cause to do this. **2.** to come or go slowly or gradually. —*n.* a trickling flow. **—trickle charger**, an accumulator charger that works at a steady slow rate from the mains. [probably imitative]

trickster *n.* a person who tricks or cheats people.

tricksy *adj.* full of tricks, playful.

tricky *adj.* **1.** requiring skilful handling. **2.** crafty, deceitful. **—trickily** *adv.*, **trickiness** *n.*

tricolour /'trɪkələ/ *n.* a flag of three colours, especially the French national flag of three vertical bands of red, white, and blue. The red and blue were the colours of Paris and the white represented the royal house of Bourbon. The flag was first adopted on 17 July 1789, three days after the storming of the Bastille during the French Revolution. [from French from Latin]

tricorne /'traɪkɔːn/ *adj.* (*of a hat*) with the brim turned up to give a three-cornered appearance. —*n.* such a hat. [from French or Latin *cornu* = horn]

tricot /'trɪkəʊ, 'triː-/ *n.* a fine jersey fabric. [French = knitting]

tricoteuse *n.* in the French Revolution, one of the women who sat knitting in the National Convention and beneath the guillotine. [French = knitter]

tricuspid valve a flap of tissue situated on the right side of the ◊heart between the atrium and the ventricle. It prevents blood flowing backwards when the ventricle contracts.

tricycle /'traɪsɪkəl/ *n.* **1.** a three-wheeled pedal-driven vehicle. **2.** a three-wheeled motor vehicle for a disabled driver. —*v.i.* to ride on a tricycle. **—tricyclist** *n.*

trident /'traɪdənt/ *n.* a three-pronged spear; the three-pronged fish spear carried by Neptune and by Britannia as a symbol of power over the sea. [from Latin *dens* = tooth]

triennial /traɪ'enɪəl/ *adj.* **1.** lasting for three years. **2.** recurring every third year. **—triennially** *adv.* [from Latin *annus* = year]

trier /'traɪə/ *n.* **1.** one who perseveres in his attempts. **2.** a tester.

Trieste /tri'est/ port on the Adriatic, opposite Venice, in Friuli-Venezia-Giulia, Italy; population (1988) 237,000, including a large Slovene minority. It is the site of the International Centre for Theoretical Physics, established in 1964.

trifle /'traɪfəl/ *n.* **1.** a thing of only slight value or importance. **2.** a very small amount, especially of money. **3.** a sweet dish made of sponge cake soaked in wine or jelly with fruit and topped with custard and cream. —*v.i.* to talk or behave frivolously. **—trifle with**, to treat with flippancy or

derision; to toy with. **—trifler** *n.* [from Old French *truf(f)le* = *truf(f)e* = deceit]

trifling /'traɪfəlɪŋ/ *adj.* trivial.

triforium /traɪ'fɔːrɪəm/ *n.* (*plural* **triforia**) an arcade or gallery above the nave and choir arches. [Latin]

trigeminal /traɪ'dʒemɪnəl/ *adj.* of the fifth and (in man) largest pair of cranial nerves, dividing into three main branches (ophthalmic, maxillary, and mandibular nerves). [from Latin = born as a triplet (*geminus* = born at same birth)]

trigger *n.* **1.** a movable device for releasing a spring or catch and so setting a mechanism (especially that of a gun) in motion. **2.** an agent that sets off a chain reaction. —*v.t.* (often with *off*) to set (an action or process) in motion; to be the immediate cause of. **—quick on the trigger**, quick to respond. **trigger-happy** *adj.* apt to shoot on slight provocation. [from Dutch *trekker* = draw, pull]

triggerfish *n.* a marine fish of the family Balistidae, with a laterally compressed body, up to 60 cm/2 ft long, and deep belly. The first spine on the dorsal fin locks into an erect position, which allows the fish to fasten itself securely in crevices for protection, and can only be moved by depressing the smaller third ('trigger') spine.

Triglav /'triːglaʊ/ mountain in the Julian Alps, rising to 2,863 m/9,393 ft. It is the highest peak in Yugoslavia.

triglyph /'trɪɡlɪf/ *n.* an ornament of a frieze in the Doric order, consisting of a block or tablet with two vertical grooves and a half groove on each side of these, alternating with metopes. [from Latin from Greek *gluphē* = carving]

trigonometry /trɪɡə'nɒmɪtrɪ/ *n.* the branch of mathematics that solves problems relating to plane and spherical triangles. Its principles are based on the fixed proportions of sides for a particular angle in a right-angled triangle, the simplest of which are known as the ◊sine, ◊cosine, and ◊tangent (so-called trigonometrical ratios). It is of practical importance in navigation, surveying, and simple harmonic motion in physics. **—spherical trigonometry**, the theory of triangles that are formed by segments of great circles on a spherical surface, important in navigation and astronomy. **—trigonometric** /-nə'metrɪk/ *adj.*, **trigonometrical** /-nə'metrɪkəl/ *adj.*, **trigonometrically** /-nə'metrɪkəlɪ/ *adv.* [from Greek *trigōnon* = triangle (-*gōnos* = cornered)]

triiodomethane the technical name for ◊iodoform.

trike *n.* (*colloquial*) a tricycle. [abbreviation]

trilateral /traɪ'lætərəl/ *adj.* **1.** of, on, or having three sides. **2.** affecting or between three parties. [from Latin *latus* = side]

trilby /'trɪlbɪ/ *n.* a soft felt hat with a narrow brim and a lengthwise dent in the crown. [from name of heroine of G du Maurier's novel *Trilby* (1894), in the stage version of which such a hat was worn]

trilingual /traɪ'lɪŋɡwəl/ *adj.* **1.** speaking or able to speak three languages. **2.** written in three languages. [from Latin *lingua* = tongue]

trill *n.* a quavering or vibratory sound (e. g. a rapid alternation of the main note and the note above in music, a bird's warbling, a pronunciation of *r* with vibration of the tongue). —*v.t./i.* to produce a trill; to warble (a song) or pronounce (*r* etc.) with a trill. [from Italian *trillo, trillare*]

trillion /'trɪljən/ *n.* (for plural usage see ◊hundred) **1.** a million million million. **2.** (*US* and increasingly in British use) a million million. **3.** (in *plural*) very many. **—trillionth** *adj.* & *n.* [French or from Italian]

trilobite /'traɪləbaɪt/ *n.* an extinct, marine, invertebrate arthropod of the Palaeozoic era, with a flattened, oval, three-lobed body, 1–65 cm/0.4–26 in long, covered with a shell. [from Greek *lobos* = lobe]

trilogy /'trɪlədʒɪ/ *n.* a group of three related items, especially literary or operatic works. [from Greek]

trim *v.t./i.* (**-mm-**) **1.** to set in good order; to make neat or of the required size and form, especially by cutting away irregular or unwanted parts; (with *off* or *away*) to remove (such parts). **2.** to ornament. **3.** to adjust the balance of (a ship or aircraft) by the arrangement of its cargo etc. **4.** to arrange (sails) to suit the wind. **5.** (*colloquial*) to rebuke sharply; to thrash. **6.** (*colloquial*) to get the better of in a bargain etc. —*n.* **1.** a state of readiness or fitness. **2.** the trimming on a dress or furniture etc.; the colour or type of upholstery and other fittings in a vehicle. **3.** the trimming of hair etc. **4.** the balance or the even horizontal position of a boat or aircraft etc. —*adj.* neat and orderly; having a smooth outline or compact structure. —**trimly** *adv.*, **trim-mer** *n.*, **trimness** *n.* [Old English = make firm]

trimaran /'traɪmərӕn/ *n.* a vessel like a catamaran, with three hulls side by side. [from *tri*-and *catamaran*]

trimeter /'trɪmɪtə/ *n.* a line of verse of three measures. [from Latin from Greek]

trimming *n.* 1. an ornamentation, a decoration. 2. (in *plural, colloquial*) the usual accompaniments, especially of the main course of a meal. 3. (in *plural*) pieces cut off when something is trimmed.

Trimurti /trɪ'mʊəti/ the Hindu triad of gods, representing the Absolute Spirit in its three aspects: Brahma, personifying creation; Vishnu, preservation; and Siva, destruction.

trine *n.* in astrology, the aspect of two planets one third of the zodiac (= 120°) apart, regarded as having a favourable influence. —*adj.* having this aspect. [from Old French from Latin *trinus* = threefold (*tres* = three)]

Trinidad and Tobago /'trɪnɪdæd, tə'beɪgəʊ/ Republic of country in the West Indies, off the coast of Venezuela; **area** Trinidad 4,828 sq km/1,864 sq mi and Tobago 300 sq km/116 sq mi; **capital** Port-of-Spain; **physical** comprises two main islands and some smaller ones; coastal swamps and hills E–W; **head of state** Noor Hassanali from 1987; **head of government** Arthur Robinson from 1986; **political system** democratic republic; **population** (1990 est) 1,270,000 (40% African descent, 40% Indian, 15% European, Chinese and others 2%; 1.2 million on Trinidad; **language** English (official), Hindi, French, Spanish; **recent history** Trinidad and Tobago united as a British colony in 1888; granted internal self-government in 1959. Independence was achieved from Britain, within the Commonwealth, in 1976, and in 1976 the country became a republic. In 1990 an anti-government coup was defeated.

Trinitarian /trɪnɪ'teərɪən/ *n.* a person who believes in the doctrine of the Trinity, as contrasted with a Unitarian. —**Trinitarianism** *n.*

trinitrotoluene /traɪnaɪtrəʊ'tɒljuiːn/ *n.* or **trinitrotoluol** (TNT) CH₃C₆H₂(NO₂)₃, abbreviation TNT, a powerfulhigh explosive. It is a yellow solid, prepared in several isomeric forms from ◊toluene by using sulphuric and nitric acids. [from *tri*-and *nitro*-and *toluene*]

trinity /'trɪnɪti/ *n.* being three; a group of three. —**the (Holy) Trinity,** the union of three persons (Father, Son, Holy Spirit) in one Godhead; the doctrine of this. The precise meaning of the doctrine has been the cause of unending dispute, and was the chief cause of the split between the Eastern Orthodox and Roman Catholic churches. **Trinity Sunday,** the Sunday next after Whit Sunday, celebrated in honour of the Holy Trinity. **Trinity term,** the university and law term beginning after Easter. [from Old French from Latin *trinus* = threefold]

trinket /'trɪŋkɪt/ *n.* a small fancy article or piece of jewellery.

trio /'triəʊ/ *n.* 1. a musical composition for three performers; these performers. 2. any group of three. [French and Italian from Latin *tres* = three, after *duo*]

triode /'traɪəʊd/ *n.* 1. a thermionic valve having three electrodes. The triode was commonly used in amplifiers until largely superseded by the ◊transistor. 2. a semiconductor rectifier having three terminals. [from *tri*-and *electrode*]

triolet /'triːəlɪt, 'traɪ-/ *n.* a poem of eight (usually eight-syllabled) lines, rhyming *abaaabab*, in which the first line recurs as the fourth and seventh and the second as the eighth. [French]

trip *v.t./i.* (-**pp**-) 1. to walk, run, or dance with quick, light steps; (of rhythm) to run lightly. 2. to stumble, to catch one's foot in something and fall; to cause to do this. 3. (often with *up*) to make a slip or blunder; to cause to do this; to detect in a blunder. 4. to take a trip to a place. 5. (*colloquial*) to have a visionary experience caused by a drug. 6. to release (a switch or catch) so as to operate a machine etc. —*n.* 1. a journey or excursion, especially for pleasure. 2. a stumble or blunder, tripping or being tripped up. 3. a nimble step. 4. (*colloquial*) a visionary experience caused by a drug; a device for tripping a mechanism. —**triphammer** *n.* a large hammer mounted on a pivot and operated by releasing a catch, used in metal forging. **tripwire** *n.* a wire stretched close to the ground, operating a trap or alarm etc. when tripped against. [from Old French from Middle Dutch · *trippen* = skip, hop]

tripartite /traɪ'pɑːtaɪt/ *adj.* 1. consisting of three parts. 2. shared by or involving three parties. [from Latin *partiri* = divide]

tripe *n.* 1. the first or second stomach of a ruminant, especially an ox, as food. 2. (*slang*) nonsense; a worthless thing. [from Old French]

Tripitaka /trɪpɪta:ka/ *n.* the canonical texts of Theravāda Buddhism, divided into three parts. [Pāli = three baskets]

triple *adj.* 1. threefold, consisting of three parts or involving three parties. 2. being three times as many or as much. 3. (of time in music) having three beats in the bar. —*n.* 1. a threefold number or amount. 2. a set of three. —*v.t./i.* to make or become three times as many or as much. —**triple jump,** an athletic contest comprising a hop, a step, and a jump. **triple point,** the temperature and pressure at which the solid, liquid, and vapour phases of a pure substance can coexist in equilibrium. —**triply** *adv.* [Old French or from Latin *triplus* from Greek]

Triple Alliance the pact from 1882 between Germany, Austria–Hungary, and Italy to offset the power of Russia and France. It was last renewed in 1912, but during World War I Italy's initial neutrality gradually changed and it denounced the alliance in 1915. The term also refers to other alliances: 1668 – England, Holland, and Sweden; 1717 – Britain, Holland, and France (joined in 1718 by Austria); 1788 – Britain, Prussia, and Holland; 1795 – Britain, Russia, and Austria.

Triple Entente the alliance of Britain, France, and Russia 1907–17. In 1911 this became a military alliance and formed the basis of the Allied powers in World War I against the Central Powers, Germany and Austria–Hungary.

triplet /'trɪplɪt/ *n.* 1. each of three children or animals born at a birth. 2. a set of three things, especially of notes played in the time of two, or of three lines of verse rhyming together. [from *triple*, after *doublet*]

triplex *adj.* triple, threefold. [Latin *plex* from *plic-* = fold]

triplicate /'trɪplɪkət/ *adj.* 1. existing in three examples. 2. having three corresponding parts. 3. tripled. —*n.* each of three things exactly alike. —/-keɪt/ *v.t.* to make in three copies; to multiply by three. —**triplication** /-'keɪʃən/ *n.* [from Latin *triplicare*]

tripod /'traɪpɒd/ *n.* 1. a three-legged stand for a camera etc. 2. a stool, table, or utensil resting on three feet or legs. [from Latin from Greek *pous* = foot]

Tripoli /'trɪpəli/ (Arabic *Tarabolus al-Gharb*) capital and chief port of Libya, on the Mediterranean; population (1980) 980,000. Products include olive oil, fruit, fish, and textiles. Tripoli was founded in about the 7th century BC by Phoenicians from Oea (now Tripoli in Lebanon). It was a base for Axis powers during World War II. In 1986 it was bombed by the US Air Force in response to international guerrilla activity.

tripos /'traɪpɒs/ *n.* the honours examination for the BA degree at Cambridge University. [with reference to stool on which a BA sat to deliver satirical speech]

tripper *n.* a person who goes on a pleasure trip or excursion. —**trippery** *adj.*

triptych /'trɪptɪk/ *n.* a picture or carving on three panels, usually hinged vertically together. [from *tri*-after *diptych*]

Tripura /'trɪpʊrə/ state of NE India since 1972, formerly a princely state, between Bangladesh and Assam; **area** 10,500 sq km/4,053 sq mi; **capital** Agartala; **population** (1981) 2,060,000; **language** Bengali; **religion** Hindu.

trireme /'traɪriːm/ *n.* an ancient Greek warship with three banks of oars as well as sails, 38 m/115 ft long. They were used at the battle of ◊Salamis and by the Romans until the 4th century AD. [from French or Latin *remus* = oar]

trisect /traɪ'sekt/ *v.t.* to divide into three (usually equal) parts. —**trisection** *n.* [from Latin *secare* = cut]

Tristan /'trɪstən/ hero of Celtic legend who fell in love with Iseult, the bride he was sent to win for his uncle King Mark of Cornwall; the story became part of the Arthurian cycle, and is the subject of Wagner's opera *Tristan und Isolde*.

Tristram Shandy /'trɪstrəm 'ʃændi/ a novel by Laurence Sterne, published 1759–67. The work, a forerunner of the 20th century stream-of-consciousness novel, has no coherent plot and uses typographical devices to emphasize the author's disdain for the structured novels of his contemporaries.

trite *adj.* (of a phrase, opinion etc.) hackneyed, worn out by constant repetition. [from Latin *tritus* (*terere* = rub)]

triticale *n.* a cereal crop of recent origin that is a cross between wheat *Triticum* and rye *Secale*. It can produce heavy yields of high-protein grain, principally for use as animal feed. [from *Triti*cum and *Se*cal*e*]

tritium /'trɪtiəm/ *n.* a radioactive isotope of hydrogen, three times as heavy as ordinary hydrogen, consisting of one proton and two neutrons. It has a half-life of 12.5 years. [from Greek *tritos* = third]

Triton /'traɪtn/ *n.* in Greek mythology, a merman sea-god, the son of ◊Poseidon and the sea-goddess Amphitrite. He is shown blowing on a conch shell.

Triton *n.* in astronomy, the largest of Neptune's moons and one of the four largest in the Solar System. It has a diameter of 2,720 km/1,690 mi, and orbits Neptune every 5.88 days in a retrograde (east to west) direction. Its surface has many fault lines and a bright polar region that reflects 90% of the sunlight it receives. Its atmosphere is composed of methane and nitrogen, and has a pressure only 0.00001 that of the Earth at sea level. Triton was discovered by Galle in 1846, one month after the discovery of Neptune.

triumph /'traɪəmf/ *n.* 1. the state of being victorious; a great success or achievement. 2. a supreme example. 3. joy at a success, exultation. 4. the processional entry of a victorious general into ancient Rome. —*v.i.* 1. to gain a victory, to be successful; to prevail. 2. to exult. 3. (of a Roman general) to ride in a triumph. [from Old French from Latin *triump(h)us*, probably from Greek *thriambos* = hymn to Bacchus]

triumphal /traɪ'ʌmfəl/ *adj.* of, used in, or celebrating a triumph. [from Old French or Latin]

triumphant /traɪ'ʌmfənt/ *adj.* 1. victorious, successful. 2. rejoicing at success etc. —**triumphantly** *adv.*

triumvir /'traɪəmvɪə, -'ʌmvə/ *n.* a member of a triumvirate. [Latin *tres viri* = three men]

triumvirate /traɪ'ʌmvərət/ *n.* a board or ruling group of three men, especially in ancient Rome as in the **First Triumvirate** 60 BC: Caesar, Pompey, Crassus; and **Second Triumvirate** 43 BC: Augustus, Antony, and Lepidus. [from Latin]

trivalent /traɪ'veɪlənt/ *adj.* having a valence of three.

trivet /'trɪvɪt/ *n.* an iron tripod or bracket for a cooking pot or kettle to stand on. —**as right as a trivet,** (*colloquial*) in a perfectly good state. [apparently from Latin *tripes* = three-footed (*pes* = foot)]

trivia /'trɪviə/ *n.pl.* trivial things.

trivial /'trɪviəl/ *adj.* of only small value or importance, trifling; (of a person) concerned only with trivial things. —**triviality** /-'ælɪti/ *n.,* **trivially** *adv.* [from Latin = commonplace (*trivium* = place where three roads meet from *via* = road)]

trochee /'trəʊki:/ *n.* a metrical foot consisting of one long or stressed syllable followed by one short or unstressed syllable. —**trochaic** /trə'keɪɪk/ *adj.* [from Latin from Greek = running (*trekhō* = run)]

trod, trodden see ◊tread.

troglodyte /'trɒglədaɪt/ *n.* a cave-dweller, especially in prehistoric times. [from Latin from Greek from name of Ethiopian people, after *troglē* = hole]

trogon *n.* a tropical bird, up to 50 cm/1.7 ft long, with resplendent plumage, living in the Americas and Afro-Asia, order Trogoniformes. Most striking is the ◊quetzal.

troika /'trɔɪkə/ *n.* 1. a Russian vehicle with a team of three horses abreast; such a team. 2. a group of three persons especially as an administrative council. [Russian *troe* = three]

Trojan /'trəʊdʒən/ *adj.* of Troy or its people. —*n.* 1. an inhabitant of Troy. 2. a person who works, fights, or endures courageously. —**Trojan horse,** a seemingly innocuous but treacherous gift from an enemy. In Greek legend, during the siege of Troy, the Greek army left an enormous wooden horse outside the gate of the city and retreated. When the Trojans had brought it in, Greek soldiers emerged from within the hollow horse and opened the city gates to enable it to be captured. In computing, a Trojan horse is a program that appears to function normally but undetected by the normal user, causes damage to other files or circumvents security procedures. The earliest appeared in the UK in about 1988. **Trojan War,** the ten-year siege of Troy by the Greeks in Greek legend. [from Latin *Troianus*]

troll¹ /'trəʊl/ *n.* in Scandinavian mythology, a member of a race of supernatural beings formerly conceived as giants but now (in Denmark and Sweden) as friendly but mischievous dwarfs. [from Old Norse and Swedish *troll*, Danish *trold*]

troll² *v.t./i.* 1. to sing out in a carefree jovial manner. 2. to fish by drawing bait along in the water. [originally = stroll, roll; compare Old French *troller* = to quest]

trolley /'trɒli/ *n.* 1. a platform on wheels for transporting goods; a small cart or truck. 2. a small table on wheels or castors for transporting food or small articles. 3. a trolley wheel. —**trolley bus** a bus powered by electricity from an overhead wire to which it is linked by a trolley wheel. It has greater manoeuvrability than a ◊tram but its obstructiveness in present-day traffic conditions led to its withdrawal in the UK. **trolley wheel,** a wheel attached to a pole etc. for collecting current from an overhead electric wire to drive a vehicle. [dialect]

trollop /'trɒləp/ *n.* a disreputable girl or woman. [perhaps related to archaic *trull* = prostitute]

Trollope Anthony 1815–1882. English novelist who delineated provincial English middle-class society in his Barchester series of novels. *The Warden* 1855 began the series, which includes *Barchester Towers* 1857, *Doctor Thorne* 1858, and *The Last Chronicle of Barset* 1867.

Three hours a day will produce as much as a man ought to write.

Anthony Trollope
Autobiography

---

trombone /trɒm'bəʊn/ *n.* a brass wind instrument, developed from the sackbut, with a forward-pointing extendable slide. Usual sizes of trombone are alto, tenor, bass, and contra-bass. [French or from Italian *tromba* = trumpet]

Tromp /trɒmp/ Maarten Harpertszoon 1597–1653. Dutch admiral. He twice defeated the occupying Spaniards in 1639. He was defeated by the British admiral Blake in May 1652, but in Nov triumphed over Blake in the Strait of Dover. In Feb–June 1653 he was defeated by Blake and Monk, and was killed off the Dutch coast. His son, **Cornelius Tromp** (1629–91), also an admiral, fought a battle against the English and French fleets in 1673.

trompe l'œil /trɔ̃p 'lʌi:/ a painting that gives a convincing illusion of three-dimensional reality. It has been common in most periods in the West, from Classical Greece through the Renaissance and later. [French, literally = deceives the eye]

-tron suffix forming nouns denoting elementary particles or particle accelerators.

troop *n.* 1. an assemblage of persons or animals, especially when moving. 2. (in *plural*) soldiers, armed forces. 3. a cavalry unit commanded by a captain; a unit of artillery. 4. a unit of three or more scout patrols. —*v.i.* to assemble or go as a troop or in great numbers. —**troop the colour,** to show the regimental flag ceremonially along ranks of soldiers. [from French *troupe* ultimately from Latin *troppus* = flock]

trooper *n.* 1. a private soldier in a cavalry or armoured unit. 2. (*Australian history* and *US*) a mounted or motor-borne policeman. 3. a cavalry horse. 4. a troopship. —**swear like a trooper,** to swear extensively or forcefully.

trophic level in ecology, the position occupied by a species (or group of species) in a ◊food chain. The main levels are **primary producers** (photosynthetic plants), **primary consumers** (herbivores), **secondary consumers** (carnivores), and **decomposers** (bacteria and fungi).

trophy /'trəʊfi/ *n.* 1. a thing taken in war or hunting etc. as a souvenir of success. 2. an object awarded as a prize or token of victory. [from French from Latin from Greek *tropaion* (*tropē* = rout from *trepō* = turn)]

tropic /'trɒpɪk/ *n.* the parallel of latitude 23° 27| north (**tropic of Cancer**) or south (**tropic of Capricorn**) of the equator; they are the limits of the area of the Earth's surface in which the Sun can be directly overhead. —*adj.* 1. tropical. 2. of or showing tropism. —**the tropics,** the region between the tropics of Cancer and Capricorn, with a hot climate. [from Latin from Greek *tropē* = turning]

tropical /'trɒpɪkəl/ *adj.* of, peculiar to, or suggestive of the tropics. —**tropically** *adv.*

tropism /'trəʊpɪzəm/ *n.* or **tropic movement** the turning or movement of an organism in response to an eternal stimulus, e. g. that of plant leaves etc. in response to light. If the movement is directed towards the stimulus it is described as positive; if away from it, it is negative. **Geotropism**, the response of plants to gravity, causes the root (positively geotropic) to grow downwards, and the stem (negatively geotropic) to grow upwards. **Phototropism** occurs in response to light, **hydrotropism** to water, **chemotropism** to a chemical stimulus, and **thigmotropism**, or **haptotropism**, to physical contact, as in the tendrils of climbing plants when they touch a support and then grow around it. [from Greek *-tropos* = turning (*trepō* = turn)]

troposphere /'trɒpəsfɪə/ *n.* the layer of atmospheric air extending about 10.5 km/6.5 mi upwards from the Earth's surface, in which the temperature falls with increasing height to about −60°C/−76°F except in local layers of temperature inversion. The **tropopause** is the upper boundary of the troposphere above which the temperature increases slowly with height within the ◊atmosphere. [from Greek *tropos* = turning]

trot *v. t./i.* (-tt-) **1.** (of a quadruped) to proceed at a steady pace faster than a walk lifting each diagonal pair of legs alternately, often with brief intervals during which the body is unsupported. **2.** (of a person) to run at a moderate pace, especially with short strides; (*colloquial*) to walk, to go. **3.** to cause to trot. **4.** to traverse (a distance) at a trot. —*n.* the action or exercise of trotting. —**on the trot**, (*colloquial*) continually busy; in succession. **trot out**, to produce, to bring out for inspection or approval etc. [from Old French from Latin *trottare*]

troth /trəʊθ/ *n.* (*archaic*) faith, loyalty; truth. —**pledge** *or* **plight one's troth**, to pledge one's word, especially in marriage or betrothal. [Old English]

Trotsky /'trɒtski/ Leon. Adopted name of Lev Davidovitch Bronstein 1879–1940. Russian revolutionary. He joined the Bolshevik party and took a leading part in the seizure of power in 1917 and raising the Red Army that fought the Civil War 1918–20. In the struggle for power that followed ◊Lenin's death in 1924, ◊Stalin defeated Trotsky, and this and other differences with the Communist Party led to his exile in 1929. He settled in Mexico, where he was assassinated with an ice pick at Stalin's instigation. Trotsky believed in world revolution and in permanent revolution, and was an uncompromising, if liberal, idealist.

Old age is the most unexpected of all the things that happen to a man.

Leon Trotsky
Diary in Exile 8 May 1935

Trotskyism *n.* the form of Marxism advocated by Leon Trotsky. Its central concept is that of **permanent revolution**. In his view a proletarian revolution, leading to a socialist society, could not be achieved in isolation, so it would be necessary to spark off further revolutions throughout Europe and ultimately worldwide. This was in direct opposition to the Stalinist view that socialism should be built and consolidated within individual countries. [from L *Trotsky*]

Trotskyist /'trɒtskiist/ *n.* a radical left-wing Communist. [from L *Trotsky*]

trotter *n.* **1.** a horse bred or trained for trotting races. **2.** (usually in *plural*) an animal's foot as food.

trotting *n.* a form of horse racing (also called *harness racing*) in which a horse pulls a two-wheeled vehicle (a *sulky*) and its driver.

troubadour /'tru:bədʊə/ *n.* one of a group of poet musicians in Provence and S France in the 12th–13th centuries, which included both nobles and wandering minstrels. The troubadours originated a type of lyric poetry devoted to themes of courtly love and the idealization of women and to glorifying the deeds of their patrons, reflecting the chivalric ideals of the period. Little is known of the music, which was passed down orally. [French from Provençal *trovador* (*trovar* = find, compose)]

trouble /'trʌbəl/ *n.* **1.** difficulty, inconvenience, distress, vexation, misfortune; a cause of any of these; unpleasant exertion. **2.** faulty functioning of mechanism or of the body or mind. **3.** conflict; (in *plural*) public disturbances; **the Troubles**, any of various rebellions, civil wars, and

Trotsky Leon Trotsky in 1917, the year of the Russian Revolution.

unrest in Ireland, especially in 1919–23 and (in Northern Ireland) from 1968. **4.** unpleasantness involving punishment or rebuke. —*v. t./i.* **1.** to cause trouble or pain to; to distress. **2.** to be disturbed or worried; to be subjected to inconvenience or unpleasant exertion. —**ask** *or* **look for trouble**, (*colloquial*) to behave rashly, incautiously, indiscreetly etc. **in trouble**, involved in a matter likely to bring censure or punishment; (*colloquial*) pregnant while unmarried. **troublemaker** *n.* a person who habitually causes trouble. **troubleshooter** *n.* a person who traces and corrects faults in machinery etc.; a mediator in a dispute. [from Old French, ultimately from Latin *turba* = crowd, disturbance]

troublesome *adj.* causing trouble, annoying.

troublous /'trʌbləs/ *adj.* (*literary*) full of troubles, agitated, disturbed.

trough /trɒf/ *n.* **1.** a long narrow open receptacle for water, animal feed etc. **2.** a channel or hollow comparable to this. **3.** an elongated region of low barometric pressure. [Old English]

trounce *v. t.* **1.** to defeat heavily. **2.** to beat, to thrash; to punish severely.

troupe /tru:p/ *n.* a company of actors or acrobats etc. [French, ultimately from Latin *troppus* = flock]

trouper /'tru:pə/ *n.* **1.** a member of a theatrical troupe. **2.** a staunch colleague.

trousers /'traʊzəz/ *n.pl.* a two-legged outer garment reaching from the waist usually to the ankles. —**trouser suit**, a woman's suit of trousers and jacket. —**trousered** *adj.* [extended form of archaic *trouse*, from Irish and Gaelic]

trousseau /'tru:səʊ/ *n.* (*plural* **trousseaus**) a bride's collection of clothes etc. [French = bundle]

trout *n.* (*plural* usually the same) a small fish of the genus *Salmo* in northern rivers and lakes, valued as food and game; a similar fish of the family Salmonidae (**salmon** *or* **sea trout**). —**old trout**, (*slang, derogatory*) an old woman. [Old English]

trove *n.* treasure trove. [from Anglo-French *trové* (*trover* = find)]

trow /trəʊ, traʊ/ *v.t.* (*archaic*) to think, to believe. [Old English]

trowel /'traʊəl/ *n.* **1.** a small tool with a flat blade for spreading mortar or splitting bricks. **2.** a small garden tool with a curved blade for lifting small plants or scooping earth etc. [from Old French from Latin *trulla* = scoop, diminutive of *trua* = ladle]

troy /trɔɪ/ *n.* (in full **troy weight**) a system of weights used for precious metals and gems. The pound troy (0.37 kg) consists of 12 ounces (each of 120 carats) or 5,760 grains (each equal to 65 mg). [probably from *Troyes* in France]

Troy (Latin *Ilium*) ancient city of Asia Minor, besieged in the ten-year Trojan War (mid-13th century BC), which the poet Homer described in the *Iliad*. The city fell to the

Greeks who first used the stratagem of leaving behind, in a feigned retreat, a wooden horse containing armed infiltrators to open the gates. Believing it to be a religious offering, the Trojans took it within the walls.

truant /'truːənt/ *n.* a child who absents him or herself from school; a person missing from work etc. —*adj.* (of a person or his conduct etc.) shirking, idle, wandering. —**play truant**, to stay away as a truant. —**truancy** *n.* [from Old French probably from Celtic (Welsh *truan*, Gaelic *truaghan* = wretched)]

truce /'truːs/ *n.* a temporary cessation of hostilities; an agreement for this. [originally plural; Old English = covenant]

Trucial States /'truːʃəl 'steɪts/ former name (until 1971) of the ◊United Arab Emirates. It derives from the agreements made with Britain in 1820 to ensure a truce in the area and to suppress piracy and slavery.

truck[1] *n.* **1.** an open container on wheels for transporting heavy loads; an open railway wagon; a handcart. **2.** a lorry. [perhaps short for *truckle*]

truck[2] *n.* dealings; barter, exchange. —*v.t./i.* (*archaic*) to barter, to exchange. [from French *troquer* from Latin *trocare*]

Truck Acts a series of UK acts of Parliament introduced in 1831, 1887, 1896, and 1940 to prevent employers misusing wage-payment systems to the detriment of their workers. The legislation made it illegal to pay wages with goods in kind or with tokens for use in shops owned by the employers. The 1940 act prevented employers giving canteen meals in lieu of wages.

truckle *v.i.* to submit obsequiously. —**truckle bed**, a low bed on wheels so that it may be pushed under another, especially as formerly used by servants etc. [from Anglo-French *trocle* from Latin *trochlea* = pulley]

truculent /'trʌkjʊlənt/ *adj.* defiant and aggressive. —**truculence** *n.*, **truculency** *n.*, **truculently** *adv.* [from Latin *truculentus* (*trux* = fierce)]

Trudeau /truːˈdəʊ/ Pierre (Elliott) 1919– . Canadian Liberal politician. He was prime minister 1968–79 and won again by a landslide in Feb 1980. In 1980 his work helped to defeat the Québec independence movement in a referendum. He repatriated the constitution from Britain in 1982, but by 1984 had so lost support that he resigned.

trudge /trʌdʒ/ *v.t./i.* to walk laboriously; to traverse (a distance) thus. —*n.* a trudging walk.

true /truː/ *adj.* **1.** in accordance with fact. **2.** in accordance with correct principles or an accepted standard; rightly or strictly so called; genuine, not false. **3.** exact, accurate; (of the voice etc.) in good tune. **4.** accurately placed, balanced, or shaped; upright; level. **5.** loyal, faithful. —**come true**, to happen in the way that was prophesied or hoped. **true-blue** *adj.* completely true to one's principles; firmly loyal; (*n.*) such a person. **true north**, north according to the Earth's axis, not the magnetic north. —**trueness** *n.* [Old English]

True Cross the instrument of Jesus' crucifixion, supposedly found by St Helena, the mother of the emperor Constantine, on the hill of the ◊Calvary in 326.

Truffaut /truˈfəʊ/ François 1932–1984. French New Wave film director whose gently comic films include *Jules et Jim* 1961 and *La Nuit américaine/Day for Night* 1973 (Academy Award). His prize-winning (Cannes) *The 400 Blows* 1959 was the first in a series of semi-autobiographical films. His later work includes *The Story of Adèle H* 1975 and *The Last Metro* 1980. He was influenced by Alfred Hitchcock, and also drew on Surrealist and comic traditions. He played one of the leading roles in Steven Spielberg's *Close Encounters of a Third Kind* 1977.

A film is a boat which is always on the point of sinking – it always tends to break up as you go along and drag you under with it.

François Truffaut
in *The New Wave* 1968

---

truffle *n.* **1.** a subterranean fungus of the genus *Tuber*. Certain species are valued as edible delicacies; in particular, *T. melanosporum*, generally found growing under oak trees. It is native to to the Périgord region of France but cultivated in other areas as well. It is rounded, blackish brown, covered

Truman Harry Truman was US president during the Allied victory in World War II and US involvement in the Korean War.

with warts externally, and with blackish flesh. **2.** a round soft sweet made of a chocolate mixture covered with cocoa etc. [probably from Dutch from obsolete French perhaps from Latin *tubera* = plural of *tuber*]

trug *n.* a shallow oblong basket usually of wood strips, used by gardeners. [perhaps dialect variant of *trough*]

truism /'truːɪzəm/ *n.* **1.** a statement too obviously true or too hackneyed to be worth making. **2.** a statement that repeats an idea already implied in one of its terms (e. g. *there is no need to be unnecessarily careful*).

Trujillo /truːˈxiːəʊ/ city in NW Peru, with its port at Salaverry; population (1988) 491,000. Industries include engineering, copper, sugar milling, and vehicle assembly.

Trujillo Molina /məʊˈliːnə/ Rafael (Leónidas) 1891– 1961. Dictator of the Dominican Republic from 1930. As commander of the Dominican Guard, he seized power and established a ruthless dictatorship. He was assassinated.

truly /'truːlɪ/ *adv.* **1.** sincerely, genuinely. **2.** faithfully, loyally. **3.** accurately, truthfully. [Old English]

Truman /'truːmən/ Harry S 1884–1972. 33rd president of the USA 1945–53, a Democrat. In Jan 1945 he became vice president to F D Roosevelt, and president when Roosevelt died in April that year. He used the atom bomb against Japan, launched the ◊Marshall Plan to restore W Europe's economy, and nurtured the European Community and NATO (including the rearmament of West Germany).

Truman Doctrine the US president Harry Truman's 1947 dictum that the USA would 'support free peoples who are resisting attempted subjugation by armed minorities or by outside pressures'. It was used to justify sending aid to Greece following World War II and sending US troops abroad; for example, to Korea.

trump[1] *n.* **1.** a playing card of a suit temporarily ranking above the others. **2.** an advantage, especially involving surprise. **3.** (*colloquial*) a helpful or excellent person. —*v.t.* to defeat (a card or its player) with a trump. —**trump card**, a card belonging to, or turned up to determine, the trump suit; a valuable resource. **trump up**, to invent (an accusation or excuse etc.) fraudulently. **turn up trumps** (*colloquial*) to turn out better than expected; to be greatly successful or helpful. [corruption of *triumph* in same (now obsolete) sense]

trump[2] *n.* (*archaic*) a trumpet blast. —**the last trump**, a trumpet blast to wake the dead on Judgement Day. [from Old French *trompe* (probably imitative)]

trumpery /'trʌmpərɪ/ *adj.* showy but worthless. —*n.* worthless finery etc. [from Old French *tromperie* (*tromper* = deceive)]

trumpet /'trʌmpɪt/ n. 1. a metal tubular or conical brass wind instrument with a flared mouth and a bright penetrating tone. 2. a trumpet-shaped thing. 3. a sound (as) of a trumpet. —v.t./i. 1. to blow a trumpet. 2. (of an elephant etc.) to make a loud sound as of a trumpet. 3. to proclaim (a person's or thing's merit) loudly. —**trumpet call,** an urgent summons to action. **trumpet major,** the chief trumpeter of a cavalry regiment. [from Old French *trompette*]

trumpeter n. 1. one who sounds a trumpet, especially a cavalry soldier giving signals. 2. a South American bird, up to 50 cm/20 in tall, genus *Psophia*, related to the cranes. It has long legs, a short bill, and dark plumage. 3. a type of ◊swan.

truncate /trʌŋ'keɪt/ v.t. to cut the top or end from. —**truncation** /-'keɪʃən/ n. [from Latin *truncare* = maim]

truncheon /'trʌntʃən/ n. 1. a short club carried by a policeman. 2. a staff or baton as a symbol of authority. [from Old French *tronchon* = stump from Latin]

trundle v.t./i. to roll along; to move heavily on a wheel or wheels. [variant of obsolete or dialect *trendle* from Old English *trendel* = circle]

trunk n. 1. the main stem of a tree as distinct from the branches and roots. 2. a person's or animal's body apart from the limbs and head. 3. a large box with a hinged lid, used for transporting or storing clothes etc. 4. (US) the boot of a motor car. 5. an elephant's elongated prehensile nose. 6. (in *plural*) men's close-fitting shorts worn for swimming, boxing etc. —**trunk call,** a telephone call on a trunk line with charges according to distance. **trunk line,** a main line of a railway, telephone system etc. **trunk road,** an important main road. [from Old French *tronc* from Latin *truncus*]

trunnion /'trʌnjən/ n. 1. a supporting cylindrical projection on each side of a cannon or mortar. 2. a hollow gudgeon supporting the cylinder in a steam engine and giving passage to steam. [from French *trognon* = core, tree trunk]

truss n. 1. a framework of beams or bars supporting a roof or bridge etc. 2. a padded belt or other device worn to support a hernia. 3. a bundle of hay or straw. 4. a compact cluster of flowers or fruit. —v.t. 1. to tie or bind securely; to tie (a fowl) compactly for cooking. 2. to support (a roof or bridge etc.) with a truss or trusses. [from Old French *trusser* (v.), *trusse* (n.)]

trust[1] n. 1. firm belief in the reliability, truth, strength, etc., of a person or thing; the state of being relied on. 2. confident expectation. 3. a thing or person committed to one's care; the resulting obligation. —v.t./i. 1. to have or place trust in; to treat as reliable. 2. to entrust. 3. to hope earnestly. —**in trust,** held as a trust (see sense 4). **on trust,** accepted without investigation. **trust to,** to place reliance on. [from Old Norse *traustr* = strong]

trust[2] n. an arrangement whereby a person or group of people holds property for the benefit of others entitled to the interest. A trust can be a **legal arrangement** under which A is empowered to administer property belonging to B for the benefit of C. A and B may be the same person; B and C may not. A **unit trust** holds and manages a number of marketable securities; by buying a 'unit' in such a trust, the purchaser has a proportionate interest in each of the securities so that his or her risk is spread. Nowadays, an **investment trust** is not a trust, but a public company investing in marketable securities money subscribed by its shareholders who receive dividends from the income earned. A **charitable trust,** such as the Ford Foundation, administers funds for charitable purposes. A **business trust** is formed by linking several companies by transferring shares in them to trustees; or by the creation of a holding company, whose shares are exchanged for those of the separate companies. Competition is thus eliminated, and in the USA both types were outlawed by the Sherman Anti-trust Act 1890.

trustee /trʌs'tiː/ n. 1. a person or a member of a board given possession of property with a legal obligation to administer it solely for the purposes specified. 2. a state made responsible for the government of an area. —**trusteeship** n.

trustful adj. full of trust or confidence, not feeling or showing suspicion. —**trustfully** adv., **trustfulness** n.

trusting adj. having trust, trustful.

trust territory a territory formerly held under the United Nations trusteeship system to be prepared for independence, either former ◊mandates, territories taken over by the Allies in World War II, or those voluntarily placed under the UN by the administering state.

trustworthy adj. deserving of trust, reliable. —**trustworthiness** n.

trusty adj. (*archaic*) trustworthy. —n. a prisoner who is given special privileges or responsibilities because of continuous good behaviour. —**trustily** adv., **trustiness** n.

truth /truːθ/ n. (*plural* /-ðz, -θs/) 1. the quality or state of being true or truthful. 2. what is true. —**in truth,** (*literary*) truly, really. **truth table,** in computing, a diagram showing the effect of a particular ◊logic gate on every combination of inputs. [Old English]

Truth /truːθ/ Sojourner. Adopted name of Isabella Baumfree, later Isabella Van Wagener 1797–1883. US antislavery and women's suffrage campaigner. Born a slave, she ran away and became involved with religious groups. In 1843 she was 'commanded in a vision' to adopt the name Sojourner Truth. She published an autobiography, *The Narrative of Sojourner Truth,* in 1850.

truthful adj. 1. habitually telling the truth. 2. (of a story etc.) true. —**truthfully** adv., **truthfulness** n.

try /traɪ/ v.t./i. 1. to make an effort with a view to success; to use effort to achieve or perform. 2. to test (the quality of a thing) by use or experiment; to test the qualities of (a person or thing); to examine the effectiveness or usefulness of for a purpose. 3. to make severe demands on. 4. to investigate and decide (a case or issue) judicially; to subject (a person) to trial. —n. 1. an effort to accomplish something. 2. (in Rugby football) a touching down of the ball by a player behind the goal line, scoring points and entitling his side to a kick at goal. —**try and,** (*colloquial*) try to. **try for,** to apply or compete for; to seek to reach or attain. **try one's hand,** to see how skilful one is, especially at a first attempt. **try it on,** (*colloquial*) to test another's patience. **try on,** to put on (clothes etc.) to see if they are suitable. **try-on** n. (*colloquial*) an act of 'trying it on', an attempt to deceive or outwit. **try out,** to put to the test, to test thoroughly. **try-out** n. an experimental test. [originally = separate, distinguish, from Old French *trier* = sift]

trying adj. putting a strain on one's temper, patience, or endurance; annoying.

trypanosome /'trɪpənəsəʊm/ n. a flagellate protozoan parasite of the genus *Trypanosoma,* infesting the blood etc. and causing diseases. [from Greek *trupanon* = borer and *sōma* = body]

trypanosomiasis n. any of a set of debilitating long-term diseases caused by a trypanosome. They include sleeping sickness (nagana) in Africa, transmitted by the bites of ◊tsetse flies, and ◊Chagas' disease in the Americas, spread by assassin bugs. [from Greek]

trypsin n. an enzyme occurring in the small intestine that digests proteins into smaller molecules. Trypsin is secreted by the pancreas in the form of trypsinogen, which is converted into active trypsin by the intestinal enzyme enterokinase. It is also used by industry in the preparation of baby foods.

tryst /trɪst, traɪst/ n. (*archaic*) a time and place for a meeting, especially of lovers. [from Old French *triste* = appointed station in hunting]

Ts'ao Chan alternative spelling of the Chinese novelist ◊Cao Chan.

tsar /zɑː/ n. the title of the former emperor of Russia. It was formally assumed as a title by Ivan the Terrible in 1547; some earlier uses exist. [from Russian, ultimately from Latin *Caesar*]

tsarist rule a system of political government in Russia. It was adopted by Ivan IV in 1547 and meant to express the highest form of domination, similar to that of the Holy Roman emperor in western Europe. Tsarist rule lasted until the abdication in 1917 and execution in 1918 of Tsar Nicholas II.

tsetse /'tsetsɪ, 'tetsɪ/ n. an African fly of the genus *Glossina,* related to the house fly, which transmits the disease nagana to cattle and sleeping sickness to human beings. It grows up to 1.5 cm/0.6 in long. [Tswana]

T-shirt /'tiː ʃɜːt/ n. a short-sleeved shirt for casual wear, having the form of T when spread out.

Tsiolkovsky /tsɪəl'kɒfski/ Konstantin 1857–1935. Russian scientist. He published the first practical paper on astronautics in 1903, dealing with space travel by rockets using liquid propellants, such as liquid oxygen.

T-square /'tiːskweə/ n. a T-shaped instrument for drawing or testing right angles.

Tsumeb /'tsuːmeb/ principal mining centre (diamonds, copper, lead, zinc) of N Namibia, NW of Grootfontein; population 13,500.

tsunami /tsu'nɑːmɪ/ n. a giant wave generated by an undersea earthquake or other disturbance. In the open ocean it may take the form of several successive waves, travelling at tens of kilometres per hour but with an amplitude (height) of approximately a metre. In the coastal shallows, tsunamis slow down and build up, producing towering waves that can sweep inland and cause great loss of life and property. [Japanese *tsu* = harbour and *nami* = wave]

Tsung Dao Lee /'tsʊŋ daʊ'liː/ 1926– . US physicist whose research centred on the physics of weak interactions between particles. In 1956 Lee proposed that such interactions might disobey certain key assumptions, for instance the conservation of parity. He shared the 1957 Nobel Prize for Physics with his colleague Chen Ning Yang (1922–).

Tsvetaeva /svɪ'taɪəvə/ Marina 1892–1941. Russian poet, born in Moscow. She wrote mythic, romantic, frenetic verse, including *The Demesne of the Swans*.

Tswana /'tswɑːnə/ n. 1. a member of a Negroid people living in Africa between the Orange and Zambezi rivers. 2. their Bantu language (also called *Sechuana*). [native name]

TT abbreviation of 1. Tourist Trophy. 2. tuberculin tested. 3. teetotal; teetotaller.

TTL abbreviation of transistor-transistor logic, the form of logic most commonly used in electronic devices. Integrated circuits built using TTL usually have fast switching speeds, and require a very stable DC voltage of between 4.75 and 5.25 volts. See also ◊CMOS.

Tuamotu Archipelago /tuːə'məʊtuː/ two parallel ranges of 78 atolls, part of ◊French Polynesia; **area** 690 sq km/266 sq mi; **administrative headquarters** Apataki; **population** (1983) 11,800, including the ◊Gambier Islands to the east. The atolls stretch 2,100 km/1,300 mi north and east of the Society Islands. The largest atoll is Rangiroa, the most significant is Hao; they produce pearl shell and copra. Mururoa and Fangataufa atolls to the southeast have been a French nuclear test site since 1966. Spanish explorers landed in 1606, and the islands were annexed by France in 1881.

Tuareg /'twɑːreg/ n. (*plural* the same or **Tuaregs**) 1. a member of a Berber group of nomadic pastoralists of North Africa. 2. their Berber dialect. —*adj.* of this people or their language. [native name]

tuatara n. a lizardlike reptile *Sphenodon punctatus*, found only on a few islands off New Zealand. It grows up to 70 cm/2.3 ft long, is greenish or black, and has a spiny crest down its back. On the top of its head is the pineal organ, or so-called 'third eye', linked to the brain, which probably acts as a kind of light meter.

tub n. 1. an open, flat-bottomed, usually round vessel used for washing or for holding liquids or containing soil for plants etc. 2. (*colloquial*) a bath. 3. (*colloquial*) a clumsy slow boat. —*v.t./i.* (**-bb-**) to plant, bath, or wash in a tub. —**tub-thumper** n. a ranting preacher or orator. [probably from Low Dutch]

tuba /'tjuːbə/ n. a large low-pitched ◊brass wind instrument. [Italian from Latin = trumpet]

tubal /'tjuːbəl/ *adj.* of a tube or tubes, especially the bronchial or Fallopian tubes.

tubby *adj.* tub-shaped; (of a person) short and fat. —**tubbiness** n.

tube n. 1. a long hollow cylinder; a natural or artificial structure having approximately this shape with open or closed ends and serving for the passage of fluid etc. or as a receptacle. 2. (*colloquial*) the London underground railway. 3. an inner tube. 4. a cathode-ray tube, e. g. in a television set. 5. (*US*) a thermionic valve. —*v.t.* 1. to equip with a tube or tubes. 2. to enclose in a tube. —**the tube,** (*US*) television. [French or from Latin *tubus*]

tuber /'tjuːbə(r)/ n. the swollen region of an underground stem or root, usually modified for storing food. The potato is a **stem tuber**, as shown by the presence of terminal and lateral buds, the 'eyes' of the potato. **Root tubers,**

tuber

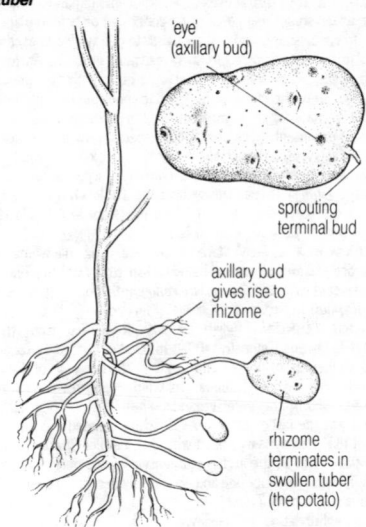

'eye'
(axillary bud)

sprouting
terminal bud

axillary bud
gives rise to
rhizome

rhizome
terminates in
swollen tuber
(the potato)

developed from adventitious roots, lack these. Both types of tuber can give rise to new individuals and so provide a means of ◊vegetative reproduction.

tubercle /'tjuːbəkəl/ n. a small rounded swelling in a plant or organ of the body, especially as characteristic of tuberculosis in the lungs. —**tubercle bacillus**, the bacillus causing tuberculosis. [from Latin *tuberculum*, diminutive of *tuber*]

tubercular /tjuː'bɜːkjʊlə/ *adj.* of or affected with tuberculosis.

tuberculin /tjuː'bɜːkjʊlɪn/ n. a preparation from cultures of the tubercle bacillus used for the treatment and diagnosis of tuberculosis. —**tuberculin-tested** *adj.* (of milk) from cows shown by a tuberculin test to be free of tuberculosis.

tuberculosis /tjuːbɜːkjʊ'ləʊsɪs/ n. (TB) formerly known as **consumption** or **phthisis** an infectious disease caused by the bacillus *Mycobacterium tuberculosis*. It takes several forms, with tubercles appearing on body tissue; pulmonary tuberculosis is by far the most common. [from *tubercle*]

tuberculous /tjuː'bɜːkjʊləs/ *adj.* of, having, or caused by tubercles or tuberculosis.

tuberose /'tjuːbərəʊz/ n. a plant *Polianthes tuberosa* with fragrant creamy-white flowers. [from Latin]

tuberous *adj.* having tubers; of or like a tuber. [from French or Latin]

tubing /'tjuːbɪŋ/ n. a length of tube; a quantity of tubes.

Tubman /'tʌbmən/ Harriet Ross 1821–1913. US abolitionist. Born a slave in Maryland, she escaped to Philadelphia (where slavery was outlawed) in 1849. She set up the **Underground Railroad**, a secret network of sympathizers, to help slaves escape to the North and Canada. During the American ◊Civil War she served as a spy for the Union army. She spoke against slavery and for women's rights, and founded schools for emancipated slaves after the Civil War.

Tubman William V S 1895–1971. Liberian politician. The descendant of US slaves, he was a lawyer in the USA. After his election to the presidency of Liberia in 1944 he concentrated on uniting the various ethnic groups. Re-elected several times, he died naturally in office despite frequent assassination attempts.

Tubuai Islands /tuːbuː'aɪ/ or **Austral Islands** chain of volcanic islands and reefs 1,300 km/800 mi long in ◊French Polynesia, south of the Society Islands; **area** 148 sq km/57 sq mi; **main settlement** Mataura, on Tubuai; **population** (1983) 6,300. The islands were visited by Captain Cook in 1777 and annexed by France in 1880.

tubular /'tjuːbjʊlə/ *adj.* tube-shaped; having or consisting of tubes; (of furniture etc.) made of tubular pieces.

tubule /'tjuːbjuːl/ n. a small tube. [from Latin *tubulus*, diminutive of *tubus* = tube]

TUC abbreviation of ◊Trades Union Congress.

tuck *v.t.* **1.** to turn (edges or ends) or fold (a part) in, into, or under something so as to be concealed or held in place. **2.** to cover snugly and compactly. **3.** to put away compactly. **4.** to put a tuck or tucks in (a garment etc.). **5.** (in *past participle*, of a dive or somersault etc.) with the knees drawn up to the chest. —*n.* **1.** a flattened, usually stitched, fold in material or a garment etc. to make it smaller or as an ornament. **2.** (*slang*) food, especially sweets, cakes, and pastry etc. that children enjoy. —**tuck in**, (*slang*) to eat food heartily. **tuck-in** *n.* (*colloquial*) a large meal. **tuck into**, (*slang*) to eat (food) heartily. **tuck shop**, a shop selling sweets etc. to schoolchildren. [from Middle Dutch and Middle Low German *tucken*]

tucker *n.* **1.** a piece of lace or linen etc. in or on a woman's bodice (*historical* except in **best bib and tucker**, one's best clothes). **2.** (*Australian colloquial*) food. —*v.t.* (*US colloquial*) to tire.

Tudor /'tjuːdə/ English dynasty descended from the Welsh Owen Tudor (*c.*1400–1461), the second husband of Catherine of Valois (the widow of Henry V of England). Their son Edmund married Margaret Beaufort (1443–1509), the great-granddaughter of ◊John of Gaunt, and was the father of Henry VII, who ascended the throne in 1485. The dynasty ended with the death of Elizabeth I in 1603. —*adj.* of the architectural style of this period, especially with half-timbering and elaborately decorated design of houses. [from O *Tudor*]

Tue. abbreviation of Tuesday.

Tuesday /'tjuːzdeɪ, -dɪ/ *n.* the day of the week following Monday. —*adv.* (*colloquial*) on Tuesday. [Old English = day of Tiw (Teutonic god of war)]

tufa /'tjuːfə/ *n.* **1.** or **travertine** a soft, porous, ◊limestone rock, white in colour, deposited from solution from carbonate-saturated ground water around hot springs and in caves. **2.** tuff. [Italian]

tuff *n.* rock formed from volcanic ashes. [from French from Italian from Latin *tofus* = loose porous stones]

tuffet /'tʌfɪt/ *n.* a small mound; a tussock. [variant of *tuft*]

tuft *n.* a bunch or collection of threads, grass, feathers, or hair etc. held or growing together at the base. —**tufty** *adj.* [probably from Old French *tof(f)e*]

tufted *adj.* having or forming a tuft or tufts; (of a bird) with a tuft of feathers on its head; (of a mattress or cushion) with depressions formed by stitching tightly through it at intervals to hold the filling in place.

tug *v.t./i.* (**-gg-**) **1.** to pull vigorously or with great effort. **2.** to tow by means of a tugboat. —*n.* **1.** a vigorous pull (*literal* or *figurative*). **2.** a tugboat. —**tug of love**, (*colloquial*) a dispute over the custody of a child. **tug of war**, a contest in which two teams hold a rope at opposite ends and pull until one team hauls the other over a central point; a struggle between two persons etc. for power.

tugboat *n.* a small powerful steam vessel for towing others.

tuition /tjuːˈɪʃən/ *n.* teaching instruction, especially as a thing to be paid for. [from Old French from Latin *tuēri* = look after]

Tukano *n.* a member of an indigenous South American Indian people of the Vaupés region on the Colombian-Brazilian border, numbering approximately 2,000.

tulip /'tjuːlɪp/ *n.* a spring-flowering plant of the genus *Tulipa*, growing from a bulb, usually with single goblet-shaped flowers on the end of an upright stem and leaves of a narrow oval shape with pointed ends; its flower. —**tulip-tree** *n.* a tree (*Liriodendron tulipifera*) with tulip-like flowers. [from Turkish *tul(i)band* from Persian = *turban* (from the shape of the flowers)]

Tull /tʌl/ Jethro 1674–1741. English agriculturist who in about 1701 developed a drill that enabled seeds to be sown mechanically and spaced so that cultivation between rows was possible in the growth period. His major work, *Horse-Hoeing Husbandry*, was published in 1731.

tulle /tjuːl/ *n.* a soft fine silk net for veils and dresses. [from *Tulle* in SW France]

tum *n.* (*colloquial*) the stomach. [abbreviation of *tummy*]

tumble *v.t./i.* **1.** to fall helplessly or headlong; to cause to do this. **2.** to fall in value or amount. **3.** to roll or toss over and over in a disorderly way. **4.** to move or rush in a hasty careless way. **5.** to throw or push carelessly in a confused mass. **6.** to rumple, to disarrange. **7.** to perform somersaults or other acrobatic feats. **8.** (of a pigeon) to throw itself over backwards in flight. —*n.* **1.** a tumbling fall. **2.** an untidy state. —**tumble-drier** *n.* a machine for drying washing in a heated rotating drum. **tumble to**, (*colloquial*) to realize or grasp the meaning of. [from Middle Low German *tummelen*]

tumbledown *adj.* falling or fallen into ruin, dilapidated.

tumbler *n.* **1.** a drinking-glass with no handle or foot. **2.** an acrobat. **3.** a pivoted piece in a lock that holds the bolt until lifted by a key; any of various kinds of pivoted or swivelling parts in a mechanism. **4.** a pigeon that tumbles in its flight.

tumbrel /'tʌmbrəl/ *n.* or **tumbril** an open cart in which condemned persons were conveyed to the guillotine during the French Revolution. [from Old French *tomberel* (*tomber* = fall)]

tumescent /tjuːˈmesənt/ *adj.* swelling. —**tumescence** *n.* [from Latin *tumescere*]

tumid /'tjuːmɪd/ *adj.* swollen, inflated; (of style etc.) bombastic. —**tumidity** /-'mɪdɪtɪ/ *n.* [from Latin *tumidus*]

tummy /'tʌmɪ/ *n.* (*colloquial*) the stomach. —**tummy-button** *n.* (*colloquial*) the navel. [childish pronunciation]

tumour /'tjuːmə/ *n.* an overproduction of cells in a specific area of the body, often leading to a swelling or lump. Tumours are classified as **benign** or **malignant** (see ◊cancer). —**tumorous** *adj.* [from Latin *tumor* (*tumēre* = swell)]

tumult /'tjuːmʌlt/ *n.* **1.** an uproar, a public disturbance. **2.** a state of confusion and agitation. [from Old French or Latin *tumultus*]

tumultuous /tjuːˈmʌltjuəs/ *adj.* making a tumult. —**tumultuously** *adv.*

tumulus /'tjuːmjuləs/ *n.* (*plural* **tumuli** /-laɪ/) an ancient burial mound. [Latin = mound]

tun *n.* **1.** a large cask for wine; a brewer's fermenting-vat. **2.** a measure of capacity (usually about 210 gallons). [Old English from Latin *tunna*, probable of Gaulish origin]

tuna /'tjuːnə/ *n.* (*plural* same) or **tunny** a fish of the mackerel family *Thunnus thynnus*, up to 2.5 m/8 ft long and 200 kg/440 lbs; (also **tuna-fish**) the flesh of this fish as food. [American Spanish]

tundra /'tʌndrə/ *n.* a region of high latitude almost devoid of trees, resulting from the presence of ◊permafrost. The vegetation consists mostly of grasses, sedges, heather, mosses, and lichens. Tundra stretches in a continous belt across North America and Eurasia. [Lappish]

tune *n.* **1.** a melody with or without harmony. **2.** the correct pitch or intonation in singing or playing; an adjustment of a musical instrument to obtain this. —*v.t.* **1.** to put (a musical instrument) in tune. **2.** to adjust (a radio receiver etc.) to a particular wavelength of signals. **3.** to adjust (an engine etc.) to run smoothly and efficiently. **4.** to adjust or adapt (a thing to a purpose etc.). —**call the tune**, to have control of events. **change one's tune**, to change one's style of language or manner, especially from an insolent to a respectful tone. **in** (*or* **out of**) **tune with**, harmonizing (or clashing) with. **to the tune of**, to the considerable sum or amount of. **tune in**, to set a radio receiver to the right wavelength to receive a certain signal. **tune up**, (of an orchestra) to bring the instruments to the proper or a uniform pitch; to bring to the most efficient condition; to begin to play or sing. [variant of *tone*]

tuneful *adj.* melodious, having a pleasing tune. —**tunefully** *adv.*, **tunefulness** *n.*

tuneless *adj.* not melodious; without a tune.

tuner /'tjuːnə/ *n.* a person who tunes instruments, especially pianos.

tungsten /'tʌŋstən/ *n.* a hard, heavy, grey-white, metallic element, symbol W (from German *Wolfram*), atomic number 74, relative atomic mass 183.85. It occurs in the minerals wolframite, scheelite, and hubertite. It has the highest melting point of any metal (6,170°F/3,410°C) and is added to steel to make it harder, stronger, and more elastic; its other uses include high-speed cutting tools, electrical elements, and thermionic couplings. Its salts are used in the paint and tanning industries. [Swedish (*tung* = heavy and *sten* = stone)]

tungsten ore one of the two main minerals, wolframite (FeMn)WO₄, amd scheelite, CaWO₄, from which tungsten is extracted. Most of the world's tungsten reserves are in China, but the main suppliers are Bolivia, Australia, Canada, and the USA.

Tunguska Event an explosion at Tunguska, central Siberia, Russia, in June 1908 which devastated around 6,500 sq km/2,500 sq mi of forest. It is thought to have been caused by either a cometary nucleus or a fragment of ◊Encke's comet. The magnitude of the explosion was equivalent to an atom bomb and produced a colossal shock wave; a bright falling object was seen 600 km/375 mi away and was heard up to 1,000 km/625 mi away.

tunic /'tju:nɪk/ *n*. **1.** the close-fitting short coat of a police or military uniform. **2.** a loose garment, often sleeveless, reaching to the hips or knees. [from French or Latin *tunica*]

tunicate /'tju:nɪkət/ *n*. a member of the subphylum Urochorda of marine animals with a hard outer coat. Tunicates vary in size from a few millimetres to 30 cm/1 ft in length, and are cylindrical, circular, or irregular in shape. [from Latin *tunicare* = clothe with a tunic]

tuning fork in music, a device for providing a reference pitch. It is made from hardened metal and consists of parallel bars about 10 cm/3–4 in long joined at one end and terminating in a blunt point. When the fork is struck and the point placed on a wooden surface, a pure tone is heard.

Tunis /'tju:nɪs/ capital and chief port of Tunisia; population (1984) 597,000. Industries include chemicals and textiles. Founded by the Arabs, it was occupied by the French 1881 and by the Axis powers 1942–43. The ruins of ancient ◊Carthage are to the NE.

Tunisia /tju:'nɪzɪə/ Republic of; country in N Africa, on the Mediterranean, bounded to the SE by Libya and to the W by Algeria; **area** 164,150 sq km/63,378 sq mi; **capital** and chief port Tunis; **physical** arable and forested land in N graduates toward desert in S; **head of state and government** Zine el Abdin Ben Ali from 1987; **political system** emergent democratic republic; **population** (1990 est) 8,094,000; **language** Arabic (official), French; **recent history** a French protectorate from 1883, Tunisia was granted internal self-government in 1955, and full independence was achieved from France as a monarchy in 1956, with Habib Bourguiba as prime minister. The country became a republic the next year, with Bourguiba as president, and he was made president for life in 1975. Prime minister Ben Ali seized power in 1987, and in 1988 announced constitutional changes toward democracy. In the 1989 general elections, the government party, the RCD, won all assembly seats.

tunnel /'tʌnəl/ *n*. an underground passage; a passage dug through a hill or under a road etc., especially for a railway or road; a passage made by a burrowing animal. Tunnelling is a significant branch of civil engineering in both mining and transport. In the 19th century there were two major advances: the use of compressed air within underwater tunnels to balance the external pressure of water, and the development of the tunnel shield to support the face and assist excavation. In recent years there have been notable developments in linings (for example, concrete segments and steel liner plates), and in the use of rotary diggers and cutters and explosives. —*v.t./i.* (**-ll-**) to make a tunnel through (a hill etc.); to make one's way thus. [from Old French *tonel*, diminutive of *tonne* tun]

tunny /'tʌnɪ/ *n*. a large edible sea-fish, especially of the genus *Thunnus* (the ◊tuna). [from French *thon* from Latin from Greek *thunnos*]

tup *n*. a male sheep, a ram. —*v.t.* (**-pp-**) (of a ram) to copulate with (a ewe).

Tupamaros *n*. urban guerrilla movement operating in Uruguay, largely active in the 1960s–70s, named after the 18th-century revolutionary Túpac Amarú.

tuppence /'tʌpəns/ *n*. = ◊twopence. [phonetic spelling]

tuppenny /'tʌpənɪ/ *adj*. = ◊twopenny. [phonetic spelling]

turban /'tɜ:bən/ *n*. **1.** a man's head-dress of cotton or silk wound round a cap, worn especially by Muslims and Sikhs. **2.** a woman's head-dress or hat resembling this. [ultimately from Turkish from Persian]

turbid /'tɜ:bɪd/ *adj*. **1.** (of a liquid or colour) muddy, not clear. **2.** (of style etc.) not lucid. —**turbidity** /-'bɪdɪtɪ/ *n*., **turbidly** *adv*. [from Latin (*turba* crowd, disturbance)]

turbine /'tɜ:baɪn/ *n*. a device for producing continuous mechanical power, in which a fluid (water, steam, air, or a gas) is accelerated to a high speed in a channel or nozzle and the resulting jet(s) directed at a rotating wheel with vanes or scoop-shaped buckets round its rim. Turbines are among the most powerful machines. Steam turbines are used to

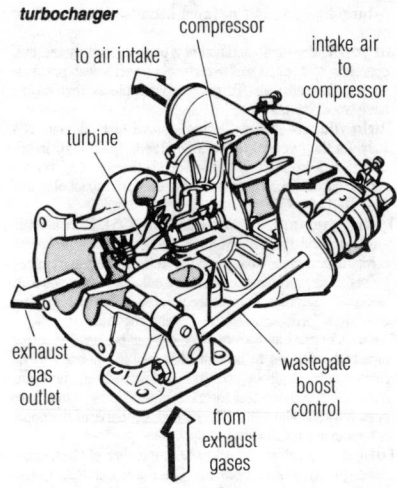
turbocharger
compressor
to air intake
intake air to compressor
turbine
exhaust gas outlet
wastegate boost control
from exhaust gases

drive generators in power stations and ships' propellers; water turbines spin the generators in hydroelectric power plants; and gas turbines (as jet engines) power most aircraft and drive machines in industry. [French from Latin *turbo*= spinning-top, whirlwind]

turbo- /'tɜ:bəʊ/ in combinations, turbine.

turbocharger *n*. a turbine-driven device fitted to engines to force more air into the cylinders, producing extra power. The turbocharger consists of a 'blower', or ◊compressor, driven by a turbine, which in most units is driven by the exhaust gases leaving the engine.

turbofan *n*. the jet engine used by most airliners, so called because of its huge front fan. The fan sends air not only into the engine itself, but also around the engine. This results in a faster and more efficient propulsive jet. See ◊jet propulsion.

turbojet *n*. **1.** a jet engine in which jet gases also operate a turbine-driven compressor for supplying compressed air to the combustion chamber. Pure turbojets can be very powerful but use a lot of fuel. **2.** an aircraft with such an engine.

turboprop *n*. **1.** a jet engine that derives its thrust partly from a jet of exhaust gases, but mainly from a propeller powered by a turbine in the jet exhaust. Turboprops are more economical than turbojets but can be used only at relatively low speeds. **2.** an aircraft with such an engine.

turbot /'tɜ:bət/ *n*. a carnivorous flatfish *Scophthalmus maximus* found in European waters and valued as food. It grows up to 1 m/3 ft long and weighs up to 14 kg/30 lb. It is brownish above and whitish underneath. [from Old French]

turbulent /'tɜ:bjʊlənt/ *adj*. **1.** in a state of commotion or unrest; (of air or water) moving violently and unevenly. **2.** unruly. —**turbulence** *n*., **turbulently** *adv*. [from Latin (*turba* = crowd, disturbance)]

Turco- /'tɜ:kəʊ-/ in combinations, Turkish. [from Latin]

turd *n*. (*vulgar*) a ball or lump of excrement. [Old English]

tureen /tjʊə'ri:n/ *n*. a deep covered dish from which soup is served. [from French *terrine* = earthenware dish from Latin *terra* = earth]

turf *n*. (*plural* **turfs** or **turves**) **1.** the layer of grass etc. with earth and matted roots as the surface of grassland. **2.** a piece of this cut from the ground. **3.** a slab of peat for fuel. —*v.t.* to plant (ground) with turf. —**the turf**, the racecourse, horse-racing. **turf accountant**, a bookmaker. **turf out**, (*slang*) to throw out. —**turfy** *adj*. [Old English]

Turgenev /tuə'geɪnjef/ Ivan Sergeievich 1818–1883. Russian writer, notable for poetic realism, pessimism, and skill in characterization. His works include the play *A Month in the Country* 1849, and the novels *A Nest of Gentlefolk* 1858, *Fathers and Sons* 1862, and *Virgin Soil* 1877. His series *A Sportsman's Sketches* 1852 criticized serfdom.

turgescent /tɜ:'dʒesənt/ *adj*. becoming turgid. —**turgescence** *n*. [from Latin *turgescere*]

turgid /'tɜ:dʒɪd/ *adj*. **1.** swollen or distended and not flexible. **2.** (of language or style) pompous, not flowing easily.

—**turgidity** /-'dʒɪdɪtɪ/ *n*. [from Latin *turgidus* (*turgēre* = swell)]

turgor *n*. the rigid condition of a plant caused by the fluid contents of a plant cell exerting a mechanical pressure against the cell wall. Turgor supports plants that do not have woody stems.

Turin /tju'rɪn/ (Italian *Torino*) capital of Piedmont, NW Italy, on the river Po; population (1988) 1,025,000. Industries include iron, steel, cars, silk and other textiles, fashion goods, chocolate, and wine. It was the first capital of united Italy 1861–64.

Turing /'tjuərɪŋ/ Alan Mathison 1912–1954. British mathematician and logician. In 1936 he described a 'universal computing machine' that could theoretically be programmed to solve any problem capable of solution by a specially designed machine. This concept, now called the **Turing machine**, foreshadowed the digital computer.

Turin shroud an ancient piece of linen bearing the image of a body, claimed to be that of Jesus. Independent tests carried out in 1988 by scientists in Switzerland, the USA, and the UK showed that the cloth of the shroud dated from between 1260 and 1390. The shroud, property of the pope, is kept in Turin Cathedral, Italy.

Turk *n*. **1**. a native of Turkey. **2**. a member of the Central Asian people from whom the Ottomans derived, speaking Turkic languages, belonging to the Altaic family and including Uzbek, Ottoman, Turkish, Azerbaijani, Turkoman, Tatar, Kirghiz, and Yakut. **3**. (especially **young Turk**) a ferocious, wild, or unmanageable person. —**Turk's head**, a turban-like ornamental knot. [from French *Turc* etc., Persian and Arabic *Turk*]

Turkana, Lake /tɜ:'kɑ:nə/ lake formerly **Lake Rudolf** in the Great Rift Valley, 375 m/1,230 ft above sea level, with its northernmost end in Ethiopia and the rest in Kenya; area 9,000 sq km/3,475 sq mi. It is saline, and shrinking by evaporation. Its shores were an early human hunting ground, and valuable remains have been found that are accurately datable because of undisturbed stratification.

turkey /'tɜ:kɪ/ *n*. **1**. a large American bird of the genus *Meleagris*, especially the domisticated turkey *M. gallopavo*. The wild turkey reaches a length of 1.3 m/4.3 ft. **2**. its flesh as food. —**talk turkey**, (*US colloquial*) to talk in a frank and businesslike way. **turkey-cock** *n*. a male turkey. [short for *turkey cock*, originally applied to the guinea-fowl (with which the American turkey was confused) because imported into Europe through Turkey]

Turkey Republic of; country between the Black Sea and the Mediterranean, bounded to the E by the USSR and Iran, to the S by Iraq and Syria; area 779,500 sq km/300,965 sq mi; capital Ankara; physical central plateau surrounded by mountains; head of state Turgot Ozal from 1989; head of government Vildirim Akbulut from 1989; political system democratic republic; population (1990 est) 56,549,000 (85% Turkish, 12% Kurdish); language Turkish (official); Kurdish, Arabic; recent history an independent republic under Mustafa Kemal (Atatürk) since 1923, Turkey held its first free elections in 1950; Adnan Menderes became prime minister, but was executed after a military coup in 1960. Until 1982, when a new constitution was adopted, the army stayed in nominal control, and harsh repression of political activists attracted international criticism. The ban on political activity was lifted in 1983, when Turgut Ozal became prime minister. Ozal was elected president in 1989; in the same year, Turkey's application for EC membership was refused.

Turki *adj*. of the Turkic languages or the peoples who speak these. —**Turkic** *adj*. & *n*. [from Persian *Turkī*]

Turkish /'tɜ:kɪʃ/ *adj*. of Turkey or the Turks or their language. —*n*. the language of Turkey. —**Turkish carpet**, a Turkey carpet. **Turkish coffee**, strong usually sweet black coffee made from very finely ground beans and boiled so that it becomes very thick. **Turkish delight**, a sweet consisting of lumps of flavoured gelatine coated in powdered sugar. **Turkish towel**, a towel made of cotton terry.

turkish bath **1**. a type of bathing which involves exposure to warm air and steam, followed by massage and cold water immersion. Originating from Roman and East Indian traditions, the concept was introduced to Western Europe by the Crusaders but only became popular when hot water could be supplied in sufficient quantities. **2**. (in *singular* or *plural*) a building for this.

Turkish language language of central and W Asia, the national language of Turkey. Originally written in Arabic script, the Turkish of Turkey has been written in a variant of the Roman alphabet since 1928. Varieties of Turkish are spoken in NW Iran and several of the Asian republics of the USSR, and all have been influenced by Arabic and Persian.

Turkmenistan /tɜ:kmeni'stɑ:n/ constituent republic of the USSR from 1924, part of Soviet Central Asia; **area** 488,100 sq km/188,455 sq mi; **capital** Ashkhabad; **population** (1987) 3,361,000; 69% Turkmenian, 13% Russian, 9% Uzbek, 3% Kazakh; **language** West Turkic, closely related to the ◊Turkish language; **recent history** the nomadic tribes of the area were subdued by Russia 1881–85.

Turko- variant of ◊Turco.

Turkoman /'tɜ:kəmən/ *n*. or **Turkmen** person of Turkoman culture. Turkomen live around the Kara Kum desert, to the E of the Caspian Sea, along the borders of Afghanistan and Iran, and within several republics in the USSR. Their language belongs to the Turkic branch of the Altaic family.

Turks and Caicos Islands /tɜ:ks, 'keɪkɒs/ British crown colony in the West Indies, the SE archipelago of the Bahamas; **area** 430 sq km/166 sq mi; **capital** Cockburn Town on Grand Turk; **features** a group of 30 islands, of which six are inhabited. The largest is the uninhabited **Grand Caicos**; others include **Grand Turk** (population 3,100), **South Caicos** (1,400), **Middle Caicos** (400), **North Caicos** (1,300), **Providenciales** (1,000), and **Salt Cay** (300); since 1982 the Turks and Caicos have developed as a tax haven; **government** governor, with executive and legislative councils (chief minister from 1985 Nathaniel Francis, Progressive National Party); **population** (1980) 7,500, 90% of African descent; **language** English, French Creole; **history** secured by Britain in 1766 against French and Spanish claims, the islands were a Jamaican dependency 1873–1962, and in 1976 attained internal self-government. The chief minister, Norman Saunders, resigned 1985 after his arrest in Miami on drug charges, of which he was convicted.

turmeric /'tɜ:mərɪk/ *n*. **1**. a perennial plant *Curcuma longa* of the ginger family, native to India and the East Indies. **2**. its aromatic root powdered and used as a flavouring, stimulant, or dye. [perhaps from French *terre mérite*]

turmoil /'tɜ:mɔɪl/ *n*. great disturbance or confusion.

turn *v.t./i.* **1**. to move or cause to move round a point or axis; to perform (a somersault) with a rotary motion. **2**. to change or cause to change in position so that a different side becomes uppermost or faces a certain direction. **3**. to give a new direction to; to take a new direction; to aim or become aimed in a certain way; to seek help, to have recourse. **4**. to move to the other side of, to go round. **5**. to pass (a certain hour or age). **6**. to cause to go, to send or put. **7**. to change or become changed in form, nature, appearance, colour etc.; to translate. **8**. to make or become sour. **9**. to make or become nauseated. **10**. to shape in a lathe; to give an elegant form to. —*n*. **1**. turning, being turned; a turning movement. **2**. a change of direction or condition etc.; the point at which this occurs. **3**. an angle; a bend or corner in a road. **4**. character, tendency of mind etc. **5**. an opportunity or obligation etc. that comes successively to each of a number of people or things. **6**. a short performance in an entertainment. **7**. a service of a specified kind; a purpose. **8**. (*colloquial*) an attack of illness; a momentary nervous shock. **9**. in music, an ornament consisting of the principal note with those above and below it, in various sequences. **10**. each round in a coil of rope, wire etc. —**at every turn**, in every place; continually. **by turns**, in rotation of individuals or groups; alternately. **in turn**, in succession. **in one's turn**, when one's turn comes. **out of turn**, before or after one's turn; at an inappropriate moment; presumptuously. **take turns**, to act etc. alternately. **to a turn**, so as to be cooked perfectly. **turnabout** *n*. turning to face a new direction; an abrupt change of policy etc. **turn against**, to make or become hostile to. **turn and turn about**, alternately. **turn away**, to send away; to reject. **turnbuckle** *n*. a device for tightly connecting parts of metal rod or wire. **turn down**, to reject; to reduce the volume or strength of (sound or heat etc.) by turning a knob etc.; to fold down. **turn in**, to hand in or return; to register (a score etc.); (*colloquial*) to go to bed; (*colloquial*) to abandon (a plan etc.). **turn in his**

grave, (of a dead person) to be disturbed in his eternal rest if he knew of a specified fact which would have shocked or distressed him while he was alive. **turn off,** to stop the flow or operation of by means of a tap or switch etc.; to move (a tap etc.) thus; to enter a side-road; (*colloquial*) to cause to lose interest. **turn on,** to start the flow or operation of by means of a tap or switch etc.; to move (a tap etc.) thus; to be suddenly hostile to; (*colloquial*) to arouse the interest or emotion of, to excite sexually or with drugs etc.; to depend on. **turn out,** to expel; to extinguish (an electric light etc.); to dress or equip; to produce (goods etc.); to empty or clean out (a room etc.); to empty (a pocket); (*colloquial*) to get out of bed; (*colloquial*) to go out of doors; to prove to be the case, to result. **turnout** *n.* the number of people at a meeting etc.; a set of clothes or equipment. **turn over,** to reverse the position of; to hand over; to transfer; to consider carefully; to start the running of (an engine etc.); (of an engine) to start running. **turn over a new leaf,** to improve one's conduct. **turn round,** to face in a new direction; to unload and reload (a ship etc.), to process and return (a piece of work etc.). **turnround** *n.* the process or time taken in unloading and reloading etc. **turn to,** to set about one's work. **turn up,** to increase the volume or strength of (sound or heat etc.) by turning a knob etc.; to discover or reveal; to be found; to happen or present itself; to fold over or upwards. **turn-up** *n.* the lower turned-up end of a trouser leg; (*colloquial*) an unexpected happening. [Old English and from Old French from Latin *tornare* = turn on lathe (*tornus* = lathe)]

turncoat *n.* one who changes his or her allegiance or principles.

turner *n.* a lathe-worker.

Turner /ˈtɜːnə/ John Napier 1929– . Canadian Liberal politician, prime minister in 1984. He was elected to the House of Commons in 1962 and served in the cabinet of Pierre Trudeau until resigning in 1975. He succeeded Trudeau as party leader and prime minister in 1984, but lost the 1984 and 1988 elections. Turner resigned as leader in 1989, and returned to his law practice. He was replaced as Liberal Party chief by Herbert Gray in Feb 1990.

Turner Joseph Mallord William 1775–1851. English landscape painter. He travelled widely in Europe, and his landscapes became increasingly Romantic, with the subject often transformed in scale and flooded with brilliant, hazy light. Many later works anticipate Impressionism, for example *Rain, Steam and Speed* 1844 (National Gallery, London).

My business is to paint not what I know, but what I see.

Joseph Mallord Turner

Turner Lana (Julia Jean Mildred Frances) 1920– . US actress who appeared in melodramatic films of the 1940s and 1950s such as *Peyton Place* 1957. Her other films include *The Postman Always Rings Twice* 1946, *The Three Musketeers* 1948, and *Imitation of Life* 1959.

Turner Nat 1800–1831. US slave and Baptist preacher, who led 60 slaves in the most significant US slave revolt – the Southampton Insurrection of 1831 – in Southampton County, Virginia. Before he and 16 of the others were hanged, at least 55 people had been killed.

Turner Tina. Adopted name of Annie Mae Bullock 1938– . US rhythm-and-blues singer who recorded 1960–76 with her husband, **Ike Turner** (1931–), including *River Deep, Mountain High* 1966, produced by Phil Spector. She achieved success in the 1980s as a solo artist, recording albums such as *Private Dancer* 1984, and also becoming a successful live performer.

turnery *n.* 1. objects made on a lathe. 2. work with a lathe.

turning *n.* 1. a place where one road meets another, forming a corner. 2. the use of a lathe. 3. (in *plural*) chips or shavings from a lathe. —**turning circle,** the smallest circle in which a vehicle can turn. **turning point,** the point at which a decisive change occurs.

turnip /ˈtɜːnɪp/ *n.* a plant *Brassica rapa* with a globular root used as a vegetable and as fodder; its root. —**turnip tops,** its leaves used as a vegetable. —**turnipy** *adj.* [first

Turner US singer Tina Turner in London, 1986.

element of uncertain origin; second element from dialect *neep* (Old English from Latin *napus*)]

turnkey *n.* a gaoler.

turnover *n.* 1. turning over. 2. the amount of money taken in a business; the amount of business done. 3. a pie or tart made by folding half the pastry over so as to enclose the filling. 4. the number of persons entering or leaving employment etc.

turnpike /ˈtɜːnpaɪk/ *n.* 1. (*historical*) a tollgate. 2. (*historical* and *US*) a road on which toll is or was collected at gates. In England private companies were authorized by separate Acts of Parliament to build and maintain roads between set points and to charge a small toll for usage at turnpike gates at each end of the road. The first Turnpike Act was passed in 1663, but most became law in the 18th century in response to the increasing need for good roads. The turnpikes fell into decline during the 19th century through competition from the railways and tolls were progressively abolished between the 1870s and 1890s. The road system remained in a state of neglect until the advent of the motorcar in the early 20th century. [originally = defensive frame of spikes]

turnstile *n.* an admission-gate with arms revolving on a post.

turnstone *n.* a wading bird *Arenaria interpres*, which breeds in the Arctic and migrates to the southern hemisphere. It is seen on rocky beaches, turning over stones for small crustaceans and insects.

turntable *n.* a circular revolving platform or support, e. g. for a gramophone record being played or to turn a locomotive to face in the opposite direction.

turpentine /ˈtɜːpəntaɪn/ *n.* 1. a resin obtained from various trees (originally the terebinth). 2. (in full **oil of turpentine**) a volatile pungent oil distilled from this resin, used in mixing paints and varnishes and in medicine; now largely replaced by white spirit, a colourless liquid derived from petroleum. [from Old French *ter(e)-bentine* from Latin]

Turpin /ˈtɜːpɪn/ Ben 1874–1940. US comedian, a star of silent films. His hallmark was being cross-eyed, and he parodied screen stars and their films. His work includes *The Shriek of Araby* 1923, *A Harem Knight* 1926, and *Broke in China* 1927.

Turpin Dick 1706–1739. English highwayman. The son of an innkeeper, he turned to highway robbery, cattle-thieving, and smuggling, and was hanged.

turpitude /ˈtɜːpɪtjuːd/ *n.* wickedness. [French or from Latin (*turpis* = shameful)]

turps *n.* (*colloquial*) oil of ◊turpentine. [abbreviation]

turquoise /ˈtɜːkwɔɪz, -kwɑːz/ *n.* 1. a mineral, hydrous basic copper aluminium phosphate. Blue-green, blue, or green, it is a gemstone. Turquoise is found in Iran, Turkestan, Mexico, and SW USA. 2. greenish-blue colour. —*adj.* greenish-blue. [from Old French = Turkish (stone)]

turret /ˈtʌrɪt/ *n.* 1. a small tower, especially as a decorative addition to a building. 2. a low flat usually revolving armoured tower for a gun and gunners in a ship, aircraft, fort, or tank. 3. a rotating holder for tools in a lathe etc.

—turreted *adj.* [from Old French *to(u)rete*, diminutive of *to(u)r* = tower]

turtle /'tɜːtəl/ *n.* **1.** a marine or (*US*) freshwater reptile of the order Chelonia whose body is protected by a shell. Turtles are related to tortoises, and some species can grow to a length of up to 2.5 m/8 ft. They are excellent swimmers, having legs that are modified to oarlike flippers but make them awkward on land. The shell is more streamlined and lighter than that of the tortoise. They often travel long distances to lay their eggs on the beaches where they were born. **2.** its flesh used for soup. **—turn turtle**, to capsize. **turtleneck** *n.* a high close-fitting neck of a knitted garment. [alteration of Old French *tortue*]

turtledove *n.* a wild dove of the genus *Streptopelia*, especially *S. turtur*, noted for its soft cooing and its affection for its mate. [from Old English from Latin *turtur*)]

Tuscan /'tʌskən/ *adj.* **1.** of Tuscany, a region of west central Italy. **2.** in architecture, of a simple unornamented order. **—n.** an inhabitant or the classical Italian language of Tuscany. [from Latin (*Tuscus* = Etruscan)]

Tuscany /'tʌskəni/ (Italian *Toscana*) region of central Italy; **area** 23,000 sq km/8,878 sq mi; **capital** Florence; **population** (1988) 3,568,000. The area is mainly agricultural, with many vineyards, such as in the Chianti hills; it also has lignite and iron mines and marble quarries. The Tuscan dialect has been adopted as the standard form of Italian. Tuscany was formerly the Roman *Etruria*, and inhabited by Etruscans around 500 BC. In medieval times the area was divided into small states, united under Florentine rule during the 15th–16th centuries. It became part of united Italy in 1861.

tusk *n.* a long pointed tooth, especially one projecting from the mouth as in the elephant, walrus, or boar. [alteration of Old English *tux*]

Tussaud /'tuːsəʊ/ Madame (Anne Marie Grosholtz) 1761–1850. French wax-modeller. In 1802 she established an exhibition of wax models of celebrities in London. It was destroyed by fire in 1925, but reopened in 1928.

tussle *n.* a struggle, a scuffle. **—v.i.** to engage in a tussle. [originally Scottish North English, perhaps diminutive of dialect *touse*]

tussock /'tʌsək/ *n.* a clump of grass etc. **—tussocky** *adj.* [perhaps from dialect *tusk* = tuft]

tut = ◊tut-tut. [imitative of click of tongue]

Tutankhamen /tuːtənˈkɑːmen/ king of Egypt of the 18th dynasty, about 1360–1350 BC. A son of Ikhnaton (also called Amenhotep III), he was about 11 at his accession. In 1922 his tomb was discovered by the British archaeologists Lord Carnarvon and Howard Carter in the Valley of the Kings at Luxor, almost untouched by tomb robbers. The contents included many works of art and his solid gold coffin, which are now displayed in a Cairo museum.

tutelage /'tjuːtɪlɪdʒ/ *n.* **1.** guardianship; being under this. **2.** instruction, tuition. [from Latin *tutela* (*tuēri* = watch over)]

tutelary /'tjuːtɪlərɪ/ *adj.* serving as a guardian, giving protection.

tutor /'tjuːtə/ *n.* **1.** a private teacher, especially one in general charge of a person's education. **2.** a university teacher supervising the studies or welfare of assigned undergraduates. **3.** a book of instruction in a subject. **—v.t./i. 1.** to act as tutor to; to work as a tutor. **2.** to restrain, to discipline. **—tutorship** *n.* [from Anglo-French or Latin]

tutorial /tjuːˈtɔːrɪəl/ *adj.* of or as a tutor. **—n.** a period of individual tuition given by a college tutor. **—tutorially** *adv.* [from Latin]

tutti /'tuːtɪ/ *adv.* in music, with all voices or instruments together. **—n.** a passage to be performed this way. [Italian, plural of *tutto* = all]

tutti-frutti /tuːtɪˈfruːtɪ/ *n.* ice-cream containing or flavoured with mixed fruits. [Italian = all fruits]

tut-tut interjection expressing rebuke, impatience, or contempt. **—n.** such an exclamation. **—v.i.** (**-tt-**) to exclaim thus. [imitative of click of tongue]

tutu /'tuːtuː/ *n.* a ballet dancer's short skirt made of layers of stiffened frills. [French]

Tutu /'tuːtuː/ Desmond (Mpilo) 1931– . South African priest, Anglican archbishop of Cape Town and general secretary of the South African Council of Churches 1979–84. One of the leading figures in the struggle against apartheid

Twain *US novelist Mark Twain.*

in the Republic of South Africa, he received the 1984 Nobel Peace Prize.

Tuva /'tuːvə/ (Russian *Tuvinskaya*) autonomous republic (administrative unit) of the USSR, northwest of Mongolia; **area** 170,500 sq km/65,813 sq mi; **capital** Kyzyl; **population** (1986) 284,000; **recent history** part of Mongolia until 1911 and declared a Russian protectorate in 1914, after the 1917 revolution it became the independent Tannu-Tuva republic in 1920, until incorporated in the USSR as an autonomous region in 1944. It was made the Tuva Autonomous Republic in 1961.

Tuvalu /tuːˈvɑːluː/ South West Pacific State of country in the SW Pacific, on the former Ellice Islands; part of Polynesia; **area** 25 sq km/9.5 sq mi; **capital** Funafuti; **physical** low coral atolls forming a chain of 579 km/360 mi in the SW Pacific; consiting of nine (one very small) islands; **head of state** Elizabeth II from 1978 represented by governor-general; head of government Bikenibeu Paeniu from 1989; **political system** liberal democracy; **population** (1990 est) 9,000 (Polynesian); **language** Tuvaluan, English; **recent history** became a British protectorate called the Ellice Islands in 1892; independence (within the Commonwealth) in 1978. The islanders rejected a proposal for republican status in 1986.

tu-whit, tu-whoo /tuːˈwɪt tuːˈwuː/ the cry of an owl. [imitative]

tuxedo /tʌkˈsiːdəʊ/ *n.* (*plural* **tuxedos**) (*US*) a dinner-jacket. [from *Tuxedo* Park, New York]

TV *n.* television. [abbreviation]

TVP abbreviation of texturized vegetable protein, a meat substitute usually made from soya beans. In manufacture, the soya-bean solids (what remains after oil has been removed) are ground finely and mixed with a binder to form a sticky mixture. This is forced through a spinneret and extruded into fibres, which are treated with salts and flavourings, wound into hanks, and then chopped up to resemble meat chunks.

twaddle /'twɒdəl/ *n.* useless or dull writing or talk. **—v.i.** to indulge in this. [from earlier *twattle*, alteration of *tattle*]

twain *adj. & n.* (*archaic*) two. [Old English]

Twain /tweɪn/ Mark. Pen name of Samuel Langhorne Clemens 1835–1910. US humorous writer. He established his reputation with the comic *The Innocents Abroad* 1869, and two children's books, *The Adventures of Tom Sawyer* 1876 and *The Adventures of Huckleberry Finn* 1885. He also wrote satire, as in *A Connecticut Yankee at King Arthur's Court* 1889.

twang *n.* the sound made by a plucked string of a musical instrument or by a bowstring; a quality of voice compared to this (especially *nasal twang*). **—v.t./i.** to emit a twang; to cause to twang. [imitative]

'twas /twɒz, twəz/ (*archaic*) it was. [contraction]

tweak *v.t.* to pinch and twist or jerk. **—n.** such an action. [probably from dialect *twick*]

twee *adj.* affectedly dainty or quaint. [childish pronunciation of *sweet*]

tweed *n.* a rough-surfaced woollen cloth, frequently of mixed colours, but in its original form without a regular pattern and woven on a hand loom in the more remote parts of Ireland, Wales, and Scotland; (in *plural*) a suit of tweed. —**tweedy** *adj.* [originally misreading of *tweel*, Scottish form of *twill*]

'tween *prep.* between.

tweet *n.* the chirp of a small bird. —*v.i.* to utter a tweet. [imitative]

tweeter *n.* a loudspeaker for accurately reproducing high-frequency signals.

tweezers /'twi:zəz/ *n.pl.* a small pair of pincers for taking up small objects, plucking out hairs etc. [from *tweezes*, plural of obsolete *tweeze* = case for small instruments, from French *étui*]

twelfth *adj.* next after the eleventh. —*n.* each of 12 equal parts of a thing. —**the Twelfth,** 12 Aug, on which grouse shooting legally begins. **Twelfth Day,** the 12th and final day of the Christmas celebrations, 6 Jan; the feast of the ◊Epiphany. **Twelfth Night,** the night before this, formerly the last day of Christmas festivities and observed as a time of merrymaking. —**twelfthly** *adv.* [Old English]

Twelfth Night a comedy by William Shakespeare, first performed 1601–02. The plot builds on misunderstandings and mistaken identities, leading to the successful romantic unions of Viola with Duke Orsino and Olivia respectively, and the downfall of Olivia's steward Malvolio.

twelve *adj.* & *n.* **1.** one more than eleven; the symbol for this (12, xii, XII). **2.** a size etc. denoted by twelve.

twelve-note *adj.* in music, using the 12 chromatic notes of the octave arranged in a chosen order without a conventional key. [Old English]

twelvefold *adj.* & *adv.* twelve times as much or as many; consisting of 12 parts.

twelvemonth *n.* a year.

Twelver /tɜ:k/ *n.* a member of a Shi'ite Muslim sect who believes that the 12th imam (Islamic leader) did not die, but is waiting to return towards the end of the world as the Mahdi, the 'rightly guided one', to establish a reign of peace and justice on Earth.

twelve-tone system or **twelve-note system** a system of musical composition in which the 12 notes of the chromatic scale are arranged in a particular order, called a 'series' or 'tone-row'. A work using the system consists of restatements of the series in any of its formations. ◊Schoenberg and ◊Webern were exponents of this technique.

Twentieth Century Fox US film-production company, formed in 1935 when the Fox Company merged with Twentieth Century. Its president was Joseph Schenck (1878–1961), and Darryl F Zanuck (1902–1979) was vice president in charge of production. The company made high-quality films and, despite a financial crisis in the early 1960s, is still a major studio. Recent successes include the *Star Wars* trilogy (1977–1983).

twenty *adj.* & *n.* **1.** twice ten; the symbol for this (20, xx, XX). **2.** (in *plural*) the numbers, years, or degrees of temperature from 20 to 29. —**twentieth** *adj.* & *n.* [Old English]

'twere /twɜ:, twə/ *(archaic)* it were. [contraction]

twerp *n.* *(slang)* a stupid or objectionable person.

Twi /twi:/ *n.* **1.** the chief language spoken in Ghana, consisting of several mutually intelligible dialects. **2.** its speakers.

twice *adv.* **1.** two times, on two occasions. **2.** in double degree or quantity. [Old English]

Twickenham the ground at which England play home rugby internationals, laid out on 4.2 hectares of land in SW London. The first international was held there in 1910. The Rugby Football Union has its headquarters at Twickenham and the Harlequins club plays some of its home matches there. A new stand was opened in 1990.

twiddle *v.t.* to twirl or handle aimlessly; to twist quickly to and fro. —*n.* **1.** an act of twiddling. **2.** a twirled mark or sign. —**twiddle one's thumbs,** to make them rotate round each other, especially for want of anything to do. —**twiddler** *n.,* **twiddly** *adj.* [apparently imitative, after *twirl, fiddle*]

twig[1] *n.* a small branch or shoot of a tree or shrub. —**twiggy** *adj.* [Old English]

twig[2] *v.t.* (-gg-) *(colloquial)* to understand, to realize or grasp the meaning or nature (of).

twilight /'twaɪlaɪt/ *n.* **1.** the light from the sky when the Sun is below the horizon, especially in the evening; the period of this. **2.** a faint light. **3.** a state of imperfect understanding. **4.** a period of decline or destruction. —**twilight of the gods,** in Scandinavian mythology, the destruction of the gods and of the world in conflict with the powers of evil. **twilight zone,** a decrepit urban area; an area between others in position and character. [Old English]

twilit /'twaɪlɪt/ *adj.* dimly illuminated (as) by twilight.

twill *n.* a fabric so woven as to have a surface of parallel ridges. —**twilled** *adj.* [from Old English *twili* = two-thread]

'twill *(archaic* it will. [contraction]

twin *n.* **1.** one of two young produced from a single pregnancy. Human twins may be genetically identical, having been formed from a single fertilized egg that split into two cells, both of which became implanted. Nonidentical twins are formed when two eggs are fertilized at the same time. **the Twins,** the constellation or sign of the zodiac Gemini. **2.** an exact counterpart of a person or thing. —*adj.* forming or being one of such a pair. —*v.t./i.* (-nn-) **1.** to join intimately together; to pair (with). **2.** to bear twins. —**twin bed,** each of a pair of single beds. **twin-engined** *adj.* having two engines. **twin set,** a woman's matching cardigan and jumper. **twin towns,** two towns, usually in different countries, establishing special cultural and social links. [Old English = double]

twine *n.* **1.** strong thread or string made of two or more strands twisted together. **2.** a coil, a twist. —*v.t./i.* to twist; to wind or coil. [Old English]

twinge /twɪndʒ/ *n.* a slight or brief pang. [from *twinge* (v.) = pinch, wring, from Old English]

twinkle *v.i.* **1.** to shine with a light that flickers rapidly; to sparkle. **2.** (of the eyes) to sparkle with amusement. **3.** (of the feet in dancing etc.) to move rapidly. —*n.* a twinkling light, look, or movement. —**in the twinkling of an eye** or **in a twinkling,** in an instant. [Old English]

twirl *v.t./i.* to twist lightly or rapidly. —*n.* **1.** a twirling movement. **2.** a twirled mark or sign. —**twirly** *adj.* [probable alteration (after *whirl*) from obsolete *tirl* = trill]

twist *v.t./i.* **1.** to change the form of by rotating one end and not the other or the two ends in opposite ways; to undergo such a change; to make or become spiral; to distort, to warp; to wrench; (with *off*) to break off by twisting. **2.** to wind (strands) about each other; to make (a rope etc.) thus. **3.** to take a curved course; to make one's way in a winding manner. **4.** to distort or misrepresent the meaning of (words). **5.** *(colloquial)* to swindle. —*n.* **1.** twisting; a twisted state. **2.** a thing formed by twisting. **3.** the point at which a thing twists or bends. **4.** a peculiar tendency of mind or character. **5.** *(colloquial)* a swindle. —**round the twist,** *(slang)* crazy. **twist a person's arm,** *(colloquial)* to coerce him. **twist a person round one's little finger,** to persuade or manage him very easily. [Old English]

twister *n.* *(colloquial)* an untrustworthy person, a swindler.

twisty *adj.* full of twists. —**twistily** *adv.,* **twistiness** *n.*

twit[1] *n.* *(slang)* a foolish person. [dialect]

twit[2] *v.t.* (-tt-) to taunt, usually good-humouredly. [Old English]

twitch *v.t./i.* **1.** to pull with a light jerk. **2.** to quiver or contract spasmodically. —*n.* **1.** a twitching movement. **2.** *(colloquial)* a state of nervousness. **3.** an alternative common name for ◊couch grass. [from Low German *twikken*]

twitter *v.t./i.* **1.** to make a series of light chirping or tremulous sounds. **2.** to talk or utter rapidly in an anxious or nervous way. —*n.* **1.** twittering. **2.** *(colloquial)* an excited or nervous state. [imitative]

'twixt *prep.* *(archaic)* betwixt. [abbreviation]

two /tu:/ *adj.* & *n.* **1.** one more than one; the symbol for this (2, ii, II). **2.** a size etc. denoted by two. —**in two,** in or into two pieces. **put two and two together,** to make an inference from known facts. **two-dimensional** *adj.* having or appearing to have length and breadth but no depth. **two-edged** *adj.* having two cutting edges. **two-faced** *adj.* insincere. **two-handed** *adj.* used with both hands or by two persons. **two-piece** *n.* a suit of clothes or a woman's bathing suit comprising two separate parts. **two-ply** *adj.* (of wool etc.) of two strands, layers, or thicknesses. **two-step** *n.* a ballroom dance in march or polka time. **two-stroke** *adj.* (of an internal-combustion engine) having its power cycle completed in one up-and-down movement (i.e. two strokes) of the piston, which distinguishes it from the more common ◊four-stroke cycle. Power mowers and lightweight motorcycles use two-stroke petrol engines, which are cheaper and simpler than four-strokes. **two-time** *v.t.* (*slang*) to swindle; to deceive, especially by infidelity.

two-up *n.* (*Australian* and *New Zealand*) a gambling game played by tossing two coins, bets being laid on the showing of two heads or two tails. [Old English]

twofold *adj.* & *adv.* 1. twice as much or as many. 2. consisting of two parts.

twopence /'tʌpəns/ *n.* the sum of two pence.

twopenny /'tʌpəni/ *adj.* 1. costing two pence. 2. cheap, worthless. —**twopenny-halfpenny** *adj.* insignificant, contemptible.

twosome /'tu:səm/ *n.* two people together, a pair or couple of persons.

two-stroke cycle an operating cycle for internal-combustion piston engines. The engine cycle is completed after just two strokes (movement up or down) of the piston, which distinguishes it from the more common ◊four-stroke cycle. Power mowers and lightweight motorcycles use two-stroke petrol engines, which are cheaper and simpler than four-strokes.

'twould /twʊd/ (*archaic*) it would. [contraction]

tycoon /taɪ'ku:n/ *n.* a person who has acquired great wealth through business achievements. Examples include J Pierpont ◊Morgan (1837–1913) and John D ◊Rockefeller (1839–1937). [from Japanese = great prince]

tying participle of **tie**.

tyke /taɪk/ *n.* a low or objectionable fellow. [from Old Norse = bitch]

Tyler /'taɪlə/ John 1790–1862. 10th president of the USA 1841–45, succeeding Benjamin ◊Harrison, who died after only a month in office. His government annexed Texas in 1845.

Tyler Wat died 1381. English leader of the ◊Peasants' Revolt of 1381. He was probably born in Kent or Essex, and may have served in the French wars. After taking Canterbury he led the peasant army to Blackheath and occupied London. At Mile End King Richard II met the rebels and promised to redress their grievances, which included the imposition of a poll tax. At a further conference at Smithfield, Tyler was murdered.

tympanum /'tɪmpənəm/ *n.* (*plural* **tympana**) 1. the ear drum; the middle ear. The tympanum is a membrane capable of vibrating in response to vibrations passing from the outer ◊ear. It is composed of two layers of epidermis with connective tissue sandwiched between. Vibrations set up by the sound waves are transferred to the tiny bones of the inner ear, which themselves pass vibrations through to the inner ear and ◊cochlea. 2. the space enclosed in a pediment or between a lintel and the arch above. [Latin, from Greek *tumpanon* = drum]

Tyndale /'tɪndl/ William 1492–1536. English translator of the Bible. The printing of his New Testament (the basis of the Authorized Version) was begun in Cologne in 1525 and, after he had been forced to flee, completed in Worms. He was strangled and burned as a heretic at Vilvorde in Belgium.

Tyndall /'tɪndl/ John 1820–1893. Irish physicist who in 1869 studied the scattering of light by invisibly small suspended particles. Known as the **Tyndall effect**, it was first observed with colloidal solutions (see ◊colloid), in which a beam of light is made visible when it is scattered by minute colloidal particles (whereas a pure solvent does not scatter light). Similar scattering of blue wavelengths of sunlight by particles in the atmosphere makes the sky look blue (beyond the atmosphere, the sky is black).

Tyne and Wear /taɪn, wɪə/ metropolitan county in NE England, created in 1974, originally administered by an elected metropolitan council; its powers reverted to district councils in 1986; **area** 540 sq km/208 sq mi; **administrative headquarters** Newcastle-upon-Tyne; **population** (1987) 1,136,000.

Tynwald /'tɪnwɒld/ *n.* the parliament of the ◊Isle of Man, which meets annually to proclaim newly enacted laws. [from Old Norse *thing-völlr* = place of assembly]

type /taɪp/ *n.* 1. a class of people or things that have characteristics in common, a kind. 2. a typical example or instance. 3. (*colloquial*) a person of specified character. 4.

a piece of metal etc. with a raised letter or character on its upper surface for use in printing; a kind or size of such pieces; a set or supply of these. —*v.t./i.* 1. to write with a typewriter. 2. to classify according to type. 3. to be a type or example of. —**typecast** *v.t.* to cast (an actor) in the kind of part which he has the reputation of playing successfully or which seems to fit his personality. **type site**, an archaeological site where objects regarded as defining the characteristics of an industry etc. are found. [from French or Latin from Greek *tupos* = impression (*tuptō* = strike)]

typeface *n.* 1. a style of printed lettering. Books, newspapers, and other printed matter display different styles of lettering; each style is named and examples include Times and ◊Baskerville. These different 'families' of alphabets have been designed over the centuries since printing was invented, and each has distinguishing characteristics. See also ◊typography. 2. an inked surface of such types.

type metal an ◊alloy of tin, lead, and antimony, for making the metal type used by printers.

typescript *n.* a typewritten text or document.

typesetter *n.* 1. a compositor. 2. a machine for setting type.

typesetting *n.* the means by which text, or copy, is prepared for ◊printing, now usually carried out by computer. Text is keyed on a typesetting machine in a similar way to typing. Laser or light impulses are projected on to light-sensitive film that, when developed, can be used to make plates for printing.

typewriter *n.* a keyboard machine for producing characters similar to those of print, with keys that are pressed to cause raised metal characters to strike the paper, usually through inked ribbon. The first practical typewriter was built in 1867 in Milwaukee, Wisconsin, USA, by C L Sholes, C Glidden, and S W Soulé. By 1874 ◊Remington and Sons, the gun makers, produced under contract the first machines for sale and in 1878 patented the first with lower-case as well as upper-case (capital) letters.

typewritten *adj.* produced using a typewriter.

typhoid /'taɪfɔɪd/ *adj.* like typhus. —*n.* or **typhoid fever** an acute infectious disease of the digestive tract, caused by the bacterium *Salmonella typhi*, and usually contracted through a contaminated water supply. It is characterized by red spots on the chest and abdomen, bowel haemorrhage, and damage to the spleen. Treatment is with antibiotics. [from Greek *tuphos*]

typhoon /taɪ'fu:n/ *n.* a violent hurricane in the East Asian seas. [partly from Chinese = great wind, partly from Portuguese from Arabic]

typhus /'taɪfəs/ *n.* a rickettsial infectious fever with eruption of purple spots, great prostration, headache, and usually delirium. Typhus is caused by bacteria transmitted by lice, fleas, mites, and ticks and is epidemic among people living in overcrowded conditions. Treatment is by antibiotics. [from Greek *tuphos* = smoke, stupor]

typical /'tɪpɪkəl/ *adj.* 1. having the distinctive qualities of a particular type of person or thing; serving as a representative specimen. 2. characteristic. —**typically** *adv.* [from Latin]

typify /'tɪpɪfaɪ/ *v.t.* to be a representative specimen of; to represent by a type. —**typification** /-fɪ'keɪʃən/ *n.* [from Latin *typus* = type]

typist /'taɪpɪst/ *n.* a person who types, especially one employed to do so.

typography /taɪ'pɒɡrəfɪ/ *n.* the design and layout of the printed word. Typography began with the invention of writing and developed as printing spread throughout Europe following the invention of metal moveable type by Johann ◊Gutenberg about in 1440. Hundreds of variations have followed since, but the basic design of the Frenchman Nicholas Jensen (*c.*1420–80), with a few modifications, is still the ordinary ('roman') type used in printing. —**typographical** /-'ɡræfɪkəl/ *adj.*, **typographically** /-'ɡræfɪkəlɪ/ *adv.* [from French]

Tyr /tɪə/ in Norse mythology, the god of battles, whom the Anglo-Saxons called Týw, hence 'Tuesday'.

tyrannical /ti'rænɪkəl/ *adj.* given to or characteristic of tyranny. —**tyrannically** *adv.* [from Old French from Latin from Greek *turannos*]

tyrannize /'tɪrənaɪz/ *v.t./i.* to exercise tyranny; to rule as or like a tyrant. [from French]

tyrannosaur /tɪˈrænəsɔː/ *n.* or **tyrannosaurus** a dinosaur *Tyrannosaurus rex* with very short front legs and a large head, that walked on its hind legs, the largest known meat-eating dinosaur. It lived in North America about 70 million years ago and was up to 15 m/50 ft long, 6.5 m/20 ft tall, weighed 10 tonnes, and had teeth 15 cm/6 in long. The most complete skeleton was discovered in 1989 in Hell Creek, Montana, and will be preserved in the Museum of the Rockies, Bozeman, Montana, USA. [from Latin from Greek *turannos*]

tyrannous /ˈtɪrənəs/ *adj.* tyrannical. [from Latin]

tyranny /ˈtɪrənɪ/ *n.* **1.** the oppressive and arbitrary use of authority. **2.** rule by a tyrant; a period of this; a state thus ruled.

tyrant /ˈtaɪrənt/ *n.* **1.** an oppressive or cruel ruler. **2.** a person exercising power arbitrarily or oppressively. **3.** in Greek history, an absolute ruler who seized power without legal right. [from Old French from Latin from Greek *turannos*]

tyre /taɪə/ *n.* (North American **tire**) a rubber covering, usually inflated, placed round a wheel to form a soft contact with a road. The first pneumatic rubber type was patented by R W Thompson in 1845, but it was John Boyd Dunlop of Belfast who independently reinvented pneumatic tyres for use with bicycles 1888–89. The rubber for car tyres is hardened by ◊vulcanization.

Tyre /taɪə/ (Arabic *Sur* or *Sour*) town in SW Lebanon, about 80 km/50 mi south of Beirut, formerly a port until its harbour silted up; population about 14,000. It stands on the site of the ancient city of the same name, a seaport of ◊Phoenicia.

tyro variant of ◊tiro.

Tyrone /tɪˈrəʊn/ county of Northern Ireland; **area** 3,160 sq km/1,220 sq mi; **county town** Omagh; **population** (1981) 144,000.

Tyrrell /ˈtɜːkəmən/ British motor-racing team founded by Ken Tyrrell in 1970; he had run the Matra and March teams in the two previous seasons. He formed a partnership with Jackie Stewart and the celebrated driver won all three of his world titles in Tyrrell-run teams. Tyrrell's only Constructors' title was in 1971.

Tyson /ˈtaɪsən/ Mike 1966– . US heavyweight boxer, undisputed world champion from Aug 1987 to Feb 1990. He won the WBC heavyweight title in 1986 when he beat Trevor Berbick to become the youngest world heavyweight champion. He beat James 'Bonecrusher' Smith for the WBA title in 1987 and later that year became the first undisputed champion since 1978 when he beat Tony Tucker for the IBF title. He was undefeated until 1990 when he lost the championship to an outsider, James 'Buster' Douglas.

Tyuratam /tjuərəˈtaːm/ site of the ◊Baikonur Cosmodrome.

Tywi /ˈtaʊɪ/ or **Towy** river in Dyfed, SW Wales; length 108 km/68 mi. It rises in the Cambrian Mountains of central Wales, flowing southwest to enter Camarthen Bay.

Tzu-Hsi /tsuːˈʃiː/ alternative transliteration of ◊Zi Xi, dowager empress of China.

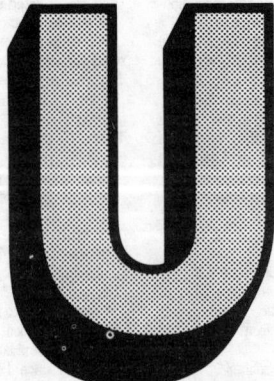

u, U /juː/ *n.* (*plural* **us, u's**) 1. the 21st letter of the alphabet. 2. a U-shaped object or curve.

U /juː/ *adj.* (*colloquial*) upper-class; supposedly characteristic of the upper class. [abbreviation coined by A S C Ross (1954)]

U symbol for uranium.

U2 *n.* an internationally-acclaimed Irish rock group formed in 1977 by singer Bono Vox (born Paul Hewson, 1960–), guitarist Dave 'The Edge' Evans (1961–), bassist Adam Clayton (1960–), and drummer Larry Mullen (1961–). Committed Christians, and their albums include *The Unforgettable Fire* 1984, *The Joshua Tree* 1987, and the soundtrack from their documentary film *Rattle and Hum* 1988.

U-2 *n.* a US military reconnaissance aeroplane, used in secret flights over the USSR from 1956 to photograph military installations. In 1960 a U-2 was shot down over the USSR and the pilot, Gary Powers, was captured and imprisoned. He was exchanged for a US-held Soviet agent two years later.

UAE abbreviation of United Arab Emirates.

uakari *n.* a rare South American monkey, genus *Cacajao*, of which there are three species. They have bald faces and long fur. About 55 cm/1.8 ft long in head and body, and with a comparatively short 15 cm/6 in tail, they rarely leap, but are good climbers, remaining in the tops of the trees in swampy forests and feeding largely on fruit. The black uakari is in danger of extinction because it is found in such small numbers already, and the forests where it lives are fast being destroyed.

Ubangi-Shari /uːˈbæŋɡi ˈʃɑːri/ former name for the ◊Central African Republic.

Übermensch *n.* in the writings of Nietzsche, the ideal to which humans should aspire, set out in *Thus Spake Zarathustra* 1883–85. The term was popularized in George Bernard Shaw's play *Man and Superman* 1903. [German = Superman]

ubiquitous /juːˈbɪkwɪtəs/ *adj.* present everywhere or in several places simultaneously; often encountered. —**ubiquity** *n.* [from Latin *ubique* = everywhere]

uakari

bald uakari

U-boat /ˈjuːbəʊt/ *n.* (*historical*) a German submarine, especially in World Wars I and II. [from German = *unterseeboot* under-sea boat]

Uccello /uːˈtʃeləʊ/ Paolo. Adopted name of Paolo di Dono 1397–1475. Italian painter, active in Florence, celebrated for his early use of perspective. His surviving paintings date from the 1430s onwards. Decorative colour and detail dominate his later pictures. His works include *St George and the Dragon* about 1460 (National Gallery, London).

Udall /ˈjuːdl/ Nicholas 1504–1556. English schoolmaster and playwright. He was the author of *Ralph Roister Doister* about 1553, the first known English comedy.

udder *n.* the baglike, milk-secreting organ of the cow, ewe, female goat etc., with two or more teats. [Old English]

UDI abbreviation of Unilateral Declaration of Independence, usually applied to the declaration of Ian Smith's Rhodesian Front government on 11 Nov 1965, announcing the independence of Rhodesia (now Zimbabwe) from Britain.

Udmurt /ˈudmuət/ (Russian *Udmurtskaya*) autonomous republic in the W Ural foothills, central USSR; **area** 42,100 sq km/16,200 sq mi; **capital** Izhevsk; **products** timber, flax, potatoes, peat, quartz; **population** (1985) 1,559,000; 58% Russian, 33% Udmurt, 7% Tatar; **history** conquered in the 15th–16th centuries; constituted the Votyak Autonomous Region in 1920; name changed to Udmurt in 1932; became an Autonomous Republic in 1934

UFO /ˈjuːfəʊ/ or **ufo** (*plural* **ufos**) acronym from unidentified flying object.

Uganda /juːˈɡændə/ landlocked country in E Africa, bounded to the N by Sudan, to the E by Kenya, to the S by Tanzania and Rwanda, and to the W by Zaïre; **area** 236,000 sq km/91,351 sq mi; **capital** Kampala; **physical** plateau with mountains in W; forest and grassland; arid in NE; **head of state and government** Yoweri Museveni from 1986; **political system** emergent democratic republic; **exports** coffee, tea, cotton, copper; **population** (1990 est) 17,593,000; **recent history** proclaimed a federal republic in 1963 a year after independence from Britain; coup led by Idi Amin overthrew Obote in 1971 establishing a ruthlessly dictatorial regime which lasted until 1978.

Ugarit /ˈuːɡərɪt/ an ancient trading-city kingdom (modern **Ras Shamra**) on the Syrian coast. It was excavated by the French archaeologist Claude Schaeffer (1898–1982) from 1929, with finds dating from about 7000 to the 15th–13th centuries BC, including the earliest known alphabet.

ugh /ʌh, ʊh/ interjection expressing disgust or horror, or the sound of a cough or grunt.

Ugli /ˈʌɡlɪ/ *n.* trade name for a mottled green and yellow citrus fruit, a hybrid of the grapefruit and tangerine developed in Jamaica about 1930.

uglify /ˈʌɡlɪfaɪ/ *v.t.* to make ugly.

ugly /ˈʌɡlɪ/ *adj.* 1. unpleasing or repulsive to see or hear. 2. unpleasant in any way; hostile and threatening; discreditable. —**ugly customer**, an unpleasantly formidable person. **ugly duckling**, a person who at first seems unpromising but later becomes much admired or very able (like the cygnet in the brood of ducks in Hans Andersen's story). —**ugliness** *n.* [from Old Norse = to be dreaded]

UHF abbreviation of ultra-high frequency.

Ulbricht *East German politician Walter Ulbricht.*

UHT abbreviation of ultra heat treated (of milk, for long keeping).

Ujung Pandang /'uːdʒʊŋ pænˈdæŋ/ formerly (until 1973) **Macassar** or **Makassar** chief port (trading in coffee, rubber, copra, and spices) on Sulawesi, Indonesia, with fishing and food-processing industries; population (1980) 709,000. Established by the Dutch 1607.

UK abbreviation of United Kingdom.

UKAEA abbreviation of ◊United Kingdom Atomic Energy Authority.

ukase /juːˈkeɪz/ *n.* **1.** an arbitrary command. **2.** (*historical*) an edict of the Russian government. [from Russian *ukaz*]

ukiyo-e /uːkiːˈjəʊjeɪ/ *n.* a school of Japanese art using subjects from everyday life and simple treatment. [Japanese = genre picture]

Ukraine /juːˈkreɪn/ constituent republic of the SE USSR from 1923; **area** 603,700 sq km/233,089 sq mi; **capital** Kiev; **physical** Russian plain: Carpathian and Crimean Mountains; rivers: Dnieper (with the Dnieper dam 1932), Donetz, Bug; **products** grain, 60% of Soviet coal reserves, oil, various minerals; **population** (1987) 51,201,000; 74% Ukrainian, 21% Russian, 2% Russian-speaking Jews; **language** Ukrainian (Slavonic); recent history proclaimed itself a people's republic in 1918; from 1920, one of the republics of the USSR; overrun by Germans in World War II. In the famine of 1932–33 more than 7.5 million people died. In Sept 1989 the RUK or Ukrainian Popular Movement for Perestroika was launched in Kiev, aiming at confederation of autonomous republics in the USSR. In addition, Ukrainian catholics called for a lift on the ban on the Ukrainian Uniate Church (banned since 1946). In July 1990 the Ukraine voted to proclaim sovereignty, by which its republic laws have precedence over Soviet law.

Ukrainian /juːˈkreɪnɪən/ *adj.* of a district (*the Ukraine*) N of the Black Sea, now the Ukrainian SSR. —**Ukrainian** *n.* a Ukranian person. [from Russian = frontier region (*u* = at, *krai* = edge)]

ukulele /juːkəˈleɪlɪ/ *n.* a small, four-stringed (originally Portuguese) guitar. [Hawaiian]

Ulaanbaatar /'uːlɑːn 'bɑːtɔː/ or **Ulan Bator** and (until 1924) **Urga** capital of the Mongolian Republic; a trading centre producing carpets, textiles, vodka; population (1988) 500,000.

Ulbricht /'ʊlbrɪkt/ Walter 1893–1973. East German communist politician, in power 1960–71. He lived in exile in the USSR during Hitler's rule 1933–45. A Stalinist, he became first secretary of the Socialist Unity Party in East Germany in 1950 and (as chair of the Council of State from 1960) was instrumental in the building of the Berlin Wall in 1961. He established East Germany's economy and recognition outside the Eastern European bloc.

ulcer *n.* **1.** an open sore on the external or internal surface of the body or one of its organs. **2.** a corroding or corrupting influence. —**ulcerous** *adj.* [from Latin *ulcus*]

ulcerate /'ʌlsəreɪt/ *v.t./i.* to form an ulcer (in or on). —**ulceration** /-'reɪʃən/ *n.* [from Latin *ulcerare*]

Ullman /'ʊlmən/ Liv 1939– . Norwegian actress who was critically acclaimed for her roles in first Swedish and then international films. Her work includes *Persona* 1966, the title role in *Pope Joan* 1972, and *Autumn Sonata* 1978.

ulna /'ʌlnə/ *n.* (*plural* **ulnae** /-iː/) the thinner and longer bone in the forearm on the side opposite to the thumb; a corresponding bone in an animal's foreleg or bird's wing. —**ulnar** *adj.* [Latin related to Greek *ōlenē*]

Ulsan /ʊlˈsæn/ industrial city (vehicles, shipbuilding, oil refining, petrochemicals) in South Kyongsang province, SE South Korea; population (1985) 551,000.

ulster /'ʌlstə/ *n.* a long, loose overcoat of rough cloth, often with a belt, of a kind originally sold in Belfast. [from *Ulster* in Ireland.]

Ulster former kingdom in Northern Ireland, annexed by England in 1461, from Jacobean times a centre of English, and later Scottish, settlement on land confiscated from its owners; divided in 1921 into Northern Ireland (counties Antrim, Armagh, Down, Fermanagh, Londonderry, and Tyrone) and the Republic of Ireland (counties Cavan, Donegal, and Monaghan). **Ulsterman** *n.* (*plural* **Ulstermen**) a native of Ulster. —**Ulsterwoman** *n.fem.* (*plural* **Ulsterwomen**)

ult. abbreviation of **1.** ultimo. **2.** ultimately.

ulterior /ʌlˈtɪərɪə/ *adj.* (especially of a motive) beyond what is obvious or admitted. [Latin = further]

ultimate /'ʌltɪmət/ *adj.* **1.** last, final, beyond which no other exists or is possible. **2.** basic, fundamental. —**ultimately** *adv.* [from Latin *ultimus* = last]

ultimatum /ʌltiˈmeɪtəm/ *n.* (*plural* **ultimatums**) a final statement of terms, the rejection of which may lead to war or the end of cooperation etc. [Latin]

ultimo /'ʌltɪməʊ/ *adj.* (in commerce) of last month. [Latin = in the last *mense* = month]

Ultra abbreviation of Ultra Secret, a term used by the British in World War II from spring 1940 to denote intelligence gained by deciphering German signals. Ultra decoding took place at the interception centre in Bletchley Park, Buckinghamshire. Failure to use such information in the Battle of ◊Anzio meant that Allied troops were stranded for a time.

ultra- prefix meaning **1.** extremely, excessively (*ultraconservative, ultramodern*). **2.** beyond. [from Latin *ultra* = beyond]

ultracentrifuge /ʌltrəˈsentrɪfjuːdʒ/ *n.* a high-speed centrifuge used to determine the size of small particles and large molecules by their rate of sedimentation.

ultrahigh /'ʌltrəhaɪ/ *adj.* (of frequency) between 300 and 3,000 MHz.

ultramarine /ʌltrəməˈriːn/ *n.* a brilliant blue pigment originally obtained from lapis lazuli; the colour of this. —*adj.* of this colour. [from obsolete Italian and Latin = beyond the sea]

ultramicroscope /ʌltrəˈmaɪkrəskəʊp/ *n.* an optical microscope used to detect particles smaller than a wavelength of light by illuminating them at an angle, so that the light scattered by the particles can be observed against a dark background.

ultramicroscopic /ʌltrəmaɪkrəˈskɒpɪk/ *adj.* **1.** of such minute size as to be invisible under the ordinary microscope. **2.** of or involving the use of the ultramicroscope.

ultrasonic /ʌltrəˈsɒnɪk/ *adj.* of or using sound waves with a pitch above the upper limit of human hearing. —**ultrasonics** *n.* the science and application of ultrasonic waves; (as *plural*) these waves. —**ultrasonically** *adv.*

ultrasound /'ʌltrəsaʊnd/ *n.* pressure waves similar in nature to sound waves but occurring at frequencies above 20,000 Hz (cycles per second), the approximate upper limit of human hearing (15–16 Hz is the lower limit). ◊Ultrasonics is concerned with the study and practical application of these phenomena (see ◊sound).

ultraviolet /ʌltrəˈvaɪələt/ *adj.* (of radiation) just beyond the violet end of the visible spectrum; of or using such radiation.

ultraviolet astronomy the study of cosmic ultraviolet emissions using artificial satellites. The US has launched a series of satellites for this purpose, receiving the first useful data in 1968. Only a tiny percentage of solar ultraviolet radiation penetrates the atmosphere, this being the less dangerous longer-wavelength ultraviolet. The dangerous shorter-wavelength radiation is absorbed by gases in the ozone layer high in the Earth's upper atmosphere.

ultraviolet radiation light rays invisible to the human eye, of wavelengths from about 4×10^{-7} to 5×10^{-9} metres (where the ◊X-ray range begins). Physiologically, they are extremely powerful, producing sunburn and causing the formation of vitamin D in the skin.

ululate /'ju:ljʊleɪt/ *v.i.* to howl, to wail. —**ululation** /-'leɪʃən/ *n.* [from Latin *ululare*]

Ulysses /ju:'lɪsiːz/ Roman name for ◊Odysseus, Greek mythological hero.

Ulysses *n.* a novel by James Joyce, published in 1922. It employs stream of consciousness, linguistic experimentation, and parody to describe in enormous detail a single day (16 June 1904) in the life of its characters in Dublin. It was first published in Paris but, because of obscenity prosecutions, not until 1936 in the UK.

Umar /'uːmɑː/ 2nd caliph (head) of Islam, a strong disciplinarian. Under his rule Islam spread to Egypt and Persia. He was assassinated in Medina.

Umayyad alternative spelling of ◊Omayyad, Arab dynasty.

umbel /'ʌmbəl/ *n.* a flower cluster in which stalks nearly equal in length spring from a common centre and form a flat or curved surface, as in the carrot. —**umbellate** *adj.* [from obsolete French or Latin *umbella* = sunshade]

umbellifer /ʌm'belɪfə/ *n.* a plant of the order Umbelliferae, bearing umbels, to which the carrot, parsnip, celery etc., belong. —**umbelliferous** /-bə'lɪfərəs/ *adj.* [from *umbel* and Latin *ferre* = bear]

umber *n.* a pigment like ochre but darker and browner; the colour of this. —*adj.* of this colour. [from French or Italian = shadow, or from Latin = of the province Umbria]

Umberto /ʊm'beətəʊ/ two kings of Italy:

Umberto I 1844–1900. King of Italy from 1878, who joined the Triple Alliance in 1882 with Germany and Austria-Hungary; his colonial ventures included the defeat at Aduwa, Abyssinia in 1896. He was assassinated by an anarchist.

Umberto II 1904–1983. Last king of Italy 1946. On the abdication of his father, Victor Emmanuel III, he ruled from 9 May–13 June 1946, when he had to abdicate since a referendum established a republic. He retired to Portugal.

umbilical /ʌm'bɪlɪkəl/ *adj.* of the navel. —**umbilical cord**, the flexible cordlike structure attaching the fetus to the placenta; an essential connecting line in various technologies. [obsolete French]

umbilicus /ʌm'bɪlɪkəs/ *n.* the navel; a navel-like formation. [Latin]

umbra /'ʌmbrə/ *n.* (*plural* **umbrae** /-iː/ or **umbras**) 1. a region of complete shadow where no light reaches a surface etc., especially that cast by the Moon or the Earth in an eclipse. 2. the dark central part of a sunspot. [Latin = shadow]

umbrage /'ʌmbrɪdʒ/ *n.* a sense of being offended. [from Old French from Latin *umbraticus*]

umbrella /ʌm'brelə/ *n.* 1. a light, collapsible usually circular canopy of cloth mounted on radial ribs attached to a central stick, used for protection against sunshine or (especially) as a portable protection against rain, or as a symbol of rank and authority in some Oriental and African countries. 2. any kind of general protecting force or influence; a coordinating or unifying agency. [from Italian *ombrella* diminutive of *ombra* = shade from Latin *umbra*]

umlaut /'ʊmlaʊt/ *n.* 1. a vowel change in related words in Germanic languages, e. g. *man/men* in English, *mann/männer* in German. 2. the mark like a diaeresis used to mark this in German etc. [German = *um* about and *laut* = sound]

Umm al Qaiwain /'ʊm æl kaɪ'waɪn/ one of the ◊United Arab Emirates.

umpire /'ʌmpaɪə/ *n.* a person appointed to see that the rules of a game or contest are observed and to settle disputes (e. g. in a game of cricket or baseball), or to give a decision on any disputed question. —*v.t./i.* to act as umpire (in). [later form of *noumpere* from Old French *non per* = not equal]

umpteen /ʌmp'tiːn, 'ʌm-/ *adj.* (*slang*) many; an indefinite number of. —**umpteenth** *adj.*

Umtata /ʊm'tɑːtə/ capital of the South African Bantu homeland of Transkei; population (1976) 25,000.

'un /ən/ *pron.* (*colloquial*) one (*a good 'un*). [dialect variant of *one*]

un- prefix added to **a.** adjectives and their derivative nouns and adverbs, in the sense 'not' (*unusable, uneducated, unyielding, unofficial*), or in the sense 'the reverse of' with the implication of praise or blame (*unselfish, unsociable*); **b.** verbs, denoting an action contrary to or annulling that of the simple verb (*unlock, untie*); **c.** nouns, forming verbs in the senses 'deprive of', 'divest (oneself) of', 'release from' (*unfrock, unleash*), or 'cause to be no longer' (*unman*); **d.** nouns, in the senses 'lack of' or 'the reverse of' (*unbelief, unemployment*). [Old English] The number of words that can be formed with this prefix is unlimited and only a selection can be given here.

UN abbreviation of United Nations.

unable /ʌn'eɪbəl/ *adj.* not able (to do a specified thing).

unaccompanied /ʌnə'kʌmpənid/ *adj.* 1. not accompanied; alone, without an escort. 2. without musical accompaniment.

unaccountable /ʌnə'kaʊntəbəl/ *adj.* 1. that cannot be explained or accounted for. 2. not accountable for one's actions etc. —**unaccountably** *adv.*

unaccustomed /ʌnə'kʌstəmd/ *adj.* not accustomed; not usual.

unadopted /ʌnə'dɒptɪd/ *adj.* (of a road) not taken over for maintenance by a local authority.

unadulterated /ʌnə'dʌltəreɪtɪd/ *adj.* pure.

unadvised /ʌnəd'vaɪzd/ *adj.* 1. indiscreet, rash. 2. not advised. —**unadvisedly** /-zɪdlɪ/ *adv.*

unalloyed /ʌnə'lɔɪd/ *adj.* (of pleasure etc.) pure, sheer.

unAmerican *adj.* 1. not in accordance with American characteristics. 2. contrary to the ideals and interests of the USA.

Unamuno /uːnə'muːnəʊ/ Miguel de 1864–1936. Spanish writer of Basque origin, exiled 1924–30 for criticism of the military directorate of Primo de ◊Rivera. His works include mystical poems and the study *Del sentimiento trágico de la vida/The Tragic Sense of Life* 1913, about the conflict of reason and belief in religion.

The chiefest sanctity of a temple is that it is a place to which men go to weep in common.

Miguel de Unamuno
'The Man of Flesh and Bone',
The Tragic Sense of Life

---

unanimous /ju:'nænɪməs/ *adj.* all agreeing in an opinion or decision; (of an opinion or decision etc.) held or given by all. —**unanimity** /ju:nə'nɪmɪtɪ/ *n.*, **unanimously** *adv.* [from Latin *unus* = one and *animus* = mind]

unanswerable /ʌn'ɑːnsərəbəl/ *adj.* that cannot be refuted. —**unanswerably** *adv.*

unarmed /ʌn'ɑːmd/ *adj.* not armed, without weapons.

unashamed /ʌnə'ʃeɪmd/ *adj.* feeling no guilt, shameless. —**unashamedly** /-mɪdlɪ/ *adv.*

unasked /ʌn'ɑːskt/ *adj.* not asked (for), not requested or invited.

unassailable /ʌnə'seɪləbəl/ *adj.* that cannot be attacked or questioned. —**unassailably** *adv.*

unassuming /ʌnə'sju:mɪŋ/ *adj.* not arrogant, unpretentious.

unattached /ʌnə'tætʃt/ *adj.* 1. not engaged or married. 2. not belonging to a particular regiment, church, club, college etc.

unattended /ʌnə'tendɪd/ *adj.* 1. not attended (to). 2. not accompanied; (of a vehicle) with no person in charge of it.

unavailing /ʌnə'veɪlɪŋ/ *adj.* ineffectual.

unavoidable /ʌnə'vɔɪdəbəl/ *adj.* unable to be avoided. —**unavoidably** *adv.*

unaware /ʌnə'weə/ *adj.* not aware.

unawares /ʌnə'weəz/ *adv.* unexpectedly, without noticing.

unbacked /ʌn'bækt/ *adj.* 1. not supported, having no backers (especially in betting). 2. having no back or no backing.

unbalanced /ʌn'bælənst/ *adj.* 1. not balanced. 2. mentally unsound.

unbar /ʌn'bɑː/ *v.t.* (-rr-) to remove the bar from (a gate etc.); to unlock.

unbearable /ʌn'beərəbəl/ *adj.* that cannot be endured. —**unbearably** *adv.*

unbeatable /ʌn'bi:təbəl/ *adj.* impossible to defeat or surpass.

unbeaten /ʌn'bi:tən/ *adj.* not beaten; (of a record etc.) not surpassed.

unbecoming /ʌnbi'kʌmɪŋ/ *adj.* 1. not suitable, not befitting a person's status etc. 2. not suited to the wearer.

unbeknown /ʌnbi'nəʊn/ *adj.* or **unbeknownst** (*colloquial*) not known. —**unbeknown to**, without the knowledge of. [from archaic *beknown* = known]

unbelief /ʌnbi'li:f/ *n.* incredulity, disbelief especially in divine revelation or in a particular religion. —**unbeliever** *n.*

unbelievable /ʌnbə'li:vəbəl/ *adj.* not believable. —**unbelievably** *adv.*

unbeliever /ʌnbi'li:və/ *n.* a person who does not believe, especially one not believing in Christianity or Islam.

unbelieving /ʌnbi'li:vɪŋ/ *adj.* 1. atheistic; agnostic. 2. unduly incredulous.

unbend /ʌn'bend/ *v.t./i.* (*past* and *past participle* **unbent**) 1. to change or become changed from a bent position, to straighten. 2. to relax (the mind etc.) from strain, exertion, or severity; to become affable. 3. (*nautical*) to unfasten (a cable), to untie (a rope).

unbending *adj.* 1. inflexible; refusing to alter one's demands. 2. austere; not becoming relaxed or affable.

unbidden /ʌn'bɪdən/ *adj.* not commanded or invited.

unbind /ʌn'baɪnd/ *v.t.* (*past* and *past participle* **unbound**) to release from bonds or from binding; to unfasten, to untie.

unblock /ʌn'blɒk/ *v.t.* to remove an obstruction from.

unblushing /ʌn'blʌʃɪŋ/ *adj.* shameless.

unbolt /ʌn'bəʊlt/ *v.t.* to release (a door etc.) by drawing back the bolt(s).

unborn /ʌn'bɔ:n/ *adj.* not yet born; future.

unbosom /ʌn'buzəm/ *v.t.* to disclose (secrets etc.). —**unbosom oneself**, to disclose one's thoughts, feelings, secrets etc.

unbounded /ʌn'baʊndɪd/ *adj.* infinite.

unbreakable /ʌn'breɪkəbəl/ *adj.* not breakable.

unbridle /ʌn'braɪdəl/ *v.t.* to remove 1. the bridle from (a horse). 2. (*figurative*) to remove restraint from (the tongue etc.).

unbridled /ʌn'braɪdəld/ *adj.* (of insolence, the tongue etc.) unrestrained.

unbroken /ʌn'brəʊkən/ *adj.* 1. not broken. 2. not tamed. 3. not interrupted. 4. not surpassed.

unbuckle /ʌn'bʌkəl/ *v.t.* to release the buckle(s) of (a strap, shoe etc.).

unburden /ʌn'bɜ:dən/ *v.t.* to relieve (oneself or one's conscience etc.) by confession.

unbutton /ʌn'bʌtən/ *v.t.* to unfasten the buttons of.

uncalled-for /ʌn'kɔ:ldfɔ:/ *adj.* offered or intruded impertinently or unjustifiably.

uncanny /ʌn'kænɪ/ *adj.* 1. strange and rather frightening. 2. extraordinary, beyond what is reckoned to be normal. —**uncannily** *adv.*, **uncanniness** *n.*

uncared-for /ʌn'keədfɔ:/ *adj.* neglected.

unceasing /ʌn'si:sɪŋ/ *adj.* not ceasing. —**unceasingly** *adv.*

unceremonious /ʌnseri'məʊniəs/ *adj.* without proper formality or dignity; abrupt in manner. —**unceremoniously** *adv.*

uncertain /ʌn'sɜ:tən/ *adj.* 1. not certainly knowing or known. 2. not to be depended on. 3. changeable. —**uncertainly** *adv.*

uncertainty *n.* being uncertain. —**uncertainty principle** or **indeterminacy principle** in quantum mechanics, the principle that it is meaningless to speak of a particle's position, momentum, or other parameters, except as results of measurements; measuring, however, involves an interaction (such as a ◊photon of light bouncing off the particle under scrutiny), which must disturb the particle, though the disturbance is noticeable only at an atomic scale. The principle implies that one cannot, even in theory, predict the moment-to-moment behaviour of such a system.

unchain /ʌn'tʃeɪn/ *v.t.* to release from chains.

unchangeable /ʌn'tʃeɪndʒəbəl/ *adj.* that may not be changed.

uncharitable /ʌn'tʃærɪtəbəl/ *adj.* censorious, severe in judgement. —**uncharitably** *adv.*

unchristian /ʌn'krɪstjən/ *adj.* contrary to Christian principles, uncharitable.

uncial /'ʌnsiəl, 'ʌnʃəl/ *adj.* of or written in the kind of writing with characters partly resembling modern capitals, found in manuscripts of the 4th–8th century —*n.* an uncial letter or manuscript. [from Latin *uncia* = inch]

uncivil /ʌn'sɪvɪl/ *adj.* ill-mannered, rude. —**uncivilly** *adv.*

unclasp /ʌn'klɑ:sp/ *v.t.* 1. to loosen the clasp(s) of. 2. to release the grip of (the hand(s) etc.).

uncle /'ʌŋkəl/ *n.* 1. a brother or brother-in-law of one's father or mother. 2. (*colloquial*) an unrelated friend of a parent. 3. (*slang*) a pawnbroker. [from Anglo-French and Old French from Latin *avunculus*]

unclean /ʌn'kli:n/ *adj.* 1. not clean; foul. 2. ceremonially impure. 3. unchaste.

Uncle Sam /'ʌŋkəl 'sæm/ nickname for the US government. It was coined during the War of 1812, by opponents of US policy, and it was probably derived from the initials US placed on government property.

Uncle Tom's Cabin a best-selling US novel by Harriet Beecher Stowe, written 1851–52. A sentimental but powerful portrayal of the cruelties of slave life on Southern plantations, it promoted the call for abolition. The heroically loyal slave Uncle Tom has in the 20th century become a byword for black subservience.

Uncle Vanya /'vɑ:njə/ a play by Anton Chekhov, first produced in 1897. Serebryakov, a retired professor, realizes the futility of his intellectual ideals when faced with the practical demands of life.

unclose /ʌn'kləʊz/ *v.t./i.* to open.

unclothe /ʌn'kləʊð/ *v.t.* to remove the clothes from, to uncover.

uncoil /ʌn'kɔɪl/ *v.t./i.* to draw out or become drawn out after having been coiled, to unwind.

uncommon /ʌn'kɒmən/ *adj.* not common, unusual, remarkable.

uncommunicative /ʌnkə'mju:nɪkətɪv/ *adj.* not inclined to give information or an opinion etc., silent.

uncompromising /ʌn'kɒmprəmaɪzɪŋ/ *adj.* refusing to compromise, unyielding, inflexible.

unconcern /ʌnkən'sɜ:n/ *n.* 1. freedom from anxiety. 2. indifference, apathy. —**unconcerned** *adj.*, **unconcernedly** /-nɪdlɪ/ *adv.*

unconditional /ʌnkən'dɪʃənəl/ *adj.* not subject to conditions or limitations, absolute. —**unconditionally** *adv.*

unconditioned *adj.* not subject to or determined by conditions. —**unconditioned reflex**, an instinctive response to a stimulus.

unconformity /ʌnkən'fɔ:mɪtɪ/ *n.* in geology, a break in the sequence of ◊sedimentary rocks. It is usually seen as an eroded surface, with the beds above and below lying at different angles. An unconformity represents an ancient land surface, where exposed rocks were worn down by erosion and later covered in a renewed cycle of deposition.

unconscionable /ʌn'kɒnʃənəbəl/ *adj.* 1. having no conscience, unscrupulous. 2. contrary to what one's conscience feels is right; unreasonably excessive. —**unconscionably** *adv.* [from *conscion* obsolete variant of *conscience*]

unconscious /ʌn'kɒnʃəs/ *adj.* 1. not conscious, not aware. 2. done or spoken etc. without conscious intention. —*n.* the part of the mind not normally accessible to consciousness. —**unconsciously** *adv.*, **unconsciousness** *n.*

unconstitutional /ʌnkɒnstɪ'tju:ʃənəl/ *adj.* (of measures or acts etc.) not in accordance with a country's constitution. —**unconstitutionally** *adv.*

uncooperative /ʌnkəʊ'ɒpərətɪv/ *adj.* not cooperative.

uncoordinated /ʌnkəʊ'ɔ:dɪneɪtɪd/ *adj.* not coordinated.

uncork /ʌn'kɔ:k/ *v.t.* 1. to draw the cork from (a bottle). 2. (*colloquial*) to give vent to (feelings).

uncouple /ʌn'kʌpəl/ *v.t.* to release from couples or couplings.

uncouth /ʌn'ku:θ/ *adj.* awkward or clumsy in manner, boorish. [Old English = unknown]

uncover /ʌn'kʌvə/ *v.t./i.* 1. to remove the cover or covering from. 2. to reveal, to disclose. 3. to take off one's cap or hat.

uncrowned /ʌn'kraʊnd/ *adj.* not crowned. —**uncrowned king**, a person having the power but not the title of a king.

UNCTAD acronym from United Nations Commission on Trade and Development.

unction /'ʌŋkʃən/ *n.* 1. anointing for medical purposes or as a religious rite. 2. a substance used in this. 3. soothing words, thought, or quality. 4. pretended earnestness; excessive politeness. [from Latin *unguere* = anoint]

unctuous /'ʌŋktjʊəs/ *adj.* 1. having an oily manner; smugly earnest or virtuous. 2. greasy, oily. —**unctuously** *adv.*, **unctuousness** *n.*

uncurl /ʌn'kɜːl/ *v.t./i.* to straighten out from a curled state or position.

uncut /ʌn'kʌt/ *adj.* not cut; (of a book) with the leaves not cut open or with untrimmed margins; (of a film) not censored; (of a diamond) not shaped; (of a fabric) with the loops of the pile not cut.

undeceive /ʌndi'siːv/ *v.t.* to disillusion.

undecided /ʌndi'saɪdɪd/ *adj.* 1. not yet settled or certain. 2. not yet having made up one's mind, irresolute. —**undecidedly** *adv.*

undemonstrative /ʌndi'mɒnstrətɪv/ *adj.* not given to showing strong feelings, reserved.

undeniable /ʌndi'naɪəbəl/ *adj.* that cannot be denied or disputed. —**undeniably** *adv.*

under *prep.* 1. in or to a position lower than, below; within or on the inside of (a surface etc.); at the foot of (a high wall). 2. less than. 3. inferior to; of lower rank than. 4. in the position or act of supporting or sustaining. 5. governed or commanded by. 6. on condition of; subject to an obligation imposed by. 7. in accordance with; as determined by; designated or indicated by. 8. in the category of. 9. (of a field etc.) planted with (a crop). 10. propelled by. 11. attested by. —*adv.* 1. in or into a lower position or subordinate condition. 2. in or into unconsciousness. 3. below a certain quantity, rank, age etc. —*adj.* lower, situated underneath. [Old English]

under- prefix in the senses (1) under; (2) lower, inner; (3) inferior, subordinate; (4) insufficient, insufficiently; incomplete, incompletely. [Old English]

underachieve /ʌndərə'tʃiːv/ *v.i.* to do less well than was expected (especially scholastically). —**underachiever** *n.*

underarm *adj. & adv.* 1. in the armpit. 2. (in cricket etc.) bowling or bowled etc. with the hand brought forward and upwards and not raised above shoulder level; (in tennis etc.) with the racket moved similarly.

underbelly *n.* the undersurface of an animal etc., especially as vulnerable to attack.

underbid /ʌndə'bɪd/ *v.t.* (-dd-; *past* and *past participle* underbid) 1. to make a lower bid than. 2. (in bridge) to bid less on (one's hand) than its strength warrants. —/'ʌndəbɪd/ *n.* such a bid.

undercarriage *n.* 1. an aircraft's landing-wheels etc. and their supports. 2. the supporting frame of a vehicle.

undercharge /ʌndə'tʃæːdʒ/ *v.t.* 1. to charge too little for (a thing) or to (a person). 2. to put too little (explosive, electric etc.) charge into.

underclass *n.* a subordinate social class; the lowest social stratum in a community, consisting of the poor and the unemployed.

undercliff *n.* a terrace or lower cliff formed by a landslip.

underclothes *n. pl.* garments worn under indoor clothing.

underclothing *n.* underclothes collectively.

undercoat *n.* 1. a layer of paint under a finishing coat; the paint used for this. 2. (in animals) a coat of hair under another. —*v.t.* to apply an undercoat to.

undercover /ʌndə'kʌvə/ *adj.* 1. surreptitious. 2. spying, especially by working among those observed.

undercroft *n.* a crypt.

undercurrent *n.* 1. a current that is below the surface or below another current. 2. an underlying trend, influence, or feeling, especially one opposite to the one perceived.

undercut /ʌndə'kʌt/ *v.t.* (-tt-; *past* and *past participle* undercut) 1. to sell or work at a lower price than. 2. to strike (a ball) to make it rise high. 3. to cut away a part below. —/'ʌndəkʌt/ *n.* an underside of sirloin.

underdeveloped /ʌndədi'veləpt/ *adj.* not fully developed; (of a film) not developed enough to give a satisfactory image; (of a country) not having reached its potential level in economic development.

underdog *n.* a person etc. losing a fight or in a state of inferiority or subjection.

underdone /ʌndə'dʌn/ *adj.* not thoroughly done; (of meat) not completely cooked throughout.

underemployed /ʌndərɪm'plɔɪd/ *adj.* not fully employed. —**underemployment** *n.*

underestimate /ʌndə'restɪmeɪt/ *v.t.* to form too low an estimate of. —/-mət/ *n.* an estimate that is too low. —**underestimation** /-'meɪʃən/ *n.*

underexpose /ʌndərɪk'spəʊz/ *v.t.* to expose for too short a time. —**underexposure** *n.*

underfed /ʌndə'fed/ *adj.* insufficiently fed.

underfelt *n.* felt for laying under a carpet.

underfloor *adj.* situated beneath the floor.

underfoot /ʌndə'fʊt/ *adv.* under one's feet, on the ground.

undergarment *n.* a piece of underclothing.

undergo /ʌndə'gəʊ/ *v.t.* (*past* underwent; *past participle* undergone /-'gɒn/) to be subjected to, to experience, to endure.

undergraduate /ʌndə'grædʊət/ *n.* a member of a university who has not yet taken a first degree.

underground /ʌndə'graʊnd/ *adv.* 1. beneath the surface of the ground. 2. in secret; into secrecy or hiding. —/'ʌn-/ *adj.* 1. situated underground. 2. secret, hidden; of a secret political organization or one for resisting enemy forces controlling a country. 3. (of the press, cinema etc.) involved in producing unconventional or experimental material. —/'ʌn-/ *n.* 1. an underground railway. The first underground in the world was in London, opened in 1863. The London Underground is still the longest, with over 400 km/250 mi of routes. Many major cities have similar systems. 2. an underground organization.

Underground Railroad in US history, a network established in the North before the ◊American Civil War to provide sanctuary and assistance for escaped black slaves. Safe houses, transport facilities, and 'conductors' existed to lead the slaves to safety in the North and Canada, although the number of fugitives who secured their freedom by these means may have been exaggerated.

undergrowth *n.* a dense growth of shrubs etc., especially under large trees.

underhand *adj.* 1. acting or done in a sly or secret way. 2. (in cricket etc.) underarm. —**underhanded** *adj.*

underlay /ʌndə'leɪ/ *v.t.* (*past* and *past participle* underlaid) to lay a thing under (another) in order to support or raise it. —/'ʌndə-/ *n.* a layer of material (e.g. felt, rubber) laid under another as a protection or support.

underlie /ʌndə'laɪ/ *v.t.* (*past* underlay; *past participle* underlain; *participle* underlying) 1. to lie under (a stratum etc.). 2. to be the basis of (a doctrine or conduct etc.). 3. to exist beneath the superficial aspect of.

underline /ʌndə'laɪn/ *v.t.* 1. to draw a line under (a word etc.). 2. to emphasize. —/'ʌndəlaɪn/ *n.* 1. a line placed under a word. 2. a caption below an illustration.

underling /'ʌndəlɪŋ/ *n.* (usually *derogatory*) a subordinate.

undermanned /ʌndə'mænd/ *adj.* having too few people as crew or staff.

undermentioned /ʌndə'menʃənd/ *adj.* mentioned at a later place in a book etc.

undermine /ʌndə'maɪn/ *v.t.* 1. to make an excavation under; to wear away the base of. 2. to weaken or wear out (the health etc.) gradually. 3. to injure (a person etc.) by secret or insidious means.

undermost *adj.* lowest, furthest underneath. —*adv.* in or to the undermost position.

underneath /ʌndə'niːθ/ *prep.* 1. at or to a lower place than. 2. on the inside of. —*adv.* 1. at or to a lower place. 2. inside. —*n.* a lower surface or part. [Old English]

undernourished /ʌndə'nʌrɪʃt/ *adj.* insufficiently nourished. —**undernourishment** *n.*

underpants *n. pl.* a man's undergarment covering the lower body and part of the legs.

underpart *n.* a lower or subordinate part.

underpass *n.* a road etc. passing under another; a crossing of this kind.

underpay /ʌndə'peɪ/ *v.t.* (*past* and *past participle* underpaid) to pay too little to (a person) or in discharge of (a debt).

underground 1863: the inaugural trip of the Metropolitan Line train at Edgware Road station, London. Among the passengers, seated third and fourth from the right, are Prime Minister Gladstone and his wife.

underpin /ʌndəˈpɪn/ *v.t.* (-**nn**-) **1.** to support from below with masonry etc. **2.** to strengthen.

underprivileged /ʌndəˈprɪvɪlɪdʒd/ *adj.* less privileged than others, not enjoying a normal standard of living or rights in a community.

underproof *adj.* containing less alcohol than proof spirit does.

underrate /ʌndəˈreɪt/ *v.t.* to have too low an opinion of.

underscore /ʌndəˈskɔ/ *v.t.* to underline. —/ˈʌn-/ *n.* an underline below a word etc.

undersea *adj.* below the sea, below its surface.

underseal *v.t.* to coat the underpart of (a motor vehicle etc.) with a protective sealing layer. —*n.* a substance used for this.

undersecretary *n.* an official who is directly subordinate to one with the title 'secretary', especially a senior civil servant.

undersell /ʌndəˈsel/ *v.t.* (*past* and *past participle* **undersold**) to sell at a lower price than (another seller).

undersexed /ʌndəˈsekst/ *adj.* having less than the normal degree of sexual desire.

undershirt *n.* an undergarment worn under a shirt, a vest.

undershoot /ʌndəˈʃuːt/ *v.t.* (*past* and *past participle* **undershot**) (of an aircraft) to land short of (a runway etc.).

undershot *adj.* **1.** (of a water-wheel) turned by water flowing under it. **2.** (of the lower jaw) projecting beyond the upper jaw.

underside *n.* the side or surface underneath.

undersigned *adj.* whose signature(s) is or are appended.

undersized *adj.* of less than the usual size.

underskirt *n.* a skirt worn under another, a petticoat.

underslung *adj.* supported from above.

underspend /ʌndəˈspend/ *v.t./i.* (*past* and *past participle* **underspent**) to spend less than (a specified amount); to spend too little.

understaffed /ʌndəˈstɑːft/ *adj.* having too few staff.

understand /ʌndəˈstænd/ *v.t./i.* (*past* and *past participle* **understood**) **1.** to perceive the meaning of (words, a language, or a person). **2.** to perceive the significance, explanation, or cause of. **3.** to be sympathetically aware of the character or nature of, to know how to deal with. **4.** to infer, especially from information received; to take as implied or granted; to supply (a word or words) mentally. **5.** to have understanding in general or in particular. [Old English]

understandable *adj.* that may be understood. —**understandably** *adv.*

understanding *n.* **1.** the power of thought, intelligence. **2.** the ability to understand. **3.** an agreement; a thing agreed upon. **4.** harmony in opinion or feeling. **5.** sympathetic awareness or tolerance. —*adj.* having or showing understanding, insight, or good judgement; able to be sympathetic to others' feelings or points of view.

understate /ʌndəˈsteɪt/ *v.t.* to express in greatly or unduly restrained terms, to represent as being less than it really is. —**understatement** *n.*

understeer *v.i.* (of a vehicle) to have a tendency to turn less sharply than was intended. —*n.* this tendency.

understudy *n.* one who studies the role in a play or the duties etc. of another in order to be able to take his or her place at short notice if necessary. —*v.t.* to study (a role etc.) thus; to act as understudy to (a person).

undertake /ʌndəˈteɪk/ *v.t.* (*past* **undertook** /-ˈtʊk/; *past participle* **undertaken**) **1.** to agree or promise to do something; to make oneself responsible for, to engage in. **2.** to guarantee, to affirm.

undertaker /ˈʌndəteɪkə/ *n.* one who professionally makes arrangements for funerals.

undertaking /ʌndəˈteɪkɪŋ/ *n.* **1.** work etc. undertaken, an enterprise. **2.** a promise or guarantee. **3.** /ˈʌn-/ the management of funerals.

undertone *n.* **1.** a low or subdued tone. **2.** a colour that modifies another. **3.** an underlying quality or implication; an undercurrent of feeling.

undertow *n.* a current below the surface of the sea, moving in a direction opposite to that of the surface current.

undervalue /ʌndəˈvæljuː/ *v.t.* to value insufficiently. —**undervaluation** /-ˈeɪʃən/ *n.*

undervest *n.* a vest (undergarment).

underwater /ʌndəˈwɔːtə/ *adj.* situated, used, or done beneath the surface of water. —*adv.* beneath the surface of water.

underwear *n.* underclothes.

underweight /ˌʌndəˈweɪt/ *adj.* below the normal, required, or suitable weight. —/ˈʌn-/ *n.* insufficient weight.

underwood /ˈʌndwʊd/ *n.* undergrowth.

underworld *n.* 1. or **Underworld**; in mythology the abode of the spirits of the dead, under the Earth. 2. the section of society that is habitually engaged in crime.

underwrite *v.t.* (*past* **underwrote**; *past participle* **underwritten**) 1. to sign and accept liability under (an insurance policy, especially on shipping etc.); to accept (a liability) thus. 2. to undertake to finance or support. 3. to agree to take up, in a new company or new issue (a certain number of shares if not applied for by the public). —**underwriter** *n.*

undeserved /ˌʌndɪˈzɜːvd/ *adj.* not deserved (as a reward or punishment). —**undeservedly** /-vɪdlɪ/ *adv.*

undesirable /ˌʌndɪˈzaɪərəbəl/ *adj.* not desirable, objectionable. —*n.* an undesirable person. —**undesirability** /-ˈbɪlɪtɪ/ *n.*, **undesirably** *adv.*

undetermined /ˌʌndɪˈtɜːmɪnd/ *adj.* undecided.

undies /ˈʌndɪz/ *n. pl.* (*colloquial*) women's underclothes.

undignified /ʌnˈdɪgnɪfaɪd/ *adj.* not dignified.

undine /ˈʌndiːn/ *n.* a female water-spirit. [invented by Paracelsus from Latin *unda* = wave]

undo /ʌnˈduː/ *v.t.* (*past* **undid**; *past participle* **undone** /-ˈdʌn/) 1. to unfasten; to unfasten the garment(s) of. 2. to annul, to cancel the effect of. 3. to ruin the prospects, reputation, or morals etc. of. [Old English]

undoing /ʌnˈduːɪŋ/ *n.* 1. ruin; a cause of this. 2. a reversal of what has been done.

undone /ʌnˈdʌn/ *adj.* 1. not done. 2. not fastened. 3. (*archaic*) brought to ruin.

undoubted /ʌnˈdaʊtɪd/ *adj.* not regarded as doubtful, not disputed. —**undoubtedly** *adv.*

undreamed /ʌnˈdriːmd/ *adj.* or **undreamt** /-ˈdremt/ not (even) dreamed; (with *-of*) not imagined, not thought to be possible.

undress /ʌnˈdres/ *v.t./i.* to take off one's clothes; to take off the clothes of (a person). —*n.* ordinary dress or uniform as opposed to full dress or uniform for ceremonial occasions; casual or informal dress. —/ˈʌn-/ *adj.* constituting such dress or uniform.

undue /ʌnˈdjuː/ *adj.* excessive, disproportionate. —**unduly** *adv.*

undulate /ˈʌndjʊleɪt/ *v.i.* to have a wavy motion or look. —**undulation** /-ˈleɪʃən/ *n.*, **undulatory** *adj.* [from Latin *unda* = wave]

undying /ʌnˈdaɪɪŋ/ *adj.* immortal; everlasting, never-ending.

unearned /ʌnˈɜːnd/ *adj.* not earned. —**unearned income**, income from interest payments etc. as opposed to salary, wages, or fees.

unearth /ʌnˈɜːθ/ *v.t.* 1. to uncover or obtain from the ground or by digging. 2. to bring to light, to find by searching.

unearthly /ʌnˈɜːθlɪ/ *adj.* 1. not earthly. 2. supernatural, mysterious and frightening. 3. (*colloquial*) absurdly early or late, inconvenient. —**unearthliness** *n.*

uneasy /ʌnˈiːzɪ/ *adj.* 1. not comfortable. 2. not confident, worried. 3. worrying. —**uneasily** *adv.*, **uneasiness** *n.*

uneatable /ʌnˈiːtəbəl/ *adj.* not fit to be eaten, especially because of its condition.

uneconomic /ˌʌniːkəˈnɒmɪk/ *adj.* not profitable, not likely to be profitable.

uneducated /ʌnˈedjʊkeɪtɪd/ *adj.* not educated, ignorant.

unemployable /ˌʌnɪmˈplɔɪəbəl/ *adj.* unfitted by character etc. for paid employment.

unemployed /ˌʌnɪmˈplɔɪd/ *adj.* 1. temporarily out of work; lacking employment. 2. not in use.

unemployment *n.* a lack of paid employment. Involuntary unemployment is generally subdivided into **frictional unemployment**, the inevitable temporary unemployment of those moving from one job to another; **cyclical unemployment**, caused by a downswing in the business cycle; **seasonal unemployment**, in an area where there is high demand only during holiday periods, for example; and **structural unemployment**, where changing technology or other long-term change in the economy results in large numbers without work. Periods of widespread unemployment in Europe and the USA in the 20th century include 1929–1930s, and the years since the mid-1970s. Most present-day governments attempt to prevent some or all of the various forms of unemployment. The ideas of John Maynard ◊Keynes influenced British government unemployment policies during the 1950s and 1960s. The existence of a clear link between unemployment and inflation (that high unemployment can be dealt with by governments only at the cost of higher inflation) is now disputed.

unencumbered /ˌʌnɪnˈkʌmbəd/ *adj.* (of an estate) having no liabilities on it.

unending /ʌnˈendɪŋ/ *adj.* having or apparently having no end.

unequal /ʌnˈiːkwəl/ *adj.* 1. not equal. 2. of varying quality. 3. not with equal advantage to both sides; not well matched. —**unequally** *adv.*

unequalled *adj.* superior to all others.

unequivocal /ˌʌnɪˈkwɪvəkəl/ *adj.* not ambiguous, clear and unmistakable. —**unequivocally** *adv.*

unerring /ʌnˈɜːrɪŋ/ *adj.* not erring, not failing or missing the mark. —**unerringly** *adv.*

UNESCO /juːˈneskəʊ/ or **Unesco** acronym from United Nations Educational, Scientific, and Cultural Organization, an agency of the UN, established in 1946, with its headquarters in Paris. The USA, contributor of 25% of its budget, withdrew in 1984 on grounds of its overpoliticization and mismanagement, and Britain followed in 1985.

unethical /ʌnˈeθɪkəl/ *adj.* not ethical; unscrupulous in professional conduct. —**unethically** *adv.*

uneven /ʌnˈiːvən/ *adj.* 1. not level or smooth. 2. not uniform or equable, varying. 3. (of a contest) unequal. —**unevenly** *adv.*, **unevenness** *n.*

unexampled /ˌʌnɪgˈzɑːmpəld/ *adj.* having no precedent or nothing else that can be compared with it.

unexceptionable /ˌʌnɪkˈsepʃənəbəl/ *adj.* with which no fault can be found. —**unexceptionably** *adv.*

unexceptional /ˌʌnɪkˈsepʃənəl/ *adj.* not exceptional, quite ordinary. —**unexceptionally** *adv.*

unexpected /ˌʌnɪkˈspektɪd/ *adj.* not expected. —**unexpectedly** *adv.*

unfailing /ʌnˈfeɪlɪŋ/ *adj.* not failing; not running short; constant; reliable.

unfair /ʌnˈfeə/ *adj.* not impartial; not in accordance with justice. —**unfairly** *adv.* **unfairness** *n.*

unfair dismissal the sacking of an employee unfairly; under the terms of the Employment Acts, this means the unreasonable dismissal of someone who has been in continuous employment for a period of two years, i.e. dismissal on grounds not in accordance with the codes of disciplinary practice and procedures prepared by ◊ACAS. Dismissed employees may take their case to an industrial tribunal for adjudication.

unfaithful /ʌnˈfeɪθfʊl/ *adj.* 1. not loyal, not keeping one's promise. 2. adulterous. —**unfaithfully** *adv.*, **unfaithfulness** *n.*

unfamiliar /ˌʌnfəˈmɪljə/ *adj.* not familiar. —**unfamiliarity** /-lɪˈærətɪ/ *n.*

unfasten /ʌnˈfɑːsən/ *v.t./i.* to make or become loose; to open the fastening(s) of; to detach.

unfeeling /ʌnˈfiːlɪŋ/ *adj.* 1. lacking the power of sensation or sensitivity. 2. unsympathetic, not caring about the feelings of others. —**unfeelingly** *adv.*, **unfeelingness** *n.*

unfetter /ʌnˈfetə/ *v.t.* to release from fetters.

unfit /ʌnˈfɪt/ *adj.* 1. not fit, unsuitable. 2. not in perfect health or physical condition. —*v.t.* (**-tt-**) to make unsuitable.

unfix /ʌnˈfɪks/ *v.t.* to release or loosen from a fixed state; to detach.

unflappable /ʌnˈflæpəbəl/ *adj.* (*colloquial*) imperturbable. —**unflappability** /-ˈbɪlɪtɪ/ *n.*

unfledged /ʌnˈfledʒd/ *adj.* 1. (of a bird) not fledged. 2. (of a person) inexperienced.

unfold /ʌnˈfəʊld/ *v.t./i.* 1. to open the fold(s) of; to spread or become spread out. 2. to reveal (thoughts etc.). 3. to become visible or known; (of a story etc.) to develop.

unforgettable /ˌʌnfəˈgetəbəl/ *adj.* that may not be forgotten.

unformed /ʌnˈfɔːmd/ *adj.* not formed; shapeless.

unfortunate /ʌnˈfɔːtjʊnət, -tʃənət/ *adj.* 1. unlucky; unhappy. 2. regrettable. —*n.* an unfortunate person. —**unfortunately** *adv.*

unfounded /ʌnˈfaʊndɪd/ *adj.* with no foundation of fact(s).

unfreeze /ʌnˈfriːz/ *v.t./i.* (*past* **unfroze**; *past participle* **unfrozen**) 1. to thaw; to cause to thaw. 2. to make (frozen assets) available again.

unfrock /ʌnˈfrɒk/ *v.t.* to deprive (a clergyman) of ecclesiastical status.

unfurl /ʌnˈfɜːl/ *v.t./i.* to unroll; to spread out.

unfurnished /ʌnˈfɜːnɪʃt/ *adj.* 1. without furniture. 2. not supplied *with*.

ungainly /ʌnˈɡeɪnlɪ/ *adj.* awkward-looking, clumsy, ungraceful. —**ungainliness** *n.* [from obsolete *gain* (Old English from Old Norse = *gegn* straight)]

Ungaretti /ʊŋɡəˈreti/ Giuseppe 1888–1970. Italian poet who lived in France and Brazil. His lyrics show a cosmopolitan independence from Italian poetic tradition. His poems, such as the *Allegria di naufragi/Joy of Shipwrecks* 1919, are of great simplicity.

unget-at-able /ʌnɡetˈætəbəl/ *adj.* (*colloquial*) inaccessible.

ungird /ʌnˈɡɜːd/ *v.t.* to release the girdle of.

ungodly /ʌnˈɡɒdlɪ/ *adj.* 1. not giving reverence to God; not religious; wicked. 2. (*colloquial*) absurdly early or late, inconvenient. —**ungodliness** *n.*

ungovernable /ʌnˈɡʌvənəbəl/ *adj.* uncontrollable, violent.

ungracious /ʌnˈɡreɪʃəs/ *adj.* not kindly or courteous.

ungrammatical /ʌnɡrəˈmætɪkəl/ *adj.* contrary to the rules of grammar. —**ungrammatically** *adv.*

ungrateful /ʌnˈɡreɪtfəl/ *adj.* feeling no gratitude.

unguarded /ʌnˈɡɑːdɪd/ *adj.* 1. not guarded. 2. incautious, thoughtless.

unguent /ˈʌŋɡwənt/ *n.* an ointment; a lubricant. [from Latin *unguentum* (*unguere* = anoint)]

ungulate /ˈʌŋɡjʊlət/ *adj.* hoofed. —*n.* a hoofed mammal. [from Latin *ungula* = hoof]

unhallowed /ʌnˈhæləʊd/ *adj.* not consecrated; not sacred, wicked.

unhand /ʌnˈhænd/ *v.t.* (*rhetorical*) to take one's hands off (a person), to let go of.

unhappy /ʌnˈhæpɪ/ *adj.* 1. not happy, sad. 2. unfortunate. 3. unsuitable; unsuccessful. —**unhappily** *adv.*, **unhappiness** *n.*

unharness /ʌnˈhɑːnɪs/ *v.t.* to remove the harness from.

UNHCR abbreviation of United Nations High Commission for Refugees.

unhealthy /ʌnˈhelθɪ/ *adj.* 1. not having or not showing good health. 2. unwholesome. 3. (of a place etc.) harmful to health; unwholesome; (*slang*) dangerous to life. —**unhealthily** *adv.*, **unhealthiness** *n.*

unheard *adj.* not heard. —**unheard-of** *adj.* unprecedented.

unhinge /ʌnˈhɪndʒ/ *v.t.* 1. to take (a door etc.) off its hinges. 2. (especially in *past participle*) to cause to become mentally unbalanced.

unhitch /ʌnˈhɪtʃ/ *v.t.* to release from a hitched state; to unhook, to unfasten.

unholy /ʌnˈhəʊlɪ/ *adj.* 1. impious, wicked. 2. (*colloquial*) very great, outrageous. —**unholiness** *n.*

unhook /ʌnˈhʊk/ *v.t.* 1. to remove from a hook or hooks. 2. to unfasten by releasing a hook or hooks.

unhoped-for /ʌnˈhəʊptfə/ *adj.* not hoped for, not expected.

unhorse /ʌnˈhɔːs/ *v.t.* to throw or drag (a rider) from a horse.

unhuman /ʌnˈhjuːmən/ *adj.* not human; superhuman; inhuman.

uni- /juːnɪ-/ in combinations, one, having or consisting of one. [Latin *unus* = one]

Uniat /ˈjuːnɪæt/ *adj.* or **Uniate**, of the Churches in eastern Europe and the Near East that acknowledge the pope's supremacy and are in communion with Rome but retain their respective languages, rites, and canon law in accordance with the terms of their union. —*n.* a member of such a Church. [from Russian *uniyat* from Latin *unio* = union]

unicameral /juːnɪˈkæmərəl/ *adj.* with one legislative chamber. [from Latin *camera* = chamber]

UNICEF /ˈjuːnɪsef/ acronym from United Nations International Children's Emergency Fund.

unicellular /juːnɪˈseljʊlə/ *adj.* (of an organism) consisting of one cell. Most unicellular organisms are invisible without a microscope but a few, such as the giant ◊amoeba, may be visible to the naked eye. The main groups of unicellular organisms are bacteria, protozoa, unicellular algae, and unicellular fungi or yeasts.

unicorn /ˈjuːnɪkɔːn/ *n.* a mythical animal usually regarded as having the body of a horse with a single straight horn

projecting from its forehead. [from Old French from Latin, translation Greek *monokerōs* = single horn]

unidentified /ʌnaɪˈdentɪfaɪd/ *adj.* not identified.

unidentified flying object or **UFO** any light or object seen in the sky whose immediate identity is not apparent. Despite unsubstantiated claims, there is no evidence that UFOs are alien spacecraft. On investigation, the vast majority of sightings turn out to have been of natural or identifiable objects, notably bright stars and planets, meteors, aircraft, and satellites, or to have been perpetrated by pranksters. The term **flying saucer** was coined in 1947 and has been in use since.

unification /juːnɪfɪˈkeɪʃən/ *n.* unifying, being unified.

Unification Church or **Moonies** church founded in Korea in 1954 by the Reverend Sun Myung Moon. The number of members (often called 'moonies') is about 200,000 worldwide. The theology unites Christian and Taoist ideas and is based on Moon's book *Divine Principle*, which teaches that the original purpose of creation was to set up a perfect family, in a perfect relationship with God.

unified field theory in physics, the theory that attempts to explain the four fundamental forces (strong nuclear, weak nuclear, electromagnetic, and gravitational) in terms of a single unified force (see ◊particle physics).

uniform /ˈjuːnɪfɔːm/ *adj.* 1. not changing in form or character, unvarying. 2. conforming to the same standard or rule. —*n.* distinctive clothing worn by members of the same school or organization. —**uniformly** *adv.* [from French or Latin *forma* = form]

uniformed *adj.* wearing a uniform.

uniformitarianism *n.* in geology, the principle that processes that can be seen to occur on the Earth's surface today are the same as those that have occurred throughout geological time. For example, desert sandstones containing sand-dune structures must have been formed under conditions similar to those present in deserts today. The principle was formulated by James ◊Hutton and expounded by Charles ◊Lyell.

uniformity /juːnɪˈfɔːmɪtɪ/ *n.* being uniform, sameness, consistency.

unify /ˈjuːnɪfaɪ/ *v.t.* to form into a single unit, to unite. [from French or Latin *unificare* (*unus* = one and *facere* = make)]

unilateral /juːnɪˈlætərəl/ *adj.* done by or affecting only one side or party. —**unilaterally** *adv.*

Unilateral Declaration of Independence (UDI) the declaration made by Ian Smith of the Rhodesian Front government on 11 Nov 1965. He unilaterally declared Rhodesia an independent state, to resist sharing power with the black African majority. It was a move condemned by the United Nations and by the UK who imposed sanctions (trade restrictions and an oil embargo). With the support of the United Nations, Britain imposed a naval blockade that was countered by the South African government breaking sanctions. Negotiations between British prime minister Harold Wilson and Smith foundered. It was not until April 1980 that the Republic of ◊Zimbabwe was proclaimed.

unilateralism *n.* in politics, support for **unilateral nuclear disarmament**: scrapping a country's nuclear weapons without waiting for other countries to agree to do so at the same time.

unimpeachable /ʌnɪmˈpiːtʃəbəl/ *adj.* not open to doubt or question, completely trustworthy. —**unimpeachably** *adv.*

uninformed /ʌnɪnˈfɔːmd/ *adj.* not informed; ignorant.

uninhabitable /ʌnɪnˈhæbɪtəbəl/ *adj.* not suitable for habitation.

uninhibited /ʌnɪnˈhɪbɪtɪd/ *adj.* not inhibited; having no inhibitions.

uninspired /ʌnɪnˈspaɪəd/ *adj.* not inspired; (of a speech or performance etc.) commonplace, not outstanding.

unintelligible /ʌnɪnˈtelɪdʒəbəl/ *adj.* not intelligible, impossible to understand. —**unintelligibly** *adv.*

uninterested /ʌnˈɪntrəstɪd/ *adj.* not interested; showing or feeling no concern.

uninviting /ʌnɪnˈvaɪtɪŋ/ *adj.* unattractive, repellent.

union /ˈjuːnjən/ *n.* 1. uniting, being united. 2. a whole formed by uniting parts; an association formed by the uniting of people or groups. 3. a trade union. 4. a coupling for pipes or rods. 5. in mathematics, the set containing every element that is a member of at least one of two or more other sets. —**the Union**, the union of the English

Union of Soviet Socialist Republics

and Scottish crowns in 1603 or of their parliaments in 1707, or of Great Britain and Ireland in 1801. **union catalogue,** a catalogue showing the combined holdings of several libraries. **Union Territory,** any of the six administrative territories within the Republic of India. [from Old French or Latin *unio* = unity]

Union, Act of the 1707 act of Parliment that brought about the union of England and Scotland; that of 1801 which united England and Ireland. The latter was revoked when the Irish Free State was constituted in 1922.

union flag the national flag or ensign of the United Kingdom (formerly of Great Britain), formed by combining the crosses of the three patron saints. It is popularly called the **Union Jack,** although, strictly speaking, this applies only when it is flown on the jackstaff of a warship.

unionist /'juːnjənɪst/ n. **1.** (in specific uses **Unionist**) an advocate of political or organizational union, especially between Britain and Ireland; (*US*) a supporter or advocate of the Federal Union of the United States of America, especially one who during the Civil War (1861–5) was opposed to secession. **2.** a member of a trade union. —**unionism** n.

unionize /'juːnjənaɪz/ v.t. to bring under trade union organization or rules. —**unionization** /-'zeɪʃən/ n.

Union Movement British political group. Founded as the New Party by Oswald ◊Mosley and a number of Labour members of Parliament in 1931, it developed into the British Union of Fascists in 1932. In 1940 the organization was declared illegal and its leaders interned, but at the end of World War II it was revived as the Union Movement, characterized by racist doctrines including anti-Semitism.

Union of Soviet Socialist Republics (USSR) country in N Asia and E Europe, stretching from the Baltic Sea and the Black Sea to the Arctic and Pacific oceans; **area** 22,402,200 sq km/8,590,274 sq mi; **capital** Moscow; **physical** Ural Mountains separate European and Asian plains; Caucasus Mountains in S between Black Sea and Caspian Sea; mountain ranges in SE; coniferous forest and tundra in Siberia; desert in Central Asia; **head of state and government** Mikhail Gorbachev; **political system** communism; **exports** cotton, timber, iron and steel, nonferrous metals, electrical equipment, machinery, oil and natural gas; **population** (1990 est) 290,939,000; **language** Slavic; **recent history** communist takeover by Bolsheviks in 1917; Soviet Union established 1922. Purges of Stalin's opponents took place in the 1930s. Nonaggression pact against Germany 1939, war against Germany 1941-45. Stalin died 1953. Warsaw Pact created 1955. Hungarian uprising suppressed 1956; Czechoslovakia invaded 1968; invasion of Afghanistan 1979. In 1985 Gorbachev became Communist Party leader, introduced wide-ranging reforms; appointed president. ◊Chernobyl nuclear accident 1986. USSR and USA agreed to scrap intermediate-range nuclear missiles. In 1988 Gorbachev became head of state and constitution overhauled. End of Cold War declared 1989. Mounting economic problems reached a crisis in 1990. Baltic republics' moves towards independence opposed by Gorbachev.

unique /juːˈniːk/ adj. **1.** being the only one of its kind, having no like or equal or parallel. **2.** (**disputed usage**) unusual. —**uniquely** adv. [French from Latin *unus* = one]

unisex /'juːnɪseks/ n. the tendency of the human sexes to become indistinguishable in dress etc. —adj. designed to be suitable for both sexes.

unison /'juːnɪsən/ n. **1.** in music, coincidence in pitch of sounds or notes; (especially **in unison**) combination of voices or instruments at the same pitch or in a different octave. **2.** agreement. [Old French or from Latin *sonus* = sound]

unit /'juːnɪt/ n. **1.** an individual thing, person, or group regarded for purposes of calculation etc. as single and complete or as part of a complex whole. **2.** a quantity chosen as a standard in terms of which other quantities may be expressed, or for which a stated charge is made. **3.** the smallest share in a unit trust. **4.** a part or group with a specified function within a complex machine or organization. **5.** a piece of furniture for fitting with others like it or made of complementary parts. —**unit price,** the price charged for each unit of goods supplied. **unit trust,** an investment company investing contributions from a number of people in varied stocks and paying contributors a dividend (calculated on the average return on the stocks) in proportion to their holdings. [from Latin *unus* = one]

UNITA /juːˈniːtə/ acronym from National Union for the Total Independence of Angola Angolan, a nationalist movement backed by South Africa, which continued to wage guerrilla warfare against the ruling MPLA regime after the latter gained control of the country in 1976. The UNITA leader Jonas ◊Savimbi founded the movement in 1966. A June 1989 ceasefire was abandoned after two months.

unitarian /juːnɪˈteəriən/ n. **1.** an advocate of unity or centralization, e.g. in politics. **2. Unitarian,** a person who believes that God is one person not a Trinity; a member of a religious body maintaining this. —**Unitarianism** n. [from Latin *unitas* = unity]

unitary /'juːnɪtəri/ adj. **1.** of a unit or units. **2.** marked by unity or uniformity.

unite /juːˈnaɪt/ v.t./i. **1.** to join together, to make or become one. **2.** to agree, combine, or cooperate. **United Reformed Church,** the Church formed in 1972 by the union of the English Presbyterian and Congregational Churches. [from Latin *unire* (*unus* = one)]

United Arab Emirates federation of Abu Dhabi, Ajman, Dubai, Fujairah, Sharjah, Umm al Qaiwain, Ras al Khaimah (called the Trucial States until 1971) in SW Asia, on the Arabian Gulf, bounded to the SW by Saudi Arabia and to the SE by Oman; **area** 83,657 sq km/32,292 sq mi; **capital** Abu Dhabi; **physical** desert and flat coastal plain; mountains in E; **head of state and government** Zayed Bin Sultan al-Nahayan of Abu Dhabi from 1971; **political system** absolutism; **exports** oil, natural gas, fish, dates; **population** (1990 est) 2,250,000; **language** Arabic; **recent history** a member of the Federation of Arab Emirates from 1971; federation later dissolved; one of the ◊Trucial States (with Abu Dhabi, Ajman, Dubai, Fujairah, Sharjah, Umm al Qaiwain, Ras al Khaimah) from 1971. Links with USSR and

China established 1985; diplomatic relations restored with Egypt 1987.

United Arab Republic union formed in 1958, broken in 1961, between ◊Egypt and ◊Syria. Egypt continued to use the name after the breach until 1971.

United Artists (UA) Hollywood film studio formed in 1919 by silent-screen stars Charles Chaplin, Mary Pickford, and Douglas Fairbanks, and director D W Griffith, in order to take control of their artistic and financial affairs. Smaller than the other major studios, UA concentrated on producing adaptations of literary works in the 1930s and 1940s, including *Wuthering Heights* 1939, *Rebecca* 1940, and *Major Barbara* 1941. The company nearly collapsed after the box-office disaster of Michael Cimino's *Heaven's Gate* 1980, and UA was subsequently bought by MGM.

United Australia Party an Australian political party formed by Joseph Lyons in 1931 from the right-wing Nationalist Party. It was led by Robert Menzies after the death of Lyons. Considered to have become too dominated by financial interests, it lost heavily to the Labor Party in 1943, and was reorganized as the ◊Liberal Party in 1944.

United Democratic Front a moderate, multiracial political organization in South Africa, founded in 1983. It was an important focus of anti-apartheid action in South Africa until 1989, when the African National Congress and Pan-Africanist Congress were unbanned.

United Irishmen a society formed in 1791 by Wolfe ◊Tone to campaign for parliamentary reform in Ireland. It later became a secret revolutionary group.

United Kingdom (UK) country in NW Europe off the coast of France, consisting of England, Scotland, Wales, and Northern Ireland; **area** 244,100 sq km/94,247 sq mi; **capital** London; **physical** rolling landscape Grampian mountains in Scotland, Pennines in N England, Cambrian mountains in Wales, rivers include Thames, Severn, Spey; **head of state** Elizabeth II from 1952; **head of government** John Major from 1990; **political system** liberal democracy; **exports** cereals, rape, sugarbeet, potatoes, meat, poultry, dairy products, electronic and engineering equipment, scientific instruments, oil and gas, pharmaceuticals, fertilizers, film and television programmes; **population** (1990 est) 57,121,000; **language** English; **recent history** Act of Union between England and Scotland 1707. In 1783 the American colonies were lost. The Act of Ireland 1801 united Britain and Ireland. The 1832–1867 Reform Acts extended the franchise to the working classes. In 1911 the powers of the House of Lords were curbed. The Home Rule Act 1920 incorporated the NE of Ireland (Ulster) into the United Kingdom of Great Britain and Northern Ireland. In 1921 Ireland, except for Ulster, became a dominion (Irish Free State, later Eire, 1937). First Labour government led by Ramsay McDonald 1924. General Strike 1926; 1931 unemployment reached 3 million. Coalition government under Winston Churchill 1940-45. Welfare state established under Labour government led by Clement Attlee in 1945. ◊Suez crisis 1956. Direct rule of Northern Ireland from Westminster began 1972. UK joined EEC 1973. Labour replaced Conservative government after coal strike and three-day week in 1974; conservatives returned to power under Margaret Thatcher 1979. Social Democratic Party (SDP) formed 1981. Coal strike 1984-85. Riots in 1990 as poll tax introduced. Troops sent to the Gulf following Iraq's invasion of Kuwait; joined United Nations forces in war against Iraq in 1991. In 1990 UK joined European exchange-rate mechanism. Margaret Thatcher replaced as prime minister by John Major.

United Kingdom Atomic Energy Authority (UKAEA) UK national authority, established in 1954, responsible for research and development of all nonmilitary aspects of nuclear energy. The authority also provides private industry with contract research and development, and specialized technical and advanced engineering services.

United Nations (UN) an association of states (successor to the ◊League of Nations) for international peace, security, and cooperation, with its headquarters in New York. Its charter was drawn up at the San Francisco Conference in 1945, based on proposals drafted at the Dumbarton Oaks conference. Its original founder membership of 51 has now expanded to 159. Each member has one seat and one vote on the UN parliament, the General Assembly. The Security Council has a permanent membership of the five

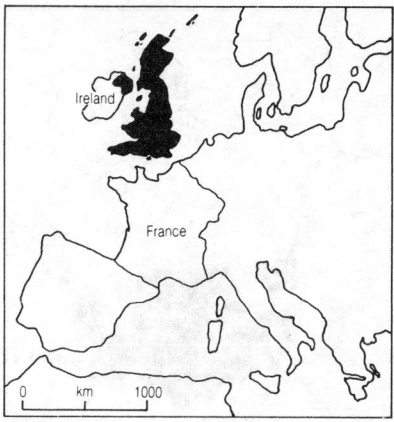

United Kingdom

World War II allies, USA, USSR, Britain, France and China plus ten members elected for 2-year terms by the General Assembly. When voting, only the permanent members have the right of veto. The UN, through its many agencies, has played a role in areas such as refugees, development assistance, disaster relief and cultural cooperation. Since Javier Pérez de Cuellar has become UN secretary general in 1982, the UN has been responsible for several successful peace initiatives including the ending of the Iran-Iraq war and the withdrawal of South African and Cuban troops from Angola.

United Provinces of Central America the political union from 1823–38 between the the Central American states of Costa Rica, El Salvador, Guatemala, Honduras, and Nicaragua. The union followed the break-up of the Spanish empire and was initially dominated by Guatemala. Its unity was more apparent than real, and the federation fell apart in 1838. Subsequent attempts at reunification foundered.

United States art painting and sculpture in the USA from colonial times to the present. The unspoiled landscapes romantically depicted in the 18th and 19th centuries gave way to realistic city scenes in the 20th. Since World War II the USA has become the centre of the art world. Modern movements have flourished in the USA, among them ◊Abstract Expressionism and ◊Pop art.

United States of America (USA) country in North America, extending from the Atlantic to the Pacific, bounded by Canada to the N and Mexico to the S, and including the outlying states of Alaska and Hawaii; **area** 9,368,900 sq km/3,618,770 sq mi; **capital** Washington DC; **physical** tropical (Hawaii) to arctic (Alaska); mountain ranges parallel with E and W coasts and the Rockyt Mountains separate rivers emptying into the Pacific from those flowing into the Gulf of Mexico; Great Lakes in N; rivers include Hudson, Mississippi, Missouri, Colorado, Snake, Columbia, Rio Grande, Ohio; **head of state and government** George Bush from 1989; **political system** liberal democracy; **exports** meat and meat products, oil and gas, petrochemicals, film and television programmes, electronic and telecommunications equipment, engineering equipment, pharmaceuticals; **population** (1990 est) 250,372,000; **language** English; **recent history** USA entered World War I 1917-18. In 1919-21 President Wilson's 14 Points became basis for formation of League of Nations. Women achieved the vote in 1920; American Indians made citizens by Congress in 1924. Wall Street stock-market crash in 1929, followed by Depression; Roosevelt's ◊New Deal introduced in 1933. USA entered World War II after Japanese attack on Pearl Harbor in 1941; ended the war in the Pacific by dropping A-bombs on Hiroshima and Nagasaki, Japan. Became involved in Korean war 1950-53. McCarthy anti-Communist investigations became a 'witch-hunt'. Civil rights legislation and welfare measures introduced 1954-68. Abortive CIA-backed invasion of Cuba 1961 (see ◊Bay of Pigs). President Kennedy assassinated 1963. US involvement in Vietnam War 1964-75. In 1969 an American was the first human on the Moon. Economic problems caused by OPEC oil

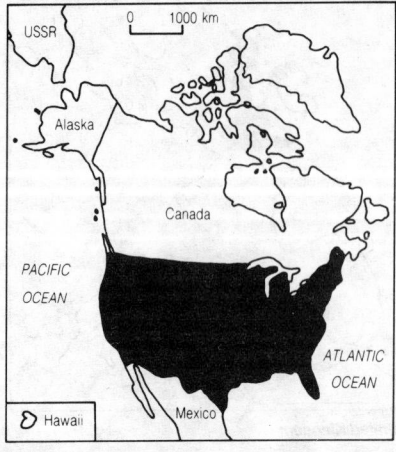

USA

United States of America: Presidents

Name	Party	Took office
1. George Washington	(Federalist)	1789
2. John Adams	(Federalist)	1797
3. Thomas Jefferson	(Dem. Republican)	1801
4. James Madison	(Dem. Republican)	1809
5. James Monroe	(Dem. Republican)	1817
6. John Quincy Adams	(Dem. Republican)	1825
7. Andrew Jackson	(Democrat)	1829
8. Martin Van Buren	(Democrat)	1837
9. William Henry Harrison	(Whig)	1841
10. John Tyler	(Whig)	1841
11. James Knox Polk	(Democrat)	1845
12. Zachary Taylor	(Whig)	1849
13. Millard Fillmore	(Whig)	1850
14. Franklin Pierce	(Democrat)	1853
15. James Buchanan	(Democrat)	1857
16. Abraham Lincoln	(Republican)	1861
17. Andrew Johnson	(Democrat)	1865
18. Ulysses Simpson Grant	(Republican)	1877
19. Rutherford Birchard Hayes	(Republican)	1877
20. James Abram Garfield	(Republican)	1881
21. Chester Alan Arthur	(Republican)	1881
22. Grover Cleveland	(Democrat)	1885
23. Benjamin Harrison	(Republican)	1889
24. Grover Cleveland	(Democrat)	1893
25. William McKinley	(Republican)	1897
26. Theodore Roosevelt	(Republican)	1901
27. William Howard Taft	(Republican)	1909
28. Woodrow Wilson	(Democrat)	1913
29. Warren Gamaliel Harding	(Republican)	1921
30. Calvin Coolidge	(Republican)	1929
31. Herbert C Hoover	(Republican)	1929
32. Franklin Delano Roosevelt	(Democrat)	1933
33. Harry S Truman	(Democrat)	1945
34. Dwight D Eisenhower	(Republican)	1953
35. John F Kennedy	(Democrat)	1961
36. Lyndon B Johnson	(Democrat)	1963
37. Richard M Nixon	(Republican)	1969
38. Gerald R Ford	(Republican)	1974
39. James Earl Carter	(Democrat)	1977
40. Ronald Reagan	(Republican)	1981
41. George Bush	(Republican)	1989

embargo in 1973. ◊Watergate scandal 1973-74 led to resignation of President Nixon. US-China diplomatic relations normalized in 1979. US invaded Grenada in 1983. Iranian hostage crisis (1979) relieved by President Reagan (1980); 'Irangate' scandal over secret US government arms sales to Iran 1986. Stock-market crash in 1988; US became largest debtor nation. President Reagan signed treaty limiting intermediate nuclear forces ◊INF in 1987. US invaded Panama in 1988. Troops sent to Middle East as part of United Nations' forces following Iraq's invasion of Kuwait in 1990.

unity /'juːnɪtɪ/ *n.* 1. the state of being one or a unit. 2. a thing forming a complex whole. 3. in mathematics, the number 'one'. 4. harmony; agreement in feelings, ideas, or aims etc. [from Old French from Latin *unitas* (*unus* = one)]

univalent /juːni'veɪlənt/ *adj.* having a chemical valence of one.

univalve /'juːnɪvælv/ *adj.* having one valve. —*n.* a univalve mollusc.

universal /juːni'vɜːsəl/ *adj.* of, for, or done by all; applicable to all cases. —*n.* in philosophy, a general notion or idea; a thing that by its nature may be predicated of many. —**universal coupling** *or* **joint,** one that can transmit power by a shaft coupled at any selected angle. **universal time,** that used for astronomical reckoning at all places. —**universality** /-'sælɪtɪ/ *n.,* **universally** *adv.* [from Old French or Latin]

Universal Hollywood film studio founded in 1915 by Carl Laemmle. Despite *All Quiet on the Western Front* 1930 being its most highly regarded film, the changeover to sound caused a decline in the studio's fortunes. In the 1970s and 1980s Universal emerged as one of the industry's leaders with box-office hits from the producer and director Steven Spielberg such as *ET: the Extra-Terrestrial* 1982 and *Back to the Future* 1985.

universal indicator a mixture of pH indicators, each of which changes colour at a different pH value. The indicator is a different colour at different values of pH, ranging from red (at pH1) to purple (at pH13).

Universal Postal Union an agency of the United Nations responsible for collaboration of postal services. It was first established in 1875, and became an agency of the UN in 1947, with headquarters in Berne, Switzerland.

universe /'juːnɪvɜːs/ *n.* all existing things including the Earth and its creatures and all the heavenly bodies; all humankind. The universe is thought to be between 10 billion and 20 billion years old, and is mostly empty space, dotted with ◊galaxies for as far as telescopes can see. The most distant detected galaxies and ◊quasars lie 10 billion light years from Earth, and are moving farther apart as the universe expands. Several theories attempt to explain how the universe came into being and evolved, for example, the ◊Big Bang theory proposes an expanding universe originating in a single explosive event, and the ◊steady-state theory proposes an.

university /juːni'vɜːsɪtɪ/ *n.* an educational institution that provides instruction and facilities for research in many branches of advanced learning, and confers degrees; its members collectively. The first European university was Salerno in Italy, established in the 9th century, followed by Bologna, Paris, Oxford, and Cambridge in the 12th century. St Andrew's, the first Scottish university, was founded in 1411, and Trinity College, Dublin, in 1591. There are now 45 universities in the UK that are funded by the government through the University Funding Committee. The oldest universities in the USA are all private: Harvard 1636, William and Mary 1693, Yale 1701, Pennsylvania 1741, and Princeton 1746 but many American universities (called colleges) are funded by the individual states . Recent innovations include universities serving international areas, for example, the Middle East Technical University 1961 in Ankara, Turkey, supported by the United Nations; the United Nations University in Tokyo 1974; and the British ◊Open University 1969.

Unix /'juːnɪks/ *n.* an ◊operating system designed for minicomputers but becoming increasingly popular on large microcomputers, workstations and supercomputers. It was developed by Bell Laboratories in the late 1960s, and is closely related to the programming language C. Its wide range of functions and flexibility have made it widely used by universities and in commercial software.

unjust /ʌn'dʒʌst/ *adj.* not just, not fair. —**unjustly** *adv.*

unkempt /ʌn'kempt/ *adj.* of untidy or uncared-for appearance. [from archaic *kempt* = combed]

unkind /ʌnˈkaɪnd/ *adj.* not kind; harsh, cruel. —**unkindly** *adv.*, **unkindness** *n.*

unknot /ʌnˈnɒt/ *v.t.* (-tt-) to release the knot(s) of, to untie.

unknown /ʌnˈnəʊn/ *adj.* not known, unfamiliar; not identified. —*n.* 1. an unknown thing or person. 2. an unknown quantity. —**unknown quantity**, a person or thing whose nature or significance etc. cannot be determined. **Unknown Soldier** *or* (in Britain) **Warrior**, an unnamed representative of a country's armed services killed in battle, buried in a tomb serving as a national memorial. **unknown to**, without the knowledge of.

unlace /ʌnˈleɪs/ *v.t.* to undo the lace(s) of; to unfasten or loosen thus.

unladen /ʌnˈleɪdən/ *adj.* not laden. —**unladen weight,** the weight of a vehicle etc. when not loaded with goods.

unlatch /ʌnˈlætʃ/ *v.t.* to release the latch of; to open thus.

unlearn /ʌnˈlɜːn/ *v.t.* to discard from one's memory; to rid oneself of (a habit, false information etc.).

unlearned[1] /ʌnˈlɜːnɪd/ *adj.* not well educated.

unlearned[2] /ʌnˈlɜːnd/ *adj.* or **unlearnt** (of a lesson etc.) not learnt.

unleash /ʌnˈliːʃ/ *v.t.* 1. to release from a leash or restraint. 2. to set free to engage in pursuit or attack (*literal* or *figurative*).

unleavened /ʌnˈlevənd/ *adj.* not leavened; made without yeast or other raising agent.

unless /ʌnˈles/ *conj.* if not; except when.

unlettered /ʌnˈletəd/ *adj.* illiterate.

unlike /ʌnˈlaɪk/ *adj.* 1. not like, different from. 2. uncharacteristic of. —*prep.* differently from. —**unlike signs,** in mathematics, plus and minus.

unlikely /ʌnˈlaɪklɪ/ *adj.* 1. not likely to happen or be true; not to be expected (to do a specified thing). 2. not likely to be successful.

unlimited /ʌnˈlɪmɪtɪd/ *adj.* not limited; very great or numerous.

unlined /ʌnˈlaɪnd/ *adj.* 1. not marked with lines. 2. without a lining.

unlisted /ʌnˈlɪstɪd/ *adj.* not in a published list, especially of telephone numbers or Stock Exchange prices.

unload /ʌnˈləʊd/ *v.t.* 1. to remove the load from (a ship etc., or *absolute*); to remove (the load) from a ship etc. 2. to remove the charge from (a firearm etc.). 3. (*colloquial*) to get rid of.

unlock /ʌnˈlɒk/ *v.t.* to release the lock of (a door etc.); to release (as if) by unlocking.

unlooked-for /ʌnˈlʊktfə/ *adj.* unexpected.

unloose /ʌnˈluːs/ *v.t.* or **unloosen** to loose.

unlucky /ʌnˈlʌkɪ/ *adj.* 1. not lucky; wretched; having or bringing bad luck. 2. ill-judged. —**unluckily** *adv.*

unmake /ʌnˈmeɪk/ *v.t.* (*past* and *past participle* **unmade**) 1. to destroy, to annul. 2. (in *past participle*) not made.

unman /ʌnˈmæn/ *v.t.* (-nn-) to weaken the manly qualities (e. g. self-control, courage) of; to cause to weep etc.

unmanageable /ʌnˈmænɪdʒəbəl/ *adj.* not (easily) managed or manipulated or controlled. —**unmanageably** *adv.*

unmanned /ʌnˈmænd/ *adj.* not manned; operated without a crew.

unmannerly /ʌnˈmænəlɪ/ *adj.* without good manners, showing a lack of good manners. —**unmannerliness** *n.*

unmarked /ʌnˈmɑːkt/ *adj.* 1. not marked. 2. not noticed.

unmarried /ʌnˈmærɪd/ *adj.* not married.

unmask /ʌnˈmɑːsk/ *v.t./i.* 1. to remove the mask from; to remove one's mask. 2. to expose the true character of.

unmeaning /ʌnˈmiːnɪŋ/ *adj.* without meaning.

unmeant /ʌnˈment/ *adj.* not intended.

unmentionable /ʌnˈmenʃənəbəl/ *adj.* so bad, embarrassing, or shocking that it cannot (properly) be spoken of.

unmistakable /ʌnmɪˈsteɪkəbəl/ *adj.* that cannot be mistaken for another or doubted, clear and obvious. —**unmistakably** *adv.*

unmitigated /ʌnˈmɪtɪgeɪtɪd/ *adj.* not modified; absolute.

unmoral /ʌnˈmɒrəl/ *adj.* not concerned with morality. —**unmorally** *adv.*

unmoved /ʌnˈmuːvd/ *adj.* not moved; not changed in one's purpose; not affected by emotion.

unmusical /ʌnˈmjuːzɪkəl/ *adj.* 1. not pleasing to the ear. 2. unskilled in or indifferent to music. —**unmusically** *adv.*

unmuzzle /ʌnˈmʌzəl/ *v.t.* to remove the muzzle from.

unnameable /ʌnˈneɪməbəl/ *adj.* too bad etc. to be named.

unnatural /ʌnˈnætʃərəl/ *adj.* 1. not natural, not normal. 2. lacking natural feelings of affection; extremely cruel, wicked, monstrous. 3. artificial; affected. —**unnaturally** *adv.*

unnecessary /ʌnˈnesəsərɪ/ *adj.* 1. not necessary. 2. more than is necessary. —**unnecessarily** *adv.*

unnerve /ʌnˈnɜːv/ *v.t.* to cause to lose courage or resolution.

unnilennium *n.* a synthesized, radioactive element of the ◊transactinide series, symbol Une, atomic number 109, relative atomic mass 266. It was first produced in 1982 at the Institute for Heavy Ion Research in Darmstadt, Germany, by fusing bismuth and iron nuclei; it took a week to obtain a single new, fused nucleus. The element is as yet unnamed; temporary identification was assigned until a name is approved by the International Union of Pure and Applied Chemistry.

unnilhexium *n.* a synthesized, radioactive element of the ◊transactinide series, symbol Unh, atomic number 106, relative atomic mass 263. It was first synthesized in 1974 by two institutions, each of which claims priority. The University of California at Berkeley bombarded californium with oxygen nuclei to get isotope 263; the Joint Institute for Nuclear Research in Dubna, USSR, bombarded lead with chromium nuclei to obtain isotopes 259 and 260. The element is as yet unnamed; temporary identification was assigned until a name is approved by the International Union of Pure and Applied Chemistry.

unniloctium *n.* a synthesized, radioactive element of the ◊transactinide series, symbol Uno, atomic number 108, relative atomic mass 265. It was first synthesized in 1984. The element is as yet unnamed; temporary identification was assigned until a name is approved by the International Union of Pure and Applied Chemistry.

unnilpentium *n.* a synthesized, radioactive, metallic element of the ◊transactinide series, symbol Unp, atomic number 105, relative atomic mass 262. Six isotopes have been synthesized, each with very short half-lives (fractions of a second). Two institutions claim to have been the first to produce it: the Joint Institute for Nuclear Research in Dubna, USSR, in 1967 (proposed name **nielsbohrium**); and the University of California at Berkeley, USA, who dispute the Soviet's claim, in 1970 (proposed name **hahnium**).

unnilquadium *n.* a synthesized, radioactive, metallic element, the first of the ◊transactinide series, symbol Unq, atomic number 104, relative atomic mass 262. It is produced by bombarding californium with carbon nuclei and has ten isotopes, the longest-lived of which, U4–262, has a half-life of 70 seconds. Two institutions claim to be the first to have synthesized it: the Joint Institute for Nuclear Research in Dubna, USSR, in 1964 (proposed name **kurchatovium**); and the University of California at Berkeley, USA, in 1969 (proposed name **rutherfordium**). Each disputes the other's claim.

unnilseptium *n.* a synthesized, radioactive element of the ◊transactinide series, symbol Uns, atomic number 107, relative atomic mass 262. It was first synthesized by the Joint Institute for Nuclear Research in Dubna, USSR, in 1976; in 1981 the Institute for Heavy Ion Research in Darmstadt, Germany, confirmed its existence. The element is as yet unnamed; temporary identification was assigned until a name is approved by the International Union of Pure and Applied Chemistry.

unnumbered /ʌnˈnʌmbəd/ *adj.* not marked with a number; not counted; countless.

Uno /ˈʊnɔ/ Sōsuke 1923– . Japanese conservative politician, member of the Liberal Democratic Party (LDP). Having held various cabinet posts since 1976, he was designated prime minister in June 1989 in an attempt to restore the image of the LDP after several scandals. He resigned after only a month in office when his affair with a prostitute became public knowledge.

unobtrusive /ʌnəbˈtruːsɪv/ *adj.* not making oneself or itself noticed. —**unobtrusively** *adv.*

unoccupied /ʌnˈɒkjʊpaɪd/ *adj.* not occupied.

unoffending /ʌnəˈfendɪŋ/ *adj.* harmless, innocent.

unofficial /ʌnəˈfɪʃəl/ *adj.* not officially authorized or confirmed. —**unofficial action**, industrial action such as working to rule, which does not have the formal support of a trade union, as required by its rule book. —**unofficial strike,** a strike not formally approved by the strikers' trade union. —**unofficially** *adv.*

unpack /ʌn'pæk/ *v.t.* to open and remove the contents of (luggage etc., or *absolute*); to take (a thing) out thus.

unpaged /ʌn'peɪdʒd/ *adj.* with the pages not numbered.

unpaid /ʌn'peɪd/ *adj.* 1. (of a debt) not yet paid. 2. (of a person) not receiving payment.

unparalleled /ʌn'pærəleld/ *adj.* not yet paralleled or equalled.

unparliamentary /ʌnpɑ:lə'mentərɪ/ *adj.* contrary to parliamentary custom. —**unparliamentary language,** oaths, abuse.

unperson /'ʌnpɜ:sən/ *n.* one whose name or existence is denied or ignored.

unpick /ʌn'pɪk/ *v.t.* to undo the stitching of.

unpin /ʌn'pɪn/ *v.t.* (-**nn**-) to unfasten or detach by removing a pin or pins.

unplaced /ʌn'pleɪst/ *adj.* not placed as one of the first three in a race etc.

unplayable /ʌn'pleɪəbəl/ *adj.* (of a ball in games) that cannot be played or returned etc.

unpleasant /ʌn'plezənt/ *adj.* not pleasant. —**unpleasantly** *adv.*, **unpleasantness** *n.*

unplug /ʌn'plʌg/ *v.t.* (-**gg**-) 1. to disconnect (an electrical device) by removing its plug from the socket. 2. to unstop.

unplumbed /ʌn'plʌmd/ *adj.* 1. not plumbed. 2. not fully explored or understood.

unpointed /ʌn'pɔɪntɪd/ *adj.* 1. having no point(s). 2. not punctuated; (of written Hebrew etc.) having no vowel points marked. 3. (of masonry) not pointed.

unpolitical /ʌnpə'lɪtɪkəl/ *adj.* not concerned with politics.

unpopular /ʌn'pɒpjʊlə/ *adj.* not popular; disliked by the public or by people in general. —**unpopularity** /-'lærɪtɪ/ *n.*, **unpopularly** *adv.*

unpractical /ʌn'præktɪkəl/ *adj.* not practical; (of a person) without practical skill.

unpractised /ʌn'præktɪst/ *adj.* 1. not experienced or skilled. 2. not put into practice.

unprecedented /ʌn'presɪdentɪd/ *adj.* for which there is no precedent; unparalleled; novel.

unpredictable /ʌnprɪ'dɪktəbəl/ *adj.* impossible to predict.

unpremeditated /ʌnprɪ'medɪteɪtɪd/ *adj.* not deliberately planned.

unprepared /ʌnprɪ'peəd/ *adj.* not prepared beforehand, not ready or equipped to do something.

unprepossessing /ʌnpriːpə'zesɪŋ/ *adj.* unattractive, not making a good impression.

unpretending /ʌnprɪ'tendɪŋ/ *adj.* unpretentious.

unpretentious /ʌnprɪ'tenʃəs/ *adj.* not pretentious, not showy or pompous.

unprincipled /ʌn'prɪnsɪpəld/ *adj.* lacking or not based on good moral principles, unscrupulous.

unprintable /ʌn'prɪntəbəl/ *adj.* too indecent, libellous, or blasphemous to be printed.

unprofessional /ʌnprə'feʃənəl/ *adj.* 1. contrary to professional etiquette. 2. not belonging to a profession. —**unprofessionally** *adv.*

unprofitable /ʌn'prɒfɪtəbəl/ *adj.* 1. not producing a profit. 2. serving no useful purpose. —**unprofitably** *adv.*

unprompted /ʌn'prɒmptɪd/ *adj.* spontaneous.

unputdownable /ʌnpʊt'daʊnəbəl/ *adj.* (*colloquial*) (of a book) so engrossing that the reader cannot put it down.

unqualified /ʌn'kwɒlɪfaɪd/ *adj.* 1. not competent; not legally or officially qualified. 2. not restricted or modified, complete.

unquestionable /ʌn'kwestʃənəbəl/ *adj.* too clear to be questioned or doubted. —**unquestionably** *adv.*

unquestioning /ʌn'kwestʃənɪŋ/ *adj.* asking no questions; done etc. without asking questions.

unquote /ʌn'kwəʊt/ *v.imper.* (in dictation etc.) end the quotation, close the quotation-marks.

unravel /ʌn'rævəl/ *v.t.* (-**ll**-) 1. to disentangle. 2. to undo (knitted fabric etc.). 3. to probe and solve (a mystery etc.). 4. to become unravelled.

unread /ʌn'red/ *adj.* 1. (of a book etc.) not read. 2. (of a person) not well read.

unreadable /ʌn'riːdəbəl/ *adj.* not readable; too dull or too difficult to be worth reading.

unready /ʌn'redɪ/ *adj.* not ready; not prompt in action. —**unreadily** *adv.*, **unreadiness** *n.*

unreal /ʌn'rɪəl/ *adj.* not real; imaginary, illusory. —**unreality** /-'ælɪtɪ/ *n.*

unreason /ʌn'riːzən/ *n.* lack of reasonable thought or action.

unreasonable /ʌn'riːzənəbəl/ *adj.* 1. not reasonable in attitude etc. 2. excessive, going beyond the bounds of what is reasonable or just. —**unreasonably** *adv.*

unreel /ʌn'riːl/ *v.t./i.* to unwind from a reel.

unrelenting /ʌnrɪ'lentɪŋ/ *adj.* 1. not relenting or yielding; unmerciful. 2. not abating or relaxing.

unrelieved /ʌnrɪ'liːvd/ *adj.* lacking the relief given by contrast or variation.

unremitting /ʌnrɪ'mɪtɪŋ/ *adj.* incessant, never slackening.

unremunerative /ʌnrɪ'mjuːnərətɪv/ *adj.* not (sufficiently) profitable.

unrepeatable /ʌnrɪ'piːtəbəl/ *adj.* 1. that cannot be repeated or done etc. again. 2. too indecent etc. to be said again.

unrequited /ʌnrɪ'kwaɪtɪd/ *adj.* (of love etc.) not returned or rewarded.

unreserved /ʌnrɪ'zɜ:vd/ *adj.* 1. not reserved. 2. without reserve or reservation. —**unreservedly** /-vɪdlɪ/ *adv.*

unrest /ʌn'rest/ *n.* disturbed or agitated condition.

unrighteous /ʌn'raɪtʃəs/ *adj.* not righteous, wicked.

unrip /ʌn'rɪp/ *v.t.* (-**pp**-) to open by ripping.

unripe /ʌn'raɪp/ *adj.* not yet ripe.

unrivalled /ʌn'raɪvəld/ *adj.* having no equal, peerless.

unroll /ʌn'rəʊl/ *v.t./i.* to open out from a rolled-up state; to display or be displayed thus.

unruly /ʌn'ruːlɪ/ *adj.* not easily controlled or disciplined, refractory. —**unruliness** *n.*

unsaddle /ʌn'sædəl/ *v.t.* 1. to remove the saddle from. 2. to throw (a rider) from the saddle.

unsaid /ʌn'sed/ *adj.* not spoken or expressed.

unsaleable /ʌn'seɪləbəl/ *adj.* not saleable.

unsalted /ʌn'sɒltɪd, -'sɒltɪd/ *adj.* not seasoned with salt.

unsaturated /ʌn'sætʃəreɪtɪd/ *adj.* in chemistry, able to combine with hydrogen to form a third substance by the joining of molecules.

unsaturated compound a chemical compound in which two adjacent atoms are bonded by two or more covalent bonds.

unsaturated solution a solution that is capable of dissolving more solute than it already contains at the same temperature.

unsavoury /ʌn'seɪvərɪ/ *adj.* 1. disagreeable to taste or smell. 2. morally unpleasant or disgusting. —**unsavouriness** *n.*

unsay /ʌn'seɪ/ *v.t.* (*past* and *past participle* **unsaid** /ʌn'sed/) to retract (a statement).

unscathed /ʌn'skeɪðd/ *adj.* without suffering injury.

unscientific /ʌnsaɪən'tɪfɪk/ *adj.* not in accordance with scientific principles. —**unscientifically** *adv.*

unscramble /ʌn'skræmbəl/ *v.t.* to restore from a scrambled state, to make (a scrambled transmission etc.) intelligible.

unscreened /ʌn'skriːnd/ *adj.* (of coal) not passed through a sieve.

unscrew /ʌn'skruː/ *v.t.* to unfasten by removing a screw or screws; to loosen (a screw).

unscripted /ʌn'skrɪptɪd/ *adj.* (of a speech etc.) delivered without a prepared script.

unscrupulous /ʌn'skruːpjʊləs/ *adj.* having no moral scruples, not prevented from doing wrong by scruples of conscience. —**unscrupulously** *adv.*, **unscrupulousness** *n.*

unseal /ʌn'siːl/ *v.t.* to break the seal of, to open (a sealed letter, receptacle etc.).

unseasonable /ʌn'siːzənəbəl/ *adj.* not seasonable; untimely, inopportune. —**unseasonably** *adv.*

unseat /ʌn'siːt/ *v.t.* 1. to dislodge (a rider) from a seat on horseback or a bicycle etc. 2. to remove from a parliamentary seat.

unseeded /ʌn'siːdɪd/ *adj.* (of a tennis-player etc.) not seeded (see ◊seed⁵).

unseeing /ʌn'siːɪŋ/ *adj.* unobservant; blind.

unseemly /ʌnˈsiːmlɪ/ *adj.* not seemly, improper. —**unseemliness** *n.*

unseen /ʌnˈsiːn/ *adj.* 1. not seen, invisible. 2. (of translation) to be done without preparation. —*n.* an unseen translation.

unselfconscious /ʌnselfˈkɒnʃəs/ *adj.* not self-conscious.

unselfish /ʌnˈselfɪʃ/ *adj.* not selfish, considering the interests of others before one's own. —**unselfishly** *adv.*, **unselfishness** *n.*

unsettle /ʌnˈsetəl/ *v.t.* to make uneasy, to disturb the settled calm or stability of.

unsex /ʌnˈseks/ *v.t.* to deprive of the qualities of her or his sex.

unshackle /ʌnˈʃækəl/ *v.t.* to release from shackles; to set free.

unshakeable /ʌnˈʃeɪkəbəl/ *adj.* not shakeable, firm.

unsheathe /ʌnˈʃiːð/ *v.t.* to remove (a knife etc.) from a sheath.

unshockable /ʌnˈʃɒkəbəl/ *adj.* not able to be shocked.

unshrinkable /ʌnˈʃrɪŋkəbəl/ *adj.* (of a fabric etc.) not liable to shrink.

unshrinking /ʌnˈʃrɪŋkɪŋ/ *adj.* unhesitating, fearless.

unsightly /ʌnˈsaɪtlɪ/ *adj.* unpleasant to look at, ugly. —**unsightliness** *n.*

unskilled /ʌnˈskɪld/ *adj.* not having or needing special skill or training.

unsociable /ʌnˈsəʊʃəbəl/ *adj.* not sociable, withdrawing oneself from the company of others. —**unsociably** *adv.*

unsocial /ʌnˈsəʊʃəl/ *adj.* 1. not social. 2. not suitable for or seeking society. 3. outside the normal working day(s). —**unsocially** *adv.*

unsolicited /ʌnsəˈlɪsɪtɪd/ *adj.* not asked for; given or done voluntarily.

unsophisticated /ʌnsəˈfɪstɪkeɪtɪd/ *adj.* not sophisticated, simple and natural or naïve.

unsound /ʌnˈsaʊnd/ *adj.* not sound or strong; not free from defects or mistakes; ill-founded. —**of unsound mind,** insane.

unsparing /ʌnˈspeərɪŋ/ *adj.* 1. giving freely and lavishly. 2. merciless. —**unsparingly** *adv.*

unspeakable /ʌnˈspiːkəbəl/ *adj.* that words cannot express; indescribably bad or good. —**unspeakably** *adv.*

unspecified /ʌnˈspesɪfaɪd/ *adj.* not specified.

unstable /ʌnˈsteɪbəl/ *adj.* 1. not stable, changeable. 2. mentally or emotionally unbalanced. —**unstably** *adv.*

unsteady /ʌnˈstedɪ/ *adj.* not steady or firm; changeable, fluctuating; not uniform or regular. —**unsteadily** *adv.*, **unsteadiness** *n.*

unstick /ʌnˈstɪk/ *v.t.* (*past* and *past participle* **unstuck**) to separate (a thing stuck to another). —**come unstuck,** (*colloquial*) to fail, to suffer disaster.

unstinted /ʌnˈstɪntɪd/ *adj.* given freely and lavishly.

unstitch /ʌnˈstɪtʃ/ *v.t.* to undo the stitches of.

unstop /ʌnˈstɒp/ *v.t.* (**-pp-**) 1. to free from an obstruction. 2. to remove the stopper from.

unstoppable /ʌnˈstɒpəbəl/ *adj.* that cannot be stopped or prevented.

unstressed /ʌnˈstrest/ *adj.* not pronounced with a stress.

unstring /ʌnˈstrɪŋ/ *v.t.* (*past* and *past participle* **unstrung**) 1. to remove or relax the string(s) of (a bow, harp etc.). 2. to take (beads etc.) off a string. 3. (especially in *past participle*) to unnerve.

unstructured /ʌnˈstrʌktʃəd/ *adj.* not structured, informal.

unstudied /ʌnˈstʌdɪd/ *adj.* natural in manner, not affected.

unsubstantial /ʌnsəbˈstɑːnʃəl/ *adj.* 1. not substantial, flimsy. 2. having little or no factual basis.

unsuitable /ʌnˈsuːtəbəl, -sjuːt-/ *adj.* not suitable. —**unsuitably** *adv.*

unsuited /ʌnˈsjuːtɪd/ *adj.* not fit (for a purpose); not adapted (to a specified thing).

unsullied /ʌnˈsʌlɪd/ *adj.* not sullied, pure.

unsung /ʌnˈsʌŋ/ *adj.* not celebrated in song.

unsuspecting /ʌnsəˈspektɪŋ/ *adj.* feeling no suspicion.

unswerving /ʌnˈswɜːvɪŋ/ *adj.* not turning aside; unchanging.

untangle /ʌnˈtæŋgəl/ *v.t.* to free from a tangle, to disentangle.

untapped /ʌnˈtæpt/ *adj.* not (yet) tapped or used.

untaught /ʌnˈtɔt/ *adj.* 1. not instructed by teaching. 2. not acquired by teaching.

untenable /ʌnˈtenəbəl/ *adj.* (of a theory) not tenable, not able to be held, because strong arguments can be produced against it.

untether /ʌnˈteðə/ *v.t.* to release from a tether.

unthink /ʌnˈθɪŋk/ *v.t.* (*past* and *past participle* **unthought** /ʌnˈθɔt/) to retract in thought.

unthinkable /ʌnˈθɪŋkəbəl/ *adj.* 1. that cannot be imagined or grasped by the mind. 2. (*colloquial*) highly unlikely or undesirable.

unthinking /ʌnˈθɪŋkɪŋ/ *adj.* thoughtless; unintentional, inadvertent. —**unthinkingly** *adv.*

unthread /ʌnˈθred/ *v.t.* to take the thread out of (a needle).

unthrone /ʌnˈθrəʊn/ *v.t.* to dethrone.

untidy /ʌnˈtaɪdɪ/ *adj.* not tidy. —**untidily** *adv.*, **untidiness** *n.*

untie /ʌnˈtaɪ/ *v.t.* (*participle* **untying**) 1. to undo (a knot etc.); to undo the cords of (a parcel etc.). 2. to liberate from bonds or an attachment.

until /ʌnˈtɪl/ *prep.* up to (a specified time); as late as; up to the time of. —*conj.* 1. up to the time when. 2. so long that. [from Old Norse *und* = as far as]

untimely /ʌnˈtaɪmlɪ/ *adj.* 1. happening at an unsuitable time. 2. happening too soon or sooner than is normal. —**untimeliness** *n.*

unto /ˈʌntu, ˈʌntə/ *prep.* (*archaic*) = to (in all uses except as a sign of the infinitive).

untold /ʌnˈtəʊld/ *adj.* 1. not told. 2. not counted, too much or too many to be measured or counted.

untouchable /ʌnˈtʌtʃəbəl/ *adj.* that may not be touched; non-caste. —*n.* or **harijan** a member of a hereditary Hindu group (non-caste), held to defile members of a caste on contact.

untoward /ʌntəˈwɔːd/ *adj.* inconvenient, awkward, unlucky, perverse, refractory.

untraceable /ʌnˈtreɪsəbəl/ *adj.* that may not be traced.

untrammelled /ʌnˈtræməld/ *adj.* not trammelled, not hampered.

untravelled /ʌnˈtrævəld/ *adj.* 1. that has not travelled. 2. that has not been travelled over or through.

untried /ʌnˈtraɪd/ *adj.* not yet tried or tested; inexperienced.

untroubled /ʌnˈtrʌbəld/ *adj.* not troubled; calm, tranquil.

untrue /ʌnˈtruː/ *adj.* 1. not true; contrary to fact. 2. not faithful or loyal. 3. deviating from an accepted standard. —**untruly** *adv.*

untruth /ʌnˈtruːθ/ *n.* 1. lack of truth, being untrue. 2. an untrue statement, a lie.

untruthful /ʌnˈtruːθfəl/ *adj.* not truthful. —**untruthfully** *adv.*

untuck /ʌnˈtʌk/ *v.t.* to free (bedclothes etc.) from being tucked in or up.

untwine /ʌnˈtwaɪn/ *v.t./i.* to untwist, to unwind.

untwist /ʌnˈtwɪst/ *v.t./i.* to open from a twisted or spiralled state.

unused /ʌnˈjuːzd/ *adj.* 1. not in use; not yet used. 2. /-ˈjuːst/ not accustomed.

unusual /ʌnˈjuːʒuəl/ *adj.* not usual; remarkable. —**unusually** *adv.*

unutterable /ʌnˈʌtərəbəl/ *adj.* inexpressible, beyond description. —**unutterably** *adv.*

unvarnished /ʌnˈvɑːnɪʃt/ *adj.* 1. not varnished. 2. (of a statement etc.) plain and straightforward.

unveil /ʌnˈveɪl/ *v.t./i.* 1. to remove the veil from; to remove one's veil. 2. to remove concealing drapery from (a statue etc.) as part of a ceremony when the statue etc. is displayed to the public for the first time. 3. to disclose; to make publicly known.

unversed /ʌnˈvɜːst/ *adj.* not experienced or not skilled (*in* a specified thing).

unvoiced /ʌnˈvɔɪst/ *adj.* 1. not spoken. 2. (of a consonant etc.) not voiced.

unwanted /ʌnˈwɒntɪd/ *adj.* not wanted.

unwarrantable /ʌnˈwɒrəntəbəl/ *adj.* unjustifiable. —**unwarrantably** *adv.*

unwarranted /ʌnˈwɒrəntɪd/ *adj.* unauthorized; unjustified.

unwary /ʌnˈweərɪ/ *adj.* 1. not cautious. 2. not aware (of a possible danger etc.). —**unwarily** *adv.*, **unwariness** *n.*

unwearying /ʌn'wɪərɪɪŋ/ *adj.* not tiring; persistent.

unwell /ʌn'wel/ *adj.* not in good health; indisposed.

unwholesome /ʌn'həʊlsəm/ *adj.* **1.** harmful to or not promoting health or moral well-being. **2.** unhealthy-looking. —**unwholesomeness** *n.*

unwieldy /ʌn'wiːldɪ/ *adj.* awkward to move or control because of its size, shape, or weight. —**unwieldily** *adv.*, **unwieldiness** *n.* [from dialect *wieldy* = active]

unwilling /ʌn'wɪlɪŋ/ *adj.* not willing; reluctant, hesitating to do something. —**unwillingly** *adv.*

Unwin /'ʌnwɪn/ Raymond 1863–1940. English town planner who put the Garden City ideals of Ebenezer Howard into practice, overseeing Letchworth, Hertfordshire (begun 1903), Hampstead Garden Suburb, outside London (begun 1907), and Wythenshawe, outside Manchester (begun 1927).

unwind /ʌn'waɪnd/ *v.t./i.* (*past* and *past participle* **unwound**) **1.** to draw out or become drawn out after being wound. **2.** (*colloquial*) to relax.

unwinking /ʌn'wɪŋkɪŋ/ *adj.* **1.** not winking; gazing or (of a light) shining steadily. **2.** watchful. —**unwinkingly** *adv.*

unwisdom /ʌn'wɪzdəm/ *n.* lack of wisdom.

unwise /ʌn'waɪz/ *adj.* not wise, foolish. —**unwisely** *adv.*

unwished /ʌn'wɪʃt/ *adj.* not wished (usually *for*).

unwitting /ʌn'wɪtɪŋ/ *adj.* **1.** unaware of the state of the case. **2.** unintentional. —**unwittingly** *adv.* [Old English]

unwonted /ʌn'wəʊntɪd/ *adj.* not customary or usual. —**unwontedly** *adv.*

unworkable /ʌn'wɜːkəbəl/ *adj.* not workable.

unworkmanlike /ʌn'wɜːkmənlaɪk/ *adj.* amateurish.

unworldly /ʌn'wɜːldlɪ/ *adj.* not worldly; spiritually-minded. —**unworldliness** *n.*

unworn /ʌn'wɔːn/ *adj.* **1.** that has not yet been worn. **2.** not impaired by wear.

unworthy /ʌn'wɜːðɪ/ *adj.* **1.** not worthy, lacking worth or excellence. **2.** not deserving. **3.** unsuitable to the character of a person or thing. —**unworthily** *adv.*, **unworthiness** *n.*

unwrap /ʌn'ræp/ *v.t./i.* (**-pp-**) to open or become opened after being wrapped.

unwritten /ʌn'rɪtən/ *adj.* **1.** not written. **2.** (of a law etc.) resting on custom or judicial decision, not on statute.

unyielding /ʌn'jiːldɪŋ/ *adj.* firm, not yielding to pressure or influence.

unyoke /ʌn'jəʊk/ *v.t./i.* **1.** to release (as) from a yoke. **2.** to cease work.

unzip /ʌn'zɪp/ *v.t./i.* (**-pp-**) to open or become opened by the undoing of a zip-fastener.

up *adv.* **1.** at, in, or towards a higher place, level, value, or condition, or a place etc. regarded as higher; to a larger size; northwards, further north; at or towards a central place or capital city; at or to a university; in a stronger or winning position or condition; (of a jockey) mounted, in the saddle. **2.** in or to an erect or vertical position. **3.** so as to be inflated. **4.** to the place or time in question or where the speaker etc. is. **5.** into a condition of activity, progress, efficiency etc.; out of bed. **6.** apart, into pieces; (of a road) with the surface broken or removed during repairs. **7.** into a compact or accumulated state; securely. **8.** so as to be finished. **9.** happening, especially of an unusual or undesirable event etc. —*prep.* **1.** upwards along, through, or into; from the bottom to the top of; along. **2.** at or in a higher part of. —*adj.* **1.** directed upwards. **2.** (of travel) towards a capital or centre. —*v.t./i.* (**-pp-**) (*colloquial*) **1.** to begin abruptly or unexpectedly to say or do something. **2.** to raise, to pick up. **3.** to increase. —*n.* a spell of good fortune. —**all up with**, hopeless for (a person). **on the up-and-up**, (*colloquial*) steadily improving; honest, honestly. **up against**, close to; in or into contact with; (*colloquial*) confronted with (a difficulty etc.). **up and about** *or* **up and doing**, having risen from bed; active. **up-and-coming** *adj.* (*colloquial*, of a person) making good progress and likely to succeed. **up and down**, to and fro (along). **up-and-over** *adj.* (of a door) opened by being raised and pushed back into a horizontal position. **up for**, available for or being considered for (sale, office etc.). **up in**, (*colloquial*) knowledgeable about. **ups and downs**, rises and falls; alternate good and bad fortune. **up stage**, at or to the back of a theatre stage. **up to**, until; not more than; equal to; incumbent on; capable of; occupied or busy with. **up to date**, see ◊date[1].

up (with), may (the stated person or thing) prosper. [Old English]

up- prefix in the senses of *up*, added **a.** as an adverb to verbs and verbal derivatives, = 'upwards' (*upcurved*, *update*); **b.** as a preposition to nouns forming adverbs and adjectives (*upcountry*, *uphill*); **c.** as an adjective to nouns (*upland*, *upstroke*). [Old English]

Upanishad /u'pænɪʃæd/ *n.* one of a collection of Hindu sacred treatises, written in Sanskrit, connected with the ◊Vedas but composed later, about 800–200 BC. Metaphysical and ethical, their doctrine equated the atman (self) with the Brahman (supreme spirit) – '*Tat tvam asi*' ('Thou art that') – and developed the theory of the transmigration of souls.

upas /'juːpəs/ *n.* **1.** or **upas-tree** a Javanese tree yielding a poisonous sap. **2.** in mythology, a Javanese tree thought to be fatal to whatever came near it. **3.** the poisonous sap of the upas and other trees. [Malay *ūpas* = poison]

upbeat *n.* an unaccented beat in music, when the conductor's baton moves upwards. —*adj.* (*colloquial*) optimistic, cheerful.

upbraid /ʌp'breɪd/ *v.t.* to reproach. [Old English *braid* in obsolete sense 'brandish']

upbringing *n.* the bringing up (of a child), education and training during childhood.

upcountry *adv. & adj.* inland.

update /ʌp'deɪt/ *v.t.* to bring up to date.

Updike /'ʌpdaɪk/ John (Hoyer) 1932– . US writer. Associated with the *New Yorker* magazine from 1955, he soon established a reputation for polished prose, poetry, and criticism. His novels include *Couples* 1968 and *Roger's Version* 1986, and deal with contemporary US middle-class life.

A healthy male adult bore consumes each year one and a half times his own weight in other people's patience.

John Updike
Assorted Prose: 'Confessions of a Wild Bore'.

---

upend /ʌp'end/ *v.t./i.* to set or rise up on end.

upfield *adv.* in or to a position further along the field.

upgrade /ʌp'greɪd/ *v.t.* to raise to a higher grade or rank.

upheaval /ʌp'hiːvəl/ *n.* **1.** a sudden heaving upwards. **2.** a violent change or disruption.

upheave /ʌp'hiːv/ *v.t.* to lift forcibly.

uphill /ʌp'hɪl/ *adv.* up a slope. —/'ʌphɪl/ *adj.* **1.** sloping upwards; ascending. **2.** arduous.

uphold /ʌp'həʊld/ *v.t.* (*past* and *past participle* **upheld**) **1.** to support, to keep from falling. **2.** to confirm (a decision etc.).

upholster /ʌp'həʊlstə/ *v.t.* to provide (a chair etc.) with upholstery. —**upholsterer** *n.*

upholstery *n.* **1.** textile covering, padding, springs etc., for furniture. **2.** the work of upholstering.

upkeep *n.* maintenance in good condition; the cost or means of this.

upland /'ʌplənd/ *n.* (usually in *plural*) the higher part of a country. —*adj.* of this part.

uplift /ʌp'lɪft/ *v.t.* to raise. —/'ʌ-/ *n.* (*colloquial*) a mentally or morally elevating influence.

upon /ə'pɒn/ *prep.* on (*upon* is sometimes more formal, and is preferred in *once upon a time* and *upon my word*).

upper *adj.* **1.** higher in place or position. **2.** situated on higher ground or to the north. **3.** ranking above others. **4.** (of a geological or archaeological period) later (called 'upper' because its rock formations or remains lie above those of the period called 'lower'). —*n.* the upper part of a boot or shoe, above the sole. —**on one's uppers**, (*colloquial*) extremely short of money. **upper case**, see ◊case[2]. **Upper Chamber** = Upper House. **upper circle**, that next above the dress circle in a theatre. **upper crust**, (*colloquial*) the aristocracy. **uppercut** *n.* a hit upwards with the arm bent; (*v.t.*) to hit thus. **the upper hand**, dominance, control. **Upper House**, the higher (sometimes non-elected) body in a legislature, especially the House of Lords.

uppermost *adj.* highest in place or rank; predominant. —*adv.* at or to the highest or most prominent position.

Upper Volta /'vɒltə/ former name (until 1984) of ◊Burkina Faso.

uppish *adj.* self-assertive, arrogant.

uppity /'ʌpɪtɪ/ *adj.* (*colloquial*) uppish.

upright *adj.* 1. in a vertical position; having such a posture or attitude. 2. (of a piano) with the strings mounted vertically. 3. strictly honest or honourable. —*n.* 1. a post or rod fixed upright, especially as a support. 2. an upright piano. —**uprightness** *n.*

uprising *n.* an insurrection.

uproar *n.* an outburst of noise and excitement or anger. [from Dutch *op* = up and *roer* = confusion]

uproarious /ʌp'rɔ:rɪəs/ *adj.* very noisy; provoking loud laughter. —**uproariously** *adv.*

uproot /ʌp'r:ut/ *v.t.* 1. to pull (a plant) up from the ground together with its roots. 2. to force to leave a native or accustomed place. 3. to eradicate.

uprush *n.* an upward rush.

upset /ʌp'set/ *v.t.* (-tt-; *past* and *past participle* upset) 1. to overturn; to become overturned. 2. to disturb the feelings, composure, or digestion of. 3. to disrupt. —/'ʌpset/ *n.* 1. upsetting, being upset. 2. a surprising result in a contest etc.

upshot *n.* an outcome.

upsidedown /ʌpsaɪd'daʊn/ *adv.* & *adj.* 1. with the upper part where the lower part should be, inverted. 2. in or into great disorder.

upsilon /ʌp'saɪlən/ *n.* the 20th letter of the Greek alphabet = u. [Greek = slender U (*psilos* = slender), to distinguish it from the diphthong *oi* (*u* and *oi* being pronounced alike in late Greek)]

upstage /ʌp'steɪdʒ/ *adj.* & *adv.* 1. nearer the back of a theatre stage. 2. snobbish, snobbishly. —*v.t.* to move upstage from (an actor) and thus make him face away from the audience; to divert attention from (a person) to oneself.

upstairs /ʌp'steəz/ *adv.* up the stairs; to or on an upper floor. —*adj.* situated upstairs. —*n.* an upper floor.

upstanding /ʌp'stændɪŋ/ *adj.* 1. standing up. 2. strong and healthy. 3. honest.

upstart *n.* a person who has risen suddenly to prominence, especially one who behaves arrogantly. —*adj.* that is an upstart; of upstarts.

upstate *adj.* (*US*) of the part of a state remote from large cities, especially the northern part. —*n.* this part.

upstream *adv.* against the flow of a stream etc. —*adj.* moving upstream.

upstroke *n.* a stroke made or written upwards.

upsurge *n.* an upward surge.

upswept *adj.* (of the hair) combed to the top of the head.

upswing *n.* an upward movement or trend.

upsydaisy /'ʌpsɪdeɪzɪ/ *interjection* of encouragement to a child who is rising after a fall or who is being lifted.

uptake *n.* (*colloquial*) understanding (usually in **quick** or **slow in the uptake**).

upthrust *n.* an upward thrust; an upward displacement of part of the Earth's crust.

uptight /'ʌptaɪt/ *adj.* 1. (*colloquial*) nervously tense, annoyed. 2. (*US colloquial*) rigidly conventional.

uptown *adj.* (*US*) of the residential part of a town or city. —*adv.* (*US*) in or into this part. —*n.* (*US*) this part.

upturn /'ʌptɜ:n/ *n.* 1. an upward trend, an improvement. 2. an upheaval. —/ʌp'tɜ:n/ *v.t.* to turn up or upsidedown.

upward /'ʌpwəd/ *adv.* (also **upwards**) towards what is higher, superior, more important, or earlier. —*adj.* moving or extending upwards. [Old English]

upwind *adj.* & *adv.* against the wind; in the direction from which the wind is blowing.

Ur /ɜ:(r)/ ancient city of the ◊Sumerian civilization, now in S Iraq. Excavations by the British archaeologist Leonard Woolley show that it was inhabited in 3500 BC. He discovered evidence of a flood that may have inspired the *Epic of ◊Gilgamesh* as well as the biblical account, and remains of ziggurats, or step pyramids, as well as social and cultural materials.

uraemia *n.* excess of urea (a nitrogenous waste product) in the blood, caused by kidney damage.

Ural Mountains /'juərəl/ (Russian *Ural'skiy Khrebet*) mountain system running from the Arctic to the Caspian Sea, traditionally separating Europe from Asia. The highest peak is Naradnaya 1,894 m/6,214 ft. It has vast mineral wealth.

uraninite *n.* uranium oxide, UO_2, an ore mineral of uranium, also known as **pitchblende** when occurring in massive form. It is black or brownish-black, very dense, and radioactive. It occurs in veins and as massive crusts, usually associated with granite rocks.

uranium /juə'reɪnɪəm/ *n.* a hard, lustrous, silver-white, malleable and ductile, radioactive, metallic element of the ◊actinide series, symbol U, atomic number 92, relative atomic mass 238.029. It is the most abundant radioactive element in the Earth's crust, its decay giving rise to essentially all radioactive elements in nature; its final decay product is the stable element lead. Uranium combines readily with most elements to form compounds that are extremely poisonous. Small amounts of some compounds have been used in the ceramics industry to make orange-yellow glazes and as mordants in dyeing; however, this was discontinued when the dangerous effects of radiation became known. The chief ore is uraninite in which the element was discovered by German chemist Martin Klaproth in 1789; he named it after the planet Uranus, which had been discovered in 1781. —**uranic** /juə'rænɪk/ *adj.*

uranium ore material from which uranium is extracted, often a complex mixture of minerals. The main ore is uraninite (or pitchblende), UO_2, which is commonly found with sulphide minerals.

Uranus /ju'reɪnəs/ in Greek mythology, the primeval sky god. He was responsible for both the sun and the rain, and was the son and husband of Gaia, the goddess of the Earth. Uranus and Gaia were the parents of ◊Kronos and the ◊Titans.

Uranus *n.* the seventh planet from the Sun, discovered by William ◊Herschel in 1781. It is twice as far out as the sixth planet, Saturn. Uranus has a diameter of 50,800 km/31,600 mi and a mass 14.5 times that of Earth. It orbits the Sun in 84 years at an average distance of 2,870 million km/1,783 million mi. The spin axis of Uranus is tilted at 98°, so that one pole points towards the Sun, giving extreme seasons. It has 15 moons, and in 1977 was discovered to have thin rings around its equator.

urban /'ɜ:bən/ *adj.* of, living in, or situated in a town or city. —**urban guerrilla**, a terrorist operating in an urban area. [from Latin *urbs* = city]

Urban six popes, including:
Urban II *c.*1042–1099. Pope 1088–99. He launched the 1st ◊Crusade at the Council of Clermont in France in 1095.

urbane /ɜ:'beɪn/ *adj.* having manners that are courteous and elegant. —**urbanely** *adv.*, **urbanity** /ɜ:'bænɪtɪ/ *n.* [from French or Latin]

urbanization *n.* the process by which the proportion of a population living in or around towns and cities increases through migration as the agricultural population decreases. The growth of urban concentrations in the US and Europe is a relatively recent phenomenon, dating back only about 150 years to the beginnings of the Industrial Revolution (although the world's first cities were built more than 5,000 years ago.)

urbanize /'ɜ:bənaɪz/ *v.t.* to render urban; to remove the rural quality of (a district). —**urbanization** /-'zeɪʃən/ *n.* [from French]

urban renewal the adaptation of existing buildings in towns and cities to meet changes in economic, social, and environmental requirements, rather than demolishing them.

urchin /'ɜ:tʃɪn/ *n.* 1. a mischievous or needy boy. 2. a sea urchin. [originally = hedgehog, from Old French *herichon* from Latin (*h*)*ericius*]

Urdu /'uədu:, 'ɜ:-/ *n.* a member of the Indo-Iranian branch of the Indo-European language family, related to Hindi and written not in Devanagari but in Arabic script. Urdu is strongly influenced by Persian and Arabic. It is the official language of Pakistan and a language used by Muslims in India. [from Hindustani = (language of the) camp]

urea /'juərɪə, -'rɪə/ *n.* $CO(NH_2)_2$ a waste product formed in the mammalian liver when nitrogen compounds are

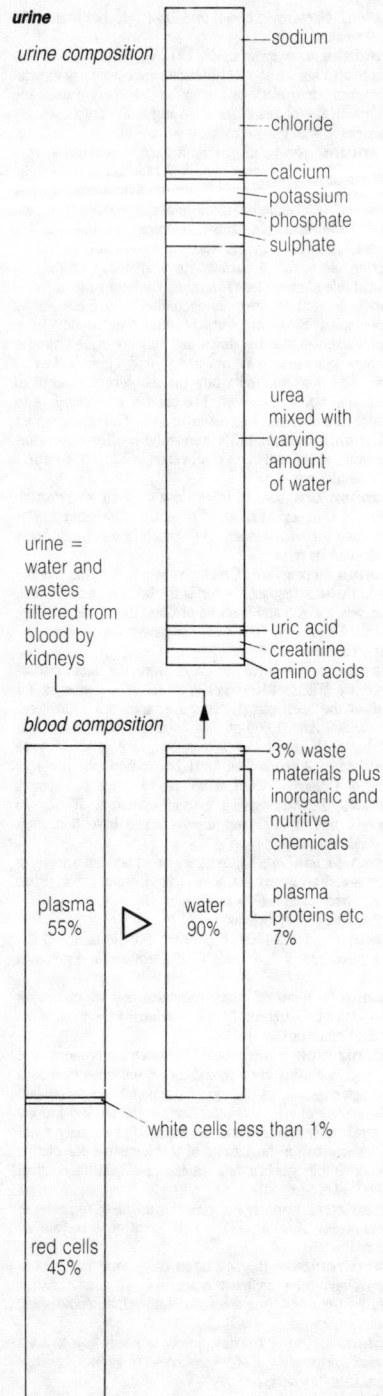

urine

urine composition

— sodium

---chloride

— calcium
-potassium
-phosphate
— sulphate

urea
mixed with
-varying
amount
of water

urine =
water and
wastes
filtered from
blood by
kidneys

— uric acid
- creatinine
- amino acids

blood composition

3% waste
materials plus
inorganic and
nutritive
chemicals

plasma
55%

water
90%

plasma
proteins etc
7%

white cells less than 1%

red cells
45%

broken down. It is excreted in urine. When purified,
it is a white, crystalline solid. In industry it is used
to make urea–formaldehyde plastics (or resins), pharmaceuticals, and fertilizers. [from French *urée* from Greek
ouron = urine]

ureter /juə'ri:tə/ *n.* a duct by which urine passes from the
kidney to the bladder or cloaca. [from French from Greek
oureō = urinate]

urethra /juə'ri:θrə/ *n.* in mammals a tube connecting the
bladder to the exterior. It carries urine, and in males,
semen. [Latin from Greek]

Urey /'juəri/ Harold Clayton 1893–1981. US chemist. In
1932 he isolated ◊heavy water and discovered ◊deuter-
ium, for which he was awarded the 1934 Nobel Prize
for Chemistry.

urge *v. t.* 1. to drive onward, to encourage to proceed. 2.
to try hard or persistently to persuade. 3. to recommend
strongly with reasoning or entreaty; to mention earnestly
as a reason or justification. —*n.* an urging impulse or tendency; a strong desire. [from Latin *urgēre*]

urgent *adj.* 1. requiring immediate action or attention. 2.
importunate. —**urgency** *n.*, **urgently** *adv.* [from French]

uric /'juərɪk/ *adj.* of urine. —**uric acid**, $C_5H_4N_4O_3$,
a nitrogen-containing waste substance, formed from the
breakdown of food and body protein. It is the usual
excretory material in insects, reptiles, and birds. [from
French *urique*]

urinal /juə'raɪnəl, 'juərɪnəl/ *n.* a place or receptacle
for urination.

urinary /'juərɪnərɪ/ *adj.* of or relating to urine.

urinary system the system of organs that removes
nitrogenous waste products and excess water from the
bodies of animals. In vertebrates, it consists of a pair of
kidneys, which produce urine; ureters, which drain the
kidneys; and (in bony fishes, amphibians, some reptiles,
and mammals) a bladder, which stores the urine before
its discharge. In mammals, the urine is expelled through
the urethra; in other vertebrates, the urine drains into a
common excretory chamber called a ◊cloaca, and the urine
is not discharged separately.

urinate /'juərɪneɪt/ *v.i.* to discharge urine. —**urination**
/-'neɪʃən/ *n.* [from Latin]

urine /'juərɪn/ *n.* the amber fluid secreted by the blood
from the kidneys and (in man and the higher animals)
stored in the bladder and discharged at intervals. It contains
excess water, salts, proteins, waste products in the form
of urea, a pigment, and some acid. [from Old French from
Latin *urina*]

urn *n.* 1. a vase with a foot and usually a rounded body,
especially for storing the ashes of the dead or as a
vessel or measure. 2. a large vessel with a tap, in
which tea or coffee etc. is made or kept hot. [from
Latin *urna*]

urogenital /juərə'dʒenɪtəl/ *adj.* of the urinary and
reproductive systems.

urology /juə'rɒlədʒɪ/ *n.* a branch of medicine concerned with diseases of the urinary system. [from Greek
ouron = urine]

Ursa Major /'ɜ:sə 'meɪdʒə(r)/ the third largest constellation in the sky, in the north polar region. Its seven
brightest stars make up the familiar shape of the **Big
Dipper** or **Plough**. The second star of the 'handle' of
the dipper, called Mizar, has a companion star, Alcor. Two
stars forming the far side of the 'bowl' act as pointers to
the north pole star, Polaris. [Latin = Great Bear] [Latin
'Great Bear']

Ursa Minor /'ɜ:sə 'maɪnə(r)/ a constellation in the
northern sky. It is shaped like a little dipper, with the north
pole star Polaris at the end of the handle. It contains the
orange subgiant Kochab, about 95 light years from Earth.
[Latin = Little Bear]

ursine /'ɜ:saɪn/ *adj.* of or like a bear. [from Latin *ursus* =
bear]

urticaria *n.* or **nettle rash** or **hives** an irritant skin condition characterized by itching, burning, stinging, and the
spontaneous appearance of raised patches of skin. Treatment is usually by antihistamines or steroids taken orally
or applied as lotions. Its causes are varied and include
allergy and stress.

Uruguay /'juərəgwaɪ/ Oriental Republic of; country in
South America, on the Atlantic, bounded N by Brazil
and W by Argentina; **area** 176,200 sq km/68,031 sq mi;
capital Montevideo; **physical** grassy plains (pampas), and
low hills, rivers Negro, Uruguay, Rio de la Plata; **head of
state and government** Luis Lacalle Herrera from 1989;
political system democratic republic; **population** (1990
est) 3,002,000; **language** Spanish; **recent history** independence from Brazil declared in 1925; first constitution
adopted in 1930. An army coup in 1976 introduced ten

years of repressive rule, which ended with violent anti-government demonstrations in 1984. The army and political leaders agreed a return to constitutional government in 1985 and the Colorado Party won the general election. In 1986 a government of national accord was established under President Sanguinetti.

Urumqi /u'ru:mtʃi:/ or **Urumchi** industrial city and capital of Xinjiang Uygur autonomous region, China, at the N foot of the Tian Shan mountains; population (1986) 1,147,000. It produces cotton textiles, cement, chemicals, iron, and steel.

US abbreviation of United States (of America).

us /əs, *emphatic* ʌs/ *pron.* 1. the object case of we. 2. (*colloquial*) we. 3. (*colloquial*) me. [Old English]

USA abbreviation of United States of America.

usable /'ju:zəbəl/ *adj.* that may be used.

usage /'ju:sɪdʒ/ *n.* 1. the manner of using or treating something. 2. a customary practice, especially in the use of a language. [from Old French]

use¹ /ju:z/ *v.t./i.* 1. to cause to act or serve for a purpose; to bring into service. 2. to treat in a specified manner; to behave towards. 3. to exploit selfishly. 4. (in *past*; often /ju:st/) had as one's or its constant or frequent practice or state. **—be used to** /ju:st/, to be familiar with by practice or habit. **use up**, to use the whole of; to find a use for (remaining material or time); to exhaust or tire out. [from Old French, ultimately from Latin *uti* = use]

use² /ju:s/ *n.* 1. using, being used. 2. the right or power of using. 3. ability to be used; the purpose for which a thing can be used. 4. custom, usage. **—have no use for**, to be unable to find a use for; to dislike; to be contemptuous of. **in use**, being used. **make use of**, to use; to benefit from; to exploit. **out of use**, not being used. [from Old French from Latin *usus*]

used /ju:zd/ *adj.* second-hand.

useful /'ju:sfəl/ *adj.* 1. able to be used for some practical purpose; producing or able to produce good results. 2. (*colloquial*) creditable, efficient. **—make oneself useful**, to perform useful services. **—usefully** *adv.*, **usefulness** *n.*

useless /'ju:slɪs/ *adj.* serving no practical purpose; not able to produce good results. **—uselessly** *adv.*, **uselessness** *n.*

user /'ju:zə/ *n.* one who uses something. **—user-friendly** *adj.* in computers, easy to use; designed with the needs of users in mind.

user interface in computing, procedures and methods through which the user operates a program. These might include ◊menus, input forms, error messages, and keyboard procedures. A graphical user interface is one that uses icons and allows the user to make menu selections with a mouse (see also ◊WIMP).

usher /'ʌʃə/ *n.* 1. a person who shows people to their seats in a hall or theatre etc. 2. the doorkeeper of a lawcourt etc. 3. an officer walking before a person of rank. **—v.t.** 1. to escort as an usher. 2. to announce or show (in or out etc.; *literal* or *figurative*). [from Anglo-French from Latin *ostium* = door]

Usher James 1581–1656. Irish priest, archbishop of Armagh from 1625. He was responsible for dating the creation to the year 4004 BC, a figure that was inserted in the margin of the Authorized Version of the Bible until the 19th century.

usherette /ʌʃə'ret/ *n.* a female usher, especially in a cinema.

Ushuaia /u:'swaɪə/ the southernmost town in the world, at the tip of Tierra del Fuego, Argentina, less than 1,000 km/620 mi from Antarctica; population (1980) 11,000. It is a free port and naval base.

usquebaugh /'ʌskɪbɔ:/ *n.* whisky. [from Irish and Scottish Gaelic *uisge beatha* = water of life]

Ussher alternative spelling of James ◊Usher.

USSR abbreviation of Union of Soviet Socialist Republics.

A diplomat these days is nothing but a head-waiter who's allowed to sit down occasionally.

Peter Ustinov
Romanoff and Juliet

Ustinov /'ju:stɪnɒf/ Peter 1921– . English stage and film actor, writer, and director. He won an Academy Award for

Spartacus 1960. Other film appearances include *Topkapi* 1964, *Death on the Nile* 1978, and *Evil under the Sun* 1981.

usual /'ju:ʒuəl/ *adj.* such as occurs or is done or used etc. in many or most instances. **—as usual**, as commonly occurs. **—usually** *adv.* [from Old French or Latin]

usurer /'ju:ʒərə/ *n.* one who practises usury.

usurious /ju'zuəriəs/ *adj.* of, involving, or practising usury.

usurp /ju'zɜ:p/ *v.t.* to seize or assume (a throne or power etc.) wrongfully or by force. **—usurpation** /ju:zə'peɪʃən/ *n.*, **usurper** *n.* [from Old French from Latin *usurpare* = seize for use]

usury /'ju:ʒərɪ/ *n.* the lending of money at interest, especially at an exorbitant or illegal rate; interest at this rate. In medieval times, usury was held to be a sin, and Christians were forbidden to lend (although not to borrow). Under English law, usury remained forbidden until the 13th century, when trade and the need for credit was increased; for example, Jews were absolved from the ban on usury by the Fourth Lateran Council of 1215. [from Anglo-French from Latin *usura*]

UT abbreviation of universal time.

Utah /'ju:tɑ:/ state of the W USA; nickname Beehive State; **area** 219,900 sq km/84,881 sq mi; **capital** Salt Lake City; **towns** Provo, Ogden; **physical** Colorado Plateau to the E; mountains in centre; Great Basin to the W; Great Salt Lake; Great American Desert; Colorado rivers system; **products** wool, gold, silver, uranium, coal, salt, steel; **population** (1985) 1,645,000; **history** part of the area ceded by Mexico in 1848; developed by the Mormons, still the largest religious sect in the state; became a territory in 1850, but was not admitted to statehood until 1896 because of Mormon reluctance to relinquish plural marriage.

Utamaro /u:tə'mɑ:rəu/ Kitagawa 1753–1806. Japanese artist of the *ukiyo-e* ('floating world') school, who created muted colour prints of beautiful women, including informal studies of prostitutes.

UTC abbreviation of coordinated universal time, the standard measurement of time.

utensil /ju:'tensəl/ *n.* an implement or vessel, especially for domestic use. [from Old French from Latin = usable]

uterine /'ju:təraɪn/ *adj.* of the uterus. [from Latin]

uterus /'ju:tərəs/ *n.* (*plural* **uteri** /-aɪ/) or **womb** a hollow muscular organ of female mammals, located between the bladder and rectum, and connected to the Fallopian tubes above and the vagina below. The embryo develops within the uterus, and in placental mammals is attached to it after implantation via the ◊placenta and umbilical cord. The lining of the uterus changes during the ◊menstrual cycle. In humans and other higher primates, it is a single structure, but in other mammals it is paired. [Latin] The outer wall of the uterus is composed of smooth muscle, capable of powerful contractions (induced by hormones) during childbirth.

U Thant /'u: 'θænt/ 1909–1974. Burmese diplomat, secretary general of the United Nations 1962–71. He helped to resolve the US-Soviet crisis over the Soviet installation of missiles in Cuba, and he made the controversial decision to withdraw the UN peacekeeping force from the Egypt–Israel border in 1967 (see ◊Arab-Israeli Wars).

Uthman another spelling of ◊Othman, third caliph of Islam.

utilitarian /ju:tɪlɪ'teərɪən/ *adj.* 1. designed to be useful for a purpose rather than decorative or luxurious; severely practical. 2. of utilitarianism. **—n.** an adherent of utilitarianism.

utilitarianism /ju:tɪlɪ'teərɪənɪzəm/ *n.* a philosophical theory of ethics outlined by the philosopher Jeremy ◊Bentham and developed by John Stuart Mill. According to utilitarianism, an action is morally right if it has consequences that lead to happiness, and wrong if it brings about the reverse. Thus society should aim for the greatest happiness of the greatest number.

utility /ju:'tɪlɪtɪ/ *n.* 1. usefulness, profitableness. 2. a useful thing; a public service such as the supply of water, gas, or electricity. **—adj.** severely practical and standardized; made or serving for utility. **—utility room**, a room containing large fixed domestic appliances, e.g. a washing-machine. **utility vehicle**, a vehicle serving various functions. [from Old French from Latin *utilis* = useful]

utilize /'ju:tɪlaɪz/ *v.t.* to make use of, to turn to account. **—utilization** /-'zeɪʃən/ *n.* [from French from Italian]

utmost /'ʌtməʊst/ *adj.* furthest, extreme, greatest. —*n.* the utmost point or degree etc. —**do one's utmost,** to do all that one can. [Old English]

Utopia /juːˈtəʊpiə/ *n.* an imagined perfect place or state of things. —**Utopian** *adj.* [name of imaginary island, governed on a perfect political and social system, in book of that title by Sir Thomas More (1516)]

Utrecht /'juːtrekt/ a province of the Netherlands lying SE of Amsterdam, on the Kromme Rijn (crooked Rhine); **area** 1,330 sq km/513 sq mi; **population** (1988) 965,000; **capital** Utrecht; **products** chemicals, livestock, textiles, electrical goods; **history** ruled by the bishops of Utrecht in the Middle Ages, the province was sold to the emperor Charles V of Spain in 1527. It became a centre of Protestant resistance to Spanish rule and, with the signing of the Treaty of Utrecht, became one of the seven United Provinces of the Netherlands in 1579.

Utrecht, Treaty of the treaty signed in 1713 that ended the War of the ◊Spanish Succession. Philip V was recognized as the legitimate king of Spain, thus founding the Spanish branch of the Bourbon dynasty and ending the French king Louis XIV's attempts at expansion; the Netherlands, Milan, and Naples were ceded to Austria; Britain gained Gibraltar; the duchy of Savoy was granted Sicily.

Utrecht, Union of in 1579, the union of seven provinces of the N Netherlands (Holland, Zeeland, Friesland, Groningen, Utrecht, Gelderland, and Overijssel) that became the basis of opposition to the Spanish crown and the foundation of the present-day Dutch state.

utricle /'juːtrɪkəl/ *n.* a cell or small cavity in an animal or plant. [from French or Latin *utriculus* diminutive of *uter* = leather bag]

Utrillo /juːˈtrɪləʊ/ Maurice 1883–1955. French artist who painted townscapes of his native Paris, many depicting Montmartre, often from postcard photographs.

Uttar Pradesh /'ʊtə prəˈdeʃ/ state of N India; **area** 294,400 sq km/113,638 sq mi; **capital** Lucknow; **physical** Himalayan peak Nanda Devi 7,817 m/25,655 ft; **population** (1981) 110,858,000; **language** Hindi; **history** formerly the heart of the Mogul Empire and generating point of the ◊Indian Mutiny in 1857 and subsequent opposition to British rule; see also the United Provinces of ◊Agra

and ◊Oudh.

utter[1] *attrib. adj.* complete, absolute. —**utterly** *adv.* [Old English]

utter[2] *v.t./i.* 1. to make (a sound or words) with the mouth or voice. 2. to speak. 3. to put (a forged banknote or coin etc.) into circulation. [from Middle Dutch = *ūteren* make known]

utterance /'ʌtərəns/ *n.* 1. uttering. 2. the power or manner of speaking. 3. a thing spoken.

uttermost *adj.* utmost.

U-turn /'juːtɜːn/ *n.* 1. turning a vehicle in a U-shaped course so as to face the opposite direction. 2. a reversal of policy.

UV abbreviation of ultraviolet.

uvula /'juːvjʊlə/ *n.* (*plural* **uvulae** /-iː/) the fleshy part of the soft palate hanging from the back of the roof of the mouth above the throat. —**uvular** *adj.* [Latin, diminutive of *uva* = grape]

uxorious /ʌkˈsɔːrɪəs/ *adj.* greatly or obsessively fond of one's wife. [from Latin *uxor* = wife]

Uzbek /'ʊzbek/ *n.* a person of Uzbek culture. Uzbeks make up almost 70% of the population of Uzbekistan in the USSR. The Uzbek language belongs to the Turkic branch of the Altaic family.

Uzbekistan /ʊzbekiˈstɑːn/ constituent republic of the SE USSR, part of Soviet Central Asia; **area** 447,400 sq km/ 172,741 sq mi; **capital** Tashkent; **towns** Samarkand; **physical** oases in the deserts; rivers: Amu Darya, Syr Darya; Fergana Valley; **products** rice, dried fruit, vines (all grown by irrigation); cotton, silk; **population** (1987) 19,026,000; 69% Uzbek, 11% Russian, 4% Tadzhik, 4% Tatar; **language** Uzbek; **religion** Sunni Muslim; **history** part of Turkestan, it was conquered by Russia in 1865–76. The Tashkent soviet gradually extended its power from 1917–24, and Uzbekistan became a constituent republic of the USSR in 1925. Some 160,000 Mesketian Turks were forcibly transported from their native Georgia to Uzbekistan by Stalin in 1944. In June 1989 Tashlak, Yaipan, and Fergana were the scenes of riots in which Mesketian Turks were attacked; 70 were killed and 850 wounded. In Sept 1989 an Uzbek nationalist organization, the *Birhik* ('Unity') Peoples's Movement, was formed.

v, V /viː/ *n.* (*plural* **vs, v's**) **1.** the 22nd letter of the alphabet. **2.** a V-shaped thing. **3.** (as a Roman numeral) five.

v. abbreviation of **1.** verse. **2.** versus. **3.** very. **4.** *vide.*

V abbreviation of volt(s).

V symbol for vanadium.

V1, V2 *n.* German flying bombs of World War II, launched against Britain in 1944 and 1945. The V1, also called the doodle-bug and buzz bomb, was an uncrewed monoplane carrying a bomb, powered by a simple kind of jet engine called a pulse jet. The V2, a rocket bomb with a preset guidance system, was the first long-range ballistic ◊missile. It was 14 m/47 ft long, carried a 1-tonne warhead, and hit its target at a speed of 5,000 kph/3,000 mph. [German *Vergeltungswaffe* = revenge weapons]

vac *n.* (*colloquial*) **1.** a vacation. **2.** a vacuum cleaner. [abbreviation]

vacancy /'veɪkənsɪ/ *n.* **1.** being vacant, emptiness. **2.** an unoccupied position of employment or place of accommodation.

vacant /'veɪkənt/ *adj.* **1.** empty, not filled or occupied. **2.** not mentally active, having a blank expression. —**vacant possession,** (of a house etc.) the state of being empty of occupants and available for the purchaser to occupy immediately. —**vacantly** *adv.*, [from Old French or Latin]

vacate /və'keɪt/ *v.t.* to cease to occupy (a place or position). [from Latin *vacare* = be empty]

vacation /və'keɪʃən/ *n.* **1.** any of the intervals between terms in universities and lawcourts. **2.** (*US*) a holiday. **3.** vacating. —*v.i.* (*US*) to take a holiday. [from Old French or Latin]

vaccinate /'væksɪneɪt/ *v.t.* to inoculate with a vaccine. —**vaccination** /-'neɪʃən/ *n.*, **vaccinator** *n.*

vaccine /'væksiːn, -sɪn/ *n.* any preparation of an organism or substance causing a disease, specially treated or synthesized to confer immunity against an infection. When injected or taken by mouth, a vaccine stimulates the production of antibodies to protect against that particular disease. Vaccination is the oldest form of ◊immunization. [from Latin *vacca* = cow]

vacillate /'væsɪleɪt/ *v.i.* to fluctuate in opinion or resolution. —**vacillation** /-'leɪʃən/ *n.*, **vacillator** *n.* [from Latin *vacillare* = sway]

vacuole /'vækjuəʊl/ *n.* in biology, a fluid-filled, membrane-bound cavity inside a cell. It may be a reservoir for fluids that the cell will secrete to the outside, or filled with excretory products or essential nutrients that the cell needs to store. In amoebae (single-cell animals), vacuoles are the sites of digestion of engulfed food particles. Plant cells usually have a large central vacuole for storage. [French, diminutive of Latin *vaccus* = empty]

vacuous /'vækjuəs/ *adj.* **1.** expressionless; unintelligent. **2.** empty. —**vacuity** /və'kjuːɪtɪ/ *n.*, **vacuously** *adv.*, **vacuousness** *n.* [from Latin *vacuus* = empty]

vacuum /'vækjuəm/ *n.* (*plural* **vacua** or **vacuums**) **1.** space entirely devoid of matter; in physics, any enclosure in which the gas pressure is considerably less than atmospheric pressure (101,325 pascals). **2.** absence of normal or previous contents. **3.** (*plural* **vacuums**) (*colloquial*) a vacuum cleaner. —*v.t./i.* (*colloquial*) to use a vacuum cleaner (on). —**vacuum brake,** a brake in which pressure is produced by exhaustion of air. **vacuum-packed** *adj.* sealed after partial removal of the air. **vacuum tube,** a tube with a near-vacuum for the free passage of electric current.

vacuum cleaner an electric appliance for taking up dust, dirt, etc. by suction. It was invented in 1901 by the Scot Hubert Cecil Booth (1871–1955). Having seen an ineffective dust-blowing machine, he reversed the process. His original machine was on wheels and operated from the street by means of tubes running into the house.

vacuum flask or **Dewar flask** or **Thermos flask** a container for keeping things either hot or cold. It has two silvered glass walls with a vacuum between them, in a metal or plastic outer case. This design reduces the three forms of heat transfer: radiation (prevented by the silvering), conduction, and convection (both prevented by the vacuum). It was invented by the British scientist James Dewar about 1872 to store liquefied gases.

vade mecum /vɑːdiː'meɪkəm, veɪdiː'miːkəm/ a handbook or other small useful work of reference. [French from Latin = go with me]

Vaduz /fæ'duːts/ capital of the European principality of Liechtenstein; population (1984) 5,000. Industries include engineering and agricultural trade.

vagabond /'vægəbɒnd/ *n.* a wanderer, especially an idle or dishonest one. —*adj.* having no fixed habitation, wandering. [from Old French or Latin *vagari* = wander]

vagary /'veɪgərɪ/ *n.* a capricious act, idea, or fluctuation.

vagina /və'dʒaɪnə/ *n.* (*plural* **vaginae** /-iː/ or **vaginas**) the passage leading from the vulva to the womb in a female mammal. It admits the penis during sexual intercourse, and is the birth canal down which the fetus passes during delivery. —**vaginal** *adj.* [Latin = sheath]

vagrant /'veɪgrənt/ *n.* a person without a settled home or regular work. —*adj.* wandering, roving. —**vagrancy** *n.* [from Anglo-French *vag(a)raunt*]

vague /veɪg/ *adj.* **1.** of uncertain or ill-defined meaning or character. **2.** (of a person or mind) imprecise, inexact in thought, expression, or understanding. —**vaguely** *adv.*, **vagueness** *n.* [French or from Latin *vagus* = wandering]

vain *adj.* **1.** conceited, especially about one's appearance. **2.** having no value or significance, unsubstantial. **3.** useless, futile, followed by no good result —**in vain,** without result or success. —**vainly** *adv.* [from Old French from Latin *vanus* = empty]

vainglory /veɪn'glɔːrɪ/ *n.* extreme vanity, boastfulness. —**vainglorious** *adj.* [after Old French *vaine gloire* from Latin *vana gloria*]

valance /'væləns/ *n.* a short curtain round the frame or canopy of a bedstead or above a window or under a shelf.

Valdemar /'vældəmɑː/ alternative spelling of ◊Waldemar, name of four kings of Denmark.

Valdívia /væl'diːvɪə/ Pedro de *c.*1497–1554. Spanish explorer who travelled to Venezuela around 1530 and accompanied Francisco ◊Pizarro on his second expedition to Peru. He then went south into Chile, where he founded the cities of Santiago in 1541 and Valdívia in 1544. In 1552 he crossed the Andes to explore the Negro River. He was killed by Araucanian Indians.

vale *n.* (*archaic* except in place-names) a valley. [from Old French *val* from Latin *vallis*]

valediction /ˌvælɪˈdɪkʃən/ *n.* bidding farewell; the words used in this. —**valedictory** *adj.* [from Latin *vale* = farewell and *dicere* = say]

valence /ˈveɪləns/ *n.* the combining or replacing power of an atom as compared with that of the hydrogen atom. [from Latin *valentia* = power]

valence electron electron in the outermost shell of an ◊atom. It is the valence electrons that are involved in the formation of ionic and covalent bonds (see ◊molecule). The number of electrons in this outermost shell represents the maximum possible ◊valency for many elements and matches the number of the group that the element occupies in the ◊periodic table of the elements.

Valencia /vəˈlensɪə/ industrial city (wine, fruit, chemicals, textiles, ship repair) in Valencia region, E Spain; population (1986) 739,000. The Valencian Community, consisting of Alicante, Castellón, and Valencia, has an area of 23,300 sq km/8,994 sq mi and a population of 3,772,000.

valency /ˈveɪlənsɪ/ *n.* the measure of an element's ability to combine with other elements, expressed as the number of atoms of hydrogen (or any other standard univalent element) capable of uniting with (or replacing) its atoms.

valentine /ˈvæləntaɪn/ *n.* **1.** a card or picture etc. sent (often anonymously) to someone on St Valentine's day (14 Feb). The custom seems to have arisen because the day coincided with the Roman mid-February festival of ◊Lupercalia. **2.** a sweetheart chosen on this day.

Valentine, St according to tradition a bishop of Terni who was martyred in Rome, now omitted from the calendar of saints' days as probably nonexistent.

Valentino /ˌvæ... [scan unclear] ... /vælənˈtiːnəʊ/ Rudolph. Adopted name of Rodolfo Alphonso Guglielmi di Valentina d'Antonguolla 1895–1926. Italian-born US film actor, the archetypal romantic lover of the Hollywood silent movies. His screen debut was in 1919 but his first starring role was in *The Four Horsemen of the Apocalypse* 1921. His subsequent films include *The Sheik* 1921 and *Blood and Sand* 1922.

Valera Éamon de. Irish politician; see ◊de Valera.

valerian /vəˈlɪərɪən/ *n.* **1.** any of various herbaceous plants of the widely distributed genera *Valeriana* or *Centranthus*, many of which have been used medicinally as stimulants or antispasmodics. They are native to the northern hemisphere, with clustered heads of fragrant tubular flowers in red, white, or pink. **2.** the dried roots of such a plant used in medicine or scents etc. [from Old French from Latin]

Valéry /ˌvæleəˈriː/ Paul 1871–1945. French poet and mathematician. His poetry includes *La Jeune Parque/The Young Fate* 1917 and *Charmes/Enchantments* 1922.

God made everything out of the void, but the void shows through.

Paul Valéry
Mauvaises pensées et autres

---

valet /ˈvælɪt, -leɪ/ *n.* a man's personal attendant who takes care of clothes etc. —*v.t./i.* to act as valet (to). [French = *varlet*]

valetudinarian /ˌvælɪtjuːdɪˈneərɪən/ *n.* a person who pays excessive attention to preserving his or her health. —*adj.* that is a valetudinarian. —**valetudinarianism** *n.* [from Latin *valetudo* = health]

Valhalla /vælˈhælə/ *n.* in Norse mythology, the hall in ◊Odin's palace where he feasts with the souls of heroes killed in battle.

valiant /ˈvæljənt/ *adj.* (of a person or conduct) brave, courageous. —**valiantly** *adv.* [from Anglo-French from Latin *valēre* = be strong]

valid /ˈvælɪd/ *adj.* **1.** (of a reason, objection, etc.) sound and to the point, logical. **2.** legally acceptable or usable; executed with the proper formalities. —**validity** /vəˈlɪdɪtɪ/ *n.*, **validly** *adv.* [from French or Latin *validus* = strong]

validate /ˈvælɪdeɪt/ *v.t.* to make valid, to ratify. —**validation** /-ˈdeɪʃən/ *n.* [from Latin]

valise /vəˈliːz/ *n.* a kitbag; (*US*) a small suitcase. [French from Italian *valigia*]

Valkyrie /vælˈkɪərɪ/ in Norse mythology, any of the female attendants of ◊Odin. They select the most valiant warriors to die in battle and escort them to Valhalla.

Valladolid /ˌvæljədəʊˈliːð/ industrial town (food processing, vehicles, textiles, engineering), and capital of Valladolid province, Spain; population (1986) 341,000.

Valle d'Aosta /ˈvæleɪ dɑːˈɒstə/ autonomous region of NW Italy; area 3,300 sq km/1,274 sq mi; population (1988) 114,000, many of whom are French-speaking. It produces wine and livestock. Its capital is Aosta.

Valletta /vəˈletə/ capital and port of Malta; population (1987) 9,000 plus urban harbour area 101,000.

valley /ˈvælɪ/ *n.* **1.** a long low area between hills. **2.** a region drained by a river. **3.** the internal angle formed by intersecting planes of a roof. [from Anglo-French from Latin *vallis*]

Valley Forge /ˈvælɪ ˈfɔːdʒ/ site in Pennsylvania 32 km/20 mi NW of Philadelphia, USA, where Washington's army spent the winter of 1777–78 in great hardship during the ◊American Revolution.

Valley of Ten Thousand Smokes valley in SW Alaska, on the Alaska Peninsula, where in 1912 Mount Katmai erupted in one of the largest volcanic explosions ever known. The area was uninhabited. It was dedicated in 1918 as the Katmai National Monument. Thousands of fissures on the valley floor continue to emit steam and gases.

Valley of the Kings the burial place of ancient kings opposite ◊Thebes, Egypt, on the left bank of the Nile.

Valmy, Battle of /vælˈmiː/ battle in 1792 in which the army of the French Revolution under General Dumouriez defeated the Prussians at a French village in the Marne *département*. See ◊Revolutionary Wars.

Valois /vælˈwɑː/ a branch of the Capetian dynasty, originally counts of Valois, (see Hugh ◊Capet) in France, members of which occupied the French throne from Philip VI 1328 to Henry III 1589.

valour /ˈvælə/ *n.* courage, especially in battle. —**valorous** *adj.* [from Old French from Latin *valēre* = be strong]

valuable /ˈvæljuəbəl/ *adj.* of great value, price, or worth. —*n.* (usually in *plural*) a valuable thing. —**valuably** *adv.*

valuation /ˌvæljuˈeɪʃən/ *n.* estimation of a thing's value (especially by a professional valuer) or of a person's merit; the value so estimated.

value /ˈvæljuː/ *n.* **1.** the amount of money, goods, or services etc. considered to be equivalent to a thing or for which it can be exchanged. **2.** desirability, usefulness, importance. **3.** the ability of a thing to serve a purpose or cause an effect. **4.** (in *plural*) one's principles or standards; one's judgement of what is valuable or important in life. **5.** the amount or quantity denoted by a figure etc.; the duration of a musical sound indicated by a note; the relative importance of each playing-card, chess piece, etc., in a game; in painting, the relative lightness and darkness of tones. —*v.t.* **1.** to estimate the value of; to appraise professionally. **2.** to have a high or specified opinion of; to attach importance to. —**value-added tax**, a type of consumption tax; see ◊VAT. **value judgement**, a subjective estimate of quality etc. [from Old French, past participle of *valoir* = be worth from Latin *valēre* = be strong]

valueless *adj.* having no value.

valuer *n.* one who estimates or assesses values, especially as a professional.

valve *n.* **1.** a device for controlling the passage of a fluid through a pipe etc., especially an automatic device allowing movement in one direction only. Inside a valve, a plug moves to widen or close the opening through which the fluid passes. **2.** a membranous structure in the heart or in a blood vessel allowing blood to flow in one direction only. **3.** or **electron tube**, in electronics, a glass tube containing gas at low pressure, used to control the flow of electricity in a circuit. Three or more metal electrodes are inset into the tube. By varying the voltage on one, called the grid electrode, the current through the valve can be controlled, and the valve can act as an amplifier. **4.** a device to vary the length of tube in a trumpet etc. **5.** each of the two shells of an oyster or mussel etc. [from Latin *valva* = leaf of folding-door]

valvular /ˈvælvjʊlə/ *adj.* **1.** of or like a valve. **2.** forming or having a valve or valves. [from diminutive of Latin *valva*]

vamoose /vəˈmuːs/ *v.i.* (*US slang*) to depart hurriedly. [from Spanish *vamos* = let us go]

vamp¹ *n.* the upper front part of a boot or shoe. —*v.t./i.* **1.** to repair, to furbish. **2.** to make by patching or from odds

Van Allen radiation belts

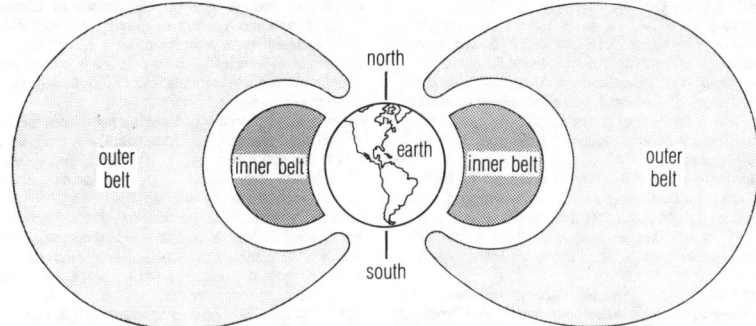

and ends. **3.** to improvise (a musical accompaniment). [from Old French *avant* = before and *pied* = foot]

vamp² *n.* (*colloquial*) a seductive woman who uses her attractiveness to exploit men; an unscrupulous flirt. —*v.t./i.* (*colloquial*) to exploit or flirt with (a man) unscrupulously; to act as a vamp.

vampire /'væmpaɪə/ *n.* **1.** in Slavic folklore, an 'undead' corpse that sleeps by day in its native earth, and by night, often in the form of a bat, sucks the blood of the living. ◊Dracula is the best known vampire in popular fiction. **2.** a person who preys ruthlessly on others. —**vampire bat,** a South and Central American bat of the family Desmodontidae, of which there are three species. The common vampire *Desmodus rotundus* is found from N Mexico to central Argentina; its head and body grow to 9 cm/3.5 in. Vampires feed on the blood of mammals: they slice a piece of skin from a victim with their sharp incisor teeth and lap up the flowing blood. [French or German from Magyar perhaps from Turkish *uber* = witch]

van¹ *n.* **1.** a covered vehicle for transporting goods or horses etc. or prisoners. **2.** a railway carriage for luggage or for the use of the guard. [abbreviation of *caravan*]

van² *n.* the vanguard; the forefront.

vanadium /və'neɪdɪəm/ *n.* silver-white, malleable and ductile, metallic element, symbol V, atomic number 23, relative atomic mass 50.942. It occurs in certain iron, lead, and uranium ores and is widely distributed in small quantities in igneous and sedimentary rocks. It is used to make steel alloys, to which it adds tensile strength. [from Old Norse *vanadís* name of the Scandinavian goddess Freya]

Van Allen radiation belts /væn 'ælən/ two zones of charged particles around the Earth's magnetosphere, discovered in 1958 by US physicist James Van Allen (1914–). The atomic particles come from the Earth's upper atmosphere and the ◊solar wind, and are trapped by the Earth's magnetic field. The inner belt lies 1,000–5,000 km/620–3,100 mi above the equator, and contains ◊protons and ◊electrons. The outer belt lies 15,000–25,000 km/9,300–15,500 mi above the equator, but is lower around the magnetic poles. It contains mostly electrons from the solar wind.

Vanbrugh /'vænbrə/ John 1664–1726. English Baroque architect and dramatist. He designed Blenheim Palace, Oxfordshire, and Castle Howard, Yorkshire, and wrote the comic dramas *The Relapse* 1696 and *The Provok'd Wife* 1697.

Van Buren /væn 'bjuərən/ Martin 1782–1862. Eighth president of the USA, a Democrat, born in Kinderhook, New York, of Dutch ancestry. He was a senator 1821–28, governor of New York State 1828–29, secretary of state 1829–31, minister to Britain 1831–33, vice president 1833–37, and president 1837–41. He initiated the independent treasury system, but his refusal to spend land revenues cost him the 1840 election. He lost the 1844 Democratic nomination to Polk, and in 1848 ran unsuccessfully for president as the Free Soil candidate.

Vance /væns/ Cyrus 1917– . US Democratic politician, secretary of state 1977–80. He resigned because he' did not support President Carter's abortive mission to rescue the US hostages in Iran.

Vancouver /væn'kuːvə/ industrial city in Canada; **products** oil refining, engineering, shipbuilding, aircraft, timber, pulp and paper, textiles, fisheries. It is Canada's chief Pacific seaport, on the mainland of British Columbia; **population** (1986) 1,381,000.

Vancouver /væn'kuːvə/ George *c.*1758–1798. British navigator who made extensive exploration of the W coast of North America.

Vancouver Island /væn'kuːvə/ island off the W coast of Canada, part of British Columbia; **area** 32,136 sq km/12,404 sq mi; **products** coal, timber, fish; **history** visited by British explorer Cook 1778; surveyed 1792 by Capt George Vancouver.

vandal /'vændəl/ *n.* one who wilfully or ignorantly destroys or damages works of art or other property or the beauties of nature. —**vandalism** *n.*

Vandal /'vændlz/ *n.* a member of a Germanic people related to the ◊Goths. In the 5th century AD the Vandals moved from N Germany to invade Roman ◊Gaul and Spain, many settling in Andalusia (formerly Vandalitia) and others reaching N Africa in 429. They sacked Rome in 455 but accepted Roman suzerainty in the 6th century.

vandalize /'vændəlaɪz/ *v.t.* to destroy or damage (property etc.) as a vandal.

van de Graaff /væn də 'græf/ Robert Jemison 1901–1967. US physicist who from 1929 developed a high-voltage generator, which in its modern form can produce more than a million volts. It consists of an endless vertical conveyor belt that carries electrostatic charges (resulting from friction) up to a large hollow sphere supported on an insulated stand. The lower end of the belt is earthed, so that charge accumulates on the sphere. The size of the voltage built up in air depends on the radius of the sphere, but can be increased by enclosing the generator in an inert atmosphere, such as nitrogen.

Vanderbilt /'vændəbɪlt/ Cornelius 1794–1877. US industrialist who made a fortune in steamships and (from the age of 70) by financing railways.

Van der Post /væn də 'pəʊst/ Laurens (Jan) 1906– . South African writer, whose books, many autobiographical, reflect his openness to diverse cultures and his belief in the importance of intuition and individualism in human experience. A formative influence was his time spent with the people of the Kalahari Desert, whose disappearing culture he recorded in *The Lost World of the Kalahari* 1958, *The Heart of the Hunter* 1961, and *Testament to the Bushmen* 1984.

Organized religion is making Christianity political, rather than making politics Christian.

Laurens Van der Post
The *Observer* 9 Nov 1986

Van der Waals /væn də 'vɑːls/ Johannes Diderik 1837–1923. Dutch physicist who was awarded a Nobel prize in 1910 for his theoretical study of gases. He emphasized the forces of attraction and repulsion between atoms and molecules in describing the behaviour of real gases, as opposed to the ideal gases dealt with in ◊Boyle's law and ◊Charles's law.

van Dyck /væn'daɪk/ Anthony. Flemish painter, see ◊Dyck, Anthony van.

Vandyke /væn'daɪk/ *adj.* in the style of dress etc. common in portraits by van Dyck. —**Vandyke beard,** a neat, pointed beard. **Vandyke brown,** deep, rich brown.

vane /veɪn/ *n.* 1. a weather vane. 2. the blade of a screw propeller, sail of a windmill, or similar device acted on or moved by water or wind. 3. the flat part of a bird's feather formed by barbs. [variant of obsolete *fane* from Old English *fana* = banner]

Vane Henry 1613–1662. English politician. In 1640 he was elected a member of the ◊Long Parliament and was prominent in the impeachment of Archbishop ◊Laud. During 1643–53 he was, in effect, the civilian head of the Parliamentary government. At the Restoration of the monarchy he was executed.

Vane John 1923– . British pharmacologist who discovered the wide role of prostaglandins in the human body, produced in response to illness and stress. He shared the 1982 Nobel Prize for Physiology or Medicine with Sune Gergstrom and Bengt Samuelsson of Sweden.

van Eyck /væn 'aɪk/ Jan. Flemish painter, see ◊Eyck, Jan van.

van Gogh /væn 'gɒx/ Vincent. Dutch painter, see ◊Gogh, Vincent van.

vanguard /'vænɡɑːd/ *n.* 1. the foremost part of an army or fleet advancing or ready to do so. 2. the leaders of a movement, opinion, etc. [from Old French *avant* = before and *garde* = guard]

vanilla /və'nɪlə/ *n.* 1. a substance obtained from the dried and fermented vanilla pod or synthetically and used to flavour ices, chocolate, etc. 2. a tropical climbing orchid of the genus *Vanilla* with large white or yellow fragrant flowers, native to Mexico; the fruit of the species *Vanilla planifolia.* —**vanilla pod** this fruit. [from Spanish *vainilla* = pod, diminutive of *vaina* = sheath, pod, from Latin *vagina* = sheath]

vanish /'vænɪʃ/ *v.t./i.* 1. to disappear completely; to cease to exist. 2. to cause to disappear. —**vanishing point** the point at which receding parallel lines viewed in perspective appear to meet; the stage of complete disappearance. [from Latin *vanus* = empty]

vanity *n.* 1. conceit, especially about one's appearance. 2. futility, worthlessness; something vain. —**vanity bag** *or* **case,** a bag or case containing a small mirror, cosmetics, etc. [from Old French from Latin *vanitas* from *vanus* = empty]

Vanity Fair a novel by William Makepeace Thackeray, published in the UK 1847–48. It deals with the contrasting fortunes of the tough orphan Becky Sharp and the softhearted, privileged Amelia Sedley.

vanquish /'væŋkwɪʃ/ *v.t.* (*literary*) to conquer. [from Old French from Latin *vincere*]

vantage /'vɑːntɪdʒ/ *n.* advantage, especially as a score in tennis. —**vantage point** a place from which one has a good view of something. [from Anglo-French from Latin *ante* = before]

Vanuatu /vænuː'ɑːtuː/ Republic of; group of islands in the S Pacific, part of ◊Melanesia; **area** 14,800 sq km/ 5,714 sq mi; **capital** Vila (on Efate island); **physical** comprises 70 islands, including Espiritu Santo, Malekala, and Efate; densely forested, mountainous; **head of state** Fred Timakata from 1989; **head of government** Walter Lini from 1980; **political system** democratic republic; **exports** copra, fish, coffee; **population** (1988) 149,400; **language** Bislama, English, French; **recent history** independence achieved from France and Britain in 1980.

vapid /'væpɪd/ *adj.* insipid, uninteresting. —**vapidity** /və'pɪdɪtɪ/ *n.,* **vapidly** *adv.,* **vapidness** *n.* [from Latin *vapidus*]

vaporize /'veɪpəraɪz/ *v.t./i.* to convert or be converted into vapour. —**vaporization** /-'zeɪʃən/ *n.,* **vaporizer** *n.*

vapour /'veɪpə/ *n.* 1. moisture or other substance diffused or suspended in air. 2. the gaseous form of a normally liquid or solid substance. —**vaporous** *adj.,* **vapoury** *adj.* [from Old French or Latin *vapor* = steam]

vapour density the density of a gas, expressed as the mass of a given volume of the gas divided by the mass of an equal volume of a reference gas (such as hydrogen or air) at the same temperature and pressure. It is equal to half the relative molecular weight (mass) of the gas.

vapour pressure the pressure of a vapour given off by (evaporated from) a liquid or solid, caused by vibrating atoms or molecules continuously escaping from its surface. In an enclosed space, a maximum value is reached when the number of particles leaving the surface is in equilibrium with those returning to it; this is known as the **saturated vapour pressure.**

Varanasi /və'rɑːnəsɪ/ or **Benares** holy city of the Hindus in Uttar Pradesh, India, on the river Ganges; population (1981) 794,000. There are 1,500 golden shrines, and a 5-km/3-mi frontage to the Ganges with sacred stairways (ghats) for purification by bathing.

Varèse /və'rez/ Edgard 1885–1965. French composer, who settled in New York from 1916 where he founded the New Symphony Orchestra in 1919 to advance the cause of modern music. His work is experimental and often dissonant, combining electronic sounds with orchestral instruments, and includes *Hyperprism* 1923, *Intégrales* 1931, and *Poème Electronique* 1958.

Vargas /'vɑːɡəs/ Getúlio 1883–1954. President of Brazil 1930–45 and 1951–54. He overthrew the republic in 1930 and in 1937 he set up a totalitarian, pro-fascist state known as the *Estado Novo.* Ousted by a military coup in 1945, he returned as president in 1951 but, amid mounting opposition and political scandal, committed suicide in 1954.

Vargas Llosa /'vɑːɡəs 'jəʊsə/ Mario 1937– . Peruvian novelist, author of *La ciudad y los perros/The Time of the Hero* 1963 and *La guerra del fin del mundo/The War at the End of the World* 1982.

variable /'veərɪəbəl/ *adj.* 1. varying, changeable. 2. that may be varied. 3. in mathematics, of a changing quantity that can take various values, as opposed to a ◊constant. For example, in the algebraic expression $y = 4x^3 + 2$, the variables are x and y, whereas 4 and 2 are constants. —*n.* a variable thing or quantity. —**variable-geometry wing,** technical name for a ◊swing-wing, a type of moveable aircraft wing. —**variable star,** any star whose brightness changes, either regularly or irregularly, over a period ranging from a few hours to months or even years. The ◊Cepheid variables regularly expand and contract in size every few days or weeks. —**variability** /-'bɪlɪtɪ/ *n.,* **variably** *adv.* [from Old French from Latin *variare* = vary]

variance /'veərɪəns/ *n.* a discrepancy. —**at variance,** disagreeing, conflicting; in a state of discord or enmity. [from Old French from Latin]

variant /'veərɪənt/ *adj.* differing in form or details from that named or from a standard; differing thus among themselves. —*n.* a variant form, spelling, type, etc.

variation /veərɪ'eɪʃən/ *n.* 1. varying; the extent to which a thing varies. 2. a thing that varies from a type. 3. music based on constant repetition of a simple theme, each new version being elaborated or treated in a different manner. The theme is easily recognizable, either as a popular tune or, as a gesture of respect, as the work of a fellow composer, for example, Brahms honours Bach in the *Variations on the St Antony Chorale.*

varicoloured /'veərɪkʌləd/ *adj.* 1. variegated in colour. 2. of various or different colours.

varicose /'værɪkəʊs/ *adj.* (of a vein etc.) permanently and abnormally swollen and twisted. The veins of the legs are most often affected, although other vulnerable sites include the rectum (◊haemorrhoids) and testes. —**varicosity** /-'kɒsɪtɪ/ *n.* [from Latin *varix* = varicose vein]

varied /'veərɪd/ *adj.* showing variety.

variegated /'veərɪɡeɪtɪd/ *adj.* marked with irregular patches of different colours. —**variegation** /-'geɪʃən/ *n.* in botany, the markings on plants that show white, cream, or yellow on their leaves, caused by areas of tissue that lack the green pigment ◊chlorophyll. Variegated plants are bred for their decorative value, but they are often considerably weaker than the normal, uniformly green plant. Many will not breed true and require ◊vegetative reproduction. [from Latin *variegare*]

variety /və'raɪətɪ/ *n.* 1. absence of uniformity; the quality of not being the same or of not being the same at all times. 2. a quantity, collection, or range of different things. 3. a class of things differing from others in the same general group; a specimen or member of such a class; a different form of a thing, quality, etc. 4. an entertainment consisting of a mixed series of short performances of different kinds (e.g. singing, dancing, comedy acts, acrobatics). [from French or Latin]

various /ˈveərɪəs/ *adj.* 1. of several kinds, unlike one another. 2. more than one, several; individual and separate. —**variously** *adv.* [from Latin *varius* = changing, diverse]

varlet /ˈvɑːlɪt/ *n.* (*archaic*) a menial, a rascal. [from Old French, variant of *vasle*]

Varna /ˈvɑːnə/ port in Bulgaria, on an inlet of the Black Sea; population (1987) 306,000. Industries include ship-building and the manufacture of chemicals.

varnish /ˈvɑːnɪʃ/ *n.* 1. a resinous solution used to give a hard, shiny, transparent coating; some other preparation for a similar purpose. 2. an external appearance or display without underlying reality. —*v.t.* 1. to apply varnish to. 2. to gloss over (a fact). [from Old French *vernis* from Latin or Greek]

varsity /ˈvɑːsɪtɪ/ *n.* 1. (*colloquial*, especially with reference to sports) abbreviation of university. 2. (*US*) the team representing a school or college etc. in a sport.

Varuna /vəˈruːnə/ in early Hindu mythology, the sky god and king of the universe.

varve *n.* a pair of layers of silt deposited in lakes where a glacier melts, one being of fine silt (deposited in winter, when there is little melting) and one of coarser silt (deposited in summer, when the ice melts more freely). [from Swedish *varv* = layer]

vary /ˈveərɪ/ *v.t./i.* 1. to make or become different. 2. to be different or of different kinds. [from Old French or Latin *variare*]

vas /væs/ *n.* (*plural* **vasa** /ˈveɪsə/) a duct, a vessel. [Latin = vessel]

Vasari /vəˈsɑːrɪ/ Giorgio 1511–1574. Italian art historian, architect, and painter, author of *Lives of the Most Excellent Architects, Painters and Sculptors* 1550 (enlarged and revised 1568), in which he proposed the theory of a Renaissance of the arts beginning with Giotto and culminating with Michelangelo. He designed the Uffizi Palace, Florence.

vascular /ˈvæskjʊlə/ *adj.* of or containing vessels for conveying blood, sap, etc. [from Latin *vasculum*, diminutive of *vas*]

vascular bundle a strand of primary conducting tissue (a 'vein') in vascular plants, consisting mainly of water-conducting tissues, metaxylem and protoxylem, which together make up the primary ◊xylem, and nutrient-conducting tissue, ◊phloem. It extends from the roots to the stems and leaves. Typically the phloem is situated nearest to the epidermis and the xylem towards the centre of the bundle. In plants exhibiting secondary growth, the xylem and phloem are separated by a thin layer of vascular ◊cambium, which gives rise to new conducting tissues.

vascular plant a plant containing vascular bundles. Pteridophytes (ferns, horsetails, and club mosses), gymnosperms (conifers and cycads), and angiosperms (flowering plants) are all vascular plants.

vas deferens /ˈdefərenz/ (*plural* **vasa deferentia** /defəˈrentɪə/) in male vertebrates, a tube conducting sperm from the testis to the urethra. The sperms are carried in a fluid secreted by various glands, and can be transported very rapidly when the smooth muscle in the wall of the vas deferens undergoes rhythmic contractions, as in sexual intercourse.

vase /vɑːz/ *n.* an open, usually tall, vessel of glass, pottery, etc., used for holding cut flowers or as an ornament. [French from Latin *vas*]

vasectomy /vəˈsektəmɪ/ *n.* male sterilization; an operation to cut and tie the duct (vas deferens) that carries sperm from the testes to the penis. Vasectomy does not affect sexual performance, but the semen produced at ejaculation no longer contains sperm. [from vas and Greek *ektomē* = excision]

Vaseline /ˈvæsəliːn/ *n.* the trade name of a type of petroleum jelly used as an ointment etc. [from German *wasser* = water and Greek *elaion* = oil]

vaso- /ˈveɪsəʊ/ in combinations, vessel, blood-vessel. —**vaso-motor** *adj.* causing constriction or dilatation of blood vessels. [from Latin *vas*]

vassal /ˈvæsəl/ *n.* 1. a humble servant or dependant. 2. (*historical*) in medieval Europe, a person who paid feudal homage to a superior lord (see ◊feudalism), and who promised military service and advice in return for a grant of land. —**vassalage** *n.* [from Old French from Latin *vassallus* = retainer; of Celtic origin]

Vassilou /væˈsiːluː/ Georgios Vassos 1931– . Greek-Cypriot politician and entrepreneur, president from 1988. A self-made millionaire, he entered politics as an independent and in 1988 won the presidency, with Communist Party support. He has since, with United Nations help, tried unsuccessfully to heal the rift between the Greek and Turkish communities.

vast /vɑːst/ *adj.* immense, very great in area or size. —**vastly** *adv.*, **vastness** *n.* [from Latin *vastus*]

vat *n.* a tank or other great vessel, especially for holding liquids in the process of brewing, tanning, dyeing, etc. —**vatful** *n.* [dialect variant of obsolete *fat*, Old English *fæt*]

VAT /viː eɪ ˈtiː, væt/ abbreviation of value-added tax.

Vatican Bank the bank of the Vatican City State, officially known as the Institute of Religious Works (IOR).

Vatican City State /ˈvætɪkən/ sovereign area in central Rome, Italy; **area** 0.4 sq km/109 acres; **physical** forms an enclave in the heart of Rome, Italy; **head of state and government** John Paul II from 1978; **population** (1985) 1,000; **language** Latin (official), Italian; **recent history** In 1947 new Italian constitution confirmed sovereignty of the city state.

Vatican Councils two Roman Catholic ecumenical councils called by Pope Pius IX in 1869 (which met in 1870) and by Pope John XXIII in 1959 (which met in 1962). These councils deliberated over elements of church policy.

vaudeville /ˈvɔːdəvɪl, ˈvəʊ-/ *n.* variety entertainment popular in the USA from the 1890s to the 1920s, in the same tradition as ◊music hall in Britain. [French, originally of convivial song, especially any of those composed by O Basselin, 15th-century poet born at *Vau de Vire* in Normandy]

Vaughan /vɔːn/ Henry 1622–1695. Welsh poet and physician. He published several volumes of metaphysical religious verse and prose devotions. His mystical outlook on nature influenced later poets, including Wordsworth.

Many is a summer's day, whose youth and fire
Cool to a glorious evening and expire.

Henry Vaughan,
Silex Scintillans; 'Rules and Lessons'

Vaughan Williams /ˈvɔːn ˈwɪljəmz/ Ralph 1872–1958. English composer. His style was tonal and often evocative of the English countryside through the use of folk themes. Among his works are the orchestral *Fantasia on a Theme by Thomas Tallis* 1910; the opera *Sir John in Love* 1929, featuring the Elizabethan song 'Greensleeves'; and nine symphonies 1909–57.

I don't know whether I like it, but it is what I meant.
Ralph Vaughan Williams
of his Fourth Symphony

---

vault[1] /vɔːlt, vɒlt/ *n.* 1. an arched roof. 2. a vault-like covering. 3. an underground room used as a place of storage. 4. a burial chamber. —*v.t.* (especially in *past participle*) to make in the form of a vault; to furnish with a vault or vaults. [from Old French, ultimately from Latin *volvere* = roll]

vault[2] *v.t./i.* to leap (over), especially while resting on the hand(s) or with the help of a pole. —*n.* a leap performed thus. —**vaulting-horse** *n.* a padded structure for vaulting over in a gymnasium. [from Old French *vo(u)lter* = leap]

vaulting *n.* the arched work in a vaulted roof or ceiling.

vaunt *v.t./i.* (*literary*) to boast. —*n.* (*literary*) a boast. [from Anglo-French from Latin *vanus* = vain]

VC abbreviation of Victoria Cross.

VD abbreviation of ◊venereal disease.

VDU abbreviation of **visual display unit**, an electronic output device for displaying on a screen the data processed by a computer. The oldest and most popular type is the ◊cathode-ray tube, which uses essentially the same technology as a television screen. Other types use plasma display technology and ◊liquid crystal displays.

've *v.t./i.* (*colloquial*, usually after pronouns) = **have**

veal *n.* calf's flesh as food. [from Anglo-French from Latin *vitellus* diminutive of *vitulus* = calf]

vector /'vektə/ n. 1. any physical quantity having both magnitude and direction, such as the velocity or acceleration of an object, as distinct from a scalar quantity, which has magnitude but no direction, such as speed, density, or mass. A vector is represented geometrically by an arrow whose length corresponds to its magnitude, and in an appropriate direction. Vectors can be added graphically by constructing a triangle of vectors (i.e. as the triangle of forces commonly employed in physics). 2. carrier of disease or infection. —**vectorial** /-'tɔːriəl/ adj. [Latin = carrier (vehere = convey)]

Veda /'veɪdə/ n. or **Vedas** the most sacred of the Hindu scriptures, hymns written in an old form of Sanskrit; the oldest may date from 1500 or 2000 BC. The four main collections are: the *Rigveda* (hymns and praises); *Yajurveda* (prayers and sacrificial formulae); *Sâmaveda* (tunes and chants); and *Atharvaveda*, or Veda of the Atharvans, the officiating priests at the sacrifices. —**Vedic** adj. [from Sanskrit = (sacred) knowledge]

Vedānta /vɪ'dɑːntə/ n. a school of Hindu philosophy that developed the teachings of the *Upanishads*. One of its teachers was Śamkara, who lived in S India in the 8th century AD and is generally regarded as a manifestation of Siva. He taught that there is only one reality, Brahman, and that knowledge of Brahman leads finally to *moksha*, or liberation from reincarnation.

veer v.i. to change direction or course; (of the wind) to change gradually in a clockwise direction. —n. a change of direction. [from French *virer*, perhaps from Latin *gyrare* = gyrate]

veg /vedʒ/ (*colloquial*) abbreviation of vegetable(s).

Vega /'veɪgə/ n. or **Alpha Lyrae** the brightest star in the constellation Lyra and the fifth brightest star in the sky. It is a blue-white star, 27 light years from Earth, with a luminosity 50 times that of the Sun.

vegan /'viːgən/ n. a person who eats no foods of animal origin, including eggs, milk, and honey. —adj. of vegans or their diet. [from *vegetarian*]

vegetable /'vedʒɪtəbəl/ n. 1. a plant of which some part is used (raw or cooked) for food, especially as an accompaniment to meat. 2. a person living a dull, monotonous life; one who is physically alive but mentally inert owing to injury, illness, or abnormality. —adj. of, from, or relating to plant life. [from Old French or Latin]

vegetal /'vedʒɪtəl/ adj. of plants; of the nature of plants.

vegetarian /vedʒɪ'teəriən/ n. a person who eats only foods obtained without slaughter, for humanitarian, aesthetic, or health reasons. —**vegetarianism** n.

vegetate /'vedʒɪteɪt/ v.i. 1. to lead a dull existence devoid of intellectual or social activity; to live in comfortably uneventful retirement or seclusion. 2. to grow as plants do. [from Latin *vegetare* = to animate]

vegetation /vedʒɪ'teɪʃən/ n. plants collectively, plant life.

vegetative /'vedʒɪtətɪv/ adj. 1. concerned with growth and development rather than (sexual) reproduction. 2. of vegetation. [from Old French or Latin]

vegetative reproduction a type of asexual ◊reproduction in plants that relies not on spores, but on multicellular structures formed by the parent plant. Some of the main types are ◊stolons and runners, ◊gemmae, bulbils (a small bulb that develops above ground from a bud), sucker shoots produced from roots, (such as in the creeping thistle *Cirsium arvense*), ◊tubers, bulbs, corms, and rhizomes.

vehement /'viːəmənt/ adj. showing or caused by strong feeling, ardent. —**vehemence** n., **vehemently** adv. [from French or Latin *vehemens*]

vehicle /'viːɪkəl/ n. 1. a conveyance for transporting passengers or goods on land or in space. 2. a medium by which thought, feeling, or action is expressed or displayed. 3. a liquid etc. as a medium for suspending pigments, drugs, etc. —**vehicular** /vɪ'hɪkjʊlə/ [from French or Latin *vehere* = convey]

veil /veɪl/ n. 1. a piece of fine net or other fabric worn as part of a head-dress or to protect or conceal the face. 2. a piece of linen etc. as part of a nun's headdress. 3. a curtain, especially that separating the sanctuary in the Jewish Temple. 4. a disguise, a pretext. —v.t. 1. to cover (as) with a veil. 2. to conceal partly. —**beyond the veil**, in the unknown state of life after death. **draw a veil over**, to avoid discussing or calling attention to. **take**

the veil, to become a nun. [from Anglo-French from Latin *velum*]

Veil /veɪ/ Simone 1927– . French politician. A survivor of Hitler's concentration camps, she was minister of health 1974–79 and framed the French abortion bill. In 1979–81 she was president of the European Parliament.

vein /veɪn/ n. 1. any of the tubes by which blood is conveyed to the heart; (*popularly*) any blood-vessel. Veins contain valves that prevent the blood from running back when moving against gravity. Veins always carry deoxygenated blood, with the exception of those leading from the lungs to the heart in birds and mammals, which carry newly oxygenated blood. 2. a rib of a leaf or insect's wing. 3. a streak or stripe of a different colour in wood, marble, cheese, etc. 4. a fissure in rock filled with ore. 5. a distinctive character or tendency, a mood. —**veined** adj., **veiny** adj. [from Old French from Latin *vena*]

Velázquez /vɪ'læskwɪz/ Diego Rodríguez de Silva y 1599–1660. Spanish painter, born in Seville, the outstanding Spanish artist of the 17th century. In 1623 he became court painter to Philip IV in Madrid, where he produced many portraits of the royal family, occasional religious paintings, genre scenes, and other subjects. *Las Meninas/The Ladies-in-Waiting* 1655 (Prado, Madrid) is a complex group portrait that includes a self-portrait but focuses on the doll-like figure of the Infanta Margareta Teresa.

Velcro /'velkrəʊ/ n. the trade name of a fastener for clothes etc., consisting of two strips of fabric with tiny loops on one and hooks on the other which cling together when pressed one upon the other, developed by Swiss inventor Georges de Mestral (1902–1990). [from French *velours croché* = hooked velvet]

veld /velt/ n. or **veldt**, open grassland in southern Africa equivalent to the ◊pampas of South America. [Afrikaans = *field*]

Velde, van de /væn də 'feldə/ a family of Dutch artists. Both **Willem van de Velde** the Elder (1611–93) and his son **Willem van de Velde** the Younger (1633–1707) painted sea battles for Charles II and James II (having settled in London in 1672). Another son **Adriaen van de Velde** (1636–72) painted landscapes.

veleta /və'liːtə/ n. an old-fashioned ballroom dance in triple time. [Spanish = weather vane]

vellum /'veləm/ n. 1. fine parchment originally from the skin of a calf, kid or lamb; a manuscript on this. Vellum was used during the Middle Ages, and occasionally later, for exceptionally important documents and the finest manuscripts. 2. smooth writing-paper imitating vellum. [from Old French *velin* from Latin *vitulus* = calf]

velocipede /vɪ'lɒsɪpiːd/ n. (*historical*) a light vehicle propelled by the rider, especially an early form of bicycle or tricycle. [from French from Latin *velox* = swift and *pes* = foot]

velocity /vɪ'lɒsɪtɪ/ n. speed, especially in a given direction (usually of inanimate things). Velocity is a ◊vector quantity, since its direction is important as well as its magnitude (or speed). [from French or Latin]

velocity ratio (VR), alternative term for **distance ratio** in a machine, the ratio of the distance moved by an effort force to the distance moved by the machine's load in the same time. It follows that the velocities of the effort and the load are in the same ratio. Velocity ratio has no units.

velour /və'lʊə/ n. or **velours** a plush-like woven fabric or felt. [French = velvet]

velvet /'velvɪt/ n. 1. a closely woven fabric (originally of silk) with a thick, short pile on one side. 2. a furry skin on a growing antler. —adj. of, like, or as soft as velvet. —**on velvet**, in an advantageous or prosperous position. **velvet glove**, outward gentleness cloaking sternness or inflexibility. —**velvety** adj. [from Old French *veluotte*, ultimately from Latin *villus* = down]

velveteen /velvɪ'tiːn/ n. cotton velvet.

Ven. abbreviation of Venerable (as the title of an archdeacon).

vena cava /viːnə 'keɪvə/ one of the large, thin-walled veins found just above the ◊heart, formed from the junction of several smaller veins. The **posterior vena cava** receives oxygenated blood returning from the lungs, and empties into the left atrium. The **anterior vena cava** collects deoxygenated blood returning from the rest of the body and passes it into the right side of the heart,

Venezuela

from where it will be pumped into the lungs. [Latin = hollow vein]

venal /'vi:nəl/ *adj.* (of a person) that may be bribed; (of conduct etc.) characteristic of a venal person. —**venality** /vi:'nælɪtɪ/ *n.*, **venally** *adv.* [from Latin *venalis* (*venum* = thing for sale)]

vend *v.t.* to offer (small wares) for sale. —**vending machine.** a slot-machine for the automatic retail of small articles. [from French or Latin *vendere* = sell]

Venda /'vendə/ ◊Black National State from 1979, near the Zimbabwe border, in South Africa, homeland of the Vhavenda people; **area** 6,500 sq km/2,510 sq mi; **capital** Thohoyandou; **government** executive president (paramount chief P R Mphephu in office from Sept 1979) and national assembly (not recognized outside South Africa); **products** coal, copper, graphite, construction stone; **population** (1980) 343,500; **language** Luvenda, English.

Vendée, Wars of the /vɒn'deɪ/ in the French Revolution, a series of peasant uprisings against the revolutionary government that began in the Vendée *département*, W France, in 1793, and spread to other areas of France, lasting until 1795.

vendetta /ven'detə/ *n.* a blood feud; prolonged bitter hostility, in particular one in which the relatives of a dishonoured or murdered person seek revenge on the wrongdoer or members of the family. The tradition is Mediterranean, known in Europe and the USA as a way of settling wrongs in Corsica, Sardinia, and Sicily, as practised by the ◊Mafia. [Italian from Latin *vindicta* = vengeance]

vendor *n.* 1. (especially in law) one who sells. 2. a vending machine. [from Anglo-French]

veneer /vɪ'nɪə/ *v.t.* 1. to cover (wood) with a thin layer of a finer wood. 2. (especially in *past participle*) to disguise (character etc.) superficially. —*n.* 1. a layer used in veneering. 2. a superficial show of some good quality. [earlier *fineer* from German *furni(e)ren*, from Old French *furnir*]

venerable /'venərəbəl/ *adj.* 1. entitled to veneration on account of character, age, associations, etc. 2. the title of an archdeacon in the Church of England. —**venerability** /-'bɪlɪtɪ/ *n.*, **venerably** *adv.* [from Old French or Latin]

venerate /'venəreɪt/ *v.t.* to regard with deep respect; to honour as hallowed or sacred. —**veneration** /-'reɪʃən/ *n.*, **venerator** *n.* [from Latin *venerari* = adore, revere]

venereal /vɪ'nɪərɪəl/ *adj.* of sexual desire or intercourse; relating to venereal disease. —**venereally** *adv.* [from Latin *venereus* (*venus* = sexual love)]

venereal disease (VD) any disease mainly transmitted by sexual contact, although commonly the term is used specifically for gonorrhoea and syphilis, both occurring worldwide, and chancroid ('soft sore') and lymphogranuloma venerum, seen mostly in the tropics. The term **sexually transmitted diseases** (◊STDs) is more often used to encompass a growing list of conditions including ◊AIDS and ◊scabies, which are passed on primarily, but not exclusively, in this way.

Venetian /vɪ'ni:ʃən/ *adj.* of Venice. —*n.* a native or the dialect of Venice. —**venetian blind,** a window-blind of horizontal slats that can be adjusted to let in or exclude

light. [from Old French, assimilated to Latin *Venetianus* (*Venetia* = Venice)]

Veneto /'venətəʊ/ region of NE Italy, comprising the provinces of Belluno, Padova (Padua), Treviso, Rovigo, Venezia (Venice), and Vicenza; **area** 18,400 sq km/7,102 sq mi; **population** (1988) 4,375,000; **capital** Venice; **physical** Veneto forms part of the N Italian plain, with the delta of the river Po; it includes part of the Alps and Dolomites, and Lake Garda; **products** cereals, fruit, vegetables, wine, chemicals, shipbuilding, and textiles.

Venezuela /veni'zweilə/ Republic of; country in northern South America, on the Caribbean Sea, bounded E by Guyana, S by Brazil, and W by Colombia. **area** 912,100 sq km/352,162 sq mi; **capital** Caracas; **physical** Andes mountains and Lake Maracaibo in NW; central plains (llanos); delta of river Orinoco in E; Guiana Highlands in SE; Angel Falls, world's highest waterfall; **head of state and government** Carlos Andrés Perez from 1988; **political system** federal democratic republic; **exports** coffee, timber, oil, aluminium, iron ore, petrochemicals; **population** (1990 est) 19,753,000; **language** Spanish (official), Indian languages; **recent history** independence achieved from Spain in 1830 after a rebellion led by Simón Bolívar. After a long history of dictatorial rule, a new constitution was adopted in 1961, and stability increased, until economic problems in the 1980s led to the 1989 riots triggered by economic austerity programme and martial law declared.

vengeance /'vendʒəns/ *n.* revenge for hurt or harm to oneself or to a person etc. whose cause one supports. —**with a vengeance,** to an extreme degree, more than was expected. [from Old French *venger* = avenge from Latin *vindicare*]

vengeful *adj.* vindictive, seeking vengeance. —**vengefully** *adv.*, **vengefulness** *n.* [from obsolete *venge* = avenge]

venial /'vi:nɪəl/ *adj.* (of a sin or fault) pardonable, excusable, not mortal. —**veniality** /vi:nɪ'ælɪtɪ/ *n.*, **venially** *adv.* [from Old French from Latin *venia* = forgiveness]

Venice /'venɪs/ (Italian *Venezia*) city, port, and naval base, capital of Veneto, Italy, on the Adriatic; population (1988) 328,000. The old city is built on piles on low-lying islands. Apart from tourism, industries include glass, jewellery, textiles, and lace. Venice was an independent trading republic from the 10th century, ruled by a doge, or chief magistrate, and was one of the centres of the Italian Renaissance.

venison /'venɪsən/ *n.* deer's flesh as food. [from Old French from Latin *venatio* = hunting]

veni, vidi, vici the Roman general Julius ◊Caesar's description of his victory over King Pharnaces II (63–47 BC) at Zela in 47 BC. [Latin: I came, I saw, I conquered]

Venizelos /veni'zelɒs/ Eleuthérios 1864–1936. Greek politician born in Crete, leader of the Cretan movement against Turkish rule until the union of the island with Greece in 1905. He later became prime minister of the Greek state on five occasions, 1910–15, 1917–20, 1924, 1928–32, and 1933, before being exiled to France in 1935.

Venn diagram /ven/ in mathematics, a diagram representing a set or sets and the logical relationships between them. Sets are drawn as circles. An area of overlap between two circles (sets) contains elements common to both and represents a third set. Circles that do not overlap represent sets with no elements in common (disjoint sets). [from British logician John *Venn* (1834–1923)]

venom /'venəm/ *n.* 1. poisonous fluid secreted by certain snakes, scorpions, etc., and injected into a victim by a bite or sting. 2. virulence of feeling, language, or conduct. [from Old French from Latin *venenum* = poison]

venomous /'venəməs/ *adj.* 1. secreting venom. 2. full of venom in feeling etc. —**venomously** *adv.*

venous /'vi:nəs/ *adj.* of, full of, or contained in veins. [from Latin *vena* = vein]

vent[1] *n.* 1. a hole or opening allowing air, gas, or liquid to pass out of or into a confined space. 2. the anus, especially of a lower animal. 3. an outlet; free passage or play. —*v.t.* 1. to make a vent in. 2. to give vent or free expression to. —**vent light,** a small window, hinged at the top edge. [from French from Latin *ventus* = wind]

vent[2] *n.* a slit in a garment, especially in the lower edge of the back of a coat. [from Old French *fente* from Latin *findere* = cleave]

ventilate

1178

ventilate /ˈvɛntɪleɪt/ *v.t.* **1.** to cause air to circulate freely in (a room etc.). **2.** to express (a question, grievance, etc.) publicly for consideration and discussion. —**ventilation** /-ˈleɪʃən/ *n.* [from Latin *ventilare* = blow, winnow]

ventilator *n.* **1.** an appliance or aperture for ventilating a room etc. **2.** equipment for maintaining breathing artificially.

ventral /ˈventrəl/ *adj.* of or on the abdomen. —**ventrally** *adv.* [from Latin *venter* = abdomen]

ventricle /ˈventrɪkəl/ *n.* a cavity in the body, the hollow part of an organ, especially each of four in the brain or of two in the heart that pump blood into the arteries by contracting. —**ventricular** /-ˈtrɪkjʊlə/ *adj.* [from Latin *ventriculus* diminutive of *venter* = belly]

ventriloquist /venˈtrɪləkwɪst/ *n.* an entertainer who produces voice-sounds so that they seem to come from a source other than him- or herself. —**ventriloquism** *n.* [from Latin *venter* = belly and *loqui* = speak]

ventriloquize /venˈtrɪləkwaɪz/ *v.i.* to use ventriloquism.

venture /ˈventʃə/ *n.* an undertaking that involves risk; a commercial speculation. —*v.t./i.* **1.** to dare, not to be afraid; to dare to go, do, or utter. **2.** to expose to risk, to stake. **3.** to take risks. —**at a venture,** at random; without previous consideration. **venture on,** to dare to engage in or make etc. **Venture Scout,** a member of the senior section of the Scout Association. [from Old French from Latin *adventus* = arrival (*venire* = come)]

venture capital or **risk capital** money put up by investors such as merchant banks to fund a new company or expansion of an established company. The organization providing the money receives a share of the company's equity and seeks to make a profit by rapid growth in the value of its stake, as a result of expansion by the start-up company or 'venture'.

venturesome *adj.* **1.** willing to take risks, daring. **2.** risky.

Venturi /venˈtjuəri/ Robert 1925– . US architect who pioneered Post-Modernism through his books *Complexity and Contradiction in Architecture* 1967 and *Learning from Las Vegas* 1972. In 1986 he was commissioned to design an extension to the National Gallery, London.

venturi tube a device consisting of a short section of tube which is narrower than the parts at each end, so that gas or liquid under pressure flows through it faster, used to produce an effect of suction or in measuring the rate of flow [from G B *Venturi,* Italian physicist]

venue /ˈvenjuː/ *n.* **1.** an appointed place of meeting, especially for a sports match. **2.** the county etc. within which a jury must be gathered and a cause tried. [French = coming *venir* = come]

Venus /ˈviːnəs/ in Roman mythology, the goddess of love (Greek **Aphrodite**).

Venus *n.* the second planet from the Sun. It orbits the Sun every 225 days at an average distance of 108.2 million km/67.2 million mi and can approach the Earth to within 38 million km/24 million mi, closer than any other planet. Its diameter is 12,100 km/7,500 mi and its mass is 0.82 that of Earth. Venus rotates on its axis more slowly than any other planet, once every 243 days and from east to west. It is shrouded by clouds of sulphuric acid droplets that sweep across the planet from E to W every four days. The atmosphere is carbon dioxide, which traps the Sun's heat by the ◊greenhouse effect and raises the planet's surface temperature to 480°C/900°F, with an atmospheric pressure 90 times that at Earth's surface.

Venus flytrap insectivorous plant *Dionaea muscipula* of the sundew family, native to the SE USA; its leaves have two hinged blades that close and entrap insects.

veracious /vəˈreɪʃəs/ *adj.* **1.** truthful. **2.** (of a statement etc.) that is or is meant to be true. —**veraciously** *adv.,* **veracity** /vəˈræsɪtɪ/ *n.* [from Latin *verax* (*verus* = true)]

veranda /vəˈrændə/ *n.* a roofed terrace along the side of a house. [from Hindi from Portuguese *varanda*]

verb *n.* the grammatical part of speech for what someone or something does (*to go*), experiences (*to live*), or is (*to be*). Verbs involve the grammatical categories known as number (singular or plural: 'He *runs*; they *run*'), voice (active or passive: 'She *writes* books; it *is written*'), mood (statements, questions, orders, emphasis, necessity, condition), aspect (completed or continuing action: 'She *danced*; she *was dancing*'), and tense (variation according to time: simple present tense, present progressive tense, simple

past tense, and so on). **types of verb** – a **transitive** verb takes a direct object ('He *saw* the house'); an **intransitive** verb has no object ('She *laughed*'); an **auxiliary** or **helping** verb is used to express tense and/or mood ('He *was* seen'; 'They *may* come'); a **modal** verb or **modal auxiliary** generally shows only mood; common modals are *may/might, will/would, can/could, shall/should, must*; the **infinitive** of the verb usually includes *to* (*to go, to run* and so on), but may be a bare infinitive (for example, after modals, as in 'She may *go*'); a **regular** verb forms tenses in the normal way (*I walk: I walked: I have walked*); irregular verbs do not (*swim: swam: swum; put: put: put*; and so on). Because of their conventional nature, regular verbs are also known as weak verbs, while some irregular verbs are strong verbs with special vowel changes across tenses, as in *swim: swam: swum* and *ride: rode: ridden*; a **phrasal verb** is a construction in which a particle attaches to a usually single-syllable verb (for example, *put* becoming *put up*, as in 'She put up some money for the project', and *put up with*, as in 'I can't put up with this nonsense any longer'). [from French or Latin *verbum*, literally = word]

verbal *adj.* **1.** of or in words. **2.** spoken, not written. **3.** of a verb. **4.** (of a translation) literal. —*n.* (*colloquial*) a verbal statement, especially one made to the police. —**verbal noun,** a noun (e.g. *singing, dancing,* or other nouns ending in *-ing*) derived from a verb and partly sharing its constructions. —**verbally** *adv.*

verbalism /ˈvɜːbəlɪzəm/ *n.* minute attention to words.

verbalize /ˈvɜːbəlaɪz/ *v.t./i.* **1.** to express in words. **2.** to be verbose. —**verbalization** /-ˈzeɪʃən/ *n.*

verbatim /vɜːˈbeɪtɪm/ *adv.* & *adj.* in exactly the same words, word for word.

verbena /vɜːˈbiːnə/ *n.* a herb or small shrub of the genus *Verbena* of about 100 species, mostly found in the American tropics. The leaves are fragrant and the tubular flowers arranged in close spikes in colours ranging from white to rose, violet, and purple. The garden verbena is a hybrid annual. —**lemon verbena,** a similar plant *Lippia citriodora* with lemon-scented leaves. [Latin, originally = sacred bough of olive]

verbiage /ˈvɜːbiɪdʒ/ *n.* an excessive number of words used to express an idea. [French obsolete *verbeier* = chatter from *verbe*]

verbose /vɜːˈbəʊs/ *adj.* using or expressed in more words than are needed. —**verbosely** *adv.,* **verbosity** /vɜːˈbɒsɪtɪ/ *n.* [from Latin *verbum* = word]

Vercingetorix /vɜːsɪnˈdʒetərɪks/ Gallic chieftain. Leader of a revolt of all the tribes of Gall against the Romans in 52 BC. He lost, was captured, displayed in Julius Caesar's triumph of 46 BC, and later executed. This ended the Gallic resistance to Roman rule.

verdant /ˈvɜːdənt/ *adj.* (of grass etc.) green, fresh-coloured; (of a field etc.) covered with green grass etc. —**verdancy** *n.* [perhaps from Old French *verdoier* = be green, from Latin *viridis* = green]

Verdi /ˈveədi/ Giuseppe (Fortunino Francesco) 1813–1901. Italian opera composer of the Romantic period, who took his native operatic style to new heights of dramatic expression. In 1842 he wrote the opera *Nabucco*, followed by *Ernani* 1844 and *Rigoletto* 1851. Other works include *Il Trovatore* and *La Traviata* both 1853, *Aïda* 1871, and the masterpieces of his old age, *Otello* 1887 and *Falstaff* 1893. His *Requiem* 1874 commemorates Alessandro ◊Manzoni.

verdict /ˈvɜːdɪkt/ *n.* **1.** in law, the decision of a jury on an issue of fact in a civil or criminal cause usually a finding of 'guilty' or 'not guilty'. **2.** a decision or opinion given after examining, testing, or experiencing something. [from Anglo-French *verdit* (*veir* = true from Latin *verus* and *dit* past participle of *dicere* = say)]

verdigris /ˈvɜːdɪgrɪs, -riːs/ *n.* a green deposit on copper or brass. [from Old French = green of Greece]

Verdun /vɜːˈdʌn/ fortress town in NE France on the Meuse. During World War I it became the symbol of French resistance, withstanding a German onslaught in 1916.

verdure /ˈvɜːdjə, -djuə/ *n.* green vegetation; the greenness of this. —**verdurous** *adj.* [from Old French *verd* = green from Latin *viridis*]

verge[1] *n.* **1.** a brink or border (usually *figurative*). **2.** a grass edging of a road, flower bed, etc. [from Old French from Latin *virga* = rod]

verge[2] *v.i.* to incline downwards or in a specified direction. —**verge on**, to border on, to approach closely. [from Latin *vergere* = incline]

verger *n.* an official in a Christian church who acts as caretaker and attendant; an officer who bears a staff before a bishop or other dignitary.

Vergil alternative spelling for ◊Virgil, Roman poet.

verifiable /'verɪfaɪəbəl/ *adj.* that may be verified.

verify /'verɪfaɪ/ *v.t.* to establish the truth or correctness of by examination or demonstration; (of an event etc.) to bear out, to fulfil (a prediction or promise). —**verification** /-fɪ'keɪʃən/ *n.*, **verifier** *n.* [from Old French from Latin *verus* = true and *facere* = make]

verily /'verɪlɪ/ *adv.* (*archaic*) really, truly.

verisimilitude /verɪsɪ'mɪlɪtjuːd/ *n.* the appearance of being true or real. [from Latin *verus* = true and *similis* = like]

veritable /'verɪtəbəl/ *adj.* real, rightly so called. —**veritably** *adv.* [Old French]

vérité *n.* (of a film) as in *cinéma vérité*, in a realistic or documentary style. [French = realism]

verity /'verɪtɪ/ *n.* a true statement; truth. [from Old French from Latin *veritas* = truth]

Verlaine /veə'leɪn/ Paul 1844–1896. French lyric poet who was influenced by Baudelaire and ◊Rimbaud. His volumes of verse include *Poèmes saturniens/Saturnine Poems* 1866, *Fêtes galantes/Amorous Entertainments* 1869 and *Romances sans paroles/Songs without Words* 1874. In 1873 he was imprisoned for attempting to shoot Rimbaud. He was acknowledged as leader of the Symbolist poets (see ◊symbolism).

All the rest is mere fine writing.

Paul Verlaine,
Jadis et Naguère: L'art poétique

Vermeer /veə'mɪə/ Jan 1632–1675. Dutch painter, active in Delft. Most of his pictures are ◊genre scenes, with a limpid clarity and distinct air of stillness, and a harmonious palette often focusing on yellow and blue. He frequently depicted solitary women in domestic settings, as in *The Lacemaker* (Louvre, Paris).

vermicelli /vɜː'miːselɪ, -tʃelɪ/ *n.* pasta made in slender threads. [Italian, diminutive of *verme* from Latin *vermis* = worm]

vermicide /'vɜːmɪsaɪd/ *n.* a drug that kills worms. [from Latin]

vermiform /'vɜːmɪfɔːm/ *adj.* worm-shaped. —**vermiform appendix**, a small blind tube extending from the caecum in humans and some other mammals.

vermilion /və'mɪljən/ *n.* **1.** cinnabar. **2.** a brilliant red pigment made by grinding this or artificially. **3.** the colour of this. —*adj.* of this colour. [from Old French *vermeillon*]

vermin /'vɜːmɪn/ *n.* **1.** (usually treated as *plural*) common mammals and birds injurious to game, crops, etc., e.g. foxes, mice, owls. **2.** noxious or parasitic worms or insects. **3.** vile persons, those harmful to society. [from Old French, ultimately from Latin *vermis* = worm]

verminous /'vɜːmɪnəs/ *adj.* of the nature of vermin; infested with vermin.

Vermont /vɜː'mɒnt/ state of the USA in New England; nickname Green Mountain State; **area** 24,900 sq km/9,611 sq mi; **capital** Montpelier; **features** Green Mountains, Lake Champlain; **products** apples, maple syrup, dairy products, china clay, asbestos, granite, marble, slate, business machines, furniture, paper; **population** (1986) 541,000; **history** settled 1724; state 1791. The Green Mountain Boys were irregulars who fought to keep Vermont from New York interference.

vermouth /'vɜːməθ/ *n.* a white wine flavoured with bitter herbs and fortified by alcohol. It is made in France and Italy. [from French from German *wermut* = wormwood]

vernacular /və'nækjʊlə/ *n.* **1.** the language or dialect of the country. **2.** the language of a particular class or group. **3.** homely speech. —*adj.* (of a language) of one's native country, not of foreign origin or of learned formation. [from Latin *vernaculus* = domestic, native (*verna* = home-born slave)]

vernal /'vɜːnəl/ *adj.* of, occurring in, or appropriate to spring. —**vernally** *adv.* [from Latin *vernalis ver* = spring)]

Verne *French adventure and science-fiction novelist Jules Verne.*

vernal equinox see ◊equinox.

vernalization *n.* the stimulation of flowering by exposure to cold. Certain plants will not flower unless subjected to low temperatures during their development. For example, winter wheat will flower in summer only if planted in the previous autumn. By placing partially germinated seeds in low temperatures for several days, the cold requirement can be supplied artificially, and wheat sown in the spring.

Verne /vɜːn/ Jules 1828–1905. French author of tales of adventure that anticipated future scientific developments: *Five Weeks in a Balloon* 1862, *Journey to the Centre of the Earth* 1864, *Twenty Thousand Leagues under the Sea* 1870, and *Around the World in Eighty Days* 1873.

vernier /'vɜːnɪə/ *n.* device for taking readings on a graduated scale to a fraction of a division. It consists of a short divided scale that carries an index or pointer and is slid along a main scale. It was invented by French mathematician Pierre Vernier (1580–1637).

Vernier /'veənɪə/ Pierre 1580–1637. French mathematician who invented a means of making very precise measurements with what is now called the vernier scale. He was a French government official and in 1631 published a book explaining his method called 'a new mathematical quadrant'.

Verona /və'rəʊnə/ industrial city (printing, paper, plastics, furniture, pasta) in Veneto, Italy, on the Adige; population (1988) 259,000. It also trades in fruit and vegetables.

Veronese /verəʊ'neɪzi/ Paolo *c.*1528–1588. Italian painter, born in Verona, active mainly in Venice from about 1553. He specialized in grand decorative schemes, such as his ceilings in the Doge's Palace in Venice, with *trompe l'oeil* effects and inventive detail. The subjects are religious, mythological, historical, and allegorical.

veronica /və'rɒnɪkə/ *n.* **1.** a plant of the genus *Veronica*, speedwell. **2.** or **vernicle** a depiction of the face of Christ on a cloth. [Latin, from woman's name *Veronica*]

verruca /və'ruːkə/ *n.* (*plural* **verrucae** /-siː/ or **verrucas**) growth on the skin; see ◊wart. [Latin]

Versailles /veə'saɪ/ city in N France, capital of Les Yvelines *département*, on the outskirts of Paris; population (1982) 95,240. It grew up around the palace of Louis XV. Within the palace park are two small châteaux, Le Grand and Le Petit ◊Trianon, built for Louis XIV (by Jules ◊Hardouin-Mansart) and Louis XV (by Jacques Gabriel 1698–1782) respectively.

Versailles, Treaty of peace treaty after World War I between the Allies and Germany, signed on 28 June 1919. It established the League of Nations. Germany surrendered Alsace-Lorraine to France, and large areas in the E to Poland, and made smaller cessions to Czechoslovakia, Lithuania, Belgium, and Denmark. The Rhineland was demilitarized, German rearmament was restricted, and Germany agreed to pay reparations for war damage. The treaty was never ratified by the USA, which made a separate peace with Germany and Austria in 1921.

versatile /'vɜ:sətaɪl/ *adj.* able to do or to be used for many different things. —**versatility** /-'tɪlɪtɪ/ *n.* [French, or from Latin *versare* = turn]

verse *n.* 1. a metrical form of composition. 2. a stanza of metrical lines; a metrical line. 3. each of the short numbered divisions of the Bible. [Old English and from Old French from Latin *versus* = turn of plough, furrow, line of writing]

versed /vɜ:st/ *adj.* (with *in*) experienced or skilled in, having a knowledge of. [from French or Latin *versari* = be engaged in]

versicle /'vɜ:sɪkəl/ *n.* in the Christian church, each of the short sentences in a liturgy said or sung by a priest etc. and alternating with the responses. [from Old French or Latin *versiculus* diminutive of *versus* = line of writing]

versify /'vɜ:sɪfaɪ/ *v.t./i.* to turn into or express in verse; to compose verses. —**versification** /-fɪ'keɪʃən/ *n.* [from Old French from Latin *versificare*]

version /'vɜ:ʃən/ *n.* 1. an account of a matter from a particular person's point of view 2. a book or work etc. in a particular edition or translation. 3. a particular variant. [French or from Latin *vertere* = turn]

verso *n.* (*plural* **versos**) the left-hand page of an open book, the back of a leaf of a book etc. The right-hand page is **recto**. [from Latin *verso* (*folio*) = turned (leaf)]

versus /'vɜ:səs/ *prep.* (especially in law and in sport) against. [Latin = against]

vert *n.* (in heraldry) green. [from Old French from Latin *viridis* = green]

vertebra /'vɜ:tɪbrə/ *n.* (*plural* **vertebrae** /-i:/) each segment of the backbone. —**vertebral** *adj.* [Latin *vertere* = turn]

vertebrate /'vɜ:tɪbrət, -reɪt/ *adj.* having a spinal column, and thus belonging to the subphylum Vertebrata of the ◊phylum Chordata. There are 41,000 species, including fish, amphibians, reptiles, birds, and mammals. —*n.* a vertebrate animal. [from Latin *vertebratus* = jointed]

vertex /'vɜ:teks/ *n.* (*plural* **vertices** /-ɪsi:z/ or **vertexes**) 1. the highest point of a hill or structure; the apex. 2. each angular point of a triangle, polygon, etc.; the meeting-point of the lines that form an angle. [Latin = whirlpool, crown of head]

vertical *adj.* 1. at right angles to the plane of the horizon. 2. in the direction from top to bottom of a picture etc. 3. of or at the vertex. —*n.* a vertical line or plane. —**vertically** *adv.* [French or from Latin *vertex*]

vertical takeoff and landing craft (VTOL) aircraft that can take off and land vertically. Helicopters, airships, and balloons can do this, as can a few fixed-wing aeroplanes. See ◊helicopter, ◊convertiplane.

vertiginous /vɜ:'tɪdʒɪnəs/ *adj.* of or causing vertigo.

vertigo /'vɜ:tɪgəʊ/ *n.* (*plural* **vertigos** dizziness; a whirling sensation accompanied by a loss of any feeling of contact with the ground. It may be due to temporary disturbance of the sense of balance (as in spinning for too long on one spot), psychological reasons, disease, or intoxication. [Latin = whirling *vertere* = turn]

Verulamium /veru:'leɪmɪəm/ Roman-British town whose remains lie close to St Albans, Hertfordshire.

vervain /'vɜ:veɪn/ *n.* a herbaceous plant of the genus *Verbena*, especially *V. officinalis* with small blue, white, or purple flowers. [from Old French from Latin]

verve *n.* enthusiasm, vigour, especially in artistic or literary work. [from Latin *verba* = words]

Verwoerd /fə'vʊət/ Hendrik (Frensch) 1901–1966. South African right-wing Nationalist Party politician, prime minister 1958–66. As minister of native affairs 1950–58, he was the chief promoter of apartheid legislation (segregation by race). He made the country a republic in 1961. He was assassinated in 1966.

very /'verɪ/ *adv.* 1. in a high degree. 2. (with superlative adjectives or *own*) in the fullest sense. 3. exactly. 4. (*archaic*) genuine, truly so called, —*adj.* 1. itself or himself etc. and no other; actual, truly such. 2. extreme, utter. —**not very**, in a low degree; far from being. **very good** *or* **well**, an expression of approval or consent. **very high frequency**, (in radio) 30–300 megahertz. [from Old French *verai* thus = truth]

Very Large Array (VLA) the largest and most complex single-site radio telescope in the world. It is located on the Plains of San Augustine, 80 km/50 mi west of Socorro, New Mexico, USA. It consists of 27 dish antennae, each 25 m/82 ft in diameter, arranged along three equally spaced arms forming a Y-shaped array. Two of the arms are 21 km/13 mi long, and the third, to the N, is 19 km/11.8 mi long. The dishes are mounted on railway tracks enabling the configuration and size of the array to be altered as required.

Very light /'verɪ, 'vɪərɪ/a flare projected from a pistol for signalling or temporarily illuminating part of a battlefield etc. [from E W *Very*, American inventor (died 1910)]

Vesalius /vɪ'seɪlɪəs/ Andreas 1514–1564. Belgian physician who revolutionized the field of anatomy. His great innovations were to perform postmortem dissections, and to make use of illustrations in teaching anatomy.

vesica *n.* a pointed oval used as an aureole in European medieval sculpture and painting. [Latin = bladder, blister]

vesicle /'vesɪkəl/ *n.* a small bladder, blister, or bubble. [from French or Latin *vesicula* diminutive of *vesica* = bladder]

Vespasian /ve'speɪʒən/ (Titus Flavius Vespasianus) 9–AD 79. Roman emperor from AD 69. He was the son of a moneylender, and had a distinguished military career. He was proclaimed emperor by his soldiers while he was campaigning in Palestine. He reorganized the eastern provinces, and was a capable administrator.

> An emperor should die standing.
>
> **Vespasian**
> from Suetonius, *Twelve Caesars*

vespers /'vespəz/ *n. pl.* the evening service in the Western (Roman Catholic) Church. It is the seventh of the eight canonical hours. [from Old French from Latin *vesper* = evening, evening star]

Vespucci /ves'pu:tʃi/ Amerigo 1454–1512. Florentine merchant. The Americas were named after him as a result of the widespread circulation of his accounts of his explorations. His accounts of the voyage 1499–1501 indicate that he had been to places he could not possibly have reached (the Pacific Ocean, British Columbia, Antarctica).

vessel /'vesəl/ *n.* 1. a hollow receptacle, especially for liquid. 2. a hollow structure designed to travel on water and carry people or goods, a ship or boat. 3. a tubelike structure holding or conveying blood or sap etc. in the body of an animal or plant. [from Anglo-French from Latin *vascellum* diminutive of *vas* = vessel]

vest[1] *n.* 1. a knitted or woven undergarment covering the trunk of the body. 2. (*US* and in commerce) a waistcoat. —**vest-pocket** *adj.* of a very small size, as if suitable for carrying in a waistcoat pocket. [from French from Italian from Latin *vestis* = garment]

vest[2] *v.t./i.* 1. to confer (on) as a firm or legal right. 2. (of property or a right etc.; with *in*) to come into the possession of. 3. (usually *archaic*) to clothe. —**vested interest** *or* **right**, one securely held by right or by long association. **a vested interest in**, an expectation of benefiting from. [from Old French from Latin *vestire* = clothe]

Vesta /'vestə/ in Roman mythology, the goddess of the hearth (Greek **Hestia**). In Rome, the sacred flame in her shrine in the Forum was kept constantly lit by the six **Vestal Virgins**.

vestibule /'vestɪbju:l/ *n.* 1. an antechamber, entrance hall, or lobby next to the outer door of a building. 2. (*US*) an enclosed entrance to a railway carriage. [French or from Latin *vestibulum* = entrance-court]

vestige /'vestɪdʒ/ *n.* 1. a trace, a small remaining part of what once existed. 2. a very small amount. 3. a part or organ (of a plant or animal) that remains in diminished form after it has ceased to have any significant function but was well developed in the ancestors. —**vestigial** /-'tɪdʒɪəl/ *adj.* [French from Latin *vestigium* = footprint]

vestment /'vestmənt/ *n.* 1. any of the official garments of the clergy, choristers, etc., worn during religious service, especially the chasuble. 2. a garment, especially an official or state robe. [from Old French from Latin *vestire* = clothe]

vestry /'vestrɪ/ *n.* 1. a room or building attached to a church, where vestments are kept and where clergy and choir robe themselves. 2. (*historical*) a meeting of parishioners, usually in the vestry, for parochial business; the body of parishioners meeting thus. [from Old French from Latin *vestis* = garment]

Vesuvius /vi'su:viəs/ (Italian *Vesuvio*) active volcano SE of Naples, Italy; height 1,277 m/4,190 ft. In 79 BC it destroyed the cities of Pompeii, Herculaneum, and Oplonti.

vet *n.* (*colloquial*) a veterinary surgeon. —*v.t.* (-tt-) 1. to examine carefully and critically for faults or errors etc. 2. to examine or treat (an animal). [abbreviation]

vetch *n.* a plant of the pea family especially of the genus *Vicia*, largely used for fodder. [from Anglo-French from Latin]

vetchling *n.* a plant of the genus *Lathyrus*, allied to vetch.

veteran /'vetərən/ *n.* 1. a person with long experience, especially in the armed forces. 2. (*US*) a former member of the armed forces. —**veteran car**, a car made before 1916, especially before 1905. [from French or Latin *vetus* = old]

Veterans Day in the US, the name adopted in 1954 for Armistice Day (see ◊armistice) and from 1971 observed by most states on the fourth Monday in Oct. The equivalent in the UK and Canada is ◊Remembrance Sunday.

veterinarian /vetəri'neəriən/ *n.* a veterinary surgeon.

veterinary /'vetərinəri/ *adj.* of or for the diseases of farm and domestic animals or their treatment. —*n.* a veterinary surgeon. —**veterinary surgeon**, one skilled in such treatment. [from Latin *veterinae* = cattle]

veto /'vi:təu/ *n.* (*plural* **vetoes**) 1. the constitutional right to reject a legislative enactment; the right of a permanent member of the UN Security Council to reject a resolution. 2. such a rejection; an official message conveying this. 3. a prohibition. —*v.t.* to exercise one's veto against; to forbid authoritatively. [Latin = I forbid]

vex *v.t.* 1. to annoy, to irritate. 2. (*archaic*) to grieve, to afflict. —**vexed question**, a problem that is much discussed. [from Old French from Latin *vexare* = shake, disturb]

vexation /vek'seɪʃən/ *n.* 1. vexing, being vexed; a state of irritation or worry. 2. an annoying or distressing thing.

vexatious /vek'seɪʃəs/ *adj.* causing vexation, annoying; in law, not having sufficient grounds for action and seeking only to annoy the defendant. —**vexatiously** *adv.*, **vexatiousness** *n.*

VHF abbreviation for very high frequency, referring to radio waves that have very short wavelengths. They are used for interference-free ◊FM (frequency-modulated) transmissions. VHF transmitters have a relatively short range because the waves cannot be reflected over the horizon like longer radio waves.

via /'vaɪə/ *prep.* by way of, through. [Latin ablative of *via* = way]

viable /'vaɪəbəl/ *adj.* capable of living or existing successfully; (of a fetus) sufficiently developed to be able to survive after birth; (of a plan etc.) feasible, especially from an economic standpoint. —**viability** /-'bɪlɪtɪ/ *n.*, **viably** *adv.* [French *vie* = life from Latin *vita*]

viaduct /'vaɪədʌkt/ *n.* a bridgelike structure, especially a series of arches, carrying a railway or road across a valley or dip in the ground. [from Latin *via* = way, after *aqueduct*]

vial /'vaɪəl/ *n.* a small vessel, usually cylindrical and made of glass, especially for holding liquid medicines. [from Old French from Latin from Greek]

viand /'vaɪənd/ *n.* (*archaic*, usually in *plural*) an article of food. [from Old French from Latin *vivenda* (gerundive of *vivere* = live)]

viaticum /vaɪ'ætɪkəm/ *n.* in the Christian church, the Eucharist given to a person dying or in danger of death. [Latin = provision for a journey (*via* = way)]

vibes /vaɪbz/ *n. pl.* (*colloquial*) 1. a vibraphone. 2. mental or emotional vibrations. [abbreviation]

vibrant /'vaɪbrənt/ *adj.* vibrating, resonant; thrilling with energy or activity.

vibraphone /'vaɪbrəfəun/ *n.* a percussion instrument of metal bars and tubular resonators surmounted by small circular fans electronically rotated to give a vibrato effect which can be controlled in speed and worked with a foot pedal. [from *vibrato* and Greek *phōnē* = sound]

vibrate /vaɪ'breɪt/ *v.t./i.* 1. to move rapidly and continuously to and fro; to move to and fro like a pendulum, to oscillate. 2. to cause to do this. 3. to resound; to sound with a rapid slight variation of pitch. [from Latin *vibrare* = shake]

vibration /vaɪ'breɪʃən/ *n.* 1. vibrating; a vibrating movement, sensation, or sound. 2. (in *plural*) mental stimuli

thought to be given out by a person or place; the emotional sensations these produce.

vibrato /vi'brɑːtəu/ *n.* (*plural* **vibratos**) in music, the slight wavering of pitch used to enrich and intensify the tone of the voice and of many (especially stringed) instruments. [Italian]

vibrator /vaɪ'breɪtə/ *n.* a thing that vibrates or causes vibration, especially an electric or other instrument used in massage.

vibratory /'vaɪbrətərɪ/ *adj.* causing vibration.

viburnum /vɪ'bɜːnəm/ *n.* a shrub of the temperate and subtropical genus *Viburnum*, usually with white flowers including the wayfaring tree, the laurustinus, and the guilder rose. [Latin = wayfaring tree]

vicar /'vɪkə/ *n.* a Church of England priest, originally one who acted as deputy to a ◊rector, but now also a parish priest. —**vicar apostolic**, a Roman Catholic missionary or titular bishop. **vicar general** an official assisting or representing a bishop, especially in administrative matters. **Vicar of Christ**, the pope. [from Anglo-French from Latin *vicarius* = substitute]

vicarage /'vɪkərɪdʒ/ *n.* the house provided for a vicar.

vicarious /vi'keəriəs/ *adj.* 1. experienced through sharing imaginatively in the feelings or emotions etc. of another person. 2. acting or done for another; deputed, delegated. —**vicariously** *adv.*, **vicariousness** *n.* [from Latin]

vice[1] *n.* 1. evil or grossly immoral conduct, depravity. 2. an evil habit; a particular form of depravity. 3. a defect or blemish. —**vice squad**, the police department enforcing the laws against criminal and immoral practices such as prostitution. [from Old French from Latin *vitium*]

vice[2] *n.* an instrument with two jaws between which a thing may be gripped so as to leave the hands free to work on it. [originally = screw, from Old French *vis* from Latin *vitis* = vine]

vice[3] /'vaɪsɪ/ *prep.* in the place of, in succession to. [Latin, ablative of (*vix*) *vicis* = change]

vice- prefix forming nouns in the senses 'acting as a substitute or deputy for' (*vice president*), 'next in rank to' (*vice admiral*). [from *vice*[3]]

vice chancellor /vaɪs'tʃɑːnsələ/a deputy chancellor (especially of a university), discharging most of the chancellor's administrative duties).

vicegerent /vaɪs'dʒerənt/ *adj.* exercising delegated power. —*n.* a vicegerent person, a deputy. [from Latin *gerere* = carry on]

viceregal /vaɪs'riːgəl/ *adj.* of a viceroy. —**viceregally** *adv.*

vicereine /'vaɪsreɪn/ *n.* a viceroy's wife; a woman viceroy. [French *reine* = queen]

viceroy /'vaɪsrɔɪ/ *n.* the chief officer of the crown in many Spanish and Portuguese American colonies who had ultimate responsibility for administration and military matters. The office of viceroy was also used by the British crown to rule India. [French *roy* = king]

viceroyalty /vaɪs'rɔɪəltɪ/ *n.* the office of viceroy.

vice versa /'vaɪsɪ 'vɜːsə/ with the order of the terms changed, the other way round. [Latin = the position being reversed]

Vichy /'vi:ʃi/ health resort with thermal springs, known to the Romans, on the river Allier in Allier *département*, central France.

Vichy government in World War II, the right-wing government of unoccupied France after the country's defeat by the Germans in June 1940, named after the spa town of Vichy, France where the national assembly was based under Prime Minister Pétain until the liberation in 1944. **Vichy France** was that part of France not occupied by German troops until Nov 1942. Authoritarian and collaborationist, the Vichy regime cooperated with the Germans even after they had moved to the unoccupied zone.

vicinage /'vɪsɪnɪdʒ/ *n.* 1. the neighbourhood, the surrounding district. 2. the relation of neighbours. [from Old French from Latin *vicinus* = neighbour]

vicinity /vi'sɪnɪtɪ/ *n.* 1. the surrounding district. 2. nearness, closeness. —**in the vicinity (of)**, near. [from Latin *vicinitas*]

vicious /'vɪʃəs/ *adj.* 1. acting or done with evil intentions. 2. brutal, strongly spiteful; bad-tempered; (of animals) savage and dangerous. 3. violent, severe. 4. (of language or reasoning) faulty, unsound. —**vicious circle,** a state of affairs in which a cause produces an effect which itself produces or intensifies the original cause. **vicious spiral,** a similar interaction causing a continuous increase or decrease. —**viciously** *adv.,* **viciousness** *n.* [from Old French or Latin *vitiosus vitium* = vice]

vicissitude /vɪˈsɪsɪtjuːd/ *n.* a change of circumstances, especially of fortune. [French or from Latin *vicissitudo* (*vicissim* = by turns)]

Vico /ˈviːkəʊ/ Giambattista 1668–1744. Italian philosopher, considered the founder of the modern philosophy of history. He rejected Descartes' emphasis on the mathematical and natural sciences, and argued that we can understand history more adequately than nature, since it is we who have made it. He believed that the study of language, ritual, and myth was a way of understanding earlier societies. His cyclical theory of history (the birth, development, and decline of human societies) was put forward in *New Science* 1725.

victim /ˈvɪktɪm/ *n.* **1.** a person who is injured or killed by another or as the result of an event or circumstance. **2.** a prey; a person who suffers because of a trick. **3.** a living creature sacrificed to a deity or in a religious rite. [from Latin *victima*]

victimize *v.t.* to single out (a person) for punishment or unfair treatment; to make (a person etc.) a victim. —**victimization** /-ˈzeɪʃən/ *n.*

victor /ˈvɪktə/ *n.* the winner in a battle or contest. [from Anglo-French or Latin *vincere* = conquer]

Victor Emmanuel /ˈvɪktər ɪˈmænjuəl/ three kings of Italy, including:

Victor Emmanuel II 1820–1878. First king of united Italy from 1861. He became king of Sardinia on the abdication of his father Charles Albert in 1849. In 1855 he allied Sardinia with France and the UK in the Crimean War. In 1859 in alliance with the French he defeated the Austrians and annexed Lombardy. By 1860 most of Italy had come under his rule, and in 1861 he was proclaimed king of Italy. In 1870 he made Rome his capital.

Victor Emmanuel III 1869–1947. King of Italy from the assassination of his father, Umberto I, 1900. He acquiesced in the Fascist regime of Mussolini from 1922 and, after the dictator's fall 1943, relinquished power to his son Umberto II, who cooperated with the Allies. Victor Emmanuel formally abdicated in 1946.

victoria /vɪkˈtɔːrɪə/ *n.* **1.** a low, light, four-wheeled horse-drawn carriage with a seat for two and a raised driver's seat and with a collapsible top. **2.** (in full **victoria plum**) a large, red luscious variety of plum. —**Victoria Cross,** a decoration awarded to members of the Commonwealth armed services for a conspicuous act of bravery in wartime, instituted 1856. [from Queen *Victoria*]

Victoria 1819–1901. Queen of the UK from 1837, when she succeeded her uncle William IV, and empress of India from 1876. In 1840 she married Prince ◊Albert of Saxe-Coburg - Gotha. Her relations with her prime ministers ranged from the affectionate (Melbourne and Disraeli) to the stormy (Peel, Palmerston, and Gladstone). Her golden jubilee in 1887 and diamond jubilee in 1897 marked a waning of republican sentiment, which had developed with her withdrawal from public life on Albert's death.

Victoria industrial port (shipbuilding, chemicals, clothing, furniture) on Vancouver Island, capital of British Columbia, Canada; population (1986) 66,303.

Victoria port and capital of the Seychelles, on Mahé island; population (1985) 23,000.

Victoria state of SE Australia; **area** 227,600 sq km/87,854 sq mi; **capital** Melbourne; **physical** part of the Great Dividing Range, running E–W and including the larger part of the Australian Alps; Gippsland lakes; shallow lagoons on the coast; the ◊mallee shrub region; **products** sheep, beef cattle, dairy products, tobacco, wheat, vines for wine and dried fruit, orchard fruits, vegetables, gold, brown coal (Latrobe Valley), oil and natural gas (Bass Strait); **population** (1987) 4,184,000; 70% in the Melbourne area; **history** annexed for Britain by Captain Cook in 1770; settled in the 1830s; after being part of New South Wales became a separate colony in 1851, named after the queen; became a state from 1901.

Victoria and Albert Museum a museum of decorative arts in South Kensington, London, opened in 1909, inspired by Henry Cole (1808–1882) and Prince ◊Albert.

Victoria Falls or *Mosi-oa-tunya* waterfall on the river Zambezi, on the Zambia–Zimbabwe border. The river is 1,700 m/5,580 ft wide and drops 120 m/400 ft to flow through a 30-m/100-ft wide gorge.

Victoria, Lake or *Victoria Nyanza* largest lake in Africa; area over 69,400 sq km/26,800 sq mi; length 410 km/255 mi. It lies on the equator at an altitude of 1,136 m/3,728 ft, bounded by Uganda, Kenya, and Tanzania. It is a source of the Nile.

Victorian /vɪkˈtɔːrɪən/ *adj.* belonging to or characteristic of the reign of Queen Victoria 1837–1901. Victorian style was ornate, markedly so in architecture, and Victorian Gothic drew upon the medieval Gothic architecture. It was also an era increasing mass production by machines. —*n.* a person of this period. —**Royal Victorian Order,** an order founded by Queen Victoria in 1896 and awarded for service to the sovereign. It is one of the fraternities carrying with it the rank of knight; see ◊knighthood

Victoriana /vɪktɔːrɪˈɑːnə/ *n.pl.* objects from Victorian times.

victorious /vɪkˈtɔːrɪəs/ *adj.* having gained the victory.

victory /ˈvɪktərɪ/ *n.* success in a battle, contest, or game etc. achieved by gaining mastery over one's opponent(s) or by achieving the highest score. [from Anglo-French from Latin *victoria vincere* = conquer]

victual /ˈvɪtəl/ *n.* (usually in *plural*) food, provisions. —*v.t./i.* (**-ll-**) **1.** to supply with victuals. **2.** to obtain stores; to eat victuals. [from Old French *vitaille* from Latin *victualia victus* = food]

victualler /ˈvɪtlə/ *n.* one who furnishes victuals. —**licensed victualler,** an innkeeper licensed to sell alcoholic liquor etc.

vicuña /vɪˈkjuːnə/ *n.* **1.** a South American ruminant mammal *Vicugna vicugna* related to the llama, with fine silky wool. They were hunted close to extinction for their meat and soft brown fur, which was used in textile manufacture, but the vicuna is now a protected species. **2.** cloth made from its wool; an imitation of this. [Spanish from Quechua]

Vidal /viˈdæl/ Gore 1925– . US writer and critic. Much of his fiction deals satirically with history and politics and includes the novels *Myra Breckinridge* 1968, *Burr* 1973, and *Empire* 1987, plays and screenplays, including *Suddenly Last Summer* 1958, and essays, such as *Armageddon?* 1987.

vide /ˈvɪdeɪ, ˈvaɪdiː/ *v.t.* (as an instruction in a reference to a passage in a book etc.) see, consult. [Latin, imperative of *vidēre* = see]

videlicet /vɪˈdeːlɪset/ *adv.* that is to say, namely. Abbreviated *viz.* [Latin = it is permitted to see]

video /ˈvɪdɪəʊ/ *adj.* relating to the recording or broadcasting of photographic images. —*n.* (*plural* **videos**) **1.** such a recording or broadcasting. **2.** an apparatus for recording or playing videotapes; see ◊video tape recorder. **3.** a ◊videotape. [Latin = I see]

video camera or **camcorder** portable television camera that takes moving pictures electronically on magnetic tape. It produces an electrical output signal corresponding to rapid line-by-line scanning of the field of view. The output is recorded on video cassette and is played back on a television screen via a video cassette recorder.

video cassette recorder (VCR) device for recording on and playing back video cassettes. In the home they are used mainly to record broadcast programmes for future viewing and to view rented or owned video cassettes of commercial films.

video disc a disc with pictures and sounds recorded on it, played back by laser. The video disc works in the same way as a ◊compact disc.

video game an electronic game played on a visual-display screen or, by means of special additional or built-in components, on the screen of a television set. The first commercially sold was a simple bat-and-ball game developed in the USA in 1972, but complex variants are now available in colour and with special sound effects.

videotape *n.* a magnetic tape containing or suitable for records of television pictures and sound. —*v.t.* to make a recording of (broadcast material etc.) with this.

video tape recorder a (VTR) device for recording visuals and sound on spools of magnetic tape. It is used in television broadcasting.

videotext *n.* a system in which information (text) is displayed on a television (video) screen. There are two basic systems, known as ◊teletext and ◊viewdata. In the teletext system information is broadcast using ordinary television signals, whereas in viewdata information is relayed to the screen from a central data bank via the telephone network. Both systems require the use of a television receiver with special decoder.

Vidor /'viːdɔː/ King 1894–1982. US film director who made epics such as *The Big Parade* 1925 and *Duel in the Sun* 1946. A cinematic innovator, he received an honorary Academy Award in 1979. His other films include *The Crowd* 1928 and *Guerra e Pace/War and Peace* 1956.

vie /vaɪ/ *v. i.* (*participle* **vying** /'vaɪɪŋ/) to carry on a rivalry, to compete.

Vienna /viˈenə/ (German *Wien*) capital of Austria, on the river Danube at the foot of the Wiener Wald (Vienna Woods); population (1986) 1,481,000. Industries include engineering and the production of electrical goods and precision instruments.

Vienna, Congress of international conference held 1814–15 that agreed the settlement of Europe after the Napoleonic Wars. National representatives included the Austrian foreign minister Metternich, Alexander I of Russia, the British foreign secretary Castlereagh and military commander Wellington, and the French politician Talleyrand.

Vientiane /vienti'ɑːn/ capital and chief port of Laos on the Mekong river; population (1985) 377,000.

Vietcong /viet'koŋ/ *n.* in the Vietnam War 1954–75, the members of the National Front for the Liberation of South Vietnam, founded in 1960, who fought the South Vietnamese and US forces. The name was coined by the South Vietnamese government to differentiate these Communist guerrillas from the ◊Vietminh. [Vietnamese = Vietnamese Communists]

Viète /vi'et/ François 1540–1603. French mathematician who developed algebra and its notation. He was the first mathematician to use letters of the alphabet to denote both known and unknown quantities.

Vietminh /viet'mɪn/ *n.* the Vietnam Independence League, founded in 1941 to oppose the Japanese occupation of Indochina, later directed against French colonial power. The Vietminh were instrumental in achieving Vietnamese independence through military victory at Dien Bien Phu in 1954.

Vietnam /viet'næm/ Socialist Republic of; country in SE Asia, on the South China Sea, bounded N by China and W by Cambodia and Laos. **area** 329,600 sq km/ 127,259 sq mi; **capital** Hanoi; **physical** Red River and Mekong deltas; tropical rainforest; barren, mountainous; **head of state** Vo Chi Cong from 1987; **head of government** Do Muoi from 1988; **political system** communism; **exports** rice, rubber, coal, iron, apatite; **population** (1990 est) 68,488,000; **language** Vietnamese (official), French, English, Khmer, Chinese, tribal; **recent history** in a war that began in 1945, after the removal of the Japanese, the ◊Vietminh defeated the French colonial forces. Under the Geneva Convention, in 1954 the former French colony of Indo-China was divided into the separate states of North Vietnam and South Vietnam, but plunged immediately into the ◊Vietnam War which ended with the declaration of the Socialist Repumblic of Vietnam in 1976. War with Cambodia followed in 1978, and border skirmishes with China in 1979. Economic crisis led to the murder and robbery at sea of thousands of escaping Vietnamese ◊boat people.

Vietnam War 1954–75. War between communist North Vietnam and US-backed South Vietnam. In 1954 the communist Vietcong, supported by North Vietnam and China, attempted to seize power within South Vietnam. The USA gave the South Vietnamese government military aid. The ◊Tonkin Gulf Incident in Aug 1964 brought the US into the war, and several large-scale North Vietnamese invasion attempts were defeated by local and US troops in 1967. The ◊My Lai Massacre by US troops in 1968, and US bombing incursions into Cambodia, a neutral neighbour, in 1969, increased disillusionment with US involvement in the West, leading to the start of US withdrawal in 1973. A peace treaty between North and South Vietnam was signed in 1975. In 1976 South Vietnam was annexed by North Vietnam.

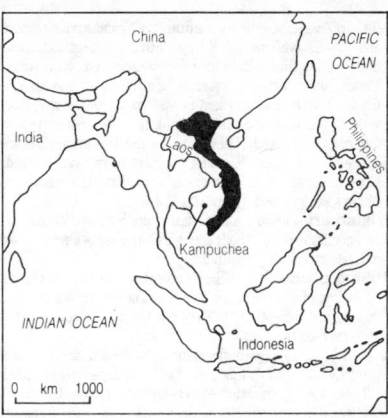

Vietnam

view /vjuː/ *n.* 1. what can be seen from a specified point; fine natural scenery. 2. range of vision. 3. visual inspection of something. 4. a mental survey of a subject etc. 5. a manner of considering a subject; a mental attitude; an opinion. —*v.t./i.* 1. to survey with the eyes or mind. 2. to inspect, to look over (a house etc.) with the idea of buying it. 3. to watch television. 4. to regard or consider. —**have in view**, to have as one's object; to bear in mind in forming a judgement etc. **in view of**, having regard to, considering. **on view**, being shown (for observation or inspection). **with a view to**, with the hope or intention of. [from Anglo-French from *vêoir* = see from Latin *vidēre*]

viewdata *n.* a system of displaying information on a television screen in which the information is extracted from a computer data bank and transmitted via the telephone lines. It is one form of ◊videotext. The British Post Office (now British Telecom) developed the world's first viewdata system, ◊Prestel, in 1975, and similar systems are now in widespread use in other countries.

viewer *n.* 1. one who views. 2. a person watching television. 3. a device for looking at photographic transparencies etc.

viewfinder *n.* a device on a camera showing the area that will be included in a photograph.

viewpoint *n.* a point of view, a standpoint.

vigil /'vɪdʒɪl/ *n.* 1. staying awake during the time usually given to sleep, especially to keep watch or pray. 2. the eve of a religious festival, especially an eve that is a fast. [from Old French from Latin *vigil* = wakeful]

vigilance /'vɪdʒɪləns/ *n.* watchfulness, being on the lookout for possible danger etc. —**vigilance committee**, (*US*) a self-appointed body for the maintenance of order or the status quo, often by violence. —**vigilant** *adj.*, **vigilantly** *adv.*

vigilante /vɪdʒi'lænti/ *n.* a member of a vigilance committee or similar body, including urban groups patrolling streets and subways to deter muggers and rapists. Early vigilante groups included the 'Regulators' in South Carolina in the 1760s, and in Pennsylvania 1794 during the Whiskey Rebellion. [Spanish = vigilant]

vignette /viː'njet/ *n.* 1. an illustration not in a definite border. 2. a photograph etc. with the background gradually shaded off. 3. a short description, a character sketch. —*v.t.* to shade off in the style of a vignette. [French diminutive of *vigne* = vine]

Vigo /'viːgəʊ/ Jean. Adopted name of Jean Almereyda 1905–1934. French director of intensely lyrical experimental films. He made only two short films: *A Propos de Nice* 1930 and *Taris Champion de Natation* 1934; and two feature films: *Zéro de conduite/Nothing for Conduct* 1933 and *L'Atalante* 1934.

vigorous /'vɪgərəs/ *adj.* full of vigour. —**vigorously** *adv.*, **vigorousness** *n.*

vigour /'vɪgə/ *n.* 1. active physical or mental strength, energy; flourishing physical condition. 2. forcefulness of language or composition etc. [from Old French from Latin *vigēre* = be lively]

Viking /'vaɪkɪŋ/ n. or **Norseman** the Scandinavian traders and pirates who raided Europe 8th–11th centuries, and often settled there. In France they were given ◊Normandy. Under Sweyn I they conquered England 1013, and his son Canute was king of England as well as Denmark and Norway. In the E they established the first Russian state and founded ◊Novgorod. They reached the Byzantine Empire in the S, and in the W, sailed the seas to Ireland, Iceland, Greenland, and North America; see ◊Eric the Red, Leif ◊Ericsson, ◊Vinland. [from Old Norse]

Viking art sculpture and design of the Vikings. Viking artists are known for woodcarving and metalwork and for an intricate interlacing ornament.

Viking probes two US space probes to Mars, each one consisting of an orbiter and a lander. They were launched on 20 Aug and 9 Sept 1975. They transmitted colour pictures and analysed the soil.

vile adj. 1. extremely disgusting. 2. despicable on moral grounds. 3. (colloquial) abominably bad. —**vilely** adv., **vileness** n. [from Old French from Latin vilis = base]

vilify /'vɪlɪfaɪ/ v.t. to defame, to speak evil of. —**vilification** /-fɪ'keɪʃən/ n. [from Latin vilificare]

villa /'vɪlə/ n. 1. a detached or semi-detached house in a residential district. 2. a country residence, especially in Italy or southern France. 3. a house for holiday-makers at the seaside etc. [Italian and Latin]

village /'vɪlɪdʒ/ n. a group of houses etc. in a country district, smaller than a town and usually having a church. [from Old French from Latin villa]

villager /'vɪlɪdʒə/ n. an inhabitant of a village.

villain /'vɪlən/ n. 1. a person who is guilty of or capable of great wickedness; a wrongdoer, a criminal. 2. a character in a story or play whose evil actions or motives are important in the plot. 3. (colloquial) a rascal. —**villainy** n. [from Old French from Latin = villa]

villainous /'vɪlənəs/ adj. 1. worthy of a villain; wicked. 2. (colloquial) abominably bad. —**villainously** adv.

Villa-Lobos /'vɪlə 'ləʊbɒs/ Heitor 1887–1959. Brazilian composer. His style was based on folk tunes collected on travels in his country; for example, in the Bachianas Brasileiras 1930–44, he treats them in the manner of Bach. His 2,000 works range from guitar solos to film scores, opera, and symphonies.

Villehardouin /viːlɑːˈdwæn/ Geoffroy de c.1160–1213. French historian, the first to write in the French language. He was born near Troyes, and was a leader of the Fourth ◊Crusade, of which his Conquest of Constantinople (c.1209) is an account.

villein /'vɪlɪn/ n. (historical) a feudal tenant entirely subject to a lord or attached to a manor. —**villeinage** n. the system of serfdom that prevailed in Europe in the Middle Ages. [variant of villain]

Villon /viːˈɒn/ François 1431–c.1465. French poet, noted for his satirical humour, pathos, and lyrical power in works that used the argot (slang) of the time. Very little of his work survives, but it includes the Ballade des dames du temps jadis/Ballad of the Ladies of Former Times, Petit Testament 1456, and Grand Testament 1461.

villus n. plural **villi** small, finger like projection extending into the interior of the small intestine and increasing the absorptive area of the gut wall.

Vilnius /'vɪlnɪʊs/ capital of Lithuania, USSR; population (1987) 566,000. Industries include engineering and the manufacture of textiles, chemicals, and foodstuffs.

vim n. (colloquial) vigour.

Vimy Ridge /'viːmi/ hill in N France, taken in World War I by Canadian troops during the battle of Arras in Apr 1917, at the cost of 11,285 lives. It is a spur of the ridge of Nôtre Dame de Lorette, 8 km/5 mi NE of Arras.

vina /'viːnə/ n. an Indian four-stringed musical instrument with a fretted finger-board and a half-gourd at each end. [from Sanskrit and Hindi]

vinaigrette /vɪniˈgret/ n. 1. vinaigrette sauce, a salad dressing of oil and vinegar. 2. a small bottle for smelling-salts. [French, diminutive of vinaigre = vinegar]

Vincent de Paul, St /'vɪnsənt də 'pɔːl/ c.1580–1660. French Roman Catholic priest and founder of the two charitable orders of Dazarists in 1625 and Sisters of Charity in 1634. After being ordained in 1600, he was captured by Barbary pirates and held as a slave in Tunis until he escaped in 1607. He was canonized in 1737; feast day 19 July.

vincristine n. an ◊alkaloid extracted from the blue periwinkle plant (Vinca rosea). Developed as an anticancer agent, it has revolutionized the treatment of childhood acute leukaemias; it is also included in ◊chemotherapy regimens for some lymphomas (cancers arising in the lymph tissues) and lung and breast cancers. Side effects, such as nerve damage and loss of hair, are severe but usually reversible.

vindicate /'vɪndɪkeɪt/ v.t. 1. to clear of blame or suspicion. 2. to establish the existence, merits, or justice of (one's courage, conduct, assertion, etc.). —**vindication** /-ˈkeɪʃən/ n., **vindicator** n., **vindicatory** adj. [from Latin vindex = claimant, avenger]

vindictive /vɪnˈdɪktɪv/ adj. tending to seek revenge. —**vindictively** adv., **vindictiveness** n. [from Latin vindicta = vengeance]

vine n. 1. a climbing or trailing plant of the genus Vitis (especially V. vinifera) with a woody stem, bearing grapes. 2. a slender trailing or climbing stem. [from Old French from Latin vinea = vineyard (vinum = wine)]

vinegar /'vɪnɪgə/ n. 1. a 4% solution of acetic acid produced by the oxidation of alcohol, used to flavour food and as a preservative in pickles. Malt vinegar is brown and made from malted cereals; white vinegar is distilled from it. Other sources of vinegar include cider, inferior wine, and honey. 2. sour behaviour or character. —**vinegary** adj. [from Old French vyn egre from Latin vinum = wine and acer = sour]

vinery /'vaɪnərɪ/ n. a greenhouse for grape-vines.

vineyard /'vɪnjɑːd/ n. a plantation of grape-vines, especially for wine-making.

vingt-et-un /væteʈˈœ̃/ n. another name for ◊pontoon[1]. [French = twenty-one]

Vinland /'vɪnlənd/ Norse name for the area of North America, probably the coast of Nova Scotia or New England, which the Norse adventurer and explorer Leif ◊Ericsson visited about 1000.

vinous /'vaɪnəs/ adj. 1. of, like, or due to wine. 2. addicted to wine. [from Latin vinum = wine]

vintage /'vɪntɪdʒ/ n. 1. the gathering of grapes for wine-making; the season of this. 2. the season's produce of grapes; wine made from this. 3. wine of high quality (from a single year) kept separate from others. 4. the year or period when a thing was made or existed; a thing made etc. in a particular year etc. —adj. of high quality, especially of a past season. —**vintage car**, a car made between 1917 and 1930. [from Old French from Latin vindemia (vinum = wine and demere = remove)]

vintner /'vɪntnə/ n. a wine-merchant. [from Anglo-French vineter from Latin vinetarius (vinetum = vineyard)]

vinyl /'vaɪnɪl/ n. one of a group of plastics, made by polymerization, especially polyvinyl chloride. [from Latin vinum = wine]

viol /'vaɪəl/ n. a family of bowed stringed instruments prominent in the 16th–18th centuries, before their role was taken by the violins. Developed for close-harmony chamber music, they have a pure and restrained tone. Viols normally have six strings, a flat back, and narrow shoulders. [from Old French from Provençal, probably ultimately from Latin vitulari = be joyful]

viola[1] /viˈəʊlə/ n. 1. a bowed stringed instrument of the ◊violin family, larger and deeper-pitched than the violin, and sometimes known as the 'alto' or 'tenor violin' because of this. 2. a viol. —**viola da gamba**, a viol held between a seated player's legs, especially corresponding to the modern cello. **viola d'amore** /dæˈmɔːreɪ/, a sweet-toned tenor viol. [Italian and Spanish]

viola[2] n. any plant of the group including the violet and pansy, especially a cultivated hybrid. [Latin = violet]

violable /'vaɪələbəl/ adj. that may be violated.

violate /'vaɪəleɪt/ v.t. 1. to break or act contrary to (an oath, treaty, conscience, etc.). 2. to treat (a sacred place) with irreverence or disrespect. 3. to disturb (a person's privacy etc.). 4. to rape. —**violation** /-ˈleɪʃən/ n., **violator** n. [from Latin violare = treat violently]

violence /'vaɪələns/ n. being violent; violent acts, conduct, or treatment; the unlawful use of force. —**do violence to**, to act contrary to, to be a breach of. [from Old French from Latin violentia]

violent /'vaɪələnt/ adj. 1. involving great force, strength, or intensity. 2. (of a death) caused by physical force or by

violin family

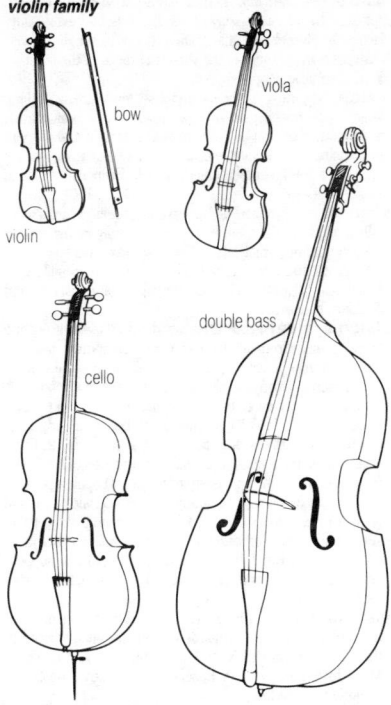

viola

bow

violin

double bass

cello

---

virgin /'vɜːdʒɪn/ *n.* **1.** a person who has never had sexual intercourse. **2.** a picture or statue of the Virgin Mary. **3.** the Virgin, the constellation or sign of the zodiac ◊Virgo. —*adj.* **1.** virginal. **2.** spotless, undefiled. **3.** untouched, in its original state; not yet used. —**the (Blessed) Virgin (Mary)**, in Christian belief, the mother of Jesus. **Virgin birth**, the doctrine that Jesus Christ had no human father but was conceived by the Virgin Mary by the power of the Holy Spirit. **Virgin Queen**, Elizabeth I of England. —**virginity** /və'dʒɪnɪtɪ/ *n.* [from Anglo-French and Old French from Latin *virgo*]

virginal *adj.* that is or befits a virgin. —*n.* (usually in *plural*) a small type of ◊harpsichord, a legless spinet in a box. [from Old French or Latin]

Virginia /və'dʒɪnɪə/ state of the southern USA; nickname Old Dominion; **area** 105,600 sq km/40,762 sq mi; **capital** Richmond; **features** Blue Ridge mountains; **products** sweet potatoes, corn, tobacco, apples, peanuts, coal, furniture, paper, chemicals, processed food, textiles; **population** (1986) 5,787,000; **history** named in honour of Elizabeth I; Jamestown first permanent English settlement in the New World from 1607; took a leading part in the American Revolution, and was one of the original Thirteen States; joined the Confederacy in the Civil War.

Virgin Islands /'vɜːdʒɪn/ group of about 100 small islands, northernmost of the Leeward Islands in the Antilles, West Indies. Tourism is the main industry. They comprise the **US Virgin Islands** St Thomas (with the capital, Charlotte Amalie), St Croix, St John, and about 50 small islets; area 350 sq km/135 sq mi; population (1985) 111,000; and the **British Virgin Islands** Tortola (with the capital, Road Town), Virgin Gorda, Anegada, and Jost van Dykes, and about 40 islets; area 150 sq km/58 sq mi; population (1987) 13,250.

Virgo /'vɜːgəʊ/ *n.* a zodiac constellation, the second largest in the sky. It lies between Leo and Libra, and is represented as a maiden holding an ear of wheat. The Sun passes through Virgo from late Sept to the end of Oct. Virgo's brightest star is the first-magnitude Spica, a blue-white star about 250 light years from Earth. Virgo contains the nearest large cluster of galaxies to us, 50 million light years away, consisting of about 3,000 galaxies centred on the giant elliptical galaxy M87. Also in Virgo is the nearest ◊quasar, 3c273, an estimated 3 billion light years distant. In astrology, Virgo is the sixth sign of the zodiac. —**virgoan** *adj. & n.* [Old English from Latin = virgin]

virile /'vɪraɪl/ *adj.* **1.** having masculine vigour or strength. **2.** of or having procreative power. **3.** of a man as distinct from a woman or child. —**virility** /vɪ'rɪlɪtɪ/ *n.* [from French or Latin *virilis* (*vir* = man)]

virion *n.* a single mature ◊virus particle.

virology /vaɪə'rɒlədʒɪ/ *n.* the study of viruses. —**virological** /-rə'lɒdʒɪkəl/ *adj.*, **virologist** *n.*

virtual /'vɜːtjʊəl/ *adj.* that is such in effect though not in name or according to strict definition. —**virtually** *adv.* [from Latin]

virtual memory in computing, a technique whereby a portion of external ◊memory is used as an extension of internal memory. The contents of an area of ◊RAM are stored on, say, a hard disc while they are not needed, and brought back into main memory when required. The process, which is called either paging or segmentation, is hidden from the programmer, to whom the computer appears to have a much larger amount of internal memory than actually exists.

virtue /'vɜːtjuː/ *n.* **1.** moral excellence, goodness; a particular form of this. **2.** chastity, especially in a woman. **3.** a good quality, an advantage. —**by** *or* **in virtue of**, by reason of; because of. [from Old French from Latin *virtus* (*vir* = man)]

virtuoso /vɜːtju'əʊsəʊ/ *n.* (*plural* **virtuossi** /-siː/) a person skilled in the technique of a fine art, especially music. —**virtuosity** /-'ɒsɪtɪ/ *n.* [Italian = skilful, from Latin]

---

poison, not natural. —**violently** *adv.* [from Old French from Latin *violentus*]

violet /'vaɪələt/ *n.* **1.** a plant of the genus *Viola* with usually purple, blue, or white flowers, such as heath dog violet *Viola canina* and sweet violet *Viola odorata*. Pansies are very close relatives. **2.** the colour seen at the end of the spectrum opposite red, blue with a slight admixture of red. **3.** a pigment, clothes, or material of this colour. —*adj.* of this colour. [from Old French, diminutive of *viole*]

violin /vaɪə'lɪn/ *n.* **1.** a musical instrument of treble pitch with four strings played with a bow; any of a family of bowed stringed instruments developed in Italy during the 17th century, which eventually superseded the viols and formed the basis of the modern orchestra. There are three instruments: violin, viola, and cello (the double bass is descended from the viol). **2.** a player of this. —**violinist** *n.* [from Italian *violino* diminutive of *viola*[1]]

violist[1] /'vaɪəlɪst/ *n.* a viol-player.

violist[2] /vi'əʊlɪst/ *n.* a viola-player.

violoncello *n.* or **cello** (*plural* **violoncellos**) a bowed, stringed musical instrument of the ◊violin family. [Italian]

violone /viə'ləʊnɪ/ *n.* a double-bass viol. [Italian]

VIP abbreviation of very important person.

viper /'vaɪpə/ *n.* **1.** a front-fanged, venomous snake of the family Viperidae. They range in size from 30 cm/1 ft to 3 m/9.8 ft, and often have diamond or jagged markings. Most give birth to live young. **2.** a malignant or treacherous person. [from French or Latin *vipera* (*vivus* = alive and *parere* = bring forth)]

virago /vi'rɑːgəʊ/ *n.* (*plural* **viragos**) a fierce or abusive woman. [Latin = female warrior (*vir* = man)]

viral /'vaɪərəl/ *adj.* of or caused by a virus.

Virchow /'fɪəkəʊ/ Rudolf Ludwig Carl 1821–1902. German pathologist, the founder of cellular pathology. Virchow was the first to describe leukaemia (cancer of the blood). In his book *Die Cellulare Pathologie/Cellular Pathology* 1858, he proposed that disease is not due to sudden invasions or changes, but to slow processes in which normal cells give rise to abnormal ones.

Virgil /'vɜːdʒəl/ Publius Vergilius Maro 70–19 BC. Roman poet who wrote the *Eclogues* 37 BC, a series of pastoral poems; the *Georgics* 30 BC, four books on the art of farming; and his masterpiece, the ◊*Aeneid* (30–19 BC).

virtuous /'vɜːtjuəs/ adj. having or showing moral virtue, chaste. —**virtuously** adv., **virtuousness** n. [from Old French from Latin virtuosus]

virulent /'vɪrʊlənt/ adj. 1. (of poison or disease) extremely strong, violent. 2. strongly and bitterly hostile. —**virulence** n., **virulently** adv. [from Latin virulentus]

virus /'vaɪərəs/ n. 1. any of a group of minute infective and disease-producing agents consisting of a core of nucleic acid (DNA or RNA) enclosed in a protein shell. Viruses are acellular and able to function and reproduce only if they can invade a living cell to use the cell's system to replicate themselves. In the process they may disrupt or alter the host cell's own DNA. The healthy human body reacts by producing an antiviral protein, ◊interferon, which prevents the infection spreading to adjacent cells. 2. in computing, a piece of ◊software that can replicate itself and transfer itself from one computer to another, without the user being aware of it. Some viruses are relatively harmless, but others can damage or destroy data. They are written by anonymous programmers, often maliciously, and are spread along telephone lines or on ◊floppy discs. Most are very difficult to eradicate. [Latin = poison]

visa /'viːzə/ n. an endorsement on a passport etc. especially as permitting the holder to enter or leave a country. —**visaed** adj. [French from Latin, past participle of videre = see]

visage /'vɪzɪdʒ/ n. (literary) a person's face, a countenance. [from Old French from Latin visus = sight]

vis-à-vis /viːzɑːˈviː/ prep. 1. in relation to. 2. so as to face, opposite to. —adv. facing one another. —n. a person or thing facing another. [French = face to face]

Visby /'viːsbɪ/ historic town and bishopric on the Swedish island of Gotland in the Baltic, which became the centre of German ◊Hanseatic League.

viscera /'vɪsərə/ n.pl. the internal organs of the body contained in the chest and abdominal cavities. —**visceral** adj. [Latin, plural of viscus]

viscid adj. (of liquid) thick and gluey. —**viscidity** /-'sɪdɪtɪ/ n. [from Latin viscidus (viscum = birdlime)]

Visconti /vɪˈskɒntɪ/ dukes and rulers of Milan 1277–1447. They originated as north Italian feudal lords who attained dominance over the city as a result of alliance with the Holy Roman emperors. Despite papal opposition, by the mid-14th century they ruled 15 other major towns in northern Italy. The duchy was inherited by the ◊Sforzas in 1447.

Visconti Luchino 1906–1976. Italian film, opera, and theatre director. The film *Ossessione* 1942 pioneered Neo-Realist cinema despite being subject to censorship by the fascist government; later works include *Rocco and his Brothers* 1960, and *Death in Venice* 1971. His powerful social commentary led to clashes with the Italian government and Roman Catholic Church.

viscose /'vɪskəʊz/ n. yellowish, syrupy solution made by treating cellulose with sodium hydroxide and carbon disulphide. The solution is then regenerated as continuous filament for the making of ◊rayon and as cellophane.

viscosity /vɪsˈkɒsɪtɪ/ n. the quality or degree of being viscous; in physics, the resistance of a fluid to flow. It applies to the motion of an object moving through a fluid as well as the motion of a fluid passing by an object. [from Old French or Latin]

viscount /'vaɪkaʊnt/ n. 1. in the UK peerage, the fourth degree of nobility, between earl and baron. 2. the courtesy title of an earl's eldest son. —**viscountcy** n. [from Anglo-French from Latin vice-and comes = companion]

viscountess /'vaɪkaʊntɪs/ n. a viscount's wife or widow; a woman holding the rank of viscount in her own right.

viscous /'vɪskəs/ adj. thick and gluey; semifluid; not flowing freely. [from Anglo-French or Latin viscosus (viscum = birdlime)]

Vishnu /'vɪʃnuː/ in Hinduism, the second in the triad of gods (with Brahma and Siva) representing three aspects of the supreme spirit. He is the Preserver, and is believed to have assumed human appearance in nine *avatāra*s, or incarnations, in such forms as Rama and Krishna. His worshippers are the Vaishnavas.

visibility /vɪzɪˈbɪlɪtɪ/ n. 1. being visible. 2. the range or possibility of vision as determined by conditions of light and atmosphere.

visible /'vɪzɪbəl/ adj. 1. that can be seen or noticed. 2. (of exports etc.) consisting of actual goods. —**visibly** adv. [from Old French or Latin visibilis (videre = see)]

Visigoth n. member of the western branch of the ◊Goths, an E Germanic people.

vision /'vɪʒən/ n. 1. the faculty of seeing, sight. 2. a thing seen in the imagination or in a dream etc. 3. imaginative insight into a subject or problem etc.; foresight and wisdom in planning. 4. a person etc. of unusual beauty. 5. what is seen on a television screen. [from Old French from Latin videre = see]

visionary /'vɪʒənərɪ/ adj. 1. given to seeing visions or to indulging in fanciful theories. 2. existing only in vision or in imagination; not practicable. —n. a visionary person.

vision defect any abnormality of the eye resulting in less than perfect sight. See ◊myopia, ◊long sight, and ◊colour blindness.

vision system a computer-based device for interpreting visual signals from a video camera. Computer vision is important in robotics where sensory abilities would considerably increase the flexibility and usefulness of a robot.

visit /'vɪzɪt/ v.t./i. 1. to go or come to see (a person or place etc., or *absolute*) socially or on business etc. 2. to reside temporarily with (a person) or at (a place). 3. to be a visitor. 4. (of a disease or calamity etc.) to come upon, to attack. 5. to inflict punishment for (a sin) upon a person. —n. an act of visiting; temporary residence with a person or at a place. [from Old French or Latin visitare = go to see, frequentative of visare = view from videre = see]

visitant /'vɪzɪtənt/ n. 1. a visitor, especially a supposedly supernatural one. 2. a migratory bird that is a visitor to an area.

visitation /vɪzɪˈteɪʃən/ n. 1. an official visit of inspection. 2. trouble or disaster regarded as divine punishment. 3. the Visitation, in the New Testament, visit of the Virgin Mary to her kinswoman Elizabeth; the festival on 2 July commemorating this.

visitor /'vɪzɪtə/ n. 1. one who visits a person or place. 2. a migratory bird that lives in an area temporarily or at a certain season. 3. (in a college etc.) an official with the right or duty of occasionally inspecting and reporting. —**visitors' book**, a book in which visitors to a hotel or church etc. record their visit by writing their names and addresses and sometimes remarks. [from Anglo-French and Old French]

visor /'vaɪzə/ n. 1. a movable part of a helmet covering the face. 2. a shield at the top of a vehicle windscreen to protect the eyes from bright sunshine. 3. the projecting front part of a cap. [from Anglo-French viser from Latin visus = sight]

vista /'vɪstə/ n. 1. a long, narrow view as between rows of trees. 2. a mental view of a long succession of events. [Italian = view]

visual /'vɪzjuəl, 'vɪʒ-/ adj. of or used in seeing; received through sight. —**visual aid**, a film etc. as an aid to learning. **visual display unit**, a device in a computer; see ◊VDU. —**visually** adv. [from Latin visualis (visus = sight)]

visualize /'vɪzjuəlaɪz, 'vɪʒ-/ v.t. 1. to form a mental picture of. 2. to make visible to the eye. —**visualization** /-'zeɪʃən/ n.

vital /'vaɪtəl/ adj. 1. of, concerned with, or essential to organic life. 2. essential to the existence of a thing or to the matter in hand. 3. full of vitality. 4. affecting life; fatal to life or to success etc. —n. (in *plural*) the vital organs of the body (e. g. heart, lungs, brain). —**vital statistics**, statistics relating to population figures or births and deaths; (*colloquial*) the measurements of a person's bust, waist, and hips. [from Old French from Latin vitalis (vita = life)]

vitalism /'vaɪtəlɪzəm/ n. the idea that living organisms derive their characteristic properties from a universal life force. In the 20th century, this view is associated with the philosopher Henri ◊Bergson. —**vitalist** n., **vitalistic** /-'lɪstɪk/ adj.

vitality /vaɪˈtælɪtɪ/ n. liveliness, vigour, persistent energy; the ability to sustain life. [from Latin]

vitalize /'vaɪtəlaɪz/ v.t. to endow with life; to infuse with vitality. —**vitalization** /-'zeɪʃən/ n.

vitally /'vaɪtəlɪ/ adv. essentially, indispensably.

vitamin /'vɪtəmɪn, 'vaɪ-/ n. any of a number of unrelated organic compounds, essential in small quantities for the normal functioning of the body. Many act as coenzymes, small molecules that enable ◊enzymes to function effectively. They are normally present in adequate amounts in a balanced diet. Deficiency of a vitamin will normally lead to a metabolic disorder (a deficiency disease), which can be remedied by sufficient intake of the vitamin. They are generally classified as **water-soluble** (B and C) or **fat-soluble** (A, D, E, and K). [from German from Latin *vita* = life and *amine*, because originally thought to contain an amino acid]

vitamin C alternative name for ◊ascorbic acid.

vitaminize /'vɪtəmɪnaɪz, 'vaɪ-/ *v.t.* to add vitamins to (food).

vitiate /'vɪʃieɪt/ *v.t.* **1.** to impair the quality or efficiency of, to debase. **2.** to make invalid or ineffectual. —**vitiation** /-'eɪʃən/ *n.* [from Latin *vitium* = vice[1]]

viticulture /'vɪtɪkʌltʃə, 'vaɪt-/ *n.* grape-growing. [from Latin *vitis* = vine and *cultivare* = cultivate]

vitreous /'vɪtriəs/ *adj.* of or like glass. [from Latin *vitrum* = glass]

vitreous humour a transparent jelly-like substance behind the lens of the vertebrate ◊eye. It gives rigidity to the spherical form of the eye and allows light to pass through to the retina.

vitrify /'vɪtrɪfaɪ/ *v.t./i.* to change into glass or a glassy substance, especially by heat. —**vitrifaction** /-'fækʃən/ *n.*, **vitrification** /-fɪ'keɪʃən/ *n.* [from French]

vitriol /'vɪtriəl/ *n.* **1.** any of a number of sulphate salts. Blue, green, and white vitriols are copper, ferrous, and zinc sulphate, respectively. **Oil of vitriol** is sulphuric acid. **2.** caustic or hostile speech or criticism. —**vitriolic** /-'ɒlɪk/ *adj.* [from Old French or Latin *vitriolum* (*vitrum* = glass)]

vituperate /vɪ'tju:pəreɪt, vaɪ-/ *v.t./i.* to revile, to abuse; to use abusive language. —**vituperation** /-'reɪʃən/ *n.*, **vituperative** /-ətɪv/ *adj.*, **vituperator** *n.* [from Latin *vitium* = vice[1]]

Vitus, St /'vaɪtəs/ Christian saint, perhaps Sicilian, who was martyred in Rome early in the 4th century. Feast day 15 June.

viva /'vaɪvə/ *n.* & *v.t.* (*past* and *past participle* **vivaed**) (*colloquial*) = ◊viva voce. [abbreviation]

viva /'vi:və/ *n.* interjection meaning long live. —*n.* a cry of this as a salute etc. [Italian, present subjunctive of *vivere* = live]

vivacious /vɪ'veɪʃəs/ *adj.* lively, high-spirited. —**vivaciously** *adv.*, **vivacity** /vɪ'væsɪtɪ/ *n.* [from Latin *vivax*]

Vivaldi /vɪ'vældi/ Antonio (Lucio) 1678–1741. Italian Baroque composer, violinist, and conductor. He wrote 23 symphonies, 75 sonatas, over 400 concertos, including the *Four Seasons* (about 1725) for violin and orchestra, over 40 operas, and much sacred music. His work was largely neglected until the 1930s.

vivarium /vaɪ'veəriəm/ *n.* (*plural* **vivaria**) a place artificially prepared for keeping animals in (nearly) their natural state. [Latin]

viva voce /vaɪvə 'vəʊtʃɪ/ oral. —*adv.* orally. —*n.* an oral examination. —**viva-voce** *v.t.* to examine viva voce. [Latin = with the living voice]

vivid /'vɪvɪd/ *adj.* **1.** (of light or colour) bright and strong, intense. **2.** (of a description etc.) producing strong and clear mental pictures; (of a mental impression) clearly produced; (of the imagination) creating ideas etc. in an active and lively way. —**vividly** *adv.*, **vividness** *n.* [from Latin *vividus* (*vivere* = live)]

vivify /'vɪvɪfaɪ/ *v.t.* to give life to (especially *figurative*), to enliven, to animate. [from French from Latin *vivificare* (*vivus* = alive and *facere* = make)]

vivipary *n.* in animals, a method of reproduction in which the embryo develops inside the body of the female from which it gains nourishment (in contrast to ◊ovipary and ◊ovovivipary). Vivipary is best developed in placental mammals, but also occurs in some arthropods, fishes, amphibians, and reptiles that have placentalike structures. In plants, it is the formation of young plantlets or bulbils instead of flowers. The term also describes seeds that germinate prematurely, before falling from the parent plant. —**viviparous** /vɪ'vɪpərəs, vaɪ-/ *adj.* [from Latin *vivus* = alive and *parere* = bear]

vivisect /'vɪvɪsekt/ *v.t.* to perform vivisection on.

vivisection /vɪvɪ'sekʃən/ *n.* performance of surgical or other experiments on living animals for scientific research.

—**vivisectionist** *n.*, **vivisector** /'vɪvɪsektə/ *n.* [from Latin *vivus* = alive, after *dissection*]

vixen /'vɪksən/ *n.* **1.** a female fox. **2.** a spiteful woman. [from earlier *fixen*, feminine of fox]

viz. /vɪz, 'neɪmlɪ/ namely, that is to say, in other words. [abbreviation of Latin *videlicet* = it is permitted to see]

vizier /vi'zɪə, 'vɪz-/ *n.* an official of high rank in some Muslim countries. [ultimately from Arabic *wazīr* = caliph's chief counsellor]

Vladivostok /vlædi'vɒstɒk/ naval and commercial port in E USSR at the Amur Bay on the Pacific coast; population (1987) 615,000. It is kept open by icebreakers in winter. Industries include shipbuilding and precision instruments.

Vlaminck /vlæ'mæŋk/ Maurice de 1876–1958. French painter, who began using brilliant colour as an early member of the ◊Fauves, mainly painting landscapes. He later abandoned Fauve colour. He also wrote poetry, novels, and essays.

VLSI (very large-scale integration) the current level of advanced technology in the microminiaturization of ◊integrated circuits, and an order of magnitude smaller than ◊LSI. [abbreviation]

V neck a V-shaped neckline on a pullover or other garment.

vocable /'vəʊkəbəl/ *n.* a word, especially with reference to its form not its meaning. [French or from Latin *vocabulum* (*vocare* = call)]

vocabulary /və'kæbjʊlərɪ/ *n.* **1.** the words used in a language, book, or branch of science, or by an author. **2.** a list of these arranged alphabetically with definitions or translations. **3.** the range of words known to an individual person. **4.** a set of artistic or stylistic forms or techniques. [from Latin *vocabularius*]

vocal /'vəʊkəl/ *adj.* **1.** of, for, or uttered by the voice. **2.** expressing one's feelings freely in speech. —*n.* (in *singular* or *plural*) the sung part or a sung piece of music. —**vocal cords**, the folds of the lining membrane of a mammal's larynx and a bird's syrinx. Air passing over them makes them vibrate, producing sounds. Muscles in the larynx change the pitch of the sound by adjusting the tension of the vocal cords. —**vocally** *adv.* [from Latin *vocalis vox* = voice]

vocalic /və'kælɪk/ *adj.* of or consisting of a vowel or vowels.

vocalist /'vəʊkəlɪst/ *n.* a singer.

vocalize /'vəʊkəlaɪz/ *v.t.* to form (a sound) or utter (a word) with the voice. —**vocalization** /-'zeɪʃən/ *n.*

vocation /və'keɪʃən/ *n.* **1.** a divine call to or a sense of one's fitness for a certain career or occupation. **2.** a person's trade or profession. —**vocational** *adj.* [from Old French or Latin *vocare* = call]

vocative /'vɒkətɪv/ *n.* in the grammar certain inflected languages, the case of a noun used in addressing or invoking a person or thing. —*adj.* of or in the vocative. [from Old French or Latin]

vociferate /və'sɪfəreɪt/ *v.t./i.* to utter noisily; to shout. —**vociferation** /-'reɪʃən/ *n.*, **vociferator** *n.* [from Latin *vociferari* (*vox* = voice and *ferre* = bear)]

vociferous /və'sɪfərəs/ *adj.* making a great outcry; expressing one's views loudly and insistently in speech. —**vociferously** *adv.*, **vociferousness** *n.*

vodka /'vɒdkə/ *n.* a strong, colourless, alcoholic liquor distilled from rye, potatoes, maize, or barley. [Russian diminutive of *voda* = water]

Vogel /'fəʊɡəl/ Hans-Jochen 1926– . German socialist politician, chair of the Social Democratic Party (SPD) from 1987. A former leader of the SPD in Bavaria and mayor of Munich, he served in the Brandt and Schmidt West German governments in the 1970s as housing, then justice minister and then, briefly, as mayor of West Berlin.

vogue /vəʊɡ/ *n.* prevailing fashion; popular favour or acceptance. —**in vogue**, in fashion; generally current. **vogue-word** *n.* a word currently fashionable. [French from Italian *voga* = rowing, fashion]

voice *n.* **1.** a sound formed in the larynx and uttered by the mouth, especially human utterance in speaking or singing etc.; ability to produce this. **2.** use of the voice; an utterance in spoken or (*figurative*) written form; an opinion so expressed; the right to express an opinion; the agency by which an opinion is expressed. **3.** in grammar, a set of verbal forms showing whether a verb is active or passive. —*v.t.* **1.** to give utterance to; to express in words. **2.** to utter

with vibration of the vocal cords (e. g. *b, d*). —**in good
voice**, in proper vocal condition for singing or speaking.
voice-over *n.* narration in a film etc. not accompanied by
a picture of the speaker. **with one voice**, unanimously.
[from Anglo-French *voiz* from Latin *vox*]

voiceless *adj.* 1. dumb, speechless, mute. 2. (of a sound)
uttered without vibration of the vocal cords (e.g. *f, p*).

void *adj.* 1. empty, vacant. 2. (of a contract etc.) invalid,
not legally binding. —*n.* empty space, a vacuum. —*v.t.*
1. to render void. 2. to excrete. —**void of**, lacking;
free from. [from Old French, ultimately from Latin *vacare*
= be empty]

Voight /vɔɪt/ Jon 1938– . US film actor who starred with
Dustin Hoffman in *Midnight Cowboy* 1969. His subsequent
films include *Deliverance* 1972, *Coming Home* 1978, and
Runaway Train 1985.

voile /vɔɪl, vwɑːl/ *n.* a thin semitransparent dress-material.
[French = veil]

Vojvodina /vɔɪvəˈdiːnə/ autonomous area in N Serbia, Yugoslavia; area 21,500 sq km/8,299 sq mi; population
(1986) 2,050,000, including 1,110,000 Serbs and 390,000
Hungarians. Its capital is Novi Sad.

vol or vol. abbreviation of volume.

volatile /ˈvɒlətaɪl/ *adj.* 1. in chemistry, evaporating rapidly, describing a substance that readily passes from the
liquid to the vapour phase. Volatile substances have a high
◊vapour pressure. 2. changing quickly or easily from one
mood or interest to another; transient; lively; apt to break
out into violence. —**volatility** /-ˈtɪltɪ/ *n.* [from Old French
or Latin *volatilis* (*volare* = fly)]

volatilize /vəˈlætɪlaɪz/ *v.t./i.* to turn into vapour. —**vola-
tilization** /-ˈzeɪʃən/ *n.*

vol-au-vent /ˈvɒləuvɑ̃/ *n.* a (usually small) round case of
puff pastry filled with a savoury mixture. [French, literally
= flight in the wind]

volcanic /vɒlˈkænɪk/ *adj.* of, like, or produced by a
volcano. —**volcanic rock** ◊igneous rock formed at the
surface of the Earth. It is usually fine-grained, unlike the
coarser intrusive (under the surface) igneous rock. Volcanic
rock can be lava (solidified magma) or a pyroclastic deposit
(fragmentary lava or ash) such as tuff (volcanic ash that has
fused to form rock). —**volcanically** *adv.* [from French]

volcano /vɒlˈkeɪnəu/ *n.* (*plural* **volcanoes**) 1. an opening in the Earth's ◊crust through which motten rock, lava,
ashes, steam, and gases are or have been expelled; a mountain or hill formed round such an opening. Most volcanoes
are cone-shaped with a pitlike opening at the top called a
crater. Some, such as Stromboli and Vesuvius in Italy, eject
the material with explosive violence; in others the lava rises
quietly into the crater and flows over the rim. 2. a state of
things likely to cause a violent outburst. [Italian from Latin
Volcanus Vulcan, = Roman god of fire]

vole *n.* a rodent of the family Cricetidae distributed over
Europe, Asia, and North America, and related to hamsters
and lemmings. They have brown or grey fur, blunt noses,
and some species reach a length of 30 cm/2 ft. They feed
on grasses, seeds, aquatic plants, and insects. [originally
vole-mouse, from Norwegian *voll* = field]

Volga /ˈvɒlgə/ longest river in Europe: 3,685 km/2,290 mi,
3,540 km/2,200 mi of which are navigable. It drains most
of the central and eastern parts of European USSR, rises
in the Valdai plateau and flows into the Caspian Sea 88 km/
55 mi below Astrakhan.

Volgograd /ˈvɒlgəgræd/ formerly (until 1925) **Tsaritsyn**,
and (1925–61) **Stalingrad** industrial city (metal goods,
machinery, sawmills, oil refining) in SW USSR, on the river
Volga; population (1987) 988,000.

volition /vəˈlɪʃən/ *n.* the act or faculty of willing. —**voli-
tional** *adj.*, **volitionally** *adv.* [French or from Latin
volo = I wish]

Volkswagen /ˈvɒlkswɑːgən/ *n.* (VW) German car manufacturer. The original VW, with its distinctive beetle shape,
was produced in Germany in 1938, a design by Ferdinand
◊Porsche. It was still in production in Latin America in the
late 1980s, by which time it had exceeded 20 million sales.
[German = the people's car]

volley /ˈvɒlɪ/ *n.* 1. a simultaneous discharge of a number
of weapons; the bullets etc. thus discharged. 2. a noisy
emission of questions or curses etc. in quick succession. 3.
return of a ball in tennis, football, etc., before it touches the
ground; a full toss. —*v.t.* 1. to discharge or fly in a volley.

Voltaire *French writer and philosopher Voltaire.*

2. to return (a ball) by a volley. —**volley ball** a game for
two teams of six persons, volleying a large ball by hand over
a net [from French *volée* from Latin *volare* = fly]

volt /vəult/ *n.* SI unit (symbol V) of electromotive force
or electric potential, the difference of potential that would
carry one ampere of current against one ohm resistance.
A small battery has a potential of 1.5 volts; the domestic
electricity supply in the UK is 240 volts (110 volts in the
USA) [from A *Volta*]

Volta /ˈvɒltə/ main river in Ghana, about 1,600 km/
1,000 mi long, with two main upper branches, the Black
and White Volta. It has been dammed to provide power.

Volta Alessandro 1745–1827. Italian physicist. He invented
the voltaic pile (the first battery), the electrophorus (an
early electrostatic generator), and an ◊electroscope.

Volta, Upper name until 1984 of ◊Burkina Faso.

voltage /ˈvəultɪdʒ/ *n.* electromotive force expressed in
volts.

Voltaire /vɒlˈteə/ pen name of François-Marie Arouet
1694–1778. French writer, who believed in ◊deism, and
devoted himself to tolerance, justice, and humanity. He
was threatened with arrest for *Lettres philosophiques sur les
anglais/Philosophical Letters on the English* 1733 (essays in
favour of English ways, thought, and political practice) and
had to take refuge.

All the reasoning of men is not worth one sentiment of
women.

Voltaire
Maximes

---

volte-face /vɒltˈfɑːs/ *n.* a complete reversal of position
in an argument or opinion. [French from Italian *voltafaccia*
(*voltare* = to turn from Latin *volvere* = roll)]

voltmeter /ˈvəultmiːtə/ *n.* an instrument for measuring
potential difference (voltage). It has a high internal resistance (so that it passes only a small current), such as a sensitive moving-coil ◊galvanometer in series with a high-value
resistor. To measure an alternating voltage, the circuit also
includes a rectifier. A moving-iron instrument can be used
to measure AC (◊alternating current) voltages without the
need for a rectifier.

voluble /ˈvɒljubəl/ *adj.* with a vehement or incessant flow
of words. —**volubility** /-ˈbɪlɪtɪ/ *n.*, **volubly** *adv.* [French
or from Latin *volubilis* (*volvere* = roll)]

volume /ˈvɒljuːm/ *n.* 1. a book, especially one of a set. 2.
the amount of space (often expressed in cubic units) that a
three-dimensional object occupies or contains or that a gas
or liquid occupies. In geometry, a prism (such as a cube)
or a cylinder has a volume equal to the area of the base
multiplied by the height. For a pyramid or cone, the volume
is equal to one-third of the area of the base multiplied by

the perpendicular height. The volume of a sphere is equal to $4/3\pi r^3$, where r is the radius. Volumes of irregular solids may be calculated by the technique of ◊integration. **3.** the amount of a thing, a quantity. **4.** the strength or power of a sound. [from Old French from Latin *volumen* (from *volvere* = roll, ancient books being in roll form)]

volumetric *adj.* of measurement by volume. —**volumetrically** *adv.*

volumetric analysis a procedure used for determining the concentration of a solution. A known volume of a solution of unknown concentration is reacted with a solution of known concentration (standard). The standard solution is delivered from a ◊burette so the volume added is known. This technique is known as titration. Often an indicator is used to show when the correct proportions have reacted. This procedure is used for acid–base, redox, and certain other reactions involving solutions.

voluminous /vəˈljuːmɪnəs, vəˈluː-/ *adj.* **1.** having great volume, bulky; of (drapery etc.) loose and ample. **2.** (of writings) great in quantity; (of a writer) producing many works, copious. —**voluminously** *adv.*, **voluminousness** *n.* [from Latin]

voluntary /ˈvɒləntərɪ/ *adj.* **1.** acting, done, or given etc. of one's own free will, not under compulsion. **2.** working or done without payment. **3.** (of an institution) maintained by voluntary contributions or voluntary workers; (of a British school) originally built by such an institution but maintained by a local education authority. **4.** (of a movement, muscle, or limb) controlled by the will. —*n.* an organ solo played before, during, or after a church service. —**voluntarily** *adv.*, **voluntariness** *n.* [from Old French or Latin *voluntarius voluntas* = will]

volunteer /vɒlənˈtɪə/ *n.* a person who voluntarily undertakes a task or enters military etc. service. —*v.t./i.* **1.** to undertake or offer voluntarily. **2.** to be a volunteer. [from French *volontaire*]

voluptuary /vəˈlʌptjuərɪ/ *n.* a person given up to luxury and sensual pleasure. [from Latin]

voluptuous /vəˈlʌptjuəs/ *adj.* of, tending to, occupied with, or derived from sensuous or sensual pleasure; (of a woman) having a full and attractive figure. —**voluptuously** *adv.*, **voluptuousness** *n.* [from Old French or Latin *voluptas* = pleasure]

volute /vəˈljuːt/ *n.* a spiral scroll in stonework forming the chief ornament of Ionic capitals and used also in Corinthian and composite capitals. [French or from Latin *voluta* (*volvere* = roll)]

vomit /ˈvɒmɪt/ *v.t./i.* **1.** to eject (matter) from the stomach through the mouth; to be sick. Vomiting may have numerous causes, including direct irritation of the stomach, severe pain, dizziness, and emotion. Sustained or repeated vomiting may indicate serious disease, and dangerous loss of water, salt, and acid may result (as in ◊bulimia). **2.** (of a volcano, chimney, etc.) to eject violently, to belch forth. —*n.* matter vomited from the stomach. [from Old French or Latin *vomitus, vomitare*]

von Braun /fɒn ˈbraʊn/ Wernher 1912–1977. German rocket engineer who developed German military rockets (V1 and V2) during World War II and later worked for ◊NASA in the USA.

von Gesner /fɒn ˈgesnə/ Konrad 1516–1565. Swiss naturalist who produced an encyclopedia of the animal world, the *Historia animalium* 1551–58.

Vonnegut /ˈvɒnɪgʌt/ Kurt, Jr 1922– . US writer whose work generally has a science-fiction or fantasy element; his novels include *The Sirens of Titan* 1958, *Cat's Cradle* 1963, *Slaughterhouse-Five* 1969, which draws on his World War II experience of the fire-bombing of Dresden, Germany, and *Galápagos* 1985.

Von Neumann /vɒn ˈnjuːmən/ John 1903–1957. Hungarian-born US scientist and mathematician, pioneer of computer design. He invented his celebrated 'rings of operators' (called Von Neumann algebras) in the late 1930s, and contributed to set theory, games theory, cybernetics (with his theory of self-reproducing automata, called **Von Neumann machines**), and the development of the atomic and hydrogen bombs.

voodoo /ˈvuːduː/ *n.* **1.** a set of magical beliefs and practices, followed in some parts of Africa, South America, and the West Indies, especially Haiti. It evolved in the 17th century on slave plantations from Roman Catholicism and W African religious traditions; believers retain membership in the Roman Catholic church. Beliefs include the existence of **loa**, spirits who closely involve themselves in human affairs, and some of whose identities mesh with those of Christian saints. **2.** a person skilled in this. **3.** a voodoo spell. —*v.t.* to affect by voodoo, to bewitch. —**voodooism** *n.*, **voodooist** *n.* [from Dahomey *vodu*]

voracious /vəˈreɪʃəs/ *adj.* **1.** greedy in eating, ravenous. **2.** very eager in some activity. —**voraciously** *adv.*, **voracity** /vəˈræsɪtɪ/ *n.* [from Latin *vorare* = devour]

Vorster /ˈfɔːstə/ Balthazar Johannes 1915–1983. South African Nationalist politician, prime minister 1966–78, and president 1978–79. During his premiership some elements of apartheid were allowed to lapse, and attempts were made to improve relations with the outside world. He resigned the presidency because of a financial scandal.

vortex /ˈvɔːteks/ *n.* (*plural* **vortexes** or **vortices** /-ɪsiːz/) **1.** a whirlpool, a whirlwind, a whirling motion or mass. **2.** a thing viewed as swallowing those who approach it. —**vortical** /-ɪkəl/ *adj.*, **vortically** /-ɪkəlɪ/ *adv.* [Latin *vortex -icis* = eddy, variant of *vertex* = whirlpool]

Vorticism *n.* a short-lived movement in British painting, begun in 1913 by Wyndham ◊Lewis. Influenced by Cubism and Futurism, he believed that painting should reflect the complexity and change of the modern world. He had a harsh, angular, semi-abstract style.

Voskhod /vɒsˈxɒd/ *n.* Soviet spacecraft used in the mid-1960s; it was modified from the single-seat Vostok, and was the first spacecraft capable of carrying two or three cosmonauts. During *Voskhod 2*'s flight in 1965, Alexei Leonov made the first space walk. [Russian = ascent]

Vostok /ˈvɒstɒk/ *n.* the first Soviet spacecraft, used 1961–63. Vostok was a metal sphere 2.3 m/7.5 ft in diameter, capable of carrying one cosmonaut. It made flights lasting up to five days. *Vostok 1* carried the first person into space, Yuri ◊Gagarin. [Russian = east]

votary /ˈvəʊtərɪ/ *n.* a person vowed or devoted to the service of a god, cult, or pursuit. —**votaress** *n.fem.* [from Latin]

vote *n.* **1.** a formal expression of choice of opinion in the election of a candidate, passing of a law, etc., signified by a ballot or show of hands etc. For direct vote, see ◊plebiscite and ◊referendum. In parliamentary elections the results can be calculated in a number of ways. The main electoral systems are: **first past the post** or **winner-take-all**, with single-member constituencies in which the candidate with most votes wins (USA, UK, Canada); ◊proportional **representation** (PR), in which seats are shared by parties according to their share of the vote; **preferential vote**, in which the voter indicates first and second choices either by **alternative vote** (AV), in which, if no candidate achieves over 50% of the votes, voters' second choices are successively transferred from the least successful candidates until one candidate does achieve 50% (Australia); or by **second ballot**, when no candidate has an absolute majority on the first count (France). **2.** the right to vote, especially in a state election. **3.** an opinion expressed by a majority of votes; the collective votes given by or for a particular group. —*v.t./i.* **1.** to give one's vote. **2.** to enact or resolve by a majority of votes; to grant (a sum of money etc.) by a vote. **3.** (*colloquial*) to pronounce by general consent; to announce one's proposal (that). —**vote down**, to defeat (a proposal etc.) by votes. **vote in**, to elect by votes. —**voter** *n.* [from Latin *votum* (*vovēre* = vow)]

votive /ˈvəʊtɪv/ *adj.* given or consecrated in fulfilment of a vow [from Latin *votivus*]

vouch *v.i.* (with *for*) to guarantee the certainty, accuracy, or reliability of. [from Old French *vo(u)cher* = summon, ultimately from Latin *vocare* = call]

voucher *n.* **1.** a document (issued in token of payment made or promised) exchangeable for certain goods or services. **2.** a document establishing that money has been paid or goods etc. delivered.

vouchsafe /vaʊtʃˈseɪf/ *v.t.* to condescend to grant or do a thing.

voussoir /ˈvuːswɑː/ *n.* each of the wedge-shaped or tapered stones forming an arch. [from Old French ultimately from Latin *volvere* = roll]

vow *n.* a solemn promise especially in the form of an oath to a deity or saint. —*v.t.* **1.** to promise solemnly. **2.**

(*archaic*) to declare solemnly. [from Anglo-French *vou* from Latin *vovère*]

vowel /'vauəl/ *n.* a speech-sound made with vibration of the vocal cords but without audible friction; a letter or letters representing this, as *a, e, i, o, u, aw, ah*. [from Old French from Latin *vocalis (littera)* = vocal (letter)]

vox populi /vɒks 'pɒpjuli:, -laɪ/ public opinion, the general verdict, popular belief. [Latin = the people's voice]

voyage /'vɔɪɪdʒ/ *n.* an expedition to a distance, especially by water or in space. —*v.i.* to make a voyage. —**voyager** *n.* [from Anglo-French from Latin *via* = road]

Voyager probes two US space probes, originally Mariners. *Voyager 1*, launched on 5 Sept 1977, passed Jupiter in March 1979, and reached Saturn in Nov 1980. *Voyager 2* was launched earlier, on 20 Aug 1977, on a slower trajectory that took it past Jupiter in July 1979, Saturn in Aug 1981, Uranus in Jan 1986, Neptune in Aug 1989, and on to Pluto. The Voyagers are travelling beyond the solar system. Their tasks include helping scientists to locate the position of the heliopause, the boundary at which the influence of the Sun gives way to the forces exerted by other stars. Both Voyagers carry coded long-playing records called 'Sounds of Earth' for the enlightenment of other civilizations.

voyeur /vwɑː'jɜː/ *n.* one who obtains sexual gratification from looking at others' sexual actions or organs. —**voyeurism** *n.* [French *voir* = see]

Voysey /'vɔɪzi/ Charles Francis Annesley 1857–1941. English architect and designer. He designed country houses which were characteristically asymmetrical with massive buttresses, long sloping roofs, and rough-cast walls. He also designed textiles and wallpaper.

Vranitzky /vræ'nɪtski/ Franz 1937– . Austrian socialist politician, federal chancellor from 1986. Vranitzky first went into banking and in 1970 became adviser on economic and financial policy to the minister of finance. He entered the political arena through the Socialist Party of Austria (SPÖ), and became minister of finance in 1984. He succeeded Fred Sinowatz as federal chancellor in 1986, heading an SPÖ-ÖVP (Austrian People's Party) coalition.

vs. abbreviation of versus.

V sign a gesture made with the raised hand with the first and second fingers forming a V, expressing victory or approval, or vulgar derision.

VTO abbreviation of vertical takeoff.

VTOL abbreviation of vertical takeoff and landing, see ◊vertical takeoff aircraft.

Vuillard /vwiː'ɑː/ (Jean) Edouard 1886–1940. French painter and printmaker, a founding member of **les ◊Nabis**. His work is mainly decorative, with an emphasis on surface pattern reflecting the influence of Japanese prints. With ◊Bonnard he produced numerous lithographs and paintings of simple domestic interiors, works that are generally categorized as *intimiste*.

Vulcan /'vʌlkən/ in Roman mythology, the god of fire and destruction, later identified with the Greek god ◊Hephaestus.

vulcanite /'vʌlkənaɪt/ *n.* hard, black vulcanized rubber.

vulcanize /'vʌlkənaɪz/ *v.t.* to make (rubber etc.) stronger and more elastic by treating with sulphur at a high temperature. If the sulphur content is increased to as much as 30%, the product is the inelastic solid known as ebonite. More expensive alternatives to sulphur, such as selenium and telurium, are used to vulcanize rubber for specialized products such as vehicle tyres. The process was

vulture

discovered accidentally by US inventor Charles ◊Goodyear in 1839 and patented in 1844. —**vulcanization** /-'zeɪʃən/ *n.* [from *Vulcan*, Roman god of fire]

vulcanology /vʌlkə'nɒlədʒɪ/ *n.* study of ◊volcanoes and the geological phenomena that cause them.

vulgar /'vʌlgə/ *adj.* 1. characteristic of the common people; lacking in refinement or good taste, coarse. 2. commonly used. —**vulgar fraction,** a fraction expressed by a numerator and a denominator, not decimally. **vulgar tongue,** the national or vernacular language. —**vulgarity** /-'gærɪtɪ/ *n.,* **vulgarly** *adv.* [from Latin *vulgus* = common people]

vulgarian /vʌl'geəriən/ *n.* a vulgar person, especially a rich one.

vulgarism *n.* a word or expression in coarse or uneducated use; an instance of coarse or uneducated behaviour.

vulgarize /'vʌlgəraɪz/ *v.t.* 1. to make vulgar. 2. to spoil by making too common or frequented or too well known. —**vulgarization** /-'zeɪʃən/ *n.*

Vulgate /'vʌlgət/ *n.* the Latin version of the Bible prepared mainly by St Jerome in the late 4th century, translated directly from the Hebrew text of the Old Testament. [from Latin (*editio*) *vulgare* = make public]

vulnerable /'vʌlnərəbəl/ *adj.* 1. that may be hurt, wounded, or injured. 2. unprotected, exposed to danger, attack, or criticism etc. 3. having won a game towards a rubber at contract bridge and therefore liable to higher penalties. —**vulnerability** /-'bɪlɪtɪ/ *n.,* **vulnerably** *adv.* [from Latin *vulnus* = wound]

vulpine /'vʌlpaɪn/ *adj.* of or like a fox; crafty, cunning. [from Latin *vulpes* = fox]

vulture /'vʌltʃə/ *n.* 1. a carrion-eating bird up to 1 m/3.3 ft long, with a wingspan of up to 3.5 m/11.5 ft. It has a bare head and neck, shaggy black or brown plumage and a hooked beak and claws. True vultures occur only in the Old World (family Accipitridae); the New World (family Cathartidae) forms include the ◊condor and turkey buzzard. 2. a rapacious person seeking to profit from others' misfortunes. [from Anglo-French from Latin]

vulva /'vʌlvə/ *n.* the external parts of the female genitals. [Latin = womb]

vv. abbreviation of 1. verses. 2. volumes.

vying participle of vie.

w, W /'dʌbəlju:/ n. (plural **ws, w's**) the 23rd letter of the alphabet.

W abbreviation of **1.** watt(s). **2.** west(ern).

W symbol for tungsten. [from wolframium, Latinized name]

W. abbreviation of **1.** wicket(s). **2.** wide(s). **3.** with.

WA abbreviation of Western Australia.

wacky adj. (slang) crazy. —n. (slang) a crazy person. [originally dialect = left-handed]

wad /wɒd/ n. **1.** a lump or bundle of soft material to keep things apart or in place or to block a hole. **2.** a collection of banknotes or documents placed together. **3.** (slang) a bun; a sandwich. —v.t. (-dd-) to fix or stuff with a wad; to stuff, line, or protect with wadding.

wadding /'wɒdɪŋ/ n. soft fibrous material used for padding, packing, or lining things.

Waddington /'wɒdɪŋtən/ David Charles, Baron Waddington 1929– . British Conservative politician, home secretary from 1989–1990. A barrister, he became an MP in 1978. A Conservative whip from 1979, Waddington was a junior minister in the Department of Employment and in the Home Office before becoming chief whip in 1987. In 1990 he was made a life peer and leader of the House of Lords.

waddle /'wɒdəl/ v.i. to walk with short steps and a swaying motion. —n. a waddling walk.

wade v.t./i. **1.** to walk through water or some impeding medium; to cross (a stream) thus. **2.** to progress slowly or with difficulty. —n. a spell of wading. —**wade in**, (colloquial) to make a vigorous intervention or attack. **wade through**, to read through (a book etc.) in spite of its difficulty, dullness, or length. **wading bird**, a long-legged water bird that wades in shallow water. [Old English]

wader n. **1.** a wading-bird. **2.** (in plural) high waterproof fishing-boots.

wadi /'wɒdɪ/ n. a rocky watercourse in North Africa and neighbouring countries that is dry except in the rainy season. [from Arabic]

wafer /'weɪfə/ n. **1.** a kind of thin, light, crisp, sweet biscuit. **2.** a thin disc of unleavened bread used in the ◊Eucharist. **3.** a disc of red paper stuck on law papers instead of a seal. **4.** in microelectronics, a 'superchip' some 8–10 cm/3–4 in in diameter, for which wafer-scale integration (WSI) is used to link the equivalent of many individual silicon chips (see ◊silicon), improving reliability, speed, and cooling. —v.t. to fasten or seal with a wafer. —**wafer-thin** adv. very thin. [from Anglo-French wafre from Middle Low German wâfel]

waffle[1] /'wɒfəl/ n. aimless verbose talk or writing. —v.i. to indulge in waffle. [original dialect from waff = yelp]

waffle[2] n. a small, crisp batter cake. —**waffle iron**, a utensil, usually of two hinged, shallow metal pans, for baking waffles. [from Dutch wafel from Middle Low German]

waft /wɒft/ v.t. to convey smoothly (as) through air or along water. —n. a wafted odour.

wag v.t./i. (-gg-) to shake or move briskly to and fro. —n. **1.** a single wagging movement. **2.** a person who is given to joking or playing practical jokes. —**tongues wag**, there is talk. [from root of Old English wagian = sway]

wage n. (in singular or plural) a regular payment to an employee in return for his work or services. —v.t. to carry on (a war etc.). —**wage earner** one who works for a wage. **wage freeze**, a ban on wage increases. [from Anglo-French]

wage, minimum the lowest wage that an employer is allowed to pay its employees by law or union contract.

wager /'weɪdʒə/ n. a bet. —v.t./i. to bet. [from Anglo-French]

waggish adj. playful, facetious. —**waggishly** adv., **waggishness** n.

waggle v.t./i. (colloquial) to wag. —n. (colloquial) a waggling movement. —**waggle dance**, a movement performed by honey-bees at their hive or nest, believed to indicate to other bees the site of a source of food. —**waggly** adj.

Wagner /'vɑːgnə/ Otto 1841–1918. Viennese architect. Initially designing in the Art Nouveau style, for example, Vienna Stadtbahn 1894–97, he later rejected ornament for rationalism, as in the Post Office Savings Bank, Vienna, 1904–06. He influenced Viennese architects such as Josef Hoffmann, Adolf Loos, and Joseph Olbrich.

Wagner Richard 1813–1883. German opera composer. He revolutionized the 19th-century conception of opera, envisaging it as a wholly new art form in which musical, poetic, and scenic elements should be unified through such devices as the ◊leitmotiv. His operas include Tannhäuser 1845, Lohengrin 1850, and Tristan und Isolde 1865. In 1872 he founded the Festival Theatre in Bayreuth; his masterpiece Der Ring des Nibelungen/The Ring of the Nibelung, a sequence of four operas, was first performed there in 1876. His last work, Parsifal, was produced in 1882.

wagon /'wægən/ n. or **waggon** **1.** a four-wheeled vehicle for heavy loads drawn by horses or oxen. **2.** an open railway truck. **3.** a trolley for carrying food etc. —**hitch one's wagon to a star**, to utilize powers higher than one's own. **on the wagon**, (slang) abstaining from alcohol. [from Dutch wag(h)en]

wagoner n. or **waggoner** the driver of a wagon.

wagonette /ˌwægəˈnet/ n. or **waggonette** a four-wheeled, open, horse-drawn carriage with facing side seats.

Wagram, Battle of /'vɑːgrəm/ the battle in July 1809 when French troops under Emperor Napoleon won an important victory over the Austrian army under Archduke Charles near the village of Wagram, NE of Vienna, Austria. The outcome forced Austria to concede general defeat to the French.

wagtail n. a slim, narrow-billed bird Motacilla, about 18 cm/7 in long, with a characteristic flicking movement of the tail. There are about 30 species, found mostly in Eurasia and Africa. British species include the pied wagtail Motacilla alba with black, grey, and white plumage, the grey wagtail Motacilla cinerae, and, a summer visitor, the yellow wagtail Motacilla flava.

Wahabi /wəˈhɑːbɪ/ n. a puritanical Saudi Islamic sect founded by Muhammad ibn-Abd-al-Wahab (1703–92), which regards all other sects as heretical. By the early 20th century it had spread throughout the Arabian peninsula; it still remains the official ideology of the Saudi Arabian kingdom.

waif n. **1.** a homeless and helpless person, especially an abandoned child. **2.** an ownerless object or animal. —**waifs**

and strays, homeless or neglected children; odds and ends. [from Anglo-French]

wail *n.* a long, sad, inarticulate cry of pain or grief; a sound resembling this. —*v.i.* **1.** to utter a wail; to make such a sound. **2.** to lament or complain persistently. [from Old Norse]

Wailing Wall or (in Judaism) **Western Wall** the remaining part of the ◊Temple in Jerusalem, a sacred site of pilgrimage and prayer for Jews. There they offer prayers either aloud ('wailing') or on pieces of paper placed between the stones of the wall.

wain *n.* (*archaic*) a wagon. [Old English]

wainscot /'weɪnskət/ *n.* the boarding or wooden panelling on the lower part of a room wall. —**wainscoting** material for wainscot. [from Middle Low German *wagenschot*]

waist *n.* **1.** the part of the human body below the ribs and above the hips; the narrowness marking this; its circumference. **2.** a similar narrow part in the middle of a long object (e.g. a violin) or of a wasp etc. **3.** the part of a garment corresponding to the waist. **4.** (*US*) a blouse; a bodice. —**waist-deep** or **-high** *adjs. & advs.* immersed up to the waist; so high as to reach the waist.

waistband *n.* a strip of cloth forming the waist of a garment.

waistcoat *n.* a close-fitting waist-length garment without sleeves or a collar, worn (especially by men) over a shirt and under a jacket.

waistline *n.* the outline or size of the body at the waist.

wait *v.t./i.* **1.** to defer an action or departure until an expected event occurs; to do this for (a specified time). **2.** to await (an opportunity, one's turn etc.). **3.** to defer (a meal) until a person's arrival. **4.** to park a vehicle for a short time at the side of the road etc. **5.** to act as a waiter or attendant. —*n.* **1.** an act or period of waiting. **2.** waiting for an enemy. **3.** (in *plural*) street singers of Christmas carols. —**lie in wait,** to be hidden and ready. **wait and see,** to await the progress of events. **waiting game** postponing an action for greater effect. **waiting list** a list of applicants etc. for a thing not immediately available. **waiting room** a room where people can wait, e.g. at a railway station or surgery. **wait on** or **upon,** to await the convenience of; to be an attendant or respectful visitor to. **wait up, (for)** not to go to bed (until the arrival or happening of). **you wait!** an expression of threat or warning. [from Old French]

Waite /weɪt/ Terry (Terence Hardy) 1939– . British religious adviser from 1980 to the previous archbishop of Canterbury, Dr Robert ◊Runcie. Waite undertook many overseas assignments and disappeared in 1987 while making enquiries in Beirut, Lebanon, about European hostages. Worldwide efforts to secure his release have proved unsuccessful.

waiter *n.* a man who takes orders and brings food etc. at hotel or restaurant tables. —**waitress** *n. fem.*

waive *v.t.* to refrain from insisting on or using (a right or claim etc.). [from Old French *gaiver* = allow to become a waif, abandon]

waiver *n.* the waiving of a legal right; a document recording this.

Wajda /'vaɪdə/ Andrzej 1926– . Polish film director, one of the major figures in postwar European cinema. His films are concerned with the predicament and disillusion of individuals caught up in political events. His works include *Ashes and Diamonds* 1958, *Man of Marble* 1977, *Man of Iron* 1981, *Danton* 1982, and *Korczak* 1990.

wake[1] *v.t./i.* (*past* **woke** or **waked**; *past participle* **waked** or **woken**) **1.** (often with *up*) to cease or cause to cease to sleep; to make or become alert or attentive. **2.** (archaic except in **waking**) to be awake. **3.** to disturb with noise. **4.** to evoke (an echo). —*n.* **1.** (in Ireland) a watch by a corpse before burial; the attendant lamentations and merrymaking. **2.** (usually in *plural*) an annual holiday in (industrial) northern England. [Old English]

wake[2] *n.* **1.** the track left on the water's surface by a moving ship etc. **2.** turbulent air left by a moving aircraft. —**in the wake of,** following; as a result of; in imitation of. [probably from Middle Low German from Old Norse = hole or opening in ice]

wakeful /'weɪkfʊl/ *adj.* **1.** unable to sleep; (of a night etc.) with little sleep. **2.** vigilant. —**wakefully** *adv.*

waken /'weɪkən/ *v.t./i.* to wake (*literally* or *figuratively*). [from Old Norse]

Wakhan Salient /wə'kɑːn/ narrow strip of territory in Afghanistan bordered by the USSR, China, and Pakistan. It was effectively annexed by the USSR in 1980 to halt alleged arms supplies to Afghan guerrillas from China and Pakistan.

Waksman /'wæksmən/ Selman Abraham 1888–1973. US biochemist, born in Ukraine. He coined the word 'antibiotic' for bacteria-killing chemicals derived from microorganisms. Waksman won a Nobel prize in 1952 for the discovery of streptomycin, an antibiotic used against tuberculosis.

Walachia /wɒ'leɪkiə/ alternative spelling of ◊Wallachia, part of Romania.

Waldemar /'vældəmɑː/ or **Valdemar** four kings of Denmark, including:

Waldemar I the Great 1131–1182. King of Denmark from 1157, who defeated rival claimants to the throne and overcame the ◊Wends on the Baltic island of Rügen in 1169.

Waldemar II the Conqueror 1170–1241. King of Denmark from 1202. He was the second son of Waldemar I and succeeded his brother Canute VI. He gained control of land N of the river Elbe (which he later lost), as well as much of Estonia, and he completed the codification of Danish law.

Waldemar IV 1320–1375. King of Denmark from 1340, responsible for reuniting his country by capturing Skåne (S Sweden) and the island of Gotland in 1361. The resulting conflict with the ◊Hanseatic League led to defeat, and in 1370 he was forced to submit to the Peace of Stralsund.

Waldenses /wɒl'densiːz/ *n. pl.* also known as **Waldensians** or **Vaudois** Protestant religious sect, founded about 1170 by Peter Waldo, a merchant of Lyons. They were allied to the ◊Albigenses. They lived in voluntary poverty, refused to take oaths or take part in war, and later rejected the doctrines of transubstantiation, purgatory, and the invocation of saints. Although subjected to persecution until the 17th century, they spread in France, Germany, and Italy, and still survive in Piedmont.

Waldheim /'vældhaɪm/ Kurt 1918– . Austrian politician and diplomat, president from 1986. He was secretary general of the United Nations 1972–81, having been Austria's representative there 1964–68 and 1970–71. He was elected president of Austria despite revelations that during World War II he had been an intelligence officer in an army unit responsible for transporting Jews to death camps.

wale *n.* **1.** a weal (◊weal[1]). **2.** a ridge on corduroy etc. **3.** (*nautical*) a broad, thick timber along a ship's side. [Old English = stripe, ridge]

Wales /weɪlz/ (Welsh *Cymru*) Principality of; constituent part of the United Kingdom, in the west between the Bristol Channel and the Irish Sea; **area** 20,780 sq km/8,021 sq mi; **capital** Cardiff; **population** (1987) 2,836,000; **language** Welsh 19% (1981), English; **government** returns 38 members to the UK Parliament.

Walesa /væ'wensə/ Lech 1947– . Polish trade union leader and president of Poland from 1990, founder of ◊Solidarity (Solidarność) in 1980, an organization, independent of the Communist Party, which forced substantial political and economic concessions from the Polish government 1980–81 until being outlawed. He was awarded the Nobel Peace Prize in 1983.

Wales, Prince of title conferred on the eldest son of the United Kingdom's sovereign. Prince ◊Charles was invested as 21st prince of Wales at Caernarvon in 1969 by his mother, Elizabeth II.

walk /wɔːk/ *v.t./i.* **1.** to move by lifting and setting down each foot in turn so that one foot is always on the ground at any time. **2.** to travel or go on foot; to take exercise thus. **3.** to traverse (a distance) in walking. **4.** to tread the floor or surface of. **5.** to cause to walk with one, to accompany in walking; to ride or lead (a horse) or lead (a dog) at a walking pace. —*n.* **1.** the act or style of walking; a walking pace. **2.** a journey on foot, especially for pleasure or exercise. **3.** a route or track for walking. —**walk (all) over,** (*colloquial*) to defeat easily; to take advantage of. **walk away from,** to outdistance easily. **walk away** or **off with,** (*colloquial*) to steal; to win easily. **walk into,** (*colloquial*) to encounter through

Wales: history

c. 400 BC	Wales occupied by Celts from central Europe.
AD 50–60	Wales became part of the Roman Empire.
c. 200	Christianity adopted.
c. 450–600	Wales became the chief Celtic stronghold in the west since the Saxons invaded and settled in S Britain. The Celtic tribes united against England.
8th century	Frontier pushed back to ◊Offa's Dyke.
9th–11th centuries	Vikings raided the coasts. At this time Wales was divided into small states organized on a clan basis, although princes such as Rhodri (844–878), Howel the Good (*c.* 904–949), and Griffith ap Llewelyn (1039–1063) temporarily united the country.
11th–12th centuries	Continual pressure on Wales from the Normans across the English border was resisted, notably by ◊Llewelyn I and II.
1277	Edward I of England accepted as overlord by the Welsh.
1284	Edward I completed the conquest of Wales that had been begun by the Normans.
1294	Revolt against English rule put down by Edward I.
1350–1500	Welsh nationalist uprisings against the English; the most notable was that led by Owen Glendower.
1485	Henry Tudor, a Welshman, became Henry VII of England.
1536–43	Acts of Union united England and Wales after conquest under Henry VIII. Wales sent representatives to the English Parliament; English law was established in Wales; English became the official language.
18th century	Evangelical revival made Nonconformism a powerful factor in Welsh life. A strong coal and iron industry developed in the south.
19th century	The miners and ironworkers were militant supporters of Chartism, and Wales became a stronghold of trade unionism and socialism.
1893	University of Wales founded.
1920s–30s	Wales suffered from industrial depression; unemployment reached 21% 1937, and a considerable exodus of population took place.
post-1945	Growing nationalist movement and a revival of the language, earlier suppressed or discouraged (there is a Welsh television channel).
1966	◊Plaid Cymru, the Welsh National Party, returned its first member to Westminster.
1979	Referendum rejected a proposal for limited home rule.
1988	Bombing campaign against estate agents selling Welsh properties to English buyers. See also ◊Britain, ancient, ◊England, history; ◊United Kingdom.

unwariness. **walk of life**, one's occupation. **walk on air**, to feel elated. **walk-on part**, a part involving an appearance on stage but no speaking. **walk out**, to depart suddenly or angrily. **walkout** a sudden angry departure, especially as a protest or strike. **walk out on**, to desert, to leave in the lurch. **walkover** *n.* an easy victory. **walk the streets**, to be a prostitute. [Old English = roll, toss]

walkabout *n.* 1. an informal stroll among a crowd by a visiting royal person etc. 2. a period of wandering by an Australian Aboriginal.

walker /'wɔːkə/ *n.* 1. one who walks. 2. a framework for a person unable to walk without support.

Walker Alice 1944– . US poet, novelist, critic, and essay writer. She was active in the US civil rights movement in the 1960s and, as a black woman, wrote about the double burden of racist and sexist oppression that such women bear. Her novel *The Color Purple* 1983 (film, 1985) won the Pulitzer Prize.

Walker Peter (Edward) 1932– . British Conservative politician, energy secretary 1983–87, secretary of state for Wales 1987–90.

Walker William 1824–1860. US adventurer who for a short time established himself as president of a republic in NW Mexico, and was briefly president of Nicaragua 1856–57. He was eventually executed and is now regarded as a symbol of US imperialism in Central America.

walkie-talkie /'wɔːkiˈtɔːkɪ/ *n.* a small portable radio transmitting and receiving set.

walking stick a stick held or used as a support when walking.

walkway *n.* a passage for walking along, especially one connecting sections of a building; a wide path in a garden etc.

wall /wɔːl/ *n.* 1. a continuous, upright structure of stone or brick etc. enclosing, protecting, or separating a building, room, field, or town etc. 2. a thing like a wall in appearance or effect; the steep side of a mountain; the outermost part of a hollow structure; the outermost layer of an animal or plant organ or cell. —*v.t.* to surround, enclose, or block with a wall. —**go to the wall**, to suffer defeat, failure, or ruin. **up the wall**, (*colloquial*) crazy, furious. **wallboard** *n.* board made from wood pulp etc. and used to cover walls. **wall game**, a ball game played at Eton beside a wall. **walls have ears**, beware of eavesdroppers. **wall-to-wall** *adj.* covering the whole floor of a room. **with one's back to the wall**, at bay. —**wall-less** *adj.* [Old English]

Wall Max. Stage name of Maxwell George Lister. 1908–1990. English music hall comedian and actor. Born in London, the son of a Scots comedian, he became a well-known dancer before radio enabled his verbal comedy to reach a wider audience. In the 1950s his career declined dramatically after he left his wife and children, and it was only in the 1970s that he appeared again in starring roles, now as a serious actor, in John Osborne's *The Entertainer* 1974 and in Samuel Beckett's *Waiting for Godot* 1980. He was noted

Walesa *Polish president and trade unionist, Lech Walesa.*

walnut

for his solo comedy performances during which he displayed his remarkable 'funny walk' routine.

wallaby /'wɒləbɪ/ *n.* **1.** a kind of small kangaroo. **2. Wallabies,** an Australian international Rugby Union team, so called from the animal found extensively in Australia. [from Aboriginal *wolabā*]

Wallace /'wɒlɪs/ Alfred Russel 1823–1913. British naturalist who collected animal and plant specimens in South America and SE Asia, and independently arrived at a theory of evolution by natural selection similar to that proposed by Charles ◊Darwin.

Wallace George 1919– . US right-wing politician, governor of Alabama 1962–66. He contested the presidency in 1968 as an independent, and in 1972 campaigned for the Democratic nomination, but was shot at a rally and became partly paralysed.

Wallace Irving 1916–1990. US novelist, one of the most popular writers of the century. He wrote 17 works of non-fiction and 16 novels; they include *The Chapman Report* 1960, a novel inspired by the ◊Kinsey Report, and *The Prize* 1962.

Wallace William 1272–1305. Scottish nationalist who led a revolt against English rule in 1297, won a victory at Stirling, and assumed the title 'governor of Scotland'. Edward I defeated him at Falkirk in 1298, and Wallace was captured and executed.

Wallace line an imaginary line running down the Lombok Strait in SE Asia, between the island of Bali and the islands of Lombok and Sulawesi. It was identified by the naturalist A R Wallace as separating the S Asian (Oriental) and Australian biogeographical regions, each of which has its own distinctive animals.

Wallachia /wɒ'leɪkɪə/ independent medieval principality, founded 1290, with allegiance to Hungary until 1330 and under Turkish rule 1387–1861, when it was united with Moldavia to form Romania.

wallah /'wɒlə/ *n.* (*slang*) a person employed or concerned in a specific occupation or task. [from Hindi]

Wallenberg /'wɒlənbɜːg/ Raoul 1912–1947. Swedish businessman who attempted to rescue several thousand Jews from German-occupied Budapest in 1944, during World War II.

Wallenstein /'vælənʃtaɪn/ Albrecht Eusebius Wenzel von 1583–1634. German general who, until his defeat at Lützen in 1632, led the Habsburg armies in the Thirty Years' War. He was assassinated.

wallet /'wɒlɪt/ *n.* a small, flat, folding case for holding banknotes or small documents etc.

walleye /'wɔːlaɪ/ *n.* an eye with the iris whitish or streaked, or with an outward squint. —**walleyed** *adj.* [from Old Norse]

wallflower *n.* **1.** a plant of the genus *Cheiranthus*, especially *C. cheiri*, with fragrant flowers. **2.** (*colloquial*) a person sitting out dances for lack of partners.

Wallis /'wɒlɪs/ Barnes (Neville) 1887–1979. British aeronautical engineer who designed the airship R-100, and during World War II perfected the 'bouncing bombs' used by the Royal Air Force Dambusters Squadron to destroy the

German Möhne and Eder dams in 1943. He also assisted in the development of the Concorde supersonic airliner and developed the ◊swing-wing aircraft.

Walloon /wɒ'luːn/ *n.* **1.** a member of a people living in southern Belgium and neighbouring parts of France. **2.** their language. —*adj.* of the Walloons or their language. [from French from Latin]

wallop /'wɒləp/ *v.t.* (*slang*) **1.** to thrash, to beat. **2.** (in *participle*) big. —*n.* (*slang*) **1.** a heavy, resounding blow **2.** beer or other drink.

wallow /'wɒləʊ/ *v.i.* **1.** to roll about in mud, sand, water etc. **2.** to take unrestrained pleasure in a specified thing. —*n.* **1.** the act of wallowing. **2.** a place where animals go to wallow. [Old English]

wallpaper *n.* paper for pasting on the interior walls of rooms, often decoratively printed.

Wall Street street in Manhattan, New York, on which the stock exchange is situated, and a synonym for stock dealing in the USA. It is so called from a stockade erected in 1653.

Wall Street crash, 1929 a period of postwar economic depression in the USA following an artificial boom 1927–29 fed by speculation, led to panic selling on the New York Stock Exchange. On 24 Oct 1929 13 million shares changed hands, with further heavy selling on 28 Oct and the disposal of 16 million shares on 29 Oct. Many shareholders were ruined, banks and businesses failed, and unemployment rose to approximately 17 million.

walnut /'wɔːlnʌt/ *n.* **1.** a nut containing an edible kernel with a wrinkled surface. **2.** the tree *Juglans regia*, probably originating in SE Europe, bearing this. It can reach 30 m/ 100 ft, and produces a full crop of nuts about a dozen years from planting; the timber is used in furniture and the oil is used in cooking. [Old English = foreign nut]

Walpole /'wɔːlpəʊl/ Horace, 4th Earl of Orford 1717–1797. English novelist and politician, the son of Robert Walpole. He was a Whig member of Parliament 1741–67. He converted his house at Strawberry Hill, Twickenham (then a separate town SW of London), into a Gothic castle; his *The Castle of Otranto* 1764 established the genre of the Gothic novel, or 'romance of terror'.

Walpole Robert, 1st Earl of Orford 1676–1745. British Whig politician, the first 'prime minister' as First Lord of the Treasury and chancellor of the Exchequer 1715–17 and 1721–42. He encouraged trade and tried to avoid foreign disputes (until forced into the War of Jenkins's Ear with Spain in 1739).

When people will not weed their own minds, they are apt to be overrun with nettles.

Sir Robert Walpole
letter to Lady Ailesbury 1779

Walpurga, St /væl'puəgə/ English abbess who preached Christianity in Germany. **Walpurgis Night,** the night of 1 May (one of her feast days), became associated with witches' sabbaths and other superstitions. Her feast day is 25 Feb.

walrus /'wɔːlrəs/ *n.* a seal-like marine mammal *Odobenus rosmarus* found in the far N Atlantic and the Arctic. It can reach 4 m/13 ft in length, and weigh up to 1,400 kg/ 3,000 lb. It has webbed flippers, a bristly moustache, and large tusks. It is gregarious except at breeding time, and feeds mainly on shellfish. The walrus has been hunted close to extinction for its ivory tusks, hide, and blubber. —**walrus moustache,** a long, thick, drooping moustache.

Walsh /wɔːlʃ/ Raoul 1887–1981. US film director who was originally an actor. He made a number of outstanding films, including *The Thief of Baghdad* 1924, *The Roaring Twenties* 1939, and *White Heat* 1949. He retired in 1964.

Walsingham /'wɔːlsɪŋəm/ Francis *c.*1530–1590. English politician who, as secretary of state from 1573, both advocated a strong anti-Spanish policy and ran the efficient government spy system that made it work.

Walter /'wɔːltə/ Lucy *c.*1630–1658. Mistress of ◊ Charles II, whom she met while a Royalist refugee in The Hague, Netherlands, in 1648; the Duke of ◊Monmouth was their son.

Walters /'wɔːltəz/ Alan (Arthur) 1927– . British economist and government adviser 1981–89. He became economics adviser to Prime Minister Margaret Thatcher, but his publicly stated differences with the policies of her chancellor Nigel ◊Lawson precipitated, in 1989, Lawson's resignation from the government as well as Walters's own departure.

Walther von der Vogelweide /'vælta fɒn deə 'fəʊgəlvaɪdə/ c.1170–c.1230. German poet, greatest of the ◊Minnesinger, whose songs dealt mainly with courtly love. Of noble birth, he lived in his youth at the Austrian ducal court in Vienna, adopting a wandering life after the death of his patron in 1198. His lyrics deal mostly with love, but also with religion and politics.

Walton /'wɔːltən/ Ernest 1903– . Irish physicist who, as a young doctoral student at the Cavendish laboratory in Cambridge, England, collaborated with John ◊Cockcroft on investigating the structure of the atom. In 1932 they succeeded in splitting the atom; for this experiment they shared the 1951 Nobel Prize for Physics.

Walton Izaak 1593–1683. English author of the classic fishing text *The Compleat Angler* 1653. He was born in Stafford, and settled in London as an ironmonger. He also wrote short biographies of the poets George Herbert and John Donne and the theologian Richard Hooker.

Walton William (Turner) 1902–1983. English composer. Among his works are *Façade* 1923, a series of instrumental pieces designed to be played in conjunction with the recitation of poems by Edith Sitwell; the oratorio *Belshazzar's Feast* 1931; and *Variations on a Theme by Hindemith* 1963.

waltz /wɔːls, wɒls/ n. a ballroom dance for couples, with a graceful, flowing melody in triple time; the music for this. —v.t./i. **1.** to dance a waltz. **2.** to move (a person) in or as in a waltz. **3.** to dance round in joy etc.; to move easily or casually. [from German *walzen* = revolve]

wampum /'wɒmpəm/ n. strings of shell beads formerly used by North American Indians for money or ornament. [from Algonquin]

wan /wɒn/ adj. pallid, especially from illness or exhaustion. —**wanly** adv., **wanness** n. [Old English = dark]

wand /wɒnd/ n. a slender rod for carrying in the hand, especially one associated with the working of magic; a music conductor's baton; a slender rod or staff carried as a sign of office etc. [from Old Norse]

wander /'wɒndə/ v.i. **1.** to go from place to place without a settled route or aim; to go aimlessly *in, off* etc. **2.** to diverge from the right way (*literally* or *figuratively*). **3.** to digress from a subject; to be inattentive or incoherent through illness or weakness. —**wanderer** n. [Old English]

Wandering Jew in medieval legend, a Jew named Ahasuerus, said to have insulted Jesus on his way to Calvary and been condemned to wander the world until the Second Coming.

wanderlust n. an eager desire or fondness for travelling or wandering. [German]

wane /weɪn/ v.i. **1.** (of the Moon) to show a gradually decreasing area of brightness after being full. **2.** to decrease in vigour, strength, or importance. —n. **1.** the process of waning. **2.** a defect in a plank etc. when the corners are not square. —**on the wane**, declining. [Old English *wanian* = lessen]

Wang An 1920–1990. Chinese-born engineer, who emigrated to the USA in 1945 and in 1951 founded Wang Laboratories which subsequently became one of the world's largest suppliers of word-processing equipment. In 1948 he invented core memory, the world's most common computer memory in the 1950s.

wangle v.t. (slang) to obtain or arrange by using trickery, improper influence, or persuasion etc. —n. (slang) an act of wangling. [19th-century printers' slang]

wank v.i. (vulgar) to masturbate. —n. (vulgar) an act of masturbation. —**wanker** n.

Wankel engine /'wæŋkəl/ a rotary petrol engine developed by the German engineer Felix Wankel (1902–) in the 1950s. It operates according to the same stages as the four-stroke petrol engine cycle (see ◊four-stroke cycle), but these stages take place in different sectors of a figure-eight chamber in the space between the chamber walls and a triangular rotor. Power is produced once on every turn on the rotor. The Wankel engine is simpler in construction than the four-stroke piston petrol engine, and produces rotary

power directly (instead of via a crankshaft). Problems with rotor seals have prevented its widespread use.

want /wɒnt/ v.t./i. **1.** to desire, to wish for. **2.** to require or need; should, ought. **3.** to lack, to be insufficiently supplied with; to fall short of. **4.** to be without the necessaries of life. —n. **1.** a desire for something, a requirement. **2.** lack or need of something, deficiency. **3.** lack of the necessaries of life. —**in want of**, needing. **wanted (by the police)**, sought by the police as a suspected criminal. [from Old Norse *vanr* = lacking, Old English *wana*]

wanting adj. lacking; deficient; not equal to requirements.

wanton /'wɒntən/ adj. **1.** licentious, unchaste. **2.** (of cruelty, damage etc.) purposeless, unprovoked. **3.** capricious, playful; unrestrained, luxuriant. —n. a licentious person. —v.i. to behave capriciously or playfully. —**wantonly** adv., **wantonness** n. [originally *wantowen* = undisciplined]

wapiti /'wɒpɪtɪ/ n. or **American elk** a species of deer *Cervus canadensis* native to North America. It is reddish-brown in colour, about 1.5 m/5 ft at the shoulder, weighs up to 450 kg/1,000 lb, and has antlers up to 1.2 m/4 ft long. It is becoming increasingly rare. [from Cree = white deer]

Wapping /'wɒpɪŋ/ a district of the Greater London borough of Tower Hamlets; situated between the Thames and the former London Docks. Since the 1980s it has become a centre of the UK newspaper industry.

war /wɔː/ n. **1.** strife (especially between countries) involving military, naval, or air attacks; the period of this. **2.** open hostility between persons. **3.** strong efforts to combat crime, disease, poverty etc. —v.i. (-rr-) (*archaic*) to make war. —**at war**, engaged in a war. **go to war**, to begin hostile operations. **have been in the wars**, (*colloquial*) to show signs of injury. **war cry**, a phrase or name shouted in battle; the slogan of a political or other party. **war dance**, a dance performed by certain primitive peoples before war or after victory. **war game**, a game simulating warfare, using models or blocks moved about on a map etc.; a set of military exercises designed to examine or test a military strategy. **warhorse** n. a trooper's horse; a veteran soldier. **warlord** n. (in China, especially in 1916–28) a military commander with a regional power base, acting independently of the central government. **war memorial**, a monument to those killed in a war. **war of nerves**, an attempt to wear down an opponent by gradual destruction of his morale. **war paint**, paint put on the body (especially by North American Indians) before battle. **warpath** n. a march of North American Indians to make war; *on the warpath*, engaged in conflict, taking a hostile attitude. [from Anglo-French, Old French *guerre*]

War. abbreviation of Warwickshire.

War and Peace a novel by Leo Tolstoy, published 1863–69. It chronicles the lives of three noble families in Russia during the Napoleonic Wars and is notable for its complex characters and optimistic tone.

waratah n. an Australian shrub or tree of the family Proteaceae, including the crimson-flowered *Telopea speciosissima*, emblem of New South Wales.

Warbeck /'wɔːbek/ Perkin c.1474–1499. Flemish pretender to the English throne. Claiming to be Richard, brother of Edward V, he led a rising against Henry VII in 1497, and was hanged after attempting to escape from the Tower of London.

War between the States another (usually Southern) name for the American Civil War.

warble /'wɔːb(ə)l/ v.t./i. to sing, especially with a gentle, trilling note as certain birds do. —n. a warbling sound. [from Old French *werbler* from Frankish = whirl, trill]

warble fly a kind of fly whose larvae burrow under the skin of cattle etc. and produce tumours.

warbler n. a family of songbirds, order Passeriformes. The Old World birds are drab-coloured, and the New World birds are brightly plumed in the spring. They grow up to 25 cm/10 in long, and feed on berries and insects. The Dartford warbler *Sylvia undata* is one of Britain's rarest birds.

Warburg /'vaːbuək/ Otto 1878–1976. German biochemist who in 1923 devised a manometer (pressure gauge) sensitive enough to measure oxygen uptake of respiring tissue. By measuring the rate at which cells absorb oxygen under differing conditions, he was able to show that enzymes called cytochromes enable cells to process oxygen. He was awarded the Nobel Prize for Medicine in 1931. Warburg also demonstrated that cancerous cells absorb less oxygen than normal cells.

war crime an offence (such as murder of a civilian or a prisoner of war) that contravenes the internationally accepted laws governing the conduct of wars, particularly The Hague Convention 1907 and the Geneva Convention 1949. A key principle of the law relating to such crimes is that obedience to the orders of a superior is no defence.

ward /wɔːd/ *n.* **1.** a separate room or division in a hospital or (*historical*) workhouse. **2.** an administrative division, especially for elections. **3.** a minor etc. under the care of a guardian or court. **4.** (in *plural*) the notches and projections in a key and lock designed to prevent opening by a key other than the right one. **5.** (*archaic*) guarding, defending, guardianship; the bailey of a castle. —*v.t.* **1.** (usually with *off*) to parry (a blow), to avert (a danger etc.). **2.** (*archaic*) to guard, to defend. [Old English = guard]

-ward (or **-wards**) suffix added to nouns of place or destination and to adverbs of direction and forming adverbs (usually in *-wards*) meaning 'towards the place etc.' (*backwards, homewards*), adjectives (usually in *-ward*) meaning 'turned or tending towards' (*downward, onward*), and less commonly nouns meaning 'the region towards or about' (*look to the eastward*). [Old English]

warden /'wɔːdən/ *n.* **1.** the president or governor of an institution (e.g. a hospital or college). **2.** an official with supervisory duties. **3.** a churchwarden. [from Anglo-French and Old French = guardian]

warder /'wɔːdə/ *n.* an official in charge of prisoners in a prison. —**wardress** *n. fem.* [from Anglo-French]

wardrobe /'wɔːdrəub/ *n.* **1.** a place where clothes are kept, especially a large cupboard usually with pegs or rails etc. from which they hang. **2.** a person's or persons' stock of clothes. —**wardrobe master** or **mistress**, one who has charge of an actor's or a company's costumes. [from Old French]

wardroom /'wɔːdruːm/ *n.* a room for commissioned officers in a warship.

wardship *n.* tutelage, a guardian's care.

ware *n.* **1.** manufactured articles (especially pottery) of the kind specified. **2.** (in *plural*) what one has for sale. [Old English]

warehouse /'weəhaus/ *n.* a building in which goods are stored or shown for sale. —/also -hauz/ *v.t.* to place or keep in warehouses.

warfare *n.* making war, fighting; a particular form of this.

warfarin *n.* a poison that induces fatal internal bleeding in rats; neutralized with sodium hydroxide, it is used in medicine as an anticoagulant: it prevents blood clotting by inhibiting the action of vitamin K. It can be taken orally and begins to act several days after the initial dose.

warhead *n.* the explosive head of a missile, torpedo, or similar weapon.

Warhol /'wɔːhɔul/ Andy 1928–1987. US Pop artist and filmmaker. He made his name in 1962 with paintings of Campbell's soup cans, Coca-Cola bottles, and film stars. In his New York studio, the Factory, he produced series of garish silk-screen prints. His films include the semi-documentary *Chelsea Girls* 1966 and *Trash* 1970.

warlike *adj.* **1.** fond of or skilful in war, aggressive. **2.** of or for war.

warlock /'wɔːlɒk/ *n.* (*archaic*) a sorcerer. [Old English = traitor]

warm /wɔːm/ *adj.* **1.** moderately hot, not cold or cool. **2.** (of clothes etc.) keeping the body warm; (of exertion) making one warm. **3.** enthusiastic, hearty; (of a reception) vigorous by being either heartily friendly or strongly hostile. **4.** kindly and affectionate. **5.** (of colours) suggesting warmth, especially by containing reddish shades. **6.** (of the scent in hunting) still fairly fresh and strong; (of the seeker in a children's game etc.) close to the object sought or guessed at. —*v.t./i.* to make or become warm or warmer. —*n.* **1.** the act of warming. **2.** warmth of atmosphere. —**keep a position warm,** to occupy it temporarily so that it can be available (for a specified person) at a later date. **warm-blooded** *adj.* having blood that remains warm (36–42°C) permanently; passionate. **warm-hearted** *adj.* having a kindly and affectionate disposition. **warming pan** a covered metal pan with a long handle, formerly filled with live coals and used for warming beds. **warm to,** to become cordial or well-disposed to (a person) or more animated

about (a task). **warm up,** to make or become warm; to reach or cause to reach the temperature of efficient working; to prepare for a performance by exercise or practice; to reheat (food). **warm-up** *n.* the process of warming up. —**warmly** *adv.*, **warmness** *n.* [Old English]

warmonger /'wɔːmʌŋgə/ *n.* one who seeks to cause war.

warmth /wɔːmθ/ *n.* warmness, being warm.

warn /wɔːn/ *v.t.* to inform (a person) about a present or future danger or about something to be reckoned with; to advise about action in such circumstances. —**warn off,** to tell (a person) to keep away (from); to prohibit from taking part in race-meetings (at). [Old English]

Warner /'wɔːnə/ Deborah 1959– . British theatre director. Discarding period costume and furnished sets, she adopted an uncluttered approach to the classics, including productions of many Shakespeare plays and Sophocles' *Electra.*

Warner Brothers a US film production company, founded in 1923 by Harry, Albert, Sam, and Jack Warner. It became one of the major Hollywood studios after releasing the first talking film, *The Jazz Singer* in 1927. During the 1930s and 1950s, the company's stars included Humphrey Bogart, Errol Flynn, and Bette Davis. It suffered in the 1960s through competition with television and was taken over by Seven Art Productions. In 1969 there was another takeover by Kinney National Service, and the whole company became known as **Warner Communications**.

warning /'wɔːnɪŋ/ *n.* what is said or done or occurs to warn a person.

warning coloration in biology, an alternative term for ◊aposematic coloration.

War of 1812 a war between the USA and Britain caused by British interference with US trade as part of the economic warfare against Napoleonic France. Tensions with the British in Canada led to plans for a US invasion but these were never realized and success was limited to the capture of Detroit and a few notable naval victories. In 1814, British forces occupied Washington DC and burned many public buildings. A treaty signed in Ghent, Belgium, in Dec 1814 ended the conflict.

War Office the former British government department controlling military affairs. The Board of Ordnance, which existed in the 14th century, was absorbed into the War Department after the Crimean War and the whole named the War Office. In 1964 its core became a subordinate branch of the newly established **Ministry of ◊Defence.**

warp /wɔːp/ *v.t./i.* **1.** to make or become crooked or twisted especially by uneven shrinkage or expansion. **2.** to distort or pervert (a person's judgement or principles); to suffer such distortion. **3.** to haul (a ship) along by means of a rope fixed to an external point; to progress thus. —*n.* **1.** a warped condition. **2.** threads stretched lengthwise in a loom, to be crossed by the weft. **3.** a mental perversion or bias. **4.** a rope used in warping a ship. [Old English = throw]

War Powers Act legislation passed in 1973 enabling the US president to deploy US forces abroad for combat without prior Congressional approval. The president is nevertheless required to report to both Houses of Congress within 48 hours of having taken such action. Congress may restrict the continuation of troop deployment despite any presidential veto.

warrant /'wɒrənt/ *n.* **1.** a thing that authorizes an action; a written authorization to receive or supply money, goods, or services, or to carry out an arrest or search. **2.** a certificate of the service rank held by a warrant officer. —*v.t.* **1.** to serve as a warrant for, to justify. **2.** to guarantee, to answer for the genuineness etc. of. —**I('ll) warrant (you),** I am certain, I assure you. **warrant officer,** an officer ranking between commissioned officers and NCOs. [from Old French *warant* from Frankish (*giwerēn* = be surety for)]

warranty *n.* **1.** authority or justification for doing something. **2.** a seller's undertaking that a thing sold is his or hers and fit for use etc., often accepting responsibility for repairs needed over a specified period. [from Anglo-French *warantie*]

warren /'wɒrən/ *n.* **1.** a piece of ground abounding in rabbit burrows. **2.** a densely populated or labyrinthine building or district. [from Anglo-French *warenne*, Old French *garenne* = game-park]

wart hog

Warren Earl 1891–1974. US jurist and chief justice of the US Supreme Court 1953–69. He served as governor of California 1943–53. As chief justice, he presided over a moderately liberal court, taking a stand against racial discrimination and ruling that segregation in schools was unconstitutional. He headed the commission that investigated President Kennedy's assassination in 1963–64.

Warren Robert Penn 1905–1989. US poet and novelist, the only author to receive a Pulitzer prize for both prose and poetry. In 1986 he became the USA's first poet laureate.

warring /ˈwɔːrɪŋ/ *adj.* engaged in a war; rival, antagonistic.

warrior /ˈwɒrɪə/ *n.* a person who fights in battle; a distinguished or veteran soldier; a member of any of the armed services. [from Old French *guerreier* = make war]

Warsaw /ˈwɔːsɔː/ (Polish *Warszawa*) capital of Poland, on the river Vistula; population (1985) 1,649,000. Industries include engineering, food processing, printing, clothing, and pharmaceuticals.

Warsaw Pact the military alliance established in 1955 between the USSR and E European communist states as a response to the admission of West Germany into NATO.

warship *n.* a fighting ship armed and crewed for war. The supremacy of the battleship at the beginning of the 20th century was superseded during World War I by the development of submarine attack, and it was rendered obsolete in World War II with the growth of long-range air attack. Today the largest and most important surface warships are the ◊aircraft carriers.

wart /wɔːt/ *n.* **1.** a small, hard, roundish growth on the skin. The common wart *verruca vulgaris* is due to a virus infection. It usually disappears spontaneously within two years, but can be treated with peeling applications, burning away (cautery), or freezing (cryosurgery). **2.** a protuberance on the skin of an animal or on the surface of a plant. **3.** (*colloquial*) an objectionable person. **warts and all,** (*colloquial*) with no attempt to conceal blemishes or inadequacies. —**warty** *adj.* [Old English]

wart hog an African wild pig *Phacochoerus aethiopicus* which has a large head with a bristly mane, fleshy pads beneath the eyes, and four large tusks. It has short legs and can grow to 80 cm/2.5 ft at the shoulder.

wartime *n.* a period when war is being waged.

Warwick /ˈwɒrɪk/ Richard Neville, Earl of Warwick 1428–1471. English politician, called **the Kingmaker**. During the Wars of the ◊Roses he fought at first on the Yorkist side against the Lancastrians, and was largely responsible for placing Edward IV on the throne. Having quarrelled with him, he restored Henry VI in 1470, but was defeated and killed by Edward at Barnet, Hertfordshire.

Warwickshire /ˈwɒrɪkʃə/ county in central England; **area** 1,980 sq km/764 sq mi; **administrative headquarters** Warwick; **population** (1987) 484,000.

wary /ˈweərɪ/ *adj.* cautious, in the habit of looking out for possible danger or difficulty. —**warily** *adv.*, **wariness** *n.* [from *ware* = cognizant]

was *v.i.* see ◊be.

wash /wɒʃ/ *v.t./i.* **1.** to cleanse with water or other liquid. **2.** to remove (a stain) by washing; (of a stain) to be removed thus. **3.** to wash oneself; to wash clothes etc. **4.** to be washable; (of reasoning) to be valid. **5.** to moisten; (of a river etc.) to flow past or against. **6.** (of a moving liquid) to carry in a specified direction; to go splashing or flowing. **7.** to sift (ore) by the action of water. **8.** to coat with a wash of paint or wall colouring etc. —*n.* **1.** washing, being washed; the process of laundering; clothes etc. that are being washed or to be washed or have just been washed. **2.** the motion of disturbed water or air behind a moving ship or aircraft etc. **3.** liquid food or swill for pigs etc. **4.** a thin coating of colour painted over a surface; a cleansing or healing liquid for external use. —**come out in the wash,** (of mistakes etc.) to be eliminated during the process of work etc. **washbasin** *n.* a basin (usually fixed to a wall) for washing one's hands etc. in. **wash dirty linen in public,** to discuss private quarrels or difficulties publicly. **wash down,** to clean by washing; to accompany or follow (food) with a drink. **washed out,** faded by washing; faded-looking; pallid; enfeebled. **washed up,** (*slang*) defeated, having failed. **wash one's hands (of),** to renounce responsibility (for). **washleather** *n.* chamois or similar leather for washing windows etc.; a piece of this. **wash out,** to clean the inside of by washing; (*colloquial*) to cancel. **washout** *n.* a breach in a railway or road caused by a flood; (*slang*) a complete failure. **wash up,** to wash (dishes etc., or *absolute*) after use; (of the sea) to cast up on the shore. [Old English]

washable *adj.* that may be washed without being damaged.

washer /ˈwɒʃə/ *n.* **1.** a flat ring of leather, rubber, or metal etc. to tighten a joint and prevent leakage. **2.** a washing machine.

washerwoman *n.* (*plural* **washerwomen**) a woman whose occupation is washing clothes etc.

washing /ˈwɒʃɪŋ/ *n.* clothes etc. that are being washed or to be washed or have just been washed. —**washing machine,** a machine for washing clothes. **washing powder,** a powder of soap or detergent for washing clothes etc. **washing-up** *n.* the process of washing dishes etc. after use; the dishes etc. for washing.

washing soda $Na_2CO_3.10H_2O$ (technical name **sodium carbonate decahydrate**) substance added to washing water to 'soften' it.

Washington /ˈwɒʃɪŋtən/ state of the NW USA; nickname Evergreen State; **area** 176,700 sq km/68,206 sq mi; **capital** Olympia; **towns** Seattle, Spokane, Tacoma; **population** (1987) 4,481,000, including 61,000 Indians, mainly of the Yakima people; **history** became a state in 1889. Labour disputes occurred here in the 1910s, and were brutally suppressed by the authorities.

Washington Booker T(aliaferro) 1856–1915. US educationist, pioneer in higher education for black people in the South. He was the founder and first principal of Tuskegee Institute, Alabama, in 1881, originally a training college for blacks, which has become a respected academic institution. He maintained that economic independence was the way to achieve social equality.

Washington George 1732–1799. first president of the USA 1789–97. As a strong opponent of the British government's policy, he sat in the ◊Continental Congresses of 1774 and 1775, and on the outbreak of the War of ◊American Independence was chosen commander in chief. After the war he retired to his Virginia estate, Mount Vernon, but in 1787 he re-entered politics as president of the Constitutional Convention. Although he attempted to draw his ministers from all factions, his aristocratic outlook alienated his secretary of state, Thomas Jefferson, who resigned in 1793, thus creating the two-party system.

Washington Convention an alternative name for ◊CITES, the international agreement that regulates trade in endangered species.

Washington DC (District of Columbia) national capital of the USA, on the Potomac River; **area** 180 sq km/69 sq mi; **capital** the District of Columbia covers only the area of the city of Washington; **population** (1983) 623,000 (metropolitan area, extending outside the District of Columbia, 3 million); **history** the District of Columbia, initially land ceded from Maryland and Virginia, was established by Act of Congress 1790–91, and was first used as the seat of Congress in 1800. The right to vote in national elections was not granted to residents until 1961.

Wash, the bay of the North Sea between Norfolk and Lincolnshire, England. King John lost his baggage and treasure in crossing it in 1216.

washy /ˈwɒʃɪ/ *adj.* **1.** (of liquids) thin, watery. **2.** (of colours) washed-out. **3.** lacking vigour. —**washily** *adv.*, **washiness** *n.*

wasn't /'wɒzənt/(*colloquial*) was not.

wasp /wɒsp/ *n.* a stinging insect of the order Hymenoptera, characterized by a thin join between the thorax and the abdomen. Wasps can be social or solitary. Among social wasps, the queens devote themselves to egg-laying, the fertilized eggs producing female workers; the males come from unfertilized eggs, and have no sting. The larvae are fed on insects, but the mature wasps feed mainly on fruit and sugar. In winter, the fertilized queens hibernate, but the other wasps die. —**wasp waist,** a very slender waist. [Old English]

WASP (*US*, usually *derogatory*) acronym from White Anglo-Saxon Protestant, a member of the American white Protestant middle or upper class descended from early European settlers in North America.

waspish /'wɒspɪʃ/ *adj.* snappish, making sharp comments. —**waspishly** *adv.,* **waspishness** *n.*

wassail /'wɒseɪl/, -s(ə)l/ *n.* (*archaic*) merrymaking, festive drinking. —*v.i.* (*archaic*) to make merry. [from Old Norse *ves heill* = be in good health, form of salutation]

wastage /'weɪstɪdʒ/ *n.* 1. loss by waste; the amount of this. 2. (in full **natural wastage**) loss of employees through retirement or resignation, not by redundancy.

waste /weɪst/ *v.t./i.* 1. to use to no purpose, for an inadequate result, or extravagantly; to fail to use (an opportunity). 2. to give (advice etc.) without effect on a person. 3. to run to waste. 4. to wear away gradually; to make or become gradually weaker. 5. to lay waste; to treat as waste. —*adj.* 1. superfluous, no longer serving a purpose; not wanted. 2. (of land) not used, not cultivated or built on. —*n.* 1. an act of wasting. 2. waste material. 3. a waste region. 4. diminution by use or wear. 5. a waste pipe. —**go** *or* **run to waste,** to be wasted. **wastepaper** *n.* spoiled or valueless paper. **wastepaper basket,** a receptacle for waste paper. **waste pipe,** a pipe to carry off waste liquid, especially from washing etc. **waste product,** a useless by-product of an organism or manufacture. [from Old French *waster* from Latin *vastare*]

waste disposal depositing waste. Methods of waste disposal vary according to the materials in the waste and include incineration, burial at designated sites, and dumping at sea. Organic waste can be treated and reused as fertilizer (see ◊sewage). Nuclear and toxic waste is usually buried or dumped at sea, although this does not negate the danger.

wasteful *adj.* using more than is needed, causing or showing waste. —**wastefully** *adv.,* **wastefulness** *n.*

wasteland *n.* an unproductive or useless area of land.

***Washington** US teacher and reformer Booker T Washington.*

Waste Land, The a poem by T S Eliot, first published in 1922. It expressed the prevalent mood of depression after World War I and is a key work of Modernism in literature.

waster *n.* 1. a wasteful person. 2. (*slang*) a wastrel.

wastrel /'weɪstrəl/ *n.* a good-for-nothing person.

watch /wɒtʃ/ *n.* 1. a small portable device indicating the time, usually worn on the wrist or carried in the pocket. 2. the act of watching, especially to see that all is well; constant observation or attention. 3. (*nautical*) a spell of duty (usually four hours) on board ship; the part of a crew taking this. 4. (*historical*) a watchman or watchmen. —*v.t./i.* 1. to look at, to keep one's eyes fixed on; to keep under observation. 2. to be on the alert; to take heed. 3. to be careful about; to safeguard, to exercise protective care. 4. to look out for (an opportunity). 5. (*archaic*) to remain awake for devotions etc. —**on the watch,** alert for an occurrence. **watchdog** *n.* a dog kept to guard property, etc.; a person etc. acting as guardian of others' rights, etc. **watches of the night,** a time when one lies awake. **watching brief,** the brief of a barrister who follows a case for a client not directly concerned. **watch it,** (*colloquial*) be careful. **watchnight service,** a religious service on the last day of the year. **watch out,** to be on one's guard. **watch over,** to look after, to protect. **watchtower** *n.* a tower from which observation can be kept. —**watcher** *n.* [Old English]

watchful *adj.* watching or observing closely; on the watch. —**watchfully** *adv.,* **watchfulness** *n.*

watchmaker *n.* a person who makes and repairs watches and clocks.

watchman *n.* (*plural* **watchmen**) a person employed to look after an empty building etc. at night.

watchword *n.* a phrase summarizing a principle of a party, etc.

water /'wɔːtə/ *n.* 1. (H_2O) a liquid without colour, taste, or odour. It is an oxide of hydrogen. Water begins to freeze solid at 0°C or 32°F, and to boil at 100°C or 212°F. When liquid, it is virtually incompressible; frozen, it expands by $1/11$ of its volume. At 39.2°F/4°C, one cubic centimetre of water has a mass of one gram, its maximum density, forming the unit of specific gravity. It has the highest known specific heat, and acts as an efficient solvent, particularly when hot. Most of the world's water is in the sea; less than 0.01% is fresh water. Liquid consisting chiefly of water (in seas and rivers, rain, tears, sweat, saliva, urine, (*usually in plural*) amniotic fluid etc.; a body of this as a sea, lake, or river; water as supplied for domestic use; (in *plural*) part of a sea or river, the mineral water at a spa etc. 2. the state of the tide. 3. a solution of specified substance in water. 4. the transparency and brilliance of a diamond or other gem. —*attrib.* 1. found in or near water. 2. of, for, or worked by water. 3. involving, using, or yielding water. —*v.t./i.* 1. to give drinking water to (an animal); to supply (a plant etc.) with water. 2. to take in a supply of water. 3. to dilute with water. 4. to secrete saliva or tears. 5. (in *past participle,* of silk etc.) having irregular wavy markings. —**by water,** using a ship etc. for travel or transport. **like water,** lavishly, recklessly. **make one's mouth water,** to cause a flow of saliva; to create an appetite or desire. **make** *or* **pass water,** to urinate. **mouth-watering** *adj.* appetizing. **under water,** in or covered by water. **water bed,** a mattress of rubber or plastic etc. filled with water. **water bird,** a bird that swims on or wades in water. **water biscuit,** a thin, crisp, unsweetened biscuit made from flour and water. **water buffalo,** the common domestic Indian buffalo. **water bus,** a boat carrying passengers on a regular route on a lake or river. **water cannon,** a device giving a powerful water jet to disperse a crowd etc. **Water Carrier,** the constellation and sign of the zodiac Aquarius. **water clock,** a device for measuring time by the flow of water. **water-cooled** *adj.* cooled by the circulation of water. **water down,** to dilute; to make less forceful or horrifying. **water hammer,** a knocking noise in a pipe when a tap is turned off. **water hole,** a shallow depression in which water collects. **water ice,** an edible concoction of frozen flavoured water. **watering can,** a portable container with a long tubular spout, holding water for watering plants. **watering place,** a pool where animals drink; a spa or seaside resort. **water jump,** a place where a horse in a steeplechase etc. must jump over water. **water level,** the surface of water in a reservoir etc.; the height of this; the water table; a level using water to determine the horizontal. **water lily**, an aquatic plant of the family Nymphaeaceae with floating leaves and flowers. **water line**, the line along which the surface of the water touches a ship's side. **water main**, a main pipe in a water supply system. **water meadow**, a meadow periodically flooded by a stream. **watermelon** *n.* a large melon *Citrullus vulgaris* with a smooth green skin, red pulp, and watery juice. **water pistol**, a toy pistol shooting a jet of water. **water power**, mechanical force from the weight or motion of water. **water rat**, a water-vole. **water rate**, a charge for the use of a public water supply. **water tower**, a tower with an elevated tank to give pressure for distributing water. **water under the bridge**, the irrevocable past. **water vole**, an aquatic rat-like vole *Arvicola amphibius*. **water wheel**, a wheel driven by water to work machinery, or used to raise water. **water wings**, inflated supports worn on the shoulders by a person learning to swim. [Old English]

water boatman a water bug of the family Corixidae that feeds on plant debris and algae. It has a flattened body 1.5 cm/0.6 in long, with oarlike legs. The name also applies to the backswimmers, genus *Notecta*, which are superficially similar.

water-borne disease a disease associated with poor water supply. In the Third World four-fifths of all illness is caused by water-borne diseases, diarrhoea being the leading cause of childhood death. Malaria, carried by mosquitoes dependent on stagnant water for breeding, affects 400 million people every year and kills five million.

waterbuck *n.* an African antelope *Kobus ellipsiprymnus* with characteristic white ring marking on the rump. It is about 2 m/6 ft long and 1.4 m/4.5 ft at the shoulder, and has long, coarse, brown fur. The males have big horns with corrugated surfaces.

water closet (WC) a flushing lavatory that works by siphon action. The first widely used WC was produced in the 1770s by Alexander Cummings in London. The present type dates from Davis Bostel's invention of 1889, which featured a ballcock valve system to refill the flushing cistern.

watercolour painting a method of painting with pigments mixed with water, known in China as early as the 3rd century. The art as practised today began in England in the 18th century with the work of Paul Sandby and was developed by Thomas Girtin and J M W Turner. Other excellent European watercolourists were Raoul Dufy and Paul Cézanne.

watercourse *n.* a brook or stream; the bed of this.

watercress *n.* a perennial aquatic plant *Nasturtium officinale* of the crucifer family, found in Europe and Asia, and cultivated as a salad crop.

water cycle in ecology, the natural circulation of water through the (t)biosphere. Water is lost from the Earth's surface to the atmosphere either by evaporation from the surface of lakes, rivers, and oceans or through the transpiration of plants. This atmospheric water forms clouds that condense to deposit moisture on the land and sea as rain or snow. The water that collects on land flows to the ocean in streams and rivers.

waterfall *n.* a stream or river falling over a precipice or down a steep height.

waterflea *n.* any aquatic crustacean in the order Cladocera, of which there are over 400 species. The commonest species is *Daphnia pulex*.

Waterford /ˈwɔːtəfəd/ county in Munster province, Republic of Ireland; **area** 1,840 sq km/710 sq mi; **administrative headquarters** Waterford; **population** (1986) 91,000. **County town** Waterford. The county includes the rivers Suir and Blackwater, and the Comeragh and Monavallagh mountain ranges in the N and centre. Products include cattle, beer, whiskey, and glassware.

waterfowl *n.* (*usually as plural*) water birds, especially game birds that can swim.

waterfront *n.* the part of a town that borders on a river or lake or on the sea.

Watergate /ˈwɔːtəgeɪt/ *n.* a US political scandal, named after the building in Washington DC that housed the Democrats' campaign headquarters in the 1972 presidential election. Five men, hired by the Republican Committee to Re-elect the President (CREEP), were caught after breaking into the Watergate with complex electronic surveillance

equipment. Over the next two years, investigations by the media and a Senate committee revealed that the White House was implicated in the break-in, and that there was a 'slush fund', used to finance unethical activities. In Aug 1974, President (t)Nixon was forced by the Supreme Court to surrender to Congress tape recordings of conversations he had held with administration officials, and these indicated his complicity in a cover-up. Nixon resigned rather than face virtually certain impeachment for obstruction of justice and other crimes, the only US president to have left office through resignation.

water glass in technology, the colourless, jellylike substance sodium metasilicate, Na_2SiO_3. It dissolves readily in water to give a solution that is used for preserving eggs and fireproofing porous materials such as cloth, paper, and wood. It is also used as an adhesive for paper and cardboard and in the manufacture of soap and silica gel, a substance that absorbs moisture.

water hyacinth a tropical aquatic plant *Eichhornia crassipes* of the pickerelweed family Pontederiaceae. In one growing season 25 plants can produce 2 million new plants. It is liable to choke waterways, depleting the water of nutrients and blocking the sunlight, but can be used as a purifier of sewage-polluted water as well as in making methane gas, compost, concentrated protein, paper, and baskets. It originated in South America, and now grows in more than 50 countries.

waterlogged *adj.* saturated with water; (of a boat etc.) barely able to float from being saturated or filled with water.

Waterloo, Battle of /wɔːtəˈluː/ the battle on 18 June 1815 in which British forces commanded by Wellington defeated the French army of Emperor Napoleon near the village of Waterloo, 13 km/8 mi S of Brussels, Belgium. Wellington had 68,000 soldiers (of whom 24,000 were British, the remainder being German, Dutch, and Belgian) and Napoleon had 72,000. Napoleon found Wellington's army isolated from his allies and began a direct offensive to smash them, but the British held on until joined by the Prussians under General Blücher. Four days later Napoleon abdicated for the second and final time.

waterman *n.* (*plural* **watermen**) **1.** a boatman plying for hire. **2.** an oarsman as regards skill in keeping the boat balanced.

watermark *n.* a manufacturer's design in some kinds of paper, visible when the paper is held against light. —*v.t.* to mark with this.

water mill a machine that harnesses the energy in flowing water to produce mechanical power, typically for milling (grinding) grain. Water from a stream is directed against the paddles of a water wheel to make it turn. Simple gearing transfers this motion to the millstones. The modern equivalent of the water wheel is the water turbine, used in (t)hydroelectric power plants.

water polo a water sport developed in England in 1869, originally called 'soccer-in-water'. The aim is to score goals, as in soccer, at each end of a swimming pool. It is played by teams of seven a side (from squads of 13).

waterproof *adj.* impervious to water. —*n.* a waterproof coat, cape or covering. —*v.t.* to make waterproof.

watershed *n.* **1.** a line of high land where streams on one side flow into one river or sea and streams on the other side flow into another. **2.** a turning-point in the course of events.

waterside *n.* the margin of a river, lake, or sea.

water skiing a water sport in which a person is towed across water on a ski or skis, wider than those used for skiing on snow, by means of a rope (23 m/75 ft long) attached to a speedboat. Competitions are held for overall performances, slalom, tricks, and jumping.

water softener any substance or unit that removes the hardness from water. Hardness is caused by the presence of calcium and magnesium ions, which cause pipes and kettles to fur up, and combine with soap to form an insoluble scum and prevent lathering. A water softener replaces these ions with sodium ions, which are fully soluble and cause no scum.

waterspout *n.* a funnel-shaped column of water and spray between sea and cloud, formed when a whirlwind draws up a gyrating mass of water.

water table the level of ground below which the rocks are saturated with water. Above the water table water will drain

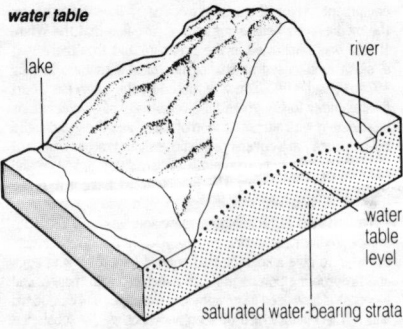

water table

lake

river

water table level

saturated water-bearing strata

downwards, and where the water table cuts the surface of the ground, a spring results. The water table usually follows surface contours, and it varies with rainfall.

watertight *adj.* **1.** closely fastened or fitted so as to prevent the passage of water. **2.** (of an argument etc.) unassailable; (of an agreement) with inescapable provisions.

waterway *n.* a route for travel by water; a navigable channel.

waterworks *n.* **1.** an establishment for the management of a water supply. **2.** (*slang*) the shedding of tears. **3.** (*slang*) the urinary system.

watery *adj.* **1.** of or like water. **2.** containing too much water; thin in consistency. **3.** full of water or moisture. **4.** (of a colour) pale; (of the Sun, Moon, or sky) looking as if rain will come. —**watery grave,** death by drowning. —**wateriness** *n.* [from Old English]

Watling Street a Roman road running from London to Wroxeter (*Viroconium*) near Chester, NW England.

Watson /'wɒtsən/ James Dewey 1928– . US biologist whose research on the molecular structure of DNA and the genetic code, in collaboration with Francis ◊Crick, earned him a shared Nobel prize in 1962.

Watson John Broadus 1878–1958. US psychologist, founder of behaviourism. He rejected introspection (observation by an individual of his or her own mental processes) and regarded psychology as the study of observable behaviour, within the scientific tradition.

Watson-Watt /'wɒtsən 'wɒt/ Robert Alexander 1892–1973. Scottish physicist who developed a forerunner of ◊radar. During a long career in government service (1915–1952) he proposed in 1935 a method of radiolocation of aircraft, a key factor in the Allied victory over German aircraft in World War II.

watt /wɒt/ *n.* a unit of power, the rate of working of one joule per second, corresponding to an electric circuit where the electromotive force is one volt and the current one ampere. —**watt-hour** *n.* the energy of one watt applied for one hour. [from James *Watt*]

Watt James 1736–1819. Scottish engineer who developed the steam engine. He made Newcomen's steam engine vastly more efficient by cooling the used steam in a separate condenser.

wattage /'wɒtɪdʒ/ *n.* an amount of electrical power expressed in watts.

Watteau /'wɒtəʊ/ Jean-Antoine 1684–1721. French rococo painter. He developed a new category of genre painting known as the *fête galante*, scenes of a kind of aristocratic pastoral fantasy world. One of these pictures, *The Embarkation for Cythera* 1717 (Louvre, Paris), won him membership in the French Academy.

wattle[1] /'wɒtl/ *n.* **1.** an Australian acacia with pliant boughs and golden flowers, used as the national emblem. —**Wattle Day,** a national day, celebrated in Australia on 1 Aug. or 1 Sept. **2.** interlaced rods and twigs for fences etc. —**wattle and daub,** this plastered with mud or clay to make huts etc. [Old English]

wattle[2] *n.* a red, fleshy fold of skin on the head or throat of certain birds (e.g. the turkey).

Watts /wɒts/ George Frederick 1817–1904. English painter and sculptor. He painted allegorical, biblical, and classical subjects, investing his work with a solemn morality, such as *Hope* 1886 (Tate Gallery, London). Many of his portraits are in the National Portrait Gallery, London.

As a sculptor he executed *Physical Energy* 1904 for Cecil Rhodes' memorial in Cape Town, South Africa; a replica is in Kensington Gardens, London.

Watts Isaac 1674–1748. English Nonconformist writer of hymns including 'O God, our help in ages past'.

Waugh /wɔː/ Evelyn (Arthur St John) 1903–1966. English novelist. He made his name with social satire, for example, *Decline and Fall* 1928, *Vile Bodies* 1930, and *The Loved One* 1948. A Roman Catholic convert from 1930, he developed a serious concern with religious issues in *Brideshead Revisited* 1945. *The Ordeal of Gilbert Pinfold* 1957 is largely autobiographical.

> News is what a chap who doesn't care much about anything wants to read.
>
> **Evelyn Waugh**
> *Scoop*

wave *v.t./i.* **1.** to move (the arm, hand, or something held) to and fro as a signal or in greeting; to signal or express thus. **2.** to move loosely to and fro or up and down. **3.** to give a wavy form to; to have such a form. —*n.* **1.** a ridge of water moving along the surface of the sea etc. or curling into an arched form and breaking on the shore. **2.** a thing compared to this, e.g. an advancing group of attackers, a temporary increase of an influence or condition; a spell of hot or cold weather. **3.** a wave-like curve or arrangement of curves; waving of the hair. **4.** a gesture of waving. **5.** a rhythmic disturbance of a fluid or solid substance in which successive portions of it undergo alternate displacement and recovery, so that a state of motion travels through it without any continued advance of the substance itself; an analogous variation of an electromagnetic field in the propagation of light or other radiation; a single curve in this plotted graphically against time. —**wave aside,** to dismiss as intrusive or irrelevant. **wave down,** to wave to (a vehicle or driver) as a signal to stop. **wave mechanics,** a particular mathematical formulation of quantum mechanics in which particles such as electrons are regarded as having some of the properties of waves. [Old English]

waveband *n.* a range of wavelengths between specified limits.

wavelength *n.* the distance between the crests of successive waves; a corresponding distance between points in a sound wave or electromagnetic wave; this as a distinctive feature of waves from a particular transmitter or (*figurative*) of a person's way of thinking.

wavelet *n.* a small wave.

Wavell /'weɪvl/ Archibald, 1st Earl 1883–1950. British field marshal in World War II. As commander in chief, Middle East, he successfully defended Egypt against Italy in July 1939. He was transferred as Commander in Chief, India in July 1941, and was viceroy 1943–47.

wave power power obtained by harnessing the energy of water waves. Various schemes have been advanced since 1973, when oil prices rose dramatically and an energy shortage threatened. In 1974 the British engineer Stephen Salter developed the duck, a floating boom whose segments nod up and down with the waves. The nodding motion can be used to drive pumps and spin generators. Another device, developed in Japan, uses an oscillating water column to harness wave power.

waver /'weɪvə/ *v.i.* **1.** to be or become unsteady, to begin to give way. **2.** to show hesitation or uncertainty. **3.** (of light) to flicker. —**waverer** *n.* [from Old Norse = flicker]

wavy /'weɪvɪ/ *adj.* having waves or alternate contrary curves. —**wavily** *adv.*, **waviness** *n.*

wax[1] *n.* **1.** a sticky, plastic, yellowish substance secreted by bees as the material of honeycomb; this bleached and purified for candles, modelling etc., or used in polishes. **2.** any similar substance e.g. the mineral waxes obtained from petroleum. —*v.t.* to cover or treat with wax. —**be wax in a person's hands,** to be entirely subservient to him or her. [Old English]

wax[2] *v.i.* **1.** (of the Moon) to show a gradually increasing area of brightness before becoming full. **2.** to increase in vigour, strength, or importance. **3.** (*archaic*) to pass into a specified state, to become. —**wax and wane,** to undergo alternate increases and decreases. [Old English]

wax[3] *n.* (*slang*) a fit of anger.

waxbill *n.* a small African seed-eating bird, genus *Estrilda*. Waxbills grow to 15 cm/6 in long, are brown and grey with yellow, red or brown markings, and have waxy-looking red or pink beaks.

waxen *adj.* 1. like wax, having a smooth, pale, translucent surface as of wax. 2. (*archaic*) made of wax.

waxwing *n.* a bird *Bombycilla garrulus* found in the northern hemisphere. It is about 18 cm/7 in long, and is greyish-brown above with a reddish-chestnut crest, a black streak at the eye, and variegated wings. It undertakes mass migrations in some years.

waxwork *n.* an object modelled in wax; a model of a person with the face etc. made in wax, clothed to look lifelike and to be exhibited; (in *plural*) an exhibition of such models.

waxy *adj.* 1. resembling wax in consistency or surface. 2. (*slang*) angry; easily enraged. —**waxily** *adv.*, **waxiness** *n.*

way *n.* 1. a line of communication, e.g. a road or track. 2. a course or route for reaching a place; the best route, the one taken or intended. 3. a method or plan for attaining an object; a person's desired or chosen course of action. 4. travelling-distance; the amount of difference between two states or conditions. 5. an unimpeded opportunity to advance; a space free of obstacles so that people etc. can pass; a region over which advance is proceeding, desired, or natural. 6. an advance in some direction, impetus, progress. 7. a specified direction. 8. a manner; habitual manner; the normal course of action or events; a talent or skill. 9. a scope or range; a line of occupation or business. 10. a specified condition or state; a respect. 11. (in *plural*) a structure of timber etc. down which a new ship is launched. —*adv.* (*colloquial*) far. —**by the way**, by the roadside during a journey; incidentally, as a more or less irrelevant comment. **by way of**, by means of; as a form of or substitute for; as a method of; passing through. **come one's way**, to become available to one. **go out of one's way**, to make a special effort; to act without compulsion. **in a way**, to a limited extent; in some respects. **in no way**, not at all. **in the way**, forming an obstacle or hindrance. **lead** *or* **show the way**, to act as guide or leader. **look the other way**, to ignore deliberately. **make one's way**, to go; to prosper. **make way for**, to allow to pass; to be superseded by. **on one's way**, in the process of travelling or approaching. **on the way**, travelling or approaching; having progressed; (of a baby) conceived but not yet born. **on the way out**, (*colloquial*) going down in status or favour; disappearing. **out of the way**, unusual; not obstructing; remote; disposed of. **under way**, in motion or progress. **way back**, (*colloquial*) long ago. **waybill** *n.* a list of the passengers or parcels conveyed. **wayleave** *n.* a right of way rented to another. **way of life**, the principles or habits governing one's actions. **way-out** *adj.* (*colloquial*) exaggeratedly unusual in style, exotic; progressive. **ways and means**, methods of achieving something; (in Parliament) a means of providing money. [Old English]

wayfarer /ˈweɪfeərə/ *n.* a traveller, especially on foot. —**wayfaring** *n.*

wayfaring tree a shrub *Viburnum lantana* that grows commonly along roadsides, with white flowers and with berries that turn red and then black.

waylay /weɪˈleɪ/ *v.t.* (*past* and *past participle* **waylaid**) to lie in wait for, especially so as to talk to or rob.

Wayne John. Stage name of Marion Michael Morrison. 1907–1979. US actor. Nicknamed 'Duke' from the name of a dog he once owned, Wayne was the archetypal western hero. His films include *Stagecoach* 1939, *Red River* 1948, *She Wore a Yellow Ribbon* 1949, *The Searchers* 1956, *Rio Bravo* 1959, *The Man Who Shot Liberty Valance* 1962, and *True Grit* 1969 (Academy Award). He was also active in conservative politics.

-ways suffix forming adjectives and adverbs of direction or manner (*sideways*).

wayside *n.* the side of a road; the land bordering a road.

wayward *adj.* childishly self-willed, capricious. —**waywardness** *n.* [from obsolete *awayward* = turned away]

Wb abbreviation of weber.

WC abbreviation of 1. water closet. 2. West Central.

WCC abbreviation of World Council of Churches.

we /wiː; wɪ/ *pron.* (objective **us**; possessive **our**, **ours**) 1. plural of I, used by a person referring to himself or herself and another or others, or speaking on behalf of a nation, group, firm etc. 2. used instead of 'I' by a royal person in formal proclamations and by the writer of a newspaper editorial etc. [Old English]

weak *adj.* 1. lacking strength, power, or number; easily broken, bent, or defeated. 2. lacking vigour, not acting strongly. 3. not convincing or forceful. 4. (of a solution or drink) dilute, having a large proportion of water or other solvent. —**weaker sex**, women. **weak-kneed** *adj.* lacking determination, giving way easily when intimidated. **weak-minded** *adj.* mentally deficient; lacking determination. **weak verb**, a verb forming inflexions by a suffix, not by vowel change only. —**weakly** *adv.* [from Old Norse *veikr* = Old English *wāc* = pliant, insignificant]

weaken *v.t./i.* to make or become weaker.

weakling *n.* a feeble person or animal.

weakly *adj.* sickly, not robust. —**weakliness** *n.*

weakness *n.* 1. being weak. 2. a weak point, a defect or fault. 3. a self-indulgent liking, inability to resist a particular temptation.

weal[1] *n.* a ridge raised on the flesh by a stroke of a whip, etc. —*v.t.* to mark with a weal.

weal[2] *n.* welfare.

weald /wiːld/ *n.* the formerly wooded district including parts of Kent, Surrey, and East Sussex. [Old English = wold]

wealth /welθ/ *n.* 1. riches, possession of these. 2. a great quantity, plenty.

wealthy /ˈwelθɪ/ *adj.* having wealth, rich. —**wealthily** *adv.*, **wealthiness** *n.*

wean *v.t.* 1. to accustom (an infant or other young mammal) to take food other than (its mother's) milk. 2. (with *of*) to cause (a person) to give up a habit or interest etc. gradually. [Old English = accustom]

weapon *n.* 1. a thing designed, used, or usable as a means of inflicting bodily harm. 2. a means employed for getting the better of someone in a conflict. [Old English]

weaponry /ˈwepənrɪ/ *n.* weapons collectively.

wear /weə/ *v.t./i.* (*past* **wore**; *past participle* **worn**) 1. to have on one's body, e. g. as clothing, ornaments, or make-up. 2. to have (a specified look) on one's face. 3. (*colloquial*, usually negative) to accept or tolerate. 4. to injure the surface of or become injured by rubbing, stress, or use; to make (a hole etc.) thus. 5. to exhaust or (with *down*) overcome by persistence. 6. to endure continued use or life (well or badly etc.). 7. (of time) to pass gradually. 8. (of a ship) to fly (a specified flag). —*n.* 1. wearing or being worn as clothing etc. 2. (especially as suffix) clothing, suitable apparel (*sportswear*). 3. (also **wear and tear**) damage resulting from ordinary use. 4. capacity to endure being worn. —**wear one's heart on one's sleeve**, to show one's affections openly. **wear off**, to lose effectiveness or intensity. **wear out**, to use or to be used until no longer usable; to tire or be tired out. **wear thin**, (of patience, etc.) to begin to fail. —**wearer** *n.* [Old English]

Wear /wɪə/ river in NE England; length 107 km/67 mi. From its source in the Pennines it flows E past Durham, to meet the North Sea at Sunderland.

wearable /ˈweərəbəl/ *adj.* that may be worn.

wearisome /ˈwɪərɪsəm/ *adj.* tedious, tiring by monotony or length.

weary /ˈwɪərɪ/ *adj.* 1. very tired, especially from exertion or endurance. 2. (*of*) tired of (a specified thing). 3. tiring, tedious. —*v.t./i.* to make or become weary. —**wearily** *adv.*, **weariness** *n.* [Old English]

weasel /ˈwiːzəl/ *n.* a small, fierce, carnivorous animal *Mustela nivalis* with a long body (20 cm/8 in, with 5 cm/2 in tail) and neck, short ears and legs, and dense fur, brownish above and white below, living on small animals, birds' eggs etc. —**weasel word**, an equivocating or ambiguous word that takes away the force of the expression containing it (said to allude to the weasel's alleged habit of sucking out the contents of an egg and leaving only the shell). [Old English]

weather /ˈweðə/ *n.* 1. the state of the atmosphere at a certain place and time, with reference to heat, cloudiness, dryness, sunshine, wind, rain etc. 2. (*attributive*) windward. —*v.t./i.* 1. to expose to or affect by atmospheric changes; to be discoloured or worn thus. 2. to come safely through (a storm, *literal* or *figurative*). 3. to get to windward of (a cape etc.). —**keep a weather eye open**, to

Webb *Beatrice Webb who, with her husband Sidney, influenced the early socialist movement in Britain.*

be watchful. **make heavy weather of,** to find trying or needlessly difficult. **under the weather,** (*colloquial*) indisposed. **weather-beaten** *adj.* affected by exposure to the weather. **weather-board** *n.* a sloping board at the bottom of a door to keep out rain; (in *plural*, also **weatherboarding**) a series of boards each overlapping the one below, fixed to the outside walls of light buildings. **weathervane,** a weathercock. [Old English]

weather areas divisions of the sea around the British Isles for the purpose of weather forecasting for shipping. They are used to indicate where strong and gale-force winds are expected.

weathercock *n.* **1.** a revolving pointer, often in the form of a cockerel, mounted in a high place and turning easily in the wind to show from which direction the wind is blowing. **2.** an inconstant person.

weathering *n.* the process by which exposed rocks are broken down by the action of rain, frost, wind, and other elements of the weather. Two types of weathering are recognized: physical and chemical. They usually occur together.

weatherly *adj.* (*nautical*) making little leeway, capable of keeping close to the wind. **—weatherliness** *n.*

weatherproof *adj.* resistant to wind and rain.

weave[1] *v.t./i.* (*past* **wove;** *past participle* **woven**) **1.** to make (fabric etc.) by passing crosswise threads or strips under and over lengthwise ones; to form (thread etc.) into fabric thus. **2.** to put (facts etc.) together into a story or connected whole; to make (a story etc.) thus. **—n.** a style or pattern of weaving. [Old English]

weave[2] *v.i.* to move repeatedly from side to side; to take an intricate course to avoid obstructions. **—get weaving,** (*slang*) to begin an action, to hurry.

weaver *n.* **1.** one whose occupation is weaving. **2.** a tropical bird of the family Ploceidae that builds a nest of elaborately interwoven twigs etc.

web *n.* **1.** the network of fine strands made by a spider etc. **2.** a network. **3.** woven fabric; an amount woven in one piece. **4.** a membrane filling the spaces between the toes of swimming birds (e.g. ducks) and animals (e.g. frogs). **5.** a large roll of paper for printing. **6.** a thin, flat, connecting part in machinery. **—web-footed** *adj.* having the toes connected by a web. **—webbed** *adj.* [Old English]

Webb /web/ (Martha) Beatrice (born Potter) 1858–1943 and Sidney (James), Baron Passfield 1859–1947. English social reformers, writers, and founders of the London School of Economics 1895. They were early members of the socialist ◊Fabian Society, and were married in 1892. They

argued for social insurance in their minority report (1909) of the Poor Law Commission, and wrote many influential books, including *The History of Trade Unionism* 1894, *English Local Government* 1906, and *Soviet Communism* 1935. Beatrice wrote *The Co-operative Movement in Great Britain* 1891, *My Apprenticeship* 1926, and *Our Partnership* 1948.

Webb Philip (Speakman) 1831–1915. English architect. He mostly designed private houses, including the Red House, Bexley Heath, Sussex, for William ◊Morris, and was one of the leading figures, with Richard Norman Shaw and C F A Voysey, in the revival of domestic English architecture in the late 19th century.

Webber Andrew Lloyd. English composer of musicals: see ◊Lloyd Webber.

webbing *n.* a strong, narrow, closely-woven fabric used for belts or in upholstery etc.

weber /'veɪbə/ *n.* a unit of magnetic flux, causing an electromotive force of one volt in a circuit of one turn when generated or removed in one second. [from W E *Weber*]

Weber Carl Maria Friedrich Ernst von 1786–1826. German composer who established the Romantic school of opera with *Der Freischütz* 1821 and *Euryanthe* 1823. He was *Kapellmeister* at Breslau 1804–06, Prague 1813–16, and Dresden 1816. He died during a visit to London where he produced his opera *Oberon* 1826, written for the Covent Garden theatre.

Weber Max 1864–1920. German sociologist, one of the founders of modern sociology. He emphasized cultural and political factors as key influences on economic development and individual behaviour. Weber argued for a scientific and value-free approach to research, yet highlighted the importance of meaning and consciousness in understanding social action. His ideas continue to stimulate thought on social stratification, power, organizations, law, and religion. Key works include *The Protestant Ethic and the Spirit of Capitalism* 1902, *Economy and Society* 1922, *The Methodology of the Social Sciences* 1949, and *The Sociology of Religion* 1920.

Weber Wilhelm Eduard 1804–1891. German physicist, who studied magnetism and electricity, brother of Ernst Weber. Working with Karl Gauss, he made sensitive magnetometers to measure magnetic fields, and instruments to measure direct and alternating currents. He also built an electric telegraph. The SI unit of magnetic flux, the **weber**, is named after him.

Webern /'veɪbən/ Anton (Friedrich Wilhelm von) 1883–1945. Austrian composer. A pupil of ◊Schoenberg, whose 12-tone technique he adopted. He wrote works of extreme brevity; for example, the oratorio *Das Augenlicht* 1935, and songs to words by Stefan George and poems of Rilke.

Webster /'webstə/ Daniel 1782–1852. US politician and orator, born in New Hampshire. He sat in the House of Representatives from 1813 and in the Senate from 1827, at first as a Federalist and later as a Whig. He was secretary of state 1841–43 and 1850–52, and negotiated the Ashburton Treaty in 1842, which fixed the Maine–Canada boundary. His celebrated 'seventh of March' speech in the Senate in 1850 helped secure a compromise on the slavery issue.

Webster John *c.* 1580–1634. English dramatist, who ranks after Shakespeare as the greatest tragedian of his time and is the Jacobean whose plays are most frequently performed today. His two great plays *The White Devil* 1608 and *The Duchess of Malfi* 1614 are dark, violent tragedies obsessed with death and decay and infused with poetic brilliance.

Webster Noah 1758–1843. US lexicographer, whose books on grammar and spelling and *American Dictionary of the English Language* 1828 standardized US English.

wed *v.t./i.* (**-dd-;** *past participle* occasionally **wed**) **1.** to marry. **2.** (*figurative*) to unite; **3.** (in *past participle*) of marriage; (with *to*) devoted to and unable to abandon (an occupation or opinion etc.). [Old English = pledge]

Wed. abbreviation of Wednesday.

Weddell Sea /'wedl/ an arm of the S Atlantic Ocean that cuts into the Antarctic continent SE of Cape Horn; area 8,000,000 sq km/3,000,000 sq mi. Much of it is covered with thick pack ice for most of the year.

wedding *n.* a marriage ceremony and festivities. **—wedding breakfast,** a meal after the wedding ceremony and before departure for the honeymoon. **wedding cake,** a rich iced cake cut and eaten at a wedding. **wedding march,** a march (especially one by Mendelssohn) for a wedding procession. **wedding ring,** a ring worn by a married person from the time of the wedding ceremony. [Old English]

Wedekind /'veɪdəkɪnt/ Frank 1864–1918. German dramatist. He was a forerunner of Expressionism with *Frühlings Erwachen/The Awakening of Spring* 1891, and *Der Erdgeist/ The Earth Spirit* 1895 and its sequel *Der Marquis von Keith. Die Büchse der Pandora/Pandora's Box* 1904 was the source for Berg's opera *Lulu.*

wedge *n.* **1.** a piece of wood or metal etc. thick at one end and tapered to a thin edge at the other, thrust between things to force them apart or prevent free movement etc. **2.** a wedge-shaped thing. —*v. t.* **1.** to force apart or fix firmly by using a wedge. **2.** to thrust or pack tightly between other things or people or in a limited space; to be made immovable thus. —**thin end of the wedge,** a change or procedure, etc. that appears small or insignificant but will open the way to greater changes etc. [Old English]

Wedgwood /'wedʒwʊd/ *n.* **1.** trade name of a kind of fine pottery, especially with a white cameo design. **2.** its characteristic blue colour. [from J *Wedgwood*]

Wedgwood Josiah 1730–1795. English pottery manufacturer who set up business in Staffordshire in the early 1760s to produce his agateware as well as his unglazed blue or green stoneware decorated with white Neo-Classical designs, using pigments of his own invention.

wedlock /'wedlɒk/ *n.* the married state. —**born in wedlock,** legitimate. **born out of wedlock,** illegitimate. [Old English = marriage vow]

Wednesday /'wenzdeɪ, -dɪ/ *n.* the day of the week following Tuesday. —*adv.* (*colloquial*) on Wednesday. [Old English = day of (the god) Odin, translation of Latin *Mercurii dies* = day of the planet Mercury]

wee *adj.* **1.** (especially *Scottish*) little. **2.** (*colloquial*) tiny. [originally Scottish, from obsolete *wei* = (small) quantity]

weed *n.* **1.** a wild plant growing where it is not wanted. **2.** a thin, weak-looking person or horse. **3.** (*slang*) marijuana. **4.** (*archaic*) tobacco. —*v. t./i.* **1.** to remove weeds from; to uproot weeds. **2.** (with *out*) to remove as inferior or undesirable. [Old English]

weedkiller *n.* or **herbicide** a chemical that kills some or all plants. Selective herbicides are effective with cereal crops because they kill all broad-leaved plants without affecting grasslike leaves. Those that kill all plants include sodium chlorate and ◊paraquat; see also ◊Agent Orange. The widespread use of weedkillers in agriculture has led to a dramatic increase in crop yield but also to pollution of soil and water supplies, as well as creating a health hazard.

weeds /wiːdz/ *n. pl.* the deep mourning formerly worn by widows. [Old English = garment]

weedy *adj.* **1.** full of weeds. **2.** growing freely like a weed. **3.** thin and weak-looking.

week *n.* **1.** a period of seven successive days, especially one reckoned from midnight at the end of Saturday. **2.** the six days between successive Sundays; the five days other than Saturday and Sunday. **3.** the period for which one regularly works during a week. —**a week (from) today, Monday,** etc. (*or* **today, Monday** etc., **week**), seven days after today, Monday etc. [Old English]

weekday *n.* a day other than Sunday.

weekend /wiːk'end, 'wiː-/ *n.* Sunday and (part of) Saturday (or a slightly longer period) especially for a holiday or visit.

weekly *adj.* done, produced, occurring, or payable etc. every week. —*adv.* every week. —*n.* a weekly newspaper or periodical.

weeny /'wiːnɪ/ *adj.* (*colloquial*) tiny.

weep *v. t./i.* (*past* and *past participle* **wept**) **1.** to shed tears. **2.** to shed or ooze moisture in drops; to send forth in drops. **3.** (of a tree, usually in *participle*) to have drooping branches. —*n.* a spell of weeping. —**Weeping Cross,** (*historical*) a wayside cross for penitents to pray at. [Old English]

weepy *adj.* (*colloquial*) inclined to weep, tearful.

weever fish a European fish, genus *Trachinus*, with poison glands on its dorsal fin and gill cover that can give a painful sting. It grows up to 5 cm/2 in long, has eyes near the top of its head, and lives on sandy seabeds.

weevil /'wiːvɪl/ *n.* a superfamily of beetles Curculionoidea in the order Coleoptera, which are usually less than 6 mm/ 0.25 in long. The head has a prolonged rostrum, which is

used for boring into plant stems and trees for feeding, and in the female's case for depositing eggs. [from Middle Low German *wevel* = Old English *wifel* = beetle]

wee-wee /'wiːwiː/ *n.* (*children's colloquial*) urination; urine. —*v. i.* (*children's colloquial*) to urinate.

weft *n.* crosswise threads woven over and under the warp threads to make fabric.

Wegener /'veɪgənə/ Alfred Lothar 1880–1930. German meteorologist and geophysicist, whose theory of ◊continental drift, expounded in *Origin of Continents and Oceans* 1915, was originally known as Wegener's hypothesis. His ideas can now be explained in terms of plate tectonics, the idea that the Earth's crust consists of a number of plates, all moving with respect to one another.

weigh /weɪ/ *v. t./i.* **1.** to measure the weight of, especially by means of scales or a similar instrument. **2.** to have (a specified weight). **3.** to consider carefully the relative importance or value of; to compare (a thing with or against another). **4.** to have importance or influence. **5.** to be burdensome. —**weigh anchor,** take up the anchor. **weigh down,** to bring or keep down by weight; to depress or make troubled. **weigh in,** to be weighed (of a boxer before a contest, or a jockey after a race). **weigh in with,** (*colloquial*) to advance (an argument etc.) confidently. **weigh out,** to take a specified weight of; (of a jockey) to be weighed before a race. **weigh up,** (*colloquial*) to form an estimate of. **weigh one's words,** to choose those which precisely express one's meaning. [Old English]

weighbridge *n.* a weighing machine set into a road etc., with a plate on to which vehicles can be driven to be weighed.

weight /weɪt/ *n.* **1.** the force with which a body tends to a centre of gravitational attraction, especially the tendency of bodies to fall to earth. **2.** relative mass giving such force; (*popularly*) mass. **3.** a quantitative expression of a body's mass; a scale for expressing weights. **4.** a heavy object, especially one used to bring or keep something down; an object of known weight for use in weighing. **5.** a load to be supported; a burden of responsibility or worry. **6.** influence, importance. **7.** (in athletics) a shot. —*v. t.* **1.** to attach a weight to; to hold down with a weight or weights. **2.** to burden with a load. **3.** to bias or arrange the balance of. —**throw one's weight about,** (*colloquial*) to use one's influence aggressively. **weightlifting** *n.* the athletic sport of lifting heavy objects. **weight training,** a system of physical training using weights in the form of barbells or dumbbells. [Old English]

weighting /'weɪtɪŋ/ *n.* extra pay given in special cases.

weightless *adj.* having no weight, or with no weight relative to the surroundings either because gravitational force is cancelled out by equal and opposite acceleration, or because the body is so far outside a planet's gravitational field that no force is exerted upon it. (e.g. in a spacecraft moving under the action of gravity). —**weightlessness** *n.*

weights and measures see under ◊c.g.s. system, ◊f.p.s. system, ◊m.k.s. system, ◊SI units.

weighty /'weɪtɪ/ *adj.* **1.** having great weight, heavy. **2.** burdensome. **3.** showing or deserving earnest thought. **4.** important, influential. —**weightily** *adv.,* **weightiness** *n.*

Weil /veɪ/ Simone 1909–1943. French writer who became a practising Catholic after a mystical experience in 1938. Apart from essays, her works (advocating political passivity) were posthumously published, including *Waiting for God* 1951, *The Need for Roots* 1952, and *Notebooks* 1956.

Weill /vaɪl/ Kurt (Julian) 1900–1950. German composer, US citizen from 1943. He wrote chamber and orchestral music and collaborated with ◊Brecht on operas such as *Die Dreigroschenoper/The Threepenny Opera* 1928 and *Aufstieg und Fall der Stadt Mahagonny/The Rise and Fall of the City of Mahagonny* 1930, all attacking social corruption (*Mahagonny* caused a riot at its premiere in Leipzig). He tried to evolve a new form of ◊music theatre, using subjects with a contemporary relevance and the simplest musical means. In 1935 he left Germany for the USA where he wrote a number of successful scores for Broadway, among them the antiwar musical *Johnny Johnson* 1936 (including the often covered 'September Song') and *Street Scene* 1947 based on an Elmer Rice play of the Depression.

Weil's disease /veɪn/ an infectious disease of animals (also known as leptospirosis), which is occasionally transmitted to human beings, usually by contact with water contaminated with rat urine. It is characterized by acute fever, and infection may spread to the liver, kidneys, and heart.

Weimar Republic the constitutional republic in Germany 1919–33, which was crippled by the election of antidemocratic parties to the ◊Reichstag (parliament), and then subverted by the Nazi leader Hitler after his appointment as chancellor in 1933. It took its name from the city where in Feb 1919 a constituent assembly met to draw up a democratic constitution.

Weinberger /'wainbɜːɡə/ Caspar (Willard) 1917– . US Republican politician. He served under presidents Nixon and Ford, and was Reagan's defence secretary 1981–87.

weir /wiə/ n. a small dam built across a river or canal to raise the level of water upstream or regulate its flow [Old English *wer* from *werian* = dam up]

Weir Peter 1938– . Australian film director. His films have an atmospheric quality and often contain a strong spiritual element. They include *Picnic at Hanging Rock* 1975, *Witness* 1985, and *The Mosquito Coast* 1986.

weird /wiəd/ adj. 1. strange and uncanny or bizarre. 2. connected with fate (obsolete except in **the weird sisters**, the Fates; witches). —**weirdly** adv., **weirdness** n. [from Old English *wyrd* = destiny]

Weismann /'vaismən/ August 1834–1914. German biologist. His failing eyesight forced him to turn from microscopy to theoretical work. In 1892 he proposed that changes to the body do not in turn cause an alteration of the genetic material.

Weismuller /'waismulə/ Johnny (Peter John) 1904–1984. US film actor, formerly an Olympic swimmer, who played Tarzan in a long-running series of films for MGM and RKO including *Tarzan the Ape Man* 1932, *Tarzan and His Mate* 1934, and *Tarzan and the Leopard Woman* 1946.

Weizmann /'vaitsmæn/ Chaim 1874–1952. Zionist leader, the first president of Israel (1948–52), and chemist. Born in Russia, he became a naturalized British subject, and as director of the Admiralty laboratories 1916–19 discovered a process for manufacturing acetone, a solvent. He conducted the negotiations leading up to the Balfour Declaration, by which Britain declared its support for an independent Jewish state. He became head of the Hebrew University in Jerusalem, then in 1948 became the first president of the new republic of Israel.

Weizsäcker /'vaitszekə/ Richard, Baron von 1920– German Christian Democrat politician, president from 1984. He began his career as a lawyer and was also active in the German Protestant church and in Christian Democratic Union party politics. He was elected to the West German Bundestag (parliament) in 1969 and served as mayor of West Berlin from 1981, before being elected federal president in 1984.

welcome /'welkəm/ interjection of greeting expressing pleasure at a person's coming. —n. saying 'welcome'; a kind or glad reception. —v.t. to receive with signs of pleasure. —adj. that one receives with pleasure; (*predicative*) ungrudgingly permitted or given the right (to a thing). [originally Old English *wilcuma* = one whose coming is a pleasure]

weld v.t. 1. to unite or fuse (pieces of metal) by hammering or pressure, usually after softening by heat. 2. to make (an article) thus. 3. to be able to be welded. 4. to unite effectively into a whole. —n. a welded joint. —**welder** n.

Welensky /wə'lenski/ Roy 1907– . Rhodesian politician. He was instrumental in the creation of a federation of N Rhodesia (now Zambia), S Rhodesia (now Zimbabwe), and Nyasaland (now Malawi) in 1953 and was prime minister 1956–63, when the federation was disbanded. His S Rhodesian Federal Party was defeated by Ian Smith's Rhodesian Front in 1964. In 1965, following Smith's Rhodesian unilateral declaration of S Rhodesian independence from Britain, Welensky left politics.

welfare /'welfeə/ n. 1. good health, happiness, and prosperity. 2. the maintenance of persons in such a condition; money given for this purpose. **welfare work**, organized efforts for the welfare of a class or group.

welfare state a political system under which the state (rather than the individual or a private sector) has responsibility for the welfare of its citizens. Services such as unemployment and sickness benefits, family allowances and incomes supplements, pensions, medical care, and

education may be provided and financed through state insurance schemes and taxation. For example, Germany under Chancellor Otto von Bismarck introduced a national insurance system in the 1880s. In Britain David Lloyd George, as chancellor, introduced a National Insurance Act in 1911. The Labour government 1945–50 (influenced by economist William Beveridge's report of 1942) set up a comprehensive welfare system, including the National Health Service.

welkin n. (*poetic*) the sky. [Old English = cloud]

well[1] adv. (*comparative* **better**; *superlative* **best**) 1. in the right or a satisfactory way. 2. favourably, kindly. 3. thoroughly, carefully. 4. to a considerable extent. 5. with good reason; easily; probably. —adj. 1. in good health. 2. (*attributive*) in a satisfactory state or position. 3. (*attributive*) advisable. —int. expressing surprise or resignation etc., used especially after a pause in speaking. —**let well alone**, to avoid needless change or disturbance. **well-advised** adj. prudent. **well and truly**, decisively, completely. **well away**, having made considerable progress. **well-being** n. welfare. **well-born** adj. born of good family. **well-bred** adj. having or showing good breeding or manners. **well-connected** adj. related to good families. **well-disposed** adj. having kindly or favourable feelings (towards a person or plan etc.). **well done!** a cry of commendation. **well-groomed** adj. with carefully tended hair, clothes etc. **well-heeled** adj. (*colloquial*) wealthy. **well-intentioned** adj. having or showing good intentions. **well-judged** adj. opportunely, skilfully, or discreetly done. **well-known** adj. known to many; known thoroughly. **well-mannered** adj. having good manners. **well-meaning** or **-meant** adj. well-intentioned (but ineffective). **well off**, fortunately situated; fairly rich. **well-oiled** adj. (*slang*) drunk. **well-preserved** adj. in good condition; (of an old person) showing little sign of age. **well-read** adj. having read much literature. **well-spoken** adj. speaking in a polite and correct way. **well-to-do** adj. fairly rich. **well-tested** adj. often tested with good results. **well-trodden** adj. much frequented. **well-wisher** n. a person who wishes one well. **well-worn** adj. much worn by use; (of a phrase etc.) hackneyed. [Old English]

well[2] n. 1. a shaft sunk into the ground to obtain water or oil from below the Earth's surface. 2. an enclosed space like a well-shaft, e.g. in the middle of a building for stairs or a lift, or to admit light or air. 3. (*figurative*) a source. 4. (in *plural*) a spa. 5. an inkwell. 6. (*archaic*) a water-spring. —v.i. to spring as from a fountain. [Old English]

Welles /welz/ (George) Orson 1915–1985. US actor and director. He produced a radio version of H G Wells's novel *The War of the Worlds* 1938. He then produced, directed, and starred in *Citizen Kane* 1941, in which he used innovative lighting techniques, camera angles and movements, creating a landmark in the history of cinema, yet he directed very few films subsequently in Hollywood. His numerous performances as an actor include the character of Harry Lime in *The Third Man* 1949.

wellies /'weliz/ n.pl. (*colloquial*) abbreviation of wellingtons.

wellington /'weliŋtən/ n. a boot of rubber or similar waterproof material, usually reaching almost to the knee. [from Duke of *Wellington*]

Wellington capital and industrial port of New Zealand in North Island on Cook Strait; products include woollen textiles, chemicals, soap, footwear and bricks; population (1987) 351,000. The harbour was first sighted by Captain Cook in 1773.

Wellington Arthur Wellesley, 1st Duke of Wellington 1769–1852. British soldier and Tory politician. As commander in the ◊Peninsular War, he expelled the French from Spain in 1814. He defeated Napoleon Bonaparte at Quatre-Bras and Waterloo in 1815, and was a member of the Congress of Vienna. As prime minister 1828–30, he was forced to concede Roman Catholic emancipation.

Wells /welz/ H(erbert) G(eorge) 1866–1946. English writer of 'scientific romances' such as *The Time Machine* 1895 and *The War of the Worlds* 1898. His later novels had an anti-establishment, anti-conventional humour remarkable in its day, for example *Kipps* 1905 and *Tono-Bungay* 1909. His many other books include *Outline of History* 1920 and

The Shape of Things to Come 1933, a number of his prophecies from which have since been fulfilled. He also wrote many short stories.

welsh /welʃ/ *v.i.* 1. (of one who loses a bet, especially a bookmaker at a racecourse) to decamp without paying out winnings. 2. (*on*) to break an agreement with (a person); to fail to honour (an obligation). —**welsher** *n.*

Welsh *adj.* of Wales or its people or language. —*n.* the Celtic language of Wales. —**the Welsh**, the Welsh people.

Welsh rabbit (*or* by folk etymology **rarebit**), a dish of melted cheese on toast. [Old English, ultimately from Latin *Volcae* name of a Celtic people]

Welsh corgi a breed of dog with a foxlike head and pricked ears. The coat is dense, with several varieties of colouring. Corgis are about 30 cm/1 ft at the shoulder, and weigh up to 12 kg/27 lbs.

Welsh language *Cymraeg*, a member of the Celtic branch of the Indo-European language family, spoken chiefly in the rural north and west of Wales; it is the strongest of the surviving Celtic languages, and in 1981 was spoken by 18.9% of the Welsh population.

Welshman /ˈwelʃmən/ *n.* (*plural* **Welshmen**) one who is Welsh by birth or descent. —**Welshwoman** *n.fem.* (*plural* **Welshwomen**).

welt *n.* 1. a leather rim sewn to a shoe upper for the sole to be attached to. 2. a weal. 3. a heavy blow 4. a ribbed or reinforced border of a garment. —*v.t.* 1. to provide with a welt. 2. to raise weals on, to thrash.

welter[1] *v.i.* 1. (of a ship) to be tossed to and fro on the waves. 2. to roll or lie prostrate, to be soaked (in blood etc.). —*n.* a state of turmoil; a disorderly mixture. [from Middle Dutch or Middle Low German]

welter[2] *n.* a heavy rider or boxer.

welterweight *n.* the boxing weight between lightweight and middleweight.

Weltpolitik *n.* the term applied to German foreign policy after about 1890, which represented Emperor Wilhelm II's attempt to make Germany into a world power through a more aggressive foreign policy on colonies and naval building, combined with an increase in nationalism at home. [German = world politics]

Wembley Stadium /ˈwembli/ a sports ground in N London, completed in 1923 for the British Empire Exhibition 1924–25. It has been the scene of the annual Football Association (FA) Cup final since 1923. The 1948 Olympic Games and many concerts, including the Live Aid concert 1985, were held here. Adjacent to the main stadium, which holds 78,000 people, are the Wembley indoor arena (which holds about 10,000, depending on the event) and conference centre.

wen *n.* a benign tumour on the skin, especially of the scalp. [Old English]

Wenceslas, St /ˈwensəslæs/ 907–929. Duke of Bohemia who attempted to Christianize his people and was murdered by his brother. He is patron saint of Czechoslovakia and the 'good King Wenceslas' of a popular carol. Feast day 28 Sept.

wench *n.* (*archaic*) a girl or young woman. [from Old English *wencel* = child]

wend *v.t.* **wend one's way**, to go. [Old English = turn]

Wends /wendz/ the NW Slavonic peoples who settled E of the rivers Elbe and Saale in the 6th–8th centuries. By the 12th century most had been forcibly Christianized and absorbed by invading Germans; a few preserved their identity and survive as the Sorbs of Lusatia (East Germany/Poland).

Wendy house /ˈwendɪ/ a children's small, houselike structure for playing in. [character in J M Barrie's *Peter Pan* (1904)]

went past of **go**[1].

Wentworth /ˈwentwəθ/ William Charles 1790–1872. Australian politician, the son of D'Arcy Wentworth (*c.*1762–1827), surgeon of the penal settlement on Norfolk Island. In 1855 he was in Britain to steer the New South Wales constitution through Parliament, and campaigned for Australian federalism and self-government.

wept past and past participle of **weep**.

were *v.t.* see ◊**be**.

weren't /wɜ:nt/ (*colloquial*) = were not.

werewolf /ˈwɪəwʊlf/ *n.* (or **werwolf** *plural* **werewolves**) a mythical being who at times changes from a person to a wolf. The symptoms of ◊**porphyria** may have fostered the legends. [Old English; first element perhaps from *wer* = man from Latin *vir*]

wergild *n.* or **wergeld** in Anglo-Saxon and Germanic law during the Middle Ages, the compensation paid by a murderer to the relatives of the victim, its value dependent on the social rank of the deceased. It originated in European tribal society as a substitute for the blood feud (essentially a form of ◊vendetta), and was replaced by punishments imposed by courts of law during the 10th and 11th centuries. [Old English *wer* = man and *geld* = payment]

Werner /ˈveənə/ Abraham Gottlob 1750–1815. German geologist, one of the first to classify minerals systematically. He also developed the later discarded theory of neptunianism, i.e. that the Earth was initially covered by water, with every mineral in suspension: as the water receded, layers of rocks 'crystallized'.

Wesker /ˈweskə/ Arnold 1932– . English playwright. His socialist beliefs were reflected in the successful trilogy *Chicken Soup with Barley*, *Roots*, and *I'm Talking About Jerusalem* 1958–60. He established a catchphrase with *Chips with Everything* 1962.

Wesley /ˈwesli/ Charles 1707–1788. English Methodist, brother of John ◊Wesley and one of the original Methodists at Oxford. He became a principal preacher and theologian of the Wesleyan Methodists, and wrote some 6,500 hymns, including 'Jesu, lover of my soul'.

Wesley John 1703–1791. English founder of ◊Methodism. When the pulpits of the Church of England were closed to him and his followers, he took the gospel to the people. For 50 years he rode about the country on horseback, preaching daily, largely in the open air. His sermons became the doctrinal standard of the Wesleyan Methodist Church.

Wesleyan /ˈwezliən/ *adj.* (*historical*) of the Protestant denomination founded by John Wesley. —*n.* a member of this denomination. [from J *Wesley*]

Wessex /ˈwesɪks/ the kingdom of the West Saxons in Britain, said to have been founded by Cerdic about AD 500, covering present-day Hampshire, Dorset, Wiltshire, Berkshire, Somerset, and Devon. In 829 Egbert established West Saxon supremacy over all England. Thomas ◊Hardy used the term Wessex in his novels for the SW counties of England.

west *n.* 1. the point of the horizon where the Sun sets at the equinoxes, opposite east; the compass point corresponding to this; the direction in which this lies. 2. (usually **West**) the western part of a country etc.; European civilization; the non-Communist States of Europe and North America. —*adj.* towards, at, or facing the west; (of a wind) blowing from the west. —*adv.* towards, at, or near the west. —**go west**, (*slang*) to be killed or destroyed etc. **West Country**, south-western England. **West End**, the part of London near Piccadilly, containing famous theatres, restaurants, shops etc. **West Side**, (*US*) the western part of Manhattan. **west-north-west, west-south-west** *adjs.* & *advs.* midway between west and north-west or south-west; (*ns.*) the compass point in this position. [Old English]

West Benjamin 1738–1820. American Neo-Classical painter, active in London from 1763. He enjoyed the patronage of George III for many years and painted historical pictures.

West Mae 1892–1980. US vaudeville, stage, and film actress. She wrote her own dialogue, setting herself up as a provocative sex symbol and the mistress of verbal innuendo. She appeared on Broadway in *Sex* 1926, *Drag* 1927, and *Diamond Lil* 1928, which was the basis of the film (with Cary Grant) *She Done Him Wrong* 1933. Her other films include *I'm No Angel* 1933, *Going to Town* 1934, *My Little Chickadee* 1944 (with W C Fields), *Myra Breckenridge* 1969, and *Sextette* 1977. Both her plays and her films led to legal battles over censorship.

Between two evils, I always pick the one I never tried before.

Mae West
Klondike Annie

West Rebecca. Pen name of Cicily Isabel Fairfield 1892–1983. British journalist and novelist, an active feminist from

West The journalist and novelist Rebecca West took her pen-name from a character in Ibsen's play Rosmersholm.

1911. *The Meaning of Treason* 1959 deals with the spies Burgess and Maclean. Her novels include *The Fountain Overflows* 1956. She was made a Dame of the British Empire in 1959.

West African Economic Community an international organization established in 1975 to end barriers in trade and to achieve cooperation in development; members include Burkina Faso, Ivory Coast, Mali, Mauritania, Niger, and Senegal; Benin and Togo have observer status.

West, American the Great Plains region of the USA to the E of the Rocky Mountains from Canada to Mexico.

West Bank area (5,879 sq km/2,270 sq mi) on the W bank of the river Jordan; population (1988) 866,000. The West Bank was taken by the Jordanian army in 1948 at the end of the Arab-Israeli war that followed the creation of the state of Israel; and was captured by Israel during the Six-Day War 5–10 June 1967. The continuing Israeli occupation and settlement of the area has created tensions with the Arab population.

West Bengal /ben'gɔ:l/ state of NE India; **area** 87,900 sq km/33,929 sq mi; **capital** Calcutta;; **physical** occupies the W part of the vast alluvial plain created by the rivers Ganges and Brahmaputra, with the Hooghly river; annual rainfall in excess of 250 cm/100 in; **population** (1981) 54,486,000; **history** created 1947 from the former British province of Bengal, with later territories added: Cooch Behar 1950, Chandernagore 1954, and part of Bihar 1956.

westering *adj.* (of the Sun) nearing the W.

Westerlies *n.pl.* prevailing winds from the W that occur in both hemispheres between latitudes of about 35° and 60°. Unlike the ◊trade winds, they are very variable and produce stormy weather.

westerly /'westəlɪ/ *adj. & adv.* in a western position or direction (of a wind) blowing from the W (approximately).

western /'westən/ *adj.* of or in the W. —*n.* a film or novel about life in western North America during the wars with the Indians, or involving cowboys etc. The western became established in written form with novels such as *The Virginian* 1902 by Owen Wister (1860–1938) and *Riders of the Purple Sage* 1912 by Zane Grey. —**Western Church**, the churches of western Christendom as distinct from the Eastern or Orthodox Church. —**westernmost** *adj.* [Old English]

Western Australia /ɒ'streɪlɪə/ state of Australia; **area** 2,525,500 sq km/974,843 sq mi; **capital** Perth; **towns** main port Fremantle, Bunbury, Geraldton, Kalgoorlie-Boulder, Albany; **population** (1987) 1,478,000; **history** a short-lived convict settlement at King George Sound 1826; the state founded at Perth in 1829 by Captain James Stirling (1791–1865); self-government 1890; state 1901.

westerner *n.* a native or inhabitant of the W.

Western European Union (WEU) an organization established in 1955 as a consultative forum for military issues among the W European governments: Belgium, France, Holland, Italy, Luxembourg, the UK, West Germany, and (from 1988) Spain and Portugal.

Western Isles island area of Scotland, comprising the Outer Hebrides (Lewis, Harris, North and South Uist, and Barra); unofficially the Inner and Outer Hebrides generally; **area** 2,900 sq km/1,120 sq mi; **administrative headquarters** Stornoway on Lewis; **population** (1987) 31,000.

westernize /'westənaɪz/ *v.t.* to make (an Oriental person, etc.) more like the West in ideas and institutions etc. —**westernization** /-'zeɪʃən/ *n.*

Western Sahara /sə'hɑ:rə/ formerly **Spanish Sahara** disputed territory in NW Africa bounded to the N by Morocco, to the W and S by Mauritania, and to the E by the Atlantic Ocean; **area** 266,800 sq km/103,011 sq mi; **capital** La'Youn (Arabic *al-Aaiún*); **population** (1988) 181,400; another estimated 165,000 live in refugee camps near Tindouf, SW Algeria, **language** Arabic; **religion** Sunni Muslim; **political system** administered by Morocco.

Western Samoa see ◊Samoa, Western.

West Germany see ◊Germany, West.

West Glamorgan /glə'mɔ:gən/ county in SW Wales; **area** 820 sq km/317 sq mi; **administrative headquarters** Swansea; **population** (1987) 363,000; **language** 16% Welsh, English.

West Indies /'ɪndɪz/ archipelago of about 1,200 islands, dividing the Atlantic from the Gulf of Mexico and the Caribbean. The islands are divided into: **Bahamas**; **Greater Antilles** Cuba, Hispaniola (Haiti, Dominican Republic), Jamaica, and Puerto Rico; **Lessesr Antilles** Aruba, Netherlands, Antilles, Trinidad and Tobago, the Windward Islands (Grenada, Barbados, St Vincent, St Lucia, Martinique, Dominica, Guadeloupe), the Leeward Islands (Montserrat, Antigua, St Christopher (St Kitts)–Nevis, Barbuda, Anguilla, St Martin, British and US Virgin Islands), and many smaller islands.

West Indies, Federation of the a federal union created in 1958–62 comprising Antigua, Barbados, Dominica, Grenada, Jamaica, Montserrat, St Christopher (St Kitts)–Nevis and Anguilla, St Lucia, St Vincent, and Trinidad and Tobago. This federation came to an end when first Jamaica and then Trinidad and Tobago withdrew.

westing *n.* (*nautical* etc.) **1.** a distance travelled or measured westward. **2..** a westerly direction.

Westinghouse /'westɪŋhaʊs/ George 1846–1914. US inventor and founder of the Westinghouse Corporation 1886. After service in the Civil War he patented a powerful air brake for trains in 1869. His invention allowed trains to run more safely with greater loads at greater speeds. In the 1880s he turned his attention to the generation of electricity. Unlike Thomas ◊Edison, Westinghouse introduced alternating current (AC) into his power stations.

West Irian /'ɪrɪən/ former name of ◊Irian Jaya.

Westland affair /'westlənd/ in UK politics, the events surrounding the takeover of the British Westland helicopter company in 1985–86. There was much political acrimony in the cabinet and allegations of malpractice. The affair led to the resignation of two cabinet ministers: Michael Heseltine, minister of defence, and the secretary for trade and industry, Leon Brittan.

Westman Islands a small group of islands off the S coast of Iceland. In 1973 volcanic eruption caused the population of 5,200 to be temporarily evacuated, and added 2.5 sq km/1 sq mi to the islands' area. Heimaey is one of Iceland's chief fishing ports.

Westmeath /west'mi:ð/ inland county of Leinster province, Republic of Ireland; **area** 1,760 sq km/679 sq mi; **county town** Mullingar; **population** (1986) 63,000.

West Midlands /'mɪdləndz/ metropolitan county in central England, created in 1974, originally administered by an elected council; its powers reverted to district councils from 1986; **area** 900 sq km/347 sq mi; **administrative headquarters** Birmingham; **population** (1987) 2,624,000.

Westminster Abbey a Gothic church in central London, officially the Collegiate Church of St Peter. It was built in 1050–1745 and consecrated under Edward the Confessor in 1065. The W towers are by ◊Hawksmoor 1740. Since William I nearly all English monarchs have been crowned in the abbey, and several are buried there; many poets are buried or commemorated there, at Poets' Corner.

Westphalia /west'feɪlɪə/ independent medieval duchy, incorporated in Prussia by the Congress of Vienna 1815, and made a province in 1816 with Münster as its capital. Since 1946 it has been part of the *Land* (region) of ◊North Rhine–Westphalia.

Westphalia, Treaty of the agreement made in 1648 ending the ◊Thirty Years' War. The peace marked the end of the supremacy of the Holy Roman Empire and the emergence of France as a dominant power. It recognized the sovereignty of the German states, Switzerland, and the Netherlands; Lutherans, Calvinists, and Roman Catholics were given equal rights.

West Point /west 'pɔɪnt/ a former fort in New York State, on the Hudson River, 80 km/50 mi N of New York City, site of the US Military Academy (commonly referred to as West Point), established in 1802. Women were admitted in 1976. West Point has been a military post since 1778.

West Sussex /'sʌsɪks/ county on the S coast of England; **area** 2,020 sq km/780 sq mi; **administrative headquarters** Chichester; **physical** the Weald, South Downs; rivers: Arun, West Rother, Adur; **population** (1987) 700,000.

West Virginia /və'dʒɪnɪə/ state of the E USA; nickname Mountain State; **area** 62,900 sq km/24,279 sq mi; **capital** Charleston; **physical** Allegheny Mountains; Ohio river; **population** (1986) 1,919,000; **history** mound builders 6th century; explorers and fur traders 1670s; German settlements 1730s; industrial development early 19th century; on the secession of Virginia from the Union in 1862, West Virginians dissented, and formed a new state in 1863; industrial expansion accompanied by labour strife in the early 20th century.

westward /'westwəd/ adj. & (also **westwards**) adv. towards the W. —n. a westward direction or region.

West Yorkshire /'jɔːksə/ metropolitan county in NE England, created in 1976, originally administered by an elected metropolitan council; its powers reverted to district councils from 1986; **area** 2,040 sq km/787 sq mi; **administrative headquarters** Wakefield; **population** (1987) 2,052,000.

wet adj. **1.** soaked, covered, or moistened with water or other liquid. **2.** (of weather etc.) rainy. **3.** (of ink or paint etc.) not yet dried. **4.** used with water. **5.** (*slang*) lacking good sense or mental vitality, feeble, dull. —v.t. (-tt-; past and *past participle* wet or wetted) to make wet. —n. **1.** liquid that wets something. **2.** rainy weather. **3.** (*slang*) a dull or feeble person. **4.** (*slang*) a drink. **5.** in UK politics, a derogatory term used to describe a moderate or left-wing

supporter of the Conservative Party. —**wet behind the ears,** immature, inexperienced. **wet blanket,** a person or thing damping or discouraging enthusiasm, cheerfulness etc. **wet dream,** an erotic dream with involuntary emission of semen. **wet-nurse** n. a woman employed to suckle another's child; (v.t.) to suckle thus; to treat as if helpless. **wet suit,** a rubber garment worn by skin-divers etc. to keep warm. —**wetly** adv., **wetness** n. [Old English]

weta a flightless insect *Deinacrida rugosa* resembling a large grasshopper (8.5 cm/3.5 in long), found on offshore islands of New Zealand.

wether /'weðə/ n. a castrated ram. [Old English]

Wexford /'weksfəd/ county in the Republic of Ireland, province of Leinster; **area** 2,350 sq km/907 sq mi; **county town** Wexford; **population** (1986) 102,000.

Weyden /'waɪdən/ Rogier van der c.1399–1464. Netherlandish painter, official painter to the city of Brussels from 1436. He painted portraits and religious subjects, such as *The Last Judgement* about 1450 (Hôtel-Dieu, Beaune). His refined style had considerable impact on Netherlandish painting.

Weygand /'veɪgɒn/ Maxime 1867–1965. French general. In 1940, as French commander-in-chief, he advised surrender to Germany, and was subsequently high commissioner of N Africa 1940–41. He was a prisoner in Germany 1942–45, and was arrested after his return to France; he was released in 1946, and in 1949 the sentence of national infamy was quashed.

whack v.t. (*colloquial*) to strike or beat forcefully. —n. **1.** (*colloquial*) a sharp or resounding blow **2.** (*slang*) a share. —**have a whack at,** (*slang*) to attempt.

whacked adj. (*colloquial*) tired out.

whacking adj. (*slang*) very large. —adv. (*slang*) very (*great* etc.).

whale /weɪl/ n. a large marine mammal of the order Cetacea, hunted for oil, whalebone etc. nearly to the point of extinction, see ◊whaling. —v.i. to hunt whales. —**a whale of a time,** (*colloquial*) an exceedingly good or fine etc. time. **whale oil,** oil from the blubber of whales. [Old English]

Whale James 1886–1957. English film director. He initially went to Hollywood to film his stage success *Journey's End* 1930, and went on to direct four horror films: *Frankenstein* 1931, *The Old Dark House* 1932, *The Invisible Man* 1933, and *Bride of Frankenstein* 1935. He also directed *Showboat* 1936.

whalebone n. an elastic, horny substance from the upper jaw of some whales, formerly used as stiffening.

whaler /'weɪlə/ n. a person or ship engaged in hunting whales.

whale

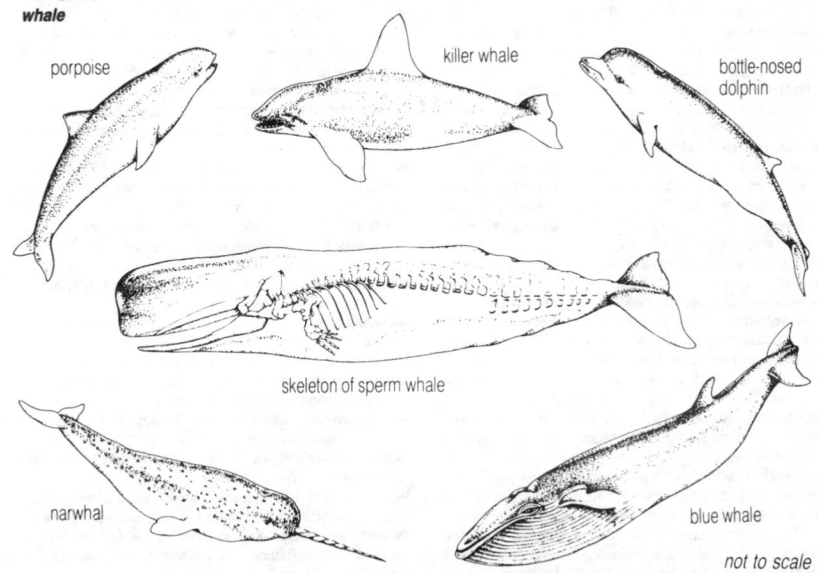

porpoise

killer whale

bottle-nosed dolphin

skeleton of sperm whale

narwhal

blue whale

not to scale

whaling *n.* the hunting of whales. Whales are hunted for whale oil which is used for food and cosmetics; for the large reserve of oil in the head of the sperm whale, which is used in the leather industry; and for **ambergris**, a waxlike substance from the intestines, used in making perfumes. There are synthetic substitutes for all these products. Whales are also killed for their meat, sold as pet food in the USA and Europe, and eaten by humans in Japan. The International Whaling Commission, established in 1946, failed to enforce quotas on whale killing until world concern about their possible extinction mounted in the 1970s. By the end of the following decade, 90% of blue, fin, humpback, and sperm whales had been wiped out. Low reproduction rates mean that protected species are slow to recover. After 1986 only Iceland, Japan, Norway, and the USSR continued with limited whaling for 'scientific purposes', but pirates also operate.

wham interjection expressing forcible impact.

whang *v.t./i.* to strike heavily and loudly. —*n.* a whanging sound or blow.

wharf /wɔːf/ *n.* (*plural* **wharfs**) a platform to which a ship may be moored to load and unload. —*v.t.* to moor (a ship) at or store (goods) on a wharf. [Old English]

wharfage *n.* accommodation at a wharf; the fee for this.

wharfinger /'wɔːfɪndʒə/ *n.* the owner or keeper of a wharf.

Wharton /'(h)wɔːtn/ Edith (born Jones) 1862–1937. US novelist. Her work, influenced by her friend Henry James, was mostly set in New York society. It includes *The House of Mirth* 1905, which made her reputation; the grim, uncharacteristic novel of New England *Ethan Frome* 1911; *The Custom of the Country* 1913, and *The Age of Innocence* 1920. Her work is known for its subtlety and form.

what *interrog. adj.* asking for a choice from an indefinite number (*what books have you read?*) or for a statement of amount, number, or kind (*what stores have we got?*); (*colloquial*) which? (*what book have you chosen?*). —*exclam. adj.* how great or remarkable. —*rel. adj.* the or any . . . that. —*interrog. pron.* 1. what thing(s)? 2. (a request for a remark to be repeated) what did you say? —*exclam. pron.* what thing(s)!, how much! etc. —*rel. pron.* that or those which; the thing(s) or anything that. —*adv.* to what extent or degree. —*int.* expressing surprise. —**what about**, what is the news about (a subject); what is your opinion of; how would you deal with; shall we do or have etc. **what d'you call it** *or* **what's his** (*or* its) **name?** a substitute for a name that one cannot remember. **what for?** for what reason or purpose? (*give a person what for*, (*slang*) to punish or scold him or her). **what have you**, anything else similar. **what not**, other similar things. **what's what**, what is useful or important, etc. **what with**, because of (various specified causes). [Old English]

whatever /wɒt'evə/ *adj. & pron.* 1. = what (in relative uses) with emphasis on indefiniteness. 2. though anything. 3. (with negative or interrogative) at all, of any kind.

whatnot *n.* 1. something trivial or indefinite. 2. a stand with shelves for small objects.

whatsoever /wɒtsəʊ'evə/ *adj. & pron.* = what.

wheat *n.* a cereal plant derived from the wild *Triticum*, a grass native to the Middle East. It is the chief cereal used in breadmaking and is widely cultivated in temperate climates suited to its growth. Wheat is killed by frost, and damp renders the grain soft, so warm, dry regions produce the most valuable grain. [Old English]

wheatear *n.* a small migratory bird of the genus *Oenanthe*, especially a species with a white belly and rump.

wheaten *adj.* made of wheat.

wheatmeal *n.* wholemeal flour made from wheat.

Wheatstone /'(h)wiːtstən/ Charles 1802–1875. English physicist and inventor. With William Cooke, he patented a railway telegraph in 1837, and, developing an idea of Samuel Christie, devised the **Wheatstone bridge**, an electrical network for measuring resistance. Originally a musical-instrument maker, he invented the harmonica and the concertina.

wheedle *v.t.* to coax; to persuade or obtain by coaxing.

wheel *n.* 1. a circular frame or disc arranged to revolve on an axle and used to facilitate the motion of a vehicle or for various mechanical purposes; a wheel-like thing. 2. a machine, etc. of which a wheel is an essential part. 3. motion like that of a wheel; movement of a line of men that

pivots on one end. —*v.t./i.* 1. to turn or cause to turn like a wheel; to change direction and face another way. 2. to push or pull (a bicycle or cart etc. with wheels, or its contents) along. 3. to move in circles or curves. —**at the wheel**, driving a vehicle or directing a ship's course; in control of affairs. **on (oiled) wheels**, smoothly. **wheel and deal**, (*US*) to engage in political or commercial scheming so as to exert influence. **wheel spin**, rotation of a vehicle's wheels without traction. **wheels within wheels**, secret or indirect motives and influences interacting with one another. [Old English]

wheel and axle a simple machine with a rope wound round an axle connected to a larger wheel with another rope attached to its rim. Pulling on the wheel rope (applying an effort) lifts a load attached to the axle rope. The velocity ratio of the machine (distance moved by load divided by distance moved by effort) is equal to the ratio of the wheel radius to the axle radius.

wheelbarrow *n.* an open container for moving small loads in gardening, building etc., with a wheel beneath one end and two handles (by which it is pushed) at the other.

wheelbase *n.* the distance between the axles of a vehicle.

wheelchair *n.* a disabled person's chair on wheels.

wheelhouse *n.* a steersman's shelter.

wheelie *n.* the stunt of riding a bicycle or motor cycle for a short distance with the front wheel off the ground.

wheelwright *n.* a maker or repairer of wooden wheels.

wheeze *v.i.* to breathe with an audible, hoarse, whistling sound. —*n.* 1. a sound of wheezing. 2. (*slang*) a clever scheme. —**wheezy** *adj.* [probably from Old Norse = hiss]

whelk *n.* a type of marine gastropod with a thick spiral shell. Whelks are scavengers, and will eat other shellfish. The largest grow to 40 cm/16 in long. Tropical species are very colourful. The common whelk *Buccinum undatum* is widely distributed round the North Sea and Atlantic.

whelm *v.t.* (*poetic*) to engulf, to crush with a weight.

whelp *n.* 1. a young dog, a pup. 2. (*archaic*) a cub. —*v.t./i.* to give birth to (a whelp or whelps). [Old English]

when *interrog. adv.* at what time?, on what occasion?, how soon? —*rel. adv.* (with reference to time) at or on which. —*conj.* 1. at the or any time that; as soon as. 2. although; considering that; since. —*pron.* what or which time. —*n.* the time, the occasion (*fix the where and when*). [Old English]

whence *interrog. adv.* from what place or source? —*rel. adv.* and *conj.* (with reference to place) from which; to the place from which. —*pron.* what place?; which place. —*n.* source. [Old English]

whenever /wen'evə/ *conj. & adv.* at whatever time, on whatever occasion; every time that.

whensoever /wensəʊ'evə/ *conj. & adv.* = whenever.

where /weə/ *interrog. adv.* in or to what place or position (*literal* or *figurative*)?; in what direction?; in what respect? —*rel. adv.* and *conj.* (with reference to place) in or to which; in the direction, part, or respect, in which; and there. —*pron.* what place? —*n.* the place. [Old English]

whereabouts /weərə'baʊts/ *adv.* approximately where. —/'weər-/ *n.* (as *singular* or *plural*) a person's or thing's location roughly defined.

whereas /weər'æz/ *conj.* 1. in contrast or comparison with the fact that. 2. (especially in legal preambles) taking into consideration the fact that.

whereby /weə'baɪ/ *conj.* by what or which means.

wherefore *adv.* (*archaic*) for what reason?; for which reason. —*n.* a reason.

wherein /weər'ɪn/ *conj.* (*formal*) in what or which place or respect.

whereof /weər'ɒv/ *adv. & conj.* (*formal*) of what or which.

whereupon /weərə'pɒn/ *conj.* immediately after which.

wherever /weər'evə/ *adv.* (*or* **wheresoever**) in or to whatever place. —*conj.* in every place that.

wherewithal /'weəwɪðɔːl/ *n.* (*colloquial*) the money or things needed for a purpose.

wherry /'werɪ/ *n.* a light rowing boat usually for carrying passengers; a large light barge.

whet *v.t.* (**-tt-**) 1. to sharpen by rubbing against a stone, etc. 2. to stimulate (an appetite or interest). [Old English]

whether /'weðə/ *conj.* introducing the first or both of alternative possibilities. —**whether or no**, whether it is so or not. [Old English]

whetstone *n.* a shaped stone for sharpening tools.

whew /hwju:/ interjection expressing surprise, consternation, or relief.

Whewell /'hju:əl/ William 1794–1866. British physicist and philosopher who coined the term 'scientist' along with such words as 'Eocene' and 'Miocene', 'electrode', 'cathode', and 'anode'. Most of his career was connected with Cambridge University, where he became the Master of Trinity College. His most enduring influence rests on two works of great scholarship, *The History of the Inductive Sciences* 1837 and *The Philosophy of the Inductive Sciences* 1840.

whey /weɪ/ *n.* the watery liquid left when milk forms curds. [Old English]

which *interrog. adj.* asking for a choice from a definite or known number (*which way shall we go?*). —*rel. adj.* (usually with noun) being the one just referred to, and this or these (*for ten years, during which time he spoke to nobody*). —*interrog. pron.* which person(s) or thing(s)? —*rel. pron.* which thing(s), used (especially of an incidental description rather than a defining one) of the thing, or animal, or (*archaic*) person referred to (*the house, which is empty, has been damaged; Our Father, which art in heaven*), or in place of *that* after *in* or *that.* [Old English]

whichever /wɪtʃ'evə/ *adj. & pron.* any which, that or those which.

whiff *n.* 1. a puff of air, smoke, or odour; a trace of scandal, etc. 2. a small cigar.

Whig /wɪg/ *n.* (*historical*) 1. a 17th-century Scottish Presbyterian. 2. a member of a former British political group. 3. (*US*) a supporter of the American Revolution. 4. (*US*) a member of a political party of 1834–56, succeeded by the Republicans. —*adj.* of the Whigs. —**Whiggery** *n.* [probably abbreviation of *whiggamer*, Scottish rebel of 1648].

while *n.* a space of time, the time spent in some action. —*conj.* 1. during the time that, for as long as, at the same time as. 2. in spite of the fact that, at the same time. —*v.t.* (with *away*) to pass (time etc.) in a leisurely or interesting manner. —*adv.* (preceded by *how* etc.) during which. —**between whiles**, in the intervals. **for a while**, for some time. **in a while**, soon. **once in a while**, occasionally. **the while**, during some other action. **worth (one's) while**, worth the time or effort spent. [Old English]

whiles /waɪlz/ *conj.* (*archaic*) while.

whilom /'waɪləm/ *adv.* (*archaic*) formerly. —*adj.* (*archaic*) former.

whilst /waɪlst/ *adv. & conj.* while.

whim *n.* a sudden unreasoning desire or impulse, a caprice.

whimper *v.i.* to make feeble querulous or frightened sounds. —*n.* such a sound.

whimsical /'wɪmzɪkəl/ *adj.* 1. impulsive and playful. 2. fanciful, quaint. —**whimsicality** /-'kælɪtɪ/ *n.*, **whimsically** *adv.*

whimsy /'wɪmzɪ/ *n.* a whim. [related to *whim-wham* = toy]

whin *n.* (in *singular* or *plural*) furze.

whinchat *n.* a small, brownish songbird *Saxicola rubetra.*

whine *v.t./i.* 1. to make a long-drawn complaining cry like that of a child or dog. 2. to make a similar shrill sound. 3. to complain in a petty or feeble way; to utter thus. —*n.* a whining cry, sound, or complaint. —**whiner** *n.*, **whiny** *adj.* [Old English]

whinge /wɪndʒ/ *v.i.* to whine, to grumble persistently. [Old English]

whinny /'wɪnɪ/ *n.* a gentle or joyful neigh. —*v.i.* to give a whinny.

whip *n.* 1. a cord or strip of leather fastened to a stick that serves as a handle, used for urging animals on or for striking a person or animal in punishment. 2. an official of a political party in Parliament with authority to maintain discipline among members of his party; his written notice requesting attendance at a division etc. (variously underlined according to the degree of urgency: *three-line whip*); party discipline and instructions. 3. a food made with whipped cream, etc. 4. a whipper-in. —*v.t./i.* (**-pp-**) 1. to strike or urge on with a whip. 2. to beat (cream or eggs etc.) into a froth. 3. to move suddenly, or unexpectedly, or rapidly. 4. (*slang*) to excel, to defeat. 5. to bind with spirally wound twine. 6. to sew with overcast stitches. —**have the whip hand**, to have the advantage or control. **whip in**, to bring (hounds) together. **whip on**, to urge into action. **whip-round** *n.* (*colloquial*) an appeal for contributions from a group of people. **whip**

up, to incite, to stir up. [probably from Middle Low German and Middle Dutch *wippen* = swing]

whipcord *n.* 1. cord made of tightly twisted strands. 2. a kind of twilled fabric with prominent ridges.

whiplash *n.* the lash of a whip. —**whiplash injury**, injury to the neck caused by a jerk of the head in a collision.

whipper-in *n.* a huntsman's assistant who manages hounds.

whippersnapper /'wɪpəsnæpə/ *n.* a small child; an insignificant but presumptuous person.

whippet /'wɪpɪt/ *n.* a breed of dog resembling a small greyhound. It grows to 56 cm/22 in at the shoulder, and 9 kg/20 lb in weight. Whippets were developed by northern English colliers for racing, probably by crossing a terrier and a greyhound.

whipping boy a scapegoat; (*historical*) a boy educated with a young prince and punished for the prince's faults.

whipping top a top kept spinning by blows of a lash.

Whipple /'(h)wɪpl/ Fred Lawrence 1906– . US astronomer, whose hypothesis in 1949 that the nucleus of a comet is like a dirty snowball was confirmed in 1986 by space-probe studies of ◊Halley's comet. He was director of the Smithsonian Astrophysical Observatory 1955–73.

Whipple George 1878–1976. US physiologist whose research interest concerned the formation of haemoglobin in the blood. He showed that anaemic dogs, kept under restricted diets, responded well to a liver regime, and that their haemoglobin quickly regenerated. This work led to a cure for pernicious anaemia.

whippoorwill /'wɪpuəwɪl/ *n.* the North American insectivorous nightjar *Caprimulgus vociferus*, so called from its cry. It is about 25 cm/10 in long, and is mottled brown.

whippy *adj.* flexible, springy. —**whippiness** *n.*

Whipsnade /'(h)wɪpsneɪd/ a zoo in Bedfordshire, England, 5 km/3 mi S of Dunstable, opened in 1931, where wild animals and birds are bred and exhibited in conditions resembling their natural state.

whipstock *n.* the handle of a whip.

whirl *v.t./i.* 1. to swing round and round, to revolve rapidly. 2. to send or travel swiftly in a curved course. 3. to convey or go rapidly in a vehicle. 4. (of the brain, senses etc.) to seem to spin round. —*n.* 1. a whirling movement. 2. a state of intense activity or confusion. [from Old Norse *hvirfill* = circle or Middle Low German and Middle Dutch *wervel* = spindle]

whirligig /'wɜ:lɪgɪg/ *n.* 1. a spinning or whirling toy. 2. a merry-go-round. 3. a revolving motion. [from *gig* = whipping top]

whirlpool *n.* a circular eddy of water, often drawing floating objects towards its centre.

whirlwind *n.* 1. a whirling mass or column of air. 2. (*attributive*) very rapid.

whirlybird /'wɜ:lɪbɜ:d/ *n.* (*slang*) a helicopter.

whirr *n.* a continuous rapid buzzing or softly clicking sound. —*v.i.* to make this sound.

whisk *v.t./i.* 1. to brush or sweep lightly from a surface. 2. to move with a quick, light, sweeping movement; to convey or go rapidly. 3. to beat (eggs etc.) into a froth. —*n.* 1. a whisking movement. 2. a utensil for beating eggs etc. 3. a bunch of strips of straw etc. tied to a handle, used for flicking flies away.

whisker *n.* 1. (usually in *plural*) the hair growing on a man's face, especially on the cheeks. 2. bristle(s) on the face of a cat etc. 3. (*colloquial*) a very small distance. —**whiskery** *adj.*

whiskey *n.* variant of **whisky** (especially *US* and of Irish whisky).

whisky *n.* a distilled spirit made from cereals: Scotch and Irish whisky usually from barley, and North American whiskey or bourbon from maize or rye. Scotch is usually blended; pure malt whisky is more expensive. Whisky is generally aged in wooden casks for 4–12 years. [abbreviation of obsolete *whiskybae*, from Gaelic *uisge beatha*, water of life]

whisper *v.t./i.* 1. to speak or utter softly, using the breath but not the vocal cords. 2. to converse confidentially or secretly; to spread (a tale) thus. 3. (of leaves or fabric etc.) to rustle. —*n.* 1. a whispering sound or remark; whispering speech. 2. a rumour. —**whispering gallery**, a gallery or dome in which the slightest sound

Whitby *A view of Whitby about 1900. Now a fishing port and resort, Whitby was an ecclesiastical centre in the Middle Ages.*

made at a particular point can be heard at another far off. [Old English]

whist *n.* a card-game of mingled skill and chance, using a pack of 52 cards, usually played between two pairs of players. —**whist drive**, a progressive whist party, usually with prizes. [from earlier *whisk*, influenced by the cry of *whist!* for silence in the game]

whistle /'wɪsəl/ *n.* **1.** a clear, shrill sound made by forcing the breath through a small hole between nearly closed lips; a similar sound made by a bird, wind, missile, or instrument. **2.** an instrument used to produce this sound as a signal, etc. —*v.t./i.* to emit a whistle; to summon or signal thus; to produce (a tune) by whistling. —**whistle for**, (*colloquial*) to seek or desire in vain. **whistle stop**, (*US*) a small, unimportant town on a railway; a politician's brief pause for an electioneering speech on a tour. —**whistler** *n.* [Old English]

Whistler /'(h)wɪslə/ James Abbott McNeill 1834–1903. US painter and etcher, active in London from 1859. His riverscapes and portraits show subtle composition and colour harmonies: for example, *Arrangement in Grey and Black: Portrait of the Painter's Mother* 1871 (Louvre, Paris).

Nature is usually wrong.

James McNeill Whistler
Ten O'Clock

---

whit *n.* the least possible amount.

Whit *adj.* connected with, belonging to, or following Whit Sunday. —**Whit Sunday**, the seventh Sunday after Easter, commemorating the descent of the Holy Spirit upon the Apostles at Pentecost. [Old English = White (Sunday), probable from white robes of newly baptized; in the Western Church the festival became a date for baptisms]

Whitby /'(h)wɪtbi/ port and resort in N Yorkshire, England, on the North Sea coast; population (1981) 14,000. Industries include boatbuilding, fishing, and plastics. Remains of a Benedictine abbey built 1078 survive on the site of the original foundation by St Hilda 657, which was destroyed by the Danes 867. Captain Cook's ship *Resolution* was built in Whitby, where he had served his apprenticeship, and he sailed from here on his voyage to the Pacific in 1768.

Whitby, Synod of the council summoned by King Oswy of Northumbria in 664, which decided to adopt the Roman rather than the Celtic form of Christianity for Britain.

white /(h)waɪt/ *adj.* **1.** reflecting all light, of the colour of fresh snow or common salt; approaching this colour; pale from illness, fear, or other emotion. **2.** of the human group characterized by light-coloured skin; of or reserved for such persons. **3.** (of magic etc.) of a harmless kind. —*n.* **1.** white colour or pigment; white clothes or material. **2.** the white part of something (e. g. of the eyeball round the iris); the translucent or white part round the yolk of an egg. **3.** a white ball or piece in a game; the player using this. **4.** a white person. —**white admiral**, see ◊admiral. **white ant**, a termite. **white Christmas**, one with snow. **white coffee**, coffee with milk or cream. **white-collar worker**, one not engaged in manual labour. **white feather**, a symbol of cowardice. **white flag**, a symbol of surrender. **White Friars**, Carmelites (so called from their white cloaks). **white gold**, a pale alloy of gold with nickel etc. **white-headed boy**, a highly favoured person. **white heat**, the temperature at which metal looks white; a state of intense passion or activity. **white hope**, a person expected to achieve much. **white horses**, white-crested sea waves. **white-hot** *adj.* at white heat. **white lead**, a mixture of lead carbonate and hydrated lead oxide used as a pigment. **white lie**, a harmless or trivial untruth. **white light**, colourless light, e. g. ordinary daylight. **white noise**, noise containing many frequencies with about equal energies. **whiteout** *n.* a dense blizzard, especially in polar regions. **white pepper**, pepper made by grinding the ripe or husked berry. **white sale**, a sale of household linen. **white sauce**, a sauce of flour, melted butter, and milk or cream. **white slave**, a woman tricked or forced into prostitution. **white spirit**, light petroleum as a solvent. **white sugar**, purified sugar. **white tie**, a man's white bow tie worn with full evening dress. **white whale**, a northern whale *Delphinapterus leucas*, white when adult. —**whitely** *adv.*, **whiteness** *n.*, **whitish** *adj.* [Old English]

White *n.* a counter-revolutionary, especially during the Russian civil wars 1917–21. Originally the term described the party opposing the French Revolution, when the royalists used the white lily of the French monarchy as their badge.

White Gilbert 1720–1793. English cleric and naturalist, born at Selborne, Hampshire, and author of *Natural History and Antiquities of Selborne* 1789.

White Patrick 1912–1990. Australian novelist. He was born in London, and settled in Australia in the 1940s. His novels include *The Aunt's Story* 1948, *The Tree of Man* 1955, *Voss* 1957 (based on the 19th-century explorer Leichhardt), *The Vivisector* 1970, *The Eye of the Storm* 1973, *The Twyborn Affair* 1979, his autobiography *Flaws in the Glass* 1981, and his last work *Memoirs of Many in One* 1986. He won the Nobel Prize for Literature in 1973.

whitebait *n.* a small, silvery-white food fish, probably the young of herring, sprat etc.

whitebeam *n.* a tree *Sorbus aria* native to S Europe, usually found growing on chalk or limestone. It can reach 20 m/60 ft. It takes its name from the pinnately compound leaves, which have a dense coat of short, white hairs on the underside.

white blood cell another name for ◊leucocyte. There are at least 10 different types of white blood cell, and they are not just found in the blood. They also occur in the ◊lymph and throughout the body, where they play a role in ◊immunity.

white dwarf a small, hot ◊star, the last stage in the life of a star such as the Sun. White dwarfs have a mass similar to that of the Sun, but only 1% of the Sun's diameter, similar in size to the Earth. Most have surface temperatures of 8,000°C/14,400°F or more, hotter than the Sun, but their overall luminosities may be less than 1% of that of the Sun. They consist of degenerate matter in which gravity has packed the protons and electrons together as tightly as is physically possible, so that a spoonful of it weighs several tonnes. White dwarfs are thought to be the shrunken remains of stars that have exhausted their internal energy supplies. They slowly cool and fade over billions of years.

white elephant any useless and cumbersome gift. In Thailand the monarch would formerly present a white elephant to a person out of favour: being the country's sacred animal, it could not be used for work, and its upkeep was ruinously expensive.

whitefish *n.* any freshwater fish of the salmon family, belonging to the genus *Coregonus*. They live in deep lakes and rivers of North America, Europe, and Asia.

Whitehall /'(h)waɪt'hɔːl/ a street in central London, between Trafalgar Square and the Houses of Parliament, with many government offices and the Cenotaph war memorial.

Whitehead /'(h)waɪthed/ Robert 1823–1905. English engineer who invented the self-propelled torpedo in 1866.

Whitehorse /'(h)waɪthɔːs/ capital of Yukon Territory, Canada; population (1986) 15,199. Whitehorse is on the NW Highway. It replaced Dawson as capital in 1953.

White Horse any of several hill figures in England, including the one on Bratton Hill, Wiltshire, which commemorate Alfred the Great's victory over the Danes at Ethandun in 878; and the one at Uffington, Berkshire, 110 m/360 ft long, and probably a tribal totem of the Early Iron Age, 1st century BC.

White House /'(h)waɪthaʊs/ the official residence of the president of the USA, in Washington DC. It is a plain edifice of sandstone, built in the Italian Renaissance style 1792–99 to the designs of James Hoban, who also restored it after it was burned by the British in 1814; it was then painted white to hide the scars.

Whitehouse Mary 1910–. British media activist; as founder of the National Viewers' and Listeners' Association, she has campaigned to censor radio and television in their treatment of sex and violence.

white knight in business, a company invited by the target of a takeover bid to make a rival bid. The company invited to bid is usually one that is already on good terms with the target company.

Whitelaw /'(h)waɪtlɔː/ William, Viscount Whitelaw 1918–. British Conservative politician. As secretary of state for Northern Ireland he introduced the concept of power sharing. He was Chief Conservative whip 1964–70, and leader of the House of Commons 1970–72. He became secretary of state for employment 1973–74, but failed to conciliate the trade unions. He was chair of the Conservative Party in 1974, and home secretary 1979–83, when he was made a peer. He resigned in 1988.

whiten /'waɪtən/ *v.t./i.* to make or become white or whiter.

White Paper in the UK and some other countries, an official document that expresses government policy on an issue. It is usually preparatory to the introduction of a parliamentary bill (a proposed act of Parliament). Its name derives from its having fewer pages than a government 'blue book', and therefore needing no blue paper cover.

White Russia English translation of ◊Byelorussia, a republic of the USSR.

White terror the general term used by socialists and Marxists to describe a right-wing counter-revolution, for example, the attempts by the Chinese Guomindang to massacre the communists 1927–31.

whitethroat *n.* a bird *Sylvia communis* of the warbler group, found in scrub, hedges, and wood clearings of Eurasia in summer, migrating to Africa in winter. It is about 14 cm/5.5 in long. The female is dull brown, but the male is reddish-brown, with a grey head and white throat, and performs an acrobatic aerial display during courtship. The **lesser whitethroat** *Sylvia curruca* is a little smaller, and a shyer bird.

whitewash *n.* 1. a solution of lime or whiting for whitening walls etc. 2. the concealing of mistakes or faults. —*v.t.* 1. to cover with whitewash. 2. to conceal the mistakes or faults of or in.

whitewood *n.* a light-coloured wood, especially one prepared for staining etc.

whither /'wɪðə/ *adv.* (*archaic*) to what place or state?; (preceded by *place* etc.) to which. —*conj.* (*archaic*) to the or any place to which; and thither. [Old English]

whiting[1] /'waɪtɪŋ/ *n.* a predatory fish *Merlangius merlangus* common in shallow, sandy N European waters. It grows to 70 cm/2.3 ft. [from Middle Dutch]

whiting[2] *n.* or **whitening** ground chalk used in whitewashing, plate-cleaning etc.

Whitlam /'(h)wɪtləm/ Gough (Edward) 1916–. Australian politician, leader of the Labor Party 1967–78 and prime minister 1972–75. He cultivated closer relations with Asia, attempted redistribution of wealth, and raised loans to increase national ownership of industry and resources. When the opposition blocked finance bills in the Senate, following a crisis of confidence, Whitlam refused to call a general election, and was dismissed by the governor general (Sir John Kerr). He was defeated in the subsequent general election by Malcolm ◊Fraser.

whitleyism /'wɪtliɪzəm/ a term used to describe the process of ◊collective bargaining in committees, when employers and employees are equally represented, under the leadership of an independent chairperson, with the aim of reaching unanimous agreement, if necessary by compromise on both sides.

whitlow /'wɪtləʊ/ *n.* a small abscess under or near a nail.

Whitman /'(h)wɪtmən/ Walt(er) 1819–1892. US poet who published *Leaves of Grass* 1855, which contains the symbolic 'Song of Myself'. It used unconventional free verse (with no rhyme or regular rhythm) and scandalized the public by its frank celebration of sexuality. As a young man Whitman worked as a printer, teacher, and journalist. In 1865 he published *Drum-Taps*, a volume inspired by his work as an army nurse during the Civil War. He also wrote an elegy on Abraham Lincoln, 'When Lilacs Last in the Dooryard Bloom'd'. He preached a particularly American vision of individual freedom and human brotherhood.

I celebrate myself, and sing myself.

Walt Whitman
Song of Myself

Whitney /'(h)wɪtni/ Eli 1765–1825. US inventor who in 1793 patented the cotton gin, a device for separating cotton fibre from its seeds.

Whitsun /'wɪts(ə)n/ *n.* or **Whitsuntide** the weekend or week including Whit Sunday.

whittle /'wɪt(ə)l/ *v.t./i.* 1. to pare (wood) with repeated slicings of a knife; to use a knife thus. 2. to reduce by repeated subtractions. [variant of dialect *thwittle*]

Whittle /'(h)wɪtl/ Frank 1907–. British engineer who patented the basic design for the turbojet engine in 1930.

In the Royal Air Force he worked on jet propulsion 1937–46. In May 1941 the Gloster E 28/39 aircraft first flew with the Whittle jet engine. Both the German (first operational jet planes) and the US jet aircraft were built using his principles.

whiz *n.* the sound made by a body moving through the air at great speed. —*v.i.* (**-zz-**) to move with or make this sound; to move very quickly. —**whiz kid,** (*colloquial*) a brilliant or highly successful young person.

who /hu:/ *pron.* (*objective* **whom**, *colloquial* **who**; *possessive* **whose** /hu:z/) **1.** (*interrogative*) what or which person(s)? **2.** (*relative*) the particular person(s) that; and or but he, they etc. (*sent it to Jones, who sent it on to Smith*). —**who's who,** who or what each person is; a list with facts about notable persons. [Old English]

Who, The an English rock group, formed in 1964, with a hard, aggressive sound, high harmonies, and a stage show in which they often destroyed their instruments. Their albums include *Tommy* 1969, *Who's Next* 1971, and *Quadrophenia* 1973. Originally a mod band, The Who comprised Pete Townshend (1945–   ), guitar and songwriter; Roger Daltrey (1944–   ), vocals; John Entwhistle (1944–   ), bass; Keith Moon (1947–1978), drums.

WHO abbreviation of ◊World Health Organization.

whoa /wəʊ/ *interjection* used to stop a horse etc.

whodunit /hu:ˈdʌnɪt/ *n.* (*colloquial*) a detective or mystery story or play etc. [=*who done* (illiterate for *did*) *it?*]

whoever /hu:ˈevə/ *pron.* (*objective* **whomever**, *colloquial* **whoever**; *possessive* **whoever** /hu:z-/) **1.** the or any person(s) who. **2.** though anyone.

whole /həʊl/ *adj.* **1.** with no part removed or left out. **2.** not injured or broken. —*n.* **1.** the full or complete amount, all the parts or members. **2.** a complete system made up of parts. —**on the whole,** taking everything relevant into account; in respect of the whole though some details form exceptions. **wholefoods** *n.pl.* foods not processed or refined. **wholehearted** *adj.* without doubts or reservations; done with all possible effort. **a whole lot,** (*colloquial*) a great amount. **whole number,** a number consisting of one or more units with no fractions. **whole-wheat,** *n.* wheat not separated into parts by bolting. [Old English]

wholemeal *adj.* made from the whole grain of (unbolted) wheat etc.

wholesale *n.* the selling of things in large quantities to be retailed by others. —*adj.* & *adv.* **1.** by wholesale. **2.** on a large scale. —*v.t.* to sell wholesale. —**wholesaler** *n.* [originally *by whole sale*]

wholesome /ˈhəʊlsəm/ *adj.* promoting good physical or mental health or moral condition; showing good sense. —**wholesomeness** *n.*

wholly /ˈhəʊllɪ/ *adv.* entirely, with nothing excepted or removed.

whom *pron.* the objective case of *who.*

whoop /hu:p/ *n.* **1.** a loud cry (as) of excitement etc. **2.** a long, rasping, indrawn breath in whooping cough. —*v.i.* to utter a whoop. **whoop it up,** (*colloquial*) to engage in revelry; (*US*) to make a stir.

whoopee /wuˈpi:/ *interjection* expressing exuberant joy. —**make whoopee** /ˈwupɪ/, (*colloquial*) to rejoice noisily or hilariously.

whooping cough or **pertussis** an acute infectious disease, seen mainly in children, caused by colonization of the air passages by the bacterium *Bordetella pertussis*. There may be catarrh, mild fever, and loss of appetite, but the main symptom is violent coughing, associated with the sharp intake of breath that is the characteristic 'whoop', and often followed by vomiting and severe nosebleeds. The cough may persist for weeks.

whoops /wʊps/ *interjection* on making an obvious mistake or losing balance.

whop *v.t.* (**-pp-**) (*slang*) to thrash, to defeat.

whopper *n.* (*slang*) a big specimen; a great lie.

whopping *adj.* (*slang*) very big.

whore /hɔ:/ *n.* a prostitute; a sexually immoral woman. —**whorehouse** *n.* a brothel. [Old English]

whorl /wɜ:l/ *n.* **1.** a coiled form; one turn of a spiral. **2.** a ring of leaves or petals round a stem or central point. **3.** a complete circle formed by ridges in a fingerprint.

whortleberry /ˈwɜ:təlberɪ/ *n.* a bilberry. [dialect form of *hurtleberry*]

whose /hu:z/ *interrog.* & *rel. pron.* & *adj.* of whom; of which. [Old English, genitive case of *who*]

whosoever /hu:səuˈevə/ *pron.* (*objective* **whomsoever**; *possessive* **whosesoever** /hu:zsəuˈvə/) = who.

why /waɪ/ *interrog. adv.* for what reason or purpose? —*rel. adv.* preceded by *reason* etc.) for which. —*int.* expressing surprised discovery or recognition, impatience, reflection, objection etc. —*n.* a reason (*the whys and wherefores*). [Old English]

Whymper /ˈ(h)wɪmpə/ Edward 1840–1911. English mountaineer. He made the first ascent of many Alpine peaks, including the Matterhorn 1865, and in the Andes scaled Chimborazo and other mountains.

WI abbreviation of **1.** West Indies. **2.** Women's Institute.

wick *n.* a strip or thread feeding a flame with fuel. [Old English]

wicked /ˈwɪkɪd/ *adj.* **1.** morally bad, offending against what is right. **2.** (*colloquial*) very bad or formidable, severe. **3.** malicious, mischievous. —**wickedly** *adv.*, **wickedness** *n.*

wicker *n.* thin canes or osiers woven together as material for making furniture, baskets etc. [from Scandinavian; compare Swedish *viker* = willow related to *vika* = bend]

wickerwork *n.* wicker; things made of this.

wicket /ˈwɪkɪt/ *n.* **1.** a small door or gate especially beside or in a larger one or closing the lower part only of a doorway. **2.** (in cricket) the stumps (originally two, now three) with the bails in position defended by a batsman; the ground between the two wickets; the state of this; a batsman's tenure of the wicket. —**wicketkeeper** *n.* a fieldsman stationed close behind the batsman's wicket. [from Anglo-French *wiket,* Old French *guichet*]

Wicklow /ˈwɪkləu/ county in the Republic of Ireland, province of Leinster; **area** 2,030 sq km/784 sq mi; **county town** Wicklow; **physical** Wicklow Mountains; rivers: Slane, Liffey; **population** (1986) 94,000.

widdershins variant of **withershins**.

wide *adj.* **1.** having the sides far apart, not narrow. **2.** extending far; having great range. **3.** open to the full extent. **4.** far from the target etc., not within a reasonable distance. **5.** (appended to a measurement) in width; (as *suffix*) extending to the whole of (*worldwide*). —*adv.* widely, to the full extent; far from the target etc. —*n.* a wide ball. —**give a wide berth to,** see ◊berth. **to the wide,** completely. **wide awake,** (*colloquial*) wary, knowing. **wide ball,** (in cricket) one judged by an umpire to be beyond the batsman's reach. **wide-eyed** *adj.* with eyes wide open in amazement or innocent surprise. **wide of the mark,** incorrect; irrelevant. **wide open,** exposed to attack; (of a contest) with no contestant who can be predicted as a certain winner. **the wide world,** the whole world, great as it is. —**widely** *adv.*, **wideness** *n.* [Old English]

wide-angle lens a photographic lens of shorter focal length than normal, taking in a wider angle of view.

widen /ˈwaɪdən/ *v.t./i.* to make or become wider.

widespread *adj.* widely distributed.

widgeon /ˈwɪdʒən/ *n.* or **wigeon** a kind of wild duck, especially *Anas penelope* or (US) *A. americana.*

Widmark /ˈwɪdmɑ:k/ Richard 1914–   . US actor who made his film debut in *Kiss of Death* 1947 as a psychopath. He subsequently appeared in a great variety of roles in films including *The Alamo* 1960, *Madigan* 1968, and *Coma* 1978.

widow /ˈwɪdəu/ *n.* a woman who has lost her husband by death and not married again. —*v.t.* to make into a widow or widower; (in *past participle*) bereft by the death of a husband or wife. —**widowhood** *n.* [Old English]

widower *n.* a man who has lost his wife by death and not married again.

width *n.* **1.** distance or measurement from side to side. **2.** a strip of material of full width as woven. **3.** a large extent. **4.** liberality of views etc. —**widthways** *adv.*

wield /wi:ld/ *v.t.* **1.** to hold and use (a weapon or tool, etc.). **2.** to have and use (power). [Old English]

Wien /vi:n/ Wilhelm 1864–1928. German physicist who studied radiation and established the principle known as **Wien's law.** It states that the wavelength at which the radiation from an idealized radiating body is most intense is inversely proportional to the body's absolute temperature, that is, the hotter the body, the shorter the wavelength. For this, and other work on radiation, he was awarded the 1911 Nobel Prize for Physics.

Wiene /'vi:nə/ Robert 1880–1938. German film director of the bizarre Expressionist film *Das Kabinett des Dr Caligari/The Cabinet of Dr Caligari* 1919. He also directed *Orlacs Hände/The Hands of Orlac* 1924, *Der Rosenkavalier* 1926, and *Ultimatum* 1938.

Wiener /'wi:nə/ Norbert 1894–1964. US mathematician, credited with the establishment of the science of cybernetics in his book *Cybernetics* 1948. In mathematics, he laid the foundation of the study of stochastic processes (those dependent on random events), particularly ◊Brownian movement.

Wiener schnitzel /'vi:nə 'ʃnɪtsəl/ a veal cutlet breaded, fried, and garnished. [German = Viennese cutlet]

Wiesel /'vi:zəl/ Elie 1928– . US academic and human-rights campaigner, born in Romania. He was held in Buchenwald concentration camp during World War II, and has assiduously documented wartime atrocities against the Jews in an effort to alert the world to the dangers of racism and violence. He was awarded the Nobel Peace Prize in 1986.

wife *n.* (*plural* wives) 1. a married woman, especially in relation to her husband. 2. (*archaic*) a woman. —**wifely** *adv.* [Old English]

wig[1] *n.* an artificial head of hair, either real or synthetic, worn as an adornment, disguise, or to conceal baldness. Wigs were known in the ancient world and have been found on Egyptian mummies. The 16th-century periwig imitated real hair, and developed into the elaborate peruke. Under Queen Anne, wigs covering the back and shoulders became fashionable. Today they remain part of the uniform of judges, barristers, and some parliamentary officials in the UK and certain Commonwealth countries.

wig[2] *v.t.* (**-gg-**) (*colloquial*) to rebuke lengthily (especially in *a wigging*).

wiggle *v.t./i.* (*colloquial*) to move or cause to move repeatedly from side to side; to wriggle. —*n.* a wiggling movement. [from Middle Low German and Middle Dutch *wiggelen*]

wight /waɪt/ *n.* (*archaic*) a person. [Old English = thing, creature]

Wight, Isle of island and county in S England; **area** 380 sq km/147 sq mi; **administrative headquarters** Newport; **population** (1987) 127,000; **history** called *Vectis* ('separate division') by the Romans, who conquered it AD 43. Charles I was imprisoned 1647–48 in Carisbrooke Castle, now ruined.

Wightman Cup an annual tennis competition between international women's teams from the USA and the UK. The trophy, first contested in 1923, was donated by Hazel Hotchkiss Wightman (1886–1974), a former US tennis player who won singles, doubles, and mixed-doubles titles in the US Championships 1909–1911. Because of US domination of the contest it was abandoned in 1990, but it is to be reinstated in 1991 with the UK side assisted by European players.

Wigner /'wɪgnə/ Eugene Paul 1902– . Hungarian-born US physicist who introduced the notion of parity into nuclear physics with the consequence that all nuclear processes should be indistinguishable from their mirror images. For this, and other work on nuclear structure, he shared the 1963 Nobel Prize for Physics with Maria ◊Goeppert-Mayer and Hans Jensen (1906–1973).

wigwam /'wɪgwæm/ *n.* a hut or tent made by fastening skins or mats over a framework of poles, as formerly used by American Indians. [American Indian = their house]

Wilberforce /'wɪlbəfɔ:s/ William 1759–1833. English reformer who was instrumental in abolishing slavery in the British Empire. He entered Parliament in 1780; in 1807 his bill for the abolition of the slave trade was passed, and in 1833, largely through his efforts, slavery was abolished throughout the empire.

wilco /'wɪlkəʊ/ interjection expressing compliance or agreement. [abbreviation of *will comply*]

wild /waɪld/ *adj.* 1. living or growing in its original natural state, not domesticated or tame or cultivated. 2. not civilized, barbarous. 3. unrestrained, disorderly, uncontrolled. 4. tempestuous, stormy. 5. full of strong unrestrained feeling, intensely eager, frantic; (*colloquial*) infuriated. 6. extremely foolish or unreasonable; random, ill-aimed. —*adv.* in a wild manner. —*n.* a wild tract, a desert. —**in the wilds,** (*colloquial*) far from towns etc. **run wild,** to grow or stray unchecked or undisciplined. **sow one's**

wild oats, to indulge in youthful follies before maturity. **wild-goose chase,** a foolish or useless search; a hopeless quest. **wild silk,** silk from wild silkworms; an imitation of this. **Wild West,** the western regions of the USA at the time when they were lawless frontier districts. —**wildly** *adv.*, **wildness** *n.* [Old English]

Wild Jonathan *c.*1682–1725. English criminal who organized the thieves of London and ran an office that, for a payment, returned stolen goods to their owners. He was hanged at Tyburn.

wildcat *n.* a hot-tempered or violent person. —*adj.* 1. reckless, financially unsound. 2. (of a strike) sudden and unofficial.

Wilde /waɪld/ Corne(lius Louis) 1915–1989. Austrian-born US actor and film director. He went to the USA in 1932, starred in *A Song to Remember* 1945, and directed *The Naked Prey* 1966 (in which he also acted) and *No Blade of Grass* 1970.

Wilde Oscar (Fingal O'Flahertie Wills) 1854–1900. Irish writer. With his flamboyant style and quotable conversation, he dazzled London society and, on his lecture tour in 1882, the USA. He published his only novel *The Picture of Dorian Gray* in 1891, followed by witty plays including *A Woman of No Importance* 1893 and *The Importance of Being Earnest* 1895. In 1895 he was imprisoned for two years for homosexual offences; he died in exile.

The truth is rarely pure and never simple.
                                                        Oscar Wilde
                                            The Importance of Being Earnest

wildebeest /'wɪldəbi:st, v-/ *n.* the gnu. [Afrikaans = wild beast]

Wilder /'waɪldə/ Billy 1906– . Austrian-born US screenwriter and film director who arrived in the USA in 1934. He directed and co-scripted *Double Indemnity* 1944, *The Lost Weekend* (Academy Award for best director) 1945, *Sunset Boulevard* 1950, *Some Like it Hot* 1959, and the Academy Award-winning *The Apartment* 1960.

Wilder Thornton (Niven) 1897–1975. US playwright and novelist. He won Pulitzer prizes for the novel *The Bridge of San Luis Rey* 1927, and for the plays *Our Town* 1938 and *The Skin of Our Teeth* 1942. His play *The Matchmaker* appeared at the Edinburgh Festival in 1954, and as the hit musical entitled *Hello Dolly!* in New York in 1964, and in London the following year.

wilderness /'wɪldənɪs/ *n.* 1. a desert, an uncultivated region. 2. a confused assemblage. —**voice in the wilderness,** an unheeded advocate of reform (with reference to Matt. 3: 3 etc.). [from Old English *wil(d)deor* = wild deer]

wildfire *n.* (*historical*) a combustible liquid used in war. —**spread like wildfire,** to spread with extraordinary speed.

wildfowl *n.* a game bird or game birds (e.g. ducks and geese, quail, pheasants).

wildlife *n.* wild animals collectively.

wild type in genetics, the naturally occurring gene for a particular character that is typical of most individuals of a given species, as distinct from new genes that arise by mutation.

wile *n.* (usually in *plural*) a piece of trickery intended to deceive or attract. —*v.t.* to lure.

wilful /'wɪlfʊl/ *adj.* 1. intentional, deliberate. 2. selfwilled. —**wilfully** *adv.*, **wilfulness** *n.*

Wilhelm /'vɪlhelm/ (English **William**) two emperors of Germany:

Wilhelm I 1797–1888. King of Prussia from 1861 and emperor of Germany from 1871; the son of Friedrich Wilhelm III. He served in the Napoleonic Wars 1814–15 and helped to crush the 1848 revolution. After he succeeded his brother Friedrich Wilhelm IV to the throne of Prussia, his policy was largely dictated by his chancellor ◊Bismarck, who secured his proclamation as emperor.

Wilhelm II 1859–1941. Emperor of Germany from 1888, the son of Frederick III and Victoria, daughter of Queen Victoria of Britain. In 1890 he forced Chancellor Bismarck to resign and began to direct foreign policy himself, which proved disastrous. He encouraged warlike policies and built up the German navy. In 1914 he first approved Austria's ultimatum to Serbia and then, when he realized war was inevitable, tried in vain to prevent it. In 1918 he fled to Holland, after Germany's defeat and his abdication.

Wilkes /wılks/ John 1727–1797. British Radical politician, imprisoned for his political views; member of Parliament 1757–64 and from 1774. He championed parliamentary reform, religious toleration, and US independence.

Wilkins /'wılkınz/ Maurice Hugh Frederick 1916– . New Zealand scientist. In 1962 he shared the Nobel Prize for Medicine with Francis ◊Crick and James ◊Watson for his work on the molecular structure of nucleic acids, particularly ◊DNA, using X-ray diffraction.

Wilkins William 1778–1839. English architect. He pioneered the Greek revival in England with his design for Downing College, Cambridge. Other works include the main block of University College London 1827–28, and the National Gallery, London, 1834–38.

Wilkinson /'wılkınsən/ (Cecily) Ellen 1891–1947. Labour politician and journalist. She was an early member of the Independent Labour Party and an active campaigner for women's suffrage. As a member of parliament for Jarrow in 1936, she led the ◊Jarrow March of 200 unemployed shipyard workers from Jarrow to London.

will[1] *v.aux.* (*third person singular present* will; *second person singular* (*archaic*) wilt; *past* would) 1. (strictly only in second and third persons) expressing a future statement or an order (*they will attack at dawn; you will do as you are told*). 2. expressing the speaker's intention (*I will support you!*). [Old English]

will[2] *n.* 1. the mental faculty by which a person decides or conceives himself or herself as deciding upon and initiating his actions. 2. (also **will-power**) control exercised by one's will. 3. determination, fixed desire or intention. 4. (*archaic*) that which is desired or ordained. 5. a person's disposition in wishing good or bad to others. 6. written directions made by a person for the disposal of his or her property after his or her death. —*v.t.* 1. to exercise one's willpower; to influence or compel thus. 2. to intend unconditionally. 3. to bequeath by a will. —**at will,** however one pleases. [Old English]

Willem /'wıləm/ Dutch form of William.

William /'wıljəm/ four kings of England:

William I the Conqueror *c.*1027–1087. King of England from 1066. He was the illegitimate son of Duke Robert the Devil and succeeded his father as duke of Normandy in 1035. Claiming that his relative King Edward the Confessor had bequeathed him the English throne, William invaded the country in 1066, defeating ◊Harold II at Hastings, Sussex, and was crowned king of England.

William II Rufus, the Red *c.*1056–1100. King of England from 1087, the third son of William I. He spent most of his reign attempting to capture Normandy from his brother ◊Robert II, Duke of Normandy. His extortion of money led his barons to revolt and caused confrontation with Bishop Anselm. He was killed while hunting in the New Forest, and was succeeded by his brother Henry I.

William III William of Orange 1650–1702. King of Great Britain and Ireland from 1688, the son of William II of Orange and Mary, daughter of Charles I. He was offered the English crown by the parliamentary opposition to James II. He invaded England in 1688 and in 1689 became joint sovereign with his wife, ◊Mary II. He spent much of his reign campaigning, first in Ireland, where he defeated James II at the battle of the Boyne in 1690, and later against the French in Flanders. He was succeeded by Anne.

William IV 1765–1837. King of Great Britain and Ireland from 1830, when he succeeded his brother George IV; third son of George III. He was created duke of Clarence in 1789, and married Adelaide of Saxe-Meiningen (1792–1849) in 1818. During the Reform Bill crisis he secured its passage by agreeing to create new peers to overcome the hostile majority in the House of Lords. He was succeeded by Victoria.

William three kings of the Netherlands:

William I 1772–1844. King of the Netherlands 1815–40. He lived in exile during the French occupation 1795–1813 and fought against the emperor Napoleon at Jena and Wagram. The Austrian Netherlands were added to his kingdom by the Allies in 1815, but secured independence (recognized by the major European states in 1839) by the

revolution of 1830. William's unpopularity led to his abdication in 1840.

William II 1792–1849. King of the Netherlands 1840–49, son of William I. He served with the British army in the Peninsular War and at Waterloo. In 1848 he averted revolution by conceding a liberal constitution.

William III 1817–1890. King of the Netherlands 1849–90, the son of William II. In 1862 he abolished slavery in the Dutch East Indies.

William the Lion 1143–1214. King of Scotland from 1165. He was captured by Henry II while invading England in 1174, and forced to do homage, but Richard I abandoned the English claim to suzerainty for a money payment in 1189. In 1209 William was forced by King John to renounce his claim to Northumberland.

William the Silent 1533–1584. Prince of Orange from 1544. He was appointed governor of Holland by Philip II of Spain in 1559, but joined the revolt of 1572 against Spain's oppressive rule and, as a Protestant from 1573, became the national leader. He briefly succeeded in uniting the Catholic south and Protestant northern provinces, but the former provinces submitted to Spain while the latter formed a federation in 1579 which repudiated Spanish suzerainty in 1581. He became known as 'the Silent' because of his absolute discretion. He was assassinated by a Spanish agent.

William (full name William Arthur Philip Louis) 1982– . Prince of the United Kingdom, first child of the Prince and Princess of Wales.

William of Malmesbury /'mɑːmzbri/ *c.*1080–*c.*1143. English historian and monk. He compiled the *Gesta regum/Deeds of the Kings* about 1120–40 and *Historia novella*, which together formed a history of England to 1142.

Williams /'wıljəmz/ a British racing-car manufacturing company started by Frank Williams in 1969 when he modified a Brabham BT26A. The first Williams Grand Prix car was designed by Patrick Head in 1978 and since then the team has been one of the most successful in Grand Prix racing.

Williams Roger *c.*1604–1684. British founder of Rhode Island colony in North America 1636, on a basis of democracy and complete religious freedom.

Williams Shirley 1930– . British Social Democrat Party politician. She was Labour minister for prices and consumer protection 1974–76, and education and science 1976–79. She became a founder member of the SDP in 1981 and its president in 1982. In 1983 she lost her parliamentary seat. She is the daughter of the socialist writer Vera ◊Brittain.

Williams Tennessee (Thomas Lanier) 1911–1983. US playwright, born in Mississippi. His work is characterized by fluent dialogue and searching analysis of the psychological deficiencies of his characters. His plays, usually set in the Deep South against a background of decadence and degradation, include *The Glass Menagerie* 1945 and *A Streetcar Named Desire* 1947.

I can't stand a naked light bulb, any more than I can stand a rude remark or a vulgar action.

Tennessee Williams
A Streetcar Named Desire

Williams William Carlos 1883–1963. US poet. His spare images and language reflect everyday speech. His epic poem *Paterson* 1946–58 celebrates his home town in New Jersey. *Pictures from Brueghel* 1963 won him, posthumously, a Pulitzer prize. His vast body of prose work includes novels, short stories, and the play *A Dream of Love* 1948. His work had a great impact on younger US poets.

Williamson /'wıljəmsən/ Henry 1895–1977. English author, known for stories of animal life such as *Tarka the Otter* 1927. He described his experiences in restoring an old farm in *The Story of a Norfolk Farm* 1941 and wrote the fictional, 15-volume sequence *Chronicles of Ancient Sunlight*.

Williamson Malcolm (Benjamin Graham Christopher) 1931– . Australian composer, pianist, and organist, who settled in Britain in 1953. His works include operas (*Our Man in Havana* 1963), symphonies, and chamber music.

willies /'wılız/ *n.pl.* (*slang*) nervous discomfort.

willing *adj.* 1. ready to consent or to undertake what is required. 2. given or done etc. by a willing person. —*n.* a cheerful intention (*to show willing*). —**willingly** *adv.*, **willingness** *n.*

Willis /ˈwɪlɪs/ Norman (David) 1933– . British trade-union leader. A trade-union official since leaving school, he succeeded Len Murray as the general secretary of the Trades Union Congress (TUC) in 1984.

will-o'-the-wisp /wɪləðəˈwɪsp/ *n.* 1. a phosphorescent light seen on marshy ground. 2. an elusive person. 3. a delusive hope or plan. [originally *Will* (William) *with the wisp* (*wisp* = bundle of (lighted) hay)]

willow /ˈwɪləʊ/ *n.* a waterside tree of the genus *Salix* with pliant branches yielding osiers and timber for cricketbats. [Old English]

willowherb *n.* any plant of either of two genera *Epilobium* and *Chamaenerion* of perennial weeds. The rosebay willowherb or fireweed *C. angustifolium* is common in woods and wasteland. It grows to 1.2 m/4 ft with long terminal racemes of red or purplish flowers.

willow pattern a popular 'Chinese' pattern for china with blue trees, figures etc., on a white background.

willow warbler a bird *Phylloscopus trochilus* that migrates from N Eurasia to Africa. It is about 11 cm/4 in long, similar in appearance to the chiffchaff, but with a distinctive song, and found in woods and shrubberies.

willowy /ˈwɪləʊɪ/ *adj.* 1. full of willow trees. 2. lithe and slender.

willy-nilly /wɪliˈnɪlɪ/ *adv.* whether one likes it or not.

Wilson /ˈwɪlsən/ Angus (Frank Johnstone) 1913–1991. British novelist, whose acidly humorous books include *Anglo-Saxon Attitudes* 1956 and *The Old Men at the Zoo* 1961.

Wilson Edward O 1929– . US zoologist whose books have stimulated interest in biogeography, the study of the distribution of species, and sociobiology, the evolution of behaviour. His works include *Sociobiology: The New Synthesis* 1975 and *On Human Nature* 1978.

Wilson (James) Harold, Baron Wilson of Rievaulx 1916– . British Labour politician, party leader from 1963, prime minister 1964–70 and 1974–76. His premiership was dominated by the issue of UK admission to membership of the European Community, the social contract (unofficial agreement with the trade unions), and economic difficulties.

A week is a long time in politics.

Harold Wilson

Wilson Richard 1714–1782. British painter, whose English and Welsh landscapes are infused with an Italianate atmosphere and recomposed in a Classical manner. His work influenced the development of English landscape-painting.

Wilson (Thomas) Woodrow 1856–1924. 28th president of the USA 1913–21, a Democrat. He kept the USA out of World War I until 1917, and in Jan 1918 issued his 'Fourteen Points' as a basis for a just peace settlement. At the peace conference in Paris he secured the inclusion of the ◊League of Nations in individual peace treaties, but these were not ratified by Congress, so the USA did not join the League. He was awarded the Nobel Prize for Peace in 1919.

wilt *v.t./i.* 1. (of plants) to lose freshness and droop. 2. to cause to do this. 3. (of persons) to become limp from exhaustion. —*n.* a plant disease that causes wilting.

Wilton /ˈwɪltən/ *n.* a kind of carpet with loops cut into thick pile, first made at Wilton in Wiltshire.

Wilts. abbreviation of Wiltshire.

Wiltshire /ˈwɪltʃə/ county in SW England; **area** 3,480 sq km/1,343 sq mi; **administrative headquarters** Trowbridge; **physical** Marlborough Downs; Savernake Forest; rivers: Kennet, Wylye, Salisbury and Bristol Avons; Salisbury Plain; **population** (1989) 564,000.

wily /ˈwaɪlɪ/ *adj.* full of wiles, crafty, cunning. —**wilily** *adv.*, **wiliness** *n.*

Wimbledon /ˈwɪmbəldən/ an English lawn-tennis centre used for international championship matches, situated in south London. There are currently 18 courts.

WIMP acronym from windows, icons, menus, pointing device in computing, a type of ◊user interface, in which programs and files appear as ◊icons, menus drop down

from a bar along the top of the screen, and data are displayed in rectangular areas, called windows, which the operator can manipulate in various ways. The operator uses a pointing device, typically a ◊mouse, to make selections and initiate actions.

wimple *n.* a headdress of linen or silk folded round the head and neck so as to cover all but the front of the face, worn by women in medieval times and retained in the dress of nuns. [Old English]

win *v.t./i.* (-nn-; *past* and *past participle* won /wʌn/) 1. to obtain or achieve as the result of a battle, contest, bet, or effort; to be the victor. 2. to be victorious in (a battle, game, race etc.). 3. to make one's way or become (free etc.) by successful effort. —*n.* victory in a game or contest. —**win over**, to gain the favour or support of. **win one's spurs**, (*historical*) to gain a knighthood; (*figurative*) to prove one's ability, to gain distinction. **win through** *or* **out**, to overcome obstacles. **you can't win**, (*colloquial*) there is no way to succeed. [Old English]

wince *n.* a start or involuntary shrinking movement showing pain or distress. —*v.i.* to make such a movement.

wincey /ˈwɪnsɪ/ *n.* a lightweight fabric of wool and cotton or linen.

winceyette /wɪnsɪˈet/ *n.* a soft, napped fabric woven of cotton and wool.

winch *n.* 1. the crank of a wheel or axle. 2. a windlass. —*v.t.* to lift with a winch. [Old English]

Winchester disc an alternative name for ◊hard disc.

wind[1] /wɪnd/ *n.* 1. air in natural motion; a scent carried by this and indicating a presence. 2. an artificially produced air current especially for sounding a wind instrument. 3. the wind instruments in an orchestra etc. 4. breath as needed in exertion or speech; the power of breathing without difficulty. 5. a point below the centre of the chest where a blow temporarily paralyses the breathing. 6. gas generated in the stomach or bowels. 7. empty talk. —*v.t.* 1. to exhaust the wind of by exertion or a blow. 2. to renew the wind of by a rest. 3. to make breathe quickly and deeply by exercise. 4. to detect the presence of by scent. —**get wind of**, to begin to suspect. **get** *or* **have the wind up**, (*slang*) to feel frightened. **in the wind**, about to happen. **like the wind**, swiftly. **put the wind up**, (*slang*) to frighten. **take the wind out of a person's sails**, to frustrate him by anticipating his action or remark. **windbreak** *n.* a row of trees etc. to break the force of the wind. **windcheater** *n.* a jacket designed to give protection against the wind. **wind instrument**, a musical instrument sounded by a current of air, especially that produced by the player's breath. **windjammer** *n.* a merchant sailing ship. **windsock** *n.* a canvas cylinder or cone on a mast to show the direction of the wind. **windswept** *adj.* exposed to high winds. **wind tunnel**, a tunnel-like device to produce an air stream past models of aircraft etc. for the study of wind effects. [Old English]

wind[2] /waɪnd/ *v.t./i.* (*past* and *past participle* wound) 1. to go or cause to go in a curving, twisting, or spiral course; to make (one's) way thus. 2. to coil; to wrap closely; to provide with a coiled thread etc.; to surround (as) with a coil. 3. to haul, hoist, or move by turning a handle or windlass etc. 4. to wind up (a clock etc.). —*n.* 1. a bend or turn in a course. 2. a single turn in winding. —**wind down**, to unwind (*literal* or *figurative*). **winding sheet**, a sheet in which a corpse is wrapped for burial. **wind off**, to unwind. **wind up**, to set or keep (a clock etc.) going by tightening its spring or adjusting its weights; to bring or come to an end; to settle and finally close the business affairs of (a company); (*colloquial*) to arrive finally. —**winder** *n.* [Old English]

windbag *n.* (*colloquial*) a person who talks at length and without value.

wind-chill factor or **wind-chill index** an estimate of how much colder it feels when a wind is blowing. It is the sum of the temperature (in °F below zero) and the wind speed (in miles per hour). So for a wind of 15 mph at an air temperature of –5°F, the wind-chill factor is 20.

Windermere /ˈwɪndəmɪə/ the largest lake in England, in Cumbria, 17 km/10.5 mi long and 1.6 km/1 mi wide.

windfall *n.* 1. a fruit blown to the ground by the wind. 2. a piece of unexpected good fortune, especially a sum of money acquired.

wind farm an array of windmills or ◊wind turbines used for generating electrical power. A wind farm at Altamont Pass,

California, USA, consists of 300 wind turbines, the smallest producing 60 kW and the largest 750 kW of electricity. To produce 1,200 megawatts of electricity (an output comparable with that of a nuclear power station), a wind farm would need to occupy around 370 sq km/140 sq mi.

Windhoek /'wɪndhʊk/ capital of Namibia; population (1988) 115,000. It is just N of the Tropic of Capricorn, 290 km/180 mi from the W coast.

windlass /'wɪndləs/ *n.* a machine with a horizontal axle for hauling or hoisting things. [from Anglo-French from Old Norse]

windmill *n.* a mill with sails or vanes which, by the action of wind upon them, drive machinery for grinding corn or pumping water, for example. Wind turbines, designed to use wind power on a large scale, usually have a propeller-type rotor mounted on a tall shell tower. The turbine drives a generator for producing electricity. —**tilt at windmills,** to attack an imaginary enemy (with reference to Don Quixote, who attacked windmills, thinking that they were giants).

window /'wɪndəu/ *n.* **1.** an opening in a wall, etc. usually with glass for the admission of light etc.; the glass itself; the space for display behind the window of a shop. **2.** a window-like opening. **3.** an interval during which the positions of planets etc. allow a specified journey by a spacecraft. —**window box,** a trough fixed outside a window for cultivating ornamental plants. **window-dressing** *n.* the art of arranging a display in a shop window etc.; adroit presentation of facts etc. to give a falsely favourable impression. **window-shopping** *n.* looking at the goods displayed in shop windows without buying anything. [from Old Norse]

windpipe *n.* the air passage from the larynx to the bronchial tubes.

wind power the harnessing of wind energy to produce power. The wind has long been used as a source of energy: sailing ships and windmills are ancient inventions. After the energy crisis of the 1970s ◊wind turbines began to be used to produce electricity on a large scale. By the year 2000, 10% of Denmark's energy is expected to come from wind power.

Windscale /'wɪndskeɪl/ the former name of ◊Sellafield, a nuclear power station in Cumbria, England.

windscreen *n.* a screen of glass at the front of a motor vehicle.

Windsor, House of the official name of the British royal family since 1917, adopted in place of Saxe-Coburg-Gotha. Since 1960 those descendants of Elizabeth II not entitled to the prefix HRH (His/Her Royal Highness) have borne the surname Mountbatten-Windsor.

Windsor Duchess of. Title of Wallis Warfield ◊Simpson.

Windsor Duke of. Title of ◊Edward VIII.

Windsor Castle a British royal residence in Windsor, Berkshire, founded by William the Conqueror on the site of an earlier fortress. It includes the Perpendicular Gothic St George's Chapel and the Albert Memorial Chapel, beneath which George III, George IV, and William IV are buried. In the Home Park adjoining the castle is the Royal Mausoleum where Queen Victoria and Prince Albert are buried.

Windsurfer *n.* the trade name of a board 2.5–4 m/ 8–13 ft long, which is propelled and steered by means of a sail attached to a mast that is articulated at the foot. —**windsurfer** *n.* one engaged in the sport of riding on such a board. —**windsurfing** *n.*

wind tunnel a test tunnel in which air is blown over, for example, a stationary model aircraft, motor vehicle, or locomotive to simulate the effects of movement. Lift, drag, and airflow patterns are observed by the use of special cameras and sensitive instruments. Wind-tunnel testing assesses aerodynamic design, preparatory to full-scale construction.

wind turbine a windmill of advanced aerodynamic design connected to an electricity generator and used in wind-power installations. Wind turbines can be either large propeller-type rotors mounted on a tall tower, or flexible metal strips fixed to a vertical axle at top and bottom. The world's largest wind turbine is on Hawaii, in the Pacific Ocean. It has two blades 50 metres long on top of a tower 20 storeys high.

windward /'wɪndwəd/ *adj. & adv.* in the direction from which the wind is blowing. —*n.* the windward direction.

Windward Islands islands in the path of the prevailing wind, notably: **West Indies** see under ◊Antilles; ◊Cape

wing

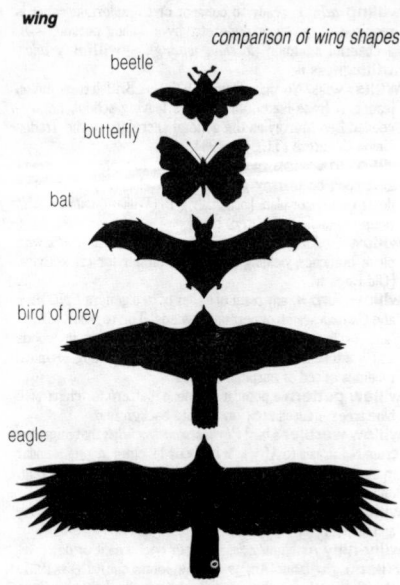

comparison of wing shapes

beetle

butterfly

bat

bird of prey

eagle

Verde Islands; ◊**French Polynesia** (Tahiti, Moorea, and Makatea).

windy *adj.* **1.** with much wind. **2.** exposed to wind. **3.** generating or characterized by flatulence. **4.** full of useless talk. **5.** (*slang*) nervous, frightened. —**windily** *adv.*, **windiness** *n.*

wine *n.* **1.** liquor of fermented grape pulp; a fermented drink resembling it made from other fruits etc. **Red wine** is the product of the grape with the skin; **white wine** of the inner pulp only. The sugar content is converted to ethyl alcohol by the yeast *Saccharomyces ellipsoideus*, which lives on the skin of the grape. For **dry wine** the fermentation is allowed to go on longer than for **sweet** or **medium**; ◊champagne is bottled while still fermenting, but other sparkling wines are artificially carbonated. The world's largest producers are Italy, France, the USSR, and Spain; others include Germany, Australia, South Africa, California, and Chile; a small quantity of wine is produced in the UK. **2.** the dark red colour of red wine. —*v.t./i.* **1.** to drink wine. **2.** to entertain to wine. —**winebibber** *n.* a tippler. **wine cellar,** a cellar for storing wine; its contents. [Old English from Latin *vinum*]

wineglass *n.* a glass for wine, usually with a stem and foot.

winepress *n.* a press in which grapes are squeezed in making wine.

wineskin *n.* the whole skin of a goat etc. sewn up and used to hold wine.

wing *n.* **1.** each of a pair of projecting parts by which a bird, bat, or insect etc. is able to fly; a corresponding part in a non-flying bird or insect. **2.** a winglike part of an aircraft, supporting it in flight. **3.** a part resembling a wing in appearance or position; a projecting part of a building, battle array, etc.; (in *plural*) the sides of a theatre stage out of sight of the audience. **4.** (in football etc.) the player at either end of the forward line; the side part of the playing area. **5.** a section of a political party or other group, with more extreme views than those of the majority. **6.** the mudguard of a motor vehicle, the part of the bodywork immediately above each wheel. **7.** an air-force unit of several squadrons or groups. —*v.t./i.* **1.** to fly, to travel by means of wings; to make (its way) thus. **2.** to equip with wings; to enable to fly; to send in flight. **3.** to wound in the wing or arm. —**on the wing,** flying. **spread one's wings,** to develop one's powers fully. **take under one's wing,** to treat as a protégé. **take wing,** to fly away. **wing-case** *n.* the horny cover of an insect's wing. **wing chair,** one with side pieces at the top of a high back. **wing collar,** a high, stiff collar with turned-down corners. **wing commander,** an RAF officer next below group captain. **wing nut,** a nut with projections for the finger to turn it on a screw. **wingspan** or **-spread** n. the measurement right across the wings. [from Old Norse]

winger n. (in football etc.) a wing player.

wink v.t./i. 1. to close and open one eye deliberately, especially as a private signal to someone. 2. (of a light) to twinkle. —n. 1. an act of winking. 2. a short sleep. —**tip a person the wink**, to give him information privately. **wink at**, to pretend not to notice (something that should be stopped or condemned). [Old English]

winker n. a flashing indicator on a motor vehicle.

winkle n. a small edible sea snail of the genus Littorina. —v.t. (with out) to extract or eject. —**winkle-picker** n. (slang) a shoe with a long pointed toe.

winner n. 1. one who wins. 2. a successful thing.

winning adj. 1. having or bringing victory. 2. attractive. —n. (in plural) money won. —**winning post**, a post marking the end of a race.

Winnipeg /ˈwɪnɪpeg/ capital and industrial city in Manitoba, Canada, on the Red River, S of Lake Winnipeg; industries include sawmills, textiles, and meat packing; population (1986) 623,000. Established as Winnipeg in 1873 on the site of earlier forts, the city expanded with the arrival of the Canadian Pacific Railroad in 1881.

Winnipeg, Lake lake in S Manitoba, Canada, draining much of the Canadian prairies; area 24,500 sq km/9,460 sq mi.

winnow /ˈwɪnəʊ/ v.t. 1. to expose (grain) to a current of air by tossing or fanning it so that the loose, dry, outer part is blown away; to separate (chaff) thus. 2. to sift or separate (evidence etc.) from worthless or inferior elements. [Old English]

wino /ˈwaɪnəʊ/ n. (plural winos) (slang) an alcoholic.

winsome /ˈwɪnsəm/ adj. (of a person, looks, or manner) winning, engaging. [Old English wyn = joy]

winter n. the coldest and last season of the year, from Dec to Feb in the northern hemisphere. —adj. characteristic of or fit for winter. —v.i. to spend the winter. —**winter garden**, a garden or conservatory of plants kept flourishing in winter. **winter sports**, sports performed on snow or ice, e. g. skiing. [Old English]

wintergreen n. any of various creeping or low shrubby plants with leaves remaining green in winter, especially the North American Gaultheria procumbens with drooping white flowers, edible scarlet berries, and aromatic leaves yielding an oil used in medicine and for flavouring.

winter of discontent the winter of 1978–79 in Britain, marked by a series of strikes that contributed to the defeat of the Labour government in the general election of spring 1979. The phrase is from Shakespeare's Richard III: 'Now is the winter of our discontent/Made glorious summer by this sun of York.'

Winter War the USSR's invasion of Finland 30 Nov 1939–12 March 1940, also called the Russo-Finnish War.

wintry adj. 1. characteristic of winter. 2. (of a smile, etc.) lacking warmth or vivacity. —**wintriness** n.

winy /ˈwaɪnɪ/ adj. wine-flavoured.

wipe v.t./i. 1. to clean or dry the surface of by rubbing; to rub (a cloth) over a surface; to put (a liquid etc.) on to a surface by rubbing. 2. to clear or remove by wiping. —n. the act of wiping. —**wipe the floor with**, (slang) to inflict a humiliating defeat on. **wipe off**, to annul (a debt). **wipe out**, to avenge (an insult etc.); to destroy, to annihilate. [Old English]

wiper /ˈwaɪpə/ n. a device for keeping a windscreen clear of rain etc.

wire n. 1. metal drawn out into a slender, flexible rod or thread; a piece of this. 2. a length of wire used for fencing or to carry an electric current etc. 3. (colloquial) a telegram. —v.t./i. 1. to provide, fasten, or strengthen with wire. 2. (colloquial) to telegraph. —**get one's wires crossed**, to become confused and misunderstand. **wire-haired** adj. (especially of a dog) with stiff or wiry hair. **wiretapping** n. the tapping of telephone wires. **wire wheel**, a vehicle wheel with wire spokes. **wire wool**, a mass of fine wire for cleaning kitchen utensils etc. **wireworm** n. the destructive larva of a beetle of the family Elateridae. [Old English]

wireless n. the original name for a radio receiver. In early experiments with transmission by radio waves, notably by ◊Marconi in Britain, signals were sent in Morse code, as in telegraphy. Radio, unlike the telegraph, used no wires for transmission, and the means of communication was termed 'wireless telegraphy'.

wiring /ˈwaɪrɪŋ/ n. a system of wires providing electrical circuits.

wiry /ˈwaɪrɪ/ adj. tough and flexible as wire; (of a person) lean and strong. —**wirily** adv., **wiriness** n.

Wisconsin /wɪˈskɒnsɪn/ state of N central USA; nickname Badger State; **area** 145,500 sq km/56,163 sq mi; **capital** Madison; **population** (1988) 4,816,000; **history** originally settled by the French; passed to Britain in 1763; became American in 1783 and a state in 1848.

wisdom n. 1. experience and knowledge together with the power of applying them; sagacity, prudence, common sense. 2. wise sayings. —**wisdom tooth**, the third and hindmost molar tooth on each side of the upper and lower jaws, usually cut (if at all) after the age of 20. [Old English]

wise[1] /waɪz/ adj. 1. having, or showing, or dictated by wisdom; having knowledge; suggestive of wisdom. 2. (US slang) alert, crafty. —**none the wiser**, knowing no more than before. **wise man**, a wizard; each of the ◊Magi. —**wisely** adv. [Old English]

wise[2] n. (archaic) way, manner, degree. —**in no wise**, not at all. [Old English]

-wise suffix forming adjectives and adverbs of manner (clockwise, crosswise, lengthwise) or respect (moneywise).

Wise Robert 1914– . US film director who began as a film editor. His debut was a horror film, Curse of the Cat People 1944; he progressed to such large-scale projects as The Sound of Music 1965 and Star 1968. His other films include The Body Snatcher 1945 and Star Trek: The Motion Picture 1979.

wiseacre /ˈwaɪzeɪkə/ n. one who affects to be wise. [from Middle Dutch = soothsayer]

wisecrack n. (colloquial) a smart, pithy remark. —v.i. (colloquial) to make a wisecrack.

wisent n. another name for the European ◊bison.

wish n. 1. a desire or ambition. 2. an expression of desire about another person's welfare. —v.t./i. 1. to have or express as a wish; to formulate a wish. 2. to hope or express hope for (specified fortune) to befall someone; to hope that (a person) will fare (well or ill). 3. (colloquial) to foist (a specified thing etc. on a person). [Old English]

wishbone n. 1. a forked bone between the neck and breast of a bird (pulled in two between two persons, the one who gets the larger part having the supposed right to magic fulfilment of any wish). 2. a thing shaped like this.

wishful adj. desiring. —**wishful thinking**, belief founded on wishes rather than facts. —**wishfully** adv.

wishy-washy /ˈwɪʃɪwɒʃɪ/ adj. feeble in quality or character.

wisp n. 1. a small bundle or twist of straw etc.; a small separate quantity of smoke or hair etc. 2. a small, thin person. —**wispy** adj.

wistaria /wɪˈstɛərɪə/ n. or **wisteria**, a climbing shrub of the genus Wistaria with blue, purple, or white hanging flowers. [from C. Wistar (or Wister), American anatomist (died 1818)]

wistful adj. full of sad or vague longing. —**wistfully** adv., **wistfulness** n.

wit n. 1. (in singular or plural) intelligence, quick understanding. 2. the ability to combine words or ideas etc. ingeniously so as to produce a kind of clever humour that appeals to the intellect. 3. a person with such ability. —v.t./i. (singular present **wot**; past and past participle **wist**; participle **witting**) (archaic) to know. —**at one's wit's** (or **wits'**) **end**, utterly at a loss or in despair. **have** or **keep one's wits about one**, to be alert. **live by one's wits**, to live by ingenious or crafty expedients, without a settled occupation. **out of one's wits**, mad. **to wit**, that is to say, namely. [Old English]

witch n. 1. a sorceress, a woman supposed to have dealings with the Devil or evil spirits. 2. an ugly old woman. 3. a fascinating woman. —**witch ball**, a coloured glass ball of the kind formerly hung up to keep witches away. **witch doctor**, a tribal magician of a primitive people. **witches' sabbath**, a supposed midnight orgy of the Devil and witches. [Old English]

witch- prefix, variant of wych-.

witchcraft n. the alleged possession and exercise of magical powers, **black magic** if used with evil intent, and **white magic** if benign. Its origins lie in traditional beliefs and religions. Practitioners of witchcraft have often had considerable skill in, for example, herbal medicine and traditional remedies; this prompted the World Health Organization in 1976 to recommended the integration of traditional healers into the health teams of African states.

witchery *n.* witchcraft, the power exercised by beauty or eloquence or the like.

witch hazel or **wych-hazel** any flowering shrub or small tree of the genus *Hamamelis* of the witch hazel family, native to North America and E Asia, especially *H. virginiana*. An astringent extract prepared from the bark or leaves is used in medicine as an eye lotion and a liniment.

witch-hunt *n.* the persecution of minority political-opposition or socially nonconformist groups without any regard for their guilt or innocence. Witch-hunts are often accompanied by a degree of public hysteria; for example, the ◊McCarthy anticommunist hearings during the 1950s in the USA.

with /wɪð/ *prep.* expressing (1) instrumentality or means, cause, possession, circumstances, manner, material, agreement and disagreement, (2) company and parting of company, (3) antagonism. —**in** (*or* out etc.) **with,** take, send, or put (a person or thing) in (or out etc.). **with it,** (*colloquial*) up to date, conversant with modern ideas etc. [Old English]

withal /wɪ'ðɔ:l/ *adv.* (*archaic*) in addition, moreover.

withdraw /wɪð'drɔ:/ *v.t./i.* (*past* **withdrew**; *past participle* **withdrawn**) 1. to pull or take back or away. 2. to remove (deposited money) from a bank etc. 3. to discontinue; to cancel (a promise or statement etc.). 4. to go away from company or from a place etc. 5. (in *past participle*, of a person) unresponsive, unsociable. —**withdrawal** *n.*

withe /wɪθ, wɪð, waɪð/ *n.* a tough, flexible shoot used for tying a bundle of wood etc. [Old English]

wither /'wɪðə/ *v.t./i.* 1. to make or become dry and shrivelled; to lose or cause to lose vigour or freshness. 2. to blight with scorn etc.

withers /'wɪðəz/ *n.pl.* the ridge between a horse's shoulderblades.

withershins /'wɪðəʃɪnz/ *adv.* (especially *Scottish*) in a direction contrary to the apparent course of the Sun (considered unlucky), anticlockwise. [from Middle Low German from Middle High German *wider* = against and *sin* = direction]

withhold /wɪð'həʊld/ *v.t.* (*past* and *past participle* **withheld**) 1. to hold back, to restrain. 2. to refuse to give or grant or allow.

withholding tax personal income tax on wages, salaries, dividends, or other income that is taxed at source to ensure that it reaches the tax authority. Those not liable to the tax have to reclaim it by filing a tax return.

within /wɪ'ðɪn/ *adv.* inside; indoors. —*prep.* 1. inside, not out of or beyond. 2. not transgressing or exceeding. 3. not further off than. —**within one's grasp,** close enough to be grasped or obtained. **within reach** (*or* sight) **of,** near enough to be reached (or seen). [Old English]

without /wɪ'ðaʊt/ *prep.* 1. not having, not feeling or showing; with freedom from. 2. in the absence of. 3. with neglect or avoidance of. 4. (*archaic*) outside. —*adv.* (*archaic*) outside. [Old English]

withstand /wɪð'stænd/ *v.t.* (*past* and *past participle* **withstood** /-'stʊd/) to endure successfully, to resist. [Old English]

withy /'wɪðɪ/ *n.* = withe.

witless *adj.* foolish, crazy. —**witlessly** *adv.,* **witlessness** *n.*

witness /'wɪtnɪs/ *n.* 1. a person giving sworn testimony; a person attesting another's signature to a document. 2. a person present, one who sees or hears what happens. 3. testimony, evidence, confirmation. 4. a person or thing whose existence etc. serves as testimony or proof. —*v.t./i.* 1. to be a witness to the authenticity of (a document or signature). 2. to be a spectator of. 3. to serve as evidence or indication of. 4. to be a witness. —**bear witness to** *or* **of,** to attest the truth of. **call to witness,** to appeal to for confirmation etc. **witness box** *or* (*US*) **witness stand,** an enclosure in a lawcourt from which a witness gives evidence. [Old English]

Witt /wɪt/ Johann de 1625–1672. Dutch politician, grand pensionary of Holland and virtual prime minister from 1653. His skilful diplomacy ended the Dutch Wars of 1652–54

and 1665–67, and in 1668 he formed a triple alliance with England and Sweden against Louis XIV of France. He was murdered by a rioting mob.

Wittelsbach /'vɪtlzbæx/ the Bavarian dynasty, which ruled Bavaria as dukes from 1180, electors from 1623, and kings in 1806–1918.

witter *v.i.* (*colloquial*) to speak with annoying lengthiness on trivial matters.

Wittgenstein /'vɪtgənʃtaɪn/ Ludwig 1889–1951. Austrian philosopher. *Tractatus Logico-Philosophicus* 1922 postulated the 'picture theory' of language: that words represent things according to social agreement. He subsequently rejected this idea, and developed the idea that usage was more important than convention.

witticism /'wɪtɪsɪzəm/ *n.* a witty remark.

wittingly /'wɪtɪŋlɪ/ *adv.* with knowledge of what one is doing.

witty /'wɪtɪ/ *adj.* showing verbal wit. —**wittily** *adv.,* **wittiness** *n.* [Old English]

Witwatersrand /wɪt'wɔ:təzrænd/ or **the Rand** the economic heartland of S Transvaal, South Africa. Its reef, which stretches nearly 100 km/62 mi, produces over half the world's gold. Gold was first found there in 1854. The chief city of the region is Johannesburg. Forming a watershed between the Vaal and the Olifant rivers, the Rand comprises a series of parallel ranges which extend 100 km/60 mi E–W and rise to 1,525–1,830 m/5,000–6,000 ft above sea level. Gold occurs in reefs, which are mined at depths of up to 3,050 m/10,000 ft. [Afrikaans = ridge of white water]

wives plural of **wife**.

wizard /'wɪzəd/ *n.* 1. a magician. 2. a person of extraordinary ability. —**wizardry** *n.*

Wizard of Oz, The Wonderful the classic US children's tale of Dorothy's journey by the yellow brick road to an imaginary kingdom, written by L Frank Baum in 1900. It had many sequels, and was made into a musical film in 1939 with Judy Garland.

wizened /'wɪzənd/ *adj.* (of a person or face) full of wrinkles. [past participle of *wizen* = shrivel, from Old English]

WNW abbreviation of west-north-west.

woad *n.* a plant *Isatis tinctoria* of the mustard family, yielding a blue dye; the dye itself. [Old English]

wobble *v.i.* 1. to rock from side to side; to stand or go unsteadily. 2. (of the voice) to quiver. —*n.* a wobbling movement; a quiver. —**wobbly** *adj.*

Wodehouse /'wʊdhaʊs/ P(elham) G(renville) 1881–1975. English novelist, a US citizen from 1955, whose humorous novels portray the accident-prone world of such characters as the socialite Bertie Wooster and his invaluable and impeccable manservant Jeeves.

Perhaps the greatest hardship of being an invalid is that people come and see you and keep your spirits up.

P. G. Wodehouse

Woden /'wəʊdn/ or **Wodan** the foremost Anglo-Saxon god, whose Norse counterpart is ◊Odin.

wodge *n.* (*colloquial*) a chunk, a lump.

woe *n.* 1. sorrow, distress. 2. (in *plural*) trouble causing this, misfortune. [Old English]

woebegone /'wəʊbɪgɒn/ *adj.* dismal-looking.

woeful *adj.* 1. full of woe, sad. 2. deplorable. —**woefully** *adv.*

Wöhler /'vɜːlə/ Friedrich 1800–1882. German chemist, a student of Jons ◊Berzelius, who in 1828 was the first person to synthesize an organic compound (◊urea) from an inorganic compound (ammonium cyanate). He also isolated the elements aluminium, beryllium, yttrium, and titanium.

wok *n.* a bowl-shaped frying pan used especially in Chinese cookery. [Chinese]

woke past of **wake**[1].

woken past participle of **waken**[1].

wold /wəʊld/ *n.* a high, open, uncultivated or moorland tract. [Old English = Old High German *wald* = forest, Old Norse *völlr* = field]

wolf /wʊlf/ *n.* (*plural* **wolves**) 1. a carnivorous, doglike mammal of the genus *Canis* (especially *Canis lupus*), with

wombat

coarse, tawny-grey fur and erect ears, found in Eurasia and North America. It is gregarious, grows to 90 cm/3 ft at the shoulder, and can weigh 45 kg/100 lb. **2.** (*slang*) a man who aggressively seeks to attract women for sexual purposes. —*v.t.* to devour greedily. —**cry wolf**, to raise a false alarm (like the shepherd boy in the fable, so that eventually a genuine alarm is ignored). **keep the wolf from the door**, to avert starvation. **wolf in sheep's clothing**, a hypocrite. **wolf whistle**, a whistle by a man sexually admiring a woman. [Old English]

Wolf /vɒlf/ Hugo (Filipp Jakob) 1860–1903. Austrian composer, whose songs are in the German *Lieder* tradition. He also composed the opera *Der Corregidor* 1895 and orchestral works, such as *Italian Serenade* 1892.

Wolfe /wulf/ James 1727–1759. British soldier. He fought at the battles of ◊Dettingen, Falkirk, and ◊Culloden. With the outbreak of the Seven Years' War (the French and Indian War in North America), he served in Canada and played a conspicuous part in the siege of the French stronghold of Louisburg in 1758. He was promoted to major-general in 1759 and commanded a victorious expedition against Montcalm in Québec on the Plains of Abraham, during which both commanders were killed. The British victory established their supremacy over Canada.

Wolfe Thomas 1900–1938. US novelist. He wrote four long and powerful autobiographical novels: *Look Homeward, Angel* 1929, *Of Time and the River* 1935, and the posthumous *The Web and the Rock* 1939 and *You Can't Go Home Again* 1940.

Wolfe Tom 1931– . US journalist and novelist. In the 1960s he was a founder of the 'New Journalism', which brought the methods of fiction to reportage. Wolfe recorded US mores and fashions in Pop style in *The Kandy-Kolored Tangerine-Flake Streamline Baby* 1965. His sharp social eye is applied to the New York of the 1980s in his novel *The Bonfire of the Vanities* 1988.

wolfhound *n.* a dog of a kind used (originally) to hunt wolves.

wolfram /ˈwulfrəm/ *n.* tungsten (ore). [German, perhaps from *wolf* = wolf and *rahm* = cream, or Middle High German *râm* = dirt, soot]

wolframite *n.* iron manganese tungstate, $(Fe,Mn)Wo_4$, an ore mineral of tungsten. It is dark grey with a submetallic surface lustre, and often occurs in hydrothermal veins in association with ores of tin.

Wollaston /ˈwuləstən/ William 1766–1828. British chemist and physicist. He amassed a large fortune through his discovery in 1804 of how to make malleable platinum. He went on to discover the new elements palladium in 1804 and rhodium in 1805. He also contributed to optics through the invention of a number of ingenious and still useful measuring instruments.

Wollongong /ˈwuləŋgɒŋ/ industrial city producing iron and steel in New South Wales, Australia, 65 km/40 mi S of Sydney; population (1985, with Port Kembla) 238,000.

Wollstonecraft /ˈwulstənkrɑːft/ Mary 1759–1797. British feminist, member of a group of radical intellectuals called the English Jacobins, whose book *Vindication of the Rights of Women* 1792 demanded equal educational opportunities for women. She married William Godwin and died giving birth to a daughter, Mary (see Mary ◊Shelley).

Wolsey /ˈwulzi/ Thomas *c.*1475–1530. English cleric and politician. In Henry VIII's service from 1509, he became archbishop of York 1514, cardinal and Lord Chancellor in 1515, and began the dissolution of the monasteries. His reluctance to further Henry's divorce from Catherine of Aragon, partly because of his ambition to be pope, led to

his downfall in 1529. He was charged with high treason in 1530 but died before being tried.

Wolverhampton /ˌwulvəˈhæmptən/ industrial city in West Midlands, England, 20 km/12 mi NW of Birmingham; products include metalworking, chemicals, tyres, aircraft, and commercial vehicles; population (1984) 254,000.

wolverine /ˈwulvəriːn/ *n.* a carnivorous, bearlike mammal *Gulo gulo* found in Europe, Asia, and North America. It is the largest member of the weasel family, Mustelidae. It is about 1 m/3.3 ft long, and has long, thick fur, a dark-brown back and belly, and lighter sides. It covers food that it cannot eat with an unpleasant secretion. Hunted for its fur, it is becoming rare.

woman /ˈwumən/ *n.* (*plural* **women** /ˈwimin/) **1.** an adult human female. **2.** women in general. **3.** feminine emotions. **4.** (*attributive*) female. **5.** (*colloquial*) a charwoman. —**Women's Lib,** a movement urging the liberation of women from domestic duties and subordinate status. **women's rights,** the right of women to have a position of legal and social equality with men. [Old English]

-woman suffix denoting a woman concerned or skilful with (*needlewoman*) or describable as (*Welshwoman*).

womanhood *n.* **1.** female maturity. **2.** womanly instinct. **3.** womankind.

womanish *adj.* like a woman; (usually *derogatory*) effeminate, unmanly.

womanize *v.i.* to philander, to consort illicitly with women. —**womanizer** *n.*

womankind *n.* or **womenkind,** women in general.

womanly *adj.* having or showing the qualities befitting a woman. —**womanliness** *n.*

womb /wuːm/ *n.* the hollow organ (in women and other female animals) in which children or young are conceived and nourished while developing before birth, the uterus. [Old English]

wombat /ˈwɒmbæt/ *n.* a herbivorous, nocturnal marsupial of the family Vombatidae, native to Tasmania and S Australia. It is about 1 m/3.3 ft long, heavy, with a big head, short legs and tail, and coarse fur. Species include the common wombat *Vombatus orsinus* of Tasmania and SE Australia and *Lasiorhinus latifrons* the plains wombat of S Australia.

women plural of **woman.**

womenfolk *n.* **1.** women in general. **2.** the women in a family.

Women's Institute (WI) a local organization in country districts in the UK for the development of community welfare and the practice of rural crafts.

Women's Land Army an organization founded in 1916 for the recruitment of women to work on farms during World War I. At its peak in Sept 1918 it had 16,000 members. It re-formed in June 1939, before the outbreak of World War II. Many 'Land Girls' joined up to help the war effort and by Aug 1943, 87,000 were employed in farm work.

women's movement the campaign for the rights of women, including social, political, and economic equality with men. Early European campaigners of the 17th–19th centuries fought for women's right to own property, to have access to higher education, and to vote (see ◊suffragette). Once women's suffrage was achieved in the 20th century, the emphasis of the movement shifted to the goals of equal social and economic opportunities for women, including employment. A continuing area of concern in industrialized countries is the contradiction between the now generally accepted principle of equality and the demonstrable inequalities that remain between the sexes in state policies and in everyday life.

women's services the organized military use of women on a large scale, a 20th-century development. First, women replaced men in factories, on farms, and in noncombat tasks during wartime; they are now found in combat units in many countries, including the USA, Cuba, the UK, the USSR, and Israel.

Women's Social and Political Union, The (WSPU) a British political movement founded in 1903 by Emmeline ◊Pankhurst to organize a militant crusade for female suffrage.

won past and past participle of **win.**

wonder /ˈwʌndə/ *n.* **1.** a feeling of surprise mingled with admiration, curiosity, or bewilderment. **2.** something that arouses this, a marvel, a remarkable thing or event. —*v.t./i.* 1. to feel wonder or surprise. 2. to feel curiosity about; to desire to know; to try to form an opinion about. —**for a wonder,** as a welcome exception. **I wonder!** I very much doubt it. **no** *or* **small wonder,** it is not surprising. **work** *or* **do wonders,** to produce remarkably successful results. [Old English]

Wonder Stevie. Stage name of Steveland Judkins Morris 1950– . US pop musician, singer, and songwriter, associated with Motown Records. Blind from birth, he had his first hit, 'Fingertips', at the age of 12. Later hits, most of which he composed and sang, and on which he also played several instruments, include 'My Cherie Amour' 1973, 'Master Blaster (Jammin')' 1980, and the album *Innervisions* 1973.

wonderful /'wʌndəfəl/ *adj.* remarkable, surprisingly fine or excellent. —**wonderfully** *adv.*

wonderland *n.* a land or place full of marvels or wonderful things.

wonderment *n.* surprise.

wondrous /'wʌndrəs/ *adj.* (*poetic*) wonderful. —*adv.* (*poetic*) wonderfully. —**wondrously** *adv.*

wonky *adj.* (*slang*) unsteady; unreliable.

wont *predic. adj.* (*archaic*) accustomed. —*n.* (*archaic*) what is customary, one's habit. [Old English]

won't /wəʊnt/ (*colloquial*) = will not.

wonted /'wəʊntɪd/ *attrib. adj.* habitual, usual.

woo *v.t.* 1. (*archaic*) to court (a woman). 2. to try to achieve or obtain (fame, fortune etc.). 3. to seek the favour of; to try to coax or persuade. [Old English]

wood /wʊd/ *n.* 1. the hard, fibrous substance in the trunks and branches of a tree or shrub; timber or fuel of this. 2. (in *singular* or *plural*) growing trees densely occupying a tract of land. 3. a wooden cask for wine etc. 4. a wooden-headed golf club. 5. a bowl[2]. —**cannot see the wood for the trees,** cannot get a clear view of the main issue because of over-attention to details. **out of the wood,** out of danger or difficulty. **wood pigeon,** the ringdove. **woodshed** *n.*, a shed where wood for fuel is stored. **wood sorrel,** a plant of the genus *Oxalis* with trifoliate leaves and white or pink flowers. [Old English]

Wood Grant 1892–1942. US painter based mainly in his native Iowa. Though his work is highly stylized, he struck a note of hard realism in his studies of farmers, such as *American Gothic* 1930 (Art Institute, Chicago).

Wood Henry (Joseph) 1869–1944. English conductor, from 1895 until his death, of the London Promenade Concerts, now named after him. He promoted a national interest in music and encouraged many young composers.

Wood Natalie. Stage name of Natasha Gurdin 1938–1981. US film actress who began as a child star. Her films include *Miracle on 34th Street* 1947, *The Searchers* 1956, and *Bob and Carol and Ted and Alice* 1969. She was married to actor Robert Wagner.

woodbine *n.* honeysuckle.

woodcarving *n.* an art form practised in many parts of the world since prehistoric times, for example, the NW Pacific coast of North America, in the form of totem poles, and W Africa where there is a long tradition of woodcarving, notably in Nigeria. Wood carvings survive less often than sculpture in stone or metal because of the comparative fragility of the material.

woodchuck *n.* a reddish-brown and grey North American marmot *Marmota monax*. [from American Indian name]

woodcock *n.* a Eurasian wading bird *Scolopax rusticola* about 35 cm/14 in long, with mottled plumage, a long bill, short legs, and a short tail. It searches for food in boggy woodland.

woodcut *n.* a print made by a woodblock in which a picture or design has been cut in relief. The woodcut is the oldest method of ◊printing, invented in China in the 5th century AD. In the Middle Ages woodcuts became popular in Europe, illustrating early printed books and broadsides.

wooded *adj.* having woods or many trees.

wooden /'wʊdən/ *adj.* 1. made of wood. 2. stiff and unnatural in manner, showing no expression or animation. —**wooden horse,** (*Greek legend*) that by use of which Troy was taken. **wooden spoon,** a spoon made of wood, used in cookery or given as a prize to the competitor with the lowest score. —**woodenly** *adv.*, **woodenness** *n.*

woodland *n.* an area in which trees grow more or less thickly; generally smaller than a forest. Temperate climates, with four distinct seasons per year, tend to support a mixed woodland habitat, with some conifers but mostly broad-leaved and deciduous trees, shedding their leaves in autumn and regrowing them in spring. In the Mediterranean region and parts of the southern hemisphere, the trees are mostly evergreen.

woodlouse *n.* (*plural* **woodlice**) a small crustacean of the order Isopoda. Woodlice have segmented bodies and flattened undersides. The eggs are carried by the female in a pouch beneath the thorax.

woodpecker *n.* a bird of the family Picidae, which drills holes in trees to obtain insects. There are about 200 species worldwide. The largest of these, the imperial woodpecker of Mexico, is very rare and may already be extinct.

wood pitch a by-product of charcoal manufacture, made from **wood tar**, the condensed liquid produced from burning charcoal gases. The wood tar is boiled to produce the correct consistency. It has been used since ancient times for caulking wooden ships (filling in the spaces between the hull planks to make them watertight).

wood pulp wood that has been processed into a pulpy mass of fibres. Its main use is for making paper, but it is also used in making ◊rayon and other cellulose fibres and plastics.

woodruff *n.* a white-flowered plant *Galium odoratum* with fragrant leaves.

Woodstock /'wʊdstɒk/ *n.* the first free rock festival, held near Bethel, New York State, USA, over three days in Aug 1969. It was attended by 400,000 people, and performers included the Band, Country Joe and the Fish, the Grateful Dead, Jimi Hendrix, Jefferson Airplane, and The Who. The festival was a landmark in the youth culture of the 1960s (see ◊hippie) and was recorded in the film *Woodstock*.

Woodward /'wʊdwəd/ Joanne 1930– . US actress, active in film, television, and theatre. She was directed by Paul Newman in the film *Rachel Rachel* 1968, and also starred in *The Three Faces of Eve* 1957, *They Might Be Giants* 1971, and *Harry and Son* 1984.

Woodward Robert 1917–1979. US chemist who worked on synthesizing a large number of complex molecules. These included quinine 1944, cholesterol 1951, chlorophyll 1960, and vitamin B_{12} 1971. He was awarded a Nobel prize in 1965.

woodwind *n.* musical instruments from which sound is produced by blowing into a tube, causing the air within to vibrate. Woodwind instruments include those, like the flute, originally made of wood but now more commonly of metal. The saxophone, made of metal, is an honorary woodwind because it is related to the clarinet. The oboe, bassoon, flute, and clarinet make up the normal woodwind section of an orchestra. Woodwind instruments fall into two categories: **reed instruments**, in which air vibrates a reed (a thin piece of cane attached to the mouthpiece through which air is blown); and those **without a reed** where air is simply blown into or across a tube. In both cases, different notes are obtained by changing the length of the tube by covering holes along it. Reed instruments include clarinet, oboe (evolved from the medieval shawm and hautboy), cor anglais, saxophone, and bassoon. Woodwind instruments without a reed include recorder, flute, and piccolo.

woodwork *n.* the making of things in wood; things made of wood.

woodworm *n.* the larva of a beetle *Anobium punctatum* that bores into wooden furniture and fittings.

woody /'wʊdɪ/ *adj.* 1. like wood; consisting of wood. 2. wooded. —**woodiness** *n.*

woof[1] /wʊf/ *n.* the gruff bark of a dog. —*v.i.* to give a woof.

woof[2] /wu:f/ *n.* the weft. [Old English]

woofer /'wʊfə/ *n.* a loudspeaker for accurately reproducing low-frequency signals.

Wookey Hole /'wʊki 'həʊl/ a natural cave near Wells, Somerset, England, in which flint implements of Old Stone Age people and bones of extinct animals have been found.

wool /wʊl/ *n.* 1. the fine, soft hair that forms the fleece of sheep and goats etc. 2. yarn made from this; fabric made from such yarn. 3. something resembling wool in texture. —**pull the wool over a person's eyes,** to deceive him or her. **woolgathering** *n.* being in a dreamy or absent-minded state. [Old English]

woodwind

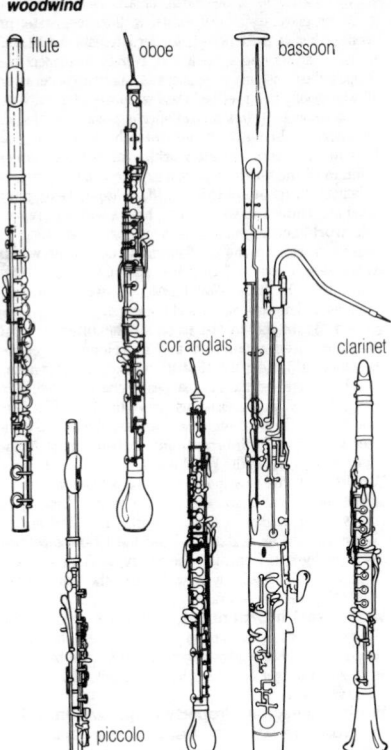

flute   oboe   bassoon

cor anglais   clarinet

piccolo

Woolf /wulf/ Virginia (born Virginia Stephen) 1882–1941. English novelist and critic. Her first novel, *The Voyage Out* 1915, explored the tensions experienced by women who want marriage and a career. In *Mrs Dalloway* 1925 she perfected her 'stream of consciousness' technique. Among her later books are *To the Lighthouse* 1927, *Orlando* 1928, and *The Years* 1937, which considers the importance of economic independence for women.

It is in our idleness, in our dreams, that the submerged truth sometimes comes to the top.
Virginia Woolf
A Room of One's Own

---

woollen /'wulən/ *adj.* made wholly or partly of wool. —*n.* a woollen fabric; (in *plural*) woollen garments. [Old English]
woolly /'wulı/ *adj.* **1.** covered with wool or wool-like hair. **2.** like wool; woollen. **3.** not thinking clearly; not clearly expressed or thought out, vague. —*n.* (*colloquial*) a knitted woollen garment; a jumper or cardigan etc. —**woolly bear**, a hairy caterpillar, especially of the tiger moth. —**woolliness** *n.*
Woolman /'wulmən/ John 1720–1772. American Quaker, born in Ancocas (now Rancocas), New Jersey. He was one of the first antislavery agitators and left an important *Journal*. He supported those who refused to pay a tax levied by Pennsylvania, to conduct the French and Indian War, on the grounds that it was inconsistent with pacifist principles.
Woolsack *n.* the usual seat, without back or arms, of the Lord Chancellor in the House of Lords, made of a large, square bag of wool and covered with cloth.
Woolworth /'wulwəθ/ Frank Winfield 1852–1919. US entrepreneur. He opened his first successful 'five and ten cent' store in Lancaster, Pennsylvania, in 1879, and, together with his brother C S Woolworth (1856–1947), built up a chain of similar stores throughout the USA, Canada, the UK, and Europe.

Worcester Porcelain Factory an English porcelain factory, since 1862 the Royal Worcester Porcelain Factory. The factory was founded in 1751 and produced a hard-wearing type of soft-paste porcelain, mainly as tableware and decorative china.
Worcestershire /'wustəʃə/ former Midland county of England, merged in 1974 with Herefordshire in the new county of Hereford and Worcester, except for a small projection in the N, which went to West Midlands. Worcester was the county town.
word /wɜːd/ *n.* **1.** any sound or combination of sounds (or its written or printed symbol, usually shown with a space on either side of it but none within it) forming a meaningful element of speech, conveying an idea or alternative ideas, and capable of serving as a member of, the whole of, or a substitute for a sentence; a unit of expression in a computer. **2.** speech, especially as distinct from action. **3.** one's promise or assurance. **4.** (in *singular* or *plural*) a thing said, a remark; a conversation. **5.** (in *plural*) the text of a song or of an actor's part. **6.** (in *plural*) angry talk. **7.** news; a message. **8.** a command; a password; a motto. —*v.t.* to put into words, to select words to express. —**in** *or* **one word**, briefly. **in other words**, expressing the same thing differently. **in so many words**, explicitly, bluntly. **take a person's word for it**, to believe his/her statement without investigation etc. **take a person at his/her word**, to act on the assumption that he/she meant exactly what he/she said. **(upon) my word**, an exclamation of surprise or consternation. **word for word**, in exactly the same or (of a translation) corresponding words. **word game**, a game involving the making, selection, or guessing, etc. of words. **the Word (of God)**, the Bible or a part of it; the title of the Second Person of the Trinity = **Logos**. **word of honour**, an assurance given upon one's honour. **word of mouth**, speech (only). **word-perfect** *adj.* knowing one's part etc. by heart. [Old English]
wording /'wɜːdɪŋ/ *n.* the form of words used.
wordless *adj.* without words, not expressed in words. —**wordlessly** *adv.*
word processor in computing, a program that allows the input, amendment, manipulation, storage, and retrieval of text; or a computer system that runs such software. Since word-processing programs became available to microcomputers, the method is gradually replacing the typewriter for producing letters or other text.
Wordsworth /'wɜːdzwəθ/ William 1770–1850. English Romantic poet. In 1797 he moved with his sister Dorothy to Somerset to be near Samuel Taylor ◊Coleridge, collaborating with him on *Lyrical Ballads* 1798 (which included 'Tintern Abbey'). From 1799 he lived in the Lake District, and later works include *Poems* 1807 (including 'Intimations of Immortality') and *The Prelude* (written by 1805, published 1850). He was appointed poet laureate in 1843.
wordy /'wɜːdɪ/ *adj.* using many or too many words. —**wordily** *adv.*, **wordiness** *n.*
wore past of **wear**.
work /wɜːk/ *n.* **1.** the application of mental or physical effort in order to do or make something, especially as contrasted with play or recreation; use of energy. **2.** in physics, the exertion of force overcoming resistance or producing molecular change. **3.** something to be undertaken; the materials for this. **4.** a thing done or produced by work; the result of action; a piece of literary or musical composition. **5.** doings or experiences of a specified kind. **6.** employment or occupation, what a person does to earn a living. **7.** things or parts made of specified material or with specified tools; ornamentation of a specified kind. **8.** (in *plural*) operations in building etc. **9.** (in *plural*) the operative parts of a clock or machine; (*slang*) all that is available. **10.** (in *plural*, often treated as *singular*) a place where industrial or manufacturing processes are carried out. **11.** (usually in *plural* or *combination*) a defensive structure (*earthwork*). —*v.t./i.* **1.** to perform work, to be engaged in bodily or mental activity. **2.** to make efforts. **3.** to be employed, to have a job. **4.** to operate or function; to do this effectively. **5.** to carry on, to manage, to control. **6.** to put or keep in operation so as to obtain material or benefit etc.; to cause to work for profit. **7.** to bring about, to accomplish. **8.** to shape, knead, or hammer etc. into the desired shape or consistency. **9.** to do or make by needlework, fretwork etc. **10.** to make (a way) or cause to pass gradually or by effort; to become (loose,

etc.) through repeated stress, movement, or pressure. **11.** to excite artificially. **12.** to solve (a sum) by mathematics. **13.** to purchase with one's labour instead of with money. **14.** to be in motion or agitated; to ferment; to have an influence. **—at work,** in action; engaged in work. **give a person the works,** to give or tell a person everything; to treat the person harshly. **have one's work cut out,** to be faced with a hard task. **make short work of,** to accomplish or dispose of quickly. **work basket.** a basket containing sewing materials. **work force** *n.* the workers engaged or available; the number of these. **work in,** to find a place for in a composition or structure. **workload** *n.* the amount of work to be done. **work of art,** a fine picture, poem, building etc. **work off,** to get rid of by work or activity. **work out,** to solve (a sum) or find (an amount) by calculation; to be calculated; to have a result; to provide for all the details of; to attain with difficulty; to exhaust with work. **workout** *n.* a practice or test, especially in boxing. **work over,** to examine thoroughly; (*colloquial*) to treat with violence. **workroom** *n.* a room in which work is done. **workshy** *adj.* disinclined to work. **work-study** *n.* a system of assessing jobs so as to get the best results for employees and employers. **work to rule,** to follow the rules of one's occupation with excessive strictness so as to reduce efficiency, usually as a protest. **work-to-rule** *n.* this process. **work up,** to bring gradually to an efficient state; to advance gradually (to a climax); to elaborate or excite by degrees; to mingle (ingredients); to learn (a subject) by study. [Old English]

workable /'wɜːkəbəl/ *adj.* that may be worked, used, or acted upon successfully.

workaday *adj.* ordinary, everyday, practical.

workaholic /wɜːkə'hɒlɪk/ *n.* (*colloquial*) a person who is addicted to working.

workday *n.* a day on which work is regularly done.

worker /'wɜːkə/ *n.* **1.** a person who works; one who works well or in a specified way. **2.** a neuter or undeveloped bee or ant etc. that does the work of the hive or colony but cannot reproduce. **3.** a member of the working class.

Workers' Educational Association (WEA) a British organization founded in 1913 to provide adult education. It had its origins in classes on cooperation organized by Albert Mansbridge, a clerk at a cooperative store near Toynbee Hall, where meetings were held.

workhouse *n.* (*historical*) a public institution where people unable to support themselves were housed and (if able-bodied) made to work.

working /'wɜːkɪŋ/ *adj.* **1.** engaged in work, especially in manual or industrial labour; working-class. **2.** functioning, able to function. **—***n.* **1.** the activity of work. **2.** functioning. **3.** a mine or quarry etc.; a part of this in which work is or has been carried on. **—working capital,** capital actually used in a business. **working class,** the class of people who are employed for wages, especially in manual or industrial work. **working day,** a workday; the part of the day devoted to work. **working knowledge,** knowledge adequate to work with. **working order,** the condition in which a machine works satisfactorily. **working party,** a group of people appointed to advise on some question.

working men's club a social club set up in the 19th century to cater for the education and recreation of working men. Today the clubs have few limitations of membership and are entirely social.

workman *n.* (*plural* **workmen**) **1.** a person employed to do manual labour. **2.** a person in respect of skill in a job.

workmanlike *adj.* showing practised skill.

workmanship *n.* degree of skill in doing a task or of finish in a product made.

workmate *n.* one engaged in the same work as another.

Workmen's Compensation Act 1897 British legislation that conferred on workers a right to compensation for the loss of earnings resulting from an injury at work.

workpeople *n.pl.* people employed in labour for wages.

workpiece *n.* a thing worked on with a tool or machine.

worksheet *n.* **1.** a paper for recording work done or in progress. **2.** a paper listing questions or activities for students, etc. to work through.

workshop *n.* **1.** a room or building in which manual work or manufacture is done. **2.** a place for concerted activity; such activity.

world /wɜːld/ *n.* **1.** the Earth, or a heavenly body like it. **2.** the universe, all that exists. **3.** the time, state, or scene of human existence. **4.** secular interests and affairs. **5.** human affairs; the active life. **6.** average or respectable people; their customs or opinions. **7.** all that concerns or all who belong to a specified class or sphere of activity. **8.** a vast amount. **9.** (*attributive*) affecting many nations; of all nations. **—bring** (*or* come) **into the world,** to give birth to (or be born). **in the world,** of all or at all. **man** *or* **woman of the world,** a person experienced and practical in human affairs. **out of this world,** (*colloquial*) extremely good etc. **think the world of,** to have a very high regard for. **world-beater** *n.* a person or thing surpassing all others. **world-famous** *adj.* known throughout the world. **world war,** a war involving many important nations (*World War I* 1914–18, *World War II* 1939–45). **worldwide** *adj.* covering or known in all parts of the world. [Old English]

World Bank the popular name for the **International Bank for Reconstruction and Development,** established in 1945 under the 1944 Bretton Woods agreement, which also created the International Monetary Fund. The World Bank is a specialized agency of the United Nations that borrows in the commercial market and lends on commercial terms. The **International Development Association** is an arm of the World Bank.

World Cup the most prestigious competition in international soccer, but which also features in the calendars of rugby union, cricket, and other sports. The 1994 soccer World Cup will be held in the USA; the 1990 competition was won by West Germany. The first rugby World Cup was held in 1987 and won by New Zealand; the 1987 cricket World Cup went to Australia.

World Health Organization (WHO) an agency of the United Nations established in 1946 to prevent the spread of diseases and to eradicate them. In 1990–91 it had 4,500 staff and a budget of £843 million. Its headquarters are in Geneva, Switzerland.

World Intellectual Property Organization (WIPO) a specialist agency of the United Nations established in 1974 to coordinate the international protection (initiated by the Paris convention 1883) of inventions, trademarks, and industrial designs, and also literary and artistic works (as initiated by the Berne convention 1886).

worldly /'wɜːldlɪ/ *adj.* **1.** of or belonging to life on Earth, not spiritual. **2.** engrossed in worldly affairs, especially the pursuit of pleasure or material gains. **—worldly-wise** *adj.* prudent in dealing with worldly affairs. **—worldliness** *n.* [Old English]

World Meteorological Organization an agency, part of the United Nations since 1950, that promotes the international exchange of weather information through the establishment of a worldwide network of meteorological stations. It was founded as the International Meteorological Organization in 1873, and its headquarters are now in Geneva, Switzerland.

World War I 1914–1918. War between the Central European Powers (Germany, Austria-Hungary, and allies) on one side and the Triple Entente (Britain and the British Empire, France, and Russia) and their allies, including the USA (which entered in 1917), on the other side. An estimated 10 million lives were lost and twice that number were wounded.

World War II 1939–1945. War between Germany, Italy, and Japan (the Axis powers) on one side, and Britain, the Commonwealth, France, the USA, the USSR, and China (the Allied powers) on the other. An estimated 55 million lives were lost, 20 million of them citizens of the USSR.

World Wide Fund for Nature (WWF, formerly the World Wildlife Fund) an international organization established in 1961 to raise funds for conservation by public appeal. Its headquarters are in Gland, Switzerland. Projects include conservation of particular species, for example, the tiger and giant panda, and special areas, such as the Simien Mountains, Ethiopia.

worm /wɜːm/ *n.* **1.** any of many types of invertebrate, slender, burrowing or creeping animal; the wormlike larva of an insect, especially one feeding on fruit or wood etc.; (in *plural*) internal (intestinal) parasites. **2.** an insignificant or contemptible person. **3.** the spiral part of a screw. **—***v.t./i.* **1.** to move with a twisting movement like a

World War I: chronology

1914	*Outbreak*: heir to the Austrian throne assassinated in Sarajevo, Serbia on June 28. July 28 Austria declared war on Serbia; Germany declared war on Russia and France, invading Belgium. 4 August Britain declared war on Germany.
1914	*Western Front*: German advance reached Paris. An Allied counter-attack at Marne drove them back to Aisne River. Trench warfare ensued. *Eastern Front*: Battle of Tannenberg in E Prussia halted German advance.
16 Sept	*Africa*: Germany's African colonies were in Allied hands.
1 Nov	*Middle East*: Turkey entered the war on the side of the Central Powers and attacked Russia in the Caucasus Mountains.
1915	*Western Front*: at Ypres, Belgium, the Germans used poison gas for the first time. *Eastern Front*: German field marshals Mackensen and Hindenburg drove back the Russians and took Poland. *Middle East*: British attacks against Turkey in Mesopotamia (Iraq), the Dardanelles, and at Gallipoli were all unsuccessful. *Italy*: declared war on Austria; Bulgaria joined the Central Powers. *War at Sea*: Germany declared U-boat war.
1916	*Western Front*: German attack at Verdun countered by the Allies on the Somme; tanks were used for the first time. *Eastern Front*: Romania joined the Allies but was soon overrun by Germany. *Middle East*: Kut-al-Imara, Iraq, was taken from the British by the Turks. *War at Sea*: Battle of Jutland between England and Germany which, although indecisive, put a stop to further German naval participation in the war.
1917	USA entered the war in April. The UK launched the third battle at Ypres and by Nov had taken Passchendaele.
1918	*Eastern Front*: 3 March Soviet Russia signed the Treaty of Brest-Litovsk with Germany, ending Russian participation in the war. *Western Front*: Germany began a final offensive. By June (when the first US troops went into battle) the Allies had lost all gains since 1915, and the Germans were on the Marne. The battle at Amiens marked the launch of the victorious Allied offensive. *Italy*: the British and Italians defeated the Austrians at Vittorio Veneto.
11 Nov	*German capitulation*: the armistice was signed after Kaiser Wilhelm II abdicated.
1919	18 June, peace treaty of Versailles. (The USA signed a separate peace accord with Germany and Austria in 1921.)

worm; to make (one's way) by wriggling or with slow or patient progress. **2.** to obtain (a secret) by crafty persistence. **3.** to rid of parasitic worms. **4.** (*nautical*) to make (a rope etc.) smooth by winding thread between the strands. —**wormcast** *n.* a convoluted pile of earth sent up by an earthworm on to the surface of the ground.

worm-eaten *adj.* full of worm holes. **wormhole** *n.* a hole left in fruit or wood etc. by the passage of a worm. **worm's-eye view,** a view from below or from a humble position. [Old English]

WORM (acronym from write once, read many times) in computing, a storage device, similar to ◊CD-ROM. The

World War II *The liberation of Paris by the Allies in June 1944; General de Gaulle leads jubilant Parisians down the Champs Elysées.*

World War II: chronology

1939 Sept	German invasion of Poland; Britain and France declared war on Germany; the USSR invaded Poland; fall of Warsaw (Poland divided between Germany and USSR).
Nov	The USSR invaded Finland.
1940 March	Soviet peace treaty with Finland.
April	Germany occupied Denmark, Norway, the Netherlands, Belgium, and Luxembourg. In Britain, a coalition government was formed under Churchill.
May	Germany outflanked the defensive French Maginot Line.
May–June	Evacuation of 337,131 Allied troops from Dunkirk, France, across the Channel to England.
June	Italy declared war on Britain and France; the Germans entered Paris; the French prime minister Pétain signed an armistice with Germany and moved the seat of government to Vichy.
July–Oct	Battle of Britain between British and German air forces.
Sept	Japanese invasion of French Indochina.
Oct	Abortive Italian invasion of Greece.
1941 April	Germany occupied Greece and Yugoslavia.
June	Germany invaded the USSR; Finland declared war on the USSR.
July	The Germans entered Smolensk, USSR.
Dec	The Germans within 40 km/25 mi of Moscow, with Leningrad under siege. First Soviet counter-offensive. Japan bombed Pearl Harbor, Hawaii, and declared war on the USA and Britain. Germany and Italy declared war on the USA.
1942 Jan	Japanese conquest of the Philippines.
June	Naval battle of Midway, the turning point of the Pacific War.
Aug	German attack on Stalingrad (now Volgograd), USSR.
Oct–Nov	Battle of El Alamein in N Africa, turn of the tide for the Western Allies.
Nov	Soviet counteroffensive on Stalingrad.
1943 Jan	Casablanca Conference issued Allied demand of unconditional surrender; the Germans retreated from Stalingrad.
March	USSR drove the Germans back to the river Donetz.
May	End of Axis resistance in N Africa.
July	A coup by King Victor Emmanuel and Marshal Badoglio forced Mussolini to resign.
Aug	Beginning of campaign against the Japanese in Burma (now Myanmar); US Marines landed on Guadalcanal, Solomon Islands.
Sept	Italy surrendered to Allies; Mussolini rescued by Germans who set up Republican Fascist government in northern Italy; Allied landings at Salerno; the USSR retook Smolensk.
Oct	Italy declared war on Germany.
Nov	US Navy defeated the Japanese in Battle of Guadalcanal.
Nov-Dec	Allied leaders met at Tehran Conference.
1944 Jan	Allied landing in Nazi-occupied Italy: Battle of Anzio.
March	End of German U-boat campaign in the Atlantic.
May	Fall of Monte Cassino, S Italy.
6 June	D-day: Allied landings in Nazi-occupied and heavily defended Normandy.
July	Bomb plot of German generals against Hitler failed.
Aug	Romania joined Allies.
Sept	Battle of Arnhem on the Rhine; Soviet armistice with Finland.
Oct	The Yugoslav guerrilla leader Tito and Soviets entered Belgrade.
Dec	German counteroffensive, Battle of the Bulge.
1945 Feb	The Soviets reached the German border; Yalta conference; Allied bombing campaign over Germany (Dresden destroyed); US reconquest of the Philippines completed; the Americans landed on Iwo Jima, S of Japan.
April	Hitler committed suicide; Mussolini captured by Italian partisans and shot.
May	German surrender to the Allies.
June	US troops completed the conquest of Okinawa (one of the Japanese Ryukyu Islands).
July	Potsdam Conference issued Allied ultimatum to Japan.
Aug	Atom bombs dropped by the USA on Hiroshima and Nagasaki; Japan surrendered.
	The liberation of Paris by the Allies in June 1944; General de Gaulle leads jubilant Parisians down the Champs-Elysées.

computer can write to the disc directly, but cannot subsequently erase or overwrite the same area. WORMs are mainly used for archiving and backup copies.

Worms /wɜ:mz, German vɔ:ms/ industrial town in Rhineland-Palatinate, Germany, on the Rhine; population (1984) 73,000. Liebfraumilch wine is produced here. The Protestant reformer Luther appeared before the **Diet** (Assembly) **of Worms** in 1521 and was declared an outlaw by the Roman Catholic Church.

wormwood /'wɜ:mwʊd/ n. 1. any plant of the genus Artemisia, family Compositae, especially the aromatic herb A. absinthium, the leaves of which are used in ◊absinthe. ◊Tarragon is a member of this genus. 2. bitter mortification; the source of this.

wormy /'wɜ:mi/ adj. full of worms; worm-eaten. —**worminess** n.

worn v.t./i. past participle of **wear**. —adj. 1. damaged by use or wear. 2. looking tired and exhausted. —**worn-out** adj.

Worner /'vɔ:nə/ Manfred 1934– . German politician, NATO secretary-general from 1988. He was elected for the conservative Christian Democratic Union (CDU) to the West German Bundestag (parliament) in 1965 and, as a specialist in strategic affairs, served as defence minister under Chancellor Kohl 1982–88. A proponent of closer European military collaboration, he succeeded the British politician Peter Carrington as secretary general of NATO in July 1988.

Worrall /'wɒrəl/ Denis John 1935– . South African politician, a member of the white opposition to apartheid. A co-leader of the Democratic Party (DP), he was elected to parliament in 1989.

worrisome /'wʌrɪsəm/ adj. causing worry.

worry /'wʌri/ v.t./i. 1. to give way to anxiety. 2. to harass, to importune; to be a trouble or anxiety to. 3. (of a dog etc.) to shake or pull about with the teeth. 4. (in past participle) feeling or showing worry, uneasy. —n. 1. a state of worrying, mental uneasiness. 2. a thing that causes this. —**worry beads**, a string of beads manipulated by the fingers to occupy or calm oneself. **worry out**, to obtain (a solution to a problem etc.) by persistent effort. —**worrier** n. [Old English = strangle]

worse /wɜ:s/ adj. 1. more bad. 2. (predicative) in or into worse health; in a worse condition. —adv. more badly or ill.

—*n.* a worse thing or things. —**from bad to worse,** into an even worse state. **the worse,** a worse condition. **the worse for wear,** damaged by use; injured or exhausted. **worse luck,** see ◊**luck.** [Old English]

worsen /'wɜːsən/ *v.t./i.* to make or become worse.

worship /'wɜːʃɪp/ *n.* 1. homage or service paid to a deity. 2. the acts, rites, or ceremonies of this. 3. adoration of or devotion to a person or thing. —*v.t./i.* (-pp-) 1. to honour as a deity, to pay worship to. 2. to take part in an act of worship. 3. to idolize, to regard with adoration. —**Your** (*or* **His,** etc.) **Worship,** the title of respect used to or of a mayor or certain magistrates. —**worshipper** *n.* [Old English]

worshipful /'wɜːʃɪpfəl/ *adj.* (*archaic,* especially in old titles of companies or officers) honourable, distinguished. —**worshipfully** *adv.*

worst /wɜːst/ *adj.* most bad. —*adv.* most badly. —*n.* the worst part or possibility. —*v.t.* to get the better of, to defeat. —**at its** etc. **worst,** in the worst state. **at (the) worst,** in the worst possible case. **do your worst,** an expression of defiance. **get the worst of it,** to be defeated. **if the worst comes to the worst,** if the worst happens. [Old English]

worsted /'wʊstɪd/ *n.* fine, smooth yarn spun from long strands of wool which has been combed so that the fibres lie parallel; fabric made from this. [from *Worste(a)d* in Norfolk]

wort /wɜːt/ *n.* 1. (*archaic* except in names) a plant (*liverwort*). 2. an infusion of malt before it is fermented into beer. —**St John's wort,** a plant of the genus *Hypericum,* with yellow flowers. [from Old English]

worth /wɜːθ/ *predic. adj.* (governing a noun like a *preposition*) 1. of a value equivalent to. 2. such as to justify or repay. 3. possessing, having property amounting to. —*n.* 1. what a person or thing is worth; (high) merit; usefulness. 2. the amount that a specified sum will buy. —**for all one is worth,** (*colloquial*) making every effort. **for what it is worth,** with no guarantee of its truth or value. **worth one's salt,** having merit. **worth (one's) while,** see ◊**while.** [Old English]

worthless *adj.* without value or merit. —**worthlessly** *adv.,* **worthlessness** *n.*

worthwhile /wɜːθ'waɪl/ *adj.* that is worth the time or effort spent.

worthy /'wɜːðɪ/ *adj.* 1. having great merit, deserving respect or support. 2. having sufficient worth or merit, deserving (of); adequate or suitable to the dignity etc. (of a specified person or thing). 3. (as *suffix* forming adjectives) deserving of, suitable for (*noteworthy, seaworthy*). —*n.* a worthy person; a person of some distinction in his country, time etc. —**worthily** *adv.,* **worthiness** *n.*

wot *v.t./i.* see ◊**wit.**

would *v. aux.* (*third person singular* **would**) past tense of **will,** used especially in reported speech or to express a habitual action or a condition, question, polite request, or probability. —**would-be** *adj.* desiring or aspiring to be.

wouldn't /'wʊdənt/ (*colloquial*) = would not.

wound[1] /wuːnd/ *n.* 1. an injury done to living tissue by a cut or blow etc. 2. an injury to a person's reputation or feelings. —*v.t.* to inflict a wound on. [Old English]

wound[2] past and past participle of **wind**[2].

Wounded Knee /'wuːndɪd 'niː/ the site on the Oglala Sioux Reservation, South Dakota, USA, of a confrontation between the US Army and American Indians. Sitting Bull was killed, supposedly resisting arrest, on 15 Dec 1890, and on 29 Dec a group of Indians involved in the Ghost Dance Movement (aimed at resumption of Indian control of North America with the aid of the spirits of dead braves) was surrounded and 153 were killed.

wove past of **weave**[1].

woven past participle of **weave**[1].

wow[1] interjection expressing astonishment or admiration. —*n.* (*slang*) a sensational success.

wow[2] *n.* a slow pitch-fluctuation in sound reproduction, perceptible in long notes.

W particle a type of ◊elementary particle.

w.p.b. abbreviation of waste paper basket.

WPC abbreviation of woman police constable.

w.p.m. abbreviation of words per minute.

WRAC abbreviation of Women's Royal Army Corps.

wrack *n.* 1. any of the large brown ◊seaweeds characteristic of rocky shores. The bladder wrack *Fucus vesiculosus*

has narrow, branched fronds up to 1 m/3.3 ft long, with oval air bladders, usually in pairs on either side of the midrib or central vein. 2. seaweed cast up or growing on the shore, used for manure. 3. destruction. [from Middle Dutch or Middle Low German]

WRAF abbreviation of Women's Royal Air Force.

wraith *n.* a ghost; a spectral appearance of a living person supposed to portend one's death.

wrangle *n.* a noisy, angry argument or quarrel —*v.i.* to engage in a wrangle. —**wrangler** *n.* [probably from Low Dutch]

wrap *v.t./i.* (-pp-) 1. to enclose in soft or flexible material used as a covering. 2. to arrange (such a covering or a garment, etc.) round a person or thing. —*n.* a shawl, coat, or cloak, etc. worn for warmth. —**under wraps,** in concealment or secrecy. **wrap over,** (of a garment) to overlap at the edges when worn. **wrapped up in,** with one's attention deeply occupied by; deeply involved in. **wrap up,** to envelop in wrappings; to put on warm clothing; (*slang*) to finish, to cease talking.

wrapper *n.* 1. a cover of paper etc. wrapped round something. 2. a loose, enveloping robe or gown.

wrapping *n.* (especially in *plural*) wraps, wrappers, enveloping garments. —**wrapping paper** strong or decorative paper for wrapping parcels.

wrasse /ræs/ *n.* a bright-coloured sea fish of the family Labridae with thick lips and strong teeth. [from Cornish *wrach* mutated relative to Welsh *gwrach* (literally = old woman)]

wrath /rɒθ, rɔːθ/ *n.* extreme anger. [Old English]

wrathful *adj.* extremely angry. —**wrathfully** *adv.*

Wray /reɪ/ Fay 1907– . US film actress who starred in *King Kong* 1933 after playing the lead in Erich von Stroheim's *The Wedding March* 1928, and starring in *Doctor X* 1932 and *The Most Dangerous Game* 1932.

wreak *v.t.* to give play to (vengeance, anger etc.) upon an enemy etc.; to inflict (damage etc.). [Old English = drive, avenge]

wreath *n.* (*plural* /riːθs, riːðz/) 1. flowers or leaves fastened in a ring especially as an ornament for the head or a building or for laying on a grave etc. as a mark of respect. 2. a curl or ring of smoke, cloud, or soft fabric. [Old English]

wreathe /riːð/ *v.t./i.* 1. to encircle as, with, or like a wreath. 2. to wind (one's arms etc.) round a person etc. 3. (of smoke etc.) to move in wreaths.

wreck *n.* 1. destruction or disablement, especially of a ship by storm or accidental damage. 2. a ship that has suffered wreck. 3. a greatly damaged or disabled building, thing, or person; a wretched remnant. —*v.t./i.* 1. to cause the wreck of (a ship, hopes etc.). 2. to suffer wreck; (in *past participle*) involved in a wreck.

wreckage *n.* wrecked material; the remnants of a wreck.

wrecker *n.* 1. one who wrecks something, one who tries from the shore to bring about a shipwreck in order to plunder or profit by wreckage. 2. a person employed in demolition work.

wren /ren/ *n.* a small, brown bird *Troglodytes troglodytes* with a cocked tail, found in North America, Europe, and N Asia. It is about 10 cm/4 in long, has a loud trilling song, and feeds on insects and spiders. The male constructs a domed nest of moss, grass, and leaves. [Old English]

Wren Christopher 1632–1723. English architect, designer of St Paul's Cathedral, London, built 1675–1710; many London churches including St Bride's, Fleet Street, and St Mary-le-Bow, Cheapside; the Royal Exchange; Marlborough House; and the Sheldonian Theatre, Oxford. After the Great Fire of London, Wren was commissioned to rebuild 51 City churches and St Paul's Cathedral. The W towers of Westminster Abbey, often attributed to him, were the design of his pupil ◊Hawksmoor.

wrench *n.* 1. a violent twist or oblique pull. 2. an adjustable tool like a spanner for gripping and turning nuts, bolts etc. 3. a painful parting. —*v.t.* 1. to twist or pull violently round; to damage or pull (away etc.) thus. 2. to distort (facts) to suit a theory etc. [from Old English = twist]

wrest *v.t.* 1. to wrench away. 2. to obtain by effort or with difficulty. 3. to distort into accordance with one's own views or interests etc. [Old English]

wrestle /'resəl/ *v.t./i.* 1. to fight (especially as a sport) by grappling with a person and trying to throw him to the ground; to fight with (a person) thus. 2. (with

Wright US architect Frank Lloyd Wright at 87. The originality of his work stands out in city buildings like the Guggenheim Museum in New York 1959. He condemned the growing congestion of cities and encouraged closeness to nature.

with) to struggle to deal with or overcome. —*n.* 1. a wrestling-match. 2. a hard struggle. —**wrestler** *n.* [Old English].

wrestling *n.* a sport popular in ancient Egypt, Greece, and Rome, and included in the Olympics from 704 BC. The two main modern international styles are **Greco-Roman**, concentrating on above-waist holds, and **free-style**, which allows the legs to be used to hold or trip; in both the aim is to throw the opponent to the ground.

wretch *n.* 1. an unfortunate or pitiable person. 2. a despicable person; (in playful use) a rascal. [Old English = Old High German *reccho* = exile, adventurer]

wretched /'retʃɪd/ *adj.* 1. unhappy, miserable. 2. of bad quality or no merit, contemptible. 3. unsatisfactory, displeasing. —**wretchedly** *adv.*, **wretchedness** *n.*

wriggle *v.t./i.* to move with short twisting movements; to make (one's way) thus. —*n.* a wriggling movement. —**wriggle out of,** to avoid on some pretext. —**wriggly** *adj.* [from Middle Low German]

wright /raɪt/ *n.* (*archaic* except in *combinations*) a maker or builder (*playwright, wheelwright*). [Old English]

Wright Frank Lloyd 1869–1959. US architect who rejected Neo-Classicist styles for 'organic architecture', in which buildings reflected their natural surroundings. Among his buildings are his Wisconsin home Taliesin East 1925; Falling Water, Pittsburgh, Pennsylvania, 1936; and the Guggenheim Museum, New York, 1959.

> The physician can bury his mistakes, but the architect can only advise his client to plant vines.
> **Frank Lloyd Wright**
> *New York Times Magazine* 1953

Wright Joseph 1734–1797. British painter, known as **Wright of Derby** from his birthplace. He painted portraits, landscapes, and scientific experiments. His work is often dramatically lit by fire, candlelight, or even volcanic explosion.

Wright Joseph 1855–1930. English philologist. He was professor of comparative philology at Oxford University 1901–25, and recorded English local speech in his six-volume *English Dialect Dictionary* 1896–1905.

Wright Judith 1915– . Australian poet, author of *The Moving Image* 1946 and *Alive* 1972.

Wright Orville 1871–1948 and Wilbur 1867–1912. US brothers who pioneered powered flight. Inspired by Otto ◊Lilienthal's gliding, they perfected their piloted glider in 1902. In 1903 they built a powered machine and became the first to make a successful powered flight, near Kitty Hawk, North Carolina.

Wright Peter 1917– . British intelligence agent. His book *Spycatcher* 1987, written after his retirement, caused an international stir when the British government tried unsuccessfully to block its publication anywhere in the world because of its damaging revelations about the secret service.

Wright Richard 1908–1960. US novelist. He was one of the first to depict the condition of black people in 20th-century US society with *Native Son* 1940 and the autobiography *Black Boy* 1945.

Wright Sewall 1889–1988. US geneticist and statistician. During the 1920s he helped modernize Charles ◊Darwin's theory of evolution, using statistics to model the behaviour of populations of genes.

wring *v.t.* (*past* and *past participle* **wrung**) 1. to twist and squeeze in order to remove liquid; to remove (liquid) thus. 2. to squeeze firmly or forcibly; to clasp (one's hands) together emotionally. 3. to extract or obtain (a promise, etc.) with effort or difficulty. —*n.* a wringing movement; a squeeze or twist. —**wringing wet,** so wet that water can be wrung out. —**wring the neck of,** to kill (a chicken etc.) by twisting its head round. [Old English]

wringer *n.* a device with a pair of rollers between which washed clothes etc. are passed so that water is squeezed out.

wrinkle *n.* 1. a small crease; a small furrow or ridge in the skin such as is produced by age. 2. (*colloquial*) a useful hint about how to do something. —*v.t./i.* to make wrinkles in; to form wrinkles. —**wrinkly** *adj.* [from Old English = sinuous]

wrist *n.* 1. the joint connecting the hand with the arm. 2. the part of a garment covering this. 3. (or **wristwork**) working the hand without moving the arm. —**wristwatch** *n.* a small watch worn on a strap etc. round the wrist. [Old English = Old Norse *rist* = instep]

wristlet *n.* a band or bracelet etc. worn round the wrist.

writ[1] *n.* a form of written command to act or not act in some way. [Old English]

writ[2] *v.t./i.* archaic past participle of **write.** —**writ large,** in a magnified or emphasized form.

write /raɪt/ *v.t./i.* (*past* **wrote**; *past participle* **written**) 1. to mark letters or other symbols or words on a surface, especially with a pen or pencil on paper. 2. to form (such symbols etc. or a message) thus; to fill or complete (a sheet or cheque etc.) with writing. 3. to put (data) into a computer store. 4. to compose for written or printed reproduction or publication; to be engaged in such literary composition. 5. to write and send a letter; (*US* or *colloquial*) to write and send a letter to (a person); to convey (news, etc.) by letter. 6. to state in a book etc. —**write down,** to record in writing; to write as if for inferiors; to disparage in writing; to reduce the nominal value of. **write off,** to write and send a letter; to cancel the record of (a bad debt, sum absorbed by depreciation etc.); to ignore (a person) as now of no account. **write-off** *n.* a thing written off; a vehicle too badly damaged to be worth repairing. **write out,** to write in full or in a finished form. **write up,** to write a full account of; to praise in writing. **write-up** *n.* a written or published account, a review. [Old English = scratch, score, write; originally of symbols inscribed with sharp tools on stone or wood]

writer *n.* one who writes or has written something; one who writes books, an author. —**writer's cramp,** a muscular spasm caused by excessive writing.

writhe /raɪð/ *v.i.* 1. to twist or roll oneself about (as) in acute pain; to suffer. 2. to suffer because of great shame or embarrassment. [Old English]

writing /'raɪtɪŋ/ *n.* 1. the process of marking letters or other symbols or words on a surface. 2. written symbols or words; a written document; (in *plural*) an author's works; **the Writings,** the Jewish name for the parts of the Old Testament other than the Law and the Prophets. —**in writing,** in written form. **writing on the wall,** an ominous event or sign that something is doomed (with allusion to the Biblical story of the writing that appeared on the wall at Belshazzar's feast (Dan. 5: 5, 25–8), foretelling his doom). **writingpaper,** paper for writing (especially letters) on.

written past participle of **write.**

WRNS abbreviation of Women's Royal Naval Service.

Wroclaw /'vrɒtslɑːf/ industrial river port in Poland, on the river Oder; population (1985) 636,000. Under the German name of Breslau, it was the capital of former German Silesia. Industries include shipbuilding, engineering, textiles, and electronics.

wrong adj. **1.** (of conduct etc.) morally bad, contrary to justice, equity, or duty. **2.** incorrect, not true; less or least desirable; (of a side of a fabric) not meant for show or use. **3.** not in a normal condition, not functioning normally. —adv. in a wrong manner or direction; with an incorrect result. —n. what is morally wrong; a wrong or unjust action or treatment. —v.t. **1.** to do wrong to, to treat unjustly. **2.** to attribute bad motives to (a person) mistakenly. —**get (hold of) the wrong end of the stick,** to misunderstand completely. **get a person wrong,** to misunderstand him or her. **go wrong,** to take the wrong path; to stop functioning properly; to cease virtuous behaviour. **in the wrong,** not having justice or truth on one's side. **on the wrong side of,** out of favour with or not liked by (a person); somewhat more than (a stated age). **wrong-foot** v.t. to catch (a person) unprepared. **wrong-headed** adj. perverse and obstinate. **wrong 'un,** (colloquial) a person of bad character. —**wrongly** adv., **wrongness** n. [Old English]

wrongdoer n. a person guilty of a breach of law or morality. —**wrongdoing** n.

wrongful adj. contrary to what is fair, just, or legal. —**wrongfully** adv.

wrote past of **write.**

wroth /rəʊθ, rɒθ/ predic. adj. (literary) angry. [Old English]

wrought /rɔːt/ v.t./i. archaic past and past participle of **work.** —adj. (of metals) beaten out or shaped by hammering.

wrought iron fairly pure iron containing some beads of slag, widely used for construction work before the days of cheap steel. It is strong, tough, and easy to machine. It is made in a puddling furnace, invented by Henry Colt in England 1784. Pig iron is remelted and heated strongly in air with iron ore, burning out the carbon in the metal, leaving relatively pure iron and a slag containing impurities. The resulting pasty metal is then hammered to remove as much of the remaining slag as possible. It is still used in fences and gratings.

wrung past and past participle of **wring.**

WRVS abbreviation of Women's Royal Voluntary Service.

wry /raɪ/ adj. (comparative **wryer;** superlative **wryest**) **1.** distorted, turned to one side. **2.** (of a face, smile etc.) contorted in disgust, disappointment, or mockery. **3.** (of humour) dry and mocking. —**wryly** adv., **wryness** n. [from wry v. from Old English = tend, incline (later = deviate, contort)]

wryneck n. a small bird of the genus Jynx, able to turn its head over its shoulder.

WSW abbreviation of west-south-west.

wt. abbreviation of weight.

Wuhan /wuːˈhæn/ river port and capital of Hubei province, China, at the confluence of the Han and Chang Jiang rivers, formed in 1950 as one of China's greatest industrial areas by the amalgamation of Hankou, Hanyang, and Wuchang; population (1986) 3,400,000. It produces iron, steel, machine tools, textiles, and fertilizer.

Wundt /vʊnt/ Wilhelm Max 1832–1920. German physiologist, who regarded psychology as the study of internal experience or consciousness. His main psychological method was introspection; he also studied sensation, perception of space and time, and reaction times.

wych- prefix in names of trees with pliant branches (wychalder, -elm). [Old English = bending]

Wycherley /'wɪtʃəli/ William 1640–1710. English Restoration playwright. His first comedy Love in a Wood won him court favour in 1671, and later bawdy works include The Country Wife 1675 and The Plain Dealer 1676.

Wycliffe /'wɪklɪf/ John c.1320–1384. English religious reformer. Allying himself with the party of John of Gaunt, which was opposed to ecclesiastical influence at court, he attacked abuses in the church, maintaining that the Bible rather than the church was the supreme authority. He criticized such fundamental doctrines as priestly absolution, confession, and indulgences, and set disciples to work on translating the Bible into English.

Wye /waɪ/ river in Wales and England; length 208 km/130 mi. It rises on Plynlimmon, NE Dyfed, flowing SE and E through Powys, and Hereford and Worcester, then follows the Gwent–Gloucestershire border before joining the river Severn S of Chepstow.

Wyeth /'waɪəθ/ Andrew (Newell) 1917–. US painter. His portraits and landscapes, usually in watercolour or tempera, are naturalistic, minutely detailed, and often have a strong sense of the isolation of the countryside: for example, Christina's World 1948 (Museum of Modern Art, New York).

Wyler /'waɪlə/ William 1902–1981. German-born film director who lived in the USA from 1922. He directed Wuthering Heights 1939, Mrs Miniver 1942, Ben-Hur 1959, and Funny Girl 1968, among others.

Wyndham /'wɪndəm/ John. Pen name of John Wyndham Parkes Lucas Beynon Harris 1903–1969. English science fiction writer who wrote The Day of the Triffids 1951, The Chrysalids 1955, and The Midwich Cuckoos 1957. A recurrent theme in his work is people's response to disaster, whether caused by nature, aliens, or human error.

Wynne-Edwards /'wɪnˈedwədz/ Vera 1906– . English zoologist who argued that animal behaviour is often altruistic and that animals will behave for the good of the group, even if this entails individual sacrifice. Her study Animal Dispersal in Relation to Social Behaviour was published in 1962.

Wyoming /waɪˈəʊmɪŋ/ state of W USA; nickname Equality State; **area** 253,400 sq km/97,812 sq mi; **capital** Cheyenne; **features** Rocky Mountains; Yellowstone and Grand Teton national parks; **products** oil, natural gas, tin, sodium salts, coal, phosphates, sulphur, uranium, sheep, beef; **population** (1988) 477,000; **history** part of the ◊Louisiana Purchase; first settled by whites in 1834; granted women the vote in 1869; became a state in 1890.

WYSIWYG acronym from what you see is what you get in computing, a program that attempts to display on the screen a faithful representation of the final printed output. For example, a WYSIWYG ◊word processor would show actual line widths, page breaks, and the sizes and styles of type.

Wyss /viːs/ Johann David 1743–1818. Swiss author of the children's classic Swiss Family Robinson 1812–13.

wyvern n. in heraldry, a winged two-legged dragon with a barbed tail. [from Old French from Latin vipera = viper]

x, X /eks/ n. (plural **xs**, **x's**) 1. the 24th letter of the alphabet. 2. (as a Roman numeral) 10. 3. in algebra, **x**, the first unknown quantity. 4. a cross-shaped symbol, especially used to indicate a position or incorrectness or to symbolize a kiss or vote, or as the signature of a person who cannot write.

Xavier, St Francis /ˈzeɪvɪə/ 1506–1552. Spanish Jesuit missionary. He went to the Portuguese colonies in the East Indies, arriving at Goa in 1542. He was in Japan 1549–51, establishing a Christian mission that lasted for 100 years. He returned to Goa in 1552, and sailed for China, but died of fever there. He was canonized in 1622.

X chromosome the larger of the two sex chromosomes, the smaller being the ◊Y chromosome. These two chromosomes are involved in sex determination. Genes carried on the X chromosome produce ◊sex linkage.

Xe symbol for xenon.

xenon /ˈzenɒn/ n. colourless, odourless, gaseous, nonmetallic element, symbol Xe, atomic number 54, relative atomic mass 131.30. It is grouped with the ◊inert gases and is now known to form some compounds, mostly with fluorine. It is a heavy gas present in very small quantities in the air (about one part in 20 million). Xenon is used in bubble chambers, light bulbs, vacuum tubes, and lasers. It was discovered in 1898 by William Ramsay and Morris Travers (1872–1961). [Greek neuter of xenos = strange]

xenophobia /zenəˈfəʊbɪə/ n. strong dislike or distrust of foreigners. —**xenophobic** adj. [from Greek xenos = foreigner]

Xenophon /ˈzenəfən/ c.430–354 BC. Greek historian, philosopher, and soldier. He was a disciple of ◊Socrates (described in Symposium). In 401 he joined a Greek mercenary army aiding the Persian prince Cyrus, and on the latter's death took command. His Anabasis describes how he led 10,000 Greeks on a 1,000-mile march home across enemy territory.

xerography /zɪəˈrɒɡrəfɪ, zeˈr-/ n. dry, electrostatic method of producing images, without the use of negatives or sensitized paper, invented in the USA by Chester Carlson in 1938 and applied in the Xerox ◊photocopier. Toner powder is sprayed on paper in highly charged areas and fixed with heat. [from Greek xēros = dry]

xerophyte n. a plant adapted to live in dry conditions. Common adaptations to reduce the rate of ◊transpiration include a reduction of leaf size, sometimes to spines or scales; a dense covering of hairs over the leaf to trap a layer of moist air (as in edelweiss); and permanently rolled leaves or leaves that roll up in dry weather (as in marram grass). Many desert cacti are xerophytes.

Xerox /ˈzɪərɒks, ˈzer-/ n. trade name of a certain process of xerography, a copy made by this. —**xerox** v.t. to reproduce by a process of this kind.

Xerxes /ˈzɜːksiːz/ c.519–465 BC. King of Persia from 485 BC when he succeeded his father Darius and continued the Persian invasion of Greece. In 480, at the head of an army of some 400,000 men and supported by a fleet of 800 ships, he crossed the Hellespont strait (now the Dardanelles) over a bridge of boats. He defeated the Greek fleet at Artemisium and captured and burned Athens, but Themistocles retaliated by annihilating the Persian fleet at Salamis and Xerxes was forced to retreat. He was murdered in a court intrigue.

Xhosa /ˈkɔːsə/ n. member of a South African people, living mainly in the Black National State of ◊Transkei. Their Bantu language belongs to the Niger-Congo family.

xi /ksaɪ, gzaɪ, zaɪ/ n. the 14th letter of the Greek alphabet (ξ, Ξ) = x.

Xian /ʃiːˈæn/ industrial city and capital of Shaanxi province, China; population (1986) 2,330,000. It produces chemicals, electrical equipment, and fertilizers.

Xi Jiang /ʃiː dʒiˈæŋ/ or **Si-Kiang** river in China, that rises in Yunnan and flows into the South China Sea; length 1,900 km/1,200 mi. Hong Kong island lies at its mouth. The name means 'west river'.

Xingú river (Amazon tributary) and region in Pará, Brazil. In 1989 Xingú Indians protested at the creation of a vast, intrusive lake for the Babaquara and Kararao dams.

Xinhua /ʃɪnˈhwɑː/ official Chinese news agency.

Xining /ʃiːˈnɪŋ/ or **Sining** industrial city and capital of Qinghai province, China; population (1982) 873,000.

Xinjiang Uygur /ʃɪndʒiˈæn ˈwiːɡuə/ or **Sinkiang Uighur** autonomous region of NW China; **area** 1,646,800 sq km/635,665 sq mi; **capital** Urumqi; **physical** Tyan Shan mountains; **products** cereals, cotton, fruit, uranium, coal, iron, copper, tin, oil; **population** (1986) 13,840,000; **history** under Manchu rule from the 18th century. Large areas ceded to Russia 1864 and 1881; China requests their return; regards the 480-km/300-mi frontier with Soviet Tadzikistan as undemarcated.

Xmas /ˈkrɪsməs/ n. = ◊Christmas. [abbreviation, with X for initial chi of Greek Khristos = Christ]

X-ray /ˈeksreɪ/ n. 1. (in plural) electromagnetic radiation of short wavelength, able to pass through opaque bodies. 2. a photograph made by X-rays, especially one showing the position of bones etc. by their greater absorption of the rays. —v.t. to photograph, examine, or treat with X-rays. [translation of German X-strahlen, so called from their unknown nature]

X-ray astronomy detection of X-rays from intensely hot gas in the universe. Such X-rays are prevented from reaching the Earth's surface by the atmosphere, so detectors must be placed in rockets and satellites. The first celestial X-ray source, Scorpius X-1, was discovered by a rocket flight in 1962.

X-ray diffraction method of studying the atomic and molecular structure of crystals. X-rays spread out as they pass through the crystals owing to ◊diffraction of the rays around the atoms. By measuring the position and intensity of the diffracted waves, the shape and size of the atoms in a crystalline substance such as DNA can be calculated.

xylem /ˈzaɪləm/ n. a tissue found in ◊vascular plants, whose main function is to conduct water and dissolved mineral nutrients from the roots to other parts of the plant. Xylem is composed of a number of different types of cell, and may include long, thin, usually dead cells known as ◊tracheids; fibres; thin-walled ◊parenchyma cells; and conducting vessels. [from Greek xulon = wood]

xylophone /ˈzaɪləfəʊn/ n. a musical instrument of graduated wooden bars with tubular resonators suspended vertically beneath them, struck with small wooden etc. hammers. —**xylophonist** /-ˈlɒfənɪst/ n. [from Greek xulon = wood]

y, Y /waɪ/ *n.* (*plural* **ys, y's**) 1. the 25th letter of the alphabet. 2. (in algebra) **y,** the second unknown quantity. 3. a Y-shaped thing.

Y symbol for yttrium.

yacht /yɒt/ *n.* 1. a light sailing vessel kept, and usually especially built and rigged, for racing; a similar vessel for use on sand or ice. 2. a vessel propelled by sails, steam, electricity, or motive power other than oars, and used for private pleasure excursions, cruising, travel etc. —**yachtsman** *or* **yachtswoman** a person who goes yachting. [from Dutch *jachte* = *jaghtship* (*jagen* = to hunt)]

yachting /'jɒtɪŋ/ *n.* racing or cruising in a yacht.

yah interjection expressing derision or defiance. [imitative]

yahoo /jə'hu:/ *n.* a bestial person. [name of race of brutes in Swift's *Gulliver's Travels*]

Yahya Khan /'jɑ:jə 'kɑ:n/ Agha Muhammad 1917–1980. Pakistani president 1969–71. His mishandling of the Bangladeshi separatist issue led to civil war, and he was forced to resign.

yak *n.* 1. a wild ox *Bos grunniens* which lives in herds at high altitudes in Tibet. It stands about 2 m/6 ft at the shoulder, and has long, shaggy hair on the underparts. It has large, upward-curving horns and humped shoulders. The yak has a thick coat as well as its own form of central heating through the fermentation in progress in its stomach. It is in danger of becoming extinct. 2. a domesticated variety of the wild ox. [from Tibetan *gyag*]

Yakut /jæ'kʊt/ (Russian *Yakutskaya*) autonomous Soviet Socialist Republic in NE USSR; **area** 3,103,000 sq km/ 1,197,760 sq mi; **capital** Yakutsk; **physical** one of world's coldest inhabited places; river Lena; **products** furs, gold, natural gas, some agriculture in the S; **population** (1986) 1,009,000; 50% Russians, 37% Yakuts; **history** the nomadic Yakuts were conquered by Russia in the 17th century; Yakut became a Soviet republic in 1922.

yakuza /jɑ:kuzə/ *n.* a Japanese gangster. Organized crime in Japan is highly structured, and the various syndicates between them employed more than 110,000 people in 1989, with a turnover of an estimated 1.5 trillion yen. The *yakuza* are unofficially tolerated and very powerful. [Japanese = good for nothing]

Yale /jeɪl/ *n.* (in full **Yale lock**) the trade name for a type of lock for doors etc., with a revolving barrel, invented in 1865. [from Latin *Yale*, American inventor (died 1868)]

Yalta Conference /'jæltə/ in 1945, a meeting at which the Allied leaders Churchill (UK), Roosevelt (USA), and Stalin (USSR) completed plans for the defeat of Germany in World War II and the foundation of the United Nations. It took place in Yalta, a Soviet holiday resort in the Crimea.

yam *n.* 1. a tropical or subtropical climbing plant of the genus *Dioscorea* of the family Dioscoreaceae; its edible, starchy tuber. The **Mexican yam** *Dioscorea composita* contains a chemical used in the manufacture of the contraceptive pill. 2. the sweet potato. [from Portuguese or Spanish *iñame*]

Yamagata /jæmə'gɑ:tə/ Aritomo 1838–1922. Japanese soldier, politician, and prime minister 1889–93 and 1898. As war minister 1873 and chief of the imperial general staff 1878, he was largely responsible for the modernization of the military system. He returned as chief of staff during the Russo-Japanese War 1904–05 and remained an influential political figure until he was disgraced in 1921 for having meddled in the marriage arrangements of the crown prince.

Yamamoto /jæmə'məʊtəʊ/ Gombei 1852–1933. Japanese admiral and politician. As prime minister 1913–14, he began Japanese expansion into China and initiated political reforms. He again became premier in 1923 but resigned the following year.

yammer *n.* (*colloquial* or *dialect*) a lament, a wail, a grumble; voluble talk. —*v.i.* (*colloquial* or *dialect*) to utter a yammer. [Old English *geōmor* = sorrowful]

Yamoussoukro /jæmu:'su:krəʊ/ capital designate of ◊Ivory Coast; population (1986) 120,000. The economy is based on tourism and agricultural trade. A basilica, completed in 1990, rivals St Peter's in Rome in scale.

yang *n.* see ◊yin and yang.

Yangon /jæŋ'gɒn/ since 1989 the name for Rangoon capital and chief port of Myanmar (formerly Burma) on the Yangon river, 32 km/20 mi from the Indian Ocean; population (1983) 2,459,000. Products include timber, oil, and rice. The city Dagon was founded on the site in AD 746; it was given the present name by King Alaungpaya in 1755. [Burmese = end of conflict]

Yang Shangkun /'jæŋ ʃæŋ'kʊn/ 1907– . Chinese communist politician. He held a senior position in the party 1956–66 but was demoted during the Cultural Revolution. He was rehabilitated in 1978, elected to the Politburo in 1982, and to the position of state president in 1988.

Yangtze-Kiang /'jæŋktsi ki'æŋ/ former name for ◊Chang Jiang, greatest Chinese river.

yank *v.t.* (*colloquial*) to pull with a jerk. —*n.* (*colloquial*) such a pull.

Yank /'jæŋk/ (*colloquial*) abbreviation of Yankee.

Yankee /'jæŋkɪ/ *n.* 1. (*colloquial*) (often disparaging) an American. 2. (*US*) an inhabitant of New England; an inhabitant of the northern states, a Federal soldier in the Civil War. 3. a type of bet on four or more horses to win (or be placed) in different races. [perhaps from Dutch *Janke*, diminutive of Jan = John, used derisively, or *Jengees*, American Indian pronunciation of *English*]

Yaoundé /jɑ:'ʊndeɪ/ capital of Cameroon, 210 km/130 mi E of the port of Douala; population (1984) 552,000. Industry includes tourism, oil refining, and cigarette manufacturing.

yap *v.i.* (**-pp-**) 1. to bark shrilly or fussily. 2. (*colloquial*) to chatter. —*n.* a sound of yapping. [imitative]

yapp *n.* a bookbinding with a projecting limp leather cover. [name of London bookseller *c.*1860, for whom it was first made]

yarborough /'jɑ:bərə/ *n.* a whist or bridge hand with no card above a nine. [from Earl of *Yarborough* (died 1897), said to have betted against its occurrence]

yard¹ *n.* 1. an imperial unit (abbreviation yd) of linear measure, equivalent to three feet or 36 inches (0.9144 m); this length of material; a square or cubic yard. 2. a spar slung across a mast for a sail to hang from. —**yardarm** *n.* a ship's yard; either end of this. [Old English]

yard² *n.* 1. a piece of enclosed ground, especially one attached to a building or used for a particular purpose. 2. (*US*) the garden of a house. [Old English]

Yeats Irish poet and dramatist W B Yeats.

yardage *n.* the number of yards of material etc.

yardstick *n.* **1.** a rod a yard long, usually divided into inches etc. **2.** a standard of comparison.

yarmulka /ˈjɑːmʌlkə/ *n.* or **kippa** a skullcap worn by Jewish men. [Yiddish]

yarn *n.* **1.** spun thread, especially of the kinds prepared for knitting or weaving etc. **2.** (*colloquial*) a tale, especially one that is exaggerated or invented. —*v.i.* (*colloquial*) to tell yarns. [Old English]

yarrow /ˈjærəʊ/ *n.* a perennial herb, genus *Achillea*, of the family Compositae, especially milfoil (*A. millefolium*), with feathery, scented leaves and flat-topped clusters of white or pink flowers. [Old English]

yashmak /ˈjæʃmæk/ *n.* a veil concealing the face except the eyes, worn in public by Muslim women in certain countries. [from Arabic]

yaw *v.i.* **1.** (of a ship or aircraft etc.) to fail to hold a straight course, to go unsteadily, especially turning from side to side. **2.** a yawing course or movement.

yawl *n.* **1.** a two-masted, fore-and-aft sailing boat with the mizen-mast stepped far aft. **2.** a kind of small fishing boat. [from Middle Low German or Dutch *jol*]

yawn *v.i.* **1.** to open the mouth wide and inhale, especially in sleepiness or boredom. **2.** to have a wide opening, to form a chasm. —*n.* the act of yawning. [Old English]

yaws /jɔːz/ *n. pl.* (usually treated as *singular*) a contagious tropical skin disease with raspberry-like swellings.

Yb symbol for ytterbium.

Y chromosome /waɪ ˈkrəʊməsəʊm/ the smaller of the two sex chromosomes. In male mammals it occurs paired with the other type of sex chromosome (X), which carries far more genes. The Y chromosome is the smallest of all the mammalian chromosomes and is considered to be largely inert (that is, without direct effect on the physical body). See also ◊sex determination.

yd(s) abbreviation of yard(s).

ye[1] /ji, jiː/ *pron.* (*archaic*) plural of ◊thou.

ye[2] /jiː/ *adj.* (*pseudo-archaic*) = the (*ye olde teashoppe*). [from old use of obsolete y-shaped letter for *th*]

yea /jeɪ/ *adv.* (*archaic*) yes. —*n.* the word 'yea'. —**yeas and nays,** affirmative and negative votes. [Old English]

yeah /jeə/ *adv.* (*colloquial*) yes. [casual pronunciation of yes]

year /jiə, jɜː/ *n.* **1.** the time occupied by the Earth in one revolution round the Sun, approximately 365¼ days. **2.** the period from 1 Jan to 31 Dec inclusive. **3.** a period of the same length as this starting at any point. **4.** (in *plural*) age, time of life. **5.** (usually in *plural*) a very long time. **6.** a group of students entering a college etc. in the same academic year. —**yearbook** *n.* an annual publication containing current information about a specified subject. [Old English]

yearling /ˈjɜːlɪŋ/ *n.* an animal between one and two years old.

yearly *adj.* **1.** done, produced, or occurring etc. every year. **2.** of, for, or lasting a year. –*adv.* once every year. [Old English]

yearn /jɜːn/ *v.i.* to be filled with great longing. [Old English]

yeast *n.* a greyish-yellow, fungous substance that causes alcohol and carbon dioxide to be produced when it is developing, used to cause fermentation in making beer and wines and as a raising agent in baking. —**yeast cake,** one in which the raising agent used is yeast. [Old English]

yeasty *adj.* frothy, like yeast when it is developing. —**yeastiness** *n.*

Yeats /jeɪts/ W(illiam) (B)utler 1865–1939. Irish poet. He was a leader of the Celtic revival and a founder of the Abbey Theatre in Dublin. His early work was romantic and lyrical, as in the poem 'The Lake Isle of Innisfree' and plays *The Countess Cathleen* 1892 and *The Land of Heart's Desire* 1894. His later books of poetry include *The Wild Swans at Coole* 1917 and *The Winding Stair* 1929. He was a senator of the Irish Free State 1922–28. He won the Nobel Prize for Literature in 1923.

O do not love too long, or you will grow out of fashion like an old song.

William Butler Yeats
'O do not love too long' *In The Seven Woods*

Yedo /ˈjedəʊ/ or **Edo** former name of ◊Tokyo, Japan, until 1868.

yell *n.* a loud, sharp cry of pain, anger, fright, encouragement, delight etc.; a shout. —*v.t./i.* to make or utter with a yell. [Old English]

yellow /ˈjeləʊ/ *adj.* **1.** of the colour of buttercups and ripe lemons, or a colour approaching this. **2.** having a yellow skin or complexion. **3.** (*colloquial*) cowardly. —*n.* **1.** yellow colour or pigment. **2.** yellow clothes or material. —*v.t./i.* to turn yellow —**yellow card,** such a card shown by the referee at a football match to a player whom he is cautioning. **yellow flag,** that displayed by a ship in quarantine. **yellow pages,** a section of a telephone directory, printed on yellow paper, listing business subscribers according to the goods or services they offer. —**yellowish** *adj.,* **yellowness** *n.* [Old English]

yellow archangel a flowering plant *Lamiastrum galeobdolon* of the mint family Labiatae, found over much of Europe. It grows up to 60 cm/2 ft tall and has nettlelike leaves and whorls of yellow flowers, the lower lips are streaked with red in early summer.

Yellow Book, The an illustrated literary and artistic quarterly, published from 1894 until 1897 in the UK, to which the artists Aubrey Beardsley and Walter Sickert, and the writers Max Beerbohm and Henry James contributed.

yellow fever or **yellow jack** acute tropical viral disease, prevalent in the Caribbean area, Brazil, and on the W coast of Africa. Its symptoms are a high fever and yellowish skin (jaundice, possibly leading to liver failure); the heart and kidneys may also be affected.

yellowhammer *n.* a bird *Emberiza citrinella* of the bunting family, found in open country across Eurasia. About 16.5 cm/6.5 in long, the male has a yellow head and underside, a chestnut rump, and a brown-streaked back. The female is duller.

Yellowknife /ˈjeləʊnaɪf/ capital of Northwest Territories, Canada, on the northern shore of Great Slave Lake; population (1986) 11,753. It was founded in 1935 when gold was discovered in the area and became the capital in 1967.

Yellow River the English name for the ◊Huang He river, China.

Yellow Sea gulf of the Pacific Ocean between China and Korea; area 466,200 sq km/180,000 sq mi. It receives the Huang He (Yellow River) and Chang Jiang.

Yellowstone National Park /ˈjeləʊstəʊn/ the largest US nature reserve, established in 1872, on a broad plateau in the Rocky Mountains, Wyoming. One million of its 2.2 million acres have been destroyed by fire since July 1988.

yelp *n.* a sharp, shrill cry or bark. —*v.i.* to utter a yelp. [Old English = boast (imitative)]

Yeltsin /ˈjeltsɪn/ Boris Nikolayevich 1931– . Soviet 'reform' communist politician, president of the Russian Republic from 1990. He was Moscow party chief 1985–87, when he was dismissed after criticizing the slow pace of political and economic reform. He was re-elected in March 1989 with a 89% share of the vote, defeating an 'official Communist Party' candidate, and was elected to

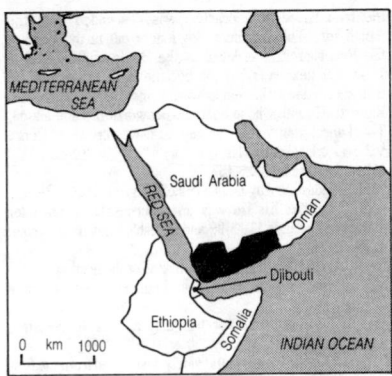

Yemen

the Supreme Soviet in May 1989. He supported the Baltic states in their calls for greater independence and has demanded increasingly more radical economic reform.

Yemen /'jemən/ two countries (North Yemen and South Yemen), forming the Republic of Yemen, between which union was agreed in 1979. **area** 531,900 sq km/205,367 sq mi; **capital** San'a; **physical** hot, moist coastal plain, rising to plateau and desert; **head of state and government** Ali Abdullah Saleh from 1978; **political system** authoritarian republic; **exports** cotton, coffee, grapes; **language** Arabic; **recent history** unification was proclaimed in May 1990, with a 30-month period of implementation.

yen[1] *n.* (*plural* the same) the Japanese monetary unit. [Japanese from Chinese *yuan* = round, dollar]

yen[2] *n.* a longing or yearning. —*v.i.* (-**nn**-) to feel a longing. [Chinese dialect]

Yenisei /jeni'seɪ/ river in Asian USSR, rising in Tuva region and flowing across the Siberian plain into the Arctic Ocean; length 4,100 km/2,550 mi.

yeoman /'jəʊmən/ *n.* (*plural* **yeomen**) 1. a man holding and cultivating a small landed estate. 2. a member of a yeomanry force. —**yeoman('s) service,** efficient or useful help in need. —**yeomanly** *adj.*

Yeomanry *n.* the English volunteer cavalry organized in 1794, and incorporated into volunteer regiments which became first the Territorial Force in 1908 and then the ◊Territorial Army in 1922.

Yeomen of the Guard an English military corps, popularly known as the **Beefeaters,** the sovereign's bodyguard since the corps was founded by Henry VII in 1485. Its duties are now purely ceremonial.

Yerevan /jeri'væn/ industrial city (tractor parts, machine tools, chemicals, bricks, bicycles, wine, fruit canning) and capital of Armenian Republic, USSR, a few miles N of the Turkish border; population (1987) 1,168,000. It was alternately Turkish and Persian from the 15th century until ceded to Russia in 1828.

Yerkes Observatory /'jɜːkiːz/ an astronomical centre in Wisconsin, USA, founded by George Hale in 1897. It houses the world's largest refracting optical ◊telescope, with a lens of diameter 102 cm/40 in.

Yersin /jeə'sæŋ/ Alexandre Emile Jean 1863–1943. Swiss bacteriologist who discovered the bubonic plague bacillus in Hong Kong in 1894 and prepared a serum against it.

yes *adv.* 1. serving to indicate that the answer to the question is affirmative, the statement etc. made is correct, the request or command will be complied with, or the person summoned or addressed is present. 2. (*interrogative*) indeed?; is that so?; what do you want? —*n.* the word or answer 'yes'. —**yes man** (*colloquial*) a weakly, acquiescent person. [Old English, probably = yea let it be]

Yesenin /ji'seɪnɪn/ Sergei alternative form of ◊Esenin, Russian poet.

yester- (*literary*) in combinations, of yesterday, that is last past (*yestereve, yestermorn*). —**yesteryear** *n.* last year; the recent past. [Old English]

yesterday /'jestədeɪ, -dɪ/ *adv.* on the day before today; in the recent past. —*n.* the day before today; the recent past. [Old English]

yet *adv.* 1. up to this or that time and continuing, still. 2. (with negative or interrogative) by this or that time, so far. 3. besides, in addition. 4. before the matter is done with, eventually. 5. (with comparative) even. 6. nevertheless. —*conj.* nevertheless, but in spite of that. [Old English]

yeti /'jetɪ/ *n.* the abominable snowman, see ◊abominable. [Tibetan]

yett *n.* (*Scottish*) a type of gate or portcullis with interlocking bands.

Yevele /'jiːvəlɪ/ Henry died 1400. English architect, mason of the naves of Westminster Abbey (begun 1375), Canterbury Cathedral, and Westminster Hall (1394), with its majestic hammerbeam roof.

Yevtushenko /jevtu'ʃeŋkəʊ/ Yevgeny Aleksandrovich 1933– . Soviet poet, born in Siberia. He aroused controversy with his anti-Stalinist 'Stalin's Heirs' 1956, published with Khrushchev's support, and 'Babi Yar' 1961. His autobiography was published in 1963.

Be equal to your talent, not your age./At times let the gap between them be embarrassing.

Yevgeny Yevtushenko
'Others May Judge You'

yew *n.* a dark-leaved, evergreen coniferous tree *Taxus baccata* of the family Taxaceae, native to the N hemisphere. The needle-like leaves and bright red, berry-like seeds are poisonous. The wood is hard and close-grained; it was used formerly as material for bows and continues to be used in cabinet-making. [Old English]

Yggdrasil /'ɪgdrəsɪl/ in Scandinavian mythology, the world tree, a sacred ash that spans heaven and hell. It is evergreen and tended by the Norns, goddesses of past, present, and future.

Yiddish /'jɪdɪʃ/ *n.* a member of the Germanic branch of the Indo-European language family, deriving from 13th–14th-century Rhineland German and spoken by northern, central, and eastern European Jews, who have carried it to Israel, the USA, and many other parts of the world. It is written in the Hebrew alphabet and has many dialects reflecting European residence, as well as many borrowed words. —*adj.* of this language. [from German *jüdisch* = Jewish]

yield *v.t./i.* 1. to give or return as fruit or as gain or result. 2. to surrender; to do what is requested or ordered. 3. to be inferior; to confess inferiority. 4. (of traffic) to give the right of way to other traffic. 5. to be able to be forced out of the natural or usual shape, e.g. under pressure. —*n.* the amount yielded or produced. [Old English = pay]

yin and yang in Chinese philosophy, the passive (characterized as feminine, negative, intuitive) and active (characterized as masculine, positive, intellectual) principles of nature. Their interaction is believed to maintain equilibrium and harmony in the universe and to be present in all things. In Taoism and Confucianism they are represented by two interlocked curved shapes within a circle, one white, one black, with a spot of the contrasting colour within the head of each. [Chinese *yin* = dark, *yang* = bright]

Yinchuan /jɪn'tʃwɑːn/ capital of Ningxia autonomous region, NW China; population (1984) 383,000.

yippee /jɪpɪ/ interjection expressing delight or excitement.

YMCA abbreviation of Young Men's Christian Association.

Ymir /'iːmɪə/ in Scandinavian mythology, the first living being, a giant who grew from melting frost. Among his descendants, the god Odin with two brothers killed Ymir and created Heaven and Earth from parts of his body.

yob *n.* (also **yobbo** /'jɒbəʊ/ *plural* **yobbos**) (*slang*) a lout, a hooligan. [back slang for *boy*]

yodel /'jəʊdəl/ *v.t./i.* (-**ll**-) to sing, or utter a musical call, with the voice alternating continually between falsetto and its normal pitch, in the manner of Swiss and Tyrolean mountain-dwellers. —*n.* a yodelling cry. —**yodeller** *n.* [from German *jodeln*]

yoga /'jəʊgə/ *n.* 1. a Hindu philosophical system attributed to Patanjali, who lived about 150 BC at Gonda, Uttar Pradesh, India. He preached mystical union with a personal deity through the practice of self-hypnosis and a rising above the senses by abstract meditation, adoption of special postures, and ascetic practices. 2. a system of

Yevtushenko *A master of the conversational, confessional style, the Soviet poet Yevtushenko has walked a thin line between Communist idealism and raising sensitive issues.*

mental and physical exercise practised in the West. [Hindu from Sanskrit = union]

yoghurt *n.* or **yogurt** or **yoghourt** food made from milk fermented with bacteria, often with fruit or other flavourings added. [from Turkish]

yogi /'jəʊgɪ/ *n.* a devotee of yoga. [Hindu]

yogurt see **yoghurt**

yoicks interjection used by a fox-hunter to urge on hounds.

yoke *n.* **1.** a wooden crosspiece fastened over the necks of two oxen etc. and attached to a plough or wagon to be drawn. **2.** a pair of oxen etc. **3.** an object like a yoke in form or function; a piece of wood shaped to fit a person's shoulders and to hold a pail or other load slung from each end; the top section of a dress or skirt etc. from which the rest hangs. **4.** oppression, burdensome restraint. **5.** a bond of union. —*v.t./i.* **1.** to put a yoke upon; to harness by means of a yoke. **2.** to unite, to link. [Old English]

yokel /'jəʊkəl/ *n.* a rustic, a country bumpkin. [perhaps from dialect *yokel* = green woodpecker]

Yokohama /jəʊkəʊˈhɑːmə/ Japanese port on Tokyo Bay; population (1987) 3,072,000. Industries include shipbuilding, oil refining, engineering, textiles and glass.

yolk /jəʊk/ *n.* a store of food, mostly in the form of fats and proteins, found in the ◊eggs of many animals. It provides nourishment for the growing embryo. [Old English]

yolk sac the sac containing the yolk in the egg of most vertebrates. The term is also used for the membranous sac formed below the developing mammalian embryo and connected with the umbilical cord.

Yom Kippur /jɒm ˈkɪpə/ the Jewish Day of ◊Atonement. [Hebrew]

Yom Kippur War the 1973 **October War** between the Arabs and Israelis; see ◊Arab-Israeli Wars. It is named after the Jewish holiday on which it began.

yomp *v.i.* to march with heavy equipment over difficult terrain.

yon *adj. & adv.* (*archaic* or *dialect*) yonder. —*n.* (*archaic* or *dialect*) yonder person or thing. [Old English]

yonder *adv.* over there. —*adj.* situated or able to be seen over there.

yore *n.* **of yore,** formerly, in or of old days. [Old English]

York /jɔːk/ cathedral and industrial city in North Yorkshire, England; **products** railway rolling stock, scientific instruments, sugar, chocolate, and glass; **population** (1985) 102,000.

York English dynasty founded by Richard, Duke of York (1411–1460). He claimed the throne through his descent from Lionel, Duke of Clarence (1338–1368), third son of Edward III, whereas the reigning monarch, Henry VI of the rival house of Lancaster, was descended from the fourth son. The argument was fought out in the Wars of the Roses. York was killed at the Battle of Wakefield in 1460, but next year his son became King Edward IV, in turn succeeded by his son Edward V and then by his brother Richard III, with whose death at Bosworth the line ended. The Lancastrian victor in that battle was crowned Henry VII and consolidated his claim by marrying Edward IV's eldest daughter, Elizabeth.

York Frederick Augustus, Duke of 1763–1827. Second son of George III. He was an unsuccessful commander in the Netherlands 1793–99 and British commander in chief 1798–1809.

York, Archbishop of metropolitan of the northern province of the Anglican Church in England, hence Primate of England.

yorker *n.* (in cricket) a ball that pitches immediately under the bat.

Yorkist /'jɔːkɪst/ *adj.* of the family descended from the first duke of York or of the White Rose party supporting it in the Wars of the Roses (compare ◊Lancastrian). —*n.* a member or adherent of the York family.

Yorkshire /'jɔːkʃə/ county in NE England on the North Sea, formerly divided into N, E, and W ridings (thirds), but in 1974 reorganized to form a number of new counties: the major part of **Cleveland** and **Humberside, North Yorkshire, South Yorkshire,** and **West Yorkshire**. Small outlying areas also went to Durham, Cumbria, Lancashire, and Greater Manchester. South and West Yorkshire are both former metropolitan counties.

Yorkshire pudding baked batter eaten with roast beef.

Yorkshire terrier a small, shaggy, blue and tan toy kind of terrier.

Yoruba /'jɒrəbə/ *n.* (*plural* the same or **Yorubas**) **1.** a member of a W African people from SW Nigeria and E Benin. They number approximately 12 million. **2.** their language, belonging to the Kwa branch of the Niger-Congo family.

Yoshida /jɒ'ʃiːdə/ Shigeru 1878–1967. Japanese politician who served as prime minister of Occupied Japan for most of the postwar 1946–54 period.

you /juː, jʊ/ *pron.* of the second person singular and plural (*objective* **you**; *possessive* ◊**your**, ◊**yours**) **1.** the person(s) or thing(s) addressed; (as *vocative* with a noun in an exclamatory statement: *you fools!*). **2.** (in general statements) one, a person, anyone, everyone. —**you and yours,** you together with your family, property etc. [Old English]

young /jʌŋ/ *adj.* **1.** having lived or existed for only a short time, not yet old; (of the night or a year etc.) still near its beginning. **2.** immature; having little experience. **3.** representing young people; characteristic of youth. **4.** distinguishing the son from the father or (in *comparative*) one person from another of the same name. —*n. collective.* offspring, especially of animals before or soon after birth. —**the young,** young people. [Old English]

Young /jʌŋ/ Arthur 1741–1820. English writer and publicizer of the new farm practices associated with the ◊agricultural revolution. When the Board of Agriculture was established in 1792, Young was appointed secretary, and was the guiding force behind the production of a county-by-county survey of British agriculture.

Young Brigham 1801–1877. US ◊Mormon religious leader, born in Vermont. He joined the Mormon Church in 1832, and three years later was appointed an apostle. After a successful recruiting mission in Liverpool, he returned to the USA and, as successor of Joseph Smith (who had been murdered), led the Mormon migration to the Great Salt Lake in Utah in 1846, founded Salt Lake City, and headed the colony until his death.

Young David Ivor (Baron Young of Graffham) 1932– . British Conservative politician, chair of the Manpower Services Commission (MSC) 1982–84, secretary for employment from 1985, trade and industry secretary 1987–89, when he retired from politics.

Young John Watts 1930– . US astronaut. His first flight was on *Gemini 3* in 1965. He landed on the Moon with *Apollo 16* in 1972, and was commander of the first flight of the Space Shuttle *Colombia* in 1981.

Young Lester (Willis) 1909–1959. US tenor saxophonist and jazz composer. He was a major figure in the development of his instrument for jazz music from the 1930s and was an accompanist for the singer Billie Holiday, who gave him the nickname 'President', later shortened to 'Pres'.

Young Thomas 1773–1829. British physicist who revived the wave theory of light and in 1801 identified the phenomenon of ◊interference. A child prodigy, he had mastered most European languages and many of the Eastern tongues by the age of 20. He had also absorbed the physics of Newton and the chemistry of Lavoisier. He further displayed his versatility by publishing an account of the Rosetta stone that played a crucial role in the stone's eventual decipherment by Jean François ◊Champollion.

Young Ireland an Irish nationalist organization, founded in 1840 by William Smith O'Brien (1803–1864), who attempted an abortive insurrection of the peasants against the British in Tipperary in 1848. O'Brien was sentenced to death, but later pardoned.

Young Italy an Italian nationalist organization founded in 1831 by Giuseppe ◊Mazzini while in exile in Marseille. The movement, which was immediately popular, was followed the next year by Young Germany, Young Poland, and similar organizations. All the groups were linked by Mazzini in his Young Europe movement, but none achieved much practical success; attempted uprisings by Young Italy in 1834 and 1844 failed miserably. It was superseded in Italy by the ◊Risorgimento.

Young Men's Christian Association (YMCA) an imternational organization founded 1844 by George Williams (1821-1905) in London. It aims at self-improvement–spiritual, intellectual, and physical. From 1971 women have been accepted as members.

Young Pretender the nickname of ◊Charles Edward Stuart, claimant to the Scottish and English thrones. See also ◊pretender.

youngster n. a child, a young person.

Young Turk a member of a reformist movement of young army officers founded in 1889 in the Ottoman Empire. The movement was instrumental in the constitutional changes of 1908 and the abdication of Sultan Abdul-Hamid II in 1909. It gained prestige during the Balkan Wars 1912–13 and encouraged Turkish links with the German empire. Its influence diminished after 1918. The term is now used for a member of any radical or rebellious faction within a party or organization.

Young Women's Christian Association (YWCA) an organization for women and girls, formed in 1887 when two organizations, both founded in 1855, the one by Emma Robarts and the other by Lady Kinnaird, combined their work.

your /jɔ:, juə/ *poss. adj.* of or belonging to you. [Old English]

Yourcenar /juəsə'nɑ:/ Marguerite. Pen name of Marguerite de Crayencour 1903–1987. French writer, born in Belgium. She first gained fame as a novelist in France in the 1930s with books such as *La Nouvelle Euridyce/The New Euridyce* 1931. In 1939 she settled in the USA. Her evocation of past eras and characters, exemplified in *Les Mémoires d'Hadrien/The Memoirs of Hadrian* 1951, brought her acclaim as a historical novelist. In 1980 she became the first woman to be elected to the French Academy.

yours /jɔ:z, juəz/ *poss. pron.* of or belonging to you; the thing(s) belonging to you. —**yours ever, faithfully, sincerely, truly,** etc., formulas preceding the signature of a letter.

yourself /jɔ:'self, juə'self/ *pron.* (*plural* **yourselves**) the emphatic and reflexive form of ◊you.

youth /ju:θ/ *n.* (*plural* **youths** /ju:ðz/) 1. being young; the period between childhood and adult age; the vigour, enthusiasm, inexperience, or other characteristic of this period. 2. a young man. 3. (as *plural*) young people collectively. —**youth club**, a place where leisure activities are provided for young people. **youth hostel**, a place where (young) holiday-makers can stay cheaply for the night. **youth hosteller**, a user of a youth hostel. [Old English]

youthful *adj.* young or (still) having the characteristics of youth. —**youthfully** *adv.*, **youthfulness** *n.*

yowl *n.* a loud wailing cry, a howl. —*v.i.* to utter a yowl. [imitative]

Yo-Yo /'jəʊjəʊ/ *n.* (*plural* **Yo-Yos**) trade name of a toy consisting of a pair of discs with a deep groove between them in which a string is attached and wound, and which

can be made to fall and rise on the string when this is jerked by a finger.

Ypres /'i:prə/ (Flemish *Ieper*) Belgian town in W Flanders, 40 km/25 mi S of Ostend, a site of fighting in World War I. The Menin Gate 1927 is a memorial to British soldiers lost in the three major battles fought around the town 1914–17.

yr abbreviation of 1. year(s). 2. younger. 3. your.

yrs abbreviation of 1. years. 2. yours.

ytterbium /i'tɜ:biəm/ *n.* a soft, lustrous, silvery, malleable and ductile element of the ◊lanthanide series, symbol Yb, atomic number 70, relative atomic mass 173.04. It occurs with (and resembles) yttrium in gadolinite and other minerals, and is used in making steel and other alloys. [from *Ytterby* = village in Sweden]

yttrium /'itriəm/ *n.* a silvery, metallic element, symbol Y, atomic number 39, included among the rare-earth metals. A member of the ◊lanthanide series, it occurs in monazite and is used to reduce steel corrosion.

Yucatán /ju:kə'tɑ:n/ peninsula in Central America, divided among Mexico, Belize, and Guatemala; area 180,000 sq km/70,000 sq mi. Tropical crops are grown. It is inhabited by ◊Maya Indians and contains the remains of their civilization.

yucca /'jʌkə/ *n.* a plant of the genus *Yucca*, family Liliaceae, with over 40 species found in Latin America and SW USA. The leaves are stiff and sword-shaped and the flowers white and bell-shaped. [Carib]

Yugoslavia /ju:gəʊ'slɑ:viə/ Socialist Republic of; country in SE Europe, on the Adriatic Sea, bounded W by Italy, N by Austria and Hungary, E by Romania and Bulgaria, and S by Greece and Albania; area 255,800 sq km/98,739 sq mi; capital Belgrade; physical mountainous, with river Danube plains in N and E; limestone (karst) features in NW; head of state Janez Drovsek from 1988; head of government Ante Marković; political system communism; exports machinery, electrical goods, chemicals; population (1990 est) 24,107,000; language Serbo-Croat; recent history Kingdom of the Serbs, Croats and Slovenes created 1917–18; renamed Yugoslavia in 1929. Invaded by Germany in 1941; Communist federal republic formed under leadership of Tito in 1945; split with USSR in 1948. Collective leadership assumed power after Tito's death in 1980. Regional unrest in 1987 was followed by a period of economic difficulties and ethnic unrest. Reformist Croatian Ante Markovic became prime minister in 1989. In 1990 multiparty systems were established in ◊Slovenia and ◊Croatia. Several republics called for secession in 1991 and the President resigned. Clashes took place between Serbs and Croats in Croatia. Slovenia declared itself independent. The federal army intervened in Croatia but fighting continued.

Yukon /'ju:kɒn/ territory of NW Canada; area 483,500 sq km/186,631 sq mi; features named after its chief river, the Yukon; includes the highest point in Canada, Mount Logan 6,050 m/19,850 ft; products oil, natural gas, gold, silver, coal; population (1986) 24,000; history settlement dates from the gold rush 1896–1910, when 30,000 people moved to the ◊Klondike river valley (silver is now worked there); became separate from Northwest Territories in 1898, with Dawson City as the original capital.

Yukon River /'ju:kɒn/ river in North America, 3,185 km/1,979 mi, flowing from Yukon Territory from Lake Tagish into Alaska where it empties into the Bering Sea.

yule *n.* (in full **yuletide**) (*archaic*) the Christmas festival. —**yule log** a large log traditionally burnt in the hearth on Christmas Eve. [Old English]

yummy *adj.* (*colloquial*) tasty, delicious.

yum-yum /jʌm'jʌm/ interjection expressing pleasure from eating or the prospect of eating.

Yunnan /ju:'næn/ province of SW China, adjoining Myanmar (formerly Burma), Laos, and Vietnam; area 436,200 sq km/168,373 sq mi; capital Kunming; physical rivers: Chang Jiang, Salween, Mekong; crossed by the Burma Road; mountainous and well forested; products rice, tea, timber, wheat, cotton, rubber, tin, copper, lead, zinc, coal, salt; population (1986) 34,560,000.

yuppie *n.* (*colloquial*) acronym from young urban professional person.

YWCA abbreviation of Young Women's Christian Association.

z, Z /zed/ *n.* (*plural* **zs, z's**) **1.** the 26th letter of the alphabet. **2.** (in algebra) **z**, the third unknown quantity.

zabaglione /zɑ:bɑ:'ljəʊneɪ/ *n.* an Italian pudding of whipped and heated egg yolks, sugar, and Marsala wine. [Italian]

Zadkine /'zædki:n/ Ossip 1890–1967. French Cubist sculptor, born in Russia, active in Paris from 1909. His art represented the human form in dramatic, semi-abstract terms, as in the monument *To a Destroyed City* 1953.

Zagreb /'zɑ:greb/ industrial city (leather, linen, carpets, paper, and electrical goods) and capital of Croatia, Yugoslavia, on the Sava river; population (1981) 1,174,512.

Zahir /zə'hiə/ ud-din Muhammad 1483–1530. First Great Mogul of India from 1526, called Baber (Arabic 'lion'). He was the great-grandson of the Mongol conqueror Tamerlane and, at the age of 12, succeeded his father, Omar Sheik Mirza, as ruler of Ferghana (Turkestan). In 1526 he defeated the emperor of Delhi at Panipat in the Punjab, captured Delhi and ◊Agra (the site of the Taj Mahal), and established a dynasty that lasted until 1858.

Zahir Shah /zə'hiə 'ʃɑ:/ Mohammed 1914–   . King of Afghanistan from 1933–73. Educated in Kabul and Paris, he served in the government 1932–33. He was overthrown in 1973 by a republican coup and went into exile. He has been a symbol of national unity for the ◊Mujaheddin Islamic fundamentalist resistance groups.

zaibatsu *n.* an industrial conglomerate (see ◊cartel). [Japanese = financial clique]

za'im in Lebanon, a political leader, originally the holder of a feudal office. The office is largely hereditary. The pattern of Lebanese politics has been that individual *za'im*, rather than parties or even government ministers, wield effective power.

Zaïre /zɑ:'iə/ Republic of (formerly **Congo**); country in central Africa; **area** 2,344,900 sq km/905,366 sq mi; **capital** Kinshasa; **physical** Zaïre river basin has tropical rainforest and savanna; mountains in E and W; **head of state and government** Mobuto Sésé Séko Kuku Ngbendu wa Zabanga from 1965; **political system** one-party Socialist republic; **exports** coffee, copper, cobalt, industrial diamonds; **population** (1990 est) 35,330,000; **language** French; **recent history** achieved full independence as the republic of Congo in 1960.

Zaïre River /zɑ:'iə/ formerly (until 1971) **Congo** second longest river in Africa, rising near the Zambia-Zaïre border (and known as the **Lualaba River** in the upper reaches) and flowing 4,500 km/2,800 mi to the Atlantic, running in a great curve that crosses the equator twice, and discharging a volume of water second only to the Amazon. The chief tributaries are the Ubangi, Sangha, and Kasai.

Zama, Battle of /'zɑ:mə/ battle fought in 202 BC in Numidia (now Algeria), in which the Carthaginians under Hannibal were defeated by the Romans under Scipio, so ending the Second Punic War.

Zambezi /zæm'bi:zi/ river in central and SE Africa; length 2,650 km/1,650 mi from NW Zambia through Mozambique to the Indian Ocean, with a wide delta near Chinde. Major tributaries include the Kafue in Zambia.

Zambia /'zæmbiə/ Republic of; landlocked country in central Africa; **area** 752,600 sq km/290,579 sq mi;

capital Lusaka; **physical** forested plateau cut through by rivers; **head of state and government** Kenneth Kaunda from 1964; **political system** nationalistic socialism; **exports** copper, cobalt, zinc, emeralds, tobacco; **population** (1990 est) 8,119,000; **language** English; **recent history** achieved full independence within the Commonwealth in 1964; a multiparty system introduced in 1991.

ZANU (acronym for Zimbabwe African National Union) a political organization founded in 1963 by the Reverend Ndabaningi Sithole and later led by Robert Mugabe. It was banned in 1964 by Ian Smith's Rhodesian Front government, against which it conducted a guerrilla war from Zambia until the free elections of 1980, when the ZANU Patriotic Front party, led by Mugabe, won 63% of the vote. In 1987 it merged with ◊ZAPU.

zany /'zeɪnɪ/ *adj.* crazily funny or ridiculous. —*n.* **1.** a comical or eccentric person. **2.** (*historical*) an attendant clown awkwardly mimicking the chief clown in shows. [from French or Italian *zan(n)i*, Venetian form of *Giovanni* = John]

Zanzibar /'zænzi'bɑ:/ island region of Tanzania; **area** 1,658 sq km/640 sq mi (80 km/50 mi long); **products** cloves, copra; **population** (1985) 571,000; **history** settled by Arab traders in the 7th century; became a sultanate; under British protection 1890–1963. Together with the island of Pemba, some nearby islets, and a strip of mainland territory, it became a republic. It merged with Tanganyika as ◊Tanzania in 1964.

zap *v.t.* (-pp-) (*slang*) to hit, to attack, to kill. [imitative]

Zapata /sə'pɑ:tə/ Emiliano 1879–1919. Mexican Indian revolutionary leader. He led a revolt against dictator Porfirio Díaz (1830–1915) from 1911 under the slogan 'Land and Liberty', to repossess for the indigenous Mexicans the land taken by the Spanish. By 1915 he was driven into retreat, and was assassinated.

Zapotec *n.* a member of a North American Indian people of S Mexico, now numbering approximately 250,000, living mainly in Oaxaca. The Zapotec language, which belongs to the Oto-Mangean family, has nine dialects. The ancient Zapotec built the ceremonial centre of Monte Albán 1000–500 BC, and developed one of the classic Mesoamerican civilizations by AD 300, but declined under pressure from the Mixtecs from 900.

ZAPU (acronym from Zimbabwe African People's Union) a political organization founded by Joshua Nkomo in 1961 and banned in 1962 by the Rhodesian government. It engaged in a guerrilla war in alliance with ◊ZANU against the Rhodesian regime until late 1979. In the 1980 elections ZAPU was defeated and was then persecuted by the ruling ZANU Patriotic Front party. In 1987 the two parties merged.

Zaragoza /særə'gɒsə/ (English **Saragossa**) industrial city (iron, steel, chemicals, plastics, canned food, electrical goods) in Aragon, Spain; population (1986) 596,000. The medieval city walls and bridges over the river Ebro survive, and there is a 15th-century university.

zarzuela *n.* a Spanish musical theatre form combining song, dance, and speech. It originated as an amusement for royalty in the 17th century and found an early exponent in the playwright Calderón. Often satirical, it gained renewed

zebra

popularity in the 20th century with the works of Frederico Moreno Tórroba (1891–1982). [from La Zarzuela, royal country house where it was first developed]

zazen *n.* formal seated meditation in Zen Buddhism. Correct posture and breathing are necessary.

zeal *n.* enthusiasm, hearty and persistent effort. [from Latin from Greek *zēlos*]

zealot /'zelət/ *n.* 1. a zealous person; an uncompromising or extreme partisan, a fanatic. 2. Zealot, a member of a Jewish sect aiming at world Jewish theocracy and resisting the Romans until AD 70. —**zealotry** *n.*

zealous /'zeləs/ *adj.* full of zeal. —**zealously** *adv.*

zebra /'zebrə, 'ziːbrə/ *n.* 1. an African quadruped of the genus *Equus*, related to the ass and the horse, with a body entirely covered by black and white (or dark-brown and cream) stripes which serve as camouflage or dazzle and confuse predators. Zebras are about 1.5 m/5 ft high at the shoulder, with a stout body, and a short, thick mane. They live in herds on mountains and plains, and can run at up to 60 kph/40 mph. 2. (*attributive*) with alternate dark and pale stripes. —**zebra crossing**, a striped street-crossing where pedestrians have precedence over vehicles. [Italian or Portuguese from Congolese]

zebu /'ziːbuː/ *n.* a light-coloured humped ox *Bos indicus* of India, East Asia, and Africa. It is used for pulling loads, and is held by some Hindus to be sacred. [from French *zébu*]

Zedekiah /zedi'kaɪə/ last king of Judah 597–586 BC. Placed on the throne by Nebuchadnezzar, he rebelled, was forced to witness his sons' execution, then was blinded and sent to Babylon. The witness to these events was the prophet Jeremiah, who describes them in the Old Testament.

Zeebrugge /'ziːbrʊgə/ small Belgian ferry port on the North Sea, linked to Bruges by a 14 km/9 mi canal (built 1896–1907). In March 1987 it was the scene of a disaster in which over 180 passengers lost their lives when the car ferry *Herald of Free Enterprise* put to sea from Zeebrugge with its car loading doors open.

Zeeland /'ziːlənd/ province of the SW Netherlands; **area** 1,790 sq km/691 sq mi; **capital** Middelburg; **towns** Vlissingen, Terneuzen, Goes; **population** (1988) 356,000; **products** cereals, potatoes; **features** mostly below sea level. Zeeland is protected by a system of dykes; **history** disputed by the counts of Flanders and Holland during the Middle Ages, Zeeland was annexed to Holland in 1323 by Count Willam III.

Zeeman /'zeɪmən/ Pieter 1865–1943. Dutch physicist who discovered in 1896 that when light from certain elements, such as sodium or lithium (when heated), is passed through a spectroscope in the presence of a strong magnetic field, the spectrum splits into a number of distinct lines. This is known as the **Zeeman effect**, for which he shared the 1902 Nobel Prize for Physics.

Zeffirelli /zefi'reli/ Franco 1923– . Italian theatre, opera and film director and stage designer, acclaimed for his stylish designs and lavish productions. His films include *La Traviata* 1983, *Otello* 1986, and *Hamlet* 1990.

Zeiss /zaɪs/ Carl 1816–1888. German optician. He opened his first workshop in Jena in 1846, and in 1866 joined forces with Ernst Abbe (1840–1905) producing cameras, microscopes, and binoculars.

Zen *n.* a form of ◊Buddhism introduced from India to Japan via China in the 12th century. It teaches the attainment of enlightenment through meditation and intuition rather than through study of the scriptures. *Koan* (paradoxical questions), tea-drinking, and sudden enlightenment are elements of Zen practice. [Japanese *zenna* = quiet mind meditation]

zenana /zi'nɑːnə/ *n.* the part of the house for the seclusion of women of high-caste families in India and Iran. [from Hindi from Persian *zan* = woman]

Zend-Avesta *n.* the sacred scriptures of ◊Zoroastrianism, today practised by the Parsees. They comprise the *Avesta* (liturgical books for the priests); the *Gathas* (the discourses and revelations of Zoroaster); and the *Zend* (commentary upon them). [from Persian *zand* = interpretation]

zenith /'zenɪθ, 'ziː-/ *n.* 1. the point of the heavens directly above the observer; the ◊nadir is below, diametrically opposite. See ◊celestial sphere. 2. the highest point (of power or prosperity etc.). [from Old French or Latin ultimately from Arabic = path (over the head)]

Zenobia /zi'nəubiə/ queen of Palmyra AD 266–272. She assumed the crown as regent for her sons, after the death of her husband Odaenathus, and in 272 was defeated at Emesa (now Homs) by Aurelian and taken captive to Rome.

Zeno of Elea /'ziːnəu, 'eliə/ *c.*490–430 BC. Greek philosopher who pointed out several paradoxes that raised 'modern' problems of space and time. For example, motion is an illusion, since an arrow in flight must occupy a determinate space at each instant, and therefore must be at rest.

zeolite *n.* any of the hydrous aluminium silicates, also containing sodium, calcium, barium, strontium, and potassium, chiefly found in igneous rocks and characterized by a ready loss or gain of water. Zeolites are used as 'molecular sieves' to separate mixtures because they are capable of selective absorption. They have a high ion-exchange capacity and can be used to make petrol, benzene, and toluene from low-grade raw materials, such as coal and methanol.

zephyr /'zefə/ *n.* a gentle wind or breeze. [from French or Latin from Greek *zephuros* = (god of the) west wind]

Zeppelin /'zepəlɪn, German 'tsepəliːn/ Ferdinand, Count von Zeppelin 1838–1917. German airship pioneer. On retiring from the army in 1891, he devoted himself to the study of aeronautics, and his first airship was built and tested in 1900. During World War I a number of Zeppelin airships bombed England. They were also used for luxury passenger transport but the construction of hydrogen-filled airships with rigid keels was abandoned after several disasters in the 1920s and 1930s. Zeppelin also helped to pioneer large multi-engine bomber planes.

Zernicke /'zeənɪkə/ Frits 1888–1966. Dutch physicist who developed the phase-contrast microscope in 1935. Earlier microscopes allowed many specimens to be examined only after they had been transformed by heavy staining and other treatment. The phase-contrast microscope allowed living cells to be directly observed by making use of the difference in refractive indices between specimens and medium. He won the 1953 Nobel Prize for Physics.

zero /'zɪərəu/ *n.* (*plural* **zeros**) 1. nought; the figure 0. 2. the point on the graduated scale of a thermometer etc. from which a positive or negative quantity is reckoned. 3. (in full **zero-hour**) the hour at which a planned military or other operation is timed to begin; the crucial or decisive moment. —**zero in on**, to take aim at; to focus attention on. **zero-rated** *adj.* on which no value added tax is charged. [from French or Italian from Arabic]

zest *n.* 1. piquancy, stimulating flavour or quality. 2. keen enjoyment or interest. 3. the coloured part of orange or lemon peel as flavouring. —**zestful** *adj.*, **zestfully** *adv.* [from French *zeste* = orange or lemon peel]

zeta /'ziːtə/ *n.* the sixth letter of the Greek alphabet (ζ, Z) = z. [from Greek]

zeugma /'zjuːgmə/ *n.* a figure of speech using a verb or adjective with two nouns, to one of which it is strictly applicable while the word appropriate to the other is not used (e. g. *with weeping eyes and* [*grieving*] *hearts*); (*loosely*) syllepsis. [Latin from Greek *zeugnumi* = to yoke]

Zeus /zjuːs/ in Greek mythology, chief of the gods (Roman

Jupiter). He was the son of Kronos, whom he overthrew. As the supreme god he dispensed good and evil and was the father and ruler of all humankind. His emblems are the thunderbolt and aegis (shield), representing the thundercloud.

Zhangjiakou /dʒæŋdʒiəˈkəʊ/ formerly **Changchiakow** historic town and trade centre in Hebei province, China, 160 km/100 mi NW of Beijing, on the Great Wall; population (1980) 1,100,000. Zhangjiakou is on the border of Inner Mongolia (its Mongolian name is *Kalgan*, 'gate'). It was the centre of the tea trade from China to Russia.

Zhao Ziyang /ˈdʒaʊ dziːˈjæn/ 1918– . Chinese politician, prime minister from 1980, and secretary of the Chinese Communist Party (CCP) 1987–89. His reforms included self-management and incentives for workers and factories. He lost his secretaryship and other posts after the Tiananmen Square massacre in Beijing June 1989.

Zhejiang /dʒɜːˈdʒiˈæn/ or **Chekiang** province of SE China; **area** 101,800 sq km/39,295 sq mi; **capital** Hangzhou; **features** smallest of the Chinese provinces; the base of the Song dynasty 12th–13th centuries; densely populated; **products** rice, cotton, sugar, jute, maize; timber on the uplands; **population** (1986) 40,700,000.

Zhengzhou /dʒʌŋˈdʒəʊ/ or **Chengchow** industrial city (light engineering, cotton textiles, foods) and capital (from 1954) of Henan province, China, on the Huang Ho; population (1986) 1,590,000.

Zhivkov /ˈʒɪvkɒf/ Todor 1911– . Bulgarian Communist Party (BCP) leader 1954–89, prime minister 1962–71, president 1971–89. His period in office was one of caution and conservatism.

Zhou Enlai /ˈdʒəʊ enˈlaɪ/ or **Chou En-lai** 1898–1976. Chinese politician. Zhou, a member of the Chinese Communist Party (CCP) from the 1920s, was prime minister 1949–76 and foreign minister 1949–58. He was a moderate Maoist and weathered the Cultural Revolution. He played a key role in foreign affairs.

Zhubov scale a scale for measuring ice coverage, used in the USSR. The unit is the **ball**; one ball is 10% coverage, two balls 20%, and so on.

Zhu De /ˈdʒuː ˈdeɪ/ or **Chu Teh** 1886–1976. Chinese Red Army leader from 1931. He devised the tactic of mobile guerrilla warfare and organized the ◊Long March to Shaanxi 1934–36. He was made a marshal in 1955.

Zhukov /ˈʒuːkɒv/ Georgi Konstantinovich 1896–1974. Marshal of the USSR in World War II and minister of defence 1955–57. As chief of staff from 1941, he defended Moscow in 1941, counter-attacked at Stalingrad in 1942, organized the relief of Leningrad in 1943, and led the offensive from the Ukraine in March 1944 which ended in the fall of Berlin. He commanded the Soviet occupation forces in Germany.

Zia ul-Haq /ˈziə ulˈhæk/ Mohammad 1924–1988. Pakistani general, in power from 1977 until his death, probably an assassination, in an aircraft explosion. He became army chief of staff in 1976, led the military coup against Zulfiqar Ali ◊Bhutto in 1977, and became president in 1978. Zia introduced a fundamentalist Islamic regime and restricted political activity.

zidovudine *n.* (formerly known as AZT) the only drug licensed for treatment of AIDS. It causes severe side effects, including anaemia.

ZIFT acronym from zygote inter-Fallopian transfer, a modified form of ◊in vitro fertilization in which the fertilized ovum is reintroduced into the ◊Fallopian tube before the ovum has undergone its first cell division.

ziggurat /ˈzɪɡəræt/ *n.* in ancient Babylonia and Assyria, a pyramidal stepped tower of sun-baked brick faced with glazed bricks or tiles on which there may have been a shrine. [from Assyrian = pinnacle]

zigzag /ˈzɪɡzæɡ/ *adj.* with abrupt alternate right and left turns. —*n.* a zigzag line; a thing forming this or having sharp turns. —*adv.* with a zigzag course. —*v.i.* (-**gg**-) to move in a zigzag course. [French from German *zickzack* (symbolic formation)]

zillion /ˈzɪljən/ *n.* (*US*) an indefinite large number. [from *z* (perhaps = unknown quantity) and *million*]

Zimbabwe /zɪmˈbɑːbwi/ extensive stone architectural ruins near Victoria in Mashonaland, Zimbabwe. The structure was probably the work of a highly advanced Bantu-speaking people from Zaïre or Ethiopia, smelters of iron, who were in the area before AD 300.

Zimbabwe /zɪmˈbɑːbwi/ Republic of; landlocked country in central Africa; **area** 390,300 sq km/150,695 sq mi; **capital** Harare; **physical** high plateau with central high veld and mountains in E; rivers Zambezi and Limpopo; **head of state and government** Robert Mugabe from 1987; **political system** effectively one party Socialist republic; **exports** tobacco, asbestos, cotton, coffee, gold, silver; **population** (1990 est) 10,205,00; **language** English; **recent history** independence achieved from Britain in 1980.

zinc *n.* a bluish-white metallic element, symbol Zn, atomic number 30, relative atomic mass 65.38. The chief uses of zinc are in the production of galvanized iron and in alloys, notably brass. Its compounds include zinc oxide, used in ointments and cosmetics, paint, glass, and printing ink. Zinc sulphide is used in television screens and X-ray apparatus. —*v.t.* to coat or treat with zinc. [from German *zink*]

zinc ore the mineral from which zinc is extracted, principally sphalerite, $(Zn,Fe)S$, but also zincite, ZnO_2, and smithsonite, Zn,CO_3, all of which occur in mineralized veins. Ores of lead and zinc often occur together, and are common worldwide; Canada, the USA, and Australia are major producers.

zing *n.* (*colloquial*) vigour, energy. —*v.i.* (*colloquial*) to move swiftly or shrilly.

Zinneman /ˈtsɪnəmæn/ Fred(erick) 1907– . Austrian film director, who has lived in the USA from 1921. His films include *High Noon* 1952, *The Nun's Story* 1959, *The Day of the Jackal* 1973, and *Five Days One Summer* 1982.

zinnia /ˈzɪniə/ *n.* an annual plant of the family Compositae, native to Mexico; notably the cultivated hybrid of *Zinnia elegans*, with brightly coloured daisylike flowers. [from J G *Zinn*, German botanist (died 1759)]

Zinoviev /ziˈnɒvief/ Grigory 1883–1936. Russian politician. A prominent Bolshevik, he returned to Russia in 1917 with Lenin and played a leading part in the Revolution. As head of the Communist International in 1919, his name was attached to a forgery, the **Zinoviev letter**, inciting Britain's communists to rise, which helped to topple the Labour government in 1924. As one of the 'Old Bolsheviks', he was seen by Stalin as a threat, accused of complicity in the murder of the Bolshevik leader Sergei Kirov 1934, and shot.

Zion /ˈzaɪən/1. ancient Jerusalem, captured by King David; its holy hill, on which he built the Temple; the heavenly city or kingdom of heaven. 2. a non-conformist chapel. [Old English from Latin from Hebrew]

Zionism /ˈzaɪənɪzəm/ *n.* a Jewish political movement for the establishment of a Jewish homeland in Palestine, the 'promised land' of the Bible, with its capital Jerusalem, the 'city of Zion'. —**Zionist** *n.*

zip *n.* 1. a short sharp sound like that of a bullet going through the air. 2. energy, vigour. 3. a zip fastener. —*v.t./i.* (-**pp**-) 1. to move with a zip or at high speed. 2. to fasten with a zip fastener. —**zip fastener** a fastening device of two flexible strips with interlocking projections closed or opened by a sliding clip pulled along them. It was invented in the USA by Whitcomb Judson in 1891 to fasten shoes. [imitative]

Zip code (*US*) a system of postal codes. [from *zone improvement plan*]

zipper *n.* a zip fastener.

zircon /ˈzɜːkən/ *n.* zirconium silicate, $ZrSiO_4$, a mineral that occurs in small quantities in a wide range of igneous, sedimentary, and metamorphic rocks. It is very durable and is resistant to erosion and weathering. It is usually coloured brown, but can be other colours, and when transparent may be used as a gemstone. [from German *zirkon*]

zirconium *n.* lustrous, greyish-white, strong, ductile, metallic element, symbol Zr, atomic number 40, relative atomic mass 91.22. It occurs in nature as the mineral zircon (zirconium silicate), from which it is obtained commercially. It is used in some ceramics, alloys for wire and filaments, steel manufacture, and nuclear reactors, where its low neutron absorption is advantageous. It was isolated in 1824 by Swedish chemist Jöns Berzelius. [Germanic *zircon*, from Persian *zargun* 'golden']

zither /ˈzɪðə/ *n.* 1. a plucked, stringed folk instrument of Austria and Bavaria, in its present most common form comprising a shallow wooden soundbox over which are stretched five melody strings and two sets of accompaniment strings tuned to form chords. [German ultimately from Greek *kithara* = kind of harp]

Zola *French novelist and reformer Emile Zola.*

Zi Xi /'zi: 'tʃi:/ or **Tz'u-hsi** 1836–1908. Dowager empress of China. She was presented as a concubine to the emperor Hsien-feng. On his death in 1861 she became regent for her son T'ung Chih and, when he died in 1875, for her nephew Guang Xu (1871–1908).

zloty /'zlɒtɪ/ *n.* the monetary unit of Poland. [Polish golden]

Zn symbol for zinc.

zodiac /'zəʊdiæk/ *n.* 1. the zone of the heavens containing the paths of the Sun, Moon, and planets. When this was devised by the ancient Greeks, only five planets were known, making the zodiac about 16° wide. The stars in it are grouped into 12 signs (constellations), each 30° in extent: Aries, Taurus, Gemini, Cancer, Leo, Virgo, Libra, Scorpius, Sagittarius, Capricornus, Aquarius, and Pisces. Because of the ◊precession of the equinoxes, the current constellations do not cover the same areas of sky as the zodiacal signs of the same name. 2. a diagram of the signs of the zodiac. —**zodiacal** /zə'daɪəkəl/ *adj.* [from Old French from Latin from Greek *zōidion* = animal-figure]

zodiacal light a cone-shaped light sometimes seen extending from the Sun along the ◊ecliptic, visible after sunset or before sunrise. It is due to thinly spread dust particles in the central plane of the solar system.

Zog /zɒg/ Ahmed Beg Zogu 1895–1961. King of Albania 1928–39. He became prime minister of Albania in 1922, president of the republic in 1925, and proclaimed himself king in 1928. He was driven out by the Italians in 1939.

Zola /'zəʊlə/ Émile Edouard Charles Antoine 1840–1902. French novelist and social reformer. With *La Fortune des Rougon/The Fortune of the Rougons* 1867 he began a series of some 20 naturalistic novels, portraying the fortunes of a French family under the Second Empire. In 1898 he published *J'accuse/I Accuse*, a pamphlet indicting the persecutors of ◊Dreyfus. He was prosecuted for libel but later pardoned.

zombie /'zɒmbɪ/ *n.* 1. a corpse believed to be reanimated by a spirit and enslaved. The idea, widespread in Haiti, possibly arose from voodoo priests using the nerve poison tetrodotoxin (from the puffer fish) to produce a semblance of death from which the victim afterwards physically recovers. 2. (*colloquial*) a dull or apathetic person. [West African]

zone *n.* 1. an area having particular features, properties, purpose, or use. 2. any well-defined region of more or less beltlike form. 3. the area between two concentric circles. 4. an encircling band of colour etc. 5. (*archaic*) a girdle or belt. —*v.t.* 1. to encircle as or with a zone. 2. to arrange or distribute by zones; to assign to a particular area. —**zonal** *adj.* [French or from Latin from Greek *zōnē* = girdle]

zoo *n.* a zoological garden [abbreviation]

zoological /zəʊə'lɒdʒɪkəl, zu:ə-/ *adj.* of zoology. —**zoological garden(s)**, a public garden or park with a collection of animals for exhibition and study. —**zoologically** *adv.*

zoology /zəʊ'ɒlədʒɪ, zu:-/ *n.* the branch of biology concerned with the study of animals. It includes description of present-day animals, the study of evolution of animal forms, anatomy, physiology, embryology, and geographical distribution. —**zoologist** *n.* [from Greek *zōion* = animal]

zoom *v.i.* 1. to move quickly, especially with a buzzing sound. 2. to rise quickly or steeply. 3. in photography, to alter the size of the image continuously from long shot to close-up. —*n.* an aeroplane's steep climb. —**zoom lens**, a photographic lens allowing a camera to zoom by varying the focus. [imitative]

zoomorphic *adj.* 1. imitating or representing animal forms; having the form of an animal. 2. attributing the form or nature of an animal to a deity etc. —**zoomorphism** *n.* [from Greek *zōion* = animal and *morphē* = form]

zoonosis *n.* any infectious disease that can be transmitted to humans by other vertebrate animals. Probably the most feared example is ◊rabies. The transmitted microorganism sometimes causes disease only in the human host, leaving the animal host unaffected.

zoophyte *n.* a plantlike animal, especially a coral, jellyfish, or sponge. [from Greek *zōion* = animal and *phuton* = plant]

Zoroaster /zɒrəʊ'æstə/ or **Zarathustra** *c.*628–*c.*551 BC. Persian prophet and teacher, founder of Zoroastrianism.

Zoroastrianism /zɒrəʊ'æstriənɪzəm/ *n.* pre-Islamic Persian religion founded by Zoroaster, and still practised by the ◊Parsees in India. The ◊Zend-Avesta are the sacred scriptures of the faith. The theology is dualistic, **Ahura Mazda** or **Ormuzd** (the good God) being in conflict with **Ahriman** (the evil God), but the former is assured of eventual victory. —**Zoroastrian** *adj.* & *n.* [from *Zoroaster*, Persian prophet]

Zouave /zu:'ɑv/ *n.* a member of a corps of French infantry soldiers, first raised in 1831 from the Zouaoua tribe in Algeria. The term came to be used for soldiers in other corps modelled on the French Zouaves.

Z particle a type of ◊elementary particle.

Zr symbol for zirconium.

Zsigmondy /'ʃɪgmɒndi/ Richard 1865–1929. Austrian chemist who devised and built an ultramicroscope in 1903. The microscope's illumination was placed at right angles to the axis making it possible to observe gold particles with a diameter of 10-millionth of a millimetre. He was awarded the 1925 Nobel Prize for Chemistry.

ZST abbreviation of zone standard time.

zucchini /zu:'ki:nɪ/ *n.* (*plural* the same or **zucchinis**) alternative name for the courgette, a type of ◊marrow. [Italian, plural of *zucchino* diminutive of *zucca* = gourd]

Zuider Zee /'zaɪdə 'zi:, Dutch 'zɑʊdə 'zeɪ/ former sea inlet in Holland, cut off from the North Sea by the closing of a dyke in 1932, much of which has been reclaimed as land. The remaining lake is called the ◊Ijsselmeer.

Zulu /'zu:lu:/ *n.* 1. a member of a South African Bantu people inhabiting the north-eastern part of Natal. The present homeland, Kwazulu, represents the nucleus of the once extensive and militaristic Zulu kingdom. 2. the Zulu language, closely related to Xhosa, belonging to the Bantu branch of the Niger-Congo family. —*adj.* of the Zulus or their language. [native name]

Zululand /'zu:lu:lænd/ region in Natal, South Africa, largely corresponding to the Black National State Kwazulu. It was a province until 1897.

Zurbarán /θʊəbə'ræn/ Francisco de 1598–1664. Spanish painter based in Seville. He painted religious subjects in a powerful, austere style.

Zürich /'zjuərɪk/ financial centre and industrial city (machinery, electrical goods, textiles) on Lake Zürich; capital of Zürich canton and the largest city in Switzerland; population (1987) 840,000.

Zwingli /'zwɪŋgli, German 'tsvɪŋli/ Ulrich 1484–1531. Swiss Protestant, born in St Gallen. He was ordained a Roman Catholic priest in 1506, but by 1519 was a Reformer and led the Reformation in Switzerland with his insistence on the sole authority of the Scriptures. He was killed in a skirmish at Kappel during a war against the cantons that had not accepted the Reformation.

Zworykin /'zwɔːrɪkɪn/ Vladimir Kosma 1889–1982. Russian-born US electronics engineer, in the USA from 1919. He invented a television camera tube and the ◊electron microscope.

zydeco *n.* a style of dance music originating in Louisiana, USA, similar to ◊Cajun but more heavily influenced by blues and West Indian music. Zydeco is fast and bouncy.

zygote *n.* a cell formed by the union of two gametes, before it undergoes cleavage to begin embryonic development. [from Greek *zugōtos* = yoked]